D1152976

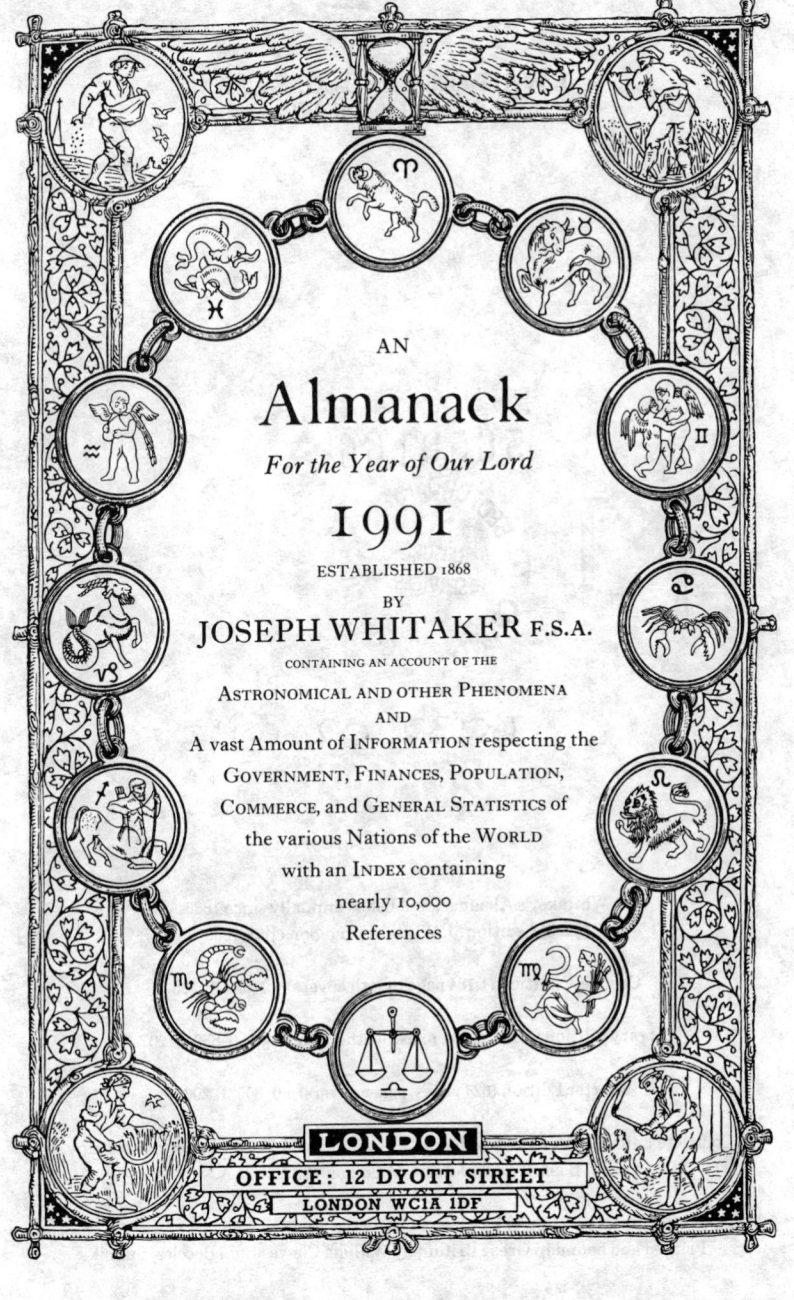

AN

Almanack

For the Year of Our Lord

1991

ESTABLISHED 1868

BY

JOSEPH WHITAKER F.S.A.

CONTAINING AN ACCOUNT OF THE

ASTRONOMICAL AND OTHER PHENOMENA

AND

A vast Amount of INFORMATION respecting the
GOVERNMENT, FINANCES, POPULATION,
COMMERCE, and GENERAL STATISTICS of
the various Nations of the WORLD
with an INDEX containing

nearly 10,000

References

LONDON

OFFICE: 12 DYOTT STREET
LONDON WC1A 1DF

J. WHITAKER AND SONS LTD.
12 Dyott Street, London WC1A 1DF

5650166

BEDFORDSHIRE
LEISURE
SERVICES
COUNTY COUNCIL

RO32·02 WHI

29 NOV 1990

Whitaker's Almanack published annually since 1868
©123rd edition. J. Whitaker and Sons Ltd. 1990

Complete Edition (1,184 pages, cloth covers) 0 85021 205 7

Library Edition (1,184 pages, maps, leather binding) 0 85021 207 3

Shorter Edition (624 pages, paper covers) 0 85021 206 5

Complete Edition distributed exclusively in the U.S.A. by Gale Research Company,
Book Tower, Detroit, Michigan 48226, U.S.A.

Typeset by Clowes Computer Composition
Printed and bound in Great Britain by William Clowes Ltd., Beccles, Suffolk

CONTENTS

CONTENTS
(of the Complete Edition and Library Edition)
continued

PREFACE
to the 123rd Annual Volume (1991)

The 123rd edition of Whitaker looks back over a particularly eventful year. The face of Europe has changed dramatically in the past eleven months; this latest edition of Whitaker lists the new governments in eastern Europe, and records and illustrates the events that brought them to power.

Sport has also been much in the news during the year. The results of the Commonwealth Games and the World Cup are included in the Sports section. The record-breaking achievements in tennis and cricket this summer are illustrated with photographs of Martina Navratilova and Graham Gooch in action.

The section containing world geographical statistics has been revised and expanded for this edition. A list of surviving recipients of the George Cross is included for the first time and, in response to requests from readers, more detailed information on forms of addressing peers has been added.

As always, we are most grateful to the many organizations and individuals who provide us with information and answer our enquiries. We also appreciate the comments and suggestions made by readers; it is very encouraging that so many responded to the questionnaire included in the last edition. Analysis of the responses has provided much helpful information, and has suggested ideas that we shall be pursuing. We would like to thank readers for taking the time to give us their views.

12 Dyott Street, London WC1A 1DF
Telephone 071–836 8911
October, 1990

HILARY MARSDEN
Editor

ABBREVIATIONS

Ψ = Seaport

A

A	Associate of.
AA	Alcoholics Anonymous; Anti-Aircraft; Automobile Association.
AAA	Amateur Athletic Association.
AB	Able-bodied seaman.
ABA	Amateur Boxing Association.
abbr(ev)	abbreviation.
ABM	Anti-ballistic missile defence system.
abr	abridged.
ac	alternating current.
a/c	account.
AC	Aircraftman; (*Ante Christum*) Before Christ; Companion, Order of Australia.
ACAS	Advisory, Conciliation and Arbitration Service.
ACT	Australian Capital Territory.
ACTT	Association of Cinematograph, Television and Allied Technicians.
AD	(*Anno Domini*) In the year of our Lord.
ADC	Aide-de-Camp.
ADC (P)	Personal ADC to The Queen.
adj	adjective.
Adjt	Adjutant.
ad lib	(*ad libitum*) at pleasure.
Adm	Admiral; Admission.
adv	adverb; advocate.
AE	Air Efficiency Award.
AEA	Atomic Energy Authority.
AEM	Air Efficiency Medal.
AERE	Atomic Energy Research Establishment.
AEU	Amalgamated Engineering Union.
AFC	Air Force Cross; Association Football Club.
AFM	Air Force Medal.
AFRC	Agricultural and Food Research Council.
AFV	Armoured fighting vehicle.
AG	Adjutant-General; Attorney-General.
AGM	air-to-ground missile; annual general meeting.
AH	(*Anno Hegirae*) In the year of the Hegira.
AIDS	Acquired Immune Deficiency Syndrome.
alt	altitude.
am	(*ante meridiem*) before noon.
AM	(*Anno mundi*) In the year of the world.
amp	ampere; amplifier.
ANC	African National Congress.
anon	anonymous(ly).
ANZAC	Australian and New Zealand Army Corps.
AO	Air Officer; Officer, Order of Australia.
AOC	Air Officer Commanding.
AFRC	Agricultural and Food Research Council.
APEX	Association of Professional, Executive, Clerical and Computer Staff.
AS	Anglo-Saxon.
ASA	Advertising Standards Authority; Amateur Swimming Association.
ASB	*Alternative Service Book.*
ASEAN	Association of South East Asian Nations.
ASH	Action on Smoking and Health.
ASLEF	Associated Society of Locomotive Engineers and Firemen.
ASLIB	Association for Information Management.
ASTMS	Association of Scientific, Technical and Managerial Staffs.
ATC	Air Training Corps.
AUC	(*ab urbe condita*) In the year from the foundation of Rome; (*anno urbis conditae*) In the year of the founding of the city.
AUT	Association of University Teachers.
AV	Audio-visual; Authorized Version.
AVR	Army Volunteer Reserve.
AWOL	Absent without leave.

B

b	born; bowled.
BA	Bachelor of Arts.
BAA	British Airports Authority; British Astronomical Association.
BAFTA	British Academy of Film and Television Arts.
BAOR	British Army of the Rhine.
Bart	Baronet.
BAS	Bachelor in Agricultural Science; British Antarctic Survey.
BB	Boys' Brigade.
BBC	British Broadcasting Corporation.
BC	Before Christ; British Columbia.
B Ch (D)	Bachelor of (Dental) Surgery.
BCL	*do*, of Civil Law.
B Com	*do*, of Commerce.
BD	*do*, of Divinity.
BDA	British Dental Association.
BDS	Bachelor of Dental Surgery.
B Ed	*do*, of Education.
BEM	British Empire Medal.
B Eng	Bachelor of Engineering.
BFI	British Film Institute.
BFPO	British Forces Post Office.
BIM	British Institute of Management.
B Litt	Bachelor of Literature *or* of Letters.
BM	*do*, of Medicine; British Museum.
BMA	British Medical Association.
B Mus	Bachelor of Music.
BOTB	British Overseas Trade Board.
Bp	Bishop.
B Pharm	Bachelor of Pharmacy.
B Phil	*do*, of Philosophy.
Br	Britain; British.
BR	British Rail.
BRCS	British Red Cross Society.
Brig	Brigadier.
Brit	Britain; British.
BSc	Bachelor of Science.
BSC	British Steel Corporation.
BSI	British Standards Institution.
BST	British Summer Time.
Bt	Baronet.
BTEC	Business and Technician Education Council.
B Th	Bachelor of Theology.
Btu	British thermal unit.
BVM	(*Beata Virgo Maria*) Blessed Virgin Mary.
BVMS	Bachelor of Veterinary Medicine and Surgery.
BWB	British Waterways Board.

C

c	(*circa*) about.
C	Celsius; Centigrade; Conservative.
CA	Chartered Accountant (*Scotland*).
CAA	Civil Aviation Authority.
CAB	Citizens' Advice Bureau.
Cantab	(of) Cambridge.
Cantuar:	of Canterbury (*Archbishop*).
CAP	Common Agricultural Policy.
Capt	Captain.
Caricom	Caribbean Community and Common Market.
Carliol:	of Carlisle (*Bishop*).
CB	Companion, Order of the Bath.
CBE	Commander, Order of the British Empire.
CBI	Confederation of British Industry.

CC	Chamber of Commerce; Companion, Order of Canada; City Council; County Council; County Court.
CCC	County Cricket Club.
C Chem	Chartered Chemist.
CD	Civil Defence; Compact Disc; Corps Diplomatique.
Cdr	Commander.
Cdre	Commodore.
CDS	Chief of the Defence Staff.
CE	Civil Engineer.
CEGB	Central Electricity Generating Board.
C Eng	Chartered Engineer.
Cento	Central Treaty Organization.
Cestr:	of Chester (*Bishop*).
CET	Central European Time; Common External Tariff.
cf	(*confer*) compare.
CF	Chaplain to the Forces.
CFC	Chlorofluorocarbon.
CGM	Conspicuous Gallantry Medal.
CGS	Centimetre-gramme-second (*system*); Chief of General Staff.
CH	Companion of Honour.
ChB/M	Bachelor/Master of Surgery.
CI	Channel Islands; The Imperial Order of the Crown of India.
CIA	Central Intelligence Agency.
Cicestr:	of Chichester (*Bishop*).
CID	Criminal Investigation Department.
CIE	Companion, Order of the Indian Empire.
cif	cost, insurance and freight.
C-in-C	Commander-in-Chief.
CIPFA	Chartered Institute of Public Finance and Accountancy.
C Lit	Companion of Literature.
CLJ	Commander, Order of St Lazarus of Jerusalem.
CM	(*Chirurgiae Magister*) Master of Surgery.
CMEA	Council for Mutual Economic Assistance.
CMG	Companion, Order of St Michael and St George.
CNAA	Council for National Academic Awards.
CND	Campaign for Nuclear Disarmament.
c/o	care of.
CO	Commanding Officer; conscientious objector.
COD	Cash on delivery.
C of E	Church of England.
COHSE	Confederation of Health Service Employees.
COI	Central Office of Information.
Col	Colonel.
Comecon	Council for Mutual Economic Assistance.
Con	Conservative.
Cpl	Corporal.
CPM	Colonial Police Medal.
CPRE	Council for the Protection of Rural England.
CPVE	Certificate of Pre-Vocational Education.
CRE	Council for Racial Equality.
CSCE	Conference on Security and Co-operation in Europe.
CSE	Certificate of Secondary Education.
CSI	Companion, Order of the Star of India.
CVO	Commander, Royal Victorian Order.

D

d	(*denarius*) penny.
DBE	Dame Commander, Order of the British Empire.
dc	direct current.
DC	District Council; District of Columbia.
DCB	Dame Commander, Order of the Bath.
D Ch	(*Doctor Chirurgiae*) Doctor of Surgery.

DCL	Doctor of Civil Law.
DCM	Distinguished Conduct Medal.
DCMG	Dame Commander, Order of St Michael and St George.
DCVO	Dame Commander, Royal Victorian Order.
DD	Doctor of Divinity.
DDS	*do*, of Dental Surgery.
DDT	dichlorodiphenyl-trichloroethane.
del	(*delineavit*) he/she drew it.
DES	Department of Education and Science.
DFC	Distinguished Flying Cross.
DFM	Distinguished Flying Medal.
DG	(*Dei gratia*) By the grace of God; Director-General.
DH	Department of Health.
DHA	District Health Authority.
DHSS	Department of Health and Social Security.
Dip Ed	Diploma in Education.
Dip H E	Diploma in Higher Education.
Dip Tech	Diploma in Technology.
DJ	Disc jockey.
DL	Deputy Lieutenant.
D Litt	Doctor of Letters *or* of Literature.
D Mus	*do*, of Music.
DNA	deoxyribonucleic acid.
DNB	*Dictionary of National Biography*.
do	(*ditto*) the same.
DoE	Department of the Environment.
DP	Data processing.
D Ph *or* D Phil	Doctor of Philosophy.
DPP	Director of Public Prosecutions.
Dr	Doctor.
DSc	Doctor of Science.
DSC	Distinguished Service Cross.
DSM	Distinguished Service Medal.
DSO	Companion, Distinguished Service Order.
DSS	Department of Social Security.
DTI	Department of Trade and Industry.
Dunelm:	of Durham (*Bishop*).
DV	(*Deo volente*) God willing.

E

E	East.
Ebor:	of York (*Archbishop*).
EC	European Community.
ECG	Electrocardiogram.
ECSC	European Coal and Steel Community.
ECU	European Currency Unit.
ED	Efficiency Decoration.
EEC	European Economic Community.
EEG	Electroencephalogram.
EETPU	Electrical, Electronic, Telecommunication and Plumbing Union.
EFTA	European Free Trade Association.
eg	(*exempli gratia*) for the sake of example.
EMS	European Monetary System.
ENEA	European Nuclear Energy Agency.
ER	Elizabetha Regina.
ERD	Emergency Reserve Decoration.
ERM	Exchange Rate Mechanism.
ERNIE	Electronic random number indicator equipment.
ESA	European Space Agency.
ESP	Extra-sensory perception.
ESRC	Economic and Social Research Council.
ETA	Euzkadi ta Askatasuna (*Basque separatist organization*).
et al	(*et alibi*) and elsewhere; (*et alii*) and others.
etc	(*et cetera*) and the other things/and so forth.
et seq	(*et sequentia*) and the following.

Euratom	European Atomic Energy Commission.
Exon:	of Exeter (*Bishop*).

F

f	(*forte*) loud.
F	Fahrenheit; Fellow of.
FA	Football Association.
FANY	First Aid Nursing Yeomanry.
FAO	Food and Agriculture Organization.
FBA	Fellow, British Academy.
FBAA	*do*, British Association of Accountants and Auditors.
FBI	Federal Bureau of Investigation.
FBIM	Fellow, British Institute of Management.
FBS	*do*, Botanical Society.
FCA	*do*, Institute of Chartered Accountants (*of England and Wales*).
FCCA	*do*, Chartered Association of Certified Accountants.
FCGI	*do*, City and Guilds of London Institute.
FCIA	*do*, Corporation of Insurance Agents.
FCIArb	*do*, Chartered Institute of Arbitrators.
FCIB	*do*, Chartered Institute of Bankers; Corporation of Insurance Brokers.
FCIBSE	*do*, Chartered Institution of Building-Services Engineers.
FCII	*do*, Chartered Insurance Institute.
FCIS	*do*, Institute of Chartered Secretaries and Administrators.
FCIT	*do*, Chartered Institute of Transport.
FCMA	*do*, Chartered Institute of Management Accountants.
FCO	Foreign and Commonwealth Office.
FCP	Fellow, College of Preceptors.
FD	(*Fidei Defensor*) Defender of the Faith.
fec	(*fecit*) made this.
FEng	Fellow, Fellowship of Engineering.
ff	(*fecerunt*) made this (*pl*); (*fortissimo*) very loud.
FFA	Fellow, Faculty of Actuaries (*Scotland*); *do*, Institute of Financial Accountants.
FFAS	*do*, Faculty of Architects and Surveyors.
FGS	*do*, Geological Society.
FHS	Fellow, Heraldry Society.
FHSM	*do*, Institute of Health Service Management.
FIA	*do*, Institute of Actuaries.
FIBiol	*do*, Institute of Biology.
FICE	*do*, Institution of Civil Engineers.
FICS	*do*, Institution of Chartered Shipbrokers.
FIEE	*do*, Institution of Electrical Engineers.
FIERE	*do*, Institution of Electronic and Radio Engineers.
FIFA	International Association Football Federation.
FIM	Fellow, Institute of Metals.
FIMM	*do*, Institution of Mining and Metallurgy.
FInstF	*do*, Institute of Fuel.
FInstP	*do*, Institute of Physics.
FIQS	*do*, Institute of Quantity Surveyors.
FIS	*do*, Institute of Statisticians.
FJI	*do*, Institute of Journalists.
fl	(*floruit*) flourished.
FLA	Fellow, Library Association.
FLS	*do*, Linnean Society.
FM	Field Marshal; frequency modulation.
fo	folio.
FO	Flying Officer.
fob	free on board.
FPA	Family Planning Association.
FPhS	Fellow, Philosophical Society.
FRAD	*do*, Royal Academy of Dancing.
FRAeS	*do*, Royal Aeronautical Society.
FRAI	*do*, Royal Anthropological Institute.
FRAM	*do*, Royal Academy of Music.

FRAS	*do*, Royal Astronomical Society.
FRBS	*do*, Royal Botanical Society; *do*, Royal Society of British Sculptors.
FRCGP	*do*, Royal College of General Practitioners.
FRCM	*do*, Royal College of Music.
FRCO	*do*, Royal College of Organists.
FRCOG	*do*, Royal College of Obstetricians and Gynaecologists.
FRCP	*do*, Royal College of Physicians, London.
FRCPath	*do*, Royal College of Pathologists.
FRCPE(d)	*do*, Royal College of Physicians, Edinburgh.
FRCPI	*do*, Royal College of Physicians, Ireland.
FRCPsych	*do*, Royal College of Psychiatrists.
FRCR	*do*, Royal College of Radiologists.
FRCS	*do*, Royal College of Surgeons of England.
FRCSE(d)	*do*, Royal College of Surgeons of Edinburgh.
FRCSGlas	*do*, Royal College of Physicians and Surgeons of Glasgow.
FRCSI	*do*, Royal College of Surgeons in Ireland.
FRCVS	*do*, Royal College of Veterinary Surgeons.
FREconS	*do*, Royal Economic Society.
FRGS	*do*, Royal Geographical Society.
FRHistS	*do*, Royal Historical Society.
FRHS	*do*, Royal Horticultural Society.
FRIBA	*do*, Royal Institute of British Architects.
FRICS	*do*, Royal Institution of Chartered Surveyors.
FRMetS	*do*, Royal Meteorological Society.
FRMS	*do*, Royal Microscopical Society.
FRNS	*do*, Royal Numismatic Society.
FRPharmS	*do*, Royal Pharmaceutical Society.
FRPS	*do*, Royal Photographic Society.
FRS	*do*, Royal Society.
FRSA	*do*, Royal Society of Arts.
FRSC	*do*, Royal Society of Chemistry.
FRSE	*do*, Royal Society of Edinburgh.
FRSL	*do*, Royal Society of Literature.
FRTPI	*do*, Royal Town Planning Institute.
FSA	*do*, Society of Antiquaries.
FSS	*do*, Statistical Society.
FSVA	*do*, Incorporated Society of Valuers and Auctioneers.
FT	*Financial Times*.
FTI	Fellow, Textile Institute.
FTII	*do*, Institute of Taxation.
FZS	*do*, Zoological Society.

G

GATT	General Agreement on Tariffs and Trade.
GBE	Dame/Knight Grand Cross, Order of the British Empire.
GC	George Cross.
GCB	Dame/Knight Grand Cross, Order of the Bath.
GCE	General Certificate of Education.
GCHQ	Government Communications Headquarters.
GCIE	Knight Grand Commander, Order of the Indian Empire.
GCLJ	Knight Grand Cross, Order of St Lazarus of Jerusalem.
GCMG	Dame/Knight Grand Cross, Order of St Michael and St George.
GCSE	General Certificate of Secondary Education.
GCSI	Knight Grand Commander, Order of the Star of India.
GCVO	Dame/Knight Grand Cross, Royal Victorian Order.
GDP	Gross domestic product.
GDR	German Democratic Republic (*E Germany*).
Gen	General.

GHQ	General Headquarters.
GM	George Medal.
GMB	General, Municipal, Boilermakers and Allied Trades Union.
GMT	Greenwich Mean Time.
GNP	Gross national product.
GOC	General Officer Commanding.
GP	General Practitioner.
Gp Capt	Group Captain.
GSO	General Staff Officer.

H

HAC	Honourable Artillery Company.
HBM	Her/His Britannic Majesty('s).
HCF	Highest common factor; Honorary Chaplain to the Forces.
HE	Her/His Excellency; His Eminence.
HGV	Heavy Goods Vehicle.
HH	Her/His Highness; Her/His Honour; His Holiness.
HIM	Her/His Imperial Majesty.
HIV	Human Immunodeficiency Virus.
HJS	(*hic jacet sepultus*) here lies buried.
HM	Her/His Majesty('s).
HMAS	Her/His Majesty's Australian Ship.
HMC	Headmasters' Conference.
HMI	Her/His Majesty's Inspector.
HML	Her/His Majesty's Lieutenant.
HMS	Her/His Majesty's Ship.
HMSO	Her/His Majesty's Stationery Office.
HNC	Higher National Certificate.
HND	Higher National Diploma.
HOLMES	Home Office Large Major Enquiry System.
Hon	Honorary; Honourable.
hp	horse power.
HP	Hire purchase.
HQ	Headquarters.
HRH	Her/His Royal Highness.
HSE	Health and Safety Executive; (*hic sepultus est*) here lies buried.
HSH	Her/His Serene Highness.
HTR	High temperature reactor.
HWM	High water mark.

I

IAAS	Incorporated Association of Architects and Surveyors.
IAEA	International Atomic Energy Agency.
IATA	International Air Transport Association.
IBA	Independent Broadcasting Authority.
Ibid	(*ibidem*) in the same place.
IBRD	International Bank for Reconstruction and Development.
ICAO	International Civil Aviation Organization.
ICBM	Inter-continental ballistic missile.
ICFTU	International Confederation of Free Trade Unions.
ICJ	International Court of Justice.
ICRC	International Committee of the Red Cross.
Id	(*idem*) the same.
IDA	International Development Association.
ie	(*id est*) that is.
IEA	International Energy Agency.
IFAD	International Fund for Agricultural Development.
IFC	International Finance Corporation.
IHS	(*Iesus Hominum Salvator*) Jesus the Saviour of Mankind.
ILEA	Inner London Education Authority.
ILO	International Labour Office/Organization.
IMF	International Monetary Fund.
IMO	International Maritime Organization.

Inc	Incorporated.
Incog	(*incognito*) unknown, unrecognized.
INF	International Nuclear Force.
INLA	Irish National Liberation Army.
In loc	(*in loco*) in its place.
Inmarsat	International Maritime Satellite Organization.
INRI	(*Iesus Nazarenus Rex Iudaeorum*) Jesus of Nazareth, King of the Jews.
Inst	(*instant*) current month.
Intelsat	International Telecommunications Satellite Consortium.
Interpol	International Criminal Police Commission.
IOM	Isle of Man.
IOU	I owe you.
IOW	Isle of Wight.
IQ	Intelligence quotient.
IRA	Irish Republican Army.
IRC	International Red Cross.
ISBN	International Standard Book Number.
ISO	Imperial Service Order.
ITU	International Telecommunication Union.
ITV	Independent Television.

J

JP	Justice of the Peace.

K

K	Köchel numeration (*of Mozart's works*).
KANU	Kenyan African National Union.
KBE	Knight Commander, Order of the British Empire.
KCB	*do*, Order of the Bath.
KCIE	*do*, Order of the Indian Empire.
KCLJ	*do*, Order of St Lazarus of Jerusalem.
KCMG	*do*, Order of St Michael and St George.
KCSI	*do*, Order of the Star of India.
KCVO	*do*, Royal Victorian Order.
KG	Knight of the Garter.
KGB	(*Komitet Gosudarstvennoi Besopasnosti*) Committee of State Security (USSR).
KKK	Ku Klux Klan.
KLJ	Knight, Order of St Lazarus of Jerusalem.
ko	knock out (*boxing*).
KP	Knight, Order of St Patrick.
KStJ	Knight, Order of St John of Jerusalem.
Kt	Knight.
KT	Knight of the Thistle.
kV	Kilovolt.
kW	Kilowatt.
kWh	Kilowatt hour.

L

L	Liberal.
Lab	Labour.
Lat	Latitude.
lbw	leg before wicket.
lc	lower case (*printing*).
LCJ	Lord Chief Justice.
LCM	Least/lowest common multiple.
LD	Liberal Democrat.
LDS	Licentiate in Dental Surgery.
LEA	Local Education Authority.
LHD	(*Literarum Humaniorum Doctor*) Doctor of Humane Letters/Literature.
Lib	Liberal.
Lic	(*Licenciado*) lawyer (*Spanish*).
Lic Med	Licentiate in Medicine.
Lit	Literary.
Lit Hum	(*Literae Humaniores*) Faculty of classics and philosophy, Oxford.
Litt D	Doctor of Letters.
LJ	Lord Justice.
LLB	Bachelor of Laws.

LLD	Doctor of Laws.
LLM	Master of Laws.
LM	Licentiate in Midwifery.
LMSSA	*do*, in Medicine and Surgery, Society of Apothecaries.
loc cit	(*loco citato*) in the place cited.
log	logarithm.
Londin:	of London (*Bishop*).
Long	Longitude.
LS	(*loco sigilli*) place of the seal.
LSA	Licentiate of Society of Apothecaries.
Lsd	(*Librae, solidi, denarii*) £, shillings and pence.
LSE	London School of Economics and Political Science.
Lt	Lieutenant.
LTA	Lawn Tennis Association.
Ltd	Limited (liability).
LTh *or* L Theol	Licentiate in Theology.
LVO	Lieutenant, Royal Victorian Order.
LWM	Low water mark.

M

M	Member of; Monsieur.
MA	Master of Arts.
MAFF	Ministry of Agriculture, Fisheries and Food.
Maj	Major.
max	maximum.
MB/D	Bachelor/Doctor of Medicine.
MBA	Master of Business Administration.
MBE	Member, Order of the British Empire.
MC	Master of Ceremonies; Military Cross.
MCC	Marylebone Cricket Club.
MCh(D)	Master of (Dental) Surgery.
MDS	*do*, of Dental Surgery.
ME	Middle English.
MEC	Member of Executive Council.
MEd	Master of Education.
mega	one million times.
MEP	Member of the European Parliament.
MFH	Master of Foxhounds.
Mgr	Monsignor.
MI	Military Intelligence.
micro	one-millionth part.
milli	one-thousandth part.
min	minimum.
MIRAS	Mortgage Interest Relief at Source.
MLA	Member of Legislative Assembly.
MLC	Member of Legislative Council.
Mlle	Mademoiselle.
MLR	Minimum lending rate.
MM	Military Medal.
Mme	Madame.
MN	Merchant Navy.
MO	Medical Officer/Orderly.
MoD	Ministry of Defence.
MoT	Ministry of Transport.
MP	Member of Parliament; Military Police.
mph	miles per hour.
MR	Master of the Rolls.
MRC	Medical Research Council.
MS	Master of Surgery; Manuscript (*pl* MSS).
MSc	Master of Science.
MSF	Manufacturing, Science and Finance Union.
MTh	Master of Theology.
Mus B/D	Bachelor/Doctor of Music.
MV	Merchant Vessel; Motor Vessel.
MVO	Member, Royal Victorian Order.
MW	Medium Wave.

N

N	North.
n/a	not applicable; not available.
NAAFI	Navy Army and Air Force Institutes.

NALGO	National and Local Government Officers' Association.
NASA	National Aeronautics and Space Administration.
NAS/UWT	National Association of Schoolmasters/ Union of Women Teachers.
NATO	North Atlantic Treaty Organization.
NB	New Brunswick; (*Nota bene*) note well.
NCO	Non-commissioned officer.
NEB	New English Bible.
NEDC	National Economic Development Council.
Nem con	(*Nemine contradicente*) no one contradicting.
NERC	Natural Environment Research Council.
nes	not elsewhere specified.
NFT	National Film Theatre.
NFU	National Farmers' Union.
NGA '82	National Graphical Association 1982.
NHS	National Health Service.
NI	National Insurance; Northern Ireland.
No	(*numero*) number.
Non seq	(*Non sequitur*) it does not follow.
Norvic:	of Norwich (*Bishop*).
NP	Notary Public.
NRA	National Rifle Association.
NS	New Style (*calendar*); Nova Scotia.
NSPCC	National Society for the Prevention of Cruelty to Children.
NSW	New South Wales.
NT	National Theatre; National Trust; New Testament.
NUCPS	National Union of Civil and Public Servants.
NUJ	*do*, of Journalists.
NUM	*do*, of Mineworkers.
NUPE	*do*, of Public Employees.
NUR	*do*, of Railwaymen.
NUS	*do*, of Seamen; *do*, of Students.
NUT	*do*, of Teachers.
NVQ	National Vocational Qualification.
NWT	Northwest Territory.
NY	New York.
NZ	New Zealand.

O

OAPEC	Organization of Arab Petroleum Exporting Countries.
OAS	Organization of American States.
OAU	Organization of African Unity.
Ob *or* obit	died.
OBE	Officer, Order of the British Empire.
OC	Officer Commanding.
ODA	Overseas Development Administration.
OE	Old English; omissions excepted.
OECD	Organization for Economic Co-operation and Development.
OED	*Oxford English Dictionary*.
Ofgas	Office of Gas Supply.
OFM	Order of Friars Minor (*Franciscans*).
Oftel	Office of Telecommunications.
OHMS	On Her/His Majesty's Service.
OM	Order of Merit.
OND	Ordinary National Diploma.
OP	Opposite prompt side (*of theatre*); Order of Preachers (*Dominicans*); out of print (*books*).
op	(*opus*) work.
op cit	(*opere citato*) in the work cited.
OPCS	Office of Population Censuses and Surveys.
OPEC	Organization of Petroleum Exporting Countries.
OS	Old Style (*calendar*); Ordnance Survey.
OSA	Order of St Augustine.
OSB	Order of St Benedict.
O St J	Officer, Order of St John of Jerusalem.

OT	Old Testament.
OTC	Officers' Training Corps.
Oxon	(of) Oxford; Oxfordshire.

P

p	page (pp pages).
p	(*piano*) softly.
PA	Personal Assistant; Press Association.
PAYE	Pay as You Earn.
pc	(*per centum*) in the hundred.
PC	Personal Computer; Police Constable; Privy Counsellor.
PCAS	Polytechnics Central Admission System.
PCFC	Polytechnics' and Colleges' Funding Council.
PDSA	People's Dispensary for Sick Animals.
PE	Physical Education.
Petriburg:	of Peterborough (*Bishop*).
PhD	Doctor of Philosophy.
pinx(it)	he/she painted it.
pl	plural.
PLA	Port of London Authority.
PLC	Public Limited Company.
PLO	Palestine Liberation Organization.
pm	(*post meridiem*) after noon.
PM	Prime Minister.
PMRAFNS	Princess Mary's Royal Air Force Nursing Service.
PO	Petty Officer; Pilot Officer; Post Office; postal order.
POW	Prisoner of War.
pp	(*per procurationem*) by proxy.
PPS	Parliamentary Private Secretary.
PR	Proportional Representation; Public Relations.
PRA	President of the Royal Academy.
Pro tem	(*pro tempore*) for the time being.
Prox	(*proximo*) next month.
PRS	President of the Royal Society.
PRSE	*do*, of Edinburgh.
Ps	Psalm.
PS	(*Post scriptum*) postscript.
PSBR	Public sector borrowing requirement.
psc	passed Staff College.
PSV	Public Service Vehicle.
Pte	Private.
PTO	Please turn over.

Q

QARANC	Queen Alexandra's Royal Army Nursing Corps.
QARNNS	Queen Alexandra's Royal Naval Nursing Service.
QB	Queen's Bench.
QC	Queen's Counsel.
QED	(*quod erat demonstrandum*) which was to be proved.
QGM	Queen's Gallantry Medal.
QHC	Queen's Honorary Chaplain.
QHDS	Queen's Honorary Dental Surgeon.
QHNS	Queen's Honorary Nursing Sister.
QHP	Queen's Honorary Physician.
QHS	Queen's Honorary Surgeon.
QMG	Quartermaster General.
QPM	Queen's Police Medal.
QS	Quarter Sessions.
QSO	Quasi-stellar object (quasar); Queen's Service Order.
quango	quasi-autonomous non-governmental organization.
qv	(*quod vide*) which see.

R

R	(*Regina*) Queen; (*Rex*) King.
RA	Royal Academy/Academician; Royal Artillery.
RAC	Royal Armoured Corps; Royal Automobile Club.

RADA	Royal Academy of Dramatic Art.
RADC	Royal Army Dental Corps.
RAE	Royal Aerospace Establishment.
RAEC	Royal Army Educational Corps.
RAeS	Royal Aeronautical Society.
RAF	Royal Air Force.
RAM	Random-access memory (*computer*); Royal Academy of Music.
RAMC	Royal Army Medical Corps.
RAN	Royal Australian Navy.
RAOC	Royal Army Ordnance Corps.
RAPC	Royal Army Pay Corps.
RAVC	Royal Army Veterinary Corps.
RBA	Royal Society of British Artists.
RBS	Royal Society of British Sculptors.
RC	Red Cross; Roman Catholic.
RCM	Royal College of Music.
RCN	Royal Canadian Navy.
RCT	Royal Corps of Transport.
RD	Refer to drawer (*banking*); Royal Naval and Royal Marine Forces Reserve Decoration; Rural Dean.
RDI	Royal Designer for Industry.
RE	Religious Education; Royal Engineers.
REME	Royal Electrical and Mechanical Engineers.
Rep	Representative; Republican.
Rev	Reverend.
RGN	Registered General Nurse.
RGS	Royal Geographical Society.
RHA	Regional Health Authority.
RHS	Royal Horticultural Society; Royal Humane Society.
RI	Rhode Island; Royal Institute of Painters in Watercolours; Royal Institution.
RIBA	Royal Institute of British Architects.
RIP	(*Requiescat in pace*) May he/she rest in peace.
RL	Rugby League.
RM	Registered Midwife; Royal Marines.
RMA	Royal Military Academy.
RMN	Registered Mental Nurse.
RN	Royal Navy.
RNIB	Royal National Institute for the Blind.
RNID	Royal National Institute for the Deaf.
RNLI	Royal National Lifeboat Institution.
RNR	Royal Naval Reserve.
RNVR	Royal Naval Volunteer Reserve.
RNXS	Royal Naval Auxiliary Service.
RNZN	Royal New Zealand Navy.
Ro	(*Recto*) on the right-hand page.
ROC	Royal Observer Corps.
Roffen:	of Rochester (*Bishop*).
ROI	Royal Institute of Oil Painters.
ROM	Read-only memory (*computer*).
RoSPA	Royal Society for the Prevention of Accidents.
RP	Royal Society of Portrait Painters.
rpm	revolutions per minute.
RRC	Lady of Royal Red Cross.
RSA	Republic of South Africa; Royal Scottish Academician; Royal Society of Arts.
RSC	Royal Shakespeare Company.
RSCN	Registered Sick Children's Nurse.
RSE	Royal Society of Edinburgh.
RSM	Regimental Sergeant Major.
RSPB	Royal Society for the Protection of Birds.
RSPCA	Royal Society for the Prevention of Cruelty to Animals.
RSV	Revised Standard Version (*of Bible*).
RSVP	(*Répondez, s'il vous plaît*) Please reply.
RSW	Royal Scottish Society of Painters in Watercolours.
RTPI	Royal Town Planning Institute.
RU	Rugby Union.
RUC	Royal Ulster Constabulary.
RV	Revised Version (*of Bible*).

RVM	Royal Victorian Medal.
RWS	Royal Water Colour Society.
RYS	Royal Yacht Squadron.

S

s	second; (*solidus*) shilling.
S	South.
SA	Salvation Army; South Africa; South America; South Australia.
SAE	Stamped addressed envelope.
Salop	Shropshire.
Sarum:	of Salisbury (*Bishop*).
SAS	Special Air Service Regiment.
SBS	Special Boat Squadron.
ScD	Doctor of Science.
SCM	State Certified Midwife.
SDI	Strategic Defence Initiative ('Star Wars').
SDLP	Social Democratic and Labour Party.
SDP	Social Democratic Party.
SEAQ	Stock Exchange Automated Quotations system.
SEN	State Enrolled Nurse.
SERC	Science and Engineering Research Council.
SERPS	State Earnings Related Pension Scheme.
SI	(*Système Internationale d'Unités*) International System of Units; Statutory Instrument.
Sic	So written.
Sig	Signature; Signor.
SJ	Society of Jesus (*Jesuits*).
SLD	Social and Liberal Democrats.
SMP	Statutory Maternity Pay.
SNP	Scottish National Party.
SOGAT	Society of Graphical and Allied Trades.
SOS	Save Our Souls (*distress signal*).
sp	(*sine prole*) without issue.
spgr	specific gravity.
SPQR	(*Senatus Populusque Romanus*) The Senate and People of Rome.
SRN	State Registered Nurse.
SS	Saints; Steamship.
SSC	Solicitor before Supreme Court (*Scotland*).
SSF	Society of St Francis.
SSP	Statutory Sick Pay.
SSSI	Site of special scientific interest.
stet	let it stand (*printing*).
STD	(*Sacrae Theologiae Doctor*) Doctor of Sacred Theology; Subscriber trunk dialling.
stp	Standard temperature and pressure.
STP	(*Sacrae Theologiae Professor*) Professor of Sacred Theology.
Sub Lt	Sub-Lieutenant.
SWAPO	South West Africa People's Organization.

T

TA	Territorial Army.
TB	Tuberculosis.
TCCB	Test and County Cricket Board.
TD	Territorial Efficiency Decoration.
temp	temperature; temporary employee.
TES	*Times Educational Supplement.*
TGWU	Transport and General Workers' Union.
TLS	*Times Literary Supplement.*
TNT	trinitrotoluene (*explosive*).
tr	transpose (*printing*).
TRH	Their Royal Highnesses.
TT	Teetotal; Tuberculin tested.
TUC	Trades Union Congress.
TVEI	Technical and Vocational Education Initiative.

U

U	Unionist.
UAE	United Arab Emirates.
uc	upper case (*printing*).
UCATT	Union of Construction, Allied Trades and Technicians.
UCCA	Universities' Central Council on Admissions.
UDI	Unilateral Declaration of Independence.
UDM	Union of Democratic Mineworkers.
UDR	Ulster Defence Regiment.
UEFA	Union of European Football Associations.
UFC	Universities' Funding Council.
UFO	Unidentified flying object.
UHF	ultra-high frequency.
UK	United Kingdom.
UKAEA	UK Atomic Energy Authority.
UN	United Nations.
UNESCO	United Nations Educational, Scientific and Cultural Organization.
UNICEF	United Nations Children's Fund.
UNIDO	United Nations Industrial Development Organization.
Unita	National Union for the Total Independence of Angola.
UPU	Universal Postal Union.
US(A)	United States (of America).
USDAW	Union of Shop, Distributive and Allied Workers.
USM	Unlisted Securities Market.
USSR	Union of Soviet Socialist Republics.

V

v	(*versus*) against.
VA	Vicar Apostolic; Victoria and Albert Order.
VAD	Voluntary Aid Detachment.
VAT	Value added tax.
VC	Victoria Cross.
VD	Venereal disease; Volunteer Officers' Decoration.
VDU	Visual display unit.
Ven	Venerable.
VHF	very high frequency.
VIP	Very important person.
Vo	(*Verso*) on the left-hand page.
VRD	Royal Naval Volunteer Reserve Officers' Decoration.
VSO	Voluntary Service Overseas.
VTOL	Vertical take-off and landing (*aircraft*).

W

W	West.
WCC	World Council of Churches.
WEA	Workers' Educational Association.
WEU	Western European Union.
WFTU	World Federation of Trade Unions.
WHO	World Health Organization.
WI	West Indies; Women's Institute.
Winton:	of Winchester (*Bishop*).
WIPO	World Intellectual Property Organization.
WMO	World Meteorological Organization.
WO	Warrant Officer.
WRAC	Women's Royal Army Corps.
WRAF	Women's Royal Air Force.
WRNS	Women's Royal Naval Service.
WRVS	Women's Royal Voluntary Service.
WS	Writer to the Signet.

Y

YMCA	Young Men's Christian Association.
YWCA	Young Women's Christian Association.

Z

ZANU	Zimbabwe African National Union.

CALENDAR FOR THE YEAR 1991

	January		February		March		April
Su.	.. — 6 13 20 27	.. — 3 10 17 24	Su.	— 3 10 17 24 31	M.	.. — 7 14 21 28	.. — 7 14 21 28
M.	.. — 7 14 21 28	.. — 4 11 18 25	M.	— 4 11 18 25 —	.. 1 8 15 22 29
Tu.	.. 1 8 15 22 29	.. — 5 12 19 26	Tu.	— 5 12 19 26 —	.. 2 9 16 23 30
W.	.. 2 9 16 23 30	.. — 6 13 20 27	W.	— 6 13 20 27 —	.. 3 10 17 24 —
Th.	.. 3 10 17 24 31	.. — 7 14 21 28	Th.	— 7 14 21 28 —	.. 4 11 18 25 —
F.	.. 4 11 18 25 —	.. 1 8 15 22 —	F.	1 8 15 22 29 —	.. 5 12 19 26 —
S.	.. 5 12 19 26 —	.. 2 9 16 23 —	S.	2 9 16 23 30 —	.. 6 13 20 27 —

	May		June		July		August
Su.	.. — 5 12 19 26	— 2 9 16 23 30	Su.	.. — 7 14 21 28	— 4 11 18 25
M.	.. — 6 13 20 27	— 3 10 17 24 —	M.	.. 1 8 15 22 29	— 5 12 19 26
Tu.	.. — 7 14 21 28	— 4 11 18 25 —	Tu.	.. 2 9 16 23 30	— 6 13 20 27
W.	.. 1 8 15 22 29	— 5 12 19 26 —	W.	.. 3 10 17 24 31	— 7 14 21 28
Th.	.. 2 9 16 23 30	— 6 13 20 27 —	Th.	.. 4 11 18 25 —	1 8 15 22 29
F.	.. 3 10 17 24 31	— 7 14 21 28 —	F.	.. 5 12 19 26 —	2 9 16 23 30
S.	.. 4 11 18 25 —	1 8 15 22 29 —	S.	.. 6 13 20 27 —	3 10 17 24 31

	September		October		November		December
Su.	.. 1 8 15 22 29	.. — 6 13 20 27	Su.	— 3 10 17 24	.. 1 8 15 22 29
M.	.. 2 9 16 23 30	.. — 7 14 21 28	M.	— 4 11 18 25	.. 2 9 16 23 30
Tu.	.. 3 10 17 24 —	.. 1 8 15 22 29	Tu.	— 5 12 19 26	.. 3 10 17 24 31
W.	.. 4 11 18 25 —	.. 2 9 16 23 30	W.	— 6 13 20 27	.. 4 11 18 25 —
Th.	.. 5 12 19 26 —	.. 3 10 17 24 31	Th.	— 7 14 21 28	.. 5 12 19 26 —
F.	.. 6 13 20 27 —	.. 4 11 18 25 —	F.	1 8 15 22 29	.. 6 13 20 27 —
S.	.. 7 14 21 28 —	.. 5 12 19 26 —	S.	2 9 16 23 30	.. 7 14 21 28 —

CALENDAR FOR THE YEAR 1992

	January		February		March		April
Su.	.. — 5 12 19 26	.. — 2 9 16 23	Su.	1 8 15 22 29	.. — 5 12 19 26
M.	.. — 6 13 20 27	.. — 3 10 17 24	M.	.. 2 9 16 23 30	— 6 13 20 27
Tu.	.. — 7 14 21 28	.. — 4 11 18 25	Tu.	.. 3 10 17 24 31	— 7 14 21 28
W.	.. 1 8 15 22 29	.. — 5 12 19 26	W.	.. 4 11 18 25 —	1 8 15 22 29
Th.	.. 2 9 16 23 30	.. — 6 13 20 27	Th.	.. 5 12 19 26 —	2 9 16 23 30
F.	.. 3 10 17 24 31	.. — 7 14 21 28	F.	.. 6 13 20 27 —	3 10 17 24 —
S.	.. 4 11 18 25 —	.. 1 8 15 22 29	S.	.. 7 14 21 28 —	4 11 18 25 —

	May		June		July		August
Su.	— 3 10 17 24 31	.. — 7 14 21 28	Su.	.. — 5 12 19 26	2 9 16 23 30
M.	.. 4 11 18 25 —	.. 1 8 15 22 29	M.	.. — 6 13 20 27	3 10 17 24 31
Tu.	.. 5 12 19 26 —	.. 2 9 16 23 30	Tu.	.. — 7 14 21 28	4 11 18 25 —
W.	.. 6 13 20 27 —	.. 3 10 17 24 —	W.	.. 1 8 15 22 29	5 12 19 26 —
Th.	.. 7 14 21 28 —	.. 4 11 18 25 —	Th.	.. 2 9 16 23 30	6 13 20 27 —
F.	1 8 15 22 29 —	.. 5 12 19 26 —	F.	.. 3 10 17 24 31	— 7 14 21 28 —
S.	2 9 16 23 30 —	.. 6 13 20 27 —	S.	.. 4 11 18 25 —	1 8 15 22 29 —

	September		October		November		December
Su.	— 6 13 20 27	.. — 4 11 18 25	Su.	1 8 15 22 29	.. — 6 13 20 27
M.	— 7 14 21 28	.. — 5 12 19 26	M.	2 9 16 23 30	.. — 7 14 21 28
Tu.	1 8 15 22 29	.. — 6 13 20 27	Tu.	3 10 17 24 —	.. 1 8 15 22 29
W.	2 9 16 23 30	.. — 7 14 21 28	W.	4 11 18 25 —	.. 2 9 16 23 30
Th.	3 10 17 24 —	.. 1 8 15 22 29	Th.	5 12 19 26 —	.. 3 10 17 24 31
F.	4 11 18 25 —	.. 2 9 16 23 30	F.	6 13 20 27 —	.. 4 11 18 25 —
S.	5 12 19 26 —	.. 3 10 17 24 31	S.	7 14 21 28 —	.. 5 12 19 26 —

PUBLIC HOLIDAYS

	1991			1992		
	ENGLAND & WALES	SCOTLAND	N. IRELAND	ENGLAND & WALES	SCOTLAND	N. IRELAND
New Year	Jan. 1	Jan. 1, 2	Jan. 1	Jan. 1	Jan. 1, 2	Jan. 1
St. Patrick's Day	—	—	March 18	—	—	March 17
Good Friday	March 29*	March 29	March 29*	April 17*	April 17	April 17*
Easter Monday..	April 1	—	April 1	April 20	—	April 20
May Day	May 6	May 6	May 6	May 4	May 4	May 4
Spring	May 27	May 6	May 27	May 25	May 4	May 25
Battle of Boyne	—	—	July 12	—	—	July 13
Summer........	Aug. 26	Aug. 5	Aug. 26	Aug. 31	Aug. 3	Aug. 31
Christmas	Dec. 25*, 26	Dec. 25, 26	Dec. 25*, 26	Dec. 25*, 26	Dec. 25, 26	Dec. 25*, 26

* In England, Wales, and Northern Ireland, Christmas Day and Good Friday are common law holidays.
In the CHANNEL ISLANDS Liberation Day (May 9) is a bank and public holiday.

NOTES FOR THE YEAR 1991

BEING THE THIRD YEAR AFTER
BISSEXTILE OR LEAP YEAR

Dominical Letter		F
Solar Cycle		12
Epact		14
Roman Indiction		14
Golden Number (Lunar Cycle)		XVI
Julian Period		6,704
Julian Day, Jan. 1 (begins at noon)		2,448,258
New Year's Day		Jan. 1
Ancient Chinese New Year (Sheep or Goat)		Feb. 15
Accession of HM The Queen (1952)		Feb. 6
Duke of York's Birthday (1960)		Feb. 19
St. David's Day		March 1
Prince Edward's Birthday (1964)		March 10
Commonwealth Day		March 11
St. Patrick's Day		March 17

Birthday of HM The Queen (1926)		April 21
St. George's Day		April 23
Coronation of HM The Queen (1953)		June 2
Duke of Edinburgh's Birthday (1921)		June 10
Queen's Official Birthday		June 15
Prince William of Wales' Birthday (1982)		June 21
Princess of Wales' Birthday (1961)		July 1
Queen Elizabeth the Queen Mother's Birthday (1900)		Aug. 4
Princess Royal's Birthday (1950)		Aug. 15
Princess Margaret's Birthday (1930)		Aug. 21
Prince Henry of Wales' Birthday (1984)		Sept. 15
Lord Mayor's Day		Nov. 9
Remembrance Sunday		Nov. 10
Prince of Wales' Birthday (1948)		Nov. 14
Wedding Day of HM The Queen (1947)		Nov. 20
St. Andrew's Day		Nov. 30

SEASONS 1991

Northern Hemisphere

					d	h	
Spring Equinox	Sun enters Sign Aries				March 21	03	
Summer Solstice	"	"	"	Cancer	June 21	21	GMT
Autumn Equinox	"	"	"	Libra	Sept. 23	13	
Winter Solstice	"	"	"	Capricornus	Dec. 22	09	

Southern Hemisphere

					d	h	
Autumn Equinox	Sun enters Sign Aries				March 21	03	
Winter Solstice	"	"	"	Cancer	June 21	21	GMT
Spring Equinox	"	"	"	Libra	Sept. 23	13	
Summer Solstice	"	"	"	Capricornus	Dec. 22	09	

British Summer Time in 1991 begins March 31d 01h GMT and ends on October 27d 01h GMT.

RELIGIOUS CALENDARS 1991

Epiphany		Jan. 6		
Ash Wednesday		Feb. 13		
Ramadan, first day		March 17		
Good Friday		March 29		
Passover, first day		March 30		
Easter Day		March 31		
Greek Orthodox Easter		April 7		
Rogation Sunday		May 5		
Ascension Day		May 9		
Feast of Weeks, first day		May 19		

Pentecost (Whit Sunday)		May 19
Trinity Sunday		May 26
Corpus Christi		May 30
Islamic New Year (1412)		July 13
Jewish New Year (5752)		Sept. 9
Day of Atonement (Yom Kippur)		Sept. 18
Feast of Tabernacles, first day		Sept. 23
First Sunday in Advent		Dec. 1
Christmas Day		Dec. 25

LAW TERMS 1991

Hilary Term begins Jan. 11 and ends March 27
Easter Term begins April 9 and ends May 24
Trinity Term begins June 4 and ends July 31
Michaelmas Term begins Oct. 1 and ends Dec. 21

QUARTER DAYS
(England, Wales, N. Ireland)

Lady Day	March 25
Midsummer	June 24
Michaelmas	Sept. 29
Christmas	Dec. 25

TERM DAYS
(Scotland)

Candlemas	Feb. 28
Whitsunday	May 28
Lammas	Aug. 28
Martinmas	Nov. 28
(*Removal Terms* are May 28 and Nov. 28).	

(*See* **Time Measurement and Calendars** sections for explanatory notes)

DAY OF		
Month	Week	

Janus, god of the portal, facing two ways, past and future.

Sun's Longitude 300° ♒ 20ᵈ 14ʰ

1	Tu.	**Naming of Jesus.** E.M. Forster *b.* 1879.
2	W.	Sir Michael Tippett *b.* 1905.
3	Th.	Clement Attlee *b.* 1883. J.R.R. Tolkien *b.* 1892.
4	F.	Albert Camus *d.* 1960. Donald Campbell *d.* 1967.
5	S.	Amy Johnson *d.* 1941.
6	S.	**The Epiphany.** Joan of Arc *b.* 1412.
7	M.	1st Balloon Crossing of English Channel 1785.
8	Tu.	Galileo *d.* 1642. Lord Baden-Powell *d.* 1941.
9	W.	Simone de Beauvoir *b.* 1908. Katherine Mansfield
10	Th.	League of Nations Founded 1920. [*b.* 1923.
11	F.	HILARY LAW SITTINGS BEGIN.
12	S.	Charles Perrault *b.* 1628. Edmund Burke *b.* 1729.
13	S.	**1st S. after Epiphany.** James Joyce *d.* 1941.
14	M.	Harold Abrahams *d.* 1978.
15	Tu.	British Museum opened 1759. Martin Luther King
16	W.	Léo Delibes *d.* 1891*. Toscanini *d.* 1957. [*b.* 1929.
17	Th.	David Lloyd George *b.* 1863.
18	F.	Capt. Scott reached South Pole 1912.
19	S.	Edgar Allen Poe *b.* 1809. Cézanne *b.* 1839.
20	S.	**2nd S. after Epiphany.** David Garrick *d.* 1779.
21	M.	Lenin *d.* 1924. Jack Nicklaus *b.* 1940.
22	Tu.	Queen Victoria *d.* 1901. Balanchine *b.* 1904 NS.
23	W.	Anna Pavlova *d.* 1931. Edvard Munch *d.* 1944.
24	Th.	Vanbrugh *bapt.* 1664. William Congreve *b.* 1670.
25	F.	**Conversion of St. Paul.** Virginia Woolf *b.* 1882.
26	S.	Gen. Gordon *b.* 1885. Jacqueline du Pré *b.* 1945.
27	S.	**9th S. before Easter.** Lewis Carroll *b.* 1832.
28	M.	Henry VIII *d.* 1547. Fyodor Dostoevsky *d.* 1881 NS.
29	Tu.	Delius *b.* 1862. H.E. Bates *d.* 1974.
30	W.	Charles I *exec.* 1649. Orville Wright *d.* 1948.
31	Th.	Guy Fawkes *exec.* 1606. A.A. Milne *d.* 1956.

*Centenary　　NS New Style

PHENOMENA

d	h	
1	20	Saturn in conjunction with Venus. Saturn 1°N.
2	22	Jupiter in conjunction with Moon. Jupiter 2°N.
3	03	Earth at perihelion (147 million km)
5	03	Neptune in conjunction with Sun.
13	20	Mercury in conjunction with Moon. Mercury 4°N.
14	09	Mercury at greatest elongation W.24°.
16	04	Saturn in conjunction with Moon. Saturn 0°.1S.
17	16	Venus in conjunction with Moon. Venus 3°S.
18	08	Saturn in conjunction with Sun.
25	14	Mars in conjunction with Moon. Mars 2°S.
29	00	Jupiter at opposition.
30	04	Jupiter in conjunction with Moon. Jupiter 2°N.

CONSTELLATIONS

The following constellations are near the meridian at

	d	h		d	h
Dec.	1	24	Dec.	16	23
Jan.	1	22	Jan.	16	21
Feb.	1	20	Feb.	15	19

Draco (below the Pole), Ursa Minor (below the Pole), Camelopardus, Perseus, Auriga, Taurus, Orion, Eridanus and Lepus.

MINIMA OF ALGOL

d	h	d	h
2	20	20	01
5	17	22	22
8	14	25	19
11	11	28	16
14	08	31	13
17	05		

MOON
Phases, Apsides & Node

	d	h	m
☾ Last Quarter	7	18	35
● New Moon	15	23	50
☽ First Quarter	23	14	22
○ Full Moon	30	6	10
Apogee (406,037 km)	12	10	57
Perigee (361,980 km)	28	8	34

Mean Longitude of Ascending Node on Jan. 1, 299°.

MONTHLY NOTES

Jan. 1. Bank Holiday in England, Wales, Scotland and Northern Ireland.

2. Bank Holiday, Scotland.

26. Australia Day. Republic Day, India.

(*See* page 64 for explanatory notes)

Day	Right Ascension	Dec. −	Equation of Time	Rise 52°	Rise 56°	Transit	Set 52°	Set 56°	Sidereal Time	Transit of First Point of Aries
	h m s	° ′	m s	h m	h m	h m	h m	h m	h m s	h m s
1	18 43 45	23 04	− 3 09	8 08	8 31	12 03	15 59	15 36	6 40 36	17 16 34
2	18 48 10	22 59	− 3 38	8 08	8 31	12 04	16 00	15 37	6 44 32	17 12 38
3	18 52 35	22 53	− 4 06	8 08	8 31	12 04	16 01	15 38	6 48 29	17 08 42
4	18 56 59	22 48	− 4 33	8 08	8 30	12 05	16 02	15 39	6 52 25	17 04 46
5	19 01 23	22 42	− 5 01	8 07	8 30	12 05	16 03	15 41	6 56 22	17 00 50
6	19 05 46	22 35	− 5 27	8 07	8 29	12 06	16 05	15 42	7 00 19	16 56 54
7	19 10 09	22 28	− 5 54	8 07	8 29	12 06	16 06	15 44	7 04 15	16 52 59
8	19 14 31	22 20	− 6 20	8 06	8 28	12 07	16 07	15 45	7 08 12	16 49 03
9	19 18 53	22 12	− 6 45	8 06	8 27	12 07	16 08	15 47	7 12 08	16 45 07
10	19 23 15	22 04	− 7 10	8 05	8 27	12 07	16 10	15 48	7 16 05	16 41 11
11	19 27 36	21 55	− 7 35	8 05	8 26	12 08	16 11	15 50	7 20 01	16 37 15
12	19 31 56	21 46	− 7 59	8 04	8 25	12 08	16 13	15 52	7 23 58	16 33 19
13	19 36 16	21 36	− 8 22	8 03	8 24	12 09	16 14	15 54	7 27 54	16 29 23
14	19 40 36	21 26	− 8 45	8 02	8 23	12 09	16 16	15 55	7 31 51	16 25 27
15	19 44 54	21 15	− 9 07	8 02	8 22	12 09	16 17	15 57	7 35 48	16 21 31
16	19 49 12	21 04	− 9 28	8 01	8 21	12 10	16 19	15 59	7 39 44	16 17 35
17	19 53 30	20 53	− 9 49	8 00	8 20	12 10	16 21	16 01	7 43 41	16 13 39
18	19 57 46	20 41	−10 09	7 59	8 18	12 10	16 22	16 03	7 47 37	16 09 43
19	20 02 02	20 29	−10 28	7 58	8 17	12 11	16 24	16 05	7 51 34	16 05 48
20	20 06 17	20 17	−10 47	7 57	8 16	12 11	16 26	16 07	7 55 30	16 01 52
21	20 10 32	20 04	−11 05	7 56	8 14	12 11	16 27	16 09	7 59 27	15 57 56
22	20 14 45	19 50	−11 22	7 55	8 13	12 12	16 29	16 11	8 03 23	15 54 00
23	20 18 58	19 37	−11 38	7 53	8 11	12 12	16 31	16 13	8 07 20	15 50 04
24	20 23 10	19 23	−11 54	7 52	8 10	12 12	16 32	16 15	8 11 17	15 46 08
25	20 27 21	19 08	−12 08	7 51	8 08	12 12	16 34	16 17	8 15 13	15 42 12
26	20 31 32	18 54	−12 22	7 50	8 07	12 12	16 36	16 19	8 19 10	15 38 16
27	20 35 41	18 38	−12 35	7 48	8 05	12 13	16 38	16 21	8 23 06	15 34 20
28	20 39 50	18 23	−12 48	7 47	8 03	12 13	16 40	16 23	8 27 03	15 30 24
29	20 43 58	18 07	−12 59	7 45	8 01	12 13	16 41	16 25	8 30 59	15 26 28
30	20 48 05	17 51	−13 10	7 44	8 00	12 13	16 43	16 28	8 34 56	15 22 33
31	20 52 12	17 35	−13 19	7 42	7 58	12 13	16 45	16 30	8 38 52	15 18 37

Duration of Civil (C), Nautical (N) and Astronomical (A) Twilight (in minutes)

Lat. °	Jan. 1 C	N	A	Jan. 11 C	N	A	Jan. 21 C	N	A	Jan. 31 C	N	A
52	41	84	125	40	82	123	38	80	120	37	78	117
56	47	96	141	45	93	138	43	90	134	41	87	130

ASTRONOMICAL NOTES

MERCURY, despite the fact that it is at greatest western elongation on the 14th, is unsuitably placed for observation.

VENUS, magnitude − 3.9, is visible in the evenings but will only be seen for a short while after sunset, low above the south-western horizon. It is slowly moving out from the Sun but even by the end of the month it is not visible for much more than an hour after sunset. On the evening of the 17th the thin crescent Moon, less than 2 days old, passes 3°N. of the planet.

MARS, its magnitude fading from −1.0 to −0.1 during January, is a prominent evening object visible through to about 03h even by the end of the month.

Mars reaches a stationary point on the 1st and then moves slowly eastward. Mars is in Taurus between the Pleiades and the Hyades. The gibbous Moon is near the planet on the 25th.

JUPITER, magnitude −2·6, is at opposition on the 29th and therefore visible throughout the hours of darkness. Jupiter is a brilliant object in Cancer. On the evening of the 2nd and again on the 29th the Full Moon passes 2°S. of the planet.

SATURN is unsuitably placed for observation, conjunction occurring on the 18th.

ECLIPSE. An annular eclipse of the Sun occurs on the 15th–16th. See page 74 for details.

(See pages 64–65 for explanatory notes)

THE MOON

Day	RA	Dec.	Hor. Par.	Semi-diam.	Sun's Co-long.	P.A. of Bright Limb	Phase	Age	Rise 52°	Rise 56°	Transit	Set 52°	Set 56°
	h m	°	′	′	°	°	%	d	h m	h m	h m	h m	h m
1	6 58	+24·1	61·1	16·7	91	73	100	14·8	16 59	16 35	0 18	8 50	9 14
2	8 01	+20·5	60·6	16·5	103	102	98	15·8	18 29	18 13	1 20	9 20	9 38
3	9 00	+15·7	59·9	16·3	115	109	93	16·8	19 56	19 46	2 16	9 42	9 54
4	9 54	+10·1	59·0	16·1	127	112	86	17·8	21 19	21 15	3 08	9 59	10 06
5	10 44	+ 4·1	58·0	15·8	139	114	77	18·8	22 37	22 39	3 55	10 14	10 15
6	11 32	− 1·8	57·1	15·5	152	115	68	19·8	23 53	23 59	4 40	10 28	10 24
7	12 19	− 7·4	56·2	15·3	164	114	58	20·8	—	—	5 24	10 42	10 33
8	13 05	−12·6	55·4	15·1	176	112	48	21·8	1 07	1 19	6 08	10 57	10 43
9	13 52	−17·1	54·8	14·9	188	109	38	22·8	2 20	2 37	6 52	11 15	10 56
10	14 40	−20·9	54·4	14·8	200	105	29	23·8	3 32	3 55	7 38	11 38	11 14
11	15 30	−23·8	54·1	14·8	212	101	21	24·8	4 41	5 09	8 26	12 07	11 39
12	16 21	−25·6	54·0	14·7	224	95	14	25·8	5 43	6 15	9 16	12 47	12 14
13	17 14	−26·3	54·0	14·7	237	89	8	26·8	6 37	7 10	10 06	13 37	13 04
14	18 07	−25·8	54·1	14·8	249	83	4	27·8	7 20	7 50	10 57	14 38	14 08
15	18 59	−24·1	54·3	14·8	261	77	1	28·8	7 53	8 19	11 46	15 46	15 21
16	19 50	−21·3	54·6	14·9	273	333	0	0·0	8 18	8 38	12 34	16 59	16 40
17	20 39	−17·5	55·0	15·0	285	251	1	1·0	8 38	8 53	13 20	18 13	18 00
18	21 27	−13·0	55·4	15·1	298	247	4	2·0	8 54	9 04	14 04	19 27	19 19
19	22 13	− 7·8	55·8	15·2	310	245	9	3·0	9 08	9 13	14 48	20 42	20 39
20	22 59	− 2·3	56·3	15·3	322	244	15	4·0	9 21	9 21	15 31	21 57	21 59
21	23 46	+ 3·5	56·9	15·5	334	244	23	5·0	9 35	9 30	16 16	23 15	23 22
22	0 34	+ 9·1	57·5	15·7	346	245	33	6·0	9 50	9 40	17 03	—	—
23	1 24	+14·5	58·1	15·8	358	247	44	7·0	10 08	9 53	17 54	0 35	0 49
24	2 18	+19·3	58·8	16·0	11	251	55	8·0	10 33	10 11	18 49	1 59	2 19
25	3 16	+23·1	59·4	16·2	23	256	66	9·0	11 07	10 39	19 49	3 23	3 50
26	4 18	+25·6	59·9	16·3	35	263	76	10·0	11 55	11 23	20 52	4 43	5 15
27	5 23	+26·3	60·3	16·4	47	270	86	11·0	13 01	12 29	21 57	5 50	6 22
28	6 29	+25·2	60·6	16·5	59	276	93	12·0	14 23	13 56	22 59	6 41	7 09
29	7 33	+22·4	60·5	16·5	71	281	98	13·0	15 52	15 32	23 58	7 17	7 38
30	8 33	+18·0	60·2	16·4	83	272	100	14·0	17 22	17 08	—	7 43	7 58
31	9 29	+12·7	59·7	16·3	96	120	99	15·0	18 48	18 41	0 52	8 02	8 12

MERCURY

Day	RA	Dec. −	Diam.	Phase	Transit		Day	RA	Dec. −	Diam.	Phase	Transit	
	h m	°			h m			h m	°			h m	
1	17 36	20·2	—	—	10 53		16	18 08	22·2	—	—	10 28	
4	17 33	20·3	—	—	10 39	Mercury is too	19	18 22	22·5	—	—	10 31	Mercury is too
7	17 36	20·7	—	—	10 31	close to the	22	18 39	22·8	—	—	10 36	close to the
10	17 44	21·2	—	—	10 27	Sun for	25	18 56	22·9	—	—	10 41	Sun for
13	17 54	21·7	—	—	10 27	observation	28	19 14	22·8	—	—	10 48	observation
16	18 08	22·2	—	—	10 28		31	19 32	22·6	—	—	10 54	

VENUS

Day	RA	Dec. −	Diam.	Phase	Transit	5° high. 52°	5° high. 56°
	h m	°	″	%	h m	h m	h m
1	19 48	22·4	10	97	13 08	16 17	15 44
6	20 14	21·3	10	96	13 15	16 34	16 04
11	20 40	19·9	10	96	13 21	16 51	16 25
16	21 06	18·2	10	95	13 27	17 09	16 46
21	21 31	16·4	11	95	13 32	17 28	17 07
26	21 55	14·3	11	94	13 37	17 46	17 29
31	22 19	12·1	11	93	13 41	18 04	17 49

MARS

Day	RA	Dec. +	Diam.	Phase	Transit	5° high. 52°	5° high. 56°
	h m	°	″	%	h m	h m	h m
1	3 40	21·9	14	95	20 56	4 24	4 40
6	3 40	22·0	13	94	20 37	4 05	4 21
11	3 42	22·1	12	93	20 19	3 48	4 04
16	3 45	22·3	12	93	20 03	3 32	3 49
21	3 49	22·5	11	92	19 47	3 18	3 35
26	3 54	22·7	11	91	19 33	3 05	3 22
31	4 00	23·0	10	91	19 19	2 53	3 10

(*See* pages 65–66 for explanatory notes)

SUNRISE AND SUNSET

Day	London 0°05' 51°30'		Bristol 2°35' 51°28'		Birmingham 1°55' 52°28'		Manchester 2°15' 53°28'		Newcastle 1°37' 54°59'		Glasgow 4°14' 55°52'		Belfast 5°56' 54°35'	
	h m	h m	h m	h m	h m	h m	h m	h m	h m	h m	h m	h m	h m	h m
1	8 06	16 02	8 16	16 12	8 18	16 04	8 25	16 00	8 31	15 49	8 47	15 53	8 46	16 08
2	8 06	16 03	8 16	16 13	8 18	16 05	8 25	16 01	8 31	15 50	8 47	15 55	8 46	16 09
3	8 06	16 04	8 16	16 14	8 18	16 06	8 25	16 02	8 31	15 51	8 47	15 56	8 46	16 11
4	8 06	16 05	8 15	16 15	8 18	16 07	8 24	16 03	8 31	15 52	8 46	15 57	8 45	16 12
5	8 05	16 06	8 15	16 16	8 17	16 09	8 24	16 05	8 30	15 54	8 46	15 59	8 45	16 13
6	8 05	16 07	8 15	16 17	8 17	16 10	8 24	16 06	8 30	15 55	8 46	16 00	8 45	16 15
7	8 05	16 09	8 14	16 19	8 17	16 11	8 23	16 07	8 29	15 56	8 45	16 01	8 44	16 16
8	8 04	16 10	8 14	16 20	8 16	16 13	8 23	16 09	8 29	15 58	8 44	16 03	8 43	16 17
9	8 04	16 11	8 14	16 21	8 16	16 14	8 22	16 10	8 28	15 59	8 44	16 05	8 43	16 19
10	8 03	16 13	8 13	16 23	8 15	16 15	8 21	16 12	8 27	16 01	8 43	16 06	8 42	16 20
11	8 03	16 14	8 12	16 24	8 14	16 17	8 21	16 13	8 26	16 03	8 42	16 08	8 41	16 22
12	8 02	16 15	8 12	16 26	8 14	16 18	8 20	16 15	8 26	16 04	8 41	16 10	8 41	16 24
13	8 01	16 17	8 11	16 27	8 13	16 20	8 19	16 16	8 25	16 06	8 40	16 11	8 40	16 25
14	8 01	16 18	8 10	16 29	8 12	16 21	8 18	16 18	8 24	16 08	8 39	16 13	8 39	16 27
15	8 00	16 20	8 10	16 30	8 11	16 23	8 17	16 20	8 23	16 09	8 38	16 15	8 38	16 29
16	7 59	16 21	8 09	16 32	8 11	16 25	8 17	16 21	8 22	16 11	8 37	16 17	8 37	16 30
17	7 58	16 23	8 08	16 33	8 10	16 26	8 16	16 23	8 21	16 13	8 36	16 19	8 36	16 32
18	7 57	16 25	8 07	16 35	8 09	16 28	8 14	16 25	8 19	16 15	8 34	16 21	8 35	16 34
19	7 56	16 26	8 06	16 36	8 08	16 30	8 13	16 26	8 18	16 17	8 33	16 22	8 33	16 36
20	7 55	16 28	8 05	16 38	8 06	16 31	8 12	16 28	8 17	16 18	8 32	16 24	8 32	16 38
21	7 54	16 30	8 04	16 40	8 05	16 33	8 11	16 30	8 16	16 20	8 30	16 26	8 31	16 40
22	7 53	16 31	8 03	16 41	8 04	16 35	8 10	16 32	8 14	16 22	8 29	16 28	8 30	16 41
23	7 52	16 33	8 02	16 43	8 03	16 37	8 08	16 34	8 13	16 24	8 28	16 30	8 28	16 43
24	7 51	16 35	8 00	16 45	8 02	16 38	8 07	16 35	8 11	16 26	8 26	16 33	8 27	16 45
25	7 49	16 36	7 59	16 47	8 00	16 40	8 06	16 37	8 10	16 28	8 24	16 35	8 25	16 47
26	7 48	16 38	7 58	16 48	7 59	16 42	8 04	16 39	8 08	16 30	8 23	16 37	8 24	16 49
27	7 47	16 40	7 57	16 50	7 58	16 44	8 03	16 41	8 07	16 32	8 21	16 39	8 22	16 51
28	7 45	16 42	7 55	16 52	7 56	16 46	8 01	16 43	8 05	16 34	8 19	16 41	8 21	16 53
29	7 44	16 44	7 54	16 54	7 55	16 47	8 00	16 45	8 03	16 36	8 18	16 43	8 19	16 55
30	7 42	16 45	7 52	16 55	7 53	16 49	7 58	16 47	8 02	16 38	8 16	16 45	8 17	16 57
31	7 41	16 47	7 51	16 57	7 52	16 51	7 57	16 49	8 00	16 40	8 14	16 47	8 16	16 59

JUPITER

Day	RA	Dec. +	Transit	5° high	
				52°	56°
	h m	° '	h m	h m	h m
1	8 58·6	17 51	2 18	19 13	19 01
11	8 54·2	18 11	1 34	18 28	18 15
21	8 49·2	18 33	0 50	17 41	17 29
31	8 43·8	18 55	0 05	16 54	16 41

Diameters—equatorial 45"; polar 43"

SATURN

Day	RA	Dec. −	Transit	
	h m	° '	h m	
1	19 50·7	21 09	13 08	Saturn is too
11	19 55·6	20 57	12 34	close to the
21	20 00·6	20 43	11 59	Sun for
31	20 05·6	20 30	11 25	observation

Diameters—equatorial 15" polar 14"
Rings—major axis 34" minor axis 13"

URANUS

Day	RA	Dec. −	Transit	
	h m	° '	h m	
1	18 42·4	23 24	12 00	Uranus is too
11	18 45·0	23 22	11 23	close to the Sun
21	18 47·6	23 19	10 46	for observation
31	18 50·0	23 16	10 10	

Diameter 4"

NEPTUNE

Day	RA	Dec. −	Transit	
	h m	° '	h m	
1	19 01·0	21 54	12 18	Neptune is too
11	19 02·6	21 52	11 41	close to the Sun
21	19 04·2	21 50	11 03	for observation
31	19 05·7	21 47	10 25	

Diameter 2"

(*See* page 66 for explanatory notes)

Februa, Roman festival
of Purification
Sun's Longitude 330°)(19ᵈ 04ʰ

Month	Week	
1	F.	Stanley Matthews *b*. 1915. Buster Keaton *d*. 1966.
2	S.	**Presentation of Christ.** Bertrand Russell *d*. 1970.
3	S.	**8th S. before Easter.** Mendelssohn *b*. 1809.
4	M.	Yalta Conference opened 1945.
5	Tu.	Sir Robert Peel *b*. 1788.
6	W.	QUEEN'S ACCESSION 1952. Fred Trueman *b*. 1931.
7	Th.	Thomas More *b*. 1478. Charles Dickens *b*. 1812.
8	F.	Mary, Queen of Scots *exec*. 1587.
9	S.	Jim Laker *b*. 1922.
10	S.	**7th S. before Easter.** Joseph Lister *d*. 1912.
11	M.	Thomas Edison *b*. 1847. John Surtees *b*. 1934.
12	Tu.	SHROVE TUESDAY. Lady Jane Grey *exec*. 1554.
13	W.	**Ash Wednesday.** Glencoe Massacre 1692.
14	Th.	VALENTINE'S DAY. Kevin Keegan *b*. 1951.
15	F.	Glinka *d*. 1857. Graham Hill *b*. 1929.
16	S.	Geraint Evans *b*. 1922. John McEnroe *b*. 1959.
17	S.	**1st S. in Lent.** Heinrich Heine *d*. 1856.
18	M.	Martin Luther *d*. 1546. Ngaio Marsh *d*. 1982.
19	Tu.	DUKE OF YORK *b*. 1960. André Gide *d*. 1951.
20	W.	Marie Rambert *b*. 1888. Enzo Ferrari *b*. 1898.
21	Th.	Andrés Segovia *b*. 1893. Douglas Bader *b*. 1910.
22	F.	John Mills *b*. 1908. Niki Lauda *b*. 1949.
23	S.	Handel *b*. 1685. Elgar *d*. 1934.
24	S.	**2nd S. in Lent.** Wilhelm Grimm *b*. 1786.
25	M.	Christopher Wren *d*. 1723. Tennessee Williams *d*. 1983.
26	Tu.	Victor Hugo *b*. 1802. Everton Weekes *b*. 1925.
27	W.	Longfellow *b*. 1807. John Steinbeck *b*. 1902.
28	Th.	John Tenniel *b*. 1820. Henry James *d*. 1916.

PHENOMENA

	d	h	
	5	21	Saturn in conjunction with Mercury. Saturn 1°N.
	12	18	Saturn in conjunction with Moon. Saturn 0°.4S.
	13	16	Mercury in conjunction with Moon. Mercury 3°S.
	16	21	Venus in conjunction with Moon. Venus 5°S.
	22	13	Mars in conjunction with Moon. Mars 2°S.
	26	08	Jupiter in conjunction with Moon. Jupiter 1°N.

CONSTELLATIONS

The following constellations are near the meridian at

	d	h		d	h
Jan.	1	24	Jan.	16	23
Feb.	1	22	Feb.	15	21
Mar.	1	20	Mar.	16	19

Draco (below the Pole), Camelopardus, Auriga, Taurus, Gemini, Orion, Canis Minor, Monoceros, Lepus, Canis Major and Puppis.

MINIMA OF ALGOL

d	h	d	h
3	09	20	14
6	06	23	11
9	03	26	08
12	00		
14	21		
17	18		

MOON
Phases, Apsides & Node

	d	h	m
☾ Last Quarter	6	13	52
● New Moon	14	17	32
☽ First Quarter	21	22	58
○ Full Moon	28	18	25

		d	h	m
Apogee (405,042 km)		9	4	19
Perigee (367,580 km)		25	1	14

Mean Longitude of Ascending Node on Feb. 1, 297°

MONTHLY NOTES

Feb.   1. Pheasant and partridge shooting ends.
       6. National Day, New Zealand.
    13. First day of Lent.
    15. Ancient Chinese New Year (Year of the Sheep or Goat).
    28. Candelmas (Scottish Term Day).

(*See* page 64 for explanatory notes)

Day	THE SUN s.d. 16′·2									Sidereal Time	Transit of First Point of Aries
	Right Ascension	Dec. −	Equation of Time	Rise		Transit	Set				
				52°	56°		52°	56°			
	h m s	° ′	m s	h m	h m	h m	h m	h m		h m s	h m s
1	20 56 17	17 18	−13 28	7 41	7 56	12 14	16 47	16 32		8 42 49	15 14 41
2	21 00 22	17 01	−13 37	7 39	7 54	12 14	16 49	16 34		8 46 46	15 10 45
3	21 04 26	16 44	−13 44	7 38	7 52	12 14	16 51	16 36		8 50 42	15 06 49
4	21 08 29	16 26	−13 50	7 36	7 50	12 14	16 52	16 38		8 54 39	15 02 53
5	21 12 31	16 08	−13 56	7 34	7 48	12 14	16 54	16 41		8 58 35	14 58 57
6	21 16 33	15 50	−14 01	7 33	7 46	12 14	16 56	16 43		9 02 32	14 55 01
7	21 20 34	15 32	−14 05	7 31	7 44	12 14	16 58	16 45		9 06 28	14 51 05
8	21 24 34	15 13	−14 09	7 29	7 42	12 14	17 00	16 47		9 10 25	14 47 09
9	21 28 33	14 54	−14 11	7 27	7 40	12 14	17 02	16 49		9 14 21	14 43 13
10	21 32 31	14 35	−14 13	7 26	7 38	12 14	17 04	16 52		9 18 18	14 39 18
11	21 36 29	14 16	−14 14	7 24	7 35	12 14	17 06	16 54		9 22 15	14 35 22
12	21 40 26	13 56	−14 15	7 22	7 33	12 14	17 07	16 56		9 26 11	14 31 26
13	21 44 22	13 36	−14 14	7 20	7 31	12 14	17 09	16 58		9 30 08	14 27 30
14	21 48 17	13 16	−14 13	7 18	7 29	12 14	17 11	17 00		9 34 04	14 23 34
15	21 52 12	12 55	−14 11	7 16	7 27	12 14	17 13	17 03		9 38 01	14 19 38
16	21 56 06	12 35	−14 08	7 14	7 24	12 14	17 15	17 05		9 41 57	14 15 42
17	21 59 59	12 14	−14 05	7 12	7 22	12 14	17 17	17 07		9 45 54	14 11 46
18	22 03 51	11 53	−14 01	7 10	7 20	12 14	17 19	17 09		9 49 50	14 07 50
19	22 07 43	11 32	−13 56	7 08	7 17	12 14	17 20	17 11		9 53 47	14 03 54
20	22 11 34	11 11	−13 51	7 06	7 15	12 14	17 22	17 14		9 57 44	13 59 58
21	22 15 25	10 49	−13 44	7 04	7 13	12 14	17 24	17 16		10 01 40	13 56 03
22	22 19 14	10 27	−13 38	7 02	7 10	12 14	17 26	17 18		10 05 37	13 52 07
23	22 23 03	10 06	−13 30	7 00	7 08	12 13	17 28	17 20		10 09 33	13 48 11
24	22 26 52	9 44	−13 22	6 58	7 05	12 13	17 30	17 22		10 13 30	13 44 15
25	22 30 39	9 21	−13 13	6 56	7 03	12 13	17 31	17 24		10 17 26	13 40 19
26	22 34 27	8 59	−13 04	6 54	7 00	12 13	17 33	17 27		10 21 23	13 36 22
27	22 38 13	8 37	−12 54	6 51	6 58	12 13	17 35	17 29		10 25 19	13 32 27
28	22 41 59	8 14	−12 43	6 49	6 55	12 13	17 37	17 31		10 29 16	13 28 31

Duration of Civil (C), Nautical (N) and Astronomical (A) Twilight (in minutes)

Lat. °	Feb. 1			Feb. 11			Feb. 21			Feb. 28		
	C	N	A	C	N	A	C	N	A	C	N	A
52	37	77	117	35	75	114	34	74	113	34	73	112
56	41	86	130	39	83	126	38	81	125	38	81	124

ASTRONOMICAL NOTES

MERCURY is unsuitably placed for observation throughout the month.

VENUS continues to be visible as a brilliant evening object, magnitude −3·9. Its rapid motion northward in declination enables it to be visible for a little longer each night, so that by the end of February it is still visible low in the western sky two hours after sunset.

MARS, magnitude +0·2, continues to be visible as a prominent object in the evening sky and even by the end of the month it is visible through to about 02h. Mars is moving eastwards in Taurus, passing 8°N. of Aldebaran on the 22nd, on the same day that it is itself overtaken by the Moon, just after First Quarter.

JUPITER is a splendid object, visible for the greater part of the night. Its magnitude is −2·6. Jupiter is in Cancer. The Moon, near Full, is near the planet on the 25th–26th.

SATURN is too close to the Sun for observation.

ZODIACAL LIGHT. The evening cone may be observed in the western sky after the end of twilight from the beginning of the month until the 15th. This faint phenomenon is only visible under good conditions, in the absence of both moonlight and artificial lighting.

(See pages 64–65 for explanatory notes)

THE MOON

Day	RA	Dec.	Hor. Par.	Semi-diam.	Sun's Co-long.	P.A. of Bright Limb	Phase	Age	Rise 52°	Rise 56°	Transit	Set 52°	Set 56°
	h m	°	′	′	°	°	%	d	h m	h m	h m	h m	h m
1	10 22	+ 6·8	58·9	16·1	108	119	96	16·0	20 11	20 09	1 43	8 19	8 22
2	11 12	+ 0·7	58·1	15·8	120	119	90	17·0	21 30	21 34	2 30	8 33	8 32
3	12 00	− 5·2	57·2	15·6	132	118	83	18·0	22 47	22 56	3 16	8 47	8 41
4	12 48	−10·7	56·4	15·4	144	116	75	19·0	—	—	4 01	9 02	8 51
5	13 36	−15·6	55·6	15·2	156	113	65	20·0	0 02	0 17	4 46	9 19	9 03
6	14 24	−19·8	55·0	15·0	168	109	56	21·0	1 16	1 37	5 32	9 41	9 19
7	15 14	−23·0	54·5	14·9	181	105	46	22·0	2 27	2 53	6 20	10 08	9 41
8	16 06	−25·2	54·2	14·8	193	100	37	23·0	3 33	4 04	7 10	10 43	10 12
9	16 58	−26·2	54·1	14·8	205	94	28	24·0	4 30	5 03	8 00	11 29	10 56
10	17 51	−26·1	54·2	14·8	217	89	20	25·0	5 17	5 49	8 50	12 26	11 55
11	18 43	−24·7	54·4	14·8	229	84	13	26·0	5 54	6 21	9 40	13 32	13 05
12	19 34	−22·2	54·7	14·9	241	80	7	27·0	6 22	6 44	10 29	14 44	14 22
13	20 24	−18·7	55·1	15·0	254	78	3	28·0	6 44	7 00	11 15	15 58	15 42
14	21 13	−14·4	55·5	15·1	266	84	1	29·0	7 01	7 12	12 01	17 13	17 03
15	22 01	− 9·3	56·0	15·3	278	209	0	0·3	7 16	7 23	12 45	18 29	18 24
16	22 47	− 3·8	56·5	15·4	290	234	2	1·3	7 30	7 31	13 30	19 45	19 46
17	23 34	+ 2·0	57·0	15·5	302	238	6	2·3	7 43	7 40	14 15	21 03	21 09
18	0 22	+ 7·8	57·5	15·7	315	241	12	3·3	7 58	7 50	15 01	22 23	22 35
19	1 13	+13·3	57·9	15·8	327	244	19	4·3	8 16	8 02	15 51	23 46	—
20	2 06	+18·2	58·4	15·9	339	248	29	5·3	8 38	8 19	16 44	—	0 04
21	3 02	+22·2	58·8	16·0	351	253	39	6·3	9 08	8 42	17 41	1 09	1 34
22	4 02	+25·0	59·1	16·1	3	259	51	7·3	9 50	9 19	18 42	2 29	2 59
23	5 05	+26·2	59·4	16·2	16	265	62	8·3	10 47	10 15	19 44	3 39	4 11
24	6 08	+25·7	59·6	16·2	28	272	73	9·3	12 01	11 31	20 45	4 34	5 04
25	7 11	+23·5	59·7	16·3	40	278	82	10·3	13 24	13 01	21 44	5 15	5 39
26	8 10	+19·8	59·6	16·2	52	282	90	11·3	14 52	14 35	22 39	5 44	6 01
27	9 07	+14·9	59·3	16·2	64	283	96	12·3	16 18	16 08	23 30	6 05	6 17
28	10 00	+ 9·3	58·9	16·1	76	275	99	13·3	17 42	17 37	—	6 23	6 29

MERCURY

Day	RA	Dec. −	Diam.	Phase	Transit		Day	RA	Dec. −	Diam.	Phase	Transit	
	h m	°			h m			h m	°			h m	
1	19 38	22·4	—	—	10 57		16	21 16	18·0	—	—	11 36	
4	19 58	22·0	—	—	11 04	Mercury is too	19	21 37	16·5	—	—	11 44	Mercury is too
7	20 17	21·3	—	—	11 12	close to the	22	21 57	14·7	—	—	11 53	close to the
10	20 37	20·4	—	—	11 20	Sun for	25	22 17	12·8	—	—	12 01	Sun for
13	20 56	19·3	—	—	11 28	observation	28	22 38	10·7	—	—	12 10	observation
16	21 16	18·0	—	—	11 36		31	22 59	8·4	—	—	12 19	

VENUS   MARS

Day	RA	Dec. −	Diam.	Phase	Transit	5° high. 52°	5° high. 56°	Day	RA	Dec. +	Diam.	Phase	Transit	5° high. 52°	5° high. 56°
	h m	°	″	%	h m	h m	h m		h m	°	″	%	h m	h m	h m
1	22 24	−11·7	11	93	13 42	18 07	17 53	1	4 01	23·0	10	91	19 16	2 50	3 08
6	22 47	− 9·3	11	92	13 45	18 25	18 13	6	4 08	23·3	9	90	19 04	2 39	2 58
11	23 10	− 6·8	11	92	13 48	18 42	18 33	11	4 16	23·6	9	90	18 52	2 29	2 48
16	23 33	− 4·3	11	91	13 51	18 59	18 52	16	4 24	23·9	9	90	18 40	2 19	2 39
21	23 56	− 1·7	11	90	13 54	19 15	19 11	21	4 33	24·2	8	90	18 30	2 10	2 30
26	0 18	+ 0·9	12	89	13 57	19 31	19 29	26	4 42	24·5	8	90	18 19	2 02	2 22
31	0 40	+ 3·5	12	88	13 59	19 47	19 47	31	4 52	24·7	8	90	18 09	1 53	2 14

(*See* pages 65–66 for explanatory notes)

SUNRISE AND SUNSET

Day	London 0°05′ 51°30′		Bristol 2°35′ 51°28′		Birmingham 1°55′ 52°28′		Manchester 2°15′ 53°28′		Newcastle 1°37′ 54°59′		Glasgow 4°14′ 55°52′		Belfast 5°56′ 54°35′	
	h m	h m	h m	h m	h m	h m	h m	h m	h m	h m	h m	h m	h m	h m
1	7 39	16 49	7 49	16 59	7 50	16 53	7 55	16 51	7 58	16 43	8 12	16 49	8 14	17 01
2	7 38	16 51	7 48	17 01	7 48	16 55	7 53	16 53	7 56	16 45	8 10	16 52	8 12	17 03
3	7 36	16 53	7 46	17 03	7 47	16 57	7 52	16 55	7 55	16 47	8 08	16 54	8 10	17 05
4	7 35	16 54	7 45	17 04	7 45	16 59	7 50	16 57	7 53	16 49	8 06	16 56	8 08	17 08
5	7 33	16 56	7 43	17 06	7 43	17 01	7 48	16 59	7 51	16 51	8 04	16 58	8 07	17 10
6	7 31	16 58	7 41	17 08	7 42	17 02	7 46	17 01	7 49	16 53	8 02	17 00	8 05	17 12
7	7 30	17 00	7 40	17 10	7 40	17 04	7 44	17 03	7 47	16 55	8 00	17 02	8 03	17 14
8	7 28	17 02	7 38	17 12	7 38	17 06	7 43	17 05	7 45	16 57	7 58	17 05	8 01	17 16
9	7 26	17 03	7 36	17 14	7 36	17 08	7 41	17 07	7 43	16 59	7 56	17 07	7 59	17 18
10	7 25	17 05	7 34	17 15	7 34	17 10	7 39	17 09	7 41	17 01	7 54	17 09	7 57	17 20
11	7 23	17 07	7 33	17 17	7 33	17 12	7 37	17 11	7 39	17 04	7 52	17 11	7 55	17 22
12	7 21	17 09	7 31	17 19	7 31	17 14	7 35	17 13	7 37	17 06	7 50	17 13	7 53	17 24
13	7 19	17 11	7 29	17 21	7 29	17 16	7 33	17 14	7 34	17 08	7 48	17 16	7 51	17 26
14	7 17	17 13	7 27	17 23	7 27	17 18	7 31	17 16	7 32	17 10	7 45	17 18	7 48	17 28
15	7 15	17 14	7 25	17 25	7 25	17 20	7 29	17 18	7 30	17 12	7 43	17 20	7 46	17 30
16	7 13	17 16	7 23	17 26	7 23	17 21	7 27	17 20	7 28	17 14	7 41	17 22	7 44	17 32
17	7 11	17 18	7 21	17 28	7 21	17 23	7 25	17 22	7 26	17 16	7 39	17 24	7 42	17 34
18	7 09	17 20	7 19	17 30	7 19	17 25	7 22	17 24	7 24	17 18	7 36	17 27	7 40	17 37
19	7 07	17 22	7 17	17 32	7 17	17 27	7 20	17 26	7 21	17 20	7 34	17 29	7 38	17 39
20	7 05	17 24	7 15	17 34	7 15	17 29	7 18	17 28	7 19	17 22	7 32	17 31	7 35	17 41
21	7 03	17 25	7 13	17 35	7 13	17 31	7 16	17 30	7 17	17 25	7 29	17 33	7 33	17 43
22	7 01	17 27	7 11	17 37	7 11	17 33	7 14	17 32	7 14	17 27	7 27	17 35	7 31	17 45
23	6 59	17 29	7 09	17 39	7 08	17 35	7 12	17 34	7 12	17 29	7 24	17 37	7 28	17 47
24	6 57	17 31	7 07	17 41	7 06	17 37	7 09	17 36	7 10	17 31	7 22	17 39	7 26	17 49
25	6 55	17 33	7 05	17 43	7 04	17 38	7 07	17 38	7 07	17 33	7 19	17 42	7 24	17 51
26	6 53	17 34	7 03	17 44	7 02	17 40	7 05	17 40	7 05	17 35	7 17	17 44	7 22	17 53
27	6 51	17 36	7 01	17 46	7 00	17 42	7 03	17 42	7 03	17 37	7 15	17 46	7 19	17 55
28	6 49	17 38	6 59	17 48	6 58	17 44	7 00	17 44	7 00	17 39	7 12	17 48	7 17	17 57

JUPITER

Day	RA	Dec. +	Transit	5° high 52°	5° high 56°
	h m	° ′	h m	h m	h m
1	8 43·3	18 57	0 00	7 17	7 20
11	8 38·0	19 18	23 11	6 24	6 38
21	8 33·1	19 37	22 27	5 42	5 56
31	8 29·2	19 51	21 44	5 00	5 14

Diameters—equatorial 45″ polar 42″

SATURN

Day	RA	Dec. −	Transit	
	h m	° ′	h m	
1	20 06·1	20 28	11 22	Saturn is too
11	20 10·9	20 14	10 47	close to the
21	20 15·5	20 00	10 12	Sun for
31	20 19·9	19 47	9 37	observation

Diameters—equatorial 15″ polar 14″
Rings—major axis 35″ minor axis 12″

URANUS

Day	RA	Dec. −	Transit	
	h m	° ′	h m	
1	18 50·2	23 16	10 06	Uranus is too
11	18 52·5	23 13	9 29	close to the Sun
21	18 54·5	23 11	8 51	for observation
31	18 56·3	23 09	8 14	

Diameter 4″

NEPTUNE

Day	RA	Dec. −	Transit	
	h m	° ′	h m	
1	19 05·9	21 47	10 21	Neptune is too
11	19 07·3	21 45	9 44	close to the Sun
21	19 08·6	21 43	9 06	for observation
31	19 09·7	21 41	8 27	

Diameter 2″

(*See* page 66 for explanatory notes)

DAY OF		
Month	Week	

Mars, Roman god of battle

Sun's Longitude 0° ♈ 21ᵈ 03ʰ

1	F.	ST. DAVID'S DAY. Dixie Dean *d.* 1980.
2	S.	Cardinal Archbishop of Westminster *b.* 1923.
3	S.	**3rd S. in Lent.** Fatima Whitbread *b.* 1961.
4	M.	Jim Clark *b.* 1936. Kenny Dalglish *b.* 1961.
5	Tu.	Rex Harrison *b.* 1908. Stalin *d.* 1953.
6	W.	Louisa M. Alcott *d.* 1888. Ivor Novello *d.* 1951.
7	Th.	Viv Richards *b.* 1952. Ivan Lendl *b.* 1960.
8	F.	Berlioz *d.* 1869. Sir Thomas Beecham *d.* 1961.
9	S.	Ernest Bevin *b.* 1881. Tamara Karsavina *b.* 1885.
10	S.	**4th S. in Lent.** PRINCE EDWARD *b.* 1964.
11	M.	Malcolm Campbell *b.* 1885. Alexander Fleming *d.*
12	Tu.	Cesare Borgia *d.* 1507. Thomas Arne *b.* 1710. [1955.
13	W.	Tsar Alexander II of Russia *assass.* 1881 NS.
14	Th.	C.P.E. Bach *b.* 1714. Tessa Sanderson *b.* 1956.
15	F.	Aristotle Onassis *d.* 1975. Rebecca West *d.* 1983.
16	S.	Aubrey Beardsley *d.* 1898. Beveridge *d.* 1963.
17	S.	**5th S. in Lent.** ST. PATRICK'S DAY.
18	M.	Ivan the Terrible *d.* 1584.
19	Tu.	**St. Joseph of Nazareth.** Dr. Livingstone *b.* 1813.
20	W.	Isaac Newton *d.* 1727. Michael Redgrave *b.* 1908.
21	Th.	Sharpeville massacre, South Africa 1960.
22	F.	Van Dyke *b.* 1599. Stephen Sondheim *b.* 1930.
23	S.	PRINCESS EUGENIE OF YORK *b.* 1990.
24	S.	**Palm Sunday.** Jules Verne *d.* 1905.
25	M.	Bartok *b.* 1881. Debussy *d.* 1918.
26	Tu.	Walt Whitman *d.* 1892. Noel Coward *d.* 1973.
27	W.	HILARY LAW SITTINGS END. James I *d.* 1625.
28	Th.	**Maundy Thursday.** Neil Kinnock *b.* 1942.
29	F.	**Good Friday.** Sir William Walton *b.* 1902.
30	S.	**Easter Eve.** Sean O'Casey *b.* 1880.
31	S.	**Easter Day.** Jesse Owens *d.* 1980.

PHENOMENA

d	h	
2	03	Mercury in superior conjunction.
12	07	Saturn in conjunction with Moon. Saturn 0°.8S.
17	11	Mercury in conjunction with Moon. Mercury 4°S.
18	21	Venus in conjunction with Moon. Venus 5°S.
21	03	Equinox.
22	16	Mars in conjunction with Moon. Mars 0°.7S.
25	12	Jupiter in conjunction with Moon. Jupiter 1°N.
27	15	Mercury at greatest elongation E. 19°.

CONSTELLATIONS

The following are near the meridian at

	d	h		d	h
Feb.	1	24	Feb.	15	23
Mar.	1	22	Mar.	16	21
Apr.	1	20	Apr.	15	19

Cepheus (below the Pole), Camelopardus, Lynx, Gemini, Cancer, Leo, Canis Minor, Hydra, Monoceros, Canis Major and Puppis.

MINIMA OF ALGOL

d	h	d	h
1	05	18	10
4	02	21	06
6	22	24	03
9	19	27	00
12	16	29	21
15	13		

NS New Style

MOON
Phases, Apsides & Node

	d	h	m
☾ Last Quarter	8	10	32
● New Moon	16	8	10
☽ First Quarter	23	6	3
○ Full Moon	30	7	17

Apogee (404,280 km) 9 0 55
Perigee (369,899 km) 22 4 37

Mean Longitude of Ascending Node on March 1, 296°.

Summer Time in 1991 (*see* p. 72).—Begins: March 31ᵈ 01ʰ GMT Ends: October 27ᵈ 01ʰ GMT.

MONTHLY NOTES

March 10. Mothering Sunday.
     11. Commonwealth Day.
     17. First day of Ramadan.
     17. Bank Holiday in Northern Ireland.
     25. Lady Day (Quarter Day).
     29. Bank Holiday in Scotland.
     30. First day of Passover. Lent ends at midnight.
     31. Financial year 1990–91 ends.

(*See* page 64 for explanatory notes)

Day	THE SUN									Sidereal Time	Transit of First Point of Aries
	Right Ascension	Dec.	Equa-tion of Time	Rise		Tran-sit	Set				
				52°	56°		52°	56°			
	h m s	° ′	m s	h m	h m	h m	h m	h m		h m s	h m s
1	22 45 45	−7 52	−12 32	6 47	6 53	12 12	17 39	17 33		10 33 13	13 24 35
2	22 49 30	−7 29	−12 21	6 45	6 50	12 12	17 40	17 35		10 37 09	13 20 39
3	22 53 14	−7 06	−12 08	6 43	6 48	12 12	17 42	17 37		10 41 06	13 16 43
4	22 56 58	−6 43	−11 56	6 40	6 45	12 12	17 44	17 39		10 45 02	13 12 48
5	23 00 42	−6 20	−11 43	6 38	6 43	12 12	17 46	17 41		10 48 59	13 08 52
6	23 04 25	−5 57	−11 29	6 36	6 40	12 11	17 48	17 44		10 52 55	13 04 56
7	23 08 07	−5 33	−11 15	6 34	6 38	12 11	17 49	17 46		10 56 52	13 01 00
8	23 11 50	−5 10	−11 01	6 32	6 35	12 11	17 51	17 48		11 00 48	12 57 04
9	23 15 32	−4 47	−10 47	6 29	6 33	12 11	17 53	17 50		11 04 45	12 53 08
10	23 19 13	−4 23	−10 32	6 27	6 30	12 10	17 55	17 52		11 08 42	12 49 12
11	23 22 54	−4 00	−10 16	6 25	6 27	12 10	17 56	17 54		11 12 38	12 45 16
12	23 26 35	−3 36	−10 01	6 22	6 25	12 10	17 58	17 56		11 16 35	12 41 20
13	23 30 16	−3 13	− 9 45	6 20	6 22	12 10	18 00	17 58		11 20 31	12 37 24
14	23 33 56	−2 49	− 9 28	6 18	6 20	12 09	18 02	18 00		11 24 28	12 33 28
15	23 37 36	−2 25	− 9 12	6 16	6 17	12 09	18 04	18 02		11 28 24	12 29 33
16	23 41 16	−2 02	− 8 55	6 13	6 14	12 09	18 05	18 04		11 32 21	12 25 37
17	23 44 56	−1 38	− 8 38	6 11	6 12	12 08	18 07	18 06		11 36 17	12 21 41
18	23 48 35	−1 14	− 8 21	6 09	6 09	12 08	18 09	18 09		11 40 14	12 17 45
19	23 52 14	−0 50	− 8 04	6 06	6 06	12 08	18 10	18 11		11 44 11	12 13 49
20	23 55 53	−0 27	− 7 46	6 04	6 04	12 08	18 12	18 13		11 48 07	12 09 53
21	23 59 32	−0 03	− 7 29	6 02	6 01	12 07	18 14	18 15		11 52 04	12 05 57
22	0 03 11	+0 21	− 7 11	5 59	5 59	12 07	18 16	18 17		11 56 00	12 02 01
23	0 06 50	+0 44	− 6 53	5 57	5 56	12 07	18 17	18 19		11 59 57	11 58 05
24	0 10 28	+1 08	− 6 35	5 55	5 53	12 06	18 19	18 21		12 03 53	11 54 09
25	0 14 06	+1 32	− 6 17	5 52	5 51	12 06	18 21	18 23		12 07 50	11 50 13
26	0 17 45	+1 55	− 5 58	5 50	5 48	12 06	18 23	18 25		12 11 46	11 46 18
27	0 21 23	+2 19	− 5 40	5 48	5 45	12 06	18 24	18 27		12 15 43	11 42 22
28	0 25 01	+2 42	− 5 22	5 46	5 43	12 05	18 26	18 29		12 19 39	11 38 26
29	0 28 40	+3 06	− 5 04	5 43	5 40	12 05	18 28	18 31		12 23 36	11 34 30
30	0 32 18	+3 29	− 4 45	5 41	5 37	12 05	18 29	18 33		12 27 33	11 30 34
31	0 35 56	+3 52	− 4 27	5 39	5 35	12 04	18 31	18 35		12 31 29	11 26 38

THE SUN s.d. 16′·1

Duration of Civil (C), Nautical (N) and Astronomical (A) Twilight (in minutes)

Lat. °	Mar. 1			Mar. 11			Mar. 21			Mar. 31		
	C	N	A	C	N	A	C	N	A	C	N	A
52	34	73	112	34	73	113	34	74	116	34	76	120
56	38	81	124	37	80	125	37	82	129	38	84	136

ASTRONOMICAL NOTES

MERCURY is too close to the Sun to be observed for the first half of the month but then becomes visible as an evening object, magnitude −1·3 to +0·5, low in the western sky around the time of the end of evening civil twilight. This evening apparition of the planet is the most favourable one of the year for observers in the northern hemisphere. On the evening of the 17th the thin crescent Moon, barely 1½ days old, may be glimpsed about 5° above Mercury.

VENUS, magnitude −4·0, is a magnificent object in the western sky in the evenings. The thin crescent Moon, only 2½ days old, will be seen about 5° to the right of the planet on the evening of the 18th.

MARS is still a prominent evening object, magnitude about +0·8, moving eastwards in the north-eastern part of Taurus. On the 22nd Mars is occulted by the Moon, at First Quarter (see pages 74–75). For observers in the British Isles this event occurs in daylight.

JUPITER, magnitude −2·4, continues to be visible as a brilliant object in the night sky, visible until the small hours of the morning. Jupiter is in Cancer. The gibbous Moon is near the planet on the 24th–25th.

SATURN is too close to the Sun for observation (though observers with telescopes should note the occultation mentioned on pages 74–75).

ZODIACAL LIGHT. The evening cone may be observed in the western sky after the end of twilight from the 2nd to the 17th. Note that the glare from Venus will prove some hindrance to observation.

(See pages 64–65 for explanatory notes)

THE MOON

Day	RA	Dec.	Hor. Par.	Semi-diam.	Sun's Co-long.	P.A. of Bright Limb	Phase	Age	Rise 52°	Rise 56°	Tran-sit	Set 52°	Set 56°
	h m	°	′	′	°	°	%	d	h m	h m	h m	h m	h m
1	10 51	+ 3·3	58·4	15·9	88	163	100	14·3	19 02	19 04	0 19	6 38	6 39
2	11 40	− 2·7	57·7	15·7	101	129	98	15·3	20 21	20 28	1 05	6 53	6 49
3	12 29	− 8·5	57·0	15·5	113	122	94	16·3	21 39	21 51	1 51	7 07	6 59
4	13 17	−13·7	56·3	15·3	125	118	88	17·3	22 55	23 13	2 37	7 24	7 10
5	14 06	−18·2	55·6	15·1	137	114	81	18·3	—	—	3 24	7 44	7 25
6	14 57	−21·8	55·0	15·0	149	109	73	19·3	0 08	0 32	4 12	8 09	7 44
7	15 48	−24·4	54·6	14·9	161	104	64	20·3	1 17	1 46	5 01	8 41	8 12
8	16 40	−25·8	54·3	14·8	173	98	54	21·3	2 19	2 51	5 52	9 23	8 51
9	17 33	−26·1	54·2	14·8	186	92	45	22·3	3 11	3 43	6 42	10 15	9 43
10	18 26	−25·2	54·3	14·8	198	87	36	23·3	3 51	4 20	7 32	11 17	10 49
11	19 17	−23·1	54·6	14·9	210	82	27	24·3	4 22	4 47	8 21	12 26	12 03
12	20 07	−19·9	55·0	15·0	222	78	19	25·3	4 47	5 05	9 08	13 39	13 21
13	20 56	−15·9	55·5	15·1	234	76	12	26·3	5 06	5 19	9 54	14 54	14 42
14	21 44	−11·1	56·1	15·3	247	75	6	27·3	5 22	5 30	10 39	16 09	16 03
15	22 32	− 5·7	56·7	15·4	259	79	2	28·3	5 37	5 40	11 24	17 26	17 25
16	23 19	+ 0·1	57·3	15·6	271	111	0	29·3	5 51	5 49	12 09	18 45	18 49
17	0 08	+ 6·0	57·9	15·8	283	217	1	0·7	6 06	5 59	12 56	20 06	20 16
18	0 58	+11·7	58·4	15·9	295	234	4	1·7	6 23	6 11	13 46	21 30	21 45
19	1 52	+16·9	58·8	16·0	308	242	9	2·7	6 44	6 27	14 39	22 55	23 17
20	2 48	+21·2	59·1	16·1	320	248	16	3·7	7 12	6 48	15 36	—	—
21	3 48	+24·3	59·2	16·1	332	255	25	4·7	7 50	7 21	16 36	0 17	0 45
22	4 51	+25·9	59·3	16·2	344	262	36	5·7	8 43	8 11	17 38	1 31	2 02
23	5 54	+25·7	59·3	16·1	356	269	47	6·7	9 51	9 21	18 39	2 30	3 01
24	6 55	+24·0	59·1	16·1	9	276	59	7·7	11 10	10 45	19 37	3 14	3 40
25	7 55	+20·7	59·0	16·1	21	281	69	8·7	12 34	12 15	20 32	3 46	4 06
26	8 51	+16·3	58·7	16·0	33	285	79	9·7	13 58	13 46	21 23	4 09	4 23
27	9 44	+11·1	58·4	15·9	45	286	88	10·7	15 20	15 14	22 11	4 28	4 37
28	10 34	+ 5·3	58·0	15·8	57	286	94	11·7	16 40	16 39	22 57	4 44	4 47
29	11 23	− 0·6	57·5	15·7	70	279	98	12·7	17 59	18 03	23 43	4 59	4 57
30	12 11	− 6·3	57·0	15·5	82	242	100	13·7	19 16	19 26	—	5 13	5 07
31	12 59	−11·7	56·4	15·4	94	143	99	14·7	20 33	20 48	0 29	5 29	5 18

MERCURY

Day	RA	Dec.	Diam.	Phase	Tran-sit		Day	RA	Dec. +	Diam.	Phase	Tran-sit	5° high. 52°	5° high. 56°
	h m	°	″	%	h m			h m	°	″	%	h m	h m	h m
1	22 45	−10·0	5	100	12 13		16	0 28	3·2	6	85	12 57	18 45	18 45
4	23 06	− 7·6	5	100	12 22	Mercury is too	19	0 47	5·9	6	76	13 04	19 06	19 08
7	23 27	− 5·0	5	99	12 31	close to the	22	1 04	8·3	6	65	13 09	19 23	19 27
10	23 48	− 2·3	5	96	12 40	Sun for	25	1 19	10·5	7	53	13 11	19 35	19 41
13	0 08	+ 0·4	5	92	12 49	observation	28	1 30	12·2	8	41	13 10	19 42	19 49
16	0 28	+ 3·2	6	85	12 57		31	1 38	13·4	8	29	13 06	19 43	19 51

VENUS

Day	RA	Dec. +	Diam.	Phase	Tran-sit	5° high. 52°	5° high. 56°
	h m	°	″	%	h m	h m	h m
1	0 31	2·5	12	88	13 58	19 41	19 40
6	0 54	5·1	12	87	14 01	19 57	19 58
11	1 16	7·6	12	86	14 04	20 12	20 16
16	1 38	10·1	12	85	14 06	20 28	20 33
21	2 01	12·5	13	83	14 09	20 44	20 51
26	2 24	14·7	13	82	14 13	20 59	21 08
31	2 48	16·9	13	81	14 17	21 14	21 26

MARS

Day	RA	Dec. +	Diam.	Phase	Tran-sit	5° high. 52°	5° high. 56°
	h m	°	″	%	h m	h m	h m
1	4 48	24·6	8	90	18 13	1 57	2 17
6	4 58	24·8	7	90	18 04	1 48	2 09
11	5 08	25·0	7	90	17 54	1 40	2 01
16	5 19	25·2	7	90	17 46	1 32	1 53
21	5 30	25·3	7	90	17 37	1 25	1 46
26	5 41	25·4	6	90	17 28	1 17	1 38
31	5 53	25·4	6	90	17 20	1 08	1 30

(*See* pages 65–66 for explanatory notes)

SUNRISE AND SUNSET

Day	London 0°05′ 51°30′		Bristol 2°35′ 51°28′		Birmingham 1°55′ 52°28′		Manchester 2°15′ 53°28′		Newcastle 1°37′ 54°59′		Glasgow 4°14′ 55°52′		Belfast 5°56′ 54°35′	
	h m	h m	h m	h m	h m	h m	h m	h m	h m	h m	h m	h m	h m	h m
1	6 47	17 40	6 57	17 50	6 55	17 46	6 58	17 46	6 58	17 41	7 10	17 50	7 14	17 59
2	6 45	17 41	6 55	17 51	6 53	17 48	6 56	17 48	6 55	17 43	7 07	17 52	7 12	18 01
3	6 42	17 43	6 52	17 53	6 51	17 49	6 53	17 50	6 53	17 45	7 05	17 54	7 10	18 03
4	6 40	17 45	6 50	17 55	6 49	17 51	6 51	17 51	6 50	17 47	7 02	17 56	7 07	18 05
5	6 38	17 47	6 48	17 57	6 46	17 53	6 49	17 53	6 48	17 49	7 00	17 59	7 05	18 07
6	6 36	17 48	6 46	17 58	6 44	17 55	6 46	17 55	6 46	17 51	6 57	18 01	7 02	18 09
7	6 34	17 50	6 44	18 00	6 42	17 57	6 44	17 57	6 43	17 53	6 54	18 03	7 00	18 11
8	6 31	17 52	6 41	18 02	6 40	17 59	6 42	17 59	6 41	17 55	6 52	18 05	6 57	18 13
9	6 29	17 54	6 39	18 04	6 37	18 00	6 39	18 01	6 38	17 57	6 49	18 07	6 55	18 15
10	6 27	17 55	6 37	18 05	6 35	18 02	6 37	18 03	6 36	17 59	6 47	18 09	6 53	18 17
11	6 25	17 57	6 35	18 07	6 33	18 04	6 35	18 05	6 33	18 01	6 44	18 11	6 50	18 19
12	6 23	17 59	6 33	18 09	6 30	18 06	6 32	18 07	6 31	18 03	6 42	18 13	6 48	18 21
13	6 20	18 01	6 30	18 11	6 28	18 08	6 30	18 08	6 28	18 05	6 39	18 15	6 45	18 23
14	6 18	18 02	6 28	18 12	6 26	18 09	6 27	18 10	6 26	18 07	6 36	18 17	6 43	18 25
15	6 16	18 04	6 26	18 14	6 23	18 11	6 25	18 12	6 23	18 09	6 34	18 19	6 40	18 27
16	6 14	18 06	6 23	18 16	6 21	18 13	6 23	18 14	6 20	18 11	6 31	18 21	6 38	18 28
17	6 11	18 07	6 21	18 17	6 19	18 15	6 20	18 16	6 18	18 13	6 29	18 23	6 35	18 30
18	6 09	18 09	6 19	18 19	6 16	18 16	6 18	18 18	6 15	18 15	6 26	18 25	6 33	18 32
19	6 07	18 11	6 17	18 21	6 14	18 18	6 15	18 20	6 13	18 17	6 23	18 28	6 30	18 34
20	6 04	18 13	6 14	18 23	6 12	18 20	6 13	18 21	6 10	18 19	6 21	18 30	6 28	18 36
21	6 02	18 14	6 12	18 24	6 09	18 22	6 11	18 23	6 08	18 21	6 18	18 32	6 25	18 38
22	6 00	18 16	6 10	18 26	6 07	18 23	6 08	18 25	6 05	18 23	6 15	18 34	6 23	18 40
23	5 58	18 18	6 08	18 28	6 05	18 25	6 06	18 27	6 03	18 25	6 13	18 36	6 20	18 42
24	5 55	18 19	6 05	18 29	6 02	18 27	6 03	18 29	6 00	18 27	6 10	18 38	6 18	18 44
25	5 53	18 21	6 03	18 31	6 00	18 29	6 01	18 31	5 58	18 29	6 08	18 40	6 15	18 46
26	5 51	18 23	6 01	18 33	5 58	18 30	5 58	18 32	5 55	18 31	6 05	18 42	6 12	18 48
27	5 48	18 24	5 58	18 34	5 55	18 32	5 56	18 34	5 52	18 33	6 02	18 44	6 10	18 50
28	5 46	18 26	5 56	18 36	5 53	18 34	5 54	18 36	5 50	18 35	6 00	18 46	6 07	18 52
29	5 44	18 28	5 54	18 38	5 51	18 36	5 51	18 38	5 47	18 37	5 57	18 48	6 05	18 54
30	5 42	18 29	5 52	18 39	5 48	18 37	5 49	18 40	5 45	18 39	5 54	18 50	6 02	18 55
31	5 39	18 31	5 49	18 41	5 46	18 39	5 46	18 41	5 42	18 40	5 52	18 52	6 00	18 57

JUPITER

Day	RA	Dec. +	Transit	5° high. 52°	5° high. 56°
	h m	° ′	h m	h m	h m
1	8 29·9	19 48	21 53	5 08	5 22
11	8 26·7	19 59	21 10	4 27	4 41
21	8 24·8	20 06	20 29	3 46	4 01
31	8 24·2	20 07	19 50	3 06	3 21

Diameters—equatorial 43″ polar 40″

SATURN

Day	RA	Dec. −	Transit
	h m	° ′	h m
1	20 19·1	19 50	9 44
11	20 23·1	19 37	9 09
21	20 26·8	19 25	8 33
31	20 30·0	19 15	7 57

Saturn is too close to the Sun for observation

Diameters—equatorial 16″ polar 14″
Rings—major axis 36″ minor axis 12″

URANUS

Day	RA	Dec. −	Transit	10° high. 52°	10° high. 56°
	h m	° ′	h m	h m	h m
1	18 55·9	23 09	8 21	6 16	7 27
11	18 57·5	23 07	7 44	5 38	6 48
21	18 58·7	23 06	7 06	5 00	6 09
31	18 59·5	23 05	6 27	4 21	5 30

Diameter 4″

NEPTUNE

Day	RA	Dec. −	Transit	10° high. 52°	10° high. 56°
	h m	° ′	h m	h m	h m
1	19 09·5	21 41	8 35	6 13	7 05
11	19 10·5	21 39	7 57	5 34	6 26
21	19 11·3	21 38	7 18	4 55	5 47
31	19 11·9	21 37	6 39	4 16	5 08

Diameter 2″

(*See* page 66 for explanatory notes)

DAY OF		

Aperire, to open. Earth opens to receive seed.

Sun's Longitude 30° ♉ 20ᵈ14ʰ

Month	Week	
1	M.	Otto von Bismarck *b*. 1815. Donizetti *d*. 1848.
2	Tu.	Comte de Mirabeau *d*. 1791. Max Ernst *b*. 1891.*
3	W.	Brahms *d*. 1897. Sir Peter Pears *d*. 1986.
4	Th.	Oliver Goldsmith *d*. 1774. Anthony Tudor *b*. 1908.
5	F.	Thomas Hobbes *b*. 1588. Chiang Kai-shek *d*. 1975.
6	S.	Danton *exec*. 1794. Igor Stravinsky *d*. 1971.
7	S.	**1st S. after Easter.** Jim Clark *d*. 1968.
8	M.	**The Annunciation.** Picasso *d*. 1973.
9	Tu.	EASTER LAW SITTINGS BEGIN. Brunel *b*. 1806.
10	W.	Swinburne *d*. 1909. Evelyn Waugh *d*. 1966.
11	Th.	Abdication of Napoleon 1814. Hallé *b*. 1819.
12	F.	Bobby Moore *b*. 1941. Joe Louis *d*. 1981.
13	S.	Edict of Nantes, 1598. Thomas Jefferson *b*. 1743.
14	S.	**2nd S. after Easter.** Simone de Beauvoir *d*. 1986.
15	M.	Joe Davis *b*. 1901. Sinking of the Titanic 1912.
16	Tu.	Goya *d*. 1828. Charlie Chaplin *b*. 1889.
17	W.	Diet of Worms 1521. Benjamin Franklin *d*. 1790.
18	Th.	John Singer Sargent *d*. 1925. Einstein *d*. 1955.
19	F.	Charles Darwin *d*. 1882. Pierre Curie *d*. 1906.
20	S.	Canaletto *d*. 1768. Bram Stoker *d*. 1912.
21	S.	**3rd S. after Easter.** QUEEN ELIZABETH II *b*. 1926.
22	M.	Kathleen Ferrier *b*. 1912. Yehudi Menuhin *b*. 1916.
23	Tu.	ST. GEORGE'S DAY. Sergei Prokofiev *b*. 1891.*
24	W.	Easter Rising began, Dublin 1916. Bill Edrich *d*. [1986.
25	Th.	**St. Mark.** Sir Stanley Rous *b*. 1895.
26	F.	Delacroix *b*. 1798. Rudolf Hess *b*. 1894.
27	S.	Samuel Morse *b*. 1791. C. Day-Lewis *b*. 1904.
28	S.	**4th S. after Easter.** League of Nations f'ded 1919.
29	M.	Thomas Beecham *b*. 1879. Duke Ellington *b*. 1899.
30	Tu.	Beatrix Potter *d*. 1943. Adolf Hitler *d*. 1945.

*Centenary

PHENOMENA

d	h	
8	20	Saturn in conjunction with Moon. Saturn 1°S.
14	20	Mercury in conjunction with Moon. Mercury 3°S.
14	21	Mercury in inferior conjunction.
17	16	Venus in conjunction with Moon. Venus 2°S.
20	00	Mars in conjunction with Moon. Mars 0°·6N.
21	19	Jupiter in conjunction with Moon. Jupiter 2°N.

CONSTELLATIONS

The following constellations are near the meridian at

	d	h		d	h
Mar.	1	24	Mar.	16	23
Apr.	1	22	Apr.	15	21
May	1	20	May	16	19

Cepheus (below the Pole), Cassiopeia (below the Pole), Ursa Major, Leo Minor, Leo, Sextans, Hydra and Crater.

MINIMA OF ALGOL

d	h		d	h
1	18		18	23
4	15		21	19
7	11		24	16
10	08		27	13
13	05		30	10
16	02			

MOON
Phases, Apsides & Node

	d	h	m
☾ Last Quarter	7	6	45
● New Moon	14	19	38
☽ First Quarter	21	12	39
○ Full Moon	28	20	59
Apogee (404,305 km)	5	21	6
Perigee (365,440 km)	17	17	6

Mean longitude of ascending node on April 1, 294°.

See note on Summer Time, p. 24.

MONTHLY NOTES

April 1. Bank Holiday in England, Wales and Northern Ireland.

5. Income tax year (1990–91) ends.

7. Greek Orthodox Easter.

(*See* page 64 for explanatory notes)

Day	Right Ascension	Dec. +	Equation of Time	Rise 52°	Rise 56°	Transit	Set 52°	Set 56°	Sidereal Time	Transit of First Point of Aries
	h m s	° '	m s	h m	h m	h m	h m	h m	h m s	h m s
1	0 39 35	4 16	− 4 09	5 36	5 32	12 04	18 33	18 37	12 35 26	11 22 42
2	0 43 13	4 39	− 3 51	5 34	5 30	12 04	18 35	18 39	12 39 22	11 18 46
3	0 46 52	5 02	− 3 33	5 32	5 27	12 03	18 36	18 41	12 43 19	11 14 50
4	0 50 31	5 25	− 3 16	5 29	5 24	12 03	18 38	18 43	12 47 15	11 10 54
5	0 54 10	5 48	− 2 58	5 27	5 22	12 03	18 40	18 45	12 51 12	11 06 59
6	0 57 49	6 11	− 2 41	5 25	5 19	12 03	18 41	18 47	12 55 08	11 03 03
7	1 01 29	6 33	− 2 24	5 23	5 16	12 02	18 43	18 49	12 59 05	10 59 07
8	1 05 08	6 56	− 2 07	5 20	5 14	12 02	18 45	18 51	13 03 02	10 55 11
9	1 08 48	7 18	− 1 50	5 18	5 11	12 02	18 46	18 53	13 06 58	10 51 15
10	1 12 28	7 41	− 1 33	5 16	5 09	12 01	18 48	18 55	13 10 55	10 47 19
11	1 16 08	8 03	− 1 17	5 14	5 06	12 01	18 50	18 57	13 14 51	10 43 23
12	1 19 49	8 25	− 1 01	5 11	5 04	12 01	18 52	19 00	13 18 48	10 39 27
13	1 23 30	8 47	− 0 46	5 09	5 01	12 01	18 53	19 02	13 22 44	10 35 31
14	1 27 11	9 09	− 0 30	5 07	4 58	12 00	18 55	19 04	13 26 41	10 31 35
15	1 30 53	9 30	− 0 16	5 05	4 56	12 00	18 57	19 06	13 30 37	10 27 39
16	1 34 35	9 52	− 0 01	5 02	4 53	12 00	18 58	19 08	13 34 34	10 23 44
17	1 38 17	10 13	+ 0 13	5 00	4 51	12 00	19 00	19 10	13 38 31	10 19 48
18	1 42 00	10 34	+ 0 27	4 58	4 48	11 59	19 02	19 12	13 42 27	10 15 52
19	1 45 43	10 55	+ 0 41	4 56	4 46	11 59	19 04	19 14	13 46 24	10 11 56
20	1 49 26	11 16	+ 0 54	4 54	4 43	11 59	19 05	19 16	13 50 20	10 08 00
21	1 53 10	11 37	+ 1 06	4 52	4 41	11 59	19 07	19 18	13 54 17	10 04 04
22	1 56 55	11 57	+ 1 19	4 50	4 39	11 59	19 09	19 20	13 58 13	10 00 08
23	2 00 39	12 17	+ 1 31	4 48	4 36	11 58	19 10	19 22	14 02 10	9 56 12
24	2 04 24	12 37	+ 1 42	4 45	4 34	11 58	19 12	19 24	14 06 06	9 52 16
25	2 08 10	12 57	+ 1 53	4 43	4 31	11 58	19 14	19 26	14 10 03	9 48 20
26	2 11 56	13 17	+ 2 04	4 41	4 29	11 58	19 15	19 28	14 14 00	9 44 24
27	2 15 42	13 36	+ 2 14	4 39	4 27	11 58	19 17	19 30	14 17 56	9 40 29
28	2 19 29	13 55	+ 2 23	4 37	4 24	11 58	19 19	19 32	14 21 53	9 36 33
29	2 23 17	14 14	+ 2 33	4 35	4 22	11 57	19 21	19 34	14 25 49	9 32 37
30	2 27 05	14 33	+ 2 41	4 33	4 20	11 57	19 22	19 36	14 29 46	9 28 41

THE SUN s.d. 16'·0

Duration of Civil (C), Nautical (N) and Astronomical (A) Twilight (in minutes)

Lat. °	Apr. 1 C	N	A	Apr. 11 C	N	A	Apr. 21 C	N	A	Apr. 30 C	N	A
52	34	76	121	35	79	128	37	84	138	39	89	152
56	38	85	137	40	90	148	42	96	167	44	105	200

ASTRONOMICAL NOTES

MERCURY continues to be visible low in the western sky around the time of the end of evening civil twilight, for the first week of the month, though it is getting noticeably fainter. On the 1st its magnitude is +1·0 but by the 7th it is only about +2·7.

VENUS continues to be visible as a magnificent object in the western sky in the evenings, magnitude −4·1. The thin crescent Moon, 3 days old, will be seen close to, and above, the planet on the 17th. Venus passes 7°N. of Aldebaran on the 21st–22nd.

MARS, magnitude +1·2, continues to be visible in the evening skies. By the end of the month it is too low above the WNW horizon to be visible after midnight. Mars passes from Taurus into Gemini at the beginning of the month. On the night of the 19th–20th the crescent Moon, just before First Quarter, will be seen passing 1°S. of the planet.

JUPITER is still a brilliant object in the evening sky and for some time after midnight. Its magnitude is −2·2. Jupiter is moving very slowly in Cancer and on the evening of the 21st the Moon, at First Quarter, passes 2°S. of the planet.

SATURN, magnitude +0·7, is slowly emerging from the morning twilight and becoming visible low above the south-eastern horizon. The Moon is near Saturn on the mornings of the 8th and 9th.

(See pages 64–65 for explanatory notes)

THE MOON

Day	RA	Dec.	Hor. Par.	Semi-diam.	Sun's Co-long.	P.A. of Bright Limb	Phase	Age	Rise 52°	Rise 56°	Transit	Set 52°	Set 56°
	h m	°	′	′	°	°	%	d	h m	h m	h m	h m	h m
1	13 48	−16·5	55·9	15·2	106	124	97	15·7	21 48	22 09	1 15	5 48	5 31
2	14 39	−20·5	55·3	15·1	118	115	92	16·7	22 59	23 26	2 03	6 11	5 49
3	15 30	−23·4	54·9	15·0	130	109	86	17·7	—	—	2 53	6 40	6 13
4	16 23	−25·2	54·5	14·9	142	102	79	18·7	0 05	0 35	3 43	7 18	6 48
5	17 15	−25·9	54·3	14·8	155	96	71	19·7	1 01	1 33	4 34	8 07	7 35
6	18 08	−25·4	54·2	14·8	167	90	62	20·7	1 46	2 16	5 24	9 05	8 35
7	19 00	−23·7	54·3	14·8	179	84	53	21·7	2 21	2 46	6 13	10 11	9 46
8	19 50	−20·9	54·6	14·9	191	79	43	22·7	2 47	3 08	7 00	11 21	11 01
9	20 39	−17·2	55·1	15·0	203	76	34	23·7	3 08	3 24	7 46	12 34	12 19
10	21 26	−12·8	55·7	15·2	216	73	25	24·7	3 26	3 36	8 31	13 48	13 39
11	22 13	− 7·7	56·4	15·4	228	72	17	25·7	3 41	3 47	9 15	15 03	15 00
12	23 01	− 2·1	57·1	15·6	240	73	10	26·7	3 56	3 57	10 00	16 21	16 22
13	23 49	+ 3·8	57·9	15·8	252	77	4	27·7	4 10	4 06	10 47	17 41	17 48
14	0 39	+ 9·6	58·6	16·0	265	91	1	28·7	4 27	4 18	11 36	19 05	19 18
15	1 33	+15·0	59·3	16·1	277	184	0	0·2	4 47	4 32	12 29	20 31	20 51
16	2 29	+19·8	59·7	16·3	289	235	2	1·2	5 13	4 52	13 26	21 58	22 23
17	3 30	+23·3	60·0	16·3	301	249	7	2·2	5 48	5 22	14 27	23 17	23 48
18	4 33	+25·4	60·0	16·3	313	258	14	3·2	6 38	6 07	15 30	—	—
19	5 38	+25·7	59·9	16·3	326	266	23	4·2	7 42	7 12	16 33	0 23	0 54
20	6 41	+24·3	59·6	16·2	338	274	33	5·2	9 00	8 33	17 32	1 13	1 40
21	7 42	+21·3	59·2	16·1	350	280	44	6·2	10 23	10 03	18 28	1 48	2 09
22	8 38	+17·2	58·7	16·0	2	285	55	7·2	11 47	11 33	19 20	2 14	2 29
23	9 31	+12·1	58·2	15·9	14	288	66	8·2	13 08	13 00	20 08	2 34	2 44
24	10 22	+ 6·6	57·7	15·7	27	289	76	9·2	14 27	14 24	20 54	2 50	2 55
25	11 10	+ 0·9	57·2	15·6	39	289	85	10·2	15 44	15 46	21 39	3 05	3 05
26	11 57	− 4·8	56·7	15·5	51	287	91	11·2	17 00	17 08	22 24	3 20	3 15
27	12 45	−10·2	56·2	15·3	63	281	96	12·2	18 16	18 29	23 10	3 35	3 26
28	13 33	−15·1	55·7	15·2	75	266	99	13·2	19 30	19 49	23 57	3 53	3 38
29	14 23	−19·2	55·3	15·1	88	182	100	14·2	20 43	21 07	—	4 14	3 54
30	15 14	−22·5	54·9	15·0	100	124	99	15·2	21 51	22 20	0 45	4 41	4 16

MERCURY

Day	RA	Dec. +	Diam.	Phase	Transit	5° high. 52°	5° high. 56°	Day	RA	Dec. +	Diam.	Phase	Transit	
	h m	°	″	%	h m	h m	h m		h m	°	″	%	h m	
1	1 40	13·7	9	26	13 03	19 42	19 50	16	1 25	10·8	12	0	11 47	
4	1 43	14·1	9	16	12 54	19 33	19 42	19	1 18	9·3	12	2	11 28	Mercury is too
7	1 42	14·0	10	9	12 40	19 18	19 27	22	1 12	7·8	12	5	11 12	close to the
10	1 38	13·4	11	4	12 24	18 58	19 05	25	1 09	6·6	11	10	10 57	Sun
13	1 32	12·2	11	1	12 06	18 33	18 39	28	1 08	5·8	11	15	10 45	for observation
16	1 25	10·8	12	0	11·47	18 06	18 11	31	1 10	5·3	10	21	10 35	

VENUS / MARS

Day	RA	Dec. +	Diam.	Phase	Transit	5° high. 52°	5° high. 56°	Day	RA	Dec. +	Diam.	Phase	Transit	5° high. 52°	5° high. 56°
	h m	°	″	%	h m	h m	h m		h m	°	″	%	h m	h m	h m
1	2 52	17·3	13	80	14 17	21 17	21 29	1	5 55	25·4	6	90	17 19	1 07	1 28
6	3 16	19·2	14	79	14 21	21 32	21 46	6	6 07	25·3	6	90	17 11	0 59	1 20
11	3 40	20·9	14	77	14 26	21 47	22 02	11	6 19	25·2	6	91	17 03	0 50	1 11
16	4 05	22·4	14	75	14 31	22 00	22 18	16	6 31	25·1	6	91	16 55	0 41	1 02
21	4 30	23·6	15	74	14 36	22 13	22 32	21	6 43	24·9	5	91	16 48	0 32	0 53
26	4 55	24·6	15	72	14 41	22 24	22 45	26	6 55	24·6	5	91	16 40	0 23	0 43
31	5 20	25·3	16	70	14 47	22 34	22 56	31	7 07	24·2	5	92	16 33	0 13	0 33

(*See* pages 65–66 for explanatory notes)

SUNRISE AND SUNSET

Day	London 0°05′ 51°30′		Bristol 2°35′ 51°28′		Birmingham 1°55′ 52°28′		Manchester 2°15′ 53°28′		Newcastle 1°37′ 54°59′		Glasgow 4°14′ 55°52′		Belfast 5°56′ 54°35′	
	h m	h m	h m	h m	h m	h m	h m	h m	h m	h m	h m	h m	h m	h m
1	5 37	18 33	5 47	18 43	5 43	18 41	5 44	18 43	5 40	18 42	5 49	18 54	5 57	18 59
2	5 35	18 34	5 45	18 44	5 41	18 43	5 41	18 45	5 37	18 44	5 47	18 56	5 55	19 01
3	5 33	18 36	5 43	18 46	5 39	18 44	5 39	18 47	5 35	18 46	5 44	18 58	5 52	19 03
4	5 30	18 38	5 40	18 48	5 36	18 46	5 37	18 49	5 32	18 48	5 41	19 00	5 50	19 05
5	5 28	18 39	5 38	18 49	5 34	18 48	5 34	18 51	5 30	18 50	5 39	19 02	5 47	19 07
6	5 26	18 41	5 36	18 51	5 32	18 50	5 32	18 52	5 27	18 52	5 36	19 04	5 45	19 09
7	5 24	18 43	5 34	18 53	5 30	18 51	5 29	18 54	5 25	18 54	5 34	19 06	5 42	19 11
8	5 21	18 44	5 31	18 54	5 27	18 53	5 27	18 56	5 22	18 56	5 31	19 08	5 40	19 13
9	5 19	18 46	5 29	18 56	5 25	18 55	5 25	18 58	5 20	18 58	5 28	19 10	5 38	19 15
10	5 17	18 48	5 27	18 58	5 23	18 57	5 22	19 00	5 17	19 00	5 26	19 12	5 35	19 16
11	5 15	18 49	5 25	18 59	5 20	18 58	5 20	19 02	5 15	19 02	5 23	19 14	5 33	19 18
12	5 12	18 51	5 23	19 01	5 18	19 00	5 18	19 03	5 12	19 04	5 21	19 16	5 30	19 20
13	5 10	18 53	5 20	19 03	5 16	19 02	5 15	19 05	5 10	19 06	5 18	19 18	5 28	19 22
14	5 08	18 54	5 18	19 04	5 14	19 04	5 13	19 07	5 07	19 08	5 16	19 20	5 25	19 24
15	5 06	18 56	5 16	19 06	5 11	19 05	5 11	19 09	5 05	19 10	5 13	19 22	5 23	19 26
16	5 04	18 58	5 14	19 08	5 09	19 07	5 08	19 11	5 02	19 12	5 11	19 24	5 21	19 28
17	5 02	18 59	5 12	19 09	5 07	19 09	5 06	19 12	5 00	19 14	5 08	19 26	5 18	19 30
18	5 00	19 01	5 10	19 11	5 05	19 11	5 04	19 14	4 58	19 16	5 06	19 28	5 16	19 32
19	4 57	19 03	5 07	19 13	5 03	19 12	5 02	19 16	4 55	19 17	5 03	19 30	5 13	19 34
20	4 55	19 04	5 05	19 14	5 00	19 14	4 59	19 18	4 53	19 19	5 01	19 32	5 11	19 36
21	4 53	19 06	5 03	19 16	4 58	19 16	4 57	19 20	4 50	19 21	4 58	19 34	5 09	19 38
22	4 51	19 08	5 01	19 18	4 56	19 18	4 55	19 22	4 48	19 23	4 56	19 36	5 06	19 39
23	4 49	19 09	4 59	19 19	4 54	19 19	4 53	19 23	4 46	19 25	4 53	19 39	5 04	19 41
24	4 47	19 11	4 57	19 21	4 52	19 21	4 50	19 25	4 43	19 27	4 51	19 41	5 02	19 43
25	4 45	19 13	4 55	19 23	4 50	19 23	4 48	19 27	4 41	19 29	4 49	19 43	5 00	19 45
26	4 43	19 14	4 53	19 24	4 48	19 25	4 46	19 29	4 39	19 31	4 46	19 45	4 57	19 47
27	4 41	19 16	4 51	19 26	4 46	19 26	4 44	19 31	4 37	19 33	4 44	19 47	4 55	19 49
28	4 39	19 18	4 49	19 28	4 44	19 28	4 42	19 32	4 34	19 35	4 42	19 49	4 53	19 51
29	4 37	19 19	4 47	19 29	4 42	19 30	4 40	19 34	4 32	19 37	4 39	19 51	4 51	19 53
30	4 35	19 21	4 45	19 31	4 40	19 31	4 38	19 36	4 30	19 39	4 37	19 53	4 49	19 55

JUPITER

Day	RA	Dec. +	Transit	5° high. 52°	5° high. 56°
	h m	° ′	h m	h m	h m
1	8 24·2	20 07	19 46	3 03	3 17
11	8 25·1	20 04	19 07	2 24	2 38
21	8 27·1	19 56	18 30	1 46	2 00
31	8 30·4	19 45	17 54	1 09	1 22

Diameters—equatorial 39″ polar 36″

SATURN

Day	RA	Dec. −	Transit	5° high. 52°	5° high. 56°
	h m	° ′	h m	h m	h m
1	20 30·3	19 14	7 54	4 21	4 46
11	20 32·9	19 06	7 17	3 43	4 08
21	20 35·0	19 00	6 40	3 05	3 30
31	20 36·4	18 56	6 02	2 27	2 51

Diameters—equatorial 16″ polar 15″
Rings—major axis 37″ minor axis 12″

URANUS

Day	RA	Dec. −	Transit	10° high. 52°	10° high. 56°
	h m	° ′	h m	h m	h m
1	18 59·6	23 05	6 23	4 17	5 26
11	19 00·1	23 05	5 44	3 38	4 47
21	19 00·2	23 05	5 05	2 59	4 08
31	18 59·9	23 05	4 25	2 20	3 29

Diameter 4″

NEPTUNE

Day	RA	Dec. −	Transit	10° high. 52°	10° high. 56°
	h m	° ′	h m	h m	h m
1	19 11·9	21 36	6 35	4 12	5 04
11	19 12·2	21 36	5 56	3 33	4 25
21	19 12·3	21 35	5 17	2 54	3 46
31	19 12·1	21 36	4 38	2 14	3 06

Diameter 2″

(*See* page 66 for explanatory notes)

DAY OF		
Month	Week	

Maia, goddess of growth and increase.

Sun's Longitude 60° II 21ᵈ 13ʰ

1	W.	**SS. Philip and James.** Khachaturyan *d.* 1978.
2	Th.	Sen. Joseph McCarthy *d.* 1957. Edgar Hoover *d.* 1972.
3	F.	Sugar Ray Robinson *b.* 1920. Henry Cooper *b.* 1934.
4	S.	First running of the Derby 1780.
5	S.	**5th S. after Easter.** Gordon Richards *b.* 1904.
6	M.	First four-minute mile run 1954.
7	Tu.	Robert Browning *b.* 1812. Tito *b.* 1892.
8	W.	V.E. DAY 1945. Gauguin *d.* 1903.
9	Th.	**Ascension Day.** Sherpa Tenzing *d.* 1986.
10	F.	Indian Mutiny began 1857. H.M. Stanley *d.* 1904.
11	S.	William Pitt *d.* 1778. Kim Philby *d.* 1988.
12	S.	**S. after Ascension (6th after Easter).**
13	M.	John Nash *d.* 1835. Sir Arthur Sullivan *b.* 1842.
14	Tu.	**St. Matthias.** Strindberg *d.* 1912.
15	W.	Edmund Kean *d.* 1833. Joseph Whitaker *d.* 1895.
16	Th.	Film Academy Awards first presented 1929.
17	F.	Satie *b.* 1866. Relief of Mafeking 1900.
18	S.	Pope John Paul II *b.* 1920. Fred Perry *b.* 1909.
19	S.	**Pentecost (Whit Sunday).** Gladstone *d.* 1898.
20	M.	Christopher Columbus *d.* 1506. Balzac *b.* 1799.
21	Tu.	Dürer *b.* 1471. Lord Rosebery *d.* 1929.
22	W.	Wagner *b.* 1813. Laurence Olivier *b.* 1907.
23	Th.	Douglas Fairbanks *b.* 1883. Ibsen *d.* 1906.
24	F.	EASTER LAW SITTINGS END.
25	S.	Lord Beaverbrook *b.* 1879. Holst *d.* 1934.
26	S.	**Trinity Sunday.** Matt Busby *b.* 1909.
27	M.	Calvin *d.* 1564. Isadora Duncan *b.* 1878.
28	Tu.	Duke of Windsor *d.* 1972.
29	W.	J.F. Kennedy *b.* 1917. Everest conquered 1953.
30	Th.	CORPUS CHRISTI. Voltaire *d.* 1778.
31	F.	Haydn *d.* 1809. Jack Dempsey *d.* 1983.

PHENOMENA

d	h	
6	06	Saturn in conjunction with Moon. Saturn 2°S.
10	03	Pluto at opposition.
12	07	Mercury in conjunction with Moon. Mercury 8°S.
12	18	Mercury at greatest elongation W.26°.
17	07	Venus in conjunction with Moon. Venus 2°N.
18	10	Mars in conjunction with Moon. Mars 2°N.
19	06	Jupiter in conjunction with Moon. Jupiter 2°N.

CONSTELLATIONS

The following constellations are near the meridian at

d	h		d	h
Apr. 1	24		Apr. 15	23
May 1	22		May 16	21
June 1	20		June 15	19

Cepheus (below the Pole), Cassiopeia (below the Pole), Ursa Minor, Ursa Major, Canes Venatici, Coma Berenices, Bootes, Leo, Virgo, Crater, Corvus, and Hydra.

ALGOL

ALGOL is inconveniently situated for observation during May.

MOON
Phases, Apsides & Node

	d	h	m
☾ Last Quarter	7	0	46
● New Moon	14	4	36
☽ First Quarter	20	19	46
○ Full Moon	28	11	37
Apogee (405,034 km)	3	14	37
Perigee (360,627 km)	15	16	40
Apogee (405,871 km)	31	2	52

Mean longitude of ascending node on May 1, 293°.

See note on Summer Time, p. 24.

MONTHLY NOTES

May   6. Bank Holiday, England, Wales, Scotland and N. Ireland.

9. Liberation Day, Channel Islands.

19. First day of Feast of Weeks.

27. Bank Holiday, England, Wales, Scotland and N. Ireland.

28. Whitsunday (Scottish Term Day and Removal Day).

(*See* page 64 for explanatory notes)

Day	THE SUN									Sidereal Time	Transit of First Point of Aries
	Right Ascension	Dec. +	Equation of Time	Rise 52°	Rise 56°	Transit	Set 52°	Set 56°			
	h m s	° ′	m s	h m	h m	h m	h m	h m		h m s	h m s
1	2 30 53	14 51	+ 2 49	4 31	4 17	11 57	19 24	19 38		14 33 42	9 24 45
2	2 34 42	15 10	+ 2 57	4 30	4 15	11 57	19 26	19 40		14 37 39	9 20 49
3	2 38 32	15 28	+ 3 04	4 28	4 13	11 57	19 27	19 42		14 41 35	9 16 53
4	2 42 22	15 45	+ 3 10	4 26	4 11	11 57	19 29	19 44		14 45 32	9 12 57
5	2 46 13	16 03	+ 3 16	4 24	4 08	11 57	19 31	19 46		14 49 29	9 09 01
6	2 50 04	16 20	+ 3 21	4 22	4 06	11 57	19 32	19 48		14 53 25	9 05 05
7	2 53 56	16 37	+ 3 26	4 20	4 04	11 57	19 34	19 50		14 57 22	9 01 09
8	2 57 48	16 53	+ 3 30	4 19	4 02	11 56	19 35	19 52		15 01 18	8 57 14
9	3 01 41	17 10	+ 3 33	4 17	4 00	11 56	19 37	19 54		15 05 15	8 53 18
10	3 05 35	17 26	+ 3 36	4 15	3 58	11 56	19 39	19 56		15 09 11	8 49 22
11	3 09 29	17 42	+ 3 39	4 13	3 56	11 56	19 40	19 58		15 13 08	8 45 26
12	3 13 24	17 57	+ 3 40	4 12	3 54	11 56	19 42	20 00		15 17 04	8 41 30
13	3 17 19	18 12	+ 3 42	4 10	3 52	11 56	19 43	20 02		15 21 01	8 37 34
14	3 21 15	18 27	+ 3 42	4 09	3 50	11 56	19 45	20 04		15 24 58	8 33 38
15	3 25 12	18 42	+ 3 42	4 07	3 48	11 56	19 47	20 06		15 28 54	8 29 42
16	3 29 09	18 56	+ 3 42	4 05	3 46	11 56	19 48	20 08		15 32 51	8 25 46
17	3 33 07	19 10	+ 3 41	4 04	3 45	11 56	19 50	20 09		15 36 47	8 21 50
18	3 37 05	19 23	+ 3 39	4 03	3 43	11 56	19 51	20 11		15 40 44	8 17 54
19	3 41 04	19 37	+ 3 37	4 01	3 41	11 56	19 53	20 13		15 44 40	8 13 59
20	3 45 03	19 50	+ 3 34	4 00	3 39	11 57	19 54	20 15		15 48 37	8 10 03
21	3 49 03	20 02	+ 3 31	3 58	3 38	11 57	19 56	20 17		15 52 33	8 06 07
22	3 53 03	20 15	+ 3 27	3 57	3 36	11 57	19 57	20 18		15 56 30	8 02 11
23	3 57 04	20 26	+ 3 23	3 56	3 35	11 57	19 58	20 20		16 00 27	7 58 15
24	4 01 05	20 38	+ 3 18	3 55	3 33	11 57	20 00	20 22		16 04 23	7 54 19
25	4 05 07	20 49	+ 3 13	3 53	3 32	11 57	20 01	20 23		16 08 20	7 50 23
26	4 09 09	21 00	+ 3 07	3 52	3 30	11 57	20 02	20 25		16 12 16	7 46 27
27	4 13 12	21 10	+ 3 01	3 51	3 29	11 57	20 04	20 26		16 16 13	7 42 31
28	4 17 16	21 21	+ 2 54	3 50	3 27	11 57	20 05	20 28		16 20 09	7 38 35
29	4 21 19	21 30	+ 2 47	3 49	3 26	11 57	20 06	20 29		16 24 06	7 34 39
30	4 25 23	21 40	+ 2 39	3 48	3 25	11 57	20 07	20 31		16 28 02	7 30 43
31	4 29 28	21 49	+ 2 31	3 47	3 24	11 58	20 09	20 32		16 31 59	7 26 48

THE SUN s.d. 15′·8

Duration of Civil (C), Nautical (N) and Astronomical (A) Twilight (in minutes)

Lat. °	May 1 C	N	A	May 11 C	N	A	May 21 C	N	A	May 31 C	N	A
52	39	90	154	41	97	179	44	106	TAN	46	116	TAN
56	45	106	209	49	121	TAN	53	143	TAN	57	TAN	TAN

ASTRONOMICAL NOTES

MERCURY is at greatest western elongation on the 12th but the long duration of twilight makes observation impossible from the latitudes of the British Isles.

VENUS, magnitude −4·1, is still a magnificent object dominating the western sky in the evenings, before setting well to the north of west. The thin crescent Moon is near the planet on the 16th to 17th. At the very end of the month Venus will be seen passing south of the Twins, Castor and Pollux.

MARS is still an evening object in the western sky, magnitude +1·5. Mars is in Gemini at first, passing 5°S. of Pollux on the 16th, and later moving eastwards into Cancer. The crescent Moon passes Mars, being seen below it on the 17th, and to the left of it on the 18th.

JUPITER, magnitude −2·0, continues to be visible

as a brilliant object in the western sky in the evenings. By the end of the month it is lost to view over the western horizon before midnight. Jupiter is in Cancer. The four Galilean satellites are readily observable with any small telescope or even a good pair of binoculars provided that they are held rigidly. The observer with binoculars will get a pleasant surprise during the middle part of the month as Jupiter passes within 1°S. of the open cluster Praesepe (the Beehive)—which is just visible to the naked eye as a misty patch of light. The Moon passes Jupiter, being seen below the planet on the 18th and to its left on the 19th.

SATURN is a morning object, magnitude +0·6, and visible in the south-eastern sky until twilight inhibits observation. On the morning of the 6th the Moon, near Last Quarter, passes 2°N. of the planet.

(*See* pages 64–65 for explanatory notes)

THE MOON

Day	RA	Dec.	Hor. Par.	Semi-diam.	Sun's Co-long.	P.A. of Bright Limb	Phase	Age	Rise 52°	Rise 56°	Transit	Set 52°	Set 56°
	h m	°	′	′	°	°	%	d	h m	h m	h m	h m	h m
1	16 06	−24·6	54·6	14·9	112	109	96	16·2	22 51	23 22	1 35	5 16	4 47
2	16 59	−25·6	54·3	14·8	124	100	91	17·2	23 40	—	2 26	6 01	5 29
3	17 51	−25·4	54·2	14·8	136	93	85	18·2	—	0 10	3 16	6 55	6 25
4	18 43	−24·1	54·1	14·8	148	86	77	19·2	0 18	0 46	4 06	7 58	7 32
5	19 34	−21·7	54·3	14·8	161	81	69	20·2	0 48	1 10	4 53	9 06	8 45
6	20 22	−18·3	54·6	14·9	173	76	60	21·2	1 11	1 28	5 39	10 17	10 01
7	21 10	−14·2	55·0	15·0	185	73	50	22·2	1 29	1 42	6 24	11 29	11 18
8	21 56	− 9·4	55·7	15·2	197	71	41	23·2	1 45	1 53	7 07	12 42	12 36
9	22 42	− 4·1	56·4	15·4	209	70	31	24·2	2 00	2 03	7 51	13 57	13 56
10	23 29	+ 1·6	57·3	15·6	222	70	22	25·2	2 14	2 12	8 36	15 14	15 19
11	0 18	+ 7·3	58·2	15·8	234	72	13	26·2	2 30	2 23	9 23	16 35	16 45
12	1 10	+12·9	59·0	16·1	246	76	7	27·2	2 48	2 36	10 14	18 01	18 17
13	2 05	+17·9	59·8	16·3	258	86	2	28·2	3 11	2 53	11 10	19 28	19 51
14	3 05	+22·0	60·4	16·5	271	133	0	29·2	3 43	3 19	12 10	20 53	21 22
15	4 09	+24·7	60·7	16·5	283	242	1	0·8	4 27	3 58	13 14	22 08	22 39
16	5 15	+25·6	60·8	16·6	295	260	5	1·8	5 27	4 56	14 20	23 06	23 34
17	6 21	+24·7	60·6	16·5	307	270	11	2·8	6 43	6 15	15 23	23 47	—
18	7 24	+22·1	60·1	16·4	320	278	20	3·8	8 07	7 45	16 22	—	0 10
19	8 24	+18·1	59·5	16·2	332	284	30	4·8	9 33	9 18	17 16	0 17	0 34
20	9 19	+13·2	58·8	16·0	344	288	41	5·8	10 57	10 47	18 06	0 39	0 50
21	10 10	+ 7·7	58·1	15·8	356	291	52	6·8	12 17	12 13	18 53	0 57	1 03
22	10 59	+ 2·0	57·4	15·6	9	292	63	7·8	13 34	13 35	19 38	1 12	1 14
23	11 46	− 3·7	56·7	15·5	21	291	73	8·8	14 50	14 56	20 22	1 27	1 23
24	12 33	− 9·1	56·2	15·3	33	289	81	9·8	16 04	16 16	21 07	1 42	1 34
25	13 21	−14·0	55·6	15·2	45	286	89	10·8	17 18	17 35	21 53	1 58	1 46
26	14 09	−18·3	55·2	15·0	57	281	94	11·8	18 31	18 54	22 41	2 18	2 00
27	15 00	−21·7	54·8	14·9	69	272	98	12·8	19 40	20 08	23 30	2 43	2 20
28	15 51	−24·1	54·5	14·8	82	247	100	13·8	20 43	21 13	—	3 15	2 47
29	16 44	−25·4	54·2	14·8	94	126	100	14·8	21 35	22 06	0 20	3 57	3 26
30	17 37	−25·5	54·1	14·7	106	100	98	15·8	22 17	22 45	1 11	4 48	4 17
31	18 29	−24·4	54·0	14·7	118	89	94	16·8	22 49	23 13	2 01	5 49	5 21

MERCURY

Day	RA	Dec. +	Diam.	Phase	Transit		Day	RA	Dec. +	Diam.	Phase	Transit	
	h m	°			h m			h m	°			h m	
1	1 10	5·3	—	—	10 35		16	1 52	8·1	—	—	10 19	
4	1 15	5·2	—	—	10 28	Mercury is too	19	2 06	9·4	—	—	10 21	Mercury is too
7	1 21	5·5	—	—	10 23	close to the	22	2 21	10·9	—	—	10 25	close to the
10	1 30	6·1	—	—	10 20	Sun for	25	2 37	12·5	—	—	10 30	Sun for
13	1 40	7·0	—	—	10 19	observation	28	2 55	14·2	—	—	10 36	observation
16	1 52	8·1	—	—	10 19		31	3 15	16·0	—	—	10 44	

VENUS / MARS

Day	RA	Dec. +	Diam.	Phase	Transit	5° high. 52°	5° high. 56°	Day	RA	Dec. +	Diam.	Phase	Transit	5° high. 52°	5° high. 56°
	h m	°	″	%	h m	h m	h m		h m	°	″	%	h m	h m	h m
1	5 20	25·3	16	70	14 47	22 34	22 56	1	7 07	24·2	5	92	16 33	0 13	0 33
6	5 45	25·8	16	68	14 52	22 42	23 04	6	7 20	23·9	5	92	16 25	0 03	0 22
11	6 10	25·9	17	66	14 57	22 48	23 10	11	7 32	23·4	5	92	16 18	23 51	0 11
16	6 34	25·8	18	64	15 02	22 52	23 14	16	7 44	22·9	5	93	16 10	23 40	0 00
21	6 58	25·4	19	62	15 06	22 53	23 14	21	7 57	22·3	5	93	16 03	23 29	23 46
26	7 22	24·8	19	59	15 10	22 52	23 13	26	8 09	21·7	5	93	15 56	23 18	23 34
31	7 45	23·9	20	57	15 13	22 49	23 08	31	8 21	21·0	5	94	15 48	23 06	23 21

(See pages 65–66 for explanatory notes)

SUNRISE AND SUNSET

Day	London 0°05′ 51°30′		Bristol 2°35′ 51°28′		Birmingham 1°55′ 52°28′		Manchester 2°15′ 53°28′		Newcastle 1°37′ 54°59′		Glasgow 4°14′ 55°52′		Belfast 5°56′ 54°35′	
	h m	h m	h m	h m	h m	h m	h m	h m	h m	h m	h m	h m	h m	h m
1	4 33	19 23	4 43	19 33	4 38	19 33	4 36	19 38	4 28	19 41	4 35	19 55	4 46	19 57
2	4 31	19 24	4 42	19 34	4 36	19 35	4 34	19 40	4 26	19 43	4 33	19 57	4 44	19 58
3	4 30	19 26	4 40	19 36	4 34	19 37	4 32	19 41	4 23	19 45	4 30	19 59	4 42	20 00
4	4 28	19 28	4 38	19 37	4 32	19 38	4 30	19 43	4 21	19 46	4 28	20 01	4 40	20 02
5	4 26	19 29	4 36	19 39	4 30	19 40	4 28	19 45	4 19	19 48	4 26	20 03	4 38	20 04
6	4 24	19 31	4 34	19 41	4 28	19 42	4 26	19 47	4 17	19 50	4 24	20 05	4 36	20 06
7	4 22	19 32	4 33	19 42	4 26	19 43	4 24	19 48	4 15	19 52	4 22	20 07	4 34	20 08
8	4 21	19 34	4 31	19 44	4 24	19 45	4 22	19 50	4 13	19 54	4 20	20 09	4 32	20 10
9	4 19	19 36	4 29	19 45	4 23	19 47	4 20	19 52	4 11	19 56	4 18	20 10	4 30	20 11
10	4 17	19 37	4 27	19 47	4 21	19 48	4 18	19 54	4 09	19 58	4 16	20 12	4 28	20 13
11	4 16	19 39	4 26	19 49	4 19	19 50	4 16	19 55	4 07	20 00	4 14	20 14	4 26	20 15
12	4 14	19 40	4 24	19 50	4 18	19 51	4 15	19 57	4 05	20 01	4 12	20 16	4 24	20 17
13	4 12	19 42	4 23	19 52	4 16	19 53	4 13	19 59	4 04	20 03	4 10	20 18	4 23	20 19
14	4 11	19 43	4 21	19 53	4 14	19 55	4 11	20 00	4 02	20 05	4 08	20 20	4 21	20 20
15	4 09	19 45	4 20	19 55	4 13	19 56	4 10	20 02	4 00	20 07	4 06	20 22	4 19	20 22
16	4 08	19 46	4 18	19 56	4 11	19 58	4 08	20 04	3 58	20 09	4 04	20 24	4 17	20 24
17	4 06	19 48	4 17	19 58	4 10	19 59	4 06	20 05	3 56	20 10	4 02	20 26	4 16	20 26
18	4 05	19 49	4 15	19 59	4 08	20 01	4 05	20 07	3 55	20 12	4 00	20 27	4 14	20 27
19	4 04	19 51	4 14	20 01	4 07	20 02	4 03	20 09	3 53	20 14	3 59	20 29	4 12	20 29
20	4 02	19 52	4 12	20 02	4 05	20 04	4 02	20 10	3 51	20 15	3 57	20 31	4 11	20 31
21	4 01	19 54	4 11	20 03	4 04	20 05	4 00	20 12	3 50	20 17	3 55	20 33	4 09	20 32
22	4 00	19 55	4 10	20 05	4 03	20 07	3 59	20 13	3 48	20 19	3 54	20 34	4 08	20 34
23	3 58	19 56	4 09	20 06	4 01	20 08	3 58	20 15	3 47	20 20	3 52	20 36	4 06	20 35
24	3 57	19 58	4 07	20 08	4 00	20 10	3 56	20 16	3 45	20 22	3 51	20 38	4 05	20 37
25	3 56	19 59	4 06	20 09	3 59	20 11	3 55	20 18	3 44	20 24	3 49	20 39	4 04	20 38
26	3 55	20 00	4 05	20 10	3 58	20 12	3 54	20 19	3 43	20 25	3 48	20 41	4 02	20 40
27	3 54	20 02	4 04	20 11	3 57	20 14	3 53	20 20	3 41	20 27	3 46	20 43	4 01	20 41
28	3 53	20 03	4 03	20 13	3 55	20 15	3 51	20 22	3 40	20 28	3 45	20 44	4 00	20 43
29	3 52	20 04	4 02	20 14	3 54	20 16	3 50	20 23	3 39	20 29	3 44	20 46	3 59	20 44
30	3 51	20 05	4 01	20 15	3 53	20 18	3 49	20 24	3 38	20 31	3 43	20 47	3 58	20 46
31	3 50	20 06	4 00	20 16	3 52	20 19	3 48	20 26	3 37	20 32	3 41	20 48	3 56	20 47

JUPITER

Day	RA	Dec. +	Transit	5° high. 52°	5° high. 56°
	h m	° ′	h m	h m	h m
1	8 30·4	19 45	17 54	1 09	1 22
11	8 34·7	19 29	17 19	0 32	0 46
21	8 39·9	19 09	16 45	23 52	0 09
31	8 45·9	18 46	16 12	23 17	23 30

Diameters—equatorial 35″ polar 33″

SATURN

Day	RA	Dec. −	Transit	5° high. 52°	5° high. 56°
	h m	° ′	h m	h m	h m
1	20 36·4	18 56	6 02	2 27	2 51
11	20 37·2	18 54	5 23	1 48	2 13
21	20 37·3	18 55	4 44	1 09	1 34
31	20 36·7	18 58	4 04	0 29	0 54

Diameters—equatorial 17″ polar 16″
Rings—major axis 39″ minor axis 13″

URANUS

Day	RA	Dec. −	Transit	10° high. 52°	10° high. 56°
	h m	° ′	h m	h m	h m
1	18 59·9	23 05	4 25	2 20	3 29
11	18 59·3	23 07	3 46	1 40	2 50
21	18 58·3	23 08	3 05	1 00	2 10
31	18 57·1	23 10	2 25	0 20	1 31

Diameter 4″

NEPTUNE

Day	RA	Dec. −	Transit	10° high. 52°	10° high. 56°
	h m	° ′	h m	h m	h m
1	19 12·1	21 36	4 38	2 14	3 06
11	19 11·7	21 36	3 58	1 35	2 27
21	19 11·1	21 37	3 18	0 55	1 47
31	19 10·4	21 38	2 38	0 15	1 07

Diameter 2″

(*See* page 66 for explanatory notes)

DAY OF		Junius, Roman gens (family). Sun's Longitude 90° ♋ 21ᵈ 21ʰ
Month	Week	
1	S.	Glinka b. 1804. Sir Hugh Walpole d. 1941.
2	S.	**2nd S. after Pentecost.** CORONATION DAY 1953.
3	M.	Bizet d. 1875. Arthur Ransome d. 1967.
4	Tu.	TRINITY LAW SITTINGS BEGIN.
5	W.	Weber d. 1826. John Maynard Keynes b. 1883.
6	Th.	Ninette de Valois b. 1898. Bjorn Borg b. 1956.
7	F.	Robert the Bruce d. 1329. Jean Harlow d. 1937.
8	S.	Thomas Paine d. 1809. Sarah Siddons d. 1831.
9	S.	**3rd S. after Pentecost.** Sybil Thorndike d. 1976.
10	M.	DUKE OF EDINBURGH b. 1921. Judy Garland b. 1922.
11	Tu.	**St. Barnabas.** Jackie Stewart b. 1939.
12	W.	Charles Kingsley b. 1819. George Bush b. 1924.
13	Th.	Dorothy L. Sayers b. 1893. Henry Segrave d. 1930.
14	F.	Emmeline Pankhurst d. 1928. G.K. Chesterton
15	S.	Wat Tyler exec. 1381. Grieg b. 1843. [d. 1936.
16	S.	**4th S. after Pentecost.** Brian Statham b. 1930.
17	M.	Joseph Addison d. 1719. Burne-Jones d. 1898.
18	Tu.	Waterloo 1815. Gorky d. 1936.
19	W.	Walter Hammond b. 1903. James Barrie d. 1937.
20	Th.	Machiavelli d. 1527. William IV d. 1837.
21	F.	PRINCE WILLIAM OF WALES b. 1982.
22	S.	Walter de la Mare d. 1956. Darius Milhaud d. 1974.
23	S.	**5th S. after Pentecost.** Len Hutton b. 1916.
24	M.	**St. John the Baptist.** Bannockburn 1314.
25	Tu.	Gustave Charpentier b. 1860. Lord Mountbatten b.
26	W.	United Nations Charter signed 1945. [1900.
27	Th.	Harriet Martineau d. 1876. Helen Keller b. 1880.
28	F.	Treaty of Versailles signed 1919.
29	S.	**St. Peter.** SS. PETER AND PAUL.
30	S.	**6th S. after Pentecost.** Margery Allingham d. 1966.

PHENOMENA

d	h	
2	13	Saturn in conjunction with Moon. Saturn 2°S.
	12 01	Mercury in conjunction with Moon. Mercury 3°S.
	13 22	Venus at greatest elongation E. 45°.
14	15	Jupiter in conjunction with Mars. Jupiter 0°.6S.
15	18	Venus in conjunction with Moon. Venus 4°N.
15	21	Jupiter in conjunction with Moon. Jupiter 3°N.
15	22	Mars in conjunction with Moon. Mars 3°N.
17	05	Mercury in superior conjunction.
18	10	Jupiter in conjunction with Venus. Jupiter 1°S.
21	21	Solstice.
23	18	Mars in conjunction with Venus. Mars 0°.2S.
29	17	Saturn in conjunction with Moon. Saturn 2°S.

CONSTELLATIONS

The following constellations are near the meridian at

	d	h		d	h
May	1	24	May	16	23
June	1	22	June	15	21
July	1	20	July	16	19

Cassiopeia (below the Pole), Ursa Minor, Draco, Ursa Major, Canes Venatici, Bootes, Corona, Serpens, Virgo and Libra.

ALGOL

ALGOL is inconveniently situated for observation during June.

MOON
Phases, Apsides & Node

		d	h	m
☾	Last Quarter	5	15	30
●	New Moon	12	12	6
☽	First Quarter	19	4	19
○	Full Moon	27	2	58

	d	h	m
Perigee (357,779 km)	13	0	24
Apogee (406,243 km)	27	7	22

Mean longitude of ascending node on June 1, 291°.

See note on Summer Time, p. 24.

MONTHLY NOTES

June 15. Queen's Official Birthday.

21. Longest day.

24. Midsummer Day (Quarter Day).

(See page 64 for explanatory notes)

Day	Right Ascension	Dec. +	Equation of Time	Rise 52°	Rise 56°	Transit	Set 52°	Set 56°	Sidereal Time	Transit of First Point of Aries
	h m s	° ′	m s	h m	h m	h m	h m	h m	h m s	h m s
1	4 33 33	21 57	+ 2 22	3 46	3 23	11 58	20 10	20 34	16 35 56	7 22 52
2	4 37 39	22 06	+ 2 13	3 46	3 21	11 58	20 11	20 35	16 39 52	7 18 56
3	4 41 45	22 13	+ 2 04	3 45	3 20	11 58	20 12	20 36	16 43 49	7 15 00
4	4 45 51	22 21	+ 1 54	3 44	3 20	11 58	20 13	20 38	16 47 45	7 11 04
5	4 49 58	22 28	+ 1 44	3 43	3 19	11 58	20 14	20 39	16 51 42	7 07 08
6	4 54 05	22 35	+ 1 34	3 43	3 18	11 59	20 15	20 40	16 55 38	7 03 12
7	4 58 12	22 41	+ 1 23	3 42	3 17	11 59	20 16	20 41	16 59 35	6 59 16
8	5 02 20	22 47	+ 1 12	3 42	3 16	11 59	20 17	20 42	17 03 31	6 55 20
9	5 06 28	22 52	+ 1 00	3 41	3 16	11 59	20 17	20 43	17 07 28	6 51 24
10	5 10 36	22 57	+ 0 49	3 41	3 15	11 59	20 18	20 44	17 11 25	6 47 28
11	5 14 45	23 02	+ 0 37	3 40	3 15	11 59	20 19	20 45	17 15 21	6 43 33
12	5 18 53	23 06	+ 0 24	3 40	3 14	12 00	20 20	20 46	17 19 18	6 39 37
13	5 23 02	23 10	+ 0 12	3 40	3 14	12 00	20 20	20 47	17 23 14	6 35 41
14	5 27 12	23 14	− 0 01	3 40	3 13	12 00	20 21	20 47	17 27 11	6 31 45
15	5 31 21	23 17	− 0 14	3 39	3 13	12 00	20 21	20 48	17 31 07	6 27 49
16	5 35 30	23 19	− 0 26	3 39	3 13	12 01	20 22	20 48	17 35 04	6 23 53
17	5 39 40	23 22	− 0 39	3 39	3 13	12 01	20 22	20 49	17 39 01	6 19 57
18	5 43 49	23 23	− 0 52	3 39	3 13	12 01	20 23	20 49	17 42 57	6 16 01
19	5 47 59	23 25	− 1 05	3 39	3 13	12 01	20 23	20 50	17 46 54	6 12 05
20	5 52 09	23 26	− 1 18	3 39	3 13	12 01	20 23	20 50	17 50 50	6 08 09
21	5 56 18	23 26	− 1 31	3 40	3 13	12 02	20 24	20 50	17 54 47	6 04 13
22	6 00 28	23 26	− 1 44	3 40	3 13	12 02	20 24	20 51	17 58 43	6 00 18
23	6 04 37	23 26	− 1 57	3 40	3 13	12 02	20 24	20 51	18 02 40	5 56 22
24	6 08 47	23 26	− 2 10	3 40	3 14	12 02	20 24	20 51	18 06 36	5 52 26
25	6 12 56	23 24	− 2 23	3 41	3 14	12 02	20 24	20 51	18 10 33	5 48 30
26	6 17 05	23 23	− 2 36	3 41	3 15	12 03	20 24	20 51	18 14 30	5 44 34
27	6 21 15	23 21	− 2 48	3 42	3 15	12 03	20 24	20 50	18 18 26	5 40 38
28	6 25 24	23 19	− 3 01	3 42	3 16	12 03	20 24	20 50	18 22 23	5 36 42
29	6 29 32	23 16	− 3 13	3 43	3 16	12 03	20 24	20 50	18 26 19	5 32 46
30	6 33 41	23 13	− 3 25	3 43	3 17	12 04	20 24	20 50	18 30 16	5 28 50

Duration of Civil (C), Nautical (N) and Astronomical (A) Twilight (in minutes)

Lat. °	June 1 C	June 1 N	June 1 A	June 11 C	June 11 N	June 11 A	June 21 C	June 21 N	June 21 A	June 30 C	June 30 N	June 30 A
52	47	117	TAN	48	125	TAN	49	128	TAN	49	125	TAN
56	58	TAN	TAN	61	TAN	TAN	63	TAN	TAN	62	TAN	TAN

ASTRONOMICAL NOTES

MERCURY is unsuitably placed for observation, superior conjunction occurring on the 17th.

VENUS continues to be visible as a magnificent object in the western skies in the evenings, magnitude −4·3. On the evening of the 15th the crescent Moon passes 4°S. of the planet. On the late evening of the 17th Venus passes 1°.2N. of Jupiter, while on the evenings of the 22nd and 23rd Venus is close to Mars.

MARS, magnitude +1·7, is an evening object, though no longer a prominent one as it draws closer to the Sun and by the end of the month it will be difficult to locate the planet above the western horizon because of the long twilight.

JUPITER is still a brilliant object in the western sky in the evenings, magnitude −1·9.

SATURN, magnitude +0·4, is a morning object and by the end of the month visible well before midnight low in the south-eastern sky. Saturn is in Capricornus. The gibbous Moon is near the planet on the 2nd–3rd and again on the 29th–30th.

EVENING SPECTACLE. The three planets Venus, Mars, and Jupiter are all close together low in the WNW sky particularly during the second part of the month, Venus being the brightest and Mars the faintest. The spectacle is enhanced on the 15th with the thin crescent Moon below the cluster of planets.

TWILIGHT. Reference to the section just above these notes shows that astronomical twilight lasts all night for some time around the summer solstice (i.e. in June and July), even in southern England. Under these conditions the sky never gets completely dark since the Sun is always less than 18° below the horizon.

(See pages 64–65 for explanatory notes)

THE MOON

Day	RA	Dec.	Hor. Par.	Semi-diam.	Sun's Co-long.	P.A. of Bright Limb	Phase	Age	Rise 52°	Rise 56°	Transit	Set 52°	Set 56°
	h m	°	′	′	°	°	%	d	h m	h m	h m	h m	h m
1	19 19	−22·3	54·1	14·7	130	82	89	17·8	23 14	23 33	2 49	6 55	6 32
2	20 08	−19·2	54·2	14·8	143	77	83	18·8	23 34	23 48	3 35	8 05	7 47
3	20 56	−15·3	54·5	14·9	155	73	75	19·8	23 50	—	4 20	9 16	9 03
4	21 42	−10·7	55·0	15·0	167	70	66	20·8	—	0 00	5 03	10 27	10 19
5	22 27	− 5·6	55·6	15·1	179	68	57	21·8	0 05	0 10	5 45	11 39	11 36
6	23 12	− 0·2	56·3	15·3	191	67	47	22·8	0 19	0 19	6 28	12 53	12 55
7	23 59	+ 5·3	57·2	15·6	204	68	36	23·8	0 33	0 29	7 13	14 10	14 17
8	0 49	+10·9	58·1	15·8	216	70	26	24·8	0 50	0 40	8 01	15 31	15 44
9	1 41	+16·0	59·0	16·1	228	73	17	25·8	1 10	0 55	8 53	16 56	17 16
10	2 39	+20·5	59·9	16·3	240	79	9	26·8	1 36	1 16	9 50	18 22	18 48
11	3 41	+23·7	60·6	16·5	253	87	4	27·8	2 14	1 47	10 53	19 43	20 13
12	4 46	+25·4	61·1	16·7	265	106	0	28·8	3 06	2 36	11 59	20 50	21 20
13	5 54	+25·3	61·3	16·7	277	255	0	0·5	4 16	3 47	13 05	21 40	22 06
14	7 00	+23·2	61·1	16·7	289	275	3	1·5	5 40	5 16	14 08	22 16	22 36
15	8 02	+19·6	60·7	16·5	302	283	9	2·5	7 09	6 51	15 06	22 42	22 55
16	9 01	+14·8	60·0	16·3	314	288	17	3·5	8 37	8 26	15 59	23 02	23 10
17	9 55	+ 9·2	59·2	16·1	326	292	27	4·5	10 01	9 56	16 49	23 18	23 21
18	10 45	+ 3·4	58·3	15·9	338	293	37	5·5	11 22	11 21	17 35	23 34	23 32
19	11 34	− 2·4	57·4	15·6	351	294	48	6·5	12 39	12 44	18 21	23 49	23 42
20	12 22	− 8·0	56·6	15·4	3	293	59	7·5	13 54	14 04	19 06	—	23 53
21	13 09	−13·0	55·9	15·2	15	290	69	8·5	15 09	15 24	19 51	0 05	—
22	13 58	−17·5	55·3	15·1	27	287	77	9·5	16 22	16 43	20 38	0 24	0 07
23	14 47	−21·0	54·8	14·9	39	283	85	10·5	17 32	17 58	21 27	0 47	0 25
24	15 38	−23·7	54·5	14·8	52	277	91	11·5	18 36	19 06	22 17	1 16	0 50
25	16 31	−25·2	54·2	14·8	64	271	96	12·5	19 32	20 03	23 07	1 54	1 24
26	17 23	−25·6	54·0	14·7	76	263	99	13·5	20 17	20 46	23 57	2 42	2 12
27	18 16	−24·8	54·0	14·7	88	222	100	14·5	20 52	21 17	—	3 40	3 12
28	19 07	−22·9	54·0	14·7	100	85	99	15·5	21 19	21 39	0 46	4 45	4 21
29	19 56	−20·0	54·1	14·7	113	77	97	16·5	21 40	21 55	1 33	5 55	5 35
30	20 44	−16·2	54·3	14·8	125	72	93	17·5	21 57	22 08	2 18	7 05	6 51

MERCURY

Day	RA	Dec. +	Diam.	Phase	Transit		Day	RA	Dec. +	Diam.	Phase	Transit	
	h m	°			h m			h m	°			h m	
1	3 22	16·6	—	—	10 47		16	5 29	24·1	—	—	11 57	
4	3 44	18·4	—	—	10 58	Mercury is too	19	5 58	24·7	—	—	12 14	Mercury is too
7	4 08	20·1	—	—	11 10	close to the	22	6 26	24·9	—	—	12 31	close to the
10	4 33	21·7	—	—	11 24	Sun for	25	6 54	24·7	—	—	12 46	Sun for
13	5 00	23·1	—	—	11 40	observation	28	7 21	24·1	—	—	13 01	observation
16	5 29	24·1	—	—	11 57		31	7 45	23·2	—	—	13 13	

VENUS

Day	RA	Dec. +	Diam.	Phase	Transit	5° high 52°	5° high 56°
	h m	°	″	%	h m	h m	h m
1	7 49	23·7	21	56	15 13	22 49	23 07
6	8 11	22·6	22	54	15 15	22 43	23 00
11	8 31	21·3	23	51	15 16	22 36	22 51
16	8 51	19·8	24	48	15 16	22 26	22 40
21	9 09	18·2	26	45	15 14	22 15	22 27
26	9 26	16·5	27	42	15 11	22 03	22 13
31	9 42	14·7	29	39	15 07	21 48	21 57

MARS

Day	RA	Dec. +	Diam.	Phase	Transit	5° high 52°	5° high 56°
	h m	°	″	%	h m	h m	h m
1	8 24	20·9	5	94	15 47	23 04	23 19
6	8 36	20·1	4	94	15 39	22 52	23 06
11	8 48	19·3	4	94	15 31	22 40	22 53
16	9 00	18·4	4	95	15 24	22 27	22 39
21	9 12	17·5	4	95	15 16	22 14	22 26
26	9 24	16·6	4	95	15 08	22 01	22 12
31	9 36	15·6	4	95	15 01	21 48	21 57

(*See* pages 65–66 for explanatory notes)

SUNRISE AND SUNSET

Day	London 0°05′ 51°30′		Bristol 2°35′ 51°28′		Birmingham 1°55′ 52°28′		Manchester 2°15′ 53°28′		Newcastle 1°37′ 54°59′		Glasgow 4°14′ 55°52′		Belfast 5°56′ 54°35′	
	h m	h m	h m	h m	h m	h m	h m	h m	h m	h m	h m	h m	h m	h m
1	3 49	20 07	3 59	20 17	3 52	20 20	3 47	20 27	3 36	20 33	3 40	20 50	3 55	20 48
2	3 48	20 09	3 59	20 18	3 51	20 21	3 46	20 28	3 35	20 35	3 39	20 51	3 54	20 49
3	3 48	20 10	3 58	20 19	3 50	20 22	3 46	20 29	3 34	20 36	3 38	20 52	3 54	20 51
4	3 47	20 11	3 57	20 20	3 49	20 23	3 45	20 30	3 33	20 37	3 37	20 54	3 53	20 52
5	3 46	20 12	3 57	20 21	3 48	20 24	3 44	20 31	3 32	20 38	3 36	20 55	3 52	20 53
6	3 46	20 12	3 56	20 22	3 48	20 25	3 43	20 32	3 31	20 39	3 36	20 56	3 51	20 54
7	3 45	20 13	3 55	20 23	3 47	20 26	3 43	20 33	3 31	20 40	3 35	20 57	3 50	20 55
8	3 45	20 14	3 55	20 24	3 47	20 27	3 42	20 34	3 30	20 41	3 34	20 58	3 50	20 56
9	3 44	20 15	3 54	20 25	3 46	20 28	3 42	20 35	3 29	20 42	3 34	20 59	3 49	20 57
10	3 44	20 16	3 54	20 26	3 46	20 29	3 41	20 36	3 29	20 43	3 33	21 00	3 49	20 58
11	3 43	20 17	3 54	20 26	3 45	20 29	3 41	20 37	3 28	20 44	3 32	21 01	3 48	20 59
12	3 43	20 17	3 53	20 27	3 45	20 30	3 40	20 37	3 28	20 45	3 32	21 02	3 48	20 59
13	3 43	20 18	3 53	20 28	3 45	20 31	3 40	20 38	3 28	20 46	3 32	21 02	3 48	21 00
14	3 43	20 18	3 53	20 28	3 45	20 31	3 40	20 39	3 27	20 46	3 31	21 03	3 47	21 01
15	3 43	20 19	3 53	20 29	3 44	20 32	3 40	20 39	3 27	20 47	3 31	21 04	3 47	21 01
16	3 42	20 19	3 53	20 29	3 44	20 32	3 39	20 40	3 27	20 47	3 31	21 04	3 47	21 02
17	3 42	20 20	3 53	20 30	3 44	20 33	3 39	20 40	3 27	20 48	3 31	21 05	3 47	21 02
18	3 42	20 20	3 53	20 30	3 44	20 33	3 39	20 41	3 27	20 48	3 31	21 05	3 47	21 03
19	3 43	20 21	3 53	20 30	3 44	20 34	3 39	20 41	3 27	20 49	3 31	21 06	3 47	21 03
20	3 43	20 21	3 53	20 31	3 44	20 34	3 39	20 41	3 27	20 49	3 31	21 06	3 47	21 03
21	3 43	20 21	3 53	20 31	3 44	20 34	3 40	20 42	3 27	20 49	3 31	21 06	3 47	21 04
22	3 43	20 21	3 53	20 31	3 45	20 34	3 40	20 42	3 27	20 49	3 31	21 06	3 47	21 04
23	3 43	20 22	3 53	20 31	3 45	20 34	3 40	20 42	3 27	20 50	3 31	21 07	3 47	21 04
24	3 44	20 22	3 54	20 31	3 45	20 35	3 40	20 42	3 28	20 50	3 32	21 07	3 48	21 04
25	3 44	20 22	3 54	20 31	3 46	20 35	3 41	20 42	3 28	20 50	3 32	21 07	3 48	21 04
26	3 44	20 22	3 54	20 31	3 46	20 35	3 41	20 42	3 29	20 50	3 33	21 07	3 49	21 04
27	3 45	20 22	3 55	20 31	3 47	20 34	3 42	20 42	3 29	20 49	3 33	21 06	3 49	21 04
28	3 45	20 21	3 55	20 31	3 47	20 34	3 42	20 42	3 30	20 49	3 34	21 06	3 50	21 04
29	3 46	20 21	3 56	20 31	3 48	20 34	3 43	20 42	3 30	20 49	3 34	21 06	3 50	21 04
30	3 46	20 21	3 57	20 31	3 48	20 34	3 43	20 41	3 31	20 49	3 35	21 06	3 51	21 03

JUPITER

Day	RA	Dec. +	Transit	5° high 52°	5° high 56°
	h m	° ′	h m	h m	h m
1	8 46·5	18 43	16 08	23 13	23 26
11	8 53·3	18 17	15 36	22 38	22 51
21	9 00·5	17 46	15 04	22 03	22 15
31	9 08·2	17 14	14 32	21 29	21 40

Diameters—equatorial 33″ polar 31″

SATURN

Day	RA	Dec. −	Transit	5° high 52°	5° high 56°
	h m	° ′	h m	h m	h m
1	20 36·6	18 58	4 00	0 25	0 50
11	20 35·4	19 04	3 19	23 41	0 11
21	20 33·5	19 12	2 38	23 01	23 27
31	20 31·2	19 22	1 57	22 21	22 47

Diameters—equatorial 18″ polar 16″
Rings—major axis 41″ minor axis 13″

URANUS

Day	RA	Dec. −	Transit	10° high 52°	10° high 56°
	h m	° ′	h m	h m	h m
1	18 57·0	23 10	2 21	0 16	1 27
11	18 55·5	23 12	1 40	23 32	0 47
21	18 53·9	23 15	0 59	22 51	0 07
31	18 52·2	23 17	0 18	22 11	23 24

Diameter 4″

NEPTUNE

Day	RA	Dec. −	Transit	10° high 52°	10° high 56°
	h m	° ′	h m	h m	h m
1	19 10·3	21 38	2 34	0 11	1 03
11	19 09·3	21 40	1 54	23 27	0 23
21	19 08·3	21 42	1 14	22 47	23 40
31	19 07·2	21 43	0 33	22 07	23 00

Diameter 2″

(See page 66 for explanatory notes)

DAY OF		
Month	Week	*Julius* Caesar, formerly *Quintilis,* 5th month (from March). Sun's Longitude 120° ♌ 23ᵈ 08ʰ

1	M.	PRINCESS OF WALES *b.* 1961. Amy Johnson *b.* 1903.
2	Tu.	Thomas Cranmer *b.* 1489. Rousseau *d.* 1778.
3	W.	St. Thomas. Janáček *b.* 1854.
4	Th.	INDEPENDENCE DAY, USA 1776. Alec Bedser *b.* 1918.
5	F.	Cecil Rhodes *b.* 1853. Georges Pompidou *b.* 1911.
6	S.	Thomas More *exec.* 1535. Aneurin Bevan *d.* 1960.
7	S.	7th S. after Pentecost. Chagall *b.* 1887.
8	M.	Edmund Burke *d.* 1797. Wilfred Rhodes *d.* 1973.
9	Tu.	Ann Radcliffe *b.* 1764. Edward Heath *b.* 1916.
10	W.	Stubbs *d.* 1806. Pissarro *b.* 1830.
11	Th.	George Gershwin *d.* 1937.
12	F.	Josiah Wedgwood *b.* 1730. Alfred Dreyfus *d.* 1935.
13	S.	Marat *assass.* 1793. Schönberg *d.* 1951.
14	S.	8th S. after Pentecost. FÊTE NATIONALE, FRANCE.
15	M.	ST. SWITHIN'S DAY. Rembrandt *b.* 1606.
16	Tu.	Roald Amundsen *b.* 1872. Hilaire Belloc *d.* 1953.
17	W.	First issue of *Punch* 1841. Whistler *d.* 1903.
18	Th.	Jane Austen *d.* 1817. W.G. Grace *b.* 1848.
19	F.	*Mary Rose* sank 1545. Degas *b.* 1834.
20	S.	Edmund Hillary *b.* 1919. Paul Valéry *d.* 1945.
21	S.	9th S. after Pentecost. 1st men on Moon 1969.
22	M.	St. Mary Magdalen. William Spooner *b.* 1844.
23	Tu.	Ulysses Grant *d.* 1885. Marshal Pétain *d.* 1951.
24	W.	Dumas (père) *b.* 1802. Matthew Webb *d.* 1883.
25	Th.	St. James. Lord Balfour *b.* 1848.
26	F.	Carl Jung *b.* 1875. Robert Graves *b.* 1895.
27	S.	Dumas (fils) *b.* 1824. Anton Dolin *b.* 1904.
28	S.	10th S. after Pentecost. Sobers *b.* 1936.
29	M.	Schumann *d.* 1856. John Barbirolli *d.* 1970.
30	Tu.	Henry Ford *b.* 1863. Bismarck *d.* 1898.
31	W.	TRINITY LAW SITTINGS END. Liszt *d.* 1886.

PHENOMENA

d	h	
4	07	Uranus at opposition.
6	15	Earth at aphelion (152 million km).
8	00	Neptune at opposition.
13	12	Mercury in conjunction with Moon. Mercury 3°N.
13	16	Jupiter in conjunction with Moon. Jupiter 3°N.
14	12	Mars in conjunction with Moon. Mars 4°N.
14	17	Venus in conjunction with Moon. Venus 3°N.
15	07	Jupiter in conjunction with Mercury. Jupiter 0°.1N.
17	06	Venus at greatest brilliancy.
25	02	Mercury at greatest elongation E.27°.
26	06	Mars in conjunction with Venus. Mars 4°N.
26	19	Saturn in conjunction with Moon. Saturn 2°S.
27	00	Saturn at opposition.

CONSTELLATIONS

The following constellations are near the meridian at

d	h		d	h
June 1	24		June 15	23
July 1	22		July 16	21
Aug. 1	20		Aug. 16	19

Ursa Minor, Draco, Corona, Hercules, Lyra, Serpens, Ophiuchus, Libra, Scorpius and Sagittarius.

MINIMA OF ALGOL

d	h		d	h
2	12		19	17
5	09		22	14
8	05		25	10
11	02		28	07
13	23		31	04
16	20			

MOON
Phases, Apsides & Node

		d	h	m
☾ Last Quarter		5	2	50
● New Moon		11	19	6
☽ First Quarter		18	15	11
○ Full Moon		26	18	24
Perigee (357,599 km)		11	10	4
Apogee (405,966 km)		24	11	10

Mean longitude of ascending node on July 1, 290°

See note on Summer Time, p. 24.

MONTHLY NOTES

July   1. National Day, Canada.

     3. Dog Days begin (end Aug. 15).

     5. Tynwald Day, Isle of Man.

    12. Bank Holiday, Northern Ireland.

    13. Islamic New Year (AH 1412).

(*See* page 64 for explanatory notes)

				THE SUN		s.d. 15'·8			Sidereal Time	Transit of First Point of Aries
Day	Right Ascension	Dec. +	Equation of Time	Rise 52°	Rise 56°	Transit	Set 52°	Set 56°		
	h m s	° ′	m s	h m	h m	h m	h m	h m	h m s	h m s
1	6 37 49	23 09	− 3 37	3 44	3 18	12 04	20 23	20 49	18 34 12	5 24 54
2	6 41 58	23 05	− 3 49	3 45	3 19	12 04	20 23	20 49	18 38 09	5 20 58
3	6 46 05	23 01	− 4 00	3 45	3 20	12 04	20 23	20 48	18 42 05	5 17 02
4	6 50 13	22 56	− 4 11	3 46	3 20	12 04	20 22	20 48	18 46 02	5 13 07
5	6 54 21	22 51	− 4 22	3 47	3 21	12 04	20 22	20 47	18 49 59	5 09 11
6	6 58 28	22 46	− 4 32	3 48	3 22	12 05	20 21	20 46	18 53 55	5 05 15
7	7 02 34	22 40	− 4 43	3 49	3 24	12 05	20 20	20 45	18 57 52	5 01 19
8	7 06 41	22 33	− 4 53	3 50	3 25	12 05	20 20	20 44	19 01 48	4 57 23
9	7 10 47	22 27	− 5 02	3 51	3 26	12 05	20 19	20 44	19 05 45	4 53 27
10	7 14 52	22 20	− 5 11	3 52	3 27	12 05	20 18	20 43	19 09 41	4 49 31
11	7 18 58	22 12	− 5 20	3 53	3 28	12 05	20 18	20 42	19 13 38	4 45 35
12	7 23 03	22 04	− 5 28	3 54	3 30	12 06	20 17	20 40	19 17 34	4 41 39
13	7 27 07	21 56	− 5 36	3 55	3 31	12 06	20 16	20 39	19 21 31	4 37 43
14	7 31 11	21 47	− 5 43	3 56	3 32	12 06	20 15	20 38	19 25 28	4 33 47
15	7 35 14	21 38	− 5 50	3 57	3 34	12 06	20 14	20 37	19 29 24	4 29 52
16	7 39 17	21 29	− 5 56	3 58	3 35	12 06	20 13	20 36	19 33 21	4 25 56
17	7 43 19	21 20	− 6 02	4 00	3 37	12 06	20 12	20 34	19 37 17	4 22 00
18	7 47 21	21 09	− 6 08	4 01	3 38	12 06	20 11	20 33	19 41 14	4 18 04
19	7 51 23	20 59	− 6 12	4 02	3 40	12 06	20 09	20 31	19 45 10	4 14 08
20	7 55 23	20 48	− 6 16	4 03	3 42	12 06	20 08	20 30	19 49 07	4 10 12
21	7 59 23	20 37	− 6 20	4 05	3 43	12 06	20 07	20 28	19 53 03	4 06 16
22	8 03 23	20 25	− 6 23	4 06	3 45	12 06	20 06	20 27	19 57 00	4 02 20
23	8 07 22	20 13	− 6 25	4 08	3 47	12 06	20 04	20 25	20 00 57	3 58 24
24	8 11 20	20 01	− 6 27	4 09	3 48	12 06	20 03	20 23	20 04 53	3 54 28
25	8 15 18	19 49	− 6 29	4 10	3 50	12 06	20 02	20 22	20 08 50	3 50 32
26	8 19 16	19 36	− 6 29	4 12	3 52	12 06	20 00	20 20	20 12 46	3 46 37
27	8 23 12	19 23	− 6 29	4 13	3 54	12 06	19 59	20 18	20 16 43	3 42 41
28	8 27 08	19 09	− 6 29	4 15	3 55	12 06	19 57	20 16	20 20 39	3 38 45
29	8 31 04	18 55	− 6 28	4 16	3 57	12 06	19 56	20 14	20 24 36	3 34 49
30	8 34 58	18 41	− 6 26	4 18	3 59	12 06	19 54	20 13	20 28 32	3 30 53
31	8 38 53	18 27	− 6 24	4 19	4 01	12 06	19 52	20 11	20 32 29	3 26 57

Duration of Civil (C), Nautical (N) and Astronomical (A) Twilight (in minutes)

Lat. °	July 1			July 11			July 21			July 31		
	C	N	A	C	N	A	C	N	A	C	N	A
52	48	124	TAN	46	116	TAN	44	107	TAN	41	98	180
56	61	TAN	TAN	58	TAN	TAN	53	144	TAN	49	122	TAN

ASTRONOMICAL NOTES

MERCURY is at greatest eastern elongation on the 25th but the long duration of twilight makes observation impossible from the latitudes of the British Isles.

VENUS, magnitude −4·5, attains its greatest brilliancy on the 17th. It is visible as a magnificent object in the western sky in the evenings but the period available for observation is shortening noticeably and it will be lost in the glare of sunset at the very end of the month. Until the end of the month Venus remains within a few degrees of Mars, though Mars is 6 magnitudes fainter and can only be detected with optical aid. Through a small telescope Venus exhibits noticeable changes during the month; its diameter increases from 29″ to 47″ while the phase changes from 39% to 14% illuminated. Venus passes 1°S. of Regulus on the 11th.

MARS is disappearing into the long evening twilight at the very beginning of the month and will not be seen again this year.

JUPITER, magnitude −1·8, is an evening object but only visible for a short while low above the western horizon. By the end of the month it is lost in the gathering twilight.

SATURN, magnitude +0·2, is at opposition on the 27th and thus visible throughout the hours of darkness.

URANUS is at opposition on the 4th, in Sagittarius. Uranus is barely visible to the naked eye since its magnitude is +5·6, but it is readily located with only small optical aid.

NEPTUNE is at opposition on the 8th, in Sagittarius. It is not visible to the naked eye since its magnitude is +7·9.

ECLIPSE. A total eclipse of the Sun occurs on the 11th. See page 74 for details.

(See pages 64–65 for explanatory notes)

THE MOON

Day	RA	Dec.	Hor. Par.	Semi- diam.	Sun's Co- long.	P.A. of Bright Limb	Phase	Age	Rise 52°	Rise 56°	Tran- sit	Set 52°	Set 56°
	h m	°	′	′	°	°	%	d	h m	h m	h m	h m	h m
1	21 30	−11·8	54·6	14·9	137	69	87	18·5	22 12	22 18	3 01	8 16	8 07
2	22 15	− 6·9	55·0	15·0	149	66	80	19·5	22 26	22 27	3 43	9 27	9 23
3	23 00	− 1·7	55·6	15·1	161	65	71	20·5	22 40	22 37	4 25	10 39	10 40
4	23 45	+ 3·8	56·2	15·3	174	65	62	21·5	22 55	22 47	5 08	11 53	11 58
5	0 32	+ 9·2	57·0	15·5	186	67	51	22·5	23 12	23 00	5 53	13 10	13 21
6	1 22	+14·4	57·9	15·8	198	69	41	23·5	23 35	23 17	6 42	14 31	14 47
7	2 16	+19·0	58·8	16·0	210	73	30	24·5	—	23 42	7 35	15 54	16 17
8	3 15	+22·6	59·7	16·3	223	78	20	25·5	0 05	—	8 34	17 16	17 45
9	4 18	+25·0	60·4	16·5	235	84	11	26·5	0 49	0 20	9 37	18 30	19 00
10	5 24	+25·6	61·0	16·6	247	91	5	27·5	1 49	1 19	10 42	19 28	19 56
11	6 30	+24·4	61·3	16·7	259	99	1	28·5	3 07	2 39	11 47	20 11	20 34
12	7 35	+21·3	61·3	16·7	272	285	0	0·2	4 35	4 14	12 49	20 42	20 58
13	8 36	+16·9	60·9	16·6	284	290	2	1·2	6 06	5 52	13 46	21 05	21 15
14	9 34	+11·4	60·3	16·4	296	293	7	2·2	7 35	7 27	14 39	21 23	21 28
15	10 27	+ 5·5	59·5	16·2	308	295	14	3·2	9 00	8 57	15 28	21 39	21 39
16	11 18	− 0·5	58·5	15·9	321	296	23	4·2	10 21	10 24	16 15	21 55	21 50
17	12 07	− 6·4	57·6	15·7	333	295	33	5·2	11 39	11 47	17 02	22 11	22 01
18	12 56	−11·7	56·7	15·4	345	294	44	6·2	12 56	13 09	17 48	22 29	22 14
19	13 45	−16·4	55·9	15·2	357	291	54	7·2	14 10	14 29	18 35	22 51	22 31
20	14 34	−20·2	55·2	15·1	10	287	64	8·2	15 22	15 47	19 23	23 18	22 53
21	15 25	−23·1	54·7	14·9	22	282	73	9·2	16 29	16 58	20 13	23 53	23 24
22	16 17	−25·0	54·4	14·8	34	277	81	10·2	17 28	17 58	21 03	—	—
23	17 08	−25·6	54·1	14·7	46	272	88	11·2	18 16	18 46	21 53	0 38	0 07
24	18 02	−25·1	54·0	14·7	58	267	93	12·2	18 54	19 21	22 42	1 33	1 03
25	18 54	−23·5	54·0	14·7	71	263	97	13·2	19 23	19 46	23 30	2 36	2 10
26	19 44	−20·8	54·1	14·7	83	263	99	14·2	19 46	20 03	—	3 44	3 23
27	20 32	−17·3	54·3	14·8	95	45	100	15·2	20 05	20 17	0 16	4 55	4 39
28	21 19	−13·0	54·6	14·9	107	62	99	16·2	20 20	20 28	1 00	6 06	5 55
29	22 04	− 8·1	54·9	15·0	119	62	95	17·2	20 34	20 37	1 43	7 17	7 12
30	22 49	− 2·9	55·3	15·1	132	62	90	18·2	20 48	20 47	2 25	8 29	8 28
31	23 34	+ 2·5	55·8	15·2	144	62	84	19·2	21 02	20 56	3 07	9 42	9 46

MERCURY

Day	RA	Dec. +	Diam.	Phase	Tran- sit		Day	RA	Dec. +	Diam.	Phase	Tran- sit	
	h m	°			h m			h m	°			h m	
1	7 45	23·2	—	—	13 13		16	9 23	15·9	—	—	13 51	
4	8 08	22·0	—	—	13 24	Mercury is too	19	9 38	14·2	—	—	13 53	Mercury is too
7	8 30	20·7	—	—	13 34	close to the	22	9 51	12·6	—	—	13 54	close to the
10	8 49	19·2	—	—	13 41	Sun for	25	10 02	11·0	—	—	13 52	Sun for
13	9 07	17·6	—	—	13 47	observation	28	10 11	9·5	—	—	13 49	observation
16	9 23	15·9	—	—	13 51		31	10 18	8·2	—	—	13 44	

VENUS

Day	RA	Dec. +	Diam.	Phase	Tran- sit	5° high. 52°	5° high. 56°
	h m	°	″	%	h m	h m	h m
1	9 42	14·7	29	39	15 07	21 48	21 57
6	9 55	12·9	31	35	15 01	21 33	21 40
11	10 07	11·1	34	32	14 53	21 15	21 21
16	10 17	9·4	37	28	14 42	20 56	21 00
21	10 24	7·7	40	23	14 30	20 35	20 37
26	10 29	6·3	43	19	14 14	20 11	20 13
31	10 30	5·0	47	14	13 55	19 46	19 47

MARS

Day	RA	Dec. +	Diam.	Phase	Tran- sit	
	h m	°	″	%	h m	
1	9 36	15·6	4	95	15 01	
6	9 48	14·6	4	96	14 53	Mars is too
11	9 59	13·5	4	96	14 45	close to the
16	10 11	12·4	4	96	14 37	Sun for
21	10 24	11·3	4	97	14 29	observation
26	10 34	10·1	4	97	14 21	
31	10 46	8·9	4	97	14 13	

(See pages 65–66 for explanatory notes)

SUNRISE AND SUNSET

Day	London 0°05′ 51°30′		Bristol 2°35′ 51°28′		Birmingham 1°55′ 52°28′		Manchester 2°15′ 53°28′		Newcastle 1°37′ 54°59′		Glasgow 4°14′ 55°52′		Belfast 5°56′ 54°35′	
	h m	h m	h m	h m	h m	h m	h m	h m	h m	h m	h m	h m	h m	h m
1	3 47	20 21	3 57	20 31	3 49	20 34	3 44	20 41	3 32	20 48	3 36	21 05	3 52	21 03
2	3 48	20 20	3 58	20 30	3 50	20 33	3 45	20 41	3 32	20 48	3 37	21 05	3 52	21 02
3	3 48	20 20	3 59	20 30	3 50	20 33	3 46	20 40	3 33	20 47	3 37	21 04	3 53	21 02
4	3 49	20 20	3 59	20 29	3 51	20 32	3 46	20 40	3 34	20 47	3 38	21 03	3 54	21 01
5	3 50	20 19	4 00	20 29	3 52	20 32	3 47	20 39	3 35	20 46	3 39	21 03	3 55	21 01
6	3 51	20 19	4 01	20 28	3 53	20 31	3 48	20 38	3 36	20 46	3 40	21 02	3 56	21 00
7	3 52	20 18	4 02	20 28	3 54	20 31	3 49	20 38	3 37	20 45	3 41	21 01	3 57	20 59
8	3 53	20 17	4 03	20 27	3 55	20 30	3 50	20 37	3 38	20 44	3 43	21 00	3 58	20 59
9	3 54	20 17	4 04	20 27	3 56	20 29	3 51	20 36	3 39	20 43	3 44	21 00	3 59	20 58
10	3 55	20 16	4 05	20 26	3 57	20 29	3 52	20 35	3 40	20 42	3 45	20 59	4 00	20 57
11	3 56	20 15	4 06	20 25	3 58	20 28	3 53	20 35	3 42	20 41	3 46	20 58	4 02	20 56
12	3 57	20 14	4 07	20 24	3 59	20 27	3 55	20 34	3 43	20 40	3 48	20 56	4 03	20 55
13	3 58	20 14	4 08	20 23	4 00	20 26	3 56	20 33	3 44	20 39	3 49	20 55	4 04	20 54
14	3 59	20 13	4 09	20 23	4 01	20 25	3 57	20 32	3 46	20 38	3 50	20 54	4 05	20 53
15	4 00	20 12	4 10	20 22	4 02	20 24	3 58	20 31	3 47	20 37	3 52	20 53	4 07	20 52
16	4 01	20 11	4 11	20 21	4 04	20 23	4 00	20 29	3 48	20 36	3 53	20 52	4 08	20 51
17	4 02	20 10	4 13	20 19	4 05	20 22	4 01	20 28	3 50	20 34	3 55	20 50	4 09	20 49
18	4 04	20 09	4 14	20 18	4 06	20 21	4 02	20 27	3 51	20 33	3 56	20 49	4 11	20 48
19	4 05	20 07	4 15	20 17	4 08	20 19	4 04	20 26	3 53	20 32	3 58	20 47	4 12	20 47
20	4 06	20 06	4 16	20 16	4 09	20 18	4 05	20 25	3 54	20 30	3 59	20 46	4 14	20 45
21	4 07	20 05	4 18	20 15	4 10	20 17	4 07	20 23	3 56	20 29	4 01	20 44	4 15	20 44
22	4 09	20 04	4 19	20 14	4 12	20 16	4 08	20 22	3 57	20 27	4 03	20 43	4 17	20 42
23	4 10	20 02	4 20	20 12	4 13	20 14	4 09	20 20	3 59	20 26	4 04	20 41	4 18	20 41
24	4 12	20 01	4 22	20 11	4 14	20 13	4 11	20 19	4 01	20 24	4 06	20 40	4 20	20 39
25	4 13	20 00	4 23	20 10	4 16	20 11	4 13	20 17	4 02	20 22	4 08	20 38	4 22	20 38
26	4 14	19 58	4 24	20 08	4 17	20 10	4 14	20 16	4 04	20 21	4 10	20 36	4 23	20 36
27	4 16	19 57	4 26	20 07	4 19	20 08	4 16	20 14	4 06	20 19	4 11	20 34	4 25	20 34
28	4 17	19 55	4 27	20 05	4 20	20 07	4 17	20 13	4 07	20 17	4 13	20 33	4 27	20 33
29	4 19	19 54	4 29	20 04	4 22	20 05	4 19	20 11	4 09	20 16	4 15	20 31	4 28	20 31
30	4 20	19 52	4 30	20 02	4 23	20 04	4 20	20 09	4 11	20 14	4 17	20 29	4 30	20 29
31	4 22	19 51	4 32	20 01	4 25	20 02	4 22	20 08	4 12	20 12	4 19	20 27	4 32	20 27

JUPITER

Day	RA	Dec. +	Transit	5° high 52°	56°
	h m	° ′	h m	h m	h m
1	9 08·2	17 14	14 32	21 29	21 40
11	9 16·3	16 38	14 01	20 54	21 05
21	9 24·6	16 00	13 30	20 19	20 30
31	9 33·0	15 20	12 59	19 45	19 54

Diameters—equatorial 31″ polar 30″

SATURN

Day	RA	Dec. −	Transit	5° high 52°	56°
	h m	° ′	h m	h m	h m
1	20 31·2	19 22	1 57	22 21	22 47
11	20 28·5	19 32	1 15	21 40	22 06
21	20 25·6	19 43	0 32	20 59	21 26
31	20 22·5	19 55	23 46	20 18	20 45

Diameters—equatorial 18″ polar 17″
Rings—major axis 42″ minor axis 14″

URANUS

Day	RA	Dec. −	Transit	10° high 52°	56°
	h m	° ′	h m	h m	h m
1	18 52·2	23 17	0 18	2 21	1 08
11	18 50·4	23 19	23 33	1 40	0 26
21	18 48·7	23 21	22 52	0 58	23 39
31	18 47·1	23 23	22 11	0 17	22 57

Diameter 4″

NEPTUNE

Day	RA	Dec. −	Transit	10° high 52°	56°
	h m	° ′	h m	h m	h m
1	19 07·2	21 43	0 33	2 55	2 02
11	19 06·0	21 45	23 48	2 14	1 21
21	19 04·9	21 47	23 08	1 33	0 40
31	19 03·8	21 49	22 28	0 52	23 55

Diameter 2″

(See page 66 for explanatory notes)

Month	Week		

Month	Week	
1	Th.	Sir Frank Worrell *b.* 1924. Blériot *d.* 1936.
2	F.	Sir Arthur Bliss *b.* 1891.* Caruso *d.* 1921.
3	S.	Casement *exec.* 1916. Joseph Conrad *d.* 1924.
4	S.	**11th S. after Pentecost.** QUEEN ELIZABETH THE QUEEN MOTHER *b.* 1900.
5	M.	Friedrich Engels *d.* 1895. Richard Burton *d.* 1984.
6	Tu.	**Transfiguration.** Alexander Fleming *b.* 1881.
7	W.	Joseph Jacquard *d.* 1834. Sidney Buller *d.* 1970.
8	Th.	PRINCESS BEATRICE OF YORK *b.* 1988.
9	F.	Herman Hesse *d.* 1962. Shostakovich *d.* 1975.
10	S.	Charles Napier *b.* 1782. Whistler *b.* 1834.
11	S.	**12th S. after Pentecost.** Andrew Carnegie *d.* 1919.
12	M.	William Blake *d.* 1827. Henry Fonda *d.* 1982.
13	Tu.	Alfred Hitchcock *b.* 1899. Ben Hogan *b.* 1912.
14	W.	William Randolph Hearst *d.* 1951.
15	Th.	ASSUMPTION. PRINCESS ROYAL *b.* 1950.
16	F.	Marvell *d.* 1678. Robert van Bunsen *d.* 1899.
17	S.	Davy Crockett *b.* 1786. Balzac *d.* 1850.
18	S.	**13th S. after Pentecost.** Godfrey Evans *b.* 1920.
19	M.	Pascal *d.* 1662. Sir Henry Wood *d.* 1944.
20	Tu.	Invasion of Czechoslovakia 1968.
21	W.	PRINCESS MARGARET *b.* 1930.
22	Th.	Cartier-Bresson *b.* 1908. Kenyatta *d.* 1978.
23	F.	Rudolf Valentino *d.* 1926. Fokine *d.* 1942.
24	S.	**St. Bartholomew.** Wilberforce *b.* 1759.
25	S.	**14th S. after Pentecost.** L. Bernstein *b.* 1918.
26	M.	Francis Chichester *d.* 1972. Charles Lindbergh *d.*
27	Tu.	Don Bradman *b.* 1908. Haile Selassie *d.* 1975. [1974.
28	W.	Burne-Jones *b.* 1833. Fantin-Latour *d.* 1904.
29	Th.	Lady Diana Cooper *b.* 1892. De Valera *d.* 1975.
30	F.	Lord Rutherford *b.* 1871.
31	S.	Clive Lloyd *b.* 1944. Rocky Marciano *d.* 1969.

PHENOMENA

d	h	
10	12	Jupiter in conjunction with Moon. Jupiter 4°N.
11	08	Mercury in conjunction with Moon. Mercury 0°·5S.
11	08	Venus in conjunction with Moon. Venus 3°S.
11	09	Venus in conjunction with Mercury. Venus 2°S.
12	04	Mars in conjunction with Moon. Mars 5°N.
14	08	Venus in conjunction with Mercury. Venus 2°S.
17	22	Jupiter in conjunction with Sun.
21	21	Mercury in inferior conjunction.
22	20	Venus in inferior conjunction.
22	22	Saturn in conjunction with Moon. Saturn 2°S.
24	16	Jupiter in conjunction with Mercury. Jupiter 4°N.
27	06	Jupiter in conjunction with Venus. Jupiter 9°N.

CONSTELLATIONS

The following constellations are near the meridian at

	d	h		d	h
July	1	24	July	16	23
Aug.	1	22	Aug.	16	21
Sept.	1	20	Sept.	15	19

Draco, Hercules, Lyra, Cygnus, Sagitta, Ophiuchus, Serpens, Aquila and Sagittarius.

MINIMA OF ALGOL

d	h	d	h
3	01	20	06
5	22	23	03
8	18	25	23
11	15	28	20
14	12	31	17
17	09		

*Centenary.

See note on Summer Time, p. 24.

MOON
Phases, Apsides & Node

	d	h	m
� Last Quarter	3	11	25
● New Moon	10	2	28
� First Quarter	17	5	1
○ Full Moon	25	9	7
Perigee (360,100 km)	8	18	12
Apogee (405,155 km)	20	22	32

Mean longitude of ascending node on Aug. 1, 288°.

MONTHLY NOTES

Aug. 5. Bank Holiday, Scotland.

12. Grouse shooting begins.

26. Bank and General Holiday, England, Wales and N. Ireland.

28. Lammas (Scottish Term Day).

(*See* page 64 for explanatory notes)

Day	Right Ascension	Dec. +	Equation of Time	Rise 52°	Rise 56°	Transit	Set 52°	Set 56°	Sidereal Time	Transit of First Point of Aries
	THE SUN s.d. 15'·8									
	h m s	° ′	m s	h m	h m	h m	h m	h m	h m s	h m s
1	8 42 46	18 12	− 6 21	4 21	4 03	12 06	19 51	20 09	20 36 26	3 23 01
2	8 46 39	17 57	− 6 17	4 22	4 05	12 06	19 49	20 07	20 40 22	3 19 05
3	8 50 32	17 42	− 6 13	4 24	4 06	12 06	19 47	20 05	20 44 19	3 15 09
4	8 54 24	17 26	− 6 08	4 25	4 08	12 06	19 46	20 02	20 48 15	3 11 13
5	8 58 15	17 10	− 6 03	4 27	4 10	12 06	19 44	20 00	20 52 12	3 07 17
6	9 02 06	16 54	− 5 57	4 29	4 12	12 06	19 42	19 58	20 56 08	3 03 21
7	9 05 56	16 37	− 5 51	4 30	4 14	12 06	19 40	19 56	21 00 05	2 59 26
8	9 09 45	16 21	− 5 44	4 32	4 16	12 06	19 39	19 54	21 04 01	2 55 30
9	9 13 34	16 04	− 5 36	4 33	4 18	12 06	19 37	19 52	21 07 58	2 51 34
10	9 17 23	15 46	− 5 28	4 35	4 20	12 05	19 35	19 50	21 11 55	2 47 38
11	9 21 11	15 29	− 5 19	4 37	4 22	12 05	19 33	19 47	21 15 51	2 43 42
12	9 24 58	15 11	− 5 10	4 38	4 24	12 05	19 31	19 45	21 19 48	2 39 46
13	9 28 44	14 53	− 5 00	4 40	4 26	12 05	19 29	19 43	21 23 44	2 35 50
14	9 32 31	14 35	− 4 50	4 41	4 28	12 05	19 27	19 40	21 27 41	2 31 54
15	9 36 16	14 17	− 4 39	4 43	4 30	12 05	19 25	19 38	21 31 37	2 27 58
16	9 40 01	13 58	− 4 27	4 45	4 32	12 04	19 23	19 36	21 35 34	2 24 02
17	9 43 46	13 39	− 4 15	4 46	4 34	12 04	19 21	19 33	21 39 30	2 20 06
18	9 47 29	13 20	− 4 02	4 48	4 36	12 04	19 19	19 31	21 43 27	2 16 11
19	9 51 13	13 01	− 3 49	4 50	4 38	12 04	19 17	19 29	21 47 24	2 12 15
20	9 54 56	12 41	− 3 35	4 51	4 39	12 03	19 15	19 26	21 51 20	2 08 19
21	9 58 38	12 21	− 3 21	4 53	4 41	12 03	19 13	19 24	21 55 17	2 04 23
22	10 02 20	12 01	− 3 07	4 54	4 43	12 03	19 10	19 21	21 59 13	2 00 27
23	10 06 01	11 41	− 2 51	4 56	4 45	12 03	19 08	19 19	22 03 10	1 56 31
24	10 09 42	11 21	− 2 36	4 58	4 47	12 02	19 06	19 16	22 07 06	1 52 35
25	10 13 23	11 00	− 2 20	4 59	4 49	12 02	19 04	19 14	22 11 03	1 48 39
26	10 17 03	10 40	− 2 03	5 01	4 51	12 02	19 02	19 11	22 14 59	1 44 43
27	10 20 43	10 19	− 1 46	5 03	4 53	12 02	19 00	19 09	22 18 56	1 40 47
28	10 24 22	9 58	− 1 29	5 04	4 55	12 01	18 57	19 06	22 22 53	1 36 52
29	10 28 01	9 37	− 1 12	5 06	4 57	12 01	18 55	19 04	22 26 49	1 32 56
30	10 31 39	9 16	− 0 54	5 07	4 59	12 01	18 53	19 01	22 30 46	1 29 00
31	10 35 18	8 54	− 0 35	5 09	5 01	12 00	18 51	18 58	22 34 42	1 25 04

Duration of Civil (C), Nautical (N) and Astronomical (A) Twilight (in minutes)

Lat. °	Aug. 1 C	N	A	Aug. 11 C	N	A	Aug. 21 C	N	A	Aug. 31 C	N	A
52	41	97	177	39	89	153	37	83	138	35	79	127
56	48	120	TAN	45	106	205	42	96	166	40	89	147

ASTRONOMICAL NOTES

MERCURY is unsuitably placed for observation, inferior conjunction occurring on the 21st.

VENUS passes through inferior conjunction on the 22nd and therefore remains too close to the Sun for observation throughout August, except possibly on the 31st, when it might be glimpsed low in the east for a few minutes before sunrise. Its magnitude is −4·1.

MARS is unsuitably placed for observation.

JUPITER passes through conjunction on the 17th

and therefore remains too close to the Sun for observation throughout the month.

SATURN continues to be visible in the southern skies, magnitude +0·2. Saturn is in Capricornus and even from southern England never gets more than 20° above the horizon. On the evening of the 22nd the gibbous Moon passes 2°N. of the planet.

METEORS. The maximum of the famous Perseid meteor shower occurs on the night of the 12th–13th. Conditions are favourable since there will be no moonlight to interfere with observations.

(See pages 64–65 for explanatory notes)

THE MOON

Day	RA	Dec.	Hor. Par.	Semi-diam.	Sun's Co-long.	P.A. of Bright Limb	Phase	Age	Rise 52°	Rise 56°	Transit	Set 52°	Set 56°
	h m	°	′	′	°	°	%	d	h m	h m	h m	h m	h m
1	0 21	+ 7·8	56·4	15·4	156	64	75	20·2	21 19	21 08	3 51	10 57	11 06
2	1 09	+13·0	57·0	15·5	168	66	66	21·2	21 39	21 23	4 38	12 14	12 29
3	2 01	+17·7	57·8	15·7	180	69	55	22·2	22 05	21 43	5 28	13 35	13 55
4	2 56	+21·6	58·5	15·9	193	74	44	23·2	22 41	22 14	6 22	14 55	15 22
5	3 55	+24·3	59·3	16·1	205	79	33	24·2	23 32	23 02	7 21	16 11	16 41
6	4 58	+25·5	59·9	16·3	217	86	23	25·2	—	—	8 24	17 14	17 44
7	6 03	+25·1	60·5	16·5	229	92	14	26·2	0 40	0 10	9 27	18 03	18 29
8	7 08	+22·8	60·8	16·6	242	97	6	27·2	2 02	1 37	10 30	18 39	18 58
9	8 10	+19·0	60·9	16·6	254	98	2	28·2	3 31	3 13	11 29	19 05	19 19
10	9 09	+14·0	60·7	16·5	266	48	0	29·2	5 02	4 50	12 24	19 26	19 34
11	10 04	+ 8·1	60·2	16·4	278	306	1	0·9	6 30	6 24	13 16	19 44	19 46
12	10 57	+ 2·0	59·5	16·2	290	301	5	1·9	7 54	7 54	14 05	20 00	19 57
13	11 48	− 4·1	58·6	16·0	303	300	11	2·9	9 16	9 21	14 53	20 16	20 09
14	12 38	− 9·8	57·7	15·7	315	297	19	3·9	10 35	10 47	15 41	20 34	20 21
15	13 28	−14·8	56·8	15·5	327	294	28	4·9	11 53	12 10	16 29	20 55	20 37
16	14 19	−19·0	56·0	15·3	339	290	38	5·9	13 07	13 30	17 17	21 20	20 57
17	15 10	−22·3	55·3	15·1	352	286	48	6·9	14 17	14 44	18 07	21 53	21 25
18	16 03	−24·5	54·8	14·9	4	281	58	7·9	15 20	15 50	18 58	22 34	22 04
19	16 55	−25·5	54·4	14·8	16	275	67	8·9	16 12	16 43	19 48	23 26	22 55
20	17 48	−25·3	54·2	14·8	28	270	76	9·9	16 54	17 22	20 38	—	23 58
21	18 40	−24·0	54·1	14·7	41	265	83	10·9	17 26	17 50	21 26	0 26	—
22	19 30	−21·6	54·2	14·8	53	262	90	11·9	17 51	18 10	22 12	1 33	1 10
23	20 19	−18·3	54·4	14·8	65	259	95	12·9	18 11	18 25	22 57	2 43	2 25
24	21 06	−14·2	54·7	14·9	77	261	98	13·9	18 28	18 37	23 41	3 54	3 41
25	21 52	− 9·5	55·0	15·0	89	287	100	14·9	18 43	18 47	—	5 06	4 58
26	22 38	− 4·3	55·4	15·1	101	39	99	15·9	18 57	18 57	0 23	6 18	6 15
27	23 23	+ 1·1	55·9	15·2	114	53	97	16·9	19 11	19 07	1 06	7 31	7 33
28	0 10	+ 6·5	56·4	15·4	126	58	93	17·9	19 27	19 18	1 50	8 46	8 53
29	0 58	+11·7	56·9	15·5	138	62	87	18·9	19 46	19 31	2 36	10 03	10 16
30	1 49	+16·5	57·4	15·6	150	66	79	19·9	20 10	19 50	3 25	11 22	11 41
31	2 43	+20·6	57·9	15·8	162	70	69	20·9	20 42	20 17	4 17	12 42	13 06

MERCURY

Day	RA	Dec. +	Diam.	Phase	Tran-sit		Day	RA	Dec. +	Diam.	Phase	Tran-sit	
	h m	°			h m			h m	°			h m	
1	10 20	7·8	—	—	13 42		16	10 13	5·9	—	—	12 34	
4	10 24	6·7	—	—	13 34	Mercury is too close to the Sun for observation	19	10 05	6·8	—	—	12 14	Mercury is too close to the Sun for observation
7	10 25	6·0	—	—	13 23		22	9 55	8·0	—	—	11 53	
10	10 24	5·5	—	—	13 09		25	9 47	9·3	—	—	11 33	
13	10 20	5·5	—	—	12 53		28	9 41	10·7	—	—	11 16	
16	10 13	5·9	—	—	12 34		31	9 39	11·8	—	—	11 02	

VENUS

Day	RA	Dec. +	Diam.	Phase	Tran-sit	
	h m	°			h m	
1	10 30	4·8	—	—	13 51	
6	10 27	3·9	—	—	13 28	
11	10 20	3·4	—	—	13 01	Venus is too close to the Sun for observation
16	10 10	3·4	—	—	12 31	
21	9 58	3·8	—	—	12 00	
26	9 46	4·5	—	—	11 29	
31	9 36	5·5	—	—	10 59	

MARS

Day	RA	Dec. +	Diam.	Phase	Tran-sit	
	h m	°			h m	
1	10 48	8·6	—	—	14 11	
6	11 00	7·4	—	—	14 03	
11	11 12	6·2	—	—	13 55	Mars is too close to the Sun for observation
16	11 23	4·9	—	—	13 47	
21	11 35	3·6	—	—	13 39	
26	11 46	2·3	—	—	13 31	
31	11 58	1·0	—	—	13 23	

(*See* pages 65–66 for explanatory notes)

SUNRISE AND SUNSET

Day	London 0°05′ 51°30′		Bristol 2°35′ 51°28′		Birmingham 1°55′ 52°28′		Manchester 2°15′ 53°28′		Newcastle 1°37′ 54°59′		Glasgow 4°14′ 55°52′		Belfast 5°56′ 54°35′	
	h m	h m	h m	h m	h m	h m	h m	h m	h m	h m	h m	h m	h m	h m
1	4 23	19 49	4 33	19 59	4 27	20 00	4 24	20 06	4 14	20 10	4 20	20 25	4 33	20 26
2	4 25	19 48	4 35	19 57	4 28	19 59	4 25	20 04	4 16	20 08	4 22	20 23	4 35	20 24
3	4 26	19 46	4 36	19 56	4 30	19 57	4 27	20 02	4 18	20 06	4 24	20 21	4 37	20 22
4	4 28	19 44	4 38	19 54	4 31	19 55	4 29	20 00	4 20	20 04	4 26	20 19	4 39	20 20
5	4 29	19 42	4 39	19 52	4 33	19 53	4 30	19 59	4 21	20 02	4 28	20 17	4 40	20 18
6	4 31	19 41	4 41	19 51	4 35	19 52	4 32	19 57	4 23	20 00	4 30	20 15	4 42	20 16
7	4 32	19 39	4 42	19 49	4 36	19 50	4 34	19 55	4 25	19 58	4 32	20 12	4 44	20 14
8	4 34	19 37	4 44	19 47	4 38	19 48	4 35	19 53	4 27	19 56	4 34	20 10	4 46	20 12
9	4 35	19 35	4 45	19 45	4 39	19 46	4 37	19 51	4 29	19 54	4 35	20 08	4 48	20 10
10	4 37	19 33	4 47	19 43	4 41	19 44	4 39	19 49	4 31	19 52	4 37	20 06	4 49	20 08
11	4 38	19 32	4 49	19 41	4 43	19 42	4 41	19 47	4 32	19 50	4 39	20 04	4 51	20 06
12	4 40	19 30	4 50	19 40	4 44	19 40	4 42	19 45	4 34	19 48	4 41	20 01	4 53	20 03
13	4 42	19 28	4 52	19 38	4 46	19 38	4 44	19 43	4 36	19 45	4 43	19 59	4 55	20 01
14	4 43	19 26	4 53	19 36	4 48	19 36	4 46	19 41	4 38	19 43	4 45	19 57	4 57	19 59
15	4 45	19 24	4 55	19 34	4 49	19 34	4 47	19 38	4 40	19 41	4 47	19 54	4 59	19 57
16	4 46	19 22	4 57	19 32	4 51	19 32	4 49	19 36	4 42	19 39	4 49	19 52	5 00	19 55
17	4 48	19 20	4 58	19 30	4 53	19 30	4 51	19 34	4 44	19 36	4 51	19 50	5 02	19 52
18	4 50	19 18	5 00	19 28	4 54	19 28	4 53	19 32	4 45	19 34	4 53	19 47	5 04	19 50
19	4 51	19 16	5 01	19 26	4 56	19 26	4 54	19 30	4 47	19 32	4 55	19 45	5 06	19 48
20	4 53	19 14	5 03	19 24	4 58	19 24	4 56	19 28	4 49	19 29	4 57	19 43	5 08	19 45
21	4 54	19 12	5 04	19 22	4 59	19 21	4 58	19 25	4 51	19 27	4 59	19 40	5 10	19 43
22	4 56	19 10	5 06	19 19	5 01	19 19	5 00	19 23	4 53	19 25	5 01	19 38	5 11	19 41
23	4 58	19 07	5 08	19 17	5 03	19 17	5 01	19 21	4 55	19 22	5 03	19 35	5 13	19 38
24	4 59	19 05	5 09	19 15	5 04	19 15	5 03	19 19	4 57	19 20	5 05	19 33	5 15	19 36
25	5 01	19 03	5 11	19 13	5 06	19 13	5 05	19 16	4 59	19 18	5 07	19 30	5 17	19 34
26	5 02	19 01	5 12	19 11	5 08	19 10	5 07	19 14	5 00	19 15	5 09	19 28	5 19	19 31
27	5 04	18 59	5 14	19 09	5 09	19 08	5 08	19 12	5 02	19 13	5 11	19 25	5 21	19 29
28	5 06	18 57	5 16	19 07	5 11	19 06	5 10	19 09	5 04	19 10	5 12	19 23	5 22	19 27
29	5 07	18 55	5 17	19 04	5 13	19 04	5 12	19 07	5 06	19 08	5 14	19 20	5 24	19 24
30	5 09	18 52	5 19	19 02	5 14	19 01	5 14	19 05	5 08	19 05	5 16	19 18	5 26	19 22
31	5 10	18 50	5 20	19 00	5 16	18 59	5 15	19 02	5 10	19 03	5 18	19 15	5 28	19 19

JUPITER

Day	RA	Dec. +	Transit	
	h m	° ′	h m	
1	9 33·8	15 16	12 56	Jupiter is
11	9 42·4	14 34	12 25	too close to
21	9 50·9	13 51	11 54	the Sun for
31	9 59·4	13 07	11 23	observation

Diameters—equatorial 31″ polar 29″

SATURN

Day	RA	Dec. −	Transit	5° high.	
				52°	56°
	h m	° ′	h m	h m	h m
1	20 22·2	19 56	23 42	3 14	2 47
11	20 19·2	20 06	22 59	2 30	2 03
21	20 16·5	20 16	22 17	1 47	1 19
31	20 14·1	20 24	21 36	1 04	0 36

Diameters—equatorial 18″ polar 17″
Rings—major axis 42″ minor axis 15″

URANUS

Day	RA	Dec. −	Transit	10° high.	
				52°	56°
	h m	° ′	h m	h m	h m
1	18 47·0	23 23	22 07	0 13	22 53
11	18 45·6	23 25	21 26	23 28	22 12
21	18 44·4	23 26	20 46	22 47	21 30
31	18 43·6	23 27	20 06	22 07	20 50

Diameter 4″

NEPTUNE

Day	RA	Dec. −	Transit	10° high.	
				52°	56°
	h m	° ′	h m	h m	h m
1	19 03·7	21 49	21 49	0 48	23 51
11	19 02·7	21 51	21 43	0 08	23 10
21	19 01·9	21 53	21 03	23 23	22 29
31	19 01·2	21 54	20 23	22 43	21 49

Diameter 2″

(See page 66 for explanatory notes)

DAY OF		
Month	Week	

Septem (seven), 7th month
of Roman (pre-Julian)
Calendar.

Sun's Longitude 180° ♎ 23ᵈ 13ʰ

1	S.	**15th S. after Pentecost.** Sassoon *d.* 1967.
2	M.	Thomas Telford *d.* 1834. Frederick Soddy *b.* 1877.
3	Tu.	Oliver Cromwell *d.* 1658.
4	W.	Third Republic proclaimed, France 1870.
5	Th.	Jesse James *b.* 1847. John Gilpin *d.* 1983.
6	F.	*Mayflower* sailed from Plymouth 1620.
7	S.	Edith Sitwell *b.* 1887. Edward Grey *d.* 1933.
8	S.	**Blessed Virgin Mary. 16th S. after Pentecost.**
9	M.	John Curry *b.* 1949. Mao Tse-tung *d.* 1976.
10	Tu.	Arnold Palmer *b.* 1929.
11	W.	David Ricardo *d.* 1823. Khrushchev *d.* 1971.
12	Th.	Jesse Owens *b.* 1913. Robert Lowell *d.* 1977.
13	F.	Montaigne *d.* 1592. Leopold Stokowski *d.* 1977.
14	S.	Fenimore Cooper *d.* 1851. Wellington *d.* 1852.
15	S.	**17th S. after Pentecost.** PRINCE HENRY OF WALES *b.* 1984.
16	M.	Gabriel Fahrenheit *d.* 1736. Bonar Law *b.* 1858.
17	Tu.	Frederick Ashton *b.* 1904. Stirling Moss *b.* 1929.
18	W.	Lord Berners *b.* 1883. Greta Garbo *b.* 1905.
19	Th.	William Golding *b.* 1911. Emil Zátopak *b.* 1922.
20	F.	Jacob Grimm *d.* 1863. Sibelius *d.* 1957.
21	S.	**St. Matthew.** Sir Walter Scott *d.* 1832.
22	S.	**18th S. after Pentecost.** Faraday *b.* 1791.*
23	M.	Wilkie Collins *d.* 1889. Sigmund Freud *d.* 1939.
24	Tu.	Horace Walpole *b.* 1717. Scott Fitzgerald *b.* 1896.
25	W.	Samuel Butler *d.* 1680. William Faulkner *b.* 1897.
26	Th.	Barnes Wallis *b.* 1887. Bartok *d.* 1945.
27	F.	Edward II *d.* 1327. Sylvia Pankhurst *d.* 1960.
28	S.	Clemenceau *b.* 1841. Herman Melville *d.* 1891.*
29	S.	**St. Michael and All Angels. 19th S. after Pentecost.**
30	M.	Corneille *d.* 1684. Rudolf Diesel *d.* 1913.

PHENOMENA

d	h	
2	13	Venus in conjunction with Mercury. Venus 7°S.
6	20	Venus in conjunction with Moon. Venus 5°S.
7	03	Mercury in conjunction with Moon. Mercury 3°N.
7	08	Jupiter in conjunction with Moon. Jupiter 4°N.
7	18	Mercury at greatest elongation W.18°.
9	21	Mars in conjunction with Moon. Mars 5°N.
10	10	Jupiter in conjunction with Mercury. Jupiter 0°·1N.
19	03	Saturn in conjunction with Moon. Saturn 2°S.
23	13	Equinox.
28	22	Venus at greatest brilliancy.

CONSTELLATIONS

The following constellations are near the meridian at

	d	h		d	h
Aug. 1	24		Aug. 16	23	
Sept. 1	22		Sept. 15	21	
Oct. 1	20		Oct. 16	19	

Draco, Cepheus, Lyra, Cygnus, Vulpecula, Sagitta, Delphinus, Equuleus, Aquila, Aquarius and Capricornus.

MINIMA OF ALGOL

d	h	d	h
3	14	17	22
6	11	20	19
9	07	23	15
12	04	26	12
15	01	29	09

* Centenary

See note on Summer Time, p. 24.

MOON
Phases, Apsides & Node

	d	h	m
☾ Last Quarter	1	18	16
● New Moon	8	11	1
☽ First Quarter	15	22	1
○ Full Moon	23	22	40

Perigee (364,662 km)   5 19 28
Apogee (404,341 km)   17 15 22

Mean longitude of ascending node
on Sept. 1, 286°

MONTHLY NOTES

Sept.   1. Partridge shooting begins.
      9. Jewish New Year (AM 5752).
   15. Battle of Britain Day.
   18. Jewish Day of Atonement (Yom Kippur).
   28. First day of Feast of Tabernacles.
   29. Michaelmas (Quarter day).

(*See* page 64 for explanatory notes)

Day	Right Ascension	Dec.	Equation of Time	Rise 52°	Rise 56°	Transit	Set 52°	Set 56°	Sidereal Time	Transit of First Point of Aries
	h m s	° ′	m s	h m	h m	h m	h m	h m	h m s	h m s
1	10 38 56	+8 33	− 0 17	5 11	5 03	12 00	18 48	18 56	22 38 39	1 21 08
2	10 42 33	+8 11	+ 0 02	5 12	5 05	12 00	18 46	18 53	22 42 35	1 17 12
3	10 46 11	+7 49	+ 0 21	5 14	5 07	11 59	18 44	18 51	22 46 32	1 13 16
4	10 49 48	+7 27	+ 0 41	5 16	5 09	11 59	18 42	18 48	22 50 28	1 09 20
5	10 53 25	+7 05	+ 1 00	5 17	5 11	11 59	18 39	18 46	22 54 25	1 05 24
6	10 57 01	+6 43	+ 1 20	5 19	5 13	11 58	18 37	18 43	22 58 22	1 01 28
7	11 00 38	+6 20	+ 1 40	5 20	5 15	11 58	18 35	18 40	23 02 18	0 57 32
8	11 04 14	+5 58	+ 2 01	5 22	5 17	11 58	18 32	18 38	23 06 15	0 53 37
9	11 07 50	+5 35	+ 2 21	5 24	5 19	11 57	18 30	18 35	23 10 11	0 49 41
10	11 11 26	+5 13	+ 2 42	5 25	5 21	11 57	18 28	18 32	23 14 08	0 45 45
11	11 15 02	+4 50	+ 3 03	5 27	5 23	11 57	18 25	18 30	23 18 04	0 41 49
12	11 18 37	+4 27	+ 3 24	5 29	5 25	11 56	18 23	18 27	23 22 01	0 37 53
13	11 22 13	+4 04	+ 3 45	5 30	5 26	11 56	18 21	18 24	23 25 57	0 33 57
14	11 25 48	+3 41	+ 4 06	5 32	5 28	11 56	18 18	18 22	23 29 54	0 30 01
15	11 29 23	+3 18	+ 4 27	5 34	5 30	11 55	18 16	18 19	23 33 51	0 26 05
16	11 32 59	+2 55	+ 4 48	5 35	5 32	11 55	18 14	18 16	23 37 47	0 22 09
17	11 36 34	+2 32	+ 5 10	5 37	5 34	11 55	18 11	18 14	23 41 44	0 18 13
18	11 40 09	+2 09	+ 5 31	5 38	5 36	11 54	18 09	18 11	23 45 40	0 14 17
19	11 43 44	+1 46	+ 5 53	5 40	5 38	11 54	18 07	18 09	23 49 37	0 10 22
20	11 47 19	+1 22	+ 6 14	5 42	5 40	11 54	18 04	18 06	23 53 33	0 06 26
21	11 50 54	+0 59	+ 6 35	5 43	5 42	11 53	18 02	18 03	23 57 30	0 02 30 / 23 58 34
22	11 54 30	+0 36	+ 6 57	5 45	5 44	11 53	18 00	18 01	0 01 26	23 54 38
23	11 58 05	+0 12	+ 7 18	5 47	5 46	11 53	17 57	17 58	0 05 23	23 50 42
24	12 01 40	− 0 11	+ 7 39	5 48	5 48	11 52	17 55	17 55	0 09 20	23 46 46
25	12 05 16	− 0 34	+ 8 00	5 50	5 50	11 52	17 53	17 53	0 13 16	23 42 50
26	12 08 52	− 0 58	+ 8 21	5 52	5 52	11 51	17 50	17 50	0 17 13	23 38 54
27	12 12 28	−1 21	+ 8 42	5 53	5 54	11 51	17 48	17 47	0 21 09	23 34 58
28	12 16 04	−1 44	+ 9 02	5 55	5 56	11 51	17 46	17 45	0 25 06	23 31 02
29	12 19 40	−2 08	+ 9 22	5 57	5 58	11 50	17 43	17 42	0 29 02	23 27 07
30	12 23 17	−2 31	+ 9 42	5 58	6 00	11 50	17 41	17 39	0 32 59	23 23 11

THE SUN   s.d. 15′·9

Duration of Civil (C), Nautical (N) and Astronomical (A) Twilight (in minutes)

Lat. °	Sept. 1 C	N	A	Sept. 11 C	N	A	Sept. 21 C	N	A	Sept. 30 C	N	A
52	35	79	127	34	76	120	34	74	115	34	73	113
56	39	89	146	38	84	135	37	82	129	37	80	126

ASTRONOMICAL NOTES

MERCURY is a morning object for the first two-thirds of the month, magnitude +1·3 to −1·2, visible low above the eastern horizon around the time of beginning of morning civil twilight. At the beginning of the month Mercury is close to Venus; the latter is passing south of Mercury as it moves rapidly outwards from the Sun. Jupiter is also emerging from the morning twilight and on the morning of the 10th passes north of Mercury, the closest distance of only 0°·06 occurring after sunrise. At the same time both planets will be passing north of the bright star Regulus, magnitude +1·3. If conditions are clear on the morning of the 7th the crescent Moon, only 1¼ days before New, may be glimpsed about 5° to the right of Jupiter and about 4° below and to the right of Mercury.

VENUS is emerging from the morning twilight and visible in the eastern sky before dawn, magnitude −4·5.

MARS is unsuitably placed for observation.

JUPITER, magnitude −1·7, has emerged from the morning twilight and become visible above the eastern horizon before dawn, to the left of Venus.

SATURN, magnitude +0·3, is an evening object, low in the SSW sky. The gibbous Moon is near the planet on the evenings of the 18th and 19th.

ZODIACAL LIGHT. The morning cone may be seen stretching up from the eastern horizon before the beginning of morning twilight from the 7th to the 21st. This faint phenomenon is only visible under good conditions, in the absence of both moonlight and artificial lighting.

(See pages 64–65 for explanatory notes)

THE MOON

Day	RA	Dec.	Hor. Par.	Semi-diam.	Sun's Co-long.	P.A. of Bright Limb	Phase	Age	Rise 52°	Rise 56°	Transit	Set 52°	Set 56°
	h m	°	'	'	°	°	%	d	h m	h m	h m	h m	h m
1	3 40	+23·6	58·5	15·9	175	76	59	21·9	21 26	20 57	5 14	13 57	14 26
2	4 41	+25·2	59·0	16·1	187	82	47	22·9	22 25	21 55	6 13	15 04	15 34
3	5 43	+25·3	59·4	16·2	199	89	36	23·9	23 40	23 13	7 15	15 57	16 24
4	6 46	+23·7	59·8	16·3	211	95	25	24·9	—	-	8 16	16 36	16 58
5	7 47	+20·5	60·1	16·4	223	100	16	25·9	1 04	0 42	9 14	17 06	17 22
6	8 46	+16·0	60·1	16·4	236	102	8	26·9	2 31	2 17	10 10	17 28	17 39
7	9 42	+10·6	60·0	16·3	248	101	3	27·9	3 59	3 50	11 03	17 47	17 52
8	10 35	+ 4·6	59·6	16·2	260	79	0	28·9	5 24	5 22	11 53	18 04	18 04
9	11 27	− 1·5	59·1	16·1	272	326	1	0·5	6 48	6 50	12 42	18 21	18 16
10	12 18	− 7·4	58·4	15·9	285	307	3	1·5	8 09	8 17	13 30	18 38	18 28
11	13 09	−12·8	57·6	15·7	297	300	8	2·5	9 29	9 43	14 19	18 58	18 43
12	14 00	−17·4	56·8	15·5	309	295	15	3·5	10 46	11 06	15 08	19 22	19 01
13	14 52	−21·1	56·0	15·3	321	290	23	4·5	12 00	12 25	15 59	19 52	19 26
14	15 45	−23·7	55·3	15·1	334	284	32	5·5	13 06	13 35	16 50	20 30	20 01
15	16 38	−25·1	54·8	14·9	346	279	41	6·5	14 03	14 34	17 41	21 18	20 48
16	17 31	−25·3	54·5	14·8	358	273	51	7·5	14 50	15 19	18 31	22 15	21 47
17	18 24	−24·3	54·3	14·8	10	267	60	8·5	15 26	15 51	19 20	23 20	22 55
18	19 14	−22·3	54·2	14·8	22	263	69	9·5	15 53	16 14	20 07	—	-
19	20 04	−19·3	54·4	14·8	35	259	78	10·5	16 15	16 31	20 52	0 28	0 09
20	20 51	−15·5	54·7	14·9	47	256	85	11·5	16 33	16 44	21 36	1 39	1 25
21	21 38	−10·9	55·0	15·0	59	255	91	12·5	16 49	16 55	22 19	2 50	2 41
22	22 24	− 5·9	55·5	15·1	71	258	96	13·5	17 04	17 06	23 03	4 03	3 58
23	23 10	− 0·6	56·1	15·3	83	268	99	14·5	17 18	17 16	23 47	5 16	5 16
24	23 56	+ 4·9	56·6	15·4	95	344	100	15·5	17 34	17 27	—	6 31	6 36
25	0 45	+10·3	57·1	15·6	108	46	99	16·5	17 53	17 40	0 33	7 48	7 59
26	1 36	+15·2	57·6	15·7	120	58	95	17·5	18 15	17 58	1 21	9 08	9 25
27	2 30	+19·5	58·1	15·8	132	66	89	18·5	18 45	18 22	2 13	10 29	10 51
28	3 27	+22·8	58·5	15·9	144	73	82	19·5	19 26	18 58	3 09	11 47	12 14
29	4 27	+24·7	58·8	16·0	156	80	72	20·5	20 20	19 51	4 08	12 56	13 26
30	5 29	+25·2	59·0	16·1	168	86	62	21·5	21 29	21 01	5 09	13 52	14 21

MERCURY

Day	RA	Dec. +	Diam.	Phase	Transit	5° high 52°	5° high 56°	Day	RA	Dec.	Diam.	Phase	Transit	
	h m	°	"	%	h m	h m	h m		h m	°	"	%	h m	
1	9 39	12·1	9	18	10 59	4 30	4 23	16	10 41	+10·0	6	79	11 04	
4	9 44	12·7	8	30	10 52	4 20	4 12	19	11 01	+ 8·2	6	87	11 13	Mercury is too
7	9 53	12·8	7	42	10 50	4 17	4 09	22	11 21	+ 6·2	5	93	11 21	close to the
10	10 06	12·4	7	56	10 52	4 21	4 14	25	11 42	+ 4·0	5	96	11 30	Sun for
13	10 22	11·4	6	68	10 57	4 31	4 25	28	12 02	+ 1·6	5	99	11 38	observation
16	10 41	10·0	6	79	11 04	4 45	4 41	31	12 21	− 0·7	5	100	11 46	

VENUS   MARS

Day	RA	Dec. +	Diam.	Phase	Transit	5° high 52°	5° high 56°	Day	RA	Dec.	Diam.	Phase	Transit	
	h m	°	"	%	h m	h m	h m		h m	°	"	%	h m	
1	9 34	5·7	56	4	10 53	4 58	4 56	1	12 00	+ 0·7	4	99	13 21	
6	9 28	6·7	53	7	10 27	4 26	4 24	6	12 12	− 0·6	4	99	13 13	
11	9 25	7·6	50	12	10 05	3 59	3 56	11	12 24	− 1·9	4	99	13 05	Mars is too
16	9 26	8·4	46	16	9 47	3 37	3 34	16	12 36	− 3·2	4	99	12 57	close to the
21	9 31	8·9	43	21	9 32	3 20	3 16	21	12 48	− 4·6	4	99	12 50	Sun for
26	9 38	9·1	40	25	9 20	3 07	3 03	26	13 00	− 5·9	4	100	12 42	observation
31	9 49	9·1	37	29	9 12	2 58	2 54	31	13 12	− 7·2	4	100	12 35	

(*See* pages 65–66 for explanatory notes)

SUNRISE AND SUNSET

Day	London 0°05′ 51°30′		Bristol 2°35′ 51°28′		Birmingham 1°55′ 52°28′		Manchester 2°15′ 53°28′		Newcastle 1°37′ 54°59′		Glasgow 4°14′ 55°52′		Belfast 5°56′ 54°35′	
	h m	h m	h m	h m	h m	h m	h m	h m	h m	h m	h m	h m	h m	h m
1	5 12	18 48	5 22	18 58	5 18	18 57	5 17	19 00	5 12	19 00	5 20	19 13	5 30	19 17
2	5 13	18 46	5 24	18 56	5 19	18 55	5 19	18 58	5 13	18 58	5 22	19 10	5 32	19 14
3	5 15	18 43	5 25	18 53	5 21	18 52	5 21	18 55	5 15	18 55	5 24	19 07	5 33	19 12
4	5 17	18 41	5 27	18 51	5 23	18 50	5 22	18 53	5 17	18 53	5 26	19 05	5 35	19 09
5	5 18	18 39	5 28	18 49	5 24	18 48	5 24	18 50	5 19	18 50	5 28	19 02	5 37	19 07
6	5 20	18 37	5 30	18 47	5 26	18 45	5 26	18 48	5 21	18 48	5 30	19 00	5 39	19 04
7	5 21	18 34	5 32	18 44	5 28	18 43	5 28	18 46	5 23	18 45	5 32	18 57	5 41	19 02
8	5 23	18 32	5 33	18 42	5 29	18 41	5 29	18 43	5 25	18 43	5 34	18 54	5 43	18 59
9	5 25	18 30	5 35	18 40	5 31	18 38	5 31	18 41	5 27	18 40	5 36	18 52	5 44	18 57
10	5 26	18 28	5 36	18 38	5 33	18 36	5 33	18 38	5 28	18 38	5 38	18 49	5 46	18 54
11	5 28	18 25	5 38	18 35	5 34	18 34	5 34	18 36	5 30	18 35	5 40	18 47	5 48	18 52
12	5 29	18 23	5 39	18 33	5 36	18 31	5 36	18 34	5 32	18 32	5 42	18 44	5 50	18 49
13	5 31	18 21	5 41	18 31	5 38	18 29	5 38	18 31	5 34	18 30	5 44	18 41	5 52	18 47
14	5 33	18 18	5 43	18 28	5 39	18 27	5 40	18 29	5 36	18 27	5 45	18 39	5 53	18 44
15	5 34	18 16	5 44	18 26	5 41	18 24	5 41	18 26	5 38	18 25	5 47	18 36	5 55	18 42
16	5 36	18 14	5 46	18 24	5 43	18 22	5 43	18 24	5 40	18 22	5 49	18 33	5 57	18 39
17	5 37	18 12	5 47	18 21	5 44	18 19	5 45	18 21	5 41	18 20	5 51	18 31	5 59	18 37
18	5 39	18 09	5 49	18 19	5 46	18 17	5 47	18 19	5 43	18 17	5 53	18 28	6 01	18 34
19	5 41	18 07	5 51	18 17	5 48	18 15	5 48	18 16	5 45	18 15	5 55	18 25	6 03	18 32
20	5 42	18 05	5 52	18 15	5 49	18 12	5 50	18 14	5 47	18 12	5 57	18 23	6 04	18 29
21	5 44	18 02	5 54	18 12	5 51	18 10	5 52	18 11	5 49	18 09	5 59	18 20	6 06	18 26
22	5 45	18 00	5 55	18 10	5 53	18 08	5 54	18 09	5 51	18 07	6 01	18 17	6 08	18 24
23	5 47	17 58	5 57	18 08	5 54	18 05	5 55	18 07	5 53	18 04	6 03	18 15	6 10	18 21
24	5 49	17 55	5 59	18 05	5 56	18 03	5 57	18 04	5 55	18 02	6 05	18 12	6 12	18 19
25	5 50	17 53	6 00	18 03	5 58	18 00	5 59	18 02	5 56	17 59	6 07	18 10	6 14	18 16
26	5 52	17 51	6 02	18 01	5 59	17 58	6 01	17 59	5 58	17 57	6 09	18 07	6 16	18 14
27	5 53	17 48	6 03	17 58	6 01	17 56	6 02	17 57	6 00	17 54	6 11	18 04	6 17	18 11
28	5 55	17 46	6 05	17 56	6 03	17 53	6 04	17 54	6 02	17 51	6 13	18 02	6 19	18 09
29	5 57	17 44	6 07	17 54	6 04	17 51	6 06	17 52	6 04	17 49	6 15	17 59	6 21	18 06
30	5 58	17 42	6 08	17 52	6 06	17 49	6 08	17 49	6 06	17 46	6 17	17 56	6 23	18 04

JUPITER

Day	RA	Dec. +	Transit	5° high. 52°	5° high. 56°
	h m	° ′	h m	h m	h m
1	10 00·2	13 03	11 20	4 46	4 39
11	10 08·5	12 19	10 49	4 19	4 12
21	10 16·5	11 35	10 18	3 52	3 45
31	10 24·3	10 52	9 46	3 24	3 18

Diameters—equatorial 31″ polar 29″

SATURN

Day	RA	Dec. −	Transit	5° high. 52°	5° high. 56°
	h m	° ′	h m	h m	h m
1	20 13·8	20 25	21 32	1 00	0 32
11	20 12·0	20 31	20 50	0 18	23 45
21	20 10·7	20 36	20 10	23 32	23 04
31	20 10·1	20 38	19 30	22 52	22 24

Diameters—equatorial 18″ polar 16″
Rings—major axis 40″ minor axis 15″

URANUS

Day	RA	Dec. −	Transit	10° high. 52°	10° high. 56°
	h m	° ′	h m	h m	h m
1	18 43·5	23 27	20 02	22 03	20 46
11	18 43·1	23 27	19 22	21 23	20 06
21	18 42·9	23 27	18 42	20 44	19 26
31	18 43·2	23 27	18 03	20 05	18 48

Diameter 4″

NEPTUNE

Day	RA	Dec. −	Transit	10° high. 52°	10° high. 56°
	h m	° ′	h m	h m	h m
1	19 01·1	21 54	20 19	22 39	21 45
11	19 00·7	21 55	19 39	21 59	21 05
21	19 00·4	21 56	19 00	21 19	20 25
31	19 00·4	21 56	18 21	20 40	19 45

Diameter 2″

(See page 66 for explanatory notes)

DAY OF		
Month	Week	

Octo (eight), 8th month
of Roman (pre-Julian)
Calendar.

Sun's Longitude 210° ♍ 23ᵈ 22ʰ

1	Tu.	MICHAELMAS LAW SITTINGS BEGIN.
2	W.	Archbishop Runcie *b.* 1921. Ghandi *b.* 1869.
3	Th.	William Morris *d.* 1896. Jean Anouilh *d.* 1987.
4	F.	First English Bible printed 1535.
5	S.	Portugal declared a Republic 1910.
6	S.	**20th S. after Pentecost.** Parnell *d.* 1891.*
7	M.	Poe *d.* 1849. Marie Lloyd *d.* 1922.
8	Tu.	Great Fire of Chicago 1871.
9	W.	Saint-Saëns *b.* 1835. John Lennon *b.* 1940.
10	Th.	Harold Pinter *b.* 1930. Ralph Richardson *d.* 1983.
11	F.	Second Boer War began 1899.
12	S.	Elizabeth Fry *d.* 1845. Ramsey MacDonald *b.* 1866.
13	S.	**21st S. after Pentecost.** Mrs. Thatcher *b.* 1925.
14	M.	Harold II *d.* 1066. Errol Flynn *d.* 1959.
15	Tu.	DUCHESS OF YORK *b.* 1959. Cole Porter *d.* 1964.
16	W.	Eugene O'Neill *b.* 1888. Edward Ardizzone *b.* 1900.
17	Th.	Chopin *d.* 1849. Arthur Miller *b.* 1915.
18	F.	**St. Luke.** Thomas Edison *d.* 1931.
19	S.	John I *d.* 1216. Jonathan Swift *d.* 1745.
20	S.	**22nd S. after Pentecost.** Palmerston *b.* 1784.
21	M.	Geoffrey Boycott *b.* 1940. Aberfan disaster 1966.
22	Tu.	Cézanne *d.* 1906. Pablo Casals *d.* 1973.
23	W.	W.G. Grace *d.* 1915. Pele *b.* 1940.
24	Th.	United Nations founded 1945.
25	F.	Macaulay *b.* 1800. Picasso *b.* 1881.
26	S.	D. Scarlatti *b.* 1685. Hogarth *d.* 1764.
27	S.	**9th S. before Christmas.** Dylan Thomas *b.* 1914.
28	M.	**SS. Simon and Jude.** Capt. Cook *b.* 1728.
29	Tu.	International Red Cross f'ded 1863.
30	W.	Angelica Kauffmann *b.* 1741. Ezra Pound *b.* 1885.
31	Th.	HALLOWMASS EVE. Vermeer *b.* 1632.

PHENOMENA

d	h	
3	17	Mercury in superior conjunction.
4	15	Venus in conjunction with Moon. Venus 0°·2N.
5	02	Jupiter in conjunction with Moon. Jupiter 4°N.
8	04	Mercury in conjunction with Moon. Mercury 5°N.
8	16	Mars in conjunction with Moon. Mars 5°N.
14	17	Mars in conjunction with Mercury. Mars 0°·2N.
15	18	Jupiter in conjunction with Venus. Jupiter 2°N.
16	11	Saturn in conjunction with Moon. Saturn 2°S.

CONSTELLATIONS

The following constellations are near the meridian at

d	h		d	h
Sept. 1	24		Sept. 15	23
Oct. 1	22		Oct. 16	21
Nov. 1	20		Nov. 15	19

Ursa Major (below the Pole), Cepheus, Cassiopeia, Cygnus, Lacerta, Andromeda, Pegasus, Capricornus, Aquarius and Piscis Austrinus.

MINIMA OF ALGOL

d	h		d	h
2	06		19	11
5	03		22	08
8	00		25	04
10	20		28	01
13	17		30	22
16	14			

*Centenary.

Summer Time in 1991 (*see* p. 72).—Ends: October 27ᵈ 01ʰ GMT.

MOON
Phases, Apsides & Node

	d	h	m
☽ Last Quarter	1	0	30
● New Moon	7	21	39
☽ First Quarter	15	17	33
○ Full Moon	23	11	8
☽ Last Quarter	30	7	11

		d	h	m
Perigee (369,418 km)		2	18	1
Apogee (404,162 km)		15	11	1
Perigee (368,398 km)		27	15	42

Mean longitude of ascending node on Oct. 1, 285°

MONTHLY NOTES

Oct.   1. Pheasant shooting begins.

(*See* page 64 for explanatory notes)

	THE SUN					s.d. 16'·1				Sidereal Time	Transit of First Point of Aries
Day	Right Ascension	Dec. −	Equation of Time	Rise		Transit	Set				
				52°	56°		52°	56°			
	h m s	° ′	m s	h m	h m	h m	h m	h m		h m s	h m s
1	12 26 53	2 54	+10 02	6 00	6 02	11 50	17 39	17 37		0 36 55	23 19 15
2	12 30 31	3 18	+10 21	6 02	6 04	11 49	17 36	17 34		0 40 52	23 15 19
3	12 34 08	3 41	+10 40	6 03	6 06	11 49	17 34	17 32		0 44 48	23 11 23
4	12 37 46	4 04	+10 59	6 05	6 08	11 49	17 32	17 29		0 48 45	23 07 27
5	12 41 24	4 27	+11 18	6 07	6 10	11 49	17 30	17 26		0 52 42	23 03 31
6	12 45 02	4 50	+11 36	6 08	6 12	11 48	17 27	17 24		0 56 38	22 59 35
7	12 48 41	5 13	+11 53	6 10	6 14	11 48	17 25	17 21		1 00 35	22 55 39
8	12 52 21	5 36	+12 11	6 12	6 16	11 48	17 23	17 19		1 04 31	22 51 43
9	12 56 00	5 59	+12 28	6 13	6 18	11 47	17 21	17 16		1 08 28	22 47 47
10	12 59 40	6 22	+12 44	6 15	6 20	11 47	17 18	17 13		1 12 24	22 43 52
11	13 03 21	6 45	+13 00	6 17	6 22	11 47	17 16	17 11		1 16 21	22 39 56
12	13 07 02	7 08	+13 16	6 19	6 24	11 47	17 14	17 08		1 20 17	22 36 00
13	13 10 43	7 30	+13 31	6 20	6 26	11 46	17 12	17 06		1 24 14	22 32 04
14	13 14 25	7 53	+13 45	6 22	6 28	11 46	17 09	17 03		1 28 11	22 28 08
15	13 18 08	8 15	+13 59	6 24	6 30	11 46	17 07	17 01		1 32 07	22 24 12
16	13 21 51	8 37	+14 13	6 25	6 32	11 46	17 05	16 58		1 36 04	22 20 16
17	13 25 35	8 59	+14 26	6 27	6 34	11 45	17 03	16 56		1 40 00	22 16 20
18	13 29 19	9 21	+14 38	6 29	6 36	11 45	17 01	16 53		1 43 57	22 12 24
19	13 33 03	9 43	+14 50	6 31	6 38	11 45	16 59	16 51		1 47 53	22 08 28
20	13 36 49	10 05	+15 01	6 32	6 40	11 45	16 57	16 48		1 51 50	22 04 32
21	13 40 35	10 26	+15 12	6 34	6 43	11 45	16 54	16 46		1 55 46	22 00 37
22	13 44 21	10 48	+15 22	6 36	6 45	11 45	16 52	16 44		1 59 43	21 56 41
23	13 48 09	11 09	+15 31	6 38	6 47	11 44	16 50	16 41		2 03 40	21 52 45
24	13 51 57	11 30	+15 40	6 40	6 49	11 44	16 48	16 39		2 07 36	21 48 49
25	13 55 45	11 51	+15 48	6 41	6 51	11 44	16 46	16 36		2 11 33	21 44 53
26	13 59 34	12 12	+15 55	6 43	6 53	11 44	16 44	16 34		2 15 29	21 40 57
27	14 03 25	12 32	+16 01	6 45	6 55	11 44	16 42	16 32		2 19 26	21 37 01
28	14 07 15	12 52	+16 07	6 47	6 57	11 44	16 40	16 30		2 23 22	21 33 05
29	14 11 07	13 13	+16 12	6 48	6 59	11 44	16 38	16 27		2 27 19	21 29 09
30	14 14 59	13 33	+16 16	6 50	7 02	11 44	16 36	16 25		2 31 15	21 25 13
31	14 18 52	13 52	+16 20	6 52	7 04	11 44	16 35	16 23		2 35 12	21 21 18

Duration of Civil (C), Nautical (N) and Astronomical (A) Twilight (in minutes)

Lat. °	Oct. 1			Oct. 11			Oct. 21			Oct. 31		
	C	N	A	C	N	A	C	N	A	C	N	A
52	34	73	113	34	73	112	34	74	113	36	75	114
56	37	80	125	37	80	124	38	81	124	40	83	126

ASTRONOMICAL NOTES

MERCURY is unsuitably placed for observation, superior conjunction occurring on the 3rd.

VENUS, magnitude −4·5, is a magnificent morning object, visible by about 03h; in fact by the end of the month it becomes visible low in the eastern sky almost 4 hours before sunrise. Venus passes 3°S. of Regulus on the morning of the 8th. During the middle of the month Venus passes south of Jupiter, the minimum separation being 2°·3.

MARS is unsuitably placed for observation.

JUPITER is a brilliant object in the morning skies, magnitude −1·8. By the end of the month it is visible low in the east by 02h. Jupiter is moving eastwards in Leo. On the morning of the 5th the old crescent Moon passes 5°S. of the planet.

SATURN continues to be visible low in the SSW sky in the evenings, magnitude +0·5. Saturn is in Capricornus. The First Quarter Moon is near the planet on the 16th.

(See pages 64–65 for explanatory notes)

THE MOON

Day	RA	Dec.	Hor. Par.	Semi-diam.	Sun's Co-long.	P.A. of Bright Limb	Phase	Age	Rise 52°	Rise 56°	Transit	Set 52°	Set 56°
	h m	°	′	′	°	°	%	d	h m	h m	h m	h m	h m
1	6 31	+24·0	59·2	16·1	181	93	50	22·5	22 48	22 25	6 09	14 35	14 59
2	7 31	+21·3	59·3	16·2	193	99	39	23·5	—	23 56	7 07	15 07	15 25
3	8 29	+17·2	59·4	16·2	205	103	28	24·5	0 12	—	8 02	15 32	15 44
4	9 24	+12·3	59·3	16·1	217	106	18	25·5	1 37	1 26	8 54	15 51	15 58
5	10 17	+ 6·6	59·1	16·1	229	106	11	26·5	3 01	2 56	9 43	16 09	16 11
6	11 08	+ 0·7	58·7	16·0	242	103	5	27·5	4 23	4 23	10 32	16 25	16 22
7	11 59	− 5·2	58·3	15·9	254	91	1	28·5	5 44	5 49	11 20	16 42	16 34
8	12 49	−10·7	57·7	15·7	266	9	0	0·1	7 04	7 15	12 08	17 01	16 48
9	13 40	−15·6	57·1	15·6	278	310	2	1·1	8 22	8 39	12 58	17 24	17 05
10	14 32	−19·7	56·4	15·4	291	297	5	2·1	9 38	10 01	13 48	17 51	17 28
11	15 26	−22·6	55·8	15·2	303	289	11	3·1	10 49	11 16	14 40	18 27	17 59
12	16 20	−24·5	55·2	15·0	315	282	17	4·1	11 51	12 20	15 32	19 11	18 41
13	17 13	−25·1	54·8	14·9	327	276	25	5·1	12 42	13 11	16 23	20 05	19 36
14	18 06	−24·5	54·4	14·8	339	270	34	6·1	13 22	13 49	17 12	21 07	20 41
15	18 58	−22·8	54·3	14·8	352	264	43	7·1	13 53	14 15	18 00	22 14	21 52
16	19 47	−20·1	54·3	14·8	4	260	53	8·1	14 17	14 35	18 46	23 23	23 07
17	20 35	−16·6	54·5	14·8	16	256	62	9·1	14 37	14 49	19 30	—	—
18	21 21	−12·4	54·8	14·9	28	253	71	10·1	14 53	15 02	20 13	0 33	0 22
19	22 07	− 7·6	55·3	15·1	40	252	79	11·1	15 09	15 12	20 56	1 44	1 38
20	22 53	− 2·4	55·9	15·2	52	252	87	12·1	15 23	15 23	21 39	2 56	2 55
21	23 39	+ 3·0	56·6	15·4	65	255	93	13·1	15 39	15 34	22 25	4 10	4 14
22	0 27	+ 8·4	57·3	15·6	77	261	97	14·1	15 57	15 46	23 13	5 27	5 36
23	1 18	+13·6	58·0	15·8	89	288	100	15·1	16 18	16 03	—	6 47	7 01
24	2 12	+18·2	58·5	16·0	101	37	99	16·1	16 46	16 25	0 05	8 10	8 29
25	3 10	+21·8	59·0	16·1	113	64	97	17·1	17 24	16 58	1 01	9 31	9 56
26	4 11	+24·2	59·3	16·2	125	75	92	18·1	18 15	17 46	2 00	10 45	11 14
27	5 14	+25·0	59·5	16·2	138	84	84	19·1	19 21	18 53	3 02	11 47	12 15
28	6 17	+24·1	59·5	16·2	150	91	75	20·1	20 38	20 14	4 03	12 34	12 59
29	7 18	+21·7	59·4	16·2	162	98	65	21·1	22 01	21 43	5 02	13 09	13 29
30	8 16	+18·0	59·2	16·1	174	103	54	22·1	23 25	23 12	5 58	13 36	13 50
31	9 11	+13·3	58·9	16·1	186	107	42	23·1	—	—	6 50	13 57	14 05

MERCURY

Day	RA	Dec. −	Diam.	Phase	Transit		Day	RA	Dec. −	Diam.	Phase	Transit	
	h m	°			h m			h m	°			h m	
1	12 21	0·7	—	—	11 46		16	13 54	11·8	—	—	12 19	
4	12 41	3·0	—	—	11 53	Mercury is too	19	14 12	13·7	—	—	12 25	Mercury is too
7	12 59	5·3	—	—	12 00	close to the	22	14 30	15·6	—	—	12 31	close to the
10	13 18	7·6	—	—	12 07	Sun for	25	14 48	17·3	—	—	12 37	Sun for
13	13 36	9·7	—	—	12 13	observation	28	15 05	18·9	—	—	12 43	observation
16	13 54	11·8	—	—	12 19		31	15 23	20·3	—	—	12 49	

VENUS   MARS

Day	RA	Dec. +	Diam.	Phase	Transit	5° high. 52°	5° high. 56°	Day	RA	Dec. −	Diam.	Phase	Transit	
	h m	°	″	%	h m	h m	h m		h m	°	″	%	h m	
1	9 49	9·1	37	29	9 12	2 58	2 54	1	13 12	7·2	4	100	12 35	
6	10 02	8·8	34	33	9 05	2 52	2 48	6	13 25	8·5	4	100	12 27	
11	10 16	8·3	32	37	9 00	2 50	2 47	11	13 37	9·8	4	100	12 20	Mars is too
16	10 32	7·5	30	40	8 56	2 50	2 47	16	13 50	11·0	4	100	12 13	close to the
21	10 49	6·5	28	43	8 53	2 53	2 51	21	14 03	12·2	4	100	12 07	Sun for
26	11 07	5·3	26	46	8 51	2 57	2 56	26	14 16	13·4	4	100	12 00	observation
31	11 26	3·9	25	49	8 50	3 03	3 03	31	14 29	14·6	4	100	11 54	

(*See* pages 65–66 for explanatory notes)

SUNRISE AND SUNSET

Day	London 0°05' 51°30'		Bristol 2°35' 51°28'		Birmingham 1°55' 52°28'		Manchester 2°15' 53°28'		Newcastle 1°37' 54°59'		Glasgow 4°14' 55°52'		Belfast 5°56' 54°35'	
	h m	h m	h m	h m	h m	h m	h m	h m	h m	h m	h m	h m	h m	h m
1	6 00	17 39	6 10	17 49	6 08	17 46	6 10	17 47	6 08	17 44	6 19	17 54	6 25	18 01
2	6 02	17 37	6 12	17 47	6 09	17 44	6 11	17 45	6 10	17 41	6 21	17 51	6 27	17 59
3	6 03	17 35	6 13	17 45	6 11	17 42	6 13	17 42	6 12	17 39	6 23	17 49	6 29	17 56
4	6 05	17 33	6 15	17 43	6 13	17 39	6 15	17 40	6 13	17 36	6 25	17 46	6 30	17 54
5	6 07	17 30	6 17	17 40	6 15	17 37	6 17	17 37	6 15	17 34	6 27	17 43	6 32	17 51
6	6 08	17 28	6 18	17 38	6 16	17 35	6 18	17 35	6 17	17 31	6 29	17 41	6 34	17 49
7	6 10	17 26	6 20	17 36	6 18	17 32	6 20	17 33	6 19	17 29	6 31	17 38	6 36	17 46
8	6 12	17 24	6 22	17 34	6 20	17 30	6 22	17 30	6 21	17 26	6 33	17 36	6 38	17 44
9	6 13	17 21	6 23	17 31	6 21	17 28	6 24	17 28	6 23	17 24	6 35	17 33	6 40	17 41
10	6 15	17 19	6 25	17 29	6 23	17 25	6 26	17 26	6 25	17 21	6 37	17 30	6 42	17 39
11	6 17	17 17	6 27	17 27	6 25	17 23	6 28	17 23	6 27	17 19	6 39	17 28	6 44	17 36
12	6 18	17 15	6 28	17 25	6 27	17 21	6 29	17 21	6 29	17 16	6 41	17 25	6 46	17 34
13	6 20	17 13	6 30	17 23	6 29	17 19	6 31	17 19	6 31	17 14	6 43	17 23	6 48	17 32
14	6 22	17 10	6 32	17 20	6 30	17 16	6 33	17 16	6 33	17 11	6 45	17 20	6 49	17 29
15	6 23	17 08	6 33	17 18	6 32	17 14	6 35	17 14	6 35	17 09	6 47	17 18	6 51	17 27
16	6 25	17 06	6 35	17 16	6 34	17 12	6 37	17 12	6 37	17 07	6 49	17 15	6 53	17 24
17	6 27	17 04	6 37	17 14	6 36	17 10	6 39	17 09	6 39	17 04	6 51	17 13	6 55	17 22
18	6 28	17 02	6 38	17 12	6 37	17 08	6 41	17 07	6 41	17 02	6 53	17 10	6 57	17 20
19	6 30	17 00	6 40	17 10	6 39	17 05	6 42	17 05	6 43	16 59	6 55	17 08	6 59	17 17
20	6 32	16 58	6 42	17 08	6 41	17 03	6 44	17 03	6 45	16 57	6 57	17 06	7 01	17 15
21	6 34	16 56	6 44	17 06	6 43	17 01	6 46	17 00	6 47	16 55	6 59	17 03	7 03	17 13
22	6 35	16 54	6 45	17 04	6 45	16 59	6 48	16 58	6 49	16 52	7 01	17 01	7 05	17 11
23	6 37	16 52	6 47	17 02	6 46	16 57	6 50	16 56	6 51	16 50	7 03	16 58	7 07	17 08
24	6 39	16 50	6 49	17 00	6 48	16 55	6 52	16 54	6 53	16 48	7 05	16 56	7 09	17 06
25	6 41	16 48	6 50	16 58	6 50	16 53	6 54	16 52	6 55	16 46	7 07	16 54	7 11	17 04
26	6 42	16 46	6 52	16 56	6 52	16 51	6 56	16 50	6 57	16 43	7 10	16 51	7 13	17 02
27	6 44	16 44	6 54	16 54	6 54	16 49	6 57	16 48	6 59	16 41	7 12	16 49	7 15	16 59
28	6 46	16 42	6 56	16 52	6 55	16 47	6 59	16 46	7 01	16 39	7 14	16 47	7 17	16 57
29	6 48	16 40	6 58	16 50	6 57	16 45	7 01	16 44	7 03	16 37	7 16	16 45	7 19	16 55
30	6 49	16 38	6 59	16 48	6 59	16 43	7 03	16 41	7 05	16 35	7 18	16 42	7 21	16 53
31	6 51	16 36	7 01	16 46	7 01	16 41	7 05	16 39	7 07	16 32	7 20	16 40	7 23	16 51

JUPITER

Day	RA	Dec. +	Transit	5° high. 52°	5° high. 56°
	h m	° '	h m	h m	h m
1	10 24·3	10 52	9 46	3 24	3 18
11	10 31·7	10 11	9 14	2 55	2 50
21	10 38·6	9 32	8 42	2 26	2 22
31	10 44·9	8 56	8 09	1 56	1 52

Diameters—equatorial 33″ polar 31″

SATURN

Day	RA	Dec. −	Transit	5° high. 52°	5° high. 56°
	h m	° '	h m	h m	h m
1	20 10·1	20 38	19 30	22 52	22 24
11	20 10·1	20 38	18 51	22 13	21 45
21	20 10·9	20 36	18 12	21 35	21 06
31	20 12·4	20 32	17 34	20 58	20 29

Diameters—equatorial 17″ polar 15″
Rings—major axis 39″ minor axis 14″

URANUS

Day	RA	Dec. −	Transit	10° high. 52°	10° high. 56°
	h m	° '	h m	h m	h m
1	18 43·2	23 27	18 03	20 05	18 48
11	18 43·8	23 26	17 25	19 26	18 09
21	18 44·8	23 25	16 46	18 48	17 32
31	18 46·1	23 23	16 08	18 10	16 55

Diameter 4″

NEPTUNE

Day	RA	Dec. −	Transit	10° high. 52°	10° high. 56°
	h m	° '	h m	h m	h m
1	19 00·4	21 56	18 21	20 40	19 45
11	19 00·7	21 56	17 41	20 01	19 06
21	19 01·1	21 56	17 03	19 22	18 28
31	19 01·8	21 55	16 24	18 44	17 49

Diameter 2″

(See page 66 for explanatory notes)

DAY OF		Novem (nine), 9th month of Roman (pre-Julian) Calendar. Sun's Longitude 240° ‡ 22ᵈ 20ʰ
Month	Week	

Month	Week	
1	F.	**All Saints.** Gary Player *b.* 1935.
2	S.	ALL SOULS. Marie Antoinette *b.* 1755.
3	S.	**8th S. before Christmas.** Matisse *d.* 1954.
4	M.	Wilfred Owen *d.* 1918. Fauré *d.* 1924.
5	Tu.	Cyprus annexed 1914. Lester Piggott *b.* 1935.
6	W.	Tchaikovsky *d.* 1893. Kate Greenaway *d.* 1901.
7	Th.	Russian Revolution 1917 NS. Gene Tunney *d.* 1978.
8	F.	Milton *d.* 1674. Munich Putsch 1923.
9	S.	Edward VII *b.* 1841. De Gaulle *d.* 1970.
10	S.	**7th S. before Christmas.** Rimbaud *b.* 1891.*
11	M.	ARMISTICE DAY. Kierkegaard *b.* 1855.
12	Tu.	Mrs. Gaskell *d.* 1865. Baroness Orczy *d.* 1947.
13	W.	Rossini *d.* 1868. Eugene Ionesco *b.* 1912.
14	Th.	PRINCE OF WALES *b.* 1948. Aaron Copland *b.* 1900.
15	F.	Brazil declared a Republic 1889.
16	S.	Hindemith *b.* 1895. Oswald Mosley *b.* 1896.
17	S.	**6th S. before Christmas.** Montgomery *b.* 1887.
18	M.	Francis Thompson *d.* 1907. Niels Bohr *d.* 1962.
19	Tu.	Schubert *d.* 1828. Basil Spence *d.* 1976.
20	W.	QUEEN'S WEDDING DAY 1947. Franco *d.* 1975.
21	Th.	Purcell *d.* 1695. Natalia Makarova *b.* 1940.
22	F.	Billie Jean King *b.* 1943. Boris Becker *b.* 1967.
23	S.	Manuel de Falla *b.* 1876. Boris Karloff *b.* 1887.
24	S.	**5th S. before Christmas.** Grace Darling *b.* 1815.
25	M.	Lilian Baylis *d.* 1937. Imran Khan *b.* 1952.
26	Tu.	William Cowper *b.* 1731. John McAdam *d.* 1836.
27	W.	Fanny Kemble *b.* 1809.
28	Th.	Jean-Baptiste Lully *b.* 1632. Enid Blyton *d.* 1968.
29	F.	Monteverdi *d.* 1643. Graham Hill *d.* 1975.
30	S.	**St. Andrew.** Oscar Wilde *d.* 1900.

*Centenary   NS New Style

PHENOMENA

d	h	
1	16	Jupiter in conjunction with Moon. Jupiter 5°N.
2	09	Venus at greatest elongation W.47°.
2	16	Venus in conjunction with Moon. Venus 5°N.
6	12	Mars in conjunction with Moon. Mars 4°N.
8	04	Mercury in conjunction with Moon. Mercury 0°·6N.
8	09	Mars in conjunction with Sun.
12	21	Saturn in conjunction with Moon. Saturn 2°S.
13	04	Pluto in conjunction with Sun.
19	02	Mercury at greatest elongation E.22°.
29	04	Jupiter in conjunction with Moon. Jupiter 5°N.

CONSTELLATIONS

The following constellations are near the meridian at

d	h		d	h
Oct. 1	24		Oct. 16	23
Nov. 1	22		Nov. 15	21
Dec. 1	20		Dec. 16	19

Ursa Major (below the Pole), Cepheus, Cassiopeia, Andromeda, Pegasus, Pisces, Aquarius and Cetus.

MINIMA OF ALGOL

d	h		d	h
2	19		17	03
5	16		20	00
8	13		22	21
11	09		25	17
14	06		28	14

MOON
Phases, Apsides & Node

	d	h	m
● New Moon	6	11	11
☽ First Quarter	14	14	2
○ Full Moon	21	22	56
☾ Last Quarter	28	15	21
Apogee (404,810 km)	12	7	31
Perigee (362,941 km)	24	2	24

Mean longitude of ascending node on Nov. 1, 283°.

MONTHLY NOTES

Nov. 1. Fox-hunting begins.

9. Lord Mayor's Show.

10. Remembrance Sunday.

28. Martinmas (Scottish Term Day and Removal Day).

(*See* page 64 for explanatory notes)

Day	Right Ascension	Dec. −	Equation of Time	Rise 52°	Rise 56°	Transit	Set 52°	Set 56°	Sidereal Time	Transit of First Point of Aries
	h m s	° ′	m s	h m	h m	h m	h m	h m	h m s	h m s
1	14 22 46	14 12	+16 22	6 54	7 06	11 44	16 33	16 21	2 39 09	21 17 22
2	14 26 41	14 31	+16 24	6 56	7 08	11 44	16 31	16 18	2 43 05	21 13 26
3	14 30 37	14 50	+16 25	6 57	7 10	11 44	16 29	16 16	2 47 02	21 09 30
4	14 34 33	15 09	+16 25	6 59	7 12	11 44	16 27	16 14	2 50 58	21 05 34
5	14 38 30	15 27	+16 24	7 01	7 14	11 44	16 25	16 12	2 54 55	21 01 38
6	14 42 28	15 46	+16 23	7 03	7 16	11 44	16 24	16 10	2 58 51	20 57 42
7	14 46 27	16 04	+16 21	7 05	7 19	11 44	16 22	16 08	3 02 48	20 53 46
8	14 50 27	16 22	+16 17	7 06	7 21	11 44	16 20	16 06	3 06 44	20 49 50
9	14 54 28	16 39	+16 13	7 08	7 23	11 44	16 19	16 04	3 10 41	20 45 54
10	14 58 29	16 56	+16 09	7 10	7 25	11 44	16 17	16 02	3 14 38	20 41 58
11	15 02 31	17 13	+16 03	7 12	7 27	11 44	16 16	16 00	3 18 34	20 38 03
12	15 06 34	17 30	+15 56	7 14	7 29	11 44	16 14	15 58	3 22 31	20 34 07
13	15 10 38	17 46	+15 49	7 15	7 31	11 44	16 12	15 57	3 26 27	20 30 11
14	15 14 43	18 02	+15 41	7 17	7 33	11 44	16 11	15 55	3 30 24	20 26 15
15	15 18 49	18 18	+15 32	7 19	7 35	11 45	16 10	15 53	3 34 20	20 22 19
16	15 22 55	18 33	+15 22	7 21	7 37	11 45	16 08	15 51	3 38 17	20 18 23
17	15 27 02	18 48	+15 11	7 22	7 40	11 45	16 07	15 50	3 42 13	20 14 27
18	15 31 10	19 03	+15 00	7 24	7 42	11 45	16 06	15 48	3 46 10	20 10 31
19	15 35 19	19 17	+14 48	7 26	7 44	11 45	16 04	15 46	3 50 07	20 06 35
20	15 39 29	19 31	+14 34	7 28	7 46	11 46	16 03	15 45	3 54 03	20 02 39
21	15 43 39	19 45	+14 20	7 29	7 48	11 46	16 02	15 43	3 58 00	19 58 43
22	15 47 50	19 58	+14 06	7 31	7 50	11 46	16 01	15 42	4 01 56	19 54 47
23	15 52 03	20 11	+13 50	7 32	7 51	11 46	16 00	15 41	4 05 53	19 50 52
24	15 56 15	20 24	+13 34	7 34	7 53	11 47	15 59	15 39	4 09 49	19 46 56
25	16 00 29	20 36	+13 17	7 36	7 55	11 47	15 58	15 38	4 13 46	19 43 00
26	16 04 44	20 48	+12 59	7 37	7 57	11 47	15 57	15 37	4 17 42	19 39 04
27	16 08 59	21 00	+12 40	7 39	7 59	11 47	15 56	15 36	4 21 39	19 35 08
28	16 13 15	21 11	+12 21	7 40	8 01	11 48	15 55	15 34	4 25 36	19 31 12
29	16 17 32	21 21	+12 01	7 42	8 03	11 48	15 54	15 33	4 29 32	19 27 16
30	16 21 49	21 31	+11 40	7 43	8 04	11 49	15 53	15 32	4 33 29	19 23 20

THE SUN s.d. 16′·2

Duration of Civil (C), Nautical (N) and Astronomical (A) Twilight (in minutes)

Lat. °	Nov. 1 C	N	A	Nov. 11 C	N	A	Nov. 21 C	N	A	Nov. 30 C	N	A
52	36	75	115	37	78	117	38	80	120	39	82	123
56	40	84	127	41	87	130	43	90	134	45	93	137

ASTRONOMICAL NOTES

MERCURY, despite the fact that it reaches greatest eastern elongation on the 19th, is unsuitably placed for observation.

VENUS continues to be visible as a magnificent object for several hours in the south-eastern sky before dawn, magnitude −4·3. On the morning of the 29th Venus passes 4°N. of Spica.

MARS is unsuitably placed for observation, conjunction occurring on the 8th.

JUPITER, magnitude −2·0, continues to be visible in the eastern sky as a brilliant morning object. By the end of the month it should be visible low in the east shortly after midnight. On the mornings of the 1st and 2nd, and again on the 29th the Moon will be seen near the planet.

SATURN, magnitude +0·6, is still an evening object, low in the south-western sky, but by the end of the month is not visible after 19h. The rings of Saturn present a beautiful spectacle to the observer with only a small telescope.

(See pages 64–65 for explanatory notes)

THE MOON

Day	RA	Dec.	Hor. Par.	Semi-diam.	Sun's Co-long.	P.A. of Bright Limb	Phase	Age	Rise 52°	Rise 56°	Transit	Set 52°	Set 56°
	h m	°	'	'	°	°	%	d	h m	h m	h m	h m	h m
1	10 03	+ 7·9	58·6	16·0	198	109	31	24·1	0 47	0 40	7 39	14 14	14 18
2	10 54	+ 2·2	58·3	15·9	211	109	22	25·1	2 07	2 06	8 27	14 31	14 30
3	11 43	− 3·6	57·8	15·8	223	108	13	26·1	3 26	3 30	9 14	14 47	14 41
4	12 33	− 9·1	57·4	15·6	235	105	7	27·1	4 45	4 54	10 01	15 05	14 54
5	13 23	−14·1	56·9	15·5	247	97	3	28·1	6 02	6 17	10 49	15 26	15 10
6	14 14	−18·3	56·4	15·4	259	70	0	29·1	7 19	7 39	11 39	15 52	15 30
7	15 07	−21·6	55·9	15·2	272	318	0	0·5	8 31	8 56	12 30	16 24	15 58
8	16 01	−23·8	55·4	15·1	284	291	2	1·5	9 37	10 05	13 22	17 05	16 36
9	16 55	−24·8	54·9	15·0	296	280	6	2·5	10 33	11 02	14 14	17 56	17 26
10	17 48	−24·6	54·6	14·9	308	273	12	3·5	11 17	11 45	15 04	18 55	18 28
11	18 40	−23·3	54·3	14·8	320	266	19	4·5	11 52	12 15	15 53	20 00	19 37
12	19 31	−20·9	54·2	14·8	333	261	27	5·5	12 18	12 37	16 39	21 08	20 50
13	20 19	−17·6	54·2	14·8	345	256	35	6·5	12 40	12 54	17 23	22 17	22 04
14	21 05	−13·7	54·4	14·8	357	253	45	7·5	12 57	13 07	18 06	23 26	23 18
15	21 51	− 9·1	54·8	14·9	9	251	54	8·5	13 13	13 18	18 48	—	—
16	22 35	− 4·2	55·3	15·1	21	249	64	9·5	13 27	13 28	19 31	0 37	0 33
17	23 21	+ 1·0	56·0	15·3	33	249	73	10·5	13 42	13 39	20 14	1 48	1 49
18	0 07	+ 6·4	56·8	15·5	46	251	82	11·5	13 59	13 51	21 01	3 03	3 09
19	0 57	+11·6	57·7	15·7	58	254	89	12·5	14 19	14 06	21 51	4 20	4 32
20	1 49	+16·4	58·5	15·9	70	259	95	13·5	14 44	14 25	22 45	5 42	5 59
21	2 46	+20·5	59·3	16·1	82	271	99	14·5	15 17	14 54	23 45	7 05	7 27
22	3 47	+23·4	59·9	16·3	94	357	100	15·5	16 04	15 36	—	8 24	8 52
23	4 51	+24·8	60·3	16·4	106	74	98	16·5	17 06	16 37	0 47	9 34	10 03
24	5 56	+24·4	60·4	16·5	118	88	94	17·5	18 22	17 56	1 51	10 29	10 55
25	7 00	+22·4	60·3	16·4	130	96	87	18·5	19 46	19 26	2 53	11 09	11 30
26	8 01	+18·9	60·0	16·4	143	103	79	19·5	21 12	20 58	3 52	11 39	11 54
27	8 58	+14·3	59·6	16·2	155	107	68	20·5	22 36	22 28	4 46	12 02	12 12
28	9 51	+ 9·0	59·0	16·1	167	110	57	21·5	23 57	23 54	5 37	12 21	12 26
29	10 42	+ 3·3	58·4	15·9	179	112	46	22·5	—	—	6 25	12 37	12 38
30	11 32	− 2·4	57·8	15·8	191	112	35	23·5	1 16	1 18	7 12	12 54	12 49

MERCURY

Day	RA	Dec. −	Diam.	Phase	Transit	Day	RA	Dec. −	Diam.	Phase	Transit	
	h m	°			h m		h m	°			h m	
1	15 29	20·8	—	—	12 51	16	16 54	25·2	—	—	13 16	
4	15 47	22·0	—	—	12 57	19	17 08	25·5	—	—	13 19	Mercury is too
7	16 04	23·1	—	—	13 03	22	17 21	25·6	—	—	13 19	close to the
10	16 22	24·0	—	—	13 08	25	17 30	25·4	—	—	13 15	Sun for
13	16 38	24·7	—	—	13 13	28	17 34	25·0	—	—	13 07	observation
16	16 54	25·2	—	—	13 16	31	17 33	24·2	—	—	12 52	

Mercury is too close to the Sun for observation

VENUS   MARS

Day	RA	Dec.	Diam.	Phase	Transit	5° high. 52°	5° high. 56°	Day	RA	Dec. −	Diam.	Phase	Transit	
	h m	°	"	%	h m	h m	h m		h m	°	"	%	h m	
1	11 29	+ 3·6	25	50	8 50	3 04	3 05	1	14 32	14·8	4	100	11 52	
6	11 49	+ 2·0	23	52	8 50	3 12	3 14	6	14 46	15·9	4	100	11 46	
11	12 08	+ 0·3	22	55	8 50	3 21	3 24	11	14 59	16·9	4	100	11 40	Mars is too
16	12 29	− 1·5	21	57	8 50	3 31	3 36	16	15 13	17·9	4	100	11 35	close to the
21	12 49	− 3·4	20	60	8 51	3 42	3 48	21	15 28	18·9	4	100	11 29	Sun for
26	13 10	− 5·3	19	62	8 53	3 53	4 01	26	15 42	19·8	4	100	11 24	observation
31	13 32	− 7·3	18	64	8 54	4 06	4 16	31	15 57	20·6	4	100	11 19	

(*See* pages 65–66 for explanatory notes)

SUNRISE AND SUNSET

Day	London 0°05′ 51°30′		Bristol 2°35′ 51°28′		Birmingham 1°55′ 52°28′		Manchester 2°15′ 53°28′		Newcastle 1°37′ 54°59′		Glasgow 4°14′ 55°52′		Belfast 5°56′ 54°35′	
	h m	h m	h m	h m	h m	h m	h m	h m	h m	h m	h m	h m	h m	h m
1	6 53	16 34	7 03	16 44	7 03	16 39	7 07	16 38	7 09	16 30	7 22	16 38	7 25	16 49
2	6 55	16 33	7 05	16 43	7 05	16 37	7 09	16 36	7 11	16 28	7 24	16 36	7 27	16 47
3	6 56	16 31	7 06	16 41	7 06	16 35	7 11	16 34	7 13	16 26	7 27	16 34	7 29	16 45
4	6 58	16 29	7 08	16 39	7 08	16 33	7 13	16 32	7 15	16 24	7 29	16 32	7 31	16 43
5	7 00	16 27	7 10	16 37	7 10	16 32	7 15	16 30	7 17	16 22	7 31	16 30	7 33	16 41
6	7 02	16 26	7 12	16 36	7 12	16 30	7 17	16 28	7 19	16 20	7 33	16 27	7 35	16 39
7	7 03	16 24	7 13	16 34	7 14	16 28	7 18	16 26	7 21	16 18	7 35	16 25	7 37	16 37
8	7 05	16 22	7 15	16 32	7 16	16 26	7 20	16 24	7 23	16 16	7 37	16 23	7 39	16 35
9	7 07	16 21	7 17	16 31	7 17	16 25	7 22	16 23	7 25	16 15	7 39	16 22	7 41	16 33
10	7 09	16 19	7 19	16 29	7 19	16 23	7 24	16 21	7 27	16 13	7 41	16 20	7 43	16 32
11	7 10	16 18	7 20	16 28	7 21	16 22	7 26	16 19	7 29	16 11	7 43	16 18	7 45	16 30
12	7 12	16 16	7 22	16 26	7 23	16 20	7 28	16 18	7 31	16 09	7 46	16 16	7 47	16 28
13	7 14	16 15	7 24	16 25	7 25	16 18	7 30	16 16	7 33	16 07	7 48	16 14	7 49	16 26
14	7 16	16 13	7 26	16 23	7 27	16 17	7 32	16 14	7 35	16 06	7 50	16 12	7 51	16 25
15	7 17	16 12	7 27	16 22	7 28	16 15	7 34	16 13	7 37	16 04	7 52	16 11	7 53	16 23
16	7 19	16 10	7 29	16 21	7 30	16 14	7 35	16 11	7 39	16 02	7 54	16 09	7 55	16 21
17	7 21	16 09	7 31	16 19	7 32	16 13	7 37	16 10	7 41	16 01	7 56	16 07	7 57	16 20
18	7 23	16 08	7 32	16 18	7 34	16 11	7 39	16 09	7 43	15 59	7 58	16 06	7 59	16 18
19	7 24	16 07	7 34	16 17	7 35	16 10	7 41	16 07	7 45	15 58	8 00	16 04	8 01	16 17
20	7 26	16 05	7 36	16 15	7 37	16 09	7 43	16 06	7 47	15 56	8 02	16 03	8 02	16 16
21	7 27	16 04	7 37	16 14	7 39	16 08	7 44	16 05	7 49	15 55	8 04	16 01	8 04	16 14
22	7 29	16 03	7 39	16 13	7 40	16 06	7 46	16 03	7 51	15 54	8 06	16 00	8 06	16 13
23	7 31	16 02	7 41	16 12	7 42	16 05	7 48	16 02	7 53	15 52	8 08	15 58	8 08	16 12
24	7 32	16 01	7 42	16 11	7 44	16 04	7 50	16 01	7 54	15 51	8 10	15 57	8 10	16 10
25	7 34	16 00	7 44	16 10	7 45	16 03	7 51	16 00	7 56	15 50	8 11	15 56	8 12	16 09
26	7 35	15 59	7 45	16 09	7 47	16 02	7 53	15 59	7 58	15 49	8 13	15 54	8 13	16 08
27	7 37	15 58	7 47	16 08	7 49	16 01	7 55	15 58	8 00	15 48	8 15	15 53	8 15	16 07
28	7 39	15 57	7 48	16 08	7 50	16 00	7 56	15 57	8 02	15 47	8 17	15 52	8 17	16 06
29	7 40	15 57	7 50	16 07	7 52	16 00	7 58	15 56	8 03	15 46	8 19	15 51	8 18	16 05
30	7 41	15 56	7 51	16 06	7 53	15 59	7 59	15 55	8 05	15 45	8 20	15 50	8 20	16 04

JUPITER

Day	RA	Dec. +	Transit	5° high. 52°	5° high. 56°
	h m	° ′	h m	h m	h m
1	10 45·5	8 53	8 05	1 53	1 49
11	10 51·1	8 21	7 31	1 22	1 19
21	10 55·9	7 54	6 57	0 50	0 47
31	10 59·8	7 33	6 21	0 16	0 13

Diameters—equatorial 35″ polar 33″

SATURN

Day	RA	Dec. −	Transit	5° high. 52°	5° high. 56°
	h m	° ′	h m	h m	h m
1	20 12·5	20 31	17 31	20 54	20 26
11	20 14·7	20 25	16 54	20 18	19 50
21	20 17·4	20 16	16 17	19 42	19 15
31	20 20·7	20 06	15 41	19 08	18 40

Diameters—equatorial 16″ polar 15″
Rings—major axis 37″ minor axis 13″

URANUS

Day	RA	Dec. −	Transit	
	h m	° ′	h m	
1	18 46·2	23 23	16 05	Uranus is too close to the Sun for observation
11	18 47·9	23 21	15 27	
21	18 49·8	23 19	14 50	
31	18 52·0	23 16	14 12	

Diameter 4″

NEPTUNE

Day	RA	Dec. −	Transit	
	h m	° ′	h m	
1	19 01·9	21 55	16 20	Neptune is too close to the Sun for observation
11	19 02·9	21 54	15 42	
21	19 04·0	21 53	15 04	
31	19 05·3	21 51	14 26	

Diameter 2″

(*See* page 66 for explanatory notes)

Month	Week	

Decem (ten), 10th month

of Roman (pre-Julian)

Calendar.

Sun's Longitude 270° ♑ 22ᵈ 09ʰ

1	S.	**Advent Sunday.** David Ben-Gurion *d.* 1973.
2	M.	St Paul's Cathedral opened 1697.
3	Tu.	R.L. Stephenson *d.* 1894. Renoir *d.* 1919.
4	W.	Hobbes *d.* 1679. Britten *d.* 1976.
5	Th.	Mozart *d.* 1791. Walt Disney *b.* 1901.
6	F.	Warren Hastings *b.* 1732. Trollope *d.* 1882.
7	S.	Lord Darnley *b.* 1545. Pearl Harbour 1941.
8	S.	**2nd S. in Advent.** Golda Meir *d.* 1978.
9	M.	Van Dyke *d.* 1641. R.A. Butler *b.* 1902.
10	Tu.	Nobel Prizes first awarded 1901.
11	W.	Alexander Solzhenitsyn *b.* 1918.
12	Th.	Frank Sinatra *b.* 1915. Hovercraft patented 1955.
13	F.	Samuel Johnson *d.* 1784. Heinrich Heine *b.* 1797.
14	S.	Prince Albert *d.* 1861. Stanley Baldwin *d.* 1947.
15	S.	**3rd S. in Advent.** Rasputin *assass.* 1916.
16	M.	Jack Hobbs *b.* 1882. Somerset Maugham *d.* 1965.
17	Tu.	First flight by Wright Brothers 1903.
18	W.	Bobby Jones *d.* 1971. Ben Travers *d.* 1980.
19	Th.	J.M.W. Turner *d.* 1851. Brezhnev *b.* 1906.
20	F.	Gen. Ludendorff *d.* 1937. Artur Rubinstein *d.* 1982.
21	S.	MICHAELMAS LAW SITTINGS END. Disraeli *b.* 1804.
22	S.	**4th S. in Advent.** Samuel Beckett *d.* 1989.
23	M.	Thomas Malthus *d.* 1834. Théophile Gautier *d.*
24	Tu.	CHRISTMAS EVE. Thackeray *d.* 1863. [1872.
25	W.	**Christmas Day.** Isaac Newton *b.* 1642.
26	Th.	**St. Stephen.** BOXING DAY. Henry Miller *b.* 1891.*
27	F.	**St. John.** Charles Lamb *d.* 1834.
28	S.	**The Holy Innocents.**
29	S.	**1st S. after Christmas.** Harvey Smith *b.* 1938.
30	M.	Robert Boyle *d.* 1691. Amelia Bloomer *d.* 1894.
31	Tu.	John Wycliffe *d.* 1384. Léon Gambetta *d.* 1882.

PHENOMENA

d	h	
2	08	Venus in conjunction with Moon. Venus 7°N.
5	10	Mars in conjunction with Moon. Mars 3°N.
6	14	Mercury in conjunction with Moon. Mercury 3°N.
8	15	Mercury in inferior conjunction.
10	09	Saturn in conjunction with Moon. Saturn 3°S.
13	09	Mars in conjunction with Mercury. Mars 3°S.
22	09	Solstice.
26	13	Jupiter in conjunction with Moon. Jupiter 6°N.
27	21	Mercury at greatest elongation W.22°.
32	09	Venus in conjunction with Moon. Venus 5°N.

CONSTELLATIONS

The following constellations are near the meridian at

	d	h		d	h
Nov.	1	24	Nov.	15	23
Dec.	1	22	Dec.	16	21
Jan.	1	20	Jan.	16	19

Ursa Major (below the Pole), Ursa Minor (below the Pole), Cassiopeia, Andromeda, Perseus, Triangulum, Aries, Taurus, Cetus and Eridanus.

MINIMA OF ALGOL

d	h	d	h
1	11	18	16
4	08	21	13
7	05	24	10
10	02	27	06
12	22	30	03
15	19		

* Centenary.

MOON
Phases, Apsides & Node

	d	h	m
● New Moon	6	3	56
☽ First Quarter	14	9	32
○ Full Moon	21	10	23
☾ Last Quarter	28	1	55

		d	h	m
Apogee (405,823 km)		10	1	50
Perigee (358,354 km)		22	9	25

Mean longitude of ascending node on Dec. 1, 281°.

MONTHLY NOTES

Dec. 10. Grouse shooting ends.

22. Shortest day.

25. Christmas Day (Quarter Day). Bank Holiday in Scotland.

26. Bank Holiday, England, Wales, Scotland and N. Ireland.

31. Various licences expire.

(See page 64 for explanatory notes)

THE SUN s.d. 16′·3

Day	Right Ascension	Dec. −	Equation of Time	Rise 52°	Rise 56°	Transit	Set 52°	Set 56°	Sidereal Time	Transit of First Point of Aries
	h m s	° ′	m s	h m	h m	h m	h m	h m	h m s	h m s
1	16 26 07	21 41	+11 18	7 45	8 06	11 49	15 53	15 31	4 37 25	19 19 24
2	16 30 26	21 51	+10 56	7 46	8 08	11 49	15 52	15 31	4 41 22	19 15 28
3	16 34 45	22 00	+10 33	7 48	8 09	11 50	15 51	15 30	4 45 18	19 11 32
4	16 39 05	22 08	+10 09	7 49	8 11	11 50	15 51	15 29	4 49 15	19 07 37
5	16 43 26	22 16	+ 9 45	7 50	8 12	11 50	15 50	15 28	4 53 11	19 03 41
6	16 47 47	22 24	+ 9 21	7 52	8 14	11 51	15 50	15 28	4 57 08	18 59 45
7	16 52 09	22 31	+ 8 55	7 53	8 15	11 51	15 49	15 27	5 01 05	18 55 49
8	16 56 32	22 38	+ 8 30	7 54	8 17	11 52	15 49	15 27	5 05 01	18 51 53
9	17 00 54	22 45	+ 8 03	7 55	8 18	11 52	15 49	15 26	5 08 58	18 47 57
10	17 05 18	22 51	+ 7 36	7 56	8 19	11 53	15 49	15 26	5 12 54	18 44 01
11	17 09 42	22 56	+ 7 09	7 57	8 20	11 53	15 48	15 25	5 16 51	18 40 05
12	17 14 06	23 01	+ 6 42	7 58	8 22	11 54	15 48	15 25	5 20 47	18 36 09
13	17 18 30	23 06	+ 6 14	7 59	8 23	11 54	15 48	15 25	5 24 44	18 32 13
14	17 22 55	23 10	+ 5 46	8 00	8 24	11 54	15 48	15 25	5 28 41	18 28 17
15	17 27 20	23 14	+ 5 17	8 01	8 25	11 55	15 48	15 25	5 32 37	18 24 22
16	17 31 45	23 17	+ 4 48	8 02	8 26	11 55	15 49	15 25	5 36 34	18 20 26
17	17 36 11	23 20	+ 4 19	8 03	8 27	11 56	15 49	15 25	5 40 30	18 16 30
18	17 40 37	23 22	+ 3 50	8 04	8 27	11 56	15 49	15 25	5 44 27	18 12 34
19	17 45 03	23 24	+ 3 21	8 04	8 28	11 57	15 49	15 26	5 48 23	18 08 38
20	17 49 29	23 25	+ 2 51	8 05	8 29	11 57	15 50	15 26	5 52 20	18 04 42
21	17 53 55	23 26	+ 2 22	8 06	8 29	11 58	15 50	15 26	5 56 16	18 00 46
22	17 58 21	23 26	+ 1 52	8 06	8 30	11 58	15 51	15 27	6 00 13	17 56 50
23	18 02 47	23 26	+ 1 22	8 07	8 30	11 59	15 51	15 27	6 04 10	17 52 54
24	18 07 14	23 26	+ 0 52	8 07	8 31	11 59	15 52	15 28	6 08 06	17 48 58
25	18 11 40	23 25	+ 0 23	8 07	8 31	12 00	15 52	15 29	6 12 03	17 45 02
26	18 16 06	23 23	− 0 07	8 08	8 31	12 00	15 53	15 29	6 15 59	17 41 06
27	18 20 33	23 21	− 0 37	8 08	8 32	12 01	15 54	15 30	6 19 56	17 37 11
28	18 24 59	23 19	− 1 06	8 08	8 32	12 01	15 55	15 31	6 23 52	17 33 15
29	18 29 25	23 16	− 1 36	8 08	8 32	12 02	15 56	15 32	6 27 49	17 29 19
30	18 33 51	23 13	− 2 05	8 08	8 32	12 02	15 57	15 33	6 31 45	17 25 23
31	18 38 16	23 09	− 2 34	8 08	8 32	12 03	15 57	15 34	6 35 42	17 21 27

Duration of Civil (C), Nautical (N) and Astronomical (A) Twilight (in minutes)

Lat. °	Dec. 1 C	N	A	Dec. 11 C	N	A	Dec. 21 C	N	A	Dec. 31 C	N	A
52	40	82	123	41	84	125	41	85	126	41	84	125
56	45	93	138	47	96	141	47	97	142	47	96	141

ASTRONOMICAL NOTES

MERCURY passes through inferior conjunction on the 8th. It then moves outwards from the Sun to become visible as a difficult morning object, magnitude about 0, low in the south-eastern sky around the time of beginning of morning civil twilight, for about the 8 days before it reaches its greatest western elongation on the 27th.

VENUS, magnitude −4·2, is still a magnificent object in the south-eastern sky in the early mornings.

MARS is unsuitably placed for observation.

JUPITER is a brilliant morning object, magnitude −2·2. It is moving slowly eastwards in Leo, reaching its first stationary point on the last day of the year.

The gibbous Moon will be seen near the planet on the mornings of the 26th and 27th.

SATURN is still an evening object low in the south-western sky, but now nearing the end of its period of visibility. Saturn, magnitude +0·7, is in Capricornus. The crescent Moon is near the planet on the evenings of the 9th and 10th.

ECLIPSE. A partial eclipse of the Moon occurs on the 21st. See page 74 for details.

METEORS. The maximum of the well-known Geminid meteor shower occurs on the night of the 13th and 14th. The Moon, at First Quarter, provides some interference until shortly before midnight.

(See pages 64–65 for explanatory notes)

THE MOON

Day	RA	Dec.	Hor. Par.	Semi-diam.	Sun's Co-long.	P.A. of Bright Limb	Phase	Age	Rise 52°	Rise 56°	Transit	Set 52°	Set 56°
	h m	°	′	′	°	°	%	d	h m	h m	h m	h m	h m
1	12 21	− 7·9	57·2	15·6	203	110	25	24·5	2 33	2 40	7 58	13 11	13 02
2	13 10	−13·0	56·7	15·4	216	108	17	25·5	3 49	4 02	8 45	13 30	13 16
3	14 00	−17·3	56·2	15·3	228	104	10	26·5	5 05	5 23	9 34	13 54	13 35
4	14 52	−20·8	55·7	15·2	240	98	5	27·5	6 18	6 41	10 24	14 23	13 59
5	15 45	−23·3	55·3	15·1	252	88	1	28·5	7 26	7 53	11 15	15 01	14 33
6	16 38	−24·6	54·9	15·0	264	44	0	29·5	8 25	8 54	12 06	15 48	15 19
7	17 32	−24·8	54·5	14·9	277	282	1	0·8	9 13	9 41	12 57	16 44	16 16
8	18 25	−23·7	54·3	14·8	289	269	3	1·8	9 51	10 16	13 47	17 48	17 23
9	19 15	−21·6	54·1	14·7	301	261	7	2·8	10 20	10 41	14 34	18 55	18 35
10	20 04	−18·6	54·0	14·7	313	256	13	3·8	10 43	10 59	15 19	20 03	19 49
11	20 51	−14·8	54·1	14·7	325	252	20	4·8	11 02	11 13	16 02	21 12	21 02
12	21 36	−10·5	54·3	14·8	337	249	28	5·8	11 18	11 25	16 43	22 21	22 16
13	22 20	− 5·7	54·7	14·9	350	248	37	6·8	11 32	11 35	17 25	23 30	23 30
14	23 05	− 0·7	55·2	15·0	2	247	46	7·8	11 47	11 45	18 07	—	—
15	23 50	+ 4·5	55·9	15·2	14	247	56	8·8	12 02	11 56	18 50	0 41	0 45
16	0 37	+ 9·7	56·7	15·4	26	249	66	9·8	12 20	12 09	19 37	1 55	2 04
17	1 26	+14·6	57·6	15·7	38	251	76	10·8	12 41	12 25	20 28	3 13	3 27
18	2 20	+18·9	58·6	16·0	50	255	84	11·8	13 10	12 48	21 24	4 33	4 53
19	3 19	+22·3	59·5	16·2	63	261	92	12·8	13 49	13 23	22 25	5 55	6 20
20	4 22	+24·4	60·3	16·4	75	268	97	13·8	14 43	14 14	23 30	7 10	7 39
21	5 27	+24·8	60·9	16·6	87	281	100	14·8	15 54	15 26	—	8 14	8 42
22	6 33	+23·4	61·2	16·7	99	92	100	15·8	17 18	16 55	0 34	9 02	9 26
23	7 37	+20·4	61·1	16·7	111	102	96	16·8	18 47	18 30	1 37	9 38	9 56
24	8 38	+15·9	60·8	16·6	123	108	90	17·8	20 15	20 05	2 36	10 04	10 16
25	9 35	+10·6	60·2	16·4	135	112	82	18·8	21 41	21 36	3 30	10 25	10 32
26	10 28	+ 4·8	59·5	16·2	147	114	73	19·8	23 03	23 03	4 21	10 44	10 45
27	11 19	− 1·1	58·6	16·0	160	114	62	20·8	—	—	5 09	11 00	10 57
28	12 09	− 6·7	57·8	15·8	172	114	51	21·8	0 22	0 28	5 56	11 17	11 10
29	12 58	−11·9	57·0	15·6	184	112	40	22·8	1 39	1 51	6 43	11 36	11 23
30	13 48	−16·5	56·3	15·3	196	109	30	23·8	2 55	3 12	7 31	11 58	11 40
31	14 39	−20·2	55·7	15·2	208	105	22	24·8	4 09	4 30	8 20	12 25	12 03

MERCURY

Day	RA	Dec. −	Diam.	Phase	Transit		Day	RA	Dec. −	Diam.	Phase	Transit	5° high 52°	5° high 56°
	h m	°	″	%	h m			h m	°	″	%	h m	h m	h m
1	17 33	24·2	9	21	12 52		16	16 29	18·9	9	20	10 50	7 14	7 39
4	17 24	23·2	9	9	12 30	Mercury is too	19	16 27	18·8	8	34	10 37	7 01	7 25
7	17 09	22·0	10	1	12 03	close to the	22	16 30	19·1	8	46	10 29	6 56	7 21
10	16 52	20·6	10	1	11 35	Sun for	25	16 38	19·7	7	56	10 26	6 57	7 24
13	16 37	19·5	9	9	11 09	observation	28	16 50	20·4	7	64	10 26	7 02	7 31
16	16 29	18·9	9	20	10 50		31	17 04	21·2	6	71	10 28	7 11	7 41

VENUS

Day	RA	Dec. −	Diam.	Phase	Transit	5° high 52°	5° high 56°
	h m	°	″	%	h m	h m	h m
1	13 32	7·3	18	64	8 54	4 06	4 16
6	13 54	9·2	18	66	8 57	4 19	4 31
11	14 16	11·1	17	68	8 59	4 33	4 47
16	14 39	13·0	17	70	9 02	4 47	5 03
21	15 02	14·8	16	71	9 06	5 02	5 20
26	15 26	16·4	15	73	9 10	5 17	5 38
31	15 50	17·9	15	75	9 15	5 32	5 55

MARS

Day	RA	Dec. −	Diam.	Phase	Transit	
	h m	°	″	%	h m	
1	15 57	20·6	4	100	11 19	
6	16 12	21·3	4	100	11 14	
11	16 27	22·0	4	100	11 10	Mars is too
16	16 42	22·5	4	100	11 05	close to the
21	16 58	23·0	4	100	11 01	Sun for
26	17 14	23·4	4	99	10 57	observation
31	17 30	23·7	4	99	10 54	

(See pages 65–66 for explanatory notes)

SUNRISE AND SUNSET

Day	London 0°05′ 51°30′		Bristol 2°35′ 51°28′		Birmingham 1°55′ 52°28′		Manchester 2°15′ 53°28′		Newcastle 1°37′ 54°59′		Glasgow 4°14′ 55°52′		Belfast 5°56′ 54°35′	
	h m	h m	h m	h m	h m	h m	h m	h m	h m	h m	h m	h m	h m	h m
1	7 43	15 55	7 53	16 05	7 55	15 58	8 01	15 54	8 07	15 44	8 22	15 49	8 22	16 03
2	7 44	15 55	7 54	16 05	7 56	15 57	8 02	15 54	8 08	15 43	8 24	15 48	8 23	16 02
3	7 46	15 54	7 55	16 04	7 58	15 57	8 04	15 53	8 10	15 42	8 25	15 47	8 25	16 02
4	7 47	15 53	7 57	16 04	7 59	15 56	8 05	15 52	8 11	15 41	8 27	15 47	8 26	16 01
5	7 48	15 53	7 58	16 03	8 00	15 56	8 07	15 52	8 13	15 41	8 28	15 46	8 28	16 00
6	7 50	15 53	7 59	16 03	8 02	15 55	8 08	15 51	8 14	15 40	8 30	15 45	8 29	16 00
7	7 51	15 52	8 01	16 02	8 03	15 55	8 09	15 51	8 15	15 40	8 31	15 45	8 30	15 59
8	7 52	15 52	8 02	16 02	8 04	15 54	8 11	15 51	8 17	15 39	8 33	15 44	8 32	15 59
9	7 53	15 52	8 03	16 02	8 05	15 54	8 12	15 50	8 18	15 39	8 34	15 44	8 33	15 59
10	7 54	15 51	8 05	16 02	8 06	15 54	8 13	15 50	8 19	15 39	8 35	15 44	8 34	15 58
11	7 55	15 51	8 05	16 01	8 07	15 54	8 14	15 50	8 20	15 38	8 37	15 43	8 35	15 58
12	7 56	15 51	8 06	16 01	8 09	15 54	8 15	15 50	8 22	15 38	8 38	15 43	8 37	15 58
13	7 57	15 51	8 07	16 01	8 10	15 54	8 16	15 49	8 23	15 38	8 39	15 43	8 38	15 58
14	7 58	15 51	8 08	16 01	8 11	15 54	8 17	15 49	8 24	15 38	8 40	15 43	8 39	15 58
15	7 59	15 51	8 09	16 02	8 11	15 54	8 18	15 50	8 25	15 38	8 41	15 43	8 40	15 58
16	8 00	15 52	8 10	16 02	8 12	15 54	8 19	15 50	8 26	15 38	8 42	15 43	8 40	15 58
17	8 01	15 52	8 11	16 02	8 13	15 54	8 20	15 50	8 26	15 38	8 43	15 43	8 41	15 58
18	8 01	15 52	8 11	16 02	8 14	15 54	8 21	15 50	8 27	15 38	8 43	15 43	8 42	15 58
19	8 02	15 53	8 12	16 02	8 14	15 55	8 21	15 50	8 28	15 39	8 44	15 43	8 43	15 58
20	8 03	15 53	8 13	16 03	8 15	15 55	8 22	15 51	8 29	15 39	8 45	15 44	8 43	15 59
21	8 03	15 53	8 13	16 03	8 16	15 55	8 23	15 51	8 29	15 39	8 45	15 44	8 44	15 59
22	8 04	15 54	8 14	16 04	8 16	15 56	8 23	15 52	8 30	15 40	8 46	15 45	8 44	16 00
23	8 04	15 54	8 14	16 04	8 17	15 56	8 24	15 52	8 30	15 41	8 46	15 45	8 45	16 00
24	8 05	15 55	8 15	16 05	8 17	15 57	8 24	15 53	8 31	15 41	8 47	15 46	8 45	16 01
25	8 05	15 55	8 15	16 06	8 17	15 58	8 24	15 53	8 31	15 42	8 47	15 47	8 46	16 02
26	8 05	15 56	8 15	16 06	8 18	15 58	8 25	15 54	8 31	15 43	8 47	15 47	8 46	16 02
27	8 06	15 57	8 16	16 07	8 18	15 59	8 25	15 55	8 31	15 43	8 48	15 48	8 46	16 03
28	8 06	15 58	8 16	16 08	8 18	16 00	8 25	15 56	8 32	15 44	8 48	15 49	8 46	16 04
29	8 06	15 58	8 16	16 09	8 18	16 01	8 25	15 57	8 32	15 45	8 48	15 50	8 46	16 05
30	8 06	15 59	8 16	16 10	8 18	16 02	8 25	15 58	8 32	15 46	8 48	15 51	8 46	16 06
31	8 06	16 00	8 16	16 11	8 18	16 03	8 25	15 59	8 32	15 47	8 48	15 52	8 46	16 07

JUPITER

Day	RA	Dec +	Transit	5° high 52°	5° high 56°
	h m	° ′	h m	h m	h m
1	10 59·8	7 33	6 21	0 16	0 13
11	11 02·7	7 17	5 45	23 38	23 35
21	11 04·5	7 09	5 07	23 01	22 58
31	11 05·2	7 08	4 29	22 22	22 19

Diameters—equatorial 38″ polar 36″

SATURN

Day	RA	Dec −	Transit	5° high 52°	5° high 56°
	h m	° ′	h m	h m	h m
1	20 20·7	20 06	15 41	19 08	18 40
11	20 24·5	19 53	15 05	18 34	18 07
21	20 28·6	19 39	14 30	18 00	17 34
31	20 33·1	19 24	13 55	17 27	17 01

Diameters—equatorial 16″ polar 14″
Rings—major axis 35″ minor axis 12″

URANUS

Day	RA	Dec −	Transit	
	h m	° ′	h m	
1	18 52·0	23 16	14 12	Uranus is too close to the Sun for observation
11	18 54·3	23 13	13 35	
21	18 56·8	23 10	12 59	
31	18 59·3	23 06	12 22	

Diameter 4″

NEPTUNE

Day	RA	Dec −	Transit	
	h m	° ′	h m	
1	19 05·3	21 51	14 26	Neptune is too close to the Sun for observation
11	19 06·7	21 49	13 48	
21	19 08·2	21 46	13 10	
31	19 09·8	21 44	12 32	

Diameter 2″

(See page 66 for explanatory notes)

NOTES ON ASTRONOMICAL SECTION

The astronomical data are given in a form suitable for those who practise naked-eye astronomy or use small telescopes. No attempt has been made to replace the *Astronomical Almanac* for professional astronomers. Positions of the heavenly bodies are given only to the degree of accuracy required by amateur astronomers for setting telescopes, or for plotting on celestial globes or star atlases. Where intermediate positions are required, linear interpolation may be employed.

All data are, unless otherwise stated, for 0^h Greenwich Mean Time (GMT), i.e. at the midnight at the beginning of the day named.

(*See also* notes on British Summer Time, p. 72).

Definitions of the terms used cannot be given in an ephemeris of this nature. They must be sought in astronomical literature and textbooks. Probably the best source for the amateur is Norton's *Star Atlas and Reference Handbook* (Longman, 18th edition, 1989; £14·95), which contains an excellent introduction to observational astronomy, and a series of star maps for showing stars visible to the naked eye. Certain more extended ephemerides are available in the British Astronomical Association Handbook, an annual popular among amateur astronomers. (Secretary: Burlington House, Piccadilly, London, W1V 9AG)

A special feature has been made of the times when the various heavenly bodies are visible in the British Isles. Since two columns, calculated for latitudes $52°$ and $56°$, are devoted to risings and settings, the range $50°$ to $58°$ can be covered by interpolation and extrapolation. The times given in these columns are GMT's for the meridian of Greenwich. An observer west of this meridian must add his longitude (in time) and vice versa.

In accordance with the usual convention in astronomy, + and − indicate respectively north and south latitudes or declinations.

PAGE ONE OF EACH MONTH

The Zodiacal signs through which the Sun is passing during each month are illustrated. The date of transition from one sign to the next, to the nearest hour, is also given.

The **festivals and holy days** in bold type in the calendar are those observed by the Church of England.

Under the heading PHENOMENA will be found particulars of the more important conjunctions of the Sun, Moon and planets with each other, and also the dates of eclipses and other astronomical phenomena of special interest.

The CONSTELLATIONS listed each month are those that are near the meridian at the beginning of the month at 22^h local mean time. Allowance must be made for Summer Time if necessary. The fact that any star crosses the meridian 4^m earlier each night or 2^h earlier each month may be used, in conjunction with the lists given each month, to find what constellations are favourably placed at any moment. The table preceding the list of constellations may be extended indefinitely at the rate just quoted.

Times of MINIMA OF ALGOL are approximate times of the middle of the period of diminished light.

The principal phases of the Moon are the GMT's when the difference between the longitude of the Moon and that of the Sun is $0°$, $90°$, $180°$ or $270°$. The times of perigee and apogee are those when the Moon is nearest to, and farthest from, the Earth, respectively. The nodes or points of intersection of the Moon's orbit and the ecliptic make a complete retrograde circuit of the ecliptic in about 19 years. From a knowledge of the longitude of the ascending node and the inclination, whose value does not vary much from $5°$, the path of the Moon among the stars may be plotted on a celestial globe or star atlas.

The MONTHLY NOTES are self-explanatory.

PAGE TWO OF EACH MONTH

The Sun's semi-diameter, in arc, is given once a month.

The right ascension given is that of the true Sun. The right ascension of the mean Sun is obtained by applying the equation of time, with the sign given, to the right ascension of the true Sun, or, more easily, by applying 12^h to the column Sidereal Time. The direction in which the equation of time has to be applied in different problems is a frequent source of confusion and error. Apparent Solar Time is equal to the Mean Solar Time plus the Equation of Time. For example at noon on Aug. 8 the Equation of Time is $-5^m 40^s$ and thus at 12^h Mean Time on that day the Apparent Time is $12^h - 5^m 40^s = 11^h 54^m 20^s$.

The Greenwich Sidereal Time at 0^h and the Transit of the First Point of Aries (which is really the mean time when the sidereal time is 0^h) are used for converting mean time to sidereal time and vice versa.

The GMT of transit of the Sun at Greenwich may also be taken as the local mean time (LMT) of transit in any longitude. It is independent of latitude. The GMT of transit in any longitude is obtained by adding the longitude to the time given if west, and vice versa.

The legal importance of SUNRISE and SUNSET is that the Road Vehicles Lighting Regulations 1989 (SI 1989 No. 1796) make the use of front and rear position lamps on vehicles compulsory during the period between sunset and sunrise. Headlamps on vehicles are required to be used during the hours of darkness, defined in these Regulations as the period between half an hour after sunset and half an hour before sunrise.

In all laws and regulations 'sunset' refers to the local sunset, i.e. the time at which the Sun sets at the place in question. This common-sense interpretation has been upheld by legal tribunals. Thus the necessity for providing for different latitudes and longitudes, as already described, is evident.

The times of SUNRISE and SUNSET are those when the Sun's upper limb, as affected by refraction, is on the true horizon of an observer at sea-level. Assuming the mean refraction to be 34', and the Sun's semi-diameter to be 16', the time given is that when the true zenith distance of the Sun's centre is $90° + 34' + 16'$ or $90° 50'$, or, in other words, when the depression of the Sun's centre below the true horizon is $50'$. The upper limb is then 34′ below the true horizon, but is brought there by refraction. It is true, of course, that an observer on a ship might see the Sun for a minute or so longer, because of the dip of the horizon, while another viewing the sunset over hills or mountains would record an earlier time. Nevertheless, the moment when the true zenith distance of the Sun's centre is 90° 50′ is a precise time dependent only on the latitude and longitude of the place, and independent of its altitude above sea-level, the contour of its horizon, the vagaries of refraction or the small seasonal change in the Sun's semi-diameter; this moment is suitable in every way as a definition of sunset (or sunrise) for all statutory purposes. (For further information *see* footnote.)

It is well known that light reaches us before sunrise and also continues to reach us for some time after sunset. The interval between darkness and sunrise or sunset and darkness is called twilight. Astronomically speaking, twilight is considered to begin or end when the Sun's centre is 18° below the horizon, as no light from the Sun can then reach the observer. As thus defined twilight may last several hours; in high latitudes at the summer solstice the depression of 18° is not reached, and twilight lasts from sunset to sunrise.

The need for some sub-division of twilight was met some years ago by dividing the gathering darkness into four steps.

(1) *Sunrise or Sunset*, defined as above.
(2) *Civil twilight*, which begins or ends when the Sun's centre is 6° below the horizon. This marks the time when operations requiring daylight may commence or must cease. In England it varies from about 30 to 60 minutes after sunset and the same interval before sunrise. 'Lighting-up time' is a crude attempt to approximate to civil twilight over the British Isles.
(3) *Nautical twilight*, which begins or ends when the Sun's centre is 12° below the horizon. This marks the time when it is, to all intent and purposes, completely dark.
(4) *Astronomical twilight*, which begins or ends when the Sun's centre is 18° below the horizon. This marks theoretical perfect darkness. It is of little practical importance, especially if nautical twilight is tabulated.

To assist observers the durations of civil, nautical and astronomical twilights are given at intervals of ten days. The beginning of a particular twilight is found by subtracting the duration from the time of sunrise, while the end is found by adding the duration to the time of sunset. Thus the beginning of astronomical twilight in latitude 52°, on the Greenwich meridian, on March 11 is found as $06^h\ 25^m - 113^m = 04^h\ 32^m$ and similarly the end of civil twilight as $17^h\ 56^m + 34^m = 18^h\ 30^m$.

The letters TAN (twilight all night) are printed when twilight lasts all night.

Under the heading ASTRONOMICAL NOTES will be found notes describing the position and visibility of all the planets and also of other phenomena; these are intended to guide naked-eye observers or those using small telescopes.

PAGE THREE OF EACH MONTH

The Moon moves so rapidly among the stars that its position is given only to the degree of accuracy that permits linear interpolation. The right ascension and declination are geocentric, i.e. for an imaginary observer at the centre of the Earth. To an observer on the surface of the Earth the position is always different, as the altitude is always less on account of parallax, which may reach 1°.

The lunar terminator is the line separating the bright from the dark part of the Moon's disk. Apart from irregularities of the lunar surface, the terminator is elliptical, because it is a circle seen in projection. It becomes the full circle forming the limb, or edge, of the Moon at New and Full Moon. The selenographic longitude of the terminator is measured from the mean centre of the visible disk, which may differ from the visible centre by as much as 8°, because of libration.

Instead of the longitude of the terminator the Sun's selenographic co-longitude is tabulated. It is numerically equal to the selenographic longitude of the morning terminator, measured eastward from the mean centre of the disk. Thus its value is approximately 270° at New Moon, 360° at First Quarter, 90° at Full Moon and 180° at Last Quarter.

The Position Angle of the Bright Limb is the position angle of the midpoint of the illuminated limb, measured eastward from the north point on the disk. The column PHASE shows the percentage of the area of the Moon's disk illuminated; this is also the illuminated percentage of the diameter at right angles to the line of cusps. The terminator is a semi-ellipse whose major axis is the line of cusps, and whose semi-minor axis is determined by the tabulated percentage; from New Moon to Full Moon the east limb is dark, and vice versa.

The times given as moonrise and moonset are those when the upper limb of the Moon is on the horizon of an observer at sea-level. The Sun's horizontal parallax is about 9″, and is negligible when considering sunrise and sunset, but that of the Moon averages about 57′. Hence the computed time represents the moment when the true zenith distance of the Moon is 90° 50′ (as for the Sun) minus the horizontal parallax. The time required for the Sun or Moon to rise or set is about four minutes (except in high latitudes). (For further information, *see* footnote on p. 71.)

SUNRISE, SUNSET and MOONRISE, MOONSET

The tables have been constructed for the meridian of Greenwich, and for latitudes 52° and 56°. They give Greenwich Mean Time (GMT) throughout the year. To obtain the GMT of the phenomenon as seen from any other latitude and longitude in the British Isles, first interpolate or extrapolate for latitude by the usual rules of proportion. To the time thus found the longitude (expressed in time) is to be *added* if west (as it usually is in Great Britain) or *subtracted* if east. If the longitude is expressed in degrees and minutes of arc, it must be converted to time at the rate of $1° = 4^m$ and $15′ = 1^m$.

A method of calculating rise and set times for other places in the world is given on pp. 70 and 71.

The GMT of transit of the Moon over the meridian of Greenwich is given; these times are independent of latitude, but must be corrected for longitude. For places in the British Isles it suffices to add the longitude if west, and vice versa. For more remote places a further correction is necessary because of the rapid movement of the Moon relative to the stars. The entire correction is conveniently determined by first finding the west longitude λ of the place. If the place is in west longitude, λ is the ordinary west longitude; if the place is in east longitude λ is the complement to 24^h (or $360°$) of the longitude and will be greater than 12^h (or $180°$). The correction then consists of two positive portions, namely λ and the fraction $\lambda/24$ (or $\lambda°/360$) multiplied by the difference between consecutive transits. Thus for Sydney, New South Wales, the longitude is $10^h\ 05^m$ east, so $\lambda = 13^h\ 55^m$ and the fraction $\lambda/24$ is 0·58. The transit on the local date 1991 September 16 is found as follows:

	d	h	m
GMT of transit at Greenwich......Sept.	15	17	41
λ		13	55
$0·58 \times (18^h\ 31^m - 17^h\ 41^m)$			29
GMT of transit at Sydney..........		16 08	05
Corr. to NSW Standard Time.......		10	00
Local standard time of transit......		16 18	05

It is evident of course, that for any given place the quantities λ and the correction to local standard time may be combined permanently, being here $23^h\ 55^m$.

Positions of Mercury are given for every third day, and those of Venus and Mars for every fifth day; they may be interpolated linearly. The diameter (Di.) is given in seconds of arc. The phase (Ph.) is the illuminated percentage of the disk. In the case of the inner planets this approaches 100 at superior conjunction and 0 at inferior conjunction. When the phase is less than 50 the planet is crescent-shaped or horned; for greater phases it is gibbous. In the case of the exterior planet Mars, the phase approaches 100 at conjunction and opposition, and is a minimum at the quadratures.

Since the planets cannot be seen when on the horizon, the actual times of rising and setting are not given; instead, the time when the planet has an apparent altitude of 5° has been tabulated. If the time of transit is between 00^h and 12^h the time refers to an altitude of 5° above the eastern horizon: if between 12^h and 24^h, to the western horizon. The phenomenon tabulated is the one that occurs between sunset and sunrise; unimportant exceptions to these rules may occur because changes are not made during a month, except in the case of Mercury. The times given may be interpolated for latitude and corrected for longitude as in the case of the Sun and Moon.

The GMT at which the planet transits the Greenwich meridian is also given. The times of transit are to be corrected to local meridians in the usual way, as already described.

PAGE FOUR OF EACH MONTH

The GMT's of Sunrise and Sunset for seven towns, whose adopted positions in longitude (W.) and latitude (N.) are given immediately below the name,

may be used not only for these phenomena, but also for lighting-up times, which, under the Road Vehicles Lighting Regulations, 1989, are from sunset to sunrise throughout the year. (*See* p. 64 for a fuller explanation.)

The particulars for the four outer planets resemble those for the planets on Page Three of each month, except that, under Uranus and Neptune, times when the planet is 10° high instead of 5° high are given; this is because of the inferior brightness of these planets. The diameters given for the rings of Saturn are those of the major axis (in the plane of the planet's equator) and the minor axis respectively. The former has a small seasonal change due to the slightly varying distance of the Earth from Saturn, but the latter varies from zero when the Earth passes through the ring plane every 15 years to its maximum opening half-way between these periods. The rings were open at their widest extent in 1988.

TIME

From the earliest ages, the natural division of time into recurring periods of day and night has provided the practical time scale for the everyday activities of mankind. Indeed, if any alternative means of time measurement is adopted, it must be capable of adjustment so as to remain in general agreement with the natural time scale defined by the diurnal rotation of the Earth on its axis. Ideally the rotation should be measured against a fixed frame of reference; in practice it must be measured against the background provided by the celestial bodies. If the Sun is chosen as the reference point, we obtain Apparent Solar Time, which is the time indicated by a sundial. It is not a uniform time, but is subject to variations which amount to as much as a quarter of an hour in each direction. Such wide variations cannot be tolerated in a practical time scale, and this has led to the concept of Mean Solar Time in which all the days are exactly the same length and equal to the average length of the Apparent Solar Day.

The positions of the stars in the sky are specified in relation to a fictitious reference point in the sky known as the First Point of Aries (or the Vernal Equinox). It is therefore convenient to adopt this same reference point when considering the rotation of the Earth against the background of the stars. The time scale so obtained is known as Apparent Sidereal Time.

Greenwich Mean Time

The daily rotation of the Earth on its axis causes the Sun and the other heavenly bodies to appear to cross the sky from East to West. It is convenient to represent this relative motion as if the Sun really performed a daily circuit around a fixed Earth. Noon in Apparent Solar Time may then be defined as the time at which the Sun transits across the observer's meridian. In Mean Solar Time, noon is similarly defined by the meridian transit of a fictitious Mean Sun moving uniformly in the sky with the same average speed as the true Sun. Mean Solar Time observed on the meridian of the transit circle telescope of the Old Royal Observatory at Greenwich is called Greenwich Mean Time (GMT). The mean solar day is divided into 24 hours and, for astronomical and other scientific purposes, these are numbered

0 to 23, commencing at midnight. Civil time is usually reckoned in two periods of 12 hours, designated a.m. (*ante meridiem*, i.e. before noon) and p.m. (*post meridiem*, i.e. after noon).

Universal Time

Before 1925 January 1, GMT was reckoned in 24 hours commencing at noon; since that date it has been reckoned from midnight. In view of the risk of confusion in the use of the designation GMT before and after 1925, the International Astronomical Union recommended in 1928 that astronomers should employ the term Universal Time, UT (or Weltzeit, WZ) to denote GMT measured from Greenwich Mean Midnight.

In precision work it is necessary to take account of small variations in Universal Time. These arise from small irregularities in the rotation of the Earth. Observed astronomical time is designated UT0. Observed time corrected for the effects of the motion of the poles (giving rise to a 'wandering' in longitude) is designated UT1. There is also a seasonal fluctuation in the rate of rotation of the Earth arising from meteorological causes, often called the annual fluctuation. UT1 corrected for this effect is designated UT2 and provides a time scale free from short-period fluctuations. It is still subject to small secular and irregular changes.

Apparent Solar Time

As has been mentioned on page 66, the time shown by a sundial is called Apparent Solar Time. It differs from Mean Solar Time by an amount known as the Equation of Time, which is the total effect of two causes which make the length of the apparent solar day non-uniform. One cause of variation is that the orbit of the Earth is not a circle, but an ellipse, having the Sun at one focus. As a consequence, the angular speed of the Earth in its orbit is not constant; it is greatest at the beginning of January when the Earth is nearest the Sun. The other cause is due to the obliquity of the ecliptic; the plane of the equator (which is at right-angles to the axis of rotation of the Earth) does not coincide with the ecliptic (the plane defined by the apparent annual motion of the Sun around the celestial sphere) but is inclined to it at an angle of 23° 26'. As a result, the apparent solar day is shorter than average at the equinoxes and longer at the solstices. From the combined effects of the components due to obliquity and eccentricity, the equation of time reaches its maximum values in February (−14 mins.) and early November (+16 mins.). It has a zero value on four dates during the year, and it is only on these dates (approx. April 15, June 14, September 1, and December 25) that a sundial shows Mean Solar Time.

Sidereal Time

A sidereal day is the duration of a complete rotation of the Earth with reference to the First Point of Aries. The term sidereal (or 'star') time is perhaps a little misleading since the time scale so defined is not exactly the same as that which would be defined by successive transits of a selected star, as there is a small progressive motion between the stars and the First Point of Aries due to the precession of the Earth's axis. This makes the length of the sidereal day shorter than the true period of rotation by 0·008 seconds. Superimposed on this steady precessional motion are small oscillations called nutation, giving rise to fluctuations in apparent sidereal time amounting to as much as 1·2 seconds. It is therefore customary to employ Mean Sidereal Time, from which these fluctuations have been removed. The conversion of GMT to Greenwich sidereal time (GST) may be performed by adding the value of the GST at 0^h on the day in question (Page Two of each month) to the GMT converted to sidereal time using the table on p. 72.

Example. To find the GST at August 8^d 02^h 41^m 11^s GMT

				h	m	s
GST at 0^h	..	..	..	21	04	01
GMT	..	..	..	2	41	11
Acceleration for 2^h	..	..	..			20
„ „ 41^m 11^s	..	..				7
Sum = GST =	..	..	..	23	45	39

If the observer is not on the Greenwich meridian then his longitude, measured positively westwards from Greenwich, must be subtracted from the GST to obtain Local Sidereal Time (LST). Thus, in the above example, an observer 5^h east of Greenwich, or 19^h west, would find his LST as 4^h 45^m 39^s.

Ephemeris Time

In the study of the motions of the Sun, Moon and planets, observations taken over an extended period are used in the preparation of tables giving the apparent position of the body each day. A table of this sort is known as an ephemeris, and may be used in the comparison of current observations with tabulated positions. A detailed examination of the observations made over the past 300 years shows that the Sun, Moon and planets appear to depart from their predicted positions by amounts proportional to their mean motions. The only satisfactory explanation is that the time scale to which the observations were referred was not uniform as had been supposed. Since the time scale was based on the rotation of the Earth, it follows that this rotation is subject to irregularities. The fact that the discrepancies between the observed and ephemeris positions were proportional to the mean motions of the bodies made it possible to secure agreement by substituting a revised time scale and recomputing the ephemeris positions. The time scale which brings the ephemeris into agreement with the observations is known as Ephemeris Time (ET).

The new unit of time has been defined in terms of the apparent annual motion of the Sun. Thus the second is now defined in terms of the annual motion of the Earth in its orbit around the Sun (1/31556925·9747 of the Tropical Year for 1900 January 0^d 12^h ET) instead of in terms of the diurnal rotation of the Earth on its axis (1/86 400 of the Mean Solar Day). In many branches of scientific work other than astronomy there has been a demand for a unit of time that is invariable, and the second of Ephemeris time was adopted by the Comité International des Poids et Mesures in 1956. The length of the unit has been chosen to provide general agreement with UT throughout the 19th and 20th centuries. During 1991 the estimated difference ET − UT is 58 seconds. The precise determination of ET from astronomical observations is a lengthy process, as the accuracy with which a single observation of the Sun can be made is far less than that obtainable in, for instance, a comparison between clocks. It is therefore necessary to average the observations over an extended period. Largely on account of its faster motion, the position of the Moon may be observed with greater accuracy, and a close approximation to Ephemeris Time may be obtained by comparing observations of the Moon with its ephemeris position. Even in this case, however, the requisite standard of accuracy can only be achieved by averaging over a number of years.

Atomic Time

The fundamental standards of time and frequency must be defined in terms of a periodic motion adequately uniform, enduring and measurable. Progress has made it possible to use natural standards, such as atomic or molecular oscillations. Continuous oscillations are generated in an electrical circuit, the frequency of which is then compared or brought into coincidence with the frequency characteristic of the absorption or emission by the atoms or molecules when they change between two selected energy levels. The National Physical Laboratory makes regular comparisons between quartz clocks of high stability and a frequency defined by atoms of caesium.

International Atomic Time (TAI) is formed by combining the readings of many caesium clocks and was set close to the astronomically-based Universal Time (UT) near the beginning of 1958. It was formally recognized in 1971 and since 1988 January 1 has been maintained by the International Bureau of Weights and Measures (BIPM). The second markers are generated according to the SI definition of the second adopted in 1967 at the 13th General Conference of Weights and Measures: 'The second is the duration of 9 192 631 770 periods of the radiation corresponding to the transition between the two hyperfine levels of the ground state of the caesium-133 atom.'

Civil time in almost all countries is now based on Co-ordinated Universal Time (UTC), established through international collaboration and based on the readings of atomic clocks and the rotation of the Earth. It was designed to make both atomic time and UT accessible with accuracies appropriate for most users.

Radio Time Signals

UTC is made generally available through time signals and standard frequency broadcasts such as MSF in the UK, CHU in Canada and WWV and WWVH in the USA. These are based on national timescales that are maintained in close agreement with UTC and provide traceability to the national timescale and to UTC. The markers of seconds in the UTC scale coincide with those of TAI.

As the rate of rotation of the Earth is variable the time signals are adjusted by the introduction of a leap second when necessary in order that UTC shall not depart from UT by more than 0·9s. For convenience leap seconds are introduced when necessary on the last second of the third, sixth, ninth or twelfth

month, but preferably on December 31 and/or June 30. In the case of a positive leap second, $23^h\ 59^m\ 60^s$ is followed one second later by $0^h\ 0^m\ 00^s$ of the first day of the month. In the case of a negative leap second, $23^h\ 59^m\ 58^s$ is followed one second later by $0^h\ 0^m\ 00^s$ of the first day of the month. Notices concerning the insertion of leap seconds in UTC are issued by the International Earth Rotation Service at the Observatoire de Paris.

To disseminate the national timescale in the UK, special signals are broadcast on behalf of the National Physical Laboratory from the British Telecom International Radio Station at Rugby. The signals are controlled from a caesium beam atomic frequency standard and consist of a standard frequency carrier of 60 kHz (MSF) which switches off for half a second to denote the passing of one minute, and for a tenth of a second to denote the passing of one second. Also transmitted are two binary coded decimal (BCD) time codes giving time of day and calendar information. Summer and winter time changes are encoded on instruction from the UK Government. Other broadcast signals in the UK include the BBC six pips signal, the British Telecom Speaking Clock and a coded time signal on the BBC 198 kHz Droitwich transmitter, which is used for timing in the electricity supply industry. From 1972 January 1 the six pips on the BBC have consisted of five short pips from second 55 to second 59 followed by one lengthened pip, the start of which indicates the exact minute. From 1990 February 5 these signals have been controlled by the BBC with respect to the broadcast MSF signal and are thus traceable to the National Physical Laboratory. Formerly they were generated by the Royal Greenwich Observatory. The British Telecom Speaking Clock is connected to the National Physical Laboratory caesium beam atomic frequency standard at the Rugby Radio Station.

Accurate timing may also be obtained from the signals of international navigation systems, such as the ground-based Loran-C or Omega, or satellite-based Global Positioning System of the USA or the GLONASS system of the USSR.

STANDARD TIME

In the year 1880 it was enacted by statute that the word 'time', when it occurred in any legal document relating to Great Britain, was to be interpreted, unless otherwise specifically stated, as the Mean Time of the Greenwich meridian. Summer Time is the 'legal' time during the period in which its use is ordained. Since the year 1883 the system of Standard Time by Zones has been gradually accepted, and now almost throughout the world a Standard Time which differs from that of Greenwich by an integral number of hours, either fast or slow, is used.

The large territories of the United States and Canada are divided into zones approximately $7\frac{1}{2}°$ on either side of central meridians. The important ones are given below; there are in addition zones from 3 to 12 hours fast in the USSR.

Variations from the standard time of some countries occurs during part of the year; they are decided annually and are usually referred to as Summer Time or Daylight Saving Time. Countries in which variations may occur are indicated with an asterisk.

Fast on Greenwich Time

In the Tonga Islands the time 13 h fast and in Chatham Is. 12 h 45 m fast on Greenwich is used, as the Date line is to the East of them.

12 hours fast
Fiji; Kiribati (Gilbert Is.); Kusaie I.; Marshall Is.; Nauru; *New Zealand; Tuvalu; *USSR (Zone 10).

11 hours 30 minutes fast
Kiribati (Banaba); Norfolk I.

11 hours fast
Kuril Is.; New Caledonia; Ponape I.; Sakhalin; Solomon Is.; *USSR (Zone 9); *Vanuatu.

10 hours fast
Admiralty Is.; *Australian Capital Territory; Guam; Mariana Is.; *New South Wales (except Broken Hill Area); Papua New Guinea; *Queensland; *Tasmania; Truk Is.; *USSR (Zone 8); *Victoria; Yap Is.

9 hours 30 minutes fast
*New South Wales (Broken Hill Area); Northern Territory (Aus); *South Australia.

9 hours fast
Irian Jaya; Japan; Korea (North and South); Molucca Is; Palau Is; *USSR (Zone 7).

8 hours fast
Bali; Brunei; *China; Hong Kong; †Kalimantan (South and East); Macao; Malaysia; *Mongolia; Philippines; Singapore; Sulawesi; Taiwan; Timor; *USSR (Zone 6); Western Australia.

7 hours fast
Christmas I. (Indian Ocean); Java; †Kalimantan (West and Middle); Kampuchea; Laos; Sumatra; Thailand; *USSR (Zone 5); Vietnam.

6 hours 30 minutes fast
Burma; Cocos (Keeling) Is.

6 hours fast
Bangladesh; Bhutan; *USSR (Zone 4).

5 hours 45 minutes fast
Nepal.

5 hours 30 minutes fast
India; Sri Lanka.

5 hours
Maldives; Pakistan; *USSR (Zone 3).

4 hours 30 minutes fast
Afghanistan.

4 hours fast
Mauritius; Oman; Réunion; Seychelles; United Arab Emirates; *USSR (Zone 2).

3 hours 30 minutes fast
Iran.

3 hours fast
Bahrain; Comoro Is.; Djibouti; Ethiopia; *Iraq; Kenya; Kuwait; Madagascar; Qatar; Saudi Arabia; Somalia; Tanzania; Uganda; *USSR (Zone 1); Yemen (North and South).

2 hours fast
Botswana; *Bulgaria; Burundi; *Crete; *Cyprus; *Egypt; *Finland; *Greece; *Israel, *Jordan, *Lebanon; Lesotho; Malawi; Mozambique; Namibia; *Romania; Rwanda; South Africa; Sudan; Swaziland; *Syria; *Turkey; Zaire (Haut-Zaire, Kasai, Kivu, Shaba); Zambia; Zimbabwe.

1 hour fast
*Albania; Algeria; *Andorra; Angola; *Austria; *Belgium; Benin; Cameroon; Central African Republic; Chad; Congo; *Czechoslovakia; *Denmark;

† The Indonesian territory on Borneo I.

Equatorial Guinea; *France; Gabon; *Germany; *Gibraltar; *Hungary; *Italy; *Libya; *Liechtenstein; *Luxembourg; *Malta; *Monaco; *Netherlands; Niger; Nigeria; *Norway; *Poland; *San Marino; *Spain; Svalbard; *Sweden; *Switzerland; *Tunisia; *Vatican City State; *Yugoslavia; Zaire (Kinshasa. Mbandaka).

Greenwich Time

Ascension I.; Burkina; *Canary Is.; *Channel Is.; Côte d'Ivoire; *Faroe Is.; Gambia; Ghana; Greenland (Danmarks Havn and Mesters Vig); Guinea; Guinea Bissau; Iceland; *Ireland (Republic); Liberia; *Madeira; Mali; Mauritania; *Morocco; *Portugal; St. Helena; São Tomé & Principe; Senegal; Sierra Leone; Togo; Tristan da Cunha; *UK (*see* p. 72).

Slow on Greenwich time

1 hour slow
*Azores; Cape Verde Is.; *Greenland (Scoresby Sound).

2 hours slow
*Fernando de Noronha I.; South Georgia.

3 hours slow
*Argentina; *Brazil (eastern); French Guiana; *Greenland (Angmagssalik and W. coast); Guyana; *St. Pierre and Miquelon; Suriname; *Uruguay.

3 hours 30 minutes slow
*Newfoundland.

4 hours slow (Atlantic time)
Anguilla; Antigua; Aruba; Barbados; *Bermuda; Bolivia; *Brazil (western); *Chile; *Dominica; Dominican Republic; *Falkland Is.; Greenland (Thule area); Grenada; Guadeloupe; *Labrador; Martinique; Montserrat; Netherlands Antilles; *New Brunswick; *Northwest Territories (E. of 68°W.); *Nova Scotia; *Quebec (E. of 63°W.); Paraguay; Puerto Rico; St. Kitts; St. Lucia; St. Vincent; Tobago; Trinidad; Venezuela; Virgin Is.

5 hours slow
*Bahamas; *Brazil (Acre territory); Cayman Is.; Colombia; *Cuba; Ecuador; *Haiti; Jamaica; *Northwest Territories (68°W. to 85°W.); *Ontario (E. of 90° W.); Panama; *Peru; *Quebec (W. of 63°W.); *Turks and Caicos Is.; *USA (*eastern time*).

6 hours slow
Belize; Costa Rica, Guatemala; Honduras; *Manitoba; Mexico (eastern); Nicaragua; Northwest Territories (85° W. to 102° W.); *Ontario (W. of 90° W.); *El Salvador; *Saskatchewan (E. of 106°W.); *USA (*central time*).

7 hours slow
*Alberta; Mexico (central); Northwest Territories (102° W. to 120° W.); *Saskatchewan (W. of 106° W.); *USA (*mountain time*).

8 hours slow
*Alaska (SE coast); *British Columbia; Mexico (western); *USA (*Pacific time*); *Yukon.

8 hours 30 minutes slow
Pitcairn I.

9 hours slow
*Alaska (E. of 169°30′W.).

10 hours slow
Aleutian Is. (W. of 169°30′ W.); Christmas I. (Pacific Ocean); French Polynesia; *Hawaii; Kiribati (Kiritimati I.); Society Is.; Tuamotu archipelago; Tubuai Is.

11 hours slow
Kiribati (Phoenix Is.); Midway Is.; Niue; Samoa.

RISING AND SETTING TIMES

Table 1. Semi-diurnal arcs (hour angles at rising/setting)

Dec.	Latitude												Dec.
	0°	10°	20°	30°	40°	45°	50°	52°	54°	56°	58°	60°	
°	h m	h m	h m	h m	h m	h m	h m	h m	h m	h m	h m	h m	°
0	6 00	6 00	6 00	6 00	6 00	6 00	6 00	6 00	6 00	6 00	6 00	6 00	0
1	6 00	6 01	6 01	6 02	6 03	6 04	6 05	6 05	6 06	6 06	6 06	6 07	1
2	6 00	6 01	6 03	6 05	6 07	6 08	6 10	6 10	6 11	6 12	6 13	6 14	2
3	6 00	6 02	6 04	6 07	6 10	6 12	6 14	6 15	6 17	6 18	6 19	6 21	3
4	6 00	6 03	6 06	6 09	6 13	6 16	6 19	6 21	6 22	6 24	6 26	6 28	4
5	6 00	6 04	6 07	6 12	6 17	6 20	6 24	6 26	6 28	6 30	6 32	6 35	5
6	6 00	6 04	6 09	6 14	6 20	6 24	6 29	6 31	6 33	6 36	6 39	6 42	6
7	6 00	6 05	6 10	6 16	6 24	6 28	6 34	6 36	6 39	6 42	6 45	6 49	7
8	6 00	6 06	6 12	6 19	6 27	6 32	6 39	6 41	6 45	6 48	6 52	6 56	8
9	6 00	6 06	6 13	6 21	6 31	6 36	6 44	6 47	6 50	6 54	6 59	7 04	9
10	6 00	6 07	6 15	6 23	6 34	6 41	6 49	6 52	6 56	7 01	7 06	7 11	10
11	6 00	6 08	6 16	6 26	6 38	6 45	6 54	6 58	7 02	7 07	7 12	7 19	11
12	6 00	6 09	6 18	6 28	6 41	6 49	6 59	7 03	7 08	7 13	7 20	7 26	12
13	6 00	6 09	6 19	6 31	6 45	6 53	7 04	7 09	7 14	7 20	7 27	7 34	13
14	6 00	6 10	6 21	6 33	6 48	6 58	7 09	7 14	7 20	7 27	7 34	7 42	14
15	6 00	6 11	6 22	6 36	6 52	7 02	7 14	7 20	7 27	7 34	7 42	7 51	15
16	6 00	6 12	6 24	6 38	6 56	7 07	7 20	7 26	7 33	7 41	7 49	7 59	16
17	6 00	6 12	6 26	6 41	6 59	7 11	7 25	7 32	7 40	7 48	7 57	8 08	17
18	6 00	6 13	6 27	6 43	7 03	7 16	7 31	7 38	7 46	7 55	8 05	8 17	18
19	6 00	6 14	6 29	6 46	7 07	7 21	7 37	7 45	7 53	8 03	8 14	8 26	19
20	6 00	6 15	6 30	6 49	7 11	7 25	7 43	7 51	8 00	8 11	8 22	8 36	20
21	6 00	6 16	6 32	6 51	7 15	7 30	7 49	7 58	8 08	8 19	8 32	8 47	21
22	6 00	6 16	6 34	6 54	7 19	7 35	7 55	8 05	8 15	8 27	8 41	8 58	22
23	6 00	6 17	6 36	6 57	7 23	7 40	8 02	8 12	8 23	8 36	8 51	9 09	23
24	6 00	6 18	6 37	7 00	7 28	7 46	8 08	8 19	8 31	8 45	9 02	9 22	24
25	6 00	6 19	6 39	7 02	7 32	7 51	8 15	8 27	8 40	8 55	9 13	9 35	25
26	6 00	6 20	6 41	7 05	7 37	7 57	8 22	8 35	8 49	9 05	9 25	9 51	26
27	6 00	6 21	6 43	7 08	7 41	8 03	8 30	8 43	8 58	9 16	9 39	10 08	27
28	6 00	6 22	6 45	7 12	7 46	8 08	8 37	8 52	9 08	9 28	9 53	10 28	28
29	6 00	6 22	6 47	7 15	7 51	8 15	8 45	9 01	9 19	9 41	10 10	10 55	29
30	6 00	6 23	6 49	7 18	7 56	8 21	8 54	9 11	9 30	9 55	10 30	12 00	30

Table 2. Correction for Refraction and Semi-diameter

	m	m	m	m	m	m	m	m	m	m	m	m	
0	3	3	4	4	4	5	5	5	6	6	6	7	0
10	3	3	4	4	4	5	5	6	6	6	7	7	10
20	4	4	4	4	5	5	6	7	7	8	8	9	20
25	4	4	4	4	5	6	7	8	8	9	11	13	25
30	4	4	4	5	6	7	8	9	11	14	21	—	30

NB: Regarding Table 1. If latitude and declination are of the same sign, take out the respondent directly. If they are of opposite signs, subtract the respondent from 12^h. *Examples.*

Lat.	Dec.	Semi-diurnal arc
$+52°$	$+20°$	7h 51m
$+52°$	$-20°$	4h 09m

SUNRISE AND SUNSET

The local mean time of sunrise or sunset may be found by obtaining the hour angle from Table 1 and applying it to the time of transit. The hour angle is negative for sunrise and positive for sunset. A small correction to the hour angle, which always has the effect of increasing it numerically, is necessary to allow for the Sun's semi-diameter (16') and for refraction (34'): it is obtained from Table 2. The resulting local mean time may be converted into the standard time of the country by taking the difference between the longitude of the standard meridian of the country and that of the place, adding it to the local mean time if the place is west of the standard meridian, and subtracting it if the place is east.

Example.—Required the New Zealand Mean Time (12^h fast on GMT) of sunset on May 24 at Auckland, latitude is 36° 50' S. (or minus), longitude 11^h 39^m E. Taking the declination as $+20°·7$ (p. 33), we find

		h m
Tabular entry for 30° Lat. and Dec. 20°, opposite signs	+	5 11
Proportional part for 6° 50' of Lat.	−	15
Proportional part for 0°·7 of Dec.	−	2
Correction (Table 2)	+	4
Hour angle		4 58
Sun transits (p. 33)		11 57
Longitudinal correction	+	21
New Zealand Mean Time		17 16

MOONRISE AND MOONSET

It is possible to calculate the times of moonrise and moonset using Table 1 though the method is more complicated because the apparent motion of the Moon is much more rapid and also more variable than that of the Sun.

The parallax of the Moon, about 57′, is near to the sum of the semi-diameter and refraction but has the opposite effect on these times. It is thus convenient to neglect all three quantities in the method outlined below.

Table 3. Longitude Correction

A \ X	40^m	45^m	50^m	55^m	60^m	65^m	70^m
h	m	m	m	m	m	m	m
1	2	2	2	2	3	3	3
2	3	4	4	5	5	5	6
3	5	6	6	7	8	8	9
4	7	8	8	9	10	11	12
5	8	9	10	11	13	14	15
6	10	11	13	14	15	16	18
7	12	13	15	16	18	19	20
8	13	15	17	18	20	22	23
9	15	17	19	21	23	24	26
10	17	19	21	23	25	27	29
11	18	21	23	25	28	30	32
12	20	23	25	28	30	33	35
13	22	24	27	30	33	35	38
14	23	26	29	32	35	38	41
15	25	28	31	34	38	41	44
16	27	30	33	37	40	43	47
17	28	32	35	39	43	46	50
18	30	34	38	41	45	49	53
19	32	36	40	44	48	51	55
20	33	38	42	46	50	54	58
21	35	39	44	48	53	57	61
22	37	41	46	50	55	60	64
23	38	43	48	53	58	62	67
24	40	45	50	55	60	65	70

Notation

φ = latitude of observer
λ = longitude of observer (measured positively towards the west)
T_{-1} = time of transit of Moon on previous day
T_0 = time of transit of Moon on day in question
T_1 = time of transit of Moon on following day
δ_0 = approximate declination of Moon
δ_R = declination of Moon at moonrise
δ_S = declination of Moon at moonset
h_0 = approximate hour angle of Moon
h_R = hour angle of Moon at moonrise
h_S = hour angle of Moon at moonset
t_R = time of moonrise
t_S = time of moonset

Method

1. With arguments φ, δ_0 enter Table 1 on p. 70 to determine h_0 where h_0 is negative for moonrise and positive for moonset.

2. Form approximate times from
$$t_R = T_0 + \lambda + h_0$$
$$t_S = T_0 + \lambda + h_0$$

3. Determine δ_R, δ_S for times t_R, t_S respectively.

4. Re-enter Table 1 on p. 70 with—
   (a) arguments φ, δ_R to determine h_R
   (b) arguments φ, δ_S to determine h_S

5. Form $t_R = T_0 + \lambda + h_R + AX$
$$t_S = T_0 + \lambda + h_S + AX$$

where $A = (\lambda + h)$

and $X = (T_0 - T_{-1})$ if $(\lambda + h)$ is negative
$X = (T_1 - T_0)$ if $(\lambda + h)$ is positive

AX is the respondent in Table 3.

Example.—To find the times of moonrise and moonset at Vancouver ($\varphi = +49°$, $\lambda = +8^h\ 12^m$) on 1991 January 11. The starting data (from p. 18) are

$$
\begin{aligned}
& \qquad\qquad\qquad\quad \text{h} \quad \text{m} \\
& T_{-1} = \quad 7 \quad 38 \\
& T_0 = \quad 8 \quad 26 \\
& T_1 = \quad 9 \quad 16 \\
& \delta = \quad -24°
\end{aligned}
$$

1. $h_0 = \quad 3^h 56^m$

2. Approximate values
$$
\begin{aligned}
t_R &= 11^d\ 08^h\ 26^m + 8^h\ 12^m + (-3^h\ 56^m) \\
&= 11^d\ 12^h\ 42^m \\
t_S &= 11^d\ 08^h\ 26^m + 8^h\ 12^m + (+3^h\ 56^m) \\
&= 11^d\ 20^h\ 34^m
\end{aligned}
$$

3. $\delta_R = -24°.8$
   $\delta_S = -25°.4$

4. $h_R = -3^h 51^m$
   $h_S = +3^h 47^m$

5. $t_R = 11^d\ 08^h\ 26^m + 8^h\ 12^m + (-3^h\ 51^m) + 9^m$
   $= 11^d\ 12^h\ 56^m$
   $t_S = 11^d\ 08^h\ 26^m + 8^h\ 12^m + (+3^h\ 47^m) + 25^m$
   $= 11^d\ 20^h\ 50^m$

To get the LMT of the phenomenon the longitude is subtracted from the GMT thus
Moonrise $= 11^d\ 12^h\ 56^m - 8^h\ 12^m = 11^d\ 04^h\ 44^m$
Moonset $= 11^d\ 20^h\ 50^m - 8^h\ 12^m = 11^d\ 12^h\ 38^m$

ASTRONOMICAL CONSTANTS

Solar Parallax .... 8″·794
Precession for the year 1991 .... 50″·288
     „   in Right Ascension .... 3ˢ·074
     „   in Declination .... 20″·044
Constant of Nutation .... 9″·202
Constant of Aberration .... 20″·496
Mean Obliquity of Ecliptic (1991)........ 23° 26′ 26″
Moon's Equatorial Hor. Parallax .... 57′ 02″·70
Velocity of light in vacuo *per sec* ...... 299792·5 km.
Solar motion *per sec* .... 20·0 km.
Equatorial radius of the Earth .... 6378·140 km.
Polar radius of the Earth .... 6356·755 km.

North Galactic Pole } RA 12ʰ 49ᵐ (1950·0).
(IAU *Standard*). } Dec. 27°·4 N.
Solar Apex .... RA 18ʰ 06ᵐ Dec. +30°
Length of Year   Tropical .... 365·24220
(*In Mean*   Sidereal .... 365·25636
  Solar Days)   Anomalistic .. 365·25964
             (*Perihelion to Perihelion*)
             Eclipse .... 346·6200

		d	h	m	s
Length of Month	New Moon to New	29	12	44	02·9
(*Mean Values*)	Sidereal	27	07	43	11·5
	Anomalistic	27	13	18	33·2

(*Perigee to Perigee*)

MEAN AND SIDEREAL TIME

Acceleration						Retardation						MEAN REFRACTION	
h	m s	h	m s	m s	s	h	m s	h	m s	m s	s	Alt. Ref.	Alt. Ref.
1	0 10	13	2 08	0 00	0	1	0 10	13	2 08	0 00	0		
2	0 20	14	2 18	3 02	1	2	0 20	14	2 18	3 03	1		
3	0 30	15	2 28	9 07	2	3	0 29	15	2 27	9 09	2	1 20 21	4 30 10
4	0 39	16	2 38	15 13	3	4	0 39	16	2 37	15 15	3	1 30 20	5 06 9
5	0 49	17	2 48	21 18	4	5	0 49	17	2 47	21 21	4	1 41 19	5 50 8
6	0 59	18	2 57	27 23	5	6	0 59	18	2 57	27 28	5	1 52 18	6 44 7
7	1 09	19	3 07	33 28	6	7	1 09	19	3 07	33 34	6	2 05 17	7 54 6
8	1 19	20	3 17	39 34	7	8	1 19	20	3 17	39 40	7	2 19 16	9 27 5
9	1 29	21	3 27	45 39	8	9	1 28	21	3 26	45 46	8	2 35 15	11 39 4
10	1 39	22	3 37	51 44	9	10	1 38	22	3 36	51 53	9	2 52 14	15 00 3
11	1 48	23	3 47	57 49	10	11	1 48	23	3 46	57 59	10	3 12 13	20 42 2
12	1 58	24	3 57	60 00		12	1 58	24	3 56	60 00		3 34 12	32 20 1
												4 00 11	62 17 1
												4 30	90 00 0

The length of a sidereal day in mean time is 23^h 56^m 04^s·09. Hence 1^h MT = 1^h + 9^s·86 ST and 1^h ST = 1^h − 9^s·83 MT.

To convert an interval of mean time to the corresponding interval of sidereal time, enter the acceleration table with the given mean time (taking the hours and the minutes and seconds separately) and add the acceleration obtained to the given mean time. To convert an interval of sidereal time to the corresponding interval of mean time, take out the retardation for the given sidereal time and subtract.

The columns for the minutes and seconds of the argument are in the form known as Critical Tables. To use these tables, find in the appropriate left-hand column the two entries between which the given number of minutes and seconds lies; the quantity in the right-hand column between these two entries is the required acceleration or retardation. Thus the

acceleration for 11^{m}26^s (which lies between the entries 9^{m}07^s and 15^{m}13^s) is 2^s. If the given number of minutes and seconds is a tabular entry, the required acceleration or retardation is the entry in the right-hand column *above* the given tabular entry, e.g. the retardation for 45^{m}46^s is 7^s.

Example.—Convert 14^{h}27^{m}35^s from ST to MT

	h m s
Given ST	14 27 35
Retardation for 14^h	2 18
Retardation for 27^{m}35^s	5
Corresponding MT	14 25 12

For further explanation, *see* p. 67. For further explanation, *see* p. 67.
The refraction table is also in the form of a critical table.

THE SUMMER TIME ACTS

In 1916 an Act ordained that during a defined period of that year the legal time for general purposes in Great Britain should be one hour in advance of Greenwich Mean Time. The Summer Time Acts, 1922 to 1925, defined the period during which Summer Time was to be in force, stabilizing practice until the war.

During the Second World War the duration of Summer Time was extended and in the years 1941–45 and in 1947, Double Summer Time (2 hrs. in advance of Greenwich Mean Time) was in force. After the war, Summer Time was extended in each year from 1948–1952 and 1961–1964 by Order in Council.

British Standard Time, during which clocks were kept one hour ahead of Greenwich Mean Time throughout the year, was in force between 1968 October 27 and 1971 October 31.

The most recent legislation is the Summer Time Act, 1972, which enacted that 'the period of summer time for the purposes of this Act is the period beginning at two o'clock, Greenwich mean time, in the morning of the day after the third Saturday in March or, if that day is Easter Day, the day after the

second Saturday in March, and ending at two o'clock, Greenwich mean time, in the morning of the day after the fourth Saturday in October.'

The duration of Summer Time can be varied by Order in Council and in recent years alterations have been made to bring the operation of Summer Time in Britain closer to similar provisions in other countries of the European Community. The latest Order in Council is the Summer Time Order 1989, stipulating that the duration of Summer Time in 1991 will be from March 31 to October 27. As in recent years, the hour of changeover will be 01^h Greenwich Mean Time.

The duration of Summer Time during the last few years is given in the following table.

1980 March 16–Oct. 26	1986 March 30–Oct. 26
1981 March 29–Oct. 25	1987 March 29–Oct. 25
1982 March 28–Oct. 24	1988 March 27–Oct. 23
1983 March 27–Oct. 23	1989 March 26–Oct. 29
1984 March 25–Oct. 28	1990 March 25–Oct. 28
1985 March 31–Oct. 27	1991 March 31–Oct. 27

PHENOMENA OF JUPITER'S SATELLITES, 1991

January

GMT (d h m)	Sat.	Phen.
1 01 38	I	Sh.I.
1 02 46	II	Sh.E.
1 03 55	I	Sh.E.
1 22 50	I	Ec.D.
2 20 07	I	Sh.I.
2 20 44	IV	Ec.D.
2 22 23	I	Sh.E.
3 01 29	IV	Ec.R.
6 05 39	III	Sh.I.
6 07 54	II	Ec.D.
7 06 16	I	Ec.D.
8 02 28	II	Sh.I.
8 03 32	I	Sh.I.
8 05 22	II	Sh.E.
8 05 49	I	Sh.E.
9 04 44	I	Ec.D.
9 19 42	III	Ec.D.
9 21 11	II	Ec.D.
9 22 00	I	Sh.I.
10 00 17	I	Sh.E.
10 19 13	I	Ec.D.
11 06 59	IV	Sh.I.
15 05 04	II	Sh.I
15 05 25	I	Sh.I.
15 07 42	I	Sh.E.
16 02 39	I	Ec.D.
16 23 41	III	Ec.D.
16 23 45	II	Ec.D.
16 23 54	I	Sh.I.
17 02 11	I	Sh.E.
17 21 07	I	Ec.D.
18 18 22	I	Sh.I.
18 20 39	I	Sh.E.
18 21 18	II	Sh.E.
20 17 11	III	Sh.E.
22 07 19	I	Sh.I.
23 04 33	I	Ec.D.
24 01 47	I	Sh.I.
24 02 19	II	Ec.D.
24 03 40	III	Ec.D.
24 04 04	I	Sh.E.
24 23 02	I	Ec.D.
25 20 16	I	Sh.I.
25 21 00	II	Sh.I.
25 22 33	I	Sh.E.
25 23 55	II	Sh.E.
27 21 09	III	Sh.E.
28 00 58	IV	Sh.I.
28 05 41	IV	Sh.E.
31 03 41	I	Sh.I.
31 05 58	I	Sh.E.

February

GMT (d h m)	Sat.	Phen.
1 03 15	I	Ec.R.
1 22 10	I	Sh.I.
1 23 37	II	Sh.I.
2 00 27	I	Sh.E.
2 02 32	II	Sh.E.
2 21 44	I	Ec.R.
3 18 55	I	Sh.E.
3 21 02	II	Ec.R.
3 21 32	III	Sh.I.
4 01 08	III	Sh.E.
7 05 35	I	Sh.I.
8 05 10	I	Ec.R.
9 00 04	I	Sh.I.
9 02 14	II	Sh.I.
9 02 21	I	Sh.E.
9 05 09	II	Sh.E.
9 23 38	I	Ec.R.
10 18 32	I	Sh.I.
10 20 49	I	Sh.E.
10 23 36	II	Ec.R.
11 01 31	III	Sh.I.
11 05 07	III	Sh.E.
11 18 07	I	Ec.R.
12 18 27	II	Sh.E.
13 18 58	IV	Sh.I.
13 23 43	IV	Sh.E.
14 19 16	III	Ec.R.
16 01 58	I	Sh.I.
16 04 15	I	Sh.E.
16 04 51	II	Sh.I.
17 01 33	I	Ec.R.
17 20 26	I	Sh.I.
17 22 44	I	Sh.E.
18 02 10	II	Ec.R.
18 05 30	III	Sh.I.
18 20 02	I	Ec.R.
19 18 09	I	Sh.I.
19 21 04	II	Sh.E.
21 23 15	III	Ec.R.
22 02 50	IV	Ec.D.
23 03 52	I	Sh.I.
23 06 09	I	Sh.E.
24 03 28	I	Ec.R.
24 22 21	I	Sh.I
25 00 38	I	Sh.E.
25 04 45	II	Sh.E.
25 21 57	I	Ec.R.
26 19 06	I	Sh.I.
26 20 47	II	Sh.I.
26 23 41	II	Sh.E.
28 18 02	II	Ec.R.

March

GMT (d h m)	Sat.	Phen.
4 00 15	I	Sh.I.
4 23 52	I	Ec.R.
5 18 44	I	Sh.I.
5 21 01	I	Sh.E.
5 23 24	II	Sh.I.
6 18 21	I	Ec.R.
7 20 37	II	Ec.R.
10 20 53	IV	Ec.D.
11 01 45	IV	Ec.R.
11 21 04	III	Sh.E.
12 01 47	I	Ec.R.
12 20 39	I	Sh.I.
12 22 55	I	Sh.E.
13 20 16	I	Ec.R.
14 23 12	II	Ec.R.
18 21 27	III	Sh.I.
19 01 03	III	Sh.E.
19 22 33	I	Sh.I
20 00 50	I	Sh.E.
20 22 11	I	Ec.R.
21 19 19	I	Sh.E.
22 01 47	II	Ec.R.
23 20 50	II	Sh.E.
26 01 26	III	Sh.I.
27 00 28	I	Sh.I.
27 19 49	IV	Ec.R.
28 00 06	I	Ec.R.
28 21 13	I	Sh.E.
29 19 15	III	Ec.R.
30 20 34	II	Sh.I.
30 23 27	II	Sh.E.

April

GMT (d h m)	Sat.	Phen.
4 20 52	I	Sh.I.
4 23 08	I	Sh.E.
5 19 36	III	Ec.D.
5 20 30	I	Ec.R.
5 23 15	III	Ec.R.
6 23 11	II	Sh.I.
8 20 16	II	Ec.R.
11 22 47	I	Sh.I.
12 22 25	I	Ec.R.
12 23 35	III	Ec.D.
15 22 52	II	Sh.I.
20 00 21	I	Ec.R.
20 21 27	I	Sh.E.
21 23 50	IV	Sh.E.
23 21 02	III	Sh.E.
24 20 35	II	Sh.E.
27 21 06	I	Sh.I.
27 23 22	I	Sh.E.
28 20 45	I	Ec.R.
30 21 25	III	Sh.I.

May

GMT (d h m)	Sat.	Phen.
1 23 11	II	Sh.E.
4 23 01	I	Sh.I.
5 22 40	I	Ec.R.
8 22 56	II	Sh.I.
13 21 41	I	Sh.E.
16 21 08	IV	Ec.D.
17 22 35	II	Ec.R.
18 23 14	III	Ec.D.
25 23 34	III	Ec.D.
28 22 53	I	Ec.R.

June

GMT (d h m)	Sat.	Phen.
2 22 53	II	Sh.E.
5 21 56	I	Sh.E.
9 22 37	II	Sh.I

November

GMT (d h m)	Sat.	Phen.
3 06 11	I	Sh.I.
19 06 43	I	Sh.E.
21 06 32	III	Ec.R.
26 06 20	I	Sh.I.
28 06 54	III	Ec.D.

December

GMT (d h m)	Sat.	Phen.
1 01 33	II	Sh.I.
4 01 56	IV	Ec.R.
8 06 55	II	Sh.E.
9 00 48	III	Sh.I.
9 04 21	III	Sh.E.
11 07 12	I	Ec.D.
12 06 51	I	Sh.E.
12 07 01	IV	Sh.I.
13 01 41	I	Ec.D.
14 01 19	I	Sh.E.
15 06 42	II	Sh.I.
17 01 49	II	Ec.D.
19 06 28	I	Sh.I.
21 00 56	I	Sh.I.
26 01 21	II	Sh.E.
27 02 18	III	Ec.R.
28 02 49	I	Sh.I.
28 05 05	I	Sh.E.
28 23 56	I	Ec.D.
29 00 58	IV	Sh.I.
29 05 12	IV	Sh.E.
29 23 33	I	Sh.I.
31 06 58	II	Ec.D.

Jupiter's satellites transit across the disk from east to west, and pass behind the disk from west to east. The shadows that they cast also transit across the disk. With the exception at times of Satellite IV, the satellites also pass through the shadow of the planet, i.e. they are eclipsed. Just before opposition the satellite disappears in the shadow to the west of the planet, and reappears from occultation on the east limb. Immediately after opposition the satellite is occulted at the west limb, and reappears from eclipse to the east of the planet. At times approximately two to four months before and after opposition, both phases of eclipses of Satellite III may be seen. When Satellite IV is eclipsed, both phases may be seen.

The list of phenomena gives most of the eclipses and shadow transits visible in the British Isles under favourable conditions.

Ec. = Eclipse	R. = Reappearance	
Sh. = Shadow transit	I. = Ingress	
D. = Disappearance	E. = Egress	

CELESTIAL PHENOMENA FOR OBSERVATION IN 1991

ECLIPSES

There will be three eclipses during 1991, two of the Sun and one of the Moon. (Penumbral eclipses are not mentioned in this section as they are difficult to observe).

1. An annular eclipse of the Sun on January 15–16 is visible as a partial eclipse from the south-eastern part of the Indian Ocean, the Southern Ocean, Oceania, Australasia, the western part of Antarctica and the Pacific Ocean. The eclipse begins on January 15 at 20^h 51^m and ends on January 16 at 02^h 55^m. The annular phase begins on January 15 at 22^h 00^m just off the west coast of Australia, crosses the extreme south-western part of Australia, Tasmania, the central part of New Zealand and ends on January 16 at 01^h 46^m in the South Pacific Ocean. The maximum duration of the annular phase is 7^m 55^s.

2. A total eclipse of the Sun on July 11. The path of totality begins in the North Pacific Ocean, crosses the Hawaiian Islands, passes along the western coast of Central America, crosses the centre of Colombia and ends in the centre of Brazil. The partial phase is visible from the Pacific Ocean, the southern half of North America, Central America, the Caribbean, South America except the extreme south, and the Atlantic Ocean. The eclipse begins at 16^h 29^m and ends at 21^h 43^m, the total phase begins at 17^h 23^m and ends at 20^h 49^m. The maximum duration of totality is 6^m 54^s.

3. A partial eclipse of the Moon on December 21 is visible from Iceland, Greenland, Arctic regions, north-west of South America, Central America, North America, the Pacific Ocean except the extreme eastern part, Australasia except the extreme west, Asia except the south-western part, and the extreme north of Scandinavia. The eclipse begins at 10^h 01^m and ends at 11^h 05^m. The time of maximum eclipse is 10^h 33^m when 0.09 of the Moon's diameter is obscured.

LUNAR OCCULTATIONS

During 1991 two planets, Mars and Saturn, and a bright star, Antares (ZC 2366), will be occulted.

Observations of the times of these occultations are made by both amateur and professional astronomers. Such observations are later analysed to yield accurate positions of the Moon; this is one method of determining the difference between ephemeris time and universal time.

Many of the observations made by amateurs are obtained with the use of a stop-watch which is compared with a time signal immediately after the observation. Thus an accuracy of about one-fifth of a second is obtainable, though the observer's personal equation may amount to one-third or one-half of a second.

The list on the opposite page includes most of the occultations visible under favourable conditions in

the British Isles. No occultation is included unless the star is at least 10° above the horizon and the Sun sufficiently far below the horizon to permit the star to be seen with the naked eye or with a small telescope. The altitude limit is reduced from 10° to 2° for stars and planets brighter than magnitude 2·0 and such occultations are also predicted in daylight.

The column Phase shows (a) whether a disappearance (D) or reappearance (R) is to be observed; and (b) whether it is at the dark limb (D) or bright limb (B). The column headed 'El. of Moon' gives the elongation of the Moon from the Sun, in degrees. The elongation increases from 0° at New Moon to 180° at Full Moon and on to 360° (or 0°) at New Moon again. Times and position angles (P), reckoned from the north point in the direction north, east, south, west, are given for Greenwich (Lat. 51° 30′, Long. 0°) and Edinburgh (Lat. 56° 00′, Long. 3° 12′ west).

The coefficients a and b are the variations in the GMT for each degree of longitude (positive to the west) and latitude (positive to the north) respectively; they enable approximate times (to within about 1^m generally) to be found for any point in the British Isles. If the point of observation is $\Delta\lambda$ degrees west and $\Delta\phi$ degrees north, the approximate time is found by adding $a.\Delta\lambda + b.\Delta\phi$ to the given GMT.

As an illustration the disappearance of Mars on March 22 at Liverpool will be found from both Greenwich and Edinburgh.

	Greenwich	Edinburgh
	°	°
Longitude	0·0	+3·2
Long. of Liverpool	+3·0	+3·0
$\Delta\lambda$	+3·0	−0·2
Latitude	+51·5	+56·0
Lat. of Liverpool	+53·4	+53·4
$\Delta\phi$	+1·9	−2·6
	h m	h m
GMT...................	15 40·9	15 33·2
$a.\Delta\lambda$.....................	−5·4	+0·3
$b.\Delta\phi$	−3·0	+0·0
	15 32·5	15 33·5

If the occultation is given for one station but not the other, the reason for the suppression is given by the following code.

N = star not occulted.

A = star's altitude less than 10° (2° for bright stars and planets).

S = Sun not sufficiently below the horizon.

G = occultation is of very short duration.

It will be noticed that in some cases the coefficients a and b are not given; this is because the occultation is so short that prediction for other places by means of these coefficients would not be reliable.

LUNAR OCCULTATIONS, 1991

Date		ZC No.	Mag.	Phase	El. of Moon	Greenwich				Edinburgh			
						UT	a	b	P	UT	a	b	P
					°	h m	m	m	°	h m	m	m	°
Jan.	19	3344	6·8	D.D.	43	18 14·6	−0·8	−0·7	66	18 10·3	−0·6	−0·3	50
	20	3482	5·7	D.D.	56	20 5·3	G	G	360	N			
	23	311	6·5	D.D.	93	19 16·9	−1·3	0·1	68	19 15·0	−1·1	0·7	52
Feb.	20	440	4·6	D.D.	77	23 14·2	0·2	−1·8	107	23 6·8	0·0	−1·7	98
	20	438	6·7	D.D.	77	23 14·3	−0·3	−0·2	42	23 12·6	−0·5	0·1	30
	21	552	3·0	D.D.	87	17 40·9	−1·3	1·2	59	17 43·8	−1·0	1·9	42
	21	553	6·8	D.D.	87	18 12·3	G	G	3	N			
	21	559	6·6	D.D.	88	18 34·0	−1·7	−3·2	135	18 20·1	−1·4	−1·1	113
	21	560	3·8	D.D.	88	18 29·8	−1·5	−0·3	88	18 25·6	−1·3	0·4	72
	21	561	5·2	D.D.	88	18 32·7	−1·4	0·3	71	18 31·4	−1·2	1·0	55
	21	552	3·0	R.B.	88	18 52·1	−1·5	−0·8	276	18 42·7	−1·4	−1·4	293
	21	570	6·8	D.D.	88	19 31·5	−1·3	−2·6	126	19 18·7	−1·2	−1·4	108
	21	587	6·4	D.D.	90	22 41·8	−0·8	−0·1	44	22 39·7	−1·0	0·6	30
	22	598	5·7	D.D.	91	1 25·3	0·9	−2·3	144	1 18·1	0·7	−2·1	136
	25	1110	3·5	D.D.	133	4 11·6	0·5	−1·5	125	4 6·1	0·4	−1·6	123
	25	1205	6·3	D.D.	141	19 2·2	−1·1	−2·5	164	18 52·8	−0·9	−0·6	143
	26	1336	5·2	D.D.	154	18 10·0	−0·6	0·2	130	18 10·7	−0·5	0·9	115
	26	1337	5·6	D.D.	154	18 14·2	−0·5	2·4	69	18 27·2	G	G	44
Mar.	12	Saturn	0·7	D.B.	312	6 46·7	−1·3	1·5	59	6 49·5	−1·1	1·5	56
	12	Saturn	0·7	R.D.	313	8 6·2	−1·6	0·7	257	8 4·8	−1·4	0·8	262
	19	399	5·7	D.D.	46	21 52·9	0·5	−1·8	114	21 46·1	0·3	−1·7	105
	20	521	6·7	D.D.	58	19 47·5	−0·5	−1·9	106	19 37·9	−0·6	−1·5	95
	21	703	6·3	D.D.	71	19 48·7	−1·0	−1·1	87	19 41·3	−1·0	−0·8	76
	22	Mars	0·9	D.D.	82	15 40·9	−1·8	−1·6	139	15 33·2	−1·3	0·0	119
	22	Mars	0·9	R.B.	83	16 29·9	−1·3	3·3	219	16 36·8	−1·2	1·8	239
	23	1050	5·8	D.D.	99	22 57·9	−1·0	−0·8	64	22 51·2	−1·1	−0·7	58
	25	1193	5·4	D.D.	113	0 46·5	−0·3	−1·6	98	0 38·3	−0·3	−1·6	95
Apr.	4	2366	1·2	D.B.	235	2 7·5	−0·9	0·0	144	A			
	4	2366	1·2	R.D.	236	3 7·3	−2·0	0·8	237	3 5·0	−1·7	0·7	239
	17	652	6·4	D.D.	41	20 58·5	0·6	−2·3	138	20 49·6	0·3	−2·2	130
	18	822	5·9	D.D.	55	21 9·2	−0·3	−1·2	77	21 2·8	−0·4	−1·2	72
	19	1017	6·8	D.D.	69	23 6·7	0·1	−1·4	93	23 0·5	0·0	−1·5	90
	20	1143	6·8	D.D.	81	20 27·5	−1·6	−0·2	60	20 22·3	G	G	50
	23	1409	5·1	D.D.	109	0 44·1	−0·4	−1·4	72	0 36·2	−0·5	−1·5	70
	24	1519	6·5	D.D.	122	1 26·2	G	G	40	N			
May	16	936	5·9	D.D.	38	21 4·2	G	G	28	N			
June	18	1670	5·1	D.D.	87	22 33·6	−0·4	−1·9	117	22 24·0	−0·4	−1·8	115
July	2	3269	4·3	R.D.	234	0 10·5	−0·7	2·0	219	0 17·2	−0·6	1·9	223
	22	2458	6·2	D.D.	138	22 13·0	−1·6	−0·7	95	A			
Aug.	17	2268	4·8	D.D.	97	20 20·2	G	G	185	S			
	17	2268	4·8	R.D.	97	20 22·4	G	G	188	A			
	17	2273	5·9	D.D.	97	20 24·7	−1·5	−1·6	131	A			
	20	2672	2·9	R.B.	129	17 54·3	−1·6	2·0	221	A			
	22	2963	5·5	D.D.	153	24 0·1	−1·6	−1·0	93	23 51·8	−1·3	−0·6	82
Sep.	17	2793	6·5	D.D.	111	21 17·7	−0·7	0·1	34	A			
	21	3269	4·3	D.D.	154	18 38·9	−0·9	1·6	86	18 43·9	−0·7	1·7	81
Oct.	16	2981	5·2	D.D.	102	19 36·9	−2·2	−1·0	108	19 27·9	−1·7	−0·4	97
	16	2990	6·7	D.D.	102	20 47·9	−1·3	−0·8	78	20 41·4	−1·1	−0·5	66
	16	2987	5·0	D.D.	102	20 45·9	−1·1	−0·4	61	20 41·7	−0·9	−0·2	50
	17	3112	6·2	D.D.	114	22 5·6	−0·3	0·7	23	22 10·1	0·2	1·6	2
	20	3482	5·7	D.D.	148	22 8·7	−1·0	1·1	41	22 11·4	−0·7	1·4	27
Dec.	10	3019	5·9	D.D.	51	19 11·1	0·1	0·9	16	A			
	11	3137	6·7	D.D.	61	18 51·5	−0·9	−0·7	66	18 46·7	−0·7	−0·3	52
	12	3248	6·6	D.D.	72	17 46·1	−1·1	0·5	46	17 46·1	−0·8	0·8	33
	17	317	6·4	D.D.	130	17 54·5	−1·6	0·6	110	17 54·5	−1·1	1·2	96

MEAN PLACES OF STARS, 1991·5

Name	Mag.	RA	Dec.	Spec-trum
		h m	° ′	
α Andromedæ *Alpheratz*	2·1	0 07·9	+29 03	A0*p*
β Cassiopeiæ *Caph*	2·3	0 08·7	+59 06	F5
γ Pegasi *Algenib*	2·8	0 12·8	+15 08	B2
α Phœnicis	2·4	0 25·9	−42 21	K0
α Cassiopeiæ *Schedar*	2·2	0 40·0	+56 29	K0
β Ceti *Diphda*	2·0	0 43·2	−18 02	K0
γ Cassiopeiæ*	Var.	0 56·2	+60 40	B0*p*
β Andromedæ *Mirach*	2·1	1 09·3	+35 35	M0
δ Cassiopeiæ	2·7	1 25·3	+60 11	A5
α Eridani *Achernar*	0·5	1 37·4	−57 17	B5
β Arietis *Sheratan*	2·6	1 54·2	+20 46	A5
γ Andromedæ *Almak*	2·3	2 03·4	+42 17	K0
α Arietis *Hamal*	2·0	2 06·7	+23 25	K2
α Ursæ Minoris *Polaris*	2·0	2 22·7	+89 14	F8
β Persei *Algol**	Var.	3 07·6	+40 55	B8
α Persei *Mirfak*	1·8	3 23·7	+49 50	F5
η Tauri *Alcyone*	2·9	3 47·0	+24 05	B5*p*
α Tauri *Aldebaran*	0·9	4 35·4	+16 30	K5
β Orionis *Rigel*	0·1	5 14·1	− 8 13	B8*p*
α Aurigæ *Capella*	0·1	5 16·1	+45 59	G0
γ Orionis *Bellatrix*	1·6	5 24·7	+ 6 21	B2
β Tauri *Elnath*	1·7	5 25·8	+28 36	B8
δ Orionis..................	2·2	5 31·6	− 0 18	B0
α Leporis..................	2·6	5 32·4	−17 50	F0
ε Orionis..................	1·7	5 35·8	− 1 12	B0
ζ Orionis..................	1·8	5 40·3	− 1 57	B0
κ Orionis..................	2·1	5 47·4	− 9 40	B0
α Orionis *Betelgeuse**	Var.	5 54·7	+ 7 24	M0
β Aurigæ *Menkalinan*	1·9	5 58·9	+44 57	A0*p*
β Canis Majoris *Mirzam*	2·0	6 22·3	−17 57	B1
α Carinæ *Canopus*	−0·7	6 23·8	−52 41	F0
γ Geminorum *Alhena*	1·9	6 37·2	+16 24	A0
α Canis Majoris *Sirius*........	−1·5	6 44·8	−16 42	A0
ε Canis Majoris..............	1·5	6 58·3	−28 58	B1
δ Canis Majoris..............	1·9	7 08·0	−26 23	F8*p*
α Geminorum *Castor*	1·6	7 34·1	+31 54	A0
α Canis Minoris *Procyon*......	0·4	7 38·9	+ 5 15	F5
β Geminorum *Pollux*	1·1	7 44·8	+28 03	K0
ζ Puppis	2·3	8 03·3	−39 59	Od
γ Velorum	1·8	8 09·3	−47 19	Oa*p*
ε Carinæ....................	1·9	8 22·3	−59 29	K0
δ Velorum	2·0	8 44·5	−54 41	A0
λ Velorum *Suhail*	2·2	9 07·7	−43 24	K5
β Carinæ...................	1·7	9 13·1	−69 41	A0
ι Carinæ....................	2·2	9 16·9	−59 14	F0
α Hydræ *Alphard*	2·0	9 27·2	− 8 37	K2
α Leonis *Regulus*............	1·3	10 07·9	+12 01	B8
γ Leonis *Algeiba*	1·9	10 19·5	+19 53	K0
β Ursæ Majoris *Merak*	2·4	11 01·3	+56 26	A0
α Ursæ Majoris *Dubhe*	1·8	11 03·2	+61 48	K0

* γ Cassiopeiæ, 1990 mag. 2·5.   β Persei, mag. 2·2 to 3·2.
  α Orionis, mag. 0·1 to 1·2.

The positions of heavenly bodies on the celestial sphere are defined by two co-ordinates, right ascension and declination, which are analogous to longitude and latitude on the surface of the Earth. If we imagine the plane of the terrestrial equator extended indefinitely, it will cut the celestial sphere in a great circle known as the celestial equator. Similarly the plane of the Earth's orbit, when extended, cuts in the great circle called the ecliptic. The two intersections of these circles are known as the First Point of Aries and the First Point of Libra. If from any star a perpendicular be drawn to the celestial equator, the length of this perpendicular is the star's declination. The arc, measured eastwards along the equator from the First Point of Aries to the foot of this perpendicular, is the right ascension. An alternative definition of right ascension is that it is the angle at the celestial pole (where the Earth's axis, if prolonged, would meet the sphere) between the great circles to the First Point of Aries and to the star.

The plane of the Earth's equator has a slow movement, so that our reference system for right ascension and declination is not fixed. The consequent alteration from year to year in these quantities is called precession. In right ascension it is an increase of about 3ˢ a year for equatorial stars, and larger or smaller changes in either direction for stars near the poles, depending on the right ascension of the star. In declination it varies between +20″ and −20″ according to the right ascension of the star.

A star or other body crosses the meridian when the sidereal time is equal to its right ascension. The altitude is then a maximum, and may be deduced by remembering that the altitude of the elevated pole is numerically equal to the latitude, while that of the equator at its intersection with the meridian is equal to the co-latitude, or complement of the latitude.

MEAN PLACES OF STARS, 1991·5

Name	Mag.	RA	Dec.	Spectrum
		h m	° ′	
δ Leonis	2·6	11 13·7	+20 34	A3
β Leonis *Denebola*	2·1	11 48·6	+14 37	A2
γ Ursæ Majoris *Phecda*	2·4	11 53·4	+53 45	A0
γ Corvi	2·6	12 15·4	−17 29	B8
α Crucis	1·0	12 26·1	−63 03	B1
γ Crucis	1·6	12 30·7	−57 04	M3
γ Centauri	2·2	12 41·0	−48 55	A0
γ Virginis	2·7	12 41·2	− 1 24	F0
β Crucis	1·3	12 47·2	−59 39	B1
ε Ursæ Majoris *Alioth*	1·8	12 53·7	+56 00	A0p
α Canum Venaticorum	2·9	12 55·6	+38 22	A0p
ζ Ursæ Majoris *Mizar*	2·1	13 23·6	+54 58	A2p
α Virginis *Spica*	1·0	13 24·7	−11 07	B2
η Ursæ Majoris *Alkaid*	1·9	13 47·2	+49 21	B3
β Centauri *Hadar*	0·6	14 03·2	−60 20	B1
θ Centauri	2·1	14 06·2	−36 20	K0
α Boötis *Arcturus*	0·0	14 15·3	+19 14	K0
α Centauri *Rigil Kent*	0·1	14 39·0	−60 48	G0
ε Boötis	2·4	14 44·6	+27 07	K0
β Ursæ Minoris *Kochab*	2·1	14 50·7	+74 11	K5
α Coronæ Borealis *Alphecca*	2·2	15 34·3	+26 45	A0
δ Scorpii	2·3	15 59·8	−22 36	B0
β Scorpii	2·6	16 04·9	−19 47	B1
α Scorpii *Antares*	1·0	16 28·9	−26 25	M0
α Trianguli Australis	1·9	16 47·8	−69 01	K2
ε Scorpii	2·3	16 49·6	−34 17	K0
α Herculis*	Var.	17 14·3	+14 24	M3
λ Scorpii	1·6	17 33·0	−37 06	B2
α Ophiuchi *Rasalhague*	2·1	17 34·5	+12 34	A5
θ Scorpii	1·9	17 36·7	−43 00	F0
κ Scorpii	2·4	17 41·9	−39 02	B2
γ Draconis	2·2	17 56·4	+51 29	K5
ε Sagittarii *Kaus Australis*	1·9	18 23·6	−34 23	A0
α Lyræ *Vega*	0·0	18 36·7	+38 47	A0
σ Sagittarii	2·0	18 54·7	−26 18	B3
β Cygni *Albireo*	3·1	19 30·4	+27 56	K0
α Aquilæ *Altair*	0·8	19 50·4	+ 8 51	A5
α Capricorni	3·8	20 17·6	−12 34	G5
γ Cygni	2·2	20 21·9	+40 14	F8p
α Pavonis	1·9	20 25·0	−56 46	B3
α Cygni *Deneb*	1·3	20 41·1	+45 15	A2p
α Cephei *Alderamin*	2·4	21 18·4	+62 33	A5
ε Pegasi	2·4	21 43·8	+ 9 50	K0
δ Capricorni	2·9	21 46·6	−16 10	A5
α Gruis	1·7	22 07·7	−47 00	B5
δ Cephei*	3·7	22 28·9	+58 22	*
β Gruis	2·1	22 42·2	−46 56	M3
α Piscis Austrini *Fomalhaut*	1·2	22 57·2	−29 40	A3
β Pegasi *Scheat*	2·4	23 03·4	+28 02	M0
α Pegasi *Markab*	2·5	23 04·3	+15 09	A0

* α Herculis, mag. 3·1 to 3·9.
δ Cephei, mag. 3·7 to 4·4, Spectrum F5 to G0.

Thus in London (Lat. 51° 30′) the meridian altitude of *Sirius* is found as follows:

	°	′
Altitude of equator	38	30
Declination south	16	42
Difference	21	48

The altitude of *Capella* (Dec. +45° 59′) at lower transit is:

	°	′
Altitude of pole	51	30
Polar distance of star	44	01
Difference	7	29

The brightness of a heavenly body is denoted by its magnitude. Omitting the exceptionally bright stars Sirius and Canopus, the twenty brightest stars are of the first magnitude, while the faintest stars visible to the naked eye are of the sixth magnitude. The magnitude scale is a precise one, as a difference of five magnitudes represents a ratio of 100 to 1 in brightness. Typical second magnitude stars are Polaris and the stars in the belt of Orion. The scale is most easily fixed in memory by comparing the stars with Norton's *Star Atlas* (*see* page 64). The stars Sirius and Canopus and the planets Venus and Jupiter are so bright that their magnitudes are expressed by negative numbers. A small telescope will show stars down to the ninth or tenth magnitude, while stars fainter than the twentieth magnitude may be photographed by long exposures with the largest telescopes.

Some of the astronomical information in this ALMANACK has been taken from *Astronomical Phenomena*, and is published here by arrangement with, and with the permission of, the Controller of HM Stationery Office.

ELEMENTS OF THE SOLAR SYSTEM

Orb	Mean Distance from Sun (Earth=1)	Mean Distance from Sun km 10⁶	Sidereal Period	Synodic Period	Incl. of Orbit to Ecliptic	Diameter	Mass (Earth=1)	Period of Rotation on Axis
			y d	Days	° '	km		d h m
Sun.............	...	...	...	...	...	1,392,000	332,948	25 09
Mercury.........	0·39	58	88	116	7 00	4,880	0·055	59
Venus............	0·72	108	225	584	3 24	12,100	0·815	243
Earth	1·00	150	1 0	...	...	12,756eq	1·00	23 56
Mars	1·52	228	1 322	780	1 51	6,790	0·107	24 37
Jupiter...........	5·20	778	11 315	399	1 18	{142,800eq / 134,200p}	318	{9 50 / 9 56}
Saturn..........	9·54	1427	29 167	378	2 29	{120,000eq / 108,000p}	95	{10 14 / 10 38}
Uranus..........	19·19	2870	84 6	370	0 46	52,000	14·6	16—28
Neptune..........	30·07	4497	164 288	367	1 46	48,400	17·2	18—20
Pluto	39·46	5950	247 255	367	17 09	2,445	0·01	6 09

eq equatorial *p* polar

THE SATELLITES

Name	Star mag.	Mean distance from Primary	Sidereal Period of Revolution	Name	Star mag.	Mean distance from Primary	Sidereal Period of Revolution
Earth		km	d	**Saturn**		km	d
Moon	—	384,400	27·322	Helene	18	377,000	2·737
				Rhea	10	527,000	4·518
Mars				Titan	8	1,222,000	15·945
Phobos	12	9,400	0·319	Hyperion	14	1,481,000	21·277
Deimos	13	23,500	1·262	Iapetus...........	11	3,561,000	79·331
				Phoebe	16	12,954,000	550·4
Jupiter							
XVI Metis	17	128,000	0·295	**Uranus**			
XV Adrastea	19	129,000	0·298	Cordelia	—	49,000	0·330
V Amalthea	14	181,000	0·498	Ophelia	—	54,000	0·372
XIV Thebe	15	222,000	0·675	Bianca	—	59,000	0·433
I Io	5	422,000	1·769	Cressida	—	62,000	0·463
II Europa	5	671,000	3·551	Desdemona	—	63,000	0·475
III Ganymede	5	1,070,000	7·155	Juliet	—	64,000	0·493
IV Callisto	6	1,880,000	16·689	Portia.............	—	66,000	0·513
XIII Leda	20	11,090,000	239	Rosalind	—	70,000	0·558
VI Himalia	15	11,480,000	251	Belinda	—	75,000	0·622
X Lysithea	18	11,720,000	259	Puck	—	86,000	0·762
VII Elara	17	11,740,000	260	Miranda	17	129,000	1·414
XII Ananke	19	21,200,000	631	Ariel.............	14	191,000	2·520
XI Carme	18	22,600,000	692	Umbriel	15	266,000	4·144
VIII Pasiphae	18	23,500,000	735	Titania	14	436,000	8·706
IX Sinope	18	23,700,000	758	Oberon	14	583,000	13·463
Saturn				**Neptune**			
Atlas.............	18	138,000	0·602	(1989N6)..........	—	48,000	0·30
Prometheus	16	139,000	0·613	(1989N5)..........	—	50,000	0·31
Pandora..........	16	142,000	0·629	(1989N3)..........	—	52,000	0·33
Janus	14	151,000	0·695	(1989N4)..........	—	62,000	0·40
Epimetheus.......	15	151,000	0·694	(1989N2)..........	—	74,000	0·55
Mimas	13	186,000	0·942	(1989N1)..........	—	118,000	1·12
Enceladus	12	238,000	1·370	Triton	14	355,000	5·877
Tethys	10	295,000	1·888	Nereid	19	5,510,000	360·21
Telesto	19	295,000	1·888				
Calypso	18	295,000	1·888	**Pluto**			
Dione	10	377,000	2·737	Charon...........	17	19,700	6·387

THE EARTH

The shape of the Earth is that of an oblate spheroid or solid of revolution whose meridian sections are ellipses not differing much from circles, whilst the sections at right angles are circles. The length of the equatorial axis is about 12,756 kilometres, and that of the polar axis is 12,714 kilometres. The mean density of the Earth is 5·5 times that of water, although that of the surface layer is less. The Earth and Moon revolve about their common centre of gravity in a lunar month; this centre in turn revolves round the Sun in a plane known as the ecliptic, that passes through the Sun's centre. The Earth's equator is inclined to this plane at an angle of 23½°. This tilt is the cause of the seasons. In mid-latitudes, and when the Sun is high above the Equator, not only does the high noon altitude make the days longer, but the

Sun's rays fall more directly on the Earth's surface; these effects combine to produce summer. In equatorial regions the noon altitude is large throughout the year, and there is little variation in the length of the day. In higher latitudes the noon altitude is lower, and the days in summer are appreciably longer than those in winter.

The average velocity of the Earth in its orbit is 30 kilometres a second. It makes a complete rotation on its axis in about $23^h 56^m$ of mean time, which is the sidereal day. Because of its annual revolution round the Sun, the rotation with respect to the Sun, or the solar day, is more than this by about four minutes (*see* p. 66). The extremity of the axis of rotation, or the North Pole of the Earth, is not rigidly fixed, but wanders over an area roughly 20 metres in diameter.

TERRESTRIAL MAGNETISM

A magnetic compass points along the horizontal component of a magnetic line of force. These directions converge on the 'magnetic dip-poles', the places where a freely suspended magnetized needle would become vertical. Not only do the positions of these poles change with time, but their exact location is ill-defined, particularly so in the case of the north dip-pole where the lines of force, on the north side of it, instead of converging radially, tend to bunch into a channel. Although it is therefore unrealistic to attempt to specify the locations of the dip-poles exactly, the present adopted positions are 77°·8 N., 103°·7W. and 64°·9 S., 139°·4 E. The two magnetic dip-poles are thus not antipodal, the line joining them passing the centre of the Earth at a distance of about 1,200 kilometres. The distances of the magnetic dip-poles from the north and south geographical poles are about 1,400 and 2,700 kilometres respectively.

There is also a 'magnetic equator', at all points of which the vertical component of the Earth's magnetic field is zero and a magnetized needle remains horizontal. This line runs between 2° and 10° north of the geographical equator in the eastern hemisphere, turns sharply south off the West African coast, and crosses South America through Brazil, Bolivia and Peru; it recrosses the geographical equator in mid-Pacific.

Reference has already been made to secular changes in the Earth's field. The following table indicates the changes in magnetic declination (or variation of the compass). Similar, though much smaller, changes have occurred in 'dip' or magnetic inclination. Secular changes differ throughout the world. Although the London observations strongly suggest a cycle with a period of several hundred years, an exact repetition is unlikely.

London			Greenwich		
1580	11°	15′ E.	1850	22°	24′ W.
1622	5	56 E.	1900	16	29 W.
1665	1	22 W.	1925	13	10 W.
1730	13	00 W.	1950	9	07 W.
1773	21	09 W.	1975	6	39 W.

In order that up-to-date information on the variation of the compass may be available, many governments publish magnetic charts on which there are lines (isogonic lines) passing through all places at which specified values of declination will be found at the date of the chart.

In the British Isles, isogonic lines now run approximately north-east to south-west. Though

there are considerable local deviations due to geological causes, a rough value of magnetic declination may be obtained by assuming that at 50° N. on the meridian of Greenwich, the value in 1991 is 4° 07′ west and allowing an increase of 10′ for each degree of latitude northwards and one of 24′ for each degree of longitude westwards. For example, at 53° N., 5° W., declination will be about 4° 07′ + 30′ + 120′, i.e. 6° 37′ west. The average annual change at the present time is about 9′ decrease.

The number of magnetic observatories is about 200, widely scattered over the globe. There are three in Great Britain run by the British Geological Survey: at Hartland, North Devon; at Eskdalemuir in Dumfriesshire, Scotland; and at Lerwick, Shetland Islands. The following are some recent annual mean values of the magnetic elements for Hartland.

Year	Declination West	Dip or Inclination	Horizontal Force	Vertical Force
	° ′	° ′	oersted	oersted
1950	11 06	66 54	0·1848	0·4334
1955	10 30	66 49	0·1859	0·4340
1960	9 59	66 44	0·1871	0·4350
1965	9 30	66 34	0·1887	0·4354
1970	9 06	66 26	0·1903	0·4364
1975	8 32	66 17	0·1921	0·4373
1980	7 44	66 10	0·1933	0·4377
1985	6 56	66 08	0·1938	0·4380
1989	6 24	66 09	0·1939	0·4386

The normal worldwide terrestrial magnetic field corresponds approximately to that of a very strong small bar magnet near the centre of the Earth but with appreciable smooth spatial departures. The origin and slow secular change of the normal field are not yet fully understood but are generally ascribed to electric currents associated with fluid motions in the Earth's core. Superimposed on the normal field are local and regional anomalies whose magnitudes may in places exceed that of the normal field; these are due to the influence of mineral deposits in the Earth's crust. A small proportion of the field is of external origin, mostly associated with electric currents in the ionosphere. The configuration of the external field and the ionization of the atmosphere depend on the incident particle and radiation flux. There are, therefore, short-term and non-periodic as well as diurnal, 27-day, seasonal and 11-year periodic changes in the magnetic field, dependent upon the position of the Sun and the degree of solar activity.

Magnetic Storms

Occasionally, sometimes with great suddenness, the Earth's magnetic field is subject for several hours to marked disturbance. In extreme cases, departures in field intensity of as much as one tenth the normal value are experienced. In many instances, such disturbances are accompanied by widespread displays of aurorae, marked changes in the incidence of cosmic rays, an increase in the reception of 'noise' from the Sun at radio frequencies together with rapid changes in the ionosphere and induced electric currents within the Earth which adversely affect radio and telegraphic communications. The disturbances are generally ascribed to changes in the stream of neutral and ionized particles which emanates from the Sun and through which the Earth is continuously passing. Some of these changes are associated with visible eruptions on the Sun, usually in the region of sunspots. There is a marked tendency for disturbances to recur after intervals of about 27 days, the apparent period of rotation of the Sun on its axis, which is consistent with the sources being located on particular areas of the Sun.

ARTIFICIAL SATELLITES

Orbits

To consider the orbit of an artificial satellite it is best to imagine that one is looking at the Earth from a distant point in space. The Earth would then be seen to be rotating about its axis inside the orbit described by the rapidly revolving satellite. The inclination of a satellite orbit to the Earth's equator (which generally remains almost constant throughout the satellite's lifetime) gives at once the maximum range of latitudes over which the satellite passes. Thus a satellite whose orbit has an inclination of 53° will pass overhead all latitudes between S. 53° and N. 53°, but would never be seen in the zenith of any place nearer the poles than these latitudes. If we consider a particular place on the earth, whose latitude is less than the inclination of the satellite's orbit then the Earth's rotation carries this place first under the northbound part of the orbit and then under the southbound portion of the orbit, these two occurrences being always less than 12 hours apart for satellites moving in direct orbits (i.e. to the east). (For satellites in retrograde orbits the words 'northbound' and 'southbound' should be interchanged in the preceding statement.) As the value of the latitude of the observer increases and approaches the value of the inclination of the orbit, so this interval gets shorter until (when the latitude is equal to the inclination) only one overhead passage occurs each day.

Observation of satellites

The regression of the orbit around the Earth causes alternate periods of visibility and invisibility, though this is of little concern to the radio or radar observer. To the visual observer the following cycle of events normally occurs (though the cycle may start in any position): invisibility, morning observations before dawn, invisibility, evening observations after dusk, invisibility, morning observations before dawn, and so on. With reasonably high satellites and for observers in high latitudes around the summer solstice the evening observations follow the morning observations without interruption as sunlight pass-ing over the polar regions can still illuminate satellites which are passing over temperate latitudes at local midnight. At the moment all satellites rely on sunlight to make them visible though a satellite with a flashing light has been suggested for a future launching. The observer must be in darkness or twilight in order to make any useful observations and the durations of twilight and the sunrise, sunset times given on Page Two of each month will be a useful guide.

Some of the satellites are visible to the naked eye and much interest has been aroused by the spectacle of a bright satellite disappearing into the Earth's shadow. The event is even more fascinating telescopically as the disappearance occurs gradually as the satellite traverses the Earth's penumbral shadow, and during the last few seconds before the eclipse is complete the satellite may change colour (under suitable atmospheric conditions) from yellow to red. This is because the last rays of sunlight are refracted through the denser layers of our atmosphere before striking the satellite.

Some satellites rotate about one or more axes so that a periodic variation in brightness is observed. This was particularly noticeable in several of the USSR satellites.

Satellite research has provided some interesting results. Among them may be mentioned a revised value of the Earth's oblateness, 1/298·2, and the discovery of the Van Allen radiation belts.

Launchings

Apart from their names, e.g. Cosmos 6 Rocket, the satellites are also classified according to their date of launch. Thus 1961 α refers to the first satellite launching of 1961. A number following the Greek letter indicated the relative brightness of the satellites put in orbit. From the beginning of 1963 the Greek letters were replaced by numbers and the numbers by roman letters e.g. 1963–01A. For all satellites successfully injected into orbit the table gives the designation and names of the main objects (in the order A, B, C ... etc.), the launch date and some initial orbital data. These are the inclination to the equator (i), the nodal period of revolution (P), the eccentricity, e, and the perigee height.

Artificial Satellites Launched in 1988–89

Designation	Satellite	Launch date	i	P	e	Perigee height (km)
1988–						
91	STS 26, TDRS3	September 29	28·5	90·7	0·002	302
92	Cosmos 1974, launcher, launcher rocket, rocket	October 3	62·9	709·1	0·736	585
93	Cosmos 1975, rocket	October 11	82·5	97·8	0·002	632
94	Cosmos 1976, rocket, engine	October 13	72·9	90·2	0·013	193
95	Raduga	October 20	1·5	1473·6	0·001	36467
96	Cosmos 1977, launcher rocket, launcher, rocket	October 25	62·9	708·2	0·734	617
97	Cosmos 1978, rocket, engine	October 27	72·9	90·2	0·013	194
98	TDF1	October 28	0·1	1436·0	0·000	35775
99	USA 33	November 6	?	?	?	?
100	VKK1	November 15	51·6	89·5	0·001	248
101	Cosmos 1979, rocket	November 18	65·0	92·8	0·001	404
102	Cosmos 1980, rocket	November 23	71·0	102·0	0·000	849
103	Cosmos 1981, rocket, engine	November 24	62·8	90·4	0·009	239
104	Soyuz TM7, rocket	November 26	51·6	89·9	0·003	252
105	Cosmos 1982, rocket	November 30	70·0	90·4	0·013	207
106	STS 27, USA 34	December 2	57·0	93·5	0·001	443
107	Cosmos 1983, rocket, engine	December 8	62·8	89·5	0·001	245
108	Ekran 19	December 10	1·4	1435·8	0·000	35766
109	Skynet 4B, Astra 1A	December 11	3·1	1403·1	0·017	34423
110	Cosmos 1984, rocket	December 16	62·8	89·6	0·010	187
111	China 25	December 22	0·6	1435·9	0·000	35781
112	Molniya 3–34, launcher rocket, launcher, rocket	December 22	62·8	702·4	0·739	458
113	Cosmos 1985, rocket	December 23	73·6	95·2	0·001	522
114	Progress 39, rocket	December 25	51·6	90·2	0·008	237
115	Molniya 1–74, launcher rocket, launcher, rocket	December 28	62·8	700·4	0·732	624
116	Cosmos 1986, rocket	December 29	64·8	89·2	0·004	212
1989–		1989				
01	Cosmos 1987–9	January 10	64·9	675·7	0·001	19117
02	Cosmos 1990, rocket	January 12	82·6	89·9	0·001	263
03	Cosmos 1991, rocket, engine	January 18	70·0	92·2	0·005	347
04	Gorizont 17	January 26	1·5	1436·1	0·000	35776
05	Cosmos 1992, rocket	January 26	74·0	100·7	0·002	772
06	Intelsat 5A F-15	January 27	0·2	1436·0	0·001	35755
07	Cosmos 1993, rocket	January 28	64·8	89·7	0·014	170
08	Progress 40, rocket	February 10	51·6	90·5	0·006	268
09	Cosmos 1994–1999, rocket	February 10	82·6	114·0	0·001	1397
10	Cosmos 2000, rocket, engine	February 10	82·4	92·0	0·004	343
11	Cosmos 2001, launcher rocket, launcher, rocket	February 14	62·8	717·7	0·736	624
12	Cosmos 2002, rocket	February 14	65·8	110·3	0·138	185
13	Navstar 2–01, rocket	February 14	55·1	713·2	0·008	19860
14	Molniya 1–75, launcher rocket, launcher, rocket	February 15	62·9	717·7	0·742	462
15	Cosmos 2003, rocket, engine	February 17	62·8	89·5	0·003	233
16	Akebono	February 21	75·1	211·2	0·433	277
17	Cosmos 2004, rocket	February 22	82·9	105·1	0·003	972
18	Meteor 2–18, rocket	February 28	82·5	104·1	0·001	941
19	Cosmos 2005, rocket	March 2	62·8	89·6	0·010	189
20	JC Sat 1, Meteosat 4	March 6	0·1	1435·6	0·002	35686
21	STS 29, TDRS4	March 13	28·5	90·7	0·002	301
22	Cosmos 2006, rocket, engine	March 16	62·8	92·0	0·006	328
23	Progress 41, rocket	March 16	51·6	91·0	0·007	276
24	Cosmos 2007, rocket	March 23	64·7	89·7	0·004	230
25	Cosmos 2008–2015, rocket	March 24	74·0	114·5	0·005	1394

Desig-nation	Satellite	Launch date	i	P	e	Perigee height (km)
1989–						
26	USA36	March 24	47·7	94·4	0·002	482
27	Tele-X	April 2	0·1	1436·0	0·000	35770
28	Cosmos 2016, rocket	April 4	83·0	104·7	0·003	956
29	Cosmos 2017, rocket, engine	April 6	62·8	89·8	0·005	231
30	Raduga 23	April 14	1·4	1473·9	0·001	36491
31	Cosmos 2018, rocket	April 20	62·8	89·4	0·009	184
32	Foton 2, rocket	April 26	62·8	90·5	0·012	216
33	STS 30	May 4	28·9	90·6	0·003	297
34	Cosmos 2019, rocket, engine	May 5	62·9	89·9	0·012	190
35	USA 37	May 10	?	?	?	?
36	Cosmos 2020, rocket	May 17	64·8	89·6	0·013	172
37	Cosmos 2021, rocket	May 24	69·9	89·4	0·005	213
38	Resurs-F, rocket	May 25	82·3	88·6	0·004	177
39	Cosmos 2022–2024	May 31	64·8	675·7	0·000	19122
40	Cosmos 2025, rocket, engine	June 1	62·8	89·0	0·011	155
41	Superbird A, DFS 1	June 5	0·1	1436·0	0·000	35769
42	Cosmos 2026, rocket	June 7	82·9	104·8	0·004	953
43	Molniya 3–35, launcher rocket, launcher, rocket	June 8	62·8	717·8	0·737	593
44	Navstar 2–02, rocket	June 10	54·6	714·2	0·005	19970
45	Cosmos 2027, rocket	June 14	65·8	94·6	0·002	482
46	USA 39	June 14	?	?	?	?
47	Cosmos 2028, rocket, engine	June 16	70·0	89·5	0·006	208
48	Raduga 24	June 21	1·4	1436·2	0·001	35768
49	Resurs-F2, rocket, engine	June 28	82·6	89·9	0·001	260
50	Nadezhda, rocket	July 4	83·0	104·9	0·004	960
51	Cosmos 2029, rocket, engine	July 5	82·4	91·6	0·001	342
52	Gorizont 18	July 5	1·5	1435·9	0·000	35774
53	Olympus 1	July 12	0·3	1437·6	0·007	35516
54	Cosmos 2030, rocket	July 12	67·1	89·6	0·014	166
55	Resurs-F3, rocket, Pion 3, Pion 4, engine	July 18	82·6	89·9	0·001	260
56	Cosmos 2031, rocket	July 18	50·6	89·0	0·005	194
57	Cosmos 2032, rocket, engine	July 20	82·3	90·0	0·013	181
58	Cosmos 2033, rocket	July 24	65·0	92·8	0·002	397
59	Cosmos 2034, rocket	July 25	82·9	105·0	0·003	968
60	Cosmos 2035, rocket, engine	August 2	82·6	90·4	0·009	230
61	STS 28, USA 40, USA 41	August 8	57·0	90·5	0·001	296
62	TV-Sat 2, Hipparcos	August 8	0·1	1429·8	0·003	35541
63	Resurs-F4, rocket	August 15	82·3	89·8	0·001	259
64	Navstar 2–03	August 18	55·0	711·9	0·004	19937
65	Cosmos 2036, rocket, engine	August 22	62·8	90·0	0·003	256
66	Progress-M, rocket	August 23	51·6	91·1	0·010	266
67	Marcopolo 1	August 27	0·1	1435·8	0·001	35777
68	Cosmos 2037, rocket	August 28	73·6	116·1	0·003	1484
69	USA 43, USA 44	September 4	?	?	?	?
70	Himawari 4	September 5	1·6	1436·1	0·002	35720
71	Soyuz TM8, rocket	September 5	51·6	91·4	0·003	325
72	USA 45	September 6	?	?	?	?
73	Resurs-F5, rocket, engine	September 6	82·3	89·9	0·001	262
74	Cosmos 2038–2043, rocket	September 14	82·6	113·9	0·001	1392
75	Cosmos 2044, rocket	September 15	82·3	89·3	0·004	206

15°

SOUTH-EAST ICELAND

FAEROES

VIKING

N UTSIRE

S UTSIRE

FAIR ISLE

BAILEY

HEBRIDES

CROMARTY

FORTIES

FISHER

FORTH

DOGGER

GERMAN BIGHT

TYNE

ROCKALL

MALIN

HUMBER

IRISH SEA

THAMES

SHANNON

FASTNET

LUNDY

DOVER

WIGHT

PLYMOUTH

PORTLAND

SOLE

BISCAY

FINISTERRE

Stations whose latest reports are broadcast in the 5 min. forecasts

A   St. Abb's Head
B   Butt of Lewis
C   Channel Light-Vessel (auto)
D   Dover
J   Jersey
K   Smith's Knoll (auto)
L   Land's End
M   Malin Head
R   Ronaldsway
RS   Royal Sovereign
S   Sumbergh
T   Tiree
V   Valentia

TIDAL CONSTANTS

The time of high water at the undermentioned ports and places may be *approximately* found by taking the appropriate Time of High Water at the Standard Port (as shown on pp. 86, 87, etc.) and adding thereto the quantities annexed. The columns headed 'Springs' and 'Neaps' show the height of the tide above datum for Mean High Water Springs and Mean High Water Neaps respectively.

EXAMPLE.—Required times of high water at Stranraer on *January* 1, 1991:—

(a) *Morning Tide.*
Appropriate time of high
    water at *Greenock* ....   0019 hrs. (*Jan.* 1)
Tidal difference .... −0020 hrs.

(b) *Afternoon Tide.*
Appropriate time of high
    water at *Greenock* ....   1226 hrs. (*Jan* 1).
Tidal difference .... −0020 hrs.

H.W at *Stranraer* ... 2359 hrs. (*Dec.* 31)

H.W. at *Stranraer* .. 1206 hrs.

Port	Diff.	Springs	Neaps	Port	Diff.	Springs	Neaps
	h.m.	metres	metres		h.m.	metres	metres
Aberdeen.......... *Leith*	−1 19	4·3	3·4	Christchurch Hbr. *L'don*	−4 53	1·8	1·4
Aberdovey..... *Liverpool*	−3 00	5·0	3·5	Cobh .... *Liverpool*	−5 55	4·2	3·3
Aberystwyth .. *Liverpool*	−3 30	5·0	3·5	Coulport ...... *Greenock*	−0 05	3·4	2·9
Aldeburgh...... *London*	−3 05	2·8	2·7	Coverack .... *Avonmouth*	−2 02	5·3	4·2
Alloa.............. *Leith*	+0 47	5·6	4·2	Cowes.......... *London*	−2 23	4·2	3·5
Amlwch .... *Liverpool*	−0 33	7·3	5·8	Cromarty.......... *Leith*	−2 56	4·3	3·4
Anstruther Easter . *Leith*	−0 22	5·5	4·4	Cromer........... *Hull*	+0 15	5·2	4·1
Antwerp (Prosper-				Dartmouth ..... *London*	+4 28	4·9	3·8
polder) .... *London*	+0 50	5·8	4·2	Deal .... *London*	−2 37	6·1	5·0
Appledore ... *Avonmouth*	−1 15	7·5	5·2	Dieppe .... *London*	−3 03	9·3	7·2
Arbroath.......... *Leith*	−0 33	5·0	4·1	Dingle Hbr..... *Liverpool*	+5 38	3·9	2·9
Ardrossan ..... *Greenock*	−0 15	3·2	2·7	Donegal Hbr. .. *Liverpool*	−5 24	3·9	3·0
†Arundel .... *London*	−2 03	3·1	2·2	Douglas (IoM).. *Liverpool*	−0 04	6·9	5·4
Avonmouth ....*A'mouth*	0 00	13·2	10·0	Dover.......... *London*	−2 52	6·7	5·3
Ayr .... *Greenock*	−0 25	3·0	2·6	Duclair......... *London*	−1 13	7·7	6·5
Baie de Lampaul . *London*	+2 30	7·5	5·8	Duddon Bar ... *Liverpool*	+0 03	8·5	6·6
Ballycotton.. *Avonmouth*	−1 43	4·2	3·3	Dunbar ....*Leith*	−0 07	5·2	4·2
Banff.............. *Leith*	−2 44	3·5	2·8	Dundalk (Sldr's Pt) *L'pool*	+0 22	5·1	4·2
Bantry .... *Liverpool*	+5 59	3·5	2·6	Dundee ....*Leith*	+0 11	5·4	4·3
Bardsey Island . *Liverpool*	−3 18	4·5	3·3	Dungeness...... *London*	−3 04	7·7	5·9
Barmouth ..... *Liverpool*	−2 57	5·0	3·5	Dunkirk ...... *London*	−1 54	5·8	4·8
Barnstaple ... *Avonmouth*	−1 00	4·1	1·4	Eastbourne ...... *London*	−2 50	7·3	5·6
Barrow (Docks) *Liverpool*	+0 15	9·1	7·1	East Loch Tarbert *G'nock*	+0 05	3·4	2·9
Barry .... *Avonmouth*	−0 22	11·4	8·7	Exmouth Dock .. *London*	+4 55	4·0	2·8
Belfast .... *London*	−2 45	3·5	3·0	Eyemouth ....*Leith*	−0 20	4·7	3·7
Berwick........... *Leith*	−0 02	4·7	3·8	Falmouth ...... *London*	+3 35	5·3	4·2
Bideford..... *Avonmouth*	−1 15	5·9	3·6	Ferryside.... *Avonmouth*	−0 58	6·7	4·5
Blackpool ..... *Liverpool*	−0 10	8·9	7·0	Filey Bay..........*Leith*	+1 50	5·8	4·9
Blacktoft .... *Hull*	+0 27	5·8	4·0	Fishguard ..... *Liverpool*	−4 01	4·8	3·4
Blakeney .... *Hull*	+0 44	3·4	2·0	Folkestone ..... *London*	−3 04	7·1	5·7
Blyth .... *Leith*	+0 50	5·0	3·9	Formby .... *Liverpool*	−0 12	9·0	7·3
Boscastle ... *Avonmouth*	−1 20	7·3	5·6	Fowey .... *London*	+3 53	5·4	4·3
Boulogne....... *London*	−2 44	8·9	7·2	Fraserburgh ....*Leith*	−2 29	3·7	2·9
Bovisand Pier... *London*	+3 55	5·3	4·3	*Freshwater Bay *London*	−4 33	2·6	2·3
Bowling....... *Greenock*	+0 15	4·0	3·4	Galway ...... *Liverpool*	−6 08	5·1	3·9
Braye .... *London*	+5 33	6·3	4·7	Glasgow....... *Greenock*	+0 28	4·7	4·1
Brest.......... *London*	+2 28	7·5	5·9	Goole .... *Hull*	+0 59	5·7	3·7
Bridgwater .. *Avonmouth*	−0 22	4·6	1·9	Gorleston ...... *London*	−5 00	2·4	2·0
Bridlington.......*Leith*	+2 03	6·1	4·7	Granton............*Leith*	0 00	5·6	4·5
Bridport (W. Bay) *London*	+4 37	4·1	3·0	Granville....... *London*	+4 25	13·0	9·8
Brighton .... *London*	−2 50	6·5	5·1	Grimsby.......... *Hull*	−0 28	7·0	5·6
Buckie .... *Leith*	−2 56	4·1	3·2	Hartlepool.........*Leith*	+0 58	5·4	4·2
Bude Haven . *Avonmouth*	−1 33	7·7	5·8	Harwich ...... *London*	−2 02	4·0	3·4
Bull Sand Fort ..... *Hull*	−0 46	6·9	5·5	Hastings ...... *London*	−2 57	7·5	5·8
Burntisland ......*Leith*	0 00	5·6	4·5	Haverfordwest . *Liverpool*	−4 50	2·2	0·3
Calais .... *London*	−2 14	7·1	5·9	Hestan Islet ... *Liverpool*	+0 25	8·3	6·3
Campbeltown .. *Greenock*	+0 07	2·9	2·6	Holyhead...... *Liverpool*	−0 48	5·7	4·5
Cape Cornwall ..*A'mouth*	−2 30	6·0	4·3	Hook of Holland . *London*	−0 01	2·1	1·7
Cardiff (Penarth)				*Hurst Point ... *London*	−3 38	2·7	2·3
Avonmouth	−0 15	12·2	9·4	Ijmuiden .... *London*	+1 12	2·0	1·7
Cardigan Port . *Liverpool*	−3 37	4·7	3·4	Ilfracombe... *Avonmouth*	−1 10	9·2	6·9
Carmarthen . *Avonmouth*	−0 48	2·6	0·4	Inveraray ..... *Greenock*	+0 11	3·3	3·0
Cayeux........ *London*	−2 55	10·2	7·9	Invergordon ....*Leith*	−2 49	4·4	3·5
Chatham .... *London*	−1 10	6·0	4·9	Ipswich ...... *London*	−1 42	4·2	3·4
Chepstow.... *Avonmouth*	+0 20	No Data		Itchenor ...... *London*	−2 23	4·8	3·8
Cherbourg...... *London*	−6 00	6·3	5·0	Kinsale .... *Liverpool*	−6 03	4·1	3·2
Chester .... *Liverpool*	+1 05	4·0	2·0	Kirkcudbright . *Liverpool*	+0 15	7·5	5·9
Chichester Hbr. . *London*	−2 25	4·9	4·0	Kirkwall ....*Leith*	−4 15	2·9	2·2

† very approximate.   * 1st High Water Springs only.

Port	Diff. h.m.	Springs metres	Neaps metres
Knights Town . *Liverpool*	+5 36	3.9	3.0
Lamlash ...... *Greenock*	-0 26	3.2	2.7
Le Havre ...... *London*	-3 55	7.9	6.6
Lerwick .... *Leith*	-3 49	2.2	1.6
Limerick Dock . *Liverpool*	-4 27	6.1	4.6
Littlehampton .. *London*	-2 38	5.8	4.6
Lizard Point . *Avonmouth*	-2 17	5.3	4.2
Llanddwyn Island *L'pool*	-1 53	5.0	4.0
Llanelli ..... *Liverpool*	-0 56	7.8	5.8
Loch Moidart .. *Greenock*	+6 00	4.8	3.5
Londonderry .. *London*	-5 37	2.7	2.1
Looe .... *London*	+3 55	5.4	4.2
Lossiemouth ...... *Leith*	-3 01	4.1	3.2
Lowestoft ...... *London*	-4 25	2.4	2.1
Lulworth Cove.. *London*	+5 00	2.3	1.5
Lundy Island *Avonmouth*	-1 23	8.0	5.9
Lyme Regis .... *London*	+4 55	4.3	3.1
*Lymington .... *London*	-3 33	3.0	2.6
Margate........ *London*	-1 52	4.8	3.9
Maryport...... *Liverpool*	+0 24	8.6	6.6
Menai Bridge .. *Liverpool*	-0 28	7.4	5.9
Mevagissey ..... *London*	+3 53	5.4	4.3
Middlesbrough .. *Leith*	+1 09	5.6	4.5
Milford Haven . *Liverpool*	-5 07	7.0	5.2
Minehead .. *Avonmouth*	-0 40	10.6	8.1
Montrose.......... *Leith*	-0 19	4.8	3.9
Morecambe .... *Liverpool*	+0 07	9.5	7.4
Mostyn Quay .. *Liverpool*	-0 17	8.5	6.7
Newburgh......... *Leith*	+0 48	4.1	3.0
Newcastle on Tyne . *Leith*	+0 54	5.3	4.1
Newhaven...... *London*	-2 48	6.6	5.2
Newlyn........ *Avonmouth*	-2 24	5.6	4.4
Newport(Gwent) *A'mouth*	-0 15	12.1	9.0
Newquay ...... *London*	-1 58	7.0	5.3
New Quay, Cardiff. *L'pool*	-3 30	4.9	3.4
North Shields ..... *Leith*	+0 51	5.0	3.9
North Sunderland .. *Leith*	+0 05	4.8	3.7
N. Woolwich .... *London*	-0 20	7.0	5.7
Oban......... *Greenock*	+5 45	4.0	2.9
Old Lynn Road..... *Hull*	+0 05	7.3	5.8
Orfordness ..... *London*	-2 50	2.8	2.7
Ostend .... *London*	-1 32	5.0	4.2
Padstow..... *Avonmouth*	-1 45	7.3	5.6
Peel (IoM) ..... *Liverpool*	-0 02	5.3	4.2
Peterhead .... *Leith*	-1 59	3.8	3.1
Plymouth ...... *London*	+4 05	5.5	4.4
Poole (Entrance) *London*	-5 03	2.0	1.6
Porlock Bay . *Avonmouth*	-0 50	10.2	7.8
Porthcawl ... *Avonmouth*	-0 53	9.9	7.5
Portmadoc..... *Liverpool*	-2 45	5.1	3.4
Portland ...... *London*	+5 10	2.1	1.4
Portpatrick.... *Liverpool*	+0 22	3.8	3.0
Portsmouth..... *London*	-2 23	4.7	3.8
Port Talbot .. *Avonmouth*	-0 53	9.6	7.3
Preston .... *Liverpool*	+0 10	5.3	3.3
Pwllheli .... *Liverpool*	-3 07	5.0	3.4
Ramsey (IoM) *Liverpool*	+0 04	7.2	5.7
Ramsgate....... *London*	-2 32	4.9	3.8
†Rosslare Hbr. . *Liverpool*	-5 23	1.9	1.4
Rosyth .... *Leith*	+0 07	5.8	4.7
Ryde .... *London*	-2 23	4.5	3.7
St. Helier ...... *London*	+4 48	11.1	8.1
St. Ives ...... *Avonmouth*	-1 55	6.6	4.9
St. Malo ...... *London*	+4 28	12.2	9.2
St. Peter Port ... *London*	+4 54	9.0	6.7
Salcombe ...... *London*	+4 10	5.3	4.1
Saltash......... *London*	+4 10	5.6	4.5
Scarborough ...... *Leith*	+1 33	5.7	4.6
Scheveningen... *London*	+0 27	2.1	1.7
Scrabster ...... *Leith*	+6 04	5.0	3.7
Seaham .... *Leith*	+0 53	5.2	4.1
Selsey Bill ...... *London*	-2 28	5.3	4.4
Sennen Cove . *Avonmouth*	-2 30	6.1	4.8
Sharpness Dock . *A'mouth*	+0 42	9.3	5.8
Sheerness ...... *London*	-1 16	5.7	4.8
Shoreham ...... *London*	-2 43	6.2	5.0
Silloth .... *Liverpool*	+0 35	9.2	7.1
Southampton (1st H.W.) ...... *London*	-2 52	4.5	3.7
Southend...... *London*	-1 22	5.7	4.8
Southwold...... *London*	-3 50	2.5	2.2
Stirling .... *Leith*	+1 13	2.9	1.6
Stonehaven....... *Leith*	-1 09	4.5	3.6
Stornoway ...... *Liverpool*	-4 15	4.8	3.7
Stranraer ..... *Greenock*	-0 20	3.0	2.5
Stromness ...... *Leith*	-5 34	3.6	2.7
Sunderland....... *Leith*	+0 51	5.2	4.2
*Swanage ...... *London*	-5 13	2.0	1.6
Swansea..... *Avonmouth*	-0 49	9.6	7.3
Tarn Point .... *Liverpool*	+0 05	8.3	6.4
Tay River (Bar) .... *Leith*	-0 19	5.2	4.2
Tees R. (Ent.) ...... *Leith*	+1 08	5.5	4.3
Teignmouth .... *London*	+4 37	4.8	3.6
Tenby .... *Avonmouth*	-1 05	8.4	6.3
Tilbury........ *London*	-0 49	6.4	5.3
Tobermory .... *Liverpool*	-5 12	4.4	3.3
Torquay........ *London*	+4 40	4.9	3.7
*Totland Bay ... *London*	-3 53	2.7	2.3
Troon .... *Greenock*	-0 25	3.2	2.7
Truro .... *London*	+3 43	5.3	4.2
Walton-on-Naze. *London*	-2 10	4.2	3.4
Waterford...... *Liverpool*	-4 54	4.6	3.6
Weston S. Mare . *A'mouth*	-0 25	12.0	9.0
†Wexford Hbr. . *Liverpool*	-5 03	1.7	1.4
Whitby........ *Leith*	+1 22	5.4	4.3
Whitehaven .... *Liverpool*	+0 10	8.0	6.3
Wick............. *Leith*	-3 26	3.4	2.7
Wisbech Cut .... *Hull*	+0 01	7.0	5.1
Workington .... *Liverpool*	+0 20	8.2	6.4
Worthing ...... *London*	-2 38	6.1	4.8
*Yarmouth (IoW) *London*	-2 53	3.1	2.5
Youghal .... *Liverpool*	-5 49	4.2	3.3

† very approximate.   * 1st High Water Springs only.

Tidal data is no longer available for a number of places which formerly appeared in the list above. These places (with the name of the substitute now recorded) are: *Devonport* (Plymouth); *Loch Long* (Coulport); *Pembroke Dock* (Milford Haven); *Penzance* (Newlyn); *Plymouth Breakwater* (Bovisand Pier); *St. Annes* (Blackpool); *Spurn Head* (Bull Sand Fort); *Ushant* (Baie de Lampaul); *Valentia Harbour* (Knights Town); *Woolwich* (N. Woolwich); *Yarmouth Roads* (Gorleston).

Tidal predictions (pp. 86–97) for London Bridge, Liverpool, Avonmouth, Hull, Dún Laoghaire and Leith are computed by the Proudman Oceanographic Laboratory, copyright reserved. Those for Greenock have been supplied by the Hydrographer of the Navy and are crown copyright.

JANUARY, 1991

High Water at the undermentioned Places (GMT*)—

†Datum of Predictions: London Bridge 3·20 m. below; Liverpool 4·93 m. below; Avonmouth 6·50 m. below; Hull (Albert Dock) 3·90 m. below; Greenock 1·62 m. below; Leith 2·90 m. below. ‡Dun Laoghaire 0·20 m. above.

Day of Month	Day of Week	LONDON BRIDGE Mn	Ht	Aft	Ht	LIVERPOOL Mn	Ht	Aft	Ht	AVONMOUTH Mn	Ht	Aft	Ht	HULL (Albert Dock) Mn	Ht	Aft	Ht	GREENOCK Mn	Ht	Aft	Ht	LEITH Mn	Ht	Aft	Ht	DUN LAOGHAIRE Mn	Ht	Aft	Ht
1	Tu	0141	6·8	1404	7·1	1118	9·6	2346	9·6	0714	13·4	1945	13·4	0621	7·5	1838	7·4	0019	3·4	1226	3·7	0223	5·6	1448	5·7	1123	4·3	2354	4·0
2	W	0229	6·9	1454	7·3	—	—	1207	9·8	0804	13·7	2033	13·6	0710	7·7	1921	7·6	0108	3·5	1312	3·9	0315	5·7	1538	5·8	—	—	1212	4·3
3	Th	0315	7·1	1542	7·5	0034	9·6	1253	9·8	0850	13·7	2118	13·5	0757	7·8	2004	7·7	0155	3·5	1356	4·0	0403	5·7	1625	5·7	0043	4·0	1301	4·3
4	F	0400	7·2	1628	7·5	0120	9·4	1338	9·6	0934	13·6	2200	13·1	0842	7·8	2044	7·8	0240	3·5	1440	4·0	0450	5·7	1713	5·7	0135	4·0	1353	4·4
5	Sa	0444	7·2	1713	7·3	0205	9·1	1423	9·3	1017	13·1	2242	12·3	0925	7·5	2124	7·6	0325	3·5	1524	3·9	0537	5·5	1803	5·5	0225	3·8	1445	4·3
6	Su	0526	7·0	1758	7·0	0249	8·7	1507	8·9	1058	12·5	2322	11·8	1007	7·1	2210	7·3	0409	3·4	1608	3·8	0626	5·2	1853	5·2	0318	3·7	1540	4·2
7	M	0610	6·7	1843	6·6	0334	8·3	1553	8·4	1139	11·7	—	—	1052	6·8	2353	6·9	0451	3·2	1653	3·6	0717	4·9	1944	4·7	0416	3·5	1639	4·1
8	Tu	0655	6·4	1933	6·2	0423	7·8	1645	7·9	0003	11·1	1221	11·0	1143	6·4	1243	6·4	0544	3·0	1742	3·4	0810	4·7	2038	4·6	0520	3·4	1746	3·8
9	W	0748	6·1	2029	6·0	0520	7·4	1749	7·4	0048	10·4	1313	10·3	0104	6·1	1354	5·9	0639	2·9	1835	3·1	0908	4·5	2139	4·5	0630	3·3	1856	3·6
10	Th	0854	5·8	2134	5·9	0631	7·3	1904	7·2	0147	9·9	1420	9·9	0225	6·1	1505	5·8	0747	2·9	1941	2·9	1012	4·5	2248	4·6	0736	3·3	2003	3·6
11	F	1010	5·8	2248	6·1	0744	7·7	2016	7·4	0304	9·9	1539	10·4	0341	5·9	1605	5·9	0902	2·9	2106	2·8	1119	4·5	2354	4·8	0832	3·4	2101	3·4
12	Sa	1127	5·9	2351	6·1	0846	7·7	2115	7·7	0420	10·2	1651	11·0	0441	5·9	1657	6·1	1007	3·2	2222	2·7	0049	4·7	1308	4·7	0919	3·5	2149	3·5
13	Su	—	—	1222	6·2	0936	8·1	2202	8·0	0522	10·9	1746	11·9	0529	6·1	1737	6·3	1100	3·1	2318	2·8	0136	4·8	1350	4·8	0959	3·7	2228	3·5
14	M	0039	6·2	1307	6·5	1019	8·3	2242	8·5	0652	11·5	1832	12·3	0608	6·3	1811	6·5	0003	3·0	1223	3·3	0219	4·8	1428	5·0	1035	3·8	2336	3·6
15	Tu	0120	6·5	1345	6·7	1057	8·7	2318	8·7	0730	12·0	1913	12·4	0642	6·5	1843	6·7	0041	3·1	1258	3·3	0255	5·0	1501	5·1	1107	3·9	1213	4·0
16	W	0157	6·7	1422	6·8	1132	8·8	2351	9·1	0804	12·5	1947	12·4	0712	6·7	1914	6·8	0115	3·2	1330	3·5	0328	5·0	1533	5·4	1140	4·0	1247	4·1
17	Th	0233	6·8	1458	7·0	—	—	1205	9·1	0910	12·7	2020	12·6	0744	6·8	1948	7·0	0148	3·3	1403	3·5	0359	5·2	1605	5·4	—	—	1325	4·1
18	F	0308	7·0	1534	7·0	0024	8·8	1239	9·2	0945	12·8	2053	12·6	0818	7·0	2023	7·1	0222	3·3	1436	3·5	0432	5·2	1640	5·4	0008	3·7	1401	4·1
19	Sa	0342	7·0	1609	7·0	0056	8·7	1313	9·2	1020	12·7	2128	12·4	0853	7·1	2058	7·1	0258	3·2	1511	3·5	0508	5·2	1717	5·2	0042	3·7	1443	4·0
20	Su	0414	7·0	1642	6·8	0130	8·5	1347	9·0	1057	12·4	2202	12·0	0929	7·1	2135	6·9	0336	3·2	1549	3·4	0546	5·2	1748	5·1	0115	3·7	1531	3·9
21	M	0445	6·8	1718	6·7	0205	8·3	1422	8·5	1134	11·4	2237	11·6	1009	6·9	2217	6·7	0417	3·3	1630	3·3	0629	5·0	1843	5·0	0153	3·7	1626	3·8
22	Tu	0518	6·7	1754	6·5	0242	8·1	1503	8·1	—	—	2312	10·8	1052	6·7	2306	6·4	0502	3·2	1714	3·2	0716	4·9	1932	4·9	0233	3·6	1733	3·6
23	W	0554	6·5	1838	6·3	0325	7·9	1550	7·9	0052	10·5	2353	10·6	1146	6·4	—	—	0550	3·2	1804	3·1	0811	4·6	2032	4·6	0318	3·5	1852	3·6
24	Th	0639	6·3	1933	6·0	0420	7·7	1651	7·7	0222	10·3	1225	11·3	0130	6·2	1259	6·0	0645	3·0	1907	3·0	0918	4·8	2146	4·8	0410	3·4	2009	3·6
25	F	0745	6·0	2050	5·9	0530	7·9	1810	8·3	0505	10·9	1342	12·1	0301	6·5	1426	6·3	0755	2·9	2044	2·9	1036	4·8	2310	4·8	0514	3·5	2115	3·7
26	Sa	0914	6·0	2213	6·3	0657	8·6	1935	8·6	0611	11·7	1512	12·8	0423	6·4	1651	6·4	0917	2·9	2216	2·9	1152	4·8	—	—	0628	3·6	2211	3·8
27	Su	1041	5·9	2330	6·4	0816	9·1	2051	9·0	0706	12·5	1633	13·4	0525	6·7	1740	6·7	1027	3·0	2321	3·1	—	—	—	—	0741	3·6	2300	3·8
28	M	—	—	1201	6·5	0924	9·6	2155	9·2	0754	13·3	1744	13·7	0615	7·0	1824	7·3	1124	3·2	—	—	0024	5·0	1258	5·1	0845	3·9	2347	4·0
29	Tu	0036	6·5	1304	6·8	1020	9·8	2249	9·5	—	—	1845	13·8	0659	7·2	1904	7·5	0014	3·4	—	—	0126	5·3	1351	5·4	0939	4·1	1202	4·3
30	W	0131	6·8	1358	7·1	1111	9·8	2337	9·6	—	—	1935	—	—	7·6	—	—	0100	3·4	1213	3·7	0219	5·5	1440	5·7	1030	4·2	—	—
31	Th	0219	7·0	1446	7·3	1156	—	—	—	—	—	2019	—	—	7·9	—	—	—	—	1258	3·8	0304	5·7	1524	5·8	1116	—	—	—

* All times shown are Greenwich Mean Time.   †Difference of height in metres from Ordnance Datum (Newlyn).   ‡Difference of height in metres from Ordnance Datum (Dublin).

FEBRUARY, 1991

High Water at the undermentioned Places (GMT*)—

Day of Month	Day of Week	London Bridge (†3·20 m. below) Mn.	Ht.	Aft.	Ht.	Liverpool (†4·93 m. below) Mn.	Ht.	Aft.	Ht.	Avonmouth (†6·50 m. below) Mn.	Ht.	Aft.	Ht.	Hull, Albert Dock (†3·90 m. below) Mn.	Ht.	Aft.	Ht.	Greenock (†1·62 m. below) Mn.	Ht.	Aft.	Ht.	Leith (†2·90 m. below) Mn.	Ht.	Aft.	Ht.	Dun Laoghaire (‡0·20 m. above) Mn.	Ht.	Aft.	Ht.
1	F	0303	7·2	1529	7·5	0021	9·6	1238	9·9	0834	14·0	2100	13·7	0740	7·6	1942	8·1	0142	3·5	1340	3·9	0347	5·7	1607	5·8	0030	4·0	1247	4·4
2	Sa	0342	7·3	1610	7·5	0100	9·5	1317	9·8	0914	13·9	2136	13·4	0819	7·5	2022	8·1	0222	3·5	1421	3·9	0427	5·7	1650	5·7	0113	4·0	1333	4·4
3	Su	0421	7·3	1649	7·3	0140	9·3	1355	9·5	0952	13·4	2213	12·9	0857	7·3	2101	7·8	0300	3·4	1501	3·8	0510	5·5	1734	5·5	0157	3·9	1418	4·2
4	M	0459	7·1	1726	7·0	0216	8·9	1432	9·0	1027	12·8	2247	12·0	0934	7·0	2141	7·5	0338	3·2	1540	3·7	0553	5·2	1817	5·2	0243	3·9	1506	4·0
5	Tu	0536	6·9	1804	6·6	0253	8·5	1510	8·5	1059	11·9	2316	11·3	1010	6·6	2221	7·0	0416	3·2	1620	3·4	0636	4·9	1903	4·9	0332	3·6	1557	3·8
6	W	0614	6·5	1843	6·3	0332	8·0	1553	8·0	1130	11·1	2347	10·5	1049	6·3	2306	6·4	0456	3·0	1745	3·2	0721	4·4	1950	4·6	0425	3·4	1656	3·5
7	Th	0702	6·1	1933	6·0	0420	7·5	1648	7·5	—	—	1205	10·2	1136	5·9	—	—	0539	2·8	1837	2·9	0810	4·3	2044	4·4	0528	3·2	1809	3·2
8	F	0802	5·8	2033	5·7	0526	7·0	1808	7·0	0032	9·6	1304	9·3	0007	5·8	1243	5·6	0631	2·8	1958	2·6	0912	4·2	2159	4·3	0642	3·1	1927	3·2
9	Sa	0914	5·5	2142	5·5	0655	6·9	1945	6·9	0157	9·1	1444	9·1	0130	5·5	1405	5·6	0751	2·6	2204	2·5	1031	4·2	2321	4·3	0753	3·3	2035	3·2
10	Su	1048	5·5	2311	5·6	0818	7·0	2056	7·3	0339	9·4	1617	9·7	0307	5·5	1528	5·8	0934	2·6	2349	2·5	1146	4·4	—	—	0848	3·3	2126	3·3
11	M	—	—	1200	5·8	0915	7·8	2145	7·8	0454	10·4	1720	10·6	0421	6·2	1630	6·6	1038	2·7	—	—	0027	4·4	1245	4·6	0934	3·5	2207	3·4
12	Tu	0012	6·0	1246	6·1	0959	8·3	2224	8·3	0546	11·3	1810	11·4	0511	6·5	1713	6·6	1125	2·8	—	—	0116	4·6	1329	4·8	1011	3·7	2242	3·6
13	W	0057	6·3	1324	6·5	1037	8·7	2258	8·6	0629	12·1	1850	12·0	0549	6·5	1750	7·3	1204	3·0	—	—	0158	4·9	1439	5·1	1044	3·9	2312	3·7
14	Th	0135	6·6	1401	6·8	1111	9·0	2330	8·9	0707	12·5	1927	12·5	0621	6·8	1822	7·5	0024	3·0	1239	3·3	0234	5·0	1510	5·3	1117	4·0	2344	3·8
15	F	0210	6·9	1436	7·0	—	—	1217	9·5	0742	13·3	1959	13·2	0650	7·0	1853	7·7	0057	3·2	1311	3·5	0305	5·3	1542	5·5	1150	3·8	—	—
16	Sa	0246	7·1	1511	7·2	0001	9·2	1250	9·5	0816	13·4	2033	13·4	0721	7·3	1927	7·7	0129	3·2	1344	3·5	0334	5·4	1615	5·6	0015	3·9	1223	4·2
17	Su	0319	7·2	1545	7·3	0034	9·2	1324	9·5	0850	13·4	2107	13·2	0754	7·4	2001	7·7	0202	3·3	1417	3·5	0406	5·4	1652	5·6	0049	3·9	1258	4·2
18	M	0352	7·2	1619	7·2	0107	9·2	1359	9·4	0924	13·3	2139	13·0	0827	7·3	2036	7·5	0237	3·3	1451	3·4	0441	5·2	1734	5·5	0125	3·8	1336	4·2
19	Tu	0423	7·1	1652	6·9	0141	9·1	1439	9·0	0959	13·0	2213	12·6	0903	7·2	2112	7·3	0313	3·3	1528	3·3	0519	5·2	1818	5·4	0203	3·7	1418	4·1
20	W	0457	6·9	1729	6·6	0218	8·8	1525	8·5	1033	12·4	2247	12·0	0939	6·9	2153	6·9	0352	3·2	1607	3·1	0600	5·0	1908	5·2	0247	3·6	1506	3·9
21	Th	0533	6·7	1810	6·3	0258	8·0	1627	8·0	1109	11·6	2325	11·3	1021	6·6	2242	6·6	0433	3·2	1650	3·1	0647	4·8	2013	5·0	0338	3·4	1601	3·7
22	F	0619	6·4	1902	6·0	0350	8·0	1754	7·9	1156	10·8	—	—	1115	6·2	2349	6·4	0518	3·0	1738	3·0	0743	4·6	2137	4·7	0440	3·3	1711	3·5
23	Sa	0727	6·0	2019	5·8	0505	7·5	1930	7·6	0021	10·0	1316	10·1	0117	6·1	1409	5·9	0610	2·9	1838	2·8	0855	4·5	2304	4·7	0559	3·6	1840	3·4
24	Su	0858	5·9	2148	5·9	0642	7·4	2049	8·1	0157	10·0	1454	10·8	0305	6·6	1538	6·4	0715	2·9	2040	2·7	1024	4·7	—	—	0722	3·6	2006	3·4
25	M	1031	6·1	2313	6·2	0809	7·9	2149	8·7	0334	10·5	1624	10·9	0421	6·6	1638	6·7	0853	2·9	2215	3·1	1146	4·9	—	—	0834	3·8	2114	3·7
26	Tu	1153	6·6	—	—	0917	8·5	2238	9·1	0458	11·5	1737	11·5	0518	7·0	1725	6·7	1012	3·4	2315	3·1	0021	5·1	1250	5·1	0932	4·0	2208	3·6
27	W	0022	6·6	1255	6·9	1010	9·1	2320	9·2	0601	12·5	1834	12·8	0601	7·3	1804	7·2	1109	3·2	—	—	0119	5·4	1342	5·4	1022	4·0	2253	3·9
28	Th	0117	6·9	1345	7·2	1057	9·6	—	—	0653	13·3	1920	13·4	—	—	—	7·6	0002	3·2	1158	3·6	0207	5·5	1425	5·7	1106	4·2	2333	3·9

* All times shown are Greenwich Mean Time.   †Difference of height in metres from Ordnance Datum (Newlyn).
‡Difference of height in metres from Ordnance Datum (Dublin).

MARCH, 1991

High Water at the undermentioned Places (GMT*)—

Datums (below/above): London Bridge †3·20 m. below · Liverpool †4·93 m. below · Avonmouth †6·50 m. below · Hull (Albert Dock) †3·90 m. below · Greenock †1·62 m. below · Leith †2·90 m. below · Dun Laoghaire ‡0·20 m. above.

For each place: **Mn** = Morning (h.m. / Ht. m.), **Aft** = Afternoon (h.m. / Ht. m.).

Day	DoW	LB Mn h.m	m	LB Aft h.m	m	LV Mn h.m	m	LV Aft h.m	m	AV Mn h.m	m	AV Aft h.m	m	HU Mn h.m	m	HU Aft h.m	m	GR Mn h.m	m	GR Aft h.m	m	LE Mn h.m	m	LE Aft h.m	m	DL Mn h.m	m	DL Aft h.m	m
1	F	0204	7·1	1430	7·4	1137	9·8	2358	9·6	0737	13·7	1959	13·7	0641	7·4	1842	7·9	0044	3·3	1240	3·7	0248	5·6	1506	5·8	1148	4·3	1229	4·3
2	Sa	0243	7·3	1510	7·5	0035	9·5	1215	9·8	0813	13·9	2036	13·9	0716	7·5	1920	8·1	0121	3·4	1320	3·8	0326	5·7	1544	5·8	0011	4·0	1310	4·3
3	Su	0321	7·3	1546	7·4	0109	9·3	1252	9·7	0849	13·8	2108	13·8	0751	7·5	1958	8·0	0157	3·4	1358	3·7	0403	5·6	1622	5·7	0047	4·0	1352	4·1
4	M	0356	7·3	1620	7·2	0141	9·3	1326	9·4	0922	13·7	2141	13·7	0826	7·4	2036	7·8	0231	3·3	1434	3·6	0440	5·4	1702	5·5	0126	3·9	1433	3·9
5	Tu	0430	7·1	1651	6·9	0215	9·0	1358	8·9	0953	12·9	2210	12·7	0900	7·3	2112	7·6	0304	3·2	1509	3·4	0518	5·2	1744	4·9	0206	3·8	1518	3·8
6	W	0502	6·9	1723	6·7	0250	8·6	1432	8·4	1021	11·9	2235	11·9	0932	6·8	2149	7·3	0338	3·1	1545	3·2	0557	4·9	1823	4·6	0247	3·6	1609	3·6
7	Th	0539	6·6	1758	6·4	0332	8·1	1511	7·7	1048	10·6	2301	10·6	1004	6·4	2227	6·8	0413	2·9	1622	3·0	0636	4·6	1907	4·3	0335	3·4	1714	3·4
8	F	0622	6·2	1841	6·1	0431	7·6	1559	7·1	1116	10·1	2333	10·1	1042	6·0	2316	6·2	0450	2·8	1702	2·7	0718	4·4	1958	4·1	0429	3·2	1841	3·1
9	Sa	0717	5·8	1935	5·7	0600	7·0	1713	6·6			1203	8·8	1137	5·6			0534	2·6	1747	2·5	0816	4·2	2110	4·1	0539	3·1	2000	3·0
10	Su	0827	5·4	2046	5·4	0737	6·7	1904	6·6	0041	8·8	1342	9·2	0042	5·2	1310	5·6	0630	2·5	1847	2·3	0933	4·1	2238	4·3	0659	3·1	2054	3·0
11	M	0955	5·3	2214	5·4	0842	7·0	2026	6·6	0254	10·3	1538	11·0	0222	5·2	1437	5·4	0839	2·5	2130	2·6	1103	4·2	2352	4·4	0806	3·4	2135	3·4
12	Tu	1122	5·6	2337	5·7	0928	7·5	2115	7·6	0417	11·1	1645	11·7	0350	5·6	1550	5·6	1003	2·7	2236	2·6			1208	4·7	0857	3·8	2209	3·6
13	W			1214	6·0			2153	8·2	0511	12·0	1736	12·6	0441	6·1	1640	6·0	1054	3·1	2319	3·0	0045	4·6	1256	4·8	0938	4·0	2242	3·6
14	Th	0025	6·2	1253	6·5	1006	8·0	2228	8·6	0557	12·6	1819	13·1	0519	6·5	1719	6·5	1134	3·2			0127	4·8	1335	5·3	1014	4·2	2323	3·9
15	F	0106	6·6	1331	6·8	1041	8·7	2301	9·3	0638	13·1	1857	13·5	0551	6·9	1753	7·0	1210	3·1			0204	5·1	1409	5·5	1047	4·2	2345	4·0
16	Sa	0142	6·9	1406	7·1	1115	9·1	2334	9·4	0714	13·5	1934	13·5	0622	7·1	1827	7·3	0028	3·2	1244	3·4	0235	5·3	1441	5·5	1120	4·0		
17	Su	0218	7·2	1443	7·3	1150	9·4			0751	13·5	2008	13·5	0653	7·2	1900	7·6	0102	3·3	1318	3·4	0305	5·5	1513	5·5	1155	3·9	1232	4·2
18	M	0251	7·3	1518	7·3	0008	9·6	1225	9·7	0826	13·5	2043	12·8	0727	7·4	1937	7·8	0146	3·3	1353	3·3	0338	5·5	1550	5·4	0019	3·8	1313	4·1
19	Tu	0325	7·3	1553	7·3	0042	9·5	1302	9·4	0901	13·5	2118	12·4	0801	7·5	2013	7·8	0211	3·3	1430	3·3	0414	5·4	1630	5·2	0056	3·7	1357	4·0
20	W	0400	7·3	1630	7·0	0119	9·4	1340	9·0	0939	13·5	2153	11·7	0837	7·4	2054	7·7	0247	3·3	1508	3·0	0456	5·3	1715	5·1	0137	3·5	1449	3·9
21	Th	0440	7·0	1708	6·6	0158	9·4	1422	8·6	1016	12·8	2230	10·7	0917	7·3	2139	7·5	0327	3·2	1548	2·8	0540	5·1	1803	4·9	0222	3·4	1549	3·8
22	F	0523	6·7	1751	6·3	0242	9·0	1514	7·8	1058	12·1	2313	10·4	1000	7·0	2233	7·0	0409	3·1	1632	2·6	0628	4·9	1859	4·6	0315	3·6	1703	3·6
23	Sa	0617	6·3	1848	5·9	0338	8·6	1621	7·6	1151	11·3			1057	6·6	2343	6·6	0453	3·0	1722	3·0	0728	4·6	2008	4·5	0420	4·0	1835	3·4
24	Su	0727	6·0	2005	5·8	0457	8·0	1751	8·1	0017	10·1	1312	10·6			1212	6·2	0544	2·9	1831	3·2	0844	4·5	2135	4·5	0541	4·1	2000	3·3
25	M	0851	5·9	2128	5·9	0632	7·5	1924	9·1	0148	10·6	1444	11·8	0124	6·2	1355	5·9	0650	2·9	2045		1013	4·5	2300		0708	4·2	2105	3·3
26	Tu	1020	6·2	2254	6·2	0757	7·5	2037	9·4	0324	11·7	1613	12·7	0303	6·0	1519	5·9	0832	3·1	2204		1133	4·8			0821		2156	3·6
27	W	1137	6·7			0901	8·1			0444	12·0	1720	13·1	0410	6·6	1619	6·3	0951	3·2	2257		0007	5·0	1235	5·1	0921		2237	3·8
28	Th	0003	6·6	1238	7·1	0952	8·7	2217	9·4	0543	12·5	1812	13·2	0501	6·9	1704	6·8	1049	3·3	2341		0101	5·2	1324	5·4	1008		2313	3·9
29	F	0057	7·0	1327	7·3	1034	9·1	2257		0632	13·1	1857	13·4	0542	7·1	1742	7·2	1136	3·5			0146	5·4	1405	5·6	1052		2347	4·0
30	Sa	0141	7·1	1408	7·4	1113	9·4	2333		0713	13·4	1934	13·5	0615	7·3	1818	7·5	0020	3·3	1218	3·5	0225	5·5	1442	5·7	1130			
31	Su	0220	7·2	1444	7·3	1150	9·5			0749		2008				1856	7·7	0055	3·3	1256	3·5	0300	5·5	1519				1208	4·2

* All times shown are Greenwich Mean Time.   † Difference of height in metres from Ordnance Datum (Newlyn).
‡ Difference of height in metres from Ordnance Datum (Dublin).

APRIL, 1991

High Water at the undermentioned Places (GMT*)—

Day of Month	Day of Week	LONDON BRIDGE †Datum of Predictions 3.20 m. below				LIVERPOOL †Datum of Predictions 4.93 m. below				AVONMOUTH †Datum of Predictions 6.50 m. below				HULL (Albert Dock) †Datum of Predictions 3.90 m. below				GREENOCK †Datum of Predictions 1.62 m. below				LEITH †Datum of Predictions 2.90 m. below				DUN LAOGHAIRE ‡Datum of Predictions 0.20 m. above			
		Mn. h.m.	Ht. m.	Aft. h.m.	Ht. m.	Mn. h.m.	Ht. m.	Aft. h.m.	Ht. m.	Mn. h.m.	Ht. m.	Aft. h.m.	Ht. m.	Mn. h.m.	Ht. m.	Aft. h.m.	Ht. m.	Mn. h.m.	Ht. m.	Aft. h.m.	Ht. m.	Mn. h.m.	Ht. m.	Aft. h.m.	Ht. m.	Mn. h.m.	Ht. m.	Aft. h.m.	Ht. m.
1	M	0256	7.2	1518	7.2	0007	9.4	1224	9.4	0822	13.4	2040	13.3	0723	7.4	1934	7.7	0129	3.2	1332	3.4	0334	5.4	1556	5.5	0021	3.9	1246	4.1
2	Tu	0329	7.2	1549	7.1	0039	9.2	1256	9.1	0853	13.0	2110	12.8	0755	7.3	2012	7.4	0201	3.2	1406	3.3	0409	5.3	1634	5.3	0056	3.9	1325	3.9
3	W	0400	7.0	1617	6.9	0110	9.0	1328	8.7	0922	12.5	2138	12.5	0827	7.1	2047	7.3	0232	3.1	1440	3.1	0444	5.1	1711	5.1	0132	3.8	1404	3.7
4	Th	0433	6.8	1647	6.7	0142	8.7	1401	8.3	0950	11.7	2203	12.1	0858	6.8	2122	6.8	0303	3.0	1513	2.9	0519	4.9	1750	4.8	0211	3.6	1446	3.5
5	F	0509	6.6	1719	6.5	0216	8.3	1439	7.8	1017	11.0	2228	11.4	0928	6.1	2157	6.1	0336	2.9	1549	2.8	0556	4.6	1833	4.5	0254	3.5	1533	3.3
6	Sa	0550	6.3	1758	6.2	0257	7.8	1524	7.3	1045	10.2	2259	10.5	1002	5.7	2242	5.7	0413	2.7	1628	2.6	0640	4.2	1924	4.3	0345	3.3	1631	3.1
7	Su	0639	5.9	1846	5.8	0350	7.2	1630	6.7	1127	9.8	2357	9.8	1049	5.6	2358	5.4	0454	2.6	1713	2.5	0734	4.1	2029	4.2	0443	3.3	1745	3.0
8	M	0741	5.6	1948	5.5	0508	6.9	1805	6.6			1246	8.8			1215	5.7	0545	2.6	1811	2.4	0844	4.1	2146	4.1	0557	3.1	1906	3.0
9	Tu	0901	5.4	2117	5.4	0638	7.0	1933	7.0	0155	8.9	1443	9.1	0133	5.5	1347	5.9	0704	2.5	2015	2.4	1002	4.2	2300	4.3	0709	3.2	2007	3.0
10	W	1023	5.6	2241	5.6	0751	7.5	2029	7.5	0327	9.8	1556	9.8	0254	5.8	1458	6.4	0904	2.6	2145	2.6	1114	4.4	2358	4.5	0809	3.2	2053	3.2
11	Th	1126	6.0	2340	6.0	0843	8.1	2112	8.1	0426	10.8	1651	11.0	0355	6.2	1553	6.9	1006	2.8	2236	2.8			1209	4.7	0854	3.4	2131	3.4
12	F			1214	6.4	0925	8.6	2150	8.5	0515	11.8	1740	12.0	0437	6.5	1638	7.1	1053	2.8	2316	2.8	0044	4.8	1254	5.3	0935	3.8	2207	3.6
13	Sa	0027	6.5	1256	6.8	1004	9.0	2227	9.0	0601	12.5	1824	12.7	0513	6.9	1718	7.5	1134	3.0	2354	3.1	0124	5.1	1332	5.5	1012	4.0	2242	3.8
14	Su	0107	6.8	1335	7.1	1042	9.3	2304	9.3	0643	13.2	1903	13.2	0550	7.1	1757	7.7	1213	3.2			0158	5.3	1408	5.7	1050	4.1	2316	4.0
15	M	0145	7.1	1413	7.2	1122	9.6	2342	9.5	0723	13.5	1942	13.6	0625	7.5	1836	7.7	0031	3.3	1251	3.3	0234	5.5	1446	5.8	1128	4.2	2352	4.1
16	Tu	0223	7.3	1451	7.3			1201	9.7	0802	13.6	2020	13.6	0702	7.6	1916	7.6	0108	3.4	1330	3.4	0351	5.5	1527	5.7			1209	4.1
17	W	0303	7.5	1529	7.3	0021	9.6	1243	9.7	0843	13.5	2100	13.4	0740	7.7	1958	7.3	0146	3.4	1410	3.4	0436	5.5	1612	5.5	0032	4.1	1254	4.1
18	Th	0345	7.4	1612	7.0	0102	9.4	1327	9.4	0925	13.1	2141	13.0	0819	7.3	2043	7.0	0225	3.3	1451	3.3	0526	5.2	1702	5.2	0115	4.0	1344	4.0
19	F	0430	7.2	1657	6.7	0145	9.1	1415	8.9	1009	12.7	2226	12.4	0901	6.7	2134	6.7	0306	3.3	1535	3.3	0620	5.0	1757	5.0	0206	3.9	1440	3.8
20	Sa	0522	6.9	1746	6.3	0236	8.7	1511	8.4	1057	11.6	2316	11.4	0950	6.3	2231	6.6	0349	3.2	1624	3.2	0723	4.7	1856	4.7	0303	3.8	1543	3.6
21	Su	0621	6.5	1845	6.1	0336	8.2	1621	7.8	1154	10.8			1047	6.3	2343	6.2	0436	3.1	1720	3.1	0836	4.7	2005	4.7	0409	3.6	1659	3.4
22	M	0727	6.3	1952	6.0	0451	7.8	1743	7.6	0019	10.3	1306	10.7	0121	6.0	1331	6.1	0529	3.0	1842	3.0	1108	4.8	2121	4.8	0525	3.5	1826	3.4
23	Tu	0840	6.2	2107	6.0	0614	7.8	1904	7.8	0138	10.4	1427	10.5	0243	6.5	1451	6.0	0636	3.0	2025	3.0			2237	5.0	0648	3.5	1944	3.4
24	W	0959	6.4	2227	6.2	0731	8.1	2012	8.1	0303	11.1	1548	11.6	0346	6.8	1550	6.4	0805	3.1	2136	3.1	0033	5.2	2341	5.3	0800	3.7	2045	3.6
25	Th	1113	6.6	2337	6.6	0830	8.5	2105	8.5	0417	11.6	1652	12.3	0435	7.0	1637	6.5	0922	3.2	2229	3.2	0119	5.3	1209	5.4	0858	3.8	2134	3.6
26	F			1212	7.0	0924	8.8	2150	8.8	0516	12.2	1744	12.9	0515	7.1	1719	6.8	1021	3.3	2313	3.3	0156	5.3	1257	5.5	0948	3.9	2214	3.8
27	Sa	0032	6.9	1302	7.1	1007	9.0	2230	9.0	0604	12.7	1829	12.7	0550	7.1	1757	7.1	1110	3.3	2352	3.3	0232	5.4	1340	5.3	1032	4.0	2250	3.9
28	Su	0117	7.0	1342	7.1	1047	9.1	2305	9.1	0646	12.7	1907	12.9	0624	7.2	1836	7.1	1154	3.2			0306	5.3	1418	5.4	1110	3.9	2321	3.9
29	M	0157	7.0	1419	7.1	1123	9.1	2340	9.0	0723	12.7	1941	12.8	0656	7.2	1914	7.2	0028	3.1	1233	3.2			1455	5.5	1147	3.9	2354	3.8
30	Tu	0232	7.0	1450	7.0	1158	9.0			0755	12.7	2013	12.8					0101	3.1	1309	3.1			1532	5.3			1223	3.8

* All times shown are Greenwich Mean Time.   †Difference of height in metres from Ordnance Datum (Newlyn).   ‡Difference of height in metres from Ordnance Datum (Dublin).

M A Y, 1 9 9 1

High Water at the undermentioned Places (GMT*)—

Datum of Predictions (below/above Ordnance Datum), times in h.m. (GMT), heights in m.:
- London Bridge †3·20 m. below
- Liverpool †4·93 m. below
- Avonmouth †6·50 m. below
- Hull (Albert Dock) †3·90 m. below
- Greenock †1·62 m. below
- Leith †2·90 m. below
- Dun Laoghaire ‡0·20 m. above

Day of Month	Day of Week	London Bridge Mn.	Ht.	Aft.	Ht.	Liverpool Mn.	Ht.	Aft.	Ht.	Avonmouth Mn.	Ht.	Aft.	Ht.	Hull Mn.	Ht.	Aft.	Ht.	Greenock Mn.	Ht.	Aft.	Ht.	Leith Mn.	Ht.	Aft.	Ht.	Dun Laoghaire Mn.	Ht.	Aft.	Ht.
1	W	0304	6·9	1519	6·8	0012	9·0	1231	8·8	0827	12·5	2043	12·4	0730	7·1	1952	6·9	0133	3·1	1342	3·0	0340	5·2	1609	5·2	0028	3·8	1300	3·7
2	Th	0336	6·8	1546	6·7	0045	8·9	1304	8·5	0857	12·1	2112	12·0	0801	6·9	2027	6·6	0204	3·1	1415	2·9	0415	5·1	1647	5·0	0104	3·8	1339	3·5
3	F	0410	6·7	1617	6·5	0117	8·7	1338	8·2	0927	11·5	2141	11·4	0830	6·7	2103	6·3	0236	3·0	1449	2·8	0450	4·9	1726	4·8	0143	3·7	1418	3·4
4	Sa	0447	6·5	1651	6·3	0154	8·4	1415	7·9	0957	10·8	2212	10·8	0901	6·5	2139	6·0	0309	3·0	1525	2·8	0528	4·7	1808	4·6	0224	3·6	1503	3·2
5	Su	0527	6·3	1729	5·9	0233	8·0	1458	7·5	1031	10·4	2248	9·8	0938	6·2	2224	5·7	0346	2·9	1606	2·7	0612	4·5	1856	4·4	0310	3·5	1554	3·1
6	M	0611	6·1	1812	5·7	0322	7·6	1555	7·1	1113	9·8	2340	9·7	1026	5·9	2323	5·5	0428	2·9	1653	2·6	0702	4·4	1951	4·3	0401	3·4	1655	3·1
7	Tu	0703	5·9	1903	5·7	0424	7·3	1706	6·9			1215	9·4	1132	5·7			0516	2·8	1751	2·6	0802	4·3	2055	4·2	0502	3·3	1804	3·1
8	W	0806	5·7	2012	5·7	0537	7·3	1824	7·1	0057	9·5	1338	9·4	0041	5·5	1255	5·7	0618	2·7	1911	2·6	0907	4·3	2200	4·3	0607	3·3	1912	3·2
9	Th	0921	5·7	2136	5·9	0648	7·5	1928	7·5	0225	10·0	1458	10·1	0152	5·6	1405	6·0	0746	2·7	2041	2·7	1013	4·5	2301	4·5	0712	3·4	2004	3·4
10	F	1030	6·0	2245	6·3	0747	8·0	2022	8·0	0332	10·8	1600	11·0	0254	6·0	1503	6·3	0906	2·8	2144	2·8	1114	4·7	2354	4·8	0807	3·6	2050	3·6
11	Sa	1127	6·4	2342	6·0	0839	8·4	2108	8·5	0428	11·6	1655	11·8	0346	6·4	1555	6·7	1006	2·9	2234	2·9			1206	5·0	0855	3·8	2131	3·8
12	Su			1218	6·7	0925	9·0	2152	9·0	0522	12·3	1746	12·5	0434	6·7	1644	7·0	1056	3·1	2318	3·1	0040	5·0	1252	5·2	0939	3·9	2209	4·0
13	M	0031	6·7	1304	6·9	1012	9·3	2235	9·3	0611	12·9	1834	13·0	0518	7·0	1730	7·3	1142	3·1			0122	5·2	1338	5·5	1022	4·0	2249	4·1
14	Tu	0116	6·9	1347	7·2	1057	9·5	2319	9·5	0657	13·3	1919	13·5	0600	7·2	1817	7·5	0001	3·2	1227	3·2	0204	5·4	1424	5·6	1105	4·1	2328	4·1
15	W	0201	7·1	1430	7·3	1143	9·6			0744	13·4	2002	13·6	0642	7·3	1903	7·5	0043	3·3	1311	3·3	0247	5·5	1511	5·7	1151	4·1		
16	Th	0246	7·3	1514	7·3	0004	9·6	1231	9·6	0830	13·4	2049	13·4	0724	7·3	1951	7·5	0124	3·4	1355	3·4	0333	5·5	1601	5·7	0012	4·1	1242	4·0
17	F	0335	7·4	1600	7·4	0050	9·6	1320	9·3	0917	13·1	2135	13·0	0808	7·3	2040	7·3	0206	3·5	1441	3·5	0422	5·5	1654	5·5	0101	4·1	1335	3·9
18	Sa	0427	7·3	1649	7·3	0140	9·3	1412	9·0	1006	12·6	2223	12·5	0854	7·1	2132	7·1	0250	3·5	1529	3·6	0516	5·3	1749	5·3	0154	4·0	1433	3·8
19	Su	0520	7·1	1742	7·1	0233	8·9	1508	8·5	1055	11·9	2315	11·9	0942	6·7	2228	6·7	0336	3·5	1621	3·6	0613	5·0	1847	5·1	0253	3·8	1535	3·6
20	M	0617	6·9	1835	6·9	0331	8·6	1612	8·1	1150	11·3			1037	6·5	2334	6·5	0424	3·4	1719	3·5	0713	5·0	1948	4·9	0356	3·7	1646	3·5
21	Tu	0716	6·6	1933	6·6	0435	8·3	1719	7·8	0012	11·4	1249	10·9	1139	6·2			0517	3·4	1829	3·4	0816	4·8	2054	4·8	0507	3·7	1803	3·5
22	W	0818	6·4	2037	6·4	0544	8·1	1829	7·8	0117	11·0	1357	10·7	0056	6·2	1256	6·4	0618	3·3	1947	3·5	0925	4·8	2204	4·8	0623	3·7	1915	3·4
23	Th	0928	6·3	2152	6·5	0655	8·1	1935	8·0	0227	11·0	1508	10·9	0209	6·4	1413	6·7	0731	3·2	2055	3·6	1032	5·0	2307	4·9	0733	3·7	2016	3·5
24	F	1040	6·5	2304	6·7	0758	8·2	2032	8·4	0338	11·3	1614	11·3	0310	6·5	1517	6·7	0845	3·2	2152	3·6	1135	5·0			0832	3·8	2107	3·6
25	Sa	1142	6·7			0853	8·3	2119	8·4	0440	11·5	1709	11·6	0402	6·5	1610	6·8	0949	3·1	2241	3·7	0000	5·1	1227	5·1	0925	3·8	2149	3·7
26	Su	0003	6·6	1232	6·6	0941	8·6	2202	8·8	0532	11·7	1757	11·9	0445	6·7	1658	6·8	1044	3·0	2324	3·8	0048	5·1	1314	5·2	1009	3·7	2226	3·8
27	M	0052	6·6	1316	6·6	1023	8·6	2241	8·8	0618	11·9	1839	12·1	0525	6·8	1742	6·9	1131	3·0			0130	5·1	1357	5·2	1052	3·7	2259	3·8
28	Tu	0133	6·7	1352	6·7	1101	8·6	2318	8·9	0657	12·0	1917	12·2	0601	6·8	1822	6·9	0003	3·1	1214	2·9	0208	5·1	1437	5·1	1128	3·8	2333	3·8
29	W	0211	6·7	1425	6·7	1137	8·6	2351	8·9	0734	12·0	1952	12·2	0636	6·9	1902	6·9	0039	3·1	1251	2·9	0244	5·1	1515	5·1				
30	Th	0246	6·7	1456	6·7			1212	8·4	0808	12·0	2025	12·1	0709	6·9	1938	6·8	0113	3·1	1326	2·8	0318	5·1	1552	5·0	0006	3·8	1204	3·6
31	F	0319	6·7	1527	6·7	0027	8·8	1246	8·4	0840	11·8	2056	11·9	0740	6·8	2012	6·8	0146	3·1	1400	2·8	0352	5·1	1630	5·0	0042	3·8	1317	3·5

* All times shown are Greenwich Mean Time.　†Difference of height in metres from Ordnance Datum (Newlyn).　‡Difference of height in metres from Ordnance Datum (Dublin).

JUNE, 1991

High Water at the undermentioned Places (GMT*)—

Datum of Predictions: London Bridge †3·20 m. below · Liverpool †4·93 m. below · Avonmouth †6·50 m. below · Hull (Albert Dock) †3·90 m. below · Greenock †1·62 m. below · Leith †2·90 m. below · Dun Laoghaire ‡0·20 m. above

Day of Month	Day of Week	London Bridge Mn. h.m.	Ht. m.	Aft. h.m.	Ht. m.	Liverpool Mn. h.m.	Ht. m.	Aft. h.m.	Ht. m.	Avonmouth Mn. h.m.	Ht. m.	Aft. h.m.	Ht. m.	Hull Mn. h.m.	Ht. m.	Aft. h.m.	Ht. m.	Greenock Mn. h.m.	Ht. m.	Aft. h.m.	Ht. m.	Leith Mn. h.m.	Ht. m.	Aft. h.m.	Ht. m.	Dun Laoghaire Mn. h.m.	Ht. m.	Aft. h.m.	Ht. m.
1	Sa	0355	6·7	1559	6·6	0100	8·7	1321	8·3	0912	11·6	2128	11·6	0812	6·8	2047	6·4	0219	3·1	1435	2·8	0428	5·0	1706	4·9	0120	3·7	1356	3·4
2	Su	0431	6·6	1634	6·5	0137	8·5	1358	8·1	0946	11·3	2203	11·3	0846	6·7	2125	6·3	0253	3·1	1512	2·8	0506	4·9	1745	4·7	0200	3·7	1438	3·3
3	M	0509	6·5	1711	6·4	0215	8·3	1439	7·8	1021	11·0	2241	11·0	0925	6·5	2206	6·1	0330	3·1	1554	2·9	0549	4·8	1828	4·6	0242	3·6	1521	3·3
4	Tu	0549	6·4	1749	6·3	0258	8·1	1524	7·6	1102	10·6	2325	10·6	1009	6·3	2254	5·9	0411	3·0	1640	2·9	0633	4·7	1915	4·5	0328	3·6	1611	3·2
5	W	0632	6·2	1832	6·1	0348	7·9	1619	7·4	1149	10·3	—	—	1059	6·1	2350	5·8	0456	3·0	1732	2·8	0723	4·6	2008	4·4	0417	3·5	1710	3·2
6	Th	0721	6·0	1923	5·9	0444	7·7	1720	7·4	0018	10·2	1246	10·3	—	—	1201	6·1	0547	2·9	1832	2·8	0819	4·6	2105	4·5	0514	3·5	1814	3·3
7	F	0823	5·9	2033	5·8	0547	7·8	1828	7·6	0124	10·3	1357	10·5	0055	5·8	1310	6·3	0648	2·9	1940	2·9	0918	4·6	2206	4·6	0617	3·6	1915	3·3
8	Sa	0935	6·0	2150	6·0	0653	8·0	1931	7·9	0237	10·7	1508	10·8	0159	6·0	1415	6·6	0802	2·8	2049	2·9	1019	4·7	2305	4·7	0720	3·6	2009	3·6
9	Su	1042	6·2	2258	6·2	0755	8·3	2029	8·4	0343	11·3	1613	11·5	0300	6·3	1515	7·0	0916	2·9	2150	3·0	1121	4·9	—	—	0818	3·6	2057	3·7
10	M	1143	6·5	2358	6·5	0853	8·7	2122	8·8	0444	11·9	1712	12·1	0357	6·6	1611	7·2	1020	3·0	2244	3·1	0000	4·9	1220	5·1	0911	3·8	2142	3·7
11	Tu	—	—	1238	6·7	0946	9·0	2213	9·2	0542	12·4	1808	12·7	0451	6·8	1711	7·4	1116	3·1	2334	3·2	0052	5·1	1315	5·3	1000	3·9	2225	4·0
12	W	0053	6·7	1328	6·8	1040	9·3	2304	9·5	0638	13·2	1900	13·4	0540	7·1	1805	7·5	1208	3·2	—	—	0141	5·3	1409	5·5	1049	4·0	2310	4·1
13	Th	0147	7·0	1416	7·1	1130	9·5	2353	9·6	0731	13·3	1951	13·5	0628	7·2	1857	7·5	0020	3·4	1258	3·3	0231	5·5	1501	5·6	1138	4·0	2358	4·2
14	F	0239	7·2	1504	7·3	—	—	1222	9·4	0822	13·5	2040	13·3	0713	7·4	1947	7·4	0106	3·5	1346	3·3	0321	5·6	1553	5·6	—	—	1226	4·2
15	Sa	0329	7·4	1552	7·4	0043	9·6	1313	9·2	0910	13·0	2128	13·0	0758	7·5	2036	7·2	0152	3·7	1434	3·3	0410	5·4	1644	5·6	0043	4·2	1326	3·9
16	Su	0420	7·5	1640	7·5	0133	9·5	1404	8·8	0957	12·9	2216	12·5	0843	7·5	2124	6·9	0237	3·7	1521	3·2	0504	5·5	1735	5·3	0143	4·2	1421	3·8
17	M	0511	7·4	1727	7·4	0223	9·3	1454	8·3	1044	12·5	2302	12·0	0929	7·3	2214	6·6	0323	3·7	1610	3·2	0556	5·2	1828	5·3	0240	4·1	1518	3·7
18	Tu	0601	7·2	1815	7·1	0314	9·0	1548	8·0	1132	11·9	2351	11·3	1017	7·1	2311	6·3	0410	3·6	1702	3·1	0652	5·0	1924	5·1	0338	4·0	1621	3·5
19	W	0652	6·8	1906	6·8	0407	8·6	1644	7·8	—	—	1221	11·3	1112	6·9	—	—	0500	3·6	1757	3·1	0749	5·0	2022	4·9	0442	3·9	1728	3·5
20	Th	0747	6·5	2002	6·4	0506	8·2	1746	8·0	0043	10·8	1316	10·5	0014	6·3	1215	6·2	0553	3·4	1859	2·9	0849	4·9	2123	4·8	0550	3·6	1838	3·4
21	F	0847	6·3	2108	6·3	0611	7·8	1852	8·1	0142	10·5	1418	10·4	0120	6·1	1328	6·1	0652	3·2	2005	2·9	0953	4·8	2226	4·8	0659	3·6	1941	3·5
22	Sa	0956	6·3	2223	6·2	0719	7·8	1955	8·3	0249	10·6	1527	10·6	0223	6·1	1440	6·2	0801	3·0	2110	2·9	1057	4·8	2325	4·8	0804	3·6	2037	3·5
23	Su	1105	6·3	2332	6·3	0822	7·9	2051	8·3	0356	10·7	1631	10·8	0322	6·1	1545	6·4	0913	2·9	2208	2·9	1158	4·8	—	—	0902	3·6	2124	3·6
24	M	—	—	1203	6·3	0917	8·1	2139	8·5	0458	10·9	1727	11·2	0416	6·3	1641	6·6	1019	2·9	2259	3·0	0020	4·8	1252	4·9	0952	3·6	2205	3·7
25	Tu	0028	6·3	1249	6·4	1004	8·3	2221	8·7	0551	11·5	1815	11·6	0502	6·5	1730	6·7	1115	2·8	2343	3·0	0107	5·0	1341	5·0	1035	3·6	2242	3·7
26	W	0113	6·4	1330	6·5	1045	8·5	2301	8·8	0638	12·0	1859	12·0	0544	6·6	1814	6·9	1201	2·8	—	—	0149	5·0	1424	5·1	1112	3·6	2314	3·8
27	Th	0154	6·5	1405	6·6	1123	8·7	2337	8·8	0719	12·1	1937	12·1	0621	6·8	1852	7·0	0023	3·1	1242	2·8	0227	5·1	1504	5·1	1148	3·5	2348	3·8
28	F	0230	6·6	1439	6·7	1158	8·9	—	—	0755	11·8	2011	11·8	0653	6·9	1924	7·0	0100	3·1	1318	2·8	0304	5·1	1539	5·1	—	—	1222	3·5
29	Sa	0305	6·7	1512	6·7	0011	8·9	1232	8·5	0827	11·9	2043	11·9	0724	7·0	1957	6·9	0134	3·2	1351	3·0	0337	5·1	1613	5·1	0023	3·8	1256	3·5
30	Su	0341	6·7	1548	6·7	0046	8·9	1306	8·9	0900	12·1	2115	12·1	0757	7·0	2029	6·8	0207	3·2	1425	3·0	0410	5·1	1645	5·0	0058	3·9	1332	3·5

* All times shown are Greenwich Mean Time.
† Difference of height in metres from Ordnance Datum (Newlyn).
‡ Difference of height in metres from Ordnance Datum (Dublin).

J U L Y , 1991

High Water at the undermentioned Places (GMT*)—

Day of Month	Day of Week	London Bridge †Datum of Predictions 3.20 m. below				Liverpool †Datum of Predictions 4.93 m. below				Avonmouth †Datum of Predictions 6.50 m. below				Hull (Albert Dock) †Datum of Predictions 3.90 m. below				Greenock †Datum of Predictions 1.62 m. below				Leith †Datum of Predictions 2.90 m. below				Dun Laoghaire ‡Datum of Predictions 0.20 m. above			
		Mn. h.m.	Ht. m.	Aft. h.m.	Ht. m.	Mn. h.m.	Ht. m.	Aft. h.m.	Ht. m.	Mn. h.m.	Ht. m.	Aft. h.m.	Ht. m.	Mn. h.m.	Ht. m.	Aft. h.m.	Ht. m.	Mn. h.m.	Ht. m.	Aft. h.m.	Ht. m.	Mn. h.m.	Ht. m.	Aft. h.m.	Ht. m.	Mn. h.m.	Ht. m.	Aft. h.m.	Ht. m.
1	M	0416	6.7	1621	6.7	0121	8.8	1340	8.4	0932	11.9	2150	12.0	0830	7.0	2105	6.7	0241	3.2	1501	3.0	0445	5.1	1722	4.9	0135	3.9	1408	3.5
2	Tu	0451	6.7	1654	6.6	0157	8.7	1415	8.3	1007	11.7	2226	11.7	0908	6.9	2142	6.5	0316	3.2	1539	3.1	0523	5.0	1800	4.8	0213	3.8	1449	3.5
3	W	0526	6.5	1727	6.5	0233	8.5	1453	8.1	1042	11.4	2302	11.0	0948	6.7	2223	6.4	0353	3.2	1621	3.1	0605	4.9	1842	4.7	0254	3.8	1533	3.4
4	Th	0603	6.4	1803	6.4	0312	8.4	1536	7.9	1120	11.1	2343	11.0	1030	6.5	2308	6.2	0434	3.1	1706	3.0	0648	4.9	1927	4.6	0339	3.7	1624	3.4
5	F	0643	6.2	1845	6.2	0400	8.2	1630	7.8			1203	10.5	1118	6.3			0519	3.1	1755	3.0	0737	4.8	2019	4.6	0432	3.7	1723	3.4
6	Sa	0735	6.0	1942	6.0	0457	8.0	1734	7.7	0032	10.7	1259	10.5	0000	6.0	1218	6.2	0609	3.0	1851	2.9	0832	4.7	2118	4.6	0533	3.6	1828	3.4
7	Su	0846	5.9	2101	6.0	0605	7.9	1849	7.8	0141	10.5	1416	10.5	0107	6.0	1330	6.2	0708	2.8	1956	2.9	0936	4.7	2223	4.8	0642	3.6	1933	3.5
8	M	1000	5.9	2221	6.1	0720	8.1	1959	8.1	0301	10.8	1535	11.0	0219	6.1	1446	6.4	0827	2.8	2108	2.9	1048	4.8	2330	4.9	0751	3.6	2030	3.7
9	Tu	1112	6.2	2334	6.4	0830	8.4	2103	8.6	0413	11.4	1644	11.7	0329	6.3	1557	6.6	0951	2.9	2214	3.1			1200	4.9	0851	3.7	2122	3.8
10	W			1217	6.6	0932	8.8	2200	9.0	0522	12.0	1750	13.0	0433	6.6	1704	6.9	1100	3.0	2312	3.3	0033	5.0	1304	5.2	0948	3.8	2211	4.0
11	Th	0042	6.6	1314	6.9	1030	9.2	2254	9.4	0625	12.6	1849	13.5	0527	7.0	1800	7.0	1157	3.2			0129	5.3	1402	5.4	1040	3.9	2258	4.1
12	F	0140	6.9	1406	7.2	1123	9.4	2344	9.6	0721	13.1	1942	13.7	0615	7.3	1850	7.5	0004	3.3	1249	3.4	0221	5.5	1455	5.6	1130	3.9	2347	4.3
13	Sa	0232	7.2	1454	7.4			1212	9.6	0812	13.4	2029	13.7	0700	7.6	1937	7.6	0052	3.5	1336	3.5	0310	5.7	1542	5.8			1221	4.0
14	Su	0321	7.4	1539	7.5	0032	9.9	1300	9.6	0858	13.5	2114	13.4	0742	7.8	2022	7.5	0139	3.7	1421	3.5	0357	5.8	1629	5.8	0037	4.0	1310	4.0
15	M	0407	7.5	1624	7.5	0119	9.8	1345	9.4	0942	13.3	2157	12.9	0825	7.8	2105	7.4	0222	3.8	1505	3.4	0445	5.7	1716	5.6	0129	4.4	1401	3.9
16	Tu	0454	7.4	1706	7.3	0204	9.6	1429	9.2	1024	12.9	2240	12.2	0908	7.7	2149	7.1	0306	3.9	1548	3.4	0535	5.4	1804	5.3	0220	4.4	1453	3.8
17	W	0537	7.2	1749	7.0	0247	9.2	1514	8.6	1105	12.3	2320	11.5	0953	7.5	2234	6.7	0350	3.8	1632	3.3	0626	5.4	1854	5.1	0313	4.3	1547	3.8
18	Th	0621	6.8	1834	6.7	0332	8.8	1600	8.2	1144	11.5			1041	7.1	2325	6.4	0435	3.6	1718	3.0	0718	5.1	1946	4.9	0410	4.2	1647	3.7
19	F	0707	6.5	1923	6.4	0421	8.4	1654	7.7	0003	10.6	1227	10.8	1134	6.6			0521	3.4	1808	3.0	0812	4.7	2041	4.7	0513	4.0	1755	3.7
20	Sa	0801	6.2	2022	6.1	0520	7.9	1800	7.4	0049	9.8	1320	10.1	0022	6.1	1243	6.2	0611	3.1	1906	2.9	0911	4.7	2143	4.5	0624	3.7	1902	3.5
21	Su	0901	6.0	2134	5.9	0635	7.6	1916	7.4	0149	9.8	1432	9.8	0128	5.9	1401	5.9	0710	2.9	2020	2.8	1020	4.5	2251	4.5	0736	3.5	2004	3.4
22	M	1014	5.8	2259	5.8	0754	7.3	2025	7.6	0308	9.8	1553	9.8	0239	5.9	1521	5.9	0832	2.7	2137	2.8	1132	4.5	2355	4.6	0841	3.6	2058	3.5
23	Tu	1130	5.9			0858	7.6	2121	8.0	0428	10.2	1702	10.7	0346	6.1	1628	6.0	1001	2.7	2238	3.0			1234	4.6	0934	3.7	2144	3.6
24	W	0005	6.0	1225	6.1	0950	7.9	2206	8.4	0530	10.8	1756	11.4	0441	6.3	1719	6.3	1105	2.8			0049	4.7	1326	4.7	1018	3.5	2222	3.8
25	Th	0055	6.2	1309	6.5	1031	8.3	2245	8.7	0619	11.3	1841	11.9	0526	6.6	1801	6.6	0010	3.1	1232	2.9	0134	4.9	1410	4.9	1053	3.5	2255	3.8
26	F	0135	6.4	1347	6.7	1108	8.5	2320	8.9	0702	11.7	1920	12.2	0603	6.8	1836	6.8	0047	3.1	1306	3.0	0214	5.0	1449	5.0	1127	3.6	2327	3.9
27	Sa	0212	6.6	1422	6.9	1142	8.6	2354	9.1	0738	12.0	1954	12.4	0635	7.0	1906	7.0	0120	3.3	1337	3.1	0247	5.1	1521	5.2	1158	3.6	2359	4.0
28	Su	0246	6.8	1456	6.9			1212	9.2	0811	12.2	2025	12.6	0704	7.2	1935	7.2	0152	3.3	1409	3.2	0318	5.3	1552	5.2			1229	3.7
29	M	0321	6.9	1529	6.9	0027	9.2	1245	9.2	0840	12.4	2056	12.7	0737	7.3	2006	7.3	0224	3.4	1442	3.2	0348	5.3	1622	5.2	0033	4.0	1301	3.7
30	Tu	0355	6.9	1602	6.9	0059	9.2	1316	9.1	0912	12.5	2129	12.6	0811	7.3	2040	7.0	0257	3.4	1518	3.3	0421	5.3	1654	5.2	0107	4.0	1337	3.7
31	W	0427	6.9	1631	6.8	0131	9.1	1348	8.7	0945	12.3	2203	12.4	0844	7.2	2114	6.9					0457	5.3	1731	5.0	0144	4.0	1414	3.7

* All times shown are Greenwich Mean Time. †Difference of height in metres from Ordnance Datum (Newlyn). ‡Difference of height in metres from Ordnance Datum (Dublin).

AUGUST, 1991

High Water at the undermentioned Places (GMT*)—

Day of Month	Day of Week	LONDON BRIDGE †Datum 3·20 m. below Mn. h.m.	Ht. m.	Aft. h.m.	Ht. m.	LIVERPOOL †Datum 4·93 m. below Mn. h.m.	Ht. m.	Aft. h.m.	Ht. m.	AVONMOUTH †Datum 6·50 m. below Mn. h.m.	Ht. m.	Aft. h.m.	Ht. m.	HULL (Albert Dock) †Datum 3·90 m. below Mn. h.m.	Ht. m.	Aft. h.m.	Ht. m.	GREENOCK †Datum 1·62 m. below Mn. h.m.	Ht. m.	Aft. h.m.	Ht. m.	LEITH †Datum 2·90 m. below Mn. h.m.	Ht. m.	Aft. h.m.	Ht. m.	DUN LAOGHAIRE ‡Datum 0·20 m. above Mn. h.m.	Ht. m.	Aft. h.m.	Ht. m.
1	Th	0459	6·7	1702	6·7	0205	8·5	1423	8·5	1017	12·0	2235	11·9	0921	7·0	2150	6·7	0332	3·4	1556	3·2	0536	5·2	1811	4·9	0222	4·0	1456	3·6
2	F	0533	6·5	1734	6·5	0242	8·8	1501	8·8	1051	11·6	2311	11·4	0959	6·8	2230	6·4	0410	3·3	1637	3·2	0618	5·1	1853	4·8	0307	3·9	1545	3·5
3	Sa	0611	6·3	1815	6·4	0324	8·3	1549	8·3	1126	11·1	2351	11·1	1044	6·3	2318	6·2	0451	3·2	1722	3·1	0705	4·9	1942	4·6	0357	3·8	1642	3·5
4	Su	0657	6·0	1907	6·1	0419	8·0	1652	8·0		10·4	1214	10·6		6·0	1257	6·1	0537	3·1	1811	3·0	0800	4·8	2042	4·5	0459	3·6	1750	3·4
5	M	0802	5·8	2027	5·9	0532	7·7	1817	7·7	0055	10·8	1333	10·3	0022	5·9	1430	5·9	0630	2·9	1910	2·9	0910	4·6	2155	4·5	0614	3·5	1903	3·6
6	Tu	0927	5·8	2157	6·0	0659	7·6	1941	7·6	0229	10·9	1507	11·4	0148	6·1	1555	6·1	0747	2·8	2028	2·9	1033	4·6	2315	4·7	0734	3·5	2010	3·6
7	W	1048	6·1	2323	6·3	0819	7·5	2053	7·4	0353	11·7	1627	12·3	0314	6·5	1659	6·6	0938	2·8	2151	3·3	1154	4·8			0844	3·6	2109	3·8
8	Th			1203	6·7	0927	7·6	2152	8·0	0511	12·3	1740	13·1	0421	7·0	1753	7·1	1053	2·9	2255	3·3	0024	4·8	1300	5·1	0942	3·6	2202	4·0
9	F	0035	6·7	1303	7·1	1023	8·4	2244	8·4	0617	13·1	1839	13·7	0515	7·5	1838	7·3	1149	3·0	2348	3·6	0121	5·3	1355	5·4	1033	3·9	2250	4·2
10	Sa	0131	7·1	1354	7·3	1112	9·0	2332	9·0	0712	13·7	1930	14·0	0600	7·8	1919	7·5	1237	3·2			0211	5·6	1444	5·6	1120	4·0	2336	4·4
11	Su	0220	7·3	1439	7·5	1157	9·5			0758	13·7	2013	14·0	0641	8·1	1959	7·7	0035	3·4	1320	3·6	0256	5·8	1527	5·8			1205	4·1
12	M	0305	7·5	1521	7·5	0015	9·9	1239	9·9	0839	13·6	2054	13·7	0721	8·1	2039	7·7	0120	3·9	1401	3·5	0340	5·7	1609	5·7	0022	4·5	1249	4·1
13	Tu	0348	7·5	1602	7·4	0056	9·7	1320	9·7	0918	13·1	2134	13·2	0802	7·9	2118	7·5	0202	3·9	1440	3·4	0423	5·4	1651	5·6	0107	4·5	1335	4·0
14	W	0428	7·4	1641	7·1	0137	9·3	1358	9·2	0956	12·7	2210	12·2	0843	7·5	2157	7·0	0243	3·8	1519	3·3	0509	5·1	1737	5·4	0156	4·4	1421	3·8
15	Th	0508	7·1	1719	6·7	0215	8·7	1436	8·7	1031	11·9	2247	11·3	0925	7·0	2238	6·4	0323	3·6	1557	3·3	0557	4·8	1823	5·1	0245	4·2	1510	3·8
16	F	0546	6·7	1758	6·4	0254	8·1	1517	8·2	1105	10·7	2319	10·2	1009	6·4	2327	5·7	0404	3·3	1637	3·0	0645	4·5	1909	4·8	0338	4·2	1603	3·6
17	Sa	0625	6·4	1842	6·1	0338	7·4	1604	7·2	1137	9·8	2354	9·8	1058	5·7			0446	3·1	1719	2·8	0735	4·3	1958	4·5	0436	4·2	1706	3·4
18	Su	0710	6·1	1940	5·8	0431	6·9	1708	7·0		9·4	1219	9·4		5·6	1200	5·6	0530	2·9	1808	2·7	0830	4·3	2056	4·3	0548	4·2	1818	3·3
19	M	0808	5·8	2049	5·6	0550	6·9	1835	7·3	0049	9·6	1335	9·6	0031	6·0	1321	6·0	0619	2·8	1914	2·6	0942	4·3	2210	4·3	0706	4·2	1930	3·3
20	Tu	0917	5·6	2221	5·6	0727	7·3	1959	7·8	0225	10·4	1521	11·3	0148	6·6	1458	6·6	0734	2·6	2101	2·7	1104	4·5	2327	4·8	0817	4·4	2031	3·5
21	W	1051	5·6	2342	6·2	0842	7·8	2100	8·4	0403	11·4	1638	12·5	0312	7·1	1612	7·1	0945	2·6	2215	2·9			1213	4·8	0914	3·9	2156	3·6
22	Th			1200	6·5	0931	8·3	2145	9·1	0506	12·4	1732	13·4	0416	7·4	1701	7·4	1051	2·7	2307	2·9	0027	4·8	1306	5·0	0955	3·5	2230	3·8
23	F	0032	6·2	1245	6·7	1010	8·6	2223	9·1	0556	12·9	1817	13·0	0502	7·5	1740	7·5	1135	2·9	2348	3·2	0114	5·0	1348	5·1	1029	3·7	2300	3·8
24	Sa	0147	6·5	1323	6·9	1045	8·8	2257	8·8	0638	12·3	1855	12·3	0539	7·2	1812	7·2	1211	3·0			0151	5·2	1426	5·3	1059	3·8	2333	3·9
25	Su	0220	6·7	1357	7·0	1116	9·0	2329	9·0	0714	12·7	1928	13·0	0610	7·1	1841	7·1	0024	3·3	1243	3·2	0223	5·4	1456	5·4	1128	3·9	2300	3·9
26	M	0253	6·9	1430	7·1	1147	9·4			0745	12·9	1959	13·2	0641	7·2	1909	7·2	0057	3·3	1313	3·3	0253	5·5	1525	5·5	1159	4·2	2333	4·2
27	Tu	0327	7·0	1503	7·1	0001	9·4	1218	9·1	0816	12·9	2032	13·2	0712	7·4	1940	7·4	0128	3·4	1344	3·4	0322	5·5	1555	5·4	0004	4·2	1230	3·9
28	W	0359	7·1	1534	7·1	0032	9·4	1249	8·6	0847	12·8	2104	12·7	0745	7·5	2011	7·5	0200	3·4	1417	3·4	0354	5·5	1627	5·3	0037	4·2	1304	3·9
29	Th	0431	7·1	1604	6·9	0104	9·1	1321	8·1	0919	12·7	2138	12·2	0819	7·4	2044	7·2	0233	3·5	1452	3·4	0430	5·5	1702	5·0	0114	4·1	1342	3·9
30	F	0505	6·9	1637	6·6	0138	8·9	1355	8·8	0952	12·4	2210	12·2	0854	7·1	2119	6·9	0308	3·4	1529	3·4	0511	5·2	1742	5·0	0154	4·1	1422	3·9
31	Sa		6·6	1713		0215	8·5	1433	8·5	1024	11·9	2245	11·6	0932	6·6	2157		0346	3·3	1609		0554	5·2	1826	4·9	0240	4·0	1511	3·7

* All times shown are Greenwich Mean Time.   † Difference of height in metres from Ordnance Datum (Newlyn).
‡ Difference of height in metres from Ordnance Datum (Dublin).

SEPTEMBER, 1991

High Water at the undermentioned Places (GMT*)—

Day of Month	Day of Week	London Bridge †Datum of Predictions 3·20 m. below				Liverpool †Datum of Predictions 4·93 m. below				Avonmouth †Datum of Predictions 6·50 m. below				Hull (Albert Dock) †Datum of Predictions 3·90 m. below				Greenock †Datum of Predictions 1·62 m. below				Leith †Datum of Predictions 2·90 m. below				Dun Laoghaire ‡Datum of Predictions 0·20 m. above			
		Mn.	Ht.	Aft.	Ht.	Mn.	Ht.	Aft.	Ht.	Mn.	Ht.	Aft.	Ht.	Mn.	Ht.	Aft.	Ht.	Mn.	Ht.	Aft.	Ht.	Mn.	Ht.	Aft.	Ht.	Mn.	Ht.	Aft.	Ht.
		h.m.	m.	h.m.	m.	h.m.	m.	h.m.	m.	h.m.	m.	h.m.	m.	h.m.	m.	h.m.	m.	h.m.	m.	h.m.	m.	h.m.	m.	h.m.	m.	h.m.	m.	h.m.	m.
1	Su	0543	6·3	1754	6·4	0257	8·5	1521	8·1	1019	11·3	2326	10·9		6·6	2245	6·2	0427	3·2	1652	3·2	0643	5·0	1917	4·7	0333	3·8	1610	3·6
2	M	0629	6·0	1852	6·1	0355	8·0	1628	7·7	1118	10·6				6·2	2351	5·9	0512	3·1	1740	3·1	0743	4·7	2021	4·5	0439	3·6	1721	3·5
3	Tu	0734	5·7	2015	5·9	0513	7·5	1800	7·5	0127	10·1	1312	10·0	0127	5·8	1432	5·8	0605	2·9	1836	3·1	0900	4·6	2142	4·5	0602	3·5	1842	3·7
4	W	0904	5·7	2148	6·0	0650	7·5	1931	7·8	0301	10·0	1453	10·4	0301	6·1	1552	6·1	0733	2·8	1958	3·0	1029	4·6	2307	4·7	0729	3·5	1958	3·9
5	Th	1031	6·0	2315	6·4	0815	8·0	2044	8·5	0346	10·7	1620	11·4	0458	6·6	1652	6·5	0938	2·9	2132	3·2	1149	4·9			0841	3·6	2100	4·1
6	F	1149	6·5			0918	8·7	2141	9·1	0504	11·8	1730	12·7	0540	7·1	1739	7·1	1135	3·1	2237	3·4	0015	5·3	1252	5·2	0937	3·8	2151	4·1
7	Sa	0022	6·9	1248	7·2	1009	9·1	2228	9·6	0540	12·7	1827	13·3	0618	7·1	1818	7·3	1218	3·2	2329	3·7	0111	5·3	1342	5·5	1023	4·0	2237	4·3
8	Su	0117	7·3	1337	7·2	1054	9·6	2312	9·9	0618	13·4	1913	13·8	0654	7·9	1855	7·5	0015	3·4	1335	3·6	0157	5·6	1426	5·7	1105	4·1	2320	4·5
9	M	0204	7·4	1419	7·3	1134	9·7	2353	10·0	0655	13·8	1952	14·0	0738	8·1	1931	7·7	0058	3·5	1411	3·5	0238	5·8	1506	5·8	1144	4·2		
10	Tu	0246	7·4	1458	7·4			1214	9·9	0738	13·7	2029	13·6	0815	8·1	2008	7·9	0137	3·8	1447	3·5	0318	5·8	1545	5·6	0002	4·2	1223	4·2
11	W	0325	7·4	1536	7·4	0031	9·9	1250	9·2	0815	13·5	2105	13·6	0858	7·8	2121	8·1	0216	3·9	1522	3·5	0359	5·8	1625	5·6	0044	4·5	1304	4·1
12	Th	0402	7·3	1613	7·3	0107	9·7	1326	8·8	0851	13·2	2139	12·9	0938	7·8	2157	8·0	0254	3·8	1558	3·3	0442	5·7	1706	5·3	0129	4·5	1346	3·9
13	F	0435	7·0	1648	7·0	0142	9·1	1401	8·3	0925	12·4	2212	12·0	1023	7·3	2237	7·3	0335	3·8	1636	3·2	0527	5·3	1748	5·0	0214	4·1	1432	3·9
14	Sa	0508	6·7	1725	6·7	0219	8·9	1437	7·8	0959	11·5	2241	11·0	1118	6·7	2334	6·7	0410	3·4	1636	2·9	0612	5·0	1831	4·7	0303	3·8	1520	3·5
15	Su	0543	6·4	1807	6·3	0258	7·9	1521	7·3	1028	10·6	2311	10·1	1223	6·1			0450	3·2	1719	2·8	0659	4·7	1916	4·5	0357	3·6	1617	3·4
16	M	0624	6·0	1900	5·9	0349	7·3	1620	6·9	1055	9·7	2366	9·2	0026	5·5	1236	6·1	0536	3·2	1813	2·7	0753	4·4	2010	4·3	0504	3·3	1725	3·3
17	Tu	0717	6·0	2008	5·7	0504	6·9	1747	6·9	1127	8·6	1236	8·8	0056	5·5	1422	5·5	0638	2·7	1636	2·6	0904	4·2	2123	4·2	0628	3·3	1845	3·4
18	W	0827	5·4	2134	5·5	0652	6·7	1923	7·2	0135	8·6	1444	9·0	0339	5·6	1623	5·6	0912	2·6	2002	2·8	1027	4·2	2245	4·3	0747	3·2	1953	3·4
19	Th	0959	5·4	2305	5·7	0812	6·7	2027	7·7	0327	10·3	1606	10·1	0428	6·5	1709	6·5	1019	2·6	2137	3·0	1138	4·2	2352	4·2	0842	3·4	2042	3·6
20	F	1122	5·8	2358	5·8	0901	7·7	2112	8·2	0433	12·0	1658	12·6	0505	7·0	1740	7·0	1103	3·0	2232	3·1	1231	4·6			0924	3·6	2124	3·8
21	Sa	0039	6·5	1250	6·6	0939	8·2	2150	8·6	0522	12·5	1743	13·0	0539	7·3	1822	7·5	1138	3·2	2315	3·4	0040	4·7	1314	5·1	0956	3·9	2158	4·0
22	Su	0116	6·6	1326	6·9	1013	8·6	2224	8·9	0604	12·9	1822	13·4	0611	7·5	1839	7·6	0026	3·2	1244	3·4	0118	5·0	1352	5·5	1026	4·0	2300	4·1
23	M	0149	6·9	1359	7·1	1045	8·9	2258	9·0	0642	13·4	1857	13·3	0645	7·6	1910	7·4	0100	3·3	1316	3·5	0152	5·5	1423	5·4	1056	4·3	2334	4·1
24	Tu	0223	7·0	1432	7·3	1116	9·2	2330	9·5	0716	13·3	1931	13·0	0719	7·6	1942	7·4	0133	3·4	1351	3·5	0223	5·5	1454	5·4	1127	4·3		
25	W	0257	7·2	1505	7·3	1149	9·6			0748	13·1	2005	13·0	0754	7·5	2016	7·2	0209	3·5	1427	3·5	0253	5·7	1525	5·3	1159	4·1		
26	Th	0331	7·2	1539	7·1	0004	9·4	1221	9·5	0820	12·7	2040	12·4	0829	7·3	2053	6·9	0246	3·5	1505	3·4	0328	5·6	1559	5·5	0009	4·3	1235	4·1
27	F	0406	7·0	1617	6·8	0039	9·3	1256	9·3	0854	12·4	2115	12·0	0907	7·3	2135	7·0	0325	3·4	1545	3·3	0407	5·5	1638	5·2	0049	4·3	1313	4·1
28	Sa	0442	7·1	1659	6·4	0116	9·0	1333	9·0	0929	12·1	2152	11·7	0945	7·0	2226	6·6	0408	3·3	1628	3·3	0449	5·5	1720	5·0	0132	4·0	1357	4·0
29	Su	0525	6·7	1749	6·3	0157	8·7	1415	8·7	1006	11·7	2231	11·4									0537	5·2	1807	5·0	0221	3·9	1449	3·9
30	M	0620	6·3			0244	8·5	1507	8·2	1047	11·4	2320	10·8									0632	4·8	1904	4·8	0318	3·7	1549	3·7

*All times shown are Greenwich Mean Time.   †Difference of height in metres from Ordnance Datum (Newlyn).
‡Difference of height in metres from Ordnance Datum (Dublin).

OCTOBER, 1991

High Water at the undermentioned Places (GMT*)—

Day of Month	Day of Week	London Bridge †3·20 m. below Mn. h.m.	Ht. m.	Aft. h.m.	Ht. m.	Liverpool †4·93 m. below Mn. h.m.	Ht.	Aft. h.m.	Ht.	Avonmouth †6·50 m. below Mn. h.m.	Ht.	Aft. h.m.	Ht.	Hull (Albert Dock) †3·90 m. below Mn. h.m.	Ht.	Aft. h.m.	Ht.	Greenock †1·62 m. below Mn. h.m.	Ht.	Aft. h.m.	Ht.	Leith †2·90 m. below Mn. h.m.	Ht.	Aft. h.m.	Ht.	Dun Laoghaire ‡0·20 m. above Mn. h.m.	Ht.	Aft. h.m.	Ht.
1	Tu	0615	5·9	1852	6·1	0346	7·8	1619	7·8	1143	10·6	1309	10·1	1109	6·2	2333	6·0	0457	3·1	1717	3·3	0738	4·7	2013	4·6	0429	3·6	1703	3·6
2	W	0724	5·7	2012	5·9	0511	7·9	1750	7·6	0032	10·1	1444	—	0110	5·9	1241	5·9	0551	2·9	1815	3·2	0858	4·6	2134	4·6	0555	3·5	1827	3·6
3	Th	0849	5·8	2138	6·2	0643	7·5	1917	8·0	0205	10·6	1609	—	0243	6·6	1427	6·6	0751	2·9	1939	3·2	1022	4·7	2255	4·8	0722	3·5	1944	3·8
4	F	1014	6·1	2259	6·6	0802	7·6	2026	8·6	0335	10·8	1713	—	0346	7·2	1539	6·7	0927	3·0	2110	3·5	1134	5·0	—	—	0831	3·7	2047	4·0
5	Sa	1129	6·6	—	—	0901	8·1	2121	8·7	0448	11·9	1805	—	0437	7·4	1634	7·2	1026	3·4	2215	3·6	0000	5·1	1233	5·3	0925	3·9	2137	4·2
6	Su	0005	7·0	1227	7·0	0949	8·7	2206	9·2	0544	12·7	1850	—	0518	7·7	1718	7·4	1113	3·4	2306	3·8	0053	5·4	1321	5·5	1008	4·1	2221	4·4
7	M	0057	7·3	1314	7·2	1031	9·2	2248	9·6	0632	13·1	1928	—	0557	7·8	1754	7·5	1154	3·6	2352	3·8	0136	5·8	1403	5·6	1047	4·2	2302	4·4
8	Tu	0142	7·4	1357	7·3	1111	9·4	2327	9·8	0713	13·5	2004	—	0636	7·9	1829	7·8	—	—	1232	3·6	0217	5·8	1442	5·7	1121	4·2	2343	4·4
9	W	0223	7·3	1436	7·3	1147	9·6	—	—	0749	13·6	2039	—	0716	7·9	1904	7·9	0033	3·8	1308	3·6	0255	5·7	1518	5·6	1158	4·2	—	—
10	Th	0258	7·3	1511	7·3	0004	9·6	1221	9·4	0823	13·5	2111	—	0757	7·8	1940	7·9	0112	3·5	1343	3·5	0335	5·7	1556	5·5	0022	4·3	1235	4·2
11	F	0332	7·1	1546	7·1	0039	9·6	1255	9·2	0857	13·0	2142	—	0836	7·5	2015	7·8	0149	3·5	1416	3·4	0415	5·5	1636	5·3	0103	4·3	1314	4·1
12	Sa	0403	6·9	1620	6·9	0113	9·3	1328	8·8	0928	11·8	2212	—	0914	7·0	2049	7·5	0225	3·5	1449	3·3	0455	5·2	1713	5·1	0146	4·0	1357	3·9
13	Su	0434	6·6	1657	6·6	0148	8·9	1405	8·4	0957	11·5	2240	—	0953	6·5	2121	7·0	0300	3·3	1523	3·1	0540	4·9	1754	4·8	0232	3·7	1443	3·8
14	M	0506	6·4	1737	6·3	0226	8·4	1447	7·9	1024	10·6	2322	—	1041	5·9	2155	6·5	0337	3·1	1600	3·0	0626	4·6	1838	4·6	0321	3·5	1533	3·6
15	Tu	0543	6·1	1825	5·9	0314	7·7	1541	7·3	1057	9·8	—	—	1150	5·5	2242	5·8	0417	3·0	1641	3·0	0718	4·2	1930	4·3	0421	3·3	1633	3·5
16	W	0631	5·8	1927	5·6	0419	7·3	1655	7·1	1153	9·1	1345	—	—	—	1317	5·1	0503	2·9	1731	3·1	0820	4·2	2035	4·3	0536	3·2	1745	3·4
17	Th	0737	5·5	2043	5·5	0551	6·7	1824	7·1	0039	8·7	1512	—	0127	5·4	1447	5·4	0602	2·7	1843	3·2	0933	4·2	2147	4·5	0656	3·4	1855	3·5
18	F	0903	5·4	2203	5·6	0719	6·9	1935	7·5	0230	8·5	1612	—	0242	5·9	1546	5·9	0759	2·7	2035	3·3	1045	4·3	2256	4·7	0757	3·6	1954	3·6
19	Sa	1024	5·6	2309	6·0	0816	7·5	2027	8·1	0342	10·0	1659	—	0339	6·4	1627	6·4	0927	2·8	2142	3·4	1142	4·6	2350	4·8	0841	3·8	2040	3·8
20	Su	1125	6·0	2357	6·4	0858	8·1	2110	8·6	0435	11·8	1743	—	0424	6·8	1701	6·8	1017	3·0	2232	3·5	0035	5·0	1230	5·1	0918	4·0	2119	4·0
21	M	0038	6·7	1249	6·8	0935	8·6	2146	9·0	0522	13·0	1824	—	0502	7·2	1733	7·2	1058	3·2	2314	3·5	0113	5·2	1310	5·3	0952	4·0	2155	4·1
22	Tu	0116	7·0	1326	7·0	1009	9·0	2223	9·3	0604	13·5	1902	—	0540	7·5	1808	7·5	1135	3·4	—	—	0149	5·5	1347	5·5	1023	4·1	2230	4·3
23	W	0152	7·1	1404	7·2	1044	9·3	2259	9·5	0643	13·5	1941	—	0618	7·6	1843	7·4	0030	3·4	1248	3·5	0225	5·6	1457	5·6	1056	4·2	2306	4·3
24	Th	0229	7·2	1442	7·4	1119	9·5	2339	9·7	0720	12·9	2019	—	0657	7·4	1919	7·5	0109	3·5	1329	3·5	0305	5·7	1535	5·6	1131	4·2	2345	4·3
25	F	0307	7·2	1521	7·4	0018	9·5	1236	9·5	0758	12·4	2100	—	0737	7·2	1957	7·4	0148	3·5	1404	3·4	0349	5·6	1618	5·6	0029	4·1	1209	4·3
26	Sa	0346	7·1	1606	7·3	0100	9·4	1319	9·3	0836	12·9	2143	—	0820	6·8	2037	7·1	0229	3·4	1444	3·3	0435	5·5	1704	5·5	0115	4·1	1251	4·2
27	Su	0430	6·8	1654	7·0	0147	9·0	1406	8·9	0917	12·4	2231	—	0908	6·3	2122	6·8	0312	3·2	1526	3·2	0529	5·1	1757	5·4	0210	4·0	1339	4·1
28	M	0518	6·4	1750	6·6	0240	8·5	1504	8·1	1000	11·7	2325	—	1000	5·9	2214	6·2	0359	3·2	1612	3·2	0627	5·1	1856	5·1	0310	3·8	1433	4·0
29	Tu	0612	6·1	1853	6·3	0345	8·0	1613	8·1	1049	11·0	—	—	1104	6·3	2319	6·1	0453	3·1	1702	3·1	0732	4·9	2003	4·8	0420	3·6	1536	3·9
30	W	0717	5·9	2004	6·2	0502	7·7	1733	8·0	1149	10·5	—	—	—	—	1232	—	0603	3·0	1802	3·5	0844	4·8	2117	4·8	0543	3·5	1807	3·8
31	Th	—	—	—	—	—	—	—	—	0031	10·6	1302	10·6	—	—	—	—	—	—	—	—	—	—	—	—	—	—	—	—

* All times shown are Greenwich Mean Time.   †Difference of height in metres from Ordnance Datum (Newlyn).
‡Difference of height in metres from Ordnance Datum (Dublin).

NOVEMBER, 1991

High Water at the undermentioned Places (GMT*)—

Datum of Predictions: London Bridge 3·20 m. below; Liverpool 4·93 m. below; Avonmouth 6·50 m. below; Hull (Albert Dock) 3·90 m. below; Greenock 1·62 m. below; Leith 2·90 m. below; Dun Laoghaire 0·20 m. above.

Day of Week	Day of Month	London Bridge				Liverpool				Avonmouth				Hull (Albert Dock)				Greenock				Leith				Dun Laoghaire			
		Mn.	Ht.	Aft.	Ht.	Mn.	Ht.	Aft.	Ht.	Mn.	Ht.	Aft.	Ht.	Mn.	Ht.	Aft.	Ht.	Mn.	Ht.	Aft.	Ht.	Mn.	Ht.	Aft.	Ht.	Mn.	Ht.	Aft.	Ht.
F	1	0830	6·0	2119	6·3	0624	7·8	1852	8·2	0149	10·5	1425	10·9	0043	6·2	1405	6·2	0740	3·0	1919	3·4	0959	4·9	2231	4·9	0705	3·6	1923	3·9
Sa	2	0949	6·2	2235	6·6	0735	8·5	1959	8·6	0311	11·0	1543	11·6	0212	6·4	1514	6·5	0900	3·2	2041	3·5	1108	5·0	2334	5·2	0810	3·7	2025	4·0
Su	3	1102	6·6	2340	6·6	0834	8·5	2054	8·9	0421	11·8	1647	12·3	0318	6·8	1607	6·8	0958	3·2	2147	3·5			1206	5·3	0904	3·9	2118	4·2
M	4			1203	7·1	0924	8·9	2142	9·2	0518	12·4	1740	12·7	0410	7·1	1652	7·1	1046	3·4	2241	3·6	0028	5·4	1255	5·4	0948	4·0	2205	4·2
Tu	5	0034	7·1	1252	7·2	1006	9·2	2224	9·3	0605	12·8	1825	13·0	0457	7·3	1730	7·3	1128	3·4	2328	3·6	0113	5·5	1338	5·5	1026	4·1	2246	4·2
W	6	0120	7·2	1335	7·1	1045	9·3	2304	9·3	0648	13·0	1904	13·0	0537	7·4	1805	7·3	1207	3·6			0155	5·6	1417	5·5	1102	4·2	2324	4·2
Th	7	0159	7·1	1413	7·0	1122	9·3	2340	9·2	0724	13·1	1941	12·9	0619	7·4	1841	7·4	0011	3·5	1243	3·5	0235	5·6	1455	5·5	1136	4·2		
F	8	0234	7·0	1450	7·0	1157	9·3			0759	13·0	2016	12·9	0659	7·4	1916	7·3	0050	3·5	1318	3·5	0314	5·6	1532	5·4	0004	4·1	1211	4·1
Sa	9	0305	7·0	1524	7·0	0017	9·0	1231	9·1	0833	12·7	2049	12·3	0740	7·3	1949	7·2	0127	3·3	1351	3·5	0354	5·3	1608	5·3	0042	4·1	1249	4·1
Su	10	0336	6·6	1559	6·9	0050	8·7	1306	8·9	0905	12·2	2121	11·7	0818	7·0	2020	6·9	0202	3·2	1424	3·5	0435	5·1	1644	5·1	0123	4·0	1329	4·0
M	11	0406	6·6	1635	6·6	0126	8·4	1341	8·5	0935	11·6	2152	11·1	0853	6·7	2051	6·7	0237	3·1	1457	3·3	0515	4·9	1724	4·9	0204	3·8	1411	3·8
Tu	12	0440	6·4	1715	6·2	0204	8·0	1420	8·1	1006	10·9	2224	10·5	0929	6·4	2127	6·4	0313	3·0	1534	3·1	0557	4·7	1808	4·7	0250	3·6	1457	3·7
W	13	0516	6·2	1758	5·9	0246	7·6	1508	7·5	1041	10·3	2304	9·9	1012	6·1	2210	6·1	0354	3·0	1614	3·0	0643	4·5	1853	4·5	0340	3·4	1547	3·6
Th	14	0558	6·0	1849	5·7	0338	7·2	1606	7·0	1127	9·8	2358	9·5	1104	5·8	2309	5·8	0440	2·9	1701	2·9	0736	4·3	1948	4·3	0438	3·3	1643	3·5
F	15	0649	5·7	1949	5·6	0445	7·0	1715	6·8			1236	9·7			1212	5·5	0537	2·9	1759	2·9	0837	4·3	2049	4·4	0546	3·2	1748	3·5
Sa	16	0755	5·5	2100	5·6	0601	7·0	1825	7·1	0114	9·3	1404	9·4	0027	5·7	1327	5·8	0651	2·9	1915	3·0	0941	4·3	2151	4·5	0654	3·3	1852	3·6
Su	17	0915	5·6	2206	5·9	0710	7·4	1927	7·9	0234	9·6	1512	10·4	0141	5·9	1434	5·9	0816	2·9	2037	3·0	1042	4·5	2252	4·7	0750	3·5	1950	3·7
M	18	1024	5·8	2305	6·2	0808	8·0	2020	8·5	0339	10·6	1609	11·2	0243	6·2	1529	6·2	0922	3·1	2141	3·1	1138	4·8	2346	4·9	0835	3·7	2038	3·9
Tu	19	1120	6·2	2356		0850	8·3	2105	8·8	0433	11·4	1659	12·0	0336	6·6	1616	6·6	1014	3·1	2234	3·2			1225	5·2	0915	3·9	2122	4·0
W	20			1210	6·9	0932	8·8	2150	9·1	0523	12·2	1749	12·6	0426	6·9	1659	6·9	1059	3·4	2321	3·3	0032	5·4	1308	5·4	0953	4·1	2203	4·1
Th	21	0042	6·8	1255	7·1	1014	9·2	2234	9·4	0611	12·8	1835	13·1	0512	7·2	1740	7·3	1141	3·4			0123	5·5	1350	5·6	1030	4·2	2244	4·2
F	22	0126	7·0	1340	7·3	1057	9·5	2319	9·6	0656	13·3	1921	13·4	0557	7·4	1821	7·4	0005	3·6	1223	3·6	0203	5·6	1432	5·6	1109	4·3	2328	4·2
Sa	23	0208	7·1	1425	7·4	1140	9·6			0740	13·5	2006	13·4	0642	7·5	1903	7·5	0050	3·5	1304	3·7	0337	5·6	1516	5·6	1151	4·3		
Su	24	0251	7·1	1511	7·4	0004	9·6	1225	9·6	0825	13·5	2053	13·3	0728	7·4	1944	7·4	0133	3·5	1345	3·8	0519	5·5	1603	5·4	0015	4·2	1236	4·3
M	25	0355	7·1	1600	7·2	0052	9·5	1313	9·4	0910	13·2	2141	12·9	0815	7·2	2027	7·2	0218	3·5	1428	3·9	0615	5·6	1653	5·2	0106	4·1	1328	4·3
Tu	26	0423	7·0	1652	7·0	0142	9·2	1404	9·2	0957	12·9	2228	12·4	0904	6·9	2114	7·2	0305	3·4	1513	3·9	0715	5·6	1748	5·1	0200	4·0	1421	4·2
W	27	0512	6·8	1746	6·7	0236	8·8	1458	8·8	1048	11·8	2320	11·8	0955	6·5	2203	6·7	0355	3·4	1600	3·8	0818	5·4	1845	5·0	0300	3·8	1521	4·1
Th	28	0604	6·5	1843	6·5	0335	8·4	1559	8·6	1142	11·2			1054	6·2	2259	6·5	0449	3·3	1650	3·8	0926	5·1	1946	5·0	0406	3·7	1628	4·0
F	29	0702	6·4	1945	6·4	0440	8·1	1705	8·3			1243	11·3			1205	6·6	0552	3·2	1747	3·6	1035	5·0	2050	5·0	0518	3·6	1742	3·9
Sa	30	0805	6·3	2051	6·4	0550	7·9	1815	8·2	0017	10·9	1352	10·9	0008	6·6	1327	6·6	0706	3·2	1852	3·5	1152	4·9	2158	5·0	0635	3·6	1855	3·9

*All times shown are Greenwich Mean Time.   †Difference of height in metres from Ordnance Datum (Newlyn).
‡Difference of height in metres from Ordnance Datum (Dublin).

DECEMBER, 1991

High Water at the undermentioned Places (GMT*)—

Day of Month	Day of Week	London Bridge †Datum of Predictions 3·20 m. below				Liverpool †Datum of Predictions 4·93 m. below				Avonmouth †Datum of Predictions 6·50 m. below				Hull (Albert Dock) †Datum of Predictions 3·90 m. below				Greenock †Datum of Predictions 1·62 m. below				Leith †Datum of Predictions 2·90 m. below				Dun Laoghaire ‡Datum of Predictions 0·20 m. above			
		Mn. h.m.	Ht. m.	Aft. h.m.	Ht. m.	Mn. h.m.	Ht. m.	Aft. h.m.	Ht. m.	Mn. h.m.	Ht. m.	Aft. h.m.	Ht. m.	Mn. h.m.	Ht. m.	Aft. h.m.	Ht. m.	Mn. h.m.	Ht. m.	Aft. h.m.	Ht. m.	Mn. h.m.	Ht. m.	Aft. h.m.	Ht. m.	Mn. h.m.	Ht. m.	Aft. h.m.	Ht. m.
1	Su	0915	6·3	2203	6·5	0700	8·0	1924	8·3	0233	10·9	1504	11·2	0130	6·5	1436	6·4	0820	3·2	2006	3·4	1033	5·0	2303	5·1	0743	3·7	2000	3·9
2	M	1028	6·4	2311	6·7	0802	8·2	2026	8·4	0343	11·2	1612	11·5	0243	6·6	1534	6·6	0923	3·3	2116	3·4	1134	5·1	—	—	0840	3·8	2058	4·0
3	Tu	1134	6·6	—	—	0857	8·5	2118	8·6	0445	11·6	1709	11·8	0343	6·8	1624	6·8	1017	3·3	2217	3·3	0000	5·2	1227	5·2	0926	3·9	2148	4·0
4	W	0008	6·7	1229	6·8	0943	8·7	2204	8·7	0537	12·0	1800	12·0	0437	6·8	1708	6·9	1103	3·4	2309	3·3	0051	5·3	1314	5·3	1008	4·0	2232	4·0
5	Th	0056	6·8	1316	6·8	1026	8·9	2247	8·8	0624	12·3	1843	12·2	0525	6·9	1747	7·0	1145	3·4	2355	3·3	0137	5·3	1356	5·3	1044	4·0	2312	4·0
6	F	0137	6·8	1355	6·8	1104	9·0	2325	8·8	0704	12·5	1924	12·3	0608	6·9	1824	7·0	1224	3·5	—	—	0220	5·3	1435	5·3	1120	4·0	2350	3·9
7	Sa	0213	6·8	1433	6·9	1140	9·1	—	—	0742	12·6	2001	12·3	0649	6·7	1857	7·0	0036	3·2	1300	3·5	0300	5·2	1513	5·3	1154	4·0	—	—
8	Su	0246	6·8	1508	6·9	0001	9·0	1215	9·0	0818	12·5	2034	12·3	0727	6·8	1930	7·0	0114	3·1	1334	3·5	0340	5·2	1548	5·3	0026	3·8	1230	4·0
9	M	0317	6·8	1545	6·8	0035	8·7	1249	8·9	0850	12·5	2105	11·9	0801	6·6	2001	7·0	0149	3·1	1407	3·4	0417	5·1	1623	5·2	0103	3·7	1307	4·0
10	Tu	0349	6·7	1620	6·7	0109	8·6	1324	8·8	0921	12·2	2136	11·6	0834	6·6	2032	6·9	0223	3·1	1441	3·4	0452	5·0	1658	5·1	0140	3·6	1346	3·9
11	W	0423	6·6	1657	6·6	0144	8·5	1401	8·5	0953	11·9	2210	11·3	0908	6·5	2108	6·6	0259	3·1	1516	3·4	0530	4·8	1738	5·0	0218	3·5	1425	3·9
12	Th	0458	6·6	1734	6·5	0220	8·3	1440	8·3	1027	11·6	2245	10·8	0946	6·3	2148	6·6	0338	3·1	1554	3·3	0610	4·6	1819	4·9	0301	3·5	1507	3·8
13	F	0534	6·4	1815	6·3	0303	7·7	1524	7·9	1106	10·7	2326	10·4	1028	5·9	2234	6·4	0421	3·1	1636	3·2	0654	4·6	1906	4·7	0347	3·3	1554	3·7
14	Sa	0614	6·1	1900	6·0	0350	7·5	1616	7·7	1150	10·4	—	—	1118	6·0	2329	6·1	0510	3·0	1724	3·2	0744	4·5	1957	4·6	0442	3·3	1649	3·6
15	Su	0700	5·9	1955	5·8	0448	7·3	1716	7·5	0014	10·1	1248	9·9	0035	6·0	1327	6·0	0606	3·0	1820	3·1	0840	4·5	2053	4·6	0546	3·3	1750	3·6
16	M	0801	5·7	2104	5·8	0556	7·4	1824	7·6	0117	9·9	1401	10·2	0147	6·0	1433	6·1	0711	3·0	1928	3·0	0941	4·6	2153	4·6	0651	3·4	1856	3·6
17	Tu	0919	5·8	2213	6·0	0704	7·6	1928	7·9	0234	10·2	1514	10·7	0251	6·1	1534	6·4	0821	3·1	2045	3·0	1042	4·6	2257	4·7	0750	3·6	1958	3·7
18	W	1030	6·0	2315	6·3	0806	8·1	2029	8·4	0343	10·9	1617	11·4	0352	6·4	1630	6·7	0927	3·1	2155	3·1	1142	4·8	2358	5·0	0841	3·7	2053	3·9
19	Th	1133	6·4	—	—	0902	8·5	2124	8·8	0445	11·6	1718	12·1	0449	6·7	1720	6·9	1023	3·4	2255	3·3	—	—	1237	5·3	0926	3·9	2142	4·0
20	F	0012	6·6	1232	6·8	0952	9·0	2216	9·2	0543	12·5	1814	12·7	0543	6·9	1807	7·2	1114	3·6	2348	3·3	0055	5·4	1327	5·5	1009	4·1	2229	4·1
21	Sa	0106	6·8	1326	7·0	1041	9·4	2306	9·5	0636	13·1	1907	13·5	0634	7·5	1850	7·5	1201	3·8	—	—	0148	5·6	1416	5·7	1053	4·2	2316	4·3
22	Su	0154	7·0	1416	7·1	1127	9·7	—	—	0728	13·5	1958	13·6	0721	7·6	1934	7·6	0037	3·7	1246	3·8	0238	5·7	1503	5·8	1137	4·3	—	—
23	M	0242	7·1	1505	7·3	0046	9·6	1306	9·8	0816	13·6	2046	13·6	0808	7·6	2016	7·7	0124	3·6	1331	3·9	0327	5·8	1552	5·8	0005	4·1	1225	4·4
24	Tu	0328	7·2	1555	7·3	0134	9·6	1354	9·8	0903	13·7	2132	13·4	0854	7·7	2100	7·5	0211	3·5	1415	3·9	0416	5·8	1640	5·8	0056	4·1	1315	4·4
25	W	0414	7·2	1644	7·3	0223	9·2	1443	9·4	0950	13·7	2219	13·0	0942	7·5	2146	7·2	0257	3·5	1500	4·0	0505	5·7	1732	5·5	0149	4·0	1408	4·4
26	Th	0501	7·1	1733	7·2	0314	8·8	1535	9·0	1037	13·1	2305	12·5	1031	6·8	2237	6·5	0344	3·5	1545	3·9	0556	5·5	1824	5·3	0243	3·9	1504	4·3
27	F	0549	6·9	1824	6·9	0406	8·3	1630	8·3	1123	12·5	2351	11·8	1127	6·5	2333	6·6	0433	3·4	1633	3·8	0650	5·3	1921	5·1	0342	3·8	1603	4·1
28	Sa	0636	6·5	1917	6·4	0506	7·9	1733	7·9	0043	11·1	1309	11·1	0045	6·6	1235	6·6	0525	3·3	1724	3·7	0746	5·1	2018	4·9	0446	3·8	1710	3·9
29	Su	0731	6·5	2015	6·3	0615	7·7	1845	7·8	0144	10·6	1415	10·6	0202	6·4	1347	6·2	0623	3·2	1820	3·6	0848	4·9	2121	4·9	0557	3·5	1823	3·8
30	M	0834	6·3	2121	6·4	0726	7·7	1957	7·8	0254	10·4	1529	10·6			1454	6·2	0730	3·2	1925	3·5	0954	4·8	2228	4·9	0708	3·5	1934	3·7
31	Tu	0948	6·1	2233	6·2													0842	3·1	2042	3·1	1102	4·8	2334	4·8	0810	3·6	2040	3·7

*All times shown are Greenwich Mean Time. †Difference of height in metres from Ordnance Datum (Newlyn). ‡Difference of height in metres from Ordnance Datum (Dublin).

WEATHER IN THE UNITED KINGDOM, 1989–90

(1989) July.—Rainfall totals were below normal except in some areas of south-east England, Northern Ireland and Shetland. Severe thunderstorms affected southern areas on the 5th–6th followed by widespread rain on the 7th and 8th causing flooding in many areas. On the 6th 85 mm (3·3 in) of rain fell at Oswestry (Shrops.) and hailstones 30 mm (1·2 in) in diameter fell near Basingstoke (Hants); 64 mm (2·5 in) of rain fell at Yeovilton (Somerset) and 52 mm (2·1 in) fell at Stanstead (Essex). On the 8th 39 mm (1·5 in) fell at Goudhurst (Kent). The weather was then mainly dry until thunderstorms developed in western Scotland, Northern Ireland and along the Thames Valley on the 25th, over Norfolk on the 29th and over the Midlands and East Anglia on the 30th. On the 21st red dust was deposited at Tiverton (Devon), Keyworth (Notts.) and Towy Castle (Dyfed). Parts of the south coast near Southampton had no measurable rain from the 8th to the end of the month and the total of 9 mm (0·3 in) at Edinburgh Royal Observatory was the lowest July rainfall ever recorded at the station. Monthly mean temperatures were above normal everywhere. Hampstead (London) had its warmest July since 1983 and its highest minimum temperature of 20·1°C (68·2°F) since 1949. The mean maximum temperature of 21·7°C (71·1°F) at Turnhouse (Lothian) was the highest since 1948. The minimum temperature of 3·5°C (38·3°F) at Glasgow Airport was the lowest since 1971. Temperatures were generally 10 to 11°C (18 to 20°F) above normal on the 6th, though during a thunderstorm at Birmingham the temperature fell from 28°C to 17°C (82·4°F to 62·6°F). The highest temperature recorded during the month was 34·4°C (93·9°F) at Mickleham (Surrey) on the 22nd and the lowest temperature recorded was 1·1°C (34°F) at Carnwath (Strathclyde) on the 2nd and at Balmoral (Grampian) on the 14th. Monthly sunshine totals were above normal everywhere except in the Western Isles. Eskdalemuir (Dumfries) had its sunniest July since 1910 and Bude (Cornwall) its sunniest since 1913. The 3rd was the sunniest July day this century at Sheffield. The highest monthly total was 326 hours at Minehead (Somerset) and the highest daily total was 16·4 hours at Prestwick (Strathclyde).

August.—Rainfall totals were below normal except in parts of northern Wales, Cumbria and western Scotland. Thunderstorms occurred in northern and eastern Scotland on the 6th, near the east coast on the 7th and in southern England on the 10th. There were gales in north-west Scotland on the 10th. Thunderstorms were widespread between the 13th and 17th. Hailstones of between 10 and 20 mm (0·4 and 0·8 in) in diameter fell at Ballywatticock (Co. Down) on the 13th. There were gales in the north and west on the 14th when gusts of 57 knots (66 mph) were recorded at Milford Haven and Brawdy (Dyfed) and Killough (Co. Down). On the 14th a holiday camp at Pwllheli (Gwynedd) was hit by a tornado which ripped the roofs off 150 chalets and caused considerable damage to other property. The damage was estimated at over £2 million. On the 23rd there was heavy rain in the Highlands; 67 mm (2·6 in) fell at Inverailort and 52 mm (2·1 in) at Onich. On the 24th and 25th rain was persistent across England. Very heavy rain in a thunderstorm caused flooding at Aldergrove (Co. Antrim) on the 25th. There were heavy showers in eastern England on the 26th. Some places on the south coast near Southampton and the Isle of Wight had no measurable rain between July 8th and the end of August. Monthly mean temperatures were above normal everywhere except the far north of Scotland. Several places in the south had temperatures around 30°C (86°F) on the 20th, and

Leuchars (Fife) recorded 25°C (77°F) on the 2nd. Kinloss (Grampian) also recorded 25°C (77°F) on the 6th. On the 26th temperatures only reached 12°C (53·6°F) in areas of eastern Scotland. The highest temperature recorded during the month was 30·4°C (86·7°F) at Coltishall (Norfolk) on the 20th and the lowest was −1·4°C (29·5°F) at Carnwath (Strathclyde) on the 28th. Monthly sunshine totals were above normal everywhere except Northern Ireland and western Scotland. Sheffield had its sunniest August since 1898 and Coventry its sunniest since 1947. Oxford had its second sunniest August for 110 years. After 1976 and 1947 it was the third sunniest August in England and Wales this century. The highest total during the month was 298 hours at Bournemouth (Dorset) and the highest daily total was 15·0 hours at Abbotsinch (Strathclyde) on the 1st and at Slapton (Devon) on the 8th.

September.—Monthly rainfall totals were below normal nearly everywhere except northern areas of Devon and Cornwall. It was the driest September in parts of eastern England since 1969 and the driest in Durham and Tynemouth since 1898. There were some severe thunderstorms in southern areas between the 10th and 13th. They occurred in Kent on the 10th, in Devon and Dorset on the 11th and in many parts of south-east England and Devon on the 12th. Houses in Wokingham and Bracknell (Berks.) were badly damaged by lightning on the 12th and in Wokingham the ambulance station was hit. In south and east London floods up to 0·5 m (1·6 ft) deep caused many motorists to abandon their cars and in Kent thousands of homes in the Faversham area were left without electricity when lightning struck power lines. A man was killed by lightning near Herne Bay, rail services were disrupted in Kent and several buildings were damaged by lightning. Rain caused a landslip on the railway line at Ruscombe (Berks.). On the 11th 98 mm (3·9 in) of rain fell at Slapton (Devon) and 64 mm (2·5 in) fell at Princetown (Devon) on the 12th. On the 13th there was extensive fog over England, Wales and southern Scotland. On the 19th 73 mm (2·9 in) of rain fell at Ardentinny (Strathclyde) and on the 20th there were gales in many places in the north and west when gusts of 60 knots (69 mph) were recorded at Edinburgh, Charter Hall (Borders), Duirinish (Highland) and Greenock Point (Strathclyde). On the 22nd 76 mm (3·0 in) of rain fell at Aber (Gwynedd). Monthly mean temperatures were above normal in England and Wales but near normal in Northern Ireland and Scotland. The mean over England and Wales was the highest since 1961, mainly because the night temperatures were unusually high. Oxford had its warmest September since 1949. The highest temperature recorded during the month was 28·0°C (82·4°F) at Gogerddan (Dyfed) on the 17th and the lowest was −6·0°C (21·2°F) at Kinbrace (Highland) on the 11th. Sunshine totals were above normal in northern and eastern Scotland and north-east and central England but below normal elsewhere. The highest monthly total was 213 hours at Guernsey and the highest daily total was 12.9 hours at Long Sutton (Hants.).

October.—Rainfall totals were generally above normal except in parts of southern and eastern Scotland, parts of eastern England and East Anglia. On the 16th 62 mm (2·4 in) of rain fell at Onich (Highland). Fog formed widely over England and Wales on the 18th and persisted all day in the Vale of York. From the 19th the weather became generally unsettled with some very heavy rain. The 20th was very wet in Wales, when 80 mm (3·1 in) of rain fell at Cwmbargoed and 77 mm (3·0 in) at Cilfynydd (Mid

Glam.); 84 mm (3·3 in) fell at Yarner Wood (Devon). Two people were killed as gales swept western areas, uprooting trees and disrupting traffic. The heavy rain caused widespread flooding. Between the 20th and 22nd 133 mm (5·2 in) of rain fell in the Brecon Beacons (Powys) area. Thunder was recorded in some part of the United Kingdom every day from the 19th to the 24th. On the 21st 66 mm (2·6 in) of rain fell at Fort William (Highland). On the 28th there was very heavy rain with gales in many areas. A gust of 88 knots (101 mph) was recorded at Portland Bill (Dorset) and 106 mm (4·1 in) of rain fell at Moel Cynnedd (Powys), while 66·5 mm (2·6 in) fell at Holme Moss (W. Yorks.). There was heavy rain in southern areas on the 30th–31st and 64 mm (2·5 in) fell at Stornoway (Western Isles) on the 30th. Snow or sleet fell in the far north of Scotland in the first half of the month and over the Scottish mountains on the 27th. Monthly mean temperatures were above normal everywhere except the extreme north of Scotland. On the 2nd the mean temperature at Cape Wrath (Highland) was 8·5°C (47·3°F) with a maximum of 8·9°C (48·0°F), while Tummell Bridge (Tayside) had a minimum of −2·6°C (27·3°F) which rose to a maximum of 15°C (59·0°F) on the 3rd. The highest temperature during the month was 23·2°C (73·8°F) at Faversham (Kent) on the 5th and the lowest was −3·0°C (26·6°F) at Grantown-on-Spey (Highland) on the 15th. Sunshine totals were below or near normal almost everywhere . On the 17th most places in the United Kingdom had between 8 and 10 hours of sunshine. The highest monthly total was 135 hours at Herne Bay (Kent) and the highest daily total was 10.7 hours at East Kilbride (Strathclyde) on the 2nd.

November.—Rainfall totals were below normal everywhere and some parts of the Moray Firth area received less than 3 mm (0·12 in) of rain during the first fortnight. However, the first few days of the month did produce some heavy rain, especially in western areas of Wales and England. On the 7th 54 mm (2·1 in) fell at St. Austell (Cornwall), 54 mm (2·1 in) at Betws-y-Coed (Gwynedd) on the 10th and 51 mm (2·0 in) at Trassey Sleivenaman (Co. Down) on the 17th. The 8th was a very windy day with many gusts over 50 knots (58 mph) being recorded in southern Wales and southern England. Gusts of 75 knots (86 mph) were recorded at Portland Bill (Dorset). The 10th brought wintry showers to the Scottish Highlands, leaving a thin covering of snow on high ground. Fog was widespread and dense in places between the 11th and 15th. Widespread fog occurred between the 18th and 22nd, especially in eastern England. On the 25th snow in north-east Scotland produced 1 cm (0·4 in) of level snow at Grantown-on-Spey (Highland). During the last week of the month dense fog occurred over central Scotland on most nights and persistent fog disrupted air and sea travel to Northern Ireland. Parts of the Midlands and central southern England were foggy on the 26th–27th and there was freezing fog in some southern areas between the 28th and 30th. Monthly mean temperatures were generally around normal. The 12th and 13th were warm in England and Wales with temperatures above 16°C (61°F) in many places. On the 13th 18·7°C (65·7°F) was recorded at Trawscoed and Cwmystwyth (Dyfed) and 18·9°C (66·0°F) at Nantmor (Gwynedd). The 25th–26th was a cold night in the south, a minimum temperature of −8·8°C (16·2°F) being recorded at Gatwick (W. Sussex). On the 25th, −8·5°C (16·7°F) was recorded at Tummel Bridge (Tayside). The highest temperature during the month was 19·1°C (66·4°F) at Aber (Gwynedd) on the 12th and the lowest was −10·3°C (13·5°F) at Grendon Underwood (Bucks.) on the 26th. Sunshine totals were mostly above normal except for a few places in north-west England, the Isle of Man, eastern

Scotland, Northern Ireland and southern Devon. Over much of southern England it was the sunniest November on record. Scotland also had a sunny month and Edinburgh had a total of 94 hours. The highest monthly total was 147 hours at Folkestone (Kent), the highest November total anywhere in the United Kingdom since records began. The highest daily total was 8·8 hours at Long Sutton (Hants.) on the 16th.

December.—Rainfall totals were generally above normal over England and Wales but below normal in Northern Ireland and Scotland. In Northern Ireland it was the driest December since 1975. There was widespread freezing fog on the 2nd and 3rd and again on the 10th and 11th. At Hampstead (London) there was no measurable rain for 31 days from November 10 to December 11, followed by 116·9 mm (4·6 in) on the 12th and 13th. On the 13th snow fell as far south as the Midlands. Drifting snow blocked the Snake and Woodhead passes in Derbyshire, roads between Shrewsbury and Much Wenlock, roads in the Ellesmere area, and the road between Ruthin and Mold in northern Wales were blocked. Snow was 13cm (5·1 ins) deep in places. There was further snow in Derbyshire on the 14th with up to 13 cm (5·1 in) lying in the Buxton area. Also on the 14th a tornado damaged more than 100 buildings at Long Stratton (Norfolk). Strong winds combined with an exceptionally high tide on the 14th brought widespread flooding to many areas on the south coast. On the 15th 24 cm (9·5 in) of level snow lay at Moel-y-Crio (Clwyd). On the 16th gales and rain in south-west England caused very severe flooding at Plymouth while 85 mm (3·3 in) of rain fell at Clatteringshaws (Galloway) and 75 mm (2·9 in) at Bryansford (Co. Down). A gust of 104 knots (120 mph) was recorded at Falmouth (Cornwall) on the 17th and 78 knots (90 mph) was recorded at Fraserburgh (Grampian) on the 18th, while snow fell over eastern Wales and the north-west Midlands. On the 21st a tornado cut through West and East Stour (Dorset), uprooting trees and causing damage to buildings. A band of heavy rain and thunder passed over southern areas on the 23rd and on the 24th a gust of 72 knots (83 mph) was recorded at Edinburgh. Monthly mean temperatures were above normal in southern areas but below normal in the north. In Scotland the coldest day was the 14th when the maximum temperature at Tummel Bridge (Tayside) was −7·0°C (19·4°F) and the minimum temperature −13°C (8·6°F). The highest temperature during the month was 15·5°C (59·9°F) at Hadlow College (Kent) on the 16th, Sparsholt (Hants.) on the 20th and Bastreet (Cornwall) on the 21st; the lowest temperature recorded was −13·6°C (7·5°F) at Kinbrace (Highland) on the 15th. Sunshine totals were below normal generally in England and Wales but above normal in most other areas. At Broom's Barn (Suffolk) it was the dullest December for 20 years with only 25 hours total for the month. Sheffield had its lowest total since 1933. The highest monthly total was 85·3 hours at Jersey and the highest daily total was 7·7 hours, also at Jersey.

Year (1989).—The main features of the weather of 1989 were the long dry period in southern England and southern Wales, and the gales of January, February, April, October and December. The lack of rainfall was a matter for concern as the dry period had really started in the late summer of 1988. Sunshine totals were above normal over most of the United Kingdom for the winter months. The 1988–89 winter was the mildest in England and Wales for 260 years and the mildest in Scotland since 1932–33. The year 1989 was the warmest in central England for 330 years. January was very mild with widespread gales in northern areas. Glasgow had its mildest

January since 1868 and Braemar had its mildest since 1856. In western Scotland it was one of the wettest Januarys on record. In Glen Shiel (Highland) 855 mm (33·7 in) of rain was recorded. Fog was widespread and slow to clear over England and Wales between the 18th and 20th. February was a month of contrasts in the north, with wet and stormy weather in western Scotland and dry weather in the east. Exceptionally heavy and prolonged rain in western Scotland on the 5th and 6th caused flooding and landslips over a wide area. Gusts reached 92 knots (106 mph) at Butt of Lewis, 93 knots (107 mph) at Benbecula, and 100 knots (115 mph) at Fair Isle on the 13th. At Fraserburgh (Grampian) a record gust of 123 knots (142 mph) was recorded with a mean speed of 66 knots (76 mph). Traffic was disrupted and trees brought down as far south as Leicestershire and Wales. On the 24th snowfall was considerable in parts of Wales, the Peak District and the southern Pennines. Southern England recorded its lowest atmospheric pressure (below 950 millibars) for over 100 years on the 25th. Bradford had its sunniest February on record. March was another generally unsettled month with rainfall above normal almost everywhere except some eastern coastal areas. Coloured dust was deposited at Keyworth (Notts.) on the 21st and at Chagford (Devon) on the 31st. Temperatures were generally above normal. On the 31st the London Weather Centre recorded 19·9°C (67·8°F), its highest March temperature for 21 years. April was a generally unsettled month with rainfall totals above normal in England, Wales and Northern Ireland but below in many parts of Scotland. There was snow or sleet on many days and on the 5th 3–6 cm (1·2–2·4 in) of snow lay in south-east England, while 40 cm (15·7 in) lay at Holme Moss (W. Yorks.). On the 13th there was a violent thunderstorm at Halstead (Essex) and on the 25th 10 cm (3·9 in) of snow lay at Nottingham. The 11th was a stormy day, particularly over south-west England and southern Wales. May was a generally warm dry month. A dust devil at Hurst (Surrey) lifted garden furniture and moved a child's metal slide nearly 12 m (39·4 ft) on the 9th and thunderstorms caused damage in a flash flood at Halifax (W. Yorks.) on the 19th. There was flooding in central and southern England, the Midlands and some northern areas after thunderstorms on the 23rd and 24th. Central London had its driest May for 300 years, and it was the driest over England and Wales since 1896. Many places had record amounts of sunshine, particularly in south-east England. June was an unusually foggy month and on the 5th and 6th thunderstorms were widespread; on the 6th traffic in Gillingham (Kent) was halted by hailstones several centimetres deep on the roads. Also on the 6th a tornado was reported near Brightlingsea (Essex). Thunder was reported in some part of the country on each of the first eight days. July was a generally warm dry month except in some areas of south-east England, Northern Ireland and Shetland where rainfall was above normal. A rainfall total of 9 mm (0·3 in) at Edinburgh was the lowest ever recorded there. Many places had the sunniest July for many years. August was generally warm and dry except in western Scotland and Northern Ireland. Sheffield had its sunniest August since 1898. September was generally warm and dry. Durham and Tynemouth had their driest September since 1898. Severe thunderstorms in the south between the 10th and 13th caused much damage. On the 12th lightning damaged houses in Wokingham and Bracknell (Berks.) and in south and east London flood water was over 1½ feet deep. In Kent a man was killed by lightning near Herne Bay. October was an unsettled month. On the 20th two people were killed and several injured as gales and heavy rain brought down trees and caused widespread flooding in western

areas. On the 28th a gust of 88 knots (101 mph) was recorded at Portland Bill. November started unsettled but became generally settled with periods of widespread fog. Over much of southern England it was the sunniest November on record and 147 hours at Folkestone (Kent) was the highest November total anywhere in the United Kingdom since sunshine records began. December was a month of contrast, dry and settled with fog at first but becoming very wet and windy. On the 13th snow fell as far south as the Midlands. Snow was 13 cm (5·1 in) deep in hilly areas of Shropshire. On the 14th gales and an exceptionally high tide brought widespread flooding to the south coast and a tornado struck Long Stratton (Norfolk). On the 16th Plymouth had its worst floods for many years and on the 17th a gust of 104 knots (120 mph) was recorded at Falmouth (Cornwall). On the 21st a tornado struck West and East Stour (Dorset); a 500 gallon oil drum was lifted and blown 200 m (656 ft) and a 17 m (56 ft) radio mast was twisted like a corkscrew before crashing to the ground.

(1990) January.—Rainfall totals were above normal except in eastern coastal areas of England. On the 3rd there was heavy rain in the Glasgow area and from the 9th rain and strong winds occurred in all areas. On the 10th 67 mm (2·6 in) of rain fell at Moel Cynnedd (Powys). On the night of the 16th–17th there were gales in northern areas with gusts of 76 knots (87 mph) at Stornoway and 79 knots (91 mph) at Benbecula (Western Isles) on the 16th, and 109 knots (125 mph), a January record, at Fair Isle (Shetland) on the 17th. The mean wind speed at Fair Isle was 72 knots (83 mph). There were heavy wintry showers in Scotland on the 17th and 18th, and on the 23rd thundery snow showers on higher ground. On the 24th there was snow as far south as the north Midlands, and snow on the 24th–25th with strong winds gave blizzards in southern Scotland. Early on the 26th 30 cm (11·8 in) of snow lay at Cairngorm (Highland) and 29 cm (11·4 in) lay at Leadhills (Borders). The 25th brought severe gales to England and Wales with gusts up to 93 knots (107 mph) at Aberporth (Dyfed) and Gwennap Head (Cornwall). Gusts above 80 knots (92 mph) were widespread on southern and western coasts, and gusts of more than 70 knots (81 mph) occurred in many areas of central and southern England and Wales. Very extensive structural damage occurred and large numbers of trees were blown down over a much greater area than that affected by the storm of October 1987. Many people were injured and several were killed. Road and rail traffic was severely disrupted and large areas were left without electricity. On the 27th heavy rain fell in a broad belt from Yorkshire and Lancashire through Wales and the Midlands to Devon and Cornwall. Heavy snow over northern England and Wales gave snow depths of 23 cm (9·1 in) at Wilsden (W. Yorks.) and 20 cm (7·9 in) at Moel-y-Crio (Clwyd). On the 29th, 30th and 31st showers and longer periods of rain were widespread. Rainfall was heavy, with thunder in the south and west and extensive flooding in many areas, particularly around the river Severn. Monthly mean temperatures were above normal everywhere and the highest temperature during the month was 16·0°C (60·8°F) at Colwyn Bay (Clwyd) on the 15th. The lowest temperature was −8·1°C (17·4°F) at Kinbrace (Highland) on the 27th. Sunshine totals were below normal in southern coastal areas, Shetland and western Scotland but above normal elsewhere. The highest monthly total was 86·7 hours at Craibstone (Grampian) and the highest daily total was 8·1 hours at East Hoathly (E. Sussex) on the 28th.

February.—Rainfall totals were above normal everywhere and were nearly four and a half times the average amount in the western Highlands. It was the wettest February since 1886 at Fort Augustus (Highland), and at Paisley (Strathclyde) it was the wettest since 1894. On the 1st heavy rain in Scotland produced a fall of 49 mm (1·9 in) at Sloy (Strathclyde). There were some severe gales on the 1st, and on the 3rd there was prolonged heavy rain south-east of a line from the Bristol Channel to the Wash, resulting in flooding in many areas. The rain turned to snow in many places. On the 4th 84 mm (3·3 in) of rain fell at Black Mount (Strathclyde). Much of England and Wales had heavy rain on the 6th and 7th; 63 mm (2·5 in) fell at Yarner Wood (Devon) on the 6th and 67 mm (2·6 in) at Pancelli (Powys) on the 7th. Cilfynydd (Mid Glam.) received 108 mm (4·3 in) over the two days. There was widespread flooding along the valleys of the rivers Wye, Severn and Thames. On the 8th and 9th there was snow in places over Scotland and over high ground in western England and Wales. On the 11th it was very wet in many areas, with heavy snow in Scotland; 57 mm (2·2 in) of rain fell at Clatteringshaws (Galloway). A gust of 81 knots (93 mph) was recorded at Burrington (Devon) on the 11th. Sleet or snow fell in northern areas on the 14th. On the 19th there were severe gales and 83 mm (3·3 in) of rain fell at Betws-y-Coed (Gwynedd). On the 22nd a gust of 113 knots (130 mph) was recorded at Cairngorm (Highland) and on the 26th there were gusts of 85 knots (98 mph) at Leeds and 86 knots (99 mph) at Hemsby (Norfolk). On the 26th and 27th very strong winds behind the spring tides caused severe flooding and wave damage along several stretches of the coast. At Towyn (Clwyd) the sea-wall was breached, causing a major disaster. Some homes were damaged beyond repair and many people were rendered homeless. Scotland had further snow showers on the 28th. Monthly mean temperatures were above normal everywhere and were more than 4°C (7°F) above normal in south-east England. The highest temperature of the month was 19·2°C (66·6°F) at March (Cambs.) on the 23rd and the lowest was −8·4°C (16·9°F) at Grantown-on-Spey (Highland) and Kinbrace (Highland) on the 15th. Sunshine totals were generally above normal in eastern areas and below in western areas. The highest monthly total was 117 hours at Folkestone (Kent) and the highest daily total was 9·9 hours at Clacton-on-Sea (Essex) on the 27th.

March.—Rainfall totals were below normal everywhere except western and northern Scotland. Fort William (Highland) had more than four times the normal amount whereas Worthing (W. Sussex) only received 7 per cent of its normal amount. It was the wettest month on record (100 years) at Fort Augustus (Highland), whereas parts of Kent had only 2 mm (0·1 in) of rain in the whole month. Over England and Wales it was the driest March since 1961. The month began with hail and snow in Scotland and 18 cm (7·1 in) of snow lay at Eskdalemuir (Dumfries) on the 2nd. On the 3rd there was persistent rain in Scotland when Fort William (Highland) had 58·6 mm (2·3 in) and Elphin (Highland) had 55 mm (2·2 in). A gust of 77 knots (89 mph) was recorded at Sumburgh (Shetland) on the 5th and 51·2 mm (2·0 in) of rain fell at Errochty (Tayside). There were stong winds in northern England on the 9th when a gust of 70 knots (81 mph) was recorded at Point of Ayre (IOM). On the 10th 65 mm (2·6 in) of rain fell at Loch Awe (Strathclyde), and gusts of 70 knots (81 mph) were recorded in Orkney and Shetland on the 11th. All areas had some rain on the 13th and on the 15th 52·3 mm (2·1 in) of rain fell at Fort William (Highland) and 78 mm (3·1 in) at Onich (Highland). The 19th was wet in parts of southern England and southern Wales, with wintry showers in the north. Coloured dust was deposited at Llanymawddwy (Gwynedd), North-

wood (London) and Woodley (Berks.) on the 19th. On the 20th 51·2 mm (2·0 in) of rain fell at Sloy (Strathclyde). There were showers of hail or snow with thunder in places on the 24th and there were showers in south-east England on the 25th. An atmospheric pressure of 1047·9 millibars in the Scilly Isles on the 3rd was the highest March pressure recorded this century. Monthly mean temperatures were above normal everywhere. Sheffield had its highest mean March temperature since 1961 and Coventry had its warmest March since 1886. The highest temperature during the month was 22·3°C (72·1°F) at Cambridge on the 18th and the lowest was −6·6°C (20·1°F) at Widdybank Fell (Co. Durham) on the 2nd. Sunshine totals were above normal in central and eastern areas but below normal in western coastal areas from Scilly to Orkney. Sheffield had its highest total since 1978 and Coventry had its highest since 1967. The highest monthly total was 185·7 hours at Guernsey and the highest daily total was 11·3 hours at Jersey on the 30th.

April.—Rainfall totals were below normal everywhere except northern and western Scotland, south-east England and East Anglia. The dry weather in most places now began to affect water levels in spite of the winter rains. Overnight on the 1st–2nd there was rain over much of Scotland, Wales and north-west England. On the 1st 25·3 mm (1·0 in) of rain fell at Lerwick (Shetland). Rain spread to other areas on the 2nd, with thunder over East Anglia and south-east England and some snow in northern areas. An earthquake shook much of England and Wales on the 2nd, the epicentre being in the Wrexham (Clwyd) area. The magnitude was 5·2 on the Richter scale but only minor damage occurred. On the 3rd there were heavy snow, sleet or hail showers, which were widespread in Scotland; Aviemore (Highland) had 11 cm (4·3 in) of level snow by the afternoon. Rain crossed most areas from the west on the 13th and 25 mm (1·0 in) fell at Holme Moss (W. Yorks.) on the 14th. Showers in eastern England on the 18th gave way to more general rain which produced 10–20 mm (0·4–0·8 in) in western areas. On the 19th there were heavy showers and thunderstorms with hail, and Hampstead Heath (London) was covered in a layer of hail. Parts of north-east England and south-east Scotland had less than 2 mm (0·1 in) of rain between the 18th and 30th. A monthly total of 7 mm (0·3 in) at Tynemouth (Tyne and Wear) was the lowest April total at the station since 1912. Monthly mean temperatures were slightly above normal in most areas. Nevertheless the 3rd saw the start of the coldest spell to affect the country in the first four months of the year. Severe frosts on the 4th and 5th damaged many plants and fruit trees which had been advanced by the earlier warm weather. The Easter Bank Holiday was cold and windy. Sheffield recorded its highest April maximum temperature since 1949. The highest temperature during the month was 25·0°C (77·0°F) at Aberdovey (Gwynedd) on the 30th and the lowest was 7·3°C (45·1°F) at St. Harmon (Powys) on the 9th. Sunshine totals were above normal everywhere except in a few areas of western Scotland and Northern Ireland. At Dyce (Grampian) a total of 209 hours for the month was the highest since 1946 and at Leuchars (Fife) a total of 217 hours was the highest since 1922. The highest total during the month was 273 hours at Eastbourne (E. Sussex) and the highest daily total was 14·7 hours at Wick (Highland) on the 4th.

May.—Rainfall totals were below normal everywhere except for a narrow band from Prestwick (Strathclyde) to Newcastle upon Tyne. Most of England and Wales had less than half the normal amount of rain, while the south Midlands, and central and southern England had less than 10 per cent of the normal amount. Benson (Oxon.) and Bracknell (Berks.) had only 6 per cent of the normal amount. There was heavy rain in northern Scotland on the 5th. The 6th was the wettest day of the month in Scotland when 28·3 mm (1·1 in) of rain fell at Kinloss (Grampian). South-west Scotland had heavy thundery showers on the 7th and 8th. On the 7th 28·3 mm (1·1 in) of rain fell at Glenlee (Galloway). There were showers and thunderstorms in most areas of England and Wales on the 9th and on the 11th there were heavy showers in eastern coastal areas of England. On the 14th–15th rain, heavy and with thunder in places, crossed much of England, Wales and southern Scotland. There were further heavy thunderstorms in Wales, northern and western England, and southern Scotland on the 15th. Also on the 15th 33·6 mm (1·3 in) of rain fell at Newcastle upon Tyne. This was the wettest day of the month in England and Wales. From the 18th to the 28th most areas were dry and some places in southern England had no rain between the 11th and the 28th. There was some significant rain in the north and west on the 29th. Monthly mean temperatures were generally above normal everywhere and the temperature reached the high 20s C (80s F) in some part of the country on each of the first five days of the month, giving the hottest start to May since 1875. At Heathrow Airport a temperature of 28·1°C (82·6°F) on the 3rd was the highest for the day since 1893. The morning of the 26th was the coldest of the month with temperatures of −2·6 and −2·7°C (27·3 and 27·1°F) being recorded in the Scottish glens. There was even a touch of ground frost in southern England. The highest temperature of the month was 28·6°C (83·5°F) at Barbourne (Worcs.) on the 3rd and the lowest was −3·0°C (26·6°F) at Covenham (Lincs.) on the 26th. Sunshine totals were mostly above normal, ranging from 98 per cent of normal in isolated places in north-east Scotland to 157 per cent to Rhoose (Mid Glam.). The highest monthly total was 331 hours at Folkestone (Kent) and the highest daily total was 16 hours at Prestwick (Strathclyde) on the 24th and at Benbecula (Western Isles) on the 25th.

June.—Rainfall totals were above normal almost everywhere except in parts of western Scotland, East Anglia, northern Devon and east Kent. A total of 127 mm (5·0 in) at Edinburgh was the highest at the station since 1928 and the second highest since 1896. On the 1st there were thunderstorms in East Anglia, Kent and the Isle of Wight, and on the 2nd there were thunderstorms in northern England. On the 3rd 39 mm (1·5 in) of rain fell at Elphin (Highland). On the 6th there was heavy rain in Scotland when 65·8 mm (2·6 in) fell at Aviemore (Highland), 51·5 mm (2·0 in) at Sloy (Strathclyde), and 49·4 mm (1·9 in) at Dalcross (Highland). At Carbridge (Highland) part of the railway embankment was washed away by a swollen stream and the Inverness–London morning express was lucky not to be derailed when it lurched over the gaps under the lines. Thunder occurred in east and south-east England on the 7th but most of East Anglia and south-east England still had little or no rain. On the 8th thunderstorms occurred in southern Scotland, the Midlands and central southern England but amounts of rain were very small. On the 10th thundery outbreaks brought small amounts of rain to central southern England and on the 11th there were some scattered showers and a wider area of rain for a time over the West Country. Boscombe Down (Wiltshire) had 15 mm (0·6 ins) of rain, the largest amount to fall in England during this period. On the 17th and 18th there was rain in all areas and on the 20th 38 mm (1·5in) fell at Cilfynnydd (Mid Glam.). Further rain fell over England and Wales on the 21st, and 67 mm (2·6 in) at Lentran (Highland). On the 22nd there were thunderstorms in East Anglia, Kent and the south Midlands but again amounts of rain were very small. On the 23rd thunderstorms crossed the country from Merseyside to East Anglia but again with very little rain. Monthly mean temperatures were below normal everywhere except the far north of Scotland, Shetland, Orkney, the Western Isles and the Channel Islands. The 9th was the warmest day in parts of Scotland and at Strathallan (Tayside) 23·9°C (75·0°F) was recorded. By contrast the maximum temperature recorded at Fylingdales (N. Yorks.) on the 12th was only 9·0°C (48·2°F). The highest temperature of the month was 26·0°C (78·8°F) at Waddington (Lincs.) on the 26th and the lowest was 0·5°C (32·9°F) at Tummel Bridge (Tayside) on the 6th. Sunshine totals were below normal everywhere except at Tiree (Strathclyde) where the total was normal. The highest monthly total was 198·5 hours at Folkestone (Kent) and the highest daily total was 15·4 hours at Boulmer (Northumberland) on the 20th.

AVERAGE AND GENERAL VALUES, 1988–1990 (June)

Month	Rainfall (mm)				Temperature (°C)				Bright Sunshine (hrs per day)			
	Aver. 1941–1970	1988	1989	1990	Aver. 1951–1980	1988	1989	1990	Aver. 1951–1980	1988	1989	1990
England and Wales												
January........	86	154	47	133	4·0	5·8	6·7	7·1	1·6	1·7	2·1	1·8
February......	65	63	88	141	4·1	5·2	6·4	7·8	2·3	3·7	3·4	2·8
March	59	94	92	24	5·9	6·6	7·8	8·7	3·6	3·1	3·4	4·4
April..........	58	42	83	38	8·2	8·5	6·9	8·5	5·1	4·6	4·7	7·1
May	67	60	21	25	11·3	12·0	13·2	12·9	6·3	6·5	8·9	8·2
June	61	37	55	70	14·3	14·6	14·7	14·0	6·7	5·8	8·0	4·4
July	73	138	38	—	16·0	15·1	18·3	—	5·9	4·9	8·5	—
August.........	90	92	58	—	15·9	15·7	17·0	—	5·5	5·8	7·6	—
September	83	66	41	—	14·0	13·8	15·1	—	4·6	4·8	4·3	—
October	83	92	98	—	11·0	11·1	12·3	—	3·3	3·3	2·9	—
November	97	49	61	—	7·1	6·2	7·2	—	2·1	3·0	2·9	—
December	90	44	134	—	5·1	7·7	5·5	—	1·5	1·3	0·9	—
YEAR	912	931	814	—	9·8	10·2	10·9	—	4·1	4·1	4·8	—
Scotland												
January........	137	193	206	247	3·5	4·2	7·3	5·7	1·3	1·4	1·3	1·3
February.......	104	149	240	292	3·4	4·5	5·2	5·6	2·4	2·2	2·7	2·1
March	92	159	188	241	5·1	5·0	5·7	7·5	3·3	3·1	3·7	3·0
April...........	90	85	63	95	7·1	7·2	6·0	7·3	5·0	4·1	4·5	5·6
May	91	55	53	55	9·9	10·5	10·7	11·0	5·7	6·5	7·0	6·6
June	92	33	76	124	12·7	13·6	12·5	12·5	5·9	6·1	6·5	4·3
July	112	202	49	—	13·9	13·7	15·6	—	4·9	4·1	7·3	—
August.........	129	187	184	—	13·9	13·9	14·1	—	4·6	4·1	4·3	—
September	137	156	96	—	12·2	12·3	12·0	—	3·7	3·9	3·7	—
October	149	177	187	—	9·8	9·3	10·4	—	2·6	2·4	2·4	—
November	142	91	60	—	6·0	6·0	6·3	—	1·7	2·1	2·3	—
December	156	150	96	—	4·5	7·3	3·2	—	1·1	0·9	1·2	—
YEAR	1431	1637	1496	—	8·5	9·0	9·1	—	3·5	3·4	3·9	—

TEMPERATURE, RAINFALL AND WIND SPEED RECORDS

WORLD: The maximum air temperature recorded is 57·8°C (136°F) at San Louis, Mexico on August 11, 1933; the minimum air temperature recorded is −89·2°C (−128·56°F) at Vostok, Antarctica on July 21, 1983. The greatest rainfall recorded in one day is 1,870 mm (73·62 in) at Cilaos, Isle de Réunion on March 16, 1952; the greatest rainfall in one calendar month is 9,300 mm (366·14 in) at Cherrapunji, Assam in July 1861, the greatest annual total being 22,990 mm (905·12 in) also at Cherrapunji in 1861. The highest gust recorded was 201 knots (231 mph) at Mount Washington Observatory, New Hampshire, USA on April 12, 1934.

UNITED KINGDOM: The maximum air temperature recorded is 38·1°C (100·5°F) at Tonbridge, Kent on July 22 1868; the minimum air temperature recorded is −27·2°C (−17°F) at Braemar (Grampian) on February 11, 1895 and January 10, 1982. The greatest rainfall recorded in one day is 280 mm (11 in) at Martinstown, Dorset on July 18, 1955. The greatest annual total is 6,528 mm (257 in) at Sprinkling Tarn, Cumbria in 1954. The highest gust recorded was 150 knots (173 mph) at Cairngorm (Highland) on March 20, 1986. The highest low-level (below 200 m (656 ft)) gust was 123 knots (141·7 mph) at Fraserburgh (Grampian) on February 13, 1989. The highest mean hourly speed was 92 knots (106 mph) at Great Dun Fell (Cumbria) in December 1974. The highest low-level mean hourly speed was 72 knots (83 mph) at Shoreham-by-Sea (Sussex) on October 16, 1987.

WIND FORCE MEASURES

The **Beaufort Scale** of wind force has been accepted internationally and is used in communicating weather conditions. Devised originally by Admiral Sir Francis Beaufort in 1805, it now consists of the numbers 0–17, each representing a certain strength or velocity of wind at 10 m (33 ft) above ground in the open.

Scale No.	Wind Force	Mph	Knots	Scale No.	Wind Force	Mph	Knots
0	Calm	1	1	9	Strong gale	47–54	41–47
1	Light air	1–3	1–3	10	Whole gale	55–63	48–55
2	Slight breeze	4–7	4–6	11	Storm	64–72	56–63
3	Gentle breeze	8–12	7–10	12	Hurricane	73–82	64–71
4	Moderate breeze	13–18	11–16	13	—	83–92	72–80
5	Fresh breeze	19–24	17–21	14	—	93–103	81–89
6	Strong breeze	25–31	22–27	15	—	104–114	90–99
7	High wind	32–38	28–33	16	—	115–125	100–108
8	Gale	39–46	34–40	17	—	126–136	109–118

TEMPERATURE, RAINFALL AND SUNSHINE
IN THE UNITED KINGDOM

The following table gives mean air temperature (°C), total monthly rainfall (mm) and mean daily bright sunshine (hrs) at a representative selection of climatological reporting stations in the United Kingdom during the year July 1989 to June 1990 and the calendar year 1989. The heights (in metres) of the reporting stations above mean sea level are also given.

| | | 1989 | | | | | | | | | | | |
| | | July | | | August | | | September | | | October | | |
Station	Ht. m	Temp. °C	Rain mm	Sun hrs	Temp. °C	Rain mm	Sun hrs	Temp. °C	Rain mm	Sun hrs	Temp. °C	Rain mm	Sun hrs
Aberdeen (Dyce) .	65	15·3	17	6·5	14·1	77	5·4	12·1	26	4·0	9·7	69	2·6
Aberporth	134	16·3	34	7·9	15·4	67	7·3	13·7	40	3·8	11·7	104	1·9
Aldergrove	68	17·1	81	8·0	14·7	111	3·8	12·5	48	3·2	10·8	112	2·3
Aspatria	61	17·1	22	9·1	15·1	130	6·1	12·7	31	3·8	11·1	102	2·5
Bala	163	16·1	28	7·7	14·9	67	6·5	12·8	41	3·4	10·9	152	2·0
Birmingham (Elmdon)	98	18·1	55	8·5	16·6	54	8·3	14·5	28	4·6	11·3	80	2·9
Boulmer	23	15·3	11	8·1	15·1	69	6·6	13·1	13	4·3	11·0	47	3·1
Bournemouth (Hurn)	10	18·7	29	9·5	16·8	41	9·2	14·9	37	4·4	12·2	88	3·2
Bradford	134	16·9	40	7·4	15·5	27	6·0	13·9	12	3·9	10·7	86	2·3
Braemar	339	15·4	12	7·5	12·8	92	5·1	10·3	69	3·9	8·3	73	2·3
Buxton..........	307	15·9	37	7·9	14·9	57	6·9	12·8	27	4·0	9·8	171	2·7
Cambridge.......	24	18·9	43	7·3	18·1	29	7·7	16·1	18	3·9	12·8	32	3·1
Cheltenham	65	19·5	48	8·1	17·5	79	7·7	15·5	57	4·3	12·5	85	2·5
Clacton-on-Sea...	16	18·2	49	7·8	17·5	40	8·4	16·0	21	4·5	12·9	36	3·8
Douglas	85	16·5	17	8·7	14·9	111	4·9	13·1	45	3·3	11·5	113	2·6
Dumfries	49	16·3	29	9·0	14·6	129	4·9	12·3	51	3·4	10·7	103	2·8
Dundee	45	16·5	15	7·9	15·1	71	5·5	12·6	38	4·2	10·7	59	3·2
Durham	102	16·9	10	7·7	15·4	61	6·5	13·3	12	4·2	10·8	49	3·0
East Malling	33	19·1	16	8·1	18·0	26	8·2	15·9	45	4·9	12·9	45	3·7
Edinburgh.......	134	16·5	9	8·6	14·7	104	5·3	12·3	24	3·6	10·7	39	3·2
Glasgow (Abbotsinch)...	5	16·5	18	9·6	14·5	120	4·5	11·9	74	3·6	10·6	119	2·8
Gogerddan	31	17·1	34	8·1	15·9	99	6·7	14·0	52	3·9	12·2	129	2·1
Hastings	45	18·8	18	8·8	17·9	19	8·9	16·5	37	4·9	13·7	77	3·9
Hull	2	18·1	53	—	17·3	34	—	15·5	27	—	12·1	48	—
Inverness	4	16·5	18	6·7	14·5	43	4·2	12·3	33	4·6	10·4	77	2·9
Leeming.........	32	17·9	25	7·6	16·2	30	7·0	14·0	5	4·4	11·4	64	3·0
Lerwick.........	82	11·7	80	4·7	11·7	89	5·0	10·5	74	4·3	8·3	130	1·8
London (Heathrow)	25	20·3	37	8·9	18·6	56	8·6	16·7	11	4·4	13·4	53	3·7
Long Ashton.....	51	18·5	36	—	16·6	49	—	14·7	54	—	12·1	111	—
Lowestoft	25	17·9	17	6·8	17·7	23	7·3	16·3	43	4·3	12·7	33	3·1
Manchester (Ringway)	75	17·7	36	7·9	15·8	59	6·1	14·1	31	4·3	11·4	84	2·7
Manston	44	18·7	38	8·5	18·3	20	7·7	16·5	24	4·7	13·4	56	4·1
Melbury.........	143	17·3	25	9·4	15·9	54	6·5	13·9	131	4·1	12·2	166	2·5
Morecambe	7	17·5	19	9·0	16·1	134	6·5	14·1	13	4·1	11·5	112	2·4
Nottingham (Watnall).....	117	17·8	31	8·3	16·5	33	8·2	14·5	22	4·2	11·4	81	3·1
Oxford	63	19·5	29	9·1	17·9	43	8·7	15·9	24	4·7	12·4	54	2·9
Penzance	19	18·6	16	9·5	17·7	43	8·6	15·9	71	5·1	13·7	127	3·2
Plymouth	27	19·2	8	10·2	17·1	41	8·7	15·3	71	4·9	13·1	109	2·9
Prestwick	16	16·1	43	9·3	14·3	144	3·8	12·5	44	2·9	10·9	103	2·2
Rhoose..........	65	18·3	53	10·2	17·0	56	8·3	14·9	82	4·3	12·1	124	2·5
St. Mawgan......	103	18·3	13	9·8	16·9	60	7·8	15·0	82	4·7	13·1	123	2·7
Shawbury	72	17·7	27	8·4	16·1	40	7·8	13·8	26	4·0	11·3	64	2·8
Sheffield........	131	18·0	41	9·2	16·5	36	7·8	14·5	23	4·5	11·7	65	2·7
Skegness	5	17·1	20	8·4	17·1	25	8·6	15·1	31	4·9	11·9	36	3·1
Southampton	3	20·1	16	9·3	18·3	27	8·8	16·5	27	4·2	13·2	94	3·0
Stornoway	15	14·1	65	5·0	12·7	173	3·5	10·9	94	4·0	9·5	231	2·0
Tenby	5	17·7	25	9·1	15·9	96	7·7	14·1	73	4·2	12·6	128	2·3
Tiree...........	9	14·3	43	7·0	13·7	219	3·8	12·0	95	3·8	10·7	215	1·9
Torbay (Torquay)	8	19·4	23	9·3	17·9	57	8·7	15·6	80	4·8	13·5	102	3·0
Trawscoed.......	63	16·7	38	7·1	15·0	99	6·3	13·4	66	3·4	11·9	180	1·8
Ventnor.........	135	18·7	18	9·8	—	—	—	16·5	45	4·3	13·9	108	4·1
Waddington	68	17·8	31	8·3	16·9	34	8·6	14·9	31	4·7	11·7	61	3·3
Weymouth	21	19·0	10	9·7	17·3	41	9·1	15·9	66	5·4	13·7	96	3·2
Whitby..........	41	16·4	25	8·3	15·9	34	7·6	14·1	18	4·4	11·5	46	3·0
Worthing	2	18·9	28	9·6	17·5	15	8·8	16·3	46	4·7	13·3	75	3·6
Writtle..........	35	18·1	79	7·9	17·4	46	8·6	15·5	15	4·5	12·5	42	3·5

TEMPERATURE, RAINFALL AND SUNSHINE IN THE UNITED KINGDOM—*contd.*

Mean temperature of the air (°C), rainfall (mm) and bright sunshine (mean hours per day) at a representative selection of reporting stations during the year July 1989 to June 1990. Fuller details of the weather are given in the *Monthly Weather Report* published by the Meteorological Office.

	1989									1990					
	November			December			Year			January			February		
Station	Temp. °C	Rain mm	Sun hrs	Temp. °C	Rain mm	Sun hrs	Temp. °C	Rain mm	Sun hrs	Temp. °C	Rain mm	Sun hrs	Temp. °C	Rain mm	Sun hrs
Aberdeen (Dyce)	6·1	25	2·4	2·9	40	1·4	8·8	500	4·4	4·8	48	2·6	5·3	64	3·6
Aberporth	7·9	74	3·2	5·5	120	1·6	10·2	785	4·8	6·9	118	1·5	7·3	91	2·3
Aldergrove	6·4	25	1·7	4·1	61	1·3	9·5	809	4·0	5·7	104	1·8	5·5	132	2·3
Aspatria	5·9	56	2·9	3·0	45	1·1	9·7	866	4·6	6·5	138	1·2	6·6	192	1·6
Bala	6·0	101	1·9	3·0	191	0·3	9·3	1204	4·0	6·0	264	1·1	7·0	263	1·4
Birmingham (Elmdon)	5·7	44	2·8	4·7	132	0·5	10·3	712	4·7	6·3	99	2·3	7·4	109	2·8
Boulmer	6·9	25	2·6	4·4	45	1·4	9·3	386	4·9	5·7	51	2·5	6·3	60	2·7
Bournemouth (Hurn)	7·1	56	3·5	5·8	204	1·2	10·9	781	5·5	7·3	130	1·5	8·3	173	3·2
Bradford	6·1	53	1·8	4·7	101	0·5	9·9	707	3·9	6·1	154	1·4	6·6	131	2·2
Braemar	3·9	36	2·2	−0·4	76	0·5	7·1	778	3·8	3·5	143	1·1	3·1	209	2·4
Buxton	4·9	90	2·1	3·3	140	0·5	5·3	1134	4·3	5·0	180	1·5	5·4	142	1·4
Cambridge	6·2	35	3·3	5·7	125	0·7	11·1	518	4·6	6·9	44	2·1	8·1	71	3·6
Cheltenham	6·7	46	3·2	5·9	139	0·7	11·2	—	4·5	7·1	106	1·8	7·6	152	2·8
Clacton-on-Sea	7·7	17	3·9	6·1	105	1·3	11·1	499	—	6·7	46	2·1	7·5	52	3·9
Douglas	7·9	101	1·7	5·5	92	0·3	10·0	987	4·4	7·1	143	1·7	6·5	120	2·0
Dumfries	6·0	37	2·6	2·9	83	0·9	9·2	906	4·2	6·0	201	1·3	6·0	243	1·9
Dundee	6·3	27	2·9	3·4	51	1·9	—	466	4·5	5·5	84	2·1	5·9	70	3·1
Durham	6·1	35	2·5	3·5	64	0·8	9·6	417	4·5	5·4	73	2·1	6·3	60	2·9
East Malling	6·5	37	3·9	6·5	116	0·5	11·3	540	5·1	6·9	92	1·7	8·3	94	3·6
Edinburgh	6·3	13	3·1	3·3	51	1·3	9·3	529	4·3	5·3	92	1·9	5·5	110	2·5
Glasgow (Abbotsinch)	5·2	37	2·7	1·9	85	0·8	9·1	1076	4·1	5·8	206	1·3	6·2	218	1·7
Gogerddan	7·6	81	2·7	4·7	134	1·2	10·4	995	4·5	7·5	151	1·3	8·1	116	2·1
Hastings	8·4	58	4·3	7·1	120	1·0	11·9	609	5·6	7·7	102	1·6	8·5	101	3·9
Hull	6·9	37	—	5·5	97	—	10·9	507	—	6·7	49	—	7·3	57	—
Inverness	6·0	6	2·7	2·9	33	1·0	9·3	622	4·0	5·5	101	1·2	5·3	141	2·6
Leeming	6·2	31	2·2	3·9	61	1·1	10·1	443	4·6	6·1	84	2·1	7·1	69	2·6
Lerwick	6·3	56	1·6	4·1	90	0·4	7·6	1226	3·4	4·9	183	0·7	4·7	199	1·7
London (Heathrow)	7·3	24	3·6	6·8	119	1·1	12·1	534	5·2	7·3	71	1·9	8·5	92	3·4
Long Ashton	6·9	65	—	5·6	145	—	10·9	868	—	7·3	142	—	8·1	145	—
Lowestoft	7·6	18	3·2	6·2	75	0·8	11·0	456	—	6·5	49	1·9	7·5	78	3·3
Manchester (Ringway)	6·4	63	2·3	4·1	70	1·1	10·3	715	4·4	6·5	116	1·9	7·2	82	2·0
Manston	7·3	30	4·1	6·7	65	0·7	11·5	450	5·3	6·6	47	1·7	7·9	64	3·9
Melbury	7·9	119	2·5	5·3	190	0·9	10·4	1259	—	7·1	219	1·3	7·9	263	2·5
Morecambe	6·9	92	2·3	4·3	67	1·1	10·4	860	4·7	6·6	153	1·5	7·1	159	2·0
Nottingham (Watnall)	5·9	31	2·7	4·5	114	0·7	10·1	641	4·7	5·9	71	1·9	6·9	111	2·5
Oxford	6·5	33	3·5	5·7	141	0·9	11·3	598	5·1	7·3	75	1·9	8·3	94	3·4
Penzance	10·2	110	3·3	8·6	183	1·3	—	979	5·4	—	—	—	9·4	181	2·5
Plymouth	9·3	85	3·3	7·8	192	1·4	11·9	905	5·5	8·5	126	1·4	9·1	198	2·6
Prestwick	5·9	35	3·1	3·3	60	1·9	9·5	885	4·2	6·3	156	1·5	6·3	181	1·5
Rhoose	7·4	68	3·2	5·6	130	1·0	10·9	882	5·2	7·3	121	1·7	7·9	120	2·9
St. Mawgan	8·9	91	3·8	7·1	142	1·8	11·5	942	5·4	8·2	170	1·8	8·5	179	2·5
Shawbury	5·7	48	2·2	3·8	116	0·5	9·9	588	4·6	6·2	107	2·3	7·4	77	2·7
Sheffield	6·5	43	1·5	4·7	159	0·4	—	736	4·7	6·4	129	1·5	7·1	115	2·2
Skegness	7·0	46	3·3	6·1	85	1·1	10·5	438	—	6·3	38	2·3	7·1	70	3·5
Southampton	8·2	52	3·5	6·8	159	1·2	12·1	675	5·3	7·7	121	1·4	8·7	168	3·1
Stornoway	6·3	58	1·9	4·7	112	1·0	8·5	1479	3·3	5·5	202	0·9	4·7	264	2·1
Tenby	8·6	111	3·1	6·6	148	1·3	10·8	1067	4·9	8·1	172	1·6	8·3	144	2·7
Tiree	6·9	68	1·8	4·9	69	1·7	9·1	1384	4·0	6·4	168	0·9	5·6	246	1·6
Torbay (Torquay)	9·4	67	2·4	7·9	234	0·9	12·1	912	5·0	8·7	155	1·7	9·0	237	2·7
Trawscoed	7·2	111	2·0	4·9	152	0·4	10·0	1181	3·7	7·3	207	0·9	7·7	155	1·4
Ventnor	9·3	56	4·0	7·5	130	1·6	—	—	—	8·1	100	1·8	8·5	129	3·4
Waddington	6·1	37	3·1	4·7	88	0·8	10·3	538	5·0	6·1	49	2·3	7·1	66	3·1
Weymouth	8·7	55	2·9	6·7	189	1·2	11·9	729	5·5	8·5	91	1·5	8·7	153	2·9
Whitby	7·1	40	2·5	5·1	60	0·9	9·9	427	4·9	6·1	74	2·4	6·9	70	2·8
Worthing	8·1	52	4·1	6·9	136	1·5	11·7	569	5·7	7·4	109	1·7	8·3	107	3·6
Writtle	5·9	25	3·2	5·6	115	0·6	10·7	560	4·9	6·7	60	1·6	7·9	85	3·6

TEMPERATURE, RAINFALL AND SUNSHINE IN THE UNITED KINGDOM—*contd.*

Mean temperature of the air (°C), rainfall (mm) and bright sunshine (mean hours per day) at a representative selection of reporting stations during the year July 1989 to June 1990. Fuller details of the weather are given in the *Monthly Weather Report* published by the Meteorological Office.

	1990											
	March			April			May			June		
Station	Temp. °C	Rain mm	Sun hrs	Temp. °C	Rain mm	Sun hrs	Temp. °C	Rain mm	Sun hrs	Temp. °C	Rain mm	Sun hrs
Aberdeen (Dyce)	3·9	19	4·7	7·3	31	6·9	9·8	49	5·6	11·9	91	4·4
Aberporth	7·9	14	3·3	7·8	21	6·2	12·3	24	8·4	12·9	64	5·3
Aldergrove	8·0	37	2·7	7·6	51	5·6	11·9	47	6·9	12·9	118	5·2
Aspatria	7·5	33	3·9	7·4	49	5·8	11·8	50	7·6	13·3	76	5·4
Bala	7·6	35	2·8	6·7	60	5·3	10·9	42	7·0	11·9	85	3·7
Birmingham (Elmdon)	8·6	14	5·3	7·9	23	6·4	12·9	15	7·8	13·9	62	4·0
Boulmer	8·3	18	5·0	7·3	11	7·3	9·7	45	6·7	12·2	57	4·9
Bournemouth (Hurn)	7·9	6	5·0	8·1	41	8·1	12·9	14	9·2	13·5	50	4·6
Bradford	7·9	32	3·6	7·5	28	5·8	11·5	37	5·5	12·8	70	3·0
Braemar	5·5	79	4·1	5·7	21	6·0	9·3	48	5·4	—	71	4·6
Buxton	6·7	45	4·0	6·3	56	6·0	11·1	45	7·2	12·3	109	3·5
Cambridge.........	8·9	23	4·9	8·5	28	6·9	12·9	6	7·3	14·5	30	3·7
Cheltenham	8·3	17	4·8	8·5	68	6·5	14·0	15	8·4	10·2	84	3·5
Clacton-on-Sea.....	8·3	11	5·4	8·8	37	8·5	12·7	24	9·5	14·5	39	5·9
Douglas	7·7	29	2·8	7·9	43	6·6	11·7	59	8·1	12·5	104	5·6
Dumfries	7·5	57	3·1	7·5	34	5·5	11·5	84	6·2	12·8	81	4·2
Dundee	8·3	17	4·9	8·1	21	—	11·0	27	6·3	13·3	107	5·1
Durham	8·1	14	4·5	7·5	10	7·1	11·2	42	6·3	12·7	46	3·8
East Malling	8·7	3	5·1	8·6	40	8·2	13·1	4	8·9	14·1	55	5·5
Edinburgh..........	7·5	29	3·5	7·5	16	5·7	10·9	30	6·8	12·5	127	5·3
Glasgow (Abbotsinch)......	7·7	151	2·5	7·5	78	4·9	11·6	49	6·8	13·0	100	5·1
Gogerddan	8·5	26	3·3	7·9	35	6·3	12·5	33	8·8	13·3	86	4·6
Hastings	8·9	4	4·8	9·2	57	8·6	13·9	12	10·4	13·9	53	5·7
Hull	9·0	11	—	8·7	19	—	12·7	36	—	14·2	62	—
Inverness	7·5	134	3·2	7·7	38	5·6	11·5	35	5·7	12·9	147	2·8
Leeming...........	8·5	11	4·1	7·9	7	6·4	12·2	30	6·7	13·6	80	3·5
Lerwick	5·1	191	2·7	5·5	143	1·1	8·3	44	5·2	10·4	134	2·9
London (Heathrow)	9·2	17	5·0	9·4	30	8·2	14·7	4	9·3	15·1	39	4·4
Long Ashton........	8·3	18	—	8·5	35	—	13·1	9	—	13·7	80	—
Lowestoft	8·5	21	5·1	8·7	49	8·2	12·9	15	8·1	14·3	41	5·0
Manchester (Ringway)........	8·2	27	3·5	8·0	37	5·9	12·7	25	7·3	13·6	84	3·5
Manston	8·7	6	5·7	8·7	41	8·2	13·3	19	10·2	14·3	56	6·4
Melbury...........	8·1	32	3·8	7·5	57	7·3	12·5	28	9·5	12·7	106	4·5
Morecambe	8·1	36	3·4	8·3	28	6·6	12·9	59	8·3	13·7	76	4·6
Nottingham (Watnall).........	8·3	14	4·6	7·9	21	6·5	12·6	15	7·9	13·6	79	3·5
Oxford	8·9	18	4·7	8·5	20	7·8	13·4	9	9·2	14·4	49	4·0
Penzance..........	9·5	25	4·2	9·3	49	8·1	13·9	15	8·1	14·0	99	5·9
Plymouth	9·1	14	4·9	9·3	34	8·0	14·1	25	9·4	13·9	80	4·9
Prestwick	7·7	89	2·7	7·3	71	5·4	11·7	68	7·6	12·9	86	5·0
Rhoose............	8·3	23	5·0	8·0	30	7·7	13·5	15	10·3	13·9	73	4·9
St. Mawgan........	8·9	26	4·5	4·9	41	8·0	13·7	27	9·6	13·4	83	5·6
Shawbury.........	8·1	13	4·0	7·4	24	6·0	12·1	22	7·7	13·6	48	4·6
Sheffield..........	8·9	22	4·4	8·5	26	6·7	12·9	19	7·1	14·0	46	3·7
Skegness	8·5	9	5·1	7·7	19	7·5	11·9	29	9·0	14·1	48	5·0
Southampton	9·1	4	4·9	9·5	36	7·9	14·5	19	9·4	14·5	54	4·5
Stornoway	6·3	206	2·1	6·5	106	5·3	9·9	57	7·5	11·6	77	3·5
Tenby............	8·6	24	3·6	8·3	25	7·5	12·9	35	8·9	13·3	81	5·4
Tiree.............	7·3	156	2·0	7·1	116	5·8	10·5	34	8·8	12·0	102	6·6
Torbay (Torquay) ...	9·2	8	5·0	9·5	32	8·1	13·9	21	9·2	14·5	46	5·0
Trawscoed.........	8·1	36	2·9	7·1	48	5·6	11·5	37	7·9	12·7	90	3·5
Ventnor...........	9·1	3	5·5	9·5	38	8·9	14·5	4	10·3	13·9	46	5·7
Waddington	8·5	13	5·4	8·1	18	7·0	12·6	16	7·9	13·7	61	3·9
Weymouth	9·0	7	5·0	9·0	25	8·1	13·2	28	10·1	14·0	47	4·8
Whitby...........	8·6	9	4·2	7·9	13	6·9	10·9	32	6·5	13·5	59	3·7
Worthing	8·5	3	5·4	9·3	42	8·5	13·6	10	10·2	13·9	53	5·2
Writtle............	8·4	8	5·2	8·1	39	8·6	12·2	16	8·2	13·9	53	4·6

METEOROLOGICAL OBSERVATIONS, LONDON (HEATHROW)

Weather Record, July, 1989

Day	Temperature Max. °C	Temperature Min. °C	Wind speed knots	Rain-fall mm	Sun-shine hrs
1	22·3	14·6	7·0	0·1	2·7
2	20·1	10·7	5·3	0·0	9·1
3	24·4	10·6	6·4	0·0	14·5
4	25·5	11·7	8·1	0·0	15·6
5	28·6	14·0	9·9	0·0	12·5
6	31·0	16·8	7·4	18·0	8·2
7	21·0	18·2	4·7	1·6	0·0
8	24·6	15·8	3·4	5·4	1·8
9	18·3	15·1	5·4	0·0	0·0
10	24·0	14·1	3·4	0·0	4·2
11	26·0	16·5	3·6	0·0	10·3
12	22·6	14·6	4·7	0·0	10·1
13	25·0	12·5	5·8	0·0	13·0
14	22·5	11·6	3·5	0·0	10·2
15	28·1	11·5	5·0	0·0	14·8
16	25·0	15·4	4·9	0·0	7·1
17	28·5	13·8	4·7	0·0	10·6
18	25·0	14·4	4·5	0·0	13·3
19	26·9	13·5	3·7	0·0	14·0
20	29·8	15·1	6·7	0·0	13·7
21	32·1	17·3	8·5	0·3	8·6
22	34·2	19·9	5·0	1·4	9·5
23	31·8	19·4	4·1	0·0	11·5
24	30·0	19·4	5·6	0·0	8·6
25	29·9	17·0	5·3	0·0	10·2
26	27·4	17·1	5·8	0·0	6·4
27	25·6	13·5	4·3	0·0	8·9
28	25·7	13·9	5·3	0·0	9·4
29	26·5	14·4	6·1	5·1	8·6
30	18·7	16·4	6·7	4·5	1·7
31	19·4	11·3	6·4	0·3	5·7
Total	—	—	—	36·7	274·8
Mean	25·8	14·8	5·5	—	—
Temp. °F	78·4	58·6		—	—
Average	22·0	12·9	8·2	51·0	189·7

Weather Record, August, 1989

Temperature Max. °C	Temperature Min. °C	Wind speed knots	Rain-fall mm	Sun-shine hrs	Day
22·1	8·5	4·9	0·0	13·5	1
23·0	10·4	4·4	0·0	9·2	2
26·4	12·9	4·5	0·0	6·3	3
25·1	11·3	4·0	0·0	13·5	4
26·9	12·0	3·3	0·0	13·5	5
29·3	14·5	4·2	0·0	11·5	6
27·0	14·8	4·7	0·0	7·2	7
26·6	14·8	4·3	0·0	7·5	8
26·1	15·8	8·3	20·6	7·6	9
20·4	16·4	3·7	18·1	0·8	10
24·2	14·6	8·7	0·0	6·2	11
24·6	14·6	6·7	0·0	6·8	12
22·2	12·9	6·8	3·1	6·5	13
24·4	14·6	9·3	1·8	7·4	14
24·2	16·0	11·5	0·0	11·3	15
23·9	16·6	6·5	0·0	6·4	16
22·4	12·7	6·3	0·3	11·0	17
23·0	10·1	4·0	0·0	13·0	18
27·0	11·1	4·3	0·0	12·6	19
28·7	13·2	6·7	0·0	13·4	20
25·8	15·8	4·4	0·0	12·9	21
24·3	11·5	4·7	0·0	7·3	22
24·9	10·0	5·0	0·0	12·7	23
26·4	11·5	6·3	0·0	11·8	24
21·5	15·8	4·2	5·8	1·0	25
23·3	14·1	3·8	5·7	2·2	26
19·1	13·1	7·7	0·0	8·7	27
19·7	8·9	4·3	0·0	12·5	28
19·7	10·1	4·8	0·0	0·0	29
26·1	14·7	6·2	0·3	6·0	30
20·1	12·0	4·7	0·0	6·8	31
—	—	—	55·7	267·2	Total
24·1	13·1	5·6	—	—	Mean
75·4	55·6		—	—	Temp. °F
21·6	12·7	8·0	58·0	176·4	Average

Weather Record, September, 1989

Day	Temperature Max. °C	Temperature Min. °C	Wind speed knots	Rain-fall mm	Sun-shine hrs
1	20·7	9·7	3·7	0·0	10·0
2	18·4	11·3	5·6	0·0	9·3
3	18·7	7·8	3·1	0·0	7·4
4	21·2	12·0	2·9	0·0	5·5
5	22·9	12·5	2·9	0·0	9·2
6	25·7	11·1	2·8	0·0	11·3
7	26·7	12·8	3·2	0·0	10·3
8	22·6	16·0	8·2	0·7	2·9
9	16·5	14·1	9·9	0·8	0·0
10	19·7	13·4	8·4	0·0	0·1
11	19·4	16·2	6·6	0·0	0·0
12	21·2	15·4	3·1	3·5	0·6
13	19·4	13·7	4·2	0·0	0·5
14	16·7	8·5	5·0	3·2	2·1
15	21·5	11·6	7·9	1·2	0·4
16	22·2	15·6	8·2	0·6	1·6
17	21·1	17·5	8·0	0·1	0·1
18	23·9	13·7	6·4	0·2	6·1
19	21·0	14·6	6·6	0·0	9·0
20	22·4	11·5	7·1	0·0	10·8
21	26·7	12·0	6·3	0·1	9·4
22	19·4	16·9	8·0	0·0	1·7
23	18·7	10·4	3·6	0·0	3·1
24	22·1	13·0	2·3	0·0	2·6
25	22·7	10·6	3·7	0·0	6·5
26	20·4	11·4	2·7	0·4	2·2
27	18·4	14·9	4·2	0·0	1·0
28	16·9	11·4	4·6	0·0	1·6
29	18·2	7·8	4·7	0·0	5·8
30	15·6	10·9	3·4	0·1	0·1
31					
Total	—	—	—	10·8	131·2
Mean	20·7	12·6	5·2	—	—
Temp. °F	69·3	54·7		—	—
Average	19·2	10·6	7·9	56·0	144·7

Weather Record, October, 1989

Temperature Max. °C	Temperature Min. °C	Wind speed knots	Rain-fall mm	Sun-shine hrs	Day
15·5	12·3	2·5	0·0	0·0	1
16·4	12·0	2·5	0·0	3·6	2
15·9	5·5	3·3	0·0	1·9	3
19·9	12·7	6·5	0·0	9·3	4
20·9	6·5	4·3	4·2	4·7	5
16·0	5·2	6·2	0·0	0·0	6
13·9	10·7	6·1	1·7	0·0	7
15·4	8·7	6·8	0·0	6·2	8
15·3	6·8	5·0	0·2	1·5	9
16·2	9·3	3·7	0·1	3·1	10
17·1	10·7	4·2	0·4	2·5	11
19·5	11·8	5·0	0·0	4·1	12
15·6	13·0	5·7	0·1	2·1	13
14·8	8·8	5·4	0·0	5·4	14
17·1	4·7	3·7	0·0	4·5	15
18·1	8·7	6·3	0·0	4·0	16
20·1	7·6	2·9	0·0	9·5	17
17·7	6·4	3·4	0·2	3·1	18
18·9	12·2	7·0	12·7	3·4	19
17·6	10·4	12·1	12·1	6·9	20
18·6	11·9	15·3	1·0	0·2	21
19·4	11·4	8·2	2·3	0·8	22
17·0	12·1	3·0	0·6	0·3	23
15·6	7·1	5·6	0·0	9·0	24
18·1	10·2	6·8	0·6	7·0	25
14·7	10·9	4·1	4·1	0·0	26
19·1	11·2	7·0	2·9	2·2	27
14·8	13·1	16·4	1·8	2·5	28
16·2	10·4	12·0	3·4	3·6	29
15·6	10·3	6·5	4·4	6·0	30
17·8	11·3	4·7	0·0	6·1	31
—	—	—	52·4	105·2	Total
17·1	9·7	5·0	—	—	Mean
62·8	49·5		—	—	Temp. °F
15·2	7·6	7·8	58·0	104·4	Average

Entries of maximum temperature cover the 24 hour period 9–9 h; minimum temperature the 24 hour period 9–9 h; rainfall is for the 24 hours commencing at 9 h on the day of entry; sunshine is for the 24 hours 0–24 h; mean wind speed is 10 metres above the ground. 100 knots = 115·1 mph; 100 mm = 3·94 in; °F = 9/5°C + 32.

Averages are for the period 1951–1980 except for mean wind speed which is for 1961–1980.

Weather Record, November, 1989

Day	Temperature Max. °C	Min. °C	Wind speed knots	Rainfall mm	Sunshine hrs
1	14·6	7·6	3·2	0·9	1·4
2	14·4	9·1	7·0	9·2	0·0
3	13·6	5·8	5·9	1·5	7·3
4	12·7	6·0	7·0	0·0	3·1
5	11·0	1·7	3·5	0·2	2·7
6	10·3	1·5	2·5	0·0	7·7
7	12·7	2·8	3·3	4·0	0·2
8	14·8	7·9	12·2	1·7	0·3
9	12·0	3·3	7·8	5·3	2·3
10	14·5	5·8	9·6	1·3	0·0
11	16·0	11·1	7·9	0·0	4·3
12	16·1	6·9	3·0	0·1	7·6
13	8·6	5·0	2·0	0·1	0·0
14	9·6	6·0	2·7	0·0	0·0
15	11·5	6·3	6·8	0·0	0·0
16	10·8	3·9	10·2	0·0	7·8
17	9·0	2·4	8·1	0·0	0·6
18	12·6	4·5	6·5	0·0	3·9
19	12·8	6·0	4·3	0·0	4·5
20	11·9	7·0	3·9	0·0	0·0
21	9·7	6·2	4·2	0·0	0·0
22	9·5	6·9	9·0	0·0	6·8
23	7·8	2·2	3·8	0·0	7·5
24	7·8	− 3·1	2·6	0·0	3·6
25	6·2	− 0·8	4·3	0·0	7·9
26	6·6	− 5·6	2·4	0·1	7·4
27	7·3	− 3·1	1·9	0·0	6·7
28	6·5	− 3·6	2·4	0·0	0·0
29	8·3	0·4	4·0	0·0	7·2
30	8·0	− 0·7	3·5	0·0	6·2
31					
Total	—	—	—	24·4	107·0
Mean	10·9	3·6	4·8	—	—
Temp. °F	51·6	38·5	—	—	—
Average	10·2	3·9	8·9	62·0	64·0

Weather Record, December, 1989

Temperature Max. °C	Min. °C	Wind speed knots	Rainfall mm	Sunshine hrs	Day
4·2	− 1·8	2·3	0·1	6·2	1
6·2	− 0·7	3·3	0·0	0·0	2
5·3	1·2	3·1	0·0	3·6	3
7·6	0·8	3·7	0·0	1·5	4
9·4	4·1	4·7	0·0	1·3	5
9·0	4·0	2·0	0·0	0·0	6
7·9	4·8	3·1	0·0	0·0	7
7·1	5·5	4·1	0·0	0·0	8
7·2	0·9	3·1	0·0	2·6	9
6·5	1·3	2·0	0·0	0·0	10
8·4	2·6	4·6	4·8	3·1	11
9·2	1·9	5·2	6·7	0·0	12
11·7	3·6	8·0	26·7	0·0	13
13·6	5·6	12·8	2·3	0·4	14
12·9	6·0	5·3	19·7	0·0	15
13·7	6·1	11·6	6·4	0·1	16
12·3	9·9	18·0	3·8	0·3	17
11·2	6·4	6·7	7·6	0·0	18
12·2	3·1	6·3	8·7	1·9	19
14·5	4·2	11·0	19·6	0·7	20
14·3	10·0	17·0	1·2	3·5	21
9·0	7·0	6·0	0·1	3·6	22
11·9	3·3	10·1	6·2	2·5	23
12·9	4·6	16·7	3·8	0·0	24
11·5	8·9	10·2	1·5	0·0	25
10·1	4·4	2·7	0·0	2·3	26
8·5	4·2	5·3	0·0	0·0	27
7·0	6·0	5·8	0·0	0·0	28
5·3	4·7	6·7	0·0	0·0	29
4·9	3·9	3·3	0·0	0·0	30
4·4	3·3	3·8	0·1	0·0	31
—	—	—	118·3	33·6	Total
9·4	4·2	6·3	—	—	Mean
48·9	39·6	—	—	—	Temp. °F
7·9	2·2	7·0	55·0	43·9	Average

Weather Record, January, 1990

Day	Temperature Max. °C	Min. °C	Wind speed knots	Rainfall mm	Sunshine hrs
1	6·4	2·6	6·3	1·5	0·0
2	9·9	0·4	5·1	0·0	0·0
3	5·5	2·4	6·6	0·0	0·0
4	8·5	2·1	3·3	0·0	2·3
5	10·2	3·1	5·7	0·5	0·0
6	12·0	6·6	6·4	12·2	0·0
7	9·7	4·0	4·2	1·0	0·2
8	10·4	3·8	3·2	0·0	6·1
9	11·0	2·7	3·6	0·1	0·0
10	11·0	8·5	9·2	0·0	0·3
11	12·0	9·0	9·3	0·0	1·6
12	8·8	5·7	7·7	3·9	1·1
13	8·1	0·5	2·6	0·1	7·1
14	10·2	0·0	4·2	0·6	0·4
15	13·2	4·3	9·4	0·0	0·0
16	12·2	9·7	12·0	1·2	0·0
17	9·7	7·2	8·5	0·0	6·4
18	9·5	0·4	5·3	0·0	7·5
19	10·2	2·5	10·8	0·3	0·0
20	11·8	3·0	6·9	0·0	1·3
21	12·3	5·7	11·1	3·1	0·0
22	12·5	10·5	9·2	4·0	3·1
23	11·1	8·5	14·3	4·1	0·0
24	12·5	3·1	9·7	3·7	6·7
25	11·8	4·1	20·0	4·8	0·5
26	7·4	3·0	11·0	0·0	3·6
27	9·9	1·6	9·4	6·5	0·0
28	8·8	3·5	11·5	1·3	6·4
29	9·5	3·2	12·7	8·4	0·0
30	11·1	6·6	15·0	10·5	2·8
31	9·7	7·3	12·5	3·3	0·1
Total	—	—	—	71·1	57·5
Mean	10·2	4·4	8·9	—	—
Temp. °F	50·4	39·9	—	—	—
Average	6·7	1·1	8·6	51·0	48·8

Weather Record, February, 1990

Temperature Max. °C	Min. °C	Wind speed knots	Rainfall mm	Sunshine hrs	Day
9·8	6·0	14·1	9·9	1·6	1
10·4	5·0	12·2	8·9	6·3	2
9·3	5·5	8·4	15·9	1·6	3
11·6	1·9	13·7	0·0	0·1	4
13·5	8·6	9·3	0·0	2·7	5
12·7	6·5	12·1	13·9	1·3	6
14·4	8·5	22·0	7·1	0·0	7
10·3	6·6	14·1	0·0	8·7	8
11·3	4·4	8·1	0·0	4·2	9
12·4	5·4	10·1	4·0	0·1	10
9·0	2·1	13·9	8·1	0·1	11
8·5	2·4	13·2	0·0	8·2	12
10·8	1·7	10·9	5·0	0·0	13
6·9	4·2	6·7	7·5	0·0	14
8·6	3·9	8·7	0·0	7·1	15
11·3	− 0·5	2·4	0·0	8·5	16
13·7	2·2	9·5	1·5	0·5	17
12·3	5·2	6·7	0·0	6·2	18
13·1	4·8	14·7	0·2	0·1	19
14·5	10·6	13·0	1·7	0·0	20
11·7	9·8	10·4	0·0	6·9	21
15·7	6·0	5·9	0·0	8·9	22
17·8	5·8	4·6	0·0	8·2	23
13·9	9·3	13·0	0·6	0·0	24
12·0	5·9	12·5	4·0	2·5	25
10·8	7·9	20·4	1·1	6·3	26
8·5	4·0	16·5	0·2	4·2	27
12·3	4·3	14·5	2·7	0·0	28
					29
					30
					31
—	—	—	92·0	94·3	Total
11·7	5·3	11·5	—	—	Mean
53·1	41·5	—	—	—	Temp. °F
7·3	− 1·3	9·3	38·0	62·2	Average

Weather Record, March, 1990

Day	Temperature Max. °C	Temperature Min. °C	Wind speed knots	Rain-fall mm	Sun-shine hrs
1	8.4	1.2	12.2	0.3	7.3
2	8.9	− 0.6	8.1	0.0	8.9
3	10.3	0.1	6.7	0.0	7.2
4	11.1	4.4	10.7	0.0	0.1
5	11.0	6.3	10.3	0.0	0.4
6	12.3	6.8	11.1	0.0	1.1
7	11.1	8.1	8.0	0.0	0.0
8	15.0	4.5	6.8	0.0	6.6
9	12.2	6.6	10.6	0.0	5.4
10	15.6	6.5	11.5	0.0	4.2
11	15.1	8.9	8.0	0.0	2.8
12	14.6	3.2	3.0	0.0	8.3
13	11.5	3.6	6.5	0.8	0.0
14	14.5	2.5	5.6	0.0	7.0
15	14.2	5.1	6.7	0.0	8.1
16	17.3	3.2	5.1	0.0	8.5
17	22.0	6.9	4.7	0.0	9.2
18	21.1	7.5	6.1	0.0	9.6
19	13.5	12.1	8.5	3.3	0.0
20	15.3	4.8	4.9	0.0	4.7
21	14.9	6.0	10.3	0.0	0.2
22	13.6	8.6	7.3	0.0	7.0
23	12.8	3.5	9.6	0.0	1.3
24	13.0	8.7	11.3	1.0	2.0
25	10.5	2.8	7.7	1.5	4.6
26	9.5	1.5	5.0	0.0	6.8
27	10.4	1.2	2.5	0.0	5.0
28	12.1	4.6	4.2	0.0	2.5
29	13.5	0.1	2.8	0.0	5.3
30	17.5	4.5	4.2	0.0	10.5
31	18.3	5.9	7.2	0.0	10.0
Total	—	—	—	6.9	154.6
Mean	13.6	4.8	7.3	—	—
Temp. °F	56.5	40.6	—	—	—
Average	10.2	2.6	9.5	43.0	110.8

Weather Record, April, 1990

Temperature Max. °C	Temperature Min. °C	Wind speed knots	Rain-fall mm	Sun-shine hrs	Day
21.2	3.8	4.8	0.2	9.2	1
17.2	8.2	5.7	6.0	1.7	2
9.6	0.7	7.9	0.1	6.2	3
8.6	− 1.2	3.5	0.0	9.5	4
10.9	− 1.8	3.5	0.0	11.5	5
11.3	− 0.5	8.5	0.0	11.6	6
12.8	3.6	11.2	0.0	9.7	7
11.2	2.9	9.3	0.0	10.0	8
11.6	0.5	4.5	0.0	11.5	9
15.3	3.7	7.2	0.0	4.3	10
15.7	5.0	5.5	0.0	5.4	11
16.1	8.4	7.9	3.0	4.1	12
9.3	7.6	4.4	7.5	3.0	13
11.2	0.3	8.8	0.6	5.2	14
12.9	3.5	9.9	0.0	9.9	15
12.2	2.2	7.2	2.2	9.6	16
12.2	1.0	7.7	3.0	9.0	17
12.5	1.8	6.8	1.9	9.1	18
12.8	5.2	6.4	0.5	6.6	19
12.9	3.0	9.0	0.9	3.4	20
16.9	7.5	8.8	3.1	7.1	21
16.1	8.4	8.2	0.0	4.2	22
17.3	7.4	7.0	0.0	7.9	23
18.2	6.1	5.8	0.0	11.5	24
20.3	5.2	3.0	0.0	10.6	25
13.8	7.7	6.6	0.7	0.3	26
14.1	4.7	5.3	0.0	12.9	27
17.9	3.2	4.2	0.0	13.1	28
22.5	6.3	3.2	0.0	13.3	29
23.1	10.9	7.0	0.0	13.6	30
					31
—	—	—	29.7	245.0	Total
14.6	4.2	6.6	—	—	Mean
58.3	39.6	—	—	—	Temp. °F
13.2	4.6	8.3	41.0	146.9	Average

Weather Record, May, 1990

Day	Temperature Max. °C	Temperature Min. °C	Wind speed knots	Rain-fall mm	Sun-shine hrs
1	24.0	11.3	8.3	0.0	13.8
2	26.2	8.9	6.7	0.0	13.9
3	28.1	12.0	5.4	0.0	13.5
4	26.9	11.3	5.6	0.0	13.9
5	27.2	10.9	3.4	0.0	13.5
6	26.0	11.8	3.6	0.0	12.7
7	18.0	8.8	4.6	0.0	11.1
8	19.4	6.8	3.7	0.0	10.5
9	15.8	10.0	4.4	1.4	0.3
10	15.4	6.8	4.0	2.7	4.1
11	14.0	6.3	4.9	0.0	0.6
12	15.9	10.0	4.8	0.0	3.8
13	17.2	7.7	3.9	0.0	4.8
14	20.2	7.3	5.1	0.0	7.8
15	22.1	12.5	9.0	0.0	12.3
16	21.0	10.7	7.4	0.0	5.3
17	21.5	7.6	5.1	0.0	12.6
18	14.5	9.5	8.4	0.0	4.4
19	16.9	7.0	6.7	0.0	12.2
20	19.5	8.6	6.3	0.0	7.2
21	20.8	6.8	8.3	0.0	7.2
22	18.7	6.4	5.7	0.0	12.9
23	21.8	6.8	3.8	0.0	8.4
24	19.0	10.3	6.8	0.0	13.8
25	17.5	5.4	6.1	0.0	13.7
26	18.3	6.1	6.0	0.0	14.7
27	21.6	5.9	3.5	0.0	13.6
28	22.0	10.4	4.8	0.0	10.7
29	21.5	11.1	6.7	0.0	1.1
30	19.0	11.8	4.0	0.0	0.1
31	24.4	12.2	5.2	0.0	12.5
Total	—	—	—	4.1	287.0
Mean	20.5	9.0	5.6	—	—
Temp. °F	68.9	48.2	—	—	—
Average	17.1	7.8	8.5	48.0	196.1

Weather Record, June, 1990

Temperature Max. °C	Temperature Min. °C	Wind speed knots	Rain-fall mm	Sun-shine hrs	Day
23.6	12.5	5.0	5.4	2.4	1
18.8	9.8	8.6	0.0	6.8	2
16.9	12.2	6.6	1.7	1.2	3
19.2	7.3	6.9	0.0	13.1	4
16.0	7.6	4.6	1.8	0.5	5
16.9	10.2	6.6	0.0	1.2	6
18.5	5.6	4.6	1.8	3.4	7
15.1	7.3	5.5	3.6	2.6	8
19.4	8.7	5.8	0.7	6.8	9
19.6	12.0	5.3	0.0	5.3	10
14.5	11.8	5.5	0.0	0.0	11
14.5	7.5	5.4	0.0	0.0	12
14.8	9.8	4.7	0.0	0.1	13
17.4	11.1	2.3	0.0	0.0	14
20.0	10.2	2.5	0.0	1.5	15
21.3	11.2	3.0	0.0	0.7	16
24.1	11.1	4.6	0.0	7.2	17
20.3	12.6	8.6	1.6	4.6	18
22.0	12.7	8.0	0.0	10.9	19
21.1	10.0	8.5	1.2	11.0	20
16.1	11.2	11.0	11.2	3.9	21
20.8	10.7	9.7	2.3	6.5	22
19.4	10.5	6.7	4.9	7.2	23
18.4	9.2	8.7	0.0	5.0	24
23.3	15.1	8.1	0.0	2.2	25
23.2	15.5	3.5	0.0	1.5	26
25.1	15.8	6.3	0.0	7.1	27
20.2	10.7	5.5	0.0	4.2	28
23.5	9.9	4.5	1.1	8.0	29
21.7	15.1	11.4	2.2	7.6	30
					31
—	—	—	39.5	132.5	Total
19.5	10.8	6.3	—	—	Mean
67.1	51.4	—	—	—	Temp. °F
20.5	10.9	8.4	51.0	206.0	Average

CHRONOLOGICAL NOTES

GEOLOGICAL TIME

The earth is thought to have come into existence approximately 4,600 million years ago, but for nearly half this time, the **Archean** era, it was uninhabited; life is generally believed to have emerged in the succeeding **Proterozoic** era. The Archean and the Proterozoic eras are often together referred to as the **Precambrian**. Although primitive forms of life e.g. algae and bacteria, existed during the Proterozoic era, it is not until the strata of Palaeozoic rocks is reached that abundant fossilized remains appear, initially of small shellfish, followed by plants, primitive fishes and, in the Devonian period (c.400 million BC), land-living plants and amphibia.

Since the Precambrian, there have been three great geological eras:

Palaeozoic ('ancient life')
*c.*570–*c.*250 million BC

(i) *Cambrian.* Mainly sandstones, slate and shales; limestones in Scotland. Shelled fossils and invertebrates, e.g. trilobites and brachiopods appear.

(ii) *Ordovician.* Mainly shales and mudstones, e.g. in N. Wales; limestones in Scotland.

(iii) *Silurian.* Shales, mudstones and some limestones, found mostly in Wales and southern Scotland.

(iv) *Devonian.* Old red sandstone, shale, limestone and slate, e.g. in S. Wales and the West Country. 'The age of fishes'—proliferation of fish fossils. First traces of land-living life.

(v) *Carboniferous.* Coal-bearing rocks, millstone grit, limestone and shale.

(vi) *Permian.* Marls, sandstones and clays, named after the area of Russia where these strata are widespread. First large-scale appearance of reptile fossils.

There were two great phases of mountain building in the Palaeozoic era: the *Caledonian*, characterized in Britain by NE–SW lines of hills and valleys; and the later *Hercyian*, widespread in W. Germany and adjacent areas, and in Britain exemplified in E.–W. lines of hills and valleys.

The end of the Palaeozoic era was marked by the extensive glaciations of the Permian period in the southern continents and the decline of amphibians; it was succeeded by an era of warm conditions.

Mesozoic ('middle forms of life')
*c.*250-*c.*65 million BC

(i) *Triassic.* Mostly sandstone, e.g. in the W. Midlands.

(ii) *Jurassic.* Mainly limestones and clays, typically displayed in the Jura Mts. and in England in a NE–SW belt from Lincolnshire and the Wash to the Severn and the Dorset coast.

(iii) *Cretaceous.* Mainly chalk, clay and sands, e.g. in Kent and Sussex.

Giant reptiles were dominant during the Mesozoic era, but it was at this time that marsupial mammals first appeared, as well as *Archaeopteryx lithographica*, the earliest known species of bird. Coniferous trees and flowering plants also developed during the era and, with the birds and the mammals, were the main species to survive into the Caenozoic (or Cenozoic) era. The giant reptiles became extinct.

Caenozoic ('recent life')
from *c.*65 million BC

(i) *Eocene.* The emergence of new forms of life, i.e. existing species.

(ii) *Oligocene.* Fossils of a few still existing species.

(iii) *Miocene.* Fossil remains show a balance of existing and extinct species.

(iv) *Pliocene.* Fossil remains show a majority of still existing species.

(v) *Pleistocene.* The majority of remains are those of still existing species.

(vi) *Holocene.* The present, post-glacial period. Existing species only, except for a few exterminated by man.

In the last 25 million years, from the Miocene through the Pliocene eras, the Alpine-Himalayan and the circum-Pacific phases of mountain building reached their climax. During the Pleistocene period ice sheets repeatedly locked up masses of water as land ice; its weight depressed the land, but the locking-up of the water lowered the sea-level by 100–200 metres. The glaciations and interglacials of the Ice Age are extremely difficult to date and classify, but recent scientific opinion considers the Pleistocene era to have begun approximately 1·7 million years ago. The last glacial retreat, merging into the Holocene period, was 10,000 years ago.

EARLY MAN

Any consideration of the history of man must start with the fact that all members of the human race belong to one species of animal, i.e. *Homo sapiens*, the definition of a species being in biological terms that all its members can interbreed. As a species of mammal it is possible to group man with other similar types, known as the primates. Amongst these is found a sub-group, the apes, which includes, in addition to man, the chimpanzees, gorillas, orang-utans and gibbons. All lack a tail, have shoulder blades at the back, and a Y-shaped chewing pattern on the surface of their molars, as well as showing the more general primate characteristics of four incisors, a thumb which is able to touch the fingers of the same hand, and finger and toe nails instead of claws. All the factors available to scientific study suggest that human beings have chimpanzees and gorillas as their nearest relatives in the animal world. However, there remains the possibility that there once lived creatures, now extinct, which were closer to modern man than the chimpanzees and gorillas, and which shared with modern man the characteristics of having flat faces (i.e. the absence of a pronounced muzzle), being bipedal, and possessing large brains.

There are two broad groups of extinct apes recognized by specialists. First the ramapithecines, the remains of which, mainly jaw fragments, have been found in East Africa, Asia, and Turkey. They lived about 14 to 8 million years ago, and from the evidence of their teeth it seems they chewed more in the manner of modern man than the other presently living apes. The second group, the australopithecines, have left much more numerous remains amongst which sub-groups may be detected, although the geographic spread is limited to South and East Africa. Living between 5 and 1·5 million years ago, they were closer relatives of modern man to the extent that they walked upright, did not have an extensive muzzle, and had similar types of pre-molars. The first australopithecine remains were recognized at Taung in South Africa in 1924, and subsequent discoveries include those at the famous site of Olduvai Gorge in Tanzania. Perhaps the most impressive discovery was made at Hadar in Ethiopia in 1974 when about half a skeleton, known as 'Lucy', was found.

Also in East Africa, between 2 million and

1·5 million years ago, lived a hominid group which not only walked upright, had a flat face, and a large brain case, but also made simple pebble and flake stone tools. On present evidence these habilines seem to have been the first people to make tools, however crude. This facility is related to the larger brain size and human beings are the only animals to make implements to be used in other processes. These early pebble tool users, because of their distinctive characteristics, have been grouped as a separate sub-species, now extinct, of the genus *Homo*, and are known as *Homo habilis*.

The use of fire, again a human characteristic, is associated with another group of extinct hominids whose remains, about a million years old, are found in South and East Africa, China, Indonesia, North Africa and Europe. No doubt the mastery of the techniques of making fire helped the colonization of the colder northern areas and in this respect the site of Vertesszollos in Hungary is of particular importance. *Homo erectus* is the name given to this group of fossils and it now includes a number of famous individual discoveries from earlier decades, for example, Solo Man, Heidelberg Man, and especially Peking Man who lived at the cave site at Choukou-tien, which has yielded evidence of fire and burnt bone.

The well known group, Neanderthal Man, or *Homo sapiens neandertalensis*, is an extinct form of modern man who lived between about 100,000 and 40,000 years ago, thus spanning the last Ice Age. Indeed, its ability to adapt to the cold climate on the edge of the ice sheets is one of its characteristic features, the remains being only found in Europe, Asia and the Middle East. Complete neanderthal skeletons were found during excavations at Tabun in Israel together with evidence of tool-making and the use of fire. Distinguished by very large brains, it seems that neanderthal man was the first to develop recognizable social customs, especially deliberate burial rites. Why the neanderthalers became extinct is not clear, but it may be connected with the climatic changes at the end of the Ice Ages which would have seriously affected their food supplies; possibly they became too specialized for their own good.

The Swanscombe skull is the only known human fossil remains found in England. Some specialists see Swanscombe Man (or, more probably, woman) as a neanderthaler. Others group these remains together with the Steinheim skull from Germany, seeing both as a separate sub-species, *Homo sapiens steinheimenses*. Unfortunately there is too little evidence as yet on which to form a final judgement.

Modern Man, *Homo sapiens sapiens*, the surviving sub-species of *Homo sapiens*, had evolved to our present physical condition and had colonized much of the world by about 30,000 years ago. There are many previously distinguished individual specimens, for example Cromagnon Man, which may now be grouped together as *Homo sapiens sapiens*. It was modern man who spread to the American continent by crossing the landbridge between Siberia and Alaska and thence moved south through North America and into South America. Equally it is modern man who over the last 30,000 years has been responsible for the major developments in technology, art and civilization generally.

One of the problems for those studying fossil man is the lack in many cases of sufficient quantities of fossil bone for analysis. It is important that theories should be tested against evidence, and not the evidence made to fit the theory. The celebrated Piltdown hoax is perhaps the best known example of 'fossils' being forged to fit what was seen in some quarters as the correct theory of man's evolution.

HUMAN CULTURAL DEVELOPMENT

The Eurocentric bias of early archaeologists meant that the search for a starting point for the development and transmission of cultural ideas, especially by migration, trade and warfare, concentrated unduly on Europe and the Near East. The Three Age System, whereby pre-history was divided into a Stone Age, Bronze Age, and Iron Age, was devised by Christian Thomsen, curator of the National Museum of Denmark in the early nineteenth century, to facilitate the classification of the Museum's collections. The descriptive adjectives referred to the materials from which the implements and weapons were made, and came to be regarded as the dominant features of the societies to which they related. The refinement of the Three Age System once dominated archaeological thought and still remains a generally accepted concept in the popular mind. However, it is now seen by archaeologists as an inadequate model for human development.

Common sense alone suggests that there were no complete breaks between one so-called 'Age' and another, any more than contemporaries would have regarded 1485 as a complete break between medieval and modern English history. Nor can the Three Age System be applied universally. In some areas it is necessary to insert a Copper Age, while in Africa south of the Sahara there would seem to be no Bronze Age at all; in Australia, Old Stone Age societies survived, while in South America, New Stone Age communities existed into modern times. The civilizations in other parts of the world clearly invalidate a Eurocentric theory of human development.

The concept of the 'Neolithic Revolution', associated with the domestication of plants and animals, was a development of particular importance in the human cultural pattern. It reflected change from the primitive hunter/gatherer economies to a more settled agricultural way of life and therefore, so the argument goes, made possible the development of urban civilization. However, it can no longer be argued that this 'Revolution' took place only in one area from which all development stemmed. Though it appears that the cultivation of wheat and barley was first undertaken, together with the domestication of cattle and goats/sheep in the Fertile Crescent, there is evidence that rice was first deliberately planted and pigs domesticated in south-east Asia; maize first cultivated in Central America and llamas first domesticated in South America. It has been recognized increasingly in recent years that cultural changes can take place independently of each other in different parts of the world at different rates and different times. There is no need for a general diffusionist theory.

Although scholars will continue to study the particular societies which interest them, it may be possible to obtain a reliable chronological framework, in absolute terms of years, against which the cultural development of any particular area may be set. The development and refinement of radio-carbon dating and other scientific methods of producing absolute chronologies is enabling the cross-referencing of societies to be undertaken. As the techniques of dating become more rigorous in application and the number of scientifically obtained dates increases, the attainment of an absolute chronology for prehistoric societies throughout the world comes closer to being achieved.

TIME MEASUREMENT AND CALENDARS

MEASUREMENTS OF TIME

Measurements of time are based on the time taken by the earth to rotate on its axis (day); by the moon to revolve round the earth (month); and by the earth to revolve round the sun (year). From these, which are not commensurable, certain average or mean intervals have been adopted for ordinary use.

The Day begins at midnight and is divided into 24 hours of 60 minutes, each of 60 seconds. The hours are counted from midnight up to 12 noon (when the sun crosses the meridian), and these hours are designated a.m. (*ante meridiem*); and again from noon up to 12 midnight, which hours are designated p.m. (*post meridiem*), except when the twenty-four hour reckoning is employed. The 24-hour reckoning ignores a.m. and p.m., and the hours are numbered 0 to 23 from midnight to midnight.

Colloquially the 24 hours are divided into day and night, day being the time while the sun is above the horizon (including the four stages of twilight defined on p. 65). Day is subdivided further into morning, the early part of daytime, ending at noon; afternoon from noon to 6 p.m. and evening, which may be said to extend from 6 p.m. until midnight. Night, the dark period between day and day, begins at the close of astronomical twilight (*see* p. 65) and extends beyond midnight to sunrise the next day.

The names of the days are derived from Old English translations or adaptations of the Roman titles.

Sunday	Sun	Sol
Monday	Moon	Luna
Tuesday	Tiw/Tyr (god of war)	Mars
Wednesday	Woden/Odin	Mercury
Thursday	Thor	Jupiter
Friday	Frigga/Freyja (goddess of love)	Venus
Saturday	Saeternes	Saturn

The Week is a period of 7 days.

The Month in the ordinary calendar is approximately the twelfth part of a year, but the lengths of the different months vary from 28 (or 29) days to 31.

The Year.—The Equinoctial or Tropical Year is the time that the earth takes to revolve round the sun from equinox to equinox, or 365·2422 mean solar days.

The Calendar Year consists of 365 days, but a year the date of which is divisible by 4, without remainder, is called bissextile (*see* Roman Calendar) or Leap Year and consists of 366 days, one day being added to the month February, so that a date 'leaps over' a day of the week. The last year of a century is not a leap year unless its number is divisible by 400 (e.g. the years 1800 and 1900 had only 365 days).

The Solstice.—A Solstice is the point in the Tropical Year at which the Sun attains its greatest distance, north or south, from the Equator. In the northern hemisphere the greatest distance north of the Equator is the Summer Solstice and the greatest distance south is the Winter Solstice.

The Summer Solstice is also the longest day of the year, measured from sunrise to sunset. At the Solstice the Sun, reaching its greatest northern declination, appears to stand still, the times of sunrise and sunset and the consequent length of the day showing no variation for several days together, before and after the longest day (June 21 or 22). For the remainder of this century the longest day in the United Kingdom will fall each year on June 21.

The date of the Solstice varies according to locality. If the Solstice falls on June 21 late in the day by

Greenwich time, that day will be the longest of the year at Greenwich even though it may be by only a second of time or a fraction thereof, but it will be on June 22, local date, in Japan, and so June 22 will be the longest day there and at places in eastern longitudes.

Leaving aside the question of locality, the date of the Solstice is also affected by the length of the Tropical Year, which is 365¼ days, less about 11 minutes. If a Solstice happens late on June 21 in one year, it will be nearly six hours later in the next, i.e. early on June 22, and that will be the longest day. This delay of the Solstice is not permitted to continue because the extra day in Leap Year brings it back a day in the Calendar.

However, because of the 11 minutes mentioned above, the additional day in Leap Year brings the Solstice back too far by 44 minutes, and the time of the Solstice in the Calendar is earlier as the century progresses. (In the year 2000 the Summer Solstice reaches its earliest date for 100 years, i.e., June 21^d 02^h.) To remedy this the last year of a century is in most cases not a Leap Year, and the omission of the extra day puts the date of the Solstice later by about six hours too much, compensation for which is made by making the fourth centennial year a Leap Year.

Similar considerations apply to the day of the Winter Solstice, the shortest day of the year. For the remainder of this century the shortest day in the United Kingdom will fall on Dec. 21 in two years of four and on Dec. 22 in the remaining two years. In the year 2000 the Winter Solstice reaches its earliest date, i.e., December 21^d 13^h. The difference due to locality also prevails in the same sense as for the longest day.

At Greenwich the Sun sets at its earliest by the clock about ten days before the shortest day, which is a circumstance that may require explanation. The daily change in the time of sunset is due in the first place to the Sun's movement southwards at this time of the year, which diminishes the interval between the Sun's transit, and its setting, and, secondly, because of the daily decrease of the Equation of Time which causes the time of Apparent noon to be continuously later, day by day, and so in a measure counteracts the first effect. The rates of the change of these two quantities are not equal, nor are they uniform, but are such that their combination causes the date of earliest sunset to be December 12 or 13 at Greenwich. In more southerly latitudes the effect of the movement of the Sun is less, and the change in the time of sunset depends on that of the Equation of Time to a greater degree, and the date of earliest sunset is earlier than it is at Greenwich.

The Equinox is the point at which the Sun crosses the Equator and day and night are of equal length all over the world. This occurs in March (Vernal Equinox—about March 21) and September (Autumnal Equinox—about September 21).

The Historical Year.—Before the year 1752, two calendar systems were in use in England. The civil or legal year began on March 25, while the historical year began on January 1. Thus the civil or legal date March 24, 1658, was the same day as the historical date March 24, 1659; and a date in that portion of the year is written as: March 24 165$\frac{8}{9}$, the lower figure showing the historical year.

The New Year.—In England in the seventh century, and as late as the thirteenth, the year was reckoned from Christmas Day, but in the twelfth century the Anglican Church began the year with the Feast of The Annunciation of the Blessed Virgin (Lady Day) on March 25 and this practice was adopted generally in the fourteenth century. The civil or legal year in the British Dominions (exclusive of Scotland) began with 'Lady Day' until 1751. But in and since 1752 the civil year has begun with January 1. Certain dividends are still paid by the Bank of England on dates based on Old Style. New Year's Day in Scotland was changed from March 25 to January 1 in 1600.

On the Continent of Europe, January 1 was adopted as the first day of the year by Venice in 1522, Germany in 1544, Spain, Portugal, and the Roman Catholic Netherlands in 1556, Prussia, Denmark and Sweden in 1559, France in 1564, Lorraine in 1579, Protestant Netherlands in 1583, Russia in 1725, and Tuscany in 1751.

The Masonic Year.—Two dates are quoted in warrants, dispensations etc., issued by the United Grand Lodge of England, those for the current year being expressed as *Anno Domini* 1991—*Anno Lucis* 5991. This *Anno Lucis* (year of light) is based on the Book of Genesis I: 3, the 4000 year difference being derived, in modified form, from *Ussher's Notation*, published in 1654, which places the Creation of the World in 4004 BC.

Regnal Years.—These are the years of a sovereign's reign, and each begins on the anniversary of his or her accession, e.g. Regnal year 40 of the present Queen begins on Feb. 6, 1991.

The system was used for dating Acts of Parliament until 1962. The Summer Time Act, 1925, for example, is quoted as 15 and 16 Geo. V. c. 64, because it became law in the Parliamentary Session which extended over part of both of these regnal years. Acts of a Parliamentary Session during which a sovereign died were usually given two year numbers, the regnal year of the deceased sovereign and the regnal year of his or her successor. Acts passed in 1952 were dated 16 Geo. VI. and 1 Elizabeth II. Since 1962 Acts of Parliament have been dated by the calendar year.

Dog Days.—The days about the heliacal rising of the Dog Star, noted from ancient times as the hottest and most unwholesome period of the year in the northern hemisphere. Their incidence has been variously calculated as depending on the Greater or Lesser Dog Star (Sirius or Procyon) and their duration has been reckoned as from 30 to 54 days. A generally accepted period is from July 3 to August 15.

Metonic (Lunar, or Minor) Cycle.—In the year 432 BC Meton, an Athenian astronomer, found that 235 lunations are very nearly, though not exactly equal in duration to 19 solar years, and, hence, after 19 years the phases of the Moon recur on the same

days of the month (nearly). The dates of Full Moon in a cycle of nineteen years were inscribed in figures of gold on public monuments in Athens, and the number showing the position of a year in the cycle is called the **Golden Number** of that year.

Roman Indiction.—A period of fifteen years, instituted for fiscal purposes about AD 300.

Solar (or Major) Cycle.—A period of twenty-eight years, in any corresponding year of which the days of the week recur on the same day of the month.

Julian Period.—Proposed by Joseph Scaliger in 1582. The period is 7980 Julian years, and its first year coincides with the year 4713 BC. 7980 is the product of the number of years in the Solar Cycle, the Metonic Cycle and the cycle of the Roman Indiction ($28 \times 19 \times 15$).

Epact.—The age of the calendar Moon, diminished by one day, on January 1, in the ecclesiastical lunar calendar.

THE FOUR SEASONS

Spring, the first season of the year, is defined astronomically to begin in the northern hemisphere at the Vernal Equinox and to end at the Summer Solstice. In Great Britain, spring in popular parlance comprises the months of March, April and May. In the southern hemisphere spring corresponds with autumn in the northern.

Summer, the second and warmest season, begins astronomically in the northern hemisphere at the Summer Solstice and ends at the Autumnal Equinox. In popular parlance summer in Great Britain includes the months of June, July and August. In the southern hemisphere summer corresponds with winter in the northern.

Autumn, the third season, begins astronomically in the northern hemisphere at the Autumnal Equinox and ends at the Winter Solstice. In Great Britain it is popularly held to include the months of September, October and November. A warm period sometimes occurs round about St. Luke's Day (October 18) and is known as 'St. Luke's Summer'. A warm period occurring round about Martinmas (November 11) is known as 'St. Martin's Summer'. In the southern hemisphere autumn corresponds with spring in the northern.

Winter, the fourth and coldest season, begins astronomically in the northern hemisphere at the Winter Solstice and ends at the Vernal Equinox. In Great Britain the season is popularly held to comprise the months of December, January and February. In the southern hemisphere it corresponds with summer in the northern.

THE CHRISTIAN CALENDAR

In the Christian chronological system the years are distinguished by cardinal numbers before or after the Incarnation, the period being denoted by the letters BC (Before Christ) or, more rarely, AC (*Ante Christum*), and AD (*Anno Domini*—In the Year of Our Lord). The correlative dates of the epoch are the 4th year of the 194th Olympiad, the 753rd year from the Foundation of Rome, AM 3761 (Jewish chronology), and the 4714th year of the Julian Period.

The system was introduced into Italy in the sixth century, and though first used in France in the seventh it was not universally established there until about the eighth century. It has been said that the system was introduced into England by St. Augustine

(AD 596), but it was probably not generally used until some centuries later. It was ordered to be used by the Bishops at the Council of Chelsea, AD 816. The actual date of the birth of Christ is somewhat uncertain.

The Julian Calendar.—In the Julian Calendar all the centennial years were leap years, and for this reason towards the close of the sixteenth century there was a difference of 10 days between the tropical and calendar years; the equinox fell on March 11 of the calendar, whereas at the time of the Council of Nicaea, (AD 325), it had fallen on March 21. In 1582 Pope Gregory ordained that October 5 should be called October 15 and that of the end-century years only the fourth should be a leap year (*see* p. 112).

The **Gregorian Calendar** was adopted by Italy, France, Spain, and Portugal in 1582, by Prussia, the German Roman Catholic States, Switzerland, Holland, and Flanders on January 1, 1583, by Poland in 1586, Hungary in 1587, the German and Netherland Protestant States and Denmark in 1700, and by Great Britain and her Dominions (including the North American Colonies) in 1752, by the omission of eleven days (September 3 being reckoned as September 14). Sweden omitted the leap day in 1700 but observed leap days in 1704 and 1708, and reverted to the Julian calendar by having two leap days in 1712; the Gregorian Calendar was adopted in 1753 by the omission of eleven days (February 18 being reckoned as March 1). Japan adopted the calendar in 1872, China in 1912, Bulgaria in 1915, Turkey and Soviet Russia in 1918, Yugoslavia and Romania in 1919, and Greece in February 1923.

In the same year that the change was made in England from the Julian to the Gregorian Calendar, the beginning of the new year was also changed from March 25 to January 1 (*see* p. 112–113).

The **Orthodox Churches.**—Some Orthodox Churches still use the Julian reckoning, but the majority of Greek Orthodox Churches and the Romanian Orthodox Church have adopted a modified 'New Calendar', observing the Gregorian Calendar for fixed feasts and the Julian for movable feasts.

The Orthodox Church year begins on September 1. There are four fast periods, and in addition to Pascha (Easter), twelve great feasts, as well as numerous commemorations of the Saints of the Old and New Testaments throughout the year.

The **Dominical Letter** is one of the letters A–G which are used to denote the Sundays in successive years. If the first day of the year is a Sunday the letter is A; if the second, B; the third, C; and so on. Leap year requires two letters, the first for January 1—February 29, the second for March 1—December 31.

Epiphany.—The Feast of the Epiphany, commemorating the manifestation of Christ, later became associated with the offering of gifts by the Magi. The day was of exceptional importance from the time of the Council of Nicaea (AD 325), as the primate of Alexandria was charged at every Epiphany Feast with the announcement in a letter to the Churches of the date of the forthcoming Easter. The day was of considerable importance in Britain as it influenced dates, ecclesiastical and lay, e.g. **Plow Monday**, when work was resumed in the fields, falls upon the Monday in the first full week after Epiphany.

Lent.—The Teutonic word *Lent*, which denotes the Fast preceding Easter, originally meant no more than the spring season; but from Anglo-Saxon times, at least, it has been used as the equivalent of the more significant Latin term **Quadragesima**, meaning the 'Forty Days' or, more literally, the fortieth day. As early as the fifth century some of the Fathers of the Church put forward the view that the forty days Fast is of Apostolic origin, but this is not supported or believed by modern scholars; and it appears to some that it dates from the early years of the fourth century. There is some suggestion that the Fast was kept originally for only forty hours. **Ash Wednesday** is the first day of Lent, which ends at midnight before Easter Day.

Sexagesima and Septuagesima.—It has been suggested that the unmeaning application of the names *Sexagesima* and *Septuagesima* to the second and third Sundays before Lent was made by analogy with the names *Quadragesima* and *Quinquagesima*.

Another less likely conjecture is that *Septuagesima* means the seventh day before the Octave of Easter. It is not certain whether the name *Quinquagesima* is due to the fact that the Sunday in question is the fiftieth day before Easter (reckoned inclusive) or was simply formed on the analogy of *Quadragesima* (*New English Dictionary*).

Mothering Sunday is the fourth Sunday in Lent.

Palm Sunday, the Sunday before Easter and the beginning of Holy Week, commemorates the triumphal entry of Christ into Jerusalem and is celebrated in Britain (when palm is not available) by branches of willow gathered for use in the decoration of churches on that day.

Maundy Thursday is the day before Good Friday, the name itself being a corruption of *dies mandati* (day of the mandate) when Christ washed the feet of the disciples and gave them the mandate to love one another.

Easter Day is the first Sunday after the Full Moon which happens upon, or next after, the 21st day of March; if the Full Moon happens upon a Sunday, Easter Day is the Sunday after. This definition is contained in an Act of Parliament (24 Geo. II., cap. 23), and explanation is given in the preamble to the Act that the day of Full Moon depends on certain tables that have been prepared. These are the tables whose essential points are given in the early pages of the Book of Common Prayer. The Moon referred to is not the real Moon of the heavens, but a hypothetical Moon on whose 'full' the date of Easter depends, and the lunations of this 'calendar' Moon consist of twenty-nine and thirty days alternately with certain necessary modifications to make the date of its full agree as nearly as possible with that of the real Moon, which is known as the **Paschal Full Moon**. As at present ordained, Easter falls on one of 35 days— (March 22–April 25).

A Fixed Easter.—On June 15, 1928, the House of Commons agreed to a motion for the third reading of the Bill that Easter Day shall, in the calendar year next but one after the commencement of the Act and in all subsequent years, be the first Sunday after the second Saturday in April. Easter would thus fall between April 9 and 15, both inclusive—that is, on the second or third Sunday in April. A clause in the Bill provided that before it shall come into operation, regard shall be had to any opinion expressed officially by the various Christian Churches. Efforts by the World Council of Churches to secure a unanimous choice of date for Easter by its member Churches have so far been unsuccessful.

Holy Days and **Saints Days** were the normal factors in early times for setting the dates of future and recurrent appointments, e.g. the **Quarter Days** in England and Wales are the Feast of the Nativity, the Feast of the Annunciation, the Feast of St. John the Baptist and the Feast of St. Michael and All Angels, while **Term Days** in Scotland are Candlemas (Feast of the Purification), Whitsunday, Lammas (Loaf Mass) and Martinmas (St. Martin's Day). **Law Sittings** in England and Wales commence on the Feast of St. Hilary and the term which begins on Old Michaelmas Day ends on the former feast of St. Thomas the Apostle.

Red-Letter Days were Holy Days and Saints Days indicated in early ecclesiastical calendars by letters printed in red ink. The days to be distinguished in this way were finally approved at the Council of Nicaea (AD 325). The judges of the Queen's Bench Division wear scarlet robes on red-letter days falling during the law sittings.

Rogation Days.—These are the Monday, Tuesday and Wednesday preceding Ascension Day (Holy Thursday) and in the fifth century were ordered by the Church to be observed as public fasts with solemn processions and supplications. The processions were discontinued as religious observances at the Reformation, but survive in the ceremony known as 'Beating the Parish Bounds'. **Rogation Sunday** is the Sunday before Ascension Day.

Ascension Day is forty days after Easter Day.

Ember Days.—The Ember Days at the four seasons are the Wednesday, Friday and Saturday (a) before the third Sunday in Advent, (b) before the second Sunday in Lent, and (c) before the Sundays nearest to the Festivals of St. Peter, and St. Michael and All Angels.

Pentecost or **Whit Sunday** is seven weeks after Easter Day. It is generally said that the name Whit

Sunday is a variant of White Sunday, and was so called from the albs or white robes of the newly baptized, but other derivations have been suggested.

Trinity Sunday is eight weeks after Easter Day, on the Sunday following Whit Sunday, and subsequent Sundays are sometimes reckoned in the Church of England as 'after Trinity'.

Thomas Becket (1118–1170) was consecrated Archbishop of Canterbury on the Sunday after Whit Sunday and his first act was to ordain that the day of his consecration should be held as a new festival in honour of the Holy Trinity. The observance thus originated spread from Canterbury throughout the whole of Christendom.

Advent Sunday is the Sunday nearest to St. Andrew's Day, November 30, which allows three Sundays between Advent and Christmas Day in all cases.

A TABLE OF THE MOVABLE FEASTS TO THE YEAR 2025

Year	Ash Wednesday	Easter	Ascension	Pentecost (Whit Sunday)	Sundays after Pentecost	Advent Sunday
1991	Feb. 13	March 31	May 9	May 19	22	Dec. 1
1992	March 4	April 19	May 28	June 7	19	Nov. 29
1993	Feb. 24	April 11	May 20	May 30	20	Nov. 28
1994	Feb. 16	April 3	May 12	May 22	21	Nov. 27
1995	March 1	April 16	May 25	June 4	20	Dec. 3
1996	Feb. 21	April 7	May 16	May 26	21	Dec. 1
1997	Feb. 12	March 30	May 8	May 18	22	Nov. 30
1998	Feb. 25	April 12	May 21	May 31	20	Nov. 29
1999	Feb. 17	April 4	May 13	May 23	21	Nov. 28
2000	March 8	April 23	June 1	June 11	19	Dec. 3
2001	Feb. 28	April 15	May 24	June 3	20	Dec. 2
2002	Feb. 13	March 31	May 9	May 19	22	Dec. 1
2003	March 5	April 20	May 29	June 8	19	Nov. 30
2004	Feb. 25	April 11	May 20	May 30	20	Nov. 28
2005	Feb. 9	March 27	May 5	May 15	22	Nov. 27
2006	March 1	April 16	May 25	June 4	20	Dec. 3
2007	Feb. 21	April 8	May 17	May 27	21	Dec. 2
2008	Feb. 6	March 23	May 1	May 11	23	Nov. 30
2009	Feb. 25	April 12	May 21	May 31	20	Nov. 29
2010	Feb. 17	April 4	May 13	May 23	21	Nov. 28
2011	March 9	April 24	June 2	June 21	18	Nov. 27
2012	Feb. 22	April 8	May 17	May 27	21	Dec. 2
2013	Feb. 13	March 31	May 9	May 19	22	Dec. 1
2014	March 5	April 20	May 29	June 8	19	Nov. 30
2015	Feb. 18	April 5	May 14	May 24	21	Nov. 29
2016	Feb. 10	March 27	May 5	May 15	22	Nov. 27
2017	March 1	April 16	May 25	June 4	20	Dec. 3
2018	Feb. 14	April 1	May 10	May 20	22	Dec. 2
2019	March 6	April 21	May 30	June 9	19	Dec. 1
2020	Feb. 26	April 12	May 21	May 31	20	Nov. 29
2021	Feb. 17	April 4	May 13	May 23	21	Nov. 28
2022	March 2	April 17	May 26	June 5	19	Nov. 27
2023	Feb. 22	April 9	May 18	May 28	21	Dec. 3
2024	Feb. 14	March 31	May 9	May 19	22	Dec. 1
2025	March 5	April 20	May 29	June 8	19	Nov. 30

NOTES CONCERNING TABLE OF MOVABLE FEASTS

Ash Wednesday (first day in Lent) can fall at earliest on February 4 and at latest on March 10.
Easter Day can fall at earliest on March 22 and at latest on April 25.
Ascension Day can fall at earliest on April 30 and at latest on June 3.
Pentecost (Whit Sunday) can fall at earliest on May 10 and at latest on June 13.
Trinity Sunday is the Sunday after Whit Sunday.
Corpus Christi falls on the Thursday after Trinity Sunday.
There are not less than 18 and not more than 23 Sundays after Pentecost.
Advent Sunday is the Sunday nearest to November 30.

A TABLE OF EASTER DAYS AND SUNDAY LETTERS, 1500 TO 2025

		1500—1599	1600—1699	1700—1799	1800—1899	1900—1999	2000—2025
d	Mar. 22	1573	1668	1761.........	1818	....	....
e	,, 23	1505-16...........	1600...........	1788...........	1845-56	1913	2008.........
f	,, 24	....	1611-95	1706-99	....	1940...........	....
g	,, 25	1543-54...........	1627-38-49.....	1722-33-44	1883-94	1951...........	....
A	,, 26	1559-70-81-92	1654-65-76......	1749-58-69-80 ..	1815-26-37......	1967-78-89.......	....
b	Mar. 27	1502-13-24-97	1608-87-92.......	1785-96.........	1842-53-64......	1910-21-32.......	2005-16 ...
c	,, 28	1529-35-40	1619-24-30.......	1703-14-25	1869-75-80......	1937-48.........	....
d	,, 29	1551-62............	1635-46-57......	1719-30-41-52..	1807-12-91......	1959-64-70.......	....
e	,, 30	1567-78-89	1651-62-73-84	1746-55-66-77 ..	1823-34	1902-75-86-97 ...	....
f	,, 31	1510-21-32-83-94	1605-16-78-89 ...	1700-71-82-93 ..	1839-50-61-72 ...	1907-18-29-91 ...	2002-13-24 ..
g	April 1	1526-37-48	1621-32	1711-16......	1804-66-77-88 ...	1923-34-45-56 ...	2018.........
A	,, 2	1553-64............	1643-48	1727-38-52(NS).	1809-20-93-99 ...	1961-72	....
b	,, 3	1575-80-86	1659-70-81......	1743-63-68-74 .	1825-31-36......	1904-83-88-94 ...	....
c	,, 4	1507-18-91	1602-13-75-86-97	1708-79-90	1847-58	1915-20-26-99 ...	2010-21 ...
d	,, 5	1523-34-45-56	1607-18-29-40 ...	1702-13-24-95..	1801-63-74-85-96	1931-42-53.......	2015.........
e	April 6	1539-50-61-72	1634-45-56.......	1729-35-40-60..	1806-17-28-90 ...	1947-58-69-80 ...	....
f	,, 7	1504-77-88	1667-72	1751-65-76 ...	1822-33-44......	1901-12-85-96 ...	....
g	,, 8	1509-15-20-99	1604-10-83-94 ...	1705-87-92-98..	1849-55-60......	1917-28	2007-12 ...
A	,, 9	1531-42............	1615-26-37-99 ...	1710-21-32	1871-82	1939-44-50.......	2023.........
b	,, 10	1547-58-69	1631-42-53-64 ...	1726-37-48-57..	1803-14-87-98 ...	1955-66-77.......	....
c	April 11	1501-12-63-74-85-96 .	1658-69-80......	1762-73-84	1819-30-41-52 ...	1909-71-82-93 ...	2004.........
d	,, 12	1506-17-28.........	1601-12-91-96 ...	1789...........	1846-57-68......	1903-14-25-36-98	2009-20 ...
e	,, 13	1533-44............	1623-28	1707-18	1800-73-79-84 ...	1941-52	....
f	,, 14	1555-60-66.........	1639-50-61......	1723-34-45-54 .	1805-11-16-95 ...	1963-68-74.......	....
g	,, 15	1571-82-93	1655-66-77-88 ...	1750-59-70-81..	1827-38	1900-06-79-90 ...	2001.........
A	April 16	1503-14-25-36-87-98 .	1609-20-82-93 ...	1704-75-86-97..	1843-54-65-76 ...	1911-22-33-95 ...	2006-17.....
b	,, 17	1530-41-52.........	1625-36	1715-20.......	1808-70-81-92 ...	1927-38-49-60 ...	2022.........
c	,, 18	1557-68............	1647-52	1731-42-56 ...	1802-13-24-97 ...	1954-65-76.......	....
d	,, 19	1500-79-84-90	1663-74-85......	1747-67-72-78 .	1829-35-40......	1908-81-87-92 ...	....
e	,, 20	1511-22-95	1606-17-79-90 ...	1701-12-83-94 .	1851-62	1919-24-30.......	2003-14-25 ..
f	April 21	1527-38-49	1622-33-44......	1717-28	1867-78-89......	1935-46-57.......	2019.........
g	,, 22	1565-76............	1660	1739-53-64 ...	1810-21-32......	1962-73-84.......	....
A	,, 23	1508	1671	....	1848	1905-16	2000.........
b	,, 24	1519	1603-14-98.....	1709-91	1859	....	2011.........
c	,, 25	1546	1641	1736...........	1886	1943...........	....

THE JEWISH CALENDAR

Origin.—The story in the Book of Genesis that the Flood began on the seventeenth day of the second month, that after the end of 150 days the waters were abated, and that on the seventeenth day of the seventh month the Ark rested on Mount Ararat, indicates a calendar of some kind and that the writers recognized 30 days as the length of a lunation. There is other mention of months by their original numbers in the Book of Genesis and in establishing the rite of the Passover Moses spoke of Abib as the month when the Israelites came out from Egypt and Abib was to be the first month of the year. In the first Book of Kings three months are mentioned by name, Ziv the second month, Ethanim the seventh and Bul the eighth, but these are not names now in use. After the dispersion, Jewish communities were left in considerable doubt as to the times of fasts and festivals. This led to the formation of the Jewish Calendar as used today, which, it is said, was done in AD 358 by Rabbi Hillel II, a descendant of Gamaliel—though some assert that it did not happen until much later. This calendar is luni-solar, and is based on the lengths of the lunation and of the tropical year

as found by Hipparchus (c. 120 BC) which differ little from those adopted at the present day. The year AM 5751 (1990–91) is the 13th year of the 303rd Metonic (Minor or Lunar) Cycle of 19 years and the 11th year of the 206th Solar (or Major) Cycle of 28 years since the Era of the Creation, which Jews hold to have occurred at the time of the Autumnal Equinox in the year known in the Christian Calendar as 3760 BC (954 of the Julian Period). The epoch or starting point of Jewish chronology corresponds to October 7, 3761 BC. At the beginning of each Solar Cycle the Tekufah of Nisan (the Vernal Equinox) returns to the same day and to the same hour.

The hour is divided into 1080 minims, and the month between one new moon and the next is reckoned as 29 days, 12 hours, 793 minims. The normal calendar year, called a Common Regular year, consists of 12 months of 30 days and 29 days alternately. Since 12 months as these comprise only 354 days, in order that each of them shall not diverge greatly from an average place in the solar year, a thirteenth month is occasionally added after the fifth month of the Civil year (which commences on the first day of the month Tishri), or as the penultimate month of the Ecclesiastical year (which commences on the first day of month Nisan), the years when this happens being called Embolismic or Leap years. Of the 19 years that form a Metonic cycle, 7 are Leap years; they occur at places in the cycle indicated by the numbers 3, 6, 8, 11, 14, 17 and 19, these places being chosen so that the accumulated excesses of the solar years should be as small as possible.

The first of each month is called the day of New Moon, though it is not necessarily the day of astronomical New Moon, that being the day on which conjunction of Sun and Moon occurs, but there is generally a difference of a day or two. In practice, in a month which follows one of 30 days, the day preceding its first day is also observed as a day of New Moon. The dates on which the first days of the months fall depend on that of the first of Tishri, which therefore controls the dates of fasts and festivals in the Jewish year. For certain ceremonial reasons connected with these, the first of Tishri must not fall on a Sunday, Wednesday or Friday, and if this should happen as the result of the computation it is postponed to the following day. Also, if the New Moon of Tishri falls on any day of the week at noon or later than noon, then the following day is to be taken for the celebration of that New Moon and is Tishri 1, provided that it is not one of the forbidden days, in which case there is a further postponement of a day.

These rules and others have been considered in detail, and a calendar scheme has been drawn up in which a Jewish year is of one of the following six types: Minimal Common (353 days), Regular Common (354 days), Full Common (355 days), Minimal Leap (383 days), Regular Leap (384 days), or Full Leap (385 days).

The Regular year has alternate months of 30 and 29 days. In a full year, whether Common or Leap, Marcheshvan, the second month of the Civil year, has 30 days instead of 29; in Minimal years Kislev, the third month, has 29 days instead of 30. The additional month in Leap years which is called Adar I, and precedes the month called Adar in Common years and Adar II, or Ve-Adar, in Leap, always has 30 days, but neither this, nor the other variations mentioned, is allowed to change the number of days in the other months which still follow the alternation of the normal twelve. In Leap years the month intercalated precedes Adar and usurps its name, but the usual Adar festivals are kept in Ve-Adar.

These are the main features of the Jewish Calendar which must be considered permanent, because as a Jewish law it cannot be altered except by a great Sanhedrin.

The Jewish day begins between sunset and nightfall. The time used is that of the meridian of Jerusalem, which is $2h.\,21m.$ in advance of Greenwich Mean Time. Rules for the beginning of Sabbaths and festivals were laid down for the latitude of London in the eighteenth century and hours for nightfall are now fixed annually by the Chief Rabbi.

Jewish Calendar 5751–52

AM 5751 (751) is a Regular Common year of 12 months, 51 Sabbaths and 354 days. AM 5752 (752) is a Full Leap year of 13 months, 55 Sabbaths and 385 days.

Jewish Month					AM 5751					AM 5752	
Tishri	1 ..	..	..	1990	September	20	..	..	1991	September	9
Marcheshvan	1 ..	..	..		October	20	..	..		October	9
Kislev	1 ..	..	..		November	18	..	..		November	8
Tebet	1 ..	..	..		December	18	..	..		December	8
Shebat	1 ..	..	..	1991	January	16	..	..	1992	January	6
*Adar	1 ..	..	..		February	15	..	..		February	5
Ve-Adar	1 ..	..	..							March	6
Nisan	1 ..	..	..		March	16	..	..		April	4
Iyar	1 ..	..	..		April	15	..	..		May	4
Sivan	1 ..	..	..		May	14	..	..		June	2
Tammuz	1 ..	..	..		June	13	..	..		July	2
Ab	1 ..	..	..		July	12	..	..		July	31
Elul	1 ..	..	..		August	11	..	..		August	30

*Known as Adar Rishon in Leap years.

Jewish Fasts and Festivals

Tishri	1–2	Rosh Hashanah (New Year).	Tebet	10	Fast of Tebet.
„	3	*Fast of Gedaliah.	†Adar	13	§Fast of Esther.
„	10	Yom Kippur (Day of Atonement).	„ „	14	Purim.
„	15–21	Succoth (Feast of Tabernacles).	„ „	15	Shushan Purim.
„	21	Hoshana Rabba.	Nisan	15–22	Pesach (Passover).
„	22	Shemini Atseret (Solemn Assembly).	Sivan	6–7	Shavuot (Feast of Weeks).
„	23	Simchat Torah (Rejoicing of the Law).	Tammuz	17	*Fast of Tammuz.
Kislev	25	Chanukah (Dedication of the Temple) begins.	Ab	9	*Fast of Ab.

* If these dates fall on the Sabbath the fast is kept on the following day.
† Ve-Adar in Leap years.
§ This fast is observed on Adar 11 (or Ve-Adar 11 in Leap years) if Adar 13 falls on a Sabbath.

THE ROMAN CALENDAR

Roman historians adopted as an epoch the Foundation of Rome, which is believed to have happened in the year 753 BC, and the ordinal number of the years in Roman reckoning is followed by the letters AUC (*ab urbe condita*), so that the year 1991 is 2744 AUC (MMDCCXLIV). The calendar that we know has developed from one established by Romulus, who is said to have used a year of 304 days divided into ten months, beginning with March. To this Numa added January and February, making the year consist of 12 months of 30 and 29 days alternately, with an additional day so that the total was 355. It is also said that Numa ordered an intercalary month of 22 or 23 days in alternate years, making 90 days in eight years, to be inserted after February 23, but there is some doubt as to the origination and the details of the intercalation in the Roman Calendar. However, it is certain that some scheme of this kind was inaugurated and not fully carried out, for in the year 46 BC Julius Caesar, who was then Pontifex Maximus, found that the calendar had been allowed to fall into some confusion. He therefore sought the help of the Egyptian astronomer Sosigenes, which led to the construction and adoption (45 BC) of the Julian Calendar, and, by a slight alteration, to the Gregorian Calendar now in use. The year 46 BC was made to consist of 445 days, and is called the Year of Confusion.

In the Roman (Julian) Calendar the days of the month were counted backwards from three fixed points, or days, and an intervening day was said to be so many days *before* the next coming point, the first and last being counted. These three points were the Kalends, the Nones, and the Ides. Their positions in the months and the method of counting from them will be seen in the table below. The year containing 366 days was called *bissextilis annus*, as it had a doubled sixth day (*bissextus dies*) before the March Kalends on February 24—*ante diem sextum Kalendas Martias*, or a.d. VI Kal. Mart.

Present days of the month	March, May, July, October have thirty-one days	January, August, December have thirty-one days	April, June, September, November have thirty days	February has twenty-eight days, and in leap year twenty-nine
1	Kalendis.	Kalendis.	Kalendis.	Kalendis.
2	VI ⎫	IV ⎫ ante	IV ⎫ ante	IV ⎫ ante
3	V ⎬ ante	III ⎭ Nonas.	III ⎭ Nonas.	III ⎭ Nonas.
4	IV ⎭ Nonas.	pridie Nonas.	pridie Nonas.	pridie Nonas.
5	III	Nonis.	Nonis.	Nonis.
6	pridie Nonas.	VIII ⎫	VIII ⎫	VIII ⎫
7	Nonis.	VII	VII	VII
8	VIII ⎫	VI ⎬ ante	VI ⎬ ante.	VI ⎬ ante
9	VII	V ⎭ Idus.	V ⎭ Idus.	V ⎭ Idus.
10	VI ⎬ ante	IV	IV	IV
11	V ⎭ Idus.	III	III	III
12	IV	pridie Idus.	pridie Idus.	pridie Idus.
13	III	Idibus.	Idibus.	Idibus.
14	pridie Idus.	XIX ⎫	XVIII ⎫	XVI ⎫
15	Idibus.	XVIII	XVII	XV
16	XVII ⎫	XVII	XVI	XIV
17	XVI	XVI	XV	XIII
18	XV	XV	XIV	XII
19	XIV	XIV	XIII	XI
20	XIII ⎬ ante Kalendas (of the month following).	XIII ⎬ ante Kalendas (of the month following).	XII ⎬ ante Kalendas (of the month following).	X ⎬ ante Kalendas Martias.
21	XII	XII	XI	IX
22	XI	XI	X	VIII
23	X	X	IX	VII
24	IX	IX	VIII	*VI
25	VIII	VIII	VII	V
26	VII	VII	VI	IV
27	VI	VI	V	III ⎭
28	V	V	IV	pridie Kalendas Martias.
29	IV	IV	III ⎭	
30	III ⎭	III ⎭	pridie Kalendas	
31	pridie Kalendas (Aprilis, Iunias, Sextilis, Novembris).	pridie Kalendas (Februarias, Septembris, Ianuarias).	(Maias, Quinctilis, Octobris, Decembris).	* (repeated in leap year).

ROMAN NUMERALS

1............I	9.........IX	17.......XVII	70.......LXX	600.......DC
2..........II	10..........X	18......XVIII	80.....LXXX	700...... DCC
3.........III	11..........XI	19........XIX	90..........XC	800.....DCCC
4.........IV	12........XII	20..........XX	100..........C	900...... CM
5..........V	13........XIII	30........XXX	200..........CC	1000........M
6.........VI	14.......XIV	40..........XL	300.......CCC	1500........MD
7........VII	15........XV	50............L	400.........CD	1900..... MCM
8....... VIII	16........XVI	60..........LX	500..........D	2000.......MM

Examples: 43 = XLIII; 66 = LXVI; 98 = XCVIII.
339 = CCCXXXIX; 619 = DCXIX; 988 = CMLXXXVIII; 996 = CMXCVI.
1674 = MDCLXXIV; 1962 = MCMLXII; 1991 = MCMXCI.
A bar placed over a numeral has the effect of multiplying the number by 1,000, e.g.

6,000 = $\overline{\text{VI}}$; 16,000 = $\overline{\text{XVI}}$; 160,000 = $\overline{\text{CLX}}$; 666,000 = $\overline{\text{DCLXVI}}$.

THE MUSLIM CALENDAR

The basic date of the Muslim Calendar is the *Hejira*, or Flight of Muhammad from Mecca to Medina, the corresponding date of which is AD 622, July 16, in the Julian Calendar. Hejira years are used principally in Iran, Turkey, Egypt, in various Arabian states, in certain parts of India and in Malaysia. The system was adopted about AD 632, commencing from the first day of the month preceding the Hejira. The years are purely lunar and consist of 12 months containing in alternate sequence 30 or 29 days, with the intercalation of one day at the end of the twelfth month at stated intervals in each cycle of 30 years. The object of the intercalation is to reconcile the date of the first of the month with the date of the actual New Moon. Some adherents still take the date of the evening of the first visibility of the crescent as that of the first of the month. In each cycle of 30 years, 19 are common and contain 354 days and 11 are intercalary (355 days), the latter being called *kabishah*.

The mean length of the Hejira year is 354 days, 8 hours, 48 minutes, and the period of mean lunation is 29 days, 12 hours, 44 minutes.

To ascertain if a Hejira year is common or *kabishah* divide it by 30; the quotient gives the number of completed cycles and the remainder shows the place of the year in the current cycle. If the remainder is 2, 5, 7, 10, 13, 16, 18, 21, 24, 26 or 29 the year is *kabishah* and consists of 355 days.

Hejira year AH 1411 (remainder 1) is a common year and AH 1412 (remainder 2) is a *kabishah* year.

Hejira Years 1411 and 1412

Name and length of month	AH 1411		AH 1412	
Muharram (30)	1990 July	24	1991 July	13
Safar (29)	Aug.	23	Aug.	12
Rabia I (30)	Sept.	21	Sept.	10
Rabia II (29)	Oct.	21	Oct.	10
Jumâda I (30)	Nov.	19	Nov.	8
Jumâda II (29)	Dec.	19	Dec.	8
Rajab (30)	1991 Jan.	17	1992 Jan.	6
Shaabân (29)	Feb.	16	Feb.	5
Ramadân (30)	March	17	March	5
Shawwâl (29)	April	16	April	4
Dhû'l-Qa'da (30)	May	15	May	3
Dhû'l-Hijja (29 or 30)	June	14	June	2

OTHER EPOCHS AND CALENDARS

China.—Until the year AD 1911 a lunar calendar was in force in China, but with the establishment of the Republic the Government adopted the Gregorian Calendar, and the new and old systems were used simultaneously by the people for several years. Since 1930 the publication and use of the old calendar have been banned by the Government, and an official Chinese Calendar, corresponding with the European or Western system, is compiled, but the old lunar calendar is still in use to some extent in China. The old Chinese Calendar, with a cycle of 60 years, is still in use in Tibet, Hong Kong, Singapore, Malaysia and elsewhere in South-East Asia.

Ethiopia.—In the Coptic Calendar, which is used by part of the population of Egypt and Ethiopia, the year is made up of 12 months of 30 days each, followed, in general, by five complementary days. Every fourth year is an Intercalary or Leap year and in these years there are six complementary days. The Intercalary year of the Coptic Calendar immediately precedes the Leap year of the Julian Calendar. The Era is that of Diocletian or the Martyrs, the origin of which is fixed at AD 284, August 29 (Julian date).

Greece.—Ancient Greek chronology was reckoned in Olympiads, cycles of 4 years corresponding with the periodic Olympic Games held on the plain of Olympia in Elis once every four years, the intervening years being the first, second, etc., of the Olympiad which received the name of the victor at the Games. The first recorded Olympiad is that of Choroebus, 776 BC.

India.—In addition to the Muslim reckoning there are six eras used in India. The principal astronomical system was the Kaliyuga Era, which appears to have been adopted in the fourth century AD. It began on February 18, 3102 BC. The chronological system of Northern India, known as the Vikrama Samvat Era, prevalent in Western India, began on February 23, 57 BC. The year AD 1991 is, therefore, the year 2048 of the Vikrama Era.

The Saka Era of Southern India dating from AD 78, March 3, was declared the uniform national calendar of the Republic of India with effect from March 22, 1957, to be used concurrently with the Gregorian Calendar. As revised, the year of the new Saka Era begins at the spring equinox, with five successive months of 31 days and seven of 30 days in ordinary years and six months of each length in leap years. The year AD 1991 is 1913 of the revised Saka Era.

In the Hills, the Saptarshi Era dates from the moment when the Saptarshi, or saints, were translated and became the stars of the Great Bear in 3076 BC.

The Buddhists reckoned from the death of Buddha in 543 BC (the actual date being 487 BC); and the epoch of the Jains was the death of Vardhamana, the founder of their faith, in 527 BC.

Iran.—The chronology of Iran is the era of Hejira, which began on AD 622, July 16. The Zoroastrian Calendar was used in pre-Muslim days and is still employed by Zoroastrians in Iran and India (Parsees) with an era beginning AD 632, June 16.

Japan.—The Japanese Calendar is essentially the same as the Gregorian Calendar in use by Western nations, the years, months and weeks being of the same length and beginning on the same days as those of the Western Calendar. The numeration of the years is different, for Japanese chronology is based on a system of epochs or periods, each of which begins at the accession of an Emperor or other important occurrence, the method being not unlike the former British system of Regnal years, but differing from it in that each year of a period closes on December 31. The Japanese scheme begins about AD 650 and the three latest epochs are defined by the reigns of Emperors, whose actual names are not necessarily used:

Epoch Taishō from 1912 Aug. 1 to 1926 Dec. 25

„ Shōwa „ 1926 Dec. 26 to 1989 Jan. 7

„ Heisei „ 1989 Jan. 8

Hence the year Heisei 3 begins on January 1, 1991. The months are not named. They are known as First Month, Second Month, etc., First Month being the equivalent to January. The days of the week are Nichiyōbi (Sun-day), Getsuyōbi (Moon-day), Kayōbi (Fire-day), Suiyōbi (Water-day), Mokuyōbi (Wood-day), Kinyōbi (Metal-day), Doyōbi (Earth-day).

To select the correct calendar for any year between 1770 and 2025, consult the Index below

* leap year

Year		Year		Year		Year		Year		Year	
1770	C	1813	K	1856	F*	1899	A	1942	I	1985	E
1771	E	1814	M	1857	I	1900	C	1943	K	1986	G
1772	H*	1815	A	1858	K	1901	E	1944	N*	1987	I
1773	K	1816	D*	1859	M	1902	G	1945	C	1988	L*
1774	M	1817	G	1860	B*	1903	I	1946	E	1989	A
1775	A	1818	I	1861	E	1904	L*	1947	G	1990	C
1776	D*	1819	K	1862	G	1905	A	1948	J*	1991	E
1777	G	1820	N*	1863	I	1906	C	1949	M	1992	H*
1778	I	1821	C	1864	L*	1907	E	1950	A	1993	I
1779	K	1822	E	1865	A	1908	H*	1951	C	1994	M
1780	N*	1823	G	1866	C	1909	K	1952	F*	1995	A
1781	C	1824	J*	1867	E	1910	M	1953	I	1996	D*
1782	E	1825	M	1868	H*	1911	A	1954	K	1997	I
1783	G	1826	A	1869	K	1912	D*	1955	M	1998	I
1784	J*	1827	C	1870	M	1913	G	1956	B*	1999	K
1785	M	1828	F*	1871	A	1914	I	1957	E	2000	N*
1786	A	1829	I	1872	D*	1915	K	1958	G	2001	E
1787	C	1830	K	1873	G	1916	N*	1959	I	2002	E
1788	F*	1831	M	1874	I	1917	C	1960	L*	2003	G
1789	I	1832	B*	1875	K	1918	E	1961	A	2004	J*
1790	K	1833	E	1876	N*	1919	G	1962	C	2005	M
1791	M	1834	G	1877	C	1920	J*	1963	E	2006	A
1792	B*	1835	I	1878	E	1921	M	1964	H*	2007	C
1793	E	1836	L*	1879	G	1922	A	1965	K	2008	F*
1794	G	1837	A	1880	J*	1923	C	1966	M	2009	I
1795	I	1838	C	1881	M	1924	F*	1967	A	2010	I
1796	L*	1839	E	1882	A	1925	I	1968	D*	2011	K
1797	A	1840	H*	1883	C	1926	K	1969	G	2012	B*
1798	C	1841	K	1884	F*	1927	M	1970	I	2013	E
1799	E	1842	M	1885	I	1928	B*	1971	K	2014	G
1800	G	1843	A	1886	K	1929	E	1972	N*	2015	I
1801	I	1844	D*	1887	M	1930	G	1973	C	2016	L*
1802	K	1845	G	1888	B*	1931	I	1974	E	2017	A
1803	M	1846	I	1889	E	1932	L*	1975	G	2018	C
1804	B*	1847	K	1890	G	1933	A	1976	J*	2019	E
1805	E	1848	N*	1891	I	1934	C	1977	M	2020	H*
1806	G	1849	C	1892	L*	1935	E	1978	A	2021	K
1807	I	1850	E	1893	A	1936	H*	1979	C	2022	M
1808	L*	1851	G	1894	C	1937	K	1980	F*	2023	A
1809	A	1852	J*	1895	E	1938	M	1981	I	2024	D*
1810	C	1853	M	1896	H*	1939	A	1982	K	2025	G
1811	E	1854	A	1897	K	1940	D*	1983	M		
1812	H*	1855	C	1898	M	1941	G	1984	B*		

A

	January	February	March
Su.	.. 1 8 15 22 29	5 12 19 26	5 12 19 26
M.	.. 2 9 16 23 30	6 13 20 27	6 13 20 27
Tu.	.. 3 10 17 24 31	7 14 21 28	7 14 21 28
W.	.. 4 11 18 25	1 8 15 22	1 8 15 22 29
Th.	.. 5 12 19 26	2 9 16 23	2 9 16 23 30
F.	.. 6 13 20 27	3 10 17 24	3 10 17 24 31
S.	.. 7 14 21 28	4 11 18 25	4 11 18 25

	April	May	June
Su.	.. 2 9 16 23 30	7 14 21 28	4 11 18 25
M.	.. 3 10 17 24	1 8 15 22 29	5 12 19 26
Tu.	.. 4 11 18 25	2 9 16 23 30	6 13 20 27
W.	.. 5 12 19 26	3 10 17 24 31	7 14 21 28
Th.	.. 6 13 20 27	4 11 18 25	1 8 15 22 29
F.	.. 7 14 21 28	5 12 19 26	2 9 16 23 30
S.	1 8 15 22 29	6 13 20 27	3 10 17 24

	July	August	September
Su.	.. 1 8 15 22 29	6 13 20 27	3 10 17 24
M.	.. 2 9 16 23 30	7 14 21 28	4 11 18 25
Tu.	.. 3 10 17 24 31	1 8 15 22 29	5 12 19 26
W.	.. 4 11 18 25	2 9 16 23 30	6 13 20 27
Th.	.. 5 12 19 26	3 10 17 24 31	7 14 21 28
F.	.. 6 13 20 27	4 11 18 25	1 8 15 22 29
S.	.. 7 14 21 28	5 12 19 26	2 9 16 23 30

	October	November	December
Su.	.. 1 8 15 22 29	5 12 19 26	3 10 17 24 31
M.	.. 2 9 16 23 30	6 13 20 27	4 11 18 25
Tu.	.. 3 10 17 24 31	7 14 21 28	5 12 19 26
W.	.. 4 11 18 25	1 8 15 22 29	6 13 20 27
Th.	.. 5 12 19 26	2 9 16 23 30	7 14 21 28
F.	.. 6 13 20 27	3 10 17 24	1 8 15 22 29
S.	.. 7 14 21 28	4 11 18 25	2 9 16 23 30

B (leap year)

	January	February	March
Su.	.. 1 8 15 22 29	5 12 19 26	4 11 18 25
M.	.. 2 9 16 23 30	6 13 20 27	5 12 19 26
Tu.	.. 3 10 17 24 31	7 14 21 28	6 13 20 27
W.	.. 4 11 18 25	1 8 15 22 29	7 14 21 28
Th.	.. 5 12 19 26	2 9 16 23	1 8 15 22 29
F.	.. 6 13 20 27	3 10 17 24	2 9 16 23 30
S.	.. 7 14 21 28	4 11 18 25	3 10 17 24 31

	April	May	June
Su.	.. 1 8 15 22 29	6 13 20 27	3 10 17 24
M.	.. 2 9 16 23 30	7 14 21 28	4 11 18 25
Tu.	.. 3 10 17 24	1 8 15 22 29	5 12 19 26
W.	.. 4 11 18 25	2 9 16 23 30	6 13 20 27
Th.	.. 5 12 19 26	3 10 17 24 31	7 14 21 28
F.	.. 6 13 20 27	4 11 18 25	1 8 15 22 29
S.	.. 7 14 21 28	5 12 19 26	2 9 16 23 30

	July	August	September
Su.	.. 1 8 15 22 29	5 12 19 26	2 9 16 23 30
M.	.. 2 9 16 23 30	6 13 20 27	3 10 17 24
Tu.	.. 3 10 17 24 31	7 14 21 28	4 11 18 25
W.	.. 4 11 18 25	1 8 15 22 29	5 12 19 26
Th.	.. 5 12 19 26	2 9 16 23 30	6 13 20 27
F.	.. 6 13 20 27	3 10 17 24 31	7 14 21 28
S.	.. 7 14 21 28	4 11 18 25	1 8 15 22 29

	October	November	December
Su.	.. 7 14 21 28	4 11 18 25	2 9 16 23 30
M.	.. 1 8 15 22 29	5 12 19 26	3 10 17 24 31
Tu.	.. 2 9 16 23 30	6 13 20 27	4 11 18 25
W.	.. 3 10 17 24 31	7 14 21 28	5 12 19 26
Th.	.. 4 11 18 25	1 8 15 22 29	6 13 20 27
F.	.. 5 12 19 26	2 9 16 23 30	7 14 21 28
S.	.. 6 13 20 27	3 10 17 24	1 8 15 22 29

Easter Days

Easter Day	Years					
March 26	1815	1826	1837	1967	1978	1989
April 2	1809	1893	1899	1961		
April 9	1871	1882	1939	1950	2023	
April 16	1775	1786	1797	1843	1854	1865 1911
	1922	1933	1995	2006	2017	
April 23	1905					

Easter Days

Easter Day	Years			
April 1	1804	1888	1956	
April 8	1792	1860	1928	2012
April 22	1832	1984		

C

	January	February	March
Su.	.. 7 14 21 28	4 11 18 25	4 11 18 25
M.	.. 1 8 15 22 29	5 12 19 26	5 12 19 26
Tu.	.. 2 9 16 23 30	6 13 20 27	6 13 20 27
W.	.. 3 10 17 24 31	7 14 21 28	7 14 21 28
Th.	.. 4 11 18 25	1 8 15 22	1 8 15 22 29
F.	.. 5 12 19 26	2 9 16 23	2 9 16 23 30
S.	.. 6 13 20 27	3 10 17 24	3 10 17 24 31

	April	May	June
Su.	.. 1 8 15 22 29	6 13 20 27	3 10 17 24
M.	.. 2 9 16 23 30	7 14 21 28	4 11 18 25
Tu.	.. 3 10 17 24	1 8 15 22 29	5 12 19 26
W.	.. 4 11 18 25	2 9 16 23 30	6 13 20 27
Th.	.. 5 12 19 26	3 10 17 24 31	7 14 21 28
F.	.. 6 13 20 27	4 11 18 25	1 8 15 22 29
S.	.. 7 14 21 28	5 12 19 26	2 9 16 23 30

	July	August	September
Su.	.. 1 8 15 22 29	5 12 19 26	2 9 16 23 30
M.	.. 2 9 16 23 30	6 13 20 27	3 10 17 24
Tu.	.. 3 10 17 24 31	7 14 21 28	4 11 18 25
W.	.. 4 11 18 25	1 8 15 22 29	5 12 19 26
Th.	.. 5 12 19 26	2 9 16 23 30	6 13 20 27
F.	.. 6 13 20 27	3 10 17 24 31	7 14 21 28
S.	.. 7 14 21 28	4 11 18 25	1 8 15 22 29

	October	November	December
Su.	.. 7 14 21 28	4 11 18 25	2 9 16 23 30
M.	.. 1 8 15 22 29	5 12 19 26	3 10 17 24 31
Tu.	.. 2 9 16 23 30	6 13 20 27	4 11 18 25
W.	.. 3 10 17 24 31	7 14 21 28	5 12 19 26
Th.	.. 4 11 18 25	1 8 15 22 29	6 13 20 27
F.	.. 5 12 19 26	2 9 16 23 30	7 14 21 28
S.	.. 6 13 20 27	3 10 17 24	1 8 15 22 29

Easter Days

March 25	1883	1894	1951				
April 1	1866	1877	1923	1934	1945	2018	
April 8	1787	1798	1849	1855	1917	2007	
April 15	1770	1781	1827	1838	1900	1906	1979
	1990	2001					
April 22	1810	1821	1962	1973			

E

	January	February	March
Su.	.. 6 13 20 27	3 10 17 24	3 10 17 24 31
M.	.. 7 14 21 28	4 11 18 25	4 11 18 25
Tu.	.. 1 8 15 22 29	5 12 19 26	5 12 19 26
W.	.. 2 9 16 23 30	6 13 20 27	6 13 20 27
Th.	.. 3 10 17 24 31	7 14 21 28	7 14 21 28
F.	.. 4 11 18 25	1 8 15 22	1 8 15 22 29
S.	.. 5 12 19 26	2 9 16 23	2 9 16 23 30

	April	May	June
Su.	.. 7 14 21 28	5 12 19 26	2 9 16 23 30
M.	.. 1 8 15 22 29	6 13 20 27	3 10 17 24
Tu.	.. 2 9 16 23 30	7 14 21 28	4 11 18 25
W.	.. 3 10 17 24	1 8 15 22 29	5 12 19 26
Th.	.. 4 11 18 25	2 9 16 23 30	6 13 20 27
F.	.. 5 12 19 26	3 10 17 24 31	7 14 21 28
S.	.. 6 13 20 27	4 11 18 25	1 8 15 22 29

	July	August	September
Su.	.. 7 14 21 28	4 11 18 25	1 8 15 22 29
M.	.. 1 8 15 22 29	5 12 19 26	2 9 16 23 30
Tu.	.. 2 9 16 23 30	6 13 20 27	3 10 17 24
W.	.. 3 10 17 24 31	7 14 21 28	4 11 18 25
Th.	.. 4 11 18 25	1 8 15 22 29	5 12 19 26
F.	.. 5 12 19 26	2 9 16 23 30	6 13 20 27
S.	.. 6 13 20 27	3 10 17 24 31	7 14 21 28

	October	November	December
Su.	.. 6 13 20 27	3 10 17 24	1 8 15 22 29
M.	.. 7 14 21 28	4 11 18 25	2 9 16 23 30
Tu.	.. 1 8 15 22 29	5 12 19 26	3 10 17 24 31
W.	.. 2 9 16 23 30	6 13 20 27	4 11 18 25
Th.	.. 3 10 17 24 31	7 14 21 28	5 12 19 26
F.	.. 4 11 18 25	1 8 15 22 29	6 13 20 27
S.	.. 5 12 19 26	2 9 16 23 30	7 14 21 28

Easter Days

March 24	1799						
March 31	1771	1782	1793	1839	1850	1861	1907
	1918	1929	1991	2002	2013		
April 7	1822	1833	1901	1985			
April 14	1805	1811	1895	1963	1974		
April 21	1867	1878	1889	1935	1946	1957	2019

D (leap year)

	January	February	March
Su.	.. 7 14 21 28	4 11 18 25	3 10 17 24 31
M.	.. 1 8 15 22 29	5 12 19 26	4 11 18 25
Tu.	.. 2 9 16 23 30	6 13 20 27	5 12 19 26
W.	.. 3 10 17 24 31	7 14 21 28	6 13 20 27
Th.	.. 4 11 18 25	1 8 15 22 29	7 14 21 28
F.	.. 5 12 19 26	2 9 16 23	1 8 15 22 29
S.	.. 6 13 20 27	3 10 17 24	2 9 16 23 30

	April	May	June
Su.	.. 7 14 21 28	5 12 19 26	2 9 16 23 30
M.	.. 1 8 15 22 29	6 13 20 27	3 10 17 24
Tu.	.. 2 9 16 23 30	7 14 21 28	4 11 18 25
W.	.. 3 10 17 24	1 8 15 22 29	5 12 19 26
Th.	.. 4 11 18 25	2 9 16 23 30	6 13 20 27
F.	.. 5 12 19 26	3 10 17 24 31	7 14 21 28
S.	.. 6 13 20 27	4 11 18 25	1 8 15 22 29

	July	August	September
Su.	.. 7 14 21 28	4 11 18 25	1 8 15 22 29
M.	.. 1 8 15 22 29	5 12 19 26	2 9 16 23 30
Tu.	.. 2 9 16 23 30	6 13 20 27	3 10 17 24
W.	.. 3 10 17 24 31	7 14 21 28	4 11 18 25
Th.	.. 4 11 18 25	1 8 15 22 29	5 12 19 26
F.	.. 5 12 19 26	2 9 16 23 30	6 13 20 27
S.	.. 6 13 20 27	3 10 17 24 31	7 14 21 28

	October	November	December
Su.	.. 6 13 20 27	3 10 17 24	1 8 15 22 29
M.	.. 7 14 21 28	4 11 18 25	2 9 16 23 30
Tu.	.. 1 8 15 22 29	5 12 19 26	3 10 17 24 31
W.	.. 2 9 16 23 30	6 13 20 27	4 11 18 25
Th.	.. 3 10 17 24 31	7 14 21 28	5 12 19 26
F.	.. 4 11 18 25	1 8 15 22 29	6 13 20 27
S.	.. 5 12 19 26	2 9 16 23 30	7 14 21 28

Easter Days

March 24	1940			
March 31	1872	2024		
April 7	1776	1844	1912	1996
April 14	1816	1968		

F (leap year)

	January	February	March
Su.	.. 6 13 20 27	3 10 17 24	2 9 16 23 30
M.	.. 7 14 21 28	4 11 18 25	3 10 17 24 31
Tu.	.. 1 8 15 22 29	5 12 19 26	4 11 18 25
W.	.. 2 9 16 23 30	6 13 20 27	5 12 19 26
Th.	.. 3 10 17 24 31	7 14 21 28	6 13 20 27
F.	.. 4 11 18 25	1 8 15 22 29	7 14 21 28
S.	.. 5 12 19 26	2 9 16 23	1 8 15 22 29

	April	May	June
Su.	.. 6 13 20 27	4 11 18 25	1 8 15 22 29
M.	.. 7 14 21 28	5 12 19 26	2 9 16 23 30
Tu.	.. 1 8 15 22 29	6 13 20 27	3 10 17 24
W.	.. 2 9 16 23 30	7 14 21 28	4 11 18 25
Th.	.. 3 10 17 24	1 8 15 22 29	5 12 19 26
F.	.. 4 11 18 25	2 9 16 23 30	6 13 20 27
S.	.. 5 12 19 26	3 10 17 24 31	7 14 21 28

	July	August	September
Su.	.. 6 13 20 27	3 10 17 24 31	7 14 21 28
M.	.. 7 14 21 28	4 11 18 25	1 8 15 22 29
Tu.	.. 1 8 15 22 29	5 12 19 26	2 9 16 23 30
W.	.. 2 9 16 23 30	6 13 20 27	3 10 17 24
Th.	.. 3 10 17 24 31	7 14 21 28	4 11 18 25
F.	.. 4 11 18 25	1 8 15 22 29	5 12 19 26
S.	.. 5 12 19 26	2 9 16 23 30	6 13 20 27

	October	November	December
Su.	.. 5 12 19 26	2 9 16 23 30	7 14 21 28
M.	.. 6 13 20 27	3 10 17 24	1 8 15 22 29
Tu.	.. 7 14 21 28	4 11 18 25	2 9 16 23 30
W.	.. 1 8 15 22 29	5 12 19 26	3 10 17 24 31
Th.	.. 2 9 16 23 30	6 13 20 27	4 11 18 25
F.	.. 3 10 17 24 31	7 14 21 28	5 12 19 26
S.	.. 4 11 18 25	1 8 15 22 29	6 13 20 27

Easter Days

March 23	1788	1856	2008
April 6	1828	1980	
April 13	1884	1952	
April 20	1924		

G

	January	February	March
Su. ..	5 12 19 26	2 9 16 23	2 9 16 23 30
M. ..	6 13 20 27	3 10 17 24	3 10 17 24 31
Tu. ..	7 14 21 28	4 11 18 25	4 11 18 25
W. .. 1	8 15 22 29	5 12 19 26	5 12 19 26
Th. .. 2	9 16 23 30	6 13 20 27	6 13 20 27
F. .. 3	10 17 24 31	7 14 21 28	7 14 21 28
S. .. 4	11 18 25	1 8 15 22	1 8 15 22 29

	April	May	June
Su. ..	6 13 20 27	4 11 18 25	1 8 15 22 29
M. ..	7 14 21 28	5 12 19 26	2 9 16 23 30
Tu. .. 1	8 15 22 29	6 13 20 27	3 10 17 24
W. .. 2	9 16 23 30	7 14 21 28	4 11 18 25
Th. .. 3	10 17 24	1 8 15 22 29	5 12 19 26
F. .. 4	11 18 25	2 9 16 23 30	6 13 20 27
S. .. 5	12 19 26	3 10 17 24 31	7 14 21 28

	July	August	September
Su. ..	6 13 20 27	3 10 17 24 31	7 14 21 28
M. ..	7 14 21 28	4 11 18 25	1 8 15 22 29
Tu. .. 1	8 15 22 29	5 12 19 26	2 9 16 23 30
W. .. 2	9 16 23 30	6 13 20 27	3 10 17 24
Th. .. 3	10 17 24 31	7 14 21 28	4 11 18 25
F. .. 4	11 18 25	1 8 15 22 29	5 12 19 26
S. .. 5	12 19 26	2 9 16 23 30	6 13 20 27

	October	November	December
Su. ..	5 12 19 26	2 9 16 23 30	7 14 21 28
M. ..	6 13 20 27	3 10 17 24	1 8 15 22 29
Tu. ..	7 14 21 28	4 11 18 25	2 9 16 23 30
W. .. 1	8 15 22 29	5 12 19 26	3 10 17 24 31
Th. .. 2	9 16 23 30	6 13 20 27	4 11 18 25
F. .. 3	10 17 24 31	7 14 21 28	5 12 19 26
S. .. 4	11 18 25	1 8 15 22 29	6 13 20 27

Easter Days

March 23	1845	1913					
March 30	1777	1823	1834	1902	1975	1986	1997
April 6	1806	1817	1890	1947	1958	1969	
April 13	1800	1873	1879	1941			
April 20	1783	1794	1851	1862	1919	1930	2003
	2014	2025					

I

	January	February	March
Su. ..	4 11 18 25	1 8 15 22	1 8 15 22 29
M. ..	5 12 19 26	2 9 16 23	2 9 16 23 30
Tu. ..	6 13 20 27	3 10 17 24	3 10 17 24 31
W. ..	7 14 21 28	4 11 18 25	4 11 18 25
Th. .. 1	8 15 22 29	5 12 19 26	5 12 19 26
F. .. 2	9 16 23 30	6 13 20 27	6 13 20 27
S. .. 3	10 17 24 31	7 14 21 28	7 14 21 28

	April	May	June
Su. ..	5 12 19 26	3 10 17 24 31	7 14 21 28
M. ..	6 13 20 27	4 11 18 25	1 8 15 22 29
Tu. ..	7 14 21 28	5 12 19 26	2 9 16 23 30
W. .. 1	8 15 22 29	6 13 20 27	3 10 17 24
Th. .. 2	9 16 23 30	7 14 21 28	4 11 18 25
F. .. 3	10 17 24	1 8 15 22 29	5 12 19 26
S. .. 4	11 18 25	2 9 16 23 30	6 13 20 27

	July	August	September
Su. ..	5 12 19 26	2 9 16 23 30	6 13 20 27
M. ..	6 13 20 27	3 10 17 24 31	7 14 21 28
Tu. ..	7 14 21 28	4 11 18 25	1 8 15 22 29
W. .. 1	8 15 22 29	5 12 19 26	2 9 16 23 30
Th. .. 2	9 16 23 30	6 13 20 27	3 10 17 24
F. .. 3	10 17 24 31	7 14 21 28	4 11 18 25
S. .. 4	11 18 25	1 8 15 22 29	5 12 19 26

	October	November	December
Su. ..	4 11 18 25	1 8 15 22 29	6 13 20 27
M. ..	5 12 19 26	2 9 16 23 30	7 14 21 28
Tu. ..	6 13 20 27	3 10 17 24	1 8 15 22 29
W. ..	7 14 21 28	4 11 18 25	2 9 16 23 30
Th. .. 1	8 15 22 29	5 12 19 26	3 10 17 24 31
F. .. 2	9 16 23 30	6 13 20 27	4 11 18 25
S. .. 3	10 17 24 31	7 14 21 28	5 12 19 26

Easter Days

March 22	1818						
March 29	1807	1891	1959	1970			
April 5	1795	1801	1863	1874	1885	1931	1942
	1953	2015					
April 12	1789	1846	1857	1903	1914	1925	1998
	2009						
April 19	1778	1829	1835	1981	1987		

H (leap year)

	January	February	March
Su. ..	5 12 19 26	2 9 16 23	1 8 15 22 29
M. ..	6 13 20 27	3 10 17 24	2 9 16 23 30
Tu. ..	7 14 21 28	4 11 18 25	3 10 17 24 31
W. .. 1	8 15 22 29	5 12 19 26	4 11 18 25
Th. .. 2	9 16 23 30	6 13 20 27	5 12 19 26
F. .. 3	10 17 24 31	7 14 21 28	6 13 20 27
S. .. 4	11 18 25	1 8 15 22 29	7 14 21 28

	April	May	June
Su. ..	5 12 19 26	3 10 17 24 31	7 14 21 28
M. ..	6 13 20 27	4 11 18 25	1 8 15 22 29
Tu. ..	7 14 21 28	5 12 19 26	2 9 16 23 30
W. .. 1	8 15 22 29	6 13 20 27	3 10 17 24
Th. .. 2	9 16 23 30	7 14 21 28	4 11 18 25
F. .. 3	10 17 24	1 8 15 22 29	5 12 19 26
S. .. 4	11 18 25	2 9 16 23 30	6 13 20 27

	July	August	September
Su. ..	5 12 19 26	2 9 16 23 30	6 13 20 27
M. ..	6 13 20 27	3 10 17 24 31	7 14 21 28
Tu. ..	7 14 21 28	4 11 18 25	1 8 15 22 29
W. .. 1	8 15 22 29	5 12 19 26	2 9 16 23 30
Th. .. 2	9 16 23 30	6 13 20 27	3 10 17 24
F. .. 3	10 17 24 31	7 14 21 28	4 11 18 25
S. .. 4	11 18 25	1 8 15 22 29	5 12 19 26

	October	November	December
Su. ..	4 11 18 25	1 8 15 22 29	6 13 20 27
M. ..	5 12 19 26	2 9 16 23 30	7 14 21 28
Tu. ..	6 13 20 27	3 10 17 24	1 8 15 22 29
W. ..	7 14 21 28	4 11 18 25	2 9 16 23 30
Th. .. 1	8 15 22 29	5 12 19 26	3 10 17 24 31
F. .. 2	9 16 23 30	6 13 20 27	4 11 18 25
S. .. 3	10 17 24 31	7 14 21 28	5 12 19 26

Easter Days

March 29	1812	1964	
April 5	1896		
April 12	1868	1936	2020
April 19	1772	1840	1908	1992

J (leap year)

	January	February	March
Su. ..	4 11 18 25	1 8 15 22 29	7 14 21 28
M. ..	5 12 19 26	2 9 16 23	1 8 15 22 29
Tu. ..	6 13 20 27	3 10 17 24	2 9 16 23 30
W. ..	7 14 21 28	4 11 18 25	3 10 17 24 31
Th. .. 1	8 15 22 29	5 12 19 26	4 11 18 25
F. .. 2	9 16 23 30	6 13 20 27	5 12 19 26
S. .. 3	10 17 24 31	7 14 21 28	6 13 20 27

	April	May	June
Su. ..	4 11 18 25	2 9 16 23 30	6 13 20 27
M. ..	5 12 19 26	3 10 17 24 31	7 14 21 28
Tu. ..	6 13 20 27	4 11 18 25	1 8 15 22 29
W. ..	7 14 21 28	5 12 19 26	2 9 16 23 30
Th. .. 1	8 15 22 29	6 13 20 27	3 10 17 24
F. .. 2	9 16 23 30	7 14 21 28	4 11 18 25
S. .. 3	10 17 24	1 8 15 22 29	5 12 19 26

	July	August	September
Su. ..	4 11 18 25	1 8 15 22 29	5 12 19 26
M. ..	5 12 19 26	2 9 16 23 30	6 13 20 27
Tu. ..	6 13 20 27	3 10 17 24 31	7 14 21 28
W. ..	7 14 21 28	4 11 18 25	1 8 15 22 29
Th. .. 1	8 15 22 29	5 12 19 26	2 9 16 23 30
F. .. 2	9 16 23 30	6 13 20 27	3 10 17 24
S. .. 3	10 17 24 31	7 14 21 28	4 11 18 25

	October	November	December
Su. .. 3	10 17 24 31	7 14 21 28	5 12 19 26
M. ..	4 11 18 25	1 8 15 22 29	6 13 20 27
Tu. ..	5 12 19 26	2 9 16 23 30	7 14 21 28
W. ..	6 13 20 27	3 10 17 24	1 8 15 22 29
Th. ..	7 14 21 28	4 11 18 25	2 9 16 23 30
F. .. 1	8 15 22 29	5 12 19 26	3 10 17 24 31
S. .. 2	9 16 23 30	6 13 20 27	4 11 18 25

Easter Days

March 28	1880	1948	
April 4	1920		
April 11	1784	1852	2004
April 18	1824	1976	

K

	January	February	March
Su.	.. 3 10 17 24 31	7 14 21 28	7 14 21 28
M.	.. 4 11 18 25	1 8 15 22	1 8 15 22 29
Tu.	.. 5 12 19 26	2 9 16 23	2 9 16 23 30
W.	.. 6 13 20 27	3 10 17 24	3 10 17 24 31
Th.	.. 7 14 21 28	4 11 18 25	4 11 18 25
F.	1 8 15 22 29	5 12 19 26	5 12 19 26
S.	2 9 16 23 30	6 13 20 27	6 13 20 27

	April	May	June
Su.	.. 4 11 18 25	2 9 16 23 30	6 13 20 27
M.	.. 5 12 19 26	3 10 17 24 31	7 14 21 28
Tu.	.. 6 13 20 27	4 11 18 25	1 8 15 22 29
W.	.. 7 14 21 28	5 12 19 26	2 9 16 23 30
Th.	1 8 15 22 29	6 13 20 27	3 10 17 24
F.	2 9 16 23 30	7 14 21 28	4 11 18 25
S.	3 10 17 24	1 8 15 22 29	5 12 19 26

	July	August	September
Su.	.. 4 11 18 25	1 8 15 22 29	5 12 19 26
M.	.. 5 12 19 26	2 9 16 23 30	6 13 20 27
Tu.	.. 6 13 20 27	3 10 17 24 31	7 14 21 28
W.	.. 7 14 21 28	4 11 18 25	1 8 15 22 29
Th.	1 8 15 22 29	5 12 19 26	2 9 16 23 30
F.	2 9 16 23 30	6 13 20 27	3 10 17 24
S.	3 10 17 24 31	7 14 21 28	4 11 18 25

	October	November	December
Su.	.. 3 10 17 24 31	7 14 21 28	5 12 19 26
M.	.. 4 11 18 25	1 8 15 22 29	6 13 20 27
Tu.	.. 5 12 19 26	2 9 16 23 30	7 14 21 28
W.	.. 6 13 20 27	3 10 17 24	1 8 15 22 29
Th.	.. 7 14 21 28	4 11 18 25	2 9 16 23 30
F.	1 8 15 22 29	5 12 19 26	3 10 17 24 31
S.	2 9 16 23 30	6 13 20 27	4 11 18 25

Easter Days

March 28	1869	1875	1937				
April 4	1779	1790	1847	1858	1915	1926	1999
	2010	2021					
April 11	1773	1819	1830	1841	1909	1971	1982
	1993						
April 18	1802	1813	1897	1954	1965		
April 25	1886	1943					

M

	January	February	March
Su.	.. 2 9 16 23 30	6 13 20 27	6 13 20 27
M.	.. 3 10 17 24 31	7 14 21 28	7 14 21 28
Tu.	.. 4 11 18 25	1 8 15 22 29	1 8 15 22 29
W.	.. 5 12 19 26	2 9 16 23	2 9 16 23 30
Th.	.. 6 13 20 27	3 10 17 24	3 10 17 24 31
F.	.. 7 14 21 28	4 11 18 25	4 11 18 25
S.	1 8 15 22 29	5 12 19 26	5 12 19 26

	April	May	June
Su.	.. 3 10 17 24	1 8 15 22 29	5 12 19 26
M.	.. 4 11 18 25	2 9 16 23 30	6 13 20 27
Tu.	.. 5 12 19 26	3 10 17 24 31	7 14 21 28
W.	.. 6 13 20 27	4 11 18 25	1 8 15 22 29
Th.	.. 7 14 21 28	5 12 19 26	2 9 16 23 30
F.	.. 1 8 15 22 29	6 13 20 27	3 10 17 24
S.	.. 2 9 16 23 30	7 14 21 28	4 11 18 25

	July	August	September
Su.	.. 3 10 17 24 31	7 14 21 28	4 11 18 25
M.	.. 4 11 18 25	1 8 15 22 29	5 12 19 26
Tu.	.. 5 12 19 26	2 9 16 23 30	6 13 20 27
W.	.. 6 13 20 27	3 10 17 24 31	7 14 21 28
Th.	.. 7 14 21 28	4 11 18 25	1 8 15 22 29
F.	1 8 15 22 29	5 12 19 26	2 9 16 23 30
S.	2 9 16 23 30	6 13 20 27	3 10 17 24

	October	November	December
Su.	.. 2 9 16 23 30	6 13 20 27	4 11 18 25
M.	.. 3 10 17 24 31	7 14 21 28	5 12 19 26
Tu.	.. 4 11 18 25	1 8 15 22 29	6 13 20 27
W.	.. 5 12 19 26	2 9 16 23 30	7 14 21 28
Th.	.. 6 13 20 27	3 10 17 24	1 8 15 22 29
F.	.. 7 14 21 28	4 11 18 25	2 9 16 23 30
S.	1 8 15 22 29	5 12 19 26	3 10 17 24 31

Easter Days

March 27	1785	1842	1853	1910	1921	2005	
April 3	1774	1825	1831	1983	1994		
April 10	1803	1814	1887	1898	1955	1966	1977
April 17	1870	1881	1927	1938	1949	2022	
April 24	1791	1859	2011				

L (leap year)

	January	February	March
Su.	.. 3 10 17 24 31	7 14 21 28	6 13 20 27
M.	.. 4 11 18 25	1 8 15 22 29	7 14 21 28
Tu.	.. 5 12 19 26	2 9 16 23	1 8 15 22 29
W.	.. 6 13 20 27	3 10 17 24	2 9 16 23 30
Th.	.. 7 14 21 28	4 11 18 25	3 10 17 24 31
F.	1 8 15 22 29	5 12 19 26	4 11 18 25
S.	2 9 16 23 30	6 13 20 27	5 12 19 26

	April	May	June
Su.	.. 3 10 17 24	1 8 15 22 29	5 12 19 26
M.	.. 4 11 18 25	2 9 16 23 30	6 13 20 27
Tu.	.. 5 12 19 26	3 10 17 24 31	7 14 21 28
W.	.. 6 13 20 27	4 11 18 25	1 8 15 22 29
Th.	.. 7 14 21 28	5 12 19 26	2 9 16 23 30
F.	1 8 15 22 29	6 13 20 27	3 10 17 24
S.	2 9 16 23 30	7 14 21 28	4 11 18 25

	July	August	September
Su.	.. 3 10 17 24 31	7 14 21 28	4 11 18 25
M.	.. 4 11 18 25	1 8 15 22 29	5 12 19 26
Tu.	.. 5 12 19 26	2 9 16 23 30	6 13 20 27
W.	.. 6 13 20 27	3 10 17 24 31	7 14 21 28
Th.	.. 7 14 21 28	4 11 18 25	1 8 15 22 29
F.	1 8 15 22 29	5 12 19 26	2 9 16 23 30
S.	2 9 16 23 30	6 13 20 27	3 10 17 24

	October	November	December
Su.	.. 2 9 16 23 30	6 13 20 27	4 11 18 25
M.	.. 3 10 17 24 31	7 14 21 28	5 12 19 26
Tu.	.. 4 11 18 25	1 8 15 22 29	6 13 20 27
W.	.. 5 12 19 26	2 9 16 23 30	7 14 21 28
Th.	.. 6 13 20 27	3 10 17 24	1 8 15 22 29
F.	.. 7 14 21 28	4 11 18 25	2 9 16 23 30
S.	1 8 15 22 29	5 12 19 26	3 10 17 24 31

Easter Days

March 27	1796	1864	1932	2016
April 3	1836	1904	1988	
April 17	1808	1892	1960	

N (leap year)

	January	February	March
Su.	.. 2 9 16 23 30	6 13 20 27	5 12 19 26
M.	.. 3 10 17 24 31	7 14 21 28	6 13 20 27
Tu.	.. 4 11 18 25	1 8 15 22 29	7 14 21 28
W.	.. 5 12 19 26	2 9 16 23	1 8 15 22 29
Th.	.. 6 13 20 27	3 10 17 24	2 9 16 23 30
F.	.. 7 14 21 28	4 11 18 25	3 10 17 24 31
S.	1 8 15 22 29	5 12 19 26	4 11 18 25

	April	May	June
Su.	.. 2 9 16 23 30	7 14 21 28	4 11 18 25
M.	.. 3 10 17 24	1 8 15 22 29	5 12 19 26
Tu.	.. 4 11 18 25	2 9 16 23 30	6 13 20 27
W.	.. 5 12 19 26	3 10 17 24 31	7 14 21 28
Th.	.. 6 13 20 27	4 11 18 25	1 8 15 22 29
F.	.. 7 14 21 28	5 12 19 26	2 9 16 23 30
S.	1 8 15 22 29	6 13 20 27	3 10 17 24

	July	August	September
Su.	.. 2 9 16 23 30	6 13 20 27	3 10 17 24
M.	.. 3 10 17 24 31	7 14 21 28	4 11 18 25
Tu.	.. 4 11 18 25	1 8 15 22 29	5 12 19 26
W.	.. 5 12 19 26	2 9 16 23 30	6 13 20 27
Th.	.. 6 13 20 27	3 10 17 24 31	7 14 21 28
F.	.. 7 14 21 28	4 11 18 25	1 8 15 22 29
S.	1 8 15 22 29	5 12 19 26	2 9 16 23 30

	October	November	December
Su.	.. 1 8 15 22 29	5 12 19 26	3 10 17 24 31
M.	.. 2 9 16 23 30	6 13 20 27	4 11 18 25
Tu.	.. 3 10 17 24 31	7 14 21 28	5 12 19 26
W.	.. 4 11 18 25	1 8 15 22 29	6 13 20 27
Th.	.. 5 12 19 26	2 9 16 23 30	7 14 21 28
F.	.. 6 13 20 27	3 10 17 24	1 8 15 22 29
S.	.. 7 14 21 28	4 11 18 25	2 9 16 23 30

Easter Days

March 26	1780		
April 2	1820	1972	
April 9	1944		
April 16	1876		
April 23	1848	1916	2000

THE WORLD

The Earth

The shape of the Earth is that of an oblate spheroid or solid of revolution whose meridian sections are ellipses, whilst the sections at right angles are circles.

Dimensions

Equatorial diameter = 12,756 km (7,926·5 miles).
Polar diameter = 12,714 km (7,899 miles).
Equatorial circumference = 40,075 km (24,901 miles).
Polar circumference = 40,008 km (24,860 miles).

The equatorial circumference is divided into 360 degrees of longitude, which is measured in degrees, minutes and seconds east or west of the Greenwich meridian (0°) to 180° (the meridian 180° E. coinciding with 180° W.).

Distance north and south of the Equator is measured in degrees, minutes and seconds of latitude. The Equator is 0°, the North Pole is 90° N. and the South Pole is 90° S. The Tropics lie at 23° 31′ N. (Tropic of Cancer) and 23° 31′ S. (Tropic of Capricorn). The Arctic Circle lies at 66° 30′ N. and the Antarctic Circle at 66° 30′ S.

Area, etc.

Surface area = 509,610,000 km²
              = 196,836,000 miles²
Land area = 148,065,120 km²
          = 57,168,000 miles²
Water area = 361,544,880 km²
           = 139,668,000 miles²

The velocity of a given point of the Earth's surface at the Equator exceeds 1,000 miles an hour (24,901·8 miles in 24 hours); the Earth's velocity in its orbit round the Sun is about 66,600 miles an hour (584,000,000 miles in 365¼ days). The Earth is distant from the Sun 93,000,000 miles, on the average.

OCEAN AREAS

	Area	
	km²	miles²
Pacific	166,240,000	64,186,300
Atlantic	86,550,000	33,420,000
Indian	73,427,000	28,350,500
Arctic	13,223,700	5,105,700

Greatest Ocean Depths

Greatest depth location	*Depth*	
	metres	feet
Mariana Trench (Pacific)	10,916	35,839
Puerto Rico Trench (Atlantic)	8,605	28,232
Java Trench (Indian)	7,125	23,376
Eurasian Basin (Arctic)	5,450	17,880

SEA AREAS

	Area	
	km²	miles²
South China	2,974,600	1,148,500
Caribbean	2,515,900	971,400
Mediterranean	2,509,900	969,100
Bering	2,226,100	873,000
Gulf of Mexico	1,507,600	582,100
Okhotsk	1,392,000	537,500
Japan	1,015,000	391,100
Hudson Bay	730,100	281,900
East China	664,600	256,600
Andaman	564,880	218,100
Black Sea	507,900	196,100
Red Sea	453,000	174,900
North Sea	427,100	164,900
Baltic Sea	382,000	147,500
Yellow Sea	294,000	113,500
Persian Gulf	230,000	88,800

THE CONTINENTS

There are six geographic continents, though America is often divided politically into North and Central America, and South America.

Africa is surrounded by sea except for the narrow isthmus of Suez in the north-east, through which is cut the Suez Canal. The Equator passes through the middle of the continent. Its extreme longitudes are 17° 20′ W. at Cape Verde, Senegal, and 51° 24′ E. at Ras Hafun, Somalia. The extreme latitudes are 37° 20′ N. at Cape Blanco, Tunisia, and 34° 50′ S. at Cape Agulhas, South Africa, about 5,000 miles apart.

America.—North America, including Mexico, is surrounded by ocean except in the south, where the isthmian states of **Central America** link North America with South America. Its extreme longitudes are 168° 5′ W. at Cape Prince of Wales, Alaska, and 55° 40′ W. at Cape Charles, Newfoundland. The extreme latitudes are 82° N. in the Arctic Ocean and 15° N. in the south of Mexico. The West Indies, about 65,000 square miles in area, extend from about 27° N. to 10° N. latitude.

South America lies mostly in the southern hemisphere; the Equator passes through the north of the continent. It is surrounded by ocean except where it is joined to Central America in the north by the narrow isthmus through which is cut the Panama Canal. Its extreme longitudes are 34° 47′ W. at Cape Branco in Brazil and 81° 20′ W. at Punta Pariña, Peru. The extreme latitudes are 12° 25′ N. at Punta Gallinas, Colombia, and 55° 59′ S. at Cape Horn, Chile.

Antarctica lies almost entirely within the Antarctic Circle (66° 33′ S.) and is the largest of the world's glaciated areas. The continent has an area of about 5·5 million square miles, 99 per cent of which is permanently ice-covered. The ice amounts to some 7·2 million cubic miles and represents more than 90 per cent of the world's fresh water. The environment is too hostile for unsupported human habitation. The staff of scientific research stations are the only people present on the continent and off-lying islands. (*See also* p. 716.)

Asia is the largest continent and occupies almost a third of the world's land surface. The extreme longitudes are about 26° E. on the west coast of Asia Minor and 169° 45′ W. at Mys Dežneva (East Cape), USSR, a distance of about 6,000 miles. Its extreme northern latitude is 77° 45′ N. at Cape Čeljuskin, USSR, and it extends over 5,000 miles south to about 1° 15′ N. of the Equator. The islands of Japan, the Philippines and Indonesia ring the continent to the east and south-east.

Australia is the smallest of the continents and lies in the southern hemisphere. It is entirely surrounded by ocean. Its extreme longitudes are 113° 9′ E. at Steep Point and 153° 38′ E. at Cape Byron. The extreme latitudes are 10° 40′ S. at Cape York and 39° S. at South East Point.

Europe, including European Russia, is the smallest continent in the northern hemisphere. Its extreme latitudes are 71° 11′ N. at North Cape in Norway, and 36° 23′ N. at Cape Matapan in southern Greece, a distance of about 2,400 miles. Its breadth from Cape da Roca in Portugal (9° 30′ W.) in the west to the Urals in the east is about 3,300 miles. The division between Europe and Asia is generally regarded as being the Ural Mountains and, in the south, the valley of the Manych, which stretches from the Caspian Sea to the mouth of the Don.

	Area	
	km²	miles²
Asia	43,998,000	16,988,000
America[1]	41,918,000	16,185,000
Africa	29,800,000	11,506,000
Antarctica	c.13,600,000	c.5,500,000
Europe[2]	9,699,000	3,745,000
Australia	7,618,493	2,941,526

[1] North and Central America has an area of 24,255,000 km² (9,365,000 miles²).
[2] Includes 5,571,000 km² (2,151,000 miles²) of USSR territory west of the Ural Mountains.

PENINSULAS

	Area	
	km²	miles²
Arabian	3,250,000	1,250,000
Southern Indian	2,072,000	800,000
Alaskan	1,500,000	580,000
Labradorian	1,300,000	500,000
Scandinavian	800,300	309,000
Iberian	584,000	225,500

LARGEST ISLANDS

Island	Ocean	Area	
		km²	miles²
Greenland	Arctic	2,175,500	840,000
New Guinea	Pacific	792,500	306,000
Borneo	Pacific	725,450	280,100
Madagascar	Indian	587,040	226,658
Baffin Island	Arctic	507,528	195,928
Sumatra	Indian	427,350	165,000
Honshu	Pacific	228,000	88,031
Great Britain[1]	Atlantic	218,040	84,186
Victoria Island	Arctic	217,290	83,895
Ellesmere Island	Arctic	196,235	75,767
Sulawesi (Celebes)	Indian	178,700	69,000
South Island, NZ	Pacific	151,010	58,305
Java	Indian	126,650	48,900
Cuba	Atlantic	114,525	44,218
North Island, NZ	Pacific	114,050	44,035
Newfoundland	Atlantic	108,855	42,030
Luzon	Pacific	105,880	40,880
Iceland	Atlantic	103,000	39,770
Mindanao	Pacific	95,247	36,775
Ireland	Atlantic	82,462	31,839

[1] Mainland only

GLACIATED AREAS

It is estimated that 15,600,000 km² (6,020,000 miles²) or about 10·4 per cent of the world's land surface is permanently covered with ice.

	Area	
	km²	miles²
South Polar regions	13,597,000	5,250,000
North Polar Regions (inc. Greenland)	1,965,000	758,500
Alaska-Canada	58,800	22,700
Asia	37,800	14,600
South America	11,900	4,600
Europe	10,700	4,128
New Zealand	984	380
Africa	238	92

LARGEST DESERTS

	Area (approx.)	
	km²	miles²
The Sahara (N. Africa)	8,400,000	3,250,000
Australian Desert	1,550,000	600,000
Arabian Desert	1,300,000	500,000
*The Gobi (Mongolia/China)	1,170,000	450,000
Kalahari Desert (Botswana)	520,000	200,000
Sonoran Desert (USA/ Mexico)	310,000	120,000
Namib Desert (Namibia)	310,000	120,000
†Kara Kum (USSR)	270,000	105,000
Thar Desert (India/Pakistan)	260,000	100,000
Somali Desert (Somalia)	260,000	100,000
Atacama Desert (Chile)	180,000	70,000
†Kyzyl Kum (USSR)	180,000	70,000
Dasht-e Lut (Iran)	52,000	20,000
Mojave Desert (USA)	35,000	13,500
Desierto de Sechura (Peru)	26,000	10,000

* Including the Takla Makan—320,000 km² (125,000 miles²)
† Together known as the Turkestan Desert

DEEPEST DEPRESSIONS

	Maximum depth below sea level	
	metres	feet
Dead Sea (Jordan/Israel)	395	1,296
Turfan Depression (Sinkiang, China)	153	505
Qattara Depression (Egypt)	132	436
Mangyshlak peninsula (Kazakh SSR)	131	433
Danakil Depression (Ethiopia)	116	383
Death Valley (California, USA)	86	282
Salton Sink (California, USA)	71	235
W. of Ustyurt plateau (Kazakh SSR)	70	230
Prikaspiyskaya Nizmennost' (Russian SFSR/Kazakh SSR)	67	220
Lake Sarykamysh (Uzbek/Turkmen SSR)	45	148
El Faiyûm (Egypt)	44	147
Valdies peninsula, Lago Enriquillo (Dominican Republic)	40	131

The world's largest exposed depression is the Prikaspiyskaya Nizmennost' covering the hinterland of the northern third of the Caspian Sea, which is itself 28 m (92 ft) below sea level.

Western Antarctica and Central Greenland largely comprise crypto-depressions under ice burdens. The Antarctic Wilkes subglacial basin has a bedrock 2,341 m (7,680 ft) below sea-level. In Greenland (lat. 73° N., long. 39° W.) the bedrock is 365 m (1,197 ft) below sea-level.

LARGEST MOUNTAIN RANGES

Range (Location)	Length	
	km	miles
Cordillera de Los Andes (W. South America)	7,200	4,500
Rocky Mountains (W. North America)	4,800	3,000
Himalaya-Karakoram-Hindu Kush (S. Central Asia)	3,800	2,400
Great Dividing Range (E. Australia)	3,600	2,250
Trans-Antarctic Mts. (Antarctica)	3,500	2,200
Atlantic Coast Range (E. Brazil)	3,000	1,900
West Sumatran-Javan Range (Indonesia)	2,900	1,800
Aleutian Range (Alaska and NW Pacific)	2,650	1,650
Tien Shan (S. Central Asia)	2,250	1,400
Central New Guinea Range (Irian Jaya— Papua New Guinea)	2,000	1,250

HIGHEST MOUNTAINS

The world's 8,000-metre mountains (with six subsidiary peaks) are in the 3,800 km (2,400 mile) long Himalaya-Karakoram-Hindu Kush range of south central Asia.

Mountain	Height	
	m	ft
Mount Everest	8,863	29,078
K2	8,607	28,238
Kangchenjunga	8,597	28,208
Lhotse	8,511	27,923
Makalu I	8,481	27,824
Lhotse Shar	8,383	27,504
Dhaulagiri I	8,167	26,795
Manaslu I (Kutang I)	8,156	26,760
Cho Oyu	8,153	26,750
Nanga Parbat (Diamir)	8,125	26,660
Annapurna I	8,091	26,546
Gasherbrum I (Hidden Peak)	8,068	26,470
Broad Peak I	8,046	26,400
Shisha Pangma (Gosainthan)	8,046	26,398
Gasherbrum II	8,034	26,360
Annapurna East	8,010	26,280
Makalu South-East	8,010	26,280
Broad Peak Central	8,000	26,246

The culminating summits in the other major mountain ranges are:—

Mountain (Range or Country)	Height	
	m	ft
Pik Pobeda (Tien Shan)	7,439	24,406
Cerro Aconcagua (Cordillera de Los Andes)	6,960	22,834
Mt. McKinley—*S. Peak* (Alaska Range)	6,194	20,320
Kilimanjaro (Tanzania)	5,894	19,340
Hkakabo Razi (Burma)	5,881	19,296
Citlaltépetl (Orizaba) (Sierra Madre Oriental, Mexico)	5,699	18,700
El'brus—*W. Peak* (Caucasus, USSR)	5,663	18,481
Vinson Massif (E. Antarctica)	4,897	16,067
Puncak Jaya (Central New Guinea Range)	4,884	16,023
Klyuchevskaya Sopka (Kamchatka peninsula, USSR)	4,850	15,910
Mt. Blanc (Alps)	4,807	15,771
Ras Dashan (Ethiopian Highlands)	4,620	15,158
Zard Kūh (Zagros Mts, Iran)	4,547	14,921
Mt. Kirkpatrick (Trans Antarctic)	4,529	14,860
Mt. Belukha (Altai Mts., USSR/ Mongolia)	4,505	14,783
Mt. Elbert (Rocky Mountains)	4,400	14,433
Mt. Rainier (Cascade Range, N. America)	4,392	14,410
Nevado de Colima (Sierra Madre Occidental, Mexico)	4,265	13,993
Jebel Toubkal (Atlas Mountains, N. Africa)	4,165	13,665
Kinabalu (Crocker Range, Borneo)	4,101	13,455
Kerinci (West Sumatran-Javan Range)	3,805	12,484
Jabal an Nabī Shu'ayb (N. Tihāmat, Yemen)	3,760	12,336
Teotepec (Sierra Madre del Sur, Mexico)	3,703	12,149
Thaban Ntlenyana (Drakensberg, South Africa)	3,482	11,425

Pico de Bandeira (Atlantic Coast Range)	2,890	9,482
Shishaldin (Aleutian Range)	2,861	9,387
Kosciusko (Great Dividing Range)	2,228	7,310

HIGHEST VOLCANOES

Volcano (last major eruption) and location	Height	
	m	ft
Guallatiri (1959), Andes, Chile	6,060	19,882
Lascar (1986), Andes, Chile	5,990	19,652
Cotopaxi (1975), Andes, Ecuador	5,897	19,347
Tupungatito (1980), Andes, Chile	5,640	18,504
Sangay (1976), Andes, Ecuador	5,230	17,159
Guagua Pichincha (1982), Andes, Ecuador	4,784	15,696
Purace (1977), Andes, Colombia	4,756	15,604
Klyuchevskaya Sopka (1985), Kamchatka peninsula, USSR	4,750	15,584
Colima (1987), Mexico	4,268	14,003
Mauna Loa (1984), Hawaii Is.	4,170	13,680
Cameroon (1982), Cameroon	4,070	13,354
Acatenango (1972), Guatemala	3,960	12,992
Fuego (1988), Guatemala	3,835	12,582
Kerinci (1987), Sumatra, Indonesia	3,800	12,467
Erebus (1988), Ross Island, Antarctica	3,794	12,450
Tacana (1988), Guatemala	3,780	12,400
Santiaguito (1902, 1988), Guatemala	3,768	12,362
Rindjani (1966), Lombok, Indonesia	3,726	12,224
Semeru (1988), Java, Indonesia	3,675	12,060
Nyirgongo (1977), Zaïre	3,475	11,400
Koryakskaya (1957), Kamchatka, USSR	3,456	11,339
Irazú (1987), Costa Rica	3,432	11,260
Slamet (1967), Java, Indonesia	3,428	11,247
Spurr (1953), Alaska, USA	3,374	11,069
Mt. Etna (1169, 1669, 1988), Sicily, Italy	3,369	11,053
Shiveluch (1964), Kamchatka, USSR	3,283	10,771
Agung (1964), Bali, Indonesia	3,142	10,308
Llaima (1988), Chile	3,128	10,239
Redoubt (1966), Alaska, USA	3,108	10,197
Tjareme (1938), Java, Indonesia	3,078	10,098
Illamna (1978), Alaska, USA	3,076	10,092
On-Taka (1980), Japan	3,063	10,049
Nyamlagira (1988), Zaire	3,056	10,028

Other notable volcanoes

Tambora (1815), Subawa, Indonesia	2,850	9,353
Mt. St. Helens (1986), Washington State, USA	2,530	8,300
Tristan da Cunha (1961), South Atlantic	2,060	6,760
Hekla (1981), Iceland	1,491	4,892
Mt. Pelée (1902), Martinique	1,397	4,583
Vesuvius (AD 79, 1944), Italy	1,280	4,198
Kilauea (1988), Hawaii, USA	1,242	4,077
Stromboli (1986), Lipari Is., Italy	926	3,038
Krakatau (1883), Sunda Strait, Indonesia	804	2,640
Santoriní (Thíra) (1628 BC), Aegean Sea, Greece	566	1,857
Vulcano (Monte Aria), Lipari Is., Italy	499	1,637
Sartsey (1867), off Iceland	173	568

LARGEST LAKES

The areas of some of these lakes are subject to seasonal variation.

Lake	Location	Area km²	Area miles²	Length km	Length miles
Caspian Sea	Iran/USSR	371,000	143,000	1,171	728
Superior	Canada/USA	82,100	31,700	563	350
Victoria	Uganda, Tanzania, Kenya	69,500	26,828	362	225
Huron	Canada/USA	59,570	23,000	331	206
Michigan	USA	57,750	22,300	494	307
Aral Sea	USSR	40,400	15,600	331	235
Tanganyika	Zaïre, Tanzania, Zambia and Burundi	32,900	12,700	675	420
*Baykal (Baikal)	USSR	31,500	12,162	635	395
Great Bear	Canada	31,328	12,096	309	192
Malawi	Tanzania, Malawi and Mozambique	28,880	11,150	580	360
Great Slave	Canada	28,570	11,031	480	298
Erie	Canada/USA	25,670	9,910	388	241
Winnipeg	Canada	24,390	9,417	428	266
Ontario	Canada/USA	19,550	7,550	310	193
Balkhash	USSR	18,427	7,115	605	376
Ladozhskoye (Ladoga)	USSR	17,700	6,835	200	124

United Kingdom

Lake	Location	Area km²	Area miles²	Length km	Length miles
Lough Neagh	N. Ireland	381·73	147·39	28·9	18
Loch Lomond	Scotland	71·12	27·46	36·44	22·64
Windermere	England	14·74	5·69	16·90	10·5
Lake Vyrnwy	Wales (artificial)	4·53	1·75	7·56	4·70
Llyn Tegid (Bala)	Wales (natural)	4·38	1·69	5·80	3·65

* World's deepest lake (1,940 m/6,365 ft)

LONGEST RIVERS

River	Length km	Length miles	Source	Outflow
Nile (Bahr-el-Nil)	6,670	4,145	R. Luvironza, Burundi	E. Mediterranean
Amazon (Amazonas)	6,648	4,007	Lago Villafro, Peru	S. Atlantic
Mississippi-Missouri	5,970	3,710	R. Red Rock, SW Montana	Gulf of Mexico
Yenisey-Angara	5,540	3,442	W. Mongolia	Kara Sea
Yangtze-Kiang (Chang Jiang)	5,530	3,436	Kunlun Mts., W. China	Yellow Sea
Ob'-Irtysh	5,410	3,362	W. Mongolia	Kara Sea
Huang He (Yellow River)	4,830	3,000	Bayan Har Shan range, central China	Yellow Sea
Zaire (Congo)	4,700	2,920	R. Lualaba, Zaire-Zambia	S. Atlantic
Amur-Argun	4,670	2,903	R. Argun, Khingan Mts., N. China	Sea of Okhotsk
Lena-Kirenga	4,345	2,700	R. Kirenga, W. of Lake Baykal, USSR	Arctic Ocean
Mackenzie-Peace	4,240	2,635	Tatlatui Lake, British Columbia	Beaufort Sea
Mekong	4,184	2,600	Lants'ang, Tibet	South China Sea
Niger	4,184	2,600	Loma Mts., Guinea	Gulf of Guinea, E. Atlantic
Rió de la Plata-Paraná	4,000	2,485	R. Paranáiba, central Brazil	S. Atlantic
Murray-Darling	3,750	2,330	SE Queensland	Lake Alexandrina, S. Australia
Volga	3,690	2,293	Valdai plateau, USSR	Caspian Sea
Zambezi	3,540	2,200	NW Zambia	S. Indian Ocean

Other notable rivers

River	Length km	Length miles	Source	Outflow
St. Lawrence	3,130	1,945	Minnesota, USA	Gulf of St. Lawrence
Ganges-Brahmaputra	2,900	1,800	R. Matsang, SW Tibet	Bay of Bengal
Indus	2,880	1,790	R. Sengge, SW Tibet	N. Arabian Sea
Danube (Donau)	2,850	1,770	Black Forest, SW Germany	Black Sea
Tigris-Euphrates	2,740	1,700	R. Murat, E. Turkey	Persian Gulf
Irrawaddy	2,090	1,300	R. Mali Hka, N. Burma	Andaman Sea
Don	1,969	1,224	SE of Novomoskovsk	Sea of Azov

British Isles

River	Length km	Length miles	Source	Outflow
Shannon	386	240	Co. Cavan, Rep. of Ireland	Atlantic
Severn	354	220	Powys, Wales	Bristol Channel
Thames	346	215	Gloucestershire, England	North Sea
Tay	188	117	Perthshire, Scotland	North Sea
Clyde	158	98½	Lanarkshire, Scotland	Forth of Clyde
Tweed	155	96¼	Peeblesshire, Scotland	North Sea
Bann (Upper and Lower)	122	76	Co. Down, N. Ireland	Atlantic

GREATEST WATERFALLS—BY HEIGHT

Waterfall	River and Location	Total drop m	ft	Greatest single leap m	ft
Angel	Carrao, Venezuela	979	3,212	807	2,648
Tugela	Tugela, S. Africa	947	3,110	410	1,350
Utigård	Jostedal Glacier, Norway	800	2,625	600	1,970
Mongefossen	Monge, Norway	774	2,540	—	—
Yosemite	Yosemite Creek, USA	739	2,425	435	1,430
Østre Mardøla Foss	Mardals, Norway	656	2,154	296	974
Tyssestrengane	Tysso, Norway	646	2,120	289	948
Kukenaam	Arabopó, Venezuela	610	2,000	—	—
Sutherland	Arthur, NZ	580	1,904	248	815
Kjellfossen[1]	Naeröfjord, Norway	561	1,841	149	490

British Isles

Eas a' Chuàl Aluinn	Glas Bheinn, Sutherland	200	658		
Powerscourt Falls	Dargle, Co. Wicklow	106	350		
Pistyll-y-Llyn	Powys-Dyfed border	c.73	230–240	(cascades)	
Pistyll Rhyadr	Clwyd-Powys border	71·5	235	(single leap)	
Caldron Snout	R. Tees, Cumbria/Durham	60	200	(cascades)	

[1] Volume often so low the fall atomizes into a 'bridal veil'.

GREATEST WATERFALLS—BY VOLUME

Waterfall (River and Location)	Mean Annual Flow m³/sec	galls/sec
Boyoma (R. Zaïre)	c.17,000	c.3,750,000
*Guaira (Alto Paraná, Brazil/ Paraguay)	13,000	2,930,000
Khône (Mekong, Laos)	11,500	2,560,000
Niagara (Horseshoe) (R. Niagara/Lake Erie–Lake Ontario)	3,000	670,000
Paulo Afonso (R. São Francisco, Brazil)	2,800	625,000
Urubu-Panga (Alto Paraná, Brazil)	2,800	625,000
Quedas do Iguaçu (R. Iguazú, Brazil/ Argentina)	1,700	385,000
Patos-Maribando (Rio Grande, Brazil)	1,500	330,000
Victoria (Mosi-oa-tunya) (R. Zambezi, Zambia/Zimbabwe)	1,100	240,000
Churchill (R. Churchill, Canada)	975	215,500
Kaieteur (R. Potaro, Guyana)	660	146,000

*Peak flow 50,000 m³/sec, 11,000,000 galls/sec.

TALLEST INHABITED BUILDINGS

Building and City	Height metres	feet
Sears Tower, Chicago	443	[1]1,454
World Trade Center, New York	412	[2]1,350
Empire State Building, New York	381	[3]1,250
Standard Oil Building, Chicago	346	1,136
John Hancock, Center, Chicago	343	1,127
Chrysler Building, New York	319	1,046
Texas Commercial Plaza, Houston	305	1,002
Allied Bank Plaza, Houston	300	985
Colombia Center, Seattle	290	954
First Bank Tower, Toronto	286	952

[1] With TV antennae 475·18 m/1,559 ft
[2] With TV antennae, 521·2 m/1,710 ft
[3] With a 67·6 m/222 ft tower (added 1950–51), 448·6 m/ 1,472 ft

TALLEST STRUCTURES

Structure and Location	Height metres	feet
Warszawa Radio Mast, Konstantynow, Poland	646	2,120
KTHI-TV Mast, Fargo, North Dakota	629	2,063
CN Tower, Metro Centre, Toronto, Canada	555	1,822

LONGEST BRIDGES—BY SPAN

Bridge and Location	Length m	ft
Suspension Spans		
Humber Estuary, Humberside, England	1,410	4,626
Verrazano Narrows, Brooklyn-Staten Is., USA	1,298	4,260
Golden Gate, San Francisco Bay, USA	1,280	4,200
Mackinac Straits, Michigan, USA	1,158	3,800
Bosphorus, Istanbul, Turkey	1,074	3,524
George Washington, Hudson River, New York City, USA	1,067	3,500
Ponte 25 Abril (Tagus), Lisbon, Portugal	1,013	3,323
Firth of Forth (road), nr. Edinburgh, Scotland	1,006	3,300
Severn River, Severn Estuary, England	988	3,240
Cantilever Spans		
Pont de Québec (rail-road), St. Lawrence, Canada	548·6	1,800
Firth of Forth (rail), nr. Edinburgh, Scotland	521·2	1,710
Minato, Osaka, Japan	510·0	1,673
Commodore Barry, Chester, Pennsylvania, USA	501·0	1,644
Greater New Orleans, Algiers, Louisiana, USA	480·0	1,575
Howrah (rail-road), Calcutta, India	457·2	1,500
Steel Arch Spans		
New River Gorge, Fayetteville, W. Virginia, USA	518·2	1,700
Bayonne (Kill van Kull), Bayonne, NJ-Staten Is., USA	503·5	1,652
Sydney Harbour, Sydney, Australia	502·9	1,650

The 'floating' bridging at Evergreen, Seattle, Washington State, USA is 3,839 m/12,596 ft long.

The longest stretch of bridgings of any kind are those between Mandeville and Jefferson, Louisiana, USA—the Lake Pontchartrain Causeway II 38·422 km/23·87 miles and I 38·352 km/23·83 miles.

LONGEST VEHICULAR TUNNELS

Tunnel and Location	Length	
	km	miles
*Seikan (rail), Tsugaru Channel, Japan	53·90	33·49
Moscow metro, Belyaevo-Medved Kovo, Moscow, USSR	30·70	19·07
Northern line tube, East Finchley-Morden, London	27·84	17·30
Oshimizu, Honshū, Japan	22·17	13·78
Simplon II (rail), Brigue, Switzerland-Iselle, Italy	19·82	12·31
Simplon I (rail), Brigue, Switzerland-Iselle, Italy	19·80	12·30
Shin-Kanmon (rail), Kanmon Strait, Japan	18·68	11·61
Great Appennine (rail), Vernio, Italy	18·49	11·49
St. Gotthard (road), Göschenen-Airolo, Switzerland	16·32	10·14
Rokko (rail), Ōsaka-Kōbe, Japan	16·09	10·00

*Sub-aqueous

The twin rail Eurotunnel under the English Channel between Cheriton, Kent and Sargette, near Calais, is due to be opened in summer 1993. The tunnels will be 49·94 km/31·03 miles in length.

The longest non-vehicular tunnelling in the world is the Delaware Aqueduct in New York State, USA, constructed in 1937–44 to a length of 168·9 km/105 miles.

British Rail

		miles	yards
Severn	Western Region	4	484
Totley	Eastern Region	3	950
Standedge	Eastern Region	3	66
Sodbury	Western Region	2	924
Disley	London Midland Region	2	346
Ffestiniog	London Midland Region	2	338
Bramhope	Eastern Region	2	241
Cowburn	London Midland Region	2	182

LONGEST SHIP CANALS

Opened	Canal		Length		Min. Depth	
			km	miles	m	ft
1933	White Sea-Baltic (formerly Stalin)	Canalized river, canal 51·5 km/32 miles	227	141·00	5·0	16·5
1869	*Suez	Links Red and Mediterranean Seas	162	100·60	12·9	42·3
1952	V. I. Lenin Volga-Don	Links Black and Caspian Seas	100	62·20	n/a	n/a
1895	Kiel (or North Sea)	Links North Sea and Baltic	98	60·90	13·7	45·0
1940	*Houston	Links inland city with sea	91	56·70	10·4	34·0
1926	Alphonse XIII	Gives Seville access to sea	85	53·00	7·6	25·0
1914	Panama	Lake chain, 78·9 km/49 miles dug	82	50·71	12·5	41·0
1894	Manchester Ship	Links city with Irish Channel	64	39·70	8·5	28·0
1931	Welland	Circumvents Niagara Falls and Rapids	45	28·00	8·8	29·0
1922	Brussels (Rupel Sea)	Renders Brussels an inland port	32	19·80	6·4	21·0

*Has no locks

The first section of China's Grand Canal, running 1,780 km/1,107 miles from Beijing to Hangchou was opened AD 610 but in undredged parts is today only 1·8 m/6 ft deep.

The longest boat canal in the world is the Volga-Baltic canal from Astrakhan to Leningrad with 2,300 route km/1,850 miles.

THE SEVEN WONDERS OF THE WORLD

I. THE PYRAMIDS OF EGYPT.—From Gizeh (near Cairo) to a southern limit 60 miles distant. The oldest is that of Zoser, at Saqqara, built about 2,700 B.C. The Great Pyramid of Cheops covers more than 12 acres and was originally 481 ft. in height and 756 × 756 ft. at the base.

II. THE HANGING GARDENS OF BABYLON.—Adjoining Nebuchadnezzar's palace, 60 miles south of Baghdad. Terraced gardens, ranging from 75 to 300 ft. above ground level, watered from storage tanks on the highest terrace.

III. THE TOMB OF MAUSOLUS.—At Halicarnassus, in Asia Minor. Built by the widowed Queen Artemisia about 350 B.C. The memorial originated the term mausoleum.

IV. THE TEMPLE OF ARTEMIS AT EPHESUS.—Ionic temple erected about 350 B.C. in honour of the goddess and burned by the Goths in A.D. 262.

V. THE COLOSSUS OF RHODES.—A bronze statue of Apollo, set up about 280 B.C. According to legend it stood at the harbour entrance of the seaport of Rhodes.

VI. THE STATUE OF ZEUS.—At Olympia in the plain of Elis, constructed of marble inlaid with ivory and gold by the sculptor Phidias, about 430 B.C.

VII. THE PHAROS OF ALEXANDRIA.—A marble watch tower and lighthouse on the island of Pharos in the harbour of Alexandria.

THE UNITED KINGDOM

The United Kingdom comprises Great Britain (England, Wales and Scotland) and Northern Ireland.

AREA
(as at March 31, 1981)

	Land		Inland Water†		Total	
	miles²	km²	miles²	km²	miles²	km²
UK*	93,005	240,882	1,242	3,218	94,247	244,100
England	50,070	129,681	293	758	50,363	130,439
Wales	7,968	20,638	50	130	8,018	20,768
Scotland	29,761	77,080	653	1,692	30,414	78,772
Northern Ireland‡ ..	5,206	13,483	246	638	5,452	14,121

* Excludes the Isle of Man (221 sq. miles) and the Channel Islands (75 sq. miles).
† Excluding tidal water.
‡ Excluding certain tidal waters that are parts of statutory areas in N. Ireland.

POPULATION

CENSUS RESULTS, 1801–1981

Before 1801 there existed no official return of the population of either England or Scotland. Estimates of the population of England at various periods, calculated from the number of baptisms, burials and marriages, are: in 1570, 4,160,221; 1600, 4,811,718; 1630, 5,600,517; 1670, 5,773,646; 1700, 6,045,008; 1750, 6,517,035.

Thousands

	United Kingdom			England and Wales			Scotland			Northern Ireland†		
	Total	Male	Female	Total	Male	Female	Total	Male	Female	Total	Male	Female
1801	—	—	—	8,893	4,255	4,638	1,608	739	869	—	—	—
1811	13,368	6,368	7,000	10,165	4,874	5,291	1,806	826	980	1,397	668	729
1821	15,472	7,498	7,974	12,000	5,850	6,150	2,092	983	1,109	1,380	665	715
1831	17,835	8,647	9,188	13,897	6,771	7,126	2,364	1,114	1,250	1,574	762	812
1841	20,183	9,819	10,364	15,914	7,778	8,137	2,620	1,242	1,378	1,649	800	849
1851	22,259	10,855	11,404	17,928	8,781	9,146	2,889	1,376	1,513	1,443	698	745
1861	24,525	11,894	12,631	20,066	9,776	10,290	3,062	1,450	1,612	1,396	668	728
1871	27,431	13,309	14,122	22,712	11,059	11,653	3,360	1,603	1,757	1,359	647	712
1881	31,015	15,060	15,955	25,974	12,640	13,335	3,736	1,799	1,936	1,305	621	684
1891	34,264	16,593	17,671	29,003	14,060	14,942	4,026	1,943	2,083	1,236	590	646
1901	38,237	18,492	19,745	32,528	15,729	16,799	4,472	2,174	2,298	1,237	590	647
1911	42,082	20,357	21,725	36,070	17,446	18,625	4,761	2,309	2,452	1,251	603	648
1921	44,027	21,033	22,994	37,887	18,075	19,811	4,882	2,348	2,535	1,258	610	648
1931	46,038	22,060	23,978	39,952	19,133	20,819	4,843	2,326	2,517	1,243	601	642
1951	50,225	24,118	26,107	43,758	21,016	22,742	5,096	2,434	2,662	1,371	668	703
1961	52,709	25,481	27,228	46,105	22,304	23,801	5,179	2,483	2,697	1,425	694	731
1971	55,515	26,952	28,562	48,750	23,683	25,067	5,229	2,515	2,714	1,536	755	781
1981	55,848	27,104	28,742	49,155	23,873	25,281	5,131	2,466	2,664	1,533*	750	783

NOTES.
1. Because of the War there was no Census in 1941.
2. The last official Census of population in respect of England and Wales, Scotland, Northern Ireland, the Isle of Man and Guernsey, was taken on the night of April 5, 1981.
3. † All figures refer to the area which is now Northern Ireland. Figures for Northern Ireland in 1921 and 1931 are estimates based on the Censuses held in 1926 and 1937.
4. *Figures include non-enumerated persons.

ISLANDS

The figures given above do not include islands of the British seas. Populations of these islands at Census years since 1900 were:—

	Isle of Man			Jersey			Guernsey		
	Total	Male	Female	Total	Male	Female	Total	Male	Female
1901............	54,752	25,496	29,256	52,576	23,940	28,636	43,042	21,140	21,902
1911............	52,016	23,937	28,079	51,898	24,014	27,884	45,001	22,215	22,786
1921............	60,284	27,329	32,955	49,701	22,438	27,263	40,529	19,303	21,226
1931............	49,308	22,443	26,865	50,462	23,424	27,038	42,743	20,675	22,068
1951............	55,123	25,749	29,464	57,296	27,282	30,014	45,747	22,094	23,380
1961............	48,151	22,060	26,091	57,200	27,200	30,000	47,178	22,890	24,288
1971............	56,289	26,461	29,828	72,532	35,423	37,109	52,708	25,382	27,326
1981............	64,679	30,901	33,778	77,000	37,000	40,000	56,000	27,000	29,000

Births and Marriages

Thousands

| | Live births | | | | | Marriages | | | |
| | United Kingdom | England and Wales | | Scotland | Northern Ireland | United Kingdom | England and Wales | | Scotland | Northern Ireland |
		Total	Wales				Total	Wales		
1982	719·2	625·9	35·7	66·2	27·0	387·0	342·2	19·0	34·9	9·9
1983	721·5	629·1	35·5	65·1	27·3	389·3	344·3	19·9	35·0	10·0
1984	729·6	636·8	35·9	65·1	27·7	395·8	349·2	19·2	36·3	10·4
1985	750·7	656·4	36·8	66·7	27·6	393·1	346·4	19·1	36·4	10·3
1986	755·0	661·0	37·0	65·8	28·2	393·9	347·9	19·5	35·8	10·2
1987	755·6	681·5	37·8	66·2	27·9	397·9	351·8	19·5	35·8	10·4
1988	787·6	693·6	38·8	66·2	27·8†	—	348·5	19·3	—	10·0†
1989†	777·3	687·7	38·0	63·5	26·1	—	—	—	—	—
1989 1st quarter†	189·4	167·0	9·3	15·9	6·5	54·7	48·3	2·9	· 5·0	1·5
2nd quarter†	199·5	176·7	9·7	16·0	6·9	110·5	98·0	5·4	9·9	2·7
3rd quarter†	198·6	175·8	9·5	16·0	6·8	—	—	—	13·0	—
4th quarter†	189·8	168·2	9·5	15·6	5·9	—	—	—	7·4	—

† Provisional.

Divorce

	1982	1983	1984	1985	1986	1987	1988
England and Wales							
Decrees absolute, granted :							
Number	146,698	147,479	144,501	160,300	153,903	151,007	152,633
Rate per 1,000 married couples	*12·0*	*12·2*	*12·0*	*13·4*	*12·9*	*12·7*	*12·8†*
Scotland							
Decrees absolute, granted :							
Number	11,288	13,238	11,906	13,371	12,800	12,133	11,472
Rate per 1,000 married couples	*9·2*	*11·0*	*9·9*	*11·2*	*10·7*	*10·2*	*9·8*
Northern Ireland							
Petitions filed :							
Nullity of marriage	5	—	6	6	6	4	1
Divorce........................	1,734	1,577	1,749	1,986	1,630	1,834	2,217
Judicial separation	2	9	5	15	17	7	6

† Provisional.

Deaths Registered*

Thousands

| | Total | | | | | Infants under one year | | | | |
| | United Kingdom | England and Wales | | Scotland | Northern Ireland | United Kingdom | England and Wales | | Scotland | Northern Ireland |
		Total	Wales				Total	Wales		
1982	662·8	581·9	35·2	65·0	15·9	7·90	6·78	0·38	0·75	0·37
1983	659·1	579·6	35·2	63·5	16·0	7·36	6·38	0·38	0·65	0·33
1984	644·9	566·9	33·7	62·3	15·7	7·00	6·04	0·31	0·67	0·29
1985	670·6	590·7	35·5	64·0	16·0	7·03	6·14	0·36	0·62	0·27
1986	660·7	581·2	34·7	63·5	16·1	7·18	6·31	0·35	0·58	0·29
1987	644·3	567·0	33·9	62·0	15·3	7·08	6·27	0·36	0·56	0·24
1988	649·2	571·4	34·0	62·0	15·8†	7·06	6·27	0·29	0·54	0·25†
1989	657·7	576·9	35·1	65·0	15·8†	6·55†	5·81	0·30	0·56	0·18†
1989 1st quarter	169·9	149·5	8·8	16·4	4·0†	1·80	1·61	0·07	0·14	0·05†
2nd quarter	155·8	136·8	8·6	15·2	3·8†	1·54	1·36	0·08	0·14	0·05†
3rd quarter	143·1	125·6	7·6	14·1	3·4†	1·42	1·26	0·07	0·12	0·04†
4th quarter	188·9	165·0	10·1	19·3	4·6†	1·78	1·58	0·08	0·15	0·05†

* Excluding stillbirths.   † Provisional.

Deaths Analysed By Cause, 1988

	England & Wales	Scotland	N. Ireland†
Total deaths	567,987	61,957	15,813
Deaths from natural causes	550,051	58,993	14,979
Infections and parasitic diseases	2,480	253	45
Intestinal infectious diseases	164	10	3
Tuberculosis of respiratory system	384	41	7
Other tuberculosis, including late effects	334	36	2
Whooping cough	—	—	—
Meningococcal infection	174	9	2
Measles	16	—	1
Malaria	6	—	—
Syphilis	29	2	1
Neoplasms	144,260	14,889	3,409
Malignant neoplasm of stomach	9,425	946	241
Malignant neoplasm of trachea, bronchus and lung	35,302	4,144	777
Malignant neoplasm of breast	13,723	1,268	317
Malignant neoplasm of uterus	3,418	313	64
Leukaemia	3,683	318	83
Benign and unspecified neoplasms	1,288	129	47
Endocrine, nutritional and metabolic diseases and immunity disorders	10,106	691	73
Diabetes mellitus	7,850	501	46
Nutritional deficiencies	106	15	1
Other metabolic and immunity disorders	1,376	126	19
Diseases of blood and blood-forming organs	2,370	175	18
Anaemias	1,245	90	8
Mental disorders	13,234	1,005	35
Diseases of nervous system and sense organs	11,220	864	152
Meningitis	230	25	4
Diseases of the circulatory system	267,927	30,511	7,774
Rheumatic heart disease	2,543	254	47
Hypertensive disease	3,578	304	49
Ischaemic heart disease	153,084	17,963	4,747
Diseases of pulmonary circulation and other forms of heart disease	21,202	2,183	834
Cerebrovascular disease	68,599	8,150	1,708
Diseases of the respiratory system	60,483	6,724	2,568
Influenza	285	25	9
Pneumonia	26,424	3,691	1,678
Bronchitis, emphysema	9,188	558	179
Asthma	2,006	152	55
Diseases of the digestive system	17,954	1,925	358
Ulcer of stomach and duodenum	4,279	359	88
Appendicitis	136	11	1
Hernia of abdominal cavity and other intestinal obstruction	1,991	193	39
Chronic liver disease and cirrhosis	2,801	429	59
Diseases of the genito-urinary system	7,589	810	250
Nephritis, nephrotic syndrome and nephrosis	4,381	525	161
Hyperplasia of prostate	483	25	4
Complications of pregnancy, childbirth, etc.	41	8	1
Abortion	7	1	1
Diseases of the skin and subcutaneous tissue	772	76	40
Diseases of the musculo-skeletal system	5,406	318	50
Congenital anomalies	1,697	237	92
Certain conditions originating in the perinatal period	248	210	100
Birth trauma, hypoxia, birth asphyxia and other respiratory conditions	90	123	37
Signs, symptoms and ill-defined conditions	4,264	297	44
Sudden infant death syndrome	1,422	134	10
Deaths from accidents and violence	17,936	2,964	834
All accidents	11,288	2,020	516
Motor vehicle accidents	4,559	561	233
Suicide and self-inflicted injury	4,220	598	153
All other external causes	2,428	346	138

† provisional.

Resident Population by Age and Sex 1988

Thousands

	0–4	5–15	16–44	45–59/64*	60/65†–79	80 and over	All ages
Males							
United Kingdom	1,920·0	4,000·0	12,347·9	6,012·8	2,944·2	588·0	27,812·7
England	1,588·9	3,290·1	10,300·0	5,029·5	2,479·4	501·6	23,189·5
Wales	95·2	202·1	595·6	307·0	156·9	29·7	1,386·5
Scotland	165·5	361·7	1,112·9	533·2	243·9	45·0	2,462·3
Northern Ireland .	70·4	146·1	339·4	143·1	64·0	11·6	774·5
Females							
United Kingdom	1,827·4	3,789·6	12,093·2	4,662·1	5,476·5	1,403·9	29,252·7
England	1,512·7	3,115·8	10,094·2	3,871·2	4,565·6	1,187·3	24,346·8
Wales	90·7	191·0	587·4	234·7	294·2	72·5	1,470·5
Scotland	157·5	343·1	1,085·7	438·0	490·4	117·0	2,631·7
Northern Ireland .	66·5	139·8	325·9	118·2	126·2	27·0	803·6

*59 for women, 64 for men.
†60 for women, 65 for men.

Birth Rates 1988

Live births per 1,000 women in age groups:

	Under 20	20–24	25–29	30–34	35–39	40 and over
United Kingdom	32	95	124	83	28	5
England	32	94	124	83	28	5
Wales	39	107	120	77	24	4
Scotland	32	89	120	72	23	3
Northern Ireland	31	115	159	114	48	12

Death Rates 1988

Deaths per 1,000 population in age groups:

	0–4	5–14	15–24	25–34	35–44	45–54	55–64	65–74	75 and over
Males									
United Kingdom	2·5	0·2	0·8	0·9	1·7	5·1	16·0	41·2	111·2
England	2·5	0·2	0·8	0·9	1·6	4·9	15·4	40·2	109·9
Wales	2·2	0·2	0·7	0·9	1·7	5·2	16·5	42·9	112·0
Scotland	2·3	0·2	1·0	1·2	2·4	6·9	19·6	47·3	119·1
Northern Ireland .	2·4	0·3	1·2	1·2	2·1	5·1	18·6	46·7	125·1
Females									
United Kingdom	1·9	0·2	0·3	0·5	1·2	3·2	9·2	23·2	84·4
England	1·9	0·1	0·3	0·4	1·1	3·0	8·9	22·6	83·7
Wales	1·5	0·1	0·3	0·4	1·2	3·4	9·2	24·1	83·2
Scotland	1·6	0·1	0·3	0·5	1·4	3·8	11·3	27·6	89·8
Northern Ireland .	2·0	0·2	0·4	0·4	1·3	4·0	10·8	24·4	90·7

ENGLISH KINGS AND QUEENS AD 827 TO 1603

Name	Dynasty	Married	Access.	Died	Age	Rgnd. Yrs.
	Saxons and Danes					
EGBERT	King of Wessex and all England		827	839	—	12
ETHELWULF	Son of Egbert		839	858	—	19
ETHELBALD	Son of Ethelwulf		858	860	—	2
ETHELBERT	Son of Ethelwulf		858	866	—	8
ETHELRED	Son of Ethelwulf		866	871	—	5
ALFRED THE GREAT	Son of Ethelwulf	Ealhswith of Gaini	871	899	52	28
EDWARD THE ELDER	Son of Alfred the Great	1st, Egwyn; 2nd, Elfled; 3rd, Eadgifu	899	925	55	26
ATHELSTAN	Eldest son of Edward the Elder by Egwyn		925	940	45	15
EDMUND	Third son of Edward the Elder by Eadgifu	1st, Elgifu; 2nd, Ethelfled	940	946	25	6
EDRED	Fourth son of Edward the Elder by Eadgifu		946	955	32	9
EDWY	Son of Edmund by Elgifu		955	959	18	3
EDGAR	Second son of Edmund by Elgifu	1st, Ethelfled; 2nd, Elfthryth	959	975	32	17
EDWARD THE MARTYR	Son of Edgar by Ethelfled		975	978	17	4
ETHELRED II	Younger son of Edgar by Elfthryth	1st, Elfgifu; 2nd, Emma, dau. of Richard, Duke of Normandy.	978	1016	48	37
EDMUND IRONSIDE	Eldest son of Ethelred II by Elfgifu		1016	1016	27	0
CANUTE THE DANE	By conquest and election	1st, Elfgifu of Deira; 2nd, Emma, widow of Ethelred II.	1017	1035	40	18
HAROLD I	Son of Canute by Elfgifu		1035	1040	—	5
HARDICANUTE	Son of Canute by Emma		1040	1042	24	2
EDWARD THE CONFESSOR	Son of Ethelred II by Emma	Edith, dau. of Earl of Godwin	1042	1066	62	24
HAROLD II	Son of Earl Godwin		1066	1066	44	0
	The House of Normandy					
WILLIAM I	Obtained the Crown by conquest	Matilda, dau. of Baldwin, Count of Flanders	1066	1087	60	21
WILLIAM II	Third son of William I	(Died unmarried)	1087	1100	43	13
HENRY I	Youngest son of William I	1st, Matilda, dau. of Malcolm Canmore, K. of Scotland; 2nd Adelicia, dau. of Godfrey, D. of Louvaine.	1100	1135	67	35
STEPHEN	Third son of Stephen, Count of Blois, by Adela, fourth dau. of William I.	Matilda, dau. of Eustace, Count of Boulogne.	1135	1154	50	19
	The House of Plantagenet					
HENRY II	Son of Geoffrey Plantagenet by Matilda, only dau. of Henry I; his grandmother, Matilda of Scotland, was a lineal descendant of Alfred and Egbert.	Eleanor, dau. of Guienne and divorced Queen of Louis VII of France.	1154	1189	56	35
RICHARD I	Eldest surviving son of Henry II	Berengaria, dau. of Sancho VI, K. of Navarre.	1189	1199	42	10
JOHN	Sixth and youngest son of Henry II	1st Avisa, dau. of E. of Gloucester, divorced upon grounds of consanguinity; 2nd Isabella dau. of Aymer, Count of Angoulême.	1199	1216	50	17
HENRY III	Elder son of John	Eleanor, dau. of Raymond, Count of Provence.	1216	1272	65	56
EDWARD I	Eldest surviving son of Henry III	1st Eleanor, dau. of Ferdinand III, K. of Castile; 2nd Margaret, dau. of Philip III, the Hardy, K. of France.	1272	1307	68	35
EDWARD II	Eldest surviving son of Edward I	Isabella, dau. of Philip IV, the Fair, K. of France	1307	1327	43	20

Name	Dynasty	Married	Access.	Died	Age	Rgnd. Yrs.
EDWARD III	Eldest son of Edward II	Philippa, dau. of William, Count of Holland and Hainault.	1327	1377	65	50
RICHARD II	Son of the Black Prince, eldest son of Edward III (died 1400).	1st Anne, dau. of Emp. Charles IV; 2nd Isabel, dau. of Charles VI, K. of France.	1377	dep. 1399	34	22
The House of Lancaster						
HENRY IV	Son of John of Gaunt, 4th son of Edward III.	1st Mary de Bohun, dau. of the E. of Hereford; 2nd Joanna of Navarre, widow of John de Montfort, D. of Brittany.	1399	1413	47	13
HENRY V	Eldest surviving son of Henry IV	Katherine, dau. of Charles VI, K. of France	1413	1422	34	9
HENRY VI	Only son of Henry V (died 1471)	Margaret of Anjou, dau. of René, D. of Anjou	1422	dep. 1461	49	39
The House of York						
EDWARD IV	Son of Richard, grandson of Edmund, fifth son of Edward III; and of Anne, great-grand-daughter of Lionel, third son of Edward III.	Elizabeth Widvile (or Woodville), dau. of Sir Richard Widvile and widow of Sir John Grey of Groby.	1461	1483	41	22
EDWARD V	Eldest son of Edward IV	(Died unmarried)	1483	1483	13	75 days
RICHARD III	Younger brother of Edward IV	Anne, dau. of the E. of Warwick, and widow of Edward, Prince of Wales, son of Henry VI.	1483	1485	32	2
The House of Tudor						
HENRY VII	Son of Edmund, eldest son of Owen Tudor, by Katherine, widow of Henry V; his mother, Margaret Beaufort, was great-grand-daughter of John of Gaunt.	Elizabeth, dau. of Edward IV	1485	1509	53	24
HENRY VIII	Only surviving son of Henry VII	1st Katherine of Aragon, widow of his elder brother Arthur, (divorced); 2nd Anne, dau. of Sir Thomas Boleyn, (beheaded); 3rd Jane, dau. of Sir John Seymour, (died in childbirth of a son, after Edward VI); 4th Anne, sister of William, D. of Cleves, (divorced); 5th Catherine Howard, niece of the Duke of Norfolk, (beheaded); 6th Catherine, dau. of Sir Thomas Parr and widow of Edward Nevill, Lord Latimer.	1509	1547	56	38
EDWARD VI	Son of Henry VIII by Jane Seymour	(Died unmarried)	1547	1553	16	6
JANE	Grand-daughter of Mary, younger sister of Henry VIII, (beheaded Feb. 12, 1554).	Lord Guildford Dudley	1553	1554	17	14 days
MARY I	Daughter of Henry VIII by Katherine of Aragon.	Philip II of Spain	1553	1558	43	5
ELIZABETH I	Daughter of Henry VIII by Anne Boleyn	(Died unmarried)	1558	1603	69	44

BRITISH KINGS AND QUEENS FROM 1603

Name	Dynasty	Married	Access.	Died	Age	Rgnd.
						Yrs.
JAMES I (VI of Scotland)	**The House of Stuart** — Son of Mary, Queen of Scots, grand-daughter of James IV and Margaret, daughter of Henry VII.	Anne, dau. of Frederick II of Denmark	1603	1625	59	22
CHARLES I	Only surviving son of James I	Henrietta-Maria, dau. of Henry IV of France	1625	Beh. 1649	48	24
Commonwealth declared May 19, 1649						
Oliver Cromwell, Lord Protector, 1653—8: Richard Cromwell, Lord Protector, 1658—9						
CHARLES II	Eldest son of Charles I (restored 1660)	Catharine, dau. of John IV, K. of Portugal, and sister of Alphonso VI.	1649	1685	55	36
JAMES II (VII of Scotland)	Second son of Charles I (died 1701) (Interregnum, Dec. 11, 1688—Feb. 13, 1689)	1st Lady Anne Hyde, dau. of Edward, E. of Clarendon, who died before James ascended the throne; 2nd Mary Beatrice Eleanor d'Este, dau. of Alphonso, D. of Modena.	1685	dep. 1688	68	3
WILLIAM III and	Son of William, Prince of Orange and grandson of Charles I	⎫ ⎬ ⎭	1689	1702	51	13
MARY II	Eldest daughter of James II			1694	33	6
ANNE	Second daughter of James II	Prince George of Denmark	1702	1714	49	12
GEORGE I	**The House of Hanover** — Son of Elector of Hanover, by Sophia, daughter of Elizabeth, daughter of James I.	Sophia, dau. of George William, D. of Celle.	1714	1727	67	13
GEORGE II	Only son of George I	Wilhelmina Caroline, dau. of John Frederick, Margrave of Brandenburg-Anspach.	1727	1760	77	33
GEORGE III	Grandson of George II	Charlotte Sophia, dau. of Charles Lewis Frederick, D. of Mecklenburg-Strelitz.	1760	1820	81	59
GEORGE IV	Eldest son of George III (Regent from February 5, 1811).	Caroline, dau. of Charles William Ferdinand, D. of Brunswick-Wolfenbuttel.	1820	1830	67	10
WILLIAM IV	Third son of George III	Adelaide, dau. of George Frederick Charles, D. of Saxe-Meiningen.	1830	1837	71	7
VICTORIA	Daughter of Edward, 4th son of George III.	Francis Albert Augustus Charles Emmanuel, D. of Saxony, Pr. of Saxe-Coburg and Gotha.	1837	1901	81	63
EDWARD VII	**The House of Saxe-Coburg** — Eldest son of Victoria	Alexandra, dau. of Christian IX, K. of Denmark.	1901	1910	68	9
GEORGE V	**The House of Windsor** — Surviving son of Edward VII	Victoria Mary, dau. of Francis, D. of Teck.	1910	1936	70	25
EDWARD VIII	Eldest son of George V (died 1972)	Mrs. Wallis Warfield (after abdication)	1936	abd. 1936	77	325 days
GEORGE VI	Second son of George V	Lady Elizabeth Bowes-Lyon, dau. of 14th Earl of Strathmore and Kinghorne (HM QUEEN ELIZABETH the QUEEN MOTHER).	1936	1952	56	15
ELIZABETH II	Elder daughter of George VI	Philip, son of Prince Andrew of Greece (HRH THE DUKE OF EDINBURGH).	1952	WHOM GOD PRESERVE.		

KINGS AND QUEENS OF SCOTS AD 1057 to 1603

Name	Sovereign	Married	Access.	Died
MALCOLM III (CANMORE)	Son of Duncan I	1st Ingibiorg, widow of Thorfinn, Earl of Orkney; 2nd Margaret, sister of Edgar the Atheling.	1057	1093
DONALD BAN	Brother of Malcolm Canmore		1093	—
DUNCAN II	Son of Malcolm Canmore, by Ingibiorg		1094	1094
DONALD BAN	(Restored)		1094	1097
EDGAR	Son of Malcolm Canmore, by Margaret	(Died unmarried)	1097	1107
ALEXANDER I (THE FIERCE)	Son of Malcolm Canmore, by Margaret	Sybilla, natural dau. of Henry I of England	1107	1124
DAVID I (THE SAINT)	Son of Malcolm Canmore, by Margaret	Matilda, dau. of Waltheof, Earl of Northumbria, widow of Simon, Earl of Northampton.	1124	1153
MALCOLM IV (THE MAIDEN)	Son of Henry, eldest son of David I	(Died unmarried)	1153	1165
WILLIAM I (THE LION)	Brother of Malcolm the Maiden	Ermengarde, dau. of Richard, Viscount of Beaumont.	1165	1214
ALEXANDER II	Son of William the Lion	1st Joanna, dau. of King John; 2nd Mary, dau. of Ingelram de Coucy (Picardy).	1214	1249
ALEXANDER III	Son of Alexander II, by Mary	1st Margaret, dau. of Henry III of England; 2nd Joleta, dau. of the Count de Dreux.	1249	1286
MARGARET (THE MAID OF NORWAY)	Daughter of Eric II of Norway, granddaughter of Alexander III.	(Died unmarried)	1286	1290
JOHN BALIOL	Grandson of eldest daughter of David, Earl of Huntingdon, brother of William the Lion.		1292	1296
ROBERT I (BRUCE)	Great-grandson of 2nd daughter of David, Earl of Huntingdon, brother of William the Lion.	1st Isabella, dau. of Donald, Earl of Mar; 2nd Elizabeth de Burgh, sister of Earl of Ulster.	1306	1329
DAVID II	Son of Robert I, by Elizabeth	1st Joanna, dau. of Edward II of England; 2nd Margaret, widow of Sir John Logie (divorced, 1369).	1329	1371
ROBERT II (STEWART)	Son of Marjorie, daughter of Robert I by first marriage, and Walter the Steward.	1st Elizabeth, dau. of Sir Robert Mure (or More) of Rowallan; 2nd Euphemia, dau. of Hugh, Earl of Ross, widow of John, Earl of Moray.	1371	1390
ROBERT III	Son of Robert II, by Elizabeth	Annabella, dau. of Sir John Drummond of Stobhall, niece of Margaret Logie.	1390	1406
JAMES I	Son of Robert III	Jane Beaufort, dau. of John, Earl of Somerset, 4th son of John of Gaunt and grandson of Edward III of England.	1406	1437
JAMES II	Son of James I	Mary, dau. of Arnold, Duke of Gueldres.	1437	1460
JAMES III	Eldest son of James II	Margaret, dau. of Christian I of Denmark, Norway and Sweden.	1460	1488
JAMES IV	Eldest son of James III	Margaret Tudor, dau. of Henry VII	1488	1513
JAMES V	Son of James IV	1st Madeleine, dau. of Francis I of France; 2nd Mary of Lorraine, dau. of Duc de Guise, widow of Duc de Longueville.	1513	1542
MARY	Daughter of James V, by Mary (died 1587)	1st Francis, Dauphin of France; 2nd Henry, Lord Darnley; 3rd James, Earl of Bothwell.	1542	abd. 1567
JAMES VI (Ascended the Throne of England 1603)	Son of Mary, by second marriage	Anne, dau. of Frederick II of Denmark	1567	1625

WELSH SOVEREIGNS AND PRINCES

WALES was ruled by Sovereign Princes from the earliest times until the death of Llywelyn in 1282. The first English Prince of Wales was the son of Edward I, and was born in Caernarvon town on April 25, 1284. According to a discredited legend, he was presented to the Welsh chieftains as their Prince, in fulfilment of a promise that they should have a Prince who 'could not speak a word of English' and should be native born. This son, who afterwards became Edward II, was created 'Prince of Wales and Earl of Chester' at the famous Lincoln Parliament on February 7, 1301. The title Prince of Wales is borne after individual conferment and is not inherited at birth, though some Princes have been declared and styled Prince of Wales but never formally so created (s.). The title was conferred on Prince Charles by HM the Queen on July 26, 1958. He was invested at Caernarvon on July 1, 1969.

Independent Princes, AD 844 to 1282

Rhodri the Great	844–878
Anarawd, son of Rhodri	878–916
Hywel Dda, the Good	916–950
Iago ab Idwal (or Ieuaf)	950–979
Hywel ab Ieuaf, the Bad	979–985
Cadwallon, his brother	985–986
Maredudd ab Owain ap Hywel Dda	986–999
Cynan ap Hywel ab Ieuaf	999–1008
Llywelyn ap Seisyll	1018–1023
Iago ab Idwal ap Meurig	1023–1039
Gruffydd ap Llywelyn ap Seisyll	1039–1063
Bleddyn ap Cynfyn	1063–1075
Trahaern ap Caradog	1075–1081
Gruffydd ap Cynan ab Iago	1081–1137
Owain Gwynedd	1137–1170
Dafydd ab Owain Gwynedd	1170–1194
Llywelyn Fawr, the Great	1194–1240
Dafydd ap Llywelyn	1240–1246
Llywelyn ap Gruffydd ap Llywelyn	1246–1282

English Princes, since AD 1301

Edward (Edward II), cr. Pr. of Wales	1301
Edward the Black Prince, s. of Edward III	1343
Richard (Richard II), s. of the Black Prince	1376
Henry of Monmouth (Henry V)	1399
Edward of Westminster, son of Henry VI	1454
Edward of Westminster (Edward V)	1471
Edward, son of Richard III (d. 1484)	1483
Arthur Tudor, son of Henry VII	1489
Henry Tudor (Henry VIII), s. of Henry VII	1504
Henry Stuart, son of James I (d. 1612)	1610
Charles Stuart (Charles I), s. of James I	1616
Charles (Charles II), son of Charles I (s.) c. 1638
James Francis Edward, 'The Old Pretender' (d. 1766)	(s.) 1688
George Augustus (George II), s. of George I	1714
Frederick Lewis, s. of George II (d. 1751)	1729
George William Frederick (George III)	1751
George Augustus Frederick (George IV)	1762
Albert Edward (Edward VII)	1841
George (George V)	1901
Edward (Edward VIII)	1910
Charles Philip Arthur George	1958

THE FAMILY OF QUEEN VICTORIA

QUEEN VICTORIA (Alexandrina Victoria) *was born* May 24, 1819; *succeeded* to the Throne June 20, 1837; *married* Feb. 10, 1840 (Francis) Albert Augustus Charles Emmanuel, Duke of Saxony, Prince of Saxe-Coburg and Gotha (**HRH Albert, Prince Consort** *born* Aug. 26, 1819, *died* Dec. 14, 1861); *died* Jan. 22, 1901. Her Majesty had *issue*:—

1. HRH Princess Victoria Adelaide Mary Louisa (*Princess Royal*) (1840–1901), *m.*, 1858, Frederic (1831–88), *Emperor of Germany* Mar.–June 1888. *Issue*:—

(1) HIM Wilhelm II (1859–1941), *Emperor of Germany* 1888–1918, *m.*, 1st, 1881, Princess Augusta Victoria of Schleswig-Holstein-Sonderburg-Augustenburg (1858–1921); 2nd, 1922, Princess Hermine of Reuss (1887–1947). *Issue*:—

(a) Prince Wilhelm (1882–1951), (*Crown Prince* 1888–1918), *m.* 1905 Duchess Cecilie of Mecklenburg-Schwerin; *issue*:—Prince Wilhelm (1906–40); Prince Ludwig Ferdinand (*b.* 1907), *m.*, 1938, Grand Duchess Kira (*see* p. 140); Prince Hubertus (1909–50); Prince Friedrich Georg (1911–66); Princess Alexandrine Irene (1915–); Princess Cecilie (1917–75).

(b) Prince Eitel-Friedrich (1883–1942), *m.* 1906 Duchess Sophie of Oldenburg (marriage dissolved 1926).

(c) Prince Adalbert (1884–1948), *m.* 1914 Duchess Adelheid of Saxe-Meiningen; *issue*:—Princess Victoria Marina (1917–81); Prince Wilhelm Victor (1919–89).

(d) Prince August Wilhelm (1887–1949), *m.* 1908 Princess Alexandra of Schleswig-Holstein-Sonderburg-Glücksburg (marriage dissolved 1920); *issue*:—Prince Alexander (1912–85).

(e) Prince Oskar (1888–1958), *m.* 1914 Countess von Ruppin; *issue*:—Prince Oskar (1915–39); Prince Burchard (1917–); Princess Herzeleide (1918–89); Prince Wilhelm (*b.* 1922).

(f) Prince Joachim (1890–1920), *m.* 1916 Princess Marie of Anhalt; *issue*:—Prince Karl (1916–75).

(g) Princess Viktoria Luise (1892–1980), *m.*, 1913, Ernst, Duke of Brunswick 1913–18 (1887–1953); *issue*:—Prince Ernst (1914–87); Prince Georg (*b.* 1915), *m.* 1946 Princess Sophie of Greece (*see* p. 139) and has issue (two sons, one daughter); Princess Frederika (1917–81), *m.* 1938 Paul I, King of the Hellenes (*see* p. 139); Prince Christian (1919–81); Prince Welf Heinrich (*b.* 1923).

(2) Princess Charlotte (1860–1919), *m.*, 1878, Bernhard, Duke of Saxe-Meiningen 1914 (1851–1914). *Issue*:—Princess Feodora (1879–1945), *m.*, 1898, Prince Heinrich XXX of Reuss.

(3) Prince Heinrich (1862–1929), *m.*, 1888, Princess Irene of Hesse (*see* p. 139). *Issue*:—

(a) Prince Waldemar (1889–1945), *m.* Princess Calixsta of Lippe.

(b) Prince Sigismund (1896–1978), *m.* Princess Charlotte of Saxe-Altenburg; *issue*:—Princess Barbe (*b.* 1920); Prince Alfred (*b.* 1924).

(4) Princess Victoria (1866–1929), *m.*, 1st, 1890, Prince Adolf of Schaumburg-Lippe (1859–1916); 2nd, 1927, Alexander Zubkov.

(5) Prince Joachim Waldemar (1868–79).

(6) Princess Sophie (1870–1932), *m.*, 1889, Constantine I (1868–1923). *King of the Hellenes*, 1913–17, 1920–23. *Issue*:—

(a) George II (1890–1947), *King of the Hellenes* 1923–24 and 1935–47, *m.*, 1921, Princess Elisabeth of Roumania (marriage dissolved 1935), (*see* p. 139).

(b) Alexander I (1893–1920), *King of the Hellenes* 1917–20, *m.*, 1919, Aspasia Manos; *issue*:—Princess Alexandra (*b.* 1921), *m.*, 1944, King Petar II of Yugoslavia (*see* p. 139).

(c) Princess Helena (1896–1982), *m.*, 1921, King Carol of Roumania (*see* below), (marriage dissolved 1928).

(d) Paul I (1901–64), *King of the Hellenes* 1947–64, *m.*, 1938, Princess Frederika of Brunswick (*see* p. 138); *issue:*—King Constantine II (*b.* 1940), *m.*, 1964, Princess Anne-Marie of Denmark (*see* p. 140), and has issue (three sons, two daughters); Princess Sophia (*b.* 1938), *m.*, 1962, Juan Carlos I of Spain (*see* p. 140); Princess Irene (*b.* 1942).

(e) Princess Irene (1904–74), *m.*, 1939, 4th Duke of Aosta; *issue:*—Prince Amedeo (*b.* 1943).

(f) Princess Katherine (*Lady Katherine Brandram*) (*b.* 1913), *m.*, 1947, Major R. C. A. Brandram, MC, TD; *issue:*—R. Paul G. A. Brandram (*b.* 1948).

(7) Princess Margarethe (1872–1954), *m.*, 1893, Prince Friedrich Karl of Hesse (1868–1940). *Issue:*—

(a) Prince Friedrich Wilhelm (1893–1916).

(b) Prince Maximilian (1894–1914).

(c) Prince Philipp (1896–1980), *m.*, 1925, Princess Mafalda of Italy; *issue:*—Prince Moritz (*b.* 1926); Prince Heinrich (*b.* 1927); Prince Otto (*b.* 1937); Princess Elisabeth (*b.* 1940).

(d) Prince Wolfgang (*b.* 1896), *m.*, 1st, 1924, Princess Marie Alexandra of Baden; 2nd, 1948, Ottilie Möller.

(e) Prince Richard (1901–).

(f) Prince Christoph (1901–43), *m.*, 1930, Princess Sophie of Greece (*see* below) and has issue (two sons, three daughters).

2. HRH Prince Albert Edward (HM KING EDWARD VII), *b.* Nov. 9, 1841, *m.* 1863 HRH Princess Alexandra of Denmark (1844–1925), *succeeded* to Throne Jan. 22, 1901, *d.* May 6, 1910. *Issue:*—

(1) Albert Victor, *Duke of Clarence and Avondale* (1864–92).

(2) George (HM KING GEORGE V) (*see* p. 140).

(3) Louise (1867–1931) *Princess Royal* 1905–31, *m.* 1889 1st Duke of Fife (1849–1912). *Issue:*—

(a) Princess Alexandra, Duchess of Fife (1891–1959), *m.* 1913 Prince Arthur of Connaught (*see* p. 140).

(b) Princess Maud (1893–1945), *m.* 1923, 11th Earl of Southesk (*b.* 1893); *issue:*—The Duke of Fife (*b.* 1929).

(4) Victoria (1868–1935).

(5) Maud (1869–1938), *m.* 1896 Prince Charles of Denmark (1872–1957), later King Haakon VII of Norway 1905–57. *Issue:*—

(a) Olav V, *King of Norway* (*b.* 1903), *m.* 1929 Princess Märtha of Sweden (1901–54); *issue:*—Princess Ragnhild (*b.* 1930); Princess Astrid (*b.* 1932); Prince Harald (*b.* 1937).

(6) Alexander (April 6–7, 1871).

3. HRH Princess Alice Maud Mary (1843–78), *m.* 1862 Prince Louis (1837–92), Grand Duke of Hesse 1877–92. *Issue:*—

(1) Victoria (1863–1950), *m.* 1884 *Admiral of the Fleet* Prince Louis of Battenberg (1854–1921), *cr.* 1st Marquess of Milford Haven 1917. *Issue:*—

(a) Alice (1885–1969), *m.*, 1903, Prince Andrew of Greece (1882–1914); *issue:*—Princess Margarita (1905–81) *m.* 1931 Prince Gottfried of Hohenlohe-Langenburg (*see* p. 140); Princess Theodora (1906–69), *m.* Prince Berthold of Baden (1906–63) and has issue (2 sons, one daughter); Princess Cecilie (1911–37), *m.* George, Grand Duke of Hesse (*see* below); Princess Sophie (*b.* 1914), *m.* 1st, 1930 Prince Christoph of Hesse (*see* above); 2nd, 1946 Prince Georg of Hanover (*see* p. 138); **Prince Philip, Duke of Edinburgh** (*b.* 1921), (*see* p. 140).

(b) Louise (1889–1965), *m.*, 1923, Gustaf VI Adolf (1882–1973), *King of Sweden* 1950–73.

(c) George, 2nd Marquess of Milford Haven (1892–1938), *m.*, 1916, Countess Nadejda, daughter of Grand Duke Michael of Russia; *issue:*—Lady Tatiana (1917–88); David Michael, 3rd Marquess (1919–70).

(d) Louis, 1st Earl Mountbatten of Burma (1900–79), *m.*, 1922, Edwina Ashley, daughter of Lord Mount Temple; *issue:*—Patricia, Countess Mountbatten of Burma (*b.* 1924), Pamela (*b.* 1929).

(2) Elizabeth (1864–1918), *m.*, 1884, Grand Duke Sergius of Russia (1857–1905).

(3) Irene (1866–1953), *m.* 1888 Prince Heinrich of Prussia (*see* p. 138).

(4) Ernst Ludwig (1868–1937), Grand Duke of Hesse 1892–1918, *m.*, 1st, 1894, Princess Victoria Melita of Saxe-Coburg (marriage dissolved 1901); 2nd, 1905, Princess Eleonore of Solms-Hohensolmslich. *Issue:*—

(a) George, Grand Duke of Hesse (1906–37), *m.* Princess Cecilie of Greece (*see* above), and had issue, 2 sons, accidentally killed with parents 1937.

(b) Ludwig, Grand Duke of Hesse (1908–68), *m.*, 1937, Margaret, daughter of 1st Lord Geddes.

(5) Frederick William (1870–73).

(6) Alix (*Tsaritsa of Russia*) (1872–1918), *m.*, 1894, Nicholas II (1868–1918) *Tsar of All the Russias* 1894–1917, assassinated July 16, 1918. *Issue:*—

(a) Grand Duchess Olga (1895–1918).

(b) Grand Duchess Tatiana (1897–1918).

(c) Grand Duchess Marie (1899–1918).

(d) Grand Duchess Anastasia (1901–18).

(e) Alexis, Tsarevitch of Russia (1904–18).

(7) Marie (1874–78).

4. HRH Prince Alfred Ernest Albert, *Duke of Edinburgh, Admiral of the Fleet* (1844–1900), *m.*, 1874, Grand Duchess Marie Alexandrovna of Russia (1853–1920); *succeeded* as *Duke of Saxe-Coburg and Gotha* Aug. 22, 1893. *Issue:*—

(1) Alfred (*Prince of Saxe-Coburg*) (1874–99).

(2) Marie (1875–1938), *m.* 1893 Ferdinand (1865–1927), *King of Roumania* 1914–27. *Issue:*—

(a) Carol II (1893–1953), *King of Roumania* 1930–40, *m.* 2nd Princess Helena of Greece (*see* above), (marriage dissolved 1928); Michael (*b.* 1921), *King of Roumania* 1927–30, 1940–47, *m.* 1948 Princess Anne of Bourbon Palma, and has issue (five daughters).

(b) Elisabeth (1894–1956), *m.* 1921 George II (1890–1947) *King of the Hellenes* (*see* p. 138).

(c) Marie (1900–61), *m.* 1922 Alexander (1888–1934), *King of Yugoslavia* 1921–34; *issue:*—Petar II (1923–70), *King of Yugoslavia* 1934–45, *m.* 1944 Princess Alexandra of Greece (*see* p. 138) and has issue (one son); Prince Tomislav (*b.* 1928), *m.*, 1st, 1957 Princess Margarita of Baden (daughter of Princess Theodora of Greece and Prince Berthold of Baden, *see* above; 2nd, 1982 Linda Bonney; and has issue (three sons, one daughter); Prince Andrej (1929–90), *m.*, 1st, Princess Christina of Hesse (daughter of Prince Christoph of Hesse and Princess Sophie of Greece, *see* above); 2nd, 1963 Princess Kira-Melita of Leiningen (*see* below); and has issue (three sons, one daughter).

(d) Prince Nicolas (1903–).

(e) Princess Ileana (*b.* 1909), *m.*, 1st, 1931, Archduke Anton of Austria; 2nd, 1954, Dr. Stefan Issarescu; *issue:*—Archduke Stefan (*b.* 1932); Archduchess Maria Ileana (1933–59); Archduchess Alexandra (*b.* 1935); Archduke Dominic (*b.* 1937); Archduchess Maria Magdalena (*b.* 1939); Archduchess Elisabeth (*b.* 1942).

(f) Prince Mircea (1913–16).

(3) Victoria Melita (1876–1936), *m.*, 1st, 1894, Grand Duke Ernst of Hesse (*see* above), (marriage dissolved 1901); 2nd, 1905, the Grand Duke Kirill of Russia (1876–1938). *Issue:*—

(a) Marie Kirillovna (1907–51), *m.*, 1925, Prince Friedrich Karl of Leiningen; *issue:*—Prince Emich (*b.* 1926); Prince Karl (*b.* 1928); Princess Kira-Melita (*b.* 1930), *m.* Prince Andrej of Yugoslavia (*see* above); Princess Margarita (*b.* 1932); Princess Mechtilde (*b.* 1936); Prince Friedrich (*b.* 1938).

(*b*) Kira Kirillovna (1909–67), *m.*, 1938, Prince Ludwig of Prussia (*see* p. 138); *issue:*—Prince Friedrich Wilhelm (*b.* 1939); Prince Michael (*b.* 1940); Princess Marie (*b.* 1942); Princess Kira (*b.* 1943); Prince Louis Ferdinand (1944–77); Prince Christian (*b.* 1946); Princess Xenia (*b.* 1949).

(*c*) Vladimir Kirillovitch (*b.* 1917), *m.*, 1948, Princess Leonida Bagration-Mukhransky; *issue:*—Grand Duchess Maria (*b.* 1953).

(4) Alexandra (1878–1942), *m.*, 1896, Ernst, Prince of Hohenlohe Langenburg. *Issue:*—

(*a*) Gottfried (1897–1960), *m.* 1931 Princess Margarita of Greece (*see* p. 139); *issue:*—Prince Kraft (*b.* 1935), Princess Beatrix (*b.* 1936), Prince George (*b.* 1938), Prince Ruprecht and Prince Albrecht (*b.* 1944).

(*b*) Maria (1899–1967), *m.* 1916 Prince Frederick of Schleswig-Holstein-Sonderburg-Glücksburg; *issue:*—Prince Peter (1922–80); Princess Marie (*b.* 1927).

(*c*) Princess Alexandra (1901–63).

(*d*) Princess Irma (1902–).

(5) Princess Beatrice (1884–1966), *m.*, 1909, Alfonso of Orleans, Infante of Spain. *Issue:*—

(*a*) Prince Alvaro (*b.* 1910), *m.* 1937 Carla Parodi-Delfino; *issue:*—Princess Gerarda (*b.* 1939); Prince Alonso (1941–75); Princess Beatriz (*b.* 1943); Prince Alvaro (*b.* 1947).

(*b*) Prince Alonso (1912–36).

(*c*) Prince Ataulfo (1913–).

5. HRH Princess Helena Augusta Victoria (1846–1923), *m.*, 1866, Prince Christian of Schleswig-Holstein-Sonderburg-Augustenburg (1831–1917). *Issue:*—

(1) Prince Christian Victor (1867–1900).

(2) Prince Albert (1869–1931), Duke of Schleswig-Holstein 1921–31.

(3) Princess Helena (1870–1948).

(4) Princess Marie Louise (1872–1956), *m.*, 1891, Prince Aribert of Anhalt (marriage dissolved 1900).

(5) Prince Harold (May 12–20, 1876).

6. HRH Princess Louise Caroline Alberta (1848–1939), *m.*, 1871, the Marquess of Lorne, afterwards *9th Duke of Argyll* (1845–1914); without issue.

7. HRH Prince Arthur William Patrick Albert, *Duke of Connaught, Field Marshal* (1850–1942), *m.*, 1879, Princess Louisa of Prussia (1860–1917). *Issue:*—

(1) Margaret (1882–1920), *m.*, 1905, Crown Prince Gustaf Adolf (1882–1973), afterwards *King of Sweden* 1950–73. *Issue:*—

(*a*) Gustaf Adolf, Duke of Västerbotten (1906–47), *m.*, 1932, Princess Sybille of Saxe-Coburg-Gotha (*see* below); *issue:*—Princess Margaretha (*b.* 1934); Princess Birgitta (*b.* 1937); Princess Désirée (*b.* 1938); Princess Christina (*b.* 1943); Carl XVI Gustaf, **King of Sweden** (*b.* 1946).

(*b*) Count Sigvard Bernadotte (*b.* 1907); *m.*, *issue:*—Count Michael (*b.* 1944).

(*c*) Princess Ingrid (*Queen Mother of Denmark*) (*b.* 1910), *m.*, 1935, Frederick IX, *King of Denmark* 1947–72 (1899–72); *issue:*—Margrethe II, **Queen of Denmark** (*b.* 1940); Princess Benedikte (*b.* 1944); Princess Anne-Marie (*b.* 1946), *m.* 1964 King Constantine II (*see* p. 139).

(*d*) Prince Bertil, Duke of Halland (*b.* 1912), *m.*, 1976, Mrs. Lilian Craig.

(*e*) Count Carl Bernadotte (*b.* 1916), *m.*, 1st, 1946, Mrs. Kerstin Johnson; 2nd, 1988 Countess Gunnila Busler.

(2) Arthur (1883–1938), *m.*, 1913, HH the Duchess of Fife (*see* p. 139). *Issue:*—

Alastair Arthur, Duke of Connaught (1914–43).

(3) (Victoria) Patricia (1886–1974), *m.*, 1919, Adm. Hon. Sir Alexander Ramsay. *Issue:*—Hon. Alexander Ramsay of Mar (*b.* 1919), *m.*, 1956, Hon. Flora Fraser, (Lady Saltoun).

8. HRH Prince Leopold George Duncan Albert, *Duke of Albany* (1853–84), *m.*, 1882, Princess Helena of Waldeck (1861–1922). *Issue:*—

(1) Alice (1883–1981), *m.*, 1904, Prince Alexander of Teck (1874–1957), *cr. 1st Earl of Athlone* 1917. *Issue:*—

(*a*) Lady May (*b.* 1906), *m.*, 1931, Sir Henry Abel-Smith, KCMG, KCVO, DSO; *issue:*—Anne (*b.* 1932); Richard (*b.* 1933); Elizabeth (*b.* 1936).

(*b*) Rupert, *Viscount Trematon* (1907–28).

(2) Charles Edward (1884–1954), *Duke of Albany* 1884 until title suspended 1917, *Duke of Saxe-Coburg-Gotha* 1900–18, *m.*, 1905, Princess Victoria Adelheid of Schleswig-Holstein-Sonderburg-Glücksburg. *Issue:*—(*a*) Prince Johann (1906–72), and has issue; (*b*) Princess Sibylle (1908–72) *m.* 1932 Prince Gustav Adolph of Sweden (*see* above); (*c*) Prince Dietmar (1909–); (*d*) Princess Caroline (1912–83); (*e*) Prince Friedrich (*b.* 1918).

9. HRH Princess Beatrice Mary Victoria Feodore (1857–1944), *m.*, 1885, Prince Henry of Battenberg (1858–96). *Issue:*—

(1) Alexander, *1st Marquess of Carisbrooke* (1886–1960), *m.*, 1917, Lady Irene Denison. *Issue:*—Lady Iris Mountbatten (1920–82).

(2) Victoria Eugénie (1887–1969), *m.*, 1906, Alfonso XIII (1886–1941) *King of Spain* 1886–1931. *Issue:*—(*a*) Prince Alfonso (1907–38); (*b*) Prince Jaime (1908–75); (*c*) Princess Beatrice (*b.* 1909); (*d*) Princess Maria (*b.* 1911); (*e*) Prince Juan (*b.* 1913) *Count of Barcelona*, and has *issue:*— Princess Maria (*b.* 1936); Juan Carlos I, **King of Spain** (*b.* 1938) *m.* 1962 Princess Sophie of Greece (*see* p. 139) and has issue (1 son, 2 daughters); Princess Margarita (*b.* 1939); (*f*) Prince Gonzale (1914–34).

(3) Major Lord Leopold Mountbatten (1889–1922).

(4) Maurice (1891–1914), died of wounds received in action.

THE HOUSE OF WINDSOR

King George V assumed by royal proclamation (June 17, 1917) for his House and family, as well as for all descendants in the male line of Queen Victoria who are subjects of these realms, the name of **Windsor.**

KING GEORGE V (George Frederick Ernest Albert), second son of King Edward VII, *born* June 3, 1865; *married* July 6, 1893, HSH Princess Victoria Mary Augusta Louise Olga Pauline Claudine Agnes of Teck (**Queen Mary**, *born* May 26, 1867; *died* March 24, 1953); *succeeded* to the Throne May 6, 1910; *died* Jan. 20, 1936. *Issue:*—

1. HRH Prince Edward Albert Christian George Andrew Patrick David, *born* June 23, 1894, *succeeded* to the Throne as **King Edward VIII**, Jan. 20, 1936; *abdicated* Dec. 11, 1936; *created Duke of Windsor*, 1936; *married* June 3, 1937, Mrs. Wallis Warfield (Her Grace The Duchess of Windsor, *born* June 19, 1896; *died* April 24, 1986), *died* May 28, 1972.

2. HRH Prince Albert Frederick Arthur George, *born* Dec. 14, 1895; *married* April 26, 1923, Lady Elizabeth Bowes-Lyon (**HM Queen Elizabeth the Queen Mother**), daughter of the 14th Earl of Strathmore and Kinghorne, *succeeded* to the Throne as **King George VI**, Dec. 11, 1936; *died* Feb. 6, 1952, having had issue (*see* pp. 142 and 143).

3. HRH Princess (Victoria Alexandra Alice) **Mary** (*Princess Royal*), *born* April 25, 1897, *married* Feb. 28, 1922, Viscount Lascelles, later the 6th Earl of Harewood (*born* Sept. 9, 1882; *died* May 24, 1947), *died* March 28, 1965. *Issue:—*

    (1) George Henry Hubert Lascelles, **7th Earl of Harewood**, KBE, *born* Feb. 7, 1923; *married* 1st, Sept. 29, 1949, Maria (Marion) Stein (marriage dissolved 1967); *issue*, (a) David Henry George, Viscount Lascelles, *born* Oct. 21, 1950; (b) James Edward, *born* Oct. 5, 1953; (c) Robert Jeremy Hugh, *born* Feb. 14, 1955; 2nd, July 31, 1967, Mrs. Patricia Tuckwell; *issue*, (d) Mark Hubert, *born* July 5, 1964.

    (2) Gerald David Lascelles, *born* Aug. 21, 1924, *married* 1st, July 15, 1952, Miss Angela Dowding (marriage dissolved, 1978); *issue*, (a) Henry Ulick, *born* May 19, 1953; 2nd, Nov. 17, 1978, Mrs. Elizabeth Colvin; *issue*, (b) Martin David, *born* Feb. 9, 1962.

4. HRH Prince Henry William Frederick Albert, Duke of Gloucester, Earl of Ulster and Baron Culloden, *born* March 31, 1900, *married* Nov. 6, 1935, Lady Alice Christabel Montagu-Douglas-Scott, daughter of the 7th Duke of Buccleuch (**HRH Princess Alice, Duchess of Gloucester**, GCB, CI, GCVO, GBE, Grand Cordon of Al Kamal, Air Chief Marshal, Colonel-in-Chief of The Royal Hussars (Prince of Wales's Own), The King's Own Scottish Borderers, Royal Corps of Transport, Royal Australian Corps of Transport, Royal New Zealand Corps of Transport, Deputy Colonel-in-Chief, The Royal Anglian Regiment, Air Chief Commandant WRAF, *born* Dec. 25, 1901); *died* June 10, 1974. *Issue:*

    (1) HRH Prince **William** Henry Andrew Frederick, *born* Dec. 18, 1941; *accidentally killed* Aug. 28, 1972.

    (2) HRH Prince **Richard** Alexander Walter George (**HRH The Duke of Gloucester**), GCVO, Colonel-in-Chief, The Gloucestershire Regiment, Royal Pioneer Corps, Honorary Colonel Royal Monmouthshire Royal Engineers (Militia), Grand Prior of the Order of St. John of Jerusalem. *Born* Aug. 26, 1944, *married* July 8, 1972, Birgitte Eva van Deurs (**HRH The Duchess of Gloucester**, GCVO), *born* June 20, Colonel-in-Chief, Royal Army Educational Corps, Royal Irish Rangers (27th (Inniskilling) 83rd and 87th), Royal Australian Army Educational Corps, Royal New Zealand Educational Corps, and has *issue:—*

      (a) Alexander Patrick Gregers Richard, Earl of Ulster, *born* Oct. 24, 1974;

      (b) Davina Elizabeth Alice Benedikte (Lady Davina Windsor), *born* Nov. 19, 1977;

      (c) Rose Victoria Birgitte Louise (Lady Rose Windsor), *born* March 1, 1980.

      Residences.—Kensington Palace, W8 4PU (Tel: 071–937 6374); Barnwell Manor, Peterborough.

5. HRH Prince George Edward Alexander Edmund, Duke of Kent, Earl of St. Andrews and Baron Downpatrick, *born* Dec. 20, 1902, *married* Nov. 29, 1934, HRH Princess Marina of Greece and Denmark (*born* Nov. 30, OS, 1906; *died* Aug. 27, 1968); *killed on active service*, Aug. 25, 1942. *Issue:—*

    (1) HRH Prince **Edward** George Nicholas Paul Patrick (**HRH The Duke of Kent**), KG, GCMG, GCVO, Personal ADC to the Queen, Major General, Hon. Air Vice-Marshal, Colonel-in-Chief The Royal Regiment of Fusiliers, The Devonshire and Dorset Regiment, The Lorne Scots Regiment (Peel, Dufferin and Hamilton Regiment), Colonel Scots Guards. *Born* Oct. 9, 1935, *married* June 8, 1961, Katharine Lucy Mary Worsley, daughter of Sir William Worsley, Bt. (**HRH The Duchess of Kent**, GCVO), *born* Feb. 22, 1933, Hon. Major General, Colonel-in-Chief 4th/7th Royal Dragoon Guards, The Prince of Wales's Own Regiment of Yorkshire, Army Catering Corps, Controller Commandant Women's Royal Army Corps, Hon. Colonel The Yorkshire Volunteers, and has *issue:—*

      (a) George Philip Nicholas, Earl of St. Andrews, *born* June 26, 1962, *married* Jan. 9, 1988, Sylvana Tomaselli and has *issue*, Edward Edmund Maximilian George, Lord Downpatrick, *born* Dec. 2, 1988;

      (b) Helen Marina Lucy (Lady Helen Windsor), *born* April 28, 1964;

      (c) Nicholas Charles Edward Jonathan (Lord Nicholas Windsor), *born* July 25, 1970.

      Residences.—York House, St. James's Palace, SW1 (Tel: 071–930 4872); Crocker End House, Nettlebed, Oxon.

    (2) HRH Princess **Alexandra** Helen Elizabeth Olga Christabel (**HRH Princess Alexandra, the Hon. Lady Ogilvy**), GCVO, Colonel-in-Chief, 17th/21st Lancers, The King's Own Royal Border Regiment, The Queen's Own Rifles of Canada, The Canadian Scottish Regiment (Princess Mary's), Deputy Colonel-in-Chief The Light Infantry, Deputy Hon. Colonel The Royal Yeomanry, Patron and Air Chief Commandant Princess Mary's Royal Air Force Nursing Service, Patron Queen Alexandra's Royal Naval Nursing Service. *Born* Dec. 25, 1936, *married* April 24, 1963, The Hon. Sir Angus Ogilvy, KCVO, 2nd son of the 12th Earl of Airlie (*born* Sept. 14, 1928) and has *issue:—*

      (a) James Robert Bruce, *born* Feb. 29, 1964, *married* July 30, 1988, Miss Julia Rawlinson;

      (b) Marina Victoria Alexandra, *born* July 31, 1966, *married* Feb. 2, 1990, Mr. Paul Mowatt and has *issue*, Zenouska, *born* May 1990.

      Residence—Thatched House Lodge, Richmond Park, Surrey. *Office*—22 Friary Court, St. James's Palace, SW1A 1BJ (Tel: 071–930 1860).

    (3) HRH Prince **Michael** George Charles Franklin (**HRH Prince Michael of Kent**), Hon. Auxiliary Commodore Royal Naval Auxiliary Service. *Born* July 4, 1942, *married* June 30, 1978, Baroness Marie-Christine Agnes Hedwig Ida von Reibnitz (**HRH Princess Michael of Kent**), and has *issue:—*

      (a) Frederick Michael George David Louis (Lord Frederick Windsor), *born* April 6, 1979;

      (b) Gabriella Marina Alexandra Ophelia (Lady Gabriella Windsor), *born* April 23, 1981.

      Residences.—Kensington Palace, W8 4PU (Tel: 071–937 9774); Nether Lypiatt Manor, Stroud, Glos.

6. HRH Prince John Charles Francis, *born* July 12, 1905; *died* Jan. 18, 1919.

THE SOVEREIGN

Her Most Excellent Majesty **ELIZABETH THE SECOND** (Elizabeth Alexandra Mary of Windsor) by the Grace of God, of the United Kingdom of Great Britain and Northern Ireland and of Her other Realms and Territories Queen, Head of the Commonwealth, Defender of the Faith, Sovereign of the British Orders of Knighthood and Sovereign Head of the Order of St. John, Lord High Admiral of the United Kingdom, Colonel-in-Chief of The Life Guards, The Blues and Royals (Royal Horse Guards and 1st Dragoons), The Royal Scots Dragoon Guards (Carabiniers and Greys), 16th/5th The Queen's Royal Lancers, Royal Tank Regiment, Corps of Royal Engineers, Grenadier Guards, Coldstream Guards, Scots Guards, Irish Guards, Welsh Guards, The Royal Welch Fusiliers, The Queen's Lancashire Regiment, The Argyll and Sutherland Highlanders (Princess Louise's), The Royal Green Jackets, Royal Army Ordnance Corps, Corps of Royal Military Police, The Queen's Own Mercian Yeomanry, The Duke of Lancaster's Own Yeomanry, The Governor General's Horse Guards, The King's Own Calgary Regiment, Canadian Forces Military Engineers Branch, Royal 22e Regiment, Governor-General's Foot Guards, The Canadian Grenadier Guards, Le Régiment de la Chaudière, 2nd Bn. Royal New Brunswick Regiment (North Shore), The 48th Highlanders of Canada, The Argyll and Sutherland Highlanders of Canada (Princess Louise's), The Calgary Highlanders, Royal Australian Engineers, Royal Australian Infantry Corps, Royal Australian Army Ordnance Corps, Royal Australian Army Nursing Corps, The Corps of Royal New Zealand Engineers, Royal New Zealand Infantry Regiment, Royal New Zealand Army Ordnance Corps, Royal Malta Artillery, The Malawi Rifles, Captain-General of Royal Regiment of Artillery, The Honourable Artillery Company, Combined Cadet Force, Royal Regiment of Canadian Artillery, Royal Regiment of Australian Artillery, Royal Regiment of New Zealand Artillery, Royal New Zealand Armoured Corps, Air-Commodore-in-Chief, Royal Auxiliary Air Force, Royal Air Force Regiment, Royal Observer Corps, Air Reserve (of Canada), Royal Australian Air Force Reserve, Territorial Air Force (New Zealand), Commandant-in-Chief, Royal Air Force College, Cranwell, Hon. Air Commodore, RAF Marham, Hon. Commissioner, Royal Canadian Mounted Police, Master of the Merchant Navy and Fishing Fleets, Head of the Civil Defence Corps.

Elder daughter of HM King George VI and of HM Queen Elizabeth the Queen Mother; *born* at 17 Bruton Street, London, W1, April 21, 1926, *succeeded* to the Throne February 6, 1952, *crowned* June 2, 1953; having *married*, November 20, 1947, in Westminster Abbey, Philip, Duke of Edinburgh, Earl of Merioneth and Baron Greenwich (**HRH The Prince Philip, Duke of Edinburgh**, *born* June 10, 1921), KG, KT, OM, GBE, AC, QSO, PC, Admiral of the Fleet, Field Marshal, Marshal of the Royal Air Force, Admiral of the Fleet, Royal Australian Navy, Field Marshal, Australian Military Forces, Marshal of the Royal Australian Air Force, Admiral of the Fleet, Royal New Zealand Navy, Field Marshal New Zealand Army, Marshal of the Royal New Zealand Air Force, Captain General, Royal Marines, Colonel-in-Chief, The Queen's Royal Irish Hussars, The Duke of Edinburgh's Royal Regiment (Berkshire and Wiltshire), The Queen's Own Highlanders (Seaforth and Camerons), Corps of Royal Electrical and Mechanical Engineers, Intelligence Corps, Army Cadet Force, The Royal Canadian Regiment, The Royal Hamilton Light Infantry (Wentworth Regiment), The Cameron Highlanders of Ottawa, The Queen's Own Cameron Highlanders of Canada, The Seaforth Highlanders of Canada, The Royal Canadian Army Cadets, The Royal Australian Electrical and Mechanical Engineers, The Australian Cadet Corps, Corps of Royal New Zealand Electrical and Mechanical Engineers, Colonel of Grenadier Guards, Hon. Colonel, Edinburgh and Heriot-Watt Universities Officers' Training Corps, The Trinidad and Tobago Regiment, Admiral, Royal Canadian Sea Cadets, Marshal, Royal New Zealand Air Force, Air Training Corps, Royal Canadian Air Cadets, Hon. Air Commodore, RAF Kinloss, Master of the Corporation of Trinity House, Ranger of Windsor Park, Admiral Sea Cadet Corps, Hon. Colonel Leicester and Derbyshire Yeomanry PAQ Sqn. *See* p. 139.

Official Residences.—Buckingham Palace, SW1 (Tel: 071–930 4832); Windsor Castle, Berks.; Palace of Holyroodhouse, Edinburgh. *Private Residences.*—Sandringham, Norfolk; Balmoral Castle, Aberdeenshire.

CHILDREN OF HER MAJESTY

HRH THE PRINCE OF WALES (CHARLES Philip Arthur George), KG, KT, GCB, AK, QSO, PC, ADC, Prince of Wales and Earl of Chester, Duke of Cornwall and Duke of Rothesay, Earl of Carrick and Baron Renfrew, Lord of the Isles and Great Steward of Scotland, Personal ADC to the Queen, Great Master of the Order of the Bath, Captain Royal Navy, Group Captain Royal Air Force, Colonel-in-Chief 5th Royal Inniskilling Dragoon Guards, The Cheshire Regiment, The Royal Regiment of Wales (24th/41st Foot), The Gordon Highlanders, The Parachute Regiment, 2nd King Edward VII's Own Gurkha Rifles (The Sirmoor Rifles), The Royal Canadian Dragoons, Lord Strathcona's Horse (Royal Canadians), Royal Regiment of Canada, Royal Winnipeg Rifles, Royal Australian Armoured Corps, The Royal Pacific Islands Regiment, Colonel, Welsh Guards, Air Commodore-in-Chief Royal New Zealand Air Force, Hon. Air Commodore, RAF Brawdy.

Born November 14, 1948, *married* July 29, 1981, Lady Diana Frances Spencer, youngest daughter of the 8th Earl Spencer and the Hon. Mrs. Shand Kydd (**HRH The Princess of Wales**, *born* July 1, 1961), Colonel-in-Chief 13th/18th Royal Hussars (Queen Mary's Own), The Royal Hampshire Regiment, The Princess of Wales's Own Regiment (of Canada), Hon. Air Commodore, RAF Wittering; and has *issue*, (*a*) William Arthur Philip Louis (**HRH Prince William of Wales**), *born* June 21, 1982; and (*b*) Henry Charles Albert David (**HRH Prince Henry of Wales**), *born* Sept. 15, 1984.

Residences.—Highgrove, Doughton, Tetbury, Glos.; Kensington Palace, W8. *Office.*—St. James's Palace, SW1 (Tel: 071–930 4832).

HRH THE PRINCESS ROYAL (ANNE Elizabeth Alice Louise), GCVO, FRS, Chief Commandant Women's Royal Naval Service, Colonel-in-Chief 14th/20th King's Hussars, Royal Corps of Signals, The Royal Scots (The Royal Regiment), The Worcestershire and Sherwood Foresters Regiment (29th/45th Foot), 8th Canadian Hussars (Princess Louise's), Canadian Forces Communications and Electronics Branch, Grey and Simcoe Foresters Militia, The Royal Regina Rifle Regiment, Royal Newfoundland Regiment, Royal Australian Corps of Signals, Royal New Zealand Corps of Signals, Royal New Zealand Nursing Corps, Hon. Colonel London University Officers' Training Corps, Hon. Air Commodore, RAF Lyneham, Commandant-in-Chief, (Ambulance and Nursing Cadets) St. John Ambulance, Commandant-in-Chief, Women's Transport Service (FANY).

Born August 15, 1950, *married* Nov. 14, 1973, Capt. Mark Anthony Peter Phillips, CVO (*born* Sept. 22, 1948), Personal ADC to the Queen, *separated* August 1989; and has *issue*, (*a*) Peter Mark Andrew, *born* Nov. 15, 1977; and (*b*) Zara Anne Elizabeth, *born* May 15, 1981.

Residence.—Gatcombe Park, Minchinhampton, Stroud, Glos. *Office.*—Buckingham Palace, SW1. (Tel: 071–930 4832).

HRH THE DUKE OF YORK (ANDREW Albert Christian Edward), Duke of York, Earl of Inverness and Baron Killyleagh, CVO, Personal ADC to the Queen, Lieutenant, Royal Navy, Colonel-in-Chief The Staffordshire Regiment (The Prince of Wales's). *Born* Feb. 19, 1960, *married* July 23, 1986, Miss Sarah Margaret Ferguson (**HRH The Duchess of York**, *born* October 15, 1959), younger daughter of Major Ronald Ferguson and Mrs. Hector Barrantes; and has *issue*, (*a*) Beatrice Elizabeth Mary (**HRH Princess Beatrice of York**), *born* Aug. 8, 1988; and (*b*) Eugenie Victoria Helena (**HRH Princess Eugenie of York**), *born* March 23, 1990.

Residences.—Sunninghill Park, Ascot, Berks.; Buckingham Palace, SW1. *Office.*—Buckingham Palace, SW1. (Tel: 071–930 4832).

HRH THE PRINCE EDWARD (Antony Richard Louis), CVO, *born* March 10, 1964.
Residence and Office.—Buckingham Palace, SW1. (Tel: 071–930 4832).

MOTHER OF HER MAJESTY

HM QUEEN ELIZABETH THE QUEEN MOTHER (Elizabeth Angela Marguerite) (daughter of the 14th Earl of Strathmore and Kinghorne), Lady of the Garter, Lady of the Thistle, CI, GMVO, GBE, Dame, Grand Cross of the Order of St. John, Royal Victorian Chain, Colonel-in-Chief 1st The Queen's Dragoon Guards, The Queen's Own Hussars, 9th/12th Royal Lancers (Prince of Wales's) The King's Regiment, The Royal Anglian Regiment, The Light Infantry, The Black Watch (Royal Highland Regiment), Royal Army Medical Corps, The Black Watch (Royal Highland Regiment) of Canada, The Toronto Scottish Regiment, Canadian Forces Medical Services, Royal Australian Army Medical Corps, Royal New Zealand Army Medical Corps, Hon. Colonel The Royal Yeomanry, The London Scottish, Inns of Court and City Yeomanry, Commandant-in-Chief RAF Central Flying School, Women's Royal Naval Service, Women's Royal Army Corps, Women's Royal Air Force, Patron St. Andrew's Ambulance Association, Commandant-in-Chief Nursing Corps and Divisions, Commandant-in-Chief (Nursing) St. John's Ambulance, Lord Warden and Admiral of the Cinque Ports and Constable of Dover Castle. *Born* August 4, 1900, *married* April 26, 1923, Prince Albert Frederick Arthur George of Windsor, Duke of York (*see* page 141).

Residences.—Clarence House, St. James's Palace, SW1 (Tel: 071–930 3141); Royal Lodge, Windsor Great Park, Berks.; Castle of Mey, Caithness, Scotland.

SISTER OF HER MAJESTY

HRH THE PRINCESS MARGARET, COUNTESS OF SNOWDON (Margaret Rose), CI, GCVO, Colonel-in-Chief, 15th/19th The King's Royal Hussars, The Royal Highland Fusiliers (Princess Margaret's Own Glasgow and Ayrshire Regiment), Queen Alexandra's Royal Army Nursing Corps, The Highland Fusiliers of Canada, The Princess Louise Fusiliers, The Bermuda Regiment, Deputy Colonel-in-Chief, The Royal Anglian Regiment, Hon. Air Commodore, RAF Coningsby, Grand President, St. John Ambulance Association and Brigade, Dame Grand Cross of the Order of St. John of Jerusalem, President of the Girl Guides Association.

Born Aug. 21, 1930; *married* May 6, 1960, Anthony Charles Robert Armstrong-Jones, GCVO (*born* March 7, 1930, son of the late Ronald Armstrong-Jones, QC and the Countess of Rosse, *created* Earl of Snowdon, 1961, Constable of Caernarvon Castle, *marriage dissolved*, 1978); and has *issue*, (*a*) David Albert Charles, Viscount Linley, *born* Nov. 3, 1961; and (*b*) Sarah Frances Elizabeth (Lady Sarah Armstrong-Jones), *born* May 1, 1964.

Residence.—Kensington Palace, W8 4PU (Tel: 071–930 3141).

Order of Succession to the Throne

1. HRH The Prince of Wales
2. HRH Prince William of Wales
3. HRH Prince Henry of Wales
4. HRH The Duke of York
5. HRH Princess Beatrice of York
6. HRH Princess Eugenie of York
7. HRH The Prince Edward
8. HRH The Princess Royal
9. Master Peter Phillips
10. Miss Zara Phillips
11. HRH The Princess Margaret, Countess of Snowdon
12. Viscount Linley
13. Lady Sarah Armstrong-Jones
14. HRH The Duke of Gloucester
15. Earl of Ulster
16. Lady Davina Windsor
17. Lady Rose Windsor
18. HRH The Duke of Kent
19. Lord Downpatrick
20. Lord Nicholas Windsor
21. Lady Helen Windsor
22. Lord Frederick Windsor
23. Lady Gabriella Windsor
24. HRH Princess Alexandra, the Hon. Lady Ogilvy
25. Mr. James Ogilvy
26. Mrs. Paul Mowatt

The Earl of St. Andrews and HRH Prince Michael of Kent are excluded from succession to the Throne, each having married a Roman Catholic. However, each transmits his right to his children.

THE QUEEN'S HOUSEHOLD

Lord Chamberlain, The Earl of Airlie, KT, PC, GCVO.
Lord Steward, The Viscount Ridley, TD.
Master of the Horse, The Earl of Westmorland, KCVO.
Treasurer of the Household, A. Goodlad, MP.
Comptroller of the Household, Sir George Young, Bt., MP.
Vice Chamberlain, D. Lightbown, MP.

Gold Stick, Maj.-Gen. Lord Michael Fitzalan Howard, GCVO, CB, CBE, MC; Gen. Sir Desmond Fitzpatrick, GCB, DSO, MBE, MC.
Vice-Adm. of the United Kingdom, Adm. Sir Anthony Griffin, GCB.
Rear-Adm. of the United Kingdom, Adm. Sir Anthony Morton, GBE, KCB.
First and Principal Naval Aide-de-Camp, Adm. Sir Julian Oswald, GCB.
Flag Aide de Camp, Adm. Sir Jeremy Black, KCB, DSO, MBE.
Aides-de-Camp General, Gen. Sir John Chapple, GCB, CBE.; Gen. Sir Charles Huxtable, KCB, CBE; Gen. Sir Robert Pascoe, KCB, MBE.
Air Aides-de-Camp, Air Chief Marshal Sir Peter Harding, GCB; Air Chief Marshal Sir Patrick Hine, GCB.

Mistress of the Robes, The Duchess of Grafton, GCVO.
Ladies of the Bedchamber, The Countess of Airlie, CVO; The Lady Farnham..
Extra Ladies of the Bedchamber, The Marchioness of Abergavenny, DCVO; The Countess of Cromer, CVO.
Women of the Bedchamber, Hon. Mary Morrison, DCVO; Lady Susan Hussey, DCVO; Mrs. John Dugdale, DCVO; The Lady Elton.
Extra Women of the Bedchamber, Mrs. John Woodroffe, CVO; Lady Rose Baring, DCVO; Mrs. Michael Wall, DCVO; Lady Abel Smith, DCVO; Mrs Robert de Pass.
Equerries, Lt.-Col. B. A. Stewart-Wilson, CVO; Wg. Cdr. D. A. Walker; Capt. J. Giles (*temp.*).
Extra Equerries, Vice-Adm. Sir Peter Ashmore, KCB, KCVO, DSC; Lt.-Col. The Lord Charteris of Amisfield, PC, GCB, GCVO, OBE, QSO; Sir Robert Fellowes, KCVO, CB; Sir Edward Ford, KCB, KCVO, ERD; Rear-Adm. John Garnier, CBE, LVO; Rear-Adm. Sir Paul Greening, KCVO; Brig. Sir Geoffrey Hardy-Roberts, KCVO, CB, CBE; The Rt. Hon. Sir William Heseltine, GCB, GCVO, QSO; Rear-Adm. Sir Hugh Janion, KCVO; Lt.-Col. Sir John Johnston, GCVO, MC; Sir Peter Miles, KCVO; Lt.-Col. Sir John Miller, GCVO, DSO, MC; Air Cdre. Sir Dennis Mitchell, KBE, CVO, DFC, AFC; The Lord Moore of Wolvercote, GCB, GCVO, CMG, QSO; Lt.-Col. Sir Eric Penn, GCVO, OBE, MC; Lt.-Col. W. H. M. Ross, OBE; Cdr. Sir Philip Row, KCVO, OBE, RN; Air Vice-Marshal Sir John Severne, KCVO, OBE, AFC; Gp. Capt. Peter Townsend, CVO, DSO, DFC; Rear Adm. Sir Richard Trowbridge, KCVO; Lt.-Col. G. West, CVO; Air Cdre. Sir Archie Winskill, KCVO, CBE, DFC, AE.

THE PRIVATE SECRETARY'S OFFICE
Buckingham Palace, SW1

Private Secretary to The Queen, Sir Robert Fellowes, KCVO, CB.
Deputy Private Secretary, Sir Kenneth Scott, KCVO, CMG.
Assistant Private Secretary, R. Janvrin, LVO.
Press Secretary, C. Anson, LVO.
Deputy Press Secretary, J. Haslam, LVO.
Assistant Press Secretaries, G. Crawford; R. W. Arbiter.
Chief Clerk, Mrs. G. S. Coulson, MVO.
Secretary to the Private Secretary, Miss E. Pearce, MVO.
Head of Information and Correspondence Section, Mrs. J. Bean, LVO.
Clerks, Mrs. J. Atwell, MVO; Mrs. P. Bachelier; Miss A. Gabbett; Mrs. C. H. Good; Miss A. Kennedy; J. Mordaunt, MVO; Miss H. Spiller.
Press Office, Miss K. McGrigor; Mrs. R. Murdo-Smith, LVO; Mrs. A. Neal, LVO.
Lady in Waiting's Office, Mrs. D. Phillips; Mrs. J. Vince.

The Queen's Archives
Round Tower, Windsor Castle.

Keeper of The Queen's Archives, Sir Robert Fellowes, KCVO, CB.
Assistant Keeper, O. Everett, LVO.
Registrar, Lady de Bellaigue, MVO.
Assistant Registrar, Miss P. Clark.
Curator of the Photographic Collection, Miss F. Dimond, MVO.

THE PRIVY PURSE AND TREASURER'S OFFICE
Buckingham Palace, SW1

Keeper of the Privy Purse and Treasurer to The Queen, Maj. Sir Shane Blewitt, KCVO.
Deputy Keeper of the Privy Purse and Deputy Treasurer, J. Parsons.
Chief Accountant and Paymaster, D. Walker, LVO.
Personnel Officer, G. Franklin, CVO.
Administrative Officer, D. Waters, CVO.
Asst. Chief Accountant and Paymaster, Miss R. Ward.
Assistant Personnel Officer, Miss C. Hall.
Superintendent of Public Enterprises, E. Hewlett.
Accountants, Mrs. J. Maitland, LVO; Mrs. D. Mowbray, MVO; Mrs. W. Johnson.
Clerks, Mrs. C. Auton, MVO; Mrs. F. Burrows; Miss C. McCarthy; Miss G. Wickham, MVO; Miss C. Robinson; Miss L. Buggé; Miss M. O'Connell; I. Biss.
Clerk of Stationery, W. Cotton.
Land Agent, Sandringham, J. Loyd, CVO.
Resident Factor, Balmoral, M. Leslie, LVO.

Royal Almonry

Lord High Almoner, The Rt. Rev. the Lord Bishop of St. Albans.
Hereditary Grand Almoner, The Marquess of Exeter.
Sub-Almoner, Rev. Canon A. D. Caesar, LVO, FRCO.
Secretary, P. Wright, CVO.
Assistant Secretary, D. Waters, CVO.

THE LORD CHAMBERLAIN'S OFFICE
Buckingham Palace, SW1

Comptroller, Lt.-Col. G. West, CVO.
Assistant Comptroller, Lt.-Col. M. Ross, OBE.
Secretary, J. E. P. Titman, CVO.
Assistant Secretary, P. D. Hartley, MVO.
State Invitations Assistant, Maj. J. C. Leech.
Registrar, J. Spencer.
Clerks, Miss S. Hay, MVO; Miss C. Britton; Mrs. J. Marsham; Miss H. Asprey; Miss L. Pears; Mrs. V. Cunningham.
Permanent Lords in Waiting, Lt. Col. The Lord Charteris of Amisfield, PC, GCB, GCVO, OBE, QSO; The Lord Moore of Wolvercote, GCB, GCVO, CMG, QSO.
Lords in Waiting, The Lord Somerleyton; The Viscount Boyne; The Viscount Long; The Lord Reay; The Earl of Strathmore and Kinghorne; The Baroness Blatch, CBE.
Gentlemen Ushers, C. Greig, CVO, CBE; Lt.-Col. Sir Julian Paget, Bt., CVO; Gp. Capt. J. Slessor; Maj. N. Chamberlayne-Macdonald, LVO, OBE; Air Marshal Sir Roy Austen-Smith, KBE, CB, DFC; Vice-Adm. Sir David Loram, KCB, LVO; Capt. M. Barrow, DSO, RN; Capt. M. Fulford-Dobson, RN; Lt. Gen. Sir Richard Vickers, KCB, LVO, OBE; Air Vice-Marshal B. Newton, CB, OBE.
Extra Gentlemen Ushers, Capt. A. Yates, LVO, RN; Maj. T. Harvey, CVO, DSO; Air Vice-Marshal Sir Ranald Reid, KCB, DSO, MC; Maj.-Gen. Sir Cyril Colquhoun, KCVO, CB, OBE; Lt.-Col. Sir John Hugo, KCVO, OBE; Vice-Adm. Sir Ronald Brockman, KCB, CSI, CIE, CVO, CBE; Air Marshal Sir Maurice Heath, KBE, CB, CVO; Sir James Scholtens, KCVO; Sir Patrick O'Dea, KCVO; Brig.-Gen. S. Cooper, CVO, OBE, CD; Adm. Sir David Williams, GCB; Capt. M. Tufnell, CVO, DSC, RN; H. Davis, CVO, CM; Maj.-Gen. R. Reid, CVO, MC, CD; Lt.-Cdr. J. Holdsworth, CVO, OBE, RN; Col. G. Leigh, CVO, CBE; Lt.-Cdr. Sir Russell Wood, KCVO, VRD; Col. D. Lawrence; Air Chief Marshal Sir Neville Stack, KCB, CVO, CBE, AFC; Maj.-Gen. Sir Desmond Rice, KCVO, CBE.
Gentleman Usher to the Sword of State, Gen. Sir Edward Burgess, KCB, OBE.
Gentleman Usher of the Black Rod, Air Chief Marshal Sir John Gingell, GBE, KCB.
Serjeants at Arms, J. E. P. Titman, CVO; M. Tims, CVO; G. Franklin, CVO.

Marshal of the Diplomatic Corps, Lt.-Gen. Sir John Richards, KCB.
Vice-Marshal, R. Hervey, CMG.

Constable & Governor of Windsor Castle, Adm. Sir David Hallifax, KCB, KBE.
Keeper of the Jewel House, Tower of London, Maj.-Gen. C. Tyler, CB.
Master of The Queen's Music, Malcolm Williamson, CBE, AO.
Poet Laureate, Ted Hughes, OBE.
Bargemaster, R. Crouch.
Keeper of the Swans, F. J. Turk, MVO.
Superintendent of the State Apartments, St. James's Palace, T. Taylor, MVO, MBE.

ROYAL COLLECTION DEPARTMENT
St. James's Palace, SW1

Director of Royal Collection and Surveyor of The Queen's Works of Art, Sir Geoffrey de Bellaigue, KCVO, FSA.
Surveyor of The Queen's Pictures, C. Lloyd.
Librarian, The Royal Library, Windsor Castle, O. Everett, LVO.
Deputy Surveyor of The Queen's Works of Art, H. Roberts.
Surveyor Emeritus of The Queen's Pictures, Sir Oliver Millar, GCVO, FBA, FSA.

Adviser for The Queen's Works of Art, Sir Francis Watson, KCVO, FBA, FSA.
Librarian Emeritus, Sir Robin Mackworth-Young, GCVO, FSA.
Curator of the Print Room, The Hon. Mrs. Roberts, MVO.
Registrar, M. Bishop, MVO.
Assistant to Registrar, Miss S. Goodbody.
Assistants to Surveyor of The Queen's Works of Art, Mrs. J. Harland, MVO; D. Rankin-Hunt.
Assistants to Surveyor of The Queen's Pictures, C. Noble, MVO; Miss C. Crichton-Stuart, MVO.
Inventory Assistant, Mrs. S. Newton.
Clerks, Miss V. Colfox; Hon. C. Neville; Miss M. Pullen; Miss S. Goodbody; Miss C. Pilkington.

ASCOT OFFICE
St. James's Palace, SW1

Her Majesty's Representative at Ascot, Col. Sir Piers Bengough, KCVO, OBE.
Secretary, Miss L. Thompson-Royd.

ECCLESIASTICAL HOUSEHOLD
The College of Chaplains.

Clerk of the Closet, Rt. Rev. Bishop of Chelmsford.
Deputy Clerk of the Closet, Rev. Canon A. D. Caesar, LVO, FRCO.
Chaplains to The Queen, Rev. J. R. W. Stott; Rev. A. H. H. Harbottle, LVO; Ven. D. N. Griffiths, RD; Canon A. Glendining, LVO; Canon J. V. Bean; Rev. K. Huxley; Ven. P. Ashford; Canon G. A. Elcoat; Canon D. C. Gray, TD; Ven. D. Scott; Canon E. James; Canon J. Hester; Rev. S. Pedley; Rev. D. Tonge; Rev. Canon C. Craston; Rev. Canon N. M. Ramm; Rev. Canon D. N. Hole; Rev. Canon M. A. Moxon; Canon R. J. W. Bevan; Canon R. T. W. McDermid; Canon G. Murphy, LVO; Canon R. H. C. Lewis; Rev. D. J. Burgess; Rev. E. R. Ayerst; Rev. R. S. Clarke; Rev. Canon C. J. Hill; Ven. K. Pound; Rev. Canon J. Haslam; Rev. Canon G. Hall.
Extra Chaplains, Rev. Canon J. S. D. Mansel, KCVO, FSA; Preb. S. A. Williams, CVO; Ven. E. J. G. Ward, LVO.

Chapels Royal

Dean of the Chapels Royal, The Bishop of London.
Sub-Dean of Chapels Royal, Rev. Canon A. D. Caesar, LVO, FRCO.
Priests in Ordinary, Rev. W. Booth; Rev. A. Ford; Rev. G. Watkins.
Organist, Choirmaster and Composer, R. J. Popplewell, FRCO, FRCM.
Domestic Chaplain—Buckingham Palace, Rev. Canon A. D. Caesar, LVO, FRCO.
Domestic Chaplain—Windsor Castle, The Dean of Windsor.
Domestic Chaplain—Sandringham, Rev. Canon G. R. Hall.
Chaplain—Royal Chapel, Windsor Great Park, Rev. Canon M. Moxon.
Chaplain—Hampton Court Palace, Rev. Canon M. Moore.
Chaplain—Tower of London, Rev. N. A. Hood.
Organist and Choirmaster—Hampton Court Palace, Gordon Reynolds, LVO.

MEDICAL HOUSEHOLD

Head of the Medical Household and Physician, A. Dawson, MD, FRCP.
Physician, R. W. Davey, MB, BS.
Serjeant Surgeon, J. Dawson, MS, FRCS.
Surgeon Oculist, P. Holmes Sellors, LVO, BM, B.Ch., FRCS.
Surgeon Gynaecologist, M. E. Setchell, FRCS, FRCOG.

Surgeon Dentist, N. A. Sturridge, CVO, LDS, BDS, DDS.
Orthopaedic Surgeon, D. R. Sweetnam, CBE, FRCS.
Physician to the Household, R. Thompson, DM, FRCP.
Surgeon to the Household, B. Jackson, MS, FRCS.
Surgeon Oculist to the Household, T. J. ffytche, FRCS.
Apothecary to The Queen and to the Household, N. R. Southward, LVO, MB, B.Chir.
Apothecary to the Household at Windsor, J. H. D. Brisco, MB, B.chir., D.obst.
Apothecary to the Household at Sandringham, H. K. Ford, LVO, MB, FRCGP.
Coroner of The Queen's Household, J. Burton, CBE, MB, BS.

CENTRAL CHANCERY OF THE ORDERS OF KNIGHTHOOD
St. James's Palace, SW1

Secretary, Lt.-Col. W. H. M. Ross, OBE.
Assistant Secretary, Sqn. Ldr. B. Sowerby, MVO.
Clerks, J. McGurk, MVO; Miss S. Koller, MVO; Miss R. Wells; Miss L. Dove; Miss F. Bean; Miss L. Marulli.

The Honorable Corps of Gentlemen at Arms
St. James's Palace, SW1

Captain, The Lord Denham, PC; Lieutenant, Maj. T. St. Aubyn; Standard Bearer, Lt.-Col. Sir James Scott, Bt.; Clerk of the Cheque & Adjutant, vacant; Harbinger, Maj. the Lord Suffield, MC.

Gentlemen of the Corps

Brigadier, A. N. Breitmeyer.
Colonels, T. Hall, OBE; Sir Piers Bengough, KCVO, OBE; Hon. N. Crossley, TD; T. Wilson; D. Fanshawe, OBE; J. Baker.
Lieutenant-Colonels, P. Hodgson; R. Mayfield, DSO; B. Lockhart; Hon. P. H. Lewis; R. Macfarlane; Hon. G. B. Norrie.
Majors, Sir Torquhil Matheson of Matheson, Bt.; F. J. H. Matheson; J. A. J. Nunn; Sir Philip Duncombe, Bt.; I. B. Ramsden, MBE; M. J. Drummond-Brady; A. Arkwright; G. M. B. Colenso-Jones; T. Gooch, MBE; J. B. B. Cockcroft; C. J. H. Gurney; J. R. E. Nelson.
Captain, The Lord Monteagle of Brandon.

The Queen's Bodyguard of the Yeoman of the Guard
St. James's Palace, SW1

Captain, The Viscount Davidson; Lieutenant, Col. A. B. Pemberton, CVO, MBE; Clerk of the Cheque and Adjutant, Col. G. W. Tufnell; Ensign, Lt.-Col. S. Longsdon; Exons., Maj. C. Marriott; Maj. C. Enderby.

MASTER OF THE HOUSEHOLD'S DEPARTMENT
Board of Green Cloth
Buckingham Palace, SW1

Master of the Household, Rear-Adm. Sir Paul Greening, KCVO.
Deputy Master of the Household, Lt.-Col. B. A. Stewart-Wilson, CVO.
Assistants to the Master of the Household, M. D. Tims, CVO; M. T. Parker, MVO.
Chief Clerk, M. C. W. N. Jephson, MVO.
Chief Housekeeper, Miss H. Colebrook.
Deputy to Assistant F, M. Bovaird.
Senior Clerk G, S. Stacey.
Administrator F, Miss J. Cartwright.
Clerks, Miss S. Derry, MVO; Miss S. Fergus, MVO; Mrs. C. Creak; K. Sharp; Miss J. Perry; Miss S. Bell; Miss L. Moran.
Palace Steward, A. Jarred, RVM.
Royal Chef, L. Mann, RVM.
Superintendent, Windsor Castle, Maj. B. Eastwood, MBE.

Assistant to Superintendent, Capt. R. McClosky, MVO.
Superintendent, The Palace of Holyroodhouse, Lt.-Col. D. Wickes.

ROYAL MEWS DEPARTMENT
Buckingham Palace, SW1

Crown Equerry, Lt.-Col. S. Gilbart-Denham.
Veterinary Surgeon, P. Scott Dunn, LVO, MRCVS.
Supt. Royal Mews, Buckingham Palace, Maj. A. Smith, MBE.
Comptroller of Stores, Maj. L. Marsham, MVO.
Chief Clerk, P. Almond, MVO.
Deputy Chief Clerk, A. Marshall.
Assistant Chief Clerk, Mrs. J. Clark.
Office Keeper, P. M. Goodman, MVO.

HER MAJESTY'S HOUSEHOLD IN SCOTLAND

Hereditary Lord High Constable, The Earl of Erroll.
Hereditary Master of the Household, The Duke of Argyll.
Lord Lyon King of Arms, Sir Malcolm Innes of Edingight, KCVO, WS.
Hereditary Bearer of the Royal Banner of Scotland, The Earl of Dundee.
Hereditary Bearer of the Scottish National Flag, The Earl of Lauderdale.
Hereditary Keepers:—
  Holyrood, The Duke of Hamilton and Brandon.
  Falkland, N. J. Crichton-Stuart.
  Stirling, The Earl of Mar and Kellie.
  Dunstaffnage, The Duke of Argyll.
Hereditary Carver, Sir Ralph Anstruther, KCVO, MC.
Keeper of Dumbarton Castle, Brig. A. S. Pearson, CB, DSO, OBE, MC, TD.
Governor of Edinburgh Castle, Lt.-Gen. Sir John MacMillan, KCB.
Historiographer, Prof. G. Donaldson, CBE, FBA, FRSE.
Botanist, Prof. D. Henderson, CBE, FRSE.
Painter and Limner, D. A. Donaldson, RSA, RP.
Sculptor in Ordinary, Prof. Sir Eduardo Paolozzi.
Astronomer, Prof. M. S. Longair, PH.D.
Heralds and Pursuivants, see p. 299-300.

Ecclesiastical Household

Dean of the Order of the Thistle, The Very Rev. G. I. Macmillan.
Dean of the Chapel Royal, Very Rev. Prof. R. A. S. Barbour, MC, DD.
Chaplains in Ordinary, Very Rev. R. A. S. Barbour, MC, DD; Rev. W. J. Morris, DD, LL.D., ph.D.; Rev. H. W. M. Cant; Rev. K. MacVicar, MBE, DFC, TD; Rev. A. J. C. Macfarlane; Rev. J. McLeod; Very Rev. G. I. Macmillan; Very Rev. W. B. Johnston, DD; Rev. M. D. Craig; Rev. W. B. R. Macmillan.
Extra Chaplains, Very Rev. the Lord MacLeod of Fuinary, MC, DD; Very Rev. Prof. J. S. Stewart, DD; Rev. Prof. E. P. Dickie, MC, DD; Very Rev. R. L. Small, CBE, DD; Very Rev. W. R. Sanderson, DD; Very Rev. R. W. V. Selby Wright, CVO, TD, DD, FRSE, FSAScot.; Rev. T. J. T. Nicol, MVO, MBE, MC, TD; Very Rev. G. T. H. Reid, MC, DD; Very Rev. Prof. J. McIntyre, CVO, DD, FRSE; Rev. C. Forrester-Paton.
Domestic Chaplain, Balmoral, Rev. J. A. K. Angus, LVO, TD.

Medical Household

Physicians in Scotland, P. Brunt, MD, FRCP; A. L. Muir, MD, FRCP.
Surgeons in Scotland, I. B. Macleod, MB, ch.B., FRCS; J. Engeset, ch.M., FRCS.

Extra Surgeons in Scotland, Prof. Sir Charles Illing-worth, CBE, MD, FRCSE; Prof. Sir Donald Douglas, MBE, ch.M., MS, D.SC., FRCS.
Apothecary to the Household at Balmoral, D. J. A. Glass, MB, ch.B.
Apothecary to the Household at the Palace of Holyrood-house, Dr. H. Gebbie, MB, ch.B.

THE QUEEN'S BODY GUARD FOR SCOTLAND

Royal Company of Archers.
Archers' Hall, Edinburgh.

Captain-General and Gold Stick for Scotland, Col. the Lord Clydesmuir, KT, CB, MBE, TD.
Captains, Maj. the Lord Home of the Hirsel, KT; The Duke of Buccleuch and Queensberry, KT, VRD; Lt.-Col. Sir John Gilmour, Bt., DSO, TD; Maj. Sir Hew Hamilton-Dalrymple, Bt., KCVO.
Lieutenants, Maj. the Earl of Wemyss and March, KT; The Earl of Airlie, KT, GCVO; The Earl of Dalhousie, KT, GCVO, GBE, MC; Capt. Sir Iain Tennant, KT.
Ensigns, Capt. N. E. F. Dalrymple-Hamilton, CVO, MBE, DSC, RN; The Marquess of Lothian, KCVO; Cdre. Sir John Clerk of Penicuik, Bt., CBE, VRD; The Earl of Elgin and Kincardine, KT.
Brigadiers, Col. G. R. Simpson, DSO, LVO, TD; Maj. D. H. Butter, MC; The Earl of Minto, OBE; Maj.-Gen. Sir John Swinton, KCVO, OBE; Gen. Sir Michael Gow, GCB; The Hon. Lord Elliott, MC; Maj. the Hon. Sir Lachlan Maclean, Bt.; The Rt. Hon. George Younger, TD, MP; Capt. G. Burnet, LVO; The Marquess of Graham; Lt.-Gen. Sir Norman Arthur, KCB; The Hon. Sir William Macpherson of Cluny, TD; Sir David Nickson, KBE.
Adjutant, Maj. the Hon. Sir Lachlan Maclean, Bt.
Surgeon, Dr. P. A. P. Mackenzie, TD.
Chaplain, Very Rev. R. Selby Wright, CVO, TD, DD, FRSE.
President of the Council and Silver Stick for Scotland, Maj. Sir Hew Hamilton-Dalrymple, Bt., KCVO.
Vice-President, The Earl of Dalhousie, KT, GCVO, GBE, MC.
Secretary, Col. H. F. O. Bewsher, OBE..
Treasurer, R. A. G. Douglas-Miller.

HOUSEHOLD OF THE PRINCE PHILIP, DUKE OF EDINBURGH

Private Secretary and Treasurer, B. H. McGrath, CVO.
Assistant Private Secretary, Brig. C. Robertson.
Equerry, Lt. Cdr, M. C. Sillars.
Extra Equerries, J. B. V. Orr, CVO; Sir Richard Davies, KCVO, CBE; Lord Buxton of Alsa.
Temporary Equerries, Capt. A. Rogers; Capt. M. Hutchings.
Chief Clerk and Accountant, V. G. Jewell, MVO.

HOUSEHOLD OF QUEEN ELIZABETH THE QUEEN MOTHER

Lord Chamberlain, Maj. the Earl of Dalhousie, KT, GCVO, GBE, MC.
Comptroller and Extra Equerry, Capt. Sir Alastair Aird, KCVO.
Private Secretary and Equerry, Lt.-Col. Sir Martin Gilliat, GCVO, MBE.
Treasurer and Equerry, Maj. Sir Ralph Anstruther, Bt., KCVO, MC.
Equerry, Maj. R. Seymour, CVO.
Press Secretary and Extra Equerry, Maj. Sir John Griffin, KCVO.
Extra Equerry, The Lord Sinclair, CVO.
Equerry, Capt. C. Morris-Adams (*temp.*).

Apothecary to the Household, Dr. N. Southward, LVO, MB, B.chir.
Surgeon-Apothecary to the Household (*Royal Lodge, Windsor*), Dr. J. Briscoe, D.obst.
Mistress of the Robes, vacant.
Ladies of the Bedchamber, The Dowager Viscountess Hambleden, GCVO; The Lady Grimthorpe, CVO.
Women of the Bedchamber, Ruth, Lady Fermoy, DCVO, OBE; Dame Frances Campbell-Preston, DCVO; Lady Elizabeth Basset, DCVO; Lady Angela Oswald.
Extra Women of the Bedchamber, Lady Victoria Wemyss, CVO; Lady Jean Rankin, DCVO; Miss Jane Walker-Okeover.
Clerk Comptroller, M. Blanch, LVO.
Clerk Accountant, J. P. Kyle, LVO.
Clerks, Mrs. R. Murphy, LVO; Miss F. Fletcher, MVO.

HOUSEHOLD OF THE PRINCE AND PRINCESS OF WALES

Private Secretary and Treasurer to The Prince and Princess of Wales, Maj.-Gen. Sir Christopher Airy, KCVO, CBE.
Assistant Private Secretary and Comptroller to The Prince and Princess of Wales, Cdr. R. J. Aylard, RN.
Assistant Private Secretaries to The Prince of Wales, P. Westmacott; G. Salter.
Secretary to the Duchy of Cornwall and Keeper of the Records, D. W. N. Landale.
Equerry to The Prince of Wales, Cdr. A. F. L. Watson.
Extra Equerries to The Prince of Wales, The Hon. Edward Adeane, CVO; Sqn. Ldr. Sir David Check-etts, KCVO; G. J. Ward, CBE; Col. J. Q. Winter, LVO; Sir John Riddle, Bt., CVO.
Assistant Private Secretary to The Princess of Wales, P. D. C. J. Jephson.
Equerry to The Princess of Wales, Sqn. Ldr. D. Barton.
Lady-in-Waiting, Miss Anne Beckwith-Smith, LVO.
Extra Ladies in Waiting, Mrs. George West; Viscountess Campden; Mrs. Max Pike; Miss Alexandra Loyd; The Hon. Mrs. Vivian Baring; Mrs. James Lonsdale.

HOUSEHOLD OF THE DUKE AND DUCHESS OF YORK

Private Secretary and Treasurer, Capt. N. Blair, RN.
Comptroller and Assistant Private Secretary, Mrs. Jonathan Mathias.
Ladies in Waiting, Mrs. John Spooner; Mrs. John Floyd.
Extra Ladies in Waiting (temp.), Miss Lucy Manners; Mrs. Harry Cotterell.
Equerry to The Duke of York, Capt. A. Buchanan-Baillie-Hamilton.
Extra Equerry, Maj. G. W. McLean.

HOUSEHOLD OF THE PRINCE EDWARD

Private Secretary and Equerry to The Prince Edward, Lt.-Col. S. G. O'Dwyer.

HOUSEHOLD OF THE PRINCESS ROYAL

Private Secretary, Lt.-Col. P. Gibbs, LVO.
Assistant Private Secretary, The Hon. Mrs. Louloudis.
Ladies in Waiting, Mrs. Richard Carew Pole, LVO; Mrs. Andrew Feilden, LVO; The Hon. Mrs. Legge-Bourke, LVO; Mrs. Malcolm Wallace, MVO; Mrs. Timothy Holderness-Roddam; Mrs. Charles Rit-chie.
Extra Ladies in Waiting, Miss Victoria Legge-Bourke, LVO; Mrs. Malcolm Innes, LVO; The Countess of Lichfield.

HOUSEHOLD OF THE PRINCESS MARGARET, COUNTESS OF SNOWDON

Private Secretary and Comptroller, The Lord Napier and Ettrick, CVO.
Personal Secretary, Miss M. Murray Brown, CVO.
Extra Ladies in Waiting, Lady Elizabeth Cavendish, LVO; Lady Aird, LVO; Mrs. Robin Benson, LVO; Lady Juliet Townsend, LVO; Mrs. Jane Stevens; The Hon. Mrs. Wills, LVO; The Lady Glenconner; The Hon. Mrs. Whitehead, LVO; The Countess Alexander of Tunis; Mrs. Charles Vyvyan.

HOUSEHOLD OF THE DUKE AND DUCHESS OF GLOUCESTER

Private Secretary, Comptroller and Equerry, Maj. N. M. L. Barne.
Assistant Private Secretary to The Duchess of Gloucester, Miss Susanne Marland.
Extra Equerry, Lt.-Col. Sir Simon Bland, KCVO.
Ladies in Waiting, Mrs. Michael Wigley, LVO; Mrs. Euan McCorquodale; Mrs. Howard Page.
Extra Lady in Waiting, Miss Jennifer Thomson.

HOUSEHOLD OF PRINCESS ALICE, DUCHESS OF GLOUCESTER

Private Secretary, Comptroller and Equerry, Maj. N. M. L. Barne.
Extra Equerry, Lt.-Col. Sir Simon Bland, KCVO.
Ladies in Waiting, Dame Jean Maxwell-Scott, DCVO; Mrs. Michael Harvey.
Extra Ladies in Waiting, Miss Dorothy Meynell, CVO; Miss Diana Harrison; The Hon. Jane Walsh, LVO; Miss Jane Egerton-Warburton, LVO.

HOUSEHOLD OF THE DUKE AND DUCHESS OF KENT

Private Secretary, Cdr. R. Walker.
Extra Equerry, Lt.-Cdr. Sir Richard Buckley, KCVO.
Equerry (temp.), Capt. the Hon. C. E. Knollys.
Ladies in Waiting, Mrs. Alan Henderson, CVO; Mrs. David Napier, LVO; Mrs Colin Marsh.
Extra Ladies in Waiting, Mrs. Peter Wilmot-Sitwell; Mrs. Julian Tomkins; Mrs. Peter Troughton.

HOUSEHOLD OF PRINCE AND PRINCESS MICHAEL OF KENT

Equerry, Lt.-Col. Sir Christopher Thompson, Bt.
Ladies in Waiting, The Hon. Mrs. Sanders; Miss Anne Frost; Lady Thompson.

HOUSEHOLD OF PRINCESS ALEXANDRA

Private Secretary and Extra Lady in Waiting, Miss Mona Mitchell, CVO.
Lady in Waiting, Lady Mary Mumford, CVO.
Extra Equerry, Maj. P. C. Clarke, CVO.
Extra Ladies in Waiting, Mrs. Peter Afia; Lady Nicholas Gordon Lennox.

ANNUITIES TO THE ROYAL FAMILY

The annuity payable to Her Majesty is known as the Civil List, and is payable out of the Consolidated Fund under the authority of a Civil List Act following the recommendation of a Parliamentary Select Committee.

The allocation for the year 1990 was as follows:—

The Queen	£5,090,000
Queen Elizabeth The Queen Mother	439,500
The Duke of Edinburgh	245,000
The Duke of York	169,000

The Prince Edward	20,000
The Princess Royal	154,500
The Princess Margaret	148,500
Princess Alice, Duchess of Gloucester	60,500
*Duke of Gloucester	119,500
*Duke of Kent	161,500
*Princess Alexandra	154,000
	6,762,000
*Refunded by The Queen	435,000
Total	6,327,000

The Prince of Wales does not receive an allocation from the Civil List, deriving his income from the revenues of the Duchy of Cornwall.

The land revenues of the Crown in England and Wales have been collected on the public account since 1760, when George III surrendered them and received a fixed annual payment or Civil List. For details of income from the Crown Estate, *see* page 309.

THE ROYAL ARMS

Quarters

1st and 4th quarters (representing England).—gules, three lions passant guardant in pale or.
2nd quarter (representing Scotland).—or, a lion rampant within a double tressure flory counterflory gules.
3rd quarter (representing Ireland).—azure, a harp or, stringed argent.
The whole shield is encircled with the Garter.
Scottish usage shows the Royal Arms with the Lion of Scotland in the 1st and 4th quarters, and the Lions of England in the 2nd quarter.

Supporters

Dexter (right).—a lion rampant guardant or, imperially crowned.
Sinister (left).—a unicorn argent, armed, crined, and unguled or, gorged with a coronet composed of crosses patées and fleurs-de-lis, a chain affixed, passing between the forelegs, and reflexed over the back.
Scottish usage shows the Royal Arms with the supporters transposed, the unicorn appearing on the right.

Badges

England.—the red and white rose united, slipped and leaved proper.
Scotland.—a thistle, slipped and leaved proper.
Ireland.—a shamrock leaf slipped vert; also a harp or, stringed argent.
United Kingdom.—the Rose of England, the Thistle of Scotland, and the Shamrock of Ireland engrafted on the same stem proper, and an escutcheon charged as the Union Flag (all ensigned with the Royal Crown).
Wales.—upon a mount vert a dragon passant, wings elevated gules.

ROYAL SALUTES

A salute of 62 guns is fired on the wharf at the Tower of London on the following occasions:
 (a) the anniversaries of the birth, accession and coronation of the Sovereign;
 (b) the anniversary of the birth of HM Queen Elizabeth the Queen Mother;
 (c) the anniversary of the birth of HRH Prince Philip, Duke of Edinburgh.
A salute of 41 guns only is fired on extraordinary and triumphal occasions, e.g. on the occasion of the Sovereign opening, proroguing or dissolving Parlia-

ment in person, or when passing through London in procession, except when otherwise ordered.

A salute of 41 guns is fired from the two saluting stations in London (the Tower of London and Hyde Park) on the occasion of the birth of a Royal infant.

Constable of the Royal Palace and Fortress of London, Field Marshal Sir John Stanier, GCB, MBE.

Lieutenant of the Tower of London, Lt.-Gen. Sir Derek Boorman, KCB.

Resident Governor and Keeper of the Jewel House, Maj.-Gen. C. Tyler, CB.

Master Gunner of St. James's Park, Gen. Sir Martin Farndale, KCB.

Master Gunner within the Tower, Col. M. Ring.

THE NATIONAL FLAG

The national flag of the United Kingdom is the Union Flag, generally known as the Union Jack. (The name 'Union Jack' derives from the use of the Union Flag on the jack-staff of naval vessels.)

The Union Flag is a combination of the cross of St. George, patron saint of England; the cross of St. Andrew, patron saint of Scotland; and a cross similar to that of St. Patrick, patron saint of Ireland.

Cross of St. George.—cross gules in a field argent (red cross on a white ground).

Cross of St. Andrew.—saltire argent in a field azure (white diagonal cross on a blue ground).

Cross of St. Patrick.—saltire gules in a field argent (red diagonal cross on a white ground).

The Union Flag was first introduced in 1606 after the union of England and Scotland. The cross of St. Patrick was added in 1801 after the union of Great Britain and Ireland.

DAYS FOR FLYING FLAGS

It is the practice to fly the Union Flag daily on some Customs Houses. In all other cases, flags are flown on government buildings by command of HM The Queen.

Days for hoisting the Union Flag are notified to the Department of the Environment by Her Majesty's command and communicated by the Department to the other government departments. On the days appointed, the Union Flag should be flown on all government buildings in London and elsewhere in the United Kingdom from 8 a.m. to sunset.

February 6.—Her Majesty's Accession.
February 19.—Birthday of The Duke of York.
March 1.—St. David's Day (in Wales only).
March 10.—Birthday of The Prince Edward.
March 11 (1991).—Commonwealth Day.
April 21.—Birthday of Her Majesty The Queen.
April 23.—St. George's Day (in England only). Where a building has two or more flagstaffs the Cross of St. George may be flown in addition to the Union Jack but not in a superior position.
June 2.—Coronation Day.
June 10.—Birthday of The Duke of Edinburgh.
June 15 (1991).—Queen's Official Birthday.
July 1.—Birthday of The Princess of Wales.
Aug. 4.—Birthday of Her Majesty Queen Elizabeth the Queen Mother.

Aug. 15.—Birthday of The Princess Royal.
Aug. 21.—Birthday of The Princess Margaret.
Nov. 10 (1991).—Remembrance Sunday.
Nov. 14.—Birthday of The Prince of Wales.
Nov. 20.—Her Majesty's Wedding Day.
Nov. 30.—St. Andrew's Day (in Scotland only).
—The occasion of the opening and closing of Parliament by the Queen, whether or not Her Majesty performs the ceremony in person (on government buildings in the Greater London area only).

Flags at half-mast

Flags will be flown at half-mast on the following occasions:

(*a*) From the announcement of the death up to the funeral of the Sovereign, except on Proclamation Day, when they are hoisted right up from 11 a.m. to sunset.

(*b*) The funerals of members of the Royal Family, subject to special commands from Her Majesty in each case.

(*c*) The funerals of foreign rulers, subject to special commands from Her Majesty in each case.

(*d*) The funerals of Prime Ministers and ex-Prime Ministers of the United Kingdom.

(*e*) Other occasions by special command of Her Majesty.

On occasions when days for flying flags coincide with days for flying flags at half-mast the following rules will be observed. Flags will be flown:

(*a*) although a member of the Royal Family, or a near relative of the Royal Family, may be lying dead, unless special commands be received from Her Majesty to the contrary;

(*b*) although it may be the day of the funeral of a Foreign Ruler.

If the body of a very distinguished subject is lying at a Government Office the flag may fly at half-mast on that office until the body has left (provided it is a day on which the flag would fly) and then the flag is to be hoisted right up. On all other Government Buildings the flag will fly as usual.

The **Royal Standard** is only to be hoisted when the Queen is actually present in the building, and never when Her Majesty is passing in procession.

RED-LETTER DAYS

Scarlet Robes are worn by the Judges of the Queen's Bench Division on Red-Letter Days and State occasions.

Jan. 25. Conversion of St. Paul.	*May* 14. St. Matthias.	*July* 25. St. James.
Feb. 2. Purification.	*June* 2. Coronation Day.	*Aug.* 4. Birthday of Queen Elizabeth the Queen Mother.
„ 6. Queen's Accession.	„ 10. Birthday of The Duke of Edinburgh.	
„ 13. Ash Wednesday.		*Oct.* 18. St. Luke.
Mar. 1. St. David.	„ 11. St. Barnabas.	„ 28. St. Simon and St. Jude.
„ 25. Annunciation.	„ 15. Queen's Official Birthday (1991).	*Nov.* 1. All Saints.
Apr. 21. Queen's Birthday.	„ 24. St. John the Baptist.	„ 9. Lord Mayor's Day.
„ 25. St. Mark.	„ 29. St. Peter.	„ 14. Birthday of The Prince of Wales.
May 1. St. Philip and St. James.	*July* 3. St. Thomas.	
„ 9. Ascension Day.		„ 30. St. Andrew.

Precedence in England

THE SOVEREIGN.
The Prince Philip, Duke of Edinburgh.
The Prince of Wales.
The Sovereign's younger Sons.
The Sovereign's Grandsons.
The Sovereign's Cousins.
Archbishop of Canterbury.
Lord High Chancellor.
Archbishop of York.
The Prime Minister.
Lord President of the Council.
Speaker of the House of Commons.
Lord Privy Seal.
Ambassadors and High Commissioners.
Lord Great Chamberlain.
Earl Marshal.
Lord Steward of the Household.
Lord Chamberlain of the Household.
Master of the Horse.
Dukes, according to their Patent of Creation: (1) of England; (2) of Scotland; (3) of Great Britain; (4) of Ireland; (5) those created since the Union.
Ministers and Envoys.
Eldest sons of Dukes of Blood Royal.
Marquesses, in same order as Dukes.
Dukes' eldest Sons.
Earls, in same order as Dukes.
Younger sons of Dukes of Blood Royal.
Marquesses' eldest Sons.
Dukes' younger Sons.
Viscounts, in same order as Dukes.
Earls' eldest Sons.
Marquesses' younger Sons.
Bishops of London, Durham and Winchester.
Other English Diocesan Bishops, according to seniority of consecration.
Suffragen Bishops, according to seniority of consecration.
Secretaries of State, if of the degree of a Baron.
Barons, in same order as Dukes.
Treasurer of the Household.
Comptroller of the Household.
Vice-Chamberlain of the Household.
Secretaries of State under the degree of Baron.
Viscounts' eldest Sons.

Earls' younger Sons.
Barons' eldest Sons.
Knights of the Garter.
Privy Counsellors.
Chancellor of the Exchequer.
Chancellor of the Duchy of Lancaster.
Lord Chief Justice of England.
Master of the Rolls.
President of the Family Division.
Vice-Chancellor.
The Lords Justices of Appeal.
Judges of the High Court.
Viscounts' younger Sons.
Barons' younger Sons.
Sons of Life Peers.
Baronets, according to date of Patent.
Knights of the Thistle.
Knights Grand Cross of the Bath.
Members of the Order of Merit.
Knights Grand Commanders of the Star of India.
Knights Grand Cross of St. Michael and St. George.
Knights Grand Commanders of the Indian Empire.
Knights Grand Cross of the Royal Victorian Order.
Knights Grand Cross of the British Empire.
Companions of Honour.
Knights Commanders of the above Orders.
Knights Bachelor.
Vice-Chancellor of the Co. Palatine of Lancaster.
Official Referees of the Supreme Court.
Circuit judges and judges of the Mayor's and City of London Court.
Companions of: (1) the Bath; (2) the Star of India; (3) St. Michael and St. George; (4) the Indian Empire.
Commanders of: (1) the Royal Victorian Order; (2) the British Empire; (3) the Distinguished Service Order.
Lieutenants of the Royal Victorian Order.
Officers of the British Empire.
Companions of the Imperial Service Order.
Eldest Sons of younger Sons of Peers.
Baronets' eldest Sons.

Eldest Sons of Knights, in the same order as their Fathers.
Members, Royal Victorian Order; Order of British Empire.
Younger Sons of the younger Sons of Peers.
Baronets' younger Sons.
Younger Sons of Knights, in the same order as their Fathers.
Naval, Military, Air, and other Esquires by Office.

Women

Women take the same rank as their husbands or as their brothers; but the daughter of a peer marrying a commoner retains her title as Lady or Honourable. Daughters of peers rank next immediately after the wives of their elder brothers, and before their younger brothers' wives. Daughters of peers marrying peers of lower degree take the same order of precedency as that of their husbands; thus the daughter of a Duke marrying a Baron becomes of the rank of Baroness only while her sisters married to commoners retain their rank and take precedence of the Baroness. Merely official rank on the husband's part does not give any similar precedence to the wife.

Peeresses in their own right take the same precedence as peers of the same rank, i.e. from their date of creation.

Local precedence

ENGLAND AND WALES.—No written code of county or city order of precedence has been promulgated, but in Counties the Lord Lieutenant stands first, and secondly (normally) the Sheriff, and therefore in Cities and Boroughs the Lord Lieutenant has social precedence over the Mayor; but at City or Borough functions the Lord Mayor or Mayor will preside. At Oxford and Cambridge the High Sheriff takes precedence of the Vice-Chancellor.
SCOTLAND.—*See* p. 613.

FORMS OF ADDRESS

It is only possible to cover here the forms of address for peers, their wife and children. Greater detail should be sought in one of the publications devoted to the subject.

Both formal and social forms of address are given where usage differs; increasingly, the social form is preferred to the formal, though this is used for official documents and on very formal occasions.

In the forms of address given below, F—— represents forename, S—— represents surname.

Baron.—*Envelope (formal)*, The Right Hon. Lord ——; *(social)*, The Lord ——. *Letter (formal)*, My Lord; *(social)*, Dear Lord ——. *Spoken*, Lord ——.

Baron's wife.—*Envelope (formal)*, The Right Hon. Lady ——; *(social)*, The Lady ——. *Letter (formal)*, My Lady; *(social)*, Dear Lady ——. *Spoken*, Lady ——.

Baron's children.—*Envelope*, The Hon. F—— S——. *Letter*, Dear Mr/Miss/Mrs S——. *Spoken*, Mr/Miss/Mrs [F——] S——.

Baroness in own right.—*Envelope*, may be addressed in same way as a Baron's wife or, if she prefers *(formal)*, The Right Hon. the Baroness ——; *(social)*, The Baroness ——. Otherwise as for a **Baron's wife**.

Baronet.—*Envelope*, Sir F—— S——, Bt. *Letter (formal)*, Dear Sir; *(social)*, Dear Sir F——. *Spoken*, Sir F——.

Baronet's wife.—*Envelope*, Lady S——. *Letter (formal)*, Dear Madam; *(social)*, Dear Lady S——. *Spoken*, Lady S——.

Countess in own right.—As for an **Earl's wife**.

Courtesy titles.—The heir apparent to a Duke, Marquess or Earl uses the highest of his father's other titles as a courtesy title. (For list, *see* page 179.) The holder of a courtesy title is not styled The Most Hon. or The Right Hon., and in correspondence 'The' is omitted before the title. The heir apparent to a Scottish title may use the title 'Master' (*see* below).

Dame.—*Envelope*, Dame F—— S——, followed by appropriate post-nominal letters. *Letter (formal)*, Dear Madam; *(social)*, Dear Dame F——. *Spoken*, Dame F——.

Duke.—*Envelope (formal)*, His Grace the Duke of ——; *(social)*, The Duke of ——. *Letter (formal)*, My Lord Duke; *(social)*, Dear Duke. *Spoken (formal)*, Your Grace; *(social)*, Duke.

Duke's wife.—*Envelope (formal)*, Her Grace the Duchess of ——; *(social)*, The Duchess of ——. *Letter (formal)*, Dear Madam; *(social)*, Dear Duchess. *Spoken*, Duchess.

Duke's eldest son.—See **Courtesy titles**.

Duke's younger sons.—*Envelope*, Lord F—— S——. *Letter (formal)*, My Lord; *(social)*, Dear Lord F——. *Spoken (formal)*, My Lord; *(social)*, Lord F——.

Duke's daughter.—*Envelope*, Lady F—— S——. *Letter (formal)*, Dear Madam; *(social)*, Dear Lady F——. *Spoken*, Lady F——.

Earl.—*Envelope (formal)*, The Right Hon. the Earl of ——; *(social)*, The Earl of ——. *Letter (formal)*, My Lord; *(social)*, Dear Lord ——. *Spoken (formal)*, My Lord; *(social)*, Lord.

Earl's wife.—*Envelope (formal)*, The Right Hon. the Countess ——; *(social)*, The Countess of ——. *Letter (formal)*, Madam; *(social)*, Lady ——. *Spoken (formal)*, Madam; *(social)*, Lady ——.

Earl's children.—*Eldest son*, see **Courtesy titles**. *Younger sons*, The Hon. F—— S—— (for forms of address, see **Baron's children**). *Daughters*, Lady F—— S—— (for forms of address, see **Duke's daughter**).

Knight (Bachelor).—*Envelope*, Sir F—— S——. *Letter (formal)*, Dear Sir; *(social)*, Dear Sir F——. *Spoken*, Sir F——.

Knight (Orders of Chivalry).—*Envelope*, Sir F—— S——, followed by appropriate post-nominal letters. Otherwise as for **Knight Bachelor**.

Knight's wife.—As for **Baronet's wife**.

Marquess.—*Envelope (formal)*, The Most Hon. the Marquess of ——; *(social)*, The Marquess of ——. *Letter (formal)*, My Lord; *(social)*, Dear Lord ——. *Spoken (formal)*, My Lord; *(social)*, Lord ——.

Marquess's wife.—*Envelope (formal)*, The Most Hon. the Marchioness of ——; *(social)*, The Marchioness of ——. *Letter (formal)*, Madam; *(social)*, Dear Lady ——. *Spoken*, Lady ——.

Marquess's children.—*Eldest son*, see **Courtesy titles**. *Younger sons*, Lord F—— S—— (for forms of address, see **Duke's younger sons**). *Daughters*, Lady F—— S—— (for forms of address, see **Duke's daughter**).

Master.—The title is used by the heir apparent to a Scottish peerage, though usually the heir apparent to a Duke, Marquess or Earl uses his courtesy title rather than 'Master'. *Envelope*, The Master of ——. *Letter (formal)*, Dear Sir; *(social)*, Dear Master of ——. *Spoken (formal)*, Master, or Sir; *(social)*, Master, or Mr S——.

Master's wife.—Addressed as for the wife of the appropriate peerage style, otherwise as **Mrs S——**.

Privy Counsellors.—*Envelope*, The Right (or Rt.) Hon. F—— S——. *Letter*, Dear Mr/Miss/Mrs S——. *Spoken*, Mr/Miss/Mrs S——. It is incorrect to use the letters PC after the name, unless the Privy Counsellor is a peer below the rank of Marquess and so is styled The Right Hon. In this case the post-nominal letters may be used in conjunction with the prefix The Right Hon.

Viscount.—*Envelope (formal)*, The Right Hon. the Viscount ——; *(social)*, The Viscount ——. *Letter (formal)*, My Lord; *(social)*, Dear Lord ——. *Spoken*, Lord ——.

Viscount's wife.—*Envelope (formal)*, The Right Hon. the Viscountess of ——; *(social)*, The Viscountess ——. *Letter (formal)*, Madam; *(social)*, Dear Lady ——. *Spoken*, Lady ——.

Viscount's children.—As for **Baron's children**.

THE PEERAGE

The rules which govern the creation and succession of Peerages are extremely complicated. There are, technically, five separate Peerages, the Peerage of England, of Scotland, of Ireland, of Great Britain, and of the United Kingdom. The Peerage of Great Britain dates from 1707 when an Act of Union combined the two Kingdoms of England and Scotland and separate Peerages were discontinued; and the Peerage of the United Kingdom from 1801 when Great Britain and Ireland were combined under an Act of Union. Some Scottish Peers have received additional Peerages of Great Britain or of the United Kingdom since 1707, and some Irish Peers additional Peerages of the United Kingdom since 1801. The Peerage of Ireland was not entirely discontinued from 1801 but holders of Irish Peerages, whether pre-dating or created subsequent to the Union of 1801, are not entitled to sit in the House of Lords if they have no additional English, Scottish, Great Britain or United Kingdom Peerage. (However, they are eligible for election to the House of Commons and to vote in Parliamentary elections, which other Peers are not.) An Irish Peer holding a Peerage of a lower grade which enables him to sit in the House of Lords is introduced there by the title which enables him to sit, though for all other purposes he is known by his higher title. In the Peerage of Scotland there is no rank of Baron; the equivalent rank is Lord of Parliament, abbreviated to 'Lord' (the female equivalent is 'Lady'). All Peers of England, Scotland, Great Britain or the United Kingdom who are of full age (21 years) and of British nationality are entitled to sit in the House of Lords. Most hereditary peerages pass on death to the nearest male heir; but certain ancient Peerages pass on death to the nearest heir, male or female, and several are held by women (*see also* pp. 172–3). Since the Peerage Act, 1963, women Peers in their own Right have been entitled to sit in the House of Lords, subject to the same qualifications as men.

Non-hereditary or Life Peerages, in the degree of Baron or Baroness, have been conferred by the Crown since 1876 on eminent judges, the Lords of Appeal or Law Lords, to enable them to carry out the judicial functions of the House of Lords, and since 1958 on men and women of distinction in public life, giving them seats in the House of Lords. Life Peers are addressed identically as an hereditary Peer, and their children have the same courtesy style as the children of an hereditary Peer.

No fees for dignities have been payable since 1937. The House of Lords surrendered the ancient right of Peers to be tried for treason or felony by their peers in 1948.

Peerages Extinct Since the Last Issue

DUKEDOMS.—Portland (*cr.* 1716).
VISCOUNTCIES.—Barrington (*cr.* 1720I*).
BARONIES.—Jessel (*cr.* 1924); Marley (*cr.* 1930).

LIFE PEERAGES.—Kilbrandon (*cr.* 1971); Trafford (*cr.* 1987); Saint Brides (*cr.* 1977); Elwyn Jones (*cr.* 1974); Irving of Dartford (*cr.* 1979); Paget of Northampton (*cr.* 1974); McAlpine of Moffat (*cr.* 1980); Gardiner (*cr.* 1963); Maclean (*cr.* 1971); Stewart of Fulham (*cr.* 1979); Heycock (*cr.* 1967); Bruce-Gardyne (*cr.* 1983); Morris of Grasmere (*cr.* 1967); Fletcher (*cr.* 1970); O'Neill of the Maine (*cr.* 1970).

Disclaimer of Peerages

The Peerage Act, 1963, enables Peers to disclaim their Peerages for life. Peers alive in 1963 could disclaim within 12 months after the passing of the Act (July 31, 1963); a person subsequently succeeding to a Peerage may disclaim within 12 months (one month if an MP) after the date of succession, or of attaining his or her majority, if later. The disclaimer is irrevocable but does not affect the descent of the Peerage after the disclaimant's death, and children of a disclaimed Peer may, if they wish, retain their precedence and any courtesy titles and styles borne as children of a Peer.

EARLS: Durham (1970); Home (1963); Sandwich (1964).
VISCOUNTS: Hailsham (1963); Stansgate (1963).
BARONS: Altrincham (1963); Archibald (1975); Merthyr (1977); Reith (1972); Sanderson of Ayot (1971); Silkin (1972); Southampton (1964).

Peers Who Are Minors

EARLS: Hardwicke (*b.* 1971).
VISCOUNTS: Dillon (*b.* 1973).
BARONS: Gretton (*b.* 1975).

Composition of the House of Lords, see p. 231

Contractions and Symbols

S. or I. appended to the date of creation denotes a *Scottish* or *Irish* title, the further addition of a * implies that the Peer in question holds also an *Imperial* title, which is specified (after the name) by its more definite description as *Engl., Brit.*, or *UK*. When both titles are alike, as in the case of Argyll, this star is appended to the conjoined date below, and it then denotes that such date is that of the imperial creation.

°.—there is no 'of' in the Marquessate or Earldom so designated.
b.—born.
s.—succeeded.
m.—married.
w.—widower or widow.
M.—minor.
†—Information on *Eldest Son or Heir* not ascertained at time of going to press.

ROYAL DUKES

Style, His Royal Highness The Duke of ——.
Addressed as, Sir, or more formally, May it please your Royal Highness.

Created
1947 *Edinburgh,* The Prince Philip, Duke of Edinburgh, KG, KT, OM, GBE, PC, *b.* 1921, *m.* (*see* p. 142).
1337 *Cornwall,* Charles, Prince of Wales, Duke of Cornwall (*Scottish Duke, Rothesay,* 1398), KG, KT, GCB, PC, *b.* 1948, *m.* (*see* p. 142).
1986 *York,* The Prince Andrew, Duke of York, CVO, *b.* 1960, *m.* (*see* p. 143).
1928 *Gloucester* (2nd), Richard, Duke of Gloucester, GCVO, *b.* 1944, *s.* 1974, *m.* (*see* p. 141).
1934 *Kent* (2nd), Edward, Duke of Kent, KG, GCMG, GCVO, *b.* 1935, *s.* 1942, *m.* (*see* p. 141).

ARCHBISHOPS

Style.—The Most Rev. and Right Hon. the Lord Archbishop of——.
Addressed as, Archbishop; *or,* Your Grace.

Introd. to House of Lords

1973   *Canterbury* (102nd), Robert Alexander Kennedy Runcie, MC, PC,
        b. 1921, *m. Consecrated Bishop of St. Albans,* 1970, *trans.* 1980.

1973   *York* (95th), John Stapylton Habgood, PC, PH.D., *b.* 1927, *m.*
        Consecrated Bishop of Durham, 1973, *trans.* 1983.

(A life peerage was conferred on Archbishop Runcie in the Queen's Birthday Honours but no title had been announced at the time of going to press. Archbishop Runcie retires in January 1991.

DUKES

Coronet.—Strawberry leaves on a circlet.
Style.—His Grace the Duke of——.
Wife's style.—Her Grace the Duchess of——.
Eldest son's style.—Takes his father's second title as a courtesy title.
Younger sons' style.—'Lord' before forename and family name.
Daughters' style.—'Lady' before forename and family name.
For forms of address, *see* page 151.

Created	Title, Order of Succession, Name, etc.	Eldest Son or Heir
1868 I.*	*Abercorn* (5th), James Hamilton (6th *Brit. Marq.,* 1790, and 14th *Scott. Earl,* 1606 both *Abercorn*), *b.* 1934, *s.* 1979, *m.*	Marquess of Hamilton, *b.* 1969.
1701 s. } 1892* }	*Argyll,* Ian Campbell (12th *Scottish* and 5th *UK Duke, Argyll*), *b.* 1937, *s.* 1973, *m.*	Marquess of Lorne, *b.* 1968.
1703 s.	*Atholl* (10th), George Iain Murray, *b.* 1931, *s.* 1957.	Godfrey P. *M.,* DSO, *b.* 1901.
1682	*Beaufort* (11th), David Robert Somerset, *b.* 1928, *s.* 1984, *m.*	Marquess of Worcester, *b.* 1952.
1694	*Bedford* (13th), John Robert Russell, *b.* 1917, *s.* 1953, *m.*	Marquess of Tavistock, *b.* 1940.
1663 s.*	*Buccleuch* (9th) & *Queensberry* (11th) (1684), Walter Francis John Montagu Douglas Scott, KT, VRD (8th *Engl. Earl, Doncaster,* 1662), *b.* 1923, *s.* 1973, *m.*	Earl of Dalkeith, *b.* 1954.
1694	*Devonshire* (11th), Andrew Robert Buxton Cavendish, MC, PC, *b.* 1920, *s.* 1950, *m.*	Marquess of Hartington, *b.* 1944.
1900	*Fife* (3rd), James George Alexander Bannerman Carnegie, *b.* 1929, *s.* 1959. *(see* p. 139).	Earl of Macduff, *b.* 1961.
1675	*Grafton* (11th), Hugh Denis Charles FitzRoy, KG, *b.* 1919, *s.* 1970, *m.*	Earl of Euston, *b.* 1947.
1643 s.*	*Hamilton* (15th) & *Brandon* (12th) (*Brit.* 1711), Angus Alan Douglas Douglas-Hamilton (*Premier Peer of Scotland*), *b.* 1938, *s.* 1973, *m.*	Marquess of Douglas and Clydesdale, *b.* 1978.
1766 I.*	*Leinster* (8th), Gerald FitzGerald (*Premier Duke, Marquess and Earl of Ireland;* 8th *Brit. Visct., Leinster,* 1747) *b.* 1914, *s.* 1976, *m.*	Marquess of Kildare, *b.* 1948.
1719	*Manchester* (12th), Angus Charles Drogo Montagu, *b.* 1938, *s.* 1985, *m.*	Viscount Mandeville, *b.* 1962.
1702	*Marlborough* (11th), John George Vanderbilt Henry Spencer-Churchill, *b.* 1926, *s.* 1972, *m.*	Marquess of Blandford, *b.* 1955.
1707 s.*	*Montrose* (7th), James Angus Graham (5th *Brit. Earl, Graham,* 1722), *b.* 1907, *s.* 1954, *m.*	Marquess of Graham, *b.* 1935.
1483	*Norfolk* (17th), Miles Francis Stapleton Fitzalan-Howard, KG, GCVO, CB, CBE, MC (*Premier Duke and Earl;* 12th *Eng. Baron Beaumont,* 1309, *s.* 1971; 4th *UK Baron Howard of Glossop,* 1869, *s.* 1972), *b.* 1915, *s.* 1975, *m.* (*Earl Marshal*).	Earl of Arundel and Surrey, *b.* 1956.
1766	*Northumberland* (11th), Henry Alan Walter Richard Percy, *b.* 1953, *s.* 1988.	Lord Ralph G.A.*P., b.* 1956.
1675	*Richmond* (10th) & *Gordon* (5th) (*UK* 1876), Charles Henry Gordon Lennox (10th *Scott. Duke, Lennox,* 1675), *b.* 1929, *s.* 1989, *m.*	Earl of March and Kinrara, *b.* 1955.
1707 s.*	*Roxburghe* (10th), Guy David Innes-Ker (5th *UK Earl, Innes,* 1837), *b.* 1954, *s.* 1974. (*Premier Baronet of Scotland*).	Marquess of Bowmont and Cessford, *b.* 1981.
1703	*Rutland* (10th), Charles John Robert Manners, CBE, *b.* 1919, *s.* 1940, *m.*	Marquess of Granby, *b.* 1959.
1684	*St. Albans* (14th), Murray de Vere Beauclerk, *b.* 1939, *s.* 1988, *m.*	Earl of Burford, *b.* 1965.
1547	*Somerset* (19th), John Michael Edward Seymour, *b.* 1952, *s.* 1984, *m.*	Lord Seymour, *b.* 1982.
1833	*Sutherland* (6th), John Sutherland Egerton, TD (5th *UK Earl Ellesmere,* 1846), *b.* 1915, *s.* 1963, *m.*	Cyril R. *E., b.* 1905.
1814	*Wellington* (8th), Arthur Valerian Wellesley, KG, LVO, OBE, MC (9th *Irish Earl, Mornington,* 1760), *b.* 1915, *s.* 1972, *m.*	Marquess of Douro, *b.* 1945.
1874	*Westminster* (6th), Gerald Cavendish Grosvenor, *b.* 1951, *s.* 1979, *m.*	None to Dukedom. To Marquessate of Westminster, Earl of Wilton, *b.* 1921 (*see* p. 159).

MARQUESSES

Coronet.—Strawberry leaves alternating with silver balls.
Style.—The Most Hon. the Marquess of——. (In Scotland the spelling 'Marquis' is
preferred for pre-Union creations.)
Wife's style.—The Most Hon. the Marchioness of——.
Eldest son's style.—Takes his father's second title as a courtesy title.
Younger sons' style.—'Lord' before forename and family name.
Daughters' style.—'Lady' before forename and family name.
For forms of address, *see* page 151.

Created	Title, Order of Succession, Name, etc.	Eldest Son or Heir
1916	*Aberdeen and Temair* (6th), Alastair Ninian John Gordon (12th Scott. Earl, Aberdeen, 1682), b. 1920, s. 1984, m.	Earl of Haddo, b. 1955.
1876	*Abergavenny* (5th), John Henry Guy Nevill, KG, OBE, b. 1914, s. 1954, m.	Guy R. G. N., b. 1945.
1821	*Ailesbury* (8th), Michael Sidney Cedric Brudenell-Bruce, b. 1926, s. 1974, m.	Earl of Cardigan, b. 1952.
1831	*Ailsa* (7th), Archibald David Kennedy, OBE, (19th Scott. Earl, Cassillis, 1509), b. 1925, s. 1957, m.	Earl of Cassillis, b. 1956.
1815	*Anglesey* (7th), George Charles Henry Victor Paget, b. 1922, s. 1947, m.	Earl of Uxbridge, b. 1950.
1789	*Bath* (6th), Henry Frederick Thynne, b. 1905, s. 1946, m.	Viscount Weymouth, b. 1932.
1826	*Bristol* (7th), (Frederick William) John Augustus Hervey, b. 1954, s. 1985.	Lord F. W. C. Nicholas W. H., b. 1961.
1796	*Bute* (6th), John Crichton-Stuart (11th Scott. Earl, Dumfries, 1633), b. 1933, s. 1956, m.	Earl of Dumfries, b. 1958.
1812	°*Camden* (6th), David George Edward Henry Pratt, b. 1930, s. 1983.	Earl of Brecknock, b. 1965.
1815	*Cholmondeley* (7th), David George Philip Cholmondeley (11th Irish Viscount, Cholmondeley, 1661), b. 1960, s. 1990. (Lord Great Chamberlain).	Charles G. C., b. 1959.
1816 I.*	°*Conyngham* (7th), Frederick William Henry Francis Conyngham (7th UK Baron, Minster, UK 1821), b. 1924, s. 1974, m.	Earl of Mount Charles, b. 1951.
1791 I.	*Donegall* (7th), Dermot Richard Claud Chichester, LVO (7th Brit. Baron, Fisherwick, 1790, 6th Brit. Baron, Templemore, 1831), b. 1916, s. to Marquessate, 1975: to Templemore Barony, 1953, m.	Earl of Belfast, b. 1952.
1789 I.*	*Downshire* (8th), (Arthur) Robin Ian Hill (8th Brit. Earl, Hillsborough, 1772), b. 1929, s. 1989, m.	Earl of Hillsborough, b. 1959.
1801 I.*	*Ely* (8th) Charles John Tottenham (8th UK Baron, Loftus, 1801), b. 1913, s. 1969, m.	Viscount Loftus, b. 1943.
1801	*Exeter* (8th), (William) Michael Anthony Cecil, b. 1935, s. 1988, m.	Lord Burghley, b. 1970.
1800 I.*	*Headfort* (6th), Thomas Geoffrey Charles Michael Taylour (4th UK Baron, Kenlis, 1831), b. 1932, s. 1960, m.	Earl of Bective, b. 1959.
1793	*Hertford* (8th), Hugh Edward Conway Seymour (9th Irish Baron, Conway, 1712), b. 1930, s. 1940, m.	Earl of Yarmouth, b. 1958.
1599 s.*	*Huntly* (13th), Granville Charles Gomer Gordon (Premier Marquess of Scotland) (5th UK Baron, Meldrum, 1815), b. 1944, s. 1987, m.	Earl of Aboyne, b. 1973.
1784	*Lansdowne* (8th), George John Charles Mercer Nairne Petty-Fitzmaurice, PC (8th Irish Earl, Kerry, 1723), b. 1912, s. 1944, w.	Earl of Shelburne, b. 1941.
1902	*Linlithgow* (4th), Adrian John Charles Hope (10th Scott. Earl, Hopetoun 1703), b. 1946, s. 1987, m.	Earl of Hopetoun, b. 1969.
1816 I.*	*Londonderry* (9th), Alexander Charles Robert Vane-Tempest-Stewart (6th UK Earl, Vane, 1823), b. 1937, s. 1955, m.	Viscount Castlereagh, b. 1972.
1701 s.*	*Lothian* (12th), Peter Francis Walter Kerr, KCVO (6th UK Baron, Kerr, 1821), b. 1922, s. 1940, m.	Earl of Ancram, b. 1945.
1917	*Milford Haven* (4th),George Ivar Louis Mountbatten,b.1961, s.1970,m.	Lord Ivar A. M. M., b. 1963.
1838	*Normanby* (4th), Oswald Constantine John Phipps, KG, CBE (8th Irish Baron, Mulgrave, 1767), b. 1912, s. 1932, m.	Earl of Mulgrave, b. 1954.
1812	*Northampton* (7th), Spencer Douglas David Compton, b. 1946, s. 1978.	Earl Compton, b. 1973.
1825 I.*	*Ormonde* (7th), James Hubert Theobald Charles Butler, MBE (7th UK Baron, Ormonde, 1821), b. 1899, s. 1971, w.	None to Marquessate. To Earldoms of Ormonde and Ossory, Viscount Mountgarret, b. 1936 (see, p. 161).
1682 s.	*Queensberry* (12th), David Harrington Angus Douglas, b. 1929, s. 1954.	Viscount Drumlanrig, b. 1967.
1926	*Reading* (4th), Simon Charles Henry Rufus Isaacs, b. 1942, s. 1980, m.	Viscount Erleigh, b. 1986.
1789	*Salisbury* (6th), Robert Edward Peter Cecil, b. 1916, s. 1972, m.	Viscount Cranborne, b. 1946.
1800 I.*	*Sligo* (10th), Denis Edward Browne (10th UK Baron, Monteagle, 1806), b. 1908, s. 1952, m.	Earl of Altamont, b. 1939.
1787	°*Townshend* (7th), George John Patrick Dominic Townshend, b. 1916, s. 1921, w.	Viscount Raynham, b. 1945.
1694 s.*	*Tweeddale* (13th), Edward Douglas John Hay (4th UK Baron, Tweeddale, 1881), b. 1947, s. 1979.	Lord Charles D. M. H., b. 1947.
1789 I.*	*Waterford* (8th), John Hubert de la Poer Beresford (8th Brit. Baron, Tyrone, 1786), b. 1933, s. 1934, m.	Earl of Tyrone, b. 1958.
1551	*Winchester* (18th), Nigel George Paulet (Premier Marquess of England), b. 1941, s. 1968, m.	Earl of Wiltshire, b. 1969.
1892	*Zetland* (4th), Lawrence Mark Dundas (6th UK Earl of Zetland, 1838, 7th Brit. Baron Dundas, 1794), b. 1937, s. 1989, m.	Earl of Ronaldshay, b. 1965.

EARLS

Coronet.—Five silver balls on stalks alternating with four gold strawberry leaves.
Style.—The Right Hon. the Earl of——.
Wife's style.—The Right Hon. the Countess of——.
Eldest son's style.—Takes his father's second title as a courtesy title.
Younger sons' style.—'The Hon.' before forename and family name.
Daughters' style.—'Lady' before forename and family name.
For forms of address, *see* page 151.

Created	Title, Order of Succession, Name, etc.	Eldest Son or Heir
1639 s.	*Airlie* (13th), David George Coke Patrick Ogilvy, KT, GCVO, PC, *b.* 1926, *s.* 1968, *m.* (*Lord Chamberlain*).	Lord Ogilvy, *b.* 1958.
1696	*Albemarle* (10th), Rufus Arnold Alexis Keppel, *b.* 1965, *s.* 1979.	Crispian W. J. K., *b.* 1948.
1952	°*Alexander of Tunis* (2nd), Shane William Desmond Alexander, *b.* 1935, *s.* 1969, *m.*	Hon. Brian J. A., *b.* 1939.
1826	°*Amherst* (5th), Jeffery John Archer Amherst, MC, *b.* 1896, *s.* 1927.	(None.)
1662 s.	*Annandale and Hartfell* (11th), Patrick Andrew Wentworth Hope Johnstone, *b.* 1941, *claim established* 1985, *m.*	Lord Johnstone, *b.* 1971.
1789 I.	°*Annesley* (10th), Patrick Annesley, *b.* 1924, *s.* 1979, *m.*	Hon. Philip H.A., *b.* 1927.
1785 I.	*Antrim* (9th), Alexander Randal Mark McDonnell, *b.* 1935, *s.* 1977, *m.* (*Viscount Dunluce.*)	Hon. Randal A. St. J. M., *b.* 1967.
1762 I.*	*Arran* (9th), Arthur Desmond Colquhoun Gore (5th *UK Baron Sudley,* 1884), *b.* 1938, *s.* 1983, *m.*	Paul A. G., CMG, CVO, *b.* 1921.
1955	°*Attlee* (2nd), Martin Richard Attlee, *b.* 1927, *s.* 1967, *m.*	Viscount Prestwood, *b.* 1956.
1714	*Aylesford* (11th), Charles Ian Finch-Knightley, *b.* 1918, *s.* 1958, *m.*	Lord Guernsey, *b.* 1947.
1937	°*Baldwin of Bewdley* (4th), Edward Alfred Alexander Baldwin, *b.* 1938, *s.* 1976, *m.*	Viscount Corvedale, *b.* 1973.
1922	*Balfour* (4th), Gerald Arthur James Balfour, *b.* 1925, *s.* 1968, *m.*	Eustace A. G. B., *b.* 1921.
1772	°*Bathurst* (8th), Henry Allen John Bathurst, *b.* 1927, *s.* 1943, *m.*	Lord Apsley, *b.* 1961.
1919	°*Beatty* (3rd), David Beatty, *b.* 1946, *s.* 1972.	Viscount Borodale, *b.* 1973.
1797 I.	*Belmore* (8th), John Armar Lowry-Corry, *b.* 1951, *s.* 1960, *m.*	Viscount Corry, *b.* 1985.
1739 I.* } 1937 }	*Bessborough,* Frederick Edward Neuflize Ponsonby (10th *Irish* and 2nd *UK Earl Bessborough*), *b.* 1913, *s.* 1956, *m.*	Arthur M. L. P., *b.* 1912 (to Irish Earldom only).
1815	*Bradford* (7th), Richard Thomas Orlando Bridgeman, *b.* 1947, *s.* 1981, *m.*	Viscount Newport, *b.*1980.
1677 s.	*Breadalbane and Holland* (10th), John Romer Boreland Campbell, *b.* 1919, *s.* 1959.	(None.)
1469 s.*	*Buchan* (17th), Malcolm Harry Erskine, (8th *UK Baron Erskine* 1806), *b.* 1930, *s.* 1984, *m.*	Lord Cardross, *b.* 1960.
1746	*Buckinghamshire* (10th), (George) Miles Hobart-Hampden, *b.* 1944, *s.* 1983, *m.*	Sir John V. Hobart, Bt., *b.* 1945.
1800	°*Cadogan* (7th), William Gerald Charles Cadogan, MC, *b.* 1914, *s.* 1933, *m.*	Viscount Chelsea, *b.* 1937.
1878	°*Cairns* (6th), Simon Dallas Cairns, *b.* 1939, *s.* 1989, *m.*	Viscount Garmoyle, *b.* 1965.
1455 s.	*Caithness* (20th), Malcolm Ian Sinclair, PC, *b.* 1948, *s.* 1965, *m.*	Lord Berriedale, *b.* 1981.
1800 I.	*Caledon* (7th), Nicholas James Alexander, *b.* 1955, *s.* 1980, *m.*	Earl Alexander of Tunis (*see* above).
1661	*Carlisle* (12th), Charles James Ruthven Howard, MC (12th *Scott. Baron, Ruthven of Freeland,* 1651), *b.* 1923, *s.* 1963, *m.*	Viscount Morpeth, *b.* 1949.
1793	*Carnarvon* (7th), Henry George Reginald Molyneux Herbert, KCVO, KBE, *b.* 1924, *s.* 1987, *m.*	Lord Porchester, *b.* 1956.
1748 I.*	*Carrick* (9th), Brian Stuart Theobald Somerset Caher Butler (3rd *UK Baron, Butler,* 1912), *b.* 1931, *s.* 1957, *m.*	Viscount Ikerrin, *b.* 1953.
1800 I.	°*Castle Stewart* (8th), Arthur Patrick Avondale Stuart, *b.* 1928, *s.* 1961, *m.*	Viscount Stuart, *b.* 1953.
1814	°*Cathcart* (6th), Alan Cathcart, CB, DSO, MC (15th *Scott. Baron, Cathcart,* 1447), *b.* 1919, *s.* 1927, *m.*	Lord Greenock, *b.* 1952.
1647 I.	*Cavan* (13th), Roger Cavan Lambart, *b.* 1944, *s.* 1988.	Arthur O. R. L., *b.* 1909.
1827	°*Cawdor* (6th), Hugh John Vaughan Campbell, *b.* 1932, *s.* 1970, *m.*	Viscount Emlyn, *b.* 1962.
1801	*Chichester* (9th), John Nicholas Pelham, *b.* 1944, *s.* 1944, *m.*	Richard A. H. P., *b.* 1952.
1803 I.*	°*Clancarty* (8th), William Francis Brinsley Le Poer Trench (7th *UK Visct. Clancarty,* 1823), *b.* 1911, *s.* 1975, *m.*	Nicholas P. R. *Le P. T.,* *b.* 1952.
1776 I.*	*Clanwilliam* (7th), John Herbert Meade (5th *UK Baron Clanwilliam,* 1828), *b.* 1919, *s.* 1989, *m.*	Lord Gillford, *b.* 1960.
1776	*Clarendon* (7th), George Frederick Laurence Hyde Villiers, *b.* 1933, *s.* 1955, *m.*	Lord Hyde, *b.* 1976.
1620 I.*	*Cork* (13th) *& Orrery* (13th)(I. 1660), Patrick Reginald Boyle (9th *Brit. Baron, Boyle of Marston,* 1711), *b.* 1910, *s.* 1967, *m.*	Hon. John W. B., DSC, *b.* 1916.
1850	*Cottenham* (8th), Kenelm Charles Everard Digby Pepys, *b.* 1948, *s.* 1968, *m.*	Viscount Crowhurst, *b.* 1983.
1762 I.*	*Courtown* (9th), James Patrick Montagu Burgoyne Winthrop Stopford (8th *Brit. Baron, Saltersford,* 1796), *b.* 1954, *s.* 1975, *m.*	Viscount Stopford, *b.* 1988.
1697	*Coventry* (11th), George William Coventry, *b.* 1934, *s.* 1940, *m.*	Viscount Deerhurst, *b.* 1957.
1857	°*Cowley* (7th), Garret Graham Wellesley, *b.* 1934, *s.* 1975, *m.*	Viscount Dangan, *b.* 1965.
1892	*Cranbrook* (5th), Gathorne Gathorne-Hardy, *b.* 1933, *s.* 1978, *m.*	Lord Medway, *b.* 1968.

Created	Title, Order of Succession, Name, etc.	Eldest Son or Heir
1801	Craven (9th), Rupert José Evelyn Craven, b. 1926, s. 1990, w.	None to Earldom. To Barony of Craven, Edmund F. C., b. 1917.
1398 s.*	Crawford (29th) & Balcarres (12th) (s. 1651), Robert Alexander Lindsay, PC, (Premier Earl on Union Roll, 5th UK Baron, Wigan, 1826, and Baron Balniel (Life Peer)), b. 1927, s. 1975, m.	Lord Balniel, b. 1958.
1861	Cromartie (5th), John Ruaridh Blunt Grant Mackenzie, b. 1948, s. 1989, m.	Viscount Tarbat, b. 1987.
1901	Cromer (3rd), George Rowland Stanley Baring, KG, GCMG, MBE, PC, b. 1918, s. 1953, m.	Viscount Errington, b. 1946.
1633 s.*	Dalhousie (16th), Simon Ramsay, KT, GCVO, GBE, MC (4th UK Baron, Ramsay, 1875), b. 1914, s. 1950, m.	Lord Ramsay, b. 1948.
1725 I.*	Darnley (11th), Adam Ivo Stuart Bligh (20th English Baron, Clifton of Leighton Bromswold, 1608), b. 1941, s. 1980, m.	Lord Clifton, b. 1968.
1711	Dartmouth (9th), Gerald Humphry Legge, b. 1924, s. 1962, m.	Viscount Lewisham, b. 1949.
1761	°De La Warr (11th), William Herbrand Sackville, b. 1948, s. 1988, m.	Lord Buckhurst, b. 1979.
1622	Denbigh (11th) & Desmond (10th) (I. 1622), William Rudolph Michael Feilding, b. 1943, s. 1966, m.	Viscount Feilding, b. 1970.
1485	Derby (18th), Edward John Stanley, MC, b. 1918, s. 1948, w.	Edward R. W. S., b. 1962.
1553	Devon (17th), Charles Christopher Courtenay, b. 1916, s. 1935, m.	Lord Courtenay, b. 1942.
1800 I.*	Donoughmore (8th), Richard Michael John Hely-Hutchinson (8th UK Visct. Hutchinson, 1821), b. 1927, s. 1981, m.	Viscount Suirdale, b. 1952.
1661 I.*	Drogheda (12th), Henry Dermot Ponsonby Moore, (3rd UK Baron, Moore, 1954), b. 1937, s. 1989, m.	Viscount Moore, b. 1983.
1837	Ducie (6th), Basil Howard Moreton, b. 1917, s. 1952, m.	Lord Moreton, b. 1951.
1860	Dudley (4th), William Humble David Ward, b. 1920, s. 1969, m.	Viscount Ednam, b. 1947.
1660 s.*	Dundee (12th), Alexander Henry Scrymgeour, (2nd UK Baron, Glassary, 1954), b. 1949, s. 1983, m.	Lord Scrymgeour, b. 1982.
1669 s.	Dundonald (15th), Iain Alexander Douglas Blair Cochrane, b. 1961, s. 1986, m.	Baron Cochrane of Cults, b. 1926 (see, p. 165).
1686 s.	Dunmore (11th), Kenneth Randolph Murray, b. 1913, s. 1981, w.	Viscount Fincastle, b. 1946.
1822 I.	Dunraven and Mount-Earl (7th), Thady Windham Thomas Wyndham-Quin, b. 1939, s. 1965, m.	(None).
1833	Durham. Disclaimed for life 1970.	
1837	Effingham (6th), Mowbray Henry Gordon Howard (16th E. Baron, Howard of Effingham, 1554), b. 1905, s. 1946, m.	Lt.-Cdr. David P. M. A. H., b. 1939.
1507 s. 1859*	} Eglinton (18th) & Winton (9th) (1600), Archibald George Montgomerie (6th UK Earl Winton, 1859), b. 1939, s. 1966, m.	Lord Montgomerie, b. 1966.
1733 I.*	Egmont (11th), Frederick George Moore Perceval (9th Brit. Baron, Lovel & Holland, 1762), b. 1914, s. 1932, m.	Viscount Perceval, b. 1934.
1821	Eldon (5th), John Joseph Nicholas Scott, b. 1937, s. 1976, m.	Viscount Encombe, b. 1962.
1633 s.*	Elgin (11th), & Kincardine (15th) (s. 1647), Andrew Douglas Alexander Thomas Bruce (4th UK Baron, Elgin, 1849), KT, b. 1924, s. 1968, m.	Lord Bruce, b. 1961.
1789 I.*	Enniskillen (7th), Andrew John Galbraith Cole (5th UK Baron, Grinstead, 1815) b. 1942, s. 1989, m.	Arthur G. C., b. 1920.
1789 I.*	Erne (6th), Henry George Victor John Crichton (3rd UK Baron, Fermanagh, 1876), b. 1937, s. 1940, m.	Viscount Crichton, b. 1971.
1452 s.	Erroll (24th), Merlin Sereld Victor Gilbert Hay (Hereditary Lord High Constable and Knight Marischal of Scotland), b. 1948, s. 1978, m.	Lord Hay, b. 1984.
1661	Essex (10th), Robert Edward de Vere Capell, b. 1920, s. 1981, m.	Viscount Malden, b. 1944.
1711	°Ferrers (13th), Robert Washington Shirley, PC, b. 1929, s. 1954, m.	Viscount Tamworth, b. 1952.
1789	°Fortescue (7th), Richard Archibald Fortescue, b. 1922, s. 1977, m.	Viscount Ebrington, b. 1951.
1841	Gainsborough (5th), Anthony Gerard Edward Noel, b. 1923, s. 1927, m.	Viscount Campden, b. 1950.
1623 s.*	Galloway (13th), Randolph Keith Reginald Stewart (6th Brit. Baron, Stewart of Garlies, 1796), b. 1928, s. 1978, m.	Andrew C. S., b. 1949.
1703 s.*	Glasgow (10th), Patrick Robin Archibald Boyle (4th UK Baron, Fairlie, 1897), b. 1939, s. 1984, m.	Viscount of Kelburn, b. 1978.
1806 I.*	Gosford (7th), Charles David Nicholas Alexander John Sparrow Acheson (5th UK Baron, Worlingham, 1835), b. 1942, s. 1966, m.	Hon. Patrick B. V. M. A., b. 1915.
1945	Gowrie (2nd), Alexander Patric Greysteil Hore-Ruthven, PC (3rd UK Baron, Ruthven of Gowrie, 1919), b. 1939, s. 1955, m.	Viscount Ruthven of Canberra, b. 1964.
1684 I.*	Granard (9th), Arthur Patrick Hastings Forbes, AFC (4th UK Baron, Granard, 1806), b. 1915, s. 1948, m.	Peter A. E. H. F., b. 1957.
1833	°Granville (5th), Granville James Leveson-Gower, MC, b. 1918, s. 1953, m.	Lord Leveson, b. 1959.
1806	°Grey (6th), Richard Fleming George Charles Grey, b. 1939, s. 1963, m.	Philip K. G., b. 1940.
1752	Guilford (9th), Edward Francis North, b. 1933, s. 1949, m.	Lord North, b. 1971.
1619 s.	Haddington (13th), John George Baillie-Hamilton, b. 1941, s. 1986, m.	Lord Binning, b. 1985.
1919	°Haig (2nd), George Alexander Eugene Douglas Haig, OBE, b. 1918, s. 1928, m.	Viscount Dawick, b. 1961.
1944	Halifax (3rd), Charles Edward Peter Neil Wood (5th UK Viscount, Halifax, 1866), b. 1944, s. 1980, m.	Lord Irwin, b. 1977.

Created	Title, Order of Succession, Name, etc.	Eldest Son or Heir
1898	*Halsbury* (3rd), John Anthony Hardinge Giffard, FRS, *b.* 1908, *s.* 1943, *w.*	Adam E. *G.*, *b.* 1934.
1754	*Hardwicke* (10th), Joseph Philip Sebastian Yorke, *b.* 1971, *s.* 1974, *M.*	Richard C. J. *Y.*, *b.* 1916.
1812	*Harewood* (7th), George Henry Hubert Lascelles, KBE, *b.* 1923, *s.* 1947, *m.* (*See also* p. 141).	Viscount Lascelles, *b.* 1950.
1742	*Harrington* (11th), William Henry Leicester Stanhope (8th *Brit. Viscount, Stanhope of Mahon,* 1717), *b.* 1922, *s.* 1929, *m.*	Viscount Petersham, *b.* 1945.
1809	*Harrowby* (7th), Dudley Danvers Granville Coutts Ryder, TD, *b.* 1922, *s.* 1987, *m.*	Viscount Sandon, *b.* 1951.
1605 s.	*Home. Disclaimed for life* 1963.	
1821	°*Howe* (7th), Frederick Richard Penn Curzon, *b.* 1951, *s.* 1984, *m.*	Charles M. P. *C.*, *b.* 1967.
1529	*Huntingdon* (16th), William Edward Robin Hood Hastings Bass, *b.* 1948, *s.* 1990, *m.*	Simon A. R. H. *H. B.*, *b.* 1950.
1885	*Iddesleigh* (4th), Stafford Henry Northcote, *b.* 1932, *s.* 1970, *m.*	Viscount St. Cyres, *b.* 1957.
1756	*Ilchester* (9th), Maurice Vivian de Touffreville Fox-Strangways, *b.* 1920, *s.* 1970, *m.*	Hon. Raymond G. *F.-S.*, *b.* 1921.
1929	*Inchcape* (3rd), Kenneth James William Mackay, *b.* 1917, *s.* 1939, *m.*	Viscount Glenapp, *b.* 1943.
1919	*Iveagh* (3rd), Arthur Francis Benjamin Guinness, *b.* 1937, *s.* 1967.	Viscount Elveden, *b.* 1969.
1925	°*Jellicoe* (2nd), George Patrick John Rushworth Jellicoe, KBE, DSO, MC, PC, *b.* 1918, *s.* 1935, *m.*	Viscount Brocas, *b.* 1950.
1697	*Jersey* (9th), George Francis Child-Villiers (12th *Irish Visct., Grandison,* 1620), *b.* 1910, *s.* 1923, *m.*	Viscount Villiers, *b.* 1948.
1822 I.	*Kilmorey* (6th), Richard Francis Needham, MP, *b.* 1942, *s.* 1977, *m.*	Viscount Newry and Morne, *b.* 1966.
1866	*Kimberley* (4th), John Wodehouse, *b.* 1924, *s.* 1941, *m.*	Lord Wodehouse, *b.* 1951.
1768 I.	*Kingston* (11th), Barclay Robert Edwin King-Tenison, *b.* 1943, *s.* 1948, *m.*	Viscount Kingsborough, *b.* 1969.
1633 s.*	*Kinnoull* (15th), Arthur William George Patrick Hay (9th *Brit. Baron, Hay of Pedwardine,* 1711), *b.* 1935, *s.* 1938, *m.*	Viscount Dupplin, *b.* 1962.
1677 s.*	*Kintore* (13th), Michael Canning William John Keith (3rd *UK Visct., Stonehaven,* 1938), *b.* 1939, *s.* 1989, *m.*	Lord Inverurie, *b.* 1976.
1914	°*Kitchener of Khartoum* (3rd), Henry Herbert Kitchener, TD, *b.* 1919, *s.* 1937.	(None.)
1756 I.	*Lanesborough* (9th), Denis Anthony Brian Butler, TD, *b.* 1918, *s.* 1950.	Henry A. B. C. *B.*, *b.* 1909.
1624 s.	*Lauderdale* (17th), Patrick Francis Maitland, *b.* 1911, *s.* 1968, *m.*	Viscount Maitland, *b.* 1937.
1837	*Leicester* (6th), Anthony Louis Lovel Coke, *b.* 1909, *s.* 1976, *m.*	Viscount Coke, *b.* 1936.
1641 s.	*Leven* (14th) *& Melville* (13th) (s. 1690), Alexander Robert Leslie Melville, *b.* 1924, *s.* 1947, *m.*	Lord Balgonie, *b.* 1954.
1831	*Lichfield* (5th), Thomas Patrick John Anson, *b.* 1939, *s.* 1960.	Viscount Anson, *b.* 1978.
1803 I.*	*Limerick* (6th), Patrick Edmund Pery, KBE (6th *UK Baron, Foxford,* 1815), *b.* 1930, *s.* 1967, *m.*	Viscount Glentworth, *b.* 1963.
1572	*Lincoln* (18th), Edward Horace Fiennes-Clinton, *b.* 1913, *s.* 1988, *m.*	Hon. Edward G. *F.-C.*, *b.* 1943.
1633 s.	*Lindsay* (16th), James Randolph Lindesay-Bethune, *b.* 1955, *s.* 1989, *m.*	Hon. John M. *L.-B.*, *b.* 1929.
1626	*Lindsey* (14th) *and Abingdon* (9th) (1682), Richard Henry Rupert Bertie, *b.* 1931, *s.* 1963, *m.*	Lord Norreys, *b.* 1958.
1776 I.	*Lisburne* (8th), John David Malet Vaughan, *b.* 1918, *s.* 1965, *m.*	Viscount Vaughan, *b.* 1945.
1822 I.*	*Listowel* (5th), William Francis Hare, GCMG, PC, (3rd *UK Baron, Hare,* 1869), *b.* 1906, *s.* 1931, *m.*	Viscount Ennismore, *b.* 1964.
1905	*Liverpool* (5th), Edward Peter Bertram Savile Foljambe, *b.* 1944, *s.* 1969, *m.*	Viscount Hawkesbury, *b.* 1972.
1945	°*Lloyd George of Dwyfor* (3rd), Owen Lloyd George, *b.* 1924, *s.* 1968, *m.*	Viscount Gwynedd, *b.* 1951.
1785 I.*	*Longford* (7th), Francis Aungier Pakenham, KG, PC (6th *UK Baron, Silchester,* 1821; 1st *UK Baron, Pakenham,* 1945), *b.* 1905, *s.* 1961, *m.*	Thomas F. D. *P.*, *b.* 1933.
1807	*Lonsdale* (7th), James Hugh William Lowther, *b.* 1922, *s.* 1953, *m.*	Viscount Lowther, *b.* 1949.
1838	*Lovelace* (5th), Peter Axel William Locke King (12th *British Baron, King,* 1725), *b.* 1951, *s.* 1964, *m.*	(None.)
1795 I.*	*Lucan* (7th), Richard John Bingham (3rd *UK Baron, Bingham,* 1934), *b.* 1934, *s.* 1964, *m.*	Lord Bingham, *b.* 1967.
1880	*Lytton* (5th), John Peter Michael Scawen Lytton (18th *English Baron, Wentworth,* 1529), *b.* 1950, *s.* 1985, *m.*	Viscount Knebworth, *b.* 1989.
1721	*Macclesfield* (8th), George Roger Alexander Thomas Parker, *b.* 1914, *s.* 1975, *m.*	Viscount Parker, *b.* 1943.
1800	*Malmesbury* (6th), William James Harris, TD, *b.* 1907, *s.* 1950, *w.*	Viscount FitzHarris, *b.* 1946.
1776 &	*Mansfield and Mansfield* (8th), William David Mungo James Murray	Viscount Stormont, *b.* 1956.
1792	(14th *Scott. Visct., Stormont,* 1621), *b.* 1930, *s.* 1971, *m.*	
1565 s.	*Mar* (13th) *& Kellie* (15th) (s. 1616), John Francis Hervey Erskine, *b.* 1921, *s.* 1955, *m.*	Lord Erskine, *b.* 1949.
1785 I.	*Mayo* (10th), Terence Patrick Bourke, *b.* 1929, *s.* 1962, *m.*	Lord Naas, *b.* 1953.
1627 I.*	*Meath* (14th), Anthony Windham Normand Brabazon (5th *UK Baron, Chaworth,* 1831), *b.* 1910, *s.* 1949, *m.*	Lord Ardee, *b.* 1941.
1766 I.	*Mexborough* (8th), John Christopher George Savile, *b.* 1931, *s.* 1980, *m.*	Viscount Pollington, *b.* 1959.
1813	*Minto* (6th), Gilbert Edward George Lariston Elliot-Murray-Kynynmound, OBE, *b.* 1928, *s.* 1975, *w.*	Viscount Melgund, *b.* 1953.

Created	Title, Order of Succession, Name, etc.	Eldest Son or Heir
1562 s.*	*Moray* (20th) Douglas John Moray Stuart (12th *Brit. Baron, Stuart of Castle Stuart*, 1796), *b.* 1928, *s.* 1974, *m.*	Lord Doune, *b.* 1966.
1815	*Morley* (6th), John St. Aubyn Parker, *b.* 1923, *s.* 1962, *m.*	Viscount Boringdon, *b.* 1956.
1458 s.	*Morton* (22nd), John Charles Sholto Douglas, *b.* 1927, *s.* 1976, *m.*	Lord Aberdour, *b.* 1952.
1789	*Mount Edgcumbe* (8th), Robert Charles Edgcumbe, *b.* 1939, *s.* 1982, *m.*	Piers V. E., *b.* 1946.
1831	*Munster* (7th), Anthony Charles FitzClarence, *b.* 1926, *s.* 1983, *m.*	(None.)
1805	°*Nelson* (9th), Peter John Horatio Nelson, *b.* 1941, *s.* 1981, *m.*	Viscount Merton, *b.* 1971.
1660 s.	*Newburgh* (12th), Prince Filippo Giambattista Francesco Aldo Maria Rospigliosi, *b.* 1942, *s.* 1986, *m.*	Princess Benedetta F. M. R., *b.* 1974.
1827 i.	*Norbury* (6th), Noel Terence Graham-Toler, *b.* 1939, *s.* 1955, *m.*	Viscount Glandine, *b.* 1967.
1806 i.*	*Normanton* (6th), Shaun James Christian Welbore Ellis Agar (9th *Brit. Baron, Mendip*, 1791) (4th *UK Baron, Somerton*, 1873), *b.* 1945, *s.* 1967, *m.*	Viscount Somerton, *b.* 1982.
1647 s.	*Northesk* (13th), Robert Andrew Carnegie, *b.* 1926, *s.* 1975, *m.*	Lord Rosehill, *b.* 1954.
1801	*Onslow* (7th), Michael William Coplestone Dillon Onslow, *b.* 1938, *s.* 1971, *m.*	Viscount Cranley, *b.* 1967.
1696 s.	*Orkney* (8th), Cecil O'Bryen Fitz-Maurice, *b.* 1919, *s.* 1951, *m.*	O. Peter St. *John*, *b.* 1938.
1925	*Oxford and Asquith* (2nd), Julian Edward George Asquith, KCMG, *b.* 1916, *s.* 1928, *m.*	Viscount Asquith, *b.* 1952.
1929	°*Peel* (3rd), William James Robert Peel (4th *UK Viscount Peel*, 1895), *b.* 1947, *s.* 1969, *m.*	Viscount Clanfield, *b.* 1976.
1551	*Pembroke* (17th) & *Montgomery* (14th) (1605), Henry George Charles Alexander Herbert, *b.* 1939, *s.* 1969.	Lord Herbert, *b.* 1978.
1605 s.	*Perth* (17th), John David Drummond, PC, *b.* 1907, *s.* 1951, *m.*	Viscount Strathallan, *b.* 1935.
1905	*Plymouth* (3rd), Other Robert Ivor Windsor-Clive (15th *English Baron, Windsor*, 1529), *b.* 1923, *s.* 1943, *m.*	Viscount Windsor, *b.* 1951.
1785 i.	*Portarlington* (7th), George Lionel Yuill Seymour Dawson-Damer, *b.* 1938, *s.* 1959, *m.*	Viscount Carlow, *b.* 1965.
1689	*Portland* (12th), Count Henry Noel Bentinck, *b.* 1919, *s.* 1990, *m.*	Viscount Woodstock, *b.* 1953.
1743	*Portsmouth* (10th), Quentin Gerard Carew Wallop, *b.* 1954, *s.* 1984, *m.*	Viscount Lymington, *b.* 1981.
1804	*Powis* (7th), George William Herbert (8th *Irish Baron, Clive*, 1762), *b.* 1925, *s.* 1988, *m.*	Viscount Clive, *b.* 1952.
1765	*Radnor* (8th), Jacob Pleydell-Bouverie, *b.* 1927, *s.* 1968, *m.*	Viscount Folkestone, *b.* 1955.
1831 i.*	*Ranfurly* (7th), Gerald Françoys Needham Knox (8th *UK Baron, Ranfurly*, 1826), *b.* 1929, *s.* 1988, *m.*	Viscount Northland, *b.* 1957.
1771 i.	*Roden* (9th), Robert William Jocelyn, *b.* 1909, *s.* 1956, *w.*	Viscount Jocelyn, *b.* 1938.
1801	*Romney* (7th), Michael Henry Marsham, *b.* 1910, *s.* 1975, *m.*	Julian C. M., *b.* 1948.
1703 s.*	*Rosebery* (7th), Neil Archibald Primrose (3rd *UK Earl, Midlothian*, 1911), *b.* 1929, *s.* 1974, *m.*	Lord Dalmeny, *b.* 1967.
1806 i.	*Rosse* (7th), William Brendan Parsons, *b.* 1936, *s.* 1979, *m.*	Lord Oxmantown, *b.* 1969.
1801	*Rosslyn* (7th), Peter St. Clair-Erskine, *b.* 1958, *s.* 1977, *m.*	Lord Loughborough, *b.* 1986.
1457 s.	*Rothes* (21st), Ian Lionel Malcolm Leslie, *b.* 1932, *s.* 1975, *m.*	Lord Leslie, *b.* 1958.
1861	°*Russell* (5th), Conrad Sebastian Robert Russell, *b.* 1937, *s.* 1987, *m.*	Viscount Amberley, *b.* 1968.
1915	°*St. Aldwyn* (2nd), Michael John Hicks Beach, GBE, TD, PC, *b.* 1912, *s.* 1916, *m.*	Viscount Quenington, *b.* 1950.
1815	*St. Germans* (10th), Peregrine Nicholas Eliot, *b.* 1941, *s.* 1988, *m.*	Lord Eliot, *b.* 1966.
1660	*Sandwich. Disclaimed for life* 1964.	
1690	*Scarbrough* (12th), Richard Aldred Lumley (13th *Irish Visct., Lumley*, 1628), *b.* 1932, *s.* 1969, *m.*	Viscount Lumley, *b.* 1973.
1701 s.	*Seafield* (13th), Ian Derek Francis Ogilvie-Grant, *b.* 1939, *s.* 1969, *m.*	Viscount Reidhaven, *b.* 1963.
1882	*Selborne* (4th), John Roundell Palmer, KBE, *b.* 1940, *s.* 1971, *m.*	Viscount Wolmer, *b.* 1971.
1646 s.	*Selkirk* (10th), (George) Nigel Douglas-Hamilton, KT, GCMG, GBE, AFC, AE, PC, QC, *b.* 1906, *s.* 1940, *m.*	The Master of Selkirk, *b.* 1939.
1672	*Shaftesbury* (10th), Anthony Ashley-Cooper, *b.* 1938, *s.* 1961, *m.*	Lord Ashley, *b.* 1977.
1756 i.*	*Shannon* (9th), Richard Bentinck Boyle (8th *Brit. Baron, Carleton* 1786), *b.* 1924, *s.* 1963.	Viscount Boyle, *b.* 1960.
1442	*Shrewsbury & Waterford* (22nd) (i. 1446), Charles Henry John Benedict Crofton Chetwynd Chetwynd-Talbot (*Premier Earl of England and Ireland; Earl Talbot*, 1784), *b.* 1952, *s.* 1980, *m.*	Viscount Ingestre, *b.* 1978.
1961	*Snowdon* (1st), Antony Charles Robert Armstrong-Jones, GCVO, *b.* 1930, *m.* (*See also* p. 143).	Viscount Linley, *b.* 1961 (*see also* p. 143).
1880	°*Sondes* (5th), Henry George Herbert Milles-Lade, *b.* 1940, *s.* 1970.	(None.)
1633 s.*	*Southesk* (11th), Charles Alexander Carnegie, KCVO (3rd *UK Baron, Balinhard*, 1869), *b.* 1893, *s.* 1941, *m.*	The Duke of Fife, *b.* 1929 (*see* pp. 139 and 153).
1765	°*Spencer* (8th), Edward John Spencer, LVO, *b.* 1924, *s.* 1975, *m.*	Viscount Althorp, *b.* 1964.
1703 s.*	*Stair* (13th), John Aymer Dalrymple, KCVO, MBE (6th *UK Baron, Oxenford*, 1841), *b.* 1906, *s.* 1961, *m.*	Viscount Dalrymple, *b.* 1961.
1984	*Stockton* (2nd), Alexander Daniel Alan Macmillan, *b.* 1943, *s.* 1986, *m.*	Viscount Macmillan of Ovenden, *b.* 1974.
1821	*Stradbroke* (6th), Robert Keith Rous, *b.* 1937, *s.* 1983, *m.*	Viscount Dunwich, *b.* 1961.
1847	*Strafford* (8th), Thomas Edmund Byng, *b.* 1936, *s.* 1984, *m.*	Viscount Enfield, *b.* 1964.
1606 s.*	*Strathmore and Kinghorne* (18th), Michael Fergus Bowes Lyon (16th *Scottish Earl, Strathmore*, 1677, & 18th *Kinghorne*, 1606; 5th *UK Earl, Strathmore & Kinghorne*, 1937), *b.* 1957, *s.* 1987, *m.*	Lord Glamis, *b.* 1986.

Created	Title, Order of Succession, Name, etc.	Eldest Son or Heir
1603	*Suffolk* (21st) *& Berkshire* (14th) (1626), Michael John James George Robert Howard, *b.* 1935, *s.* 1941, *m.*	Viscount Andover, *b.* 1974.
1955	*Swinton* (2nd), David Yarburgh Cunliffe-Lister, *b.* 1937, *s.* 1972, *m.*	Hon. Nicholas J. C.-L., *b.* 1939.
1714	*Tankerville* (10th), Peter Grey Bennet, *b.* 1956, *s.* 1980.	Rev. the Hon. George A. G. B., *b.* 1925.
1822	°*Temple of Stowe* (8th), (Walter) Grenville Algernon Temple-Gore-Langton, *b.* 1924, *s.* 1988, *m.*	Hon. James G. T.-G.-L., *b.* 1955.
1815	*Verulam* (7th), John Duncan Grimston (11th *Irish Visct., Grimston,* 1719; 16th *Scott. Baron, Forrester of Corstorphine,* 1633), *b.* 1951, *s.* 1973, *m.*	Viscount Grimston, *b.* 1978.
1729	°*Waldegrave* (12th), Geoffrey Noel Waldegrave, KG, GCVO, TD, *b.* 1905, *s.* 1936, *m.*	Viscount Chewton, *b.* 1940.
1759	*Warwick & *°*Brooke* (8th) (*Brit.* 1746), David Robin Francis Guy Greville (8th *Earl Brooke* and 8th *Earl of Warwick*), *b.* 1934, *s.* 1984.	Lord Brooke, *b.* 1957.
1633 s.*	*Wemyss* (12th) *& March* (8th) (s. 1697), Francis David Charteris, KT (5th *UK Baron, Wemyss,* 1821), *b.* 1912, *s.* 1937, *w.*	Lord Neidpath, *b.* 1948.
1621 I.	*Westmeath* (13th), William Anthony Nugent, *b.* 1928, *s.* 1971, *m.*	Hon. Sean C. W. N., *b.* 1965.
1624	*Westmorland* (15th), David Anthony Thomas Fane, KCVO, *b.* 1924, *s.* 1948, *m.* (*Master of the Horse*).	Lord Burghersh, *b.* 1951.
1876	*Wharncliffe* (5th), Richard Alan Montagu Stuart Wortley, *b.* 1953, *s.* 1987, *m.*	Viscount Carlton, *b.* 1980.
1801	*Wilton* (7th), Seymour William Arthur John Egerton, *b.* 1921, *s.* 1927, *m.*	Baron Ebury, *b.* 1934 (*see* p. 165).
1628	*Winchilsea* (16th) *& Nottingham* (11th) (1675), Christopher Denys Stormont Finch Hatton, *b.* 1936, *s.* 1950, *m.*	Viscount Maidstone, *b.* 1967.
1766 I.	°*Winterton* (7th), Robert Chad Turnour, *b.* 1915, *s.* 1962, *m.*	N. Cecil T., DFM, CD, *b.* 1919.
1956	*Woolton* (3rd), Simon Frederick Marquis, *b.* 1958, *s.* 1969, *m.*	(None.)
1837	*Yarborough* (7th), John Edward Pelham, *b.* 1920, *s.* 1966, *m.*	Lord Worsley, *b.* 1963.

VISCOUNTS

Coronet.—Nine silver balls on a circlet.
Style.—The Right Hon. the Viscount——.
Wife's style.—The Right Hon. the Viscountess——.
Children's style.—'The Hon.' before forename and family name. (In Scotland the heir apparent to a Viscount may be styled 'The Master of—— (title of peer)'.)
For forms of address, *see* page 151.

Created	Title, Order of Succession, Name, etc.	Eldest Son or Heir
1945	*Addison* (3rd), Michael Addison, *b.* 1914, *s.* 1976, *m.*	Hon. William M. W. A., *b.* 1945.
1946	*Alanbrooke* (3rd), Alan Victor Harold Brooke, *b.* 1932, *s.* 1972.	(None.)
1919	*Allenby* (3rd), Lt.-Col. Michael Jaffray Hynman Allenby, *b.* 1931, *s.* 1984, *m.*	Hon. Henry J. H. A., *b.* 1968.
1911	*Allendale* (3rd), Wentworth Hubert Charles Beaumont, *b.* 1922, *s.* 1956, *m.*	Hon. Wentworth P. I. B., *b.* 1948.
1642 s.	*of Arbuthnott* (16th), John Campbell Arbuthnott, CBE, DSC, *b.* 1924, *s.* 1966, *m.*	Master of Arbuthnott, *b.* 1950.
1751 I.	*Ashbrook* (10th), Desmond Llowarch Edward Flower, KCVO, MBE, *b.* 1905, *s.* 1936, *m.*	Hon. Michael L. W. F., *b.* 1935.
1917	*Astor* (4th), William Waldorf Astor, *b.* 1951, *s.* 1966, *m.*	Hon. William W. A., *b.* 1979.
1781 I.	*Bangor* (7th), Edward Henry Harold Ward, *b.* 1905, *s.* 1950, *m.*	Hon. William M. D. W., *b.* 1948.
1925	*Bearsted* (4th), Peter Montefiore Samuel, MC, TD, *b.* 1911, *s.* 1986, *m.*	Hon. Nicholas A. S., *b.* 1950.
1963	*Blakenham* (2nd), Michael John Hare, *b.* 1938, *s.* 1982, *m.*	Hon. Caspar J. H., *b.* 1972.
1935	*Bledisloe* (3rd), Christopher Hiley Ludlow Bathurst, QC, *b.* 1934, *s.* 1979, *m.*	Hon. Rupert E. L. B., *b.* 1964.
1712	*Bolingbroke* (7th) *& St. John* (8th) (1716), Kenneth Oliver Musgrave St. John, *b.* 1927, *s.* 1974, *m.*	Hon. Henry F. St. J., *b.* 1957.
1960	*Boyd of Merton* (2nd), Simon Donald Rupert Neville Lennox-Boyd, *b.* 1939, *s.* 1983, *m.*	Hon. Benjamin A. L.-B., *b.* 1964.
1717 I.*	*Boyne* (10th), Gustavus Michael George Hamilton-Russell (4th *UK Baron, Brancepeth,* 1866), *b.* 1931, *s.* 1942, *m.*	Hon. Gustavus M. S. H.-R., *b.* 1965.
1929	*Brentford* (4th), Crispin William Joynson-Hicks, *b.* 1933, *s.* 1983, *m.*	Hon. Paul W. J.-H., *b.* 1971.
1929	*Bridgeman* (3rd), Robin John Orlando Bridgeman, *b.* 1930, *s.* 1982, *m.*	Hon. William O. C. B., *b.* 1968.
1868	*Bridport* (4th), Alexander Nelson Hood (7th *Duke of Brontë in Sicily,* 1799, *and* 6th *Irish Baron, Bridport* 1794), *b.* 1948, *s.* 1969, *m.*	Hon. Peregrine A. N. H., *b.* 1974.
1952	*Brookeborough* (3rd), Alan Henry Brooke, *b.* 1952, *s.* 1987, *m.*	Hon. Christopher A. B., *b.* 1954.
1933	*Buckmaster* (3rd), Martin Stanley Buckmaster, OBE, *b.* 1921, *s.* 1974.	Hon. Colin J. B., *b.* 1923.
1939	*Caldecote* (2nd), Robert Andrew Inskip, KBE, DSC, *b.* 1917, *s.* 1947, *m.*	Hon. Piers J. H. I., *b.* 1947.
1941	*Camrose* (2nd), (John) Seymour Berry, TD, *b.* 1909, *s.* 1954, *m.*	Baron Hartwell, MBE, TD, *b.* 1911 (*see* p. 175).

Created	Title, Order of Succession, Name, etc.	Eldest Son or Heir

1954   *Chandos* (3rd), Thomas Orlando Lyttelton, *b.* 1953, *s.* 1980, *m.*   Hon. Oliver A. *L.*, *b.* 1986.

1665 I.   *Charlemont* (14th), John Day Caulfeild (18th *Irish Baron, Caulfeild of Charlemont*, 1620), *b.* 1934, *s.* 1985, *m.*   Hon. John D. *C.*, *b.* 1966.

1921   *Chelmsford* (3rd), Frederic Jan Thesiger, *b.* 1931, *s.* 1970, *m.*   Hon. Frederic C. P. *T.*, *b.* 1962.

1717 I.   *Chetwynd* (10th), Adam Richard John Casson Chetwynd, *b.* 1935, *s.* 1965, *m.*   Hon. Adam D. *C.*, *b.* 1969.

1911   *Chilston* (4th), Alastair George Akers-Douglas, *b.* 1946, *s.* 1982, *m.*   Hon. Oliver I. *A.-D.*, *b.* 1973.

1902   *Churchill* (3rd), Victor George Spencer (5th *UK Baron Churchill*, 1815), *b.* 1934, *s.* 1973.   None to Viscountcy. To Barony, R. Harry R. *S.*, *b.* 1926.

1718   *Cobham* (11th), John William Leonard Lyttelton (8th *Irish Baron, Westcote*, 1776), *b.* 1943, *s.* 1977, *m.*   Hon. Christopher C. *L.*, *b.* 1947.

1902   *Colville of Culross* (4th), John Mark Alexander Colville, QC (13th *Scott. Baron, Colville of Culross*, 1604), *b.* 1933, *s.* 1945, *m.*   Master of Colville, *b.* 1959.

1826   *Combermere* (5th), Michael Wellington Stapleton-Cotton, *b.* 1929, *s.* 1969, *m.*   Hon. Thomas R. W. *S.-C.*, *b.* 1969.

1917   *Cowdray* (3rd), Weetman John Churchill Pearson, TD (3rd *UK Baron, Cowdray*, 1910), *b.* 1910, *s.* 1933, *m.*   Hon. Michael O. W. *P.*, *b.* 1944.

1927   *Craigavon* (3rd), Janric Fraser Craig, *b.* 1944, *s.* 1974.   (None.)

1886   *Cross* (3rd), Assheton Henry Cross, *b.* 1920, *s.* 1932.   (None.)

1943   *Daventry* (3rd), Francis Humphrey Maurice FitzRoy Newdegate, *b.* 1921, *s.* 1986, *m.*   Hon. James E. *F.N.*, *b.* 1960.

1937   *Davidson* (2nd), John Andrew Davidson, *b.* 1928, *s.* 1970, *m.*   Hon. Malcolm W. M. *D.*, *b.* 1934.

1956   *De L'Isle* (1st), William Philip Sidney, VC, KG, GCMG, GCVO, PC, (6th *Baron De L'Isle and Dudley*, 1835), *b.* 1909, *s.* to Barony 1945, *m.*   Maj. Hon. Philip J. A. *S.*, MBE, *b.* 1945.

1776 I.   *De Vesci* (7th), Thomas Eustace Vesey (8th *Irish Baron, Knapton*, 1750), *b.* 1955, *s.* 1983, *m.*   Hon. Damian B. J. *V.*, *b.* 1985.

1917   *Devonport* (3rd), Terence Kearley, *b.* 1944, *s.* 1973.   Chester D. H. *K.*, *b.* 1932.

1964   *Dilhorne* (2nd), John Mervyn Manningham-Buller, *b.* 1932, *s.* 1980, *m.*   Hon. James E. *M.-B.*, *b.* 1956.

1622 I.   *Dillon* (22nd), Henry Benedict Charles Dillon, *b.* 1973, *s.* 1982, *M.*   Hon. Richard A. L. *D.*, *b.* 1948.

1785 I.   *Doneraile* (10th), Richard Allen St. Leger, *b.* 1946, *s.* 1983, *m.*   Hon. Nathaniel W. R. St. J. St. L., *b.* 1971.

1680 I.*   *Downe* (11th), John Christian George Dawnay (4th *UK Baron, Dawnay*, 1897), *b.* 1935, *s.* 1965, *m.*   Hon. Richard H. *D.*, *b.* 1967.

1959   *Dunrossil* (2nd), John William Morrison, CMG, *b.* 1926, *s.* 1961, *m.*   Hon. Andrew W. R. *M.*, *b.* 1953.

1964   *Eccles* (1st), David McAdam Eccles, CH, KCVO, PC, *b.* 1904, *m.*   Hon. John D. *E.*, CBE, *b.* 1931.

1897   *Esher* (4th), Lionel Gordon Baliol Brett, CBE, *b.* 1913. *s.* 1963, *m.*   Hon. Christopher L. B. *B.*, *b.* 1936.

1816   *Exmouth* (10th), Paul Edward Pellew, *b.* 1940, *s.* 1970, *m.*   Hon. Edward F. *P.*, *b.* 1978.

1620 S.   *Falkland* (15th), Lucius Edward William Plantagenet Cary (*Premier Scottish Viscount on the Roll*), *b.* 1935, *s.* 1984.   Master of Falkland, *b.* 1963.

1720   *Falmouth* (9th), George Hugh Boscawen (26th *Eng. Baron, Le Despencer*, 1264), *b.* 1919, *s.* 1962.   Hon. Evelyn A. H. *B.*, *b.* 1955.

1918   *Furness* (2nd), William Anthony Furness, *b.* 1929, *s.* 1940.   (None.)

1720 I.*   *Gage* (7th), George John St. Clere Gage, (6th *Brit. Baron, Gage*, 1790), *b.* 1932, *s.* 1982.   Hon. Henry N. *G.*, *b.* 1934.

1727 I.   *Galway* (12th), George Rupert Monckton-Arundell, *b.* 1922, *s.* 1980, *m.*   Hon. John P. *M.*, *b.* 1952.

1478 I.*   *Gormanston* (17th), Jenico Nicholas Dudley Preston (*Premier Viscount of Ireland*; 5th *UK Baron, Gormanston*, 1868), *b.* 1939, *s.* 1940, *w.*   Hon. Jenico F. T. *P.*, *b.* 1974.

1816 I.   *Gort* (8th), Colin Leopold Prendergast Vereker, *b.* 1916, *s.* 1975, *m.*   Hon. Foley R.S.P. *V.*, *b.* 1951.

1900   *Goschen* (4th), Giles John Harry Goschen, *b.* 1965, *s.* 1977.   (None.)

1849   *Gough* (5th), Shane Hugh Maryon Gough, *b.* 1941, *s.* 1951.   (None.)

1937   *Greenwood* (2nd), David Henry Hamar Greenwood, *b.* 1914, *s.* 1948.   Hon. Michael G. H. *G.*, *b.* 1923.

1929   *Hailsham. Disclaimed for life* 1963.

1891   *Hambleden* (4th), William Herbert Smith, *b.* 1930, *s.* 1948, *m.*   Hon. William H. B. *S.*, *b.* 1955.

1884   *Hampden* (6th), Anthony David Brand, *b.* 1937, *s.* 1975, *m.*   Hon. Francis A. *B.*, *b.* 1970.

1936   *Hanworth* (2nd), David Bertram Pollock, *b.* 1916, *s.* 1936, *m.*   Hon. David S. G. *P.*, *b.* 1946.

1791 I.   *Harberton* (10th), Thomas de Vautort Pomeroy, *b.* 1910, *s.* 1980, *m.*   Hon. Robert W. *P.*, *b.* 1916.

1846   *Hardinge* (6th), Charles Henry Nicholas Hardinge, *b.* 1956, *s.* 1984, *m.*   Hon. Andrew H. *H.*, *b.* 1960.

1791 I.   *Hawarden* (8th), Robert Leslie Eustace Maude, *b.* 1926, *s.* 1958, *m.*   Hon. Robert C. W. L. *M.*, *b.* 1961.

1960   *Head* (2nd), Richard Antony Head, *b.* 1937, *s.* 1983, *m.*   Hon. Henry J. *H.*, *b.* 1980.

1550   *Hereford* (18th), Robert Milo Leicester Devereux (*Premier Viscount of England*), *b.* 1932, *s.* 1952.   Hon. Charles R. de B. *D.*, *b.* 1975.

1842   *Hill* (8th), Antony Rowland Clegg-Hill, *b.* 1931, *s.* 1974.   Peter D. R. C. *C.-H.*, *b.* 1945.

1796   *Hood* (7th), Alexander Lambert Hood (7th *Irish Baron, Hood*, 1782), *b.* 1914, *s.* 1981, *m.*   Hon. Henry L. A. *H.*, *b.* 1958.

1956   *Ingleby* (2nd), Martin Raymond Peake, *b.* 1926, *s.* 1966, *m.*   (None.)

1945   *Kemsley* (2nd), (Geoffrey) Lionel Berry, *b.* 1909, *s.* 1968, *m.*   Richard G. *B.*, *b.* 1951.

Created	Title, Order of Succession, Name, etc.	Eldest Son or Heir
1911	*Knollys* (3rd), David Francis Dudley Knollys, *b.* 1931, *s.* 1966, *m.*	Hon. Patrick N. M. K., *b.* 1962.
1895	*Knutsford* (6th), Michael Holland-Hibbert, *b.* 1926, *s.* 1986, *m.*	Hon. Henry T. H.-H., *b.* 1959.
1945	*Lambert* (3rd), Michael John Lambert, *b.* 1912, *s.* 1989, *m.*	(None.)
1954	*Leathers* (2nd), Frederick Alan Leathers, *b.* 1908, *s.* 1965, *m.*	Hon. Christopher G. L., *b.* 1941.
1922	*Leverhulme* (3rd), Philip William Bryce Lever, KG, TD, *b.* 1915, *s.* 1949, *w.*	(None.)
1781 I.	*Lifford* (9th), (Edward) James Wingfield Hewitt, *b.* 1949, *s.* 1987, *m.*	Hon. James T. W. H., *b.* 1979.
1921	*Long* (4th), Richard Gerard Long, *b.* 1929, *s.* 1967, *m.*	Hon. James R. L., *b.* 1960.
1957	*Mackintosh of Halifax* (3rd), (John) Clive Mackintosh, *b.* 1958, *s.* 1980, *m.*	Hon. Thomas H. G. M., *b.* 1985.
1955	*Malvern* (3rd), Ashley Kevin Godfrey Huggins, *b.* 1949, *s.* 1978.	Hon. M. James H., *b.* 1928.
1945	*Marchwood* (3rd), David George Staveley Penny, *b.* 1936, *s.* 1979, *m.*	Hon. Peter G. W. P., *b.* 1965.
1942	*Margesson* (2nd), Francis Vere Hampden Margesson, *b.* 1922, *s.* 1965, *m.*	Capt. Hon. Richard F. D. M., *b.* 1960.
1660 I.*	*Massereene* (13th) & *Ferrard* (6th) (1797), John Clotworthy Talbot Foster Whyte-Melville Skeffington (6th *UK Baron, Oriel*, 1821), *b.* 1914, *s.* 1956, *m.*	Hon. John D. C. W.-M. F. S., *b.* 1940.
1802	*Melville* (9th), Robert David Ross Dundas, *b.* 1937, *s.* 1971, *m.*	Hon. Robert H. K. D., *b.* 1984.
1916	*Mersey* (4th), Richard Maurice Clive Bigham, *b.* 1934, *s.* 1979, *m.*	Hon. Edward J. H. B., *b.* 1966.
1717 I.*	*Midleton* (12th), Alan Henry Brodrick (9th *Brit. Baron, Brodrick of Peper Harow*, 1796), *b.* 1949, *s.* 1988, *m.*	Hon. Ashley R. B., *b.* 1980.
1962	*Mills* (3rd), Christopher Philip Roger Mills, *b.* 1956, *s.* 1988, *m.*	(None.)
1716 I.	*Molesworth* (11th), Richard Gosset Molesworth, *b.* 1907, *s.* 1961, *w.*	Hon. Robert B. K. M., *b.* 1959.
1801 I.*	*Monck* (7th), Charles Stanley Monck (4th *UK Baron, Monck*, 1866), *b.* 1953, *s.* 1982.	Hon. George S. M., *b.* 1957.
1957	*Monckton of Brenchley* (2nd), Gilbert Walter Riversdale Monckton, CB, OBE, MC, *b.* 1915, *s.* 1965, *m.*	Hon Christopher W. M., *b.* 1952.
1935	*Monsell* (2nd), Henry Bolton Graham Eyres Monsell, *b.* 1905, *s.* 1969.	(None.)
1946	*Montgomery of Alamein* (2nd), David Bernard Montgomery, CBE, *b.* 1928, *s.* 1976, *m.*	Hon. Henry D. M., *b.* 1954.
1550 I.*	*Mountgarret* (17th), Richard Henry Piers Butler (4th *UK Baron, Mountgarret*, 1911), *b.* 1936, *s.* 1966, *m.*	Hon. Piers J. R. B., *b.* 1961.
1964	*Muirshiel* (1st), John Scott Maclay, KT, CH, CMG, PC, *b.* 1905, *w.*	(None.)
1952	*Norwich* (2nd), John Julius Cooper, *b.* 1929, *s.* 1954, *m.*	Hon. Jason C. D. B. C., *b.* 1959.
1651 s.	*of Oxfuird* (13th), George Hubbard Makgill, *b.* 1934, *s.* 1986, *m.*	Master of Oxfuird, *b.* 1969.
1873	*Portman*, (9th), Edward Henry Berkeley Portman, *b.* 1934, *s.* 1967, *m.*	Hon. Christopher E. B. P., *b.* 1958.
1743 I.*	*Powerscourt* (10th), Mervyn Niall Wingfield (4th *UK Baron, Powerscourt*, 1885), *b.* 1935, *s.* 1973, *m.*	Hon. Mervyn A. W., *b.* 1963.
1900	*Ridley* (4th), Matthew White Ridley, TD, *b.* 1925, *s.* 1964, *m.* (*Lord Steward*).	Hon. Matthew W. R., *b.* 1958.
1960	*Rochdale* (1st), John Durival Kemp, OBE, TD (2nd *UK Baron, Rochdale*, 1913), *b.* 1906, *s.* to Barony 1945, *m.*	Hon. St. John D. K., *b.* 1938.
1919	*Rothermere* (3rd), Vere Harold Esmond Harmsworth, *b.* 1925, *s.* 1978, *m.*	Hon. Harold J. E. V. H., *b.* 1967.
1937	*Runciman of Doxford* (3rd), Walter Garrison Runciman, CBE, FBA (4th *UK Baron, Runciman*, 1933), *b.* 1934, *s.* 1989, *m.*	Hon. David W. R., *b.* 1967.
1918	*St. Davids* (2nd), Jestyn Reginald Austen Plantagenet Philipps (19th *English Baron Strange of Knokin*, 1299, 7th *English Baron Hungerford*, 1426, *and De Moleyns*, 1445), *b.* 1917, *s.* to Viscountcy 1938, to Baronies 1974, *m.*	Hon. Colwyn J. J. P., *b.* 1939.
1801	*St. Vincent* (7th), Ronald George James Jervis, *b.* 1905, *s.* 1940, *m.*	Hon. Edward R. J. J., *b.* 1951.
1937	*Samuel* (3rd), David Herbert Samuel, PH.D., *b.* 1922, *s.* 1978, *m.*	Hon. Dan J. S., *b.* 1925.
1911	*Scarsdale* (3rd), Francis John Nathaniel Curzon (7th *Brit. Baron, Scarsdale*, 1761), *b.* 1924, *s.* 1977, *m.*	Hon. Peter G. N. C., *b.* 1949.
1905	*Selby* (4th), Michael Guy John Gully, *b.* 1942, *s.* 1959, *m.*	Hon. Edward T. W. G., *b.* 1967.
1805	*Sidmouth* (7th), John Tonge Anthony Pellew Addington, *b.* 1914, *s.* 1976, *w.*	Hon. Jeremy F. A., *b.* 1947.
1940	*Simon* (2nd), John Gilbert Simon, CMG, *b.* 1902, *s.* 1954, *m.*	Hon. Jan D. S., *b.* 1940.
1960	*Slim* (2nd), John Douglas Slim, OBE, *b.* 1927, *s.* 1970, *m.*	Hon. Mark W. R. S., *b.* 1960.
1954	*Soulbury* (2nd), James Herwald Ramsbotham, *b.* 1915, *s.* 1971, *w.*	Hon. Sir Peter E. R., GCMG, GCVO, *b.* 1919.
1776 I.	*Southwell* (7th), Pyers Anthony Joseph Southwell, *b.* 1930, *s.* 1960, *m.*	Hon. Richard A. P. S., *b.* 1956.
1942	*Stansgate. Disclaimed for life* 1963.	
1959	*Stuart of Findhorn* (2nd), David Randolph Moray Stuart, *b.* 1924, *s.* 1971, *m.*	Hon. James D. S., *b.* 1948.
1957	*Tenby* (3rd), William Lloyd George, *b.* 1927, *s.* 1983, *m.*	Hon. Timothy H. G. L. G., *b.* 1962.
1952	*Thurso* (2nd), Robin Macdonald Sinclair, *b.* 1922, *s.* 1970, *m.*	Hon. John A. S., *b.* 1953.
1983	*Tonypandy* (1st), (Thomas) George Thomas, PC, *b.* 1909.	(None.)
1721	*Torrington* (11th), Timothy Howard St. George Byng, *b.* 1943, *s.* 1961, *m.*	John L. B., MC, *b.* 1919.

Created	Title, Order of Succession, Name, etc.	Eldest Son or Heir
1936	*Trenchard* (3rd), Hugh Trenchard, *b.* 1951, *s.* 1987, *m.*	Hon. Alexander T. *T.*, *b.* 1978.
1921	*Ullswater* (2nd), Nicholas James Christopher Lowther, *b.* 1942, *s.* 1949, *m.*	Hon. Benjamin J. *L.*, *b.* 1975.
1621 I.	*Valentia* (15th), Richard John Dighton Annesley, *b.* 1929, *s.* 1983, *m.*	Hon. Francis W. D. *A.*, *b.* 1959.
1964	*Watkinson* (1st), Harold Arthur Watkinson, CH, PC, *b.* 1910, *m.*	(None.)
1952	*Waverley* (3rd), John Desmond Forbes Anderson, *b.* 1949, *s.* 1990.	(None.)
1938	*Weir* (3rd), William Kenneth James Weir, *b.* 1933, *s.* 1975, *m.*	Hon. James W. H. *W.*, *b.* 1965.
1983	*Whitelaw* (1st), William Stephen Ian Whitelaw, CH, MC, PC, *b.* 1918, *m.*	(None.)
1918	*Wimborne* (3rd), Ivor Fox-Strangways Guest (4th *UK Baron, Wimborne,* 1880), *b.* 1939, *s.* 1967, *m.*	Hon. Ivor M.V.*G.*, *b.* 1968.
1923	*Younger of Leckie* (3rd), Edward George Younger, OBE, TD, *b.* 1906, *s.* 1946, *w.*	Rt. Hon. George K. H. *Y.*, TD, MP, *b.* 1931.

BISHOPS

Style.—The Right Rev. The Lord Bishop of ——. *Addressed as,* My Lord.
The Bishops of London, Durham and Winchester always have seats in the
House of Lords; the other 21 seats are filled by the remaining diocesan Bishops in
order of seniority. The Bishop of Sodor and Man and the Bishop of Gibraltar are
not eligible to sit in the House of Lords.

Introd. to House of Lords		Election as Diocesan Bp. confirmed	Trans. to present See
1977	*London* (130th), Graham Douglas Leonard, PC, *b.* 1921, *cons.* 1964, *m.*	1973	1981
1984	*Durham* (92nd), David Edward Jenkins, *b.* 1925, *cons.* 1984, *m.*	1984	—
1982	*Winchester* (95th), Colin Clement Walter James, *b.* 1926, *cons.* 1973, *m.*	1977	1985
1976	*Southwark* (7th), Ronald Oliver Bowlby, *b.* 1926, *cons.* 1973, *m.*	1973	1980
1979	*Chichester* (102nd), Eric Waldram Kemp, DD, *b.* 1915, *cons.* 1974, *m.*	1974	
1980	*Liverpool* (6th), David Stuart Sheppard, *b.* 1929, *cons.* 1969, *m.*	1975	
1981	*Gloucester* (37th), John Yates, *b.* 1925, *cons.* 1972, *m.*	1975	
1984	*Ripon* (11th), David Nigel de Lorentz Young, *b.* 1931, *cons.* 1977, *m.*	1977	
1985	*Chelmsford* (7th), John Waine, *b.* 1930, *cons.* 1975, *m.*	1978	1986
1985	*Manchester* (9th), Stanley Eric Francis Booth-Clibborn, *b.* 1924, *cons.* 1979, *m.*	1979	
1985	*Leicester* (4th), Cecil Richard Rutt, CBE, *b.* 1925, *cons.* 1966, *m.*	1979	
1985	*Sheffield* (5th), David Ramsay Lunn, *b.* 1930, *cons.* 1980.	1980	
1985	*St. Albans* (8th), John Bernard Taylor, *b.* 1929, *cons.* 1980, *m.*	1980	
1985	*Newcastle* (10th), Andrew Alexander Kenny Graham, *b.* 1929, *cons.* 1977.	1981	
1986	*Salisbury* (76th), John Austin Baker, *b.* 1928, *cons.* 1982, *m.*	1982	
1987	*Worcester* (111th), Philip Harold Ernest Goodrich, *b.* 1929, *cons.* 1973, *m.*	1982	
1987	*Chester* (39th), Michael Alfred Baughen, *b.* 1930, *cons.* 1982, *m.*	1982	
1988	*Guildford* (7th), Michael Edgar Adie, *b.* 1929, *cons.* 1983, *m.*	1983	
1988	*Bradford* (7th), Robert Kerr Williamson, *b.* 1932, *cons.* 1984, *m.*	1984	
1989	*Lichfield* (97th), Keith Norman Sutton, *b.* 1934, *cons.* 1978, *m.*	1984	
1989	*Peterborough* (36th), William John Westwood, *b.* 1925, *cons.* 1975, *m.*	1984	
1990	*Portsmouth* (7th), Timothy John Bavin, *b.* 1935, *cons.* 1974.	1985	
1990	*Exeter* (69th), (Geoffrey) Hewlett Thompson, *b.* 1929, *cons.* 1974, *m.*	1985	
1990	*Bristol* (54th), Barry Rogerson, *b.* 1936, *cons.* 1979, *m.*	1985	

Bishops awaiting seats, in order of seniority

Wakefield (10th), David Michael Hope, D.Phil., *b.* 1940, *cons.* 1985.	1985	
Coventry (7th), Simon Barrington-Ward, *b.* 1930, *cons.* 1985, *m.*	1985	
Norwich (70th), Peter John Nott, *b.* 1933, *cons.* 1977, *m.*	1985	
St. Edmundsbury and Ipswich (8th), John Dennis, *b.* 1931, *cons.* 1979, *m.*	1986	
Lincoln (70th), Robert Maynard Hardy, *b.* 1936, *cons.* 1980, *m.*	1986	
Oxford (41st), Richard Douglas Harries, *b.* 1936, *cons.* 1987, *m.*	1987	
Birmingham (7th), Mark Santer, *b.* 1936, *cons.* 1981, *m.*	1987	
†*Bath and Wells* (75th), George Leonard Carey, PH.D., *b.* 1935, *cons.* 1987	1987	
Derby (5th), Peter Spencer Dawes, *b.* 1928, *cons.* 1988, *m.*	1988	
Southwell (9th), Patrick Burnet Harris, *b.* 1934, *cons.* 1973, *m.*	1988	
Rochester (105th), (Anthony) Michael (Arnold) Turnbull, *b.* 1935, *cons.* 1988, *m.*	1988	
Blackburn (7th), Alan David Chesters, *b.* 1937, *cons.* 1989, *m.*	1989	
Carlisle (65th), Ian Harland, *b.* 1932, *cons.* 1985, *m.*	1989	
Truro (13th), Michael Thomas Ball, *b.* 1932, *cons.* 1980.	1990	

Introd. to House of Lords		Election as Diocesan Bp. confirmed	Trans. to present See
	Ely (67th), Stephen Whitefield Sykes, *b.* 1939, *cons.* 1990, *m.*	1990	
	Hereford (103rd), John Keith Oliver, *b.* 1935, *cons.* 1990, *m.*	1990	

* The Bishop of Leicester retires in October 1990.
† George Carey is to become Archbishop of Canterbury when Archbishop Runcie retires in January 1991.

BARONS

Coronet.—Four silver balls.
Style.—The Right Hon. the Lord ——.
Wife's style.—The Right Hon. the Lady ——.
Children's style.—'The Hon.' before forename and family name. (In Scotland the heir apparent to a Lord may be styled 'The Master of —— (title of peer)'.)
For forms of address, *see* page 151.

Created	Title, Order of Succession, Name, etc.	Eldest Son or Heir
1911	*Aberconway* (3rd), Charles Melville McLaren, *b.* 1913, *s.* 1953, *m.*	Hon. Henry C. M., *b.* 1948.
1873	*Aberdare* (4th), Morys George Lyndhurst Bruce, KBE, PC, *b.* 1919, *s.* 1957, *m.*	Hon. Alastair J. L. B., *b.* 1947.
1835	*Abinger* (8th), James Richard Scarlett, *b.* 1914, *s.* 1943, *m.*	Hon. James H. S., *b.* 1959.
1869	*Acton* (4th), Richard Gerald Lyon-Dalberg-Acton, *b.* 1941, *s.* 1989, *m.*	Hon. John C. F. H. L.-D.-A., *b.* 1966.
1887	*Addington* (6th), Dominic Bryce Hubbard, *b.* 1963, *s.* 1982.	Hon. Michael W. L. H., *b.* 1965.
1955	*Adrian* (2nd), Richard Hume Adrian, FRS, *b.* 1927, *s.* 1977, *m.*	(None.)
1907	*Airedale* (4th), Oliver James Vandeleur Kitson, *b.* 1915, *s.* 1958.	(None.)
1896	*Aldenham* (6th), and *Hunsdon of Hunsdon* (4th) (1923), Vicary Tyser Gibbs, *b.* 1948, *s.* 1986, *m.*	Hon. Humphrey W. F. G., *b.* 1989.
1962	*Aldington* (1st), Toby Austin Richard William Low, KCMG, CBE, DSO, TD, PC, *b.* 1914, *m.*	Hon Charles H. S. L., *b.* 1948.
1902	*Allerton* (3rd), George William Lawies Jackson, *b.* 1903, *s.* 1925, *w.*	(None.)
1945	*Altrincham. Disclaimed for life* 1963.	
1929	*Alvingham* (2nd), Maj.-Gen. Robert Guy Eardley Yerburgh, CBE, *b.* 1926, *s.* 1955, *m.*	Capt. Hon. Robert R. G. Y., *b.* 1956.
1892	*Amherst of Hackney* (4th), William Hugh Amherst Cecil, *b.* 1940, *s.* 1980, *m.*	Hon. Hugh W. A. C., *b.* 1968.
1881	*Ampthill* (4th), Geoffrey Denis Erskine Russell, CBE, *b.* 1921, *s.* 1973.	Hon. David W. E. R., *b.* 1947.
1947	*Amwell* (2nd), Frederick Norman Montague, *b.* 1912, *s.* 1966, *m.*	Hon. Keith N. M., *b.* 1943.
1863	*Annaly* (5th), Luke Robert White, *b.* 1927, *s.* 1970, *m.*	Hon. Luke R. W., *b.* 1954.
1949	*Archibald. Disclaimed for life* 1975.	
1885	*Ashbourne* (4th), Edward Barry Greynville Gibson, *b.* 1933, *s.* 1983, *m.*	Hon. Edward C. d'O. G., *b.* 1967.
1835	*Ashburton* (6th), Alexander Francis St. Vincent Baring, KG, KCVO, *b.* 1898, *s.* 1938, *w.*	Hon. Sir John F. H. B., KCVO, *b.* 1928.
1892	*Ashcombe* (4th), Henry Edward Cubitt, *b.* 1924, *s.* 1962, *m.*	M. Robin C., *b.* 1936.
1911	*Ashton of Hyde* (3rd), Thomas John Ashton, TD, *b.* 1926, *s.* 1983, *m.*	Hon. Thomas H. A., *b.* 1958.
1800 I.	*Ashtown* (6th), Christopher Oliver Trench, *b.* 1931, *s.* 1979.	Sir Nigel C. C. T., KCMG, *b.* 1916.
1956	*Astor of Hever* (3rd), John Jacob Astor, *b.* 1946, *s.* 1984.	Hon. Philip D. P. A., *b.* 1959.
1789 I. 1793*	*Auckland* (9th), Ian George Eden (9th *Brit. Baron, Auckland*), *b.* 1926, *s.* 1957, *m.*	Hon. Robert I. B. E., *b.* 1962.
1313	*Audley* (25th), Richard Michael Thomas Souter, *b.* 1914, *s.* 1973, *m.*	Three co-heiresses.
1900	*Avebury* (4th), Eric Reginald Lubbock, *b.* 1928, *s.* 1971, *m.*	Hon. Lyulph A. J. L., *b.* 1954.
1718 I.	*Aylmer* (13th), Michael Anthony Aylmer, *b.* 1923, *s.* 1982, *m.*	Hon. A. Julian A., *b.* 1951.
1929	*Baden-Powell* (3rd), Robert Crause Baden-Powell, *b.* 1936, *s.* 1962, *m.*	Hon. David M. B.-P., *b.* 1940.
1780	*Bagot* (9th), Heneage Charles Bagot, *b.* 1914, *s.* 1979, *m.*	Hon. Charles H. S. B., *b.* 1944.
1953	*Baillieu* (3rd), James William Latham Baillieu, *b.* 1950, *s.* 1973, *m.*	Hon. Robert L. B., *b.* 1979.
1607 S.	*Balfour of Burleigh* (8th), Robert Bruce, *b.* 1927, *s.* 1967, *m.*	Hon. Victoria B., *b.* 1973.
1945	*Balfour of Inchrye* (2nd), Ian Balfour, *b.* 1924, *s.* 1988, *m.*	(None.)
1924	*Banbury of Southam* (3rd), Charles William Banbury, *b.* 1953, *s.* 1981, *m.*	(None.)
1698	*Barnard* (11th), Harry John Neville Vane, TD, *b.* 1923, *s.* 1964, *m.*	Hon. Henry F. C. V., *b.* 1959.
1887	*Basing* (5th), Neil Lutley Sclater-Booth, *b.* 1939, *s.* 1983, *m.*	Hon. Stuart W. S.-B., *b.* 1969.
1917	*Beaverbrook* (3rd), Maxwell William Humphrey Aitken, *b.* 1951, *s.* 1985, *m.*	Hon. Maxwell F. A, *b.* 1977.
1647 S.	*Belhaven and Stenton* (13th), Robert Anthony Carmichael Hamilton, *b.* 1927, *s.* 1961, *m.*	Master of Belhaven, *b.* 1953.
1848 I.	*Bellew* (7th), James Bryan Bellew, *b.* 1920, *s.* 1981, *m.*	Hon. Bryan E. B., *b.* 1943.
1856	*Belper* (4th), (Alexander) Ronald George Strutt, *b.* 1912, *s.* 1956.	Hon. Richard H. S., *b.* 1941.
1938	*Belstead* (2nd), John Julian Ganzoni, PC, *b.* 1932, *s.* 1958.	(None.)
1922	*Bethell* (4th), Nicholas William Bethell, MEP, *b.* 1938, *s.* 1967.	Hon. James N. B., *b.* 1967.
1938	*Bicester* (3rd), Angus Edward Vivian Smith, *b.* 1932, *s.* 1968.	Hugh C. V. S., *b.* 1934.

Created	Title, Order of Succession, Name, etc.	Eldest Son or Heir
1903	*Biddulph* (5th), (Anthony) Nicholas Colin Maitland Biddulph, *b.* 1959, *s.* 1988.	Hon. William I. R. *M.B.*, *b.* 1963.
1938	*Birdwood* (3rd), Mark William Ogilvie Birdwood, *b.* 1938, *s.* 1962, *m.*	(None.)
1958	*Birkett* (2nd), Michael Birkett, *b.* 1929, *s.* 1962, *m.*	Hon. Thomas *B.*, *b.* 1982.
1907	*Blyth* (4th), Anthony Audley Rupert Blyth, *b.* 1931, *s.* 1977, *m.*	Hon. Riley A. J. *B.*, *b.* 1955.
1797	*Bolton* (7th), Richard William Algar Orde-Powlett, *b.* 1929, *s.* 1963, *m.*	Hon. Harry A. N. *O.-P.*, *b.* 1954.
1452 s.	*Borthwick* (23rd), John Henry Stuart Borthwick, TD, *b.* 1905, *claim succeeded* 1986, *w.*	Master of Borthwick, *b.* 1940.
1922	*Borwick* (4th), James Hugh Myles Borwick, MC, *b.* 1917, *s.* 1961, *m.*	Hon. George S. *B.*, *b.* 1922.
1761	*Boston* (10th), Timothy George Frank Boteler Irby, *b.* 1939, *s.* 1978, *m.*	Hon. George W. E. B. *I.*, *b.* 1971.
1942	*Brabazon of Tara* (3rd), Ivon Anthony Moore-Brabazon, *b.* 1946, *s.* 1974, *m.*	Hon. Benjamin R. *M.-B.*, *b.* 1983.
1880	*Brabourne* (7th), John Ulick Knatchbull, *b.* 1924, *s.* 1943, *m.*	Lord Romsey, *b.* 1947 (*see* p. 172).
1925	*Bradbury* (2nd), John Bradbury, *b.* 1914, *s.* 1950, *m.*	Hon. John *B.*, *b.* 1940.
1962	*Brain* (2nd), Christopher Langdon Brain, *b.* 1926, *s.* 1966, *m.*	Hon. Michael C. *B.*, DM, *b.* 1928.
1938	*Brassey of Apethorpe* (3rd), David Henry Brassey, *b.* 1932, *s.* 1967, *m.*	Hon. Edward *B.*, *b.* 1964.
1788	*Braybrooke* (10th), Robin Henry Charles Neville, *b.* 1932, *s.* 1990, *m.*	Richard N., *b.* 1922.
1957	*Bridges* (2nd), Thomas Edward Bridges, GCMG, *b.* 1927, *s.* 1969, *m.*	Hon. Mark T. *B.*, *b.* 1954.
1945	*Broadbridge* (3rd), Peter Hewett Broadbridge, *b.* 1938, *s.* 1972, *m.*	Martin H. *B.*, *b.* 1929.
1933	*Brocket* (3rd), Charles Ronald George Nall-Cain, *b.* 1952, *s.* 1967, *m.*	Hon. Alexander C. C. *N.-C.*, *b.* 1984.
1860	*Brougham and Vaux* (5th), Michael John Brougham, *b.* 1938, *s.* 1967.	Hon. Charles W. *B.*, *b.* 1971.
1945	*Broughshane* (2nd), Patrick Owen Alexander Davison, *b.* 1903, *s.* 1953, *m.*	Hon. W. Kensington *D.*, DSO, DFC, *b.* 1914.
1776	*Brownlow* (7th), Edward John Peregrine Cust, *b.* 1936, *s.* 1978, *m.*	Hon. Peregrine E. Q. *C.*, *b.* 1974.
1942	*Bruntisfield* (1st), Victor Alexander George Anthony Warrender, MC, *b.* 1899, *m.*	Col. Hon. John R. *W.*, OBE, MC, TD, *b.* 1921.
1950	*Burden* (2nd), Philip William Burden, *b.* 1916, *s.* 1970, *m.*	Hon. Andrew P. *B.*, *b.* 1959.
1529	*Burgh* (7th), Alexander Peter Willoughby Leith, *b.* 1935, *s.* 1959, *m.*	Hon. Alexander G. D. *L.*, *b.* 1958.
1903	*Burnham* (5th), William Edward Harry Lawson, *b.* 1920, *s.* 1963, *m.*	Hon. Hugh J. F. *L.*, *b.* 1931.
1897	*Burton* (3rd), Michael Evan Victor Baillie, *b.* 1924, *s.* 1962, *m.*	Hon. Evan M. R. *B.*, *b.* 1949.
1643	*Byron* (13th), Robert James Byron, *b.* 1950, *s.* 1989, *m.*	(None.)
1937	*Cadman* (3rd), John Anthony Cadman, *b.* 1938, *s.* 1966, *m.*	Hon. Nicholas A. J. *C.*, *b.* 1977.
1796	*Calthorpe* (10th), Peter Waldo Somerset Gough-Calthorpe, *b.* 1927, *s.* 1945, *m.*	(None.)
1945	*Calverley* (3rd), Charles Rodney Muff, *b.* 1946, *s.* 1971, *m.*	Hon. Jonathan E. *M.*, *b.* 1975.
1383	*Camoys* (7th), (Ralph) Thomas Campion George Sherman Stonor, *b.* 1940, *s.* 1976, *m.*	Hon. R. William R. T. *S.*, *b.* 1974.
1715 I.	*Carbery* (11th), Peter Ralfe Harrington Evans-Freke, *b.* 1920, *s.* 1970, *m.*	Hon. Michael P. *E.-F.*, *b.* 1942.
1834 I. 1838* }	*Carew* (6th), William Francis Conolly-Carew, CBE (6th *UK. Baron,* *Carew*, 1838), *b.* 1905, *s.* 1927, *m.*	Hon. Patrick T. *C.-C.*, *b.* 1938.
1916	*Carnock* (4th), David Henry Arthur Nicolson, *b.* 1920, *s.* 1982.	Nigel *N.*, MBE, *b.* 1917.
1796 I. 1797* }	*Carrington* (6th), Peter Alexander Rupert Carington, KG, GCMG, CH, MC, PC, (6th *Brit. Baron, Carrington*, 1797), *b.* 1919, *s.* 1938, *m.*	Hon. Rupert F. J. C., *b.* 1948.
1812 I.	*Castlemaine* (8th), Roland Thomas John Handcock, MBE, *b.* 1943, *s.* 1973.	Terence R. *H.*, *b.* 1902.
1936	*Catto* (2nd), Stephen Gordon Catto, *b.* 1923, *s.* 1959, *m.*	Hon. Innes G. *C.*, *b.* 1950.
1918	*Cawley* (3rd), Frederick Lee Cawley, *b.* 1913, *s.* 1954, *m.*	Hon. John F. *C.*, *b.* 1946.
1937	*Chatfield* (2nd), Ernle David Lewis Chatfield, *b.* 1917, *s.* 1967, *m.*	(None.)
1858	*Chesham* (6th), Nicholas Charles Cavendish, *b.* 1941, *s.* 1989, *m.*	Hon. Charles G. C. *C.*, *b.* 1974.
1945	*Chetwode* (2nd), Philip Chetwode, *b.* 1937, *s.* 1950, *m.*	Hon. Roger *C.*, *b.* 1968.
1945	*Chorley* (2nd), Roger Richard Edward Chorley, *b.* 1930, *s.* 1978, *m.*	Hon. Nicholas R. D. *C.*, *b.* 1966.
1858	*Churston* (4th), Richard Francis Roger Yarde-Buller, VRD, *b.* 1910, *s.* 1930, *m.*	Hon. John F. *Y.-B.*, *b.* 1934.
1946	*Citrine* (2nd), Norman Arthur Citrine, *b.* 1914, *s.* 1983, *m.*	Hon. Ronald E. *C.*, *b.* 1919.
1800 I.	*Clanmorris* (8th), Simon John Ward Bingham, *b.* 1937, *s.* 1988, *m.*	John T. *B.*, *b.* 1923.
1672	*Clifford of Chudleigh* (14th), Thomas Hugh Clifford, *b.* 1948, *s.* 1988, *m.*	Hon. Alexander T. H. *C.*, *b.* 1985.
1299	*Clinton* (22nd), Gerard Nevile Mark Fane Trefusis, *b.* 1934, *title called out of abeyance* 1965, *m.*	Hon. Charles P. R. F. *T.*, *b.* 1962.
1955	*Clitheroe* (2nd), Ralph John Assheton, *b.* 1929, *s.* 1984, *m.*	Hon. Ralph C. *A.*, *b.* 1962.
1919	*Clwyd* (3rd), (John) Anthony Roberts, *b.* 1935, *s.* 1987, *m.*	Hon. John M. *R.*, *b.* 1971.
1948	*Clydesmuir* (2nd), Ronald John Bilsland Colville, KT, CB, MBE, TD, *b.* 1917, *s.* 1954, *m.*	Hon. David R. *C.*, *b.* 1949.
1960	*Cobbold* (2nd), David Antony Fromanteel Lytton Cobbold, *b.* 1937, *s.* 1987, *m.*	Hon. Henry F. L. *C.*, *b.* 1962.

Created	Title, Order of Succession, Name, etc.	Eldest Son or Heir
1919	*Cochrane of Cults* (4th), (Ralph Henry) Vere Cochrane, b. 1926, s. 1990, m.	Hon. Thomas H. V. C., b. 1957.
1954	*Coleraine* (2nd), (James) Martin (Bonar) Law, b. 1931, s. 1980, m.	Hon. James P. B. L., b. 1975.
1873	*Coleridge* (5th), William Duke Coleridge, b. 1937, s. 1984, m.	Hon. James D. C., b. 1967.
1946	*Colgrain* (3rd), David Colin Campbell, b. 1920, s. 1973, m.	Hon. Alastair C. L. C., b. 1951.
1917	*Colwyn* (3rd), (Ian) Anthony Hamilton-Smith, CBE, b. 1942, s. 1966, m.	Hon. Craig P. H.-S., b. 1968.
1956	*Colyton* (1st), Henry Lennox d'Aubigné Hopkinson, CMG, PC, b. 1902, m.	Hon. Nicholas H. E. H., b. 1932.
1841	*Congleton* (8th), Christopher Patrick Parnell, b. 1930, s. 1967, m.	Hon. John P. C. P., b. 1959.
1927	*Cornwallis* (3rd), Fiennes Neil Wykeham Cornwallis, OBE, b. 1921, s. 1982, m.	Hon. F. W. Jeremy C., b. 1946.
1874	*Cottesloe* (4th), John Walgrave Halford Fremantle, GBE, TD, b. 1900, s. 1956, m.	Hon. John T. F., b. 1927.
1929	*Craigmyle* (3rd), Thomas Donald Mackay Shaw, b. 1923, s. 1944, m.	Hon. Thomas C. S., b. 1960.
1899	*Cranworth* (3rd), Philip Bertram Gurdon, b. 1940, s. 1964, m.	Hon. Sacha W. R. G., b. 1970.
1959	*Crathorne* (2nd), Charles James Dugdale, b. 1939, s. 1977, m.	Hon. Thomas A. J. D., b. 1977.
1892	*Crawshaw* (4th), William Michael Clifton Brooks, b. 1933, s. 1946.	Hon. David G. B., b. 1934.
1940	*Croft* (2nd), Michael Henry Glendower Page Croft, b. 1916, s. 1947, w.	Hon. Bernard W. H. P. C., b. 1949.
1797 I.	*Crofton* (7th), Guy Patrick Gilbert Crofton, b. 1951, s. 1989, m.	Hon. Arthur B. A. C., b. 1957.
1375	*Cromwell* (7th), Godfrey John Bewicke-Copley, b. 1960, s. 1982.	Hon. Thomas D. B.-C., b. 1964.
1947	*Crook* (2nd), Douglas Edwin Crook, b. 1926, s 1989, m.	Hon. Robert D. E. C., b. 1955.
1920	*Cullen of Ashbourne* (2nd), Charles Borlase Marsham Cokayne, MBE, b. 1912, s. 1932, m.	Hon. Edmund W. M. C., b. 1916.
1914	*Cunliffe* (3rd), Roger Cunliffe, b. 1932, s. 1963, m.	Hon. Henry C., b. 1962.
1927	*Daresbury* (3rd), Edward Gilbert Greenall, b. 1928, s. 1990, m.	Hon. Peter G. G., b. 1953.
1924	*Darling* (2nd), Robert Charles Henry Darling, b. 1919, s. 1936, m.	Hon. Robert J. H. D., b. 1944.
1946	*Darwen* (3rd), Roger Michael Davies, b. 1938, s. 1988, m.	Hon. Paul D., b. 1962.
1923	*Daryngton* (2nd), Jocelyn Arthur Pike Pease, b. 1908, s. 1949.	(None.)
1932	*Davies* (3rd), David Davies, b. 1940, s. 1944, m.	Hon. David D. D., b. 1975.
1812 I.	*Decies* (6th), Arthur George Marcus Douglas de la Poer Beresford, b. 1915, s. 1944, m.	Hon. Marcus H. T. *de la P.B.*, b. 1948.
1299	*de Clifford* (27th), John Edward Southwell Russell, b. 1928, s. 1982, m.	Hon. William S. R., b. 1930.
1851	*De Freyne* (7th), Francis Arthur John French, b. 1927, s. 1935, m.	Hon. Fulke C. A. J. F., b. 1957.
1821	*Delamere* (5th), Hugh George Cholmondeley, b. 1934, s. 1979, m.	Hon. Thomas P. G. C., b. 1968.
1838	*de Mauley* (6th), Gerald John Ponsonby, b. 1921, s. 1962, m.	Col. Hon. Thomas M. P., TD, b. 1930.
1937	*Denham* (2nd), Bertram Stanley Mitford Bowyer, PC, b. 1927, s. 1948, m.	Hon. Richard G. G. B., b. 1959.
1834	*Denman* (5th), Charles Spencer Denman, CBE, MC, TD, b. 1916, s. 1971, w.	Hon. Richard T. S. D., b. 1946.
1885	*Deramore* (6th), Richard Arthur de Yarburgh-Bateson, b. 1911, s. 1964, m.	(None.)
1887	*De Ramsey* (3rd), Ailwyn Edward Fellowes, KBE, TD, b. 1910, s. 1925, w.	Hon. John A. F., b. 1942.
1264	*de Ros* (28th), Peter Trevor Maxwell, b. 1958, s. 1983, m. *(Premier Baron of England).*	Hon. Diana E. M., b. 1957.
1881	*Derwent* (5th), Robin Evelyn Leo Vanden-Bempde-Johnstone, LVO, b. 1930, s. 1986, m.	Hon. Francis P. H. V.-B.-J., b. 1965.
1831	*De Saumarez* (6th), James Victor Broke Saumarez, b. 1924, s. 1969, m.	Hon. Eric D. S., b. 1956.
1910	*de Villiers* (3rd), Arthur Percy de Villiers, b. 1911, s. 1934.	Hon. Alexander C. *de V.*, b. 1940.
1930	*Dickinson* (2nd), Richard Clavering Hyett Dickinson, b. 1926, s. 1943, m.	Hon. Martin H. D., b. 1961.
1620 I. 1765*	} *Digby* (12th), Edward Henry Kenelm Digby, (6th *Brit. Baron, Digby*), b. 1924, s. 1964, m.	Hon. Henry N. K. D., b. 1954.
1615	*Dormer* (16th), Joseph Spencer Philip Dormer, b. 1914, s. 1975.	Geoffrey H. D., b. 1920.
1943	*Dowding* (2nd), Derek Hugh Tremenheere Dowding, b. 1919, s. 1970, m.	Hon. Piers H. T. D., b. 1948.
1800 I.	*Dufferin and Clandeboye* (10th), Francis George Blackwood, b. 1916, s. 1988, m.	Hon. John F. B., b. 1944.
1929	*Dulverton* (2nd), (Frederick) Anthony Hamilton Wills, CBE, TD, b. 1915, s. 1956, m.	Hon. G. Michael H. W., b. 1944.
1800 I.	*Dunalley* (6th), Henry Desmond Graham Prittie, b. 1912, s. 1948, m.	Hon. Henry F. C. P., b. 1948.
1324 I.	*Dunboyne* (28th), Patrick Theobald Tower Butler, VRD, b. 1917, s. 1945, m.	Hon. John F. B., b. 1951.
1802	*Dunleath* (4th), Charles Edward Henry John Mulholland, TD, b. 1933, s. 1956, m.	Sir Michael H. M., Bt., b. 1915.
1439 I.	*Dunsany* (19th), Randal Arthur Henry Plunkett (20th *Irish Baron Killeen*, 1449), b. 1906, s. 1957, m.	Hon. Edward J. C. P., b. 1939.
1780	*Dynevor* (9th), Richard Charles Uryan Rhys, b. 1935, s. 1962.	Hon. Hugo G. U. R., b. 1966.
1928	*Ebbisham* (2nd), Rowland Roberts Blades, TD, b. 1912, s. 1953, m.	(None.)
1857	*Ebury* (6th), Francis Egerton Grosvenor, b. 1934, s. 1957, m.	Hon. Julian F. M. G., b. 1959.

Created	Title, Order of Succession, Name, etc.	Eldest Son or Heir
1963	*Egremont* (2nd), & *Leconfield* (7th) (1859), John Max Henry Scawen Wyndham, b. 1948, s. 1972, m.	Hon. George R. V. W., b. 1983.
1643	*Elibank* (14th), Alan D'Ardis Erskine-Murray, b. 1923, s. 1973, m.	Master of Elibank, b. 1964.
1802	*Ellenborough* (8th), Richard Edward Cecil Law, b. 1926, s. 1945, w.	Maj. Hon. Rupert E. H. L., b. 1955.
1509 s.*	*Elphinstone* (18th), James Alexander Elphinstone (4th *UK Baron Elphinstone*, 1885), b. 1953, s. 1975, m.	Master of Elphinstone, b. 1980.
1934	*Elton* (2nd), Rodney Elton, TD, b. 1930, s. 1973, m.	Hon. Edward P. E., b. 1966.
1964	*Erroll of Hale* (1st), Frederick James Erroll, TD, PC, b. 1914, m.	(None.)
1964	*Erskine of Rerrick* (2nd), Iain Maxwell Erskine, b. 1926, s. 1980, m.	(None.)
1627 s.	*Fairfax of Cameron* (14th), Nicholas John Albert Fairfax, b. 1956, s. 1964, m.	Hon. Edward N. T. F., b. 1984.
1961	*Fairhaven* (3rd), Ailwyn Henry George Broughton, b. 1936, s. 1973, m.	Hon. James H. A. B., b. 1963.
1916	*Faringdon* (3rd), Charles Michael Henderson, b. 1937, s. 1977, m.	Hon. James H. H., b. 1961.
1756 I.	*Farnham* (12th), Barry Owen Somerset Maxwell, b. 1931, s. 1957, m.	Hon. Simon K. M., b. 1933.
1856 I.	*Fermoy* (6th), Patrick Maurice Burke Roche, b. 1967, s. 1984.	Hon. E. Hugh B. R., b. 1972.
1826	*Feversham* (6th), Charles Antony Peter Duncombe, b. 1945, s. 1963, m.	Hon. Jasper O. S. D., b. 1968.
1798 I.	*ffrench* (8th), Robuck John Peter Charles Mario ffrench, b. 1956, s. 1986.	Hon. John C. M. J. F. ff., b. 1928.
1909	*Fisher* (3rd), John Vavasseur Fisher, DSC, b. 1921, s. 1955, m.	Hon. Patrick V. F., b. 1953.
1295	*Fitzwalter* (21st), (Fitzwalter) Brook Plumptre, b. 1914, *called out of abeyance*, 1953, m.	Hon. Julian B. P., b. 1952.
1776	*Foley* (8th), Adrian Gerald Foley, b. 1923, s. 1927, m.	Hon. Thomas H. F., b. 1961.
1445 s.	*Forbes* (22nd), Nigel Ivan Forbes, KBE (*Premier Baron of Scotland*), b. 1918, s. 1953, m.	Master of Forbes, b. 1946.
1821	*Forester* (8th), (George Cecil) Brooke Weld-Forester, b. 1938, s. 1977, m.	Hon. Charles R. G. W.-F., b. 1975.
1922	*Forres* (4th), Alastair Stephen Grant Williamson, b. 1946, s. 1978, m.	Hon. George A. M. W., b. 1972.
1917	*Forteviot* (3rd), Henry Evelyn Alexander Dewar, MBE, b. 1906, s. 1947, w.	Hon. John J. E. D., b. 1938.
1951	*Freyberg* (2nd), Paul Richard Freyberg, OBE, MC, b. 1923, s. 1963, m.	Hon. Valerian B. F., b. 1970.
1917	*Gainford* (3rd), Joseph Edward Pease, b. 1921, s. 1971, m.	Hon. George P., b. 1926.
1818 I.	*Garvagh* (5th), (Alexander Leopold Ivor) George Canning, b. 1920, s. 1956, m.	Hon. Spencer G. S. de R. C., b. 1953.
1942	*Geddes* (3rd), Euan Michael Ross Geddes, b. 1937, s. 1975, m.	Hon. James G. N. G., b. 1969.
1876	*Gerard* (4th), Robert William Frederick Alwyn Gerard, b. 1918, s. 1953.	Anthony R. H. G., b. 1949.
1824	*Gifford* (6th), Anthony Maurice Gifford, QC, b. 1940, s. 1961, m.	Hon. Thomas A. G., b. 1967.
1917	*Gisborough* (3rd), Thomas Richard John Long Chaloner, b. 1927, s. 1951, m.	Hon. Thomas P. L. C., b. 1961.
1960	*Gladwyn* (1st), (Hubert Miles) Gladwyn Jebb, GCMG, GCVO, CB, b. 1900, m.	Hon. Miles A. G. J., b. 1930.
1899	*Glanusk* (4th), David Russell Bailey, b. 1917, s. 1948, m.	Hon. Christopher R. B., b. 1942.
1918	*Glenarthur* (4th), Simon Mark Arthur, b. 1944, s. 1976, m.	Hon. Edward A. A., b. 1973.
1911	*Glenconner* (3rd), Colin Christopher Paget Tennant, b. 1926, s. 1983, m.	Hon. Charles E. P. T., b. 1957.
1964	*Glendevon* (1st), John Adrian Hope, PC, b. 1912, m.	Hon. Julian J. S. H., b. 1950.
1922	*Glendyne* (3rd), Robert Nivison, b. 1926, s. 1967, m.	Hon. John N., b. 1960.
1939	*Glentoran* (2nd), Daniel Stewart Thomas Bingham Dixon, KBE, PC (NI), b. 1912, s. 1950, w.	Hon. Thomas R. V. D., MBE, b. 1935.
1909	*Gorell* (4th), Timothy John Radcliffe Barnes, b. 1927, s. 1963, m.	Hon. Ronald A. H. B., b. 1931.
1953	*Grantchester* (2nd), Kenneth Bent Suenson-Taylor, CBE, QC, b. 1921, s. 1976, m.	Hon. Christopher J. S-.T., b. 1951.
1782	*Grantley* (7th), John Richard Brinsley Norton, MC, b. 1923, s. 1954, m.	Hon. Richard W. B. N., b. 1956.
1794 I.	*Graves* (8th), Peter George Wellesley Graves, b. 1911, s. 1963, m.	Evelyn P. G., b. 1926.
1445 s.	*Gray* (22nd), Angus Diarmid Ian Campbell-Gray, b. 1931, s. 1946, w.	Master of Gray, b. 1964.
1950	*Greenhill* (3rd), Malcolm Greenhill, b. 1924, s. 1989.	(None.)
1927	*Greenway* (4th), Ambrose Charles Drexel Greenway, b. 1941, s. 1975, m.	Hon. Mervyn S. K. G., b. 1942.
1902	*Grenfell* (3rd), Julian Pascoe Francis St. Leger Grenfell, b. 1935, s. 1976, m.	Francis P. J. G., b. 1938.
1944	*Gretton* (4th), John Lysander Gretton, b. 1975, s. 1989, M.	(None.)
1397	*Grey of Codnor* (5th), Charles Legh Shuldham Cornwall-Legh, CBE, AE, b. 1903, *title called out of abeyance* 1989, m.	Hon. Richard H. C.-L., b. 1936.
1955	*Gridley* (2nd), Arnold Hudson Gridley, b. 1906, s. 1965, m.	Hon. Richard D. A. G., b. 1956.
1964	*Grimston of Westbury* (2nd), Robert Walter Sigismund Grimston, b. 1925, s. 1979, m.	Hon. Robert J. S. G., b. 1951.
1886	*Grimthorpe* (4th), Christopher John Beckett, OBE, b. 1915, s. 1963, m.	Hon. Edward J. B., b. 1954.
1945	*Hacking* (3rd), Douglas David Hacking, b. 1938, s. 1971, m.	Hon. Douglas F. H., b. 1968.
1950	*Haden-Guest* (4th), Peter Haden Haden-Guest, b. 1913, s. 1987, m.	Hon. Christopher H.-G., b. 1948.
1886	*Hamilton of Dalzell* (4th), James Leslie Hamilton, b. 1938, s. 1990, m.	Hon. Gavin G. H., b. 1968.

Created	Title, Order of Succession, Name, etc.	Eldest Son or Heir
1874	*Hampton* (6th), Richard Humphrey Russell Pakington, *b.* 1925, *s.* 1974, *m.*	Hon. John H. A. P., *b.* 1964.
1939	*Hankey* (2nd), Robert Maurice Alers Hankey, KCMG, KCVO, *b.* 1905, *s.* 1963, *m.*	Hon. Donald R. A. H., *b.* 1938.
1958	*Harding of Petherton* (2nd), John Charles Harding, *b.* 1928, *s.* 1989, *m.*	Hon. William A. J. H., *b.* 1969.
1910	*Hardinge of Penshurst* (3rd), George Edward Charles Hardinge, *b.* 1921, *s.* 1960, *m.*	Hon. Julian A. H., *b.* 1945.
1876	*Harlech* (6th), Francis David Ormsby-Gore, *b.* 1954, *s.* 1985, *m.*	Hon. Jasset D. C. O.-G., *b.* 1986.
1939	*Harmsworth* (3rd), Thomas Harold Raymond Harmsworth, *b.* 1939, *s.* 1990, *m.*	Hon. Dominic M. E. H., *b.* 1973.
1815	*Harris* (6th), George Robert John Harris, *b.* 1920, *s.* 1984.	Derek M. H., *b.* 1916.
1954	*Harvey of Tasburgh* (2nd), Peter Charles Oliver Harvey, *b.* 1921, *s.* 1968, *m.*	Hon. John W. H., *b.* 1923.
1295	*Hastings* (22nd), Edward Delaval Henry Astley, *b.* 1912, *s.* 1956, *m.*	Hon. Delaval T. H. A., *b.* 1960.
1835	*Hatherton* (8th), Edward Charles Littleton, *b.* 1950, *s.* 1985, *m.*	Hon. Thomas E. L., *b.* 1977.
1776	*Hawke* (10th), (Julian Stanhope) Theodore Hawke, *b.* 1904, *s.* 1985, *m.*	Hon. Edward G. H., *b.* 1950.
1927	*Hayter* (3rd), George Charles Hayter Chubb, KCVO, CBE, *b.* 1911, *s.* 1967, *m.*	Hon. G. William M. C., *b.* 1943.
1945	*Hazlerigg* (2nd), Arthur Grey Hazlerigg, MC, TD, *b.* 1910, *s.* 1949, *w.*	Hon. Arthur G. H., *b.* 1951.
1797 I.	*Headley* (7th), Charles Rowland Allanson-Winn, *b.* 1902, *s.* 1969, *m.*	Hon. Owain G. A.-W., *b.* 1906.
1943	*Hemingford* (3rd), (Dennis) Nicholas Herbert, *b.* 1934, *s.* 1982, *m.*	Hon. Christopher D. C. H., *b.* 1973.
1906	*Hemphill* (5th), Peter Patrick Fitzroy Martyn Martyn-Hemphill, *b.* 1928, *s.* 1957, *m.*	Hon. Charles A. M. M.-H., *b.* 1954.
1799 I.*	*Henley* (8th), Oliver Michael Robert Eden (6th *UK Baron, Northington*, 1885), *b.* 1953, *s.* 1977, *m.*	Hon. John W. O. E., *b.* 1988.
1800 I.*	*Henniker* (8th), John Patrick Edward Chandos Henniker-Major, KCMG, CVO, MC (4th *UK Baron, Hartismere*, 1866), *b.* 1916, *s.* 1980, *m.*	Hon. Mark I. P. C. H.-M., *b.* 1947.
1886	*Herschell* (3rd), Rognvald Richard Farrer Herschell, *b.* 1923, *s.* 1929, *m.*	(None.)
1935	*Hesketh* (3rd), Thomas Alexander Fermor-Hesketh, *b.* 1950, *s.* 1955, *m.*	Hon. Robert F.-H., *b.* 1951.
1828	*Heytesbury* (6th), Francis William Holmes à Court, *b.* 1931, *s.* 1971, *m.*	Hon. James W. H. à C., *b.* 1967.
1886	*Hindlip* (5th), Henry Richard Allsopp, *b.* 1912, *s.* 1966, *m.*	Hon. Charles H. A., *b.* 1940.
1950	*Hives* (2nd), John Warwick Hives, CBE, *b.* 1913, *s.* 1965, *m.*	Matthew P. H., *b.* 1971.
1912	*Hollenden* (3rd), Gordon Hope Hope-Morley, *b.* 1914, *s.* 1977, *m.*	Hon. Ian H. H.-M., *b.* 1946.
1897	*HolmPatrick* (3rd), James Hans Hamilton, *b.* 1928, *s.* 1942, *m.*	Hon. Hans J. D. H., *b.* 1955.
1933	*Horder* (2nd), Thomas Mervyn Horder, *b.* 1910, *s.* 1955.	(None.)
1797 I.	*Hotham* (8th), Henry Durand Hotham, *b.* 1940, *s.* 1967, *m.*	Hon. William B. H., *b.* 1972.
1881	*Hothfield* (5th), George William Anthony Tufton, TD, *b.* 1904, *s.* 1986, *w.*	Hon. Anthony C. S. T., *b.* 1939.
1597	*Howard de Walden* (9th), John Osmael Scott-Ellis, TD (5th *UK Baron, Seaford*, 1826), *b.* 1912, *s.* 1946, *m.*	To Barony of Howard of Walden, four co-heiresses. To Barony of Seaford, Colin H. F. *Ellis*, *b.* 1946.
1930	*Howard of Penrith* (2nd), Francis Philip Howard, *b.* 1905, *s.* 1939, *m.*	Hon. Philip E. H., *b.* 1945.
1960	*Howick of Glendale* (2nd), Charles Evelyn Baring, *b.* 1937, *s.* 1973, *m.*	Hon. David E. C. B., *b.* 1975.
1796 I.	*Huntingfield* (6th), Gerard Charles Arcedeckne Vanneck, *b.* 1915, *s.* 1969, *m.*	Hon. Joshua C. V., *b.* 1954.
1866	*Hylton* (5th), Raymond Hervey Jolliffe, *b.* 1932, *s.* 1967, *m.*	Hon. William H. M. J., *b.* 1967.
1933	*Iliffe* (2nd), Edward Langton Iliffe, *b.* 1908, *s.* 1960, *m.*	Robert P. R. I., *b.* 1944.
1543 I.	*Inchiquin* (18th), Conor Myles John O'Brien, *b.* 1943, *s.* 1982.	Murrough R. O'B., *b.* 1910.
1962	*Inchyra* (2nd), Robert Charles Reneke Hoyer Millar, *b.* 1935, *s.* 1989, *m.*	Hon. Christian J. C. H. M., *b.* 1962.
1964	*Inglewood* (2nd), (William) Richard Fletcher-Vane, MEP, *b.* 1951, *s.* 1989, *m.*	Hon. Christopher J. F.-V., *b.* 1953.
1919	*Inverforth* (4th), Andrew Peter Weir, *b.* 1966, *s.* 1982.	Hon. John V. W., *b.* 1935.
1941	*Ironside* (2nd), Edmund Oslac Ironside, *b.* 1924, *s.* 1959, *m.*	Hon. Charles E. G. I., *b.* 1956.
1952	*Jeffreys* (3rd), Christopher Henry Mark Jeffreys, *b.* 1957, *s.* 1986, *m.*	Hon. Alexander C. D. J., *b.* 1959.
1906	*Joicey* (4th), Michael Edward Joicey, *b.* 1925, *s.* 1966, *m.*	Hon. James M. J., *b.* 1953.
1937	*Kenilworth* (4th), (John) Randle Siddeley, *b.* 1954, *s.* 1981.	(None.)
1935	*Kennet* (2nd), Wayland Hilton Young, *b.* 1923, *s.* 1960, *m.*	Hon. William A. T. Y., *b.* 1957.
1776 I. 1886* }	*Kensington* (8th), Hugh Ivor Edwardes (5th *UK Baron, Kensington*), *b.* 1933, *s.* 1981, *m.*	Hon. William O. A. E., *b.* 1964.
1951	*Kenswood* (2nd), John Michael Howard Whitfield, *b.* 1930, *s.* 1963, *m.*	Hon. Michael C. W., *b.* 1955.
1788	*Kenyon* (5th), Lloyd Tyrell-Kenyon, CBE, *b.* 1917, *s.* 1927, *m.*	Hon. Lloyd T.-K., *b.* 1947.
1947	*Kershaw* (4th), Edward John Kershaw, *b.* 1936, *s.* 1962, *m.*	Hon. John C. E. K., *b.* 1971.
1943	*Keyes* (2nd), Roger George Bowlby Keyes, *b.* 1919, *s.* 1945, *m.*	Hon. Charles W. P. K., *b.* 1951.
1909	*Kilbracken* (3rd), John Raymond Godley, DSC, *b.* 1920, *s.* 1950, *m.*	Hon. Christopher J. G., *b.* 1945.

Created	Title, Order of Succession, Name, etc.	Eldest Son or Heir
1900	*Killanin* (3rd), Michael Morris, MBE, TD, b. 1914, s. 1927, m.	Hon. G. Redmond F. M., b. 1947.
1943	*Killearn* (2nd), Graham Curtis Lampson, b. 1919, s. 1964, m.	Hon. Victor M. G. A. L., b. 1941.
1789 I.	*Kilmaine* (7th), John David Henry Browne, b. 1948, s. 1978, m.	Hon. John F. S. B., b. 1983.
1831	*Kilmarnock* (7th), Alastair Ivor Gilbert Boyd, b. 1927, s. 1975, m.	Hon. Robin J. B., b. 1941.
1941	*Kindersley* (3rd), Robert Hugh Molesworth Kindersley, b. 1929, s. 1976.	Hon. Rupert J. M. K., b. 1955.
1223 I.	*Kingsale* (35th), John de Courcy (*Premier Baron of Ireland*), b. 1941, s. 1969.	Nevinson R. de C., b. 1920.
1682 s. ⎫ 1860* ⎭	*Kinnaird* (13th), Graham Charles Kinnaird (5th *UK. Baron, Kinnaird*), b. 1912, s. 1972, m.	(None.)
1902	*Kinross* (5th), Christopher Patrick Balfour, b. 1949, s. 1985, m.	Hon. Alan I. B., b. 1978.
1951	*Kirkwood* (3rd), David Harvie Kirkwood, PH.D., b. 1931, s. 1970, m.	Hon. James S. K., b. 1937.
1800 I.	*Langford* (9th), Geoffrey Alexander Rowley-Conwy, OBE, b. 1912, s. 1953, m.	Hon. Owain G. R.-C., b. 1958.
1942	*Latham* (2nd), Dominic Charles Latham, b. 1954, s. 1970.	Anthony M. L., b. 1954.
1431	*Latymer* (8th), Hugo Nevill Money-Coutts, b. 1926, s. 1987, m.	Hon. Crispin J. A. N. M.-C., b. 1955.
1869	*Lawrence* (5th), David John Downer Lawrence, b. 1937, s. 1968.	(None.)
1947	*Layton* (3rd), Geoffrey Michael Layton, b. 1947, s. 1989, m.	Hon. David L., MBE, b. 1914.
1839	*Leigh* (5th), John Piers Leigh, b. 1935, s. 1979, m.	Hon. Christopher D. P. L., b. 1960.
1962	*Leighton of St. Mellons* (2nd), (John) Leighton Seager, b. 1922, s. 1963, m.	Hon. Robert W. H. L. S., b. 1955.
1797	*Lilford* (7th), George Vernon Powys, b. 1931, s. 1949, m.	Hon. Mark V. P., b. 1975.
1945	*Lindsay of Birker* (2nd), Michael Francis Morris Lindsay, b. 1909, s. 1952, m.	Hon. James F. L., b. 1945.
1758 I.	*Lisle* (7th), John Nicholas Horace Lysaght, b. 1903, s. 1919, m.	Patrick J. L., b. 1931.
1895	*Loch* (4th), Spencer Douglas Loch, MC, b. 1920, s. 1982, m.	(None.)
1850	*Londesborough* (9th), Richard John Denison, b. 1959, s. 1968, m.	(None.)
1541 I.	*Louth* (16th), Otway Michael James Oliver Plunkett, b. 1929, s. 1950, m.	Hon. Jonathan O. P., b. 1952.
1458 s. ⎫ 1837* ⎭	*Lovat* (15th), Simon Christopher Joseph Fraser, DSO, MC, TD (4th *UK Baron, Lovat*), b. 1911, s. 1933, m.	Master of Lovat, b. 1939.
1946	*Lucas of Chilworth* (2nd), Michael William George Lucas, b. 1926, s. 1967, m.	Hon. Simon W. L., b. 1957.
1929	*Luke* (2nd), Ian St. John Lawson-Johnston, KCVO, TD, b. 1905, s. 1943, m.	Hon. Arthur C. St. J. L.-J., b. 1933.
1839	*Lurgan* (5th), John Desmond Cavendish Brownlow, OBE, b. 1911, s. 1984.	(None.)
1914	*Lyell* (3rd), Charles Lyell, b. 1939, s. 1943.	(None.)
1859	*Lyveden* (6th), Ronald Cecil Vernon, b. 1915, s. 1973, m.	Hon. Jack L. V., b. 1938.
1959	*MacAndrew* (3rd), Christopher Anthony Colin MacAndrew, b. 1945, s. 1989, m.	Hon. Oliver C. J. M., b. 1983.
1776 I.	*Macdonald* (8th), Godfrey James Macdonald of Macdonald, b. 1947, s. 1970, m.	Hon. Godfrey E. H. T. M., b. 1982.
1949	*Macdonald of Gwaenysgor* (2nd), Gordon Ramsay Macdonald, b. 1915, s. 1966, m.	Hon. Kenneth L. M., b. 1921.
1937	*McGowan* (3rd), Harry Duncan Cory McGowan, b. 1938, s. 1966, m.	Hon. Harry J. C. M., b. 1971.
1922	*Maclay* (3rd), Joseph Paton Maclay, b. 1942, s. 1969, m.	Hon. Joseph P. M., b. 1977.
1955	*McNair* (3rd), Duncan James McNair, b. 1947, s. 1989.	Hon. William S. A. M., b. 1958.
1951	*Macpherson of Drumochter* (2nd), (James) Gordon Macpherson, b. 1924, s. 1965, m.	Hon. James A. M., b. 1979.
1937	*Mancroft* (3rd), Benjamin Lloyd Stormont Mancroft, b. 1957, s. 1987.	(None.)
1807	*Manners* (5th), John Robert Cecil Manners, b. 1923, s. 1972, m.	Hon. John H. R. M., b. 1956.
1922	*Manton* (3rd), Joseph Rupert Eric Robert Watson, b. 1924, s. 1968, m.	Capt. Hon. Miles R. M. W., b. 1958.
1908	*Marchamley* (3rd), John William Tattersall Whiteley, b. 1922, s. 1949, m.	Hon. William F. W., b. 1968.
1964	*Margadale* (1st), John Granville Morrison, TD, b. 1906, w.	Hon. James I. M., TD, b. 1930.
1961	*Marks of Broughton* (2nd), Michael Marks, b. 1920, s. 1964.	Hon. Simon R. M., b. 1950.
1964	*Martonmere* (2nd), John Stephen Robinson, b. 1963, s. 1989.	David A. R., b. 1965.
1776 I.	*Massy* (9th), Hugh Hamon John Somerset Massy, b. 1921, s. 1958, m.	Hon. David H. S. M., b. 1947.
1935	*May* (3rd), Michael St. John May, b. 1931, s. 1950, m.	Hon. Jasper B. St. J. M., b. 1965.
1928	*Melchett* (4th), Peter Robert Henry Mond, b. 1948, s. 1973.	(None.)
1925	*Merrivale* (3rd), Jack Henry Edmond Duke, b. 1917, s. 1951, m.	Hon. Derek J. P. D., b. 1948.
1911	*Merthyr. Disclaimed for life* 1977.	
1919	*Meston* (3rd), James Meston, b. 1950, s. 1984, m.	Hon. Thomas J. D. M., b. 1977.
1838	*Methuen* (6th), Anthony John Methuen, b. 1925, s. 1975.	Hon. Robert A. H. M., b. 1931.
1711	*Middleton* (12th), (Digby) Michael Godfrey John Willoughby, MC, b. 1921, s. 1970, m.	Hon. Michael C. J. W., b. 1948.
1939	*Milford* (2nd), Wogan Philipps, b. 1902, s. 1962, m.	Hon. Hugo J. L. P., b. 1929.

Created	Title, Order of Succession, Name, etc.	Eldest Son or Heir
1933	*Milne* (2nd), George Douglass Milne, TD, *b.* 1909, *s.* 1948, *m.*	Hon. George A. *M.*, *b.* 1941.
1951	*Milner of Leeds* (2nd), Arthur James Michael Milner, AE, *b.* 1923, *s.* 1967, *m.*	Hon. Richard J. *M.*, *b.* 1959.
1947	*Milverton* (2nd), Rev. Fraser Arthur Richard Richards, *b.* 1930, *s.* 1978, *m.*	Hon. Michael H. *R.*, *b.* 1936.
1873	*Moncreiff* (5th), Harry Robert Wellwood Moncreiff, *b.* 1915, *s.* 1942, *w.*	Hon. Rhoderick H. W. *M.*, *b.* 1954.
1884	*Monk Bretton* (3rd), John Charles Dodson, *b.* 1924, *s.* 1933, *m.*	Hon. Christopher M. *D.*, *b.* 1958.
1885	*Monkswell* (5th), Gerard Collier, *b.* 1947, *s.* 1984, *m.*	Hon. James A. *C.*, *b.* 1977.
1728	*Monson* (11th), John Monson, *b.* 1932, *s.* 1958, *m.*	Hon. Nicholas J. *M.*, *b.* 1955.
1885	*Montagu of Beaulieu* (3rd), Edward John Barrington Douglas-Scott-Montagu, *b.* 1926, *s.* 1929, *m.*	Hon. Ralph *D.-S.-M.*, *b.* 1961.
1839	*Monteagle of Brandon* (6th), Gerald Spring Rice, *b.* 1926, *s.* 1946, *m.*	Hon. Charles J. S. *R.*, *b.* 1953.
1943	*Moran* (2nd), (Richard) John (McMoran) Wilson, KCMG, *b.* 1924, *s.* 1977, *m.*	Hon. James M. *W.*, *b.* 1952.
1918	*Morris* (3rd), Michael David Morris, *b.* 1937, *s.* 1975, *m.*	Hon. Thomas A. S. *M.*, *b.* 1982.
1950	*Morris of Kenwood* (2nd), Philip Geoffrey Morris, *b.* 1928, *s.* 1954, *m.*	Hon. Jonathan D. *M.*, *b.* 1968.
1945	*Morrison* (2nd), Dennis Morrison, *b.* 1914, *s.* 1953.	(None.)
1831	*Mostyn* (5th), Roger Edward Lloyd Lloyd-Mostyn, MC, *b.* 1920, *s.* 1965, *m.*	Hon. Llewellyn R. L. *L.-M.*, *b.* 1948.
1933	*Mottistone* (4th), David Peter Seely, CBE, *b.* 1920, *s.* 1966, *m.*	Hon. Peter J. P. *S.*, *b.* 1949.
1945	*Mountevans* (3rd), Edward Patrick Broke Evans, *b.* 1943, *s.* 1974, *m.*	Hon. Jeffrey de C. R. *E.*, *b.* 1948.
1283	*Mowbray* (26th), *Segrave* (27th) (1283), & *Stourton* (23rd) (1448), Charles Edward Stourton, CBE, *b.* 1923, *s.* 1965, *m.*	Hon. Edward W. S. *S.*, *b.* 1953.
1932	*Moyne* (2nd), Bryan Walter Guinness, *b.* 1905, *s.* 1944, *m.*	Hon. Jonathan B. *G.*, *b.* 1930.
1929	*Moynihan* (3rd), Antony Patrick Andrew Cairnes Berkeley Moynihan, *b.* 1936, *s.* 1965, *m.*	Hon. Colin B. *M.*, MP, *b.* 1955.
1781 I.	*Muskerry* (9th), Robert Fitzmaurice Deane, *b.* 1948, *s.* 1988, *m.*	Hon. Jonathan F. *D.*, *b.* 1986.
1627 s.	*Napier* (14th) & *Ettrick* (5th) (UK 1872), Francis Nigel Napier, CVO, *b.* 1930, *s.* 1954, *m.*	Master of Napier, *b.* 1962.
1868	*Napier of Magdala* (6th), Robert Alan Napier, *b.* 1940, *s.* 1987, *m.*	Hon. James R. *N.*, *b.* 1966.
1940	*Nathan* (2nd), Roger Carol Michael Nathan, *b.* 1922, *s.* 1963, *m.*	Hon. Rupert H. B. *N.*, *b.* 1957.
1960	*Nelson of Stafford* (2nd), Henry George Nelson, *b.* 1917, *s.* 1962, *m.*	Hon. Henry R. G. *N.*, *b.* 1943.
1959	*Netherthorpe* (3rd), James Frederick Turner, *b.* 1964, *s.* 1982, *m.*	Hon. Patrick A. *T.*, *b.* 1971.
1946	*Newall* (2nd), Francis Storer Eaton Newall, *b.* 1930, *s.* 1963, *m.*	Hon. Richard H. E. *N.*, *b.* 1961.
1776 I.	*Newborough* (7th), Robert Charles Michael Vaughan Wynn, DSC, *b.* 1917, *s.* 1965, *m.*	Hon. Robert V. *W.*, *b.* 1949.
1892	*Newton* (4th), Peter Richard Legh, *b.* 1915, *s.* 1960, *m.*	Hon. Richard T. *L.*, *b.* 1950.
1930	*Noel-Buxton* (3rd), Martin Connal Noel-Buxton, *b.* 1940, *s.* 1980, *m.*	Hon. Charles C. *N.-B.*, *b.* 1975.
1957	*Norrie* (2nd), (George) Willoughby Moke Norrie, *b.* 1936, *s.* 1977, *m.*	Hon. Mark W. J. *N.*, *b.* 1972.
1884	*Northbourne* (5th), Christopher George Walter James, *b.* 1926, *s.* 1982, *m.*	Hon. Charles W. H. *J.*, *b.* 1960.
1866	*Northbrook* (5th), Francis John Baring, *b.* 1915, *s.* 1947, *m.*	Hon. Francis T. *B.*, *b.* 1954.
1878	*Norton* (7th), John Arden Adderley, OBE, *b.* 1915, *s.* 1961, *m.*	Hon. James N. A. *A.*, *b.* 1947.
1906	*Nunburnholme* (4th), Ben Charles Wilson, *b.* 1928, *s.* 1974, *m.*	Hon. Charles T. *W.*, *b.* 1935.
1950	*Ogmore* (2nd), Gwilym Rees Rees-Williams, *b.* 1931, *s.* 1976, *m.*	Hon. Morgan *R.-W.*, *b.* 1937.
1870	*O'Hagan* (4th), Charles Towneley Strachey, MEP, *b.* 1945, *s.* 1961, *m.*	Hon. Richard T. *S.*, *b.* 1950.
1868	*O'Neill* (4th), Raymond Arthur Clanaboy O'Neill, TD, *b.* 1933, *s.* 1944, *m.*	Hon. Shane S. C. *O'N.*, *b.* 1965.
1836 I.*	*Oranmore and Browne* (4th), Dominick Geoffrey Edward Browne (2nd UK Baron Mereworth, 1926), *b.* 1901, *s.* 1927, *m.*	Hon. Dominick G. T. *B.*, *b.* 1929.
1933	*Palmer* (4th), Adrian Bailie Nottage Palmer, *b.* 1951, *s.* 1990, *m.*	Hon. Hugo B. R. *P.*, *b.* 1980.
1914	*Parmoor* (4th), (Frederick Alfred) Milo Cripps, *b.* 1929, *s.* 1977.	M. Anthony L. *C.*, CBE, DSO, TD, QC, *b.* 1913.
1937	*Pender* (3rd), John Willoughby Denison-Pender, *b.* 1933, *s.* 1965, *m.*	Hon. Henry J. R. *D.-P.*, *b.* 1968.
1866	*Penrhyn* (6th), Malcolm Frank Douglas-Pennant, DSO, MBE, *b.* 1908, *s.* 1967, *m.*	Hon. Nigel *D.-P.*, *b.* 1909.
1603	*Petre* (18th), John Patrick Lionel Petre, *b.* 1942, *s.* 1989, *m.*	Hon. Dominic W. *P.*, *b.* 1966.
1918	*Phillimore* (4th), Claud Stephen Phillimore, *b.* 1911, *s.* 1990, *m.*	Hon. Francis S. *P.*, *b.* 1944.
1945	*Piercy* (3rd), James William Piercy, *b.* 1946, *s.* 1981.	Hon. Mark E. P. *P.*, *b.* 1953.
1827	*Plunket* (8th), Robin Rathmore Plunket, *b.* 1925, *s.* 1975, *m.*	Hon. Shaun A. F. S. *P.*, *b.* 1931.
1831	*Poltimore* (7th), Mark Coplestone Bampfylde, *b.* 1957, *s.* 1978, *m.*	Hon. Henry A. W. *B.*, *b.* 1985.
1690 s.	*Polwarth* (10th), Henry Alexander Hepburne-Scott, TD, *b.* 1916, *s.* 1944, *m.*	Master of Polwarth, *b.* 1947.
1930	*Ponsonby of Shulbrede* (4th), Frederick Matthew Thomas Ponsonby, *b.* 1958, *s.* 1990.	(None.)
1958	*Poole* (1st), Oliver Brian Sanderson Poole, CBE, TD, PC, *b.* 1911, *m.*	Hon. David C. *P.*, *b.* 1945.
1852	*Raglan* (5th), FitzRoy John Somerset, *b.* 1927, *s.* 1964.	Hon. Geoffrey *S.*, *b.* 1932.
1932	*Rankeillour* (4th), Peter St. Thomas More Henry Hope, *b.* 1935, *s.* 1967.	Michael R. *H.*, *b.* 1940.

Created	Title, Order of Succession, Name, etc.	Eldest Son or Heir
1953	*Rathcavan* (2nd), Phelim Robert Hugh O'Neill, PC (NI), b. 1909, s. 1982, m.	Hon. Hugh D. T. *O'N.*, b. 1939.
1916	*Rathcreedan* (3rd), Christopher John Norton, b. 1949, s. 1990, m.	Hon. Adam G. *N.*, b. 1952.
1868 I.	*Rathdonnell* (5th), Thomas Benjamin McClintock–Bunbury, b. 1938, s. 1959, m.	Hon. William L. *M.-B.*, b. 1966.
1911	*Ravensdale* (3rd), Nicholas Mosley, MC, b. 1923, s. 1966, m.	Hon. Shaun N. *M.*, b. 1954.
1821	*Ravensworth* (8th), Arthur Waller Liddell, b. 1924, s. 1950, m.	Hon. Thomas A. H. *L.*, b. 1954.
1821	*Rayleigh* (6th), John Gerald Strutt, b. 1960, s. 1988.	Hon. Hedley V. *S.*, b. 1915.
1937	*Rea* (3rd), John Nicolas Rea, MD, b. 1928, s. 1981, m.	Hon. Matthew J. *R.*, b. 1956.
1628 S.	*Reay* (14th), Hugh William Mackay, b. 1937, s. 1963, m.	Master of Reay, b. 1965.
1902	*Redesdale* (5th), Clement Napier Bertram Mitford, b. 1932, s. 1963, m.	Hon. Rupert B. *M.*, b. 1967.
1940	*Reith. Disclaimed for life* 1972.	
1928	*Remnant* (3rd), James Wogan Remnant, CVO, b. 1930, s. 1967, m.	Hon. Philip J. *R.*, b. 1954.
1806 I.	*Rendlesham* (8th), Charles Anthony Hugh Thellusson, b. 1915, s. 1943, w.	Hon. Charles W. B. *T.*, b. 1954.
1933	*Rennell* (3rd), (John Adrian) Tremayne Rodd, b. 1935, s. 1978, m.	Hon. James R. D. T. *R.*, b. 1978.
1964	*Renwick* (2nd), Harry Andrew Renwick, b. 1935, s. 1973, m.	Hon. Robert J. *R.*, b. 1966.
1885	*Revelstoke* (4th), Rupert Baring, b. 1911, s. 1934.	Hon. John *B.*, b. 1934.
1905	*Ritchie of Dundee* (5th), (Harold) Malcolm Ritchie, b. 1919, s. 1978, m.	Hon. Charles R. R. *R.*, b. 1958.
1935	*Riverdale* (2nd), Robert Arthur Balfour, b. 1901, s. 1957, m.	Hon. Mark R. *B.*, b. 1927.
1961	*Robertson of Oakridge* (2nd), William Ronald Robertson, b. 1930, s. 1974, m.	Hon. William B. E. *R.*, b. 1975.
1938	*Roborough* (2nd), Massey Henry Edgcumbe Lopes, b. 1903, s. 1938, m.	Hon. Henry M. *L.*, b. 1940.
1931	*Rochester* (2nd), Foster Charles Lowry Lamb, b. 1916, s. 1955, m.	Hon. David C. *L.*, b. 1944.
1934	*Rockley* (3rd), James Hugh Cecil, b. 1934, s. 1976, m.	Hon. Anthony R. C., b. 1961.
1782	*Rodney* (9th), John Francis Rodney, b. 1920, s. 1973, m.	Hon. George B. *R.*, b. 1953.
1651 S.*	*Rollo* (13th), Eric John Stapylton Rollo (4th *UK Baron, Dunning*, 1869), b. 1915, s. 1947, m.	Master of Rollo, b. 1943.
1959	*Rootes* (2nd), William Geoffrey Rootes, b. 1917, s. 1964, m.	Hon. Nicholas G. *R.*, b. 1951.
1796 I. } 1838* }	*Rossmore* (7th), William Warner Westenra (6th *UK Baron, Rossmore*), b. 1931, s. 1958, m.	Hon. Benedict W. *W.*, b. 1983.
1939	*Rotherwick* (2nd), (Herbert) Robin Cayzer, b. 1912, s. 1958, w.	Hon. H. Robin *C.*, b. 1954.
1885	*Rothschild* (4th), (Nathaniel Charles) Jacob Rothschild, b. 1936, s. 1990, m.	Hon. Nathaniel P. V. J. *R.*, b. 1971.
1911	*Rowallan* (3rd), Arthur Cameron Corbett, b. 1919, s. 1977.	Hon. John P. C. *C.*, b. 1947.
1947	*Rugby* (3rd), Robert Charles Maffey, b. 1951, s. 1990, m.	Hon. Timothy J. H. *M.*, b. 1975.
1919	*Russell of Liverpool* (3rd), Simon Gordon Jared Russell, b. 1952, s. 1981, m.	Hon. Edward C. S. *R.*, b. 1985.
1876	*Sackville* (6th), Lionel Bertrand Sackville-West, b. 1913, s. 1965, m.	Hugh R. I. *S.-W.*, MC, b. 1919.
1964	*St. Helens* (2nd), Richard Francis Hughes-Young, b. 1945, s. 1980, m.	Hon. Henry T. *H.-Y.*, b. 1986.
1559	*St. John of Bletso* (21st), Anthony Tudor St. John, b. 1957, s. 1978.	Edmund O. *St. J.*, b. 1927.
1887	*St. Levan* (4th), John Francis Arthur St. Aubyn, DSC, b. 1919, s. 1978, m.	Hon. O. Piers *St. A.*, MC, b. 1920.
1885	*St. Oswald* (5th), Derek Edward Anthony Winn, b. 1919, s. 1984, m.	Hon. Charles R. A. *W.*, b. 1959.
1960	*Sanderson of Ayot. Disclaimed for life* 1971.	
1945	*Sandford* (2nd), Rev. John Cyril Edmondson, DSC, b. 1920, s. 1959, m.	Hon. James J. M. *E.*, b. 1949.
1871	*Sandhurst* (5th), (John Edward) Terence Mansfield, DFC, b. 1920, s. 1964, m.	Hon. Guy R. J. *M.*, b. 1949.
1802	*Sandys* (7th), Richard Michael Oliver Hill, b. 1931, s. 1961, m.	Marcus T. *H.*, b. 1931.
1888	*Savile* (3rd), George Halifax Lumley-Savile, b. 1919, s. 1931.	Hon. Henry L. T. *L.-S.*, b. 1923.
1447	*Saye and Sele* (21st), Nathaniel Thomas Allen Fiennes, b. 1920, s. 1968, m.	Hon. Richard I. *F.*, b. 1959.
1932	*Selsdon* (3rd), Malcolm McEacharn Mitchell-Thomson, b. 1937, s. 1963, m.	Hon. Callum M. M. *M.-T.*, b. 1969.
1916	*Shaughnessy* (3rd), William Graham Shaughnessy, b. 1922, s. 1938, m.	Hon. Michael J. *S.*, b. 1946.
1946	*Shepherd* (2nd), Malcolm Newton Shepherd, PC, b. 1918, s. 1954, m.	Hon. Graeme G. *S.*, b. 1949.
1964	*Sherfield* (1st), Roger Mellor Makins, GCB, GCMG, FRS, b. 1904, w.	Hon. Christopher J. *M.*, b. 1942.
1902	*Shuttleworth* (5th), Charles Geoffrey Nicholas Kay-Shuttleworth, b. 1948, s. 1975, m.	Hon. Thomas E. *K.-S.*, b. 1976.
1950	*Silkin. Disclaimed for life* 1972.	
1963	*Silsoe* (2nd), David Malcolm Trustram Eve, QC, b. 1930, s. 1976, m.	Hon. Simon R. T. *E.*, b. 1966.
1947	*Simon of Wythenshawe* (2nd), Roger Simon, b. 1913, s. 1960, m.	Hon. Matthew *S.*, b. 1955.
1449 S.	*Sinclair* (17th), Charles Murray Kennedy St. Clair, CVO, b. 1914, s. 1957, m.	Master of Sinclair, b. 1968.
1957	*Sinclair of Cleeve* (3rd), John Lawrence Robert Sinclair, b. 1953, s. 1985.	(None.)
1919	*Sinha* (3rd), Sudhindro Prosanno Sinha, b. 1920, s. 1967, m.	Hon. Sushanto *S.*, b. 1953.
1828	*Skelmersdale* (7th), Roger Bootle-Wilbraham, b. 1945, s. 1973, m.	Hon. Andrew *B.-W.*, b. 1977.
1916	*Somerleyton* (3rd), Savile William Francis Crossley, b. 1928, s. 1959, m.	Hon. Hugh F. S. *C.*, b. 1971.
1784	*Somers* (8th), John Patrick Somers Cocks, b. 1907, s. 1953, m.	Philip S. *S. C.*, b. 1948.

Created	Title, Order of Succession, Name, etc.	Eldest Son or Heir
1780	Southampton. Disclaimed for life 1964.	
1917	Southborough (4th), Francis Michael Hopwood, b. 1922, s. 1982, w.	(None.)
1959	Spens (3rd), Patrick Michael Rex Spens, b. 1942, s. 1984, m.	Hon. Patrick N. G. S., b. 1968.
1640	Stafford (15th), Francis Melfort William Fitzherbert, b. 1954, s. 1986, m.	Hon. Benjamin J. B. F., b. 1983.
1938	Stamp (4th), Trevor Charles Bosworth Stamp, MD, FRCP, b. 1935, s. 1987, m.	Hon. Nicholas C. T. S., b. 1978.
1839	Stanley of Alderley (8th) & Sheffield (8th) (1738 I.), Thomas Henry Oliver Stanley (7th UK Baron Eddisbury, 1848), b. 1927, s. 1971, m.	Hon. Richard O. S., b. 1956.
1318	Strabolgi (11th), David Montague de Burgh Kenworthy, b. 1914, s. 1953, m.	Rev. Hon. Jonathan M. A. K., b. 1916.
1954	Strang (2nd), Colin Strang, b. 1922, s. 1978, m.	(None.)
1955	Strathalmond (3rd), William Roberton Fraser, b. 1947, s. 1976, m.	Hon. William G. F., b. 1976.
1936	Strathcarron (2nd), David William Anthony Blyth Macpherson, b. 1924, s. 1937, m.	Hon. Ian D. P. M., b. 1949.
1955	Strathclyde (2nd), Thomas Galloway Dunlop du Roy de Blicquy Galbraith, b. 1960, s. 1985.	Hon. Charles W. du R. de B. G., b. 1962.
1900	Strathcona and Mount Royal (4th), Donald Euan Palmer Howard, b. 1923, s. 1959, m.	Hon. Donald A. S. H., b. 1961.
1836	Stratheden & Campbell (1841) (6th), Donald Campbell, b. 1934, s. 1987, m.	Hon. David A. C., b. 1963.
1884	Strathspey (5th), Donald Patrick Trevor Grant of Grant, b. 1912, s. 1948, m.	Hon. James P. G., b. 1943.
1838	Sudeley (7th), Merlin Charles Sainthill Hanbury-Tracy, b. 1939, s. 1941, m.	Desmond A. J. H-T., b. 1928.
1786	Suffield (11th), Anthony Philip Harbord-Hamond, MC, b. 1922, s. 1951, m.	Hon. Charles A. A. H.-H., b. 1953.
1893	Swansea (4th), John Hussey Hamilton Vivian, b. 1925, s. 1934, m.	Hon. Richard A. H. V., b. 1957.
1907	Swaythling (4th), David Charles Samuel Montagu, b. 1928, s. 1990, m.	Hon. Charles E. S. M., b. 1954.
1919	Swinfen (3rd), Roger Mynors Swinfen Eady, b. 1938, s. 1977, m.	Hon. Charles R. P. S. E., b. 1971.
1935	Sysonby (3rd), John Frederick Ponsonby, b. 1945, s. 1956.	(None.)
1831 I.	Talbot of Malahide (10th), Reginald John Richard Arundell, b. 1931, s. 1987, w.	Hon. Richard J. T. A., b. 1957.
1946	Tedder (2nd), John Michael Tedder, SC.D., PH.D., D.SC., b. 1926, s. 1967, m.	Hon. Robin J. T., b. 1955.
1884	Tennyson (4th), Harold Christopher Tennyson, b. 1919, s. 1951.	Hon. Mark A. T., DSC, b. 1920.
1918	Terrington (4th), (James Allen) David Woodhouse, b. 1915, s. 1961, m.	Hon. C. Montague W., DSO, OBE, b. 1917.
1940	Teviot (2nd), Charles John Kerr, b. 1934, s. 1968, m.	Hon. Charles R. K., b. 1971.
1616	Teynham (20th), John Christopher Ingham Roper-Curzon, b. 1928, s. 1972, m.	Hon. David J. H. I. R.-C., b. 1965.
1964	Thomson of Fleet (2nd), Kenneth Roy Thomson, b. 1923, s. 1976, m.	Hon. David K. R. T., b. 1957.
1792	Thurlow (8th), Francis Edward Hovell-Thurlow-Cumming-Bruce, KCMG, b. 1912, s. 1971, m.	Hon. Roualeyn R. H.-T.-C.-B., b. 1952.
1876	Tollemache (5th), Timothy John Edward Tollemache, b. 1939, s. 1975, m.	Hon. Edward J. H. T., b. 1976.
1564 S.	Torphichen (15th), James Andrew Douglas Sandilands, b. 1946, s. 1975, m.	Douglas R. A. S., b. 1926.
1947	Trefgarne (2nd), David Garro Trefgarne, PC, b. 1941, s. 1960, m.	Hon. George G. T., b. 1970.
1921	Trevethin (4th), and Oaksey (2nd), John Geoffrey Tristram Lawrence, OBE (2nd UK Baron, Oaksey, 1947), b. 1929, s. 1971, m.	Hon. Patrick J. T. L., b. 1960.
1880	Trevor (4th), Charles Edwin Hill-Trevor, b. 1928, s. 1950, m.	Hon. Marke C. H.-T., b. 1970.
1461 I.	Trimlestown (19th), Charles Aloysius Barnewall, b. 1899, s. 1937, w.	Hon. Anthony E. B., b. 1928.
1940	Tryon (3rd), Anthony George Merrik Tryon, b. 1940, s. 1976, m.	Hon. Charles G. B. T., b. 1976.
1935	Tweedsmuir (2nd), John Norman Stuart Buchan, CBE, CD, b. 1911, s. 1940, m.	Hon. William B., b. 1916.
1523	Vaux of Harrowden (10th), John Hugh Philip Gilbey, b. 1915, s. 1977, m.	Hon. Anthony W. G., b. 1940.
1800 I.	Ventry (8th), Andrew Wesley Daubeny de Moleyns, b. 1943, s. 1987, m.	Hon. Francis W. D. de M., b. 1965.
1762	Vernon (10th), John Lawrance Vernon, b. 1923, s. 1963, m.	Robert Vernon-Harcourt, b. 1918.
1922	Vestey (3rd), Samuel George Armstrong Vestey, b. 1941, s. 1954, m.	Hon. William G. V., b. 1983.
1841	Vivian (5th), Anthony Crespigny Claude Vivian, b. 1906, s. 1940, w.	Hon. Nicholas C. L. V., b. 1935.
1934	Wakehurst (3rd), (John) Christopher Loder, b. 1925, s. 1970, m.	Hon. Timothy W. L., b. 1958.
1723	Walpole (10th), Robert Horatio Walpole, b. 1938, s. 1989, m. (8th Brit. Baron Walpole of Wolterton, 1756).	Hon. Jonathan R. H. W., b. 1967.
1780	Walsingham (9th), John de Grey, MC, b. 1925, s. 1965, m.	Hon. Robert de G., b. 1969.
1936	Wardington (2nd), Christopher Henry Beaumont Pease, b. 1924, s. 1950, m.	Hon. William S. P., b. 1925.
1792 I.	Waterpark (7th), Frederick Caryll Philip Cavendish, b. 1926, s. 1948, m.	Hon. Roderick A. C., b. 1959.

Created	Title, Order of Succession, Name, etc.	Eldest Son or Heir
1942	*Wedgwood* (4th), Piers Anthony Weymouth Wedgwood, *b.* 1954, *s.* 1970, *m.*	John W., CBE, MD, *b.* 1919.
1861	*Westbury* (5th), David Alan Bethell, MC, *b.* 1922, *s.* 1961, *m.*	Hon. Richard N. B., MBE, *b.* 1950.
1944	*Westwood* (2nd), William Westwood, *b.* 1907, *s.* 1953, *m.*	Hon. William G. W., *b.* 1944.
1935	*Wigram* (2nd), (George) Neville (Clive) Wigram, MC, *b.* 1915, *s.* 1960, *w.*	Maj. Hon. Andrew F. C. W., MVO, *b.* 1949.
1491	*Willoughby de Broke* (21st), Leopold David Verney, *b.* 1938, *s.* 1986, *m.*	Hon. Rupert G. V., *b.* 1966.
1946	*Wilson* (2nd), Patrick Maitland Wilson, *b.* 1915, *s.* 1964, *w.*	(None.)
1937	*Windlesham* (3rd), David James George Hennessy, CVO, PC, *b.* 1932, *s.* 1962, *w.*	Hon. James H., *b.* 1968.
1951	*Wise* (2nd), John Clayton Wise, *b.* 1923, *s.* 1968, *m.*	Hon. Christopher J. C. W., PH.D., *b.* 1949.
1869	*Wolverton* (7th), Christopher Richard Glyn, *b.* 1938, *s.* 1988, *m.*	Hon. Andrew J. G., *b.* 1943.
1928	*Wraxall* (2nd), George Richard Lawley Gibbs, *b.* 1928, *s.* 1931.	Hon. Sir Eustace H. B. G., KCVO, CMG, *b.* 1929.
1915	*Wrenbury* (3rd), John Burton Buckley, *b.* 1927, *s.* 1940, *m.*	Hon. William E. B., *b.* 1966.
1838	*Wrottesley* (6th), Clifton Hugh Lancelot de Verdon Wrottesley, *b.* 1968, *s.* 1977.	Hon. Mark W., *b.* 1951.
1919	*Wyfold* (3rd), Hermon Robert Fleming Hermon-Hodge, *b.* 1915, *s.* 1942.	(None.)
1829	*Wynford* (8th), Robert Samuel Best, MBE, *b.* 1917, *s.* 1943, *m.*	Hon. John P. B., *b.* 1950.
1308	*Zouche* (18th), James Assheton Frankland, *b.* 1943, *s.* 1965, *m.*	Hon. William T. A. F., *b.* 1984.

WOMEN PEERS IN THEIR OWN RIGHT

Peerages falling under this heading are the result of regular inheritance in lines which are open to females in default of males. A woman peer in her own right retains her title after marriage, and if her husband's rank is the superior she is designated by the two titles jointly, the inferior one last; her hereditary claim still holds good in spite of any marriage whether higher or lower. No rank held by a woman can confer any title or even precedence upon her husband but the rank of a woman peer in her own right is inherited by her eldest son (or perhaps daughter), to whomsoever she may have been married.
Where marked ° the 'of' is not used.

COUNTESSES IN THEIR OWN RIGHT
Style.—The Right Hon. the Countess (of) ——.
Husband.—Untitled.
Children's style.—As for children of an Earl.
For forms of address, *see* page 151.

Created	Title, Name, etc.	Eldest Son or Heir
1643 s.	*Dysart* (11th in line), Rosamund Agnes Greaves, *b.* 1914, *s.* 1975.	Lady Katherine *Grant of Rothiemurchus, b.* 1918.
1633 s.	*Loudoun* (13th in line), Barbara Huddleston Abney-Hastings, *b.* 1919, *s.* 1960, *m.*	Lord Mauchline, *b.* 1942.
c.1115s.	*Mar* (31st in line), Margaret of Mar (*Premier Earldom of Scotland*), *b.* 1940, *s.* 1975, *m.*	Mistress of Mar, *b.* 1963.
1947	°*Mountbatten of Burma* (2nd in line), Patricia Edwina Victoria Knatchbull, *b.* 1924, *s.* 1979, *m.*	Lord Romsey, *b.* 1947 (*see also* p. 164).
c.1235 s.	*Sutherland* (24th in line), Elizabeth Millicent Sutherland, *b.* 1921, *s.* 1963, *m.*	Lord Strathnaver, *b.* 1947.

BARONESSES IN THEIR OWN RIGHT
Style.—The Right Hon. the Lady ——, or The Right Hon. the Baroness ——, according to her preference.
Husband.—Untitled.
Children's style.—As for children of a Baron.
For forms of address, *see* page 151.

Created	Title, Name, etc.	Eldest Son or Heir
1421	*Berkeley* (17th in line), Mary Lalle Foley Berkeley, *b.* 1905, *title called out of abeyance,* 1967.	Hon. Cynthia E. *Gueterbock, b.* 1909.
1455	*Berners* (15th in line), Vera Ruby Williams, *b.* 1901, *s.* 1950, *m.*	Two co-heiresses.
1529	*Braye* (8th in line), Mary Penelope Aubrey–Fletcher, *b.* 1941, *s.* 1985, *m.*	Two co-heiresses.
1321	*Dacre* (27th in line), Rachel Leila Douglas-Home, *b.* 1929, *title called out of abeyance,* 1970, *m.*	Hon. James T. A. *D.-H., b.* 1952.
1332	*Darcy de Knayth* (18th in line), Davina Marcia Ingrams, *b.* 1938, *s.* 1943, *w.*	Hon. Caspar D. *I., b.* 1962.
1439	*Dudley* (14th in line), Barbara Amy Felicity Hamilton, *b.* 1907, *s.* 1972, *m.*	Hon. Jim A. H. *Wallace, b.* 1930.

Created	Title, Name, etc.	Eldest Son or Heir
1490 s.	*Herries of Terregles* (14th in line), Anne Elizabeth Fitzalan-Howard, *b.* 1938, *s.* 1975, *m.*	Lady Mary *Mumford*, CVO, *b.* 1940.
1602 s.	*Kinloss* (12th in line), Beatrice Mary Grenville Freeman-Grenville, *b.* 1922, *s.* 1944, *m.*	Master of Kinloss, *b.* 1953.
1663	*Lucas of Crudwell* (10th in line) *& Dingwall* (7th in line) (Scottish Lordship 1609), Anne Rosemary Palmer, *b.* 1919, *s.* 1958, *m.*	Hon. Ralph M. *P.*, *b.* 1951.
1681 s.	*Nairne* (12th in line), Katherine Evelyn Constance Bigham (*Katherine, Viscountess Mersey*), *b.* 1912, *s.* 1944, *w.*	Viscount Mersey, *b.* 1934 (*see* p. 161).
1945	*Portal of Hungerford* (2nd in line), Rosemary Ann Portal, *b.* 1923, *s.* 1971.	(None.)
1445 s.	*Saltoun* (20th in line), Flora Marjory Fraser, *b.* 1930, *s.* 1979, *m.*	Hon. Katharine I. M. I. *F.*, *b.* 1957.
1489 s.	*Sempill* (20th in line), Ann Moira Sempill, *b.* 1920, *s.* 1965, *m.*	Master of Sempill, *b.* 1949.
1628	*Strange* (16th in line), (Jean) Cherry Drummond of Megginch, *b.* 1928, *title called out of abeyance,* 1986, *m.*	Hon. Adam H. *D. of M.*, *b.* 1953.
1544–5	*Wharton* (11th in line), Myrtle Olive Felix Robertson, *b.* 1934, *title called out of abeyance,* 1990, *m.*	Hon. Myles C. D. *R.*, *b.* 1964.
1313	*Willoughby de Eresby* (27th in line), (Nancy) Jane Marie Heathcote-Drummond-Willoughby, *b.* 1934, *s.* 1983.	Two co-heiresses.

LIFE PEERS

Created under the Appellate Jurisdiction Act, 1876 (as amended)

BARONS

Created		
1986	*Ackner*, Desmond James Conrad Ackner, PC, *b.* 1920, *m.*	Lord of Appeal in Ordinary.
1981	*Brandon of Oakbrook*, Henry Vivian Brandon, MC, PC, *b.* 1920, *m.*	Lord of Appeal in Ordinary.
1980	*Bridge of Harwich*, Nigel Cyprian Bridge, PC, *b.* 1917, *m.*	Lord of Appeal in Ordinary.
1982	*Brightman*, John Anson Brightman, PC, *b.* 1911, *m.*	Lord of Appeal (retired).
1957	*Denning*, Alfred Thompson Denning, PC, *b.* 1899, *m.*	Lord of Appeal (retired).
1961	*Devlin*, Patrick Arthur Devlin, PC, FBA, *b.* 1905, *m.*	Lord of Appeal (retired).
1974	*Edmund-Davies*, (Herbert) Edmund Edmund-Davies, PC, *b.* 1906, *m.*	Lord of Appeal (retired).
1986	*Goff of Chieveley*, Robert Lionel Archibald Goff, PC, *b.* 1926, *m.*	Lord of Appeal in Ordinary.
1985	*Griffiths*, (William) Hugh Griffiths, MC, PC, *b.* 1923, *m.*	Lord of Appeal in Ordinary.
1987	*Jauncey of Tullichettle*, Charles Eliot Jauncey, PC, *b.* 1925, *m.*	Lord of Appeal in Ordinary.
1977	*Keith of Kinkel*, Henry Shanks Keith, PC, *b.* 1922, *m.*	Lord of Appeal in Ordinary.
1979	*Lane*, Geoffrey Dawson Lane, AFC, PC, *b.* 1918, *m.*	Lord of Appeal (Lord Chief Justice).
1986	*Oliver of Aylmerton*, Peter Raymond Oliver, PC, *b.* 1921, *m.*	Lord of Appeal in Ordinary.
1962	*Pearce*, Edward Holroyd Pearce, PC, *b.* 1901, *w.*	Lord of Appeal (retired).
1980	*Roskill*, Eustace Wentworth Roskill, PC, *b.* 1911, *m.*	Lord of Appeal (retired).
1972	*Salmon*, Cyril Barnet Salmon, PC, *b.* 1903, *w.*	Lord of Appeal (retired).
1977	*Scarman*, Leslie George Scarman, OBE, PC, *b.* 1911, *m.*	Lord of Appeal (retired).
1982	*Templeman*, Sydney William Templeman, MBE, PC, *b.* 1920, *w.*	Lord of Appeal in Ordinary.
1964	*Wilberforce*, Richard Orme Wilberforce, CMG, OBE, PC, *b.* 1907, *m.*	Lord of Appeal (retired).

Created under Life Peerages Act, 1958

Life Peerages were conferred on the following: in the New Years Honours List 1990, Admiral of the Fleet Sir John Fieldhouse, Miss Daphne Park, Sir Francis Tombs; in the Queen's Birthday Honours List 1990, Rt. Hon. Barbara Castle, the Hon. Dame Lydia Dunn, Sir Robert Haslam, Sir Peter Lane, Sir George Porter, Rt. Rev. Robert Runcie.

In April 1990, 14 life peerages were conferred, to create more 'working' peers in the House of Lords, on the following: Heather Brigstocke, Richard Cavendish, Julia Cumberlege, Stanley Clinton Davis, Diana Eccles, Shreela Flather, Patricia Hollis, Richard Holme, Brian Morris, Malcolm Pearson, Ivor Richard, Ernest Soulsby, the Rt. Hon. Eric Varley, Sir Oulton Wade.

BARONS

Created	
1974	*Alexander of Potterhill*, William Picken Alexander, PH.D., *b.* 1905, *m.*
1988	*Alexander of Weedon*, Robert Scott Alexander, QC, *b.* 1936, *m.*
1976	*Allen of Abbeydale*, Philip Allen, GCB, *b.* 1912, *m.*
1961	*Alport*, Cuthbert James McCall Alport, TD, PC, *b.* 1912, *w.*
1965	*Annan*, Noel Gilroy Annan, OBE, *b.* 1916, *m.*
1970	*Ardwick*, John Cowburn Beavan, *b.* 1910, *m.*
1988	*Armstrong of Ilminster*, Robert Temple Armstrong, GCB, CVO, *b.* 1927, *m.*
1973	*Ashby*, Eric Ashby, D.SC., FRS, *b.* 1904, *m.*

Created

1967 *Aylestone*, Herbert William Bowden, CH, CBE, PC, *b.* 1905, *m.*
1982 *Bancroft*, Ian Powell Bancroft, GCB, *b.* 1922, *m.*
1974 *Banks*, Desmond Anderson Harvie Banks, CBE, *b.* 1918, *m.*
1974 *Barber*, Anthony Perrinott Lysberg Barber, TD, PC, *b.* 1920, *m.*
1983 *Barnett*, Joel Barnett, PC, *b.* 1923, *m.*
1982 *Bauer*, Prof. Peter Thomas Bauer, D.SC., *b.* 1915.
1967 *Beaumont of Whitley*, Rev. Timothy Wentworth Beaumont, *b.* 1928, *m.*
1979 *Bellwin*, Irwin Norman Bellow, *b.* 1923, *m.*
1981 *Beloff*, Max Beloff, *b.* 1913, *m.*
1981 *Benson*, Henry Alexander Benson, GBE, *b.* 1909, *m.*
1969 *Bernstein*, Sidney Lewis Bernstein, *b.* 1899, *m.*
1971 *Blake*, Robert Norman William Blake, FBA, *b.* 1916, *m.*
1983 *Blanch*, Rt. Rev. Stuart Yarworth Blanch, PC, *b.* 1918, *m.*
1978 *Blease*, William John Blease, *b.* 1914, *m.*
1980 *Boardman*, Thomas Gray Boardman, MC, TD, *b.* 1919, *m.*
1986 *Bonham-Carter*, Mark Raymond Bonham Carter, *b.* 1922, *m.*
1976 *Boston of Faversham*, Terence George Boston, QC, *b.* 1930, *m.*
1984 *Bottomley*, Arthur George Bottomley, OBE, PC, *b.* 1907, *m.*
1972 *Boyd-Carpenter*, John Archibald Boyd-Carpenter, PC, *b.* 1908, *m.*
1987 *Bramall*, Edwin Noel Westby Bramall, KG, GCB, OBE, MC, *Field Marshal, b.* 1923, *m.*
1976 *Briggs*, Asa Briggs, *b.* 1921, *m.*
1974 *Briginshaw*, Richard William Briginshaw, *b.* 19–, *m.*
1976 *Brimelow*, Thomas Brimelow, GCMG, OBE, *b.* 1915, *m.*
1975 *Brookes*, Raymond Percival Brookes, *b.* 1909, *m.*
1979 *Brooks of Tremorfa*, John Edward Brooks, *b.* 1927, *m.*
1983 *Broxbourne*, Derek Colclough Walker-Smith, TD, QC, PC, *b.* 1910, *m.*
1974 *Bruce of Donington*, Donald William Trevor Bruce, *b.* 1912, *m.*
1976 *Bullock*, Alan Louis Charles Bullock, FBA, *b.* 1914, *m.*
1988 *Butterfield*, (William) John (Hughes) Butterfield, OBE, DM, *b.* 1920, *m.*
1985 *Butterworth*, John Blackstock Butterworth, CBE, *b.* 1918, *m.*
1978 *Buxton of Alsa*, Aubrey Leland Oakes Buxton, MC, *b.* 1918, *m.*
1965 *Caccia*, Harold Anthony Caccia, GCMG, GCVO, *b.* 1905, *m.*
1987 *Callaghan of Cardiff*, (Leonard) James Callaghan, KG, PC, *b.* 1912, *m.*
1984 *Cameron of Lochbroom*, Kenneth John Cameron, PC, *b.* 1931, *m.*
1981 *Campbell of Alloway*, Alan Robertson Campbell, QC, *b.* 1917, *m.*
1974 *Campbell of Croy*, Gordon Thomas Calthrop Campbell, MC, PC, *b.* 1921, *m.*
1966 *Campbell of Eskan*, John (Jock) Middleton Campbell, *b.* 1912, *w.*
1964 *Caradon*, Hugh Mackintosh Foot, GCMG, KCVO, OBE, PC, *b.* 1907, *w.*
1987 *Carlisle of Bucklow*, Mark Carlisle, QC, PC, *b.* 1929, *m.*
1983 *Carmichael of Kelvingrove*, Neil George Carmichael, *b.* 1921.
1975 *Carr of Hadley*, (Leonard) Robert Carr, PC, *b.* 1916, *m.*
1987 *Carter*, Denis Victor Carter, *b.* 1932, *m.*
1977 *Carver*, (Richard) Michael (Power) Carver, GCB, CBE, DSO, MC, *Field Marshal, b.* 1915, *m.*
1990 *Cavendish of Furness*, (Richard) Hugh Cavendish, *b.* 19–, *m.*
1982 *Cayzer*, (William) Nicholas Cayzer, *b.* 1910, *m.*
1964 *Chalfont*, (Alun) Arthur Gwynne Jones, OBE, MC, PC, *b.* 1919, *m.*
1985 *Chapple*, Frank Joseph Chapple, *b.* 1921, *m.*
1978 *Charteris of Amisfield*, Martin Michael Charles Charteris, GCB, GCVO, OBE, PC, *b.* 1913, *m.*
1963 *Chelmer*, Eric Cyril Boyd Edwards, MC, TD, *b.* 1914, *m.*
1987 *Chilver*, (Amos) Henry Chilver, FRS, *b.* 1926, *m.*
1977 *Chitnis*, Pratap Chidamber Chitnis, *b.* 1936, *m.*
1979 *Cledwyn of Penrhos*, Cledwyn Hughes, CH, PC, *b.* 1916, *m.*
1990 *Clinton-Davis*, Stanley Clinton Davis, *b.* 1928, *m.*
1978 *Cockfield*, (Francis) Arthur Cockfield, PC, *b.* 1916, *m.*
1987 *Cocks of Hartcliffe*, Michael Francis Lovell Cocks, PC, *b.* 1929, *m.*
1980 *Coggan*, Rt. Rev. (Frederick) Donald Coggan, PC, Royal Victorian Chain, *b.* 1909, *m.*
1964 *Collison*, Harold Francis Collison, CBE, *b.* 1909, *m.*
1987 *Colnbrook*, Humphrey Edward Gregory Atkins, KCMG, PC, *b.* 1922, *m.*
1981 *Constantine of Stanmore*, Theodore Constantine, CBE, AE, *b.* 1910, *m.*
1959 *Craigton*, Jack Nixon Browne, CBE, PC, *b.* 1904, *m.*
1987 *Crickhowell*, (Roger) Nicholas Edwards, PC, *b.* 1934, *m.*
1978 *Croham*, Douglas Albert Vivian Allen, GCB, *b.* 1917, *m.*
1974 *Cudlipp*, Hugh Cudlipp, OBE, *b.* 1913, *m.*
1979 *Dacre of Glanton*, Hugh Redwald Trevor-Roper, *b.* 1914, *m.*
1986 *Dainton*, Frederick Sydney Dainton, PH.D., SC.D., FRS, *b.* 1914, *m.*
1974 *Davies of Penrhys*, Gwilym Elfed Davies, *b.* 1913, *m.*
1983 *Dean of Beswick*, Joseph Jabez Dean, *b.* 1922.
1986 *Deedes*, William Francis Deedes, MC, PC, *b.* 1913, *m.*
1976 *Delfont*, Bernard Delfont, *b.* 1909, *m.*
1970 *Diamond*, John Diamond, PC, *b.* 1907, *m.*
1967 *Donaldson of Kingsbridge*, John George Stuart Donaldson, OBE, *b.* 1907, *m.*
1988 *Donaldson of Lymington*, John Francis Donaldson, PC, *b.* 1920, *m. (Master of the Rolls)*.
1985 *Donoughue*, Bernard Donoughue, D.Phil., *b.* 1934, *m.*
1987 *Dormand of Easington*, John Donkin Dormand, *b.* 1919, *m.*
1983 *Eden of Winton*, John Benedict Eden, PC, *b.* 1925, *m.*
1985 *Elliott of Morpeth*, Robert William Elliott, *b.* 1920, *m.*

Created
1972 *Elworthy*, (Samuel) Charles Elworthy, KG, GCB, CBE, DSO, LVO, DFC, AFC, *Marshal of the Royal Air Force*, b. 1911, w.
1981 *Elystan-Morgan*, Dafydd Elystan Elystan-Morgan, b. 1932, m.
1980 *Emslie*, George Carlyle Emslie, MBE, PC, b. 1919, m.
1983 *Ennals*, David Hedley Ennals, PC, b. 1922, m.
1978 *Evans of Claughton*, (David Thomas) Gruffydd Evans, b. 1928, m.
1983 *Ezra*, Derek Ezra, MBE, b. 1919, m.
1983 *Fanshawe of Richmond*, Anthony Henry Fanshawe Royle, KCMG, b. 1927, m.
1958 *Ferrier*, Victor Ferrier Noel-Paton, ED, b. 1900, w.
1990 *Fieldhouse*, John David Elliott Fieldhouse, GCB, GBE, *Admiral of the Fleet*, b. 1928, m.
1983 *Fitt*, Gerard Fitt, b. 1926, m.
1979 *Flowers*, Brian Hilton Flowers, FRS, b. 1924, m.
1967 *Foot*, John Mackintosh Foot, b. 1909, m.
1982 *Forte*, Charles Forte, b. 1908, m.
1962 *Franks*, Oliver Shewell Franks, OM, GCMG, KCB, KCVO, CBE, PC, FBA, b. 1905, w.
1989 *Fraser of Carmyllie*, Peter Lovat Fraser, QC, PC, b. 1945, m.
1974 *Fraser of Kilmorack*, (Richard) Michael Fraser, CBE, b. 1915, m.
1982 *Gallacher*, John Gallacher, b. 1920, m.
1979 *Galpern*, Myer Galpern, b. 1903.
1975 *Gibson*, (Richard) Patrick (Tallentyre) Gibson, b. 1916, m.
1979 *Gibson-Watt*, (James) David Gibson-Watt, MC, PC, b. 1918, m.
1977 *Glenamara*, Edward Watson Short, CH, PC, b. 1912, m.
1965 *Goodman*, Arnold Abraham Goodman, CH, b. 1913.
1987 *Goold*, James Duncan Goold, b. 1934, m.
1982 *Gormley*, Joseph Gormley, OBE, b. 1917, m.
1976 *Grade*, Lew Grade, b. 1906, m.
1983 *Graham of Edmonton*, (Thomas) Edward Graham, b. 1925, m.
1967 *Granville of Eye*, Edgar Louis Granville, b. 1899, m.
1983 *Gray of Contin*, James (Hamish) Hector Northey Gray, PC, b. 1927, m.
1974 *Greene of Harrow Weald*, Sidney Francis Greene, CBE, b. 1910, m.
1974 *Greenhill of Harrow*, Denis Arthur Greenhill, GCMG, OBE, b. 1913, m.
1975 *Gregson*, John Gregson, b. 1924.
1968 *Grey of Naunton*, Ralph Francis Alnwick Grey, GCMG, GCVO, OBE, b. 1910, m.
1983 *Grimond*, Joseph Grimond, TD, PC, b. 1913, m.
1970 *Hailsham of St. Marylebone*, Quintin McGarel Hogg, KG, CH, PC, b. 1907, m.
1983 *Hanson*, James Edward Hanson, b. 1922, m.
1974 *Harmar-Nicholls*, Harmar Harmar-Nicholls, b. 1912, m.
1974 *Harris of Greenwich*, John Henry Harris, b. 1930, m.
1979 *Harris of High Cross*, Ralph Harris, b. 1924, m.
1968 *Hartwell*, (William) Michael Berry, MBE, TD, b. 1911, w.
1971 *Harvey of Prestbury*, Arthur Vere Harvey, CBE, b. 1906, m.
1974 *Harvington*, Robert Grant Grant-Ferris, AE, PC, b. 1907, m.
1990 *Haslam*, Robert Haslam, b. 1923, m.
1978 *Hatch of Lusby*, John Charles Hatch, b. 1917.
1987 *Havers*, (Robert) Michael (Oldfield) Havers, PC, b. 1923, m.
1984 *Henderson of Brompton*, Peter Gordon Henderson, KCB, b. 1922, m.
1979 *Hill-Norton*, Peter John Hill-Norton, GCB, *Admiral of the Fleet*, b. 1915, m.
1967 *Hirshfield*, Desmond Barel Hirshfield, b. 1913, m.
1979 *Holderness*, Richard Frederick Wood, PC, b. 1920, m.
1990 *Holme of Cheltenham*, Richard Gordon Holme, CBE, b. 1936, m.
1974 *Home of the Hirsel*, Alexander Frederick Douglas-Home, KT, PC, b. 1903, w.
1979 *Hooson*, (Hugh) Emlyn Hooson, QC, b. 1925, m.
1974 *Houghton of Sowerby*, (Arthur Leslie Noel) Douglas Houghton, CH, PC, b. 1898, m.
1978 *Howie of Troon*, William Howie, b. 1924, m.
1961 *Hughes*, William Hughes, CBE, PC, b. 1911, m.
1966 *Hunt*, (Henry Cecil) John Hunt, KG, CBE, DSO, b. 1910, m.
1980 *Hunt of Tanworth*, John Joseph Benedict Hunt, GCB, b. 1919, m.
1978 *Hunter of Newington*, Robert Brockie Hunter, MBE, FRCP, b. 1915, m.
1978 *Hutchinson of Lullington*, Jeremy Nicolas Hutchinson, QC, b. 1915, m.
1982 *Ingrow*, John Aked Taylor, OBE, TD, b. 1917, m.
1987 *Irvine of Lairg*, Alexander Andrew Mackay Irvine, QC, b. 1940, m.
1968 *Jacques*, John Henry Jacques, b. 1905, m.
1988 *Jakobovits*, Immanuel Jakobovits, b. 1921, m.
1959 *James of Rusholme*, Eric John Francis James, b. 1909, m.
1987 *Jay*, Douglas Patrick Thomas Jay, PC, b. 1907, m.
1987 *Jenkin of Roding*, (Charles) Patrick (Fleeming) Jenkin, PC, b. 1926, m.
1987 *Jenkins of Hillhead*, Roy Harris Jenkins, PC, b. 1920, m.
1981 *Jenkins of Putney*, Hugh Gater Jenkins, b. 1908, w.
1981 *John-Mackie*, John John-Mackie, b. 1909, m.
1987 *Johnston of Rockport*, Charles Collier Johnston, TD, b. 1915, m.
1987 *Joseph*, Keith Sinjohn Joseph, CH, PC, b. 1918, m.
1983 *Kaberry of Adel*, Donald Kaberry, TD, b. 1907, m.
1981 *Kadoorie*, Lawrence Kadoorie, CBE, b. 1899, m.
1976 *Kagan*, Joseph Kagan, b. 1915, m.
1970 *Kearton*, (Christopher) Frank Kearton, OBE, FRS, b. 1911, m.
1980 *Keith of Castleacre*, Kenneth Alexander Keith, b. 1916, m.

Created

1985   *Kimball*, Marcus Richard Kimball, *b.* 1928, *m.*
1983   *King of Wartnaby*, John Leonard King, *b.* 1918, *m.*
1965   *Kings Norton*, Harold Roxbee Cox, PH.D., *b.* 1902, *m.*
1975   *Kirkhill*, John Farquharson Smith, *b.* 1930, *m.*
1974   *Kissin*, Harry Kissin, *b.* 1912, *m.*
1987   *Knights*, Philip Douglas Knights, CBE, QPM, *b.* 1920, *m.*
1990   *Lane of Horsell*, Peter Stewart Lane, *b.* 1925, *w.*
1964   *Leatherland*, Charles Edward Leatherland, OBE, *b.* 1898, *w.*
1979   *Lever of Manchester*, Harold Lever, PC, *b.* 1914, *m.*
1982   *Lewin*, Terence Thornton Lewin, KG, GCB, LVO, DSC, *Admiral of the Fleet*, *b.* 1920, *m.*
1989   *Lewis of Newnham*, Jack Lewis, FRS, *b.* 1928, *m.*
1965   *Lloyd of Hampstead*, Dennis Lloyd, QC, ll.D., *b.* 1915, *m.*
1973   *Lloyd of Kilgerran*, Rhys Gerran Lloyd, CBE, QC, *b.* 1907, *m.*
1974   *Lovell-Davis*, Peter Lovell Lovell-Davis, *b.* 1924, *m.*
1979   *Lowry*, Robert Lynd Erskine Lowry, PC, PC(NI), *b.* 1919, *w.* (*Lord of Appeal in Ordinary*).
1984   *McAlpine of West Green*, (Robert) Alistair McAlpine, *b.* 1942, *m.*
1988   *Macaulay of Bragar*, Donald Macaulay, QC, *b.* 1933.
1975   *McCarthy*, William Edward John McCarthy, *b.* 1925, *m.*
1976   *McCluskey*, John Herbert McCluskey, *b.* 1929, *m.*
1989   *McColl of Dulwich*, Ian McColl, FRCS, FRCSE, *b.* 1933, *m.*
1966   *McFadzean*, William Hunter McFadzean, KT, *b.* 1903, *m.*
1980   *McFadzean of Kelvinside*, Francis Scott McFadzean, *b.* 1915, *w.*
1978   *McGregor of Durris*, Oliver Ross McGregor, *b.* 1921, *m.*
1982   *McIntosh of Haringey*, Andrew Robert McIntosh, *b.* 1933, *m.*
1979   *Mackay of Clashfern*, James Peter Hymers Mackay, PC, *b.* 1927, *m.* (*Lord High Chancellor*).
1988   *Mackenzie-Stuart*, Alexander John Mackenzie Stuart, , *b.* 1924, *m.*
1974   *Mackie of Benshie*, George Yull Mackie, CBE, DSO, DFC, *b.* 1919, *w.*
1982   *MacLehose of Beoch*, (Crawford) Murray MacLehose, KT, GBE, KCMG, KCVO, *b.* 1917, *m.*
1967   *MacLeod of Fuinary*, Very Rev. George Fielden MacLeod, MC, DD, *b.* 1895, *w.*
1967   *Mais*, Alan Raymond Mais, GBE, TD, ERD, *b.* 1911, *m.*
1981   *Marsh*, Richard William Marsh, PC, *b.* 1928, *m.*
1985   *Marshall of Goring*, Walter Charles Marshall, CBE, FRS, *b.* 1932, *m.*
1980   *Marshall of Leeds*, Frank Shaw Marshall, *b.* 1915, *m.*
1987   *Mason of Barnsley*, Roy Mason, PC, *b.* 1924, *m.*
1980   *Matthews*, Victor Collin Matthews, *b.* 1919, *m.*
1983   *Maude of Stratford-upon-Avon*, Angus Edmund Upton Maude, TD, PC, *b.* 1912, *m.*
1981   *Mayhew*, Christopher Paget Mayhew, *b.* 1915, *m.*
1985   *Mellish*, Robert Joseph Mellish, PC, *b.* 1913, *m.*
1979   *Miles*, Bernard James Miles, CBE, *b.* 1907, *m.*
1978   *Mishcon*, Victor Mishcon, *b.* 1915, *m.*
1981   *Molloy*, William John Molloy, *b.* 1918, *m.*
1961   *Molson*, (Arthur) Hugh (Elsdale) Molson, PC, *b.* 1903, *m.*
1986   *Moore of Wolvercote*, Philip Brian Cecil Moore, GCB, GCVO, CMG, PC, *b.* 1921, *m.*
1990   *Morris of Castle Morris*, Brian Robert Morris, D.phil., *b.* 1930, *m.*
1985   *Morton of Shuna*, Hugh Drennan Baird Morton, *b.* 1930, *m.*
1971   *Moyola*, James Dawson Chichester-Clark, PC (NI), *b.* 1923, *m.*
1984   *Mulley*, Frederick William Mulley, PC, *b.* 1918, *m.*
1985   *Murray of Epping Forest*, Lionel Murray, OBE, PC, *b.* 1922, *m.*
1964   *Murray of Newhaven*, Keith Anderson Hope Murray, KCB, PH.D., *b.* 1903.
1979   *Murton of Lindisfarne*, (Henry) Oscar Murton, OBE, TD, PC, *b.* 1914, *m.*
1975   *Northfield*, (William) Donald Chapman, *b.* 1923.
1966   *Nugent of Guildford*, (George) Richard (Hodges) Nugent, PC, *b.* 1907, *m.*
1973   *O'Brien of Lothbury*, Leslie Kenneth O'Brien, GBE, PC, *b.* 1908, *m.*
1976   *Oram*, Albert Edward Oram, *b.* 1913, *m.*
1971   *Orr-Ewing*, (Charles) Ian Orr-Ewing, OBE, *b.* 1912, *m.*
1975   *Parry*, Gordon Samuel David Parry, *b.* 1925, *m.*
1990   *Pearson of Rannoch*, Malcolm Everard MacLaren Pearson, *b.* 19–.
1967   *Penney*, William George Penney, OM, KBE, Ph.D., D.SC., FRS, *b.* 1909, *m.*
1982   *Pennock*, Raymond William Pennock, *b.* 1920, *m.*
1979   *Perry of Walton*, Walter Laing Macdonald Perry, OBE, FRS, FRSE, *b.* 1921, *m.*
1987   *Peston*, Maurice Harry Peston, *b.* 1931, *m.*
1983   *Peyton of Yeovil*, John Wynne William Peyton, PC, *b.* 1919, *m.*
1975   *Pitt of Hampstead*, David Thomas Pitt, *b.* 1913, *m.*
1959   *Plowden*, Edwin Noel Plowden, GBE, KCB, *b.* 1907, *m.*
1987   *Plumb*, (Charles) Henry Plumb, MEP, *b.* 1925, *m.*
1981   *Plummer of St. Marylebone*, (Arthur) Desmond (Herne) Plummer, TD, *b.* 1914, *m.*
1973   *Porritt*, Arthur Espie Porritt, GCMG, GCVO, CBE, *b.* 1900, *m.*
1990   *Porter of Luddenham*, George Porter, OM, FRS, *b.* 1920, *m.*
1987   *Prior*, James Michael Leathes Prior, PC, *b.* 1927, *m.*
1975   *Pritchard*, Derek Wilbraham Pritchard, *b.* 1910, *m.*
1982   *Prys-Davies*, Gwilym Prys Prys-Davies, *b.* 1923, *m.*
1987   *Pym*, Francis Leslie Pym, MC, PC, *b.* 1922, *m.*
1982   *Quinton*, Anthony Meredith Quinton, *b.* 1925, *m.*
1978   *Rawlinson of Ewell*, Peter Anthony Grayson Rawlinson, PC, QC, *b.* 1919, *m.*
1976   *Rayne*, Max Rayne, *b.* 1918, *m.*
1983   *Rayner*, Derek George Rayner, *b.* 1926.

Created

1987 *Rees*, Peter Wynford Innes Rees, PC, QC, b. 1926, m.
1988 *Rees-Mogg*, William Rees-Mogg, b. 1928, m.
1970 *Reigate*, John Kenyon Vaughan-Morgan, PC, b. 1905, m.
1978 *Reilly*, Paul Reilly, b. 1912, m.
1979 *Renton*, David Lockhart-Mure Renton, KBE, TD, PC, QC, b. 1908, w.
1990 *Richard*, Ivor Seward Richard, QC, b. 1932, m.
1979 *Richardson*, John Samuel Richardson, LVO, MD, FRCP, b. 1910, m.
1983 *Richardson of Duntisbourne*, Gordon William Humphreys Richardson, KG, MBE, TD, PC, b. 1915, m.
1987 *Rippon of Hexham*, (Aubrey) Geoffrey (Frederick) Rippon, PC, QC, b. 1924, m.
1961 *Robens of Woldingham*, Alfred Robens, PC, b. 1910, m.
1977 *Roll of Ipsden*, Eric Roll, KCMG, CB, b. 1907, m.
1987 *Ross of Newport*, Stephen Sherlock Ross, b. 1926, m.
1975 *Ryder of Eaton Hastings*, Sydney Thomas Franklin (Don) Ryder, b. 1916, m.
1962 *Sainsbury*, Alan John Sainsbury, b. 1902, m.
1989 *Sainsbury of Preston Candover*, John Davan Sainsbury, b. 1927, m.
1987 *St. John of Fawsley*, Norman Antony Francis St. John-Stevas, PC, b. 1929.
1985 *Sanderson of Bowden*, Charles Russell Sanderson, b. 1933, m.
1979 *Scanlon*, Hugh Parr Scanlon, b. 1913, m.
1976 *Schon*, Frank Schon, b. 1912, m.
1972 *Seebohm*, Frederic Seebohm, TD, b. 1909, m.
1978 *Sefton of Garston*, William Henry Sefton, b. 1915, m.
1958 *Shackleton*, Edward Arthur Alexander Shackleton, KG, OBE, PC, b. 1911, m.
1989 *Sharp of Grimsdyke*, Eric Sharp, CBE, b. 1916, m.
1959 *Shawcross*, Hartley William Shawcross, GBE, PC, QC, b. 1902, w.
1980 *Sieff of Brimpton*, Marcus Joseph Sieff, OBE, b. 1913, m.
1971 *Simon of Glaisdale*, Jocelyn Edward Salis Simon, PC, b. 1911, m. (*Lord of Appeal, retired*).
1978 *Smith*, Rodney Smith, KBE, FRCS, b. 1914, m.
1965 *Soper*, Rev. Donald Oliver Soper, PH.D., b. 1903, m.
1990 *Soulsby*, Ernest Jackson Lawson Soulsby, PH.D., b. 1926, m.
1983 *Stallard*, Albert William Stallard, b. 1921, m.
1987 *Stevens of Ludgate*, David Robert Stevens, b. 1936, m.
1981 *Stodart of Leaston*, James Anthony Stodart, PC, b. 1916, m.
1983 *Stoddart of Swindon*, David Leonard Stoddart, b. 1926, m.
1969 *Stokes*, Donald Gresham Stokes, TD, b. 1914, m.
1979 *Strauss*, George Russell Strauss, PC, b. 1901, m.
1981 *Swann*, Michael Meredith Swann, PH.D., FRS, b. 1920, m.
1971 *Tanlaw*, Simon Brooke Mackay, b. 1934, m.
1978 *Taylor of Blackburn*, Thomas Taylor, CBE, b. 1929, m.
1968 *Taylor of Gryfe*, Thomas Johnston Taylor, b. 1912, m.
1982 *Taylor of Hadfield*, Francis Taylor, b. 1905, m.
1966 *Taylor of Mansfield*, Harry Bernard Taylor, CBE, b. 1895, w.
1987 *Thomas of Gwydir*, Peter John Mitchell Thomas, PC, QC, b. 1920, w.
1981 *Thomas of Swynnerton*, Hugh Swynnerton Thomas, b. 1931, m.
1977 *Thomson of Monifieth*, George Morgan Thomson, KT, PC, b. 1921, m.
1967 *Thorneycroft*, (George Edward) Peter Thorneycroft, CH, PC, b. 1909, m.
1962 *Todd*, Alexander Robertus Todd, OM, D.SC., D.Phil., FRS, b. 1907, w.
1990 *Tombs*, Francis Leonard Tombs, b. 1924, m.
1981 *Tordoff*, Geoffrey Johnson Tordoff, b. 1928, m.
1974 *Tranmire*, Robert Hugh Turton, KBE, MC, PC, b. 1903, m.
1979 *Underhill*, (Henry) Reginall Underhill, CBE, b. 1914, m.
1990 *Varley*, Eric Graham Varley, PC, b. 1932, m.
1985 *Vinson*, Nigel Vinson, LVO, b. 1931, m.
1990 *Wade of Chorlton*, (William) Oulton Wade, b. 1932, m.
1974 *Wallace of Campsie*, George Wallace, b. 1915, m.
1974 *Wallace of Coslany*, George Douglas Wallace, b. 1906, m.
1961 *Walston*, Henry David Leonard George Walston, CVO, b. 1912, m.
1989 *Walton of Detchant*, John Nicholas Walton, TD, FRCP, b. 1922, m.
1977 *Wedderburn of Charlton*, Kenneth William Wedderburn, QC, b. 1927, m.
1976 *Weidenfeld*, (Arthur) George Weidenfeld, b. 1919.
1980 *Weinstock*, Arnold Weinstock, b. 1924, m.
1965 *Wells-Pestell*, Reginald Alfred Wells-Pestell, CBE, b. 1910, m.
1978 *Whaddon*, (John) Derek Page, b. 1927, m.
1974 *Wigoder*, Basil Thomas Wigoder, QC, b. 1921, m.
1985 *Williams of Elvel*, Charles Cuthbert Powell Williams, CBE, b. 1933, m.
1963 *Willis*, Edward Henry Willis, b. 1918, m.
1969 *Wilson of Langside*, Henry Stephen Wilson, PC, QC, b. 1916, m.
1983 *Wilson of Rievaulx*, (James) Harold Wilson, KG, OBE, PC, FRS, b. 1916, m.
1975 *Winstanley*, Michael Platt Winstanley, b. 1918, m.
1965 *Winterbottom*, Ian Winterbottom, b. 1913, m.
1985 *Wolfson*, Leonard Gordon Wolfson, b. 1927, m.
1987 *Wyatt of Weeford*, Woodrow Lyle Wyatt, b. 1918, m.
1978 *Young of Dartington*, Michael Young, PH.D., b. 1915, m.
1984 *Young of Graffham*, David Ivor Young, PC, b. 1932, m.
1971 *Zuckerman*, Solly Zuckerman, OM, KCB, FRS, MD, D.SC., b. 1904, m.

BARONESSES

Created

1979 *Airey of Abingdon*, Diana Josceline Barbara Neave Airey, *b.* 1919, *w.*
1970 *Bacon*, Alice Martha Bacon, CBE, PC, *b.* 1911.
1967 *Birk*, Alma Birk, *b.* 1921, *m.*
1987 *Blackstone*, Tessa Ann Vosper Blackstone, PH.D., *b.* 1942.
1987 *Blatch*, Emily May Blatch, CBE, *b.* 1937, *m.*
1990 *Brigstocke*, Heather Renwick Brigstocke, *b.* 1929, *w.*
1964 *Brooke of Ystradfellte*, Barbara Muriel Brooke, DBE, *b.* 1908, *w.*
1962 *Burton of Coventry*, Elaine Frances Burton, *b.* 1904.
1982 *Carnegy of Lour*, Elizabeth Patricia Carnegy of Lour, *b.* 1925.
1990 *Castle of Blackburn*, Barbara Anne Castle, PC, *b.* 1910, *w.*
1982 *Cox*, Caroline Anne Cox, *b.* 1937, *m.*
1990 *Cumberlege*, Julia Frances Cumberlege, CBE, *b*, 1943, *m.*
1978 *David*, Nora Ratcliff David, *b.* 1913, *m.*
1974 *Delacourt-Smith of Alteryn*, Margaret Rosalind Delacourt-Smith, *b.* 1916, *m.*
1978 *Denington*, Evelyn Joyce Denington, DBE, *b.* 1907, *m.*
1990 *Dunn*, Lydia Selina Dunn, DBE, MLC, MEC, *b.* 1940, *m.*
1990 *Eccles of Moulton*, Diana Catherine Eccles, *b.* 19–, *m.*
1972 *Elles*, Diana Louie Elles, *b.* 1921, *m.*
1958 *Elliot of Harwood*, Katharine Elliot, DBE, *b.* 1903, *w.*
1981 *Ewart-Biggs*, (Felicity) Jane Ewart-Biggs, *b.* 1929, *w.*
1975 *Faithfull*, Lucy Faithfull, OBE, *b.* 1910.
1974 *Falkender*, Marcia Matilda Falkender, CBE, *b.* 1932.
1974 *Fisher of Rednal*, Doris Mary Gertrude Fisher, *b.* 1919, *w.*
1990 *Flather*, Shreela Flather, *b.* 19–, *m.*
1981 *Gardner of Parkes*, (Rachel) Trixie (Anne) Gardner, *b.* 1927, *m.*
1988 *Hart of South Lanark*, Judith Constance Mary Hart, DBE, PC, *b.* 1924, *m.*
1990 *Hollis of Heigham*, Patricia Lesley Hollis, D.PHIL., *b.* 1941, *m.*
1985 *Hooper*, Gloria Dorothy Hooper, *b.* 1939.
1965 *Hylton-Foster*, Audrey Pellew Hylton-Foster, DBE, *b.* 1908, *w.*
1979 *Jeger*, Lena May Jeger, *b.* 1915, *w.*
1967 *Llewelyn-Davies of Hastoe*, (Annie) Patricia Llewelyn-Davies, PC, *b.* 1915, *w.*
1978 *Lockwood*, Betty Lockwood, *b.* 1924, *w.*
1979 *McFarlane of Llandaff*, Jean Kennedy McFarlane, *b.* 1926.
1971 *Macleod of Borve*, Evelyn Hester Macleod, *b.* 1915, *w.*
1970 *Masham of Ilton*, Susan Lilian Primrose Cunliffe-Lister, *b.* 1935, *m.* (*Countess of Swinton*).
1982 *Nicol*, Olive Mary Wendy Nicol, *b.* 1923, *m.*
1989 *Oppenheim-Barnes*, Sally Oppenheim-Barnes, PC, *b.* 1930, *m.*
1990 *Park of Monmouth*, Daphne Margaret Sybil Désirée Park, CMG, OBE, *b.* 1921.
1964 *Phillips*, Norah Phillips, *b.* 1910, *w.*
1974 *Pike*, (Irene) Mervyn (Parnicott) Pike, *b.* 1918.
1981 *Platt of Writtle*, Beryl Catherine Platt, CBE, *b.* 1923, *m.*
1974 *Robson of Kiddington*, Inga-Stina Robson, *b.* 1919, *w.*
1979 *Ryder of Warsaw*, (Margaret) Susan Cheshire, CMG, OBE, *b.* 1924, *m.*
1971 *Seear*, (Beatrice) Nancy Seear, PC, *b.* 1913.
1967 *Serota*, Beatrice Serota, *b.* 1919, *m.*
1973 *Sharples*, Pamela Sharples, *b.* 1923, *m.*
1974 *Stedman*, Phyllis Stedman, OBE, *b.* 1916, *m.*
1980 *Trumpington*, Jean Alys Barker, *b.* 1922, *w.*
1985 *Turner of Camden*, Muriel Winifred Turner, *b.* 1927, *m.*
1974 *Vickers*, Joan Helen Vickers, DBE, *b.* 1907.
1985 *Warnock*, Helen Mary Warnock, DBE, *b.* 1924, *m.*
1970 *White*, Eirene Lloyd White, *b.* 1909, *w.*
1971 *Young*, Janet Mary Young, PC, *b.* 1926, *m.*

COURTESY TITLES

Holders of courtesy titles are addressed in the same manner as holders of substantive titles.

From this list it will be seen that, for example, the Marquess of Blandford is heir to the Dukedom of Marlborough, and Viscount Althorp to the Earldom of Spencer. Titles of second heirs are also given, and the courtesy title of the father of a second heir is indicated by *; e.g., Earl of Burlington, eldest son of *Marquess of Hartington.

Marquesses

Blandford—*Marlborough*, D.
Bowmont—*Roxburghe*, D.
Douglas and Clydesdale—*Hamilton*, D.
*Douro—*Wellington*, D.
*Graham—*Montrose*, D.
Granby—*Rutland*, D.
Hamilton—*Abercorn*, D.
*Hartington—*Devonshire*, D.
*Kildare—*Leinster*, D.
Lorne—*Argyll*, D.
*Tavistock—*Bedford*, D.
Worcester—*Beaufort*, D.

Earls

*Aboyne—*Huntly*, M.
Altamont—*Sligo*, M.
Ancram—*Lothian*, M.
Arundel and Surrey—*Norfolk*, D.
Bective—*Headfort*, M.
Belfast—*Donegall*, M.
*Brecknock—*Camden*, M.
Burford—*St. Albans*, D.
Burlington—**Hartington*, M.
Cardigan—*Ailesbury*, M.
Cassillis—*Ailsa*, M.
Compton—*Northampton*, M.
Dalkeith—*Buccleuch*, D.
Dumfries—*Bute*, M.
*Euston—*Grafton*, D.
Haddo—*Aberdeen and Temair*, M.
Hillsborough—*Downshire*, M.
*Hopetoun—*Linlithgow*, M.
Macduff—*Fife*, D.
*March and Kinrara—*Richmond*, D.
*Mount Charles—*Conyngham*, M.
Mornington—**Douro*, M.
Mulgrave—*Normanby*, M.
Offaly—**Kildare*, M.
*Ronaldshay—*Zetland*, M.
*St. Andrews—*Kent*, D.
*Shelburne—*Lansdowne*, M.
*Tyrone—*Waterford*, M.
Ulster—*Gloucester*, D.
Uxbridge—*Anglesey*, M.
Wiltshire—*Winchester*, M.
Yarmouth—*Hertford*, M.

Viscounts

Althorp—*Spencer*, E.
Amberley—*Russell*, E.

Andover—*Suffolk and Berkshire*, E.
Anson—*Lichfield*, E.
Asquith—*Oxford & Asquith*, E.
Boringdon—*Morley*, E.
Borodale—*Beatty*, E.
Boyle—*Shannon*, E.
Brocas—*Jellicoe*, E.
Calne and Calstone—**Shelburne*, E.
Campden—*Gainsborough*, E.
Carlow—*Portarlington*, E.
Carlton—*Wharncliffe*, E.
Castlereagh—*Londonderry*, M.
Chelsea—*Cadogan*, E.
Chewton—*Waldegrave*, E.
Clanfield—*Peel*, E.
Clive—*Powis*, E.
Coke—*Leicester*, E.
Corry—*Belmore*, E.
Corvedale—*Baldwin of Bewdley*, E.
Cranborne—*Salisbury*, M.
Cranley—*Onslow*, E.
Crichton—*Erne*, E.
Crowhurst—*Cottenham*, E.
Dalrymple—*Stair*, E.
Dangan—*Cowley*, E.
Dawick—*Haig*, E.
Deerhurst—*Coventry*, E.
Drumlanrig—*Queensberry*, M.
Dunwich—*Stradbroke*, E.
Dupplin—*Kinnoull*, E.
Ebrington—*Fortescue*, E.
Ednam—*Dudley*, E.
Elveden—*Iveagh*, E.
Emlyn—*Cawdor*, E.
Encombe—*Eldon*, E.
Ennismore—*Listowel*, E.
Enfield—*Strafford*, E.
Erleigh—*Reading*, M.
Errington—*Cromer*, E.
Feilding—*Denbigh*, E.
Fincastle—*Dunmore*, E.
FitzHarris—*Malmesbury*, E.
Folkestone—*Radnor*, E.
Garmoyle—*Cairns*, E.
Glandine—*Norbury*, E.
Glenapp—*Inchcape*, E.
Glentworth—*Limerick*, E.
Grimstone—*Verulam*, E.
Gwynedd—*Lloyd George of Dwyfor*, E.
Hawkesbury—*Liverpool*, E.
Ikerrin—*Carrick*, E.
Ingestre—*Shrewsbury*, E.
Ipswich—**Euston*, E.
Jocelyn—*Roden*, E.
Kelburn—*Glasgow*, E.
Kingsborough—*Kingston*, E.

Knebworth—*Lytton*, E.
Lascelles—*Harewood*, E.
Lewisham—*Dartmouth*, E.
Linley—*Snowdon*, E.
Loftus—*Ely*, M.
Lowther—*Lonsdale*, E.
Lumley—*Scarbrough*, E.
Lymington—*Portsmouth*, E.
Macmillan of Ovenden—*Stockton*, E.
Maidstone — *Winchilsea and Nottingham*, E.
Maitland—*Lauderdale*, E.
Malden—*Essex*, E.
Mandeville—*Manchester*, D.
Melgund—*Minto*, E.
Merton—*Nelson*, E.
Moore—*Drogheda*, E.
Morpeth—*Carlisle*, E.
Newport—*Bradford*, E.
Newry and Mourne—*Kilmorey*, E.
Northland—*Ranfurly*, E.
Parker—*Macclesfield*, E.
Perceval—*Egmont*, E.
Petersham—*Harrington*, E.
Pollington—*Mexborough*, E.
Prestwood—*Attlee*, E.
Quenington—*St. Aldwyn*, E.
Raynham—*Townshend*, M.
Reidhaven—*Seafield*, E.
Ruthven of Canberra—*Gowrie*, E.
St. Cyres—*Iddesleigh*, E.
Sandon—*Harrowby*, E.
Slane—**Mount Charles*, E.
Somerton—*Normanton*, E.
Stopford—*Courtown*, E.
Stormont—*Mansfield*, E.
Strathallan—*Perth*, E.
Stuart—*Castle Stewart*, E.
Suirdale—*Donoughmore*, E.
Tamworth—*Ferrers*, E.
Tarbat—*Cromartie*, E.
Tiverton—*Halsbury*, E.
Vaughan—*Lisburne*, E.
Villiers—*Jersey*, E.
Weymouth—*Bath*, M.
Windsor—*Plymouth*, E.
Wolmer—*Selborne*, E.
Woodstock—*Portland*, E.

Barons (Lord—)
Aberdour—*Morton*, E.
Apsley—*Bathurst*, E.
Ardee—*Meath*, E.
Ashley—*Shaftesbury*, E.

Balgonie—*Leven & Melville*, E.
Balniel—*Crawford and Balcarres*, E.
Berriedale—*Caithness*, E.
Bingham—*Lucan*, E.
Binning—*Haddington*, E.
Brooke—*Warwick*, E.
Bruce—*Elgin*, E.
Buckhurst—*De La Warr*, E.
Burghersh—*Westmorland*, E.
Burghley—*Exeter*, M.
Cardross—*Buchan*, E.
Clifton—*Darnley*, E.
Courtenay—*Devon*, E.
Dalmeny—*Rosebery*, E.
Doune—*Moray*, E.
Downpatrick—**St. Andrews*, E.
Eliot—*St. Germans*, E.
Erskine—*Mar & Kellie*, E.
Fintrie—**Graham*, M.
Gillford—*Clanwilliam*, E.
Glamis—*Strathmore*, E.
Greenock—*Cathcart*, E.
Guernsey—*Aylesford*, E.
Hay—*Erroll*, E.
Herbert—*Pembroke*, E.
Howland—**Tavistock*, M.
Hyde—*Clarendon*, E.
Inverurie—*Kintore*, E.
Irwin—*Halifax*, E.
Johnstone—*Annandale and Hartfell*, E.
La Poer—**Tyrone*, E.
Leslie—*Rothes*, E.
Leveson—*Granville*, E.
Loughborough—*Rosslyn*, E.
Mauchline—*Loudoun*, C.
Medway—*Cranbrook*, E.
Montgomerie—*Eglinton and Winton*, E.
Moreton—*Ducie*, E.
Naas—*Mayo*, E.
Neidpath—*Wemyss & March*, E.
Norreys—*Lindsey & Abingdon*, E.
North—*Guilford*, E.
Ogilvy—*Airlie*, E.
Oxmantown—*Rosse*, E.
Porchester—*Carnarvon*, E.
Ramsay—*Dalhousie*, E.
Romsey—*Mountbatten of Burma*, C.
Rosehill—*Northesk*, E.
Scrymgeour—*Dundee*, E.
Settrington—**March and Kinrara*, E.
Seymour—*Somerset*, D.
Strathnaver—*Sutherland*, C.
Wodehouse—*Kimberley*, E.
Worsley—*Yarborough*, E.

Surnames of Peers differing from their Titles

The following symbols indicate the rank of the peer holding each title: *C.* Countess; *D.* Duke; *E.* Earl; *M.* Marquess; *V.* Viscount; *Life Peer/Peeress. Where no designation is given, the title is that of an hereditary Baron or Baroness.

Abney-Hastings—*Loudoun, C.*
Acheson—*Gosford, E.*
Adderley—*Norton*
Addington—*Sidmouth, V.*
Agar—*Normanton, E.*
Airey—*A. of Abingdon**
Aitken—*Beaverbrook*
Akers-Douglas—*Chilston, V.*
Alexander—*A. of Potterhill**
Alexander—*A. of Tunis, E.*
Alexander—*A. of Weedon**
Alexander—*Caledon, E.*
Allen—*A. of Abbeydale**
Allen—*Croham**
Allanson-Winn—*Headley*
Allsopp—*Hindlip*
Anderson—*Waverley, V.*
Annesley—*Valentia, V.*
Anson—*Lichfield, E.*
Armstrong—*A. of Ilminster**
Armstrong-Jones—*Snowdon, E.*
Arthur—*Glenarthur*
Arundell—*Talbot of Malahide*
Ashley-Cooper—*Shaftesbury, E.*
Ashton—*A. of Hyde*
Asquith—*Oxford & Asquith, E.*
Assheton—*Clitheroe*
Astley—*Hastings*
Astor—*A. of Hever*
Atkins—*Colnbrook**
Aubrey-Fletcher—*Braye*
Bailey—*Glanusk*
Baillie—*Burton*
Baillie Hamilton—*Haddington, E.*
Baldwin—*B. of Bewdley, E.*
Balfour—*B. of Inchrye*
Balfour—*Kinross*
Balfour—*Riverdale*
Bampfylde—*Poltimore*
Banbury—*B. of Southam*
Baring—*Ashburton*
Baring—*Cromer, E.*
Baring—*Howick of Glendale*
Baring—*Northbrook*
Baring—*Revelstoke*
Barker—*Trumpington**
Barnes—*Gorell*
Barnewall—*Trimlestown*
Bathurst—*Bledisloe, V.*
Beauclerk—*St. Albans, D.*
Beaumont—*Allendale, V.*
Beaumont—*B. of Whitley**
Beavan—*Ardwick**
Beckett—*Grimthorpe*
Bellow—*Bellwin**
Bennet—*Tankerville, E.*

Bentinck—*Portland, E.*
Beresford—*Decies*
Beresford—*Waterford, M.*
Berry—*Camrose, V.*
Berry—*Hartwell**
Berry—*Kemsley, V.*
Bertie—*Lindsey, E.*
Best—*Wynford*
Bethell—*Westbury*
Bewicke-Copley—*Cromwell*
Bigham—*Mersey, V.*
Bigham—*Nairne*
Bingham—*Clanmorris*
Bingham—*Lucan, E.*
Blackwood—*Dufferin & Clandeboye*
Blades—*Ebbisham*
Bligh—*Darnley, E.*
Boote-Wilbraham—*Skelmersdale*
Boscawen—*Falmouth, V.*
Boston—*Boston of Faversham**
Bourke—*Mayo, E.*
Bowden—*Aylestone**
Bowes Lyon—*Strathmore, E.*
Bowyer—*Denham*
Boyd—*Kilmarnock*
Boyle—*Cork & Orrery, E.*
Boyle—*Glasgow, E.*
Boyle—*Shannon, E.*
Brabazon—*Meath, E.*
Brand—*Hampden, V.*
Brandon—*B. of Oakbrook**
Brassey—*B. of Apethorpe*
Brett—*Esher, V.*
Bridge—*B. of Harwich**
Bridgeman—*Bradford, E.*
Brodrick—*Midleton, V.*
Brooke—*Alanbrooke, V.*
Brooke—*Brookeborough, V.*
Brooke—*B. of Ystradfellte**
Brooks—*B. of Tremorfa**
Brooks—*Crawshaw*
Brougham—*Brougham and Vaux*
Broughton—*Fairhaven*
Browne—*Craigton**
Browne—*Kilmaine*
Browne—*Oranmore and Browne*
Browne—*Sligo, M.*
Brownlow—*Lurgan*
Bruce—*Aberdare*
Bruce—*Balfour of Burleigh*
Bruce—*B. of Donington**
Bruce—*Elgin and Kincardine, E.*
Brudenell-Bruce—*Ailesbury, M.*
Buchan—*Tweedsmuir*
Buckley—*Wrenbury*
Burton—*B. of Coventry**
Butler—*Carrick, E.*
Butler—*Dunboyne*
Butler—*Lanesborough, E.*

Butler—*Mountgarret, V.*
Butler—*Ormonde, M.*
Buxton—*B. of Alsa**
Byng—*Strafford, E.*
Byng—*Torrington, V.*
Callaghan—*C. of Cardiff**
Cameron—*C. of Lochbroom**
Campbell—*Argyll, D.*
Campbell—*Breadalbane and Holland, E.*
Campbell—*C. of Alloway**
Campbell—*C. of Croy**
Campbell—*C. of Eskan**
Campbell—*Cawdor, E.*
Campbell—*Colgrain*
Campbell—*Stratheden and Campbell*
Campbell-Gray—*Gray*
Canning—*Garvagh*
Capell—*Essex, E.*
Carington—*Carrington*
Carlisle—*C. of Bucklow**
Carmichael—*C. of Kelvingrove**
Carnegie—*Fife, D.*
Carnegie—*Northesk, E.*
Carnegie—*Southesk, E.*
Carr—*C. of Hadley**
Cary—*Falkland, V.*
Castle—*C. of Blackburn**
Caulfeild—*Charlemont, V.*
Cavendish—*C. of Furness**
Cavendish—*Chesham*
Cavendish—*Devonshire, D.*
Cavendish—*Waterpark*
Cayzer—*Rotherwick*
Cecil—*Amherst of Hackney*
Cecil—*Exeter, M.*
Cecil—*Rockley*
Cecil—*Salisbury, M.*
Chaloner—*Gisborough*
Chapman—*Northfield**
Charteris—*C. of Amisfield**
Charteris—*Wemyss and March, E.*
Cheshire—*Ryder of Warsaw**
Chetwynd-Talbot—*Shrewsbury, E.*
Chichester—*Donegall, M.*
Chichester-Clark—*Moyola**
Child-Villiers—*Jersey, E.*
Cholmondeley—*Delamere*
Chubb—*Hayter*
Clegg-Hill—*Hill, V.*
Clifford—*Clifford of Chudleigh*
Cochrane—*C. of Cults*
Cochrane—*Dundonald, E.*
Cocks—*C. of Hartcliffe**
Cocks—*Somers*
Cokayne—*Cullen of Ashbourne*
Coke—*Leicester, E.*

Cole—*Enniskillen, E.*
Collier—*Monkswell*
Colville—*Clydesmuir*
Colville—*C. of Culross, V.*
Compton—*Northampton, M.*
Conolly-Carew—*Carew*
Constantine—*C. of Stanmore**
Cooper—*Norwich, V.*
Corbett—*Rowallan*
Courtenay—*Devon, E.*
Cox—*Kings Norton**
Craig—*Craigavon, V.*
Crichton—*Erne, E.*
Crichton-Stuart—*Bute, M.*
Cripps—*Parmoor*
Crossley—*Somerleyton*
Cubitt—*Ashcombe*
Cunliffe-Lister—*Masham of Ilton**
Cunliffe-Lister—*Swinton, E.*
Curzon—*Howe, E.*
Curzon—*Scarsdale, V.*
Cust—*Brownlow*
Dalrymple—*Stair, E.*
Daubeny de Moleyns—*Ventry*
Davies—*Darwen*
Davies—*D. of Penrhys**
Davis—*Clinton-Davis**
Davison—*Broughshane*
Dawnay—*Downe, V.*
Dawson-Damer—*Portarlington, E.*
Dean—*D. of Beswick**
Deane—*Muskerry*
de Courcy—*Kingsale*
de Grey—*Walsingham*
Delacourt-Smith—*Delacourt Smith of Alteryn**
Denison—*Londesborough*
Denison-Pender—*Pender*
Devereux—*Hereford, V.*
Dewar—*Forteviot*
De Yarburgh-Bateson—*Deramore*
Dixon—*Glentoran*
Dodson—*Monk Bretton*
Donaldson—*D. of Kingsbridge**
Donaldson—*D. of Lymington**
Dormand—*D. of Easington**
Douglas—*Morton, E.*
Douglas—*Queensberry, M.*
Douglas-Hamilton—*Hamilton, D.*
Douglas-Hamilton—*Selkirk, E.*
Douglas-Home—*Dacre*
Douglas-Home—*Home of the Hirsel**
Douglas-Pennant—*Penrhyn*
Douglas-Scott-Montagu—*Montagu of Beaulieu*

Drummond—*Perth, E.*
Drummond—*Strange*
Dugdale—*Crathorne*
Duke—*Merrivale*
Duncombe—*Feversham*
Dundas—*Melville, V.*
Dundas—*Zetland, M.*
Eady—*Swinfen*
Eccles—*E. of Moulton**
Eden—*Auckland*
Eden—*E. of Winton**
Eden—*Henley*
Edgcumbe—*Mount Edgcumbe, E.*
Edmondson—*Sandford*
Edwardes—*Kensington*
Edwards—*Chelmer**
Edwards—*Crickhowell**
Egerton—*Sutherland, D.*
Egerton—*Wilton, E.*
Eliot—*St. Germans, E.*
Elliot—*E. of Harwood**
Elliot-Murray-Kynynmound—*Minto, E.*
Elliott—*E. of Morpeth**
Erroll—*E. of Hale*
Erskine—*Buchan, E.*
Erskine—*E. of Rerrick*
Erskine—*Mar & Kellie, E.*
Erskine-Murray—*Elibank*
Evans—*E. of Claughton**
Evans—*Mountevans*
Evans-Freke—*Carbery*
Eve—*Silsoe*
Eyres Monsell—*Monsell, V.*
Fairfax—*F. of Cameron*
Fane—*Westmorland, E.*
Feilding—*Denbigh, E.*
Fellowes—*De Ramsey*
Fermor-Hesketh—*Hesketh*
Fiennes—*Saye & Sele*
Fiennes-Clinton—*Lincoln, E.*
Finch Hatton—*Winchilsea, E.*
Finch-Knightley—*Aylesford, E.*
Fisher—*F. of Rednal**
Fitzalan-Howard—*Herries of Terregles*
Fitzalan-Howard—*Norfolk, D.*
FitzClarence—*Munster, E.*
FitzGerald—*Leinster, D.*
Fitzherbert—*Stafford*
Fitz-Maurice—*Orkney, E.*
FitzRoy—*Grafton, D.*
FitzRoy Newdegate—*Daventry, V.*
Fletcher-Vane—*Inglewood*
Flower—*Ashbrook, V.*
Foley Berkeley—*Berkeley*
Foljambe—*Liverpool, E.*
Foot—*Caradon**
Forbes—*Granard, E.*
Fox-Strangways—*Ilchester, E.*
Frankland—*Zouche*

Fraser—*F. of Carmyllie**
Fraser—*F. of Kilmorack**
Fraser—*Lovat*
Fraser—*Saltoun*
Fraser—*Strathalmond*
Freeman-Grenville—*Kinloss*
Fremantle—*Cottesloe*
French—*De Freyne*
Galbraith—*Strathclyde*
Ganzoni—*Belstead*
Gardner—*G. of Parkes**
Gathorne-Hardy—*Cranbrook, E.*
Gibbs—*Aldenham*
Gibbs—*Wraxall*
Gibson—*Ashbourne*
Giffard—*Halsbury, E.*
Gilbey—*Vaux of Harrowden*
Glyn—*Wolverton*
Godley—*Kilbracken*
Goff—*G. of Chieveley**
Gordon—*Aberdeen, M.*
Gordon—*Huntly, M.*
Gordon Lennox—*Richmond, D.*
Gore—*Arran, E.*
Gough-Calthorpe—*Calthorpe*
Graham—*G. of Edmonton**
Graham—*Montrose, D.*
Graham-Toler—*Norbury, E.*
Grant of Grant—*Strathspey*
Grant-Ferris—*Harvington**
Granville—*G. of Eye**
Gray—*G. of Contin**
Greaves—*Dysart, C.*
Greenall—*Daresbury*
Greene—*G. of Harrow Weald**
Greenhill—*G. of Harrow**
Greville—*Warwick, E.*
Grey—*G. of Naunton**
Grimston—*G. of Westbury*
Grimston—*Verulam, E.*
Grosvenor—*Ebury*
Grosvenor—*Westminster, D.*
Guest—*Wimborne, V.*
Guinness—*Iveagh, E.*
Guinness—*Moyne*
Gully—*Selby, V.*
Gurdon—*Cranworth*
Gwynne Jones—*Chalfont**
Hamilton—*Abercorn, D.*
Hamilton—*Belhaven and Stenton*
Hamilton—*Dudley*
Hamilton—*H. of Dalzell*
Hamilton—*Holm Patrick*
Hamilton-Russell—*Boyne, V.*
Hamilton-Smith—*Colwyn*
Hanbury-Tracy—*Sudeley*
Handcock—*Castlemaine*
Harbord-Hamond—*Suffield*
Harding—*H. of Petherton*

Hardinge—*H. of Penshurst*
Hare—*Blakenham, V.*
Hare—*Listowel, E.*
Harmsworth—*Rothermere, V.*
Harris—*H. of Greenwich**
Harris—*H. of High Cross**
Harris—*Malmesbury, E.*
Hart—*H. of South Lanark**
Harvey—*H. of Prestbury**
Harvey—*H. of Tasburgh*
Hastings Bass—*Huntingdon, E.*
Hatch—*H. of Lusby**
Hay—*Erroll, E.*
Hay—*Kinnoull, E.*
Hay—*Tweeddale, M.*
Heathcote-Drummond-Willoughby—*Willoughby de Eresby*
Hely-Hutchinson—*Donoughmore, E.*
Henderson—*Faringdon*
Henderson—*H. of Brompton**
Hennessy—*Windlesham*
Henniker-Major—*Henniker*
Hepburne-Scott—*Polwarth*
Herbert—*Carnarvon, E.*
Herbert—*Hemingford*
Herbert—*Pembroke, E.*
Herbert—*Powis, E.*
Hermon-Hodge—*Wyfold*
Hervey—*Bristol, M.*
Hewitt—*Lifford, V.*
Hicks Beach—*St. Aldwyn, E.*
Hill—*Downshire, M.*
Hill—*Sandys*
Hill-Trevor—*Trevor*
Hobart-Hampden—*Buckinghamshire, E.*
Hogg—*Hailsham of St. Marylebone**
Holland-Hibbert—*Knutsford, V.*
Hollis—*H. of Heigham**
Holme—*H. of Cheltenham**
Holmes à Court—*Heytesbury*
Hood—*Bridport, V.*
Hope—*Glendevon*
Hope—*Linlithgow, M.*
Hope—*Rankeillour*
Hope Johnstone—*Annandale and Hartfell, E.*
Hope-Morley—*Hollenden*
Hopkinson—*Colyton*
Hopwood—*Southborough*
Hore Ruthven—*Gowrie, E.*
Houghton—*H. of Sowerby**
Hovell-Thurlow-Cumming-Bruce—*Thurlow*
Howard—*Carlisle, E.*
Howard—*Effingham, E.*
Howard—*H. of Penrith*
Howard—*Strathcona*

Howard—*Suffolk and Berkshire, E.*
Howie—*H. of Troon**
Hubbard—*Addington*
Huggins—*Malvern, V.*
Hughes—*Cledwyn of Penrhos**
Hughes-Young—*St. Helens*
Hunt—*H. of Tanworth**
Hunter—*H. of Newington**
Hutchinson—*H. of Lullington**
Ingrams—*Darcy de Knayth*
Innes-Ker—*Roxburghe, D.*
Inskip—*Caldecote, V.*
Irby—*Boston*
Irvine—*I. of Lairg**
Isaacs—*Reading, M.*
Jackson—*Allerton*
James—*J. of Rusholme**
James—*Northbourne*
Jauncey—*J. of Tullichettle**
Jebb—*Gladwyn*
Jenkin—*J. of Roding**
Jenkins—*J. of Hillhead**
Jenkins—*J. of Putney**
Jervis—*St. Vincent, V.*
Jocelyn—*Roden, E.*
Johnston—*J. of Rockport**
Jolliffe—*Hylton*
Joynson-Hicks—*Brentford, V.*
Kaberry—*K. of Adel**
Kay-Shuttleworth—*Shuttleworth*
Kearley—*Devonport, V.*
Keith—*K. of Castleacre**
Keith—*K. of Kinkel**
Keith—*Kintore, E.*
Kemp—*Rochdale, V.*
Kennedy—*Ailsa, M.*
Kenworthy—*Strabolgi*
Keppel—*Albemarle, E.*
Kerr—*Lothian, M.*
Kerr—*Teviot*
King—*Lovelace, E.*
King—*K. of Wartnaby**
King-Tenison—*Kingston, E.*
Kitchener—*K. of Khartoum, E.*
Kitson—*Airedale*
Knatchbull—*Brabourne*
Knatchbull-Mountbatten of Burma, C.*
Knox—*Ranfurly, E.*
Lamb—*Rochester*
Lambart—*Cavan, E.*
Lampson—*Killearn*
Lane—*L. of Horsell**
Lascelles—*Harewood, E.*
Law—*Coleraine*
Law—*Ellenborough*
Lawrence—*Trevethin and Oaksey*
Lawson—*Burnham*
Lawson-Johnston—*Luke*

Legge—*Dartmouth, E.*
Legh—*Grey of Codnor*
Legh—*Newton*
Leith—*Burgh*
Lennox-Boyd—*Boyd of Merton, V.*
Le Poer Trench—*Clancarty, E.*
Leslie—*Rothes, E.*
Leslie Melville—*Leven and Melville, E.*
Lever—*Leverhulme, V.*
Lever—*L. of Manchester*
Leveson-Gower—*Granville, E.*
Lewis—*L. of Newnham*
Liddell—*Ravensworth*
Lindesay-Bethune—*Lindsay, E.*
Lindsay—*Crawford, E.*
Lindsay—*L. of Birker*
Littleton—*Hatherton*
Llewelyn-Davies—*Llewelyn-Davies of Hastoe**
Lloyd—*L. of Hampstead**
Lloyd—*L. of Kilgerran**
Lloyd George—*Lloyd George of Dwyfor, E.*
Lloyd George—*Tenby, V.*
Lloyd-Mostyn—*Mostyn*
Loder—*Wakehurst*
Lopes—*Roborough*
Low—*Aldington*
Lowry-Corry—*Belmore, E.*
Lowther—*Lonsdale, E.*
Lowther—*Ullswater, V.*
Lubbock—*Avebury*
Lucas—*L. of Chilworth*
Lumley—*Scarbrough, E.*
Lumley-Savile—*Savile*
Lyon-Dalberg-Acton—*Acton*
Lysaght—*Lisle*
Lyttelton—*Chandos, V.*
Lyttelton—*Cobham, V.*
Lytton Cobbold—*Cobbold*
McAlpine—*M. of West Green**
Macaulay—*M. of Bragar**
McClintock-Bunbury—*Rathdonnell*
McColl—*M. of Dulwich**
Macdonald—*M. of Gwaenysgor*
Macdonald of Macdonald—*Macdonald*
McDonnell—*Antrim, E.*
McFadzean—*M. of Kelvinside**
McFarlane—*M. of Llandaff**
McGregor—*M. of Durris**
McIntosh—*M. of Haringey**
Mackay—*Inchcape, E.*
Mackay—*M. of Clashfern**
Mackay—*Reay*
Mackay—*Tanlaw**
Mackenzie—*Cromartie, E.*
Mackie—*John-Mackie**

Mackie—*M. of Benshie**
Mackintosh—*M. of Halifax, V.*
McLaren—*Aberconway*
Maclay—*Muirshiel, V.*
MacLehose—*M. of Beoch**
Macleod—*M. of Borve**
MacLeod—*M. of Fuinary**
Macmillan—*Stockton, E.*
Macpherson—*M. of Drumochter*
Macpherson—*Strathcarron*
Maffey—*Rugby*
Maitland—*Lauderdale, E.*
Makgill—*Oxfuird, V.*
Makins—*Sherfield*
Manners—*Rutland, D.*
Manningham-Buller—*Dilhorne, V.*
Mansfield—*Sandhurst*
Marks—*M. of Broughton*
Marquis—*Woolton, E.*
Marshall—*M. of Goring**
Marshall—*M. of Leeds**
Marsham—*Romney, E.*
Martyn-Hemphill—*Hemphill*
Mason—*M. of Barnsley**
Maude—*Hawarden, V.*
Maude—*M. of Stratford-upon-Avon**
Maxwell—*de Ros*
Maxwell—*Farnham*
Meade—*Clanwilliam, E.*
Mercer Nairne Petty-Fitzmaurice—*Lansdowne, M.*
Millar—*Inchyra*
Milles-Lade—*Sondes, E.*
Milner—*M. of Leeds*
Mitchell-Thomson—*Selsdon*
Mitford—*Redesdale*
Monckton—*M. of Brenchley, V.*
Monckton-Arundell—*Galway, V.*
Mond—*Melchett*
Money-Coutts—*Latymer*
Montagu—*Manchester, D.*
Montagu—*Swaythling*
Montagu Douglas Scott—*Buccleuch, D.*
Montagu Stuart Wortley—*Wharncliffe, E.*
Montague—*Amwell*
Montgomerie—*Eglinton, E.*
Montgomery—*M. of Alamein, V.*
Moore—*Drogheda, E.*
Moore—*M. of Wolvercote**
Moore-Brabazon—*Brabazon of Tara*
Moreton—*Ducie, E.*
Morris—*Killanin*
Morris—*M. of Castle Morris**
Morris—*M. of Kenwood*

Morrison—*Dunrossil, V.*
Morrison—*Margadale*
Morton—*M. of Shuna**
Mosley—*Ravensdale*
Mountbatten—*Milford Haven, M.*
Muff—*Calverley*
Mulholland—*Dunleath*
Murray—*Atholl, D.*
Murray—*Dunmore, E.*
Murray—*Mansfield and Mansfield, E.*
Murray—*M. of Epping Forest**
Murray—*M. of Newhaven**
Murton—*M. of Lindisfarne**
Nall-Cain—*Brocket*
Napier—*Napier and Ettrick*
Napier—*N. of Magdala*
Needham—*Kilmorey, E.*
Nelson—*N. of Stafford*
Nevill—*Abergavenny, M.*
Neville—*Braybrooke*
Nicolson—*Carnock*
Nivison—*Glendyne*
Noel—*Gainsborough, E.*
Noel-Paton—*Ferrier**
North—*Guilford, E.*
Northcote—*Iddesleigh, E.*
Norton—*Grantley*
Norton—*Rathcreedan*
Nugent—*N. of Guildford**
Nugent—*Westmeath, E.*
O'Brien—*Inchiquin*
O'Brien—*O'Brien of Lothbury**
Ogilvie-Grant—*Seafield, E.*
Ogilvy—*Airlie, E.*
Oliver—*O. of Aylmerton**
O'Neill—*Rathcavan*
Orde-Powlett—*Bolton*
Ormsby-Gore—*Harlech*
Page—*Whaddon**
Paget—*Anglesey, M.*
Pakenham—*Longford, E.*
Pakington—*Hampton*
Palmer—*Lucas of Crudwell*
Palmer—*Selborne, E.*
Park—*P. of Monmouth**
Parker—*Macclesfield, E.*
Parker—*Morley, E.*
Parnell—*Congleton*
Parsons—*Rosse, E.*
Paulet—*Winchester, M.*
Peake—*Ingleby, V.*
Pearson—*Cowdray, V.*
Pearson—*P. of Rannoch**
Pease—*Daryngton*
Pease—*Gainford*
Pease—*Wardington*
Pelham—*Chichester, E.*
Pelham—*Yarborough, E.*
Pellew—*Exmouth, V.*
Penny—*Marchwood, V.*
Pepys—*Cottenham, E.*
Perceval—*Egmont, E.*
Percy—*Northumberland, D.*
Perry—*P. of Walton**
Pery—*Limerick, E.*

Peyton—*P. of Yeovil**
Philipps—*Milford*
Philipps—*St. Davids, V.*
Phipps—*Normanby, M.*
Pitt—*P. of Hampstead**
Platt—*P. of Writtle**
Pleydell-Bouverie—*Radnor, E.*
Plummer—*P. of St. Marylebone**
Plumptre—*Fitzwalter*
Plunkett—*Dunsany*
Plunkett—*Louth*
Pollock—*Hanworth, V.*
Pomeroy—*Harberton, V.*
Ponsonby—*Bessborough, E.*
Ponsonby—*de Mauley*
Ponsonby—*P. of Shulbrede*
Ponsonby—*Sysonby*
Portal—*P. of Hungerford*
Porter—*P. of Luddenham**
Powys—*Lilford*
Pratt—*Camden, M.*
Preston—*Gormanston, V.*
Primrose—*Rosebery, E.*
Prittie—*Dunalley*
Ramsay—*Dalhousie, E.*
Ramsbotham—*Soulbury, V.*
Rawlinson—*R. of Ewell**
Rees-Williams—*Ogmore*
Rhys—*Dynevor*
Richards—*Milverton*
Richardson—*R. of Duntisbourne**
Rippon—*R. of Hexham**
Ritchie—*R. of Dundee*
Robens—*R. of Woldingham**
Roberts—*Clwyd*
Robertson—*R. of Oakridge*
Robertson—*Wharton*
Robinson—*Martonmere*
Robson—*R. of Kiddington**
Roche—*Fermoy*
Rodd—*Rennell*
Roll—*R. of Ipsden**
Roper-Curzon—*Teynham*
Rospigliosi—*Newburgh, E.*
Ross—*R. of Newport**
Rous—*Stradbroke, E.*
Rowley-Conwy—*Langford*
Royle—*Fanshawe of Richmond**
Runciman—*R. of Doxford, V.*
Russell—*Ampthill*
Russell—*Bedford, D.*
Russell—*de Clifford*
Russell—*R. of Liverpool*
Ryder—*Harrowby, E.*
Ryder—*R. of Eaton Hastings**
Sackville—*De La Warr, E.*
Sackville-West—*Sackville*
Sainsbury—*S. of Preston Candover**

C. Countess; D. Duke; E. Earl; M. Marquess; V. Viscount; * Life Peer.

St. Aubyn—*St. Levan*
St. Clair—*Sinclair*
St. Clair-Erskine—*Rosslyn, E.*
St. John—*Bolingbroke and St. John, V.*
St. John—*St. John of Blesto*
St. John-Stevas—*St. John of Fawsley**
St. Leger—*Doneraile, V.*
Samuel—*Bearsted, V.*
Sanderson—*S. of Bowden**
Sandilands—*Torphichen*
Saumarez—*De Saumarez*
Savile—*Mexborough, E.*
Scarlett—*Abinger*
Sclater-Booth—*Basing*
Scott—*Eldon, E.*
Scott-Ellis—*Howard de Walden*
Scrymgeour—*Dundee, E.*
Seager—*Leighton of St. Mellons*
Seely—*Mottistone*
Sefton—*S. of Garston**
Seymour—*Hertford, M.*
Seymour—*Somerset, D.*
Sharp—*S. of Grimsdyke**
Shaw—*Craigmyle*
Shirley—*Ferrers, E.*
Short—*Glenamara**
Siddeley—*Kenilworth*
Sidney—*De L'Isle, V.*
Sieff—*S. of Brimpton**
Simon—*S. of Glaisdale**
Simon—*S. of Wythenshawe*
Sinclair—*Caithness, E.*
Sinclair—*S. of Cleeve*
Sinclair—*Thurso, V.*
Skeffington—*Massereene, V.*
Smith—*Bicester*
Smith—*Hambleden, V.*

Smith—*Kirkhill**
Somerset—*Beaufort, D.*
Somerset—*Raglan*
Souter—*Audley*
Spencer—*Churchill, V.*
Spencer-Churchill—*Marlborough, D.*
Spring Rice—*Monteagle of Brandon*
Stanhope—*Harrington, E.*
Stanley—*Derby, E.*
Stanley—*Stanley of Alderley & Sheffield*
Stapleton-Cotton-Combermere, V.*
Stevens—*S. of Ludgate**
Stewart—*Galloway, E.*
Stodart—*S. of Leaston**
Stoddart—*S. of Swindon**
Stonor—*Camoys*
Stopford—*Courtown, E.*
Stourton—*Mowbray*
Strachey—*O'Hagan*
Strutt—*Belper*
Strutt—*Rayleigh*
Stuart—*Castle Stewart, E.*
Stuart—*Moray, E.*
Stuart—*S. of Findhorn, V.*
Suenson-Taylor—*Grantchester*
Taylor—*Ingrow**
Taylor—*T. of Blackburn**
Taylor—*T. of Gryfe**
Taylor—*T. of Hadfield**
Taylor—*T. of Mansfield**
Taylour—*Headfort, M.*
Temple-Gore-Langton—*Temple of Stowe, E.*
Tennant—*Glenconner*
Thellusson—*Rendlesham*
Thesiger—*Chelmsford, V.*
Thomas—*T. of Gwydir**
Thomas—*T. of Swynnerton**

Thomas—*Tonypandy, V.*
Thomson—*T. of Fleet*
Thomson—*T. of Monifieth**
Thynne—*Bath, M.*
Tottenham—*Ely, M.*
Trefusis—*Clinton*
Trench—*Ashtown*
Trevor-Roper—*Dacre of Glanton**
Tufton—*Hothfield*
Turner—*Netherthorpe*
Turner—*T. of Camden**
Turnour—*Winterton, E.*
Turton—*Tranmire**
Tyrell-Kenyon—*Kenyon*
Vanden-Bempde-Johnstone—*Derwent*
Vane—*Barnard*
Vane—*Inglewood*
Vane-Tempest-Stewart—*Londonderry, M.*
Vanneck—*Huntingfield*
Vaughan—*Lisburne, E.*
Vaughan-Morgan—*Reigate**
Vereker—*Gort, V.*
Verney—*Willoughby de Broke*
Vernon—*Lyveden*
Vesey—*De Vesci, V.*
Villiers—*Clarendon, E.*
Vivian—*Swansea*
Wade—*W. of Chorlton**
Walker-Smith—*Broxbourne**
Wallace—*W. of Campsie**
Wallace—*W. of Coslany**
Wallop—*Portsmouth, E.*
Walton—*W. of Detchant**
Ward—*Bangor, V.*
Ward—*Dudley, E.*
Warrender—*Bruntisfield*
Watson—*Manton*
Wedderburn—*W. of Charlton**

Weir—*Inverforth*
Weld-Forester—*Forester*
Wellesley—*Cowley, E.*
Wellesley—*Wellington, D.*
Westenra—*Rossmore*
White—*Annaly*
Whiteley—*Marchamley*
Whitfield—*Kenswood*
Williams—*Berners*
Williams—*W. of Elvel**
Williamson—*Forres*
Willoughby—*Middleton*
Wills—*Dulverton*
Wilson—*Moran*
Wilson—*Nunburnholme*
Wilson—*W. of Langside**
Wilson—*W. of Rievaulx**
Windsor—*Gloucester, D.*
Windsor—*Kent, D.*
Windsor-Clive—*Plymouth, E.*
Wingfield—*Powerscourt, V.*
Winn—*St. Oswald*
Wodehouse—*Kimberley, E.*
Wood—*Halifax, E.*
Wood—*Holderness**
Woodhouse—*Terrington*
Wyatt—*W. of Weeford**
Wyndham—*Egremont & Leconfield*
Wyndham-Quin—*Dunraven, E.*
Wynn—*Newborough*
Yarde-Buller—*Churston*
Yerburgh—*Alvingham*
Yorke—*Hardwicke, E.*
Young—*Kennet*
Young—*Y. of Dartington**
Young—*Y. of Graffham**
Younger—*Y. of Leckie, V.*

C. Countess; *D.* Duke; *E.* Earl; *M.* Marquess; *V.* Viscount; * Life Peer.

ORDERS OF CHIVALRY

The Most Noble Order of the Garter (1348)—KG

Ribbon, Garter Blue. *Motto*, Honi soit qui mal y pense (*Shame on him who thinks evil of it*). The number of Knights Companions is limited to 24.

SOVEREIGN OF THE ORDER—THE QUEEN

Lady of the Garter—HM QUEEN ELIZABETH THE QUEEN MOTHER, 1936.

Royal Knights

HRH The Duke of Edinburgh, 1947.
HRH The Prince of Wales, 1958.
HRH The Duke of Kent, 1985.

Extra Knights Companions and Ladies

Princess Juliana of the Netherlands, 1958.
HM The King of Norway, 1959.
HM The King of The Belgians, 1963.
HRH The Grand Duke of Luxemburg, 1972.
HM The Queen of Denmark, 1979.
HM The King of Sweden, 1983
HM The King of Spain, 1988.
HM The Queen of the Netherlands, 1989.

Knights and Lady Companions

The Viscount De L'Isle, 1968.
The Lord Ashburton, 1969.
Sir Cennydd Traherne, 1970.
The Earl Waldegrave, 1971.
The Earl of Longford, 1971.
The Lord Shackleton, 1974.
The Marquess of Abergavenny, 1974.
The Lord Wilson of Rievaulx, 1976.
The Duke of Grafton, 1976.
The Earl of Cromer, 1977.
The Lord Elworthy, 1977.
The Lord Hunt, 1979.
Sir Paul Hasluck, 1979.
The Duke of Norfolk, 1983.
The Lord Lewin, 1983.
The Lord Richardson of Duntisbourne, 1983.

The Marquess of Normanby, 1985.
The Lord Carrington, 1985.
The Lord Callaghan of Cardiff, 1987.
The Viscount Leverhulme, 1988.
The Lord Hailsham of St. Marylebone, 1988.
Lavinia, Duchess of Norfolk, 1990.
The Duke of Wellington, 1990.
Field Marshal Lord Bramall, 1990.
Prelate, The Bishop of Winchester.
Chancellor, The Marquess of Abergavenny, KG, OBE.
Register, The Dean of Windsor.
Garter King of Arms, Sir Colin Cole, KCVO, TD.
Gentleman Usher of the Black Rod, Air Chief Marshal Sir John Gingell, GBE, KCB.
Secretary, D. H. B. Chesshyre, LVO.

The Most Ancient and Most Noble Order of the Thistle (revived 1687)—KT

Ribbon, Green. *Motto*, Nemo me impune lacessit (*No one provokes me with impunity*). The number of Knights is limited to 16.

SOVEREIGN OF THE ORDER—THE QUEEN

Lady of the Thistle—HM QUEEN ELIZABETH THE QUEEN MOTHER, 1937

Royal Knights

HRH The Duke of Edinburgh, 1952.
HRH The Prince of Wales (*Duke of Rothesay*), 1977.

Extra Knight

HM The King of Norway, 1962.

Knights

The Lord Home of the Hirsel, 1962.
The Earl of Wemyss and March, 1966.

The Earl of Dalhousie, 1971.
The Lord Clydesmuir, 1972.
The Viscount Muirshiel, 1973.
Sir Donald Cameron of Lochiel, 1973.
The Earl of Selkirk, 1976.
The Lord McFadzean, 1976.
The Hon. Lord Cameron, 1978.
The Duke of Buccleuch and Queensberry, 1978.
The Earl of Elgin and Kincardine, 1981.
The Lord Thomson of Monifieth, 1981.

The Lord MacLehose of Beoch, 1983.
The Earl of Airlie, 1985.
Capt. Sir Iain Tennant, 1986.
Chancellor, The Lord Home of the Hirsel.
Dean, The Very Rev. G. I. Macmillan.
Secretary and Lord Lyon King of Arms, Sir Malcolm Innes of Edingight, KCVO, WS.
Usher of the Green Rod, Rear-Admiral D.A. Dunbar-Nasmith, CB, DSC.

The Most Honourable Order of the Bath (1725)

GCB, Knight (or Dame) Grand Cross; KCB, Knight Commander; DCB, Dame Commander; CB, Companion

GCB Mil.   *Ribbon*, Crimson. *Motto*, Tria juncta in uno (*Three joined in one*).   GCB Civ.

Remodelled 1815, and enlarged many times since. The Order is divided into civil and military divisions. Women became eligible for the Order from Jan. 1, 1971.

THE SOVEREIGN; *Great Master and First or Principal Knight Grand Cross*, HRH The Prince of Wales, KG, KT, GCB; *Dean of the Order*, The Dean of Westminster; *Bath King of Arms*, Air Chief Marshal Sir David Evans, GCB, CBE; *Registrar and Secretary*, Rear-Adm. D. E. Macey, CB; *Genealogist*, Dr. C. Swan, CVO, Ph.D.; *Gentleman Usher of the Scarlet Rod*, Air Vice-Marshal Sir Richard Peirse, KCVO, CB; *Deputy Secretary*, The Secretary of the Central Chancery of the Orders of Knighthood; *Chancery*, Central Chancery of the Orders of Knighthood, St. James's Palace, SW1A 1BH.

The Order of Merit (1902)—OM
Ribbon, Blue and Crimson.

OM il.   This Order is designed as a special distinction for eminent men and women without conferring a knighthood upon them. The Order is limited in numbers to 24, with the addition of foreign honorary members. Membership is of two kinds, Military and Civil,   OM Civ. the badge of the former having crossed swords, and the latter oak leaves. Membership is denoted by the suffix OM, which follows the first class of the Order of the Bath and precedes the letters designating membership of the inferior classes of the Bath and all classes of the lesser Orders of Knighthood.

THE SOVEREIGN
HRH THE DUKE OF EDINBURGH (1968)

Dorothy Hodgkin, 1965.
The Lord Zuckerman, 1968.
The Lord Penney, 1969.
Dame Veronica Wedgwood, 1969.
Sir Isaiah Berlin, 1971.
Sir George Edwards, 1971.
Sir Alan Hodgkin, 1973.
The Lord Todd, 1977.
The Lord Franks, 1977.

Gp. Capt. Leonard Cheshire, VC, 1981.
Sir Andrew Huxley, 1983.
Sir Sidney Nolan, 1983.
Sir Michael Tippett, 1983.
Rev. Prof. Owen Chadwick, KBE, 1983.
Graham Greene, 1986.
Frederick Sanger, 1986.

Air Commodore Sir Frank Whittle, 1986.
Sir Yehudi Menuhin, 1987.
Prof. Sir Ernst Gombrich, 1988.
Dr. Max Perutz, 1988.
Dame Cicely Saunders, 1989.
The Lord Porter of Luddenham, 1990.
Honorary Member, Mother Teresa, 1983.

Secretary and Registrar, Sir Edward Ford, KCB, KCVO.
Chancery, Central Chancery of the Orders of Knighthood, St. James's Palace, SW1A 1BH.

The Most Exalted Order of the Star of India (1861)
GCSI, Knight Grand Commander; KCSI, Knight Commander; CSI, Companion
Ribbon, Light Blue, with White Edges. *Motto,* Heaven's Light our Guide.

THE SOVEREIGN; *Registrar,* The Secretary of the Central Chancery of the Orders of Knighthood. No conferments have been made since 1947.

The Most Distinguished Order of St. Michael and St. George (1818)

GCMG, Knight (or Dame) Grand Cross; KCMG, Knight Commander; DCMG, Dame Commander; CMG, Companion

GCMG   *Ribbon,* Saxon Blue, with Scarlet centre. *Motto,* Auspicium melioris aevi (Token of   KCMG
a better age)

THE SOVEREIGN; *Grand Master,* HRH The Duke of Kent, KG, GCMG, GCVO, ADC; *Prelate,* The Rt. Rev. the Bishop of Coventry; *Chancellor,* The Lord Carrington, KG, GCMG, CH, MC, PC; *Secretary,* Sir Patrick Wright, GCMG; *Registrar,* Sir John Graham, Bt., GCMG; *King of Arms,* Sir Oliver Wright, GCMG, GCVO, DSC; *Gentleman Usher of the Blue Rod,* Sir John Moreton, KCMG, KCVO, MC; *Dean,* The Dean of St. Paul's; *Deputy Secretary,* The Secretary of the Central Chancery of the Orders of Knighthood; *Chancery,* Central Chancery of the Orders of Knighthood, St. James's Palace, SW1A 1BH.

The Most Eminent Order of the Indian Empire (1868)
GCIE, Knight Grand Commander; KCIE, Knight Commander; CIE, Companion
Ribbon, Imperial Purple. *Motto,* Imperatricis auspiciis (*Under the auspices of the Empress*).

THE SOVEREIGN; *Registrar,* The Secretary of the Central Chancery of the Orders of Knighthood. No conferments have been made since 1947.

The Imperial Order of the Crown of India (for Ladies)—CI
Instituted 1877. *Badge,* the royal cipher in jewels within an oval, surmounted by an Heraldic Crown and attached to a bow of light blue watered ribbon, edged white. The honour does not confer any rank or title upon the recipient. No conferments have been made since 1947.

HM THE QUEEN, 1947.
HM Queen Elizabeth the Queen Mother, 1931.

HRH The Princess Margaret, Countess of Snowdon, 1947.

HRH The Princess Alice, Duchess of Gloucester, 1937.
HH Maharani of Travancore, 1929.

The Royal Victorian Order (1896)
GCVO, Knight or Dame Grand Cross; KCVO, Knight Commander; DCVO, Dame Commander; CVO, Commander; LVO, Lieutenant; MVO, Member
Ribbon, Blue, with Red and White Edges. *Motto,* Victoria.

GCVO   THE SOVEREIGN; *Grand Master,* HM Queen Elizabeth The Queen Mother; *Chancellor,*   KCVO
The Lord Chamberlain; *Secretary,* The Keeper of the Privy Purse; *Registrar,* The Secretary of the Central Chancery of the Orders of Knighthood; *Chaplain,* The Rev. J. Robson. *Hon. Genealogist,* D. H. B. Chesshyre, LVO.

The Most Excellent Order of the British Empire (1917)

(The Order was divided into *Military* and *Civil* divisions in Dec. 1918)
GBE, Knight or Dame Grand Cross; KBE. Knight Commander; DBE, Dame Commander;
CBE, Commander; OBE, Officer; MBE, Member

GBE   *Ribbon,* Rose pink edged with pearl grey with vertical pearl stripe in centre (Military   KBE
Division); without vertical pearl stripe (Civil Division). *Motto,* For God and the Empire.

THE SOVEREIGN: *Grand Master,* HRH The Prince Philip, Duke of Edinburgh, KG, PC, KT, OM, GBE, FRS; *Prelate,* The Bishop of London; *King of Arms,* Admiral Sir Anthony Morton, GBE, KCB; *Registrar,* The Secretary of the Central Chancery of the Orders of Knighthood; *Secretary,* Sir Robin Butler, KCB, CVO; *Dean,* The Dean of St. Paul's; *Gentleman Usher of the Purple Rod,* Sir Robin Gillett, Bt., GBE; *Chancery,* Central Chancery of the Orders of Knighthood, St. James's Palace, SW1A 1BH.

Order of the Companions of Honour (1917)—CH

Ribbon, Carmine, with Gold Edges.

This Order consists of one Class only and carries with it no title. It ranks after the 1st Class of the Order of the British Empire, i.e. Knights and Dames Grand Cross (Military and Civil Divisions). The number of awards is limited to 65 (excluding honorary members) and the Order is open to both sexes.

Anthony, Rt. Hon. John, 1982.
Ashley, Rt. Hon. Jack, 1975.
Aylestone, The Lord, 1975.
Brenner, Sydney, 1987.
Carrington, The Lord, 1983.
Casson, Sir Hugh, 1985.
Cledwyn of Penrhos, The Lord, 1977.
de Valois, Dame Ninette, 1982.
Eccles, The Viscount, 1984.
Fraser, Rt. Hon. Malcolm, 1977.
Freud, Lucian, 1983.
Gielgud, Sir John, 1977.
Glenamara, The Lord, 1976.
Goodman, The Lord, 1972.
Gorton, Rt. Hon. Sir John, 1971.
Greene, Graham, 1966.

Hailsham of St. Marylebone, The Lord, 1974.
Hawking, Prof. Stephen, 1989.
von Hayek, Prof. Friedrich, 1984.
Healey, Rt. Hon. Denis, 1979.
Houghton of Sowerby, The Lord, 1967.
Jones, James, 1978.
Joseph, The Lord, 1986.
Lange, Rt. Hon. David, 1989.
Muirshiel, The Viscount, 1962.
Muldoon, Rt. Hon. Sir Robert, 1977.
Pasmore, Victor, 1981.
Perutz, Prof. Max, 1975.
Piper, John, 1972.
Popper, Prof. Sir Karl, 1982.
Powell, Anthony, 1987.

Powell, Sir Philip, 1984.
Rahman, Tunku Abdul, 1960.
Runciman, Hon. Sir Steven, 1984.
Rylands, George, 1987.
Sanger, Frederick, 1981.
Smith, Arnold Cantwell, 1975.
Somare, Rt. Hon. Sir Michael, 1978.
Summerson, Sir John, 1987.
Talboys, Rt. Hon. Brian, 1981.
Tebbit, Rt. Hon. Norman, 1987.
Thorneycroft, The Lord, 1980.
Tippett, Sir Michael, 1979.
Trudeau, Rt. Hon. Pierre, 1984.
Watkinson, The Viscount, 1962.
Whitelaw, The Viscount, 1974.
Honorary Members, Lee Kuan Yew, 1970; Dr. Joseph Luns, 1971.

Secretary and Registrar, The Secretary of the Central Chancery of the Orders of Knighthood.

The Distinguished Service Order (1886)—DSO

Ribbon, Red, with Blue Edges.

Bestowed in recognition of especial services in action of commissioned officers in the Navy, Army and Royal Air Force and (since 1942) Mercantile Marine. The members are Companions only and rank immediately before the 4th Class of the Royal Victorian Order. A Bar may be awarded for any additional act of service.

The Imperial Service Order (1902)—ISO

Ribbon, Crimson, with Blue Centre.

Appointment of Companion of this Order shall be open to those members of the Civil Services whose eligibility shall be determined by the grade held by such persons. The Order consists of THE SOVEREIGN and Companions (not exclusively male) to a number not exceeding 1,700, of whom 1,100 may belong to the Home Civil Services and 600 to Overseas Civil Services. *Secretary,* Sir Robin Butler, KCB, CVO. *Registrar,* The Secretary of the Central Chancery of the Orders of Knighthood, St. James's Palace, SW1A 1BH.

The Royal Victorian Chain (1902)

Founded by King Edward VII, in 1902. It confers no precedence on its holders.
HM THE QUEEN
HM QUEEN ELIZABETH THE QUEEN MOTHER, 1937.

Princess Juliana of the Netherlands, 1950.
HM The King of Norway, 1955.
HM The King of Thailand, 1960.
HIH The Crown Prince of Ethiopia, 1965.
HM The King of Jordan, 1966.

HM King Zahir Shah of Afghanistan, 1971.
Rt. Hon. Roland Michener, 1973.
HM The Queen of Denmark, 1974.
HM The King of Nepal, 1975.
HM The King of Sweden, 1975.
The Right Rev. The Lord Coggan, 1980.

HM The Queen of the Netherlands, 1982.
General Antonio Eanes, 1985.
HM The King of Spain, 1986.
HM The King of Saudi Arabia, 1987.
HRH The Princess Margaret, Countess of Snowdon, 1990.

BARONETAGE AND KNIGHTAGE

Badge of Baronets
of the United Kingdom

Badge of Ulster

Badge of Baronets
of Nova Scotia

BARONETS

Style.—'Sir' before forename and surname, followed by 'Bt.' *Wife's style.*—'Lady' followed by surname.
For forms of address, *see* page 151.

There are five different creations of Baronetcies: Baronets of England (creations dating from 1611); Baronets of Ireland (creations dating from 1611); Baronets of Scotland or Nova Scotia (creations dating from 1625); Baronets of Great Britain (creations after the Act of Union 1707 which combined the Kingdoms of England and Scotland); and Baronets of the United Kingdom (creations after the union of Great Britain and Ireland in 1801).

The Official Roll of Baronets is kept at the Home Office by the Registrar of the Baronetage. Anyone who considers that he is entitled to be entered on the Roll may petition the Crown through the Home Secretary. Every person succeeding to a Baronetcy must exhibit proofs of succession to the Home Secretary. A person whose name is not entered on the Official Roll will not be addressed or mentioned by the title of Baronet in any official document, nor will he be accorded precedence as a Baronet.

KNIGHTS

Style.—'Sir' before forename and surname, followed by appropriate post-nominal initials if a Knight Grand Cross, Knight Grand Commander or Knight Commander. *Wife's style.*—'Lady' followed by surname.
For forms of address, *see* page 151.

The prefix 'Sir' is not used by knights who are clerics of the Church of England, who do not receive the accolade. (Their wives are entitled to precedence as the wife of a knight but not to the style of 'Lady'.)

Orders of Knighthood

Knight Grand Cross, Knight Grand Commander, and Knight Commander are the higher classes of the Orders of Chivalry (*see* pp. 184–186). Honorary knighthoods of these orders may be conferred on men who are citizens of countries of which the Queen is not head of state. As a rule, the prefix 'Sir' is not used by honorary knights.

Knights Bachelor

The Knights Bachelor do not constitute a Royal Order, but comprise the surviving representation of the ancient State Orders of Knighthood. The Register of Knights Bachelor, instituted by James I in the 17th century, lapsed, and in 1908 a voluntary association under the title of The Society of Knights (now The Imperial Society of Knights Bachelor by Royal command) was formed with the primary objects of continuing the various registers dating from 1257 and obtaining the uniform registration of every created Knight Bachelor. In 1926 a design for a badge to be worn by Knights Bachelor was approved and adopted, a miniature reproduction being shown above; in 1974 a neck badge and miniature were added.

The Officers of the Society are: *Knight Principal*, Sir Colin Cole, KCVO, TD; *Chairman of Council*, Sir David Napley; *Prelate*, Rt. Rev. and Rt. Hon. The Bishop of London; *Hon. Registrar*, Sir Roger Falk, OBE; *Hon. Treasurer*, The Lord Lane of Horsell; *Clerk to the Council*, R. M. Esden; *Deputy Clerk*, Lt.-Col. G. H. H. Coles; *Office*, 21 Old Buildings, Lincoln's Inn, WC2A 3UJ.

LIST OF BARONETS AND KNIGHTS
(Revised to Aug. 31, 1990)
Peers are not included in this list

When an obelisk (†) precedes a name it indicates that, at the time of going to press, the Baronet concerned has not been registered on the Official Roll of the Baronetage. The date of creation of the Baronetcy is given in parenthesis ( ).

A full entry in italic type indicates that the recipient of a Knighthood died during the year in which the honour was conferred. The name is included for purposes of record.

I. Baronet of Ireland; NS Baronet of Nova Scotia; s. Baronet of Scotland.

Aarvold, *Hon.* Sir Carl Douglas, Kt., OBE, TD.

Abal, Sir Tei, Kt., CBE.

Abbott, Sir Albert Francis, Kt., CBE.

Abdy, Sir Valentine Robert Duff, Bt. (1850).

Abel, Sir Seselo (Cecil) Charles Geoffrey, Kt., OBE.

Abeles, Sir (Emil Herbert) Peter, Kt.

Abell, Sir Anthony Foster, KCMG.

Abercromby, Sir Ian George, Bt. (s. 1636).

Abraham, Sir Edward Penley, Kt., CBE, FRS.

Acheson, *Prof.* Sir (Ernest) Donald, KBE.

Ackers, Sir James George, Kt.

Ackroyd, Sir John Robert Whyte, Bt. (1956).

Acland, Sir Antony Arthur, GCMG, KCVO.

Acland, *Maj.* Sir (Christopher) Guy (Dyke), Bt. (1890).

Acland, *Maj.-Gen.* Sir John Hugh Bevil, KCB, CBE.

Acland, Sir Richard Thomas Dyke, Bt. (1644).

Acton, Sir Harold Mario Mitchell, Kt., CBE.

Adam, Sir Christopher Eric Forbes, Bt. (1917).

Adams, Sir Philip George Doyne, KCMG.

Adams-Schneider, *Rt. Hon.* Sir Lancelot Raymond, KCMG.

Adamson, Sir (William Owen) Campbell, Kt.

Adcock, Sir Robert Henry, Kt., CBE.

Addison, Sir William Wilkinson, Kt.

Ademola, *Rt. Hon.* Sir Adetokunbo Adegboyega, KBE.

Adrien, *Hon.* Sir Maurice Latour-, Kt.

Agnew, Sir Crispin Hamlyn, Bt. (s. 1629).

Agnew, Sir (John) Anthony Stuart, Bt. (1895).

Agnew, Sir (William) Godfrey, KCVO, QB.

Ah-Chuen, Sir Moi Lin Jean Etienne, Kt.

Aiken, *Air Chief Marshal* Sir John Alexander Carlisle, KCB.

Ainley, Sir (Alfred) John, Kt., MC.

Ainsworth, Sir (Thomas) David, Bt. (1916).

Aird, *Capt.* Sir Alastair Sturgis, KCVO.

Aird, Sir (George) John, Bt. (1901).

Airey, Sir Lawrence, KCB.

Airy, *Maj.-Gen.* Sir Christopher John, KCVO, CBE.

Aisher, Sir Owen Arthur, Kt.

Aitchison, Sir Charles Walter de Lancey, Bt. (1938).

Aitken, Sir Robert Stevenson, Kt., MD, D.Phil.

Akehurst, *Gen.* Sir John Bryan, KCB, CBE.

Akers-Jones, Sir David, KBE, CMG.

Albert, Sir Alexis François, Kt., CMG, VRD.

Albu, Sir George, Bt. (1912).

Aldington, Sir Geoffrey William, KBE, CMG.

Aldous, *Hon.* Sir William, Kt.

Alexander, Sir Alexander Sandor, Kt.

Alexander, Sir Charles Gundry, Bt. (1945).

Alexander, Sir Claud Hagart-, Bt. (1886).

Alexander, *Hon.* Sir Darnley Arthur Raymond, Kt., CBE.

Alexander, Sir Douglas, Bt. (1921).

Alexander, Sir (John) Lindsay, Kt.

Alexander, *Prof.* Sir Kenneth John Wilson, Kt.

Alexander, Sir Michael O'Donal Bjarne, KCMG.

Alexander, Sir Norman Stanley, Kt., CBE.

†Alexander, Sir Patrick Desmond William Cable-, Bt. (1809).

Allan, Sir Anthony James Allan Havelock-, Bt. (1858).

Allan, Sir Colin Hamilton, KCMG, OBE.

Allard, Sir Gordon Laidlaw, Kt.

Allen, *Prof.* Sir Geoffrey, Kt., Ph.D., FRS.

Allen, *Hon.* Sir Peter Austin Philip Jermyn, Kt.

Allen, Sir Peter Christopher, Kt.

Allen, Sir Richard Hugh Sedley, KCMG.

Allen, Sir William Guilford, Kt.

Allen, Sir (William) Kenneth (Gwynne), Kt.

Alleyne, Sir George Allanmoore Ogarren, Kt.

Alleyne, *Rev.* Sir John Olpherts Campbell, Bt. (1769).

Alliance, Sir David, Kt., CBE.

Allinson, Sir (Walter) Leonard, KCVO, CMG.

Alliott, *Hon.* Sir John Downes, Kt.

Alment, Sir (Edward) Anthony John, Kt.

Althaus, Sir Nigel Frederick, Kt.

Alun-Jones, Sir (John) Derek, Kt.

Ambo, *Rt. Rev.* George, KBE.

Amies, Sir (Edwin) Hardy, KCVO.

Amis, Sir Kingsley William, Kt., CBE.

Anderson, *Prof.* Sir (James) Norman (Dalrymple), Kt., OBE, QC, FBA.

Anderson, *Maj.-Gen.* Sir John Evelyn, KBE.

Anderson, Sir John Muir, Kt., CMG.

Anderson, Sir Kenneth, KBE, CB.

Anderson, *Hon.* Sir Kevin Victor, Kt.

Anderson, *Vice-Adm.* Sir Neil Dudley, KBE, CB.

Anderson, *Prof.* Sir (William) Ferguson, Kt., OBE.

Andrew, Sir Robert John, KCB.

Andrews, *Hon.* Sir Dormer George, Kt.

Angus, Sir Michael Richardson, Kt.

Ansell, *Col.* Sir Michael Picton, Kt., CBE, DSO.

Anson, *Vice-Adm.* Sir Edward Rosebery, KCB.

Anson, Sir John, KCB.

Anson, *Rear-Adm.* Sir Peter, Bt., CB (1831).

Anstey, *Brig.* Sir John, Kt., CBE, TD.

Anstruther, Sir Ralph Hugo, Bt. KCVO, MC (s. 1694).

Anthony, Sir (Michael) Mobolaji Bank-, KBE.

Antico, Sir Tristan Venus, Kt.

Antrobus, Sir Philip Coutts, Bt. (1815).

Appleyard, Sir Raymond Kenelm, KBE.

Arbuthnot, Sir John Sinclair-Wemyss, Bt., MBE, TD (1964).

Arbuthnot, Sir Keith Robert Charles, Bt. (1823).

Archdale, *Cdr.* Sir Edward Folmer, Bt., DSC, RN (1928).

Archer, *Gen.* Sir (Arthur) John, KCB, OBE.

Archer, Sir Clyde Vernon Harcourt, Kt.

Arculus, Sir Ronald, KCMG, KCVO.

Armitage, *Air Chief Marshal* Sir Michael John, KCB, CBE.

Armstrong, Sir Andrew Clarence Francis, Bt., CMG (1841).

Armstrong, Sir Thomas Henry Wait, Kt., D.Mus..

Armytage, Sir John Martin, Bt. (1738).

Arnold, *Rt. Hon.* Sir John Lewis, Kt.

Arnold, Sir Thomas Richard, Kt., MP.

Arnott, Sir Alexander John Maxwell, Bt. (1896).

Arnott, *Prof.* Sir (William) Melville, Kt., TD, MD.

Arrindell, Sir Clement Athelston, GCMG, GCVO, QC.

Arrowsmith, Sir Edwin Porter, KCMG.

Arthur, *Lt.-Gen.* Sir (John) Norman Stewart, KCB.

Arthur, Sir Stephen John, Bt. (1841).

Ash, *Prof.* Sir Eric Albert, Kt., CBE, FRS.

Ashburnham, Sir Denny Reginald, Bt. (1661).

Ashe, Sir Derick Rosslyn, KCMG.

Ashley, Sir Bernard Albert, Kt.

Ashmore, *Admiral of the Fleet* Sir Edward Beckwith, GCB, DSC.

Ashmore, *Vice-Adm.* Sir Peter William Beckwith, KCB, KCVO, DSC.

Ashworth, Sir Herbert, Kt.

Aske, *Rev.* Sir Conan, Bt. (1922).

Askew, Sir Bryan, Kt.

Astley, Sir Francis Jacob Dugdale, Bt. (1821).

Aston, Sir Harold George, Kt., CBE.

Aston, *Hon.* Sir William John, KCMG.

Astor, *Hon.* Sir John Jacob, Kt., MBE.

Astwood, *Hon.* Sir James Rufus, Kt.

Astwood, *Lt.-Col.* Sir Jeffrey Carlton, Kt., CBE, ED.

Atcherley, Sir Harold Winter, Kt.

Atiyah, Sir Michael Francis, Kt., Ph.D., FRS.

Atkinson, *Air Marshal* Sir David William, KBE.

Atkinson, Sir Frederick John, KCB.

Atkinson, Sir John Alexander, KCB, DFC.

Atkinson, Sir Robert, Kt., DSC.

Attenborough, Sir David Frederick, Kt., CBE, FRS.

Attenborough, Sir Richard Samuel, Kt., CBE.

Atwell, Sir John William, Kt., CBE, FRSE.

Atwill, Sir (Milton) John (Napier), Kt.

Audland, Sir Christopher John, KCMG.

Audley, Sir George Bernard, Kt.

Auld, *Hon.* Sir Robin Ernest, Kt.

†Austin, Sir Michael Trescawen, Bt. (1894).

Austin, *Vice-Adm.* Sir Peter Murray, KCB.

Aykroyd, Sir Cecil William, Bt. (1929).

Aykroyd, Sir William Miles, Bt., MC (1920).

Aylmer, Sir Richard John, Bt. (I. 1622).

Backhouse, Sir Jonathan Roger, Bt. (1901).

Bacon, Sir Nicholas Hickman Ponsonby, Bt. *Premier Baronet of England* (1611 and 1627).

Bacon, Sir Sidney Charles, Kt., CB.

Baddeley, Sir John Wolsey Beresford, Bt. (1922).

Baddiley, *Prof.* Sir James, Kt., PH.D., D.SC., FRS, FRSE.

Badenoch, Sir John, Kt., DM, FRCP.

Badger, Sir Geoffrey Malcolm, Kt.

†Bagge, Sir (John) Jeremy Picton, Bt. (1867).

Bagnall, *Field Marshal* Sir Nigel Thomas, GCB, CVO, MC.

Bailey, Sir Alan Marshall, KCB.

Bailey, Sir Brian Harry, Kt., OBE.

Bailey, Sir Derrick Thomas Louis, Bt., DFC (1919).

Bailey, *Prof.* Sir Harold Walter, Kt., D.Phil., FBA.

Bailey, Sir John Bilsland, KCB.

Bailey, Sir Richard John, Kt., CBE.

Bailey, Sir Stanley Ernest, Kt., CBE, QPM.

Baillie, Sir Gawaine George Hope, Bt. (1823).

Baines, *Prof.* Sir George Grenfell-, Kt., OBE.

Baird, Sir David Charles, Bt. (1809).

Baird, *Lt.-Gen.* Sir James Parlane, KBE, MD.

Baird, Sir James Richard Gardiner, Bt., MC (s. 1695).

Baird, *Vice-Adm.* Sir Thomas Henry Eustace, KCB.

Bairsto, *Air Marshal* Sir Peter Edward, KBE, CB.

Baker, Sir (Allan) Ivor, Kt., CBE.

Baker, Sir Robert George Humphrey Sherston-, Bt. (1796).

Baker, *Hon.* Sir (Thomas) Scott (Gillespie), Kt.

Balcombe, *Rt. Hon.* Sir (Alfred) John, Kt.

Balderstone, Sir James Schofield, Kt.

Baldwin, Sir Peter Robert, KCB.

Balfour, *Gen.* Sir (Robert George) Victor FitzGeorge-, KCB, CBE, DSO, MC.

Ball, *Air Marshal* Sir Alfred Henry Wynne, KCB, DSO, DFC.

Ball, Sir Charles Irwin, Bt. (1911).

Ball, Sir Christopher John Elinger, Kt.

Ball, *Prof.* Sir Robert James, Kt., PH.D.

Balmer, Sir Joseph Reginald, Kt.

Bamford, Sir Anthony Paul, Kt.

Banks, Sir Maurice Alfred Lister, Kt.

Banner, Sir George Knowles Harmood-, Bt. (1924).

Bannerman, Sir Alexander Patrick, Bt. (s. 1682).

Bannerman, Sir David Gordon, OBE, Bt. (s. 1682).

Bannister, Sir Roger Gilbert, Kt., CBE, DM, FRCP.

Barber, Sir Derek Coates, Kt.

Barber, *Hon.* Sir (Edward Hamilton) Esler, Kt.

Barber, Sir William Francis, Bt., TD (1960).

Barclay, Sir Colville Herbert Sanford, Bt. (s. 1668).

Barclay, Sir Roderick Edward, GCVO, KCMG.

Barford, Sir Leonard, Kt.

†Baring, Sir John Francis, Bt. (1911).

Baring, *Hon.* Sir John Francis Harcourt, Kt., KCVO.

Barker, Sir Alwyn Bowman, Kt., CMG.

Barker, Sir Harry Heaton, Kt., KBE.

Barker, Sir William, KCMG, OBE.

Barlow, Sir Christopher Hilaro, Bt. (1803).

Barlow, Sir (George) William, Kt.

Barlow, Sir John Kemp, Bt. (1907).

Barlow, Sir Thomas Erasmus, Bt., DSC (1902).

Barnard, Sir (Arthur) Thomas, Kt., CB, OBE.

Barnard, *Capt.* Sir George Edward, Kt.

Barnard, Sir Joseph Brian, Kt.

Barnes, Sir Denis Charles, KCB.

Barnes, Sir (Ernest) John (Ward), KCMG, MBE.

Barnes, Sir James George, Kt., MBE.

Barnes, Sir Kenneth, KCB.

Barnett, *Air Chief Marshal* Sir Denis Hensley Fulton, GCB, CBE, DFC.

Barnett, Sir Oliver Charles, Kt., CBE, QC.

Barnewall, Sir Reginald Robert, Bt. (I. 1623).

Barraclough, *Air Chief Marshal* Sir John, KCB, CBE, DFC, AFC.

Barraclough, Sir Kenneth James Priestley, Kt., CBE, TD.

Barran, Sir David Haven, Kt.

Barran, Sir John Napoleon Ruthven, Bt. (1895).

Barratt, Sir Lawrence Arthur, Kt.

Barratt, Sir Richard Stanley, Kt., CBE, QPM.

Barrett, *Lt.-Gen.* Sir David William Scott-, KBE, MC.

Barrett, *Lt.-Col.* Sir Dennis Charles Titchener, Kt., TD.

Barrington, Sir Alexander (Fitzwilliam Croker), Bt. (1831).

Barrington, Sir Nicholas John, KCMG, CVO.

Barron, Sir Donald James, Kt.

Barrow, *Capt.* Sir Richard John Uniacke, Bt. (1835).

Barrowclough, Sir Anthony Richard, Kt., QC.

Barry, Sir (Lawrence) Edward (Anthony Tress), Bt. (1899).

Barry, Sir (Philip) Stuart Milner-, KCVO, CB, OBE.

Bartlett, Sir John Hardington, Bt. (1913).

Barton, *Prof.* Sir Derek Harold Richard, Kt., FRS, FRSE.

Barttelot, *Lt.-Col.* Sir Brian Walter de Stopham, Bt., OBE (1875).

Barwick, *Rt. Hon.* Sir Garfield Edward John, GCMG.

Basten, Sir Henry Bolton, Kt., CMG.

Batchelor, Sir Ivor Ralph Campbell, Kt., CBE.

Bate, Sir David Lindsay, KBE.

Bate, Sir (Walter) Edwin, Kt., OBE.

Bateman, Sir Cecil Joseph, KBE.

Bateman, Sir Geoffrey Hirst, Kt., FRCS.

Bateman, Sir Ralph Melton, KBE.

Bates, *Prof.* Sir David Robert, Kt., D.SC., FRS.

Bates, *Maj.-Gen.* Sir (Edward) John (Hunter), KBE, CB, MC.

Bates, Sir Geoffrey Voltelin, Bt., MC (1880).

Bates, Sir John David, Kt., CBE, VRD.

Bates, Sir (John) Dawson, Bt., MC (1937).

Batho, Sir Peter Ghislain, Bt. (1928).

Bathurst, *Adm.* Sir (David) Benjamin, KCB.

Bathurst, Sir Frederick Peter Methuen Hervey-, Bt. (1818).

Bathurst, Sir Maurice Edward, Kt., CMG, CBE, QC.

Batsford, Sir Brian Caldwell Cook, Kt.

Batten, Sir John Charles, KCVO.

Battishill, Sir Anthony Michael William, KCB.

Batty, Sir William Bradshaw, Kt., TD.

Baxendell, Sir Peter Brian, Kt., CBE.

Bayliss, *Prof.* Sir Noel Stanley, Kt., CBE.

Bayliss, Sir Richard Ian Samuel, KCVO, MD, FRCP.

Bayly, *Vice-Adm.* Sir Patrick Uniacke, KCB, CB, DSC.

Baynes, Sir John Christopher Malcolm, Bt. (1801).

Bazley, Sir Thomas Stafford, Bt. (1869).

Beach, *Gen.* Sir (William Gerald) Hugh, GBE, KCB, MC.

Beale, Sir William Francis, Kt., OBE.

Beament, Sir James William Longman, Kt., SC.D., FRS.

Beattie, *Hon.* Sir Alexander Craig, Kt.

Beattie, *Hon.* Sir David Stuart, GCMG, GCVO.

Beauchamp, Sir Christopher Radstock Proctor-, Bt. (1745).

Beaumont, Sir George (Howland Francis), Bt. (1661).

Beaumont, Sir Richard Ashton, KCMG, OBE.

Beavis, *Air Chief Marshal* Sir Michael Gordon, KCB, CBE, AFC.

Becher, Sir William Fane Wrixon, Bt., MC (1831).

Beck, Sir Edgar Charles, Kt., CBE.

Beck, Sir Edgar Philip, Kt.

Beckett, *Capt.* Sir (Martyn) Gervase, Bt., MC (1921).

Beckett, Sir Terence Norman, Kt., KBE.

Bedbrook, Sir George Montario, Kt., OBE.

Bedingfeld, *Capt.* Sir Edmund George Felix Paston-, Bt. (1661).

Beecham, Sir John Stratford Roland, Bt. (1914).

Beeley, Sir Harold, KCMG, CBE.

Beetham, *Marshal of the Royal Air Force* Sir Michael James, GCB, CBE, DFC, AFC.

Beevor, Sir Thomas Agnew, Bt. (1784).

Begg, Sir Neil Colquhoun, KBE.

Begg, *Admiral of the Fleet* Sir Varyl Cargill, GCB, DSO, DSC.

Beit, Sir Alfred Lane, Bt. (1924).

Beith, Sir John Greville Stanley, KCMG.

Beldam, *Rt. Hon.* Sir (Alexander) Roy (Asplan), Kt.

Bell, Sir Gawain Westray, KCMG, CBE.

Bell, Sir (George) Raymond, KCMG, CB.

Bell, Sir John Lowthian, Bt. (1885).

Bell, Sir (William) Ewart, KCB.

Bell, Sir William Hollin Dayrell Morrison-, Bt. (1905).

Bellew, Hon. Sir George Rothe, KCB, KCVO, FSA.

Bellew, Sir Henry Charles Gratton-, Bt. (1838).

Bellinger, Sir Robert Ian, GBE.

Bellingham, Sir Noel Peter Roger, Bt. (1796).

Bengough, *Col*, Sir Piers, KCVO, OBE.

Benn, Sir James Jonathan, Bt. (1914).

Benn, *Capt.* Sir (Patrick Ion) Hamilton, Bt. (1920).

Bennett, Sir Charles Moihi Te Arawaka, Kt., DSO.

Bennett, *Air Vice-Marshal* Sir Erik Peter, KBE, CB.

Bennett, *Rt. Hon.* Sir Frederic Mackarness, Kt.

Bennett, Sir Hubert, Kt.

Bennett, Sir John Mokonuiarangi, Kt.

Bennett, *Gen.* Sir Phillip Harvey, KBE, DSO.

Bennett, Sir Reginald Frederick Brittain, Kt., VRD.

Bennett, Sir Ronald Wilfrid Murdoch, Bt. (1929).

Benson, Sir Christopher John, Kt.

Benson, Sir (William) Jeffrey, Kt.

Benthall, Sir (Arthur) Paul, KBE.

Bentley, Sir William, KCMG.

Beresford, Sir Alexander Paul, Kt.

Berger, *Vice-Adm.* Sir Peter Egerton Capel, KCB, MVO, DSC.

Berghuser, *Hon.* Sir Eric, Kt., MBE.

Berlin, Sir Isaiah, Kt., OM, CBE.

Bernard, Sir Dallas Edmund, Bt. (1954).

Berney, Sir Julian Reedham Stuart, Bt. (1620).

Berrill, Sir Kenneth Ernest, GBE, KCB.

Berriman, Sir David, Kt.

Berthon, *Vice-Adm.* Sir Stephen Ferrier, KCB.

Berthoud, Sir Martin Seymour, KCVO, CMG.

Best, Sir Richard Radford, KCVO, CBE.

Bethune, Sir Alexander Maitland Sharp, Bt. (s. 1683).

Bethune, *Hon.* Sir (Walter) Angus, Kt.

Bevan, Sir Martyn Evan Evans, Bt. (1958).

Bevan, Sir Timothy Hugh, Kt.

Beynon, *Prof.* Sir (William John) Granville, Kt., CBE, PH.D., D.SC., FRS.

Bibby, Sir Derek James, Bt., MC (1959).

Bickersteth, *Rt. Rev.* John Monier, KCVO.

Biddulph, Sir Ian D'Olier, Bt. (1664).

Bide, Sir Austin Ernest, Kt.

Bidwell, Sir Hugh Charles Philip, GBE.

Biggs, Sir Norman Paris, Kt.

Billiere, *Lt.-Gen.* Sir Peter Edgar de la Cour de la, KCB, CBE, DSO, MC.

Bing, Sir Rudolf Franz Josef, KBE.

Bingham, *Hon.* Sir Eardley Max, Kt., QC.

Bingham, *Rt. Hon.* Sir Thomas Henry, Kt.

Bird, *Col.* Sir Richard Dawnay Martin-, Kt., CBE, TD.

Bird, Sir Richard Geoffrey Chapman, Bt. (1922).

Birkin, Sir John Christian William, Bt. (1905).

Birkin, Sir John Derek, Kt., TD.

Birkmyre, Sir Henry, Bt. (1921).

Birley, Sir Derek Sydney, Kt.

Birtwistle, Sir Harrison, Kt.

Bishop, Sir Frederick Arthur, Kt., CB, CVO.

Bishop, Sir George Sidney, Kt., CB, OBE.

Bishop, *Instructor Rear-Adm.* Sir William, KBE, CB.

Bjelke-Petersen, *Hon.* Sir Johannes, KCMG.

Black, Sir Cyril Wilson, Kt.

Black, *Prof.* Sir Douglas Andrew Kilgour, Kt., MD, FRCP.

Black, Sir James Whyte, Kt., FRCP, FRS.

Black, *Adm.* Sir (John) Jeremy, KCB, DSO, MBE.

Black, Sir Robert Brown, GCMG, OBE.

Black, Sir Robert David, Bt. (1922).

Blacker, *Gen.* Sir Cecil Hugh, GCB, OBE, MC.

Blackett, Sir George William, Bt. (1673).

Blackman, Sir Frank Milton, KCVO, OBE.

Blackwell, Sir Basil Davenport, Kt.

Blair, Sir Alastair Campbell, KCVO, TD, WS..

Blair, *Lt.-Gen.* Sir Chandos, KCVO, OBE, MC.

Blair, Sir Edward Thomas Hunter, Bt. (1786).

Blair-Kerr, *Hon.* Sir Alastair, Kt.

Blake, Sir Alfred Lapthorn, KCVO, MC.

Blake, Sir Francis Michael, Bt. (1907).

Blake, Sir (Thomas) Richard (Valentine), Bt. (I. 1622).

Blaker, Sir John, Bt. (1919).

Blaker, *Rt. Hon.* Sir Peter Allan Renshaw, KCMG, MP.

Blakiston, Sir Ferguson Arthur James, Bt. (1763).

Bland, Sir Henry Armand, Kt., CBE.

Bland, *Lt.-Col.* Sir Simon Claud Michael, KCVO.

Blaxter, Sir Kenneth Lyon, Kt., FRS, FRSE.

Blelloch, Sir John Nial Henderson, KCB.

Blennerhassett, Sir (Marmaduke) Adrian Francis William, Bt. (1809).

Blewitt, *Maj.* Sir Shane Gabriel Basil, KCVO.

Blois, Sir Charles Nicholas Gervase, Bt. (1686).

Blomefield, Sir Thomas Charles Peregrine, Bt. (1807).

Bloomfield, *Hon.* Sir John Stoughton, Kt., QC.

Bloomfield, Sir Kenneth Percy, Kt.

Blosse, *Capt.* Sir Richard Hely Lynch-, Bt. (1622).

Blount, Sir Walter Edward Alpin, Bt., DSC (1642).

Blundell, Sir Michael, KBE.

Blunden, Sir George, Kt.

Blunden, Sir Philip Overington, Bt. (I. 1766).

Blunt, Sir David Richard Reginald Harvey, Bt. (1720).

Blyth, Sir James, Kt.

Boardman, *Prof.* Sir John, Kt., FSA, FBA.

Boardman, Sir Kenneth Ormrod, Kt.

Bodily, *Hon.* Sir Jocelyn, Kt., VRD.

Bodmer, Sir Walter Fred, Kt., PH.D., FRS.

Body, Sir Richard Bernard Frank Stewart, Kt., MP.

Boevey, Sir Thomas Michael Blake Crawley-, Bt. (1784).

Boileau, Sir Guy (Francis), Bt. (1838).

Boles, Sir Jeremy John Fortescue, Bt. (1922).

Boles, Sir John Dennis, Kt., MBE.

Bolland, Sir Edwin, KCMG.

Bollers, *Hon.* Sir Harold Brodie Smith, Kt.

Bolton, Sir Frederic Bernard, Kt., MC.

Bonallack, Sir Richard Frank, Kt., CBE.

Bonar, Sir Herbert Vernon, Kt., CBE.

Bond, Sir Kenneth Raymond Boyden, Kt.

Bondi, *Prof.* Sir Hermann, KCB, FRS.

Bonham, *Maj.* Sir Antony Lionel Thomas, Bt. (1852).

Bonsall, Sir Arthur Wilfred, KCMG, CBE.

Bonsor, Sir Nicholas Cosmo, Bt., MP (1925).

Boolell, Sir Satcam, Kt.

Boon, Sir Peter Coleman, Kt.

Boord, Sir Nicolas John Charles, Bt. (1896).

Boorman, *Lt.-Gen.* Sir Derek, KCB.

Booth, Sir Angus Josslyn Gore-, Bt. (I. 1760).

Booth, Sir Christopher Charles, Kt., MD, FRCP.

Booth, Sir Douglas Allen, Bt. (1916).

Booth, Sir Gordon, KCMG, CVO.

Booth, Sir Robert Camm, Kt., CBE, TD.

Boothby, Sir Brooke Charles, Bt. (1660).

Boreel, Sir Francis David, Bt. (1645).

Boreham, Sir (Arthur) John, KCB.

Boreham, *Hon.* Sir Leslie Kenneth Edward, Kt.

Bornu, The Waziri of, KCMG, CBE.

Borrie, Sir Gordon Johnson, Kt., QC.

Borthwick, Sir John Thomas, Bt. MBE (1908).

Bossom, *Hon.* Sir Clive, Bt. (1953).

Boswall, Sir (Thomas) Alford Houstoun-, Bt. (1836).

Boswell, *Lt.-Gen.* Sir Alexander Crawford Simpson, KCB, CBE.

Bosworth, Sir Neville Bruce Alfred, Kt., CBE.

Bottomley, Sir James Reginald Alfred, KCMG.

Boughey, Sir John George Fletcher, Bt. (1798).

Boulton, Sir Clifford John, KCB.

Boulton, Sir (Harold Hugh) Christian, Bt. (1905).

Boulton, Sir William Whytehead, Bt., CBE, TD (1944).

Bourne, Sir (John) Wilfrid, KCB.

Bovell, *Hon.* Sir (William) Stewart, Kt.

Bowater, Sir Euan David Vansittart, Bt. (1939).

Bowater, Sir (John) Vansittart, Bt. (1914).

Bowden, Sir Frank, Bt. (1915).

Bowen, Sir Geoffrey Fraser, Kt.

Bowen, Sir Mark Edward Mortimer, Bt. (1921).

Bowen, *Hon.* Sir Nigel Hubert, KBE.

Bower, *Air Marshal* Sir Leslie William Clement, KCB, DSO, DFC.

Bowlby, Sir Anthony Hugh Mostyn, Bt. (1923).

Bowman, Sir George, Bt. (1961).

Bowman, Sir John Paget, Bt. (1884).

Bowman-Shaw, Sir (George) Neville, Kt.

Bowmar, Sir Charles Erskine, Kt.

Bowness, Sir Alan, Kt., CBE.

Bowness, Sir Peter Spencer, Kt., CBE.

Boxer, *Air Vice-Marshal* Sir Alan Hunter Cachemaille, KCVO, CB, DSO, DFC.

Boyce, Sir Robert Charles Leslie, Bt. (1952).

Boyd, Sir Alexander Walter, Bt. (1916).

Boyd, *Prof.* Sir Robert Lewis Fullarton, Kt., CBE, D.SC., FRS.

Boyes, Sir Brian Gerald Barratt-, KBE.

Boyle, *Marshal of the Royal Air Force* Sir Dermot Alexander, GCB, KCVO, KBE, AFC.

Boyle, Sir Stephen Gurney, Bt. (1904).

Boyne, Sir Henry Brian, Kt., CBE.

Boynton, Sir John Keyworth, Kt., MC.

Boyson, *Rt. Hon.* Sir Rhodes, Kt., MP.

Brabham, Sir John Arthur, Kt., OBE.

Bradbeer, Sir John Derek Richardson, Kt., OBE, TD.

Bradbury, *Surgeon Vice-Adm.* Sir Eric Blackburn, KBE, CB.

Bradford, Sir Edward Alexander Slade, Bt. (1902).

Bradlaw, *Prof.* Sir Robert Vivian, Kt., CBE.

Bradley, Sir Burton Gyrth Burton-, Kt., OBE.

Bradman, Sir Donald George, Kt.

Bradshaw, Sir Kenneth Anthony, KCB.

Bradshaw, *Lt.-Gen.* Sir Richard Phillip, KBE.

Brain, Sir (Henry) Norman, KBE, CMG.

Braine, *Rt. Hon.* Sir Bernard Richard, Kt., MP.

Braithwaite, Sir (Joseph) Franklin Madders, Kt.

Braithwaite, Sir Rodric Quentin, KCMG.

Bramall, Sir (Ernest) Ashley, Kt.

Bramley, *Prof.* Sir Paul Anthony, Kt.

Branch, Sir William Allan Patrick, Kt.

Brancker, Sir (John Eustace) Theodore, Kt., QC.

Branigan, Sir Patrick Francis, Kt., QC.

Bray, Sir Theodor Charles, Kt., CBE.

Braynen, Sir Alvin Rudolph, Kt.

Brearley, Sir Norman, Kt., CBE, DSO, MC, AFC.

Bremridge, Sir John Henry, KBE.

Brennan, *Hon.* Sir (Francis) Gerard, KBE.

Brett, Sir Charles Edward Bainbridge, Kt., CBE.

Brett, Sir Lionel, Kt.

Brickwood, Sir Basil Greame, Bt. (1927).

Bridges, *Hon.* Sir Phillip Rodney, Kt., CMG.

Brierley, Sir Ronald Alfred, Kt.

Brierley, Sir Zachry, Kt., CBE.

Briggs, *Hon.* Sir Geoffrey Gould, Kt.

Bright, Sir Keith, Kt.

Brinckman, Sir Theodore George Roderick, Bt. (1831).

Brisco, Sir Donald Gilfrid, Bt. (1782).

Briscoe, Sir John Leigh Charlton, Bt., DFC (1910).

Brise, Sir John Archibald Ruggles-, Bt., CB, OBE, TD (1935).

Bristow, *Hon.* Sir Peter Henry Rowley, Kt.

Brittan, *Rt. Hon.* Sir Leon, Kt., QC.

Britton, Sir Edward Louis, Kt., CBE.

Broackes, Sir Nigel, Kt.

Broadbent, Sir Ewen, KCB, CMG.

Broadbent, Sir George Walter, Bt. (1893).

Broadhurst, *Air Chief Marshal* Sir Harry, GCB, KBE, DSO, DFC, AFC.

Brockhoff, Sir Jack Stuart, Kt.

Brocklebank, Sir Aubrey Thomas, Bt. (1885).

Brockman, *Vice-Adm.* Sir Ronald Vernon, KCB, CVO, CSI, CIE, CBE.

Brockman, *Hon.* Sir Thomas Charles Drake-, Kt., DFC.

Brodie, Sir Benjamin David Ross, Bt. (1834).

Brogan, *Lt.-Gen.* Sir Mervyn Francis, KBE, CB.

Bromhead, Sir John Desmond Gonville, Bt. (1806).

Bromley, Sir Rupert Charles, Bt. (1757).

Bromley, Sir Thomas Eardley, KCMG.

Brook, Sir Robin, Kt., CMG, OBE.

†Brooke, Sir Alistair Weston, Bt. (1919).

Brooke, Sir Francis George Windham, Bt. (1903).

Brooke, *Hon.* Sir Henry, Kt.

Brooke, Sir Richard Neville, Bt. (1662).

Brookes, Sir Wilfred Deakin, Kt., CBE, DSO.

Brooksbank, Sir (Edward) Nicholas, Bt. (1919).

Broom, *Air Marshal* Sir Ivor Gordon, KCB, CBE, DSO, DFC, AFC.

Broughton, *Air Marshal* Sir Charles, KBE, CB.

Broughton, Sir Evelyn Delves, Bt. (1661).

Broun, Sir Lionel John Law, Bt. (s. 1686).

Brown, Sir Allen Stanley, Kt., CBE.

Brown, Sir (Arthur James) Stephen, KBE.

Brown, *Adm.* Sir Brian Thomas, KCB, CBE.

Brown, *Lt.-Col.* Sir Charles Frederick Richmond, Bt. (1863).

Brown, Sir (Cyril) Maxwell Palmer, KCB, CMG.

Brown, Sir David, Kt.

Brown, *Vice-Adm.* Sir David Worthington, KCB.

Brown, Sir Derrick Holden-, Kt.

Brown, Sir Douglas Denison, Kt.

Brown, *Hon.* Sir Douglas Dunlop, Kt.

Brown, Sir Edward Joseph, Kt., MBE.

Brown, *Prof.* Sir (Ernest) Henry Phelps, Kt., MBE, FBA.

Brown, Sir (Frederick Herbert) Stanley, Kt., CBE.

Brown, *Prof.* Sir (George) Malcolm, Kt., FRS.

Brown, Sir John Douglas Keith, Kt.

Brown, Sir John Gilbert Newton, Kt., CBE.

Brown, Sir Mervyn, KCMG, OBE.

Brown, *Hon.* Sir Ralph Kilner, Kt., OBE, TD.

Brown, Sir Raymond Frederick, Kt., OBE.

Brown, Sir Robert Crichton-, KCMG, CBE, TD.

Brown, *Hon.* Sir Simon Denis, Kt.

Brown, *Rt. Hon.* Sir Stephen, Kt.

Brown, Sir Thomas, Kt.

Brown, Sir William Brian Piggott-, Bt. (1903).

Browne, *Rt. Hon.* Sir Patrick Reginald Evelyn, Kt., OBE, TD.

Brownrigg, Sir Nicholas (Gawen), Bt. (1816).

Bruce, Sir Arthur Atkinson, KBE, MC.

Bruce, Sir (Francis) Michael Ian, Bt. (s. 1628).

Bruce, Sir Hervey James Hugh, Bt. (1804).

Bruce, *Rt. Hon.* Sir (James) Roualeyn Hovell-Thurlow-Cumming-, Kt.

Brunner, Sir John Henry Kilian, Bt. (1895).

Brunton, Sir (Edward Francis) Lauder, Bt. (1908).

Brunton, Sir Gordon Charles, Kt.

Bryan, Sir Arthur, Kt.

Bryan, Sir Paul Elmore Oliver, Kt., DSO, MC.

Bryce, *Hon.* Sir (William) Gordon, Kt., CBE.

Bryson, *Vice-Adm.* Sir Lindsay Sutherland, KCB.

Buchan, Sir John, Kt., CMG.

Buchanan, Sir Andrew George, Bt. (1878).

Buchanan, Sir Charles Alexander James Leith-, Bt. (1775).

Buchanan, *Prof.* Sir Colin Douglas, Kt., CBE.

Buchanan, *Vice-Adm.* Sir Peter William, KBE.

Buck, Sir (Philip) Antony (Fyson), Kt., QC, MP.

Buckley, *Rt. Hon.* Sir Denys Burton, Kt., MBE.

Buckley, Sir John William, Kt.

Buckley, *Rear-Adm.* Sir Kenneth Robertson, KBE.

Buckley, *Lt.-Cdr.* Sir (Peter) Richard, KCVO.

Buckley, *Hon.* Sir Roger John, Kt.

Bulkeley, Sir Richard Harry David Williams-, Bt., TD (1661).

Bull, Sir Simeon George, Bt. (1922).

Bull, Sir Walter Edward Avenon, KCVO.

Bullard, Sir Giles Lionel, KCVO, CMG.

Bullard, Sir Julian Leonard, GCMG.

Bullus, Sir Eric Edward, Kt.

Bulmer, Sir William Peter, Kt.

Bultin, Sir Bato, Kt., MBE.

Bunbury, Sir Michael William, Bt. (1681).

Bunbury, Sir (Richard David) Michael Richardson-, Bt. (I. 1787).

Bunch, Sir Austin Wyeth, Kt., CBE.

Bunting, Sir (Edward) John, KBE.

Burbidge, Sir Herbert Dudley, Bt. (1916).

Burbury, *Hon.* Sir Stanley Charles, KCMG, KCVO, KBE.

Burdett, Sir Savile Aylmer, Bt. (1665).

Burgen, Sir Arnold Stanley Vincent, Kt., FRS.

Burgess, *Gen.* Sir Edward Arthur, KCB, OBE.

Burgh, Sir John Charles, KCMG, CB.

Burke, Sir James Stanley Gilbert, Bt. (I. 1797).

Burke, *Prof.* Sir Joseph Terence, KBE.

Burke, Sir (Thomas) Kerry, Kt.

Burley, Sir Victor George, Kt., CBE.

Burman, Sir (John) Charles, Kt.

Burman, Sir Stephen France, Kt., CBE.

Burnet, Sir James William Alexander (Sir Alastair Burnet), Kt.

Burnett, *Air Chief Marshal* Sir Brian Kenyon, GCB, DFC, AFC.

Burnett, Sir David Humphery, Bt., MBE, TD (1913).

Burnett, Sir John Harrison, Kt.

Burnett, Sir Walter John, Kt.

Burney, Sir Cecil Denniston, Bt. (1921).

Burns, Sir Charles Ritchie, KBE, MD.

Burns, Sir John Crawford, Kt.

Burns, Sir Terence, Kt.

Burns, *Maj.-Gen.* Sir (Walter Arthur) George, KCVO, CB, DSO, OBE, MC.

Burrell, Sir John Raymond, Bt. (1774).

Burrenchobay, Sir Dayendranath, KBE, CMG, CVO.

Burrows, Sir Bernard Alexander Brocas, GCMG.

Burston, Sir Samuel Gerald Wood, Kt., OBE.

Burt, *Hon.* Sir Francis Theodore Page, KCMG.

Burton, Sir Carlisle Archibald, Kt., OBE.

Burton, Sir George Vernon Kennedy, Kt., CBE.

Burton, *Air Marshal* Sir Harry, KCB, CBE, DSO.

Burton-Chadwick, Sir Joshua Kenneth, Bt. (1935).

Busby, Sir Matthew, Kt., CBE.

Bush, *Adm.* Sir John Fitzroy Duyland, GCB, DSC.

Busk, Sir Douglas Laird, KCMG.

Butler, *Rt. Hon.* Sir Adam Courtauld, Kt.

Butler, Sir Clifford Charles, Kt., Ph.D., FRS.

Butler, Sir (Frederick) (Edward) Robin, KCB, CVO.

Butler, Sir Michael Dacres, GCMG.

Butler, Sir (Reginald) Michael (Thomas), Bt. (1922).

Butler, *Hon.* Sir Richard Clive, Kt.

Butler, *Col.* Sir Thomas Pierce, Bt., CVO, DSO, OBE (1628).

Butt, Sir (Alfred) Kenneth Dudley, Bt. (1929).

Butterworth, Sir (George) Neville, Kt.

Buxton, Sir Thomas Fowell Victor, Bt. (1840).

Buzzard, Sir Anthony Farquhar, Bt. (1929).

Byatt, Sir Hugh Campbell, KCVO, CMG.

Byers, Sir Maurice Hearne, Kt., CBE, QC.

Byford, Sir Lawrence, Kt., CBE, QPM.

Byrne, Sir Clarence Askew, Kt., OBE, DSC.

Cable, Sir James Eric, KCVO, CMG.

Cadbury, Sir (George) Adrian (Hayhurst), Kt.

Cadell, *Vice-Adm.* Sir John Frederick, KBE.

Cadwallader, Sir John, Kt.

Cahn, Sir Albert Jonas, Bt. (1934).

Cain, Sir Edward Thomas, Kt., CBE.

Cain, Sir Henry Edney Conrad, Kt.

Caine, Sir Michael Harris, Kt.

Caine, Sir Sydney, KCMG.

Cairncross, Sir Alexander Kirkland, KCMG.

Calderwood, Sir Robert, Kt.

Caldwell, *Surgeon Vice-Adm.* Sir (Eric) Dick, KBE, CB.

Callaghan, Sir Allan Robert, Kt., CMG.

Callaghan, Sir Bede Bertrand, Kt., CBE.

Callard, Sir Eric John, Kt.

Callaway, *Prof.* Sir Frank Adams, Kt., CMG, OBE.

Calley, Sir Henry Algernon, Kt., DSO, DFC.

Callinan, Sir Bernard James, Kt., CBE, DSO, MC.

Calne, *Prof.* Sir Roy Yorke, Kt., FRS.

Calthorpe, Sir Euan Hamilton Anstruther-Gough-, Bt. (1929).

Cameron of Lochiel, Sir Donald Hamish, KT, CVO, TD.

Cameron, Sir (Eustace) John, Kt., CBE.

Cameron, Sir James Clark, Kt., CBE, TD.

Cameron, *Hon.* Sir John, KT, DSC, QC (Lord Cameron).

Cameron, Sir John Watson, Kt., OBE.

Campbell, Sir Alan Hugh, GCMG.

Campbell, Sir Clifford Clarence, GCMG, GCVO.

Campbell, Sir Colin Moffat, Bt., MC (s. 1668).

Campbell, *Col.* Sir Guy Theophilus Halswell, Bt., OBE, MC (1815).

Campbell, *Maj.-Gen.* Sir Hamish Manus, KBE, CB.

Campbell, Sir Ian Tofts, Kt., CBE, VRD.

Campbell, Sir Ilay Mark, Bt. (1808).

Campbell, Sir Matthew, KBE, CB, FRSE.

Campbell, Sir Niall Alexander Hamilton, Bt. (1831).

Campbell, Sir Robin Auchinbreck, Bt. (s. 1628).

Campbell, Sir Thomas Cockburn-, Bt. (1821).

Campbell, *Hon.* Sir Walter Benjamin, Kt.

Campbell, *Hon.* Sir William Anthony, Kt.

Campion, Sir Harry, Kt., CB, CBE.

Cantley, *Hon.* Sir Joseph Donaldson, Kt., OBE.

Carden, *Lt.-Col.* Sir Henry Christopher, Bt., OBE (1887).

Carden, Sir John Craven, Bt. (I. 1787).

Carew, Sir Rivers Verain, Bt. (1661).

Carey, Sir Peter Willoughby, GCB.

Carlill, *Vice-Adm.* Sir Stephen Hope, KBE, CB, DSO.

Carlisle, Sir John Michael, Kt.

Carmichael, Sir David Peter William Gibson-Craig-, Bt. (s. 1702 and 1831).

Carmichael, Sir John, KBE.

Carnac, *Rev. Canon* Sir (Thomas) Nicholas Rivett-, Bt. (1836).

Carnegie, *Lt.-Gen.* Sir Robin Macdonald, KCB, OBE.

Carnegie, Sir Roderick Howard, Kt.

Carnwath, Sir Andrew Hunter, KCVO.

Caro, Sir Anthony Alfred, Kt., CBE.

Carpenter, *Very Rev.* Edward Frederick, KCVO.

Carr, Sir (Albert) Raymond (Maillard), Kt.

Carr, *Air Marshal* Sir John Darcy Baker-, KBE, CB, AFC.

Carrick, *Hon.* Sir John Leslie, KCMG.

Carsberg, *Prof.* Sir Bryan Victor, Kt.

Carswell, *Hon.* Sir Robert Douglas, Kt.

Carter, Sir Charles Frederick, Kt., FBA.

Carter, Sir Derrick Hunton, Kt., TD.

Carter, Sir John, Kt., QC.

Carter, Sir John Alexander, Kt.

Carter, Sir William Oscar, Kt.

Cartland, Sir George Barrington, Kt., CMG.

Cartledge, Sir Bryan George, KCMG.

Cary, Sir Roger Hugh, Bt. (1955).

Cash, Sir Gerald Christopher, GCMG, GCVO, OBE.

Cass, Sir John Patrick, Kt., OBE.

Cassel, Sir Harold Felix, Bt., TD, QC (1920).

Cassels, *Field Marshal* Sir (Archibald) James Halkett, GCB, KBE, DSO.

Cassels, Sir John Seton, Kt., CB.

Cassels, *Adm.* Sir Simon Alastair Cassillis, KCB, CBE.

Cassidi, *Adm.* Sir (Arthur) Desmond, GCB.

Casson, Sir Hugh Maxwell, CH, KCVO, PPRA, FRIBA.

Cater, Sir Jack, KBE.

Cater, Sir John Robert, Kt.

Catherwood, Sir (Henry) Frederick (Ross), Kt., MEP.

Catling, Sir Richard Charles, Kt., CMG, OBE.

Cato, *Hon.* Sir Arnott Samuel, KCMG.

Caughey, Sir Thomas Harcourt Clarke, KBE.

Caulfield, *Hon.* Sir Bernard, Kt.

Cave, Sir Charles Edward Coleridge, Bt. (1896).

Cave, Sir (Charles) Philip Haddon-, KBE, CMG.

Cave, Sir Robert Cave-Browne-, Bt. (1641).

Cawley, Sir Charles Mills, Kt., CBE, Ph.D.

Cayley, Sir Digby William David, Bt. (1661).

Cayzer, Sir James Arthur, Bt. (1904).

Cazalet, *Hon.* Sir Edward Stephen, Kt.

Cazalet, Sir Peter Grenville, Kt.

Cecil, *Rear-Adm.* Sir (Oswald) Nigel Amherst, KBE, CB.

Chacksfield, *Air Vice-Marshal* Sir Bernard Albert, KBE, CB.

Chadwick, *Rev. Prof.* Henry, KBE.

Chadwick, *Rev. Prof.* (William) Owen, OM, KBE, FBA.

Chalk, *Hon.* Sir Gordon William Wesley, KBE.

Chamberlain, *Hon.* Sir Reginald Roderic St. Clair, Kt.

Chan, *Rt. Hon.* Sir Julius, KBE.

Chance, Sir (George) Jeremy ffolliott, Bt. (1900).

Chandler, Sir Colin Michael, Kt.

Chandler, Sir Geoffrey, Kt., CBE.

Chaney, *Hon.* Sir Frederick Charles, KBE, AFC.

Chapman, Sir David Robert Macgowan, Bt. (1958).

Chapman, Sir George Alan, Kt.

Chapman, *Hon.* Sir Stephen, Kt.

Chapple, *Gen.* Sir John Lyon, GCB, CBE.

Charles, Sir Joseph Quentin, Kt.

Charnley, Sir (William) John, Kt., CB.

Chaytor, Sir George Reginald, Bt. (1831).

Cheadle, Sir Eric Wallers, Kt., CBE.

Checketts, *Sqn. Ldr.* Sir David John, KCVO.

Cheetham, Sir Nicolas John Alexander, KCMG.

Chesterman, Sir (Dudley) Ross, Kt., Ph.D.

Chesterton, Sir Oliver Sidney, Kt., MC.

Chetwood, Sir Clifford Jack, Kt.

Chetwynd, Sir Arthur Ralph Talbot, Bt. (1795).

Cheung, Sir Oswald Victor, Kt., CBE.

Cheyne, Sir Joseph Lister Watson, Bt., OBE (1908).

Chichester, Sir (Edward) John, Bt. (1641).

Child, Sir (Coles John) Jeremy, Bt. (1919).

Chilton, *Air Marshal* Sir (Charles) Edward, KBE, CB.

Chilton, *Brig.* Sir Frederick Oliver, Kt., CBE, DSO.

Chilwell, *Hon.* Sir Muir Fitzherbert, Kt.

Chinn, Sir Trevor Edwin, Kt., CVO.

Chitty, Sir Thomas Willes, Bt. (1924).

Cholmeley, Sir Montague John, Bt. (1806).

Christie, Sir George William Langham, Kt.

Christie, *Hon.* Sir Vernon Howard Colville, Kt.

Christie, Sir William, Kt., MBE.

Christison, *Gen.* Sir (Alexander Frank) Philip, Bt., GBE, CB, DSO, MC (1871).

Christofas, Sir Kenneth Cavendish, KCMG, MBE.

Christopherson, Sir Derman Guy, Kt., OBE, D.Phil., FRS.

Chung, Sir Sze-yuen, Kt., GBE.

Clapham, Sir Michael John Sinclair, KBE.

Claringbull, Sir (Gordon) Frank, Kt., Ph.D.

Clark, Sir George Anthony, Bt. (1917).

Clark, Sir John Allen, Kt.

Clark, Sir John Douglas, Bt. (1886).

Clark, Sir John Stewart-, Bt., MEP (1918).

Clark, Sir Robert Anthony, Kt., DSC.

Clark, Sir Robin Chichester-, Kt.

Clark, Sir Terence Joseph, KBE, CMG, CVO.

Clark, Sir Thomas Edwin, Kt.

Clark, *Rt. Hon.* Sir William Gibson, Kt., MP.

Clarke, Sir (Charles Mansfield) Tobias, Bt. (1831).

Clarke, *Prof.* Sir Cyril Astley, KBE, MD, SC.D., FRS, FRCP.

Clarke, Sir Ellis Emmanuel Innocent, GCMG.

Clarke, Sir (Henry) Ashley, GCMG, GCVO.

Clarke, Sir Jonathan Dennis, Kt.

Clarke, Sir Rupert William John, Bt., MBE (1882).

Clay, Sir Richard Henry, Bt. (1841).

Clayton, Sir David Robert, Bt., (1732).

Clayton, *Air Marshal* Sir Gareth Thomas Butler, KCB, DFC.

Clayton, Sir Robert James, Kt., CBE.

Cleary, Sir Joseph Jackson, Kt.

Clegg, Sir Walter, Kt.

Cleminson, Sir James Arnold Stacey, KBE, MC.

Clerk, Sir John Dutton, Bt., CBE, VRD (s. 1679).

Clerke, Sir John Edward Longueville, Bt. (1660).

Clifford, Sir Roger Joseph, Bt. (1887).

Clothier, Sir Cecil Montacute, KCB, QC.

Clowes, *Col.* Sir Henry Nelson, KCVO, DSO, OBE.

Clucas, Sir Kenneth Henry, KCB.

Clutterbuck, *Vice-Adm.* Sir David Granville, KBE, CB.

Coates, Sir Ernest William, Kt., CMG.

Coates, Sir Frederick Gregory Lindsay, Bt. (1921).

Coats, Sir Alastair Francis Stuart, Bt. (1905).

Coats, Sir William David, Kt.

Cobban, Sir James Macdonald, Kt., CBE, TD.

Cochrane, Sir (Henry) Marc (Sursock), Bt. (1903).

Cockburn, Sir John Elliot, Bt. (s. 1671).

Cockburn, Sir Robert, KBE, CB, Ph.D.

Cockcroft, Sir Wilfred Halliday, Kt., D.Phil.

Cockerell, Sir Christopher Sydney, Kt., CBE, FRS.

Cockram, Sir John, Kt.

Codrington, Sir Simon Francis Bethell, Bt. (1876).

Codrington, Sir William Alexander, Bt. (1721).

Coghill, Sir Egerton James Nevill Tobias, Bt. (1778).

Cohen, Sir Bernard Nathaniel Waley-, Bt. (1961).

Cohen, Sir Edward, Kt.

Coldstream, Sir George Phillips, KCB, KCVO, QC.

Cole, Sir (Alexander) Colin, KCVO, TD.

Cole, Sir David Lee, KCMG, MC.

Cole, Sir (Robert) William, Kt.

Coles, Sir (Arthur) John, KCMG.

Colfox, Sir (William) John, Bt. (1939).

Collett, Sir Christopher, GBE.

Collett, Sir Ian Seymour, Bt. (1934).

Collins, Sir Arthur James Robert, KCVO.

Collyear, Sir John Gowen, Kt.

Colman, Sir Michael Jeremiah, Bt. (1907).

Colquhoun, *Maj.-Gen.* Sir Cyril Harry, KCVO, CB, OBE.

Colquhoun of Luss, Sir Ivar Iain, Bt. (1786).

Colt, Sir Edward William Dutton Bt. (1694).

Colthurst, Sir Richard La Touche, Bt. (1744).

Combs, Sir Willis Ide, KCVO, CMG.

Compston, *Vice-Adm.* Sir Peter Maxwell, KCB.

Compton, Sir Edmund Gerald, GCB, KBE.

Compton Miller, Sir John (Francis), Kt., MBE, TD.

Comyn, *Hon.* Sir James, Kt.

Conant, Sir John Ernest Michael, Bt. (1954).

Conran, Sir Terence Orby, Kt.

Cons, *Hon.* Sir Derek, Kt.

Constable, Sir Robert Frederick Strickland-, Bt. (1641).

Constantine, *Air Chief Marshal* Sir Hugh Alex, KBE, CB, DSO.

Cook, *Prof.* Sir Alan Hugh, Kt.

Cook, Sir Christopher Wymondham Rayner Herbert, Bt. (1886).

Cook, Sir (Philip) Halford, Kt., OBE.

Cooke, Sir Charles Fletcher-, Kt., QC.

Cooke, *Lt.-Col.* Sir David William Perceval, Bt. (1661).

Cooke, *Rt. Hon.* Sir Robin Brunskill, KBE.

Cooley, Sir Alan Sydenham, Kt., CBE.

Coop, Sir Maurice Fletcher, Kt.

Cooper, *Rt. Hon.* Sir Frank, GCB, CMG.

Cooper, *Gen.* Sir George Leslie Conroy, GCB, MC.

Cooper, Sir Patrick Graham Astley, Bt. (1821).

Cooper, Sir Richard Powell, Bt. (1905).

Cooper, Sir William Daniel Charles, Bt. (1863).

Cooper, Sir William Henry, Kt., CBE.

Cooper, *Prof.* Sir (William) Mansfield, Kt.

Coote, Sir Christopher John, Bt., *Premier Baronet of Ireland* (I. 1621).

Copas, *Most Rev.* Virgil, KBE, DD.

Copisarow, Sir Alcon Charles, Kt.

Corbet, Sir John Vincent, Bt., MBE (1808).

Corby, Sir (Frederick) Brian, Kt.

Corfield, *Rt. Hon.* Sir Frederick Vernon, Kt., QC.

Corfield, Sir Kenneth George, Kt.

Cork, Sir Kenneth Russell, GBE.

Corley, Sir Kenneth Sholl Ferrand, Kt.

Cormack, Sir Magnus Cameron, KBE.

Corness, Sir Colin Ross, Kt.

Cornford, Sir (Edward) Clifford, KCB.

Cornforth, Sir John Warcup, Kt., CBE, D.Phil., FRS.

Corry, Sir William James, Bt. (1885).

Cortazzi, Sir (Henry Arthur) Hugh, GCMG.

Cory, Sir Clinton James Donald, Bt. (1919).

Costar, Sir Norman Edgar, KCMG.

Cotter, *Lt.-Col.* Sir Delaval James Alfred, Bt., DSO (I. 1763).

Cotterell, Sir John Henry Geers, Bt. (1805).

Cotton, Sir John Richard, KCMG, OBE.

Cotton, *Hon.* Sir Robert Carrington, KCMG.

Cottrell, Sir Alan Howard, Kt., ph.D., FRS.

Cotts, Sir (Robert) Crichton Mitchell, Bt. (1921).

Coulson, Sir John Eltringham, KCMG.

Couper, Sir (Robert) Nicholas (Oliver), Bt. (1841).

Court, *Hon.* Sir Charles Walter Michael, KCMG, OBE.

Couzens, Sir Kenneth Edward, KCB.

Covacevich, Sir (Anthony) Thomas, Kt., DFC.

Cowan, Sir Robert, Kt.

Coward, *Vice-Adm.* Sir John Francis, KCB, DSO.

Cowen, *Rt. Hon. Prof.* Sir Zelman, GCMG, GCVO, QC.

Cowley, *Lt.-Gen.* Sir John Guise, GC, KBE, CB.

Cowperthwaite, Sir John James, KBE, CMG.

Cox, Sir Anthony Wakefield, Kt., CBE, FRIBA.

Cox, *Prof.* Sir David Roxbee, Kt., FRS.

Cox, Sir (Ernest) Gordon, KBE, TD, D.SC., FRS.

Cox, Sir Geoffrey Sandford, Kt., CBE.

Cox, Sir (George) Trenchard, Kt., CBE, FSA.

Cox, *Vice-Adm.* Sir John Michael Holland, KCB.

Cox, Sir John William, Kt., CBE.

Cox, Sir Mencea Ethereal, Kt., Cradock, Sir Percy, GCMG.

Craig, Sir (Albert) James (Macqueen), GCMG.

Craig, *Marshal of the Royal Air Force* Sir David Brownrigg, GCB, OBE.

Cramer, *Hon.* Sir John Oscar, Kt.

Crane, Sir James William Donald, Kt., CBE.

Craufurd, Sir Robert James, Bt. (1781).

Craven, *Air Marshal* Sir Robert Edward, KBE, CB, DFC.

Crawford, *Prof.* Sir Frederick William, Kt.

Crawford, *Hon.* Sir George Hunter, Kt.

Crawford, Sir (Robert) Stewart, GCMG, CVO.

Crawford, *Prof.* Sir Theodore, Kt.

Crawford, *Vice-Adm.* Sir William Godfrey, KBE, CB, DSC.

Crawshaw, *Hon.* Sir (Edward) Daniel (Weston), Kt.

Crawshay, *Col.* Sir William Robert, Kt., DSO, ERD, TD.

Creagh, *Maj.-Gen.* Sir (Kilner) Rupert Brazier-, KBE, CB, DSO.

Crichton, Sir Andrew James Maitland-Makgill-, Kt.

Crill, Sir Peter Leslie, Kt., CBE.

Cripps, Sir Cyril Humphrey, Kt.

Cripps, Sir John Stafford, Kt., CBE.

Crisp, Sir (John) Peter, Bt. (1913).

Critchett, Sir Ian (George Lorraine), Bt. (1908).

Croft, Sir John Archibald Radcliffe, Bt. (1818).

Croft, Sir Owen Glendower, Bt. (1671).

†Crofton, Sir Hugh Denis, Bt. (1801).

Crofton, *Prof.* Sir John Wenman, Kt.

Crofton, Sir Malby Sturges, Bt. (1838).

Croker, Sir Walter Russell, KBE.

Crookenden, *Lt.-Gen.* Sir Napier, KCB, DSO, OBE.

Croom-Johnson, *Rt. Hon.* Sir David Powell, Kt., DSC, VRD.

Cross, Sir Barry Albert, Kt., CBE, FRS.

Cross, *Air Chief Marshal* Sir Kenneth Brian Boyd, KCB, CBE, DSO, DFC.

Crossland, Sir Bernard, Kt., CBE.

Crossland, Sir Leonard, Kt.

Crossley, Sir Nicholas John, Bt. (1909).

Crouch, Sir David Lance, Kt.

Cruthers, Sir James Winter, Kt.

Cubbon, Sir Brian Crossland, GCB.

Cubitt, Sir Hugh Guy, Kt., CBE.

Cuckney, Sir John Graham, Kt.

Cumber, Sir John Alfred, Kt., CMG, MBE, TD.

Cumming, Sir William Gordon Gordon-, Bt. (1804).

Cuninghame, Sir John Christopher Foggo Montgomery-, Bt. (NS 1672).

†Cuninghame, Sir William Henry Fairlie-, Bt. (s. 1630).

Cunliffe, Sir David Ellis, Bt. (1759)

Cunningham, Sir Charles Craik, GCB, KBE, CVO.

Cunningham, *Lt.-Gen.* Sir Hugh Patrick, KBE.

Cunynghame, Sir Andrew David Francis, Bt. (s. 1702).

Curle, Sir John Noel Ormiston, KCVO, CMG.

Curran, Sir Samuel Crowe, Kt., D.SC., ph.D., FRS, FRSE.

Currie, *Prof.* Sir Alastair Robert, Kt., FRCP, FRCPE, FRSE.

†Currie, Sir Donald Scott, Bt. (1847).

Currie, Sir Neil Smith, Kt., CBE.

Curtis, Sir (Edward) Leo, Kt.

Curtis, Sir William Peter, Bt. (1802).

Curtiss, *Air Marshal* Sir John Bagot, KCB, KBE.

Curwen, Sir Christopher Keith, KCMG.

Cuthbertson, Sir Harold Alexander, Kt.

Cutler, Sir (Arthur) Roden, VC, KCMG, KCVO, CBE.

Cutler, Sir Charles Benjamin, KBE, ED.

Cutler, Sir Horace Walter, Kt., OBE.

Dacie, *Prof.* Sir John Vivian, Kt., MD, FRS.

Dalais, Sir Adrien Pierre, Kt.

Dale, Sir William Leonard, KCMG.

Dalrymple, *Maj.* Sir Hew Fleetwood Hamilton-, Bt., KCVO (s. 1697).

Dalton, Sir Alan Nugent Goring, Kt., CBE.

Dalton, *Vice-Adm.* Sir Geoffrey Thomas James Oliver, KCB.

Dalton, *Vice-Adm.* Sir Norman Eric, KCB, OBE.

Daly, *Lt.-Gen.* Sir Thomas Joseph, KBE, CB, DSO.

Dalyell, Sir Tam, Bt., MP (NS 1685).

Daniel, Sir Goronwy Hopkin, KCVO, CB, D.Phil.

Daniell, Sir Peter Averell, Kt., TD.

Danks, Sir Alan John, KBE.

Darby, *Prof.* Sir Henry Clifford, Kt., CBE.

Darby, Sir Peter Howard, Kt., CBE, QFSM.

Darell, Sir Jeffrey Lionel, Bt., MC (1795).

Dargie, Sir William Alexander, Kt., CBE.

Darling, Sir Clifford, Kt.

Darling, Sir James Ralph, Kt., CMG, OBE.

Darling, *Gen.* Sir Kenneth Thomas, GBE, KCB, DSO.

Darlington, *Rear-Adm.* Sir Charles Roy, KBE.

Darvall, Sir (Charles) Roger, Kt., CBE.

Dashwood, Sir Francis John Vernon Hereward, Bt., *Premier Baronet of Great Britain* (1707).

Dashwood, Sir Richard James, Bt. (1684).

Daunt, Sir Timothy Lewis Achilles, KCMG.

David, Sir Jean Marc, Kt., CBE, QC.

Davidson, Sir Robert James, Kt.

Davie, Sir Antony Francis Ferguson-, Bt. (1847).

Davies, *Air Marshal* Sir Alan Cyril, KCB, KBE.

Davies, *Hon.* Sir (Alfred William) Michael, Kt.

Davies, Sir Alun Talfan, Kt., QC.

Davies, Sir (David) Arthur, KBE.

Davies, Sir David Henry, Kt.

Davies, *Hon.* Sir (David Herbert) Mervyn, Kt., MC, TD.

Davies, Sir David Joseph, Kt.

Davies, *Vice-Adm.* Sir Lancelot Richard Bell, KBE.

Davies, Sir Oswald, Kt., CBE.

Davies, Sir Peter Maxwell, Kt., CBE.

Davies, Sir Richard Harries, KCVO, CBE.

Davies, Sir Victor Caddy, Kt., OBE.

Davis, Sir Charles Sigmund, Kt., CB.

Davis, Sir Colin Rex, Kt., CBE.

Davis, *Hon.* Sir (Dermot) Renn, Kt., OBE.

Davis, Sir (Ernest) Howard, Kt., CMG, OBE.

Davis, Sir John Gilbert, Bt. (1946).

Davis, Sir John Henry Harris, Kt.

Davis, Sir Maurice Herbert, Kt., OBE.

Davis, Sir Rupert Charles Hart-, Kt.

Davis, *Hon.* Sir Thomas Robert Alexander Harries, KBE.

Davis, Sir (William) Allan, GBE.

Davison, *Rt. Hon.* Sir Ronald Keith, GBE, CMG.

Dawbarn, Sir Simon Yelverton, KCVO, CMG.

Dawson, *Hon.* Sir Daryl Michael, KBE, CB.

Dawson, Sir Hugh Michael Trevor, Bt. (1920).

Dawson, *Air Chief Marshal* Sir Walter Lloyd, KCB, CBE, DSO.

Dawtry, Sir Alan (Graham), Kt., CBE, TD.

Day, Sir Derek Malcolm, KCMG.

Day, Sir (Judson) Graham, Kt.

Day, Sir Robin, Kt.

Deakin, Sir (Frederick) William (Dampier), Kt., DSO.

Dean, Sir (Arthur) Paul, Kt., MP.

Dean, Sir Patrick Henry, GCMG.

Deane, *Hon.* Sir William Patrick, KBE.

Dearing, Sir Ronald Ernest, Kt., CB.

de Bellaigue, Sir Geoffrey, KCVO.

Debenham, Sir Gilbert Ridley, Bt. (1931).

Deer, Sir (Arthur) Frederick, Kt., CMG.

de Hoghton, Sir (Richard) Bernard (Cuthbert), Bt. (1611).

De la Bère, Sir Cameron, Bt. (1953).

Delacombe, *Maj.-Gen.* Sir Rohan, KCMG, KCVO, KBE, CB, DSO.

de la Mare, Sir Arthur James, KCMG, KCVO.

Delamere, Sir Monita Eru, KBE.

de la Rue, Sir Andrew George Ilay, Bt. (1898).

Dellow, Sir John Albert, Kt., CBE.

de Lotbinière, *Lt.-Col.* Sir Edmond Joly, Kt.

Delve, Sir Frederick William, Kt., CBE.

de Montmorency, Sir Arnold Geoffroy, Bt. (I. 1631).

Denholm, Sir John Ferguson (Ian), Kt., CBE.

Denman, Sir (George) Roy, KCB, CMG.

Denny, Sir Alistair Maurice Archibald, Bt. (1913).

Denny, Sir Anthony Coningham de Waltham, Bt. (I. 1782).

Dent, Sir John, Kt., CBE.

Denton, *Prof.* Sir Eric James, Kt., CBE, FRS.

Derbyshire, Sir Andrew George, Kt.

Derham, Sir Peter John, Kt..

de Trafford, Sir Dermot Humphrey, Bt. (1841).

Deverell, Sir Colville Montgomery, GBE, KCMG, CVO.

Devesi, Sir Baddeley, GCMG, GCVO.

De Ville, Sir Harold Godfrey Oscar, Kt.

Devitt, Sir Thomas Gordon, Bt. (1916).

de Waal, Sir (Constant Henrik) Henry, KCB, QC.

Dewey, Sir Anthony Hugh, Bt. (1917).

Dewhurst, *Prof.* Sir (Christopher) John, Kt.

†d'Eyncourt, Sir Mark Gervais Tennyson-, Bt. (1930).

Dhenin, *Air Marshal* Sir Geoffrey Howard, KBE, AFC, GM, MD.

Dhrangadhra, HH the Maharaja Raj Saheb of, KCIE.

Dibela, *Hon.* Sir Kingsford, GCMG.

Dick, Sir John Alexander, Kt., MC, QC.

Dickinson, Sir Harold Herbert, Kt.

Dickinson, Sir Samuel Benson, Kt.

Dilbertson, Sir Geoffrey, Kt., CBE.

Dilke, Sir John Fisher Wentworth, Bt. (1862).

Dill, Sir Nicholas Bayard, Kt., CBE.

Dillon, *Rt. Hon.* Sir (George) Brian (Hugh), Kt.

Dillon, Sir John Vincent, Kt., CMG.

Dillon, Sir Max, Kt.

Diver, *Hon.* Sir Leslie Charles, Kt.

Dixon, Sir John George, Bt. (1919).

Dobson, Sir Denis William, KCB, OBE, QC.

Dobson, *Gen.* Sir Patrick John Howard-, GCB.

Dobson, Sir Richard Portway, Kt.

Dodds, Sir Ralph Jordan, Bt. (1964).

Dodson, Sir Derek Sherborne Lindsell, KCMG, MC.

Dodsworth, Sir John Christopher Smith-, Bt. (1784).

Doll, *Prof.* Sir (William) Richard (Shaboe), Kt., OBE, FRS, DM, MD, D.SC.

Dollery, Sir Colin Terence, Kt.

Donald, Sir Alan Ewen, KCMG.

Donald, *Air Marshal* Sir John George, KBE.

Donne, *Hon.* Sir Gaven John, KBE.

Donne, Sir John Christopher, Kt.

Dookun, Sir Dewoonarain, Kt.

Dorman, *Lt.-Col.* Sir Charles Geoffrey, Bt., MC (1923).

Dorman, Sir Maurice Henry, GCMG, GCVO.

Dos Santos, Sir Errol Lionel, Kt., CBE.

Dougherty, *Maj.-Gen.* Sir Ivan Noel, Kt., CBE, DSO, ED.

Doughty, Sir William Roland, Kt.

Douglas, *Prof.* Sir Donald Macleod, Kt., MBE.

Douglas, Sir (Edward) Sholto, Kt.

Douglas, Sir Robert McCallum, Kt., OBE.

Douglas, *Rt. Hon.* Sir William Randolph, KCMG.

Dover, *Prof.* Sir Kenneth James, Kt., D.Litt., FBA, FRSE.

Down, Sir Alastair Frederick, Kt., OBE, MC, TD.

Downey, Sir Gordon Stanley, KCB.

Downs, Sir Diarmuid, Kt., CBE.

Downward, Sir William Atkinson, Kt.

Dowson, Sir Philip Manning, Kt., CBE, ARA.

Doyle, Sir Reginald Derek Henry, Kt., CBE.

†D'Oyly, Sir Nigel Hadley Miller, Bt. (1663).

Drake, Sir (Arthur) Eric (Courtney), Kt., CBE.

Drake, *Hon.* Sir (Frederick) Maurice, Kt., DFC.

Drew, Sir Arthur Charles Walter, KCB.

Drew, *Lt.-Gen.* Sir (William) Robert (Macfarlane), KCB, CBE, FRCP.

Dreyer, *Adm.* Sir Desmond Parry, GCB, CBE, DSC.

Dring, *Lt.-Col.* Sir Arthur John, KBE, CIE.

Drinkwater, Sir John Muir, Kt., QC.

Driver, Sir Antony Victor, Kt.

Driver, Sir Eric William, Kt.

Drury, Sir (Victor William) Michael, Kt., OBE.

Dryden, Sir John Stephen Gyles, Bt. (1733 and 1795).

du Cann, *Rt. Hon.* Sir Edward Dillon Lott, KBE.

Duckmanton, Sir Talbot Sydney, Kt., CBE.

Duckworth, *Maj.* Sir Richard Dyce, Bt. (1909).

du Cros, Sir Claude Philip Arthur Mallet, Bt. (1916).

Duff, *Rt. Hon.* Sir (Arthur) Antony, GCMG, CVO, DSO, DSC.

Duffus, *Hon.* Sir William Algernon Holwell, Kt.

Dugdale, Sir William Stratford, Bt., MC (1936).

Duke, *Maj.-Gen.* Sir Gerald William, KBE, CB, DSO.

Dunbar, Sir Archibald Ranulph, Bt. (s. 1700).

Dunbar, Sir David Hope-, Bt. (s. 1664).

Dunbar, Sir Drummond Cospatrick Ninian, Bt., MC (s. 1698).

Dunbar, Sir Jean Ivor, Bt. (s. 1694).

Dunbar of Hempriggs, Dame Maureen Daisy Helen (Lady Dunbar of Hempriggs), Btss. (s. 1706).

Duncan, Sir James Blair, Kt.

Duncombe, Sir Philip Digby Pauncefort-, Bt. (1859).

Dundas, Sir Hugh Spencer Lisle, Kt., CBE, DSO, DFC.

Dunham, Sir Kingsley Charles, Kt., Ph.D., FRS, FRSE.

Dunlop, Sir (Ernest) Edward, Kt., CMG, OBE.

Dunlop, Sir Thomas, Bt. (1916).

Dunlop, Sir William Norman Gough, Kt.

Dunn, *Air Marshal* Sir Eric Clive, KBE, CB, BEM.

Dunn, *Lt.-Col.* Sir (Francis) Vivian, KCVO, OBE.

Dunn, *Air Marshal* Sir Patrick Hunter, KBE, CB, DFC.

Dunn, *Rt. Hon.* Sir Robin Horace Walford, Kt., MC.

Dunnett, Sir (Ludovic) James, GCB, CMG.

Dunning, Sir Simon William Patrick, Bt. (1930).

Dunphie, *Maj.-Gen.* Sir Charles Anderson Lane, Kt., CB, CBE, DSO.

Dunstan, *Lt.-Gen.* Sir Donald Beaumont, KBE, CB.

†Duntze, Sir Daniel Evans, Bt. (1774).

Dupree, Sir Peter, Bt. (1921).

Dupuch, Sir (Alfred) Etienne (Jerome), Kt., OBE.

Durand, *Rev.* Sir (Henry Mortimer) Dickon, Bt. (1892).

Durham, Sir Kenneth, Kt.

Durie, Sir Alexander Charles, Kt., CBE.

Durkin, *Air Marshal* Sir Herbert, KBE, CB.

Durrant, Sir William Henry Estridge, Bt. (1784).

Duthie, *Prof.* Sir Herbert Livingston, Kt.

Duthie, Sir Robert Grieve (Robin), Kt., CBE.

Duval, Sir (Charles) Gaetan, Kt.

Duxbury, *Air Marshal* Sir (John) Barry, KCB, CBE.

Dyer, *Prof.* Sir (Henry) Peter (Francis) Swinnerton-, Bt., KBE, FRS (1678).

Dyke, Sir David William Hart, Bt. (1677).

Earle, Sir (Hardman) George (Algernon), Bt. (1869).

East, Sir (Lewis) Ronald, Kt., CBE.

Eastham, *Hon.* Sir (Thomas) Michael, Kt.

Easton, *Air Cdre.* Sir James Alfred, KCMG, CB, CBE.

Easton, Sir Robert William Simpson, Kt., CBE.

Eastwood, Sir John Bealby, Kt..

Eaton, *Vice-Adm.* Sir Kenneth John, KCB.

Eberle, *Adm.* Sir James Henry Fuller, GCB.

Ebrahim, Sir (Mahomed) Currimbhoy, Bt. (1910).

Eburne, Sir Sidney Alfred William, Kt., MC.

Eccles, Sir John Carew, Kt., D.Phil., FRS.

Echlin, Sir Norman David Fenton, Bt. (I. 1721).

Eckersley, Sir Donald Payze, Kt., OBE.

Edden, *Vice-Adm.* Sir (William) Kaye, KBE, CB.

†Edge, Sir William, Bt. (1937).

Edmenson, Sir Walter Alexander, Kt., CBE.

Edmonstone, Sir Archibald Bruce Charles, Bt. (1774).

Edwardes, Sir Michael Owen, Kt.

Edwards, Sir Christopher John Churchill, Bt. (1866).

Edwards, Sir George Robert, Kt., OM, CBE, FRS.

Edwards, Sir (John) Clive (Leighton), Bt. (1921).

Edwards, Sir Llewellyn Roy, Kt.

Edwards, *Prof.* Sir Samuel Frederick, Kt., FRS.

Egan, Sir John Leopold, Kt.

Egerton, Sir John Alfred Roy, Kt.

Egerton, Sir (Philip) John (Caledon) Grey-, Bt. (1617).

Egerton, Sir Seymour John Louis, GCVO.

Egerton, Sir Stephen Loftus, KCMG.

Eggleston, *Hon.* Sir Richard Moulton, Kt.

Eichelbaum, *Rt. Hon.* Sir Thomas, GBE.

†Eliott of Stobs, Sir Charles Joseph Alexander, Bt. (s 1666).

Elliot, Sir Gerald Henry, Kt.

†Elliott, Sir Clive Christopher Hugh, Bt. (1917).

Elliott, Sir Norman Randall, Kt., CBE.

Elliott, Sir Randal Forbes, KBE.

Elliott, *Prof.* Sir Roger James, Kt., FRS.

Elliott, Sir Ronald Stuart, Kt.

Ellis, Sir John Rogers, Kt., MBE, MD, FRCP.

Ellis, Sir Ronald, Kt.

Ellison, *Rt. Rev.* and *Rt. Hon.* Gerald Alexander, KCVO.

Ellison, *Col.* Sir Ralph Harry Carr-, Kt., TD.

Ellwood, *Air Marshal* Sir Aubrey Beauclerk, KCB, DSC.

Elphinstone, Sir John, Bt. (s 1701).

Elphinstone, Sir (Maurice) Douglas (Warburton), Bt., TD (1816).

Elton, Sir Arnold, Kt., CBE.

Elton, Sir Charles Abraham Grierson, Bt. (1717).

Elton, *Prof.* Sir Geoffrey Rudolph, Kt., FBA.

Elwood, Sir Brian George Conway, Kt., CBE.

Elworthy, Sir Peter Herbert, Kt.

Elyan, Sir (Isadore) Victor, Kt.

Emery, Sir Peter Frank Hannibal, Kt., MP.

Empson, *Adm.* Sir (Leslie) Derek, GBE, KCB.

Emson, *Air Marshal* Sir Reginald Herbert, KBE, CB, AFC.

Engineer, Sir Noshirwan Phirozshah, Kt.

Engle, Sir George Lawrence Jose, KCB, QC.

English, Sir Cyril Rupert, Kt.

English, Sir David, Kt.

Entwistle, Sir (John Nuttall) Maxwell, Kt.

Ereaut, Sir (Herbert) Frank Cobbold, Kt.

Eri, Sir Vincent Serei, GCMG.

Errington, *Col.* Sir Geoffrey Frederick, Bt. (1963).

Errington, Sir Lancelot, KCB.

Erskine, Sir (Thomas) David, Bt. (1821).

Esmonde, Sir Thomas Francis Grattan, Bt. (I. 1629).

Espie, Sir Frank Fletcher, Kt., OBE.

Esplen, Sir John Graham, Bt. (1921).

Eustace, Sir Joseph Lambert, GCMG, GCVO.

Evans, Sir Anthony Adney, Bt. (1920).

Evans, *Hon.* Sir Anthony Howell Meurig, Kt., RD.

Evans, *Air Chief Marshal* Sir David George, GCB, CBE.

Evans, Sir Francis Loring Gwynne-, Bt. (1913).

Evans, Sir Geraint Llewellyn, Kt., CBE.

Evans, Sir Richard Mark, KCMG, KCVO.

Evans, Sir (Robert) Charles, Kt.

Evans, Sir (William) Vincent (John), GCMG, MBE, QC.

Eveleigh, *Rt. Hon.* Sir Edward Walter, Kt., ERD.

Everard, *Maj.-Gen.* Sir Christopher Earle Welby-, KBE, CB.

Everard, Sir Robin Charles, Bt. (1911).

Everson, Sir Frederick Charles, KCMG.

Every, Sir Henry John Michael, Bt. (1641).

Ewans, Sir Martin Kenneth, KCMG.

Ewart, Sir (William) Ivan (Cecil), Bt., DSC (1887).

Ewbank, *Hon.* Sir Anthony Bruce, Kt.

Ewin, Sir (David) Ernest Thomas Floyd, Kt., OBE, MVO.

Ewing, *Vice-Adm.* Sir (Robert) Alastair, KBE, CB, DSC.

Ewing, Sir Ronald Archibald Orr-, Bt. (1886).

Eyre, Sir Graham Newman, Kt., QC.

Eyre, *Maj.-Gen.* Sir James Ainsworth Campden Gabriel, KCVO, CBE.

Eyre, Sir Reginald Edwin, Kt.

Faber, Sir Richard Stanley, KCVO, CMG.

Fadahunsi, Sir Joseph Odeleye, KCMG.

Fagge, Sir John William Frederick, Bt. (1660).

Fairbairn, *Hon.* Sir David Eric, KBE, DFC.

Fairbairn, Sir (James) Brooke, Bt. (1869).

Fairbairn, Sir Nicholas Hardwick, Kt., QC, MP.

Fairclough, Sir John Whitaker, Kt.

Fairfax, Sir Vincent Charles, Kt., CMG.

Fairgrieve, Sir (Thomas) Russell, Kt., CBE, TD.

Fairhall, *Hon.* Sir Allen, KBE.

Falconer, *Hon.* Sir Douglas William, Kt., MBE.

Falk, Sir Roger Salis, Kt., OBE.

Falkiner, Sir Edmond Charles, Bt. (l. 1778).

Falkner, Sir (Donald) Keith, Kt.

Falle, Sir Samuel, KCMG, KCVO, DSC.

Fareed, Sir Djamil Sheik, Kt.

Faridkot, *Col.* HH the Raja of, KCSI.

Farmer, Sir (Lovedin) George Thomas, Kt.

Farndale, *Gen.* Sir Martin Baker, KCB.

Farquhar, Sir Michael Fitzroy Henry, Bt. (1796).

Farquharson, *Rt. Hon.* Sir Donald Henry, Kt.

Farquharson, Sir James Robbie, KBE.

Farr, Sir John Arnold, Kt., MP.

Farrar-Hockley, *Gen.* Sir Anthony Heritage, GBE, KCB, DSO, MC.

Farrer, Sir Charles Matthew, KCVO.

Farrington, Sir Henry Francis Colden, Bt. (1818).

Faulkner, Sir Eric Odin, Kt., MBE.

Faulkner, Sir Percy, KBE, CB.

Fawcus, Sir (Robert) Peter, KBE, CMG.

Fawkes, Sir Randol Francis, Kt.

Fawcett, Sir James Edmund Sandford, Kt., DSC, QC.

Fay, Sir (Humphrey) Michael Gerard, Kt.

Fayrer, Sir John Lang Macpherson, Bt. (1896).

Feilden, Sir Bernard Melchior, Kt., CBE.

Feilden, Sir Henry Wemyss, Bt. (1846).

Feldman, Sir Basil Samuel, Kt.

Fell, Sir Anthony, Kt.

Fellowes, *Rt. Hon.* Sir Robert, KCVO, CB.

Fenn, Sir Nicholas Maxted, KCMG.

Fennell, *Hon.* Sir (John) Desmond Augustine, Kt., OBE.

Fennessy, Sir Edward, Kt., CBE.

Ferens, Sir Thomas Robinson, Kt., CBE.

Ferguson, *Lt.-Col.* Sir Neil Edward Johnson-, Bt., TD (1906).

Fergusson of Kilkerran, Sir Charles, Bt. (s. 1703).

Fergusson, Sir Ewan Alastair John, KCMG.

Fergusson, Sir James Herbert Hamilton Colyer-, Bt. (1866).

Feroze, Sir Rustam Moolan, Kt., FRCS.

Ferris, *Hon.* Sir Francis Mursell, Kt., TD.

ffolkes, Sir Robert Francis Alexander, Bt, OBE (1774).

Fieldhouse, Sir Harold, KBE, CB.

Fielding, Sir Colin Cunningham, Kt., CB.

Fielding, Sir Leslie, KCMG.

Fiennes, Sir John Saye Wingfield Twisleton-Wykeham-, KCB, QC.

Fiennes, Sir Maurice Alberic Twisleton-Wykeham-, Kt.

Fiennes, Sir Ranulph Twisleton-Wykeham-, Bt. (1916).

Figg, Sir Leonard Clifford William, KCMG.

Figgess, Sir John George, KBE, CMG.

Figgures, Sir Frank Edward, KCB, CMG.

Figures, Sir Colin Frederick, KCMG, OBE.

Fingland, Sir Stanley James Gunn, KCMG.

Finlay, Sir David Ronald James Bell, Bt. (1964).

Finley, Sir Peter Hamilton, Kt., OBE, DFC.

Finniston, Sir (Harold) Montague, Kt., Ph.D., FRS.

Finsberg, Sir Geoffrey, Kt., MBE, MP.

Firth, *Prof.* Sir Raymond William, Kt., Ph.D., FBA.

Fish, Sir Hugh, Kt., CBE.

Fisher, Sir George Read, Kt., CMG.

Fisher, *Hon.* Sir Henry Arthur Pears, Kt.

Fisher, Sir Nigel Thomas Loveridge, Kt., MC.

Fison, Sir (Richard) Guy, Bt., DSC (1905).

Fitch, *Adm.* Sir Richard George Alison, KCB.

Fitzgerald, *Rev.* (Sir) Edward Thomas, Bt. (1903).

FitzGerald, Sir George Peter Maurice, Bt., MC (*The Knight of Kerry*) (1880).

FitzHerbert, Sir Richard Ranulph, Bt. (1784).

Fitzmaurice, *Lt.-Col.* Sir Desmond FitzJohn, Kt., CIE.

Fitzpatrick, *Gen.* Sir (Geoffrey Richard) Desmond, GCB, DSO, MBE, MC.

Fitzpatrick, *Air Marshal* Sir John Bernard, KBE, CB.

Flanagan, Sir James Bernard, Kt., CBE.

Flavelle, Sir (Joseph) David Ellsworth, Bt. (1917).

Fleming, *Instructor Rear-Adm.* Sir John, KBE, DSC.

Fletcher, *Hon.* Sir Alan Roy, Kt.

Fletcher, Sir James Muir Cameron, Kt.

Fletcher, Sir John Henry Lancelot Aubrey-, Bt. (1782).

Fletcher, Sir Leslie, Kt., DSC.

Fletcher, *Air Chief Marshal* Sir Peter Carteret, KCB, OBE, DFC, AFC.

Floyd, Sir Giles Henry Charles, Bt. (1816).

Foley, Sir (Thomas John) Noel, Kt., CBE.

Foot, Sir Geoffrey James, Kt.

Foots, Sir James William, Kt.

Forbes, *Hon.* Sir Alastair Granville, Kt.

Forbes of Pitsligo, Sir Charles Edward Stuart-, Bt. (s. 1626).

Forbes of Brux, *Hon.* Sir Ewan, Bt. (s. 1630).

Forbes, *Maj.* Sir Hamish Stewart, Bt., MBE, MC (1823).

Forbes, *Vice-Adm.* Sir John Morrison, KCB.

Ford, Sir Andrew Russell, Bt. (1929).

Ford, *Capt.* Sir Aubrey St. Clair-, Bt., DSO, RN (1793).

Ford, Sir David Robert, KBE, LVO, OBE.

Ford, *Maj.* Sir Edward William Spencer, KCB, KCVO.

Ford, *Air Marshal* Sir Geoffrey Harold, KBE, CB.

Ford, *Prof.* Sir Hugh, Kt., FRS.

Ford, Sir John Archibald, KCMG, MC.

Ford, Sir Richard Brinsley, Kt., CBE.

Ford, *Gen.* Sir Robert Cyril, GCB, CBE.

Foreman, Sir Philip Frank, Kt., CBE.

Forman, Sir John Denis, Kt., OBE.

Forrest, *Prof.* Sir (Andrew) Patrick (McEwen), Kt.

Forrest, Sir James Alexander, Kt.

Forrest, *Rear-Adm.* Sir Ronald Stephen, KCVO.

Forster, Sir Archibald William, Kt.

Forster, Sir Oliver Grantham, KCMG, MVO.

Forwood, Sir Dudley Richard, Bt. (1895).

Foster, *Prof.* Sir Christopher David, Kt.

Foster, Sir John Gregory, Bt. (1930).

Foster, Sir Norman Robert, Kt.

Foster, Sir Robert Sidney, GCMG, KCVO.

Foulis, Sir Ian Primrose Liston-, Bt. (s. 1634).

Foulkes, Sir Nigel Gordon, Kt.

Fowden, Sir Leslie, Kt., FRS.

†Fowke, Sir David Frederick Gustavus, Bt. (1814).

Fowler, Sir (Edward) Michael Coulson, Kt.

Fowler, *Rt. Hon.* Sir (Peter) Norman, Kt., MP.

Fox, Sir (Henry) Murray, GBE.

Fox, Sir (John) Marcus, Kt., MBE, MP.

Fox, *Rt. Hon.* Sir Michael John, Kt.

Frame, Sir Alistair Gilchrist, Kt.

France, Sir Arnold William, GCB.

France, Sir Christopher Walter, KCB.

Francis, Sir Horace William Alexander, Kt., CBE.

Francis, Sir Richard Trevor Langford, KCMG.

Frank, Sir Douglas George Horace, Kt., QC.

Frank, Sir (Frederick) Charles, Kt., OBE, FRS.

Frank, Sir Robert Andrew, Bt. (1920).

Frankel, Sir Otto Herzberg, Kt., D.SC., FRS.

Franklin, Sir Eric Alexander, Kt., CBE.

Franklin, Sir Michael David Milroy, KCB, CMG.

Franks, Sir Arthur Temple, KCMG.

Fraser, Sir Angus McKay, KCB, TD.

Fraser, Sir Basil Malcolm, Bt. (1921).

Fraser, Sir Bruce Donald, KCB.

Fraser, Sir Charles Annand, KCVO.

Fraser, *Gen.* Sir David William, GCB, OBE.

Fraser, Sir Douglas Were, Kt., ISO.

Fraser, *Air Marshal Rev.* Sir (Henry) Paterson, KBE, CB, AFC.

Fraser, Sir Ian, Kt., DSO, OBE.

Fraser, Sir Ian James, Kt., CBE, MC.

Fraser, Sir (James) Campbell, Kt.

Fraser, *Prof.* Sir James David, Bt. (1943).

Fraser, Sir William Kerr, GCB.

Frederick, Sir Charles Boscawen, Bt. (1723).

Freeland, Sir John Redvers, KCMG.

Freeman, *His Eminence Cardinal* James Darcy, KBE.

Freeman, Sir James Robin, Bt. (1945).

Freeman, Sir Ralph, Kt., CVO, CBE.

Freer, *Air Chief Marshal* Sir Robert William George, GBE, KCB.

Freeth, *Hon.* Sir Gordon, KBE.

French, *Hon.* Sir Christopher James Saunders, Kt.

Fretwell, Sir George Herbert, KBE, CB.

Fretwell, Sir (Major) John (Emsley), GCMG.

Freud, Sir Clement Raphael, Kt.

Froggatt, Sir Leslie Trevor, Kt.

Froggatt, Sir Peter, Kt.

Frossard, Sir Charles Keith, Kt.

Frost, *Hon.* Sir (Thomas) Sydney, Kt.

Fry, *Hon.* Sir William Gordon, Kt.

Fryberg, Sir Abraham, Kt., MBE.

Fuchs, Sir Vivian Ernest, Kt., Ph.D.

Fuller, *Hon.* Sir John Bryan Munro, Kt.

Fuller, Sir John William Fleetwood, Bt. (1910).

Fung, *Hon.* Sir Kenneth Ping-Fan, Kt., CBE.

Furness, Sir Stephen Roberts, Bt. (1913).

Gadsden, Sir Peter Drury Haggerston, GBE.

Gage, Sir Berkeley Everard Foley, KCMG.

Gairy, *Rt. Hon.* Sir Eric Matthew, Kt.

Gaius, *Rt. Rev.* Saimon, KBE.

Gallwey, Sir Philip Frankland Payne-, Bt. (1812).

Galsworthy, Sir John Edgar, KCVO, CMG.

Gamble, Sir David Hugh Norman, Bt. (1897).

Ganilau, *Ratu* Sir Penaia Kanatabatu, GCMG, KCVO, KBE, DSO.

Gardner, Sir Douglas Bruce Bruce-, Bt. (1945).

Gardner, Sir Edward Lucas, Kt., QC.

Gardner-Thorpe, *Col.* Sir Ronald, GBE, TD.

Garland, *Hon.* Sir Patrick Neville, Kt.

Garland, *Hon.* Sir Ransley Victor, KBE.

Garlick, Sir John, KCB.

Garner, Sir Anthony Stuart, Kt.

Garnier, *Rear-Adm.* Sir John, KCVO, CBE, LVO.

Garran, Sir (Isham) Peter, KCMG.

Garrett, *Hon.* Sir Raymond William, Kt., AFC.

Garrioch, Sir (William) Henry, Kt.

Garrod, *Lt.-Gen.* Sir (John) Martin Carruthers, KCB, OBE.

Garthwaite, Sir William Francis Cuthbert, Bt., DSC (1919).

Garvey, Sir Ronald Herbert, KCMG, KCVO, MBE.

Gaskell, Sir Richard Kennedy Harvey, Kt.

Gatehouse, *Hon.* Sir Robert Alexander, Kt.

Geddes, Sir (Anthony) Reay (Mackay), KBE.

Gentry, *Maj.-Gen.* Sir William George, KBE, CB, DSO.

George, Sir Arthur Thomas, Kt.

Gerken, *Vice-Adm.* Sir Robert William Frank, KCB, CBE.

Gethin, Sir Richard Joseph St. Lawrence, Bt. (I. 1665).

Ghurburrun, Sir Rabindrah, Kt.

Gibb, Sir Francis Ross (Frank), Kt., CBE.

Gibbings, Sir Peter Walter, Kt.

Gibbon, *Gen.* Sir John Houghton, GCB, OBE.

Gibbons, Sir (John) David, KBE.

Gibbons, Sir William Edward Doran, Bt. (1752).

Gibbs, *Hon.* Sir Eustace Hubert Beilby, KCVO, CMG.

Gibbs, *Air Marshal* Sir Gerald Ernest, KBE, CIE, MC.

Gibbs, *Rt. Hon.* Sir Harry Talbot, GCMG, KBE.

Gibbs, *Rt. Hon.* Sir Humphrey Vicary, GCVO, KCMG, OBE.

Gibbs, *Field Marshal* Sir Roland Christopher, GCB, CBE, DSO, MC.

Gibson, Sir Alexander Drummond, Kt., CBE.

Gibson, Sir Christopher Herbert, Bt. (1931).

Gibson, *Rev.* Sir David, Bt. (1926).

Gibson, *Vice-Adm.* Sir Donald Cameron Ernest Forbes, KCB, DSC.

Gibson, Sir Donald Evelyn Edward, Kt., CBE.

Gibson, *Hon.* Sir Peter Leslie, Kt.

Gibson, *Rt. Hon.* Sir Ralph Brian, Kt.

Giddings, *Air Marshal* Sir (Kenneth Charles) Michael, KCB, OBE, DFC, AFC.

Gielgud, Sir (Arthur) John, Kt., CH.

Giffard, Sir (Charles) Sydney (Rycroft), KCMG.

Gilbert, *Air Chief Marshal* Sir Joseph Alfred, KCB, CBE.

Gilbertson, Sir Geoffrey, Kt., CBE.

Gilbey, Sir (Walter) Derek, Bt. (1893).

Gilchrist, Sir Andrew Graham, KCMG.

Gilkison, Sir Alan Fleming, Kt., CBE.

Gillett, Sir Robin Danvers Penrose, Bt., GBE, RD (1959).

Gilliat, *Lt.-Col.* Sir Martin John, GCVO, MBE.

Gillmore, Sir David Howe, KCMG.

Gilmour, *Col.* Sir Allan Macdonald, KCVO, OBE, MC.

Gilmour, *Rt. Hon.* Sir Ian Hedworth John Little, Bt., MP (1926)..

Gilmour, Sir John Edward, Bt., DSO, TD (1897).

Gina, Sir Lloyd Maepeza, KBE.

Gingell, *Air Chief Marshal* Sir John, GBE, KCB.

Girolami, Sir Paul, Kt.

Gladstone, Sir (Erskine) William, Bt. (1846).

Glasspole, Sir Florizel Augustus, GCMG, GCVO.

Glen, Sir Alexander Richard, KBE, DSC.

Glenn, Sir (Joseph Robert) Archibald, Kt., OBE.

Glidewell, *Rt. Hon.* Sir Iain Derek Laing, Kt.

Glock, Sir William Frederick, Kt., CBE.

Glover, *Gen.* Sir James Malcolm, KCB, MBE.

Glover, Sir Victor Joseph Patrick, Kt.

Glyn, Sir Alan, Kt., ERD, MP.

Glyn, Sir Anthony Geoffrey Leo Simon, Bt. (1927).

Glyn, Sir Richard Lindsay, Bt. (1759 and 1800).

Goad, Sir (Edward) Colin (Viner), KCMG.

Godber, Sir George Edward, GCB, DM.

Goff, Sir Robert (William) Davis-, Bt. (1905).

Gohel, Sir Jayvantsinhji Kayaji, Kt., CBE.

Gold, Sir Arthur Abraham, Kt., CBE.

Gold, Sir Joseph, Kt.

Goldberg, *Prof.* Sir Abraham, Kt., MD, DSC, FRCP.

Golding, Sir John Simon Rawson, Kt., OBE.

Golding, Sir William Gerald, Kt., CBE.

Goldman, Sir Samuel, KCB.

Goldsmith, Sir James Michael, Kt.

Gombrich, *Prof.* Sir Ernst Hans Josef, Kt., OM, CBE, PH.D., FBA, FSA.

Gooch, Sir (Richard) John Sherlock, Bt. (1746).

Gooch, Sir Robert Douglas, Bt. (1866).

Goodall, Sir (Arthur) David Saunders, KCMG.

Goodenough, Sir Richard Edmund, Bt. (1943).

Goodhart, Sir Philip Carter, Kt., MP.

Goodhart, Sir Robert Anthony Gordon, Bt. (1911).

Goodhart, Sir William Howard, Kt., QC.

Goodhew, Sir Victor Henry, Kt.

Goodison, Sir Alan Clowes, KCMG.

Goodison, Sir Nicholas Proctor, Kt.

Goodson, Sir Mark Weston Lassam, Bt. (1922).

Goodwin, Sir Matthew Dean, Kt., CBE.

Goody, *Most Rev.* Launcelot John, KBE.

Goold, Sir George Leonard, Bt. (1801).

Gordon, Sir Alexander John, Kt., CBE.

Gordon, Sir Andrew Cosmo Lewis Duff-, Bt. (1813).

Gordon, Sir Charles Addison Somerville Snowden, KCB.

Gordon, Sir Keith Lyndell, Kt., CMG.

Gordon, Sir (Lionel) Eldred (Peter) Smith-, Bt. (1838).

Gordon, Sir Robert James, Bt. (s. 1706).

Gordon, Sir Sidney Samuel, Kt., CBE.

Gordon Lennox, Lord Nicholas Charles, KCMG, KCVO.

Gore, Sir Richard Ralph St. George, Bt. (I. 1622).

Goring, Sir William Burton Nigel, Bt. (1627).

Gorton, *Rt. Hon.* Sir John Grey, GCMG, CH.

Goschen, Sir Edward Christian, Bt., DSO (1916).

Gosling, Sir (Frederick) Donald, Kt.

Goulding, Sir (Ernest) Irvine, Kt.

Goulding, Sir (William) Lingard Walter, Bt. (1904).

Gourlay, *Gen.* Sir (Basil) Ian (Spencer), KCB, OBE, MC, RM.

Gourlay, Sir Simon Alexander, Kt.

Govan, Sir Lawrence Herbert, Kt.

Gow, *Gen.* Sir (James) Michael, GCB.

Gowans, Sir James Learmonth, Kt., CBE, FRCP, FRS.

Gowans, *Hon.* Sir (Urban) Gregory, Kt.

Gowing, *Prof.* Sir Lawrence Burnett, Kt., CBE.

Graaff, Sir de Villiers, Bt., MBE (1911).

Grabham, Sir Anthony Henry, Kt.

Graesser, *Col.* Sir Alastair Stewart Durward, Kt., DSO, OBE, MC, TD.

Graham, Sir Charles Spencer Richard, Bt. (1783).

Graham, Sir James Bellingham, Bt. (1662).

Graham, Sir James Thompson, Kt., CMG.

Graham, Sir John Alexander Noble, Bt., GCMG (1906).

Graham, Sir John Moodie, Bt. (1964).

Graham, Sir (John) Patrick, Kt.

Graham, Sir Norman William, Kt., CB.

Graham, Sir Peter Alfred, Kt., OBE.

Graham, Sir Ralph Wolfe, Bt. (1629).

Graham, *Hon.* Sir Samuel Horatio, Kt., CMG, OBE.

Grandy, *Marshal of the Royal Air Force* Sir John, GCB, GCVO, KBE, DSO.

Grant, Sir Archibald, Bt. (s. 1705).

Grant, Sir Clifford, Kt.

Grant, Sir (John) Anthony, Kt., MP.

Grant, Sir Patrick Alexander Benedict, Bt. (s. 1688).

Grantham, *Adm.* Sir Guy, GCB, CBE, DSO.

Gray, Sir (Francis) Anthony, KCVO.

Gray, Sir John Archibald Browne, Kt., SC.D., FRS.

Gray, *Vice-Adm.* Sir John Michael Dudgeon, KBE, CB.

Gray, *Lt.-Gen.* Sir Michael Stuart, KCB, OBE.

Gray, Sir William Hume, Bt. (1917).

Gray, Sir William Stevenson, Kt.

Graydon, *Air Marshal* Sir Michael James, KCB, CBE.

Grayson, Sir Rupert Stanley Harrington, Bt. (1922).

Green, Sir (Edward) Stephen (Lycett), Bt., CBE (1886).

Green, Sir George Ernest, Kt.

Green, *Hon.* Sir Guy Stephen Montague, KBE.

Green, Sir Kenneth, Kt.

Green, Sir Owen Whitley, Kt.

Green, Sir Peter James Frederick, Kt.

Greenaway, Sir Derek Burdick, Bt., CBE (1933).

Greenborough, Sir John, KBE.

Greene, Sir (John) Brian Massy-, Kt.

Greengross, Sir Alan David, Kt.

Greening, *Rear-Adm.* Sir Paul Woollven, KCVO.

Greenwell, Sir Edward Bernard, Bt. (1906).

Greeves, *Maj.-Gen.* Sir Stuart, KBE, CB, DSO, MC.

Gregson, Sir Peter Lewis, KCB.

Grenside, Sir John Peter, Kt., CBE.

Gretton, *Vice-Adm.* Sir Peter William, KCB, DSO, OBE, DSC.

Grey, Sir Anthony Dysart, Bt. (1814).

Grey, Sir Paul Francis, KCMG.

Grierson, Sir Michael John Bewes, Bt. (s. 1685).

Grierson, Sir Ronald Hugh, Kt.

Grieve, *Prof.* Sir Robert, Kt.

Griffin, *Adm.* Sir Anthony Templer Frederick Griffith, GCB.

Griffin, *Maj.* Arthur John Stewart, KCVO.

Griffin, Sir (Charles) David, Kt., CBE.

Griffin, Sir John Bowes, Kt., QC.

Griffiths, Sir Eldon Wylie, Kt., MP.

Griffiths, Sir (Ernest) Roy, Kt.

Griffiths, Sir John Norton-, Bt. (1922).

Griffiths, Sir Percival Joseph, KBE, CIE.

Griffiths, Sir Reginald Ernest, Kt., CBE.

Grimwade, Sir Andrew Sheppard, Kt., CBE.

Grindrod, *Most Rev.* John Basil Rowland, KBE.

Grinstead, Sir Stanley Gordon, Kt.

Groom, *Air Marshal* Sir Victor Emmanuel, KCVO, KBE, CB, DFC.

Grose, *Vice-Adm.* Sir Alan, KBE.

Grotrian, Sir Philip Christian Brent, Bt. (1934).

Grove, Sir Charles Gerald, Bt. (1874).

Grove, Sir Edmund Frank, KCVO.

Groves, Sir Charles Barnard, Kt., CBE.

Grugeon, Sir John Drury, Kt..

Guinness, Sir Alec, Kt., CBE.

Guinness, Sir Howard Christian Sheldon, Kt., VRD.

Guinness, Sir Kenelm Ernest Lee, Bt. (1867).

Guise, Sir John, GCMG, KCB.

Guise, Sir John Grant, Bt. (1783).

Gujadhur, Sir Radhamohun, Kt., CMG.

Gull, Sir Rupert William Cameron, Bt. (1872).

Gunn, *Prof.* Sir John Currie, Kt., CBE.

Gunn, Sir William Archer, KBE, CMG.

†Gunning, Sir Charles Theodore, Bt. (1778).

Gunston, Sir Richard Wellesley, Bt. (1938).

Guthrie, *Lt.-Gen.* Sir Charles Ronald Llewelyn, KCB, LVO, OBE.

Guthrie, Sir Malcolm Connop, Bt., (1936)

Guthrie, *Hon.* Sir Rutherford Campbell, Kt., CMG.

Guy, *Gen.* Sir Roland Kelvin, GCB, CBE, DSO.

Habakkuk, Sir John Hrothgar, Kt., FBA.

Hackett, *Gen.* Sir John Winthrop, GCB, CBE, DSO, MC.

Hadlee, Sir Richard John, Kt., MBE.

Hadley, Sir Leonard Albert, Kt.

Hadow, Sir Gordon, Kt., CMG, OBE.

Hadow, Sir (Reginald) Michael, KCMG.

Hague, *Prof.* Sir Douglas Chalmers, Kt., CBE.

Halberg, Sir Murray Gordon, Kt., MBE.

Hale, *Prof.* Sir John Rigby, Kt.

Hall, Sir Arnold Alexander, Kt., FRS.

Hall, Sir Basil Brodribb, KCB, MC, TD.

Hall, *Air Marshal* Sir Donald Percy, KCB, CBE, AFC.

Hall, Sir Douglas Basil, Bt., KCMG (s. 1687).

Hall, Sir (Frederick) John (Frank), Bt. (1923).

Hall, Sir John Bernard, Bt. (1919).

Hall, Sir Peter Reginald Frederick, Kt., CBE.

Hall, Sir Robert de Zouche, KCMG.

Hall, *Brig.* Sir William Henry, KBE, DSO, ED.

Halliday, Sir George Clifton, Kt.

Halliday, *Vice-Adm.* Sir Roy William, KBE, DSC.

Hallifax, *Adm.* Sir David John, KCB, KBE.

Hallinan, Sir (Adrian) Lincoln, Kt.

Halpern, Sir Ralph Mark, Kt.

Halsey, *Rev.* Sir John Walter Brooke, Bt. (1920).

Halstead, Sir Ronald, Kt., CBE.

Hambling, Sir (Herbert) Hugh, Bt. (1924).

Hamburger, Sir Sidney Cyril, Kt., CBE.

Hamer, *Hon.* Sir Rupert James, KCMG, ED.

Hamill, Sir Patrick, Kt., QPM.

Hamilton, Sir Edward Sydney, Bt. (1776 and 1819).

Hamilton, Sir James Arnot, KCB, MBE.

Hamilton, *Adm.* Sir John Graham, GBE, CB.

†Hamilton, Sir Malcolm William Bruce Stirling-, Bt. (s. 1673).

Hamilton, Sir Michael Aubrey, Kt.

Hamilton, Sir Patrick George, Bt. (1937).

Hamilton, Sir (Robert Charles) Richard Caradoc, Bt. (s. 1646).

Hammett, *Hon.* Sir Clifford James, Kt.

Hammick, Sir Stephen George, Bt. (1834).

Hampshire, Sir Stuart Newton, Kt., FBA.

Hanbury, Sir John Capel, Kt., CBE.

Hancock, *Lt.-Col.* Sir Cyril Percy, KCIE, OBE, MC.

Hancock, Sir David John Stowell, KCB.

Hancock, *Air Marshal* Sir Valston Eldridge, KBE, CB, DFC.

Hand, *Most Rev.* Geoffrey David, KBE.

Handley, Sir David John Davenport-, Kt., OBE.

Hanham, Sir Michael William, Bt., DFC (1667).

Hanley, Sir Michael Bowen, KCB.

Hanmer, Sir John Wyndham Edward, Bt. (1774).

Hannay, Sir David Hugh Alexander, KCMG.

Hanson, Sir Anthony Leslie Oswald, Bt. (1887).

Hanson, Sir (Charles) John, Bt. (1918).

Harcourt-Smith, *Air Chief Marshal* Sir David, GBE, KCB, DFC.

Harders, Sir Clarence Waldemar, Kt., OBE.

Hardie, Sir Charles Edgar Mathewes, Kt., CBE.

Hardie, Sir Douglas Fleming, Kt., CBE.

Harding, Sir George William, KCMG, CVO.

Harding, *Air Chief Marshal* Sir Peter Robin, GCB.

Harding, Sir Roy Pollard, Kt., CBE.

Hardinge, Sir Robert Arnold, Bt. (1801).

Hardingham, Sir Robert Ernest, Kt., CMG, OBE.

Hardman, Sir Fred, Kt., MBE.

Hardman, Sir Henry, KCB.

Hardy, Sir James Gilbert, Kt., OBE.

Hardy, Sir Rupert John, Bt. (1876).

Hare, Sir Thomas, Bt. (1818).

Harford, Sir James Dundas, KBE, CMG.

Harford, Sir (John) Timothy, Bt. (1934).

Hargroves, *Brig.* Sir Robert Louis, Kt., CBE.

Harington, *Gen.* Sir Charles Henry Pepys, GCB, CBE, DSO, MC.

Harington, Sir Nicholas John, Bt. (1611).

Harland, *Air Marshal* Sir Reginald Edward Wynyard, KBE, CB.

Harley, Sir Thomas Winlack, Kt., MBE, MC.

Harman, *Gen.* Sir Jack Wentworth, GCB, OBE, MC.

Harman, *Hon.* Sir Jeremiah LeRoy, Kt.

Harmer, Sir Frederic Evelyn, Kt., CMG.

Harmer, Sir (John) Dudley, Kt., OBE.

Harmsworth, Sir Hildebrand Harold, Bt. (1922).

Harper Gow, Sir Leonard Maxwell, Kt., MBE.

Harpham, Sir William, KBE, CMG.

Harris, *Prof.* Sir Alan James, Kt., CBE.

Harris, Sir Anthony Kyrle Travers, Bt. (1953).

Harris, *Prof.* Sir Charles Herbert Stuart-, Kt., CBE, MD.

Harris, *Lt.-Gen.* Sir Ian Cecil, KBE, CB, DSO.

Harris, Sir Jack Wolfred Ashford, Bt. (1932).

Harris, Sir Philip Charles, Kt.

Harris, Sir Ronald Montague Joseph, KCVO, CB.

Harris, Sir William Gordon, KBE, CB.

Harrison, Sir Donald Frederick Norris, Kt., FRCS.

Harrison, Sir Ernest Thomas, Kt., OBE..

Harrison, Sir Francis Alexander Lyle, Kt., MBE, QC.

Harrison, *Surgeon Vice-Adm.* Sir John Albert Bews, KBE.

Harrison, *Hon.* Sir (John) Richard, Kt., ED.

Harrison, Sir Michael James Harwood, Bt. (1961).

Harrison, *Prof.* Sir Richard John, Kt., FRS.

Harrison, Sir (Robert) Colin, Bt. (1922).

Harrop, Sir Peter John, KCB.

Hart, Sir Byrne, Kt., CBE, MC.

Hart, Sir Francis Edmund Turton-, KBE.

Hartley, *Air Marshal* Sir Christopher Harold, KCB, CBE, DFC, AFC.

Hartley, Sir Frank, Kt., CBE, Ph.D.

Hartopp, Sir John Edmund Cradock-, Bt. (1796).

Hartwell, Sir Brodrick William Charles Elwin, Bt. (1805).

Harvey, Sir Charles Richard Musgrave, Bt. (1933).

Harvey-Jones, Sir John Henry, Kt., MBE.

Haskard, Sir Cosmo Dugal Patrick Thomas, KCMG, MBE.

Haslam, *Hon.* Sir Alec Leslie, Kt.

Haslam, *Rear-Adm.* Sir David William, KBE, CB.

Hasluck, *Rt. Hon.* Sir Paul Meernaa Caedwalla, KG, GCMG, GCVO.

Hassan, Sir Joshua Abraham, GBE, KCMG, LVO, QC.

Hassett, *Gen.* Sir Francis George, KBE, CB, DSO, MVO.

Hastings, Sir Stephen Lewis Edmonstone, Kt., MC.

Hatty, *Hon.* Sir Cyril James, Kt.

Haughton, Sir James, Kt., CBE, QPM.

Havelock, Sir Wilfrid Bowen, Kt.

Hawker, Sir (Frank) Cyril, Kt.

Hawkings, Sir (Francis) Geoffrey, Kt.

Hawkins, Sir Arthur Ernest, Kt.

Hawkins, Sir Humphry Villiers Caesar, Bt. (1778).

Hawkins, Sir Paul Lancelot, Kt., TD.

Hawley, Sir Donald Frederick, KCMG, MBE.

†Hawley, Sir Henry Nicholas, Bt. (1795).

Haworth, Sir Philip, Bt. (1911).

Hawthorne, *Prof.* Sir William Rede, Kt., CBE, SC.D., FRS.

Hay, Sir Arthur Thomas Erroll, Bt., ISO (s. 1663).

Hay, Sir David Osborne, Kt., CBE, DSO.

Hay, Sir Hamish Grenfell, Kt.

Hay, Sir James Brian Dalrymple-, Bt. (1798).

†Hay, Sir Ronald Frederick Hamilton, Bt. (s. 1703).

Hayday, Sir Frederick, Kt., CBE.

Haydon, Sir Walter Robert, KCMG.

Hayes, Sir Brian David, GCB.

Hayes, Sir Claude James, KCMG.

Hayes, *Vice-Adm.* Sir John Osier Chattock, KCB, OBE.

Hayhoe, *Rt. Hon.* Sir Bernard John (Barney), Kt., MP.

Hayman, Sir Peter Telford, KCMG, CVO, MBE.

Hayr, *Air Marshal* Sir Kenneth William, KCB, CBE, AFC.

Hone, *Maj.-Gen.* Sir (Herbert) Ralph, KCMG, KBE, MC, TD, QC.

Honeycombe, *Prof.* Sir Robert William Kerr, Kt., FRS.

Honywood, Sir Filmer Courtenay William, Bt. (1660).

Hood, Sir Alexander William Fuller-Acland-, Bt. (1806).

Hood, Sir Harold Joseph, Bt., TD (1922).

Hookway, Sir Harry Thurston, Kt.

Hoole, Sir Arthur Hugh, Kt.

Hooper, Sir Leonard James, KCMG, CBE.

Hope, Sir (Charles) Peter, KCMG, TD.

Hope, Sir John Carl Alexander, Bt. (s. 1628).

Hope, Sir Robert Holms-Kerr, Bt. (1932).

Hopkin, Sir David Armand, Kt.

Hopkin, Sir (William Aylsham) Bryan, Kt., CBE.

Hopkins, Sir James Sidney Rawdon Scott-, Kt., MEP.

Hordern, Sir Michael Murray, Kt., CBE.

Hordern, Sir Peter Maudslay, Kt., MP.

Horlick, *Vice-Adm.* Sir Edwin John, KBE.

Horlick, Sir John James Macdonald, Bt. (1914).

Hornby, Sir Derek Peter, Kt.

Hornby, Sir Simon Michael, Kt.

Horne, Sir Alan Gray Antony, Bt. (1929).

Horsfall, Sir John Musgrave, Bt., MC, TD (1909).

Horsley, *Air Marshal* Sir (Beresford) Peter (Torrington), KCB, CBE, MVO, AFC.

Hort, Sir James Fenton, Bt. (1767).

Hoskyns, Sir Benedict Leigh, Bt. (1676).

Hoskyns, Sir John Austin Hungerford Leigh, Kt.

†Houldsworth, Sir Richard Thomas Reginald, Bt. (1887).

Hounsfield, Sir Godfrey Newbold, Kt., CBE.

House, *Lt.-Gen.* Sir David George, GCB, KCVO, CBE, MC.

Houssemayne du Boulay, Sir Roger William, KCVO, CMG.

Howard, Sir (Hamilton) Edward de Coucey, Bt., GBE (1955).

Howard, *Prof.* Sir Michael Eliot, Kt., CBE, MC.

Howard, *Maj.-Gen.* Lord Michael Fitzalan-, GCVO, CB, CBE, MC.

Howard, Sir Walter Stewart, Kt., MBE.

Howe, *Rt. Hon.* Sir (Richard Edward) Geoffrey, Kt., QC, MP.

Howie, Sir James William, Kt., MD.

Howlett, *Gen.* Sir Geoffrey Hugh Whitby, KBE, MC.

Hoyle, *Prof.* Sir Fred, Kt., FRS.

Hoyos, *Hon.* Sir Fabriciano Alexander, Kt.

Huckle, Sir (Henry) George, Kt., OBE.

Huddie, Sir David Patrick, Kt.

Hudleston, *Air Chief Marshal* Sir Edmund Cuthbert, GCB, CBE.

Hudson, Sir Havelock Henry Trevor, Kt.

Hudson, *Lt.-Gen.* Sir Peter, KCB, CBE.

Huggins, *Hon.* Sir Alan Armstrong, Kt.

Hugh-Jones, Sir Wynn Normington, Kt., MVO.

Hughes, Sir David Collingwood, Bt. (1773).

Hughes, *Prof.* Sir Edward Stuart Reginald, Kt., CBE.

Hughes, Sir Jack William, Kt.

Hughes, *Air Marshal* Sir (Sidney Weetman) Rochford, KCB, CBE, AFC.

Hughes, Sir Trevor Denby Lloyd-, Kt.

Hughes, Sir Trevor Poulton, KCB.

Hugo, *Lt.-Col.* Sir John Mandeville, KCVO, OBE.

Hulme, *Hon.* Sir Alan Shallcross, KBE.

Hulse, Sir (Hamilton) Westrow, Bt. (1739).

Hulton, Sir Geoffrey Alan, Bt. (1905).

Hume, Sir Alan Blyth, Kt., CB.

Humphreys, Sir Olliver William, Kt., CBE.

Humphreys, Sir (Raymond Evelyn) Myles, Kt.

Hunn, Sir Jack Kent, Kt., CMG.

Hunt, Sir David Wathen Stather, KCMG, OBE.

Hunt, Sir John Leonard, Kt., MP.

Hunt, *Adm.* Sir Nicholas John Streynsham, GCB, LVO.

Hunt, Sir Rex Masterman, Kt., CMG.

Hunt, Sir Robert Frederick, Kt., CBE.

Hunter, *Hon.* Sir Alexander Albert, KBE.

Hunter, Sir Ian Bruce Hope, Kt., MBE.

Hurley, Sir John Garling, Kt., CBE.

Hurrell, Sir Anthony Gerald, KCVO, CMG.

Hutchinson, *Hon.* Sir Ross, Kt., DFC.

Hutchison, *Lt.-Cdr.* Sir (George) Ian Clark, Kt., RN.

Hutchison, *Hon.* Sir Michael, Kt.

Hutchison, Sir Peter, Bt. (1939).

Hutchison, Sir Peter Craft, Bt. (1956).

Hutson, Sir Francis Challenor, Kt., CBE.

Hutton, *Rt. Hon.* Sir (James) Brian Edward, Kt.

Hutton, Sir Leonard, Kt.

Huxley, *Prof.* Sir Andrew Fielding, Kt., OM, FRS.

Huxtable, *Gen.* Sir Charles Richard, KCB, CBE.

Hyatali, *Hon.* Sir Isaac Emanuel, Kt.

Ibbs, Sir (John) Robin, KBE.

Ihaka, *Ven.* Sir Kingi Matutaera, Kt., MBE.

Illingworth, *Prof.* Sir Charles Frederick William, Kt., CBE.

Imbert, Sir Peter Michael, Kt., QPM.

Inch, Sir John Ritchie, Kt., CVO, CBE.

Inge, *Gen.* Sir Peter Anthony, KCB.

Ingilby, Sir Thomas Colvin William, Bt. (1866).

Inglefield, Sir Gilbert Samuel, GBE, TD.

Inglis, Sir Brian Scott, Kt.

Inglis of Glencorse, Sir Roderick John, Bt. (s. 1703).

Ingram, Sir James Herbert Charles, Bt. (1893).

Innes, Sir Charles Kenneth Gordon, Bt. (NS 1686).

Innes of Edingight, Sir Malcolm Rognvald, KCVO.

Innes, Sir Peter Alexander Berowald, Bt. (s. 1628).

Inniss, *Hon.* Sir Clifford de Lisle, Kt.

Irish, Sir Ronald Arthur, Kt., OBE.

Irvine, *Rt. Hon.* Sir Bryant Godman, Kt.

Irvine, *Dr.* Sir Robin Orlando Hamilton, Kt.

Irving, Sir Charles Graham, Kt., MP.

Irving, *Rear-Adm.* Sir Edmund George, KBE, CB.

Irwin, Sir James Campbell, Kt., OBE, ED.

Isham, Sir Ian Vere Gyles, Bt. (1627).

Jack, *Hon.* Sir Alieu Sulayman, Kt.

Jackman, *Air Marshal* Sir (Harold) Douglas, KBE, CB.

Jackson, *Air Chief Marshal* Sir Brendan James, KCB.

Jackson, Sir (John) Edward, KCMG.

Jackson, *Hon.* Sir Lawrence Walter, KCMG.

Jackson, Sir Michael Roland, Bt. (1902).

Jackson, Sir Nicholas Fane St. George, Bt. (1913).

Jackson, *Air Vice-Marshal* Sir Ralph Coburn, KBE, CB.

Jackson, Sir Robert, Bt. (1815).

Jackson, *Cdr.* Sir Robert Gillman Allen, KCVO, CMG, OBE.

Jackson, *Gen.* Sir William Godfrey Fothergill, GBE, KCB, MC.

Jackson, Sir William Thomas, Bt. (1869)

Jacob, *Lt.-Gen.* Sir (Edward) Ian (Claud), GBE, CB.

Jacob, Sir Isaac Hai, Kt., QC.

Jacobi, *Dr.* Sir James Edward, Kt., OBE.

Jacobs, Sir David Anthony, Kt.

Jacobs, *Hon.* Sir Kenneth Sydney, KBE.

Jacobs, Sir Piers, KBE.

Jacobs, Sir Wilfred Ebenezer, GCMG, GCVO, OBE, QC.

Jacomb, Sir Martin Wakefield, Kt.

Jaffray, Sir William Otho, Bt. (1892).

Jakeway, Sir (Francis) Derek, KCMG, OBE.

James, Sir Cynlais Morgan, KCMG.

James, Sir Gerard Bowes Kingston, Bt. (1823).

Jamieson, *Air Marshal* Sir David Ewan, KBE, CB.

Janion, *Rear-Adm.* Sir Hugh Penderel, KCVO.

Jansen, Sir Ross Malcolm, KBE.

Janvrin, *Vice-Adm.* Sir (Hugh) Richard Benest, KCB, DSC.

Jardine, Sir Andrew Colin Douglas, Bt. (1916).

Jardine, *Maj.* Sir (Andrew) Rupert (John) Buchanan-, Bt., MC (1885).

Jardine of Applegirth, Sir Alexander Maule, Bt. (s. 1672).

Jarratt, Sir Alexander Anthony, Kt., CB.

Jarrett, Sir Clifford George, KBE, CB.

Jawara, *Hon.* Sir Dawda Kairaba, Kt.

Jay, Sir Antony Rupert, Kt.

Jeewoolall, Sir Ramesh, Kt.

Jeffcoate, Sir (Thomas) Norman (Arthur), Kt., MD, FRCS.

Jefferson, Sir George Rowland, Kt., CBE.

Jefferson, Sir Mervyn Stewart Dunnington-, Bt. (1958).

Jehangir, Sir Hirji, Bt. (1908).

Jejeebhoy, Sir Rustom, Bt. (1857).

Jellicoe, Sir Geoffrey Alan, Kt., CBE, FRIBA.

Jenkins, Sir Michael Romilly Heald, KCMG.

Jenkins, Sir Owain Trevor, Kt.

Jenkinson, Sir John Banks, Bt. (1661).

Jenks, Sir Richard Atherley, Bt. (1932).

Jennings, Sir Albert Victor, Kt.

Jennings, Sir Raymond Winter, Kt., QC.

Jennings, *Prof.* Sir Robert Yewdall, Kt., QC.

Jenour, Sir (Arthur) Maynard (Chesterfield), Kt., TD.

Jephcott, *Hon.* Sir Bruce Reginald, Kt., CBE.

Jephcott, Sir (John) Anthony, Bt. (1962).

Jessel, Sir Charles John, Bt. (1883).

Jewkes, Sir Gordon Wesley, KCMG.

Joel, *Hon.* Sir Asher Alexander, KBE.

John, Sir Rupert Godfrey, Kt.

Johnson, *Lt.-Gen.* Sir Garry Dene, KCB, OBE, MC.

Johnson, Sir John Rodney, KCMG.

Johnson, Sir Peter Colpoys Paley, Bt. (1755).

Johnson, *Hon.* Sir Robert Lionel, Kt.

†Johnson, Sir Robin Eliot, Bt. (1818).

Johnson, Sir Ronald Ernest Charles, Kt., CB.

Johnson Smith, Sir Geoffrey, Kt., MP.

Johnston, Sir Alexander, GCB, KBE.

Johnston, Sir (David) Russell, Kt., MP.

Johnston, Sir Edward Alexander, KBE, CB.

Johnston, Sir John Baines, GCMG, KCVO.

Johnston, *Lt.-Col.* Sir John Frederick Dame, GCVO, MC.

Johnston, *Lt.-Gen.* Sir Maurice Robert, KCB, OBE.

Johnston, Sir Thomas Alexander, Bt. (s. 1626).

Johnstone, Sir Frederic Allan George, Bt. (s. 1700).

Jolliffe, Sir Anthony Stuart, GBE.

Jones, *Lt.-Gen.* Sir (Charles) Edward Webb, KCB, CBE.

Jones, Sir Christopher Lawrence-, Bt. (1831).

Jones, *Air Marshal* Sir Edward Gordon, KCB, CBE, DSO, DFC.

Jones, Sir (Edward) Martin Furnival, Kt., CBE.

Jones, *Rt. Hon.* Sir Edward Warburton, Kt.

Jones, Sir Ewart Ray Herbert, Kt., D.SC., Ph.D., FRS.

Jones, Sir Francis Avery, Kt., CBE, FRCP.

Jones, *Air Marshal* Sir George, KBE, CB, DFC.

Jones, Sir Glyn Smallwood, GCMG, MBE.

Jones, Sir Gordon Pearce, Kt.

Jones, Sir Harry Ernest, Kt., CBE.

Jones, Sir James Duncan, KCB.

Jones, Sir (John) Kenneth (Trevor), Kt., CBE, QC.

Jones, Sir John Lewis, KCB, CMG.

Jones, Sir John Prichard-, Bt. (1910).

Jones, Sir Keith Stephen, Kt.

Jones, *Hon.* Sir Kenneth George Illtyd, Kt.

Jones, *Air Marshal* Sir Laurence Alfred, KCB, CB, AFC.

Jones, Sir (Owen) Trevor, Kt.

Jones, Sir Robert Edward, Kt.

Jones, Sir Simon Warley Frederick Benton, Bt. (1919).

Jones, Sir (Thomas) Philip, Kt., CB.

Jones, Sir (William) Emrys, Kt.

Jordan, *Air Marshal* Sir Richard Bowen, KCB, DFC.

Joseph, *Maj.* Sir (Herbert) Leslie, Kt.

Jowitt, *Hon.* Sir Edwin Frank, Kt.

Judge, *Hon.* Sir Igor, Kt.

Jugnauth, *Rt. Hon.* Sir Aneerood, KCMG, QC.

Jungius, *Vice-Adm.*, Sir James George, KBE.

Junor, Sir John Donald Brown, Kt.

Jupp, *Hon.* Sir Kenneth Graham, Kt., MC.

Kadoorie, Sir Horace, CBE.

Kalo, Sir Kwamala, Kt., MBE.

Kan Yuet-Keung, Sir, GBE.

Kapi, *Hon.* Sir Mari, Kt., CBE.

Karimjee, Sir Tayabali Hassanali Alibhoy, Kt.

Katsina, The Emir of, KBE, CMG.

Katz, Sir Bernard, Kt., FRS.

Kavali, Sir Thomas, Kt., OBE.

Kawharu, *Prof.* Sir Ian Hugh, Kt.

Kay, *Prof.* Sir Andrew Watt, Kt.

Kaye, Sir David Alexander Gordon, Bt. (1923).

Kaye, Sir Emmanuel, Kt., CBE.

Kaye, Sir John Phillip Lister Lister-, Bt. (1812).

Keane, Sir Richard Michael, Bt. (1801).

Keatinge, Sir Edgar Mayne, Kt., CBE.

Keeble, Sir (Herbert Ben) Curtis, GCMG.

Keith, *Prof.* Sir James, KBE.

Kellett, Sir Brian Smith, Kt.

Kellett, Sir Stanley Charles, Bt. (1801).

Kelliher, Sir Henry Joseph, Kt.

Kelly, *Rt. Hon.* Sir (John William) Basil, Kt.

Kelly, Sir William Theodore, Kt., OBE.

Kemball, *Air Marshal* Sir (Richard) John, KCB, CBE.

Kemsley, *Col.* Sir Alfred Newcombe, KBE, CMG, ED.

Kendrew, Sir John Cowdery, Kt., CBE, SC.D., FRS.

Kenilorea, *Rt. Hon.* Sir Peter, KBE.

Kennard, *Lt.-Col.* Sir George Arnold Ford, Bt. (1891).

Kennaway, Sir John Lawrence, Bt. (1791).

Kennedy, Sir Albert Henry, Kt.

Kennedy, Sir Clyde David Allen, Kt.

Kennedy, Sir Francis, KCMG, CBE.

Kennedy, *Hon.* Sir Ian Alexander, Kt.

Kennedy, Sir Michael Edward, Bt. (1836).

Kennedy, *Hon.* Sir Paul Joseph Morrow, Kt.

Kennedy, *Air Chief Marshal* Sir Thomas Lawrie, GCB, AFC.

Kennedy-Good, Sir John, KBE.

Kennon, *Vice-Adm.* Sir James Edward Campbell, KCB, CBE.

Kenny, *Gen.* Sir Brian Leslie Graham, KCB, CBE.

Kent, Sir Harold Simcox, GCB, QC.

Kenyon, Sir George Henry, Kt.

Kermode, Sir Ronald Graham Quale, KBE.

Kerr, *Vice-Adm.* Sir John Beverley, KCB.

Kerr, *Rt. Hon.* Sir (John) Robert, GCMG, GCVO.

Kerr, *Rt. Hon.* Sir Michael Robert Emanuel, Kt.

Kerruish, Sir (Henry) Charles, Kt., OBE.

Kerry, Sir Michael James, KCB, QC.

Kershaw, Sir (John) Anthony, Kt., MC.

Keville, Sir (William) Errington, Kt., CBE.

Kidd, Sir Robert Hill, KBE, CB.

Kidu, *Hon.* Sir Buri (William), Kt.

Kikau, *Ratu* Sir Jone Latianara, KBE.

Kiki, *Hon.* Sir (Albert) Maori, KBE.

Killen, *Hon.* Denis James, KCMG.

Killick, Sir John Edward, GCMG.

Kilpatrick, *Prof.* Sir Robert, Kt., CBE.

Kimber, Sir Charles Dixon, Bt. (1904).

Kinahan, Sir Robert George Caldwell, Kt., ERD.

King, Sir Albert, Kt., OBE.

King, *Gen.* Sir Frank Douglas, GCB, MBE.

King, Sir John Christopher, Bt. (1888).

King, *Vice-Adm.* Sir Norman Ross Dutton, KBE.

King, Sir Richard Brian Meredith, KCB, MC.

King, Sir Sydney Percy, Kt., OBE.

King, Sir Wayne Alexander, Bt. (1815).

Kingman, *Prof.* Sir John Frank Charles, Kt., FRS.

Kingsland, Sir Richard, Kt., CBE, DFC.

Kingsley, Sir Patrick Graham Toler, KCVO.

Kinloch, Sir David, Bt. (s. 1686).

Kinloch, Sir John, Bt. (1873).

Kirby, *Hon.* Sir Richard Clarence, Kt.

Kirkpatrick, Sir Ivone Elliott, Bt. (s. 1685).

Kirwan, Sir (Archibald) Laurence Patrick, KCMG, TD.

Kitson, *Gen.* Sir Frank Edward, GBE, KCB, MC.

Kitson, Sir Timothy Peter Geoffrey, Kt.

Kitto, *Rt. Hon.* Sir Frank Walters, KBE.

Kleinwort, Sir Kenneth Drake, Bt. (1909).

Klug, Sir Aaron, Kt.

Knight, Sir Allan Walton, Kt., CMG.

Knight, Sir Arthur William, Kt.

Knight, Sir Harold Murray, KBE, DSC.

Knight, *Air Chief Marshal* Sir Michael William Patrick, KCB, AFC.

Knill, Sir John Kenelm Stuart, Bt. (1893).

Knipe, Sir Leslie Francis, Kt., MBE.

Knott, Sir John Laurence, Kt., CBE.

Knowles, Sir Charles Francis, Bt. (1765).

Knowles, Sir Leonard Joseph, Kt., CBE.

Knowles, Sir Richard Marchant, Kt.

Knox, Sir Bryce Muir, KCVO, MC, TD.

Knox, *Hon.* Sir John Leonard, Kt.

Knox, *Hon.* Sir William Edward, Kt.

Kornberg, *Prof.* Sir Hans Leo, Kt., D.SC., SC.D., Ph.D., FRS.

Krusin, Sir Stanley Marks, Kt., CB.

Kurongku, *Most. Rev.* Peter, KBE.

Labouchere, Sir George Peter, GBE, KCMG.

Lacon, Sir Edmund Vere, Bt. (1818).

Lacy, Sir Hugh Maurice Pierce, Bt. (1921).

Lagesen, *Air Marshal* Sir Philip Jacobus, KCB, DFC, AFC.

Laidlaw, Sir Christophor Charles Fraser, Kt.

Laing, Sir Hector, Kt.

Laing, Sir (John) Maurice, Kt.

Laing, Sir (William) Kirby, Kt.

Lake, Sir (Atwell) Graham, Bt. (1711).

Laker, Sir Frederick Alfred, Kt.

Lakin, Sir Michael, Bt. (1909).

Laking, Sir George Robert, KCMG.

Lamb, Sir Albert (Larry), Kt.

Lamb, Sir Albert Thomas, KBE, CMG, DFC.

Lamb, Sir Lionel Henry, KCMG, OBE.

Lambert, Sir Anthony Edward, KCMG.

Lambert, Sir Edward Thomas, KBE, CVO.

Lambert, Sir John Henry, KCVO, CMG.

†Lambert, Sir Peter John Biddulph, Bt. (1711).

Lampl, Sir Frank William, Kt.

Lancaster, *Vice-Adm.* Sir John Strike, KBE, CB.

Landau, Sir Dennis Marcus, Kt.

Lane, Sir David William Stennis Stuart, Kt.

Lang, *Lt.-Gen.* Sir Derek Boileau, KCB, DSO, MC.

Langham, Sir James Michael, Bt. (1660).

Langley, *Maj.-Gen.* Sir Henry Desmond Allen, KCVO, MBE.

Langrishe, Sir Hercules Ralph Hume, Bt. (I. 1777).

Lapsley, *Air Marshal* Sir John Hugh, KBE, CB, DFC, AFC.

Lapun, *Hon.* Sir Paul, Kt.

Larcom, Sir (Charles) Christopher Royde, Bt. (1868).

Larmour, Sir Edward Noel, KCMG.

Lartigue, Sir Louis Cools-, Kt., OBE.

Lasdun, Sir Denys Louis, Kt., CBE, FRIBA.

Latey, *Rt. Hon.* Sir John Brinsmead, Kt., MBE.

Latham, Sir Richard Thomas Paul, Bt. (1919).

Latimer, Sir (Courtenay) Robert, Kt., CBE.

Latimer, Sir Graham Stanley, KBE.

Laucke, *Hon.* Sir Condor Louis, KCMG.

Lauder, Sir Piers Robert Dick-, Bt. (s. 1690).

Laughton, Sir Anthony Seymour, Kt.

Laurantus, Sir Nicholas, Kt., MBE.

Laurence, Sir Peter Harold, KCMG, MC.

Laurie, Sir Robert Bayley Emilius, Bt. (1834).

Lavan, *Hon.* Sir John Martin, Kt.

Law, *Adm.* Sir Horace Rochfort, GCB, OBE, DSC.

Lawes, Sir (John) Michael Bennet, Bt. (1882).

Lawler, Sir Peter James, Kt., OBE.

Lawrence, Sir David Roland Walter, Bt. (1906).

Lawrence, Sir Guy Kempton, Kt., DSO, OBE, DFC.

Lawrence, Sir John Patrick Grosvenor, Kt., CBE.

Lawrence, Sir John Waldemar, Bt., OBE (1858).

Lawrence, Sir William Fettiplace, Bt. (1867).

Lawson, Sir Christopher Donald, Kt.

Lawson, *Col.* Sir John Charles Arthur Digby, Bt., DSO, MC (1900).

†Lawson, Sir John Philip Howard, Bt. (1841).

Lawson, *Hon.* Sir Neil, Kt.

Lawson, *Gen.* Sir Richard George, KCB, DSO, OBE.

Lawton, *Prof.* Sir Frank Ewart, Kt.

Lawton, *Rt. Hon.* Sir Frederick Horace, Kt.

Layden, Sir John (Jack), Kt.

Layfield, Sir Frank Henry Burland Willoughby, Kt., QC.

Lazarus, Sir Peter Esmond, KCB.

Lea, *Lt.-Gen.* Sir George Harris, KCB, DSO, MBE.

Lea, *Vice-Adm.,* Sir John Stuart Crosbie, KBE.

Lea, Sir (Thomas) Julian, Bt. (1892).

Leach, *Admiral of the Fleet* Sir Henry Conyers, GCB.

Leach, Sir Ronald George, GBE.

Leahy, Sir John Henry Gladstone, KCMG.

Lean, Sir David, Kt., CBE.

Learmont, *Lt.-Gen.* Sir John Hartley, KCB, CBE.

Leask, *Lt.-Gen.* Sir Henry Lowther Ewart Clark, KCB, DSO, OBE.

Leather, Sir Edwin Hartley Cameron, KCMG, KCVO.

Leaver, Sir Christopher, GBE.

Le Bailly, *Vice-Adm.* Sir Louis Edward Stewart Holland, CB.

Le Cheminant, *Air Chief Marshal* Sir Peter de Lacey, GBE, KCB, DFC.

Lechmere, Sir Berwick Hungerford, Bt. (1818).

Ledger, Sir Frank, (Joseph Francis), Kt.

Ledwidge, Sir (William) Bernard (John), KCMG.

Lee, Sir Arthur James, KBE, MC.

Lee, *Air Chief Marshal* Sir David John Pryer, GBE, CB.

Lee, Sir (Henry) Desmond (Pritchard), Kt.

Lee, *Brig.* Sir Leonard Henry, Kt., CBE.

Lee, Sir Quo-wei, Kt., CBE.

Lee, *Col.* Sir William Allison, Kt., OBE, TD.

Leeds, Sir Christopher Anthony, Bt. (1812).

Lees, *Air Marshal* Sir Ronald Beresford, KCB, CBE, DFC.

Lees, Sir Thomas Edward, Bt. (1897).

Lees, Sir Thomas Harcourt Ivor, Bt. (1804).

Lees, Sir (William) Antony Clare, Bt. (1937).

Leese, Sir John Henry Vernon, Bt. (1908).

Le Fanu, *Maj.* Sir (George) Victor (Sheridan), KCVO.

le Fleming, Sir Quintin John, Bt. (1705).

Legard, Sir Charles Thomas, Bt. (1660).

Leggatt, *Rt. Hon.* Sir Andrew Peter, Kt.

Leggatt, Sir Hugh Frank John, Kt.

Leggett, Sir Clarence Arthur Campbell, Kt., MBE.

Leigh, Sir John, Bt. (1918).

Leigh, Sir Neville Egerton, KCVO.

Leighton, Sir Michael John Bryan, Bt. (1693).

Leitch, Sir George, KCB, OBE.

Leith, Sir Andrew George Forbes-, Bt. (1923).

Le Marchant, Sir Francis Arthur, Bt. (1841).

Le Masurier, Sir Robert Hugh, Kt., DSC.

Lemon, Sir (Richard) Dawnay, Kt., CBE.

Leng, *Gen.* Sir Peter John Hall, KCB, MBE, MC.

Lennard, *Rev.* Sir Hugh Dacre Barrett-, Bt. (1801).

Leon, Sir John Ronald, Bt. (1911).

Leonard, *Hon.* Sir (Hamilton) John, Kt.

Lepping, Sir George Geria Dennis, GCMG, MBE.

Le Quesne, Sir (Charles) Martin, KCMG.

Le Quesne, Sir (John) Godfray, Kt., QC.

Leslie, Sir Colin Alan Bettridge, Kt.

Leslie, Sir John Norman Ide, Bt. (1876).

†Leslie, Sir (Percy) Theodore, Bt. (s. 1625).

Lethbridge, Sir Thomas Periam Hector Noel, Bt. (1804).

Leuchars, Sir William Douglas, KBE.

Leupena, Sir Tupua, GCMG, MBE.

Levene, Sir Peter Keith, KBE.

Lever, Sir (Tresham) Christopher Arthur Lindsay, Bt. (1911).

Levey, Sir Michael Vincent, Kt., MVO.

Levine, Sir Montague Bernard, Kt.

Levinge, Sir Richard George Robin, Bt. (I. 1704).

Levy, Sir Ewart Maurice, Bt. (1913).

Lewando, Sir Jan Alfred, Kt., CBE.

Lewis, Sir Allen Montgomery, GCMG, GCVO, QC.

Lewis, *Adm.* Sir Andrew Mackenzie, KCB.

Lewis, Sir Kenneth, Kt.

Lewis, Sir Terence Murray, Kt., OBE, QPM.

Lewis, Sir William Arthur, Kt.

Lewthwaite, Sir William Anthony, Bt. (1927).

Ley, Sir Francis Douglas, Bt., MBE, TD (1905).

Leyland, Sir Philip Vyvyan Naylor-, Bt. (1895).

Lickley, Sir Robert Lang, Kt., CBE.

Lidbury, Sir John Towersey, Kt.

Lidderdale, Sir David William Shuckburgh, KCB.

Liddle, Sir Donald Ross, Kt.

Liggins, Sir Edmund Naylor, Kt., TD.

Lighthill, Sir (Michael) James, Kt., FRS.

Lighton, Sir Christopher Robert, Bt., MBE (I. 1791).

Lim, Sir Han-Hoe, Kt., CBE.

Linacre, Sir (John) Gordon (Seymour), Kt., CBE, AFC, DFM.

Lincoln, Sir Anthony Handley, KCMG, CVO.

Lincoln, *Hon.* Sir Anthony Leslie Julian, Kt.

Lindley, Sir Arnold Lewis George, Kt.

Lindop, Sir Norman, Kt.

Lindsay, Sir James Harvey Kincaid Stewart, Kt.

Lindsay, Sir Ronald Alexander, Bt., (1962).

Lintott, Sir Henry John Bevis, KCMG.

Lithgow, Sir William James, Bt. (1925).

Little, *Hon.* Sir Douglas Macfarlan, Kt.

Little, *Most Rev.* Thomas Francis, KBE.

Littler, Sir (James) Geoffrey, KCB.

Livesay, *Vice-Adm.* Sir Michael Howard, KCB.

Llewellyn, Sir David Treharne, Kt.

Llewellyn, Sir Henry Morton, Bt., CBE (1922).

Llewellyn, *Lt.-Col.* Sir Michael Rowland Godfrey, Bt. (1959).

Llewelyn, Sir John Michael Dillwyn-Venables-, Bt. (1890).

Lloyd, *Rt. Hon.* Sir Anthony John Leslie, Kt.

Lloyd, Sir Ian Stewart, Kt., MP.

Lloyd, Sir (John) Peter (Daniel), Kt.

Lloyd, Sir Richard Ernest Butler, Bt. (1960).

Lloyd-Jones, Sir (Peter) Hugh (Jefferd), Kt.

Lloyd Jones, Sir Richard Anthony, KCB.

Loader, Sir Leslie Thomas, Kt., CBE.

Loane, *Most Rev.* Marcus Lawrence, KBE.

Lobo, Sir Rogerio Hyndman, Kt., CBE.

Lock, *Cdr.* Sir (John) Duncan, Kt.

Lockhart, Sir Simon John Edward Francis Sinclair-, Bt. (s. 1636).

Lockspeiser, Sir Ben, KCB, FRS.

Lockwood, Sir Joseph Flawith, Kt.

Loder, Sir Giles Rolls, Bt. (1887).

Lodge, Sir Thomas, Kt.

Loehnis, Sir Clive, KCMG.

Logan, Sir Donald Arthur, KCMG.

Logan, Sir Raymond Douglas, Kt.

Lokoloko, Sir Tore, GCMG, GCVO, OBE.

Longden, Sir Gilbert James Morley, Kt., MBE.

Longland, Sir John Laurence, Kt.

Longley, Sir Norman, Kt., CBE.

Looker, Sir Cecil Thomas, Kt.

Loram, *Vice-Adm.* Sir David Anning, KCB, MVO.

Lorimer, Sir (Thomas) Desmond, Kt.

Lousada, Sir Anthony Baruh, Kt.

Love, Sir Makere Rangiatea Ralph, Kt.

Lovell, Sir (Alfred Charles) Bernard, Kt., OBE, FRS.

Lovelock, Sir Douglas Arthur, KCB.

Loveridge, Sir John Henry, Kt., CBE.

Loveridge, Sir John Warren, Kt.

Lovill, Sir John Roger, Kt., CBE.

Low, Sir Alan Roberts, Kt.

Low, Sir James Richard Morrison-, Bt. (1908).

Lowe, *Air Chief Marshal* Sir Douglas Charles, GCB, DFC, AFC.

Lowe, *Air Vice-Marshal* Sir Edgar Noel, KBE, CB.

Lowe, Sir Thomas William Gordon, Bt. (1918).

Lowry, Sir John Patrick, Kt., CBE.

Lowson, Sir Ian Patrick, Bt. (1951).

Lowther, *Maj.* Sir Charles Douglas, Bt. (1824).

Loyd, Sir Francis Alfred, KCMG, OBE.

Lu, Sir Tseng Chi, Kt.

Lucas, Sir Cyril Edward, Kt., CMG, FRS.

Lucas, Sir Thomas Edward, Bt. (1887).

Luckhoo, *Hon.* Sir Joseph Alexander, Kt.

Luckhoo, Sir Lionel Alfred, KCMG, CBE, QC.

Lucy, Sir Edmund John William Hugh Cameron-Ramsay-Fairfax-, Bt. (1836).

Luddington, Sir Donald Collin Cumyn, KBE, CMG, CVO.

Lumsden, Sir David James, Kt.

Lus, *Hon.* Sir Pita, Kt., OBE.

Lush, *Hon.* Sir George Hermann, Kt.

Lushington, Sir John Richard Castleman, Bt. (1791).

Lusty, Sir Robert Frith, Kt.

Luyt, Sir Richard Edmonds, GCMG, KCVO, DCM.

Lyell, *Rt. Hon.* Sir Nicholas Walter, Kt., QC, MP.

Lygo, *Adm.* Sir Raymond Derek, KCB.

Lyle, Sir Gavin Archibald, Bt. (1929).

Lyons, Sir Edward Houghton, Kt.

Lyons, Sir (Isidore) Jack, Kt., CBE.

Lyons, Sir James Reginald, Kt.

Lyons, Sir John, Kt.

Lyons, *His Hon.* Sir Rudolph, Kt., QC.

McAdam, Sir Ian William James, Kt., OBE.

Macadam, Sir Peter, Kt.

McAlpine, Sir Robin, Kt., CBE.

McAlpine, Sir William Hepburn, Bt. (1918).

Macara, Sir (Charles) Douglas, Bt. (1911).

Macartney, Sir John Barrington, Bt. (I. 1799).

McAvoy, Sir (Francis) Joseph, Kt., CBE.

McCaffrey, Sir Thomas Daniel, Kt.

McCall, Sir (Charles) Patrick Home, Kt., MBE, TD.

McCallum, Sir Donald Murdo, Kt., CBE.

McCamley, Sir Graham Edward, Kt., MBE.

McCarthy, *Rt. Hon.* Sir Thaddeus Pearcey, KBE.

McCaw, *Hon.* Sir Kenneth Malcolm, Kt., QC.

McClellan, *Col.* Sir Herbert Gerard Thomas, Kt., CBE, TD.

McClintock, Sir Eric Paul, Kt.

McColl, Sir Colin Hugh Verel, KCMG.

McCollum, *Hon.* Sir William, Kt.

McConnell, *Cdr.* Sir Robert Melville Terence, Bt., VRD (1900).

McCowan, *Rt. Hon.* Sir Anthony James Denys, Kt..

McCowan, Sir Hew Cargill, Bt. (1934).

McCrea, *Prof.* Sir William Hunter, Kt., FRS.

McCrindle, Sir Robert Arthur, Kt., MP.

McCullough, *Hon.* Sir (Iain) Charles (Robert), Kt.

McCusker, Sir James Alexander, Kt.

MacDermott, *Rt. Hon.* Sir John Clarke, Kt.

McDermott, Sir (Lawrence) Emmet, KBE.

MacDougall, *Gen.* Sir Arthur Leslie, KBE, CB.

McDonald, *Air Chief Marshal* Sir Arthur William Baynes, KCB, AFC.

McDonald, Sir Duncan, Kt., CBE.

Macdonald, Sir Herbert George deLorme, KBE.

Macdonald of Sleat, Sir Ian Godfrey Bosville, Bt. (s. 1625).

Macdonald, Sir Kenneth Carmichael, KCB.

Macdonald, *Vice-Adm.* Sir Roderick Douglas, KBE.

McDonald, *Hon.* Sir William John Farquhar, Kt.

MacDougall, Sir (George) Donald (Alastair), Kt., CBE, FBA.

McDowell, Sir Eric Wallalce, Kt., CBE.

McDowell, Sir Henry McLorinan, KBE.

Mace, *Lt.-Gen.* Sir John Airth, KBE, CB.

McEvoy, *Air Chief Marshal* Sir Theodore Newman, KCB, CBE.

McEwen, Sir John Roderick Hugh, Bt. (1953).

McFarland, Sir John Talbot, Bt. (1914).

Macfarlane, Sir (David) Neil, Kt., MP.

Macfarlane, Sir George Gray, Kt., CB.

McFarlane, Sir Ian, Kt.

Macfarlane, Sir James Wright, Kt.

Macfarlane, Sir Norman Somerville, Kt.

McGeoch, *Vice-Adm.* Sir Ian Lachlan Mackay, KCB, DSO, DSC.

Macgregor, Sir Edwin Robert, Bt. (1828).

MacGregor of MacGregor, Sir Gregor, Bt. (1795).

McGregor, Sir Ian Alexander, Kt., CBE, FRS.

MacGregor, Sir Ian Kinloch, Kt.

McGrigor, *Capt.* Sir Charles Edward, Bt. (1831).

McInerney, *Hon.* Sir Murray Vincent, Kt.

McIntosh, *Vice-Adm.* Sir Ian Stewart, KBE, CB, DSO, DSC.

McIntosh, Sir Ronald Robert Duncan, KCB.

McKaig, *Adm.* Sir (John) Rae, KCB, CBE.

McKay, *Hon.* Sir Donald Norman, KCMG.

Mackay, Sir (George Patrick) Gordon, Kt., CBE.

McKay, Sir James Wilson, Kt.

McKay, Sir John Andrew, Kt., CBE.

Mackay, Sir William Calder, Kt., OBE, MC.

McKee, *Maj.* Sir (William) Cecil, Kt., ERD.

McKenzie, Sir Alexander, KBE.

Mackenzie, Sir Alexander Alwyne Henry Charles Brinton Muir-, Bt. (1805).

Mackenzie, Sir (Alexander George Anthony) Allan, Bt. (1890).

Mackenzie, *Vice-Adm.* Sir Hugh Stirling, KCB, DSO, DSC.

†Mackenzie, Sir Peter Douglas, Bt. (s. 1673).

†Mackenzie, Sir Roderick McQuhae, Bt. (s. 1703).

McKenna, Sir Roy Allan, KBE.

Mackeson, Sir Rupert Henry, Bt. (1954).

Mackie, Sir Maitland, Kt., CBE.

MacKinlay, Sir Bruce, Kt., CBE.

McKinnon, *Hon.* Sir Stuart Neil, Kt.

McKissock, Sir Wylie, Kt., OBE, FRCS.

Macklin, Sir Bruce Roy, Kt., OBE.

Mackworth, *Cdr.* Sir David Arthur Geoffrey, Bt. (1776).

Maclaren, Sir Hamish Duncan, KBE, CB, DFC.

MacLaurin, Sir Ian Charter, Kt.

Maclean, Sir Donald Og Grant, Kt.

Maclean, Sir Fitzroy Hew, Bt., CBE (1957).

McLean, Sir Francis Charles, Kt., CBE.

MacLean, *Vice-Adm.* Sir Hector Charles Donald, KBE, CB, DSC.

Maclean, Sir Lachlan Hector Charles, Bt. (NS 1631).

Maclean, Sir Robert Alexander, KBE.

MacLellan, Sir (George) Robin (Perronet), Kt., CBE.

McLennan, Sir Ian Munro, KCMG, KBE.

McLeod, Sir Charles Henry, Bt. (1925).

MacLeod, Sir (Hugh) Roderick, Kt.

McLeod, Sir Ian George, Kt.

McLintock, Sir Michael William, Bt. (1934).

Maclure, Sir John Robert Spencer, Bt. (1898).

McMahon, Sir Brian Patrick, Bt. (1817).

McMahon, Sir Christopher William, Kt.

McMichan, Sir John, Kt., MD, FRS, FRCP.

Macmillan, Sir Alexander McGregor Graham, Kt.

Macmillan, Sir (James) Wilson, KBE.

MacMillan, *Lt.-Gen.* Sir John Richard Alexander, KCB, CBE.

MacMillan, Sir Kenneth, Kt.

McMullin, *Rt. Hon.* Sir Duncan Wallace, Kt.

Macnab, *Brig.* Sir Geoffrey Alex Colin, KCMG, CB.

Macnaghten, Sir Patrick Alexander, Bt. (1836).

McNair-Wilson, Sir Patrick Michael Ernest David, Kt., MP.

McNair-Wilson, Sir (Robert) Michael Conal, Kt., MP.

McNamara, *Air Chief Marshal* Sir Neville Patrick, KBE.

Macnaughton, *Prof.* Sir Malcolm Campbell, Kt.

McNee, Sir David Blackstock, Kt., QPM.

McNeice, Sir (Thomas) Percy (Fergus), Kt., CMG, OBE.

McPetrie, Sir James Carnegie, KCMG, OBE.

MacPherson, Sir Keith Duncan, Kt.

Macpherson of Cluny, *Hon.* Sir William Alan, Kt., TD.

McQuarrie, Sir Albert, Kt.

Macrae, *Col.* Sir Robert Andrew Scarth, KCVO, MBE.

Macready, Sir Nevil John Wilfrid, Bt. (1923).

Macrory, Sir Patrick Arthur, Kt.

McShine, *Hon.* Sir Arthur Hugh, Kt.

Mactaggart, Sir John Auld, Bt. (1938).

Madden, *Adm.* Sir Charles Edward, Bt., GCB (1919).

Maddocks, Sir Kenneth Phipson, KCMG, KCVO.

Maddox, Sir (John) Kempson, Kt., VRD, MD.

Madigan, Sir Russel Tullie, Kt., OBE.

Magarey, Sir James Rupert, Kt.

Magnus, Sir Laurence Henry Philip, Bt. (1917).

Maguire, *Air Marshal* Sir Harold John, KCB, DSO, OBE.

Mahon, Sir (John) Denis, Kt., CBE.

Mahon, Sir William Walter, Bt. (1819).

Main, Sir Peter Tester, Kt., ERD.

Maini, Sir Amar Nath, Kt., CBE.

Mais, *Hon.* Sir (Robert) Hugh, Kt.

Maitland, Sir Donald James Dundas, GCMG, OBE.

Maitland, Sir Richard John, Bt. (1818).

Makins, Sir Paul Vivian, Bt. (1903).

Malcolm, Sir David Peter Michael, Bt. (s. 1665).

Malet, *Col.* Sir Edward William St. Lo, Bt., OBE (1791).

Mallaby, Sir Christopher Leslie George, KCMG.

Mallinson, Sir William John, Bt. (1935).

Malone, *Hon.* Sir Denis Eustace Gilbert, Kt.

Mamo, Sir Anthony Joseph, Kt., OBE.

Manchester, Sir William Maxwell, KBE.

Mander, Sir Charles Marcus, Bt. (1911).

Manduell, Sir John, Kt., CBE.

Mann, *Rt. Hon.* Sir Michael, Kt.

Mann, *Rt. Rev.* Michael Ashley, KCVO.

Mann, Sir Rupert Edward, Bt. (1905).

Mansel, *Rev. Canon* James Seymour Denis, KCVO.

Mansel, Sir Philip, Bt. (1622).

Mansfield, *Vice-Adm.* Sir (Edward) Gerard (Napier), KBE, CVO.

Mansfield, Sir Philip (Robert Aked), KCMG.

Mant, Sir Cecil George, Kt., CBE.

Mantell, *Hon.* Sir Charles Barrie Knight, Kt.

Manzie, Sir (Andrew) Gordon, KCB.

Mara, *Rt. Hon. Ratu* Sir Kamisese Kapaiwai Tuimacilai, GCMG, KBE.

March, Sir Derek Maxwell, KBE.

Margetson, Sir John William Denys, KCMG.

Marjoribanks, Sir James Alexander Milne, KCMG.

Mark, Sir Robert, GBE.

Markham, Sir Charles John, Bt. (1911).

Marking, Sir Henry Ernest, KCVO, CBE, MC.

Marling, Sir Charles William Somerset, Bt. (1882).

Marr, Sir Leslie Lynn, Bt. (1919).

Marriner, Sir Neville, Kt., CBE.

Marriott, Sir Hugh Cavendish Smith-, Bt. (1774).

Marsden, Sir Nigel John Denton, Bt. (1924).

Marshall, Sir Arthur Gregory George, Kt., OBE.

Marshall, Sir Colin Marsh, Kt.

Marshall, Sir Denis Alfred, Kt.

Marshall, *Prof.* Sir (Oshley) Roy, Kt., CBE.

Marshall, Sir Peter Harold Reginald, KCMG.

Marshall, Sir Robert Braithwaite, KCB, MBE.

Marshall, Sir (Robert) Michael, Kt., MP.

Mars-Jones, *Hon.* Sir William Lloyd, Kt., MBE.

Martell, *Vice-Adm.* Sir Hugh Colenso, KBE, CB.

Martin, *Rear-Adm. Sir David James*, KCMG.

Martin, *Vice-Adm.* Sir John Edward Ludgate, KCB, DSC.

Martin, *Prof.* Sir (John) Leslie, Kt., Ph.D.

Martin, Sir John Miller, KCMG, CB, CVO.

Martin, *Col.* Sir Robert Andrew St. George, KCVO, OBE.

Martin, Sir Sidney Launcelot, Kt.

Marwick, Sir Brian Allan, KBE, CMG.

Marychurch, Sir Peter Harvey, KCMG.

Masefield, Sir Peter Gordon, Kt.

Mason, *Hon.* Sir Anthony Frank, KBE.

Mason, Sir (Basil) John, Kt., CB, D.SC., FRS.

Mason, Sir Frederick Cecil, KCVO, CMG.

Mason, Sir John Charles Moir, KCMG.

Mason, *Prof.* Sir Ronald, KCB, FRS.

Matane, Sir Paulias Nguna, Kt., CMG, OBE.

Mather, Sir (David) Carol (Macdonell), Kt., MC.

Mather, Sir William Loris, Kt., CVO, OBE, MC, TD.

Mathers, Sir Robert William, Kt.

Matheson, Sir (James Adam) Louis, KBE, CMG.

Matheson of Matheson, Sir Torquhil Alexander, Bt. (1882).

Mathias, Sir Richard Hughes, Bt. (1917).

Matthews, Sir Peter Alec, Kt.

Matthews, Sir Peter Jack, Kt., CVO, OBE, QPM.

Matthews, Sir Stanley, Kt., CBE.

Mavor, *Air Marshal* Sir Leslie Deane, KCB, AFC.

†Maxwell, Sir Michael Eustace George, Bt. (s. 1681).

Maxwell, Sir Nigel Mellor Heron-, Bt. (s. 1683).

Maxwell, Sir Robert Hugh, KBE.

May, *Rt. Hon.* Sir John Douglas, Kt.

May, Sir Kenneth Spencer, Kt., CBE.

Mayall, Sir (Alexander) Lees, KCVO, CMG.

Mayhew, *Rt. Hon.* Sir Patrick Barnabas Burke, Kt., QC, MP.

Mayhew-Sanders, Sir John Reynolds, Kt.

Maynard, *Hon.* Sir Clement Travelyan, Kt.

Maynard, *Air Chief Marshal* Sir Nigel Martin, KCB, CBE, DFC, AFC.

Meade, Sir (Richard) Geoffrey (Austin), KBE, CMG, CVO.

Meaney, Sir Patrick Michael, Kt.

Medlycott, Sir Mervyn Tregonwell, Bt. (1808).

Megarry, *Rt. Hon.* Sir Robert Edgar, Kt., FBA.

Megaw, *Rt. Hon.* Sir John, Kt., CBE, TD.

Meinertzhagen, Sir Peter, Kt., CMG.

Mellon, Sir James, KCMG.

Mellor, Sir John Francis, Bt. (1924).

Melville, Sir Harry Work, KCB, Ph.D., D.SC., FRS.

Melville, Sir Leslie Galfreid, KBE.

Melville, Sir Ronald Henry, KCB.

Mensforth, Sir Eric, Kt., CBE, F.Eng.

Menter, Sir James Woodham, Kt., Ph.D., SC.D., FRS.

Menteth, Sir James Wallace Stuart-, Bt. (1838).

Menuhin, Sir Yehudi, OM, KBE.

Menzies, Sir Peter Thomson, Kt.

Messervy, Sir (Roney) Godfrey (Collumbell), Kt.

Meyer, Sir Anthony John Charles, Bt., MP (1910).

Meyjes, Sir Richard Anthony, Kt.

Meyrick, Sir David John Charlton, Bt. (1880).

Meyrick, Sir George Christopher Cadafael Tapps-Gervis-, Bt. (1791).

Miakwe, *Hon.* Sir Akepa, KBE.

Michael, Sir Peter Colin, Kt., CBE.

Micklethwait, Sir Robert Gore, Kt., QC.

Middleton, Sir George Humphrey, KCMG.

Middleton, Sir Peter Edward, GCB.

Middleton, Sir Stephen Hugh, Bt. (1662).

Miers, Sir (Henry) David Alastair Capel, KBE, CMG.

Milbank, Sir Anthony Frederick, Bt. (1882).

Milburn, Sir Anthony Rupert, Bt. (1905).

Miles, Sir Peter Tremayne, KCVO.

Miles, Sir William Napier Maurice, Bt. (1859).

Millais, Sir Ralph Regnault, Bt. (1885).

Millar, Sir Oliver Nicholas, GCVO, FBA.

Millar, Sir Ronald Graeme, Kt.

Millard, Sir Guy Elwin, KCMG, CVO.

Miller, Sir Donald John, Kt., FRSE.

Miller, Sir Douglas Sinclair, KCVO, CBE.

Miller, Sir Hilary Duppa (Hal), Kt., MP.

Miller, Sir (Ian) Douglas, Kt.

Miller, Sir John Holmes, Bt. (1705).

Miller, *Lt.-Col.* Sir John Mansel, GCVO, DSO, MC.

Miller, Sir (Joseph) Holmes, Kt., OBE.

Miller, Sir (Oswald) Bernard, Kt.

Miller, Sir Peter North, Kt.

Miller, Sir Stephen James Hamilton, KCVO, MD, FRCS.

Miller of Glenlee, Sir (Frederick William) Macdonald, Bt. (1788).

Millett, *Hon.* Sir Peter Julian, Kt.

Milling, *Air Marshal* Sir Denis Crowley-, KCB, CBE, DSO, DFC.

Mills, *Vice-Adm.* Sir Charles Piercy, KCB, CBE, DSC.

Mills, Sir Frank, KCVO, CMG.

Mills, Sir John Lewis Ernest Watts, Kt., CBE.

Mills, Sir Peter Frederick Leighton, Bt. (1921).

Mills, Sir Peter McLay, Kt.

†Milman, *Lt.-Col.* Sir Derek, Bt. (1800).

Milne, Sir John Drummond, Kt.

Milner, Sir (George Edward) Mordaunt, Bt. (1717).

Milnes Coates, Sir Anthony Robert, Bt. (1911).

Milton-Thompson, *Surgeon Vice-Adm.* Sir Godfrey James, KBE.

Minhinnick, Sir Gordon Edward George, KBE.

Minogue, *Hon.* Sir John Patrick, Kt., QC.

Miskin, *Hon.* Sir James William, Kt., QC.

Mitchell, *Air Cdre.* Sir (Arthur) Dennis, KBE, CVO, DFC, AFC.

Mitchell, Sir David Bower, Kt., MP.

Mitchell, Sir Derek Jack, KCB, CVO.

Mitchell, *Prof.* Sir Edgar William John, Kt., CBE, FRS.

Mitchell, Sir Hamilton, KBE.

Mobbs, Sir (Gerald) Nigel, Kt.

Moberly, Sir John Campbell, KBE, CMG.

Moberly, Sir Patrick Hamilton, KCMG.

Mocatta, Sir Alan Abraham, Kt., OBE.

Moffat, *Lt.-Gen.* Sir (William) Cameron, KBE.

Mogg, *Gen.* Sir (Herbert) John, GCB, CBE, DSO.

Moir, Sir Ernest Ian Royds, Bt. (1916).

Moller, *Hon.* Sir Lester Francis, Kt.

†Molony, Sir Thomas Desmond, Bt. (1925).

Monro, Sir Hector Seymour Peter, Kt., MP.

Monson, Sir (William Bonnar) Leslie, KCMG, CB.

Montgomery, Sir (Basil Henry) David, Bt. (1801).

Montgomery, Sir (William) Fergus, Kt., MP.

Mookerjee, Sir Birendra Nath, Kt.

Moollan, Sir Abdool Hamid Adam, Kt.

Moollan, *Hon.* Sir Cassam (Ismael), Kt.

Moon, Sir Peter James Scott, KCVO, CMG.

Moon, Sir Peter Wilfred Giles Graham-, Bt. (1855).

†Moon, Sir Roger, Bt. (1887).

Moore, Sir Edward Stanton, Bt., OBE (1923).

Moore, Sir Francis Thomas, Kt.

Moore, Sir Henry Roderick, Kt., CBE.

Moore, *Hon.* Sir John Cochrane, Kt.

Moore, *Maj.-Gen.* Sir (John) Jeremy, KCB, OBE, MC.

Moore, Sir John Michael, KCVO, CB, DSC.

Moore, *Prof.* Sir Norman Winfrid, Bt. (1919).

Moore, Sir William Roger Clotworthy, Bt., TD (1932).

Moores, Sir John, Kt., CBE.

Mootham, Sir Orby Howell, Kt.

Mordaunt, Sir Richard Nigel Charles, Bt. (1611).

Moreton, Sir John Oscar, KCMG, KCVO, MC.

Morgan, *Maj.-Gen.* Sir David John Hughes-, Bt., CB, CBE (1925).

Morgan, Sir Ernest Dunstan, KBE.

Morgan, Sir John Albert Leigh, KCMG.

Morgan-Giles, *Rear-Adm.* Sir Morgan Charles, Kt., DSO, OBE, GM.

Morland, *Hon.* Sir Michael, Kt.

Morland, Sir Robert Kenelm, Kt.

Morpeth, Sir Douglas Spottiswoode, Kt., TD.

Morris, *Air Marshal* Sir Arnold Alec, KBE, CB.

Morris, Sir Robert Byng, Bt. (1806).

Morrison, *Hon.* Sir Charles Andrew, Kt., MP.

Morrison, Sir Howard Leslie, Kt., OBE.

Morritt, *Hon.* Sir (Robert) Andrew, Kt., CVO.

Morrow, Sir Ian Thomas, Kt.

Morse, Sir Christopher Jeremy, KCMG.

Morton, *Adm.* Sir Anthony Storrs, GBE, KCB.

Morton, Sir Brian, Kt.

Morton, Sir William David, Kt., CBE.

Moseley, Sir George Walker, KCB.

Moser, *Prof.* Sir Claus Adolf, KCB, CBE, FBA.

†Moss, Sir David John Edwards-, Bt. (1868).

Mostyn, *Gen.* Sir (Joseph) David Frederick, KCB, CBE.

†Mostyn, Sir William Basil John, Bt. (1670).

Mott, Sir John Harmer, Bt. (1930).

Mott, Sir Nevill Francis, Kt., FRS.

Mount, Sir James William Spencer, Kt., CBE, BEM.

Mount, Sir William Malcolm, Bt. (1921).

Mountain, Sir Denis Mortimer, Bt. (1922).

Mowbray, Sir John, Kt.

Mowbray, Sir John Robert, Bt. (1880).

Moynihan, Sir Noel Henry, Kt.

Muir, Sir John Harling, Bt. (1892).

Muir, Sir Laurence Macdonald, Kt.

Muir Wood, Sir Alan Marshall, Kt., FRS.

Muirhead, Sir David Francis, KCMG, CVO.

Muldoon, *Rt. Hon.* Sir Robert David, GCMG, CH.

Mulholland, Sir Michael Henry, Bt. (1945).

Mullens, *Lt.-Gen.* Sir Anthony Richard Guy, KCB, OBE.

Mummery, *Hon.* Sir John Frank, Kt.

Munn, Sir James, Kt., OBE.

Munro, Sir Alan Gordon, KCMG.

Munro, Sir Alasdair Thomas Ian, Bt. (1825).

Munro, Sir Ian Talbot, Bt. (s. 1634).

Munro, *Hon.* Sir Robert Lindsay, Kt., CBE.

Munro, Sir Sydney Douglas Gun-, GCMG, MBE.

Murley, Sir Reginald Sydney, KBE, TD, FRCS.

Murphy, Sir Leslie Frederick, Kt.

Murray, *Rear-Adm.* Sir Brian Stewart, KCMG.

Murray, *Rt. Hon.* Sir Donald Bruce, Kt.

Murray, Sir Donald Frederick, KCVO, CMG.

Murray, Sir James, KCMG.

Murray, Sir John Antony Jerningham, Kt., CBE.

Murray, Sir Nigel Andrew Digby, Bt. (s. 1628).

Murray, Sir Patrick Ian Keith, Bt. (s. 1673).

Murray, Sir Rowland William Patrick, Bt. (s. 1630).

Murrie, Sir William Stuart, GCB, KBE.

Mursell, Sir Peter, Kt., MBE.

Musgrave, Sir Christopher Patrick Charles, Bt. (1611).

Musgrave, Sir Richard James, Bt. (I. 1782).

Musker, Sir John, Kt.

Musson, *Gen.* Sir Geoffrey Randolph Dixon, GCB, CBE, DSO.

Mustill, *Rt. Hon.* Sir Michael John, Kt.

Myers, Sir Kenneth Ben, Kt., MBE.

Myers, Sir Philip Alan, Kt., OBE, QPM.

Myers, *Prof.* Sir Rupert Horace, KBE.

Mynors, Sir Richard Baskerville, Bt. (1964).

Nabarro, Sir John David Nunes, Kt., MD, FRCP.

Naipaul, Sir Vidiadhar Surajprasad, Kt.

Nairn, Sir Michael, Bt. (1904).

Nairn, Sir Robert Arnold Spencer-, Bt. (1933).

Nairne, *Rt. Hon.* Sir Patrick Dalmahoy, GCB, MC.

Nalder, *Hon.* Sir Crawford David, Kt.

Nall, Sir Michael Joseph, Bt., RN (1954).

Napier, Sir Oliver John, Kt.

Napier, Sir Robin Surtees, Bt. (1867).

Napier, Sir William Archibald, Bt. (s. 1627).

Napley, Sir David, Kt.

Narain, Sir Sathi, KBE.

Neal, Sir Eric James, Kt.

Neal, Sir Leonard Francis, Kt., CBE.

Neale, Sir Alan Derrett, KCB, MBE.

Neave, Sir Arundell Thomas Clifton, Bt. (1795).

Nedd, *Hon.* Sir Robert Archibald, Kt.

Neill, *Rt. Hon.* Sir Brian Thomas, Kt.

Neill, Sir Francis Patrick, Kt., QC.

Neill, *Rt. Hon.* Sir Ivan, Kt.

Nelson, *Maj.-Gen.* Sir (Eustace) John (Blois), KCVO, CB, DSO, OBE, MC.

Nelson, *Air Marshal* Sir (Sidney) Richard (Carlyle), KCB, OBE, MD.

Nelson, *Maj.* Sir William Vernon Hope, Bt., OBE (1912).

Nepean, *Lt.-Col.* Sir Evan Yorke, Bt. (1802).

Ness, *Air Marshal* Sir Charles Ernest, KCB, CBE.

Neville, Sir Richard Lionel John Baines, Bt. (1927).

New, *Maj.-Gen.* Sir Laurence Anthony Wallis, Kt., CB, CBE.

Newbold, Sir Charles Demorée, KBE, CMG, QC.

Newman, Sir Francis Hugh Cecil, Bt. (1912).

Newman, Sir Geoffrey Robert, Bt. (1836).

Newman, Sir Jack, Kt., CBE.

Newman, Sir Kenneth Leslie, GBE.

Newns, Sir (Alfred) Foley (Francis Polden), KCMG, CVO.

Newsam, Sir Peter Anthony, Kt.

Newton, Sir (Harry) Michael (Rex), Bt. (1900).

Newton, Sir Kenneth Garnar, Bt., OBE, TD (1924).

Newton, Sir (Leslie) Gordon, Kt.

Ngata, Sir Henare Kohere, Kt.

Niall, Sir Horace Lionel Richard, Kt., CBE.

Nicholas, Sir David, Kt., CBE.

Nicholas, Sir Herbert Richard, Kt., OBE.

Nicholas, Sir John William, KCVO, CMG.

Nicholls, *Rt. Hon.* Sir Donald James, Kt.

Nicholls, *Air Marshal* Sir John Moreton, KCB, CBE, DFC, AFC.

Nichols, Sir Edward Henry, Kt., TD.

Nicholson, Sir Bryan Hubert, Kt.

Nicholson, *Hon.* Sir David Eric, Kt.

Nicholson, Sir Godfrey, Bt. (1958).

Nicholson, Sir John Norris, Bt., KBE, CIE (1912).

Nicholson, *Hon.* Sir Michael, Kt.

Nicholson, Sir Robin Buchanan, Kt., Ph.D., FRS.

Nickson, Sir David Wigley, KBE.

Nicolson, Sir David Lancaster, Kt.

Nield, Sir Basil Edward, Kt., CBE, QC.

Nield, Sir William Alan, GCMG, KCB.

Nightingale, Sir Charles Manners Gamaliel, Bt. (1628).

Nightingale, Sir John Cyprian, Kt., CBE, BEM, QPM.

Nimmo, *Hon.* Sir John Angus, Kt., CBE.

Niven, Sir (Cecil) Rex, Kt., CMG, MC.

Nixon, Sir Edwin Ronald, Kt., CBE.

Nixon, *Rev.* Sir Kenneth Michael John Basil, Bt. (1906).

Noad, Sir Kenneth Beeson, Kt., MD.

Noble, Sir Iain Andrew, Bt., OBE (1923).

Noble, Sir Marc Brunel, Bt. (1902).

Noble, Sir (Thomas Alexander) Fraser, Kt., MBE.

Nock, Sir Norman Lindfield, Kt.

Nolan, *Hon.* Sir Michael Patrick, Kt.

Nolan, Sir Sidney Robert, Kt., OM, CBE.

Nombri, Sir Joseph Karl, Kt., ISO, BEM.

Norman, Sir Arthur Gordon, KBE, DFC.

Norman, *Vice-Adm.* Sir (Horace) Geoffrey, KCVO, CB, CBE.

Norman, Sir Mark Annesley, Bt. (1915).

Norman, *Prof.* Sir Richard Oswald Chandler, KBE, FRS.

Norman, Sir Robert Henry, Kt., OBE.

Norman, Sir Robert Wentworth, Kt.

Normanton, Sir Tom, Kt., TD.

Norris, *Air Chief Marshal* Sir Christopher Neil Foxley-, GCB, DSO, OBE.

Norris, Sir Eric George, KCMG.

Norris, *Hon.* Sir John Gerald, Kt., ED.

North, Sir Thomas Lindsay, Kt.

North, Sir (William) Jonathan (Frederick), Bt. (1920).

Norton, Sir Clifford John, KCMG, CVO.

Norwood, Sir Walter Neville, Kt.

Nossal, Sir Gustav Joseph Victor, Kt., CBE.

Nosworthy, Sir John Reeve, Kt., CBE.

Nott, *Rt. Hon.* Sir John William Frederic, KCB.

Nourse, *Rt. Hon.* Sir Martin Charles, Kt.

Nugent, Sir John Edwin Lavallin, Bt. (I. 1795).

Nugent, *Maj.* Sir Peter Walter James, Bt. (1831).

Nugent, Sir Robin George Colborne, Bt. (1806).

Nuttall, Sir Nicholas Keith Lillington, Bt. (1922).

Nutting, *Rt. Hon.* Sir (Harold) Anthony, Bt. (1903).

Oakeley, Sir John Digby Atholl, Bt. (1790).

Oakes, Sir Christopher, Bt. (1939).

Oakshott, Hon. Sir Anthony Hendrie, Bt. (1959).

Oates, Sir Thomas, Kt., CMG, OBE.

Oatley, Sir Charles William, Kt., OBE, FRS.

Obolensky, *Prof.* Sir Dimitri, Kt.

O'Brien, Sir Frederick William Fitzgerald, Kt.

O'Brien, Sir Richard, Kt., DSO, MC.

O'Brien, Sir Timothy John, Bt. (1849).

O'Brien, *Adm.* Sir William Donough, KCB, DSC.

O'Connell, Sir Maurice James Donagh MacCarthy, Bt. (1869).

O'Connor, *Rt. Hon.* Sir Patrick McCarthy, Kt.

O'Dea, Sir Patrick Jerad, KCVO.

Odell, Sir Stanley John, Kt.

Ogden, Sir (Edward) Michael, Kt., QC.

Ogilvie, Sir Alec Drummond, Kt.

Ogilvy, Hon. Sir Angus James Bruce, KCVO.

Ogilvy, Sir David John Wilfrid, Bt. (s. 1626).

Ognall, *Hon.* Sir Harry Henry, Kt.

O'Halloran, Sir Charles Ernest, Kt.

Ohlson, Sir Brian Eric Christopher, Bt. (1920).

Okeover, *Capt.* Sir Peter Ralph Leopold Walker-, Bt. (1886).

Olewale, *Hon.* Sir Niwia Ebia, Kt.

Oliphant, Sir Mark (Marcus Laurence Elwin), KBE, FRS.

Oliver, Sir (Frederick) Ernest, Kt., CBE, TD.

O'Loghlen, Sir Colman Michael, Bt. (1838).

Olver, Sir Stephen John Linley, KBE, CMG.

O'Neil, *Hon.* Sir Desmond Henry, Kt.

Ongley, *Hon.* Sir Joseph Augustine, Kt.

Onslow, Sir John Roger Wilmot, Bt. (1797).

Oppenheim, Sir Alexander, Kt., OBE, D.SC., FRSE.

Oppenheim, Sir Duncan Morris, Kt.

Oppenheimer, Sir Michael Bernard Grenville, Bt. (1921).

Oppenheimer, Sir Philip Jack, Kt.

Opperman, *Hon.* Sir Hubert Ferdinand, Kt., OBE.

Orde, Sir John Alexander Campbell-, Bt. (1790).

O'Regan, *Hon.* Sir John Barry, Kt.

Ormond, Sir John Davies Wilder, Kt., BEM.

Ormrod, *Rt. Hon.* Sir Roger Fray Greenwood, Kt.

Orr, *Rt. Hon.* Sir Alan Stewart, Kt., OBE.

Orr, Sir David Alexander, Kt., MC.

Orr, Sir John Henry, Kt., OBE, QPM.

Osborn, Sir John Holbrook, Kt.

Osborn, Sir Richard Henry Danvers, Bt. (1662).

Osborne, Sir Peter George, Bt. (I. 1629).

Osifelo, Sir Frederick Aubarua, Kt., MBE.

Osman, Sir (Abdool) Raman Mahomed, GCMG, CBE.

Osmond, Sir Douglas, Kt., CBE.

Osmond, Sir (Stanley) Paul, Kt., CB.

Oswald, *Adm.* Sir (John) Julian Robertson, GCB.

Otton, Sir Geoffrey John, KCB.

Otton, *Hon.* Sir Philip Howard, Kt.

Oulton, Sir Antony Derek Maxwell, GCB, QC.

Outram, Sir Alan James, Bt. (1858).

Overall, Sir John Wallace, Kt., CBE, MC.

Overton, Sir Hugh Thomas Arnold, KCMG.

Owen, Sir Geoffrey, Kt.

Owen, Sir Hugh Bernard Pilkington, Bt. (1813).

†Owen, Sir Hugo Dudley Cunliffe-, Bt. (1920).

Owen, *Hon.* Sir John Arthur Dalziel, Kt.

Owo, The Olowo of, Kt.

Oxford, Sir Kenneth Gordon, Kt., CBE, QPM.

Packard, *Lieut.-Gen.* Sir (Charles) Douglas, KBE, CB, DSO.

Padmore, Sir Thomas, GCB.

Page, Sir Alexander Warren, Kt., MBE.

Page, Sir (Arthur) John, Kt.

Page, Sir Frederick William, Kt., CBE.

Page, Sir John Joseph Joffre, Kt., OBE.

Paget, Sir John Starr, Bt. (1886).

Paget, Sir Julian Tolver, Bt., CVO (1871).

Pain, *Lt.-Gen.* Sir (Horace) Rollo (Squarey), KCB, MC.

Pain, *Hon.* Sir Peter Richard, Kt.

Palin, *Air Marshal* Sir Roger Hewlett, KCB, OBE.

Palliser, *Rt. Hon.* Sir (Arthur) Michael, GCMG.

Palmar, Sir Derek James, Kt.

Palmer, Sir (Charles) Mark, Bt. (1886).

Palmer, *Gen.* Sir (Charles) Patrick (Ralph), KBE.

Palmer, Sir Geoffrey Christopher John, Bt. (1660).

Palmer, Sir John Chance, Kt.

Palmer, Sir John Edward Somerset, Bt. (1791).

Palmer, *Maj.-Gen.* Sir (Joseph) Michael, KCVO.

Pao, Sir Yue-Kong, Kt., CBE.

Paolozzi, Sir Eduardo Luigi, Kt., CBE, RA.

Pape, *Hon.* Sir George Augustus, Kt.

Pararajasingam, Sir Sangarapillai, Kt.

Parbo, Sir Arvi Hillar, Kt.

Parham, *Adm.* Sir Frederick Robertson, GBE, KCB, DSO.

Parish, Sir David Elmer Woodbine, Kt., CBE.

Park, *Hon.* Sir Hugh Eames, Kt.

Parker, Sir (Arthur) Douglas Dodds-, Kt.

Parker, Sir Karl Theodore, Kt., CBE, Ph.D., FBA.

Parker, Sir Peter, Kt., LVO.

Parker, Sir Richard (William) Hyde, Bt. (1681).

Parker, *Rt. Hon.* Sir Roger Jocelyn, Kt.

Parker, *Vice-Adm.* Sir (Wilfred) John, KBE, CB, DSC.

Parker, Sir (William) Alan, Bt. (1844).

Parkes, Sir Basil Arthur, Kt., OBE.

Parkes, Sir Edward Walter, Kt.

Parkinson, Sir Nicholas Fancourt, Kt.

Parry, Sir Ernest Jones-, Kt.

Parry, Sir (Frank) Hugh (Nigel), Kt., CBE.

Parry-Evans, *Air Chief Marshal* Sir David, KCB, CBE.

Parsons, Sir Anthony Derrick, GCMG, MVO, MC.

Parsons, Sir (John) Michael, Kt.

Parsons, Sir Richard Edmund (Clement Fownes), KCMG.

Partridge, Sir Michael John Anthony, KCB.

Pascoe, *Gen.* Sir Robert Alan, KCB, MBE.

Pasley, Sir John Malcolm Sabine, Bt. (1794).

Paterson, Sir Dennis Craig, Kt.

Paterson, Sir George Mutlow, Kt., OBE, QC.

Paterson, Sir John Valentine Jardine, Kt.

Paton, Sir (Thomas) Angus (Lyall), Kt., CMG, FRS.

Paton, *Prof.* Sir William Drummond Macdonald, Kt., CBE, DM, FRS, FRCP.

Pattie, *Rt. Hon.* Sir Geoffrey Edwin, Kt., MP.

Pattinson, *Hon.* Sir Baden, KBE.

Pattinson, Sir (William) Derek, Kt.

Paul, Sir John Warburton, GCMG, OBE, MC.

Paul, *Air Marshal* Sir Ronald Ian Stuart-, KBE.

Payne, Sir Norman John, Kt., CBE.

Peach, Sir Leonard Harry, Kt.

Peacock, *Prof.* Sir Alan Turner, Kt., DSC.

Peacock, Sir Geoffrey Arden, Kt., CVO.

Pearce, Sir Austin William, Kt., CBE, Ph.D.

Pearce, Sir (Daniel Norton) Idris, Kt., CBE, TD.

Pearce, Sir Eric Herbert, Kt., OBE.

Peard, *Rear-Adm.* Sir Kenyon Harry Terrell, KBE.

Pearman, *Hon.* Sir James Eugene, Kt., CBE.

Pearson, Sir Francis Fenwick, Bt., MBE (1964).

Pearson, Sir (James) Denning, Kt.

Pearson, *Gen.* Sir Thomas Cecil Hook, KCB, CBE, DSO.

Peart, *Prof.* Sir William Stanley, Kt., MD, FRS.

Pease, Sir (Alfred) Vincent, Bt. (1882).

Pease, Sir Richard Thorn, Bt. (1920).

Peat, Sir Gerrard Charles, KCVO.

Peat, Sir Henry, KCVO, DFC.

Peck, Sir Edward Heywood, GCMG.

Peck, Sir John Howard, KCMG.

Pedder, *Vice-Adm.* Sir Arthur Reid, KBE, CB.

Pedder, *Air Marshal* Sir Ian Maurice, KCB, OBE, DFC.

Pedler, Sir Frederick Johnson, Kt.

Peek, Sir Francis Henry Grenville, Bt. (1874).

Peek, *Vice-Adm.* Sir Richard Innes, KBE, CB, DSC.

Peel, Sir John Harold, KCVO.

Peel, Sir (William) John, Kt.

Peierls, Sir Rudolf Ernst, Kt., CBE, D.SC., D.Phil., FRS.

Peirse, Sir Henry Grant de la Poer Beresford-, Bt. (1814).

Peirse, *Air Vice-Marshal* Sir Richard Charles Fairfax, KCVO, CB.

Pelly, Sir John Alwyne, Bt. (1840).

Pemberton, Sir Francis Wingate William, Kt., CBE.

Penn, *Lt.-Col.* Sir Eric Charles William Mackenzie, GCVO, OBE, MC.

Percival, Sir Anthony Edward, Kt., CB.

Percival, *Rt. Hon.* Sir (Walter) Ian, Kt., QC.

Pereira, Sir (Herbert) Charles, Kt., D.SC., FRS.

Perkins, *Surgeon Vice-Adm.* Sir Derek Duncombe Steele-, KCB, KCVO.

Perring, Sir Ralph Edgar, Bt. (1963).

Perris, Sir David (Arthur), Kt., MBE.

Perry, Sir David Howard, KCB.

Perry, Sir (David) Norman, Kt., MBE.

Pestell, Sir John Richard, KCVO.

Peterkin, Sir Neville, Kt.

Petersen, Sir Jeffrey Charles, KCMG.

Petit, Sir Dinshaw Manockjee, Bt. (1890).

Peto, Sir Henry George Morton, Bt. (1855).

Peto, Sir Michael Henry Basil, Bt. (1927).

Petrie, Sir Peter Charles, Bt., CMG (1918).

Pettigrew, Sir Russell Hilton, Kt.

Pettit, Sir Daniel Eric Arthur, Kt.

Philips, *Prof.* Sir Cyril Henry, Kt.

Philipson, Sir Robert James, (Sir Robin Philipson), Kt., RA.

Phillips, *Prof.* Sir David Chilton, KBE, Ph.D., FRS.

Phillips, Sir Fred Albert, Kt., CVO.

Phillips, Sir Henry Ellis Isidore, Kt., CMG, MBE.

Phillips, Sir Horace, KCMG.

Phillips, *Hon.* Sir Nicholas Addison, Kt.

Phillips, Sir Peter John, Kt., OBE.

Phillips, Sir Robin Francis, Bt. (1912).

Pickard, Sir Cyril Stanley, KCMG.

Pickering, Sir Edward Davies, Kt.

Pickthorn, Sir Charles William Richards, Bt. (1959).

Pidgeon, Sir John Allan Stewart, Kt.

Piers, Sir Charles Robert Fitzmaurice, Bt. (I. 1661).

Pigot, Sir George Hugh, Bt. (1764).

Pigott, Sir Berkeley Henry Sebastian, Bt. (1808).

Pike, Sir Michael Edmund, KCVO, CMG.

Pike, Sir Philip Ernest Housden, Kt., QC.

Pike, *Lt.-Gen.* Sir William Gregory Huddleston, KCB, CBE, DSO.

Pilcher, Sir (Charlie) Dennis, Kt., CBE.

Pilditch, Sir Richard Edward, Bt. (1929).

Pile, Sir Frederick Devereux, Bt. MC (1900).

Pile, Sir William Dennis, GCB, MBE.

Pilkington, Sir Antony Richard, Kt.

Pilkington, Sir Lionel Alexander Bethune, (Sir Alastair), Kt., FRS.

Pilkington, Sir Thomas Henry Milborne-Swinnerton-, Bt. (s. 1635).

Pill, *Hon.* Sir Malcolm Thomas, Kt.

Pillar, *Adm.* Sir William Thomas, GBE, KCB.

Pindling, *Rt. Hon.* Sir Lynden Oscar, KCMG.

Pinker, Sir George Douglas, KCVO.

Pinsent, Sir Christopher Roy, Bt. (1938).

Piper, Sir David Towry, Kt., CBE.

Pippard, *Prof.* Sir (Alfred) Brian, Kt., FRS.

Pirbhai, Sir Eboo, Kt., OBE.

Pirie, *Gp. Capt.* Sir Gordon Hamish, Kt., CVO, CBE.

Pitblado, Sir David Bruce, KCB, CVO.

Pitoi, Sir Sere, Kt., CBE.

Pitt, Sir Harry Raymond, Kt., Ph.D., FRS.

Pitts, Sir Cyril Alfred, Kt.

Pixley, Sir Neville Drake, Kt., MBE, VRD.

Pizey, *Adm.* Sir (Charles Thomas) Mark, GBE, CB, DSO.

Plaister, Sir Sydney, Kt., CBE.

Plastow, Sir David Arnold Stuart, Kt.

†Platt, Sir (Frank) Lindsey, Bt. (1958).

Platt, *Prof.* Hon. Sir Peter, Bt. (1959).

Playfair, Sir Edward Wilder, KCB.

Pliatzky, Sir Leo, KCB.

Plowman, Sir (John) Anthony, Kt.

Plowman, *Hon.* Sir John Robin, Kt., CBE.

Plumb, *Prof.* Sir John Harold, Kt.

Poett, *Gen.* Sir (Joseph Howard) Nigel, KCB, DSO.

Pole, *Col.* Sir John Gawen Carew, Bt., DSO, TD (1628).

Pole, Sir Peter Van Notten, Bt. (1791).

Pollen, Sir John Michael Hungerford, Bt. (1795).

Pollock, Sir George, Kt., QC.

Pollock, Sir George Frederick, Bt. (1866).

Pollock, Sir Giles Hampden Montagu-, Bt. (1872).

Pollock, *Admiral of the Fleet* Sir Michael Patrick, GCB, MVO, DSC.

Pollock, Sir William Horace Montagu-, KCMG.

Ponsonby, Sir Ashley Charles Gibbs, Bt., MC (1956).

Pontin, Sir Frederick William, Kt.

Poore, Sir Herbert Edward, Bt. (1795).

Pope, *Vice-Adm.* Sir (John) Ernle, KCB.

Pope, Sir Joseph Albert, Kt., D.SC., Ph.D.

Popper, *Prof.* Sir Karl Raimund, Kt., CH, Ph.D., FRS.

Popplewell, *Hon.* Sir Oliver Bury, Kt.

Portal, Sir Jonathan Francis, Bt. (1901).

Porter, Sir John Simon Horsbrugh-, Bt. (1902).

Porter, Sir Leslie, Kt.

Porter, *Air Marshal* Sir (Melvin) Kenneth (Drowley), KCB, CBE.

Porter, *Hon.* Sir Murray Victor, Kt.

Porter, *Rt. Hon.* Sir Robert Wilson, Kt., QC.

Posnett, Sir Richard Neil, KBE, CMG.

Potter, Sir (Joseph) Raymond (Lynden), Kt.

Potter, *Hon.* Sir Mark Howard, Kt.

Potter, *Maj.-Gen.* Sir (Wilfrid) John, KBE, CB.

Potter, Sir (William) Ian, Kt.

Potts, *Hon.* Sir Francis Humphrey, Kt.

Pound, Sir John David, Bt. (1905).

Pountain, Sir Eric John, Kt.

Powell, Sir (Arnold Joseph) Philip, Kt., CH, OBE, RA, FRIBA.

Powell, Sir Nicholas Folliott Douglas, Bt. (1897).

Powell, Sir Richard Royle, GCB, KBE, CMG.

Power, Sir Alastair John Cecil, Bt. (1924).

Powles, Sir Guy Richardson, KBE, CMG, ED.

Poynton, Sir (Arthur) Hilton, GCMG.

Prain, Sir Ronald Lindsay, Kt., OBE.

Prendergast, Sir John Vincent, KBE, CMG, GM.

Prentice, *Rt. Hon.* Sir Reginald Ernest, Kt.

Prentice, *Hon.* Sir William Thomas, Kt., MBE.

Prescott, Sir Mark, Bt. (1938).

Preston, Sir Kenneth Huson, Kt.

Preston, Sir Peter Sansome, KCB.

Preston, Sir Ronald Douglas Hildebrand, Bt. (1815).

Prevost, Sir Christopher Gerald, Bt. (1805).

Price, Sir Charles Keith Napier Rugge-, Bt. (1804).

Price, Sir David Ernest Campbell, Kt., MP.

Price, Sir Francis Caradoc Rose, Bt. (1815).

Price, Sir Frank Leslie, Kt.

Price, Sir (James) Robert, KBE.

Price, Sir Leslie Victor, Kt., OBE.

Price, Sir Norman Charles, KCB.

Price, Sir Robert John Green-, Bt. (1874).

Prichard, Sir Montague Illtyd, Kt., CBE, MC.

Prickett, *Air Chief Marshal* Sir Thomas Other, KCB, DSO, DFC.

Prideaux, Sir Humphrey Povah Treverbian, Kt., OBE.

Prideaux, Sir John Francis, Kt., OBE.

†Primrose, Sir John Ure, Bt. (1903).

Pringle, *Air Marshal* Sir Charles Norman Seton, KBE.

Pringle, *Lt.-Gen.* Sir Steuart (Robert), Bt., KCB, RM (s. 1683).

Pritchard, Sir Asa Hubert, Kt.

Pritchard, Sir Neil, KCMG.

Pritchett, Sir Victor Sawdon, Kt., CBE.

Proby, Sir Peter, Bt. (1952).

Proctor, Sir Roderick Consett, Kt., MBE.

Proud, Sir John Seymour, Kt.

Prout, Sir Christopher James, Kt., TD, QC, MEP.

Pryke, Sir David Dudley, Bt. (1926).

Pugh, Sir Idwal Vaughan, KCB.

Pugsley, *Prof.* Sir Alfred Grenvile, Kt., OBE, D.SC., FRS.

Pullen, Sir William Reginald James, KCVO.

Pullinger, Sir (Francis) Alan, Kt., CBE.

Pumphrey, Sir (John) Laurence, KCMG.

Purchas, *Rt. Hon.* Sir Francis Brooks, Kt.

Quicke, Sir John Godolphin, Kt., CBE.

Quilliam, *Hon.* Sir (James) Peter, Kt.

Quilter, Sir Anthony Raymond Leopold Cuthbert, Bt. (1897).

Quinlan, Sir Michael Edward, KCB.

Quinton, Sir James Grand, Kt.

Quirk, *Prof.* Sir (Charles)Randolph, Kt., CBE, FBA.

Rabukawaqa, Sir Josua Rasilau, KBE, MVO.

Raby, Sir Victor Harry, KBE, CB, MC.

Radcliffe, Sir Sebastian Everard, Bt. (1813).

Radclyffe, Sir Charles Edward Mott-, Kt.

Radford, Sir Ronald Walter, KCB, MBE.

Radzinowicz, *Prof.* Sir Leon, Kt., LL.D.

Rae, *Hon.* Sir Wallace Alexander Ramsay, Kt.

Raeburn, Sir Michael Edward Norman, Bt. (1923).

Raeburn, *Maj.-Gen.* Sir (William) Digby (Manifold), KCVO, CB, DSO, MBE.

Raffray, Sir Piat Joseph Raymond Andre, Kt.

Raikes, *Vice-Adm.* Sir Iwan Geoffrey, KCB, CBE, DSC.

Ralli, Sir Godfrey Victor, Bt., TD (1912).

Ramdanee, Sir Mookteswar Baboolall Kailash, Kt.

Ramphal, Sir Shridath Surendranath, Kt., GCMG.

Ramphul, Sir Baalkhristna, Kt.

Rampton, Sir Jack Leslie, KCB.

Ramsay, Sir Alexander William Burnett, Bt. (1806).

Ramsay, Sir Thomas Meek, Kt., CMG.

Ramsbotham, *Lt.-Gen.* Sir David John, KCB, CBE.

Ramsbotham, *Hon.* Sir Peter Edward, GCMG, GCVO.

Ramsden, Sir John Charles Josslyn, Bt. (1689).

Ramsey, Sir Alfred Ernest, Kt.

Randle, *Prof.* Sir Philip John, Kt.

Ranger, Sir Douglas, Kt., FRCS.

Rank, Sir Benjamin Keith, Kt., CMG.

†Rankin, Sir Ian Niall, Bt. (1898).

Raper, *Vice-Adm.* Sir (Robert) George, KCB.

Rasch, *Maj.* Sir Richard Guy Carne, Bt. (1903).

Rashleigh, Sir Richard Harry, Bt. (1831).

Rattee, *Hon.* Sir Donald Keith, Kt.

Rault, Sir Louis Joseph Maurice, Kt.

Rawlins, *Surgeon Vice-Adm.* Sir John Stuart Pepys, KBE.

Rawlinson, Sir Anthony Henry John, Bt. (1891).

Rayne, Sir Edward, Kt., CVO.

Read, *Air Marshal* Sir Charles Frederick, KBE, CB, DFC, AFC.

Read, *Gen.* Sir (John) Antony (Jervis), GCB, CBE, DSO, MC.

Read, Sir John Emms, Kt.

Reade, Sir Clyde Nixon, Bt. (1661).

Reay, *Lt.-Gen.* Sir (Hubert) Alan John, KBE.

Redgrave, *Maj.-Gen.* Sir Roy Michael Frederick, KBE, MC.

Redmayne, Sir Nicholas, Bt. (1964).

Redmond, Sir James, Kt.

Redwood, Sir Peter Boverton, Bt. (1911).

Reece, Sir Charles Hugh, Kt.

Reece, Sir James Gordon, Kt.

Reed, *Hon.* Sir Nigel Vernon, Kt., CBE.

Rees, Sir (Charles William) Stanley, Kt., TD.

Reeve, Sir (Charles) Trevor, Kt.

Reeves, *Most Rev.* Paul Alfred, GCMG, GCVO.

Reffell, *Adm.* Sir Derek Roy, KCB.

Refshauge, *Maj.-Gen.* Sir William Dudley, Kt., CBE.

Reid, Sir Alexander James, Bt. (1897).

Reid, *Hon.* Sir George Oswald, Kt., QC.

Reid, *Air Vice-Marshal* Sir (George) Ranald Macfarlane, KCB, DSO, MC.

Reid, Sir (Harold) Martin (Smith), KBE, CMG.

Reid, Sir Hugh, Bt. (1922).

Reid, Sir John James Andrew, KCMG, CB, TD.

Reid, Sir Norman Robert, Kt.

Reid, Sir Robert Basil, Kt., CBE.

Reid, Sir Robert Paul, Kt.

Reilly, Sir (D'Arcy) Patrick, GCMG, OBE.

Reilly, *Lt.-Gen.* Sir Jeremy Calcott, KCB, DSO.

Renals, Sir Stanley, Bt. (1895).

Rendell, Sir William, Kt.

Rennie, Sir John Shaw, GCMG, OBE.

Renouf, Sir Clement William Bailey, Kt.

Renouf, Sir Francis Henry, Kt.

Renshaw, Sir (Charles) Maurice Bine, Bt. (1903).

Renwick, Sir Richard Eustace, Bt. (1921).

Renwick, Sir Robin William, KCMG.

Reporter, Sir Shapoor Ardeshirji, KBE.

Rex, *Hon.* Sir Robert Richmond, KBE, CMG.

Reynolds, Sir David James, Bt. (1923).

Reynolds, Sir Peter William John, Kt., CBE.

Rhodes, Sir Basil Edward, Kt., CBE, TD.

Rhodes, Sir John Christopher Douglas, Bt. (1919).

Rhodes, Sir Peregrine Alexander, KCMG.

Rice, *Maj.-Gen.* Sir Desmond Hind Garrett, KCVO, CBE.

Richards, *Hon.* Sir Edward Trenton, Kt., CBE.

Richards, Sir (Francis) Brooks, KCMG, DSC.

Richards, Sir James Maude, Kt., CBE.

Richards, *Lt.-Gen.* Sir John Charles Chisholm, KCB, RM.

Richards, Sir Rex Edward, Kt., D.SC., FRS.

Richardson, Sir Anthony Lewis, Bt. (1924).

Richardson, *Gen.* Sir Charles Leslie, GCB, CBE, DSO.

Richardson, *Air Marshal* Sir (David) William, KBE.

Richardson, Sir Egerton Rudolf, Kt., CMG.

Richardson, *Rt. Hon.* Sir Ivor Lloyd Morgan, Kt.

Richardson, Sir (John) Eric, Kt., CBE.

Richardson, Sir (Lionel) Earl George, Kt.

Richardson, Sir Michael John de Rougemont, Kt.

Richardson, *Lt.-Gen.* Sir Robert Francis, KCB, CVO, CBE.

Richardson, Sir Simon Alaisdair Stewart-, Bt. (s. 1630).

Riches, Sir Derek Martin Hurry, KCMG.

Riches, *Gen.* Sir Ian Hurry, KCB, DSO.

Richmond, Sir Alan James, Kt.

Richmond, *Rt. Hon.* Sir Clifford Parris, KBE.

Richmond, Sir John Frederick, Bt. (1929).

Richmond, *Prof.* Sir Mark Henry, Kt., FRS.

Rickett, Sir Denis Hubert Fletcher, KCMG, CB.

Rickett, Sir Raymond Mildmay Wilson, Kt., CBE, PH.D.

Ricketts, Sir Robert Cornwallis Gerald St. Leger, Bt. (1828).

Ricks, Sir John Plowman, Kt.

Riddell, Sir John Charles Buchanan, Bt., CVO (s. 1628).

Ridley, Sir Adam (Nicholas), Kt.

Ridley, Sir Sidney, Kt.

Ridsdale, Sir Julian Errington, Kt., CBE, MP.

Rigby, *Lt.-Col.* Sir (Hugh) John (Macbeth), Bt. (1929).

Riley, Sir Ralph, Kt., FRS.

Ring, Sir Lindsay Roberts, GBE.

Ringadoo, *Hon.* Sir Veerasamy, GCMG.

Ripley, Sir Hugh, Bt. (1880).

Risk, Sir Thomas Neilson, Kt.

Risson, *Maj.-Gen.* Sir Robert Joseph Henry, Kt., CB, CBE, DSO, ED.

Ritchie, Sir James Edward Thomson, Bt., TD (1918).

Rix, Sir Brian Norman Roger, Kt., CBE.

Rix, Sir John, Kt., MBE.

Roberts, Sir Bryan Clieve, KCMG, QC.

Roberts, *Hon.* Sir Denys Tudor Emil, KBE, QC.

Roberts, Sir (Edward Fergus) Sidney, Kt., CBE.

Roberts, Sir Frank Kenyon, GCMG, GCVO.

Roberts, Sir Geoffrey Newland, Kt., CBE, AFC.

Roberts, *Brig.* Sir Geoffrey Paul Hardy-, KCVO, CB, CBE.

Roberts, Sir Gilbert Howland Rookehurst, Bt. (1809).

Roberts, Sir Gordon James, Kt., CBE.

Roberts, Sir (Ieuan) Wyn Pritchard, Kt., MP.

Roberts, Sir Samuel, Bt. (1919).

Roberts, Sir Stephen James Leake, Kt.

Roberts, Sir William James Denby, Bt. (1909).

Robertson, *Prof.* Sir Alexander, Kt., CBE.

Robertson, *Prof.* Sir Rutherford Ness, Kt., CMG.

Robins, Sir Ralph Harry, Kt.

Robinson, Sir Albert Edward Phineas, Kt.

†Robinson, Sir Christopher Philipse, Bt. (1854).

Robinson, *Prof.* Sir (Edward) Austin (Gossage), Kt., CMG, OBE, FBA.

Robinson, Sir John James Michael Laud, Bt. (1660).

Robinson, *Rt. Hon.* Sir Kenneth, Kt.

Robinson, Sir Niall Bryan Lynch-, Bt., DSC (1920).

Robinson, Sir Wilfred Henry Frederick, Bt. (1908).

Robotham, *Hon.* Sir Lascelles Lister, Kt.

Robson, *Prof.* Sir James Gordon, Kt., CBE.

Robson, Sir John Adam, KCMG.

Robson, Sir Thomas Buston, Kt., MBE.

Roch, *Hon.* Sir John Ormond, Kt.

Roche, Sir David O'Grady, Bt. (1838).

Rodger, Sir William Glendinning, Kt., OBE.

Rodgers, Sir John Charles, Bt. (1964).

Rodrigues, Sir Alberto Maria, Kt., CBE, ED.

Roe, *Air Chief Marshal* Sir Rex David, GCB, AFC.

Rogers, Sir Frank Jarvis, Kt.

Rogers, *Air Chief Marshal* Sir John Robson, KCB, CBE.

Rogers, Sir Philip James, Kt., CBE.

Roll, *Rev.* Sir James William Cecil, Bt. (1921).

Rooke, Sir Denis Eric, Kt., CBE.

Roper, *Hon.* Sir Clinton Marcus, Kt.

Ropner, Sir John Bruce Woollacott, Bt. (1952).

Ropner, Sir Robert Douglas, Bt. (1904).

Roscoe, Sir Robert Bell, KBE.

Rose, Sir Alec Richard, Kt.

Rose, *Hon.* Sir Christopher Dudley Roger, Kt.

Rose, Sir Clive Martin, GCMG.

Rose, Sir David Lancaster, Bt. (1874).

Rose, Sir Julian Day, Bt. (1872 and 1909).

Rosier, *Air Chief Marshal* Sir Frederick Ernest, GCB, CBE, DSO.

Roskill, Sir Ashton Wentworth, Kt., QC.

Ross, Sir Alexander, Kt.

Ross, Sir Archibald David Manisty, KCMG.

Ross, Sir (James) Keith, Bt., RD, FRCS (1960).

Ross, Sir Lewis Nathan, Kt., CMG.

Rosser, Sir Melvyn Wynne, Kt.

Rossi, Sir Hugh Alexis Louis, Kt., MP.

Rostron, Sir Frank, Kt., MBE.

Roth, *Prof.* Sir Martin, Kt., MD, FRCP.

Rothenstein, Sir John Knewstub Maurice, Kt., CBE, PH.D.

Rothnie, Sir Alan Keir, KCVO, CMG.

Rothschild, Sir Evelyn Robert Adrian de, Kt.

Rougier, *Hon.* Sir Richard George, Kt.

Rous, Sir Anthony Gerald Roderick, KCMG, OBE.

Row, *Hon.* Sir John Alfred, Kt.

Row, *Cdr.*, Sir Philip John, KCVO, OBE, RN.

Rowe, Sir Henry Peter, KCB, QC.

Rowe-Ham, Sir David Kenneth, GBE.

Rowell, Sir John Joseph, Kt., CBE.

Rowland, *Air Marshal* Sir James Anthony, KBE, DFC, AFC.

Rowlands, *Air Marshal* Sir John Samuel, GC, KBE.

Rowley, Sir Charles Robert, Bt. (1836).

Rowley, Sir Joshua Francis, Bt. (1786).

Rowling, *Rt. Hon.* Sir Wallace Edward, KCMG.

Rowntree, Sir Norman Andrew Forster, Kt.

Roxburgh, *Vice-Adm.* Sir John Charles Young, KCB, CBE, DSO, DSC.

Royden, Sir Christopher John, Bt. (1905).

Rucker, Sir Arthur Nevil, KCMG, CB, CBE.

Rumbold, Sir Henry John Sebastian, Bt. (1779).

Rumbold, Sir (Horace) Algernon (Fraser), KCMG, CIE.

Rumbold, Sir Jack Seddon, Kt.

Runciman, *Hon.* Sir James Cochran Stevenson (Sir Steven Runciman), Kt., CH.

Rusby, *Vice-Adm.* Sir Cameron, KCB, MVO.

Russell, Sir Archibald Edward, Kt., CBE, FRS.

Russell, Sir Charles Ian, Bt. (1916).

Russell, Sir Evelyn Charles Sackville, Kt.

Russell, Sir George Michael, Bt. (1812).

Russell, Sir (Robert) Mark, KCMG.

Russell, Sir Spencer Thomas, Kt.

Russell, *Rt. Hon.* Sir (Thomas) Patrick, Kt.

Rutter, Sir Frank William Eden, KBE.

†Ryan, Sir Derek Gerald, Bt. (1919).

Rycroft, Sir Richard Newton, Bt. (1784).

Ryrie, Sir William Sinclair, KCB.

Sainsbury, Sir Robert James, Kt.

St. Aubyn, Sir (John) Arscott Molesworth-, Bt. (1689).

†St. George, Sir George Bligh, Bt. (I. 1766).

St. Johnston, Sir Kerry, Kt.

Sainty, Sir John Christopher, KCB.

Sakzewski, Sir Albert, Kt.

Salt, Sir Anthony Houlton, Bt. (1869).

Salt, Sir (Thomas) Michael John, Bt. (1899).

Samuel, Sir Jon Michael Glen, Bt. (1898).

Samuelson, Sir (Bernard) Michael (Francis), Bt. (1884).

Sandberg, Sir Michael Graham Ruddock, Kt., CBE.

Sanders, Sir Robert Tait, KBE, CMG.

Sanderson, Sir (Frank Philip) Bryan, Bt. (1920).

Sandilands, Sir Francis Edwin Prescott, Kt., CBE.

Sarei, Sir Alexis Holyweek, Kt., CBE.

Sarell, Sir Roderick Francis Gisbert, KCMG, KCVO.

Sargant, Sir (Henry) Edmund, Kt.

Saunders, *Hon.* Sir John Anthony Holt, Kt., CBE, DSO, MC.

Saunders, Sir Owen Alfred, Kt., D.SC., FRS.

Saunders, Sir Peter, Kt.

Sauzier, Sir (André) Guy, Kt., CBE, ED.

Savage, Sir Ernest Walter, Kt.

Savile, Sir James Wilson Vincent, Kt., OBE.

Saville, *Hon.* Sir Mark Oliver, Kt.

Savory, Sir Reginald Charles Frank, Kt., CBE.

Say, *Rt. Rev.* Richard David, KCVO.

Schiemann, *Hon.* Sir Konrad Hermann Theodor, Kt.

Scholey, Sir David Gerald, Kt., CBE.

Scholey, Sir Robert, Kt., CBE.

Scholtens, Sir James Henry, KCVO.

Schubert, Sir Sydney, Kt.

Schultz, Sir (Joseph) Leopold, Kt., OBE.

Schuster, Sir (Felix) James Moncrieff, Bt., OBE (1906).

Scipio, Sir Hudson Rupert, Kt.

Scoon, Sir Paul, GCMG, GCVO, OBE.

Scoones, *Maj.-Gen.* Sir Reginald Laurence, KBE, CB, DSO.

Scopes, Sir Leonard Arthur, KCVO, CMG, OBE.

Scott, Sir Anthony Percy, Bt. (1913).

Scott, Sir (Charles) Hilary, Kt.

Scott, Sir (Charles) Peter, KBE, CMG.

Scott, Sir David Aubrey, GCMG.

†Scott, Sir Dominic James Maxwell, Bt. (1642).

Scott, Sir Ian Dixon, KCMG, KCVO, CIE.

Scott, Sir James Walter, Bt. (1962).

Scott, Sir Kenneth Bertram Adam, KCVO, CMG.

Scott, Sir Michael, KCVO, CMG.

Scott, Sir Oliver Christopher Anderson, Bt. (1909).

Scott, *Prof.* Sir Philip John, KBE.

Scott, *Hon.* Sir Richard Rashleigh Folliott, Kt.

Scott, Sir Terence Charles Stuart Morrison-, Kt., DSC, D.SC.

Scott, Sir Walter, Bt. (1907).

Scott, *Rear-Adm.* Sir (William) David (Stewart), KBE, CB.

Scowen, Sir Eric Frank, Kt., MD, D.SC., Ll.D., FRCP, FRCS.

Scrivenor, Sir Thomas Vaisey, Kt., CMG.

Seale, Sir John Henry, Bt. (1838).

Seaman, Sir Keith Douglas, KCVO, OBE.

Sebright, Sir Peter Giles Vivian, Bt. (1626).

Seccombe, Sir (William) Vernon Stephen, Kt.

Secombe, Sir Harry Donald, Kt., CBE.

Seconde, Sir Reginald Louis, KCMG, CVO.

Seely, Sir Nigel Edward, Bt. (1896).

Seeto, Sir Ling James, Kt., MBE.

Seeyave, Sir Rene Sow Choung, Kt., CBE.

Selby, Sir Kenneth, Kt.

Seligman, Sir Peter Wendel, Kt., CBE.

Sells, Sir David Perronet, Kt.

Senior, Sir Edward Walters, Kt., CMG.

Sergeant, Sir Patrick, Kt.

Series, Sir (Joseph Michel) Emile, Kt., CBE.

Serpell, Sir David Radford, KCB, CMG, OBE.

Seton, Sir Iain Bruce, Bt. (s. 1663).

Seton, Sir Robert James, Bt. (s. 1683).

Severne, *Air Vice-Marshal* Sir John de Milt, KCVO, OBE, AFC.

Sewell, Sir (John) Allan, Kt., ISO.

Seymour, *Cdr.* Sir Michael Culme-, Bt., RN (1809).

Shakerley, Sir Geoffrey Adam, Bt. (1838).

Shakespeare, Sir William Geoffrey, Bt. (1942).

Shapland, Sir William Arthur, Kt.

Sharp, Sir Adrian, Bt. (1922).

Sharp, Sir George, Kt., OBE.

Sharp, Sir Kenneth Johnston, Kt., TD.

Sharp, Sir Milton Reginald, Bt. (1920).

Sharp, Sir Richard Lyall, KCVO, CB.

Sharp, Sir (William Harold) Angus, KBE, QPM.

Sharpe, *Hon.* Sir John Henry, Kt., CBE.

Sharpe, Sir Reginald Taaffe, Kt., QC.

Shattock, Sir Gordon, Kt.

Shaw, Sir Brian Piers, Kt.

Shaw, Sir (Charles) Barry, Kt., CB, QC.

Shaw, Sir (John) Giles (Dunkerley), Kt., MP.

Shaw, Sir John Michael Robert Best-, Bt. (1665).

Shaw, Sir Michael Norman, Kt., MP.

Shaw, Sir Robert, Bt. (1821).

Shaw, Sir Roy, Kt.

Shaw, Sir Run Run, Kt., CBE.

Sheen, *Hon.* Sir Barry Cross, Kt.

Sheffield, Sir Reginald Adrian Berkeley, Bt. (1755).

Shehadie, Sir Nicholas Michael, Kt., OBE.

Sheil, *Hon.* Sir John, Kt.

Shelbourne, Sir Philip, Kt.

Sheldon, *Hon.* Sir (John) Gervase (Kensington), Kt.

Shelley, Sir John Richard, Bt. (1611).

Shelton, Sir William Jeremy Masefield, Kt., MP.

Shepheard, Sir Peter Faulkner, Kt., CBE.

Shepherd, Sir Peter Malcolm, Kt., CBE.

Sheppard, Sir Allen John George, Kt.

Shepperd, Sir Alfred Joseph, Kt.

Sherlock, Sir Philip Manderson, KBE.

Sherman, Sir Alfred, Kt.

Sherman, Sir Louis, Kt., OBE.

Shields, Sir Neil Stanley, Kt., MC.

Shields, Sir Robert, Kt., MD.

Shiffner, Sir Henry David, Bt. (1818).

Shillington, Sir (Robert Edward) Graham, Kt., CBE.

Shock, Sir Maurice, Kt.

Sholl, *Hon.* Sir Reginald Richard, Kt.

Shone, Sir Robert Minshull, Kt., CBE.

Short, *Brig.* Sir Noel Edward Vivian, Kt., MBE, MC.

Shuckburgh, Sir (Charles Arthur) Evelyn, GCMG, CB.

Shuckburgh, Sir Rupert Charles Gerald, Bt. (1660).

Siaguru, Sir Anthony Michael, KBE.

Sich, Sir Rupert Leigh, Kt., CB.

Siddall, Sir Norman, Kt., CBE.

Sidey, *Air Marshal* Sir Ernest Shaw, KBE, CB, MD.

Sie, Sir Banja Tejan-, GCMG.

Simeon, Sir John Edmund Barrington, Bt. (1815).

Simmons, *Air Marshal* Sir Michael George, KCB, AFC.

Simonet, Sir Louis Marcel Pierre, Kt., CBE.

Simpson, *Hon.* Sir Alfred Henry, Kt.

Simpson, Sir Joseph Trevor, KBE.

Simpson, Sir William James, Kt.

Sinclair, Sir Clive Marles, Kt.

Sinclair, Sir George Evelyn, Kt., CMG, OBE.

Sinclair, Sir Ian McTaggart, KCMG, QC.

Sinclair, *Prof.* Sir Keith, Kt., CBE.

Sinclair, *Air Vice-Marshal* Sir Laurence Frank, GC, KCB, CBE, DSO.

†Sinclair, Sir Patrick Robert Richard, Bt. (s. 1704).

Sinclair, Sir Ronald Ormiston, KBE.

Singh, *Hon.* Sir Vijay Raghubir, Kt.

Singhania, Sir Padampat, Kt.

Singleton, Sir Edward Henry Sibbald, Kt.

Sinnamon, Sir Hercules, Kt., OBE.

Sisson, Sir Roy, Kt.

Sitwell, Sir (Sacheverell) Reresby, Bt. (1808).

Skeet, Sir Trevor Herbert Harry, Kt., MP.

Skeggs, Sir Clifford George, Kt.

Skingsley, *Air Chief Marshal* Sir Anthony Gerald, KCB.

Skinner, Sir Thomas Edward, KBE.

Skinner, Sir (Thomas) Keith (Hewitt), Bt. (1912).

Skipwith, Sir Patrick Alexander d'Estoteville, Bt. (1622).

Skyrme, Sir (William) Thomas (Charles), KCVO, CB, CBE, TD.

Slack, Sir William Willatt, KCVO, FRCS.

Slade, Sir Benjamin Julian Alfred, Bt. (1831).

Slade, *Rt. Hon.* Sir Christopher John, Kt.

Slaney, *Prof.* Sir Geoffrey, KBE.

Slater, *Vice-Adm.* Sir John Cunningham Kirkwood, KCB, LVO.

†Sleight, Sir Richard, Bt. (1920).

Slimmings, Sir William Kenneth MacLeod, Kt., CBE.

Sloman, Sir Albert Edward, Kt., CBE.

Slynn, *Hon.* Sir Gordon, Kt.

Smallpeice, Sir Basil, KCVO.

Smallwood, *Air Chief Marshal* Sir Denis Graham, GBE, KCB, DSO, DFC.

Smart, *Prof.* Sir George Algernon, Kt., MD, FRCP.

Smart, Sir Jack, Kt., CBE.

Smedley, Sir Harold, KCMG, MBE.

Smeeton, *Vice-Adm.* Sir Richard Michael, KCB, MBE.

Smiley, Sir Hugh Houston, Bt. (1903).

Smirk, Sir (Frederick) Horace, KBE, MD.

Smith, Sir Alan, Kt., CBE, DFC.

Smith, Sir Alexander Mair, Kt., Ph.D.

Smith, Sir Charles Bracewell-, Bt. (1947).

Smith, Sir Christopher Sydney Winwood, Bt. (1809).

Smith, Sir Cyril, Kt., MBE, MP.

Smith, *Prof.* Sir David Cecil, Kt., FRS.

Smith, Sir David Iser, KCVO.

Smith, Sir Dudley (Gordon), Kt., MP.

Smith, *Maj.-Gen.* Sir (Francis) Brian Wyldbore-, Kt., CB, DSO, OBE.

Smith, *Prof.* Sir (Francis) Graham, Kt., FRS.

Smith, Sir (Frank) Ewart, Kt.

Smith, *Col.* Sir Henry Abel, KCMG, KCVO, DSO.

Smith, Sir Howard Frank Trayton, GCMG.

Smith, *Hon.* Sir James Alfred, Kt., CBE, TD.

Smith, Sir (James) Eric, Kt., CBE, SC.D., FRS.

Smith, Sir John Hamilton-Spencer-, Bt. (1804).

Smith, Sir John Kenneth Newson-, Bt. (1944).

Smith, Sir John Lindsay Eric., Kt., CBE.

Smith, Sir John Wilson, Kt., CBE.

Smith, Sir Leslie Edward George, Kt.

Smith, Sir Raymond Horace, KBE.

Smith, Sir Reginald Beaumont, Kt.

Smith, Sir Richard Rathbone Vassar-, Bt., TD (1917).

Smith, Sir (Richard) Robert Law-, Kt., CBE, AFC.

Smith, Sir Robert Courtney, Kt., CBE.

Smith, Sir Robert Hill, Bt. (1945).

Smith, *Air Marshal* Sir Roy David Austen-, KBE, CB, DFC.

Smith, Sir (Thomas) Gilbert, Bt. (1897).

Smith, *Adm.* Sir Victor Alfred Trumper, KBE, CB, DSC.

Smith, Sir William Reardon Reardon-, Bt. (1920).

Smith, Sir (William) Reginald Verdon, Kt.

Smith, Sir (William) Richard Prince-, Bt. (1911).

Smithers, *Prof.* Sir David Waldron, Kt., MD.

Smithers, Sir Peter Henry Berry Otway, Kt., VRD, D.Phil.

Smithers, *Hon.* Sir Reginald Allfree, Kt.

Smyth, Sir Thomas Weyland Bowyer-, Bt. (1661).

Smyth, Sir Timothy John, Bt. (1955).

Snelling, Sir Arthur Wendell, KCMG, KCVO.

Snelson, Sir Edward Alec Abbott, KBE.

Soame, Sir Charles John Buckworth-Herne-, Bt. (1697).

Sobell, Sir Michael, Kt.

Sobers, Sir Garfield St. Auburn, Kt.

Solomon, Sir David Arnold, Kt., MBE.

Solomons, *Hon.* Sir (Louis) Adrian, Kt.

Solti, Sir Georg, KBE.

Somare, *Rt. Hon.* Sir Michael Thomas, GCMG, CH.

Somers, *Rt. Hon.* Sir Edward Jonathan, Kt.

Somerset, Sir Henry Beaufort, Kt., CBE.

Somerville, *Brig.* Sir John Nicholas, Kt., CBE.

†Somerville, Sir Quentin Charles Somerville Agnew-, Bt. (1957).

Somerville, Sir Robert, KCVO.

Sopwith, Sir Charles Ronald, Kt.

Soutar, *Air Marshal* Sir Charles John Williamson, KBE.

South, Sir Arthur, Kt.

Southby, Sir John Richard Bilbe, Bt. (1937).

Southern, Sir Richard William, Kt., FBA.

Southern, Sir Robert, Kt., CBE.

Southey, Sir Robert John, Kt., CMG.

Southward, Sir Leonard Bingley, Kt., OBE.

Southward, Sir Ralph, KCVO, FRCP.

Southwood, *Prof.* Sir (Thomas) Richard (Edmund), Kt., FRS.

Southworth, Sir Frederick, Kt., QC.

Souyave, *Hon.* Sir (Louis) Georges, Kt.

Sowrey, *Air Marshal* Sir Frederick Beresford, KCB, CBE, AFC.

Soysa, Sir Warusahennedige Abraham Bastian, Kt., CBE.

Sparkes, Sir Robert Lyndley, Kt.

Sparrow, Sir John, Kt.

Spearman, Sir Alexander Young Richard Mainwaring, Bt. (1840).

Speed, Sir Robert William Arney, Kt., CB, QC.

Speelman, Sir Cornelis Jacob, Bt. (1686).

Speight, *Hon.* Sir Graham Davies, Kt.

Speir, Sir Rupert Malise, Kt.

Spencer, Sir Kelvin Tallent, Kt., CBE, MC.

Spender, *Prof.* Sir Stephen Harold, Kt., CBE.

Spicer, Sir James Wilton, Kt., MP.

Spicer, Sir Peter James, Bt. (1906).

Spooner, Sir James Douglas, Kt.

Spotswood, *Marshal of the Royal Air Force* Sir Denis Frank, GCB, CBE, DSO, DFC.

Spratt, *Col.* Sir Greville Douglas, GBE, TD.

Spreckley, Sir (John) Nicholas (Teague), KCVO, CMG.

Springer, Sir Hugh Worrell, GCMG, GCVO, CBE.

Spry, *Brig.* Sir Charles Chambers Fowell, Kt., CBE, DSO.

Spry, *Hon.* Sir John Farley, Kt.

Stabb, *Hon.* Sir William Walter, Kt., QC.

Stack, *Air Chief Marshal* Sir (Thomas) Neville, KCB, CVO, CBE, AFC.

Stainton, Sir (John) Ross, Kt., CBE.

Stakis, Sir Reo Argiros, Kt.

Stallard, Sir Peter Hyla Gawne, KCMG, CVO, MBE.

Stallworthy, Sir John Arthur, Kt., FRCS.

Stamer, Sir (Lovelace) Anthony, Bt. (1809).

Stanbridge, *Air Vice-Marshal* Sir Brian Gerald Tivy, KCVO, CBE, AFC.

Stanford, *Adm.* Sir Peter Maxwell, GCB, LVO.

Stanier, *Brig.* Sir Alexander Beville Gibbons, Bt., DSO, MC (1917).

Stanier, *Field Marshal* Sir John Wilfred, GCB, MBE.

Stanley, *Rt. Hon.* Sir John Paul, Kt., MP.

†Staples, Sir Thomas, Bt. (I. 1628).

Stapleton, Sir (Henry) Alfred, Bt. (1679).

Stark, Sir Andrew Alexander Steel, KCMG, CVO.

Starke, *Hon.* Sir John Erskine, Kt.

Starkey, Sir John Philip, Bt. (1935).

Starrit, Sir James, KCVO.

Statham, Sir Norman, KCMG, CVO.

Staughton, *Rt. Hon.* Sir Christopher Stephen Thomas Jonathan Thayer, Kt.

Staveley, Sir John Malfroy, KBE, MC.

Staveley, *Admiral of the Fleet* Sir William Doveton Minet, GCB.

Stear, *Air Marshal* Sir Michael James Douglas, KCB, CBE.

Steedman, *Air Chief Marshal* Sir Alasdair (Alexander McKay Sinclair), GCB, CBE, DFC.

Steel, Sir David Edward Charles, Kt., DSO, MC, TD.

Steel, *Rt. Hon.* Sir David Martin Scott, KBE, MP.

Steel, *Maj.* Sir (Fiennes) William Strang, Bt. (1938).

Steel, Sir James, Kt., CBE.

Steele, Sir (Philip John) Rupert, Kt.

Steere, Sir Ernest Henry Lee-, KBE.

Stenhouse, Sir Nicol, Kt.

Stening, *Col.* Sir George Grafton Lees, Kt., ED.

Stephen, *Rt. Hon.* Sir Ninian Martin, GCMG, GCVO, KBE.

Stephenson, Sir Henry Upton, Bt. (1936).

Stephenson, *Rt. Hon.* Sir John Frederick Eustace, Kt.

Sterling, Sir Jeffrey Maurice, Kt., CBE.

Sternberg, Sir Sigmund, Kt.

Stevens, Sir Laurence Houghton, Kt., CBE.

Stevenson, *Vice-Adm.* Sir (Hugh) David, KBE.

Stevenson, Sir Simpson, Kt.

Stewart, Sir Alan, KBE.

Stewart, Sir Alan d'Arcy, Bt. (l. 1623).

Stewart, Sir David Brodribb, Bt., TD (1960).

Stewart, Sir David James Henderson-, Bt. (1957).

Stewart, Sir Edward Jackson, Kt.

Stewart, *Prof.* Sir Frederick Henry, Kt., ph.D., FRS, FRSE.

Stewart, Sir Houston Mark Shaw-, Bt., MC, TD (s. 1667).

Stewart, Sir Hugh Charlie Godfray, Bt. (1803).

Stewart, Sir James Douglas, Kt.

Stewart, Sir John Keith Watson, Bt. (1920).

Stewart, Sir Michael Norman Francis, KCMG, OBE.

Stewart, Sir Robertson Huntly, Kt., CBE.

Stewart, Sir Ronald Compton, Bt. (1937).

Steyn, *Hon.* Sir Johan Van Zyl, Kt.

Stibbon, *Gen.* Sir John James, KCB, OBE.

Stinson, Sir Charles Alexander, KBE.

Stirling, Sir Alexander John Dickson, KBE, CMG.

Stirling, *Col.* Sir (Archibald) David, Kt., DSO, OBE.

Stockdale, Sir Arthur Noel, Kt.

Stockdale, Sir Thomas Minshull, Bt. (1960).

Stocker, *Rt. Hon.* Sir John Dexter, Kt., MC, TD.

Stoddart, *Wg. Cdr.* Sir Kenneth Maxwell, KCVO, AE.

Stoker, *Prof.* Sir Michael George Parke, Kt., CBE, FRCP, FRS, FRSE.

Stokes, Sir John Heydon Romaine, Kt., MP.

Stone, *Prof.* Sir (John) Richard (Nicholas), Kt., CBE.

Stones, Sir William Frederick, Kt., OBE.

Stonhouse, Sir Philip Allan, Bt. (1628).

Stonor, *Air Marshal* Sir Thomas Henry, KCB.

Storey, *Hon.* Sir Richard, Bt. (1960).

Stormonth Darling, Sir James Carlisle, Kt., CBE, MC, TD.

Stott, Sir Adrian George Ellingham, Bt. (1920).

Stow, Sir Christopher Philipson-, Bt., DFC (1907).

Stow, Sir John Montague, GCMG, KCVO.

Stowe, Sir Kenneth Ronald, GCB, CVO.

Stracey, Sir John Simon, Bt. (1818).

Strachey, Sir Charles, Bt. (1801).

Stradling Thomas, Sir John, Kt., MP.

Straker, Sir Michael Ian Bowstead, Kt., CBE.

Strawson, *Prof.* Sir Peter Frederick, Kt., FBA.

Street, *Hon.* Sir Laurence Whistler, KCMG.

Streeton, Sir Terence George, KBE, CMG.

Strong, Sir Roy Colin, Kt., ph.D., FSA.

Stronge, Sir James Anselan Maxwell, Bt. (1803).

Stroud, *Prof.* Sir (Charles) Eric, Kt., FRCP.

Strutt, Sir Nigel Edward, Kt., TD.

Stuart, Sir James Keith, Kt.

Stuart, Sir Kenneth Lamonte, Kt.

†Stuart, Sir Phillip Luttrell, Bt. (1660).

Stuart-Smith, *Rt. Hon.* Sir Murray, Kt.

Stubblefield, Sir (Cyril) James, Kt., D.SC., FRS.

Stubbs, Sir James Wilfrid, KCVO, TD.

Stucley, *Lt.* Sir Hugh George Coplestone Bampfylde, Bt. (1859).

Studd, Sir Edward Fairfax, Bt. (1929).

Studd, Sir Peter Malden, GBE, KCVO.

Studholme, Sir Henry William, Bt. (1956).

Style, *Lt. Cdr.* Sir Godfrey William, Kt., CBE, DSC, RN.

†Style, Sir William Frederick, Bt. (1627).

Suffield, Sir (Henry John) Lester, Kt.

Sugden, Sir Arthur, Kt.

Sullivan, Sir Desmond John, Kt.

Sullivan, Sir Richard Arthur, Bt. (1804).

Summerfield, *Hon.* Sir John Crampton, Kt., CBE.

Summers, Sir Felix Roland Brattan, Bt. (1952).

Summerson, Sir John Newenham, Kt., CH, CBE, FBA, FSA.

Sunderland, *Prof.* Sir Sydney, Kt., CMG.

Surridge, Sir (Ernest) Rex (Edward), Kt., CMG.

Sutherland, Sir John Brewer, Bt. (1921).

Sutherland, Sir Maurice, Kt.

Sutherland, Sir William George MacKenzie, Kt.

Suttie, Sir (George) Philip Grant-, Bt. (s. 1702).

Sutton, Sir Frederick Walter, Kt., OBE.

Sutton, *Air Marshal* Sir John Matthias Dobson, KCB.

Sutton, Sir Richard Lexington, Bt. (1772).

Sutton, Sir Stafford William Powell Foster-, KBE, CMG, QC.

Swaffield, Sir James Chesebrough, Kt., CBE, RD.

Swallow, Sir William, Kt.

Swan, Sir John William David, KBE.

Swan, *Lt.-Col.* Sir William Bertram, KCVO, CBE, TD.

Swann, Sir Anthony Charles Christopher, Bt., CMG, OBE (1906).

Swanwick, Sir Graham Russell, Kt., MBE.

Swartz, *Hon.* Sir Reginald William Colin, KBE, ED.

Swayne, Sir Ronald Oliver Carless, Kt., MC.

Swinson, Sir John Henry Alan, Kt., OBE.

Swinton, *Maj.-Gen.* Sir John, KCVO, OBE.

Swire, Sir Adrian Christopher, Kt.

Swire, Sir John Anthony, Kt., CBE.

Swiss, Sir Rodney Geoffrey, Kt., OBE.

Swynnerton, Sir Roger John Massy, Kt., CMG, OBE, MC.

†Sykes, Sir Francis John Badcock, Bt. (1781).

Sykes, Sir John Charles Anthony le Gallais, Bt. (1921).

Sykes, Sir Tatton Christopher Mark, Bt. (1783).

Symington, *Prof.* Sir Thomas, Kt., MD, FRSE.

Symons, *Vice-Adm.* Sir Patrick Jeremy, KBE.

Synge, Sir Robert Carson, Bt. (1801).

Tait, *Adm.* Sir (Allan) Gordon, KCB, DSC.

Tait, Sir James Sharp, Kt., D.SC., LlD., ph.D.

Tait, Sir Peter, KBE.

Talbot, *Vice-Adm.* Sir (Arthur Allison) FitzRoy, KBE, CB, DSO.

Talbot, *Hon.* Sir Hilary Gwynne, Kt.

Tancred, Sir Henry Lawson-, Bt. (1662).

Tangaroa, *Hon.* Sir Tangoroa, Kt., MBE.

Tange, Sir Arthur Harold, Kt., CBE.

Tansley, Sir Eric Crawford, Kt., CMG.

Tapp, *Maj.-Gen.* Sir Nigel Prior Hanson, KBE, CB, DSO.

Tapsell, Sir Peter Hannay Bailey, Kt., MP.

Tate, *Lt.-Col.* Sir Henry, Bt. (1898).

Taukala, Sir David Dawea, Kt., MBE.

Tavaiqia, *Ratu* Sir Josaia, KBE.

Tavare, Sir John, Kt., CBE.

Taylor, *Lt.-Gen.* Sir Allan Macnab, KBE, MC.

Taylor, Sir Alvin Burton, Kt.

Taylor, Sir (Arthur) Godfrey, Kt.

Taylor, Sir Cyril Julian Hebden, Kt.

Taylor, Sir George, Kt., D.SC., FRS, FRSE.

Taylor, Sir Henry Milton, Kt.

Taylor, Sir James, Kt., MBE, D.SC.

Taylor, Sir John Lang, KCMG.

Taylor, Sir Michael Goodiff, Kt., CBE.

Taylor, Sir Nicholas Richard Stuart, Bt. (1917).

Taylor, *Rt. Hon.* Sir Peter Murray, Kt.

Taylor, *Prof.* Sir William, Kt., CBE.

Tebbit, Sir Donald Claude, GCMG.

Te Heuheu, Sir Hepi Hoani, KBE.

Telford, Sir Robert, Kt., CBE.

Temple, Sir Ernest Sanderson, Kt., MBE, QC.

Temple, Sir John Meredith, Kt.

Temple, Sir Rawden John Afamado, Kt., CBE, QC.

Temple, *Maj.* Sir Richard Anthony Purbeck, Bt., MC (1876).

Templeton, Sir John Marks, Kt.

Tennant, *Capt.* Sir Iain Mark, KT.

Tennant, Sir Peter Frank Dalrymple, Kt., CMG, OBE.

Teo, Sir Fiatau Penitala, GCMG, GCVO, ISO, MBE.

Terry, Sir George Walter Roberts, Kt., CBE, QPM.

Terry, Sir John Elliott, Kt.

Terry, Sir Michael Edward Stanley Imbert-, Bt. (1917).

Terry, *Air Chief Marshal* Sir Peter David George, GCB, AFC.

Tetley, Sir Herbert, KBE, CB.

Tett, Sir Hugh Charles, Kt.

Thiess, Sir Leslie Charles, Kt., CBE.

Thomas, Sir Derek Morison David, KCMG.

Thomas, Sir Frederick William, Kt.

Thomas, Sir (Godfrey) Michael (David), Bt. (1694).

Thomas, Sir Jeremy Cashel, KCMG.

Thomas, Sir John Maldwyn, Kt.

Thomas, Sir Keith Vivian, Kt.

Thomas, Sir Robert Evan, Kt.

Thomas, *Hon.* Sir Swinton Barclay, Kt.

Thomas, Sir William James Cooper, Bt., TD (1919).

Thomas, Sir (William) Michael (Marsh), Bt. (1918).

Thomas, *Adm.* Sir (William) Richard Scott, KCB, OBE.

Thompson, Sir Christopher Peile, Bt. (1890).

Thompson, Sir Edward Hugh Dudley, Kt., MBE, TD.

Thompson, *Vice-Adm.* Sir Hugh Leslie Owen, KBE.

Thompson, Sir (Humphrey) Simon Meysey-, Bt. (1874).

Thompson, *Hon.* Sir John, Kt.

Thompson, Sir Paul Anthony, Bt. (1963).

Thompson, Sir Peter Anthony, Kt.

Thompson, Sir Ralph Patrick, Kt.

Thompson, Sir Richard Hilton Marler, Bt. (1963).

Thompson, Sir Robert Grainger Ker, KBE, CMG, DSO, MC.

Thompson, Sir (Thomas) Lionel Tennyson, Bt. (1806).

Thomson, Sir Adam, Kt., CBE.

Thomson, Sir Evan Rees Whitaker, Kt.

Thomson, Sir (Frederick Douglas) David, Bt. (1929).

Thomson, Sir Ivo Wilfrid Home, Bt. (1925).

Thomson, Sir John, KBE, TD.

Thomson, Sir John Adam, GCMG.

Thomson, Sir John (Ian) Sutherland, KBE, CMG.

Thorn, Sir John Samuel, Kt., OBE.

Thorne, *Maj.-Gen.* Sir David Calthrop, KBE.

Thorne, Sir Peter Francis, KCVO, CBE.

Thornton, *Lt.-Gen.* Sir Leonard Whitmore, KCB, CBE.

Thornton, Sir Peter Eustace, KCB.

Thorold, Sir Anthony Henry, Bt., OBE, DSC (1642).

Thorpe, *Hon.* Sir Mathew Alexander, Kt.

Thouron, Sir John Rupert Hunt, KBE.

†Throckmorton, Sir Anthony John Benedict, Bt. (1642).

Thwaites, Sir Bryan, Kt., Ph.D.

Thwin, Sir U, Kt.

Tibbits, *Capt.* Sir David Stanley, Kt., DSC.

Tickell, Sir Crispin Charles Cervantes, GCMG, KCVO.

Tidbury, Sir Charles Henderson, Kt.

Tikaram, Sir Moti, KBE.

Tilney, Sir John Dudley Robert Tarleton, Kt., TD.

Tippet, *Vice-Adm.* Sir Anthony Sanders, KCB.

Tippett, Sir Michael Kemp, Kt., OM, CH, CBE.

Tirvengadum, Sir Harry Krishnan, Kt.

Tizard, Sir John Peter Mills, Kt.

Tod, *Air Marshal* Sir John Hunter Hunter-, KBE, CB.

Todd, Sir Ian Pelham, KBE, FRCS.

Todd, *Hon.* Sir (Reginald Stephen) Garfield, Kt.

†Tollemache, Sir Lyonel Humphry John, Bt. (1793).

Tololo, Sir Alkan, KBE.

Tomkins, Sir Alfred George, Kt., CBE.

Tomkins, Sir Edward Emile, GCMG, CVO.

Tomlinson, *Prof.* Sir Bernard Evans, Kt., CBE.

Tomlinson, Sir (Frank) Stanley, KCMG.

Tooley, Sir John, Kt.

Tooth, Sir (Hugh) John Lucas-, Bt. (1920).

Tooth, *Hon.* Sir (Seymour) Douglas, Kt.

ToRobert, Sir Henry Thomas, KBE.

Tory, Sir Geofroy William, KCMG.

Touche, Sir Anthony George, Bt. (1920).

Touche, Sir Rodney Gordon, Bt. (1962).

Tovey, Sir Brian John Maynard, KCMG.

ToVue, Sir Ronald, Kt., OBE.

Townsend, *Rear-Adm.* Sir Leslie William, KCVO, CBE.

Townsing, Sir Kenneth Joseph, Kt., CMG.

Traherne, Sir Cennydd George, KG, TD.

Traill, Sir Alan Towers, GBE.

Trant, *Gen.* Sir Richard Brooking, KCB.

Travancore, *Maj.-Gen.* HH the Maharajah of, GCSI, GCIE.

Travers, Sir Thomas à'Beckett, Kt.

Treacher, *Adm.* Sir John Devereux, KCB.

Trehane, Sir (Walter) Richard, Kt.

Trelawny, Sir John Barry Salusbury-, Bt. (1628).

Trench, Sir Nigel Clive Cosby, KCMG.

Trench, Sir Peter Edward, Kt., CBE, TD.

Trescowthick, Sir Donald Henry, KBE.

Trethowan, Sir (James) Ian (Raley), Kt.

Trethowan, *Prof.* Sir William Henry, Kt., CBE, FRCP.

Trevelyan, Sir George Lowthian, Bt. (1874).

Trevelyan, Sir Norman Irving, Bt. (1662).

Trewby, *Vice-Adm.* Sir (George Francis) Allan, KCB.

Tritton, Sir Anthony John Ernest, Bt. (1905).

†Trollope, Sir Anthony Simon, Bt. (1642).

Trotman-Dickenson, Sir Aubrey Fiennes, Kt.

Trotter, Sir Ronald Ramsay, Kt.

Troubridge, Sir Thomas Richard, Bt. (1799).

Troughton, Sir Charles Hugh Willis, Kt., CBE, MC, TD.

Troup, *Vice-Adm.* Sir (John) Anthony (Rose), KCB, DSC.

Trowbridge, *Rear-Adm.* Sir Richard John, KCVO.

Truscott, Sir George James Irving, Bt. (1909).

Tuck, Sir Bruce Adolph Reginald, Kt. (1910).

Tucker, *Hon.* Sir Richard Howard, Kt.

Tudor, *Hon.* Sir James Cameron, KCMG.

Tudor Evans, *Hon.* Sir Haydn, Kt.

Tugendhat, Sir Christopher Samuel, Kt.

Tuite, Sir Christopher Hugh, Bt., Ph.D. (1622).

Tuivaga, Sir Timoci Uluiburotu, Kt.

Tuke, Sir Anthony Favill, Kt.

Tupper, Sir Charles Hibbert, Bt. (1888).

Turbott, Sir Ian Graham, Kt., CMG, CVO.

Turing, Sir John Dermot, Bt. (s. 1638).

Turnbull, Sir George Henry, Kt.

Turnbull, Sir Richard Gordon, GCMG.

Turner, *Rt. Hon.* Sir Alexander Kingcome, KBE.

Turner, *Adm.* Sir (Arthur) Francis, KCB, DSC.

Turner, *Hon.* Sir Michael John, Kt.

Tuti, *Rev.* Dudley, KBE.

Tuzo, *Gen.* Sir Harry Craufurd, GCB, OBE, MC.

Twiss, *Adm.* Sir Frank Roddam, KCB, KCVO, DSC.

Tyler, *Maj.-Gen.* Sir Leslie Norman, KBE, CB.

Tyree, Sir (Alfred) William, Kt., OBE.

Tyrrell, Sir Murray Louis, KCVO, CBE.

Tyrwhitt, Sir Reginald Thomas Newman, Bt. (1919).

Udoma, *Hon.* Sir (Egbert) Udo, Kt.

Unsworth, Hon. Sir Edgar Ignatius Godfrey, Kt., CMG.

Unwin, Sir (James) Brian, KCB.

Ure, Sir John Burns, KCMG, LVO.

Urquhart, Sir Brian Edward, KCMG, MBE.

Urwick, Sir Alan Bedford, KCVO, CMG.

Usher, Sir Leonard Gray, KBE.

†Usher, Sir Robert Edward, Bt. (1899).

Ustinov, Sir Peter Alexander, Kt., CBE.

Vallat, Sir Francis Aimé, GBE, KCMG, QC.

Vallings, *Vice-Adm.* Sir George Montague Francis, KCB.

Vanderfelt, Sir Robin Victor, KBE.

van der Post, Sir Laurens Jan, Kt., CBE.

Vane, Sir John Robert, Kt., D.Phil., D.SC., FRS.

Vangeke, *Most Rev.* Louis, KBE.

Vanneck, *Air Cdre.* Hon. Sir Peter Beckford Rutgers, GBE, CB, AFC.

van Straubenzee, Sir William Radcliffe, Kt., MBE.

Vasquez, Sir Alfred Joseph, Kt., CBE, QC.

Vaughan, Sir (George) Edgar, KBE.

Vaughan, Sir Gerard Folliott, Kt., MP, FRCP.

Vavasour, *Cdr.* Sir Geoffrey William, Bt., DSC, RN (1828).

Veale, Sir Alan John Ralph, Kt.

Veira, Sir Philip Henry, KBE.

Verco, Sir Walter John George, KCVO.

Verney, Sir John, Bt., MC, TD (1946).

Verney, Sir Ralph Bruce, Bt., KBE (1818).

Vernon, Sir James, Kt., CBE.

Vernon, Sir Nigel John Douglas, Bt. (1914).

Vesey, Sir (Nathaniel) Henry (Peniston), Kt., CBE.

Vestey, Sir (John) Derek, Bt. (1921).

Vial, Sir Kenneth Harold, Kt., CBE.

Vick, Sir (Francis) Arthur, Kt., OBE, Ph.D.

Vickers, *Lt.-Gen.* Sir Richard Maurice Hilton, KCB, MVO, OBE.

Victoria, Sir (Joseph Aloysius) Donatus, Kt., CBE.

Villiers, Sir Charles Hyde, Kt., MC.

Vincent, *Gen.* Sir Richard Frederick, GBE, KCB, DSO.

Vincent, Sir William Percy Maxwell, Bt. (1936).

Vinelott, *Hon.* Sir John Evelyn, Kt.

Vines, Sir William Joshua, Kt., CMG.

Vyse, *Lt.-Gen.* Sir Edward Dacre Howard-, KBE, CB, MC.

Vyvyan, Sir John Stanley, Bt. (1645).

Waddell, Sir Alexander Nicol Anton, KCMG, DSC.

Waddell, Sir James Henderson, Kt., CB.

Wade, *Prof.* Sir Henry William Rawson, Kt., QC, FBA.

Wade, *Air Chief Marshal* Sir Ruthven Lowry, KCB, DFC.

Wade-Gery, Sir Robert Lucian, KCMG, KCVO.

Wagner, Sir Anthony Richard, KCB, KCVO.

Waite, *Hon.* Sir John Douglas, Kt.

Wake, Sir Hereward, Bt. MC (1621).

Wakefield, Sir (Edward) Humphry (Tyrell), Bt. (1962).

Wakefield, Sir Norman Edward, Kt.

Wakefield, Sir Peter George Arthur, KBE, CMG.

Wakeford, *Air Marshal* Sir Richard Gordon, KCB, OBE, MVO, AFC.

Wakeley, Sir John Cecil Nicholson, Bt., FRCS (1952).

Wakeman, Sir (Offley) David, Bt. (1828).

Walker, *Rev.* Alan Edgar, Kt., OBE.

Walker, Sir Allan Grierson, Kt., QC.

Walker, *Gen.* Sir Antony Kenneth Frederick, KCB.

Walker, Sir Baldwin Patrick, Bt. (1856).

Walker, Sir (Charles) Michael, GCMG.

Walker, Sir Edward Ronald, Kt., CBE.

Walker, Sir Gervas George, Kt.

Walker, *Maj.* Sir Hugh Ronald, Bt. (1906).

Walker, Sir James Graham, Kt., MBE.

Walker, Sir James Heron, Bt. (1868).

Walker, Sir Michael Leolin Forestier-, Bt. (1835).

Walker, Sir Patrick Jeremy, KCB.

Walker, *Gen.* Sir Walter Colyear, KCB, CBE, DSO.

Wall, *Dr. Hon.* Sir Gerard Aloysius, Kt.

Wall, Sir Patrick Henry Bligh, Kt., MC, VRD.

Wall, Sir Robert William, Kt., OBE.

Wallace, Sir Ian James, Kt., CBE.

Waller, *Hon.* Sir (George) Mark, Kt.

Waller, *Rt. Hon.* Sir George Stanley, Kt., OBE.

Waller, Sir (John) Keith, Kt., CBE.

Waller, Sir John Stainer, Bt. (1815).

Waller, Sir Robert William, Bt. (I. 1780).

Walley, Sir John, KBE, CB.

Walsh, Sir Alan, Kt., D.SC., FRS.

Walsh, Prof. Sir John Patrick, KBE.

Walsham, *Rear-Adm.* Sir John Scarlett Warren, Bt., CB, OBE (1831).

Walter, Sir Harold Edward, Kt.

Walters, *Prof.* Sir Alan Arthur, Kt.

Walters, Sir Dennis Murray, Kt., MBE, MP.

Walters, Sir Frederick Donald, Kt.

Walters, Sir Peter Ingram, Kt.

Walters, Sir Roger Talbot, KBE, FRIBA.

Walton, Sir John Robert, Kt.

Wan, Sir Wamp, Kt., MBE.

Wanstall, *Hon.* Sir Charles Gray, Kt.

Ward, *Hon.* Sir Alan Hylton, Kt.

Ward, Sir Arthur Hugh, KBE.

Ward, *Gen.* Sir Dudley, GCB, KBE, DSO.

Ward, Sir John Guthrie, GCMG.

Ward, Sir Joseph James Laffey, Bt. (1911).

Ward, *Maj.-Gen.* Sir Philip John Newling, KCVO, CBE.

Ward, Sir Terence George, Kt., CBE.

Wardale, Sir Geoffrey Charles, KCB.

Wardlaw, Sir Henry (John), Bt. (s. 1631).

Wardle, Sir Thomas Edward Jewell, Kt.

Waring, Sir (Alfred) Holburt, Bt. (1935).

Warmington, *Lt.-Cdr.* Sir Marshall George Clitheroe, Bt., RN (1908).

Warner, Sir (Edward Courtenay) Henry, Bt. (1910).

Warner, Sir Edward Redston, KCMG, OBE.

Warner, Sir Frederick Archibald, GCVO, KCMG.

Warner, Sir Frederick Edward, Kt., FRS.

Warner, *Hon.* Sir Jean-Pierre Frank Eugene, Kt.

Warnock, Sir Geoffrey James, Kt.

Warren, Sir Brian Charles Pennefather, Bt. (1784).

Warren, Sir Frederick Miles, KBE.

Warren, Sir (Harold) Brian (Seymour), Kt.

Wass, Sir Douglas William Gretton, GCB.

Waterhouse, *Hon.* Sir Ronald Gough, Kt.

Waterlow, Sir Christopher Rupert, Bt. (1873).

Waterlow, Sir (James) Gerard, Bt. (1930).

Waters, *Lt.-Gen.* Sir (Charles) John, KCB, CBE.

Wates, Sir Christopher Stephen, Kt.

Watkins, *Rt. Hon.* Sir Tasker, VC, GBE.

Watson, Sir Bruce Dunstan, Kt.

Watson, Sir Francis John Bagott, KCVO, FBA, FSA.

Watson, Sir (James) Andrew, Bt. (1866).

Watson, Sir John Forbes Inglefield-, Bt. (1895).

Watson, Sir Michael Milne-, Bt., CBE (1937).

Watson, Sir (Noel) Duncan, KCMG.

Watson, *Vice-Adm.* Sir Philip Alexander, KBE, MVO.

Watt, *Surgeon Vice-Adm.* Sir James, KBE, FRCS.

Watt, Sir James Harvie-, Bt. (1945).

Watts, Sir Arthur Desmond, KCMG.

Watts, *Lt.-Gen.* Sir John Peter Barry Condliffe, KBE, CB, MC.

Wauchope, Sir Roger (Hamilton) Don-, Bt. (s. 1667).

Way, Sir Richard George Kitchener, KCB, CBE.

Weatherall, *Prof.* Sir David John, Kt., FRS.

Weatherall, *Vice-Adm.* Sir James Lamb, KBE.

Weatherstone, Sir Dennis, KBE.

Weaver, Sir Tobias Rushton, Kt., CB.

Webb, *Lt.-Gen.* Sir Richard James Holden, KBE, CB.

Webb, Sir Thomas Langley, Kt.

Webster, *Very Rev.* Alan Brunskill, KCVO.

Webster, *Vice-Adm.* Sir John Morrison, KCB.

Webster, *Hon.* Sir Peter Edlin, Kt.

Wedderburn, Sir Andrew John Alexander Ogilvy-, Bt. (1803).

Wedgwood, Sir (Hugo) Martin, Bt. (1942).

Weeks, Sir Hugh Thomas, Kt., CMG.

Weinberg, Sir Mark Aubrey, Kt.

Weipers, *Prof.* Sir William Lee, Kt.

Weir, Sir Michael Scott, KCMG.

Weir, Sir Roderick Bignell, Kt.

Welby, Sir (Richard) Bruno Gregory, Bt. (1801).

Welch, Sir John Reader, Bt. (1957).

Weld, *Col.* Sir Joseph William, Kt., OBE, TD.

Weldon, Sir Anthony William, Bt. (I. 1723).

Welensky, *Rt. Hon.* Sir Roy, (Roland), KCMG.

Wellings, Sir Jack Alfred, Kt., CBE.

Wells, Sir Charles Maltby, Bt., TD (1944).

Wells, Sir John Julius, Kt.

West-Russell, *Hon.* Sir David Sturrock, Kt.

Westbrook, Sir Neil Gowanloch, Kt., CBE.

Westerman, Sir (Wilfred) Alan, Kt., CBE.

Wheatley, Sir (George) Andrew, Kt., CBE.

Wheeler, Sir Ernest Richard, KCVO, MBE.

Wheeler, Sir Frederick Henry, Kt., CBE.

Wheeler, Sir Harry Anthony, Kt., OBE.

Wheeler, *Air Chief Marshal* Sir (Henry) Neil (George), GCB, CBE, DSO, DFC, AFC.

Wheeler, Sir John Daniel, Kt., MP.

Wheeler, Sir John Hieron, Bt. (1920).

Wheeler, *Hon.* Sir Kenneth Henry, Kt.

Wheler, Sir Edward Woodford, Bt. (1660).

Whishaw, Sir Charles Percival Law, Kt.

Whitaker, *Maj.* Sir James Herbert Ingham, Bt. (1936).

White, Sir Christopher Robert Meadows, Bt. (1937).

White, Sir Dick Goldsmith, KCMG, KBE.

White, Sir Frederick William George, KBE, ph.D., FRS.

White, Sir George Stanley James, Bt. (1904).

White, Sir Harold Leslie, Kt., CBE.

White, *Wg-Cdr.* Sir Henry Arthur Dalrymple-, Bt., DFC (1926).

White, *Hon.* Sir John Charles, Kt., MBE.

White, Sir John Woolmer, Bt. (1922).

White, Sir Lynton Stuart, Kt., MBE. TD.

White, *Adm.* Sir Peter, GBE.

White, Sir Thomas Astley Woollaston, Bt. (1802).

White, Sir (Vincent) Gordon (Lindsay), KBE.

Whitehead, Sir John Stainton, KCMG, CVO.

Whitehead, Sir Rowland John Rathbone, Bt. (1889).

Whiteley, Sir Hugo Baldwin Huntington-, Bt. (1918).

Whiteley, *Gen.* Sir Peter John Frederick, GCB, OBE, RM.

Whitford, *Hon.* Sir John Norman Keates, Kt.

Whitley, *Air Marshal* Sir John René, KBE, CB, DSO, AFC.

Whitmore, Sir Clive Anthony, GCB, CVO.

Whitmore, Sir John Henry Douglas, Bt. (1954).

Whitteridge, Sir Gordon Coligny, KCMG, OBE.

Whittle, *Air Cdre.* Sir Frank, OM, KBE, CB, FRS.

Wickerson, Sir John Michael, Kt.

Wicks, Sir James Albert, Kt.

Wigan, Sir Alan Lewis, Bt. (1898).

Wiggin, Sir John Henry, Bt., MC (1892).

Wigglesworth, Sir Vincent Brian, Kt., CBE, MD, FRS.

Wigram, *Rev. Canon* Sir Clifford Woolmore, Bt. (1805).

Wilbraham, Sir Richard Baker, Bt. (1776).

Wilford, Sir (Kenneth) Michael, GCMG.

Wilkins, Sir Graham John, Kt.

Wilkins, *Lt.-Gen.* Sir Michael Compton Lockwood, KCB, OBE.

Wilkinson, Sir (David) Graham (Brook) Bt. (1941).

Wilkinson, *Prof.* Sir Denys Haigh, Kt., FRS.

Wilkinson, *Prof.* Sir Geoffrey, Kt., FRS.

Wilkinson, *Rt. Hon.* Sir Nicolas Christopher Henry Browne-, Kt.

Wilkinson, Sir Peter Allix, KCMG, DSO, OBE.

Wilkinson, Sir Philip William, Kt.

Wilkinson, Sir William Henry Nairn, Kt.

Willatt, Sir (Robert) Hugh, Kt.

Willcocks, Sir David Valentine, Kt., CBE, MC.

Williams, Sir Alastair Edgcumbe James Dudley-, Bt. (1964).

Williams, Sir Alwyn, Kt., ph.D., FRS.

Williams, Sir (Arthur) Gareth Ludovic Emrys Rhys, Bt. (1918).

Williams, *Prof.* Sir Bruce Rodda, KBE.

Williams, *Adm.* Sir David, GCB.

Williams, Sir David Innes, Kt.

Williams, *Hon.* Sir Denys Ambrose, Kt.

Williams, Sir Donald Mark, Bt. (1866).

Williams, Sir Edgar Trevor, Kt., CB, CBE, DSO.

Williams, *Prof.* Sir (Edward) Dillwyn, Kt., FRCP.

Williams, *Hon.* Sir Edward Stratten, KCMG, KBE.

Williams, Sir Francis John Watkin, Bt., QC (1798).

Williams, Sir Henry Sydney, Kt., OBE.

Williams, Sir (John) Leslie, Kt., CBE.

Williams, Sir John Robert, KCMG.

Williams, Sir Leonard, KBE, CB.

Williams, Sir Osmond, Bt., MC (1909).

Williams, Sir Peter Watkin, Kt.

Williams, *Prof.* Sir Robert Evan Owen, Kt., MD, FRCP.

Williams, Sir (Robert) Philip Nathaniel, Bt. (1915).

Williams, Sir Robin Philip, Bt. (1953).

Williams, Sir (William) Maxwell (Harries), Kt.

Williamson, *Marshal of the Royal Air Force* Sir Keith Alec, GCB, AFC.

Williamson, Sir (Nicholas Frederick) Hedworth, Bt. (1642).

Willink, Sir Charles William, Bt. (1957).

Willis, *Hon.* Sir Eric Archibald, KBE, CMG.

Willis, *Vice-Adm.* Sir (Guido) James, KBE.

Willison, *Lt.-Gen.* Sir David John, KCB, OBE, MC.

Willison, Sir John Alexander, Kt., OBE.

Willoughby, *Maj.-Gen.* Sir John Edward Francis, KBE, CB.

Wills, Sir David Seton, Bt. (1904).

Wills, Sir (Hugh) David Hamilton, Kt., CBE, TD.

Wills, Sir John Spencer, Kt.

Wills, Sir John Vernon, Bt., TD (1923).

Wilmot, Sir Henry Robert, Bt. (1759).

Wilmot, *Cdr.* Sir John Assheton Eardley-, Bt., MVO, DSC, RN (1821).

Wilson, Sir Alan Herries, Kt., FRS.

Wilson, *Lt.-Gen.* Sir (Alexander) James, KBE, MC.

Wilson, Sir Angus Frank Johnstone, Kt., CBE.

Wilson, Sir Anthony, Kt.

Wilson, Sir Austin George, Kt., OBE.

Wilson, *Vice-Adm.* Sir Barry Nigel, KCB.

Wilson, Sir Charles Haynes, Kt.

Wilson, Sir David, Bt. (1920).

Wilson, Sir David Clive, KCMG.

Wilson, Sir David Mackenzie, Kt.

Wilson, Sir Geoffrey Masterman, KCB, CMG.

Wilson, Sir James William Douglas, Bt. (1906).

Wilson, Sir John Foster, Kt., CBE.

Wilson, Sir John Gardiner, Kt., CBE.

Wilson, Sir John Martindale, KCB.

Wilson, Sir (Mathew) Martin, Bt. (1874).

Wilson, Sir Reginald Holmes, Kt.

Wilson, Sir Robert, Kt., CBE.

Wilson, Sir Robert Donald, Kt.

Wilson, *Rt. Rev.* Roger Plumpton, KCVO, DD.

Wilson, Sir Roland, KBE.

Wilson, *Hon.* Sir Ronald Darling, KBE, CMG.

Wilton, Sir (Arthur) John, KCMG, KCVO, MC.

Wiltshire, Sir Frederick Munro, Kt., CBE.

Windeyer, Sir Brian Wellingham, Kt.

Wingate, *Capt.* Sir Miles Buckley, KCVO.

Winnifrith, Sir (Alfred) John (Digby), KCB.

Winnington, Sir Francis Salwey William, Bt. (1755).

Winskill, *Air Cdre.* Sir Archibald Little, KCVO, CBE, DFC.

Winterbottom, Sir Walter, Kt., CBE.

Wiseman, Sir John William, Bt. (1628).

Wolfson, Sir Brian Gordon, Kt.

Wolfson, Sir David, Kt.

Wolfson, Sir Isaac, Bt., FRS (1962).

Wolseley, Sir Charles Garnet Richard Mark, Bt. (1628).

Wolseley, Sir Garnet, Bt. (I 1745).

Wolstenholme, Sir Gordon Ethelbert Ward, Kt., OBE.

Wombwell, Sir George Philip Frederick, Bt. (1778).

Womersley, Sir Peter John Walter, Bt. (1945).

Wontner, Sir Hugh Walter Kingwell, GBE, CVO.

Wood, Sir Anthony John Page, Bt. (1837).

Wood, Sir David Basil Hill-, Bt. (1921).

Wood, Sir Frederick Ambrose Stuart, Kt.

Wood, Sir Henry Peart, Kt., CBE.

Wood, *Prof.* Sir John Crossley, Kt., CBE.

Wood, *Hon.* Sir John Kember, Kt., MC.

Wood, Sir Martin Francis, Kt., OBE.

Wood, Sir Russell Dillon, KCVO, VRD.

Wood, Sir William Alan, KCVO, CB.

Woodcock, Sir John, Kt., CBE, QPM.

Woodfield, Sir Philip John, KCB, CBE.

Woodhouse, *Rt. Hon.* Sir (Arthur) Owen, KBE, DSC.

Woodroffe, *Most Rev.* George Cuthbert Manning, KBE.

Woodroofe, Sir Ernest George, Kt., Ph.D.

Woodruff, *Prof.* Sir Michael Francis Addison, Kt., D.SC., FRS, FRCS.

Woods, Sir Colin Philip Joseph, KCVO, CBE.

Woods, *Most Rev.* Frank, KBE, DD.

Woods, *Rt. Rev.* Robert Wilmer, KCMG, KCVO.

Woodward, *Hon.* Sir (Albert) Edward, Kt., OBE.

Woodward, *Adm.* Sir John Forster, GBE, KCB.

Woolf, *Rt. Hon.* Sir Harry Kenneth, Kt.

Woolf, Sir John, Kt.

Woollaston, Sir (Mountford) Tosswill, Kt.

Wordie, Sir John Stewart, Kt., CBE, VRD.

Worsley, *Gen.* Sir Richard Edward, GCB, OBE.

Worsley, Sir (William) Marcus (John), Bt. (1838).

Worthington, *Air Vice-Marshal* Sir Geoffrey Luis, KBE, CB.

Wraight, Sir John Richard, KBE, CMG.

Wraxall, Sir Charles Frederick Lascelles, Bt. (1813).

Wrey, Sir (Castel Richard) Bourchier, Bt. (1628).

Wright, Sir Allan Frederick, KBE.

Wright, Sir Denis Arthur Hepworth, GCMG.

Wright, Sir Edward Maitland, Kt., D.Phil.,Ll.D., D.SC., FRSE.

Wright, *Hon.* Sir (John) Michael, Kt.

Wright, Sir (John) Oliver, GCMG, GCVO, DSC.

Wright, Sir Patrick Richard Henry, GCMG.

Wright, Sir Paul Hervé Giraud, KCMG, OBE.

Wright, Sir Richard Michael Cory-, Bt. (1903).

Wright, Sir Rowland Sydney, Kt., CBE.

Wrightson, Sir Charles Mark Garmondsway, Bt. (1900).

Wykeham, *Air Marshal* Sir Peter Guy, KCB, DSO, OBE, DFC, AFC.

Wylie, Sir Campbell, Kt., ED, QC.

Wynn, Sir David Watkin Williams-, Bt. (1688).

Yang, *Hon.* Ti Liang, Kt.

Yapp, Sir Stanley Graham, Kt.

Yarrow, Sir Eric Grant, Bt., MBE (1916).

Yeend, Sir Geoffrey John, Kt., CBE.

Yellowlees, Sir Henry, KCB.

Yocklunn, Sir John (Soong Chung), KCVO.

Youens, Sir Peter William, Kt., CMG, OBE.

Young, Sir Brian Walter Mark, Kt.

Young, *Lt.-Gen.* Sir David Tod, KBE, CB, DFC.

Young, Sir George Samuel Knatchbull, Bt., MP (1813).

Young, *Hon.* Sir Harold William, KCMG.

Young, Sir John Kenyon Roe, Bt. (1821).

Young, *Hon.* Sir John McIntosh, KCMG.

Young, Sir Leslie Clarence, Kt., CBE.

Young, Sir Norman Smith, Kt.

Young, Sir Richard Dilworth, Kt.

Young, Sir Robert Christopher Mackworth-, GCVO.

Young, Sir Roger William, Kt.

Young, Sir Stephen Stewart Templeton, Bt. (1945).

Young, Sir William Neil, Bt. (1769).

Younger, *Maj.-Gen.* Sir John William, Bt., CBE (1911).

Younger, Sir William McEwan, Bt., DSO (1964).

Zeidler, Sir David Ronald, Kt., CBE.

Zoleveke, Sir Gideon Pitabose, KBE.

Zunz, Sir Gerhard Jacob (Jack), Kt.

Zurenuo, *Rt. Rev.* Zurewe Kamong, Kt., OBE.

Baronetcies Extinct (since last issue).—Houldsworth (UK, 1956); Jessel (UK, 1917) by the death of Baron Jessel.

DAMES GRAND CROSS AND DAMES COMMANDERS

Style.—'Dame' before forename and surname, followed by appropriate post-nominal initials. Where such an award is made to a lady already in enjoyment of a higher title, the appropriate initials follow her name.
Husband.—Untitled.
For forms of address, *see* page 151.

Dame Grand Cross and Dames Commander are the higher classes for women of the Order of the Bath, the Order of St. Michael and St. George, the Royal Victorian Order, and the Order of the British Empire. Dames Grand Cross rank after the wives of Baronets and before the wives of Knights Grand Cross. Dames Commanders rank after the wives of Knights Grand Cross and before the wives of Knights Commanders.

Honorary Dame Commanders may be conferred on women who are citizens of countries of which the Queen is not head of state.

LIST OF DAMES

(Revised to Aug. 31, 1990)
Women Peers in their own right and Life Peers are not included in this list.

HM Queen Elizabeth The Queen Mother, KG, KT, CI, GMVO.
HRH The Princess Royal, GCVO.
HRH The Princess Margaret, Countess of Snowdon, CI, GCVO.
HRH The Duchess of Gloucester, GCVO.
HRH The Princess Alice, Duchess of Gloucester, GCB, CI, GCVO, GBE.
HRH The Duchess of Kent, GCVO.
HRH The Princess Alexandra of Kent, GCVO.
Abaijah, Dame Josephine, DBE.
Abel Smith, Lady, DCVO.
Abergavenny, The Marchioness of, DCVO.
Albemarle, The Countess of, DBE.
Anderson, Dame Judith, DBE.
Anderson, *Brig.* Hon. Dame Mary Mackenzie (Mrs. Pihl), DBE.
Anglesey, The Marchioness of, DBE.
Ashcroft, Dame Peggy, DBE.
Baker, Dame Janet Abbott (Mrs. Shelley), DBE.
Baring, Lady Rose Gwendolen Louisa, DCVO.
Barnes, Dame (Alice) Josephine (Mary Taylor), DBE, FRCP, FRCS.
Barrow, Dame (Ruth) Nita, GCMG.
Basset, Lady Elizabeth, DCVO.
Beaurepaire, Dame Beryl Edith, DBE.
Berry, Dame Alice Miriam, DBE.
Bishop, Dame (Margaret) Joyce, DBE.
Blaize, Dame Venetia Ursula, DBE.
Blaxland, Dame Helen Frances, DBE.
Booth, *Hon.* Dame Margaret Myfanwy Wood, DBE.
Bottomley, Dame Bessie Ellen, DBE.
Boyd, Dame Vivienne Myra, DBE.
Brazill, Dame Josephine (Sister Mary Philippa), DBE.
Breen, Dame Marie Freda, DBE.
Bridges, Dame Mary Patricia, DBE.
Brown, Dame Beryl Paston, DBE.
Brown, Dame Gillian Gerda, DCVO, CMG.
Browne, Lady Moyra Blanche Madeleine, DBE.
Bryans, Dame Anne Margaret, DBE.
Bryce, Dame Isabel Graham, DBE.
Burnside, Dame Edith, DBE.
Butler-Sloss, *Rt. Hon.* Dame (Ann) Elizabeth (Oldfield), DBE.
Buttfield, Dame Nancy Eileen, DBE.
Bynoe, Dame Hilda Louisa, DBE.

Cartwright, Dame Mary Lucy, DBE, SC.D., D.Phil., FRS.
Cartwright, Dame Silvia Rose, DBE.
Cayford, Dame Florence Evelyn, DBE.
Chesterton, Dame Elizabeth Ursula, DBE.
Clay, Dame Marie Mildred, DBE.
Clayton, Dame Barbara Evelyn (Mrs. Klyne), DBE.
Cleland, Dame Rachel, DBE.
Clode, Dame (Emma) Frances (Heather), DBE.
Coles, Dame Mabel Irene, DBE.
Conan Doyle, *Air Cmdt.* Dame Jean Lena Annette (Lady Bromet), DBE.
Cooper, Dame Whina, DBE.
Coulshed, Dame (Mary) Frances, DBE, TD.
Cozens, *Brig.* Dame (Florence) Barbara, DBE, RRC.
Crowe, Dame Sylvia, DBE.
Daws, Dame Joyce Margaretta, DBE.
De La Warr, Sylvia, Countess, DBE.
Dell, Dame Miriam Patricia, DBE.
Dench, Dame Judith Olivia (Mrs. Williams), DBE.
de Valois, Dame Ninette, CH, DBE.
Dickson, Dame Violet Penelope, DBE.
Donaldson, Dame (Dorothy) Mary (Lady Donaldson of Lymington), GBE.
Dugdale, Kathryn Edith Helen (Mrs. John Dugdale), DCVO.
Durack, Dame Mary (Mrs. H. C. Miller), DBE.
Emerton, Dame Audrey Caroline, DBE.
Fenner, Dame Peggy Edith, DBE, MP.
Fermoy, Ruth Sylvia, Lady, DCVO, OBE.
Fitton, Dame Doris Alice (Mrs. Mason), DBE.
Fonteyn, Dame Margot, DBE.
Fookes, Dame Janet Evelyn, DBE, MP.
Fraser, Dame Dorothy Rita, DBE.
Friend, Dame Phyllis Muriel, DBE.
Frink, Dame Elisabeth, DBE, RA.
Frost, Dame Phyllis Irene, DBE.
Fry, Dame Margaret Louise, DBE.
Gallagher, Dame Monica Josephine, DBE.
Gardiner, Dame Helen Louisa, DBE, MVO.
Gibbs, Dame Molly Peel, DBE.

Giles, *Air Cmdt.* Dame Pauline (Mrs. Parsons), DBE, RRC.
Godwin, Dame (Beatrice) Anne, DBE.
Golding, Dame (Cecilie) Monica, DBE.
Goodman, Dame Barbara, DBE.
Gordon, Dame Minita Elmira, GCMG, GCVO.
Grafton, The Duchess of, GCVO.
Green, Dame Mary Georgina, DBE.
Grey, Dame Beryl Elizabeth (Mrs. Svenson), DBE.
Guilfoyle, Dame Margaret Georgina Constance, DBE.
Hall, Dame Catherine Mary, DBE.
Hambleden, Patricia, Viscountess, GCVO.
Hammond, Dame Joan Hood, DBE.
Hedley-Miller, Dame Mary Elizabeth, DCVO, CB.
Heilbron, *Hon.* Dame Rose, DBE.
Henrison, Dame Anne Elizabeth Rosina, DBE.
Herbison, Dame Jean Marjory, DBE, CMG.
Hercus, *Hon.* Dame (Margaret) Ann, DCMG.
Hill, Dame Elizabeth Mary, DBE.
Hill, *Air Cdre.* Dame Felicity Barbara, DBE.
Hiller, Dame Wendy (Mrs. Gow), DBE.
Holland-Martin, Rosamund Mary, Lady, DBE.
Horsman, Dame Dorothea Jean, DBE.
Howard, Dame Rosemary Christian, DBE.
Hunter, Dame Pamela, DBE.
Hurley, *Prof.* Dame Rosalinde (Mrs. Gortvai), DBE.
Hussey, Lady Susan Katharine, DCVO.
Isaacs, Dame Albertha Madeline, DBE.
James, Dame Naomi Christine, DBE.
Jenkins, Dame (Mary) Jennifer (Lady Jenkins of Hillhead), DBE.
Jessel, Dame Penelope, DBE.
Jones, Dame Gwyneth (Mrs. Haberfeld-Jones), DBE.
Kekedo, Dame Mary, DBE, BEM.
Kelleher, Dame Joan, DBE.
Kellett-Bowman, Dame (Mary) Elaine, DBE, MP.
Kettlewell, *Cmdt.* Dame Marion Mildred, DBE.

Kilroy, Dame Alix Hester Marie (Lady Meynell), DBE.

Kirk, Dame (Lucy) Ruth, DBE.

Knight, Dame (Joan Christabel) Jill, DBE, MP.

Kramer, *Prof.* Dame Leonie Judith, DBE.

Lancaster, Dame Jean, DBE.

Lister, Dame Unity Viola, DBE.

Litchfield, Dame Ruby Beatrice, DBE.

Lloyd, *Prof.* Dame June Kathleen, DBE, FRCP.

Lowrey, *Air Cmdt.* Dame Alice, DBE, RRC.

Lynn, Dame Vera (Mrs. Lewis), DBE.

Mackinnon, Dame (Una) Patricia, DBE.

Macknight, Dame Ella Annie Noble, DBE, MD.

Macmillan of Ovenden, Katharine, Viscountess, DBE.

Maconchy, Dame Elizabeth Violet (Mrs. Le Fanu), DBE.

Mann, Dame Ida Caroline, DBE, D.SC., FRCS.

Markova, Dame Alicia, DBE.

Maxwell-Scott, Dame Jean Mary Monica, DCVO.

Menzies, Dame Pattie Maie, GBE.

Metge, Dr. Dame (Alice) Joan, DBE.

Miles, Dame Margaret, DBE.

Miller, Dame Mabel Flora Hobart, DBE.

Mitchell, *Hon.* Dame Roma Flinders, DBE.

Morrison, *Hon.* Dame Mary Anne, DCVO.

Mueller, Dame Anne Elisabeth, DCB.

Munro, Dame Alison, DBE.

Murdoch, Dame Elisabeth Joy, DBE.

Murdoch, Dame (Jean) Iris (Mrs. Bayley), DBE.

Murray, Dame (Alice) Rosemary, DBE, D.Phil.

Niccol, Dame Kathleen Agnes, DBE.

Norris, Dame Ada May, DBE, CMG.

Ollerenshaw, Dame Kathleen Mary, DBE, D.Phil.

Park, Dame Merle Florence (Mrs. Bloch), DBE.

Parker, Dame Marjorie Alice Collett, DBE.

Paterson, Dame Betty Fraser Ross, DBE.

Pepys, Lady (Mary) Rachel, DCVO.

Plowden, The Lady, DBE.

Prendergast, Dame Simone Ruth, DBE.

Prentice, Dame Winifred Eva, DBE.

Preston, Dame Frances Olivia Campbell-, DCVO.

Purves, Dame Daphne Helen, DBE.

Pyke, Lady, DBE.

Quinn, Dame Sheila Margaret Imelda, DBE.

Railton, *Brig.* Dame Mary, DBE.

Railton, Dame Ruth (Mrs. King), DBE.

Rankin, Lady Jean Margaret Florence, DCVO.

Raven, Dame Kathleen Annie (Mrs. Ingram), DBE.

Reader-Harris, Dame (Muriel) Diana, DBE.

Riddelsdell, Dame Mildred, DCB, CBE.

Ridley, Dame (Mildred) Betty, DBE.

Rivett-Drake, *Brig.* Dame Jean Elizabeth Rivett, DBE.

Roberts, Dame Joan Howard, DBE.

Roberts, Dame Shelagh Marjorie, DBE.

Robertson, *Cmdt.* Dame Nancy Margaret, DBE.

Roe, Dame Raigh Edith, DBE.

Rue, Dame (Elsie) Rosemary, DBE.

Salas, Dame Margaret Laurence, DBE.

Saunders, Dame Cicely Mary Strode, OM, DBE, FRCP.

Scott, Dame Catherine Campbell, DBE.

Scott, Dame Margaret, (Dame Catherine Margaret Mary Denton), DBE.

Seccombe, Dame Joan Anna Dalziel, DBE.

Shenfield, Dame Barbara Estelle, DBE.

Sherlock, *Prof.* Dame Sheila Patricia Violet, DBE, MD, FRCP.

Smieton, Dame Mary Guillan, DBE.

Smith, Dame Margaret Natalie (Maggie) (Mrs. Cross), DBE.

Smith, Dame Margot, DBE.

Snagge, Dame Nancy Marion, DBE.

Soames, Mary, Lady, DBE.

Stark, Dame Freya (Mrs. Perowne), DBE.

Stephens, *Air Cmdt.* Dame Anne, DBE.

Stewart, Dame Muriel Acadia, DBE.

Sutherland, Dame Joan (Mrs. Bonynge), DBE.

Szaszy, Dame Miraka Petricevich, DBE.

Taylor, Dame Jean Elizabeth, DCVO.

Te Atairangikaahu, Te Arikinui, Dame, DBE.

Te Kanawa, Dame Kiri Janette (Mrs. Park), DBE.

Tilney, Dame Guinevere (Lady Tilney), DBE.

Tizard, Dame Catherine Anne, DBE.

Tokiel, Dame Rosa, DBE.

Turner, *Brig.* Dame Margot, DBE, RRC.

Tyrwhitt, *Brig.* Dame Mary Joan Caroline, DBE, TD.

Uatioa, Dame Mere, DBE.

Uvarov, Dame Olga, DBE.

Varley, Dame Joan Fleetwood, DBE.

Vaughan, Dame Janet Maria (Mrs. Gourlay), DBE, FRS.

Wakehurst, Margaret, Lady, DBE.

Walker, Dame Susan Armour, DBE.

Wall, (Alice) Anne, (Mrs. Michael Wall), DCVO.

Warburton, Dame Anne Marion, DCVO, CMG.

Waterhouse, Dame Rachel Elizabeth, DBE, Ph.D.

Wedega, Dame Alice, DBE.

Wedgwood, Dame (Cicely) Veronica, OM, DBE.

Weston, Dame Margaret Kate, DBE.

Williamson, Dame (Elsie) Marjorie, DBE, Ph.D.

Winstone, Dame Dorothy Gertrude, DBE, CMG.

Wormald, Dame Ethel May, DBE.

Yonge, Dame (Ida) Felicity (Ann), DBE.

THE ORDER OF ST. JOHN

The Most Venerable Order of the Hospital of St. John of Jerusalem

St. John's Gate, Clerkenwell, EC1M 4DA

Grand Prior, HRH The Duke of Gloucester, GCVO.

Lord Prior, The Lord Grey of Naunton, GCMG, GCVO, OBE.
Chancellor, The Lord Vestey.

CHIEFS OF CLANS AND NAMES IN SCOTLAND

Only chiefs of whole Names or Clans are included, except certain special instances (marked *), who though not chiefs of a whole name, were, or are, for some reason, (e.g. the Macdonald forfeiture), independent. Under decision (*Campbell-Gray*, 1950) that a bearer of a 'double or triple-barrelled' surname cannot be held chief of a part of such, several others cannot be included in the list at present.

THE ROYAL HOUSE: HM The Queen

AGNEW: Sir Crispin Agnew of Lochnaw, Bt., 6 Palmerston Road, Edinburgh.

ANSTRUTHER: Sir Ralph Anstruther of that Ilk, Bt., KCVO, MC, Balcaskie, Pittenweem, Fife.

ARBUTHNOTT: The Viscount of Arbuthnott, CBE, DSC, Arbuthnott House, Laurencekirk, Kincardineshire.

BARCLAY: Peter C. Barclay of that Ilk, Gatemans, Stratford St. Mary, Colchester, Essex.

BORTHWICK: The Lord Borthwick, TD, Crookston, Heriot, Midlothian.

BOYD: The Lord Kilmarnock, Casa de Mondragon, Ronda (Malaga), Spain.

BOYLE: The Earl of Glasgow, Kelburn, Fairlie, Ayrshire.

BRODIE: Ninian Brodie of Brodie, Brodie Castle, Forres, Morayshire.

BRUCE: The Earl of Elgin and Kincardine, KT, Broomhall, Dunfermline, Fife.

BUCHAN: David S. Buchan of Auchmacoy, Auchmacoy, Ellon, Aberdeenshire.

BURNETT: J. C. A. Burnett of Leys, Crathes Castle, Kincardineshire.

CAMERON: Col. Sir Donald Cameron of Lochiel, KT, CVO, TD, Achnacarry, Spean Bridge, Inverness-shire.

CAMPBELL: The Duke of Argyll, Inveraray, Argyll.

CARMICHAEL: Richard J. Carmichael of Carmichael, Carmichael, Thankerton, Biggar, Lanarkshire.

CARNEGIE: The Earl of Southesk, KCVO, Kinnaird Castle, Brechin.

CATHCART: Maj.-Gen. The Earl Cathcart, CB, DSO, MC, 2 Pembroke Gardens, W8.

CHARTERIS: The Earl of Wemyss and March, KT, Gosford House, Longniddry, East Lothian.

CLAN CHATTAN: M. K. Mackintosh of Clan Chattan, Maxwell Park, Gwelo, Zimbabwe.

CHISHOLM: Alastair Chisholm of Chisholm (*The Chisholm*), Silver Willows, Bury St. Edmunds.

COCHRANE: The Earl of Dundonald, Lochnell Castle, Ledaig, Argyllshire.

COLQUHOUN: Sir Ivar Colquhoun of Luss, Bt., Camstraddan, Luss, Dunbartonshire.

CRANSTOUN: vacant.

CRICHTON: Charles Crichton of that Ilk, Monzie, Perth.

DARROCH: Capt. Duncan Darroch of Gourock, The Red House, Branksome Park Road, Camberley, Surrey.

DEWAR: Kenneth M. J. Dewar of that Ilk and Vogrie, The Dower House, Grayshott, Nr. Hindhead, Surrey.

DRUMMOND: The Earl of Perth, PC, Stobhall, Perth.

DUNBAR: Sir Jean Dunbar of Mochrum, Bt., 45–55 39th Street, Long Island City, New York.

DUNDAS: David D. Dundas of Dundas, 8 Derna Road, Kenwyn 7700, South Africa.

DURIE: Raymond V. D. Durie of Durie, Court House, Pewsey, Wilts.

ELIOTT: Mrs. Margaret Eliott of Redheugh, Redheugh, Newcastleton, Roxburghshire.

ERSKINE: The Earl of Mar and Kellie, Claremont House, Alloa.

FARQUHARSON: Capt. A. A. C. Farquharson of Invercauld, MC, Invercauld, Braemar.

FERGUSSON: Sir Charles Fergusson of Kilkerran, Bt., Kilkerran, Maybole, Ayrshire.

FORBES: The Lord Forbes, KBE, Balforbes, Alford, Aberdeenshire.

FORSYTH: Alistair Forsyth of that Ilk, Ethie Castle, by Arbroath, Angus.

FRASER: The Lady Saltoun, Cairnbulg Castle, Fraserburgh, Aberdeenshire.

FRASER (OF LOVAT)*: The Lord Lovat, DSO, MC, TD, Balblair House, Beauly, Inverness-shire.

GAYRE: Lt.-Col. Robert Gayre of Gayre and Nigg, 1–3 Gloucester Lane, Edinburgh.

GORDON: The Marquess of Huntly, Aboyne Castle, Aberdeenshire.

GRAHAM: The Duke of Montrose, Auchmar, Drymen, Stirlingshire.

GRANT: The Lord Strathspey, 111 Elms Ride, West Wittering, W. Sussex.

GRIERSON: Sir Michael Grierson of Lag, Bt., 40C Palace Road, London.

HAIG: The Earl Haig, OBE, Bemersyde, Melrose, Roxburghshire.

HALDANE: Alexander N. C. Haldane of Gleneagles, Auchterarder, Perthshire.

HANNAY: Ramsey W. R. Hannay of Kirkdale and of that Ilk, Cardoness House, Gatehouse-of-Fleet, Kirkcudbrightshire.

HAY: The Earl of Erroll, Wolverton Farm, Wolverton, Basingstoke, Hants.

HENDERSON: John W. P. Henderson of Fordell, 7 Owen Street, Toowoomba, Queensland, Australia.

HUNTER: Neil A. Hunter of Hunterston, Tour d'Escas, Carretera d'Escas, La Massana, Andorra.

IRVINE OF DRUM: C. F. Irvine of Drum, 29 Forest Road, Hoylake, Wirral, Merseyside.

JARDINE: Sir Alexander Jardine of Applegirth, Bt., Ash House, Thwaites, Millom, Cumbria.

JOHNSTONE: The Earl of Annandale and Hartfell, Raehills, Lockerbie, Dumfriesshire.

KEITH: The Earl of Kintore, Glenton House, Rickarton, Stonehaven, Kincardineshire.

KENNEDY: The Marquess of Ailsa, OBE, Blanefield, Kirkoswald, Ayrshire.

KERR: The Marquess of Lothian, KCVO, Monteviot, Ancrum, Roxburghshire.

KINCAID: Mrs. Heather V. Kincaid of Kincaid, 4A Bristol Gardens, Brighton, E. Sussex.

LAMONT: Peter N. Lamont of that Ilk, St. Patrick's College, Manley, NSW 2095, Australia.

LEASK: Madam Leask of Leask, 1 Vincent Road, Sheringham, Norfolk.

LENNOX: Edward J. H. Lennox of that Ilk, Pools Farm, Downton on the Rock, Ludlow, Shropshire.

LESLIE: The Earl of Rothes, Tanglewood, West Tytherley, Salisbury, Wilts.

LINDSAY: The Earl of Crawford and Balcarres, PC, Balcarres, Colinsburgh, Fife.

LOCKHART: Angus H. Lockhart of the Lee, Newholme, Dunsyre, Lanark.

LUMSDEN: Gillem Lumsden of that Ilk and Blanerne, Kindersleigh, Bois Avenue, Chesham Bois, Amersham, Bucks.

MCBAIN: J. H. McBain of McBain, 7025, North Finger Rock Place, Tucson, Arizona, USA.

MALCOLM (MACCALLUM): Robin N. L. Malcolm of Poltalloch, Duntrune Castle, Lochgilphead, Argyll.

MACDONALD: The Lord Macdonald (*The Macdonald of Macdonald*), Ostaig House, Skye.

MACDONALD OF CLANRANALD*: Ranald A. Macdonald of Clanranald, 55 Compton Road, N1.

MACDONALD OF SLEAT (CLAN HUSTEAIN)*: Sir Ian Bosville Macdonald of Sleat, Bt., Thorpe Hall, Rudston, Driffield, N. Humberside.

MacDonell of Glengarry*: Air Cdre. Aeneas R. MacDonell of Glengarry, CB, DFC, Elonbank, Castle Street, Fortrose, Ross-shire.

MacDougall: vacant.

MacDowell: Fergus D. H. Macdowell of Garthland, 16 Tower Road, Nepean, Ontario, Canada.

MacGregor: Sir Gregor MacGregor of MacGregor, Bt., Bannatyne, Newtyle, Angus.

Mackay: The Lord Reay, 11 Wilton Crescent, SW1.

Mackenzie: The Earl of Cromartie, MC, TD, Castle Leod, Strathpeffer, Ross-shire.

Mackinnon: Madam Anne Mackinnon of Mackinnon, 16 Purleigh Road, Bridgewater, Somerset.

Mackintosh: The Mackintosh of Mackintosh, OBE, Moy Hall, Inverness.

MacLachlan: Madam Marjorie MacLachlan of MacLachlan, Castle Lachlan, Argyll.

MacLaren: Donald MacLaren of MacLaren and Achleskine, c/o Foreign and Commonwealth Office, London SW1.

Maclean: The Hon. Sir Lachlan Maclean of Duart, Bt., Duart Castle, Mull.

MacLennan: vacant.

MacLeod: J. MacLeod of MacLeod, Dunvegan Castle, Skye.

MacMillan: George MacMillan of MacMillan, Finlaystone, Langbank, Renfrewshire.

Macnab: J. C. Macnab of Macnab (*The Macnab*), Finlarig, Killin, Perthshire.

Macnaghten: Sir Patrick Macnaghten of Macnaghten and Dundarave, Bt., Dundarave, Bushmills, Co. Antrim.

Macneacail: Iain Macneacail of Macneacail and Scorrybreac, 12 Fox Street, Ballina, NSW, Australia.

MacNeil of Barra: Ian R. Macneil of Barra (*The Macneil of Barra*), Kisimul Castle, Barra.

Macpherson: The Hon. Sir William Macpherson of Cluny, TD, Newtown Castle, Blairgowrie, Perthshire.

MacThomas: Andrew P. C. MacThomas of Finegand, c/o The Clan MacThomas Society, 19 Warriston Avenue, Edinburgh 3.

Maitland: The Earl of Lauderdale, 12 St. Vincent Street, Edinburgh.

Makgill: The Viscount of Oxfuird, Hill House, St. Mary Bourne, Andover, Hants.

Mar: The Countess of Mar, St. Michael's Farm, Great Witley, Worcs.

Marjoribanks: William Marjoribanks of that Ilk, Kirklands of Forglen, Turriff, Aberdeenshire.

Matheson: Sir Torquhil Matheson of Matheson, Bt., Sanderwick Court, Frome, Somerset.

Menzies: David R. Menzies of Menzies, 20 Nardina Crescent, Dalkeith, Western Australia.

Moffat: Francis Moffat of that Ilk, Redacres, Moffat, Dumfriesshire.

Moncreiffe: vacant.

Montgomerie: The Earl of Eglinton and Winton, The Dutch House, West Green, Hartley Wintney, Hants.

Morrison: Dr. Iain M. Morrison of Ruchdi, Todhurst Farm, Lake Lane, Barnham, W. Sussex.

Munro: Patrick G. Munro of Foulis, TD, Foulis Castle, Ross.

Murray: The Duke of Atholl, Blair Castle, Blair Atholl, Perthshire.

Nicolson: The Lord Carnock, 90 Whitehall Court, SW1.

Ogilvy: The Earl of Airlie, KT, GCVO, PC, Cortachy Castle, Kirriemuir, Angus.

Ramsay: The Earl of Dalhousie, KT, GCVO, GBE, MC, Brechin Castle, Angus.

Rattray: James S. Rattray of Rattray, Craighall, Rattray, Perthshire.

Robertson: Alexander G. H. Robertson of Struan (*Struan-Robertson*), The Breach Farm, Goudhurst Road, Cranbrook, Kent.

Rollo: The Lord Rollo, Pitcairns, Dunning, Perthshire.

Rose: Miss Elizabeth Rose of Kilravock, Kilravock Castle, Croy, Inverness.

Ross: David C. Ross of that Ilk, The Old Schoolhouse, Fettercairn, Kincardineshire.

Ruthven: The Earl of Gowrie, PC, Castlemartin, Kilcullen, Co. Kildare, Republic of Ireland.

Scott: The Duke of Buccleuch and Queensberry, KT, VRD, Bowhill, Selkirk.

Scrymgeour: The Earl of Dundee, Birkhill, Cupar, Fife.

Sempill: The Lady Sempill, Druminnor Castle, Rhynie, Aberdeenshire.

Shaw: John Shaw of Tordarroch, Newhall, Balblair, By Conon Bridge, Ross-shire.

Sinclair: The Earl of Caithness, Finstock Manor, Finstock, Oxon.

Stirling: Fraser J. Stirling of Cader, 17 Park Row, Farnham, Surrey.

Sutherland: The Countess of Sutherland, House of Tongue, Brora, Sutherland.

Swinton: vacant.

Urquhart: Kenneth T. Urquhart of that Ilk, 4713 Orleans Boulevard, Jefferson, Louisiana, USA.

Wallace: Lt.-Col. M. R. Wallace of that Ilk, Hilton of Gask, Auchterarder, Perthshire.

Wedderburn of that Ilk: The Master of Dundee, Birkhill, Cupar, Fife.

Wemyss: David Wemyss of that Ilk, Invermay, Forteviot, Perthshire.

PRINCIPAL DECORATIONS AND MEDALS (in order of Precedence)

Victoria Cross (VC)—1856.

George Cross (GC)—1940.

British Orders of Knighthood, Etc. (for order in which worn, *see* pp. 184–86).

Baronet's Badge

Knight Bachelor's Badge

Decorations

Royal Red Cross (Class I—RRC)—1883.—For ladies.

Distinguished Service Cross (DSC)—1914.—For officers of RN below the rank of Captain, and Warrant Officers.

Military Cross (MC)—Dec. 1914.—Awarded to Captains, Lieutenants, and Warrant Officers (I and II) in the Army and Indian and Colonial Forces.

Distinguished Flying Cross (DFC)—1918.—For officers and Warrant Officers in the RAF (and Fleet Air Arm from April 9, 1941) for acts of gallantry when flying in active operations against the enemy.

Air Force Cross (AFC)—1918.—Instituted as preceding but not in active operations against the enemy when flying, although not in active operations against the enemy (extended to Fleet Air Arm since April 9, 1941).

Royal Red Cross (Class II—ARRC).

Order of British India.

Kaisar-i-Hind Medal.

Order of St. John.

Medals for Gallantry and Distinguished Conduct

Union of South Africa Queen's Medal for Bravery, in Gold.

Distinguished Conduct Medal (DCM)—1854.—Awarded to warrant officers, non-commissioned officers and men of the Army and RAF.

Conspicuous Gallantry Medal (CGM)—1874.—Is bestowed upon warrant officers and men of the RN and since 1942 of Mercantile Marine and RAF.

The George Medal (GM)—1940.

Queen's Police Medal for Gallantry.

Queen's Fire Service Medal for Gallantry.

Royal West African Frontier Force Distinguished Conduct Medal.

King's African Rifles Distinguished Conduct Medal.

Indian Distinguished Service Medal.

Union of South Africa Queen's Medal for Bravery, in Silver.

Distinguished Service Medal (DSM)—1914.—For chief petty officers, petty officers and men, of all branches of the Royal Navy, and since 1942 of Mercantile Marine; non-commissioned officers and men of the Royal Marines; all other persons holding corresponding positions in Her Majesty's service afloat.

Military Medal (MM)—1916.—For warrant and non-commissioned officers and men and serving women.

Distinguished Flying Medal (DFM)—1918.—and the Air Force Medal (AFM)—For warrant and non-commissioned officers and men for equivalent services as for DFC and AFC (extended to Fleet Air Arm, 1941).

Constabulary Medal (Ireland).

Medal for Saving Life at Sea.

Indian Order of Merit (Civil).

Indian Police Medal for Gallantry.

Ceylon Police Medal for Gallantry.

Sierra Leone Police Medal for Gallantry.

Sierra Leone Fire Brigades Medal for Gallantry.

Colonial Police Medal for Gallantry (CPM)

Queen's Gallantry Medal.—1974.

Royal Victorian Medal (RVM)—(Gold, Silver and Bronze).

British Empire Medal (BEM)—(formerly the Medal of the Order of the British Empire, for Meritorious Service; also includes the Medal of the Order awarded before Dec. 29, 1922).

Queen's Police (QPM) and Fire Services Medals for Distinguished Service (QFSM).

Queen's Medal for Chiefs.

War Medals and Stars (in order of date).

Polar Medals (in order of date).

Imperial Service Medal.

Police Medals for Valuable Service.

Badge of Honour.

Jubilee, Coronation and Durbar Medals.

King George V, King George VI and Queen Elizabeth II Long and Faithful Service Medals.

Efficiency and Long Service Decorations and Medals.

Medal for Meritorious Service.

Long Service and Good Conduct Medal—(Military).

Naval Long Service and Good Conduct Medal.

Royal Marine Meritorious Service Medal.

Royal Air Force Meritorious Service Medal.

Royal Air Force Long Service and Good Conduct Medal.

Medal for Long Service and Good Conduct (Ulster Defence Regiment).

Police Long Service and Good Conduct Medal.

Fire Brigade Long Service and Good Conduct Medal.

Colonial Police and Fire Brigades Long Service Medal.

Colonial Prison Service Medal.

Army Emergency Reserve Decoration (ERD)—1952.

Volunteer Officer's Decoration (VD).

Volunteer Long Service Medal.

Volunteer Officer's Decoration (for India and the Colonies).

Volunteer Long Service Medal (for India and the Colonies).

Colonial Auxiliary Forces Officer's Decoration.

Colonial Auxiliary Forces Long Service Medal.

Medal for Good Shooting (Naval).

Militia Long Service Medal.

Imperial Yeomanry Long Service Medal.

Territorial Decoration (TD)—1908.

Efficiency Decoration (ED).

Territorial Efficiency Medal.

Efficiency Medal.

Special Reserve Long Service and Good Conduct Medal.

Decoration for Officers, Royal Navy Reserve (RD)—1910.

Decoration for Officers, RNVR (VRD)

Royal Naval Reserve Long Service and Good Conduct Medal.

RNVR Long Service and Good Conduct Medal.

Royal Naval Auxiliary Sick Berth Reserve Long Service and Good Conduct Medal.

Royal Fleet Reserve Long Service and Good Conduct Medal.

Royal Naval Wireless Auxiliary Reserve Long Service and Good Conduct Medal.

Air Efficiency Award (AE)—1942.

Ulster Defence Regiment Medal.

The Queen's Medal.—(For champion shots in the RN, RM, RNZN, Army, RAF).

Cadet Forces Medal.—1950.

Coast Life Saving Corps Long Service Medal.—1911.

Special Constabulary Long Service Medal.

Royal Observer Corps Medal.

Civil Defence Long Service Medal.

Royal Ulster Constabulary Service Medal.

Service Medal of the Order of St. John.

Badge of the Order of the League of Mercy.

Voluntary Medical Service Medal.—1932.

Women's Royal Voluntary Service Medal.

Colonial Special Constabulary Medal.

Foreign Orders, Decorations and Medals (in order of date).

THE VICTORIA CROSS, VC

For Conspicuous Bravery

Ribbon, Crimson, for all Services (until 1918 it was *Blue* for Royal Navy).

Instituted on January 29, 1856, the Victoria Cross was awarded retrospectively to 1854, the first being held by Lt. C. D. Lucas, RN for bravery in the Baltic Sea on June 21, 1854 (gazetted Feb. 24, 1857). The first 62 Crosses were presented by Queen Victoria in Hyde Park, London, on June 26, 1857.

The VC is worn before all other decorations, on the left breast, and consists of a cross-pattée of bronze, 1½ inches in diameter, with the Royal Crown surmounted by a lion in the centre, and beneath there is the inscription 'For Valour'. Holders of the VC receive a tax-free annuity of £100, irrespective of need or other conditions. In 1911, the right to receive the Cross was extended to Indian soldiers, and in 1920 a Royal Warrant extended the right to Matrons, Sisters and Nurses, and the staff of the Nursing Services and other services pertaining to hospitals and nursing, and to civilians of either sex regularly or temporarily under the orders, direction or supervision of the Naval, Military, or Air Forces of the Crown.

Surviving Recipients of the Victoria Cross
(as at Aug. 31, 1990)

Agansing Rai, *Havildar*, MM (Gurkha Rifles), *World War* 1944
Ali Haidar, *Jemadar* (Frontier Force Rifles), *World War* 1945
Annand, *Capt.* R. W. (Durham Light Infantry), *World War* 1940
Bhan Bhagta Gurung, *Capt.* (2nd Gurkha Rifles), *World War* 1945
Bhandari Ram, *Capt.* (Baluch R.), *World War* ..1944
Burton, *Cpl.* R. H. (Duke of Wellington's R.), *World War* 1944
Campbell, *Brig.* L. M., DSO, OBE, TD (Argyll & Sutherland Highlanders), *World War* 1943
Chapman, *Sgt.* E. T., BEM (Monmouthshire R.), *World War* 1945
Cheshire, *Group Capt.* G. L., OM, DSO, DFC (RAF), *World War* 1944
Cruickshank, *Flt. Lt.* J. A. (RAFVR), *World War* 1944
Cutler, Sir Roden, AK, KCMG, KCVO, CBE (Australia), *World War* 1941
De L'Isle, *Maj.* The Viscount, KG, PC, GCMG, GCVO (*Hon.* W. P. Sidney) (Grenadier Guards), *World War* 1944
Eardley, *Sgt.* G. H., MM (KSLI), *World War* 1944
Ervine-Andrews, *Lt.-Col.* H. M. (E. Lancs. R.), *World War* 1940
Foote, *Maj.-Gen.* H. R. B., CB, DSO (R. Tank R.), *World War* 1942
Fraser, *Lt. Cdr.* I. E., DSC (RNR), *World War* 1945
Gaje Ghale, *Subedar* (Gurkha Rifles), *World War* 1943
Ganju Lama, *Jemadar*, MM (Gurkha Rifles), *World War* 1944
Gardner, *Capt.* P. J., MC (RTR), *World War* 1941
Gian Singh, *Jemadar* (Punjab R.), *World War* ..1945
Gould, *Lt.* T. W. (RN), *World War* 1942
Hinton, *Sgt.* J. D. (NZMF), *World War* 1941

Jackson, *WO* N. C. (RAFVR), *World War* 1944
Jamieson, *Maj.* D. A., CVO (R. Norfolk R.), *World War* 1944
Kenna, *Pte.* E. (Australian M. F.), *World War* ..1945
Kenneally, *C-Q-M-S* J. P. (Irish Guards), *World War* 1943
Lachiman Gurung, *Rifleman* (Gurkha Rifles), *World War* 1945
Learoyd, *Wing-Cmdr.* R. A. B. (RAF), *World War* 1940
Mahony, *Lt.-Col.* J. K., CD (Westminster R., Canada), *World War* 1944
Merritt, *Lt.-Col.* C. C. I., CD (S. Saskatchewan R.), *World War* 1942
Norton, *Capt.* G. R., MM (SAMF), *World War* 1944
Parkash Singh, *Maj.* (Punjab R.), *World War* ...1943
Payne, *WO* K. (Australian Army), *Vietnam* 1969
Place, *Rear-Adm.* B. C. G., CB, DSC (RN), *World War* 1943
Porteous, *Col.* P. A. (RA), *World War* 1942
Rambahadur Limbu, *Lt.*, MVO (Gurkha Rifles), *Sarawak* 1965
Reid, *Flt.-Lt.* W. (RAFVR), *World War* 1943
Smith, *Sgt.* E. A., CD (Seaforth Highlanders of Canada), *World War* 1944
Smythe, *Capt.* Q. G. M. (SAMF), *World War* 1942
Speakman-Pitt, *Sgt.* W. (Black Watch), *Korea* ..1951
Tilston, *Maj.* F. A., CD (Essex Scottish, Canada), *World War* 1945
Tulbahadur Pun, *WO1* (Gurkha Rifles), *World War* 1944
Umrao Singh, *Sub-Major* (IA), *World War* 1944
Upham, *Capt.* C. H. (and Bar, 1942), (NZMF), *World War* 1941
Watkins, *Maj. Rt. Hon.* Sir Tasker, GBE (Welch R.), *World War* 1944
Wilson, *Lt.-Col.* E. C. T. (E. Surrey R.), *World War* 1940

THE GEORGE CROSS, GC (1940)

For Gallantry

Ribbon, Dark Blue, threaded through a bar adorned with laurel leaves.

Instituted September 24th, 1940 (with amendments, November 3rd, 1942).

The George Cross is worn before all other decorations (except the VC) on the left breast (when worn by a woman it may be worn on the left shoulder from a ribbon of the same width and colour fashioned into a bow). It consists of a plain silver cross with four equal limbs, the cross having in the centre a circular medallion bearing a design showing St. George and the Dragon. The inscription 'For Gallantry' appears round the medallion and in the angle of each limb of the cross is the Royal cypher 'G VI' forming a circle concentric with the medallion. The reverse is plain and bears the name of the recipient and the date of the award. The cross is suspended by a ring from a bar adorned with laurel leaves on dark blue ribbon 1½ inches wide.

The cross is intended primarily for civilians; awards to the fighting services are confined to actions for which purely military honours are not normally granted. It is awarded only for acts of the greatest heroism or of the most conspicuous courage in circumstances of extreme danger. From April 1, 1965, holders of the Cross have received a tax-free annuity of £100.

Empire Gallantry Medal.—The Royal Warrant which ordained that the grant of the Empire Gallantry Medal should cease authorized holders of that medal to return it to the Central Chancery of the Orders of Knighthood and to receive in exchange the George Cross. A similar provision applied to posthumous awards of the Empire Gallantry Medal made after the outbreak of war in 1939.

In October 1971 all surviving holders of the Albert Medal and the Edward Medal exchanged those decorations for the George Cross.

Surviving Recipients of the George Cross
(as at Aug. 31, 1990)

(If the recipient originally received the Empire Gallantry Medal, the Albert Medal or the Edward Medal, this is indicated by the initials in parenthesis after the name.)

Archer, *Col.* B. S. T., GC, OBE, ERD 1941
Ashburnham Ruffner, Mrs. D., GC (AM) 1917
Atkinson, T., GC (EGM) 1939
Babington, J. H., GC, OBE 1940
Baker, J. T., GC (EM) 1929
Baldwin, W. C. G., GC, Ph.D. (EM) 1943
Bamford, J., GC 1952
Barkat Singh, *Ex. Sub.*, GC (EGM) 1938
Baxter, W. F., GC (EM) 1942
Beaton, J., GC 1974
Biggs, *Maj.* K. A., GC 1946
Blackburn, R., GC (EGM) 1936
Blackburn, S., GC (EM) 1947
Bridge, *Cdr.* J., GC, GM 1944
Butson, *Col.* A. R. C., GC, CD, MD (AM) 1948
Bywater, R. A. S., GC, GM 1944
Cobham, *Cdr.* A. J., GC, MBE (EGM) 1930
Copperwheat, *Lt. Cdr.* D. A., GC 1942
Cowley, *Lt.-Gen.* Sir John, GC, KCB, CBE (AM) 1935
Durrani, *Lt.-Col.* M. K., GC 1946
Easton, J. M. C., GC 1941
Errington, H., GC 1941
Fairfax, F. W., GC 1953
Farrow, K., GC (AM) 1948
Fisher, B., GC (EM) 1939
Flintoff, H. H., GC (EM) 1944
Gibbs, S., GC (AM) 1927
Gledhill, A. J., GC 1967
Goad, W., GC (AM) 1943
Goldsworthy, *Lt. Cdr.* L. V., GC, DSC, GM 1944
Gregson, J. S., GC (AM) 1943
Hallowes, Mrs. O. M. C., GC, MBE, Legion
    d'Honneur 1946
Hawkins, E., GC (AM) 1943
Hodge, *Capt.* A. M., GC, VRD (EGM) 1940
Idris, Shawish Taha, GC (EGM) 1934

Kinne, D. G., GC 1954
Lowe, A. R., GC (AM) 1949
Lynch, J., GC, BEM (AM) 1948
McAloney, *Gp. Capt.* W. S., GC, OBE (AM) 1938
McClymont, J. M., GC (EGM) 1940
Manwaring, T. G., GC (EM) 1949
May, P. R. S., GC (AM) 1947
Miller, *Lt. Cdr.* J. B. P., GC 1941
Moore, R. V., GC 1940
Moss, B., GC 1940
Naughton, F., GC (EGM) 1937
Nix, F. E., GC (EM) 1944
Omara, Eduardo, GC (EGM) 1934
Patton, The Hon. John, GC, CBE 1940
Pearson, Miss J. D. M., GC (EGM) 1940
Pratt, M. K., GC 1978
Purves, Mrs. M., GC (AM) 1949
Purvis, J. S., GC (EM) 1929
Raweng, Awang anak, GC 1951
Riley, G., GC (AM) 1944
Rimmer, R., GC (EGM) 1931
Rogerson, S., GC 1946
Rowlands, *Air Marshal* Sir John, GC, KBE 1943
Sinclair, *Air Vice-Marshal* Sir Laurence, GC,
    KCB, CBE, DSO 1941
Stevens, H. W., GC 1958
Stronach, *Capt.* G. P., GC 1943
Styles, *Lt.-Col.* S. G., GC 1972
Sylvester, W. G., GC (EGM) 1940
Taylor, *Lt. Cdr.* W. H., GC, MBE 1941
Walker, C., GC 1972
Walker, C. H., GC (AM) 1942
Walton, E. W. K., GC (AM) 1948
Wastie, G. C., GC (EM) 1930
Watt-Bonar, E., GC (EGM) 1932
Western, D., GC (AM) 1948
Wilcox, C., GC (EM) 1949
Wiltshire, S. N., GC (EGM) 1930
Yates, P. W., GC (EM) 1932
Younger, W., GC (EM) 1948

THE MILITARY KNIGHTS OF WINDSOR

The Military Knights of Windsor take part in all ceremonies of the Noble Order of the Garter and attend Sunday morning service in St. George's Chapel, Windsor Castle, as representatives of the Knights of the Garter. The Knights receive a small stipend in addition to their army pensions and quarters in Windsor Castle.

The Knights of Windsor were originally founded in 1348 after the Wars in France to assist English Knights, who, having been prisoners in the hands of the French, had become impoverished by the payments of heavy ransoms. When Edward III founded the Order of the Garter later the same year, he incorporated the Knights of Windsor and the College of St. George into its foundation and raised the number of Knights to 26 to correspond with the number of the Knights of the Garter. Known later as the Alms Knights or Poor Knights of Windsor, their establishment was reduced under the will of King Henry VIII to 13 and Statutes were drawn up by Queen Elizabeth I.

In 1833 King William IV changed their designation to The Military Knights and granted them their present uniform which consists of a scarlet tail-coat with white cross sword-belt, crimson sash and cocked hat with plume. The badges are the Shield of St. George and the Star of the Order of the Garter.

Governor, Maj.-Gen. Peter Downward, CB, DSO, DFC.

Military Knights, Maj. H. Smith, MBE, RVM; Maj. A. E. Wollaston, MVO; Brig. A. L. Atkinson, OBE; Brig. J. F. Lindner, OBE, MC; Brig. A. C. Tyler, CBE, MC; Maj. W. L. Thompson, MVO, MBE, DCM; Maj. L. W. Dickerson; Maj. J. C. Cowley, DCM; Lt.-Col. N. L. West; Maj. G. R. Mitchell; MBE, BEM; Lt.-Col. R. L. C. Tamplin; Maj. P. H. Bolton, MBE.

Supernumerary, Lt.-Col. A. R. Clark, MC.

THE PRIVY COUNCIL

Apart from Cabinet Ministers, who must be Privy Counsellors and are sworn in on first assuming office, membership of the Council (retained for life) is accorded by the Sovereign on the recommendation of the Prime Minister to eminent people in independent monarchical countries of the Commonwealth.

HRH The Duke of Edinburgh.............	1951
HRH The Prince of Wales .	1977
Aberdare, Lord	1974
Ackner, Lord	1980
Adams-Schneider, Sir Lancelot	1980
Ademola, Sir Adetokunbo .	1963
Airlie, Earl of	1984
Aldington, Lord..........	1954
Alebua, Ezekiel	1988
Alison, Michael	1981
Alport, Lord	1960
Amery, Julian	1960
Anthony, Douglas	1971
Archer, Peter	1977
Armstrong, Ernest	1979
Arnold, Sir John	1979
Ashdown, Paddy	1989
Ashley, Jack	1979
Avonside, Lord	1962
Aylestone, Lord	1962
Azikiwe, Nnamdi.........	1960
Bacon, Baroness	1966
Baker, Kenneth	1984
Balcombe, Sir John	1985
Barber, Lord	1963
Barnett, Lord	1975
Barwick, Sir Garfield	1964
Beldam, Sir Roy	1989
Belstead, Lord	1983
Benn, Anthony	1964
Bennett, Sir Frederic	1985
Bevins, John.............	1959
Biffen, John	1979
Bingham, Sir Thomas.....	1986
Bird, Vere	1982
Bisson, Gordon	1987
Blaker, Sir Peter	1983
Blanch, Rt. Rev. Lord	1975
Booth, Albert	1976
Bottomley, Lord..........	1952
Boyd-Carpenter, Lord	1954
Boys, Michael............	1990
Boyson, Sir Rhodes	1987
Braine, Sir Bernard	1985
Brandon of Oakbrook, Lord	1978
Bridge of Harwich, Lord ..	1975
Brightman, Lord	1979
Brittan, Sir Leon.........	1981
Brooke, Peter	1988
Brown, Sir Stephen	1983
Browne, Sir Patrick	1974
Browne-Wilkinson, Sir Nicolas.................	1983
Broxbourne, Lord	1957
Buchanan-Smith, Alick ...	1981
Buckley, Sir Denys	1970
Butler, Sir Adam	1984
Butler-Sloss, Dame Elizabeth	1988
Caithness, Earl of	1990
Callaghan of Cardiff, Lord .	1964
Cameron of Lochbroom, Lord	1984
Campbell of Croy, Lord ...	1970
Canterbury, The Archbishop of	1980
Caradon, Lord	1968
Carlisle of Bucklow, Lord .	1979
Carr of Hadley, Lord......	1963
Carrington, Lord.........	1959
Casey, Maurice	1986
Castle of Blackburn, Baroness	1964
Cato, Robert	1981
Chalfont, Lord	1964
Chalker, Lynda	1987
Chan, Sir Julius	1981
Channon, Paul	1980
Charteris of Amisfield, Lord	1972
Chataway, Christopher ...	1970
Clark, Helen	1990
Clark, Sir William	1990
Clarke, Kenneth	1984
Cledwyn of Penrhos, Lord .	1966
Cockfield, Lord...........	1982
Cocks of Hartcliffe, Lord ..	1976
Coggan, Rt. Rev. Lord	1961
Colman, Fraser	1986
Colnbrook, Lord	1973
Colyton, Lord	1952
Compton, John...........	1983
Concannon, John	1978
Cooke, Sir Robin	1977
Cooper, Sir Frank	1983
Cope, John	1988
Corfield, Sir Frederick	1970
Cowen, Sir Zelman	1981
Craigton, Lord	1961
Crawford and Balcarres, Earl of	1972
Crickhowell, Lord	1979
Cromer, Earl of	1966
Croom-Johnson, Sir David	1984
Cumming-Bruce, Sir Roualeyn...............	1977
Davies, Denzil	1978
Davison, Sir Ronald	1978
Deedes, Lord	1962
De L'Isle, Viscount	1951
Dell, Edmund	1970
Denham, Lord	1981
Denning, Lord	1948
Devlin, Lord	1960
Devonshire, Duke of	1964
Diamond, Lord	1965
Dillon, Sir Brian	1982
Donaldson of Lymington, Lord	1979
Douglas, Sir William......	1977
du Cann, Sir Edward	1964
Duff, Sir Antony	1980
Dunn, Sir Robin..........	1980
Eccles, Viscount	1951
Eden of Winton, Lord	1972
Edmund-Davies, Lord.....	1966
Eichelbaum, Sir Thomas ..	1989
Ellison, Rt. Rev. Gerald ...	1973
Emslie, Lord	1972
Ennals, Lord.............	1970
Erroll of Hale, Lord	1960
Esquivel, Manuel.........	1986
Eveleigh, Sir Edward	1977
Farquharson, Sir Donald..	1989
Fellowes, Sir Robert	1990
Fernyhough, Ernest	1970
Ferrers, Earl	1982
Foot, Michael	1974
Fowler, Sir Norman	1979
Fox, Sir Michael	1981
Franks, Lord	1949
Fraser, Malcolm	1976
Fraser of Carmyllie, Lord .	1989
Freeman, John...........	1966
Freeson, Reginald	1976
Gairy, Sir Eric	1977
Georges, Telford	1986
Gibbs, Sir Harry	1972
Gibbs, Sir Humphrey	1969
Gibson, Sir Ralph	1985
Gibson-Watt, Lord	1974
Gilbert, John	1978
Gilmour, Sir Ian, Bt	1973
Glenamara, Lord	1964
Glendevon, Lord	1959
Glidewell, Sir Iain	1985
Goff of Chieveley, Lord ...	1982
Gordon, John	1978
Gorton, Sir John	1968
Gowrie, Earl of	1984
Gray of Contin, Lord	1982
Griffiths, Lord	1980
Grimond, Lord	1961
Gummer, John	1985
Hailsham of St. Marylebone, Lord	1956
Harrison, Walter	1977
Hart of South Lanark, Baroness	1967
Harvington, Lord	1971
Hasluck, Sir Paul	1966
Hattersley, Roy	1975
Havers, Lord.............	1977
Hayhoe, Sir Barney	1985
Healey, Denis	1964
Heath, Edward	1955
Herbison, Margaret	1964
Heseltine, Michael	1979
Heseltine, Sir William ...	1986
Higgins, Terence	1979
Holderness, Lord	1959
Home of the Hirsel, Lord ..	1951
Hope, *Hon.* Lord	1989
Houghton of Sowerby, Lord	1964
Howard, Michael.........	1990
Howe, Sir Geoffrey (*Lord President*)	1972
Howell, David............	1979
Howell, Denis	1976
Hughes, Lord	1970
Hunt, David	1990
Hunt, Jonathan	1989
Hurd, Douglas	1982
Hutton, Sir Brian	1988
Irvine, Sir Bryant Godman	1982
Jauncey of Tullichettle, Lord	1988

Wilberforce, Lord	1964	Windlesham, Lord	1973	Wylie, *Hon.* Lord	1970
Williams, Alan	1977	Wingti, Paias	1987	York, The Archbishop of ..	1983
Williams, Shirley	1974	Withers, Reginald	1977	Young, Baroness	1981
Wilson of Langside, Lord ..	1967	Woodhouse, Sir Owen	1974	Young of Graffham, Lord ..	1984
Wilson of Rievaulx, Lord ..	1947	Woolf, Sir Harry	1986	Younger, George	1979

Clerk of the Council, G. I. de Deney, cvo   *Deputy Clerk of the Council,* R. P. Bulling.

PRIME MINISTERS SINCE 1782

Marquess of Rockingham, *Whig,* March 27, 1782.
Earl of Shelburne, *Whig,* July 13, 1782.
Duke of Portland, *Coalition,* April 4, 1783.
William Pitt, *Tory,* Dec. 7, 1783.
Henry Addington, *Tory,* March 21, 1801.
William Pitt, *Tory,* May 16, 1804.
Lord Grenville, *Whig,* Feb. 10, 1806.
Duke of Portland, *Tory,* March 31, 1807.
Spencer Perceval, *Tory,* Dec. 6, 1809.
Earl of Liverpool, *Tory,* June 16, 1812.
George Canning, *Tory,* April 30, 1827.
Viscount Goderich, *Tory,* Sept. 8, 1827.
Duke of Wellington, *Tory,* Jan. 26, 1828.
Earl Grey, *Whig,* Nov. 24, 1830.
Viscount Melbourne, *Whig,* July 13, 1834.
Sir Robert Peel, *Tory,* Dec. 26, 1834.
Viscount Melbourne, *Whig,* March 18, 1835.
Sir Robert Peel, *Tory,* Sept. 6, 1841.
Lord John Russell, *Whig,* July 6, 1846.
Earl of Derby, *Tory,* Feb. 28, 1852.
Earl of Aberdeen, *Peelite,* Dec. 28, 1852.
Viscount Palmerston, *Liberal,* Feb. 10, 1855.
Earl of Derby, *Conservative,* Feb. 25, 1858.
Viscount Palmerston, *Liberal,* June 18, 1859.
Earl Russell, *Liberal,* Nov. 6, 1865.
Earl of Derby, *Conservative,* July 6, 1866.
Benjamin Disraeli, *Conservative,* Feb. 27, 1868.
W. E. Gladstone, *Liberal,* Dec. 9, 1868.
Benjamin Disraeli, *Conservative,* Feb. 21, 1874.
W. E. Gladstone, *Liberal,* April 28, 1880.
Marquess of Salisbury, *Conservative,* June 24, 1885.

W. E. Gladstone, *Liberal,* Feb. 6, 1886.
Marquess of Salisbury, *Conservative,* Aug. 3, 1886.
W. E. Gladstone, *Liberal,* Aug. 18, 1892.
Earl of Rosebery, *Liberal,* March 3, 1894.
Marquess of Salisbury, *Conservative,* July 2, 1895.
A. J. Balfour, *Conservative,* July 12, 1902.
Sir H. Campbell-Bannerman, *Liberal,* Dec. 5, 1905.
H. H. Asquith, *Liberal,* April 8, 1908.
H. H. Asquith, *Coalition,* May 26, 1915.
D. Lloyd-George, *Coalition,* Dec. 7, 1916.
A. Bonar Law, *Conservative,* Oct. 23, 1922.
S. Baldwin, *Conservative,* May 22, 1923.
J. R. MacDonald, *Labour,* Jan. 22, 1924.
S. Baldwin, *Conservative,* Nov. 4, 1924.
J. R. MacDonald, *Labour,* June 8, 1929.
J. R. MacDonald, *Coalition,* Aug. 25, 1931.
S. Baldwin, *Coalition,* June 7, 1935.
N. Chamberlain, *Coalition,* May 28, 1937.
W. S. Churchill, *Coalition,* May 11, 1940.
W. S. Churchill, *Conservative,* May 23, 1945.
C. R. Attlee, *Labour,* July 26, 1945.
Sir W. S. Churchill, *Conservative,* Oct. 26, 1951.
Sir Anthony Eden, *Conservative,* April 6, 1955.
H. Macmillan, *Conservative,* Jan. 13, 1957.
Sir Alec Douglas-Home, *Conservative,* Oct. 19, 1963.
J. H. Wilson, *Labour,* Oct. 16, 1964.
E. R. G. Heath, *Conservative,* June 19, 1970.
J. H. Wilson, *Labour,* March 4, 1974.
L. J. Callaghan, *Labour,* April 5, 1976.
Mrs. M. H. Thatcher, *Conservative,* May 4, 1979.

SPEAKERS OF THE COMMONS SINCE 1660

Parliament of England

1660 Sir Harbottle Grimston.
1661 Sir Edward Turner.
1673 Sir Job Charlton.
1673 Sir Edward Seymour.
1678 Sir Robert Sawyer.
1679 Sir William Gregory.
1680 Sir William Williams.
1685 Sir John Trevor.
1688 Henry Powle.
1694 Paul Foley.
1698 Sir Thomas Lyttelton.
1700 Robert Harley (*Earl of Oxford and Mortimer*).
1702 John Smith.

Parliament of Great Britain

1708 Sir Richard Onslow (*Lord Onslow*).
1710 William Bromley.
1713 Sir Thomas Hanmer.
1715 Spencer Compton (*Earl of Wilmington*).
1727 Arthur Onslow.
1761 Sir John Cust.
1770 Sir Fletcher Norton.
1780 Charles Cornwall.

1788 Hon. William Grenville (*Lord Grenville*).
1789 Henry Addington (*Viscount Sidmouth*).

Parliament of United Kingdom

1801 Sir John Mitford (*Lord Redesdale*).
1802 Charles Abbot (*Lord Colchester*).
1817 Charles M. Sutton (*Viscount Canterbury*).
1835 James Abercromby (*Lord Dunfermline*).
1839 Charles Shaw-Lefevre (*Viscount Eversley*).
1857 J. Evelyn Denison (*Viscount Ossington*).
1872 Sir Henry Brand (*Viscount Hampden*).
1884 Arthur Wellesley Peel (*Viscount Peel*).
1895 William C. Gully (*Viscount Selby*).
1905 James W. Lowther (*Viscount Ullswater*).
1921 John H. Whitley.
1928 Hon. Edward A. FitzRoy.
1943 Col. D. Clifton Brown (*Viscount Ruffside*).
1951 William S. Morrison (*Viscount Dunrossil*).
1959 Sir Harry Hylton-Foster.
1965 Horace M. King (*Lord Maybray-King*).
1971 Selwyn Lloyd (*Lord Selwyn-Lloyd*).
1976 George Thomas (*Viscount Tonypandy*).
1983 (Bruce) Bernard Weatherill.

THE UNITED KINGDOM CONSTITUTION

The United Kingdom constitution is not contained in any single document but has evolved in the course of time, formed partly by statute, partly by common law and partly by convention. A constitutional monarchy, the United Kingdom is governed by Ministers of the Crown in the name of the Sovereign, who is head both of the state and the government.

The organs of government are the *legislature* (Parliament), the *executive* and the *judiciary*. The executive consists of Her Majesty's Government (Cabinet and other Ministers), government departments (*see* pp. 295–375), local authorities (*see* Index), and public corporations operating nationalized industries or social or cultural services (*see* pp. 295–375). The judiciary (*see* **Law Courts and Offices**) pronounces on the law, both written and unwritten, interprets statutes and is responsible for the enforcement of the law; the judiciary is independent of both the legislature and the executive.

THE MONARCHY

The Sovereign personifies the state and is, in law, an integral part of the legislature, head of the executive, head of the judiciary, the Commander-in-Chief of all armed forces of the Crown and the 'Supreme Governor' of the Church of England. The seat of the monarchy is in the United Kingdom. In the Channel Islands and the Isle of Man, which are Crown dependencies, the Sovereign is represented by a Lieutenant-Governor; in the member states of the Commonwealth of which the Sovereign is head of state, her representative is a Governor-General (*see also* p. 625); in United Kingdom dependencies the Sovereign is usually represented by a Governor, who is responsible to the British Government.

Although the powers of the monarchy are now very limited, restricted mainly to the advisory and ceremonial, there are important acts of government which require the participation of the Sovereign. These include summoning, proroguing and dissolving Parliament, giving Royal Assent to Bills passed by Parliament, appointing important office-holders, e.g. government ministers, judges, bishops, and governors, conferring peerages, knighthoods and other honours, and granting pardon to a person wrongly convicted of a crime. An important function is appointing a Prime Minister, by convention the leader of the political party which enjoys, or can secure, a majority of votes in the House of Commons. In international affairs the Sovereign as head of State has the power to declare war and make peace, to recognize foreign states and governments, to conclude treaties and to annex or cede territory. However, as the Sovereign entrusts executive power to Ministers of the Crown and acts on the advice of her Ministers, which she cannot ignore, in practice royal prerogative powers are exercised by Ministers, who are responsible to Parliament.

Ministerial responsibility does not diminish the Sovereign's importance to the smooth working of government. She holds meetings of the Privy Council, gives audiences to her Ministers and other officials at home and overseas, receives accounts of Cabinet decisions, reads dispatches and signs state papers; she must be informed and consulted on every aspect of national life; and she must show complete impartiality.

Counsellors of State

In the event of the Sovereign's absence abroad, it is necessary to appoint Counsellors of State under Letters Patent to carry out the chief functions of the Monarch, including the holding of Privy Councils

and giving Royal Assent to Acts passed by Parliament. The normal procedure is to appoint as Counsellors three or four members of the Royal Family among those remaining in the United Kingdom. In the event of the Sovereign on accession being under the age of eighteen years, or at any time unavailable or incapacitated by infirmity of mind or body for the performance of the royal functions, provision is made for a Regency.

THE PRIVY COUNCIL

The Sovereign in Council, or Privy Council, was the chief source of executive power until the system of Cabinet government developed. Now its main function is to advise the Sovereign to approve Orders in Council and to advise on the issue of royal proclamations. The Council's own statutory responsibilities (independent of the powers of the Sovereign in Council) include powers of supervision over the registering bodies for the medical and allied professions. A full Council is summoned only on the death of the Sovereign or when the Sovereign announces his or her intention to marry (for full list of Counsellors, *see* pp. 227–9).

There are a number of advisory Privy Council committees, whose meetings the Sovereign does not attend. Some are prerogative committees, such as those dealing with legislative matters submitted by the legislatures of the Channel Islands and the Isle of Man or with applications for charters of incorporation; and some are provided for by statute, e.g. those for the universities of Oxford and Cambridge and the Scottish universities.

The Judicial Committee of the Privy Council is the final court of appeal from courts of the United Kingdom dependencies, courts of independent Commonwealth countries which have retained the right of appeal, courts of the Channel Islands and the Isle of Man, some professional and disciplinary committees, and church sources. The Committee is composed of all Privy Counsellors who hold, or have held, high judicial office, although usually only three or five hear each case.

Administrative work is carried out by the Privy Council Office under the direction of the Lord President of the Council, a Cabinet Minister.

PARLIAMENT

Parliament is the supreme law-making authority and can legislate for the United Kingdom as a whole or for any parts of it separately (the Channel Islands and the Isle of Man are Crown dependencies and not part of the United Kingdom). The main functions of Parliament are to pass laws, to provide (by voting taxation) the means of carrying on the work of government and to scrutinize government policy and administration, particularly proposals for expenditure. International treaties and agreements are by custom presented to Parliament before ratification.

Parliament emerged during the late thirteenth and early fourteenth centuries. The nucleus of early Parliaments were the officers of the King's household and the King's judges, joined by such ecclesiastical and lay magnates as the King might summon to form a prototype 'House of Lords', and occasionally by the knights of the shires, burgesses and proctors of the lower clergy. By the end of Edward III's reign a 'House of Commons' was beginning to appear; the first known Speaker was elected in 1377.

Parliamentary procedure is based on custom and precedent, partly formulated in the Standing Orders of both Houses (*see* **Standing Orders**, p. 236), and each House has the right to control its own internal proceedings and to commit for contempt. The system of debate in the two Houses is similar; when a motion has been moved, the Speaker proposes the question as the subject of a debate. Members speak from wherever they have been sitting. Questions are decided by a vote on a simple majority. Draft legislation is introduced, in either House, as a Bill. Bills can be introduced by a Government Minister or a private Member, but in practice the majority of Bills which become law are introduced by the Government. To become law, a Bill must be passed by each House (for parliamentary stages, *see* Bill, p. 234) and then sent to the Sovereign for the Royal Assent, after which it becomes an Act of Parliament.

Proceedings of both Houses are public, except on extremely rare occasions. The minutes (called Votes and Proceedings in the Commons, and Minutes of Proceedings in the Lords) and the speeches (The Official Report of Parliamentary Debates, *Hansard*) are published daily. Proceedings are also recorded for transmission on radio and television and preserved by the Parliamentary Sound Archive. Television cameras have been allowed into the House of Lords since January 1985, and into the House of Commons since November 1989; committee meetings may also be televised.

By the Parliament Act of 1911, the maximum duration of a Parliament is five years, if not previously dissolved, the term being reckoned from the date given on the writs for the new Parliament. The maximum life has been prolonged by legislation in such rare circumstances as the two world wars (Jan. 31, 1911–Nov. 25, 1918; Nov. 26, 1935–June 15, 1945). Dissolution and writs for a general election are ordered by the Queen on the advice of the Prime Minister. The life of a Parliament is divided into sessions, usually of one year in length, beginning and ending most often in October or November.

THE HOUSE OF LORDS

The House of Lords consists of the Lords Spiritual and Temporal. The Lords Spiritual are the Archbishops of Canterbury and York, the Bishops of London, Durham and Winchester, and the 21 senior diocesan bishops of the Church of England. The Lords Temporal consist of all hereditary Peers and Peeresses of England, Scotland, Great Britain and the United Kingdom who have not disclaimed their Peerages, Life Peers and Peeresses created under the Life Peerages Act 1958, and those Lords of Appeal in Ordinary created Life Peers under the Appellate Jurisdiction Act 1876, as amended (Law Lords). Disclaimants of an hereditary Peerage lose their right to sit in the House of Lords but gain the right to vote at Parliamentary elections and to offer themselves for election to the House of Commons. (*See also* p. 152.) Peers who do not wish to attend sittings of the House of Lords may apply for leave of absence for the duration of a Parliament.

Until the beginning of this century the House of Lords had considerable power, being able to veto any Bill submitted to it by the House of Commons, but those powers were greatly reduced by the Parliament Act of 1911 and subsequently by the Parliament Act of 1949 (*see* **Parliament Acts 1911 and 1949,** p. 235).

Combined with its legislative role, the House of Lords has judicial powers as the ultimate Court of Appeal for Courts in Great Britain and Northern Ireland, except for criminal cases in Scotland. These powers are exercised by the Lord Chancellor and the Law Lords.

Members of the House of Lords are unpaid. However, they are entitled to reimbursement of travelling expenses on parliamentary business within the UK and certain other expenses incurred for the purpose of attendance at sittings of the House, within a maximum for each day of £64·00 for overnight subsistence, £24·00 for day subsistence and incidental travel, and £25·00 for secretarial costs, postage and certain additional expenses.

Composition
(as at July 31, 1990)

Archbishops and Bishops	26
Peers by succession	764
	(21 women)
Hereditary Peers of first creation (including the Prince of Wales)	20
Life Peers under the Appellate Jurisdiction Act 1876	19
Life Peers under the Life Peerages Act 1958	360
	(52 women)
TOTAL	1,189
Of whom:	
Peers without Writs of Summons	89
Peers on leave of absence from the House	142

State of Parties
(as at July 1990)

About half of the members of the House of Lords take the whip of one of the political parties. The other members sit on the cross-benches or as independents.

Conservative	429
Labour	109
Liberal Democrats	54
Archbishops and Bishops	26
Cross-Bench	243

Officers

The House is presided over by the Lord Chancellor, who is ex officio Speaker of the House. A panel of deputy Speakers is appointed by Royal Commission. The first deputy Speaker is the Chairman of Committees, appointed at the beginning of each session, a salaried officer of the House who takes the chair in Committee of the whole House and in some Select Committees. He is assisted by a panel of Deputy Chairmen, headed by the salaried Principal Deputy Chairman of Committees, who is also Chairman of the European Communities Committee of the House. The permanent officers include the Clerk of the Parliaments, who is in charge of the administrative staff collectively known as the Parliament Office; the Gentleman Usher of the Black Rod, who is also Serjeant-at-Arms in attendance upon the Lord Chancellor and is responsible for security and for accommodation and services in the House of Lords; and the Yeoman Usher who is Deputy Serjeant-at-Arms and assists Black Rod in his duties.

OFFICERS

Speaker, The Rt. Hon. the Lord Mackay of
 Clashfern £12,810
  Private Secretary, Ms J. Rowe.
Chairman of Committees, The Rt. Hon. the
 Lord Aberdare, KBE. £40,863
Principal Deputy Chairman of Committees,
 The Baroness Serota £37,353
Clerk of the Parliaments, M. A. J. Wheeler-
 Booth £77,000
Clerk Assistant and Clerk of the Journals,
 J. M. Davies .... £54,900–£64,300
Reading Clerk, P. D. G. Hoyter ..... £47,000–£54,100
Counsel to Chairman of Committees,
 D. Rippengal, CB, QC. .... £54,900–£64,300
Second Counsel, Mrs. E. Denza, CMG.
 £47,000–£54,100

Assistant Counsel, N. J. Adamson, CB, QC.
£35,741–£48,069
Principal Clerks, J. A. Vallance White
(*Judicial Office and Fourth Clerk at the
Table*); M. G. Pownall (*Committees*)
£40,004–£54,100
Chief Clerks, C. A. J. Mitchell; B. P. Keith;
R. H. Walters, D.Phil.; D. R. Beamish;
Mrs. F. M. Martin .... £33,026–£43,046
Senior Clerks, D. F. Slater (*Seconded as
Secretary to the Leader of the House
and Chief Whip*); Dr. F. P. Tudor;
E. C. Ollard; Miss M. E. De Groose;
A. Makower; E. J. J. Wells;
T. V. Hohan .... £22,848–£31,751
Clerk of the Records, H. S. Cobb, FSA £33,026–£43,046
Deputy Clerk of the Records, D. J. Johnson,
FSA............................ £25,825–£38,568
Assistant Clerks of the Records, J. C.
Morgan (*Sound Archives*); S. K. Ellison
£22,848–£31,751
Accountant, C. Preece............. £22,848–£31,751
Assistant Accountant, Miss J. M.
Lansdown .... £17,536–£24,520
Judicial Taxing Clerk, C. G. Osborne
£17,536–£24,520
Librarian, R. H. V. C. Morgan .... £33,026–£43,046
Deputy Librarian, D. L. Jones. .... £25,825–£38,568
Library Clerks, P. G. Davis, Ph.D.; Miss I. L.
Victory, Ph.D. .... £22,848–£31,751
Examiners of Petitions for Private Bills,
M. G. Pownall; R. J. Willoughby.
*Gentleman Usher of the Black Rod and
Serjeant-at-Arms,* Air Chief Marshal Sir
John Gingell, GBE, KCB. .... £47,000–£54,100
*Yeoman Usher of the Black Rod and Deputy
Serjeant-at-Arms,* Air Cdre. A. C. Curry,
OBE............................ £22,848–£31,751
Staff Superintendent, Maj. F. P. Horsfall, MBE.
Shorthand Writer, Mrs. E. M. C. Holland ...... *fees*
Editor, Official Report (*Hansard*), Mrs.
M. E. Villiers .... £31,149–£40,568
Deputy Editor, Official Report, G. R. Good-
barne .... £23,418–£34,886

THE HOUSE OF COMMONS

The Members of the House of Commons are elected
by universal adult suffrage. For electoral purposes,
the United Kingdom is divided into constituencies,
each of which returns one Member to the House of
Commons, the Member being the candidate who
obtains the largest number of votes cast in the
constituency. To ensure equitable representation
the four Boundary Commissions keep constituency
boundaries under review and recommend any redis-
tribution of seats which may seem necessary due to
population movements, etc. The number of seats was
raised to 640 in 1945, then reduced to 625 in 1948, and
subsequently rose to 630 in 1955, 635 in 1970 and 650
in 1983. Of the present 650 seats there are 523 for
England, 38 for Wales, 72 for Scotland and 17 for
Northern Ireland.

Elections

Elections are by secret ballot, each elector casting
one vote: voting is not compulsory. When a seat
becomes vacant between General Elections, a by-
election is held.

British subjects and citizens of the Irish Republic
can stand for election as Members of Parliament
(MPs) provided they are 21 or over and not subject to
disqualification. Those disqualified from sitting in
the House include undischarged bankrupts, people
sentenced to more than one year's imprisonment,
clergy of the Church of England, Church of Scotland,

Church of Ireland and Roman Catholic Church,
members of the House of Lords, and holders of certain
offices listed in the House of Commons Disqualification Act 1975 (e.g. members of the judiciary, Civil
Service, regular armed forces, police forces, some
local government officers and some members of public
corporations and government commissions).

A candidate does not require any party backing
but his or her nomination for election must be
supported by the signatures of ten people registered
in the constituency. A candidate must also deposit
with the returning officer £500, which is forfeit
if the candidate does not receive more than
5 per cent of the votes cast. All election expenses,
except the candidate's personal expenses, are subject
to a statutory limit of £3,648, plus 3·1 pence for each
elector in a borough constituency or 4·1 pence for
each elector in a county constituency. (*See* pp. 241–
248 for an alphabetical list of MPs, and pp. 249–276
for the results of the last General Election and
subsequent by-elections.)

Business

The week's business of the House is outlined each
Thursday by the Leader of the House, after consultation between the Chief Government Whip and the
Chief Opposition Whip. A quarter to a third of the
time will be taken up by the Government's legislative
programme, and the rest by other business, e.g.
question time. As a rule Bills likely to raise political
controversy are introduced in the Commons before
going on to the Lords, and the Commons claims
exclusive control in respect of national taxation and
expenditure. Bills such as the Finance Bill, which
imposes taxation, and the Consolidated Fund Bills,
which authorize expenditure, must begin in the
Commons. A Bill of which the financial provisions
are subsidiary may begin in the Lords; and the
Commons may waive its rights in regard to Lords'
amendments affecting finance.

The Commons has a public register of MPs'
financial, and certain other, interests. Members must
also disclose any relevant financial interest or benefit
in a matter before the House when taking part in a
debate, in certain other proceedings of the House or
in consultations with other Members, with Ministers
or civil servants.

Members pay, etc.

Since 1911 Members of the House of Commons have
received salary payments; facilities for free travel
were introduced in 1924. Members are entitled to
claim income tax relief on expenses incurred in the
course of their Parliamentary duties. Salary rates
since 1911 were as follows:

	p.a.		p.a.
1911..........	£400	1978 June	£6,897
1931..........	360	1979 June	9,450
1934..........	380	1980 June	11,750
1935..........	400	1981 June	13,950
1937..........	600	1982 June	14,510
1946..........	1,000	1983 June	15,308
1954..........	1,250	1984 Jan......	16,106
1957..........	1,750	1985 Jan......	16,904
1964..........	3,250	1986 Jan......	17,702
1972 Jan......	4,500	1987 Jan......	18,500
1975 June	5,750	1988 Jan......	22,548
1976 June	6,062	1989 Jan......	24,107
1977 July	6,270	1990 Jan......	26,701

In October 1969 Members were granted an allowance for secretarial and research expenses. In 1987
this became known as the Office Costs Allowance,
and in April 1989 rose to £24,903 a year.

Since January 1972 Members can claim reimbursement for the additional cost of staying overnight away from their main residence while on Parliamentary business. This was set at £10,138 for the 1990–91 financial year. Since 1984 this has been non-taxable.

From March 1980 provision was made enabling each Member in receipt of Office Costs Allowance to contribute sums to an approved pension scheme for the provision of a pension, or other benefits, for or in respect of persons whose salary is met by him/her from the Office Costs Allowance.

The cost of travel allowances for 1989–90 was stated in June 1990 to be £6,777,595 (car mileage claims £4,368,079, rail travel £818,768 and air travel £718,279, spouse/children travel £484,562, extended travel within the UK £105,724, and secretarial/staff travel £282,183).

Members pensions

The Ministerial Salaries and Members' Pensions Act 1965 established a contributory pension fund providing pensions for former Members of Parliament and for dependants of deceased former Members. The Fund was reconstituted and the scheme restructured to bring it into line with pension schemes in the public sector by the Parliamentary and Other Pensions Acts 1972: further Acts modifying the arrangements for Members, Ministers and certain officeholders were passed in 1976, 1978, 1981, 1984 and 1987. The Parliamentary and Other Pensions Act 1987 is an enabling measure which provides that the detailed provisions may be contained in subordinate legislation.

The arrangements now provide a pension of one-fiftieth of salary for each year of pensionable service with a maximum of two-thirds of salary at age 65. Pension is normally payable at age 65, for men and women, or on later retirement. Pensions may be paid earlier e.g. on ill-health retirement. The widow/widower of a former Member receives a pension of one-half of the late Member's pension. Pensions are index-linked. Members contribute 9 per cent of salary to the pension fund; there is an Exchequer contribution, currently slightly less than half the amount contributed by Members.

The House of Commons Members' Fund provides for annual or lump sum grants to ex-Members, their widows or widowers, and children whose incomes are below certain limits. Alternatively, payments of £1,698 per annum to ex-Members with at least ten years service and who left the House of Commons before October 1964, and £849 per annum to their widows or widowers are made as of right. Members contribute £24 per annum and the Exchequer £115,000 per annum to the Fund. The income of the Fund in 1987–88 was £220,922 and estimated expenditure on grants and payments was £141,056. The net assets of the Fund as at September 30, 1987 amounted to £1,490,633.

Officers

The House of Commons is presided over by the Speaker, who has considerable powers to maintain order in the House. His deputy, the Chairman of Ways and Means, and two Deputy Chairmen may preside over sittings of the House of Commons; they are elected by the House, and, like the Speaker, neither speak nor vote other than in their official capacity. The staff of the House are employed by a Commission chaired by the Speaker. The Heads of House of Commons Departments (*see* below) are permanent officers of the House, not MPs. The Clerk of the House is the principal adviser to the Speaker on the privileges and procedures of the House, the conduct of the business of the House, and Committees. The Serjeant-at-Arms is responsible for security,

ceremonial, and for accommodation in the Commons part of the Palace of Westminster.

OFFICERS AND OFFICIALS

Speaker, The Rt. Hon. Bernard Weatherill, MP for Croydon North East £55,221
Chairman of Ways and Means, The Rt. Hon. Harold Walker, MP for Doncaster Central . £44,951
First Deputy Chairman of Ways and Means, Sir Paul Dean, MP for Woodspring £41,941
Second Deputy Chairman of Ways and Means, Miss Betty Boothroyd, MP for West Bromwich West £41,941

Offices of the Speaker and Chairman of Ways and Means

Speaker's Secretary, P. J. Kitcatt, CB.
£33,026–£37,186
Speaker's Counsel, H. Knorpel, CB, QC;
G. E. Gammie, CB, QC. £45,350
Assistant to Speaker's Counsel, P. Harvey, CB. . . . . £24,789–£29,224
Chaplain to the Speaker, The Rev. Canon D. Gray, TD.
Secretary to the Chairman of Ways and Means, R. I. S. Phillips.

Department of the Clerk of the House

Clerk of the House of Commons, Sir Clifford Boulton, KCB. £76,320
Clerk Asst., D. W. Limon £53,420
Clerk of Committees, J. F. Sweetman, TD £53,420
Principal Clerks (£40,004–£45,350):—
  Public Bills, H. M. Barclay.
  Journal Office, W. R. McKay.
  Table Office, C. B. Winnifrith.
  Overseas Office, R. B. Sands.
  Select Committees, G. Cubie.
  Second Clerk of Select Committees, A. J. Hastings.
  Private Bills, R. J. Willoughby.
  Standing Committees, J. R. Rose.
  Financial Committees, D. G. Millar.
Deputy Principal Clerks, S. A. L. Panton; M. R. Jack, PH.D.; Mrs. J. Sharpe; Ms. A. Milner-Barry; R. W. G. Wilson; W. A. Proctor; F. A. Cranmer; R. J. Rogers; C. R. M. Ward, PH.D.; Ms. H. E. Irwin; D. W. N. Doig; A. Sandall; D. L. Natzler; E. P. Silk; D. F. Harrison . . . . £33,026–£37,186
Senior Clerks, A. R. Kennon; D. W. Robson; L. C. Laurence-Smyth; S. J. Patrick; D. J. Gerhold; C. J. Poyser; S. J. Priestley; A. H. Doherty; P. A. Evans; R. I. S. Phillips; R. G. James; Mrs E. J. Flood; Ms P. A. Helme; D. R Lloyd; R. A. Lambert; J. M. Hope (*acting*); H. R. Neilson (*acting*); D. Steel (*acting*) . . . . £22,848–£26,910
Clerk of Services Sub-Committees, K. J. Brown . . . . £21,793–£25,652
Examiners of Petitions for Private Bills, R. J. Willoughby; M. G. Pownall.
Registrar of Members' Interests, A. J. Hastings.
Taxing Officer, R. J. Willoughby.

Department of the Serjeant at Arms

Serjeant-at-Arms, Sir Alan Urwick, KCVO, CMG. £45,350
Deputy Serjeant-at-Arms, P. N. W. Jennings
£33,026–£37,186
Assistant Serjeant-at-Arms, M. J. A. Cummins . . . . £24,621–£31,462
Deputy Assistant Serjeants-at-Arms, P. A. J. Wright; J. F. Collins . . . . £22,848–£26,910

Department of the Library

Librarian, D. Menhennet, D.Phil £45,350
Deputy Librarian, D. J. T. Englefield
£40,004–£41,496

Library and Information Service

Assistant Librarians, G. F. Lock; Miss
J. B. Tanfield . . . . £33,026–£37,186
Deputy Assistant Librarians, S. Z. Young;
Mrs. H. R. Coates; Miss P. J. Baines; K. G.
Cuninghame; Mrs. J. M. Wainwright;
C. C. Pond, PH.D.; Mrs. C. B. Andrews; R.
C. Clements; Mrs. J. M. Lourie . . £25,825–£33,026
Senior Library Clerks, Ms. F. Poole; Mrs. J.
M. Fiddick; C. R. Barclay; Mrs. C. M.
Gillie; R. J. Ware, D.Phil; Ms. D. Gore,
PH.D; R. J. Twigger; B. K. Winetrobe; T.
N. Edmonds; R. J. Cracknell; Miss O. M.
Gay; Miss E. M. McInnes; Mrs. G. L. Allen;
Miss M. Baber; Ms A. Muir . . . . . £22,848–£26,910

Vote Office

Deliverer of the Vote, G. R. Russell . £25,825–£33,026
Deputy Deliverer of the Vote, H. C. Foster
£22,848–£26,910

Administration Department

Head of Administration Department, G. A.
Roberts £45,350
Accountant, J. L. G. Dobson . . . . £40,004–£41,496

Deputy Accountant, A. J. Lewis . . . . £33,026–£37,186
Senior Assistant Accountant, A. R. Marskell
£25,825–£33,026
Assistant Accountants, M. J. Barram; Miss
M. M. McColl; M. Fletcher; R. H. A. Rus-
sell . . . . £22,848–£26,910
Head of Establishments Office, B. A. Wilson
£33,026–£37,186
Deputy Head of Establishments Office, J. A.
Robb . . . . £25,825–£33,026
Computer Officer, R. S. Morgan . . . . £33,026–£37,186
Internal Auditor, A. A. Cameron . . . £22,848–£26,910
Staff Inspector, R. C. Collins . . . . . . £22,848–£26,910

Department of the Official Report

Editor, I. D. Church . . . . £40,004–£41,496
Deputy Editor, P. Walker . . . . £25,825–£33,026
Principal Assistant Editors, R. V. Hadlow;
J. Gourley; J. Withers; W. G. Garland
£24,140–£30,837
Assistant Editors, Miss V. Grainger; J. Led-
gerwood; Miss V. A. A. Clarke; Miss H.
Hales; Miss G. L. Sutherland . . . . £21,732–£27,709

Refreshment Department

General Manager, W. J. J. Smillie . . £25,825–£33,026
Deputy General Manager, E. J. Nash
£22,848–£26,910
Catering Accountant, D. R. W. Wood
£22,848–£26,910

PARLIAMENTARY INFORMATION
The following is a short glossary of aspects of work of Parliament
(Unless otherwise stated, references are to House of Commons procedures.)

Adjournment Debate.—Usually a half-hour debate introduced by a backbencher at the end of
business for the day. The subjects raised are often
local or personal issues.

Bill.—Proposed legislation is termed a Bill. The
stages of a Public Bill (for **Private Bills**, *see* below)
in the House of Commons are as follows:

First Reading: There is no debate at this stage,
which nowadays merely constitutes an order to have
the Bill printed.

Second Reading: The debate on the principles of
the Bill.

Committee Stage: The detailed examination of a
Bill, clause by clause. In most cases this takes place
in a Standing Committee, or the whole House may
act as a Committee. A Special Standing Committee
may take evidence before embarking on detailed
scrutiny of the Bill. Very rarely, a Bill may be
examined by a Select Committee (*see* below).

Report Stage: Detailed review of a Bill as amended
in Committee.

Third Reading: Final debate on a Bill.

Public Bills go through the same stages in the
House of Lords, except that in almost all cases the
Committee stage is taken in Committee of the Whole
House.

A Bill may start in either House, and has to pass
through both Houses to become law.

Both Houses have to agree the same text of a Bill,
so that the amendments made by the second House
are then considered in the originating House and if
not agreed, sent back or themselves amended, until
agreement is reached.

Chiltern Hundreds.—A legal fiction, a nominal
office of profit under the Crown, the acceptance of

which requires a Member to vacate his seat. The
Manor of Northstead is similar. These are the only
means by which an MP may resign.

Closure & Guillotine.—To prevent deliberate
waste of time of either House, a motion may be made
that the question be now put. In the House of
Commons, if the Speaker decides that the rights of a
minority are not being prejudiced and 100 members
support the closure motion in a division, if carried,
the original motion is put to the House without
further debate.

The Guillotine represents a more rigorous and
systematic application of the Closure. Under this
system, a Bill proceeds in accordance with a rigid
timetable and discussion is limited to the time allotted
to each group of clauses. The Closure is hardly ever
used in the Lords, and there is no procedure for a
guillotine. The completion of business in the Lords
is ensured by agreement from all sides of the House.

Consolidated Fund Bill.—A Bill to authorize
issue of money to maintain Government services.
The Bill is dealt with without debate, but afterwards
members may raise topics of public or local importance.

Delegated Legislation.—Many Statutes empower Ministers to make delegated legislation, with
little or no reference back to Parliament, usually by
means of Statutory Instruments. These fall into four
broad categories:—

(i) Affirmative Instruments, which are subject to
approval by resolutions of both Houses before they
can come into or remain in force;

(ii) Negative Instruments, which are subject to
annulment by resolution of either House;

(iii) General Instruments, which include those not required to be laid before Parliament and those which are required to be so laid but are not subject to approval or annulment;

(iv) Special Procedure Orders, against which parties outside Parliament may lodge petitions.

Dissolution.—Parliament comes to an end either by dissolution by the Sovereign, on the advice of the Prime Minister, or on the expiration of the term of five years for which the House of Commons was elected. Dissolution is normally effected by a Royal Proclamation.

Early Day Motion.—A motion put on the Notice Paper by an MP without in general the real prospect of its being debated. Such motions are expressions of backbench opinion.

Emergency Debate.—In the Commons a method of obtaining prompt discussion of a matter of urgency is by moving the adjournment under Standing Order No. 20 for the purpose of discussing a specific and important matter that should have urgent consideration. A member may ask leave to make this motion by giving written notice to the Speaker, usually before 12 noon, and if the Speaker considers the matter of sufficient importance and the House agrees, it is discussed usually at 7 p.m. on the following day.

Father of the House.—The Member whose continuous service in the House of Commons, is the longest. The present Father of the House is the Rt. Hon. Sir Bernard Braine, elected first in 1950.

General Synod Measure.—A measure passed by the national assembly of the Church of England under the Church of England Assembly (Powers) Act 1919. These measures are considered by the Joint Ecclesiastical Committee, who make a report. They are then considered by both Houses, and if approved, sent for the Royal Assent.

Hansard.—The official report of debates in both Houses (and in Standing Committees) published by HMSO, normally on the day after the sitting concerned.

Hours of Meeting.—The House of Commons meets on Monday, Tuesday, Wednesday and Thursday at 2.30 p.m., and on Friday at 9.30 a.m. The House of Lords normally meets at 2.30 p.m. on Monday, Tuesday and Wednesday and at 3 p.m. on Thursday. In the latter part of the session, the House of Lords sometimes sits on Fridays at 11 a.m.

Hybridity.—A Public Bill which is considered to affect specific private or local interests, as distinct from all such interests of a single category, is called a Hybrid Bill and is subject to a special form of scrutiny to enable people affected to object. In the House of Lords, affirmative instruments (*see* **Delegated Legislation**) may also be treated as hybrid.

Leader of the Opposition.—In 1937 the office of Leader of the Opposition was recognized and a salary of £2,000 per annum was assigned to the post, thus following a practice which had prevailed in the Dominion of Canada since 1906. From January 1990 the salary was £52,301. The present Leader of the Opposition is the Rt. Hon. Neil Kinnock.

The Lord Chancellor.—The Lord High Chancellor of Great Britain is (ex officio) the Speaker of the House of Lords. Unlike the Speaker of the House of Commons, he is a member of the Government, takes part in debates and votes in divisions. He has none of the powers to maintain order that the Speaker in the Commons has, these powers being exercised in the Lords by the House as a whole. The Lord Chancellor sits in the Lords on one of the Woolsacks, couches covered with red cloth and stuffed with wool. If he wishes to address the House in any way except formally as Speaker, he leaves the Woolsack.

Naming.—When a member has been named by the Speaker for a breach of order, i.e. contrary to the practice of the House, called by surname and not addressed as the 'Hon. Member for ... (her/his constituency)', the Leader of the House moves that the offender 'be suspended from the service of the House' for (in the case of a first offence) a period of five sitting days. Should the member offend again, the period of suspension is increased.

Opposition Day.—A day on which the topic for debate is chosen by the Opposition. There are 20 such days in a normal session. On 17 days, subjects are chosen by the Leader of the Opposition; on the remaining three days by the leader of the next largest opposition party.

Parliament Acts 1911 and 1949.—Under these Acts Bills may become law without the consent of the Lords.

Since at least the 18th century the Commons have had the privilege of having bills concerned with supply (i.e. taxation and money matters) passed without amendment by the Lords, though until 1911 the Lords retained the right to reject such bills outright.

By the Parliament Act 1911 a Bill which has been endorsed by the Speaker of the House of Commons as a Money Bill, and has been passed by the Commons and sent up to the Lords at least one month before the end of a session, can become law without the consent of the Lords if it is not passed by them without amendment within a month.

Under the Parliament Acts 1911 and 1949, if the Lords reject any other Public Bill (except one to prolong the life of a Parliament) which has been passed by the Commons in two successive sessions then that Bill shall (unless the Commons direct to the contrary) become law without the consent of the Lords. The Lords have power, therefore, to delay a Public Bill for thirteen months from its first Second Reading in the House of Commons.

Prime Minister's Questions.—The Prime Minister answers questions from 3.15 to 3.30 p.m. on Tuesdays and Thursdays. Nowadays the 'open question' predominates. Members tend to ask the Prime Minister what are her or his official engagements for the day; a supplementary question on virtually any topic can then be put.

Private Bill.—A Bill promoted by a body or an individual to give powers additional to, or in conflict with, the general law, and to which a special procedure applies to enable people affected to object.

Private Members' Bill.—A Public Bill promoted by a Member who is not a member of HM Government.

Private Notice Question.—A question adjudged of urgent importance on submission to the Speaker (in the Lords, the Leader of the House), answered at the end of oral questions—usually at 3.30 p.m.

Privilege.—The following are covered by the privilege of Parliament:—

(i) freedom from interference in going to, attending at, and going from, Parliament;

(ii) freedom of speech in Parliamentary proceedings;

(iii) the printing and publishing of anything relating to the proceedings of the two Houses is subject to privilege;

(iv) each House is the guardian of its dignity and may punish any insult to the House as a whole.

Prorogation.—The bringing to an end, by the Sovereign on the advice of the Government, of a session of Parliament. Public Bills which have not completed all their stages lapse on Prorogation.

Queen's Speech.—The Speech delivered by HM The Queen at the State Opening of Parliament, in which the Government's programme for the session is set forth. The Speech is, in fact, drafted by Civil Servants and approved by the Cabinet.

Question Time.—Oral questions are answered by Ministers in the Commons from 2.30 to 3.30 p.m. every day except Friday. They are also taken at the start of the Lords sittings, with a daily limit of four oral questions.

Royal Assent.—The Royal Assent is signified by Letters Patent to such Bills and Measures as have passed both Houses of Parliament (or Bills which have been passed under the Parliament Acts 1911 and 1949). The Sovereign has not given Royal Assent in person since 1854. On occasion, for instance in the Prorogation of Parliament, Royal Assent may be pronounced to the two Houses by Lords Commissioners; but more usually Royal Assent is notified to each House sitting separately in accordance with the Royal Assent Act 1967. The old French formulae for Royal Assent are then endorsed on the Acts by the Clerk of the Parliaments.

The power to withhold assent resides with the Sovereign, but has not been exercised in the United Kingdom since 1707, in the reign of Queen Anne.

Select Committees consisting usually of 10–15 members of all parties are a means used by both Houses in order to investigate certain matters.

Most Select Committees in the House of Commons are now tied to departments; each Committee investigates subjects within a government department's remit (*see* below).

There are other House of Commons Select Committees dealing with Public Accounts (i.e. the spending by HM Government of money voted by Parliament) and European Legislation, and also domestic committees dealing, for example, with Privilege and Services. Major Select Committees usually take evidence in public; their evidence and reports are published by HMSO.

The principal Select Committee in the House of Lords is that on the European Communities, which has, at present, six sub-committees dealing with all areas of Community policy. The House of Lords also has a Select Committee on Science and Technology, which appoints sub-committees to deal with specific subjects. In addition, *ad hoc* Select Committees have been set up from time to time to investigate specific subjects, e.g. overseas trade, murder and life imprisonment. There are also some Joint Committees of the two Houses, e.g. the Joint Committee on Statutory Instruments.

Departmental Committees

Agriculture.—*Chair*, J. Wiggin, MP; *Clerk*, D. W. Robson.

Defence.—*Chair*, M. Mates, MP; *Clerk*, D. L. Natzler.

Education, Science and Arts.—*Chair*, M. Thornton, MP; *Clerk*, A. Sandall.

Employment.—*Chair*, R. Leighton, MP; *Clerk*, S. J. Patrick.

Energy.—*Chair*, Dr. M. Clark, MP; *Clerk*, D. J. Gerhold.

Environment.—*Chair*, Sir Hugh Rossi, MP; *Clerk*, F. A. Cranmer.

Foreign Affairs.—*Chair*, D. Howell, MP; *Clerk*, R. W. G. Wilson.

Home Affairs.—*Chair*, Sir John Wheeler, MP; *Clerk*, E. P. Silk.

Scottish Affairs.—Committee not appointed.

Social Services.—*Chair*, F. Field, MP; *Clerk*, Ms H. E. Irwin.

Trade and Industry.—*Chair*, K. Warren, MP; *Clerk*, A. R. Kennon.

Transport.—*Chair*, D. Marshall, MP; *Clerk*, A. H. Doherty.

Treasury and Civil Service.—*Chair*, T. Higgins, MP; *Clerk*, D. G. Millar.

Welsh Affairs.—*Chair*, G. Wardell, MP; *Clerk*, D. F. Harrison.

Non-departmental Committees

European Legislation.—*Chair*, N. Spearing, MP; *Clerk*, C. R. M. Ward.

Members' Interests.—*Chair*, Sir Geoffrey Smith, MP; *Clerk*, A. J. Hastings.

Parliamentary Commissioner for Administration.—*Chair*, Sir Anthony Buck, MP; *Clerk*, C. G. Lee.

Privileges.—*Chair*, Sir Geoffrey Howe, MP; *Clerk*, W. R. McKay.

Procedure.—*Chair*, Sir Peter Emery, MP; *Clerk*, D. W. N. Doig.

Public Accounts.—*Chair*, R. Sheldon, MP; *Clerk*, Mrs E. J. Flood.

The Speaker.—The Speaker of the House of Commons is the spokesman and president of the Chamber. He is elected by the House at the beginning of each Parliament or when the previous Speaker retires or dies. He neither speaks in debates nor votes in divisions except when the voting is equal.

Standing Orders.—Rules which have from time to time been agreed by each House of Parliament to regulate the conduct of its business. These orders may be amended or repealed, and are from time to time suspended or dispensed with.

State Opening.—This marks the start of each new session of Parliament. Parliament is normally opened, in the presence of both Houses, by the Queen in person, who makes the Speech from the Throne which outlines the Government's policies for the coming session (*see* **Queen's Speech**). In the absence of the Queen, Parliament is opened by Royal Commission, and the Queen's Speech is read by one of the Lords Commissioners specially appointed by Letters Patent for the occasion.

Strangers.—Anyone who is not a Member or Officer of the House is a stranger. Visitors are generally admitted to debates of both Houses but may be excluded if the House so decides. In practice this happens only in time of war.

Ten Minute Rule.—A colloquial term for Standing Order No. 19, under which backbenchers have an opportunity on Tuesdays and Wednesdays to state for about ten minutes why a Bill on a certain subject should be introduced. Time is also available for a short opposing speech.

Vacant Seats.—When a vacancy occurs in the House of Commons during a session of Parliament, the Writ for the by-election is moved by a Whip of the party to which the member whose seat has been vacated belonged. If the House is in recess, the Speaker can issue a warrant for a writ, should two members certify to him that a seat is vacant.

Whips.—In order to secure the attendance of Members of a particular party in Parliament on all occasions, and particularly on the occasion of an important vote, Whips (originally known as 'Whippers-in') are appointed. The written appeal or circular letter issued by them is also known as a 'whip', its urgency being denoted by the number of times it is underlined. Failure to respond to a three-line whip, headed 'Most important', is tantamount in the Commons to secession (at any rate temporarily) from the party. Whips are officially recognized by Parliament and are provided with office accommodation in both Houses. In both Houses, Government and some Opposition Whips receive salaries from public funds.

Public Information Service.—Enquiries from the general public and organizations of all kinds

about the work, practices, composition and history of the House of Commons are answered by the Public Information Office, House of Commons, SW1A 0AA (Tel: 071–219 4272). This office also edits the House of Commons Weekly Information Bulletin (published by HMSO). A series of factsheets on the work and processes of the House is available.

The Journal and Information Office, House of Lords, SW1A 0PW (Tel: 071–219 3107) answers queries relating to the procedure and practice of the Lords.

THE GOVERNMENT

The Government is the body of Ministers responsible for the administration of national affairs, determining policy and introducing into Parliament any legislation necessary to give effect to government policy. The majority of Ministers are members of the House of Commons but members of the House of Lords or of neither House may also hold Ministerial responsibility. The Lord Chancellor is always a member of the House of Lords. The Prime Minister is, by current convention, always a member of the House of Commons.

THE PRIME MINISTER

The office of Prime Minister, which had been in existence for nearly 200 years, was officially recognized in 1905 and its holder was granted a place in the Table of Precedence. The Prime Minister, by tradition also First Lord of the Treasury and Minister for the Civil Service, is appointed by the Sovereign and is usually the leader of the party which enjoys, or can secure, a majority in the House of Commons. Other Ministers are appointed by the Sovereign on the recommendation of the Prime Minister, who also allocates functions amongst Ministers and has the power to obtain their resignation or dismissal individually.

The Prime Minister informs the Sovereign of state and political matters, advises on the dissolution of Parliament, and makes recommendations for important Crown appointments, the award of honours, etc.

As the chairman of Cabinet meetings and leader of a political party, the Prime Minister is responsible for translating party policy into government activity. As leader of the Government, the Prime Minister is responsible to Parliament and to the electorate for the policies and their implementation.

The Prime Minister also represents the nation in international affairs, e.g. summit conferences.

THE CABINET

The Cabinet developed during the 18th century as an inner committee of the Privy Council, which was the chief source of executive power until that time. The Cabinet is composed of about 20 Ministers chosen by the Prime Minister, usually the heads of government departments (generally known as Secretaries of State unless they have a special title, e.g. Chancellor of the Exchequer), the leaders of the two Houses of Parliament, and the holders of various traditional offices.

The Cabinet's functions are the final determination of policy, control of government and co-ordination of government departments. The exercise of its functions is dependent upon enjoying majority support in the House of Commons. Cabinet meetings are held in private, taking place once or twice a week during parliamentary sittings and less often during a recess. Proceedings are confidential, the members being bound by their oath as Privy Counsellors not to disclose information about the proceedings.

The convention of collective responsibility means that the Cabinet acts unanimously even when Cabinet Ministers do not all agree on a subject. The policies of departmental Ministers must be consistent with the policies of the Government as a whole, and once the Government's policy has been decided, each Minister is expected to support it or resign.

The convention of Ministerial responsibility holds a Minister, as the political head of his or her department, accountable to Parliament for the department's work. Departmental Ministers usually decide all matters within their responsibility, although on matters of political importance they normally consult their colleagues collectively. A decision by a departmental Minister is binding on the Government as a whole.

HER MAJESTY'S GOVERNMENT

(*See also* **Occurrences during printing**)

THE CABINET

Prime Minister, First Lord of the Treasury and Minister for the Civil Service, THE RT. HON. MARGARET HILDA THATCHER, MP, *born* Oct. 13, 1925.

Lord President of the Council and Leader of the House of Commons, The Rt. Hon. Sir (Richard Edward) Geoffrey Howe, QC, MP, *born* Dec. 20, 1926.

Lord High Chancellor, The Rt. Hon. the Lord Mackay of Clashfern, *born* July 2, 1927.

Secretary of State for Foreign and Commonwealth Affairs, The Rt. Hon. Douglas Richard Hurd, CBE, MP, *born* March 8, 1930.

Chancellor of the Exchequer, The Rt. Hon. John Major, MP, *born* March 29, 1943.

Secretary of State for the Home Department, The Rt. Hon. David Charles Waddington, QC, MP, *born* Aug. 2, 1929.

Secretary of State for Defence, The Rt. Hon. Thomas Jeremy King, MP, *born* June 13, 1933.

Chancellor of the Duchy of Lancaster, The Rt. Hon. Kenneth Wilfred Baker, MP, *born* Nov. 3, 1934.

Secretary of State for Health, The Rt. Hon. Kenneth Henry Clarke, QC, MP, *born* July 2, 1940.

Secretary of State for Education and Science, The Rt. Hon. John Roddick Russell MacGregor, OBE, MP, *born* Feb. 14, 1937.

Secretary of State for Scotland, The Rt. Hon. Malcolm Leslie Rifkind, QC, MP, *born* June 21, 1946.

Secretary of State for Transport, The Rt. Hon. Cecil Edward Parkinson, MP, *born* Sept. 1, 1931.

Secretary of State for Energy, The Rt. Hon. John Wakeham, MP, *born* June 22, 1932.
Lord Privy Seal and Leader of the House of Lords, The Rt. Hon. The Lord Belstead, *born* Sept. 30, 1932.
Secretary of State for Social Security, The Rt. Hon. Antony Harold Newton, OBE, MP, *born* Aug. 29, 1937.
Secretary of State for the Environment, The Rt. Hon. Christopher Francis Patten, MP, *born* May 12, 1944.
Secretary of State for Northern Ireland, The Rt. Hon. Peter Leonard Brooke, MP, *born* March 3, 1934.
Minister of Agriculture, Fisheries and Food, The Rt. Hon. John Selwyn Gummer, MP, *born* Nov. 26, 1939.
Chief Secretary to the Treasury, The Rt. Hon. Norman Stewart Hughson Lamont, MP, *born* May 8, 1942.
Secretary of State for Employment, The Rt. Hon. Michael Howard, QC, MP, *born* July 7, 1941.
Secretary of State for Wales, The Rt. Hon. David James Fletcher Hunt, MBE, MP, *born* May 21, 1942.
Secretary of State for Trade and Industry, The Rt. Hon. Peter Bruce Lilley, MP, *born* Aug. 23, 1943.

LAW OFFICERS

Attorney-General, The Rt. Hon. Sir Patrick Barnabas Burke Mayhew, QC, MP.
Lord Advocate, The Rt. Hon. The Lord Fraser of Carmyllie, QC.
Solicitor-General, The Rt. Hon. Sir Nicholas Walter Lyell, QC, MP.
Solicitor-General for Scotland, Alan Ferguson Rodger, QC*
   (* not a member of the House of Commons)

OTHER MINISTERS

Parliamentary Secretary to the Treasury, Timothy Renton, MP.
Paymaster General, Richard Ryder, OBE, MP.
Financial Secretary to the Treasury, The Hon. Francis Maude, MP.

Transport, Roger Freeman, MP; The Lord Brabazon of Tara.
Treasury, John Maples, MP (*Economic Secretary*).
Welsh Office, Sir Wyn Roberts, MP.

MINISTERS OF STATE

Agriculture, Fisheries and Food, The Baroness Trumpington.
Defence, The Hon. Archibald Hamilton, MP (*Armed Forces*); The Hon. Alan Clark, MP (*Defence Procurement*).
Education and Science, Timothy Eggar, MP.
Employment, (no appointment made).
Energy, (no appointment made).
Environment, Michael Spicer, MP (*Housing, Planning*); Michael Portillo, MP (*Local Government, Inner Cities*); David Trippier, RD, MP (*Environment and Countryside*).
Foreign and Commonwealth Affairs, The Rt Hon. Lynda Chalker, MP (*Minister for Overseas Development*); The Rt. Hon. William Waldegrave, MP; Tristan Garel-Jones, MP; The Earl of Caithness, PC.
Health, Mrs. Virginia Bottomley, MP.
Home Office, The Earl Ferrers, PC; The Rt. Hon. John Patten, MP; Mrs. Angela Rumbold, CBE, MP.
Northern Ireland, The Rt. Hon. John Cope, MP.
Privy Council Office, David Mellor, QC, MP (*Minister for the Arts*).
Scottish Office, Ian Lang, MP; Michael Forsyth, MP.
Social Security, The Rt. Hon. Nicholas Scott, MBE, MP.
Trade and Industry, The Hon. Douglas Hogg, QC, MP; The Hon. Timothy Sainsbury, MP; The Lord Hesketh.

UNDER-SECRETARIES OF STATE

Agriculture, Fisheries and Food, David Maclean, MP; David Curry, MP.
Defence, The Earl of Arran (*Armed Forces*); Kenneth Carlisle (*Defence Procurement*).
Education and Science, Alan Howarth, CBE, MP; Michael Fallon, MP.
Employment, Robert Jackson, MP; Eric Forth, MP; The Viscount Ullswater.
Energy, The Hon. Colin Moynihan, MP; Anthony Baldry, MP.
Environment, David Heathcoat-Amory, MP; Robert Atkins, MP (*Minister for Sport*); Patrick Nicholls, MP; The Lord Strathclyde.
Foreign and Commonwealth Affairs, Mark Lennox-Boyd, MP.
Health, The Baroness Hooper; Stephen Dorrell, MP.
Home Office, Peter Lloyd, MP.
Northern Ireland Office, Dr. Brian Mawhinney, MP; Richard Needham, MP; The Lord Skelmersdale.
Scottish Office, Lord James Douglas-Hamilton, MP.
Social Security, The Lord Henley; Mrs. Gillian Shephard, MP.
Trade and Industry, John Redwood, MP.
Transport, Patrick McLoughlin, MP; Christopher Chope, MP.
Treasury, The Lords Commissioners (*see* Government Whips).
Welsh Office, Ian Grist, MP.

GOVERNMENT WHIPS

HOUSE OF LORDS

Captain of the Honourable Corps of Gentlemen-at-Arms (Chief Whip), The Rt. Hon. The Lord Denham.
Captain of the Queen's Bodyguard of the Yeoman of the Guard (Deputy Chief Whip), The Viscount Davidson.
Lords in Waiting, The Viscount Long; The Lord Reay; The Earl of Strathmore and Kinghorne.
Baroness in Waiting, The Baroness Blatch, CBE.

HOUSE OF COMMONS

Parliamentary Secretary to the Treasury (Chief Whip), Timothy Renton, MP.

Treasurer of HM Household (Deputy Chief Whip), Alastair Goodlad, MP.
Comptroller of HM Household, Sir George Young, Bt., MP.
Vice-Chamberlain of HM Household, David Lightbown, MP.
Lords Commissioners, John Taylor, MP; The Hon. Thomas Sackville, MP; Sydney Chapman, MP; Gregory Knight, MP; Irvine Patnick, OBE, MP.
Assistant Whips, Nicholas Baker, MP; Timothy Wood, MP; Neil Hamilton, MP; Timothy Boswell, MP; Timothy Kirkhope, MP.

GOVERNMENT BY PARTY

Before the reign of William and Mary the principal Officers of State were chosen by and were responsible to the Sovereign alone and not to Parliament or the nation at large. Such officers acted sometimes in concert with one another, but more often independently, and the fall of one did not, of necessity, involve that of others, although all were liable to be dismissed at any moment.

In 1693 the Earl of Sunderland recommended to William III the advisability of selecting a Ministry from the political party which enjoyed a majority in the House of Commons and the first united Ministry was drawn in 1696 from the Whigs, to which party the King owed his throne. This group became known as the Junto and was regarded with suspicion as a novelty in the political life of the nation, being a small section meeting in secret apart from the main body of Ministers. It may be regarded as the forerunner of the Cabinet and in course of time it led to the establishment of the principle of joint responsibility of Ministers, so that internal disagreement caused a change of personnel or resignation of the whole body of Ministers.

The accession of George I, who was unfamiliar with the English language, led to a disinclination on the part of the Sovereign to preside at meetings of his Ministers and caused the appearance of a Prime Minister, a position first acquired by Robert Walpole in 1721 and retained without interruption for 20 years and 326 days.

In 1828 the old party of the Whigs became known as **Liberals**, a name originally given to it by its opponents to imply laxity of principles, but gradually accepted by the party to indicate its claim to be pioneers and champions of political reform and progressive legislation. In 1861 a Liberal Registration Association was founded and Liberal Associations became widespread. In 1877 a National Liberal Federation was formed, with headquarters in London. The Liberal Party was in power for long periods during the second half of the nineteenth century and for several years during the first quarter of the twentieth century, but after a split in the party the numbers elected were small from 1931. In March 1988, the Liberals and the Social Democratic Party merged under the title **Social and Liberal Democrats**. Since October 1989 they have been known as the **Liberal Democrats**.

Soon after the change from Whig to Liberal the Tory Party became known as **Conservative**, a name traditionally believed to have been invented by John Wilson Croker in 1830 and to have been generally adopted about the time of the passing of the Reform Act of 1832 to indicate that the preservation of national institutions was the leading principle of the party. After the Home Rule crisis of 1886 the dissentient Liberals entered into a compact with the Conservatives, under which the latter undertook not to contest their seats, but a separate **Liberal Unionist** organization was maintained until 1912, when it was united with the Conservatives.

Labour candidates for Parliament made their first appearance at the General Election of 1892, when there were 27 standing as Labour or Liberal-Labour. In 1900 the Labour Representation Committee was set up in order to establish a distinct Labour group in Parliament, with its own whips, its own policy, and a readiness to co-operate with any party which might be engaged in promoting legislation in the direct interest of labour. In 1906 the LRC became known as The Labour Party.

The Council for Social Democracy was announced by four former Labour Cabinet Ministers on January 25, 1981. Subsequently a number of sitting Labour Members of Parliament, together with one Conservative, joined the new group, and on March 26, 1981 the **Social Democratic Party** was launched. Later in the year the SDP and the Liberal Party formed an electoral alliance. In 1988 a majority of the SDP agreed on a merger with the Liberal Party (*see* above) but a minority continued as a separate party under the SDP title. In June 1990 it was decided to wind up the party organization.

The government of the day is formed by the party which wins the largest number of seats in the House of Commons at a General Election, or which has the support of a majority of members in the House of Commons. By tradition, the leader of the majority party is asked by the Sovereign to form a government, while the largest minority party becomes the official Opposition with its own leader and 'Shadow Cabinet'. Leaders of the Government and Opposition sit on the front benches of the Commons with their supporters (the back-benchers) sitting behind them.

When a party is in Opposition and its leadership becomes vacant, it makes its free choice among the various personalities available; but if the party is in office, the Sovereign's choice may anticipate, and in a certain sense forestall, the decision of the party.

POLITICAL PARTIES

(*See also* **Occurrences during printing**)

The parties included here are those with MPs sitting in the House of Commons.

CONSERVATIVE AND UNIONIST PARTY, Central Office, 32 Smith Square, SW1P 3HH. (Tel: 071-222 9000).—*Party Chairman*, The Rt. Hon. K. Baker, MP; *Deputy Chairman*, D. Trippier, RD, MP; *Vice Chairmen*, Sir Thomas Arnold, MP; Dame Joan Seccombe, OBE; Sir James Spicer, MP; The Rt. Hon. Sir Geoffrey Pattie, MP; *Hon. Treasurers*, Sir Hector Laing; Lord Beaverbrook.

SCOTTISH CONSERVATIVE PARTY, Central Office, 3 Chester Street, Edinburgh EH3 7RF. (Tel: 031-226 4426).—*Chairman*, M. B. Forsyth, MP; *Deputy Chairman*, W. Hughes; *Hon. Treasurer*, D. Mitchell; *Dir. of Organization*, S. Turner.

LABOUR PARTY, 150 Walworth Road, SE17 1JT. (Tel: 071-703 0833).—*Chair*, Ms J. Richardson, MP; *Vice Chair*, T. Sawyer; *Treasurer*, S. McCluskie; *Gen. Sec.*, L. Whitty; *Parliamentary Party Leader*, The Rt. Hon. N. Kinnock, MP; *Deputy Leader*, The Rt. Hon. R. Hattersley, MP; *Leader of the Labour Peers*, Lord Cledwyn of Penrhos, CH.

Shadow Cabinet 1989–90

Leader, The Rt. Hon. N. Kinnock.
Deputy Leader and Shadow Home Secretary, The Rt. Hon. R. Hattersley.
Chief Whip, D. Foster.
Chair, Parliamentary Party, The Rt. Hon. S. Orme.
Trade and Industry, G. Brown.
Shadow Chancellor, The Rt. Hon. J. Smith.
Health, R. Cook.
Employment, A. Blair.
Shadow Foreign Secretary, The Rt. Hon. G. Kaufman.
Children, Miss J. Lestor.
Women's Rights, Ms J. Richardson.
Campaigns Co-ordinator and Leader of the House, Dr. J. Cunningham.
Environment, B. Gould.
Energy, F. Dobson.
Transport, J. Prescott.
Social Security, M. Meacher.
Food, Agriculture and Rural Affairs, Dr. D. Clark.
Development and Co-operation, Mrs. A. Clwyd.
Scotland, D. Dewar.
Wales, B. Jones.
Chief Secretary to the Treasury, Mrs. M. Beckett.
Education, J. Straw.
Leader of the Labour Peers, The Rt. Hon. Lord Cledwyn of Penrhos, CH.
Opposition Chief Whip, Lords (*acting*), Lord Graham of Edmonton.
Peers Representative, Lord Dean of Beswick.
Acting Labour Chief Whip in the House of Lords is Lord Graham of Edmonton. Labour Chief Whip in the House of Commons is D. Foster, MP.

LIBERAL DEMOCRATS, 4 Cowley Street, SW1P 3NB. (Tel: 071-222 7999).—*President*, C. Kennedy, MP; *Deputy Chair*, T. C. Jones; *Hon. Treasurer*, T. Razzall; *Gen. Sec.*, G. Elson; *Leader of the Party*, The Rt. Hon. Paddy Ashdown, MP; *Leader in the Lords*, The Rt. Hon. the Lord Jenkins of Hillhead.

SCOTTISH LIBERAL DEMOCRATS, 4 Clifton Terrace, Edinburgh EH12 5DR. (Tel: 031-337 2314).—*Chairman*, R. Thomson; *Hon. Treasurer*, K. Smith; *Party President*, Sir Russell Johnston, MP; *Party Leader*, M. G. Bruce, MP.

WELSH LIBERAL DEMOCRATS, 91 St. Mary Street, Cardiff CF1 1DW. (Tel: 0222-382210).—*Chairman*, G. Griffiths; *Treasurer*, Dr. G. Morrison; *Party President*, Rev. R. Roberts; *Party Leader*, R. Livsey, MP.

Party Spokesmen

Agriculture, G. Howells, MP.
Defence, M. Campbell, MP.
Education, S. Hughes, MP.
Employment, J. Wallace, MP.
Environment, M. Bruce, MP.
Europe, Sir Russell Johnston, MP.
Foreign Affairs, The Rt. Hon. Sir David Steel, MP.
Health, C. Kennedy, MP.
Home Office, R. Maclennan, MP.
Legal Affairs, A. Carlile, MP.
N. Ireland, The Rt. Hon. P. Ashdown, MP.
Scotland, Mrs. R. Michie, MP.
Social Security, A. Kirkwood, MP.
Trade and Industry, M. Taylor, MP.
Transport, R. Fearn, MP.
Treasury, A. Beith, MP.
Wales, R. Livsey, MP.

Liberal Democrat Whips in the House of Lords are: *Chief Whip*, Lord Tordoff; *Deputy Whip*, Viscount Falkland. Whips in the House of Commons are: *Chief Whip*, J. R. Wallace, MP; *Deputy Whips*, S. Hughes, MP; A. Kirkwood, MP.

PLAID CYMRU, 51 Cathedral Road, Cardiff CF1 9HD. (Tel: 0222-231944).—*Chairman*, D. Huws; *Deputy Chairman*, I. W. Jones, MP; *Hon. Treasurer*, S. R. Morgan; *Sec.*, D. Williams; *Party President*, D. E. Thomas, MP; *Vice-President*, D. Iwan.

SCOTTISH NATIONAL PARTY, 6 North Charlotte Street, Edinburgh EH2 4JH. (Tel: 031-226 3661).—*National Convener*, G. Wilson; *Deputy Vice Convener*, A. Salmond, MP; *National Treasurer*, A. Morgan; *National Sec.*, J. Swinney; *Parliamentary Party Leader*, Mrs. M. Ewing, MP; *Chief Whip*, A. Welsh, MP.

NORTHERN IRELAND

SOCIAL DEMOCRATIC AND LABOUR PARTY, 24 Mount Charles, Belfast BT7 1NZ. (Tel: 0232-323428).—*Chairman*, A. Maginness; *Deputy Chairmen*, Ms. A. Hegarty; T. Kelly; *Hon. Treasurer*, P. Brannigan; *Gen. Sec.*, P. McGlone; *Parliamentary Party Leader*, J. Hume, MP; *Deputy Leader*, S. Mallon, MP; *Chief Whip*, E. McGrady, MP.

ULSTER DEMOCRATIC UNIONIST PARTY, 296 Albertbridge Road, Belfast BT5 4GX. (Tel: 0232-458597).—*Chairman*, J. McClure; *Deputy Chairman*, S. Gibson; *Hon. Treasurer*, D. Herron; *Sec.*, A. Kane; *Parliamentary Party Leader*, Dr. I. Paisley, MP; *Deputy Leader*, P. Robinson, MP.

ULSTER UNIONIST COUNCIL, 3 Glengall Street, Belfast BT12 5AE. (Tel: 0232-324601).—*Chairman*, J. Nicholson, MEP; *Vice Chairman*, A. J. Wilson; *Hon. Treasurer*, J. Allen; *Party Sec.*, J. Wilson; *Party Leader*, The Rt. Hon. J. H. Molyneaux, MP.

MEMBERS OF THE HOUSE OF COMMONS
(as at Aug. 7 1990)

Lib. Dem. = Liberal Democrat. *SD* = Independent Social Democrat. For other abbreviations, *see* page 249
* Denotes membership of the last Parliament.

A *full entry in italic type* denotes that a Member died during the year in which he was elected. The name is included for purposes of record.

	Maj.
Abbott, Ms. Diane J. (*b.* 1953), *Lab., Hackney N. and Stoke Newington*	7,678
*Adams, Allen S. (*b.* 1946), *Lab., Paisley N.*	14,442
*Adams, Gerard (*b.* 1948), *SF, Belfast W.*	2,221
*Adley, Robert J. (*b.* 1935), *C., Christchurch*	22,374
*Aitken, Jonathan W. P. (*b.* 1942), *C., Thanet S.*	13,683
*Alexander, Richard T. (*b.* 1934), *C., Newark*	13,543
*Alison, Rt. Hon. Michael J. H. (*b.* 1926), *C., Selby*	13,779
Allason, Rupert W. S. (*b.* 1951), *C., Torbay*	8,820
Allen, Graham W. (*b.* 1953), *Lab., Nottingham N.*	1,665
*Alton, David P. P. (*b.* 1951), *Lib. Dem., Liverpool, Mossley Hill*	2,226
*Amery, Rt. Hon. H. Julian (*b.* 1919), *C., Brighton, Pavilion*	9,142
*Amess, David A. A. (*b.* 1952), *C., Basildon*	2,649
Amos, Alan T. (*b.* 1952), *C., Hexham*	8,066
*Anderson, Donald (*b.* 1939), *Lab., Swansea E.*	19,338
Arbuthnot, James N. (*b.* 1952), *C., Wanstead and Woodford*	16,412
*Archer, Rt. Hon. Peter K., QC (*b.* 1926), *Lab., Warley W.*	5,393
Armstrong, Ms. Hilary J. (*b.* 1945), *Lab., Durham NW*	10,162
Arnold, Jacques A. (*b.* 1947), *C., Gravesham*	8,792
*Arnold, Sir Thomas (*b.* 1947), *C., Hazel Grove*	1,840
*Ashby, David G. (*b.* 1940), *C., Leicestershire NW*	7,828
*Ashdown, Rt. Hon. J. J. D. (Paddy) (*b.* 1941), *Lib. Dem., Yeovil*	5,700
*Ashley, Rt. Hon. Jack, CH (*b.* 1922), *Lab., Stoke-on-Trent S.*	5,053
*Ashton, Joseph W. (*b.* 1933), *Lab., Bassetlaw*	5,613
*Aspinwall, Jack H. (*b.* 1933), *C., Wansdyke*	16,144
*Atkins, Robert J. (*b.* 1946), *C., S. Ribble*	8,430
*Atkinson, David A. (*b.* 1940), *C., Bournemouth E.*	14,683
*Baker, Rt. Hon. Kenneth W. (*b.* 1934), *C., Mole Valley*	16,076
*Baker, Nicholas B. (*b.* 1938), *C., Dorset N.*	11,907
*Baldry, Antony B. (*b.* 1950), *C., Banbury*	17,330
*Banks, Robert G. (*b.* 1937), *C., Harrogate*	11,902
*Banks, Tony L. (*b.* 1943), *Lab., Newham NW*	8,496
Barnes, Harold (*b.* 1936), *Lab., Derbyshire NE*	3,720
*Barnes, Mrs. Rosemary S. (*b.* 1946), *SD, Greenwich*	2,141
*Barron, Kevin J. (*b.* 1946), *Lab., Rother Valley*	15,790
*Batiste, Spencer L. (*b.* 1945), *C., Elmet*	5,356
Battle, John D. (*b.* 1951), *Lab., Leeds W.*	4,692
*Beaumont-Dark, Anthony M. (*b.* 1932), *C., Birmingham, Selly Oak*	2,584
*Beckett, Mrs. Margaret M. (*b.* 1943), *Lab., Derby S.*	1,516
*Beggs, J. Roy (*b.* 1936), *OUP, Antrim E.*	15,360
*Beith, Alan J. (*b.* 1943), *Lib. Dem., Berwick-upon-Tweed*	9,503
*Bell, Stuart (*b.* 1938), *Lab., Middlesbrough*	14,958
*Bellingham, Henry C. (*b.* 1955), *C., Norfolk NW*	10,825

	Maj.
*Bendall, Vivian W. H. (*b.* 1938), *C., Ilford N.*	12,090
*Benn, Rt. Hon. Anthony N. W. (*b.* 1925), *Lab., Chesterfield*	8,577
*Bennett, Andrew F. (*b.* 1939), *Lab., Denton and Reddish*	8,250
Bennett, Nicholas J. (*b.* 1949), *C., Pembroke*	5,700
*Benyon, William R. (*b.* 1930), *C., Milton Keynes*	13,701
*Bermingham, Gerald E. (*b.* 1940), *Lab., St. Helens S.*	13,801
*Bevan, A. David G. (*b.* 1928), *C., Birmingham, Yardley*	2,522
*Bidwell, Sydney J. (*b.* 1917), *Lab., Ealing, Southall*	7,977
*Biffen, Rt. Hon. W. John (*b.* 1930), *C., Shropshire N.*	14,415
*Blackburn, John G. (*b.* 1933), *C., Dudley W.*	10,244
*Blair, Anthony C. L. (*b.* 1953), *Lab., Sedgefield*	13,058
*Blaker, Rt. Hon. Sir Peter KCMG (*b.* 1922), *C., Blackpool S.*	6,744
Blunkett, David (*b.* 1947), *Lab., Sheffield, Brightside*	24,191
Boateng, Paul Y. (*b.* 1951), *Lab., Brent S.*	7,931
*Body, Sir Richard (*b.* 1927), *C., Holland with Boston*	17,595
*Bonsor, Sir Nicholas, Bt. (*b.* 1942), *C., Upminster*	16,857
*Boothroyd, Miss Betty (*b.* 1929), *Lab., West Bromwich W.*	5,253
*Boscawen, Hon. Robert T., MC (*b.* 1923), *C., Somerton and Frome*	9,538
Boswell, Timothy E. (*b.* 1942), *C., Daventry*	19,690
*Bottomley, Peter J. (*b.* 1944), *C., Eltham*	6,460
*Bottomley, Mrs. Virginia H. B. M. (*b.* 1948), *C., Surrey SW*	14,343
*Bowden, Andrew, MBE (*b.* 1930), *C., Brighton, Kemptown*	9,260
*Bowden, Gerald F., TD (*b.* 1935), *C., Dulwich*	180
Bowis, John C. (*b.* 1945), *C., Battersea*	857
*Boyes, Roland (*b.* 1937), *Lab., Houghton and Washington*	20,193
*Boyson, Rt. Hon. Sir Rhodes (*b.* 1925), *C., Brent N.*	15,720
Bradley, Keith J. C. (*b.* 1950), *Lab., Manchester, Withington*	3,391
*Braine, Rt. Hon. Sir Bernard (*b.* 1914), *C., Castle Point*	19,248
*Brandon-Bravo, Martin M. (*b.* 1932), *C., Nottingham S.*	2,234
*Bray, Dr. Jeremy W. (*b.* 1930), *Lab., Motherwell S.*	16,930
Brazier, Julian W. H. (*b.* 1953), *C., Canterbury*	14,891
*Bright, Graham F. J. (*b.* 1942), *C., Luton S.*	5,115
*Brooke, Rt. Hon. Peter L. (*b.* 1934), *C., City of London and Westminster S.*	12,042
*Brown, Dr. J. Gordon (*b.* 1951), *Lab., Dunfermline E.*	19,589
*Brown, Michael R. (*b.* 1951), *C., Brigg and Cleethorpes*	12,248
*Brown, Nicholas H. (*b.* 1950), *Lab., Newcastle upon Tyne E.*	12,500
*Brown, Ronald D. M. (*b.* 1940), *Lab., Edinburgh, Leith*	11,327

	Maj.
*Browne, John E. D. D. (b. 1938), C., Winchester	7,479
Bruce, Ian C. (b. 1947), C., Dorset S.	15,067
*Bruce, Malcolm G. (b. 1944), Lib. Dem., Gordon	9,519
*Buchan, Norman F. (b. 1922), Lab., Paisley S.	15,785
*Buchanan-Smith, Rt. Hon. Alick L. (b. 1932), C., Kincardine and Deeside	2,063
*Buck, Sir Antony, QC (b. 1928), C., Colchester N.	13,623
Buckley, George J. (b. 1935), Lab., Hemsworth	20,700
*Budgen, Nicholas W. (b. 1937), C., Wolverhampton SW	10,318
Burns, Simon H. M. (b. 1952), C., Chelmsford	7,761
*Burt, Alistair J. H. (b. 1955), C., Bury N.	6,911
*Butcher, John P. (b. 1946), C., Coventry SW	3,210
Butler, Christopher J. (b. 1950), C., Warrington S.	3,609
*Butterfill, John V. (b. 1941), C., Bournemouth W.	12,651
*Caborn, Richard G. (b. 1943), Lab., Sheffield, Central	19,342
*Callaghan, James (b. 1927), Lab., Heywood and Middleton	6,848
Campbell, Ronald (b. 1943), Lab., Blyth Valley	853
Campbell W. Menzies, CBE, QC (b. 1941), Lib. Dem., Fife NE	1,447
*Campbell-Savours, Dale N. (b. 1943), Lab., Workington	7,019
*Canavan, Dennis A. (b. 1942), Lab., Falkirk W.	13,552
*Carlile, Alexander C., QC (b. 1948), Lib. Dem., Montgomery	2,558
*Carlile, John R. (b. 1942), C., Luton N.	15,573
*Carlisle, Kenneth M. (b. 1941), C., Lincoln	7,483
Carr, Michael (b. 1947, elected May, d. July 1990) Lab., Bootle	23,517
Carrington, Matthew H. M. (b. 1947), C., Fulham	6,322
*Carttiss, Michael R. H. (b. 1938), C., Great Yarmouth	10,083
*Cartwright, John C. (b. 1933), SD, Woolwich	1,937
*Cash, William N. P. (b. 1940), C., Stafford	13,707
*Chalker, Rt. Hon. Mrs. Lynda (b. 1942), C., Wallasey	279
*Channon, Rt. Hon. H. Paul G. (b. 1935), C., Southend W.	8,400
*Chapman, Sydney B. (b. 1935), C., Chipping Barnet	14,871
*Chope, Christopher R., OBE (b. 1947), C., Southampton, Itchen	6,716
*Churchill, Winston S. (b. 1940), C., Davyhulme	8,199
*Clark, Hon. Alan K. M. (b. 1928), C., Plymouth, Sutton	4,013
*Clark, Dr. David G. (b. 1939), Lab., South Shields	13,851
*Clark, Dr. Michael (b. 1935), C., Rochford	19,694
*Clark, Rt. Hon. Sir William (b. 1917), C., Croydon S.	19,063
*Clarke, Rt. Hon. Kenneth H., QC (b. 1940), C., Rushcliffe	20,839
*Clarke, Thomas, CBE (b. 1941), Lab., Monklands W.	18,333
*Clay, Robert A. (b. 1946), Lab., Sunderland N.	14,672
*Clelland, David G. (b. 1943), Lab., Tyne Bridge	15,573
*Clwyd, Mrs. Ann (b. 1937), Lab., Cynon Valley	21,571
*Cohen, Harry M. (b. 1949), Lab., Leyton	4,641

	Maj.
*Coleman, Donald R., CBE (b. 1925), Lab., Neath	20,578
*Colvin, Michael K. B. (b. 1932), C., Romsey and Waterside	15,272
*Conway, Derek L. (b. 1953), C., Shrewsbury and Atcham	9,064
*Cook, Francis (b. 1935), Lab., Stockton N.	8,801
*Cook, R. F. (Robin) (b. 1946), Lab., Livingston	11,105
Coombs, Anthony M. V. (b. 1952), C., Wyre Forest	7,224
*Coombs, Simon C. (b. 1947), C., Swindon	4,857
*Cope, Rt. Hon. John A. (b. 1937), C., Northavon	14,270
*Corbett, Robin (b. 1933), Lab., Birmingham, Erdington	2,467
*Corbyn, Jeremy B. (b. 1949), Lab., Islington N.	9,657
*Cormack, Patrick T. (b. 1939), C., Staffordshire S.	25,268
*Couchman, James R. (b. 1942), C., Gillingham	12,549
Cousins, James M. (b. 1944), Lab., Newcastle upon Tyne, Central	2,483
*Cox, Thomas M. (b. 1930), Lab., Tooting	1,441
Cran, James D. (b. 1944), C., Beverley	12,595
*Critchley, Julian M. G. (b. 1930), C., Aldershot	17,784
*Crowther, J. Stanley (b. 1925), Lab., Rotherham	16,012
Cryer, G. Robert (b. 1934), Lab., Bradford S.	309
Cummings, John S. (b. 1943), Lab., Easington	24,639
*Cunliffe, Lawrence F. (b. 1929), Lab., Leigh	16,606
*Cunningham, Dr. John A. (b. 1939), Lab., Copeland	1,894
*Currie, Mrs. Edwina (b. 1946), C., Derbyshire S.	10,311
Curry, David M. (b. 1944), C., Skipton and Ripon	17,174
*Dalyell, Tam (Sir Thomas Dalyell of the Binns, Bt.) (b. 1932), Lab., Linlithgow	10,373
Darling, Alistair M. (b. 1953), Lab., Edinburgh, Central	2,262
*Davies, Rt. Hon. D. J. Denzil (b. 1938), Lab., Llanelli	20,935
Davies, J. Quentin (b. 1944), C., Stamford and Spalding	13,991
*Davies, Ronald (b. 1946), Lab., Caerphilly	19,167
Davis, David M. (b. 1948), C., Boothferry	18,970
*Davis, Terence A. G. (b. 1938), Lab., Birmingham, Hodge Hill	4,789
Day, Stephen R. (b. 1948), C., Cheadle	10,631
*Dean, Sir Paul (b. 1924), C., Woodspring	17,852
Devlin, Timothy R. (b. 1959), C., Stockton S.	774
*Dewar, Donald C. (b. 1937), Lab., Glasgow, Garscadden	18,977
*Dickens, Geoffrey K. (b. 1931), C., Littleborough and Saddleworth	6,202
*Dicks, Terence P. (b. 1937), C., Hayes and Harlington	5,965
*Dixon, Donald (b. 1929), Lab., Jarrow	18,795
*Dobson, Frank G. (b. 1940), Lab., Holborn and St. Pancras	8,853
Doran, Frank (b. 1949), Lab., Aberdeen S.	1,198
*Dorrell, Stephen J. (b. 1952), C., Loughborough	17,648
*Douglas, Richard G. (b. 1932), Independent, Dunfermline W.	9,402
*Douglas-Hamilton, Lord James (b. 1942), C., Edinburgh W.	1,234
*Dover, Densmore R. (b. 1938), C., Chorley	8,057
*Duffy, A. E. Patrick (b. 1920), Lab., Sheffield, Attercliffe	17,191
*Dunn, Robert J. (b. 1946), C., Dartford	14,929

Maj.

*Haselhurst, Alan G. B. (b. 1937), C., Saffron Walden 16,602

*Hattersley, Rt. Hon. Roy S. G. (b. 1932), Lab., Birmingham, Sparkbrook 11,859

*Hawkins, Christopher J. (b. 1937), C., High Peak 9,516

Hayes, Jeremy J. J. (b. 1953), C., Harlow .. 5,877

*Hayhoe, Rt. Hon. Sir Barney (b. 1925), C., Brentford and Isleworth 7,953

*Haynes, D. F. (Frank) (b. 1926), Lab., Ashfield 4,400

*Hayward, Robert A. (b. 1949), C., Kingswood 4,393

Heal, Mrs Sylvia Lloyd (b. 1942), Lab., Staffordshire Mid 9,449

*Healey, Rt. Hon. Denis W., CH, MBE (b. 1917), Lab., Leeds E. 9,526

*Heath, Rt. Hon. Edward R. G., MBE (b. 1916), C., Old Bexley and Sidcup 16,274

*Heathcoat-Amory, David P. (b. 1949), C., Wells 8,541

*Heffer, Eric S. (b. 1922), Lab., Liverpool, Walton 23,253

Henderson, Douglas J. (b. 1949), Lab., Newcastle upon Tyne N. 5,243

*Heseltine, Rt. Hon. Michael R. D. (b. 1933), C., Henley 17,082

Hicks, Mrs. Maureen P. (b. 1948), C., Wolverhampton NE 204

*Hicks, Robert A. (b. 1938), C., Cornwall SE 6,607

*Higgins, Rt. Hon. Terence L. (b. 1928), C., Worthing 18,501

*Hill S. James A. (b. 1926), C., Southampton, Test 6,954

Hinchliffe, David M. (b. 1948), Lab., Wakefield 2,789

*Hind, Kenneth H. (b. 1949), C., Lancashire W. 1,353

Hoey, Catharine (Kate) L. (b. 1946), Lab., Vauxhall 9,766

*Hogg, Hon. Douglas M. (b. 1945), C., Grantham 21,303

*Hogg, Norman (b. 1938), Lab., Cumbernauld and Kilsyth 14,403

*Holt, J. Richard (b. 1931), C., Langbaurgh 2,088

*Home Robertson, John D. (b. 1948), Lab., E. Lothian 10,105

Hood, James (b. 1949), Lab., Clydesdale ... 10,502

*Hordern, Sir Peter (b. 1929), C., Horsham 23,907

*Howard, Rt. Hon. Michael, QC (b. 1941), C., Folkestone and Hythe 9,126

*Howarth, Alan T., CBE (b. 1944), C., Stratford-upon-Avon 21,165

*Howarth, George E. (b. 1949), Lab., Knowsley N. 21,098

*Howarth, J. Gerald D. (b. 1947), C., Cannock and Burntwood 2,689

*Howe, Rt. Hon. Sir Geoffrey, QC (b. 1926), C., Surrey E. 18,126

*Howell, Rt. Hon. David A. R. (b. 1936), C., Guildford 12,607

*Howell, Rt. Hon. Denis H. (b. 1923), Lab., Birmingham, Small Heath 15,521

*Howell, Ralph F. (b. 1923), C., Norfolk N. .. 15,310

*Howells, Geraint W. (b. 1925), Lib. Dem., Ceredigion and Pembroke N. 4,700

Howells, Dr. Kim S. (b. 1946), Lab., Pontypridd 10,794

*Hoyle E. Douglas H. (b. 1930), Lab., Warrington N. 8,013

Hughes, John (b.1925), Lab., Coventry NE 11,867

*Hughes, Robert (b. 1932), Lab., Aberdeen N. 16,278

Hughes, Robert G. (b. 1951), C., Harrow W. 15,444

*Hughes, Royston J. (b. 1925), Lab., Newport E. 7,064

Maj.

*Hughes, Simon H. W. (b. 1951), Lib. Dem., Southwark and Bermondsey 2,779

*Hume, John (b. 1937), SDLP, Foyle 9,860

*Hunt, Rt. Hon. David J. F., MBE (b. 1942), C., Wirral W. 12,723

*Hunt, Sir John (b. 1929), C., Ravensbourne 16,919

*Hunter, Andrew R. F. (b. 1943), C., Basingstoke 17,893

*Hurd, Rt. Hon. Douglas R., CBE (b. 1930), C., Witney 18,464

Illsley, Eric E. (b. 1955), Lab., Barnsley, Central 19,051

Ingram, Adam P. (b. 1947), Lab., East Kilbride 12,624

Irvine, Michael F. (b. 1939), C., Ipswich ... 874

*Irving, Sir Charles G. (b. 1926), C., Cheltenham 4,896

Jack, J. Michael (b. 1946), C., Fylde 17,772

*Jackson, Robert V. (b. 1946), C., Wantage . 12,156

Janman, Timothy S. (b. 1957), C., Thurrock 690

*Janner, Hon. Greville E., QC (b. 1928), Lab., Leicester W. 1,201

*Jessel, Toby F. H. (b. 1934), C., Twickenham 7,127

*Johnson Smith, Sir Geoffrey (b. 1924), C., Wealden 20,110

*Johnston, Sir Russell (b. 1932), Lib. Dem., Inverness, Nairn and Lochaber 5,431

*Jones, Gwilym H. (b. 1947), C., Cardiff N. . 8,234

Jones, Ieuan W. (b. 1949), PC, Ynys Môn . 4,298

Jones, Martyn D. (b. 1947), Lab., Clwyd SW 1,028

*Jones, Robert B. (b. 1950), C., Hertfordshire W. 14,924

*Jones S. Barry (b. 1938), Lab., Alyn and Deeside 6,416

*Jopling, Rt. Hon. T. Michael (b. 1930), C., Westmorland and Lonsdale 14,920

*Kaufman, Rt. Hon. Gerald B. (b. 1930), Lab., Manchester, Gorton 14,065

*Kellett-Bowman, Dame Elaine, DBE (b. 1924), C., Lancaster 6,453

*Kennedy, Charles P. (b. 1959), Lib. Dem., Ross, Cromarty and Skye 11,319

*Key, S. Robert (b. 1945), C., Salisbury 11,443

*Kilfedder, James A. (b. 1928), UPUP, Down N. 3,953

*King, Roger D. (b. 1943), C., Birmingham, Northfield 3,135

*King, Rt. Hon. Thomas J. (b. 1933), C., Bridgwater 11,195

*Kinnock, Rt. Hon. Neil G. (b. 1942), Lab., Islwyn 22,947

Kirkhope, Timothy J. R. (b. 1945), C., Leeds NE 8,419

*Kirkwood, Archibald J. (b. 1946), Lib. Dem., Roxburgh and Berwickshire 4,008

Knapman, Roger M. (b. 1944), C., Stroud .. 12,375

*Knight, Gregory (b. 1949), C., Derby N. ... 6,325

*Knight, Dame Jill, DBE (b. 1923), C., Birmingham, Edgbaston 8,581

*Knowles, Michael (b. 1942), C., Nottingham E. 456

*Knox, David L. (b. 1933), C., Staffordshire, Moorlands 14,427

*Lambie, David (b. 1925), Lab., Cunninghame S. 16,633

*Lamond, James A. (b. 1928), Lab., Oldham Central and Royton 6,279

*Lamont, Rt. Hon. Norman S. H. (b. 1942), C., Kingston upon Thames 11,186

*Lang, Ian B. (b. 1940), C., Galloway and Upper Nithsdale 3,673

*Latham, Michael A. (b. 1942), C., Rutland and Melton 23,022

*Lawrence, Ivan J., QC (b. 1936), C., Burton 9,830

*Lawson, Rt. Hon. Nigel (b. 1932), C., Blaby 22,176

	Maj.
*Leadbitter, Edward (b. 1919), Lab., Hartlepool	7,289
*Lee, John R. L. (b. 1942), C., Pendle	2,639
*Leigh, Edward J. E. (b. 1950), C., Gainsborough and Horncastle	9,723
*Leighton, Ronald (b. 1930), Lab., Newham NE	8,236
*Lennox-Boyd, Hon. Mark A. (b. 1943), C., Morecambe and Lunesdale	11,785
*Lester, James T. (b. 1932), C., Broxtowe	16,651
Lestor, Miss Joan (b. 1931), Lab., Eccles	9,699
*Lewis, Terence (b. 1935), Lab., Worsley	7,337
*Lightbown, David L. (b. 1932), C., Staffordshire SE	10,885
*Lilley, Rt. Hon. Peter B. (b. 1943), C., St. Albans	10,881
*Litherland, Robert K. (b. 1930), Lab., Manchester, Central	19,867
Livingstone, Ken R. (b. 1945), Lab., Brent E.	1,653
*Livsey, Richard A. L. (b. 1935), Lib. Dem., Brecon and Radnor	56
*Lloyd, Anthony J. (b. 1950), Lab., Stretford	9,402
*Lloyd, Sir Ian (b. 1921), C., Havant	16,510
*Lloyd, Peter R. C. (b. 1937), C., Fareham	18,795
*Lofthouse, Geoffrey (b. 1925), Lab., Pontefract and Castleford	21,626
*Lord, Michael N. (b. 1938), C., Suffolk, Central	16,290
*Loyden, Edward (b. 1923), Lab., Liverpool, Garston	13,777
*Luce, Rt. Hon. Richard N. (b. 1936), C., Shoreham	17,070
*Lyell, Rt. Hon. Sir Nicholas, QC (b. 1938), C., Bedfordshire, Mid.	22,851
McAllion, John (b. 1948), Lab., Dundee E.	1,015
McAvoy, Thomas (b. 1943), Lab., Glasgow, Rutherglen	13,995
McCartney, Ian (b. 1951), Lab., Makerfield	15,558
*McCrea, Rev. Robert T. W. (b. 1948), DUP, Ulster, Mid.	9,360
*McCrindle, Sir Robert (b. 1929), C., Brentwood and Ongar	18,921
MacDonald, Calum A. (b. 1956), Lab., Western Isles	2,340
McFall, John (b. 1944), Lab., Dumbarton	5,222
*Macfarlane, Sir Neil (b. 1936), C., Sutton and Cheam	15,718
McGrady, Edward K. (b. 1943), SDLP, Down S.	731
*MacGregor, Rt. Hon. John R. R., OBE (b. 1937), C., Norfolk S.	12,418
*McKay, Allen (b. 1927), Lab., Barnsley W. and Penistone	14,191
*MacKay, Andrew J. (b. 1949), C., Berkshire E.	22,626
*McKelvey, William (b.1934), Lab., Kilmarnock and Loudoun	14,127
*Maclean, David J. (b. 1953), C., Penrith and the Border	17,366
McLeish, Henry B. (b. 1948), Lab., Fife, Central	15,709
*Maclennan, Robert A. R. (b. 1936), Lib. Dem., Caithness and Sutherland	8,494
*McLoughlin, Patrick A. (b. 1957), C., Derbyshire W.	10,527
*McNair-Wilson, Sir Patrick (b. 1929), C., New Forest	21,732
*McNair-Wilson, Sir Michael (b. 1930), C., Newbury	16,658
*McNamara, J. Kevin (b. 1934), Lab., Kingston upon Hull N.	12,169
*McWilliam, John D. (b.1941), Lab., Blaydon	12,488
*Madden, Maxwell F. (b. 1941), Lab., Bradford W.	7,551

	Maj.
*Madel, William D. (b.1938), C., Bedfordshire SW	22,305
*Maginnis, Kenneth (b. 1938), OUP, Fermanagh and S. Tyrone	12,823
Mahon, Mrs. Alice (b. 1937), Lab., Halifax	1,212
*Major, Rt. Hon. John (b. 1943), C., Huntingdon	27,044
*Malins, Humfrey J. (b. 1945), C., Croydon NW	3,988
*Mallon, Seamus (b. 1936), SDLP, Newry and Armagh	5,325
Mans, Keith D. R. (b. 1946), C., Wyre	14,661
*Maples, John C. (b. 1943), C., Lewisham W.	3,772
*Marek, Dr. John (b. 1940), Lab., Wrexham	4,152
*Marland, Paul (b. 1940), C., Gloucestershire W.	11,679
*Marlow, Antony R. (b. 1940), C., Northampton N.	9,256
*Marshall, David (b. 1941), Lab., Glasgow, Shettleston	18,981
Marshall, James (b. 1941), Lab., Leicester S.	1,877
Marshall, John L. (b. 1940), C., Hendon S.	11,124
*Marshall, Sir Michael (b. 1930), C., Arundel	18,880
Martin, David J. P. (b. 1945), C., Portsmouth S.	205
*Martin, Michael J. (b. 1945), Lab., Glasgow, Springburn	22,063
Martlew, Eric A. (b. 1949), Lab., Carlisle	916
*Mates, Michael J. (b. 1934), C., Hampshire E.	23,786
*Maude, Hon. Francis A. A. (b. 1953), C., Warwickshire N.	2,829
*Mawhinney, Dr. Brian S. (b. 1940), C., Peterborough	9,784
*Maxton, John A. (b. 1936), Lab., Glasgow, Cathcart	11,203
*Maxwell-Hyslop, R. J. (Robin) (b. 1931), C., Tiverton	9,212
*Mayhew, Rt. Hon. Sir Patrick B. B., QC (b. 1929), C., Tunbridge Wells	16,122
*Meacher, Michael H. (b. 1939), Lab., Oldham W.	5,967
Meale, J. Alan (b. 1949), Lab., Mansfield	56
*Mellor, Rt. Hon. David J., QC (b. 1949), C., Putney	6,907
*Meyer, Sir Anthony, Bt. (b. 1920), C., Clwyd NW	11,781
Michael, Alun E. (b. 1943), Lab., Cardiff S. and Penarth	4,574
Michie, Mrs. J. Ray (b. 1934), Lib. Dem., Argyll and Bute	1,394
*Michie, William (b. 1935), Lab., Sheffield, Heeley	14,440
*Miller, Sir Hilary (Hal) (b. 1929), C., Bromsgrove	16,685
*Mills, Iain C. (b. 1940), C., Meriden	16,820
*Miscampbell, Norman A., QC (b. 1925), C., Blackpool N.	7,321
Mitchell, Andrew J. B. (b. 1956), C., Gedling	16,539
*Mitchell, Austin V. (b. 1934), Lab., Great Grimsby	8,784
*Mitchell, Sir David (b. 1928), C., Hampshire NW	13,437
*Moate, Roger D. (b. 1938), C., Faversham	13,978
*Molyneaux, Rt. Hon. James H. (b. 1920), OUP, Lagan Valley	23,373
*Monro, Sir Hector (b. 1922), C., Dumfries	7,493
*Montgomery, Sir Fergus (b. 1927), C., Altrincham and Sale	14,228
Moonie, Dr. Lewis G. (b. 1947), Lab., Kirkcaldy	11,570
*Moore, Rt. Hon. John E. M. (b. 1937), C., Croydon, Central	12,617
Morgan, H. Rhodri (b. 1939), Lab., Cardiff W.	4,045

Maj.

Morley, Elliot A. (b. 1952), *Lab., Glanford and Scunthorpe* 512
*Morris, Rt. Hon. Alfred (b. 1928), *Lab., Manchester, Wythenshawe* 11,855
*Morris, Rt. Hon. John, QC (b. 1931), *Lab., Aberavon* 20,609
*Morris, Michael W. L. (b. 1936), *C., Northampton S.* 17,803
*Morrison, Hon. Sir Charles A. (b. 1932), *C., Devizes* 17,830
*Morrison, Rt. Hon. Peter H. (b. 1944), *C., City of Chester* 4,855
Moss, Malcolm D. (b. 1943), *C., Cambridgeshire NE* 1,428
Mowlam, Dr. Marjorie (b. 1949), *Lab., Redcar* 7,735
*Moynihan, Hon. Colin B. (b. 1955), *C., Lewisham E.* 4,814
*Mudd W. David (b. 1933), *C., Falmouth and Camborne* 5,039
Mullin, Christopher J. (b. 1947), *Lab., Sunderland S.* 12,613
Murphy, Paul P. (b. 1948), *Lab., Torfaen* .. 17,550
*Neale, Gerrard A. (b. 1941), *C., Cornwall N.* 5,682
*Needham, Richard F. (b. 1942), *C., Wiltshire N.* 10,939
*Nellist, David J. (b. 1952), *Lab., Coventry SE.* 6,653
*Nelson, R. Anthony (b. 1948), *C., Chichester* 20,177
*Neubert, Michael J. (b. 1933), *C., Romford* 13,471
*Newton, Rt. Hon. Antony H., OBE (b. 1937), *C., Braintree* 16,857
*Nicholls, Patrick C. M. (b. 1948), *C., Teignbridge* 10,425
Nicholson, David J. (b. 1944), *C., Taunton* 10,380
Nicholson, Miss Emma H. (b. 1941), *C., Devon W. and Torridge* 6,468
Norris, Steven J. (b. 1945), *C., Epping Forest* 4,504
*Oakes, Rt. Hon. Gordon J. (b. 1931), *Lab., Halton* 14,578
*O'Brien, William F. (b. 1929), *Lab., Normanton* 7,287
*O'Neill, Martin J. (b. 1945), *Lab., Clackmannan* 12,401
*Onslow, Rt. Hon. Cranley G. D. (b. 1926), *C., Woking* 16,544
*Oppenheim, Phillip A. C. L. (b. 1956), *C., Amber Valley* 9,500
*Orme, Rt. Hon. Stanley (b. 1923), *Lab., Salford E.* 12,056
*Owen, Dr. the Rt. Hon. David A. L. (b. 1938), *SD, Plymouth, Devonport* 6,470
*Page, Richard L. (b. 1941), *C., Hertfordshire SW* 15,784
Paice, James E. T. (b. 1949), *C., Cambridgeshire SE* 17,502
*Paisley, Rev. Ian R. K. (b. 1926), *DUP, Antrim N.* 23,234
*Parkinson, Rt. Hon. Cecil E. (b. 1931), *C., Hertsmere* 18,106
*Parry, Robert (b. 1933), *Lab., Liverpool, Riverside* 20,689
*Patchett, Terry (b. 1940), *Lab., Barnsley E.* 23,511
Patnick, C. Irvine, OBE, (b. 1929), *C., Sheffield, Hallam* 7,637
*Patten, Rt. Hon. Christopher F. (b. 1944), *C., Bath* 1,412
*Patten, Rt. Hon. John H. C. (b. 1945), *C., Oxford W. and Abingdon* 4,878
*Pattie, Rt. Hon. Sir Geoffrey (b. 1936), *C., Chertsey and Walton* 17,469
*Pawsey, James F. (b. 1933), *C., Rugby and Kenilworth* 16,264

Maj.

*Peacock, Mrs. Elizabeth J. (b. 1937), *C., Batley and Spen* 1,362
*Pendry, Thomas (b. 1934), *Lab., Stalybridge and Hyde* 5,663
*Pike, Peter L. (b. 1937), *Lab., Burnley* 7,557
Porter, David J. (b. 1948), *C., Waveney* 11,783
*Porter, George B. (b. 1939), *C., Wirral S.* .. 10,963
*Portillo, Michael D. X. (b. 1953), *C., Enfield, Southgate* 18,345
*Powell, Raymond (b. 1928), *Lab., Ogmore* . 22,292
*Powell, William R. (b. 1948), *C., Corby* 1,805
*Prescott, John L. (b. 1938), *Lab., Kingston upon Hull E.* 14,689
*Price, Sir David (b. 1924), *C., Eastleigh* .. 13,355
Primarolo, Ms. Dawn (b. 1954), *Lab., Bristol S.* 1,404
Quin, Miss Joyce G. (b. 1944), *Lab., Gateshead E.* 17,228
*Radice, Giles H. (b. 1936), *Lab., Durham N.* 18,433
*Raffan, Keith W. T. (b. 1949), *C., Delyn* ... 1,224
*Raison, Rt. Hon. Timothy H. F. (b. 1929), *C., Aylesbury* 16,558
*Randall, Stuart J. (b. 1938), *Lab., Kingston upon Hull W.* 8,130
*Rathbone, J. R. (Tim) (b. 1933), *C., Lewes* . 13,620
*Redmond, Martin (b. 1937), *Lab., Don Valley* 11,467
Redwood, John A. (b. 1951), *C., Wokingham* 20,387
*Rees, Rt. Hon. Merlyn (b. 1920), *Lab., Leeds S. and Morley* 6,711
Reid, Dr. John (b. 1947), *Lab., Motherwell N.* 23,595
*Renton, Rt. Hon. R. Timothy (b. 1932), *C., Sussex, Mid* 18,292
*Rhodes James, Robert V. (b. 1933), *C., Cambridge* 5,060
*Richardson, Ms. Josephine (b. 1923), *Lab., Barking* 3,409
Riddick, Graham E. G. (b. 1955), *C., Colne Valley* 1,677
*Ridley, Rt. Hon. Nicholas (b. 1929), *C., Cirencester and Tewkesbury* 12,662
*Ridsdale, Sir Julian, CBE (b. 1915), *C., Harwich* 12,082
*Rifkind, Rt. Hon. Malcolm L., QC (b. 1946), *C., Edinburgh, Pentlands* 3,745
*Roberts, Sir Wyn P. (b. 1930), *C., Conwy* .. 3,024
*Robertson, George I. M. (b. 1946), *Lab., Hamilton* 21,662
*Robinson, Geoffrey (b. 1939), *Lab., Coventry NW* 5,663
*Robinson, Peter D. (b. 1948), *DUP, Belfast E.* 9,798
*Roe, Mrs. Marion A. (b. 1936), *C., Broxbourne* 22,995
*Rogers, Allan R. (b. 1932), *Lab., Rhondda* . 30,754
*Rooker, Jeffrey W. (b. 1941), *Lab., Birmingham, Perry Barr* 6,933
*Ross, Ernest (b. 1942), *Lab., Dundee W.* ... 16,526
*Ross, William (b. 1936), *OUP, Londonderry E.* 20,157
*Rossi, Sir Hugh (b. 1927), *C., Hornsey and Wood Green* 1,779
*Rost, Peter L. (b. 1930), *C., Erewash* 9,754
*Rowe, Andrew J. B. (b. 1935), *C., Kent, Mid.* 14,768
*Rowlands, Edward (b. 1940), *Lab., Merthyr Tydfil and Rhymney* 28,130
Ruddock, Ms. Joan M. (b. 1943), *Lab., Lewisham, Deptford* 6,771
*Rumbold, Mrs. Angela C. R., CBE (b. 1932), *C., Mitcham and Morden* 6,183
*Ryder, Richard A., OBE (b. 1949), *C., Norfolk, Mid* 18,008
*Sackville, Hon. Thomas G. (b. 1950), *C., Bolton W.* 4,593

Maj.

*Sainsbury, Hon. Timothy A. D. (*b.* 1932), C.,
Hove 18,218
Salmond, Alexander E. A. (*b.* 1954), SNP,
Banff and Buchan 2,441
*Sayeed, Jonathan (*b.* 1948), C., Bristol E. . 4,123
*Scott, Rt. Hon. Nicholas P., MBE (*b.* 1933),
C., Chelsea 13,319
*Sedgemore, Brian C. J. (*b.* 1937), Lab.,
Hackney S. and Shoreditch 7,522
Shaw, David L. (*b.* 1950), C., Dover 6,541
*Shaw, Sir Giles (*b.* 1931), C., Pudsey 6,436
*Shaw, Sir Michael (*b.* 1920), C., Scarborough 13,626
*Sheerman, Barry J. (*b.* 1940), Lab., Hud-
dersfield 7,278
*Sheldon, Rt. Hon. Robert E. (*b.* 1923), Lab.,
Ashton-under-Lyne 9,286
*Shelton, Sir William (*b.* 1929), C., Streatham 2,407
Shephard, Mrs. Gillian P. (*b.* 1940), C.,
Norfolk SW 20,436
*Shepherd, Colin R. (*b.* 1938), C., Hereford . 1,413
*Shepherd, Richard C. S. (*b.* 1942), C.,
Aldridge-Brownhills 12,396
*Shersby, J. Michael (*b.* 1933), C., Uxbridge 15,970
*Shore, Rt. Hon. Peter D. (*b.* 1924), Lab.,
Bethnal Green and Stepney 5,284
*Short, Ms. Clare (*b.* 1946), Lab., Birming-
ham, Ladywood 10,028
Sillars, James (*b.* 1937), SNP, Glasgow
Govan 3,554
*Sims, Roger E. (*b.* 1930), C., Chislehurst ... 14,507
*Skeet, Sir Trevor (*b.* 1918), C., Bedfordshire
N. 16,505
*Skinner, Dennis E. (*b.* 1932), Lab., Bolsover 14,120
Smith, Andrew D. (*b.* 1951), Lab., Oxford E. 1,288
*Smith, Christopher R. (*b.* 1951), Lab., Isling-
ton S. and Finsbury 805
*Smith, Sir Cyril, MBE (*b.* 1928), Lib. Dem.,
Rochdale 2,779
*Smith, Sir Dudley (*b.* 1926), C., Warwick
and Leamington 13,982
*Smith, Rt. Hon. John, QC (*b.* 1938), Lab.,
Monklands E. 16,389
Smith, John W. P. (*b.* 1951), Lab., Vale of
Glamorgan 6,028
*Smith, Timothy J. (*b.* 1947), C., Beaconsfield 21,339
*Smyth, Rev. W. Martin (*b.* 1931), OUP,
Belfast S. 11,954
*Snape, Peter C. (*b.* 1942), Lab., West Brom-
wich E. 983
*Soames, Hon. A. Nicholas W. (*b.* 1948), C.,
Crawley 12,138
*Soley, Clive S. (*b.* 1939), Lab., Hammersmith 2,415
*Spearing, Nigel J. (*b.* 1930), Lab., Newham
S. 2,766
*Speed, H. Keith, RD (*b.* 1934), C., Ashford . 15,488
*Speller, Antony (*b.* 1929), C., Devon N. .. 4,469
*Spicer, Sir James (*b.* 1925), C., Dorset W. ... 12,364
*Spicer W. Michael H. (*b.* 1943), C., Worces-
tershire S. 13,645
*Squire, Robin C. (*b.* 1944), C., Hornchurch 10,694
*Stanbrook, Ivor R. (*b.* 1924), C., Orpington 12,732
*Stanley, Rt. Hon. Sir John (*b.* 1942), C.,
Tonbridge and Malling 16,429
*Steel, Rt. Hon. Sir David (*b.* 1938), Lib.
Dem., Tweeddale, Ettrick and Lauder-
dale 5,942
*Steen, Anthony D. (*b.* 1939), C., South Hams 13,146
Steinberg, Gerald N. (*b.* 1945), Lab., Dur-
ham, City of 6,125
*Stern, Michael C. (*b.* 1942), C., Bristol NW 6,952
*Stevens, Lewis D., MBE (*b.* 1936), C., Nun-
eaton 5,655
*Stewart, Andrew S. (*b.* 1937), C., Sherwood 4,495
*Stewart, Rt. Hon. B. H. Ian H., RD (*b.* 1935),
C., Hertfordshire N. 11,442
*Stewart, J. Allan (*b.* 1942), C., Eastwood .. 6,014

Maj.

*Stokes, Sir John (*b.* 1917), C., Halesowen
and Stourbridge 13,808
*Stott, Roger, CBE (*b.* 1943), Lab., Wigan ... 20,462
*Stradling Thomas, Sir John (*b.* 1925), C.,
Monmouth 9,350
*Strang, Gavin S. (*b.* 1943), Lab., Edinburgh
E. 9,295
*Straw, J. W. (Jack) (*b.* 1946), Lab., Black-
burn 5,497
*Sumberg, David A. G. (*b.* 1941), C., Bury S. 2,679
Summerson, Hugo H. F. (*b.* 1950), C.,
Walthamstow 1,512
*Tapsell, Sir Peter (*b.* 1930), C., Lindsey E. . 8,616
*Taylor, Edward M. (*b.* 1937), C., Southend
E. 13,847
Taylor, Ian C., MBE, (*b.* 1945), C., Esher ... 19,068
*Taylor, Rt. Hon. John D. (*b.* 1937), OUP,
Strangford 20,646
*Taylor, John M. (*b.* 1941), C., Solihull 21,786
*Taylor, Matthew O. J. (*b.* 1963), Lib. Dem.,
Truro 4,753
Taylor, Mrs. W. Ann (*b.* 1947), Lab., Dews-
bury 445
*Tebbit, Rt. Hon. Norman B., CH (*b.* 1931),
C., Chingford 17,955
*Temple-Morris, Peter (*b.* 1938), C., Leomin-
ster 14,075
*Thatcher, Rt. Hon. Mrs. Margaret H. (*b.*
1925), C., Finchley 8,913
*Thomas, Dafydd E. (*b.* 1946), PC, Meirion-
nydd Nant Conwy 3,026
*Thompson, Donald (*b.* 1931), C., Calder
Valley 6,045
*Thompson, H. Patrick (*b.* 1935), C., Norwich
N. 7,776
*Thompson, John (*b.* 1928), Lab., Wansbeck 16,789
*Thorne, Neil G., OBE, TD (*b.* 1932), C., Ilford
S. 4,572
*Thornton, G. Malcolm (*b.* 1939), C., Crosby 6,847
*Thurnham, Peter G. (*b.* 1938), C., Bolton
NE 813
*Townend, John E. (*b.* 1934), C., Bridlington 17,321
*Townsend, Cyril D. (*b.* 1937), C., Bexley-
heath 11,687
*Tracey, Richard P. (*b.* 1943), C., Surbiton . 9,741
Tredinnick, David A. S. (*b.* 1950), C.,
Bosworth 17,016
Trimble W. David (*b.* 1944), OUP, Upper
Bann 13,849
*Trippier, David A., RD (*b.* 1946), C., Rossen-
dale and Darwen 4,982
*Trotter, Neville G. (*b.* 1932), C., Tynemouth 2,583
*Twinn, Dr. Ian D. (*b.* 1950), C., Edmonton . 7,286
Turner, Dennis (*b.* 1942), Lab., Wolver-
hampton SE 6,398
*Vaughan, Sir Gerard (*b.* 1923), C., Reading
E. 16,217
Vaz, N. Keith A. S. (*b.* 1956), Lab., Leicester
E. 1,924
*Viggers, Peter J. (*b.* 1938), C., Gosport 13,723
*Waddington, Rt. Hon. David C., QC (*b.*
1929), C., Ribble Valley 19,528
*Wakeham, Rt. Hon. John (*b.* 1932), C.,
Colchester S. and Maldon 15,483
*Waldegrave, Rt. Hon. William A. (*b.* 1946),
C., Bristol W. 7,703
*Walden, George G. H., CMG (*b.* 1939), C.,
Buckingham 18,526
*Walker, A. Cecil (*b.* 1924), OUP, Belfast N. 8,560
*Walker, Rt. Hon. Harold (*b.* 1927), Lab.,
Doncaster, Central 8,196
*Walker, Rt. Hon. Peter E., MBE (*b.* 1932), C.,
Worcester 10,453
*Walker, William C. (*b.* 1929), Tayside N. .. 5,016
*Wallace, James R. (*b.* 1954), Lib. Dem.,
Orkney and Shetland 3,922

	Maj.		Maj.
*Waller, Gary P. A. (b. 1945), C., Keighley ..	5,606	*Wilkinson, John A. D. (b. 1940), C., Ruislip-	
Walley, Ms. Joan L. (b. 1949), Lab., Stoke-		Northwood	16,971
on-Trent N.	8,513	*Williams, Rt. Hon. Alan J. (b. 1930), Lab.,	
*Walters, Sir Dennis, MBE (b. 1928), C.,		Swansea W.	7,062
Westbury	10,097	Williams, Alan W. (b. 1945), Lab., Carmar-	
*Ward, John D., CBE (b. 1925), C., Poole	14,808	then	4,317
*Wardell, Gareth L. (b. 1944), Lab., Gower .	5,764	Wilshire, David (b. 1943), C., Spelthorne ..	20,050
*Wardle, Charles F. (b. 1939), C., Bexhill and		Wilson, Brian D. H. (b. 1948), Lab., Cun-	
Battle	20,519	ninghame N.	4,467
*Wareing, Robert N. (b. 1930), Lab., Liver-		*Winnick, David J. (b. 1933), Lab., Walsall	
pool, West Derby	20,496	N.	1,790
*Warren, Kenneth R. (b. 1926), C., Hastings		*Winterton, Mrs. J. Ann (b. 1941), C.,	
and Rye	7,347	Congleton	7,969
Watson, Michael (b. 1949), Lab., Glasgow		*Winterton, Nicholas R. (b. 1938), C., Mac-	
Central	6,462	clesfield	19,092
*Watts, John A. (b. 1947), C., Slough	4,090	Wise, Mrs. Audrey (b. 1935), Lab., Preston	10,645
*Weatherill, Rt. Hon. B. Bernard (b. 1920),		*Wolfson, G. Mark (b. 1934), C., Sevenoaks .	17,345
The Speaker, Croydon NE	12,519	*Wood, Timothy J. R. (b. 1940), C., Steven-	
*Wells, Bowen (b. 1935), C., Hertford and		age	5,340
Stortford	17,140	*Woodcock, Michael (b. 1943), C., Ellesmere	
Welsh, Andrew (b. 1944), SNP, Angus E.	1,544	Port and Neston	1,853
*Welsh, Michael C. (b. 1926), Lab., Doncaster		Worthington, Anthony (b. 1941), Lab.,	
N.	19,935	Clydebank and Milngavie	16,304
*Wheeler, Sir John D. (b. 1940), C., West-		Wray, James (b. 1938), Lab., Glasgow,	
minster N.	3,310	Provan	18,372
*Whitney, Raymond W., OBE (b. 1930), C.,		*Yeo, Timothy S. K. (b. 1945), C., Suffolk	
Wycombe	13,819	S.	16,243
Widdecombe, Miss Ann N. (b. 1947), C.,		*Young, David W. (b. 1930), Lab., Bolton SE	11,381
Maidstone	10,364	*Young, Sir George, Bt. (b. 1941), C., Ealing,	
*Wiggin, A. W. (Jerry), TD (b. 1937), C.,		Acton	12,243
Weston-super-Mare	7,998	*Younger, Rt. Hon. George K. H., TD (b.	
*Wigley, Dafydd W. (b.1943), PC, Caernarfon	12,802	1931), C., Ayr	182

SMALL MAJORITIES

The following Members were returned in June 1987 with majorities of fewer than 1,000 votes.

*Richard Livsey (L/All., Brecon and Radnor) .	56	Elliott Morley (Lab., Glanford and	
Alan Meale (Lab., Mansfield)	56	Scunthorpe)	512
*Conal Gregory (C., York)	147	Timothy Janman (C., Thurrock)	690
*Gerald Bowden (C., Dulwich)	180	Edward McGrady (SDLP, Down S.)	731
*Rt. Hon. George Younger (C., Ayr)	182	Timothy Devlin (C., Stockton S.)	774
Mrs. Maureen Hicks (C., Wolverhampton		*Christopher Smith (Lab., Islington S. and	
NE)	204	Finsbury)	805
David Martin (C., Portsmouth S.)	205	*Peter Thurnham (C., Bolton NE)	813
*Mrs. Lynda Chalker (C., Wallasey)	279	Ronald Campbell (Lab., Blyth Valley)	853
Robert Cryer (Lab., Bradford S.)	309	John Bowis (C., Battersea)	857
John Garrett (Lab., Norwich S.)	336	Michael Irvine (C., Ipswich)	874
Mrs. Ann Taylor (Lab., Dewsbury)	445	Eric Martlew (Lab., Carlisle)	916
*Michael Knowles (C., Nottingham E.)	456	*Michael Forsyth (C., Stirling)	948
		*Peter Snape (Lab., West Bromwich E.)	983

WOMEN MEMBERS

The number of women MPs returned in June 1987 (41) was the highest ever.

Ms. Diane Abbott (Lab., Hackney N. and Stoke Newington); Ms. Hilary Armstrong (Lab., Durham, NW); *Mrs. Rosemary Barnes (SDP/All., Greenwich); *Mrs. Margaret Beckett (Lab., Derby S.); *Miss Betty Boothroyd (Lab., West Bromwich W.); *Mrs. Virginia Bottomley (C., Surrey, SW); *Mrs. Lynda Chalker (C., Wallasey); *Mrs. Ann Clwyd (Lab., Cynon Valley); *Mrs. Edwina Currie (C., Derbyshire S.); *Hon. Mrs. Gwyneth Dunwoody (Lab., Crewe and Nantwich); Mrs. Margaret Ewing (SNP, Moray); *Dame Peggy Fenner (C., Medway); *Miss Janet Fookes (C., Plymouth Drake); Mrs. Maria Fyfe (Lab., Glasgow Maryhill); Mrs. Llinos Golding (Lab., Newcastle under Lyme); Mrs. Mildred Gordon (Lab., Bow and Poplar); Mrs. Theresa Gorman (C., Billericay); *Ms. Harriet Harman (Lab., Peckham); Mrs. Maureen Hicks (C., Wolverhampton NE); *Mrs. Elaine Kellett-Bowman (C., Lancaster); *Dame Jill Knight (C., Birmingham Edgbaston); Miss Joan Lestor (Lab., Eccles); Mrs. Alice Mahon (Lab., Halifax); Mrs. Ray Michie (L./All., Argyll and Bute); Dr. Marjorie Mowlam (Lab., Redcar); Miss Emma Nicholson (C., Devon W. and Torridge); *Mrs. Elizabeth Peacock (C., Batley and Spen); Ms. Dawn Primarolo (Lab., Bristol S.); Miss Joyce Quin (Lab., Gateshead E.); *Ms. Jo Richardson (Lab., Barking); *Mrs. Marion Roe (C., Broxbourne); Ms. Joan Ruddock (Lab., Lewisham Deptford); *Mrs. Angela Rumbold (C., Mitcham and Morden); Mrs. Gillian Shephard (C., Norfolk SW); *Ms. Clare Short (Lab., Birmingham Ladywood); Mrs. Ann Taylor (Lab., Dewsbury); *Rt. Hon. Mrs. Margaret Thatcher (C., Finchley); Ms. Joan Walley (Lab., Stoke-on-Trent); Miss Ann Widdecombe (C., Maidstone); *Mrs. Ann Winterton (C., Congleton); Mrs. Audrey Wise (Lab., Preston).

The number of women MPs was 43 in July 1990 following the election of Kate Hoey (Lab., Vauxhall) and Sylvia Heal (Lab., Staffordshire Mid).

THE HOUSE OF COMMONS BY CONSTITUENCIES, JUNE 1987

The figures following the name of each Constituency denote the total number of *Electors* in the Parliamentary Division at the General Election of June 11, 1987.

An asterisk * denotes membership of the last Parliament. The majority in the 1983 General Election (and in any subsequent by-election) is shown below the 1987 result. For **by-elections** since the 1987 General Election, *see* p. 275-6.

Abbreviations — *C.* = Conservative; *DUP* = Democratic Unionist Party; *Ind.* = Independent; *L./All., SDP/ All.* = Liberal and Social Democratic Alliance; *Lab.* = Labour; *OUP* = Official Unionist Party; *PC* = Plaid Cymru; *SDLP* = Social Democratic and Labour Party; *SDP* = Social Democratic Party; *SF* = Sinn Fein; *SLD* = Social and Liberal Democrats; *SNP* = Scottish National Party; *UPUP* = Ulster Popular Unionist Party; *All.* = Alliance Party (NI); *BN* = British Nationalist; *Bread* = Creek Road Fresh Bread Party; *BT* = Blancmange Thrower; *CD* = Christian Democrat; *CMNHY* = Common Market No, Hanging Yes; *Comm.* = Communist Party; *CPRP* = Capital Punishment Referendum Party; *CPWSML* = Capital Punishment Will Save More Lives; *CS* = Christian Socialist Opposing Secret Masonic Government; *DC* = Democratic Commonwealth Party; *Dem.* = Independent Democrat; *Ecol.* = Ecology (NI); *Ex. Lab. Mod.* = Ex Labour Moderate; *Falk.* = Right of Falkland Islands to elect Westminster MP; *FDP* = Fancy Dress Party; *Fell.* = Fellowship Party; *FP* = Feudal Party; *Gait. Lab.* = Gaitskell Labour; *Gold* = Gold Party; *Grem.* = Gremloid; *Grn.* = Green Party; *HP* = Human Party; *ICC* = Independent Community Campaigner, East Oxford People; *ICN* = Independent Christian Nationalist; *LAO* = Law and Order; *LAPP* = Let's Have Another Party Party; *LM* = Loony Official Monster Raving Party; *ML* = Moderate Labour Party; *NFFG* = National Front Flag Group; *NPR* = National People's Rally; *OFP* = Official Fidgeyitous Party; *OOBPC* = Only Official Best Party Candidate; *OSM* = Orkney and Shetland Movement; *PIP* = Public Independent Plaintiff; *Prot. U.* = Protestant Unionist; *PRP* = Protestant Reformation Party; *RABIES* = Rainbow Alliance Brixton Insane Extremist Section; *RCP* = Return Capital Punishment; *Real U.* = Real Unionist; *RF* = Red Front; *Ret.* = Retired; *RRPRC* = Revolutionary Reform Party Representative of Christ; *SE* = Spare the Earth; *SPGB* = Socialist Party of Great Britain; *WP* = Workers' Party (NI); *WRP* = Workers' Revolutionary Party.

ENGLAND

Aldershot (Hants)
E. 80,797

*J. M. G. Critchley, C.	35,272
R. A. Hargreaves, L./All.	17,488
I. H. Pearson, Lab.	7,061
C. maj.	17,784
(June '83, C. maj. 12,218)	

Aldridge-Brownhills
(W. Midlands)
E. 62,129

*R. C. S. Shepherd, C.	26,434
C. Duncan, Lab.	14,038
G. Betteridge, SDP/All.	9,084
C. maj.	12,396
(June '83, C. maj. 12,284)	

Altrincham and Sale
(Gtr. Manchester)
E. 67,611

*Sir F. Montgomery, C.	27,746
J. Mulholland, L./All.	13,518
D. Hinder, Lab.	10,617
C. maj.	14,228
(June '83, C. maj. 10,911)	

Amber Valley (Derbys)
E. 68,478

*P. A. C. L. Oppenheim, C.	28,603
D. M. Bookbinder, Lab.	19,103
S. Reynolds, L./All.	7,904
C. maj.	9,500
(June '83, C. maj. 3,318)	

Arundel (W. Sussex)
E. 78,683

*R. M. Marshall, C.	34,356
Dr. J. M. M. Walsh, L./All.	15,476
P. Slowe, Lab.	6,177
C. maj.	18,880
(June '83, C. maj. 15,705)	

Ashfield (Notts)
E. 70,937

*D. F. Haynes, Lab.	22,812
B. G. Coleman, C.	18,412
Mrs. F. B. Stein, L./All.	13,542
Lab. maj.	4,400
(June '83, Lab. maj. 6,087)	

Ashford (Kent)
E. 70,052

*H. K. Speed, C.	29,978
N. N. Macmillan, SDP/All.	14,490
M. J. Wiggins, Lab.	7,775
Dr. C. A. Porter, Grn.	778
C. maj.	15,488
(June '83, C. maj. 13,911)	

Ashton-under-Lyne
(Gtr. Manchester)
E. 58,440

*Rt. Hon. R. E. Sheldon, Lab.	22,389
H. L. Cadman, C.	13,103
M. J. Hunter, L./All.	7,760
Lab. maj.	9,286
(June '83, Lab. maj. 7,697)	

Aylesbury (Bucks)
E. 76,919

*Rt. Hon. T. H. F. Raison, C.	32,970
M. A. Soole, SDP/All.	16,412
Ms. J. Larner, Lab.	7,936
C. maj.	16,558
(June '83, C. maj. 14,920)	

Banbury (Oxon)
E. 69,455

*A. B. Baldry, C.	29,716
D. C. Rowland, SDP/All.	12,386
J. A. Honeybone, Lab.	10,789
C. maj.	17,330
(June '83, C. maj. 13,025)	

Barking (Gtr. London)
E. 51,639

*Ms. J. Richardson, Lab.	15,307
W. K. Sharp, C.	11,898
J. K. Gibb, L./All.	7,336
Lab. maj.	3,409
(June '83, Lab. maj. 4,026)	

Barnsley (S. Yorks)

CENTRAL E. 55,902

E. E. Illsley, Lab.	26,139
Mrs. V. Prais, C.	7,088
Mrs. S. A. M. Holland, L./All.	5,928
Lab. maj.	19,051
(June '83, Lab. maj. 14,173)	

EAST E. 53,505

*T. Patchett, Lab.	28,948
W. J. Clappison, C.	5,437
G. J. Griffiths, L./All.	4,482
Lab. maj.	23,511
(June '83, Lab. maj. 17,492)	

WEST AND PENISTONE E. 61,091

*A. McKay, Lab.	26,498
A. J. C. Duncan, C.	12,307
R. Hall, SDP/All.	7,409
Lab. maj.	14,191
(June '83, Lab. maj. 10,342)	

Barrow and Furness (Cumbria)
E. 69,288

*C. S. Franks, C.	25,431
P. Phizacklea, Lab.	21,504
R. W. Phelps, SDP/All.	7,799
C. maj.	3,927
(June '83, C. maj. 4,577)	

Basildon (Essex)
E. 68,500

*D. A. A. Amess, C.	21,858
J. G. H. Fulbrook, Lab.	19,209
R. M. Auvray, L./All.	9,139
C. maj.	2,649
(June '83, C. maj. 1,379)	

Basingstoke (Hants)
E. 78,003

*A. R. F. Hunter, C.	33,657
D. Bennett, SDP/All.	15,764
P. Daden, Lab.	10,632
C. maj.	17,893
(June '83, C. maj. 12,450)	

Bassetlaw (Notts)
E. 68,043

*J. W. Ashton, *Lab.*		25,385
D. R. J. Selves, *C.*		19,772
W. G. Smith, *SDP/All.*		7,616
Lab. maj.		5,613
(June '83, Lab. maj. 3,831)		

Bath (Avon)
E. 65,246

*C. F. Patten, *C.*		23,515
J. M. Dean, *SDP/All.*		22,103
Mrs. J. Smith, *Lab.*		5,507
D. N. Wall, *Grn.*		687
C. maj.		1,412
(June '83, C. maj. 5,304)		

Batley and Spen (W. Yorks)
E. 74,347

*Mrs. E. J. Peacock, *C.*		25,512
K. J. Woolmer, *Lab.*		24,150
K. Burke, *SDP/All.*		8,372
A. Harrison, *ML.*		689
C. maj.		1,362
(June '83, C. maj. 870)		

Battersea (Gtr. London)
E. 66,979

J. C. Bowis, *C.*		20,945
*A. Dubs, *Lab.*		20,088
D. I. Harries, *SDP/All.*		5,634
Ms. S. G. Willington, *Grn.*		559
A. B. Bell, *WRP.*		116
C. maj.		857
(June '83, Lab. maj. 3,276)		

Beaconsfield (Bucks)
E. 67,713

*T. J. Smith, *C.*		33,324
D. H. Ive, *L./All.*		11,985
K. J. Harper, *Lab.*		5,203
C. maj.		21,339
(June '83, C. maj. 18,300)		

Beckenham (Gtr. London)
E. 60,110

*Sir P. C. Goodhart, *C.*		24,903
C. G. Darracott, *L./All.*		11,439
K. G. Ritchie, *Lab.*		7,888
C. maj.		13,464
(June '83, C. maj. 12,670)		

Bedfordshire

MID E. 80,673

*N. W. Lyell, QC, *C.*		37,411
N. C. Hills, *SDP/All.*		14,560
J. Heywood, *Lab.*		11,463
C. maj.		22,851
(June '83, C. maj. 17,381)		

NORTH E. 73,536

*Sir T. H. H. Skeet, *C.*		29,845
Mrs. J. V. Lennon, *L./All.*		13,340
C. B. Henderson, *Lab.*		13,140
C. D. Slee, *OOBPC*		435
C. maj.		16,505
(June '83, C. maj. 13,849)		

SOUTH WEST E. 78,956

*W. D. Madel, *C.*		36,140
J. R. Burrow, *SDP/All.*		13,835
P. H. Dimoldenberg, *Lab.*		11,352
P. J. Rollings, *Grn.*		822
C. maj.		22,305
(June '83, C. maj. 15,731)		

Berkshire East
E. 87,820

*A. J. MacKay, *C.*		39,094
Mrs. L. A. Murray, *SDP/All.*		16,468
R. J. E. Evans, *Lab.*		9,287
C. maj.		22,626
(June '83, C. maj. 16,099)		

Berwick-upon-Tweed (Nthmb)
E. 54,378

*A. J. Beith, *L./All.*		21,903
T. Middleton, *C.*		12,400
S. Lambert, *Lab.*		7,360
N. Pamphilion, *Grn.*		379
L./All. maj.		9,503
(June '83, L./All. maj. 8,215)		

Bethnal Green and Stepney
(Gtr. London)
E. 55,769

*Rt. Hon. P. D. Shore, *Lab.*		15,490
J. A. Shaw, *L./All.*		10,206
Lady O. H. Maitland, *C.*		6,176
Ms. S. Gasquoine, *Comm.*		232
Lab. maj.		5,284
(June '83, Lab. maj. 6,358)		

Beverley (Humberside)
E. 78,923

J. D. Cran, *C.*		31,459
J. Bryant, *L./All.*		18,864
M. Shaw, *Lab.*		9,901
C. maj.		12,595
(June '83, C. maj. 13,869)		

Bexhill and Battle
(E. Sussex)
E. 65,288

*C. F. Wardle, *C.*		33,570
R. Kiernan, *SDP/All.*		13,051
D. K. Watts, *Lab.*		3,903
C. maj.		20,519
(June '83, C. maj. 19,746)		

Bexleyheath
(Gtr. London)
E. 59,448

*C. D. Townsend, *C.*		24,866
B. C. Standen, *L./All.*		13,179
J. F. Little, *Lab.*		8,218
C. maj.		11,687
(June '83, C. maj. 10,258)		

Billericay (Essex)
E. 79,535

*Mrs. T. E. Gorman, *C.*		33,741
M. Birch, *SDP/All.*		15,755
R. Howitt, *Lab.*		11,942
C. maj.		17,986
(June '83, C. maj. 14,615)		

Birkenhead (Merseyside)
E. 65,662

*F. Field, *Lab.*		27,883
K. J. Costa, *C.*		12,511
R. Kemp, *L./All.*		7,095
Lab. maj.		15,372
(June '83, Lab. maj. 9,714)		

Birmingham (W. Midlands)

EDGBASTON E. 54,416

*Dame J. C. J. Knight, DBE, *C.*		18,595
J. Wilton, *Lab.*		10,014
J. C. Binns, *SDP/All.*		7,843
P. Simpson, *Grn.*		559
S. T. Hardwick, *Ind. C.*		307
C. maj.		8,581
(June '83, C. maj. 11,418)		

ERDINGTON E. 54,179

*R. Corbett, *Lab.*		17,037
P. J. Johnston, *C.*		14,570
N. Biddlestone, *SDP/All.*		5,530
Lab. maj.		2,467
(June '83, Lab. maj. 231)		

HALL GREEN E. 61,148

A. R. Hargreaves, *C.*		20,478
Mrs. E. Brook, *Lab.*		12,857
M. Wilkes, *SDP/All.*		12,323
C. maj.		7,621
(June '83, C. maj. 9,373)		

HODGE HILL E. 59,296

*T. A. G. Davis, *Lab.*		19,872
S. Eyre, *C.*		15,083
K. G. Hardeman, *L./All.*		5,868
Lab. maj.		4,789
(June '83, Lab. maj. 5,092)		

LADYWOOD E. 58,761

*Ms. C. Short, *Lab.*		21,971
S. T. Lee, *C.*		11,943
G. S. Sangha, *SDP/All.*		3,532
Ms. J. Millington, *Grn.*		650
Lab. maj.		10,028
(June '83, Lab. maj. 9,030)		

NORTHFIELD E. 73,319

*R. D. King, *C.*		24,024
J. F. Spellar, *Lab.*		20,889
J. Gordon, *SDP/All.*		8,319
C. maj.		3,135
(June '83, C. maj. 2,760)		

PERRY BARR E. 73,767

*J. W. Rooker, *Lab.*		25,894
J. D. B. Taylor, *C.*		18,961
D. D. Webb, *L./All.*		6,514
Lab. maj.		6,933
(June '83, Lab. maj. 7,402)		

SELLY OAK E. 72,213

*A. M. Beaumont-Dark, *C.*		23,305
A. Bore, *Lab.*		20,721
Mrs. C. Cane, *L./All.*		8,128
Ms. M. Hackett, *Grn*		611
C. maj.		2,584
(June '83, C. maj. 5,396)		

SMALL HEATH E. 56,722
*Rt. Hon. D. H. Howell, Lab. 22,787
P. Nischal, C. 7,266
J. A. M. Hemming, L./All. 3,600
A. Clawley, Grn. 559
P. R. Sheppard, Comm. 154
  Lab. maj. 15,521
  (June '83, Lab. maj. 15,252)

SPARKBROOK E. 53,093
*Rt. Hon. R. S. G. Hattersley,
  Lab. 20,513
N. A. Khan, C. 8,654
R. Dimmick, SDP/All. 3,803
R. Ambler, Grn. 526
P. Khan, RF. 229
  Lab. maj. 11,859
  (June '83, Lab. maj. 10,548)

YARDLEY E. 56,957
*A. D. G. Bevan, C. 17,931
G. Edge, Lab. 15,409
L. Smith, L./All. 8,734
  C. maj. 2,522
  (June '83, C. maj. 2,865)

Bishop Auckland (Durham)
E. 72,147

*D. Foster, Lab. 25,648
R. Wight, C. 18,613
G. Irwin, L./All. 9,195
  Lab. maj. 7,035
  (June '83, Lab. maj. 4,306)

Blaby (Leics)
E. 77,094

*Rt. Hon. N. Lawson, C. 37,732
R. E. Lustig, L./All. 15,556
J. M. Roberts, Lab. 9,046
  C. maj. 22,176
  (June '83, C. maj. 17,116)

Blackburn (Lancs)
E. 74,801

*J. W. Straw, Lab. 27,965
Mrs. A. C. Cheetham, C. 22,468
M. A. Ali, SDP/All. 5,602
  Lab. maj. 5,497
  (June '83, Lab. maj. 3,055)

Blackpool (Lancs)

NORTH E. 58,893
*N. A. Miscampbell, QC, C. 20,680
E. Kirton, Lab. 13,359
C. J. Heyworth, L./All. 9,032
  C. maj. 7,321
  (June '83, C. maj. 10,152)

SOUTH E. 57,567
*Rt. Hon. Sir P. A. R. Blaker,
  KCMG, C. 20,312
Mrs. S. Baugh, Lab. 13,568
J. Allitt, SDP/All. 8,405
  C. maj. 6,744
  (June '83, C. maj. 10,138)

Blaydon (Tyne & Wear)
E. 66,301

*J. D. McWilliam, Lab. 25,277
V. P. Nunn, SDP/All. 12,789
P. R. Pescod, C. 12,147
  Lab. maj. 12,488
  (June '83, Lab. maj. 7,222)

Blyth Valley (Nthmb)
E. 59,104

R. Campbell, Lab. 19,604
Miss R. M. Brownlow,
  SDP/All. 18,751
Dr. R. Kinghorn, C. 7,823
  Lab. maj. 853
  (June '83, Lab. maj. 3,243)

Bolsover (Derbys)
E. 65,452

*D. E. Skinner, Lab. 28,453
M. R. Lingens, C. 14,333
M. H. Fowler, SDP/All. 7,836
  Lab. maj. 14,120
  (June '83, Lab. maj. 13,848)

Bolton (Gtr. Manchester)

NORTH EAST E. 59,382
*P. G. Thurnham, C. 20,742
F. R. White, Lab. 19,929
J. H. Alcock, SDP/All. 6,060
  C. maj. 813
  (June '83, C. maj. 2,443)

SOUTH EAST E. 65,932
*D. W. Young, Lab. 26,791
S. Windle, C. 15,410
F. Harasiwka, L./All. 7,161
  Lab. maj. 11,381
  (June '83, Lab. maj. 8,753)

WEST E. 69,843
*T. G. Sackville, C. 24,779
G. J. Harkin, Lab. 20,186
D. T. Eccles, SDP/All. 10,936
  C. maj. 4,593
  (June '83, C. maj. 7,152)

Boothferry (Humberside)
E. 75,176

D. M. Davis, C. 31,716
Mrs. J. D. Davies, L./All. 12,746
R. Donson, Lab. 12,498
  C. maj. 18,970
  (June '83, C. maj. 17,420)

Bootle (Merseyside)
E. 71,765

*A. Roberts, Lab. 34,975
P. R. Papworth, C. 10,498
P. Denham, SDP/All. 6,820
  Lab. maj. 24,477
  (June '83, Lab. maj. 15,139)
  (See also p. 276)

Bosworth (Leics)
E. 77,186

D. A. S. Tredinnick, C. 34,145
D. C. Bill, L./All. 17,129
R. S. Hall, Lab. 10,787
Mrs. D. Freer, Grn 660
  C. maj. 17,016
  (June '83, C. maj. 17,294)

Bournemouth (Dorset)

EAST E. 75,232
*D. A. Atkinson, C. 30,925
Dr. J. Millward, L./All. 16,242
I. A. Taylor, Lab. 5,885
  C. maj. 14,683
  (June '83, C. maj. 11,416)

WEST E. 74,444
*J. V. Butterfill, C. 30,117
P. G. M. Craven, SDP/All. 17,466
R. W. Jones, Lab. 7,018
  C. maj. 12,651
  (June '83, C. maj. 13,331)

Bow and Poplar (Gtr. London)
E. 59,178

Ms. M. Gordon, Lab. 15,746
E. Flounders, L./All. 11,115
D. C. Hughes, C. 6,810
P. S. Chappell, WRP 274
  Lab. maj. 4,631
  (June '83, Lab. maj. 5,861)

Bradford (W. Yorks)

NORTH E. 67,430
C. P. Wall, Lab. 21,009
*G. J. Lawler, C. 19,376
A. M. Berkeley, SDP/All. 8,656
  Lab. maj. 1,633
  (June '83, C. maj. 1,602)

SOUTH E. 69,588
G. R. Cryer, Lab. 21,230
G. T. Hall, C. 20,921
T. Lindley, SDP/All. 9,109
  Lab. maj. 309
  (June '83, Lab. maj. 110)

WEST E. 70,763
*M. F. Madden, Lab. 25,775
I. Duncan-Smith, C. 18,224
M. Moghal, SDP/All. 5,657
  Lab. maj. 7,551
  (June '83, Lab. maj. 3,337)

Braintree (Essex)
E. 76,994

*A. H. Newton, OBE, C. 32,978
I. G. Bing, SDP/All. 16,121
B. Stapleton, Lab. 11,764
  C. maj. 16,857
  (June '83, C. maj. 13,441)

Brent (Gtr. London)

EAST E. 61,020
K. R. Livingstone, Lab. 16,772
Miss H. S. Crawley, C. 15,119
D. W. Finkelstein, SDP/
  All. 5,710
R. Q. Dooley, Ind. Lab. 1,035
M. Litvinoff, Grn. 716
  Lab. maj. 1,653
  (June '83, Lab. maj. 4,834)

NORTH E. 63,081
*Dr. R. Boyson, C. 26,823
P. Patel, Lab. 11,103
C. Mularczyk, SDP/All. 6,868
  C. maj. 15,720
  (June '83, C. maj. 14,651)

SOUTH E. 62,772
P. Y. Boateng, Lab. 21,140
A. J. Paterson, C. 13,209
M. T. Harskin, L./All. 6,375
  Lab. maj. 7,931
  (June '83, Lab. maj. 10,519)

Brentford and Isleworth
(Gtr. London)
E. 71,715

**Rt. Hon. Sir B. J. Hayhoe,
C.* 26,230
Ms. A. Keen, *Lab.* 18,277
Dr. D. M. W. Wilks, *SDP/
All.* 9,626
T. Cooper, *Grn.* 849
C. maj. 7,953
(June '83, C. maj. 9,387)

Brentwood and Ongar (Essex)
E. 67,521

*R. A. McCrindle, C. 32,258
N. R. Amor, *L./All.* 13,337
J. W. Orpe, *Lab.* 7,042
Mrs. M. E. Willis, *Grn.* ... 686
C. maj. 18,921
(June '83, C. maj. 14,202)

Bridgwater (Somerset)
E. 67,480

*Rt. Hon. T. J. King, C. 27,177
C. Clarke, *SDP/All.* 15,982
J. Turner, *Lab.* 9,594
C. maj. 11,195
(June '83, C. maj. 10,697)

Bridlington (Humberside)
E. 80,126

*J. E. Townend, C. 32,351
E. I. Marshall, *SDP/All.* 15,030
L. M. Bird, *Lab.* 10,653
R. D. Myerscough, *Grn.* ... 983
C. maj. 17,321
(June '83, C. maj. 16,609)

Brigg and Cleethorpes
(Humberside)
E. 80,096

*M. R. Brown, C. 29,723
I. Powney, *L./All.* 17,475
T. Geraghty, *Lab.* 13,876
C. maj. 12,248
(June '83, C. maj. 12,189)

Brighton (E. Sussex)

KEMPTOWN *E.* 60,271
*A. Bowden, MBE, *C.* 24,031
J. S. Bassam, *Lab.* 14,771
C. Berry, *L./All.* 6,080
C. maj. 9,260
(June '83, C. maj. 9,378)

PAVILION *E.* 58,910
*Rt. Hon. H. J. Amery, C. .. 22,056
D. S. Hill, *Lab.* 12,914
K. F. Carey, *SDP/All.* 8,459
C. maj. 9,142
(June '83, C. maj. 11,132)

Bristol (Avon)

EAST *E.* 63,840
*J. Sayeed, C. 21,906
R. R. Thomas, *Lab.* 17,783
D. M. E. Foster, *L./All.* 10,247
P. M. Kingston, *NFFG* ... 286
C. maj. 4,123
(June '83, C. maj. 1,789)

NORTH WEST *E.* 72,876
*M. C. Stern, C. 26,953
T. W. Walker, *Lab.* 20,001
J. M. G. Kirkaldy, *SDP/
All.* 10,885
C. maj. 6,952
(June '83, C. maj. 6,327)

SOUTH *E.* 68,733
Ms. D. Primarolo, *Lab.* ... 20,798
P. S. Cutcher, *C.* 19,394
Mrs. H. S. Long, *SDP/All.* 9,952
G. R. Vowles, *Grn.* 600
Ms. C. M. Meghji, *RF* ... 149
Lab. maj. 1,404
(June '83, Lab. maj. 4,419)

WEST *E.* 72,357
*Hon. W. A. Waldegrave, C. 24,695
G. R. P. Ferguson, *L./All.* . 16,992
Mrs. M. C. Georghiou, *Lab.* 11,337
Mrs. G. A. Dorey, *Grn.* ... 1,096
Ms. V. Ralph, *Comm.* 134
C. maj. 7,703
(June '83, C. maj. 10,178)

Bromsgrove (H & W)
E. 69,494

*H. D. Miller, C. 29,051
J. D. Ward, *Lab.* 12,366
D. L. Cropp, *SDP/All.* 11,663
C. maj. 16,685
(June '83, C. maj. 17,175)

Broxbourne (Herts)
E. 70,631

*Mrs. M. A. Roe, C. 33,567
Mrs. E. Yates, *L./All.* 10,572
P. Parry, *Lab.* 8,984
C. maj. 22,995
(June '83, C. maj. 17,466)

Broxtowe (Notts)
E. 71,780

*J. T. Lester, C. 30,462
K. Fleet, *Lab.* 13,811
K. M. Melton, *L./All.* 12,562
C. maj. 16,651
(June '83, C. maj. 15,078)

Buckingham
E. 70,036

*G. G. H. Walden, CMG, *C.* . 32,162
C. M. Burke, *L./All.* 13,636
M. Groucutt, *Lab.* 9,053
C. maj. 18,526
(June '83, C. maj. 13,968)

Burnley (Lancs)
E. 65,956

*P. L. Pike, Lab. 25,140
H. Elletson, *C.* 17,583
R. H. Baker, *SDP/All.* 9,241
Lab. maj. 7,557
(June '83, Lab. maj. 770)

Burton (Staffs)
E. 73,252

*I. J. Lawrence, QC, *C.* 29,160
D. Heptonstall, *Lab.* 19,330
K. A. Hemsley, *L./All.* 9,046
C. maj. 9,830
(June '83, C. maj. 11,647)

Bury (Gtr. Manchester)

NORTH *E.* 67,961
*A. J. H. Burt, C. 28,097
D. Crausby, *Lab.* 21,186
D. Vasmer, *L./All.* 6,804
C. maj. 6,911
(June '83, C. maj. 2,792)

SOUTH *E.* 65,039
*D. A. G. Sumberg, C. 23,878
D. Boden, *Lab.* 21,199
D. A. Eyre, *SDP/All.* 6,772
C. maj. 2,679
(June '83, C. maj. 3,720)

Bury St. Edmunds (Suffolk)
E. 76,619

*Sir E. W. Griffiths, C. 33,672
Sir R. Harland, *SDP/All.* . 12,214
C. L. Greene, *Lab.* 9,841
Ms. I. M. J. Wakelam, *Grn.* 1,057
C. maj. 21,458
(June '83, C. maj. 16,122)

Calder Valley (W. Yorks)
E. 73,398

*D. Thompson, C. 25,892
D. M. Chaytor, *Lab.* 19,847
D. T. Shutt, *L./All.* 13,761
C. maj. 6,045
(June '83, C. maj. 7,999)

Cambridge
E. 69,336

*R. V. Rhodes James, C. ... 21,624
Mrs. S. V. T. B. Williams,
SDP/All. 16,564
C. J. Howard, *Lab.* 15,319
Ms. M. E. Wright, *Grn.* 597
C. maj. 5,060
(June '83, C. maj. 5,968)

Cambridgeshire

NORTH EAST *E.* 74,231
M. D. Moss, C. 26,983
*C. R. Freud, L./All. 25,555
R. J. Harris, *Lab.* 4,891
C. maj. 1,428
(June '83, L./All. maj. 5,195)

SOUTH EAST *E.* 73,216
J. E. T. Paice, C. 32,901
P. C. Lee, *SDP/All.* 15,399
T. G. Ling, *Lab.* 7,694
C. maj. 17,502
(June '83, C. maj. 13,764)

SOUTH WEST *E.* 81,658
*Sir J. A. Grant, C. 36,622
D. C. Nicholls, *L./All.* 18,371
Ms. J. Billing, *Lab.* 8,434
C. maj. 18,251
(June '83, C. maj. 13,867)

Cannock and Burntwood (Staffs)
E. 68,137

*J. G. D. Howarth, C. 24,186
G. E. Roberts, *Lab.* 21,497
N. Stanley, *L./All.* 8,698
C. maj. 2,689
(June '83, C. maj. 2,045)

Canterbury (Kent)
E. 76,062

J. W. H. Brazier, *C.*		30,273
J. Purchese, *L./All.*		15,382
Ms. L. A. Keen, *Lab.*		9,494
S. Dawe, *Grn.*		947
Miss J. M. White, *ICN*		157
C. maj.		14,891

(June '83, C. maj. 15,742)

Carlisle (Cumbria)
E. 55,053

E. A. Martlew, *Lab.*		18,311
W. G. Hodgson, *C.*		17,395
R. S. Hunt, *SDP/All*		7,655
Lab. maj.		916

(June '83, Lab. maj. 71)

Carshalton and Wallington
(Gtr. London)
E. 69,120

*F. N. Forman, *C.*		27,984
J. D. Grant, *SDP/All.*		13,575
Mrs. J. G. Baker, *Lab.*		9,440
R. W. Steel, *Grn.*		843
C. maj.		14,409

(June '83, C. maj. 10,755)

Castle Point (Essex)
E. 65,992

Rt. Hon. Sir B. R. Braine, C.		29,681
Miss A. P. Bastow, *SDP/All.*		10,433
W. A. Deal, *Lab.*		9,422
C. maj.		19,248

(June '83, C. maj. 15,417)

Cheadle
(Gtr. Manchester)
E. 68,332

S. R. Day, *C.*		30,484
A. B. Leah, *L./All.*		19,853
Ms. A. Coffey, *Lab.*		5,037
C. maj.		10,631

(June '83, C. maj. 9,380)

Chelmsford (Essex)
E. 82,564

S. H. M. Burns, *C.*		35,231
S. G. Mole, *L./All.*		27,470
C. E. Playford, *Lab.*		4,642
A. C. Slade, *Grn.*		486
C. maj.		7,761

(June '83, C. maj. 378)

Chelsea
(Gtr. London)
E. 49,534

*N. P. Scott, MBE, *C.*		18,443
Mrs. J. M. Ware, *L./All.*		5,124
D. J. Ward, *Lab.*		4,406
Ms. N. Kortvelyessy, *Grn.*		587
C. maj.		13,319

(June '83, C. maj. 12,021)

Cheltenham (Glos)
E. 79,234

*C. G. Irving, *C.*		31,371
R. G. Holme, *L./All.*		26,475
M. Luker, *Lab.*		4,701
C. maj.		4,896

(June '83, C. maj. 5,518)

Chertsey and Walton (Surrey)
E. 71,448

*G. E. Pattie, *C.*		32,119
Mrs. S. K. Stapely, *SDP/All.*		14,650
H. G. Trace, *Lab.*		7,185
C. maj.		17,469

(June '83, C. maj. 15,699)

Chesham and Amersham
(Bucks)
E. 71,751

*Rt. Hon. Sir I. H. J. L. Gilmour, Bt., *C.*		34,504
A. T. Ketteringham, *L./All.*		15,064
P. A. Goulding, *Lab.*		5,170
Mrs. A. G. Darnbrough, *Grn.*		760
C. maj.		19,440

(June '83, C. maj. 15,879)

Chester, City of
E. 65,845

*Hon. P. H. Morrison, *C.*		23,582
D. Robinson, *Lab.*		18,727
R. A. Stunell, *L./All.*		10,262
C. maj.		4,855

(June '83, C. maj. 9,099)

Chesterfield (Derbys)
E. 70,357

*Rt. Hon. A. N. W. Benn, *Lab.*		24,532
A. H. Rogers, *L./All.*		15,955
R. P Grant, *C.*		13,472
Lab. maj.		8,577

(June '83, Lab. maj. 7,763)
(March '84, Lab. maj. 6,264)

Chichester (W. Sussex)
E. 81,019

*R. A. Nelson, *C.*		37,274
P. F Weston, *L./All.*		17,097
D. Morrison, *Lab.*		4,751
I. F. N. Bagnall, *Grn.*		1,196
C. maj.		20,177

(June '83, C. maj. 20,117)

Chingford (Gtr. London)
E. 56,797

*Rt. Hon. N. B. Tebbit, *C.*		27,110
J. G. Williams, *L./All.*		9,155
Ms. M. I. Cosin, *Lab.*		6,650
Ms. E. Newton, *Grn.*		634
C. maj.		17,955

(June '83, C. maj. 12,414)

Chipping Barnet (Gtr. London)
E. 60,876

*S. B. Chapman, *C.*		24,686
J. Skinner, *L./All.*		9,815
D. Perkin, *Lab.*		8,115
C. maj.		14,871

(June '83, C. maj. 12,393)

Chislehurst (Gtr. London)
E. 55,535

*R. E. Sims, *C.*		24,165
R. A. Younger-Ross, *L./All.*		9,658
S. H. Ward, *Lab.*		8,115
C. maj.		14,507

(June '83, C. maj. 12,061)

Chorley (Lancs)
E. 78,541

*D. R. Dover, *C.*		29,015
A. J. Watmough, *Lab.*		20,958
I. A. Simpson, *L./All.*		9,706
A. S. Holgate, *Grn.*		714
C. maj.		8,057

(June '83, C. maj. 10,275)

Christchurch (Dorset)
E. 70,964

*R. J. Adley, *C.*		35,656
Miss H. J. McKenzie, *SDP/All.*		13,282
Ms. C. E. Longhurst, *Lab.*		5,174
C. maj.		22,374

(June '83, C. maj. 19,738)

Cirencester and Tewkesbury
(Glos)
E. 84,071

*Rt. Hon. N. Ridley, *C.*		36,272
P. T. Beckerlegge, *L./All.*		23,610
J. D. Naysmith, *Lab.*		5,342
M. A. Curtis, *Male OAP*		283
C. maj.		12,662

(June '83, C. maj. 13,827)

The City of London and
Westminster South
E. 57,428

*Hon. P. L. Brooke, *C.*		19,333
Ms. J. C. G. Smithard, *SDP/All*		7,291
Ms. R. E. Bush, *Lab.*		6,821
C. maj.		12,042

(June '83, C. maj. 13,387)

Colchester (Essex)
E. 82,420

*Sir P. A. F. Buck, QC, *C.*		32,747
A. Hayman, *SDP/All.*		19,124
R. A. Green, *Lab.*		10,768
C. maj.		13,623

(June '83, C. maj. 15,048)

SOUTH, AND MALDON E. 84,392

*Rt. Hon. J. Wakeham, *C.*		34,894
J. W. Stevens, *SDP/All.*		19,411
Ms. S. Bigwood, *Lab.*		9,229
C. maj.		15,483

(June '83, C. maj. 12,165)

Colne Valley (W. Yorks)
E. 70,199

G. E. G. Riddick, *C.*		20,457
N. J. Priestley, *L./All.*		18,780
J. A. Harman, *Lab.*		16,353
M. R. Mullany, *Grn.*		614
C. maj.		1,677

(June '83, L./All. maj. 3,146)

Congleton (Cheshire)
E. 68,172

*Mrs. J. A. Winterton, *C.*		26,513
I. M. Brodie-Browne, *L./All.*		18,544
M. Knowles, *Lab.*		9,810
C. maj.		7,969

(June '83, C. maj. 8,459)

Copeland (Cumbria)
E. 54,695

*Dr. J. A. Cunningham,
Lab. 20,999
A. R. M. Toft, *C.* 19,105
E. T. Colgan, *SDP/All.* 4,052
R. A. Gibson, *Grn.* 319
Lab. maj. 1,894
(June '83, Lab. maj. 1,837)

Corby (Northants)
E. 66,119

*W. R. Powell, C. 23,323
H. A. Feather, *Lab.* 21,518
T. G. Whittington, *L./All.* 7,805
C. maj. 1,805
(June '83, C. maj. 3,168)

Cornwall

NORTH E. 72,375
*G. A. Neale, C. 29,862
M. N. Mitchell, *L./All.* ... 24,180
Ms. C. Herries, *Lab.* 3,719
C. maj. 5,682
(June '83, C. maj. 5,059)

SOUTH EAST E. 70,248
*R. A. Hicks, C. 28,818
I. P. Tunbridge, *L./All.* ... 22,211
P. A. Clark, *Lab.* 4,847
C. maj. 6,607
(June '83, C. maj. 8,354)

Coventry (W. Midlands)

NORTH EAST E. 67,479
J. Hughes, *Lab.* 25,832
C. Prior, *C.* 13,965
S. Wood, *L./All.* 7,502
A. McNally, *Comm.* 310
Lab. maj. 11,867
(June '83, Lab. maj. 8,775)

NORTH WEST E. 53,090
*G. Robinson, Lab. 19,450
J. Powell, *C.* 13,787
T. Jones, *SDP/All.* 6,455
Lab. maj. 5,663
(June '83, Lab. maj. 3,038)

SOUTH EAST E. 51,880
*D. J. Nellist, Lab. 17,969
A. Grant, *C.* 11,316
F. Devine, *SDP/All.* 8,095
N. Hutchinson, *Grn.* 479
Lab. maj. 6,653
(June '83, Lab. maj. 2,682)

SOUTH WEST E. 65,567
*J. P. Butcher, C. 22,318
R. E. G. Slater, *Lab.* 19,108
R. Wheway, *L./All.* 10,166
C. maj. 3,210
(June '83, C. maj. 6,447)

Crawley (W. Sussex)
E. 72,076

*Hon. A. N. W. Soames, C. . 29,259
P. J. Leo, *Lab.* 17,121
D. N. Simmons, *SDP/All.* 12,674
C. maj. 12,138
(June '83, C. maj. 11,814)

Crewe and Nantwich (Cheshire)
E. 72,961

*Hon. Mrs. G. P. Dunwoody,
Lab. 25,457
Mrs. A. F. Browning, *C.* ... 24,365
Dr. K. N. Roberts, *SDP/All.* 8,022
Lab. maj. 1,092
(June '83, Lab. maj. 290)

Crosby (Merseyside)
E. 83,914

*G. M. Thornton, C. 30,836
A. F. S. Donovan, *SDP/All.* 23,989
C. W. Cheetham, *Lab.* 11,992
C. maj. 6,847
(June '83, C. maj. 3,401)

Croydon (Gtr. London)

CENTRAL E. 55,410
*Rt. Hon. J. E. M. Moore, C. 22,133
Ms. B. T. Prentice, *Lab.* .. 9,516
T. Burgess, *SDP/All.* 7,435
C. maj. 12,617
(June '83, C. maj. 11,821)

NORTH EAST E. 63,129
*Rt. Hon. B. B. Weatherill,
(The Speaker) 24,188
Miss C. Patrick, *Lab.* 11,669
J. D. Goldie, *SDP/All.* 8,128
The Speaker maj. 12,519
(June '83, C. maj. 11,627)

NORTH WEST E. 57,369
*H. J. Malins, C. 18,665
M. H. Wicks, *Lab.* 14,677
L. A. Rowe, *L./All.* 6,363
C. maj. 3,988
(June '83, C. maj. 4,092)

SOUTH E. 65,085
*Sir W. G. Clark, C. 30,732
I. Morrison, *L./All.* 11,669
G. R. Davies, *Lab.* 4,679
P. C. Baldwin, *Grn.* 900
C. maj. 19,063
(June '83, C. maj. 17,440)

Dagenham (Gtr. London)
E. 61,714

*B. C. Gould, Lab. 18,454
R. J. M. Neill, *C.* 15,985
J. Carter, *SDP/All* 7,088
Lab. maj. 2,469
(June '83, Lab. maj. 2,997)

Darlington (Durham)
E. 65,940

*M. Fallon, C. 24,831
O. O'Brien, *Lab.* 22,170
A. Collinge, *L./All.* 6,289
C. maj. 2,661
(June '83, C. maj. 3,438)

Dartford (Kent)
E. 72,632

*R. J. Dunn, C. 30,685
B. J. Clarke, *Lab.* 15,756
M. G. Bruce, *SDP/All.* ... 10,449
K. J. Davenport, *FDP* 491
C. maj. 14,929
(June '83, C. maj. 13,563)

Daventry (Northants)
E. 69,241

T. E. Boswell, *C.* 31,353
I. R. Miller, *L./All.* 11,663
Mrs. L. M. A. W. Koumi,
Lab. 11,097
C. maj. 19,690
(June '83, C. maj. 13,136)

Davyhulme (Gtr. Manchester)
E. 65,558

*W. S. Churchill, C. 23,633
J. Nicholson, *Lab.* 15,434
D. I. Wrigley, *L./All.* 11,637
C. maj. 8,199
(June '83, C. maj. 9,014)

Denton and Reddish
(Gtr. Manchester)
E. 69,533

*A. F. Bennett, Lab. 26,023
P. Slater, *C.* 17,773
T. I. Huffer, *SDP/All.* 8,697
Lab. maj. 8,250
(June '83, Lab. maj. 5,125)

Derby

NORTH E. 71,738
*G. Knight, C. 26,561
P. Whitehead, *Lab.* 20,236
S. F. Connolly, *L./All.* 7,268
E. Wall, *Grn.* 291
C. maj. 6,325
(June '83, C. maj. 3,506)

SOUTH E. 68,825
*Mrs. M. M. Beckett, Lab. . 21,003
P. F. Leighton, *C.* 19,487
Ms. P. N. Mellor, *SDP/All.* 7,608
Lab. maj. 1,516
(June '83, Lab. maj. 421)

Derbyshire

NORTH EAST E. 70,314
H. Barnes, *Lab.* 24,747
J. H. Hayes, *C.* 21,027
S. P. Hardy, *SDP/All.* 9,985
Lab. maj. 3,720
(June '83, Lab. maj. 2,006)

SOUTH E. 80,045
*Mrs. E. Currie, C. 31,927
J. D. Whitby, *Lab.* 21,616
J. Edgar, *SDP/All.* 11,509
C. maj. 10,311
(June '83, C. maj. 8,613)

WEST E. 70,782
*P. A. McLoughlin, C. 31,224
C. R. Walmsley, *L./All.* ... 20,697
W. Moore, *Lab.* 6,875
C. maj. 10,527
(June '83, C. maj. 15,325)
(May '86, C. maj. 100)

Devizes (Wilts)
E. 86,047

*Hon. C. A. Morrison, C. .. 36,372
Mrs. L. E. Siegle, *L./All.* .. 18,542
R. W. Buxton, *Lab.* 11,487
C. maj. 17,830
(June '83, C. maj. 15,624)

Devon

NORTH E. 67,474
*A. Speller, C	. .	28,071
M. A. Pinney, L./All.	. . . . .	23,602
Ms. A. Marjoram, Lab.	. . .	3,467
C. maj.	. . . .	4,469
(June '83, C. maj. 8,727)

WEST AND TORRIDGE E. 74,550
Miss E. H. Nicholson, C. . .	29,484
J. P. A. Burnett, L./All. . .	23,016
D. G. Brenton, Lab.	4,990
F. Williamson, Grn.	1,168
C. maj.	6,468
(June '83, C. maj. 12,351)

Dewsbury (W. Yorks)
E. 70,836
Mrs. W. A. Taylor, Lab. . .	23,668
*J. Whitfield, C.	23,223
A. Mills, SDP/All.	8,907
Lab. maj.	445
(June '83, C. maj. 2,086)

Doncaster (S. Yorks)

CENTRAL E. 69,699
*Rt. Hon. H. Walker, Lab. .	26,266
Miss P. E. Rawlings, C. . . .	18,070
J. A. Gore-Browne, SDP/	
All.	7,004
Lab. maj.	8,196
(June '83, Lab. maj. 2,508)

NORTH E. 72,986
*M. C. Welsh, Lab.	32,950
R. J. Shepherd, C.	13,015
P. Norwood, SDP/All.	7,394
Lab. maj.	19,935
(June '83, Lab. maj. 12,711)

Don Valley (S. Yorks)
E. 74,500
*M. Redmond, Lab.	29,200
C. H. Gallagher, C.	17,733
W. K. Whitaker, L./All. . .	8,027
Lab. maj.	11,467
(June '83, Lab. maj. 6,466)

Dorset

NORTH E. 72,844
*N. B. Baker, C.	32,854
Dr. G. W. Tapper, L./All. .	20,947
J. Hanley, Lab.	3,819
C. maj.	11,907
(June '83, C. maj. 11,380)

SOUTH E. 72,855
I. C. Bruce, C.	30,184
B. Ellis, L./All.	15,117
Ms. B. Dench, Lab.	9,494
A. Hayler, Ind.	244
C. maj.	15,067
(June '83, C. maj. 15,098)

WEST E. 64,360
*J. W. Spicer, C.	28,305
T. Jones, L./All.	15,941
D. Watson, Lab.	6,123
C. maj.	12,364
(June '83, C. maj. 13,952)

Dover (Kent)
E. 68,997
D. L. Shaw, C.	25,343
S. S. E. W. Love, Lab.	18,802
G. Nice, SDP/All.	10,942
C. maj.	6,541
(June '83, C. maj. 9,220)

Dudley (W. Midlands)

EAST E. 75,206
*Rt. Hon. Dr. J. W. Gilbert,	
Lab.	24,942
Mrs. E. Jones, C.	21,469
K. Monks, SDP/All.	7,965
Lab. maj.	3,473
(June '83, Lab. maj. 5,816)

WEST E. 81,789
*J. G. Blackburn, C.	32,224
G. Titley, Lab.	21,980
G. P. T. Lewis, L./All.	10,477
C. maj.	10,244
(June '83, C. maj. 8,723)

Dulwich (Gtr. London)
E. 56,355
*G. F. Bowden, C.	16,563
Miss C. L. Hoey, Lab.	16,383
Dr. A. N. G. Harris, SDP/	
All.	5,664
A. Goldie, Grn.	432
C. maj.	180
(June '83, C. maj. 1,859)

Durham

CITY OF E. 66,567
G. N. Steinberg, Lab.	23,382
D. Stoker, SDP/All.	17,257
C. M. Colquhoun, C.	11,408
Lab. maj.	6,125
(June '83, Lab. maj. 1,973)

NORTH E. 72,115
*G. H. Radice, Lab.	30,798
Dr. D. Jeary, SDP/All. . . .	12,365
N. C. Gibbon, C.	11,602
Lab. maj.	18,433
(June '83, Lab. maj. 13,437)

NORTH WEST E. 61,302
Ms. H. J. Armstrong, Lab.	22,947
D. Iceton, C.	12,785
C. Foote Wood, L./All. . . .	9,349
Lab. maj.	10,162
(June '83, Lab. maj. 6,356)

Ealing (Gtr. London)

ACTON E. 67,176
*Sir G. S. K. Young, Bt., C. . .	25,499
P. J. Portwood, Lab.	13,256
S. R. D. Brooks, SDP/All.	8,973
C. maj.	12,243
(June '83, C. maj. 10,092)

NORTH E. 71,634
*H. Greenway, C.	30,100
H. J. Benn, Lab.	14,947
A. H. J. Miller, L./All. . . .	8,149
Mrs. K. Fitzherbert, Grn. .	577
C. maj.	15,153
(June '83, C. maj. 6,291)

Southall E. 74,843
*S. J. Bidwell, Lab.	26,480
M. A. Truman, C.	18,503
Mrs. M. Howes, L./All. . . .	6,947
R. F. Lugg, WRP	256
Lab. maj.	7,977
(June '83, Lab. maj. 11,116)

Easington (Durham)
E. 64,863
J. S. Cummings, Lab.	32,396
W. J. Perry, C.	7,757
G. Morpeth, L./All.	7,447
Lab. maj.	24,639
(June '83, Lab. maj. 14,792)

Eastbourne (E. Sussex)
E. 74,144
*I. Gow, TD, C.	33,587
P. G. Driver, L./All.	16,664
A. Patel, Lab.	4,928
Ms. R. Addison, Grn.	867
C. maj.	16,923
(June '83, C. maj. 13,486)

Eastleigh (Hants)
E. 87,552
*Sir D. E. C. Price, C.	35,584
M. J. Kyrle, L./All.	22,229
D. J. C. Bull, Lab.	11,599
C. maj.	13,355
(June '83, C. maj. 13,008)

Eccles (Gtr. Manchester)
E. 66,961
Miss J. Lestor, Lab.	25,346
Mrs. M. E. J. Packalow, C.	15,647
P. C. W. Beatty, SDP/All.	8,924
Lab. maj.	9,699
(June '83, Lab. maj. 6,005)

Eddisbury (Cheshire)
E. 73,894
*A. R. Goodlad, C.	29,474
R. I. Fletcher, L./All.	13,639
Mrs. C. Grigg, Lab.	13,574
A. Basden, Grn.	976
C. maj.	15,835
(June '83, C. maj. 14,846)

Edmonton (Gtr. London)
E. 66,080
*Dr. I. D. Twinn, C.	24,556
B. G. Grayston, Lab.	17,270
M. Lawson, SDP/All.	6,115
C. maj.	7,286
(June '83, C. maj. 1,193)

Ellesmere Port and Neston
(Cheshire)
E. 71,344
*M. Woodcock, C.	25,664
Miss H. M. Jones, Lab. . . .	23,811
S. A. Holbrook, SDP/All. .	8,143
D. J. E. Carson, PRP	185
C. maj.	1,853
(June '83, C. maj. 7,087)

Elmet (W. Yorks)
E. 69,024

*S. L. Batiste, C.	25,658
C. Burgon, *Lab.*	20,302
J. D. Macarthur, *SDP/All.*	8,755
C. maj.	5,356
(June '83, C. maj. 7,856)	

Eltham (Gtr. London)
E. 54,063

*P. J. Bottomley, C.	19,752
D. Vaughan, *Lab.*	13,292
E. J. Randall, *L./All.*	8,542
C. maj.	6,460
(June '83, C. maj. 7,592)	

Enfield (Gtr. London)

NORTH *E.* 69,488

*T. J. C. Eggar, C.	28,758
M. Upham, *Lab.*	14,743
Ms. H. Leighter, *SDP/All.*	7,633
M. Chantler, *Grn.*	644
C. maj.	14,015
(June '83, C. maj. 11,716)	

SOUTHGATE *E.* 66,600

*M. D. X. Portillo, C.	28,445
N. Harvey, *L./All.*	10,100
R. Course, *Lab.*	9,114
S. Rooney, *Grn.*	696
C. maj.	18,345
(June '83, C. maj. 15,819)	
(Dec. '84, C. maj. 4,711)	

Epping Forest (Essex)
E. 67,804

*Sir J. A. Biggs-Davison, C.	31,536
A. Humphris, *SDP/All.*	10,023
S. Murray, *Lab.*	9,499
R. Denhard, *Grn.*	695
C. maj.	21,513
(June '83, C. maj. 15,378)	
(*See also* p. 276)	

Epsom and Ewell (Surrey)
E. 70,683

*Hon. A. G. Hamilton, C.	33,145
Mrs. M. J. Joachim, *L./All.*	12,384
Mrs. D. B. Follett, *Lab.*	7,751
C. maj.	20,761
(June '83, C. maj. 17,195)	

Erewash (Derbys)
E. 76,545

*P. L. Rost, C.	28,775
R. W. Jones, *Lab.*	19,021
Ms. C. P. Moss, *SDP/All.*	11,442
C. maj.	9,754
(June '83, C. maj. 11,319)	

Erith and Crayford
(Gtr. London)
E. 59,292

*D. A. Evennett, C.	20,203
C. F. Hargrave, *Lab.*	13,209
A. J. Wellbeloved, SDP/ All.	11,300
C. maj.	6,994
(June '83, C. maj. 920)	

Esher (Surrey)
E. 62,117

I. C. Taylor, MBE, *C.*	31,334
A. J. Barnett, *L./All.*	12,266
N. J. V. Lucas, *Lab.*	4,197
C. maj.	19,068
(June '83, C. maj. 15,912)	

Exeter (Devon)
E. 75,208

*J. G. Hannam, C.	26,922
M. S. Thomas, *SDP/All.*	19,266
J. A. Vincent, *Lab.*	13,643
R. J. Vail, *Grn.*	597
N. D. Byles, *LAPP*	209
C. maj.	7,656
(June '83, C. maj. 9,880)	

Falmouth and Camborne
(Cornwall)
E. 68,612

*W. D. Mudd, C.	23,725
J. C. Marks, *SDP/All.*	18,686
J. Cosgrove, *Lab.*	11,271
F. Zapp, *LM*	373
C. maj.	5,039
(June '83, C. maj. 11,025)	

Fareham (Hants)
E. 76,974

*P. R. C. Lloyd, C.	36,781
T. Slack, *L./All.*	17,986
M. Merritt, *Lab.*	5,451
C. maj.	18,795
(June '83, C. maj. 16,316)	

Faversham (Kent)
E. 79,039

*R. D. Moate, C.	31,074
E. M. Goyder, *SDP/All.*	17,096
P. Dangerfield, *Lab.*	12,616
C. maj.	13,978
(June '83, C. maj. 14,597)	

Feltham and Heston
(Gtr. London)
E. 81,062

*R. P. Ground, QC, C.	27,755
C. Hinds, *Lab.*	22,325
J. Daly, *SDP/All.*	9,623
C. maj.	5,430
(June '83, C. maj. 2,148)	

Finchley (Gtr. London)
E. 57,727

*Rt. Hon. Mrs. M. H. Thatcher, C.	21,603
J. Davies, *Lab.*	12,690
D. Howarth, *L./All.*	5,580
'Lord' Buckethead, *Grem.*	131
Miss M. St. Vincent, *Gold*	59
C. maj.	8,913
(June '83, C. maj. 9,314)	

Folkestone and Hythe (Kent)
E. 64,406

*M. Howard, QC, C.	27,915
J. R. MacDonald, *L./All.*	18,789
V. S. Anand, *Lab.*	3,720
C. maj.	9,126
(June '83, C. maj. 11,670)	

Fulham (Gtr. London)
E. 54,498

M. H. M. Carrington, *C.*	21,752
W. R. N. Raynsford, Lab.	15,430
P. A. C. Marshall, *SDP/All.*	4,365
Ms. J. Grimes, *Grn.*	465
C. maj.	6,322
(June '83, C. maj. 4,789)	
(April '86, Lab. maj. 3,503)	

Fylde (Lancs)
E. 63,246

J. M. Jack, *C.*	29,559
Mrs. E. A. Smith, *L./All.*	11,787
G. Smith, *Lab.*	6,955
H. Fowler, *RCP*	405
C. maj.	17,772
(June '83, C. maj. 17,102)	

Gainsborough and Horncastle
(Lincs)
E. 69,760

*E. J. E. Leigh, C.	28,621
D. A. Grace, *L./All.*	18,898
R. Naylor, *Lab.*	6,156
C. maj.	9,723
(June '83, C. maj. 5,067)	

Gateshead East (Tyne & Wear)
E. 67,953

Miss J. G. Quin, *Lab.*	28,895
F. W. Rogers, *C.*	11,667
N. G. Rippeth, *SDP/All.*	8,231
Lab. maj.	17,228
(June '83, Lab. maj. 10,322)	

Gedling (Notts)
E. 68,398

A. J. B. Mitchell, *C.*	29,492
V. R. Coaker, *Lab.*	12,953
D. Morton, *SDP/All.*	11,684
C. maj.	16,539
(June '83, C. maj. 14,664)	

Gillingham (Kent)
E. 71,847

*J. R. Couchman, C.	28,711
L. R. Andrews, *L./All.*	16,162
D. J. Bishop, *Lab.*	9,230
C. maj.	12,549
(June '83, C. maj. 10,843)	

Glanford and Scunthorpe
(Humberside)
E. 72,816

E. A. Morley, *Lab.*	24,733
*R. S. Hickmet, C.	24,221
C. Nottingham, *SDP/All.*	7,762
K. S. Trivedi, *Ind.*	104
Lab. maj.	512
(June '83, C. maj. 637)	

Gloucester
E. 76,910

D. C. French, *C.*	29,826
D. Hulme, *Lab.*	17,791
J. Hilton, *L./All.*	12,417
C. maj.	12,035
(June '83, C. maj. 12,537)	

Gloucestershire West
E. 77,994

*P. Marland, *C.*	....	29,257
P. E. S. Nielson, *Lab.*	.....	17,578
J. T. Watkinson, *SDP/All.*		16,440
C. maj.	....	11,679
(June '83, C. maj. 9,652)		

Gosport (Hants)
E. 68,113

*P. J. Viggers, *C.*	....	29,804
P. J. Chegwyn, *L./All.*	.....	16,081
A. Lloyd, *Lab.*	....	5,053
C. maj.	....	13,723
(June '83, C. maj. 14,451)		

Grantham (Lincs)
E. 79,434

*Hon. D. M. Hogg, *C.*	.....	33,988
J. P. Heppell, *L./All.*	.....	12,685
M. B. Gent, *Lab.*	....	12,197
Mrs. P. A. Hewis, *Grn.*	....	700
C. maj.	....	21,303
(June '83, C. maj. 18,911)		

Gravesham (Kent)
E. 72,759

J. A. Arnold, *C.*	....	28,891
M. A. Coleman, *Lab.*	.....	20,099
R. I. Crawford, *L./All.*	....	8,724
C. maj.	....	8,792
(June '83, C. maj. 8,463)		

Great Grimsby (Humberside)
E. 68,501

*A. V. Mitchell, *Lab.*	.....	23,463
C. F. Robinson, *C.*	....	14,679
P. W. Genney, *SDP/All.*		13,457
Lab. maj.	....	8,784
(June '83, Lab. maj. 731)		

Great Yarmouth
(Norfolk)
E. 65,770

*M. R. H. Carttiss, *C.*	.....	25,336
J. Cannell, *Lab.*	....	15,253
S. D. Maxwell, *SDP/All.*		8,387
C. maj.	....	10,083
(June '83, C. maj. 11,200)		

Greenwich (Gtr. London)
E. 50,830

*Mrs. R. S. Barnes, *SDP/ All.*		15,149
Mrs. D. F. M. Wood, *Lab.*	..	13,008
J. G. C. Antcliffe, *C.*	......	8,695
Ms. J. Thomas, *Grn.*	.....	346
R. Mallone, *Fell.*	....	59
Ms. P. Clinton, *Comm.*	...	58
SDP/All. maj.	....	2,141
(June '83, Lab. maj. 1,211)		
(Feb. '87, SDP/All. maj. 6,611)		

Guildford (Surrey)
E. 77,872

*Rt. Hon. D. A. R. Howell, *C.*		32,504
Mrs. M. L. Sharp, *SDP/All.*		19,897
R. J. Wolverson, *Lab.*	....	6,216
C. maj.	....	12,607
(June '83, C. maj. 11,824)		

Hackney (Gtr. London)
NORTH AND STOKE NEWINGTON
E. 66,771

Ms. D. J. Abbott, *Lab.*	....	18,912
O. Letwin, *C.*	....	11,234
S. H. Taylor, *SDP/All.*	...	7,446
D. J. Fitzpatrick, *Grn.*	....	997
Ms. Y. T. Anwar, *RF.*	....	228
Lab. maj.	....	7,678
(June '83, Lab. maj. 8,545)		

SOUTH AND SHOREDITCH E. 70,873

*B. C. J. Sedgemore, *Lab.*	..	18,799
M. C. Northcroft-Brown, *C.*	11,277
J. D. Roberts, *L./All.*	.....	8,812
D. Green, *Comm.*	......	403
Lab. maj.	....	7,522
(June '83, Lab. maj. 7,691)		

Halesowen and Stourbridge
(W. Midlands)
E. 78,017

*J. H. R. Stokes, *C.*	....	31,037
T. J. Sunter, *Lab.*	....	17,229
D. C. A. Simon, *SDP/All.*		13,658
C. maj.	....	13,808
(June '83, C. maj. 13,316)		

Halifax (W. Yorks)
E. 73,392

Mrs. A. Mahon, *Lab.*	.....	24,741
*R. Galley, *C.*	....	23,529
F. L. Cockcroft, *SDP/All.*		8,758
Lab. maj.	....	1,212
(June '83, C. maj. 1,869)		

Halton (Cheshire)
E. 73,848

*Rt. Hon. G. J. Oakes, *Lab.*	.	32,065
J. Hardman, *C.*	....	17,487
Ms. H. Clucas, *SDP/All.*		8,272
Lab. maj.	....	14,578
(June '83, Lab. maj. 6,829)		

Hammersmith (Gtr. London)
E. 48,285

*C. S. Soley, *Lab.*	....	15,811
N. J. A. Deva, *C.*	....	13,396
S. H. J. A. Knott, *L./All.*	..	5,241
D. P. Kirk, *Grn.*	....	453
P. J. F. Fitzpatrick, *RF*	...	125
Miss M. M. A. Carrick, *Humanist*	....	98
Lab. maj.	....	2,415
(June '83, Lab. maj. 1,954)		

Hampshire
EAST E. 86,363

*M. J. Mates, *C.*	....	43,093
R. Booker, *L./All.*	....	19,307
C. Lloyd, *Lab.*	....	4,443
C. maj.	....	23,786
(June '83, C. maj. 18,327)		

NORTH WEST E. 69,965

*D. B. Mitchell, *C.*	....	31,470
I. H. Wills, *L./All.*	....	18,033
Ms. A. Burnage, *Lab.*	....	4,980
C. maj.	....	13,437
(June '83, C. maj. 12,122)		

Hampstead and Highgate
(Gtr. London)
E. 63,301

*Sir G. Finsberg, MBE, *C.*	..	19,236
P. J. Turner, *Lab.*	....	17,015
Mrs. A. Sofer, *SDP/All.*		8,744
G. Weiss, *Rainbow*	....	137
Ms. S. Ellis, *Humanist*	...	134
C. maj.	....	2,221
(June '83, C. maj. 3,370)		

Harborough (Leics)
E. 74,700

*Sir J. A. Farr, *C.*	....	35,216
T. J. Swift, *L./All.*	....	16,406
P. Harley, *Lab.*	....	7,646
C. maj.	....	18,810
(June '83, C. maj. 18,485)		

Harlow (Essex)
E. 70,286

*J. J. J. Hayes, *C.*	....	26,017
A. S. Newens, *Lab.*	......	20,140
Mrs. M. C. Eden-Green, *SDP/All.*	....	8,915
C. maj.	....	5,877
(June '83, C. maj. 3,674)		

Harrogate (N. Yorks)
E. 75,761

*R. G. Banks, *C.*	....	31,167
J. R. Leach, *SDP/All.*	....	19,265
A. J. Wright, *Lab.*	....	5,671
C. maj.	....	11,902
(June '83, C. maj. 15,888)		

Harrow (Gtr. London)
EAST E. 81,124

*H. J. M. Dykes, *C.*	....	32,302
D. J. Brough, *Lab.*	....	14,029
Mrs. Z. Gifford, *L./All.*	...	13,251
C. maj.	....	18,273
(June '83, C. maj. 12,668)		

WEST E. 74,041

R. G. Hughes, *C.*	....	30,456
S. P. Bayliss, *SDP/All.*	...	15,012
C. Bastin, *Lab.*	....	9,665
C. maj.	....	15,444
(June '83, C. maj. 11,021)		

Hartlepool (Cleveland)
E. 68,686

*E. Leadbitter, *Lab.*	......	24,296
P. C. Catchpole, *C.*	....	17,007
A. Preece, *L./All.*	....	7,047
I. J. Cameron, *Ind.*	....	1,786
Lab. maj.	....	7,289
(June '83, Lab. maj. 3,090)		

Harwich (Essex)
E. 77,149

*Sir J. E. Ridsdale, CBE, *C.*		29,344
Miss E. Lynne, *L./All.*	....	17,262
R. Knight, *Lab.*	....	9,920
C. A. Humphrey, *OFP*	...	161
C. maj.	....	12,082
(June '83, C. maj. 12,502)		

Hastings and Rye (E. Sussex)
E. 72,758

*K. R. Warren, C.		26,163
D. J. Amies, *L./All.*		18,816
Ms. J. Hurcombe, *Lab.*		6,825
D. Howell, *LM.*		242
S. P. Davies, *NPR*		194
C. maj.		7,347
(June '83, C. maj. 10,980)		

Havant (Hants)
E. 76,344

*Sir I. S. Lloyd, C.		32,527
Mrs. E. E. Cleaver, *SDP/All.*		16,017
J. A. Phillips, *Lab.*		8,030
G. W. Fuller, *Bread*		373
C. maj.		16,510
(June '83, C. maj. 11,956)		

Hayes and Harlington
(Gtr. London)
E. 58,240

*T. P. Dicks, C.		21,355
P. F. Fagan, *Lab.*		15,390
Ms. S. Slipman, *SDP/All.*		6,641
C. maj.		5,965
(June '83, C. maj. 4,234)		

Hazel Grove (Gtr. Manchester)
E. 65,717

*T. R. Arnold, C.		24,396
A. M. Vos, *L./All.*		22,556
J. G. Ford, *Lab.*		6,354
Ms. F. K. Chapman, *Grn.*		346
C. maj.		1,840
(June '83, C. maj. 2,022)		

Hemsworth (W. Yorks)
E. 54,951

G. J. Buckley, *Lab.*		27,859
E. H. Garnier, *C.*		7,159
J. D. Wooffindin, *L./All.*		6,568
Lab. maj.		20,700
(June '83, Lab. maj. 14,190)		

Hendon (Gtr. London)

NORTH *E.* 55,095

*J. M. Gorst, C.		20,155
Ms. J. Manson, *Lab.*		9,223
Ms. E. Davies, *SDP/All.*		6,859
C. maj.		10,932
(June '83, C. maj. 9,025)		

SOUTH *E.* 54,560

J. L. Marshall, *C.*		19,341
M. O. Palmer, *L./All.*		8,217
Miss L. Christian, *Lab.*		7,261
C. maj.		11,124
(June '83, C. maj. 6,433)		

Henley (Oxon)
E. 65,443

*Rt. Hon. M. R. D. Heseltine, C.		29,978
J. Madeley, *L./All.*		12,896
M. B. Barber, *Lab.*		6,173
C. maj.		17,082
(June '83, C. maj. 13,781)		

Hereford
E. 67,075

*C. R. Shepherd, C.		24,865
C. F. Green, *L./All.*		23,452
V. S. Woodell, *Lab.*		4,031
C. maj.		1,413
(June '83, C. maj. 2,277)		

Hertford and Stortford
E. 75,508

*B. Wells, C.		33,763
R. E. Wotherspoon, *SDP/All.*		16,623
Mrs. P. R. E. Sumner, *Lab.*		7,494
G. C. Cole, *Grn.*		814
C. maj.		17,140
(June '83, C. maj. 12,929)		

Hertfordshire

NORTH *E.* 78,694

*B. H. I. H. Stewart, RD, C.		31,750
G. W. Binney, *L./All.*		20,308
A. Gorst, *Lab.*		11,782
C. maj.		11,442
(June '83, C. maj. 9,943)		

SOUTH WEST *E.* 75,643

*R. L. Page, C.		32,791
I. M. Blair, *L./All.*		17,007
I. Willmore, *Lab.*		8,966
C. maj.		15,784
(June '83, C. maj. 12,194)		

WEST *E.* 78,966

*R. B. Jones, C.		31,760
N. A. Hollinghurst, *SDP/All.*		16,836
A. McBrearty, *Lab.*		15,317
C. maj.		14,924
(June '83, C. maj. 9,576)		

Hertsmere (Herts)
E. 73,367

*Rt. Hon. C. E. Parkinson, C.		31,278
L. S. Brass, *L./All.*		13,172
F. Ward, *Lab.*		10,835
C. maj.		18,106
(June '83, C. maj. 14,870)		

Hexham (Nthmb)
E. 56,360

A. T. Amos, *C.*		22,370
E. M. Robson, *L./All.*		14,304
M. R. Wood, *Lab.*		8,103
Mrs. S. M. Wood, *Grn.*		336
C. maj.		8,066
(June '83, C. maj. 8,308)		

Heywood and Middleton
(Gtr. Manchester)
E. 59,487

*J. Callaghan, Lab.		21,900
R. E. Walker, *C.*		15,052
I. Greenhalgh, *SDP/All.*		6,953
Lab. maj.		6,848
(June '83, Lab. maj. 3,974)		

High Peak (Derbys)
E. 69,926

*C. J. Hawkins, C.		25,715
Mrs. J. McCrindle, *Lab.*		16,199
Dr. J. Oldham, *SDP/All.*		14,389
C. maj.		9,516
(June '83, C. maj. 9,940)		

Holborn and St. Pancras
(Gtr. London)
E. 70,589

*F. G. Dobson, Lab.		22,966
P. J. Luff, *C.*		14,113
S. McGrath, *L./All.*		7,994
M. J. Gavan, *RF*		300
Lab. maj.		8,853
(June '83, Lab. maj. 7,259)		

Holland with Boston (Lincs)
E. 65,539

*Sir R. B. F. S. Body, C.		27,412
Mrs. C. Le Brun, *L./All.*		9,817
J. D. Hough, *Lab.*		9,734
D. James, *Local Voice*		405
C. maj.		17,595
(June '83, C. maj. 11,736)		

Honiton (Devon)
E. 77,259

*Sir P. F. H. Emery, C.		34,931
G. Tatton-Brown, *SDP/All.*		18,369
S. Pollentine, *Lab.*		4,988
S. Hughes, *LM*		747
C. maj.		16,562
(June '83, C. maj. 14,769)		

Hornchurch (Gtr. London)
E. 62,397

*R. C. Squire, C.		24,039
A. R. Williams, *Lab.*		13,345
M. L. C. Long, *L./All.*		9,609
C. maj.		10,694
(June '83, C. maj. 9,184)		

Hornsey and Wood Green
(Gtr. London)
E. 80,594

*Sir H. A. L. Rossi, C.		25,397
Mrs. B. M. R. Roche, *Lab.*		23,618
D. Eden, *SDP/All.*		8,928
Ms. E. Crosbie, *Grn.*		1,154
C. maj.		1,779
(June '83, C. maj. 3,899)		

Horsham (W. Sussex)
E. 86,135

*Sir P. M. Hordern, C.		39,775
Mrs. J. Pearce, *SDP/All.*		15,868
M. Shrimpton, *Lab.*		5,435
T. Metheringham, *Grn.*		1,383
C. maj.		23,907
(June '83, C. maj. 21,785)		

Houghton and Washington
(Tyne & Wear)
E. 77,906

*R. Boyes, Lab.		32,805
J. M. Callanan, *C.*		12,612
R. F. Kenyon, *SDP/All.*		10,090
Lab. maj.		20,193
(June '83, Lab. maj. 13,821)		

Hove (E. Sussex)
E. 72,626

*Hon. T. A. D. Sainsbury, C. 28,952
Mrs. M. E. Collins, *SDP/*
 All. 10,734
D. K. Turner, *Lab.* 9,010
T. A. Layton, *SE* 522
 C. maj. 18,218
(June '83, C. maj. 17,219)

Huddersfield (W. Yorks)
E. 66,413

B. J. Sheerman, Lab. 23,019
N. J. Hawkins, *C.* 15,741
J. Smithson, *L./All.* 10,773
N. A. L. Harvey, *Grn.* 638
 Lab. maj. 7,278
(June '83, Lab. maj. 3,955)

Huntingdon (Cambs)
E. 86,186

Rt. Hon. J. Major, C. 40,530
A. J. Nicholson, *SDP/All.* 13,486
D. M. Brown, *Lab.* 8,883
B. Lavin, *Grn.* 874
 C. maj. 27,044
(June '83, C. maj. 20,348)

Hyndburn (Lancs)
E. 60,529

J. K. Hargreaves, C. 21,606
K. Coombes, *Lab.* 19,386
J. Strak, *SDP/All.* 7,423
F. Smith, *Grn.* 297
 C. maj. 2,220
(June '83, C. maj. 21)

Ilford (Gtr. London)

NORTH E. 60,433
V. W. H. Bendall, C. 24,110
P. Jeater, *Lab.* 12,020
G. Tobbell, *SDP/All.* 7,757
 C. maj. 12,090
(June '83, C. maj. 11,201)

SOUTH E. 58,572
N. G. Thorne, OBE, TD, C. 20,351
K. Jones, *Lab.* 15,779
R. J. Scott, *L./All.* 5,928
 C. maj. 4,572
(June '83, C. maj. 4,566)

Ipswich (Suffolk)
E. 68,165

M. F. Irvine, *C.* 23,328
K. T. Weetch, Lab. 22,454
H. P. Nicholson, *SDP/All.* 6,596
D. T. Lettice, *WRP* 174
 C. maj. 874
(June '83, Lab. maj. 1,077)

Isle of Wight
E. 98,694

B. J. A. Field, *C.* 40,175
M. Young, *L./All.* 33,733
K. Pearson, *Lab.* 4,626
 C. maj. 6,442
(June '83, L./All. maj. 3,503)

Islington (Gtr. London)

NORTH E. 58,917
J. B. Corbyn, Lab. 19,577
E. G. Noad, *C.* 9,920
A. Whelan, *SDP/All.* 8,560
C. Ashby, *Grn.* 1,131
 Lab. maj. 9,657
(June '83, Lab. maj. 5,607)

SOUTH AND FINSBURY E. 57,910
C. R. Smith, Lab. 16,511
G. Cunningham, *SDP/All.* 15,706
A. Mitchell, *C.* 8,482
P. Powell, *Grn.* 382
S. Dowsett, *SPGB* 81
Ms. J. Early, *HP* 56
 Lab. maj. 805
(June '83, Lab. maj. 363)

Jarrow (Tyne & Wear)
E. 62,845

D. Dixon, Lab. 29,651
P. Yeoman, *C.* 10,856
P. Freitag, *L./All.* 6,230
 Lab. maj. 18,795
(June '83, Lab. maj. 13,877)

Keighley (W. Yorks)
E. 65,831

G. P. A. Waller, C. 23,903
A. Rye, *Lab.* 18,297
J. H. Wells, *L./All.* 10,041
 C. maj. 5,606
(June '83, C. maj. 2,774)

Kensington (Gtr. London)
E. 48,212

Sir B. M. Rhys Williams,
 Bt., *C.* 14,818
B. T. Bousquet, *Lab.* 10,371
W. H. Goodhart, *SDP/All.* 5,379
R. E. Shorter, *Grn.* 528
Miss L. Carrick, *Humanist* 65
Mrs. M. Hughes, *PIP* 30
 C. maj. 4,447
(June '83, C. maj. 5,101)
(*See also* p. 275)

Kent Mid
E. 72,456

A. J. B. Rowe, C. 28,719
G. D. Colley, *L./All.* 13,951
J. A. Hazelgrove, *Lab.* 9,420
 C. maj. 14,768
(June '83, C. maj. 12,543)

Kettering (Northants)
E. 65,965

R. N. Freeman, C. 26,532
Mrs. C. M. Goodhart, *SDP/*
 All. 15,205
A. M. Minto, *Lab.* 10,229
 C. maj. 11,327
(June '83, C. maj. 8,586)

Kingston upon Hull

EAST E. 68,657
J. L. Prescott, Lab. 27,287
P. Jackson, *C.* 12,598
T. Wright, *L./All.* 8,572
 Lab. maj. 14,689
(June '83, Lab. maj. 10,074)

NORTH E. 73,288
J. K. McNamara, Lab. ... 26,123
Miss A. O'Brien, *C.* 13,954
S. W. Unwin, *SDP/All.* 10,962
 Lab. maj. 12,169
(June '83, Lab. maj. 6,028)

WEST E. 55,636
S. J. Randall, Lab. 19,527
M. R. C. Humphrys, *C.* ... 11,397
M. Bond, *SDP/All.* 6,669
 Lab. maj. 8,130
(June '83, Lab. maj. 3,654)

Kingston upon Thames
(Gtr. London)
E. 54,839

Rt. Hon. N. S. H. Lamont,
 C. 24,198
R. M. Hayes, *L./All.* 13,012
R. Markless, *Lab.* 5,676
J. Baker, *CPWSML* 175
 C. maj. 11,186
(June '83, C. maj. 8,872)

Kingswood (Avon)
E. 73,089

R. A. Hayward, C. 26,300
R. L. Berry, *Lab.* 21,907
Mrs. P. Whittle, *SDP/All.* 10,382
 C. maj. 4,393
(June '83, C. maj. 1,797)

Knowsley (Merseyside)

NORTH E. 52,960
G. E. Howarth, Lab. 27,454
Ms. R. Cooper, *L./All.* 6,356
R. C. A. Brown, *C.* 4,922
D. Hallsworth, *RF* 538
 Lab. maj. 21,098
(June '83, Lab. maj. 17,191)
(Nov. '86, Lab. maj. 6,724)

SOUTH E. 65,643
S. F. Hughes, Lab. 31,378
A. J. Hall, *C.* 10,532
Mrs. R. Watmough, *SDP/*
 All. 6,760
 Lab. maj. 20,846
(June '83, Lab. maj. 11,769)
(*See also* p. 276)

Lancashire West
E. 76,094

K. H. Hind, C. 26,500
C. Pickthall, *Lab.* 25,147
R. Jermyn, *SDP/All.* 8,972
 C. maj. 1,353
(June '83, C. maj. 6,858)

Lancaster (Lancs)
E. 57,229

Mrs. M. E. Kellett-Bow-
 man, *C.* 21,142
J. Gallacher, *Lab.* 14,689
Mrs. K. C. Brooks, *L./All.* 9,003
P. F. F. Jones, *Grn.* 473
 C. maj. 6,453
(June '83, C. maj. 10,636)

Langbaurgh (Cleveland)
E. 79,193

*J. R. Holt, C.		26,047
P. Harford, *Lab.*		23,959
R. A. J. Ashby, *L./All.*		12,405
C. maj.		2,088
(June '83, C. maj. 6,024)		

Leeds (W. Yorks)

CENTRAL   E. 59,019

D. J. Fatchett, Lab.		21,270
D. Schofield, *C.*		9,765
Dr. Karen Lee, *SDP/All.*		6,853
W. Innis, *Comm.*		355
Lab. maj.		11,505
(June '83, Lab. maj. 8,222)		

EAST   E. 61,178

Rt. Hon. D. W. Healey, CH, MBE, Lab.		20,932
J. S. W. Sheard, *C.*		11,406
Miss M. G. Clay, *L./All.*		10,630
Lab. maj.		9,526
(June '83, Lab. maj. 6,095)		

NORTH EAST   E. 64,631

T. J. R. Kirkhope, *C.*		22,196
P. M. Crystal, *SDP/All.*		13,777
O. B. Glover, *Lab.*		12,292
Ms. C. D. Nash, *Grn.*		416
C. maj.		8,419
(June '83, C. maj. 8,995)		

NORTH WEST   E. 68,227

Dr. K. Hampson, C.		22,480
B. Peters, *L./All.*		17,279
Ms. J. Thomas, *Lab.*		11,210
A. Stevens, *Grn.*		663
C. maj.		5,201
(June '83, C. maj. 8,537)		

SOUTH AND MORLEY   E. 60,726

Rt. Hon. M. Rees, Lab.		21,551
Mrs. T. C. Holdroyd, *C.*		14,840
E. J. V. Dawson, *SDP/All.*		7,099
Lab. maj.		6,711
(June '83, Lab. maj. 5,854)		

WEST   E. 66,344

J. D. Battle, *Lab.*		21,032
M. J. Meadowcroft, L./All.		16,340
P. D. Allott, *C.*		11,276
Lab. maj.		4,692
(June '83, L./All. maj. 2,048)		

Leicester

EAST   E. 66,372

N. K. A. S. Vaz, *Lab.*		24,074
P. N. E. Bruinvels, C.		22,150
Mrs. A. M. Ayres, *SDP/All.*		5,935
Lab. maj.		1,924
(June '83, C. maj. 933)		

SOUTH   E. 73,236

J. Marshall, *Lab.*		24,901
D. H. Spencer, QC, C.		23,024
R. Pritchard, *L./All.*		7,773
B. Fewster, *Grn.*		390
M. M. Mayat, *Ind. Lab.*		192
Ms. R. F. Manners, *WRP*		96
Lab. maj.		1,877
(June '83, C. maj. 7)		

WEST   E. 67,829

G. E. Janner, QC, Lab.		22,156
J. S. W. Cooper, *C.*		20,955
W. Edgar, *SDP/All.*		6,708
Lab. maj.		1,201
(June '83, Lab. maj. 1,712)		

Leicestershire North West
E. 70,633

D. G. Ashby, C.		27,872
Mrs. S. A. Waddington, *Lab.*		20,044
D. S. Emmerson, *L./All.*		10,034
Miss H. T. Michetschlager, *Grn.*		570
C. maj.		7,828
(June '83, C. maj. 6,662)		

Leigh (Gtr. Manchester)
E. 69,155

L. F. Cunliffe, Lab.		30,064
L. B. A. Browne, *C.*		13,458
S. D. Jones, *SDP/All.*		7,743
Lab. maj.		16,606
(June '83, Lab. maj. 12,314)		

Leominster (H & W)
E. 69,977

P. Temple-Morris, C.		31,396
S. C. Morris, *L./All.*		17,321
A. C. R. Chappell, *Lab.*		4,444
Mrs. F. M. Norman, *Grn.*		1,102
C. maj.		14,075
(June '83, C. maj. 9,786)		

Lewes (E. Sussex)
E. 73,181

J. R. Rathbone, C.		32,016
D. F. Bellotti, *L./All.*		18,396
R. P. Taylor, *Lab.*		4,973
A. G. P. Sherwood, *Grn.*		970
C. maj.		13,620
(June '83, C. maj. 13,904)		

Lewisham (Gtr. London)

DEPTFORD   E. 58,151

Ms. J. M. Ruddock, *Lab.*		18,724
M. C. Punyer, *C.*		11,953
Ms. A. M. E. Braun, *SDP/All.*		6,513
P. K. Makepeace, *Grn.*		568
Lab. maj.		6,771
(June '83, Lab. maj. 6,032)		

EAST   E. 59,627

Hon. C. B. Moynihan, C.		19,873
M. R. Profitt, *Lab.*		15,059
Mrs. V. W. Stone, *SDP/All.*		9,118
C. maj.		4,814
(June '83, C. maj. 1,909)		

WEST   E. 62,923

J. C. Maples, C.		20,995
J. P. Dowd, *Lab.*		17,223
Ms. S. C. Titley, *L./All.*		7,247
C. maj.		3,772
(June '83, C. maj. 2,506)		

Leyton (Gtr. London)
E. 57,662

H. M. Cohen, Lab.		16,536
S. Banks, *L./All.*		11,895
D. N. Gilmartin, *C.*		11,692
Lab. maj.		4,641
(June '83, Lab. maj. 4,516)		

Lincoln
E. 77,049

K. M. Carlisle, C.		27,097
N. J. Butler, *Lab.*		19,614
P. Zentner, *SDP/All.*		11,319
T. B. Kyle, *RRPRC*		232
C. maj.		7,483
(June '83, C. maj. 10,286)		

Lindsey East (Lincs)
E. 74,027

Sir P. H. B. Tapsell, C.		29,048
J. C. L. Sellick, *L./All.*		20,432
K. Stevenson, *Lab.*		6,206
C. maj.		8,616
(June '83, C. maj. 7,517)		

Littleborough and Saddleworth
(Gtr. Manchester)
E. 66,074

G. K. Dickens, C.		22,027
C. Davies, *L./All.*		15,825
P. Stonier, *Lab.*		13,299
C. maj.		6,202
(June '83, C. maj. 5,650)		

Liverpool

BROADGREEN   E. 63,091

T. Fields, Lab.		23,262
R. Pine, *L./All.*		17,215
M. R. G. Seddon, *C.*		7,413
Lab. maj.		6,047
(June '83, Lab. maj. 3,800)		

GARSTON   E. 61,280

E. Loyden, Lab.		24,848
P. B. Feather, *C.*		11,071
R. Isaacson, *SDP/All.*		10,370
K. Timlin, *WRP*		98
Lab. maj.		13,777
(June '83, Lab. maj. 4,002)		

MOSSLEY HILL   E. 60,954

D. P. P. Alton, L./All.		20,012
J. A. Devaney, *Lab.*		17,786
W. M. Lightfoot, *C.*		8,005
L./All. maj.		2,226
(June '83, L./All. maj. 4,195)		

RIVERSIDE   E. 53,328

R. Parry, Lab.		25,505
S. Fitzsimmons, *C.*		4,816
B. S. Chahal, *SDP/All.*		3,912
Ms. C. A. Gardner, *Comm.*		601
Lab. maj.		20,689
(June '83, Lab. maj. 17,378)		

WALTON   E. 73,118

E. S. Heffer, Lab.		34,661
P. R. Clark, *L./All.*		11,408
I. A. Mays, *C.*		7,738
Lab. maj.		23,253
(June '83, Lab. maj. 14,115)		

West Derby *E.* 60,522

R. N. Wareing, Lab.	29,021
J. E. Backhouse, *C.*	8,525
M. Ferguson, *SDP/All.*	6,897
Lab. maj.	20,496
(June '83, Lab. maj. 11,843)	

Loughborough (Leics)
E. 73,660

S. J. Dorrell, C.	31,931
C. J. Wrigley, *Lab.*	14,283
R. G. Fox, *SDP/All.*	11,499
R. Gupta, *Grn.*	656
C. maj.	17,648
(June '83, C. maj. 16,180)	

Ludlow (Salop)
E. 66,187

C. J. F. Gill, RD, *C.*	27,499
D. Phillips, *L./All.*	15,800
K. Harrison, *Lab.*	7,724
C. maj.	11,699
(June '83, C. maj. 11,303)	

Luton (Beds)

North *E.* 74,235

J. R. Carlisle, C.	30,997
M. Wright, *Lab.*	15,424
J. D. Stephen, *SDP/All.*	11,166
C. maj.	15,573
(June '83, C. maj. 11,981)	

South *E.* 71,231

G. F. J. Bright, C.	24,762
W. D. McKenzie, *Lab.*	19,647
P. Chapman, *L./All.*	9,146
C. maj.	5,115
(June '83, C. maj. 4,621)	

Macclesfield (Cheshire)
E. 76,093

N. R. Winterton, C.	33,208
A. B. Haldane, *L./All.*	14,116
Ms. C. Pinder, *Lab.*	11,563
C. maj.	19,092
(June '83, C. maj. 20,679)	

Maidstone (Kent)
E. 72,987

Miss *A. N. Widdecombe, C.*	29,100
C. J. Sutton-Mattocks, *L./All.*	18,736
K. P. Brooks, *Lab.*	6,935
Mrs. P. A. Kemp, *Grn.*	717
C. maj.	10,364
(June '83, C. maj. 7,226)	

Makerfield (Gtr. Manchester)
E. 70,819

I. McCartney, *Lab.*	30,190
L. A. Robertson, *C.*	14,632
B. Hewer, *L./All.*	8,838
Lab. maj.	15,558
(June '83, Lab. maj. 10,876)	

Manchester

Blackley *E.* 58,814

K. Eastham, Lab.	22,476
K. Nath, *C.*	12,354
H. Showman, *SDP/All.*	8,041
Lab. maj.	10,122
(June '83, Lab. maj. 6,456)	

Central *E.* 62,928

R. K. Litherland, Lab.	27,428
M. R. W. Banks, *C.*	7,561
B. W. McColgan, *SDP/All.*	5,250
Lab. maj.	19,867
(June '83, Lab. maj. 18,485)	

Gorton *E.* 64,243

Rt. Hon. G. B. Kaufman, Lab.	24,615
J. Kershaw, *C.*	10,550
K. A. Whitmore, *L./All.*	9,830
Ms. P. Lawrence, *RF*	253
Lab. maj.	14,065
(June '83, Lab. maj. 9,965)	

Withington *E.* 65,343

K. J. C. Bradley, *Lab.*	21,650
F. J. Silvester, C.	18,259
Mrs. A. Jones, *L./All.*	9,978
M. T. Abberton, *Grn.*	524
Lab. maj.	3,391
(June '83, C. maj. 2,373)	

Wythenshawe *E.* 58,287

Rt. Hon. A. Morris, Lab.	23,881
D. G. Sparrow, *C.*	12,026
Ms. J. Butterworth, *SDP/All.*	5,921
Ms. S. Connelly, *RF*	216
Lab. maj.	11,855
(June '83, Lab. maj. 10,684)	

Mansfield (Notts)
E. 66,764

J. A. Meale, *Lab.*	19,610
C. Hendry, *C.*	19,554
B. Answer, *SDP/All.*	11,604
B. Marshall, *ML*	1,580
Lab. maj.	56
(June '83, Lab. maj. 2,216)	

Medway (Kent)
E. 64,103

Dame P. Fenner, DBE, *C.*	23,889
V. Hull, *Lab.*	13,960
Mrs. J. Horne-Roberts, *SDP/All.*	8,450
Ms. J. V. Rosser, *Grn.*	504
C. maj.	9,929
(June '83, C. maj. 8,656)	

Meriden (W. Midlands)
E. 78,444

I. C. Mills, C.	31,935
R. H. Burden, *Lab.*	15,115
Ms. C. E. Parkinson, *SDP/All.*	10,896
C. maj.	16,820
(June '83, C. maj. 15,018)	

Middlesbrough (Cleveland)
E. 60,789

S. Bell, Lab.	25,747
R. J. Orr-Ewing, *C.*	10,789
P. A. Hawley, *L./All.*	6,594
Lab. maj.	14,958
(June '83, Lab. maj. 9,669)	

Milton Keynes (Bucks)
E. 97,041

W. R. Benyon, C.	35,396
W. T. Rodgers, *SDP/All.*	21,695
Ms. Y. V. A. Brownfield-Pope, *Lab.*	16,111
A. H. Francis, *Grn.*	810
C. maj.	13,701
(June '83, C. maj. 11,522)	

Mitcham and Morden
(Gtr. London)
E. 63,089

Mrs. A. C. R. Rumbold, CBE, *C.*	23,002
Ms. S. McDonagh, *Lab.*	16,819
B. L. H. Douglas-Mann, *SDP/All.*	7,930
C. maj.	6,183
(June '83, C. maj. 6,451)	

Mole Valley (Surrey)
E. 67,715

Rt. Hon. K. W. Baker, C.	31,689
Mrs. S. P. Thomas, *L./All.*	15,613
C. M. B. King, *Lab.*	4,846
C. maj.	16,076
(June '83, C. maj. 14,718)	

Morecambe and Lunesdale
(Lancs)
E. 55,718

Hon. M. A. Lennox-Boyd, C.	22,327
Mrs. J. Greenwell, *SDP/All.*	10,542
D. Smith, *Lab.*	9,535
C. maj.	11,785
(June '83, C. maj. 12,194)	

Newark (Notts)
E. 67,555

R. T. Alexander, C.	28,070
D. Barton, *Lab.*	14,527
G. A. Emerson, *SDP/All.*	9,833
C. maj.	13,543
(June '83, C. maj. 14,283)	

Newbury (Berks)
E. 75,187

R. M. C. McNair-Wilson, C.	35,266
D. D. Rendel, *L./All.*	18,608
R. C. Stapley, *Lab.*	4,765
C. maj.	16,658
(June '83, C. maj. 13,038)	

Newcastle under Lyme (Staffs)
E. 66,053

Mrs. L. Golding, Lab.	21,618
A. L. Thomas, *L./All.*	16,486
P. C. J. Ridgway, *C.*	14,863
M. J. Nicklin, *Ex Lab. Mod.*	397
Lab. maj.	5,132
(June '83, Lab. maj. 2,804)	
(July '86, Lab. maj. 799)	

Newcastle upon Tyne

Central *E.* 63,682

J. M. Cousins, *Lab.*	20,416
P. R. G. Merchant, C.	17,933
Dr. N. Martin, *SDP/All.*	7,304
R. J. Bird, *Grn.*	418
K. Williams, *RF*	111
Lab. maj.	2,483
(June '83, C. maj. 2,228)	

EAST *E.* 59,369
**N. H. Brown, Lab. 23,677
Miss J. G. A. Riley, *C.* 11,177
P. J. Arnold, *L./All.* 6,728
J. Keith, *Comm.* 362
   Lab. maj. 12,500
   (June '83, Lab. maj. 7,492)

NORTH *E.* 69,178
D. J. Henderson, *Lab.* 22,424
J. W. Shipley, *L./All.* 17,181
J. W. Tweddle, *C.* 12,915
   Lab. maj. 5,243
   (June '83, Lab. maj. 2,556)

New Forest (Hants)
E. 75,083

*P. M. E. D. McNair-Wilson,
  C. 37,188
R. Karn, *L./All.* 15,456
J. I. Hampton, *Lab.* 4,856
   C. maj. 21,732
   (June '83, C. maj. 20,925)

Newham (Gtr. London)

NORTH EAST *E.* 60,787
**R. Leighton, Lab. 20,220
P. Davis, *C.* 11,984
Ms. H. Steele, *L./All.* 6,772
   Lab. maj. 8,236
   (June '83, Lab. maj. 8,509)

NORTH WEST *E.* 47,568
**T. L. Banks, Lab. 15,677
J. C. Wylie, *C.* 7,181
R. H. Redden, *SDP/All.* .. 4,920
Ms. A. V. Degrandis-
  Harrison, *Grn.* 497
   Lab. maj. 8,496
   (June '83, Lab. maj. 6,918)

SOUTH *E.* 50,244
**N. J. Spearing, Lab. 12,935
J. Fairrie, *C.* 10,169
A. J. Kellaway, *SDP/All.* 6,607
   Lab. maj. 2,766
   (June '83, Lab. maj. 7,311)

Norfolk

MID *E.* 73,893
**R. A. Ryder, OBE, C. 32,758
G. J. E. Graham, *SDP/All.* 14,750
K. Luckey, *Lab.* 10,272
   C. maj. 18,008
   (June '83, C. maj. 15,515)

NORTH *E.* 69,790
**R. F. Howell, C. 28,822
N. R. Anthony, *SDP/All.* 13,512
A. Earle, *Lab.* 10,765
M. G. Filgate, *Grn.* 960
   C. maj. 15,310
   (June '83, C. maj. 13,223)

NORTH WEST *E.* 73,739
**H. C. Bellingham, C. 29,393
C. Brocklebank-Fowler,
  SDP/All. 18,568
F. Dignan, *Lab.* 10,184
   C. maj. 10,825
   (June '83, C. maj. 3,147)

SOUTH *E.* 78,372
**Rt. Hon. J. R. R. Mac-
  Gregor,* OBE, *C.* 33,912
R. A. P. Carden, *L./All.* ... 21,494
L. Addison, *Lab.* 8,047
   C. maj. 12,418
   (June '83, C. maj. 12,135)

SOUTH WEST *E.* 74,240
Mrs. G. P. Shephard, *C.* .. 32,519
M. Scott, *L./All.* 12,083
Ms. M. Page, *Lab.* 11,844
   C. maj. 20,436
   (June '83, C. maj. 14,910)

Normanton (W. Yorks)
E. 62,899

**W. O'Brien, Lab. 23,303
M. D. M. Smith, *C.* 16,016
R. J. Macey, *SDP/All.* 7,717
   Lab. maj. 7,287
   (June '83, Lab. maj. 4,183)

Northampton

NORTH *E.* 69,294
**A. R. Marlow, C. 24,816
O. J. Granfield, *Lab.* 15,560
A. S. Rounthwaite, *L./All.* 10,690
M. Green, *Grn.* 471
S. Colling, *WRP* 156
   C. maj. 9,256
   (June '83, C. maj. 9,860)

SOUTH *E.* 76,071
**M. W. L. Morris, C. 31,864
J. Dickie, *Lab.* 14,061
G. Hopkins, *SDP/All.* 10,639
Mrs. M. Hamilton, *Grn.* .. 647
   C. maj. 17,803
   (June '83, C. maj. 15,126)

Northavon (Avon)
E. 78,483

**J. A. Cope, C. 34,224
Mrs. C. Willmore, *L./All.* . 19,954
D. Norris, *Lab.* 8,762
   C. maj. 14,270
   (June '83, C. maj. 12,983)

Norwich (Norfolk)

NORTH *E.* 62,725
**H. P. Thompson, C. 22,772
Miss M. H. R. Honeyball,
  Lab. 14,996
T. P. Nicholls, *L./All.* 11,922
   C. maj. 7,776
   (June '83, C. maj. 5,879)

SOUTH *E.* 64,421
J. L. Garrett, *Lab.* 19,666
**J. A. Powley, C. 19,330
C. J. M. Hardie, *SDP/All.* 12,896
   Lab. maj. 336
   (June '83, C. maj. 1,712)

Norwood (Gtr. London)
E. 56,602

**J. D. Fraser, Lab. 18,359
D. C. R. Grieve, *C.* 13,636
M. M. Noble, *SDP/All.* ... 12,579
F. M. Jackson, *RABIES* 171
R. J. Hammond, *CD.* 151
   Lab. maj. 4,723
   (June '83, Lab. maj. 2,883)

Nottingham

EAST *E.* 68,266
**M. Knowles, C. 20,162
M. Aslam, *Lab.* 19,706
S. Parkhouse, *L./All.* 6,887
K. Malik, *RF* 212
   C. maj. 456
   (June '83, C. maj. 1,464)

NORTH *E.* 69,620
G. W. Allen, *Lab.* 22,713
**R. G. J. Ottaway, C. 21,048
S. C. Fernando, *SDP/All.* 5,912
J. H. Peck, *Comm.* 879
   Lab. maj. 1,665
   (June '83, C. maj. 362)

SOUTH *E.* 72,807
*M. M. Brandon-Bravo, C. . 23,921
A. Simpson, *Lab.* 21,687
L. V. Williams, *SDP/All.* 7,517
   C. maj. 2,234
   (June '83, C. maj. 5,715)

Nuneaton (Warwicks)
E. 68,287

**L. D. Stevens, MBE, C. ... 24,630
Mrs. V. A. Veness, *Lab.* .. 18,975
A. Trembath, *SDP/All.* ... 10,550
Dr. J. Morrissey, *Grn.* 719
   C. maj. 5,655
   (June '83, C. maj. 5,061)

Old Bexley and Sidcup
(Gtr. London)
E. 50,831

*Rt. Hon. E. R. G. Heath,
  MBE, *C.* 24,350
T. H. Pearce, *L./All.* 8,076
H. J. A. Stoate, *Lab.* 6,762
   C. maj. 16,274
   (June '83, C. maj. 12,718)

Oldham (Gtr. Manchester)

CENTRAL AND ROYTON
E. 65,277
**J. A. Lamond, Lab. 21,759
J. A. Farquhar, *C.* 15,480
Mrs. A. Dunn, *SDP/All.* 7,956
   Lab. maj. 6,279
   (June '83, Lab. maj. 3,312)

WEST *E.* 57,178
**M. H. Meacher, Lab. 20,291
Mrs. J. M. Jacobs, *C.* 14,324
Miss M. R. Mason, *L./All.* 6,478
   Lab. maj. 5,967
   (June '83, Lab. maj. 3,180)

Orpington (Gtr. London)
E. 59,608

**I. R. Stanbrook, C. 27,261
J. H. Fryer, *L./All.* 14,529
S. J. Cowan, *Lab.* 5,020
   C. maj. 12,732
   (June '83, C. maj. 10,151)

Oxford

EAST *E.* 62,145
A. D. Smith, *Lab.* 21,103
**S. J. Norris, C. 19,815
Mrs. M. Godden, *L./All.* .. 7,648
D. Dalton, *Grn.* 441
P. S. Mylvaganam, *ICC* .. 60
   Lab. maj. 1,288
   (June '83, C. maj. 1,267)

WEST AND ABINGDON *E.* 69,193

*J. H. C. Patten, C.	......	25,171
C. M. P. Huhne, *SDP/All.*		20,293
J. G. Power, *Lab.*	....	8,108
D. Smith, *Grn.*	....	695
C. maj.	....	4,878

(June '83, C. maj. 7,151)

Peckham (Gtr. London)
E. 59,261

*Ms. H. Harman, Lab.	....	17,965
Mrs. L. K. F. Ingram, *C.*	....	8,476
R. H. Shearman, *L./All.*	....	5,878
Miss D. Robinson, *Grn.*	....	628
Lab. maj.		9,489

(June '83, Lab. maj. 8,824)

Pendle (Lancs)
E. 63,588

*J. R. L. Lee, C.	....	21,009
Mrs. S. Renilson, *Lab.*	....	18,370
A. G. Lishman, *L./All.*	....	12,662
C. maj.		2,639

(June '83, C. maj. 6,135)

Penrith and the Border
(Cumbria)
E. 70,994

*D. J. Maclean, C.	....	33,148
D. J. Ivison, *L./All.*	....	15,782
J. M. P. Hutton, *Lab.*	....	6,075
C. maj.		17,366

(June '83, C. maj. 15,421)
(July '83, C. maj. 552)

Peterborough (Cambs)
E. 84,284

*Dr. B. S. Mawhinney, C.	..	30,624
A. MacKinlay, *Lab.*	......	20,840
D. W. Green, *L./All.*	....	9,984
N. A. Callaghan, *Grn.*	....	506
C. maj.		9,784

(June '83, C. maj. 10,439)

Plymouth (Devon)

DEVONPORT *E.* 64,741

*Rt. Hon. Dr. D. A. L. Owen,		
SDP/All.	....	21,039
T. Jones, *C.*		14,569
I. Flintoff, *Lab.*	....	14,166
SDP/All. maj.	..	6,470

(June '83, SDP/All. maj. 4,936)

DRAKE *E.* 51,186

*Miss J. E. Fookes, C.	.....	16,195
D. Astor, *SDP/All.*	.....	13,070
D. Jamieson, *Lab.*	......	9,451
Ms. P. Barber, *Grn.*	......	493
C. maj.		3,125

(June '83, C. maj. 8,585)

SUTTON *E.* 64,120

*Hon. A. K. M. Clark, C.	..	23,187
B. Tidy, *L./All.*	....	19,174
R. D. Maddern, *Lab.*	.....	8,310
C. maj.		4,013

(June '83, C. maj. 11,687)

Pontefract and Castleford
(W. Yorks)
E. 64,414

*G. Lofthouse, Lab.	....	31,656
J. H. Mallins, *C.*	......	10,030
M. F. Taylor, *L./All.*	......	5,334
D. M. Lees, *RF*	....	295
Lab. maj.		21,626

(June '83, Lab. maj. 13,691)

Poole (Dorset)
E. 76,673

*J. D. Ward, CBE, C.	....	34,159
R. J. Whitley, *SDP/All.*		19,351
M. Shutler, *Lab.*	....	5,901
C. maj.		14,808

(June '83, C. maj. 14,429)

Portsmouth (Hants)

NORTH *E.* 80,501

*P. H. S. Griffiths, C.	....	33,297
Mrs. E. Mitchell, *SDP/All.*		14,896
D. Miles, *Lab.*	....	12,016
C. maj.	....	18,401

(June '83, C. maj. 17,999)

SOUTH *E.* 76,292

*D. Martin, C.	....	23,534
*M. T. Hancock, *SDP/All.*		23,329
K. Gardiner, *Lab.*	....	7,047
R. Hughes, *657 Party*	.....	455
C. maj.		205

(June '83, C. maj. 12,335)
(June '84, SDP/All. maj. 1,341)

Preston (Lancs)
E. 64,459

*Mrs. A. Wise, Lab.	....	23,341
Dr. R. T. Chandran, *C.*	....	12,696
J. P. Wright, *L./All.*	.....	8,452
Lab. maj.	....	10,645

(June '83, Lab. maj. 6,978)

Pudsey (W. Yorks)
E. 71,681

*J. G. D. Shaw, C.	....	25,457
J. P. F. Cummins, *L./All.*		19,021
N. Taggart, *Lab.*	....	11,461
C. maj.		6,436

(June '83, C. maj. 5,314)

Putney (Gtr. London)
E. 63,108

*D. J. Mellor, C.	....	24,197
P. G. Hain, *Lab.*	....	17,290
Ms. S. Harlow, *L./All.*	.....	5,934
S. Desorgher, *Grn.*	....	508
C. maj.	....	6,907

(June '83, C. maj. 5,019)

Ravensbourne (Gtr. London)
E. 59,365

*J. L. Hunt, C.	....	28,295
G. Campbell, *SDP/All.*	...	11,376
M. D'Arcy, *Lab.*	....	5,087
A. Waide, *BN*	....	184
C. maj.	....	16,919

(June '83, C. maj. 15,512)

Reading (Berks)

EAST *E.* 72,311

*Sir G. Vaughan, C.	......	28,515
Mrs. S. M. Baring, *SDP/*		
All.	....	12,298
M. J. Salter, *Lab.*	....	11,371
P. J. Unsworth, *Grn.*	.....	667
A. B. Shone, *CS*		125
C. maj.		16,217

(June '83, C. maj. 11,508)

WEST *E.* 70,391

*R. A. B. Durant, C.	......	28,122
K. H. Lock, *L./All.*	......	11,369
M. E. Orton, *Lab.*	......	10,819
E. P. Wilson, *Grn.*	......	542
C. maj.		16,753

(June '83, C. maj. 11,399)

Redcar (Cleveland)
E. 63,393

Dr. Marjorie Mowlam, Lab.		22,824
P. J. Bassett, *C.*	....	15,089
G. Nightingale, *SDP/All.*		10,298
Lab. maj.		7,735

(June '83, Lab. maj. 3,104)

Reigate (Surrey)
E. 71,940

*G. A. Gardiner, C.	....	30,925
Mrs. E. A. Pamplin, *SDP/*		
All.	....	12,752
R. P. Spencer, *Lab.*	......	7,460
G. Brand, *Grn.*	....	1,026
C. maj.		18,173

(June '83, C. maj. 16,307)

Ribble Valley (Lancs)
E. 62,644

*Rt. Hon. D. C. Waddington,		
QC, C.	....	30,136
M. Carr, *SDP/All.*	....	10,608
G. Pope, *Lab.*	....	8,781
C. maj.		19,528

(June '83, C. maj. 18,591)

Richmond and Barnes
(Gtr. London)
E. 54,700

*J. J. Hanley, C.	....	21,729
A. J. Watson, *L./All.*	......	19,963
M. D. Gold, *Lab.*	....	3,227
Miss C. M. Matthews, *Grn.*		610
C. maj.		1,766

(June '83, C. maj. 74)

Richmond (N. Yorks)
E. 79,277

*Rt. Hon. L. Brittan, QC,		
C.	....	34,995
D. Lloyd-Williams, *L./All.*		15,419
F. Robson, *Lab.*	....	6,737
C. maj.		19,576

(June '83, C. maj. 18,066)
(*See also* p. 276)

Rochdale (Gtr. Manchester)
E. 68,703

*C. Smith, MBE, L./All.	....	22,245
D. Williams, *Lab.*	....	19,466
C. Condie, *C.*	....	9,561
L./All. maj.		2,779

(June '83, L./All. maj. 7,587)

Rochford (Essex)
E. 76,048

Dr. M. Clark, C.	....	35,872
P. Young, *L./All.*	....	16,178
D. Weir, *Lab.*	....	7,308
C. maj.	....	19,694
(June '83, C. maj. 13,102)		

Romford (Gtr. London)
E. 55,668

M. J. Neubert, C.	....	22,745
N. J. M. Smith, *Lab.*	.....	9,274
J. H. Bates, *L./All.*	......	8,195
F. J. Gibson, *Grn.*	....	385
C. maj.	....	13,471
(June '83, C. maj. 10,574)		

Romsey and Waterside (Hants)
E. 79,136

M. K. B. Colvin, C.	....	35,303
A. T. Bloss, *SDP/All.*	......	20,031
S. J. Roberts, *Lab.*	....	7,213
C. maj.	....	15,272
(June '83, C. maj. 13,690)		

Rossendale and Darwen (Lancs)
E. 75,038

D. A. Trippier, C.	....	28,056
Mrs. J. Anderson, *Lab.*	...	23,074
P. J. Hulse, *L./All.*	....	9,097
C. maj.	....	4,982
(June '83, C. maj. 8,821)		

Rotherham (S. Yorks)
E. 61,521

J. S. Crowther, Lab.	......	25,422
J. C. C. Stevens, *C.*	....	9,410
P. J. Bowler, *L./All.*	......	7,766
Lab. maj.	....	16,012
(June '83, Lab. maj. 11,709)		

Rother Valley (S. Yorks)
E. 66,416

K. J. Barron, Lab.	....	28,292
P. R. Rayner, *C.*	....	12,502
J. R. Boddy, *SDP/All.*	....	9,240
M. R. Driver, *WRP*	....	145
Lab. maj.	....	15,790
(June '83, Lab. maj. 8,625)		

Rugby and Kenilworth
(Warwicks)
E. 76,654

J. F. Pawsey, C.	....	31,485
J. Airey, *Lab.*	....	15,221
D. R. Owen-Jones, *L./All.*	.	14,343
C. maj.	....	16,264
(June '83, C. maj. 14,241)		

Ruislip-Northwood
(Gtr. London)
E. 56,365

J. A. D. Wilkinson, C.	....	27,418
Mrs. D. Darby, *L./All.*	....	10,447
Ms. H. A. Smith, *Lab.*	....	5,913
C. maj.	....	16,971
(June '83, C. maj. 12,982)		

Rushcliffe (Notts)
E. 72,797

Rt. Hon. K. H. Clarke, QC,		
C.	....	34,214
L. George, *SDP/All.*	.....	13,375
P. Tipping, *Lab.*	....	9,631
Ms. H. Wright, *Grn.*	.....	991
C. maj.	....	20,839
(June '83, C. maj. 20,220)		

Rutland and Melton (Leics)
E. 77,846

M. A. Latham, C.	....	37,073
R. C. Renold, *L./All.*	.....	14,051
L. C. Burke, *Lab.*	....	8,680
C. maj.	....	23,022
(June '83, C. maj. 18,353)		

Ryedale (N. Yorks)
E. 83,205

J. R. Greenway, C.	....	35,149
Mrs. E. L. Shields, L./All.	.	25,409
J. Beighton, *Lab.*	....	5,340
C. maj.	....	9,740
(June '83, C. maj. 16,142)		
(May '86, L./All. maj. 4,940)		

Saffron Walden (Essex)
E. 73,185

A. G. B. Haselhurst, C.	...	33,354
M. P. Hayes, *L./All.*	......	16,752
R. Gifford, *Lab.*	....	6,674
G. B. Hannah, *Grn.*	......	816
W. O. Smedley, *CMNHY*	....	217
C. maj.	....	16,602
(June '83, C. maj. 15,363)		

St. Albans (Herts)
E. 75,281

P. B. Lilley, C.	....	31,726
A. S. B. Walkington, *L./All.*	20,845
A. McWalter, *Lab.*	....	6,922
Ms. E. V. Field, *Grn.*	.....	788
W. H. Pass, *CPRP*	....	110
C. maj.	....	10,881
(June '83, C. maj. 8,561)		

St. Helens (Merseyside)

NORTH *E.* 70,836

J. Evans, Lab.	....	28,989
Miss M. J. Libby, *C.*	......	14,729
N. P. Derbyshire, *L./All.*	...	10,300
Lab. maj.	....	14,260
(June '83, Lab. maj. 9,259)		

SOUTH *E.* 69,449

G. E. Bermingham, Lab.	..	27,027
A. J. Brown, *C.*	....	13,226
P. J. Briers, *SDP/All.*	....	9,252
Lab. maj.	....	13,801
(June '83, Lab. maj. 9,662)		

St. Ives (Cornwall)
E. 67,448

D. A. Harris, C.	....	25,174
H. H. J. Carter, *SDP/All.*	..	17,619
I. Hope, *Lab.*	....	9,275
C. maj.	....	7,555
(June '83, C. maj. 7,859)		

Salford East
(Gtr. Manchester)
E. 58,087

Rt. Hon. S. Orme, Lab.	...	22,555
C. W. H. McFall, *C.*	......	10,499
P. Keaveney, *SDP/All.*	...	5,105
S. G. Murray, *WRP*	......	201
Lab. maj.	....	12,056
(June '83, Lab. maj. 9,541)		

Salisbury (Wilts)
E. 76,221

S. R. Key, C.	....	31,612
P. A. Mitchell, *SDP/All.*		20,169
Ms. T. E. Seabourne, *Lab.*	.	5,455
S. W. Fletcher, *Ind.*	......	372
C. maj.	....	11,443
(June '83, C. maj. 7,174)		

Scarborough (N. Yorks)
E. 74,612

Sir M. N. Shaw, C.	....	27,672
Mrs. H. Callan, *SDP/All.*		14,046
M. Wolstenholme, *Lab.*	..	12,913
C. maj.	....	13,626
(June '83, C. maj. 13,929)		

Sedgefield (Durham)
E. 60,866

A. C. L. Blair, Lab.	......	25,965
N. B. S. Hawkins, *C.*	......	12,907
R. I. Andrew, *SDP/All.*	....	7,477
C. maj.	....	13,058
(June '83, Lab. maj. 8,281)		

Selby (N. Yorks)
E. 71,378

Rt. Hon. M. J. H. Alison,		
C.	....	28,611
J. T. Grogan, *Lab.*	....	14,832
J. E. F. Longman, *L./All.*	.	12,010
C. maj.	....	13,779
(June '83, C. maj. 15,965)		

Sevenoaks (Kent)
E. 73,179

G. M. Wolfson, C.	....	32,945
S. R. Jakobi, *L./All.*	......	15,600
G. A. Green, *Lab.*	....	7,379
C. maj.	....	17,345
(June '83, C. maj. 15,706)		

Sheffield (S. Yorks)

ATTERCLIFFE *E.* 67,051

A. E. P. Duffy, Lab.	......	28,266
G. J. Perry, *C.*	....	11,075
Ms. H. E. Woolley, *SDP/*		
All.	....	9,549
Lab. maj.	....	17,191
(June '83, Lab. maj. 11,612)		

BRIGHTSIDE *E.* 64,982

D. Blunkett, *Lab.*	....	31,208
Miss M. C. Glyn, *C.*	......	7,017
J. A. Leeman, *L./All.*	.....	6,434
Lab. maj.	....	24,191
(June '83, Lab. maj. 15,209)		

CENTRAL *E.* 61,156
*R. G. Caborn, *Lab.* 25,872
B. Oxley, *C.* 6,530
Ms. F. C. Hornby, *SDP/All.* 5,314
C. T. Dingle, *RF.* 278
K. E. Petts, *Comm.* 203
   Lab. maj. 19,342
   (June '83, Lab. maj. 16,790)

HALLAM *E.* 74,158
C. I. Patnick, *C.* 25,649
P. J. Gold, *L./All.* 18,012
M. C. Savani, *Lab.* 11,290
Ms. L. M. Spencer, *Grn.* .. 459
   C. maj. 7,637
   (June '83, C. maj. 11,774)

HEELEY *E.* 73,931
*W. Michie, *Lab.* 28,425
N. P. Mearing-Smith, *C.* .. 13,985
P. Moore, *SDP/All.* 10,811
   Lab. maj. 14,440
   (June '83, Lab. maj. 8,368)

HILLSBOROUGH *E.* 76,312
*M. H. Flannery, *Lab.* ... 26,208
D. Chadwick, *L./All.* 22,922
J. D. Sykes, *C.* 10,396
   Lab. maj. 3,286
   (June '83, Lab. maj. 1,546)

Sherwood (Notts)
E. 71,378

*A. S. Stewart, *C.* 26,816
W. S. G. Bach, *Lab.* 22,321
S. R. Thompstone, *SDP/
  All.* 9,343
   C. maj. 4,495
   (June '83, C. maj. 658)

Shipley (W. Yorks)
E. 68,705

*Sir J. M. Fox, MBE, *C.* 26,941
W. J. L. Wallace, *L./All.* .. 14,311
C. R. B. Butler, *Lab.* 12,669
C. M. Harris, *Grn.* 507
   C. maj. 12,630
   (June '83, C. maj. 11,445)

Shoreham (W. Sussex)
E. 71,318

*Rt. Hon. R. N. Luce, *C.* ... 33,660
J. A. Ingram, *L./All.* 16,590
P. Godwin, *Lab.* 5,053
   C. maj. 17,070
   (June '83, C. maj. 15,766)

Shrewsbury and Atcham (Salop)
E. 70,689

*D. L. Conway, *C.* 26,027
R. Hutchison, *L./All.* 16,963
Mrs. E. Owen, *Lab.* 10,797
G. Hardy, *Grn.* 660
   C. maj. 9,064
   (June '83, C. maj. 8,624)

Shropshire North
E. 77,122

*Rt. Hon. W. J. Biffen, *C.* .. 30,385
G. Smith, *L./All.* 15,970
R. Hawkins, *Lab.* 11,866
   C. maj. 14,415
   (June '83, C. maj. 11,667)

Skipton and Ripon
(N. Yorks)
E. 72,199

D. M. Curry, *C.* 33,128
S. J. Cooksey, *L./All.* 15,954
T. L. Whitfield, *Lab.* 6,264
Ms. L. S. Williams, *Grn.* .. 825
   C. maj. 17,174
   (June '83, C. maj. 15,046)

Slough (Berks)
E. 73,424

*J. A. Watts, *C.* 26,166
E. Lopez, *Lab.* 22,076
M. Goldstone, *SDP/All.* .. 7,490
   C. maj. 4,090
   (June '83, C. maj. 3,106)

Solihull (W. Midlands)
E. 78,123

*J. M. Taylor, *C.* 35,844
G. E. Gadie, *L./All.* 14,058
Mrs. S. E. Knowles, *Lab.* . 8,791
   C. maj. 21,786
   (June '83, C. maj. 17,394)

Somerton and Frome
(Somerset)
E. 68,773

*Hon. R. T. Boscawen, MC,
  C. 29,351
R. G. Morgan, *L./All.* 19,813
I. S. Kelly, *Lab.* 5,461
   C. maj. 9,538
   (June '83, C. maj. 9,227)

Southampton (Hants)

ITCHEN *E.* 72,687
*C. R. Chope, OBE, *C.* 24,419
J. Y. Denham, *Lab.* 17,703
R. C. Mitchell, *SDP/All.* .. 13,006
   C. maj. 6,716
   (June '83, C. maj. 5,290)

TEST *E.* 73,918
*S. J. A. Hill, *C.* 25,722
A. P. V. Whitehead, *Lab.* . 18,768
Mrs. V. Rayner, *L./All.* ... 11,950
   C. maj. 6,954
   (June '83, C. maj. 9,346)

Southend (Essex)

EAST *E.* 59,073
*E. M. Taylor, *C.* 23,753
H. J. Berkeley, *SDP/All.* .. 9,906
D. R. Scully, *Lab.* 7,296
   C. maj. 13,847
   (June '83, C. maj. 10,691)

WEST *E.* 68,415
*Rt. Hon. H. P. G. Channon,
  C. 28,003
G. Grant, *L./All.* 19,603
Mrs. A. Smith, *Lab.* 3,899
   C. maj. 8,400
   (June '83, C. maj. 8,033)

South Hams (Devon)
E. 78,583

*A. D. Steen, *C.* 34,218
R. F. Chave, *L./All.* 21,072
*W. W. Hamilton, *Lab.* ... 5,060
C. G. Titmuss, *Grn.* 1,178
T. C. Langsford, *LM* 277
   C. maj. 13,146
   (June '83, C. maj. 12,401)

Southport (Merseyside)
E. 71,443

R. C. Fearn, *L./All.* 26,110
N. M. Thomas, *C.* 24,261
Mrs. A. Moore, *Lab.* 3,483
J. R. G. Walker, *Grn.* 653
   L./All. maj. 1,849
   (June '83, C. maj. 5,039)

South Ribble (Lancs)
E. 72,177

*R. J. Atkins, *C.* 28,133
D. F. Roebuck, *Lab.* 19,703
J. A. Holleran, *L./All.* 11,746
   C. maj. 8,430
   (June '83, C. maj. 12,659)

South Shields (Tyne & Wear)
E. 60,754

*Dr. D. G. Clark, *Lab.* 24,882
M. L. D. Fabricant, *C.* 11,031
Ms. M. Meling, *SDP/All.* . 6,654
E. G. Dunn, *Dem.* 408
   Lab. maj. 13,851
   (June '83, Lab. maj. 6,402)

Southwark and Bermondsey
(Gtr. London)
E. 55,438

*S. H. W. Hughes, *L./All.* .. 17,072
J. Bryan, *Lab.* 14,293
O. Heald, *C.* 4,522
P. N. Power, *Comm.* 108
   L./All. maj. 2,779
   (June '83, L./All. maj. 5,164)

Spelthorne (Surrey)
E. 72,967

D. Wilshire, *C.* 32,440
Mrs. M. Cunningham,
  SDP/All. 12,390
D. F. J. Welfare, *Lab.* 9,227
   C. maj. 20,050
   (June '83, C. maj. 13,506)

Stafford
E. 72,431

*W. N. P. Cash, *C.* 29,541
C. B. Phipps, *SDP/All.* ... 15,834
Ms. N. Hafeez, *Lab.* 12,177
   C. maj. 13,707
   (June '83, C. maj. 14,277)
   (May '84, C. maj. 3,980)

Staffordshire

MID *E.* 71,252
*B. J. Heddle, *C.* 28,644
C. R. St. Hill, *Lab.* 13,990
T. A. Jones, *L./All.* 13,114
J. G. Bazeley, *Ind. C.* 836
   C. maj. 14,654
   (June '83, C. maj. 13,880)
   (*See also* p. 276)

MOORLANDS E. 74,302
*D. L. Knox, C. 31,613
Mrs. V. Ivers, *Lab.* 17,186
J. P. Corbett, *SDP/All.* 10,950
C. maj. 14,427
(June '83, C. maj. 16,566)

SOUTH E. 79,261
*P. T. Cormack, C. 37,708
Mrs. F. Oborski, *L./All.* .. 12,440
P. Bateman, *Lab.* 11,805
C. maj. 25,268
(June '83, C. maj. 19,760)

SOUTH EAST E. 66,176
*D. L. Lightbown, C. 25,115
Miss E. Gluck, *SDP/All.* ... 14,230
D. Spilsbury, *Lab.* 13,874
C. maj. 10,885
(June '83, C. maj. 10,898)

Stalybridge and Hyde
(Gtr. Manchester)
E. 67,983

*T. Pendry, Lab. 24,401
R. N. Greenwood, *C.* 18,738
P. J. Ashenden, *SDP/All.* .. 7,311
Lab. maj. 5,663
(June '83, Lab. maj. 4,362)

Stamford and Spalding (Lincs)
E. 70,560

*J. Q. Davies, C. 31,000
Miss R. Bryan, *L./All.* 17,009
P. E. Lowe, *Lab.* 6,882
C. maj. 13,991
(June '83, C. maj. 11,756)

Stevenage (Herts)
E. 69,525

*T. J. R. Wood, C. 23,541
B. R. M. Stoneham, *SDP/
All.* 18,201
M. R. C. Withers, *Lab.* ... 14,229
C. maj. 5,340
(June '83, C. maj. 1,755)

Stockport (Gtr. Manchester)
E. 60,059

*A. R. Favell, C. 19,410
Mrs. S. Haines, *Lab.* 16,557
J. L. Begg, *SDP/All.* 10,365
M. Shipley, *Grn.* 573
C. maj. 2,853
(June '83, C. maj. 5,786)

Stockton (Cleveland)
NORTH E. 70,329
*F. Cook, Lab. 26,043
D. J. C. Faber, *C.* 17,242
N. F. G. Bosanquet, *SDP/
All.* 9,712
Lab. maj. 8,801
(June '83, Lab. maj. 1,870)

SOUTH E. 75,279
T. R. Devlin, C. 20,833
*I. W. Wrigglesworth, SDP/
All.* 20,059
J. M. Scott, *Lab.* 18,600
C. maj. 774
(June '83, SDP/All. maj. 102)

Stoke-on-Trent (Staffs)
CENTRAL E. 65,987
*M. Fisher, Lab. 23,842
D. Stone, *C.* 14,072
I. Cundy, *SDP/All.* 7,462
Lab. maj. 9,770
(June '83, Lab. maj. 8,250)

NORTH E. 74,184
Ms. J. L. Walley, *Lab.* 25,459
R. Davies, *C.* 16,946
S. J. Simmonds, *SDP/All.* .. 11,665
Lab. maj. 8,513
(June '83, Lab. maj. 8,203)

SOUTH E. 70,806
*Rt. Hon. J. Ashley, CH, Lab. 24,794
D. Hartshorne, *C.* 19,741
P. Wild, *L./All.* 7,669
Lab. maj. 5,053
(June '83, Lab. maj. 7,105)

Stratford-upon-Avon (Warwicks)
E. 81,263

*A. T. Howarth, CBE, C. ... 38,483
D. G. Cowcher, *L./All.* 17,318
R. H. Rhodes, *Lab.* 6,335
C. maj. 21,165
(June '83, C. maj. 17,917)

Streatham (Gtr. London)
E. 60,519

*W. J. M. Shelton, C. 18,916
Ms. A. Tapsall, *Lab.* 16,509
M. Tuffrey, *L./All.* 6,663
C. maj. 2,407
(June '83, C. maj. 5,902)

Stretford (Gtr. Manchester)
E. 57,568

*A. J. Lloyd, Lab. 22,831
D. Dougherty, *C.* 13,429
D. Lee, *SDP/All.* 5,125
Lab. maj. 9,402
(June '83, Lab. maj. 4,342)

Stroud (Glos)
E. 81,275

R. M. Knapman, C. 32,883
A. A. Walker-Smith, *L./All.* 20,508
T. Levitt, *Lab.* 12,145
C. maj. 12,375
(June '83, C. maj. 11,714)

Suffolk
CENTRAL E. 79,199
*M. N. Lord, C. 32,422
T. Dale, *L./All.* 16,132
M. Walker, *Lab.* 11,817
C. maj. 16,290
(June '83, C. maj. 14,731)

COASTAL E. 75,684
*Rt. Hon. J. S. Gummer, C. 32,834
Mrs. J. M. Miller, *SDP/All.* 17,554
Mrs. S. A. Reeves, *Lab.* ... 7,534
J. W. Holloway, *Grn.* 1,049
C. maj. 15,280
(June '83, C. maj. 15,622)

SOUTH E. 81,954
*T. S. K. Yeo, C. 33,972
C. M. N. Bradford, *L./All.* .. 17,729
A. C. Bavington, *Lab.* 11,876
C. maj. 16,243
(June '83, C. maj. 11,269)

Sunderland
(Tyne & Wear)
NORTH E. 75,674
*R. A. Clay, Lab. 29,767
I. S. Picton, *C.* 15,095
T. Jenkinson, *L./All.* 8,518
Lab. maj. 14,672
(June '83, Lab. maj. 7,196)

SOUTH E. 74,947
C. J. Mullin, *Lab.* 28,823
G. E. Howe, *C.* 16,210
K. Hudson, *SDP/All.* 7,768
D. N. Jacques, *Grn.* 516
Lab. maj. 12,613
(June '83, Lab. maj. 5,548)

Surbiton (Gtr. London)
E. 45,428

*R. P. Tracey, C. 19,861
D. T. Burke, *SDP/All.* 10,120
A. McGowan, *Lab.* 5,111
Ms. J. Vidler, *Grn.* 465
C. maj. 9,741
(June '83, C. maj. 8,749)

Surrey
EAST E. 59,528
*Rt. Hon. Sir R. E. G. Howe,
QC, C. 29,126
M. A. J. Anderson, *L./All.* 11,000
M. Davis, *Lab.* 4,779
D. Newell, *Grn.* 1,044
C. maj. 18,126
(June '83, C. maj. 15,436)

NORTH WEST E. 83,083
*W. M. J. Grylls, C. 38,535
C. Brodie, *L./All.* 14,960
J. Cooper, *Lab.* 6,751
C. maj. 23,575
(June '83, C. maj. 21,018)

SOUTH WEST E. 73,018
*Mrs. V. H. B. M. Bottomley,
C. 34,024
G. D. Scott, *L./All.* 19,681
J. K. P. Evers, *Lab.* 3,224
M. J. Green, *Ind. C.* 299
C. maj. 14,343
(June '83, C. maj. 14,351)
(May '84, C. maj. 2,599)

Sussex Mid
E. 80,147

*R. T. Renton, C. 37,781
N. S. E. Westbrook, *L./All.* 19,489
R. Hughes, *Lab.* 4,573
C. maj. 18,292
(June '83, C. maj. 16,744)

Sutton and Cheam
(Gtr. London)
E. 63,850

*D. N. Macfarlane, C. 29,710
R. D. Grieg, *L./All.* 13,992
Ms. L. Monk, *Lab.* 5,202
C. maj. 15,718
(June '83, C. maj. 10,264)

Sutton Coldfield (W. Midlands)
E. 72,329

*Rt. Hon. P. N. Fowler, C.	.	34,475
T. Bick, L./All.	....	13,292
P. McLoughlin, Lab.	......	6,104
C. maj.	....	21,183
(June '83, C. maj. 18,984)		

Swindon (Wilts)
E. 86,150

*S. C. Coombs, C.	....	29,385
Ms. G. Johnston, Lab.	.....	24,528
D. J. Scott, SDP/All.	.....	13,114
C. maj.	....	4,857
(June '83, C. maj. 1,395)		

Tatton (Cheshire)
E. 71,904

*M. N. Hamilton, C.	....	30,128
Ms. B. Gaskin, SDP/All.		13,034
Ms. H. A. Blears, Lab.	....	11,760
M. G. Gibson, FP.	....	263
C. maj.	....	17,094
(June '83, C. maj. 13,960)		

Taunton (Somerset)
E. 74,145

D. J. Nicholson, C.	....	30,248
M. A. K. Cocks, SDP/All.		19,868
Dr. G. Reynolds, Lab.	....	8,754
C. maj.	....	10,380
(June '83, C. maj. 12,567)		

Teignbridge (Devon)
E. 71,872

*P. C. M. Nicholls, C.	.....	30,693
R. D. Ryder, L./All.	.....	20,268
J. Greenwood, Lab.	.....	6,413
A. Hope, LM	....	312
C. maj.	....	10,425
(June '83, C. maj. 8,218)		

Thanet (Kent)

NORTH   E. 69,723

*R. J. Gale, C.	....	29,225
N. R. M. Cranston, SDP/		
All.	....	11,745
A. M. Bretman, Lab.	.....	8,395
D. R. Condor, Grn.	....	996
C. maj.	....	17,480
(June '83, C. maj. 14,545)		

SOUTH   E. 62,761

*J. W. P. Aitken, C.	......	25,135
W. H. Pitt, L./All.	....	11,452
C. Wright, Lab.	....	9,673
C. maj.	....	13,683
(June '83, C. maj. 14,051)		

Thurrock (Essex)
E. 67,594

T. S. Janman, C.	....	20,527
*Dr. O. A. McDonald, Lab.		19,837
D. S. Benson, SDP/All.	...	7,970
C. maj.	....	690
(June '83, Lab. maj. 1,722)		

Tiverton (Devon)
E. 68,210

*R. J. Maxwell-Hyslop, C.	.	29,875
D. J. Morrish, L./All.	....	20,663
Mrs. J. A. Northam, Lab.	.	3,400
W. J. Jones, LAO	....	434
C. maj.	....	9,212
(June '83, C. maj. 7,886)		

Tonbridge and Malling (Kent)
E. 76,797

*Rt. Hon. J. P. Stanley, C.	.	33,990
M. J. Ward, SDP/All.	....	17,561
D. G. Still, Lab.	....	7,803
M. D. S. Easter, BN.	.....	369
C. maj.	....	16,429
(June '83, C. maj. 13,520)		

Tooting (Gtr. London)
E. 68,116

*T. M. Cox, Lab.	....	21,457
M. A. Winter, C.	....	20,016
J. N. Ambache, SDP/All.		6,423
Ms. M. Vickery, Grn.	...	621
Lab. maj.	....	1,441
(June '83, Lab. maj. 2,659)		

Torbay (Devon)
E. 70,435

R. W. S. Allason, C.	......	29,029
N. D. Bye, L./All.	....	20,209
G. R. Taylor, Lab.	....	4,538
C. maj.	....	8,820
(June '83, C. maj. 6,555)		

Tottenham (Gtr. London)
E. 76,092

B. A. L. Grant, Lab.	......	21,921
P. L. Murphy, C.	....	17,780
S. Etherington, L./All.	...	8,983
D. Nicholls, Grn.	....	744
P. Nealon, Gait. Lab.	.....	638
Ms. C. L. Dixon, WRP	.....	205
Lab. maj.	....	4,141
(June '83, Lab. maj. 9,396)		

Truro (Cornwall)
E. 72,432

*M. O. J. Taylor, L./All.	...	28,368
N. F. St. Aubyn, C.	......	23,615
J. R. King, Lab.	....	5,882
L./All. maj.	....	4,753
(June '83, L./All. maj. 10,480)		
(March '87, L./All. maj. 14,617)		

Tunbridge Wells (Kent)
E. 76,291

*Sir P. B. B. Mayhew, QC, C.		33,111
Mrs. D. A. Buckrell, L./All.		16,989
P. L. Sloman, Lab.	......	6,555
C. maj.	....	16,122
(June '83, C. maj. 15,126)		

Twickenham (Gtr. London)
E. 64,661

*T. F. H. Jessel, C.	......	27,331
J. Waller, L./All.	....	20,204
Ms. V. C. M. Vaz, Lab.	...	4,415
D. S. Batchelor, Grn.	.....	746
C. maj.	....	7,127
(June '83, C. maj. 4,792)		

Tyne Bridge
(Tyne & Wear)
E. 58,152

*D. G. Clelland, Lab.	......	23,131
M. W. Bates, C.	....	7,558
J. C. Mansfield, SDP/All.		6,005
Lab. maj.	....	15,573
(June '83, Lab. maj. 11,693)		
(Dec '85, Lab. maj. 6,575)		

Tynemouth
(Tyne & Wear)
E. 74,407

*N. G. Trotter, C.	....	25,113
P. Cosgrove, Lab.	....	22,530
D. F. Mayhew, L./All.	...	10,446
C. maj.	....	2,583
(June '83, C. maj. 9,609)		

Upminster (Gtr. London)
E. 66,613

*Sir N. C. Bonsor, Bt., C.	..	27,946
J. Martin, SDP/All.	.....	11,089
D. R. O'Flynn, Lab.	......	11,069
C. maj.	....	16,857
(June '83, C. maj. 12,814)		

Uxbridge (Gtr. London)
E. 63,157

*J. M. Shersby, C.	....	27,292
D. Keys, Lab.	....	11,322
A. Goodman, SDP/All.	...	9,164
I. Flindall, Grn.	....	549
C. maj.	....	15,970
(June '83, C. maj. 12,837)		

Vauxhall (Gtr. London)
E. 66,538

*S. K. Holland, Lab.	......	21,364
D. R. Lidington, C.	......	12,345
S. H. V. Acland, SDP/All.		7,764
Ms. J. Owens, Grn.	......	770
D. J. S. Cook, Comm.	.....	223
K. Oluremi, RF.	....	117
Lab. maj.	....	9,019
(June '83, Lab. maj. 7,780)		
(See also p. 276)		

Wakefield (W. Yorks)
E. 69,580

D. M. Hinchliffe, Lab.	....	24,509
N. J. Hazell, C.	....	21,720
Dr. L. Kamal, SDP/All	...	6,350
Lab. maj.	....	2,789
(June '83, Lab. maj. 360)		

Wallasey (Merseyside)
E. 67,216

*Mrs. L. Chalker, C.	......	22,791
L. Duffy, Lab.	....	22,512
J. K. Richardson, SDP/		
All.	....	8,363
C. maj.	....	279
(June '83, C. maj. 6,708)		

Wallsend (Tyne & Wear)
E. 76,688

*W. E. Garrett, Lab.	....	32,709
D. Milburn, C.	....	13,325
Mrs. J. Phylactou, SDP/		
All.	....	11,508
Lab. maj.	....	19,384
(June '83, Lab. maj. 12,514)		

Walsall (W. Midlands)

NORTH E. 68,331
*D. J. Winnick, Lab.	......	21,458
Mrs. L. Hertz, C.		19,668
I. Shires, L./All.	....	9,285
Lab. maj.	....	1,790

(June '83, Lab. maj. 2,824)

SOUTH E. 66,746
*B. T. George, Lab.	....	22,629
G. E. Postles, C.		21,513
L. A. King, L./All.	....	6,241
Lab. maj.	....	1,116

(June '83, Lab. maj. 702)

Walthamstow (Gtr. London)
E. 48,691
H. H. F. Summerson, C.	..	13,748
*E. P. Deakins, Lab.	......	12,236
P. L. Leighton, SDP/All.		8,852
Dr. Z. I. Malik, DC	......	396
C. maj.	....	1,512

(June '83, Lab. maj. 1,305)

Wansbeck (Nthmb)
E. 62,639
*J. Thompson, Lab.	....	28,080
Mrs. S. Mitchell, L./All.	..	11,291
D. Walton, C.	....	9,490
Lab. maj.	....	16,789

(June '83, Lab. maj. 7,831)

Wansdyke (Avon)
E. 75,239
*J. H. Aspinwall, C.	......	31,537
R. B. Blackmore, L./All.	..	15,393
I. White, Lab.	....	14,231
C. maj.	....	16,144

(June '83, C. maj. 13,066)

Wanstead and Woodford
(Gtr. London)
E. 57,921
J. N. Arbuthnot, C.	......	25,701
J. R. Bastick, L./All.	.....	9,289
Mrs. L. Hilton, Lab.	.....	6,958
C. maj.	....	16,412

(June '83, C. maj. 14,354)

Wantage (Oxon)
E. 66,499
*R. V. Jackson, C.	....	27,951
Mrs. W. Tumin, SDP/All.		15,795
S. Ladyman, Lab.	....	8,055
C. maj.	....	12,156

(June '83, C. maj. 10,125)

Warley (W. Midlands)

EAST E. 55,706
*A. M. W. Faulds, Lab.	...	19,428
A. Antoniou, C.	....	13,843
J. J. Jordan, SDP/All.	...	5,396
Lab. maj.	....	5,585

(June '83, Lab. maj. 3,391)

WEST E. 57,526
*Rt. Hon. P. K. Archer, QC, Lab.	....	19,825
W. Williams, C.	....	14,432
Miss E. Todd, L./All.	.....	6,027
Lab. maj.	....	5,393

(June '83, Lab. maj. 5,268)

Warrington (Cheshire)

NORTH E. 75,627
*E. D. H. Hoyle, Lab.	......	27,422
L. Jones, C.	....	19,409
C. Bithel, SDP/All.	......	10,046
Lab. maj.	....	8,013

(June '83, Lab. maj. 5,277)

SOUTH E. 76,219
C. J. Butler, C.	....	24,809
A. Booth, Lab.	....	21,200
I. Marks, L./All.	....	13,112
C. maj.	....	3,609

(June '83, C. maj. 6,465)

Warwick and Leamington
E. 72,763
*Sir D. G. Smith, C.	......	27,530
K. P. O'Sullivan, SDP/All.		13,548
Ms. A. Christina, Lab.	....	13,019
Ms. J. A. Alty, Grn.	......	1,214
C. maj.	....	13,982

(June '83, C. maj. 13,032)

Warwickshire

NORTH E. 70,687
*Hon. F. A. A. Maude, C.	..	25,453
M. O'Brien, Lab.	....	22,624
Mrs. S. J. Neale, SDP/All.		8,382
C. maj.	....	2,829

(June '83, C. maj. 2,585)

Watford (Herts)
E. 73,540
*W. A. T. T. Garel-Jones, C.		27,912
M. J. Jackson, Lab.	......	16,176
Mrs. F. M. Beckett, SDP/All.	....	13,202
C. maj.	....	11,736

(June '83, C. maj. 12,006)

Waveney (Suffolk)
E. 81,889
D. J. Porter, C.	....	31,067
J. A. Lark, Lab.	....	19,284
D. Beaven, SDP/All.	.....	13,845
C. maj.	....	11,783

(June '83, C. maj. 14,298)

Wealden (E. Sussex)
E. 73,057
*Sir G. J. Johnson Smith, C.	....	35,154
D. Sinclair, SDP/All.	....	15,044
C. Ward, Lab.	....	4,563
C. maj.	....	20,110

(June '83, C. maj. 17,185)

Wellingborough (Northants)
E. 70,450
*P. D. Fry, C.	....	29,038
J. Currie, Lab.	....	14,968
L. E. Stringer, L./All.	....	11,047
C. maj.	....	14,070

(June '83, C. maj. 12,056)

Wells (Somerset)
E. 67,195
*D. P. Heathcoat-Amory, C.		28,624
A. A. S. Butt Philip, L./All.		20,083
P. James, Lab.	....	4,637
J. S. Fish, Falk.	....	134
C. maj.	....	8,541

(June '83, C. maj. 6,575)

Welwyn Hatfield (Herts)
E. 73,607
D. J. Evans, C.	....	27,164
Miss L. P. Granshaw, SDP/All.	....	16,261
C. R. Pond, Lab.	....	15,699
B. I. Dyson, Ind. C.	......	401
C. maj.	....	10,903

(June '83, C. maj. 12,246)

Wentworth (S. Yorks)
E. 63,886
*P. Hardy, Lab.	....	30,205
W. J. Hague, C.	....	10,113
D. M. Eglin, SDP/All.	....	6,031
Lab. maj.	....	20,092

(June '83, Lab. maj. 15,935)

West Bromwich (W. Midlands)

EAST E. 58,239
*P. C. Snape, Lab.	....	18,162
R. F. Woodhouse, C.	.....	17,179
M. G. Smith, L./All.	.....	7,268
Lab. maj.	....	983

(June '83, Lab. maj. 298)

WEST E. 58,944
*Miss B. Boothroyd, Lab.	..	19,925
F. A. Betteridge, C.	......	14,672
A. Collingbourne, SDP/All.	....	4,877
Lab. maj.	....	5,253

(June '83, Lab. maj. 6,639)

Westbury (Wilts)
E. 84,860
*D. M. Walters, MBE, C.	....	34,256
D. J. Hughes, L./All.	.....	24,159
H. W. Thomas, Lab.	......	7,982
C. maj.	....	10,097

(June '83, C. maj. 8,506)

Westminster North
(Gtr. London)
E. 59,263
*J. D. Wheeler, C.	....	19,941
Ms. J. F. Edwards, Lab.	..	16,631
R. J. De Ste Croix, SDP/All.	....	5,116
D. Stutchfield, Grn.	......	450
C. maj.	....	3,310

(June '83, C. maj. 1,710)

Westmorland and Lonsdale
(Cumbria)
E. 70,237
*Rt. Hon. T. M. Jopling, C.	..	30,259
S. Collins, L./All.	....	15,339
C. Halfpenny, Lab.	......	6,968
C. maj.	....	14,920

(June '83, C. maj. 16,587)

Weston-super-Mare (Avon)
E. 76,341
*A. W. Wiggin, TD, C.	.....	28,547
J. R. Crockford-Hawley, SDP/All.	....	20,549
P. J. Loach, Lab.	....	6,584
Dr. R. H. Lawson, Grn.	...	2,067
C. maj.	....	7,998

(June '83, C. maj. 9,491)

Wigan (Gtr. Manchester)
E. 72,064

*R. Stott, CBE, *Lab.*	....	33,955
K. R. Wade, *C.*	....	13,493
K. J. White, *L./All.*	....	7,732
Lab. maj.	....	20,462

(June '83, Lab. maj. 17,305)

Wiltshire North
E. 80,712

R. F. Needham, C.	....	35,309
C. S. M. Graham, *L./All.*	..	24,370
Mrs. C. Reid, *Lab.*	....	4,343
C. maj.	....	10,939

(June '83, C. maj. 7,232)

Wimbledon (Gtr. London)
E. 63,353

Dr. C. Goodson-Wickes, *C.*		24,538
A. C. Slade, *L./All.*	....	13,237
Ms. C. M. Bickerstaff, *Lab.*		10,428
C. maj.	....	11,301

(June '83, C. maj. 11,546)

Winchester (Hants)
E. 76,507

J. E. D. D. Browne, C.	....	32,195
J. L. MacDonald, *SDP/All.*		24,716
F. C. Inglis, *Lab.*	....	4,028
Ms. J. P. Walker, *Grn.*	....	565
C. maj.	....	7,479

(June '83, C. maj. 13,047)

Windsor and Maidenhead
(Berks)
E. 79,319

Dr. A. Glyn, ERD, C.	......	33,980
S. J. Jackson, *L./All.*	.....	16,144
Ms. H. B. De Lyon, *Lab.*	..	6,678
W. O. Board, *Ind. C.*	.....	1,938
P. Gordon, *Grn.*	....	711
Ms. P. H. Stephenson, *BT*		328
C. maj.	....	17,836

(June '83, C. maj. 18,203)

Wirral (Merseyside)

SOUTH E. 62,251

G. B. Porter, C.	....	24,821
J. S. Swarbrooke, *Lab.*	...	13,858
P. N. Gilchrist, *L./All.*	...	10,779
C. maj.	....	10,963

(June '83, C. maj. 13,838)

WEST E. 63,597

D. J. F. Hunt, MBE, C.	....	25,736
A. H. Dunn, *Lab.*	....	13,013
A. J. Brame, *L./All.*	......	10,015
D. Burton, *Grn.*	....	806
C. maj.	....	12,723

(June '83, C. maj. 15,151)

Witney (Oxon)
E. 75,284

*Rt. Hon. D. R. Hurd, CBE,		
C.	....	33,458
Miss M. E. Burton, *L./All.*		14,994
Ms. C. Collette, *Lab.*	.....	9,733
C. maj.	....	18,464

(June '83, C. maj. 12,712)

Woking (Surrey)
E. 82,476

C. G. D. Onslow, C.	......	35,990
P. Goldenberg, *L./All.*	....	19,446
Miss A. J. Pollack, *Lab.*	..	6,537
C. maj.	....	16,544

(June '83, C. maj. 16,237)

Wokingham (Berks)
E. 85,474

J. A. Redwood, *C.*	....	39,808
J. C. Leston, *L./All.*	......	19,421
P. J. Morgan, *Lab.*	....	5,622
C. maj.	....	20,387

(June '83, C. maj. 15,698)

Wolverhampton (W. Midlands)

NORTH EAST E. 63,464

Mrs. M. P. Hicks, *C.*	.....	19,857
K. Purchase, *Lab.*	....	19,653
M. Pearson, *L./All.*	......	7,623
C. maj.	....	204

(June '83, Lab. maj. 214)

SOUTH EAST E. 55,710

D. Turner, *Lab.*	....	19,760
J. P. Mellor, *C.*	....	13,362
R. F. Whitehouse, *L./All.*	.	7,258
Lab. maj.	....	6,398

(June '83, Lab. maj. 5,012)

SOUTH WEST E. 68,586

N. W. Budgen, C.	....	26,235
R. Lawrence, *Lab.*	....	15,917
B. Lamb, *SDP/All.*	....	9,616
C. maj.	....	10,318

(June '83, C. maj. 11,520)

Woodspring (Avon)
E. 76,289

Sir P. Dean, C.	....	34,134
Mrs. C. R. Coleman, *L./All.*		16,282
D. L. T. Chapple, *Lab.*	....	8,717
Dr. B. R. Keeble, *Grn.*	....	1,208
C. maj.	....	17,852

(June '83, C. maj. 15,132)

Woolwich (Gtr. London)
E. 58,071

J. C. Cartwright, SDP/All.		17,137
J. Austin Walker, *Lab.*	....	15,200
A. Salter, *C.*	....	8,723
SDP/All. maj.		1,937

(June '83, SDP/All. maj. 2,725)

Worcester
E. 68,980

*Rt. Hon. P. E. Walker, MBE,		
C.	....	25,504
M. J, Webb, *Lab.*	....	15,051
J. J. Caiger, *SDP/All.*	....	12,386
C. maj.	....	10,453

(June '83, C. maj. 10,871)

Worcestershire

MID E. 80,591

M. E. Forth, C.	....	31,854
P. Pinfield, *Lab.*	....	16,943
E. Harwood, *SDP/All.*	....	12,954
C. maj.	....	14,911

(June '83, C. maj. 14,205)

SOUTH E. 77,237

W. M. H. Spicer, C.	......	32,277
P. J. Chandler, *L./All.*	....	18,632
R. J. Garnett, *Lab.*	....	6,374
G. M. H. Woodford, *Grn.*	.	1,089
C. maj.	....	13,645

(June '83, C. maj. 11,389)

Workington (Cumbria)
E. 56,911

*D. N. Campbell-Savours,		
Lab.	....	24,019
Miss A. C. B. McIntosh, *C.*		17,000
G. W. Badger, *L./All.*	.....	4,853
Lab. maj.	....	7,019

(June '83, Lab. maj. 7,128)

Worsley (Gtr. Manchester)
E. 73,208

*T. Lewis, *Lab.*	....	27,157
Mrs. V. Horman, *C.*	......	19,820
D. Cowpe, *L./All.*	....	9,507
Lab. maj.	....	7,337

(June '83, Lab. maj. 4,139)

Worthing (W. Sussex)
E. 77,000

*Rt. Hon. T. L. Higgins, C.	.	34,573
B. A. Clare, *L./All.*	....	16,072
J. Deen, *Lab.*	....	5,387
C. maj.	....	18,501

(June '83, C. maj. 15,253)

The Wrekin (Salop)
E. 82,520

B. J. Grocott, *Lab.*	....	27,681
*P. W. Hawksley, *C.*	......	26,225
G. Cook, *SDP/All.*	....	10,737
Lab. maj.	....	1,456

(June '83, C. maj. 1,331)

Wycombe (Bucks)
E. 71,918

R. W. Whitney, OBE, C.	...	28,209
T. E. G. Hayhoe, *SDP/All.*		14,390
J. R. W. Huddart, *Lab.*	...	9,773
C. maj.	....	13,819

(June '83, C. maj. 13,197)

Wyre (Lancs)
E. 67,066

K. D. R. Mans, *C.*	....	26,800
I. C. Murdoch, *SDP/All.*	..	12,139
P. Ainscough, *Lab.*	......	10,725
R. Brown, *Grn.*	....	874
C. maj.	....	14,661

(June '83, C. maj. 14,811)

Wyre Forest (H & W)
E. 70,784

A. M. V. Coombs, *C.*	.....	25,877
A. J. Batchelor, *L./All.*	...	18,653
N. Knowles, *Lab.*	....	10,365
C. maj.	....	7,224

(June '83, C. maj. 8,177)

Yeovil (Somerset)
E. 70,390

J. J. D. Ashdown, L./All.	.	28,841
G. D. S. Sandeman, *C.*	....	23,141
J. Fitzmaurice, *Lab.*	......	4,099
L./All. maj.	....	5,700

(June '83, L./All. maj. 3,406)

York (N. Yorks)
E. 79,297

*C. R. Gregory, C.		25,880
H. Bayley, *Lab.*		25,733
J. V. Cable, *SDP/All.*		9,898
A. D. Dunnett, *Grn.*		637
C. maj.		147

(June '83, C. maj. 3,647)

WALES

Aberavon (W. Glam)
E. 52,280

*Rt. Hon. J. Morris, QC, *Lab.*	27,126
Mrs. M. Harris, *L./All.*		6,517
P. Warrick, *C.*		5,861
Miss A. Howells, *PC.*		1,124
Lab. maj.		20,609

(June '83, Lab. maj. 15,539)

Alyn and Deeside (Clwyd)
E. 58,674

*S. B. Jones, *Lab.*		22,916
N. J. Twilley, *C.*		16,500
E. C. H. Owen, *SDP/All.*		7,273
J. D. Rogers, *PC.*		478
Lab. maj.		6,416

(June '83, Lab. maj. 1,368)

Blaenau Gwent
E. 56,011

*Rt. Hon. M. M. Foot, *Lab.*		32,820
A. R. Taylor, *C.*		4,959
D. I. McBride, *L./All.*		3,847
S. Morgan, *PC.*		1,621
Lab. maj.		27,861

(June '83, Lab. maj. 23,705)

Brecon and Radnor (Powys)
E. 49,394

*R. A. L. Livsey, *L./All.*		14,509
J. P. Evans, *C.*		14,453
F. R. Willey, *Lab.*		12,180
J. H. Davies, *PC*		535
L./All. maj.		56

(June '83, C. maj. 8,784)
(July '84, L./All. maj. 559)

Bridgend (Mid Glam)
E. 57,389

W. J. Griffiths, *Lab.*		21,893
*P. C. Hubbard-Miles, *C.*		17,513
R. Smart, *SDP/All.*		5,590
Miss L. McAllister, *PC*		1,065
Lab. maj.		4,380

(June '83, C. maj. 1,327)

Caernarfon (Gwynedd)
E. 45,661

*D. W. Wigley, *PC.*		20,338
F. F. E. Aubel, *C.*		7,536
D. Rhys Williams, *Lab.*		5,632
J. H. Parsons, *L./All.*		2,103
PC maj.		12,802

(June '83, PC maj. 10,989)

Caerphilly (Mid Glam)
E. 64,154

*R. Davies, *Lab.*		28,698
M. E. Powell, *C.*		9,531
M. G. Butlin, *L./All.*		6,923
L. G. Whittle, *PC*		3,955
Lab. maj.		19,167

(June '83, Lab. maj. 11,553)

Cardiff (S. Glam)

CENTRAL E. 52,980

*I. Grist, *C.*		15,241
J. O. Jones, *Lab.*		13,255
M. J. German, *L./All.*		12,062
Ms. S. M. Caiach, *PC*		535
C. maj.		1,986

(June '83, C. maj. 3,452)

NORTH E. 54,704

*G. H. Jones, *C.*		20,061
S. H. Tarbet, *Lab.*		11,827
A. W. Jeremy, *SDP/All.*		11,725
Ms. E. M. Bush, *PC*		692
C. maj.		8,234

(June '83, C. maj. 6,848)

SOUTH AND PENARTH E. 58,714

A. E. Michael, *Lab.*		20,956
G. J. J. Neale, *C.*		16,382
Mrs. J. E. Randerson, *L./All.*		6,900
Ms. S. A. Edwards, *PC*		599
Lab. maj.		4,574

(June '83, Lab. maj. 2,276)

WEST E. 57,363

H. R. Morgan, *Lab.*		20,329
*S. Terlezki, *C.*		16,284
R. G. Drake, *SDP/All.*		7,300
P. J. Keelan, *PC*		736
Lab. maj.		4,045

(June '83, C. maj. 1,774)

Carmarthen (Dyfed)
E. 65,252

A. W. Williams, *Lab.*		19,128
R. Richards, *C.*		14,811
H. T. Edwards, *PC*		12,457
G. G. Jones, *SDP/All.*		7,203
G. E. Oubridge, *Grn.*		481
Lab. maj.		4,317

(June '83, Lab. maj. 1,154)

Ceredigion and Pembroke North
(Dyfed)
E. 63,141

*G. W. Howells, *L./All.*		17,683
O. J. Williams, *C.*		12,983
J. R. Davies, *Lab.*		8,965
C. G. Davis, *PC*		7,848
Mrs. M. A. Wakefield, *Grn.*		821
L./All. maj.		4,700

(June '83, L./All. maj. 5,639)

Clwyd

NORTH WEST E. 66,118

*Sir A. J. C. Meyer, Bt., *C.*	.	24,116
K. L. Thomas, *Lab.*		12,335
O. G. Griffiths, *L./All.*		11,279
R. K. Davies, *PC*		1,966
C. maj.		11,781

(June '83, C. maj. 9,989)

SOUTH WEST E. 58,158

M. D. Jones, *Lab.*		16,701
*R. L. Harvey, *C.*		15,673
R. T. Ellis, *SDP/All.*		10,778
E. L. Jones, *PC*		3,987
Lab. maj.		1,028

(June '83, C. maj. 1,551)

Conwy (Gwynedd)
E. 52,862

*I. W. P. Roberts, *C.*		15,730
J. R. Roberts, *L./All.*		12,706
Ms. E. Williams, *Lab.*		9,049
R. Davies, *PC*		3,177
C. maj.		3,024

(June '83, C. maj. 4,268)

Cynon Valley (Mid Glam)
E. 49,621

*Mrs. A. Clwyd, *Lab.*		26,222
K. D. Butler, *SDP/All.*		4,651
M. A. Bishop, *C.*		4,638
Mrs. D. L. Richards, *PC*	.	2,549
Lab. maj.		21,571

(June '83, Lab. maj. 13,074)
(May '84, Lab. maj. 12,835)

Delyn (Clwyd)
E. 63,541

*K. W. T. Raffan, *C.*		21,728
D. G. Hanson, *Lab.*		20,504
D. J. Evans, *L./All.*		8,913
D. J. Owen, *PC*		1,329
C. maj.		1,224

(June '83, C. maj. 5,944)

Gower (W. Glam)
E. 58,871

*G. L. Wardell, *Lab.*		22,138
G. A. L. Price, *C.*		16,374
D. H. O. Elliott, *SDP/All.*		7,645
J. G. M. Edwards, *PC*		1,341
Lab. maj.		5,764

(June '83, Lab. maj. 1,205)

Islwyn (Gwent)
E. 50,414

*Rt. Hon. N. G. Kinnock, *Lab.*		28,901
J. Twitchen, *C.*		5,954
Ms. J. Gasson, *SDP/All.*		3,746
A. Richards, *PC*		1,932
Lab. maj.		22,947

(June '83, Lab. maj. 14,380)

Llanelli (Dyfed)
E. 63,845

*Rt. Hon. D. J. D. Davies, *Lab.*		29,506
P. J. Circus, *C.*		8,571
M. J. Shrewsbury, *L./All.*	.	6,714
A. Price, *PC*		5,088
Lab. maj.		20,935

(June '83, Lab. maj. 13,606)

Meirionnydd Nant Conwy
(Gwynedd)
E. 31,632

*D. E. Thomas, *PC*		10,392
D. T. Jones, *C.*		7,366
H. G. Roberts, *Lab.*		4,397
D. L. Roberts, *SDP/All.*		3,847
PC maj.		3,026

(June '83, PC maj. 2,643)

Merthyr Tydfil and Rhymney
(Mid Glam)
E. 58,285

*E. Rowlands, Lab.	....	33,400
N. M. Walters, *C.*	....	5,270
P. Verma, *L./All.*	....	3,573
Mrs. J. Davies, *PC*	....	2,085
Lab. maj.	....	28,130

(June '83, Lab. maj. 22,730)

Monmouth (Gwent)
E. 58,468

*Sir J. Stradling Thomas, C.		22,387
Ms. K. Gass, *Lab.*	....	13,037
C. Lindley, *SDP/All.*	....	11,313
Mrs. S. Meredudd, *PC*	....	363
C. maj.	....	9,350

(June '83, C. maj. 9,343)

Montgomery (Powys)
E. 39,808

*A. C. Carlile, QC L./All.	....	14,729
D.M. Evans, *C.*	....	12,171
E. D. W. Llewellyn Jones,		
Lab.	....	3,304
C. Clowes, *PC*	....	1,412
L./All. maj.	....	2,558

(June '83, L./All. maj. 668)

Neath (W. Glam)
E. 55,261

*D. R. Coleman, Lab.	.....	27,612
M. R. T. Howe, *C.*	....	7,034
J. Warman, *SDP/All.*	....	6,132
H. John, *PC*	....	2,792
Lab. maj.	....	20,578

(June '83, Lab. maj. 13,604)

Newport (Gwent)

EAST *E.* 52,199

*R. J. Hughes, Lab.	....	20,518
G. R. Webster-Gardiner, *C.*		13,454
Mrs. F. A. David, *SDP/All.*		7,383
G. Butler, *PC*	....	458
Lab. maj.	....	7,064

(June '83, Lab. maj. 2,630)

WEST *E.* 55,455

P. P. Flynn, *Lab.*	....	20,887
*M. N. F. Robinson, C.	.....	18,179
G. W. Roddick, *L./All.*	....	5,903
D. J. Bevan, *PC*	....	377
Lab. maj.	....	2,708

(June '83, C. maj. 581)

Ogmore (Mid Glam)
E. 51,255

*R. Powell, Lab.	....	28,462
M. F. Barratt, *C.*	....	6,170
Ms. M. James, *SDP/All.*	....	3,954
J. G. Jones, *PC*	....	1,791
T. H. Spence, *Ind. Lab.*	...	652
Lab. maj.	....	22,292

(June '83, Lab. maj. 17,364)

Pembroke (Dyfed)
E. 70,360

N. J. Bennett, *C.*	....	23,314
B. J. Rayner, *Lab.*	....	17,614
P. E. C. Jones, *L./All.*	....	14,832
O. Osmond, *PC*	....	1,119
C. maj.	....	5,700

(June '83, C. maj. 9,356)

Pontypridd (Mid Glam)
E. 61,255

*B. T. John, Lab.	....	26,422
D. Swayne, *C.*	....	9,145
P. G. Sain-Ley-Berry, *SDP/*		
All.	....	8,865
D. L. Bowen, *PC*	....	2,498
Lab. maj.	....	17,277

(June '83, Lab. maj. 8,744)
(See also p. 276)

Rhondda (Mid Glam)
E. 60,931

*A. R. Rogers, Lab.	....	35,015
G. R. Davies, *PC*	....	4,261
J. R. YorkWilliams, *SDP/*		
All.	....	3,930
S. H. Reid, *C.*	....	3,611
A. True, *Comm.*	....	869
Lab. maj.	....	30,754

(June '83, Lab. maj. 21,370)

Swansea (W. Glam)

EAST *E.* 57,200

*D. Anderson, Lab.	....	27,478
R. D. Lewis, *C.*	....	8,140
Rev. D. W. Thomas, *L./All.*		6,380
C. Reid, *PC*	....	1,145
Lab. maj.	....	19,338

(June '83, Lab. maj. 13,535)

WEST *E.* 59,836

*Rt. Hon. A. J. Williams,		
Lab.	....	22,089
N. M. Evans, *C.*	....	15,027
M. Ford, *L./All.*	....	7,019
N. Williams, *PC*	....	902
Mrs. J. V. Harman, *Grn.*	..	469
Lab. maj.	....	7,062

(June '83, Lab. maj. 2,350)

Torfaen (Gwent)
E. 59,896

P. P. Murphy, *Lab.*	......	26,577
G. R. Blackburn, *L./All.*	..	9,027
R. Gordon, *C.*	....	8,632
J. Evans, *PC*	....	577
M. Witherden, *Grn.*	....	450
Lab. maj.	....	17,550

(June '83, Lab. maj. 8,285)

Vale of Glamorgan (S. Glam)
E. 65,310

*Sir H. R. Gower, C.	......	24,229
J. W. P. Smith, *Lab.*	......	17,978
D. K. Davies, *SDP/All.*	...	8,633
P. G. Williams, *PC*	......	946
C. maj.	....	6,251

(June '83, C. maj. 10,393)
(See also p. 276)

Wrexham (Clwyd)
E. 62,401

*Dr. J. C. Marek, Lab.	....	22,144
R. H. W. Graham-Palmer,		
C.	....	17,992
M. Thomas, *L./All.*	......	9,808
D. Watkins, *PC*	....	539
Lab. maj.	....	4,152

(June '83, Lab. maj. 424)

Ynys Môn/Anglesey
(Gwynedd)
E. 52,633

I. W. Jones, PC	....	18,580
R. Evans, *C.*	....	14,282
C. Parry, *Lab.*	....	7,252
I. L. Evans, *SDP/All.*	.....	2,863
PC maj.	....	4,298

(June '83, C. maj. 1,684)

SCOTLAND

Aberdeen (Grampian)

NORTH *E.* 63,214

*R. Hughes, Lab.	....	24,145
R. Smith, *SDP/All.*	......	7,867
Mrs. G. E. C. Scanlan, *C.*	..	6,330
P. Greenhorn, *SNP*	......	5,827
Lab. maj.	....	16,278

(June '83, Lab. maj. 9,144)

SOUTH *E.* 62,943

F. Doran, *Lab.*	....	15,917
*G. P. Malone, C.	....	14,719
I. G. Philip, *SDP/All.*	.....	8,844
M. F. Weir, *SNP*	....	2,776
Lab. maj.	....	1,198

(June '83, C. maj. 3,581)

Angus East (Tayside)
E. 61,060

A. Welsh, *SNP*	....	19,536
*P. L. Fraser, QC, C.	....	17,992
R. Mennie, *Lab.*	....	4,971
I. Mortimer, *SDP/All.*	.....	3,592
SNP maj.	....	1,544

(June '83, C. maj. 3,527)

Argyll and Bute (S'clyde)
E. 48,700

Mrs. J. R. Michie, *L./All.*	.	13,726
*J. J. MacKay, C.	....	12,332
R. Shaw, *SNP*	....	6,297
D. Tierney, *Lab.*	....	4,437
L./All. maj.	....	1,394

(June '83, C. maj. 3,844)

Ayr (S'clyde)
E. 66,450

*Rt. Hon. G. K. H. Younger,		
TD, *C.*	....	20,942
K. MacDonald, *Lab.*	.....	20,760
K. M. Moody, *L./All.*	.....	7,859
C. Weir, *SNP*	....	3,548
C. maj.	....	182

(June '83, C. maj. 7,987)

Banff and Buchan (Grampian)
E. 62,149

A. E. A. Salmond, *SNP*	..	19,462
*A. McQuarrie, C.	....	17,021
G. M. Burness, *SDP/All.*	...	4,211
J. Livie, *Lab.*	....	3,281
SNP maj.	....	2,441

(June '83, C. maj. 937)

Caithness and Sutherland
(H'land)
E. 31,279

*R. A. R. Maclennan, SDP/
All. 12,338
R. L. Hamilton, *C.* 3,844
A. Byron, *Lab.* 3,437
K. MacGregor, *SNP* 2,371
W. A. Mowat, *Ind. L.* 686
B. Planterose, *Grn.* 333
SDP/All. maj. 8,494
(June '83, SDP/All. maj. 6,843)

Carrick, Cumnock and Doon
Valley (S'clyde)
E. 56,360

*G. Foulkes, Lab. 25,669
S. Stevenson, *C.* 8,867
Mrs. M. Ali, *SDP/All.* 4,106
C. D. Calman, *SNP* 4,094
Lab. maj. 16,802
(June '83, Lab. maj. 11,370)

Clackmannan (Central)
E. 49,083

*M. J. O'Neill, Lab. 20,317
Dr. A. Macartney, *SNP* .. 7,916
J. Parker, *C.* 5,620
Mrs. A. Watters, *SDP/All.* 3,961
Lab. maj. 12,401
(June '83, Lab. maj. 9,639)

Clydebank and Milngavie
(S'clyde)
E. 50,152

A. Worthington, *Lab.* 22,528
K. Hirstwood, *C.* 6,224
R. Ackland, *SDP/All.* 5,891
S. Fisher, *SNP* 4,935
Lab. maj. 16,304
(June '83, Lab. maj. 7,715)

Clydesdale (S'clyde)
E. 61,620

J. Hood, *Lab.* 21,826
R. Robertson, *C.* 11,324
J. Boyle, *SDP/All.* 7,909
M. Russell, *SNP* 7,125
Lab. maj. 10,502
(June '83, Lab. maj. 4,866)

Cumbernauld and Kilsyth
(S'clyde)
E. 45,427

*N. Hogg, Lab. 21,385
T. Johnston, *SNP* 6,982
C. S. Deans, *SDP/All.* 4,059
Mrs. A. E. Thomson, *C.* ... 3,227
Lab. maj. 14,403
(June '83, Lab. maj. 9,928)

Cunninghame (S'clyde)

NORTH *E.* 54,817
B. D. H. Wilson, *Lab.* 19,061
*J. A. Corrie, C. 14,594
D. J. Herbison, *SDP/All.* 5,185
M. Brown, *SNP* 4,076
Lab. maj. 4,467
(June '83, C. maj. 1,637)

SOUTH *E.* 49,842
*D. Lambie, Lab. 22,728
E. R. Gibson, *C.* 6,095
J. A. Boss, *L./All.* 4,426
Mrs. K. Ullrich, *SNP* 4,115
Lab. maj. 16,633
(June '83, Lab. maj. 11,768)

Dumbarton (S'clyde)
E. 58,968

J. McFall, *Lab.* 19,778
R. F. Graham, *C.* 14,556
R. Mowbray, *SDP/All.* ... 6,060
Ms. J. Herriot, *SNP* 5,564
Lab. maj. 5,222
(June '83, Lab. maj. 2,115)

Dumfries (D & G)
E. 59,347

*Sir H. S. P. Monro, C. 18,785
Ms. C. W. Phillips, *Lab.* ... 11,292
J. R. McCall, *SDP/All.* 8,064
T. McAlpine, *SNP* 6,391
P. M. Thomas, *Grn.* 349
C. maj. 7,493
(June '83, C. maj. 8,694)

Dundee (Tayside)

EAST *E.* 60,805
J. McAllion, *Lab.* 19,539
*R. G. Wilson, SNP 18,524
P. Cook, *C.* 5,938
Mrs. M. von Romberg, *L./*
All. 2,143
Lab. maj. 1,015
(June '83, SNP maj. 5,016)

WEST *E.* 61,926
*E. Ross, Lab. 24,916
J. A. Donnelly, *C.* 8,390
A. N. Morgan, *SNP* 7,164
Ms. R. Lonie, *SDP/All.* ... 5,922
S. R. Mathewson, *Comm.* . 308
Lab. maj. 16,526
(June '83, Lab. maj. 10,150)

Dunfermline (Fife)

EAST *E.* 51,175
*Dr. J. G. Brown, Lab. 25,381
C. Shenton, *C.* 5,792
Ms. E. Harris, *L./All.* 4,122
Mrs. A. McGarny, *SNP* .. 3,901
Lab. maj. 19,589
(June '83, Lab. maj. 11,301)

WEST *E.* 51,063
*R. G. Douglas, Lab. 18,493
P. R. Gallie, *C.* 9,091
F. A. Moyes, *SDP/All.* 8,288
G. Hughes, *SNP* 3,435
Lab. maj. 9,402
(June '83, Lab. maj. 2,474)

East Kilbride (S'clyde)
E. 63,097

A. P. Ingram, *Lab.* 24,491
D. R. E. Sullivan, *SDP/All.* 11,867
P. M. Walker, *C.* 7,344
J. H. Taggart, *SNP* 6,275
Lab. maj. 12,624
(June '83, Lab. maj. 4,336)

East Lothian
E. 65,046

*J. D. Home Robertson,
Lab. 24,583
S. M. Langdon, *C.* 14,478
A. Robinson, *L./All.* 7,929
A. Burgon-Lyon, *SNP* ... 3,727
A. Marland, *Grn.* 451
Lab. maj. 10,105
(June '83, Lab. maj. 6,241)

Eastwood (S'clyde)
E. 61,872

*J. A. Stewart, C. 19,388
R. Leishman, *SDP/All.* ... 13,374
P. A. Grant-Hutchison,
Lab. 12,305
J. Findlay, *SNP* 4,033
C. maj. 6,014
(June '83, C. maj. 8,595)

Edinburgh (Lothian)

CENTRAL *E.* 59,529
A. M. Darling, *Lab.* 16,502
*Sir A. Fletcher, C. 14,240
A. Myles, *L./All.* 7,333
B. Shaw, *SNP* 2,559
Mrs. L. M. Hendry, *Grn.* . 438
Lab. maj. 2,262
(June '83, Lab. maj. 2,566)

EAST *E.* 48,895
*G. S. Strang, Lab. 18,257
J. F. Renz, *C.* 8,962
Mrs. J. Aitken, *L./All.* ... 5,592
M. Bovey, *SNP* 3,434
Lab. maj. 9,295
(June '83, Lab. maj. 5,866)

LEITH *E.* 60,359
*R. D. M. Brown, Lab. 21,104
D. A. Y. Menzies, *C.* 9,777
Mrs. S. Wells, *SDP/All.* .. 7,843
W. Morrison, *SNP* 4,045
Lab. maj. 11,327
(June '83, Lab. maj. 4,973)

PENTLANDS *E.* 58,125
*Rt. Hon. M. L. Rifkind, QC,
C. 17,278
M. Lazarowicz, *Lab.* 13,533
K. A. Smith, *SDP/All.* 11,072
D. N. MacCormick, *SNP* .. 3,264
C. maj. 3,745
(June '83, C. maj. 4,309)

SOUTH *E.* 63,842
N. Griffiths, *Lab.* 18,211
*M. A. F. J. K. Ancram (Earl
of Ancram), *C.* 16,352
D. A. Graham, *SDP/All.* .. 10,900
Mrs. R. Moore, *SNP* 2,455
Mrs. R. Clark, *Grn.* 440
Lab. maj. 1,859
(June '83, C. maj. 3,655)

WEST *E.* 62,214
*Lord James Douglas-Ham-
ilton, *C.* 18,450
D. G. King, *L./All.* 17,216
M. McGregor, *Lab.* 10,957
N. Irons, *SNP* 2,774
C. maj. 1,234
(June '83, C. maj. 498)

Falkirk (Central)

EAST *E.* 52,564
* *H. Ewing, *Lab.* 21,379
* K. H. Brookes, *C.* 7,356
* R. N. F. Halliday, *SNP* ... 6,056
* Mrs. E. G. Dick, *SDP/All.* .. 4,624
  * *Lab. maj.* 14,023
  * (June '83, Lab. maj. 10,061)

WEST *E.* 50,222
* *D. A. Canavan, *Lab.* 20,256
* D. R. D. Thomas, *C.* 6,704
* I. R. Goldie, *SNP* 6,696
* M. J. Harris, *L./All.* 4,841
  * *Lab. maj.* 13,552
  * (June '83, Lab. maj. 8,978)

Fife

CENTRAL *E.* 56,090
* H. B. McLeish, *Lab.* 22,827
* R. E. Aird, *C.* 7,118
* Mrs. T. M. Little, *L./All.* .. 6,487
* D. Hood, *SNP* 6,296
  * *Lab. maj.* 15,709
  * (June '83, Lab. maj. 7,794)

NORTH EAST *E.* 52,266
* W. M. Campbell, CBE, QC,
  L./All. 17,868
* *J. S. B. Henderson, *C.* 16,421
* A. M. E. Gannon, *Lab.* ... 2,947
* F. D. Roche, *SNP* 2,616
  * *L./All. maj.* 1,447
  * (June '83, C. maj. 2,185)

Galloway and Upper Nithsdale
(D & G)
E. 53,429
* *I. B. Lang, *C.* 16,592
* S. F. Norris, *SNP* 12,919
* J. McKercher, *L./All.* 6,001
* J. Gray, *Lab.* 5,298
* D. Kenny, *Ret.* 230
  * *C. maj.* 3,673
  * (June '83, C. maj. 5,461)

Glasgow (S'clyde)

CATHCART *E.* 49,307
* *J. A. Maxton, *Lab.* 19,623
* W. A. Harvey, *C.* 8,420
* Miss M. Craig, *SDP/All.* ... 5,722
* W. A. Steven, *SNP* 3,883
  * *Lab. maj.* 11,203
  * (June '83, Lab. maj. 4,230)

CENTRAL *E.* 51,137
* *R. McTaggart, *Lab.* 21,619
* B. Jenkin, *C.* 4,366
* Dr. J. Bryden, *L./All.* 3,528
* A. Wilson, *SNP* 3,339
* A. Brooks, *Grn.* 290
* J. P. McGoldrick, *Comm.* .. 265
* D. Owen, *RF* 126
  * *Lab. maj.* 17,253
  * (June '83, Lab. maj. 10,962)
  * (*See also* p. 276)

GARSCADDEN *E.* 47,958
* *D. C. Dewar, *Lab.* 23,178
* A. Brophy, *SNP* 4,201
* T. N. A. Begg, *C.* 3,660
* S. Callison, *SDP/All.* 3,211
  * *Lab. maj.* 18,977
  * (June '83, Lab. maj. 13,474)

GOVAN *E.* 50,616
* *Rt. Hon. B. Millan, *Lab.* .. 24,071
* A. Ferguson, *SDP/All.* 4,562
* Mrs. J. R. Girsman, *C.* 4,411
* F. McCabe, *SNP* 3,851
* D. Chalmers, *Comm.* 237
  * *Lab. maj.* 19,509
  * (June '83, Lab. maj. 13,057)
  * (*See also* p. 275)

HILLHEAD *E.* 57,836
* G. Galloway, *Lab.* 17,958
* *Rt Hon. R. H. Jenkins,
  SDP/All. 14,707
* B. D. Cooklin, *C.* 6,048
* W. Kidd, *SNP* 2,713
* A. Whitelaw, *Grn.* 443
  * *Lab. maj.* 3,251
  * (June '83, SDP/All. maj. 1,164)

MARYHILL *E.* 52,371
* Mrs. M. Fyfe, *Lab.* 23,482
* Miss E. M. A. Attwooll, *L./
  All.* 4,118
* G. Roberts, *SNP* 3,895
* S. R. R. Kirk, *C.* 3,307
* D. Spaven, *Grn.* 539
  * *Lab. maj.* 19,364
  * (June '83, Lab. maj. 11,203)

POLLOK *E.* 51,396
* J. Dunnachie, *Lab.* 23,239
* Mrs. G. French, *C.* 5,256
* J. Shearer, *L./All.* 4,445
* A. Doig, *SNP* 3,528
* D. Fogg, *Grn.* 362
  * *Lab. maj.* 17,983
  * (June '83, Lab. maj. 11,532)

PROVAN *E.* 43,744
* J. Wray, *Lab.* 22,032
* W. Ramsay, *SNP* 3,660
* Miss A. Strutt, *C.* 2,336
* J. Morrison, *SDP/All.* 2,189
  * *Lab. maj.* 18,372
  * (June '83, Lab. maj. 15,385)

RUTHERGLEN *E.* 57,313
* T. McAvoy, *Lab.* 24,790
* R. E. Brown, *L./All.* 10,795
* G. Hamilton, *C.* 5,088
* J. Higgins, *SNP* 3,584
  * *Lab. maj.* 13,995
  * (June '83, Lab. maj. 9,126)

SHETTLESTON *E.* 53,604
* *D. Marshall, *Lab.* 23,991
* J. M. S. Fisher, *C.* 5,010
* J. MacVicar, *SNP* 4,807
* Miss P. Clarke, *L./All.* 3,942
  * *Lab. maj.* 18,981
  * (June '83, Lab. maj. 12,416)

SPRINGBURN *E.* 51,563
* *M. J. Martin, *Lab.* 25,617
* B. O'Hara, *SNP* 3,554
* M. Call, *C.* 2,870
* D. Rennie, *L./All.* 2,746
  * *Lab. maj.* 22,063
  * (June '83, Lab. maj. 17,599)

Gordon (Grampian)
E. 73,479
* *M. G. Bruce, *L./All.* 26,770
* P. R. Leckie, *C.* 17,251
* Mrs. M. C. Morrell, *Lab.* .. 6,228
* G. E. Wright, *SNP* 3,876
  * *L./All. maj.* 9,519
  * (June '83, L./All. maj. 850)

Greenock and Port Glasgow
(S'clyde)
E. 57,756
* *Dr. N. A. Godman, *Lab.* .. 27,848
* J. H. Moody, *L./All.* 7,793
* T. J. D. Pearson, *C.* 4,199
* T. Lenehan, *SNP* 3,021
  * *Lab. maj.* 20,055
  * (June '83, Lab. maj. 4,625)

Hamilton (S'clyde)
E. 62,205
* *G. I. M. Robertson, *Lab.* .. 28,563
* G. S. Mond, *C.* 6,901
* T. Mackay, *L./All.* 6,302
* C. Crossley, *SNP* 6,093
  * *Lab. maj.* 21,662
  * (June '83, Lab. maj. 15,019)

Inverness, Nairn and Lochaber
(H'land)
E. 66,743
* *Sir D. R. Johnston, *L./All.* 17,422
* D. Stewart, *Lab.* 11,991
* Mrs. A. T. Keswick, *C.* ... 10,901
* N. P. Johnson, *SNP* 7,001
  * *L./All. maj.* 5,431
  * (June '83, L./All. maj. 7,298)

Kilmarnock and Loudoun
(Grampian)
E. 62,648
* *W. McKelvey, *Lab.* 23,713
* Mrs. A. K. Bates, *C.* 9,586
* G. Leslie, *SNP* 8,881
* P. Kerr, *SDP/All.* 6,698
  * *Lab. maj.* 14,127
  * (June '83, Lab. maj. 8,800)

Kincardine and Deeside
(Grampian)
E. 63,587
* *Rt. Hon. A. L. Buchanan-
  Smith, *C.* 19,438
* N. R. Stephen, *L./All.* 17,375
* J. K. Thomaneck, *Lab.* ... 7,624
* Mrs. F. E. Duncan, *SNP* .. 3,082
* Mrs. L. M. Perica, *Grn.* ... 299
  * *C. maj.* 2,063
  * (June '83, C. maj. 7,796)

Kirkcaldy (Fife)
E. 53,439
* Dr. L. G. Moonie, *Lab.* ... 20,281
* I. G. Mitchell, *C.* 8,711
* D. Stewart, *SDP/All.* 7,118
* W. A. R. Mullin, *SNP* 4,794
  * *Lab. maj.* 11,570
  * (June '83, Lab. maj. 5,331)

Linlithgow (Lothian)
E. 59,542

*T. Dalyell, *Lab.*	21,869
J. Sillars, *SNP*	11,496
T. R. Armstrong Wilson, *C.*	6,828
Mrs. H. McDade, *SDP/All.*	5,840
J. Glassford, *Comm.*	154
Lab. maj.	10,373
(June '83, Lab. maj. 11,361)	

Livingston (Lothian)
E. 56,583

*R. F. Cook, *Lab.*	19,110
R. McCreadle, *L./All.*	8,005
Dr. M. N. A. Mayall, *C.*	7,860
K. MacAskill, *SNP*	6,959
Lab. maj.	11,105
(June '83, Lab. maj. 4,951)	

Midlothian
E. 60,549

*A. Eadie, bem, *Lab.*	22,553
A. R. Dewar, *SDP/All.*	10,300
Dr. F. Riddell, *C.*	8,527
I. Chisholm, *SNP*	4,947
I. Smith, *Grn.*	412
Lab. maj.	12,253
(June '83, Lab. maj. 6,156)	

Monklands (S'clyde)
E. 49,644

*Rt. Hon. J. Smith, qc, *Lab.*	22,649
J. Love, *C.*	6,260
K. Gibson, *SNP*	4,790
Mrs. S. Grieve, *L./All.*	3,442
Lab. maj.	16,389
(June '83, Lab. maj. 9,799)	

West *E.* 50,874

*T. Clarke, cbe, *Lab.*	24,499
G. Lind, *C.*	6,166
Ms. A. McQueen, *SDP/All.*	4,408
K. Bovey, *SNP*	4,260
Lab. maj.	18,333
(June '83, Lab. maj. 12,264)	

Moray (Grampian)
E. 62,201

Mrs. M. Ewing, *SNP*	19,510
*A. Pollock, *C.*	15,825
C. R. C. Smith, *Lab.*	5,118
D. G. M. Skene, *L./All.*	4,724
SNP maj.	3,685
(June '83, C. maj. 1,713)	

Motherwell (S'clyde)
North *E.* 57,632

Dr. J. Reid, *Lab.*	29,825
A. Currie, *SNP*	6,230
R. Hargrave, *C.*	4,939
G. Swift, *L./All.*	3,558
Lab. maj.	23,595
(June '83, Lab. maj. 17,894)	

South *E.* 52,127

*Dr. J. W. Bray, *Lab.*	22,957
J. Wright, *SNP*	6,027
J. S. Bercow, *C.*	5,702
W. R. MacGregor, *SDP/All.*	4,463
R. Somerville, *Comm.*	223
Lab. maj.	16,930
(June '83, Lab. maj. 12,349)	

Orkney and Shetland
E. 31,047

*J. R. Wallace, *L./All.*	8,881
R. W. A. Jenkins, *C.*	4,959
J. H. Aberdein, *Lab.*	3,995
J. Goodlad, *OSM*	3,095
G. K. Collister, *Grn.*	389
L./All. maj.	3,922
(June '83, L./All. maj. 4,150)	

Paisley (S'clyde)
North *E.* 49,487

*A. S. Adams, *Lab.*	20,193
Mrs. E. F. Laing, *C.*	5,751
Miss E. P. McCartin, *SDP/All.*	5,741
I. Taylor *SNP*	4,696
Lab. maj.	14,442
(June '83, Lab. maj. 7,587)	

South *E.* 51,127

*N. F. Buchan, *Lab.*	21,611
A. M. Carmichael, *L./All.*	5,826
Miss D. A. Williamson, *C.*	5,644
J. R. Mitchell, *SNP*	5,398
Lab. maj.	15,785
(June '83, Lab. maj. 6,529)	

Perth and Kinross (Tayside)
E. 63,443

*N. H. Fairbairn, qc, *C.*	18,716
J. M. Fairlie, *SNP*	13,040
S. Donaldson, *L./All.*	7,969
J. W. McConnell, *Lab.*	7,490
C. maj.	5,676
(June '83, C. maj. 6,733)	

Renfrew West and Inverclyde (S'clyde)
E. 56,189

T. Graham, *Lab.*	17,525
*Mrs. A. A. McCurley, *C.*	13,472
Dr. J. D. Mabon, *SDP/All.*	9,669
C. Campbell, *SNP*	4,578
Lab. maj.	4,053
(June '83, C. maj. 1,322)	

Ross, Cromarty and Skye (H'land)
E. 52,369

*C. P. Kennedy, *SDP/All.*	18,809
F. Spencer Nairn, *C.*	7,490
M. M. MacMillan, *Lab.*	7,287
R. M. Gibson, *SNP*	4,492
S.D.P./All. maj.	11,319
(June '83 SDP/All. maj. 1,704)	

Roxburgh and Berwickshire (Borders)
E. 43,140

*A. J. Kirkwood, *L./All.*	16,388
Dr. L. Fox, *C.*	12,380
T. Luckhurst, *Lab.*	2,944
M. Douglas, *SNP*	1,586
L./All. maj.	4,008
(June '83, L./All. maj. 3,396)	

Stirling (Central)
E. 57,836

*M. B. Forsyth, *C.*	17,591
M. Connarty, *Lab.*	16,643
I. McFarlane, *L./All.*	6,804
I. M. Lawson, *SNP*	4,897
C. maj.	948
(June '83, C. maj. 5,133)	

Strathkelvin and Bearsden (S'clyde)
E. 62,676

S. L. Galbraith, *Lab.*	19,639
*M. W. Hirst, *C.*	17,187
J. Bannerman, *L./All.*	11,034
G. Paterson, *SNP*	3,654
Lab. maj.	2,452
(June '83, C. maj. 3,700)	

Tayside North
E. 53,985

*W. C. Walker, *C.*	18,307
K. J. N. Guild, *SNP*	13,291
P. F. Regent, *L./All.*	5,201
J. Whytock, *Lab.*	3,550
C. maj.	5,016
(June '83, C. maj. 10,099)	

Tweeddale, Ettrick and Lauderdale (Borders)
E. 37,875

*Rt. Hon. D. M. S. Steel, *L./All.*	14,599
Mrs. S. Finlay-Maxwell, *C.*	8,657
N. Glen, *Lab.*	3,320
A. Lumsden, *SNP*	2,660
L./All. maj.	5,942
(June '83, L./All. maj. 8,539)	

Western Isles
E. 23,507

C. A. MacDonald, *Lab.*	7,041
I. Smith, *SNP*	4,701
K. MacIver, *SDP/All.*	3,419
M. Morrison, *C.*	1,336
Lab. maj.	2,340
(June '83 SNP maj. 3,712)	

NORTHERN IRELAND

Antrim
East *E.* 60,587

*J. R. Beggs, *OUP*	23,942
S. Neeson, *All.*	8,582
A. Kelly, *WP*	936
OUP maj.	15,360
(June '83, OUP maj. 367)	
(Jan. '86, OUP maj. 24,981)	

North *E.* 65,733

*Rev. I. R. K. Paisley, *DUP*	28,383
S. Farren, *SDLP*	5,149
G. Williams, *All.*	5,140
S. Reagan, *SF*	2,633
DUP maj.	23,234
(June '83, DUP maj. 13,173)	
(Jan. '86, DUP maj. 33,024)	

South *E.* 61,649

*C. Forsythe, *OUP*	25,395
G. Mawhinney, *All.*	5,808
D. McClelland, *SDLP*	3,611
H. Cushinan, *SF*	1,592
OUP maj.	19,587
(June '83, OUP maj. 6,792)	
(Jan. '86, OUP maj. 28,217)	

Belfast

EAST *E.* 54,628
*P. D. Robinson, DUP 20,372
Dr. J. Alderdice, *All.* 10,574
F. Cullen, *WP* 1,314
J. O'Donnell, *SF* 649
   DUP maj. 9,798
   (June '83, DUP maj. 7,989)
   (Jan. '86, DUP maj. 21,690)

NORTH *E.* 59,124
*A. C. Walker, OUP 14,355
A. Maginness, *SDLP* 5,795
G. Seawright, *Prot. U.* ... 5,671
P. McManus, *SF* 5,062
S. Lynch, *WP* 3,062
T. Campbell, *All.* 2,871
   OUP maj. 8,560
   (June '83, OUP maj. 7,079)
   (Jan. '86, OUP maj. 16,577)

SOUTH *E.* 54,208
*Rev. W. M. Smyth, OUP 18,917
D. Cook, *All.* 6,963
Dr. A. McDonnell, *SDLP* 4,268
G. Carr, *WP* 1,528
S. McKnight, *SF* 1,030
   OUP maj. 11,954
   (June '83, OUP maj. 9,724)
   (Jan. '86, OUP maj. 14,136)

WEST *E.* 59,324
*G. Adams, SF 16,862
Dr. J. G. Hendron, *SDLP* 14,641
F. Miller, *OUP* 7,646
Mrs. M. McMahon, *WP* .. 1,819
   SF maj. 2,221
   (June '83, SF maj. 5,445)

Down

NORTH *E.* 65,018
*J. A. Kilfedder, UPUP ... 18,420
R. McCartney, *Real U.* ... 14,467
J. Cushnahan, *All.* 7,932
   UPUP maj. 3,953
   (June '83, UPUP maj. 13,846)
   (Jan. '86, UPUP maj. 22,727)

SOUTH *E.* 71,235
E. K. McGrady, *SDLP* ... 26,579
*Rt. Hon. J. E. Powell, MBE,
  OUP 25,848
Ms. G. Ritchie, *SF* 2,363
Miss S. E. Laird, *All.* 1,069
D. O'Hagan, *WP* 675
   SDLP maj. 731
   (June '83, OUP maj. 548)
   (Jan. '86, OUP maj. 1,842)

Fermanagh and South Tyrone
E. 68,979
*K. Maginnis, OUP 27,446
P. Corrigan, *SF* 14,623
Mrs. R. Flanagan, *SDLP* . 10,581
D. Kettyles, *WP* 1,784
J. Haslett, *All.* 941
   OUP maj. 12,823
   (June '83, OUP maj. 7,676)
   (Jan. '86, OUP maj. 12,579)

Foyle
E. 70,519
*J. Hume, SDLP 23,743
G. Campbell, *DUP* 13,883
M. McGuiness, *SF* 8,707
Mrs. E. Zammitt, *All.* 1,276
E. Melaugh, *WP* 1,022
   SDLP maj. 9,860
   (June '83, SDLP maj. 8,148)

Lagan Valley
E. 64,873
*Rt. Hon. J. H. Molyneaux,
  OUP 29,101
S. A. Close, *All.* 5,728
B. McDonnell, *SDLP* 2,888
P. J. Rice, *SF* 2,656
J. T. Lowry, *WP* 1,215
   OUP maj. 23,373
   (June '83, OUP maj. 17,216)
   (Jan. '86, OUP maj. 29,186)

Londonderry East
E. 71,031
*W. Ross, OUP 29,532
A. Doherty, *SDLP* 9,375
J. Davey, *SF* 5,464
P. McGowan, *All.* 3,237
F. Donnelly, *WP* 935
M. H. Samuel, *Ecol.* 281
   OUP maj. 20,157
   (June '83, OUP maj. 7,262)
   (Jan. '86, OUP maj. 28,921)

Newry and Armagh
E. 66,027
*S. Mallon, SDLP 25,137
J. F. Nicholson, *OUP* 19,812
J. McAllister, *SF* 6,173
W. H. Jeffrey, *All.* 664
J. O'Hanion, *WP* 482
   SDLP maj. 5,325
   (June '83, OUP maj. 1,554)
   (Jan. '86, SDLP maj. 2,583)

Strangford
E. 64,429
*Rt. Hon. J. D. Taylor, OUP 28,199
A. J. Morrow, *All.* 7,553
Miss I. E. Hynds, *WP* 1,385
   OUP maj. 20,646
   (June '83, OUP maj. 7,370)
   (Jan. '86, OUP maj. 30,634)

Ulster, Mid-
E. 67,256
*Rev. R. T. W. McCrea, DUP 23,004
P. D. Haughey, *SDLP* 13,644
S. Begley, *SF* 12,449
P. Bogan, *All.* 1,846
P. J. McClean, *WP* 1,133
   DUP maj. 9,360
   (June '83, DUP maj. 78)
   (Jan. '86, DUP maj. 9,697)

Upper Bann
E. 64,540
*J. H. McCusker, OUP 26,037
Mrs. B. Rodgers, *SDLP* .. 8,676
B. P. Curran, *SF* 3,126
Mrs. M. F. A. Cook, *All.* .. 2,487
T. French, *WP* 2,004
   OUP maj. 17,361
   (June '83, OUP maj. 17,081)
   (Jan. '86, OUP maj. 22,333)
   (*See also* p. 276)

BY-ELECTIONS
(Since 1987 General Election)

Kensington (Gtr. London)
(July 14, 1988)

J. D. Fishburn, *C.* 9,829
Mrs. A. Holmes, *Lab.* 9,014
W. Goodhart *SLD* 2,546
J. Martin *SDP* 1,190
P. Hobson, *Grn Party* 572
Mrs. C. Payne, *Rainbow Alliance Payne and Pleasure Party* 193
'Lord' Sutch, *Monster Raving Loony Rock Music Party* 61
J. Duignan, *London Class War* 60
B. Goodier, *Anti Left Wing Fascist* 31
B. McDermott, *Free Trade Liberal Party–Europe Out* 31
R. Edey, *Fair Wealth Distribution Fair Housing Provision* 30
W. Scola, *The Leveller Party* 27
J. Crowley, *Anti-Yuppie Revolutionary Crowleyist Vegetarian Visionary* .. 24
J. Connell, *Peace—Stop ITN Manipulation* 20
Dr. K. Trivedi, *Independent Janata Party* 5
   C. maj. 815

Glasgow Govan (S'clyde)
(Nov. 10, 1988)

J. Sillars, *SNP* 14,677
R. Gillespie, *Lab.* 11,123
C. Hamilton, *C.* 2,207
B. Ponsonby, *SLD* 1,246
G. Campbell, *Grn.* 345
D. Chalmers, *Comm.* 281
'Lord' Sutch, *Monster Raving Loony Party* 174
F. Clark, *Rainbow Zippy Alliance* 51
   SNP maj. 3,554

Epping Forest (Essex)
(Dec. 15, 1988)

S. J. Norris, C.	13,183
A. J. Thompson, SLD	8,679
S. W. Murray, Lab.	6,261
M. G. Pettman, SDP	4,077
A. M. Simms, Grn.	672
Ms. T. Wingfield, Independent National Front	286
'Lord' Sutch, Monster Raving Loony Liberal Christmas	208
J. Moore, Rainbow Alliance Change the World	33
B. G. Goodier, Vote No Belsen for South Africans ...	16
C. maj.	4,504

Pontypridd (Mid Glam)
(Feb. 23, 1989)

Dr. K. Howells, Lab.	20,549
S. Morgan, PC	9,755
N. Evans, C.	5,212
T. Ellis, SLD	1,500
T. Thomas, SDP	1,199
D. Richards, Comm.	239
D. Black, Ind.	57
Lab. maj.	10,794

Richmond (N. Yorks.)
(Feb. 23, 1989)

W. Hague, C.	19,543
M. Potter, SDP	16,909
Mrs. B. Pearce, SLD	11,589
F. Robson, Lab.	2,591
Dr. R. Upsall, Grn.	1,473
'Lord' Sutch, Monster Raving Loony Party	167
A. Mills, University Information Officer	113
Miss L. St. Claire, Corrective Party	107
N. Watkins, Official Liberal	70
C. maj.	2,634

Vale of Glamorgan (S. Glam)
(May 4, 1989)

J. Smith, Lab.	23,342
R. Richards, C.	17,314
F. Leavers, SLD	2,017
J. Dixon, PC	1,672
K. Davies, SDP	1,098
Miss M. Wakefield, Grn. ...	971
C. Tiarks, Protect the NHS	847
'Lord' Sutch, Monster Raving Loony Party	266
E. Roberts, Welsh Independence	148

Miss L. St. Claire, *Corrective*

Party	39
D. Black, Ind.	32
Lab. maj.	6,028

Glasgow Central (S'clyde)
(June 15, 1989)

M. Watson , Lab.	14,480
A. Neil, SNP	8,018
A. Hogarth, C.	2,028
Ms. I. Brandt, Grn.	1,019
R. McCreadie, SLD	411
P. Kerr, SDP	253
Ms. L. Murdoch, Revolutionary Communist	141
W. Kidd, Scottish Socialist .	137
D. Lettice, Workers Revolutionary	48
Lab. maj.	6,462

Vauxhall (Gtr. London)
(June 15, 1989)

Miss C. L. Hoey, Lab.	15,191
M. Keegan, C.	5,425
M. Tuffrey, SLD	5,043
H. Bewley, Grn.	1,767
H. Andrew, People's Candidate	302
D. Allen, The Greens	264
R. Narayan, Barrister, Civil Liberties Activist in Brixton	179
D. Milligan, Revolutionary Communist	177
P. Harrington, Official National Front	127
'Lord' Sutch, Monster Raving Loony Mad Hatters ..	106
D. Black, Christian Alliance	86
E. Budden, National Front .	83
G. Rolth, Fellowship	21
W. Scola, Leveller	21
Lab. maj.	9,766

Staffordshire, Mid
(March 22, 1990)

Mrs. S. Heal, Lab.	27,649
C. C. L. Prior, C.	18,200
T. A. Jones, Lib. Dem.	6,315
I. W. Wood, SDP	1,422
R. Saunders, Grn.	1,215
J. G. Bazeley, Anti-Thatcher C.	547
'Lord' Sutch, Monster Raving Loony Green Teeth ...	336
C. J. G. Hill, National Front	311
C. A. Abell, NHS Supporters	102

N. Parker-Jervis, *Against*

Immigration C. Green ...	71
S. B. F. Hughes, Raving Loony Green Giant Supercalafragalistic	59
L. St. C. Love, National Independent Correct Edification	51
B. R. A. Mildwater, Save the 2CV	42
D. M. Black, Christian Patriotic Alliance/Save Britain Campaign	39
Lab. maj.	9,449

Upper Bann
(May 17, 1990)

D. Trimble, OUP	20,547
Mrs. B. Rodgers, SDLP ...	6,698
Ms S. Campbell, SF	2,033
Rev. H. Ross, Ulster Independence	1,534
T. French, Workers' Party .	1,083
Mrs. C. Jones, C.	1,038
Dr. W. Ramsay, All.	948
G. McMichael, DUP	600
P. Doran, Grn.	576
E. Holmes, Right to Vote Labour	235
A. Dunn, SDP	154
OUP maj.	13,849

Bootle
(May 24, 1990)

M. Carr, Lab.	26,737
J. Clappison, C.	3,220
J. Cunningham, Lib. Dem. ..	3,179
S. Brady, Grn.	1,267
K. White, Lib.	474
D. Sutch, Monster Raving Loony Cavern Rock	418
J. Holmes, SDP	155
T. Schofield, Ind.	27
Lab. maj.	23,517

Vacant
(as at Aug. 7, 1990)

Knowsley South—through the death of Sean Hughes, MP, on June 24, 1990.

Bootle—through the death of Michael Carr, MP, on July 20, 1990.

Eastbourne—through the death of Ian Gow, TD, MP, on July 30, 1990.

Bradford North—through the death of Pat Wall, MP, on Aug. 6, 1990.

(See also **Occurrences during printing**)

EUROPEAN PARLIAMENT—UK MEMBERS
(as at end July 1990)

An asterisk* denotes membership of the last Parliament.

	Maj.
*Adam, Gordon J. (*b.* 1934), *Lab., Northumbria*	60,040
*Balfe, Richard A. (*b.* 1944), *Lab. Co-op, London S. Inner*	45,018
Barton, Roger (*b.* 1945), *Lab., Sheffield*	69,276
*Beazley, Christopher J. P. (*b.* 1952), *C., Cornwall and Plymouth*	19,817
*Beazley, Peter G. (*b.* 1922), *C., Bedfordshire S.*	2,977
*Bethell, The Lord (*b.* 1938), *C., London NW*	7,400
*Bird, John A. W. (*b.* 1926), *Lab. Co-op, Midlands W.*	42,364
Bowe, David (*b.* 1955), *Lab., Cleveland and Yorkshire N.*	24,092
*Buchan, Mrs. Janey O. (*b.* 1926), *Lab., Glasgow*	59,232
*Cassidy, Bryan M. D. (*b.* 1934), *C., Dorset E. and Hampshire W.*	61,774
*Catherwood, Sir Frederick (*b.* 1925), *C., Cambridge and Bedfordshire N.*	32,321
Coates, Kenneth (*b.* 1939), *Lab., Nottingham*	14,513
*Collins, Kenneth D. (*b.* 1939), *Lab., Strathclyde E.*	60,317
Crampton, Peter D. (*b.* 1932), *Lab., Humberside*	16,328
*Crawley, Mrs. Christine M. (*b.* 1950), *Lab., Birmingham E.*	46,948
*Daly, Mrs. Margaret E. (*b.* 1938), *C., Somerset and Dorset W.*	52,220
David, Wayne (*b.* 1957), *Lab., Wales S.*	62,557
Donnelly, Alan J. (*b.* 1957), *Lab., Tyne and Wear*	95,780
*Elles, James E. M. (*b.* 1949), *C., Oxford and Buckinghamshire*	47,518
*Elliott, Michael N. (*b.* 1932), *Lab., London W.*	14,808
*Ewing, Mrs. Winifred M. (*b.* 1929), *SNP, Highlands and Islands*	44,695
*Falconer, Alec (*b.* 1940), *Lab., Scotland Mid and Fife*	52,157
*Ford, J. Glyn (*b.* 1950), *Lab., Greater Manchester E.*	34,501
Green, Ms. Pauline (*b.* 1948), *Lab. Co-op, London N.*	5,837
Harrison, Lyndon (*b.* 1947), *Lab., Cheshire W.*	23,201
*Hindley, Michael J. (*b.* 1947), *Lab., Lancashire E.*	39,148
*Hoon, Geoffrey W. (*b.* 1953), *Lab., Derbyshire*	33,388
*Howell, Paul F. (*b.* 1951), *C., Norfolk*	20,907
*Hughes, Stephen S. (*b.* 1952), *Lab., Durham*	86,848
*Hume, John, MP (*b.* 1937), *SDLP, N. Ireland*	—
Inglewood, The Lord (Richard Fletcher-Vane) (*b.* 1951), *C., Cumbria and Lancashire N.*	2,391
*Jackson, Mrs. Caroline F. (*b.* 1946), *C., Wiltshire*	46,313
*Jackson, Christopher M. (*b.* 1935), *C., Kent E.*	28,961
*Kellett-Bowman, Edward T. (*b.* 1931), *C., Hampshire Central*	27,674
*Lomas, Alfred (*b.* 1928), *Lab., London NE*	47,767
*McGowan, Michael (*b.* 1940), *Lab., Leeds*	42,518
McCubbin, Henry (*b.* 1942), *Lab., Scotland NE*	2,613
McIntosh, Miss Anne C. B. (*b.* 1954), *C., Essex NE*	39,398
*McMahon, Hugh R. (*b.* 1938), *Lab., Strathclyde W.*	39,591
*McMillan-Scott, Edward H. C. (*b.* 1949), *C., York*	15,102
*Martin, David W. (*b.* 1954), *Lab., Lothians*	38,826
*Megahy, Thomas (*b.* 1929), *Lab., Yorkshire SW*	65,901
*Moorhouse, C. James O. (*b.* 1924), *C., London S. and Surrey E.*	30,816
*Morris, Rev. David R. (*b.* 1930), *Lab., Wales Mid and W.*	51,912
*Newens, A. Stanley (*b.* 1930), *Lab. Co-op, London Central*	11,542
*Newman, Edward (*b.* 1953), *Lab., Greater Manchester Central*	38,867
*Newton Dunn, William F. (*b.* 1941), *C., Lincolnshire*	20,650
Nicholson, James F. (*b.* 1945), *OUP, N. Ireland*	—
Oddy, Ms. Christine M. (*b.* 1955), *Lab., Midlands Central*	5,093
*O'Hagan, The Lord (*b.* 1945), *C., Devon*	57,298
*Paisley, Rev. Ian R. K., MP (*b.* 1926), *DUP, N. Ireland*	—
*Patterson, G. Benjamin (Ben) (*b.* 1939), *C., Kent W.*	24,050
*Plumb, The Lord (*b.* 1925), *C., The Cotswolds*	45,678
Pollack, Ms. Anita J. (*b.* 1946), *Lab., London SW*	518
*Prag, Derek (*b.* 1923), *C., Hertfordshire*	43,342
*Price, Peter N. (*b.* 1942), *C., London SE*	7,590
*Prout, Sir Christopher, TD, QC (*b.* 1942), *C., Shropshire and Stafford*	2,544
Rawlings, Miss Patricia (*b.* 1939), *C., Essex SW*	9,403
Read, Ms. Mel (*b.* 1939), *Lab., Leicester*	15,322
*Scott-Hopkins, Sir James (*b.* 1921), *C., Hereford and Worcester*	25,665
*Seal, Barry H. (*b.* 1937), *Lab., Yorkshire W.*	37,927
*Seligman, R. Madron (*b.* 1918), *C., Sussex W.*	46,233
*Simmonds, Richard J. (*b.* 1944), *C., Wight and Hampshire E.*	39,430
*Simpson, Anthony M. H., TD (*b.* 1935), *C., Northamptonshire*	20,447
Simpson, Brian (*b.* 1953), *Lab., Cheshire E.*	1,864
Smith, Alexander (*b.* 1943), *Lab., Scotland S.*	15,693
*Smith, Llewellyn T. (*b.* 1944), *Lab., Wales SE*	108,488
Spencer Thomas N. B. (*b.* 1948), *C., Surrey W.*	49,342
Stevens, John C. C. (*b.* 1955), *C., Thames Valley*	26,491
*Stevenson, George W. (*b.* 1938), *Lab., Staffordshire E.*	31,769
*Stewart, Kenneth A. (*b.* 1925), *Lab., Merseyside W.*	49,817
*Stewart-Clark, Sir John, Bt. (*b.* 1929), *C., Sussex E.*	53,294
Titley, Gary (*b.* 1950), *Lab., Greater Manchester W.*	50,135
*Tomlinson, John E. (*b.* 1939), *Lab., Birmingham W.*	30,860
*Tongue, Miss Carole (*b.* 1955), *Lab., London E.*	27,385
*Turner, Amédée E., QC (*b.* 1929), *C., Suffolk*	25,693
*Welsh, Michael J. (*b.* 1942), *C., Lancashire Central*	5,688
*West, Norman (*b.* 1935), *Lab., Yorkshire S.*	91,784
White, Ian (*b.* 1947), *Lab., Bristol*	9,982
Wilson, Joseph (*b.* 1937), *Lab., Wales N.*	4,460
Wynn, Terence (*b.* 1946), *Lab., Merseyside E.*	76,867

UNITED KINGDOM ELECTIONS TO EUROPEAN PARLIAMENT (June 15, 1989)

(*Corr.* = Corrective Party; *Hum.* = Humanist Party; *ICP* = International Communist Party; *Lab. RG* = Labour for Regional Government; *MK* = Mebyon Kernow; *W. Reg.* = Wessex Regionalists. For other abbreviations, see p. 249)

Bedfordshire South
E. 569,506

*P. G. Beazley, C.	73,406
T. McWalter, *Lab.*	70,429
D. Everett, *Grn.*	34,508
W. M. Johnston, *SLD*	8,748
R. Muller, *SDP*	3,067
C. maj.	*2,977*
(June '84, C. maj. 14,982)	

Birmingham East
E. 531,081

*Mrs. C. M. Crawley, *Lab.*	96,588
M. J. C. Harbour, *C.*	49,640
P. M. Simpson, *Grn.*	22,589
J. C. Binns, *SDP*	5,424
J. M. E. C. Roodhouse, *SLD*	4,010
M. Wingfield, *NF*	1,471
Lab. maj.	*46,948*
(June '84, Lab. maj. 21,383)	

Birmingham West
E. 515,817

*J. E. Tomlinson, *Lab.*	86,545
C. F. Robinson, *C.*	55,685
J. D. Bentley, *Grn.*	21,384
S. Reynolds, *SLD*	7,673
Lab. maj.	*30,860*
(June '84, Lab. maj. 6,244)	

Bristol
E. 562,277

I. White, *Lab.*	87,753
*R. J. Cottrell, *C.*	77,771
D. N. Wall, *Grn.*	39,436
C. Boney, *SLD.*	16,309
G. McEwen *W. Reg.*	1,017
Lab. maj.	*9,982*
(June '84, C. maj. 17,644)	

Cambridge and Bedfordshire North
E. 562,539

*Sir F. Catherwood, *C.*	84,044
M. Strube, *Lab.*	51,723
Ms. M. E. Wright, *Grn.*	37,956
A. N. Duff, *SLD*	15,052
C. maj.	*32,321*
(June '84, C. maj. 47,216)	

Cheshire East
E. 518,311

B. Simpson, *Lab.*	74,721
*Sir T. Normanton, *C.*	72,857
C. C. White, *Grn.*	21,456
Mrs. B. Fraenkel, *SLD*	12,344
Lab. maj.	*1,864*
(June '84, C. maj. 18,376)	

Cheshire West
E. 543,256

L. Harrison, *Lab.*	102,962
*A. Pearce, *C.*	79,761
G. L. Nicholls, *Grn.*	25,933
J. Rankin, *SLD*	9,333
Lab. maj.	*23,201*
(June '84, C. maj. 9,692)	

Cleveland and Yorkshire North
E. 571,254

D. Bowe, *Lab.*	94,953
*Sir P. Vanneck, *C.*	70,861
O. Dumpleton, *Grn.*	17,225
T. M. Mawston, *SLD*	8,470
R. I. Andrew *SDP*	7,970
Lab. maj.	*24,092*
(June '84, C. maj. 2,625)	

Cornwall and Plymouth
E. 542,527

*C. J. P. Beazley, *C.*	88,376
P. A. Tyler, *SLD*	68,559
Ms. D. Kirk, *Lab.*	41,466
H. Hoptrough, *Grn.*	24,581
C. Lawry, *MK*	4,224
C. maj.	*19,817*
(June '84, C. maj. 17,751)	

The Cotswolds
E. 558,115

*Lord Plumb, *C.*	94,852
Mrs. S. Limb, *Grn.*	49,174
T. Levitt, *Lab.*	48,180
L. A. Rowe, *SLD*	18,196
C. maj.	*45,678*
(June '84, C. maj. 48,942)	

Cumbria and Lancashire North
E. 561,263

W. R. Fletcher Vane, *C.*	84,035
J. M. P. Hutton, *Lab.*	81,644
Mrs. C. E. Smith, *Grn.*	21,262
E. E. Hill, *SLD*	12,590
J. Bates, *SDP*	4,206
C. maj.	*2,391*
(June '84, C. maj. 23,795)	

Derbyshire
E. 564,429

*G. W. Hoon, *Lab.*	105,018
P. Jenkinson, *C.*	72,630
E. Wall, *Grn.*	20,781
S. Molloy, *SLD*	4,613
Mrs. A. M. Ayres, *SDP*	3,858
Lab. maj.	*33,388*
(June '84, Lab maj. 6,853)	

Devon
E. 596,671

*Lord O'Hagan, *C.*	110,518
P. S. Christie, *Grn.*	53,220
W. J. Cairns, *Lab.*	40,675
M. Edmunds, *SLD*	23,306
R. Edwards, *SDP*	7,806
S. B. F. Hughes, *LM*	2,241
Lady Rous *W. Reg.*	385
C. maj.	*57,298*
(June '84, C. maj. 56,610)	

Dorset East and Hampshire West
E. 608,895

*B. M. D. Cassidy, *C.*	111,469
Ms. K. I. Bradbury, *Grn.*	49,695
H. R. White, *Lab.*	38,011
H. R. Legg, *SLD*	21,809
C. maj.	*61,774*
(June '84, C. maj. 59,891)	

Durham
E. 530,137

*S. S. Hughes, *Lab.*	124,448
R. Hull, *C.*	37,600
Ms. H. I. Lennox, *Grn.*	18,770
P. Freitag, *SLD*	8,369
Lab. maj.	*86,848*
(June '84, Lab. maj. 61,227)	

Essex North East
E. 598,542

Miss A. C. B. McIntosh, *C.*	92,758
Ms. H. J. Bryan, *Lab.*	53,360
C. R. Keene, *Grn.*	45,163
Miss D. P. Wallis, *SLD.*	16,939
C. maj.	*39,398*
(June '84, C. maj. 54,302)	

Essex South West
E. 569,011

Miss P. E. Rawlings, *C.*	77,408
J. W. Orpe, *Lab.*	68,005
Mrs. M. E. Willis, *Grn.*	32,242
T. P. Allen, *SLD*	10,618
C. maj.	*9,403*
(June '84, C. maj. 16,021)	

Glasgow
E. 487,199

*Mrs. J. O. Buchan, *Lab.*	107,818
A. Brophy, *SNP*	48,586
Mrs. A. K. Bates, *C.*	20,761
D. L. Spaven, *Grn.*	12,229
J. Morrison, *SLD.*	3,887
D. Chalmers, *Comm.*	1,164
J. Simons, *ICP*	193
Lab. maj.	*59,232*
(June '84, Lab. maj. 65,733)	

Greater Manchester Central
E. 481,023

*E. Newman, *Lab.*	86,914
Miss C. E. Gillan, *C.*	48,047
B. Candeland, *Grn.*	19,742
J. H. Mulholland, *SLD*	9,437
S. M. Millson, *SDP*	2,769
S. Knight, *Hum.*	1,045
Lab. maj.	*38,867*
(June '84, Lab. maj. 28,077)	

Greater Manchester East
E. 506,930

*J. G. Ford, *Lab.*	93,294
R. N. Greenwood, *C.*	58,793
M. J. Shipley, *Grn.*	19,090
A. B. Leah, *SLD*	16,645
Lab. maj.	*34,501*
(June '84, Lab. maj. 8,651)	

Greater Manchester West
E. 522,476

G. Titley, *Lab.*	109,228
P. H. Twyman, *C.*	59,093
D. W. Milne, *Grn.*	22,778
A. H. Cruden, *SLD*	6,940
Mrs. B. Archer, *SDP*	4,526
Lab. maj.	*50,135*
(June '84, Lab. maj. 37,698)	

Hampshire Central
E. 546,630

E. T. Kellett-Bowman, C. .	78,651
Ms. A. Mawle, *Lab.*	50,977
Mrs. S.J. Penton, *Grn.* ...	33,186
D. W. G. Chidgey, *SLD* ..	18,418
C. maj.	*27,674*
(June '84, C. maj. 44,821)	

Hereford and Worcester
E. 595,504

Sir J. Scott-Hopkins, C. ..	87,898
C. A. Short, *Lab.*	62,233
Ms. F. M. Norman, *Grn.*..	49,296
Mrs. J. D. Davies, *SLD.*	13,569
C. maj.	*25,665*
(June '84, C. maj. 39,934)	

Hertfordshire
E. 517,137

D. N. Prag, C.	86,898
V. S. Anand, *Lab.*	43,556
M. F. Ames, *Grn.*	37,277
M. D. Phelan, *SLD*	13,456
Mrs. C. Treves Brown,	
SDP	5,048
C. maj.	*43,342*
(June '84, C. maj. 45,932)	

Highlands and Islands
E. 313,877

Mrs. W. M. Ewing SNP	66,297
Sir A. McQuarrie, *C.*	21,602
N. MacAskill, *Lab.*	17,848
M. Gregson, *Grn.*	12,199
N. Michison, *SLD*	10,644
SNP maj.	*44,695*
(June '84, SNP maj. 16,277)	

Humberside
E. 504,219

P. D. Crampton *Lab.*	74,163
R. C. Battersby, C.	57,835
Mrs. J. C. Clark, *Grn.*....	23,835
F. L. Parker, *SLD*	3,989
S. W. Unwin, *SDP*	3,419
Lab. maj.	*16,328*
(June '84, C. maj. 8,015)	

Kent East
E. 575,789

C. M. Jackson, C.	85,667
G. N. J. Perry, *Lab.*	56,706
Ms. P. A. Kemp, *Grn.*	36,931
A. F. C. Morris, *SLD*	15,470
C. maj.	*28,961*
(June '84, C. maj. 48,867)	

Kent West
E. 569,725

G. B. Patterson, C.	82,519
P. L. Sloman, *Lab.*	58,469
J. Tidy, *Grn.*	33,202
J. B. Doherty, *SLD.*	16,087
C. maj.	*24,050*
(June '84, C. maj. 34,630)	

Lancashire Central
E. 537,610

M. J. Welsh, C...........	81,125
G. W. T. Smith, *Lab.*......	75,437
Mrs. H. Ingham, *Grn.*....	28,777
Ms. J. Ross-Mills, *SLD.*..	7,378
C. maj.	*5,688*
(June '84, C. maj. 26,195)	

Lancashire East
E. 529,740

M. J. Hindley, Lab.	96,926
R. W. Sturdy, *C.*	57,778
S. Barker, *Grn.*	20,728
M. Hambley, *SLD*	12,661
Lab. maj.	*39,148*
(June '84, Lab. maj. 7,905)	

Leeds
E. 519,631

M. McGowan, Lab.	97,385
J. W. Tweddle, *C.*	54,867
C. R. Lord, *Grn.*	22,558
Mrs. J. Ewens, *SLD*	11,720
Lab. maj.	*42,518*
(June '84, Lab. maj. 10,457)	

Leicester
E. 579,050

Ms. I. M. Read, *Lab.*	90,798
F. A. Tuckman, C........	75,476
C. J. Davis, *Grn.*	33,081
A. G. Barrett, *Ind. C.*	6,996
G. W. Childs, *SLD*	6,791
Lab. maj.	*15,322*
(June '84, C. maj. 2,892)	

Lincolnshire
E. 586,156

W. F. Newton Dunn, C. ..	92,043
S. Taggart, *Lab.*	71,393
Ms. J. Steranka, *Grn.*	24,908
J. P. Heppell, *SLD*	14,341
C. maj.	*20,650*
(June '84, C. maj. 45,445)	

London Central
E. 486,558

A. S. Newens, Lab. Co-op.	78,561
Ms. H. S. Crawley, *C.*	67,019
Ms. N. Kortvelyessy, *Grn.*	28,087
Miss S. A. Ludford, *SLD*	7,864
W. D. E. Mallinson, *SDP*	2,957
'Lord' D. E. Sutch, *LM* ..	841
Ms. L. St-Claire, *Corr.* ..	707
J. S. Swinden, *Hum.*	304
Lab. Co-op maj.	*11,542*
(June '84, Lab. maj. 13,297)	

London East
E. 530,548

Miss C. Tongue, Lab.	92,803
A. R. Tyrrell, *C.*.........	65,418
Ms. E. L. Crosbie, *Grn.* ...	21,388
J. K. Gibb, *SLD*	7,341
D. A. O'Sullivan, *ICP*	717
Lab. maj.	*27,385*
(June '84, Lab. maj. 12,159)	

London North
E. 573,043

Ms. P. Green, *Lab. Co-op.*	85,536
R. M. Lacey, *C.*	79,699
S. Clark, *Grn.*............	30,807
Ms. H. F. Leighter, *SLD*	8,917
P. Burns, *Ind.*	2,016
Ms. L. Reith, *Comm.*	850
Lab. Co-op. maj.	*5,837*
(June '84, C. maj. 4,853)	

London North East
E. 510,138

A. Lomas, Lab.	76,085
M. Trend, *C.*.............	28,318
Mrs. J. D. Lambert, *Grn.* ..	25,949
S. Banks, *SLD*	9,575
Ms. N. C. Temple, *Comm.*..	1,129
Lab. maj.	*47,767*
(June '84, Lab. maj. 52,665)	

London North West
E. 506,707

Lord Bethell, C.	74,900
A. K. Toms, *Lab.*.........	67,500
I. E. Flindall, *Grn.*	28,275
C. D. Noyce, *SLD*	10,553
C. maj.	*7,400*
(June '84, C. maj. 7,422)	

London South and Surrey East
E. 495,942

C. J. O. Moorhouse, C. ...	78,256
R. J. E. Evans, *Lab.*	47,440
G. F. Brand, *Grn.*	31,854
P. H. Billenness, *SLD*....	14,967
C. maj.	*30,816*
(June '84, C. maj. 44,657)	

London, South East
E. 558,815

P. N. Price, C.	80,619
D. J. Earnshaw, *Lab.*	73,029
Dr. E. C. McPhee, *Grn.*....	37,576
A. A. Kinch, *SDP*	10,196
Mrs. M. C. Williams, *SLD*	9,052
W. E. Turner, *Ind.*	456
C. maj.	*7,590*
(June '84, C. maj. 20,015)	

London, South Inner
E. 528,188

R. A. Balfe, Lab. Co-op ...	90,378
R. J. Wheatley, *C.*	45,360
Ms. P. A. Shepherd, *Grn.* ..	26,230
M. J. Pindar, *SLD.*	10,277
P. N. Power, *Comm.*	1,277
Ms. D. Weppler, *Comm.*	
League	323
Lab. Co-op maj.	*45,018*
(June '84, Lab. maj. 31,481)	

London South West
E. 486,412

Ms A. J. Pollack, *Lab.* ...	74,298
Dame S. M. Roberts, C. ..	73,780
Ms. M. A. Elson, *Grn.*	35,476
J. C. Field, *SLD*	10,400
Lab. maj.	*518*
(June '84, C. maj. 6,867)	

London West
E. 515,581

M. N. Elliott, Lab.	92,959
B. Donnelly, *C.*	78,151
J. R. Hywell-Davies, *Grn.* ..	32,686
J. G. Parry, *SLD.*	9,309
J. Rogers-Davies, *SDP*...	2,877
Lab. maj.	*14,808*
(June '84, Lab. maj. 5,229)	

Lothians
E. 523,506

*D. W. Martin, Lab.	90,840
Mrs. C. M. Blight, C.	52,014
J. Smith, SNP	44,935
R. C. M. Harper, Grn	22,983
K. Leadbetter, SLD	9,222
Lab. maj.	*38,826*

(June '84, Lab. maj. 25,924)

Merseyside East
E. 519,514

T. Wynn, Lab.	107,288
E. N. Farthing, C.	30,421
R. L. Georgeson, Grn.	20,018
R. M. Clayton, SLD	5,658
Lab. maj.	*76,867*

(June '84, Lab. maj. 49,039)

Merseyside West
E. 508,722

*K. A. Stewart, Lab.	93,717
M. D. Byrne, C.	43,900
L. Brown, Grn.	23,052
Mrs. H. F. Clucas, SLD	16,327
D. J. E. Carson, PRP	1,747
Lab. maj.	*49,817*

(June '84, Lab. maj. 13,197)

Midlands Central
E. 539,211

Ms. C. M. Oddy, Lab.	76,736
*J. de Courcy Ling, C.	71,643
Ms. J. A. Alty, Grn.	42,622
I. Cundy, SLD.	8,450
Lab. maj.	*5,093*

(June '84, C. maj. 12,729)

Midlands West
E. 529,505

*J. A. W. Bird, Lab. Co-op.	105,529
M. J. Whitby, C.	63,165
J. Raven, Grn.	21,787
Mrs. F. M. Oborski, SLD	6,974
Lab. Co-op maj.	*42,364*

(June '84, Lab. maj. 19,685)

Norfolk
E. 577,576

*P. F. Howell, C.	92,385
Ms. M. Page, Lab.	71,478
M. Macartney-Filgate, Grn.	40,575
R. A. Lawes, SLD	8,902
S. D. Maxwell, SDP	4,934
C. maj.	*20,907*

(June '84, C. maj. 36,857)

Northamptonshire
E. 587,733

*A. M. H. Simpson, C.	86,695
M. Coyne, Lab.	66,248
Ms. A. T. Bryant, Grn.	43,071
R. Church, SLD.	11,619
C. maj.	*20,447*

(June '84, C. maj. 39,859)

Northumbria
E. 514,083

*G. J. Adam, Lab.	110,688
P. Yeoman, C.	50,648
Ms. A. Lipman, Grn.	24,882
Viscount Morpeth, SLD	10,983
Lab. maj.	*60,040*

(June '84, Lab. maj. 15,700)

Nottingham
E. 565,354

K. Coates, Lab.	92,261
*M. L. Kilby, C.	77,748
Mrs. S. E. Blount, Grn.	34,097
A. Swift, SLD	6,693
Lab. maj.	*14,513*

(June '84, Lab. maj. 16,126)

Oxford and Buckinghamshire
E. 560,730

*J. E. M. Elles, C.	92,483
R. Gifford, Lab.	44,965
T. H. Andrewes, Grn.	42,058
R. Johnston, SLD	14,405
R. C. Turner, Ind.	3,696
C. maj.	*47,518*

(June '84, C. maj. 49,081)

Scotland Mid and Fife
E. 534,638

*A. Falconer, Lab.	102,246
K. W. MacAskill, SNP	50,089
A. Christie, C.	46,505
G. Moreton, Grn.	14,165
M. Black, SLD	8,857
Lab. maj.	*52,157*

(June '84, Lab. maj. 27,166)

Scotland North East
E. 554,408

H. McGubbin, Lab.	65,348
Dr. A. Macartney, SNP	62,735
*J. L. C. Provan, C.	56,835
M. Hill, Grn.	15,584
S. Horner, SLD	12,704
Lab. maj.	*2,613*

(June '84, C. maj. 9,171)

Scotland South
E. 491,865

A. Smith, Lab.	81,366
*A. H. Hutton, C.	65,673
M. Brown, SNP	35,155
J. Button, Grn.	11,658
J. E. McKercher, SLD	10,368
Lab. maj.	*15,693*

(June '84, C. maj. 3,137)

Sheffield
E. 564,409

R. Barton, Lab.	109,677
T. S. R. Mort, C.	40,401
P. L. Scott, Grn.	26,844
A. H. Rogers, SLD	10,910
D. E. Hyland, ICP	657
Lab. maj.	*69,276*

(June '84, Lab. maj. 46,283)

Shropshire and Stafford
E. 597,554

*C. J. Prout, C.	85,896
D. J. A. Hallam, Lab.	83,352
R. T. C. Saunders, Grn.	29,637
C. Hards, SLD	10,568
C. maj.	*2,544*

(June '84, C. maj. 24,932)

Somerset and Dorset West
E. 582,098

*Mrs. M. E. Daly, C.	106,716
Dr. R. H. Lawson, Grn.	54,496
Ms. D. M. Organ, Lab.	46,210
M. Mactaggart, SLD	28,662
A. P. B. Mockler W. Reg.	930
C. maj.	*52,220*

(June '84, C. maj. 40,251)

Staffordshire East
E. 581,127

*G. W. Stevenson, Lab.	94,873
M. F. Spungin, C.	63,104
S. Parker, Grn.	23,415
R. C. Dodson, SLD	7,046
Lab. maj.	*31,769*

(June '84, Lab. maj. 7,867)

Strathclyde East
E. 494,274

*K. D. Collins, Lab.	109,170
G. A. Leslie, SNP	48,853
M. Dutt, C.	22,233
A. Whitelaw, Grn.	9,749
G. Lait, SLD	4,276
Lab. maj.	*60,317*

(June '84, Lab. maj. 63,462)

Strathclyde West
E. 493,067

*H. R. McMahon, Lab.	89,627
C. M. Campbell, SNP	50,036
S. J. Robin, C.	45,872
G. Campbell, Grn.	16,461
D. J. Herbison, SLD.	8,098
Lab. maj.	*39,591*

(June '84, Lab. maj. 23,038)

Suffolk
E. 550,131

*A. E. Turner, C.	82,481
M. D. Cornish, Lab.	56,788
A. C. Slade, Grn.	37,305
P. R. Odell, SLD	12,660
C. maj.	*25,693*

(June '84, C. maj. 47,098)

Surrey West
E. 515,881

T. N. B. Spencer, C.	89,674
E. Haywood, Grn.	40,332
H. G. Trace, Lab.	28,313
A. Davies, SLD	18,042
B. M. Collignon, SDP	3,676
C. maj.	*49,342*

(June '84, C. maj. 52,588)

Sussex East
E. 553,536

*Sir J. Stewart-Clark, Bt., C.	96,388
Ms. G. Roles, Lab..	43,094
Ms. R. Addison, Grn	42,316
Mrs. D. Venables, SLD	16,810
D. Howells, LM	1,181
C. maj.	*53,294*

(June '84, C. maj. 65,621)

Sussex West
E. 554,664

*R. M. Seligman, C.	95,821
I. F. N. Bagnall, Grn.	49,588
M. Shrimpton, Lab.	32,006
Dr. J. M. M. Walsh, SLD.	24,855
C. maj.	*46,233*

(June '84, C. maj. 57,502)

Thames Valley
E. 542,855

J. C. C. Stevens, C.	73,070
Ms. H. B. de Lyon, Lab.	46,579
P. Gordon, Grn.	36,865
D. B. Griffiths, SLD	14,603
C. maj.	*26,491*

(June '84, C. maj. 38,805)

Tyne and Wear
E. 530,953

A. J. Donnelly, *Lab.*	.....	126,682
N. C. Gibbon, *C.*	....	30,902
R. Stather, *Grn.*	....	18,107
P. J. Arnold, *SLD*	......	6,101
T. P. Kilgallon, *SPGB*	...	919
Lab. maj.	....	*95,780*

(June '84, Lab. maj. 49,414)

Wales Mid and West
E. 547,740

*Rev. D. R. Morris, *Lab.*	..	105,670
O. J. Williams, *C.*	......	53,758
Ms. B. I. McPake, *Grn.*	....	29,852
Dr. P. J. S. Williams, *PC*		26,063
G. A. Sinclair, *SLD*	....	10,031
Lab. maj.	....	*51,912*

(June '84, Lab. maj. 36,452)

Wales North
E. 540,230

J. Wilson, *Lab.*	....	83,638
*Miss B. A. Brookes, *C.*	...	79,178
Dr. D. E. Thomas, *PC*	...	64,120
P. H. W. Adams, *Grn.*	....	15,832
R. K. Marshall, *SLD*	....	10,056
Lab. maj.	....	*4,460*

(June '84, C. maj. 12,278)

Wales South
E. 520,911

W. David, *Lab.*	....	108,550
A. R. Taylor, *C.*	....	45,993
G. P. Jones, *Grn.*	....	25,993
P. J. Keelan, *PC*	....	10,727
P. K. Verma, *SLD*	....	4,037
D. A. T. Thomas, *SDP*	...	3,513
Lab. maj.	....	*62,557*

(June '84, Lab. maj. 44,258)

Wales South East
E. 561,068

*L. T. Smith, *Lab.*	......	138,872
R. J. Young, *C.*	....	30,384
M. J. Witherden, *Grn.*	...	27,869
Ms. J. Evans, *PC*	....	14,152
P. Nicholls-Jones, *SLD*	..	4,661
Lab. maj.	....	*108,488*

(June '84, Lab. maj. 95,557)

Wight and Hampshire East
E. 574,332

*R. J. Simmonds, *C.*	......	90,658
Dr. A. D. Burnett, *Lab.*	..	51,228
S. L. Rackett, *Grn.*	......	40,664
Ms. V. A. Rayner, *SLD*	..	19,569
C. maj.	....	*39,430*

(June '84, C. maj. 42,928)

Wiltshire
E. 568,875

*Mrs. C. F. Jackson, *C.*	...	93,200
G. A. Harris, *Lab.*	....	46,887
J. V. Hughes, *Grn.*	......	46,735
P. N. Crossley, *SLD*	.....	18,302
J. A. Cade, *Ind.*	....	4,809
C. maj.	....	*46,313*

(June '84, C. maj. 26,469)

York
E. 542,998

*E. H. C. McMillan-Scott, *C.*	....	81,453
J. T. Grogan, *Lab.*	......	66,351
R. Bell, *Grn.*	....	27,525
A. Collinge, *SLD*	....	12,542
C. maj.	....	*15,102*

(June '84, C. maj. 36,402)

Yorkshire South
E. 518,995

*N. West, *Lab.*	....	121,060
W. J. Clappison, *C.*	......	29,276
A. Grace, *Grn.*	....	19,063
B. Boulton, *SLD*	....	5,039
Lab. maj.	....	*91,784*

(June '84, Lab. maj. 67,749)

Yorkshire South West
E. 523,322

*T. Megahy, *Lab.*	....	108,444
G. T. Horton, *C.*	....	42,543
Mrs. S. Leyland, *Grn.*	....	25,677
J. A. D. Ridgway, *SLD*	...	10,352
Lab. maj.	....	*65,901*

(June '84, Lab. maj. 44,173)

Yorkshire West
E. 564,001

*B. H. Seal, *Lab.*	....	108,644
G. T. Hall, *C.*	....	70,717
N. Parrott, *Grn.*	....	28,308
P. Wrigley, *SLD*	....	9,765
Lab. maj.	....	*37,927*

(June '84, Lab. maj. 20,854)

Northern Ireland
E. 1,105,551

*Rev. I. R. K. Paisley, MP, *DUP*	....	160,110
*J. Hume, MP, *SDLP*	.....	136,335
J. F. Nicholson, *OUP*	....	118,785
D. Morrison *SF*	....	48,914
J. T. Alderdice, *All.*	......	27,905
A. Kennedy, *C.*	....	25,789
M. H. Samuel, *Ecol.*	......	6,569
S. Lynch, *WP*	....	5,590
M. Langhammer, *Lab. RG*		3,540
B. Caul, *Lab. 87*	....	1,274

Rev. I. R. K. Paisley, J. Hume and
J. F. Nicholson were elected by the
single transferable voting system.

PARLIAMENTARY ASSOCIATIONS

COMMONWEALTH PARLIAMENTARY ASSOCIATION (1911)

The Commonwealth Parliamentary Association consists of 115 branches in the national, state, provincial or territorial parliaments in the countries of the Commonwealth. Commonwealth Parliamentary conferences and general assemblies are held every year in different countries of the Commonwealth.

President (1989–90), D. N. E. Mutasa, MP, Senior Minister for Political Affairs (*Zimbabwe*).
Vice-President (1989–90), Hon. Rabi Ray, MP, Speaker of the Lok Sabha (*India*).
Secretary-General, D. Tonkin, 7 Old Palace Yard, SW1P 3JY.

United Kingdom Branch

Hon. Presidents, The Lord Chancellor; Mr. Speaker.
Chairman of Branch, The Rt. Hon. Margaret Thatcher, MP.

Chairman of Executive Committee, Sir Peter Hordern, MP.
Secretary, P. Cobb, OBE, Westminster Hall, Palace of Westminster, SW1.

THE INTER-PARLIAMENTARY UNION (1889)

To facilitate personal contact between members of all Parliaments in the promotion of representative institutions, peace and international co-operation.
Secretary General, P. Cornillon, Place du Petit-Saconnex, BP 99, 1211 Geneva 19, Switzerland.

British Group
Palace of Westminster, SW1A 0AA

Hon. Presidents, The Lord Chancellor; Mr. Speaker.
President, The Rt. Hon. Margaret Thatcher, MP.
Chairman, M. Marshall, MP.
Secretary, D. Ramsay.

PARLIAMENTARY SUMMARY 1989–90

The House of Lords re-assembled after the summer recess on October 9, 1989, and the House of Commons on October 17.

On October 9 in the House of Lords, the Government was defeated on an Opposition amendment to the Local Government and Housing Bill relating to the treatment of bad or doubtful debtors in respect of uncollected rents after April 1, 1989. On October 11 Lord Hesketh, Parliamentary Under-Secretary of State for the Environment, announced details of the arrangements for the transitional period for the introduction of the community charge—the so-called safety net.

On October 19 the Home Secretary (Douglas Hurd) made a statement giving the Government's response to the quashing by the Court of Appeal of the convictions of the four people found guilty of the pub bombings in Guildford and Woolwich in 1974. He described the convictions as a serious miscarriage of justice which had resulted in wrongful imprisonment for many years. He also announced the setting up of an inquiry into these convictions and into the conviction of the Maguire family in 1976, for possessing explosives. The Shadow Home Secretary (Roy Hattersley) welcomed the statement and stressed that Parliament and the country should do everything possible to ensure that there was no repetition of such cases.

On October 23 an Opposition amendment to the Children Bill calling for the setting up of Family Courts was unsuccessful but the Solicitor General (Sir Nicholas Lyell) gave an undertaking to introduce some reforms in this area, short of the creation of family courts *per se*. On October 24 the Government moved a closure motion on the debate on the remaining stages of this Bill to avoid a threatened filibuster by Labour MPs. On October 25 the Government suffered two further defeats on Opposition amendments in the House of Lords on the Local Government and Housing Bill. One amendment proposed to prevent the sale of certain housing association properties (111 votes to 38), and the other to prevent the sale of houses specifically converted for the elderly (94 votes to 36); on November 1 the Government gave an undertaking that it would not overturn this amendment. On October 25 the Secretary of State for Social Security (Tony Newton) gave the details of the increases in social security benefits for the coming year, confirming that child benefit would remain at the existing level again. The Shadow Health Secretary (Robin Cook) welcomed some elements of the statement, especially the introduction of a carer's premium on income support, but claimed that the comparatively minor changes announced by Mr Newton were not the comprehensive review that had been promised.

On October 31 the Secretary of State for Trade and Industry (Nicholas Ridley) announced that the Government was prepared to waive its 'golden share' in Jaguar PLC, provided that the requisite 75 per cent of shareholders backed this move, to enable the Ford company to purchase a controlling share of the company. The Shadow Trade Secretary (Bryan Gould) called this 'another victim of the Government's destructive policy towards manufacturing ... the disappearance of the last vestige of what had remained of the indigenous British car industry'.

On November 6 the Secretary of State for the Environment (Chris Patten) made a statement about the local authority grant settlement in England for 1990–91. In this he estimated that the national non-domestic rate multiplier would be 36p, yielding an estimated £10.4 million. He also gave details of how the standard spending assessments (SSA) were to be calculated, estimating that this should produce an average community charge of £278 per person. The new Shadow Environment Secretary (Bryan Gould) responded by reiterating that the Opposition had long attacked the community charge proposals as being 'inherently complicated and unworkable, and fundamentally unfair'. On November 7 the Secretary of State for Transport (Cecil Parkinson) announced the publication of the report by Sir Anthony Hidden into the Clapham Junction rail disaster of December 1988. The report concluded that the accident was caused by faulty wiring work. The Shadow Transport Secretary (John Prescott) claimed that the report revealed the dangers of policies that led to the presence of overworked, exhausted staff, many of whom lacked proper training, and who suffered from low pay and poor morale. The Secretary of State for Health (Kenneth Clarke) announced that he had asked the armed forces to assist in providing accident and emergency services in London as the pay dispute in the ambulance service worsened. Robin Cook, the Shadow Health Secretary, suggested that a more sensible course would be for the matter to be referred to arbitration. The Opposition was able to force a rare emergency debate on the worsening state of the dispute.

On 9 November the Secretary of State for Energy (John Wakeham) announced to the Commons that no nuclear power stations would now be included in the plans for the privatization of the electricity supply industry. These stations will be part of a Government-owned company. Consideration would have to be given to the plans to construct any new nuclear stations. The Opposition Energy spokesman (Frank Dobson) said that this was one of the most extraordinary statements the House had ever heard and accused the Government of making a shambles of the electricity industry. The Secretary of State for Scotland (Malcolm Rifkind) made a similar statement to the effect that Scottish nuclear power assets would be held by Scottish Nuclear Ltd., which would remain publicly owned. On November 13 the Minister for Agriculture (John Gummer) answered a question in the House on the risk of lead contamination in milk and meat following the discovery of lead in cattle feed. He also outlined the Government's plans to eliminate any danger to the consumer.

FINANCIAL STATEMENT

On November 15 John Major, who replaced Nigel Lawson as Chancellor of the Exchequer in October, presented his autumn financial statement. Mr. Major told the Commons that public expenditure was likely to be £168,000 million in the current year, some £1,000 million higher than the original total. This he attributed partly to lower than expected proceeds from the privatization programme but principally to overspending by local authorities. In the current year the ratio of public spending to Gross Domestic Product (GDP) was likely to be 38.75 per cent, significantly below the level forecast.

PUBLIC EXPENDITURE

Mr. Major said 'Tight control of Government expenditure remains a central element of the Government's economic strategy.... For 1990–91, the new planning total has been set at £179,000 million and, in the following two years, at £192,000 million and £203,000 million respectively. Within that, the estimates of privatization proceeds are unchanged, at £5,000 million a year. There are also substantial reserves, rising from £3,000 million in 1990–91 to £6,000 million and £9,000 million in the following two years.'

SPENDING PROGRAMMES

The Chancellor went on to detail the increased expenditure by departments: 'The new plans also show continued real growth in spending on the Government's priorities. Thus, between this year and next, spending on the National Health Service will rise by £2,400 million ... the clearest possible evidence of the Government's practical commitment to improving the care available in the NHS.

'Spending on national roads is planned to double between 1988–89 and 1992–93. Extra financing of £400 million to £500 million a year is being made available for the railways and London Regional Transport ... In total we have added £1,800 million to the planned spending on transport in the next two years.

'The plans provide an extra £250 million over the next two years for a new initiative to tackle homelessness ... Central Government support for the provision of new homes by housing associations will more than double from £800 million in 1989–90 to £1,700 million in 1992–93.

'There will be a further increase of over £500 million in the total resources available to higher education in 1990–91 compared with this year. It will provide for the continuing growth in the number of students, which has risen by 30 per cent since 1979 and is now at a record level ... There is provision for more environmental research, including the new climate change centre and the doubling of our contribution to the United Nations environmental programme.

'The plans include the money central Government provides to support local authority spending ... The cost to the taxpayer of these measures will be nearly £700 million in 1990–91, with further substantial sums in each of the following two years.

'The Government's new plans demonstrate their continuing commitment to two vital principles: first, to maintain firm control over total spending; and secondly, to increase efficiency in order to provide more resources where they are most needed.'

NATIONAL INSURANCE

Turning to national insurance contributions, the Chancellor said, 'Next year, the initial class 1 rate payable on earnings up to the lower earnings limit will remain at 2 per cent ... On additional earnings, up to the upper earnings limit, the rate will remain unchanged at 9 per cent. For employers, the main rate will also be unchanged at 10.45 per cent. The lower earnings limit will be increased to £46 a week, in line with the single person's pension, and the upper earnings limit for the three reduced bands will be increased broadly in line with prices.'

Mr. Major concluded, 'The Government's fiscal position is also very strong. I now expect this year's fiscal surplus to be about £12,500 million, equivalent to 2.5 per cent of GDP. That represents a very tight fiscal stance by any standards.

'As domestic demand slows, import growth should moderate. At the same time, the strong rise in imports, which has been one of the most welcome developments in 1989, is forecast to continue. Non-oil visible exports are expected to rise by over 11 per cent this year, the highest rate since 1973, and we expect a further substantial increase next year. As a result, we now forecast that the current account deficit will fall from some £20,000 million in the current year to about £15,000 million in 1990.

'We will also see a further reduction in inflation. The headline measure of retail price inflation has already peaked at over 8 per cent in May and June this year, and has since come down a little. Following the recent rise in mortgage rates, it will remain high for some months, but our forecast is for it to fall to

5.75 per cent by the fourth quarter of 1990, and I expect to see it fall still further after that.

'Our priority must be to bring inflation down decisively, and keep it down. To achieve this, the economy must slow down for a while. This does mean that 1990 may not be an easy year, but the economy enters the 1990s in incomparably better shape than it entered the 1980s.'

THE QUEEN'S SPEECH

On November 16 the Parliamentary session ended. The Queen opened the new session of Parliament on November 21 and in her speech, which outlined the Government's legislative programme for the session, said:

'I look forward to visiting New Zealand next February for the 150th anniversary of the treaty of Waitangi and for the Commonwealth Games, and, in June, to paying a State visit to Iceland and a visit to Canada.

'My Government will continue to attach the highest priority to national and Western security and to the preservation of peace with freedom and justice. They will stand by their obligations to the NATO Alliance and will continue to sustain the United Kingdom's contribution to Western defence by maintaining adequate and effective nuclear and conventional forces.

'My Government will work for balanced and verifiable measures of arms control. They will continue to play an active part in the Vienna negotiations on the reduction of conventional forces in Europe and the multilateral negotiations in Geneva on the abolition of chemical weapons.

'My Government will continue to promote improved relations between East and West, and to work for further progress on human rights. They will aim to strengthen still further the present positive relations between the United Kingdom and the Soviet Union, and to encourage reform in that country. They will lend every possible encouragement and support to the remarkable changes taking place in Poland, Hungary and now in East Germany. They will work to ensure that these take place within a stable Europe.

'My Government will continue to support the right of the Afghan people to choose for themselves a fully representative government. They will continue to work for a peaceful solution to the conflicts in the middle east and to play their part in the search for a settlement in Cambodia. They look forward to the independence of Namibia and will continue to encourage the forces for peaceful change and reconciliation in southern Africa.

'My Government will work vigorously and with determination to restore confidence in Hong Kong, building on the foundation of the Sino-British Joint Declaration. They will honour their commitment to the people of the Falkland Islands while seeking further progress in normalizing relations with Argentina.

'My Government will continue to pursue firm financial policies designed to reduce inflation and foster the conditions necessary for sustained economic growth. They will continue to promote enterprise and to facilitate the growth of employment.

'A Bill will be introduced to assist the financial restructuring of the British Coal Corporation.

'A Bill will be introduced to facilitate the sale of the Crown Suppliers and other parts of the Property Services Agency.

'My Government will continue to attach very great importance to protecting the national and international environment. A Bill be introduced to provide new powers to control pollution and waste. My

Government will work with business, local government, the voluntary sector and local people to regenerate our cities.

'A Bill will be introduced to strengthen the law on food safety and consumer protection.

'My Government will continue to develop training and enterprise councils. Legislation will be introduced to make further reforms in industrial relations and trade union law.

'My Government will vigorously pursue their policies for reducing crime and combating the trafficking and abuse of drugs. A Bill will be introduced to improve the ability of the United Kingdom to co-operate with other countries in the investigation of crime.

'A Bill will be brought forward to provide for a wider choice of broadcast services, to strengthen the oversight of programme standards, to reform the independent television and radio systems and to implement the other proposals in the broadcasting White Paper.

'A Bill will be introduced to improve the administration of civil justice and to increase choice in the provision of legal services.

'My Government will continue to take action to raise standards in education. A Bill will be introduced to supplement students' grants with loans.

'A Bill will be brought forward to improve the National Health Service and the management of community care.

'A Bill will be introduced to institute a legal framework for scientific developments on human fertilization and embryology.

'For Scotland, legislation will be introduced to establish Scottish Enterprise and Highlands and Islands Enterprise, to prepare for the winding up of the new town development corporations, to increase choice in the provision of legal services and to effect certain other law reform measures.

'In Northern Ireland, my Government will maintain its support for the enforcement of the law and the defeat of terrorism. They will continue to encourage the greater involvement of locally elected representatives in the affairs of Northern Ireland, to improve the economic and social well-being of the Province, and to work within the framework of the Anglo-Irish Agreement.

'A Bill will be brought forward to improve aviation and maritime security.

'Legislation will be introduced to make changes to the law relating to social security and occupational pensions.

'Other measures will be laid before you.'

Debate on the Queen's Speech

The Leader of the Opposition (Neil Kinnock) welcomed some of the measures outlined in the Queen's Speech and gave qualified support to other elements. But he opposed certain measures 'root and branch', especially the proposed reforms of the National Health Service. He was also critical of the Government's record on inflation (7 per cent and rising) and the lack of any serious measures in the speech to combat this. He concluded, 'The Government have ruled the 1980s and have made it a decade of deceit, division and debt. They are out of touch, they are running out of time, and they will soon be out of power'. There was the usual six days of debate on the contents of the speech.

On November 30 the Trade Secretary (Nicholas Ridley) announced details of the Comptroller and Auditor General's report into the sale of the Rover Group to British Aerospace (BAe). The report covered the exclusivity of the negotiations, the adequacy of the agreed sum (£150 million) and the

way the deal was concluded. The Shadow Trade Secretary (Gordon Brown) accused the Secretary of State of having to be 'dragged to the House' to explain the sudden appearance of additional subsidies of some £38 million given to BAe.

On December 1 Nicholas Ridley introduced the Landlord and Tenant (Licensed Premises) Bill. The Bill had not been mentioned in the Queen's Speech, but is intended to repeal section 43 (1) (d) of the Landlord and Tenant Act 1954, thereby enabling the introduction of measures recommended by the Monopolies and Mergers Commission report on the brewing industry. On December 4 the Coal Industry Bill, which restructures the finances of the British Coal Corporation received its second reading in the House of Commons by 272 votes to 184. On December 5 the Food Safety Bill, intended to strengthen protection of the consumer, received its second reading in the House of Lords. In the Commons the Defence Secretary (Tom King) announced that, in order to increase production, full contractorization would be introduced into the Atomic Weapons Research Establishment (AWRE), though the land, facilities and other assets would remain in Government ownership. The Opposition Defence spokesman (Martin O'Neill) expressed particular concern over the safety aspects of such an arrangement. On December 6 the Agriculture Minister, John Gummer, answered a private notice question from his Labour opposite number (Dr David Clark) about his decision not to publish a list of microwave ovens that fail to cook foods to the minimum temperature required to kill bacteria. The Property Services Agency and Crown Suppliers Bill, to enable privatization to take place, received its second reading in the Commons by 237 votes to 189. On December 7 the Human Fertilization and Embryology Bill, which clarifies the law relating to research on human embryos and establishes a Human Fertilization and Embryology Authority, received its second reading in the Lords; the Government promised a free vote in both Houses on the issues of both embryology research and abortion. In the Commons the National Health Service and Community Care Bill, designed to implement the Government's NHS reforms and to set up the structure for care in the community, received its second reading (completed on December 11) by 323 votes to 247.

On December 11 Tom King announced that the Government had agreed to treat pre-1973 war widows on the same basis as those widowed after that date and that they would receive a special payment of £40 a week. The Minister's statement followed a public campaign. On December 12 the Foreign Secretary (Douglas Hurd) made a statement about the forcible repatriation of 51 Vietnamese boat people from Hong Kong. The Opposition had criticized the policy itself and the way in which it was carried out. On December 14 Transport Secretary Cecil Parkinson published a series of consultation papers containing proposals designed to relieve traffic congestion in London, such as a system of priority red routes and the enforcement of traffic and parking regulations. John Prescott criticized the plans for concentrating on roads rather than on public transport.

On December 18 the Broadcasting Bill, which will deregulate the broadcasting industry, received its second reading in the Commons by 310 votes to 238. On December 19 the Courts and Legal Services Bill received its second reading in the Lords. The Bill contains proposals to allow solicitors rights of audience in the higher courts, to allow building societies and banks to offer conveyancing (subject to safeguards), to permit 'no win, no fee' agreements between litigants and legal advisers, and to establish a new legal services ombudsman. In the Commons the Trade Secretary, Nicholas Ridley, made a statement on the publication of the report of the Parliamentary Commissioner on the Barlow Clowes affair. He announced that the Government had agreed that shareholders could claim 90 per cent of their investment up to £50,000; 80 per cent of investments between £50,000 and £100,000; and 60 per cent of investments over that. Gordon Brown wanted to know what action would be taken over the five significant areas of maladministration by the Department of Trade and Industry identified by the Commissioner.

On December 20 Douglas Hurd announced that in 1997, when Hong Kong is due to be handed back to the Chinese, 50,000 households and up to 250,000 Hong Kong citizens would be given full British passports. Recipients will be decided on the basis of a points system. The Shadow Foreign Secretary (Gerald Kaufman) described this system as inherently unworkable, invidious and divisive. Douglas Hurd also made a statement about the American invasion of Panama, welcoming the establishment of democratic government there. On December 21 the Education Secretary (John MacGregor) announced that the major banks had pulled out of the Student Loans Company, set up to handle the new student loans scheme currently under discussion in Parliament. Mr MacGregor said that the Government would continue with the introduction of student loans and would move the company to Government ownership. The Shadow Education Secretary (Jack Straw) felt that the measure should be withdrawn in its entirety.

On January 9 the Enterprise and New Towns (Scotland) Bill received its second reading in the Commons. It is intended to set up Scottish Enterprise and to improve arrangements for training and development in Scotland, partly through new private sector enterprise companies. On January 10 Tony Newton announced that a disability allowance would be introduced for people of working age and below. The Disability Employment Credit is intended to make it easier for the disabled to take up jobs, and an age-related addition will be added to the Severe Disablement Allowance. The Opposition Social Services spokesman (Michael Meacher) said that the proposals fell short of a comprehensive disability income, which was the real answer to the problem. The Aviation and Maritime Security Bill designed to combat international terrorism in the skies and at sea received an unopposed second reading in the Commons.

On January 15 the Environmental Protection Bill, which introduces the concept of integrated pollution control and the idea that the 'polluter pays', received its second reading in the Commons. On January 22 the Social Security Bill received its second reading in the Commons by 278 votes to 217. It proposes to amend the law relating to social security and to occupational and personal pensions, and to establish a Pensions Ombudsman and a registrar of Occupational and Personal Pension Schemes. It will also introduce the payment of grants for the improvement of energy efficiency in certain dwellings.

On January 29 the Home Secretary (David Waddington) announced the Government's response to the publication of the report by Lord Justice Taylor into the Hillsborough Stadium disaster in April 1989. Mr Waddington said that the Government would not be proceeding with the establishment of the Football Membership Authority and identity cards for supporters, as planned in the Football Spectators Act 1989. The Employment Bill, which outlaws the closed shop, received its second reading in the Commons by 255 votes to 198. On January 30 the Law Reform (Miscellaneous Provisions) (Scotland) Bill, a catch-all bill covering legal reforms, conveyancing, divorce and licensing, received its second reading in the Lords. On February 1 Tom King told the Commons

that there would be an inquiry into the dismissal of the former Army press officer Colin Wallace. Mr King said that the inquiry would not be investigating specifically Mr Wallace's claim to be the victim of a 'dirty tricks' operation. This limitation was criticized by Opposition MPs. In the Lords the Government was defeated (31 votes to 30) on an amendment moved by Lord Mischon (Lab.) to the Courts and Legal Services Bill. The amendment will require solicitors to account for the commissions charged on conveyancing, rather than simply disclosing them without detailed explanation.

In the Lords the Government was defeated on an amendment to the Human Fertilization and Embryology Bill moved by Lady Saltoun of Abernathy (Ind.) to prohibit the provision of artificial insemination by donors and in vitro fertilization to unmarried women. On February 8, on a free vote, the Lords approved Clause 11 of the Bill (embryo research) by 234 votes to 80.

On February 12 William Waldegrave, Minister of State at the Foreign and Commonwealth Office, answered a private notice question from Gerald Kaufman on the Government's policy towards Nelson Mandela following his release from prison in South Africa after 25 years. Mr Waldegrave welcomed the release, saying that Mr Mandela symbolized the aspirations of millions of South Africans to a non-racial and democratic South Africa. On February 13 the Employment Secretary (Michael Howard) told the Commons of the proposed sale of part of the Skills Training Agency to a management buyout team, Astra Training Services Ltd. The sale was criticized by Labour's Employment spokesman (Tony Blair), who felt that training should not be put into private hands but that the Government should invest more money in it. On February 16 Douglas Hurd told the Commons of plans to increase the number of directly elected seats to the Hong Kong legislature. The aim is to hold full direct elections by 2007, provided those drafting the Basic Law for the post-1997 period agree.

On February 27 the Education (Student Loans) Bill received its second reading in the Lords, despite an amendment moved by Lord Russell (Lib. Dem.) to the effect that the Government had not given the Lords sufficient information to enable them to judge whether the proposals in the bill were capable of being put into effect. The amendment was defeated by 174 votes to 124.

On March 7 the Trade Secretary, Nicholas Ridley, made a statement on the report of the inspectors investigating the take-over of Harrods by House of Fraser Holdings PLC. Mr Ridley reiterated the Government's decision not to refer the take-over to the Monopolies and Mergers Commission and the decision not to disqualify any director under section 8 of the Company Directors Disqualification Act 1986. He said he would not be publishing the report. The Commons debated the case of John Browne, the Conservative MP for Winchester, whom a select committee found had failed to inform the House of all his outside interests. The Commons endorsed the findings of the committee and voted (237 to 67) that Mr Browne be suspended from the House for four weeks without pay.

On March 12 William Waldegrave answered a private notice question from Gerald Kaufman on the Government's response to the 'unjustified sentence' imposed on Mr Farzad Bazoft and Mrs Daphne Parish for alleged spying in Iraq. On March 15, following the carrying out of the death sentence passed on Mr Bazoft, Douglas Hurd told the Commons that he had recalled the British ambassador in Iraq and had cancelled all military training provided in the UK for Iraqis. On March 13 the Northern Ireland Secretary (Peter Brooke) said the Government was deeply disappointed at the decision of the Supreme

Court in Dublin to overrule extradition orders on two convicted terrorists who had escaped from the Maze prison in Northern Ireland in 1983.

THE BUDGET

On March 20 John Major presented his first budget, which was also the first budget to be televised. The Chancellor began with an account of the performance of the economy in the past year (1989) and the prospects for the coming year (1990) but beforehand he paid a fulsome tribute to his predecessor, Nigel Lawson: 'He has left the public finances stronger than at any time in living memory and he was also the architect of as comprehensive a tax reform as any other Chancellor this century. That will be an enduring record.'

Outlining his proposals, which he claimed would include incentives both to save and to give, Mr Major said, 'The Government's economic policy has two main objectives. The first is to bring down inflation again. Until that happens, we cannot reduce interest rates and keep them down. The second is to enable the country to take the opportunities of the 1990s. In western Europe, the single market is nearly on us. And the whole of eastern Europe, where there is great good will for Britain, has opened up in a most dramatic way. We need to make sure that British business can take advantage of these changes.

'The general tightening of monetary policy is likely to mean lower growth in 1990 than last year and, in due course, a fall in inflation. We are likely, therefore, also to see slower growth in world trade in the current year, although the astonishing developments in eastern Europe improve the long-term prospects.

'High interest rates also reflect very strong investment growth over the last two years in all major industrialized economies. This rise in investment is to be welcomed but it also emphasizes the need for a healthy level of savings to finance it.

'During the last year, business confidence in Britain has remained a good deal stronger than many people expected. New businesses have outnumbered closures, by around 1,500 every week; a larger figure than we expected and a record never before approached. Employment has continued to rise and unemployment to fall. Almost 27 million men and women are in work today—a larger number than ever before and 1.5 million more than at the beginning of the 1980s. Business investment has risen by a further 9 per cent in the last year, making a total rise of 40 per cent over three years and taking it to its highest level ever, and a great part of this investment has been financed from rising company profits. In the last few years, profitability has recovered to the levels of 20 years ago.

INFLATION

'These are all favourable developments which reflect well on businesses' preparation for the future, but recently, they have been accompanied by the return of inflationary pressures. That, beyond any doubt, is the most urgent problem before us today. To a degree, it is a problem common to all nations. Since its low point in 1986 and 1987, inflation has risen significantly throughout the Group of Seven—the leading economies of the western world—but our affliction has been sharper. There are a number of reasons for this—some welcome and some not. The record rise in business investment is obviously welcome; but it has been accompanied by a rapid growth in borrowing and consumer spending ... Policy was therefore tightened, and interest rates have now been in double figures for 20 months ... Squeezing inflation is always difficult, but there is now clear evidence that demand is slowing down.

High street sales are now only 2 per cent up on a year ago. The housing market has cooled off noticeably. New car and vehicle registrations are down, and import growth has been sharply reduced.

'No one likes to see the economy slow, but it is inevitable if we are to push inflation downwards. I now expect the economy to grow by only 1 per cent this year, compared with the above-trend growth of 4.5 per cent in 1987 and 1988. The size of this slowdown shows the extent of the downward pressure on inflation. But growth should return in 1991 towards its sustainable rate of around 2.75 per cent.

'We cannot afford to relax policy ... the buoyancy of past demand means that inflation has been far more stubborn than expected. A significant fall is some months away and a number of factors will mean that the position will worsen noticeably before it improves. This will be reflected in the retail price index (RPI) during the next few months.

'The largest single factor is the increase of some £5,000 million in local authority revenue spending next year. This is mainly responsible for the expected growth of more than 30 per cent in average community charges compared to domestic rates. This will add more than 1 per cent to the RPI next month. Similarly, the further rise in mortgage rates last month will also increase the RPI. As a result I now expect that RPI inflation may still be a little over 7 per cent by the fourth quarter of this year, compared to the 5.75 per cent I had previously expected. Beyond that, as the effects of these one-off increases drop out and the lagged effect of monetary tightening builds up, I expect inflation to fall below 5 per cent during 1991.'

MONETARY POLICY

The Chancellor went on to deal with monetary policy and interest rates. 'In recent months, I have looked carefully to see whether there is any effective alternative to interest rates. I have done so because I am very conscious of the burden they place on business and on individuals purchasing their own homes.

'However, having looked at the matter, I have concluded that it is extremely unlikely that credit controls would work in the modern world in anything other than the very short term. They were becoming less and less effective even before exchange controls were abolished over ten years ago. Their main impact now would be to replace domestic borrowing with overseas borrowing. That, of course, applies to other countries too, and it is for that reason that governments of all persuasions throughout the western world are abolishing credit controls and are relying on interest rates to control money.'

Turning to the question of Britain joining the exchange rate mechanism, Mr Major said, 'Progress on reducing inflation is also a vital precondition of our commitment to take sterling into the exchange rate mechanism of the European monetary system. Our commitment to do so was set out at Madrid. It remains firm, and conditions for entry remain unchanged. When we join the exchange rate mechanism, it will provide a new framework for interest rate decisions, but even then, no one should suppose it will bring a dispensation from the need for strong domestic monetary control—indeed, quite the reverse. Commitment to the one will reinforce commitment to the other.

'My judgement is that interest rates will stay high for some time to come. The moment I judge that I can safely lower them, I shall, but to reduce them prematurely only to increase them again would be extremely damaging. When I bring them down, it will be because I believe that they are likely to stay down.'

FISCAL POLICY

The Chancellor turned to public sector finances, outlining the 'dramatic improvement' in their state over the past ten years. 'In the past three [years] we have repaid around £25,000 million, reducing the burden of Government debt to levels that we have not seen since before the first world war ... As a result of the debt repayments, we are saving over £2,500 million a year in debt interest.

'The fall in the surplus owes less to the slowdown in growth than to a number of special factors. We have seen a fall in privatization proceeds from the very high level achieved in 1988–89. There has also been a sharp and unwelcome increase in local authority spending. This has been particularly marked in their capital spending, as local authorities have sought to forestall the new controls which will take effect in April. As a result, we now expect the public expenditure planning total this year to be overshot by £2,250 million.

'Another, but much more welcome, factor in reducing the surplus has been the higher national insurance rebates which have resulted from the huge success of personal pensions ... Over 3.5 million people have now taken out personal pensions.

'Next year some of these factors will be partially reversed, but we will see the effect of slower growth on the debt repayment. In particular, corporation tax receipts are likely to fall a little after six years of rapid growth, not least because of the higher investment of recent years which can be set off against tax.

'Accordingly, I am budgeting next year for a further public sector debt repayment of £7,000 million—the same as this year.'

TAXATION ON BUSINESS

Turning to business taxation, the Chancellor began by announcing two measures designed to help cash flow. 'From April next year, all debts that are over two years old and written off in the trader's accounts will qualify automatically for relief from Value Added Tax (VAT). This will be worth about £150 million to business next year. I also propose to help companies by simplifying the rule for traders registering for VAT ... this will be based on actual turnover in the preceding 12 months and not unknown turnover in the distant future ... it will save businesses £35 million in 1990–91 and £75 million the year after that.

'I have two further VAT changes. First, I propose to increase the VAT threshold to £25,400, a modest sum, but the maximum permitted under European Community law. The second change ... I propose is that VAT paid on directors' accommodation should no longer be deductible.

'I also have some changes to corporation tax. While the main rate ... will remain at 35 per cent, I propose to reduce the burden of tax for smaller companies. At present, companies with profits below £150,000 pay a reduced rate of corporation tax of 25 per cent. I propose to raise this ceiling by one third, to £200,000. For companies with profits above this limit, the average rate of tax gradually rises until their profits reach the upper profits limit of £750,000 a year. I propose to raise this limit, again by a third, to £1 million ... These changes mean that we will have the most favourable structure of corporation tax for small companies anywhere in the European Community.

'I also have a specific tax to help training ... In future, over £2,000 million of our public expenditure on training will be spent through training and enterprise councils (TECs), most of which will be coming into operation over the next year. The Government has already promised to match local business donations to TECs pound for pound within certain limits. I now propose to encourage businesses to maximize the money they put into training by providing tax relief on business donations to TECs for five years until April 1995. I propose to extend the same concession to local enterprise agencies until the same date.

'My next announcement has implications for one in four of the adult population, for that is the number of people—nearly 11 million—who now own shares in the United Kingdom ... I therefore decided to abolish stamp duty on securities late in 1991–92 to coincide as closely as I can manage with the introduction of paperless trading. Stamp duty reserve tax will also be abolished at the same time. Both the abolition of the tax and the introduction of a more modern dealing system will help to secure the United Kingdom's position as a leading financial centre in an increasingly competitive world market.

'The Finance Bill will also include a number of measures on life assurance ... These measures, which flow from the changes in the Finance Act 1989, followed extensive consultation with the industry. They put the taxation of life assurance companies' unit trust holdings on a sounder footing, and make a number of technical improvements. They will yield £50 million in 1990–91. A further measure will be introduced to ring-fence long-term business assets. Without this there could be a significant loss of tax.

'I also have a measure to announce that will clarify the tax regime for banks ... I have decided to remove the uncertainties of the present law. Banks will continue to be able to offset their losses on sovereign loans fully against tax, but under a clearer mechanism than previously, which will be broadly based on the Bank of England's present guidelines. There will be a limit on future increases in the cost of this tax relief between years. For the 12 months starting today, banks' tax relief on such provisions will be limited to the same high proportion of debts as this mechanism indicates for 1989. Thereafter, the ceiling will be increased in steps of 5 per cent a year so that the banks will, in time, get all the tax relief to which they are entitled. If the banks sell their debt to a third party and crystallize their losses, their tax relief on them will be similarly phased, but where the debt is sold back to the foreign state, to reduce its debt once and for all, tax relief on that loss will be available in full and immediately. This measure will produce a yield of around £200 million in 1991–92.'

TAXES ON SPENDING

Turning to excise duties, Mr Major told the Commons that, taken as a whole, they must rise broadly in line with inflation but that he did have some modest adjustments. 'First for vehicle excise duty (VED) ... Last year's budget removed 80 different VED rates, and I propose to eliminate a further 188 today. VED on cars will be unchanged once again this year at £100. Nor will there be any change in VED for public or private sector buses, coaches, taxis and many lorries. I will recoup the cost of this by increasing petrol and DERV duties by rather more than strict revalorization. These will rise by 10 per cent. This will add 9p to a gallon of DERV and almost 11p to a gallon of leaded petrol. For unleaded, the cash increase will be smaller, at around 9p per gallon. This will widen the tax differential even further in favour of unleaded petrol. This will amount to almost 16p a gallon.

'For alcohol, with one exception, I propose to raise the duties in line with inflation. This will put 7p on a bottle of table wine, but only 2p on a pint of beer. Spirits, however, have enjoyed a duty standstill since 1985. I propose therefore an increase of 10 per cent, which will increase the price of a bottle of spirits by 54p.

'Cigarettes also were not increased last year. This year I propose a 10 per cent increase in duty, which will put 10p on a packet of 20 cigarettes. The duty on cigars will rise similarly, and will add 5p to the cost of a packet of five small cigars. But I do not this year propose any increase in the duty on pipe tobacco.'

FOOTBALL

The Chancellor now turned to Lord Justice Taylor's report into football ground safety following the disaster at Hillsborough, which had recommended improvements to both comfort and safety at football league grounds over the next ten years. The Chancellor outlined the fiscal assistance which the Government was proposing to give football clubs to implement the programme of work envisaged. He said, 'Much of the expenditure required . . . is eligible for capital allowances or full offset against tax . . . and I have asked the Inland Revenue to provide urgent guidance to clarify the tax position. However, tax allowances cannot help where there is no profit to set costs against. This is the case with many clubs. I have therefore reviewed the rate of pool betting duty—the tax which is paid by the pools companies on the stakes they receive. This currently stands at 42.5 per cent. I propose to reduce it to 40 per cent, on the clear understanding that the full amount saved is passed by the pools promoters to the Football Trust, and is used by it to improve safety and comfort of fans at English and Scottish football league grounds . . . The duty will be reduced, in the first instance for five years. At the end of that period, I will review the position again. This reduction will yield around £100 million for football over five years.'

INCOME TAX

The Chancellor had no change to announce to either the basic or the higher rate of income tax but he did confirm that it remained the Government's objective to move towards a basic rate of 20p when it was possible to do so. He did announce some changes to personal tax allowances: 'This year I propose to uprate the main income tax allowances by the statutory indexation factor of 7.7 per cent rounded up. The personal allowances will rise by £220 to £3,005. The new married couple's allowance will be set at £1,720, as will the additional personal allowance for single parents and the widow's bereavement allowance. However, the basic rate limit, the level at which higher rate liability begins, will be unchanged, at £20,700 of taxable income.

'The allowances for the elderly will similarly be fully uprated in line with inflation. For those aged 65 to 74, the personal allowance goes up by £270 to £3,670 and the married couple's allowance goes up by £160 to £2,145. For those aged 75 and over, the personal allowance goes up by £280 to £3,820 and the married couple's allowance will rise to £2,185. The income limit for these allowances will also be fully indexed to £12,300.

'I also propose to raise the inheritance tax threshold by £10,000 to £128,000, in line with inflation.

'The capital gains tax exemption currently stands at £5,000. However, from April, the introduction of independent taxation means that married couples will be entitled to . . . two amounts rather than having to share one between them as at present. I have therefore decided to leave the exempt amount at £5,000 per person, which effectively gives a married couple an exemption of £10,000 in total.

'I also have to set the scales for the taxation of the private use of company cars . . . I propose an increase—but a smaller one than in previous years—of 20 per cent. The yield from this will be £160 million in 1990–91. There will be no change in the fuel scales.

'The tax allowance for the blind, although anomalous, has long been accepted as a proper recognition of the special difficulties faced by blind people. This allowance is modest, but welcome, at £540 a year. I propose to make it less modest and more welcome and to double it. From April 6, it will stand at £1,080.

'Before I leave income tax, I have a small supply-side measure to announce that will help the labour market to work better. We have always made it clear that it is not for the Government to encourage or discourage women with children to go out to work . . . However, it is undeniable that an increasing number of mothers do want to return to work, and many employers, in private industry and in public services . . ., are keen to encourage them to do so. If an employer provides a nursery for his staff . . ., he can set out the full cost against corporation tax. However, any employee who benefits and who earns more than £8,500 a year is required to pay tax on the value of the benefit in kind. Many employers have argued that this is an obstacle to growth and many women see that as a positive disincentive to return to work. For those reasons, I have decided to exempt the value of workplace nurseries and playgroups from taxation as benefit in kind. That will take effect from April 6 this year.'

CHARITIES

Mr Major praised the British for their generous instinct towards causes that appealed to them. Whilst he felt that the tax system already offered a great deal of help to charities, he had further proposals to help. He continued, 'We have been considering how covenants can be made easier for charities and donors to use and the Inland Revenue will therefore be issuing new guidance to simplify them. Since 1987, relief for covenants has been complemented by the payroll giving scheme. The scheme has been doing well since its launch, and I now propose to increase the annual limit from £480 to £600.

'These reliefs are focused mainly on regular giving, which is of great importance to charities. However, they are ill suited to encourage the one-off gift which, for a variety of reasons, many people find more convenient. Therefore, I propose a gift aid scheme that will, for the first time, give tax relief for large money donations . . . The lower qualifying limit for gift aid will be £600 per donation—the new ceiling for payroll giving. The relief will be available on one-off gifts up to an annual ceiling of £5 million per individual donor. The tax relief will be reclaimable by the charity, and payable to it at basic rate. As with covenants, the donor will get any higher rate tax relief that is due direct from the tax office . . . This will come into operation from October 1 this year.

'I have a further measure to help charities. This is a package of VAT reliefs, giving help especially to organizations engaged in sea rescue, medical care and research. These will come into effect on May 1 and give an additional benefit of about £5 million a year.'

SAVINGS

Turning to the taxation of savings, the Chancellor began with shares. 'I am pleased to report that last year was a record one for personal equity plans (PEPs), with 300,000 plans taken out to a value of some £750 million. To build on this success, I propose to raise the overall annual limit on investment in PEPs by a quarter, from £4,800 to £6,000. Within that, the annual limit on investment in unit and investment trusts will be increased by the same percentage to £3,000. I am also sympathetic to the problems that investment and unit trusts face in qualifying for PEP treatment. This arises from the requirement that 75 per cent of their portfolio should be invested in ordinary UK equities. I propose to relax this rule to 50 per cent. I also propose to raise the PEP limit for those trusts that do not satisfy this rule from the present £750 to £900.

'Last year [the Chancellor] put employee share ownership plans or ESOPs ... on the statute book. One impediment to their growth has been that the transfer of shares to the work-force can mean that the company owner faces an immediate tax charge. To prevent this, I propose to introduce a rollover relief from capital gains tax for sales of shares to ESOPs. I believe that this will remove an obstacle to their development and give this form of employee share ownership the fillip that it deserves.'

Mr Major then turned to discuss the effect of independent taxation of women, which had been announced in the 1988 budget. He said, 'In future, a husband and wife will be taxed entirely separately. Every married woman will have a tax allowance of her own to set against her income. Three and three quarter million people will gain. One million elderly married couples will pay less tax, and 200,000 pensioner couples will be taken out of tax altogether. No one will be sorry to see the old system go. One of its worst features was its treatment of the savings of married women. Whether they had other income or not, the interest on their savings was added to their husband's income and taxed at his rate. This was a clear penalty on thrift. From April, all that will end.

However, independent taxation has thrown into sharp relief another aspect of the tax system that affects all savers, and which no longer deserves to survive. Some women will see the benefit of independent taxation automatically, if they have their money invested in national savings, or other accounts which pay interest gross of tax, but many women with only small savings prefer to save with high street banks or building societies, and so, frankly, do many other small savers. For all these savers, income tax—or rather, a proxy for it, called the composite rate—is deducted before the interest ever gets to the saver, and whether or not the saver is liable to pay tax.

'The scale of the problem is compelling. Once independent taxation is implemented, there will be 14 million people who have savings income that does not merit taxation, but which is taxed under present legislation. There is no way out of this problem other than to abolish composite rate tax entirely. This I propose to do with effect from April 6, 1991, the earliest practicable date. From then on, tax will fall on those who should pay it, and not on those who should not pay it. We shall discuss with the banks and building societies how to effect this enormous organizational change.

'Meanwhile the Department of National Savings also has a part to play in encouraging the savings habit. I am therefore announcing today a 1 per cent increase in the interest paid on national savings investment account and income bonds, where interest is already paid gross.'

Having recapped on the measures already taken by the Government to encourage the saving habit among taxpayers, Mr Major went on to outline a new scheme: 'I propose to introduce a wholly new tax incentive which will reward saving and encourage people to build up a stock of capital. Every adult will be entitled to one tax exempt special savings account, TESSA for short. All commercial banks or building societies will be able to offer such an account. The essence of the scheme is to encourage people to save regularly over a five-year period. The incentive for them to do so is that all the interest earned on their capital will be entirely free of tax, provided only that the capital itself is left undisturbed over the five-year period. The annual limit on the amount that can be invested will be £1,800 or £150 a month. In the first year, anyone who has capital that they are willing to tie up for longer can put this money in their account from the outset, up to a limit of £3,000, but the overall limit of £9,000 for the whole plan applies nonetheless.

'To cope with the circumstances of many small savers who use their interest on their savings for their everyday expenses, it will be possible to withdraw interest, but only up to the net-of-tax level. At the end of the five years, the depositor then gets a bonus representing the money which would otherwise have gone in tax. The depositor will get this provided none of the capital has been withdrawn before the five years is up. They can, of course, withdraw the capital at any time, but without tax relief.

'This scheme is convenient, flexible and simple. The new relief will be available from January next year. Its costs will depend on take-up, but could be at least £200 million in the first full year, and rising thereafter.'

SOCIAL SECURITY SYSTEM

Mr Major, having completed the passage on savings incentives, then began to discuss the anomalies in the system that appeared to penalize those who held savings, in particular the social security claimants affected by the so-called 'capital rule'. During this passage of the Chancellor's speech there were interruptions from Scottish Opposition MPs, who were incensed that the reforms being suggested for community charge relief were not to be applied retrospectively to Scotland, where the charge had already been in operation for a year.

The changes that provoked this disruption were outlined by the Chancellor: 'People with capital over £3,000 start to have their benefits reduced, and those with more than a certain level of savings—£6,000 in the case of income support and family credit and £8,000 in the case of housing benefit and community charge benefit—become completely ineligible for all means-tested benefits, however low their incomes. There must, of course, be some upper limits above which help is no longer given, but the present limits are widely resented as a penalty on thrift and self-provision. I have therefore reviewed the present limits with ... the Secretary of State for Social Services and we have decided that they should be raised. The limit for income support and family credit, where the stress is less great, will rise from £6,000 to £8,000, but the problem is most acute for those whose savings disqualify them from housing benefit and from community charge benefit. I propose, therefore, to double the capital cut-off for both these benefits, from £8,000 to £16,000. This measure will benefit around a quarter of a million people, two thirds of them pensioners who are at present wholly excluded from benefit. The total cost will be £120 million a year, which will be met from the reserve and will not increase the public expenditure levels. The necessary regulations will be laid today so that the limits will be increased when the benefits are uprated at the beginning of April.'

The Chancellor concluded, 'This is a saver's budget. It takes no risks with inflation. It further strengthens the public finances. It helps the less well-off. It gives women a better deal. It offers help to charities and sport, and it reduces the tax burden on growing companies. It is the right budget for this year, and it sets the right course for the 90s.'

Debate on the Budget

The ensuing debate was dominated by the row over the failure to apply community charge relief to Scotland. Neil Kinnock, the Leader of the Opposition, congratulated the Chancellor on his maiden budget and agreed that there was much in it that the Opposition could welcome and support. But he went on to say, 'The Budget yet again completely fails to address the necessity of actively promoting the objective of a commitment to long-termism, yet we know that it is the course that must be followed, not only because it makes sense for our under-invested and debt-ridden economy but because commitment to the long term so obviously works in practice for competitor countries.' Dr David Owen, the SDP leader, wondered whether the Chancellor had grappled with the basic problem of the British economy, the underlying rate of inflation. After the usual four days of debate the Budget motion was carried by 320 votes to 218.

On March 27 the Transport Secretary (Cecil Parkinson) told the Commons that the Government had dropped the majority of the road proposals issued in *Traffic in London* in December following the representations that had been received in the consultation period. He said that the Government would still be looking for improved rail links, however. Martyn Jones (Lab., Clwyd SW), who had secured top place in the ballot for Private Members' Bills, had introduced the Consumer Guarantees Bill, which was intended to strengthen the rights of the consumer. On March 30 Mr Jones was forced to withdraw all the elements of his Bill relating to the consumer guarantee in the Remaining Stages debate in the Commons, because the Consumer Affairs Minister (Eric Forth) had made it clear that the Government would not accept the proposals to their present form.

On April 2 the Home Secretary (David Waddington) made a statement about the weekend's disturbances in central London during a protest march about the community charge; 339 people had been arrested. MPs from all sides of the House defended the right of free people to demonstrate peacefully but condemned outright the violence of this march. On April 3 the Environment Secretary (Chris Patten) announced the details of his plans to 'charge cap' some 20 high spending councils, all Labour. This was condemned by Bryan Gould, the Shadow Environment Minister, as an overtly political move that was not based on any defensible principle. On April 4 the Scottish Secretary (Malcolm Rifkind) announced details of a scheme to introduce retrospectively an increased upper limit for community charge benefit in Scotland, in line with the Budget proposals for England and Wales.

On April 18 the Trade Secretary (Nicholas Ridley) made a statement in the Commons about the seizure on April 10 of metal tubes which were bound for Iraq and which could be used for making a 'supergun.' This incident followed the seizure of nuclear trigger devices in March. On April 19 the British Nationality (Hong Kong) Bill received its second reading in the Commons by 313 votes to 216. On April 23, in a free vote, the Commons voted by 362 votes to 189 in favour of Clause 11 of the Human Fertilization and Embryology Bill allowing regulated research using embryos. The next day, after a series of late night votes, the Commons voted by 409 to 152 to reduce the time limit for legal abortions to 24 weeks. On April 23 David Waddington announced that the siege at Strangeways prison in Manchester had finally ended after more than three weeks and that an inquiry would be set up under Lord Justice Woolf.

On May 1 the Government was defeated in the House of Lords on a cross-party amendment to the Law Reform (Miscellaneous Provisions) (Scotland) Bill. The amendment, to prevent the use of video evidence in cases of alleged war crimes committed in German-held territory, was passed, by 137 votes to 62, removing the proposal from the Bill.

On May 8 the Government was defeated in the Lords on an amendment to the NHS and Community Care Bill. Moved by Lord Allen of Abbeydale (Ind.) with all-party support, the amendment would prevent grants for the provision of community care services being put to any other purpose, and was passed by 127 votes to 119. An Opposition amendment to make community care proposals subject to an Order by the Secretary of State after consultation with local authorities, users and carers was passed by 114 votes to 113. On May 10 the Government was defeated again (by 67 votes to 66) on an amendment moved by Lord Seebohm (Ind.) which would compel local councils to explain how they were going to find homes for schizophrenics, the mentally and physically handicapped and the disabled needing care.

On May 16 Malcolm Rifkind, the Scottish Secretary, made a statement to the House regretting the proposed closure of the Ravenscraig strip mill by British Steel. His comment that he hoped to persuade the company to reconsider its decision angered many free-market Conservative MPs who felt that this should not be Government policy. The issue was debated on an Opposition motion on May 21. On May 17 the Agriculture Minister (John Gummer) made a statement about bovine spongiform encephalopathy (BSE) and reiterated that the 'clear and consistent advice of the best scientific opinion is that British beef is safe'. This subject was also debated on an Opposition motion on May 21. On May 17 the Northern Ireland Secretary (Peter Brooke) announced the results of the Stevens inquiry into allegations of collusion between members of the security forces in Northern Ireland and loyalist paramilitaries. The inquiry found a few cases of collusion involving a very small number of members of the UDR, and made recommendations to ensure that this would not happen again.

In the Lords on May 21 the Government experienced four defeats on the Social Security Bill: an amendment was successfully moved by Baroness Darcy de Knayth (Ind.) to allow deaf and dyslexic students to claim income support and housing benefit (87 votes to 86); and two amendments were moved by Baroness David (Lab.) to prevent the Government from removing grants to students (86 votes to 53, and 77 votes to 53). A new Government clause to change the system to allow the recovery of benefit from accident victims who eventually receive compensation was rejected by 69 votes to 58.

On June 4 the second reading of the War Crimes Bill, intended to enable the prosecution of Nazi war criminals now resident in the UK, was rejected by the Lords. An amendment moved by Lord Campbell of Alloway (Con.), declining to give the Bill a second reading on the grounds of retrospection and the impossibility of a fair trial, was passed by 207 votes to 74. On June 7 John Gummer came straight to the Commons from Brussels to announce the outcome of negotiations with the European Commission over import bans on British beef because of fears of BSE. The negotiations resulted in the lifting of import bans imposed by some European countries in return for higher safety standards.

On June 14 Cecil Parkinson, the Transport Secretary, announced that the Government would not be putting any money towards the high-speed rail link between London and the Channel Tunnel, a move condemned by John Prescott as one that meant Britain would enter the 21st century with an inadequate 19th century railway system. On June 21 the Home Secretary (David Waddington) made a statement on the report of the Calcutt inquiry into the press's respect for privacy, and related matters. He announced the setting up of new standards for protecting the privacy of individuals.

On June 26 David Waddington gave the Commons details of the bombing of the Carlton Club in London by the IRA, in which several people had been injured but only two had been detained in hospital. There was some criticism of the Government for making the statement at all, because this was seen as elevating the incident and giving publicity to the bombers. On June 27 the Commons reversed all the defeats the Government had experienced in the Lords on the NHS and Community Care Bill. However, the Commons did ensure the safeguarding of grants for the treatment of drug and alcohol dependants. On the same day the Commons select committee on energy produced its report on the cost of nuclear power, in which it criticized Cecil Parkinson, the former Energy Secretary, Malcolm Rifkind (the Scottish Secretary) and the industry itself for failing to disclose the true costs of nuclear power generation. On June 28 the Trade Secretary (Nicholas Ridley) made a statement about the European Commission ruling on the arrangements agreed between the British Government and British Aerospace (BAe) over the sale to BAe of the Government shareholding in the Rover Group. The Commission ruled on June 27 that BAe should repay the £44.4 million of 'sweeteners' it received from the Government as inducement to buy Rover. Mr Ridley told the Commons that the Government accepted the Commission's ruling but felt that the repayment figure was too high by at least £11 million. Gordon Brown, the Shadow Trade and Industry Secretary, called the deal a 'sorry and shameful tale of incompetence and deception'. The Commons select committee on trade and industry announced that it would carry out its own inquiry into the sale.

On July 2 the Environment Minister (Chris Patten) told the Commons of the outcome of the conference on the environment held in London. This had resulted in an agreement to phase out harmful chlorofluorocarbons (CFCs) by the year 2000, with intermediate cuts of 50 per cent by 1995 and 85 per cent by 1997, compared to 1986. It had also been agreed that halons should be phased out by the year 2000, except for essential uses, with an intermediate cut of 50 per cent by 1995. On July 3 a dispute in the Commons over the announcement of details of the first hospitals to opt out and form independent NHS trusts led to the Speaker suspending the Commons for ten minutes owing to 'unruly behaviour'. The Health Secretary (Kenneth Clarke) had to return to the Commons on July 4 to give the details. On July 5 the Government was defeated in the Lords on an amendment to the Environmental Protection Bill moved by Lord Stanley of Alderley (Con.) which will require owners of dogs to register them. The Government indicated that it might not overturn this amendment when the Bill returns to the Commons.

On July 10, in the committee stage of the Law Reform (Miscellaneous Provisions) (Scotland) Bill, the Scottish Secretary was obliged to withdraw several of the clauses relating to licensing reform and divorce. Because of the lack of co-operation from Scottish Conservative backbench MPs on the committee, who were concerned at the wide scope of the Bill and the shortage of time to discuss it, there was a danger of the Bill not completing its committee stage on schedule. On July 14 Nicholas Ridley resigned as Trade and Industry Secretary following the publication in the *Spectator* of an interview in which he questioned the role and motives of a united Germany in the European Community. The views expressed in the interview had led to a row in Prime Minister's question time on July 12 when Mrs Thatcher distanced herself from her Minister but refused to sack him, causing Labour MP Dawn Primarolo to ask if there was 'anything the Secretary of State could do or say that would get him the sack?'

On July 17 the Lords passed the report stage of the Landlord and Tenant (Licensed Premises) Bill only after accepting a codicil moved by Lord Williams of Elvel (Labour's spokesman on trade) criticizing the Government for failing to honour a commitment made by Trade Minister (Lord Trefgarne) in the second reading debate. Lord Trefgarne had undertaken to bring forward an amendment to provide for special arrangements for compensation of tenants of licensed premises during a transitional period. On July 18 Kenneth Clarke, the Health Secretary, announced that the Government intended to phase in its new community care proposals over two years, rather than introduce them immediately, as had been expected. On July 19 Chris Patten, the Environment Secretary, made a statement outlining the Government's package of community charge reforms. These will include increased assistance offered through the transitional relief scheme, extended for a year, amounting to some £300 million of extra Government money. Other adjustments would also be made, including a change to the business rate for bed and breakfast accommodation, to be based on the amount of accommodation rather than the length of time the rooms were available. Announcements about the arrangements for Wales and Scotland were made separately by the Welsh Secretary (David Hunt) on July 23 and the Scottish Secretary (Malcolm Rifkind) on July 25. On July 18 the Government was defeated in the Lords on an amendment to the Broadcasting Bill moved by Baroness David requiring television to maintain public service programmes (91 votes to 64). Late on July 19 the Commons voted to make permanent the experimental televising of the proceedings of the House. An amendment moved by Dale Campbell-Savours (Lab.) to set up a dedicated channel to broadcast the Commons' proceedings was defeated by 94 votes to 67. On July 20 the Energy Minister (Peter Morrison) announced that the Government had decided to redeem their remaining 'golden share' in Britoil. Opposition MPs protested that it was too important a statement to be made on a Friday when most MPs, especially those Scottish MPs most affected by the decision, were not at Westminster.

On July 23 the Independent Labour MP Dick Douglas (Dunfermline W), who had resigned the Labour whip over the party's policy on non-payment of the community charge, was suspended from the Commons for five days for obstructing the business of the House. The Energy Secretary (John Wakeham) announced that Hanson PLC had expressed an interest in acquiring PowerGen, the smaller of the two electricity generating companies to be privatized in 1991, and that the Government was following up this expression of interest. He said that if Hanson did bid, the Government would be looking for an auction involving other potential purchasers. Frank Dobson, the Shadow Energy Minister, derided this as the end of popular capitalism and an example of the Government rewarding its friends. On July 24 the Prime Minister announced changes to the funding of the Civil List (which makes an annual grant to members of the Royal Family), in effect reverting to the system that was in operation under the Civil List Act 1972. On July 25 the Defence Secretary (Tom King) made a statement outlining the Government's proposed cuts in the armed forces following the recent events in Eastern Europe. These were welcomed on all sides of the House. Later, in a debate on an Opposition motion on the Government's 'mismanagement' of the economy, the Shadow Chancellor (John Smith) criticized the Chancellor's proposal of a 'hard ECU'. Mr Major had put forward this proposal at the economic summit in Houston earlier in July. He suggested that the European Community should have a two-tier financial system, based on national currencies and the european currency unit (ECU) which would work in tandem.

Both Houses rose for the summer recess on July 26.

THE PRINCIPAL PARTIES IN PARLIAMENT (1931–1987)

General Election	Conservative	Liberal	Labour
1931............	471	72 (a)	65 (b)
1935............	387	54 (c)	166 (d)
1945............	189	25 (e)	396 (f)
1950............	298 (g)	9	315 (h)
1951............	320 (i)	6	296 (h)
1955............	344 (i)	6	277 (j)
1959............	365 (i)	6	258 (k)
1964............	303 (i)	9	317
1966............	253 (i)	12	363 (l)
1970............	330 (m)	6	287 (n)
1974 (February)	296	14	301 (o)
1974 (October) ..	276	13	319 (p)
1979............	339	11	268 (q)
1983............	397	23 (r)	209 (s)
1987............	376	22 (t)	229 (u)

NOTES.—(a) Liberal National 35 (Simon); Liberal 33 (Samuel); 4 (Lloyd George). (b) National Labour 13 (MacDonald); Labour 52 (Henderson). (c) Liberal National 33; Liberal 21. (d) National Labour 8; Labour 154; ILP 4. (e) Liberal National 13; Liberal 12. (f) Labour 393; ILP 3. (g) Incl. Nat. Liberal. (h) Irish Nationalists (2) and Speaker make total of 625.

(i) Including associates. (j) Sinn Fein (2) and Speaker make total of 630. (k) Independent (1) makes total of 630. (l) Republican Labour (1) makes total of 630. (m) Including Ulster Unionists. (n) Scottish Nationalist (1); Independent (5) and Speaker make total of 630. (o) United Ulster Unionist Council (11), Scottish Nationalist (7), Plaid Cymru (2); Social Democratic and Labour Party (1); Social Democrat (1); Independent Labour (1); and Speaker make total of 635. (p) Scottish Nationalist (11); United Ulster Unionist (10); Plaid Cymru (3); Social Democratic and Labour Party (1); Independent (1) and Speaker make a total of 635. (q) Ulster Unionist (5); Democratic Unionist (3); Plaid Cymru (2); Scottish Nationalist (2); Social Democratic and Labour (1); United Ulster Unionist (1); Independent (2) and Speaker make a total of 635. (r) Liberal 17; SDP 6. (s) Official Unionist (11); Democratic Unionist (3); Scottish Nationalist (2); Plaid Cymru (2); Ulster Popular Unionist (1); Social Democratic and Labour Party (1) and Provisional Sinn Fein (1) make a total of 650. (t) Liberal 17; SDP 5. (u) Ulster Unionist (9); Scottish Nationalist (3); Plaid Cymru (3); Democratic Unionist (3); Social Democratic and Labour Party (3); Ulster Popular Unionist (1); Sinn Fein (1) make a total of 650.

PARLIAMENTS SINCE 1945

Assembled	Dissolved	Duration yrs. m. d.	Assembled	Dissolved	Duration yrs. m. d.
1945 Aug. 1	1950 Feb. 3	4 6 2	1970 June 29	1974 Feb. 8	3 7 10
1950 March 1	1951 Oct. 5	1 7 4	1974 March 6	1974 Sept. 20	0 6 14
1951 Oct. 31	1955 May 6	3 6 6	1974 Oct. 22	1979 April 7	4 5 16
1955 June 7	1959 Sept. 18	4 3 11	1979 May 9	1983 May 13	4 0 4
1959 Oct. 20	1964 Sept. 25	4 11 5	1983 June 15	1987 May 18	3 11 3
1964 Oct. 27	1966 March 10	1 4 11	1987 June 17		
1966 April 18	1970 May 29	4 1 11			

MAJORITIES IN THE HOUSE OF COMMONS SINCE 1945

Year	Party	Majority	Year	Party	Majority
1945	Labour	146	1970	Conservative	31
1950	Labour	8	1974 (Feb.)	No majority	
1951	Conservative	16	1974 (Oct.)	Labour	5
1955	Conservative	59	1979	Conservative	43
1959	Conservative	100	1983	Conservative	144
1964	Labour	5	1987	Conservative	102
1966	Labour	99			

VOTES CAST AT UK GENERAL ELECTIONS, 1974–87

General Election, October, 1974*

Labour	11,456,597
Conservative	10,464,675
Liberal	5,346,800
Scottish Nationalist	839,628
Plaid Cymru	166,321
Others	195,065

General Election, 1983*

Conservative	13,012,602
Labour	8,457,124
Liberal/SDP Alliance	7,780,587
Scottish Nationalist	331,975
Plaid Cymru	125,309
Others	198,383

General Election, 1979*

Conservative	13,697,753
Labour	11,506,741
Liberal	4,305,324
Scottish Nationalist	504,259
National Front	191,706
Plaid Cymru	132,544
Others	188,063

General Election, 1987*

Conservative	13,760,525
Labour	10,029,944
Liberal/SDP Alliance	7,341,152
Scottish Nationalist	416,873
Plaid Cymru	123,589
Green†	89,753
Others	37,576

*Excluding Northern Ireland seats   †Excluding Ecology candidate in Northern Ireland

PUBLIC ACTS OF PARLIAMENT 1989–90

This list is of Public Acts which all received the Royal Assent after August 1989. The date stated after each Act is the date it came into force.

Brunei (Appeals) Act 1989, c. 36 (Feb. 1, 1990) provides for the making of Orders in Council conferring jurisdiction on the Judicial Committee of the Privy Council in respect of appeals from the Supreme Court of Brunei Darussalam in order to give effect to arrangements between the UK and the Brunei Darussalam governments.

Football Spectators Act 1989, c. 37 (various dates, some to be appointed) introduces a national membership scheme and licences to control the admission of spectators at football matches, and provides for the safety of spectators.

Employment Act 1989, c. 38 (various dates) amends the Sex Discrimination Act 1975 by implementing the principle of equal treatment for men and women with regards to access to employment, vocational training, promotion and working conditions.

Self-Governing Schools etc. (Scotland) Act 1989, c. 39 (various dates, some to be appointed) makes provisions for the acquisition of self-governing status by certain public schools in Scotland and makes further provisions with regard to education in Scotland generally.

Companies Act 1989, c. 40 (various dates, some to be appointed) amends the law relating to company accounts. It makes new provision with respect to the registration of company charges and the doctrine of constructive notice. It abolishes the *ultra vires* rule and makes amendments to the objects clause. It creates a new definition for groups of companies and enlarges the powers of DTI inspectors.

Children Act 1989, c. 41 (various dates, some to be appointed) reforms the law relating to children; provides for local authority services for children in need, amends the law relating to children's homes, community homes, voluntary homes and voluntary organizations; makes provision with respect to fostering, child minding and adoption.

Local Government and Housing Act 1989, c. 42 (various dates, some to be appointed) establishes a new framework for the improvement of housing in terms of area renewal and grant aid; amends existing law on, *inter alia*, community charges, unfit housing, right to buy and public and private sector security of tenure; makes provision with respect to the members, officers and other staff and the procedure of local authorities and concerning the finances and expenditure of local authorities.

Statute Law (Repeals) Act 1989, c. 43 (most provisions on Nov. 16, 1989) repeals certain enactments which (except insofar as their effect is prescribed) are no longer of practical utility.

Opticians Act 1989, c. 44 (Feb. 16, 1990) consolidates certain enactments relating to opticians with amendments to give effect to recommendations of the Law Commission and the Scottish Law Commission.

Prisons (Scotland) Act 1989, c. 45 (Feb. 16, 1990) consolidates certain enactments relating to prisons and other institutions for offenders in Scotland.

Consolidated Fund (No. 2) Act 1989, c. 46 (Dec. 21, 1989) applies certain sums out of the Consolidated Fund to the service of the years ending March 31, 1990 and 1991.

Capital Allowances Act 1990, c. 1 (March 19, 1990) consolidates certain enactments relating to capital allowances.

Civil Aviation Authority (Borrowing Powers) Act 1990, c. 2 (March 19, 1990) increases the CAA's statutory borrowing limit with power to make further increases by order; extends the CAA's power to borrow in currencies other than sterling.

Coal Industry Act 1990, c. 3 (part on March 19, the rest on May 19, 1990) makes new provision with respect to grants and loans under existing powers and makes new provision with respect to grants by the Secretary of State to the British Coal Corporation; makes provision as to the licensing of coal working, searching and boring, and the preservation of amenity in connection with opencast coal working.

Consolidated Fund Act 1990, c. 4 (March 28, 1990) applies certain sums out of the Consolidated Fund to the service of the years ending March 31, 1989, 1990 and 1991.

Criminal Justice (International Co-operation) Act 1990, c. 5 (day or days to be appointed) enables the UK to co-operate with other countries in criminal proceedings and investigations; enables the UK to sign the Vienna Convention against Illicit Traffic in Narcotic Drugs and Psychotropic Substances and provides for the seizure, detention and forfeiture of drug-trafficking money imported or exported in cash.

Education (Student Loans) Act 1990, c. 6 (April 26, 1990) makes provision for students in higher education to be granted loans towards their maintenance.

Pensions (Miscellaneous Provisions) Act 1990, c. 7 (various dates) amends enactments relating to certain public service pension schemes.

Town and Country Planning Act 1990, c. 8 (except as provided in Part II and Schedule 4 to c. 9 below, Aug. 24, 1990) consolidates certain enactments relating to town and country planning (excluding special controls in respect of buildings and areas of special architectural or historic interest and in respect of hazardous substances).

Planning (Listed Buildings and Conservation Areas) Act 1990, c. 9 (except as provided in Schedule 4, Aug. 24, 1990) consolidates certain enactments relating to special controls in respect of buildings and areas of special architectural or historic interest.

Planning (Hazardous Substances) Act 1990, c. 10 (day or days to be appointed) consolidates certain enactments relating to special controls in respect of hazardous substances.

Planning (Consequential Provisions) Act 1990, c. 11 (Aug. 24, 1990) makes provisions for repeals, consequential amendments, transitional and transitory matters, and savings in connection with the consolidation of enactments in the Town and Country Planning Act 1990, the Planning (Listed Buildings and Conservation Areas) Act 1990 and the Planning (Hazardous Substances) Act 1990.

Property Services Agency and Crown Suppliers Act 1990, c. 12 (June 29, 1990) makes provision for the transfer of the Crown Services (known as the Property Services Agency and the Crown Suppliers).

Greenwich Hospital Act 1990, c. 13 (June 29, 1990) makes provision to enable the Royal Hospital School to admit children of either sex and without regard to any seafaring family connection.

Pakistan Act 1990, c. 14 (Oct. 1, 1990) makes provisions to modify certain enactments to take account of the readmission of Pakistan as a member of the Commonwealth.

Agricultural Holdings (Amendment) Act 1990, c. 15 (July 29, 1990) amends certain provisions of the 1986 Act.

Food Safety Act 1990, c. 16 (day or days to be appointed) makes provisions to amend and replace certain enactments relating to food, establishing a number of offences in relation to the safety of food and the protection of consumer interests.

Australian Constitution (Public Record Copy) Act 1990, c. 17 (June 29, 1990) makes provisions to exclude one of the record copies of the Commonwealth of Australia Constitution Act 1900 from the public records to which the Public Records Act 1958 applies.

Computer Misuse Act 1990, c. 18 (Aug. 29, 1990) makes provisions for securing material against unauthorized access or modification and for purposes connected to it.

National Health Service and Community Care Act 1990, c. 19 (June 29, 1990) makes provision concerning health authorities and other bodies; provides for the establishment of NHS trusts and makes additional provisions about financing of medical practitioners' practices, accommodation and welfare services provided by local authorities and the Secretary of State's powers in respect of these functions; amends other enactments relating to the NHS and repeals the Health Services Act 1976.

Entertainments (Increased Penalties) Act 1990, c. 20 (July 13, 1990) increases the penalties for certain offences under enactments relating to the licensing of premises or places which are used for dancing, music and similar types of entertainment.

Licensing (Low Alcohol Drinks) Act 1990, c. 21 (day or days to be appointed, failing which Jan. 1, 1994) amends the definition of 'intoxicating liquor' in the Licensing Act 1964 and of 'alcoholic liquor' in the Licensing (Scotland) Act 1976 with respect to alcohol in low alcohol drinks.

Term and Quarter Days (Scotland) Act 1990, c. 22 (with exceptions, July 13, 1991) regulates in relation to Scotland the dates of Whitsunday (May 28), Martinmas (Nov. 28), Candlemas (Feb. 28) and Lammas (Aug. 28) and for connected purposes.

Access to Health Records Act 1990, c. 23 (Nov. 1, 1991) establishes a right of access to health records by the person to whom they relate and others; provides for the correction of inaccurate health records and for the avoidance of certain contractual obligations relating to supplying another person with a copy of a health record.

Rights of Way Act 1990, c. 24 (Aug. 13, 1990) amends the law in relation to rights of way and the restoration of the surface of land over which rights of way pass; keeps the line of rights of way clear of crops, enables local authorities to act in connection with such offences.

Horses (Protective Headgear for Young Riders) Act 1990, c. 25 (various dates) secures the wearing of protective headgear by children whilst horse-riding and prescribes offences and penalties for failing so to do.

Gaming (Amendment) Act 1990, c. 26 (various dates) amends provisions of the 1968 Act relating to premises licensed or registered under Part II of that Act.

Social Security Act 1990, c. 27 (day or days to be appointed) amends the law relating to social security, occupational and personal pension schemes; establishes and confers functions on a Pensions Ombudsman and a Registrar of Occupational and Personal Pension Schemes; provides for the improvement of energy efficiency in certain dwellings.

Finance Act 1990, c. 29 (July 26, 1990) grants certain duties, alters others and amends the law relating to the National Debt and Public Revenue. *Inter alia*, it brings in provisions to abolish composite rate tax on building society and bank interest so that tax deducted at source can be reclaimed by low taxpayers, alters the registration requirements for VAT, makes provision for workplace nurseries and provides for the abolition of stamp duty on securities.

Government Trading Act 1990, c. 30 (July 26, 1990) amends the Government Trading Funds Act 1973 and the Exchequer and Audit Departments Act 1921, s. 5; repeals the Borrowing (Control and Guarantees) Act 1946.

Representation of the People Act 1990, c. 32 (day or days to be appointed) makes provision to enable a person who is no longer at his/her qualifying address or at any other address in the same area to be eligible for an absent vote for an indefinite period at Parliamentary and local elections.

Marriage (Registration of Buildings) Act 1990, c. 33 (Sept. 26, 1990) allows a building to be registered for the solemnization of marriages under the Marriage Act 1949, s. 41, notwithstanding that it forms part of another building.

British Nationality (Hong Kong) Act 1990, c. 34 (day or days to be appointed) provides for the acquisition of British citizenship by up to 50,000 selected Hong Kong residents, their spouses and minor children.

Enterprise and New Towns (Scotland) Act 1990, c. 35 (day or days to be appointed) establishes Scottish Enterprise and Highlands and Islands Enterprise and makes provision for their functions; dissolves the Scottish Development Agency and the Highland and Islands Development Board; makes further provision as regards new towns in Scotland; and for connected purposes.

Contracts (Applicable Law) Act 1990, c. 36 (day or days to be appointed) provides for effect to be given to the Rome Convention on Law applicable to Contractual Obligations, the first protocol thereto, and the associated Luxembourg Convention of 1984 in the case of conflict in order to enable the convention to determine the law of which country is to govern the contract in question.

Appropriation Act 1990.

Aviation and Maritime Security Act 1990.

GOVERNMENT AND PUBLIC OFFICES

SALARIES 1990–91

Ministerial Salaries
(as at Jan. 1, 1990)

Prime Minister £35,120*
Secretary of State £35,120
Minister of State (Lords) £39,641
Minister of State (Commons) £24,850
Parliamentary Under Secretary £18,860

* The Prime Minister's salary is £46,750 but since July 1980 she has drawn the same salary as a Cabinet Minister.

(Ministers who are Members of the House of Commons receive a (reduced) Parliamentary salary (£20,101 in 1990) in addition to this ministerial salary.)

Civil Service (Basic) Salaries
(from April 1, 1990)

+ Secretary to the Cabinet and Head of the
    Home Civil Service.................. £95,750
+ Permanent Secretary to the Treasury ... £89,500
+ Head of the Diplomatic Service £89,500
+ Grade 1 .... £77,000
+ Grade 1A £70,500
+ Grade 2 .... £54,900
   Grade 3 .... £43,350–£47,000*
   Grade 4 .... £36,818–£42,907
   Grade 5 .... £30,001–£35,436
   Grade 6 .... £23,039–£31,276
   Grade 7 .... £20,189–£25,160
   Senior Executive Officer .... £15,156–£20,152
   Higher Executive Officer (D) ... £13,022–£16,336
   Higher Executive Officer ...... £12,367–£16,441
   Executive Officer .... £7,286–£13,145
   Administration Trainee .... £10,246–£12,074

* Including £2,000 London allowance.
+ These grades do not attract London Weighting.
London Weighting, since July 1, 1989, is:

   Inner zone .... £1,750 a year
   Intermediate zone .... £1,000 a year
   Outer zone .... £725 a year

The Home Civil Service's unified pay and grading structure for senior personnel represents the following:

Grade	Title
1	Permanent Secretary.
1A	Second Permanent Secretary.
2	Deputy Secretary.
3	Under Secretary.
4	Chief Scientific Officer B, Professional and Technology Directing A.
5	Assistant Secretary, Deputy Chief Scientific Officer, Professional and Technology Directing B.
6	Senior Principal, Senior Principal Scientific Officer, Professional and Technology Superintending Grade.
7	Principal.

ADVISORY, CONCILIATION AND ARBITRATION SERVICE
27 Wilton Street, SW1X 7AX
[071–210 3000]

The Advisory, Conciliation and Arbitration Service (ACAS) is an independent organization set up under the Employment Protection Act, 1975, under the management of a Council appointed by the Secretary of State for Employment. The functions of the Service are to provide facilities for conciliation, mediation and arbitration as a means of avoiding and resolving industrial disputes; and to provide advisory services to industry on industrial relations and matters affecting the quality of working life.

ACAS also has offices in Birmingham, Bristol, Cardiff, Fleet, Glasgow, Leeds, Liverpool, Manchester, Newcastle upon Tyne and Nottingham.

Chairman, D. B. Smith, CB.
Chief Conciliation Officer (G4), D. G. Boyd, CBE.
Director of Resources and General Policy Branch (G5), E. Norcross.

MINISTRY OF AGRICULTURE, FISHERIES AND FOOD
Whitehall Place, SW1A 2HH†
[071–270 3000]

The Ministry of Agriculture, Fisheries and Food is responsible for administering government policy for agriculture, horticulture, fisheries and food in England and for many food matters in the United Kingdom as a whole. In association with the other Agricultural Departments in the UK and the Intervention Board for Agricultural Produce, the Ministry is responsible for the negotiation and administration of the EC common agricultural and fisheries policies and for various national support schemes.

The Ministry administers arrangements for the control and eradication of plant diseases and for assistance to capital investment in farm and horticultural businesses and flood defence; it exercises responsibilities relating to the protection of the countryside and the marine environment as well as other rural issues and appropriate research and development.

The Ministry has certain responsibilities for ensuring public health standards in the manufacture, preparation and distribution of basic foods, and planning to safeguard essential food supplies in times of emergency. The Ministry is responsible for government relations with the UK food and drink manufacturing industries, and the food and drink importing, distributive and catering trades.

The Food Safety Directorate is responsible for many aspects of food safety and quality. These include analytical and research work, pesticide safety approval, biotechnology, meat hygiene, animal health and welfare, and the related public health issues.

The Agricultural Development and Advisory Service (ADAS) provides scientific, technical and professional services in support of the Ministry's statutory functions, and advice to farmers, growers and ancillary industries.

Minister, THE RT. HON. JOHN GUMMER, MP.
  Principal Private Secretary (G7), A. J. Lebrecht.
  Asst. Private Secretary, M. D. K. Harrison.
  Parliamentary Private Secretaries, J. M. Jack, MP; J. Paice, MP.
  Special Adviser, R. Gueterbock.
Minister of State (Lords), THE BARONESS TRUMPINGTON (*Countryside*).
  Private Secretary, L. D. Harris.
Parliamentary Secretary, DAVID CURRY, MP (*Farming and Fisheries*).
  Private Secretary, Mrs. L. Reay.
Parliamentary Secretary, DAVID MACLEAN, MP (*Food*).
  Private Secretary, D. North.
Parliamentary Clerk, R. L. Alderton.
Permanent Secretary (G1), D. H. Andrews, CB, CBE.
  Private Secretary, A. F. Robinson.

---

†Unless otherwise stated, this is the main address of Divisions of the Ministry.

ESTABLISHMENT DEPARTMENT
Director of Establishments (G3), D. H. Griffiths.

Staff Resources and Organization
Victory House, 30–34 Kingsway, WC2B 6TU
[071–405 4310]
Head of Division (G5), A. G. Kuyk.

Establishments (General) Division
Victory House, 30–34 Kingsway, WC2B 6TU
[071–405 4310]
Head of Division (G5), Mrs. A. M. Pickering.

Staff Training Branch*
Principal (G7), Miss E. M. Berthoud.

Welfare Branch
Victory House, 30–34 Kingsway, WC2B 6TU
[071-405 4310]
Chief Welfare Officer (SEO), D. J. Jones.

Personnel Division
Victory House, 30–34 Kingsway, WC2B 6TU
[071–405 4310]
Head of Division (G5), Mrs. K. J. A. Brown.

FINANCE DEPARTMENT
Principal Finance Officer (G3), A. R. Cruickshank.

Financial Planning Division*
Head of Division (G5), H. B. Brown.

Financial Guidance Division*
Head of Division (G5), R. C. McIvor.

Financial Management Division*
Head of Division (G5), C. J. Lawson.

Audit Division*
Director of Audit (G5), D. V. Fisher.
Deputy Director of Audit (G6), D. J. Littler.

Purchasing and Supply Unit*
Director (G5), G. Lander.

LEGAL DEPARTMENT
55 Whitehall, SW1A 2EY
[071–270 3000]
Legal Adviser and Solicitor (G2), G. J. Jenkins, QC.
Principal Assistant Solicitors (G3), A. E. Munir; B. T. Atwood.

Legal Division A1
Assistant Solicitor (G5), P. D. Davis.

Legal Division A2
Assistant Solicitor (G5), A. Yavash.

Legal Division A3
Assistant Solicitor (G5), M. C. P. Thomas.

Legal Division A4
Assistant Solicitor (G5), Miss E. A. Stephens.

Legal Division A5
Assistant Solicitor (G5), J. E. G. Vaux.

Legal Division A6
Assistant Solicitor (G5), Mrs. C. Davis.

Legal Division B1
Assistant Solicitor (G5), J. F. McCleary.

Legal Division B2
Assistant Solicitor (G5), D. J. Pearson.

Legal Division B3
Assistant Solicitor (G5), A. I. Corbett.

*At Nobel/Ergon House, 17 Smith Square, SW1P 3JR [071-238 3000].

Legal Division B4
Assistant Solicitor (G5), L. Gunatilleke.

Investigation Unit
Chief Investigation Officer (SEO), A. F. N. Maloney.

MANAGEMENT SERVICES
Under Secretary (G3), M. T. Haddon.

Information Technology Directorate
Government Buildings, Epsom Road,
Guildford, Surrey GU1 2LD
[0483-68121]
Director (G4), D. Selwood.
Assistant Directors (G5), A. G. Matthews; D. J. Dunthorne; (G6), D. D. Brown; R. F. Syrett.

Building Projects Unit
Eastbury House, 30–34 Albert
Embankment, SE1 7TL
[071-238 3000]
Head of Division (G5), J. S. Buchanan.

Office Services Division*
Head of Division (G6), J. E. Nunn, DFC.

Departmental Health and Safety Unit
Head of Unit (G7), P. A. Greatorex.

Management Services Division
Eastbury House, 30–34 Albert
Embankment, SE1 7TL
[071-238 3000]
Head of Division (G5), P. A. Cocking.

Information Division
Chief Information Officer (G5), S. Dugdale.
Chief Press Officer, M. Smith.
Principal Librarian (G7), T. Cullen.

AGRICULTURAL COMMODITIES
Deputy Secretary (G2), R. J. Packer.

EUROPEAN COMMUNITY AND EXTERNAL TRADE POLICY
Under Secretary (G3), R. J. D. Carden.

European Community Division I
Head of Division (G5), C. I. Llewelyn.

European Community Division II
Head of Division (G6), D. Maskell.

External Trade Policy Division
Head of Division (G5), D. P. Hunter.

ARABLE CROPS
Under Secretary (G3), C. J. Barnes.

Cereals, Set-Aside and Extensification Division
Head of Division (G5), R. E. Melville.

Sugar, Oils and Fats Division
Head of Division (G5), R. S. Thomas.

Horticulture and Potatoes Division
Head of Division (G5), Miss V. A. Smith.

LIVESTOCK PRODUCTS
Under Secretary (G3), S. Wentworth.

Beef Division
Head of Division (G5), J. R. Cowan.

Sheep and Livestock Subsidies Division
Head of Division (G5), G. Belchamber.

Pigs, Eggs and Poultry Division
Head of Division (G5), M. Ring.

Milk and Milk Products
Head of Division (G5), P. Elliott.

FOOD, DRINK AND MARKETING POLICY

Under Secretary (G3), J. W. Hepburn.

Food Industry, Marketing and Competition Policy Division
Head of Division (G5), J. D. Garnett.

Alcoholic Drinks Division
Head of Division (G5), D. V. Orchard.

External Relations and Trade Promotion Division I
Head of Division (G5), R. J. Dalton.

External Relations and Trade Promotion Division II
Head of Division (G5), A. H. Abbott.

Tropical Foods
Head of Division (G5), R. J. Dalton.

COUNTRYSIDE, MARINE ENVIRONMENT AND FISHERIES

Deputy Secretary (G2), B. J. G. Hilton.

LANDS

Under Secretary (G3), J. A. Anderson.*

Rural Structures and Grants Division*
Head of Division (G5), T. E. D. Eddy.

Land Use and Tenure Division*
Head of Division (G5), G. P. McLachlan.

Environmental Protection Division*
Head of Division (G5), P. P. Nash.

Conservation Policy Division*
Head of Division (G5), C. R. Bodrell.

FISHERIES DEPARTMENT*

Fisheries Secretary (G3), C. R. Cann.

Marine Environmental Protection Division
Head of Division (G5), P. M. Boyling.

Fisheries Division I
Head of Division (G5), G. W. Noble.

Fisheries Division II
Head of Division (G5), A. R. Burne.

Fisheries Division III
Head of Division (G5), Mrs. A. M. Blackburn.

Fisheries Division IV
Head of Division (G5), I. C. Redfern.

Sea Fisheries Inspectorate
Chief Inspector (G6), M. G. Jennings.

Fisheries Research
Director of Fisheries Research and Development for Great Britain (G4), D. J. Garrod, ph.d.
Deputy Directors of Fisheries Research (G5), Dr. J. G. Shepherd; Dr. C. E. Purdom.

Fisheries Laboratory
Pakefield Road, Lowestoft, Suffolk NR33 0HT
[0502–62244]

Fisheries Laboratory
Remembrance Avenue, Burnham-on-Crouch,
Essex CM0 8HA
[0621–782658]

————————————

*At Nobel/Ergon House, 17 Smith Square, SW1P 3JR [071–238 3000].

Fisheries Experiment Station
Benarth Road, Conwy, Gwynedd LL32 8UB
[049–263 3883]

Fish Diseases Laboratory
The Nothe, Weymouth, Dorset DT4 8UB
[03057–72137]
Officer-in-Charge (Principal Scientific Officer) (G7),
B. J. Hill, ph.d.

FLOOD DEFENCE, PLANT PROTECTION AND AGRICULTURAL RESOURCES

Under Secretary (G3), M. Madden.

Agricultural Resources Policy Division
Head of Division (G5), G. R. Waters.

Plant Variety, Rights Office and Seeds
White House Lane, Huntingdon Road,
Cambridge CB3 0LF
[0223–277151]
Head of Division (G5), J. Harvey.

Plant Health Division*
Head of Division (G5), J. C. Edwards.

Flood Defence Division*
Eastbury House, 30–34 Albert
Embankment, SE1 7TL
[071-238 3000]
Head of Division (G5), J. R. Park, ph.d.

ECONOMICS AND STATISTICS

Under Secretary (G3), R. E. Mordue.

Economics (Farm Business) Division
Senior Economic Adviser (G5), Mrs. S. M. Dickinson.

Economics (International) Division
Senior Economic Adviser (G5), R. W. Irving.

Economics (Resource Use) Division
Senior Economic Adviser (G5), A. P. Power, ph.d.

Statistics (Agricultural Commodities) Division*
Chief Statistician (G5), P. J. Lund, ph.d.

Statistics (Census and Prices) Division
Government Buildings, Epsom Road,
Guildford GU1 2LD
[0483–68121]
Chief Statistician (G5), D. E. Bradbury.

Economics and Statistics (Food)
Senior Economic Adviser (G5), J. M. Slater, ph.d.

FOOD SAFETY

Deputy Secretrary (G2), C. W. Capstick, cmg.

ANIMAL HEALTH

Under Secretary (G3), Mrs. E. A. J. Attridge.

Animal Health Division
Government Buildings, Hook Rise South,
Tolworth, Surbiton, Surrey KT6 7NF
[081–330 4411]
Head of Division (G5), R. C. Lowson.

Animal Welfare Division
Government Buildings, Hook Rise South,
Tolworth, Surbiton, Surrey KT6 7NF
[081–330 4411]
Head of Division (G5), A. J. Perrins.

Meat Hygiene Division
Tolworth Tower, Surbiton, Surrey KT6 7DX
[081–330 4411]
Head of Division (G5), M. J. Griffiths.

FOOD SAFETY

Under Secretary (G3), B. H. B. Dickinson.

Food Safety, Fertilizers and Feedstuffs Standards Division*
Head of Division (G5), R. C. McKinley.

Food Standards Division*
Head of Division (G5), C. A. Cockbill.

Microbiological Safety of Food Division
Head of Division (G5), J. C. Suich.

CHIEF SCIENTIST'S GROUP

Chief Scientist (Fisheries and Food) (G3), M. E. Knowles, ph.d.
Chief Scientist (Agriculture and Horticulture) (G3), D. W. F. Shannon, ph.d.*

Research and Development Requirements Division*
Head of Division (G5), A. T. Cahn.

Food Science Division I*
Head of Division (G5), J. Bell.

Food Science Division II*
Head of Division (G5), W. H. B. Denner, ph.d.

Food Science Laboratory
Colney Lane,
Norwich NR4 7UQ
[0603–501102]
Head of Laboratory (G6), D. J. McWeeny.

Torry Research Station
PO Box 31, 135 Abbey Road,
Aberdeen AB9 8DG
[0224–877071]
Director (G5), G. Hobbs, ph.d.

PESTICIDES, VETERINARY MEDICINES AND EMERGENCIES

Under Secretary (G3), P. W. Murphy.

Emergencies and Food Protection Division
Head of Division (G5), G. F. Meekings.

Pesticides Safety Division
Head of Division (G5), G. A. Hollis.

Biotechnology Unit
Head of Unit (G7), J. A. Bainton.

AGRICULTURAL DEVELOPMENT AND ADVISORY SERVICE (ADAS) AND REGIONAL ORGANIZATION

Director General of ADAS and Regional Organization/Chief Scientific Adviser (G2), P. J. Bunyan, d.sc., ph.d.

ADAS AND REGIONAL ADMINISTRATION

Director of Regional Administration (G3), D. J. Coates.*

Eastern, Block C, Government Buildings, Brooklands Avenue, Cambridge CB2 2DR (0223–358911).—*Regional Director (G4)*, G. K. Bruce.

Northern, Block 2, Government Buildings, Lawnswood, Leeds LS16 5PY (0532–611223).—*Regional Director (G4)*, A. F. Baines.

South Eastern, Block A, Government Offices, Coley Park, Reading RG1 6DT (0734–581222).—*Regional Director (G4)*, G. M. Trevelyan.

---

*At Nobel/Ergon House, 17 Smith Square, SW1P 3JR [071–238 3000].

South Western, Block 3, Government Buildings, Burghill Road, Westbury-on-Trym, Bristol BS10 6NJ (0272–500000).—*Regional Director (G4)*, B. F. Shorney.

Midlands and Western, Woodthorne, Wolverhampton WV6 8TQ (0902–754190).—*Regional Director (G4)*, A. D. Bailey.

Wales, Plas Crug, Aberystwyth SY23 1PQ.—*Chief ADAS Officer (G5)*, T. M. K. Evans.

ADAS and Regional Management Division
Head of Division (G5), B. J. Harding.*

FARM AND COUNTRYSIDE SERVICE

Director of Service (G3), P. Needham.*
Head of Product Services (G4), J. B. Finney, cbe.
Staff Officer (G5), I. M. Tring.

ADAS Marketing Unit
Head of Unit (G5), D. E. Bawcutt.*

ADAS Information Services Unit
Rivershill House, St. Georges Road
Cheltenham
Head of Unit (G5), R. W. Swain.

RESEARCH AND DEVELOPMENT SERVICE

Director of Service (G3), vacant.
Director of Field Research and Development (G4), A. D. Hughes.*
Director ADAS Central Science Laboratory (G4), P. I. Stanley, phd.
Staff Officer (G6), W. J. Stubbs.*

ADAS Central Science Laboratory Slough
London Road, Slough, Berks. SL3 7HJ
[0753–34626]

ADAS Central Science Laboratory Harpenden
Hatching Green, Harpenden, Herts. AL5 2BD
[0582–75241]
Director of Harpenden Laboratory (G5), A. R. Hardy.

STATE VETERINARY SERVICE
Government Buildings, Hook Rise South,
Tolworth, Surbiton, Surrey KT15 3NB
[081–330 4411]

Chief Veterinary Officer (G3A), K. C. Meldrum.
Director of Veterinary Field Services (G3), I. Crawford.
Staff Officer (G5), W. A. Edwards.

Lasswade Veterinary Laboratory,
East of Scotland College of Agriculture,
The Bush Estate, Penicuik,
Midlothian EH26 09N
[031–445 4811]

Cattle Breeding Centre,
Shinfield, Reading, Berks. RG2 9BZ
[0734–883157]

EXECUTIVE AGENCIES

Central Veterinary Laboratory
New Haw, Weybridge, Surrey KT15 3NB
[09323–41111]
The Central Veterinary Laboratory provides scientific and technical expertise in animal and public health.
Director of Laboratory (G3), T. W. A. Little, ph.d.

Veterinary Medicines Directorate
New Haw, Weybridge, Surrey KT15 3NB
[09323–36911]

The Veterinary Medicines Directorate is responsible for all aspects of licensing and control of animal medicines, including the protection of the consumer from hazardous or unacceptable residues.
Director (G4), J. M. Rutter, Ph.D.

AGRICULTURAL AND FOOD RESEARCH COUNCIL
Central Office, Wiltshire Court,
Farnsby Street, Swindon SN1 5AT
[0793-514242]

The Agricultural and Food Research Council (AFRC) is an independent body established by Royal Charter. It is funded from the Science Budget of the Department of Education and Science, receives commissions from the Ministry of Agriculture, Fisheries and Food, and does research for industry and other bodies.

The Council is responsible for research done in its institutes and in UK university departments funded through its research grants scheme. It advises the Department of Agriculture and Fisheries for Scotland (DAFS) on research in the Scottish Agricultural Research Institutes.

The institutes funded through AFRC and DAFS, and the university groups supported, form the Agricultural and Food Research Service.

Chairman, A. Grant.
Deputy Chairman and Secretary, Prof. W. D. P. Stewart, FRSE, FRS (until Oct. 1990).
Members, Prof. T. L. Blundell, FRS; T. E. Boswell, MP; Dr. P. J. Bunyan; Prof. J. M. M. Cunningham, CBE; Prof. A. W. Cuthbert, FRS; Dr. D. A. Evans; D. F. R. George; D. F. Goodwin; L. P. Hamilton, CB; Prof. J. L. Harper, FRS; B. J. G. Hilton; Prof. W. F. H. Jarrett, FRS; Dr. M. Knowles; Prof. J. R. Krebs, FRS; M. MacKie, jnr; Prof. T. Mansfield; Prof. A. Nienow; Prof. J. R. Norris; G. T. Pryce; Dr. D. W. F. Shannon; Prof. R. Whittenbury.
Assessors, Dr. R. F. Coleman, FRSE; J. I. Davies, MBE; K. Meldrum; Dr. C. McMurray; Prof. H. Smith, FRS.
Deputy Secretary (G2), vacant.
Director of Central Office (G3), B. G. Jamieson, Ph.D.
Heads of Divisions (G5), S. H. Visscher (*Finance*); J. M. Y. Dickens (*Personnel*); Dr. J. N. Wingfield (*Research*); Dr. A. V. Harrison (*Policy*).
Commercial Policy Section (G7), S. M. Lawrie.
Principal Information Officer (G7), M. A. Winstanley.
For institutes and units of the Agricultural and Food Research Service, *see* Index.

COLLEGE OF ARMS OR HERALDS COLLEGE
Queen Victoria Street, EC4V 4BT
[071–248 2762]

The College is the official repository of the Arms and pedigrees of English, Northern Irish, and Commonwealth families and their descendants, and its records include official copies of the records of Ulster King of Arms, the originals of which remain in Dublin. The 13 officers of the College specialize in genealogical and heraldic work for their respective clients.

Arms have been and still are granted by Letters Patent from the Kings of Arms under authority delegated to them by the Sovereign, such authority having been expressly conferred on them since at least the fifteenth century. A right to Arms can only be established by the registration in the official records of the College of Arms of a pedigree showing direct male line descent from an ancestor already appearing therein as being entitled to Arms, or by making application through the College of Arms for a Grant of Arms.

The College of Arms is open Mon.–Fri. 10–4, when an Officer of Arms is in attendance to deal with enquiries by the public, though such enquiries may also be directed to any of the Officers of Arms, either personally or by letter.

Earl Marshal, His Grace the Duke of Norfolk, KG, GCVO, CB, CBE, MC.

Kings of Arms

Garter, Sir Colin Cole, KCVO, TD, FSA.
Clarenceux, Sir Anthony Wagner, KCB, KCVO, FSA.
Norroy and Ulster, J. P. B. Brooke-Little, CVO, FSA.

Heralds

York (and Registrar), C. M. J. F. Swan, CVO, Ph.D., FSA.
Chester, D. H. B. Chesshyre, LVO, FSA.
Windsor, T. D. Mathew.
Lancaster, P. L. Gwynn-Jones.
Somerset, T. Woodcock.
Richmond, P. L. Dickinson, FSA.

Earl Marshal's Secretary, Sir Walter Verco, KCVO, Surrey Herald Extraordinary.

Pursuivants

Portcullis, P. B. Spurrier.
Bluemantle, T. D. McCarthy.
Rouge Croix, H. E. Paston-Bedingfeld.
Rouge Dragon, T. H. S. Duke.

COURT OF THE LORD LYON
HM New Register House, Edinburgh EH1 3YT
[031–556 7255]

The Court of the Lord Lyon is the Scottish Court of Chivalry, (including the genealogical jurisdiction of the *Ri-Sennachie* of Scotland's Celtic Kings) and adjudicates rights to arms and administration of the Scottish Public Register of All Arms and Bearings and Public Register of All Genealogies. The Lord Lyon presides and judicially establishes rights to existing arms or succession to Chiefship, or for cadets with scientific 'differences' showing position in clan or family. Pedigrees are also established by decrees of Lyon Court and by Letters Patent. As Royal Commissioner in Armory, he grants Patents of Arms (which constitute the grantee and heirs noble in the Noblesse of Scotland) to 'virtuous and well-deserving' Scotsmen, and petitioners (personal or corporate) in Her Majesty's overseas realms of Scottish connection, and issues birthbrieves.
Lord Lyon King of Arms, Sir Malcolm Innes of Edingight, KCVO, WS, FSA Scot.

Heralds

Albany, J. A. Spens, RD, WS.
Rothesay, Sir Crispin Agnew of Lochnaw, Bt.
Ross, C. J. Burnett, FSA Scot.

Pursuivants

Kintyre, J. C. G. George, FSA Scot.
Unicorn, Alastair Campbell of Airds, younger, FSA Scot.

Lyon Clerk and Keeper of Records, Mrs. C. G. W. Roads, MVO, FSA Scot.

Procurator-Fiscal, I. R. Guild, CBE, WS.
Herald Painter, Mrs. J. Phillips.
Macer, T. C. Gray.

OFFICE OF ARTS AND LIBRARIES
Horse Guards Road, SW1P 3AL
[071–270 3000]

The Office of Arts and Libraries, formerly part of the Department of Education and Science, was established in its present form in 1983. It has general responsibilities for government arts policy and its objectives are to assist the development of artistic and cultural activity throughout the country and to promote public interest in, and appreciation of, the arts and cultural heritage.

It directly funds over 20 bodies including the Arts Council, the eleven national museums and galleries, the British Library and its St. Pancras project. The Office of Arts and Libraries also has policy responsibilities towards the public library and local museum services. The Government Art Collection, which is responsible for the acquisition, maintenance and display of works of art in major government buildings in this country and abroad, also forms part of the Office.

Minister for the Arts, THE RT. HON. DAVID MELLOR, QC, MP.
Private Secretary, M. Le Jeune.
Head of the Office of Arts and Libraries (G2), C. E. Henderson.

Arts and Heritage
Assistant Secretary (G5), Miss S. E. Brown.
Principals (G7), P. J. Fallon; S. J. Alcock; Miss C. R. Morrison; Miss J. C. Mole.

Museums, Galleries, Finance and Establishments
Assistant Secretary (G5), N. Pittman.
Principals (G7), I. D. Baxter; E. A. Yeo; K. Gray.

Libraries and Information Services
Assistant Secretary (G7), C. C. Leamy.
Principal (G7), A. Poulter.
Library Advisers, P. J. Beauchamp; Miss C. R. Lutyens.

British Library Project St. Pancras
Project Director (G5), J. R. W. Pardey.

Government Art Collection
Curator, Dr. W. Baron.

ARTS COUNCIL OF GREAT BRITAIN
14 Great Peter Street, SW1P 3NQ
[071-333 0010]

The Arts Council, an independent body established in 1946, is the principal channel for the Government's support of the arts. It funds the major arts organizations in England, the Regional Arts Associations and the Scottish and Welsh Arts Councils. It also provides a service of advice, information and help to artists, arts organizations and the general public.

Its objectives are to develop and improve the understanding and practice of the arts and to increase their accessibility to the public.

The Council distributes an annual grant from the Office of Arts and Libraries, and for the year 1990–91 the amount is £174·95 million.
Chairman, P. Palumbo.
Secretary-General, A. Everitt.

ART GALLERIES, ETC.

ROYAL FINE ART COMMISSION
7 St. James's Square, SW1Y 4JU
[071–839 6537]

Established in 1924, the Commission is an autonomous authority on the aesthetic implications of any project or development, primarily but not exclusively architectural, which affects the visual environment.
Chairman, The Lord St. John of Fawsley, PC.
Commissioners, R. D. Carter, CBE,; Dame Elizabeth Chesterton, DBE; Sir Philip Dowson, CBE, RA; M. Girouard, PH.D.; Sir Alexander Gordon, CBE; The Duke of Grafton, KG, FSA; M. J. Hopkins, CBE; R. MacCormac; P. Nuttgens, CBE, PH.D.; Mrs. J. Nutting; D. Hamilton Fraser, RA; Sir Philip Powell, CH, OBE, RA; J. Sutherland; Miss W. Taylor, CBE; W. Whitfield, CBE; J. Winter, MBE; H. T. Moggridge, OBE; S. A. Lipton.
Secretary (G6), S. Cantacuzino, CBE.

ROYAL FINE ART COMMISSION FOR SCOTLAND
9 Atholl Crescent,
Edinburgh EH3 8HA
[031–229 1109]

Chairman, The Hon. Lord Prosser.
Commissioners, Miss K. Borland; J. Boys, FRIBA; W. D. Campbell; Dr. Deborah Howard, PH.D., FSA; W. K. Mackay; A. S. Matheson, FRIBA; G. Ogilvie-Laing; R. R. Steedman, RSA; Mrs. F. M. E. Walker; Prof. R. Walker; R. Wedgwood.
Secretary, C. Prosser.

NATIONAL GALLERY
Trafalgar Square, WC2N 5DN
[071–839 3321]

Hours of opening.—Weekdays 10–6, Sun. 2–6. Closed on Good Friday, Christmas Eve, Christmas Day, Boxing Day, New Year's Day and May Day Bank Holiday.

The National Gallery was founded in 1824, following a Parliamentary grant of £60,000 for the purchase and exhibition of the Angerstein collection of pictures. The present site was first occupied in 1838 and enlarged and improved at various times throughout the years. A substantial extension to the north of the building with a public entrance in Orange Street was opened in 1975, and a new wing, the Sainsbury wing, opens in spring 1991. Expenses for 1990–91 are estimated at £22,953,000.

Board of Trustees
Chairman, The Lord Rothschild.
Trustees, HRH The Prince of Wales, KG, KT, GCB, PC; Mrs. C. Hubbard, CBE; Lord Alexander of Weedon, QC; F. St. J. Gore, CBE; B. Gascoigne; P. Troughton; Sir Rex Richards, FRS; The Countess of Airlie, CVO; Sir Derek Oulton, KCB, QC; N. Baring; E. Uglow.

Officers
Director, R. N. MacGregor.................£50,120
Chief Curator (G5), Dr. C. P. H. Brown.
Senior Curators (G5), Dr. A. J. W. Braham; *(G6)*, Dr. N. Penny; *(G7)*, Dr. S. Foister; Dr. D. Gordon; M. Helston.
Chief Restorer (G5), M. H. Wyld.
Scientific Adviser (G6), Dr. A. Roy.
Bursar (G5), Ms. C. E. Macready.
Head of Building, Mrs. J. Evans.

NATIONAL PORTRAIT GALLERY
St. Martin's Place, WC2H 0HE
[071–306 0055]

Open Mon.–Fri. 10–5. Sat. 10–6. Sun. 2–6.

A grant was made in 1856 to form a gallery of the portraits of the most eminent persons in British history. The present building was opened in 1896, £80,000 being contributed to its cost by Mr. W. H. Alexander; an extension erected at the expense of Lord Duveen was opened in 1933. An outstation was opened at Bodelwyddan Castle in 1988.

Chairman, The Rev. Prof. W. O Chadwick, OM, KBE, FBA.
Trustees, The Lord President of the Council (*ex officio*); The President of the Royal Academy of Arts (*ex officio*); The Duke of Grafton, KG, FSA; Sir Oliver Millar, GCVO, FBA, FSA; J. Roberts, D.Phil.; The Lord Morris of Castle Morris, D.Phil.; Mrs. S. Crosland; Prof. M. Gowing, CBE, FBA; The Marquess of Anglesey, FSA; H. Keswick; Prof. N. Lynton; The Lord Sieff of Brimpton, OBE; The Lord Weidenfeld; Sir Eduardo Paolozzi; J. Tusa.

Director, J. T. Hayes, CBE, Ph.D., FSA £39,746
Keeper and Deputy Director, M. Rogers, D.Phil.
£35,436

TATE GALLERY
Millbank, SW1P 4RG
[071–821 1313]

Hours of opening.—Weekdays 10–5.50. Sun. 2–5.50. Closed on New Year's Day, Good Friday, May Day Holiday, Christmas Eve, Christmas Day and Boxing Day.

The Tate Gallery comprises the National Collections of British painting and 20th century painting and sculpture. The Gallery was opened in 1897, the cost of erection (£80,000) being defrayed by Sir Henry Tate, who also contributed the nucleus of the present collection. The Turner Wing, built at the expense of Sir Joseph Duveen was opened in 1920. Lord Duveen defrayed the cost of galleries to contain the collection of modern foreign painting, completed in 1926, and a new sculpture hall, completed in 1937. The latest extension to the Tate Gallery, the Clore Gallery for the Turner Collection, was opened by HM The Queen on April 1, 1987. The Tate Gallery Liverpool, sited in the Albert Dock opened in May 1988. Total government funding for 1990–91 is £13,761,000.

Board of Trustees

Chairman, D. Stevenson.
Trustees, The Countess of Airlie, CVO; G. de Botton; J. Golding; C. LeBrun; D. Puttnam, CBE; Sir Mark Weinberg; Mrs. C. Hubbard; W. Govett; Mrs. P. Ridley; M. Craig-Martin.

Officers
Salaries

Director £50,120
Grade 5 .... £31,276–£35,436
Grade 6 .... £24,075–£31,276

Director, N. Serota.
Keeper of the British Collection (G5), A. Wilton.
Keeper of the Modern Collection (G5), R. Morphet.
Keeper of Conservation (G5), The Viscount Dunluce.
Deputy Keepers (G6), L. A. Parris; J. Lewison; Miss R. Rattenbury; R. Perry.
Secretary and Head of Administration (G6), R. Aylward.

Tate Gallery Liverpool
Albert Dock, Liverpool L3 4BB
[051–709 3223]
Open Tues.–Sun., 11–7. Admission free.
Curator (G6), R. Francis.

WALLACE COLLECTION
Hertford House, Manchester Square, W1M 6BN
[071–935 0687]

Admission free. Open on weekdays 10–5: Sun. 2–5. Closed on Good Friday, December 24–26, January 1 and May Day.

The Wallace Collection was bequeathed to the nation by the widow of Sir Richard Wallace, Bt., on her death in 1897, and Hertford House was subsequently acquired by the Government. The collection includes pictures, drawings and miniatures, French furniture, sculpture, bronzes, porcelain, armour and miscellaneous *objets d'art.* The total net expenses for 1990–91 were estimated at £1,898,000.

Director, J. A. S. Ingamells.
Assistants to Director, P. Hughes; Miss R. J. Savill.
Head of Administration, A. W. Houldershaw.

NATIONAL GALLERIES OF SCOTLAND
The Mound, Edinburgh EH2 2EL
[031–556 8921]

Chairman of the Trustees, A. M. Grossart, CBE.
Trustees, The Countess of Rosebery; J. Packer, OBE; A. R. Cole-Hamilton; Mrs. L. W. Gibbs; Sir Norman Macfarlane; R. W. Begg; Dr. T. Johnston; Prof. A. A. Tait.

Salaries 1990

Director .... £36,818–£38,254
Keeper .... £23,039–£30,001
Assistant Keeper/Curator .... £21,189–£24,075

Director, T. Clifford.
Keeper of Conservation, J. P. Dick.
Keeper of Information (Asst. Keeper), Miss L. S. Callander.
Keeper of Education (Asst. Keeper), Ms. L. B. Shaw.
Registrar (Asst. Keeper), J. P. Mason.
Secretary (Keeper), W. J. Sinclair.
Buildings (Asst. Keeper), C. P. Fotheringham.

Comprising:

National Gallery of Scotland
The Mound, Edinburgh
[031–556 8921]

Open: Mon.–Sat. 10–5; Sun. 2–5; Closed December 25, 26, 31; January 1, 2, 3.
Keeper, M. Clarke.
Assistant Keepers, Miss L. M. Errington, Ph.D.; Ms. J. Lloyd Williams.
Keeper of Prints and Drawings, H. Macandrew.
Assistant Keeper, R. M. M. Campbell.

Scottish National Portrait Gallery
1 Queen Street, Edinburgh
[031–556 8921]

Hours—as for National Gallery of Scotland.
Keeper, D. Thomson, Ph.D.
Assistant Keepers, Miss R. K. Marshall, Ph.D.; J. E. Holloway.
Curator of Photography, Miss S. F. Stevenson.

Scottish National Gallery of Modern Art
Belford Road, Edinburgh EH4 3DR
[031–556 8921]

Hours—as for National Gallery of Scotland.
Keeper, R. Calvocoressi.
Assistant Keepers, K. S. Hartley; P. Elliott.

(For other British Art Galleries, *see* Index.)

UNITED KINGDOM ATOMIC ENERGY AUTHORITY
11 Charles II Street, SW1Y 4QP
[071–930 5454]

The UKAEA was established by the Atomic Energy Authority Act, 1954, and is responsible for research and development support for the UK nuclear power programme and for public information. Since April 1986 the UKAEA has been required by the Government to operate on a quasi-commercial footing and in 1990 it adopted the trading name AEA Technology. It provides scientific and technical knowledge and services, products and consultancy on a commercial basis to governments, utilities and industries worldwide. The UKAEA has eight laboratories.
Chairman, J. N. Maltby, CBE *(part-time)* £50,000
Chief Executive and Deputy Chairman, Dr. B. L. Eyre £81,000
Members (full-time), Dr. G. G. E. Low, CBE; A. W. Hills; Dr. R. S. Nelson .... £64,660–£67,800
Members (part-time) Prof. Sir Peter Hirsch, FRS; A. Bullock; R. Sanderson, OBE; Prof. Sir Roger Elliott, FRS; J. A. Gardiner *(each £6,800).*
Secretary, J. R. Bretherton.

THE AUDIT COMMISSION FOR LOCAL AUTHORITIES AND THE NATIONAL HEALTH SERVICE IN ENGLAND AND WALES
1 Vincent Square, SW1P 2PN
[071–828 1212]

The Audit Commission was set up in 1983 with responsibility for the external audit of local authorities. This remit was extended from October 1990 to include the audit of the National Health Service bodies in England and Wales. The Commission appoints the auditors, who may be from the District Audit Service or from a private firm of accountants. The Commission also has responsibility to promote value for money in the services provided by local authorities and health bodies.

The Commission has 15–17 members appointed by the Secretary of State for the Environment in consultation with the Secretaries of State for Wales and for Health. Though appointed by the Secretary of State the Commissioners are responsible to Parliament.
Chairman, D. J. S. Cooksey.
Deputy Chairman, H. S. Axton.
Controller of Audit, H. J. Davies.
Deputy Controller, J. C. Nicholson, CBE.

THE COMMISSION FOR LOCAL AUTHORITY ACCOUNTS IN SCOTLAND
18 George Street, Edinburgh EH2 2QU
[031–226 7346]

The Commission was set up in 1975. It is responsible for securing the audit of the accounts of Scottish local authorities and certain joint boards and joint committees. Amongst its duties the Commission is required to deal with reports made by the Controller of Audit on items of account contrary to law; incorrect accounting; and losses due to misconduct, negligence and failure to carry out statutory duties. Since 1988 the Commission has had responsibility for value-for-money audits of authorities.

Members are appointed by the Secretary of State for Scotland.
Chairman, Prof. J. R. Small.
Controller of Audit, J. Broadfoot.
Secretary, J. Ritchie.

THE BANK OF ENGLAND
Threadneedle Street, EC2R 8AH
[071–601 4444]

The Bank of England was incorporated in 1694 under Royal Charter. It is the banker of the Government on whose behalf it manages the Note Issue and the National Debt. As central reserve bank of the country, the Bank keeps the accounts of British banks, who maintain with it a proportion of their cash resources, and of most overseas central banks.
Governor, Rt. Hon. Robin Leigh-Pemberton.
Deputy Governor, E. A. J. George.
Directors, Dr. D. V. Atterton, CBE; Hon. Sir John Baring, CVO; Sir Adrian Cadbury; A. L. Coleby; F. B. Corby; Sir Colin Corness; A. D. Crockett; J. S. Flemming; Sir Robert Haslam; Sir Martin Jacomb; Prof. M. A. King; Sir Hector Laing; G. H. Laird; B. Quinn; Sir David Scholey, CBE; D. A. Walker.
Associate Directors, P. H. Kent; H. C. E. Harris; I. Plenderleith.
Advisers to the Governor, J. P. Charkham; A. L. Coleby; Sir Peter Petrie.
Assistant Director, R. A. Barnes.
Chief of Banking Department (Chief Cashier), G. M. Gill.
Chief Registrar, D. A. Bridger.
General Manager, Printing Works, A. W. Jarvis.
Secretary, G. A. Croughton.
Head of Information Division, J. R. E. Footman.
The Auditor, J. Bartlett.

BOUNDARY COMMISSIONS

The Commissions are constituted under the Parliamentary Constituencies Act, 1986. The Speaker of the House of Commons is ex-officio chairman of all four Commissions in the United Kingdom. Each of the four Commissions is required by law to keep the parliamentary constituencies in their part of the United Kingdom under review. Each of the three Commissions in Great Britain is required by law to keep the European Parliamentary constituencies in their part of Great Britain under review.

England
St. Catherines House, 10 Kingsway, WC2B 6JP
[071–242 0262]

Deputy Chairman, The Hon. Mr. Justice Knox.
Joint Secretaries, R. McLeod; Mrs. J. S. Morris.

Wales
St. Catherines House, 10 Kingsway, WC2B 6JP
[071–242 0262]

Deputy Chairman, The Hon. Mr. Justice Anthony Evans.
Joint Secretaries, R. McLeod; Mrs. J. S. Morris.

Scotland
St. Andrew's House, Edinburgh EH1 3DE
[031–244 2196-8]

Deputy Chairman, The Hon. Lord Davidson.
Secretary, D. K. C. Jeffrey.

Northern Ireland
c/o Northern Ireland Office,
Whitehall, SW1A 2AZ
[071–210 6569]

Deputy Chairman, Mr. Justice Higgins.
Secretary, J. R. Fisher.

BRITISH BROADCASTING CORPORATION
Broadcasting House, W1A 1AA
[071–580 4468]

The BBC was incorporated under Royal Charter as successor to the British Broadcasting Company, Ltd., whose licence expired Dec. 31, 1926. Its present Charter came into force Aug. 1, 1981, for 15 years. The Chairman, Vice-Chairman and other Governors are appointed by the Queen in Council. The BBC is financed by revenue from receiving licences for the Home services and by grant-in-aid from Parliament for the External services. The total number of receiving licences in the UK at March 31, 1990 was 19,644,599, of which 1,680,618 were for monochrome receivers and 17,963,981 for colour receivers. Annual television fees are: monochrome £24; colour £71. Television licence fees became index-linked from April 1, 1988.

Board of Governors
(as at Aug. 1, 1990)

Chairman, M. Hussey. £39,200
Vice-Chairman, The Lord Barnett, PC £10,085
Governors, J. Kincade, CBE, Ph.D. (*N. Ireland*); J. Parry, CBE (*Wales*); Sir Graham Hills, FRSE (*Scotland*) . . . . (*each*) £10,085
Dr. J. Roberts; W. B. Jordan; J. K. Oates; Miss P. D. James, OBE; Miss J. Glover, D.Phil; Mrs. S. Sadeque; Lord Nicholas Gordon Lennox, KCMG, KCVO . . . . (*each*) £5,030

Board of Management

Director-General, M. Checkland.
Deputy Director-General, J. Birt.
Managing Directors, P. Fox (*Network Television*); D. Hatch (*Network Radio*); J. Tusa (*External Broadcasting*); R. Neil (*Regional Broadcasting*).
Directors, W. Dennay (*Engineering*); H. James (*Corporate Affairs*); I. Phillips (*Finance*); R. Chase (*Personnel*).

Other Senior Staff

Director, News and Current Affairs, I. Hargreaves.
Director, Resources, Radio, D. Thomas.
Director, Resources, Television, C. Taylor.
Deputy Managing Director, External Broadcasting, D. Witherow.
Deputy Director of Engineering, C. Sandbank.
Head of Policy and Planning Unit, Ms. P. Hodgson.
Controller, BBC-1, J. Powell.
Controller, BBC-2, A. Yentob.
Assistant Managing Director, Network Television, W. Wyatt.
Controller, Radio 1, J. Beerling.
Controller, Radio 2, Ms. F. Line.
Controller, Radio 3, J. Drummond.
Controller, Radio 4, M. Green.
Controller, Radio 5, Ms. P. Ewing.
Controller, Scotland, P. Chalmers.
Controller, Wales, G. Talfan Davies.
Controller, N. Ireland, Rev. Dr. C. Morris.
Chief Political Adviser, Ms. M. Douglas.
Controller, Editorial Policy, J. Wilson.
Controller, Information Services, M. Bunce.
The Secretary, J. McCormick.

Legal Adviser, G. Roscoe.
Chief Executive, BBC Enterprises, J. Arnold-Baker.

BRITISH COAL CORPORATION
Hobart House, Grosvenor Place, SW1X 7AE
[071–235 2020]

The British Coal Corporation (formerly the National Coal Board) was constituted in 1946 and took over the mines on January 1, 1947.
Chairman, Lord Haslam.
Deputy Chairman and Operations Director, J. H. Northard, CBE.
Deputy Chairman, D. W. Kendall.
Executive Members, M. J. Edwards, CBE (*Commercial Director*); M. H. Butler (*Finance Director*); K. Moses, CBE (*Technical Director*).
Non-Executive Members, C. Baker; Dr. D. V. Atterton, CBE; Dr. T. J. Parker; Sir Ronald Dearing, CB; D. B. Walker; J. P. Erbé.
Secretary, M. S. Shelton.
Industrial Relations Director, K. Hunt.
Regional Director (*North*), L. Harris, OBE.
Regional Director (*Midlands and South*), A. Wheeler.

THE BRITISH COUNCIL
10 Spring Gardens, SW1A 2BN
[071–930 8466]

The British Council was established in 1934 and incorporated by Royal Charter in 1940.
It is an independent, non-political organization which promotes Britain abroad. It provides access to British ideas, talents and experience in education and training, books and periodicals, the English language, the arts, the sciences and technology.
The Council is represented in 90 countries and runs 145 offices, 116 libraries and 52 English language schools around the world.
The Council's annual turnover in 1990–91 is estimated at £348 million, including grants from the Foreign and Commonwealth Office and the Overseas Development Administration. The Council's own earnings now exceed £72 million.
Chairman, Sir David Orr, MC.
Director-General, Sir Richard Francis, KCMG.
£69,960

BRITISH RAILWAYS BOARD
Euston House, 24 Eversholt Street,
PO Box 100, NW1 1DZ
[071–928 5151]

The British Railways Board came into being on Jan. 1, 1963 under the terms of the Transport Act, 1962. The Board became responsible for the provision of railway services in Great Britain and for catering and other services formerly carried on by the British Transport Commission.
Chairman, Sir Robert Reid £112,244
Vice-Chairman, D. Fowler, CBE.
Members, Sir Oscar DeVille, CBE*; Sir Derek Hornby*; Sir Allen Sheppard*; R. W. Tookey, CBE*; Ms. A. Biss*; Miss K. T. Kantor*; J. B. Cameron, CBE; J. K. WELSBY, CBE; D. E. Rayner; J. C. P. Edmonds.
* Part-time members, paid *pro rata*.

BSI (BRITISH STANDARDS INSTITUTION)
2 Park Street, W1A 2BS
[Enquiry Section: BSI, Linford Wood, Milton Keynes, MK14 6LE. Tel. 0908–221166]

BSI (the British Standards Institution) is the recognized authority in the UK for the preparation and publication of national standards for industrial and consumer products. In consultation with the interests concerned, BSI prepares standards relating to nearly every sector of the nation's industry and trade.

British Standards are issued for voluntary adoption, though in a number of cases compliance with a British Standard is required by legislation. BSI operates certification schemes under which industrial and consumer products are certified as complying with the relevant British Standard and may carry the Institution's certification trade marks, known as the 'Kitemark' and the 'Safety Mark'. BSI runs one of the largest testing laboratories in Europe and has an advisory service for exporters, Technical Help to Exporters.

BSI is financed by voluntary subscriptions, an annual Government grant, the sale of its publications, and fees for testing and certification. There are more than 20,000 subscribing members of BSI.

Director General, Dr. I. Dunstan.

BRITISH TECHNOLOGY GROUP
101 Newington Causeway, SE1 6BU
[071–403 6666]

British Technology Group (BTG) is a self-financing technology transfer organization. It searches for new technology worldwide, licenses new scientific and engineering products to industry, and provides finance for the development of new technology.

Chairman, C. Barker.
Chief Executive, I. A. Harvey.

BRITISH TOURIST AUTHORITY
Thames Tower, Black's Road, W6 9EL
[071–846 9000]

The British Tourist Authority has specific responsibility for promoting tourism to Great Britain from overseas. It also has a general responsibility for the promotion and development of tourism and tourist facilities within Great Britain as a whole. With the agreement of the corresponding bodies in Northern Ireland, the Channel Islands and the Isle of Man, the Authority may also carry out promotion overseas on behalf of those territories.

Chairman, W. Davis (*part-time*).
Chief Executive, M. G. Medlicott.

BRITISH WATERWAYS BOARD
Greycaine Road, Watford, Herts. WD2 4JR
[0923–226422]

The British Waterways Board is the navigational authority for nearly 2,000 miles of canals and river navigations in England, Scotland and Wales. Some 340 miles are maintained and are being developed as commercial waterways for use by freight-carrying vessels, and another 1,200 miles, the cruising waterways, are being developed for boating, fishing and other leisure activities. The remaining 500 miles, the remainder waterways, are maintained with due regard to safety, public health and the preservation of amenities. Over a third of this remaining mileage is navigable and a further third is being, or has been, restored to navigation over the last twenty years.

Chairman, D. C. Ingman (*part-time*).
Vice-Chairman, Sir Peter Hutchison, Bt. (*part-time*).
Members (*all part-time*), J. Gordon; Dr. B. Goodman; M. Golder; D. H. R. Yorke.
Chief Executive, B. C. Dice.
Secretary and Solicitor, R. J. Duffy.

BROADCASTING STANDARDS COUNCIL
5–8 The Sanctuary, SW1P 3JS
[071–233 0544]

The Council was set up in 1988 to consider the portrayal of sex and of violence and matters of taste and decency in any television or radio programme or advertisement. The Council's main tasks are: to draw up a code of practice; to consider complaints; to monitor programmes; and to undertake relevant research. Members of the Council are appointed by the Home Secretary. (The appointments are part-time.)

Chairman, The Lord Rees-Mogg £31,500
Deputy Chairman, Miss J. Barrow, OBE £24,000
Members, R. Barker, OBE, RD; The Bishop of Peterborough; A. Dubs; Dr. R. Brinley Jones; Dr. Jean Curtis-Raleigh; Rev. C. Robertson £9,500
Director, C. Shaw.
Deputy Director, D. Houghton.

THE BROADS AUTHORITY
Thomas Harvey House, 18 Colegate,
Norwich NR3 1BQ
[0603–610734]

The Broads Authority is a special statutory authority set up under the Norfolk and Suffolk Broads Act 1988, with powers and responsibilities similar to those of National Park Authorities. The functions of the Authority, as set out in the Act, are: to conserve and enhance the natural beauty of the Broads; to promote the enjoyment of the Broads by the public; and to protect the interests of navigation.

The Authority comprises 35 members, appointed by Norfolk County Council (4); Suffolk County Council (2); Broadland District Council (2); Great Yarmouth Borough Council (2); North Norfolk District Council (2); Norwich City Council (2); South Norfolk District Council (2); Waveney District Council (2); the Countryside Commission (2); the Nature Conservancy Council (1); the Great Yarmouth Port Authority (2); National Rivers Authority (Anglian Region) (1); the Secretary of State for the Environment (9); and two from amongst members of the Authority's statutory Navigation Committee who are not already members of the Authority.

Chairman, J. S. Peel, MC.
Chief Executive, M. A. Clark.

CABINET OFFICE

The Cabinet Office comprises the Secretariat, who support Ministers collectively in the conduct of Cabinet business; and the Office of the Minister for the Civil Service (OMCS) which is responsible for the management and organization of the Civil Service and recruitment into it, efficiency, and senior appointments. Other functions are from time to time laid on the Office, some ephemerally and some permanently. Non-departmental Ministers may be attached to the Office.

The functions of the Cabinet Office (OMCS) are in support of the Prime Minister in her capacity as Minister for the Civil Service, with responsibility for day-to-day supervision delegated to the Minister of State, Privy Council Office.

(For **Salaries**, *see* page 295)

PRIME MINISTER'S OFFICE

Prime Minister and Minister for the Civil Service, THE RT. HON. MARGARET THATCHER, MP.
Principal Private Secretary to the Prime Minister, (*G3*), A. Turnbull.
Private Secretaries to the Prime Minister, C. D. Powell (*Overseas Affairs*); B. Potter (*Economic Affairs*); D. Morris (*Parliamentary Affairs*); Miss C. A. Slocock (*Home Affairs*).
Personal Assistant to the Prime Minister, Mrs. A. Ponsonby.

Secretary for Appointments (G5), J. R. Catford.
Foreign Affairs Adviser, Sir Percy Cradock, GCMG.
Political Secretary, J. Whittingdale.
Policy Unit, G. Guise; Miss C. Sinclair; J. Mills; Prof.
B. Griffiths; A. Dunlop; I. K. Whitehead; H. Harris-
Hughes; R. Harris.
Chief Press Secretary, B. Ingham.
Deputy Chief Press Secretary, T. J. Perks.
Assistant Private Secretaries to Prime Minister, Miss
J. Drever; Miss J. L. Wilkinson.
Parliamentary Private Secretary, P. Morrison, MP.
Adviser on Efficiency, Sir Angus Fraser, KCB, TD.

Efficiency Unit
70 Whitehall, SW1A 2AS

Head of Unit (G3), D. Brereton.
Assistant Secretaries (G5), Mrs. S. Hughes; Dr. G. D.
Coley; P. J. R. Jarvis; Dr. I. V. Howell.

Cabinet Office

*Secretary to the Cabinet and Head of Home Civil Ser-
vice*, Sir Robin Butler, KCB, CVO.

Ceremonial Branch

Ceremonial Officer (G5), J. H. Thompson, CB.

SECRETARIAT
70 Whitehall, SW1A 2AS
[071–270 3000]

Deputy Secretaries (G2), Sir Christopher Curwen,
KCMG; D. Hadley; L. V. Appleyard; P. F. Owen, CB.
Chief Scientific Adviser, Prof. W. P. D. Stewart.
Under Secretaries (G3), A. C. D. Macrae; W. D.
Reeves; T. J. Burr; C R. Walker; M. Russell; B. G.
Bender.
Assistant Secretaries (G5), Brig. J. A. J. Budd; M.
Nicholson; R. P. Short; L. Parker; Mrs. G. Craig;
P. I. Bailey; G. Barrass; D. Gowan; Dr. D. J. W.
Lumley; Air Cdre. N. J. G. Hednett, MBE; P. L.
Thomas; M. B. Nicholson; S. H. D. Hawker.
Senior Principals (G6), C. K. Davies; P. C. F. Gilbert;
P. F. Tero; Dr. J. N. Wingfield; J. Reynolds; Dr. J.
A. Leather; M. G. Foster; J. C. Dilling.

ESTABLISHMENT OFFICER'S GROUP

Principal Establishment and Finance Officer, (G3), S.
R. Davie.

Information Services

Chief Press Officer (G6), J. P. Lawson.

Establishment Division

Deputy Establishment Officer (G5), G. S. Royston.

Finance Division

Senior Finance Officer (G6), Miss J. M. E. Buchan.

Internal Audit

Principal (G7), I. C. R. Boulton.

Historical Section
Hepburn House, Marsham Street, SW1P 4HW
[071–217 6032]

Departmental Records Adviser (G6), Miss. P. M.
Andrews.

OFFICE OF THE MINISTER FOR THE
CIVIL SERVICE
Horse Guards Road, SW1P 3AL
[071–270 3000]

Second Permanent Secretary (G1A), E. P. Kemp, CB.
*Director of Management Development and Training
(G2)*, B. T. Gilmore.
Security Adviser, Air Cdre. P. V. Mayall, CBE.

Management and Development Group

Assistant Secretaries (G5), R. D. J. Wright; Miss S.
Haird.

Senior Staff and Europe Division

*Under Secretary and Director, Public Appointments
Unit (G3)*, G. T. Morgan.
Assistant Secretary (G5), A. Phillips.

Machinery of Government

Assistant Secretary (G5), A. D. Whetnall.

Security Division

Assistant Secretary (G5), H. H. Taylor.

Information Officer Management Unit

Chief Information Officer A (G5), Ms. A. Nash.

Civil Service Commission
Alencon Link, Basingstoke, Hants. RG21 1JB
[0256–29222]

First Commissioner (G2), J. H. Holroyd.
Commissioners (G3), B. Walmsley; (G4), J. K. Moore
(*Director, Civil Service Selection Board*).
Commissioners (part-time), G. L. Dennis; Miss D.
Whittingham; Miss U. Prashar.
Assistant Secretary (G5), C. J. Parry.
Senior Principals (G6), P. Cook; R. B. M. Payne; P. J.
Wiggett.

Civil Service Selection Board
24 Whitehall, SW1A 2ED

Director (G4), J. K. Moore.
Deputy Director (G6), A. S. Halford.
Chief Psychologist (G6), F. D. Bedford.

Top Management Programme

Director (G2), B. T. Gilmore.
Deputy Directors (G5), W. D. Harding; Mrs. S. R.
Street.

EXECUTIVE AGENCIES

Occupational Health Service
18–20 Hill Street, Edinburgh EH2 3NB

Medical Adviser and Director, Dr. G. S. Sorrie.
Deputy Medical Advisers, Dr. P. J. Constable; Dr. A.
N. Hepburn.

Civil Service College
Sunningdale Park, Ascot, Berks. SL5 0QE
[0990–23444]
11 Belgrave Road, SW1V 1RB
[071–834 6644]

Chief Executive (G3), Miss M. T. Neville-Rolfe.
Director of Services and Resources (G5), I. Cameron.
Directors (G5), J. Allen; A. A. Carter; Dr. R. J. Smith;
Ms. C. M. Bentley.
College Secretary (G6), Miss M. A. Wood.

CABLE AUTHORITY
Gillingham House, 38–44 Gillingham Street,
SW1V 1HU
[071–821 6161]

The Cable Authority is the statutory body established by the Cable and Broadcasting Act 1984 to
grant franchises for the operation of new cable
systems and to licence the provision of and regulate
the content of cable programme services, including
those satellite television channels which are carried
on cable networks. Its functions will be absorbed by
the Independent Television Commission on Jan. 1,
1991.

Chairman, R. Burton.

Deputy Chairman, Prof. J. Ring, CBE.
Members, Mrs. A. Ballard; P. Johnson; Mrs. E. MacDonald-Brown; P. Paine, CBE, DFC; P. Darwin.
Director-General, J. Davey.
Secretary, A. Hewitt.

CENTRAL STATISTICAL OFFICE
Great George Street, SW1P 3AQ
[071–270 6363/6364]

The work of the Central Statistical Office encompasses data collection from businesses and the preparation of macro-economic statistics; statistics relating to institutional sectors and financial statistics; the retail prices index and the family expenditure survey; liaison with international statistical bodies and central management of the Government Statistical Services (GSS).
Director and Head of the Government Statistical Service (G1A), Sir Jack Hibbert, KCB.
Private Secretary, Miss I. Shirley.
Deputy Director (G3), M. J. Erritt.
Principal Establishment Officer (G5), F. Martin.
Head of Information (G5), J. B. Wright.
National Accounts Quality Control (G5), R. J. Scott.

Directorate A
Millbank Tower, Millbank, SW1P 4QU
[071–217 4363]

Deputy Director of the CSO (G3), M. J. Erritt.
Heads of Branches (G5):
International and social statistics, T. J. Griffin.
GSS management and policy, P. P. Altobell.
Methodology, survey control and classifications, P. B. Kenny.

Directorate B
Cardiff Road, Newport, Gwent NP9 1XG
[0633–815696]

Director (G3), N. Harvey.
Heads of Branches (G5):
Short term production and products, D. R. Lewis.
Censuses, stocks, capital expenditure, C. J. Spiller.
Distribution and services; prices; purchases, R. M. Norton.
Registers, legal, statistical computing, Dr. R. L. Butchart.

Directorate C

Assistant Director (G3), R. G. Ward.
Heads of Branches (G5):
National accounts co-ordination, Miss S. P. Carter.
Total domestic expenditure, K. Mansell.
GDP(Output), IOP and industrial statistics, D. C. K. Stirling.

Directorate D

Assistant Director (G3), J. E. Kidgell.
Heads of Branches (G5):
Balance of payments current account, G. Jenkinson.
Financial accounts, B. J. Buckingham.
Private sector accounts, Dr. G. A. Keenay.
Overseas transactions; research and development statistics, P. H. Richardson.

Directorate E

Assistant Director (G3), P. D. Dworkin.
Heads of Branches (G5):
Information systems and strategy, Dr. J. H. Ludley.

Retail prices, family expenditure, taxes and benefits, D. J. Sellwood.
Press, publications, publicity, J. B. Wright.

CERTIFICATION OFFICE FOR TRADE UNIONS AND EMPLOYERS' ASSOCIATIONS
27 Wilton Street, SW1X 7AZ
[071–210 3733/4]

The Certification Officer is an independent statutory authority appointed by the Secretary of State for Employment. He is responsible for receiving and scrutinizing annual returns from trade union and employers' associations; for reimbursing certain costs of trade unions' postal ballots; for dealing with complaints concerning trade union elections; for ensuring observance of statutory requirements governing political funds and trade union mergers; and for certifying the independence of trade unions.
Certification Officer, M. Wake.
Assistant Certification Officer, G. S. Osborne.

Scotland
58 Frederick Street, Edinburgh EH2 1LN
[031–226 3224]

Assistant Certification Officer for Scotland, J. L. J. Craig.

CHARITY COMMISSION
St. Alban's House, 57–60 Haymarket, SW1Y 4QX
[071–210 3000]
Graeme House, Derby Square, Liverpool L2 7SB
[051–227 3191]
The Deane, Tangier, Taunton, Somerset TA1 4AY
[0823–321102]

The Charity Commissioners are appointed under the Charities Act, 1960, principally to further the work of charities in England and Wales by giving advice and information, and by investigating and checking abuses. The Commissioners maintain a register of charities; give consent to land transactions; help to modernize the purposes and administrative machinery of charities; and, in the name of one of their staff, the Official Custodian for Charities, hold investments for charities.
At the end of 1989 the total number of registered charities was 168,170.

Chief Commissioner, R. I. L Guthrie.
Commissioners, J. Farquharson; R. M. Venables.
Commissioners (part-time), M. Webber; Mrs. D. H. Yeo.
(Commissioners .... £36,818–£47,600)
Deputy Commissioners (G5), J. A. Dutton; J. F. Claricoat; G. S. Goodchild; K. M. Dibble; S. Slack.
Secretary and Asst. Commissioner (G5), D. Forrest.
Director of Operations and Asst. Commissioner (G5), J. H. Vining.
Grade 6, Mrs. H. M. Phillips; Miss D. F. Taylor; S. K. Sen; P. P. White; N. M. Mackenzie; D. C. Raikes; M. J. Harbottle; I. M. Davies; P. W. Somerfield; C. Noon; V. Mitchell.
Grade 7, R. E. Hatton; A. O. Polak; Miss S. M. St. C. Smith; M. C. T. Seymour; Miss C. F. Byrne; K. M. Dickin; M. J. McManus; R. E. Edwards; G. B. Ward; R. Kilby; Mrs. A. Ireland; T. Le Grice; Miss V. A. Nuttall.
Official Custodian for Charities (G6), R. J. Crick.
Deputy Official Custodian (G7), Mrs. S. E. Gillingham.
Establishment Officer (G6), J. M. Samuels.

OFFICE OF THE
CHIEF ADJUDICATION OFFICER
Cumberland House,
15–17 Cumberland Place, Southampton SO9 2DD
[0703–330066]

The Chief Adjudication Officer is an independent authority under the Social Security Act, 1975 (as amended) appointed by the Secretary of State for Social Services to give advice to adjudication officers (who make decisions of first instance on all claims for Social Security cash benefits), to keep under review the operation of the system of adjudication and to report annually to the Secretary of State on adjudication standards. The Office also enters written observations on all appeals made to the Social Security Commissioners.

Chief Adjudication Officer, M. E. H. Platt.

CHURCH COMMISSIONERS
1 Millbank, SW1P 3JZ
[071–222 7010]

The Church Commissioners were established on April 1, 1948, by the amalgamation of Queen Anne's Bounty (established 1704) and the Ecclesiastical Commissioners (established 1836).

The Commissioners' main task is to improve the stipends and housing of the Church of England clergy and to provide them and their widows with adequate pensions and assistance with housing in retirement. They also carry out administrative duties in connection with pastoral reorganization and redundant churches, and have been designated by the General Synod as the central stipends authority of the Church of England.

The Commissioners' income for the year ended Dec. 31, 1989, was derived from the following sources:—

	£ million
Stock exchange investments	62·8
Land and property	58·8
Mortgages, loans, etc.	19·2
Trust income, and diocesan/parish contributions for stipends	60·4
	£201·2

This income, plus £1·7m from balances brought forward, was applied as follows:—

Clergy stipends	108·2
Clergy and widows' pensions	49·5
Clergy houses	20·1
Episcopal administration and payments to Chapters	7·5
Church buildings	6·3
Administrative expenses of the Commissioners and related bodies	11·3
	£202·9

Constitution

The Archbishops of Canterbury and of York; the 41 diocesan Bishops; 5 deans or provosts, 10 other clergy and 10 laymen appointed by the General Synod; 4 laymen nominated by the Queen; 4 persons nominated by the Archbishop of Canterbury; The Lord Chancellor; The Lord President of the Council; the First Lord of the Treasury; The Chancellor of the Exchequer; The Secretary of State for the Home Department; The Speaker of the House of Commons; The Lord Chief Justice; The Master of the Rolls; The Attorney-General; The Solicitor-General; The Lord Mayor and two Aldermen of the City of London; The Lord Mayor of York and one representative from each of the Universities of Oxford and Cambridge.

Church Estates Commissioners

First, Sir Douglas Lovelock, KCB.
Second, Rt. Hon. Michael Alison, MP.
Third, Mrs. M. H. Laird.

Officers

Secretary, J. E. Shelley.
Deputy Secretary, P. Locke.
Under Secretary (Pastoral), D. J. Day.
Assistant Secretaries:
Chief Accountant, D. I. Archer.
Deputy Accountant and Trust Officer, G. C. Baines.
Bishoprics, C. P. Canton.
Commercial Property, R. M. Hutchings.
Computer Manager, J. W. Ferguson.
Establishment Officer, W. R. Herbert.
Estates, P. H. P. Shaw.
General Purposes, M. D. Elengorn.
Houses, D. J. B. Long.
Investments Manager, P. G. Brealey.
Pastoral, D. N. Goodwin.
Redundant Churches, J. M. Davies.
Stipends and Allocations, R. S. Hopgood.
Senior Principals, M. G. S. Farrell; A. S. Hardy; B. J. Hardy; E. G. Peacock.
Principals, A. W. Atkins; P. D. Chadwick; Miss A. M. Mackie; G. Wills; J. A. W. Elloy; C. R. Bullen; N. M. Waring; D. W. H. Lewis; N. J. Neil-Smith.

Legal Department

Official Solicitor, E. W. Wills.
Deputy Solicitor, J. P. Guy.
Solicitors, Miss J. M. Bland; J. D. Carter; Miss J. A. Egar; Miss S. M. S. Jones; R. D. C. Murray; Mrs. S. E. Prosser; T. Tayleur.

CIVIL AVIATION AUTHORITY
CAA House, 45–59 Kingsway, WC2B 6TE
[071–379 7311]

The CAA is responsible for the economic regulation of UK airlines by licensing air routes, air travel organizers and approving fares; for the safety regulation of UK civil aviation by the certification of airlines and aircraft, and by licensing aerodromes, flight crew and aircraft engineers; and, through the National Air Traffic Services, for the provision of air traffic control and telecommunications services.

Chairman, Sir Christopher Tugendhat (*part-time*) £48,375
Managing Director, T. Murphy.
Secretary, Miss G. M. E. White.

CLYDE PORT AUTHORITY
16 Robertson Street, Glasgow G2 8DS
[041-221 8733]

The Authority is a self-governing statutory body established by individual Act of Parliament and provides sea port facilities within a 450 sq. mile area of jurisdiction which encompasses the River Clyde, its estuary and sea lochs.

Chairman, Sir Robert Easton, CBE.
Managing Director, J. Mather.
Director and Secretary, G. P. Johnston.
Director and Marine Operations, Capt. D. B. McMurray.

COMMONWEALTH DEVELOPMENT CORPORATION
1 Bessborough Gardens, SW1V 2JQ
[071–828 4488]

The Corporation's area of operations covers British dependent territories and, with Ministerial approval, any Commonwealth or other developing country. At present, the Corporation is authorized to operate in 36 Commonwealth and 16 non-Commonwealth countries in addition to the British dependent territories. The Corporation is authorized to borrow up to £750,000,000.

Chairman (part-time), P. Leslie.
Deputy Chairman (part-time), Sir Michael Caine.
Members (part-time), Mrs. A. Wright; V. Robertson, OBE; M. D. Nightingale, OBE; Prof. M. Faber; M. Robinson; E. B. Waide, OBE; M. D. McWilliam.
General Manager, J. D. Eccles, CBE.

COMMONWEALTH SECRETARIAT
(*see* p. 626)

COMMONWEALTH WAR GRAVES COMMISSION
2 Marlow Road, Maidenhead, Berkshire SL6 7DX
[0628–34221]

The Commonwealth War Graves Commission (formerly Imperial War Graves Commission) was founded by Royal Charter in 1917. It is responsible for the commemoration of 1,695,000 members of the forces of the Commonwealth who fell in the two world wars. More than one million graves are maintained in 23,102 burial grounds throughout the world. Over three-quarters of a million men and women who have no known grave or who were cremated are commemorated by name on memorials built by the Commission.

The funds of the Commission are derived from the six Governments participating in its work—the UK, Australia, Canada, India, New Zealand and South Africa.

President, HRH The Duke of Kent, KG, GCMG, GCVO, ADC.
Chairman, The Secretary of State for Defence in the UK.
Vice-Chairman, Gen. Sir Robert Ford, GCB, CBE.
Members, The Secretary of State for the Environment in the UK; The High Commissioners in London for Australia, Canada, India, and New Zealand; the Ambassador in London for the Republic of South Africa; Air Chief Marshal Sir John Gingell, GBE, KCB; Capt. Sir Miles Wingate, KCVO; Maj.-Gen. D. Smith, CBE, DSO, CD; The Rt. Hon. J. D. Concannon; Dame Janet Fookes, DBE, MP; Sir Derek Day, KCMG; Sir Nigel Mobbs; Adm. Sir Nicholas Hunt, GCB, LVO.
Director-General, J. Saynor.
Deputy Director-Generals, D. Kennedy (*Administration*); N. B. Osborn, OBE (*Operations*).
Directors, R. D. Wilson (*Finance*); A. Coombe (*Works*); P. J. Noakes (*Horticulture*); H. Mackay (*Management Services*); T. F. Penfold (*Personnel*); J. P. D. Gee (*Information and Secretariat*).
Legal Adviser and Solicitor, G. C. Reddie.
Hon. Artistic Adviser, Prof. Sir Peter Shepheard, CBE.
Hon. Botanical Adviser, Prof. G. T. Prance, D.Phil., FLS.

Imperial War Graves Endowment Fund
Trustees, Gen. Sir Robert Ford, GCB, CBE; H. U. A. Lambert; The Lord Remnant, CVO.
Hon. Secretary to the Trustees, R. D. Wilson.

COUNTRYSIDE COMMISSION
John Dower House, Crescent Place,
Cheltenham, Glos. GL50 3RA
[0242–521381]

The Countryside Commission is an independent agency set up in 1968 to promote the conservation and enhancement of landscape beauty in England and Wales, to encourage the provision and improvement of facilities in the countryside for enjoyment, including the need to secure access for open air recreation. Since April 1982 the Commission has been funded by annual grant from the Department of the Environment. Members of the Commission are appointed by the Secretary of State for the Environment and the Secretary of State for Wales acting jointly.

From April 1, 1991, the Countryside Commission's responsibilities in Wales will be discharged by the new Countryside Council for Wales, subject to parliamentary approval.

Chairman, Sir Derek Barber.
Director General (G3), A. A. C. Phillips.
Directors (G5), R. Clarke (*Policy*); M. J. Kirby (*Regions*); M. Taylor (*Resources*).
National Heritage Adviser, P. Walsh.
Head of Corporate Planning (G7), T. Robinson.
Head of Conservation Branch (G7), R. Roberts.
Head of Recreation and Access Branch (G7), J. W. B. Worth.
Head of Communications Branch (G7), C. Pugsley.
Head of Finance and Establishments (G7), V. Ellis.
Head of National Parks and Planning Branch (G7), R. Lloyd.
Head of Training and Voluntary Action Branch (G7), I. Mitchell.
Regional Officers (G7), G. Taylor (*Newcastle*); K. Buchanan (*Cambridge*); Dr. S. A. Bucknall (*Leeds*); E. Holdaway (*Bristol*); R. T. Thomas (*Manchester*); D. E. Coleman (*London*); F. S. Walmsley (*Birmingham*); Dr. M. Carroll (*Task Force Trees*).

Office for Wales
Ladywell House, Newtown, Powys, SY16 1RD
[0686–626799]

(For situation after April 1, 1991, *see* above.)
Chairman, R. E. M. Rees.
Principal Officer (G7), A. M. H. Fitton.

COUNTRYSIDE COMMISSION FOR SCOTLAND
Battleby, Redgorton, Perth, PH1 3EW
[0738–27921]

Established under the Countryside (Scotland) Act, 1967, with functions for the provision, development and improvement of facilities for the enjoyment of the Scottish countryside, and for the conservation and enhancement of its natural beauty and amenity.

Chairman, J. R. Carr (*part-time*).
Commissioners, J. M. S. Arnott (*Vice-Chairman*); Prof. C. H. Gimingham; Q. Brown; R. B. Cowe, MBE; R. D. Cramond, CBE; Mrs. S. Harvey; A. W. Henry; E. Langmuir, MBE; I. Miller; Dr. W. E. S. Mutch; Prof. J. C. Smyth, OBE; W. M. Turnbull; Dr. A. Watson.
Director, D. Campbell.
Asst. Directors, J. M. Fladmark (*Planning*); J. R. Turner (*Research and Development*); M. A. Payne (*Communications and Training*); W. T. Band (*Finance and Administration*); R. I. Fairley (*Policy Officer*).

COVENT GARDEN MARKET AUTHORITY
Covent House, New Covent Garden Market,
SW8 5NX
[071–720 2211]

The Covent Garden Market Authority is constituted under the Covent Garden Market Acts, 1961 to 1966, the members being appointed by the Minister of Agriculture, Fisheries and Food. The Authority owns and operates the 56-acre New Covent Garden Markets (fruit, vegetable, flowers) which have been trading since 1974.
Chairman, W. P. Bowman, OBE (*part-time*).
Members (*part-time*), P. J. Hunt; E. I. Kingston; J. A. Harvey; R. Smith, OBE; Sir Peter Reynolds, OBE.
General Manager, Dr. P. M. Liggins.
Secretary, P. R. Taylor.

CRIMINAL INJURIES COMPENSATION BOARD
Blythswood House, 200 West Regent Street,
Glasgow G2 4SW
[041–221 0945]

LONDON OFFICE: Whittington House,
19 Alfred Place, WC1E 7LG
[071–636 9501 and 071–636 2812]

The Board was constituted in 1964 to administer the Government scheme for *ex gratia* payments of compensation to victims of crimes of violence.
Chairman, The Lord Carlisle of Bucklow, PC, QC £53,400
Members, J. F. A. Archer, QC; Sir Derek Bradbeer, OBE; D. Brennan, QC; D. Calcutt, QC; H. Carlisle, QC; B. W. Chedlow, QC; J. Cherry, QC; Miss B. Cooper, QC; Miss D. Cotton, QC; J. D. Crowley, QC; T. Dawson, QC; T. A. K. Drummond, QC; C. Fawcett, QC; W. Gage, QC; B. Green, QC; G. M. Hamilton, QC; Sir Arthur Hoole; J. Law, QC; M. E. Lewer, QC; J. Leighton Williams, QC; C. Lindsay, QC; Lord Macaulay of Bragar, QC; D. MacKay, QC; Sir Denis Marshall; Mrs. B. Mills, QC; Sir John Palmer; I. M. S. Park, CBE; T. Preston, QC; Miss S. Ritchie, QC; D. B. Robertson, QC; C. Seagroatt, QC; L. S. Shields, QC; Mrs. J. Smith, QC; R. Smith, QC; E. Stone, QC; D. M. Thomas, OBE, QC; D. O. Thomas, QC; P. Weitzman, QC; C. H. Whitby, QC.
Secretary and Solicitor, D. M. North.
Deputy Secretary, D. J. White.

CROFTERS COMMISSION
4–6 Castle Wynd, Inverness IV2 3EQ
[0463–237231]

The Crofters Commission was established by Act of Parliament in 1955 and is responsible for re-organizing, developing and regulating crofting in the seven crofting (and former county) areas of Argyll, Caithness, Inverness, Orkney, Ross and Cromarty, Shetland and Sutherland. The Commission keeps under review all matters relating to crofting, advises the Secretary of State for Scotland on crofting matters and liaises with other relevant bodies. The Commission also administers the Crofting Counties Agricultural Grants (Scotland) Scheme 1972.
Chairman, H. A. M. Maclean.
Members (*part-time*), A. I. Macarthur; B. T. Hunter; D. A. Morrison; P. Morrison; I. G. Munro; D. Macdonald.
Secretary (*G6*), A. Johnston.

CROWN AGENTS FOR OVERSEA GOVERNMENTS AND ADMINISTRATIONS
St. Nicholas House, St. Nicholas Road, Sutton,
Surrey, SM1 1EL
[081–643 3311]

The Crown Agents act on behalf of governments and public authorities in the developing world. Incorporated by Act of Parliament, they provide commercial, financial and professional services to public sector authorities and the major international development agencies. They do not act for individuals or for commercial concerns in the private sector.
Chairman, Sir Peter Graham, OBE.
Managing Director, P. F. Berry.

CROWN ESTATE COMMISSIONERS
16 Carlton House Terrace, SW1Y 5AH
[071–210 3000]

The Land Revenues of the Crown in England and Wales have been collected on the public account since 1760, when George III surrendered them and received a fixed annual payment or Civil List. At the time of the surrender the gross revenues amounted to about £89,000 and the net return to about £11,000.
In the year ended March 31, 1990, the gross income from the Crown Estate totalled £101,000,000. The total expenditure was £27,000,000. The sum of £55,000,000 was paid to the Exchequer in 1989–90 as Surplus Revenue.
The Land Revenues in Ireland have been carried to the Consolidated Fund since 1820; from April 1, 1923, as regards Southern Ireland, they have been collected and administered by the Irish Government.
The Land Revenues in Scotland were transferred to the Commissioners in 1833.
First Commissioner and Chairman (*part-time*), The Earl of Mansfield and Mansfield.
Second Commissioner and Chief Executive (*G2*), C. K. Howes.
Commissioners (*part-time*), R. B. Caws, CBE; P. Sober; G. D. I. Lillingston, CBE; J. N. C. James, CBE; A. S. Macdonald, CBE.
Deputy Chief Executive (*G3*), H. B. Clarke.
Clerk to the Commissioners and Corporate Services Manager (*G6*), M. E. Beckwith.
Crown Estate Surveyor (*G5*), C. F. Hynes.
Asset Managers (*Urban Estates*) (*G7*), M. W. Dillon; J. S. Ellingford; B. T. O'Connoll; M. Tree.
Housing Manager (*G7*), R. Wyatt.
Property Services and Technical Manager (*G6*), P. Shearmur.
Head of Valuation and Investment Analysis (*G7*), R. Spence.
Head of Building Services (*G7*), R. Turner.
Business Manager, Agricultural Estates (*G5*), R. J. Mulholland.
Asset Manager (*G7*), J. Stumbke.
Business Manager, Marine Estates (*G6*), F. G. Parrish.
Accountant and Receiver-General (*G5*), D. E. G. Griffiths.
Information Systems Manager (*G6*), D. Kingston-Smith.
Head of Internal Audit (*G7*), J. E. Ford.
Head of Finance Branch (*G7*), J. G. Lelliott.
Legal Adviser (*G4*), M. L. Davies.
Deputy Legal Adviser (*G6*), H. Turnsek.
Solicitors (*G6*), A. S. Dawson; J. B. Postgate; R. T. Hayward; M. Drayton; (*G7*), P. Horner.
Senior Legal Assistant, M. A. J. Cordingley.
Head of Personnel Group (*G7*), R. J. Blake.

Scotland
10 Charlotte Square, Edinburgh
[031–226 2741]

Crown Estate Receiver for Scotland (*G6*), M. J. Gravestock.
Solicitor, D. F. Stewart.
Planning Adviser (*G7*), Dr. P. McGovern.
Glenlivit Estate Development Manager (*G7*), N. Sutherland.

Windsor Estate

Surveyor and Deputy Ranger (G4), A. R. Wiseman, MVO.
Crown Estate Forestry Officer and Chief Forester, Windsor (G7), J. J. Taylor.
Keeper of Gardens (G7), J. Bond.

BOARD OF CUSTOMS AND EXCISE
New King's Beam House, 22 Upper Ground, SE1 9PJ
[071-620 1313]

Commissioners of Customs were first appointed in 1671 and housed by the King in London. The present 'Long Room' in the Custom House, Lower Thames Street, EC3, replaced that built by Charles II and was rebuilt after destruction by fire in 1718 and 1814. The Excise Department was formerly under the Inland Revenue Department and was amalgamated with the Customs Department on April 1, 1909.

HM Customs and Excise is responsible for collecting and administering customs and excise duties and value added tax and advises the Chancellor of the Exchequer on any matters connected with them. The Department is also responsible for preventing and detecting the evasion of revenue laws and for enforcing a range of prohibitions and restrictions on the importation of certain classes of goods. In addition, the Department undertakes certain agency work on behalf of other departments, including the compilation of UK overseas trade statistics from customs import and export documents.
(For **Salaries,** *see* page 295.)

The Board
Chairman (G1), Brian Unwin, KCB.
  Private Secretaries, Miss J. E. Andrews; Miss J. H. Daniels.
Deputy Chairmen (G2), Mrs. V. P. M. Strachan; P. Jefferson Smith.
Commissioners (G3), R. Craggs; D. J. Howard; A. W. Russell; Ms. D. J. Seammen; P. R. H. Allen; D. F. O. Battle.

Headquarters Office
Assistant Secretaries (G5), I. D. Savins; P. Kent; D. A. Walton; B. J. Cockerell; J. W. Tracey; J. C. Stevenson; D. Gaw; M. R. Brown; N. Hodson; R. Shepard; I. Walton; A. Killikelly; M. J. Eland; M. Peach; K. M. Romanski; Ms. D. Barrett; B. E. G. Banks; J. P. Bone; D. C. Hewett; A. Ferguson; R. D. Goddard; A. F. Cross-Rudkin; C. J. Holloway; P. Trevett; B. G. Dawbarn; Mrs. M. Smith; J. Campbell; V. C. Whittington; P. A. Blomfield.
Head of Information (G7), Ms. L. J. Sinclair.

VAT Central Unit
Controller (G5), M. J. Wardle.
Deputy Controller (G6), B. Smith.

Solicitor's Office
Solicitor (G2), M. L. Saunders, CB.
Principal Assistant Solicitors (G3), G. F. Butt; D. E. J. Nissen.
Assistant Solicitors (G5), P. Breuer; P. J. C. Ellis; M. Michael; R. D. S. Wylie; M. A. Cooper; D. E. T. S. Keefe; M. C. K. Gasper; Miss A. E. Bolt; D. Pratt; Miss S. G. Linton; J. A. Quin; I. D. Napper.

Accountant and Comptroller-General's Office
Accountant and Comptroller-General (G5), P. A. Blomfield.
Deputy Accountants-General (G6), J. E. Ebery; L. J. Haugh.

Statistical Office
Controller (G5), M. E. Pratt.

Investigation Division
Chief Investigation Officer (G5), F. D. Tweddle.

Collectors of Customs and Excise (G5)
England and Wales
Birmingham, M. W. Summers.
Dover, R. Crossley.
East Anglia, R. N. Lewis.
East Midlands, C. J. Packman.
Leeds, W. J. G. Prollins.
Liverpool, C. Roberts.
London Airports, J. Bugge.
London Central, Mrs. F. Boardman.
London North and West, C. A. Bray.
London Port, P. J. Webb.
London South, T. S. Archer.
Manchester, J. C. Barnard.
Northampton, P. E. St. Quentin.
Northern England, J. McKenzie.
Reading, A. Bowen.
Southampton, R. I. Bolt.
South Wales and the Borders, W. I. Stuttle.
South West England, M. W. G. Lloyd.

Scotland
Edinburgh, W. F. Coghill.
Glasgow & Clyde, T. F. Jessop.

Northern Ireland
Belfast, R. N. McAfee.

OFFICE OF THE DATA PROTECTION REGISTRAR
Springfield House, Water Lane, Wilmslow, Cheshire SK9 5AX
[Admin.: 0625–535711; Enquiries: 0625–535777]

The Office of the Data Protection Registrar was created by the Data Protection Act, 1984. It is the Registrar's duty to compile and maintain the Register of Data Users and Computer Bureaux and provide facilities for members of the public to examine the Register; to promote observance of the data protection principles; to consider complaints made by data subjects; to disseminate information about the Act; to encourage the production of codes of practice by trade associations and other bodies, to guide data users in complying with the data protection principles; to co-operate with other parties to the Council of Europe Convention and act as UK authority for the purposes of Article 13 of the Convention; to report annually to Parliament on the performance of his functions under the Act.
Registrar, E. J. Howe, CBE.

MINISTRY OF DEFENCE
See Armed Forces Section

DESIGN COUNCIL
28 Haymarket, SW1Y 4SU
[071–839 8000]

The Design Council's aim is to improve the design of British products by: advising companies on up-to-date practice in engineering and industrial design; the annual British Design Awards; publishing information to help manufacturers, designers, and others professionally involved in design; and promoting improvements in design education at all levels. There is a Design Centre in London and offices in Glasgow, Cardiff, Belfast, Wolverhampton and Manchester. The Design Council is funded partly by a Government grant-in-aid and partly by earned revenues.

Chairman, Sir Simon Hornby.
Director, I. Owen.

THE DUCHY OF CORNWALL
10 Buckingham Gate, SW1E 6LA
[071-834 7346]

The Duchy of Cornwall was instituted by Edward III in 1337 for the support of his eldest son, Edward, the Black Prince, and since 1503 the eldest surviving son of the Sovereign has, as heir apparent, succeeded to the dukedom by inheritance. As the oldest of the English duchies, it has enjoyed a long association with the Crown. Before elevation to a dukedom, it was an earldom from 1227, when Richard, King of the Romans and younger brother of Henry III, was created Earl of Cornwall.

The Prince's Council

HRH The Prince of Wales, KG, KT, GCB; Sir Nicholas Henderson, GCMG (*Lord Warden of the Stannaries*); Hon. Sir John Baring, KCVO (*Receiver General*); R. J. A. Carnwath, QC (*Attorney-General to the Prince of Wales*); D. W. N. Landale (*Secretary and Keeper of the Records*); Sir John Riddell, Bt.; J. E. Pugsley; J. N. C. James, CBE; A. M. J. Galsworthy; Maj.-Gen. Sir Christopher Airy, KCVO, CBE; C. Howes.

Other Officers of the Duchy of Cornwall

Auditors, J. H. Bowman; P. L. Ainger; H. Hughes.
Solicitor, M. H. Boyd-Carpenter.
Deputy Secretary, K. J. S. Knott.
Sheriff (1990–91), J. M. Williams.

THE DUCHY OF LANCASTER
Lancaster Place, Strand, WC2E 7ED
[071-836 8277]

The estates and jurisdiction known as the Duchy and County Palatine of Lancaster have been attached to the Crown since 1399, when John of Gaunt's son came to the throne as Henry IV. As the Lancaster inheritance it goes back to 1265. Edward III erected Lancashire into a County Palatine in 1351.

Chancellor of the Duchy of Lancaster, THE RT. HON. KENNETH BAKER, MP.

Private Secretary, R. Cannif.

Attorney-General and Attorney and Serjeant within the County Palatine of Lancaster, J. F. Parker, QC.
Receiver-General, Maj. Sir Shane Blewitt, KCVO.
Vice-Chancellor, The Hon. Mr. Justice Scott.
Clerk of the Council and Keeper of Records, M. K. Ridley.
Solicitor, W. O. Farrer.
Asst. Solicitor, I. J. Dicker.
Chief Clerk, P. C. Clarke, CVO.

ECONOMIC AND SOCIAL RESEARCH COUNCIL
Cherry Orchard East, Kembrey Park, Swindon SN2 6UQ
[0793–513838]

The ESRC is an independent, Government-funded body established by Royal Charter in 1965. It supports research into economic life and social behaviour carried out in universities, polytechnics and research centres in Britain. The Council carries out its role by awarding research grants, by initiating research and research contracts, by funding designated research centres, and by awarding postgraduate studentships and bursaries. In addition, the Council provides advice and disseminates knowledge on the social sciences.

Chairman, Prof. H. Newby.
Secretary, W. Solesbury.

For research centres of the Economic and Social Science Research Council, *see* Index.

DEPARTMENT OF EDUCATION AND SCIENCE
Elizabeth House, York Road, SE1 7PH
[071–934 9000]

The Government Department of Education was, until the establishment of a separate office, a Committee of the Privy Council appointed in 1839 to supervise the distribution of certain grants which had been made by Parliament since 1834. The Act of 1899 established the Board of Education, with a President and Parliamentary Secretary, and created a Consultative Committee. The Education Act of 1944 established the Ministry of Education. In April 1964 the office of the Minister of Science was combined with the Ministry to form the Department of Education and Science. The cost of administration for the financial year 1990–91 is estimated at £90,400,000. (For **Salaries,** *see* page 295).

Secretary of State for Education and Science, THE RT. HON. JOHN MACGREGOR, OBE, MP.
Private Secretary, S. T. Crowne.
Parliamentary Private Secretary, A. Stewart, MP.
Minister of State, TIMOTHY EGGAR, MP.
Private Secretary, Mrs. L. J. Chapman.
Parliamentary Under Secretaries of State, ALAN HOWARTH, CBE, MP; MICHAEL FALLON, MP.
Permanent Secretary (G1), J. Caines, CB.
Private Secretary, P. G. Cohen.
Deputy Secretaries (G2), E. J. Bolton, CBE (*SCI*); N. W. Stuart, CB; J. M. M. Vereker; A. J. Wiggins; Sir David Phillips, KBE, FRS.
Under Secretaries (G3), M. M. Capey (*Director of Establishments*); A. E. D. Chamier; C. A. Clark; J. E. Coleman (*Legal Adviser*); D. M. Forester; N. T. Hardyman; J. C. Hedger; R. D. Horne; D. G. Libby; B. M. Norbury; N. J. Sanders (*Accountant General*); C. H. Saville; N. Summers; W. B. Wakefield, CB (*Director of Statistics*); D. A. Wilkinson.
Chief Architect (G4), P. Benwell.

Schools Branch 1

Assistant Secretaries (G5), Miss C. E. Hodkinson; M. J. Richardson; Miss S. L. Scales; A. D. Adamson.
Principals (G7), D. H. Griffiths; D. K. Timms; Miss C. Bienkowska; B. C. Willett; M. E. Mout; C. P. Barnham; A. G. Short; T. C. Tarrant; Miss L. M. Clarke; N. R. Flint; J. Browning; D. F. Miller; P. V. D. Swift; B. D. Glickman.

Schools Branch 2

Assistant Secretaries (G5), Miss D. C. Fordham; Ms. J. F. Cramphorn; A. J. Shaw.
Senior Principal (G6), P. S. Lewis.
Principals (G7), C. Dowe; I. C. Loveless; Mrs. P. A. Masters; Mrs. J. D. Nisbet; N. Cornwell; C. Dee; D. Noble; G. A. Holley; I. M. Hughes; A. W. Wilshaw; Mrs. S. C. West.

Schools Branch 3

Assistant Secretaries (G5), Mrs. H. M. Williams; Miss A. J. Benham; A. J. Wye; M. B. Baker.
Principals (G7), C. De Grouchy; Mrs. S. G. Evans; Miss K. J. Fleay; Mrs. S. Jetha; W. A. Smyth; A. B. Thompson; L. B. Webb; Miss J. D. Worsfold; Mrs. M. E. P. Farthing; R. A. V. Jacobs; J. F. Birds.

Schools Branch 4

Assistant Secretaries (G5), Miss A. Stewart; A. G. B. Woollard; Miss P. Laidlaw; P. A. Shaw; R. C. Frost (*Staff Inspector*).
Principals (G7), S. Kershaw; Miss N. Bartman; D. Foster; S. Hillier; M. F. Neale; N. Roberts (*Accoun-*

tant); R. Troedson; S. E. Burt; J. P. Moore; N. C. Jackson; J. A. Lawrence; Mrs. D. T. Wood; M. McBride.

Architects and Building Branch

Chief Architect (*G4*), P. Benwell.
Deputy Chief Architect (*G5*), A. J. Branton.
Chief Quantity Surveyor (*G5*), B. G. Whitehouse.
Superintending Architects, M. S. Hacker; G. J. Parker; J. J. Wilson; D. H. Griffin.
Principals (*G7*), K. L. R. English; A. G. Myatt.
Principal Research Officer, Dr. G. B. Kenny.
Principal Architects, E. C. Bissell; Mrs. D. Holt; Miss E. J. Lloyd-Jones; P. Lenssen; D. S. Nightingale; Miss B. M. T. Sanders; D. F. Wicks; A. J. Benson-Wilson; J. R. C. Brooke; A. C. Thompson.
Principal Quantity Surveyors, A. A. Jones; J. L. S. Sinclair; M. E. H. Sturt.
Principal Engineer, M. J. Patel.
Principal Furniture Designer, N. J. Carter.
SPTO Architects, S. Aswat; G. E. Hughes; Miss L. Watson; T. J. Williamson; W. Beading; T. W. Prosser; R. H. Bishop; W. A. Fletcher.
SPTO Quantity Surveyors, T. W. A. Carden; G. Wonnacott.
SPTO Engineer, R. L. Daniels.

Further and Higher Education Branch 1

Assistant Secretaries (*G5*), A. Clarke; E. R. Morgan; D. M. Williams.
Senior Principal (*G6*), Dr. E. J. Herbert.
Principals (*G7*), K. Baxter; Ms G. Beauchamp; M. F. Hipkins; P. J. Hodgman; W. A. Irvine; A. Callaghan; P. F. Curran; A. Sevier.

Further and Higher Education Branch 2

Assistant Secretaries (*G5*), Mrs. C. M. Chattaway; R. D. Hull; Mrs. J. Ledger.
Principals (*G7*), A. J. Coles; K. Davey; G. H. N. Evans; P. W. Fulford-Jones; Miss C. E. Treen; D. Barwick; Mrs. J. M. Baxter; M. P. Howarth; E. G. Hartman; Ms. S. P. Gane.

Further and Higher Education Branch 3

Assistant Secretaries (*G5*), Miss M. d'Armenia; T. B. Jeffery; M. J. G. Smith; M. D. Phipps.
Senior Principal (*G6*), D. I. B. Hardy.
Principals (*G7*), Miss A. Barlow; M. J. Jubb; M. L. Lyons; S. Lee; D. D. Cook; P. S. Sharples; J. K. Bushnell; Ms. C. M. R. Jones; D. M. Carter; R. S. H. Frost; Dr. G. Ingle; C. T. Moorcroft; Ms. S. A. Gray; R. H. Campbell; J. Abbott; P. V. Chorley; J. S. Streat.

Science Branch

Assistant Secretaries (*G5*), R. P. Ritzema; P. J. Thorpe; Miss J. P. Partington.
Senior Principal (*G6*), K. D. J. Root.
Principals (*G7*), L. J. R. Dando; D. M. Mainwood; Mrs. C. Hadjimatheou; S. F. Denning; P. B. Long; P. J. Hodgson; M. H. Sharpe.

Information Branch

Assistant Secretary (*G5*), J. W. Coe.
Senior Principal Information Officer (*G6*), K. B. Kerslake.
Chief Information Officer (*G7*), A. M. J. Marre.

Teachers Pay and General Branch

Assistant Secretaries (*G5*), R. W. Chattaway; B. D. Cullen (*Senior Economic Adviser*); H. W. B. Davies; R. B. Ladley (*Scientific Officer*).
Principals (*G7*), M. Barker; T. P. Franklin; A. J. Sargent; Mrs. A. C. Jeffery; M. Thompson; J. A. Tarsh.

Pensions Branch
Mowden Hall, Staindrop Road,
Darlington, Co. Durham DL3 9BG
[0325–460155]

Assistant Secretary (*G5*), J. Wilde.
Principals (*G7*), D. G. Halladay; P. M. Bleasdale; A. Allison.

Teachers Supply, Training and International Relations Branch

Assistant Secretaries (*G5*), B. Bekhradnia; S. R. C. Jones; J. W. Whitaker.
Principals (*G7*), J. C. Sheridan; Ms. E. Slater; M. Wardle; Mrs. S. G. Murton; D. A. Jones; Mrs. A. M. Curtis; Mrs. G. W. Dishart; S. A. Mellor; R. J. Wood; Miss L. Hanmer.

Information Systems Branch

Assistant Secretary (*G5*), F. M. Scott.
Senior Principals (*G6*), A. Cowan; A. H. Tyler; P. D. Gott.
Principals (*G7*), B. Lillburn; Mrs. N. A. T. Malt; R. E. J. Denness; Mrs. J. M. Craggs; M. Midwood; A. P. Thompson; D. Craggs; E. J. Simpson.

Statistics Branch

Chief Statisticians (*G5*), J. W. Gardner; H. M. Dale.
Statisticians (*G7*), A. J. Barnett; Miss A. C. Brown; R. M. Ellison; R. K. Jain; S. N. Kew; J. Pascoe; T. C. Knight; M. J. Davidson.

Legal Branch

Assistant Legal Advisers (*G5*), D. J. Aries; F. L. Croft; M. Harris.
Assistant Solicitor (*G6*), A. D. Preston.
Senior Legal Assistant (*G6*), N. P. Beach.

Library

Chief Librarian, D. N. Allum.

Finance Branch

Assistant Secretaries (*G5*), R. L. Smith; P. Smith; M. C. Stark.
Senior Principal (*G6*), P. J. Edwards (*Assistant Accountant General*).
Principals (*G7*), E. A. Alcock; P. L. Jones; Ms. R. M. King; D. R. Pollard; G. D. S. Sandeman; B. G. Townsend; C. Walker; J. J. Watson; Miss S. A. Clarke; R. J. Gardner; S. A. Marston; S. N. Jardine; P. Swinbank.

HM Inspectorate (England)

Senior Chief Inspector (*G2*), E. J. Bolton, CB.
Chief Inspectors (*G4*), J. A. Everson; T. P. Melia; Miss A. C. Millett; A. J. Rose; B. D. Short; M. J. Tomlinson; Mrs. S. P. Twite.
Divisional Inspectors (*G5*), R. G. Booth; R. J. Brake; B. A. Chaplin; E. Scott; K. W. Thomas; D. E. Walker.
Staff Inspectors (*G5*), Mrs. C. A. Agambar; T. H. Bennetts; P. L. Bradbury; P. Brown; R. A. Callender; B. J. Chopping; P. R. Clarke; M. J. Convey; D. A. Cormican; A. T. Cox; Miss K. Cross; L. S. Crickmore; D. A. Denegri; Mrs. G. M. Dolden; P. D. Edwards; Mrs. V. E. Emmett; Mrs. G. Everson; J. H. Fairhurst; D. Fraser; G. R. Frater; R. C. Frost; A. Gibson; G. Goldstein; V. Green; J. A. Hamer; R. A. S. Hennessey; G. A. Hicks; P. Highfield; M. W. Himsworth; D. G. Labon; Miss B. J. Lewis; C. P. Marshall; M. R. E. Mealing; R. W. Mycock; Ms. S. M. Nicholls; G. T. Peaker; P. J. Pearson; Miss J. M. Phillips; C. Potts; W. J. Rea; C. M. Richards; G. Robson; P. Singh; Mrs. M. M. Smart; D. E. Soulsby; Mrs. B. Staniland; J. Stanyer; D. W. Taylor; A. F. Thomas; D. R. Trainor; A. F. Turberfield, CBE; A. D. J. Turner; Mrs. J. W.

Turner; J. R. Ungoed-Thomas; D. L. West; C. C. B. Wightwick; J. B. Willcock; T. Wylie; F. P. Young; R. E. Young.

HM Inspectors (G6), W. Agnew; D. W. Airey; Mrs. G. M. V. Alexander; Ms. J. C. Andrae; K. J. Anglesey; P. L. Armitage; D. G. Arrell; A. Ashworth; D. Baillie; W. G. Bakehouse; Mrs. C. A. Baker; Mrs. E. M. Baker; Mrs. M. T. Banbury; C. Banks; Miss D. M. L. Barlow; J. H. Barnes; Mrs. J. M. Barnes; G. Barratt; R. E. Barrett; Ms. E. P. Baxell; Mrs. I. M. B. Beckett; P. E. B. Belshaw; J. F. Bennett; Miss. V. Blackburn; Ms. S. B. Blatton; A. J. Boddington; Mrs. C. M. Bond; Mrs. E. J. Boucher; Miss E. Bourne; Mrs. M. T. Boyd-Clarke; D. J. Bradbury; M. H. Bradley; Miss P. A. Brain; T. E. Brand; Mrs. H. S. Bridge; E. F. H. Brittain; F. Brook; Mrs. J. M. Brookes; Miss C. M. Brooks; A. W. Brown; Mrs. M. A. Buckingham; M. J. Buckley; Miss K. Bull; J. M. Burgess; Mrs. G. M. Burke; Ms. M. E. Caistor; M. J. Campbell; P. Candlish; N. Carr; Mrs. J. Carswell; M. J. Caton; B. Chandler; M. Charnley; Ms. J. A. Cheong; Miss D. H. Chorley; Mrs. M. S. Christie; D. Clare; C. R. Clark; P. Clarke; G. Clay; R. S. W. Clements; D. G. Close; D. A. Coe; J. E. M. Cohn; B. Colbeck; Mrs. M. E. Coleman; M. J. Collier; Mrs. P. M. Collins; Mrs. A. Cooke; P. Cradock; G. Cranmer; Mrs. G. K. Crawford; J. Creedy; M. Cribb; Ms. O. Cupid; Ms. B. J. Cusdin; D. K. Dana; C. M. Davies; M. C. Davis; J. Dawson; T. Dickinson, OBE; T. Dillon; A. Dobson; Ms. C. R. Donoughue; J. A. S. Dossett; P. W. Dougill; M. A. Dowling; R. G. Dyke; K. H. Dyson; Mrs. M. E. Eade; Mrs. C. Elliott; D. L. Elliott; J. A. Elliott; L. J. Ellis; M. A. Emery; Mrs. J. E. Ensing; C. B. L. Evans; Ms. C. Farrell; Mrs. B. E. Fawcett; Ms. F. D. Findlay; B. P. Fitzgerald; J. Fitzpatrick; I. G. Forrest; D. H. M. Foster; Ms. M. C. Fraser; P. S. Friend; Mrs. C. Frisby; B. Frost; C. C. Frost; D. J. Frost; B. S. Furness; P. Gannon; D. A. Gardiner; V. Gardiner; P. H. W. Garwood; I. Gera; Mrs. P. Gibbon; Mrs. J. E. A. Gifford; G. A. Gill; C. R. Gillings; C. Goodhead; Mrs E. M. Goodwin; C. D. Gould; C. Goulding; D. I. Grant; J. D. Green; B. Gregson-Allcott; N. Grenyer; P. Griffiths; R. H. Griffiths; Mrs. F. Hadley; Mrs. C. E. Hague; E. E. J. Haidon; D. S. Hale; M. Halle; D. J. Halligan; N. J. Hallmark; P. G. Hancock; Ms. S. C. Hands; J. N. Hardwick; J. S. Hardwick; R. A. Hargreaves; B. R. Harris; S. M. Harrison; D. J. Hart; R. Hartley; A. Harvey; R. C. Harvey; Mrs. G. M. Hayes; G. M. Hearnshaw; Miss L. M. Hencher; M. L. Hening; Mrs. J. S. Herbert; J. A. Hertrich; P. M. Hesketh; D. Hibbert; J. M. Hibbs; J. F. H. Hilbourne; Mrs. E. M. Hill; I. A. E. Hill; W. J. Hill; Mrs. G. A. Hindhaugh; D. G. Holford; T. Holland; Ms. M. H. Hollingsworth; J. R. Holmes; C. Hooper; F. X. Horan; J. E. Hosegood; D. J. House; B. A. F. Hubbard; B. R. Hudson; V. C. Hughes; Ms D. M. Hunt; J. E. Hunt; P. J. Hunt; J. B. Huskins; Mrs. M. A. V. Huxley; J. S. Ingleson; P. F. J. Irvine; A. R. Ivatts; M. J. Ive; H. A. James; R. K. James; T. M. Jardine; B. D. Jelly; Miss S. H. Johns; P. W. R. Johnson; H. B. Joicey; B. Jones; Mrs. M. E. Jones; M. G. Jones; P. R. Jones; M. Jutsum; Mrs. G. N. Kanji; R. Kapadia; W. D. Kaye; Mrs. A. C. Keelan-Towner; M. Kerrigan; T. J. Key; M. A. Khan; B. L. King; D. P. King; K. King; A. V. Kirwan; D. Knighton; J. B. Knox; A. J. Lacey; G. N. E. Lageard; Miss E. J. M. Layson; J. P. Leigh; D. Lewis; D. F. Lewis; D. J. Lewis; Mrs. J. M. Lingard; E. R. B. Little; G. R. Little; A. W. Littlewood; W. K. G. Lloyd; A. B. Lomax; R. Long; J. A. Low; T. L. Lusty; J. A. Mabey; Mrs. E. M. McAndrew; B. McCafferty; C. McCall; Mrs. H. M. Macdonald; D. G. McEnhill; D. C. McIntosh; Ms J. D. McKenley; M. McLaughlin; Mrs. P. R. Maclay; Mrs. J. McLean; I. A. McNally; M. E. Madden; Mrs. J. P. Maddick; J. R. Marriott; G. D. Marrow; E. S. Martin; Mrs. M. M. Martin; W. P. Massam; Miss E. M. Matthews; J. E. Mattick; B. R. Meech; G. Merlane; B. E. Merton; K. Miller; H. Millington; P. Milton; Miss H. A. Moffat; Ms. J. L. Mokades; A. R. H. Monk; D. Moon; D. L. Moore; P. R. Moore; S. H. Morris; Mrs. A. M. Mukhopadhyay; Miss F. A. Munday; P. Muschamp; C. Needham; A. J. Nisbett; P. M. Nixon; M. Norman; Mrs. G. I. Oldham; P. I. Orr; B. C. O'Sullivan; Mrs. S. O'Sullivan; W. E. Owen; H. M. Page; E. K. Page-Jones; A. C. Parfitt; K. Parker; D. J. Parks; J. M. Parsons; Miss E. L. Passmore; I. M. Paterson; P. Piddock; M. W. A. Pitts; E. A. Pollard; M. R. Potter; C. P. Power; Mrs. B. F. Pratley; A. E. Price; Mrs. M. P. Pryce; M. E. Pullee; P. C. Purdy; C. J. Redman; J. D. Reid; J. C. Richardson; A. S. Robertson; C. Robinson; I. A. Rodger; S. J. A. Rogers; A. C. Rowe; C. Rowe; M. J. Ryder; W. H. Salaman; Mrs. J. Sartain; Mrs. K. J. Saunders; B. Sayer; Ms. M. Sayer; J. C. W. Schenk; D. J. Scott; Ms. S. M. Scott; P. L. Seaborne; G. W. Searle; Mrs. P. J. Sellwood; R. V. L. Shannon; D. T. V. Sharman; D. I. Shelton; R. Shippam; A. R. Shirley; Mrs. V. M. Sida; P. J. Silvester; Mrs. D. E. Simmonds; D. Singleton; G. Sleightholme; B. J. Smeaton; B. J. Smith; P. J. C. Smith; P. R. Smith; Ms. S. P. Soul-Grey; Mrs. M. F. Spence; J. D. Stannard; Ms. O. M. Stannard; D. Starling; J. W. Steel, OBE; J. M. Steels; J. B. Stevenson; Mrs. M. T. Stiles; R. W. Stockdale, OBE; M. M. Stone; R. Storrs; Ms. M. E. Stride; R. Summersby; D. P. Swain; A. Sykes; D. W. Sylvester; F. Taylor; J. A. Taylor; R. S. Taylor; M. D. Thirkell; D. L. Thorburn; J. Tierney; M. J. Todd; P. N. Toft; Ms. E. Tombs; B. D. Tomkins; J. V. Townshend; J. E. Trickey; Ms. L. J. Tumman; G. C. Turner; T. Turner; E. A. Vallis; M. Wardlow; Mrs. A. P. Warren; R. K. Warren; N. G. Warwick; J. M. Watson; M. R. Webb; Mrs. J. M. Webberley; R. R. Weir; D. J. Wells; K. J. Wheeldon; R. Whitburn; Miss F. White; J. White; F. Whiteman; D. G. Whittaker; Ms. S. M. Wiles; D. G. Williams; J. R. Williams; K. G. Williams; Mrs. S. A. Williams; G. R. Wilson; J. D. Woodhouse; Mrs. S. A. Woodroffe; R. D. Woods; J. I. Wragg; Miss B. M. Wright; D. Wynne; Miss A. P. Yeomans; R. E. Yorke; A. J. Youngs.

HM Inspectorate Support Services

Principals (G7), C. Boxall; N. D. Rudoe; R. C. Knight.

HM Inspectorate (Wales)

(See Welsh Office)

Establishments and Organization Branch

Assistant Secretaries (G5), E. B. Granshaw; Miss J. Gilbey; A. N. Brown; Mrs. B. Morris *(Accountancy Adviser)*.

Senior Principals (G6), H. H. Barrick; N. J. Beggs.

Principals (G7), C. Bramley; Miss A. F. Brown; R. S. Daruwalla; K. R. Fitzgerald; K. M. Miles; D. A. Robins; Mrs. M. J. Lawrence.

OFFICE OF ELECTRICITY REGULATION
Hagley House, Hagley Road,
Birmingham B16 8QG
[021–456 2100]

The Office of Electricity Regulation (Offer) is a regulatory body set up under the Electricity Act 1989. It is headed by the Director General of Electricity Supply, who is independent of Ministerial control.

Director General, Prof. S. C. Littlechild.
Deputy Director General, Ms. P. A. Boys.
Deputy Director General for Scotland, R. N. Irvine.

DEPARTMENT OF EMPLOYMENT
Caxton House, Tothill Street, SW1H 9NF
[071–273 3000]

The Department of Employment is responsible for the Government policy of promoting a competitive and efficient labour market conducive to the growth of employment and the reduction of unemployment. Its main tasks are to help people acquire and improve their skills and competence for work, to help unemployed people, to promote the creation and growth of small firms and self-employment, to encourage industries to train their workforce, and to develop tourism.

Many of the executive functions carried out in the Department's area of policy interest are exercised by separate public agencies reporting to the Secretary of State for Employment. These include the Health and Safety Commission and ACAS and, within the Department, the Employment Service and the Training Agency.

(For **Salaries**, *see* page 295).

Secretary of State for Employment, THE RT. HON. MICHAEL HOWARD, QC, MP.
  Principal Private Secretary (G5), C. M. Norris.
  Parliamentary Private Secretary, R. King, MP.
Under Secretaries of State, ROBERT JACKSON, MP; ERIC FORTH, MP; THE VISCOUNT ULLSWATER.
  Private Secretaries, Mrs G. Tayleur; Ms. C. Rainey.
Parliamentary Clerk, S. J. Loach.
Permanent Secretary (G1), Sir Geoffrey Holland, KCB.
  Private Secretary, Ms. M. Niven.
Deputy Secretaries (G2), I. Manley, CB; G. Reid.
Legal Adviser (G3), H. R. L. Purse.
Special Advisers, T. Collins; Miss C. Stratton.

The Employment Service
(An executive agency within the Department of Employment.)
Chief Executive (G3+), M. E. G. Fogden.
Deputy Chief Executive (G3), J. Turner.
Director of Field Operations (G4), J. W. Cooper, CBE.
Director of Personnel and Business Services (G4), D. B. Price.
Director of Programmes (G4), M. Emmott.

The Training Agency
(*See* entry on pages 367–8)

Industrial Relations
Grade 3, C. F. Tucker, R. Hillier.
Grade 5, D. W. Brown; A. G. Johnson; P. A. L. Parker; D. A. Roberts; M. C. Davey.
Chief Wages Inspector (G6), J. A. Dyble.
Secretary of Wages Councils, G. Knorpel.

International and Tourism Division
Grade 3, R. A. David.
Grade 5, Mrs. R. Le Guen; P. Brannen; Mrs. J. Whitaker; P. Gregory.

Economic Research and Briefing
Chief Economic Adviser (G3), D. Stanton.
Grade 5, Ms. H. Canter; Ms. P. Meadows; Mrs. Z. Hornstein; D. Bower.

Employment and Training Policy Division
Grade 3, D. J. Normington.
Grade 5, M. J. Brimmer; I. Fair; Miss M. C. Fahey; Dr. P. Buley (*Small Firms*); J. W. Dewsbury (*Careers Service*).

Personnel and Business Services Division
Director of Personnel (G3), E. G. Whybrew.
Head of Business Services (G4), M. H. Davies.
Head of Group Personnel Unit (G5), R. K. Harrison.
Director of Computing (G5), vacant.
Head of Personnel Services Branch (G5), D. Lifton.

Information Division
Head of Information (G5), B. Sutlieff.
Deputy Head of Information (G6), M. Helm.

Finance and Resource Management Division
Director of Finance and Resource Management (G3), Miss J. H. Bacon.
Grade 5, Mrs. A. V. Wheatcroft; P. Robson; Miss W. A. C. Harris.

Solicitor's Office
Legal Adviser (G3), H. R. L. Purse.

Statistics Division
Director of Statistics (G3), P. J. Stibbard.
Chief Statisticians (G5), M. J. N. Hughes; D. J. Sellwood; D. Fenwick; Ms. M. Rout.

DEPARTMENT OF ENERGY
1 Palace Street, SW1E 5HE
[071–238 3000]

The Department of Energy is responsible for the development of government policy in relation to all forms of energy. It also discharges governmental functions connected with the coal and electricity industries. It is responsible for the UK Atomic Energy Authority; is the sponsoring department for the nuclear power industry and is responsible for the development of oil and gas resources on the British sector of the continental shelf. It is the sponsoring department for the oil industry and is responsible for international aspects of energy problems, including relations and co-operation with oil producing countries. The Department is the co-ordinating body for energy efficiency policy and for encouraging the development of new sources of energy.

(For **Salaries**, *see* page 295).

Secretary of State for Energy, THE RT. HON. JOHN WAKEHAM, MP.
  Principal Private Secretary, J. S. Neilson.
  Parliamentary Private Secretary, A. Mitchell, MP.
Parliamentary Under-Secretaries of State, TONY BALDRY, MP; THE HON. COLIN MOYNIHAN, MP.
Permanent Under Secretary of State (G1), G. H. Chipperfield, CB.
  Private Secretary, Ms M. Jackson.
Deputy Secretaries (G2), J. R. S. Guinness; R. J. Priddle.
Chief Scientific Adviser, Prof. Sir Richard Norman, KBE, FRS.
Parliamentary Clerk, T. Collingridge.

Establishment and Finance Division
Principal Establishment and Finance Officer (G3), M. S. Buckley.
Director of Resource Management (G4), A. J. Dorken.
Assistant Secretaries (G5), R. Beasley; J. Morris; P. D. Atkinson; Dr. D. P. Hauser; B. Hampton.

Electricity Division A
Under Secretary (G3), C. C. Wilcock.
Assistant Secretaries (G5), G. W. Thynne; S. F. Powell.

Electricity Division B
Under Secretary (G3), W. I. Macintyre.
Assistant Secretary (G5), M. Higson.
Grade 4, W. F. S. Rickett; Mrs M. Thompson.
Chief Electrical Engineering Inspector (G7), J. G. Lindsay.

Coal Division
Under Secretary (G3), R. Heathcote.

Assistant Secretaries (G5), Dr. D. H. Metz; J. A. V. Collett.

Atomic Energy Division

Under Secretary (G3), Dr. T. Walker.
Assistant Secretaries (G5), P. H. Agrell; A. J. T. Steele; Dr. C. Myerscough; S. H. Haddrill; Mrs J. Britton; Mrs P. Sellers.

Energy Technology Division

Chief Scientist (G3), Dr. W. D. Evans.
Deputy Chief Scientific Officers (G5), Dr. A. Eggington; G. Bevan.
Assistant Secretary (G5), Dr. W. D. Evans.
Senior Principal Scientific Officers (G6), H. F. Ferguson; R. A. Meir; Dr. S. E. R. Hiscocks; W. Macpherson; Dr. D. Fairmaner; B. T. Mould.

International Unit

Assistant Secretary (G5), S. W. Freemantle.

Energy Efficiency Office

Director General (G3), Dr. E. G. Finer.
Directors (G5), J. E. P. Miles; Dr. N. Williams; H. E. Miller.
Director (G6), Mrs. A. Wadsworth.

Economics and Statistics Division

Under Secretary (G3), E. H. M. Price.
Chief Statistician (G5), G. White.
Senior Economic Advisers (G5), S. A. Price; S. F. D. Powell; G. R. Horton.

Oil and Gas Division

Under Secretary (G3), D. R. Davis.
Assistant Secretaries (G5), W. C. F. Butler; Ms. A. Beaton; N. A. C. Hirst; J. R. Wakely.

Gas and Oil Measurement Branch
Government Buildings, Saffron Road, Wigston, Leicester
[0533–785354]

Director (G5), J. Plant.
Senior Chief Examiner (G6), G. A. Paul-Clark.

Petroleum Engineering Division

Director (G3), P. T. Harding.
Reservoir Evaluation Specialists I, I. W. G. Hughes; J. R. Petrie.
Reservoir Evaluation Specialists II, J. H. Aitken; D. W. Mann.
Petroleum Specialists II, R. Giles; D. R. Clementson; B. B. Moore; T. F. Kimber.
Senior Principal Scientific Officer (G6), J. N. Mansfield.
Assistant Director Engineer (G6), G. N. Marriott.

Offshore Supplies Office
Alhambra House, 45 Waterloo Street, Glasgow G2 6AS
[041–221 8777]

Director General (G3), J. E. d'Ancona.
Director Industry (G5), W. E. Allison.
Director Policy and Administration (G5), A. E. Maule.
Director Research and Development (G5), C. P. Carter.
Director China Unit (G6), Dr. K. P. Forrest.
Senior Principal Business Development (G6), H. Holden.
Senior Principal Scientific Officer (G6), Dr. K. Tregonning.
Assistant Director Engineers (G6), H. M. Whiteside; P. R. Taylor.

Information Division

Head of Information (G5), N. W. Hayes.
Deputy Head of Information and Chief Press Officer (G7), J. P. Stubbs.

DEPARTMENT OF THE ENVIRONMENT
2 Marsham Street, SW1P 3EB
[071–276 3000]

The Department of the Environment is responsible for planning and land use; local government; housing, construction; inner city areas; new towns; environmental protection; conservation areas and countryside affairs; royal parks and palaces; historic buildings and ancient monuments; sport and recreation. The Property Services Agency is responsible for all construction activities, supplies and transport at home and abroad for all Government departments including the Ministry of Defence and some repayment clients including British Telecom.
(For *Salaries, see* page 295)

Secretary of State for the Environment, THE RT. HON. CHRISTOPHER PATTEN, MP.
  Private Secretary, P. Ward.
  Special Adviser, P. R. J. Rock.
  Parliamentary Private Secretary, R. Key, MP.
Minister for Local Government and Inner Cities, MICHAEL PORTILLO, MP.
  Private Secretary, T. F. Beattie.
  Parliamentary Private Secretary, D. Ames, MP.
Minister for Environment and Countryside, DAVID TRIPPIER, RD, MP.
  Private Secretary, Mrs. S. Bishop.
Minister for Housing and Planning, MICHAEL SPICER, MP.
  Private Secretary, A. G. Riddell.
  Parliamentary Private Secretary, G. Howarth, MP.
Parliamentary Under Secretaries of State, DAVID HEATHCOAT-AMORY, MP; PATRICK NICHOLLS, MP; ROBERT ATKINS, MP (*Minister for Sport*); THE LORD STRATHCLYDE.
  Private Secretaries, Mrs. T. Vokes; S. Hoggan; S. F. Eden; S. Stringer.
Lord in Waiting, Lord Reay.
Parliamentary Clerk, Ms. K. Jennings.
Permanent Secretary (G1), Sir Terence Heiser, KCB.
  Private Secretary, M. J. Bailey.
Second Permanent Secretary and Chief Executive, PSA (G1A), A. P. Brown.
  Private Secretary, K. E. Lloyd.

ORGANIZATION, ESTABLISHMENTS AND HERITAGE
2 Marsham Street, SW1P 3EB
[071–276 3000]

Director General (G2), P. C. McQuail.

Personnel

Director (G3), Mrs. M. McDonald.
Grade 5, Mrs. A. Heath; R. Bayly; L. B. Hicks.
Chief Librarian (G6), P. Kirwan.
Chief Welfare Officer (G7), R. J. Lintern.

Administrative Resources

Director (G3), D. A. R. Peel.
Grade 4, B. G. Rosser.
Grade 5, Miss P. E. Alexander; I. C. McBrayne; J. P. Channing.
Grade 6, R. H. Cheeseman; D. Tridgell; R. Bendall.

Heritage and Royal Estate

Director (G3), J. A. L. Gunn.
Grade 5, J. J. Rendell; T. E. Radice.

Historic Royal Palaces Agency
The Birdwood Annexe, Hampton Court Palace, East Molesey, Surrey KT8 9AU

(An Executive Agency within the Department of the Environment.)
Chief Executive (G3), D. C. Beeton.

Director of Finance and Resources (G5), Ms. S. A. Booth.
Administrator, Hampton Court Palace (G5), J. Yarnall *(acting)*.
Resident Governor, HM Tower of London (G5), Maj.-Gen. C. Tyler (retd.).

PLANNING INSPECTORATE

Chief Planning Inspector (G3), H. S. Crow.
Deputy Chief Planning Inspector (G4), J. R. Mossop.
Director of Operations (G4), A. J. M. Morgan.
Assistant Chief Planning Inspectors (G5), Miss G. M. Pain; J. T. Graham; M. I. Montague-Smith; J. Acton; J. T. Dunlop; M. C. Hurley; D. F. Harris; R. E. Wilson.
Head of Administration (G5), D. A. C. Marshall.

REGIONAL OFFICES

West Midlands, Birmingham.—*Regional Director (G3)*, D. R. Ritchie. *Regional Controllers (G5)*, J. E. Northover; D. L. Saunders; Mrs. P. M. Holland.
Yorkshire and Humberside, Leeds.—*Regional Director (G3)*, J. P. Henry. *Regional Controllers (G5)*, I. H. Crowther; Mrs. E. A. Kenry.
North West, Manchester.—*Regional Director (G3)*, D. C. Renshaw. *Regional Controllers (G5)*, B. C. Isherwood; P. Styche.
Northern, Newcastle upon Tyne.—*Regional Director (G3)*, J. A. Owen. *Regional Controllers (G5)*, Ms. D. Caudle; R. G. Bell.
South West, Bristol.—*Regional Director (G3)*, Mrs. E. A. Hopkins. *Regional Controller (G5)*, S. McQuillin.
East Midlands, Nottingham.—*Regional Director (G4)*, D. J. Morrison. *Regional Controller (G6)*, G. Meynell, MBE; R. J. Smith.
South East, London W14.—*Regional Director (G3)*, D. Gruffydd Jones. *Regional Controllers (G5)*, Mrs. J. A. Bridges; R. Williams; J. A. Colley; *(G6)*, E. G. Everett.
Eastern, Bedford.—*Regional Director (G3)*, P. F. Emms. *Regional Controllers (G5)*, A. Z. Levy; R. A. Bird.

LONDON REGIONAL OFFICE

Under Secretary (G3), A. A. Pelling.
Grade 5, A. Buchanan; B. Strong; B. H. Leonard; Miss E. Poole.

Information

Director (G4), R. S. J. Bright.
Grade 5, J. Gee.
Grade 6, vacant.

PLANNING, INNER CITIES, REGIONAL DEVELOPMENT, LAND AND PROPERTY

Deputy Secretary (G2), D. J. Burr.

Inner Cities

Director (G3), Miss E. C. Turton.
Head of Divisions (G5), C. P. Evans; A. C. B. Ramsay; Mrs. L. A. C. Simcock; G. L. Laufer; Mrs. J. Peretz.

Land and Property

Director (G4), vacant.
Grade 6, J. C. White.

Planning and Development Control

Director (G3), P. J. Fletcher.
Grade 5, D. N. Donaldson; A. H. Corner; R. S. Horsman.

Planning Services

Director (G4), J. B. Wilson.

Grade 5, R. C. Mabey; J. A. Zetter; A. F. Richardson.
Grade 6, D. C. Stroud.
Grade 7, P. Morgan.

MERSEYSIDE TASK FORCE

Director (G3), Dr. R. C. Dobbie.
Controllers (G5), S. P. Sage; I. Urquhart.

CHIEF ARCHITECTURAL ADVISER ON THE BUILT ENVIRONMENT

Grade 2, J. B. Jefferson, CB, CBE.
Grade 5, J. E. Turner.

HOUSING AND CONSTRUCTION

Deputy Secretary (G2), K. E. C. Sorenson.

Housing Associations and Private Rented Sector

Under Secretary (G3), J. F. Ballard.
Heads of Divisions (G5), R. J. Gibson; M. J. C. Faulkner; J. W. M. Rogers; A. H. Davis.
Grade 6, J. S. Gill.

Housing Monitoring and Analysis

Under Secretary (G3), D. C. L. Wroe.
Grade 5, J. E. Turner; A. E. Holmans, CBE; R. F. Sellwood; D. T. I. G. Davies; N. Dorling; Mrs. J. Littlewood; D. E. Allnut.

Public Housing Management and Resources

Under Secretary (G3), A. G. Watson.
Heads of Divisions (G5), J. Stevens; D. V. Teasdale; I. H. Nicol; J. Jacobs; P. F. Everall; P. J. Radley.

Construction Industry

Under Secretary (G3), D. A. McDonald.
Heads of Divisions (G5), A. D. Fagin; G. I. Fuller; I. C. Macpherson; F. D. Sando.

Sports and Recreation Directorate

Under Secretary (G3), D. A. McDonald.
Head of Division (G5), N. A. J. Kinghan.

Building Research Establishment

Director (G3), R. G. Courtney.
Deputy Director (G4), J. M. Baker.
Heads of Departments and Stations (G5), Dr. J. B. Menzies; N. O. Milbank; B. O. Hall; Dr. W. D. Woolley.
Heads of Services/Research (G6), A. J. M. Harrison; Dr. J. F. A. Moore; Dr. A. B. Birties; R. E. Baldwin; Dr. V. A. C. Crisp; B. B. Pigott; C. R. Durham; P. A. MacDermott; H. W. Harrison; J. R. Britten; R. M. C. Driscoll; Dr. P. J. Nixon; Dr. J. R. F. Burdett; Dr. J. P. Cornish; A. J. Butler; Dr. P. R. Warren; H. Gulvanessian; Dr. A. J. Bravery; Dr. J. W. Llewellyn.
Heads of Laboratories and Services (G7), P. W. Staff; J. Hartup; T. W. Payne; A. J. Newman.

FINANCE AND LOCAL GOVERNMENT

Principal Finance Officer (G2), C. J. S. Brearley.

Local Government Finance Policy

Under Secretary (G3), N. W. Summerton.
Heads of Divisions (G5), P. J. J. Britton; J. E. Roberts;

R. Jones; P. Rowsell; Mrs. C. Wells; I. J. Scotter; P. F. Unwin.

Housing, Water and Central Finance

Under Secretary (G3), R. S. Dudding.
Heads of Divisions (G5), J. Adams; B. Redfern; D. A. C. Heigham; (*G6*), G. Knowles.
Head of Internal Audit (G6), M. R. Haselip.

Local Government

Under Secretary (G3), R. J. A. Sharp.
Heads of Divisions (G5), R. D. Compton; A. J. C. Simcock; H. C. T. Fawcett; (*G6*), P. G. Iredale.

Economics

Chief Economic Adviser (G3), Dr. J. H. Rickard.

LEGAL

Solicitor and Legal Adviser (G2), M. J. Ware, CB.
Deputy Solicitors (G3), J. G. Medcalf; J. A. Catlin.
Assistant Solicitors (G5), J. L. Comber; Mrs. J. L. Weinberg; P. J. Szell; D. J. Serjeant; I. D. Day; C. M. Vine; Mrs. S. Headley; Miss R. A. Lester; Mrs. P. J. Conlon; Mrs. G. Hedley-Dent.

CHIEF ENVIRONMENTAL SCIENTIST

Chief Scientist (G3), Dr. D. J. Fisk.
Head of Division (G5), C. L. Robson.

ENVIRONMENT PROTECTION

Deputy Secretary (G2), F. A. Osborn.

Directorate of Rural Affairs

Under Secretary (G3), R. J. Green.
Grade 5, R. Bunce; D. R. Lewis; R. M. Pritchard; P. Leonard.
Grade 6, C. Folland.

HM Inspectorate of Pollution

Director and Chief Inspector (G3), Dr. F. S. Feates.
Deputy Chief Inspector (G4), Dr. A. J. Duncan.
Heads of Division (G5), M. F. Tunnicliffe; A. Windsor; L. N. Stuffins; L. Packer; (*G6*), Dr. M. W. Jones.

Directorate of Air, Climate and Toxic Substances

Under Secretary (G3), Dr. D. J. Fisk.
Heads of Division (G5), N. Sanders; A. Davis; Dr. N. J. King.
Grade 6, Dr. A. J. Apling; D. L. Pounder; Dr. D. K. Bryce; Dr. P. J. Corcoran.

Central Directorate of Environmental Protection

Under Secretary (G3), J. Hobson.
Heads of Division (G5), Miss F. McConnell; G. N. Bendon; J. Grevatt; J. W. Smith.

Environmental Policy and Analysis

Director (G3), R. H. Young.
Heads of Division (G5), J. Stoker; P. S. MacCormack; N. J. Hartley.

Water Directorate

Director (G3), Miss D. A. Nichols.
Heads of Divisions (G5), M. G. Healey; C. R. Hook; D. L. H. Roberts; D. R. Lewis; J. Jacobs; Ms L. Bell.

PSA SERVICES

Chief Executive (G1A), A. P. Brown.
Private Secretary, Mrs. N. Baxter.

Chief Executive's Strategy Unit

Grade 3, Mrs. J. Williams.
Grade 5, D. Miles.

Directorate of Corporate Affairs

Grade 3, A. S. Kennedy.

Group Personnel Directorate

Director (G3), P. D. Draper.
Grade 5, J. Bird; A. Hazeldine.

Finance

Principal Finance Officer (G3), R. A. Gomme, CB.
Grade 5, Mrs. H. Parker-Brown.
Head of Internal Audit (G5), M. Reece.
Group Management Accountant (G5), J. Tomlinson.

Group Finance Directorate

Director (G3), A. Marson.
Grade 5, M. Taylor.

Information Technology

Grade 4, D. Evans.
Computing:
Grade 5, A. J. Spires.
Grade 6, J. Scott; B. Edgill.

PSA PROJECTS

Managing Director (G2), J. P. G. Rowcliffe.

Operations Directorate 1

Director (G3), S. G. D. Duguid.

Managing Directors, Projects Offices
London A.—(*G4*), K. Jeavons; (*G5*), A. Bell; C. Crooke.
London B.—(*G4*), F. Rymill; (*G5*), A. Porteous; J. Chisnall; M. Chammings.
London C.—(*G4*), M. R. Sutton; (*G5*), G. Skene; W. H. Clark; B. Brown; R. Holland.

Operations Directorate 2

Director (G3), A. G. Gosling.

Managing Directors, Projects Offices
Edinburgh.—(*G4*), J. T. Wilson.
Leeds.—(*G4*), G. Sowden.
Birmingham.—(*G4*), A. Towers.
Cardiff.—(*G4*), J. Clemits.

Directorate of Marketing & Planning

Grade 3, R. Gray.
Grade 5, Mrs. B. Riddell.
Grade 6, A. Hogger.

Projects Personnel Director (G5), R. G. Jones.
Projects Finance Director (G5), B. Neale.

PSA INTERNATIONAL

Managing Director (G3), R. G. S. Johnston.
Grade 5, M. Latham; A. Sannia; vacant.

Germany

Grade 4, R. B. Perry.
Grade 5, Dr. J. T. Fulton.
Grade 6, C. G. W. Wilkes.

PSA SPECIALIST SERVICES

Managing Director (G2), J. B. Jefferson, CB, CBE.

Building and Quantity Surveying

Grade 4, M. Barnes.

Civil Engineering Services

Grade 4, H. Webber.
Grade 5, J. K. Chatterjee.

Mechanical & Electrical Engineering Services

Grade 4, R. C. Cracknell.
Grade 5, J. Fisher.

PSA BUILDING MANAGEMENT

Managing Director (G2), M. R. Rumball.
Director of Operations (G3), P. Butter.
Finance Director (G5), D. Cheal.
Personnel Director (G5), Dr. M. Barratt.
Director of Development (G4), E. Turtle.

Managing Directors/Heads of Regional Businesses

London (G4), P. Livesey.
Scotland (G4), B. Taylor.
Wales (G5), R. Kent.
Southern (G4), M. Newey.
South West (G4), S. Todd.
South East (G4), P. Pryke.
Midland (G4), B. Jordan.
North East (G4), G. Flanagan.
North West (G4), M. Harrison.
Eastern (G4), A. Staveley.

ROYAL COMMISSION ON ENVIRONMENTAL POLLUTION
Church House, Great Smith Street, SW1P 3BL
[071–276 2080]

The Commission was set up in 1970, to advise on matters, both national and international, concerning the pollution of the environment; on the adequacy of research in this field; and the future possibilities of danger to the environment.
Chairman, The Lord Lewis of Newnham, FRS.
Members, Prof. H. Charnock, FRS; Prof. Dame Barbara Clayton, DBE; The Earl of Cranbrook; H. R. Fell; P. R. A. Jacques, CBE; Prof. J. H. Lawton, FRS; J. J. R. Pope, OBE; D. A. D. Reeve, CBE; W. N. Scott, OBE; Dr. C. W. Suckling, CBE; Prof. E. M. Rothschild; Prof. Z. A. Silberston, OBE.
Secretary, B. Glicksman.

EQUAL OPPORTUNITIES COMMISSION
Overseas House, Quay Street, Manchester M3 3HN
[061–833 9244]

Press Office: Swan House, 53 Poland Street, W1V 3DF
(071–287 3953)

Regional Offices: St. Andrew House, 141 West Nile Street, Glasgow G1 2RN (041–332 8018); Caerwys House, Windsor Place, Cardiff (0222–43552)

The Commission was set up by Parliament in 1975 as a result of the passing of the Sex Discrimination Act. It works towards the elimination of discrimination by virtue of sex or marital status and to promote equality of opportunity between men and women generally.
Chair, Mrs. J. Foster...........................£44,300
Deputy Chair, Mrs. J. O'Dell, OBE £18,590
Members, K. Boardman; A. Simpkin; Mrs. P. Turner; Miss M. Monk; Mrs. M. Prosser; Lady Brittan; Mrs. A. Hasan; N. Cowan; Ms. B. Hillon; Lady Scott; Ms. A. Watts.
Chief Executive, Miss V. Amos.

EXCHEQUER AND AUDIT DEPARTMENT
See National Audit Office

ECGD (EXPORT CREDITS GUARANTEE DEPARTMENT)
PO Box 272, Export House,
50 Ludgate Hill, EC4M 7AJ
[071–382 7000]
Crown Building, Cathays Park,
Cardiff CF1 3NH
[0222–824000]

ECGD (Export Credits Guarantee Department), the official export credit insurer, is a separate government department responsible to the Secretary of State for Trade and Industry and functions under the Export Guarantees and Overseas Investment Act 1978. This enables ECGD to encourage UK exports by making available export credit insurance to British firms engaged in selling overseas and to guarantee repayment to banks in Britain providing finance for export credit for goods sold on credit terms of two years or more. Guarantees under Section 1 of the Act are given after consultation with an Advisory Council of bankers and businessmen.

The Act also empowers ECGD to insure British private investment overseas against political risks, such as war, expropriation and restrictions on remittances.
Chief Executive, M. G. Stephens.
Directors (G3), G. E. J. Breach; R. G. Codd; C. Foxall; M. T. Hawtin; R. Wild (T).
Heads of Divisions (G5), C. M. Bossom; A. J. Bray; G. Bromley; R. P. Burnett; P. J. Callagham; J. G. M. Cochrane; D. R. Coombe; D. C. Cooper; R. I. Fear; A. P. Fowell; T. M. Jaffray; R. F. Lethbridge; K. G. Lockwood; M. J. Long; V. P. Lunn Rockliffe; R. W. MacGregor; M. D. Pentecost; Mrs. V. A. Randall; R. A. Ranson; J. K. Sedman; J. R. Weiss.
Senior Principals (G6), Miss J. Albutt; G. C. Bird; D. Q. Bryars; J. D. Cameron; D. Collins; J. M. Foster (T); D. A. Green; A. P. G. Hare; G. G. Jones; L. S. W. Montgomery; B. M. Sidwell, TD; J. S. Snowden; B. Southwell; Miss J. West.
Principals (G7), J. S. Astruc; J. E. Atkinson; D. M. Beaton; D. I. Calvert; A. L. Childs; Mrs. H. V. Cieslik; Mrs. A. C. Cowie; D. M. Cox; G. P. Cox; A. B. Coyne; M. J. Crane; R. P. D. Crick; J. C. W. Croall; S. R. Dodgson; L. Easterbrook; R. X. Fear; G. C. Fisher; Mrs. J. A. Fulwood; P. C. Gaudoin; N. F. George; R. Gotts; J. E. F. Grafton; R. T. Griffiths; P. Hambleton; R. Hardy; C. J. Hatton; R. Holloway; B. S. Hooper; P. Jackson; P. F. Jennings; Miss S. J. Johnson; C. D. Jones; K. Jones; R. Jones; N. A. Lambert; Mrs. F. M. Lewis; D. J. M. Lucas; I. Mackay; Mrs. M. Maddox; S. Merchack; D. W. Miller; D. J. Morris; A. J. E. Muckersie; P. L. Neal; G. A. Newhouse; R. C. Parry; R. J. Pomeroy; S. C. Pond; P. J. Radford; A. B. Redmayne; Miss S. E. Rice; S. Rosenthal; M. Russell; M. Scales; R. Scott; K. R. Smith; R. G. Smith; R. J. Stafford; R. S. Summers; J. Sweeney; Miss V. M. Taylor; A. V. Thomas; C. M. Thorogood; D. A. H. Tickner; R. N. Tolliday; J. A. Tyler; E. J. Walsby; A. R. Watt; R. A. Watt; T. West; F. Whitehead; J. M. Willis; D. L. Wyatt; J. A. Youd; G. A. Young.
Principal Information Officer, vacant.

Regional Offices

Belfast: Windsor House, 9–15 Bedford Street, BT2 7EG (0232–231743); *Birmingham*: Colmore Centre, 115 Colmore Row, B3 3SB (021–233 1771); *Bristol*: 3 Buckingham Court, Beaufort Office Park, Woodlands Lane, Almondsbury, BS12 4NF (0454–616999); *Cambridge*: Three Crowns House, 72–80 Hills Road, CB2

1NJ (0223–68801); *City of London:* Export House, 50 Ludgate Hill, EC4M 7AY (071–382 7000); *Croydon:* Sunley House, Bedford Park, Croydon, CR9 4HL (081–680 5030); *Glasgow:* Berkeley House, 285 Bath Street, G2 4JL (041–332 8707); *Leeds:* West Riding House, 67 Albion Street, LS1 5AA (0532–450631); *Manchester:* Townbury House, Blackfriars Street, M3 5AL (061–834 8181).

Export Guarantees Advisory Council

Chairman, P. E. Leslie.
Deputy Chairman, vacant.
Other Members, E. L. Brooks; The Hon. D. Douglas-Home; D. Eustace; R. H. George, CBE; A. G. Gormly; S. M. F. Harris; M. Riding; Prof. K. Scholes.

OFFICE OF FAIR TRADING
Field House, Bream's Buildings, EC4A 1PR
[071–242 2858]

The Office of Fair Trading is a non-Ministerial government department, headed by the Director General of Fair Trading. It keeps commercial activities in the UK under review and seeks to protect consumers against unfair trading practices. The Director General's consumer protection duties under the Fair Trading Act 1973, together with his responsibilities under the Consumer Credit Act 1974, the Estate Agents Act 1979, and Control of Misleading Advertisements Regulations 1988, are administered by the Office's Consumer Affairs Division. The Competition Policy Division is concerned with monopolies and mergers (under the Fair Trading Act 1973), and the Director General's other responsibilities for competition matters, including those under the Restrictive Trade Practices Act 1976, the Resale Prices Act 1976, the Competition Act 1980 and the Financial Services Act 1986. The Office is the UK competent authority on the application of the European Commission's competition rules, and also liaises with the Commission on consumer protection initiatives.

Director General, Sir Gordon Borrie, QC.
Deputy Director General (G2), J. W. Preston, CB.

Consumer Affairs Division

Director (G3), R. J. Thomas.
Assistant Directors (G5), H. J. Charman; M. Lanyon; D. W. Lightfoot.

Competition Policy Division

Director (G3), Dr. M. Howe.
Assistant Directors (G5), Dr. A. Marshall; P. E. Mason; A. J. White; A. G. Atkinson.

Legal Division

Director (G3), R. Woolman.
Assistant Directors (G5), M. A. Khan; P. T. Rostron.

Senior Economic Adviser (G5), D. Elliot.
Establishment and Finance Officer (G5), Miss C. Banks.
Chief Information Officer (G6), J. E. Perry, OBE.

FOREIGN AND COMMONWEALTH OFFICE
Downing Street, SW1A 2AL
[071-270 3000]

The Foreign and Commonwealth Office provides, mainly through diplomatic missions, the means of communication between the British Government and other governments and international governmental organizations for the discussion and negotiation of all matters falling within the field of international relations. It is responsible for alerting the British Government to the implications of developments overseas; for protecting British interests overseas; for protecting British citizens abroad; for explaining British policies to, and cultivating friendly relations with, Governments overseas and for the discharge of British responsibilities to the dependent territories.

Salaries

For Ministerial salaries, *see* page 295.

Diplomatic Service
(since April 1, 1990)

Permanent Under Secretary and Head of the Diplomatic Service	£83,780
Senior Grade Salary Point 1 (SP1)	£76,320
Senior Grade Salary Point 2 (SP2)	£63,390
Senior Grade Salary Point 3 (SP3)	£53,420
Senior Grade Salary Point 4 (SP4)	£50,120
Senior Grade Salary Point 5 (SP5)	£43,350
Diplomatic Service Grade 4 (DS4)	£31,276–£35,436
Diplomatic Service Grade 5 (DS5)	£21,098–£25,160

Secretary of State, THE RT. HON. DOUGLAS HURD, CBE, MP.
  Private Secretary, J. S. Wall, LVO.
  Assistant Private Secretaries, R. H. T. Gozney; S. L. Gass.
  Social Secretary, Miss D. J. Pearey, MBE.
  Parliamentary Private Secretary, T. Yeo, MP.
Ministers of State for Foreign and Commonwealth Affairs, THE RT. HON. WILLIAM WALDEGRAVE, MP; THE EARL OF CAITHNESS, PC; TRISTAN GAREL-JONES, MP.
  Private Secretaries, R. V. Court; Hon. D. Asquith; Ms. N. M. Brewer.
Minister of State for Foreign and Commonwealth Affairs (Minister for Overseas Development), THE RT. HON. LYNDA CHALKER, MP.
  Private Secretary, E. C. N. Taylor.
  Parliamentary Private Secretary, D. Nicholson, MP.
Parliamentary Under Secretary of State, THE HON. MARK LENNOX-BOYD, MP.
  Private Secretary, M. A. Hatfull.
Parliamentary Relations Unit, M. C. Bates. (*Head*); S. W. Gregson (*Deputy Head and Parliamentary Clerk*).
Permanent Under Secretary of State and Head of the Diplomatic Service, Sir Patrick Wright, GCMG
  Private Secretary, G. D. Adams.
Deputy Under Secretaries (SP2), J. D. I. Boyd, CMG, (*Chief Clerk*); W. R. Tomkys, CMG; N. P. Bayne, CMG; P. J. Weston, CMG (*Political Director*); N. H. R. A. Broomfield, CMG; R.J.T. McLaren, CMG.
HM Vice-Marshal of the Diplomatic Corps, R. Hervey, CMG.
Assistant Under Secretaries (SP5), A. J. Beamish, CMG; P. J. Goulden, CMG; Mrs. V. E. Sutherland; (*Deputy Chief Clerk*); D. E. S. Blatherwick, CMG, OBE (*Principal Finance Officer and Chief Inspector*); The Hon. D. Gore-Booth, CMG; P. S. Fairweather, CMG; D. Slater, CMG; R. A. Burns; J. Ling (*Director of Communications & Technical Services*); Miss R. J. Spence; M. L. Tait, CMG, LVO; J. Q. Greenstock; R. O. Miles; M. H. Jay.
Legal Adviser, Sir Arthur Watts, KCMG, QC.
Second Legal Adviser, D. H. Anderson, CMG.
Deputy Legal Advisers, F. D. Berman, CMG; D. M. Edwards.
Legal Counsellors, M. C. Wood; I. D. Hendry; K. J. Chamberlain; Mrs. A. Glover.
International Labour Adviser, A. E. Smith.
Overseas Police Adviser (DS4), J. W. Kelland, LVO, QPM.

Signals Department (Government Communications Headquarters)
Priors Road, Cheltenham, Glos. GL52 5AJ
[0242–221491]

Heads of Departments (DS4) and Assistant Heads of Department (DS5)

Aid Policy Dept., C. Raleigh; *Asst.*, D. Lyscom.
Arms Control and Disarmament Dept., P. D. R. Davies; *Asst.*, Dr. R. Pullen.
Aviation and Maritime Dept., E. J. Hughes.
Central African Dept., M. E. Cook; *Asst.*, C. Jennings.
Claims Dept., J. Thomas; *Asst.*, R. Miller.
Commercial Management and Exports Dept., R. Reeve; *Asst.*, Miss P. M. Kelly, MBE.
Commonwealth Co-ordination Dept., T. C. S. Stitt; *Asst.*, M. W. Powles.
Conference on Security and Co-operation in Europe Unit, D. J. Johnson.
Consular Dept., C. J. A. Denne; *Asst.*, J. W. Mac-Donald.
Cultural Relations Dept., J. N. Elam; *Assts.*, I. Rawlinson, OBE; S. F. Howarth.
Defence Dept., P. Yarnold; *Asst.*, J. Noakes.
East African Dept., R. Edis; *Asst.*, M. R. Crompton.
Eastern European Dept., C. Hulse, OBE; *Assts.*, Miss A. W. Lewis; J. C. R. Gray.
Economic Advisers, S. H. Broadbent; *Asst.*, N. R. Chrimes.
Economic Relations Dept., R. Bone; *Asst.*, S. Chard.
Environment Science and Energy Dept., A. R. Brenton.
European Community Dept. (External), E. Jones Parry; *Asst.*, C. Prentice.
European Community Dept. (Internal), M. Arthur; *Asst.*, N. Sheinwald.
Falkland Islands Dept., J. Dew.
Far Eastern Dept., H. L. Davies; *Asst.*, D. Warren.
Finance Dept., G. F. Griffiths; *Asst.*, F. Calleghan.
Home Estate and Services Dept., D. Brown; *Asst.*, P. McDermott, MVO.
Hong Kong Dept., A. R. Paul; *Asst.*, Miss R. Marsden.
Information Dept., R. J. S. Muir; *Assts.*, C. J. Ingham; D. Wyatt.
Information Systems Division (Operations), R. Cowling; *Assts.*, D. Carrol; C. Ford.
Information Systems Division (Projects), K. Willis.
Information Systems Division (Resources), D. Wright, OBE; *Assts.*, D. Briggs; J. Bambrough.
Information Systems Division (Services), P. Piddington; *Asst.*, N. Paget.
Library and Records Dept., R. Bone; *Assts.*, R. L. E. Foreman; I. S. Lockhart, MBE; B. Barrett.
Management Review Staff, A. F. Smith; *Deputy Head*, J. Anning.
Medical and Staff Welfare Unit, E. A. Burner; *Deputy Head*, F. Scutt.
Mexico and Central America Dept., A. L. S. Coltman; *Asst.*, R. W. Sindon.
Middle East Dept., J. R. Young; *Asst.*, S. Lamport.
Migration and Visa Dept., A. E. Montgomery; *Asst.*, J. Smith-Laittan.
Narcotics Control and Aids Dept., T. J. David.
Nationality and Treaty Dept., H. McQuade; *Asst.*, A. Harrington.
Near East and North Africa Dept., S. W. J. Fuller; *Asst.*, E. Glover.
News Dept., B. Mower.
Non-Proliferation Dept., R. H. Smith.
North America Dept., D. A. Burns.
Overseas Estate Dept., M. H. R. Bertram; *Deputy Head*, J. Owen.

---

*Joint Foreign and Commonwealth Office/Overseas Development Administration Dept.

Overseas Inspectorate, D. E. S. Blatherwick, CMG, OBE (*Chief Inspector and Principal Finance Officer*); *Inspectors*, D. I. Lewty; Miss M. I. Rothwell; S. D. M. Jack; R. Bedford.
Permanent Under Secretary's Dept., P. M. Nixon, CMG; *Deputy Head*, N. W. Browne.
Personnel Operations Dept., E. Clay; *Deputy Head*, H. J. S. Pearce; *Assts.*, P. A. Heald, MBE; Miss D. Symes; V. Fean.
Personnel Policy Dept., D. Walker.
Personnel Services Dept., A. P. F. Bache; *Assts.*, J. Long; M. Greenstreet.
Policy Planning Staff, R. Cooper, MVO; *Asst.*, J. Powell.
Protocol Dept., D. C. B. Beaumont; *Assts.*, T. C. Almond, OBE; S. W. F. Martin, LVO (*First Assistant Marshal of the Diplomatic Corps*).
Republic of Ireland Dept., T. J. B. George.
Research and Analysis Dept., *Director*, A. St. J. Figgis; *Regional Directors*, C. J. S. Rundle, OBE (*Africa & Middle East*); K. C. Walker (*Asia*); Miss S. Morphet (*Atlantic*); J. R. Banks (*Soviet Union & E. Europe*).
Resource Management Dept., R. J. Chase; *Asst.*, M. C. Clements.
Security Dept., J. W. Hodge; *Asst.*, M. Hickson, LVO.
Security Policy Dept., S. J. Gomersall; *Asst.*, P. Ricketts.
South America Dept., M. S. Baker-Bates; *Asst.*, J. M. Cresswell.
South Asian Dept., M. J. Williams; *Asst.*, R. Codrington.
South-East Asian Dept., D. H. Colvin; *Asst.*, J. W. Guy, OBE.
Southern African Dept., R. Dales; *Asst.*, G. Berg.
Southern European Dept., D. C. A. Madden; *Asst.*, H. B. Warren-Gash.
South Pacific Dept., R. Thomas; *Asst.*, A. C. Walder.
Soviet Dept., S. N. P. Hemans, CVO; *Asst.*, D. Gowan.
Technical Security Dept., M. J. B. Smith; *Assts.*, R. Read; J. Gould.
Training Dept., T. D. Curran; *Director of Language Centre*, J. Moore.
United Nations Dept., Miss M. G. D. Evans; *Asst.*, J. Watt.
West African Dept., vacant.
West Indian and Atlantic Dept., R. S. Gorham; *Asst.*, P. A. Penfold, OBE.
Western European Dept., H. N. H. Synnott; *Assts.*, N. Cox; E. Callway.

CORPS OF QUEEN'S MESSENGERS
Foreign and Commonwealth Office, SW1A 2AH

Superintendent of the Corps of Queen's Messengers, Maj. I. G. M. Bamber.
Queen's Messengers, Maj. J. E. A. Andre; Cdr. R. D. D. Bamford; Cdr. D. H. Barraclough; Lt.-Cdr. B. R. Bezance; Maj. A. N. D. Bols; Lt. Cdr. K. E. Brown; Lt.-Col. W. P. A. Bush; Lt.-Col. M. B. de S. Clayton; Lt.-Col. J. B. B. Clee; Capt. G. Courtauld; Maj. F. C. W. Courtenay-Thompson; Col. J. M. Deans; Maj. P. C. H. Dening-Smitherman; Maj. P. T. Dunn; Capt. N. C. E. Gardner; Cdr. P. G. Gregson; Maj. D. A. Griffiths; Wg. Cdr. J. O. Jewiss; Lt.-Col. P. S. Kerr-Smiley; Lt.-Col. J. M. C. Kimmins; Lt.-Col. R. C. Letchworth; G. F. Miller; Lt.-Col. A. R. Murray; Maj. D. R. Nevile; Maj. K. J. Rowbottom; Maj. M. R. Senior; Cdr. K. M. C. Simmons, AFC; Maj. P. M. O. Springfield; Maj. J. S. Steele; Col. D. W. F. Taylor.

FOREIGN COMPENSATION COMMISSION
Alexandra House, Kingsway, WC2B 6TT
[071–438 7045]

The Commission was set up by the Foreign

Compensation Act 1950 primarily to distribute under Orders in Council funds received from other governments in accordance with agreements to pay compensation for expropriated British property and other losses sustained by British nationals.

The Commission has the further duty of registering claims for British-owned property in contemplation of agreements with other countries, and it has done so in seven instances since 1950.

Chairman, A. W. E. Wheeler, CBE.
Commissioner, J. A. S. Hall, DFC, QC.
Secretary and Chief Examiner, D. H. Wright.

FORESTRY COMMISSION
231 Corstorphine Road, Edinburgh EH12 7AT
[031–334 0303]

The Forestry Commission has the legal status of, and functions as a Government department. It reports directly to Forestry Ministers (i.e. the Minister of Agriculture, Fisheries and Food, the Secretary of State for Scotland, and the Secretary of State for Wales), to whom it is responsible for advice on forestry policy and for the implementation of that policy in Great Britain. There is a statutorily-appointed Chairman and Board of Commissioners (four full-time and six part-time) with prescribed duties and powers. The full-time Commissioners form the Executive Board.

As the Forestry Authority for Great Britain, the Commission is also responsible for carrying out certain regulatory functions in connection with plant health and felling licensing, for conducting forestry research, and administering grant-aid schemes for private woodlands. As the Forestry Enterprise, the Commission has a primary responsibility to provide timber for industry. In discharging their functions, the Forestry Commissioners are charged with endeavouring to achieve a reasonable balance between the needs of forestry and conservation.

Chairman, J. R. Johnstone, CBE *(part-time)*
            £28,742
Director-General and Deputy Chairman, T. R.
 Cutler.................................£53,420
Commissioner for Private Forestry and Development,
 R. T. Bradley.........................£43,350
Commissioner for Administration and Finance,
 D. S. Grundy.........................£43,350
Commissioner for Operations, D. L. Foot £43,350
Secretary to the Commissioners, P. J. Clarke . £39,746

REGISTRY OF FRIENDLY SOCIETIES
15 Great Marlborough Street, W1V 2AX
[071–437 9992]

The Registry of Friendly Societies is a Government department serving two statutory bodies, the Building Societies Commission, and the Central Office of the Registry of Friendly Societies, together with the Assistant Registrar of Friendly Societies for Scotland.

The Building Societies Commission was established by the Building Societies Act, 1986. The Commission is responsible for the supervision of building societies, and administers the system of regulation. It also advises the Treasury and other Government departments on matters relating to building societies.

The Central Office of the Registry of Friendly Societies provides a public registry for mutual organizations registered under the Building Societies Act, 1986, Friendly Societies Act, 1974, and the Industrial and Provident Societies Act, 1965. It is responsible for the supervision of friendly societies and credit unions, and advises the Government on issues affecting those societies. The Chief Registrar

has certain powers to arbitrate in disputes between members and registered societies. He also acts as the Industrial Assurance Commissioner.
(For **Salaries**, *see* page 295)

Building Societies Commission

Chairman, J. M. Bridgeman, CB..
Deputy Chairman, Mrs. R. E. J. Gilmore.
Commissioners, D. Hobson; T. F. Mathews; S. Proctor, CBE; G. Sammons; H. R. C. Walden, CBE.

Central Office

Chief Registrar, J. M. Bridgeman, CB.
Assistant Registrars, A. Wilson; D. W. Lee; A. J. Perrett; R. N. Williams.

The Registry

First Commissioner and Chief Registrar (G2), J. M. Bridgeman, CB.

Staff serving the Building Societies Commission:
Grade 3, Mrs. R. E. J. Gilmore.
Grade 5, T. F. Mathews; D. A. W. Stevens; Mrs. A. M. Halsey; J. M. Palmer.
Grade 6, N. F. Digance.
Grade 7, A. G. Tebbutt; Mrs. S. A. Russell; D. A. W. Stevens; E. Engstrom; M. E. Duff; N. J. Lock; S. M. Uttley; D. S. Bobker.

Staff serving the Central Office:
Assistant Registrar (G4), A. Wilson.
Assistant Registrar (G5), D. W. Lee.
Grade 7, F. da Rocha; N. J. F. Fawcett; C. T. Martyn.

Central Services
Assistant Registrar (G5), A. J. Perrett.
Legal Staff (G6), Mrs. V. Edwards; P. G. Ashcroft; P. V. H. Smith.
Establishment and Finance Officer (G6), M. L. Battenti.

Registry of Friendly Societies, Scotland
58 Frederick Street, Edinburgh, EH2 1NB
[031–226 3224]

Assistant Registrar (G5), J. L. J. Craig, WS.

GAMING BOARD FOR GREAT BRITAIN
Berkshire House, 168–173 High Holborn,
WC1V 7AA
[071–240 0821]

The Board was established on October 25, 1968, to maintain a broad oversight of developments in gaming in Great Britain, to check prospective gaming licensees management and staff, and to advise the Home Secretary on making regulations which may be needed for the further control of gaming.
Chairman (part-time), N. A. Ward Jones, CBE, VRD
            £26,578
Members (part-time), P. B. Kavanagh, CBE, QPM; Lady Ibbs; W. N. Hunter Smart; M. H. Hogan. £10,659
Secretary, P. R. Burleigh.

OFFICE OF GAS SUPPLY
Southside, 105 Victoria Street, SW1E 6QT
[071–828 0898]

The Office of Gas Supply (Ofgas) is a regulatory body set up under the Gas Act 1986. It is headed by the Director General of Gas Supply, who is independent of Ministerial control.

The principal function of Ofgas is to monitor British Gas' activities as a public gas supplier and, where necessary, enforce the conditions of that company's authorization to act as a public gas supplier. Other functions are to grant authorizations to other suppliers of gas through pipes; to investigate complaints on matters where enforcement powers may be exercisable; to fix and publish maximum charges for reselling gas; to publish information and advice for the benefit of tariff customers; to keep under review developments concerning the gas supply industry, including competition; to settle the terms on which other suppliers have access to British Gas' pipelines in the event of disagreement.

Director General, J. McKinnon.
Deputy Director General, M. R. Keay.
Legal Adviser, D. R. M. Long.
Business Adviser, G. McGregor.
Public Affairs Adviser, I. Cooke.
Consumer Affairs Adviser, W. Macleod.

THE GOVERNMENT ACTUARY
22 Kingsway, WC2B 6LE
[071–242 6828]

The Government Actuary provides a consulting service to Government departments, nationalized industries and Commonwealth Governments. His actuaries advise on social security schemes and superannuation arrangements within the public sector at home and abroad, on population and other statistical studies, and on Government supervision of insurance companies and friendly societies.

Government Actuary, C. D. Daykin.
Directing Actuaries, D. H. Loades; G. G. Newton, CB; M. A. Pickford.
Chief Actuaries, D. G. Ballantine; P. L. Burt; J. L. Field; R. T. Foster; T. W. Hewitson; P. H. Hinton; A. G. Young.
Actuaries, E. I. Battersby; A. B. Chughtai; W. H. P. Davies; A. P. Gallop; T. A. Grant; C. A. Harris; F. A. Honeysett; A. I. Johnston; V. P. Knowles; Mrs. I. W. Lane; J. M. MacLeod; A. J. Macnair; P. Merricks; A. P. Pavelin; J. W. Peers; H. J. Prescott; D. F. Renn; J. G. Spain.

GOVERNMENT HOSPITALITY FUND
8 Cleveland Row, SW1A 1DH
[071–210 3000]

Instituted in 1908 for the purpose of organizing official hospitality on a regular basis, with a view to the promotion of international goodwill.
Minister in Charge, The Earl of Caithness, PC.
Secretary, Brig. A. Cowan, MBE.

DEPARTMENT OF HEALTH
Richmond House, 79 Whitehall, SW1A 2NS
[071–210 3000]

The Department of Health was formed in July 1988 by the division of the Department of Health and Social Security into two separate departments.

The Department of Health is responsible for the administration of the National Health Service in England and for the personal social services run by local authorities in England for children, the elderly, infirm, handicapped and other persons in need. It has functions relating to food hygiene and welfare foods. The Department is also concerned with the medical treatment of war pensioners, and is responsible for the ambulance and first aid services in emergency, under the Civil Defence Act 1948. The Department represents the UK on the World Health Organization.

(For **Salaries,** *see* page 295)

Secretary of State for Health, THE RT. HON. KENNETH CLARKE, QC, MP.
Private Secretary, A. J. McKeon.
Special Adviser to the Secretary of State, Mrs. T. Keswick.

Minister of State, MRS. VIRGINIA BOTTOMLEY, MP.
Private Secretary, T. Sands.
Parliamentary Under Secretaries of State, THE BARONESS HOOPER; STEPHEN DORRELL, MP.
Private Secretary, Mrs. Y. Baxter.
Permanent Secretary (G1), Sir Christopher France, KCB.
Private Secretary (G7), E. Waterhouse.
Chief Medical Officer (G1A), Prof. Sir Donald Acheson, KBE.
Chief Scientist, Prof. F. W. O'Grady, CBE, TD.

NATIONAL HEALTH SERVICE POLICY BOARD

Chairman, The Secretary of State.
Deputy Chairman, Sir Roy Griffiths.
Members, Sir Donald Acheson, KBE (*Chief Medical Officer*); Sir James Ackers; Prof. C. Chantler; Baroness Cumberledge, CBE; Sir Graham Day; Sir Kenneth Durham; Sir Christopher France, KCB (*Permanent Secretary*); S. Dorrell, MP (*Parliamentary Under Secretary*); Mrs. V. Bottomley, MP (*Minister of State*); D. Nichol, CBE; Sir Robert Scholey, CBE.

NATIONAL HEALTH SERVICE MANAGEMENT EXECUTIVE

Chief Executive, D. Nichol, CBE.
Deputy Chief Executive and Director of Operations, M. Malone-Lee.
Director of Planning & Information, M. J. Fairey.
Director of Personnel, E. Caines.
Director of Financial Management, Ms. S. Masters.
Medical Director, Dr. D. Walford.
Director, Family Practitioner Services, B. Rayner, CB.
Deputy Chief Nursing Officer, Ms. C. McLoughlin.
Property Adviser, I. Oddy.

HEALTH AND PERSONAL SOCIAL SERVICES GROUP

Deputy Secretary (G2), T. S. Heppell, CB

Environmental Health and Food Safety

Under Secretary (G3), Miss R. O. B. Pease.
Assistant Secretaries (G5), J. C. Dobson; J. A. Parker.
Senior Principal (G6), P. W. Otley.

Hotel and Dietetic Services Branch

Chief Officer, Mrs. M. Fry.
Deputy Chief Officer, Hotel and Dietetic Services (G7), R. E. Brown.

Priority Care Division

Under Secretary (G3), C. H. Wilson.
Assistant Secretaries (G5), A. D. Bacon; K. Jacobsen; Miss P. M. C. Winterton; J. C. Stopes-Roe; S. J. Catling.

Community Services Division

Under Secretary (G3), J. Halliday.
Assistant Secretaries (G5), C. E. Stone; N. Boyd; R. P. S. Hughes; Miss J. Morgan.

Child Health, Maternity and Prevention Division and Aids Unit

Under Secretary (G3), N. M. Hale.
Assistant Secretaries (G5), J. C. Middleton; W. Burroughs; R. Cunningham; A. Barton.

FAMILY PRACTITIONERS SERVICES AND MEDICINES

Deputy Secretary (G2), B. R. Rayner.

Division FPS1

Under Secretary (G3), J. F. Shaw.
Assistant Secretaries (G5), D. Walden; J. Sharpe; D. Wild; B. A. R. Smith, CBE; G. J. F. Podger.

Division FPS2

Under Secretary (G3), B. Bridges.
Assistant Secretaries (G5), Miss I. Nisbet; K. J. Guinness; B. A. Harrison, CBE.

Medicines Control Agency

Director (G3), Dr. K. H. Jones.
Grade 4, D. O. Hagger; R. Alder.
Grade 5, W. Robertson.

NHS MANAGEMENT BOARD OPERATIONS GROUP

Director of Operations (G2), M. Malone-Lee.

Regional Liaison Division

Under Secretary (G3), A. J. Merifield.
Assistant Secretaries (G5), Ms. L. Lockyer; Ms. P. A. Stewart; Mrs. A. de Peyer.

ESTATES DIRECTORATE

Director (G3), M. A. Meager.

ED1

Assistant Secretary (G5), T. Whiteley.
Superintending Estate Surveyor (G6), J. C. Ellis.
Superintending Architect (G6), W. R. Hyslop.

ED2

Assistant Director (G5), G. G. Mayers.
Superintending Estate Surveyor (G6), M. J. Bridgford.
Superintending Engineer (G6), G. D. Fisher.
Superintending Architect (G6), B. Hitchcox.

ED3

Assistant Secretary (G5), P. R. Gant.

ED4

Assistant Director and Chief Surveyor (G5), D. A. Butler.
Superintending Surveyor (G6), R. W. Davis.
Superintending Engineer (G6), R. H. Lawton.
Superintending Surveyor (G6), K. J. McSweeney.
Superintending Engineer (G6), R. J. Tuthill.

ED5

Assistant Director and Chief Engineer (G5), L. W. M. Arrowsmith.
Superintending Surveyor (G6), D. W. Luscombe.
Superintending Engineer (G6), B. C. Oliver.
Superintending Engineer (G6), T. Wagstaff.

ED6

Assistant Director & Chief Architect (G5), P.L. Ward.
Superintending Architect (G6), L. Bartholomew.
Superintending Surveyor (G6), D. A. Eastwood.
Superintending Engineer (G6), J. M. Singh.

ED7

Assistant Director (G5), C. Davies.
Superintending Architect (G6), M. F. Kemp.
Superintending Architect (G6), A. Noakes.

NHS PROCUREMENT DIRECTORATE

Acting Director of Procurement and Distribution (G3), E. M. Sutherland.
Assistant Directors (G5), Miss M. N. Duncan; Dr. D. C. Potter; E. H. W. Luxton; B. J. Love.
Product Group Heads (G6), C. Bray; R. W. B. Allen; A. D. C. Shipley; Dr. N. A. Slark.
Commercial Executives (G6), F. G. Doyle; A. Doveston; T. Bird; R. Buchanan; K. Gill; J. Smith; R. G. Hale.

NHS MANAGEMENT BOARD PERSONNEL GROUP

Director of Operations (Personnel) (G2), E. Caines.

Division HAP

Under Secretary (G3), R. W. D. Venning.
Assistant Secretaries (G4), R. M. Drury; (G5), R. M. Orton; I. Jewesbury; Mrs. P. Hurley.

Information Systems Directorate

Director of Information Systems (G2), M. J. Fairey, CB.
Deputy Director (G4), R. T. Rogers.
Assistant Secretaries (G5), M. A. O'Flynn; vacant.
Senior Principals (G6), M. C. McCurry; P. Mason.

Research Management Division

Chief Scientist (G2), Prof. F. W. O'Grady, CBE, TD.
Director of Research Management (G4), J. Barnes.
Assistant Secretaries (G5), D. M. Woolley; Mrs. J. Griffin.
Senior Medical Officers (G5), Dr. M. B. Dastgir; Dr. E. Wilson; Dr. M. Cuthbert; Dr. J. Lloyd.
Senior Principal Research Officers (G6), P. J. Hennessy; Ms. H. Canter; Ms. A. Kauder.

Social Services Inspectorate

Chief Inspector (G2), W. B. Utting.
Deputy Chief Inspectors (G4), D. C. Brand; Miss C. Hey.
Assistant Chief Inspectors (HQ), Miss J. Baraclough; Mrs. P. K. Hall; S. Mitchell; J. G. Smith; Mrs. W. Rose.
Assistant Chief Inspectors (Regions), S. Allard; P. Brearley; J. K. Corcoran; J. Cypher; B. Gilroy; B. D. Harrison; A. Jones; D. G. Lambert; Miss A. Taylor.

MEDICAL DIVISIONS (HEALTH AND PERSONAL SOCIAL SERVICES)

Chief Medical Officer (G1A), Sir Donald Acheson, KBE.
Deputy Chief Medical Officers (G2), Dr. M. E. Abrams; Dr. J. S. Metters; Dr. D. Walford.

MEDICAL DIVISIONS UNDER DR. ABRAMS

Division HPS

Senior Principal Medical Officer (G3), Dr. N. P. Halliday.
Senior Medical Officers (G5), Dr. P. J. Bourdillon; Dr. N. P. Melia; Dr. M. J. Prophet; Dr. J. Hangartner; Dr. D. Rothman.

Division MCD

Senior Principal Medical Officer (G3), Dr. E. Rubery.
Principal Medical Officers (G4), Dr. G. Lewis; Dr. R. Skinner.
Senior Medical Officers (G5), Dr. P. E. Exon; Dr. D. Salisbury; Dr. A. Dawson; Dr. G. Greenberg; Dr. L. Robinson; Dr. M. Dunne; Dr. S. Lader; Dr. C. Swinson; Dr. J. Hilton.

Division TEH

Senior Principal Medical Officer (G3), Dr. J. H. S. Steadman.
Principal Medical Officers (G4), Dr. G. K. Matthew; Dr. G. E. Diggle.
Senior Medical Officers (G5), Dr. F. A. Chandra; Dr. M. Waring; Dr. R. B. Singh; Dr. E. Smales; Dr. N. Lazarus; Dr. T. Meredith; Dr. R. L. Maynard.

Division E

Principal Medical Officer (G4), Dr. J. D. F. Bellamy.

MEDICAL DIVISIONS UNDER DR. METTERS

Division CPNM

Senior Principal Medical Officer (G3), Dr. P. R. Greenfield.
Principal Medical Officer (G4), Dr. J. M. Graham.
Senior Medical Officers (G5), Dr. E. Cloake; Dr. D. Ernaelsteen; Dr. W. J. Modle; Dr. I. A. Lister-Cheese; Dr. P. Clarke; Dr. M. J. Wiseman; Dr. H. Markowe; Dr. S. Leff; Dr. F. Harvey.
Medical Officer (G6), Dr. J. G. Ablett.

Division MHIE

Senior Principal Medical Officer (G3), Dr. J. L. Reed.
Principal Medical Officers (G4), Dr. J. E. Shanks; Dr. R. Jenkins.
Senior Medical Officers (G5), Dr. P. Mason; Dr. J. Brooksbank; Dr. D. Jones.

Division MCA

Director (G3), Dr. K. H. Jones.
Principal Medical Officers (G4), Dr. D. Jefferys; Dr. P. N. Adams; Dr. S. Wood.
Senior Medical Officers (G5), Dr. L. K. Fowler; Dr. A. Nath; Dr. J. A. Nicholson; Dr. J. Raine; Dr. F. Rotblat; Dr. K. Winship; Dr. D. Looi; Dr. R. Shah; Dr. K. McGovern; Dr. P. Tsintis; Dr. J. Dunne; Dr. S. Eisen; Dr. B. Davis; Dr. P. Waller; Dr. J. J. T. Herbert; Dr. P. C. Sharpe; Dr. S. A. W. Shakir.

Division ISD

Senior Principal Medical Officer (G3), Dr. G. Jones.
Principal Medical Officers (G4), Dr. H. Pickles; Dr. P. A. Hyzler.
Senior Medical Officers (G5), Dr. S. A. Munday; Dr. A. Rawson; Dr. P. R. Dendy; Dr. P. Furnell; Dr. S. P. Vahl; Dr. H. Sutton; Dr. A. Rejman; Dr. C. Collier.

MEDICAL DIVISIONS UNDER DR. WALFORD

Division MPO

Principal Medical Officer (G4), Dr. D. Cunningham.
Senior Medical Officers (G5), Dr. A. L. J. Martin; Dr. W. Thorne; Dr. G. N. Brown; Dr. D. Holt; Dr. D. MacPherson; Dr. I. H. Nicholas.

Division PCR

Senior Principal Medical Officer (G3), Dr. G. C. Rivett.
Senior Medical Officers (G5), Dr. W. G. Griffiths; Dr. W. Miller; Dr. V. Press; Dr. P. Leech; Dr. T. Mann; Dr. A. Hepburn.

Division MME

Senior Principal Medical Officer (G3), Dr. A. J. Isaacs.
Senior Medical Officers (G5), Dr. P. Mason; Dr. M. Smith; Dr. B. Ely; Dr. P. J. Doyle; Dr. J. Ashwell.
Assistant Secretary (G5), N. F. Duncan.
Principals (G7), Ms. J. Needham; A. L. Perl; J. Gooderham.

Dental Division

Chief Dental Officer, R. B. Mouatt.

Senior Dental Officers, C. Howard; J. M. G. Hunt; G. A. Wells.

Nursing Division

Director of Nursing/Deputy Chief Nursing Officer, Miss C. McLoughlin.
Principal Nursing Officers, Ms. M. A. Clark; Mrs. D. A. Patey; Ms. J. Tait; Miss C. Clifford; Miss D. J. Dolman; P. Gibbons.

Pharmaceutical Division

Chief Pharmaceutical Officer, B. H. Hartley.
Deputy Chief Pharmaceutical Officer (G5), Dr. P. R. Noyce.
Superintending Pharmaceutical Officers (G6), J. R. V. Merrills; P. E. Green.

Information Division

Director of Information (G4), Miss R. Christopherson.
Deputy Directors (G6), C. P. Wilson (*news*); G. Meredith (*publicity*).

NATIONAL HEALTH SERVICE
Regional Health Authorities

The chairmen, and members of Regional Health Authorities are appointed by the Secretary of State for Health.

Northern, Benfield Road, Walker Gate, Newcastle upon Tyne. *Chairman*, Prof. Sir Bernard Tomlinson, CBE, MD. *Regional General Manager*, D. Hague.

Yorkshire, Park Parade, Harrogate. *Chairman*, Sir Bryan Askew. *Regional General Manager*, A. Foster.

Trent, Fulwood House, Old Fulwood Road, Sheffield. *Chairman*, Sir Michael Carlisle. *Regional General Manager*, B. Edwards, CBE.

East Anglia, Union Lane, Chesterton, Cambridge. *Chairman*, C. Walker. *Regional General Manager*, A. Liddell.

North East Thames, 40 Eastbourne Terrace, W2 3QR. *Chairman*, Sir David Berriman. *Regional General Manager*, T. Hunt.

North West Thames, 40 Eastbourne Terrace, W2 3QR. *Chairman*, Sir William Doughty. *Regional General Manager*, D. J. Kenny.

South East Thames, Thrift House, Collington Avenue, Bexhill-on-Sea, E. Sussex. *Chairman*, Sir Peter Baldwin, KCB. *Regional General Manager*, G. N. V. Green.

South West Thames, 40 Eastbourne Terrace, W2 3QR. *Chairman*, Baroness Cumberlege, CBE. *Regional General Manager*, C. Spry.

Wessex, Highcroft, Romsey Road, Winchester, Hants. *Chairman*, R. Buchanan. *Regional General Manager*, K. Jarrold.

Oxford, Old Road, Headington, Oxford. *Chairman*, Sir Gordon Roberts, CBE. *Regional General Manager*, R. M. Nicholls.

South Western, King Square House, 26–27 King Square, Bristol. *Chairman*, Sir Vernon Seccombe. *Regional General Manager*, Miss C. E. Hawkins.

West Midlands, Arthur Thompson House, 146–150 Hagley Road, Birmingham. *Chairman*, Sir James Ackers. *Regional General Manager*, K. F. Bales, CBE.

Mersey, Hamilton House, 24 Pall Mall, Liverpool L3 6AL. *Chairman*, Sir Donald Wilson. *Regional General Manager*, G. Scaife.

North Western, Gateway House, Piccadilly South, Manchester M60 7LP. *Chairman*, R. B. Martin, QC. *Regional General Manager*, D. Allison, CB.

Special Health Authorities

Health Education Authority, Hamilton House, Mabledon Place, WC1H 9TX. *Chairman*, Sir Donald

Maitland, GCMG, OBE; *Chief Executive*, Dr. Spencer Hagard.

Disablement Services Authority, 14 Russell Square, WC1. *Chairman*, Lord Holderness, PC; *Chief Executive*, M. G. Jeremiah.

Special Hospitals Service Authority
Charles House, Kensington High Street, W14

The Special Hospitals Service is provided by four hospitals: Rampton; Broadmoor; Moss Side; and Park Lane.

Chairman, Dr. D. E. Edmond.
Chief Executive, C. Kaye.

NATIONAL HEALTH SERVICE, SCOTLAND
See Scottish Office

DEPARTMENTS OF HEALTH AND SOCIAL SECURITY—COMMON SERVICES ADMINISTRATION AND FINANCE GROUP

Principal Establishments and Finance Officer (G2), Mrs. A. E. Bowtell, CB.

FINANCE GROUP

Finance Division A

Director of Finance (Health) (G3), T. R. H. Luce.
Assistant Secretaries (G5), M. R. Harris; P. Garland.

Finance Division B

Under Secretary (Health) (G4), Ms. M. E. Stuart.
Assistant Secretaries (G5), Mrs. R. Grimshaw; H. Jones; P. F. Slade; Miss A. Mithani.

Financial Management Directorate

Director of Finance NHSHE (G2), Ms. S. V. Master.
Deputy Directors (G3), R. Jefferies; R. J. Kerr; R. J. Peters; T. Scott.

Finance Division D

Under Secretary (Social Security) (G3), Mrs. E. A. Woods.
Assistant Secretaries (G5), J. T. Hughes; J. R. Simpson; C. N. Leivers; Mrs. J. Clayton.

NHS Superannuation Branch

Executive Director (Personnel) (G4), R. M. Drury.
Senior Principal (G6), D. Napier.

Statistics and Management Information Division (SMI)

Director of Statistics and Management Information (G3), Dr. R. Gibbs.
Chief Statisticians (G5), Miss P. W. Annesley; J. N. Lithgow; R. K. Willmer; T. J. Orchard; G. J. O. Philpotts.

Economic Adviser's Office (Health)

Chief Economic Adviser (G3), C. H. Smee.
Senior Economic Advisers (G5), M. A. Parsonage; A. Burchell.

Operational Research Service (Health)

Under Secretary (G3), C. H. Smee.
Branch Heads (G5), Dr. G. H. D. Royston; A. P. G. Hare; (G6), F. M. Gayton.

Central Resource Management

Assistant Secretary (G5), M. Brown.
Senior Principal (G6), T. Thorne.

Departmental Personnel Management

Principal Establishment Officer (G3), Miss A. Perkins.

Assistant Secretaries (G5), R. J. Tilney; P. E. Turner; I. Magee; B. K. Gilbert.

Solicitor's Office

Solicitor (G2), P. K. J. Thompson.
Principal Assistant Solicitors (G3), Mrs. M. A. Morgan; A. D. Roberts.
Proceedings Operational Director (G4), G. E. Beaven.

HEALTH AND SAFETY COMMISSION
Baynards House, 1 Chepstow Place,
Westbourne Grove, W2 4TF
[071–243 6000]

The Health and Safety Commission was created under the Health and Safety at Work etc. Act 1974 with duties to reform health and safety law, to propose new regulations and generally to promote the protection of people at work and of the public from hazards arising from industrial (including commercial) activity including major industrial accidents and the transportation of hazardous materials.

The Commission members are appointed by the Secretary of State for Employment, although the Commission assists a number of Secretaries of State concerned with aspects of its functions. It is made up of representatives of employers, trades unions and local authorities. The Chairman is full time.

The Commission can appoint agents, and it works in due conjunction with local authorities who enforce the Act in such premises as offices and warehouses. Its position as a statutory body guarantees the day-to-day independence from Government necessary to enable it to fulfil its functions and command public confidence.

Chairman, Dr. E. J. Cullen.
Members, Dr. M. C. Shannon; Dr. C. M. Thomas; P. Jacques; A. Tuffin; R. Symons; P. Gallagher; J. Marvin; E. Carrick, Dame Rachel Waterhouse, DBE, Ph.D.
Secretary, M. F. Downing.

HEALTH AND SAFETY EXECUTIVE
Baynards House, 1 Chepstow Place,
Westbourne Grove, W2 4TF
[071–221 0870]

The Health and Safety Executive is the Health and Safety Commission's major instrument. Through its inspectorates it enforces health and safety law in the majority of industrial premises, to protect both workpeople and the public. The Executive advises the Commission in its major task of laying down safety standards through regulations and practical guidance for very large numbers of industrial processes, liaising as necessary with government departments and other institutions. The Executive is also the licensing authority for nuclear installations. In carrying out its functions the Executive acts independently of Government guided only by the Commission as to general health and safety policy.

Director General (G2), J. D. Rimington, CB.
Deputy Director General (G2), D. C. T. Eves.
Member of the Executive, D. J. Hodgkins.

HM Factory Inspectorate
HM Chief Inspector of Factories (G3), A. J. Linehan.

HM Agricultural Inspectorate
HM Chief Agricultural Inspector (G3), C. Boswell.

HM Mines Inspectorate
HM Chief Inspector of Mines (G3), Dr. M. D. Jones.

HM Nuclear Installations Inspectorate
HM Chief Inspector of Nuclear Installations (G3), E. A. Ryder.

Safety and General Policy Division
Director (G3), D. J. Hodgkins.

Technology Division
(includes HM Explosives Inspectorate and Major Hazards Unit).
Director (G3), A. C. Barrell.

Research and Laboratory Services Division
Director (G3), Dr. J. McQuaid.

Health Policy Division
(includes the Employment Medical Advisory Service).
Director of Medical Services (G3), Dr. J. T. Carter.

Solicitor's Office
Solicitor (G4), B. J. Ecclestone.

Resources and Planning Division
(including the Accident Prevention Advisory Unit).
Director (G3), A. W. Brown.

HIGHLANDS AND ISLANDS DEVELOPMENT BOARD
Bridge House, 20 Bridge Street,
Inverness IV1 1QR
[0463–234171]

The Board, a grant-aided body, responsible to the Secretary of State for Scotland, has two broad objectives. These are: to assist the people of the Highlands and Islands to improve their economic and social conditions; to enable the Highlands and Islands to play a more effective part in the economic and social development of the nation.
The Board is to be wound up and replaced on April 1, 1991 by a new body, Highlands and Islands Enterprise. The new body will bring together the powers of the HIDB, the Training Agency in the HIDB area, and the land renewal functions of the Scottish Development Agency in the HIDB area.
Chairman, Sir Robert Cowan.
Secretary, J. A. MacAskill.

HISTORIC BUILDINGS AND MONUMENTS COMMISSION FOR ENGLAND (ENGLISH HERITAGE)
Fortress House,
23 Savile Row, W1X 2HE
[071–973 3000]

Under the National Heritage Act, 1983, the duties of the Commission are: to secure the preservation of ancient monuments and historic buildings; to promote the preservation and enhancement of conservation areas; to promote the public's enjoyment of, and advance their knowledge of, ancient monuments and historic buildings and their preservation. The Commission has advisory committees on historic buildings, ancient monuments, historic areas, and London.
Chairman, The Lord Montagu of Beaulieu.
Commissioners, HRH The Duke of Gloucester; Dr. R. W. Brunskill; M. B. Caroe; Viscountess Cobham; Dr. N. Cossons; Sir Hugh Cubitt; Prof. B. Cunliffe; The Baroness Hollis of Heigham; Sir George Moseley; J. Newman; D. Somerset.
Chief Executive, Miss J. A. Page.

WELSH HISTORIC MONUMENTS (CADW)
Brunel House, 2 Fitzalan Road,
Cardiff CF2 1UY
[0222–465511]

Chairman, The Marquess of Anglesey, FSA, FRS.
Members, W. Lindsay Evans; Prof. J. Eynon, OBE,

FRIBA, FSA; The Earl Lloyd George of Dwyfor; T. Lloyd; Prof. G. Williams, CBE, D.Litt., FBA, FSA; R. Haslam.
Secretary, R. W. Hughes.

HISTORIC BUILDINGS COUNCIL FOR SCOTLAND
20 Brandon Street, Edinburgh EH3 5RA
[031–556 8400]

Chairman, Sir Nicholas Fairbairn, QC, MP.
Members, Sir Ilay Campbell, Bt.; Mrs P. Chalmers; R. Clow; Prof. J. D. Dunbar-Nasmith, CBE, FRSA, FRSE; M. Ellington; I. Hutchison, OBE; The Lord Jauncey, PC; K. Martin; J. A. M. Mitchell, CB, CVO, MC; Rev. K. Nugent, SJ; Mrs. M. Richards; Prof. A. J. Rowan.
Secretary, I. G. Dewar.

ROYAL COMMISSION ON THE HISTORICAL MONUMENTS OF ENGLAND
Fortress House, 23 Savile Row, W1X 2JQ
[071–973 3500]

The Royal Commission on the Historical Monuments of England was established in 1908. The Royal Commission is the national body charged with the recording and analysing of ancient and historical monuments and buildings. It compiles, preserves and makes publicly available the national archive of such material, which is housed in the National Monuments Record.
Chairman, The Baroness Park of Monmouth, CMG, OBE.
Commissioners, Prof. M. W. Beresford, FBA; Prof. R. Bradley, FSA; R. A. Buchanan, Ph.D.; Prof. J. D. Evans, Ph.D., Litt.D., FBA, FSA; D. J. Keene, Ph.D.; Prof. G. H. Martin, CBE, D.Phil., FSA; Prof. G. I. Meirion-Jones, Ph.D., FSA; Prof. J. K. Downes, Ph.D., FSA; Prof. A. C. Thomas, D.Litt., FSA; Prof. M. Biddle, FBA, FSA; Prof. P. E. Lasko, CBE, FBA, FSA; Prof. M. Todd, FSA; Mrs. B. K. Cherry, FSA; R. D. H. Gem, Ph.D., FSA; T. R. M. Longman.
Secretary, T. G. Hassall, FSA.

ROYAL COMMISSION ON ANCIENT AND HISTORICAL MONUMENTS IN WALES
The Crown Building, Plas Crug,
Aberystwyth SY23 2HP
[0970–624381]

The Commission was appointed in 1908 to make an inventory of the ancient and historical monuments in Wales and Monmouthshire. The Commission also includes the National Monuments Record for Wales.
Chairman, Prof. G. Williams CBE, FBA, FSA.
Commissioners, M. R. Apted, Ph.D., FSA; G. C. Boon, FSA; R. W. Brunskill, Ph.D.; Prof. D. Ellis Evans, D.Phil., FBA; R. M. Haslam, FSA; J. B. Smith; G. J. Wainwright, Ph.D., FSA; Prof. J. G. Williams.
Secretary, P. Smith, FSA.

ROYAL COMMISSION ON ANCIENT AND HISTORICAL MONUMENTS OF SCOTLAND
54 Melville Street, Edinburgh EH3 7HF
[031–225 5994]

The Commission was appointed in 1908 to make an inventory of the ancient and historical monuments of Scotland and to specify those that seem most worthy of preservation. The Commission also includes the National Monuments Record of Scotland.
Chairman, The Earl of Crawford and Balcarres, PC.
Commissioners, Prof. A. A. M. Duncan, FBA, FRSE; Prof. J. D. Dunbar-Nasmith, CBE, FRIBA; Prof. Rosemary Cramp, CBE, FSA; Prof. L. Alcock, FSA,

FRSE; Mrs. P. E. Durham; Prof. T. C. Smout, PH.D.; The Hon. Lord Cullen.
Secretary, R. J. Mercer, FSA.

ANCIENT MONUMENTS BOARD FOR WALES
Brunel House, 2 Fitzalan Road, Cardiff CF2 1UY
[0222–465511]

Chairman, Prof. G. Williams, CBE, FBA, FSA.
Members, R. B. Heaton, FRIBA; Prof. R. R. Davies, D.Phil.; Dr. H. S. Green, FSA; R. G. Keen; Miss F. Lynch, FSA; Prof. W. H. Manning, FSA; D. Moore, RD, FSA; P. Smith, FSA.
Secretary, S. Morris.

ANCIENT MONUMENTS BOARD FOR SCOTLAND
20 Brandon Street, Edinburgh EH3 5RA
[031–244 3076]

Chairman, Prof. E. C. Fernie, FSA, FSA SCOT.
Members, Dr. A. Fenton, CBE, FRSE, FSA SCOT.; J. Simpson, FSA SCOT.; Sir Jamie Stormonth Darling, CBE, MC, TD, WS; Prof. J. J. Wilkes, PH.D., FSA, FSA SCOT.; Mrs. E. V. W. Proudfoot, FSA, FSA SCOT.; Mrs. K. Dalyell; R. J. Mercer, FSA, FSA SCOT.; Prof. I. B. Cowan, PH.D.; J. H. A. Gerrard, FRSA; T. R H. Godden, CB; L. J. Masters; Dr. A. Ritchie, FSA.
Secretary, Ms J. Hutchison.

HOME-GROWN CEREALS AUTHORITY
Hamlyn House, Highgate Hill, N19 5PR
[071–263 3391]

Constituted under the Cereals Marketing Act, 1965, the Authority consists of nine members representing UK cereal growers, nine representing dealers in, or processors of, grain and three independent members. The purpose of the Authority is to improve the production and marketing of UK grain. The Authority also provides certain agency services to the Intervention Board for Agricultural Produce in connection with the application of the Common Agricultural Policy in the UK.
Chairman, G. B. Nelson.
General Manager, C. J. Ames.

British Cereal Exports
Chairman, R. J. Cherrington.
Manager, J. B. Rose.

HOME OFFICE
50 Queen Anne's Gate, SW1H 9AT
[071–273 3000]

The Home Office deals with those internal affairs in England and Wales which have not been assigned to other Government Departments. The Home Secretary is particularly concerned with the administration of justice; criminal law; the treatment of offenders including probation and the prison service; the police; immigration and nationality; passport policy matters; community relations; certain public safety matters; fire and civil emergencies services and also with broad questions of national broadcasting policy. He personally is the link between The Queen and the public and exercises certain powers on her behalf including that of the Royal Pardon.

Other subjects dealt with include electoral arrangements; addresses and petitions to The Queen; ceremonial and formal business connected with honours; requests for extradition of criminals; scrutiny of local authority byelaws; grant of licences for scientific procedures involving animals; cremations, burials and exhumations; firearms; dangerous drugs and poisons, general policy on laws relating to shops, liquor licensing, gaming and lotteries, charitable collections and marriage; theatre and cinema licensing; co-ordination of government action in relation to the voluntary social services; and sex discrimination and race relations policy.

The Home Secretary is also the link between the UK Government and the governments of the Channel Islands and the Isle of Man.

(For **Salaries**, *see* page 295)

Secretary of State for the Home Department, THE RT. HON. DAVID WADDINGTON, QC, MP.
 Principal Private Secretary (G5), C. J. Walters.
 Private Secretaries, Ms. S. J. Dent; P. R. C. Storr.
 Parliamentary Private Secretary, M. Brandon-Bravo, MP.
Ministers of State, THE EARL FERRERS, PC; THE RT. HON. JOHN PATTEN, MP; MRS. ANGELA RUMBOLD, CBE, MP.
Parliamentary Under Secretary of State, PETER LLOYD, MP.
 Parliamentary Private Secretaries:
 To Mrs. Rumbold, J. Q. Davies, MP.
 To Mr. Patten, E. Leigh, MP.
Parliamentary Clerk, B. E. R. Kinney.
Permanent Under Secretary of State (G1), Sir Clive Whitmore, GCB, CVO.
 Private Secretary, R. G. Yates.
Chief Medical Officer (at Department of Health), Prof. Sir Donald Acheson, KBE.

Legal Adviser's Branch
Legal Adviser (G2), A. H. Hammond.
Principal Assistant Legal Advisers (G3), D. J. Bentley; Miss P. A. Edwards.
Assistant Legal Advisers, R. J. Clayton; Mrs. S. A. Evans; A. M. C. Inglese; D. Seymour; A. W. D. Wilson.
Senior Principal Legal Assistants, Mrs. J. M. Jones; J. O'Meara; C. M. L. Osborne; Mrs. C. Price.

CRIMINAL AND STATISTICS DEPARTMENTS
Deputy Under Secretary (G2), J. F. Halliday.

Criminal Policy Department
Assistant Under Secretary of State (G3), G. L. Angel.
Heads of Divisions (G5), R. J. Baxter; A. Cogbill; P. C. Edwards; Mrs. E. France; P. R. A. Fulton; Miss J. M. Goose; Miss S. Marshall.
Senior Principal (G6), A. Norbury.
Principals (G7), Miss D. Collins; F. E. Cook; R. G. W. Dyce; Ms. J. M. Hawkes; L. D. Hay; L. T. Hughes; Ms. H. Jackson; N. Jordon; Mrs. C. Lehman; K. MacKenzie; Mrs. R. M. Mitev; T. C. Morris; A. Pickersgill; Ms. S. A. Rex; D. Rigby; Ms. L. Rogerson; G. Sutton; Ms. F. Taylor; R. J. Weatherill; R. B. Woodland.
Chief Inspector, Drugs Branch (G6), A. McFarlane.

Research and Planning Unit
Head of Unit (G5), R. Tarling.
Grade 6, P. J. Jordan; G. R. Walmsley.
Principals (G7), A. C. Barton; D. C. Brown; J. A. Ditchfield; Dr. P. J. Ekblom; Dr. S. Field; J. H. Graham; Dr. P. Grove; Dr. T. Hope; Mrs. K. E. Howard; Mrs. P. Mayhew; Ms. P. M. Morgan; Miss J. W. Mott; Dr. G. I. U. Mair; J. F. Mcleod; Mrs. M. Manolias; A. D. Moxon; W. E. Saulsbury; Dr. L. J. F. Smith; F. P. E. Southgate; Ms. J. Vennard; Dr. I. P. Williamson.

Statistics Department
Assistant Under Secretary of State (G3), C. P. Nuttall.

Chief Statisticians (G5), C. G. Lewis; J. L. Walker; P. W. Ward.
Statisticians (G7), Ms. A. Barber; G. G. Barclay; W. D. Burns; K. Childs; L. Davidoff; Mrs. P. Dowdeswell; P. F. Collier; Miss G. Goddard; M. Lock; Mrs. R. Passmore; Z. J. Frosztega; K. M. Jackson; Miss A. Marshall; Ms. C. D. Morgan; R. Pape; Mrs. P. A. Penneck; P. E. Ramell; Ms. K. Shaw; R. M. Taylor.

Criminal Justice and Constitutional Department

Assistant Under Secretary of State (G3), M. E. Head.
Heads of Divisions (G5), S. S. Bampton; E. A. Grant; Miss P. C. Drew; A. Harding.
Principals (G7), Mrs. P. A. Almond; Ms. S. Bailey; R. M. Bradley; N. M. Clowes; Ms. J. Cooke; P. Duffin; J. Gilhespy; H. D. Hillier; J. M. Hough; D. Massey; W. E. Porter-Hodges; Mrs. E. A. Sandars; K. W. Smalldon; G. Underwood; P. F. Vallance; J. Wake; Mrs. J. S. Waters; S. M. K. Willmington.
Chief Inspector of Probation (G4), C. H. Thomas, OBE.
Deputy Chief Inspector of Probation (G6), D. F. Duchemin, TD.

Animals (Scientific Procedure) Inspectorate

Chief Inspector, Dr. R. M. Watt.
Superintending Inspectors, C. B. Hart; Dr. W. D. Tavernor.

POLICE DEPARTMENT

Deputy Under Secretary (G2), I. M. Burns.

Police Department

Assistant Under Secretaries of State (G3), S. W. Boys Smith; S. G. Norris; G. J. Wasserman.
Heads of Divisions (G5), M. J. Addison; Mrs. P. G. W. Catto; J. W. Cane; Miss A. M. Edwards; J. L. Goddard; K. H. Heal; J. Le Vay; C. B. J. Sutton.
Senior Principals (G6), D. R. Birleson; R. A. Giman; Dr. H. Goldman; M. P. Gore; Dr. P. Young.
Principals (G7), D. W. A. Cole; M. P. Cook; T. P. R. Crompton; P. R. Curwen; N. Hancock; M. J. I. Hill; C. C. R. Hudson; R. Korniki; Dr. G. K. Laycock; Mrs. S. G. Mann; M. R. Matthews; Mrs. G. I. Moody; J. F. Nicholson; D. Pooley; M. Phillips; P. W. Pugh; R. P. Rhodes; S. J. Rimmer; Miss J. B. Rumble; Ms. A. M. Rutherford; A. C. Sinfield; R. E. Smith; F. Smith; D. Theobald; P. Tomlinson; Mrs. A. Underhill; J. Ward; S. C. Wells; Ms. A. E. Wickington; A. Wolfenden; Miss M. S. Wooldridge.

Police Scientific Development Branch
Sandridge Laboratories, Woodcock Hill, Sandridge, St. Albans, Herts. AL4 9HQ
[0727–65051]

Head of Laboratory (G6), Dr. P. A. Young.
Principal Scientific Officers (G7), C. J. Aldridge; E. C. Brown; R. Harry; T. Kent; Dr. R. J. Lacey; Dr. S. R. Lewis; C. D. Payne; A. Ford; Dr. J. Tan.

Langhurst House, Langhurstwood Road, Nr. Horsham, Sussex RH12 4WX
[0403–55451]

Principal Scientific Officers, (G7), Dr. N. D. Custance; A. G. Lindfield; M. J. Thompson.

Headquarters Forensic Science Service
Horseferry House
Dean Ryle Street, SW1
[071–217 3000]

Director General (G4), Dr. J. Thompson.
Head of Administration (G6), J. P. Emery.
Head of Quality Management (G6), Dr. A. Moffat.
Head of Support (G6), Dr. D. Werrett.

Principals (G7), J. Glaze; T. Howitt; C. Passey; Dr. R. Totty.

Police National Computer Organization
Horseferry House,
Dean Ryle Street, SW1
[071–217 3000]

Technical Development Director (G5), A. Holt.
Deputy Assistant Commissioner, J. F. Newing, QPM.
Senior Principals (G6), G. M. Cole; T. R. Mann; D. W. Punshon; Dr. G. Turnball.
Principals (G7), B. J. Blain; E. L. Brannan; Mrs. P. Cocks; G. T. Coulthard; D. H. Faulks; J. A. Henderson; P. D. Hill-Jones; A. F. G. Hitchman; D. C. Moulton; Dr. F. Preston; D. A. Quarmby; R. J. Reason; B. G. Stocking; R. H. Watt.

Directorate of Telecommunications
Horseferry House,
Dean Ryle Street, SW1
[071–217 3000]

Head of Directorate (G5), A. J. Pearson.
Assistant Director (G6), N. K. Finlayson.
Head of Operations (G6), I. Aitken.
Head of Marketing (G6), J. H. A. Sharpley.
Principals (G7), B. Albon; F. W. Catterall; W. Hogg; A. Hulme; A. N. Kent; J. Leary; T. J. Logan; J. L. Mumford; K. O'Sullivan; M. A. Parker; R. J. Sanders; A. A. Sipson; K. Staves; D. C. J. Theobald; P. M. Tomlinson.

HM Inspectorate of Constabulary

HM Chief Inspector of Constabulary, Sir John Woodcock, CBE, QPM..........................£61,502
HM Inspectors, J. H. Brownlow, CBE, QPM; C. J. Dear, QPM; D. Elliott, CBE, QPM; T. A. Morris, QPM; Sir Philip Myers, OBE, QPM; C. Sampson, CBE, QPM; J. Smith ....£55,608.

Police Staff College
Bramshill House, Basingstoke, Hampshire
RG27 0JW
[025 126–2931]

Commandant, R. S. Bunyard, CBE, QPM.
Deputy Commandant and Director of Courses, P. J. Lewis.
Secretary (G7), K. J. Sheehan.

BROADCASTING, EQUAL OPPORTUNITIES, IMMIGRATION AND NATIONALITY DEPARTMENTS

Deputy Under Secretary (G2), A. J. Langdon.

Broadcasting and Miscellaneous Department

Assistant Under Secretary of State (G3), C. L. Scoble.
Heads of Divisions (G5), S. B. Hickson; N. M. Johnson; L. P. Wright.
Principals (G7), D. A. L. Cooke; R. Eagle; Miss G. F. Harrison; N. M. McLean; G. H. Marriage; J. Sibson; R. B. Snow; C. P. Stevens; R. Thew; A. J. Townsend.

Equal Opportunities and General Department

Assistant Under Secretary of State (G3), R. J. Fries.
Heads of Divisions (G5), Mrs. P. A. Lee, CBE; G. P. Pratt.
Senior Principal (G6), J. Daly.
Principals (G7), Dr. S. R. E. Atkins; J. P. Casey; Mrs. D. Grice; C. Harnett; Mrs. E. Moody; Mrs. J. S. Morris; S. Pike; D. J. Rigby.

Voluntary Services Unit

Assistant Secretary (G5), Mrs. B. H. Fair.
Principals (G7), A. C. Crook; Miss C. Dale; A. V. H. Stainer; Ms. J. Thorpe.

Immigration and Nationality Department
Lunar House, 40 Wellesley Road, Croydon, Surrey,
CR9 2BY
[081–760 plus ext.]

Assistant Under Secretaries of State (G3), R. M. Morris; T. C. Platt.
Heads of Divisions (G5), J. I. Chisholm; Miss V. R. Dews; R. A. Harrington; T. J. Kavanagh; E. B. Nicholls; N. C. Sanderson; N. R. Varney.
Senior Principals (G6), G. Boiling; D. M. McQueen; C. J. Saunders.
Principals (G7), C. A. Allison; Mrs. H. Bayne; B. D. Bishop; W. F. Bryant; J. G. Burgess; J. Casey; A. D. Cory; J. Gilbert; Miss G. M. Griffith; Mrs. C. Kellas; R. W. Knight; C. R. Miller; D. A. Peters; R. P. Ritchie; S. Spence; P. A. Stanton; P. N. Wrench.

Immigration Service

Chief Inspector (G4), P. Tompkins, CBE.
Deputy Chief Inspectors (G6), Miss K. Collins; T. Farrage; D. J. McDonough.
Assistant Chief Inspectors (G7), J. M. Durose; V. Hogg; G. Maguire; K. Rogers.

Passport Department
Clive House, Petty France, SW1H 9HD
[071–271 3000]

Heads of Divisions (G5), N. S. Benger; J. E. Hayzelden.
Deputy Head of Division (Director of Operations) (G6), C. B. Manchip.
Principals (G7), M. Copley; E. Downham; R. G. Le Marechal; R. I. Henderson; T. Lonsdale.

PRISON SERVICE
Cleland House, Page Street, SW1P 4LN
[071–217 3000]

Non-Civil Service grade salaries

HM Chief Inspector of Prisons	£51,000
Prison Service Governor I	£36,633
Prison Service Governor II	£33,079
Prison Service Governor III	£28,440
Prison Service Governor IV	£22,636–£24,377

Director-General of the Prison Service (G2), C. J. Train, CB.
Deputy Director-General of the Prison Service (G3), B. A. Emes.

Prisons Department

Assistant Under Secretaries of State (Directors) (G3), J. G. Pilling (*Personnel and Finance*); W. J. A. Innes (*Operational Policy*); Mrs. J. E. Reisz (*Directorate of Services*); Dr. R. J. Wool (*Medical Services*).
Non-Executive Members, Mrs. U. Banerjee; Miss P. Downs.
Heads of Divisions (G5), B. O. Bubbear; B. M. Caffarey; W. R. Fittall; G. E. Guy; Mrs. V. V. R. Harris; J. A. Ingman; W. A. Jeffrey; J. Lynch; Miss C. J. Stewart; R. R. Tilt.
Deputy Director of Prison Medical Services (G4), Dr. P. J. Hynes.
Principal Medical Officers (G4), Dr. P. Arrowsmith; Dr. P. B. Pattison; Dr. J. M. Sinclair.
Senior Principals (G6), T. K. Cobley; P. Cook; R. E. Corrigan; C. F. Drewitt; G. E. Dunkley; M. Ireson; B. Johnson; R. W. Lockett; B. S. Luetchford; P. Sleightholme; Miss A. Smith.
Governors (I), D. A. Brown; R. Jacques; J. E. Simmons.
Principals (G7), A. J. Adams; Ms. S. F. Adams; D. Aldridge; Miss M. V. A. Allibone; O. P. Astaniotis; J. H. Attridge; A. J. Beadle; W. M. Black; P. Broadhurst; M. J. Brown; A. D. Burgess; B. G. Chaplin; B. Charlson; Ms. R. Collins-Rice; H. M. C. Crudge; J. Davies; P. Dawson; B. J. Derry; P. Done; D. H. Gannon; Ms. V. Gray; S. Hadjipavlon;

N. F. M. Home; S. S. Horlock; Ms. L. M. Jackson; M. W. Jarvis; F. N. Jasper; R. S. H. Kettle; Miss B. Latimer; C. J. Lawton; Ms. P. Lowe; K. Marshall; D. Neal; K. R. North; J. S. Nottingham; M. J. A. Prowse; Miss G. Romney; J. Simpson; R. E. Smith; G. H. Thomas; A. G. Thomson; P. Ward; T. A. Ward; Miss S. Weinel; W. F. Whiteing; R. L. Williams; T. J. Wilson; Mrs. H. Wood; D. I. M. Wright; E. Wright; P. Wright; R. A. Wright.
Governors (II), Miss M. A. Carden; A. J. Fitzpatrick; M. R. J. Gander; P. J. Leonard; Miss S. F. McCormick; B. McLuckie; J. Marriott; M. Mogg; M. Newell; S. C. A. Pryor.
Prison Service Chaplaincy (G6), Ven. K. S. Pound.
Director of Psychological Services, P. H. Shapland.
Chief Education Officer (G6), I. G. Benson.
Chief Physical Education Officer (G6), M. W. Denton.
Governors (III), N. D. Clifford; R. Daly; J. R. Dovell; Miss U. M. B. McCollam; W. R. Quirie; I. Truffet; J. Uzzell; C. P. Welsh; I. G. Windebank.

Directorate of Works
Abell House, John Islip Street, SW1P 4LH
[071–217 3000]

Director of Works (G4), W. L. Sparks.
Group Managers:
  Superintending Architects (G6), J. H. Cooper; S. Mahraj.
  Chief Civil Structural Engineer (G6), R. W. T. Haines.
  Chief Mechanical and Electrical Engineer (G6), R. Putland.
  Chief Quantity Surveyor (G6), A. W. Gillman.
Principals (G7), P. J. Attwater; B. J. Bleet; J. K. Chamberlain; A. Dick; J. A. Doohan; J. V. Gleed; M. C. Hayes; G. E. Hickey; J. V. R. Hillyer; R. T. Lewis; D. Manning; A. A. Newman; M. Ryland; K. T. Stannard; B. A. Stickley; M. Sweeny; N. L. Wilson.

Prison Service Industries and Farms
Lunar House, Wellesley Road, Croydon,
Surrey CR9 2BY
[081–760 plus ext.]

Director (G5), Miss J. MacNaughton.
Group Managers (G6), J. D. Cleary; M. Codd; G. C. Robertson; A. Sweeney; J. Weller.
Principals (G7), C. Allars; J. A. Byrd; J. Cairns; B. D. Feist; R. Fisher; A. Gillcrist; W. Heppolette; N. F. Montgomery-Pott; D. E. Neville; T. Senior; A. S. Wilson.

Supply and Transport Branch
Crown House, 52 Elizabeth Street,
Corby, Northants.
[0536–202101]

Director (G5), D. J. Hardwick.
Principals (G7), R. C. Brett; D. J. Brown; M. Fitzgerald; S. Sirikanda; A. S. Thompson.

Prison Service Regional Offices

Midland, Birmingham:
Regional Director (G5), J. R. Sandy.
Deputy Regional Director, A. M. E. de Frisching.
Assistant Regional Directors (G7), W. L. Mowbray (*Administration*); (II), J. O'Neill (*Young Offenders*); (II) J. R. Wilkinson (*Operations*).

South West, Bristol:
Regional Director (G5), I. M. Dunbar.
Deputy Regional Director, (I), J. Hunter.
Assistant Regional Directors (G7), S. E. Bass (*Administration*); (G7), J. W. Plumb (*Young Offenders*); (II), R. D. Dixon (*Adult Offenders*).

North, Manchester:
Regional Director (G5), A. H. Papps.
Deputy Regional Director (I), T. Bone.

Assistant Regional Directors (II), F. V. Weigh (*Operation I Division*); (II), A. Stapleton (*Operation II Division*); (G7), L. Edgar (*Management Support I Division*); (II), R. Halward (*Regimes I Division*); P. J. Rudgard (*Management Support II Division*).

South East, Woking:
Regional Director (G5), G. Dadds.
Deputy Regional Director, (I), W. Abbott.
Assistant Regional Directors (II) T. Abbott; J. Thomas-Ferrand; K. M. Brewer; C. Lambert.
Assistant Regional Director (G7), K. P. Wallace (*Administration*).

PRISONS
Governors

Acklington, Northumberland, C. Harder.
Albany, IOW, P. J. Kitteridge.
Aldington, Kent, J. Hone.
Ashwell, Leics., H. Reid.
Askham Grange, Yorks., P. M. Quin.
Bedford, R. B. Clark.
Belmarsh, H. D. Jones.
Birmingham, C. B. Scott.
Blantyre House, J. Semple.
Blundeston, Suffolk, Miss J. M. Fowler.
Bristol, R. Smith.
Brixton, SW2, R. E. Withers.
Bullwood Hall, P. B. Tucker.
Camp Hill, IOW, D. M. Morrison.
Canterbury, D. Twiner.
Cardiff, A. K. Rawson.
Channings Wood, Devon, J. C. Mullens.
Chelmsford, D. B. Sinclair.
Coldingley, Surrey, R. Clarke.
Cookham Wood, P. J. Meakings.
Dartmoor, R. J. May.
Dorchester, B. Coatsworth.
Downview, Surrey, D. Aram.
Drake Hall, Stafford, R. J. Crouch.
Durham, M. Mogg.
East Sutton Park, G. Gibson.
Erlestoke Park, R. S. Brandon.
Exeter, D. Alderson.
Featherstone, Wolverhampton, L. M. Wiltshire.
Ford, Sussex, Maj. B. Smith.
Frankland, Durham, P. Buxton.
Full Sutton, B. V. Smith.
Garth, D. Curtis.
Gartree, Leics., R. S. Duncan.
Gloucester, J. Alldridge.
Grendon and Spring Hill, Bucks., M. F. G. Selby.
Haslar, S. O'Neill.
Haverigg, Cumbria, D. I. Lockwood.
Highpoint, Newmarket, R. Curtis.
Hindley, Lancs., A. F. Jennings.
Holloway, N7, T. M. O'Sullivan.
Hull, P. M. Wheatley.
Kingston, Portsmouth, R. Merricks.
Kirkham, Lancs., Maj. R. B. Coombs.
Lancaster, W. J. Ginn.
Leeds, C. J. Jones.
Leicester, C. J. Williams.
Lewes, T. M Turner.
Leyhill, Glos., N. W. A. Wall.
Lincoln, W. J. MacGowan.
Lindholme, Doncaster, vacant.
Littlehey, S. J. Twinn.
Liverpool, A. N. Joseph.
Long Lartin, Worcs., A. H. Rayfield
Maidstone, G. Gregory-Smith.
Manchester, F. B. O'Friel.
Morton Hall, Lincoln, M. F. Clarke.
New Hall, H. G. Owen.
Northeye, Sussex, D. A. Godfrey.
North Sea Camp, M. L. Knight.
Norwich, A. J. Barclay.

Nottingham, L. Lavender.
Oxford, R. J. Talbot.
Parkhurst, IOW, J. Blakey.
Pentonville, N7, R. J. Kendrick.
Preston, B. A. Wilson.
Ranby, F. Abbott.
Reading, D. Myers.
Rochester, D. Wilson.
Rudgate, W. Yorks., D. Whitehead.
Send, Surrey, A. C. Smith.
Shepton Mallet, C. T. Nellins.
Shrewsbury, G. Ross.
Stafford, D. Shaw.
Standford Hill, W. J. Cooper.
Stocken, R. P. Feeney.
Styal, Cheshire, G. Walker.
Sudbury Fosten, Derbys., L. Stones.
Swaleside, Kent, B. W. Sutton.
Swansea, C. T. Erickson.
Thorp Arch, W. Yorks, G. Barnard.
The Verne, Dorset, D. G. Longley.
Wakefield, T. J. Gadd.
Wakefield Service College, J. W. Staples.
Wandsworth, SW18, C. G. Clarke.
Wayland, T. C. H. Newth.
Wellingborough, M. Selby.
Winchester, J. C. Newell.
Wormwood Scrubs, W12, J. F. Perriss.
Wymott, Preston, W. J. Mansfield.

YOUNG OFFENDER INSTITUTIONS
Governors

Aylesbury, J. W. Dring.
Bullwood Hall, Essex, P. B. Tucker.
Castington, R. Mitchell.
Deerbolt, P. A. Whitehouse.
Dover, T. G. Murtagh.
Drake Hall, R. J. Crouch.
East Sutton Park, Kent, G. Gibson.
Eastwood Park, Glos., M. A. Cook.
Everthorpe, Humberside, T. Davies.
Feltham, J. Whitty.
Glen Parva, Leics., J. H. Rumball.
Grendon/Spring Hill, M. F. G. Selby.
Guys Marsh, Dorset, G. Brunskill.
Hatfield, Yorks., W. J. Clark.
Hewell Grange, Worcs., D. W. Bamber.
Hollesley Bay Colony, Suffolk, Miss J. M. King.
Huntercombe and Finnamore Wood, Oxon., Miss A. W. Hair.
Kirklevington, Cleveland, C. R. Griffiths.
Lowdham Grange, Notts., R. S. Radcliffe.
The Mount, Mrs. M. Donnelly.
New Hall, H. G. Owen.
Northallerton, J. N. Brooke.
Onley, Warwicks., R. Doughty.
Oxford, R. J. Talbot.
Portland, Dorset, M. Langdon.
Rochester, D. Wilson.
Stoke Heath, Salop, J. L. Harrison.
Styal, Cheshire, G. Walker.
Swinfen Hall, Staffs., C. Scott.
Thorn Cross, D. Hall.
Usk and Prescoed, Gwent, D. T. Williams.
Werrington, Staffs., P. E. Salter.
Wetherby, Yorks., A. Holman.
Whatton, Notts., M. A. Lewis.

REMAND CENTRES
Governors

Brockhill, Worcs., P. T. Hanglin.
Cardiff, A. K. Rawson.
Exeter, D. Alderson.
Feltham, J. Whitty.
Glen Parva, J. H. Rumball.
Latchmere House, Surrey, P. B. Wailen.
Low Newton, Co. Durham, K. Forster.

Norwich, A. J. Barclay.
Pucklechurch, Bristol, D. C. Leach.
Risley, Cheshire, I. A. E. Boon.

Inspectorate of Prisons

HM Chief Inspector of Prisons, His Hon. Judge Tumim.
HM Deputy Chief Inspector of Prisons (G5), M. D. Jenkins.
HM Inspectors (Gov. I), C. Allen; D. M. Brooke; D. J. Jarvis; *(Gov. IV)*, A. Lucas; *(G7)*, J. J. Courtney; B. J. Wells.
Principal (G7), S. C. Handley.

ESTABLISHMENT, FINANCE AND MANPOWER, FIRE AND EMERGENCY PLANNING DEPARTMENTS

Deputy Under Secretary (G2), D. E. R. Faulkner.

Establishment Department

Assistant Under Secretary of State (G3), A. R. Rawsthorne *(Personnel, Organization and Management Services)*.
Heads of Divisions (G5), B. W. Buck; P. Canovan; Mrs. C. Crawford; T. J. Flesher; Mrs. E. I. France; R. M. Whalley.
Senior Principals (G6), D. J. Grant; F. R. Hayhurst; M. H. Rumble.
Principals (G7), K. Aylen; F. Bannister; W. Black; D. J. Blackwood; Mrs. M. E. Bowden; J. W. Bradley; G. Brown; M. Carr; R. C. Case; Mrs. E. Cook; G. J. Edwards; B. Elliott; A. Fishwick; J. Fleming; I. C. Gaskell; J. A. Greenland; R. A. Hemmings; D. G. Jones; B. J. Jordan; J. A. Leake; Mrs. J. Morgan; Mrs. M. E. Moxon; K. E. R. Rogers; D. G. Ross; G. R. Sampher; J. S. Sarjantson; A. Silver; S. E. Wharton; Mrs. V. M. Wilsdon.

Home Office Unit at Civil Service Selection Board
Kirkland House, 24 Whitehall, SW1A 2ED
[071–210 plus extension]

Head of Division (G5), R. J. Miles.
Principal Psychologist (G7), D. J. Murray.

Public Relations Branch

Director of Information Services (G4), A. M. Moorey.
Deputy Director, J. Haslam.
Information Officers (G6), R. Windsor; *(G7)*, C. T. T. Whitehead.

Finance and Manpower Department

Assistant Under Secretary of State (Principal Finance Officer) (G3), A. J. Butler.
Heads of Divisions (G5), M. P. Bolt; N. A. Nagler; G. K. Sandiford.
Senior Principals (G6), T. A. S. Devon; D. W. Diamond; A. K. Holman.
Principals (G7), I. J. Acton; Ms. J. Bonelle; R. Braganza; G. Brindle; G. Cassell; K. I. Cole; Mrs. M. Cooper; T. A. S. Daniels; C. I. Dickinson; P. Durbin; F. H. Eggleston; G. B. Fox; B. R. Gange; P. W. Jones; D. J. Kent; Miss D. London; D. Mullarky; S. S. Munday; P. T. Quibell; I. F. Smith; G. L. Thomas.

Fire and Emergency Planning Department

Assistant Under Secretary of State (G3), A. H. Turney.
Civil Emergencies Adviser, D. C. G. Brook, CB, CBE.
Heads of Divisions (G5), P. E. Bolton; E. Soden; P. G. Spurgeon.
Grade 6, D. R. Dewick; Dr. D. M. S. Pearce; Dr. J. R. Stealey.
Principals (G7), F. J. Archer; Mrs. P. R. Atkins; B. R. Barrett; Dr. G. A. Carr-Hill; N. M. Clowes; E. Cook; D. H. Evans; Dr. J. A. Harwood; R. Haugh;

A. J. Lewis; A. E. Mantle; D. J. Mould; Miss S. E. Paul; Mrs. I. Posen; T. E. Russell; Dr. G. E. Scott.

HM Fire Service Inspectorate

HM Chief Inspector, Sir Reginald Doyle, CBE.
HM Inspectors, D. A. Buswell; S. D. Christian; B. T. A. Collins, OBE; T. Greenwold; A. F. Kilford; P. A. Kilshaw; W. Lumb; D. N. McCallum, OBE; N. Musselwhite, QFSM; W. C. Perry, MBE; K. T. Phillips; H. V. Reed; D. F. Robins; N. F. Roundell, CBE, QFSM; G. J. Tinley.
Senior Engineering Inspector, R. M. Simpson, OBE.
Principal (G7), R. G. W. Cooke.

Fire Service College
Moreton-in-Marsh, Gloucestershire GL56 0RH
[0608–50831]

Commandant, B. Fuller.
Deputy Commandant, A. Salisbury.
Secretary (G7), J. A. Gundersen.

Emergency Planning College
The Hawkhills, Easingwold, Yorks. YO6 3EG
[0347–21406]

Head of College (G5), J. B. Bettridge, CBE.
Vice-Principal, Col. D. W. Smith, DFC.

Home Office HQ UK Warning and Monitoring Organization
James Wolfe Road, Cowley, Oxford OX4 2PT
[0865–776005]

Director (G6), R. F. Cooke.
Deputy Director I (G7), W. P. Lawrie.
Deputy Director II (G7), D. L. Warden.

HORSERACE TOTALISATOR BOARD
74 Upper Richmond Road, SW15 2SU
[081–874 6411]

Established by the Betting, Gaming and Lotteries Act, 1963, as successor in title to the Racecourse Betting Control Board established by the Racecourse Betting Act, 1928.

Its function is to operate totalisators on approved racecourses in Great Britain, and it also provides on- and off-course cash and credit offices. Under the Horserace Totalisator and Betting Levy Board Act, 1972, it is further empowered to offer bets at starting price (or other bets at fixed odds) on any sporting event.

Chairman, Lord Wyatt of Weeford £73,000
Members, The Lord Chapple; Mrs. P. Hastings; Hon. D. Montagu; P. S. Winfield; J. F. Sanderson; HRH Prince Michael of Kent.

HOUSING CORPORATION
149 Tottenham Court Road, W1P 0BN
[071–387 9466]

Established by Parliament in 1964, the Housing Corporation registers, promotes, funds and supervises housing associations. There are over 2,400 registered associations in England providing more than half a million homes. Housing associations are non-profit making bodies run by voluntary committees.

The Corporation's duties have been extended under the provisions of the Housing Act 1988 to cover responsibilities for the payments of capital and revenue grants to housing associations, for helping tenants interested in Tenants' Choice, and the approval and revocation of potential new landlords under this policy.

Chairman, Sir Christopher Benson.

INDEPENDENT BROADCASTING AUTHORITY
70 Brompton Road, SW3
[071–584 7011]

The Authority was created by Parliament in 1954 as the Independent Television Authority, to provide a comprehensive television service additional to that of the BBC. Under the terms of the Sound Broadcasting Act, 1972 the Authority was renamed the Independent Broadcasting Authority, and its functions were extended to cover the provisions of independent local radio. The Broadcasting Act 1980 provided for the setting up of the Fourth Channel. The Broadcasting Act 1981 consolidated a number of Acts relating to the IBA.

A new Broadcasting Bill is due to receive Royal Assent during 1990, its provisions coming into force at the beginning of 1991. Two new bodies will replace the IBA, the Independent Television Commission (*see* below) and the Radio Authority (*see* p. 354).

The IBA transmission system will be privatized early in 1991.

Chairman, G. Russell, CBE.
Deputy Chairman, The Lord Chalfont, OBE, MC, PC.
Members, Prof. J. F. Fulton; R. A. Grantham; Lady Popplewell; Mrs. P. Mathias; P. Sheth.
Director General, Lady Littler.
Director of Television, D. Glencross.
Director of Radio, P. A. C. Baldwin.
Director of Engineering, Dr. J. Forrest.
Director of Finance, P. Rogers.
Controller of Advertising, F. Willis.
Controller of Public Affairs, Miss S. Thane.
Secretary, K. Blyth.
Regional Officers, M. J. Fay *(Yorkshire)*; E. Lewis *(Wales and West of England)*; D. Anderson *(Northern Ireland)*; S. Perkins *(East of England)*; D. Lee *(North-West England)*; B. Marjoribanks *(Scotland)*; J. Dougray *(North-East England and the Borders)*; N. J. Reedy *(East and West Midlands)*; J. B. Scott *(South of England and Channel Islands)*.

INDEPENDENT TELEVISION COMMISSION
70 Brompton Road, SW3 1EY
[071–584 7011]

The Independent Television Commission will replace the Independent Broadcasting Authority at the beginning of 1991. The Commission will be responsible for licensing and regulating all commercially funded UK television services.

Chairman-designate, G. Russell, CBE.
Members-designate, The Earl of Dalkeith; Prof. J. F. Fulton; Ms P. Mathias; Lady Popplewell; Prof. J. Ring; P. Sheth.
Chief-Executive-designate, D. Glencross.

INDUSTRIAL INJURIES ADVISORY COUNCIL
The Adelphi, 1–11 John Adam Street, WC2N 6HT
[071–962 8000]

The Industrial Injuries Advisory Council is a statutory body under the Social Security Act, 1975, which considers and advises the Secretary of State for Social Services on Regulations and other questions relating to industrial injuries benefits or their administration.

Chairman, Prof. J. M. Harrington.
Members, G. Appleby; Dr. J. Asherson; Miss J. C. Brown; Prof. M. J. Cinnamond; Dr. D. Coggon; Prof. A. Dayan; J. Henry; P. R. A. Jacques; Dr. C. P. Juniper; T. W. Mawer; Dr. A. J. Newman Taylor; Mrs. M. Prosser; Dr. E. Roman; Dr. A. Sinclair; Miss B. Swiadkowska.
Secretary, A. L. Perl.

CENTRAL OFFICE OF INFORMATION
Hercules Road, SE1 7DU
[071–928 2345]

The Central Office of Information is an executive agency which produces information and publicity material, and supplies publicity services, for other Government departments on a repayment basis. In the UK it conducts Government display press, television, radio and poster advertising, produces and distributes booklets, leaflets, films, television and radio material, exhibitions, photographs and other visual material; and distributes departmental press notices. For the overseas departments it supplies British information posts overseas with press, radio and television material, booklets, magazines, reference services, films, exhibitions, photographs, display and reading room material.

Administrative responsibility for the Central Office of Information rests with HM Treasury Ministers, while the ministers whose departments it serves are responsible for the policy expressed in its work. (For **Salaries**, *see* page 295)

Director-General (G4), G. M. Devereau.
Private Secretary, Ms. R. Leech.
Deputy Director-General (G5), J. Bolitho.

Films, Television and Radio
Director (G6), C. E. Skinner.

Exhibitions
Director (G6), J. Marshall.

MARKETING GROUP
Group Director (G5), R. N. Hooper.

Client Services
Director (G6), Miss J. Luke.

Communications Services
Director (G6), J. A. Leys.

OVERSEAS PUBLICITY GROUP
Group Director (G5), R. Smith.

Overseas Press Services
Director (G6), G. L. Stickland.

Overseas Publications
Director (G6), D. Benyon.

Overseas Visitors & Information Studies
Director (G6), D. A. Smith.

HOME PUBLICITY GROUP
Group Director (G5), D. A. Low.

Advertising
Director (G6), M. Brodie.

Home Publications
Director (G6), M. Jacobson.

Research
Director (G6), M. C. Warren.

REGIONAL SERVICES AND EMERGENCY PLANNING
Group Director (G5), P. T. Brazier.

ADMINISTRATION SERVICES GROUP
Principal Establishment and Finance Officer (G5), D. A. Truman.

Personnel and Office Services Director (G6), W. J. Colwill, OBE.

Finance and Management Services Director (G6), K. E. Williamson.

REGIONAL OFFICES

North Eastern, Wellbar House, Gallowgate, Newcastle upon Tyne.—*Regional Director (G7)*, R. P. Haslam.

Yorkshire and Humberside, City House, New Station Street, Leeds.—*Regional Director (G6)*, A. S. Poole, LVO.

Eastern, Three Crowns House, 72–80 Hills Road, Cambridge.—*Regional Director (G7)*, Mrs. V. Burdon.

London and South Eastern, Hercules Road, SE1 7DU.—*Regional Director (G6)*, D. Smith.

South Western, The Pithay, Bristol.—*Regional Director (G7)*, P. D. Yorke.

Midlands, Five Ways Tower, Frederick Road, Edgbaston, Birmingham.—*Regional Director (G6)*, O. J. B. Prince-White.

North Western, Sunley Building, Piccadilly Plaza, Manchester.—*Regional Director (G7)*, Mrs. E. Jones.

BOARD OF INLAND REVENUE
Somerset House, WC2R 1LB
[071–438 6622]

The Board of Inland Revenue was constituted under the Inland Revenue Board Act, 1849, by the consolidation of the Board of Excise and the Board of Stamps and Taxes. In 1909 the administration of excise duties was transferred to the Board of Customs. The Board of Inland Revenue administers and collects direct taxes—mainly income tax, corporation tax, capital gains tax, inheritance tax, stamp duty, development land tax and petroleum revenue tax—and advises the Chancellor of the Exchequer on policy questions involving them. The Head Office is in London and there are Inspectors of Taxes offices and Collection offices throughout the United Kingdom. The Department's Valuation Office is responsible for valuing property for tax purposes, for compensation and for compulsory purchase and (in England and Wales) for local rating purposes. In 1988–89 Inland Revenue collected over £69,000 million tax.

(For **Salaries,** *see* page 295)

The Board

Chairman (G1), Sir Anthony Battishill, KCB.
  Private Secretary, Miss J. McClatchey.
Deputy Chairmen (G2), A. J. G. Isaac, CB; T. J. Painter, CB.
  Private Secretary, Miss J. M. Goold.
Directors General (G2), L. J. H. Beighton; S. C. T. Matheson.
Commissioner: Chief Valuer (G2), R. R. B. Shutler.

Subject Divisions

Directors (G3), P. Lewis; B. T. Houghton; E. McGivern; D. Y. Pitts; M. A. Johns; K. V. Deacon; J. H. Roberts; B. A. Mace.
Senior Principal Inspector of Taxes (G4), J. C. Campbell; K. A. Skinner, CBE; R. E. Creed; J. Moule; M. D. E. Newstead; E. K. Pearson; G. F. Hamilton; W. Northend; J. M. L. Davenport; D. W. Hugo; I. N. Hunter; B. Sadler; J. F. Hall; J. M. Phalp; R. M. Elliss.
Grade 5, J. D. Farmer; D. L. Shaw; R. Warden; A. J. O'Brien; M. F. Cayley; J. H. Reed; M. J. G. Elliott; J. P. B. Bryce; P. W. Fawcett; J. B. Shepherd; B. O'Connor; L. E. Jaundoo; C. Stewart; A. W. Kuczys; C. R. Massingale; C. D. Sullivan; M. O. R.

Haigh; D. E. Pipe; Miss R. A. Dyall; M. T. Evans; S. P. Norris.
Principal Inspectors of Taxes (G5), R. C. Mountain; M. L. Gordon; J. W. Calder; J. Potter; T. R. Evans; J. F. Leverington; I. S. Gerrie; A. J. Wardrop; A. Cummins; A. Beauchamp; R. E. Haigh; A. Harrison; D. F. Parratt; D. A. Smith; J. T. Cawdron; A. C. Williams.
Controller of Oil Taxation Office (G4), M. Templeman.

Central Division

Grade 3, C. W. Corlett.
Grade 5, R. B. Willis; I. Fraser.
Senior Economic Adviser (G5), W. M. McNie.

Management Divisions

Director of Personnel (G3), P. B. G. Jones.
Assistant Directors (G4), G. Findley; G. F. Hamilton; (G5) R. Neilson; N. C. Munro; Mrs. C. Hubbard; R. A. Hutton; J. T. Tudor; M. K. Robins.
Director of Manpower and Support Services (G3), J. M. Crawley.
Assistant Directors (G5), D. Ward; Miss M. A. Hill; A. W. Bryant.
Head of Operational Research (G5), R. P. R. Tilley.
Director of Information Technology (G3), G. H. Bush.
Deputy Director of Information Technology (G4), C. J. Thompson.
Assistant Directors (G5), A. M. Paterson; R. A. Hamilton; I. P. Crump; E. Wilson; D. Topple; B. T. Glassberg; R. Assirati.
Director of Operations (G3), C. Cherry.
Deputy Directors of Operations (G4), D. W. Muir; E. J. Gribbon; J. E. Yard.
Assistant Directors (G5), J. H. Keelty; E. C. Jones; Miss M. James; J. M. Thomas; R. S. Hurcombe; D. J. Timmons; S. J. McManus; C. H. Coleman; J. P. Gilbody; S. H. Banyard; Miss M. Boulton.
BROCS Project Office (G5), R. W. Skelley.
Controller, Enforcement Office (G5), R. F. Bruford.
Head of Communications Group (G5), P. C. Tharby.
Press Secretary (G7), D. I. Richardson.

Finance Division

Principal Finance Officer (G3), J. M. Crawley.
Assistant Secretaries (G5), I. R. Spence; R. R. Martin.
Controller, Central Accounting Office (G6), D. Easey.
Chief Internal Auditor (G6), N. Buckley.

Statistics Division

Director (G3), J. R. Calder.
Chief Statisticians (G5), J. B. Dearman; F. A. Fitzpatrick; G. A. Keenay; I. Stewart.
Computing (G6), R. James.

The Stamp Office
South-West Wing, Bush House, Strand, WC2B 4QN and Barrington Road, Worthing, W. Sussex BN12 4XH

Controller (G6), K. S. Hodgson.

Capital Taxes Office
Minford House, Rockley Road, W14 0DF

Controller (G4), G. A. Spencer.
Deputy Controllers/Assistant Secretaries (G5), B. D. Kent; R. J. Draper; A. G. Nield.
Asst. Controllers (G6), D. J. Ferley; C. A. Oldridge; H. V. Capon; R. T. Kablean; J. Blagden; T. J. Plumb; R. Shanks; N. Tant; F. A. Cook.
Boards Actuarial Adviser (G6), D. R. Erasmus.
Senior Principal (G6), P. Twiddy.

Solicitor of Inland Revenue
Somerset House, WC2R 1LB

Solicitor (G2), R. K. Miller, CB.
Principal Assistant Solicitors (G3), B. E. Cleave; J. D. H. Johnston; P. L. Ridd.

Assistant Solicitors (G5), R. J. Alderman; C. J. C. Baron; J. C. H. Bates; Miss M. P. Boland; S. Bousher; K. Brown; K. O. Butterfield; A. J. Gunz; N. R. Phillips; A. K. S. Shaw; R. W. Thornhill; R. Waterson; Miss A. E. Wyman.

Superannuation Funds Office
Lynwood Road, Thames Ditton, Surrey KT7 0DP

Controller (G5), R. G. Lusk.
Assistant Controllers (G6), R. C. Fullbrook; P. E. P. Berry.

Inspector of Foreign Dividends Office
Lynwood Road, Thames Ditton, Surrey KT7 0DP

Inspector of Foreign Dividends (G6), J. Steele.

Office of the Chief Valuer
New Court, Carey Street, WC2A 2JE

Chief Valuer (G2), R. R. B. Shutler.
Deputy Chief Valuers (G3), A. J. Langford; R. J. Pawley.
Assistant Chief Valuers (G4), R. A. Dales; P. Upton.
Superintending Valuers (G5), G. I. Coe; P. Crease; A. Dixen; M. J. Loveridge; W. J. Reed; A. B. Prior.
Assistant Directors (G5), J. H. Ebdon; D. N. Huckle; R. F. Moore; D. K. Park.

INLAND REVENUE (SCOTLAND)
80 Lauriston Place, Edinburgh EH3 9SL

Controller (G4), O. J. D. Clarke.
Group Controllers (G5), J. Brown; J. McCloskey; G. Watson; B. Ritchie.

The Stamp Office (Scotland)
16 Picardy Place, Edinburgh EH1 3NB

Controller, D. G. Hunter.

Capital Taxes Office
Mulberry House, 16 Picardy Place, Edinburgh EH1 3NB

Registrar (G5), P. G. Bruce, MBE.
Deputy Registrar (G7), W. Young.
Chief Examiners (G7), G. Mackie; Mrs. J. A. Templeton; W. Young; J. Telford; T. E. Naysmith; C. G. Hogg; Miss A. Forbes; Miss K. M. Patrick; D. M. Paterson.

Solicitor's Office
80 Lauriston Place, Edinburgh EH3 9SL

Solicitor, T. H. Scott.
Senior Principals (Legal) (G6), I. K. Laing; D. S. Wishart.
Principal (Legal), H. M. Milne.

Office of the Chief Valuer, Scotland
15 Drumsheugh Gardens, Edinburgh EH3 7UN

Chief Valuer (G4), J. A. Sutherland.
Assistant Chief Valuer (G5), M. A. Newbury.

INTERVENTION BOARD
Fountain House, Queen's Walk, Reading RG1 7QW
[0734–583626]

The Intervention Board was formed as a Government department in 1972, becoming operational on Feb. 1, 1973. The Board became an executive agency in April 1990. The Board is responsible for the implementation of European Community regulations covering the market support arrangements of the Common Agricultural Policy. Members of the Board are appointed by and are responsible to the Minister of Agriculture and the Secretaries of State for Scotland, Wales and Northern Ireland.
(For **Salaries**, *see* page 295)

Chairman, A. J. Ellis, CBE.
Chief Executive (G3), G. Stapleton.

Heads of Divisions
Finance Division (G5), J. N. Diserens.
External Trade Division (G5), G. N. Dixon.
Crops Division (G5), H. MacKinnon.
Livestock Products Division (G5), R. A. Saunderson.
Corporate Services Division (G5), J. W. M. Peffer.
Accountancy Services (G6), R. Bryant.
Procurement and Supply Services (G6), P. J. Offer.
Establishments Services (G6), R. J. Lovell.
Computer Services (G6), T. T. Simpson.

UK Seeds Executive
Chairman, Prof. J. C. Murdoch, OBE, PH.D.
Members, T. M. Clucas; J. M. Harley; J. Harvey; Prof. J. D. Hayes, PH.D.; P. R. Hayward, OBE; I. C. Henderson; D. R. Thomas; I. M. Whitelaw.

LAND AUTHORITY FOR WALES
The Custom House, Custom House Street, Cardiff CF1 5AP
[0222–223444]

The Authority is responsible for acquiring and disposing of land needed for private development in Wales.
Chairman, G. D. Inkin, OBE (part-time) £23,688
Chief Executive, B. Ryan.

LAND REGISTRIES

HM LAND REGISTRY
Lincoln's Inn Fields, WC2A 3PH
[071–405 3488]

The registration of title to land was first introduced in England and Wales by the Land Registry Act, 1862; HM Land Registry operates today under the Land Registration Acts, 1925 to 1986. The object of registering title to land is to create and maintain a register of land owners whose title is guaranteed by the State and so to simplify the transfer, mortgage and other dealings with real property. Compulsory registration on sale was introduced in stages affecting only certain areas. However, from December 1, 1990 registration of title will be compulsory on sale throughout England and Wales. The register, which has hitherto been private and could only be inspected with the consent of the registered proprietor, becomes open to inspection by the public on December 3, 1990.

HM Land Registry is an executive agency administered under the Lord Chancellor by the Chief Land Registrar. The work is decentralized to a number of regional offices. The Chief Land Registrar is also responsible for the Land Charges Department and the Agricultural Credits Department.
(For **Salaries**, *see* page 295)

Headquarters Office
Chief Land Registrar and Chief Executive (G2), E. J. Pryer.
Chief Land Registrar and Chief Executive designate (G2), J. J. Manthorpe.
Senior Land Registrar (G5), Mrs. J. G. Totty.
Principal Establishment Officer (G5), E. G. Beardsall.
Controller (Registration) (G5), G. N. French.
Controller (Information Technology) (G5), R. J. Fenn.
Controller (Management Services) (G6), P. J. Smith.
Land Registrar (G5), C. J. West.

Birkenhead District Land Registry
Old Market House, Hamilton Street,
Birkenhead L41 5JW
[051–647 2377]

District Land Registrar (G5), M. G. Garwood.
Area Manager (G6), J. Eccles.

Coventry District Land Registry
Greyfriars Business Centre,
2 Eaton Road, Coventry CV1 2SD
[0203–632442]

District Land Registrar (G5), S. P. Kelway.
Area Manager (G6), J. C. Lillistone.

Croydon District Land Registry
Sunley House, Bedford Park, Croydon CR9 3LE
[081–686 8833]

District Land Registrar (G5), D. M. J. Moss.
Area Manager (G6), V. J. C. Shorney.

Durham District Land Registry
Southfield House, Southfield Way,
Durham DH1 5TR
[091–3866151]

District Land Registrar (G5), P. H. Curnow.
Area Manager (G6), D. J. Long.

Gloucester District Land Registry
Twyver House, Bruton Way,
Gloucester GL1 1DQ
[0452–28666]

District Land Registrar (G5), W. W. Budden.
Area Manager (G6), D. Thomas.

Harrow District Land Registry
Lyon House, Lyon Road, Harrow,
Middx. HA1 2EU
[081–427 8811]

District Land Registrar (G5), M. L. Wood.
Area Manager (G6), M. J. Wyatt.

Kingston upon Hull District Land Registry
Earle House, Portland Street, Hull HU2 8JN
[0482–223244]

District Land Registrar (G5), S. R. G. Coveney.
Area Manager (G7), E. Howard.

**Land Charges and Agricultural Credits
Department**
Burrington Way, Plymouth PL6 3LP
[0752–779831]

Superintendent of Land Charges (G7), H. Myers.

Leicester District Land Registry
Thames Tower, 99 Burleys Way,
Leicester LE1 3UB
[0533–510010]

District Land Registrar (G5), P. J. Timothy.
Area Manager (G7), B. Warriner.

Lytham District Land Registry
Birkenhead House, Lytham St. Annes,
Lancs. FY8 5AB
[0253–736999]

District Land Registrar (G5), J. G. Cooper.
Area Manager (G6), E. J. Stringer.

Nottingham District Land Registry
Chalfont Drive, Nottingham NG8 3RN
[0602–291166]

District Land Registrar (G5), P. J. Timothy.
Area Manager, (G6), W. Whitaker.

Peterborough District Land Registry
Touthill Close, City Road,
Peterborough PE1 1XN
[0733–555666]

District Land Registrar (G5), M. Avens.
Area Manager (G6), B. J. Andrews.

Plymouth District Land Registry
Plumer House, Tailyour Road,
Crownhill, Plymouth PL6 5HY
[0752–701234]

District Land Registrar (G5), A. J. Pain.
Area Manager(G6), K. Robinson.

Portsmouth District Land Registry
St. Andrews Court, St. Michael's Way,
Portsmouth PO1 2JH
[0705–865022]

District Land Registrar (G5), Mrs. P. M. Reeson.
Area Manager (G7), A. W. Howarth.

Stevenage District Land Registry
Brickdale House, Danestrete, Stevenage,
Herts. SG1 1XG
[0438–313003]

District Land Registrar (G5), D. M. T. Mullett.
Area Manager (G6), A. D. Gould.

Swansea District Land Registry
Tybryn Glas High Street,
Swansea SA1 1PW
[0792–458877]

District Land Registrar (G5), G. A. Hughes.
Area Manager (G6), B. E. G. Martin.

Telford District Land Registry
Stafford Park 15, Telford,
Shropshire TF3 3BB
[0952–290355]

District Land Registrar (G5), M. A. Roche.
Area Manager (G6), R. D. Moseley.

Tunbridge Wells District Land Registry
Curtis House, Hawkenbury, Tunbridge Wells,
Kent TN2 5AQ
[0892–510015]

District Land Registrar (G5), G. R. Tooke.
Area Manager (G6), B. E. Kitching.

Weymouth District Land Registry
1 Cumberland Drive, Weymouth,
Dorset DT4 9TT
[03057–776161]

District Land Registrar (G5), Mrs. P. M. Reeson.
Area Manager (G6), R. R. C. Green.

Computer Services Division
Burrington Way,
Plymouth PL5 3LP
[0752–779831]

Head of Division (G6), A. A. Restorick.

**DEPARTMENT OF THE REGISTERS OF
SCOTLAND (EXECUTIVE AGENCY)**
Meadowbank House, 153 London Road,
Edinburgh EH8 7AU
[031–659 6111]

The Registers of Scotland consist of: General
Register of Sasines and Land Register of Scotland;
Register of Deeds in the Books of Council and
Session; Register of Protests; Register of English and
Irish Judgments; Register of Service of Heirs;
Register of the Great Seal; Register of the Quarter
Seal; Register of the Prince's Seal; Register of Crown
Grants; Register of Sheriffs' Commissions; Register

of the Cachet Seal; Register of Inhibitions and Adjudications; Register of Entails; Register of Hornings.

The General Register of Sasines and the Land Register of Scotland form the chief security in Scotland of the rights of land and other heritable (or real) property.

Keeper of the Registers of Scotland (G4), J. W. Barron.
Deputy Keeper (G5), R. C. Brown.
Senior Assistant Keepers (G6), A. G. Rennie; A. A. Snowdon; G. C. Warrender.
Assistant Keepers (G7), J. Anderson; R. C. Clark; J. Cogle; B. J. Corr; A. M. Falconer; A. B. Farmer; R. Glen; H. Hosken; J. Knox; D. Lorimer; D. McCallum; Mrs. A. McDonald; D. Manson; A. G. T. New; A. W. Ramage; J. Rynn; Mrs. P. M. Stewart; I. M. Tainsh; M. J. Wilczynski.

LAW COMMISSION
(England and Wales)
Conquest House, 37–38 John Street,
Theobalds Road, WC1N 2BQ
[071–242 0861]

Set up on June 16, 1965, under the Law Commissions Act, 1965, to make proposals to the Government for the examination of the law and for its revision where it is unsuited for modern requirements, obscure, or otherwise unsatisfactory. It recommends to the Lord Chancellor programmes for the examination of different branches of the law and suggests whether the examination should be carried out by the Commission itself or by some other body. The Commission is also responsible for the preparation of Consolidation and Statute Law (Repeals) Bills.

Chairman, The Hon. Mr. Justice Gibson.
Members, T. M. Aldridge; J. Beatson; R. Buxton, QC; Prof. B. M. Hoggett, QC.
Secretary, M. H. Collon.

SCOTTISH LAW COMMISSION
140 Causewayside, Edinburgh EH9 1PR
[031–668 2131]

Chairman, The Hon. Lord Davidson.
Commissioners, Dr. E. M. Clive; I. D. MacPhail, QC (*full-time*); Prof. P. N. Love, CBE; W. Nimmo Smith, QC (*part-time*).
Secretary, K. F. Barclay.

LAW OFFICERS' DEPARTMENTS
Attorney-General's Chambers,
9 Buckingham Gate, SW1E 6JP
[071–828 7155]
Attorney General's Chambers,
Royal Courts of Justice, Belfast BT1 3JY
[0232–235111]

The Law Officers of the Crown for England and Wales are the Attorney General and the Solicitor General. The Attorney General is the Minister responsible for the work of the Law Officers' Departments: the Treasury Solicitor's Department, the Crown Prosecution Service, the Serious Fraud Office, and the Legal Secretariat to the Law Officers. The Director of Public Prosecutions (who is head of the Crown Prosecution Service), the Director of Public Prosecutions for Northern Ireland, and the Director of the Serious Fraud Office are responsible to the Attorney General for the performance of their duties.

The Attorney General is the Government's principal legal adviser, dealing with questions of law arising on Bills, issues of legal policy, and major international and domestic litigation involving the Government. The Solicitor General is responsible for such matters as the Attorney General delegates to him.

Attorney General, THE RT. HON. SIR PATRICK MAYHEW, QC, MP . . . . £37,320†
    Parliamentary Private Secretary, D. A. Sumberg, MP.
Solicitor General, THE RT. HON SIR NICHOLAS LYELL, QC, MP . . . . £30,600†
    Parliamentary Private Secretary, P. Ground, QC, MP.
Legal Secretary (G3), Miss J. L. Wheldon.
Asst. Legal Secretary (G4), M. L. Carpenter.

† Excluding reduced Parliamentary salary of £20,101.

THE LAY OBSERVER'S OFFICE
Royal Courts of Justice, Strand, WC2A 2LL
[071–210 4598]

The Lay Observer's Office was established in 1975 and is funded by the Lord Chancellor's Department. The function of the Lay Observer is to monitor the Solicitor's Complaints Bureau's handling of complaints made to it about the conduct of solicitors or solicitors' employees. The Lay Observer is independent and is appointed by the Lord Chancellor.

The Lay Observer is to be replaced in January 1991 by the Legal Services Ombudsman.

Lay Observer (G5), L. Lightman.
Clerk, J. S. Twist.

LEGAL AID BOARD
5th Floor, Newspaper House,
8–16 Great New Street, EC4A 3BN
[071–353 7411]

The Legal Aid Board has the general function of ensuring that advice, assistance and representation are available, in accordance with the Legal Aid Act 1988. It took over from the Law Society on April 1, 1989 responsibility for administering legal aid. The Board is a non-departmental government body whose members are appointed by the Lord Chancellor.

Chairman, J. Pitts.
Members, M. Acland; Ms. D. Beale; A. Blake; Ms. H. Bradley; L. Devonald; K. Farrow; Ms. S. Harold; G. Hibbert; D. Sinker; J. Smith; P. Soar.
Chief Executive, S. Orchard.

SCOTTISH LEGAL AID BOARD
44 Drumsheugh Gardens,
Edinburgh EH3 7SW
[031–226 7061]

The Scottish Legal Aid Board was set up under the Legal Aid (Scotland) Act 1986. It is responsible for ensuring that advice, assistance and representation are available, in accordance with the Act. The Board is a non-departmental government body whose members are appointed by the Secretary of State for Scotland.

Chairman, D. B. Grant, CBE, TD.
Members, G. Barrie; Prof. T. F. Carbery, OBE; Miss L. Clark, QC; Mrs. C. Davies; B. G. Donald; A. Gilchrist; G. D. Holmes, CB; D. A. Leitch; R. J. Livingstone; Mrs. I. McColl; C. N. McEachran, QC; R. G. McEwan, QC; G. H. Speirs; Mrs. M. Tait.
Chief Executive, A. M. Douglas.

LIBRARIES

OFFICE OF ARTS AND LIBRARIES
(*see* entry on page 300)

THE BRITISH LIBRARY
2 Sheraton Street, W1V 4BH
[071–636 1544]

The British Library is the UK's national library
and occupies the central position in the library and
information network. The Library aims to serve
scholarship, research, industry, commerce and all
other major users of information. Its services are
based on collections which include over 18 million
volumes (books, manuscripts, maps, newspapers and
other serials, stamps and music), 1 million discs,
55,000 hours of tape recordings, in more than 20
buildings in London and one complex in West
Yorkshire.

The British Library was established on July 1, 1973
under the British Library Act, 1972. It brought
together the library departments of the British
Museum, the National Central Library, the National
Lending Library for Science and Technology, the
British National Bibliography Ltd and, in 1974, the
functions of the Office for Scientific and Technical
Information. Subsequently the Library took responsibility for other organizations: the India Office
Library and Records and the HMSO Binderies in
1982; and the National Sound Archive in 1983. Since
1985 they have all been regrouped into three service
areas, a Research and Development Department plus
a corporate administrative centre.

Access to the Humanities and Social Sciences
reading rooms in Great Russell Street is limited to
holders of a British Library Reader's Pass, and
information about eligibility (basically, academic
researchers and investigative professionals) is available from the Reader Admissions Office. The Aldwych
and Holborn reading rooms of the Science Reference
and Information Service are open to the general
public without charge or formality.

The Library's exhibition galleries are housed in
the British Museum building in Great Russell Street.
On permanent display are famous items from the
national written archive including the Magna Carta,
the Lindisfarne Gospels and Shakespeare's First
Folio.

The British Library will be moving to purpose-
built accommodation at St. Pancras, London NW1 in
1991 (open to the public in 1993).

Board Members
Chairman, Cdr. L. M. M. Saunders Watson.
Chief Executive and Deputy Chairman, K. R. Cooper.
Directors General, J. M. Smethurst; D. Russon.
Part-time Members, The Lord Adrian, MD, FRS; The
Lord Windlesham, CVO, PC; Prof. A. S. Forty, Ph.D.,
D.SC.; The Lord Morris of Castle Morris; Sir Robin
Mackworth-Young, KCVO, FSA; R. E. Utiger, CBE;
T. J. Rix; Dame Anne Warburton, DCVO, CMG; H.
Heaney; D. Peake.

HUMANITIES AND SOCIAL SCIENCES
Director General, J. M. Smethurst.

Preservation Service
Great Russell Street, WC1B 3DG
[071–323 7619]

Director, Dr. D. W. Clements.

Collection Development

Director, B. C. Bloomfield.

Oriental Collections
Store Street, WC1E 7DG
[071–323 7642]

India Office Library and Records
197 Blackfriars Road, SE1 8NG
[071–928 9531]

*English Language, Western, Eastern European
Printed Books*
Great Russell Street, WC1B 3DG
[071–323 7676]

Special Collections

Director, Mrs. S. J. Tyacke.

*Western Manuscripts, Maps, Manuscript and
Printed Music, Stamps*
Great Russell Street, WC1B 3DG
[071–323 7513]

Public Services, Planning and Administration

Director, A. Phillips.

*Reading rooms for Great Russell Street collections,
Official Publications*
Great Russell Street, WC1B 3DG
[071–323 7676]

Information Sciences Service
7 Ridgmount Street, WC1E 7AE
[071–323 7688]

The National Sound Archive
29 Exhibition Road, SW7 2AS
[071–589 6603]

Newspaper Library
Colindale Avenue, NW9 5HE
[071–323 7357]

SCIENCE, TECHNOLOGY AND INDUSTRY

Director General, D. Russon.

Document Supply Centre
Boston Spa, Wetherby, W. Yorks. LS23 7BQ
[0937–843434]

Director, D. Bradbury.

Science Reference and Information Service
25 Southampton Buildings, Chancery Lane,
WC2A 1AW
[071–323 7494]
9 Kean Street WC2B 4AT
[071–323 7288]

Director, A. Gomersall.

Acquisitions Processing and Cataloguing
2 Sheraton Street, W1V 4BH
[071–323 7077]

Director, Mrs. J. Butcher.

Computing and Telecommunications
2 Sheraton Street, W1V 4BH
[071–323 7077]

Director, J. Mahoney.

National Bibliographic Service
2 Sheraton Street, W1V 4BH
[071–323 7077]

Director, S. Ede.

RESEARCH AND DEVELOPMENT
DEPARTMENT
2 Sheraton Street, W1V 4BH
[071–323 7060]

Director, B. J. Perry.

CENTRAL ADMINISTRATION
2 Sheraton Street, WC1V 4BH
[071–323 7132]

Director, L. Bell.

NATIONAL LIBRARY OF SCOTLAND
George IV Bridge, Edinburgh EH1 1EW
[031–226 4531]

Open free. Reading Room, weekdays, 9.30–8.30; Sat. 9.30–1. Map Library, weekdays, 9.30–5; Sat. 9.30–1. Exhibition, weekdays, 9.30–5; Sat. 9.30–1; Sun. 2–5.

The Library, which was founded as the Advocates' Library in 1682, became the National Library of Scotland by Act of Parliament in 1925. It continues to share the rights conferred by successive Copyright Acts since 1710. Its collections of printed books and MSS, augmented by purchase and gift, are very large and it has an unrivalled Scottish collection. The present building was opened by The Queen in 1956.

The Reading Room is for reference and research which cannot conveniently be pursued elsewhere. Admission is by ticket issued to an approved applicant.

Salaries

Librarian .... £36,818–£41,296
Keeper .... £23,039–£35,436
Curator Grade C .... £20,189–£28,710

Chairman of the Trustees, M. F. Strachan, CBE, FRSE.
Librarian and Secretary to the Trustees, vacant.
Secretary of the Library, I. D. McGowan.
Curators Grade C, M. C. Graham; J. E. McIntyre.
Keepers of Printed Books, A. M. Marchbank, PH.D.; Ms. A. Matheson, PH.D.
Curators Grade C, T. A. Cherry; R. Duce; Ms. A. E. Harvey Wood; B. P. Hillyard, D.Phil.; S. Holland; Ms. R. I. Hope; W. A. Kelly; J. M. Morris; Ms. J. M. Wilkes.
Keeper of Manuscripts, P. M. Cadell.
Curators Grade C, L. G. Brown, PH.D., FSA; I. C. Cunningham; I. F. Maciver; S. M. Simpson; Ms. E. D. Yeo.
Director of Computer Services and Research (Keeper), B. Gallivan.
Curator Grade C, R. F. Guy.
Director of Scottish Science Library (Keeper), Ms. A. J. Bunch.

THE NATIONAL LIBRARY OF WALES
Llyfrgell Genedlaethol Cymru
Aberystwyth, Dyfed SY23 3BU
[0970–623816]

Readers' room open on weekdays, 9.30 a.m. to 6 p.m. (Saturdays, 5 p.m.); closed on Sundays, Bank Holidays and first week of October. Admission by Reader's Ticket.

Founded by Royal Charter, 1907, and maintained by annual grant from the Treasury. One of the six libraries entitled to privileges under Copyright Act. Contains about 15,000,000 printed books, 40,000 manuscripts, 4,000,000 deeds and documents, and numerous maps, prints and drawings, and audio-visual collection. Specializes in manuscripts and books relating to Wales and the Celtic peoples. Repository for pre-1858 Welsh probate records. Approved by the Master of the Rolls as a repository for manorial records and tithe documents, and by the Lord Chancellor for certain legal records. Bureau of the Regional Libraries Scheme for Wales.
Librarian, B. F. Roberts, PH.D., FSA.
Secretary, D. B. Lloyd.

Heads of Departments, D. Huws (*Manuscripts and Records*); J. L. Madden (*Printed Books*); D. H. Owen (*Pictures and Maps*).

LIGHTHOUSE AUTHORITIES

CORPORATION OF TRINITY HOUSE
Trinity House, Tower Hill, EC3N 4DH
[071–480 6601]

Trinity House, the first general lighthouse and pilotage authority in the Kingdom, was a body of importance when Henry VIII granted the institution its first charter in 1514. The Corporation is the general lighthouse authority for England, Wales and the Channel Islands, with certain statutory jurisdiction over aids to navigation maintained by local harbour authorities. It is also responsible for dealing with wrecks dangerous to navigation, except those occurring within port limits or wrecks of HM ships. The Trinity House Lighthouse Service is maintained out of the General Lighthouse Fund which is provided from light dues levied on ships at ports of the UK and Republic of Ireland. The Corporation is also a deep-sea pilotage authority and a charitable organization.

The affairs of the Corporation are controlled by a board of Elder Brethren, who are master mariners with long experience of command in the Royal and Merchant Navy together with figures from the world of commerce, and the Secretary. A separate board, which comprises Elder Brethren, senior staff and outside representatives currently controls the Lighthouse Service. The Board is assisted by administrative and technical staff. The Elder Brethren also act as nautical assessors in marine cases in the Admiralty Division of the High Court of Justice.

Elder Brethren

Master, HRH the Duke of Edinburgh, KG, KT.
Deputy Master, Capt. P. M. Edge.
Elder Brethren, Capt. I. R. C. Saunders; Capt. P. F. Mason, CBE; HRH the Prince of Wales, KG, KT; Capt. Sir George Barnard, FRSA; Capt. R. N. Mayo, CBE; Capt. Sir David Tibbits, DSC, RN; Capt. D. A. G. Dickens; Capt. J. E. Bury; Capt. J. A. N. Bezant, DSC, RD, RNR (*ret.*); Capt. D. J. Cloke; The Lord Wilson of Rievaulx, KG, OBE, FRS; Capt. Sir Miles Wingate, KCVO; Rt. Hon. Edward Heath, MBE, MP; Capt. T. Woodfield, OBE; Sir Arthur Drake, CBE; The Lord Simon of Glaisdale, PC; Admiral of the Fleet the Lord Lewin, KG, GCB, LVO, DSC; Capt. D. T. Smith, RN; Commander Sir Robin Gillett, GBE, RD, RNR; The Lord Shackleton, KG, OBE, PC; Sir John Cuckney; Capt. D. J. Orr; The Lord Carrington, KG, GCMG, CH, MC, PC; Sir Brian Shaw; The Lord Mackay of Clashfern, PC; Sir Adrian Swire; Capt. N. M. Turner, RD.

Officers

Secretary, J. B. Fuller.
Deputy Secretary, M. J. Faulkner.
Director of Engineering, D. A. S. Vennings.
Director of Finance, K. W. Clark.
Personnel and General Services Manager, Mrs. B. C. Heesom.
Navigation Manager, N. J. Cutmore.
Legal and Information Manager, D. I. Brewer.
General Manager Operations, Capt. J. H. Barnes.
Operations Administration Manager, S. J. W. Dunning.
Deputy Director of Engineering, F. E. J. Holden.
Senior Inspector of Shipping, J. Sedgwick.
Manager, Corporate Department, R. Dobb.
Information Officer, H. L. Cooper.

COMMISSIONERS OF NORTHERN LIGHTHOUSES
84 George Street, Edinburgh EH2 3DA.
[031-226 7051]

The Commissioners of Northern Lighthouses are the general lighthouse authority for Scotland and the Isle of Man. The present board owes its origin to an Act of Parliament passed in 1786. At present the Commissioners operate under the Merchant Shipping Act, 1894 and are 19 in number.

The Commissioners control 25 major manned lighthouses, 59 major automatic lighthouses, 112 minor lights and many lighted and unlighted buoys. They have a fleet of two motor vessels.

Commissioners

The Lord Advocate, the Solicitor General for Scotland, the Lord Provosts of Edinburgh, Glasgow and Aberdeen; the Provost of Inverness; the Chairman of Argyll and Bute District Council; the Sheriffs-Principal of North Strathclyde, Tayside, Central, Fife, Grampian, Highlands and Islands, South Strathclyde, Dumfries and Galloway, Lothians and Borders, and Glasgow and Strathkelvin; T. Macgill; Capt. A. F. Dickson, OBE; Capt. W. B. Kinley; A. J. Struthers; W. F. Hay, CBE; J. Hann, CBE.

Officers

General Manager, Cdr. J. M. Mackay, MBE.
Secretary, I. A. Dickson.
Engineer-in-Chief, W. Paterson.

LOCAL COMMISSIONERS

COMMISSION FOR LOCAL ADMINISTRATION IN ENGLAND
21 Queen Anne's Gate, SW1H 9BU
[071-222 5622]

Local Commissioners (local ombudsmen) are responsible for investigating complaints from members of the public against local authorities (but not town and parish councils); police authorities; the Commission for New Towns and new town development corporations (housing functions); and urban development corporations (town and country planning functions). The Commissioners are appointed by the Crown on the recommendation of the Secretary of State for the Environment.

Certain types of action are excluded from investigation, particularly personnel matters and commercial transactions unless they relate to the purchase or sale of land. Complaints can be sent direct to the local ombudsman or through a councillor, although the local ombudsman will not consider a complaint unless the Council has had an opportunity to investigate and reply to a complainant.

A free booklet *Complaint about the Council? How to Complain to your Local Ombudsman* is available from the Commission's office.

Chairman of the Commission and Local Commissioner, D. C. M. Yardley, D.Phil. £76,320
Vice Chairman and Local Commissioner, F. G. Laws
.... £54,420
Local Commissioner, Mrs. P. A. Thomas £53,420
Member, The Parliamentary Commissioner for Administration
Secretary, G. D. Adams £36,735

COMMISSION FOR LOCAL ADMINISTRATION IN WALES
Derwen House, Court Road, Bridgend CF31 1BN
[0656-661325/6]

The Local Commissioner for Wales has similar powers to the Local Commissioners in England. The Commissioner is appointed by the Crown on the recommendation of the Secretary of State for Wales. A free booklet *Your Local Ombudsman in Wales* is available from the Commission's office.
Local Commissioner, H. F. Jones.
Secretary, D. Bowen.

COMMISSIONER FOR LOCAL ADMINISTRATION IN SCOTLAND
5 Shandwick Place, Edinburgh EH2 4RG
[031-229 4472]

The Local Commissioner for Scotland has similar powers to the Local Commissioners in England, and is appointed by the Crown on the recommendation of the Secretary of State for Scotland.
Local Commissioner, R. G. E. Peggie, CBE.
Secretary, K. Bratton.

LONDON REGIONAL TRANSPORT
55 Broadway, SW1H 0BD
[071-222 5600]

Subject to the financial objectives and principles approved by the Secretary of State for Transport, London Regional Transport has a general duty to provide or secure the provision of public transport services for Greater London.
Chairman, C. W. Newton £80,000
Members, J. Telford Beasley; M. Marsh £60,000

LORD ADVOCATE'S DEPARTMENT
Fielden House, 10 Great College Street,
SW1P 3SL
[071-276 3000]

The Law Officers for Scotland are the Lord Advocate and the Solicitor-General for Scotland. The Lord Advocate's Department is responsible for drafting Scottish legislation, for providing legal advice to other departments on Scottish questions and for assistance to the Law Officers for Scotland in certain of their legal duties.
Lord Advocate, THE LORD FRASER OF CARMYLLIE, PC,
QC £44,661
Solicitor-General for Scotland, ALAN F. RODGER, QC.
£39,109
Legal Secretary and First Scottish Parliamentary Counsel, J. C. McCluskie, QC £53,420
Assistant Legal Secretaries and Scottish Parliamentary Counsel, G. M. Clark; D. J. S. Duncan; G. Kowalski; P. J. Layden, TD ...... £45,350–£52,460
Asst. Legal Secs. and Depute Scottish Parliamentary Counsel, J. D. Harkness; D. C. Macrae; C. A. M. Wilson .... £35,741–£43,046
Asst. Legal Sec. and Asst. Scottish Parliamentary Counsel, Miss M. Mackenzie £24,500

LORD CHANCELLOR'S DEPARTMENT
House of Lords, SW1A 0PW
[071-219 3000]

The Lord Chancellor is responsible for promoting general reforms in the civil law, for the procedure of the civil courts and for the administration of the Supreme Court (Court of Appeal, High Court and Crown Court) and county courts in England and Wales, and for legal aid schemes. He is responsible for advising the Crown on the appointment of judges and certain other officers and is himself responsible for the appointment of Masters and Registrars of the High Court and District and County Court Registrars and magistrates. He is responsible for ensuring that letters patent and other formal documents are passed in the proper form under the Great Seal of the Realm, of which he is the custodian. The work in connection with this is carried out under his direction in the Office of the Clerk of the Crown in Chancery. (For **Salaries**, *see* page 295)

Lord Chancellor, THE LORD MACKAY OF CLASHFERN, PC £91,500
  Private Secretary, Miss J. Lowe.
Permanent Secretary (G1), T. S. Legg, CB, QC.
  Private Secretary, Ms. E. Hutchinson.

Crown Office

Clerk of the Crown in Chancery (G1), T. S. Legg, CB, QC.
Deputy Clerk of the Crown in Chancery (G2), R. Potter, CB.
Clerk of the Chamber, Miss J. L. Waine.

POLICY AND LEGAL SERVICES
Trevelyan House, 30 Great Peter Street,
SW1P 2BY
[071–210 8872]

Deputy Secretary (G2), R. Potter, CB.

Court Service Management Group

Head of Group (G4), J. F. Brindley.
Heads of Divisions (G5), R. Stoate; R. A. Vincent; R. J. Clark.

Policy and Legal Services Group

Head of Group (G3), J. G. H. Gasson, CB.
Heads of Divisions (G5), W. Arnold; M. Kron; R. H. H. White.

JUDICIAL APPOINTMENTS AND LEGISLATION
House of Lords, SW1A 0PW
[071–219 4311]

Deputy Secretary (G2), M. D. Huebner.

Judicial Appointments Group
House of Lords, SW1A 0PW
[071–219 3000]

Head of Group (G3), J. L. Heritage.
Heads of Divisions (G5), D. E. Staff; M. Sayers.

26–28 Old Queen Street, SW1H 2HP
[071–210 3537]
Grade 5, R. V. Grobler; G. Norman.

Legislation Group
26–28 Old Queen Street, SW1H 2HP
[071–210 3128]

Head of Group (G3), L. Oates.
Heads of Divisions (G5), P. Graham Harris; M. H. Collon; M. C. L. Carpenter.

Establishment and Finance Group
Trevelyan House, 30 Great Peter Street, SW1P 2BY
[071–210 8503]

Principal Establishment and Finance Officer (G3), B. Cousins, CBE.
Heads of Divisions (G5), L. W. V. Everett; D. S. Mortimer; D. Nooney; Mrs. N. A. Oppenheimer.
Principal Information Officer (G7), vacant.

Public Trust Office
See p. 354

Ecclesiastical Patronage
10 Downing Street, SW1
[071–930 4433]

Secretary for Ecclesiastical Patronage, J. R. Catford.
Assistant Secretary for Ecclesiastical Patronage (G7), N. Wheeler.

Statutory Publications Office
Queen Anne's Chambers, 28 Broadway, SW1H 9JS
[071–210 3000]

Editor (G5), J. M. Gibson.
Grade 6, C. E. J. Carey.
  See also Law Courts and Offices

LORD GREAT CHAMBERLAIN'S OFFICE
House of Lords, SW1A 0PW
[071–219 3100]

The Lord Great Chamberlain is a Great Officer of State, the office being hereditary since the grant of Henry I to the family of De Vere, Earls of Oxford.
Lord Great Chamberlain, The Marquess of Cholmondeley.
Secretary to the Lord Great Chamberlain, Air Chief Marshal Sir John Gingell, GBE, KCB.
Clerk to the Lord Great Chamberlain, Mrs. S. E. Douglas.

LORD PRIVY SEAL'S OFFICE
Privy Council Office,
Whitehall, SW1A 2AT
[071–270 3000]

As leader of the House of Lords, the Lord Privy Seal is responsible to the Prime Minister for the arrangement of government business in the House. He also has a responsibility to the House itself to advise it on procedural matters and other difficulties which arise.
Lord Privy Seal, and Leader of the House of Lords, THE LORD BELSTEAD, PC.
Private Secretary, Miss G. M. Kirton.
Assistant Private Secretary, W. Hawkins.

OFFICE OF MANPOWER ECONOMICS
22 Kingsway, WC2B 6JY
[071–405 5944]

The Office of Manpower Economics was set up in 1971. It is an independent non-statutory organization which is responsible for servicing independent review bodies which advise on the pay of various public service groups (*see* **Review Bodies**, p. 356), the Pharmacists Review Panel, the Police Negotiating Board and the Civil Service Arbitration Tribunal. The Office is also responsible for servicing *ad hoc* bodies of inquiry and for undertaking research into pay and associated matters as requested by Government.
Director, D. G. Talintyre.
Assistant Secretaries (G5), D. W. R. Lewis; P. J. H. Edwards; Dr. M. E. McDowall.

MEDICAL RESEARCH COUNCIL
20 Park Crescent, W1N 4AL
[071–636 5422]

The Medical Research Council is the main Government agency for the promotion of medical and related biological research. The Council employs its own research staff and also provides grants for other institutions and for individuals who are not members of its own staff, thus complementing the research resources of the universities and hospitals.
Chairman, Sir David Plastow.

Deputy Chairman and Secretary, D. A. Rees, Ph.D., D.SC., FRS.

Members, Sir Donald Acheson, KBE, DM, FRCP; Prof. I. V. Allen, D.SC., MD; Prof. C. L. Berry, Ph.D.; Prof. M. Bobrow, D.SC.; K. C. Calman, MD, Ph.D., FRCS Glas., FRCP; J. T. Carter, FRCP; P. Doyle, Ph.D.; Prof. Sir Aaron Klug, SC.D., FRS; Prof. C. D. Marsden, D.SC., FRCP, FRS; Prof. T. J. McElwain, FRCP; Prof. F. W. O'Grady, CBE, TD, MD, FRCP; Prof. G. K. Radda, D.Phil., FRS; Prof. R. Shields, MD, FRCS, FRCSE; Mrs R. Short; J. W. G. Smith, MD, FRCP.

Administrative Secretary, Ms. N. Morris.

Neurobiology and Mental Health Board

Chairman, A. D. Baddeley, Ph.D.

Cell Biology and Disorders Board

Chairman, Prof. G. Radda.

Physiological Systems and Disorders Board

Chairman, Prof. D. K. Peters, FRCP.

Tropical Medicine Research Board

Chairman, Dr. J. W. B. Smith.

Health Services Research Committee

Chairman, Prof. J. K. Wing, MD, Ph.D.

HEADQUARTERS OFFICE

Second Secretary, D. Evered, D.SC., MD, FRCP.

Medical Division

Heads of Division, D. James, Ph.D.; J. Alwen, Ph.D.

Administrative Division

Administrative Secretary, Ms. N. Morris.
Assistant Secretaries, B. C. Dodd; J. E. A. Hay; D. Smith, Ph.D.

Secretariat

Assistant Secretary, N. H. Winterton.

For units of Medical Research Council, *see* Index.

MONOPOLIES AND MERGERS COMMISSION
New Court, 48 Carey Street, WC2A 2JT
[071-324 1467]

The Commission was established in 1948 as the Monopolies and Restrictive Practices Commission and was reconstituted on subsequent occasions. It became the Monopolies and Mergers Commission in 1973. The Commission has the duty of investigating and reporting on questions referred to it with respect to: the existence or possible existence of monopolies not registrable under the Restrictive Trade Practices Act, 1976, and relating to the supply of goods or services in the UK or part of the UK or to the supply of goods for export; the transfer of a newspaper or newspaper's assets; the creation or possible creation of a merger qualifying for investigation within the meaning of the Fair Trading Act, 1973.

References may be made to the Commission on the general effect on the public interest of specified monopoly or other uncompetitive practices and of restrictive labour practices.

The Competition Act, 1980, provides for the reference to the Commission of particular anti-competitive practices and of questions of efficiency, costs, service provided and possible abuse of monopolies in the public sector. In respect of recently-privatized industries, references to the Commission may be made in certain circumstances, with regard to their respective industries, by the Director General of Telecommunications, the Civil Aviation Authority, the Director General of Gas Supply, the Director General of Water Services and the Director General of Electricity Supply.

Chairman, M. S. Lipworth £77,000
Deputy Chairmen, H. H. Hunt, CBE; H. H. Liesner, CB;
P. H. Dean £26,990
Members, A. G. Armstrong; C. C. Baillieu; I. Barter; Prof. M. E. Beesley, CBE; Mrs. C. Blight; F. E. Bonner, CBE; *P. Brenan; L. Britz; K. S. Carmichael, CBE; R. Davies; Prof. S. Eilon; J. Evans; A. Ferry, MBE; P. S. G. Flint; D. G. Goyder; M. R. Hoffman; J. D. Keir, QC; *L. Kingshott; Miss P. K. R. Mann; G. C. S. Mather; L. A. Mills; Prof. P. Minford; J. D. Montgomery; B. C. Owens; *Prof. J. Pickering; D. P. Thomson; C. A. Unwin, MBE; S. Wainwright, CBE; Prof. G. Whittington; R. Young.
each £10,866 (*£7,244)

Secretary, S. N. Burbridge.

MUSEUMS

MUSEUMS AND GALLERIES COMMISSION
7 St. James's Square, SW1Y 4JU
[071-839 9341]

Established in February 1931 as the Standing Commission on Museums and Galleries, the Commission was re-named and took up new functions in September 1981. Its sponsor department is the Office of Arts and Libraries. The Commission advises the Government, including the Department of Education for Northern Ireland, the Scottish Education Department and Welsh Office, on museum affairs. There are 15 Commissioners, appointed by the Prime Minister.

The Commission's executive functions include the services of the National Museums Security Adviser; allocation of grants to the seven Area Museum Councils in England; funding and monitoring of the work of the Museum Documentation Association; directly administering a capital grant scheme for non-national museums, and various other grant schemes. The Commission administers the arrangements for government indemnities and the acceptance of works of art in lieu of Inheritance Tax, and it has responsibility for the two purchase grant funds for local museums managed on its behalf by the Victoria and Albert and Science Museums. The Commission's Conservation Unit advises on conservation and operates grants schemes for conservators. The Travelling Exhibitions Unit promotes and encourages travelling exhibitions. A registration scheme for museums in the UK is being implemented with the assistance of the Commission.

Chairman, Lord Morris of Castle Morris, D.Phil.
Members, The Marchioness of Anglesey, DBE; F. Atkinson, OBE; R. Begg, CBE; L. Brandes, CB; The Lord Dainton, FRS; F. Dunning, OBE; Prof. Sir John Hale, FBA; J. Last, CBE; Sir Hugh Leggatt; The Lord O'Neill, TD; The Lord Rees, PC, QC; R. H. Smith; Dame Margaret Weston, DBE; Adm. Sir David Williams, GCB.

Director and Secretary, P. Longman.

THE BRITISH MUSEUM
Great Russell Street, WC1B 3DG
[071-636 1555]

Antiquities collections, coins and medals, prints and drawings. Open weekdays (including Bank Holidays) 10–5 and Sun. 2.30–6. Closed on Good Friday, Christmas Eve, Christmas Day, Boxing Day, New Year's Day and the first Monday in May. The ethnographical collections are displayed in the Museum of Mankind at 6 Burlington Gardens, W1. Opening times as above.

The British Museum may be said to date from 1753,

when Parliament granted funds to purchase the collections of Sir Hans Sloane and the Harleian manuscripts, and for their proper housing and maintenance. The building (Montagu House) was opened in 1759. The present buildings were erected between 1823 and the present day, and the original collection has increased to its present dimensions by gifts and purchases. Government grants for running costs and works and building projects were estimated at £26,600,000 in 1990–91.

Board of Trustees

Appointed by the Sovereign: HRH The Duke of Gloucester, GCVO. *Appointed by the Prime Minister:* The Lord Windlesham, CVO, PC (*Chairman*); Sir Matthew Farrer, KCVO; G. C. Greene, CBE; Prof. E. T. Hall, D.Phil., FSA, FBA; C. E. A. Hambro; Sir Peter Harrop, KCB; S. Keswick; Hon. Mrs. Marten, OBE; Mrs. M. Moore; Prof. G. H. Treitel, DCL., FBA, QC; S. Towneley, PH.D.; Sir Ian Trethowan; The Lord Weinstock; Prof. W. Whitfield, CBE; Sir Oliver Wright, GCMG, GCVO, DSC.
Nominated by the learned Societies: The Lord Adrian, MD, FRS (*Royal Society*); A. Jones, RA (*Royal Academy*); Sir Claus Moser, KCB, CBE (*British Academy*); vacant (*Society of Antiquaries*)
Appointed by the Trustees of the British Museum: Sir David Attenborough, CBE, FRS; Prof. Rosemary Cramp, CBE, FSA; Prof. Sir John Hale, FSA, FBA; Prof. P. Lasko, CBE, FSA, FBA; The Lord Egremont.

Salaries

Grade 2	£53,420
Grade 4	£38,284–£39,746
Grade 5	£31,276–£35,436
Grade 6	£24,075–£31,276
Grade 7	£21,095–£25,160
Head of Press and PR	£14,909–£18,864
Press and PR Officer	£11,709–£15,504

Officers

Director (G2), Sir David Wilson.
Deputy Director (G4), Ms. J. M. Rankine.
Secretary (G6), G. B. Morris.
Assistant to the Director (G7), Ms. M. L. Caygill.
Head of Public Services (G6), G. A. L. House.
Head of Design (G6), Margaret Hall, OBE.
Head of Education (G7), J. F. Reeve.
Head of Press and Public Relations, A. E. Hamilton.
Press and Public Relations Officer, Miss A. F. Dunkels.
Head of Administration (G5), C. E. I. Jones.
Head of Building and Security Services (G6), K. T. Stannard.
Head of Architectural and Building Services (G7), C. J. Walker.
Head of Finance (G7), D. E. Williams.
Head of Personnel and Office Services (G7), Miss B. A. Hughes.
Keeper of Prints and Drawings (G5), J. K. Rowlands.
Deputy Keeper (G6), A. V. Griffiths.
Assistant Keepers (G7), Ms. F. A. Carey; N. J. L. Turner; Ms. L. Stainton; M. B. Royalton-Kisch.
Keeper of Coins and Medals (G5), M. Jones.
Deputy Keeper (G6), M. J. Price.
Assistant Keepers (G7), M. G. Powell-Jones; Ms. M. M. Archibald; A. M. Burnett; B. J. Cook.
Keeper of Egyptian Antiquities (G5), W. V. Davies.
Assistant Keepers (G7), M. L. Bierbrier; A. J. Spencer.
Keeper of Western Asiatic Antiquities (G5), J. E. Curtis.
Assistant Keepers (G7), C. B. F. Walker; I. L. Finkel.
Keeper of Greek and Roman Antiquities (G5), B. F. Cook.
Deputy Keeper (G6), vacant.

Assistant Keepers (G7), Ms. S. E. C. Walker; Ms. V. Tatton-Brown; D. J. R. Williams.
Keeper of Medieval and Later Antiquities (G5), N. M. Stratford.
Deputy Keepers (G6), G. H. Tait; J. Cherry; Ms. L. E. Webster.
Assistant Keepers (G7), D. Kidd; D. Buckton; T. H. Wilson.
Keeper of Prehistoric and Romano-British Antiquities (G5), I. H. Longworth.
Deputy Keepers (G6), I. M. Stead; T. W. Potter.
Assistant Keepers (G7), I. A. Kinnes; Ms. J. M. Cook.
Keeper of Japanese Antiquities (G5), L. R. H. Smith.
Keeper of Oriental Antiquities (G5), Ms. J. M. Rawson.
Deputy Keeper (G6), J. M. Rogers.
Assistant Keepers (G7), W. Zwalf; Ms. A. S. L. Farrer; J. R. Knox.
Keeper of Ethnography (G5), M. D. McLeod.
Deputy Keeper (G6), B. Durrans.
Assistant Keepers (G7), Ms. E. M. Carmichael; Ms. S. G. Weir; Ms. D. Starzecka; J. C. H. King; J. B. Mack; N. F. Barley.
Keeper of Scientific Research (G5), Ms S. G. E. Bowman.
Principal Scientific Officers (G7), P. T. Craddock; M. J. Hughes; I. C. Freestone; A. P. Middleton; E. J. Neville; M. Cowell.
Keeper of Conservation (G5), W. A. Oddy.
Principal Scientific Officers (G7), V. D. Daniels; Ms S. M. Bradley.
Principal Conservator (G7), Ms. H. P. Lane.

THE NATURAL HISTORY MUSEUM
Cromwell Road, SW7 5BD
[071–938 9123]

Open Mon.–Sat. (except New Year's Day, Good Friday, May Day, Christmas Eve, Christmas Day and Boxing Day) 10–6, Sun. 1–6. Admission, £3.00.

The Natural History Museum originates from the natural history departments of the British Museum. During the 19th century the natural history collections grew extensively and in 1881 they were moved to South Kensington. In 1963 the Natural History Museum became completely independent with its own body of Trustees. The Zoological Museum, Tring, bequeathed by the second Lord Rothschild, has formed part of the Museum since 1938. The Geological Museum merged with the Natural History Museum in 1985 (opening times are as given above). Research workers are admitted to the libraries and study collections by Student's Ticket, applications for which should be made in writing to the Director.

The administrative expenses were estimated at £21,680,000 in 1989–90.
(For **Salaries,** *see* page 295).

Board of Trustees

Chairman, Sir Walter Bodmer, FRS.
Appointed by the Prime Minister: Sir Owen Green; Prof. J. M. Thomas, FRS; G. M. Ronson; E. N. K. Clarkson, FRSE; Mrs. J. M. D'Abo; D. H. Henderson; Prof. R. May, FRS.
Nominated by the Royal Society: Prof. Sir Andrew Huxley, OM, FRS.
Appointed by the Trustees of the British Museum (Natural History): R. J. Carter; Prof. B. K. Follett, FRS; Sir Anthony Laughton, FRS.
Director (G3), N. R. Chalmers, PH.D.
Associate Director (Scientific Development) (G5), J. F. Peake.
Secretary (G5), C. J. E. Legg.
Assistant to the Director (G7), Miss R. P. Baillon.

Marketing and Development Department
Head (G6), A. P. Harvey.

Deputy Head and Corporate Communications Manager (G7), C. E. Metcalf.
Marketing Manager (G7), Mrs. J. A. Nadolski.

Department of Zoology

Keeper (G5), C. R. Curds, D.SC.
Deputy Keepers (G6), R. J. Lincoln, Ph.D.; I. R. Bishop, OBE (acting).
Grade 6 , J. D. Taylor, Ph.D.
Grade 7, E. N. Arnold, Ph.D.; G. A. Boxhall, Ph.D.; R. A. Bray, Ph.D.; P. F. S. Cornelius, Ph.D.; J. D. George, Ph.D.; D. I. Gibson, Ph.D.; R. W. Ingle, Ph.D.; Mrs. J. Jewell, Ph.D.; N. R. Merrett; C. B. Moncrieff; P. B. Mordan, Ph.D.; H. M. Platt, Ph.D.; D. G. Reid, Ph.D.; D. M. Roberts, Ph.D.; D. Rollinson, Ph.D.; V. R. Southgate, Ph.D.

Bird Section
Park Street, Tring, Herts.
[044 282-4181]

Grade 6, I. R. Bishop, OBE.

Department of Entomology

Keeper (G5), L. A. Mound, D.SC.
Deputy Keeper (G6), I. D. Gauld, Ph.D.
Grade 6, R. L. Blackman Ph.D.; R. I. Vane-Wright.
Grade 7, P. C. Barnard, Ph.D.; B. Bolton; Mrs. J. M. Cox, Ph.D.; M. G. Fitton, Ph.D.; P. M. Hammond; D. Hollis; W. J. Knight, Ph.D.; C. H. C. Lyal, Ph.D.; J. S. Noyes, Ph.D.; G. S. Robinson, Ph.D.; K. S. O. Sattler, Ph.D.; M. J. Scobie, Ph.D.; A. J. Shelley, Ph.D.; N. E. Stork, Ph.D.; R. T. Thompson; W. G. Tremewan.
Principal Research Fellow, P. D. Ready, Ph.D.

Department of Botany

Keeper (G5), S. Blackmore, Ph.D.
Deputy Keeper (G6), D. A. Sutton, Ph.D.
Grade 6, C. J. Humphries, Ph.D.
Grade 7, A. Eddy; D. J. Galloway, Ph.D.; C. J. Jarvis, Ph.D.; A. C. Jermy; D. M. John, Ph.D.; R. J. Pankhurst; J. H. Price; I. Tittley.

Department of Palaeontology

Keeper (G5), L. R. M. Cocks, D.SC.
Deputy Keepers (G6), M. K. Howarth, Ph.D.; H. G. Owen, Ph.D.
Grade 6, C. Patterson, Ph.D.; R. A. Fortey, SC.D.; P. J. Andrews, Ph.D.
Grade 7, C. H. C. Brunton, Ph.D.; P. L. Forey, Ph.D.; A. W. Gentry, D.Phil.; R. P. S. Jefferies, Ph.D.; Mrs. A. C. Milner, Ph.D.; Miss T. I. Molleson; N. J. Morris, D.Phil.; C. P. Nuttall; J. B. Richardson, Ph.D.; B. R. Rosen, Ph.D.; A. B. Smith, Ph.D.; C. B. Stringer, Ph.D.; P. D. Taylor, Ph.D.; J. E. P. Whittaker, Ph.D.

Department of Mineralogy

Keeper (G5), P. Henderson, D.Phil.
Deputy Keeper (G6), A. L. Graham, Ph.D.
Grade 6, R. Hutchison, Ph.D.; A. R. Woolley, Ph.D.
Grade 7, A. M. Clark, Ph.D.; G. Cressey, Ph.D.; A. J. Criddle; R. F. Symes, Ph.D.

Department of Administrative Services

Head of Finance and Establishment Officer (G5), C. J. E. Legg.
Building Manager (G6), R. H. Essex.
Personnel Officer (G7), Mrs. P. H. I. Orchard.
Head of Finance and Accounts (G6), P. M. Hockwell.
Publications Officer (G6), C. A. P. Reynard.
Grade 7, B. S. Martin; N. H. Thomson.

Department of Library Services

Head (G6), R. E. R. Banks.
Deputy Head (G7), Miss P. Gilbert.

Department of Public Services

Head (G5), R. S. Miles, D.SC.
Deputy Head (G6), G. C. S. Clarke, Ph.D.
Operations Manager (G6), M. B. McBratney.
Contracts and Production Manager (G7), R. G. Nash.
Technical Services Manager (G7), J. Furlong.
Head of Exhibition and Design (G7), R. M. Bloomfield, Ph.D.

Geological Museum
Exhibition Road, South Kensington, SW7 2DE
[071-938 8932]

The Museum's three public galleries have major displays of gems and basic earth science.

MUSEUM OF LONDON
London Wall, EC2Y 5HN
[071-600 3699]

The Museum of London opened in 1976. It is based on the amalgamation of the former Guildhall Museum and London Museum. The Museum is controlled by a Board of Governors, appointed (nine each) by the Government and the Corporation of London. The exhibition illustrates the history of London from prehistoric times to the present day.
Chairman of Board of Governors, R. M. Robbins, CBE, FSA.
Director, M. G. Hebditch, FSA.

THE SCIENCE MUSEUM
South Kensington, SW7 2DD
[071-938 8000]

Open on Mon.–Sat. 10–6; Sun. 11–6. Closed on New Year's Day, Good Friday, Christmas Eve, Christmas Day and Boxing Day. Admission charge.
The Science Museum, part of the National Museum of Science & Industry, houses the national collections of science, technology, industry and medicine. The Museum began as the Science Collection of the South Kensington Museum and first opened in 1857. In 1883 it acquired the collections of the Patent Museum and in 1909 the Science Collections were transferred to the new Science Museum, leaving the Art Collections with the Victoria and Albert Museum.
Some of the Museum's commercial aircraft, agricultural machinery, and road and rail transport collections are at Wroughton, near Swindon, Wilts., and are open for public viewing on selected weekends during the summer.
The Museum is responsible for the Concorde Exhibition at the Fleet Air Arm Museum, Yeovilton.
The running expenses, including building costs, of the Museum, the Science Museum Library, the National Railway Museum and the National Museum of Photography, Film and Television are estimated at £20,634,000 for 1990–91.
(For **Salaries**, see page 295.)
Director, Dr. N. Cossons, OBE.

RESOURCE MANAGEMENT DIVISION

Assistant Director (G5), J. J. Defries.
Head of Personnel and Training (G7), C. Gosling.
Head of Finance (G7), J. Reid.
Estate Development Manager (SPTO), R. Maisey.
Building Manager (SEO), J. Bevin.

COLLECTIONS MANAGEMENT DIVISION

Assistant Director (G5), Dr. T. Wright.

Science Group

Head of Group (G5), Dr. D. A. Robinson.

Curators (G7), Dr. D. Vaughan; Dr. A. Q. Morton; C. N. Brown; Dr. J. Darius.

Life Sciences and the Environment Group

Head of Group (G5), vacant.
Curators (G7), Dr. G. M. Lawrence; P. R. Mann; A. Nahum.

Technology Group

Head of Group (G5), Dr. E. J. S. Becklake.
Curators (G7), Dr. B. P. Bowers; D. D. Swade.

Services Group

Head of Group (G6), Dr. R. F. Bud.
Curators (G7), Dr. R. Price; Dr. A. K. Newmark.

MARKETING DIVISION

Assistant Director (G5), C. M. Pemberton.
Marketing Manager (G7), M. Sullivan.

PUBLIC SERVICES DIVISION

Assistant Director (G5), T. Suthers.
Head of Operations and House Management (G6), I. M. Ball.
Head of Interpretation (G7), Dr. G. Farmelo.

RESEARCH AND INFORMATION SERVICES DIVISION
[071–938 8234]

A national library of science, specializing in the history of science and technology. Bibliographies supplied.Photocopying and microfilm service. Open Mon.–Sat. 10–5.30. Closed on Sundays and Bank Holiday weekends.
Assistant Director (G5), Prof. J. R. Durant.
Head of Library and Information Services (G6), Dr. L. D. Will.

NATIONAL RAILWAY MUSEUM
Leeman Road, York YO2 4XJ
[0904–621261]

The Museum, opened in 1975, houses the national rail transport collection. Locomotives, rolling stock and carriages are displayed to illustrate the technical, social and economic story of the development of railways in Britain. Open Mon.–Sat. 10–6, Sun. 11–6.
Head of Museum (G5), Dr. J. A. Coiley.
Deputy Head (G7), R. Shorland-Ball.

NATIONAL MUSEUM OF PHOTOGRAPHY, FILM AND TELEVISION
Prince's View, Bradford BD5 0TR
[0274–727488]

The Museum, opened in 1983, collects, conserves and displays photography, film and television materials and equipment. The Museum has the only IMAX cinema in the UK. Open Tues.–Sun. 11–6, with special exhibition galleries open to 7.30.
Head of Museum (G5), C. J. Ford.

THE VICTORIA AND ALBERT MUSEUM
South Kensington, SW7 2RL
[071–938 8500]

Open Mon.–Sat. 10–5.50, Sun. 2.30–5.50. Closed Christmas Eve, Christmas Day, Boxing Day, New Year's Day and May Day. The National Art Library is open Tues.–Sat. 10–5 (closed 1–2 Sat.) and the Print Room Tues.–Fri. 10–5, Sat. 10–1, 2–4.30. Donations are invited.

A museum of all branches of fine and applied art, the Victoria and Albert Museum descends directly

from the Museum of Manufactures, which opened in Marlborough House in 1852 after the Great Exhibition of 1851. The Museum was moved in 1857 to become part of the collective South Kensington Museum. It was renamed the Victoria and Albert Museum in 1899. The branch museum at Bethnal Green was opened in 1872 and the building is the most important surviving example of the type of glass and iron construction used by Paxton for the Great Exhibition. The Victoria and Albert Museum also administers the Wellington Museum (Apsley House), Ham House, Osterley Park, and the Theatre Museum.

Director and Secretary (G3), Mrs. E. A. L. Esteve-Coll.
Assistant Directors (G5), J. D. W. Murdoch (*Collections*); J. W. Close (*Administration*).

Ceramics Collection

Curator (G5), Dr. O. Watson.

Department of Conservation

Keeper (G5), Dr. J. Ashley-Smith.

Far Eastern Collection

Curator (G6), Miss R. Kerr.
Deputy Curator (G7), A. C. Clunas.

Furniture and Woodwork Collection

Curator (G6), S. S. Jervis (*acting*).

Indian and South East Asian Collection

Curator (G6), Dr. D. Swallow.
Deputy Curator (G7), J. S. Guy.

National Art Library

Librarian (G5), J. F. van den Wateren.
Head of Special Collections (G7), Dr. R. Watson.
Head of Public Services (G7), Mrs G. Varley.
Head of Collections Management (G7), D. Dodds.

Metalwork Collection

Curator (G6), Mrs. P. Glanville (*acting*).
Deputy Curator (G7), Miss M. Campbell; E. R. Edgecumbe.

Prints, Drawings, Photographs and Paintings Collection

Curator (G6), Miss S. B. Lambert (*acting*).
Deputy Curators (G7), L. S. Lambourne; M. Haworth-Booth; M. Snodin.

Sculpture Collection

Curator (G6), P. E. D. Williamson.
Deputy Curator (G7), M. Baker.

Textile Furnishings and Dress Collection

Curator (G6), Mrs. V. D. Mendes.
Deputy Curator (G7), Miss W. Hefford.

Presentation and Marketing

Head of Public Affairs (G5), B. Hooper.

BETHNAL GREEN MUSEUM OF CHILDHOOD
Cambridge Heath Road, Bethnal Green, E2 9PA
[081–980 3204]

Open Mon.–Thurs. and on Sat. 10–6, Sun. 2.30–6. Closed every Friday, May Day, Christmas Eve, Christmas Day, Boxing Day and New Year's Day.
Curator (G6), A. P. Burton.
Deputy Curator (G7), Dr. S. Laurence.

THEATRE MUSEUM
1E Tavistock Street, WC2E 7PA
[071–836 7891]

Open Tues.–Sun. 11–7. Closed Mon. except Bank Holidays. Admission £2.25, concessions £1.25.
Curator (G6), Ms M. Benton.

THE COMMONWEALTH INSTITUTE
Kensington High Street, W8 6NQ
[071–603 4535]

The Commonwealth Institute is a centre for information about the Commonwealth. It is funded by the British Government with contributions from other Commonwealth Governments. The Institute is controlled by a Board of Governors which includes the High Commissioners of all Commonwealth countries represented in London. The Institute has permanent exhibitions on all Commonwealth nations, plus educational resource, information and conference centres.

Open Mon.–Sat. 10–5, Sun. 2–5. Admission free. Closed Good Friday, May Day, Christmas Eve, Christmas Day, Boxing Day and New Year's Day.
Director General, J. F. Porter.
Director of Education, G. Brandt.
Chief Administrative Officer, P. Kennedy.
Head of Exhibitions and Information, J. Stevenson.

IMPERIAL WAR MUSEUM
Lambeth Road, SE1 6HZ
[071–735 8922]

Open daily 10–6. Closed Christmas Eve, Christmas Day, Boxing Day and New Year's Day. Admission, £3·00; concessions, £1·50; free day on Fridays. The Reference departments are open Mon.–Sat. 10–5, Sat. by appointment only.

The Museum, founded in 1917, illustrates and records all aspects of the two world wars and other military operations involving Britain and the Commonwealth since 1914. It was opened in its present home, formerly Bethlem Hospital or Bedlam, in 1936. The Museum also administers HMS *Belfast* in the Pool of London, Duxford Airfield near Cambridge and The Cabinet War Rooms in Westminster.

Expenses for 1990–91 are estimated at £16,075,000. (For Salaries, *see* page 295.)

Director General (G4), A. C. N. Borg, Ph.D., FSA.
Deputy Director General (G5), R. W. K. Crawford.
Secretary (G6), J. J. Chadwick.
Personnel Officer (G7), P. L. Cracknell.
Finance Officer (G7), Mrs. P. A. Whitfield.
Museum Superintendent (G7), D. A. Needham.
Senior Keeper and Keeper of Audio-Visual Records (G5), G. T. C. Coultass.
Director of Duxford Airfield (G5), E. O. Inman.
Director of HMS Belfast (G5), Capt. F. A. Collins, RN.

Keepers

Department of Museum Services (G6), C. Dowling, D.Phil.
Department of Documents (G6), R. W. A. Suddaby.
Department of Exhibits and Firearms (G6), D. J. Penn.
Department of Printed Books (G6), G. M. Bayliss, Ph.D.
Department of Art (G6), Miss A. H. Weight.
Department of Film (G6), Miss A. E. Fleming.
Department of Information Retrieval (G6), R. B. N. Smither.
Department of Photographs (G6), Miss K. J. Carmichael.
Department of Sound Records (G6), Mrs. M. A. Brooks.
Department of Marketing and Training (G6), Miss A. Godwin.
Curator of the Cabinet War Rooms (G7), E. J. Wenzel.

NATIONAL MARITIME MUSEUM
Greenwich, SE10 9NF
[081–858 4422]

Open Mon.–Sat., 10–6 (10–5 in winter); Sun. 2–6 (2–5 in winter). Closed Jan. 1, Good Friday and Dec. 24–26. Admission charge.

Reading Room open Mon.–Fri., 10–5; readers' tickets available on written application to Reader Services Section.

Established by Act of Parliament in 1934, the National Maritime Museum illustrates the maritime history of Great Britain in the widest sense, underlining the importance of the sea and its influence on the nation's power, wealth, culture, technology and institutions. The Museum is in two groups of buildings in Greenwich Park—the main buildings centred around the Queen's House (built by Inigo Jones, 1616–35) and the Old Royal Observatory (including Wren's Flamsteed House) to the south—and also includes the *Cutty Sark*. The collections include paintings, actual craft and ship models, ships' lines, prints and drawings, atlases and charts, navigational and astronomical instruments, uniforms and relics, books and MSS.
Director, R. L. Ormond.

NATIONAL ARMY MUSEUM
Royal Hospital Road, SW3 4HT
[071–730 0717]

Established by Royal Charter (1960). History of five centuries of the British Army, including the story of the Indian Army up to Independence in 1947. Open, Mon.–Sat., 10–5.30; Sun. 2–5.30. The Indian Army room at the Royal Military Academy Sandhurst, Camberley, Surrey may be viewed by appointment.
Director, I. G. Robertson.
Personal Assistant to the Director, Mrs E. Carpenter.
Assistant Directors, D. K. Smurthwaite; A. J. Guy; M. L. Nyman.
Museum Secretary, Maj. P. R. Bateman.

ROYAL AIR FORCE MUSEUM
Grahame Park Way,
Hendon, NW9 5LL
[081–205 2266]

Situated on the former airfield at Hendon, the Museum illustrates the development of aviation from before the Wright brothers to the present-day RAF. Over 60 historic aircraft are on display from the Museum's collection. The complex includes Battle of Britain and Bomber Command halls.

Open daily, 10–6. Closed Dec. 24, 25, 26, Jan. 1, Admission charge.
Director, Dr. M. A. Fopp.
Deputy Director, J. D. Freeborn.
Keepers, D. C. R. Elliott; P. G. Murton; A. C. Harold; D. F. Lawrence.

THE NATIONAL MUSEUMS AND GALLERIES ON MERSEYSIDE
William Brown Street, Liverpool L3 8EN
[051–207 0001]

The Board of Trustees of the National Museums and Galleries on Merseyside was established in 1986 to take over responsibility for the museums and galleries previously administered by Merseyside County Council. Various stores ancillary to the collections are also the responsibility of the body. It is grant-aided by the Minister for Arts.

All properties are open all year except Jan. 1, Dec. 24–26 and Good Friday. Opening times for all properties (except the Maritime Museum) are Mon.–Sat. 10–5, Sun. 2–5. Opening times for the Merseyside Maritime Museum are daily 10.30–5.30. Admission charge.
Chairman of the Board of Trustees, Sir Leslie Young, CBE.
Director, R. Foster.
Head of Central Services, P. Sudbury, Ph.D.

Keeper of Art Galleries, J. Treuherz.
Keeper of Conservation, J. France.

Liverpool Museum
William Brown Street, Liverpool

Keeper, E. Greenwood.

Merseyside Maritime Museum
Albert Dock, Liverpool
[051–709 1551]

Keeper, M. Stammers.

Museum of Labour History
County Sessions House, Islington, Liverpool

Walker Art Gallery
William Brown Street, Liverpool

Lady Lever Art Gallery
Port Sunlight Village, Bebington, Wirral

Sudley Art Gallery
Mossley Hill Road, Liverpool

(For other Museums in England, *see* Index)

THE NATIONAL MUSEUM OF WALES
(Amgueddfa Genedlaethol Cymru)
Cathays Park, Cardiff CF1 3NP
[0222–397951]

Open Tues.–Sat., 10–5. Sun. 2.30–5. Closed on
Mondays (except Bank Holidays), Christmas Eve,
Christmas Day, Boxing Day, New Year's Day and
Good Friday. Admission charge.
President, Hon. J. Davies.
Vice-President, C. R. T. Edwards.
Director, A. Wilson.
Chief of Administration, T. Arnold.
Keepers, M. G. Bassett, ph.d. (*Geology*); B. A. Thomas,
ph.d. (*Botany*); P. M. Morgan (*Zoology*); H. S.
Green, ph.d. (*Archaeology*); T. J. Stevens (*Art*).

Welsh Folk Museum
(Amgueddfa Werin Cymru)
St. Fagans, Nr. Cardiff

Open April–Oct., daily 10–5; Nov.–March, Mon.–
Sat. 10–5. Admission charge. Closed on Christmas
Eve, Christmas Day, Boxing Day, New Year's Day
and Good Friday.
Curator, J. G. Jenkins, ph.d.
Keepers, E. Scourfield, ph.d.; E. William, ph.d.; D. R.
Saer.

Roman Legionary Museum, Caerleon
Caerleon, Gwent.

Contains material found on the site of the Roman
fortress of Isca and its suburbs. Open Mon.–Sat. 10–
6, Sun. 2–6 (closes 4.30 p.m. mid–Oct. to mid-March).
Closed Dec. 24–26, Jan. 1, May Day and Good Friday.
Admission charge.

Turner House Art Gallery
Plymouth Road, Penarth, Nr. Cardiff

Open Tues.–Fri. 11–12.45 and 2–5, Sun. 2–5. Closed
Mondays, except Bank Holidays, Saturdays and on
Christmas Eve, Christmas Day, Boxing Day, New
Year's Day, Good Friday, and May Day.

Museum of the North
Llanberis, Gwynedd

A multi-media presentation of the history of Wales,
and about the electricity supply industry. Open June
to mid-Sept. 9.30–6; mid-Sept.–May, 10–5. Closed Dec.
24–26, Jan. 1 and Good Friday. Admission charge.

Welsh Slate Museum
Llanberis, Gwynedd

Open Easter–Sept. 30 daily 9.30–5.30. Admission
charge.

Segontium Roman Fort Museum
Beddgelert Road, Caernarfon, Gwynedd

Open weekdays at 9.30, Sundays at 2. Closes at 6
from May to September, at 5.30 in March, April and
October, at 4 from November to February. Closed
Christmas Eve, Christmas Day, Boxing Day, New
Year's Day and Good Friday. On the site of the fort,
the museum is in the guardianship of the Welsh
Office. Contains mostly material excavated there.

Museum of the Welsh Woollen Industry
Dre-fach Felindre, nr. Llandysul, Dyfed

It occupies part of a working mill. Open April–
Sept., Mon.–Sat. 10–5; Oct.–March, Mon.–Fri. 10–5.
Admission charge.

Welsh Industrial and Maritime Museum
Bute Street, Cardiff

Open Tues.–Sat. 10–5; Sun. 2.30–5. Closed Mon-
days, Christmas Eve, Christmas Day, Boxing Day,
New Year's Day and Good Friday. Admission charge.
Keeper, S. Owen-Jones, ph.d.

The Graham Sutherland Gallery
and Picton Castle Grounds
The Rhos, Haverfordwest
[0437–751296]

Open March 31–Sept. 30, Tues.–Sun. 10.30–12.30,
1.30–5.00. Closed Mondays (except Bank Holidays).
Admission charge.

NATIONAL MUSEUMS OF SCOTLAND
Chambers Street, Edinburgh EH1 1JF
[031–225 7534]

Open, Mon.–Sat., 10–5 and Sun., 2–5. Closed Dec.
25 and 26 and Jan. 1 and 2.

The National Museums of Scotland include the
Royal Museum of Scotland, Chambers Street, and the
Royal Museum of Scotland, Queen Street in Edin-
burgh, as well as the Scottish United Services
Museum at Edinburgh Castle, the Scottish Agricul-
tural Museum at Ingliston, the Museum of Flight at
East Fortune, Shambellie House Museum of Costume
near Dumfries and Biggar Gasworks Museum. The
Museums are governed by a board of Trustees.

Director, R. G. W. Anderson, d.phil.
Museums Administrator, I. Hooper.
Keeper, Department of History & Applied Art (G5),
Miss D. Idiens.
Keeper, Department of Archaeology, D. V. Clarke,
d.phil.
Keeper, Department of Geology (G5), W. D. I. Rolfe
ph.d.
Keeper, Department of Natural History (G5), M. Shaw,
d.phil.
*Keeper, Department of Science, Technology and Work-
ing Life (G5)*, D. J. Bryden.
Head, Department of Public Affairs (G6), Ms S. Brock,
ph.d.
Head, Department of Museum Services (G6), S. R.
Elson.
Keeper, Scottish United Services Museum (G6), S. C.
Wood.

NATIONAL AUDIT OFFICE
157–197 Buckingham Palace Road, SW1W 9SP
[071–798 7000]

The National Audit Office came into existence
under the National Audit Act 1983, to replace and

continue the work of the former Exchequer and Audit Department. The Act reinforced the Office's total financial and operational independence from the Government and brought its head, the Comptroller and Auditor General, into a closer relationship with Parliament as an officer of the House of Commons.

The National Audit Office provides independent information, advice and assurance to Parliament and the public about all aspects of the financial operations of government departments and many other bodies receiving public funds. This it does by examining and certifying the accounts of these organizations; and by regularly publishing reports to Parliament on the results of its value for money investigations of the economy, efficiency and effectiveness with which public resources have been used. The National Audit Office is also the auditor by agreement of the accounts of certain international and other organizations. In addition, the office authorizes the issue of public funds to Government departments.

Comptroller and Auditor General, J. B. Bourn, CB.
  Private Secretary, M. Sinclair.
Deputy Comptroller and Auditor General, R. N. Le Marechal.
Assistant Auditor Generals, D. A. Dewar; M. J. Goodson; J. A. Higgins; P. J. C. Keemer; L. H. Hughes.
Directors, M. R. J. Paul; P. J. Beck; J. A. Davies; I. R. W. Hargest; R. W. Locke; P. O'Keefe; A. G. Brown; T. J. Lovett; G. J. S. Frith; C. L. Press; B. D. Baker; C. K. Beauchamp; M. C. Pfleger; R. M. Bennett; B. Hogg; G. G. Jones; R. J. McCourt; J. Marshall; A. R. Murray; J. Parsons; J. M. Pearce; A. G. Roberts; R. A. Skeen; R. E. Spurgeon.
Deputy Directors, E. J. Weeks; C. J. Day; D. C. Page; J. E. Smith; W. L. Ewing; G. J. McKeown; M. V. Pettet; A. Cunningham; K. Maclean; M. L. Daynes; D. R. Corsby; R. W. Tycer; J. J. Jones; D. J. Woodward; A. Burchell; J. B. Cavanagh; J. Darling; P. R. Duncombe; R. J. Eales; D. A. Ferguson; N. Gale; T. Griffiths; K. Hawkswell; J. Hirst; Mrs. H. Jackson; Miss J. Lawler; J. S. McEwen; Miss C. Mawhood; R. Parker; R. A. Pocock; M. J. Reeves; N. Sloan; J. O. A. Thompson; P. G. Woodward.

NATIONAL CONSUMER COUNCIL
20 Grosvenor Gardens, SW1W 0DH
[071–730 3469]

The National Consumer Council was set up by the Government in 1975 to give an independent voice to consumers in the UK. Its job is to advocate the consumer interest to decision-makers in business, industry, the public utilities, the professions, and central and local government. It does this through a combination of research and campaigning. It is funded by a grant-in-aid from the Department of Trade and Industry.
Chairman, Lady Wilcox.
Director, M. Healy.

NATIONAL DEBT OFFICE
see **National Investment and Loans Office.**

NATIONAL ECONOMIC DEVELOPMENT COUNCIL
Millbank Tower, Millbank, SW1P 4QX
[071–217 4000]

The National Economic Development Council brings together Government, management and unions to tackle issues vital to jobs and economic growth, by identifying obstacles to economic development and promoting change.

Council
Government Members, The Chancellor of the Exchequer (*Chairman*); the Secretaries of State for Education and Science, Employment, Energy, Environment, and Trade and Industry.
Management Members, J. M. M. Banham; Sir Brian Corby; Adm. Sir Raymond Lygo, KCB; D. A. G. Monk; T. J. O'Connor; Sir Thomas Risk.
Trade Union Members, R. Bickerstaffe; Miss B. Dean; J. Edmonds; W. Jordan, R. Todd; N. Willis.
Independent Members, Sir James Ackers; E. A. Hammond, OBE; The Rt. Hon. Robin Leigh-Pemberton; Sir Bryan Nicholson; Dame Rachel Waterhouse, DBE; G. B. Wolfson.

Office
Director-General, W. A. Eltis.
Secretary to the Council, M. Couchman.
Industrial Director, D. Fraser.
Economic Director, K. Mayhew.

NATIONAL GALLERIES
See **Art Galleries**

NATIONAL HERITAGE MEMORIAL FUND
10 St James's Street, SW1A 1EF
[071–930 0963]

The National Heritage Memorial Fund was established in 1980 as an independent body, and is intended as a memorial to those who have died for the UK. The Fund is empowered, by the National Heritage Act 1980, to give financial assistance towards the cost of acquiring, maintaining or preserving land, buildings, works of art and other objects of outstanding interest which are also of importance to the national heritage. The Fund is administered by up to eleven Trustees, appointed by the Prime Minister.

The Fund's major sources of money are the Department of the Environment and the Office of Arts and Libraries, each of which gives annual grants. In its first ten years, the Fund spent £120 million in carrying out its responsibilities.

Trustees
The Lord Charteris of Amisfield (*Chairman*); The Marquess of Anglesey; Sir Nicholas Goodison; Prof. F. G. T. Holliday; Sir Martin Jacomb; C. Kinahan; Sir Oliver Millar; The Lord Morris of Castle Morris; Sir Norman Macfarlane; M. McCrum; Cdr. L. M. M. Saunders Watson.
Director, Miss G. Nayler.

NATIONAL INSURANCE JOINT AUTHORITY
The Adelphi, 1–11 John Adam Street, WC2N 6HT
[071–962 8000]

The Authority's function is to co-ordinate the operation of social security legislation in Great Britain and Northern Ireland, including the necessary financial adjustments between the two National Insurance Funds.
Members, The Secretary of State for Social Security; the Head of the Department of Health and Social Services for Northern Ireland.
Secretary, Mrs. D. M. Joannou.

NATIONAL INVESTMENT AND LOANS OFFICE
Royex House, Aldermanbury Square, EC2V 7LR
[071–606 7321]

The National Investment and Loans Office was set up on April 1, 1980 by merging the staffs of the

National Debt Office and the Public Works Loan Board. The Department provides staff and services for the National Debt Commissioners and the Public Works Loan Commissioners.
Director, I. H. Peattie.
Establishment Officer, A. G. Ladd.

National Debt Office

Comptroller General, I. H. Peattie.

Public Works Loan Board

Chairman, R. J. Dent.
Deputy Chairman, Miss F. M. Cook.
Other Commissioners, Miss V. J. Di Palma, OBE; G. Ross Russell; P. Brackfield; D. H. Adams; R. A. Chapman; R. Emmott; B. Fieldhouse; A. Morton; I. C. Wilson, OBE; G. G. Williams.
Secretary, I. H. Peattie.
Assistant Secretary, D. L. Hammond.

NATIONAL RADIOLOGICAL PROTECTION BOARD
Chilton, Didcot, Oxon. OX11 0RQ
[0235–831600]

The National Radiological Protection Board is an independent statutory body created by the Radiological Protection Act 1970. The Government's purpose was to establish a national point of authoritative reference in radiological protection.
Chairman, Sir Richard Southwood, FRS.
Director, Dr. R. H. Clarke.

NATIONAL RIVERS AUTHORITY
Rivers House, 30–34 Albert Embankment, SE1 7TL
[071–820 0101]

The National Rivers Authority (NRA) is an independent body set up under the Water Act 1989 to take over the regulatory and other river functions of the former water authorities in England and Wales. Its responsibilities include monitoring the quality of water and controlling pollution, and the management of water resources, flood defence and fisheries.

The NRA has a board of 15 members, two of whom are appointed by the Minister of Agriculture, Fisheries and Food, one by the Secretary of State for Wales, and the rest by the Secretary of State for the Environment.
Chairman, The Lord Crickhowell, PC.
Chief Executive, Dr. J. Bowman, CBE.
Chief Scientist, Dr. J. Pentreath.
Technical Director, Dr. C. Swinnerton.
Finance Director, P. Partridge.
Personnel Director, P. Humphreys.
Corporate Affairs Director, Ms. M. Evans.

DEPARTMENT FOR NATIONAL SAVINGS
Charles House, 375 Kensington High Street, W14 8SD
[071–605 9300]

The Department for National Savings was established as a Government Department in 1969. The Department is responsible for the administration of a wide range of schemes for personal savers. (For details of schemes, *see* **National Savings** section). (For **Salaries**, *see* page 295)

Director of Savings (G2), J. A. Patterson, CB.
Deputy Director (G3), C. D. Butler.
Establishment Officer (G5), D. S. Speedie.
Finance Officer (G5), C. Ward.
Controllers (G5), Mrs. S. Cullum (*Marketing & Information*); R. S. Watts; J. Stamp; E. B. Senior; P. N. S. Hickman Robertson.

Senior Principals (G6), D. W. Kellaway; I. T. Standen; R. H. Lee; I. Forsyth; A. S. McGill; D. H. Monaghan; M. A. Nicholls.
Principals (G7), A. G. Muir; W. J. Herd; D. K. Paterson; A. J. V. Cummings; Dr. A. Fort; W. J. Ferrier; H. Johnson; J. W. Davison; D. Newton; A. B. Wood; P. Finnie; C. E. Funk; I. Jordinson; A. Brown; T. Threlfall; B. Paley; A. T. Stevenson; H. Webster; J. Wheatley; T. J. F. McMahon; C. McVey; R. A. Nichol; N. Thistlethwaite; J. B. Dunphy; J. C. Foreman; D. Wilson; P. B. Robinson; G. V. Wise; A. S. Lamond; D. Jeffrey; R. H. Mitchell; J. Bolam; R. W. Day; I. S. Campbell; C. Dodsworth; J. C. Foreman; R. R. Hesketh; J. C. Lunn; R. J. McLelland; M. J. Tan.

NATIONAL TRAINING TASK FORCE
214 Gray's Inn Road, WC1X 8HL
[071–278 0363]

The National Training Task Force was established by the Government to advise the Secretary of State for Employment and to assist him in carrying out his training responsibilities throughout Great Britain.
Chairman, Sir Brian Wolfson.
Members, R. Dawe; Sir Peter Bowness; L. Spencer; Sir Eric Pountain; Sir Melvyn Rosser; Sir Peter Thompson; T. Cleaver; Mrs. P. Leith; M. Rowarth; Ms. S. Mirman; Sir David Nickson; Sir James Ackers; W. Jordan; A. Sheppard; A. Collier.

NATURAL ENVIRONMENT RESEARCH COUNCIL
Polaris House, North Star Avenue, Swindon SN2 1EU
[0793–411500]

The Natural Environment Research Council was established in 1965, to encourage, plan and conduct research in the physical and biological sciences which relate to man's natural environment and its resources.

The Council carries out research and training through its own institutes and grant-aided institutes, and by grants, fellowships and post-graduate awards to universities and other institutions of higher education.
Chairman, Prof. J. Knill, Ph.D., D.Sc.
Secretary, Dr. Eileen Buttle.
Director of Earth Sciences, Prof. J. C. Briden, Ph.D.
Director of Terrestrial and Fresh Water Sciences, P. B. Tinker, D.Sc., Ph.D.
Director of Marine and Atmospheric Sciences, J. D. Woods, Ph.D.

CENTRAL SERVICES

NERC Scientific Services
Polaris House, North Star Avenue, Swindon, Wilts. SN2 1EU
[0793–411000]

Director, B. J. Hinde.

Research Vessel Services
No. 1 Dock, Barry, S. Glamorgan
[0446–737451]

Head, Dr. C. Fay.

NERC Computer Service
Holbrook House, Station Road, Swindon, Wilts. SN1 1DE
[0793–411000]

Director, H. J. Down.

For research institutes and units of the Natural Environment Council, *see* Index.

NATURE CONSERVANCY COUNCIL
Northminster House, Peterborough PE1 1UA
[0733-40345]

The Nature Conservancy Council establishes, maintains and manages National Nature Reserves, advises generally on nature conservation, gives advice to the Government on nature conservation policies and on how other policies may affect nature conservation, and supports, commissions and undertakes relevant research.

Under the Environmental Protection Bill currently before Parliament, the Council is to be divided into three separate bodies, with responsibility for England, Scotland and Wales respectively.
Chairman, Sir William Wilkinson.
Director General, T. R. Hornsby.
Chief Scientist, Dr. D. R. Langslow.
Director, Policy Planning and Services, Dr. F. B. O'Connor.
Director, Organizational Planning, Miss C. E. M. Wood.
Country Headquarters:
England: Northminster House, Peterborough PE1 1UA.—*Director*, E. Idle.
Scotland: 12 Hope Terrace, Edinburgh EH9 2AS.—*Director*, Dr. J. Francis.
Wales: Plas Penrhos, Penrhos Road, Bangor, Gwynedd LL57 2LQ.—*Director*, Dr. T. Pritchard.

NORTHERN IRELAND OFFICE

The Northern Ireland Office is the UK government department in which the Secretary of State for Northern Ireland has overall responsibility for the government of Northern Ireland. The Secretary of State is directly responsibile for constitutional developments, law and order, security and electoral matters. Under the Northern Ireland Act 1974, the Northern Ireland departments are also subject to the direction and control of the Secretary of State during direct rule.

Whitehall, SW1A 2AZ
[071-210 3000]
Secretary of State for Northern Ireland, THE RT. HON. PETER BROOKE, MP.
Minister of State, THE RT. HON. JOHN COPE, MP.
Parliamentary Under Secretaries of State, RICHARD NEEDHAM, MP; DR. BRIAN MAWHINNEY, MP; THE LORD SKELMERSDALE.
Permanent Under Secretary of State, J. A. Chilcot, CB.
Second Permanent Under Secretary of State, Head of the NICS, Sir Kenneth Bloomfield, KCB.

Northern Ireland Civil Service
Stormont Castle, Belfast BT4 3TT
[0232-63011]

Department of Agriculture for Northern Ireland
Dundonald House, Upper Newtownards Road, Belfast BT4 3SB
[0232-650111]

Department of Economic Development Northern Ireland
Netherleigh, Massey Avenue, Belfast BT4 2JP
[0232-63244]

Department of Education for Northern Ireland
Rathgael House, Balloo Road, Bangor, Co. Down BT19 2PR
[0247-270077]

Department of the Environment for Northern Ireland
Parliament Buildings, Stormont, Belfast BT4 3SS
[0232-63210]

Department of Finance and Personnel
Parliament Buildings, Stormont, Belfast BT4 3SW
[0232-63210]

Department of Health and Social Services Northern Ireland
Dundonald House, Upper Newtownards Road, Belfast BT4 3SF
[0232-650111]

OMBUDSMAN, *see* LOCAL COMMISSIONERS, and PARLIAMENTARY COMMISSIONER
(For non-statutory Ombudsmen, *see* Index)

ORDNANCE SURVEY
Romsey Road, Maybush, Southampton SO9 4DH
[0703-792000]

The Ordnance Survey is the national mapping agency for Britain. It became an executive agency in May 1990 and reports to the Secretary of State for the Environment.

The Ordnance Survey has military origins. It produces over 220,000 large scale maps of the country at three basic scales. These are 1:1,250 (50 inches to 1 mile) for urban areas; 1:2,500 (25 inches to 1 mile) for rural areas; and 1:10,000 (6 inches to 1 mile) for mountain and moorland. Additionally, Ordnance Survey produces a range of small scale maps and other products for general use.
Director-General, P. McMaster.
Directors:
Surveys and Production, A. S. Macdonald.
Marketing, Planning and Development, J. Leonard.
Establishments and Finance, K. Nolan.
Heads of Functions:
Production, D. Davies.
Topographic Surveys, P. Wesley.
Marketing, D. Toft.
Research and Development, M. Sowton.
Finance, J. Evenett.
Establishments, I. Lock.
Information and Computer Service, B. W. Nanson.
Overseas Surveys, E. Gilbert.

OVERSEAS DEVELOPMENT ADMINISTRATION
Eland House, Stag Place, SW1E 5DH
[071-273 3000]
Abercrombie House, Eaglesham Road, East Kilbride, Glasgow G75 8EA
[03552-41199]

The Overseas Development Administration deals with British development assistance to overseas countries. This includes both capital aid on concessional terms and technical assistance (mainly in the form of specialist staff abroad and training facilities in the United Kingdom), whether provided directly to developing countries or through the various multilateral aid organizations, including the United Nations and its specialized agencies.
(For **Salaries**, *see* page 295)

Minister for Overseas Development, THE RT. HON. LYNDA CHALKER, MP.
Private Secretary (G7), E. C. N. Taylor.
Parliamentary Private Secretary, D. Nicholson, MP.

Permanent Secretary (G1A), T. P. Lankester.
Private Secretary, Ms. S. A. Howes.
Deputy Secretary (G2), R. M. Ainscow, CB.
Under Secretaries (G3), N. B. Hudson; J. A. L. Faint; B. R. Ireton; J. V. Kerby; R. G. Manning; A. J. Bennett; J. B. Wilmshurst.

Economic and Social Division

Head of the Economic Service (G3), J. B. Wilmshurst.
Senior Economic Advisers (G5), J. C. H. Morris; G. P. Sandersley; A. G. Coverdale; B. P. Thomson; R. J. Moberly.
Economic Advisers (G7), P. J. Ackroyd; P. D. Balacs; Dr. F. C. Clift; J. G. Clarke; P. J. Dearden; D. Donaldson; K. E. Gubbins; Dr. G. Haley; E. Hawthorn; P. G. Hill; J. L. Hoy; W. Kingsmill; P. J. A. Landymore; M. Lewis; A. Moon; P. L. Owen; J. N. Stevens; Ms R. Turner.
Chief Statistician (G5), R. M. Allen.
Statisticians (G7), A. B. Williams; Miss M. O'Connor; J. R. B. King; P. J. Crook; Mrs. M. E. Frosztega.
Principal Finance Management and Administration Adviser (G5), K. L. Sparkhall.
Senior Finance Management and Administration Adviser (G6), E. A. Gill.
Senior Finance and Management Advisor (G6), D. W. Heffer.
Senior Social Development Advisers (G6), E. Hanley; Dr. R. J. Eyben.
Social Development Adviser (G7), Ms P. Holden.

Information Department

Head of Information Dept. (G5), J. C. Machin.
Principal Information Officer (G7), R. W. Fosker.

Development Divisions

Heads of Divisions (G5):
Caribbean (Bridgetown), M. G. Bawden.
East Africa (Nairobi), D. Sands Smith.
Pacific (Suva), Mrs. P. M. Wilkinson.
South-East Asia (Bangkok), M. J. Dinham.
Southern Africa (Lilongwe), Ms. S. E. Unsworth.
Assistant Secretaries (G5), Miss A. M. Archbold; G. A. Beattie; P. D. M. Freeman; W. Hobman; Mrs. B. M. Kelly; M. C. McCulloch; J. C. Machin; V. J. McLean; Dr. D. Nabarro; R. G. Pettitt; M. A. Power; C. P. Raleigh; D. L. Stanton; G. M. Stegmann; D. F. Turner; M. Wickstead; R. J. Wilson; R. W. Wootton.
Senior Principals (G6), D. G. Bell; J. H. S. Chard; F. Crampsey; B. W. Hammond; S. Ray; D. Richards; G. A. Williams.
Principals (G7), J. D. Aitken; R. Allen; J. A. Anning; G. A. Armstrong; C. B. Austin; Ms S. Bailey; D. W. Baker; D. G. Bell; H. Britton; W. A. Brownlie; P. J. Burton; R. T. Calvert; P. H. Charters; D. J. Church; T. F. G. Connor; G. Crabtree; Ms N. E. Cund; A. D. Davis; P. Dean; J. R. Drummond; J. R. Gilbert; M. A. Hammond; Ms. V. M. Harris; B. Hefferon; Ms. P. J. Hilton; M. I. Holland; N. Hoult; W. Jardine; Mrs. J. Laurence; D. Lawless; G. G. Leader; J. Lingham; M. A. B. Lowcock; G. H. Malley; P. S. Mason; C. A. Metcalf; J. C. H. Millett; J. D. Moye; G. A. Mustard; C. Myhill; P. T. Perris; B. G. Peskett; G. M. Porter; Mrs. J. Radice; S. Ray; S. R. J. Robbins; P. T. Rose; C. R. Roth; Dr. P. W. K. Rundell; Ms P. Schofield; J. M. Scoular; S. J. Sharpe; R. J. Smith; Miss R. B. Stevenson; M. J. Sexton; I. F. Stickels; I. D. Stuart; A. J. Sutherland; C. M. Taylor; E. C. N. Taylor; N. Thomas; B. A. Thorpe; R. G. Toulmin; N. A. Tranter; D. Trotter; Miss M. H. Vowles; C. W. Warren; C. J. White; R. S. White; D. M. Whitecross; J. M. Winter; A. K. C. Wood; M. S. S. Wyatt.

Advisory and Specialist Staff

Chief Education Adviser (G5), Dr. R. O. Iredale.
Senior Education Advisers (G6), M. D. Francis; Ms. M. Harrison; M. E. Seath; Dr. D. G. Swift.
Chief Engineering Adviser (G5), T. D. Pike.
Senior Engineering Advisers (G6), J. N. Bulman; A. G. Colley; C. I. Ellis; D. Gillett; B. Dolton; P. H. Hilton; H. B. Jackson; D. Pagan; M. F. Sergeant.
Engineering Advisers (G7), R. J. Cadwallader; P. W. D. H. Roberts; A. Coulthart; A. Barker; A. Smallwood.
Senior Renewable Energy and Research Adviser (G6), Dr. J. L. D. Harrison.
Senior Electrical and Mechanical Engineering Adviser (G6), R. P. Jones.
Senior Architectural and Physical Planning Advisers (G6), M. W. Parkes; W. M. Housego-Woolgar.
Senior Medical Adviser (G6), Dr. P. Key, OBE.
Principal Nursing and Health Services Adviser, Miss M. Pollock.
Nursing and Health Services Adviser, Miss J. Isard.
Chief Natural Resources Adviser (G3), A. J. Bennett.
Deputy Chief Natural Resources and Principal Agricultural Adviser (G5), J. M. Scott.
Deputy Chief Natural Resources Adviser (G5), Dr. J. C. Davies, OBE (Research).
Senior Natural Resources Advisers (G6), J. R. F. Hansell; A. J. Tainsh; R. L. Waddell; J. B. Warren; M. J. Wilson.
Senior Agricultural Advisers (G6), M. F. Watson; D. J. Salmon.
Agricultural Advisers (G7), Dr. H. Potter; D. A. Trotman.
Animal Health Advisers (G6), G. G. Freeland; Dr. A. D. Irvin.
Fisheries Advisers (G6), Dr. J. Tarbit; R. W. Beales.
Forestry Advisers (G6), W. J. Howard; R. Jenkin.
Senior Procurement Adviser (G6), R. C. Morgan.

Natural Resources Institute
Central Avenue, Chatham Maritime,
Chatham, Kent ME4 4TB
[0634–880088]

Director (G5), G. A. Beattie.

OFFICE OF THE PARLIAMENTARY COMMISSIONER AND HEALTH SERVICE COMMISSIONER
Church House, Great Smith Street, SW1P 3BW
[071–276 3000]

The Parliamentary Commissioner for Administration is responsible for investigating complaints referred to him by Members of the House of Commons from members of the public who claim to have sustained injustice in consequence of maladministration in connection with administrative action taken by or on behalf of Government departments and certain non-departmental public bodies. Certain types of action by Government departments or bodies are excluded from investigation. Actions taken by other public bodies (such as local authorities, the police, the Post Office and nationalized industries) are outside the Commissioner's scope.

The Health Service Commissioners for England, for Scotland and for Wales are responsible for investigating complaints against National Health Service authorities that are not dealt with by those authorities to the satisfaction of the complainant. Complaints can be referred direct by the member of the public who claims to have sustained injustice or hardship in consequence of the failure in a service provided by a relevant body; failure of that body to provide a service or in consequence of any other action by that body. Certain types of action are excluded, in particular, action taken solely in consequence of the exercise of clinical judgment. The three offices are presently held by the Parliamentary Commissioner.

Parliamentary Commissioner and Health Service Commissioner, W. K. Reid, CB............£72,000

Deputy Parliamentary Commissioner (G3), J. E. Avery.

Deputy Health Service Commissioner, R. A. Oswald.

Directors (G5), K. H. Green; Mrs. J. M. Fowler; M. D. Randall; J. C. Bateman; M. A. Johnson; M. P. Cornwell-Kelly.

Principals (G7), P. J. Belsham; G. M. Keil; Mrs. C. Bentley; Miss D. M. Pace; T. J. Corkett; R. A. Bourley; D. S. Burn; A. C. Beer (*Establishment Officer*); Mrs. E. A. Cooper; S. J. Drummond; J. D. Jarvis; D. Hall; B. P. Jones; D. G. Tempest.

PARLIAMENTARY COUNSEL
36 Whitehall, SW1A 2AY
[071–210 6633]

Parliamentary Counsel draft all Government Bills (i.e. primary legislation) except common form ones and those relating exclusively to Scotland. They also advise on all aspects of parliamentary procedure in connection with such Bills and draft Government amendments to them as well as any motions (including financial resolutions) necessary to secure their introduction into, and passage through, Parliament.

First Counsel, Sir Henry de Waal, KCB, QC . . . £76,320
Second Counsel, P. Graham, CB, QC £63,390
Counsel, J. D. M. Rennie, CB; J. C. Jenkins, CB; J. S. Mason, CB; Miss S. P. Burns, CB; D. W. Saunders, CB; E. G. Caldwell, CB; E. G. Bowman; G. B. Sellers; E. R. Sutherland . . . . *up to* £53,420

PAROLE BOARD
Abell House, John Islip Street, SW1P 4LH
[071–217 5705]

The Board was constituted under section 59 of the Criminal Justice Act, 1967.

The function of the Board is to advise the Secretary of State for the Home Department with respect to: Release on licence under section 60 (i) or 61 and recall under section 62 of the Criminal Justice Act, 1967 of persons whose cases have been referred to the Board by the Secretary of State; the conditions of such licences, and the variation and cancellation of such conditions; and any other matter so referred which is connected with release on licence or recall of persons to whom section 60 or 61 of the Act applies.

Chairman, The Viscount Colville of Culross, QC.
Vice-Chairman, The Hon. Mr. Justice Ognall.
Secretary, T. J. Wilkie.

PATENT OFFICE
State House, 66–71 High Holborn,
WC1R 4TP
[071–831 2525]

The Patent Office is an executive agency of the Department of Trade and Industry. The duties of the Patent Office consist in the administration of the Patent Acts, the Registered Designs Act and the Trade Marks Act and in dealing with questions relating to the Copyright Designs and Patents Act 1988. The Search and Advisory Service will carry out commercial searches through patent information. In 1989 the Office granted 10,138 patents and registered 8,945 designs and 22,374 trade and service marks.

Comptroller-General (G3), P. R. S. Hartnack.
Assistant Comptroller Industrial Property & Copyright Dept. (G4), V. Tarnofsky.
Assistant Comptroller Patents & Designs (G4), T. W. Sage.

Assistant Registrar, Trade Marks (G4), J. M. Myall.
Head of Marketing and Information Services (Supt. Examiner), E. F. Blake.
Head of Administration and Resources (G5), P. Bunn.
Head of ADP Unit (G6), G. Bennett.

PAYMASTER GENERAL'S OFFICE
HM Treasury, Parliament Street, SW1P 3AG
[071–270 4350]
Sutherland House, Russell Way, Crawley, West
Sussex RH10 1UH
[0293–560999]

The Paymaster General's Office was formed by the consolidation in 1835 of various separate pay departments then existing, some of which dated back at least to the Restoration of 1660. Its function is that of paying agent for Government departments, other than the Revenue departments. Most of its payments are made through banks, to whose accounts the necessary transfers are made at the Bank of England. The payment of over one million public service pensions is an important feature of its work.

Paymaster General, RICHARD RYDER, OBE, MP.
Assistant Paymaster General (G5), L. A. Andrews.
Senior Principals (G6), K. Sullens; G. Thomas.
Principals (G7), D. R. Alexander; Mrs. D. F. Ambrose; T. R. George; R. G. Hollands; J. A. Payne; C. A. Ulph; M. D. West.

POLICE COMPLAINTS AUTHORITY
10 Great George Street, SW1P 3AB
[071–273 6450]

The Police Complaints Authority was established under the Police and Criminal Evidence Act 1984 to introduce a further independent element into the procedure for dealing with complaints by members of the public against police officers in England and Wales. The Authority has powers to supervise the investigation of certain categories of serious complaints and certain statutory functions in relation to the disciplinary aspects of complaints.

Chairman, His Hon. Judge Petre.
Deputy Chairman (Discipline), Brig. J. Pownall.
Deputy Chairman (Investigations), Rt. Hon. R. Moyle.
Members, Air Vice-Marshal D. Clark; V. Clements; J. Crawford; B. A. Gillman; G. V. Marsh; B. V. Moore; P. W. Moorhouse; K. Singh; Capt. N. Taylor; Mrs. R. Vickers; Mrs. R. Wolff.

POLITICAL HONOURS SCRUTINY
COMMITTEE
Cabinet Office, 53 Parliament Street, SW1A 2NG
[071–210 3000]

The function of the Political Honours Scrutiny Committee is set out in an Order in Council dated May 31, 1979. The Prime Minister submits certain particulars to the Committee about persons proposed to be recommended for honour for their political services. The Committee, after such enquiry as they think fit, report to the Prime Minister whether, so far as they believe, the persons whose names are submitted to them are fit and proper persons to be recommended.

Chairman, The Lord Shackleton, KG, OBE, PC, FRS.
Members, The Lord Grimond, TD, PC; The Lord Pym, MC, PC.
Secretary, J. H. Thompson, CB.

THE POLYTECHNICS AND COLLEGES
FUNDING COUNCIL
Metropolis House, 22 Percy Street, W1P 9FF
[071–637 1132]

The Polytechnics and Colleges Funding Council (PCFC) was established as a result of the Education

Act 1988 to oversee the sector of higher education formerly controlled by local authorities. The Council consists of 15 members appointed by the Secretary of State for Education and Science and meets five times a year.

The PCFC distributes over £1,000 million of public funds in England each year to all the polytechnics, the largest colleges of higher education, and a number of specialist colleges. It also funds certain higher education courses in further education colleges. The PCFC sector comprises 84 institutions serving nearly 360,000 students. The PCFC also advises the Secretary of State on the funding of higher education. For this it has established Programme Advisory Groups to review provision in nine subject areas. It also establishes *ad hoc* committees of enquiry on particular issues.

Chairman, Sir Ronald Dearing.
Chief Executive, W. H. Stubbs.
Director of Finance, N. Brown.
Secretary, Dr. R. Brown.

OFFICE OF POPULATION CENSUSES AND SURVEYS
St. Catherine's House, 10 Kingsway,
WC2B 6JP
[071–242 0262]

The Office of Population Censuses and Surveys was created by a merger in May 1970 of the General Register Office and the Government Social Survey Department. The Registrar General controls the local registration service in England and Wales in the exercise of its registration and marriage duties. Copies of the original registrations of births, stillbirths, marriages and deaths are kept in London. A register of adopted children is held at Titchfield. Central indexes are compiled annually and certified copies of entries may be obtained on payment of certain fees. Since 1841 the Registrar General has been responsible for taking the census of population. He also prepares and publishes a wide range of statistics and appropriate commentary relating to population, fertility, births, still-births, marriages, deaths and cause of death and infectious diseases. The Registrar General is also responsible for conducting surveys on a range of subjects for other Government departments. He maintains, at Southport, the National Health Service Central Register.

Hours of access to Public Search Room, St Catherine's House, Mon.–Fri., 8.30 a.m.–4.30 p.m.
Director and Registrar General (G2), P. J. Wormald, CB.
Deputy Director (G3), E. J. Thompson.
Chief Medical Statistician (G3), A. J. Fox, ph.D.
Grade 5, R. Barnes; J. Craig; J. V. Ribbins *(Deputy Registrar General)*; I. K. G. Arnold; J. A. Rowntree; B. H. Mahon; B. S. Smith.
Senior Statisticians (Medical), J. S. A. Ashley; A. G. McCormick; A. J. Swerdlow.
Grade 6, B. S. T. Alcock; E. Barton; Mrs. M. Bone; R. J. Butcher; A. M. Clark; J. Denton; Mrs. K. H. Dunnell; W. Jenkins; I. B. Knight; D. L. Pearce; R. K. Thomas; R. McLeod.
Grade 7, R. I. Armitage; F. L. Ashwood; Mrs. P. E. Astbury; Ms J. Atkinson; N. E. Auckland; R. A. P. Bailey; N. Bateson; R. J. Beacham; D. E. Birch; Mrs. B. J. Botting; M. J. Bradley; J. A. Brown; T. B. Bryson; L. Bulusu; D. Capron; R. J. Carpenter; J. Cloyne; Mrs. J. Cooper; C. J. Denham; T. L. F. Devis; J. M. Dixie; Mrs. J. C. Dobbs; Miss C. M. Ellis; Ms. E. M. Goddard; I. Golds; Mrs. H. A. Green; Mrs. J. R. Gregory; P. C. Gregory; J. Haskey; A. J. H. Hay; P. J. Heady; Mrs. J. Humby; A. F. Jones; B. G. Little; Miss C. S. J. Lloyd; D. Lockyer; W. F. Loomes; Mrs. S. M. McCartney;

Miss E. M. McCrossan; Mrs. I. MacDonald-Davies; Miss M. Machin; A. J. Manners; Mrs. J. Martin; R. Massingham; Ms. J. Matheson; B. W. Meakings; I. D. Mills; D. J. Mountjoy; R. M. Nicholls; A. Parr *(Chief Inspector of Registration)*; M. Quinn; Mrs. I. Rauta; R. U. Redpath; Miss J. M. R. Rosenbaum; T. A. Russell; J. A. Salvetti; C. Savage; Ms J. M. Sharp; D. Stewart; Mrs. L. M. Street; A. W. Tester; Miss J. Todd; Mrs. M. J. Waggett; Miss S. Wallace *(Press Officer)*; P. H. White.

PORT OF LONDON AUTHORITY
International House, World Trade Centre,
E1 9UN
[071–481 1954]

The Port of London Authority is a public trust constituted under the Port of London Act 1968 (as amended) and a Harbour Revision Order of 1975. The Board comprises a Chairman and up to ten non-executive members appointed by the Secretary of State for Transport, and up to six executive members appointed by the Board.

The Port of London Authority is the governing body for the Port of London, covering the tidal portion of the River Thames from Teddington to the seaward limit. The enclosed dock at Tilbury is wholly-owned by the PLA. Some cargo-handling facilities along the river are owned by the PLA.

Chairman, Sir Brian Kellett.
Vice-Chairman, R.Crawford, CBE.
Chief Executive, River, D. Jeffery.
Chief Executive, Property, J. C. Jenkinson, MVO.
Chief Executive Tilbury, J. S. McNab.
Secretary, G. E. Ennals.

THE POST OFFICE
30 St. James's Square, SW1Y 4PY
[071–490 2888]

Crown services for the carriage of Government despatches were set up about 1516. The conveyance of public correspondence began in 1635 and the mail service was made a Parliamentary responsibility with the setting up of a Post Office in 1657. Telegraphs came under the Post Office control in 1870 and the Post Office Telephone Service began in 1880. The National Girobank service of the Post Office began in 1968. The Post Office ceased to be a Government department on October 1, 1969 and responsibility for the running of the postal, telecommunications, and giro and remittance services was transferred to a public authority called the Post Office. The 1981 British Telecommunications Act separated the functions of the Post Office, making it solely responsible for postal services and Girobank (privatized in 1990).

The Chairman and members of the Post Office Board are appointed by the Secretary of State but responsibility for the running of the Post Office as a whole rests with the Board in its corporate capacity.

Financial Results

	1988–89 £m.	1989–90 £m.
Post Office Group		
Turnover	3,914·8	4,459·4
Trading profit before tax	170·1	116·4
Royal Mail and Parcel force		
Turnover	3,125·2	3,615·1
Trading profit before tax and interest on long-term loans	97·4	32·1

Post Office Counters
Turnover................... 798·4 875·1
Trading profit before tax and
interest on long-term loans . 46·1 21·7

Post Office Board

Chairman, Sir Bryan Nicholson.
Deputy Chairman, K. M. Young, CBE.
Members, W. Cockburn, CBE, TD (*Managing Director, Royal Mail*); N. Nelson (*Managing Director, Parcelforce*); A. J. Roberts (*Managing Director, Counters*); R. Close (*Corporate Finance and Planning*).
Secretary, Miss M. MacDonald.

PRIVY COUNCIL OFFICE
Whitehall, SW1A 2AT
[071-270 3000]

The Office is responsible for the arrangements leading to the making of all Royal Proclamations and Orders in Council; for certain formalities connected with Ministerial changes; for considering applications for the grant (or amendment) of Royal Charters; the scrutiny and approval of by-laws and statutes of Chartered Bodies; for the appointment of High Sheriffs and many Crown and Privy Council appointments to governing bodies.

Lord President of the Council (and Leader of the House of Commons), THE RT. HON. SIR GEOFFREY HOWE, QC, MP.
Private Secretary, T. Sutton.
Minister of State, THE RT. HON. DAVID MELLOR, MP.
Clerk of the Council, G. I. de Deney, CVO £45,350
Deputy Clerk of the Council, R. P. Bulling £33,026
Senior Clerk, Miss J. Fairbairn £20,323

PUBLIC HEALTH LABORATORY SERVICE
61 Colindale Avenue, NW9 5DF
[071-200 1295]

The Public Health Laboratory Service comprises 52 regional or area laboratories distributed through England and Wales, the Central Public Health Laboratory and the Communicable Disease Surveillance Centre at Colindale, and the Centre for Applied Microbiology and Research, Porton Down. The PHLS gives a diagnostic microbiological service to hospitals, and provides reference facilities that are available nationally. It collates information on the incidence of infection, and when necessary it institutes special enquiries into outbreaks and the epidemiology of infectious disease. It also undertakes bacteriological surveillance of the quality of food and water for local authorities and others. The PHLS is often called upon to advise central and local government and the hospital service on many aspects of infectious disease. It maintains close contact with veterinary organizations in areas of mutual interest, and collaborates with the World Health Organization and with national laboratory and epidemiological services overseas.

The Board

Chairman, Dr. M. P. W. Godfrey, CBE, FRCP.
Members, D. F. R. Crofton; E. Doorbar; A. E. Eames; Dr. J. M. Forsythe; J. Godfrey; A. Graham-Dixon, QC; Prof. P. R. Grob, MD; Dr. E. L. Harris, CB, FRCP; Prof. Dame Rosalinde Hurley, DBE, MD; Dr H. H. John; Prof. M. D. Lilly; Dr. M. J. Painter; Prof. J. R. Pattison; Prof. C. S. Peckham; Prof. I. Phillips; J. J. Skehel, Ph.D., FRS.
Staff Assessors, J. P. Alexander; R. Gross; Dr. A. T. Willis.

Head Office
Colindale Avenue, NW9 5DF

Director, Dr. J. W. G. Smith.
Deputy Directors, Dr. E. M. Cooke; Dr. C. Roberts.
Secretary, K. M. Saunders.
Deputy Secretary, J. M. Harker.

Central Public Health Laboratory
Colindale Avenue, NW9 5HT

Director, Dr. M. C. Timbury.
Division of Enteric Pathogens, B. Rowe, TD.
Division of Hospital Infection, B. D. Cookson.
Division of Microbiological Reagents and Quality Control, A. G. Taylor, Ph.D.
Food Hygiene Laboratory, R. J. Gilbert, Ph.D.
Mycological Reference Laboratory, Prof. D. W. R. Mackenzie, Ph.D.
National Collection of Type Cultures, L. R. Hill, D.SC.
Virus Reference Laboratory, P. P. Mortimer, MD.

Communicable Diseases Surveillance Centre
Colindale Avenue, NW9 5EQ

Director, Dr. C. L. R. Bartlett.

Centre for Applied Microbiology and Research
Porton Down, Salisbury,
Wilts, SP4 0JG

Director, Dr. P. M. Sutton.
Director of Pathology Division, Dr. A. Baskerville.
Director of Biologics Division, Prof. J. Melling, Ph.D.
Director of Biotechnology Division, Prof. A. Atkinson, Ph.D.

Other Special Laboratories and Units

Anaerobe Reference Unit, Public Health Laboratory, Luton.—A. T. Willis, MD.
Gonococcus Reference Unit, Public Health Laboratory, Bristol.—A. E. Jephcott, MD.
Malaria Reference Laboratory, London School of Hygiene and Tropical Medicine, WC1—Prof. D. J. Bradley, DM; Prof. W. Peters, MD, D.SC.
Mycobacterium Reference Unit, Public Health Laboratory, Cardiff.—P. A. Jenkins, Ph.D.

Regional Laboratories

Birmingham, I. D. Farrell, MD; *Bristol,* A. E. Jephcott, MD; *Cambridge,* A. M. Rampling (*acting*); *Cardiff,* C. D. Ribeiro (*acting*); *Leeds,* R. N. Peel; *Liverpool,* J. H. Pennington, MD; *Manchester,* D. M. Jones, MD; *Newcastle,* N. F. Lightson; *Oxford,* J. B. Selkon, TD; *Portsmouth,* O. A. Okubadejo, MD; *Sheffield,* P. Norman.

Area Laboratories

Ashford, C. Dulake; *Bath,* D. G. White; *Brighton,* B. T. Thom; *Carlisle,* M. A. Knowles; *Carmarthen,* H. D. S. Morgan; *Chelmsford,* R. E. Tettmar, D.Path.; *Chester,* P. Hunter; *Coventry,* P. R. Mortimer, MD; *Dorchester,* P. Burden; *Epsom,* S. A. Chambers; *Exeter,* J. G. Cruickshank; *Gloucester,* K. A. V. Cartwright; *Guildford,* Prof. R. Y. Cartwright; *Hereford,* I. R. Ferguson; *Hull,* S. L. Mawer; *Ipswich,* P. H. Jones; *Leicester,* C. J. Mitchell; *Lincoln,* E. R. Youngs; LONDON: *Central Middlesex Hospital,* D. A. McSwiggan; *Dulwich,* A. H. C. Uttley, Ph.D.; *Tooting,* R. Holliman (*acting*); *Whipps Cross,* B. Chattopadhyay, MD; *Luton,* A. T. Willis, MD; *Middlesbrough,* E. McKay-Ferguson, MD; *Norwich,* P. M. B. White; *Nottingham,* M. J. Lewis, MD; *Peterborough,* R. S. Jobanputra, MD; *Plymouth,* P. J. Wilkinson; *Poole,*

W. L. Hooper; *Preston*, D. N. Hutchinson; *Reading*, J. V. Dadswell; *Rhyl*, D. N. Looker; *Salisbury*, S. Patrick; *Shrewsbury*, C. A. Morris, MD; *Southampton*, J. A. Lowes; *Stoke-on-Trent*, J. Gray; *Swansea*, D. H. M. Joynson; *Taunton*, J. V. S. Pether; *Truro*, W. A. Telfer Brunton; *Watford*, M. T. Moulsdale; *Wolverhampton*, R. G. Thompson.

REGISTRAR OF PUBLIC LENDING RIGHT
Bayheath House, Prince Regent Street,
Stockton-on-Tees, TS18 1DF
[0642–604699]

Under the Public Lending Right system, in operation since January 1983, payment is made from public funds to authors whose books are lent out from public libraries. Payment is made once a year (in February) and the amount each author receives is proportionate to the number of times (established from a sample) that each registered book was lent out during the previous year.

The Registrar of PLR, who is appointed by the Minister for the Arts, compiles the register of authors and books. Only living authors resident in the UK or West Germany are eligible to apply. (The term 'author' covers writers, illustrators, translators, and some editors/compilers.)

A payment of 1·39 pence was made in 1989–90 for each estimated loan of a registered book, up to a top limit of £6,000 for the books of any one registered author; the money for loans above this level is used to augment the remaining PLR payments.

In February 1990, the sum of £3,063,000 was made available for distribution to 14,200 registered authors and assignees as the annual payment of PLR.

The PLR Advisory Committee advises the Minister for the Arts and the Registrar of Public Lending Right. Its members are appointed by the Minister.
Chairman of Advisory Committee, D. H. Whitaker.
Registrar, J. W. Sumsion.

PUBLIC RECORD OFFICE
See Record Offices

PUBLIC TRUST OFFICE
Stewart House, 24 Kingsway, WC2B 6JX
[071–269 7000]

The Public Trustee is a trust Corporation created to undertake the business of executorship and trusteeship; he can act as executor or administrator of the estate of a deceased person, or as trustee of a will or settlement. The Public Trustee is also responsible for the performance of all the administrative, but not the judicial, tasks required of the Court of Protection under Part VII of the Mental Health Act, 1983, relating to the management and administration of the property and affairs of persons suffering from mental disorder. The Public Trustee also acts as Receiver when so directed by the Court, usually where there is no other person willing or able to so act.

The Accountant General of the Supreme Court, through the Court Funds Office, is responsible for the investment and accounting of funds in court for persons under a disability, monies in Court subject to litigation and statutory deposits.

The Court Funds Office is at 22 Kingsway, WC2B 6LE (071-936 6000).
Public Trustee and Accountant General, J. A. Boland.
Assistant Public Trustee (Administration) and Deputy Accountant General, P. J. Farmer.
Assistant Public Trustee (Legal), H. N. Mather.
Investment Manager, H. Stevenson.
Chief Property Adviser, A. Nightingale.

Client Services Sector

Head, E. J. Dober.
Receivership Division, R. A. Cunningham, TD.
Protection Division, I. S. Price.

Internal Services Sector

Head, I. J. MacBean.
Court Funds Office, F. J. Eddy.

PUBLIC WORKS LOAN BOARD
see **National Investment and Loans Office.**

COMMISSION FOR RACIAL EQUALITY
Elliot House, 10–12 Allington Street, SW1E 5EH
[071–828 7022]

Established on June 13, 1977, under the Race Relations Act 1976, to work towards elimination of discrimination and promote equality of opportunity and good relations between different racial groups generally.
Chairman, M. Day, OBE.
Deputy Chairmen, J. Abrams, OBE; R. Singh.
Members, L. Crawford; Mrs. S. Sadeque; M. Skillicorn; K. R. Whitesides; Q. S. Anisuddin; Prof. B. Hepple; Mrs. E. Nam; D. A. C. Lambert; Dr. D. Ray; R. Kent.
Chief Executive, Dr. P. Sanders.

THE RADIO AUTHORITY
70 Brompton Road, SW3 1EY
[071-584 7011]

The Radio Authority will be established by the Broadcasting Bill currently before Parliament as one of the two successor bodies to the Independent Broadcasting Authority. The function of the Authority is to assign frequencies, to grant licences to provide independent radio services, and to regulate the output of the services in accordance with published codes dealing with standards for programming, advertising and sponsorship.

Members of the Authority are appointed by the Secretary of State for the Home Department. Senior executive staff are appointed by the Authority.
Chairman, The Lord Chalfont OBE, MC, PC.
Deputy Chairman, Mrs. J. McIvor.
Members, Mrs. M. Corrigan; J. Grant; R. Hooper; R. Sondhi.
Chief Executive, P. Baldwin.
Deputy Chief Executive and Head of Regulation, P. Brown.
Head of Development, D. Vick.
Head of Finance, Ms M. Turner.
Head of Engineering, M. Thomas.
Secretary to the Authority, J. Norrington.

RECORD OFFICES, ETC.

ADVISORY COUNCIL ON PUBLIC RECORDS
Public Record Office, Chancery Lane, WC2A 1LR
[081–878 3666]

Council members are appointed by the Lord Chancellor, under the Public Records Act 1958, to advise him on matters concerning public records in general and, in particular, on those aspects of the work of the Public Record Office which affect members of the public who make use of the facilities provided by the Public Record Office. The Council meets quarterly and produces an annual report which is published alongside the Report of the Keeper of Public Records as a House of Commons sessional paper.

Chairman, The Master of the Rolls.

Members, Prof. B. W. E. Alford; Miss S. Beesley; A. C. Carlile, QC, MP; Rt. Hon. Sir Frank Cooper, GCB, CMG; Miss V. Cromwell; T. A. G. Davis, MP; Prof. R. B. Dobson; J. S. W. Gibson; M. A. Latham, MP; Prof. Shula Marks; Sir George Moseley, KCB; Prof. H. Roseveare; Prof. W. Saunders; Prof. R. Skidelsky; D. G. Vaisey.

Assessors, B. Cousins, CBE; M. Roper.

Secretary, Dr. M. R. Foster.

THE PUBLIC RECORD OFFICE
Chancery Lane, WC2A 1LR
[081-876 3444]
Ruskin Avenue, Kew,
Richmond, Surrey TW9 4DU
[081-876 3444]

The Office, originally established in 1838 under the Master of the Rolls, was placed by the Public Records Act 1958 under the direction of the Lord Chancellor. He appoints a Keeper of Public Records, whose duties are to co-ordinate and supervise the selection of records of government departments and the English Law Courts for permanent preservation, to safeguard the records under his charge, and to make them available to the public.

The Office holds records of central government dating from *Domesday Book* (1086) to the present. Under the Public Records Act 1967 they are normally open to inspection when 30 years old, and are then available, without charge, in the reading rooms, Mon.–Fri., 9.30–5. The museum at Chancery Lane is open Mon.–Fri., 10–5.

Keeper of Public Records (G3), M. Roper.

Deputy Keeper (G5), C. D. Chalmers.

Records Administration Officer (G5), Dr. N. G. Cox.

Establishment Officer (G7), J. A. Keene.

Principal Assistant Keepers (G6), Miss G. L. Beech; N. E. Evans; Dr. A. A. H. Knightbridge; Mrs. A. E. Morton; Mrs. A. N. Nicol; Dr. J. B. Post; Dr. D. L. Thomas; J. L. Walford.

Assistant Keepers (G7), Mrs. M. K. Banton; Dr. A. S. Bevan; Dr. T. M. Chalmers; Miss M. M. Condon; C. R. H. Cooper; Miss A. Crawford; Dr. D. Crook; Dr. H. Forde; Dr. M. R. Foster; Dr. E. M. Hallam Smith; Ms. S. M. F. Healy; Dr. E. J. Higgs; Mrs. H. E. Jones; A. H. Lawes; A. J. McDonald; J. Murray; T. R. Padfield; Dr. N. A. M. Rodger; Miss J. A. V. Rose.

Head, Repository and Reprographic Services (G7), K. J. Smith.

Principal Inspecting Officer (G7), A. W. H. Medlicott.

Inspecting Officers, D. Barlow; R. A. Blake; Miss C. J. Dimmer; J. S. Harley; F. McCall; Mrs. E. J. Baldwin; C. J. Edwards; Mrs. H. R. Saw; Miss L. R. Hoare .... £15,786–£20,152

Head of Information Technology Unit (G7), Miss J. K. Lawlor.

HOUSE OF LORDS RECORD OFFICE
House of Lords, SW1A 0PW
[071-219 3074]

Since 1497, the records of Parliament have been kept within the Palace of Westminster. They are in the custody of the Clerk of the Parliaments. In 1946 a record department was established to supervise their preservation and their production to students. The Search Room of this office is open to the public Mon.–Fri., 9.30–5.

The records preserved number some 3,000,000 documents, and include Acts of Parliament from 1497, Journals of the House of Lords from 1510, Minutes and Committee proceedings from 1610, and Papers laid before Parliament from 1531. Amongst the records are the Petition of Right, the Death Warrant of Charles I, the Declaration of Breda, and the Bill of Rights. The House of Lords Record Office also has charge of the Journals of the House of Commons (from 1547), and other surviving records of the Commons (from 1572), which include plans and annexed documents relating to Private Bill legislation from 1818. Among other documents are the records of the Lord Great Chamberlain, the political papers of certain members of the two Houses (including the papers of Lloyd George, Bonar Law and other statesmen previously preserved in the Beaverbrook Library), and documents relating to Parliament acquired on behalf of the nation. All the manuscripts and other records are preserved in the Victoria Tower of the Houses of Parliament. A permanent exhibition was established in the Royal Gallery in 1979.

Clerk of the Records, H. S. Cobb, FSA.
£33,026–£43,046

Deputy Clerk of the Records, D. J. Johnson, FSA.
£25,825–£38,568

Assistant Clerks of the Records, J. C. Morgan (*Sound Archives*); S. K. Ellison .... £22,848–£31,751

ROYAL COMMISSION ON HISTORICAL MANUSCRIPTS
Quality House, Quality Court, Chancery Lane, WC2A 1HP
[071-242 1198]

The Commission was set up by Royal Warrant in 1869 to enquire and report on collections of papers of value for the study of history in private hands. In 1959 a new warrant enlarged these terms of reference to include all historical records, wherever situated, outside the Public Records and gave it added responsibilities, as a central co-ordinating body, to promote, assist and advise on their proper preservation and storage. The Commission has published over 200 volumes of reports. It holds a further 33,000 unpublished reports and computerized indices in the National Register of Archives, available for consultation in its search room. It also administers the Manorial and Tithe Documents Rules on behalf of the Master of the Rolls.

Chairman, G. E. Aylmer, FBA.

Commissioners, The Lord Kenyon, CBE, FSA; The Lord Fletcher, PC, FSA; The Lord Blake, FBA; J. P. W. Ehrman, FBA, FSA; Prof. S. F. C. Milsom, FBA; Sir John Habakkuk, FBA; P. T. Cormack, FSA, MP; Prof. G. W. S. Barrow, FBA; Mrs. V. L. Pearl, FSA; The Marquess of Anglesey; Prof. Owen Chadwick, OM, KBE, FBA; D. G. Vaisey, FSA; The Viscount of Arbuthnott, CBE, DSC; The Lord Camoys; The Lord Egremont and Leconfield; Mrs. J. Thirsk, FBA.

Secretary, B. S. Smith, FSA.

SCOTTISH RECORD OFFICE
HM General Register House, Edinburgh EH1 3YY
[031-556 6585]

The history of the national archives of Scotland can be traced back to the 13th century. The present headquarters of the Scottish Record Office, the General Register House, was founded in 1774. Here are preserved the administrative records of pre-Union Scotland, the registers of central and local courts of law, the public registers of property rights and legal documents, and many collections of local and church records and private archives. Certain groups of records, mainly the modern records of government departments in Scotland, the Scottish railway records, the plans collection, and private archives of an industrial or commercial nature are preserved in the branch repository at the West

Register House in Charlotte Square. The Search Rooms in both buildings open Mon.–Fri., 9–4.45. A permanent exhibition at the West Register House and changing exhibitions at the General Register House are open to the public on weekdays, 10–4. The National Register of Archives (Scotland), which is a branch of the Scottish Record Office, is based in the West Register House.
Keeper of the Records of Scotland, P. M. Cadell.

CORPORATION OF LONDON RECORDS OFFICE
Guildhall, EC2P 2EJ
[071–260 1251]

Contains the municipal archives of the City of London which are regarded as the most complete collection of ancient municipal records in existence. Includes charters of William the Conqueror, Henry II, and later Kings and Queens to 1957; ancient custumals: Liber Horn, Dunthorne, Custumarum, Ordinacionum, Memorandorum and Albus, Liber de Antiquis Legibus, and collections of Statutes; continuous series of judicial rolls and books from 1252 and Council minutes from 1275; records of the Old Bailey and Guildhall Sessions from 1603, and financial records from the 16th century, together with the records of London Bridge from the 12th century and numerous subsidiary series and miscellanea of historical interest. A Guide was published in 1951. Readers' Room open Mon.–Fri., 9.30–4.45.
Keeper of the City Records, The Town Clerk.
City Archivist, J. R. Sewell.
Deputy City Archivist, Mrs. J. M. Bankes.

RED DEER COMMISSION
Knowsley, 82 Fairfield Road, Inverness IV3 5LH
[0463–231751]

The Red Deer Commission has the general functions of furthering the conservation and control of red and sika deer in Scotland and of keeping under review all matters relating to roe deer. It has the statutory duty, with powers, to prevent damage to agriculture and forestry by red and sika deer. The Commission also has the power to advise in the interest of conservation any owner of land, on questions relating to the carrying of stocks of red deer, sika deer and roe deer on that land and to carry out research into matters of scientific importance relating to deer.
Chairman, I. K. Mackenzie, OBE (*part time*) .. £15,173
Secretary, A. Rinning .... £15,156–£19,348
Senior Field Officer, L. A. H. K. Stewart, MBE.

REVIEW BODIES

The secretariat for these bodies is provided by the Office of Manpower Economics (see page 340).

ARMED FORCES PAY

The Review Body on Armed Forces Pay was appointed in September 1971 to advise the Prime Minister on the pay and allowances of members of Naval, Military and Air Forces of the Crown and of any women's service administered by the Defence Council.
Chairman, Sir Peter Cazalet.
Members, P. Ball; G. M. Hourston; D. P. M. Hudson; Mrs. J. Hughes; R. Sanderson, OBE; Gen. Sir Richard Trant, KCB; Prof. J. White, CBE.

DOCTORS' AND DENTISTS' REMUNERATION

The Review Body on Doctors' and Dentists' Remuneration was appointed in July 1971 to advise the Prime Minister on the remuneration of doctors and dentists taking any part in the National Health Service.
Chairman, Sir Trevor Holdsworth.
Members, Mrs. J. d'Arbo; D. G. Boyd; D. F. Johns, MBE; Prof. G. F. Thomason, CBE; J. K. Warburton, CBE.

NURSING STAFF, MIDWIVES, HEALTH VISITORS AND PROFESSIONS ALLIED TO MEDICINE

The Review Body for nursing staff, midwives, health visitors and professions allied to medicine was set up in July 1983 to advise the Prime Minister on the remuneration of nursing staff, midwives and health visitors employed in the National Health Service; and physiotherapists, radiographers, remedial gymnasts, occupational therapists, orthoptists, chiropodists, dietitians and related grades employed in the National Health Service.
Chairman, M. Bett, CBE.
Deputy Chairman, Sir John Herbecq, KCB.
Members, Mrs. M. Cameron; J. Hildreth; Miss A. Mackie, OBE; I. H. Phillipps; Mrs. R. Pickvance; Prof. G. F. Thomason, CBE; Miss D. Whittingham.

TOP SALARIES

The Review Body on Top Salaries was appointed in May 1971 to advise the Prime Minister on the remuneration of the higher judiciary and other judicial appointments, senior civil servants, and senior officers of the armed forces. The Review Body has also been asked on a number of occasions to advise on the remuneration of Members of Parliament and of Ministers and on the level of parliamentary allowances.
Chairman, Sir David Nickson, KBE.
Members, Sir Terence Beckett, KBE; Ms. L. Botting; Sir Peter Cazalet; Sir Cecil Clothier, KCB; A. G. Gormley; H. S. Pigott; J. J. R. Pope, OBE; Sir Anthony Wilson.

ROYAL BOTANIC GARDEN EDINBURGH
Inverleith Row, Edinburgh EH3 5LR
[031–552 7171]

The Royal Botanic Garden Edinburgh, which originated as the Physic Garden established in 1670 beside the Palace of Holyroodhouse, became the direct responsibility of the Commissioners of Her Majesty's Works and Public Buildings (later the Department of Public Works) in 1889, transferring to the Department of Agriculture and Fisheries for Scotland in 1969. Since 1986, RBG Edinburgh has been administered by a Board of Trustees established under the National Heritage (Scotland) Act 1985.

RBG Edinburgh is an international centre for scientific research on plant diversity, maintaining collections of living plants and reference resources, including a herbarium of some 2 million specimens of preserved plants. Other statutory functions of RBG Edinburgh include provision of education and information on botany and horticulture, and the provision of public access to the living plant collections.

The Garden moved to its present site at Inverleith, Edinburgh in 1821. There are also three specialist gardens: Younger Botanic Garden, Benmore, near Dunoon, Argyllshire; Logan Botanic Garden, near Stranraer, Wigtownshire; Dawyck Botanic Garden, near Stobo, Peeblesshire. Public opening hours: RBG

Edinburgh – daily (except Dec. 25, Jan 1) 9 to sunset
(1 hour earlier in summer) (Sun. 11 to sunset);
specialist gardens – April–Oct. 10–6.

Chairman of the Board of Trustees, Sir Peter Hutchison, Bt.
Regius Keeper, Dr. D. S. Ingram.
Assistant Keeper, Dr. D. J. Mann.

ROYAL BOTANIC GARDENS KEW
Richmond, Surrey TW9 3AB
[081-940 1171]
Wakehurst Place, Ardingly, near Haywards Heath,
West Sussex RH17 6TN
[0444–892701]

The Royal Botanic Gardens (RBG), Kew were
founded in 1759 by HRH Princess Augusta. In 1841,
they became a public institution; in 1847 the Museums
of Economic Botany were opened, and in 1852 the
Herbarium and Library were established. The Jodrell
Laboratory opened in 1876. In 1965, the garden at
Wakehurst Place was acquired; it is owned by the
National Trust and managed by RBG Kew. From
1903 to 1984, RBG Kew was part of the Ministry of
Agriculture, Fisheries and Food. Under the National
Heritage Act 1983, a Board of Trustees was set up to
administer the Gardens which in 1984 became an
independent body supported by a grant-in-aid.

The functions of RBG Kew are to carry out
research into plant sciences, to disseminate knowledge about plants and to provide the public with the
opportunity to gain knowledge and enjoyment from
the Gardens' collections. There are extensive national reference collections of living and preserved
plants and a comprehensive library and archive. The
main emphasis is on tropical and subtropical plants.

Open daily, except Christmas Day and New Year's
Day, from 9.30 a.m. The closing hour varies from 4
p.m. in mid-winter to 6.30 p.m. on week-days, and 8
p.m. on Sundays and Bank Holidays, in mid-summer.
Admission (1990), £1. Museums open 9.30 a.m.; Glasshouses, 9.30–4.30 (weekdays); to 5.30 p.m. (Sundays).
No dogs except guide-dogs for the blind.

BOARD OF TRUSTEES

Chairman, Hon. J. D. Eccles, CBE.
Members, Sir Leslie Fowden, FRS; Sir David Attenborough, CBE, FRS; Prof. W. G. Chaloner, FRS; Prof.
E. C. D. Cocking, FRS; Sir Philip M. Dowson, CBE;
Prof. G. E. Fogg, CBE; R. A. E. Herbert; Mrs. A.
Lennox-Boyd; P. J. D. Marshall; Prof. Elizabeth B.
Robson, PH.D.; Cdr. L. M. Saunders Watson.
Director, Dr. G. T. Prance.

ROYAL COMMISSION FOR THE
EXHIBITION OF 1851
Sherfield Building,
Imperial College of Science and Technology,
SW7 2AZ
[071-225 6110]

Incorporated by Supplemental Charter as a permanent Commission after winding up the affairs of
the Great Exhibition of 1851. It has for its object the
promotion of scientific and artistic education by
means of funds derived from its Kensington estate,
purchased with the surplus left over from the Great
Exhibition.
President, HRH The Duke of Edinburgh, KG, KT, PC.
Chairman, Board of Management, Sir Denis Rooke,
CBE, FRS.
Secretary to Commissioners, M. C. Neale, CB.

THE ROYAL MINT
Llantrisant, nr. Pontyclun,
Mid-Glamorgan CF7 8YT
[0443–222111]

The Royal Mint became an executive agency in
April 1990, the Minister to whom the Mint is
responsible being the Chancellor of the Exchequer.

The prime responsibility of the Royal Mint is the
provision of United Kingdom coinage, but it actively
competes in world markets for a share of the available
circulating coin business and, on average, two-thirds
of the 15,000 tonnes of coins produced annually are
exported to over 100 countries. The Mint also
manufactures special proof and uncirculated quailty
coins in gold, silver and other metals; military and
civil decorations and medals; commemorative and
prize medals; and royal and official seals.
Master Worker and Warden, The Chancellor of the
Exchequer (ex officio).
Deputy Master and Comptroller, A. D. Garrett.

ROYAL NATIONAL THEATRE BOARD
South Bank, SE1 9PX
[071–928 2033]

Chairman, The Lady Soames, DBE.
Members, R. Baird; The Lord Chorley; R. Clutton;
M. Codron, CBE; Dame Judi Dench, DBE; J. Hannam,
MP; Sarah Hogg; S. Lipton; Sonia Melchett; R. M.
Mills; The Lord Mishcon; Sir Derek Mitchell, KCB,
CVO; Sir Michael Palliser, GCMG; Lois Sieff, OBE; J.
Whitney; Sir Peter Parker, LVO.
Secretary, A. Blackstock.

RURAL DEVELOPMENT COMMISSION
11 Cowley Street, SW1P 3NA
[071-276 6969]

The Rural Development Commission was formed
in 1988 by the merger of the Development Commission
for Rural England and the Council for Small Industries in Rural Areas. It is a statutory body funded by
Government grant-in-aid which undertakes to alleviate economic and social problems in rural areas and
advises the Government on related rural matters in
England. It concentrates its resources in Rural
Development Areas but some assistance is available
both within and outside the RDAs.
Chairman, The Lord Shuttleworth.
Other Commissioners, Mrs. P. Batty Shaw, CBE; R.
Best, OBE; Prof. M. D. I. Chisholm; D. J. C.
Davenport, CBE; M. Schreiber; R. Thompson; A.
Leavett; J. L. Thompson; G. P. Gray; M. B. Ferris;
J. M. Galsworthy.
Chief Executive, R. Butt.

SCIENCE AND ENGINEERING
RESEARCH COUNCIL
Polaris House, North Star Avenue,
Swindon, Wilts. SN2 1ET
[0793–411000]

The Science and Engineering Research Council
(SERC) is one of five research councils funded
through the Department of Education and Science.
Its purpose is to develop the natural and social
sciences, including engineering, to maintain a fundamental capacity of research and scholarship and to
support relevant postgraduate education. SERC's
role is to encourage and support research and
advanced training in UK universities and polytechnics in all the basic areas of science and engineering.
Chairman, Sir Mark Richmond, FRS.
Members, Prof. T. L. Blundell; Prof. P. G. Burke; D.
A. Davis; Prof. A. Donnachie; G. N. Fairtlough;
Prof. B. E. F. Fender; C. A. P. Foxell; Dr. G. R.

Higginson; Prof. C. J. Humphreys; Dr. C. Jordan; Dr. A. Ledwith; D. Nash; Prof. E. R. Oxburgh; Prof. J. T. Stuart; Prof. J. M. Thomas; Prof. A. Wolfendale.

SCOTTISH OFFICE

The Secretary of State for Scotland is responsible in Scotland for a wide range of statutory functions which in England and Wales are the responsibility of a number of departmental ministers. He also works closely with ministers in charge of Great Britain departments on topics of special significance to Scotland within their fields of responsibility. His statutory functions are administered by five main departments: the Department of Agriculture and Fisheries for Scotland, the Scottish Development Department, the Scottish Education Department, the Scottish Home and Health Department, and the Industry Department for Scotland. These Departments (plus Central Services embracing the Solicitor's Office, the Scottish Information Office, Establishment, Liaison and Finance Divisions) are collectively known as the Scottish Office. In addition there are a number of other Scottish Departments for which the Secretary of State has some degree of responsibility; these include the Scottish Courts Administration, the Department of the Registrar General for Scotland (the General Register Office), the Scottish Record Office and the Department of the Registers of Scotland. The Secretary of State also bears Ministerial responsibility for the activities in Scotland of several statutory bodies whose functions extend throughout Great Britain such as the Training Agency and the Forestry Commission.
(For **Salaries**, *see* page 295)

Dover House, Whitehall, SW1A 2AU
[071–270 3000]

Secretary of State for Scotland, THE RT. HON. MALCOLM RIFKIND, QC, MP.
Private Secretary (G5), J. D. Gallagher
Assistant Private Secretaries, Miss U. M. Jamieson; L. Wright.
Ministers of State, IAN LANG, MP (*Industry and Education*); THE LORD SANDERSON OF BOWDEN (*Agriculture and Fisheries, Forestry, the Highlands and Islands, Tourism, and Rural Policy Co-ordination*).
Private Secretaries, K. A. L. Thomson (*I. Lang*); Dr. P. J. Rycroft (*Lord Sanderson of Bowden*).
Parliamentary Under Secretaries of State, LORD JAMES DOUGLAS–HAMILTON, MP; MICHAEL FORSYTH, MP*
Private Secretaries, Miss J. F. Waterman (*Lord James Douglas–Hamilton*); D. B. Binnie (*M. Forsyth*)*.
Parliamentary Clerk, I. D. Stage.
Permanent Under Secretary of State (G1), R. R. Hillhouse.
Private Secretary, A. I. Wilson.
Liaison Staff;
Assistant Secretary (G5), E. W. Ferguson.

St. Andrew's House,
Edinburgh EH1 3DG
[031–556 8400]

MANAGEMENT GROUP SUPPORT STAFF

Principal (G7), G. S. Pearson.

---

*Based at New St. Andrew's House.

CENTRAL SERVICES

Deputy Secretary (*Central Services*) (G2), I. D. Penman, CB.

Establishment Division
16 Waterloo Place Edinburgh, EH1 3DN
[031–556 8400]

Principal Establishment Officer (G3), J. Hamill.
Assistant Secretaries (G5), D. J. Chalmers; R. S. B. Gordon; D. Stevenson.
Senior Principals (G6), A. B. Fairweather, OBE, TD; I. C. Henderson; A. Stephenson; R. Tait.

Directorate of Information Technology
Broomhouse Drive, Edinburgh EH11 3XD
[031–556 8400]
Computer Services
Director (G5), J. Duffy.
Deputy Director (G6), I. W. Goodwin.

Telecommunications
St. Andrew's House, Edinburgh EH1 3DE
[031–556 8400]

Director (G6), A. F. Harrison.

Finance Division
New St. Andrew's House, Edinburgh EH1 3SX
[031–556 8400]
Finance Group
Principal Finance Officer (G3), H. H. Mills.
Assistant Secretaries (G5), T. A. Cameron; J. S. Graham; L. Mosco; B. Naylor; A. J. Rushworth; W. T. Tait.

Local Government Finance Group
Assistant Secretaries (G5), C. M. Baxter; K. W. McKay.

Solicitor's Office
(*For the Scottish Departments and certain UK services, including HM Treasury, in Scotland.*)

Solicitor (G2), R. Brodie, CB.
Deputy Solicitor (G3), N. W. Boe.
Divisional Solicitors (G5), J. B. Allan; †K. F. Barclay; G. C. Duke; R. M. Henderson; G. Jackson; J. L. Jamieson; †Mrs. L. A. Lilliker; H. F. Macdiarmid; T. G. Walters.
†Seconded to Scottish Law Commission

Scottish Information Office
(*For the Scottish Departments and certain UK services*)

Director (G5), C. F. Corbett.
Deputy Director (G6), D. C. M. Beveridge, OBE.

Statistics
Chief Statistician (G5), Dr. J. R. Cuthbert.

DEPARTMENT OF AGRICULTURE AND FISHERIES FOR SCOTLAND
Pentland House, 47 Robb's Loan, Edinburgh
EH14 1TW
[031–556 8400]

Dover House, Whitehall, London, SW1A 2AU
[071–270 3000]

Secretary (G2), L. P. Hamilton, CB.
Under Secretary (G3), D. J. Essery.
Fisheries Secretary (G3), G. Robson.
Assistant Secretaries (G5), P. S. Collings; E. C. Davison; I. W. Gordan; T. J. Kelly; A. K. MacLeod; J. A. Rennie; N. E. Sharp; I. M. Whitelaw.
Chief Agricultural Officer (G4), J. F. Hutcheson.
Deputy Chief Agricultural Officer (G5), W. A. Macgregor.
Assistant Chief Agricultural Officers (G6), D. R. J.

Craven; J. A. Hardie; J. G. Muir; A. Robb; J. I. Woodrow.
Chief Agricultural Economist (G6), J. M. Dunn, D.Phil.
Chief Meat and Livestock Inspector (G7), J. Miller.
Chief Food and Dairy Officer (G7), D. J. MacDonald.
Chief Surveyor (G6), N. Taylor.
Scientific Adviser (G5), T. W. Hegarty, Ph.D.
Senior Principal Scientific Officers (G6), R. J. Dowdell, Ph.D.; D. Thornton.

Agricultural Scientific Services
East Craigs, Edinburgh EH12 8NJ
[031–556 8400]

Director (G5), Dr. R. K. M. Hay.
Deputy Director (G6), J. R. Cutler.
Senior Principal Scientific Officers (G6), S. R. Cooper; M. J. Richardson.

Fisheries Research Services
Marine Laboratory, PO Box 101,
Victoria Road, Torry, Aberdeen AB9 8DB
[0224–876544]

Director and Co-ordinator of Fisheries Research and Development (G4), Prof. A. D. Hawkins, Ph.D., FRSE.
Deputy Director (G5), D. N. MacLennan.
Senior Principal Scientific Officers (G6), R. M. Cook, Ph.D.; J. M. Davies, Ph.D.; A. L. S. Munro, Ph.D.; P. A. M. Stewart, Ph.D.; C. S. Wardle, Ph.D.

Freshwater Fisheries Laboratory
Faskally, Pitlochry, Perthshire PH16 5LB
[0796–2060]

Senior Principal Scientific Officers (G6), R. G. J. Shelton, Ph.D.; J. E. Thorpe, Ph.D.

Sea Fisheries Inspectorate

Chief Inspector of Sea Fisheries (G6), J. F. Fenton.
Inspector of Salmon and Freshwater Fisheries for Scotland (G7), R. B. Williamson.
Marine Superintendent, Capt. R. M. Mill Irving.

SCOTTISH DEVELOPMENT DEPARTMENT
St. Andrew's House, Edinburgh EH1 3DG
[031–556 8400]
Dover House, Whitehall, London, SW1A 2AU
[071–270 3000]

Secretary and Chief Economic Adviser (G2), Dr. R. C. L. McCrone, CB, FRSE.
Under Secretaries (G3), J. F. Laing; Miss E. A. MacKay.
Director, Historic Buildings and Monuments Scotland (G4), G. N. Munro.
Assistant Secretaries (G5), Ms. L. Clare; R. S. Crofts; Mrs. M. B. Gunn; C. C. MacDonald; J. S. B. Martin; K. W. Moore; J. N. Randall; E. C. Reavley; R. E. S. Robinson; Mrs. G. M. Stewart; J. A. Thomson.

Professional Staff

Chief Engineer (G3), R. MacGillivray.
Deputy Chief Engineer (G5), A. C. Paton.
Assistant Chief Engineers (G6), T. Bolton; T. D. Macdonald; N. G. Semple.
Director of Building and Chief Architect (G3), J. E. Gibbons, Ph.D.
Deputy Director of Building and Deputy Chief Architect (G5), M. R. Miller.
Deputy Director of Building and Chief Quantity Surveyor (G5), D. C. Russell.
Deputy Director (G5), T. Birley.
Assistant Directors (G6), G. Gray; H. R. McCallum.
Chief Planner (G3), A. Mackenzie.
Deputy Chief Planner (G5), D. R. Dare.
Assistant Chief Planners (G6), T. Williamson; A. W. Denham; I. R. Duncan; S. G. Fulton.
Chief Research Officer (G5), Dr. C. P. A. Levein.

Senior Principal Research Officers (G6), Mrs. B. Doig; Dr. Jacqueline Tombs.
Director of Roads and Chief Engineer (G4), J. A. L. Dawson.
Deputy Chief Engineer (Roads) (G5), G. S. Marshall.
Deputy Chief Engineer (Bridges) (G5), J. Innes.
Assistant Chief Engineers (G6), R. D. Udall; J. A. Howison.
HM Chief Industrial Pollution Inspector (G5), I. W. W. Wright.
Chief Estates Officer (G6), R. I. K. White.
Chief Inspector of Ancient Monuments for Scotland, Dr. D. J. Breeze.
Chief Inspector of Historic Buildings, D. M. Walker.

Inquiry Reporters
16 Waterloo Place, Edinburgh EH1 3DN
[031–556 8400]

Chief Reporter (G3), A. G. Bell.
Deputy Chief Reporter (G5), R. M. Hickman.

INDUSTRY DEPARTMENT
FOR SCOTLAND
New St. Andrew's House, Edinburgh EH1 3TA
[031–556 8400]
and
Dover House, Whitehall, SW1A 2AU
[071–270 3000]

Secretary (G2), P. MacKay.
Under Secretaries (G3), A. D. F. Findlay; E. J. Weeple.
Assistant Secretaries (G5), D. A. Brew; G. D. Calder; D. A. Campbell; J. W. Elvidge; Miss I. M. Low; Mrs. N. S. Munro; D. N. G. Reid; Mrs. A. Robson.
Senior Economic Advisers (G5), A. Goudie; J. A. Peat.

Industrial Expansion
Alhambra House, 45 Waterloo Street, Glasgow
G2 6AT
[041–248 2855]

Under Secretary (G3), H. Morison.
Industrial Adviser, Dr. C. K. Benington.
Scientific Adviser, Prof. J. Lamb.
Assistant Secretaries (G5), A. W. Fraser; S. F. Hampson.
Senior Principal (G6), J. McGhee.

Locate in Scotland
120 Bothwell Street, Glasgow G2 7JP
[041–248 2700]

Director (G4), E. Frizzell.
Senior Principal (G6), W. Malone.
Principal (G7), R. Whyte.
Director (North America), R. Crawford.

SCOTTISH EDUCATION DEPARTMENT
New St. Andrew's House,
Edinburgh EH1 3SY
[031–556 8400]
and
Dover House, Whitehall, London, SW1A 2AU
[071–270 3000]

Secretary (G2), G. R. Wilson.
Under Secretaries (G3), N. G. Campbell; W. A. P. Weatherston; H. Robertson, MBE.
Assistant Secretaries (G5), D. A. Bennett; P. Brady; M. J. P. Cunliffe; M. Ewart; J. W. L. Lonie; G. McHugh; Miss M. MacLean; K. Macrae; D. Salmond, Ph.D. *(Chief Statistician);* J. W. Sinclair; D. Wishart.
Senior Principal (G6), D. Wann.

HM Inspectors of Schools
Senior Chief Inspector (G3), T. N. Gallacher.

Deputy Senior Chief Inspectors (G4), D. W. Mack; S. E. McCelland, Ph.D.

Chief Inspectors (G5), W. T. Beveridge; W. F. L. Bigwood; J. P. Donaldson; G. P. D. Gordon; J. Howgego; J. J. McDonald; A. S. McGlynn; D. A. Osler; A. M. Rankin; D. B. Young.

Inspectors (G6), J. N. Alison; D. T. G. Allan; M. T. J. Axford; P. Banks; Mrs. W. Binnie; A. D. Blair; Mrs. J. M. Bowen; J. Boyes; Miss C. L. Boyle; M. J. Brown; Mrs. M. M. Browning; J. W. Burdin; D. C. Burgess; T. N. Carr; W. Clark; M. Q. Cramb; Mrs. A. D. Craw; F. Crawford; A. H. B. Davidson; R. F. Dick; J. C. Dignan; G. H. C. Donaldson; D. W. Duncan; Miss K. M. Fairweather; B. Fryer; A. R. Gallon; I. K. Gamble; W. Geddes; M. Gibson, Ph.D.; A. B. Giovanazzi; G. D. Gray, Ph.D.; T. O. Greig; R. A. Hawke; K. A. Hope; L. A. Hunter; M. Jack; J. Jackson, Ph.D.; E. S. Kelly; D. E. Kelso; Ms. A. Kennedy; D. G. Kirkpatrick; I. Lawson; M. McAllan; I. M. MacAskill; L. McCallum; H. K. McCorkindale; Mrs. M. A. Macfarlane; Ms. I. S. McGregor; R. E. McKinstry; H. M. MacLaren; C. R. MacLean; A. J. Macpherson; D. MacQuarrie; A. Maltby; R. H. Manser; A. F. Marquis; D. Martin; H. L. Martin; G. Mathison; W. M. Mein; Mrs. J. M. Millar; J. Mitchell; Miss E. R. Mowat; B. Nickerson, Ph.D.; F. S. O'Hagan, Ph.D.; I. P. Pascoe; W. M. Patterson; N. A. Pepin; J. Picken; T. A. Rankin; M. C. Rhodes; S. A. Ritchie; I. D. S. Robertson; Mrs. M. A. Robertson; Mrs. P. A. Robertson; S. M. Robertson; A. L. Robson; M. Roebuck; I. S. Rowley; D. M. Russell; A. L. Small; E. P. Spencer; K. Srinivassan; H. M. Stalker; A. M. Steel; W. Stevenson; A. Stewart; Mrs. J. A. Stewart; W. P. Stewart; T. Straiton, Ph.D.; J. W. Thomson; R. M. S. Tuck; R. S. Weir; Miss G. A. White; J. G. L. Wright; R. W. J. Young, Ph.D.

Social Work Services Group
43 Jeffrey Street, Edinburgh EH1 1DN
[031–556 8400]

The Social Work Services Group, which is attached to the Scottish Education Department, administers the provisions of the Social Work (Scotland) Act, 1968.

Under Secretary (G3), N. G. Campbell.
Assistant Secretaries (G5), D. A. Bennet; M. J. P. Cunliffe; J. W. Sinclair.
Chief Social Work Adviser, D. Colvin.
Senior Advisers, Ms. M. L. Hunt; F. A. O'Leary; I. C. Robertson; A. R. Sabine; J. I. Smith.

SCOTTISH HOME AND HEALTH DEPARTMENT
St. Andrew's House,
Edinburgh EH1 3DE
[031–556 8400]
Dover House, Whitehall, London, SW1A 2AU
[071–270 3000]

Secretary (G2), G. A. Hart, CB.
Under Secretaries (G3), D. Belfall; J. E. Fraser, CB; K. J. MacKenzie.

National Health Service in Scotland Management Executive

Chief Executive, D. Cruickshank.
  Private Secretary, Ms. J. A. Stirton.
Director of Strategic Management, G. A. Anderson.
Director of Finance, M. Collier.
Director of Administration, D. Steel.
Assistant Secretaries (G5), A. M. Burnside; D. J. Crawley; I. G. F. Gray; R. D. Jackson; C. M. A. Lugton; C. K. McIntosh; A. J. Matheson; W. Moyes; P. M. Russell; R. H. Scott; G. M. D. Thomson; G. W. Tucker.
Senior Principal (G6), N. MacLeod.

Medical Services

Chief Medical Officer (G2), K. C. Calman.
Deputy Chief Medical Officer (G3), Dr. A. B. Young.
Principal Medical Officers, J. V. Basson; C. F. Fleming; G. Gilray; Margaret Hennigan; A. D. McIntyre; A. Rourke.
Senior Medical Officers, R. E. G. Aitken, TD; I. R. Bashford; P. W. Brooks; S. Capewell; W. Dodd; Dr. Margaret Halley; D. U. Sinclair; R. D. Skinner, Dr. Elisabeth Sowler; M. A. R. Thomson; O. A. Thores.
Senior Regional Medical Officers, I. G. Conn; H. McBain.
Regional Medical Officers, I. Arthurson; P. I. Brown; J. E. Durkacz; T. E. S. Fergusson; G. W. G. Hunter; K. Inglis; G. McKay; A. S. Mackenzie; Ms. E. M. Melville; J. P. Reid; P. I. T. Walker.
Chief Scientist, Prof. R. D. Weir, OBE.
Chief Dental Officer, N. K. Colquhoun.
Deputy Chief Dental Officer, J. R. Wild.
Regional Dental Officers, M. G. Platt; Miss A. J. Power; G. A. Reid.
Chief Nursing Officer, Mrs. Y. Moores.
Chief Pharmacist (G6), G. Calder.

Miscellaneous Appointments

HM Chief Inspector of Constabulary, C. Sampson, CBE, QPM.
HM Chief Inspector of Prisons, T. B. Buyers, OBE.
Commandant, Scottish Police College, T. J. Whitson, OBE.
HM Chief Inspector of Fire Services, A. Winton, QFSM.
Commandant, Scottish Fire Service Training School, C. F. McManus, QFSM.
Secretary, Scottish Health Service Advisory Council, W. J. Farquhar.

Prisons Group
Calton House, 5 Redheughs Rigg,
Edinburgh EH12 9HW
[031–556 8400]

Director of Scottish Prison Service (G4), P. McKinlay.
Deputy Director (Administration) (G5), F. H. Orr.
Deputy Director (Operations) (G5), W. McVey.
Deputy Director, Personnel (G5), A. R. Walker.
Deputy Director, Regime Services and Supplies (G6), N. Harvey.
Deputy Director, Planning and Development (G5), J. W. H. Irvine.
Deputy Director, Estates (G6), D. D. Sutherland.
Deputy Director, Training (G5), W. J. Fearnley.

Prison Governors

Aberdeen, L. C. McBain.
Barlinnie, P. Withers.
Barlinnie Special Unit, D. E. Gunn.
Castle Huntly Young Offenders Institution, E. J. Brownsmith.
Cornton Vale, A. Thomson.
Dumfries Young Offenders Institution, G. Taylor.
Dungavel, A. P. Spencer.
Edinburgh, J. Pearce.
Friarton, J. A. Harker.
Glenochil Prison and Young Offenders Institution, J. Milne.
Greenock, I. A. Bannatyne.
Inverness, L. W. G. Hewitson.
Longriggend Remand Institution, A. F. King.
Low Moss, W. Davidson.
Noranside, J. C. Stuart.
Penninghame, Mrs. M. Wood.
Perth, R. Kite.
Peterhead, M. J. Milne.
Polmont Young Offenders Institution, G. R. Bond.
Shotts, A. G. Coyle.
Shotts Alternative Unit, P. A. J. Roberts.
Scottish Prison Service College, R. L. Houchin.

Mental Welfare Commission for Scotland
25 Drumsheugh Gardens, Edinburgh EH3 7NS
[031–225 7034]

Chairman, P. C. Millar, OBE.
Commissioners, Mrs. A. Baxter; Dr. D. Blaney; P. H.
Brodie; R. G. Davis; Mrs. A. M. Glen; Ms. A. M.
Green; Mrs. H. L. Grieve; Mrs. J. I. D. Isbister; D.
A. Macdonald, OBE; Mrs. H. S. Mein; Sir David
Montgomery; M. O'Reilly; J. G. Sutherland.
Medical Commissioners, W. Boyd; A. A. McKechnie.
Social Work Commissioner, J. H. L. Richards.
Secretary, D. Wishart.

*Counsel to the Secretary of State for Scotland under
the Private Legislation Procedure (Scotland) Act,
1936* (50 Frederick Street, Edinburgh.—(031–226
6499)).
Senior Counsel, G. S. Douglas, QC.
Junior Counsel, N. M. P. Morrison.

NATIONAL HEALTH SERVICE, SCOTLAND

Health Boards

Argyll and Clyde, Gilmour House, Paisley. *Chairman*, J. D. Ryan, CBE. *General Manager*, I. C. Smith.

Ayrshire and Arran, PO Box 13, Hunters Avenue,
Ayr. *Chairman*, W. S. Fyfe, OBE. *General Manager*,
J. M. Eckford.

Borders, Huntlyburn, Melrose, Roxburghshire.
Chairman, Dr. D. H. Pringle, CBE. *General Manager*, D. A. Peters.

Dumfries and Galloway, Nithbank, Dumfries.
Chairman, J. A. M. McIntyre, OBE. *General Manager*, M. D. Cook.

Fife, Glenrothes House, North Street, Glenrothes.
Chairman, Mrs. P. A. H. Ferguson. *General Manager*, F. F. Gibb.

Forth Valley, 33 Spittal Street, Stirling. *Chairman*,
Mrs. J. D. Isbister. *General Manager*, A. R.
Robertson.

Grampian, 1–7 Albyn Place, Aberdeen. *Chairman*,
J. Kyle, CBE. *General Manager*, H. Fullerton.

Greater Glasgow, The Royal Beatson Memorial
Hospital, 132 Hill Street, Glasgow. *Chairman*, Dr.
T. J. Thomson, CBE. *General Manager*, L. Peterken,
CBE.

Highland, Reay House, 17 Old Edinburgh Road,
Inverness. *Chairman*, J. McWilliam, OBE. *General Manager*, R. R. W. Stewart.

Lanarkshire, 14 Beckford Street, Hamilton, Lanarkshire. *Chairman*, Mrs. B. M. Gunn, OBE. *General Manager*, F. Clark.

Lothian, 11 Drumsheugh Gardens, Edinburgh.
Chairman, Dr. J. W. Baynham. *General Manager*,
F. Clark (until end 1990).

Orkney, Balfour Hospital, New Scapa Road, Kirkwall, Orkney. *Chairman*, J. D. M. Robertson, OBE.
General Manager, Dr. J. I. Cromarty.

Shetland, 28 Burgh Road, Lerwick. *Chairman*, Mrs.
F. Grains. *General Manager*, B. J. Atherton.

Tayside, PO Box 75, Vernonholme, Riverside Drive,
Dundee. *Chairman*, D. B. Grant, CBE, TD. *General
Manager*, Dr. R. C. Graham.

Western Isles, 37 South Beach Street, Stornoway,
Isle of Lewis. *Chairman*, Mrs. M. A. MacMillan.
General Manager, J. J. Glover.

Common Services Agency
Trinity Park House, South Trinity Road,
Edinburgh EH5 3SE

Chairman, D. F. McQuaker.
General Manager, J. T. Donald.

GENERAL REGISTER OFFICE (Scotland)
New Register House, Edinburgh EH1 3YT
[031–556 3952]

The General Register Office for Scotland is the
Scottish equivalent of the Office of Population
Censuses and Surveys. The main records in the
custody of the Registrar General for Scotland are:
the statutory registers of births, deaths, marriages,
still-births, adoptions and divorces; the old parish
registers (recording births, marriages, deaths, etc.
before civil registration began in 1855); and records
of censuses of the population in Scotland.

Hours of public access: Mon.–Thurs. 9–4.30; Fri.
9–4.

Registrar General (G4), Dr. C. M. Glennie.
Deputy Registrar General (G5), B. V. Philp.
Senior Principal (G6), D. A. Orr.
Principals (G7), I. G. Bowie; R. C. Lawson; D. M.
Robertson.
Statisticians (G7), J. Arrundale; G. W. L. Jackson; F.
G. Thomas.

SEA FISH INDUSTRY AUTHORITY
Sea Fisheries House, 10 Young Street,
Edinburgh EH2 4JQ
[031–225 2515]

Chairman, B. Davies, CBE.
Chief Executive, C. H. Davies.
Deputy Chief Executive, P. D. Chaplin.
Secretary and Administration Director, R. A. Davie.
Technical Director, A. G. Hopper.
Marketing Director, R. M. Kennedy.
Training Director, K. Waind.

SECURITIES AND INVESTMENTS BOARD
3 Royal Exchange Buildings, EC3V 3NL
[071–283 2474]
[*Central register of authorized firms*: 071–929 3652]

The Securities and Investments Board became in
1987 the designated agency, under the Financial
Services Act 1986, to regulate the activities of
investment businesses in the UK. Although not a
statutory body, the Board has powers under the 1986
Act to recognize self-regulating organizations,
professional bodies, investment exchanges and clearing houses, and directly to authorize firms to do
investment business in the UK. The Board also has
the power to act as a prosecuting authority in respect
of persons carrying on investment business without
being authorized.

Members of the Board are appointed by agreement
between the Secretary of State for Trade and Industry
and the Governor of the Bank of England. The
Chairman and Executive Directors are full-time
Board members; the others are part-time and nonexecutive.

The Board

Chairman, D. A. Walker.
Deputy Chairmen, Sir Mark Weinberg; R. N. Quartano, CBE.
Executive Director and Chief Operating Officer, R. H.
F. Croft, CBE.
Executive Director, D. E. Fellows.
Members (part-time), D. M. Child, CBE; J. A. Gardiner;
N. Lessels; P. J. Manser; E. E. Ray, CBE; G. R.
Russell; Viscount Runciman of Doxford, CBE; L.

Warwick; Dame Rachel Waterhouse, DBE; R. B. Williamson, CBE.
Executive Directors, R. H. F. Croft, CBE; D. E. Fellows.

Management

The Chairman.
The Executive Directors.
Directors of Divisions:
  Authorization, Compliance and Enforcement, J. D. Orme.
  Finance, R. B. A. Purcell.
  Financial Regulation, A. J. Thrall.
  Futures and Options, M. B. Gittins.
  Information Services, B. W. Smith.
  Intermediaries, A. Selman.
  International Securities, R. J. Britton.
  Investment Management and Public Affairs, C. Bowe.
  Legal Services, M. C. Blair.
Deputy Directors:
  Authorization, Compliance and Enforcement, R. L. Devlin; J. M. Thomas.
  Futures and Options, P.E. Thompson.
  Intermediaries, R. B. Ferguson.
  International Securities, A. C. Pirie.
  Investment Management, M. Borland.
  Legal Services, A. Whittaker; J. Welch.
  Personnel and Administration, R. J. Woodley.
Secretary to the Board, T. E. Allen.
Special Adviser, P. Jackson.

RECOGNIZED BODIES
(as at July 1, 1990)

Self-regulating Organizations

The Association of Futures Brokers and Dealers Ltd. (AFBD).
The Financial Intermediaries, Managers and Brokers Regulatory Association Ltd. (FIMBRA).
*The Investment Management Regulatory Organization Ltd. (IMRO).
*The Life Assurance and Unit Trust Regulatory Organization Ltd. (LAUTRO).
The Securities Association Ltd. (TSA).
*These two bodies are also recognized self-regulating organizations for friendly societies.

International Securities Self-regulating Organization
(recognized by DTI)

The Association of International Bond Dealers (AIBD)

Recognized Investment Exchanges

UK Exchanges
The Baltic Futures Exchange (BFE).
The International Petroleum Exchange of London Ltd. (IPE).
The International Stock Exchange of Great Britain and the Republic of Ireland Ltd. (ISE).
The London Commodity Exchange (1986) Ltd. (London FOX).
The London International Financial Futures Exchange Ltd. (LIFFE).
The London Metal Exchange Ltd. (LME).
OM London Ltd.

Overseas Exchanges (recognized by the Secretary of State for Trade and Industry)
The National Association of Securities Dealers Automated Quotations System.
Sydney Futures Exchange Ltd.

Recognized Professional Bodies

The Institute of Chartered Accountants in England and Wales.
The Institute of Chartered Accountants of Scotland.
The Institute of Chartered Accountants in Ireland.
The Chartered Association of Certified Accountants.
The Institute of Actuaries.
The Insurance Brokers Registration Council.
The Law Society of England and Wales.
The Law Society of Scotland.
The Law Society of Northern Ireland.

Recognized Clearing Houses

International Commodities Clearing House Ltd. (ICCH).
GAFTA Clearing House Company Ltd.

THE SECURITY SERVICE COMMISSIONER
c/o The Home Office, 50 Queen Anne's Gate,
SW1H 9AT

The Commissioner is appointed by the Prime Minister. He keeps under review the issue of warrants by the Secretary of State under the Security Service Act 1989 and is required to give the Security Service Tribunal all such assistance in discharging its functions as it may require. He is also required to submit an annual report on the discharge of his functions to the Prime Minister.
Commissioner, The Rt. Hon. Lord Justice Stuart-Smith.

SECURITY SERVICE TRIBUNAL
PO Box 18, SE1 0TZ

The Security Service Act 1989 established a Tribunal of three to five senior members of the legal profession, independent of the Government and appointed by HM The Queen, to investigate complaints from any person about anything which they believe the Security Service has done to them or to their property.
President, The Hon. Mr Justice Simon Brown.
Vice President, Sheriff J. McInnes, QC.
Member, Sir Richard Gaskell.

SERIOUS FRAUD OFFICE
Elm House, 10–16 Elm Street, WC1X 0BJ
[071–239 7272]

The Serious Fraud Office is an independent department under the superintendence of the Attorney General. Its remit is to investigate and prosecute serious and complex fraud. The scope of its powers covers England, Wales and Northern Ireland. The staff includes lawyers, accountants and other support staff, and investigating teams work closely with the police.
Director (G2), Mrs. B. Mills, QC.
Deputy Director (G3), M. Chance.
Chief Accountant (G3), J. Knox.

DEPARTMENT OF SOCIAL SECURITY
Richmond House, 79 Whitehall, SW1A 2NS
[071-210 3000]

The Department was formed in July 1988 by the division of the Department of Health and Social Security into two separate departments. The Department of Social Security is responsible for the social security services in England, Wales and Scotland.
(For **Salaries**, *see* page 295)

Secretary of State for Social Security, THE RT. HON.
ANTONY NEWTON, OBE, MP.
Private Secretary, J. S. Lord.
Minister of State, RT. HON. NICHOLAS SCOTT, MBE, MP.
(Social Security and Disabled People).
Private Secretary, S. Willis.
Parliamentary Under Secretary of State (Lords), THE
LORD HENLEY.
Private Secretary, T. Lowe.
Parliamentary Under Secretary of State (Commons),
MRS. GILLIAN SHEPHARD, MP.
Private Secretary, Miss C. Edwards.
Permanent Secretary (G1), Sir Michael Partridge,
KCB.
Private Secretary, Mrs. V. Andrews.

SOCIAL SECURITY OPERATIONS GROUP

Deputy Secretary (G2), N. L. J. Montagu.

Regional Directorate

Under Secretary (G3), Mrs. M. A. Robinson.
Assistant Secretaries (G5), O. C. L. Thorpe; J. F.
Jones; J. C. Eversfield; K. Bellamy; Mrs. C. Souter.

Information Technology Services Agency

Chief Executive, F. J. Kenworthy.
Deputy Chief Executive, P. G. Dunn.
Directors, A. Smith; Ms. A. Cleveland; R. Tilney; A.
Stott; K. Caldwell; G. McCorkell.
Non-Executive Directors, J. M. Bankier, CBE; J. Y.
Marshall.

North Fylde Central Office

Controller (G5), E. Boyd.

Newcastle upon Tyne Central Office

Controller, NCO Benefits Division (G5), A. J. Laur-
ance.
Head of Contributions Unit (G5), Miss A. Chant (Chief
Executive from April 1991).

SOCIAL SECURITY POLICY GROUP

Deputy Secretary (G2), R. A. Birch.

Social Security Division A

Under Secretary (G3), Mrs. S. Maunsell.
Assistant Secretaries (G5), Mrs. U. Brennan; P. L.
Adeane; A. Baker; J. W. White.

Social Security Division B

Under Secretary (G3), B. W. Taylor.
Assistant Secretaries (G5), D. Allsop; Miss K. E. W.
Blunt; B. Merkel; Miss M. Moodie.

Social Security Division C

Under Secretary (G3), Mrs. J. M. Firth.
Assistant Secretaries (G5), G. C. Fiegehen; S. Hewitt.
Senior Principal (G6), A. Thompson.

Social Security Division D

Under Secretary (G3), M. L. Whippman.
Assistant Secretaries (G5), Mrs. R. J. Butler; R. P.
Cleasby; Mrs. L. M. Richards; M. Street.

Medical Division (Social Security)

Chief Medical Adviser (G3), Dr. W. R. O. Eggington.
Principal Medical Officers, Dr. K. A. Cameron; Dr. P.
Castaldi; T. J. G. Phillips; Dr. D. R. Findlay.

Information Division

Head of Information (G5), S. Reardon.
Press Officer (G7), J. Bretherton.

REGIONAL ORGANIZATION

Scotland and Northern England
3 Lady Lawson Street, Edinburgh

Controller (G4), A. Laurence.

Wales and Central England
Five Ways Tower, Frederick Road,
Edgbaston, Birmingham

Director (G4), J. T. Green.

Southern England
Sutherland House, 29–37 Brighton Road,
Sutton, Surrey

Director (G4), I. Magee.

SOCIAL SECURITY ADVISORY COMMITTEE
New Court, Carey Street, WC2A 2LS
[071–972 1507]

The Social Security Advisory Committee (SSAC)
was established by the Social Security Act 1980 to
advise the Secretary of State for Social Security and
the Department of Health and Social Services for
Northern Ireland on all Social Security matters
except those relating to benefits for industrial
injuries and diseases and occupational pensions. The
Social Security Housing Benefit Act 1982 added
housing benefit to the Committee's responsibilities.
Chairman, P. M. Barclay, CBE.
Members, Mrs. J. Anelay; Mrs. E. A. Denholm; Rev.
G. H. Good, OBE; H. Hodge; J. Hughes; P. Jacques;
P. F. Naish; Hon. Mrs. R. H. P. Price; A. M. Sealey;
Dr. A. V. Stokes, OBE; Prof. Olive Stevenson; R. G.
Wendt; D. L. Willetts.
Secretary, L. C. Smith.

SPORTS COUNCIL
16 Upper Woburn Place, WC1H 0QP
[071–388 1277]

The Sports Council, created under Royal Charter,
promotes the development of sport and fosters the
provision of facilities for sport and recreation in
Great Britain.
Chairman, P. G. Yarranton.

HMSO (HER MAJESTY'S STATIONERY
OFFICE)
St. Crispins, Duke Street, Norwich NR3 1PD
[0603–622211]

HMSO (Her Majesty's Stationery Office) was
established in 1786 and is the UK Government
executive agency that provides printing, binding,
office supplies and office machinery to the public
service. HMSO is also the Government's publisher
and has bookshops for the sale of Government
publications in London, Edinburgh, Manchester,
Bristol, Birmingham and Belfast, as well as appointed
agents in other cities. HMSO obtains most of its
supplies and printing from commercial sources by
competitive tender, apart from about 20 per cent of
its printing requirement, such as Hansard and Bills
and Acts of Parliament, which are produced in its
own printing works. HMSO is a self-financing
Government trading fund and competes for its
business with other commercial suppliers.
(For **Salaries**, *see* page 295)

Controller and Chief Executive (G2), P. I. Freeman.
Executive Assistant, Mrs. J. B. Ward.
Deputy Chief Executive (G4), M. D. Lynn.
Director General of Corporate Services (G4), D. W.
Ray.

Heads of Divisions

Publications (G5), C. J. Penn.
Supply (G5), P. J. Macdonald.
Production (G5), D. G. Forbes.
Print Procurement (G5), B. Ekers.
Corporate Development (G5), C. N. Southgate.
Finance (G5), V. G. Bell.
Personnel Services (G5), A. J. Davies.
Industrial Personnel (G5), D. J. Wintle.
Marketing (G6), G. A. H. Turner.
Information Technology (G5), D. C. Kerry.

Scotland
Bankhead Avenue, Edinburgh EH11 4AB

Bookshop: 71 Lothian Road, Edinburgh EH3 9AZ
Director Edinburgh (G7), G. W. Bedford.

Northern Ireland
IDB House, Chichester Street, Belfast BT1 4PS

Retail and Trade Bookshop: 80 Chichester Street,
Belfast BT1 4JY
Director Belfast (G7), Miss V. J. Wilson, OBE.

London
Publications Centre: 51 Nine Elms Lane, SW8 5DR.
Bookshop: 49 High Holborn, WC1V 6HB.

Manchester
Broadway, Chadderton, Oldham, Lancs. OL9 9QH

Bookshop: 9–21 Princess Street, Manchester
M60 8AS.

Bristol
Ashton Vale Road, Bristol BS3 2HN

Bookshop: Southey House, Wine Street, Bristol
BS1 2BH.

Birmingham
Bookshop: 258 Broad Street, Birmingham B1 2HE.

STATUTE LAW COMMITTEE
House of Lords, SW1A 0PW

The Committee exercises a general supervision
over the form of the statute law and of Statutory
Instruments. It is also responsible for the publication
of amended editions of the Statutes, including the
current official revised edition of the Statutes in
Force.
Chairman, The Lord Chancellor.
Vice-Chairman, The Hon. Mr. Justice Gibson.
Members, The Attorney General; The Lord Advo-
cate; The Hon. Lord Davidson; The Rt. Hon. J.
Morris, QC, MP; The Rt. Hon. P. Archer, QC, MP; Sir
Anthony Buck, QC, MP; T. S. Legg, CB, QC; D.
Rippengal, CB, QC; H. Knorpel, CB; Sir Henry de
Waal, KCB, QC; J. C. McCluskie, QC; Sir John Sainty,
KCB; Sir Terence Heiser, KCB; H. W. Gamon, CBE,
MC; Sir Nicholas Lyell, QC, MP; Sir Robin Butler,
KCB, CVO; C. Boulton, CB; T. R. Erskine, CB; K. F.
Barclay; M. H. Collon; R. Brodie, CB; Sir Clive
Whitmore, GCB, CVO; J. Nursaw, CB, QC; H. M.
Barclay; Rt. Hon. Sir Brian Hutton; The Lord
Jauncey of Tullichettle, PC; Dr. P. Freeman.
Secretary, B. P. Keith.

OFFICE OF TELECOMMUNICATIONS
Export House, 50 Ludgate Hill, EC4M 7JJ
[071–822 1600]

Oftel is a non-Ministerial Government department
headed by a Director General, which is responsible
for supervising telecommunications activities in the
UK.
Its principal functions are to ensure that holders
of telecommunications licences comply with their
licence conditions; to maintain and promote effective
competition in telecommunications; to promote, in
respect of prices, quality and variety the interests of
consumers, purchasers and other users of telecommunication services and apparatus.
The Director General has powers to deal with anti-
competitive practices and monopoly situations. He
also has a duty to consider all reasonable complaints
and representations about telecommunication apparatus and services.
Director General, Prof. Sir Brian Carsberg.
Deputy Director General, W. R. B. Wigglesworth.
Director of PTO Licensing, G. P. Knight.
Director of Apparatus Approval, Dr. H. Stewart.
Head of Information, D. C. Redding.

TOURIST BOARDS

The English Tourist Board, the Scottish Tourist
Board and the Wales Tourist Board are responsible
for developing and marketing the tourist industry in
their respective countries. The Boards' main objectives are to promote holidays and to encourage the
provision and improvement of tourist amenities.

English Tourist Board
Thames Tower, Black's Road, W6 9EL
[081–846 9000]

Chief Executive, J. East.

Scottish Tourist Board
23 Ravelston Terrace, Edinburgh EH4 3EU
[031–332 2433]

Chief Executive, T. M. Band.

Wales Tourist Board
Brunel House, 2 Fitzalan Road, Cardiff CF2 1UY
[0222–499909]

Chief Executive, P. Loveluck.

DEPARTMENT OF TRADE AND INDUSTRY
1–19 Victoria Street, SW1H 0ET
[071–215 5000]
[*Enterprise Initiative*: 0800–500200]
[*Single European Market*: 081–200 1992]

The Department is responsible for:
(a) international trade policy, including the promotion of UK trade interests in the European
Community, GATT, OECD, UNCTAD and other
international organizations.
(b) the promotion of UK exports and assistance to
exporters.
(c) policy in relation to industry, including the
promotion of enterprise, open markets and measures
to help industry strengthen its competitiveness;
specific interest in all markets, apart from those
covered by other departments; regional policy, Inner
Cities Initiative, enterprise and deregulation, and
regional industrial assistance (some of this applying
only to England); and policy in relation to British
Shipbuilders and the Post Office.
(d) competition policy and consumer protection,
including relations with the Office of Fair Trading
and the Monopolies and Mergers Commission.
(e) policy on science and technology and research
and development matters, space, standards, quality
and design, support for innovation; and the National
Engineering Laboratory, and the following executive
agencies: the Laboratory of the Government Chemist; the National Physical Laboratory; the National
Weights and Measures Laboratory; Warren Springs
Laboratory.
(f) company legislation and Companies House executive agency; the Insolvency Service executive
agency; the regulation of financial services and the

insurance industries; the regulation of radio frequencies; and the Patent Office executive agency.
(For Salaries, *see* page 295).

Secretary of State for Trade and Industry and President of the Board of Trade, THE RT. HON. PETER LILLEY, MP.
Principal Private Secretary, M. Stanley.
Minister for Industry and Enterprise, THE HON. DOUGLAS HOGG, QC, MP.
Private Secretary, K. Phillips.
Minister for Trade, THE HON. TIMOTHY SAINSBURY, MP.
Private Secretary, A. Walker.
Minister of State (Lords), THE LORD HESKETH.
Parliamentary Under Secretary of State for Corporate Affairs, JOHN REDWOOD, MP.
Private Secretary, Mrs. H. Dunstan.
Permanent Secretary (G1), Sir Peter Gregson, KCB.
Private Secretary, T. Medawar.
Deputy Secretaries (G2), D. M. Dell, CB; Dr. R. F. Coleman (*Chief Engineer and Scientist*); R. Mountfield, CB; C. W. Roberts, CB; R. Williams, CB; A. Lane, CB; G. A. Hosker, CB (*The Solicitor*); W. M. Knighton, CB (*Principal Establishment and Finance Officer*).
Parliamentary Clerk, T. Williams.

LINE DIVISION ORGANIZATION

Business Task Forces Division 1
Ashdown House, 123 Victoria Street, SW1E 6RB
[071–215 5000]

Under Secretary (G3), R. W. Simpson.
Heads of Branch (G5), C. L Jackson; M. R. Cohen; Miss S. E. Harding; B. D. Winkett.

Business Task Forces Division 2
Ashdown House, 123 Victoria Street, SW1E 6RB
[071–215 5000]

Under Secretary (G3), A. J. Nieuduszynski.
Heads of Branch (G5), D. Richardson; D. Marsh; Dr. M Sutton; C. A. Palmer; (*G6*), M. O. Ralph; Dr. G. T. Coleman.

Enterprise Initiative Division
Kingsgate House, 66–74 Victoria Street,
SW1E 6SW
[071–215 5000]

Under Secretary (G3), A. R. Titchener.
Heads of Branches (G5), H. P. Brown; S. Pride; Mrs. E. Ryle; R. M. Upson.

Manufacturing Technology Division
Kingsgate House, 123 Victoria Street, SW1E 6SW
[071–215 5000]

Under Secretary (G3), J. E. Cammell.
Heads of Branch (G5), H. M. Lanyon; J. Octon; B. N. Steele; A. Berry; Dr. K. Poulter.

Information Technology Division
Kingsgate House, 66–74 Victoria Street,
SW1E 6SW
[071–215 5000]

Under Secretary (G3), Dr. J. C. J. Thynne, CB.
Heads of Branches (G5), R. C. Louth; B. L. Nuttall; J. T. Cast; Prof. J. N. Buxton; Dr. A. J. Wallard; J. P. Hobday; P. J. Casey; H. J. Ivey.

British National Space Centre
Millbank Tower, Millbank, SW1P 4QU
[071–217 3000]

Director General (G2), A. J. Pryor.
Deputy Director General, L. Jones.
Heads of Branch (G5), Dr. J. E. Harries; Dr. R. Jude;

K. Inglis; (*G6*), Miss V. Bowell; Dr. D. Williams; J. Thomas.

Telecommunications and Posts Division
Kingsgate House, 66–74 Victoria Street,
SW1E 6SW
[071–215 5000]

Under Secretary (G3), P. Salvidge.
Heads of Branch (G5), Mrs. E. C. Jones; J. Phillips; D. D. Sibbick; P. Smith; S. R. Temple.

Research and Technology Policy Division
Ashdown House, 123 Victoria Street, SW1E 6RB
[071–215 5000]

Under Secretary (G3), Dr. C. Hicks.
Heads of Branch (G5), Mrs. M. Bloom; J. H. Chapman; R. Foster; J. D. Howarth.

National Physical Laboratory
Teddington, Middx. TW11 0LW
[081–977 3222]

(An executive agency of the Department of Trade and Industry.)
Director (G3), Dr. P. B. Clapham.

Laboratory of the Government Chemist
Queens Road, Teddington, Middx. TW11 0LY
[081–943 7000]

(An executive agency of the Department of Trade and Industry.)
Government Chemist (G3), A. Williams.

National Engineering Laboratory
East Kilbride, Glasgow G75 0QU
[03552–20222]

Chief Executive (G3), W. Edgar.

Warren Spring Laboratory
Gunnels Wood Road, Stevenage, Herts SG1 2BX
[0438–741122]

(An executive agency of the Department of Trade and Industry.)
Director (G3), Dr. J. S. S. Reay.

National Weights and Measures Laboratory
Stanton Avenue, Teddington, Middx. TW11 0JZ
[081–943 7272]

(An executive agency of the Department of Trade and Industry.)
Director (G5), vacant.

Competition Policy Division
1–19 Victoria Street, SW1H 0ET
[071–215 5000]

Under Secretary (G3), H. V. B. Brown.
Heads of Branch (G5), Dr. C. E. D. Bell; G. C. Riggs; Mrs. A. Walker.

Inner Cities Unit
1–19 Victoria Street, SW1H 0ET
[071–215 5000]

Director (G4), M. Gahagan.
Deputy Director (G5), Ms. S. Seymour.

Investment, Development and Accountancy Services Division
Kingsgate House, 66–74 Victoria Street,
SW1E 6SW
[071–215 5000]

Director (G3), P. M. S. Corley.
Directors, IDU (G3), J. G. Chastney; C. Crombie.
Heads of Branch (G5), R. H. S. Wells; G. M. Field; J. C. S. Priston; Dr. C. P. Hicks; K. Holt; Mrs. A. Taylor; (*G6*), K. R. Timmins.

Deregulation Unit
1–19 Victoria Street, SW1H 0ET
[071–215 5000]

Director (G3), J. A. Cooke.
Heads of Branch (G5), I. Freeman; R. Allpress.

Overseas Trade Divisions
1–19 Victoria Street, SW1H 0ET
[071–215 5000]

Division 1 (*Projects and Export Policy*)

Under Secretary (G3), C. C. W. Adams.
Heads of Branch (G5), R. I. Rogers; C. E. Blundell; N. Worman; A. P. Vinall.

Division 2
(*N. America, NE and SE Asia, China, Hong Kong and Export Licensing Operation*)

Under Secretary (G3), R. J. Meadway.
Heads of Branch (G5), J. V. Hagestadt; D. E. Love; M. V. Coolican.

Division 3
Under Secretary (G3), P. Bryant.

Administration and Finance
Head of Branch (G5), I. Jones.

Exports to Europe Branch
Head of Branch (G5), K. D. Levinson.

Export Data Branch
Director (G6), A. Reynolds.

Fairs and Promotions Branch
Head of Branch (G5), G. J. Bradshaw.

Eastern Europe Branch
Director (G4), K. W. N. George.

Division 4
Under Secretary (G3), M. M. Baker.

Middle East and N. Africa Branch
Head of Branch (G5), M. G. Petter.

Mexico, Central America, Caribbean, S. America and Australasia Branch
Head of Branch (G5), J. M. Bowder.

Sub-Saharan Africa and S. Asia Branch
Head of Branch (G5), M. A. S. Garrod.

Internal European Policy Division
1–19 Victoria Street, SW1H 0ET
[071–215 5000]

Under Secretary (G3), N. R. Thornton.
Heads of Branch (G5), Dr. A. W. C. Keddie; R. T. King; W. L. Stow.

External European Policy Division
1–19 Victoria Street, SW1H 0ET
[071–215 5000]

Under Secretary (G3), T. Muir.
Heads of Branch (G5), M. D. C. Johnson; R. Allen; Miss A. E. Stoddart.

Consumer Affairs Division
10–18 Victoria Street, SW1H 0NN
[071–215 5000]

Under Secretary (G3), C. T. Newton.
Heads of Branch (G5), D. Jones; M. A. R. Lunn; R. E. Palmer.
Trading Standards Adviser (G5), M. Oldham.

Companies Division
10–18 Victoria Street, SW1H 0NN
[071–215 5000]

Under Secretary (G3), Mrs. S. E. Brown.
Heads of Branch (G5), M. J. C. Butcher; C. W. Johnston; J. Healey.
Grade 6, F. C. Jenkins.

Companies House
Companies House, Crown Way, Cardiff
CF4 3UZ
[0222–388588]

(An executive agency of the Department of Trade and Industry).
Registrar of Companies for England and Wales (G4), D. Durham.
London Search Room, 55–71 City Road, EC1Y 1BB
[071–253 9393]

102 George Street, Edinburgh EH2 3DJ
[031–225 5774]
Registrar for Scotland, J. D. Leithead.

Financial Services Division
10–18 Victoria Street, SW1H 0NN
[071–215 5000]

Under Secretary (G3), W. B. Willott.
Heads of Branch (G5), Dr. J. P. Compton; S. J. Bowen; Miss R. M. Thompson.

The Insolvency Service
Bridge Place, 88–89 Eccleston Square, SW1V 1PT
[071–215 5000]

(An executive agency of the Department of Trade and Industry.)
Inspector General of the Insolvency Service and Chief Executive, P. R. Joyce.
Deputy Inspectors General, D. J. Flynn; J. R. Donnison.
Head of Branch (G5), Miss A. J. Brimelow.

Insurance Division
10–18 Victoria Street, SW1H 0NN
[071–215 5000]

Under Secretary (G3), A. C. Russell.
Heads of Branch (G5), D. W. Hellings; D. G. Hyde; M. G. Roberts.

Patent Office and Industrial Property and Copyright Department
see entry on p. 351

Radiocommunications Division
Waterloo Bridge House, Waterloo Road, SE1 8UA
[071–215 5000]

(An executive agency of the Department of Trade and Industry.)
Under Secretary (G3), M. J. Michell.
Director (G4), Dr. K. C. Shotton.
Heads of Branch (G5), M. Goddard; S. Spivey; R. A. Bedford; P. Loughead; (G6) B. A. Maxwell.

SERVICE DIVISION ORGANIZATION

Finance and Resource Management Division
Ashdown House, 123 Victoria Street, SW1E 6RB
[071–215 5000]

Under Secretary (G3), A. Whiting.
Heads of Branch (G5), D. M. Hoddinott; M. O'Shea; D. T. Smith.

Accounts Branch
PO Box 100, Government Buildings, Cardiff Road,
Newport, Gwent NP9 1ZA
[0633–810636]

Director of Accounts, D. M. Hoddinott.

Internal Audit
29 Bressenden Place, SW1E 5DT
[071–215 5000]

Head of Internal Audit, A. C. Elkington.

Management Services and Manpower Division
29 Bressenden Place, SW1E 5DT
[071–215 5000]

Under Secretary (G3), R. M. Rumbelow.
Director of Administrative Information Technology Services (G4), R. J. Wheeler.
Heads of Branch (G5), Miss D. Gane; K. M. Long.

Personnel Management Division
Allington Towers,
19 Allington Street, SW1E 5EB
[071–215 5000]

Under Secretary (G3), A. C. Hutton.
Heads of Branch (G5), J. P. Spencer; D. W. F. Johnson; J. F. Bailes; T. Bryan.

Information Division
1–19 Victoria Street, SW1H 0ET
[071–215 5000]

Head of Information (G4), Ms. J. M. Caines.
Deputy Heads of Information Division (G5), S. Lyle-Smythe; (G6), Miss A. MacLean.

Investigations Division
Ashdown House, 123 Victoria Street, SW1E 6RB
[071–215 5000]

Head of Branch (G3), D. R. C. Durie.
Head of Legal Services (G4), Mrs. T. J. Dunstan.
Assistant Solicitors (G5), H. H. Bradshaw; A. W. G. Catto; E. A. Thompson; B. J. Welch; Mrs. B. Chase.

Solicitor's Office
10–18 Victoria Street, SW1H 0NN
[071–215 5000]

The Solicitor (G2), G. A Hosker, CB.
Grade 3, P. H. Bovey; C. S. Kerse; J. M. Stanley.
Assistant Solicitors (G5), H. D. M. Bailey; Mrs. N. M. P. Chappell; Mrs. E. M. Drage; R. D. Fayers; Miss P. A. E. Granados; R. Higgins, CBE; D. S. Mangat; I. K. Mathers; Miss K. Morton; Miss E. N. O'Flynn; S. A. Parker; Miss J. Richardson; J. W. Roberts; Miss J. V. Stokes; A. M. Susman; Miss V. C. Woodbridge.

Economics, Market Intelligence and Statistics Division
1–19 Victoria Street, SW1H 0ET
[071–215 5000]

Under Secretary (G3), D. R. Coates.
Head of Industrial and Regional Economics (G4), Dr. J. A. S. Robertson.
Heads of Branch (G5), Dr. D. S. Higham; P. J. Goate; B. M. Nonhebel; J. M. Barber; M. S. Bradbury; Dr. R. Van Slooten; P. G. Waller; J. A. Astin.

Central Unit
1–19 Victoria Street, SW1H 0ET
[071–215 5000]

Head of Unit (G3), J. A. Cooke.
Grade 5, J. Green.

BRITISH OVERSEAS TRADE BOARD
1–19 Victoria Street, SW1H 0ET
[071–215 5000]

President, The Secretary of State for Trade and Industry.
Chairman, Sir James Cleminson, KBE, MC.
Vice-Chairman, HRH The Duke of Kent, KG, GCMG, GCVO.

Members, J. M. Banham; N. P. Bayne, CMG; A. B. Cleaver; D. M. Dell, CB; T. P. Frost; A. G. Gormly; Dr. A. Hayes; Sir Derek Hornby; The Earl of Limerick, KBE; J. W. Parsons, CBE; M. S. Perry, OBE; M. G. Stephens; B. D. Taylor.
Chief Executive, D. M. Dell, CB.
Secretary (G5), D. Saunders.

REGIONAL OFFICES

DTI North East, Stanegate House, 2 Groat Market, Newcastle upon Tyne NE1 1YN. (091–232 4722).—*Regional Director (G3),* Mrs. P. A. Denham.

DTI North West, Sunley Tower, Piccadilly Plaza, Manchester M1 4BA. (061–236 2171).—*Regional Director (G3),* J. H. Pownall.

DTI Yorkshire and Humberside, 25 Queen Street, Leeds LS1 2TV. (0532 443171).—*Regional Director (G3),* E. Wright.

DTI West Midlands, Ladywood House, Stephenson Street, Birmingham B2 4DT. (021–631 6181).—*Regional Director (G3),* N. H. Perry.

DTI East Midlands, Severns House, 20 Middle Pavement, Nottingham NG1 7DW. (0602 506181).—*Regional Director (G5),* R. M. Anderson.

DTI South West, The Pithay, Bristol BS1 2PB. (0272–272666).—*Regional Director (G5),* D. B. Lodge.

DTI South East, Bridge Place, 88–89 Eccleston Square, SW1V 1PT. (071–215 5000).—*Regional Director (G5),* I. Jones.

DTI East, Westbrook Centre, Milton Road, Cambridge CB4 1YG. (0223–461939).—*Regional Director (G5),* W. J. Hall.

TRAINING AGENCY
Head Office: Moorfoot, Sheffield S1 4PQ
[0742–753275]

The Training Agency is the UK national training authority. It operates as an executive agency within the Department of Employment and reports to the Secretary of State for Employment. The Agency develops and organizes the provision of the Government's training and vocational education programmes.
(For **Salaries,** *see* page 295)

Director General, R. J. Dawe, CB, OBE.

Resources and Personnel Division

Director (G3), Mrs. V. Bayliss.
Heads of Branches (G5):
Resource Control, K. C. G. White.
Internal Audit (G6), C. Williams.
Finance Control, N. L. Gregory.
Information Systems and Management Services, I. E. Turl.
Personnel and Staff Development, J. West.

Training Development Directorate

Director, and Chief Inspector of Training Standards Advisory Service (G4), J. D. Tinsley.

Information Services

Head (G5), M. Evans.

POLICY AND PROGRAMMES DIVISION

Deputy Director General and Director, Policy and Programmes Division, I. Johnston.

Quality Standards and Methods

Director (G4), G. Kendall.

Heads of Branches (G5):
Learning Technology Unit, C. M. King.
Qualifications and Standards, J. K. Fuller.
Psychological Service, Dr. M. Killcross.
Qualifications Standards and Methods Learning Systems and Access, C. P. Thomas.
Standards Methodology Unit (G6), G. Debling.

Education Programmes

Director (G3), Mrs. A. Jones.
Heads of Branches (G5):
TVEI Unit, M. Fahey.
Higher Education, G. Macnair.
Further Education, K. Franklin.
Compacts Support Unit, D. H. Duff.

Systems and Strategy

Director (G3), D. Grover.
Heads of Branches (G5):
Business Communications, P. Keen.
Evaluation and Research, Mrs. J. Marquand.
Industry Bodies, J. Wiltshire.

Field Operations

Director (G4), J. Lambert.
Heads of Branches (G5):
Business and Enterprise, B. Heatley.
Field Planning, I. Randall.
Labour Market Information, A. G. Davies.
Special Needs, Miss S. Newton.

Training and Enterprise Programmes

Director (G3), S. Loveman.
Programme Support (G5), J. Franklin.
Employment Training (G6), D. Tansley.

Directorate of Operations and TEC Development

Director (G3), J. Surr.
Head of TEC Policy (G5), P. Launer.
Head of Field Systems Branch (G5), M. Christie.

DEPARTMENT OF TRANSPORT
2 Marsham Street, SW1P 3EB
[071–276 3000]

The Department of Transport is responsible for land, sea and air transport, including sponsorship of the rail and bus industries; airports; domestic and international civil aviation; shipping and the ports industry; navigational lights, pilotage, HM Coastguard and marine pollution; motorways and other trunk roads; oversight of road transport including vehicle standards, registration and licensing, driver testing and licensing, bus and road freight licensing, regulation of taxis and private hire cars, road safety; and oversight of local authorities transport planning including payment of Transport Supplementary Grant.

(For **Salaries,** *see* page 295).

Secretary of State for Transport, THE RT. HON. CECIL PARKINSON, MP.
  Private Secretary, S. C. Whiteley.
  Special Advisers, Miss E. Buchanan; Prof. B. J. Hoskins.
  Parliamentary Private Secretary, J. Butterfill, MP.
Minister of State for Public Transport, ROGER FREEMAN, MP.
  Private Secretary, S. L. Gooding.
Minister of State, THE LORD BRABAZON OF TARA.
Parliamentary Under Secretaries, CHRISTOPHER CHOPE, OBE, MP *(Road and Traffic)*; PATRICK MCLOUGHLIN, MP *(Aviation and Shipping).*
  Private Secretaries, G. Pendlebury; S. L. J. Buck.
  Parliamentary Private Secretary to Minister of State

and Parliamentary Under Secretaries, N. Bennett, MP.
Lord in Waiting, The Viscount Davidson.
  Private Secretary. Miss S. J. Smith.
Parliamentary Clerk, Mrs. L. C. Jones.
Permanent Under Secretary of State (G1), Sir Alan Bailey, KCB.
  Private Secretary, S. Ghagan.

Information

Head of Information (G5), Miss G. P. Samuel.

PUBLIC TRANSPORT AND RESEARCH

Deputy Secretary (G2), E. B. C. Osmotherly.

Railways

Under Secretary (G3), J. R. Coates.
Heads of Division (G5), A. Fortnam; S. K. Reeves; Mrs. C. M. Dixon; R. S. Peal; A. S. D. Whybrow.
Chief Inspecting Officer (G4), R. J. Seymour.
Deputy Chief Inspecting Officer (G5), A Cooksey.

Public Transport

Under Secretary (G3), R. E. Clarke.
Heads of Division (G4), F. Gale; *(G5),* Miss S. J. Lambert; M. N. Lambirth.

Transport and Road Research Laboratory

Director (G3), D. F. Cornelius.
Deputy Director *(G4),* D. I. Robertson.
Grade 5, P. H. Bly; G. Maycocks; J. Porter; Dr. G. P. Tilly; D. R. Hinsley; Dr. R. M. Kimber.
Grade 6, J. S. Yerrell; G. F. Salt.

Science and Research Policy and Programmes

Grade 5, P. G. O'Neill.

ESTABLISHMENT AND FINANCE OFFICER
2 Marsham Street, SW1 3EB

Principal Establishment and Finance Officer (G2), J. W. S. Dempster.

Personnel
Lambeth Bridge House, SE1 7SB
[071–238 3000]

Director of Personnel (G3), R. A. Allan.
Grade 5, P. Stringfellow; Mrs. M. Clare; R. T. Bishop.
Chief Welfare Officer (G7), R. J. Lintern.
Grade 6, G. Bray; K. Wight; C. Payne; I. R. Heawood.
Chief Librarian (G6), P. Kirwan.

Finance

Under Secretary (G3), H. M. G. Stevens.
Heads of Division (G5), Mrs. G. M. Ashmore; D. M. Smith; P. G. Davies; M. J. Fuhr; J. S. Parker.
Accounting Adviser (G5), A. R. Allum.

Internal Audit

Head of Branch (G6), P. Houston.

Freight

Under Secretary (G3), D. J. Lyness.
Grade 5, L. Moyle.
Grade 6, J. Winder; D. J. Blackman.

Traffic Area Offices
Traffic Commissioners and Licensing Authorities

Eastern (Nottingham and Cambridge), Brig. C. M. Boyd.
Metropolitan (London), Air Vice-Marshal R. G. Ashford, CBE.
North Eastern (Newcastle upon Tyne and Leeds), F. Whalley.
North Western (Manchester), M. S. Albu.

Scottish (Edinburgh), K. R. Waterworth.
South Eastern (Eastbourne), Brig. M. H. Turner.
West Midlands (Birmingham), J. M. C. Pugh.
Western (Bristol), Maj.-Gen. V. H. J. Carpenter, CB, MBE.
South Wales (Cardiff), J. M. C. Pugh.

Economics and Statistics

Chief Economic Adviser (G3), Dr. J. H. Rickard.
Grade 5, C. T. B. Smith; M. C. Mann.

Statistics

Under Secretary (G3), D. W. Flaxen.
Grade 5, Miss B. J. Wood; H. Collings; G. R. Emes; R. P. Donachie.

Vehicle Inspectorate Executive Agency

Chief Executive (G4), R. J. Oliver.
Deputy Chief Executive (G5), J. A. T. David.
Director of Administration (G6), K. Walton.

Driving Standards Executive Agency

Chief Executive (G5), Dr. C. M. Woodman.

Transport Policy Unit

Grade 5, A. J. Nichols.

HIGHWAYS, SAFETY AND TRAFFIC

Deputy Secretary (G2), D. Holmes, CB.

Driver and Vehicle Licensing Executive Agency

Director (G3), S. R. Curtis.
Deputy Director (G4), M. A. Robinson.
Heads of Division (G5), R. J. Verge; P. G. Collis; J. K. Griffiths.
Grade 6, T. J. Horton.

Highways Programme Support Services

Under Secretary (G3), D. A. Holland.
Heads of Division (G5), Ms. A. Munro; J. B. W. Robins; M. R. Nevard.
Grade 7, Mrs. G. M. Holt.

Motorway Widening Unit

Director (G4), Dr. J. H. Denning.
Grade 5, N. E. Firkins.

Construction Programme Division

Eastern.—Director (G4), B. A. Sperring; *G5,* J. P. Boud.
North West.—Director (G4), G. E. Hancock; *G5,* E. A. Sherwin.
South East.—Director (G4), J. W. Fellows; *G5,* M. G. Quinn.
South West.—Director (G4), W. E. Gallagher; *G5,* G. D. Rowe.
West Midlands.—Director (G4), T. A. Rochester; *G5,* J. M. Bradley.
Yorkshire and Humberside.—Director (G5), A. J. Homer.
East Midlands.—Director (G5), S. Rose.
Northern.—Director (G5), M. B. Constable.

Network Management and Maintenance

Under Secretary (G3), P. Critchley, CB.
Heads of Division (G5), P. R. Smith; B. J. Billington; N. T. Rees; P. R. Smith.

Highways Policy and Resources

Grade 3, P. Wood.
Grade 5, B. R. A. Blaxall; P. J. Coby; D. J. Kershaw; P. E. Pickering; Miss P. M. Williams.

Engineering Policy

Director and Chief Highway Engineer (G3), F. J. Parker.
Grade 5, P. H. Dawe; J. A. Kerman; N. S. Organ.

Road and Vehicle Safety

Under Secretary (G3), R. Bird.
Heads of Division (G5), D. R. Instone; I. R. Jordan; Dr. P. H. Martin.

Chief Mechanical Engineer's Office

Chief Mechanical Engineer (G4), E. Dunn.

Vehicle Certification Executive Agency

Chief Executive (G5), D. W. Harvey.

Departmental Medical Adviser, Dr. J. F. Taylor.
Head of Medical Advisory Board (G5), Dr. R. J. M. Irvine.

London Region

Under Secretary (G3), I. Yass.
Grade 4, P. R. Smethurst.
Heads of Division (G5), R. M. C. Edridge; J. D. Wells; P. E. Butler; Dr. S. Chatterjee.

REGIONAL OFFICES

West Midlands, Birmingham.—*Regional Director (G3),* D. R. Ritchie; *Director (G5),* W. S. C. Wadrup.
Yorkshire and Humberside, Leeds.—*Regional Director (G3),* J. P. Henry; *Director (G5),* J. R. Wilkins.
North West, Manchester.—*Regional Director (G3),* D. C. Renshaw; *Director (G5),* D. York.
Northern, Newcastle upon Tyne.—*Regional Director (G3),* J. A. Owen; *Director (G5),* M. B. Constable.
South West, Bristol.—*Regional Director (G3),* Ms. E. A. Hopkins; *Director (G5),* A. P. Moss.
East Midlands, Nottingham.—*Regional Director (G4),* D. J. Morrison; *Director (G5),* S. Rose.
South East, London.—*Regional Director (G3),* D. Gruffydd Jones; *Director (G5),* A. D. Rowland.
Eastern, London.—*Regional Director (G3),* P. F. Emms; *Director (G5),* P. E. Nutt.

AVIATION, SHIPPING AND INTERNATIONAL

Deputy Secretary (G2), G. R. Sunderland.

Civil Aviation Policy Directorate

Under Secretary (G3), A. J. Goldman.
Grade 5, D. S. Evans; W. E. Kelly; E. C. Neve.
Grade 6. J. K. Adams.

International Aviation Directorate

Under Secretary (G3), D. C. Moss.
Heads of Division (G5), D. B. Cooke; M. L. Fielder; G. J. Skinner; F. A. Neal.

Air Accidents Investigation Branch

Chief Inspector of Air Accidents (G4), K. P. R. Smart.
Deputy Chief Inspector of Accidents (G5), vacant.

International Transport Directorate

Under Secretary (G3), J. D. Henes.
Grade 5, P. D. Burgess; A. J. Hunt.

Channel Tunnel Safety Unit

Grade 3, A. B. Martin.

Shipping Policy, Emergencies and Security Directorate

Under Secretary (G3), D. J. Rowlands.
Heads of Division (G5), R. G. Jones; P. Kitchen; C. J. Harris.
Grade 6 J. R. Perrett.

Marine Directorate

Under Secretary (G3), H. B. Wenban-Smith.
Heads of Division (G5), J. R. Fells; Mrs. A. M. Moss; M. W. Jackson.

Marine Emergency Operations and Marine Pollution Control Unit

Director (G4), Capt. W. H. H. McLeod, OBE.
Chief Coastguard (G5), Cdr. D. T. Ascona.
Surveyor General (G4), G. Thompson.
Deputy Surveyors General (G5), P. J. Hambling; W. A. Graham; N. W. Scully.

Marine Accidents Investigation Branch

Chief Inspector of Marine Accidents (G5), Capt. P. B. Marriott.

THE TREASURY
Parliament Street, SW1P 3AG
[071–233 3000]

The Office of the Lord High Treasurer has been continuously in commission for well over 200 years. The Lord High Commissioners of HM Treasury consist of the First Lord of the Treasury (who is also the Prime Minister), the Chancellor of the Exchequer and five Junior Lords. This Board of Commissioners is assisted at present by the Chief Secretary, a Parliamentary Secretary who is the Chief Whip, a Financial Secretary, an Economic Secretary, a Minister of State, and by the Permanent Secretary.

The Prime Minister and First Lord is not primarily concerned in the day to day aspects of Treasury business. The Parliamentary Secretary and the Junior Lords are Government whips in the House of Commons. The management of the Treasury devolves upon the Chancellor of the Exchequer and, under him, the Chief Secretary, the Financial Secretary, the Economic Secretary and the Paymaster General.

The Chief Secretary is responsible for the control of public expenditure; public services and industry groups; overseas aid and export credit; and efficiency in the public sector.

The Financial Secretary discharges the traditional responsibility of the Treasury for the largely formal procedure for the voting of funds by Parliament. He also has responsibility for other Parliamentary financial business, Inland Revenue duties and taxes, privatization policy, and industrial casework.

The Economic Secretary has responsibility for monetary policy; the Royal Mint; the financial system (including banks, building societies and other financial institutions); HMSO, the Central Office of Information, the Government Actuary's Department, and the Civil Service catering organization; international financial business; the Central Computer and Telecommunications Agency; North Sea fiscal regime; Department for National Savings, Registry of Friendly Societies and the National Loans Office; and the Treasury research budget. The Paymaster General deals with European Community business; civil service pay; Customs and Excise matters; procurement policy and the Central Unit on Purchasing; charities (non-tax aspects), profit-related pay, and the Paymaster General's Office. All Treasury Ministers are concerned in tax matters.

Prime Minister and First Lord of the Treasury, THE RT. HON. MARGARET THATCHER, MP.
Chancellor of the Exchequer, THE RT. HON. JOHN MAJOR, MP £35,120
Principal Private Secretary, vacant.
Private Secretary, J. M. G. Taylor.
Parliamentary Private Secretary, A. Favell, MP.
Parliamentary Clerk, B. O. Dyer.
Chief Secretary to the Treasury, THE RT. HON. NORMAN LAMONT, MP £35,120

Private Secretary, Miss G. C. Evans.
Assistant Private Secretary, P. T. Wanless.
Paymaster General, RICHARD RYDER, OBE, MP £24,850
Private Secretary, M. R. Buckler.
Financial Secretary to the Treasury, THE HON. FRANCIS MAUDE, MP £24,850
Private Secretary, S. Flanagan.
Economic Secretary, JOHN MAPLES, MP £18,860
Private Secretary, Miss. S. M. A. James.
Parliamentary Secretary to the Treasury and Government Chief Whip, THE RT. HON. TIMOTHY RENTON, MP £29,230
Private Secretary, M. Maclean.
Treasurer of HM Household and Deputy Chief Whip, ALASTAIR GOODLAD, MP £24,850
Lord Commissioners of the Treasury, J. Taylor, MP; The Hon. T. Sackville, MP; S. Chapman, MP; G. Knight, MP; I. Patnick, OBE, MP £15,990
Assistant Whips, N. Baker, MP; T Wood, MP; N. Hamilton, MP; T. Boswell, MP; T. Kirkhope, MP £15,990
(NOTE.—All salaries shown above do not include Parliamentary salary.)
(For Civil Service **Salaries**, *see* page 295).

Permanent Secretary of the Treasury, Sir Peter Middleton, GCB.
Private Secretary, R. J. Evans.
Second Permanent Secretaries (G1A), N. L. Wicks, CVO, CBE *(Overseas Finance)*; N. J. Monck *(Public Expenditure)*; G. H. Phillips, CB *(Civil Service Management and Pay)*.
Head of Government Economics Service and Chief Economic Adviser to the Treasury, Sir Terence Burns.
Head of Government Accountancy Service, A. J. Hardcastle.
Deputy Secretaries (G2), M. C. Scholar *(Public Finance)*; H. P. Evans *(Overseas Finance)*; A. J. C. Edwards *(Public Services, and General Expenditure)*; R. Wilson *(Industry)*.
Deputy Chief Economic Adviser to the Treasury (G2), J. C. Odling-Smee.

INDUSTRY

Industry, Agriculture and Employment Group

Under Secretary (G3), G. Monger.
Assistant Secretaries (G5), Miss J. Barber; Miss M. O'Mara; D. Revolta.

Public Enterprises Group

Under Secretary (G3), S. A. Robson.
Assistant Secretaries (G5), R. Bent; M. L. Williams.

Home Transport and Education Group

Under Secretary (G3), Mrs. A. F. Case.
Assistant Secretaries (G5), C. Farthing; J. E. Mortimer.

PUBLIC SERVICES AND GENERAL EXPENDITURE

Management Policy Group

Under Secretary (G3), W. L. St. Clair.
Assistant Secretaries (G5), P. M. Rayner; N. M. Hansford.

Social Services and Territorial Group

Under Secretary (G3), Miss M. E. Peirson.
Assistant Secretaries (G5), J. P. McIntyre; R. B. Saunders; A. M. White.

Local Government Group

Under Secretary (G3), D. J. Bostock.
Assistant Secretaries (G5), N. J. Ilett; S. N. Wood.

Central Unit on Purchasing

Director, P. Forshaw.
Deputy Director, M. J. Hoare.

Accounts and Purchasing

Under Secretary (G3), J. S. Beastall.
Assistant Secretary (G5), J. R. Colling.

Central Computer and Telecommunications Agency

Under Secretary (G3), I. P. Wilson.
Assistant Secretaries (G5), W. Houldsworth; C. R. Muid; I. S. Thomson; R. E. Dibble; J. Winup; A. R. Williams.

GENERAL EXPENDITURE
General Expenditure Policy Group

Under Secretary (G3), Mrs. J. R. Lomax.
Assistant Secretaries (G5), J. F. Gilhooly; F. K. Jones; I. W. V. Taylor.

Defence Policy, Manpower and Material Group

Under Secretary (G3), D. J. L. Moore.
Assistant Secretaries (G5), H. J. Bush; T. R. Fellgett.

OVERSEAS FINANCE
International Finance Group

Under Secretary (G3), A. C. S. Allan.
Assistant Secretaries (G5), C. L. Melliss; C. R. Pickering.

Aid and Export Finance Group

Under Secretary (G3), P. Mountfield.
Assistant Secretaries (G5), A. R. M. Bottrill; Mrs. S. D. Brown.

European Community Group

Under Secretary (G3), R. I. G. Allen.
Assistant Secretaries (G5), Mrs. M. E. Brown; M. C. Mercer.

Accountancy Advice Group

Grade 4, D. Cooke.
Assistant Secretary (G5), D. Jamieson.
Senior Principals (G6), K. E. Bradley; J. L. Constantine.

DEPUTY CHIEF ECONOMIC ADVISER'S SECTOR
Deputy Secretary (G2), J. C. Odling-Smee.
Assistant Secretary (G5), vacant.

Economics Assessment Group

Under Secretary (G3), P. N. Sedgewick.
Senior Economic Advisers (G5), J. S. Hibberd; D. E. Owen.

Medium Term and Policy Analysis Group

Under Secretary (G3), C. Riley.
Assistant Secretaries (G5), S. J. Davies; C. Kelly.

Economics of Industry Division

Under Secretary (G3), M. J. Spackman.
Assistant Secretaries (G5), A. J. Meyrick; R. Weeden.

PUBLIC FINANCE
Fiscal Policy Group

Under Secretary (G3), R. P. Culpin.
Assistant Secretary (G5), Miss J. K. Rutter.

Monetary Group

Under Secretary (G3), P. R. C. Gray.
Assistant Secretaries (G5), J. W. Grice; J. P. McIntyre.

Financial Institutions and Markets Group

Under Secretary (G3), H. G. Walsh.
Assistant Secretaries (G5), L. Watts (*Accounts*); Miss G. M. Noble; J. M. G. Taylor.

Public Sector Finance

Assistant Secretary (G5), C. J. Mowl.
Economic Adviser (G7), Ms. C. Turk.
Statistician (G7), Mrs. H. Wright.

CIVIL SERVICE MANAGEMENT AND PAY
Pay and Industrial Relations Group

Deputy Secretary (G3), C. W. Kelly.
Assistant Secretaries (G5), J. S. Cunliffe; I. Strachan; Ms. E. I. Young.
Grade 6, F. S. G. Easton.

Personnel Policy Group

Under Secretary (G3), L. J. Harris.
Assistant Secretaries (G5), J. Dixon; Mrs. N. F. Haworth; G. H. B. Jordan.
Grade 6, J. A. Barker; D. G. Pain; D. W. Rayson.

CENTRAL DIVISIONS
Establishment and Organization Division

Under Secretary (G3), B. M. Fox.
Assistant Secretaries (G5), E. I. Cooper; A. J. T. MacAuslan; D. Todd.
Senior Principals (G6), R. N. Edwards; J. H. Edwards; B. J. Porteus; D. Rampton.

Economic Briefing Division

Assistant Secretary (G5), A. W. Ritchie.

Information Division

Assistant Secretary (G5), A. T. O'Donnell.
Deputy Head of Division (G6), Miss J. C. Simpson.

TREASURY REPRESENTATIVES IN USA
Economic Minister and UK Representative IMF/ IBRD, D. L. C. Peretz.

CIVIL SERVICE CATERING ORGANIZATION
Executive Director (G4), D. S. B. Simpson.

RATING OF GOVERNMENT PROPERTY DEPARTMENT
Jameson House, 69 Notting Hill Gate, W11 3JU
(Transfers to Inland Revenue in Spring 1991).

Treasury Valuer, T. J. Cundall.
Deputy Treasury Valuer, B. G. Jones.

THE TREASURY SOLICITOR
Department of HM Procurator-General and Treasury Solicitor
Queen Anne's Chambers, 28 Broadway, SW1H 9JS
[071–210 3000]

The Treasury Solicitor's Department provides legal services for many Government departments. Those that do not have their own lawyers are given legal advice, and both they and many other departments are provided with litigation and conveyancing services. The Department also deals with Bona Vacantia. The Treasury Solicitor is also the Queen's Proctor.
(For **Salaries**, *see* page 295).

Procurator-General and Treasury Solicitor (G1), J. Nursaw, CB, QC.
Deputy Treasury Solicitor (G2), T. J. G. Pratt.

Central Advisory Division
Principal Assistant Solicitor (G3), M. A. Blythe.
Assistant Solicitors (G5), F. L. Croft; M. J. Hemming.
Grade 6, Mrs. P. Dayer; C. J. Gregory; Miss P. F. Henderson; Ms. V. Selzer.

Litigation Divisions
Principal Assistant Solicitors (G3), R. N. Ricks; J. H. Wilkinson.
Assistant Solicitors (G5), D. Brummell; I. Hood; A. Leithead; R. Lines; A. J. Sandal; S. Sargant; G. F. Sills.
Grade 6, A. P. M. Aylett; Mrs. D. Babar; M. R. M. Davis; J. N. Desai; A. K. Fraser; P. D. F. Grant; J. D. Howes; A. D. Lawton; P. Messer; D. Palmer; D. A. Stalker; A. Turek.
Senior Legal Assistant, Miss P. J. Carroll.
Principals (G7), N. Ash; Mrs. J. Bonsey; Miss R. M. Caudwell; N. M. Fleischman; Mrs. G. Fuller; Miss E. Long; Miss M. A. McNally; N. Magyar; F. G. O'Connell; R. C. J. Opie; H. O. J. R. Shepheard; C. Stephens; M. G. Truran; R. J. Walters; J. C. Youdell.

Queen's Proctor Division
Queen's Proctor, J. Nursaw, CB, QC.
Assistant Queen's Proctor, I. Hood.

Property Division
Principal Assistant Solicitor (G3), A. D. Osborne.
Assistant Solicitors (G5), R. W. M. Cooper; Miss G. Gilder; P. L. Noble; P. F. Nockles; M. F. Rawlins; A. M. Scarfe; J. Wyer.
Grade 6, R. L. Coward; M. Drayton; D. J. C. Garnett; R. D. Harris; J. B. Howe; C. L. Oastler; R. M. Pierce; A. W. Prior; S. W. Rock; M. R. Rosenfeld; Miss P. E. Slatter; R. J. B. Stenhouse; T Sylvester-Jones; B. D. Thurley.
Senior Legal Assistants, M. V. Cooper; T. Forrester; A. R. Lilleystone; S. A. Tobin; W. F. Williams.
Grade 7, I. Adams; D. G. Ager; H. S. Davis; Mrs. A. M. Foxhuntley; C. R. Irving; R. S. Lugg; J. H. McFarland; G. J. Norris; P. Page; D. A. Reid; N. P. Rex; G. T. Tuttle; J. M. Williamson.

Establishment, Finance and General Services Division
Establishment and Legal Personnel Officer (G5), D. F. W. Pickup.

Deputy Establishment Officer (G7), Mrs. P. L. Woods.
Head of Costs Branch (G6), P. Moran.
Chief Accountant (G7), B. C. Shephard.

Bona Vacantia Division
Assistant Solicitor (G5), Miss S. L. Sargant.
Senior Legal Assistant, M. R. M. Davies.
Grade 7, Miss H. Donnelly.

Ministry of Defence Branch
Neville House, Page Street, SW1P 4LS
[071–218 4691]

Grade 4, R. P. Ellis.
Grade 5, J. R. G. Braggins.
Grade 6, R. A. D. Jackson; A. L. Norris; M. B. Sturdy.

Department of Education and Science Branch
Elizabeth House, York Road, SE1 7PH
[071–934 9000]

Principal Assistant Solicitor (G3), J. E. Coleman, CB.
Assistant Solicitors (G5), D. J. Aries; M. Harris; A. D. Preston.
Grade 6, Miss J. L. C. Brooks; S. T. Harker.
Senior Legal Assistant, N. P. Beach.

Department of Employment Branch
Caxton House, Tothill Street, SW1H 9NF
[071–273 3000]

Principal Assistant Solicitor (G3), H. R. L. Purse.
Assistant Solicitors (G5), R. J. Baker; Mrs. A. Leale; S. G. Milligan; Miss V. Rice-Pyle.
Grade 6, R. H. Britten; G. W. M. Galliford; C. House; N. A. D. Lambert; Miss M. Trefgarne; J. K. Winayak.
Senior Legal Assistant, J. Hall.
Grade 7, P. H. Kilgarriff.

Department of Energy Branch
1 Palace Street, SW1E 5HE
[071–238 3000]

Principal Assistant Solicitor (G3), G. B. Claydon.
Assistant Solicitors (G5), D. Hogg; D. H. M. Ingham; S. G. Milligan; D. F. Pascho.
Grade 6, M. R. Brocklehurst; F. D. W. Clarke; Miss V. F. Dewhurst; Mrs. C. V. Fox; R. C. Perkins.

Department of Transport Branch
2 Marsham Street, SW1P 3EB
[071–276 3000]

Principal Assistant Solicitor (G3), G. H. Beetham.
Assistant Solicitors (G5), R. G. Bellis; P. D. Coopman; C. W. M. Ingram; B. W. James; A. G. Jones.
Grade 6, Miss A. Lind-Smith; B. McHenry; N. C. Thomas,.
Senior Legal Assistants, B. J. Hammersley; A. K. Johnston.
Grade 7, Mrs. A. Heilpern; Miss A. Lancaster; A. W. Stewart.

COUNCIL ON TRIBUNALS
7th Floor, 22 Kingsway, WC2B 6LE
[071-936 7045]

The Council on Tribunals is an independent statutory body. It keeps under review the constitution and working of the various tribunals which have been placed under its general supervision, and considers and reports on administrative procedures relating to statutory inquiries. It is consulted by Government departments on proposals for legislation affecting tribunals and inquiries, and on proposals where the need for an appeals procedure may arise. It also offers advice on draft primary legislation.

Some 60 tribunals are currently under the Council's supervision. The matters with which they deal range from agriculture to immigration, pensions, road traffic, taxation, and the allocation of school places.

The Scottish Committee of the Council generally considers Scottish tribunals and matters relating only to Scotland.

Members of the Council are appointed by the Lord Chancellor and the Lord Advocate. The Scottish Committee is composed partly of members of the Council designated by the Lord Advocate and partly others appointed by him. The Parliamentary Commissioner for Administration is *ex officio* a member of both the Council and the Scottish Committee.

Chairman, Sir Cecil Clothier, KCB, QC.

Members, The Parliamentary Commissioner for Administration; G. M. Anderson; T. N. Biggart, CBE; M. Dempsey; Prof. D. L. Foulkes; T. R. H. Godden, CB; B. Hill; Miss J. Horsham, CB; G. V. Hyde; W. N. Hyde; Mrs. J. U. Kellock; L. F. Read, QC; M. E. J. Rush, CBE; Mrs. S. H. Spence; Prof. A. Webb.

Secretary, C. W. Dyment.

Scottish Committee
20 Walker Street, Edinburgh EH3 7HR
[031–220 1236]

Chairman, T. N. Biggart, CBE.

Members, The Parliamentary Commissioner for Administration; D. Bruce; W. J. Campbell; Mrs. C. A. M. Davies; T. R. H. Godden; J. Langan; Lady Scott.

Secretary, Ms. L. Wilkie.

TRIBUNALS
(*see* pages 388–89)

UNIVERSITIES FUNDING COUNCIL
14 Park Crescent, W1N 4DH
[071–636 7799]

The Universities Funding Council was established under the provisions of the Education Reform Act 1988, and came into existence formally on April 1, 1989.

Chairman, The Lord Chilver, FRS.

Chief Executive, Sir Peter Swinnerton-Dyer, Bt., KBE, FRS.

Members, Prof. J. P. Barron; Prof. Gillian Brown; Mrs. R. Chapman; Prof. D. Dilks; Prof. Sir Colin Dollery; Prof. B. Follett, FRS; Sir Kenneth Green; Prof. Marian Hicks; R. B. Horton; Sir Donald McCallum; Sir Charles Reece; Prof. G. Roberts, FRS; Prof. H. Wood.

Secretary, N. T. Hardyman, CB.

Assistant Secretaries (G5), E. C. Appleyard; J. H. Farrant; M. S. Hedges.

OFFICE OF WATER SERVICES
Centre City Tower, 7 Hill Street,
Birmingham B5 4UA
[021–625 1300]

The Office of Water Services (Ofwat) was set up under the Water Act 1989 and came into being on Sept. 1, 1989. Its role is to support the Director General of Water Services who regulates the economic framework of the water industry in England and Wales. His main duties are to ensure that water companies comply with the terms of their appointments (or licences) and to protect the interests of water consumers. The Director General has established ten customer service committies who investigate complaints and identify customer concerns. The Director General is independent of Ministerial control and directly accountable to Parliament.

Director General of Water Services, I. Byatt.

WELSH OFFICE

The Welsh Office has responsibility in Wales for ministerial functions relating to health and personal social services; education, except for terms and conditions of service, student awards and the University; the Welsh language and culture; local government; housing; water and sewerage; environmental protection; sport; agriculture and fisheries; forestry; land use, including town and country planning, countryside and nature conservation; new towns; ancient monuments and historic buildings; roads; tourism; a range of matters affecting the careers service and the activities of the Training Agency in Wales; financial assistance to industry; the urban programme in Wales; the operation of the European Regional Development Fund in Wales and other European Community matters; civil emergencies, and all financial aspects of these matters, including Welsh rate support grant. It has oversight responsibilities for economic affairs and regional planning in Wales.

(For **Salaries,** *see* page 295).

Gwydyr House, Whitehall, SW1A 2ER
[071–270 300]

Secretary of State for Wales, THE RT. HON. DAVID HUNT, MBE, MP.

  Private Secretary, L. Conway.

  Assistant Private Secretaries, A. G. Aggett; A. E. Coleman.

  Parliamentary Private Secretary, J. Bowis, MP.

Minister of State, SIR WYN ROBERTS, MP.

  Private Secretary, M. C. Hum.

Parliamentary Under-Secretary, IAN GRIST, MP.

  Private Secretary, W. H. Rees.

Parliamentary Clerk, V. R. Watkin.

Permanent Secretary (G1), Sir Richard Lloyd Jones, KCB.

  Private Secretary, I. R. Miller.

Cathays Park, Cardiff CF1 3NQ
[0222–825111]

Deputy Secretaries (G2), J. W. Lloyd; F. J. Craig.

Establishment Group

Principal Establishment Officer (G3), G. C. G. Craig.

Heads of Divisions (G5), R. M. Abel; W. L. Chapman.

Senior Economic Adviser (G5), O. T. Hooker.

Chief Statistician (G5), Dr. M. P. G. Pepper.

Head of Health Intelligence Unit (G6), G. J. Cockell.

Principals (G7), R. J. Callen; P. Davenport; C. Tudor.

Economic Adviser (G7), V. W. F. McPherson.

Principal Research Officers (G7), I. I. Thomas; E. Darwin; Mrs. M. A. J. Gronow.

Statisticians (G7), D. D. Baird; M. R. Brand; G. P. Davies; J. T. Fletcher; K. Francombe; Ms. C. Fullerton; P. J. Fullerton; E. Swires Hennessy; J. D. James; H. M. Jones; R. Jones; J. D. Kinder; Mrs. S. Stansfield.

Cadw: Welsh Historic Monuments
Brunel House, Fitzalan Road, Cardiff CF2 1UY
[0222–465511]

Director, E. A. J. Carr.

Conservation Architect (G6), J. D. Hogg.

Principal Inspector of Ancient Monuments and Historic Buildings, J. R. Avent.

Cathays Park, Cardiff CF1 3NQ

Inspectors of Ancient Monuments and Historic Buildings, J. K. Knight; A. D. McLees; Dr. S. E. Rees; R. C. Turner; M. J. Yates.

Finance Group

Principal Finance Officer (G3), R. A. Wallace.

Heads of Divisions (G5), C. L. Jones; L. A. Pavelin; J. Shortridge; B. Wilcox.

Grade 6, M. G. Horlock.
Principals (G7), B. R. Davies; Dr. M. Dunn; J. Kilner; P. G. C. Lunn; R. D. Macey; H. Rawlings; D. T. Richards; B. O. Valentine.
Head of Internal Audit (G7), D. Howarth.
Head of NHS Audit (G7), P. Brown.

Housing, Health and Social Services Policy Group

Head of Group (G3), R. W. Jarman.
Heads of Divisions (G5), D. Adams; R. J. Davies; S. H. Martin; A. Thornton.
Chief Social Work Service Officer (G5), D. G. Evans.
Chief Architect (G6), C. Eyres (*acting*).
Deputy Chief Social Work Service Officer, J. K. Fletcher.
Principals (G7), Mrs. N. Barry; C. Coombs; A. C. Elmer; P. Godden-Kent; D. B. Hilbourne; A. G. Huws; Miss E. M. Jones; Mrs. C. Peat; M. Shannahan; A. C. Wood.
Social Work Service Officers (G7), D, Barker; D. A. Brushett; G. H. Davies; Miss R. E. Evans; I. Forster; J. F. Mooney; C. D. Vyvyan; Mrs. P. White; R. C. Woodward.
Principal Professional and Technology Officers (G7), R. Broad; T. A. Campden; G. N. Harding; W. Ross.

Health Professional Group

Medical Officer .... £24,997–£33,970
Dental Officer .... £24,997–£33,970
Chief Medical Officer (G3), Dr. D. J. Hine.
Deputy Chief Medical Officer (G4), Dr. H. G. Penrhyn-Jones.
Senior Medical Officers (G5), D. Ferguson Lewis; Ms. M. Cotter; D. Owen; Ms. R. Jacobs; J. K. Richmond; Ms. A. K. Thomas.
Chief Dental Officer, D. M. Heap.
Medical Officers, J. D. Andrews; J. W. Crossley; T. I. Evans; Dr. L. Hamilton-Kirkwood; N. E. Thomas.
Dental Officers, T. M. Davies; J. D. O. Parkholm; T. A. Williams.
Scientific Adviser (G5), Dr. J. A. V. Pritchard.
Pharmaceutical Adviser (G6), Dr. G. B. A. Veitch.
Environmental Health Adviser (G6), R. J. Alexander.

National Health Service Directorate

Director of the NHS in Wales, J. W. Owen.
Heads of Divisions (G5), W. G. Davies; G. T. Evans; D. A. Pritchard; N. E. Thomas; Mrs. B. J. M. Wilson.
Principals (G7), Mrs. J. Annand; C. J. Burdett; J. Duggan; M. H. Harper; T. W. Hunter; R. J. Keveren; D. McGlinn; Mrs C. Maddocks; K. Orchard; D. M. Rolph; K. S. Sleight; G. P. Thomas; M. F. Webb.
Ambulance Adviser (G7), P. J. Hunt.
Principal Professional and Technology Officer (G7), M. W. Grist.

Nursing Division

Chief Nursing Officer (G3), Miss M. Bull.
Deputy Chief Nursing Officer (G4), Mrs. B. Melvin.
Nursing Officers (G6), Mrs. R. Cohen; Miss G. Harris; Dr. D. Keyzer; M. F. Tonkin; Mrs. D. J. Vass.

Legal Division

Legal Adviser (G3), A. J. Beale.
Assistant Solicitors (G5), D. G. Lambert; P. J. Murrin.
Grade 6, J. D. H. Evans; A. K. Gillard; C. P. Jones; C. G. Longville; Mrs. T. C. Shellens; J. H. Turnbull; A. J. Watkins; A. Widdrington.
Senior Legal Assistants (G7), A. J. Park; Mrs. A. T. Parkes; D. H. J. Williams.

Information Division

Director of Information (G5), H. G. Roberts.
Chief Press Officer (G7), E. M. Bowen, MVO.

Economic and Regional Policy Group

Head of Group (G3), M. J. Cochlin.
Heads of Divisions (G5), M. E. Bevan; Miss E. N. M. Davies; B. J. Mitchell; D. T. Richards; F. G. Watson.
Principals (G7), D. Beames; M. H. Bendon; M. C. Berenson; R. O. Evans; Ms. J. M. Gordon; Miss J. E. Paulett; D. C. Quinlan; Ms. J. H. Roberts; J. N. Roberts.

Industry Department

Director (G3), C. D. Stevens.
Industrial Director (G4), T. E. Morgan, MBE.
Heads of Divisions (G5), D. Jones; R. C. Williams.
Senior Principal Scientific Officer (G6), Dr. R. J. Loveland.
Principals (G7), P. Bishop; J. A. Grimes; D. Pugh (at Colwyn Bay); K. Smith; R. Waller; J. W. Wallington.
Principal Scientific Officers (G7), P. Bragg; G. A. Madden.

Education Department

Head of Department (G3), R. H. Jones, CVO.
Chief Inspector (G4), R. L. Jones.
Heads of Divisions (G5), H. Evans; M. L. Evans.
Heads of Divisions (G5), R. C. Simpson; W. S. Jones.
Principals (G7), Mrs. J. Booker; D. A. Bullen; R. O. Evans; B. Hayward-Blake; Mrs. J. Hopkins; J. R. Howells; Mrs. J. Milligan; M. G. Richards; Mrs. H. Thomas; A. Whittaker.

HM Inspectorate

Chief Inspector (G4), R. L. Jones.
Staff Inspectors (G5), S. J. Adams; W. R. Jenkins; T. E. Parry; P. Thomas; R. Thomas; M. J. F. Wynn.
HM Inspectors (G6), C. Abbott; G. Adams; R. A. Charles; Mrs. G. Briwnant Jones; R. G. Davies; D. G. Evans; J. R. N. Evans; N. B. Evans; Mrs. L. Gainsbury; G. C. Griffiths; J. Griffiths; M. G. Haines; A. Hamilton Jones; I. G. Higginbotham; A. Higgins; I. L. James; Mrs. R. James; M. John; G. D. Jones; A. R. Large; G. T. J. Jones; O. E. Jones; Mrs A. Keane; J. M. Laugharne; M. J. Law; J. R. Lewis; Miss S. Lewis; Mrs. M. E. R. Lloyd; A. Lowndes; A. Morgan; I. G. Morgan; Miss P. A. Nicholas; Miss E. Ogwen; T. G. Prosser; W. H. Raybould; D. G. H. Rees; Miss D. Selleck; Mrs. V. Scott; R. I. Swain; R. Taylor; G. Thomas; Mrs. I. Thomas; Miss L. Thomas; P. B. Walker; B. Wigley; E. L. Williams; D. P. Williams.

Transport, Planning, Water and Environment Group

Head of Group (G3), P. R. Gregory.
Director of Highways (G4), K. J. Thomas°.
Heads of Divisions (G5), A. H. H. Jones; D. I. Westlake°; C. J. Curry (*Chief Planner*); H. R. Bollington°; Mrs. E. Taylor°; (G6), D. M. Timlin.
Superintending Engineers (G6), J. G. Evans°; B. H. Hawker*.
Superintending Estates Officer (G6), G. K. Hoad.
Senior Principal (G6), P. R. Marsden.
Principals (G7), W. M. P. Cooper; G. Davies; R. W. Jenkins°; Miss C. M. Owen; A. V. Price; D. Powell°; G. R. Jones; D. Hadfield°; W. P. Roderick; D. Simpson; B. Smith.
Principal Planning Officers (G7), D. B. Courtier; J. O. Pryce; J. V. Spear.
Principal Research Officers (G7), A. S. Dredge; Ms. L. J. Roberts.
Principal Estates Officer (G7), R. W. Wilson.
Principal Professional and Technology Officers (G7), J. A. Atkins; H. R. Payne; J. E. Saunders.
Principal Professional and Technology Officers, Highways Directorate (G7), P. Dunstan°; J. A. L.

Harries*; A. L. Howcraft°; B. J. W. Martin°; R. H. Powell°; J. R. Rees°; D. P. Soane°; C. W. W. Smart°; J. Fitch*; J. Collins°; K. J. Alexander°; R. H. Hooper*.

Planning Inspectorate

Principal Planning Inspectors (G5), R. Pierce; D. Sheers.

Senior Housing and Planning Inspectors (G6), T. W. B. Barnes; J. H. Chadwick; R. Davies; P. V. Farrow; M. Griffin; G. Sloan; A. H. Vaughan; S. B. Wild.

HM Inspectorate of Pollution for Wales

Inspector, Radiation and Chemicals (G7), Dr. C. Hardman.

Inspector, Water (G7), A. A. Houlden.

Agriculture Department

Head of Department (G3), O. Rees.

Heads of Divisions (G5), G. Podmore; D. R. Thomas; L. K. Walford.

Principals (G7), P. Finnigan†; J. C. Alexander; J. C. Carter (*acting*); R. A. Norris; R. F. Patterson; C. E. Taylor°; D. R. Davies; B. E. Price°; P. N. S. Wolfenden†.

Divisional Executive Officers (G7), W. K. Griffiths (*Carmarthen*); E. Hughes (*Caernarfon*); R. J. E. Wilcox (*Llandrindod Wells*).

Based at:

°Ty Glas Road, Llanishen, Cardiff CF4 5PL (022–753271)

*Government Buildings, Pinerth Road, Rhos on Sea, Colwyn Bay LL28 4UL (0492–44261)

†Plas Crug, Aberystwyth SY23 1NG (0970–3162)

WOMEN'S NATIONAL COMMISSION
Government Offices, Horse Guards Road, SW1P 3AL
[071–270 5903]

The Women's National Commission is an advisory committee to Government whose terms of reference are to ensure by all possible means that the informed opinions of women are given their due weight in the deliberations of Government. The Commission's fifty members are all women who are elected or appointed by national organizations with a large and active membership of women. The organizations include the women's sections of the major political parties, trades unions, religious groups, professional women's organizations and other bodies broadly representative of women.

Government Co-Chairman, Mrs. Gillian Shephard, MP (*nominated by the Prime Minister* 1990).

Elected Co-Chairman, Mrs. Margaret Morrison, BEM (*elected* 1989).

Secretary, Ms. M. Jones.

WOMEN'S ROYAL VOLUNTARY SERVICE
234–244 Stockwell Road, SW9 9SP
[071–733 3388]

The Women's Royal Voluntary Service (WRVS) assists Government departments, local authorities and voluntary bodies in organizing and carrying out welfare and emergency work for the community on a nationwide network operated through area, county, district and London borough organizers. Activities include work for the elderly and handicapped, for young families and for prisoners and their families; non-medical work in hospitals; welfare work for HM Forces and for Service families; and trained teams to assist in national and local emergencies. Administrative costs are met from an annual Home Office grant.

National Chairman, The Hon. Mrs. Mary Corsar.

LAW COURTS AND OFFICES

THE JUDICIAL COMMITTEE OF THE PRIVY COUNCIL

The Judicial Committee of the Privy Council is the final court of appeal from courts of the United Kingdom dependencies, courts of independent Commonwealth countries which have retained the right of appeal, courts of the Channel Islands and the Isle of Man, some professional and disciplinary committees, and church sources.

The Judicial Committee includes the Lord Chancellor, the Lords of Appeal in Ordinary (*see* below) and other members of the Privy Council who hold or have held high judicial office, and certain judges from the Commonwealth. Usually, only three or five hear each case.

Privy Council Office (Judicial Department), Downing Street, SW1A 2AJ.
Registrar of the Privy Council, D. H. O. Owen.
Chief Clerk, D. Rushton.

THE JUDICATURE OF ENGLAND AND WALES

The legal system of England and Wales is separate from those of Scotland and Northern Ireland and differs from them in law, judicial procedure and court structure, although there is a common distinction between civil law (disputes between individuals) and criminal law (acts harmful to the community).

The supreme judicial authority for England and Wales is the House of Lords, which is the ultimate Court of Appeal from all courts in Great Britain and Northern Ireland (except criminal courts in Scotland). As a Court of Appeal it consists of the Lord Chancellor and the Lords of Appeal in Ordinary (Law Lords).

The Supreme Court of Judicature comprises the Court of Appeal, the Crown Court and the High Court of Justice. The High Court of Justice is the superior civil court and is divided into three Divisions. The Chancery Division is concerned mainly with equity, bankruptcy and contentious probate business; the Queen's Bench Division deals with commercial and maritime law, with civil cases not assigned to other courts, and hears appeals from lower courts; and the Family Division, which deals with matters relating to family law. Sittings are held at the Royal Courts of Justice in London or at 24 Crown Court centres outside the capital. High Court judges sit alone to hear cases at first instance. Appeals from lower courts are heard by two or three judges, or by single judges of the appropriate Division.

The decision to prosecute in cases tried on indictment and in summary cases of a serious nature rests with the Crown Prosecution Service, an independent prosecuting body established in 1986 to serve all of England and Wales (*see* p. 383–4). At the head of the Service is the Director of Public Prosecutions, who discharges his duties under the superintendence of the Attorney General. Certain categories of offence continue to require the consent for prosecution of the Attorney General.

Minor criminal offences (summary offences) are dealt with in magistrates' courts, which usually consist of three unpaid lay magistrates (justices of the peace) sitting without a jury, who are advised on points of law and procedure by a legally-qualified clerk to the justices. In busier courts a full-time, salaried and legally-qualified stipendiary magistrate presides alone. Cases involving people under 17 are heard in juvenile courts, specially constituted magistrates' courts which sit apart from other courts.

Preliminary proceedings in a serious case to decide whether there is evidence to justify committal for trial in the Crown Court are also held in the magistrates' courts. Appeals from magistrates' courts against sentence or conviction are made to the Crown Court. Appeals upon a point of law are made to the High Court, and may go on to the House of Lords.

The Crown Court sits in about 90 centres, divided into six circuits, and is presided over by High Court judges, full-time circuit judges, and part-time recorders, sitting with a jury in all trials which are contested. It deals with trials of the more serious criminal offences, the sentencing of offenders committed for sentence by magistrates' courts (when the magistrates consider their own power of sentence inadequate), and appeals from lower courts. Magistrates usually sit with a circuit judge or recorder to deal with appeals and committals for sentence. Appeals from the Crown Court, either against sentence or conviction, are made to the Court of Appeal (Criminal Division), presided over by the Lord Chief Justice. A further appeal from the Court of Appeal to the House of Lords can be brought if a point of law of general public importance is considered to be involved.

Most minor civil cases are dealt with by the county courts, of which there are about 300. For cases involving small claims there are special arbitration facilities and simplified procedures; cases involving claims which exceed set limits may be tried in the county courts with the consent of the parties, or in certain circumstances on transfer from the High Court. Undefended divorce cases and, outside London, bankruptcy proceedings can be heard in designated county courts. Magistrates' courts can deal with certain classes of civil case, mostly those relating to the family, and committees of magistrates licence public houses, clubs and betting shops. Appeals in matrimonial, adoption and guardianship proceedings heard in the magistrates' courts go to the Family Division of the High Court; affiliation appeals and appeals from decisions of the licensing committees of magistrates to the Crown Court. Appeals from the High Court and county courts are heard in the Court of Appeal (Civil Division), presided over by the Master of the Rolls, and may go on to the House of Lords, the final court of appeal in civil cases.

Coroners' courts investigate violent and unnatural deaths or sudden deaths where the cause is unknown. Cases may be brought before a local coroner (a senior lawyer or doctor) by doctors, the police, various public authorities or members of the public. Where a death is sudden and the cause is unknown, the coroner may order a post-mortem examination to determine the cause of death rather than holding an inquest in court.

THE HOUSE OF LORDS
(as final Court of Appeal)

The Lord High Chancellor
The Rt. Hon. the Lord Mackay of Clashfern
(*born 1927, apptd. 1987*).
Lords of Appeal in Ordinary (each £88,500)

	Apptd.
Rt. Hon. Lord Keith of Kinkel, *born 1922*	1977
Rt. Hon. Lord Bridge of Harwich, *born 1917* . .	1980
Rt. Hon. Lord Brandon of Oakbrook, MC, *born 1920*	1981
Rt. Hon. Lord Templeman, MBE, *born 1920*	1982
Rt. Hon. Lord Griffiths, MC, *born 1923*	1985
Rt. Hon. Lord Ackner, *born 1920*	1986
Rt. Hon. Lord Oliver of Aylmerton, *born 1921*	1986

Rt. Hon. Lord Goff of Chieveley, *born* 1926 ... 1986
Rt. Hon. Lord Jauncey of Tullichettle, *born*
1925...................................... 1987
Rt. Hon. Lord Lowry, *born* 1919............. 1988
Registrar (The Clerk of the Parliaments), Sir John
Sainty, KCB.

SUPREME COURT OF JUDICATURE
COURT OF APPEAL

Ex officio Judges.—The Lord High Chancellor, the
Lord Chief Justice of England, the Master of the
Rolls, the President of the Family Division, and the
Vice-Chancellor.
The Master of the Rolls (£88,500)
The Rt. Hon. the Lord Donaldson of Lymington
(*born* 1920, *apptd*. 1982)
Secretary, Miss V. Seymour; *Clerk*, G. Corimmett.

Lords Justices of Appeal (each £85,000)

	Apptd.
Rt. Hon. Sir Tasker Watkins, GBE, VC, *born* 1918......................................	1980
Rt. Hon. Sir Patrick O'Connor, *born* 1914	1980
Rt. Hon. Sir Michael Fox, *born* 1921	1981
Rt. Hon. Sir Christopher Slade, *born* 1927 ...	1982
Rt. Hon. Sir Francis Purchas, *born* 1919	1982
Rt. Hon. Sir Brian Dillon, *born* 1923	1982
Rt. Hon. Sir Roger Parker, *born* 1923	1983
Rt. Hon. Sir Anthony Lloyd, *born* 1929	1984
Rt. Hon. Sir Brian Neill, *born* 1923	1985
Rt. Hon. Sir Michael Mustill, *born* 1931	1985
Rt. Hon. Sir Martin Nourse, *born* 1932........	1985
Rt. Hon. Sir Iain Glidewell, *born* 1924	1985
Rt. Hon. Sir John Balcombe, *born* 1925......	1985
Rt. Hon. Sir Ralph Gibson, *born* 1922	1985
Rt. Hon. Sir John Stocker, MC, TD, *born* 1918	1986
Rt. Hon. Sir Harry Woolf, *born* 1933	1986
Rt. Hon. Sir Donald Nicholls, *born* 1933	1986
Rt. Hon. Sir Thomas Bingham, *born* 1933	1986
Rt. Hon. Sir Patrick Russell, *born* 1926	1986
Rt. Hon. Dame Elizabeth Butler-Sloss, DBE, *born* 1933	1988
Rt. Hon. Sir Peter Taylor, *born* 1930	1988
Rt. Hon. Sir Murray Stuart-Smith, *born* 1927.	1988
Rt. Hon. Sir Christopher Staughton, *born* 1933	1988
Rt. Hon. Sir Michael Mann, *born* 1930	1988
Rt. Hon. Sir Donald Farquharson, *born* 1928 .	1989
Rt. Hon. Sir Anthony McCowan, *born* 1928 ..	1989
Rt. Hon. Sir Roy Beldam, *born* 1925..........	1989
Rt. Hon. Sir Andrew Leggatt, *born* 1930	1990

Court of Appeal (Criminal Division)

Judges, The Lord Chief Justice of England, The
Master of the Rolls, Lords Justices of Appeal and
the Judges of the High Court of Justice.

Courts-Martial Appeal Court

Judges, The Lord Chief Justice of England, The
Master of the Rolls, Lords Justices of Appeal, and
Judges of the High Court of Justice.

HIGH COURT OF JUSTICE
CHANCERY DIVISION
President, The Lord High Chancellor

The Vice-Chancellor (£85,000)
The Rt. Hon. Sir Nicolas Browne-Wilkinson
(*born* 1930, *apptd*. 1985)
Secretary (vacant); *Clerk*, W. Northfield, BEM.

Judges (each £77,000)

	Apptd.
Hon. Sir John Vinelott, *born* 1923	1978
Hon. Sir Jean-Pierre Warner, *born* 1924	1981
Hon. Sir Peter Gibson, *born* 1934	1981
Hon. Sir Mervyn Davies, MC, TD, *born* 1918 ...	1982

Hon. Sir Jeremiah Harman, *born* 1930	1982
Hon. Sir Richard Scott, *born* 1934	1983
Hon. Sir Leonard Hoffman, *born* 1934........	1985
Hon. Sir John Knox, *born* 1925	1985
Hon. Sir Peter Millett, *born* 1932	1986
Hon. Sir Andrew Morritt, *born* 1938 1988
Hon. Sir William Aldous, *born* 1936 1988
Hon. Sir John Mummery, *born* 1938 1989
Hon. Sir Francis Ferris, TD, *born* 1932 1990

High Court of Justice in Bankruptcy

Judges, The Master of the Rolls, The Vice-Chancellor,
the Lords Justices, and other members of the Court
of Appeal.

Companies Court

Judges, The Vice Chancellor and judges of the
Chancery Division of the High Court.

Patent Court (Appellate Section)

Judges, The Hon. Mr. Justice Aldous; The Hon. Mr.
Justice Mummery; The Hon. Mr. Justice Morritt;
The Hon. Mr. Justice Hoffman.

QUEEN'S BENCH DIVISION
The Lord Chief Justice of England (£95,750)
The Rt. Hon. the Lord Lane, AFC
(*born* 1918, *apptd*. 1980)
Secretary, Mrs. J. Simpson; *Clerk*, J. Bond.

Judges (each £77,000)

	Apptd.
Hon. Sir Leslie Boreham, *born* 1918..........	1972
Hon. Sir Michael Davies, *born* 1921..........	1973
Hon. Sir Haydn Tudor Evans, *born* 1920	1974
Hon. Sir Kenneth Jupp, MC, *born* 1917	1975
Hon. Sir Derek Hodgson, *born* 1917..........	1977
Hon. Sir Ronald Waterhouse, *born* 1926......	1978
Hon. Sir Maurice Drake, DFC, *born* 1923......	1978
Hon. Sir Barry Sheen, *born* 1918	1978
Hon. Sir Christopher French, *born* 1925	1979
Hon. Sir Peter Webster, *born* 1924...........	1980
Hon. Sir Charles McCullough, *born* 1931	1981
Hon. Sir John Leonard, *born* 1926	1981
Hon. Sir David Hirst, *born* 1925	1982
Hon. Sir John Stewart Hobhouse, *born* 1932..	1982
Hon. Sir Michael Nolan, *born* 1928	1982
Hon. Sir Oliver Popplewell, *born* 1927........	1983
Hon. Sir William Macpherson, TD, *born* 1926 .	1983
Hon. Sir Philip Otton, *born* 1933	1983
Hon. Sir Paul Kennedy, *born* 1935	1983
Hon. Sir Michael Hutchison, *born* 1933	1983
Hon. Sir Simon Brown, *born* 1937	1984
Hon. Sir Anthony Evans, *born* 1934	1984
Hon. Sir Mark Saville, *born* 1936	1985
Hon. Sir Johan Steyn, *born* 1932	1985
Hon. Sir Christopher Rose, *born* 1937........	1985
Hon. Sir Richard Tucker, *born* 1931	1985
Hon. Sir Robert Gatehouse, *born* 1924	1985
Hon. Sir Patrick Garland, *born* 1929.........	1985
Hon. Sir John Roch, *born* 1934	1985
Hon. Sir Michael Turner, *born* 1931	1985
Hon. Sir John Alliott, *born* 1932	1986
Hon. Sir Harry Ognall, *born* 1934	1986
Hon. Sir Konrad Schiemann, *born* 1937	1986
Hon. Sir John Owen, *born* 1925	1986
Hon. Sir Denis Henry, *born* 1931	1986
Hon. Sir Humphrey Potts, *born* 1931.........	1986
Hon. Sir Richard Rougier, *born* 1932	1986
Hon. Sir Ian Kennedy, *born* 1930	1986
Hon. Sir Nicholas Phillips, *born* 1938	1987
Hon. Sir Robin Auld, *born* 1937	1988
Hon. Sir Malcolm Pill, *born* 1938	1988
Hon. Sir Stuart McKinnon, *born* 1938	1988
Hon. Sir Mark Potter, *born* 1937	1988

Hon. Sir Henry Brooke, *born* 1936 1988
Hon. Sir Igor Judge, *born* 1941 1988
Hon. Sir Edwin Jowitt, *born* 1929 1988
Hon. Sir Michael Morland, *born* 1929 1989
Hon. Sir Mark Waller, *born* 1940 1989
Hon. Sir Roger Buckley, *born* 1939 1989
Hon. Sir Anthony Hidden, *born* 1936 1989
Hon. Sir Desmond Fennell, OBE, *born* 1933 1989
Hon. Sir Michael Wright, *born* 1932 1990
Hon. Sir Charles Mantell, *born* 1937 1990

FAMILY DIVISION
President (£85,000)
Rt. Hon. Sir Stephen Brown
(*born* 1929, *apptd.* 1988).
Secretary, Mrs. S. Leung; *Clerk*, Mrs. S. Bell.

Judges (each £77,000)	Apptd.
Hon. Sir Kenneth Hollings, MC, *born* 1918	1971
Hon. Sir John Wood, MC, *born* 1922	1977
Hon. Sir Michael Eastham, *born* 1920	1978
Hon. Dame Margaret Booth, DBE, *born* 1933 . .	1979
Hon. Sir Anthony Lincoln, *born* 1920	1979
Hon. Sir Anthony Ewbank, *born* 1925	1980
Hon. Sir John Waite, *born* 1932	1982
Hon. Sir Anthony Hollis, *born* 1927	1982
Hon. Sir Swinton Thomas, *born* 1931	1985
Hon. Sir Mathew Thorpe, *born* 1938	1988
Hon. Sir Edward Cazalet, *born* 1936	1988
Hon. Sir Alan Ward, *born* 1938	1988
Hon. Sir Scott Baker, *born* 1937	1988
Hon. Sir Robert Johnson, *born* 1933	1989
Hon. Sir Douglas Brown, *born* 1931	1989
Hon. Sir Donald Rattee, *born* 1937	1989

RESTRICTIVE PRACTICES COURT

President, The Hon. Mr. Justice Lincoln. *Judicial Members*, The Hon. Mr. Justice Warner; The Hon. Lord Sutherland; The Hon. Mr. Justice Murray.
Lay Members, N. L. Salmon; I. G. Stewart; B. M. Currie; L. Robertson; R. Garrick.

OFFICIAL REFEREES' COURTS
St. Dunstan's House,
133–137 Fetter Lane,
EC4A 1HD

His Hon. Judge Newey, QC; His Hon. Judge Lewis, QC; His Hon. Judge Davies, QC; His Hon. Judge Fox-Andrews, QC; His Hon. Judge Bowsher, QC; His Hon. Judge Loyd, QC; His Hon. Judge Forbes, QC £67,000

LORD CHANCELLOR'S DEPARTMENT
See **Government and Public Offices.**

SUPREME COURT DEPARTMENTS AND OFFICES
Royal Courts of Justice, WC2A 2LL
[071–936 6000]

Administrator, J. R. A. Hanratty, TD.
£31,276–£35,436

Central Office of the Supreme Court
Royal Courts of Justice, WC2A 2LL

Senior Master of the Supreme Court (QBD), and Queen's Remembrancer, W. K. Topley £53,050
Masters of the Supreme Court (QBD), P. B. Creight-more; D. L. Prebble; A. A. Grant; G. H. Hodgson; R. L. Turner; J. Trench; M. Tennant; P. Miller
£43,450
Chief Clerk (Central Office), C. F. Jones
£20,189–£24,075
Chief Clerk to the Queen's Bench Judges in Chambers, A. Foley . . . . £20,189–£24,075

Court of Appeal (Civil Division) Office
Royal Courts of Justice, WC2A 2LL
[071–936 6000]

Registrar, J. D. R. Adams £53,050

Criminal Appeal Office
Royal Courts of Justice, WC2A 2LL
[071–936 6000]

Registrar, M. McKenzie £53,050
Deputy Registrar, J. P. Stockton . . . £31,276–£35,436
Chief Clerk, J. Read . . . . £20,189–£24,075

Courts-Martial Appeals Office
Royal Courts of Justice, WC2A 2LL
[071–936 6000]

Registrar, M. McKenzie £53,050
Chief Clerk, J. Read.

Crown Office of the Supreme Court
Royal Courts of Justice, WC2A 2LL
[071–936 6000]

Master of the Crown Office, and Queen's Coroner and Attorney, M. McKenzie £53,050
Head of Crown Office, Mrs. L. Knapman
£31,276–£35,436

Supreme Court Taxing Office

Chief Master, F. G. Berkeley £53,050
Masters of the Supreme Court, A. J. Wright; C. R. N. Martyn; M. N. Devonshire, TD; P. T. Hurst; C. A. Prince; M. Ellis £43,450
Chief Clerk, A. J. Burroughs . . . . £20,189–£24,075
Principal Taxing Officer, T. J. Ryan £20,189–£24,075

Examiners of the Court
(Empowered to take Examination of Witnesses in all Divisions of the High Court)
M. F. Meredith-Hardy; B. Rathbone; N. W. Briggs; R. Jacobs.

Chancery Chambers,
Royal Courts of Justice, WC2A 2LL
[071–936 6000]

Chief Master of the Supreme Court, R. D. Munrow
£53,050
Masters of the Supreme Court, M. B. Cholmondeley Clarke; J. M. Dyson; J. S. Gowers; G. A. Barratt
£43,450
Chief Clerk, G. Robinson . . . . £20,189–£24,075
Conveyancing Counsel of the Supreme Court, J. Monckton; S. G. Maurice; M. J. Roth.

Bankruptcy Department
Thomas More Building, Royal
Courts of Justice, Strand, WC2A 2LL
[071–936 6000]

Chief Registrar, T. L. Dewhurst £53,050
Chief Clerk, T. Palmer.

Official Receivers' Department
21 Bloomsbury Street, WC1B 3SS
[071–323 3090]

Senior Official Receiver, J. R. Donnison.
Official Receivers, M. J. Pugh; L. T. Cramp; M. W. A. Sanderson; G. J. A. Harp.

Companies Court
Thomas More Building,
Royal Courts of Justice, WC2A 2LL
[071–936 6000]

Registrar, M. Buckley.
Chief Clerk, C. A. N. Edinboro . . . . . £20,189–£24,075
Senior Official Receiver, Companies Department, J. R. Donnison.

Restrictive Practices Court
Thomas More Building,
Royal Courts of Justice, WC2A 2LL
[071–936 6000]

Clerk of the Court, M. Buckley.
Chief Clerk, C. A. N. Edinboro.

Principal Registry (Family Division)
Somerset House, WC2R 1LP
[071–936 6000]

Senior Registrar, C. F. Turner £53,050
Registrars, T. G. Guest; D. E. Morris; J. E. Artro-
Morris; R. B. Rowe; G. B. N. A. Angel; B. P. F.
Kenworthy-Browne; Mrs. K. T. Moorhouse; D. T.
A. Davies; Mrs. N. Pearce; M. J. Segal; R. Conn
.... £43,450
Secretary, G. J. Maple .... £20,189–£24,075

District Probate Registrars

Birmingham and Stoke-on-Trent, C. Marsh.
Brighton and Maidstone, M. N. Emery.
Bristol, Exeter and Bodmin, P. L. Speyer.
Ipswich, Norwich and Peterborough, E. R. Alexander.
Leeds, Lincoln and Sheffield, A. P. Dawson.
Liverpool, Lancaster and Chester, B. J. Thomas.
Llandaff, Bangor, Carmarthen and Gloucester,
D. W. Jones.
Manchester and Nottingham, M. A. Moran.
Newcastle, Carlisle, York and Middlesbrough, A.
Bertram.
Oxford, Miss M. L. Farmborough.
Winchester, A. K. Biggs.

**Admiralty and Commercial Registry and
Marshal's Office**
Royal Courts of Justice, WC2A 2LL
[071–936 6000]

Registrar, W. K. Topley £43,450
Marshal and Chief Clerk, V. E. Ricks
.... £20,189–£24,075

Court of Protection
Stewart House, 24 Kingsway, WC2B 6HD

Master, Mrs. A. B. Macfarlane £53,050

Official Solicitor's Department
81 Chancery Lane, WC2A 1DD

Official Solicitor to the Supreme Court, H. D. S.
Venables .... £43,800–£50,900
Deputy Official Solicitor, H. J. Baker £33,491–£46,319
Chief Clerk, Mrs. V. J. Carter ...... £20,189–£24,075

**OFFICE OF THE LORD CHANCELLOR'S
VISITORS**
Trevelyan House, 30 Great Peter Street, SW1
[071–210 8563]

Legal Visitor, M. H. Fauvelle.
Medical Visitors, A. G. Fullerton; F. E. Kenyon; R.
J. Kerry; K. Khan; P. A. Morris; D. Parr; J.
Roberts.

**OFFICE OF THE JUDGE ADVOCATE OF
THE FLEET**
The Law Courts, Barker Road, Maidstone ME16
8EQ

Judge Advocate of the Fleet, His Hon. Judge Waley,
VRD, QC.

**OFFICE OF THE JUDGE ADVOCATE
GENERAL OF THE FORCES**
(*Joint Service for the Army and the Royal Air Force*)
22 Kingsway, WC2B 6LE

Judge Advocate General, J. Stuart-Smith, CB, QC.
.... £58,900
Vice Judge Advocate General, G. L. Chapman
.... £51,000
Assistant Judge Advocates General, E. G. Moelwyn-
Hughes; A. P. Pitts; S. B. Spence; D. M. Berkson;
M. A. Hunter; T. R. King........ £34,500–£39,800
Deputy Judge Advocates, J. P. Camp; T. G. Pontius;
Miss S. E. Woollam .... £24,150–£33,850

**HIGH COURT AND
CROWN COURT CENTRES**

First-tier centres deal with both civil and criminal
cases and are served by High Court and Circuit
Judges. Second-tier centres deal with criminal cases
only and are served by High Court and Circuit
Judges. Third-tier centres deal with criminal cases
only and are served only by Circuit Judges.

Midland and Oxford Circuit

First-tier—Birmingham, Lincoln, Nottingham, Ox-
ford, Stafford, Warwick. *Second-tier*—Leicester,
Northampton, Shrewsbury, Worcester. *Third-tier*—
Coventry, Derby, Grimsby, Hereford, Peterborough,
Stoke-on-Trent, Wolverhampton.
Circuit Administrator, R. E. K. Holmes, 2 Newton
Street, Birmingham B4 7LU.
Courts Administrators, Birmingham Group, V. C.
Grove; *Nottingham Group,* Mrs. E. A. Folman;
Stafford Group, A. F. Parker.

North Eastern Circuit

First-tier—Leeds, Newcastle upon Tyne, Sheffield,
Teesside. *Second-tier*—York. *Third-tier*—Beverley,
Doncaster, Durham, Huddersfield, Wakefield.
Circuit Administrator, S. W. L. James, West Riding
House, 17th Floor, Albion Street, Leeds LS1 5AA.
Courts Administrators, Leeds Group, P. Delany;
Newcastle upon Tyne Group, F. I. Lance; *Sheffield
Group,* G. Bingham.

Northern Circuit

First-tier—Carlisle, Liverpool, Manchester, Pres-
ton. *Third-tier*—Barrow-in-Furness, Bolton, Burn-
ley, Lancaster.
Circuit Administrator, P. M. Harris, Aldine House,
West Riverside, New Bailey Street, Salford
M3 5EU.
Courts Administrators, Manchester Group, A. H.
Howard; *Liverpool Group,* D. A. Beaumont; *Preston
Group,* Mrs. A. Prior.

South Eastern Circuit

First-tier—Chelmsford, Lewes, Norwich. *Second-
tier*—Ipswich, London (Central Criminal Court),
Maidstone, Reading, St. Albans. *Third-tier*—Ayles-
bury, Bury St. Edmunds, Cambridge, Canterbury,
Chichester, Guildford, King's Lynn, London (Acton,
Croydon, Inner London Session House, Isleworth,
Kingston upon Thames, Knightsbridge, Middlesex
Guildhall, Snaresbrook, Southwark and Wood
Green), Southend.
The High Court in Greater London sits at the
Royal Courts of Justice.
Circuit Administrator, B. Cooke, New Cavendish
House, 18 Maltravers Street, WC2.
Deputy Circuit Administrator, G. E. Calvett.
Courts Administrators, Chelmsford Group, P. Hand-
cock; *Maidstone Group,* Mrs. H. Hartwell; *Kingston
Group,* P. M. Thomas; *London (Civil),* K. Winberg;
London (Crime), G. F. Addicott.

Wales and Chester Circuit

First-tier—Caernarfon, Cardiff, Chester, Mold, Swansea. *Second-tier*—Carmarthen, Newport, Welshpool. *Third-tier*—Dolgellau, Haverfordwest, Knutsford, Merthyr Tydfil, Warrington.
Circuit Administrator, D. Howe, Churchill House, Churchill Way, Cardiff.
Courts Administrators, Cardiff Group, G. Jones; *Chester Group*, E. R. Walter.

Western Circuit

First-tier—Bristol, Exeter, Truro, Winchester. *Second-tier*—Dorchester, Gloucester, Plymouth. *Third-tier*—Barnstaple, Bournemouth, Devizes, Newport (IOW), Portsmouth, Salisbury, Southampton, Swindon, Taunton.
Circuit Administrator, G. Jones, Bridge House, Clifton, Bristol BS8 4BN.
Courts Administrators, Bristol Group, A. C. Butler; *Exeter Group*, J. Ardern; *Winchester Group*, P. Matthews.

CIRCUIT JUDGES

(*Senior Circuit Judges, £62,500; Circuit Judges, £56,300)

Midland and Oxford Circuit

W. A. L. Allardice; F. A. Allen; B. J. Appleby, QC; M. J. Astill; I. J. Black, QC; J. F. Blythe, TD; D. W. Brunning; F. L. Clark, QC; P. N. R. Clark; R. R. B. Cole; J. M. Coulson; P. F. Crane; P. J. Crawford, QC; R. H. Curtis, QC; I. T. R. Davidson, QC; A. C. H. de Piro, QC; T. M. Dillon, QC; J. F. Evans, QC; B. A. Farrer, QC; Miss E. N. Fisher; J. E. Fletcher; R. J. H. Gibbs, QC; H. G. A. Gosling; J. Hall; M. K. Harrison-Hall; T. R. Heald; J. R. Hopkin; R. H. Hutchinson; J. E. M. Irvine; R. P. V. Jenkins; J. G. Jones; T. O. Kellock, QC; J. T. C. Lee; M. H. Mander; K. Matthewman; R. G. May; P. W. Medd, OBE, QC; K. S. W. Mellor, QC; N. Micklem; A. J. H. Morrison; M. D. Mott; A. J. D. Nicholl; J. F. F. Orrell; C. J. Pitchers; F. M. Potter; J. R. Pyke; D. E. Roberts; J. A. O. Shand; J. R. S. Smyth; P. J. Stretton; C. S. Stuart-White; H. C. Tayler, QC; K. J. Taylor; R. J. Toyn; M. B. Ward; R. L. Ward, QC; D. J. R. Wilcox; D. H. Wild; H. Wilson; J. W. Wilson; B. Woods; G. H. Wootton; C. G. Young.

Northern Circuit

H. H. Andrew, QC; J. R. Arthur, DFC; A. W. Bell; R. C. W. Bennett; M. S. Blackburn; A. S. Booth, QC; R. Brown; I. B. Campbell; F. B. Carter, QC; D. Clark; G. P. Crowe, QC; J. M. Davies, QC; *R. E. Davies, QC (*Recorder of Manchester*); Miss A. E. Downey; B. Duckworth; S. B. Duncan; Miss A. M. Ebsworth; A. A. Edmondson; D. M. Evans, QC; S. J. D. Fawcus; D. G. F. Franks; R. G. Hamilton; J. A. Hammond; R. J. Hardy; F. D. Hart,QC; T. D. T. Hodson; Miss M. Holt; G. W. Humphries; A. C. Jolly; H. A. Kershaw; P. M. Kershaw, QC; H. L. Lachs; C. N. Lees; J. M. Lever, QC; R. Lockett; J. H. Lord; D. Lynch; B. C. Maddocks; C. J. Mahon; I. H. Morris-Jones, QC; G. K. Naylor, TD; M. O'Donoghue; F. D. Paterson; R. E. I. Pickering; D. A. Pirie; A. J. Proctor; M. A. G. Sachs; N. W. M. Sellers, VRD; H. S. Singer; J. A. Stannard; Miss A. H. Steel; I. R. Taylor, QC; *Sir Sanderson Temple, MBE, QC (*Recorder of Liverpool*); J. P. Townend; I. S. Webster; W. R. Wickham.

North Eastern Circuit

T. G. F. Atkinson; G. Baker, QC; P. M. Baker, QC; J. M. A. Barker; G. N. Barr Young; H. G. Bennett, QC; D. R. Bentley, QC; D. M. A. Bryant; B. Bush; M. C. Carr; P. J. Charlesworth; G. J. K. Coles, QC; J. A. Cotton; J. Crabtree; M. T. Cracknell; W. H. R. Crawford, QC; P. J. Fox, QC; A. N. Fricker, QC; M. S.

Garner; H. G. Hall; W. Hannah; G. F. R. Harkins; J. A. Henham; D. Herrod, QC; R. Hunt; V. R. Hurwitz; A. E. Hutchinson, QC; J. R. Johnson; G. M. Lightfoot; A. C. Macdonald; Miss M. B. M. MacMurray, QC; A. L. Myerson, QC; D. A. Orde; Miss H. E. Paling; R. A. Percy; J. Pickles; D. M. Savill, QC; A. Simpson; J. Stephenson; R. A. R. Stroyan, QC; R. C. Taylor; G. M. Vos; M. Walker; P. H. C. Walker.

South Eastern Circuit

M. F. Addison; F. J. Aglionby; A. K. Allen, OBE; M. J. Anwyl-Davies, QC; J. A. Baker; J. B. Baker, QC; M. J. D. Baker; P. V. Baker, QC; A. F. Balston; R. M. N. Band, MC, QC; C. J. A. Barnett, QC; R. A. Barr; N. G. A. Bathurst; P. T. S. Batterbury, TD; P. J. L. Beaumont, QC; N. E. Beddard; F. E. Beezley; G. J. Binns; M. Birks; J. C. C. Blofeld, QC; J. Bolland; P. C. Bowsher, QC; P. N. Brandt; L. J. Bromley, QC; A. E. Brooks; G. N. Butler, QC; *N. M. Butter, QC; H. J. Byrt, QC; C. V. Callman; B. E. Capstick, QC; B. L. Charles, QC; A. W. Clark; D. J. Clarkson, QC;; P. C. Clegg; M. Cohen, QC; Patricia Coles, QC; C. C. Colston, QC; C. D. Compston; M. J. Cook; R. A. Cooke; R. K. Cooke, OBE; G. H. Coombe; M. R. Coombe; Margaret D. Cosgrave; R. C. Cox; P. V. Crocker; D. L. Croft, QC; I. H. Davies, TD; L. J. Davies, QC; W. L. M. Davies, QC; W. N. Denison, QC; K. M. Devlin; A. E. J. Diamond; G. L. S. Dobry, CBE, QC; C. M. Edwards; Q. T. Edwards, QC; F. P. L. Evans; J. K. Q. Evans; A. L. Figgis; J. J. Finney; T. J. Forbes, QC; P. Ford; J. J. Fordham; G. C. F. Forrester; J. Fox-Andrews, QC.

A. Garfitt; L. Gerber; S. A. Goldstein; P. W. Goldstone; M. B. Goodman; J. H. Gower, QC; M. Graham, QC; P. B. Greenwood; D. J. Griffiths; G. D. Grigson; R. B. Groves, TD, VRD; N. T. Hague, QC; P. J. Halnan; J. Hamilton; R. E. Hammerton; J. P. Harris, DSC, QC; R. G. Hawkins, QC; J. D. W. Hayman; A. H. Head; M. R. Hickman; J. C. Hicks, QC; A. N. Hitching; D. Holden; A. C. W. Hordern, QC; Sir David Hughes-Morgan, Bt., CB, CBE; J. Hunter; M. J. Hyam; C. P. James; W. Kee; M. Kennedy, QC; A. M. Kenny; J. F. Kingham; C. F. Kolbert; L. G. Krikler; L. H. C. Lait; G. F. B. Laughland, Q.C.; R. Laurie; T. Lawrence; E. Lewis, QC; A. C. L. Lewisohn; A. Lipfriend; D. T. Lloyd; F. R. Lockhart; G. D. Lovegrove, QC; D. B. D. Lowe; R. H. Lownie; Mrs. N. M. Lowry; R. J. Lowry, QC; J. A. T. Loyd, QC; R. D. Lymbery, QC (*Common Serjeant*); K. M. McHale; K. A. Machin, QC; I. G. McLean; J. L. E. MacManus, TD, QC; M. B. McMullan; M. J. P. Macnair; K. C. Macrae; J. R. Main, QC; B. A. Marder, QC; O. S. Martin, QC; N. A. Medawar, QC; D. J. Mellor; J. H. E. Mendl; A. L. Mildon, QC; D. Q. Miller; S. G. Mitchell, QC; E. F. Monier-Williams; D. Morton Jack; J. I. Murchie.

Mrs. N. F. Negus; J. H. R. Newey, Q.C.; C. W. F. Newman, QC; Mrs. M. F. Norrie; Suzanne F. Norwood; C. R. Oddie; A. Owen; D. A. Paiba; R. H. S. Palmer; Miss V. A. Pearlman; F. H. L. Petre; A. J. Phelan; D. C. Pitman; P. B. Pollock; H. C. Pownall, QC; R. J. C. V. Prendergast; J. E. Pullinger; J. W. Rant, QC; E. V. P. Reece; G. K. Rice; K. A. Richardson, QC; G. Rivlin, QC; D. A. H. Rodwell, QC; G. H. Rooke, TD, QC; P. C. R. Rountree; K. W. R. Rubin; J. H. Rucker; T. R. G. Ryland; R. B. Sanders; J. D. Sheerin; *G. J. Shindler, QC; D. R. A. Sich; K. T. Simpson; P. R. Simpson; M. Singh, QC; J. K. E. Slack, TD; P. M. J. Slot; R. J. Southan; *R. O. C. Stable, QC; E. Stockdale; C. J. Sumner; W. F. C. Thomas; A. G. Y. Thorpe; A. H. Tibber; C. H. Tilling; A. M. Troup; S. Tumim; J. T. Turner; C. J. M. Tyrer; J. E. Van der Werff; L. J. Verney, TD (*Recorder of London*); A. O. R. Vick, QC; Miss M. S. Viner, QC; B. J. Wakley, MBE; A. F. Waley, VRD, QC; R. Walker; D. B. Watling, QC; V. B. Watts; Sir David West-Russell; F. J. White; J. E. Williams; S. M. Willis; G. N. Worthington; E. G. Wrintmore; K. H. Zucker, QC.

Wales and Chester Circuit

T. R. Crowther, QC; G. H. M. Daniel; R. D. G. David, QC; J. B. S. Diehl, QC; D. E. H. Edwards; Lord Elystan-Morgan; T. M. Evans, QC; W. N. Francis; M. Gibbon, QC; D. M. Hughes; G. J. Jones; G. E. Kilfoil; T. E. I. Lewis-Bowen; D. G. Morgan; T. H. Moseley, QC; D. A. Phillips; D. W. Powell; E. J. Prosser, QC; H. W. J. ap Robert; H. E. P. Roberts, QC; *J. C. Rutter; S. M. Stephens, QC; D. B. Williams, TD, QC; H. V. Williams, QC; R. G. Woolley.

Western Circuit

S. T. Bates, QC; G. B. Best; C. L. Boothman; Miss J. W. Bracewell, QC; M. J. L. Brodrick; R. D. H. Bursell, QC; Sir Jonathan Clarke; Hazel Counsell; J. A. Cox; J. W. Da Cunha; M. Dyer; *P. Fallon, QC; P. D. Fanner; B. J. F. Galpin; D. L. Griffiths; I. S. Hill, QC; G. B. Hutton; J. H. Inskip, QC; A. C. Lauriston, QC; D. McCarraher, VRD; H. E. L. McCreery, QC; Miss S. M. D. McKinney; I. S. McKintosh; J. G. McNaught; E. G. Neville; S. K. O'Malley; J. N. P. Rudd; D. A. Smith, QC; K. C. L. Smithies; W. E. M. Taylor; H. J. M. Tucker, QC; D. M. Webster, QC; J. R. Whitley; J. A. J. Wigmore; K. M. Willcock, QC; J. H. Wroath.

RECORDERS

J. R. S. Adams; I. D. G. Alexander, QC; J. Altman; Miss C. Alton; W. P. Andreae-Jones, QC; P. J. Andrews; Ms L. E. Appleby, QC; J. F. Appleton; J. F. A. Archer, QC; Rt. Hon. P. K. Archer, QC, MP; A. J. Arlidge, QC; E. K. Armitage; R. Ashton; P. Ashworth, QC; J. M. Aspinall; N. J. Atkinson; M. G. Austin-Smith, QC; W. S. Aylen, QC; P. Back, QC; J. F. Badenoch, QC; P. G. N. Badge; A. B. Baillie; N. R. J. Baker, QC; T. W. Barber; G. S. Barham; A. Barker, QC; B. J. Barker, QC; D. Barker, QC; R. O. Barlow; D. M. W. Barnes, QC; T. P. Barnes, QC; W. E. Barnett, QC; Sir Anthony Barrowclough, QC; J. E. Barry; G. R. Bartlett, QC; J. C. T. Barton, QC; K. Bassingthwaite; R. J. A. Batt; S. D. Batten, QC; J. J. Baughan, QC; J. F. Beashel; C. H. Beaumont; C. O. M. Bedingfield, TD, QC; R. W. Belben; R. Bell, QC; The Hon. M. J. Beloff, QC; D. P. Bennett; H. P. D. Bennett, QC; P. Bennett, QC; K. C. Bentall; H. L. Bentham; D. M. Berkson; Miss I. Bernstein; R. H. Bernstein, DFC, QC; M. Bethel, QC; J. P. V. Bevan; J. C. Beveridge, QC; P. V. Birkett, QC; P. W. Birts, QC; J. W. Black, QC; J. A. Blair-Gould; A. N. H. Blake; C. Bloom, QC; D. J. Blunt; J. G. Boal; G. T. K. Boney, QC; D. J. Boulton; P. H. Bowers; J. J. Boyle; A. V. Bradbury; R. W. A. Bray; D. J. Brennan, QC; M. L. Brent, QC; J. J. B. G. Brice, QC; J. N. W. Bridges-Adams; A. J. Brigden; A. N. J. Briggs; P. J. Briggs; D. K. Brown; R. G. Brown; A. Bueno, QC; J. M. Bull, QC; J. W. M. Bullimore; D. L. Bulmer; J. P. Burgess; J. K. Burke, QC; J. P. Burke, QC; M. A. B. Burke-Gaffney, QC; H. W. Burnett, QC; M. R. Burr; M. J. Burton, QC; A. J. Butcher, QC; A. N. L. Butterfield; R. J. Buxton, QC.

Mrs. B. A. Calvert, QC; D. Calvert-Smith; Miss S. M. C. Cameron; A. N. B. Campbell; The Lord Campbell of Alloway, QC; J. Q. Campbell; B. J. Canham; G. M. C. Carey; A. C. Carlile, QC, MP; The Lord Carlisle of Bucklow, PC, QC; H. B. H. Carlisle, QC; R. C. L. Carr; M. L. Cartlidge; B. I. Caulfield; J. Cavell; J. M. Chadwick, QC; J. A. Chadwin, QC; J. R. Chalkley; N. M. Chambers, QC; F. A. Chapman; B. W. Chedlow, QC; J. M. Cherry, QC; C. H. Clark, QC; A. P. Clarke, QC; C. S. C. S. Clarke, QC; D. C. Clarke, QC; R. N. B. Clegg, QC; G. M. Clifton; C. D. Cochrane, QC; P. J. Cockcroft; D. J. Cocks, QC; J. J. Coffey; T. A. Coghlan; W. J. Coker; J. R. Cole; N. J. Coleman; N. B. C. Coles, QC; S. H. Colgan; P. N. Collier; A. D. Collins, QC; J. M. Collins; P. H. Collins; A. D. Colman, QC; S. S. Coltart; Ms. M. Colton; Viscount Colville of Culross, QC; J. S. Colyer, QC; P. R. C. Coni, QC; T. A. C. Coningsby, QC; M. B. Connell, QC; J. G. Connor; R.

D. Connor; C. S. Cook; Miss B. P. Cooper, QC; A. Cooray; S. M. Corkhill; T. G. E. Corrie; E. Cotran; M. G. Cotterill; G. W. A. Cottle; Miss D. R. Cotton, QC; J. S. Coward, QC; B. R. E. Cox, QC; P. J. Cox, DSC, QC; C. J. Crespi, QC; P. J. Cresswell, QC; D. I. Crigman, QC; M. L. S. Cripps; I. W. Crompton; F. P. Crowder, QC; J. D. Crowley, QC; E. J. R. Crowther, OBE; W. R. H. Crowther, QC; Miss E. A. M. Curnow, QC; M. J. Curwen; Ms. J. M. P. Daley; S. C. Darwall-Smith; Mrs. S. P. Darwall-Smith; G. W. Davey; D. T. A. Davies; G. L. Davies; Ms L. H. Davies; A. W. Dawson; D. H. Day, Q.C.; M. Dean, QC; J. J. Deave; J. B. Deby, QC; C. F. Dehn, QC; P. A. de la Piquerie; P. N. De Mille; M. A. de Navarro, QC; W. E. Denny, CBE, QC; R. L. Denyer, QC; S. C. Desch, QC; J. E. Devaux; M. N. Devonshire; A. D. Dinkin; I. J. Dobkin; Ms B. Dohmann, QC; A. M. Donne, QC; D. P. Draycott, QC; R. Du Cann, QC; S. M. Duffield; P. R. Dunkels; W. H. Dunn, QC; C. H. Durman; A. H. Durrant; J. A. Dyson, QC.

D. Eady, QC; Ms D. B. Eaglestone; T. K. Earnshaw; J. S. Eastwood; H. W. P. Eccles, QC; G. O. Edwards, QC; D. F. Elfer, QC; G. Elias, QC; B. J. Elliott; R. M. Englehart, QC; G. A. Ensor; D. A. Evans, QC; D. R. Evans, QC; Miss M. A. P. Evans; S. J. Evans; E. C. Evans-Lombe, QC; Sir Graham Eyre, QC; W. D. Fairclough; J. D. Farnworth; D. J. Farrer, QC; E. J. Faulks; M. H. Fauvelle; R. Fernyhough, QC; P. Fingret; G. D. Flather, QC; P. E. J. Focke, QC; J. D. Foley; R. A. Fordham; J. R. Foster, QC; R. M. Foster; Ms. D. A. Freedman; R. H. K. Frisby, QC.

W. M. Gage, QC; M. Gale, QC; J. R. B. Geake; A. C. Geddes; A. H. Gee, QC; R. Gee; J. A. D. Gilliland, QC; L. N. H. George; L. Giovene; A. T. Glass, QC; W. J. Glover, QC; Miss A. F. Goddard, QC; H. K. Goddard, QC; Ms. L. S. Godfrey; J. B. Goldring, QC; A. R. Goldsack, QC; A. J. J. Gompertz, QC; A. A. Gordon; C. G. M. Gordon; J. P. Gorman, QC; J. B. Gosschalk; C. O. G. Gould; T. J. C. Goudie, QC; A. S. Grabiner, QC; The Lord Grantchester, QC; C. A. St. J. Gray, QC; G. Gray, QC; J. M. Gray; R. I. Gray, QC; R. M. K. Gray, QC; B. S. Green, QC; H. Green, QC; S. P. Grenfell; R. D. Grey, QC; J. C. Griffiths, CMG, QC; L. Griffiths; J. D. Griggs; M. G. Grills; Mrs. H. M. Grindrod, QC; M. A. W. Grundy; S. J. Gullick.

A. S. Hacking, QC; Mrs. C. M. A. Hagen; M. F. Haigh; J. W. Haines; J. C. Hall; V. E. Hall; Ms. H. C. Hallett, QC; A. B. R. Hallgarten, QC; G. Hallon; A. W. Hamilton, QC; G. M. Hamilton, TD, QC; S. T. Hammond; J. Hampton; C. R. H. Hardy; Miss R. S. A. Hare, QC; B. Hargrove, OBE, QC; R. D. Harman, QC; D. M. Harris, QC; G. C. W. Harris, QC; M. F. Harris; M. G. V. Harrison, QC; R. M. Harrison, QC; C. P. Hart-Leverton, QC; C. S. Harvey, MBE, TD; M. L. T. Harvey, QC; R. O. Havery, QC; T. S. A. Hawkesworth, QC; R. J. Haworth; R. W. P. Hay; R. Hayward-Smith, QC; M. Hedley; T. B. Hegarty; G. E. Heggs; R. A. Henderson, QC; R. H. Q. Henriques, QC; P. J. M. Heppel; R. B. Hickman; B. J. Higgs, QC; E. M. Hill, QC; J. W. Hillyer; A. J. H. Hilton, QC; Ms. E. J. Hindley; J. D. Hitchen; S. A. Hockman, QC; C. R. Hodson; P. M. L. Hoffman; The Hon. Mary Hogg, QC; A. J. C. Hoggett, QC; Ms. B. M. Hoggett, QC; D. A. Hollis, VRD, QC; F. R. B. Holloway; C. J. Holmes; A. T. Hoolahan, QC; A. Hooper, QC; The Lord Hooson, QC; C. P. Hotten; R. Houlker, QC; M. Howard, QC, MP; N. J. G. Howarth; R. W. Howe; M. J. Hubbard, QC; A. P. G. Hughes, QC; J. Hugill, QC; J. G. Hull, QC; P. J. Hunt, QC; I. G. A. Hunter, QC; M. Hussain; B. A. Hytner, QC.

N. J. Inglis-Jones, QC; D. A. Inman; The Lord Irvine of Lairg, QC; R. E. Jack, QC; M. R. Jackson; P. J. E. Jackson; R. M. Jackson, QC; I. E. Jacob; C. E. F. James; N. F. B. Jarman, QC; D. A. Jeffreys, QC; J. Jeffs, QC; D. B. Johnson, QC; M. H. Johnson; A. G. H. Jones; E. S. Jones, QC; G. R. Jones; H. D. H. Jones; N. H. Jones, QC; S. E. Jones; T. G. Jones; W. H. Joss; P. S. L. Joyce; M. D. L. Kalisher, QC; M. L. Kallipetis,

QC; J. W. Kay, QC; M. R. Kay, QC; D. St. J. Keane, QC; M. L. Keane; R. W. M. Keeling; K. R. Keen; D. W. Keene, QC; D. A. M. Kemp, QC; T. D. Kent-Jones; M. Khayat; R. I. Kidwell, QC; A. W. P. King; A. T. H. Kirkwood, QC; R. C. Klevan, QC.

L. P. Laity; C. A. Lamb; D. G. Lane; P. Langan, QC; J. B. R. Langdon; G. J. H. Langley, QC; D. N. R. Latham, QC; R. B. Latham; S. W. Lawler; I. J. Lawrence, QC, MP; J. G. M. Laws; M. H. Lawson; G. S. Lawson Rogers; L. D. Lawton, QC; D. Lederman, QC; M. K. Lee, QC; R. T. L. Lee; I. Leeming, QC; C. H. de V. Leigh, QC; Sir Godfrey Le Quesne, QC; A. P. Lester, QC; B. H. Leveson, QC; S. Levine; D. M. Levy, QC; M. E. Lewer, QC; A. K. Lewis, QC; M. ap G. Lewis, QC; R. S. Lewis; C. C. D. Lindsay, QC; S. J. Linehan; J. S. Lipton; B. J. E. Livesey, QC; R. J. D. Livesey, QC; C. G. Llewellyn-Jones, QC; H. J. Lloyd, QC; J. Lloyd-Eley, QC; A. J. C. Lodge, Q.C.; A. G. Longden; D. C. Lovell-Pank; R. P. Lowden; G. W. Lowe; G. W. Lowther; F. D. L. Loy; G. Lumley; Sir Nicholas Lyell, QC, MP; E. Lyons, QC.

A. G. McCallum; A. W. McCreath; A. G. MacDuff; D. D. McEvoy, QC; R. D. Machell, QC; E. A. Machin, QC; D. I. Mackay; T. N. MacKean; N. R. B. Macleod, QC; N. J. C. McLusky; J. B. MacMillan; T. Maher; Miss V. H. Mairants; A. R. Malcolm; Miss A. Mallalieu, QC; A. C. B. Markham-David; J. H. Mance, QC; M. E. Mann, QC; F. J. M. Marr-Johnson; L. A. Marshall; R. G. Marshall-Andrews, QC; D. N. N. Martineau; H. R. A. Martineau; C. G. Masterman; D. Matheson, QC; W. D. Matthews; P. B. Mauleverer, QC; R. B. Mawrey, QC; A. T. K. May, QC; H. R. Mayor, QC; M. Meggerson; G. D. Mercer; M. K. Mettyear; J. T. Milford, QC; R. A. Miller; T. J. Milligan; Mrs. B. J. L. Mills, QC; J. B. M. Milmo, QC; N. A. Miscampbell, QC, MP; J. E. Mitting, QC; H. J. Montlake; E. G. Moelwyn-Hughes; M. J. Moore-Bick, QC; H. M. Morgan; J. A. Morgan; L. J. J. Morgan; W. G. O. Morgan, QC; G. E. Moriarty, QC; T. R. A. Morison, QC; P. R. Morrell; A. P. Morris; D. G. Morris; The Rt. Hon. J. Morris, QC, MP; J. I. Morris; W. P. Morris; D. C. Morton; A. G. Moses, QC; R. T. Moss; P. C. Mott; J. Mulcahy, QC; F. J. Muller, QC; M. J. A. Murphy; N. J. Mylne, QC.

T. M. E. Nash; M. H. D. Neligan; R. F. Nelson, QC; D. E. Neuberger, QC; R. E. Newbold; G. M. Newman, QC; J. D. Newton; G. Nice, QC; C. V. Nicholls, QC; C. A. A. Nicholls, QC; M. C. Nicholson; A. S. T. E. Nicol; B. Nolan; J. G. Nutting; D. P. O'Brien, QC; P. W. O'Brien; E. M. Ogden, QC; B. R. Oliver; S. J. L. Oliver, QC; C. P. L. Openshaw; M. A. Oppenheimer; R. T. N. Orme; R. C. C. O'Rorke; S. K. Overend; F. D. Owen; G. V. Owen, QC; R. M. Owen, QC; S. R. Page; D. C. J. Paget; A. W. Palmer, QC; A. D. W. Pardoe, QC; S. A. B. Parish; A. E. W. Park, QC; J. F. Parker, QC; T. C. Parkin; G. C. Parkins, QC; G. E. Parkinson; M. P. Parroy; E. O. Parry; N. S. K. Pascoe, QC; A. Patience, QC; J. G. Paulusz; Mrs. N. Pearce; D. H. Penry-Davey, QC; J. R. Peppitt, QC; Sir Ian Percival, QC; D. S. Perrett, QC; M. Pert; W. B. Phillips; N. A. J. Philpot; C. J. Pitchford, QC; A. P. Pitts; Miss E. F. Platt, QC; J. R. Platt; J. R. Playford, QC; R. F. D. Pollard; A. G. S. Pollock, QC; D. A. Poole, QC; L. R. Portnoy; M. J. Pratt, QC; S. Pratt; T. W. Preston, QC; J. E. Previté, QC; J. A. Price, QC; N. P. L. Price; P. J. Price, QC; R. N. M. Price; R. C. Pryor, QC; A. C. Pugh, QC; G. V. Pugh, QC; C. P. B. Purchas, QC; R. M. Purchas, QC; N. R. Purnell, QC; P. O. Purnell, QC.

D. A. Radcliffe; A. Rankin, QC; A. D. Rawley, QC; L. F. Read, QC; A. R. F. Redgrave; P. Rees; J. R. Reid, QC; R. E. Rhodes, QC; M. S. Rich, QC; D. W. Richards; H. A. Richardson; Miss S. A. Ritchie, QC; B. A. Rix, QC; S. D. Robbins; J. A. Roberts, QC; J. D. Roberts; J. H. Roberts; J. H. P. Roberts; J. M. G. Roberts, QC; P. B. Roberts; P. E. Robertshaw; V. Robinson, QC; D. E. H. Robson, QC; G. W. Roddick, QC; J. M. T. Rogers, QC; J. W. Rogers, QC; K. S. Rokison, QC; J. J. Rowe,

QC; R. J. Royce, QC; A. A. Rumbelow, QC; R. R. Russell; G. C. Ryan, QC.

J. E. A. Samuels, QC; J. H. B. Saunders; M. P. Sayers, QC; R. J. Scholes, QC; R. M. Scott; A. F. B. Scrivener, QC; R. J. Seabrook, QC; C. Seagroatt, QC; H. M. Self, QC; M. R. Selfe; D. H. D. Selwood; D. Serota, QC; J. L. Sessions; R. M. Shawcross; P. P. Shears; S. J. Sher, QC; M. D. Sherrard, QC; L. S. Shields, QC; J. M. Shorrock, QC; S. R. Silber, QC; A. G. Simmons; J. P. Singer, QC; P. F. Singer; J. C. N. Slater, QC; S. P. Sleeman; A. T. Smith, QC; C. M. Smith, QC; J. H. Smith, QC; R. S. Smith, QC; S. A. R. Smith; R. E. Snape; S. M. Solley, QC; R. F. Solman; P. C. E. Southwell; Miss J. M. Southworth, QC; M. H. Spence, QC; S. B. Spence; D. H. Spencer, QC; J. Spencer; M. G. Spencer, QC; S. M. Spencer, QC; L. Spittle; J. A. C. Spokes, QC; R. W. Spon-Smith; S. A. Stamler, QC; D. P. Stanley; Ms E. M. Steel; M. T. Steiger; D. H. Stembridge, QC; Mrs L. J. Stern; J. S. H. Stewart, QC; R. M. Stewart, QC; G. J. C. Still; D. M. A. Stokes, QC; M. G. T. Stokes; E. D. R. Stone, QC; P. L. Storr; T. M. F. Stow, QC; D. M. A. Strachan, QC; M. Stuart-Moore, QC; J. Stuart-Smith, QC; G. C. Styler; F. R. C. Such; A. B. Suckling, QC; J. M. Sullivan, QC; Ms. L E. Sullivan; L. Swift, QC; M. R. Swift, QC.

J. A. Tackaberry, QC; G. F. Tattersall; A. B. Taylor; E. Taylor; N. Taylor, QC; J. J. Teare; A. D. Temple, QC; V. B. A. Temple; M. I. Tennant; K. J. Tetley; Lord Thomas of Gwydir, PC, QC; D. M. Thomas, OBE, QC; D. O. Thomas, QC; P. M. Thomas; R. J. L. Thomas, QC; R. L. Thomas; R. U. Thomas, QC; A. A. R. Thompson, QC; J. Tiley; M. B. Tillett; R. N. Titheridge, QC; J. K. Toulmin, QC; R. G. Toulson, QC; J. B. S. Townend, QC; H. B. Trethowan; A. D. H. Trollope; S. L. Tuckey, QC; H. W. Turcan; P. A. Twigg, QC; C. J. M. Tyrer; A. R. Tyrrell, QC; J. G. G. Ungley; Mrs. A. P. Uziell-Hamilton; N. P. Valios; A. R. Vandermeer, QC; M. J. D. Vere-Hodge; C. D. Voelcker.

Rt. Hon. D. C. Waddington, QC, MP; J. P. Wadsworth, QC; D. St. J. Wagstaff; R. M. Wakerley, QC; W. H. Waldron, QC; J. D. G. Walford; R. Walker; R. J. Walker, QC; T. E. Walker, QC; J. J. Walker-Smith; N. P. R. Wall, QC; B. Walsh, QC; D. E. B. Waters; Sir James Watson, Bt.; C. D. G. Waud; P. A. Webster; M. Weisman; P. Weitzman, QC; C. P. C. Whelon; G. Whitburn, QC; C. H. Whitby, QC; W. J. M. White; P. G. Whiteman, QC; D. R. B. Whitehouse, QC; P. J. M. Whiteman, TD; A. Whitfield, QC; D. G. Widdicombe, QC; A. D. F. Wilcken; S. R. Wilkinson; D. B. Williams; G. H. G. Williams, QC; G. W. Williams, QC; J. G. Williams, QC; J. L. Williams, QC; The Hon. J. M. Williams, QC; S. W. Williamson, QC; J. C. Willis; A. M. Wilson, QC; N. A. R. Wilson, QC; C. Wilson-Smith, QC; G. W. Wingate-Saul, QC; M. E. Wolff; H. Wolton, QC; D. A. Wood, QC; D. R. Wood; W. R. Wood; C. G. P. Woodford; L. G. Woodley, QC; S. Woodley; B. Woodward; W. C. Woodward, QC; Ms. A. F. W. Woolley; D. R. Woolley, QC; N. G. Wootton; A. M. Worrall, QC; N. J. Worsley; P. F. Worsley, QC; D. E. M. Young, QC.

STIPENDIARY MAGISTRATES
PROVINCIAL
(each £43,450)

Greater Manchester, W. D. Fairclough (1982); C. T. Latham, OBE (1976).

Hampshire, T. G. Cowling (1989).

Humberside, N. H. White (1985).

Merseyside, N. G. Wootton (1976).

Middlesex, N. A. McKittrick (1989).

Mid Glamorgan, B. R. Oliver (1983); J. T. Curran (1990).

South Glamorgan, Sir Lincoln Hallinan (1976).

South Yorkshire, I. W. Crompton (1983); J. E. Barry (1985); W. D. Thomas (1989).

West Midlands, F. H. Hatchard (1981); W. M. Probert (1983); B. Morgan (1989).

West Yorkshire, F. D. L. Loy (1972); Mrs. P. A. Hewitt (1990); G. H. Kamil (1990).

METROPOLITAN

Chief Metropolitan Stipendiary Magistrate and Chairman of Committee of Magistrates for Inner London Area, Sir David Hopkin (*Bow Street*) £51,000

Committee of Magistrates for Inner London Area

3rd Floor, North West Wing,
Bush House, Aldwych, WC2B 4PJ

Principal Chief Clerk and Clerk to the Committee, I. Fowler £41,448
Chief Clerk (Training), J. W. Greenhill £37,218

Magistrates
(each £41,750)

Bow Street, The Chief Magistrate; R. D. Bartle; J. G. Connor; Miss D. Wickham.

Camberwell Green, R. D. Connor; C. P. M. Davidson; P. Fingret; Mrs. H. Mitcham; J. R. D. Phillips.

Clerkenwell, M. L. R. Romer; C. J. Bourke; M. A. Johnstone.

Greenwich and Woolwich, Mrs. K. R. Keating; B. Loosley; I. Bing.

Highbury Corner, D. Barr; G. E. Parkinson; Miss D. Quick; G. Wicks.

Horseferry Road, Miss P. A. Long; A. R. Davies; R. T. Moss; T. Maher.

Marlborough Street, K. J. H. Nichols; J. Q. Campbell.

Marylebone, G. L. J. Noel; Miss D. A. Freedman; Sir Bryan Roberts, KCMG, QC; B. Black.

Old Street, D. B. Meier; Miss D. Quick.

South Western, S. G. Clixby; A. Cooray; M. H. D. Neligan.

Thames, P. G. N. Badge; B. J. Canham; N. Crichton.

Tower Bridge, C. D. Voelcker; Mrs. J. R. Comyns; T. M. English.

Wells Street, Miss A. M. Jennings; D. M. Fingleton; K. L. Maitland-Davies.

West London, H. J. Cook; D. Kennett Brown.

Unattached Magistrates, T. H. Workman; G. B. Breen; A. W. Ormerod.

CROWN PROSECUTION SERVICE

Headquarters: 4/12 Queen Anne's Gate, SW1H 9AZ
[071-273 8152: *Casework sections,* 071-222 7944]

Fraud Divisions
10 Furnival Street, EC4A 1PE
[071-831 3038]

The Crown Prosecution Service (CPS) handles the prosecution of criminal proceedings instituted by police forces (excluding certain minor road traffic offences). The head of the CPS is the Director of Public Prosecutions; day-to-day administration of the CPS is handled by the Deputy Director. There are 31 areas, each headed by a Chief Crown Prosecutor.

Salaries

Grade 1	£77,000
Grade 2	£54,900
Grade 3	£43,350–£47,000
Grade 4	£36,818–£42,907
Grade 5	£30,001–£35,436

London Weighting=£1,750 p.a.

Director of Public Prosecutions (G1), A. D. Green, QC.
Deputy Director and Chief Executive (G2), D. S. Gandy, CB, OBE.

Principal Establishment and Finance Officer (G3), D. J. Wiblin.
Director, Headquarters Casework (G3), C. Newell.
Field Director, Operations (G3), G. Duff.
Field Director, Resources (G3), G. D. Etherington.
Head, Policy Division (G3), K. Ashken.
Head, General Casework (G5), D. Kyle.
Head, Special Casework (G5), M. Bibby.
Heads, Fraud Divisions (G5), T. Waring; G. Adams.
Head, Police Complaints Division (G5), C. Cleugh.
Head, Planning and Finance (G5), R. M. Prideaux.
Head, Personnel (G5), W. R. Mann.
Head, Management Services Division (G5), R. J. Caider.
Head, Training (G6), A. B. Machray.

CPS AREAS

AVON/SOMERSET, Froomsgate House, Rupert Street, Bristol BS1 2PS.—*Chief Crown Prosecutor (G5),* C. T. Jones.

CAMBRIDGESHIRE/LINCOLNSHIRE, Justinian House, Spitfire Close, Ermine Business Park, Cambs. PE18 6XY.—*Chief Crown Prosecutor (G5),* D. G. Lewis.

CHESHIRE, 2nd Floor, Windsor House, Pepper Street, Chester CH1 1TD.—*Chief Crown Prosecutor (G5),* Mrs. N. E. Hollingsworth.

CLEVELAND/NORTH YORKSHIRE, Rydale Building, 60 Piccadilly, York YO1 1NS.—*Chief Crown Prosecutor (G5),* D. M. Sharp.

DERBYSHIRE, Celtic House, Heritage Gate, Friary Street, Derby DE1 1QX.—*Chief Crown Prosecutor (G5),* D. R. K. Seddon.

DEVON/CORNWALL, Bradninch Hall, Castle Street, Exeter EX4 3PL.—*Chief Crown Prosecutor (G5),* R. J. Green.

DORSET/HAMPSHIRE, Black Horse House, 8–10 Leigh Road, Eastleigh, Hants. SO5 4FH.—*Chief Crown Prosecutor (G5),* P. Boeuf.

ESSEX, Gemini Centre, 88 New London Road, Chelmsford, Essex CM2 0BR.—*Chief Crown Prosecutor (G5),* J. J. Goodwin.

GLOUCESTERSHIRE/WILTSHIRE, 7 Avon Reach, Monkton Hill, Chippenham, Wilts. SN15 1EE.—*Chief Crown Prosecutor (G5),* R. A. Prickett.

GREATER MANCHESTER, PO Box 377, Sunlight House, Quay Street, Manchester M60 3LU.—*Chief Crown Prosecutor (G4),* A. R. Taylor.

HERTFORDSHIRE/BEDFORDSHIRE, Queens House, 58 Victoria Street, St. Albans AL1 3HZ.—*Chief Crown Prosecutor (G5),* C. Ingham.

HUMBERSIDE, Queens House, Paragon Street, Hull HU3 3DA.—*Chief Crown Prosecutor (G5),* L. M. Bell.

KENT, Kent House, Lower Stone Street, Maidstone, Kent ME15 6JT.—*Chief Crown Prosecutor (G5),* R. A. Crabb.

LANCASHIRE/CUMBRIA, Robert House, 2 Starkie Street, Preston, Lancs. PR1 3NY.—*Chief Crown Prosecutor (G5),* J. V. Bates.

LEICESTERSHIRE/NORTHAMPTONSHIRE, Leicester House, Lee Circle, Leicester LE1 3RE.—*Chief Crown Prosecutor (G5),* P. J. M. Hollingworth.

LONDON (INNER), Portland House, Stag Place, SW1E 5BH.—*Chief Crown Prosecutor (G4),* B. McArdle.

LONDON (NORTH), Solar House, 1 Romford Road, Stratford E15 4LJ.—*Chief Crown Prosecutor (G4),* R. J. Chronnell.

LONDON (SOUTH)/SURREY, Tolworth Tower, Surbiton KT6 7DS.—*Chief Crown Prosecutor (G4),* D. E. Dracup.

MERSEYSIDE, 7th Floor (South), Royal Liver Building, Liverpool L3 1HN.—*Chief Crown Prosecutor (G4),* E. C. Woodcock.

NORFOLK/SUFFOLK, Saxon House, 1 Cromwell Square, Ipswich, Suffolk IP1 1TS.—*Chief Crown Prosecutor (G5)*, M. F. C. Harvey.

NORTHUMBRIA/DURHAM, Cuthbert House, All Saints Centre, Newcastle upon Tyne NE1 2DW.—*Chief Crown Prosecutor (G5)*, D. A. Farmer.

NORTH WALES/DYFED/POWYS, 491 Abergele Road, Old Colwyn, Colwyn Bay, Clwyd LL29 9AE.—*Chief Crown Prosecutor (G5)*, A. S. R. Clarke.

NOTTINGHAMSHIRE, 2 King Edward Court, King Edward Street, Nottingham NG1 1EL.—*Chief Crown Prosecutor (G5)*, D. C. Beal.

SOUTH WALES/GWENT, Pearl Assurance House, Greyfriars Road, Cardiff CF1 3PL.—*Chief Crown Prosecutor (G4)*, H. G. Wallace.

SOUTH YORKSHIRE, Belgrave House, 47 Bank Street, Sheffield S1 2EH.—*Chief Crown Prosecutor (G4)*, M. J. Rose.

STAFFORDSHIRE/WARWICKSHIRE, Government Buildings, 11A Princes Street, Stafford ST16 2EU.—*Chief Crown Prosecutor (G5)*, D. V. Dickenson.

SUSSEX, Unit 3, Clifton Mews, Clifton Hill, Brighton, E. Sussex BN1 3HR.—*Chief Crown Prosecutor (G5)*, D. Thompson.

THAMES VALLEY, The Courtyard, Lombard Street, Abingdon, Oxon. OX14 5SE.—*Chief Crown Prosecutor (G5)*, vacant.

WEST MERCIA, Orchard House, Victoria Square, Droitwich, Worcester WR9 8QT.—*Chief Crown Prosecutor (G5)*, D. R. Stott.

WEST MIDLANDS, The McClaren Building, Dale End, Birmingham B4 7NR.—*Chief Crown Prosecutor (G3)*, P. D. F. Higginbottom.

WEST YORKSHIRE, Grove Hall, College Grove Road, Wakefield WF1 3RA.—*Chief Crown Prosecutor (G4)*, R. Otley.

THE SCOTTISH JUDICATURE

Scotland has a legal system separate and differing greatly from the English legal system in enacted law, judicial procedure and the structure of courts.

There is in Scotland a system of public prosecution headed by the Lord Advocate which is independent of the police, who have no say in the decision to prosecute. The Lord Advocate, discharging his functions through the Crown Office in Edinburgh, is responsible for prosecutions in the High Court, sheriff courts and district courts. Prosecutions in the High Court are prepared by the Crown Office and conducted in court by one of the Law Officers or an advocate-depute. In the inferior courts the decision to prosecute is made and prosecution is preferred by procurators fiscal, who are lawyers and full-time civil servants, subject to the directions of the Crown Office. A permanent legally-qualified civil servant known as the Crown Agent is responsible for the running of the Crown Office and the organization of the Procurator Fiscal Service, of which he is the head.

Scotland is divided into six Sheriffdoms, each with a full-time Sheriff Principal. The Sheriffdoms are further divided into sheriff court districts, each of which has a legally-qualified, resident sheriff or sheriffs, who are the judges of the court.

In criminal cases sheriffs principal and sheriffs have the same powers; sitting with a jury of 15 members, they may try more serious cases on indictment, or, sitting alone, may try lesser cases under summary procedure. Minor summary offences are dealt with in district courts which are administered by the district and the islands local government authorities and presided over by lay justices of the peace, and, in Glasgow only, by stipendiary magistrates. Juvenile offenders (children under 16) may be brought before an informal children's hearing comprising three local lay people. The superior criminal court is the High Court of Justiciary which is both a trial and an appeal court. Cases on indictment are tried by a High Court Judge, sitting with a jury of 15, in Edinburgh and on circuit in other towns. Appeals from the lower courts against conviction or sentence are heard also by the High Court, which sits as an appeal court only in Edinburgh. There is no further appeal to the House of Lords in criminal cases.

In civil cases the jurisdiction of the sheriff court extends to most kinds of action. Appeal against decisions of the sheriff may be made to the Sheriff Principal and thence to the Court of Session, or direct to the Court of Session, which sits only in Edinburgh. The Court of Session is divided into the Inner and the Outer House. The Outer House is a court of first instance in which cases are heard by judges sitting singly, sometimes with a jury of 12. The Inner House, itself subdivided into two Divisions of equal status, is mainly an appeal court. Appeals may be made to the Inner House from the Outer House as well as from the sheriff court. An appeal may be made from the Inner House to the House of Lords.

The Judges of the Court of Session are the same as those of the High Court of Justiciary, the Lord President of the Court of Session also holding the office of Lord Justice General in the High Court.

The office of coroner does not exist in Scotland. The local procurator fiscal inquires privately into sudden and suspicious deaths and may report findings to the Crown Agent. In some cases a fatal accident inquiry may be held before the sheriff.

COURT OF SESSION and HIGH COURT OF JUSTICIARY

The Lord President and Lord Justice General,
(£87,700)
The Rt. Hon. Lord Hope
(born 1938, *apptd.* 1989)

INNER HOUSE

Lords of Session (each £84,250)

FIRST DIVISION

	Apptd.
The Lord President.	
Hon. Lord Allanbridge (William Ian Stewart), *born* 1925	1977
Hon. Lord Cowie (William Lorn Kerr Cowie), *born* 1926	1977
Hon. Lord Mayfield (Ian MacDonald, MC), *born* 1921	1981

SECOND DIVISION

Lord Justice Clerk (£85,250), The Rt. Hon. Lord Ross, (Donald MacArthur Ross), *born* 1927	1985
Hon. Lord Dunpark (Alastair McPherson Johnston, TD), *born* 1915	1971
Rt. Hon. Lord Wylie (Norman Russell Wylie, VRD), *born* 1923	1974
Rt. Hon. Lord Murray (Ronald King Murray), *born* 1922	1979

OUTER HOUSE

Lords of Session (each £76,300)

Hon. Lord Davidson (Charles Kemp Davidson), *(seconded to Scottish Law Commission) born* 1929	1983

Hon. The Lord McCluskey, *born* 1929 1984
Hon. Lord Morison (Alastair Malcolm Morison), *born* 1931 1985
Hon. Lord Sutherland (Ranald Iain Sutherland), *born* 1932 1985
Hon. Lord Weir (David Bruce Weir), *born* 1931 1985
Hon. Lord Clyde (James John Clyde), *born* 1932 1985
Hon. Lord Cullen (William Douglas Cullen), *born* 1935 1986
Hon. Lord Prosser (William David Prosser), *born* 1934 1986
Hon. Lord Kirkwood (Ian Candlish Kirkwood), *born* 1932 1987
Hon. Lord Coulsfield (John Taylor Cameron), *born* 1934 1987
Hon. Lord Milligan (James George Milligan), *born* 1934 1988
Hon. The Lord Morton of Shuna, *born* 1930 .. 1988
Hon. Lord Caplan (Philip Isaac Caplan), *born* 1929.................................... 1989
Rt. Hon. The Lord Cameron of Lochbroom, *born* 1931 1989
Hon. Lord Marnoch (Michael Stewart Rae Bruce), *born* 1938........................ 1990
Hon. Lord MacLean (Ranald Norman Munro MacLean), *born* 1938.................... 1990

COURT OF SESSION AND HIGH COURT OF JUSTICIARY
Parliament House, Parliament Square, Edinburgh

Principal Clerk of Session and Justiciary, H. S. Foley .... £30,001–£39,746
Deputy Principal Clerk of Justiciary and Administration, J. Robertson .... £20,189–£28,710
Deputy Principal Clerk of Session and Principal Extractor, M. Weir .... £20,189–£28,710
Deputy Principal Clerk (Keeper of the Rolls), M. G. Bonar .... £20,189–£28,710
Depute Clerks of Session and Justiciary, W. Gillon; T. D. McIntosh; A. Hogg; N. J. Dowie; J. M. Clark; I. Smith; J. A. R. Cowie; E. G. Appelbe; T. Higgins; T. B. Cruickshank; Q. Oliver; F. Shannly; R. D. Sinclair; Mrs. A. Leighton; T. M. Thomson; D. D. Mackay; A. S. Moffat; J. Atkinson; D. J. Shand; G. Ellis; Mrs. G. McKeand .... £15,156–£21,862

SCOTTISH COURTS ADMINISTRATION
26–27 Royal Terrace, Edinburgh EH7 5AH

Director, G. Murray.

SHERIFF COURT OF CHANCERY
16 North Bank Street, Edinburgh EH1 2NJ

Sheriff of Chancery, C. G. B. Nicholson, QC.

HM COMMISSARY OFFICE
16 North Bank Street, Edinburgh EH1 2NJ

Commissary Clerk, D. B. White.

SCOTTISH LAND COURT
1 Grosvenor Crescent, Edinburgh

Chairman, The Hon. Lord Elliott, MC £56,600
Members, A. B. Campbell, OBE; D. D. McDiarmid; R. MacDonald.

SHERIFFDOMS
Salaries
Sheriff Principal £56,600
Sheriff £51,000
Regional Sheriff Clerk .... £23,039–£39,746
Sheriff Clerk .... £15,786–£39,746

GRAMPIAN, HIGHLAND AND ISLANDS
Sheriff Principal, R. D. Ireland, QC
Regional Sheriff Clerk, J. S. Doig.

Sheriffs and Sheriff Clerks

Aberdeen and Stonehaven, A. M. G. Russell, CBE, QC; D. J. Risk; D. W. Bogie, D. Kelbie; *Sheriff Clerks,* J. Rodden; W. A. Mouser.
Banff and Peterhead, A. J. Murphy; *Sheriff Clerk,* A. H. Hempseed.
Elgin, N. McPartlin; *Sheriff Clerk,* A. Lynch.
Inverness, Lochmaddy, Portree, Stornoway, Dingwall, Tain, Wick and Dornoch, W. J. Fulton; D. Booker-Milburn; J. O. A. Fraser; E. Stewart; *Sheriff Clerks,* J. S. Doig; J. S. McMillan.
Kirkwall and Lerwick, A. A. MacDonald; *Sheriff Clerk,* J. Rodden.
Fort William, D. Noble (also *Oban and Campbeltown*); *Sheriff Clerk,* J. S. Doig.

TAYSIDE, CENTRAL AND FIFE
Sheriff Principal, R. R. Taylor, QC, Ph.D.
Regional Sheriff Clerk, B. J. Young.

Sheriffs and Sheriff Clerks

Arbroath and Forfar, S. O. Kermack; *Sheriff Clerks,* B. T. McCabe; P. Dougan.
Dundee, G. L. Cox; A. L. Stewart; *Sheriff Clerk,* B. J. Young.
Perth, J. F. Wheatley; C. Smith*; *Sheriff Clerk,* Miss J. Telfer.
Falkirk, A. V. Sheehan; A. B. Wilkinson; *Sheriff Clerk,* D. Nicoll.
Stirling, W. C. Henderson; R. E. G. Younger; *Sheriff Clerk,* K. MacKenzie.
Alloa, R. E. G. Younger; *Sheriff Clerk,* R. G. Young.
Cupar, J. C. McInnes (also *Perth*); *Sheriff Clerk,* B. Sullivan.
Dunfermline, J. S. Forbes; W. M. Reid; *Sheriff Clerk,* J. Ross.
Kirkcaldy, W. J. Christie; C. R. Macarthur, QC; *Sheriff Clerk,* T. Fyffe.

LOTHIAN AND BORDERS
Sheriff Principal, C. G. B. Nicholson, QC
Regional Sheriff Clerk, D. B. White.

Sheriffs and Sheriff Clerks

Edinburgh, N. E. D. Thomson; J. L. M. Mitchell; P. G. B. McNeill, Ph.D.; Miss H. J. Aronson; R. G. Craik, QC; G. I. W. Shiach; Miss I. A. Poole; R. J. D. Scott; A. M. Bell; J. M. S. Horsburgh; G. W. S. Presslie; J. A. Farrell*; I. A. Cameron; *Sheriff Clerk,* D. B. White.
Peebles, N. E. D. Thomson (also *Edinburgh*); *Sheriff Clerk,* D. B. White.
Linlithgow, M. Stone; H. R. MacLean; *Sheriff Clerk,* R. Sinclair.
Haddington, G. W. S. Presslie (also *Edinburgh*); *Sheriff Clerk,* B. W. S. Manthorpe.
Jedburgh and Duns, J. V. Paterson; *Sheriff Clerk,* A. G. Pryde.
Selkirk, J. V. Paterson; *Sheriff Clerk,* A. G. Pryde.

NORTH STRATHCLYDE
Sheriff Principal, R. C. Hay, CBE
Regional Sheriff Clerk, A. A. Brown.

Sheriffs and Sheriff Clerks

Oban and Campbeltown, D. Noble (also *Fort William*); *Sheriff Clerks,* N. R. Weir; A. A. Brown.

---

*Floating Sheriff

Dumbarton, J. T. Fitzsimons; T. Scott; S. W. H. Fraser; *Sheriff Clerk*, N. R. Weir.
Paisley, R. G. Smith; C. N. Stoddart; J. Spy; C. K. Higgins; C. W. Palmer; C. G. McKay*; *Sheriff Clerk*, A. A. Brown.
Greenock, J. Irvine Smith (also *Rothesay*); Sir Stephen Young; *Sheriff Clerk*, A. P. MacPherson.
Kilmarnock, T. M. Croan; D. B. Smith; T. F. Russell; *Sheriff Clerk*, J. Shaw.
Dunoon, C. W. Palmer (also *Dumbarton*); *Sheriff Clerk*, A. P. MacPherson.

GLASGOW AND STRATHKELVIN

Sheriff Principal, N. D. MacLeod, QC
Regional Sheriff Clerk, C. McLay.

Sheriffs and Sheriff Clerks

Glasgow, A. C. Horsfall (*seconded to Scottish Lands Tribunal*); J. J. Maguire; A. A. Bell, QC; B. Kearney; G. H. Gordon, QC; A. C. McKay; A. Lothian; J. C. M. Jardine; Mrs. D. J. B. Robertson; B. A. Lockhart; I. G. Pirie; Miss A. L. A. Smith; W. G. Stevenson, QC; G. J. Evans; E. H. Galt; F. J. Keane; A. C. Henry; J. K. Mitchell; A. G. Johnston; J. P. Murphy; M. Sischy; *Sheriff Clerk*, C. McLay.

SOUTH STRATHCLYDE, DUMFRIES AND GALLOWAY

Sheriff Principal, J. S. Mowat, QC
Regional Sheriff Clerk, H. Findlay.

Sheriffs and Sheriff Clerks

Hamilton, L. S. Lovat; A. C. MacPherson; W. F. Lunny; I. A. MacMillan, CBE; V. J. Canavan (also *Airdrie*); W. E. Gibson; I. C. Simpson*; *Sheriff Clerk*, J. Cumming.
Lanark, J. D. Allan; *Sheriff Clerk*, D. M. Cameron.
Ayr, N. Gow, QC; R. G. McEwan, QC; *Sheriff Clerk*, E. A. Cumming.
Stranraer and Kirkcudbright, J. R. Smith; *Sheriff Clerk*, N. L. Hodgson.
Dumfries, K. G. Barr; L. Cameron; *Sheriff Clerk*, P. McGonigle.
Airdrie, J. H. Stewart; J. S. Boyle; V. J. Canavan (also *Hamilton*); R. H. Dickson; *Sheriff Clerk*, H. Findlay.

*Floating Sheriff

CROWN OFFICE

Regent Road, Edinburgh EH7 5BL
[031-557 3800]

Crown Agent, I. Dean, CB £54,900
Deputy Crown Agent, A. C. Normand £38,254

PROCURATOR FISCAL SERVICE

Grampian, Highlands and Islands Region

Regional Procurator Fiscal, S. W. Lockhart, CBE (*Aberdeen*).
Procurators Fiscal, J. D. McNaughton (*Stonehaven*); A. J. M. Colley (*Banff*); I. S. McNaughtan (*Peterhead*); A. Wither (*Elgin*); A. C. P. Reith (*Wick*); C. B. McClory (*Portree and Lochmaddy*); C. S. Mackenzie (*Stornoway*); H. T. Westwater (*Dornoch* and *Tain*); B. Heywood (*Inverness*); A. C. P. Reith (*Kirkwall*); Miss A. Thom (*Lerwick*); J. I. M. MacGillivray (*Fort William*); D. R. Hingston (*Dingwall*).

Tayside, Central and Fife Region

Regional Procurator Fiscal, D. R. Smith (*Dundee*).
Procurators Fiscal, C. D. G. Hillary (*Arbroath*); A. L. Ingram (*Forfar*); M. MacPhail (*Perth*); G. E. Scott (*Falkirk*); K. Valentine (*Stirling*); I. D. Douglas (*Alloa*); R. A. S. Brown (*Cupar*); R. T. Hamilton (*Dunfermline*); Mrs. I. Guild (*Kirkcaldy*).

Lothian and Borders Region

Regional Procurator Fiscal, J. D. Lowe (*Edinburgh*).
Procurators Fiscal, F. J. M. Brown (*Peebles*); H. R. Annan (*Linlithgow*); A. N. MacDonald (*Haddington*); J. C. Whitelaw (*Duns* and *Jedburgh*); D. McNeill (*Selkirk*).

North Strathclyde Region

Regional Procurator Fiscal, R. F. Lees (*Paisley*).
Procurators Fiscal, I. Henderson (*Campbeltown* and *Oban*); J. Cardle (*Dumbarton*); P. Docherty (*Greenock*); D. L. Webster (*Dunoon* and *Rothesay*); J. G. MacGlennan (*Kilmarnock*).

Glasgow and Strathkelvin Region

Regional Procurator Fiscal, A. S. Jessop (*Glasgow*).

South Strathclyde, Dumfries and Galloway Region

Regional Procurator Fiscal, W. G. Carmichael (*Hamilton*).
Procurators Fiscal, S. R. Houston (*Lanark*); N. G. O'Brien (*Ayr*); F. Walkinshaw (*Stranraer*); J. T. MacDougall (*Dumfries* and *Kirkcudbright*); A. T. Wilson (*Airdrie*).

NORTHERN IRELAND JUDICATURE

In Northern Ireland the legal system and the structure of courts closely resemble those of England and Wales; there are, however, often differences in enacted law.

The Supreme Court of Judicature of Northern Ireland comprises the Court of Appeal, the High Court of Justice and the Crown Court. The practice and procedure of these Courts is similar to those in England. The superior civil court is the High Court of Justice, from which an appeal lies to the Court of Appeal; the House of Lords is the final civil appeal court.

The decision to prosecute in cases tried on indictment and in summary cases of a serious nature rests in Northern Ireland with the Director of Public Prosecutions, who is responsible to the Attorney General. Minor summary offences are prosecuted by the police.

Minor criminal offences are dealt with in magistrates' courts by a full-time, legally qualified resident magistrate and, where an offender is under 17, by juvenile courts consisting of the resident magistrate and two lay members specially qualified to deal with juveniles (at least one of whom must be a woman). Appeals from magistrates' courts are heard by the county court. The Crown Court, served by High Court and county court judges, deals with criminal trials on indictment. Cases are heard before a judge and, except those involving offences specified under emergency legislation, a jury. Appeals from the Crown Court against conviction or sentence are heard by the Northern Ireland Court of Appeal; the House of Lords is the final court of appeal.

Magistrates' courts in Northern Ireland can deal with certain classes of civil case but most minor civil cases are dealt with in county courts. Judgments of all civil courts are enforceable through a centralized procedure administered by the Enforcement of Judgments Office.

SUPREME COURT OF JUDICATURE
The Royal Courts of Justice
Belfast

Lord Chief Justice of Northern Ireland (£88,500)
The Rt. Hon. Sir Brian Hutton
(*born* 1931, *apptd.* 1988)

Lords Justices of Appeal (each £85,000)

		Apptd.
Rt. Hon. Sir Basil Kelly, *born* 1920	....	1984
Rt. Hon. Sir John MacDermott, *born* 1927	....	1987
Rt. Hon. Sir Donald Murray, *born* 1923	......	1975

Puisne Judges (each £77,000)

Hon. Sir John Higgins, *born* 1927	....	1984
Hon. Sir Robert Carswell, *born* 1934	....	1984
Hon. Sir Michael Nicholson, *born* 1933	....	1986

Hon. Sir William McCollum, *born* 1933	......	1987
Hon. Sir William Campbell, *born* 1936	....	1988
Hon. Sir John Sheil, *born* 1938	....	1989

Lord Chief Justice's Office

Principal Secretary to the Lord Chief Justice and Clerk of the Crown for Northern Ireland, J. A. L. McLean, QC.
Legal Secretary to the Lord Chief Justice, Mrs. D. M. Kennedy.

Masters of Supreme Court (£43,450):
Master, Central Office, V. A. Care, QC.
Master, High Court, J. W. Wilson, QC.
Master, Office of Care and Protection, F. B. Hall.
Master, Chancery Office, V. G. Bridges.
Master, Bankruptcy and Companies Office, J. B. C. Glass.
Master, Probate and Matrimonial Office, R. T. Hillar.
Master, Taxing Office, J. C. Napier.

Accountant, Court Funds Office, J. Jackson.

Recorders

Belfast, Judge Pringle, QC £58,900
Londonderry, Judge Hart, QC.

County Court Judges

Judge Babington, DSC, QC; Judge Chambers, QC; Judge Curran, QC; Judge Gibson, QC; Judge McKee, QC; Judge Petrie, QC; Rt. Hon. Judge Sir Robert Porter, QC; Judge Russell, QC; Judge Higgins, QC; Judge Smyth, QC; Judge Martin, QC £58,900

Crown Solicitor's Office
Royal Courts of Justice, Belfast

Crown Solicitor, H. A. Nelson.

Department of the Director of Public Prosecutions
Royal Courts of Justice, Belfast

Director of Public Prosecutions, A. Fraser, QC.
Deputy Director of Public Prosecutions, D. Magill.

ECCLESIASTICAL COURTS

Original jurisdiction is exercised by the Consistory Court of each diocese in England, presided over by the Chancellor of that diocese. Appellate jurisdiction is exercised by the Provincial Courts detailed below, and by the Court for Ecclesiastical Causes Reserved, and by Commissions of Review (the membership of these being newly constituted for each case).

Court of Arches
(Province of Canterbury)
Registry, 16 Beaumont Street, Oxford OX1 2LZ

Dean of the Arches, The Rt. Worshipful Sir John Owen.

Court of the Vicar-General of the Province of Canterbury
Registry, 16 Beaumont Street, Oxford OX1 2LZ
Vicar-General, The Rt. Worshipful Miss S. Cameron, QC.

Chancery Court of York
Registry, 1 Peckitt Street, York YO1 1SG
Auditor, The Rt. Worshipful Sir John Owen.

The Vicar-General of the Province of York
Registry, 1 Peckitt Street, York YO1 1SG

Vicar-General, The Rt. Worshipful T. A. C. Coningsby, QC.

Court of Faculties
Registry, 1 The Sanctuary, SW1P 3JT

Office for the issue of special and ordinary marriage licences, appointment of notaries public, etc. Office hours, Mon.–Fri., 10–4.
Master of the Faculties, The Rt. Worshipful Sir John Owen.

TRIBUNALS

COMMONS COMMISSIONERS
Golden Cross House, Duncannon Street
WC2N 4JF
[071–210 4584]

The Commons Commissioners are responsible for deciding disputes arising under the Commons Registration Act 1965 and the Common Land (Rectification of Registers) Act 1989. They also enquire into the ownership of unclaimed common land. Commissioners are appointed by the Lord Chancellor.

Chief Commons Commissioner, P. G. Langdon-Davies.
Commissioners, M. Roth; I. L. R. Romer; D. M. Burton.
Clerk, Miss W. G. E. George.

COPYRIGHT TRIBUNAL
Room 1509, State House, 66–71 High Holborn,
WC1R 4TP
[071–831 2525]

Chairman, J. M. Bowers.
Secretary, C. Brook.

EMPLOYMENT APPEAL TRIBUNAL
Central Office, 4 St. James's Square, SW1Y 4JU
Divisional Office, 11 Melville Crescent, Edinburgh, EH3 7LU.
President, The Hon. Mr. Justice Wood.
Registrar, Miss V. J. Selio.

IMMIGRATION APPELLATE AUTHORITIES
Thanet House, 231 Strand, WC2R 1DA

Immigration Appeal Tribunal
President, D. L. Neve £51,000
Vice-Presidents, G. W. Farmer; Prof. D. C. Jackson £51,000

Immigration Appeal Adjudicators
Chief Adjudicator, M. Patey, MBE £51,000

THE INDUSTRIAL TRIBUNALS
Central Office (England and Wales)
93 Ebury Bridge Road, SW1W 8RE

President, His Honour Judge Sir David West-Russell
£53,400

Central Office (Scotland)
St. Andrew House, 141 West Nile Street,
Glasgow G1 2RU

President, I. M. Thomson, WS £56,600

LANDS TRIBUNAL
48–49 Chancery Lane, WC2A 1JR
[071–936 7200]

President, V. G. Wellings, QC £60,000
Members, C. R. Mallett; W. Hall, DFC, Dr. T. Hoyes; His Hon. Judge B. Marder, QC £54,000
Member (part-time), J. C. Hill, TD ...... £219 per day
Registrar, C. A. McMullan.

LANDS TRIBUNAL FOR SCOTLAND
1 Grosvenor Crescent, Edinburgh EH12 5ER
[031–225 7996]

President, The Hon. Lord Elliott, MC........ £56,600
Members, W. Hall, DFC; Sheriff A. C. Horsfall, QC; A. R. MacLeary *(full-time)*; W. D. C. Andrews, CBE, WS *(part-time)*.......................... £51,000
Clerk, D. Pentland.

NHS TRIBUNAL

Inquires into representations that the continued inclusion of a family practitioner (doctor, dentist, pharmacist or optician) on a Family Practitioner Committee's list would be prejudicial to the efficiency of the services concerned. The Tribunal sits when required, about eight times a year, and usually in London.

Chairman, B. Hargrove, QC.
Clerk, I. D. Keith, 1–2 Judges Terrace, East Grinstead, W. Sussex RH19 3AA (Tel: 0342–321111).

PENSIONS APPEAL TRIBUNALS
Central Office (England and Wales)
48–49 Chancery Lane, WC2A 1JR

Responsibility for hearing appeals in connection with War Pensions.

President, M. H. Fauvelle £44,300

Pensions Appeal Tribunals for Scotland

20 Walker Street, Edinburgh EH3 7HS

President, J. A. Cameron.

OFFICE OF THE PRESIDENT OF SOCIAL SECURITY APPEAL TRIBUNALS, MEDICAL APPEAL TRIBUNALS AND VACCINE DAMAGE TRIBUNALS
Clements House, Gresham Street, EC2V 7DN
[071–606 2106]

An independent statutory authority which exercises judicial and administrative control over social security appeal tribunals, medical appeal tribunals and vaccine damage tribunals.

President, His Hon. Judge D. Holden £56,000
Secretary, J. Read.

OFFICE OF THE SOCIAL SECURITY COMMISSIONERS
London: Harp House, 83–86 Farringdon Street, EC4A 4DH (Tel: 071–353 5145)
Edinburgh: 23 Melville Street, EH3 7PW

The final statutory authority to decide social security and medical claims.

Chief Commissioner, His Hon. Judge K. Machin, QC.
Secretary, Mrs. M. White *(London)*; R. Lindsay *(Edinburgh)*.

OFFICE OF THE SOCIAL SECURITY COMMISSIONERS FOR NORTHERN IRELAND
Lancashire House, 5 Linenhall Street,
Belfast BT2 8AA
[0232–332344]

Chief Commissioner, Hon. Judge Chambers, QC.
Secretary, J. E. P. Millar.

THE SOLICITORS' DISCIPLINARY TRIBUNAL
60 Carey Street, WC2A 2JB
[071–242 0219]

Independent body with members appointed by the Master of the Rolls.

President, G. B. Marsh.
Clerk, Mrs. S. C. Elson.

SPECIAL COMMISSIONERS OF INCOME TAX
Turnstile House, 98 High Holborn, WC1V 6LQ
[071–831 5253]

Independent body appointed by the Lord Chancellor to hear appeals concerning income taxes, etc.

Presiding Special Commissioner, His Hon. Judge Medd, OBE, QC £48,100
Special Commissioners, B. M. F. O'Brien; T. H. K. Everett; D. A. Shirley £41,150
Deputy Special Commissioners, D. C. Potter, QC; R. H. Widdows, CB.
Clerk, R. P. Lester £19,611

TRANSPORT TRIBUNAL
48–49 Chancery Lane, WC2A 1JR

President, Judge Inskip, QC.
Secretary, E. J. Thomas.

VAT TRIBUNALS
15–17 Great Marlborough Street, W1V 2AP
[071–437 8330]

VAT Tribunals are administered by the Lord Chancellor's Department (the Secretary of State in Scotland) and determine disputes concerning VAT.

President, His Hon. Judge Medd, OBE, QC ... £48,100
Vice-President, Scotland, R. A. Bennett, CBE, QC.
£39,400

Registrar, J. M. Busby.

Tribunal Centres

London (including Belfast), 15–17 Great Marlborough Street, W1V 2AP.
Edinburgh, 44 Palmerston Place, Edinburgh EH12 5BJ.
Manchester, Warwickgate House, Warwick Road, Old Trafford, Manchester M16 0GP.

Parliamentary and Local Government Election Petitions Office
Room 120, Royal Courts of Justice, Strand, WC2A 2LL

Prescribed Officer, K. W. Topley.
Chief Clerk, C. I. P. Denyer.

THE POLICE SERVICE

There are 52 police forces in the United Kingdom, each responsible for law enforcement in its area. Most forces' area is conterminous with an English or Welsh county or Scottish region, though there are several combined forces. Law enforcement in London is carried out by the Metropolitan Police and the City of London Police; in Northern Ireland by the Royal Ulster Constabulary; and by the Isle of Man, States of Jersey, and Guernsey forces in their respective islands and bailiwicks.

Each police force is maintained by a police authority. The authorities of English and Welsh forces comprise committees of local councillors and magistrates; in Scotland, the regional and islands councils are the authorities. The authority for the Metropolitan Police is the Home Secretary. In Northern Ireland the Secretary of State appoints the police authority.

Police authorities are financed by central and local government. Subject to the approval of the Home Secretary and to regulations, they appoint the chief constable, decide the maximum size of the force and provide buildings and equipment.

The Home Secretary and the Secretaries of State for Scotland and Northern Ireland are responsible for the organization, administration and operation of the police service. They make regulations covering matters such as police ranks, discipline, hours of duty, and pay and allowances.

All police forces (including the Metropolitan Police at the request of the Commissioner) are subject to inspection by HM Inspectors of Constabulary, who report to the respective Secretary of State.

The investigation of a serious complaint against a police officer is supervised by the Police Complaints Authority in England and Wales. In Scotland, complaints are investigated by independent public prosecutors.

Basic rates of police pay
(since Sept. 1, 1990)

Chief Constable	£48,015–£61,029
Deputy Chief Constable	£42,291–£48,822
Assistant Chief Constable	£40,278
Chief Superintendent...........	£34,167–£36,276
Superintendent	£30,729–£33,369
Chief Inspector	£22,590–£25,128
Inspector	£19,896–£22,590
Sergeant	£17,346–£19,896
Constable	£10,866–£18,132

Metropolitan Police
(Including London Weighting and London Allowance for ranks below Commissioner)

Metropolitan Commissioner	£76,320*
Deputy Commissioner	£65,025
Assistant Commissioner	£57,366
Deputy Assistant Commissioner	£45,894
Commander	£40,278
Chief Superintendent...........	£35,337–£37,446
Superintendent	£32,682–£34,539
Chief Inspector	£24,843–£27,375
Inspector	£22,137–£24,843
Sergeant	£18,516–£21,066
Constable	£12,036–£19,302

*Since April 1, 1990.

POLICE AUTHORITIES IN THE UNITED KINGDOM

Police Force	Headquarters	Actual Strength	Chief Constable (a) Chief Officer	Chairman of Police Authority/Committee
England				
Avon and Somerset	Bristol	3,149	D. Shattock, QPM	R. Mullett
Bedfordshire	Bedford	1,049	A. Dyer, QPM	(Elected at each meeting)
Cambridgeshire	Huntingdon	1,217	I. H. Kane, QPM	K. Spink, OBE
Cheshire	Chester	1,865	D. J. Graham, QPM	J. H. Collins, OBE
Cleveland	Middlesbrough	1,477	K. Hellawell	I. Jeffrey
Cumbria	Penrith	1,166	L. Sharp, QPM	R. Watson
Derbyshire	Ripley	1,794	J. F. Newing, QPM	R. W. Jones
Devon and Cornwall	Exeter	2,846	J. S. Evans, QPM	D. L. C. Roberts
Dorset	Dorchester	1,265	B. H. Weight, QPM	Maj. Gen. H. M. G. Bond
Durham	Durham	1,372	F. W. Taylor, QPM	Mrs. J. Parkin
Essex	Chelmsford	2,889	J. H. Burrow, OBE	G. C. Waterer, MBE
Gloucestershire	Cheltenham	1,164	A. H. Pacey, QPM	C. P. Hay
Greater Manchester	Manchester 16	6,990	C. J. Anderton, CBE, QPM	S. Murphy
Hampshire	Winchester	3,162	J. C. Hoddinott, QPM	B. L. P. Blacker
Hertfordshire	Welwyn Garden City	1,669	B. H. Skitt, BEM, QPM	F. Cogan, CBE
Humberside	Hull	1,992	D. Hall, CBE, QPM	S. J. Bayes
Kent	Maidstone	3,059	P. Condon, QPM	C. R. Carr
Lancashire	Preston	3,175	R. B. Johnson, CBE, QPM	Mrs. R. B. Henig
Leicestershire	Leicester	1,775	M. J. Hirst, QPM	R. R. Angrave
Lincolnshire	Lincoln	1,197	N. G. Ovens, QPM	M. D. Kennedy
Merseyside	Liverpool 69	4,695	J. Sharples, QPM	G. Bundred
Norfolk	Norwich	1,383	P. J. Ryan	R. Chase
Northamptonshire	Northampton	1,130	D. J. O'Dowd, QPM	A. A. Morby
Northumbria	Newcastle upon Tyne	3,588	Sir Stanley Bailey, CBE, QPM	G. Gill
North Yorkshire	Northallerton	1,371	D. M. Burke, QPM.	J. H. G. Parfect, MBE
Nottinghamshire	Nottingham	2,320	D. Crompton, QPM	C. Winterton
South Yorkshire	Sheffield	2,925	R. Wells, QPM	Sir John Layden
Staffordshire	Stafford	2,202	C. H. Kelly, CBE, QPM	Miss I. H. Moseley

Police Force	Headquarters	Actual Strength	Chief Constable (a) Chief Officer	Chairman of Police Authority/Committee
Suffolk	Ipswich	1,197	A. T. Coe, QPM	Capt. R. J. Sheepshanks, CBE
Surrey	Guildford	1,694	B. Hayes, QPM	Mrs. D. James
Sussex	Lewes	2,950	R. Birch, CBE, QPM	Mrs. P. A. Drake
Thames Valley	Oxford	3,682	C. Smith, CVO, QPM	Lt. Col. J. C. Walton
Warwickshire	Warwick	991	P. D. Joslin, QPM	J. L. Findon
West Mercia	Worcester	1,995	A. A. Mullett, QPM	R. A. H. Lloyd, TD
West Midlands	Birmingham 4	6,818	R. Hadfield, QPM	L. J. Jones
West Yorkshire	Wakefield	5,240	P. J. Nobes, QPM	T. Brennan
Wiltshire	Devizes	1,074	W. R. Girven, QPM	Lt.-Col. D. B. W. Jarvis, DFC
Wales				
Dyfed-Powys	Carmarthen	937	R. White	A. L. Pritchard
Gwent	Cwmbran	1,002	J. E. Over, QPM, CPM	B. Sutton
North Wales	Colwyn Bay	1,335	D. Owen, QPM	T. M. Hughes
South Wales	Bridgend	3,123	W. R. Lawrence	H. J. Gough
Scotland				
Central Scotland	Stirling	633	I. T. Oliver, QPM, Ph.D.	H. Brown
Dumfries and Galloway	Dumfries	344	G. Esson, QPM	R. L. Brown
Fife	Kirkcaldy	754	W. M. Moodie, CBE, QPM	C. J. Groom
Grampian	Aberdeen	1,099	A. G. Lynn, CVO, CBE, QPM	J. K. A. Thomaneck
Lothian and Borders	Edinburgh 4	2,426	Sir William Sutherland, QPM	J. Cook
Northern	Inverness	631	H. C. MacMillan, QPM	Mrs I. Rhind
Strathclyde	Glasgow 2	6,884	A. K. Sloan, QPM	J. Jennings
Tayside	Dundee	1,016	J. W. Bowman, QPM	W. Smith
Northern Ireland				
Royal Ulster Constabulary	Belfast 5	8,250	H. N. Annesley, QPM	T. Rainey
Islands				
Isle of Man	Douglas	209	R. E. N. Oake	†Hon. E. G. Lowey, MLC
States of Jersey	St. Helier	222	(a) D. Parkinson	R. J. Shenton
Guernsey	St. Peter Port	149	(a) M. Le Moignan	M. W. Torode

† Minister for Department of Home Affairs

METROPOLITAN POLICE FORCE
New Scotland Yard, Broadway, SW1H 0BG
[071–230 1212]
Establishment, 28,565

Commissioner, Sir Peter Imbert, QPM
Deputy Commissioner, Sir John Dellow, CBE
Receiver, D. H. J. Hilary £54,900
Deputy Receiver, R. M. Gregory £39,746

Territorial Operations Department

Assistant Commissioner, R. A. Hunt, QPM.
Deputy Assistant Commissioner, D. N. Meynell, OBE.
Commanders, G. E. Howlett, OBE, QPM; R. G. Monk; A. J. Speed.
Head of Administration, Miss B. Arnold
£24,075–£31,276

Area Headquarters

Deputy Assistant Commissioners, C. J. Rideout, QPM; C. Pollard, QPM; W. E. E. Boreham, OBE; M. B. Taylor; D. J. Osland, QPM; J. E. Metcalfe.
Commanders, C. A. Couch; G. M. Ness, QPM; J. A. Coo; H. N. L. Blenkin; M. G. Farbrother; D. N. Stevens; D. A. Ray; J. F. Purnell, GM; E. D. Humphrey; D. Flanders; D. M. T. Kendrick; B. G. Moss; B. J. Luckhurst; T. D. Laidlow.

Specialist Operations Department

Assistant Commissioner, J. A. Smith, QPM.
Deputy Assistant Commissioners, J. H. Cracknell, LVO; S. R. A. Crawshaw, QPM; P. Phelan, QPM.

Commanders, M. R. Campbell; K. G. Churchill-Coleman, QPM; D. G. Gunn; R. A. Penrose; D. C. Stockley; A. G. Fry, QPM; J. P. O'Connor; D. Buchanan; R. C. Marsh.

Metropolitan Police Laboratory

Director, Dr. B. Sheard £39,000
Deputy Directors, G. J. O. Lee; M. R. Loveland; P. D. Martin; Dr. W. D. C. Wilson .... £24,075–£31,276
Senior Principal Scientific Officer, B. B. Wheals
£24,075–£31,276

Personnel and Training Department

Assistant Commissioner, G. W. Jones, QPM.
Deputy Assistant Commissioners, E. Mitchell, QPM; Miss J. Hilton, QPM (*temp.*)
Commanders, M. J. Sullivan, QPM; M. Briggs; L. T. Roach, QPM.
Welfare Officer, K. F. T. Rivers, MBE £21,098–£25,160

Metropolitan Police Cadet Corps

Commander, M. Briggs.

Medical and Dental Branch

Chief Medical Officer, Dr. E. C. A. Bott, CBE £43,350

Management Support Department

Assistant Commissioner, P. J. J. Winship, QPM.
Deputy Assistant Commissioner, J. A. Howey.

Complaints Investigation Bureau

Commander, J. G. Taylor.

Directorate of Public Affairs
Director of Public Affairs, M. S. D. Granatt
£31,276–£35,436
Deputy Director of Public Affairs, D. H. Dowle
£24,075–£31,276

Directorate of Management Services
Director, Mrs S. M. Merchant (*temp.*)
£31,276–£35,436
Deputy Directors, P. I. May . . . . £24,075–£31,276

Force Inspectorate

Deputy Assistant Commissioner, T. J. Siggs, OBE
Commanders, J. J. Allison; R. C. Adams, BEM

Solicitor's Department

Solicitor, C. S. Porteous £42,907
Assistant Solicitors, R. E. Marsh; P. A. Shawdon; D.
S. Hamilton . . . . £36,818–£41,296

The following departments are responsible to the
Receiver through the Deputy Receiver.

'E' Department

Establishment Officer, R. B. Jones . . £31,276–£35,436
Deputy Establishment Officers, D. F. F. Hannaford;
D. Wilson . . . . £24,075–£31,276

'F' Department

Director of Finance, J. A. Crutchlow £31,276–£35,436
Deputy Directors of Finance, D. H. Burr; J. N.
Nicholson; M. W. Maidment . . . . . £24,075–£31,276

Supplies and Services Department

Director, N. N. I. Batten . . . . £24,075–£31,276

Catering Department

Director of Catering, A. Thompson . . £24,075–£31,276

Property Services Department

Director of Property Services, T. G. Lawrence
£31,276–£35,436
Deputy Directors, R. M. Boa; K. R. Sewell; D. F.
Hobart . . . . £24,075–£31,276

Chief Engineer's Department

Chief Engineer, N. Boothman . . . . . . £31,276–£35,436
Deputy Chief Engineers, D. A. Woolgar; G. C.
Sudbury; J. T. Clifton; R. J. Perham
£24,075–£31,276

Department of Computing Services

Director, DCS, D. K. Dunkin . . . . . . £31,276–£35,436
Deputy Directors, DCS, K. G. Daly; T. Egan
£24,075–£31,276

CITY OF LONDON POLICE
26 Old Jewry, EC2R 8DJ
[071-601 2222]
Strength of Force (June 1990), 811

Commissioner, O. Kelly, QPM £57,498
Assistant Commissioner, C. Coxall £44,820
Commander, H. J. Moore £36,699
Chief Superintendents (£31,131–£33,528):
  '*B' Division*, G. Marshall.
  '*C' Division*, R. Knevett.
  CID, P. Gwynn.
  CID/Fraud, P. Nove.
  Management Support, E. Aggar.
  Operational Support, T. Hillier.

BRITISH TRANSPORT POLICE
15 Tavistock Place, WC1H 9SJ
[071–388 7541]
Strength of Force (May 1990), 1,893

The Force provides a policing service to the British
Railways Board and London Underground Ltd.
Police posts are located throughout England, Wales
and Scotland.
The Chief Constable reports to the British Trans-
port Police Committee, a statutory body set up under
the Transport Act 1962. The members of the Commit-
tee are appointed by the British Railways Board and
London Regional Transport.
Chief Constable, D. O'Brien, OBE.
Deputy Chief Constable, G. E. Coles.
Assistant Chief Constables:
  London Underground Division, W. Palmer.
  Management Services, A. Parker.
  Operations, W. I. McGregor.
  Scotland Division, A. M. Mackenzie.

MINISTRY OF DEFENCE POLICE
Ministry of Defence, Empress State Building,
Lillie Road, SW6 1TR
[071–385 1244]
Strength of Force (May 1990), 4,600

The Ministry of Defence Police is a statutory police
force directly responsible to the Secretary of State
for Defence for the policing of all military land,
stations and establishments in the United Kingdom.
Chief Constable, J. Reddington, QPM
Deputy Chief Constable, N. L. Chapple, QPM
Head of MDP Secretariat, B. Aves.
Assistant Chief Constables:
  Inspectorate and Firearms, S. G. Edwards.
  Operations, R. E. Murray.
  Personnel and Training, A. A. J. Scales.
  Scotland, A. F. Grant.
  Support, C. Bucke.

ROYAL PARKS CONSTABULARY
2 Marsham Street, SW1P 3EB
[071-276 3761/3]
Strength of Force (June 1990), 158

The Royal Parks Constabulary is maintained by
the Department of the Environment and is responsible, through the Bailiff of the Royal Parks, for the
policing of twenty Royal Parks and Gardens in and
around London. These comprise an area in excess of
6,000 acres. Officers of the Force are appointed under
the Parks Regulations Act 1872, as amended by the
Parks Regulations (Amendment) Act 1974.
Chief Officer, P. H. Gilbert.
Deputy Chief Officer, M. J. Loader.

UNITED KINGDOM ATOMIC ENERGY
AUTHORITY CONSTABULARY
11 Charles II Street, SW1Y 4QP
[071-389-6565]
Strength of Force (June 1990), 603

The Constabulary is responsible for policing United
Kingdom Atomic Energy Authority and British
Nuclear Fuels PLC establishments and for escorting
nuclear material between establishments.
The Chief Constable is responsible, through the
Atomic Energy Authority Police Committee, to the
Secretary of State for Energy.
Chief Constable, H. J. McMorris, QPM
Deputy Chief Constable, E. H. Miller.

STAFF ASSOCIATIONS

ASSOCIATION OF CHIEF POLICE OFFICERS OF ENGLAND, WALES AND NORTHERN IRELAND, Room 1133, New Scotland Yard, Broadway, SW1H 0BG.—Represents the Chief Constables, Deputy Chief Constables and Assistant Chief Constables of England, Wales and N. Ireland, and officers of the rank of Commander and above in the Metropolitan and City of London Police. *Gen. Sec.*, Miss M. C. E. Barton.

THE POLICE SUPERINTENDENTS' ASSOCIATION OF ENGLAND AND WALES, 67A Reading Road, Pangbourne RG8 7JD.—Represents officers of the rank of Superintendent and Chief Superintendent. *Sec.*, Chief Supt. T. G. Hewitt.

THE POLICE FEDERATION OF ENGLAND AND WALES, 15–17 Langley Road, Surbiton, Surrey KT6 6LP.—Represents officers up to and including the rank of Chief Inspector. *Gen. Sec.*, Insp. V. Nield (Miss).

ASSOCIATION OF CHIEF POLICE OFFICERS (SCOTLAND), Police Headquarters, Fettes Avenue, Edinburgh EH4 1RB.—Represents the Chief Constables, Deputy Chief Constables and Assistant Chief Constables of the Scottish police forces. *Hon. Sec.*, Chief Constable Sir William Sutherland, QPM.

THE ASSOCIATION OF SCOTTISH POLICE SUPERINTENDENTS, Hon. Secretary's Office, Strathclyde Police, 'P' Division, Divisional Headquarters, 217 Windmillhill Street, Motherwell ML1 1RZ.—Represents officers of the rank of Superintendent and Chief Superintendent. *Hon. Sec.*, Chief Supt. J. Urquhart.

THE SCOTTISH POLICE FEDERATION, 5 Woodside Place, Glasgow G3 7PD.—Represents officers up to and including the rank of Chief Inspector. *Gen. Sec.*, A. W. A. Wallace.

THE SUPERINTENDENTS ASSOCIATION OF NORTHERN IRELAND, Ormiston House, Hawthornden Road, Belfast BT4 3JW.—Represents Superintendents and Chief Superintendents in the RUC. *Hon. Sec.*, W/Chief Supt. A. Donald.

THE POLICE FEDERATION FOR NORTHERN IRELAND, Royal Ulster Constabulary, Garnerville, Garnerville Road, Belfast BT4 2NX.—Represents officers up to and including the rank of Chief Inspector. *Gen. Sec.*, J. Elder.

THE ARMED FORCES

MINISTRY OF DEFENCE
Main Building, Whitehall, SW1A 2HB
[01–218 9000]

Salaries
Secretary of State £35,120
Minister of State, Commons £24,850
Minister of State, Lords £39,641
Parliamentary Under Secretaries £18,860
Grade 1 .... £76,320
Grade 1a £69,960
Grade 2 .... £53,420–£63,390
Grade 3 .... £43,350–£52,460
Grade 4 .... £36,818–£38,254
Grade 5 .... £30,001–£38,991
(For Services salaries, *see* pp. 404–9.)

Secretary of State for Defence, THE RT. HON. THOMAS KING, MP.
  Private Secretary (*G5*), S. Webb.
Minister of State for the Armed Forces, HON. ARCHIBALD HAMILTON, MP.
  Private Secretary, Miss P. M. Aldred.
Parliamentary Under Secretary of State for the Armed Forces, THE EARL OF ARRAN.
  Private Secretary, P. A. Wilson.
Minister of State for Defence Procurement, THE HON. ALAN CLARK, MP.
  Private Secretary, J. Scoopes.
Parliamentary Under Secretary of State for Defence Procurement, KENNETH CARLISLE, MP.
  Private Secretary, C. R. C. Holderness.
Permanent Under Secretary of State (*G1*), Sir Michael Quinlan, KCB.
  Private Sec., T. C. McKane.
Chief of Defence Staff, Marshal of the RAF Sir David Craig, GCB, OBE.

Defence Staff
Vice Chief of the Defence Staff, Gen. Sir Richard Vincent, GBE, KCB, DSO.
Deputy Under Sec. (*Policy*) (*G2*), R. C. Mottram.
Deputy Chief of the Defence Staff (*Commitments*), Air Marshal Sir Kenneth Hayr, KCB, CBE, AFC.
Asst. Under Sec. (*Commitments*) (*G3*), N. Bevan.
Asst. CDS (*NATO/UK*), Rear-Adm. M. G. T. Harris.
Asst. CDS (*Overseas*), Rear-Adm. E. S. J. Larken, DSO.
Asst. CDS (*Logistics*), Air Vice-Marshal J. H. Harris, CBE.
Deputy CDS (*Systems*), Lt.-Gen. Sir Anthony Mullens, KCB, OBE.
Asst. CDS (*Concepts*), Air Vice-Marshal A. L. Roberts, CBE, AFC.
Asst. CDS, Operational Requirements (*Sea*), Rear-Adm. C. L. Wood.
Asst. CDS, Operational Requirements (*Land*), Maj.-Gen. A. S. J. Blacker, CBE.
Asst. CDS, Operational Requirements (*Air*), Air Vice-Marshal J. S. Allison, CBE.
Asst. CDS (*CIS*), Rear-Adm. R. Walmsley.
Asst. CDS (*Policy and Nuclear*), Air Vice-Marshal J. F. Willis, CBE.
Asst. Under Sec. (*Policy*) (*G3*), H. Griffiths.
Deputy CDS (*Programmes and Personnel*), Vice-Adm. Sir Barry Wilson, KCB.
Asst. CDS (*Programmes*), Maj.-Gen. the Hon. T. P. J. Boyd-Carpenter, MBE.
Surgeon Gen. and Dir. Gen. Medical Services (*RAF*), Air Marshal N. H. Mills, QHP.
Deputy Surgeon Gen. (*Ops.*) *and Medical Dir. Gen.* (*Naval*), Surgeon Rear-Adm. D. A. Lammiman, LVO, QHS.
Deputy Surgeon Gen. (*Health Services*) *and Dir. Gen. Army Medical Services*, Maj.-Gen. P. J. Beale, QHP.

Naval Department
Chief of Naval Staff and First Sea Lord, Adm. Sir Julian Oswald, GCB, ADC.
Asst. Chief of Naval Staff, Rear-Adm. H. M. White, CBE.
Hydrographer of the Navy, Rear-Adm. J. A. L. Myres.
Cmdt. Gen. Royal Marines, Lt.-Gen. H. Y. La R. Beverley, OBE.
Chief of Naval Personnel and Second Sea Lord, Adm. Sir Brian Brown, KCB, CBE.
Naval Secretary, Rear-Adm. D. S. Dobson.
Dir. Gen., Naval Manpower and Training, Rear-Adm. N. Purvis.
Dir. Gen., Naval Personal Services, Rear-Adm. D. M. Dow.
Asst. Under Sec. (*Naval Personnel*) (*G3*), J. M. Moss.
Chief of Fleet Support, Vice-Adm. Sir Jock Slater, KCB, LVO.
Asst. Under Sec. (*Fleet Support*) (*G3*), N. D. Paren.
Dir. Gen., Ship Refitting (*G3*), G. A. Allin.
Dir. Gen., Supplies and Transport (*G3*), J. T. Baugh.
  Principal Dir., Supplies and Transport (*Ops.*) (*G4*), W. N. Cooke.
  Principal Dir., Supplies and Transport (*Stores and Victualling*) (*G4*), G. E. Miller.
  Principal Dir. Supplies and Transport (*Armaments*) (*G4*), M. A. Holder.
Dir. Gen., Fleet Support (*Policy and Services*), Rear-Adm. R. T. Frere.
Dir. Gen., Aircraft (*Navy*), Rear-Adm. R. H. Burn, AFC.
Chaplain of The Fleet, Ven. M. H. G. Henley, QHC.

Army Department
Chief of the General Staff, Gen. Sir John Chapple, GCB, CBE, ADC (*Gen.*).
Asst. Chief of the General Staff, Maj.-Gen. R. N. Wheeler.
Dir., Military Survey, Maj.-Gen. P. F. Fagan, MBE.
Dir. Gen., TA and Organization, Maj.-Gen. D. M. Naylor, MBE.
Dir. Gen., Training and Doctrine (*Army*), Maj.-Gen. A. A. Denison-Smith, MBE.
Dir., Royal Armoured Corps, Maj.-Gen. R. E. Barron.
Dir., Royal Artillery, Maj.-Gen. B. T. Pennicott.
Dir., Infantry, Maj.-Gen. R. J. Hodges, CB, OBE.
Dir., Army Air Corps, Maj.-Gen. R. D. Grist, OBE.
Engineer in Chief (*Army*), Maj.-Gen. R. L. Peck.
Signal Officer in Chief (*Army*), Maj.-Gen. R. F. L. Cook.
Military Secretary, Lt.-Gen. Sir John Learmont, KCB, CBE.
Adjutant-General, Gen. Sir Robert Pascoe, KCB, MBE, ADC (*Gen.*).
Asst. Under Sec. (*Adjutant General*) (*G3*), M. Gainsborough.
Dir. Gen., Army Manning & Recruiting, Maj.-Gen. J. F. J. Johnston, CBE.
Paymaster in Chief, Maj.-Gen. P. S. Bray.
Dir. Gen., Personal Services (*Army*), Maj.-Gen. P. P. D. Stone, CBE.
Dir. Security (*Army*), Maj.-Gen. P. D. Alexander, CB, MBE (retd).
Dir., Army Legal Services, Maj.-Gen. D. H. D. Selwood.
Dir., Army Education, Maj.-Gen. C. A. Kinvig.
Quartermaster General, Lt.-Gen. Sir Edward Jones, KCB, CBE.
Asst. Under Sec. (*Quartermaster*) (*G3*), N. J. Beaumont.
Dir. Gen., Logistic Policy (*Army*), Maj.-Gen. G. W. Field, OBE.
Dir. Gen., Transport and Movements, Maj.-Gen. C. E. G. Carrington, CBE.

Dir. Gen., Ordnance Services, Maj.-Gen. D. F. E. Botting, CBE.
Dir. Gen., Electrical and Mechanical Engineering, Maj.-Gen. D. Shaw, CBE.
Chaplain General, Rev. J. Harkness, OBE, QHC.

Air Force Department

Chief of the Air Staff, Air Chief Marshal Sir Peter Harding, GCB.
Asst. Chief of Air Staff, Air Vice-Marshal C. J. Thomson, CBE, AFC.
Cmdt. Gen. (RAF Regt.) and Dir. Gen. of Security, Air Vice-Marshal G. C. Williams, AFC.
Controller of National Air Traffic Services, Air Marshal Sir Thomas Stonor, KCB.
Air Member for Personnel, Air Chief Marshal Sir David Parry-Evans, KCB, CBE.
Air Secretary, Air Vice-Marshal R. J. Honey, CBE.
Dir. Gen., RAF Personal Services, Air Vice-Marshal D. O. Crwys-Williams, CB.
Dir. Gen., Training, Air Vice-Marshal E. H. Macey, CBE.
Dir. Legal Services (RAF) Air Vice-Marshal R. T. Dawson, CBE.
Asst. Under Sec. (Personnel (Air)) (G3), M. J. Harte, PH.D.
Air Member for Supply and Organization, Air Chief Marshal Sir Brendan Jackson, KCB.
Dir. Gen., Support Systems, Air Vice-Marshal J. P. R. Browne, CBE.
Chief Engineer, Air Marshal Sir Frank Holroyd, KBE, CB.
Dir. Gen. Support Management, Air Vice-Marshal C. P. Baker.
Ass. Under Sec. (Supply and Organization (Air)) (G3), T. F. W. Knapp.
Chaplain-in-Chief, Rev. B. N. Halfpenny, CB, QHC.

Defence Scientific Staff

Chief Scientific Adviser (G1A), Prof. E. R. Oxburgh, PH.D.
Deputy Chief Scientific Adviser (G2), Dr. G. G. Pope, CB.
Director, Chemical Defence Establishment (G3), Dr. G. S. Pearson, CB.
Asst. Chief Scientific Advisers (G3), D. E. Humphries *(Projects and Research)*; Mrs. M. J. Bourne, OBE *(Capabilities)*; *(G4)* Dr. R. G. Ridley *(Nuclear)*.
Dir., Defence Operational Analysis Establishment (G3), Dr. D. Leadbeater.
Dir. Gen., Strategic Defence Initiative Participation Office (G3), Dr. S. Orman.

Office of Management and Budget

Second Permanent Under Secretary of State (G1A), J. M. Stewart, CB.
Deputy Under Secs. (G2), M. J. V. Bell *(Finance)*; R. M. Hastie-Smith, CB *(Civilian Management)*; R. L. L. Facer *(Personnel and Logistics)*; C. T. McDonnell *(Resources and Programmes)*.
Asst. Under Secs. of State (G3), T. J. Brack *(General Finance)*; M. J. Culham *(Civilian Management (Administrators))*; I. D. Dawson *(Resources)*; M. J. Dimond *(Dir. Gen. Defence Accounts)*; A. G. Rucker *(Security and Common Services)*; D. C. R. Heyhoe *(Dir. Gen. of Management Audit)*; J. F. Howe *(Personnel and Logistics)*; R. Jackling, CBE *(Programmes)*; D. B. Ormand *(Management Strategy)*; N. H. Nicholls *(Systems)*; B. F. Rule *(Dir. Gen. Information Technology Systems)*; D. J. L. Smith, PH.D. *(Civilian Management (Specialists))*.
Head, States (G4), M. V. Wilde.

Public Relations

Chief of Public Relations (G4), H. B. Colver.
Deputy Chief of Public Relations (G5), C. Verey.
Dir. of Public Relations (Navy), Capt. P. A. Voute, RN.
Dir. of Public Relations (Army), Brig. B. H. Dutton.
Dir. of Public Relations (RAF), Air Cdre. M. Barnes.

PROCUREMENT EXECUTIVE

Chief of Defence Procurement, Sir Peter Levene, KBE
Private Secretary, Miss S. Scholefield.

Procurement Executive Policy and Administration

Deputy Under Secretary (Defence Procurement) (G2), A. J. P. Macdonald, CB.
Asst. Under Secretary (International and Domestic Procurement) (G3), J. A. Galvin.
President of the Ordnance Board, Air Vice-Marshal J. M. P. Calnan.
Dir. Gen. Defence Quality Assurance (G3), B. Miller.
Dir. Gen. Defence Contracts (G3), B. J. Slade.
Principal Dir. Accountancy, Estimating and Pricing Services (G4), J. V. A. Crawford.
Principal Dir. of Patents (G4), E. J. Mansfield.

Research and Development Controllerate

Chief Executive (designate), N. H. Hughes.
Asst. Under Sec. Defence Research Agency Implementation Team (G3), P. E. Chamberlain.
Asst. Under Sec. Research & Development Establishments and Research Admin (G3), A. J. Cragg.
Deputy Controller (Nuclear) (G3), J. C. Mabberley.
Deputy Controller (Research) (G3), T. Buckley, PH.D.
Cmdt. Aeroplane & Armament Experimental Establishment, Air Cdre. D. L. Bywater.
Dir. Admiralty Research Establishment (G3), P. D. Ewins.
Deputy Directors (G3), P. M. Sutcliffe; *(G4)* B. P. Blaydes.
Dir. Atomic Weapons Establishment (G2), Dr. T. P. McLean, CB.
Dir. Royal Aerospace Establishment (G2), M. T. Peters.
Deputy Directors (G3), F. W. Armstrong; J. M. Flood.
Dir. Royal Armament Research & Development Establishment (G2/3).
Dir. Royal Signals & Radar Establishment (G2), S. J. Robinson, OBE.
Deputy Directors (G3), Dr. A. L. Mears; Dr. J. Prior.

Sea Systems Controllerate

Controller of the Navy, Vice-Adm. Sir Kenneth Eaton, KCB.
Asst. Under Sec. (Material Naval) (G3), B. R. Hawtin.
Principal Dir., Navy and Nuclear Contracts (G4), A. J. Figes.
Chief Abovewater Systems Executive and Deputy Controller, Vice-Adm. R. C. F. Hill.
Dir. Gen. Surface Ships (G3), H. Perkins.
Dir. Gen. Surface Weapons (G4), Cdre. F. P. Scourse, MBE.
Dir. Gen. Marine Engineering, Cdre. R. F. James.
Naval Ships Acceptance, Cdre. P. Dalrymple Smith.
Chief Underwater Systems Executive (G3), A. J. Creighton.
Dir. Gen. Submarines (G3), W. G. Sanders.
Dir. Gen. Underwater Weapons (G4), R. McCaughan.
Chief Naval Architect (G3), B. O. Wall.
Chief Strategic Systems Executive, Rear-Adm. I. H. Pirnie.
Deputy Chief Strategic Systems Executive, Cdre. J. S. Kelly, OBE.
Dir. Gen. Strategic Weapons Systems, Cdre. T. W. Craven.

Land Systems Controllerate

Master General of the Ordnance, Gen. Sir John Stibbon, KCB, OBE.
Dir. Gen. Policy and Special Projects, Maj.-Gen. A. C. P. Stone.
Vice Master General of the Ordnance, Maj.-Gen. G. M. Hutchinson, CB.
Asst. Under Sec. (Ordnance) (G3), Dr. A. Fox.
Principal Dir., Contracts (Ordnance) (G4), R. C. Harford.
Dir. Gen., Guided Weapons and Electronics (G3), J. D. Maines.
Dir. Gen., Land Fighting Systems, Maj.-Gen. R. J. Hayman-Joyce, CBE.
Dir. Gen., Weapons (Army), Maj.-Gen. E. G. Willmott, OBE.

Air Systems Controllerate

Controller Aircraft, D. M. Spiers, CB, TD.
Dep. Controller Aircraft, Air Marshal Sir Michael Simmons, KCB, AFC.
Asst. Under Sec. (Air (Procurement Executive)) (G3), B. A. Taylor.
Principal Dir., Contracts (Air) (G4), D. A. Oakley.
Dir. Gen. Aircraft 1, (G3), J. A. Gordon.
Dir. Gen. Aircraft 2, Air Vice-Marshal D. Cousins, AFC.
Dir. Gen. Aircraft 3, (G3), J. W. Britton.
Dir. Gen., Air Weapons Electronic Systems (G3), K. G. Hambleton.

Dir. Gen., Strategic Electronic Systems, Air Vice-Marshal M. J. D. Brown.

Defence Export Services Organization

Head of Defence Export Services (G2), A. Thomas.
Military Deputy to Head of DES, Rear-Adm. P. B. Rowe, CBE, LVO.
Dir. Gen. Saudi Airforce Projects, Air Marshal Sir Ronald Stuart-Paul, KBE.
Dir. Gen., Marketing (G3), R. J. Harding, CMG.
Asst. Under Sec. of State (DES Admin.) (G3), M. D. Tidy.

METEOROLOGICAL OFFICE
London Road, Bracknell, Berks.
[0344-420242]

The Meteorological Office is the state meteorological service. It became an executive agency within the Ministry of Defence in April 1990. It provides meteorological services for the Services departments and civilian aviation, shipping, public services, the press, industry and the general public. It collects, distributes and publishes meteorological information from all parts of the world and undertakes research related to meteorology and climate.
Chief Executive (G2), Dr. J. T. Houghton, CBE, FRS.
Dir. of Operations (G3), P. Ryder.
Dir. of Research (G4), Dr. K. A. Browning.

THE ROYAL NAVY

THE QUEEN

Admirals of the Fleet

HRH The Prince Philip, Duke of Edinburgh, KG, KT, OM, GBE, AC, QSO, PC, *born* June 10, 1921		Jan. 15, 1953
Sir Varyl Begg, GCB, DSO, DSC, *born* Oct. 1, 1908		Aug. 12, 1968
The Lord Hill-Norton, GCB, *born* Feb. 8, 1915		March 12, 1971
Sir Michael Pollock, GCB, LVO, DSC, *born* Oct. 19, 1916		March 1, 1974
Sir Edward Ashmore, GCB, DSC, *born* Dec. 11, 1919		Feb. 9, 1977
The Lord Lewin, KG, GCB, LVO, DSC, *born* Nov. 19, 1920		July 6, 1979
Sir Henry Leach, GCB, *born* Nov. 18, 1923		Dec. 1, 1982
The Lord Fieldhouse, GCB, GBE, *born* Feb. 12, 1928		Aug. 2, 1985
Sir William Staveley, GCB, *born* Nov. 10, 1928		May 25, 1989

Admirals

Oswald, Sir Julian, GCB, ADC (*Chief of Naval Staff and First Sea Lord*).
Bathurst, Sir Benjamin, KCB (*C.-in-C. Fleet, Allied C.-in-C. Channel and C-in-C. Eastern Atlantic Area*).
Black, Sir Jeremy, KCB, DSO, MBE, ADC (*C.-in-C. Naval Home Command*).
Thomas, Sir Richard, KCB, OBE (*UK Military Rep. HQ NATO*).
Brown, Sir Brian, KCB, CBE (*Chief of Naval Personnel, and Second Sea Lord*).

Vice-Admirals

Symons, Sir Patrick, KBE (*Representative to Supreme Allied Command Atlantic in Europe*).
Slater, Sir Jock, KCB, LVO (*Chief of Fleet Support*).
Kerr, Sir John, KCB.
King, Sir Norman, KBE (*Chief of Staff to Commander, Allied Naval Forces Southern Europe*).
Livesay, Sir Michael, KCB (*Flag Officer Scotland and N. Ireland, Commander Northern Atlantic, and Commander NORE Sub. Area Channel*).
Grose, Sir Alan, KBE (*Flag Officer Plymouth and Naval Base Comd. Devonport*).

Coward, Sir John, KCB, DSO (*Flag Officer Submarines & Comd. Sub. Area Eastern Atlantic*).
Weatherall, Sir James, KBE (*Deputy Supreme Allied Commander Atlantic*).
Wilson, Sir Barry, KCB (*Deputy CDS (Programmes and Personnel)*).
Eaton, Sir Kenneth, KCB (*Controller of the Navy*).
Hill, R. C. F. (*Chief Abovewater Systems Executive*).

Rear-Admirals

Garnier, J., CBE, LVO (*Flag Officer Royal Yachts*).
Balfour, H. M., CB, LVO (*Commander, Sultan of Oman's Navy*).
Wood, C. L., (*Asst. CDS Operational Requirements (Sea Systems)*).
Layman, C. H., DSO, LVO (*Asst. Dir. (Communications and Information Systems) on the IMS*).
Purvis, N., (*Dir. Gen. Naval Manpower and Training*).
White, H. M., CBE (*Asst. Chief of Naval Staff*).
Hill-Norton, The Hon. N. J. (*Flag Officer Third Flotilla*).
Larken, E. S. J., DSO (*Asst. CDS (Overseas)*).
Dobson, D. S. (*Naval Secretary*).
Woodhead, A. P. (*Flag Officer First Flotilla*).

Allen, D., CBE (*Defence Services Secretary*).

Pirnie, I. H., (*Chief Strategic Systems Executive*).

Salt, J. F. T. G. (*Senior Directing Staff (Naval)*).

Newman, R. T. (*Chief of Staff*).

Frere, R. T. (*Dir. Gen. Fleet Support (Policy and Services)*).

Layard, M. H. G., CBE (*Flag Officer Naval Air Command*).

Dow, D. M. (*Dir. Gen. Naval Personal Services*).

Cooke-Priest, C. H. D. (*Deputy Asst. Chief of Staff (Operations) on the Staff of the Supreme Allied Commander Europe*).

Carine, J. (*Chief of Staff to C.-in-C. Naval Home Command*).

Tod, J. J. R., CBE (*Flag Officer Portsmouth & Naval Base Commander Portsmouth*).

Harris, M. G. T. (Asst. CDS (*NATO/UK*)).

Abbott, P. C. (*Flag Officer Second Flotilla*).

Richardson, A. B. (*Flag Officer Sea Training & Naval Base Commander Portland*).

Middleton, J. P. W. (*Chief Staff Officer (Engineering)*).

Biggs, G. W. R. (*Flag Officer Gibraltar, Gibraltar Naval Base Commander & COMGIBMED*).

Walmsley, R. (*Asst. CDS (CIS)*).

Rowe, P. B., CBE, LVO (*Military Deputy to Head of DES*).

Myres, J. A. L. (*Hydrographer of the Navy*).

Hoddinott, A. P., OBE (*Commander British Naval Staff Washington, Naval Attaché Washington and UK National Liaison Representative to SACLANT*).

Burn, R. H., AFC (*Dir. Gen. Aircraft (Naval)*).

HER MAJESTY'S FLEET
(as at April 1, 1990)

Type/Class	No.	Operational or engaged in preparing for service or trials or training	No.	Undergoing refit or on standby etc.
Submarines				
Polaris	3	*Repulse, Resolution, Revenge*	1	*Renown*
Fleet	14	*Conqueror, Courageous, Sovereign, Swiftsure, Superb, Sceptre, Spartan, Talent*, Trafalgar, Turbulent, Tireless, Torbay, Trenchant, Valiant*	3	*Warspite, Churchill, Splendid*
Type 2400	2	*Upholder*, Unseen*		
Oberon Class	8	*Onslaught, Otter, Otus, Ocelot, Onyx, Osiris, Oracle, Opossum*	2	*Odin, Opportune*
ASW Carriers	2	*Ark Royal, Invincible*	1	*Illustrious*
Assault Ships	2	*Fearless†, Intrepid*		
Guided-Missile Destroyers				
Type 82	1	*Bristol*		
Type 42	11	*Birmingham, Cardiff, Edinburgh, Exeter, Glasgow, Gloucester, Liverpool, Manchester, Newcastle, Nottingham, York*	1	*Southampton*
Frigates				
Type 23	2	*Norfolk†, Argyll**		
Type 22	13	*Battleaxe, Beaver, Brave, Brazen†, Brilliant, Broadsword, Campbeltown, Chatham†, Cornwall, Coventry, Cumberland, London, Sheffield*	1	*Boxer*
Type 21	6	*Amazon, Ambuscade, Active, Avenger, Alacrity, Arrow*		
Leander Class	11	*Argonaut, Charybdis, Penelope, Phoebe, Danae, Andromeda, Ariadne, Cleopatra, Jupiter, Minerva, Hermione*	2	*Sirius, Scylla*
Navigation Training Ship	1	*Juno*		
Offshore Patrol				
Castle Class	2	*Leeds Castle, Dumbarton Castle*		
Island Class	6	*Alderney, Guernsey, Orkney, Shetland, Anglesey, Jersey*	1	*Lindisfarne*
MCMVs				
Minesweepers Ton Class	3	*Cuxton, Soberton, Upton*		
River Class**	12	*Waveney, Carron, Dovey, Helford, Humber, Blackwater, Itchen, Helmsdale, Orwell, Ribble, Spey, Arun*		
Minehunters Ton Class	8	*Brereton, Iveston, Kedleston, Kellington, Hubberston, Nurton, Sheraton, Wilton*	3	*Brinton, Kirkliston, Gavinton*
Hunt Class	13	*Brecon, Brocklesby, Ledbury, Cottesmore†, Dulverton†, Middleton, Chiddingford, Hurworth, Bicester, Atherstone, Berkeley, Quorn, Cattistock*		
Single Role Minehunter	2	*Sandown†, Inverness**		

Type/Class	No.	Operational or engaged in preparing for service or trials or training	No.	Undergoing refit or on standby etc.
Patrol Craft				
Bird Class	4	*Kingfisher, Peterel, Sandpiper, Redpole*	1	*Cygnet*
Coastal Training Craft†	15	*Attacker, Fencer, Hunter, Chaser, Striker, Archer, Biter, Smiter, Pursuer, Blazer, Dasher, Puncher, Charger, Ranger, Trumpeter*		
Peacock Class	2	*Peacock, Plover*	1	*Starling*
Gibraltar Search and Rescue Craft	2	*Cormorant, Hart*		
Support Ships				
Submarine Tender	1	*Sentinel*		
Seabed Operations Vessel	1	*Challenger*		
Royal Yacht/Hospital Ship	1	*Britannia*		
Training Ships				
Fleet Tenders	6	*Manly, Mentor, Messina, Milbrook*		
Ice Patrol Ship	1	*Endurance*		
Survey Ships	6	*Bulldog†, Hecate, Herald, Gleaner†, Hecla, Roebuck*	2	*Beagle, Fawn*

Notes:
(1) Strengths at April 1, 1990. This table includes ships due for completion or disposal during the course of 1990–91; the numbers of each type are not therefore an accurate indication of the ships available at any one time. Ships solely engaged in harbour training duties are not included.
(2) All submarines, ASW Carriers, Assault Ships, Guided Missile Destroyers, Frigates, Offshore Patrol Ships and MCMVs are assigned to NATO, or will be so assigned on becoming operational. Other ships could be made available in support of NATO operations if national requirements permitted.
(3) Ships marked * were under construction on April 1, 1990 and are planned to enter service during 1990–91.
(4) Ships marked † are engaged in trials or training.
(5) River Class vessels, marked **, apart from HMS *Blackwater*, are operated by the Royal Naval Reserve.
(6) Coastal Training Craft are operated by the Royal Naval Reserve and the University Royal Naval Units.
(7) Ships approved for disposal or sale during 1989–90: Achilles, Olympus. Disposals announced July 1990: Conqueror, Onslaught, Odin, Phoebe, Gavinton, Kirkliston, Peterel, Sandpiper, Challenger.

The Royal Naval Reserve (RNR).—The Royal Naval Reserve is a totally integrated part of the Royal Navy. It comprises around 6,000 men and women who volunteer to train in their spare time for a variety of sea and shore tasks which they would carry out in time of tension or war. With units spread nationwide, the Service is currently expanding.
Chief of Staff, Capt. C. W. Pile.

Royal Naval Auxiliary Service (RNXS).—The Royal Naval Auxiliary Service is a uniformed civilian volunteer service, administered by the Ministry of Defence and trained by the Royal Navy to operate at ports and anchorages, for duty in emergencies and war. RNXS units are situated on the coasts of the United Kingdom and organized and run by the Area Flag Officers. The role of the RNXS is to assist with the defence of ports and anchorages by manning local headquarters and supporting the Naval Control of Shipping Organization. The strength is 3,000.
Patron and Hon. Auxiliary Commodore, HRH Prince Michael of Kent.
Captain, Capt. R. S. Stenlare, RN.

ROYAL MARINES

The Corps of Royal Marines was first formed in 1664 and is part of the Naval Service. The Royal Marines provide Britain's sea soldiers and in particular 3 Commando Brigade Royal Marines, two thirds of which is trained and equipped for arctic warfare. Royal Marines also serve in HM Ships, provide landing craft crews, special boat sections and other detachments for naval and amphibious operations. They also provide the Naval Band Service.
The Corps is about 7,000 strong.
Commandant General, Royal Marines, Lt.-Gen. H. Y. La R. Beverley, OBE.
Major-Generals, A. F. Whitehead, DSO (*Chief of Staff*); R. J. Ross, OBE (*Commando Forces*); P. T. Stevenson; M. P. J. Hunt, OBE (*British Forces Falkland Is.*).
Brigadier, R. C. van der Horst, OBE (*Comd, Training and Reserve Forces*).

Royal Marines Reserve (RMR).—The Royal Marines Reserve is a force of commando-trained volunteers who train to combat-readiness in order to support the regular Royal Marines, should the need arise. About 50 per cent are trained and equipped for arctic warfare and most regular Royal Marine specializations are open to the reservist. There are RMR centres in London, Glasgow, Bristol, Liverpool and Newcastle, each with a number of outlying detachments. The present strength of the RMR is around 1,200.
Director, Brig. R. C. van der Horst, OBE.

QUEEN ALEXANDRA'S ROYAL NAVAL NURSING SERVICE

The first nursing sisters were appointed to naval hospitals in 1884 and the Queen Alexandra's Royal Naval Nursing Service (QARNNS) gained its current title under the patronage of Queen Alexandra in 1902. Nursing ratings were introduced in 1960 and from 1982 a number of men have taken the opportunity to join QARNNS as both officers and ratings. Still largely based at the Royal Naval Hospitals, QARNNS continue their responsibility for the health and fitness of naval personnel. The strength is about 430.

Patron, HRH Princess Alexandra, the Hon. Lady Ogilvy.

Matron-in-Chief, Miss J. Titley.

WOMEN'S ROYAL NAVAL SERVICE

Originally founded in 1917, the Women's Royal Naval Service (WRNS) was temporarily disbanded between World Wars I and II. The contribution of the Service is now firmly established as a professional and integral part of the Royal Navy with personnel serving in the United Kingdom and abroad in a wide range of specialist roles. As of February 6, 1990, members of the WRNS can serve at sea on Royal Navy warships, although the majority still serve as shore-based personnel. The strength of the WRNS is about 3,000.

Chief Commandant, HRH The Princess Royal.

Director, Commandant A. Larken, ADC.

THE ARMY

THE QUEEN

Field Marshals

HRH The Prince Philip, Duke of Edinburgh, KG, KT, OM, GBE, AC, QSO, PC, *born* June 10, 1921 . . . . . Jan. 15, 1953
Sir James Cassels, GCB, KBE, DSO, *born* Feb. 28, 1907 . . . . Feb. 29, 1968
The Lord Carver, GCB, CBE, DSO, MC, *born* April 24, 1915 . . . . July 18, 1973
Sir Roland Gibbs, GCB, CBE, DSO, MC, *born* June 22, 1921 . . . . July 13, 1979
The Lord Bramall, KG, GCB, OBE, MC, *born* Dec. 18, 1923 . . . . Aug. 1, 1982
Sir John Stanier, GCB, MBE, *born* Oct. 6, 1925 . . . . July 10, 1985
Sir Nigel Bagnall, GCB, CVO, MC, *born* Feb. 10, 1927 . . . . Sept. 9, 1988

Generals

Vincent, Sir Richard, GBE, KCB, DSO, Col. Cmdt. RA (*Vice Chief of the Defence Staff*).

Chapple, Sir John, GCB, CBE, ADC (*Gen.*), Col. 2 GR (*Chief of the General Staff*).

Huxtable, Sir Charles, KCB, CBE, ADC (*Gen.*), Col. DWR (*C.-in-C. UKLF*).

Kenny, Sir Brian, KCB, CBE, Col. Cmdt. RAVC, Col. QRIH, Col. Cmdt. RAC (*D. SACEUR*).

Pascoe, Sir Robert, KCB, MBE, ADC (*Gen.*), Col. Cmdt. 1 RGJ, Col. Cmdt. ALC (*Adjutant General*).

Palmer, Sir Patrick, KBE, Col. A. & S. H. (*C.-in-C. AFNORTH*).

Stibbon, Sir John, KCB, OBE, Col. Cmdt. RAPC, Col. Cmdt. RPC, Col. Cmdt. RE, (*Master General of the Ordnance*).

Inge, Sir Peter, KCB, Col. Green Howards, Col. Cmdt. RMP, Col. Cmdt. APTC (*C.-in-C. BAOR and Comd. Northern Army Group*).

Walker, Sir Anthony, KCB, Col. Cmdt. RTR (*Comdt. Royal College of Defence Studies*).

Lieutenant-Generals

Ramsbotham, Sir David, KCB, CBE, Col. Cmdt. 2 RGJ (*Comd. UK Fd. Army and Inspec. Gen. TA*).

Billiere, Sir Peter de la, KCB, CBE, DSO, MC.

MacMillan, Sir John, KCB, CBE, Col. Cmdt. The Scottish Division (*GOC Scotland and Governor Edinburgh Castle*).

Waters, Sir John, KCB, CBE, Col. Glosters, Col. Cmdt. POW Division (*GOC & D. Mil. Ops. Northern Ireland*).

Jones, Sir Edward, KCB, CBE, Col. Cmdt. RAEC, Col. Cmdt. 3 RGJ (*Quartermaster General*).

Learmont, Sir John, KCB, CBE, Col. Cmdt. AAC, Col. Cmdt. RA (*Military Secretary*).

Mullens, Sir Anthony, KCB, OBE (*Deputy Chief of the Defence Staff (Systems*)).

Johnson, Sir Garry, KCB, OBE, MC, Col. Cmdt. The Light Division (*Comd. Training and Arms Directors*).

Guthrie, Sir Charles, KCB, LVO, OBE, Col. Cmdt. Int. Corps (*Comd. 1 (Br) Corps*).

Swinburn, R. H. (*GOC SE District*).

Major-Generals

Cooper, S. C. (*GOC London District and Maj.-Gen. Comd. The Household Divn.*).

Beckett, E. H. A., CB, MBE, Col. Cmdt. The King's Division, (*Head of British Defence Staff, Washington*).

Shaw, A. J., CB, CBE, QHP (*DGAMS and DSG (Ops.)*).

Willmott, E. G., CB, OBE, Col. Cmdt. RE (*Dir. Gen. Weapons (Army*)).

Fawcus, G. B. (*Chief of Staff LIVE OAK*).

Bonnet, P. R. F., MBE (*GOC W District*).

Crowfoot, A. B., CBE (*GOC NW District*).

Graham, P. W., CBE, Col. Gordons (*Cmdt. RMAS*).

Pollard, A. J. G., CBE, Col. Comdt. SASC, Dep. Col. R. Anglian (*GOC SW District*).

Ansell, N. G. P., OBE (*Senior Army Member, Royal College of Defence Studies*).

Davies, P. R., Col. King's (*GOC Wales*).

Hodges, R. J., CB, OBE, Col. Kings Own Border (*Dir. Infantry*).

Lee, J. S., CB, MBE.

Blacker, A. S. J., CBE, Col. Cmdt. REME, Col. Cmdt. RTR (*Asst. Chief of the Defence Staff OR (Land*)).

Carlier, A. N., OBE (*Chief Joint Services Liaison Organization Bonn*).

Fagan, P. F., CB, MBE (*Dir. Gen. Military Survey.*).

Friedberger, J. P. W., CBE (*Cdr. British Forces Cyprus and Admin. Sovereign Base Areas*).

Llewellyn, R. M., OBE (*Chief of Staff HQ UKLF*).

Naylor, D. M., MBE (*Dir. Gen. TA and Organization*).

Rous, The Hon. W. E., OBE (*Cmdt. Staff College*).

Boyd-Carpenter, The Hon. T. P. J., MBE (*Asst. Chief of Defence Staff (Programmes*)).

Hulme, J. A., CB, Col. Cmdt. RAOC.

Peck, R. L. (*Engineer-in-Chief (Army*)).

Shaw, D., CBE (*Dir. Gen. Electrical and Mechanical Engineering*).

Carrington, C. E. G., CBE (*Dir. Gen. Transport and Movements*).

Stone, P. P. D., CBE, Col. Cmdt. MPSC, Dep. Col. R. Anglian (*Dir. Gen. Personal Services (Army*)).

Corbett, R. J. S. (*GOC Berlin (Br. Sector*)).

Hayman-Joyce, R. J., CBE (*Dir. Gen. Land Fighting Systems*).

Wilkes, M. J., CBE.

Beale, P. J., QHP (*Comd. Med. UKLF*).

Bray, P. S. (*Paymaster in Chief (Army*)).

Cowan, S., CBE, Col. QGS (*Cmdt. RMCS*).
Hutchinson, G. M., CB (*Vice Master General of the Ordnance*).
Pennicott, B. T. (*Dir. Royal Artillery*).
Macphie, D. L., QHS (*Comd. Med. BAOR*).
Brown, M., QHP (*DA Med.*).
MacKenzie, J. J. G., OBE (*Cmdt. 4 Armd Division*).
Coull, J. T., QHS (*DA Surg.*).
Barr, J. A. J. P., CBE (*Dep. Chief of Staff (Support) AFNORTH*).
Cook, R. F. L. (*Signal Officer in Chief (Army)*).
Duffell, P. R., CBE, MC (*CBF Hong Kong*).
Evans, W. A. (*GOC E. District*).
Sugden, F. G. CBE (*Chief of Staff HQ BAOR*).
Wheeler, R. N., CBE (*Asst. Chief of General Staff*).
Crawford, I. P., GM (*Cmdt. Royal Army Medical College*).

Rose, H. M., OBE, QGM (*GOC NE District Comd. 2 Inf. Divn.*).
Barron, R. E. (*Dir. Royal Armoured Corps*).
Grist, R. D., OBE (*Dir. Army Air Corps*).
Shellard, M. F. L., CBE (*Comd. Artillery 1 (Br) Corps*).
Thomson, D. P., CBE, MC (*CLF & DD Ops. N. Ireland*).
Selwood, D. H. D. (*Dir. Army Legal Services*).
Denison-Smith, A. A., MBE (*Dir. Gen. Training & Doctrine*).
Johnston, J. F. J., CBE (*Dir. Gen. Army Manning & Recruiting*).
Makepeace-Warne, A., MBE (*Cmdt. Joint Services Defence College*).
Alexander, J. O. C., OBE (*Comd. Comms. BAOR*).
Field, G. W., OBE (*Dir. Gen. Logistic Policy (Army)*).

CONSTITUTION OF THE BRITISH ARMY

The Regular Forces include the following Arms, Branches and Corps. Soldiers' record offices are shown at the end of each group; records of officers are maintained at the Ministry of Defence.

The Arms

Household Cavalry.—The Life Guards; The Blues and Royals (Royal Horse Guards and 1st Dragoons). *Records*, Horse Guards, London, SW1.

Royal Armoured Corps.—Cavalry Regiments: 1st The Queen's Dragoon Guards; The Royal Scots Dragoon Guards (Carabiniers and Greys); 4th/7th Royal Dragoon Guards; 5th Royal Inniskilling Dragoon Guards; The Queen's Own Hussars; The Queen's Royal Irish Hussars; 9th/12th Royal Lancers (Prince of Wales's); The Royal Hussars (Prince of Wales's Own), 13th/18th Royal Hussars (Queen Mary's Own); 14th/20th King's Hussars; 15th/19th The King's Royal Hussars; 16th/5th The Queen's Royal Lancers; 17th/21st Lancers; Royal Tank Regiment comprising four regular regiments. *Records*, Queen's Park, Chester.

Artillery.—Royal Regiment of Artillery. *Records*, Imphal Barracks, Fulford Road, York.

Engineers.—Corps of Royal Engineers. *Records*, Kentigern House, Brown Street, Glasgow.

Signals.—Royal Corps of Signals. *Records*, Kentigern House, Brown Street, Glasgow.

The Infantry

The Foot Guards and Regiments of Infantry of the Line are grouped in Divisions as follows:—

Guards Division.—Grenadier, Coldstream, Scots, Irish and Welsh Guards. *Divisional HQ*, HQ Household Division, Horse Guards, SW1. *Depot*, Pirbright Camp, Brookwood, Surrey. *Records*, Imphal Barracks, Fulford Road, York.

Scottish Division.—The Royal Scots (The Royal Regiment); The Royal Highland Fusiliers (Princess Margaret's Own Glasgow and Ayrshire Regiment); The King's Own Scottish Borderers; The Black Watch (Royal Highland Regiment); Queen's Own Highlanders (Seaforth and Camerons); The Gordon Highlanders; The Argyll and Sutherland Highlanders (Princess Louise's). *Divisional HQ*, The Castle, Edinburgh. *Depots*, Scottish Divisional Depots, Glencorse, Milton Bridge, Midlothian; Albemarle Barracks, Ouston, Newcastle. *Records*, Imphal Barracks, Fulford Road, York.

Queen's Division.—The Queen's Regiment, The Royal Regiment of Fusiliers, The Royal Anglian Regiment. *Divisional HQ*, Bassingbourn Barracks, Royston, Herts. *Depot*, Bassingbourn Barracks, Royston, Herts. *Records*, Higher Barracks, Exeter, Devon.

King's Division.—The King's Own Royal Border Regiment; The King's Regiment; The Prince of Wales's Own Regiment of Yorkshire; The Green Howards (Alexandra, Princess of Wales's Own Yorkshire Regiment); The Royal Irish Rangers (27th (Inniskilling) 83rd and 87th); The Queen's Lancashire Regiment; The Duke of Wellington's Regiment (West Riding). *Divisional HQ*, Imphal Barracks, York. *Depots*, The King's Division Depot (Yorkshire), Queen Elizabeth Barracks, Strensall, Yorks.; Albemarle Barracks, Ouston, Newcastle. The King's Division Depot (Royal Irish Rangers), St. Patrick's Barracks, Ballymena, Northern Ireland. *Records*, Imphal Barracks, Fulford Road, York.

Prince of Wales's Division.—The Devonshire and Dorset Regiment; The 22nd (Cheshire) Regiment; The Royal Welch Fusiliers; The Royal Regiment of Wales (24th/41st Foot); The Gloucestershire Regiment; The Worcestershire and Sherwood Foresters Regiment (29th/45th Foot); The Royal Hampshire Regiment; The Staffordshire Regiment (The Prince of Wales's); The Duke of Edinburgh's Royal Regiment (Berkshire and Wiltshire). *Divisional HQ*, Whittington Barracks, Lichfield, Staffs. *Depot*, The Prince of Wales's Division Depot, Whittington Barracks, Lichfield, Staffs. *Records*, Imphal Barracks, Fulford, York.

Light Division.—The Light Infantry; The Royal Green Jackets. *Divisional HQ*, Sir John Moore Barracks, Winchester, Hants. *Depot*, Sir John Moore Barracks, Winchester, Hants. *Records*, Higher Barracks, Exeter.

Brigade of Gurkhas.—2nd King Edward VII's Own Gurkha Rifles (The Sirmoor Rifles); 6th Queen Elizabeth's Own Gurkha Rifles; 7th Duke of Edinburgh's Own Gurkha Rifles; 10th Princess Mary's Own Gurkha Rifles; The Queen's Gurkha Engineers; Queen's Gurkha Signals; Gurkha Transport Regt. *Brigade HQ*, HMS *Tamar*, Hong Kong, BFPO 1. *Depot*, Training Depot, Brigade of Gurkhas, Malaya Lines, Sek Kong, BFPO 1. *Records*, Record Office, Brigade of Gurkhas, Hong Kong, BFPO 1.

The Parachute Regiment (Three regular battalions).—*Depot*, Browning Barracks, Aldershot, Hants. *Records*, Higher Barracks, Exeter.

Special Air Service Regiment.—*Regimental HQ*, Duke of York's Headquarters, Sloane Square, SW3. *Depot*, Stirling Lines, Hereford. *Records*, Higher Barracks, Exeter, Devon.

Army Air Corps.—*Regimental HQ* and *Depot*, Middle Wallop, Hants. *Records*, Higher Barracks, Exeter.

The Services

Royal Army Chaplain's Department.—*Regimental HQ* and *Depot*, Bagshot Park, Surrey.

Royal Corps of Transport.—*Records*, Kentigern House, Brown Street, Glasgow.

Royal Army Medical Corps, Royal Army Dental Corps, Queen Alexandra's Royal Army Nursing Corps, and Women's Royal Army Corps.—*Records*, Queen's Park, Chester.

Royal Army Ordnance Corps, Corps of Royal Electrical and Mechanical Engineers.—*Records*, Glen Parva Barracks, Saffron Road, Wigston, Leicester.

Small Arms School Corps.—*Records*, Higher Barracks, Exeter.

General Service Corps.—*Records*, Imphal Barracks, Fulford Road, York.

Corps of Royal Military Police, Royal Army Pay Corps, Royal Army Veterinary Corps, Royal Pioneer Corps, Intelligence Corps, Army Catering Corps, Military Provost Staff Corps, Royal Army Educational Corps, Army Physical Training Corps, Army Legal Corps, Sandhurst, Officers Training Corps.—*Records*, Higher Barracks, Exeter, Devon.

The Ulster Defence Regiment (UDR) was raised under authority of the UDR Act 1969 and assists the Regular Army in Northern Ireland.—*HQ*, Magheralave Road, Lisburn, Co. Antrim. *Records*, Imphal Barracks, Fulford Road, York.

The Territorial Army (TA).—The Territorial Army is designed to provide a highly trained and well equipped force which will complete the Regular Army order of battle in a time of national emergency. Its establishment is approximately 91,000. A new element of the TA, the Home Service Force, designed to produce a low cost guard force, is currently being expanded to some 4,500 posts.

QUEEN ALEXANDRA'S ROYAL ARMY NURSING CORPS

The Queen Alexandra's Royal Army Nursing Corps (QARANC) was founded in 1902 as Queen Alexandra's Imperial Military Nursing Service (QAIMNS) and gained its present title in 1949. The QARANC has trained nurses for the register and roll since 1950 and has eight other employment categories. There was an introduction of a non-nursing officer element in 1959 for personnel work. The QARANC provides service in military hospitals world-wide—United Kingdom (including Northern Ireland), BAOR, Hong Kong, Cyprus, Falkland Islands and Belize.

Colonel-in-Chief, HRH Princess Margaret.
Matron-in-Chief (Army) and Director of Defence Nursing Services, Brig. J. M. Field, QHNS.

WOMEN'S ROYAL ARMY CORPS

The Women's Royal Army Corps (WRAC) was formed on February 1, 1949 as a Corps of the Regular Army. The Corps predecessors were Queen Mary's Army Auxiliary Corps (QMAAC) in World War I, and the Auxiliary Territorial Service (ATS) in World War II. The present role of the WRAC is to be organized and trained, as an integral part of the Army, to carry out those tasks for which its members are best suited and qualified, so that it will contribute to the maximum efficiency of the Army as a whole. The Corps is approximately 8,500 (Regular and TA) and is employed by 36 sponsors in 30 employments in 500 units worldwide in the British Army.

Commandant-in-Chief, HM Queen Elizabeth The Queen Mother.
Controller Commandant, HRH The Duchess of Kent, GCVO.
Deputy Controller Commandant, Brig. A. Field, CB.
Director, Women's Royal Army Corps, Brig. G. K. Ramsey, MBE, ADC.

THE ROYAL AIR FORCE

THE QUEEN

Marshals of the Royal Air Force

HRH The Prince Philip, Duke of Edinburgh, KG, KT, OM, GBE, AC, QSO, PC, *born* June 10, 1921	Jan. 15, 1953
Sir Dermot A. Boyle, GCB, KCVO, KBE, AFC, *born* Oct. 2, 1904	Jan 1, 1958
The Lord Elworthy, KG, GCB, CBE, DSO, MVO, DFC, AFC, *born* March 23, 1911	April 1, 1967
Sir John Grandy, GCB, GCVO, KBE, DSO, *born* Feb. 8, 1913	April 1, 1971
Sir Denis Spotswood, GCB, CBE, DSO, DFC, *born* Sept. 26, 1916	March 31, 1974
Sir Michael Beetham, GCB, CBE, DFC, AFC, *born* May 17, 1923	Oct. 15, 1982
Sir Keith Williamson, GCB, AFC, *born* Feb. 25, 1928	Oct. 15, 1985
Sir David Craig, GCB, OBE (*Chief of Defence Staff*), *born* Sept. 17, 1929	Nov. 14, 1988

Air Chief Marshals

Harding, Sir Peter, GCB (*Chief of the Air Staff*).
Hine, Sir Patrick, GCB (*AOC.-in-C. Strike Command*).
Skingsley, Sir Anthony, KCB (*Deputy C.-in-C., Allied Forces Central Europe*).
Parry-Evans, Sir David, KCB, CBE (Air Member for Personnel).
Jackson, Sir Brendan, KCB (*Air Member for Supply and Organization*).

Air Marshals

Hayr, Sir Kenneth, KCB, CBE, AFC (*Deputy CDS (Commitments)*).
Holroyd, Sir Frank, KBE, CB (*Chief Engineer (RAF)*).

Stonor, Sir Thomas, KCB (*Controller National Air Traffic Services*).
Simmons, Sir Michael, KCB, AFC (*Deputy Controller Aircraft*).
Graydon, Sir Michael, KCB, CBE (*AOC.-in-C. RAF Support Command*).
Palin, Sir Roger, KCB, OBE (*C.-in-C. RAF Germany and Cmdr. 2 ATAF*).
Stear, Sir Michael, KCB, CBE (*AOC No. 18 Group*).
Stuart-Paul, Sir Ronald, KBE (*Dir. Gen. Saudi Armed Forces Project*).
Kemball, Sir John, KCB, CBE (*Chief of Staff & Deputy C.-in-C. Strike Command*).
Mills, N. H., QHP (*Surgeon General and Dir. Gen. Medical Services (RAF)*).

Air Vice-Marshals

Bennet, Sir Erik, KBE (*Commander Sultan of Oman's Air Force*).

Macey, E. H., OBE (*Dir. Gen. of Training (RAF)*).

Alcock, R. J. M., CB (*Air Officer Engineering Strike Command*).

Walker, J. R., CBE, AFC (*Dir. Gen. Management and Support Intelligence*).

Pilkington, M. J., CBE (*Air Officer Training RAF Support Command*).

Brown, M. J. D. (*Dir. Gen. of Strategic Electronic Systems*).

Roberts, A. L., CBE, AFC (*Asst. Chief of Defence Staff (Concepts)*).

Wilson, R. A. F., CB, AFC (*Air Officer Commanding No. 1 Group*).

Thomson, C. J., CBE, AFC (*Asst. Chief of the Air Staff*).

Honey, R. J., CBE (*Air Secretary and Air Officer Commanding RAF Personnel Management Centre*).

Williams, G. C., AFC (*Cmdt. Gen. RAF Regt. & Dir. Gen. Security (RAF)*).

Austin, R. M., AFC (*Air Officer Commanding and Cmdt. RAF College, Cranwell*).

Woodford, A. A. G., CB (*Asst. Chief of Staff (Policy) Supreme HQ Allied Powers Europe*).

Harris, J. H., CBE (*Asst. CDS (Logistics)*).

Crwys-Williams, D. O., CB (*Dir. Gen. of Personal Services (RAF)*).

Blackley, A. B., CBE, AFC (*Deputy Chief of Staff (Operations) Allied Air Forces Central Europe*).

Johns, R. E., CBE, LVO (*Senior Air Staff Officer, Strike Command*).

Evans, C. E., CBE (*Senior Directing Staff, Royal College of Defence Studies*).

Willis, J. F., CBE (*Asst. Chief of the Defence Staff (Policy and Nuclear)*).

Harding, P. J., CBE, AFC (*Dep. Comd. RAF Germany*).

Robinson, B. L. (*Air Officer Administration, Strike Command*).

Wratten, W. J., CBE, AFC (*Air Officer Commanding No. 11 Group*).

Hunter, A. F. C., CBE, AFC (*Comd. British Forces Cyprus*).

Browne, J. P. R., CBE (*Dir. Gen. Support Systems (RAF)*).

Dicken, M. J. C. W., CB (*Air Officer Administration, RAF Support Command*).

Morris, J., CBE (*Air Officer Scotland and Northern Ireland*).

Cousins, D., AFC (*Dir. Gen. Aircraft 2*).

Emmerson, D., CBE, AFC (*Chief of Staff HQ No. 18 Group*).

Moran, M. F., QHP (*Senior Consultant*).

Johnson, A. T., QHS (*Principal Medical Officer, Strike Command*).

Davies, D. B. A. L., QHP (*Principal Medical Officer RAF Support Command*).

Halfpenny, B. N., CB, QHC (*Chaplain-in-Chief*).

Dawson, R. T., CBE (*Dir. of Legal Services (RAF)*).

Campbell, D. G. (*Air Officer Maintenance RAF Support Command*).

Allison, J. S., CBE (*Asst. CDS (Operational Requirements)*).

Baker, C. P. (*Dir. Gen. of Support Management (RAF)*).

Calnan, J. M. P. (*President of the Ordnance Board*).

Peters, R. G. (*Cmdt. RAF Staff College, Bracknell*).

Ernsting, J., OBE, QHS (*Dean of Air Force Medicine*).

CONSTITUTION OF THE ROYAL AIR FORCE

The Royal Air Force consists of three Commands: Strike Command and Support Command in the United Kingdom, and RAF Germany. Strike Command is responsible for providing the air defence of the United Kingdom and reinforcement forces for NATO; its roles include strike/attack, air defence, control and reporting, maritime surveillance, air reconnaissance, air-to-air refuelling, offensive support, air transport, aero-medical facilities, and search and rescue. Support Command is responsible for air and ground training, communications, engineering support, logistics, hospitals and for providing a range of administrative support. RAF Germany provides tactical air support in NATO's Central Region; its roles include strike/attack, interdiction, counter air operations, air defence, close air support of land forces, tactical reconnaissance and helicopter support.

To carry out its tasks, the Royal Air Force is equipped with Victor, Tornado, Buccaneer, Phantom, Harrier, Jaguar, Canberra, Nimrod, Shackleton, VC10, Tristar, Hercules, Hawk, Jet Provost, Tucano, Chipmunk and Bulldog aircraft; Puma, Wessex, Sea King and Chinook helicopters; miscellaneous communications aircraft, etc.; Bloodhound and Rapier missiles, and the Skyguard system.

Royal Auxiliary Air Force (RAUXAF).—Formed in 1924, the Auxiliary Air Force served with great distinction in the Second World War and in recognition of its war record King George VI conferred the prefix 'Royal' in 1947. Following a major reduction of units in the late 1950s, the benefits to be gained by using auxiliary forces in certain roles has resulted in a subsequent expansion. Today, the Royal Auxiliary Air Force supports the RAF in maritime air operations, air and ground defence of major airfields, air movements and aeromedical evacuation.

Air Commodore-in-Chief, HM The Queen.

Director of Reserve Forces (RAF), Air Cdre. R. P. Skelley.

Royal Air Force Volunteer Reserve (RAFVR).—The Royal Air Force Volunteer Reserve was created in 1936 with the object of providing training for the increased number of aircrew who were seen as necessary for the forthcoming conflict. The RAFVR was reconstituted in 1947 following war service and today is a small but important part of the Air Force Reserve. There are RAFVR aircrew with the Harrier, Nimrod and Tornado Forces, and RAFVR units specializing in intelligence-orientated duties and public relations.

Director of Reserve Forces (RAF), Air Cdre. R. P. Skelley.

PRINCESS MARY'S ROYAL AIR FORCE NURSING SERVICE

The Princess Mary's Royal Air Force Nursing Service (PMRAFNS) is open to suitable male and female candidates. Commissions are offered to those who are Registered General Nurses (RGN) and possess a second qualification suitable to the needs of the service. RGNs with no additional experience or qualification are also recruited as non-commissioned officers in the grade of Staff Nurse.

Air Chief Commandant, HRH Princess Alexandra, the Hon. Lady Ogilvy, GCVO.

Matron-in-Chief, Group Captain E. A. I. Sandison.

WOMEN'S ROYAL AIR FORCE

Formed on April 1, 1918, the Women's Royal Air Force (WRAF) was disbanded on April 1, 1920 and reformed on February 1, 1949 from the Women's Auxiliary Air Force, the World War II Service which had been formed on June 28, 1939, and from the RAF Companies of the Auxiliary Territorial Service.

WRAF officers and airwomen, respectively, serve in most of the RAF ground branches and trades and also as Air Loadmaster aircrew. WRAF personnel are employed at RAF stations and higher formations at home and abroad, and they compete, on equal terms, with their RAF counterparts for appointments, promotion and places on training courses.

Commandant-in-Chief, HM Queen Elizabeth the Queen Mother.
Air Chief Commandant, HRH Princess Alice, Duchess of Gloucester.
Director, Air Commodore, M. B. R. Montague, ADC.

ROYAL OBSERVER CORPS
Bentley Priory, Stanmore, Middlesex

Established 1925, the Royal Observer Corps is a uniformed voluntary civilian organization originally set up to identify and track the movement of aircraft in war. In 1955 the Corps assumed the modern role of detecting nuclear bursts and monitoring radioactive fall-out in support of the United Kingdom Warning and Monitoring Organization. The Corps is affiliated to the Royal Air Force and is administered by the Ministry of Defence.

Air Commodore-in-Chief, HM The Queen.
Commandant, Air Commodore G. M. Boddy, OBE.

RELATIVE RANK—SEA, LAND AND AIR

Royal Navy	Army	Royal Air Force
1. Admiral of the Fleet.	1. Field Marshal.	1. Marshal of the RAF.
2. Admiral (Adm.).	2. General (Gen.).	2. Air Chief Marshal.
3. Vice-Admiral (Vice-Adm.).	3. Lieutenant-General (Lt.-Gen.).	3. Air Marshal.
4. Rear-Admiral (Rear-Adm.).	4. Major-General (Maj.-Gen.).	4. Air Vice-Marshal.
5. Commodore (1st & 2nd Class) (Cdre.).	5. Brigadier (Brig.).	5. Air Commodore (Air Cdre.).
6. Captain (Capt.).	6. Colonel (Col.).	6. Group Captain (Gp. Capt.).
7. Commander (Cdr.).	7. Lieutenant-Colonel (Lt.-Col.).	7. Wing Commander (Wg. Cdr.).
8. Lieutenant Commander (Lt. Cdr.).	8. Major (Maj.).	8. Squadron Leader (Sqn. Ldr.).
9. Lieutenant (Lt.).	9. Captain (Capt.).	9. Flight Lieutenant (Flt.-Lt.).
10. Sub-Lieutenant (Sub-Lt.).	10. Lieutenant (Lt.).	10. Flying Officer (FO).
11. Acting Sub-Lieutenant (Acting Sub-Lt.).	11. Second Lieutenant (2nd. Lt.).	11. Pilot Officer (PO).

SERVICE SALARIES AND PENSIONS

The following rates of pay have been introduced as part of the 1990 pay award for Service personnel.

Salaries for the Women's Services (*see* pp. 407–9) reflect equal pay for equal work and conditions, but because the X-Factor addition for women is lower than for men (9 per cent compared to 10 per cent), women's rates approximate to 99·08 per cent of the rates for men.

Since 1970 the determining factor of the Review Bodies' recommendations has been the relation of forces' salaries to civilian earnings by a carefully detailed process of job evaluation.

ROYAL NAVY AND ROYAL MARINES
Normal Rates

Rank	Daily	Annual
	£	£
Midshipman		
On appointment.............	20·29	7,406
After 1 year.................	25·21	9,202
Sub-Lieutenant and Acting Lieutenant RM		
On appointment...............	28·90	10,549
After 2 years in rank	38·04	13,885
After 3 years in rank	41·04	14,980
Lieutenant		
On appointment.............	48·42	17,673
After 1 year in rank	49·73	18,151
After 2 years in rank	51·04	18,630
After 3 years in rank	52·35	19,108
After 4 years in rank	53·66	19,586
After 5 years in rank	54·97	20,064
After 6 years in rank	56·28	20,542
Lieutenant Commander/Captain RM		
On appointment.............	61·03	22,276
After 1 year in rank	62·54	22,827
After 2 years in rank	64·05	23,378
After 3 years in rank	65·56	23,929
After 4 years in rank	67·07	24,481
After 5 years in rank	68·58	25,032
After 6 years in rank	70·09	25,583
After 7 years in rank	71·60	26,134
After 8 years in rank	73·11	26,685
Commander/Major RM		
On appointment with less than 19 years service	83·90	30,624
After 2 years in rank or with 19 years service	86·11	31,430
After 4 years in rank or with 21 years service	88·32	32,237
After 6 years in rank or with 23 years service	90·53	33,043
After 8 years in rank or with 25 years service	92·74	33,850
Captain/Lieutenant-Colonel RM		
On appointment.............	96·59	35,255
After 2 years in rank	99·13	36,182
After 4 years in rank	101·67	37,110
With 6 years seniority/Colonel RM	116·05	42,358
Rear-Admiral/Major-General RM	129·59	47,358
Vice-Admiral/Lieutenant-General RM	151·51	55,301
Admiral/General RM	210·96	77,000
Admiral of the Fleet	262·33	95,750

ARMY
Normal Rates

Rank	Daily	Annual
	£	£
Second Lieutenant	28·90	10,549
Lieutenant		
On appointment...............	38·04	13,885
After 1 year in rank	39·04	14,250
After 2 years in rank	40·04	14,615
After 3 years in rank	41·04	14,980
After 4 years in rank	42·04	15,345
Captain		
On appointment.............	48·02	17,527
After 1 year in rank	49·73	18,151
After 2 years in rank	51·04	18,630
After 3 years in rank	52·35	19,108
After 4 years in rank	53·66	19,586
After 5 years in rank	54·97	20,064
After 6 years in rank	56·28	20,542
Major		
On appointment.............	61·03	22,276
After 1 year in rank	62·54	22,827
After 2 years in rank	64·05	23,378
After 3 years in rank	65·56	23,923
After 4 years in rank	67·07	24,481
After 5 years in rank	68·58	25,032
After 6 years in rank	70·09	25,582
After 7 years in rank	71·60	25,773
After 8 years in rank	73·11	26,685
Special List Lieutenant-Colonel	83·16	30,353
Lieutenant-Colonel		
On appointment with less than 19 years service	83·90	30,624
After 2 years in rank or with 19 years service	86·11	31,430
After 4 years in rank or with 21 years service	88·32	32,237
After 6 years in rank or with 23 years service	90·53	33,043
After 8 years or with 25 years service	92·74	33,850
Colonel		
On appointment.............	96·59	35,244
After 2 years in rank	99·13	36,182
After 4 years in rank	101·67	37,110
After 6 years in rank	102·21	38,037
After 8 years in rank	106·75	38,964
Brigadier......................	116·05	42,358
Major-General	129·59	47,300
Lieutenant-General	151·41	55,301
General	210·96	77,000
Field Marshal..................	262·33	95,750

ROYAL AIR FORCE, Normal Rates

Rank	Daily	Annual	Rank	Daily	Annual
	£	£		£	£
Acting Pilot Officer—			Squadron Leader (*cont.*)—		
On appointment	25·21	9,202	After 7 years in rank	71·60	26,134
After 6 months in the rank (aircrew officers only)	25·79	9,413	After 8 years in rank	73·11	26,685
Pilot Officer	28·90	10,549	Wing Commander—		
Flying Officer—			On appointment with less than 19 years service	83·90	30,624
On appointment	38·04	13,885	After 2 years in rank or with 19 years service	86·11	31,430
After 1 year in rank	39·04	14,250	After 4 years in rank or with 21 years service	88·32	32,237
After 2 years in rank	40·04	14,615	After 6 years in rank or with 23 years service	90·53	33,043
After 3 years in rank	41·04	14,980	After 8 years in rank or with 25 years service	92·74	33,850
After 4 years in rank	42·04	15,345	Group Captain—		
Flight Lieutenant—			On appointment	96·59	35,255
On appointment	48·42	17,673	After 2 years in rank	99·13	36,182
After 1 year in rank	49·73	18,151	After 4 years in rank	101·67	37,110
After 2 years in rank	51·04	18,630	After 6 years in rank	104·21	38,037
After 3 years in rank	52·35	19,108	After 8 years in rank	106·75	38,964
After 4 years in rank	53·66	19,586	Air Commodore	116·05	42,358
After 5 years in rank	54·97	20,064	Air Vice-Marshal	129·59	47,300
After 6 years in rank	56·28	20,542	Air Marshal	151·51	55,301
Squadron Leader—			Air Chief Marshal	210·96	77,000
On appointment	61·03	22,276	Marshal of the Royal Air Force	262·33	95,750
After 1 year in rank	62·54	22,872			
After 2 years in rank	64·05	23,378			
After 3 years in rank	65·56	23,929			
After 4 years in rank	67·07	24,481			
After 5 years in rank	68·58	25,032			
After 6 years in rank	70·09	25,583			

ROYAL NAVY AND ROYAL MARINES SPECIAL DUTIES LIST OFFICERS, ARMY MALE OFFICERS COMMISSIONED FROM THE RANKS, ROYAL AIR FORCE BRANCH OFFICERS

Years of Commissioned Service	Years of Non-Commissioned Service from age 18					
	Less than 12 years		12 years but less than 15 years		15 years or more	
	Daily	Annual	Daily	Annual	Daily	Annual
	£	£	£	£	£	£
On appointment	51·59	18,830	54·35	19,838	57·11	20,845
After 1 year service	52·97	19,334	55·73	20,341	58·11	21,225
After 2 years service	54·35	19,838	57·11	20,845	59·19	21,604
After 3 years service	55·73	20,341	58·15	21,225	60·23	21,984
After 4 years service	57·11	20,845	59·19	21,604	61·27	22,364
After 5 years service	58·15	21,225	60·23	21,984	62·31	22,743
After 6 years service	59·19	21,604	61·27	22,364	63·35	23,123
After 8 years service	60·23	21,984	62·31	22,743	64·39	23,502
After 10 years service	61·27	22,364	63·35	23,123	64·39	23,502
After 12 years service	62·31	22,743	64·39	23,502	64·39	23,502
After 14 years service	63·35	23,123	64·39	23,502	64·39	23,502
After 16 years service	64·39	23,502	64·39	23,502	64·39	23,502

ROYAL NAVY ARTIFICERS, MEDICAL AND COMMUNICATIONS TECHNICIANS
Daily rates of pay for those committed to serve for:

Rank	Less than 6 years Scale A	6 years but less than 9 years Scale B	9 years or more Scale C
	£	£	£
FCPO Artificer/Technician	54·12	54·42	54·87
CCPO Artificer/Technician	52·11	52·41	52·86
CPO Artificer/1st Class Technician—Scale I	50·10	50·40	50·85
—Scale II	48·18	48·48	48·93
PO Artificer/2nd Class Technician	42·69	42·99	43·44
Probationary or Acting PO Artificer/3rd Class Technician	40·72	41·02	41·47
4th Class Technician (Leading)	35·65	35·95	36·40
Leading Artificer/Acting 4th Class Technician	33·43	33·73	34·18
Acting Leading Artificer	30·17	30·47	30·92
5th Class Technician (Able)	28·33	28·63	29·08

ROYAL NAVY AND ROYAL MARINES—OTHER BRANCHES

Daily rates of pay for those committed to serve for:

Rank	Less than 6 years Scale A	6 years but less than 9 years Scale B	9 years or more Scale C
	£	£	£
Fleet Chief Petty Officer/Warrant Officer Class I—Scale I ..	49·96	50·26	50·71
Chief Petty Officer—Scale I	44·22	44·52	44·97
—Scale II	43·42	43·72	44·17
Petty Officer/Sergeant—Scale I	39·55	39·85	40·30
—Scale II	38·34	39·14	39·59
Leading Rating/Corporal—Scale I	35·65	35·95	36·40
—Scale II	33·43	33·73	34·18
Able Rating/Marine 1st Class—Scale I	28·33	28·63	29·08
—Scale II	26·61	26·91	27·36
—Scale III	23·19	23·49	23·94
Ordinary Rating/Marine 2nd Class—Scale I	19·54	19·84	20·29
—Scale II	17·96	18·26	18·71

ARMY

Daily rates of pay for those committed to serve for:

Rank	Less than 6 years Scale A			6 years but less than 9 years Scale B			9 years or more Scale C		
	Band 1	Band 2	Band 3	Band 1	Band 2	Band 3	Band 1	Band 2	Band 3
	£	£	£	£	£	£	£	£	£
Private Class IV ...	17·96	—	—	18·26	—	—	18·71	—	—
Class III ...	19·93	23·19	26·73	20·23	23·49	27·03	20·68	23·94	27·48
Class II ...	22·31	25·57	29·11	22·61	25·87	29·41	23·06	26·32	29·86
Class I	24·21	27·47	31·01	24·51	27·77	31·31	24·96	28·22	31·76
Lance Corporal									
Class III ...	24·21	27·47	31·01	24·51	27·77	31·31	24·96	28·22	31·76
Class II ...	26·08	29·34	32·88	26·38	29·64	33·18	26·83	30·09	33·63
Class I	28·09	31·35	34·89	28·39	31·65	35·19	28·84	32·10	35·64
Corporal Class II ...	30·17	33·43	36·97	30·47	33·73	37·27	30·92	34·18	37·72
Class I	32·39	35·65	39·19	32·69	35·95	39·47	33·14	36·40	39·94

	Band 4	Band 5	Band 6	Band 7	Band 4	Band 5	Band 6	Band 7	Band 4	Band 5	Band 6	Band 7
	£	£	£	£	£	£	£	£	£	£	£	£
Sergeant	35·32	38·84	42·69	—	35·62	39·14	42·99	—	36·07	39·59	42·44	—
Staff Sergeant	37·35	40·87	44·72	48·88	37·65	41·17	45·02	49·18	38·10	41·62	45·47	49·63
Warrant Officer												
Class II	39·94	43·46	47·31	51·47	40·24	43·76	47·61	51·77	40·69	44·21	48·06	52·22
Class I	42·59	46·11	49·96	54·12	42·89	46·41	50·26	54·72	43·34	46·86	50·71	54·87

ROYAL AIR FORCE AIRMEN (GROUND TRADES, APPRENTICES AND PMRAFNS)

Daily rates of pay for those committed to serve for:

Rank/Category	Less than 6 years Scale A			6 years but less than 9 years Scale B			9 years or more Scale C		
	Band 1	Band 2	Band 3	Band 1	Band 2	Band 3	Band 1	Band 2	Band 3
	£	£	£	£	£	£	£	£	£
Aircraftman over 17 on entry.	17·96	17·96	17·96	18·26	18·26	18·26	18·71	18·71	18·71
Leading Aircraftman	19·93	23·19	26·73	20·23	23·49	27·03	20·68	23·94	27·48
Senior Aircraftman	24·21	27·47	31·01	24·51	27·77	31·31	24·96	28·22	31·76
Junior Technician	28·09	31·35	34·89	28·39	31·65	35·19	28·84	32·10	35·64
Corporal	32·00	35·26	39·19	32·30	35·56	39·49	32·75	36·01	39·94

	Band 4	Band 5	Band 6	Band 7	Band 4	Band 5	Band 6	Band 7	Band 4	Band 5	Band 6	Band 7
	£	£	£	£	£	£	£	£	£	£	£	£
Sergeant	34·32	38·84	42·69	—	35·62	39·14	42·99	—	36·07	39·59	43·44	—
Chief Technician............	36·96	40·48	44·33	48·49	37·26	40·78	44·63	48·79	37·71	41·23	45·08	49·24
Flight Sergeant	38·61	42·13	45·98	50·14	38·91	42·43	46·28	50·44	39·36	42·88	46·73	50·89
Warrant Officer	42·59	46·11	49·96	54·12	42·89	46·41	50·26	54·42	43·34	46·86	50·71	54·87

ROYAL AIR FORCE—AIRMEN (AIRCREW)
Daily rates for those committed to serve for:

Rank	Less than 6 years Scale A			6 years but less than 9 years Scale B			9 years or more Scale C		
	Band 5	Band 6	Band 7	Band 5	Band 6	Band 7	Band 5	Band 6	Band 7
	£	£	£	£	£	£	£	£	£
Pilot, Navigator, Air Engineer (A) and Air Signallers (A)									
Sergeant	—	42·69	—	—	42·99	—	—	43·44	—
Flight Sergeant ..	—	—	50·14	—	—	50·44	—	—	50·89
Master Aircrew ..	—	—	54·12	—	—	54·42	—	—	54·87
Air Electronics Operators									
Sergeant	42·69	—	—	42·99	—	—	43·44	—	—
Flight Sergeant ..	—	45·98	—	—	46·28	—	—	46·73	—
Master Aircrew ..	—	49·96	—	—	50·26	—	—	50·71	—

WOMEN'S SERVICES

OFFICERS OF WRNS

Rank	Daily	Annual
	£	£
Probationary 3rd Officer	28·64	10,454
Third Officer		
On confirmation	31·66	11,556
After 2 years..................	37·70	13,761
Second Officer		
On appointment................	47·98	17,513
After 1 year in rank	49·28	17,987
After 2 years in rank	50·58	18,462
After 3 years in rank	51·88	18,936
After 4 years in rank	53·17	19,407
After 5 years in rank	54·47	19,882
After 6 years in rank	55·77	20,356
First Officer		
On appointment................	60·48	22,075
After 1 year in rank	61·97	22,619
After 2 years in rank	63·47	23,167
After 3 years in rank	64·97	23,714
After 4 years in rank	66·46	24,258
After 5 years in rank	67·96	24,805
After 6 years in rank	69·46	25,353
After 7 years in rank	70·95	25,897
After 8 years in rank	72·45	26,644
Chief Officer		
On appointment with less than 19 years service	83·14	30,346
After 2 years in rank or with 19 years service................	85·33	31,145
After 4 years in rank or with 21 years service................	87·52	31,945
After 6 years in rank or with 23 years service................	89·73	32,751
After 8 years in rank or with 25 years service................	91·94	33,558
Superintendent		
On appointment................	96·05	35,058
After 2 years in rank	98·59	35,985
After 4 years in rank	101·13	36,912
After 6 years in rank	103·13	37,840
After 8 years in rank	106·21	38,767
Director, WRNS	115·78	42,260

FEMALE OFFICERS OF QARNNS

Rank	Daily	Annual
	£	£
Nursing Officer		
On appointment..............	35·97	13,129
After 1 year in rank	36·92	13,476
After 2 years in rank	37·87	13,823
After 3 years in rank	38·81	14,166
After 4 years in rank	39·76	14,512
Senior Nursing Officer		
On appointment..............	45·79	16,713
After 1 year in rank	47·03	17,166
After 2 years in rank	48·27	17,619
After 3 years in rank	49·51	17,706
After 4 years in rank	50·75	18,524
After 5 years in rank	51·99	18,976
After 6 years in rank	53·22	19,425
Superintending Nursing Officer		
On appointment..............	57·72	21,068
After 1 year in rank	59·14	21,586
After 2 years in rank	60·57	22,108
After 3 years in rank	62·00	22,630
After 4 years in rank	63·43	23,152
After 5 years in rank	64·86	23,674
After 6 years in rank	66·28	24,192
After 7 years in rank	67·71	24,714
After 8 years in rank	69·14	25,236
Chief Nursing Officer		
On appointment with less than 19 years service	83·14	30,346
After 2 years in rank or with 19 years service................	85·14	31,145
After 4 years in rank or with 21 years service................	87·52	31,945
After 6 years in rank or with 23 years service................	89·73	32,751
After 8 years in rank or with 25 years service................	91·94	33,558
Principal Nursing Officer		
On appointment................	96·05	35,058
After 2 years in rank	98·59	35,985
After 4 years in rank	101·13	36,912
After 6 years in rank	103·67	37,839
After 8 years in rank	106·21	38,767
Matron-in-Chief	115·78	42,260

OFFICERS OF WRAC AND QARANC

Rank	Daily	Annual
	£	£
Second-Lieutenant	28·64	10,454
Lieutenant—On appointment	37·70	13,761
After 1 year in rank	38·69	14,122
After 2 years in rank	39·68	14,483
After 3 years in rank	40·67	14,845
After 4 years in rank	41·66	15,206
Captain—On appointment	47·98	17,513
After 1 year in rank	49·28	17,987
After 2 years in rank	50·58	18,462
After 3 years in rank	51·88	18,936
After 4 years in rank	53·17	19,407
After 5 years in rank	54·47	19,882
After 6 years in rank	55·77	20,356
Major—On appointment	60·48	22,075
After 1 year in rank	61·97	22,619
After 2 years in rank	63·47	23,167
After 3 years in rank	64·97	23,714
After 4 years in rank	66·46	24,258
After 5 years in rank	67·96	24,805
After 6 years in rank	69·46	25,353
After 7 years in rank	70·95	25,897
After 8 years in rank	72·45	26,444
Lieutenant-Colonel— On appointment with less than 19 years service	83·14	30,346
After 2 years in rank or with 19 years service	85·33	31,145
After 4 years in rank or with 21 years service................	87·52	31,945
After 6 years in rank or with 23 years service................	89·73	32,751
After 8 years in rank or with 25 years service................	91·94	35,748
Colonel—On appointment........	96·05	35,058
After 2 years in rank	98·59	35,985
After 4 years in rank	101·13	36,912
After 6 years in rank	103·67	37,840
After 8 years in rank	106·21	38,767
Brigadier.......................	115·78	42,260

OFFICERS OF WRAF AND FEMALE OFFICERS OF THE PMRAFNS

Rank	Daily	Annual
	£	£
Acting Pilot Officer..............	24·98	9,118
Pilot Officer	28·64	10,454
Flying Officer—On appointment ..	37·70	13,761
After 1 year in rank	38·69	14,122
After 2 years in rank	39·68	14,483
After 3 years in rank	40·67	14,845
After 4 years in rank	41·66	15,206
Flight Lieutenant— On appointment................	47·98	17,513
After 1 year in rank	49·28	17,989
After 2 years in rank	50·58	18,462
After 3 years in rank	51·88	18,936
After 4 years in rank	53·17	19,407
After 5 years in rank	54·47	19,882
After 6 years in rank	55·77	20,356
Squadron Leader— On appointment................	60·48	22,075
After 1 year in rank	61·97	22,619
After 2 years in rank	63·47	23,167
After 3 years in rank	64·97	23,714
After 4 years in rank	66·46	24,258
After 5 years in rank	67·96	24,805
After 6 years in rank	69·46	25,353
After 7 years in rank	70·95	25,897
After 8 years in rank	72·45	26,444
Wing Commander— On appointment with less than 19 years service	83·14	30,346
After 2 years in rank or with 19 years service................	85·33	31,266
After 4 years in rank or with 21 years service................	87·52	31,945
After 6 years in rank or with 23 years service................	89·73	32,751
After 8 years in rank or with 25 years service................	91·94	33,558
Group Captain—On appointment .	96·05	35,058
After 2 years in rank	98·59	35,985
After 4 years in rank	101·13	36,912
After 6 years in rank	103·67	37,840
After 8 years in rank	106·21	38,761
Air Commodore	115·78	42,260

WRNS RATINGS AND NAVAL NURSES
Daily rates for those who have served for:

Rank	Less than 6 years Scale A			6 years but less than 9 years Scale B			9 years or more Scale C		
	Band 1	Band 2	Band 3	Band 1	Band 2	Band 3	Band 1	Band 2	Band 3
	£	£	£	£	£	£	£	£	£
Ordinary Rating under 17.........	13·46	—	—	—	—	—	—	—	—
Ordinary Rating at 17...............	17·79	17·79	—	18·09	18·09	—	18·54	18·54	—
Able Rating Scale C	19·75	22·98	26·49	20·05	23·28	26·79	20·50	23·73	27·24
Scale B	23·14	26·37	29·88	23·44	26·67	30·18	23·84	27·12	30·63
Scale A	24·84	28·07	31·58	25·14	28·37	31·88	25·59	28·32	32·33
Leading Rating Scale B	29·89	33·12	36·63	30·19	33·42	36·93	30·64	33·87	37·38
Scale A	32·09	35·32	38·83	22·39	25·62	39·13	32·84	36·07	39·58

	Band 4	Band 5	Band 6	Band 7	Band 4	Band 5	Band 6	Band 7	Band 4	Band 5	Band 6	Band 7
	£	£	£	£	£	£	£	£	£	£	£	£
Petty Officer Scale B	34·62	38·11	41·93	46·05	34·92	38·41	42·23	46·35	35·37	38·82	42·68	46·80
Scale A	35·37	38·86	42·68	46·80	35·67	39·16	42·98	47·10	36·12	39·61	43·43	47·55
CPO Scale B	37·27	40·76	44·58	48·70	37·57	41·06	44·88	49·00	38·02	41·51	45·33	49·45
Scale A	38·18	41·67	45·49	49·61	38·48	41·97	45·79	49·91	38·93	42·42	46·24	50·36
Warrant Officer	42·20	45·69	49·51	53·63	42·50	45·99	49·81	53·93	42·95	46·44	50·26	54·38

WRAC and QARANC
Daily rates of pay for those who have served for:

Rank	Less than 6 years			6 years but less than 9 years			9 years or more		
	Band 1	Band 2	Band 3	Band 1	Band 2	Band 3	Band 1	Band 2	Band 3
	£	£	£	£	£	£	£	£	£
Private Class IV Age 17–17½ ..	13·46								
Class IV	17·79	—		18·09	—		18·54	—	
Class III	19·75	22·98	26·49	20·05	23·28	26·79	20·50	23·73	27·24
Class II	22·11	25·34	28·84	22·41	25·64	29·14	22·86	26·09	29·59
Class I	23·99	27·22	30·73	24·29	27·52	31·03	24·74	27·97	31·48
Lance Corporal Class III	23·99	27·22	30·73	24·29	27·52	31·03	24·74	27·97	31·48
Class II	25·84	29·07	32·58	26·14	29·37	32·88	26·59	29·82	33·33
Class I	27·83	31·06	34·57	28·13	31·36	34·87	28·58	31·81	35·32
Corporal Class II	29·89	33·12	36·63	30·19	33·42	36·93	30·64	33·87	37·38
Class I	32·09	35·32	38·83	32·39	34·62	39·13	32·84	36·07	39·58

Rank	Band 4	Band 5	Band 6	Band 7	Band 4	Band 5	Band 6	Band 7	Band 4	Band 5	Band 6	Band 7
	£	£	£	£	£	£	£	£	£	£	£	£
Sergeant	35·00	38·49	42·30	—	35·50	38·79	42·60	—	35·75	39·24	43·05	—
Staff Sergeant	37·01	40·50	44·31	48·43	37·31	40·80	44·61	48·73	37·76	41·25	45·06	49·18
Warrant Officer Class II	39·58	43·06	46·88	51·00	39·88	43·36	47·18	51·30	40·33	43·81	47·63	51·75
Class I	42·20	45·69	49·51	53·63	42·50	45·99	49·81	53·93	42·95	46·44	50·26	54·38

WRAF AIRWOMEN (Ground Trades) and PMRAFNS
Daily rates of pay for those who have served for:

Rank/Category	Less than 6 years			6 years but less than 9 years			9 years or more		
	Band 1	Band 2	Band 3	Band 1	Band 2	Band 3	Band 1	Band 2	Band 3
	£	£	£	£	£	£	£	£	£
Aircraftwoman under age 17 .	13·46								
Aircraftwoman at age 17 .	17·79	17·79							
Leading Aircraftwoman	19·75	22·98	26·49	20·05	23·28	26·79	20·50	23·73	27·24
Senior Aircraftwoman	23·99	27·22	30·73	24·29	27·52	31·03	24·74	27·97	31·48
Junior Technician	27·83	31·06	34·57	28·13	31·36	34·87	28·58	31·81	35·32
Corporal	31·70	34·93	38·83	32·00	35·23	39·13	32·45	35·68	39·58

Rank/Category	Band 4	Band 5	Band 6	Band 7	Band 4	Band 5	Band 6	Band 7	Band 4	Band 5	Band 6	Band 7
	£	£	£	£	£	£	£	£	£	£	£	£
Sergeant	35·00	38·49	42·30	—	35·30	38·79	42·60	—	35·75	39·24	43·05	—
Chief Technician	36·63	40·11	43·93	48·05	36·93	40·41	44·23	48·35	37·38	40·86	44·68	48·80
Flight Sergeant	38·25	41·74	45·56	49·68	38·55	42·04	45·86	49·98	39·00	42·49	46·31	50·43
Warrant Officer	42·20	45·69	49·51	53·63	42·50	45·99	49·81	53·93	42·95	46·44	50·26	54·38

SERVICE RETIREMENT BENEFITS, ETC.

Those who leave the Forces having served at least five years, but not long enough to qualify for the appropriate immediate pension, now qualify for a preserved pension and terminal grant both of which are payable at age 60. The tax-free resettlement grants shown below are payable on release to those who qualify for a preserved pension and who have completed nine years service from age 21 (officers) or 12 years from age 18 (other ranks). The annual rates for the Army are given; these apply to the equivalent ranks in all Services, including the Nursing Services.

RETIREMENT BENEFITS (MEN) Officers*—All Services

No. of years reckonable service over age 21	Capt. (incl. QM) and below	Major (incl. QM)	Lt.-Col.	Col. (incl. Deputy Chaplain General)	Brigadier	Major-General	Lieutenant-General	General
	£p.a.	£p.a.	£p.a.	£p.a.	£p.a.	£p.a.	£p.a.	£p.a.
16	5,855	6,977	8,958	10,312				
17	6,123	7,308	9,372	10,789				
18	6,391	7,640	9,787	11,266				
19	6,659	7,971	10,201	11,743				
20	6,972	8,303	10,616	12,220				
21	7,196	8,634	11,030	12,697				
22	7,464	8,965	11,444	13,174	14,896			
23	7,732	9,297	11,859	13,651	15,367			
24	8,000	9,628	12,273	14,128	15,837	17,685		
25	8,268	9,960	12,688	14,604	16,308	18,211		
26	8,536	10,291	13,102	15,081	16,779	18,736		
27	8,804	10,622	13,516	15,558	17,249	19,262	22,519	
28	9,072	10,954	13,931	16,035	17,720	19,787	23,134	
29	9,340	11,285	14,345	16,512	18,190	20,313	23,748	
30	9,609	11,616	14,759	16,989	18,661	20,839	24,363	33,923
31	9,877	11,948	15,174	17,466	19,132	21,364	24,977	33,779
32	10,145	11,279	15,588	17,943	19,603	21,890	25,592	35,634
33	10,413	12,611	16,003	18,420	20,073	22,415	26,206	36,490
34	10,681	12,942	16,417	18,897	20,544	22,941	26,821	37,345

* Including those male officers holding equivalent ranks in the QARNNS.

Ratings, Soldiers and Airmen*

Number of years reckonable service	Below Corporal	Corporal	Sergeant	Staff Sergeant	Warrant Officer Class II	Warrant Officer Class I
	£p.a.	£p.a.	£p.a.	£p.a.	£p.a.	£p.a.
22	3,383	4,351	4,780	5,416	5,570	6,101
23	3,501	4,503	4,947	5,605	5,767	6,320
24	3,619	4,655	5,114	5,794	5,965	6,540
25	3,737	4,807	5,281	5,983	6,162	6,759
26	3,856	4,959	5,447	6,172	6,360	6,979
27	3,974	5,111	5,614	6,361	6,557	7,198
28	4,092	5,263	5,781	6,550	6,754	7,418
29	4,210	5,415	5,948	6,739	6,952	7,637
30	4,328	5,566	6,115	6,928	7,149	7,857
31	4,446	5,718	6,282	7,117	7,347	8,075
32	4,564	5,870	6,449	7,306	7,544	8,296
33	4,682	6,022	6,616	7,495	7,741	8,515
34	4,801	6,174	6,782	7,684	7,936	8,735
35	4,919	6,326	6,949	7,873	8,136	8,954
36	5,037	6,478	7,116	8,062	8,334	9,174
37	5,155	6,630	7,283	8,251	8,531	9,393

* Including male nurses serving in the QARNNS holding equivalent rank.

RETIREMENT BENEFITS (WOMEN)

The annual rates for WRAC are given; these apply to equivalent ranks in all Services, including the Nursing Services.

OFFICERS (16–34 years' service).—Captain, £5,811–£10,601; Major, £6,925–£12,845; Lt.-Col., £8,891–£16,294; Colonel, £11,210–£18,803; Brigadier, £14,859–£20,493.

SERVICEWOMEN (22–37 years' service).—Below Corporal, £3,358–£5,116; Corporal, £4,318–£6,580; Sergeant, £4,744–£7,228; Staff Sergeant, £5,375–£8,189; Warrant Officer II, £5,528–£8,467; Warrant Officer I, £6,055–£9,323.

NOTES

Terminal grants are in each case three times the rate of retired pay or pension. There are special rates of retired pay for Chaplains, Flight Lieutenants (Specialist Aircrew), and certain other ranks not shown above. Lower rates are payable in cases of voluntary retirement.

The normal rates of gratuity for officers with short service commissions are £1,990 (men) and £1,975 (women) for each year completed. Resettlement grants are: officers £6,847 (men) and £6,796 (women); non-commissioned ranks £4,538 (men), £4,504 (women).

THE CHURCHES

THE CHURCH OF ENGLAND

THE GENERAL SYNOD OF THE CHURCH OF ENGLAND
Offices.—Church House, Dean's Yard, SW1P 3NZ

The General Synod was constituted in 1970, under the Synodical Government Measure 1969, in succession to the former Church Assembly. There are in total some 574 members of the General Synod, divided into three distinct houses: the House of Bishops, the House of Clergy and the House of Laity. It is presided over jointly by the Archbishops of Canterbury and York and normally meets three times each year, in February, July and November.

The function of the General Synod is to consider and make provision for all matters concerning the Church of England, and to consider and express opinion on any other matters of religious or public interest. The Synod appoints a number of Committees, Boards and Councils which deal with, or advise the Synod on, a wide range of matters affecting the Church and its Ministry.

Under the Church of England Assembly (Powers) Act 1919 the General Synod has the power, delegated by Parliament, to frame Statute Law on any matter concerning the Church of England, which are known as Measures. A Measure, once approved by General Synod, must be laid before both Houses of Parliament who may accept or reject it but may not amend it. If the Measure is accepted it is then submitted for Royal Assent and when this has been given, the Measure has the full force of law just as an Act of Parliament.

The Synod also has the power to make Canons and other ecclesiastical regulations provided that they do not conflict with statutory law. Canons have to be submitted to the Crown before they can come into effect.

Presidents, The Archbishop of Canterbury; The Archbishop of York.
Sec. Gen., P. Mawer.
THE HOUSE OF BISHOPS.—*Chairman*, The Archbishop of Canterbury; *Vice Chairman*, The Archbishop of York.
THE HOUSE OF CLERGY.—*Joint Chairmen*, The Archdeacon of Leicester; Canon P. H. Boulton.
THE HOUSE OF LAITY, *Chairman*, Prof. J. D. McClean; *Vice Chairman*, Mrs. J. Dann.

Stipends 1990–91

Archbishop of Canterbury	£37,800
Archbishop of York	£33,080
Bishop of London	£30,805
Bishop of Durham	£27,150
Bishop of Winchester	£22,585
Diocesan Bishop	£20,650
Suffragan Bishop	£16,980
Dean or Provost	£16,980
Canons Residentiary	£13,880

Province of Canterbury

CANTERBURY

Stipendiary Male Clergy, 198
Stipendiary Women Deacons, 10.
102*nd Archbishop and Primate of All England*,
Most Rev. and Rt. Hon. Robert Alexander
Kennedy Runcie, MC, *cons.* 1970, *trs.* 1980
(Lambeth Palace, SE1 7JU) [Signs Robert Cantuar:] 1980
(Archbishop Runcie retires in January 1991 and will be replaced by George Carey, Bishop of Bath and Wells.)

Bishops Suffragan

Dover, Rt. Rev. Richard Henry McPhail Third, *cons.* 1976 (Upway, St. Martin's Hill, Canterbury, CT1 1PR) 1980
Maidstone, Rt. Rev. David James Smith, *cons.* 1987 (Bishop's House, Pett Lane, Charing, Ashford TN27 0DL) 1987

Assistant Bishops

Rt. Rev. Ross Hook, MC (*cons.* 1965), 1986; Rt. Rev. William Franklin, OBE (*cons.* 1972), 1987; Rt. Rev. Richard Say, KCVO (*cons.* 1961), 1988.

Dean

Very Rev. John Arthur Simpson 1986

Canons Residentiary

J. H. R. De Sausmarez (1981); P. Brett (1983); Ven. M. Till (1986); C. A. Lewis (1987).
Organist, D. Flood (1988).

Archdeacons

Canterbury, Ven. M. Till 1986
Maidstone, Ven. P. Evans 1989

Vicar-General of Province and Diocese, Miss S. Cameron, QC.

Commissary General, J. H. R. Newey, QC (1971).
Joint Registrars of the Province, F. E. Robson, 16 Beaumont Street, Oxford; B. J. T. Hanson, Church House, Dean's Yard, SW1P 3NZ.
Registrar of the Diocese of Canterbury, A. O. E. Davies, 9 The Precincts, Canterbury CT1 2EQ.

LONDON

Stipendiary Male Clergy, 568
Stipendiary Women Deacons, 49.
130*th Bishop*, Rt. Rev. and Rt. Hon. Graham Douglas Leonard, *cons.* 1964, *trs.* 1973 and 1981 (8 Barton Street, SW1P 3NE) [Signs Graham Londin:] 1981

Area Bishops

Edmonton, Rt. Rev. Brian John Masters, *cons.* 1982 (13 North Audley Street, W1Y 1FW) 1984
Kensington, Rt. Rev. John Hughes, PH.D., *cons.* 1987 (19 Campden Hill Square, W8 7JY) 1987
Stepney, Rt. Rev. James Lawton Thompson, *cons.* 1978 (63 Coborn Road, E3 2DB) 1978
Willesden, Rt. Rev. Thomas Frederick Butler, PH.D., *cons.* 1985 (173 Willesden Lane, NW6 7YN) 1985

Bishop Suffragan

Fulham, Rt. Rev. (Charles) John Klyberg, *cons.* 1985 (4 Cambridge Place, W8 5PB) 1985

Assistant Bishops

Rt. Rev. Maurice Wood, DSC (*cons.* 1971), 1985; Rt. Rev. Michael Marshall (*cons.* 1975) 1984.

Dean of St. Paul's

Very Rev. Thomas Eric Evans 1988

Canons Residentiary

Ven. G. Cassidy (1987); C. J. Hill (1989).
Organist, J. Scott.
Receiver of St. Paul's, M. Postgate.

Archdeacons

Charing Cross, Rt. Rev. C. J. Klyberg 1989
Hackney, Ven. R. E. D. Sharpley 1981
Hampstead, Ven. R. A. W. Coogan 1985
London, Ven. G. Cassidy 1987
Middlesex, Ven. T. J. Raphael 1983
Northolt, Ven. E. Shirras 1985

*Chancellor and Commissary of the Dean and
Chapter,* G. H. Newsom, QC (1971).
Registrar, D. W. Faull, 35 Great Peter Street,
SW1P 3LR.

WESTMINSTER

*The Collegiate Church of St. Peter (A Royal
Peculiar)*
Dean, Michael Clement Otway Mayne 1986
Sub Dean and Archdeacon, A. E. Harvey (1987).

Canons of Westminister

A. E. Harvey (1982); D. C. Gray (1987); C. D.
Semper (1987); P. S. Bates (1990).
Chapter Clerk and Receiver General, Rear-Adm.
K. A. Snow, CB (1987).
Organist, M. Neary, FRCO (1988).
Legal Secretary, C. L. Hodgetts (1973).
Registrar, S. J. Holmes (1984), 20 Dean's Yard,
SW1P 3PA.

WINCHESTER

Stipendiary Male Clergy, 260
Stipendiary Women Deacons, 5.
95th Bishop, Rt. Rev. Colin Clement Walter
James, *cons.* 1973, *trs.* 1977 and 1985 (Wolvesey,
Winchester SO23 9ND) [Signs Colin
Winton:] 1985

Bishops Suffragan

Basingstoke, Rt. Rev. Michael Richard John
Manktelow, *cons.* 1977 (1 The Close, Winches-
ter SO23 9LS) 1977
Southampton, Rt. Rev. John Freeman Perry,
cons. 1989 (Jollers, Sparsholt SO21 2NS) 1989

Assistant Bishops

Rt. Rev. Hassan Dehqani-Tafti (*cons.* 1961), 1982;
Rt. Rev. Leslie Rees (*cons.* 1980), 1986.

Dean

Very Rev. Trevor Randall Beeson 1987

Dean of Jersey (A Peculiar), Very Rev. Basil
Arthur O'Ferrall, CB 1985
Dean of Guernsey (A Peculiar), Very Rev. Jeffery
Fenwick 1989

Canons Residentiary

E. G. Job (1979); P. A. Britton (1980); A. K.
Walker (1987).
Organist, D. Hill, FRCO (1988).

Archdeacons

Basingstoke, Ven. A. F. Knight 1990
Winchester, Ven. A. G. Clarkson 1984

Chancellor, J. Spokes, QC (1985).
Registrar and Legal Secretary, P. M. White, 19
St. Peter Street, Winchester SO23 8BU.

BATH AND WELLS

Stipendiary Male Clergy, 255
Stipendiary Women Deacons, 4.
75th Bishop, Rt. Rev. George Leonard Carey,
PH.D., *cons.* 1987 (The Palace, Wells BA5 2PD)
[Signs George Bath & Wells] 1987
(Bishop Carey is to become Archbishop of Canterbury
following the retirement of Archbishop Runcie in
January 1991.)

Bishop Suffragan

Taunton, Rt. Rev. Nigel Simeon McCulloch, *cons.*
1986 (Sherford Farm House, Sherford, Taunton
TA1 3RF) 1986

Dean

Very Rev. Richard Lewis 1990

Canons Residentiary

S. R. Cutt (1979); C. E. Thomas (1983); P. de N.
Lucas (1988).
Organist, A. Crossland, FRCO (1970).

Archdeacons

Bath, Ven. J. E. Burgess 1975
Taunton, Ven. L. E. Olyott 1977
Wells, Ven. C. E. Thomas .1983

Chancellor, G. H. Newsom, QC (1970).
Registrar, Sec. & Chapter Clerk, N. M. Cavender,
Diocesan Registry, Market Place, Wells
BA5 2RE.

BIRMINGHAM

Stipendiary Male Clergy, 220
Stipendiary Women Deacons, 11.
7th Bishop, Rt. Rev. Mark Santer, *cons.* 1981
(Bishop's Croft, Harborne, Birmingham
B17 0BG) [Signs Mark Birmingham] 1987

Bishop Suffragan

Aston, (vacant).

Assistant Bishop

Rt. Rev. Michael Whinney (*cons.* 1982) 1989

Provost

Very Rev. Peter Austin Berry 1986

Canons Residentiary

D. McLean (1972); L. M. Davies (1981); Ven. C. J.
G. Barton (1990).
Organist, M. R. Huxley, FRCO (1986).

Archdeacons

Aston, Ven. C. J. G. Barton 1990
Birmingham, Ven. J. F. Duncan 1985
Coleshill, Ven. J. L. Cooper 1990

Chancellor, His Hon. Judge Aglionby (1970).
Registrar and Legal Secretary, M. B. Shaw, St.
Philip's House, St. Philip's Place, Birmingham
B3 2PP.

BRISTOL

Stipendiary Male Clergy, 164
Stipendiary Women Deacons, 19.
54th Bishop, Rt. Rev. Barry Rogerson, *cons.* 1979
(Bishop's House, Clifton Hill, Bristol BS8 1BW)
[Signs Barry Bristol] 1985

Bishop Suffragan

Malmesbury, Rt. Rev. Peter James Firth, *cons.*
1983 (7 Ivywell Rd., Bristol BS9 1NX) 1983

Dean

Very Rev. Wesley Arthur Carr 1987

Canons Residentiary

J. Rogan (1983); A. L. J. Redfern (1987); J. L. Simpson (1989).
Organist, C. Brayne, FRCO (1990).

Archdeacons

Bristol, Ven. D. J. Banfield 1990
Swindon, Ven. K. J. Clark 1982

Chancellor, D. C. Calcutt, QC (1971).
Registrar and Sec., T. R. Urquhart, 30 Queen Charlotte Street, Bristol BS13 8HE.

CHELMSFORD

Stipendiary Male Clergy, 474
Stipendiary Women Deacons, 18.
7th Bishop, Rt. Rev. John Waine, *cons.* 1975 (Bishopscourt, Margaretting, Ingatestone CM4 0HD) [Signs John Chelmsford] 1986

Bishops Suffragan

Barking, vacant.
Bradwell, Rt. Rev. Charles Derek Bond, *cons.* 1976 (21 Elmhurst Avenue, Benfleet SS7 5RY) 1976
Colchester, Rt. Rev. Michael Edwin Vickers, *cons.* 1988, (1 Fitzwalter Road, Lexden, Colchester CO3 3SS) 1988

Provost

Very Rev. John Henry Moses, PH.D. 1982

Canons Residentiary

P. G. Brett (1985); P. G. Southwell-Sander (1985); T. Thompson (1988).
Organist, G. Elliott, Ph.D., FRCO (1981).

Archdeacons

Colchester, Ven. E. C. F. Stroud 1983
Southend, Ven. J. S. Bailey 1982
West Ham, Ven. R. F. Sainsbury 1988

Chancellor, Miss S. M. Cameron, QC (1970).
Diocesan Registrar, B. Hood, Guy Harlings, New Street, Chelmsford CM1 1NG.

CHICHESTER

Stipendiary Male Clergy, 358
Stipendiary Women Deacons, 5.
102nd Bishop, Rt. Rev. Eric Waldram Kemp, DD, *cons.* 1974 (The Palace, Chichester PO19 1PY) [Signs Eric Cicestr:] 1974

Bishops Suffragan

Horsham, Rt. Rev. Ivor Colin Docker, *cons.* 1975 (Bishop's Lodge, Worth, nr. Crawley RH10 4RT) 1975
Lewes, Rt. Rev. Peter John Ball, *cons.* 1977 (Litlington Rectory, nr. Polegate BN26 5RB) . 1977

Assistant Bishops

Rt. Rev. William Hunt (*cons.* 1955), 1980; Rt. Rev. Mark Green (*cons.* 1972), 1982; Rt. Rev. Simon Phipps (*cons.* 1968), 1987; Rt. Rev. Edward Knapp-Fisher (*cons.* 1960), 1987; Rt. Rev. Morris Maddocks (*cons.* 1972), 1987.

Dean

Very Rev. John David Treadgold, LVO 1989

Canons Residentiary

R. T. Greenacre (1975); J. F. Hester (1985).
Organist, A. J. Thurlow, FRCO (1980).

Archdeacons

Chichester, Ven. K. Hobbs 1981
Horsham, Ven. W. C. L. Filby 1983
Lewes and Hastings, Rt. Rev. C. C. Luxmoore .. 1989

Chancellor, His Honour Judge Q. T. Edwards, QC (1978).
Legal Secretary to the Bishop, and Diocesan Registrar, C. L. Hodgetts, 5 East Pallant, Chichester PO19 1TS.

COVENTRY

Stipendiary Male Clergy, 173
Stipendiary Women Deacons, 10.
7th Bishop, Rt. Rev. Simon Barrington-Ward, *cons.* 1985 (The Bishop's House, 23 Davenport Road, Coventry CV5 6PW) [Signs Simon Coventry] 1985

Bishop Suffragan

Warwick, Rt. Rev. George Clive Handford, *cons.* 1990 (139 Kenilworth Road, Coventry CV4 7AF) 1990

Assistant Bishops

Rt. Rev. John Daly (*cons.* 1935), 1968; Rt. Rev. Vernon Nicholls (*cons.* 1974), 1984.

Provost

Very Rev. John Fitzmaurice Petty 1987

Canons Residentiary

P. Oestreicher (1986); M. Sadgrove (1987); D. A. Carrette (1988).
Organist, A. P. Wright, FRCO (1984).

Archdeacons

Coventry, Ven. H. I. L. Russell 1989
Warwick, Ven. M. J. J. Paget-Wilkes 1990

Chancellor, W. M. Gage (1980).
Registrar, D. J. Dumbleton, 8 The Quadrant, Coventry CV1 2EL.

DERBY

Stipendiary Male Clergy, 217
Stipendiary Women Deacons, 14.
5th Bishop, Rt. Rev. Peter Spencer Dawes, *cons.* 1988 (The Bishop's House, 6 King Street, Duffield, Derby DE6 4EU) [Signs Peter Derby] 1988

Bishop Suffragan

Repton, Rt. Rev. Francis Henry Arthur Richmond, *cons.* 1986 (Repton House, Lea, Matlock DE4 5JP) 1986

Provost

Very Rev. Benjamin Hugh Lewers 1981

Canons Residentiary

Ven. R. S. Dell (1981); I. Gatford (1984); G. R. Orchard (1986); G. A. Chesterman (1989).
Organist, P. Gould, FRCO (1982).

Archdeacons

Chesterfield, Ven. G. R. Phizackerley 1978
Derby, Ven. R. S. Dell 1973

Chancellor, J. W. M. Bullimore (1981).
Registrar, J. S. Battie, Derby Church House, Full Street, Derby DE1 3DR.

ELY

Stipendiary Male Clergy, 166
Stipendiary Women Deacons, 5.
67th *Bishop*, Rt. Rev. Stephen Whitfield Sykes, *cons.* 1990 (The Bishop's House, Ely CB7 4DW)
[Signs Stephen Ely].........................1990

Bishop Suffragan

Huntingdon, Rt. Rev. William Gordon Roe, D.Phil., *cons.* 1980 (14 Lynn Road, Ely, Cambs. CB6 1DA) 1980

Dean, vacant.

Canons Residentiary

D. J. Green (1980); J. Rone (1989).
Organist, P. Trepte.

Archdeacons

Ely, Ven. D. Walser 1981
Huntingdon, Ven. R. K. Sledge...............1978
Wisbech, Ven. D. Fleming 1984

Chancellor, W. Gage, QC.
Registrar, W. H. Godfrey, 18 The Broadway, St. Ives, Huntingdon PE17 4BS.
Joint Registrar, P. F. B. Beesley, 1 The Sanctuary, SW1P 3JT.

EXETER

Stipendiary Male Clergy, 291
Stipendiary Women Deacons, 9.
69th *Bishop*, Rt. Rev. Geoffrey Hewlett Thompson, *cons.* 1974 (The Palace, Exeter EX1 1HY)
[Signs Hewlett Exon:] 1985

Bishops Suffragan

Crediton, Rt. Rev. Peter Everard Coleman, *cons.* 1984 (10 The Close, Exeter EX1 1EZ) 1984
Plymouth, Rt. Rev. Richard Stephen Hawkins, *cons.* 1988 (31 Riverside Walk, Tamerton Foliot, Plymouth PL5 4AQ).................1988

Assistant Bishops

Rt. Rev. Ronald Goodchild (*cons.* 1964), 1983; Rt. Rev. Philip Pasterfield (*cons.* 1974), 1984; Rt. Rev. Richard Cartwright (*cons.* 1972), 1988.

Dean

Very Rev. Richard Montague Stephens Eyre ...1981

Canons Residentiary

J. A. Thurmer (1973); A. C. Mawson (1979); Ven. J. Richards (1981).
Organist, L. Nethsingha, FRCO (1972).

Archdeacons

Barnstaple, Ven. T. Lloyd 1989
Exeter, Ven. J. Richards 1981
Plymouth, Ven. R. G. Ellis 1982
Totnes, Ven. A. F. Tremlett...................1988

Chancellor, D. C. Calcutt, QC (1971).
Registrar, J. F. G. Michelmore, TD, 18 Cathedral Yard, Exeter EX1 1HE.
Diocesan Secretary, Rev. R. R. Huddleson, Diocesan House, Palace Gate, Exeter EX1 1HX.

GIBRALTAR IN EUROPE

1st *Bishop*, Rt. Rev. John Richard Satterthwaite, *cons.* 1970 (5A Gregory Place, W8 4NG) [Signs John Gibraltar] 1970

Bishop Suffragan

In Europe, Rt. Rev. Edward Holland 1986

Auxiliary Bishops

Rt. Rev. E. M. H. Capper, OBE, (*cons.* 1967), 1973; Rt. Rev. D. de Pina Cabral, (*cons.* 1967), 1976; Rt. Rev. A. W. M. Weeks, CB, (*cons.* 1977), 1988.

Vicar-General, Rev. Canon P. O. Deacon.
Bishop's Commissaries, Canon L. Tyzack; Canon J. D. Beckwith; Canon D. H. Palmer; A. M. Apostol.
Dean, Cathedral Church of the Holy Trinity, Gibraltar, Very Rev. B. W. Horlock, OBE.
Chancellor, Pro-Cathedral of St. Paul, Valletta, Malta, Canon P. Cousins.
Chancellor, Pro-Cathedral of the Holy Trinity, Brussels, Belgium, Ven. J. Lewis.

Archdeacons

Aegean, Ven. G. B. Evans.
North-west Europe, Ven. J. Lewis.
North France, Ven. M. B. Lea.
Gibraltar, Rt. Rev. D. de Pina Cabral.
Italy, Ven. G. L. C. Westwell.
Riviera, Ven. J. Livingstone.
Scandinavia, Ven. G. A. C. Brown.
Switzerland, Ven. P. J. Hawker.

Chancellor, D. Calcutt, QC.
Diocesan Registrar and Legal Secretary, J. G. Underwood, 37A Walbrook, EC4 8BS.

GLOUCESTER

Stipendiary Male Clergy, 185
Stipendiary Women Deacons, 7.
37th *Bishop*, Rt. Rev. John Yates, *cons.* 1972 (Bishopscourt, Gloucester GL1 2BQ) [Signs John Gloucestr] 1975

Bishop Suffragan

Tewkesbury, Rt. Rev. Geoffrey David Jeremy Walsh, *cons.* 1986 (Green Acre, Hempsted, Gloucester GL2 6LS) 1986

Dean

Very Rev. Kenneth Neal Jennings 1982

Canons Residentiary

D. C. St. V. Welander (1975); A. L. Dunstan (1978); R. D. M. Grey (1982); P. R. Greenwood (1986).
Organist, J. D. Sanders, FRCO (1967).

Archdeacons

Cheltenham, Ven. J. A. Lewis.................1988
Gloucester, Ven. C. J. H. Wagstaff 1982

Chancellor & Vicar-Gen., vacant.
Registrar, C. G. Peak, 34 Brunswick Road, Gloucester GL1 1JW.
Diocesan Secretary, R. Anderton, Church House, College Green, Gloucester GL1 2LY.

GUILDFORD

Stipendiary Male Clergy, 201
Stipendiary Women Deacons, 12.
7th *Bishop*, Rt. Rev. Michael Edgar Adie, *cons.* 1983 (Willow Grange, Woking Road, Guildford GU4 7QS) [Signs Michael Guildford] 1983

Bishop Suffragan

Dorking, Rt. Rev. David Peter Wilcox, *cons.* 1986 (13 Pilgrims Way, Guildford GU4 8AD) 1986

Dean

Very Rev. Alexander Gillan Wedderspoon 1987

Canons Residentiary

F. S. Telfer (1973); P. G. Croft (1983).
Organist, A. T. S. Millington, FRCO (1983).

Archdeacons

Dorking, Ven. C.W. Herbert 1990
Surrey, Ven. J. S. Went 1989
Chancellor, M. B. Goodman.
Legal Secretary and Registrar, P. F. B. Beesley, 1
The Sanctuary, SW1P 3JT.

HEREFORD

Stipendiary Male Clergy, 140
Stipendiary Women Deacons, 3.
103*rd Bishop*, Rt. Rev. John Oliver, *cons.* 1990
(The Palace, Hereford HR4 9BN) [signs John
Hereford] 1990

Bishop Suffragan

Ludlow, Rt. Rev. Ian MacDonald Griggs, *cons.*
1987 (Halford Vicarage, Craven Arms, Shropshire SY7 9BT)............................1987

Dean

Very Rev. Peter Haynes......................1982

Canons Residentiary

Ven. A. H. Woodhouse (1982); P. Iles (1983); J.
Tiller (1984).
Organist, R. Massey, FRCO (1974).

Archdeacons

Hereford, Ven. A. H. Woodhouse 1982
Ludlow, Ven. J. H. R. Lewis 1987
Chancellor, J. M. Henty.
Joint Registrars, V. T. Jordan, 44 Bridge Street,
Hereford; P. Beesley, 1 The Sanctuary, West-
minster, SW1P 3JT.

LEICESTER

Stipendiary Male Clergy, 178
Stipendiary Women Deacons, 12.
Bishop, vacant.

Assistant Bishops

Rt. Rev. John Mort, CBE (*cons.* 1952) 1972; Rt.
Rev. Godfrey Ashby, (*cons.* 1980) 1988.

Provost

Very Rev. Alan Christopher Warren 1978

Canons Residentiary

M. T. H. Banks (1988); M. Wilson (1988).
Organist, P. White, FRCO (1968).

Archdeacons

Leicester, Ven. R. D. Silk 1980
Loughborough, Ven. T. H. Jones 1986
Chancellor, N. Seed (1989).
Registrar, G. K. J. Moore, 10 Friar Lane, Leicester
LE1 5QD.

LICHFIELD

Stipendiary Male Clergy, 426
Stipendiary Women Deacons, 24.
97*th Bishop*, Rt. Rev. Keith Norman Sutton,
cons. 1978 (Bishop's House, The Close, Lichfield
WS13 7LG) [Signs Keith Lichfield] 1984

Bishops Suffragan

Shrewsbury, Rt. Rev. John Dudley Davies, *cons.*
1987 (Athlone House, 68 London Road, Shrewsbury SY2 6PG) 1987
Stafford, Rt. Rev. Michael Charles Scott-Joynt,
cons. 1987 (Ash Garth, Broughton Crescent,
Barlaston ST12 9DD)......................1987
Wolverhampton, Rt. Rev. Christopher John Mayfield, *cons.* 1985 (61 Richmond Road, Wolverhampton WV3 9JH) 1985

Dean

Very Rev. John Harley Lang 1980

Canons Residentiary

Ven. R. B. Ninis (1974); A. N. Barnard (1977);
W. J. Turner (1983); J. Howe (1988).
Organist, J. Rees-Williams, FRCO (1978).

Archdeacons

Lichfield, Ven. R. B. Ninis 1974
Salop, Ven. G. Frost 1987
Stoke-on-Trent, Ven. D. Ede 1989
Chancellor, Judge J. A. O. Shand.
Diocesan Registrar, J. P. Thorneycroft, St.
Mary's House, The Close, Lichfield WS13 7LD.

LINCOLN

Stipendiary Male Clergy, 258
Stipendiary Women Deacons, 15.
70*th Bishop*, Rt. Rev. Robert Maynard Hardy,
cons. 1980 (Bishop's House, Eastgate, Lincoln
LN2 1QQ) [Signs Robert Lincoln] 1987

Bishops Suffragan

Grantham, Rt. Rev. William Ind, *cons.* 1987
(Fairacre, Barrowby High Road, Grantham
NG31 8NP) 1987
Grimsby, Rt. Rev. David Tustin, *cons.* 1979 (43
Abbey Park Road, Grimsby DN32 0HS) 1979

Assistant Bishops

Rt. Rev. Gerald Colin (*cons.* 1966), 1979; Rt. Rev.
Harold Darby (*cons.* 1975) 1989.

Dean

Very Rev. Brandon Donald Jackson 1989

Canons Residentiary

D. C. Rutter (1965); B. R. Davis (1977); J. S.
Nurser, PH.D. (1977); Ven. J. H. C. Laurence
(1985).
Organist, C. Walsh, FRCO (1988).

Archdeacons

Lincoln, Ven. M. P. Brackenbury 1988
Lindsey, Ven. J. H. C. Laurence 1985
Stow, Ven. R. J. Wells 1989
Chancellor, His Honour Judge M. B. Goodman (1971).
Registrar and Legal Secretary, D. M. Wellman, 28
West Parade, Lincoln LN1 1JT.

NORWICH

Stipendiary Male Clergy, 238
Stipendiary Women Deacons, 7.
70*th Bishop*, Rt. Rev. Peter John Nott, *cons.* 1977
(Bishop's House, Norwich, NR3 1SB) [Signs
Peter Norvic:] 1985

Bishops Suffragan

Lynn, Rt. Rev. David Edward Bentley, *cons.* 1986
(The Old Vic, Castle Acre, King's Lynn PE32
2AA) 1986
Thetford, Rt. Rev. Timothy Dudley-Smith, *cons.*
1981 (Rectory Meadow, Bramerton, Norwich
NR14 7DW)...............................1981

Dean

Very Rev. John Paul Burbridge...............1983

Canons Residentiary

D. H. Bishop (1980); C. Beswick (1984); M. S.
McLean (1986).
Organist, M. B. Nicholas, FRCO (1971).

Archdeacons

Lynn, Ven. A. C. Foottit 1987
Norfolk, Ven. P. Dawson 1977
Norwich, Ven. A. M. Handley 1981

Chancellor, His Hon. J. H. Ellison, VRD (1955).
Registrar and Sec., B. O. L. Prior, MBE, TD, 74 The Close, Norwich NR1 4DE.

OXFORD

Stipendiary Male Clergy, 449
Stipendiary Women Deacons, 23.
41*st Bishop*, Rt. Rev. Richard Douglas Harries, *cons.* 1987 (Diocesan Church House, North Hinksey, Oxford OX2 0NB) [Signs Richard Oxon:] 1987

Area Bishops

Buckingham, Rt. Rev. Simon Hedley Burrows, *cons.* 1974 (Sheridan, Grimms Hill, Great Missenden HP16 9BD) 1974
Dorchester, Rt. Rev. Anthony Russell, *cons.* 1988 Holmby House, Sibford Ferris, Banbury, Oxon. OX15 5RG. 1988
Reading, Rt. Rev. John Frank Ewan Bone, *cons.* 1989 (Greenbanks, Old Bath Road, Sonning, Reading RG4 0SY).........................1989

Assistant Bishops

Rt. Rev. Albert Cragg, DD, (*cons.* 1970), 1982; Rt. Rev. Eric Wild, (*cons.* 1972), 1982; Rt. Rev. Leonard Ashton, CB, (*cons.* 1974), 1984; Rt. Rev. Richard Watson (*cons.* 1970), 1988; Rt. Rev. Peter Walker (*cons.* 1972), 1990.

Dean of Christ Church

Very Rev. Eric William Heaton 1979

Canons Residentiary

M. F. Wiles, (1970); J. C. Fenton (1978); Ven. F. V. Weston (1982); O. M. T. O'Donovan, D.Phil. (1982); R. D. Williams, D.Phil. (1985); J. M. Pierce (1987).
Organist, S. Darlington, FRCO.

Archdeacons

Berkshire, Ven. D. Griffiths....................1987
Buckingham, Ven. J. A. Morrison 1989
Oxford, Ven. F. V. Weston 1982

Chancellor, P. T. S. Boydell, QC (1958).
Registrar and Legal Secretary, F. E. Robson, 16 Beaumont Street, Oxford OX1 2LZ.

WINDSOR

The Queen's Free Chapel of St. George within Her Castle of Windsor (A Royal Peculiar)
Dean, Very Rev. Patrick Reynolds Mitchell, FSA......................................1989

Canons Residentiary

J. A. White (1982); D. M. Stanesby (1985); A. A. Coldwells (1987); D. M. Moxon (1990).
Organist, C. J. Robinson, LVO, FRCO (1975).
Chapter Clerk, Lt.-Col. N. J. Newman (1990).

PETERBOROUGH

Stipendiary Male Clergy, 183
Stipendiary Women Deacons, 9.
36*th Bishop*, Rt. Rev. William John Westwood, *cons.* 1975 (The Palace, Peterborough PE1 1YA) [Signs William Petriburg:] 1984

Bishop Suffragan

Brixworth, Rt. Rev. Paul Everard Barber, *cons.* 1989 (4 The Avenue, Dallington, Northampton NN1 4RZ) 1989

Dean

Very Rev. Randolph George Wise 1981

Canons Residentiary

T. R. Christie (1980); J. Higham (1983); T. Willmott (1989).
Organist, C. S. Gower, FRCO (1977).

Archdeacons

Northampton, Ven. B. R. Marsh 1964
Oakham, Ven. B. Fernyhough 1977

Chancellor, T. A. C. Coningsby, QC (1989).
Registrar and Legal Secretary, R. Hemingray, 10 Queen Street, Peterborough PE1 1PH.

PORTSMOUTH

Stipendiary Male Clergy, 135
Stipendiary Women Deacons, 9.
7*th Bishop*, Rt. Rev. Timothy John Bavin, *cons.* 1974 (Bishopswood, Fareham, Hants. PO14 1NT) [Signs Timothy Portsmouth] 1985

Provost

Very Rev. David Staffurth Stancliffe 1982

Canons Residentiary

R. Eckersley (1984); M. D. Doe (1989); C. J. Bradley (1990); D. T. Isaac (1990).
Organist, A. Froggatt, FRCO.

Archdeacons

Isle of Wight, Ven. A. H. M. Turner 1986
Portsmouth, Ven. N. H. Crowder 1985

Chancellor, His Honour Judge Aglionby (1978).
Registrar, Miss H. A. G. Tyler, 132 High Street, Portsmouth PO1 2HR.

ROCHESTER

Stipendiary Male Clergy, 227
Stipendiary Women Deacons, 13.
105*th Bishop*, Rt. Rev. Anthony Michael Arnold Turnbull, *cons.* 1988 (Bishopscourt, Rochester ME1 1TS) [Signs Michael Roffen:] 1988

Bishop Suffragan

Tonbridge, Rt. Rev. David Henry Bartleet, *cons.* 1982 (Bishop's Lodge, St. Botolph's Road, Sevenoaks TN13 3AG) 1982

Dean

Very Rev. Edward Frank Shotter 1990

Canons Residentiary

E. R. Turner (1981); R. J. R. Lea (1988); J. Armson (1989); N. Warren (1989).
Organist, B. Ferguson, FRCO (1977).

Archdeacons

Bromley, Ven. E. R. Francis 1979
Rochester, Ven. N. L. Warren 1989
Tonbridge, Ven. R. J. Mason 1977

Chancellor, His Honour Judge M. B. Goodman (1971).
Registrar, O. R. Woodfield, The Precinct, Rochester ME1 1SZ.
Secretary, D. W. Faull, 35 Great Peter Street, SW1P 3LR.

ST. ALBANS

Stipendiary Male Clergy, 309
Stipendiary Women Deacons, 23.
8th *Bishop*, Rt. Rev. John Bernard Taylor, *cons.*
1980 (Abbey Gate House, St. Albans AL3 4HD)
[Signs John St. Albans] 1980

Bishops Suffragan

Bedford, Rt. Rev. David John Farmbrough, *cons.*
1981 (168 Kimbolton Road, Bedford MK41
8DN)......................................1981
Hertford, Rt. Rev. Robin Jonathan Norman
Smith, *cons.* 1990 (Hertford House, Abbey Mill
Lane, St. Albans AL3 4HE) 1990

Dean

Very Rev. Peter Clement Moore, D.Phil.........1973

Canons Residentiary

B. C. E. Pettifer; C. B. Slee (1982); C. Garner
(1984); G. R. S. Ritson (1987); M. Sansom (1988).
Organist, B. Rose, FRCO (1988).

Archdeacons

Bedford, Ven. M. G. Bourke 1986
St. Albans, Ven. P. B. Davies 1987
Chancellor, G. H. Newsom, QC (1958).
Registrar and Legal Sec., D. N. Cheetham,
Holywell Lodge, 41 Holywell Hill, St. Albans
AL1 1HE.

ST. EDMUNDSBURY AND IPSWICH

Stipendiary Male Clergy, 187
Stipendiary Women Deacons, 8.
8th *Bishop*, Rt. Rev. John Dennis, *cons.* 1979
(Bishop's House, Ipswich IP1 3ST) [Signs John
St. Edmunds & Ipswich] 1986

Bishop Suffragan

Dunwich, Rt. Rev. Eric Nash Devenport, *cons.*
1980 (The Old Vicarage, Stowupland, Stow-
market IP14 4BQ) 1980

Provost

Very Rev. Raymond Furnell..................1981

Canons Residentiary

G. J. Tarris (1982); R. Garrard (1987); A. M.
Shaw (1989).

Archdeacons

Ipswich, Ven. T. A. Gibson 1987
Sudbury, Ven. D. J. Smith 1984
Suffolk, Ven. N. Robinson 1987
Chancellor, His Honour Judge Blofeld, QC (1974).
Registrar, J. D. Mitson, 22–28 Museum Street,
Ipswich IP1 1JA.

SALISBURY

Stipendiary Male Clergy, 264
Stipendiary Women Deacons, 7.
76th *Bishop*, Rt. Rev. John Austin Baker, *cons.*
1982 (South Canonry, The Close, Salisbury SP1
2ER) [Signs John Sarum]...................1982

Bishops Suffragan

Ramsbury, Rt. Rev. Peter St. George Vaughan,
cons. 1989 (Bishop's House, Urchfont, Devizes,
Wilts. SN10 4QU) 1989
Sherborne, Rt. Rev. John Dudley Galtrey Kirk-
ham, *cons.* 1976 (Little Bailie, Sturminster
Marshall, Wimborne BH21 4AD) 1976

Assistant Bishop

Rt. Rev. John Cavell, (*cons.* 1972) 1988

Dean

Very Rev. the Hon. Hugh Geoffrey Dickinson ..1986

Canons Residentiary

I. G. D. Dunlop, FSA (1972); D. J. C. Davies (1985);
J. R. Stewart (1990).
Organist, R. G. Seal, FRCO (1968).

Archdeacons

Dorset, Ven. G. E. Walton 1982
Sarum, Ven. B. J. Hopkinson 1986
Sherborne, Ven. J. K. Oliver 1985
Wilts, Ven. B. J. Smith 1980
Chancellor of the Diocese, His Hon. J. H. Ellison,
VRD (1955).
Registrar and Legal Secretary, F. M. Broadbent,
42 Castle Street, Salisbury SP1 3TX.

SOUTHWARK

Stipendiary Male Clergy, 396
Stipendiary Women Deacons, 31.
7th *Bishop*, Rt. Rev. Ronald Oliver Bowlby, *cons.*
1973, *trs.* 1980 (Bishop's House, 38 Tooting Bec
Gardens, SW16 1QZ) [Signs Ronald South-
wark] 1980

Bishops Suffragan

Croydon, Rt. Rev. Wilfred Denniston Wood, DD,
cons. 1985 (St. Matthew's House, George
Street, Croydon CR0 1PE) 1985
Kingston upon Thames, Rt. Rev. Peter Stephen
Maurice Selby, PH.D., *cons.* 1984 (*Office.—*
Whitelands College, West Hill, SW15 3SN) ...1984
Woolwich, Rt. Rev. Albert Peter Hall, *cons.* 1984
(8B Hillyfields Crescent, SE4 1QA) 1984

Assistant Bishops

Rt. Rev. Edmund Capper, OBE (*cons.* 1967), 1981;
Rt. Rev. Archibald Gordon (*cons.* 1975), 1984;
Rt. Rev. John Hughes (*cons.* 1956), 1986; Rt.
Rev. Hugh Montefiore (*cons.* 1970), 1987; Rt.
Rev. Simon Phipps (*cons.* 1976), 1987; Rt. Rev.
Colin Buchanan (*cons.* 1985), 1989; Rt. Rev.
Michael Nazir-Ali (*cons.* 1984), 1990.

Provost

Very Rev. David Lawrence Edwards 1983

Canons Residentiary

P. H. Penwarden (1971); I. G. Smith-Cameron
(1972); J. S. Cox (1983); P. B. Price (1988).
Organist, P. Wright (1989).

Archdeacons

Croydon, Ven. F. R. Hazell....................1984
Lambeth, Ven. C. R. B. Bird 1988
Lewisham, Ven. G. Kuhrt 1989
Reigate, Ven. P. B. Coombs 1988
Southwark, Ven. D. L. Bartles-Smith 1985
Wandsworth, Ven. D. Gerrard 1989
Chancellor, vacant.
Registrar, D. W. Faull, 35 Great Peter Street,
SW1P 3LR.

TRURO

Stipendiary Male Clergy, 149
Stipendiary Women Deacons, 2.
13th *Bishop*, Rt. Rev. Michael Thomas Ball, *cons.*
1980 (Lis Escop, Truro, TR3 6QQ) [Signs
Michael Truron] 1990

Bishop Suffragan

St. Germans, Rt. Rev. Richard Llewellin, *cons.*
1986 (32 Falmouth Road, Truro TR1 2HX) ...1985

Assistant Bishop

Rt. Rev. Richard Cartwright (*cons.* 1972) 1982

Dean

Very Rev. David John Shearlock...............1982

Canons Residentiary

W. J. P. Boyd, ph.D. (1985); Ven. R. L. Ravenscroft
(1988); R. O. Osborne (1988).
Organist, D. J. Briggs, FRCO (1989).

Archdeacons

Cornwall, Ven. R. L. Ravenscroft 1988
Bodmin, Ven. R. D. C. Whiteman 1989

Chancellor, P. T. S. Boydell, QC (1957).
Registrar and Secretary, M. J. Follett, 2 Princes
Street, Truro TR1 2EZ.

WORCESTER

Stipendiary Male Clergy, 150
Stipendiary Women Deacons, 14.
111th *Bishop*, Rt. Rev. Philip Harold Ernest
Goodrich, *cons.* 1973 (The Bishop's House,
Hartlebury Castle, Kidderminster DY11 7XX)
[Signs Philip Worcester] 1982

Bishop Suffragan

Dudley, Rt. Rev. Anthony Charles Dumper, *cons.*
1977 (The Bishop's House, Brooklands, Halesowen Road, Cradley Heath B64 7JF).........1977

Assistant Bishops

Rt. Rev. David Allenby (*cons.* 1962), 1968; Rt.
Rev. Oliver Tomkins (*cons.* 1959), 1975; Rt.
Rev. John Maund, CBE, MC (*cons.* 1950), 1984;
Rt. Rev. Kenneth Woollcombe (*cons.* 1971),
1989; Rt. Rev. George Briggs (*cons.* 1973), 1990.

Dean

Very Rev. Robert Martin Colquhoun Jeffery ...1987

Canons Residentiary

Ven. F. Bentley (1984); D. G. Thomas (1987); I.
M. MacKenzie (1989).
Organist, D. Hunt, MUS.D., FRCO (1975).

Archdeacons

Dudley, Ven. J. Gathercole 1987
Worcester, Ven. F. Bentley 1984

Chancellor, P. T. S. Boydell, QC (1959).
Registrar, Rev. Canon J. A. Dale, Diocesan
Registry, The Old Palace, Deansway, Worces-
ter WR1 2JE.

Province of York

YORK

Stipendiary Male Clergy, 322
Stipendiary Women Deacons, 17.
95th *Archbishop and Primate of England* Most
Rev. and Rt. Hon. John Stapylton Habgood,
ph.D., *cons.* 1973, *trs.* 1983 (Bishopthorpe, York
YO2 1QE) [Signs John Ebor:] 1983

Bishops Suffragan

Hull, Rt. Rev. Donald George Snelgrove, TD,
cons. 1981 (Hullen House, Woodfield Lane,
Hessle, Hull HU13 0ES) 1981
Selby, Rt. Rev. Clifford Conder Barker, TD, *cons.*
1976 (8 Bankside Close, Upper Poppleton, York
YO2 6LH) 1983
Whitby, Rt. Rev. Gordon Bates, *cons.* 1983 (60
West Green, Stokesley, Middlesbrough
TS9 5BD) 1983

Assistant Bishops

Rt. Rev. George Cockin (*cons.* 1959), 1969; Rt.
Rev. Richard Wimbush (*cons.* 1963), 1977; Rt.
Rev. Richard Wood (*cons.* 1973), 1985; Rt. Rev.
Ronald Foley (*cons.* 1982), 1989.

Dean

Very Rev. John Eliot Southgate 1984

Canons Residentiary

R. A. Hockley (1976); R. Mayland (1982); J. Toy,
ph.D. (1983); R. Metcalfe (1988).
Organist, P. J. Moore, FRCO.

Archdeacons

Cleveland, Ven. R. J. Woodley 1984
East Riding, Ven. H. F. Buckingham 1988
York, Ven. G. B. Austin 1988

*Official Principal and Auditor of the Chancery
Court*, J. A. D. Owen, QC.
Chancellor of the Diocese, T. A. C. Coningsby, QC
(1977).

*Vicar-General of the Province and Official Prin-
cipal of the Consistory Court*, T. A. C. Coningsby, QC.
Registrar and Legal Secretary, L. P. M. Lennox,
1 Peckitt Street, York YO1 1SG.

DURHAM

Stipendiary Male Clergy, 285
Stipendiary Women Deacons, 17.
92nd *Bishop*, Rt. Rev. David Edward Jenkins,
cons. 1984 (Auckland Castle, Bishop Auckland
DL14 7NR) [Signs David Dunelm] 1984

Bishop Suffragan

Jarrow, Rt. Rev. Alan Smithson, *cons.* 1990.....1990

Dean

Very Rev. John Robert Arnold 1989

Canons Residentiary

Ven. M. C. Perry (1970); R. L. Coppin (1974);
Ven. J. D. Hodgson (1983); T. Hart (1983).
Organist, J. B. Lancelot, FRCO (1985).

Archdeacons

Auckland, Ven. J. D. Hodgson 1983
Durham, Ven. M. C. Perry 1970

Chancellor, Judge R. D. H. Bursell, QC (1989).
Registrar and Legal Secretary, D. M. Robertson,
Diocesan Registry, Auckland Castle, Bishop
Auckland DL14 7QJ (1988).

BLACKBURN

Stipendiary Male Clergy, 267
Stipendiary Women Deacons, 3.
7th *Bishop*, Rt. Rev. Alan David Chesters, *cons.*
1989 (Bishop's House, Ribchester Road, Blackburn BB1 9EF) [Signs Alan Blackburn] 1989

Bishops Suffragan

Burnley, Rt. Rev. Ronald James Milner, *cons.* 1988 (Dean House, 449 Padiham Road, Burnley BB12 6TE) 1988

Lancaster, Rt. Rev. John Nicholls, *cons.* 1990 (Wheatfields, 7 Dallas Road, Lancaster LA1 1TN) 1990

Provost

Very Rev. Lawrence Jackson 1973

Canons Residentiary

J. M. Taylor (1976); B. M. Beaumont (1977); G. I. Hirst (1987); M. A. Kitchener (1990).
Organist, D. A. Cooper, FRCO (1983).

Archdeacons

Blackburn, Ven. W. D. Robinson 1986
Lancaster, Ven. K. H. Gibbons 1989

Chancellor, J. W. M. Bullimore (1990).
Registrar, D. A. Smith, Diocesan Registry, Cathedral Close, Blackburn BB1 5AB (1990).

BRADFORD

Stipendiary Male Clergy, 136
Stipendiary Women Deacons, 8.
7th Bishop, Rt. Rev. Robert Kerr Williamson, *cons.* 1984 (Bishopscroft, Ashwell Road, Heaton, Bradford BD9 4AU) [Signs Robert Bradford]..................................1984

Assistant Bishop

Rt. Rev. David Evans (*cons.* 1978) 1988

Provost

Very Rev. John Stephen Richardson 1990

Canons Residentiary

K. H. Cook (1977); C. J. Hayward (1983).
Organist, A. Horsey (1986).

Archdeacons

Bradford, Ven. D. H. Shreeve 1984
Craven, Ven. B. A. Smith 1987

Chancellor, D. M. Savill, QC (1976).
Registrar and Secretary, J. G. H. Mackrell, 6–14 Devonshire Street, Keighley BD21 2AY (1977).

CARLISLE

Stipendiary Male Clergy, 191
Stipendiary Women Deacons, 4.
65th Bishop, Rt. Rev. Ian Harland, *cons.* 1985 (Rose Castle, Dalston, Carlisle CA5 7BZ), [Signs Ian Carliol:] 1989

Bishop Suffragan

Penrith, Rt. Rev. George Lanyon Hacker, *cons.* 1979 (The Rectory, Great Salkeld, Penrith CA11 9NA) 1979

Dean

Very Rev. Henry Edward Champneys Stapleton 1988

Canons Residentiary

R. A. Chapman (1978); Ven. C. P. Stannard (1984); R. C. Johns (1989).
Organist, R. A. Seivewright (1960).

Archdeacons

Carlisle, Ven. C. P. Stannard 1984
West Cumberland, Ven. T. R. B. Hodgson 1979
Westmorland and Furness, Ven. L. J. Peat 1989

Chancellor, His Hon. D. J. Stinson (1971).
Registrar and Secretary, I. S. Sutcliffe, Castle Street, Carlisle CA3 8TW (1964).

CHESTER

Stipendiary Male Clergy, 312
Stipendiary Women Deacons, 9.
39th Bishop, Rt. Rev. Michael Alfred Baughen, *cons.* 1982 (Bishop's House, Chester CH1 2JD) [Signs Michael Cestr:] 1982

Bishops Suffragan

Birkenhead, Rt. Rev. Ronald Brown, *cons.* 1974 (Trafford House, Queen's Park, Chester CH4 7AX) 1974

Stockport, Rt. Rev. Frank Pilkington Sargeant, *cons.* 1984 (32 Park Gate Drive, Cheadle Hulme, Cheshire SK8 7DF) 1984

Dean

Very Rev. Stephen Stewart Smalley 1986

Canons Residentiary

W. H. Vanstone (1978); C. D. Biddell (1986); R. M. Rees (1990); C. J. Bennetts (1990).
Organist, R. A. Fisher, FRCO (1967).

Archdeacons

Chester, Ven. M. F. Gear 1988
Macclesfield, Ven. J. S. Gaisford 1986

Chancellor, H. H. Lomas (1977).
Registrar and Legal Secretary, A. K. McAllester, Friars, 20 White Friars, Chester CH1 1XS.

LIVERPOOL

Stipendiary Male Clergy, 274
Stipendiary Women Deacons, 23.
6th Bishop, Rt. Rev. David Stuart Sheppard, *cons.* 1969 (Bishop's Lodge, Woolton Park, Liverpool L25 6DT) [Signs David Liverpool] 1975

Bishop Suffragan

Warrington, Rt. Rev. Michael Henshall, *cons.* 1976 (Martinsfield, Elm Avenue, Great Crosby, Liverpool L23 2SX) 1976

Assistant Bishops

Rt. Rev. William Baker (*cons.* 1943), 1968; Rt. Rev. Graham Chadwick (*cons.* 1976), 1990.

Dean

Very Rev. Rhys Derrick Chamberlain Walters ..1983

Canons Residentiary

M. M. Wolfe (1982); D. J. Hutton (1983); K. J. Riley (1983); H. Thomas (1988).
Organist, I. Tracey (1980).

Archdeacons

Liverpool, Ven. G. H. G. Spiers 1979
Warrington, Ven. C. D. S. Woodhouse 1981

Chancellor, R. G. Hamilton.
Registrar and Cathedral Chapter Clerk, R. H. Arden, 1 Hanover Street, Liverpool L1 3DW.

MANCHESTER

Stipendiary Male Clergy, 366
Stipendiary Women Deacons, 17.
9th Bishop, Rt. Rev. Stanley Eric Francis Booth-Clibborn, *cons.* 1979 (Bishopscourt, Bury New Road, Manchester M7 0LE) [Signs Stanley Manchester] 1979

Bishops Suffragan

Bolton, Rt. Rev. David George Galliford, *cons.* 1984 (4 Sandfield Drive, Lostock, Bolton BL6 4DU)..................................1984

Hulme, Rt. Rev. Colin John Fraser Scott, *cons.*
1984 (1 Raynham Avenue, Didsbury, Manchester M20 0BW) 1984
Middleton, Rt. Rev. Donald Alexander Tytler, *cons.* 1982 (The Hollies, Manchester Road, Rochdale OL11 3QY) 1982

Assistant Bishop

Rt. Rev. Edward Wickham (*cons.* 1959) 1982

Dean

Very Rev. Robert Murray Waddington 1984

Canons Residentiary

Ven. R. B. Harris (1980); J. R. Atherton, PH.D. (1984); B. Duncan (1986); R. E. H. Johnson (1990).
Organist, G. Stewart.

Archdeacons

Bolton, Ven. W. S. Brison 1985
Manchester, Ven. R. B. Harris 1980
Rochdale, Ven. D. Bonser 1982
Chancellor, G. C. H. Spafford (1976).
Registrar and Bishop's Secretary, M. Darlington, 90 Deansgate, Manchester M3 2GH (1986).

NEWCASTLE

Stipendiary Male Clergy, 179
Stipendiary Women Deacons, 3.
10*th Bishop*, Rt. Rev. Andrew Alexander Kenny Graham, *cons.* 1977 (Bishop's House, 29 Moor Road South, Gosforth, Newcastle upon Tyne NE3 1PA) [Signs A. Newcastle]..............1981

Assistant Bishop

Rt. Rev. Kenneth Gill (*cons.* 1972)..............1980

Provost

Very Rev. Nicholas Guy Coulton 1990

Canons Residentiary

W. J. Thomas (1983); R. Langley (1985); P. R. Strange (1986); I. F. Bennett (1988).
Organist, T. Hone (1987).

Archdeacons

Lindisfarne, Ven. M. E. Bowering 1987
Northumberland, Ven. W. J. Thomas...........1983
Chancellor, His Hon. A. J. Blackett-Ord, CVO (1971).
Registrar and Secretary, R. R. V. Nicholson, 46 Grainger Street, Newcastle upon Tyne NE1 5LB.

RIPON

Stipendiary Male Clergy, 177
Stipendiary Women Deacons, 13.
11*th Bishop*, Rt. Rev. David Nigel de Lorentz Young, *cons.* 1977 (Bishop Mount, Ripon HG4 5DP) [Signs David Ripon] 1977

Bishop Suffragan

Knaresborough, Rt. Rev. Malcolm James Mennin, *cons.* 1986 (16 Shaftesbury Avenue, Roundhay, Leeds LS8 1DT).............................1986

Assistant Bishops

Rt. Rev. John Howe (*cons.* 1955) 1985; Rt. Rev. Ralph Emmerson (*cons.* 1972) 1986.

Dean

Very Rev. Christopher Russell Campling 1984

Canons Residentiary

R. B. McFadden (1979); D. G. Ford (1980); P. J. Marshall (1985).
Organist, R. Perrin, FRCO (1966).

Archdeacons

Leeds, Ven. A. J. Comber 1982
Richmond, Ven. N. G. L. R. McDermid 1983
Chancellor, D. M. Savill, QC (1987).
Registrar and Legal Secretary, J. R. Balmforth, York House, York Place, Knaresborough HG5 0AD.

SHEFFIELD

Stipendiary Male Clergy, 216
Stipendiary Women Deacons, 16.
5*th Bishop*, Rt. Rev. David Ramsay Lunn, *cons.* 1980 (Bishopscroft, Snaithing Lane, Sheffield S10 3LG) [Signs David Sheffield]............1980

Bishop Suffragan

Doncaster, Rt. Rev. William Michael Dermot Persson, *cons.* 1982 (Bishops Lodge, Rotherham S65 4PF)...................................1982

Assistant Bishops

Rt. Rev. Kenneth Skelton, CBE (*cons.* 1962), 1984; Rt. Rev. Kenneth Pillar (*cons.* 1982), 1989.

Provost

Very Rev. John Warren Gladwin 1988

Canons Residentiary

T. M. Page (1982); Ven. S. R. Lowe (1988); J. R. Giles (1988).
Organist, G. Matthews, FRCO (1967).

Archdeacons

Doncaster, Ven. D. Carnelley...................1985
Sheffield, Ven. S. R. Lowe 1988
Chancellor, G. B. Graham, QC (1971).
Registrar and Legal Secretary, C. P. Rothwell, 30 Bank Street, Sheffield S1 2DS.

SODOR AND MAN

Stipendiary Male Clergy, 25.
79*th Bishop*, Rt. Rev. Noel Debroy Jones, CB, *cons.* 1989 (The Bishop's House, Quarterbridge Road, Douglas, IOM) [Signs Noel Sodor and Man] ...1989

Canons Residentiary

B. H. Kelly (1980); D. Baggaley (1980); J. D. Gelling (1980); B. H. Partington (1985).

Archdeacon

Isle of Man, Ven. D. A. Willoughby 1982
Vicar-General and Registrar, P. W. S. Farrant, 24 Athol Street, Douglas.

SOUTHWELL

Stipendiary Male Clergy, 212
Stipendiary Women Deacons, 9.
9*th Bishop*, Rt. Rev. Patrick Burnet Harris, *cons.* 1973 (Bishop's Manor, Southwell NG25 0JR) [Signs Patrick Southwell] 1988

Bishop Suffragan

Sherwood, Rt. Rev. Alan Wyndham Morgan, *cons.* 1989 (Dunham House, Westgate, Southwell NG25 0JL)................................1989

Provost

Very Rev. John Murray Irvine 1978

Canons Residentiary

D. P. Keene (1981); I. G. Collins (1985).
Organist, P. R. Hale, FRCO (1989).

Archdeacons

Newark, Ven. D. Leaning 1980
Nottingham, vacant.

Chancellor, J. Shand (1981).
Registrar, P. H. Mellors, Diocesan Office, Westgate, Southwell NG25 0JL (1970).

WAKEFIELD

Stipendiary Male Clergy, 211
Stipendiary Women Deacons, 11.
10th Bishop, Rt. Rev. David Michael Hope, D.Phil., *cons.* 1985 (Bishop's Lodge, Woodthorpe Lane, Wakefield WF2 6JJ) [Signs David Wakefield]...............................1985

Bishop Suffragan

Pontefract, Rt. Rev. Thomas Richard Hare, *cons.* 1971 (306 Barnsley Road, Wakefield WF26AX)
1971

Provost

Very Rev. John Edward Allen. 1982
Organist, J. L. Bielby, FRCO (1971).

Archdeacons

Halifax, Ven. D. Hallett 1989
Pontefract, Ven. K. Unwin 1981

Chancellor, G. B. Graham, QC (1959).
Registrar and Sec., E. Chapman, Burton Street, Wakefield WF1 2DA (1979).

THE CHURCH IN WALES

9th Archbishop of Wales, Most Rev. George Noakes (Bishop of St. David's), *elected* 1987.

BANGOR

79th Bishop, Rt. Rev. John Cledan Mears, *b.* 1922, *cons.* 1982 (Tŷ'r Esgob, Bangor LL57 2SS) [Signs Cledan Bangor] 1982

LLANDAFF

101st Bishop, Rt. Rev. Roy Thomas Davies, *b.* 1934, *cons.* 1985 (Llys Esgob, The Cathedral Green, Llandaff, Cardiff CF5 2YE) [Signs Roy Landav]
1985

MONMOUTH

7th Bishop, Rt. Rev. Royston Clifford Wright, *b.* 1922, *cons.* 1986 (Bishopstow, Stow Hill, Newport NP9 4EA) [Signs Clifford Monmouth] 1986

ST. ASAPH

74th Bishop, Rt. Rev. Alwyn Rice Jones, *b.*, 1934, *cons.* 1982 (Esgobty, St. Asaph, Clwyd LL17 0TW) [Signs Alwyn St. Asaph] 1982

ST. DAVID'S

124th Bishop and 9th Archbishop of Wales, Most Rev. George Noakes, *b.* 1924, *cons.* 1982 (Llys Esgob, Abergwili, Dyfed SA31 2JG) [Signs George Cambrensis] 1982

SWANSEA AND BRECON

7th Bishop, Rt. Rev. Dewi Morris Bridges, *b.* 1933, *cons.* 1988 (Ely Tower, Brecon, Powys LD3 9DE) [Signs Dewi Swansea & Brecon] 1988

(Stipend of diocesan bishop of the Church in Wales is £21,025 p.a. from Jan. 1, 1991)

THE EPISCOPAL CHURCH IN SCOTLAND

Primus of the Episcopal Church in Scotland, Most Rev. George Henderson (Bishop of Argyll and the Isles), *elected* 1990.

The Rt. Rev. Bishops

Aberdeen and Orkney, Frederick Charles Darwent, *b.* 1927, *cons.* 1978, *apptd.* 1978. *Clergy* 14.
Argyll and the Isles, George Kennedy Buchanan Henderson, *b.* 1921, *cons.* 1977, *apptd.* 1977. *Clergy* 10.
Brechin, Robert Taylor Halliday, *b.* 1932, *cons.* 1990, *apptd.* 1990. *Clergy* 17.
Edinburgh, Richard Frederick Holloway, *b.* 1933, *cons.* 1986, *apptd.* 1986. *Clergy* 65.

Glasgow and Galloway, Derek Alec Rawcliffe, OBE, *b.* 1921, *cons.* 1974, *apptd.* 1981. *Clergy* 42.
Moray, Ross and Caithness, George Minshull Sessford, *b.* 1928, *cons.* 1970, *apptd.* 1970. *Clergy* 17.
St. Andrews, Dunkeld and Dunblane, Michael Geoffrey Hare-Duke, *b.* 1925, *cons.* 1969, *apptd.* 1969. *Clergy* 30.

Registrar of the Episcopal Synod, I.R. Guild, 16 Charlotte Square, Edinburgh EH2 4YS. Churches, Mission Stations, etc., 341. Clergy 206; Communicants, 35,281.

(Stipend of diocesan bishop of the Episcopal Church in Scotland is £13,860.)

THE CHURCH OF IRELAND

Central Office.—Church of Ireland House, Church Avenue, Rathmines, Dublin 6.

PROVINCE OF ARMAGH

Archbishop of Armagh and Primate of All Ireland, Most Rev. Robert Henry Alexander Eames, Ph.D., *b.* 1937, *cons.* 1975, *trs.* 1986: *Clergy* 51.

The Rt. Rev. Bishops

Clogher, Brian Desmond Anthony Hannon, *b.* 1936, *apptd.* 1986: *Clergy* 33.

Connor, Samuel Greenfield Poyntz, Ph.D., *b.* 1926, *apptd.* 1978, *trs.* 1987: *Clergy* 117.

Derry and Raphoe, James Mehaffey, Ph.D., *b.* 1931, *apptd.* 1980: *Clergy* 56.

Down and Dromore, Gordon McMullan, Ph.D., *b.* 1934, *apptd.* 1980, *trs.* 1986: *Clergy* 110.

Kilmore, Elphin and Ardagh, William Gilbert Wilson, Ph.D., *b.* 1918, *apptd.* 1981: *Clergy* 25.

Tuam, Killala and Achonry, John Robert Winder Neill, *b.* 1945, *apptd.* 1986: *Clergy* 11.

PROVINCE OF DUBLIN

Archbishop of Dublin, Bishop of Glendalough, and Primate of Ireland, Most Rev. Donald Arthur Caird, DD, *b.* 1925, *cons.* 1970, *apptd.* 1985: *Clergy* 91.

The Rt. Rev. Bishops

Cashel and Ossory, Noel Vincent Willoughby, *b.* 1926, *apptd.* 1980: *Clergy* 34.

Cork, Cloyne and Ross, Robert Alexander Warke, *b.* 1930, *apptd.* 1988: *Clergy* 26.

Limerick and Killaloe, Edward Flewett Darling, *b.* 1933, *apptd.* 1985: *Clergy* 19.

Meath and Kildare, Most Rev. Walton Newcombe Francis Empey, *b.* 1934, *cons.* 1981, *trs.* 1985: *Clergy* 21.

St. Patrick's National Cathedral, Dublin: *Dean and Ordinary,* Very Rev. V. G. B. Griffin, Ph.D.

ANGLICAN COMMUNION OVERSEAS

ANGLICAN CHURCH OF AUSTRALIA

Primate of Australia, vacant.

Sees	Apptd.

Province of New South Wales

Metropolitan

Archbishop of Sydney, The Most Rev. Donald William Bradley Robinson, *cons.* 1973 1982
Asst. Bps., J. R. Reid, (1972); E. D. Cameron, (1975); R. H. Goodhew, (1982); P. R. Watson (1989); P. W. Barnett (1990).

The Rt. Rev. Bishops

Armidale, P. Chiswell, *cons.* 1976 1976	
Bathurst, B. W. Wilson, *cons.* 1984 1989	
Canberra and Goulburn, O. D. Dowling, *cons.* 1981 1983	
Grafton B. A. Schultz, *cons.* 1985 1985	
Newcastle, A. C. Holland, *cons.* 1970 1978	
Riverina, B. R. Hunter, *cons.* 1971 1971	

Province of Queensland

Metropolitan

Archbishop of Brisbane, The Most Rev. Peter Hollingworth, *cons.* 1985 1990
Asst. Bps., A. O. Charles, (1983); G. V. Browning, (1985).

The Rt. Rev. Bishops

Carpentaria, A. F. B. Hall-Matthews 1984	
North Queensland, H. J. Lewis 1971	
Northern Territory, C. M. Wood.	
Rockhampton, G. A. Hearn 1981	

Province of South Australia

Metropolitan

Archbishop of Adelaide, The Most Rev. Keith Rayner, AO, Ph.D., *cons.* 1969 1975

The Rt. Rev. Bishops

The Murray, G. H. Walden, *cons.* 1981 1989	
Willochra, W. D. H. McCall, *cons.* 1987 1987	

Sees	Apptd.

Province of Victoria

Metropolitan

Archbishop of Melbourne, vacant.
Asst. Bps., J. A. Grant (1970); J. C. Stewart (1984); R. L. Butterss (1985); J. W. Wilson (1985); J. Bayton (1989).

The Rt. Rev. Bishops

Ballarat, J. Hazlewood, *cons.* 1975 1975	
Bendigo, O. S. Heyward, *cons.* 1975 1975	
Gippsland, C. D. Sheumack, *cons.* 1987 1987	
Wangaratta, R. G. Beal, *cons.* 1985 1985	

Province of Western Australia

Metropolitan

Archbishop of Perth, The Most Rev. Peter Frederick Carnley, Ph.D., *cons.* 1981 1981
Asst. Bps., M. B. Challen (1978); B. R. Kyme (1982); B. Wright (1988).

The Rt. Rev. Bishops

Bunbury, H. J. U. Jamieson, *cons.* 1974 1984	
North-west Australia, G. B. Muston, *cons.* 1971 . 1982	
Asst. Bp., B.R. Buckland (1988).	

Extra-Provincial Diocese

Tasmania, P. K. Newell, *cons.* 1982 1982

EPISCOPAL CHURCH OF BRAZIL
(Igreja Episcopal Do Brasil)

Primate, The Most Rev. Olavo Ventura Luiz (Bishop of South Western Brazil), *cons.* 1976 . 1986

The Rt. Rev. Bishops

Brasilia, A. Santos, *cons.* 1989 1989	
Central Brazil, S. A. Ruiz, *cons.* 1985 1985	
Northern Brazil, C. E. Rodrigues, *cons.* 1985 . . . 1986	
Pelotas, L. O. P. Prado, *cons.* 1987 1989	
South Central Brazil, G. Soares de Lima, *cons.* 1989 1989	
Southern Brazil, C. V. S. Gastal, *cons.* 1984 1984	
South Western Brazil, (*see* above) 1976	

Sees	Apptd.

CHURCH OF THE PROVINCE OF BURMA

Archbishop of Province, The Most Rev. Andrew
Mya Han (Bishop of Rangoon), *cons.* 1988 1988

The Rt. Rev. Bishops

Mandalay, T. Mya Wah, *cons.* 1984 1984
Myitkyina, A. Hla Aung, *cons.* 1988 1988
Pa'an, G. Kyaw Mya, *cons.* 1979 1979
Rangoon, (see above).
Sittwe, B. Theaung Hawi, *cons.* 1978 1980

CHURCH OF THE PROVINCE OF BURUNDI, RWANDA AND ZAIRE

Archbishop of Province, The Most Rev. Samuel
Sindamuka (Bishop of Bujumbura) 1989

The Rt. Rev. Bishops

Boga Zaire, B. Njojo 1980
Bujumbura, (see above) 1975
Bukavu, B. Dirokpa 1982
Butare, Justin Ndandali, *cons.* 1975 1975
Buye, S. Ndayisenga 1979
Gitega, J. Nduwayo 1985
Kigali, A. Sebununguri, *cons.* 1965.
Kisangani, S. T. Mugera 1980
Shaba, E. M. Kolini.
Shyira, A. Nshamihigo, *cons.* 1984 1984

ANGLICAN CHURCH OF CANADA

Primate The Most Rev. Michael Geoffrey Peers,
cons. 1977 1986

Province of British Columbia

Metropolitan

Archbishop of New Westminster, The Most Rev.
Douglas Walter Hambidge, *cons.* 1969 1981

The Rt. Rev. Bishops

British Columbia R. F. Shepherd, *cons.* 1984 1984
Caledonia, J. E. Hannen, *cons.* 1981 1981
Cariboo, J. S. P. Snowden, *cons.* 1975 1975
Kootenay, D. P. Crawley, *cons.* 1990 1990
Yukon, R. C. Ferris, *cons.* 1981 1981

Province of Canada

Metropolitan

Archbishop of Montreal, vacant.

The Rt. Rev. Bishops

Central Newfoundland, E. Marsh, *cons.* 1990 ...1990
Eastern Newfoundland and Labrador, M. Mate,
cons. 1980..................................1980
Fredericton, G. C. Lemon, *cons.* 1989 1989
Montreal, A. S. Hutchison.
Nova Scotia, A. G. Peters, *cons.* 1981 1982
Quebec, vacant.
Western Newfoundland, S. S. Payne, *cons.* 1978 .1978

Province of Ontario

Metropolitan

Archbishop of Niagara, The Most Rev. John
Charles Bothwell, *cons.* 1971 1985

The Rt. Rev. Bishops

Algoma, L. E. Peterson, *cons.* 1983 1983
Huron, D. D. Jones, *cons.* 1982 1984
Moosonee, C. J. Lawrence, *cons.* 1980 1980
Ontario, A. A. Read, *cons.* 1972 1981
Ottawa, E. K. Lackey, *cons.* 1981 1981
Toronto T. E. Finlay, *cons.* 1986 1990

Province of Rupert's Land

Metropolitan

Archbishop of Rupert's Land, The Most Rev.
Walter Heath Jones, *cons.* 1970 1988

Sees	Apptd.

The Rt. Rev. Bishops

Arctic, vacant.
Athabasca , G. F. Woolsey, *cons.* 1983 1983
Brandon, J. F. S. Conlin, *cons.* 1975.............1975
Calgary, J. B. Curtis, *cons.* 1983 1983
Edmonton, K. L. Genge, *cons.* 1988 1988
Keewatin, H. J. P. Allan, *cons.* 1974 1974
Qu' Appelle, E. Bays, *cons.* 1986 1986
Rupert's Land (see above).
Saskatchewan, T. O. Morgan, *cons.* 1985 1985
Saskatoon, R. A. Wood, *cons.* 1981 1981

CHURCH OF THE PROVINCE OF CENTRAL AFRICA

Archbishop of Province, The Most Rev. Walter
P. K. Makhulu (Bishop of Botswana), *cons.*
1979 1980

The Rt. Rev. Bishops

Botswana (see above).
Central Zambia, C. W. H. Shaba, *cons.* 1984 1984
Harare, R. P. Hatendi, *cons.* 1979 1981
Lake Malawi, P. N. Nyanja, *cons.* 1978 1978
The Lundi, J. Siyachitema, *cons.* 1981 1981
Lusaka, S. S. Mumba, *cons.* 1981...............1981
Manicaland, E. Masuko, *cons.* 1981.............1981
Matabeleland, T. T. Naledi, *cons.* 1987 1987
Northern Zambia, B. Malango, *cons.* 1988 1988
Southern Malawi, B. N. Aipa, *cons.* 1987 1987

CHURCH OF THE PROVINCE OF THE INDIAN OCEAN

Archbishop of Province, The Most Rev. French
Chang-Him (Bishop of Seychelles) 1984

The Rt. Rev. Bishops

Antananarivo, R. Rabenirina, *cons.* 1984 1984
Antsiranana, K. Benzies, *cons.* 1982 1982
Mauritius, R. Donat, *cons.* 1984 1984
Seychelles, (see above).
Toamasina, vacant.

THE HOLY CATHOLIC CHURCH IN JAPAN (Nippon Sei Ko Kai)

Primate

The Most Rev. Christopher Ichiro Kikawada
(Bishop of Osaka), *cons.* 1975................1986

The Rt. Rev. Bishops

Chubu, S. W. Hoyo, *cons.* 1987 1987
Hokkaido, A. H. Amagi, *cons.* 1987.............1987
Kita Kanto, J. T. Yashiro, *cons.* 1985...........1985
Kobe, P. K. Yashiro, *cons.* 1984 1984
Kyoto, vacant.
Kyushu, J. N. Iida, *cons.* 1982 1982
Okinawa, P. S. Nakamura, *cons.* 1972 1972
Osaka, (see above) 1975
Tohoku, C. Y. Tazaki, *cons.* 1979 1979
Tokyo, J. M. Takeda, *cons.* 1988 1988
Yokohama, R. S. Kajiwara, *cons.* 1984 1984

THE EPISCOPAL CHURCH IN JERUSALEM AND THE MIDDLE EAST

President-Bishop, Rt. Rev. S. Kafity 1986
Jerusalem, S. Kafity 1984
Iran, I. Mottahedeh 1990
Egypt, G. Abdel Malik 1984
Cyprus and the Gulf, J. Brown 1986

CHURCH OF THE PROVINCE OF KENYA

Archbishop of Province, The Most Rev. Manasses
Kuria (Bishop of Nairobi), *cons.* 1970 1980

Sees	Apptd.

The Rt. Rev. Bishops
Eldoret, vacant.
Machakos, B. N. P. Nzimbi, *cons.* 1985 1985
Maseno North, J. Mundia, *cons.* 1970 1970
Maseno South, J. H. Okullu, *cons.* 1974.........1974
Maseno West, D. J. Omolo, *cons.* 1982 1985
Mombasa, C. Nzano, *cons.* 1975 1981
Mount Kenya Central, J. Mahiaini, *cons.* 1984 ..1984
Mount Kenya East, D. Gitari, *cons.* 1975 1975
Mount Kenya South, G. M. Njuguna, *cons.* 1984 .1985
Nairobi, (see above).
Nakuru, S. N. Mwangi, *cons.* 1990 1990
Nambale, I. Namango, *cons.* 1984 1987

CHURCH OF THE PROVINCE
OF MELANESIA

Archbishop of Province, The Most Rev. Amos
Stanley Waiaru (Bishop of Central Melanesia),
cons. 1981 1988

The Rt. Rev. Bishops
Central Melanesia, (see above).
Malaita, R. O. Aumae 1990
Temotu, L. S. Munamua, *cons.* 1987.............1987
Vanuatu, M. H. Tavoa 1990
Ysabel, E. L. Pogo, *cons.* 1981 1981

CHURCH OF THE PROVINCE
OF NEW ZEALAND

Primate

Archbishop of New Zealand, The Most Rev.
Brian Newton Davis (Bishop of Wellington),
cons. 1980...................................1986

The Rt. Rev. Bishops
Aotearoa, W. Vercoe, *cons.* 1981 1981
Auckland, B. C. Gilberd, *cons.* 1985 1985
Christchurch, D. J. Coles, *cons.* 1990 1990
Dunedin, Ms A. P. Jamieson, *cons.* 1990 1990
Nelson, D. L. Eaton, *cons.* 1990 1990
Polynesia, J. L. Bryce, *cons.* 1975 1975
Waiapu, P. G. Atkins, *cons.* 1983 1983
Waikato, R. A. Herft, *cons.* 1986 1986
Wellington, (see above).

CHURCH OF THE PROVINCE OF NIGERIA

Archbishop of the Province, The Most Rev.
Abiodun Adetiloye 1988

The Rt. Rev. Bishops
Aba, A. O. Iwuagwu 1985
Abuja, P. J. Akinola 1989
Akoko, J. O. K. Olowokure 1986
Akure, E. B. Gbonigi 1983
Asaba, R. N. C. Nwosu 1977
Awka, M. S. C. Anikwenwa 1987
Bauchi, E. O. Chukwuma 1990
Benin, J. K. George 1985
Egba-Egbado, T. I. Akintayo 1977
Ekiti, C. A. Akinbola 1986
Enugu, G. N. Otubelu 1969
Ibadan, G. I. O. Olajide 1988
Ijebu, I. B. O. Akintemi 1976
Ijebu Remo, E. O. I. Ogundana 1984
Ilesha, E. A. Ademowo 1989
Jos, T. E. I. Adesola 1985
Kaduna, T. Ogbonyomi 1975
Kafanchan, W. Diya 1990
Kano, B. O. Omoseibi 1990
Katsina, J. S. Kwasu 1990
Kwara, H. Haruna 1974
Lagos, J. A. Adetiloye 1985
Maiduguri, E. K. Mani 1990
Makurdi, J. T. Iyangemar 1990
Minna, J. A. Yisa..............................1990

Sees	Apptd.

The Niger, J. A. Onyemelukwe.................1975
Niger Delta, S. O. Elenwa 1981
Okigwe/Orlu, S. C. N. Ebo 1984
Ondo, S. O. Aderin 1981
Osun, S. O. Fagbemi 1987
Owerri, B. C. Nwankiti.......................1968
Owo, A. O. Awosan 1983
Sokoto, J. A. Idowu-Fearon 1990
Warri, J. O. Dafiewhare 1980
Yola, C. O. Efobi 1990

ANGLICAN CHURCH OF
PAPUA NEW GUINEA

Archbishop of Province, The Most Rev. B. S.
Meredith (Bishop of New Guinea Is.), *cons.*
1967 1990

The Rt. Rev. Bishops
Aipo Rongo, P. Richardson, *cons.* 1987 1987
Dogura, B. Kerina, *cons.* 1981.................1990
New Guinea Is., (see above).
Popondota, W. Siba, *cons.* 1990 1990
Port Moresby, I. R. Gadebo, *cons.* 1983 1983

CHURCH OF THE PROVINCE
OF SOUTHERN AFRICA

Metropolitan

Archbishop of Cape Town, The Most Rev. Desmond Mpilo Boy Tutu, *cons.* 1976 1986
Bps. *Suff.*, C. H. Albertyn, *cons.* 1983 (1983); A. G.
Quinlan, *cons.* 1988 (1988); E. Mackenzie, *cons.*
1988 (1988).

The Rt. Rev. Bishops
Bloemfontein, T. S. Stanage, *cons.* 1978.......1982
Christ the King, P. J. Lee, *cons.* 1990 1990
George, D. G. Damant, *cons.* 1985 1985
Grahamstown, D. P. H. Russell, *cons.* 1986 1986
Johannesburg, D. Buchanan, *cons.* 1986........1986
Kimberley & Kuruman, G. A. Swartz, *cons.*
1972..1983
Lebombo, D. S. Sengulane, *cons.* 1976 1976
Lesotho, P. S. Mokuku, *cons.* 1978 1978
Namibia, J. H. Kauluma, *cons.* 1978 1981
Natal, M. Nuttall, *cons.* 1975 1982
Niassa, P. T. Manhique, *cons.* 1986 1986
Port Elizabeth, B. R. Evans, *cons.* 1975 1976
Pretoria, R. A. Kraft, *cons.* 1982 1982
St. Helena, J. N. Johnson, *cons.* 1985 1985
St. John's, J. Z. Dlamini, *cons.* 1980 1985
St. Mark the Evangelist, R. P. J. Le Feuvre,
cons. 1987.
South Eastern Transvaal, D. A. Beetge, *cons.*
1990...1990
Swaziland, B. L. N. Mkhabela, *cons.* 1975 1975
Zululand, M. B. Zulu, *cons.* 1975 1975
Order of Ethiopia, S. Dwane, *cons.* 1983 1983

ANGLICAN CHURCH OF THE
SOUTHERN CONE OF AMERICA

Presiding Bishop, Rt. Rev. Colin Bazley.

The Rt. Rev. Bishops
Argentina, David Leake.
Chile, C. F. Bazley, *cons.* 1969 1977
Northern Argentina, vacant.
Paraguay, J. Ellison.
Peru, A. Winstanley.
Uruguay, H. W. Godfree.

CHURCH OF THE PROVINCE
OF THE SUDAN

Archbishop of Province, The Most Rev. Benjamina
Wani Yugusuk (Bishop of Juba).

Sees	Apptd.

The Rt. Rev. Bishops

Bor, N. Garang.
Juba, (see above).
Kadugli, M. Khamis.
Kajo-Kaji, M. B. Dawidi.
Khartoum, B. I. Tia.
Maridi, J. Marona.
Mundri, E. Munda.
Rumbek, G. R. Jur (*acting*).
Yei, S. Solomona.
Yambio, D. Zindo, cons. 1984 1984
Wau, G. R. Jur.

CHURCH OF THE PROVINCE OF TANZANIA

Archbishop of Province The Most Rev. John
   Acland Ramadhani (Bishop of Zanzibar and
   Tanga), cons. 1980 1984

The Rt. Rev. Bishops

Central Tanganyika, G. Mhogolo, cons. 1989 . . .1989
Dar es Salaam, C. Mlangwa, cons. 1984 1984
Kagera, C. Ruhuza, cons. 1985 1985
Mara, G. Nyaronga, cons. 1985 1985
Masasi, C. R. Norgate, cons. 1984 1984
Morogoro, D. Mageni, cons. 1987 1987
Mount Kilimanjaro, A. Mohamed, cons. 1982 . . .1982
Ruvuma, Stanford Shauri 1989
South West Tanganyika, C. Mwaigoga, cons.
   1983 1983
Tabora, F. Ntiruka, cons. 1989 1989
Victoria Nyanza, J. Rusibamayila, cons. 1976 . . .1976
Western Tanganyika, G. E. Mpango, cons. 1983 .1983
Zanzibar and Tanga, (see above).

CHURCH OF THE PROVINCE OF UGANDA

Archbishop of the Province, The Most Rev. Dr.
   Yona Okoth (Bishop of Kampala), cons. 1972 .1984

The Rt. Rev. Bishops

Bukedi, N. E. Okille 1984
Bunyoro-Kitara, Y. Rwakaikara 1981
Busoga, C. Bamwoze 1972
East Ankole, A. Betungura 1970
Kampala, (see above).
Karamoja, P. Lomongin .1987
Kigezi, William Rukirande.
Lango, M. Otim 1976
Madi and West Nile, E. Adrale.
Mbale, A. M. Wesonga 1981
Mityana, Y. Mukasa 1977
Mukono, L. Mpalanyi-Nkoyoyo 1985
Namirembe, M. Kauma 1985
North Kigezi, Y. Ruhindi 1981
Northern Uganda, B. Ogwal-Abwang 1974
Ruwenzori, E. Kamanyire 1981
Soroti, G. Ilukor 1976
South Ruwenzori, Zebidee Masereka.
West Ankole, Y. Bamunoba 1977
West Buganda, C. Senyonjo 1974

EPISCOPAL CHURCH IN THE USA

Presiding Bishop and Primate, Most Rev. Edmond Lee Browning, DD, cons. 1968 1986

Rt. Rev. Bishops
(*Missionary Diocese)

Province I

Connecticut, Arthur E. Walmsley, cons. 1979 . . .1981
Maine, Edward C. Chalfant, cons. 1984 1986
Massachusetts, David E. Johnson, cons. 1985 . .1986
New Hampshire, Douglas E. Theuner, cons.
   1986 1986
Rhode Island, George N. Hunt, cons. 1980 1980

Sees	Apptd.

Vermont, Daniel L. Swensen, cons. 1986 1987
Western Massachusetts, Andrew F. Wissemann,
   cons. 1984 1984

Province II

Albany, David S. Ball, cons. 1984 1984
Central New York, O'Kelley Whitaker, cons.
   1981 1983
Europe, Convocation of American Churches in,
   M. P. Bigliardi.
Haiti, Luc A. J. Garnier, cons. 1971 1971
Long Island, Robert C. Witcher, cons. 1975 1977
New Jersey, G. P. Mellick Belshaw, cons. 1975 . .1983
New York, Richard Grein, cons. 1981 1989
Newark, John S. Spong, cons. 1976 1979
Rochester, William G. Burrill, cons. 1984 1984
Virgin Islands, Don. E. Taylor, cons. 1987 1987
Western New York, David C. Bowman, cons.
   1986 1987

Province III

Bethlehem, J. Mark Dyer, cons. 1982 1983
Central Pennsylvania, Charles F. McNutt, cons.
   1980 1982
Delaware, C. Cabell Tennis, cons. 1986 1986
Easton, Elliott L. Sorge, cons. 1971 1983
Maryland, A. Theodore Eastman, cons. 1982 . . .1986
Northwestern Pennsylvania, Donald. J. Davis,
   cons. 1973 1974
Pennsylvania, Allen L. Bartlett, cons. 1986 1987
Pittsburgh, Alden M. Hathaway, cons. 1981 1983
Southern Virginia, C. Charles Vaché, cons.
   1976 1978
Southwestern Virginia, Arthur H. Light, cons.
   1979 1979
Virginia, Peter J. Lee, cons. 1984 1985
Washington, vacant.
West Virginia, John H. Smith, cons. 1989 1989

Province IV

Alabama, Robert O. Miller, cons. 1988 1988
Atlanta, Frank K. Allan, cons. 1988 1989
Central Florida, William H. Folwell, cons. 1970 .1970
Central Gulf Coast, Charles F. Duvall, cons.
   1981 1981
East Carolina, B. Sidney Sanders, cons. 1979 . .1983
East Tennessee, William E. Sanders, cons. 1979 .1985
Florida, Frank S. Cerveny, cons. 1974 1975
Georgia, Harry W. Shipps, cons. 1984 1985
Kentucky, David B. Reed, cons. 1964 1974
Lexington, Don A. Wimberley, cons. 1984 1985
Louisiana, James B. Brown, cons. 1976 1976
Mississippi, Duncan M. Gray jun., cons. 1974 . . .1974
North Carolina, Robert W. Estill, cons. 1980 1983
South Carolina, C. FitzSimons Allison, cons.
   1980 1982
Southeast Florida, Calvin O. Schofield jun.,
   cons. 1979 1980
Southwest Florida, Roger Harris, cons. 1989 1989
Tennessee, George L. Reynolds, cons. 1985 1985
Upper South Carolina, William A. Beckham,
   cons. 1979 1979
West Tennessee, Alex D. Dickson jun., cons.
   1983 1983
Western Louisiana, Willis R. Henton, cons. 1980 .1980
Western North Carolina, William G. Weinhauer,
   cons. 1973 1975

Province V

Chicago, Frank T. Griswold III, cons. 1985 1987
Eau Claire, William C. Wantland, cons. 1980 . . .1980
Fond Du Lac, William L. Stevens, cons. 1980 . . .1980

Sees	Apptd.
Indianapolis, Edward W. Jones, *cons.* 1977 1977	
Michigan, R. Stewart Wood, *cons.* 1990 1990	
Milwaukee, Roger J. White, *cons.* 1984 1985	
Missouri, William A. Jones jun., *cons.* 1975 1975	
Northern Indiana, Francis C. Gray, *cons.* 1986 ..1987	
Northern Michigan, Thomas K. Ray, *cons.* 1982 .1982	
Ohio, James R. Moodey, *cons.* 1983 1984	
Quincy, Donald J. Parsons, *cons.* 1973..........1973	
Southern Ohio, William G. Black, *cons.* 1979 1980	
Springfield, Donald M. Hultstrand, *cons.* 1982 ..1982	
Western Michigan, Edward L. Lee jun., *cons.*	
1989.......................................1989	

Province VI

Colorado, vacant.
Iowa, C. Christopher Epting, *cons.* 1988 1988
Minnesota, Robert M. Anderson, *cons.* 1978 1978
Montana, Charles I. Jones, *cons.* 1986..........1986
Nebraska, James E. Krotz, *cons.* 1989 1989
North Dakota, Andrew H. Fairfield, *cons.* 1990 ..1990
South Dakota, Craig B. Anderson, *cons.* 1984 ...1984
Wyoming, Bob G. Jones, *cons.* 1977 1977

Province VII

Arkansas, Herbert A. Donovan jun., *cons.*
1980.......................................1981
Dallas, Donis D. Patterson, *cons.* 1983 1983
Fort Worth, Clarence C. Pope jun., *cons.* 1985 ..1986
Kansas, William E. Smalley, *cons.* 1989 1989
Northwest Texas, Sam B. Hulsey, *cons.* 1980 1980
Oklahoma, Robert M. Moody, *cons.* 1988 1989
Rio Grande, Terence Kelshaw, *cons.* 1989 1989
Texas, Maurice M. Benitez, *cons.* 1980 1980
West Missouri, John C. Buchanan, *cons.* 1989...1989
West Texas, John H. MacNaughton, *cons.* 1986 .1987
Western Kansas, John F. Ashby, *cons.* 1981.....1981

Province VIII

Alaska, George C. Harris, *cons.* 1981..........1981
Arizona, Joseph T. Heistand, *cons.* 1976........1979
California, William E. Swing, *cons.* 1979 1980
Eastern Oregon, Rustin R. Kimsey, *cons.* 1980 ..1980
El Camino Real, Richard L. Skimpfky (*elect.*)
Hawaii, Donald P. Hart, *cons.* 1986 1986
Idaho, vacant.
Los Angeles, Frederick L. Borsch, *cons.* 1988 ...1988
Navajoland Area Mission, Steven T. Plummer,
cons. 1989.................................1989
Nevada, Stewart C. Zabriskie, *cons.* 1986 1986
Northern California, John L. Thompson III, *cons.*
1978.......................................1978
Olympia, Vincent W. Warner, *cons.* 1989.......1990
Oregon, Robert L. Ladehoff, *cons.* 1985 1986
San Diego, C. Brinkley Morton, *cons.* 1982 1982
San Joaquin, John D. Schofield, *cons.* 1988 1989
Spokane, Leigh A. Wallace, *cons.* 1979 1979
Taiwan, John C. T. Chien, *cons.* 1988 1988
Utah, George E. Bates, *cons.* 1986 1986

*Province IX

Cuernavaca, Jose G. Saucedo, *cons.* 1958 1989
Colombia, Bernardo Merino-Botero, *cons.* 1979 .1979
Dominican Republic, Telesforo A. Isaac, *cons.*
1972.......................................1972
Ecuador, Adrian D. Caceres-Villavicencio, *cons.*
1971.......................................1971
Guatemala, Armando Guerra-Soria, *cons.* 1982 .1982
Honduras, Leopold Frade, *cons.* 1984 1984
Mexico, Sergio Cananga-Gomez, *cons.* 1989 1989
Nicaragua, Sturdie W. Downs-Higgs, *cons.*
1985.......................................1985
Northern Mexico, German Martinez-Marquez,
cons. 1987................................1987

Sees	Apptd.
Panama, James H. Ottley, *cons.* 1984 1984	
El Salvador, James H. Ottley, *cons.* 1984 1989	
Southeastern Mexico, Claro Huerta-Rames, *cons.*	
1980.......................................1989	
Western Mexico, Samuel Espinoza-Venegas, *cons.*	
1981.......................................1983	

Extra-Provincial

Costa Rica, Cornelius J. Wilson, *cons.* 1978 1978
Puerto Rico, David Alvarez.
Venezuela, Onell A. Soto, *cons.* 1987 1987

CHURCH OF THE (ON-GOING) PROVINCE OF WEST AFRICA

Archbishop of Province, The Most Rev. George
Daniel Browne, DD, (Bishop of Liberia), *cons.*
1970.......................................1982
Bp. Suff., Rt. Rev. Edward W. Neufville (1984).

The Rt. Rev. Bishops

Accra, F. W. B. Thompson, *cons.* 1983 1983
Bo, M. Keili, OBE, *cons.* 1981 1981
Cape Coast, K. Quashie.
Freetown, P. E. S. Thompson, *cons.* 1981 1981
Gambia, T. Johnson, *cons.* 1990 1990
Guinea, vacant.
Koforidua, R. G. Okine, *cons.* 1981.............1981
Kumasi, E. K. Yeboah, *cons.* 1985..............1985
Liberia, (see above)
Sekondi, T. Annobil, *cons.* 1981 1981
Sunyani/Tamale, J. K. Dadson, *cons.* 1981 1981

The Anglican Church of Cameroon is a missionary
area of the Province.

CHURCH IN THE PROVINCE OF THE WEST INDIES

Archbishop of Province, The Most Rev. Orland
Lindsay (Bishop of North Eastern Caribbean
and Aruba), *cons.* 1970 1986

The Rt. Rev. Bishops

Barbados, D. W. Gomez, *cons.* 1972 1972
Belize, D. M. Smith, *cons.* 1989 1989
Guyana, R. O. George, *cons.* 1976 1980
Jamaica, N. W. de Souza, *cons.* 1973 1979
Bps. Suff., W. A. Murray (1976) (Mandeville);
A. C. Reid (1980) (Montego Bay); H. V.
Spence (*Kingston*).
Nassau and the Bahamas, M. H. Eldon, CMG,
cons. 1971 1972
NE Caribbean and Aruba (see above).
Trinidad and Tobago, C. O. Abdulah, *cons.*
1970.......................................1970
Windward Islands, P. Elder, *cons.* 1966.

OTHER CHURCHES AND EXTRA-PROVINCIAL DIOCESES

Under the Archbishop of Canterbury

The Rt. Rev. Bishops

Bermuda, W. J. D. Down 1990
Kuching, John Leong Chee Yun.
Lusitanian Church in Portugal, F. Soares 1971
Pusan, Bundo Kim 1988
Sabah, Yong Ping Chung.
Seoul, S. S. Kim.
Singapore, M. Tay 1982
Spanish Reformed Episcopal Church, A.
Sanchez 1982
Taejon, Paul Hwan Yoon 1988
West Malaysia, J. G. Savarimuthu 1973

NON-CONFORMIST AND FREE CHURCHES, ETC.

THE CHURCH OF SCOTLAND

Church Office, 121 George Street, Edinburgh
EH2 4YN

THE CHURCH OF SCOTLAND is Presbyterian in constitution, and is governed by Kirk Sessions, Presbyteries, Synods, and the General Assembly, which consists of representative ministers and elders, in equal numbers, from each of the Presbyteries. It is presided over by a Moderator chosen annually by the Assembly. The Sovereign, if not present in person, is represented by a Lord High Commissioner, who is appointed each year by the Crown.

The country, for Church purposes, is divided into 12 Synods and 46 Presbyteries, and there are about 1,300 ministers and licentiates engaged in ministerial and other work. There are 131 ministers and other personnel working with partner Churches and in overseas charges in 26 countries. At Dec. 31, 1989, congregations numbered 1,700, with a total membership of 804,468.

Lord High Commissioner (1990), The Rt. Hon. Lord Ross.
Moderator of the General Assembly (1990), Rt. Rev. Prof. R. Davidson.
Principal Clerk, Rev. J. L. Weatherhead.
Deputy Clerk, Rev. A. G. McGillivray.
Procurator, G. Penrose, QC.
Law Agent and Solicitor of the Church, R. A. Paterson.
Parliamentary Agent, I. McCulloch (London).
General Treasurer, W. G. P. Colledge.

THE PRESBYTERIAN CHURCH IN IRELAND

The largest of the Presbyterian churches in Ireland consists of 21 presbyteries, 432 ministers, 564 congregations, with 131,471 communicants, 123,283 families and 6,100 Sunday-school teachers. During the 12 months ended Dec. 31, 1989, there was contributed by congregational effort £4,214,060 plus IR£281,432 for religious, charitable, and missionary purposes. The total income for the period raised by congregations for all purposes was £25,278,847 plus IR£1,549,421.

General Sec., Very Rev. Dr. T. J. Simpson, Church House, Belfast BT1 6DW.

FREE CHURCHES
The Baptist Union of Great Britain

The Baptists have over 35,000,000 members in all countries. In Britain they are for the most part grouped in Associations of churches, and the majority of these belong to the Baptist Union, which was formed in 1812. Current statistics show that there are 2,155 churches and 164,095 members. There also exist separate Baptist Unions of Scotland (166 churches and 14,600 members); Wales (586 churches and 29,593 members); Ireland (92 churches and 8,550 members).

President of the Baptist Union of Great Britain (1990–91), Rev. Dr. D. J. Tidball.
General Secretary, Rev. B. Green. *Office*, Baptist House, PO Box 44, 129 Broadway, Didcot, Oxon. OX11 8RT.

The Congregational Federation

The majority of those members of the Congregational Church who did not join the United Reformed Church comprise the Congregational Federation. This has about 9,696 members, 117 ministers and 282 churches.

Gen. Sec., G. M. Adams, The Congregational Centre, 4 Castle Gate, Nottingham NG1 7AS.

The Free Church of England

The Free Church of England (otherwise called The Reformed Episcopal Church) has 30 churches and 1,700 adherents in England.
Gen. Sec., Rt. Rev. A. Ward, 28 Sedgebrook, Liden, Swindon, Wilts. SN3 6EY.

Independent Methodist Church

Independent Methodists.—This body is Congregational in its organization, with an unpaid Ministry. Its first Conference was held in 1805. In 1990 there were in Great Britain 131 Ministers, 3,820 Members, 106 Churches and 2,950 Sunday scholars.
Gen. Sec., Rev. J. M. Day, The Old Police House, Croxton, Stafford ST21 6PE.

The Methodist Church

THE METHODIST CHURCH was founded in 1739 by the two brothers Wesley and rapidly spread throughout the British Isles and to America before 1770. The Methodist Church in Great Britain was united in 1932 by the fusion of the Wesleyan Methodist Church (the original section), the Primitive Methodist Church (1810) and the United Methodist Church (a 1907 fusion of the Methodist New Connexion (1797), the Bible Christian Methodist Church (1815) and the United Methodist Free Churches (1828 and 1849)).

The World Methodist Council, founded 1881, reorganized 1951, associates Methodism throughout the world in 90 countries.

The Methodist Church in Great Britain is governed primarily by the Conference; secondarily by the District Synods (held in the autumn and the spring), consisting of all the ministers and of selected laypeople in each district, over which a chairman, who is a minister, is appointed by the Conference; and thirdly by the circuit meeting of the ministers and lay officers of each circuit. The authority of both Synods and Circuit Meetings is subordinate to the Conference, which has the supreme legislative and judicial power in Methodism.

President of the Conference (July 1990–91), Rev. Dr. D. English.
Vice-President of the Conference (July 1990–91), Mrs. R. Wass.
Secretary of the Conference, Rev. B. E. Beck, 1 Central Buildings, Westminster, SW1H 9NH.
Statistics.—In 1989 in association with the Conference in Great Britain there were 3,514 Ministers, 10,359 Local Preachers, 431,549 Members in 7,207 churches. (Statistics are published triennially.)

The Methodist Church in Ireland has 195 Ministers, 295 Lay Preachers, 19,782 adult and 12,269 junior members.

President (1990–91), Rev. W. T. Buchanan.
Secretary, Rev. E. T. I. Mawhinney. 3 Upper Malone Road, Belfast BT9 6TD.

The Presbyterian Church of Wales

THE PRESBYTERIAN or CALVINISTIC METHODIST CHURCH OF WALES is the only Church of purely Welsh origin, and embraces a large section of the Welsh-speaking population. Its form of government is Presbyterian, and it is a constituent of the World Alliance of Reformed Churches.

In 1989 the body numbered: chapels and other buildings, 1,050; ministers in pastoral charge, 146; elders, 4,554; communicants, 65,237; Sunday scholars, 20,949.

The *Association in the East* which includes nine of the English Presbyteries was formed in 1947.
Moderator of General Assembly (1990–1), Rev. R. L. Jones, Cardiff.
Moderators of Associations (1990–1), *South Wales*, Rev. D. J. Jones, Llanelli; *North Wales*, Rev. I. Lloyd, Prestatyn; *East Wales*, G. Dixey, Newport.
General Secretary, Rev. D. H. Owen, 53 Richmond Road, Cardiff CF2 3UP

The Salvation Army

First known as the Christian Mission, the Salvation Army was founded by William Booth in the East End of London in 1865. In 1878 it took its present name and adopted a quasi-military method of government. Since then it has become established in 94 countries of the world. The world leader, known as the General, is elected by a High Council, consisting of all active Commissioners and Territorial Commanders who have held the rank of Colonel for at least two years. In 1990 there were in Great Britain, 1,037 Corps (Churches), 135 Social Services Centres and 1,648 Officers engaged in evangelistic and social work. The latest world statistics (1988) are 14,397 Corps, 4,975 Social Services Centres (including institutions and schools) and 25,056 Officers.
General, Eva Burrows. *International Headquarters*, 101 Queen Victoria Street, EC4P 4EP.

United Reformed Church

THE UNITED REFORMED CHURCH was formed by the union of the Congregational Church in England and Wales and the Presbyterian Church of England on October 5, 1972. The Re-formed Association of Churches of Christ were joined to the URC on September 26, 1981. It is divided into 12 Provinces, each with a Provincial Moderator, and 70 Districts. There are 126,000 members and 1,000 serving ministers of whom 190 are auxiliary and give voluntary service. It shares an international mission through the Council for World Mission and is a member of the British and World Council of Churches. Its ministers are trained at five recognized colleges.
General Sec., Rev. B. G. Thorogood, 86 Tavistock Place, WC1H 9RT

Wesleyan Reform Union

The Union is Methodist in doctrine, Congregational in government, with, if any church desires it, a paid ministry. It is the remnant of the original Reformers expelled from Wesleyan Methodism in 1849. The adherents are mainly in the Midland and Northern counties. In 1990 there were in Great Britain 20 Ministers, 139 Lay Preachers, 2,996 Members, 130 Churches and 1,746 Sunday School scholars.
President, Rev. M. Nicholls.
General Secretary, Rev. E. W. Downing, Wesleyan Reform Church House, 123 Queen Street, Sheffield 1.

LUTHERAN CHURCH

The Lutheran Church is one of the largest Protestant churches, with over 70 million members worldwide, although there are only about 27,000 adherents in Great Britain. The government and organization of the Lutheran Church varies from country to country, some having an episcopal and some a more congregational form.
Very few British people are Lutherans and services in Great Britain are held in many languages to serve members of different nationalities. English-language congregations in Great Britain are members either of the Lutheran Church in Great Britain–United Synod or of the Evangelical Lutheran Church of England. The United Synod and most of the 'national churches' are members of the Lutheran Council of Great Britain and through the Council are related to the Lutheran World Federation.
LUTHERAN COUNCIL OF GREAT BRITAIN, 8 Collingham Gardens, SW5 0HW.—*Chairman*, Very Rev. R. J. Patkai.

ORTHODOX CHURCH

Greek Orthodox Church (*Archdiocese of Thyateira and Great Britain*), Most Rev. Archbishop Gregorios, 5 Craven Hill, W2 3EN.

Serbian Orthodox Church (*Patriarchate of Serbia*) Right Rev. Bishop Lavrentije, 89 Lancaster Road, W11 1QQ.

Russian Orthodox Church (*Patriarchate of Moscow*), Most Rev. Metropolitan Anthony of Sourozh, Russian Cathedral, Ennismore Gardens, SW7 1NH.

Russian Orthodox Church Abroad, Parish of the Dormition, 57 Harvard Road, W3 7NA; All Saints Church House, 14 St. Dunstan's Road, NW6.

The Poles, Ukrainians, Latvians, Byelorussians and Romanians also have congregations in this country.

OTHER DENOMINATIONS

The General Assembly of Unitarian and Free Christian Churches has about 95 ministers, 230 chapels and other places of worship in Great Britain and Ireland.
Gen. Sec., Dr. R. W. Smith, Essex Hall, 1–6 Essex Street, Strand, WC2R 3HY.

The Religious Society of Friends (Quakers), founded in the 17th century, has no separated ministry. There are in Great Britain 464 places of worship and 18,070 members (world membership 213,800). *Central Offices (Great Britain)*, Friends House, Euston Road, NW1 2BJ; (*Ireland*), Swanbrook House, Morehampton Road, Dublin 4.

The First Church of Christ, Scientist, in Boston Massachusetts, USA, has about 230 branch churches and societies in Great Britain and Ireland.
District Manager, Committees on Publication for Great Britain and Ireland, 108 Palace Gardens Terrace, W8 4RT.

The Seventh Day Adventists (*HQ*, Stanborough Park, Watford, Herts. WD2 6JP), have more than 235 organized churches and companies and more than 17,000 members in the British Isles. *Executive Sec.*, D. W. McFarlane.

THE ROMAN CATHOLIC CHURCH

HIS HOLINESS POPE JOHN PAUL II (Karol Wojtyla), *born* in Wadowice, Poland, May 18, 1920; *ordained priest* November 1, 1946; appointed *Archbishop of Krakow* January 13, 1964, created *Cardinal* at a Consistory on June 26, 1967. Formally assumed Pontificate October 16, 1978.

THE SACRED COLLEGE OF CARDINALS, when complete, consisted of six Cardinal Bishops, fifty Cardinal Priests and fourteen Cardinal Deacons. This number was fixed by Pope Sixtus V in 1586. The number was increased by Pope John XXIII, who created 52 new Cardinals, and by Pope Paul VI, who created 141 new Cardinals; Pope John Paul II has created 86 new Cardinals (15 on June 30, 1979, 18 on Feb. 2, 1983, 28 on May 25, 1985, 25 on June 28, 1988). On July 2, 1990 there were 145 Cardinals.

The Cardinals are advisers and assistants of the Sovereign Pontiff and form the supreme council or Senate of the Church. On the death of the Pope they elect his successor. The assembly of the Cardinals at the Vatican for the election of a new Pope is known as the Conclave in which, in complete seclusion, the Cardinals elect by secret ballot; a two-thirds majority is necessary before the vote can be accepted as final. When a Cardinal receives the necessary votes the Dean of the Sacred College formally asks him if he will accept election and the name by which he wishes to be known. On his acceptance of the office the Conclave is dissolved and the First Cardinal Deacon announces the election to the assembled crowd in St. Peter's Square. On the first Sunday or Holyday following the election the new Pope assumes the pontificate at High Mass in St. Peter's Square. A new pontificate is dated from the assumption of the pontificate.

FORMS OF ADDRESS: *Cardinal.*—His Eminence Cardinal—(if an Archbishop, His Eminence the Cardinal Archbishop of—); *Archbishop.*—The Most Revd. Archbishop of—; *Bishop.*—The Rt. Revd. Bishop of—.

THE CURIA

The Curia or governing body of the Roman Catholic Church is made up of various administrative departments headed by the Secretariat of State and the Sacred Council for the Public Affairs of the Church. Below these are congregations, secretariats and tribunals assisted by commissions and offices. All are headed by Cardinals. (A British equivalent would be the Ministers or Secretaries of State heading the various government departments.)

The Vatican State has, as with any nation, its own diplomatic service although its representatives are officially acknowledged in different ways throughout the countries of the world. Where the representation is only to the local churches and not to the government of that country, the man appointed is an Apostolic Delegate. However, where the representative is recognized as having diplomatic status by a particular government, he is known as either a nuncio, pro nuncio or inter nuncio. Nuncios are Papal Ambassadors who are given precedence over all other ambassadors by their appointed country and are the doyens of the diplomatic corps. In countries where precedence is not recognized, as in Britain, the papal representative is known as a pro nuncio.

THE BISHOPS' CONFERENCES

The Roman Catholic church in England and Wales is governed by:

1. **The Bishops' Conference** which consists of the local ordinaries (the diocesan bishops) of any rite; coadjutor bishops and auxiliaries; and titular bishops with special tasks. They are headed by the President (Cardinal Basil Hume) and Vice President (Archbishop Worlock, Archbishop of Liverpool).

2. **The Bishops' Standing Committee** made up of the Metropolitans (Archbishops) and department heads. It has general responsibility for continuity and policy between the plenary sessions of the Conference and for the preparation of the agenda and implementation of Conference decisions. This committee is serviced by the General Secretariat.

There are five departments, each with an episcopal chairman, which look after the life of the church within England and Wales. The departments and their heads are:

(a) Department for Christian Life and Worship: Archbishop Bowen (*Southwark*).

(b) Department for Mission and Unity: Bishop Clark (*East Anglia*).

(c) Department for Christian Doctrine and Formation: Bishop Konstant (*Leeds*).

(d) Department for Christian Responsibility and Citizenship: Bishop Harris (*Middlesbrough*).

(e) Department for International Affairs: Bishop Kelly (*Salford*).

As well as the above, the Conference has agencies and consultative bodies affiliated to it and all are serviced by the General Secretariat headed by a General Secretary namely:

England and Wales—Mgr. Vincent Nichols, 39 Eccleston Square, SW1V 1PD.

Scotland—Rt. Revd. Maurice Taylor, Bishop of Galloway, Candida Casa, 8 Corsehill Road, Ayr, Scotland, KA7 26T.

Ireland—(Executive Secretary) Revd. Gerard Clifford, Iona, 67 Newry Road, Dundalk, Co. Louth.

GREAT BRITAIN

Apostolic Pro-Nuncio to the United Kingdom of Great Britain and Northern Ireland, The Most Revd. Luigi Barbarito.

England and Wales

The Most Revd. Archbishops	Cons.	Clgy.
Westminster, HE Cardinal Basil Hume		
(1976)	1976	839
Auxil., John Crowley	1986	
Auxil., Victor Guazzelli	1970	
Auxil., Gerald Mahon	1970	
Auxil., James J. O'Brien	1977	
Birmingham, Maurice Couve de Murville		
(1982)	1982	426
Auxil., Joseph Cleary	1965	
Auxil., Philip Pargeter	1989	
Cardiff, John A. Ward (1983)	1981	163
Liverpool, Derek Worlock (1976)	1965	515
Auxil., Kevin O'Connor	1979	
Auxil., John Rawsthorne	1981	
Auxil., Vincent Malone	1989	
Southwark, Michael Bowen (1977)	1970	518
Auxil., Charles Henderson	1972	
Auxil., Howard Tripp	1980	
Auxil., John Jukes	1980	

The Rt. Revd. Bishops		
Arundel and Brighton, Cormac Murphy-		
O'Connor	1977	255
Brentwood, Thomas McMahon (1980)	1980	188
Clifton, Mervyn Alexander (1975)	1972	242
East Anglia, Alan Clark (1976)	1969	112

	Cons.	Clgy.
Hallam, Gerald Moverley (1980) 1968		100
Hexham and Newcastle, Hugh Lindsay		
(1974) 1969		309
Auxil., Owen Swindelhurst 1977		
Lancaster, John Brewer (1985)..........1971		228
Leeds, David Konstant (1985)...........1977		225
Menevia (*Wales*), Daniel Mullins (1987) ..1970		59
Middlesbrough, Augustine Harris (1978) .1966		201
Auxil., Thomas O'Brien..............1981		
Northampton, Patrick Leo McCartie 1977		
Nottingham, James McGuinness (1975) ..1972		224
Plymouth, Christopher Budd 1986		168
Portsmouth, F. Crispian Hollis (1989) ...1987		282
Salford, Patrick Kelly 1984		455
Shrewsbury, Joseph Gray (1980) 1969		226
Wrexham (*Wales*), James Hannigan		
(1987) 1983		94

Scotland

The Most Revd. Archbishops

St. Andrews and Edinburgh, Keith Patrick O'Brian 1985		213
Auxil., James Monaghan............1970		
Auxil., Kevin Rafferty 1990		
Glasgow, Thomas Winning (1974) 1972		338
Auxil., Charles Renfrew 1977		

The Rt. Revd. Bishops

Aberdeen, Mario Conti 1977		59
Argyll and the Isles, vacant.............		35
Dunkeld, Vincent Logan 1981		67
Galloway, Maurice Taylor.............1981		75
Motherwell, Joseph Devine (1983) 1977		190
Paisley, John A. Mone (1988) 1984		98

IRELAND

There is one hierarchy for the whole of Ireland. Several of the dioceses have territory partly in the Republic of Ireland and partly in Northern Ireland. *Nuncio to Ireland*, Most Revd. Emanuele Gerada (titular Archbishop of Nomenta).

The Most Revd. Archbishops

Armagh, (vacant)		271
Cashel, Dermot Clifford 1986		122
Dublin, Desmond Connell (1988) 1988		994
Auxil., Joseph Carroll 1968		
Auxil., James Kavanagh 1973		
Auxil., Donal Murray...............1982		
Auxil., Dermot O'Mahony............1975		
Auxil., Eamonn Walsh 1990		
Auxil., Desmond Williams 1985		
Tuam, Joseph Cassidy (1987) 1979		165

The Rt. Revd. Bishops

Achonry, Thomas Flynn 1975		55
Ardagh and Clonmacnois, Colm O'Reilly 1983		108
Clogher, Joseph Duffy.................1979		124
Clonfert, Joseph Kirby 1988		76
Cloyne, John Magee 1987		155
Cork and Ross, Michael Murphy 1976		360
Auxil., John Buckley 1984		
Derry, Edward Daly 1974		149
Auxil., Francis Lagan 1988		
Down and Connor, Cahal Daly 1967		324
Auxil., Anthony Farquhar 1983		
Auxil., Patrick Walsh 1983		
Dromore, Francis Brooks...............1976		71
Elphin, Dominic Conway 1970		104
Ferns, Brendon Comiskey 1980		148
Galway and Kilmacduagh, Eamonn		
Casey 1969		134

	Cons.	Clgy.
Kerry, Dermot O'Sullivan 1985		143
Kildare and Leighlin, Laurence Ryan ...1984		225
Killala, Thomas Finnegan..............1970		51
Killaloe, Michael Harty 1967		186
Kilmore, Francis McKiernan 1972		103
Limerick, Jeremiah Newman 1974		234
Meath, Michael Smith (1990) 1984		270
Ossory, Laurence Forristal 1980		125
Raphoe, Seamus Hegarty 1984		102
Waterford and Lismore, Michael Russell .1965		206

RESIDENTIAL ARCHBISHOPRICS
THROUGHOUT THE WORLD

This list is set out with the name of the relevant country first; then the name of the diocese; and finally the Archbishop's name. It does not include England and Wales, Scotland or Ireland which are above.

Albania

Durrës, vacant. (Apostolic Administrator, Mgr. Nicola Troshani).
Shkodër, vacant. (Apostolic Administrator, Mgr. Ernesto Coba).

Algeria

Algiers, Henri Teissier.

Angola

Huambo, Francisco Viti.
Luanda, HE Cardinal Alexandre do Nascimento.
Lubango, Manuel Franklin da Costa.

Argentina

Bahia Blanca, Jorge Mayer.
Buenos Aires, HE Cardinal Juan Carlos Aramburu.
Córdoba, HE Cardinal Raúl Francisco Primatesta.
Corrientes, Fortunato A. Rossi.
La Plata, Antonio Quarracino.
Mendoza, Candido Genaro Rubiolo.
Paraná, Estanislao Esteban Karlich.
Resistencia, Juan J. Iriarte.
Rosario, Jorge Manuel López.
Salta, Moises J. Blanchoud.
San Juan de Cuyo, Italo Severino Di Stefano.
Santa Fe, Edgardo Gabriel Storni.
Tucumán, Horatio A. Bozzoli.

Australia

Adelaide, Leonard Anthony Faulkner.
Brisbane, Francis Roberts Rush.
Canberra, Francis P. Carroll.
Hobart, Joseph E. D'Arcy.
Melbourne, Thomas Francis Little.
Perth, William J. Foley.
Sydney, HE Cardinal Edward B. Clancy.

Austria

Salzburg, Georg Eder.
Vienna, HE Cardinal Hans Hermann Groer.

Bangladesh

Dhaka, Michael Rozario.

Belgium

Malines-Bruxelles, HE Cardinal Godfried Danneels.

Benin

Cotonou, Christophe Adimou.

Bolivia

Cochabamba, Rene Fernandez Apaza.
La Paz, Luis Sainz Hinojosa.
Santa Cruz de la Sierra, Luis Rodriguez Pardo.
Sucre, Jesus G. Pérez Rodriguez.

Brazil

Aparacida, Geraldo Maria de Morais Penido.
Aracaju, Luciano José Cabral Duarte.
Bélem do Pará, Vicente Joaquim Zico.
Belo Horizonte, Serafim Fernandes de Araújo.
Botucatu, Antonio M. Mucciolo.
Brasilia, HE Cardinal Jose Freire Falcao.
Campinas, Gilberto Pereira Lopes.
Campo Grande, Vitorio Pavanello.
Cascavel, Armando Cirio.
Cuiaba, Bonifacio Piccinini.
Curitiba, Pedro Antonio Fedalto.
Diamantina, Geraldo Majelo Reis.
Florianópolis, Alfonso Niehues.
Fortaleza, HE Cardinal Aloisio Lorscheider.
Goiania, Antonio Ribeiro de Oliveira.
Juiz de Fora, vacant.
Londrina, Geraldo Majela Agnelo.
Maceió, Edvaldo G. Amaral.
Manaus, Clovis Frainer.
Mariana, Luciano Mendes de Almeida.
Maringá, Jaime Luis Coelho.
Natal, Alair V. Fernandes de Melo.
Niteroi, Carlos A. Navarro.
Olinda & Recife, José Cardoso Sobrinho.
Paraiba, José M. Pires.
Porto Alegre, Claudio Colling.
Porto Velho, José Martins da Silva.
Pouso Alegre, José D'Angelo Neto.
Ribeirão Preto, Arnaldo Ribeiro.
São Luis do Maranhão, Paulo Eduardo Andrade Ponte.
São Paulo, HE Cardinal Paulo Evaristo Arns.
São Salvador da Bahia, HE Cardinal Lucas Moreira Neves.
São Sebastião do Rio de Janeiro, HE Cardinal Eugenio de Araújo Sales.
Teresina, Miguel F. Camara Filho.
Uberaba, Benedito de Ulhôa Vieira.
Vitória, Silvestre L. Scandian.

Burkina

Ouagadougou, HE Cardinal Paul Zoungrana.

Burundi

Gitega, Joachim Ruhuna.

Cameroon

Bamenda, Paul Verdzekov.
Douala, Simon Tonyé.
Garoua, HE Cardinal Christian W. Tumi.
Yaoundé, Jean Zoa.

Canada

Edmonton, Joseph N. MacNeil.
Grouard-McLennon, Henri Légaré.
Halifax, James Martin Hayes.
Keewatin-Le Pas, Peter Alfred Sutton.
Kingston, Francis John Spence.
Moncton, Donat Chiasson.
Montreal, Jean-Claude Turcotte.
Ottawa, Marcel A. Gervais.
Quebec, Maurice Couture.
Regina, Charles Halpin.
Rimouski, Gilles Ouellet.
St. Boniface, Antoine Hacault.
St. Johns, Newfoundland, Alphonsus L. Penney.
Sherbrooke, Jean Marie Fortier.
Toronto, Aloysius Matthew Ambrozie.
Vancouver, James Francis Carney.
Winnipeg, Latin Rite–Adam Exner; Ukrainian Rite–Maxim Hermaniuk.

Central African Republic

Bangui, Joachim N'Dayen.

Chad

Ndjamena, Charles Vandame.

Chile

Antofagasta, vacant.
Concepción, Antonio M. Casamitjana.
La Serena, Bernardino Pinera Carvallo.
Puerto Montt, Savino B. C. Bertollo.
Santiago de Chile, Carlos Oviedo Cavada.

China

Anking, Huai-Ning, vacant.
Canton, Dominic Tang Yee-Ming.
Changsha, vacant.
Chungking, vacant.
Foochow, Min-Hou, vacant.
Hangchow, vacant.
Hankow, vacant.
Kaifeng, vacant.
Kunming, vacant.
Kweiyang, vacant.
Lanchow, vacant.
Mukden, vacant.
Nanchang, vacant.
Nanking, vacant.
Nanning, vacant.
Peking, vacant.
Sian, vacant.
Suiyüan, Francis Wang Hsueh-Ming.
Taiyuan, vacant; Bishop Emeritus Dominic Luke Capozi (expelled April 11, 1946, now living in Nazareth, Israel).
Tsinan, vacant.

Colombia

Antioquia, Eladio Acosta Arteaga.
Barranquilla, Felix Maria Torres Parra.
Bogotá, HE Cardinal Mario Revollo Bravo.
Bucaramanga, Hector Rueda Hernández.
Cali, Pedro Rubiano Sáenz.
Cartagena, Carlos Jose Ruiseco Vieira.
Ibague, José Joaquin Flórez Hernández.
Manizales, José de Jesús Pimiento Rodriguez.
Medellin, HE Cardinal Alfonso López Trujillo.
Nueva Pamplona, Rafael Sarmiento Peralta.
Popayán, Samuel Silverio Buitrago Trujillo.
Tunja, Augusto Trujillo Arango.

Congo

Brazzaville, Barthélémy Batantu.

Costa Rica

San José, Román Arrieta Villalobos.

Côte d'Ivoire

Abidjan, HE Cardinal Bernard Yago.

Cuba

San Cristóbal de la Habana, Jaime Lucas Ortega y Alamino.
Santiago de Cuba, Pedro Meurice Estiu.

Cyprus

Cyprus (Maronite Seat at Nicosia), Boutros Gemayel.

Czechoslovakia

Olomouc, František Vanak.
Praha, HE Cardinal František Tomášek.
Trnava, Jan Sokol.

Dominican Republic

Santo Domingo, Nicolás de Jesús López Rodriguez.

Ecuador

Cuenca, Alberto Luna Tobar.
Guayaquil, Ignacio Larrea Holguin.
Quito, Antonio J. González Zumárraga.

Equatorial Guinea
Malabo, Rafael Nze Abuy.

Ethiopia
Addis Ababa, HE Cardinal Paul Tzadua.

France
Aix, Bernard Panafieu.
Albi, Roger Meindre.
Auch, Gabriel Vanel.
Avignon, Raymond Bouchex.
Besançon, Lucien Daloz.
Bordeaux, Pierre Eyt.
Bourges, Pierre Plateau.
Cambrai, Jacques Delaporte.
Chambéry, Claude Feidt.
Lyon, HE Cardinal Albert Decourtray.
Marseilles, Robert Coffy.
Paris, HE Cardinal J. M. Lustiger.
Reims, Jean Balland.
Rennes, Jacques Jullien.
Rouen, Joseph Duval.
Sens, Eugene Ernoult.
Strasbourg, Charles Amarin Brand.
Toulouse, André Collini.
Tours, Jean Honoré.

French Polynesia
Papeete, Michel Coppenrath.

Gabon
Libreville, André Fernand Anguilé.

Germany (Federal Republic)
Bamberg, Elmar Maria Kredel.
Cologne, HE Cardinal Joachim Meisner.
Essen, HE Cardinal Franz Hengsbach.
Freiburg im Breisgau, Oskar Saier.
Munich & Freising, HE Cardinal Friedrich Wetter.
Paderborn, Johannes Joachim Degenhardt.

Ghana
Cape Coast, John Kodwo Amissah.
Tamale, Peter Poreiku Dery.

Greece
Athens, Nicholaos Foscolos.
Corfu, Antonio Varthalitis.
Naxos, Jean Perris.
Rhodes, vacant (Apostolic administrator, Michel Pierre Franzidis).

Guatemala
Guatemala, Prospero Penandos del Barrio.

Guinea
Conakry, Robert Sarah.

Haiti
Cap-Haitien, François Gayot.
Port au Prince, François-Wolff Ligondé.

Honduras
Tegucigalpa, Hector Enrique Santos Hernández.

Hong Kong
Hong Kong, HE Cardinal J. B. Wu Cheng Chung.

Hungary
Eger, Istvan Seregely.
Esztergom, HE Cardinal Laslo Paskai.
Kalocsa, Laszlo Danko.

India
Agra, Cecil de Sa.
Bangalore, Alphonsus Mathias.
Bhopal, Eugene D'Souza.
Bombay, Thomas Dabre.
Calcutta, Henry Sebastian D'Souza.
Changanacherry, Joseph Powathil.
Cuttack-Bhubaneswar, Raphael Cheenath.
Delhi, Angelo Innocent Fernandes.
Ernakulam, HE Cardinal Anthony Padiyara.
Goa and Daman, Raul Nicolau Gonsalves.
Hyderabad, Saminini Arulappa.
Madras and Mylapore, Casimir Gnanadickam.
Madurai, Marianus Arokiasamy.
Nagpur, Leobard D'Souza.
Pondicherry and Cuddalore, Venmani S. Selvanather.
Ranchi, Telesphore P. Toppo.
Shillong-Gauhati, Hubert D'Rosario.
Trivandrum (Syrian Melekite Rite), Benedict Varghese Mar Gregorios Thangalathil.
Verapoly, Cornelius Elanjikal.

Indonesia
Ende, Donatus Djagom.
Jakarta, Leo Soekoto.
Kupang, Gregorius Manteiro.
Medan, Alfred Gonti Pius Datubara.
Merauke, Jacobus Duivenvoorde.
Pontianak, Hieronymus Herculanus Bumbun.
Semarang, Julius R. Darmaatmadja.
Ujung Pandang, R. P. Francis van Roessel.

Iran
Ahváz, Hanna Zora.
Tehran, Youhannan Semaan Issayi.
Urmyä, Thomas Meram.

Iraq
Arbil, Stephane Babaca.
Baghdad: Latin Rite, Paul Dahdah; Syrian Rite, Athanase M. S. Matoka; Armenian Rite, Paul Coussa.
Basra, Yousif Thomas.
Kirkuk, André Sana.
Mosul, Georges Garmo.

Israel
Akka (Greek Melekite Catholic Rite), Maximos Salloum.

Italy
Acerenza, Michele Scandiffio.
Amalfi, Ferdinand Palatucci.
Ancona, Dionigi Tettamanzi.
Bari, Mariano Magrassi.
Benevento, Carlo Minchiatti.
Bologna, HE Cardinal Giacomo Biffi.
Brindisi, Settimio Todisco.
Cagliari, Otterino Pietro Alberti.
Camerino, Francesco Gioia.
Campobasso-Boiano, Ettore Di Filippo.
Capua, Luigi Diligenza.
Catania, Luigi Bommarito.
Catanzaro, Antonio Cantisani.
Chieti, Antonio Valentini.
Conza, Mario Milano.
Cosenza, Dino Trabalzini.
Crotone-Santa Severina, Giuseppi Agostino.
Fermo, Cleto Bellucci.
Ferrara, Luigi Maverna.
Florence, HE Cardinal Silvano Piovanelli.
Foggia, Giuseppe Casale.
Gaeta, Vincenzo Farano.
Genoa, HE Cardinal Giovanni Canestri.
Gorizia and Gradisca, Antonio Vitale Bommarco.
Lanciano, Enzio d'Antonio.
L'Aquila, Mario Peressin.
Lecce, Cosmo F. Ruppi.
Lucca, Giuliano Agresti.

Manfredonia, Vincenzo D'Addario.
Matera, Ennio Appignanesi.
Messina, Ignazio Cannavó.
Milan, HE Cardinal Carlo Maria Martini.
Modena, Santo B. Quadri.
Monreale, Salvatore Cassisa.
Naples, HE Cardinal Michele Giordano.
Oristano, Pier Luigi Tiddia.
Otranto, Vincenzo Franco.
Palermo, HE Cardinal Salvatore Pappalardo.
Perugia, Ennio Antonelli.
Pescara-Penne, Francesco Cuccarese.
Pisa, Alessandro Plotti.
Potenza, Guiseppe Vairo.
Ravenna, Ersilio Tonini.
Reggio Calabria, Aurelio Sorrentino.
Rossano, Serafino Sprovieri.
Salerno, Guerino Grimaldi.
Sassari, Salvatore Isgrò.
Siena, Gaetano Bonicelli.
Siracusa, Giuseppe Costanzo.
Sorrento, Felice Cece.
Spoleto, Antonio Ambrosanio.
Taranto, Luigi Papa.
Turin, Giovanni Saldarini.
Trani and Barletta, Giuseppe Carata.
Trento, Giovanni Sartori.
Udine, Alfredo Battisti.
Urbino, Donato U. Bianchi.
Vercelli, Albino Mensa.

Jamaica
Kingston, Samuel Emmanuel Carter.

Japan
Nagasaki, Francis Xavier Shimamoto.
Osaka, Paul Hisao Yasuda.
Tōkyō, Peter Seiichi Shirayanagi.

Jordan
Petra and Filadelfia (Greek Melekite Catholic Rite), Saba Youakim.

Kenya
Kisumu, Zaccharus Okoth.
Mombasa, John Njenga.
Nairobi, HE Cardinal Maurice Otunga.
Nyeri, Nicodemus Kirima.

Korea
Kwangju, Victorinus Kong-Hi Youn.
Seoul, HE Cardinal Stephen Sou Hwan Kim.
Taegu, Paul Moun-Hi Ri.

Lebanon
Antelias (Maronite Rite), Joseph Mohsen Bechara.
Baalbek, Eliopoli (Greek Melekite Catholic Rite), Salim Bustros.
Baniyas (Greek Melekite Catholic Rite), Antoine Hayek.
Beirut (Greek Melekite Catholic Rite), Habib Bacha; (Maronite Rite), Khalil Abinader.
Saïda (Greek Melekite Catholic Rite), Georges Kwaiter.
Tripoli (Maronite Rite), Antoine Joubeir; (Greek Melekite Catholic Rite), Joseph Khoury.
Tyre (Greek Melekite Catholic Rite), Jean A. Haddad; (Maronite Rite), Joseph Khoury.
Zahle and Furzol (Greek Melekite Catholic Rite), Andre Haddad.

Lesotho
Maseru, Bernard Mohlalisi.

Liberia
Monrovia, Michael Kpakala Francis.

Lithuania
Kaunas, HE Cardinal Vincentas Sladkevicius.
Vilnius, Julijonas Steponavicius.

Luxembourg
Luxembourg, Jean Hengen.

Madagascar
Diego Suarez, Albert Joseph Tsiahoana.
Fianarantsoa, Gilbert Ramanantoanina.
Tananarive, HE Cardinal Victor Razafimahatratra.

Malaysia
Kuching, Peter Chung Hoan Ting.

Mali
Bamako, Luc Auguste Sangaré.

Malta
Malta, Joseph Mercieca.

Martinique
Fort de France, Maurice Marie-Sainte.

Mauritius
Port Louis, HE Cardinal Jean Margeot.

Mexico
Acapulco, Rafael Bello Ruiz.
Antequera, Bartolomé Carrasco Briseno.
Chihuahua, Adalberto Almeida Merino.
Durango, Antonio L. Avina.
Guadalajara, Juan J.P. Ocampo.
Hermosillo, Carlos Quintero Arce.
Jalapa, Sergio Obeso Rivero.
Mexico City, HE Cardinal Ernesto Corripio Ahumada.
Monterrey, Adolfo Suarez Rivera.
Morelia, Estanislao Alcarez Figueroa.
Puebla de los Angeles, Rosendo Huesca Pacheco.
San Luis Potosi, Arturo A. Szymanski Ramirez.
Tlalnepantla, Manuel P. Gil Gonzalez.
Yucatán, Manuel Castro Ruiz.

Monaco
Monaco, Joseph-Marie Sardou.

Morocco
Rabat, Hubert Michon.
Tanger, Antonio J. Peteiro Freire.

Mozambique
Beira, Jaime P. Goncalves.
Maputo, HE Cardinal Alexandre José Maria dos Santos.
Nampula, Manuel Vieira Pinto.

Myanmar (Burma)
Mandalay, Alphonse U. Than Aung.
Rangoon, Gabriel Thohey Mahn Gaby.

Netherlands
Utrecht, HE Cardinal Adrianus J. Simonis.

New Zealand
Wellington, HE Cardinal Thomas Stafford Williams.

Nicaragua
Managua, HE Cardinal Miguel Obando Bravo.

Nigeria
Kaduna, Peter Yariyok Jatau.
Lagos, Anthony Okogie.
Onitsha, Stephen Nweke Ezeanya.

Oceania
Agaña, Anthony Sablan Apuron.
Honiara, Adrian Thomas Smith.

Nouméa, Michel-Marie-Bernard Calvet.
Samoa, Apia and Tokelau, HE Cardinal Pio Taofino'u.
Suva, Petero Mataca.

Pakistan

Karachi, HE Cardinal Joseph Cordeiro.

Panama

Panama, Marcos Gregorio McGrath.

Papua New Guinea

Madang, Benedict To Varpin.
Mount Hagen, Michael Meier.
Port Moresby, Peter Kurongku.
Rabaul, Karl Hesse.

Paraguay

Asuncion, Felipe Santiago B. Avalos.

Peru

Arequipa, Fernando Vargas Ruiz de Somocurcio.
Ayacucho o Huamanga, Federico Richter Fernandez-Prada.
Cuzco, Alcides Mendoza Castro.
Huancayo, Emilio Vallebuona Merea.
Lima, Augusto Vargas Alzamora.
Piura, Oscar Rolando Cantuarias Pastor.
Trujillo, Manuel Prado Pérez-Rosas.

Philippines

Caceres, Leonardo Legazpi.
Cagayan de Oro, Jesus B. Tuquib.
Capiz, Onesimo C. Gordoncillo.
Cebu, Nome di Gesù, HE Cardinal Ricardo Vidal.
Cotabato, Philip Frances Smith.
Davao, Antonio Mabutas.
Jaro, Alberto J. Piamonte.
Lingayan-Dagupen, Federico G. Limon.
Lipa, Mariano Gaviola.
Manila, HE Cardinal Jaime L. Sin.
Nueva Segovia, Orlando Quevedo.
Ozamiz, Jesus Dosado.
Palo, Pedro R. Dean.
San Fernando, Paciano Aniceto.
Tuguegarao, Diosdado A. Talamayan.
Zamboanga, Francisco Raval Cruces.

Poland

Gniezno, HE Cardinal Józef Glemp. (See also Warsaw).
Kraków, HE Cardinal Franciszek Macharski.
Lwów, vacant (Apostolic Administrator, Mgr. Marian Jaworski).
Poznan, Jerzy Stroba.
Warsaw, HE Cardinal Józef Glemp.
Wroclaw, HE Cardinal Henryk Roman Gulbinowicz.

Portugal

Braga, Eurico Dias Nogueira.
Evora, Maurilio Jorge Quintal de Gouveia.

Puerto Rico

San Juan, HE Cardinal Luis Aponte Martinez.

Romania

Bucarest, vacant (Apostolic Administrator, Mgr. Ioan Robu).
Fagaras and Alba Julia (Romanian Byzantine Rite), Alexandru Todea.

Rwanda

Kigali, Vincent Nsengiyumva.

El Salvador

San Salvador, Arturo Rivera Damas.

Senegal

Dakar, HE Cardinal Hyacinthe Thiandoum.

Sierra Leone

Freetown & Bo, Joseph Ganda.

Singapore

Singapore, Gregory Yong Sooi Nghean.

South Africa

Bloemfontein, Peter John Butelezi.
Cape Town, Lawrence Patrick Henry.
Durban, Denis Eugene Hurley.
Pretoria, George Francis Daniel.

Spain

Barcelona, Ricardo Maria Carles Gordó.
Burgos, Theodoro C. Fernandez.
Granada, José Méndez Asensio.
Madrid, HE Cardinal Angel Suquia Goicoechea.
Oviedo, Gabino Diaz Merchán.
Pamplona, José Mariá Cirardo Lachiondo.
Santiago de Compostela, Antonio Rouco Varela.
Sevilla, Carlos Amigo Vallejo.
Tarragona, Ramon Torrella Cascante.
Toledo, HE Cardinal Marcelo González Martin.
Valencia, Miguel Roca Cabanellas.
Valladolid, José Delicado Baeza.
Zaragoza, Eliaz Yanez Alvarez.

Sri Lanka

Colombo, Nicholas Marcus Fernando.

Sudan

Khartoum, Gabriel Zubeir Wako.

Syria

Alep, Beroea, Halab (Greek Melekite Catholic Rite), Néophytes Edelby; (Syrian Rite), Denys P. Beiloune; (Maronite Rite), Pierre Callaos; (Armenian Rite), Boutros Marayati.
Baniyas (Greek Melekite Catholic Rite), Antoine Hayek.
Bosra, Bostra, Boulos Nassif Borkhoche.
Damascus (Greek Melekite Catholic Rite), vacant; (Syrian Rite), Eustache J. Mounayer; (Maronite Rite), Hamid A. Mourany.
Hassaké-Nisibi, Georges Habib Hafouri.
Homs, Emesa (Syrian Catholic Rite), Jean Dahi.
Laodicea (Greek Melekite Catholic Rite), Michel Yatim.

Taiwan

Taipei, Joseph Ti-Kang.

Tanzania

Dar es Salaam, HE Cardinal Laurean Rugambwa.
Mwanza, Antony Mayala.
Tabora, Mario E. A. Mgulunde.

Thailand

Bangkok, HE Cardinal Michael Michai Kitbunchu.
Tharé and Nonseng, Lawrence Khai Saen-Phon-On.

Togo

Lomé, Robert Casimir Dosseh-Anyron.

Trinidad

Port of Spain, Gordon Anthony Pantin.

Turkey

Diarbekir, Paul Karatas.
Istanbul (*Constantinople*), Jean Tcholakian.
Izmir, Giuseppe G. Bernardini.

Uganda

Kampala, Emmanuel Wamala.

Uruguay
Montevideo, José Gottardi Cristelli.

USA
Anchorage, Francis Thomas Hurley.
Atlanta, vacant.
Baltimore, William Henry Keeler.
Boston, HE Cardinal Bernard F. Law.
Chicago, HE Cardinal Joseph L. Bernardin.
Cincinnati, Daniel E. Pilarczyk.
Denver, James Francis Stafford.
Detroit, Adam J. Maida.
Dubuque, Daniel W. Kucera.
Hartford, John F. Whealon.
Indianapolis, Edward T. O'Meara.
Kansas City, Ignatius J. Strecker.
Los Angeles, Roger M. Mahony.
Louisville, Thomas C. Kelly.
Miami, Edward A. McCarthy.
Milwaukee, Rembert G. Weakland.
Mobile, Oscar H. Lipscomb.
Newark, Theodore E. McCarrick.
New Orleans, Francis B. Schulte.
New York, HE Cardinal John J. O'Connor.
Oklahoma City, Charles A. Salatka.
Omaha, Daniel E. Sheehan.
Philadelphia, Anthony J. Beuilacqua.
Pittsburgh, Stephen J. Kocisko.
Portland (Oregon), William J. Levada.
St Louis (Missouri), John L. May.
St Paul & Minneapolis, John Robert Roach.
San Antonio, Patrick F. Flores.
San Francisco, John R. Quinn.
Santa Fe, Robert F. Sanchez.
Seattle, Raymond G. Hunthausen.
Washington, HE Cardinal James A. Hickey.

USSR
Armenia (Catholic Armenian Rite), Boutros Marayati.

There is an unnamed Apostolic Administrator in the following Russian dioceses: Mohilev, Moscow, Leningrad, Kharkov, Kazan, Samara and Simbirsk.

Venezuela
Barquisimeto, Julio Manuel Chirivella Varela.
Caracas, HE Cardinal José Ali Lebrún Moratinos; (Greek Melekite Catholic Rite), Pierre Rai.
Ciudad Bolivar, Medardo Luzardo Romero.
Maracaibo, Domingo Roa Pérez.
Mérida, Miguel Antonio Salas Salas.
Valencia, Jorge Liberato Urosa Savino.

Vietnam
Hanoi, vacant.
Hue, vacant.
Thanh-Phô Hôchiminh, Paul Nguyên Van Binh.

West Indies
Castries, Kelvin Edward Felix.

Yugoslavia
Bar, Petar Perkolić.
Belgrade, Franc Perko.
Ljubljana, Alojzij Suštar.
Rijeka-Senj, Anton Tamarut.
Split-Makarska, Ante Juric.
Vrhbosna, vacant. (Apostolic Administrator, Ciril Kos).
Zadar, Marijan Oblak.
Zagreb, HE Cardinal Franjo Kuharić.

Zaire
Bukavu, Mulindwa Mutabesha.
Kananga, Bakole wa Ilunga.
Kinshasa, vacant.

Kisangani, Laurent Monsengwo Pasinya.
Lubumbashi, Kabanga Songasonga.
Mbandaka-Bikoro, Etsou-Nzabi-Bamungwabi.

Zambia
Kasama, Elias Mutale.
Lusaka, Adrian Mungandu.

Zimbabwe
Harare, Patrick Chakaipa.

ARCHBISHOPS OF TITULAR SEES
Acrida, Mario Schierano.
Adana (Greek Melekite Catholic Rite), Gregoire Haddad.
Amantia, Edward Idris Cassidy.
Amasya, James Patrick Carroll.
Amida, Flavien Zacharie Melkie.
Aquileia, Michele Cecchini.
Beroe, Victor Sartre.
Cadi, Stefan M. Marusyn.
Celene, Gabriel Montaluo.
Cesariana, HE Cardinal Angelo Felici.
Cesarea in Palaestina (Greek Melekite Catholic Rite), Hilarion Capucci.
Claudiopolis in Honoriade, Alfredo Bruniera.
Corinthus, Gennaro Verolino.
Dara, Nicholas T. Elko.
Doclea, Pier Luigi Celata.
Drivastum, Traian Crisan.
Edessa in Osrhoëne (Syrian Catholic Rite), Gregoire Ephrem Jarjour.
Egina, Raffaele Forni.
Ephesus, John Henry Boccella.
Fiorentino, Luigi Barbarito.
Forum Novum, Giovanni Battista Re.
Gabala, Gérard de Milleville.
Gangra, Antonio Ferreira de Macedo.
Gradum, José López Ortiz.
Hadrianopolis in Haemimonto, Lino Zanini.
Heraclea, Jozef Kowalczyk.
Idicra, HE Cardinal Ferdinando Giuseppe Antonelli.
Kaškar, Emmanuel-Karim Delly.
Macra, John Dooley.
Madaurus, Janusz Bolonek.
Marcianopolis, Teofilo Camomot Bastida.
Mesembria, Loris Francesco Capovilla.
Meta, Audrys J. Backis.
Nazareth, Giuseppe Carata.
Neapoli, HE Cardinal Jacques Martin.
Nicaea Parva, Paolino Limongi.
Nicosia, Aurelio Signora.
Novaliciana, Faustino Sainz Munoz.
Nubia, Paul Antaki.
Octava, Blasco Francisco Collaco.
Otriculum, Pietro Biggio.
Razia Ria, Marian Oles.
Rebellum, Giovanni Marray.
Rusellae, Lorenzo Antonetti.
Salamis, Joseph Kuo.
Satrianum, Patrick Coveney.
Scytopolis, Joseph Raya.
Selymbria, Emile Socquet.
Severiana, Luigi Bressan.
Silli, Jan Schotte.
Sinna, Paul F. Tabet.
Soteropolis, Ettore Cunial.
Tagase, Giovanni Ceirano.
Tagora, HE Cardinal Eduardo M. Somalo.
Tarsus (Maronite Rite), Abdallah Bared; (Greek Melekite Catholic Rite), Loutfi Laham.
Tharros, Giuseppe Uhač.
Tiburnia, Donato Squicciarini.
Turris, Vincenzo Moreni.
Velebusdo, Jose M. Estepa Llaurens.

Villamagna, Giulio Einaudi.
Viminacium, Franco Brambilla.
Volsinium, Justin Francis Rigali.

PATRIARCHS IN COMMUNION WITH THE ROMAN CATHOLIC CHURCH

Alexandria, HB Stephanos II Ghattas (Patriarch for Catholic Copts).
Antioch, HB Ignace Antoine II Hayek (Patriarch for Syrian Rite Catholics); HB Maximos V. Hakim (Patriarch for Greek Melekite Rite Catholics); HB Nasrallah Piere Sfeir (Patriarch for Maronite Rite Catholics).
Jerusalem, HB Michel Sabbah (Patriarch for Latin Rite Catholics).
Babilonia of the Chaldeens, HB Raphael I Bidawid.
Cilicia of the Armenians, HB Jean Pierre XVIII Kasparian (Patriarch for Armenian Rite Catholics).
Oriental India, Archbishop Raul Nicolau Gonsalves.
Lisbon, HE Cardinal Antonio Ribeiro.
Venice, HE Cardinal Marco Ce.

POPES FROM 1800

Sovereign Pontiff	Family Name	Elected
Pius VII	Chiaramonti	1800
Leo XII	della Genga	1823
Pius VIII	Castiglioni	1829
Gregory XVI	Cappellari	1831
Pius IX	Mastai-Ferretti	1846
Leo XIII	Pecci	1878
Pius X	Sarto	1903
Benedict XV	della Chiesa	1914
Pius XI	Ratti	1922

Sovereign Pontiff	Family Name	Elected
Pius XII	Pacelli	1939
John XXIII	Roncalli	1958
Paul VI	Montini	1963
John Paul I	Luciani	1978
John Paul II	Wojtyla	1978

Adrian IV (Nicholas Breakspear, the only Englishman elected Pope) was born at Langley, near St. Albans; elected Pope, on the death of Anastasius IV, 1154; died 1159.

THE JEWS

CHIEF RABBI—The Lord Jakobovits, PH.D.
Office, Adler House, Tavistock Square, WC1H 0EP.   *Executive Officer*, A. Greenbat.

It is estimated that about 360,000 Jews are resident in the UK, some 280,000 in Greater London.

The *Board of Deputies of British Jews*, established in 1760, is the representative body of British Jewry and is recognized by HM Government. The basis of representation is mainly synagogal, but secular organizations are also represented. It is a deliberative body and its objects are to watch over the interests of British Jewry, to protect Jews against any disability which they may suffer by reason of their creed and to take such action as may be conducive to their welfare.

President, Dr. Lionel Kopelowitz.

Secretary General, H. Pinner, OBE, Woburn House, Tavistock Square, WC1H 0EP.

The *Beth Din* (Court of Judgment) is a rabbinic body consisting of *Dayanim* (Assessors) and the Chief Rabbi, who is President of the Court. The Court arbitrates when requested in cases between Jew and Jew, and Jew and non-Jew, and gives decisions on religious questions. The decisions are based on Jewish Law and practice and do not conflict with the law of the land. The *Beth Din* also deals with matters concerning dietary law and marriages and divorces, according to Jewish Law.

Dayanim, Rabbi C. Ehrentreu; Rabbi Dr. I. Lerner; Rabbi C. D. Kaplin; Rabbi I. D. Berger.

EDUCATION IN THE UNITED KINGDOM

(For addresses of national education departments, *see* **Government and Public Offices**. For other addresses, *see* **Education Directory**.)

The Government's stated aims in education are to raise standards of achievement at all levels of ability; to increase parental choice; to secure the best possible return from the resources invested in the education service; and to widen access to further and higher education while linking them more closely to the needs of the economy. To achieve these objectives three major pieces of educational legislation have been introduced over the past four years.

Recent legislation

The first of the recent measures was the Education Act 1986 which legislated for changes in the management of schools and the terms of employment of teachers.

The Education (No. 2) Act 1986 extended the legislation by requiring appraisal and more effective in-service training for teachers. It also made changes in the management and accountability of schools, introducing new arrangements for the composition of governing bodies which increased the influence of parents.

The Education Reform Act 1988 provided for: the introduction of a national curriculum supported by attainment targets and systems of assessment; local education authorities to delegate control for their budgets to all secondary schools and larger primary schools; all secondary schools and the larger primary schools to have the choice to opt out of local authority control and achieve grant-maintained (GM) status; and the establishment of City Technology Colleges and City Colleges for the Technology of the Arts.

These provisions apply to schools in England and Wales and similar measures have been implemented for Northern Ireland. These include: a curriculum common to all schools with six broad areas of study incorporating certain compulsory subjects; formal assessment of pupils; the introduction of measures to facilitate the growth of integrated schools (*see* also p. 440); schools (initially secondary schools) and further education colleges to have control over their own budgets; changes to the composition of further education college boards to reflect the community served by the college.

In Scotland, the School Boards (Scotland) Act 1988 increased parental involvement in school management by instituting school boards with parent representation for state schools in Scotland. The Self-Governing Schools etc. (Scotland) Act 1989 created two new types of schools: self-governing schools, which opt to withdraw from local authority control while remaining in the public sector; and Technology Academies, to be set up in partnership with industry in deprived urban areas.

National administration of education

In the United Kingdom responsibility for education is largely decentralized. The Secretary of State for Education and Science has overall responsibility for all aspects of education in England, and for government policy and support for universities throughout Britain in consultation with the Secretaries of State for Wales and Scotland. Responsibility in Wales for nursery, primary and secondary education, and for all non-university institutions of higher and further education, the youth and community services, and adult education lies with the Secretary of State for Wales. The general supervision of the national system of education in Scotland, except for the universities, is the responsibility of the Secretary of State for Scotland acting through the Scottish Education Department. All aspects of education in

Northern Ireland, schools, further education and universities, are the responsibility of the Secretary of State for Northern Ireland.

The main concerns of the education departments (the Department of Education and Science (DES), the Welsh Office, the Scottish Education Department (SED), and the Department of Education for Northern Ireland (DENI)) are the formulation of national policies for education, and the maintenance of consistency in educational standards. They are responsible for the broad allocation of resources for education, for the rate and distribution of educational building and for the supply, training and superannuation of teachers. Hitherto, none of the education departments have run any schools or colleges directly, nor employed any teachers. However, under the provisions of the Education Reform Act 1988 and the Self-Governing Schools etc. (Scotland) Act 1989, the Department of Education and Science in England and Wales and the Scottish Education Department will fund individual schools which have opted out of local education authority control and applied for direct funding from the Secretaries of State. In addition, the Department of Education and Science, in association with sponsors from industry, will fund the new City Technology Colleges and City Colleges for the Technology of the Arts. Technology Academies are to be instituted on a similar basis in Scotland.

Schools in Northern Ireland providing integrated education will be able to apply for grant-maintained status from the Department of Education for Northern Ireland.

The Inspectorate

In England, Wales and Scotland Her Majesty's Inspectors (HMIs) inspect state and independent schools and all other educational establishments apart from universities. The same function is performed in Northern Ireland by the Education and Training Inspectorate of the Department of Education. The Inspectors assess standards and trends and advise the Secretaries of State on the performance of the system in the United Kingdom. They identify and make more widely known good practice and promising developments, and draw attention to weaknesses. They provide advice and help to those with responsibilities for, or in, the institutions through day-to-day contacts, contributions to training, and their publications. Inspection visits are the main way in which the Inspectors perform their functions. There were, in 1990–91, 480 HMIs in England, 56 in Wales, 106 in Scotland, and 62 members of the Inspectorate in Northern Ireland.

Expenditure

The Department of Education and Science, the Welsh Office, the Scottish Office and the Northern Ireland Office act within a framework of estimates approved by Parliament.

In real terms expenditure on education by the Departments was as follows (£ million):

	1989–90 estimated outturn	1990–91 planned
DES	18,052	19,577
Welsh Office	960	1,017
SED	2,466	2,543
DENI	893	987

In the United Kingdom in 1987–88, central government expenditure on education was apportioned as follows (£million):

Schools.................................. 12,026
Further and higher education 5,214
Other education and related expenditure .. 940

Most of this expenditure is incurred by local authorities which make their own expenditure decisions according to their local situations and needs and which are also responsible for funding most further education courses. The bulk of direct expenditure by central government is by the DES, which supports the universities in England, Wales and Scotland through the Universities Funding Council (UFC). It also supports higher education courses in polytechnics and colleges of higher education, and prescribed higher education courses in local education authority colleges in England through the Polytechnics and Colleges Funding Council (PCFC), and grant-maintained schools and CTCs.

The Welsh Office funds grants for adult, higher and further education and supports bilingual education and the Welsh language.

In Scotland, as in England and Wales, the bulk of expenditure on education is at a local level by the regional and islands councils. The main elements of central government expenditure are grant-aided special schools, self-governing schools, one TA, student awards, and the capital and recurrent grants to central institutions and colleges of education.

The Department of Education for Northern Ireland finances higher education, teacher education, teacher salaries and superannuation, student awards and voluntary grammar schools. Remaining expenditure is by education and library boards at local level.

Local administration of education

The education service at present is a national service in which the provision of school education and post-school further education is locally administered and its administration is still largely decentralized.

England and Wales.—In England and Wales the education service is administered by local education authorities (LEAs), which carry the day-to-day responsibility for providing most state primary and secondary education and some further education to meet the needs of their areas.

Each local education authority is required by statute to appoint an education committee, or committees, authorized to exercise on its behalf any of the authority's functions with respect to education except the power to borrow money. Members of the council make up a majority of these committees, but a number of people with experience in education and knowledge of the local education situation are also included.

The LEAs own and maintain schools and colleges, build new ones and provide equipment. Most of the public money spent on education is disbursed by the local authorities. LEAs are financed largely from the community charge and Aggregate External Finance (AEF) from the Department of the Environment in England and the Welsh Office in Wales.

The powers of local education authorities as regards the control of their schools have been modified in recent years. The Education (No. 2) Act 1986 legislated for equal numbers of parents and local authority representatives as governors in most maintained schools. This modification was continued by the Education Reform Act 1988, which delegated control of their budgets directly to secondary and larger primary schools. It also provided for schools with over 300 pupils to opt out of local authority control and to be funded directly by central government.

Scotland.—The duty of providing education locally in Scotland rests with the nine regional and three island councils. They are responsible for the construction of buildings, the employment of teachers and other staff, and the provision of equipment and materials. Their responsibility for the curricula taught in schools is delegated at the moment to individual headteachers, but discussions are taking place on the standardization of curricula to allow for new assessment procedures.

The powers of local authorities in educational institutions under their control have been reduced in Scotland as in England and Wales. Under the School Boards (Scotland) Act 1988, education authorities are required to establish school boards consisting of parents and teachers as well as co-opted members, responsible among other things for the appointment of staff. The Self-Governing Schools etc. (Scotland) Act 1989 provides for schools to withdraw from local authority control and become self-governing; for the institution of Technology Academies (TAs) directly funded by central government; and for the composition of further education college councils on which at least half the members are employers, and for the delegation of substantial functions to these new councils.

Northern Ireland.—Education is administered locally in Northern Ireland by five education and library boards. All grant-aided schools include elected parents and teachers on their boards of governors. Provision is being made for schools wishing to provide integrated education to be grant-maintained from the outset. All secondary schools and colleges of further education will have full responsibility for their own budgets, including staffing costs, by April 1991. Primary and nursery schools will have partly delegated budgets, although the Boards will be able to delegate fully if they wish.

The Council for Catholic Maintained Schools forms an upper tier of management for Catholic schools and provides advice on matters relating to management and administration.

SCHOOLS AND PUPILS

Schooling is compulsory in the United Kingdom for all children between 5 and 16 years. Some provision is made for children under 5 and many pupils remain at school after the minimum leaving age. No fees are charged in any publicly maintained school in England, Wales and Scotland. In Northern Ireland, however, fees are paid by pupils in preparatory departments of grammar schools. Prior to 1990 a small number of pupils was admitted to the secondary departments of grammar schools on a fee-paying basis, as a result of the existence of a fixed quota for pupils transferring to these departments. From 1990, with the abolition of this quota, any pupil resident in Northern Ireland who is admitted to the secondary department of a grammar school will not pay fees.

In the United Kingdom, parents have a right to express a preference for a particular school and have a right to appeal if dissatisfied. Parental choice has been increased by the introduction of a policy known as more open enrolment whereby schools are required to admit children up to the limit of their capacity if there is a demand for places and to publish their criteria for selection if they are over-subscribed.

Schools are now required to make available information about themselves and their examination results. Corporal punishment is no longer legal in publicly maintained schools in the United Kingdom.

Fall and rise in numbers

In primary education, and increasingly in secondary education, pupil numbers in the United Kingdom have declined. In primary schools pupil numbers peaked at around 5·9 million in 1975–76 and reached their lowest figure of 4·3 million in 1985–86. Numbers stood at 4·6 million in 1987–88 and are expected to increase gradually year by year until by 1998 they reach about 4·7 million. In secondary schools pupil numbers rose from 3·5 million in 1971 to 4·6 million in 1981. They stood at 3·7 million in 1987–88 and are projected to decrease to 3·4 million in 1991, before rising to 3·6 million in 1998.

England and Wales

There are two main categories of school in England and Wales: those maintained by local education authorities (27,351), which charge no fees; and independent schools (2,422), which charge fees (*see* p. 441). To these categories may be added two more as a result of the Education Reform Act 1988, consisting of institutions funded directly by the Secretary of State. These comprise primary and secondary schools with over 300 pupils which, although still providing free education, have applied to opt out of local education authority control in favour of grant-maintained (GM) status; and City Technology Colleges (*see* below).

Maintained schools.—These are of two types: (i) county schools (15,760 in 1989) which are owned by LEAs and wholly funded by them. They are non-denominational and provide primary and secondary education; (ii) voluntary schools (7,507 in 1989) which also provide primary and secondary education. Although the buildings are in many cases provided by the voluntary bodies (mainly religious denominations) they are financially maintained by an LEA.

All publicly maintained schools have a governing body usually made up of an equal number of parent representatives and governors appointed by the LEA, the headteacher (unless he or she chooses otherwise), and serving teachers. Parental involvement in the running of their children's schools has increased considerably in recent years, and parents have also been given the power to decide by ballot whether their child's school should opt out of local authority control. The responsibilities of governors under the Education (No. 2) Act 1986 were extended to cover the overall policies of schools and their academic aims and objectives. The governors also now control matters of school discipline and the appointment and dismissal of staff. The Education Reform Act 1988 delegated control of the administration of the major part of school budgets, including staffing costs, from LEAs directly to the larger primary and secondary schools under an initiative known as Local Management of Schools (LMS).

Voluntary schools are of three kinds: controlled (3,090), aided (4,339) and special agreement (78). In *controlled* schools the LEA bears all costs. In *aided* schools the building is usually provided by the voluntary body. The managers or governors are responsible for repairs to the outside of the school building and for improvements and alterations to it, though the Department of Education and Science may reimburse part of approved capital expenditure. The LEA pays for internal maintenance and other running costs. *Special agreement* schools are those where the LEA may, by special agreement, pay between one-half and three-quarters of the cost of building a new, or extending an existing, voluntary school, almost always a secondary school. There are no special agreement schools in Wales. In voluntary schools the majority of the managers or governors are appointed by the voluntary body and at least one by the LEA. The managers or governors control the

appointment of teachers. Expenditure is normally apportioned between the authority and the voluntary body.

Grant-Maintained (GM) Schools.—All secondary schools and larger primary schools are eligible to apply for grant-maintained status, subject to a ballot of parents. GM schools are maintained directly by the Secretary of State, not the LEA, and are wholly run by their own governing body. By September 1990 there were at least 42 GM schools, of which about 60 per cent were comprehensive schools.

City Technology Colleges (CTCs) and City Colleges for the Technology of the Arts (CCTAs).—These schools are state-aided but independent of LEAs. Their aim is to widen the choice of secondary education in disadvantaged urban areas and to teach a broad curriculum with an emphasis on science, technology, business understanding and arts technologies. Capital costs are shared by government and sponsors from industry and commerce, and running costs will be covered by a per capita grant from the DES in line with comparable costs in an LEA maintained school.

The first city technology college opened in September 1988 in Solihull. By September 1991 there will be at least thirteen. The first CCTA will open in Croydon in 1990.

Scotland

Schools in Scotland fall into three main categories: (a) *education authority* schools (3,779) (known as public schools) which are financed and managed by the regional and islands councils; (b) *grant aided* schools (7), conducted by voluntary managers who receive grants direct from the Scottish Education Department; and (c) *independent* schools (117), which receive no direct grant and charge fees, but are subject to inspection and registration. An additional category is created under the provisions of the Self-Governing Schools etc. (Scotland) Act 1989, of schools opting to be managed entirely by a board of management consisting of the headmaster, parent and staff representatives and co-opted members. The change of status will require a ballot of parents and the publication of proposals by the board, and the achievement of self-government is subject to a final decision by the Secretary of State. These schools will remain in the public sector and will be funded by direct government grant set to match the resources the school would have received under education authority management.

Under the School Boards (Scotland) Act 1988, education authorities are required to establish school boards to participate in the administration and management of schools. These boards consist of elected parents and staff members as well as co-opted members.

Technology Academies (TAs).—The Self-Governing Schools etc. (Scotland) Act 1989 provides for setting up technology academies in areas of urban deprivation. These secondary schools are intended to be so placed as to draw on a wide catchment, and will offer a broad curriculum with an emphasis on science and technology. They are to be founded and managed in partnership with industrial sponsors, with central government meeting the running costs by grant-aid thereafter. It is planned to have one academy established and operating in 1990–91.

Northern Ireland

There are three main categories of grant-aided school in Northern Ireland: (a) *controlled* schools (718), which are controlled by the education and library boards with all costs paid from public funds; (b) *voluntary maintained* schools (591), mainly under Roman Catholic management, which receive grants towards capital costs and running costs in whole or in part; and (c) *voluntary grammar* schools (57), which may be under Roman Catholic or non-denominational management and receive grants from the Department of Education for Northern Ireland. All grant-aided schools include elected parents and teachers on their boards of governors, whose responsibilities also include financial management under the Local Management of Schools (LMS) initiative. There also are 16 independent schools in Northern Ireland.

The majority of children in Northern Ireland are educated in schools which in practice are segregated on religious lines. The Education Reform (Northern Ireland) Order 1989, however, makes provision for parents to opt for integrated education more easily. These provisions include arrangements to fund new integrated schools from the outset and procedures for balloting parents in existing segregated schools to determine whether they want instead to have integrated schools.

THE STATE SYSTEM

Nursery education.—Nursery education is for children from 2 to 5 years and is not compulsory. In the United Kingdom it takes place in nursery schools or nursery classes in primary schools. In 1987–88, 700,000 pupils under 5 years of age were receiving education in maintained nursery and primary schools, an increase of 19,000 on the previous year. Of the total, 97,600 were in nursery schools, 557,400 in nursery classes in primary schools, and 39,700 in non-maintained nursery schools. Expressed as a percentage of the population aged 3 and 4 years, the 700,000 represented 48·4 per cent, compared to 47·6 per cent in the previous year.

Many children also attend pre-school playgroups organized by parents and voluntary bodies such as the Pre-School Playgroups Association.

Primary education.—Primary education begins at 5 years and is almost always co-educational. In England, Wales and Northern Ireland the transfer to secondary school is generally made at 11 years. In Scotland, the primary school course lasts for seven years and pupils transfer to secondary courses at about the age of 12.

Primary schools consist mainly of *infants' schools* for children aged 5 to 7, *junior schools* for those aged 7 to 11, and combined *junior and infant schools* for both age groups. In addition, *first schools* in some parts of England cater for ages 5 to 8, 9 or 10. (They are the first stage of a three-tier system: first, middle and secondary). Many primary schools provide nursery classes for children under 5 (*see* above).

The number of primary schools in the United Kingdom in 1987–88 was 24,482, which was 127 fewer than in 1986–87, with 4,598,000 full- and part-time pupils, of which 766,800 were under five. Between 1988 and 1998 primary school pupil numbers are projected to rise by about 10 per cent.

Pupil-teacher ratios in maintained primary schools in the United Kingdom are:

	1986–87	1987–88
England	21·9	22·0
Wales	22·1	22·1
Scotland	20·4	20·4
N. Ireland	23·4	23·5
UK..............	21·8	21·9

The average size of classes 'as taught' has fallen slightly from 25·5 in 1981 to 25·4 in 1988.

Middle schools.—Middle schools (which take children from first schools), mostly in England, cover varying age ranges between 8 and 14 and usually lead on to comprehensive upper schools.

Secondary education.—Secondary schools are for children aged 11 to 16 and for those who choose to stay on to 18. At 16, many students prefer to move on

to tertiary or sixth form colleges (*see* p. 445). Most secondary schools in England, Wales and Scotland are co-educational. The largest secondary schools have over 2,000 pupils but only 21·7 per cent of the schools take over 1,000 pupils.

In England and Wales the main types of secondary schools are: (a) *comprehensive* schools (85·7 per cent of pupils in England, 98·3 in Wales), whose admission arrangements are without reference to ability or aptitude; (b) *middle deemed secondary* schools for children aged variously between 8–14 years who then move on to senior comprehensive schools at 12, 13 or 14 (6·5 per cent of pupils in England, 0·1 per cent in Wales); (c) *secondary modern* schools (4·0 per cent of pupils in England, 0·5 per cent in Wales) providing a general education with a practical bias; (d) *secondary grammar* schools (3·2 per cent of pupils in England, 0·5 per cent in Wales) with selective intake providing an academic course from 11 to 16–18 years; and (e) *technical* schools (0·1 per cent) in England only providing an integrated academic and technical education.

In January 1989 there were in England and Wales 3,136,699 pupils in maintained secondary schools, including 10·4 per cent (England) and 11·3 per cent (Wales) who were 16 or over. After falling by 12 per cent between 1987 and 1991, numbers are projected to rise by 8·7 per cent by 1998.

Pupil-teacher ratios have improved steadily from 16·1 in 1985–86 to 15·3 in 1989 in England and Wales. A steady annual decrease in class sizes in England resumed, after a rise in 1985 (to 21·4), from 20·9 in 1984 to 20·6 in 1989. In Wales the average class size in 1989 was 19·0.

In Scotland 99·3 per cent of pupils in education authority secondary schools attend schools with a comprehensive intake. Most of these schools provide a full range of courses appropriate to all levels of ability from first to sixth year. In 1988–89 there were 312,600 pupils in education authority schools, of whom 24·1 per cent were 16 or over. Numbers are not expected to increase much between 1990 and 1995. Pupil-teacher ratios have improved from 14·4 in 1981–82 to 12·4 in 1989. The average class size in 1987 was 18·8.

In most areas of Northern Ireland there is a selective system of secondary education with pupils transferring either to grammar schools or secondary schools at 11–12 years of age. Parents can choose the school they would like their children to attend and all those who apply must be admitted. If a school is over-subscribed beyond its statutory admissions number, selection is on the basis of published criteria. In drawing up their criteria most grammar schools place emphasis on performance in the transfer procedure tests which are centrally administered by the Department of Education. When parents consider that a school has not applied its criteria fairly they have access to independent appeals tribunals. Grammar schools provide an academic type of secondary education with A-levels at the end of the seventh year, while secondary non-grammar schools follow a curriculum suited to a wider range of aptitudes and abilities.

In 1987–88 there were 145,000 pupils in public sector secondary schools, of whom 92,534 (63·8 per cent) attended non-grammar secondary and 52,466 (56·2 per cent) attended grammar schools. Of these 21·8 per cent were 16 or over. Pupil-teacher ratios in Northern Ireland have improved from 15·5 in 1982 to 14·9 in 1988.

Special education.—Special education is provided for children with special educational needs, usually because they have a disability which either prevents or hinders them from making use of educational facilities of a kind generally provided for children of their age in schools within the area of the local authority concerned. Maintained special schools are run by education authorities which pay all the costs of maintenance. Non-maintained special schools are run by voluntary bodies; they may receive some grant from central government for capital expenditure and for equipment, but their current expenditure is met primarily from the fees charged to the education authorities for pupils placed in the schools. Some independent schools provide education wholly or mainly for children with special educational needs. The national curriculum also applies to children with a statement of special needs, but there is provision for them to be exempt from it, or for it to be modified to suit the individual child's capabilities.

In January 1988 in the United Kingdom there was a total of 117,700 full-time pupils in special schools (of whom 3,000 were in hospital schools in England, Wales and Northern Ireland). Of the total, 100,500 were in England, 3,900 in Wales, 9,400 in Scotland and 3,800 in Northern Ireland. Numbers have gone down since 1975–76 as education authorities in England, Wales and Northern Ireland must now ensure that children with special needs are educated as far as possible in ordinary schools with support teaching.

In Scotland, school placing is a matter of agreement between education authorities and parents. Parents have the right to say which school they want their child to attend, and a right of appeal where their wishes are not being met. Whenever possible, children with special needs are integrated into ordinary schools. However, for those who require a different environment or specialized facilities, there are special schools, both grant-aided and independent, and special classes within ordinary schools. The Self-Governing Schools etc. (Scotland) Act 1989 obliges education authorities to respond to reasonable requests for independent special schools, and provides for them to send children with special needs to schools outside Scotland if appropriate provision is not available within the country.

Alternative provision

There is no legal obligation on parents in the United Kingdom to educate their children at school provided that the local education authority is satisfied that the child is receiving full-time education suited to its age, abilities and aptitudes. The education authority need not be informed that a child is being educated at home unless the child is already registered at a state school. In this case the parents must arrange for the child's name to be removed from the school's register (by writing to the headteacher) before education at home can begin. Failure to de-register a child leaves the parents liable to prosecution for condoning non-attendance.

In most cases an initial visit is made by an education adviser or education welfare officer, and sometimes subsequent inspections are made, but practice varies according to the individual education authority. There is no requirement for parents educating their children at home to be in possession of a teaching qualification.

Further advice on educating children other than at school can be obtained from Education Otherwise (see p. 453).

INDEPENDENT SCHOOLS

Independent schools receive no grants from public funds. They charge fees, and are owned and managed under special trusts, with profits being used for the benefit of the schools concerned. There is a wide variety of provision, from kindergartens to large day and boarding schools, and from experimental schools to traditional institutions. A number of independent schools have been instituted recently by religious and ethnic minorities.

All independent schools in the United Kingdom are open to inspection by the Inspectorate (see above) and must register with the appropriate government education department. The education departments lay down certain minimum standards and can make schools remedy any unacceptable features of their building or instruction and exclude any unsuitable teacher or proprietor. Most independent schools offer a similar range of courses to state schools and enter pupils for the same public examinations. Introduction of the national curriculum and the associated education targets and assessment procedures is not obligatory in the independent sector.

The term public schools is often applied to those independent schools in membership of the Headmasters' Conference, the Governing Bodies Association or the Governing Bodies of Girls' Schools Association. Most public schools are single-sex (about half of them for girls) but there are some mixed schools and an increasing number of schools have mixed sixth forms.

Preparatory schools are so called because they prepare children for the Common Entrance Examination to senior independent schools. Most cater for boys from about 7 to 13 years, but some are for girls and an increasing number are co-educational. The Common Entrance Examination is set by the Common Entrance Examination Board, but marked by the independent school to which the pupil intends to go. It is taken at 13 by boys, and from 11 to 13 by girls.

In 1989 there were in England 2,270 independent schools with 540,102 full-time pupils and a pupil-teacher ratio of 11·2.

In Wales in 1988–89 there were 66 independent schools, with 11,804 pupils and a pupil-teacher ratio of 10·0.

In Scotland in 1988–89 there were 117 registered independent schools with 32,400 pupils. Most independent schools in Scotland follow the English examination system, i.e. GCSE followed by A-levels, although some take the Scottish Education Certificate at Ordinary/Standard grade followed by Highers.

There are 16 independent schools in Northern Ireland with 1,119 pupils and a pupil-teacher ratio of 13·2.

Assisted Places Scheme

The Assisted Places Scheme enables children to attend independent secondary schools which their parents could not otherwise afford. The scheme provides help with tuition fees and other expenses, except boarding costs, on a sliding scale depending on the family's income. The take-up rate for places available at age 11 to 13 at the 302 participating schools in England and Wales is over 90 per cent, and the proportion of pupils receiving full fee remission is 33·5 per cent. Some 34,000 places were offered in England and Wales in the academic year 1989–90. The 49 participating schools in Scotland admitted 2,684 pupils on the scheme, which, unlike that in England and Wales, is cash-limited. The proportion of pupils receiving full fee remission is 44 per cent.

The scheme is administered and funded in England by the Department of Education and Science, in Wales by the Welsh Office, and in Scotland by the Scottish Education Department.

The scheme does not operate in Northern Ireland as the independent sector admits non-fee paying pupils. There is, however, a similar scheme known as the Talented Children's Scheme to help pupils gifted in music and dance.

Further information can be obtained from the Independent Schools Information Service.

THE CURRICULUM
England and Wales

Headteachers in England and Wales were entirely responsible for determining the curriculum in their schools with due reference to their local education authority and their school governors until the Education Reform Act 1988 legislated for the progressive introduction from autumn 1989 of a national curriculum in primary and secondary schools. During the period of compulsory schooling for children aged 5 to 16 the curriculum will include mathematics, English and science as core subjects; and history, geography, technology, music, art, physical education and (for pupils in secondary schools) a modern foreign language as foundation subjects. For the core and foundation subjects there will be attainment targets and assessment procedures at the ages of 7, 11 and 14; at 16 the GCSE will be the main form of assessment. It is intended that pupils with special educational needs should have access to as much of the national curriculum as possible. Religious education is required to be available in schools, with the curriculum devised locally, but parents will have the right to remove their children if they wish.

In Wales in 1988 the Welsh language was in use as the main or secondary medium of instruction in 13·4 per cent of primary and over 11 per cent of secondary schools. Following the introduction of the national curriculum it will constitute a core subject in Welsh-speaking schools and a foundation subject in the others.

In England the National Curriculum Council, funded by the Department of Education and Science, is responsible for the promotion and support of curriculum development in addition to advising the Secretary of State on the national curriculum. In Wales this function is performed by the Curriculum Council for Wales, funded by the Welsh Office.

Scotland

The content and management of the curriculum in Scotland is the responsibility of education authorities and individual headteachers. Advice and guidance is provided by the Scottish Education Department and the Scottish Consultative Council on the Curriculum. Scotland effectively has a national curriculum for 14–16 year-olds, who are required to study English, mathematics and a science subject plus five other subjects. These form the core area, supplemented by other activities forming the elective area. There is a recommended percentage of class time to be devoted to each area over the two years. Provision is made for teaching in Gaelic in Gaelic-speaking areas.

The Scottish Consultative Council on the Curriculum, which is responsible for development and advisory work on the curriculum in Scotland, has been asked to undertake a major review of the balance of the primary curriculum, and to produce new guidelines for each of the subject areas for the age group 5–14. There will be new guidelines on assessment across the whole curriculum, and standardized tests will be introduced in English and mathematics for 9 and 12 year-olds. For 16–18 year-olds, there is available a modular system of vocational courses in addition to academic courses.

Northern Ireland

Major programmes of curriculum review and development are in progress in primary and secondary schools. A curriculum common to all schools is being introduced over a three year period to 1992–93, with six broad areas of study within which ten subjects will be compulsory; religious education will also be a compulsory part of the curriculum. The Irish language will be a compulsory subject in Irish

medium primary schools and can be chosen as the compulsory foreign language in secondary schools. Arrangements for the assessment of pupils, broadly in line with those in England and Wales, are proposed at the ages of 8, 11, 14 and 16.

The Northern Ireland Curriculum Council advises the Government on all matters concerning the curriculum for grant-aided schools in Northern Ireland.

Records of achievement

Records of achievement are documents which set down the range of pupils' achievements and activities both inside and outside the classroom, including those not tested by examination. It is intended that by 1991 parents in England and Wales will receive a yearly progress report on their children. There is a similar commitment for Northern Ireland. In Scotland the report card system is being reformed to give parents more information on their children's progress.

Technical and Vocational Initiative

The Technical and Vocational Initiative (TVEI) operates across the curriculum within a framework of general education in England, Wales and Scotland. It aims to make the secondary curriculum more relevant to adult life and work. Following pilot projects, it is now a national scheme with newly established criteria which complement and are compatible with the requirements of the new national curriculum in England and Wales. Participation is voluntary, and is open to all maintained schools and colleges providing for young people of all abilities aged 14–18. TVEI is not an examination or a qualification.

THE EXAMINATION SYSTEM
England, Wales and Northern Ireland

Until the end of 1987 secondary school pupils at the end of compulsory schooling around the age of 16, and others, took the General Certificate of Education (GCE) Ordinary-level or the Certificate of Secondary Education (CSE). From 1988 these were replaced by a single system of examinations, the General Certificate of Secondary Education (GCSE), which is usually taken after five years of secondary education. The first examinations took place in summer 1988.

The GCSE differs from its predecessors in that there are: syllabuses based on national criteria covering course objectives, content and assessment methods; differentiated assessment (i.e. different papers or questions for different ranges of ability); and grade-related criteria (i.e. grades awarded on absolute rather than relative performance).

The GCSE certificates are awarded on a seven point scale, A to G. Grades A to C are the equivalent of the corresponding O-level grades A to C, or CSE grade 1. Grades D, E, F and G record achievement at least as high as that represented by CSE grades 2 to 5. There is no restriction on entry to any examination. All GCSE syllabuses, assessments and grading procedures are monitored by the School Examinations and Assessment Council (*see* below) to ensure that they conform to the national criteria.

Of school leavers in the United Kingdom who left school without A-levels or SCE H-grades in 1987–88, 34·1 per cent had achieved one or more graded GCE O-level, CSE, SCE O-grade results, compared to 24 per cent in 1980–81.

Certificate of Extended Education.—The Certificate of Extended Education (CEE) comprises a number of single-subject examinations set and awarded by a number of GCSE examining boards and taken a year after GCSE. Apart from English and mathematics, subjects are non-traditional and include social, environmental, technological, business and health studies.

Advanced levels and Advanced Supplementary levels.—Advanced (A-level) examinations, taken by those who choose to continue their education two years after GCSE, continue as before although changes have been made to the grading system.

A-level courses last two years, and have traditionally provided the foundation for entry to higher education. A-levels are marked on a seven point scale, from A to E, N (narrow failure) and U (unclassified), which latter grade will not be certificated.

As an alternative to, and to complement, A-level examinations, Advanced Supplementary level (AS-level) examinations were introduced in September 1987, with the first examinations taking place in summer 1989. AS-levels are for full-time A-level students but also open to other students. An AS-level syllabus covers not less than half the amount of ground covered by the corresponding A-level syllabus and, where possible, is related to it. An AS-level course lasts two years and requires not less than half the teaching time of the corresponding A-level course, and two AS-levels are equivalent to one A-level. AS-level courses are intended to supplement and broaden A-level studies, and examinations are held at the same time as A-levels. AS-level passes are graded A to E, with grade standards related to the A-level grades.

A mixture of A-level courses in the subjects to be specialized in and AS-levels will form the standard for admission to higher education.

In the United Kingdom in 1987–88, 24 per cent of all 17 year olds (23 per cent of boys, 25 per cent of girls) achieved one or more A-level or SCE H-grade result, compared to 20 per cent in 1980–81. This figure includes those continuing their education in maintained further education establishments including tertiary colleges, as well as school leavers.

Of school leavers alone (797,000), 18·8 per cent achieved at least one A-level or SCE H-grade (18·6 per cent of boys, 19·1 per cent of girls). Of those in Great Britain obtaining two or more A-levels, or three or more SCE H-grades, 25 per cent studied sciences (34 per cent of boys, 16 per cent of girls), 40 per cent studied arts/social studies (31 per cent of boys, 40 per cent of girls), and 35·5 per cent (36 per cent of boys, 35 per cent of girls) studied science and arts/social studies.

S-levels.—Most examining boards allow the option of an additional paper of greater difficulty to be taken by A-level candidates to obtain what is known as a Special-level or Scholarship-level qualification. S-level papers are available in most of the traditional academic subjects and are marked on a three point scale, grade A or 1, grade B or 2, and unclassified.

Co-ordination and advisory body.—The School Examinations and Assessment Council (SEAC) has been set up to advise the Government on all school examinations and assessment matters in England and Wales. It is also responsible for the development of the assessment system for the national curriculum. The Council is funded wholly by the Department of Education and Science.

The Northern Ireland Schools Examinations and Assessment Council performs the same function in Northern Ireland, funded by the Department of Education for Northern Ireland.

The Certificate of Pre-Vocational Education.—The Certificate of Pre-Vocational Education (CPVE) is a one-year full-time (or two years part-time) course available at schools and colleges in England, Wales and Northern Ireland. It is intended for a wide ability range at 16+, including pupils who might not go on to A-levels but would like to continue their education on completion of their secondary schooling. The qualification is offered by the Business and Technician Training Council and the City and Guilds of London Institute operating together as the Joint Board for Pre-Vocational Education.

There are no formal examinations but credits for work achieved during CPVE can be built up towards further study. Within guidelines laid down by the Board, schools and colleges design their own courses, which stress activity-based learning, basic numeracy and work experience. The CPVE is mainly for those who want to find out what aptitudes they may have and to prepare themselves for work, but who are not yet committed to a particular occupation.

Scotland

The system of public examinations in Scotland is different from that elsewhere in the United Kingdom. At the end of the fourth year of secondary education (equivalent to the fifth year in the rest of the United Kingdom), at about the age of 16, pupils take either the Ordinary grade of the Scottish Certificate of Education Examination (corresponding to the old GCE Ordinary level) or the Standard grade. The Ordinary grade is gradually being replaced by the new Standard grade courses and examinations, which have been designed to suit every level of ability, with assessment against nationally determined standards of performance.

For most courses there are three separate examination papers at the end of the two-year Standard grade course. They are set at Credit (leading to awards at grade 1 or 2), General (leading to awards at grade 3 or 4) and Foundation (leading to awards at grade 5 or 6) levels. Grade 7 is available to those who, although they have completed the course, have shown no significant level of attainment. Normally pupils will take examinations covering two pairs of grades, either grades 1–4 or grades 3–6.

Pupils may attempt as many of a wide range of subjects as they are capable of, on either the Ordinary/Standard grades, or on the Higher grade which is normally taken one year after Ordinary/Standard grades, at the age of 17 or thereabouts. The shorter length of course means that Higher grades are normally studied to a lesser depth than A-levels; on the other hand it is common for pupils to be presented for four or more Higher grades at a single diet of the examination.

The Certificate of Sixth Year Studies (CSYS) is designed to give direction and purpose to sixth-year work by encouraging pupils who have completed their main subjects at Higher grade to study a maximum of three of these subjects in depth. Pupils may also use the sixth year to gain improved or additional Higher grades or Ordinary/Standard grades.

The Scottish Certificate of Education Examination and the Certificate of Sixth Year Studies are conducted by the Scottish Examination Board.

National Certificate.—The National Certificate was introduced in 1984–85 as an alternative to, and to complement, Highers and CSYS. It is awarded to pupils over the age of 16 who have successfully completed a programme of vocational courses based on modular study units. It replaces the profusion of courses and certificates available in non-advanced further education, and the assessment system is based on national criteria. The modules are now being introduced in schools for pupils aged 14–16, and other short courses are being devised for use in schools. The National Certificate is validated by the Scottish Vocational Education Council (*see* also p. 445).

The International Baccalaureate

The International Baccalaureate is an internationally recognized two-year pre-university course and examination designed to facilitate the mobility of students and to promote international understanding. Candidates must offer one subject from each of six subject groups, at least three at higher level and the remainder at subsidiary level. Single subjects can be offered, for which a certificate is received. There are 22 schools and colleges in the United Kingdom which offer the International Baccalaureate diploma. Further information can be obtained from International Baccalaureate London.

TEACHERS
England and Wales

Teachers are appointed by local education authorities, school governing bodies, or school managers. Those in publicly maintained schools must be approved as 'qualified' by the Department of Education and Science. To become a qualified teacher it is necessary to have successfully completed a course of initial teacher training, usually either a Bachelor of Education (B.Ed.) degree or the Postgraduate Certificate of Education (PGCE). Teacher training has hitherto been largely integrated with the rest of higher education, with training places concentrated in universities, polytechnics and institutes or colleges of education, but under the articled teacher scheme graduates will be paid a bursary in addition to a salary to complete a school-based PGCE course over two years involving a progressively increasing teaching load.

With certain exceptions the profession now has an all-graduate entry. Teachers in further education are not required to have qualified teacher status, though roughly half have a teaching qualification and most have industrial, commercial or professional experience.

The licensed teacher scheme is designed to attract into the teaching profession mature entrants without formal teaching qualifications but with relevant training and experience. All licensees will be required to have the equivalent of two years higher education in the United Kingdom in addition to the equivalent of grade C in GCSE maths and English. Local education authorities will be involved in devising a suitable two-year training programme for any licensed teachers they may appoint to their schools; for grant-maintained schools and City Technology Colleges this will be a matter for the school itself.

Scotland

All teachers in maintained schools must be registered with the General Teaching Council for Scotland. They are registered provisionally for a two-year probationary period which can be extended if necessary. Only graduates are accepted as entrants to the teaching profession in Scotland.

Northern Ireland

Teacher training in Northern Ireland is provided by the two universities and two colleges of education. The colleges are concerned with teacher education mainly for the primary school sector. They also provide B.Ed. courses for intending secondary school teachers of religious education, commercial studies, and craft, design and technology. With these excep-

tions, the training of teachers for secondary schools is provided in the education departments of the universities.

Accreditation of training courses

The Council for the Accreditation of Teacher Education (CATE) advises on course accreditation in England, Wales and Northern Ireland and monitors and disseminates good practice. In Scotland all training courses in colleges of education must be approved by the Scottish Education Department and a validating body.

Newly-trained teachers

Of teachers who in 1987 had successfully completed initial training courses in the United Kingdom, 8,700 had completed a postgraduate course and 7,700 a course for non-graduates.

In the year to January 1989, 12,857 teachers took up first full-time appointments, either permanently or for at least one term's duration, in maintained nursery, primary and secondary schools in England and Wales. In Scotland and Northern Ireland, figures for 1989 were 922 and 522 respectively.

Shortage subjects.—Because of a shortage of teachers in a number of secondary subjects, a tax-free bursary scheme for trainee teachers on one- or two-year courses has been introduced. The subjects are mathematics, chemistry, modern languages (including Welsh in Wales), and technology, which attract a bursary of £1,500, and physics, which attracts a bursary of £2,000.

Serving teachers

In 1987–88 there were 621,000 teachers (full-time and full-time equivalent) in public sector schools and establishments of further education in the United Kingdom. Of these, 500,000 were in maintained schools and 121,000 in further education. There were 206,000 full-time teachers in public sector primary schools, 253,000 in public sector secondary schools and 20,000 in special schools.

Salaries

All qualified teachers in England, Wales and Northern Ireland other than heads and deputy heads, are paid on an 11 point scale ranging from £9,000 to £16,002 (January 1991 figures). Entry points vary depending on qualification and according to the discretion of the appointing authority. In addition, incentive allowances are payable on a range of five rates. Headteachers' salaries range from £19,200 to £37,902; deputy headteachers' salaries range from £18,300 to £27,600. There is a statutory superannuation scheme in maintained schools.

Teachers in Scotland are paid (1990 figures) on a ten point scale from £9,840 to £16,356. As in the rest of the United Kingdom, the entry point depends on type of qualification, and additional allowances are payable under certain circumstances. Headteachers are paid on a scale from £18,450 to £33,825 and depute headteachers from £19,371 to £25,827 depending on whether the school is primary or secondary and the size of school roll.

FURTHER EDUCATION

The Education Reform Act 1988 defines further education as all provision outside schools to people aged over 16 of education up to and including A-level and its equivalent; the term non-advanced further education (NAFE) applied

to courses up to A-level standard is no longer employed in England and Wales. All education authorities have a duty to secure provision for adequate facilities for further education in their area.

England and Wales

Responsibility for co-ordinating further education provision rests with ten **Regional Advisory Councils** set up by the local education authorities (LEAs) in each region. There are nine for England, and the Welsh Joint Committee acts as the council for Wales. The councils operate in accordance with terms of reference agreed between the participating LEAs, which meet staffing and other expenses. Members include representatives from LEAs, polytechnics and universities, further education institutions, employers and employees in industry and commerce. HM Inspectors attend as assessors.

In England and Wales further education courses are taught at a variety of institutions. These range from polytechnics and colleges of further and higher education (most of which also offer higher education courses) to tertiary colleges and sixth form colleges, which concentrate on the provision of normal sixth form school courses as well as a range of vocational courses. A number of institutions specific to a particular form of training, e.g. the Royal College of Music, are also involved. All such courses are funded by local education authorities, including further education courses in polytechnics and colleges of higher education.

Every institution maintained by a local education authority and providing full-time further education under a further education scheme is required to appoint a board of governors. At least half the governors must represent employment interests or be independent of local authority or college interests. Local authorities must delegate to these bodies extensive powers over the appointment of staff and the management of college budgets under the local management of further and higher education colleges initiative.

The position of teaching staff in further education establishments is similar to that in schools with respect to qualifications and regular appraisal of teachers' performance.

Much of the post-school provision outside the higher education sector is broadly vocational in purpose. It extends from lower level technical and commercial courses through courses for those aiming at higher level posts in industry, commerce and administration, to professional courses. Facilities for GCSE courses, CEE (Certificate of Extended Education), CPVE (Certificate of Pre-Vocational Education), AS-levels and A-level courses are also provided (*see* pp. 442–3). These courses can form the foundation for progress to higher education qualifications (*see* below).

The main courses and examinations in the vocational field are offered by the following bodies, but there are also many others:

Business and Technician Education Council (BTEC) provides awards across a wide range of subject areas and three main qualifications. The BTEC First Certificate can be taken over one year part-time and the BTEC First Diploma over one year full-time or two years part-time. Neither requires any formal academic qualifications for entry. The BTEC National Certificate is taken over two years part-time and the BTEC National Diploma over two years full-time or over three years part-time or as a sandwich course. Both require certain academic qualifications for entry.

City and Guilds of London Institute (C&G) offers a wide range of technical and vocational qualifications. Courses are usually run at colleges of further education, training centres and by large companies. Most courses are part-time for students already in employment, but some full-time courses are available.

The City and Guilds of London Institute and the Business and Technician Education Council, operating together as the **Joint Board for Pre-Vocational Education**, are responsible for administering the Certificate of Pre-Vocational Education (*see* p. 443).

RSA (Royal Society of Arts) Examinations Board schemes cover a wide range of vocational qualifications, including business and administration, language schemes and teaching qualifications. Many schemes are offered at levels matching those established by the NCVQ (*see* below). There are no set entry requirements and a policy operates of credit accumulation, so that candidates can take a single unit or complete qualifications.

There are 516 further education establishments in England and Wales with 2,632 adult education centres. In 1988–89 there were 356,735 full-time and sandwich students and 753,237 part-time students on further education courses.

Scotland

Education authorities in Scotland provide further education comprising non-advanced courses up to SCE Highers grade, GCE A-level and SCOTVEC vocational courses. Courses are taught mainly at colleges of further education, including technical colleges, and in some schools.

The Self-Governing Schools (Scotland) Act 1989 legislated for Further Education College Councils to be set up with extensive powers to run their colleges. The Act specifies that at least half the members of college councils must be private or public sector employers and not more than one-fifth local authority representatives; that education authorities must delegate substantial functions to the new councils; and that colleges must be allowed to earn income from commercial activities.

The Scottish Vocational Education Council (SCOTVEC) provides national qualifications, known as the National Certificate, across a similar range of occupational sectors to the Business and Technician Education Council in England and Wales. The system is completely comprehensive and covers the whole range of non-advanced further education provision in Scotland. Students may study for the National Certificate on a full-time, part-time, or day- or block-release basis. The system is based on modules and National Certificate modules and modular programmes can be taken in further education colleges, central institutions or in secondary schools from the age of 16 onwards. Scottish Vocational Qualifications (SVQS) combine programmes of SCOTVEC's National Certificate modules or Higher National Units with skills gained in the work-place.

In 1987–88 there were 29,065 full-time and sandwich students, 163,462 part-time students on non-advanced vocational courses of further education in the 50 further education colleges, 12 central institutions and five colleges of education.

Northern Ireland

Education and library boards are obliged to prepare and submit for approval to the Department of Education for Northern Ireland, schemes setting out the principles to be applied by the boards in planning the further education provision to be made by colleges under their management.

Although the colleges of further education are maintained by the education and library boards, proposals along the lines of those in England and Wales are to be implemented in 1991 for the delegation of financial powers and responsibilities to the boards of governors of the colleges. The composition of the boards themselves is to be changed to include 50 per cent membership from the professions, local business or industry, or other fields of employment relevant to the activities of the college.

On reaching school-leaving age, pupils may attend colleges of further education to pursue the same type of vocational courses as are provided in colleges in England and Wales, administered by the same examining bodies.

Northern Ireland has 26 institutions of further education with 231 out-centres. In 1988–89 there were 15,037 full-time students and 32,269 part-time students on non-advanced vocational courses of further education.

Course Information

Applications for further education courses are generally made directly to the colleges concerned. Information on further education courses in the United Kingdom and addresses of colleges can be found in the *Directory of Further Education* published annually by the Careers Research and Advisory Council.

National Council for Vocational Qualifications

The National Council for Vocational Qualifications (NCVQ) was set up by the Government in October 1986 to achieve a coherent national framework for vocational qualifications. The Council does not award qualifications but works with and through the established examining and awarding bodies to reform the existing vocational qualifications system and introduce simplified arrangements. The new system should be fully operational in England, Wales and Northern Ireland by 1992. It does not apply to Scotland, where a reformed framework already exists under the SCOTVEC National Certificate (*see* above).

The name and style *National Vocational Qualification* will be accorded to qualifications accredited by NCVQ and awarded by bodies it has approved. The NVQ framework is currently based on four levels incorporating qualifications up to and including the Higher National standard.

A *National Record of Vocational Achievement* has been introduced which allows small elements of competence acquired at different times and in different ways to be recorded in a standard form and to be built up into a full NVQ.

HIGHER EDUCATION

The term higher education is used to describe education above A-level and Higher grade or their equivalent, which is provided in universities, polytechnics and colleges of higher education.

The Education Reform Act 1988 legislated for important changes in the structure, national planning and funding of higher education (*see* below).

Students

In 1987–88, there were 626,000 full-time and sandwich students in higher education in the United Kingdom, of whom 61,500 were from overseas. The number of part-time students in the United Kingdom, including the Open University, was 366,000. The proportion of 18 and 19 year-olds entering full-time higher education in Great Britain rose from 13·2 per cent in 1983–84 to 14·6 per cent in 1987–88. The number of mature entrants to full-time higher education in 1987 (excluding those at the Open University) was up by 34 per cent on 1981–82. The number of full-time students on science courses in 1987–88 was 132,600, of which 45,300 were female, compared to 139,700 (47,600 female) in 1986–87.

Academic staff

Each university appoints its own academic staff on its own conditions, though there is a common salary structure and, except for Oxford and Cambridge, a common career structure. The University Commissioners were appointed under the Education Reform Act 1988 to secure changes in university statutes to abolish the granting of tenure, thus enabling staff to be dismissed for good cause and for redundancy.

The Education Reform Act 1988 has taken polytechnics and higher education colleges in England and Wales out of local education authority control, turning them into employers on their own account. The Polytechnics and Colleges Employers Forum has been set up to look after salary structures, which are being re-negotiated.

Teaching staff in higher education require no formal teaching qualification, but teacher trainers are required to spend a certain amount of time in schools to ensure that they have sufficient recent practical experience.

In 1988–89 there were 51,036 full-time and part-time academic staff in universities in the United Kingdom and 116,350 in public sector further and higher education.

The 1990–91 salary scales for non-clinical academic staff in universities were: lecturer grade A £11,399–£16,755; lecturer grade B £17,455–£22,311; senior lecturer £23,423–£28,616; professor £27,013 (minimum). The salaries of clinical academic staff are kept broadly comparable to those of doctors and dentists in the National Health Service.

UNIVERSITIES

Universities are self-governing institutions, usually established by Royal Charter, which are responsible for their own academic appointments, curricula and student admissions. The universities have freedom in academic matters but the Government, through the University Funding Council, determines the total size of the university student population, its distribution between arts, science, medicine, etc., and the part which the university sector plays in the whole higher education system.

Overall responsibility for universities throughout Great Britain rests with the Secretary of State for Education and Science, who consults with the Secretaries of State for Scotland and Wales as necessary. Universities in Northern Ireland are the responsibility of the Secretary of State for Northern Ireland.

Advice to the Government on university matters is provided by the Universities Funding Council (UFC). The UFC acts as a buffer between the Government, from which it receives a block grant of money, and the universities, to which it allocates its grant. Its brief is to secure more effective use of public funds allocated to higher education.

There are 46 universities in the United Kingdom. Of these, 35 are in England, one (a federal institution) in Wales, eight in Scotland and two in Northern Ireland. In 1988–89 there was a total of 333,547 full-time students at universities in the United Kingdom (39,321 of these from overseas) and 50,097 part-time students. Women form 42·2 per cent of the full-time total and 42·1 per cent of the part-time total.

The non-residential **Open University** provides courses leading to degrees nationally. Teaching is through a combination of television and radio programmes, correspondence, tutorials, short residential courses and local audio-visual centres. No qualifications are needed for entry. The Open University offers undergraduate, post-experience and postgraduate courses. The University also has a programme of higher degrees: B.Phil., M.Phil. and

Ph.D. through research, and MA and M.Sc. through taught courses. A Master of Business Administration (MBA) degree course was introduced in 1989.

The Open University is grant-aided directly by the Department of Education and Science and does not come under the Universities Funding Council. For Open University purposes Northern Ireland is administered as a separate section of the United Kingdom and the cost is met by the Department of Education for Northern Ireland.

In 1989, 71,017 undergraduates were registered at the Open University, of whom 32,668 were women and 38,349 were men. Estimated cost (1990) of a BA general degree was around £2,000 and of a BA Hons. degree over £2,500. Applications should be made direct to The Open University, PO Box 71, Milton Keynes MK7 6AG.

The independent **University of Buckingham** provides a two-year course leading to a bachelor's degree and its tuition fees were £6,790 for 1990. It receives no capital or recurrent income from the Government but its students are eligible for mandatory awards from local education authorities. Its academic year consists of four terms of ten weeks each.

Courses

All universities award their own degrees and sometimes act as awarding and validating bodies for neighbouring colleges of higher education, though this function is increasingly being taken on by the Council for National Academic Awards (*see* below). With the exception of certain Scottish universities where Master is sometimes used for a first degree in arts subjects, undergraduate courses lead to the title of Bachelor—Bachelor of Arts (BA) and Bachelor of Science (B.Sc.) being the most common—and for a higher degree Master of Arts (MA), Master of Science (M.Sc.) (usually taught courses) and the research degrees of Master of Philosophy (M.Phil.) and Doctor of Philosophy (Ph.D. or, at a few universities, D.Phil.).

Most undergraduate programmes at British universities run for three years, except in Scotland and at the University of Keele where they may take four years. Professional courses in subjects such as medicine, dentistry and veterinary science take longer. Details of courses on offer and of entry requirements to first degree courses can be found in the annual handbook produced co-operatively by the universities, *University Entrance: The Official Guide,* published by the Association of Commonwealth Universities (for address, *see* p. 454).

Postgraduate programmes vary in length. Taught courses which lead to certificates, diplomas or master's degrees usually take one year full-time or two years part-time. Research degrees take from two to three years full-time and much longer if completed on a part-time basis. Details of taught courses and research degree opportunities can be found in *Graduate Studies* published annually for the Careers Research and Advisory Centre by Hobsons Publishing PLC (for address, *see* p. 454).

Post-experience short courses are forming an increasing part of university provision, reflecting the need to update professional and technical training. Most of these courses finance themselves.

Admissions

Constraints are imposed by the Government on the number of home students which a university is able to admit, but the individual university decides which students to accept and which to reject. Students applying for admission to a first degree course at most universities do not apply direct but through a clearing-house, the Universities' Central Council on Admissions (UCCA). All universities in the United Kingdom participate in the UCCA scheme except the Open University which conducts its own admissions direct. The *UCCA handbook* is issued free for use in completing UCCA application forms, and is available from schools, colleges, or direct from the Universities' Central Council on Admissions (for address, *see* p. 455).

For admission as a postgraduate student, universities normally require a good first degree in a subject related to the proposed course of study or research, but each candidate is considered on his or her merits. Application is normally to the institution direct.

Finance

Universities are being expected to look to a much wider range of funding sources than before, and to generate additional revenue in collaboration with industry.

In the academic year 1988–89 the total recurrent income of universities in the United Kingdom was £3,193 million. The exchequer grant was £1,693 million, forming 53·0 per cent of total income compared to 1976–77 when it formed 75 per cent. The total non-recurrent exchequer grant for 1987–88 was £121 million. Income from contracts with industry, commerce and public corporations was £638,680, an increase of 15·8 per cent on the previous year.

NON-UNIVERSITY SECTOR

England and Wales

Polytechnics, colleges of higher education, and other major establishments provide both further and higher education courses (*see* Further Education above) in England and Wales. Higher education courses comprise courses for the further training of teachers, and other courses which last full-time for at least four weeks or, if part-time, involve more than 60 hours of instruction. They include first degree and postgraduate courses (including research) leading to the same qualifications as those awarded by universities, courses for Diploma of Higher Education, Higher National Diploma and Higher National Certificate courses, courses in preparation for professional examinations and other courses of above GCE A-level or Ordinary National Certificate standard. Facilities are available for full-time and part-time study, and day release, sandwich or block release courses are more commonly available than in universities. Higher education courses are offered in some 400 institutions outside the universities.

The **Diploma of Higher Education** (Dip.H.E.) is a two-year diploma usually intended to serve as a stepping-stone to a degree course or other further study. It has a normal entry requirement of two A-levels. The Dip.H.E. is usually awarded by the Council for National Academic Awards (*see* below).

The **BTEC Higher National Certificate** (HNC) is awarded after two years part-time study. The **BTEC Higher National Diploma** (HND) is awarded after two years full-time, or three years sandwich or part-time study. Entry is with either a BTEC National Certificate or Diploma; or at least one GCE A-level pass plus appropriate supporting GCSEs/GCE O-levels or CSE grade 1 passes; or BTEC Certificates of Achievement at appropriate levels and in relevant subjects; and/or appropriate on- or off-the-job training.

The **Council for National Academic Awards** (CNAA) was established by Royal Charter in 1964 as a self-governing body to award degrees to students taking courses approved by it in non-university institutions. However, academic responsibility is now increasingly being devolved to accredited institutions which control the academic standards of their taught courses as well as having the authority to validate new courses and to modify existing ones. Thirty eight institutions, including all the polytechnics, have so far been accredited.

More than 140 colleges in Britain conduct courses leading to CNAA degrees: BA, B.Ed., B.Sc., and higher degrees including MA and M.Sc. (for postgraduate course work) and M.Phil. and Ph.D. (for research which may be undertaken jointly in industry and an academic institution). Some colleges of higher education have retained their traditional links with a university which validates and awards their degrees.

Until April 1989 all public sector higher education establishments were under local education authority control, except for institutions for teacher training and a few others which were grant-maintained directly from central government. However, the Education Reform Act 1988 legislated for the 31 polytechnics and 55 higher education colleges in England to be removed from local education authority control and incorporated as independent institutions, each run by a Higher Education Corporation (HEC). The HECs are responsible for providing higher education and carrying out research in these institutions. HECs are controlled by boards of governors appointed by the Secretary of State. At least half the members of each board must be drawn from industry, business, commerce and the professions.

The HECs are funded by the Polytechnics and Colleges Funding Council (PCFC), which allocates funds between individual institutions for the provision of higher education, both in its own sector, and in colleges under local education authority control. The PCFC also advises the Secretary of State for Education on matters relevant to its sector. The Wales Advisory Body for Local Authority Higher Education (WAB) performs the same function for the Secretary of State for Wales. The independent higher education institutions are, like the universities, expected to supplement their income by undertaking consultancy work and exploiting commercial possibilities.

In November 1987, there was a total of 261,867 students enrolled at polytechnics: 248,006 (42 per cent of them women) were on higher education courses, and of this number, 170,870 (44 per cent of them women) were full-time or sandwich course students. In those colleges of higher education now in the PCFC sector, there were (1987) 94,900 students, of which 75,700 were full-time or sandwich course students.

There are 340 major establishments of higher education (maintained, assisted by LEAs, in receipt of direct grant from the DES, or voluntary) in addition to the polytechnics. In England and Wales in 1987 they catered for 110,000 students on higher education courses including 22,900 on full-time or sandwich courses.

Admissions

Information on all higher education courses in polytechnics including postgraduate courses, can be found in the *Polytechnic Courses Handbook* available from the Committee of Directors of Polytechnics (for address, *see* p. 455). Postgraduate courses in all PCFC institutions are included in *Graduate Studies* (*see* above).

The entry requirements in this sector are much the same as those for universities, i.e. two or three GCSEs at grades A to C, or equivalent, and two or three A-levels for first degrees, and a good first degree in a related subject for postgraduate study, although each candidate is considered on his or her merits. Polytechnics and colleges are, however, often more flexible than universities in accepting alternative entry qualifications, particularly technician-level awards.

The Polytechnics Central Admissions System (PCAS) acts as a clearing-house for all full-time and sandwich first degree, HND and Dip.H.E. courses at participating polytechnics and colleges, except for art and design courses (*see* p. 454). Applicants can obtain a copy of the *Guide for Applicants* and the PCAS application form either from their school or college or from PCAS.

For CNAA first degree and postgraduate courses in art and design and BTEC HND courses in design and associated studies, applications should be made through the Art and Design Admissions Registry.

For polytechnic courses other than the above, applications are made to the institution direct, using the Polytechnic Standard Application Form, available in schools or colleges or from the Committee of Directors of Polytechnics. Applications for courses at colleges of higher education outside the clearing-house schemes are also made direct to the institutions.

Scotland

Advanced full-time courses outside the universities in Scotland are provided by the twelve central institutions, five colleges of education, the agricultural college, and 49 local education authority colleges. These are funded by central government mainly through the Scottish Education Department. Each is managed by an independent governing body which includes representatives of industrial, commercial, professional and educational interests. Most of the courses at the central institutions have a vocational orientation and are of the sandwich type. They are intended to complement provision in the universities. Most of the degrees are validated by the CNAA, though some degree courses such as agriculture, fine art and planning are run in collaboration with nearby universities which validate and award the degrees.

In 1987–88, 69,030 students were enrolled on advanced courses of higher education (43 per cent of them women): 31,680 at central institutions, 5,360 at colleges of education, and 31,990 at education authority colleges. Of the total number, 35,210 were on full-time or sandwich courses (48 per cent of them women).

Applications to the central institutions are made direct to the college concerned, with the exception of those courses offered by certain agricultural and art central institutions which are run in conjunction with universities. Application for these courses is made through UCCA. Application for teacher training courses is made to TEACH (*see* p. 454). Further information can be obtained from the institutions themselves or from the Conference of Scottish Centrally-Funded Colleges (*see* p. 454).

Northern Ireland

In Northern Ireland advanced courses are provided by 26 institutions of further education and by the University of Ulster. As well as offering first and postgraduate degrees, the University runs courses leading to the BTEC Higher National Diploma and professional qualifications. Applications to undertake courses other than degree courses are made to the institutions direct.

In 1988–89, 3,117 students were enrolled on advanced courses of higher education in the institutions of further education (44·8 per cent of them women). There were 582 students on full-time or sandwich courses, including 363 women.

FEES

The tuition fees for students with mandatory awards (*see* p. 449) are paid by the grant-awarding body. Students from member states of the European

Community pay fees at home student rates. Since 1980–81 students from outside the EC have paid fees that are meant to cover the cost of their education, but financial help is available under a number of schemes. Information about these schemes is available from British Council offices worldwide.

The recommended minimum fees at universities in England, Wales and Scotland for students from non-EC countries in 1990–91 are £4,560 (£3,370 in Northern Ireland) for arts students, £6,050 (£4,495–£6,050 in Northern Ireland) for science students and £11,150 throughout the UK for students following clinical courses in medicine, dentistry and veterinary science. These compare with undergraduate fees for home and EC students of £1,675 for all courses in the academic year 1990–91. From 1991–92 differential fees will be introduced, broadly on the same basis as those for overseas students.

At polytechnics and higher education colleges the same fees apply as at universities for home students and EC nationals. No recommended minimum fees have been set for non-EC overseas students for 1990–91.

For postgraduate students, the maximum tuition fee that will be reimbursed through the awards system is £1,985 in 1990–91.

GRANTS FOR STUDENTS

Students in the United Kingdom who plan to take a full-time or sandwich course of further study after leaving school may be eligible for a grant. A parental contribution is deductible on a sliding scale dependent on income. For married students this may be deducted from their spouse's income instead. However, parental contribution is not deducted from the grant to students over 25 years of age who have been self-supporting for at least three years. Tuition fees are paid in full for all students in receipt of a grant regardless of parental income.

Grants are paid by education authorities in England, Wales and Northern Ireland, and by the Scottish Education Department in Scotland. Applications are made to the authority in the area in which the student normally lives. Applications should not, however, be made earlier than the January preceding the start of the course.

Types of grant

Grants are of two kinds: mandatory and discretionary. *Mandatory* grants are those which awarding authorities must pay to students who are attending designated courses (*see* below) and who can satisfy certain other conditions. Such a grant is awarded normally to enable the student to attend only one designated course and there is no general entitlement to an award for any particular number of years. *Discretionary* grants are those for which each awarding authority has discretion to decide its own policy.

Designated courses are those full-time or sandwich courses leading to: a university or CNAA degree; the Diploma of Higher Education (Dip.H.E.); the Higher National Diploma (HND) of the Business and Technician Education Council; initial teacher-training courses including those for the postgraduate certificate of education and the art teachers' certificate or diploma; a university certificate or diploma course lasting at least three years; other qualifications which are specifically designated as being comparable to first degree courses; and the SCOTVEC Higher National Diploma.

Eligibility.—To be eligible for a mandatory grant, students admitted to a designated course must usually have been ordinarily resident in the United Kingdom for the three years immediately preceding the academic year in which the course begins; have not previously attended a course of advanced further education of more than two years' duration; and

apply for the grant before the end of the first term of the course. (The local education authority should be consulted for advice about eligibility.)

Students taking designated courses who do not satisfy the residency condition may be eligible for a mandatory grant if they come from other member states of the EC and can establish migrant worker status, or their parents are migrant workers; or if they, or their spouse and children, are asylees or refugees.

Value.—A means-tested maintenance grant, usually paid once a term, covers periods of attendance during term as well as the Christmas and Easter vacations, but not the summer vacation. It is subject to deduction on account of the student's own income and her/his parents' or spouse's income. The basic grant rates (1990–91) are: £2,845 if living in a hall of residence or lodgings and studying within the London area; £2,265 as above but outside the London area; £1,795 if living at the parental home. Tuition fees in full are usually paid direct to the university or college by the education authority. Additional allowances are available if, for example, the course requires a period of study abroad.

Cost.—Education authority and Scottish Education Department expenditure on student maintenance in 1987–88 was £728·3 million.

Student loans.—The Education (Student Loans) Act 1990 legislates for interest-free but indexed top-up loans of up to £460 in 1990–91 to be made available to students in the United Kingdom from autumn 1990. This will increase the resources available to students by 25 per cent. The government expects to make at least £178 million available for loans in 1990–91.

Students will apply direct to the Student Loans Company Ltd., which has been set up to administer the scheme, and which will require a certificate of eligibility from their place of study. Loans are available to students on designated courses within the scope of mandatory awards and the same residency conditions apply. Repayment will normally be over five to seven years, although it can be deferred if income is low.

Postgraduate awards

Unlike funding for undergraduates, which is mandatory for most degree and equivalent level courses, grants for postgraduate study are usually discretionary. Grants are also often dependent on the class of first degree, especially for research degrees.

A number of schemes of postgraduate bursaries or studentships for residents in England and Wales are funded by the Department of Education and Science, the five Government research councils, the Ministry of Agriculture, Fisheries and Food, and the British Academy which awards grants for study in the humanities.

In Scotland postgraduate funding is provided by the Department of Agriculture and Fisheries for Scotland, the Scottish Education Department, and the research councils as in England and Wales.

Awards in Northern Ireland are made by the Department of Education for Northern Ireland, the Department of Agriculture for Northern Ireland, and the Medical Research Council.

In 1987–88 in the United Kingdom 23,300 awards were made.

Value.—The national rates for twelve-month studentships in 1990–91 were: £4,690 in college or lodgings in London; £3,725 in college or lodgings outside London; £2,750 for those living with parents or spouse's parents. The rates for 30-week bursaries for 1990–91 were: £2,775 in college or lodgings in London; £2,195 in college or lodgings outside London; £1,655 if living with parents or spouse's parents.

ADULT AND CONTINUING EDUCATION

The term adult education covers a broad spectrum of educational activities ranging from non-vocational courses of general interest, through the acquiring of special vocational skills needed in industry or commerce, to study for a degree at the Open University.

Providers

Courses specifically for adults are funded and/or provided by many bodies. They include, in the statutory sector: local education authorities in England and Wales; the regional and islands education authorities in Scotland and the Scottish Education Department; education and library boards in Northern Ireland; the Open University; the extramural departments of other universities and Birkbeck College of the University of London; residential colleges; the Open College; the BBC, IBA and local radio stations. There are, in addition, a number of voluntary bodies.

The local education authorities in England and Wales operate through 'area' adult education centres (2,632 in 1988), institutes or colleges, and the adult studies departments of colleges of further education. The regional and islands education authorities in Scotland fund adult education including that provided by the universities and the Workers' Educational Association at vocational further education colleges (50 in 1989). In addition, the Scottish Education Department provides grants to a number of voluntary organizations. Provision in the statutory sector in Northern Ireland is the responsibility of the universities and the education and library boards which operate 26 further education colleges and a number of community schools.

More than 30 universities have extra-mural, adult education or continuing education departments which serve their local areas or regions, and Birkbeck College in the University of London caters solely for part-time students. The Open University, in partnership with the BBC, provides distance teaching leading to ordinary or honours first degrees, and also offers post-experience and higher degree courses (*see* p. 446–7). Institutions in the PCFC sector in England and Wales, because of their range of courses and flexible patterns of student attendance, provide substantial opportunities in the field of adult and continuing education. The Polytechnic Association for Continuing Education (PACE) exists to promote collaboration between polytechnics and colleges of higher education active in this area. The Open College uses radio and television to provide open learning courses in areas of vocational and technical competence, leading to nationally recognized qualifications or credits towards them.

Of the voluntary bodies, the biggest is the **Workers' Educational Association** (WEA) which operates throughout the United Kingdom and comprises about 900 branches, organized into 19 districts, and nearly 1,500 affiliated educational and workers' organizations. It aims to stimulate and to satisfy the demands of workers for education, and to further the advancement of education generally, reaching about 180,000 adult students annually. The Department of Education and Science (DES), Welsh Office, Scottish Education Department, Department of Education for Northern Ireland and local education authorities make grants towards provision.

The **National Institute of Adult Continuing Education (England and Wales)** (NIACE) provides information and advice to organizations and individuals on all aspects of adult continuing education. It conducts inquiries into problems, organizes conferences and issues publications. NIACE manages a number of agencies and special units, including the Adult Literacy and Basic Skills Unit, which receive funding from the DES and the Welsh Office. The Welsh committee, NIACE Cymru, receives financial support from the Welsh Office Education Department, support in kind from the Welsh Joint Education Committee, and advises government, voluntary bodies and education providers on adult continuing education and training matters in Wales.

The **Scottish Institute of Adult and Continuing Education** (SIACE) advises on policy, conducts research, provides information, arranges conferences and produces publications. Its membership comprises all the major funders and providers of adult and continuing education in Scotland.

The **Northern Ireland Council for Continuing Education** has an advisory role. Its membership includes representatives of most organizations involved in the field, together with appointees of the Northern Ireland Minister responsible for education.

The **Universities Council for Adult and Continuing Education** consists of one or two representatives from each university in the United Kingdom. It was established in 1947 for the interchange of ideas and the formulation of common policies on extramural education.

Courses

Although lengths vary, most courses are part-time. Long-term residential colleges, which are grant-aided by the DES, the Welsh Office or the Scottish Office, provide full-time courses lasting one or two years.

Some colleges and centres offer short-term residential courses, lasting from a day or two to a few weeks, in a wide range of subjects. Local education authorities directly sponsor many of the colleges while others are sponsored by universities or voluntary organizations. A booklet listing courses, *Residential Short Courses*, is published by NIACE.

Grants

Although full-time courses at degree level attract mandatory awards regardless of the age of the student, for courses below that level all students over the age of 19 must pay a fee. However, discretionary grants may be available. Adult education bursaries for students at the long-term residential colleges of adult education are the responsibility of the colleges themselves. The awards are administered for the colleges by the Awards Officer of the Residential Colleges Committee for students resident in England; by the Welsh Office Education Department for those resident in Wales; by the Scottish Education Department for those resident in Scotland; and by the Department of Education for Northern Ireland for students resident there. The bursaries are paid in accordance with the rates and conditions set from time to time by the DES. *Adult Education Bursaries* can be obtained from the Awards Officer, Adult Education Bursaries, c/o Ruskin College (*see* p. 463).

Numbers

There are no comprehensive statistics covering all aspects of adult education. However, it is known that enrolments on evening courses in further education establishments in the United Kingdom numbered 2,117,000 in 1987–88 (75 per cent women). This number included 1,443,100 students at adult education centres in England and Wales. In 1987–88, 304,408 students attended courses of liberal adult education provided by university extra-mural departments including joint courses with the WEA in the United Kingdom.

EDUCATION DIRECTORY

LOCAL EDUCATION AUTHORITIES

ENGLAND

County Councils

Avon, PO Box 57, Avon House North, St. James Barton, Bristol BS99 7EB. (Tel: 0272-290777).—*Dir.*, Dr. C. Saville.

Bedfordshire, County Hall, Cauldwell Street, Bedford MK42 9AP. (Tel: 0234-63222).—*Dir.*, D. G. Wadsworth.

Berkshire, Shire Hall, Shinfield Park, Reading RG2 9XD. (Tel: 0734-233400).—*Chief Education Officer*, S. R. Goodchild.

Buckinghamshire, County Hall, Aylesbury HP20 1UZ. (Tel: 0296-395000).—*Dir.*, E. S. Sharp.

Cambridgeshire, Castle Court, Castle Hall, Cambridge CB3 0AP. (Tel: 0223-317111).—*Chief Education Officer*, G. H. Morris.

Cheshire, County Hall, Chester CH1 1SQ. (Tel: 0244-602424).—*Dir.*, N. J. Fitton.

Cleveland, Woodlands Road, Middlesbrough TS1 3BN. (Tel: 0642-248155).—*County Education Officer*, A. H. R. Calderwood.

Cornwall, New County Hall, Truro TR1 3AY. (Tel: 0872-74282).—*Sec. of Education*, D. W. Fryer.

Cumbria, 5 Portland Square, Carlisle CA1 1PU. (Tel: 0228-23456).—*Dir.*, Miss P. Black.

Derbyshire, County Offices, Matlock DE4 3AG. (Tel: 0629-580000).—*Dir.*, G. Lennox.

Devon, County Hall, Exeter EX2 4QG. (Tel: 0392-272039).—*Chief Education Officer*, S. W. Jenkin.

Dorset, County Hall, Dorchester DT1 1XJ. (Tel: 0305-251000).—*Dir.*, P. L. Gedling.

Durham, County Hall, Durham DH1 5UJ. (Tel: 091-386 4411).—*Dir.*, K. B. Grimshaw.

East Sussex, PO Box 4, County Hall, St. Anne's Crescent, Lewes BN7 1SG. (Tel: 0273-481000).—*County Education Officer*, D. Mallen.

Essex, Threadneedle House, Market Road, Chelmsford CM1 1LD. (Tel: 0245-492211).—*County Education Officer*, R. M. Sharp.

Gloucestershire, Shire Hall, Gloucester GL1 2TP. (Tel: 0452-425300).—*Dir.*, K. D. Anderson.

Hampshire, The Castle, Winchester SO23 8UJ. (Tel: 0962-841841).—*County Education Officer*, P. J. Coles.

Hereford and Worcester, Castle Street, Worcester WR1 3AG. (Tel: 0905-763763).—*County Education Officer*, J. W. Turnbull.

Hertfordshire, County Hall, Hertford SG13 8DE. (Tel: 0992-555700).—*County Education Officer*, Mrs. H. du Quesnay.

Humberside, County Hall, Beverley HU17 9BA. (Tel: 0482-867131).—*Dir.*, Dr. M. W. Garnett.

Isle of Wight, County Hall, Newport PO30 1UD. (Tel: 0983-821000).—*Dir.*, J. D. Williams.

Kent, Springfield, Maidstone ME14 2LJ. (Tel: 0622-671411).—*Dir.*, R. Pryke.

Lancashire, County Hall, Preston PR1 8XJ. (Tel: 0772-263701).—*Chief Education Officer*, A. J. Collier.

Leicestershire, County Hall, Glenfield, Leicester LE3 8RF. (Tel: 0533-323232).—*Dir.*, K. H. Wood-Allum.

Lincolnshire, County Offices, Newland, Lincoln LN1 1YQ. (Tel: 0522-552222).—*Dir.*, A. M. Ridings, frsa.

Norfolk, County Hall, Martineau Lane, Norwich NR1 2DH. (Tel: 0603-222146).—*Dir.*, M. H. Edwards.

Northamptonshire, Northampton House, Northampton NN1 2HX. (Tel: 0604-236250).—*County Education Officer*, J. R. Atkinson.

Northumberland, County Hall, Morpeth NE61 2EF. (Tel: 0670-514343).—*Dir.*, C. C. Tipple.

North Yorkshire, County Hall, Racecourse Lane, Northallerton DL7 8AE. (Tel: 0609-780780).—*Dir.*, F. F. Evans.

Nottinghamshire, County Hall, West Bridgford, Nottingham NG2 7QP. (Tel: 0602-823823).—*Dir.*, A. J. Fox.

Oxfordshire, Macclesfield House, New Road, Oxford OX1 1NA. (Tel: 0865-792422).—*Chief Education Officer*, Mrs. J. Stephens.

Shropshire, The Shirehall, Abbey Foregate, Shrewsbury SY2 6ND. (Tel: 0743-254301).—*County Education Officer*, P. B. Cates.

Somerset, County Hall, Taunton TA1 4DY. (Tel: 0823-333451).—*Chief Education Officer*, Mrs. J. Wisker.

Staffordshire, Tipping Street, Stafford ST16 2DH. (Tel: 0785-223121).—*Chief Education Officer*, Dr. P. J. Hunter.

Suffolk, St. Andrew House, County Hall, Ipswich IP4 1LJ. (Tel: 0473-230000).—*County Education Officer*, T. R. Cornthwaite.

Surrey, County Hall, Penrhyn Road, Kingston upon Thames KT1 2DJ. (Tel: 081-541 9999).—*County Education Officer*, M. C. Pinchin.

Warwickshire, PO Box 24, 22 Northgate Street, Warwick CV34 4SR. (Tel: 0926-410410).—*Dir.*, Ms. M. Maden.

West Sussex, County Hall, Chichester PO19 1RH. (Tel: 0243-777100).—*Dir.*, R. D. C. Bunker.

Wiltshire, County Hall, Bythesea Road, Trowbridge BA14 8JN. (Tel: 0225-753641).—*Dir.*, I. M. Slocombe.

Metropolitan District Councils

Barnsley, Berneslai Close, Barnsley. (Tel: 0226-733252).—*Dir.*, T. Brooks.

Birmingham, Council House, Margaret Street, B3 3BU. (Tel: 021-235 2540).—*Dir.*, D. Hammond.

Bolton, Paderborn House, Civic Centre, BL1 1JW. (Tel: 0204-22311).—*Education Officer*, B. Hughes.

Bradford, Provincial House, BD1 1NP. (Tel: 0274-752500).—*Dir.*, W. R. Knight, cbe.

Bury, Athenaeum House, Market Street, BL9 0BN. (Tel: 061-705 5000).—*Education Officer*, M. Gray.

Calderdale.—Northgate House, Halifax HX1 1UN. (Tel: 0422-57257).—*Education Officer*, A. Pickvance.

Coventry, New Council Offices, Earl Street, CV1 5RR. (Tel: 0203-831500).—*Education Officer*, C. Farmer.

Doncaster, Princegate, Doncaster. (Tel: 0302-734102).—*Education Officer*, A. M. Taylor.

Dudley, Westox House, 1 Trinity Road, DY1 1JB. (Tel: 0384-456000).—*Education Officer*, R. K. Westerby.

Gateshead, Civic Centre, Regent Street, NE8 1HH. (Tel: 091-477 1011).—*Dir.*, D. Arbon.

Kirklees, Oldgate House, 2 Oldgate, Huddersfield HD1 6QW. (Tel: 0484-422123).—*Education Officer*, Ms. J. Devlin.

Knowsley, Huyton Hey Road, Huyton, Merseyside L36 5YM. (Tel: 051-480 5111).—*Education Officer*, A. Culley.

Leeds, Merrion House, Woodhouse Lane, LS2 8DT. (Tel: 0532-463000).—*Chief Education Officer*, R. S. Johnson, cbe.

Liverpool, 14 Sir Thomas Street, L1 6BJ. (Tel: 051-227 3911).—*Dir.*, M. F. Cogley.

MANCHESTER, Cumberland House, Crown Square, M60 3BB. (Tel: 061-234 5000).—*Education Officer*, R. Jobson.

NEWCASTLE UPON TYNE, Civic Centre, NE1 8PU. (Tel: 091-232 8520).—*Education Officer*, W. B. Downer.

NORTH TYNESIDE, The Chase, North Shields NE29 0RW. (Tel: 091-257 6621).—*Education Officer*, J. F. Partington.

OLDHAM, Chadderton Town Hall, Middleton Road, Chadderton, OL9 6JW. (Tel: 061-624 0505).—*Education Officer*, W. R. Kneen, PH.D.

ROCHDALE, PO Box 70, Municipal Offices, Smith Street, OL16 1YD. (Tel: 0706-47474).—*Education Officer*, A. N. Naylor.

ROTHERHAM, Norfolk House, Walker Place, Rotherham. (Tel: 0709-382121).—*Education Officer*, K. Snowden.

ST. HELENS, Century House, Hardshaw Street, St. Helens WA10 1RN. (Tel: 0744-24061).—*Dir.*, N. D. Nelson.

SALFORD, Chapel Street, M3 5LT. (Tel: 061-832 9751).—*Chief Education Officer*, A. Lockhart.

SANDWELL, PO Box 41, Shaftesbury House, 402 High Street, West Bromwich B70 9LT. (Tel: 021-525 7366).—*Dir.*, G. A. Brinsdon.

SEFTON, Town Hall, Bootle, Merseyside L20 7AE. (Tel: 051-922 4040).—*Education Officer*, J. A. Marsden.

SHEFFIELD, PO Box 67, Leopold Street, S1 1RJ. (Tel: 0742-726341).—*Chief Education Officer*, Mrs. A. Muller (*acting*).

SOLIHULL, PO Box 18, Council House, B91 3QS. (Tel: 021-704 6000).—*Dir.*, M. E. Sweet.

SOUTH TYNESIDE, Town Hall and Civic Offices, South Shields, NE33 2RL. (Tel: 091-427 1717).—*Education Officer*, I. L. Reid.

STOCKPORT, Town Hall, SK1 3XE (Tel: 061-480 4949).—*Education Officer*, J. E. Hendy.

SUNDERLAND, PO Box 101, Town Hall and Civic Centre, SR2 7DN. (Tel: 091-567 6161).—*Education Officer*, D. A. Bowers.

TAMESIDE, Council Offices, Wellington Road, Ashton-under-Lyne OL6 6DL. (Tel: 061-330 8355).—*Dir*, A. M. Webster.

TRAFFORD, PO Box 19, Tatton Road, Sale M33 1YR. (Tel: 061-872 2101).—*Chief Education Officer*, C. J. Radley.

WAKEFIELD, County Hall, WF1 2QW. (Tel: 0924-290900).—*Education Officer*, A. Lenney.

WALSALL, Civic Centre, Darwall Street, WS1 1DQ. (Tel: 0922-650000).—*Education Officer*, Mrs D. M. Tuck.

WIGAN, Gateway House, Standishgate, WN1 1XL. (Tel: 0942-44991).—*Education Officer*, J. K. Hampson.

WIRRAL, Hamilton Building, Conway Street, Birkenhead L41 4FD. (Tel: 051-666 2121).—*Dir.*, D. Rigby.

WOLVERHAMPTON, Civic Centre, St. Peter's Square, WV1 1RR. (Tel: 0902-27811).—*Education Officer*, Ms. C. Adams.

London

The ILEA was abolished on April 1, 1990 and from that date the inner London boroughs(*) and the Corporation of the City of London assumed responsibility for the provision of education within their own areas.

BARKING AND DAGENHAM, Town Hall, Barking, Essex IG11 7LU. (Tel: 081-592 4500).—*Education Officer*, A. Larbalestier.

BARNET, Town Hall, Friern Barnet, N11 3DL. (Tel: 081-368 1255).—*Education Officer*, N. M. Gill.

BEXLEY, Hill View, Hill View Drive, Welling, Kent DA16 3RY. (Tel: 081-303 7777).—*Education Officer*, G. Hall.

BRENT, PO Box 1, 9 Park Lane, Wembley, Middx. HA9 7RW. (Tel: 081-900 5443).—*Dir.*, G. Benham.

BROMLEY, Town Hall, Widmore Road, Bromley, Kent BR1 1SB. (Tel: 081-464 3333).—*Dir.*, G. Grainge.

*CAMDEN, Crowndale Centre, 216–220 Eversholt Street, NW1 1BE (Tel: 071-860 5882).—*Education Officer*, P. Mitchell.

*CITY OF LONDON, Clements House, 14–18 Gresham Street, EC2P 2EJ. (Tel: 071-260 1750).—*City Education Officer*, D. Smith.

*CITY OF WESTMINSTER, City Hall, PO Box 240, Victoria Street, SW1E 6QP. (Tel: 071-828 8070).—*Education Officer*, G. Robins.

CROYDON, Taberner House, Park Lane, CR9 3JS. (Tel: 081-686 4433).—*Dir.*, P. Benians.

EALING, Hadley House, 79–81 Uxbridge Road, W5 2BU. (Tel: 081-579 2424).—*Dir.*, Ms. U. Barlow.

ENFIELD, PO Box 56, Civic Centre, Silver Street, EN1 3XQ. (Tel: 081-366 6565).—*Education Officer*, G. Hutchinson.

*GREENWICH, Riverside House, 9th Floor, Beresford Street, Woolwich, SE18 6DF.—*Dir.*, N. McClelland.

*HACKNEY, 727 East Road, N1 6AH. (Tel: 071-490 8838).—*Dir.*, G. John.

*HAMMERSMITH AND FULHAM, Banda House, Cambridge Grove, W6 9JU. (Tel: 081-748 3020).—*Dir.*, Ms. C. Whatford.

HARINGEY, 48 Station Road, N22 6UX. (Tel: 081-975 9700).—*Education Officer*, R. L. Jones.

HARROW, Civic Centre, Station Road, Harrow HA1 2UH. (Tel: 081-863 5611).—*Dir.*, H. Fielding.

HAVERING, Mercury House, Mercury Gardens, Romford RM1 3DR. (Tel: 0708-766999).—*Dir.*, B. H. Laister.

HILLINGDON, Civic Centre, Uxbridge, Middx. UB8 1UW. (Tel: 0895-50528).—*Education Officer*, Mrs. J. Greenfield (*acting*).

HOUNSLOW, Civic Centre, Lampton Road, Hounslow, Middx. TW3 4DN. (Tel: 081-570 7728).—*Dir.*, J. D. Trickett.

*ISLINGTON, Former Barnsbury School for Girls, Barnsbury Park, N1 1HJ. (Tel: 071-226 1234).—*Education Officer*, C. Webb.

*KENSINGTON AND CHELSEA, Town Hall, Hornton Street, W8 7NX. (Tel: 071-937 5464).—*Education Officer*, M. Stoten.

KINGSTON UPON THAMES, Guildhall, KT1 1EU. (Tel: 081-546 2121).—*Dir.*, W. Dickinson.

*LAMBETH, 50 Acre Lane, SW2 5SS. (Tel: 071-274 6288).—*Education Officer*, B. Burchell.

*LEWISHAM, 1 Aitken Road, SE6 2UL. (Tel: 081-697 8166).—*Education Officer*, L. Fullick.

MERTON, Crown House, London Road, Morden, Surrey SM4 5DX. (Tel: 081-543 2222).—*Dir.*, R. Davies.

NEWHAM, Broadway House, 322 High Street, E15 1AJ. (Tel: 081-534 4545).—*Education Officer*, S. Lawless.

REDBRIDGE, Lynton House, 255–259 High Road, Ilford, IG1 1NN. (Tel: 081-478 3030).—*Dir.*, K. G. M. Ratcliffe.

RICHMOND UPON THAMES, Civic Centre, 44 York Street, TW1 3BZ. (Tel: 081-891 1411).—*Education Officer*, G. Alexander.

*SOUTHWARK, 19 Grange Road, SE16 3BE. (Tel: 071-237 4551).—*Education Officer*, G. Mott.

SUTTON, The Grove, Carshalton, Surrey SM5 3AL. (Tel: 081-770 6500).—*Dir.*, C. Blurton.

*TOWER HAMLETS, Bow House Annexe, 153–159 Bow Road, E3 2SE. (Tel: 081-980 4414).—*Education Officer*, Ms. A. Sofer.

WALTHAM FOREST, Municipal Offices, High Road, Leyton E10 5QJ. (Tel: 081-527 5544).—*Dir.*, J. M. Shepherd.

*WANDSWORTH, Town Hall, Wandsworth High Street, SW18 2PU. (Tel: 081-871 7890).—*Education Officer*, D. Naismith.

WALES
County Councils

CLWYD, Shire Hall, Mold CH7 6NB. (Tel: 0352-2121).—*Dir.*, H. K. Evans.

DYFED, Pibwrlwyd, Carmarthen SA31 2NH. (Tel: 0267-233333).—*Dir.*, W. J. Phillips.

GWENT, County Hall, Cwmbran NP44 2XG. (Tel: 0633-838838).—*Dir.*, G. V. Drought.

GWYNEDD, County Offices, Caernarfon LL55 1SH. (Tel: 0286-4121).—*Dir.*, G. E. Humphreys.

MID GLAMORGAN, County Hall, Cathays Park, Cardiff CF1 3NF. (Tel: 0222-820820).—*Dir.*, E. Roberts.

POWYS, County Hall, Llandrindod Wells LD1 5LG. (Tel: 0597-826000).—*Dir.*, R. W. Bevan.

SOUTH GLAMORGAN, County Hall, Atlantic Wharf, Cardiff CF1 5UW. (Tel: 0222-872000).—*Dir.*, D. Orrell.

WEST GLAMORGAN, County Hall, Swansea SA1 3SN. (Tel: 0792-471111).—*Dir.*, J. Beale.

SCOTLAND
Regional and Islands Councils

BORDERS, Regional Headquarters, Newtown St. Boswells, Melrose TD6 0SA. (Tel: 0835-23301).—*Dir.*, I. Dutton.

CENTRAL, Regional Council Offices, Viewforth, Stirling FK8 2ET. (Tel: 0786-73111).—*Dir.*, I. Collie.

DUMFRIES AND GALLOWAY, 30 Edinburgh Road, Dumfries DG1 1JQ. (Tel: 0387-61234).—*Dir.*, W. C. Fordyce.

FIFE, Rothesay House, North Street, Glenrothes KY7 5LT. (Tel: 0592-754411).—*Dir.*, M. More.

GRAMPIAN, Woodhill House, Westburn Road, Aberdeen AB9 2LU. (Tel: 0224-682222).—*Dir.*, J. Graham.

HIGHLAND, Regional Buildings, Glenurquhart Road, Inverness IV3 5NX. (Tel: 0463-234121).—*Dir.*, Dr. C. E. Stewart.

LOTHIAN, 40 Torphichen Street, Edinburgh EH3 8JJ. (Tel: 031-225 1399).—*Dir.*, W. D. C. Semple.

ORKNEY, Council Offices, Kirkwall KW15 1NY. (Tel: 0856-3535).—*Dir.*, Mrs. M. J. B. Crichton.

SHETLAND, 1 Harbour Street, Lerwick. (Tel: 0595-3535).—*Dir.*, R. A. B. Barnes.

STRATHCLYDE, 20 India Street, Glasgow G2 4PF. (Tel: 041-204 2900).—*Dir.*, F. Pignatelli.

TAYSIDE, Tayside House, 28 Crichton Street, Dundee DD1 3RA. (Tel: 0382-23281).—*Dir.*, A. B. Watson.

WESTERN ISLES, Council Offices, Sandwick Road, Stornoway, Isle of Lewis PA87 2BW. (Tel: 0851-3773).—*Dir.*, N. R. Galbraith.

NORTHERN IRELAND
Education and Library Boards

BELFAST, Board Headquarters, 40 Academy Street, Belfast BT1 2NQ. (Tel: 0232-329211).—*Chief Exec.*, T. G. J. Moag.

NORTH EASTERN, County Hall, 182 Galgorm Road, Ballymena, Co. Antrim BT42 1HN. (Tel: 0266-653333).—*Chief Exec.*, R. A. Hamilton.

SOUTH EASTERN, 18 Windsor Avenue, Belfast BT9 6EF. (Tel: 0232-381188).—*Chief Exec.*, T. Nolan, OBE.

SOUTHERN, 3 Charlemont Place, The Mall, Armagh BT61 9AX. (Tel: 0861-523811).—*Chief Exec.*, J. G. Kelly.

WESTERN, 1 Hospital Road, Omagh, Co. Tyrone BT79 0AW. (Tel: 0662-240240).—*Chief Exec.*, M. H. F. Murphy, OBE.

ISLANDS, ETC.

GUERNSEY, PO Box 32, Grange Road, St. Peter Port. (Tel: 0481-710821).—*Dir.*, M. D. Hutchings.

JERSEY, PO Box 142, St. Saviour. (Tel: 0534-71065).—*Dir.*, B. Grady.

ISLE OF MAN, Government Offices, Buck's Road, Douglas. (Tel: 0624-26262).—*Dir.*, A. Davies.

ISLES OF SCILLY, Town Hall, St. Mary's TR21 0LW. (Tel: 0720-22537).—*Sec. for Education*, L. W. Michell.

ADVISORY BODIES
Schools

EDUCATION OTHERWISE, 25 Common Lane, Hemmingford Abbots, Cambridge PE18 9AN. *Helpline*, tel: 0480-63130.

INTERNATIONAL BACCALAUREATE LONDON, 18 Woburn Square, WC1H 0NS. (Tel: 071-637 1682).—*Deputy Dir.-Gen.*, vacant.

SCHOOLS EXAMINATION AND ASSESSMENT COUNCIL, Newcombe House, 4 Notting Hill Gate, W11 3JB. (Tel: 071-229 1234).—*Chief Exec.*, P. Halsey, CB, LVO; *Sec.*, P. Dines.

Independent Schools

ASSISTED PLACES COMMITTEE, 26 Queen Anne's Gate, SW1H 9AN. (Tel: 071-222 9595).—*Sec.*, Mrs. L. Shaw.

COMMON ENTRANCE BOARD, Drax House, Tilshead, Salisbury, Wilts. SP3 4SJ. (Tel: 0980-620473).—*Sec.*, Mrs. E. J. Twiston-Davies.

GOVERNING BODIES ASSOCIATION, Windleshaw Lodge, Withyham, Nr. Hartfield, E. Sussex TN7 4DB.—*Sec.*, D. G. Banwell.

GOVERNING BODIES OF GIRLS' SCHOOLS ASSOCIATION, Windleshaw Lodge, Withyham, Nr. Hartfield, E. Sussex TN7 4DB.—*Sec.*, D. G. Banwell.

INDEPENDENT SCHOOLS INFORMATION SERVICE, 56 Buckingham Gate, SW1E 6AG. (Tel: 071-630 8793/4).—*National Dir.*, D. J. Woodhead.

Further Education

FURTHER EDUCATION UNIT, 2–6 Orange Street, WC2H 7WE. (Tel: 071-321 0433).—*Chief Officer*, G. Stanton.

NATIONAL COUNCIL FOR VOCATIONAL QUALIFICATIONS, 222 Euston Road, NW1 2BZ. (Tel. 071-387 9898).

Regional Advisory Councils

CENTRA (NORTH WESTERN REGIONAL ADVISORY COUNCIL FOR FURTHER EDUCATION), Town Hall, Walkden Road, Worsley, Manchester M28 4QE. (Tel: 061-702 8700).—*Manager*, R. S. Welsh.

EAST ANGLIAN REGIONAL ADVISORY COUNCIL FOR FURTHER EDUCATION, 2 Looms Lane, Bury St. Edmunds, Suffolk IP33 1HE. (Tel: 0284-764977).—*Dir.*, Mrs. H. Herrington.

EAST MIDLAND FURTHER EDUCATION COUNCIL, Robins Wood House, Robins Wood Road, Aspley, Nottingham NG8 3NH. (Tel: 0602-293291).—*Sec.*, R. Ainscough.

REGIONAL ADVISORY COUNCIL FOR FURTHER EDUCATION, LONDON AND SOUTH EASTERN REGION, 232 Vauxhall Bridge Road, SW1V 1AU. (Tel: 071-233 6199).—*Dir.*, L. South.

NORTHERN COUNCIL FOR FURTHER EDUCATION, 5 Grosvenor Villas, Grosvenor Road, Newcastle upon Tyne NE2 2RU. (Tel: 091-281 3242).—*Sec.*, J. F. Pearce.

SOUTHERN REGIONAL COUNCIL FOR FURTHER EDUCATION, 26 Bath Road, Reading RG1 6NT. (Tel: 0734-572120).—*Sec.*, B. J. Knowles.

REGIONAL COUNCIL FOR FURTHER EDUCATION FOR THE SOUTH WEST, Bishops Hull House, Bishops Hull, Taunton, Somerset TA1 5RA. (Tel: 0823-335491).—*Sec.*, F. S. Fisher.

WELSH JOINT EDUCATION COMMITTEE, 245 Western Avenue, Cardiff CF5 2YX. (Tel: 0222-571102).—*Sec.*, C. Heycock.

WEST MIDLANDS ADVISORY COUNCIL FOR FURTHER EDUCATION AND TRAINING, Norfolk House, Smallbrook Queensway, Birmingham B5 4NB. (Tel: 021-643 8924).—*Chief Officer*, C. H. Smith.

YORKSHIRE AND HUMBERSIDE ASSOCIATION FOR FURTHER AND HIGHER EDUCATION, Bowling Green Terrace, Leeds LS11 9SX. (Tel: 0532-440751).—*Sec.*, M. J. Hudson.

Higher Education

THE ASSOCIATION OF COMMONWEALTH UNIVERSITIES, John Foster House, 36 Gordon Square, WC1H 0PF. (Tel: 071-387 8572).—*Sec.-Gen.*, A. Christodoulou, CBE.

COMMITTEE OF VICE-CHANCELLORS AND PRINCIPALS OF THE UNIVERSITIES OF THE UNITED KINGDOM, 29 Tavistock Square, WC1H 9EZ. (Tel: 071-387 9231).—*Dir.*, Ms. A. Stevens.

POLYTECHNICS AND COLLEGES FUNDING COUNCIL, Metropolis House, 22 Percy Street, W1P 9FF (*see* also **Government Offices**).

UNIVERSITIES' FUNDING COUNCIL, 14 Park Crescent, W1N 4DH (*see* also **Government Offices**).

WALES ADVISORY BODY FOR LOCAL AUTHORITY HIGHER EDUCATION, 24 Cathedral Road, Cardiff CF1 9LJ. (Tel: 0222-397844).—*Sec.*, vacant.

Curriculum Councils, etc.

NATIONAL CURRICULUM COUNCIL, Albion Wharf, 25 Skeldergate, York YO1 2XL. (Tel: 0904-622533).—*Chief Exec.*, M. R. Davies.

NORTHERN IRELAND CURRICULUM COUNCIL, Stranmillis College, Stranmillis Road, Belfast BT9 5DY. (Tel: 0232-381414).—*Chief Exec.*, Mrs. C. Coxhead.

SCOTTISH CONSULTATIVE COUNCIL ON THE CURRICULUM, 17 St. John Street, Edinburgh EH8 8DG. (Tel: 031-557 4888).—*Chief Exec.*, D. R. McNicoll.

CURRICULUM COUNCIL FOR WALES, Castle Buildings, Womanby Street, Cardiff CF1 9SX. (Tel: 0222-344946/388150).—*Chief Exec.*, B. Jones.

TRAINING AGENCY, TVEI Unit, Moorfoot, Sheffield S1 4PQ. (Tel: 0742-758316).

EXAMINING BODIES
GCSE

LONDON EAST ANGLIAN GROUP, The Lindens, 139 Lexden Road, Colchester CO3 3RL. (Tel: 0206-549595); Stewart House, 32 Russell Square, WC1B 5DN. (Tel: 071-436 5351).—*Chief Exec.*, A. Smith.

NORTHERN EXAMINING ASSOCIATION, c/o Joint Matriculation Board, Manchester M15 6EU. (Tel: 061-273 2565).—*Joint Sec.*, C. Vickerman.

NORTH REGIONAL EXAMINATIONS BOARD, Wheatfield Road, Westerhope, Newcastle upon Tyne NE5 5JZ. (Tel: 091-286 2711).—*Sec.*, D. Kelly.

NORTH WEST REGIONAL EXAMINATIONS BOARD,Orbit House, Albert Street, Eccles, Manchester M30 0WL. (Tel: 061-788 9521).—*Sec.*, Ms. K. Tattersall.

SOUTHERN EXAMINING GROUP, Stag Hill House, Guildford, Surrey GU2 5XJ. (Tel. 0483-506506).—*Joint Secs.*, J. A. Day; J. Pailing.

WEST MIDLANDS EXAMINATIONS BOARD, Norfolk House, Smallbrook Queensway, Birmingham B5 4NJ. (Tel: 021-631 2151).—*Sec.*, B. Swift.

NORTHERN IRELAND SCHOOLS EXAMINATIONS COUNCIL, Beechill House, 42 Beechill Road, Belfast BT8 4RS. (Tel. 0232-704666).—*Chief Officer*, J. Caves.

WELSH JOINT EDUCATION COMMITTEE, 245 Western Avenue, Cardiff CF5 2YX. (Tel. 0222-571102).—*Sec.*, C. Heycock.

A-level

ASSOCIATED EXAMINING BOARD, Stag Hill House, Guildford, Surrey GU2 5XJ. (Tel: 0483-506506).—*Sec-Gen.*, J. A. Day.

CAMBRIDGE UNIVERSITY LOCAL EXAMINATIONS SYNDICATE, Syndicate Buildings, 1 Hills Road, Cambridge CB1 2EU. (Tel: 0223-61111).—*Sec.*, J. L. Reddaway.

JOINT MATRICULATION BOARD, Manchester M15 6EU. (Tel: 061-273 2565).—*Sec.*, Ms. K. Tattersall.

OXFORD AND CAMBRIDGE SCHOOLS EXAMINATION BOARD, Purbeck House, Purbeck Road, Cambridge CB2 2PU. (Tel: 0223-411211).—*Sec.*, H. F. King.

OXFORD AND CAMBRIDGE SCHOOLS EXAMINATION BOARD, Elsfield Way, Oxford OX2 8EP. (Tel: 0865-54421).—*Sec.*, K. Schoenenberger.

SOUTHERN UNIVERSITIES' JOINT BOARD, Cotham Road, Bristol BS6 6DD. (Tel: 0272-736042).—*Sec.*, Dr. S. T. Smith.

UNIVERSITY OF LONDON SCHOOL EXAMINATIONS BOARD, Stewart House, 32 Russell Square, WC1B 5DN. (Tel: 071-636 8000).—*Sec.*, A. R. Stephenson.

UNIVERSITY OF OXFORD DELEGACY OF LOCAL EXAMINATIONS, Ewert House, Ewert Place, Summertown, Oxford OX2 7BZ. (Tel: 0865-54291).—*Sec.*, J. Pailing.

Scotland

SCOTTISH EXAMINATION BOARD, Ironmills Road, Dalkeith, Midlothian EH22 1LE. (Tel: 031-663 6601).—*Dir.*, H. A. Long, PH.D.

SCOTTISH VOCATIONAL EDUCATION COUNCIL, Hanover House, 24 Douglas Street, Glasgow G2 7NQ. (Tel: 041-248 7900).—*Chief Exec.*, T. J. McCool.

Further Education

BUSINESS AND TECHNICIAN EDUCATION COUNCIL, Central House, Upper Woburn Place, WC1H 0HH. (Tel: 071-388 3288).—*Chief Exec.*, J. E. Sellars.

CITY AND GUILDS OF LONDON INSTITUTE, 76 Portland Place, W1N 4AA. (Tel: 071-278 2468).— *Dir. Gen.*, J. Barnes.

JOINT BOARD FOR PRE-VOCATIONAL EDUCATION, The CPVE Unit, 46 Britannia Street, WC1X 9RG. (Tel: 071-278 3344).—*Chairman*, M. Boxall; *Head of Unit*, Ms. S. Fifer.

RSA EXAMINATIONS BOARD, Westwood Business Park, Coventry CV4 8HS. (Tel: 0203-470033).—*Chief Exec.*, M. F. Cross.

Higher Education

COUNCIL FOR NATIONAL ACADEMIC AWARDS, 344–354 Gray's Inn Road, WC1X 8BP. (Tel: 071-278 4411).—*Chairman*, Sir Bryan Nicholson; *Chief Exec.*, M. Frazer, PH.D.

ADMISSIONS INFORMATION

ART AND DESIGN ADMISSIONS REGISTRY, Penn House, 9 Broad Street, Hereford HR4 9AP. (Tel: 0432-266653).—*Registrar*, T. W. M. Gourdie.

CAREERS RESEARCH AND ADVISORY CENTRE, Sheraton House, Castle Park, Cambridge CB3 0AX. (Tel: 0223-460277).—*Dir.*, D. Blandford. *Publishers*, Hobsons Publishing PLC, Bateman Street, Cambridge CB2 1LZ.

THE CENTRAL INSTITUTIONS INFORMATION OFFICE, Conference of Scottish Centrally-Funded Colleges, Room 54, Moray House College, Holyrood Road, Edinburgh EH8 8AQ. (Tel: 031-557 6309).—*Sec.*, Dr. J. Robinson.

CENTRAL REGISTER AND CLEARING HOUSE LTD., 3 Crawford Place, W1H 2BN.—*Registrar*, Lt.-Col. O. J. Massey.

COMMITTEE OF DIRECTORS OF POLYTECHNICS, Kirkman House, 12–14 Whitfield Street, W1P 6AX. (Tel: 071-637 9939).—*Sec.*, Dr. M. S. Lewis.

POLYTECHNICS CENTRAL ADMISSIONS SYSTEM, Fulton House, Jessop Avenue, Cheltenham, Glos. GL50 3SH. (Tel: 0242-227788).—*Chief Exec.*, M. A. Higgins.

TEACHER EDUCATION ADMISSIONS CLEARING HOUSE (TEACH), (Scotland only), PO Box 165, Holyrood Road, Edinburgh EH8 8AT.—*Registrar*, Miss R. C. Williamson.

UNIVERSITIES' CENTRAL COUNCIL ON ADMISSIONS, PO Box 28, Cheltenham, Glos. GL50 3SA. (Tel: 0242-222444).—*Gen. Sec.*, P. A. Oakley.

UNIVERSITIES

ASTON UNIVERSITY (1966)
Aston Triangle, Birmingham B4 7ET
[021-359 3611]

Full-time Students (1989–90), 3,630.
Chancellor, Sir Adrian Cadbury (1979).
Vice-Chancellor, Prof. Sir Frederick Crawford, PH.D., D.Eng., D.SC.
Registrar and Secretary, R. D. A. Packham.

UNIVERSITY OF BATH (1966)
Claverton Down, Bath BA2 7AY
[0225-826826]

Full-time Students (1989–90), 4,360.
Chancellor, The Lord Kearton, OBE, FRS (1980).
Vice-Chancellor, Prof. J. R. Quayle, PH.D., FRS.
Secretary and Registrar, R. M. Mawditt, OBE, FRSA.

THE UNIVERSITY OF BIRMINGHAM (1900)
Edgbaston, Birmingham B15 2TT
[021-414 3344]

Full-time Students (1989-90), 10,000.
Chancellor, Sir Alexander Jarratt, CB (1983).
Vice-Chancellor, Prof. M. W. Thompson, D.SC.
Registrar and Secretary, D. R. Holmes.

UNIVERSITY OF BRADFORD (1966)
Bradford BD7 1DP

Full-time Students (1989–90), 4,850.
Chancellor, Sir John Harvey-Jones, MBE (1986).
Vice-Chancellor, Prof. D. J. Johns, PH.D., D.SC. (1989).
Registrar and Secretary, D. W. Granger, MBE.

THE UNIVERSITY OF BRISTOL (1909)
Bristol BS8 1TH
[0272-303030]

Full-time Students (1989–90), 7,760.
Chancellor, Sir Jeremy Morse, KCMG (1989).
Vice-Chancellor, Sir John Kingman, FRS.
Registrar, Mrs. C. M. Cunningham.
Secretary, J. H. M. Parry.

BRUNEL UNIVERSITY (1966)
Uxbridge, Middx. UB8 3PH

Full-time Students (1988–89), 3,740.
Chancellor, The Earl of Halsbury, FRS (1966).
Vice-Chancellor, Prof. M. J. H. Sterling.
Registrar and Secretary, D. Neave.

UNIVERSITY OF BUCKINGHAM (1983)
(Founded 1976 as University College at
Buckingham). Independent of state finance.
Buckingham MK18 1EG
[0280-814080]

Full-time Students (1989–90), 755.
Chancellor, The Lord Hailsham of St. Marylebone, KG, CH, PC, FRS (1983).
Vice-Chancellor, Dr. A. M. Barrett, PH.D., FRSA.
Registrar and Secretary, M. Lavis, PH.D.

THE UNIVERSITY OF CAMBRIDGE
FULL TERMS, 1991
Lent, Jan. 15 to March 15; *Easter*, April 23 to June 14; *Michaelmas*, Oct. 8 to Dec. 6

Number of Undergraduates in Residence 1989–90:
Men, 6,048; *Women*, 4,195

UNIVERSITY OFFICERS, etc.†   Elect.

Chancellor, HRH The Duke of Edinburgh, KG, KT, OM, GBE, PC	1977
Vice-Chancellor, Prof. D. G. T. Williams (*Wolfson*)	1989
High Steward, The Lord Devlin, PC, FBA (*Christ's*)	1966
Deputy High Steward, The Lord Richardson of Duntisbourne, PC, MBE, TD.	1983
Commissary, The Lord Oliver, PC (*Trinity Hall*)	1989
Proctors, R. H. Christie (*Trinity Hall*); T. G. A. Ram (*Gonville & Caius*)	1990
Orator, J. Diggle, LITT.D. (*Queens'*)	1982
Registrary, S. G. Fleet, PH.D. (*Downing*)	1983
Deputy Registrary, R. F. Holmes (*Darwin*)	1972
Librarian, F. W. Ratcliffe, PH.D. (*Corpus Christi*)	1980
Treasurer, M. P. Halstead, PH.D. (*Gonville & Caius*)	1985
Secretary General of the Faculties, J. R. G. Wright (*St. Catharine's*)	1987
Director of the Fitzwilliam Museum, S. S. Jervis (*Corpus Christi*)	1990

Cambridge Colleges and Halls, etc.
(With dates of foundation)

Christ's (1505), *Master*, Prof. Sir Hans Kornberg, PH.D., D.SC., SC.D., FRS (1983).
Churchill (1960), *Master*, Prof. A. N. Broers, PH.D., FRS (1990).
Clare (1326), *Master*, Prof. R. C. O. Matthews, CBE, FBA (1975).
Clare Hall (1966), *President*, Prof. D. A. Low, PH.D. (1987).
Corpus Christi (1352), *Master*, M. W. McCrum (1980).
Darwin (1964), *Master*, Prof. G. E. R. Lloyd, PH.D., FBA (1989).
Downing (1800), *Master*, P. Mathias, CBE, LITT.D., FBA (1987).
Emmanuel (1584), *Master*, C. P. Wroth, PH.D. (1990).
Fitzwilliam (1966), *Master*, vacant.
Girton (1869), *Mistress*, The Baroness Warnock, DBE (1984).
Gonville & Caius (1348), *Master*, Prof. P. Gray, SC.D., FRS (1988).
Homerton (1824) (for B. Ed. Students), *Principal*, A. G. Bamford (1985).
Hughes Hall (1885), (for post-graduate students), *President*, T. D. Hawkins (1989).
Jesus (1496), *Master*, Prof. A. C. Renfrew, SC.D. (1986).

---

† Correspondence for the Vice-Chancellor and other administrative officers should be sent to the University Offices, The Old Schools, Cambridge CB2 1TN. (Tel: 0223-337733).

King's (1441), *Provost*, Prof. P. P. G. Bateson, sc.D.,
   FRS (1987).
Lucy Cavendish College (1965) (for women research
   students and mature and affiliated undergradu-
   ates), *President*, Dame Anne Warburton, DCVO,
   CMG (1985).
Magdalene (1542), *Master*, D. Calcutt, QC (1985).
*New Hall (1954), *President*, Mrs. V. L. Pearl, PH.D.
   (1981).
*Newnham (1871), *Principal*, Miss S. J. Browne, CB
   (1983).
Pembroke (1347), *Master*, Prof. the Lord Adrian, MD,
   FRS (1981).
Peterhouse (1284), *Master*, Prof. H. Chadwick, KBE,
   DD, FBA (1987).
Queens' (1448), *President*, Rev. J. C. Polkinghorne,
   SC.D., FRS (1989).
Robinson (1977), *Warden*, Prof. the Lord Lewis of
   Newnham, SC.D., FRS (1977).
St. Catharine's (1473), *Master*, Prof. B. E. Supple,
   Ph.D. (1984).
St. Edmund's (1896), *Master*, R. M. Laws, CBE, PH.D.
   (1986).
St. John's (1511), *Master*, Prof. R. A. Hinde, SC.D., FRS
   (1989).
Selwyn (1882), *Master*, Prof. Sir Alan Cook, SC.D., FRS
   (1983).
Sidney Sussex (1596), *Master*, Prof. D. H. Northcote,
   Ph.D., SC.D., FRS (1976).
Trinity (1546), *Master*, Michael Atiyah, PH.D., FRS,
   FRSE (1990).
Trinity Hall (1350), *Master*, Sir John Lyons, PH.D.
   (1984).
Wolfson (1965), *President*, Prof. D. G. T. Williams
   (1980).

* Colleges for women only.

CITY UNIVERSITY (1966)
Northampton Square, EC1V 0HB
[071-253 4399]

Full-time Students (1989–90), 3,785.
Chancellor, The Rt. Hon. Lord Mayor of London.
Vice-Chancellor and Principal, Prof. R. N. Franklin,
   D.Phil., D.SC.
Registrar, A. H. Seville, PH.D.
Secretary, M. M. O'Hara.

THE UNIVERSITY OF DURHAM
(Founded 1832; re-organized 1908, 1937 and 1963)
Old Shire Hall, Durham DH1 3HP
[091-374 2000]

Full-time Students (1989–90), 5,331.
Chancellor, Dame Margot Fonteyn de Arias (1982).
Vice-Chancellor and Warden, Prof. E. A. V. Ebsworth,
   D.SC., FRSE.
Registrar and Secretary, J. C. F. Hayward.

Colleges
Collingwood.—Principal, G. H. Blake, PH.D.
Graduate Society.—Principal, M. Richardson, PH.D.
Grey.—Master, V. E. Watts.
Hatfield.—Master, J. P. Barber, PH.D.
St. Aidan's.—Principal, vacant.
St. Chad's.—Principal, Rev. D. Jasper, PH.D.
St. Cuthbert's Society.—Principal, S. G. C. Stoker.
St. Hild and St. Bede.—Principal, J. V. Armitage,
   PH.D.
St. John's.—Principal, Rev. A. C. Thiselton, PH.D.
St. Mary's.—Principal, Miss J. M. Kenworthy.
Trevelyan.—Principal, Miss D. Lavin.
University.—Master, E. C. Salthouse, PH.D.
Ushaw.—President, Rt. Rev. Mgr. P. F. J. Walton.
Van Mildert.—Principal, Ms. J. Turner, PH.D.

THE UNIVERSITY OF EAST ANGLIA (1963)
Norwich NR4 7TJ
[0603-56161]

Full-time Students (1989–90), 4,680.
Chancellor, Rev. Prof. W. O. Chadwick, OM, KBE, FBA
   (1985).
Vice-Chancellor, Prof. D. C. Burke, PH.D.
Registrar and Secretary, M. G. E. Paulson-Ellis.

THE UNIVERSITY OF ESSEX (1964)
Wivenhoe Park, Colchester CO4 3SQ
[0206-873333]

Full-time Students (1989–90), 3,486.
Chancellor, The Rt. Hon. Sir Patrick Nairne, GCB, MC
   (1983).
Vice-Chancellor, Prof. M. Harris, PH.D.
Registrar, E. Newcomb.

THE UNIVERSITY OF EXETER (1955)
Exeter EX4 4QJ
[0392-263263]

Full-time Students (1989–90), 6,100.
Chancellor, Sir Rex Richards, D.SC., FRS (1981).
Vice-Chancellor, D. Harrison, CBE, PH.D., SC.D.
Academic Registrar and Secretary, I. H. C. Powell.

THE UNIVERSITY OF HULL (1954)
Cottingham Road, Hull HU6 7RX

Full-time Students (1987–88), 4,910.
Chancellor, The Lord Wilberforce, CMG, OBE, PC (1978).
Vice-Chancellor, Prof. Sir William Taylor, CBE, PH.D.
Registrar and Secretary, F. T. Mattison.

THE UNIVERSITY OF KEELE (1962)
Keele, Newcastle under Lyme, Staffs. ST5 5BG
[0782-621111]

Full-time Students (1989–90), 3,450.
Chancellor, Sir Claus Moser, KCB, CBE, FBA (1986).
Vice-Chancellor, Prof. B. E. Fender, CMG, PH.D.
Registrar, D. Cohen, PH.D.

UNIVERSITY OF KENT AT CANTERBURY (1965)
Canterbury CT2 7LX
[0227-764000]

Full-time Students (1989–90), 4,891.
Chancellor, R. Horton (1990).
Vice-Chancellor, D. J. E. Ingram, D.Phil., D.SC.
Registrar, A. D. Linfoot.

THE UNIVERSITY OF LANCASTER (1964)
Lancaster LA1 4YW
[0524-65201]

Full-time Students (1989–90), 5,300.
Chancellor, HRH Princess Alexandra, the Hon. Lady
   Ogilvy, GCVO (1964).
Vice-Chancellor, Prof. H. J. Hanham, PH.D.
Secretary, G. M. Cockburn.

THE UNIVERSITY OF LEEDS (1904)
Leeds LS2 9JT
[0532-431751]

Full-time Students (1989–90), 10,842.
Chancellor, HRH The Duchess of Kent, GCVO (1966).
Vice-Chancellor, Sir Edward Parkes, PH.D., SC.D.
Registrar, J. J. Walsh.

THE UNIVERSITY OF LEICESTER (1957)
Leicester LE1 7RH
[0533-522522]

Full-time Students (1989–90), 5,671.
Chancellor, Prof. Sir George Porter, FRS, Ph.D., SC.D. (1985).
Vice-Chancellor, K. J. R. Edwards, Ph.D.
Registrar, Prof. G. Bernbaum.

THE UNIVERSITY OF LIVERPOOL (1903)
PO Box 147, Liverpool L69 3BX
[051-794 2000]

Full-time Students (1989–90), 8,717.
Chancellor, The Viscount Leverhulme, KG, TD (1980).
Vice-Chancellor, Prof. G. J. Davies, Ph.D., SC.D.
Registrar, P. H. Gayward, OBE.
Academic Secretary, M. D. Carr.

THE UNIVERSITY OF LONDON (1836)
Senate House, WC1E 7HU
[071-636 8000]

Internal Students (1988–89), 54,521, External Students, 24,856.
Visitor, HM The Queen in Council.
Chancellor, HRH The Princess Royal, GCVO, FRS (1981).
Vice-Chancellor, Prof. S. R. Sutherland.
Chairman of the Court, The Lord Goff of Chieveley, PC, DCL.
Chairman of Convocation, Prof. C. D. Cowan, CBE, Ph.D.
Principal, P. Holwell.

Principal Officers

Clerk of the Court, P. J. Griffiths.
Clerk of the Senate, J. R. Davidson.
Academic Registrar, Mrs. G. F. Roberts.
Secretary to School Examinations Council, A. R. Stephenson.

Schools of the University

Birkbeck College, Malet Street, WC1E 7HX.—*Master*, The Baroness Blackstone, Ph.D.
Goldsmiths' College, Lewisham Way, New Cross, SE14 6NW.—*Warden*, Prof. A. Rutherford.
Imperial College of Science, Technology and Medicine, Prince Consort Road, SW7 2AZ.—*Rector*, Prof. Sir Eric Ash, CBE, Ph.D., FRS.
Institute of Education, 20 Bedford Way, WC1H 0AL.—*Dir.*, Sir Peter Newsam.
King's College London (includes former Chelsea College and Queen Elizabeth College), Strand, WC2R 2LS.—*Principal*, Prof. J. D. E. Beynon, Ph.D.
London School of Economics and Political Science, Houghton Street, WC2A 2AE.—*Dir.*, Prof. J. M. Ashworth, Ph.D., D.SC.
Queen Mary and Westfield College, Mile End Road, E1 4NS.—*Principal*, Prof. I. Butterworth, CBE, Ph.D., FRS.
Royal Holloway and Bedford New College, Egham Hill, Egham, Surrey TW20 0EX.—*Principal*, Prof. N. Gowar.
Royal Veterinary College, Royal College Street, NW1 0TU.—*Principal and Dean*, Prof. L. E. Lanyon, Ph.D.
School of Oriental and African Studies, Malet Street, WC1E 7HP.—*Dir.*, Prof. M. D. McWilliam.
School of Pharmacy, 29–39 Brunswick Square, WC1N 1AX.—*Dean*, Prof. A. T. Florence, Ph.D., FRSE.
University College, Gower Street, WC1E 6BT.—*Provost*, Dr. D. H. Roberts, CBE, FRS.
Wye College, Wye, Ashford, Kent TN25 5AH.—*Principal*, Prof. J. H. D. Prescott, Ph.D.

*Heythrop College, 11–13 Cavendish Square, W1M 0AN.—*Principal*, Rev. B. A. Callaghan, SJ.

Medical Schools

Charing Cross and Westminster Medical School, The Reynolds Building, St. Dunstan's Road, W6 8RP.—*Dean*, J. E. H. Pendower; *Sec.*, G. K. Buckley.
Royal Free Hospital School of Medicine, Rowland Hill Street, NW3 2PF.—*Dean*, Prof. A. J. Zuckerman, MD, FRCP; *Sec.*, B. A. Blatch.
The Royal London Hospital Medical College, Turner Street, E1 2AD.—*Dean*, Prof. R. Duckworth, CBE, MD, FRCS, FRCPath; *Sec.*, J. W. Walmsley.
St. Bartholomew's Hospital Medical College, West Smithfield, EC1A 7BE.—*Dean*, Prof. L. H. Rees, MD, FRCP; *Sec.*, Dr. J. C. Axe.
St. George's Hospital Medical School, Cranmer Terrace, SW17 0RE.—*Dean*, Prof. A. W. Asscher, MD, FRCP; *Sec.*, R. B. Hill.
United Medical and Dental Schools of Guy's and St. Thomas's Hospitals, Guy's: London Bridge, SE1 9RT; St. Thomas's: Lambeth Palace Road, SE1 7EH.—*Dean*, Prof. I. R. Cameron, DM, FRCP; *Sec.*, C. S. Argles.

Postgraduate Medical Institutions

London School of Hygiene and Tropical Medicine, Keppel Street, WC1E 7HT.—*Dean*, Prof. R. G. Feachem, Ph.D.
Royal Postgraduate Medical School, Du Cane Road, W12 0SH.—*Dean*, Prof. D. N. S. Kerr, FRCP.
British Postgraduate Medical Federation (University of London), 33 Millman Street, WC1N 3EJ.—*Dir.*, Prof. M. J. Peckham, MD, FRCP(G), FRCR.
Comprises:—
Institute of Cancer Research, Royal Cancer Hospital, 17A Onslow Gardens, SW7 3AL.—*Dir.*, Prof. R. A. Weiss, Ph.D.
Institute of Child Health, 30 Guilford Street, WC1N 1EH.—*Dean*, vacant.
Institute of Dental Surgery, Eastman Dental Hospital, Gray's Inn Road, WC1X 8LD.—*Dean*, Prof. G. B. Winter, D.Ch., FDS.
National Heart and Lung Institute, Fulham Road, SW3 6HP.—*Dean*, M. Green, DM, FRCP.
Hunterian Institute, Royal College of Surgeons of England, Lincoln's Inn Fields, WC2A 3PN.—*Master*, Prof. Sir Stanley Peart, FRS, FRCP; *Academic Dean*, Prof. G. P. Lewis, Ph.D.
Institute of Neurology, National Hospital, Queen Square, WC1N 3BG.—*Dean*, D. N. Landon.
Institute of Ophthalmology, Judd Street, WC1H 9QS.—*Dean*, R. K. Blatch, MD, FRCS.
Institute of Psychiatry, De Crespigny Park, Denmark Hill, SE5 8EF.—*Dean*, D. S. Checkley, MD.

Senate Institutes

British Institute in Paris, 9–11 Rue de Constantine, 75007, Paris.—*Dir.*, Prof. C. L. Campos, L-ès-L., Ph.D. *London office:* Senate House, Malet Street, WC1E 7HU.
Courtauld Institute of Art, North Block, Somerset House, Strand, WC2R 2LS.—*Dir.*, Prof. C. M. Kauffman, Ph.D.
Institute of Advanced Legal Studies, Charles Clore House, 17 Russell Square, WC1B 5DR.—*Dir.*, Prof. T. C. Daintith.
Institute of Classical Studies, 31–34 Gordon Square, WC1H 0PY.—*Dir.*, Prof. J. P. Barron, D.Phil., FSA.
Institute of Commonwealth Studies, 27–28 Russell Square, WC1B 5DS.—*Dir.*, Prof. Shula E. Marks, Ph.D.

*Not in receipt of UFC grants.

Institute of Germanic Studies, 29 Russell Square, WC1B 5DP.—*Hon. Dir.*, Prof. M. W. Swales, PH.D.

Institute of Historical Research (including the Institute of United States Studies), Senate House, Malet Street, WC1E 7HU.—*Dir.*, Prof. P. K. O'Brien, D.PHIL.

Institute of Latin American Studies, 31 Tavistock Square, WC1H 9HA.—*Dir.*, Prof. L. M. Bethell, PH.D.

Institute of Romance Studies, Senate House, Malet Street, WC1E 7HU.—*Dir.*, Prof. M. M. Bowie, D.Phil.

School of Slavonic and East European Studies, Senate House, Malet Street, WC1E 7HU.—*Dir.*, Prof. M. A. Branch, PH.D.

Warburg Institute, Woburn Square, WC1H 0AB.— *Dir.*, Dr. N. Mann.

Institute of Zoology, Royal Zoological Society, Regent's Park, NW1 4RY.—*Dir.*, Prof. A. P. F. Flint, PH.D., D.SC.

Institutions having Recognized Teachers

Jews' College, 44A Albert Road, NW4 2SJ.—*Principal*, vacant.

London Business School, Sussex Place, NW1 4SA.— *Principal*, Prof. G. Bain, D.PHIL.

Royal Academy of Music, Marylebone Road, NW1 5HT.—*Principal*, Sir David Lumsden, D.Phil., FRCM.

Royal College of Music, Prince Consort Road, SW7 2BS.—*Dir.*, M. G. Matthews, FRSA, FRCM.

Trinity College of Music, Mandeville Place, W1M 6AQ.—*Principal*, P. Jones, CBE, FRCM.

LOUGHBOROUGH UNIVERSITY OF TECHNOLOGY (1966)
Loughborough LE11 3TU

Full-time Students (1988–89), 5,800.
Chancellor, Sir Denis Rooke, CBE, FRS (1989).
Vice-Chancellor, Prof. D. E. N. Davies, CBE, PH.D., D.SC., FRS.
Registrar, D. E. Fletcher, PH.D.

THE UNIVERSITY OF MANCHESTER
(Founded 1851; re-organized 1880 and 1903).
Oxford Road, Manchester MI3 9PL

Full-time Students (1988–89), 16,372.
Chancellor, Prof. J. A. G. Griffith, FBA (1986).
Vice-Chancellor, Sir Mark Richmond, PH.D., SC.D., FRS.
Registrar and Secretary, K. E. Kitchen.

UNIVERSITY OF MANCHESTER INSTITUTE OF SCIENCE AND TECHNOLOGY (1824)
PO Box 88, Manchester M60 1QD
[061-2363311]

Full-time Students (1989–90), 4,707.
President, Sir John Mason, CB, D.SC., FRS (1986).
Principal, Prof. H. C. A. Hankins, PH.D.
Secretary and Registrar, P. C. C. Stephenson.

THE UNIVERSITY OF NEWCASTLE UPON TYNE
(Founded 1852; re-organized 1908, 1937 and 1963)
6 Kensington Terrace, Newcastle upon Tyne
NE1 7RU
[091-222 6000]

Full-time Students (1989–90), 8,317.
Chancellor, The Viscount Ridley, TD (1989).
Vice-Chancellor, Prof. L. W. Martin, PH.D.
Registrar, D. E. T. Nicholson.

THE UNIVERSITY OF NOTTINGHAM (1948)
University Park, Nottingham NG7 2RD
[0602-484848]

Full-time Students (1989–90), 8,400.
Chancellor, Sir Gordon Hobday, PH.D. (1979).
Vice-Chancellor, Prof. C. M. Campbell.
Registrar, G. E. Chandler.

THE UNIVERSITY OF OXFORD

FULL TERMS, 1991

Hilary, Jan. 13 to March 9; *Trinity*, April 21 to June 15; *Michaelmas*, Oct. 13 to Dec. 7

Number of Undergraduates in Residence 1989–90: *Men*, 6,122; *Women*, 4,053

UNIVERSITY OFFICERS, etc.†	Elect.
Chancellor, The Lord Jenkins of Hillhead, PC (*Balliol*)	1987
High Steward, The Lord Goff of Chieveley (*Lincoln* and *New College*)	1990
Vice-Chancellor, Sir Richard Southward, D.SC., FRS (*Merton*)	1989
Proctors, J. M. Innes (*Somerville*); C. J. Crouch, D.Phil. (*Trinity*)	1990
Assessor, P. J. Waller (*Merton*)	1990
Public Orator, G. W. Bond (*Pembroke*)	1980
Bodley's Librarian, D. G. Vaisey (*Exeter*)	1986
Keeper of Archives, J. Hackney (*Wadham*)	1988
Director of the Ashmolean Museum, C. J. White (*Worcester*)	1985
Registrar of the University, A. J. Dorey, D.Phil. (*Linacre*)	1979
Surveyor to the University, D. W. Bending	1985
Secretary of Faculties, A. P. Weale (*Worcester*)	1984
Secretary of the Chest and Chief Accountant, I. G. Thompson (*Merton*)	1986
Deputy Registrar (Admin.), D. W. Roberts (*Pembroke*)	
Deputy Registrar (General), P. W. Jones (*Green*)	1989

Oxford Colleges and Halls
(With dates of foundation)

All Souls (1438), *Warden*, Sir Patrick Neill, QC (1977).
Balliol (1263), *Master*, B. S. Blumberg (1989).
Brasenose (1509), *Principal*, The Lord Windlesham, CVO, PC (1989).
Christ Church (1546), *Dean*, Very Rev. E. W. Heaton (1979).
Corpus Christi (1517), *President*, Prof. Sir Keith Thomas, FBA (1986).
Exeter (1314), *Rector*, Sir Richard Norman, KBE, D.SC., FRS (1987).
Green (1979), *Warden*, Sir Crispin Tickell, GCMG, KCVO (1990).
Hertford (1874), *Principal*, Prof. E. C. Zeeman, FRS (1988).
Jesus (1571), *Principal*, Dr. P. M. North, CBE, DCL (1984).
Keble (1868), *Warden*, G. B. Richardson, CBE (1989).
Lady Margaret Hall (1878), *Principal*, D. M. Stewart (1979).
Linacre (1962), *Principal*, Sir Bryan Cartledge, KCMG (1988).
Lincoln (1427), *Rector*, Sir Maurice Shock (1987).
Magdalen (1458), *President*, A. D. Smith, CBE (1988).
Merton (1264), *Warden*, J. M. Roberts, D.Phil. (1985).

† Correspondence for the Vice-Chancellor and other administrative officers should be sent to the University Offices, Wellington Square, Oxford OX1 2JD. (Tel: 0865-270001).

New College (1379), *Warden*, H. McGregor, QC, DCL (1985).

Nuffield (1937), *Warden*, Sir David Cox, FRS (1988).

Oriel (1326), *Provost*, E. W. Nicholson, DD, FBA (1990).

Pembroke (1624), *Master*, Sir Roger Bannister, CBE, DM, FRCP (1985).

Queen's (1340), *Provost*, J. Moffatt, D.Phil. (1987).

Rewley House (1990), *President*, G. P. Thomas, Ph.D. (1990).

St. Anne's (1952) (Originally Society of Oxford Home-Students (1879)), *Principal*, Claire Palley, Ph.D. (1984).

St. Antony's (1950), *Warden*, R. Dahrendorf, HON. KBE, Ph.D., FBA (1987).

St. Catherine's (1962), *Master*, E. B. Smith, D.Sc. (1988).

St. Cross (1965), *Master*, R. C. Repp, D.Phil. (1987).

St. Edmund Hall (c. 1278), *Principal*, J. C. B. Gosling (1983).

*St. Hilda's (1938), *Principal*, Miss E. Llewellyn-Smith, CB (1990).

St. Hugh's (1886), *Principal*, Miss M. R. Trickett (1973).

St. John's (1555), *President*, W. Hayes, D.Phil. (1987).

St. Peter's (1929), *Master*, Prof. G. E. Aylmer, D.Phil., FBA (1978).

*Somerville (1879), *Principal*, Miss C. E. Pestell, CMG (1989).

Trinity (1554), *President*, Sir John Burgh, KCMG, CB (1987).

University (1249), *Master*, W. J. Albery, D.Phil., FRS (1989).

Wadham (1612), *Warden*, Sir Claus Moser, KCB, CBE, FBA (1984).

Wolfson (1966), *President*, Sir Raymond Hoffenberg, KBE, FRCP (1985).

Worcester (1714), *Provost*, The Lord Briggs, FBA (1976).

Campion Hall (1896), *Master*, Rev. J. A. Munitiz (1989).

St. Benet's Hall (1897), *Master*, Rev. P. F. Cowper, OSB (1989).

Mansfield (1886), *Principal*, D. J. Trevelyan, CB (1989).

Regent's Park (1810), *Principal*, Rev. P. S. Fiddes, D.Phil. (1989).

Greyfriars (1910), *Warden*, Rev. M. W. Sheehan, D.Phil. (1990).

Manchester (1990), *Principal*, Rev. R. Waller, Ph.D. (1990).

* Colleges for women only.

THE UNIVERSITY OF READING (1926)
Whiteknights, PO Box 217, Reading RG6 2AH
[0734-875123]

Full-time Students (1989–90), 7,473.
Chancellor, The Lord Sherfield, GCB, GCMG, FRS (1970).
Vice-Chancellor, E. S. Page, Ph.D.
Registrar, T. Bottomley.

UNIVERSITY OF SALFORD (1967)
Salford M5 4WT
[061-745 5000]

Full-time Students (1989–90), 4,096.
Chancellor, HRH The Duchess of York (1990).
Vice-Chancellor, Prof. T. M. Husband, Ph.D.
Registrar, S. R. Bosworth, OBE.

THE UNIVERSITY OF SHEFFIELD (1905)
Western Bank, Sheffield S10 2TN

Full-time Students (1987–88), 7,914.
Chancellor, The Lord Dainton, Ph.D., Sc.D., FRS (1979).
Vice-Chancellor, Prof. G. G. Roberts.
Registrar and Secretary, Dr. J. S. Padley.

THE UNIVERSITY OF SOUTHAMPTON (1952)
Highfield, Southampton SO9 5NH
[0703-595000]

Full-time Students (1989–90), 7,396.
Chancellor, The Earl Jellicoe, KBE, DSO, MC, PC (1984).
Vice-Chancellor, G. R. Higginson, Ph.D.
Secretary and Registrar, D. A. Schofield.
Academic Registrar, Miss A. E. Clarke.

UNIVERSITY OF SURREY (1966)
Guildford, Surrey GU2 5XH
[0483-571281]

Full-time Students (1989–90), 4,285.
Chancellor, HRH The Duke of Kent, KG, GCMG, GCVO (1977).
Vice-Chancellor, Prof. A. Kelly, CBE, SC.D., FRS.
Secretary, L. J. Kail.

THE UNIVERSITY OF SUSSEX (1961)
Falmer, Brighton BN1 9RH

Full-time Students (1988–89), 4,935.
Chancellor, The Earl of March and Kinrara (1985).
Vice-Chancellor, Sir Leslie Fielding, KCMG.
Registrar and Secretary, G. Lockwood, D.Phil.

THE UNIVERSITY OF WARWICK (1965)
Coventry CV4 7AL

Full-time Students (1989–90), 9,029.
Chancellor, Sir Shridath Surendranath Ramphal, GCMG, QC (1989).
Vice-Chancellor, C. L. Brundin, Ph.D.
Registrar, M. L. Shattock, OBE.

THE UNIVERSITY OF YORK (1963)
Heslington, York YO1 5DD
[0904-430000]

Full-time Students (1988–89), 4,098.
Chancellor, The Lord Swann, Ph.D., FRS, FRSE (1979).
Vice-Chancellor, Prof. S. B. Saul, Ph.D.
Registrar, D. J. Foster.

CRANFIELD INSTITUTE OF TECHNOLOGY (1969)
Cranfield, Bedford MK43 0AL
[0908-672974]

Under Royal Charter (1969) the Cranfield Institute of Technology grants degrees in applied science, engineering, technology and management.
Full-time Students (1989–90), 2,040.
Chancellor, The Lord Kings Norton, Ph.D. (1969).
Vice-Chancellor, Prof. F. R. Hartley, D.SC.
Secretary and Registrar, J. K. Pettifer.

THE OPEN UNIVERSITY (1969)
Walton Hall, Milton Keynes MK7 6AA
[0908-274066]

Students and clients (1990), 200,000.
Tuition by correspondence linked with special radio and television programmes, video and audio cassettes, residential schools and a locally-based tutorial and counselling service. Under Royal Charter the University awards degrees of BA, B.Phil., MA, MBA, M.SC., M.Phil., Ph.D., D.SC. and D.Litt. There are seven faculties—arts, education, mathematics, science, social sciences, technology and management and a wide range of continuing education courses and study packs.
Chancellor, The Lord Briggs, FBA (1978).
Vice-Chancellor, Dr. J. S. Daniel.
Secretary, D. J. Clinch.

ROYAL COLLEGE OF ART (1837)
Kensington Gore, SW7 2EU
[071-584 5020]

Under Royal Charter (1967) the Royal College of Art grants the degrees of Doctor, Doctor of Philosophy, Master of Arts, Master of Design and Master of Design (Engineering) (RCA).
Students (1989–90), 600 (all postgraduate).
Provost, The Earl of Gowrie, PC (1986).
Registrar, K. Reid.

THE UNIVERSITY OF WALES (1893)
King Edward VII Avenue, Cathays Park,
Cardiff CF1 3NS
[0222-382656]

Chancellor, HRH The Prince of Wales, KG, KT, GCB, PC (1976).
Pro-Chancellor, The Lord Cledwyn of Penrhos, CH, PC (1985).
Vice-Chancellor, Prof. E. Sutherland, PH.D.
Registrar, M. A. R. Kemp, PH.D.

Colleges

University College of Wales, Aberystwyth.—*Princ.*, Prof. K. O. Morgan, D.phil. (1979).
University College of North Wales, Bangor.—*Princ.*, Prof. E. Sunderland, PH.D. (1984).
University of Wales College of Cardiff, Cardiff.—*Princ.*, Sir Aubrey Trotman-Dickenson, PH.D., D.SC. (1968).
St. David's College, Lampeter.—*Princ.*, The Lord Morris of Castle Morris (1990).
University College, Swansea.—*Princ.*, Prof. B. L. Clarkson, PH.D., (1982).
University of Wales College of Medicine, Cardiff.—*Provost*, Prof. Sir Herbert Duthie, MD, ch.M., FRCS (1979).

SCOTLAND

UNIVERSITY OF ABERDEEN (1495)
Regent Walk, Aberdeen AB9 1FX
[0224-272000]

Full-time Students (1989–90), 6,701.
Chancellor, Sir Kenneth Alexander, FRSE (1987).
Principal, Prof. G. P. McNicol, MD, PH.D., FRSE (1981).
Secretary, N. R. D. Begg.
Rector, vacant.

UNIVERSITY OF DUNDEE (1967)
Dundee DD1 4HN
[0382-23181]

Full-time Students (1989–90), 4,369.
Chancellor, The Earl of Dalhousie, KT, GCVO, GBE, MC (1977).
Vice-Chancellor, Prof. M. J. Hamlin, Ll.D.
Secretary, R. Seaton.
Rector, P. H. Scott, CMG (1989–92).

UNIVERSITY OF EDINBURGH (1583)
Old College, South Bridge, Edinburgh EH8 9YL
[031-667 1011]

Full-time Students (1989–90), 11,221.
Chancellor, HRH The Prince Philip, Duke of Edinburgh, KG, KT, OM, GBE, PC, FRS (1952).
Vice-Chancellor and Principal, Sir David Smith, D.Phil., FRS.
Secretary, Dr. M. J. B. Lowe.
Rector, Ms. M. Gray (1988–91).

UNIVERSITY OF GLASGOW (1451)
Glasgow G12 8QQ
[041-339 8855]

Full-time Students (1989–90), 12,100.
Chancellor, Sir Alexander Cairncross, KCMG, FBA (1972).
Vice-Chancellor, Sir William Fraser, GCB, FRSE.
Registrar, J. M. Black.
Secretary, R. Ewen, OBE, TD.
Rector, P. Kane (1990–1993).

HERIOT-WATT UNIVERSITY (1966)
Riccarton, Edinburgh EH14 4AS
[031-449 5111]

Full-time Students (1989–90), 5,016.
Chancellor, The Lord Thomson of Monifieth, KT, PC, FRSE (1977).
Principal and Vice-Chancellor, Prof. A. G. J. Mac-Farlane, CBE, PH.D., FRS (1989).
Secretary, P. L. Wilson.
Registrar, D. Sturgeon.

UNIVERSITY OF ST. ANDREWS (1411)
College Gate, St. Andrews KY16 9AJ
[0334-76161]

Full-time Students (1989–90), 3,983.
Chancellor, Sir Kenneth Dover, D.Litt., FRSE, FBA (1981).
Vice-Chancellor, Prof. S. Arnott, PH.D., FRS, FRSE.
Secretary of Court, D. P. Dorward.
Rector, N. Parsons (1989–91).

UNIVERSITY OF STIRLING (1967)
Stirling FK9 4LA
[0786-73171]

Full-time Students (1989–90), 3,500.
Chancellor, The Lord Balfour of Burleigh, FRSE (1988).
Principal and Vice-Chancellor, Prof. A. J. Forty, PH.D., D.SC., FRSE.
Registrar, D. J. Farrington, D.phil.
Secretary, R. G. Bomont.

UNIVERSITY OF STRATHCLYDE (1964)
16 Richmond Street, Glasgow G1 1XQ
[041-552 4400]

Full-time Students (1989–90), 8,098.
Chancellor, The Lord Todd, OM, D.SC., D.phil., FRS (1965).
Principal and Vice-Chancellor, Sir Graham Hills, PH.D., D.SC., FRSE.
Secretary, P. W. A. West.

NORTHERN IRELAND

THE QUEEN'S UNIVERSITY OF BELFAST (1908)
Belfast BT7 1NN
[0232-245133]

Full-time Students (1989–90), 8,500.
Chancellor, Sir Rowland Wright, CBE, D.SC. (1984).
President and Vice-Chancellor, G. Beveridge, PH.D., FRSE.
Secretary, D. Wilson.

UNIVERSITY OF ULSTER (1984)
(Amalgamation of New University of Ulster and
Ulster Polytechnic)
Cromore Road, Coleraine BT52 1SA
[0232-852926]

Full-time Students (1989–90), 10,490.
Chancellor, The Lord Grey of Naunton, GCMG, GCVO,
OBE (1985).
Vice-Chancellor, Sir Derek Birley.
Academic Registrar, P. J. Conway.
Secretary, J. A. Hunter.

NON-UNIVERSITY SECTOR
POLYTECHNICS

The number of students (full-time equivalent) for
the academic year 1989–90 are shown in parenthesis.

BIRMINGHAM POLYTECHNIC, Perry Barr, Birmingham
B42 2SU (8,300).—*Dir.*, P. C. Knight, D.Phil.;
Registrar, Ms. M. Penlington.

BOURNEMOUTH POLYTECHNIC, Poole House, Talbot
Campus, Fern Borough, Dorset BH12 5BB. (Tel:
0202-524111). (4,000).—*Dir.*, B. R. MacManus, PH.D.;
Registrar, Miss B. Chamberlain.

BRIGHTON POLYTECHNIC, Lewes Road, Brighton BN2
4AT. (Tel: 0273-600900). (6,325).—*Dir.*, Prof. D.
Watson; *Registrar*, A. F. Hussey.

BRISTOL POLYTECHNIC, Coldharbour Lane, Frenchay,
Bristol BS16 1QY. (Tel: 0272-656261). (8,170).—*Dir.*,
A. C. Morris; *Registrar*, Mrs. H. K. Croft.

CITY OF LONDON POLYTECHNIC, 117–119 Houndsditch,
EC3 7BU. (Tel: 071-283 1030). (c. 7,256).—*Dir.*, Prof.
R. Floud, D.Phil.; *Registrar*, B. High.

COVENTRY POLYTECHNIC, Priory Street, Coventry
CV1 5FB. (Tel: 0203-631313). (7,281).—*Dir.*, M.
Goldstein, PH.D., D.SC., FRSC; *Registrar*, Ms. S.
Haselgrove.

HATFIELD POLYTECHNIC, College Lane, Hatfield, Herts
AL10 9AB. (Tel: 0707-279000). (5,869).—*Dir.*, Prof.
N. K. Buxton, PH.D.; *Registrar*, P. G. Jeffreys.

HUDDERSFIELD POLYTECHNIC, Queensgate, Huddersfield HD1 3DH. (Tel: 0484-422288). (6,250).—*Rector*,
Prof. K. J. Durrands; *Registrar*, M. Bond.

HUMBERSIDE POLYTECHNIC, Cottingham Road, Hull
HU6 7RT. (Tel: 0482-440550). (c. 4,500).—*Principal*,
R. P. King; *Registrar*, Mrs. P. Jackson.

KINGSTON POLYTECHNIC, Penrhyn Road, Kingston
upon Thames KT1 2EE. (Tel: 081-549 1366).
(6,900).—*Dir.*, R. C. Smith, CBE, PH.D.; *Registrar*,
Miss A. Hynes.

LANCASHIRE POLYTECHNIC, Preston PR1 2TQ. (Tel:
0772-201201). (6,500).—*Rector*, B. G. Booth; *Registrar*, D. Sharrocks.

LEEDS POLYTECHNIC, Calverley Street, Leeds LS1
3HE. (Tel: 0532-832600). (6,968).—*Dir.*, C. Price.

LEICESTER POLYTECHNIC, PO Box 143, Leicester LE1
9BH. (Tel: 0533-551551). (c. 7,500).—*Dir.*, K. Barker;
Registrar, H. E. J. Woolls.

LIVERPOOL POLYTECHNIC, Rodney House, 70 Mount
Pleasant, Liverpool L3 5UX. (Tel: 051-207 3581).
(9,321).—*Rector*, Prof. P. Toyne; *Registrar*, Miss P.
Eastwood.

MANCHESTER POLYTECHNIC, All Saints, Man-
chester M15 6BH. (Tel: 061-247 2000). (14,563)—
Dir., Sir Kenneth Green; *Registrar*, J. D. M.
Karczewski-Slowikowski.

MIDDLESEX POLYTECHNIC, Trent Park, Bramley Road,
N14 4XS. (Tel: 081-368 1299). (8,145).—*Dir.*, Sir
Raymond Rickett, CBE, PH.D.; *Registrar*, G. Jones.

NEWCASTLE UPON TYNE POLYTECHNIC, Newcastle
upon Tyne NE1 8ST. (Tel: 091-232 6002). (9,520)—
Dir., Prof. L. Barden, CBE, PH.D., D.SC.; *Registrar*, R.
A. Bott.

NOTTINGHAM POLYTECHNIC, Burton Street, Nottingham NG1 4BU. (Tel: 0602-418418). (9,924).—
Dir., Prof. R. Cowell, PH.D.; *Registrar*, A. E. Foster.

OXFORD POLYTECHNIC, Headington, Oxford OX3 0BP.
(Tel: 0865-741111). (6,575).—*Dir.*, Dr. C. Booth;
Registrar, R. Tulloch.

POLYTECHNIC OF CENTRAL LONDON, 309 Regent Street,
W1R 8AL. (Tel: 071-580 2020). (4,828).—*Rector*,
Prof. T. E. Burlin, D.SC., PH.D.; *Registrar*, Ms. J.
Worner.

POLYTECHNIC OF EAST LONDON, Romford Road, E15
4LZ. (Tel: 081-590 7722). (6,700).—*Rector*, Prof. G.
T. Fowler; *Registrar*, G. D. Miller.

POLYTECHNIC OF NORTH LONDON, Holloway Road,
N7 8DB. (Tel: 071-607 2789). (5,500)—*Dir.*, L. Wagner; *Registrar*, Dr. P. Holiday.

POLYTECHNIC SOUTH WEST, Drake Circus, Plymouth
PL4 8AA. (Tel: 0752-600600). (7,940).—*Dir.*, R. J.
Bull; *Registrar*, Dr. C. J. Sparrow.

PORTSMOUTH POLYTECHNIC, Ravelin House, Museum
Road, Portsmouth PO1 2QQ. (Tel: 0705-827681).
(7,343).—*Pres.*, vacant; *Registrar*, Brig. B. R. Biggs.

SHEFFIELD CITY POLYTECHNIC, Pond Street, Sheffield
S1 1WB. (Tel: 0742-720911). (10,300).—*Principal*, J.
M. Stoddart; *Registrar*, Ms. J. Tory.

SOUTH BANK POLYTECHNIC, 103 Borough Road, SE1
0AA. (Tel: 071-928 8989). (7,255).—*Dir.*, Mrs. P.
Perry; *Registrar*, N. Andrew.

STAFFORDSHIRE POLYTECHNIC, College Road, Stoke-
on-Trent, ST4 2DE. (Tel: 0782-744531). (c. 8,000).—
Dir., K. A. B. Thompson; *Academic Registrar*, Mrs. F.
Francis.

SUNDERLAND POLYTECHNIC, Langham Tower, Ryhope
Road, Sunderland SR2 7EE. (Tel: 091-515 2000).
(6,342).—*Rector*, Ms. A. Wright, PH.D.; *Registrar*, S.
Porteous.

TEESSIDE POLYTECHNIC, Middlesbrough, Cleveland
TS1 3BA (4,487)—*Dir.*, M. D. Longfield, PH.D.;
Registrar, M. McClintock.

THAMES POLYTECHNIC, Wellington Street, Woolwich,
SE18 6PF. (Tel: 081-316 8000). (6,500).—*Dir.*, N.
Singer, CBE, PH.D.; *Registrar*, A. I. Mayfield.

WOLVERHAMPTON POLYTECHNIC, Molineux Street,
Wolverhampton WV1 1SB. (Tel: 0902-321000).
(8,980).—*Dir.*, Prof. M. J. Harrison; *Registrar*, A.
M. Cooper.

POLYTECHNIC OF WALES, Pontypridd, Mid Glamorgan
CF37 1DL (4,500).—*Dir.*, J. D. Davies, OBE, PH.D.,
D.SC.

SCOTTISH CENTRAL INSTITUTIONS

DUNCAN OF JORDANSTONE COLLEGE OF ART, Perth
Road, Dundee DD1 4HT. (Tel: 0382-23261).—*Principal*, R. Miller-Smith.

DUNDEE INSTITUTE OF TECHNOLOGY, Bell Street,
Dundee DD1 1HG. (Tel: 0382-27225).—*Principal*, H.
G. Cuming, CBE, PH.D.

EDINBURGH COLLEGE OF ART, Lauriston Place, Edinburgh EH3 9DF. (Tel: 031-229 9311).—*Principal*,
Prof. A. J. Rowan, PH.D.

GLASGOW COLLEGE, Cowcaddens Road, Glasgow G4
0BA. (Tel: 041-331 3000).—*Principal*, Dr. J. S.
Mason.

GLASGOW SCHOOL OF ART, 167 Renfrew Street,
Glasgow G3 6RQ. (Tel: 041-332 9797).—*Dir.*, W.
Buchanan (*acting*).

NAPIER COLLEGE, 219 Colinton Road, Edinburgh
EH14 1DJ. (Tel: 031-444 2266).—*Principal*, W. A.
Turmeau, CBE, PH.D.

PAISLEY COLLEGE OF TECHNOLOGY, High Street,
Paisley PA1 2BE. (Tel: 041-848 3000).—*Principal*,
Prof. R. W. Shaw.

QUEEN MARGARET COLLEGE, Clerwood Terrace, Edinburgh EH12 8TS. (Tel: 031-317 3000).—*Principal*, D. F. Leach.

THE QUEEN'S COLLEGE, GLASGOW, 1 Park Drive, Glasgow G3 6LP.—*Principal*, G. A. Richardson, PH.D.

ROBERT GORDON'S INSTITUTE OF TECHNOLOGY, Schoolhill, Aberdeen AB9 1FR. (Tel: 0224-633611).—*Principal*, D. A. Kennedy, PH.D.

ROYAL SCOTTISH ACADEMY OF MUSIC AND DRAMA, 100 Renfrew Street, Glasgow G2 3BD. (Tel: 041-332 4101).—*Principal*, Dr. P. Ledger, CBE.

SCOTTISH AGRICULTURAL COLLEGE, Cleeve Gardens, Oakbank Road, Perth PH1 1HF. (Tel: 0738-36611). Campuses at Aberdeen, Auchincruive, and Edinburgh.—*Principal*, Prof. P. C. Thomas.

SCOTTISH COLLEGE OF TEXTILES, Netherdale, Galashiels, Selkirkshire, TD1 3HF. (Tel: 0896-3351).—*Principal*, C. E. R. Maddox, PH.D.

COLLEGES

It is not possible to name here all the colleges offering courses of higher or further education. The list of English colleges that follows is confined to those in the PCFC sector; there are many more colleges in England providing higher education courses, some with PCFC funding. The list of colleges in Wales, Scotland and Northern Ireland includes institutions providing at least one full-time course leading to a first degree granted by a university or by the Council for National Academic Awards (CNAA). It does not include colleges forming part of a polytechnic or a university, nor does it include Scottish central institutions.

ENGLAND

PCFC Sector

ANGLIA HIGHER EDUCATION COLLEGE, Victoria Road South, Chelmsford CM1 1LL. (Tel: 0245-493131).—*Dir.*, M. Salmon.

BATH COLLEGE OF HIGHER EDUCATION, Newton Park, Newton St. Loe, Bath BA2 9BN. (Tel: 0225-873701).—*Dir.*, B. L. Gomes da Costa.

BISHOP GROSSETESTE COLLEGE, Lincoln LN1 3DY. (Tel: 0522-527347).—*Principal*, Prof. L. Marsh, D.PHIL.

BOLTON INSTITUTE OF HIGHER EDUCATION, Deane Road, Bolton BL3 5AB. (Tel: 0204-28851).—*Principal*, R. Oxtoby, PH.D.

BRETTON HALL COLLEGE OF HIGHER EDUCATION, West Bretton, Wakefield, W. Yorks. WF4 4LG. (Tel: 0924-830261).—*Principal*, Prof. J. L. Taylor, OBE.

BUCKINGHAMSHIRE COLLEGE OF HIGHER EDUCATION, Queen Alexandra Road, High Wycombe, Bucks. HP11 2JZ. (Tel: 0494-22141).—*Dir.*, D. J. Everett, LL.D.

CAMBORNE SCHOOL OF MINES, Pool, Redruth, Cornwall TR15 3SE. (Tel: 0209-714866).—*Principal*, P. Hackett, OBE, PH.D.

THE CENTRAL SCHOOL OF SPEECH AND DRAMA, Embassy Theatre, Eton Avenue, London NW3 3HY. (Tel: 071-722 8183).—*Principal*, R. S. Fowler.

CHARLOTTE MASON COLLEGE OF EDUCATION, Rydal Road, Ambleside, Cumbria LA22 9BB. (Tel: 05394-33066).—*Principal*, Prof. J. Thorley, PH.D.

CHELTENHAM AND GLOUCESTER COLLEGE OF HIGHER EDUCATION, PO Box 220, The Park, Cheltenham GL50 2QF. (Tel: 0242-513836).—*Principal*, Miss J. O. Trotter.

CHESTER COLLEGE, Cheyney Road, Chester CH1 4BJ.—*Principal*, Rev. E. V. Binks.

CHRIST CHURCH COLLEGE, North Holmes Road, Canterbury, Kent CT1 1QU. (Tel: 0227-762444).—*Principal*, M. H. A. Berry, TD.

COLLEGE OF RIPON AND YORK ST. JOHN, Lord Mayor's Walk, York YO3 7EX. (Tel: 0904-656771).—*Principal*, Dr. G. P. McGregor.

COLLEGE OF ST. MARK AND ST. JOHN, Derriford Road, Plymouth PL6 8BH. (Tel: 0752-777188).—*Principal*, J. E. Anderson.

CREWE AND ALSAGER COLLEGE OF HIGHER EDUCATION, Crewe Road, Crewe CW1 1DU. (Tel: 0270-500661).—*Dir.*, Miss B. P. R. Ward, CBE.

DARTINGTON COLLEGE OF ARTS, Totnes, Devon TQ9 6EJ.—*Principal*, G. Dowrick.

DERBYSHIRE COLLEGE OF HIGHER EDUCATION, Kedleston Road, Derby DE3 1GB.—*Dir.*, J. May, TD, PH.D.

EALING COLLEGE OF HIGHER EDUCATION, St. Mary's Road, Ealing, London W5 5RF. (Tel: 081-579 5000).—*Dir.*, Prof. N. Merritt.

EDGE HILL COLLEGE OF HIGHER EDUCATION, St. Helens Road, Ormskirk, Lancs. L39 4QP. (Tel: 0695-575171).—*Dir.*, Prof. R. Gee.

FALMOUTH SCHOOL OF ART AND DESIGN, Woodlane, Falmouth, Cornwall TR11 4RA. (Tel: 0326-211077).—*Principal*, Prof. A. G. Livingston.

HARPER ADAMS AGRICULTURAL COLLEGE, Newport, Shropshire TF10 8NB. (Tel: 0952-820280).—*Principal*, A. G. Harris.

HOMERTON COLLEGE, Cambridge CB2 2PH. (Tel: 0223-411141).—*Principal*, A. G. Bamford, CBE.

INSTITUTE OF ADVANCED NURSING, Royal College of Nursing, 20 Cavendish Square, W1M 0AB.—*Principal (acting)*, J. C. A. Wells.

KENT INSTITUTE OF ART AND DESIGN, Oakwood Park, Oakwood Road, Maidstone ME16 8AG (*also* New Dover Road, Canterbury CT1 3AN; and Fort Pitt, Rochester ME1 1DZ). (Tel: 0622-757286).—*Dir.*, P. I. Williams.

KING ALFRED'S COLLEGE, Sparkford Road, Winchester SO22 4NR. (Tel: 0962-841515).—*Principal*, J. A. Cranmer.

LIVERPOOL INSTITUTE OF HIGHER EDUCATION, PO Box 6, Stand Park Road, Liverpool L16 9JD. (Tel: 051-722 2361).—*Rector*, J. Burke, OBE, PH.D.

THE LONDON INSTITUTE, 388–396 Oxford Street, W1R 1FE.—*Rector*, J. McKenzie. Comprising:
Camberwell College of Arts, Peckham Road, SE5 8UF.
Central St. Martins College of Art and Design, Southampton Row, WC1B 4AP.
Chelsea College of Art and Design, Manresa Road, SW3 6LS.
College for the Distributive Trades, 30 Leicester Square, WC2H 7LE.
London College of Fashion, 20 John Prince's Street, W1M 9HE.
London College of Printing, Elephant and Castle, SE1 6SB.

LOUGHBOROUGH COLLEGE OF ART AND DESIGN, Radmoor, Loughborough, Leics. LE11 3BT. (Tel: 0509-261515).—*Principal*, I. Pugh.

LSU COLLEGE OF HIGHER EDUCATION, The Avenue, Southampton SO9 5HB. (Tel: 0703-228761).—*Principal*, Dr. A. C. Chitnis.

LUTON COLLEGE OF HIGHER EDUCATION, Park Square, Luton LU1 3JU. (Tel: 0582-34111).—*Dir.*, A. J. Wood, PH.D.

NENE COLLEGE, Moulton Park, Northampton NN2 7AL. (Tel: 0604-715000).—*Dir.*, Dr. S. M. Gaskell.

NEWMAN COLLEGE, Genners Lane, Bartley Green, Birmingham B32 3NT. (Tel: 021-476 1181).—*Principal*, Joan S. Cuming, PH.D.

NORTH RIDING COLLEGE, Filey Road, Scarborough, N. Yorks. YO11 3AZ. (Tel: 0723-362392).—*Principal*, F. W. Wright.

RAVENSBOURNE COLLEGE OF DESIGN AND COMMUNICATION, Walden Road, Chislehurst, Kent BR7 5SN. (Tel: 081-468 7071).—*Dir.*, N. J. Frewing.

ROEHAMPTON INSTITUTE, Senate House, Roehampton Lane, London SW15 5PU. Comprises Digby Stuart

College, Froebel Institute, Southlands College and Whitelands College. (Tel: 081-878 8117).—*Rector*, Prof. S. C. Holt, Ph.D.

ROSE BRUFORD COLLEGE OF SPEECH AND DRAMA, Lamorbey Park, Burnt Oak Lane, Sidcup, Kent DA15 9DF. (Tel: 081-300 3024).—*Principal*, P. Robins.

ROYAL ACADEMY OF MUSIC, Marylebone Road, London NW1 5HT. (071-935 5461).—*Principal*, Sir David Lumsden, D.Phil.

ROYAL COLLEGE OF MUSIC, Prince Consort Road, London SW7 2BS. (Tel: 071-589 3643).—*Dir.*, M. G. Matthews.

ROYAL NORTHERN COLLEGE OF MUSIC, 124 Oxford Road, Manchester M13 9RD.—*Principal*, Sir John Manduell, CBE.

S. MARTIN'S COLLEGE OF HIGHER EDUCATION, Bowerham, Lancaster LA1 3JD. (Tel: 0524-63446).—*Principal*, D. Edynbry, Ph.D.

ST. MARY'S COLLEGE, Strawberry Hill, Twickenham TW1 4SX. (Tel: 081-892 0051).—*Principal*, Rev. Father D. A. Beirne.

SALFORD COLLEGE OF TECHNOLOGY, Frederick Road, Salford M6 6PU. (Tel: 061-736 6541).—*Principal*, Dr. R. Allerton.

SOUTHAMPTON INSTITUTE OF HIGHER EDUCATION, East Park Terrace, Southampton SO9 4WW. (Tel: 0703-229381).—*Principal*, D. G. Leyland.

SOUTH WEST LONDON COLLEGE, Centre for Higher Business Studies, Tooting Broadway, SW17 0TQ. (Tel: 081-672 2441).—*Principal*, L. H. Jones.

THE THAMES VALLEY COLLEGE OF HIGHER EDUCATION, Wellington Street, Slough SL1 1YG. (Tel: 0753-34585).—*Principal*, I. Wallis.

TRINITY AND ALL SAINTS' COLLEGE, Brownberrie Lane, Horsforth, Leeds LS18 5HD. (Tel: 0532-584341).—*Principal*, Dr. G. L. Turnbull.

TRINITY COLLEGE OF MUSIC, 11–13 Mandeville Place, W1M 4AQ. (Tel: 071-935 5773).—*Principal*, P. Jones, CBE.

WESTHILL COLLEGE, Hamilton Building, Weoley Park Road, Selly Oak, Birmingham B29 6LL. (Tel: 021-472 7245).—*Principal*, Rev. G. Benfield.

WEST LONDON INSTITUTE OF HIGHER EDUCATION, Lancaster House, Borough Road, Isleworth, Middx. TW7 5DU.—*Principal*, J. E. Kane, OBE, Ph.D.

WESTMINSTER COLLEGE, North Hinksey, Oxford OX2 9AT. (Tel: 0865-247644).—*Principal*, Rev. Dr. K. B. Wilson.

WEST SURREY COLLEGE OF ART AND DESIGN, Falkner Road, The Hart, Farnham, Surrey GU9 7DS. (Tel: 0252-722441).—*Dir.*, N. J. Taylor.

WEST SUSSEX INSTITUTE OF HIGHER EDUCATION, The Dome, Upper Bognor Road, Bognor Regis, West Sussex PO21 1HR. (Tel: 0243-865581).—*Dir.*, J. F. Wyatt.

WINCHESTER SCHOOL OF ART, Park Avenue, Winchester, Hants. SO23 8DL. (Tel: 0962-842500).—*Principal*, M. Sadler-Forster.

WORCESTER COLLEGE OF HIGHER EDUCATION, Henwick Grove, Worcester WR2 6AJ. (Tel: 0905-748080).—*Principal*, D. R. Shadbolt, OBE, D.Phil.

WALES

GWENT COLLEGE OF HIGHER EDUCATION, Clarence Place, Newport, Gwent NP9 0UW. (Tel: 0633-421292).—*Principal*, M. I. Harris, OBE.

NORMAL COLLEGE, Bangor, Gwynedd LL57 2PX. (Tel: 0248-370171).—*Principal*, R. Williams.

THE NORTH EAST WALES INSTITUTE OF HIGHER EDUCATION, Kelsterton Road, Connah's Quay, Deeside, Clwyd CH5 4BR. (Tel: 0244-831531).—*Principal*, Prof. G. O. Phillips, Ph.D., D.SC.

SOUTH GLAMORGAN INSTITUTE OF HIGHER EDUCATION, Western Avenue, Llandaff, Cardiff CF5 2YB.—*Principal*, E. J. Brent, Ph.D.

TRINITY COLLEGE, Carmarthen, Dyfed, SA31 3EP. (Tel: 0267-236234).—*Principal*, D. C. Jones-Davies.

WELSH AGRICULTURAL COLLEGE, Llanbadarn Fawr, Aberystwyth, Dyfed SY23 3AL. (Tel: 0970-624471).—*Principal*, J. R. Gill.

WELSH COLLEGE OF MUSIC AND DRAMA, Castle Grounds, Cathays Park, Cardiff CF1 3ER. (Tel: 0222-342854).—*Principal*, E. Fivet.

WEST GLAMORGAN INSTITUTE OF HIGHER EDUCATION, Townhill Road, Swansea SA2 0UT. (Tel: 0792-203482).—*Principal*, G. Stockdale, Ph.D.

SCOTLAND

CRAIGIE COLLEGE OF EDUCATION, Ayr KA8 0SR. (Tel: 0292-260321).—*Principal*, G. M. Wilson, Ph.D.

GLASGOW COLLEGE OF BUILDING AND PRINTING, 60 North Hanover Street, Glasgow G1 2BP. (Tel: 041-332 9969).—*Principal*, T. B. Wilson.

JORDANHILL COLLEGE OF EDUCATION, 73 Southbrae Drive, Jordanhill, Glasgow G13 1PP. (Tel: 041-959 1232).—*Principal*, T. R. Bone, CBE, Ph.D.

MORAY HOUSE COLLEGE OF EDUCATION, Holyrood Road, Edinburgh EH8 8AQ. (Tel: 031-556 8455).—*Principal*, G. Kirk.

NORTHERN COLLEGE OF EDUCATION, Hilton Place, Aberdeen AB9 1FA. (Tel: 0224-283500); Gardyne Road, Dundee DD5 1NY. (Tel: 0382-453433).—*Principal*, D. A. Adams.

ST. ANDREW'S COLLEGE OF EDUCATION, Duntocher Road, Bearsden, Glasgow G61 4QA. (Tel: 041-943 1424).—*Principal*, B. J. McGettrick.

NORTHERN IRELAND

ST. MARY'S COLLEGE, 191 Falls Road, Belfast BT12 6FE. (Tel: 0232-327678).—*Principal*, J. I. O'Connell.

STRANMILLIS COLLEGE, Stranmillis Road, Belfast BT9 5DY. (Tel: 0232-381271).—*Principal*, R. J. Rodgers, Ph.D.

ADULT AND CONTINUING EDUCATION

NATIONAL INSTITUTE OF ADULT CONTINUING EDUCATION, 19B De Montfort Street, Leicester LE1 7GE. (Tel: 0533-551451).—*Dir.*, A. Tuckett.

NIACE CYMRU, 245 Western Avenue, Cardiff CF5 2YX. (Tel: 0222-571201).—*Admin. Officer*, Ms. A. Poole.

NORTHERN IRELAND COUNCIL FOR CONTINUING EDUCATION, Department of Education for Northern Ireland, Rathgael House, Balloo Road, Bangor BT19 2PR. (Tel: 0247-270077).—*Sec.*, Miss S. Pidduck.

OPEN COLLEGE, 101 Wigmore Street, W1H 9AA. (Tel: 071-935 8088).

THE POLYTECHNIC ASSOCIATION FOR CONTINUING EDUCATION, Educational Development Officer, Polytechnic of Wales, Pontypridd, Mid Glam. CF37 1DL. (Tel: 0443-480480).—*Sec.*, P. Race.

THE RESIDENTIAL COLLEGES COMMITTEE, c/o Ruskin College, Oxford OX1 2HE. (Tel: 0865-56360).—*Awards Officer*, Mrs. C. A. Gregory.

SCOTTISH INSTITUTE OF ADULT AND CONTINUING EDUCATION, 30 Rutland Square, Edinburgh EH1 2BW. (Tel: 031-229 0331).—*Dir.*, Mrs. H. Johnston.

THE UNIVERSITIES COUNCIL FOR ADULT AND CONTINUING EDUCATION, Department of Continuing Education, The University of Warwick, Coventry CV4

7AL. (Tel: 0203-523835).—*Hon. Sec.*, Prof. C. Duke, Ph.D.

THE WORKER'S EDUCATIONAL ASSOCIATION, Temple House, 9 Upper Berkeley Street, W1H 8BY. (Tel: 071-402 5608).—*Gen. Sec.*, R. Lochrie.

Long-term Residential Colleges for Adult Education

COLEG HARLECH, Harlech, Gwynedd LL46 2PU. (Tel: 0766-780363).—*Warden*, J. W. England.

CO-OPERATIVE COLLEGE, Stanford Hall, Loughborough, Leics. LE12 5QR. (Tel: 0509-852333).—*Principal*, Dr. R. Houlton.

FIRCROFT COLLEGE, 1018 Bristol Road, Selly Oak, Birmingham B29 6LH. (Tel: 021-472 0116).—*Principal*, K. Jackson.

HILLCROFT COLLEGE, South Bank, Surbiton, Surrey KT6 6DF. (Tel: 081-399 2688). (For women only).—*Principal*, Ms. E. Aird.

NEWBATTLE ABBEY COLLEGE, Dalkeith, Midlothian EH22 3LL. (Tel: 031-662 1921).—*Principal*, A. D. Reid.

NORTHERN COLLEGE, Wentworth Castle, Stainborough, Barnsley, S. Yorks. S75 3ET. (Tel: 0226-285426).—*Principal*, R. H. Fryer.

PLATER COLLEGE, Pullens Lane, Oxford OX3 0DT. (Tel: 0865-741676).—*Principal*, D. G. Chiles.

RUSKIN COLLEGE, Walton Street, Oxford OX1 2HE. (Tel: 0865-54331).—*Principal*, S. Yeo, D.Phil.

PROFESSIONAL EDUCATION
(excluding postgraduate study)

NOTE.—References to courses at universities, polytechnics and colleges in the sections following are not claimed to be comprehensive and cover only full-time courses leading to first degrees. Full lists appear in *University Entrance: The Official Guide* and in the *CNAA Directory of First Degree and Diploma of Higher Education Courses*. Both are published annually.

Postgraduate study and research are not covered here.

ACCOUNTANCY

(*See also* Business, Management and Administration).

First degrees in *Accounting* or *Accountancy* are granted by most universities. At several universities one of these subjects can be combined, e.g. with Financial Administration, Finance or Economics.

Courses leading to first degrees in *Accounting*, *Accountancy* or *Accounting and Finance* granted by the CNAA are provided by most polytechnics.

The main bodies granting membership on examination after a period of practical work are:

INSTITUTE OF CHARTERED ACCOUNTANTS IN ENGLAND AND WALES, Chartered Accountants' Hall, PO Box 433, Moorgate Place, EC2P 2BJ.—*Sec.*, A. J. Colquhoun.

INSTITUTE OF CHARTERED ACCOUNTANTS OF SCOTLAND, 27 Queen Street, Edinburgh EH2 1LA.—*Sec.*, P. W. Johnston.

CHARTERED ASSOCIATION OF CERTIFIED ACCOUNTANTS, 29 Lincolns Inn Fields, WC2A 3EE.—*Sec.*, A. W. Sansom.

CHARTERED INSTITUTE OF MANAGEMENT ACCOUNTANTS, 63 Portland Place, W1N 4AB.—*Sec.*, Sir George Vallings, KCB.

CHARTERED INSTITUTE OF PUBLIC FINANCE AND ACCOUNTANCY, 3 Robert Street, WC2N 6BH.—*Sec.*, N. P. Hepworth, OBE.

ACTUARIAL SCIENCE

First degrees in *Actuarial Science* are granted by the City University and the Universities of Kent and London (London School of Economics and Political Science); and in *Actuarial Studies* and either *Mathematics* or *Economics* by Southampton University.

Two professional organizations grant qualifications after examination:

INSTITUTE OF ACTUARIES, Staple Inn Hall, High Holborn, WC1V 7QJ.—*Sec. Gen.*, C. D. A. Mackie.

FACULTY OF ACTUARIES IN SCOTLAND, 23 St. Andrew Square, Edinburgh EH2 1AQ.—*Sec.*, W. W. Mair.

AERONAUTICS
and Aeronautical Engineering

First degrees in *Aeronautical Engineering* are granted by the Universities of Bath, Belfast, Bristol, Cambridge, the City University (also *Air Transport Engineering*), Cranfield Institute of Technology (Shrivenham College), the Universities of Glasgow, London (Imperial College of Science and Technology, Queen Mary and Westfield College, also *Avionics—Aeronautical/Electrical*), Loughborough, Manchester, Salford and Southampton (*Aeronautics and Astronautics* and *Aerospace Systems Engineering*).

First degrees in *Aeronautical Engineering* granted by the CNAA are provided at Hatfield Polytechnic and Kingston Polytechnic.

AGRICULTURE

First degrees in *Agriculture* or *Agricultural Science(s)* are granted by the Universities of Aberdeen, Belfast, Edinburgh, London (Wye College), Newcastle upon Tyne, Nottingham, Reading and Wales (University Colleges of Aberystwyth and Bangor); and in *Horticulture* by London (Wye College), Nottingham, Reading and Strathclyde.

First degrees in *Agriculture* granted by the CNAA are provided at Harper Adams College, Hatfield, Middlesex, South West and Wolverhampton Polytechnics.

ARCHAEOLOGY

First degrees in *Archaeology* or *Archaeological Sciences/Studies* are granted by the Universities of Belfast, Birmingham, Bradford, Cambridge, Durham, Edinburgh, Exeter, Glasgow, Leicester, Liverpool, London (University College, Queen Mary and Westfield College, King's College, School of Oriental and African Studies), Manchester, Newcastle upon Tyne, Nottingham, Reading, Sheffield, Southampton, Wales (University College Cardiff, Bangor UC, St. David's UC) and York. At several of the above universities archaeology must be combined with another subject, e.g. ancient history or anthropology.

ARCHITECTURE

(*See also* Building, and Town and Country Planning).

First degrees in *Architecture/Architectural Studies* are granted by the Universities of Bath, Belfast, Cambridge, Dundee, Edinburgh, Glasgow, Heriot-Watt, Leeds, Liverpool, London (University College), Manchester, Newcastle upon Tyne, Nottingham, Sheffield, Strathclyde, Wales (Cardiff).

First degrees in *Architecture/Architectural Studies* granted by the CNAA are provided by the Polytechnics of Birmingham, Brighton, Humberside, Kingston, Leeds, Leicester, Liverpool, Manchester, Oxford, Central London, East London, Huddersfield, North London, Polytechnic South West, Portsmouth, South Bank and Thames, and by Kent Institute and Robert Gordon's Institute.

Other schools of architecture include THE ARCHITECTURAL ASSOCIATION, 34–36 Bedford Square, WC1B 2ES.—*Sec.*, E. A. Le Maistre.

THE ROYAL INSTITUTE OF BRITISH ARCHITECTS
66 Portland Place, W1N 4AD

The Education and Professional Development Committee of the Royal Institute of British Architects sets standards and guides the whole system of architectural education throughout the United Kingdom. Courses at Schools recognized by the RIBA exempt students from the RIBA's own examinations.
Pres., M. Hutchison.
Dir.-Gen. The Rt. Hon. W. Rodgers.

ART AND DESIGN

First degrees in *Art, Fine Art* or *History of Art* are granted by the Universities of Aberdeen, Cambridge, East Anglia, Edinburgh, Essex, Glasgow, Lancaster (*Visual Arts*), Leeds, Leicester, London (Courtauld Institute of Art, Birkbeck, University and Queen Mary and Westfield Colleges, School of Oriental and African Studies, Goldsmiths' College), Loughborough (*Design and Technology*), Manchester, Manchester Institute of Science and Technology (*Textile Design*), Newcastle upon Tyne, Nottingham, Oxford, Reading, St. Andrews, Sussex, Wales (University College, Aberystwyth) and Warwick. At several other universities art or history of art can be combined with another subject. The degrees in *Art* granted by the Royal College of Art are higher degrees.

Courses leading to first degrees in *Art and Design, Fine Art, Graphic Design, Textiles/Fashion* or *Three-Dimensional Design* granted by the CNAA are provided by more than 40 colleges/schools of art and polytechnics, some of which also offer CNAA degree courses in other subjects in the field of Art and Design, including *Furniture Design, Industrial Design* and *Interior Design*.

ASTRONOMY

First degrees in *Astronomy* are granted by the Universities of Glasgow, London (University and Queen Mary and Westfield Colleges), Newcastle, St. Andrew's, Sheffield; in *Astrophysics* by the Universities of Edinburgh, London (Queen Mary and Westfield College, University College), Newcastle, St. Andrews and Wales (University College, Cardiff); and in *Physics and Astronomy/Astrophysics* at the Universities of Birmingham, Glasgow, Kent, Leeds, Leicester, London (King's College, Royal Holloway & Bedford New College, University College), Manchester and Sussex. Various combinations of Astronomy and Astrophysics with other subjects are also available.

Astronomy may be taken as part of a CNAA degree course at certain polytechnics.

BANKING

First degrees with specialization in *Banking and Finance* are granted by the Universities of Birmingham (*Money, Banking and Finance*), Loughborough, Ulster, Wales (University College, Cardiff and Bangor UC), and the City University (*Banking and International Finance*).

Finance may be taken as part of a CNAA degree course at many polytechnics/colleges.

Professional organizations granting qualifications after examination:—

CHARTERED INSTITUTE OF BANKERS, 10 Lombard Street, EC3V 9AS.—*Sec. Gen.*, E. Glover.
INSTITUTE OF BANKERS IN SCOTLAND, 19 Rutland Square, Edinburgh EH1 2DE.—*Sec.*, Dr. C. W. Munn.

BIOLOGY, CHEMISTRY, PHYSICS

First degrees in these subjects are granted by many universities. Courses leading to first degrees granted by the CNAA are provided by many polytechnics. Professional qualifications are awarded by:—

INSTITUTE OF BIOLOGY, 20 Queensberry Place, SW7 2DZ.—*Gen. Sec.*, Dr. R. H. Priestley.
ROYAL SOCIETY OF CHEMISTRY, Burlington House, Piccadilly, W1V 0BN.—*Pres.*, Sir Rex Richards, FRS; *Sec.*, J. S. Gow, Ph.D., FRSC, FRSE.
INSTITUTE OF PHYSICS, 47 Belgrave Square, SW1X 8QX.—*Chief Exec.*, Dr. A. Jones.

BREWING

First degrees in *Brewing and Distilling* are granted by Heriot-Watt University.

BUILDING
(*See also* Architecture, Estate and Land Management and Surveying)

First degrees in *Building, Building Engineering, Building Services Engineering* or *Building Technology* are granted by the following Universities: Bath, Heriot-Watt, Liverpool, London (University College), Loughborough, Manchester (Manchester Institute of Science and Technology, Reading, Salford (*Building Surveying, Quantity Surveying*), Strathclyde (*Building Design Engineering*), and Ulster. Courses covering other aspects of building and construction are also available.

First degrees in *Building, Building Management, Building Engineering, Construction, Construction Management* and *Residential Development* granted by the CNAA are provided by Brighton, Bristol, Coventry, Lancashire, Leeds, Newcastle, Nottingham, Central London, Sheffield, South Bank and Thames and Wolverhampton Polytechnics, the Polytechnic of Wales, Anglia HE College, Glasgow College and Napier Polytechnic of Edinburgh.

Examinations are also conducted by:—

CHARTERED INSTITUTE OF BUILDING, Englemere, King's Ride, Ascot, Berks. SL5 8BJ.—*Chief Exec.*, K. Banbury.
INSTITUTE OF BUILDING CONTROL, 21 High Street, Ewell, Epsom, Surrey KT17 1SB.—*Sec.*, Ms. R. Raywood.
INSTITUTE OF CLERKS OF WORKS OF GREAT BRITAIN, 41 The Mall, W5 3TJ.—*Sec.*, A. P. Macnamara.

BUSINESS, MANAGEMENT AND ADMINISTRATION

First degrees in *Business, Management, Administration* or various aspects or combinations of these subjects are granted by all Universities.

Courses leading to first degrees in *Business Studies, Business Administration*, or other aspects of business, granted by the CNAA, are provided by all polytechnics. The CNAA also grants first degrees in *Marketing*.

Professional bodies conducting training and/or examinations in *Business, Administration, Management* or *Commerce* include:

ROYAL INSTITUTE OF PUBLIC ADMINISTRATION, 3 Birdcage Walk, SW1H 9JH.—*Dir.-Gen.*, D. Falcon.

CAM FOUNDATION, Abford House, 15 Wilton Road, SW1V 1NJ.—*Registrar*, Ms. K. Eastlake.

CHARTERED INSTITUTE OF MARKETING, Moor Hall, Cookham, Maidenhead, Berks. SL6 9QH.—*Dir. Gen.*, T. J. Nash.

CHARTERED INSTITUTE OF TRANSPORT, 80 Portland Place, W1N 4DP.—*Dir. Gen.*, R. P. Botwood.

FACULTY OF SECRETARIES AND ADMINISTRATORS, 15 Church Street, Godalming, Surrey GU7 1EL.—*Sec.*, Mrs. D. M. Rummery.

INSTITUTE OF ADMINISTRATIVE MANAGEMENT, 40 Chatsworth Parade, Petts Wood, Orpington, Kent BR5 1RW.—*Chief Exec.*, M. J. Ainsworth.

INSTITUTE OF CHARTERED SECRETARIES AND ADMINISTRATORS, 16 Park Crescent, W1N 4AH.—*Sec.*, M. J. Ainsworth

INSTITUTE OF CHARTERED SHIPBROKERS, 24 St. Mary Axe, EC3A 8DE.—*Sec.*, J. H. Parker.

INSTITUTE OF EXPORT, Export House, 64 Clifton Street, EC2A 4HB.—*Sec.*, D. J. Langham.

INSTITUTE OF HEALTH SERVICES MANAGEMENT, 75 Portland Place, W1N 4AN.—*Dir.*, Ms. M. Dixon, ph.D.

INSTITUTE OF HOUSING, 9 White Lion Street, N1 9XJ.—*Asst. Dir., Education and Training*, Ms. A. Paterson.

INSTITUTION OF INDUSTRIAL MANAGERS, Rochester House, 66 Little Ealing Lane, W5 4XX.—*Chief Exec.*, G. J. Rawlins, OBE

INSTITUTE OF PERSONNEL MANAGEMENT, IPM House, Camp Road, SW19 4UX.—*Dir. Gen.*, K. B. Ward Lilley.

INSTITUTE OF PRACTITIONERS IN ADVERTISING, 44 Belgrave Square, SW1X 8QS.—*Sec.*, J. Raad.

INSTITUTE OF PURCHASING AND SUPPLY, Easton House, Easton on the Hill, Stamford, Lincs. PE9 3NZ.—*Dir. Gen.*, P. Thomson.

HENLEY—THE MANAGEMENT COLLEGE, Greenlands, Henley on Thames, Oxon., RG9 3AU.—*Princ.*, Prof. R. Wild.

LONDON BUSINESS SCHOOL, Sussex Place, Regent's Park, NW1 4SA.—*Princ.*, Prof. G. Bain, ph.D.

MANCHESTER BUSINESS SCHOOL, Booth Street West, Manchester M15 6PB.—*Dir.*, Prof. T. Cannon.

SCOTTISH BUSINESS SCHOOLS, CONFEDERATION OF.—*Dir.*, M. Makower, c/o University of Stirling, Department of Business and Management, Stirling SK9 4LA.

LONDON CHAMBER OF COMMERCE AND INDUSTRY EXAMINATIONS BOARD, Marlowe House, Station Road, Sidcup, Kent DA15 7BJ.—*Dir.*, C. Bateson.

COMPUTER SCIENCE

First degrees covering various aspects of *Computer/ Computing Science, Data Processing, Information Systems* and *Information Technology* are available at all universities.

Courses leading to first degrees in computer science subjects granted by the CNAA are provided by all the polytechnics.

These subjects also form part of other degree courses, often as *Mathematics/Statistics and Computer Science*, at many universities, polytechnics and colleges.

DANCE

(*See also* Recreation, Sport, etc.)

First degrees in *Dance in Society* are granted by the University of Surrey.

The University of Kent grants a first degree in *Contemporary Dance* for which courses are provided at the London Contemporary Dance School.

First degrees in *Dance Theatre* are granted by the CNAA for which courses are provided at the Laban Centre for Movement and Dance; dance also forms part of other CNAA degree courses, often called *Performing Arts* or *Creative Arts*, at several polytechnics and colleges.

ROYAL ACADEMY OF DANCING, 48 Vicarage Crescent, SW11 3LT.—*Dirs*, D. Wall, CBE; Ms. P. Yates.

ROYAL BALLET SCHOOL, 155 Talgarth Road, W14 9DE, and White Lodge, Richmond Park, Surrey TW10 5HR.—*Dir.*, Dame Merle Park, DBE.

IMPERIAL SOCIETY OF TEACHERS OF DANCING, Euston Hall, Birkenhead Street, WC1H 8BE.—*Gen. Sec.*, M. J. Browne.

DEFENCE

First degrees in *Peace Studies* are granted by the Universities of Bradford and Ulster, and in *Strategic Studies* by the Universities of Lancaster and Wales (University College, Aberystwyth).

Royal Naval Colleges

ROYAL NAVAL COLLEGE, Greenwich, SE10 9NN.—*Admiral President*, Adm. Sir Brian Brown, KCB, CBE; *Dean of the College*, Prof. G. Till.

BRITANNIA ROYAL NAVAL COLLEGE, Dartmouth, Devon TQ6 0HJ.—Initial officer training. *Captain*, Capt. J. R. Shiffner.

ROYAL NAVAL ENGINEERING COLLEGE, Manadon, Plymouth PL5 3AQ.—BA, B.Eng., M.Sc. and specialist training in naval engineering. Students are selected uniformed officers of the Royal Navy, Commonwealth and foreign navies, and civilians. *Captain*, Capt. T. J. England. *Dean*, Capt. J. N. McGrath. *Exec. Officer*, Cdr. B. V. C. Reeves, LVO.

INSTITUTE OF NAVAL MEDICINE, Alverstoke, Gosport, Hants. PO12 2DL.—Higher professional and postgraduate training for officers of all three services, and some civilians. *Medical Officer in Charge*, Surgeon Capt. A. Craig.

Military Colleges

STAFF COLLEGE, Camberley, Surrey GU15 4NP.—*Commandant*, Maj.-Gen. The Hon. W. E. Rous.

ROYAL MILITARY ACADEMY, Sandhurst, Camberley, Surrey GU15 4PQ.—*Commandant*, Maj.-Gen. P. W. Graham, CBE.

ROYAL MILITARY COLLEGE OF SCIENCE, Shrivenham, Swindon, Wilts. SN6 8LA.—Students from UK and overseas study from degree to postgraduate levels in management, science and technology. There is an increasing range of research and consultancy activity as the College is now a Faculty of the Cranfield Institute of Technology. *Commandant*, Maj.-Gen. S. Cowan, CBE. *Principal*, Prof. A. C. Baynham, ph.D.

INSTITUTE OF ARMY EDUCATION, Court Road, Eltham, SE9 5NR.—*Director*, Maj.-Gen. C. A. Kinvig.

Royal Air Force Colleges

ROYAL AIR FORCE STAFF COLLEGE, Bracknell, Berks. RG12 3DD.—Prepares selected senior officers for high-grade command and staff appointments. The majority of students are RAF officers but officers from the other UK services and from foreign air forces also attend.

Air Officer Commanding and Commandant, Air Vice-Marshal R. G. Peters.

ROYAL AIR FORCE COLLEGE, Cranwell, Sleaford, Lincs NG34 8HB.—Initial officer training for officers of the RAF, WRAF and PMRAFNS, and initial specialist training for officers of the Engineer and Supply Branches. Advanced specialist training is provided for officers of the General Duties, Engineer and Supply Branches and basic flying training for pilots of the General Duties Branch.

Air Officer Commanding and Commandant, Air Vice-Marshal R. M. Austin, AFC.

ROYAL AIR FORCE SCHOOL OF EDUCATION AND TRAINING SUPPORT, RAF Newton, Nottingham NG13 8HL.—*Commanding Officer*, Gp. Capt. R. S. R. Lloyd.

DENTISTRY

First degrees in Dentistry are granted by the Universities of Belfast, Birmingham, Bristol, Dundee, Glasgow, Leeds, Liverpool, London (United Medical and Dental Schools of Guy's and St. Thomas's Hospitals, King's College School of Medicine and Dentistry, London Hospital Medical College), Manchester, Newcastle upon Tyne, Sheffield, Wales (College of Medicine).

To be entitled to be registered in the Dentists Register, a person must hold the degree or diploma in dental surgery of a University in the United Kingdom or Republic of Ireland or the diploma of any of the licensing authorities (The Royal College of Surgeons of England, of Edinburgh and in Ireland, and the Royal College of Physicians and Surgeons of Glasgow). Nationals of an EC member state holding an appropriate European diploma, and holders of certain overseas diplomas, may also be registered. The Dentists Register is maintained by THE GENERAL DENTAL COUNCIL, 37 Wimpole Street, W1M 8DQ. *Registrar*, N. T. Davies.

DIETETICS

(*See also* Food and Nutrition Science)

Courses in *Nutrition and Dietetics* leading to first degrees granted by the University of Wales are provided by South Glamorgan Institute of Higher Education. The Universities of Bradford, London (King's College), Nottingham, Southampton, Surrey and Ulster grant first degrees in *Nutrition* and related subjects.

First degrees in *Dietetics* and *Nutrition and Dietetics* granted by the CNAA are provided by Glasgow College, Huddersfield Polytechnic, Queen Margaret College, Edinburgh, and Robert Gordon's Institute.

The professional association is THE BRITISH DIETETIC ASSOCIATION, 7th Floor, Elizabeth House, 22 Suffolk Street, Queensway, Birmingham B1 1LS. Full membership is open to dietitians holding a recognized qualification, who may also become State Registered Dietitians through the Council for Professions Supplementary to Medicine (*q.v.*).

DRAMA

First Degrees in *Drama* are granted by the Universities of Birmingham (*Drama and Theatre Arts*), Bristol, East Anglia, Exeter, Glasgow (*Theatre Studies*), Hull, Kent (*Drama and Theatre Studies*), Lancaster (*Theatre Studies*), London (Royal Holloway and Bedford New College, *Drama and Theatre Studies*, Goldsmiths', *Drama and Theatre Arts*), Loughborough, Manchester and Wales (University College of Aberystwyth) and Warwick (*Theatre Studies and Dramatic Arts*). Drama also forms part of degree courses in other universities.

First degrees in *Drama Studies, Theatre, Theatre Arts* and *Drama, Theatre and TV Studies* granted by the CNAA are provided at a number of polytechnics and colleges.

The national validating body for courses providing training in drama is THE NATIONAL COUNCIL FOR DRAMA TRAINING, 5 Tavistock Place, WC1H 9SS. *Chief Exec.*, Miss E. M. McKay. It currently has accredited courses at the following: Academy of Live and Recorded Arts; Arts Educational Schools; Birmingham School of Speech Training & Dramatic Art; Bristol Old Vic Theatre School; Central School of Speech and Drama; Drama Centre, London; Drama Studio; Guildford School of Acting; Guildhall School of Music and Drama; London Academy of Music and Dramatic Art; Manchester Polytechnic School of Theatre; Mountview Theatre School; Rose Bruford College of Speech and Drama; Royal Academy of Dramatic Art; Royal Scottish Academy of Music and Drama; Webber Douglas Academy of Dramatic Art; Welsh College of Music and Drama. (The accreditation of a course in a school does not necessarily imply that other courses of different type or duration in the same school are also accredited.)

ECONOMICS

Almost all universities grant first degrees in *Economics*. Courses leading to first degrees in *Economics* granted by the CNAA are provided by many polytechnics and colleges.

ENGINEERING

(*See separate subjects below*)

THE ENGINEERING COUNCIL, 10 Maltravers Street, WC2R 3ER, supervises the engineering profession through the 47 nominated engineering institutions who are represented on its system of a Board for Engineers' Registration. Working with and through the institutions, the Council sets the standards for the registration of individuals, and also the accreditation for academic courses in universities, polytechnics and technical colleges and the practical training in industry.—*Sec.*, L. Chelton. The principal qualifying bodies are:—

BRITISH COMPUTER SOCIETY, 13 Mansfield Street, W1M 0BP.—*Chief Exec.*, J. R. Brookes.

CHARTERED INSTITUTION OF BUILDING SERVICES ENGINEERS, Delta House, 222 Balham High Road, SW12 9BS.—*Sec.*, A. V. Ramsay.

INSTITUTION OF CHEMICAL ENGINEERS, George E. Davis Building, 165–171 Railway Terrace, Rugby, Warks. CV21 3HQ.—*Gen. Sec.*, Dr. T. J. Evans.

INSTITUTION OF CIVIL ENGINEERS, Great George Street, SW1P 3AA.—*Sec.*, R. Dobson.

INSTITUTION OF ELECTRICAL ENGINEERS, Savoy Place, WC2R 0BL.—*Sec.*, Dr. J. C. Williams.

INSTITUTE OF ENERGY, 18 Devonshire Street, W1N 2AU.—*Sec.* C. Rigg, TD.

INSTITUTION OF GAS ENGINEERS, 17 Grosvenor Crescent, SW1X 7ES.—*Sec.*, D. J. Chapman.

INSTITUTE OF MARINE ENGINEERS, The Memorial Building, 76 Mark Lane, EC3R 7JN.—*Sec.*, J. E. Sloggett.

INSTITUTE OF MEASUREMENT AND CONTROL, 87 Gower Street, WC1E 6AA.—*Sec.*, M. J. Yates.

INSTITUTION OF MECHANICAL ENGINEERS, 1 Birdcage Walk, SW1H 9JJ.—*Sec.* R. Mellor, CBE.

INSTITUTE OF METALS, 1 Carlton House Terrace, SW1Y 5DB.—*Sec.*, Dr. J. A. Catterall.

INSTITUTION OF MINING ENGINEERS, Danum House, 6A South Parade, Doncaster DN1 2DY.—*Sec.*, W. J. W. Bourne, OBE.

INSTITUTION OF MINING AND METALLURGY, 44 Portland Place, W1N 4BR.—*Sec.*, M. J. Jones.

INSTITUTION OF PRODUCTION ENGINEERS, Rochester House, 66 Little Ealing Lane, W5 4XX.—*Sec.*, Brig. P. V. Crooks.
INSTITUTION OF STRUCTURAL ENGINEERS, 11 Upper Belgrave Street, SW1X 8BH.—*Sec.*, D. J. Clark.
ROYAL AERONAUTICAL SOCIETY, 4 Hamilton Place, W1V 0BQ.—*Sec.*, R. J. Kennett.
ROYAL INSTITUTION OF NAVAL ARCHITECTS, 10 Upper Belgrave Street, SW1X 8BQ.—*Sec.*, J. Rosewarn.

ENGINEERING, GENERAL AND ENGINEERING SCIENCE

First degrees in *General Engineering* or *Engineering Science* are granted by the Universities of Aberdeen, Aston, Cambridge, Durham, Edinburgh, Exeter, Hull, Lancaster, Leicester, Liverpool, London (Queen Mary and Westfield College), Loughborough, Manchester (foundation year), University of Manchester Institute of Science and Technology (*Integrated Engineering*), Oxford, Reading, Stirling, Sussex, Ulster, Wales (University College, Cardiff and Swansea), and Warwick.
Courses leading to first degrees in *Engineering* granted by the CNAA are provided by some 12 polytechnics and colleges.

Aeronautical Engineering

See main heading: AERONAUTICS AND AERONAUTICAL ENGINEERING

Agricultural Engineering

First degrees in *Agricultural Engineering* and *Agricultural Mechanization Management* are granted by the University of Newcastle upon Tyne. Courses in *Agricultural Engineering* and *Agricultural Technology & Management* leading to degrees granted by Cranfield Institute of Technology are provided at Silsoe College.

Chemical Engineering

First degrees are granted by the Universities of Aston (*Chemical Process Engineering*), Bath, Belfast, Birmingham, Bradford, Cambridge, Edinburgh, Exeter, Heriot-Watt, Leeds, London (Imperial College of Science and Technology, University College), Loughborough, Manchester (Manchester Institute of Science and Technology), Newcastle upon Tyne (*Chemical & Process Engineering*), Nottingham, Sheffield (*Chemical Process Engineering*), Strathclyde, Surrey and Wales (University College, Swansea).
Courses leading to first degrees in *Chemical Engineering* granted by the CNAA are provided by Paisley College of Technology, Polytechnic of East London, Polytechnic of the South Bank, Teesside Polytechnic and Polytechnic of Wales.

Civil and Mechanical Engineering

First degrees in *Civil* (or *Civil and Structural*), and *Mechanical Engineering* are granted by the Universities of Aberdeen, Aston, Bath (*M.*), Belfast, Birmingham, Bradford, Bristol, Brunel, Cambridge, the City University, Cranfield Institute, the Universities of Dundee, Edinburgh, Exeter, Glasgow, Heriot-Watt, Lancaster (*M.*), Leeds, Leicester (*M.*), Liverpool, London (Imperial College of Science and Technology, King's College (*M.*), Queen Mary and Westfield College, University College), Loughborough, Manchester, Manchester Institute of Science and Technology, Newcastle upon Tyne, Nottingham, Reading (*M.*), Salford, Sheffield, Southampton, Strathclyde, Surrey, Sussex (*M.*), Ulster, Wales (University Colleges at Cardiff and Swansea) and Warwick.

Many polytechnics and colleges provide courses in *civil engineering* or *mechanical engineering*, or both, leading to first degrees granted by the CNAA.

Electrical and Electronic Engineering and Electronics

First degrees in *Electronic Engineering* or *Electronics* or *Electrical and Electronic Engineering* or *Electrical Engineering (including Electronics)* are granted by all universities.
Courses leading to first degrees in *Electronic Engineering* or in *Electrical and Electronic Engineering*, granted by the CNAA are provided by many polytechnics and colleges.

Marine Engineering and Naval Architecture

First degrees in *Marine Engineering* and *Naval Architecture* are granted by the University of Newcastle upon Tyne; in *Naval Architecture* by the Universities of Glasgow, London (University College) and Strathclyde; in *Offshore Engineering* by Heriot-Watt University; and in *Ship Science* by the University of Southampton.
First degrees in *Mechanical Engineering (Marine)* granted by the CNAA are provided at Liverpool Polytechnic.

Nuclear Engineering

First degrees in *Nuclear Engineering* are granted by the University of Manchester.

Production Engineering

First degrees in *Production Engineering*, *Manufacturing Engineering* or *Industrial Engineering* are granted by the Universities of Aston, Bath, Belfast, Birmingham, Brunel, Cambridge, Exeter (*Engineering (Operations & Manufacturing)*), Hull (*Engineering Design and Manufacture*), Loughborough, Strathclyde and Warwick (*Engineering (Manufacturing Systems)*).
First degrees in *Production Engineering*, *Industrial Engineering*, *Manufacturing Engineering*, *Manufacturing Systems Engineering*, and *Plant Engineering* granted by the CNAA are provided by nearly all polytechnics.

Structural Engineering

First degrees in *Civil and Structural Engineering* are granted by the Universities of Aberdeen, Bradford, Heriot-Watt (*Structural Engineering*), Liverpool, London (University College, *Civil, Structural and Environmental Engineering*), and Sheffield.

ESTATE AND LAND MANAGEMENT
(*See also* **Building** and **Surveying**)

First degrees are granted by the Universities of Aberdeen (*Land Economy*), Reading (*Land Management* and *Rural Land Management*) and Ulster (*Estate Management*).
First degrees in *Estate Management, Housing, Housing Studies, Land Administration, Land Economics, Land Management, Minerals Estate Management, Urban Estate Management, Urban Land Administration, Urban Land Economics* and *Valuation and Estate Management* granted by the CNAA are provided at most polytechnics.

FOOD AND NUTRITION SCIENCE
(*See also* **Dietetics** and **Home Economics**)

First degrees in *Food Science* are granted by the Universities of Belfast (also *Food Technology*), Leeds, London (King's College), Newcastle (*Agricultural &*

Food Marketing), Nottingham, Reading, Strathclyde, Surrey, Ulster (*Food Technology Management*) and Wales (University College, Aberystwyth, *Agricultural & Food Marketing*); in *Nutrition* by the Universities of London (King's College), Nottingham and Surrey; and in *Human Nutrition* by the University of Ulster.

First degrees in *Food Science*; *Catering and Applied Nutrition*; *Food and Accommodation Studies*; *Food Marketing Sciences*; *Industrial Food Technology*; *Nutrition and Dietetics* granted by the CNAA are provided at many polytechnics.

Scientific and professional bodies include:

INSTITUTE OF FOOD SCIENCE & TECHNOLOGY, 5 Cambridge Court, 210 Shepherd's Bush Road, W6 7NL.—*Exec. Sec.*, Ms. H. G. Wild.

NUTRITION SOCIETY, Grosvenor Gardens House, 35–37 Grosvenor Gardens, SW1W 0BS.—*Hon. Sec.*, Dr. R. F. Grimble.

FORESTRY AND TIMBER STUDIES

First degrees in *Forestry* are granted by the Universities of Aberdeen, Edinburgh (also *Agriculture, Forestry & Rural Economy*), and Wales (University College, Bangor, also *Wood Science* and *Agroforestry*).

First degrees in *Timber Technology* granted by the CNAA are provided at Buckinghamshire HE College.

Professional organizations include:

ROYAL FORESTRY SOCIETY OF ENGLAND, WALES AND NORTHERN IRELAND, 102 High Street, Tring, Herts., HP23 4AF.—*Dir.*, J. E. Jackson, PH.D.

ROYAL SCOTTISH FORESTRY SOCIETY, 11 Atholl Crescent, Edinburgh EH3 8HE.—*Sec.*, W. B. C. Walker.

INSTITUTE OF CHARTERED FORESTERS, 22 Walker Street, Edinburgh EH3 7HR.—*Sec.*, Mrs. M. W. Dick.

COMMONWEALTH FORESTRY ASSOCIATION, c/o Oxford Forestry Institute, South Parks Road, Oxford OX1 3RB.—*Sec.*, M. T. Rogers.

FUEL AND ENERGY STUDIES

(*See also* Nuclear Engineering)

First degrees in *Fuel and Combustion Science* and in *Fuel and Energy Engineering* are granted by the University of Leeds; in *Petroleum Engineering* by London (Imperial College of Science and Technology); and in *Chemical Process Engineering and Fuel Technology* by the University of Sheffield. These subjects may also form part of other degree courses.

First degrees in *Energy Engineering* are granted by the CNAA.

The principal professional bodies are:—

INSTITUTE OF ENERGY, 18 Devonshire Street, W1N 2AU.—*Sec.*, C. Rigg, TD.

INSTITUTION OF GAS ENGINEERS, 17 Grosvenor Crescent, SW1X 7ES.—*Sec.*, D. J. Chapman.

INSTITUTE OF PETROLEUM, 61 New Cavendish Street, W1M 8AR.—*Dir. Gen.*, A. E. H. Williams.

GEOLOGY

First degrees in *Geology* or *Geological Sciences* or *Applied Geology* are granted by the Universities of Aberdeen (with *Petroleum Geology*), Belfast, Birmingham, Bristol, Cambridge, Durham, Edinburgh, Exeter, Glasgow, Keele, Leeds, Leicester, Liverpool, London (Birkbeck College, Imperial College of Science and Technology (also *Mining Geology*), Royal Holloway & Bedford New College, University College), Manchester, Newcastle upon Tyne, Oxford (*Earth Sciences*), St. Andrews (*Geoscience*), Southampton, Wales (University Colleges at Aberystwyth and Cardiff).

Degree courses in *Geophysics* and *Geophysical Sciences* are provided by the Universities of East Anglia, Edinburgh, Lancaster, Leeds, Leicester, Liverpool, Newcastle and Southampton.

First degrees in *Geology, Earth Sciences*, etc. granted by the CNAA are provided by some 11 polytechnics and colleges.

HOME ECONOMICS AND CATERING, HOTELKEEPING AND INSTITUTIONAL MANAGEMENT

(*See also* Dietetics, and Food)

First degrees in *Home Economics* are granted by the University of Wales (University College, Cardiff); in *Hotel and Catering Management* by the Universities of Strathclyde, Surrey (also *Hotel Management*), Ulster (*Hotel and Tourism Management*, also *Hospitality Management*) and Wales (University College, Cardiff, *Hotel and Institutional Management*).

First degrees are granted by the CNAA in *Home Economics, Hotel and Catering Administration/Management/Studies, Applied Consumer Science, Hospitality Management, International Hotel Management* and combinations of these subjects. Courses are available at over 20 polytechnics and colleges.

Qualifying professional body in the subjects is:

HOTEL CATERING AND INSTITUTIONAL MANAGEMENT ASSOCIATION, 191 Trinity Road, SW17 7HN.—*Dir.*, Ms. E. Gadsby.

INDUSTRIAL RELATIONS

First degrees in *Industrial Relations* are granted by the University of Kent. *Industrial relations* also forms part of degree courses at other universities.

INSURANCE

First degrees in *Banking, Insurance and Finance* are granted by the University of Wales (University College, Bangor).

First degrees in *Risk Management* granted by the CNAA are provided at Glasgow College.

Organizations conducting examinations and awarding diplomas:—

ASSOCIATION OF AVERAGE ADJUSTERS, HQS *Wellington*, Temple Stairs, Victoria Embankment, WC2R 2PN.—*Sec.*, Mrs. P. J. Albano.

CHARTERED INSURANCE INSTITUTE, 20 Aldermanbury, EC2V 7HY.—*Dir. Gen.*, Dr. D. E. Bland.

CHARTERED INSTITUTE OF LOSS ADJUSTERS, Manfield House, 376 The Strand, WC2R 0LR.—*Dir.*, A. F. Clack.

JOURNALISM

Courses for trainee newspaper journalists are available at 11 centres. One-year full-time courses are available for selected students. Particulars of all these courses are available from the Director of the NATIONAL COUNCIL FOR TRAINING OF JOURNALISTS, Carlton House, Hemnall Street, Epping, Essex CM16 4NL.—*Dir.*, D. K. Hall. Short courses for experienced journalists are also arranged by the National Council.

For periodical journalists, there are four centres running courses approved by THE PERIODICALS TRAINING COUNCIL, Imperial House, 15–19 Kingsway, WC2B 6UN.—*Dir.*, D. Longbottom.

LANGUAGES

First Degrees in *English* and in a wide range of other languages are granted by all universities. Degrees in *Linguistics* are awarded by the Universities of Cambridge, East Anglia, Essex (also *Language*

Studies and *Psycholinguistics*), Lancaster, Leeds (*Linguistics and Phonetics*), London (School of Oriental and African Studies, University College), Newcastle upon Tyne, Reading, Sussex and Wales (University College, Bangor, *Applied Linguistics* and *Theoretical Linguistics*); in *Applied Languages* by the University of Ulster; and in *Modern Languages and Linguistics* by the University of York. These subjects also form part of degree courses at many other universities.

Courses leading to first degrees in *English* and other languages granted by the CNAA are provided by many polytechnics and colleges.

LAW

First Degrees in *Law* are granted by most universities.

Courses leading to first degrees in *Law* granted by the CNAA are provided by most polytechnics.

THE BAR

Admission to the Bar of England and Wales is controlled by the Inns of Court, and admission to the Bar of Northern Ireland by the Honorable Society of the Inn of Court of Northern Ireland. Admission as an Advocate of the Scottish Bar is controlled by the Faculty of Advocates.

England and Wales

THE GENERAL COUNCIL OF THE BAR
11 South Square, Gray's Inn, WC1R 5EL

The governing body of the Barristers' branch of the legal profession, established in 1987 in succession to the Senate of the Inns of Court and the Bar.
Chairman, P. Creswell, QC.
Chief Executive, J. Mottram, CB, LVO, OBE.

THE INNS OF COURT

THE INNER TEMPLE, EC4Y 7HL.—*Treasurer*, F. Petre Crowder, QC; *Sub-Treasurer*, Capt. P. T. Sheehan, CBE, RN.
THE MIDDLE TEMPLE, EC4Y 9AT.—*Treasurer*, L. Price, QC; *Deputy Treasurer*, G. Darling, QC.
GRAY'S INN, WC1R 5EU.—*Treasurer*, Sir Patrick Neill, QC; *Under-Treasurer*, D. Machin.
LINCOLN'S INN, WC2A 3TL.—*Treasurer*, The Hon. Mr. Justice Michael Davies; *Under-Treasurer*, Capt. P. M. Carver, RN.

The education and examination of students for the Bar of England and Wales is superintended by the COUNCIL OF LEGAL EDUCATION, Inns of Court School of Law, 4 Gray's Inn Place, WC1R 5DX.
Chairman, The Hon. Mr. Justice Hoffmann.
Dean, Inns of Court School of Law, Mrs. M. A. Phillips.

Scotland

FACULTY OF ADVOCATES, Advocates Library, Parliament House, Edinburgh EH1 1RF.—*Dean*, A. C. M. Johnston, QC; *Clerk*, P. B. Cullen.

Northern Ireland

THE HONORABLE SOCIETY OF THE INN OF COURT OF NORTHERN IRELAND, Royal Courts of Justice, Belfast BT1 3JF.—*Treasurer* (1990), The Hon. Mr. Justice Nicholson; *Under-Treasurer*, J. A. L. McLean, QC.

SOLICITORS

Qualifications for Solicitor are obtainable only from one of the Law Societies, which control the education and examination of articled clerks, and the admission of solicitors.

LAW SOCIETY OF ENGLAND AND WALES, 113 Chancery Lane, WC2A 1PL.—*President* (1990–91), J. A. Holland; *Vice-Pres.* (1990–91), P. T. Ely; *Sec.-Gen.*, J. W. Hayes.
Courses for The Law Society examinations are provided by THE COLLEGE OF LAW, at Braboeuf Manor, St. Catherine's, Guildford, Surrey GU3 1HA; 33–35 Lancaster Gate, W2 3LU; 2 Breams Buildings, Chancery Lane, EC4A 1DP; Christleton Hall, Chester CH3 7AB; and Bishopthorpe Road, York YO2 1QA.
The SOLICITORS COMPLAINTS BUREAU, Portland House, Stag Place, SW1E 5BL, is an independent arm of the Law Society set up to handle complaints about solicitors.
LAW SOCIETY OF SCOTLAND, Law Society's Hall, 26 Drumsheugh Gardens, Edinburgh EH3 7YR.—*Pres.* (1990–91), A. T. F. Gibb; *Sec.*, K. W. Pritchard.
LAW SOCIETY OF NORTHERN IRELAND, Law Society House, 90–106 Victoria Street, Belfast BT1 3JZ.—*Sec.*, M. C. Davey.

LIBRARIANSHIP AND INFORMATION SCIENCE

First degrees are granted by the University of Belfast (*Information Science*), Loughborough (*Library Studies*), and the University of Wales (Aberystwyth) (*Librarianship* with another subject) (jointly with the College of Librarianship, Wales).

First degrees in *Librarianship* or *Librarianship/ Library Studies and Information Studies/Science* granted by the CNAA are provided at some nine polytechnics and colleges.

Two-thirds of entrants into librarianship are graduates in other subjects, who must take a one-year postgraduate course.

THE LIBRARY ASSOCIATION, 7 Ridgmount Street, WC1E 7AE, maintains the professional register of Chartered Members. A full list of accredited degree and postgraduate courses is available from the Education Department.—*Chief Exec.*, G. Cunningham.

MATERIALS STUDIES (including Metallurgy)

First degrees in *Materials Science, Materials Technology, or Materials Science and Technology* are granted by the Universities of Bath, Birmingham, Brunel, Cambridge (*Materials Science and Metallurgy*), Leeds, Liverpool, London (Imperial College of Science and Technology, Queen Mary and Westfield College), Manchester and Manchester Institute of Science and Technology, Sheffield (*Science and Engineering of Materials*), Strathclyde (*Science of Engineering Materials*), Surrey and Wales (University College, Swansea, *Materials Engineering*). First degrees in *Polymer Science and Engineering* are granted by London (Queen Mary and Westfield College) and Manchester Institute of Science and Technology (*Polymer Science and Technology*). First degrees in *Ceramics Science and Engineering* are granted by the Universities of Leeds and Sheffield; and in *Science and Engineering of Glasses* by the University of Sheffield. First degrees in *Metallurgy* and/or *Metallurgical Engineering* are granted by the Universities of Birmingham (*Metallurgy/Materials Engineering*), Brunel, Cambridge (*Materials Science and Metallurgy*), Leeds, Liverpool (*Metallurgy and Materials Science*), Manchester and Manchester Institute of Science and Technology, Oxford (*Metallurgy and Science of Materials*), Sheffield (*Science and Engineering of Metals*), Strathclyde and Surrey.

First degrees in *Materials Science/Technology* or

Metallurgy or *Metallurgy and Materials* or *Polymer Science* granted by the CNAA are provided at Manchester, North London, Sheffield, Sunderland, Thames and Wolverhampton Polytechnics, and at Robert Gordon's Institute.

INSTITUTE OF METALS, 1 Carlton House Terrace, SW1Y 5DB, is a qualifying body.—*Sec.*, Dr. J. A. Catterall.

MATHEMATICS

First degrees in *Mathematics* and/or *Applied Mathematics* are granted by all universities.

Courses leading to first degrees in *Mathematics* granted by the CNAA are provided by about 16 polytechnics and colleges.

MEDICINE

First degrees in *Medicine* are granted by the Universities of Aberdeen, Belfast, Birmingham, Bristol, Cambridge (*Medical Sciences*), Dundee, Edinburgh, Glasgow, Leeds, Leicester, Liverpool, London medical schools/colleges (University College and Middlesex SM, King's College SMD, St. Mary's HMS, and those listed on p. 457), Manchester, Newcastle upon Tyne, Nottingham, Oxford, St. Andrews (*Medical Science*), Sheffield, Southampton, and University of Wales College of Medicine.

Licensing Corporations granting Diplomas

ROYAL COLLEGE OF PHYSICIANS OF LONDON AND THE ROYAL COLLEGE OF SURGEONS OF ENGLAND, Examining Board in England, 35–43 Lincoln's Inn Fields, WC2A 3PN.

SOCIETY OF APOTHECARIES OF LONDON, Black Friars Lane, EC4V 6EJ.—*Clerk*, Maj. J. C. O'Leary; *Registrar*, D. H. C. Barrie.

SCOTTISH TRIPLE QUALIFICATION BOARD, Nicolson Street, Edinburgh EH8 9DW and 242 St. Vincent Street, Glasgow.

Colleges holding postgraduate membership and diploma examinations

ROYAL COLLEGE OF GENERAL PRACTITIONERS, 14 Princes Gate, SW7 1PU.—*Pres.*, Dr. S. Carne.

ROYAL COLLEGE OF OBSTETRICIANS AND GYNAECOLOGISTS, 27 Sussex Place, Regent's Park, NW1 4RG.— *Pres.*, S. Simmons; *Sec.*, P. A. Barnett.

ROYAL COLLEGE OF PATHOLOGISTS, 2 Carlton House Terrace, SW1Y 5AF.—*Pres.*, Prof. P. J. Lachmann.

ROYAL COLLEGE OF PHYSICIANS OF ENGLAND, 11 St. Andrews Place, NW1 4LE.—*Sec.*, D. B. Lloyd.

ROYAL COLLEGE OF PSYCHIATRISTS, 17 Belgrave Square, SW1X 8PG.—*Pres.*, Prof. A. Sims.

ROYAL COLLEGE OF RADIOLOGISTS, 38 Portland Place, W1N 3DG.—*Pres.*, Dr. O. Craig.

ROYAL COLLEGE OF SURGEONS OF ENGLAND, 35 Lincoln's Inn Fields, WC2A 3PN.—*Pres.*, Sir Ian Todd, KBE; *Sec.*, R. S. Johnston-Gilbert, OBE.

ROYAL COLLEGE OF PHYSICIANS OF EDINBURGH, 9 Queen Street, Edinburgh EH2 1JQ.—*Pres.*, Prof. J. Richmond, MD; *Sec.*, Dr. J. L. Anderton.

ROYAL COLLEGE OF SURGEONS OF EDINBURGH, Nicolson Street, Edinburgh EH8 9DW.—*Pres.*, Prof. G. D. Chisholm; *Sec.*, Prof. A. G. D. Maran.

ROYAL COLLEGE OF PHYSICIANS AND SURGEONS OF GLASGOW, 234–242 St. Vincent Street, Glasgow G2 5RJ.—*Pres.*, J. McArthur; *Hon. Sec.*, Dr. A. D. Beattie.

PROFESSIONS SUPPLEMENTARY TO MEDICINE

The standard of professional education in chiropody, dietetics, medical laboratory sciences, occupational therapy, orthoptics, physiotherapy and radiography is the responsibility of seven professional boards, which also publish an annual register of qualified practitioners. The work of the Boards is coordinated by THE COUNCIL FOR PROFESSIONS SUPPLEMENTARY TO MEDICINE, Park House, 184 Kennington Park Road, SE11 4BU. *Registrar*, R. Pickis.

Biomedical/Medical Laboratory Sciences

First degrees in *Biomedical Sciences* are granted by the Universities of Bradford and Ulster.

First degrees in *Biomedical Sciences* and *Medical Laboratory Science* granted by the CNAA are provided at Liverpool, Portsmouth and Wolverhampton Polytechnics, and combinations including these subjects are available at other polytechnics and colleges.

Qualifications from higher or further education establishments and training in medical laboratories are required for progress to the professional examinations and qualifications of the INSTITUTE OF MEDICAL LABORATORY SCIENCES, 12 Queen Anne Street, W1M 0AU.

Chiropody

Professional qualifications are granted by THE SOCIETY OF CHIROPODISTS, 53 Welbeck Street, W1M 7HE, to students who have passed the qualifying examination after attending a course of full-time training for three years at one of the 14 recognized schools in the UK (11 in England and Wales, two in Scotland and one in Northern Ireland). Qualifications granted by the Society are approved by the Chiropodists Board for the purpose of State Registration, which is a condition of employment within the National Health Service. *Gen. Sec.*, J. G. C. Trouncer.

Dietetics
(*See* main heading, p. 467)

Occupational Hygiene

First degrees in *Occupational Hygiene* granted by the CNAA are provided at South Bank Polytechnic.

Occupational Therapy

First degrees in *Occupational Therapy* are granted by the University of Ulster; first degrees in *Occupational Therapy* granted by the CNAA are provided by Queen Margaret College, Edinburgh.

Professional qualifications are awarded by THE COLLEGE OF OCCUPATIONAL THERAPISTS, 6–8 Marshalsea Road, SE1 1HL, upon completion of one of the 25 training courses approved by the College. *Sec.*, Air Cdre. G. J. B. Claridge, CBE.

Orthoptics

Orthoptists undertake the diagnosis and treatment of all types of squint and other anomalies of binocular vision, working in close collaboration with ophthalmologists. The training and maintenance of professional standards are the responsibility of the Orthoptists Board of the Council for the Professions Supplementary to Medicine. The examining and qualifying body is the BRITISH ORTHOPTIC SOCIETY, Tavistock House North, Tavistock Square, WC1H 9HX. *Sec.*, Ms. J. Voller. Training consists of a three-year course at one of nine approved Orthoptic Schools in England and Wales and one in Scotland.

(*See also* main heading Ophthalmic Optics, p. 473)

Physiotherapy

First degrees in *Physiotherapy* are granted by the University of Ulster; first degrees in *Physiotherapy* granted by the CNAA are provided at Coventry, East London, Sheffield and Teesside Polytechnics, and at

Queen Margaret College, Edinburgh, and Queen's College, Glasgow.

Full-time three- or four-year degree or diploma courses are available at 30 recognized Schools in the UK. Information about courses leading to eligibility for Membership of The Chartered Society of Physiotherapy and to State Registration is available from THE CHARTERED SOCIETY OF PHYSIOTHERAPY, 14 Bedford Row, London WC1R 4ED.—*Sec.*, T. Simon.

Radiography and Radiotherapy

Examinations leading to qualification are conducted by THE COLLEGE OF RADIOGRAPHERS, 14 Upper Wimpole Street, W1M 8BN.

There are recognized training centres in radiography and radiotherapy throughout the UK.

METEOROLOGY

First degrees in *Meteorology* are granted by the University of Reading. The subject is also included in degree courses at some other universities.

MINING AND MINING ENGINEERING

First degrees in *Mining* or *Mining Engineering* are granted by the following universities: Leeds (also *Mineral Engineering*), London (Imperial College of Science and Technology) and Nottingham.

First degrees granted by the CNAA in *Mining Engineering* and *Mineral Engineering* are provided at Camborne School of Mines.

Miscellaneous Authorities

ENGINEERING COUNCIL, 10 Maltravers Street, WC2R 3ER. *See* p. 467.

INSTITUTION OF MINING ENGINEERS, Danum House, 6A South Parade, Doncaster DN1 2DY—*Sec.*, W. J. W. Bourne, OBE.

MUSIC

First degrees in *Music* are granted by the Universities of Belfast, Birmingham, Bristol, Cambridge, the City University, the Universities of Durham, East Anglia, Edinburgh, Exeter, Glasgow, Hull, Lancaster, Leeds, Liverpool, London (King's College, Royal Holloway and Bedford New College; *also* Goldsmiths' College, Royal Academy of Music, Royal College of Music, and Trinity College of Music), Manchester, Newcastle upon Tyne, Nottingham, Oxford, Reading, Sheffield, Southampton, Surrey (*Academic & Practical Applications of Music; Music & Sound Recording (Tonmeister)*), Sussex, Ulster, Wales (University Colleges at Bangor and Cardiff) and York.

Courses leading to first degrees in *Music* granted by the CNAA are provided by several polytechnics and colleges.

ASSOCIATED BOARD OF THE ROYAL SCHOOLS OF MUSIC, 14 Bedford Square, WC1B 3JG.—Conducts the local examinations in centres throughout the world in music and speech for the Royal Academy of Music and the Royal College of Music in London, the Royal Northern College of Music, Manchester and the Royal Scottish Academy of Music and Drama, Glasgow.

Chief Exec. and Dir. of Examinations, R. Smith.

ROYAL ACADEMY OF MUSIC, Marylebone Road, NW1 5HT.—*Principal,* Sir David Lumsden, D.Phil.

ROYAL COLLEGE OF MUSIC, Prince Consort Road, SW7 2BS.—*Director,* M. G. Matthews.

ROYAL NORTHERN COLLEGE OF MUSIC, 124 Oxford Road, Manchester M13 9RD.—*Principal,* Sir John Manduell, CBE.

ROYAL SCOTTISH ACADEMY OF MUSIC AND DRAMA, 100 Renfrew Street, Glasgow G2 3DB.—*Principal,* Dr. P. Ledger, CBE.

ROYAL COLLEGE OF ORGANISTS, Kensington Gore, SW7 2QS.—*Clerk,* K. B. Lyndon.

GUILDHALL SCHOOL OF MUSIC AND DRAMA, Silk Street, EC2Y 8DT.—*Principal,* I. Horsbrugh.

LONDON COLLEGE OF MUSIC, 47 Great Marlborough Street, W1V 2AS.—*Director,* J. McCabe, CBE.

TRINITY COLLEGE OF MUSIC, 11–13 Mandeville Place, W1M 6AQ.—*Principal,* P. Jones, CBE.

NAUTICAL STUDIES
(*See also* Marine Engineering)

The University of Wales grants first degrees in *Maritime Studies, Maritime Commerce* and *Maritime Geography* (courses at University College, Cardiff and at the Institute of Science and Technology).

First degrees in *Maritime Studies* and *Fishery Studies* granted by the CNAA are provided at Humberside and Liverpool Polytechnics and Polytechnic South West.

Merchant Navy Training Schools
For Officers

THE COLLEGE OF MARITIME STUDIES, Warsash, Southampton SO3 6ZL. *Dean,* Capt. M. Longman.

For Seamen

INDEFATIGABLE AND NATIONAL SEA TRAINING SCHOOL FOR BOYS, Plas Llanfair, Llanfairpwllgwyngyll, Gwynedd LL61 6NT.—*Captain Headmaster,* Capt. T. R. Beggs.

NATIONAL SEA TRAINING COLLEGE, Denton, Gravesend, Kent DA12 2HR.—*Princ.,* Capt. C. G. W. Hunter.

NURSING

Courses in which academic study leading to a degree at a University may be combined with nursing training/practical nursing in hospitals are provided by the Universities of Birmingham, Bradford, the City University, Edinburgh, Glasgow, Hull, Lancaster, Liverpool, London (King's College), Manchester, Nottingham, Southampton, Surrey, Ulster and Wales (College of Medicine).

First degrees in *Nursing* granted by the CNAA are provided at many polytechnics and at Anglia HE college, Buckinghamshire College, Dundee Institute, Glasgow College, NE Surrey College and Queen Margaret College.

Three-year courses are undertaken for State Registration in general, sick children's, mental and mental deficiency nursing. Two-year courses lead to State enrolment. There are training schools in many parts of Great Britain.

THE ROYAL COLLEGE OF NURSING
OF THE UNITED KINGDOM
20 Cavendish Square, W1M 0AB

The Royal College of Nursing, within its Institute of Advanced Nursing Education, provides education at post-basic level in hospital, occupational health and community health fields. Advanced courses are held in preparation for senior posts in management and teaching; and other short and special courses.

Gen. Sec. (designate), Miss C. Hancock.

Director of Education and Principal of the Institute of Advanced Nursing Education, J. C. A. Wells (*acting*).

ENGLISH NATIONAL BOARD FOR NURSING, MIDWIFERY AND HEALTH VISITING, Victory House, 170 Totten-

ham Court Road, W1P 0HA.—*Chief Exec. Officer,*
D. Jones, OBE.

WELSH NATIONAL BOARD FOR NURSING, MIDWIFERY
AND HEALTH VISITING, Floor 13, Pearl Assurance
House, Greyfriars Road, Cardiff CF1 3AG.—*Chief
Exec. Officer,* D. A. Ravey.

NATIONAL BOARD FOR NURSING, MIDWIFERY AND
HEALTH VISITING FOR SCOTLAND, 22 Queen Street,
Edinburgh EH2 1JX.—*Chief Exec. Officer.,* Mrs. E.
C. Mitchell.

NATIONAL BOARD FOR NURSING, MIDWIFERY AND
HEALTH VISITING FOR NORTHERN IRELAND, RAC
House, 79 Chichester Street, Belfast BT1 4JE.—
Chief Exec. Officer, J. J. Walsh.

OPHTHALMIC OPTICS

First degrees in *Ophthalmic Optics* or *Optometry*
are granted by the Universities of Aston, Bradford,
the City University, Manchester (Manchester Institute of Science and Technology), and Wales (University College, Cardiff).

First degrees in *Optometry* granted by the CNAA
are provided at Glasgow College.

THE BRITISH COLLEGE OF OPTOMETRISTS, 10 Knaresborough Place, SW5 0TG, grants qualifications as
an optometrist.—*Gen. Sec.,* T. H. Collingridge.

THE ASSOCIATION OF BRITISH DISPENSING OPTICIANS,
6 Hurlingham Business Park, Sulivan Road, SW6
3DU, grants qualifications as a dispensing optician.—*Registrar,* D. G. Baker.

PHARMACY

First degrees in *Pharmacy* are granted by the
Universities of Aston, Bath, Belfast, Bradford, London (King's College and the School of Pharmacy),
Manchester, Nottingham, Strathclyde, Wales (University College, Cardiff).

First degrees in *Pharmacy* and *Pharmacology*
granted by the CNAA are provided at Brighton,
Leicester, Liverpool, East London, Portsmouth and
Sunderland Polytechnics, and Robert Gordon's Institute.

Information may be obtained from The Secretary
and Registrar, ROYAL PHARMACEUTICAL SOCIETY OF
GREAT BRITAIN, 1 Lambeth High Street, SE1 7JN.
Sec. and Registrar, J. Ferguson.

PHOTOGRAPHY, FILM AND TV STUDIES

First degrees are awarded by the Universities of
Glasgow (*Theatre Studies/Film & TV Studies*), Kent
(*Drama/Film Studies*) and Reading (*Film & Drama*).
At some other universities these subjects may be
studied as part of a first degree course.

First degrees in *Photography, Photographic Arts/
Sciences/Studies* and various aspects of film, video
and television are granted by the CNAA and courses
are available at some 11 polytechnics and colleges.

BRITISH INSTITUTE OF PROFESSIONAL PHOTOGRAPHY,
Amwell End, Ware, Herts. SG12 9HN.—*Chief
Exec.,* A. M. Berkeley.

PRINTING

First degrees in *Typography and Graphic Communication* are awarded by the University of Reading.

First degrees in *Graphic Design* granted by the
CNAA are provided at many polytechnics and
colleges. First degrees in *Printing and Packaging
Technology* granted by the CNAA are provided by
Watford College in association with Hatfield Poly-
technic.

Courses in general and technical design and
administrative aspects of printing are available at

technical colleges throughout the United Kingdom.
Details can be obtained from the Institute of Printing
and the British Printing Industries Federation (*see
below*).

In addition to the examining and organizing bodies
listed below, examinations are held by various
independent regional examining boards in further
education.

BRITISH PRINTING INDUSTRIES FEDERATION, 11 Bedford Row, WC1R 4DX.—*Dir.-Gen.,* C. Stanley.

INSTITUTE OF PRINTING, 8 Lonsdale Gardens, Tunbridge Wells, Kent TN1 1NU.—*Sec.,* C. F. Partridge.

RECREATION, SPORT, AND HUMAN MOVEMENT STUDIES

(See also Dance)

First degrees are granted by the University of
Birmingham (*Sport and Recreation Studies*), Lancaster (*Physical Education*), Leeds, (*Physical Education*), Liverpool (*Physical Education*), Loughborough
(*Physical Education and Sports Science*; also *Physical
Education, Sports Science and Recreation Management*) and Ulster (*Sport and Leisure Studies*). *Physical Education* and various aspects of recreation may
also be studied as part of other first degree courses at
several universities.

First degrees in various aspects of physical education, recreation and sports science/studies are
granted by the CNAA; *Physical Education and
Sports Science/Studies* also form part of a degree
course at many other colleges/polytechnics.

ROBOTICS

First degrees in *Electronic Control and Robot
Engineering* are granted by the University of Hull.

SOCIAL WORK

First degrees in *Social Studies* or in *Social Sciences*
are granted by most universities. Courses leading to
first degrees in *Social Science* or *Social Sciences/
Applied Social Science* or *Sociology* granted by the
CNAA are provided by many polytechnics and
colleges.

CENTRAL COUNCIL FOR EDUCATION AND TRAINING
IN SOCIAL WORK, Derbyshire House, St. Chad's Street,
WC1H 8AD.—*Dir.,* A. Hall. The Council promotes
education and training for social work and social
care throughout the UK. It approves training programmes, including those leading to one of three
social work qualifying awards: the Certificate of
Qualification in Social Work, the Certificate in Social
Service, and the Diploma in Social Work.

SPEECH SCIENCE

(See also Languages)

First degrees are awarded in *Speech Science* by the
University of Sheffield; in *Speech Sciences* by the
University of London (University College); in *Speech
Pathology* by the University of Manchester; and in
Speech Therapy by the University of Ulster.

First degrees in various aspects of speech therapy
and speech pathology granted by the CNAA are
provided at Birmingham, Leeds, Leicester and
Manchester Polytechnics, and at the Central School
of Speech and Drama and Queen Margaret College.

THE COLLEGE OF SPEECH THERAPISTS, Harold Poster
House, 6 Lechmere Road, NW2 5BU, provides details
of courses leading to qualification as a speech
therapist. The College also sponsors advanced clinical courses. Associate Membership is available for
professionals in other disciplines. A Directory of
Members of the College is published triennially. *Gen.
Sec.,* D. J. C. Wiseman.

SURVEYING
(*See also* Building and Estate and Land Management)

First degrees in *Surveying Science* are granted by the University of Newcastle upon Tyne; in *Building Economics and Quantity Surveying* and in *Building Surveying* by Heriot-Watt University; in *Quantity Surveying* by Ulster University; in *Property Valuation and Finance* by the City University; in *Quantity Surveying* and *Building Surveying* by the Universities of Reading and Salford.

First degrees in *Quantity Surveying, Surveying and Mapping Sciences* and *Urban Estate Surveying* granted by the CNAA are provided by most polytechnics.

Qualifying professional bodies include:

ROYAL INSTITUTION OF CHARTERED SURVEYORS (incorporating The Institute of Quantity Surveyors), 12 Great George Street, SW1P 3AD.—*Sec. Gen.*, M. Pattison.

ARCHITECTS AND SURVEYORS INSTITUTE, 15 St. Mary Street, Chippenham, Wilts. SN15 3JN.—*Chief Exec.*, B. A. Hunt.

INCORPORATED ASSOCIATION OF ARCHITECTS AND SURVEYORS, Jubilee House, Billing Brook Road, Weston Favell, Northampton NN3 4NW.—*Administrator*, B. D. Hughes.

RATING AND VALUATION ASSOCIATION, 41 Doughty Street, WC1N 2LF.—*Dir.*, C. Farrington.

INCORPORATED SOCIETY OF VALUERS AND AUCTIONEERS, 3 Cadogan Gate, SW1X 0AS.—*Sec.*, M. Astbury.

TEACHING

To become a qualified teacher it is necessary to have successfully completed a course of initial teacher training.

Non-graduates usually qualify by way of a three- or four-year course leading to a Bachelor of Education (B.Ed.) honours degree, but some universities offer first degree courses (BA, B.Sc.) taken concurrently with a certificate of education. Graduates take a one-year postgraduate certificate of education (PGCE).

Details of courses in England and Wales are contained in the *Handbook of Degree and Advanced Courses* published annually by the National Association of Teachers in Further and Higher Education.

Applications for B.Ed. courses in England and Wales at institutions other than universities are made through the Central Register and Clearing House Ltd., from which application forms can be obtained. For all PGCE courses in England and Wales, applications are handled by the Graduate Teacher Training Registry at the same address. (For address, *see* p. 454).

Details of courses in Scotland can be obtained from the colleges of education and from TEACH (*see* p. 454). Details of courses in Northern Ireland can be obtained from the Department of Education for Northern Ireland. Applications for teacher training courses in Scotland and Northern Ireland are made to the institutions direct.

TECHNICAL EDUCATION

First degrees in one or more technologies are awarded by almost all universities; and many polytechnics and colleges of technology provide courses leading to first degrees granted by the CNAA. Details are given under individual subject headings.

Industry Training Boards

AGRICULTURAL, Stoneleigh Park Pavilion, National Agricultural Centre, Kenilworth, Warks. CV8 2UG.—*Chief Exec.*, N. M. Snook.

CLOTHING AND ALLIED PRODUCTS, 80 Richardshaw Lane, Pudsey, Leeds LS28 6BN.—*Chief Exec.*, J. W. Dearden.

CONSTRUCTION, Bircham Newton, Nr. King's Lynn, Norfolk PE31 6RH.— *Sec.*, M. Smith.

ENGINEERING, 54 Clarendon Road, Watford, Herts. WD1 1LB.—*Sec.*, E. P. Jones.

HOTEL AND CATERING, International House, High Street, W5 5DB.—*Sec.*, C. Kingshott.

LOCAL GOVERNMENT TRAINING BOARD, Arndale House, Arndale Centre, Luton, Beds. LU1 2TS.—*Chief Exec.*, M. G. Clarke.

MAN-MADE FIBRES INDUSTRY TRAINING ADVISORY BOARD, Central House, Gate Lane, Sutton Coldfield, W. Midlands B73 5TS.—*Sec.*, P. Grice.

OFFSHORE PETROLEUM, Offshore Training Centre, Forties Road, Montrose, Angus DD10 9ET.—*Sec.*, G. A. R. Stark.

PLASTICS PROCESSING, Coppice House, Halesfield 7, Telford, Shropshire, TF7 4NA.—*Chief Exec.*, J. C. Shearman.

ROAD TRANSPORT, Capitol House, Empire Way, Wembley, Middx. HA9 0NG.—*Dir. Gen.*, D. C. Barnett.

TEXTILES

First degrees are awarded by the Universities of Leeds (*Textile Chemistry* and *Textile Studies*) and Manchester (Manchester Institute of Science and Technology, *Textile Science and Technology*).

Courses leading to first degrees granted by the CNAA in various aspects of Textiles, Clothing Studies, and Textile Marketing are provided by many polytechnics and colleges.

THE TEXTILE INSTITUTE, 10 Blackfriars Street, Manchester M3 5DR.—*Gen. Sec.*, R. G. Denyer.

THEOLOGY

First degrees in *Theology, Divinity, Religious Studies*, or combinations of these subjects are granted by most universities.

Courses leading to first degrees in *Theology* or *Theological Studies* granted by the CNAA are provided by about half a dozen polytechnics and colleges.

Theological Colleges
Anglican

CHICHESTER THEOLOGICAL COLLEGE, Chichester, W. Sussex PO19 1SG. (45).—*Princ.*, Rev. Canon J. Hind.

COATES HALL, Rosebery Crescent, Edinburgh EH12 5JT. (23).—*Princ.*, Rev. Canon K. Mason.

CRANMER HALL, St. John's College, Durham DH1 3RJ. (80).—*Warden*, Rev. I. P. M. Cundy.

LINCOLN THEOLOGICAL COLLEGE, Drury Lane, Lincoln LN1 3BP. (65).—*Warden*, Rev. Canon W. M. Jacob, PH.D.

OAK HILL COLLEGE, Chase Side, N14 4PS. (134).—*Princ.*, Rev. Canon G. Bridger.

COLLEGE OF THE RESURRECTION, Mirfield, W. Yorks. WF14 0BW. (30).—*Princ.*, Rev. Fr. D. Lloyd.

RIDLEY HALL, Cambridge CB3 9HG. (56).—*Princ.*, Rev. Canon H. F. de Waal.

RIPON COLLEGE, Cuddesdon, Oxford OX9 9EX. (70).—*Princ.*, Rev. Canon J. H. Garton.

ST. DEINIOL'S LIBRARY, Hawarden, Deeside, Clwyd CH5 3DF.—*Princ.*, Rev. P. J. Jagger.

ST. JOHN'S COLLEGE, Bramcote, Nottingham NG9 3DS. (110).—*Princ.*, Rev. Dr. J. Goldingay.

ST. MICHAEL'S THEOLOGICAL COLLEGE, Llandaff, Cardiff CF5 2YJ. (40).—*Warden.*, Rev. Canon J. H. L. Rowlands.

ST. STEPHEN'S HOUSE, 16 Marston Street, Oxford OX4 1JX. (58).—*Princ.*, Rev. E. R. Barnes.

SALISBURY AND WELLS THEOLOGICAL COLLEGE, 19 The Close, Salisbury SP1 2EE. (62).—*Princ.*, Rev. P. A. Crowe.

TRINITY COLLEGE, Stoke Hill, Bristol BS9 1JP. (120).—*Princ.*, Rev. D. Gillett.

WESTCOTT HOUSE, Jesus Lane, Cambridge CB5 8BP. (50).—*Princ.*, Rev. Dr. R. W. N. Hoare.

WYCLIFFE HALL, 54 Banbury Road, Oxford OX2 6PW. (78).—*Princ.*, Rev. Dr. R. T. France.

Church of Scotland

CHRIST'S COLLEGE, Aberdeen AB1 1YD. (186).—*Master*, Rev. H. R. Sefton, PH.D.

NEW COLLEGE, Mound Place, Edinburgh EH1 2LU. (307).—*Princ.*, Rev. Prof. D. B. Forrester.

TRINITY COLLEGE, 4 The Square, University of Glasgow, Glasgow G12 8QQ. (130).—*Princ.*, Very Rev. Prof. R. Davidson, DD.

Presbyterian Church of Wales

UNITED THEOLOGICAL COLLEGE, Aberystwyth SY23 2LT. (42).—*Princ.*, Rev. Prof. E. ap Nefydd Roberts.

Presbyterian

UNION THEOLOGICAL COLLEGE, Belfast BT7 1JT. (96).—*Princ.*, R. F. G. Holmes.

Methodist

EDGHILL THEOLOGICAL COLLEGE, 9 Lennoxvale, Belfast BT9 5BY. (87).—*Princ.*, Rev. W. D. D. Cooke, PH.D.

WESLEY COLLEGE, College Park Drive, Henbury Road, Bristol BS10 7QD. (65).—*Princ.*, Dr. H. McKeating.

WESLEY HOUSE, Cambridge CB5 8BJ. (35).—*Princ.*, Rev. Dr. I. H. Jones.

Baptist

BRISTOL BAPTIST COLLEGE, Woodland Road, Bristol BS8 1UN. (40).—*Princ.*, Rev. Dr. J. E. Morgan-Wynne.

NORTHERN BAPTIST COLLEGE, Luther King House, Brighton Grove, Rusholme, Manchester M14 5JP. (43).—*Princ.*, Rev. Dr. B. Haymes.

NORTH WALES BAPTIST COLLEGE, Ffordd Ffriddoedd, Bangor, Gwynedd LL57 2EH. (5).—*Princ.*, Rev. J. R. Rowlands.

REGENT'S PARK COLLEGE, Oxford OX1 2LB. (75).—*Princ.*, Rev. Dr. P. S. Fiddes.

THE SCOTTISH BAPTIST COLLEGE, 12 Aytoun Road, Glasgow G41 5RT. (20).—*Princ.*, Rev. I. J. N. Oakley.

SOUTH WALES BAPTIST COLLEGE, 54 Richmond Road, Cardiff CF2 3UR. (20).—*Princ.*, Rev. N. Clark.

SPURGEON'S COLLEGE, South Norwood Hill, SE25 6DJ. (67).—*Princ.*, P. Beasley-Murray, PH.D.

United Reformed

BALA-BANGOR INDEPENDENT COLLEGE, Bangor LL57 2EH. (15).—*Princ.*, R. T. Jones, D.Phil., DD.

MANSFIELD COLLEGE, Mansfield Road, Oxford OX1 3TF. (185).—*Princ.*, D. J. Trevelyan, CB.

NORTHERN COLLEGE, Luther King House, Brighton Grove, Rusholme, Manchester M14 5JP. (45).—*Princ.*, Rev. R. J. McKelvey, PH.D.

WESTMINSTER COLLEGE, Madingley Road, Cambridge CB3 0AA. (40).—*Princ.*, Rev. M. H. Cressey.

Congregational

COLLEGE OF THE WELSH INDEPENDENTS, 38 Pier Street, Aberystwyth, Dyfed.—*Princ.*, Rev. Dr. E. S. John.

SCOTTISH CONGREGATIONAL COLLEGE, Rosebery Crescent, Edinburgh EH12 5YN. (5).—*Princ.*, Rev. Dr. J. W. S. Clark.

Unitarian

MANCHESTER COLLEGE, Mansfield Road, Oxford OX1 3TF.—*Princ.*, R. Waller.

UNITARIAN COLLEGE, Luther King House, Brighton Grove, Rusholme, Manchester M14 5JP. (4).—*Principal*, Rev. G. Murphy.

Ecumenical

QUEEN'S COLLEGE, Somerset Road, Edgbaston, Birmingham B15 2QH. (75).—*Princ.*, Rev. Dr. J. B. Walker.

Non-Denominational

ST. MARY'S COLLEGE, The University, St. Andrews, Fife KY16 9JU. (188).—*Princ.*, Very Rev. D. W. D. Shaw.

Roman Catholic

ALLEN HALL COLLEGE, 28 Beaufort Street, SW3 5AA. (75).—*Rector*, Rt. Rev. Mgr. P. O'Donoghue.

CAMPION HOUSE COLLEGE, 112 Thornbury Road, Isleworth, Middx. TW7 4NN. (35).—*Princ.*, Rev. M. Barrow, SJ.

CHESTERS COLLEGE, 2 Chesters Road, Bearsden, Glasgow. (45).—*Rector*, Very Rev. P. Tartaglia.

OSCOTT COLLEGE, Chester Road, Sutton Coldfield, W. Midlands B73 5AA. (76).—*Rector*, Rt. Rev. Mgr. P. McKinney.

ST. JOHN'S SEMINARY, Wonersh, Guildford, Surrey GU5 0QX. (50).—*Rector*, Rt. Rev. Mgr. P. Smith.

USHAW COLLEGE, Durham DH7 9RH. (130).—*Princ.*, Rt. Rev. Mgr. P. Walton.

Jewish

JEWS' COLLEGE, Albert Road, NW4 2SJ. (130).—*Princ.*, Rabbi Dr. J. Sacks.

LEO BAECK COLLEGE, Sternberg Centre for Judaism, 80 East End Road, N3 2SY (20).—*Princ.* Rabbi Dr. J. Magonet.

TOWN AND COUNTRY PLANNING

First degrees are granted by the Universities of Belfast (*Environmental Planning*), Dundee (*Town and Regional Planning*), Heriot-Watt (*Town Planning*), Kent (*Urban Studies*), London (University College, *Environmental Studies* and *Town and Country Planning*), Manchester (*Town and Country Planning*), Newcastle upon Tyne (*Town and Country Planning*), Sheffield (*Urban Studies*), Strathclyde (*Planning*), Sussex (*Urban Studies*), and Wales (University College, Cardiff, *Town Planning Studies*).

First degrees in *Town Planning*, *Town and Country Planning*, *Environmental/Urban Planning*, and other aspects of planning granted by the CNAA are provided at Birmingham, Bristol, Leeds, Oxford, Central London and South Bank Polytechnics.

The ROYAL TOWN PLANNING INSTITUTE, 26 Portland Place, W1N 4BE, recognizes a number of degree and diploma courses in town planning. *Sec. Gen.*, D. Fryer.

TRANSPORT

First degrees are granted by the Universities of Aston (*Transport Management*), Loughborough (*Transport Management and Planning*), and Wales (University College, Cardiff, *International Transport*). The City University awards a first degree in *Air Transport Engineering*.

First degrees in *Transportation Engineering* granted by the CNAA are provided by Napier Polytechnic of Edinburgh.

THE CHARTERED INSTITUTE OF TRANSPORT, 80 Portland Place, London W1N 4DP, conducts qualifying examinations in transport management leading to chartered professional status. *Dir. Gen.*, R. P. Botwood.

VETERINARY STUDIES

First degrees in *Veterinary Science/Medicine and Surgery* are granted by the Universities of Bristol, Cambridge, Edinburgh, Glasgow, Liverpool and London (Royal Veterinary College).

INDEPENDENT SCHOOLS

The following pages list those independent schools whose Head is a member of the Headmasters' Conference, the Society of Headmasters and Headmistresses of Independent Schools or the Girls Schools Association.

THE HEADMASTERS' CONFERENCE

Chairman (1991), J. G. Parker (Manchester GS); *Sec.*, V. S. Anthony, 130 Regent Road, Leicester LE1 7PG; *Membership Sec.*, R. N. P. Griffiths, 1 Russell House, Bepton Road, Midhurst, W. Sussex GU29 9NB. The annual meetings are, as a rule, held at the end of September.

The Headmasters of some maintained schools are by invitation Additional Members of the HMC. These include the following: Aylesbury Grammar School; The Cavendish School; Easingwold School; Haberdashers' Aske's Hatcham Boys' School; Haywards Heath Sixth Form College; The John Fisher School; The Judd School; Liskeard School; The London Oratory School; Longsands Community College; Prescot School; The Richard Huish College; Richmond School; The Royal Grammar School, High Wycombe; The Royal Grammar School, Lancaster; St. Bartholomew's School; Sir Roger Manwood's School; Watford Grammar School.

Name of School	Founded	No. of Pupils	Annual Fees B'ding	Annual Fees Day	Headmaster *(With date of Appointment)*
England and Wales					
Abbotsholme School, Staffs.	1889	250‡	£8,370	£5,580	D. J. Farrant (1984)
Abingdon School, Oxon.	1256	730	£7,278	£3,831	M. St. J. Parker (1975)
Aldenham School, Herts.	1597	380†	£9,102	£5,781	M. Higginbottom (1983)
Alleyn's School, SE22	1619	921‡	......	£4,035	D. A. Fenner (1976)
Allhallows School, Dorset	1515	300‡	£8,424	£4,212	P. S. Larkman, LVO (1983)
Ampleforth College (*RC*), Yorks. ...	1802	620	£8,820	......	Rev. Dr. D. L. Milroy, OSB (1980)
*Ardingly College, W. Sussex	1858	475‡	£8,670	£6,825	J. W. Flecker (1980)
Arnold School, Blackpool	1896	827‡	£5,300	£2,640	J. A. B. Kelsall (1987)
Ashville College, Harrogate	1877	650‡	£6,537	£3,555	M. H. Crosby (1987)
Bancroft's School, Essex	1727	720‡	......	£3,984	Dr. P. C. D. Southern (1985)
Barnard Castle School, Co. Durham	1883	509†	£4,326°°	£2,316°°	F. S. McNamara (1980)
Bedales School, Hants.	1893	393‡	£9,375	£6,720	E. A. M. MacAlpine (1981)
Bedford School	1552	750	£7,593	£4,785	Dr. I. P. Evans (1990)
Bedford Modern School	1566	987	£6,055	£3,060	P. J. Squire (1977)
Berkhamsted School, Herts.	1541	500	£7,374	£4,827	Rev. K. H. Wilkinson (1989)
Birkenhead School, Merseyside	1860	756	......	£2,595	S. J. Haggett (1988)
Bishop's Stortford College, Herts. ..	1868	356	£6,078°°	£4,317°°	S. G. G. Benson (1984)
*Bloxham School, Oxon.	1860	359†	£8,100	£5,574	M. W. Vallance (1982)
Blundell's School, Devon	1604	475†	£8,400	£5,100	A. J. D. Rees (1980)
Bolton School	1524	850	......	£2,937	A. W. Wright (1983)
Bootham School, York.	1823	335‡	£6,222°	£3,837°	I. M. Small (1988)
Bradfield College, Berks.	1850	560†	£9,300	£6,975	P. B. Smith (1985)
Bradford Grammar School	1662	1,020†	......	£2,686	D. A. G. Smith (1975)
Brentwood School, Essex	1557	880†	£7,269	£4,152	J. A. E. Evans (1981)
Brighton College, E. Sussex	1845	490‡	£8,685	£5,715	J. D. Leach (1987)
Bristol Cathedral School	1542	460†	......	£2,997	R. A. Collard (1990)
Bristol Grammar School	1532	980‡	......	£2,688	C. E. Martin (1986)
Bromsgrove School, Worcs.	1553	550‡	£7,485	£4,692	T. M. Taylor (1986)
Bryanston School, Dorset	1928	670‡	£9,750	......	T. D. Wheare (1983)
Bury Grammar School, Lancs.	1634	650	......	£2,400	J. Robson (1969)
Canford School, Dorset	1923	530†	£9,260	£6,665	M. Marriott (1976)
Caterham School, Surrey	1811	450†	£7,380	£4,020	S. R. Smith (1976)
Charterhouse, Surrey	1611	700†	£9,795	£8,100	P. J. Attenborough (1982)
Cheadle Hulme School, Cheshire ...	1855	1,080‡	£6,195	£2,685	D. J. Wilkinson (1990)
Cheltenham College, Glos.	1841	560†	£9,450	£7,110	P. D. V. Wilkes (1990)
Chigwell School, Essex	1629	344†	£6,192	£4,071	A. R. M. Little (1989)
Christ College, Brecon	1541	360†	£6,249	£4,737	S. W. Hockey (1982)
Christ's Hospital, W. Sussex	1553	850‡	varies	......	R. C. Poulton (1987)
Churcher's College, Hants.	1722	460‡	£6,780	£3,663	G. W. Buttle (1988)
City of London, EC4	1442	850	......	£4,248	B. G. Bass (1990)
City of London Freemen's School, Surrey	1854	360‡	£6,624	£4,248	D. C. Haywood (1987)
Clifton College, Bristol	1862	700‡	£9,300	£6,510	H. Monro (1990)
Colfe's School, SE12	1652	700†	......	£3,375	Dr. D. Richardson (1990)
Colston's School, Bristol	1710	322‡	£6,585	£3,975	S. B. Howarth (1988)
Coventry School	—	1,644‡	......	£2,541	R. Cooke (*Director*) (1977)
Cranleigh School, Surrey	1863	560†	£9,585	£7,200	A. Hart (1984)
Culford School, Suffolk	1881	680‡	£7,065	£4,593	D. Robson (1971)
Dame Allan's School, Newcastle upon Tyne....................	1705	450†	......	£2,550	T. A. Willcocks (*Principal*) (1988)
Dauntsey's School, Wiltshire	1543	593‡	£7,800	£4,830	C. R. Evans (1985)

* Woodard Corporation School.   ‡ Co-educational.   † Girls in VI form.   ° 1990 figure.   °°1989 figure.

Name of School	Founded	No. of Pupils	Annual Fees B'ding	Annual Fees Day	Headmaster *(With date of Appointment)*
Dean Close School, Cheltenham....	1884	440‡	£7,695°	£5,025°	C. J. Bacon (1979)
*Denstone College, Staffs..........	1873	345‡	£8,070	£5,748	H. C. K. Carson (1990)
Douai School (*RC*), Berks.........	1903	300	£7,800	£4,920	Dom. G. Scott, OSB (1987)
Dover College, Kent...............	1871	300‡	£7,650	£5,055	J. K. Ind (1981)
Downside School (*RC*), Somerset..	1607	424	£8,280	£5,298	Dom. P. Jebb, OSB (1980)
Dulwich College, SE21	1619	1,395	£8,790	£4,395	A. C. F. Verity (*Master*) (1986)
Durham School	1414	387†	£8,700	£5,799	M. A. Lang (1982)
Eastbourne College, E. Sussex	1867	540†	£8,757	£6,474	C. J. Saunders (1981)
*Ellesmere College, Shropshire	1884	400†	£7,920	£5,610	D. R. du Croz (1988)
Eltham College, SE9	1842	530†	£7,296	£3,456	D. M. Green (1990)
Emanuel School, W11..............	1594	760		£3,492	P. F. Thomson (1984)
Epsom College, Surrey	1855	650†	£8,550	£6,000	Dr. J. B. Cook (1982)
Eton College, Berks...............	1440	1,260	£9,396	......	Dr. W. E. K. Anderson (1980)
Exeter School	1633	710†	£5,565	£2,985	G. T. Goodall (1979)
Felsted School, Essex	1564	470†	£9,090	£7,170	E. J. H. Gould (1983)
Forest School, E17...............	1834	442†	£6,099	£4,044	J. C. Gough (*Warden*) (1983)
Framlingham College, Suffolk	1864	440‡	£7,119	£4,569	J. F. X. Miller (1989)
Frensham Heights, Surrey	1925	266‡	£8,160°	£5,130°	A. L. Pattinson (1973)
Giggleswick School, N. Yorks......	1512	320‡	£8,550	£5,670	P. Hobson (1986)
Gresham's School, Norfolk	1555	484‡	£8,895	£6,225	H. R. Wright (1985)
Haberdashers' Aske's School, Herts.	1690	1,103		£4,143	K. Dawson (1987)
Haileybury, Herts.................	1862	660†	£9,585	£6,450	D. J. Jewell (1987)
Hampton School, Middx............	1557	850		£3,300	G. G. Able (1988)
Harrow School, Middx.	1571	770	£10,200	......	I. D. S. Beer (1981)
Hereford Cathedral School	1384	600‡	£5,655	£3,285	Dr. H. C. Tomlinson (1987)
Highgate School, N6	1565	585	£7,410	£4,380	R. P. Kennedy (1989)
Hulme Grammar School, Oldham ..	1611	740		£2,430	G. F. Dunkin (1987)
*Hurstpierpoint College, W. Sussex .	1849	415	£8,595	£6,870	S. A. Watson (1986)
Hymers College, Hull	1889	900‡		£2,535	J. C. Morris (1990)
Ipswich School, Suffolk	1390	621†	£5,780	£3,540	Dr. J. M. Blatchly (1972)
John Lyon School, Middx..........	1876	508		£3,390	Rev. T. J. Wright (1986)
Kelly College, Devon	1877	360‡	£8,475	£4,680	C. H. Hirst (1985)
Kent College, Canterbury	1885	550‡	£6,426°	£3,600°	R. J. Wicks (1980)
Kimbolton School, Cambs..........	1600	540‡	£5,985	£3,357	R. V. Peel (1987)
King Edward VI School, Southampton	1553	961†	......	£3,300	T. R. Cookson (1990)
King Edward VII School, Lytham ..	1908	552		£2,361	D. Heap (1982)
King Edward's School, Bath.......	1552	680†		£2,970	J. P. Wroughton (1982)
King Edward's School, Birmingham	1552	800	......	£2,880	M. J. W. Rogers (*Chief Master*) (1982)
King Edward's School, Witley, Surrey	1553	525‡	£6,711	£4,956	R. J. Fox (1988)
*King's College, Taunton	1880	475	£8,640	£6,450	R. S. Funnell (1988)
King's College School, SW19.......	1829	660		£4,485	R. M. Reeve (1980)
King's School, Bruton, Somerset ...	1519	332†	£8,460	£5,985	A. H. Beadles (1985)
King's School, Canterbury	600	704‡	£8,085	£5,655	Rev. Canon A. C. J. Phillips (1986)
King's School, Chester	1541	476	......	£3,063	A. R. D. Wickson (1981)
King's School, Ely, Cambs.	970	430‡	£8,688	£5,538	H. Ward (1970)
King's School, Macclesfield.......	1502	865†	......	£3,135	A. G. Silcock (1987)
King's School, Rochester, Kent	604	380†	£7,605	£4,560	Dr. I. R. Walker (1986)
King's School, Worcester	1541	710†	£6,249	£3,828	Dr. J. M. Moore (1983)
Kingston Grammar School, Surrey.	1561	590‡	......	£3,765	A. B. Creber (1987)
Kingswood School, Bath	1748	487‡	£7,150	£4,700	G. M. Best (1987)
*Lancing College, W. Sussex........	1848	555†	£9,027	£6,417	J. S. Woodhouse (1981)
Latymer Upper School, W6	1624	1,000	......	£3,795	M. C. Pavey (1988)
Leeds Grammar School	1552	1,027		£2,700	B. W. Collins (1986)
Leighton Park School, Reading	1890	350†	£2,385	£1,750	J. A. Chapman (1986)
The Leys School, Cambridge.......	1875	400†	£8,880	£6,570	Rev. J. C. A. Barrett (1990)
Liverpool College	1840	371†	......	£2,760	R. V. Haygarth (1979)
Llandovery College, Dyfed	1848	240‡	£6,000	£4,035	Dr. C. E. Evans (*Warden*) (1988)
Lord Wandsworth College, Hants. .	1912	440‡	£7,056	£5,508	G. A. G. Dodd (1982)
Loughborough Grammar School ...	1495	900	£5,997	£3,099	D. N. Ireland (1984)
Magdalen College School, Oxford ..	1480	500	£6,342	£3,342	W. B. Cook (*Master*) (1972)
Malvern College, Worcs.	1865	600	£9,210	£6,705	R. de C. Chapman (1983)
Manchester Grammar School	1515	1,450	......	£3,000	J. G. Parker (*High Master*) (1985)
Marlborough College, Wilts........	1843	900‡	£9,495	£7,122	D. R. Cope (*Master*) (1986)
Merchant Taylors' School, Liverpool......................	1620	700	......	£2,889	S. J. R. Dawkins (1986)
Merchant Taylors' School, Middx. .	1561	720	£8,040	£5,040	D. J. Skipper (1982)

* Woodard Corporation School.   ‡ Co-educational.   † Girls in VI form.   ° 1990 figure.

Name of School	Founded	No. of Pupils	Annual Fees		Headmaster (With date of Appointment)
			B'ding	Day	
Mill Hill School, NW7	1807	535†	£8,550	£5,625	A. C. Graham (1979)
Monkton Combe School, Bath	1868	330†	£8,685	£6,405	M. J. Cuthbertson (1990)
Monmouth School, Gwent	1614	540	£6,099	£3,570	R. D. Lane (1982)
Mount St. Mary's College (RC), Derbys.	1842	288‡	£6,486	£4,380	Rev. J. F. Grumitt, SJ (1976)
Newcastle under Lyme School	1874	1,220†	......	£2,361°	J. W. Donaldson (Principal) (1974)
Norwich School	1250	600	£5,925	£3,225	C. D. Brown (1984)
Nottingham High School	1513	830	......	£2,835	D. T. Witcombe, PH.D. (1970)
Oakham School, Rutland	1584	980‡	£7,827	£4,191	G. Smallbone (1985)
The Oratory School (RC), Berks.	1859	395	£7,518°	£5,259°	M. K. Lynn (1989)
Oundle School, Northants	1556	780‡	£9,700	......	D. B. McMurray (1984)
Pangbourne College, Berks.	1917	325	£8,340	£5,850	A. B. E. Hudson (1988)
Perse School, Cambridge	1615	488	£5,430°	£2,688°	Dr. G. M. Stephen (1987)
Plymouth College	1877	685	£6,030	£3,165	A. M. Joyce (1983)
Pocklington School, York.	1514	584‡	£6,519	£3,336	A. D. Pickering (1981)
Portsmouth Grammar School	1732	750†	......	£2,955	A. C. V. Evans (1983)
Prior Park College (RC), Bath	1830	385‡	£7,770	£4,296	J. W. R. Goulding (1989)
Queen Elizabeth GS, Wakefield	1591	740†	£4,926	£3,021	R. P. Mardling (1985)
Queen Elizabeth's GS, Blackburn	1567	1,086†	......	£2,799	P. F. Johnston (1978)
Queen Elizabeth's Hospital, Bristol.	1590	480	£5,256	£2,994	Dr. R. Gliddon (1985)
Queen's College, Taunton	1843	450‡	£6,765	£4,425	A. P. Hodgson (1979)
Radley College, Oxon.	1847	606	£9,300	......	D. R. W. Silk (Warden) (1968)
Ratcliffe College (RC), Leicester	1844	430‡	£6,600	£4,410	Rev. L. G. Hurdidge (1985)
Reed's School, Surrey	1813	360†	£6,900	£5,200	D. E. Prince (1983)
Reigate Grammar School, Surrey	1675	850†	......	£3,600	J. G. Hamlin (1982)
Rendcomb College, Glos.	1920	263†	£7,400	......	J. Tolputt (1987)
Repton School, Derby	1557	570†	£8,820	£6,540	G. E. Jones (1986)
RNIB New College, Worcester	1987	117‡	£14,361°	£9,576°	Rev. B. R. Manthorp (1980)
Rossall School, Lancs.	1844	500‡	£8,628	£6,021	R. D. W. Rhodes (1987)
Royal Grammar School, Guildford	1552	800	......	£3,540°	J. Daniel (1972)
Royal Grammar School, Newcastle upon Tyne	1545	966	......	£2,550	A. S. Cox (1972)
Royal Grammar School, Worcester	1291	775	£6,750	£2,925	T. E. Savage, TD (1978)
Rugby School, Warwicks.	1567	700†	£9,660	£5,595	M. B. Mavor, CVO (1990)
Rydal School, Clwyd	1885	350‡	£6,885	£5,235	P. F. Watkinson (1968)
Ryde School, Isle of Wight	1921	416‡	£5,874	£2,877	M. D. Featherstone (1990)
St. Albans School, Herts.	1570	665	......	£3,720	S. C. Wilkinson (1984)
St. Ambrose College, Cheshire	1946	640	......	£2,298	T. D. Coleman (1984)
St. Anselm's College (RC), Birkenhead.	1933	650	......	£2,322	Rev. Br. C. J. Sreenan, OBE (1988)
St. Bede's College (RC), Manchester	1876	880‡	......	£2,562°	J. Byrne (1983)
St. Bees School, Cumbria	1583	360‡	£7,800	£5,460	P. A. Chamberlain (1988)
St. Benedict's School (RC), W5	1902	580†	......	£3,165	Dr. A. J. Dachs (1987)
St. Dunstan's College, SE6	1888	650	......	£3,450	B. D. Dance (1973)
St. Edmund's College (RC), Herts.	1568	386‡	£6,792	£4,365	D. J. J. McEwen (1984)
St. Edmund's School, Canterbury	1749	315‡	£8,370	£5,490	J. V. Tyson (1978)
St. Edward's College (RC), Liverpool	1853	639†	......	£2,539	Rev. Br. B. D. Sassi (1984)
St. Edward's School, Oxford	1863	585†	£7,350°°	£5,520°°	D. Christie (1988)
St. George's College (RC), Surrey	1869	565†	£6,930	£4,590	Rev. J. W. Munton (1987)
St. John's School, Surrey	1851	460†	£7,500	£5,250	D. E. Brown (1985)
St. Lawrence College, Kent	1879	380‡	£8,010	£5,370	J. H. Binfield (1983)
St. Mary's College (RC), Merseyside	1919	575‡	......	£2,514	Rev. Br. P. E. Ryan (1987)
St. Paul's School, SW13	1509	761	£9,120	£5,727	Rev. Canon P. Pilkington (High Master) (1986)
St. Peter's School, York	627	471‡	£6,753	£3,930	R. N. Pittman (1985)
Sedbergh School, Cumbria	1525	495	£7,650	£5,310	Dr. R. G. Baxter (1982)
Sevenoaks School, Kent	1418	910‡	£8,685	£5,274	R. P. Barker (1981)
Sherborne School, Dorset	1550	660	£9,450	£7,185	P. H. Lapping (1988)
Shrewsbury School	1552	670	£9,120	£6,435	F. E. Maidment (1988)
Silcoates School, W. Yorks.	1820	420†	£6,480	£3,690	J. C. Baggaley (1979)
Solihull School, Warwicks	1560	986†	......	£2,650	A. Lee (1983)
Stamford School, Lincs.	1532	792	£5,880	£2,940	G. J. Timm (1978)
Stockport Grammar School	1487	1,010‡	......	£2,898	D. R. J. Bird (1985)
Stonyhurst College (RC), Lancs.	1593	435	£8,286	£4,467	Dr. R. G. G. Mercer (1985)
Stowe School, Bucks.	1923	590†	£8,658°	£6,060°	J. G. L. Nichols (1989)
Sutton Valence School, Kent	1576	420‡	£8,500	£5,350	M. R. Haywood (1980)
Taunton School	1847	600‡	£7,680°	£4,975°	B. B. Sutton (1987)
Tettenhall College, Staffs.	1863	300‡	£6,126	£3,774	W. J. Dale (1968)

‡ Co-educational.   † Girls in VI form.   ° 1990 figure.   °°1989 figure.

Name of School	Founded	No. of Pupils	Annual Fees B'ding	Annual Fees Day	Headmaster (With date of Appointment)
Tonbridge School, Kent...........	1553	650	£9,150	£6,450	J. M. Hammond (1990)
Trent College, Derbys.............	1868	523†	£6,255°	£3,726°	J. S. Lee (1988)
Trinity School, Surrey............	1596	825	......	£3,762	R. J. Wilson (1972)
Truro School	1879	850‡	£6,150	£3,270	B. K. Hobbs (1986)
University College School, NW3 ...	1830	520	......	£5,070	G. D. Slaughter (1983)
Uppingham School, Leics.	1584	680†	£9,750	......	N. R. Bomford (1982)
Warwick School	914	794	£6,960	£3,210	P. J. Cheshire (1989)
Wellingborough School, Northants.	1595	440‡	£6,735	£4,095	G. Garrett (1973)
Wellington College, Berks.	1856	839†	£9,375	£6,825	C. J. Driver (1989)
Wellington School, Somerset	1841	800†	£5,835	£3,135	A. Rogers (1990)
Wells Cathedral School, Somerset ..	1180	595‡	£6,552	£3,705	J. S. Baxter (1986)
West Buckland School, Devon	1858	461‡	£6,513	£1,964	M. Downward (1979)
Westminster School, SW1	1560	605†	£8,850	£5,925	D. M. Summerscale (1986)
Whitgift School, Surrey...........	1596	920	......	£3,876	D. A. Raeburn (1970)
William Hulme's GS, Manchester ..	1887	794‡	......	£3,090	P. D. Briggs (1987)
Winchester College, Hants.........	1382	646	£9,900	£7,425	J. P. Sabben-Clare (1985)
Wolverhampton Grammar School ..	1512	625†	......	£3,393	B. St. J. Trafford (1990)
Woodbridge School, Suffolk	1662	546‡	£6,750	£4,110	Dr. D. Younger (1985)
Woodhouse Grove School, Bradford	1812	575	£6,105	£3,735	D. A. Miller (1972)
*Worksop College, Notts..........	1895	420‡	£7,875	£5,400	R. D. V. Knight (1990)
Worth School (*RC*), W. Sussex	1959	311	£8,550	......	Rev. R. S. Ortiger (1983)
Wrekin College, Shropshire	1880	390‡	£7,395	£5,058	J. H. Arkell (1983)
Wycliffe College, Glos.	1882	330‡	£7,194°	£4,683°	A. P. Millard (1987)
Scotland					
Daniel Stewart's and Melville College, Edinburgh	1832	780	£5,868	£3,036	P. F. J. Tobin (1989)
Dollar Academy, Clackmannanshire	1818	887†	£5,046°°	£2,352°°	L. Harrison (*Rector*) (1984)
Dundee High School, Tayside	1239	750‡	......	£2,400	R. Nimmo (*Rector*) (1977)
The Edinburgh Academy...........	1824	580†	£7,770	£3,795	L. E. Ellis (*Rector*) (1977)
Fettes College, Edinburgh	1870	380‡	£9,360	£6,285	M. T. Thyne (1988)
George Heriot's School, Edinburgh.	1659	1,329‡	......	£2,580°	K. P. Pearson (1983)
George Watson's College, Edinburgh..	1741	1,230‡	£5,868	£3,036	F. E. Gerstenberg (*Principal*) (1985)
Glasgow Academy	1845	500	......	£2,760	C. W. Turner (*Rector*) (1983)
Glenalmond College, Perth.	1841	350‡	£9,300	......	S. R. D. Hall (*Warden*) (1987)
Gordonstoun School, Moray	1934	490‡	£8,700	£5,580	M. C. S.-R. Pyper (1990)
The High School of Glasgow	1124	580‡	......	£3,030	R. G. Easton (1983)
Hutcheson's Grammar School, Glasgow....................	1641	1,053‡	......	£2,593	D. R. Ward (*Rector*) (1987)
Kelvinside Academy, Glasgow	1878	500	......	£2,915	J. H. Duff (*Rector*) (1980)
Loretto School, E. Lothian	1827	300†	£6,300°°	£3,945°°	Rev. N. W. Drummond (1984)
Merchiston Castle School, Edinburgh......................	1833	370	£8,580	£5,520	D. M. Spaworth (1981)
Morrison's Academy, Perthshire....	1860	600‡	£6,330	£2,175	H. A. Ashmall (*Rector*) (1979)
Robert Gordon's College, Aberdeen	1729	850‡	£5,900	£2,290	G. A. Allan (1978)
Strathallan School, Perth	1913	400‡	£8,655	£5,770	C. D. Pighills (1975)
Northern Ireland					
Bangor Grammar School, Co. Down	1856	880	......	£1,700	T. W. Patton (1979)
Belfast Royal Academy	1785	1,270‡	......	£1,800	W. M. Sillery (1980)
Campbell College, Belfast..........	1894	450	£6,200	£2,725	Dr. R. J. I. Pollock (1987)
Coleraine Academical Institution ..	1856	850	£4,200	£1,800	R. S. Forsythe (1984)
Methodist College, Belfast.........	1868	1,600‡	£4,000°	£1,850°	T. W. Mulryne (1988)
Portora Royal School, Enniskillen .	1618	350‡	£4,700	£2,300	R. L. Bennett (1983)
Royal Belfast Academical Institution	1810	900	......	£2,000	R. M. Ridley (1990)
Channel Islands and Isle of Man					
Elizabeth College, Guernsey	1563	550	£4,305	£1,545	J. H. F. Doulton (1988)
Victoria College, Jersey...........	1852	570	£6,324	£1,290	M. H. Devenport (1967)
King William's College, Isle of Man	1668	338‡	£7,590	£5,370	S. A. Westley (1989)

* Woodard Corporation School.   ‡ Co-educational.   † Girls in VI form.   ° 1990 figure.   °°1989 figure.

HMC SCHOOLS OVERSEAS
Fees are given in local currency

Name of School	Founded	No. of Pupils	Annual Fees B'ding	Annual Fees Day	Headmaster *(With date of Appointment)*
Africa					
Falcon College, Esigodini, Zimbabwe	1954	450	Z$6,600	....	P. N. Todd (1985)
Hilton College, Natal, SA	1872	490	R16,300	....	P. Marsh (1987)
Michaelhouse, Natal, SA	1896	485	R16,300	....	J. Pluke (1987)
Peterhouse, Marondera, Zimbabwe	1955	737†	Z$7,200	Z$3,930	Rev. Dr. A. J. Megahey (*Rector*) (1984)
St. George's College, Harare, Zimbabwe	1896	840	Z$3,930°	Z$1,560°	J. C. Berry (1983)
St. John's College, Johannesburg, SA	—	604†	R14,250	R8,250	W. W. MacFarlane (1983)
St. Stithian's College, Randburg, SA	1953	650	R11,667	R6,465	D. B. Wylde (1989)
Australia					
Anglican Church GS, Queensland	1912	1,283	$A8,900	$A3,950	C. V. Ellis (1987)
Brighton GS, Victoria	1882	750	....	$A6,330	R. L. Rofe (1967)
Camberwell GS, Victoria	1886	975	....	$A6,066	C. F. Black (1987)
Canberra GS, ACT	1929	921	$A10,540	$A4,600	T. C. Murray (1986)
Caulfield GS, Victoria	1881	1,530‡	$A12,075	$A6,180	Rev. A. S. Holmes (*Principal*) (1977)
Cranbrook School, NSW	1918	772	$A12,290	$A6,080	Dr. B. N. Carter (1985)
The Geelong College, Victoria	1861	986‡	$A13,332	$A6,572	A. P. Sheahan (1986)
Geelong GS, Victoria	1855	1,220‡	$A13,206	$A6,168	J. E. Lewis (1980)
Guildford GS, W. Australia	1896	785	$A10,304	$A4,776	J. M. Moody (1979)
Haileybury College, Victoria	1892	1,800	....	$A6,360	A. M. H. Aikman (*Principal*) (1974)
Hale School, W. Australia	1858	700	$A10,500	$A5,000	J. Inverarity, MBE (1989)
King's School, Parramatta, NSW	1831	900	$A13,000	$A7,500	J. A. Wickham (1984)
Kinross Wolaroi School, NSW	1886	640‡	$A10,865	$A5,050	A. E. S. Anderson (1978)
Knox, GS, NSW	1924	1,250	$A12,500	$A6,080	Dr. I. W. Paterson (1969)
Melbourne C. of E. GS, Victoria	1856	970	$A12,340	$A7,100	A. J. de V. Hill (1988)
Newington College, NSW	1863	1,110	$A12,000	$A5,550	A. J. Rae (1972)
The Peninsula School, Victoria	1961	993	$A11,226	$A5,820	H. A. Macdonald (1971)
St. Peter's College, S. Australia	1847	770	$A11,880	$A5,480	Dr. A. J. Shinkfield (1978)
Scotch College, Adelaide, S. Australia	1919	670‡	$A13,160	$A6,160	W. M. Miles (1975)
Scotch College, Hawthorn, Victoria	1851	1,366	$A12,840	$A6,480	Dr. F. G. Donaldson (1983)
Scotch College, Swanbourne, W. Australia	1897	727	$A10,480	$A4,960	W. R. Dickinson (1972)
Scots College, Sydney, NSW	1893	1,100	$A13,605	$A7,095	G. A. W. Renney (*Principal*) (1980)
Sydney C. of E. GS, NSW	1889	970	$A12,165	$A6,204	R. A. I. Grant (1983)
Sydney GS, NSW	1857	1,120	....	$A7,485	Dr. R. D. Townsend, D. Phil. (1989)
Wesley College, Melbourne, Victoria	1866	2,048‡	....	$A6,190	D. H. Prest (*Principal*) (1972)
Canada					
Brentwood College School, Vancouver	1961	375‡	C$13,675°°	C$6,800°°	W. T. Ross (1976)
Glenlyon-Norfolk School, BC	—	275‡	C$12,670	C$5,570	D. S. S. Brooks (1987)
Hillfield Strathallan College, Ontario	1901	975‡	....	C$7,550	M. B. Wansbrough (1969)
Pickering College, Ontario.	1842	175	C$14,850	C$7,400	S. H. Clark (1978)
St. Andrew's College, Ontario	1899	393	C$16,150°	C$9,350°	R. P. Bedard (1981)
Toronto French School, Ontario	1962	1,240‡	C$14,950	C$7,600	A. S. Troubetzkoy (1987)
Trinity College School, Ontario.	1865	403	C$16,350°	C$9,000°	R. C. N. Wright (1983)
Upper Canada College, Toronto	1829	635	C$18,200	C$9,950	E. A. Barton (*Principal*) (1988)
Europe					
Aiglon College, Switzerland	1949	257‡	Frs.40,725	Frs.25,620°	P. Parsons (1976)
British School in the Netherlands	1935	470‡	....	Fl.14,310°°	B. D. Davidson (1979)
British School of Brussels	1970	1,075‡	....	Frs.390,000	Dr. J. Jackson (1983)
British School of Paris, France	1954	284‡	Frs.93,915	Frs.63,165	A. W. Livingstone-Smith (1986)
The English School, Nicosia, Cyprus	1900	825‡°	....	C£1,100	A. M. Hudspeth (1988)

† Girls in VI form.　　‡ Co-educational.　　° 1990 figure.　　°° 1989 figure.

Name of School	Founded	No. of Pupils	Annual Fees B'ding	Annual Fees Day	Headmaster (With date of Appointment)
The International School of Paris	1964	240‡	....	Frs.69,000	N. M. Prentki (1988)
St. Columba's College, Dublin	1843	278‡	IR£4,500°	IR£2,850°	T. E. Macey (*Warden*) (1988)
St. George's English School, Rome	1958	750‡	....	L13,500,000	Dr. C. H. R. Niven (1988)
Hong Kong					
The Island School	1967	1,170‡	....	HK$35,000	D. J. James (1988)
King George V School	1900	1,050‡	....	HK$36,300	M. J. Behennah (1989)
India					
Birla Public School, Pilani	—	344	Rs.10,600	Rs.3,400	B. K. Sood (1973)
Lawrence School, Ootacamund ..	1858	450‡	Rs.14,000	....	B. S. Bhatnagar (1986)
Lawrence School, Sanawar	1847	550‡	Rs.20,000	....	S. B. Singh (1988)
The Scindia School, Gwalior	1897	750	Rs.15,500	....	Dr. S. D. Singh (1978)
New Zealand					
Christ's College, Christchurch ...	1850	600	NZ$9,270	NZ$5,175	Dr. M. J. Rosser (1985)
Collegiate School, Wanganui	1854	510†	NZ$11,215	NZ$6,280	T. S. McKinlay (1988)
King's College, Auckland	1896	800†	NZ$10,620	NZ$6,285	J. S. Taylor (1988)
Rathkeale College, Masterton ...	1964	300†	NZ$12,000	NZ$5,550	R. G. Nethercote (1988)
St. Andrew's College, Christchurch	1916	569	NZ$10,797	NZ$6,318	Dr. A. J. Rentoul (*Rector*) (1982)
South America					
Academia Britanica Cuscatleca, El Salvador	1971	1,350‡	....	C10,000	A. J. McQuiggan (1986)
Markham College, Peru	1946	750	....	I117,000	W. J. Baker (1990)
St. Andrew's Scots School, Argentina	—	590‡	....	US$5,000	K. Prior (1982)
St. George's College, Argentina .	1898	228‡	US$7,200	US$5,400	G. R. Sims (1986)
St. Paul's School, Brazil	1926	700‡	....	US$5,000	C. McCann (1990)
United Arab Emirates					
Dubai College	1855	511†	....	Dh.18,000°	H. J. Deelman (1987)
USA					
The Rivers School, Massachusetts	1915	260‡	....	$10,000°	R. A. Bradley (1981)

‡ Co-educational.   † Girls in VI form.   ° 1990 figure.

SOCIETY OF HEADMASTERS AND HEADMISTRESSES OF INDEPENDENT SCHOOLS

Hon. Secretary, A. E. R. Dodds, Mantons, Park Road, Winchester, Hants. SO23 7BE.

The Society was founded in 1961 and, in general, represents smaller boarding schools. A Headmaster may be a member of both HMC and SHMIS. This is the case for the Headmasters of the following schools, details of which appear in the HMC list:

Abbotsholme School, Bedales School, Churcher's College, City of London Freemen's School, Colston's School, Frensham Heights, Lord Wandsworth College, Pangbourne College, Reed's School, Rendcomb College, Ryde School, St. George's College, Silcoates School, Tettenhall College, Wells Cathedral School, West Buckland School and Woodbridge School.

Name of School	Founded	No. of Pupils	Annual Fees B'ding	Annual Fees Day	Headmaster (With date of Appointment)
Ackworth School, W. Yorks	1779	420‡	£6,579	£3,696	D. S. Harris (1989)
Austin Friars School (RC), Carlisle	1951	300‡	£5,400	£3,075	Rev. T. Lyons, OSA (1981)
Bearwood College, Berks.	1827	340	£7,275	£4,125	The Hon. M. C. Penney (1980)
Bedstone College, Shropshire	1948	220‡	£5,295°°	.....	G. S. Wilson (1971)
Belmont Abbey (RC), Hereford	1926	220	£6,300	£3,825	Rev. D. C. Jenkins, OSB (1988)
Bembridge School, Isle of Wight ...	1919	173‡	£5,295°	£2,850°	J. High (1986)
Bentham School, N. Yorks	1726	254‡	£5,850	£2,955	J. E. Rigg (1988)
Bethany School, Kent	1866	255	£6,840	£4,440	W. M. Harvey (1988)

‡ Co-educational.   ° 1990 figure.   °° 1989 figure.

Name of School	Founded	No. of Pupils	Annual Fees B'ding	Annual Fees Day	Headmaster (With date of Appointment)
Box Hill School, Surrey	1959	280‡	£7,488	£4,362	Dr. R. A. S. Atwood (1987)
Carmel College (*Jewish*), Oxon.	1948	284‡	£10,125	£6,000	P. D. Skelker (1984)
Clayesmore School, Dorset	1896	300‡	£8,340	£5,880	D. J. Beeby (1986)
Cokethorpe School, Oxon.	1957	170	£7,320	£5,010	D. G. Crawford (1989)
Ewell Castle School, Surrey	1926	355†	......	£2,640°	R. A. Fewtrell (1983)
Friends' School, Essex	1702	280‡	£6,654	£3,972	Miss S. H. Evans (1989)
Fulneck Boys' School, W. Yorks.	1753	312†	£5,550°	£2,865°	I. D. Cleland (1980)
*Grenville College, Devon	1954	372	£7,200	£3,555	Dr. D. C. Powell-Price, TD (1975)
Halliford School, Middx.	1956	325†	......	£3,120	J. R. Crook (1984)
Keil School, Dumbarton	1915	209‡	£6,507	£3,450	C. H. Tongue (1984)
Kingham Hill School, Oxon.	1886	240	£6,600	£3,660	M. Payne (1990)
King's School, Gloucester	1541	530‡	£6,000	£3,000	Rev. A. C. Charters (1983)
King's School, Tynemouth	1860	500†	......	£2,550	W. T. Gillen (1987)
Kirkham Grammar School, Lancs.	1549	512‡	£4,080°	£2,220°	M. J. Summerlee (1972)
Lord Mayor Treloar College, Hants.	1908	283‡	£20,958	£15,717	H. Heard (1990)
Milton Abbey School, Dorset	1954	280	£8,568	......	R. H. Hardy (1987)
Oswestry School, Shropshire	1407	300‡	£6,675	£3,960	I. G. Templeton (1985)
Pierrepont School, Surrey	1947	265‡	£5,964°°	£3,579°°	J. D. Payne (1983)
The Purcell School (music), Middx.	1962	160‡	£10,464	£6,189	K. J. Bain (1983)
Rannoch School, Perthshire	1959	250‡	£7,260	£4,470	M. Barratt (1982)
Reading Blue Coat School, Berks.	1646	530†	£6,513	£3,570	Rev. A. C. E. Sanders (1974)
Rishworth School, W. Yorks.	1724	481‡	£6,690	£3,585	A. J. Morsley (1986)
Rougemont School, Gwent	1919	280‡	......	£2,720	R. Ham (1989)
Royal Hospital School, Ipswich	1712	660‡	£4,500	......	M. A. B. Kirk (1983)
Royal Russell School, Surrey	1853	430‡	£7,455	£3,915	R. D. Balaam (1981)
Royal School, Dungannon, N. Ireland	1614	600‡	£2,200	£1,600	P. D. Hewitt (1984)
Royal Wolverhampton School	1850	330‡	£6,330	£3,660	P. Gorring (1985)
Ruthin School, Clwyd	1574	170‡	£7,005	£4,575	F. R. Ullmann (1986)
St. David's College, Gwynedd	1965	250	£6,360°	£4,110°	B. T. C. Morris (1989)
Scarborough College, N. Yorks.	1898	436‡	£7,179	£3,864	D. S. Hempsall, ph.D. (1985)
Seaford College, W. Sussex	1884	400	£6,840	......	R. C. Hannaford (1990)
Shebbear College, Devon	1841	290†	£6,472	£3,582	R. J. Buley (1983)
Shiplake College, Oxon.	1959	335	£8,610	£5,655	N. V. Bevan (1988)
Sidcot School, Avon	1808	290‡	£7,185	£4,185	C. J. Greenfield (1986)
Stanbridge Earls School, Hants.	1952	165‡	£8,850	£6,600	H. Moxon (1984)
Warminster School, Wilts.	1707	330‡	£6,435	£3,870	T. D. Holgate (1990)
Wisbech GS, Cambs.	1379	600‡	......	£3,270	R. S. Repper (1988)

*Woodard Corporation School.   ‡Co-educational.   †Girls in VI form.   °1990 figure.   °°1989 figure.

GIRLS' SCHOOLS ASSOCIATION

THE GIRLS' SCHOOLS ASSOCIATION, 130 Regent Road, Leicester LE1 7PG. (Tel: 0533-541619).—*President* (1990–91), Miss E. Castle; *Sec.*, Miss A. C. Parkin.

Name of School	Founded	No. of Pupils	Annual Fees B'ding	Annual Fees Day	Headmistress (a) Headmaster (With date of Appointment)
Abbey School, Reading	1887	750	......	£3,090	Miss S. M. Hardcastle, MBE (1960)
Abbot's Hill, Herts.	1912	150	£7,500	£4,425	Mrs. J. Kingsley (1979)
Adcote School, Shropshire	1907	120	£6,450	£3,825	Mrs. S. B. Cecchet (1979)
Alice Ottley School, Worcester	1883	570	£6,210	£3,240	Miss C. Sibbit (1986)
All Hallows School, Suffolk	1864	97	£5,103°	£3,213°	Miss A. C. Harris (1984)
Amberfield School, Ipswich	1952	350	......	£2,775	Mrs. P. F. Webb (1979)
Ashford School, Kent	1910	542	£6,801	£3,893	Mrs. A. T. D. Macaire (1984)
Assumption School, N. Yorks.	1852	150	£5,940	£3,330	Mrs. V. Fisher (1990)
Atherley School, Southampton (CSC)	1926	320	......	£3,036	Mrs. M. Williams (1988)
Badminton School, Bristol	1858	300	£6,150°°	£3,450°°	(a) C. J. T. Gould (1981)
‡Bath High School	1875	389	......	£2,724	Miss M. A. Winfield (1985)
Battle Abbey School, E. Sussex	1912	147††	£6,870	£4,140	(a) D. J. A. Teall (1982)

‡Girls' Public Day School Trust.   CSC Church Schools Company.   ††Co-educational.   °°1989 figure.
°1990 figure.

Name of School	Founded	No. of Pupils	B'ding	Day	Headmistress (a) Headmaster (With date of Appointment)
Bedford High School	1882	793	£6,645	£3,465	Mrs. D. M. Willis (1987)
Bedgebury School, Kent	1860	330	£7,929	£4,800	Mrs. M. E. A. Kaye (1987)
‡Belvedere School, Liverpool	1880	426	......	£2,724	Miss S. Downs (1972)
‡Benenden School, Kent	1923	400	£9,450	......	Mrs. G. D. duCharme (1985)
Beresford House School, E. Sussex	1902	185	£7,500°	£3,945°	Miss S. B. Jackson (1988)
Berkhamsted School, Herts.	1888	461	£6,150	£3,423	Miss V. E. M. Shepherd (1980)
‡Birkenhead High School	1901	756	......	£2,724	Mrs. K. R. Irving (1986)
‡Blackheath High School, SE3	1880	361	......	£3,072	Miss R. K. Musgrave (1989)
Bolton School, Lancs.	1877	928	......	£2,937	Mrs. M. A. Spurr (1979)
Bradford Girls' Grammar School	1875	690	......	£2,796	Mrs. L. J. Warrington (1987)
‡Brighton and Hove High School	1876	554	£5,724	£2,724	Miss R. A. Woodbridge (1989)
Brigidine Convent, Windsor	1948	325	......	£2,985	Mrs. M. B. Cairns (1986)
‡Bromley High School, Kent	1883	519	......	£3,072	Mrs. E. J. Hancock (1989)
Bruton School, Somerset	1900	500	£4,740	£2,595	Mrs. J. M. Wade (1987)
Burgess Hill School, W. Sussex	1906	308	£6,558	£3,777	Mrs. B. H. Webb (1979)
Bury Grammar School, Lancs.	1884	813	......	£2,400	Miss J. M. Lawley (1987)
Casterton School, Cumbria	1823	340	£6,378	£3,924	(a) A. F. Thomas (1990)
‡Central Newcastle High School	1895	559	......	£2,724	Mrs. A. M. Chapman (1985)
Channing School, N6	1885	300	......	£4,020	Mrs. I. R. Raphael (1984)
‡Charters-Ancaster School, E. Sussex	1906	179	£5,910	£2,910	Mrs. K. Lewis (1990)
Cheltenham Ladies' College, Glos.	1853	850	£9,075	£5,760	Miss E. Castle (*Principal*) (1987)
City of London School for Girls, EC2	1894	550	......	£3,375°	Lady France (1986)
Clarendon School, Bedford	1898	198	£7,425	£4,305	Mrs. M. Crane (1990)
Clifton High School, Bristol	1877	457	£6,000	£3,075	Mrs. J. D. Walters (1985)
Cobham Hall, Kent	1962	285	£8,700	£5,820	Mrs. R. J. McCarthy (1989)
Collegiate School, Bristol	1902	105	£5,565	£2,655	Mrs. L. Sharland (1980)
Colston's Girls' School, Bristol	1891	642	......	£2,619	Mrs. J. P. Franklin (1989)
Combe Bank School, Kent	1868	250	£6,450	£3,900	Mrs. A. J. K. Austin (1982)
Commonweal Lodge School, Surrey	1916	200	......	£2,340	Miss J. M. Brown (1982)
Cranford House School, Oxon.	1931	118	......	£3,330	Miss T. A. Spencer (1980)
Croft House School, Dorset	1941	198	£7,050	£4,905	Mrs. S. Rawlinson (1985)
Croham Hurst School, Surrey	1899	352	......	£3,090	Miss J. M. Shelmerdine (1986)
‡Croydon High School, Surrey	1874	719	......	£3,072	Mrs. P. E. Davies (1990)
Dame Alice Harpur School, Bedford	1882	824	......	£2,487°	Mrs. R. Randle (1990)
Dame Allan's Girls' School, Newcastle upon Tyne	1705	450†	......	£2,550	(a) T. A. Willcocks (*Principal*) (1988)
Derby High School	1892	280	......	£3,285	(a) Dr. G. H. Goddard (1983)
Downe House, Berks.	1907	470	£8,760	£6,345	Miss S. Cameron (1989)
Dunottar School, Surrey	1926	309	......	£3,000	Miss J. Burnell (1985)
Durham High School	1884	287	......	£2,583	Miss B. E. Stephenson (1978)
Edgbaston Church of England College	1886	300	......	£2,775	(a) I. J. Walkley (1979)
Edgbaston High School	1876	540	......	£3,120	Mrs. S. J. Horsman (1987)
Edgehill College, Devon	1884	370	£6,810	£3,735	Mrs. E. M. Burton (1987)
Ellerslie, Worcs.	1922	240	£7,902	£5,148	Mrs. E. M. Baker (1988)
Elmslie Girls' School, Lancs.	1918	350	......	£2,574	Miss E. M. Smithies (1978)
Eothen School, Surrey (*CSC*)	1892	190	......	£3,366	Miss D. C. Raine (1973)
Farlington School, W. Sussex	1896	235	£6,450	£3,975	Mrs. P. Metham (1987)
Farnborough Hill, Hants.	1889	510	......	£3,189	Sr. E. McCormack (1988)
Farringtons, Kent	1911	300	£6,540	£3,579	Mrs. B. J. Stock (1986)
Felixstowe College, Suffolk	1929	300	£7,125°	£4,365°	Mrs. A. F. Woodings (1989)
Fernhill Manor School, Hants.	1890	187	£5,985	£3,810	(a) Rev. A. J. Folks (1985)
Francis Holland School, NW1	1878	350	......	£3,636	Mrs. P. H. Parsonson (1988)
Francis Holland School, SW1	1881	181	......	£3,888	Mrs. J. A. Anderson (1982)
Gateways School, Leeds	1941	220	......	£4,230°	Miss L. M. Brown (1984)
Godolphin School, Wilts.	1726	335	£7,920	£4,710	Mrs. H. Fender (1990)
Godolphin and Latymer School, W6	1905	700	......	£3,795	Miss M. Rudland (1986)
Greenacre School, Surrey	1933	375	£6,360	£3,345	Mrs. P. M. Wood (1990)
The Grove School, Hindhead, Surrey	1877	180	£5,743	£3,073	(a) C. Brooks (1984)
Guildford High School (*CSC*)	1888	446	......	£3,171°	J. E. Dutton (1977)
Haberdashers' Aske's School for Girls, Herts.	1873	835	......	£2,400°	Mrs. S. Wiltshire (1974)
Haberdashers' Monmouth School, Gwent	1891	535	£5,451	£2,886	Miss H. L. Gichard (1986)
Harrogate Ladies' College	1893	400	£6,690	£4,455	Mrs. J. C. Lawrance (1974)
Headington School, Oxford	1915	560	£6,228	£3,180	Miss E. M. Tucker (1982)
‡Heathfield School, Ascot, Berks.	1900	220	£9,150	......	Mrs. S. E. Watkins (1982)

‡Girls' Public Day School Trust.   *CSC* Church Schools Company.   †Boys in VI form.   °1990 figure.

Name of School	Founded	No. of Pupils	Annual Fees B'ding	Annual Fees Day	Headmistress (a) Headmaster (With date of Appointment)
‡Heathfield School, Pinner, Middx. . .	1900	350		£3,072	Mrs. J. Merritt (1988)
Hethersett Old Hall School, Norwich	1928	223	£5,670	£2,940	Mrs. V. M. Redington (1983)
Highclare School, W. Midlands	1932	340†	. . . . . .	£2,376	Mrs. C. A. Hanson (1974)
Hollygirt School, Nottingham	1877	320	. . . . . .	£2,580	Mrs. M. R. Banks (1985)
Holy Child School, Birmingham . . .	1933	223	£5,445	£2,895	Miss J. M. Johnson (1987)
Holy Trinity Convent School, Bromley	1886	380	. . . . . .	£2,670°	Sr. B. Wetz (1986)
Holy Trinity School, Kidderminster	1903	385	. . . . . .	£2,070°	Mrs. K. S. Butwilowska (1986)
Howell's School, Denbigh, Clwyd . . .	1859	300	£7,500	£4,692	Miss P. Dixon (1990)
‡Howell's School, Llandaff, Cardiff . .	1860	579	£5,724	£2,724	Miss J. P. Turner (1978)
Hull High School (CSC)	1890	232	£3,867	£2,232	Miss C. M. B. Radcliffe (1976)
Hulme Grammar School, Oldham . . .	1895	476	. . . . . .	£2,436	Mrs. A. Groom (1985)
Hunmanby Hall School, N. Yorks. . .	1928	210	£6,510	£3,510	Miss J. Rutherford (1986)
Huyton College, Liverpool	1894	207	£6,720	£2,955	Miss W. E. Edwards (1984)
‡Ipswich High School	1878	408	. . . . . .	£2,724	Miss P. M. Hayworth (1971)
James Allen's Girls' School, SE22 . .	1741	720	. . . . . .	£3,750	Mrs. B. Davies (1984)
School of Jesus and Mary, Suffolk . .	1860	186	. . . . . .	£2,790	Mrs. E. A. McKay (1982)
Kent College	1885	293	£7,395	£4,410	Miss B. Crompton (1990)
King Edward VI High School for Girls, Birmingham	1883	556	. . . . . .	£2,940	Miss E. W. Evans (1977)
King's HS for Girls, Warwick	1879	530	. . . . . .	£2,745	Mrs. J. M. Anderson (1987)
Kingsley School, Warwicks.	1884	412	£6,420	£2,970	Mrs. M. A. Webster (1988)
Lady Eleanor Holles School, Middx.	1711	620	. . . . . .	£3,375	Miss E. M. Candy (1981)
La Retraite School, Wilts.	1953	220	. . . . . .	£3,120	Mrs. M. Paisey (1986)
La Sagesse Convent High School, Newcastle upon Tyne	1906	500	. . . . . .	£2,176	Mrs. D. C. Parker (1988)
La Sagesse Convent School, Hants. .	1896	160	£4,116°	£1,900°	Sr. Thomas Cox (1977)
Lavant House School, W. Sussex	1952	150	£6,705	£3,990	Mrs. Y. Graham (1990)
Lawnside, Worcs.	1818	130	£7,860	£4,500	Miss J. Harvey (1991)
Leeds Girls' High School	1876	600	. . . . . .	£3,129	Miss P. A. Randall (1977)
Leicester High School	1906	300	. . . . . .	£2,550°	Mrs. D. Buchan (1982)
Loughborough High School	1850	530	£4,566	£2,790	Miss J. E. L. Harvatt (1978)
Luckley-Oakfield School, Berks. . . .	1895	290	£5,385	£3,375	(a) R. C. Blake (1984)
Malvern Girls' College, Worcs.	1893	520	£6,480°	£4,320°	Dr. V. B. Payne (1986)
Manchester High School	1874	737	. . . . . .	£2,775	Miss M. M. Moon (1983)
Maynard School, Exeter	1877	461	. . . . . .	£2,859	Miss F. Murdin (1980)
Merchant Taylors' School, Liverpool	1888	551	. . . . . .	£2,889	Miss E. J. Panton (1988)
Micklefield School, E. Sussex	1910	170	£7,200	£4,200	(a) E. Reynolds (1987)
Moira House School, E. Sussex	1875	300	£7,701	£3,771	(a) A. R. Underwood (1975)
More House School, SW1	1953	240	. . . . . .	£3,840	Mrs. M. E. Dodds (1989)
Moreton Hall, Shropshire	1913	350	£8,205	£5,445	(a) E. J. Cussell (1976)
Mount School, York	1831	275	£6,834	£4,575	Miss B. J. Windle (1986)
Newcastle upon Tyne Church HS . .	1885	370	. . . . . .	£2,700	Miss P. E. Davies (1974)
New Hall, Essex	1642	555	£8,175	£5,235	Sr. M. M. Horton (1986)
Northampton High School	1878	510	. . . . . .	£2,376°	Mrs. L. A. Mayne (1988)
North Foreland Lodge, Hants.	1909	187	£7,200	. . . . . .	Miss D. L. Matthews (1983)
North London Collegiate School . . .	1850	700	. . . . . .	£3,405	Mrs. J. L. Clanchy (1986)
Northwood College, Middx.	1878	478	£4,923°	£2,919°	Mrs. D. K. Dalton (1986)
‡Norwich High School	1875	609	. . . . . .	£2,724	Mrs. V. C. Bidwell (1985)
‡Nottingham High School	1875	801	. . . . . .	£2,724	Mrs. C. Bowering (1984)
‡Notting Hill and Ealing High School	1873	568	. . . . . .	£3,072	Mrs. C. J. Fitz (1983)
Oakdene, Beaconsfield, Bucks.	1911	240	£6,600	£3,870	Miss A. M. Tippett (1987)
Ockbrook School, Derby	1799	210	£4,461	£2,322	Dr. M. Rennie (1987)
Old Palace School, Surrey	1887	600	. . . . . .	£2,799	Miss K. L. Hilton (1974)
‡Oxford High School	1875	553	. . . . . .	£2,724	Mrs. J. Townsend (1981)
Palmers Green High School, N21 . . .	1905	130	. . . . . .	£2,790	Mrs. S. Grant (1989)
Park School, Somerset	1851	95	£5,280°	£3,150°	Mrs. M. J. Hannon (1987)
Parsons Mead, Surrey	1897	490	£6,405	£3,450	Miss E. B. Plant (1990)
Penrhos College, Clwyd	1880	280	£7,140	£4,890	(a) N. C. Peacock (1974)
Perse School for Girls, Cambridge . .	1881	550	. . . . . .	£3,144	Miss H. S. Smith (1989)
Pipers Corner School, Bucks.	1930	263	£6,456	£3,420	Dr. M. M. Wilson (1986)
Polam Hall, Co. Durham	1848	350	£6,180	£3,030	Mrs. H. C. Hamilton (1987)
‡Portsmouth High School	1882	504	. . . . . .	£2,724	Mrs. J. M. Dawtrey (1984)
Princess Helena College, Herts.	1820	183	£7,440	£5,250	Miss H. Davidson-Wall (1990)
Prior's Field, Surrey	1902	230	£6,225°	£3,885°	Mrs. J. M. McCallum (1987)
‡Putney High School, SW15	1893	605	. . . . . .	£3,072	Mrs. P. A. Penney (1987)

‡ Girls' Public Day School Trust. *CSC* Church Schools Company. † Boys in VI form. ° 1990 figure.

Name of School	Founded	No. of Pupils	B'ding	Day	Headmistress (a) Headmaster (With date of Appointment)
			Annual Fees		
Queen Anne's School, Berks.	1698	400	£8,136	£5,085	Miss A. M. Scott (1977)
*Queen Ethelburga's School, Harrogate	1912	135	£6,930	£4,080	Mrs. J. M. Town (1988)
*Queen Margaret's School, York	1901	360	£7,350	£4,650	(a) C. S. McGarrigle (1983)
Queen Mary School, Lytham, Lancs.	1930	600	......	£2,361	Miss M. C. Ritchie (1981)
Queen's College, W1	1848	410	£5,625	£3,825	Mrs. P. J. Fleming (1983)
Queen's Gate School, SW7.........	1891	170	......	£4,000	Mrs. A. M. Holyoak (1987)
Queen's School, Chester	1878	420	......	£2,568	Miss D. M. Skilbeck (1989)
Queenswood, Herts.	1894	389	£8,370	......	Mrs. A. M. B. Butler (1981)
Redland High School, Bristol	1882	437	......	£2,775	Mrs. C. Lear (1989)
Red Maids' School, Bristol	1634	470	£5,712	£2,856	Miss S. Hampton (1987)
Rickmansworth Masonic School, Herts.......................	1788	520	£5,760	£3,300	(a) D. L. Curtis (1980)
Roedean School, Brighton.........	1885	470	£9,585	......	Mrs. A. R. Longley (1984)
Rosemead, W. Sussex	1919	150	£6,675	£3,810	Mrs. J. Bevis (*Principal*) (1987)
Royal Naval School, Surrey	1840	297	£6,795	£4,650	Dr. J. L. Clough (1987)
Royal School, Bath	1864	320	£6,561°	£4,125°	Dr. J. McClure (1987)
Runton and Sutherland School, Norfolk	1911	170	£5,805	£3,186	Miss A. Ritchie (1990)
Rye St. Anthony School (*RC*), Oxford	1930	390	£5,796	£3,162	Miss A. M. Jones (1990)
Sacred Heart School (*RC*), Kent ...	1915	213	£7,935	£4,560	(a) Dr. J. A. Fallon (1979)
St. Albans High School, Herts.	1889	710	......	£3,375	Miss E. M. Diggory (1983)
St. Andrew's School, Bedford	1897	186	......	£2,190	Mrs. S. E. Cooke (1987)
St. Anne's School, Cumbria........	1863	300	£7,590	£5,190	(a) M. P. Hawkins (1986)
St. Antony's-Leweston School, Dorset	1891	400	£7,440	£4,725	Mrs. P. Cartwright (1983)
St. Audries School, Somerset	1906	150	£6,960	£4,065	Mrs. A. N. Smith (1988)
St. Brandon's School, Avon	1831	250	£6,885	£3,345	(a) Mrs. S. Cooke (Jan. 1991)
St. Catherine's School, Surrey	1885	455	£6,300	£3,840	(a) J. R. Palmer (1982)
*School of St. Clare, Penzance	1889	130	£5,901	£3,261	(a) I. Halford (1986)
St. David's School, Middx..........	1716	260	£5,769°	£3,348°	Mrs. J. G. Osborne (1985)
St. Dunstan's Abbey, Devon	1850	240	£4,845	£2,985	Miss H. L. Abley (1970)
St. Elphin's School, Derbys.	1844	250	£7,188	£4,185	(a) A. P. C. Pollard (1979)
St. Felix School, Suffolk	1897	350	£7,248	£4,482	Miss M. A. Claydon (1987)
St. Francis' College (*RC*), Herts.	1933	239	£7,005	£3,600	Mrs. J. Frith (1987)
S. Gabriel's School, Berks.........	1929	160	......	£3,273	(a) D. Cobb (1990)
St. George's School, Ascot, Berks. ..	1923	280	£8,850	£4,950	Mrs. A. M. Griggs (1989)
School of S. Helen and S. Katharine, Oxon.....................	1903	500	£4,560°	£2,385°	Miss Y. Paterson (1973)
St. Helen's School, Middx........	1899	568	£5,115°	£2,715°	Mrs. Y. A. Burne, PH.D. (1987)
*S. Hilary's School, Cheshire	1880	340	......	£2,400	Mrs. J. Tracey (1985)
St. Hilary's School, Sevenoaks, Kent	1942	200	......	£3,420	Mrs. P. Miles (1977)
St. James's and the Abbey, Worcs...	1896	168	£7,350	£4,899	Miss E. M. Mullenger (1986)
St. Joseph's Convent School (*RC*), Berks.......................	1909	536	......	£2,565°	Miss M. Ball (1986)
St. Joseph's School, Lincoln	1905	200	£5,550	£2,775	Mrs. A. Scott (1983)
St. Leonards-Mayfield School, E. Sussex	1850	552	£7,335	£4,890	Sr. J. Sinclair (1980)
St. Margaret's School, Bushey, Herts.....................	1749	380	£6,210	£3,870	Mrs. S. K. Law (1985)
*St. Margaret's School, Exeter	1904	380	£4,608	£2,817	Mrs. J. M. Giddings (1984)
St. Martin's School, Solihull	1941	260	......	£3,585	Mrs. S. J. Williams (1988)
School of St. Mary and St. Anne, Abbots Bromley, Staffs	1874	260	£8,120	£5,400	(a) A. Grigg (1989)
St. Mary's Hall, Brighton	1836	251	£6,996	£4,383	Mrs. M. T. Broadbent (1988)
St. Mary's School (*RC*), Ascot, Berks.......................	1885	320	£8,940	£5,364	Sr. M. M. Orchard (1982)
St. Mary's School, Calne, Wilts.....	1872	320	£8,175	£5,085	Miss D. H. Burns (1985)
St. Mary's School, Cambridge......	1898	460	£4,770	£2,673	Miss M. Conway (1989)
St. Mary's School, Colchester	1908	300	......	£2,655	Mrs. G. M. G. Mouser (1981)
St. Mary's School, Gerrards Cross ..	1872	206	......	£3,540	Mrs. J. P. G. Smith (1984)
St. Mary's School (*RC*), Shaftesbury	1945	310	£7,065	£4,425	Sr. M. Campion Livesey (1985)
St. Mary's School, Wantage, Oxon..	1873	300	£7,725	......	Mrs. P. H. Johns (1980)
*S. Michaels Burton Park, W. Sussex	1844	200	£7,440	£4,905	Miss V. G. Bolton (1988)
St. Michael's, Limpsfield, Surrey ...	1850	150	£6,720	£3,690	M. J. Hustler, PH.D. (1989)
St. Paul's Girls' School, W6	1904	615	......	£4,536	Mrs. H. Williams (*High Mistress*) (1989)

*Woodard Corporation School.   °1990 figure.

Name of School	Founded	No. of Pupils	Annual Fees B'ding	Day	Headmistress (a) Headmaster (With date of Appointment)
St. Stephen's College, Kent	1867	87	£5,490°°	£3,390°°	Miss M. de Villiers (1987)
St. Swithun's School, Winchester ..	1884	420	£8,100	£4,890	Miss J. E. Jefferson (1986)
St. Teresa's Convent School, Dorking	1928	340	£6,705	£3,426	(a) L. Allan (1987)
Selwyn School, Glos.	—	262	£5,025	£2,925	(a) A. Beatson (1990)
‡Sheffield High School	1878	510	......	£2,724	Mrs. M. A. Houston (1989)
Sherborne School for Girls, Dorset .	1899	464	£8,280	£5,520	Miss J. M. Taylor (1985)
‡Shrewsbury High School	1885	369	......	£2,724	Miss S. Gardner (1990)
Sir William Perkins's School, Surrey	1725	495		£2,745	Mrs. A. F. Darlow (1982)
‡South Hampstead High School, NW3	1876	514	......	£3,072	Mrs. D. A. Burgess (1975)
Stamford High School, Lincs.	1876	745	£5,880	£2,940	Miss G. K. Bland (1978)
Stonar School, Wilts.	1921	395	£6,825	£3,021	Mrs. S. Hopkinson (1985)
Stover School, Devon	1932	265	£5,265°	£2,742°	Mrs. W. E. Lunel (1984)
Stratford House School, Kent	1912	250	......	£3,255	Mrs. A. A. Williamson (1974)
‡Streatham Hill and Clapham High School, SW2	1887	384	......	£3,072	Miss G. M. Ellis (1979)
Sunderland Church High School (*CSC*)	1884	223†	......	£3,018	Mrs. M. Thrush (1980)
Surbiton High School (*CSC*), Surrey	1884	457	......	£3,390	Mrs. R. A. Thynne (1979)
‡Sutton High School, Surrey	1884	577	......	£3,072	Miss A. E. Cavendish (1980)
‡Sydenham High School, SE26	1887	436	......	£3,072	Mrs. G. Baker (1988)
Talbot Heath, Dorset	1886	475	£5,395	£2,809	Miss C. E. Austin-Smith (1976)
Teesside High School, Cleveland ...	1970	540	......	£2,850	Mrs. H. Coles (1982)
Tormead School, Surrey	1905	365	......	£3,435	Mrs. J. Crouch-Smith (1977)
Truro High School	1880	408†	£4,905°	£2,715°	Mrs. J. F. Marshall (1982)
*Tudor Hall School, Oxon.	1850	250	£7,950	£5,070	Miss N. Godfrey (1984)
Upper Chine, Isle of Wight	1799	186	£5,790°	£3,030°	Dr. H. Harvey (1990)
Ursuline Convent School, Kent	1904	302	£6,738	£3,651	Sr. M. Murphy (1977)
Ursuline High School, Ilford	1903	410	......	£3,060	Miss J. Reddington (1990)
Wadhurst College, E. Sussex	1930	186	£7,485	£4,710	(a) R. Purdom (1989)
Wakefield Girls' High School	1878	900	......	£2,520	Mrs. P. A. Langham (1987)
Walthamstow Hall, Kent	1838	400	£7,635	£4,140	Mrs. J. S. Lang (1984)
Wentworth Milton Mount, Dorset .	1962	328	£6,465	£4,020	Miss S. Coe (Jan. 1991)
Westfield School, Newcastle upon Tyne	1962	212	......	£2,958	(a) J. S. Taylor (1990)
West Heath, Kent	1867	169	£8,250	£5,790	Mrs. D. Cohn-Sherbok (1988)
Westholme School, Lancs.	1923	600	......	£2,415	Mrs. L. Croston (1988)
Westonbirt, Glos.	1928	275	£8,034	£5,169	Mrs. G. Hylson-Smith (1986)
Westwood House School, Peterborough	1939	240	£5,640	£2,805	Mrs. A. J. V. Storey (1977)
‡Wimbledon High School, SW19	1880	464	......	£3,072	Mrs. R. A. Smith (1982)
Wispers School, Surrey	1946	190	£5,775	£3,600	(a) L. H. Beltran (1978)
Withington Girls' School, Manchester....................	1890	460	......	£2,715	Mrs. M. Kenyon (1986)
Woldingham School, Surrey	1842	446	£7,935	£4,800	Dr. P. Dineen (1985)
Wroxall Abbey School, Warwick ..	1872	130	£6,570	£3,876	Mrs. I. D. M. Iles (1980)
Wychwood School, Oxford	1897	160	£5,445	£3,210	Mrs. M. L. Duffill (1981)
Wycombe Abbey School, Bucks.	1896	490	£9,072	......	Mrs. J. M. Goodland (1989)
Wykeham House School, Fareham, Hants	1913	190	......	£2,766	Mrs. E. M. Moore (1983)
York College for Girls (*CSC*)	1908	250	......	£3,070	Mrs. J. L. Clare (1982)
Scotland					
Laurel Bank School, Glasgow	1903	380	......	£2,619°	Miss L. G. Egginton (1984)
Mary Erskine School, Edinburgh ..	1694	560	£5,868	£3,036	P. F. J. Tobin (*Principal*) (1989)
Oxenfoord Castle School, Midlothian	1931	70	£7,026	£2,595	Miss M. Carmichael (1979)
Park School, Glasgow	1880	251	......	£2,673	Mrs. M. E. Myatt (1986)
St. Denis and Cranley School, Edinburgh...................	1858	200	£6,360	£3,165	Mrs. J. M. Munro (1984)
St. George's School, Edinburgh	1888	570	£6,180	£3,150	Mrs. J. G. Scott (1986)
St. Leonards School, St. Andrews ..	1877	363	£8,850	£4,650	Mrs. L. E. James (1988)
St. Margaret's School, Aberdeen ...	1846	216	......	£2,508	Miss L. M. Ogilvie (1989)
St. Margaret's School, Edinburgh ..	1890	500	£6,195	£3,095	Mrs. M. J. Cameron (1984)
Wellington School for Girls, Ayr ...	1849	300	£5,850	£2,895	Mrs. D. A. Gardner (1988)
Channel Islands					
The Ladies' College, Guernsey	1872	325	......	£1,425	Miss J. Honey (1976)

‡ Girls' Public Day School Trust, 26 Queen Anne's Gate, SW1H 9AN.   * Woodard Corporation School.
CSC Church Schools Company, 1A Doughty Street, WC1N 2PH.   † Boys in VI form.   ° 1990 figure.
°° 1989 figure.

EVENTS OF THE YEAR
SEPT. 1, 1989—AUG. 31, 1990

ROYAL HOUSE

(1989). Sept. 5. The Prince of Wales attended the Rare Breeds Survival Trust conference at Warwick University. 24. The Duke of Edinburgh visited the Royal Marines School of Music, Deal, following an IRA bomb attack there.

Oct. 8. The Queen and the Duke of Edinburgh left Heathrow Airport to visit Singapore and attend the Commonwealth Heads of Government conference in Malaysia. 12. The Duchess of York opened the Food for Thought Gallery at the Science Museum. 13. Prince Edward attended a greyhound race meeting at Canterbury in aid of the Royal Marines School of Music disaster fund. 20. Prince Edward attended the memorial service for Lord Olivier at Westminster Abbey. 22. The Queen arrived at Heathrow Airport from Malaysia. 24. The Queen started the XIVth Commonwealth Games relay from the forecourt of Buckingham Palace.

Nov. 2. The Prince and Princess of Wales left Heathrow Airport for Indonesia and Hong Kong. 10. The Princess of Wales arrived at Gatwick Airport from Hong Kong. 11. The Queen, accompanied by other members of the Royal Family, attended the Royal British Legion Festival of Remembrance at the Royal Albert Hall. 12. The Queen and the Duke of Edinburgh, along with the Duke of York, laid wreaths at the Cenotaph on Remembrance Day. 13. The Prince of Wales arrived at RAF Lyneham from Hong Kong. 20. The Queen and the Duke of Edinburgh attended the Royal Variety Performance at the London Palladium. The Prince and Princess of Wales attended a dinner in their honour at 10 Downing Street. 21. The Queen opened the new session of Parliament. 22. The Duke of Edinburgh attended the memorial service at Canterbury Cathedral for those who died in the bomb attack at the Royal Marines School of Music in Deal.

Dec. 2. The Princess Royal attended a greyhound gala night at Blunsdon Stadium, Swindon. 5. The Duchess of York presented the *Times*/Shell UK Museum Awards at the National Gallery. 8. The Prince of Wales represented the Queen at the Sovereign's Parade at the Royal Military Academy, Sandhurst. 11. The Princess of Wales presented the 1989 ABSA/*Daily Telegraph* awards for Business Sponsors of the Arts at the Royal National Theatre.

(1990). Jan. 12. The Princess of Wales opened the new headquarters of Child-Line,

London. 21. Prince Edward left Heathrow Airport for New Zealand, where he opened the Commonwealth Games on behalf of the Queen. 30. The Queen and the Duke of Edinburgh left Heathrow Airport for New Zealand, to visit the Commonwealth Games.

Feb. 6. Prince Edward arrived at Heathrow Airport from Australia. 7. The Princess of Wales opened the Natural History Museum's Activity Centre. 18. The Queen and the Duke of Edinburgh arrived at Heathrow Airport from New Zealand. The Princess Royal left RAF Lyneham for a visit to The Gambia, Senegal and Mali. 27. The Princess Royal arrived at RAF Lyneham at the conclusion of her visit to West Africa.

March 1. The Prince and Princess of Wales visited Clwyd to meet people affected by the severe flooding at Towyn and those involved in the rescue and evacuation operations. 12. The Queen and the Duke of Edinburgh attended the Commonwealth Day Observance Service in Westminster Abbey. 15. The Prince and Princess of Wales left Heathrow Airport for a visit to Nigeria and the Republic of Cameroon. 19. The Queen and the Duke of Edinburgh attended the Royal Film Performance of *Always* at the Odeon, Leicester Square. 23. The Duchess of York gave birth to a 7lb 1½oz baby daughter at the Portland Hospital, London. On March 30 it was announced that the Princess would be called Eugenie Victoria Helena. 25. The Princess Royal visited Berne, Switzerland, for a meeting of the Fédération Équestre Internationale. 27. The Prince of Wales attended the International Council of United World Colleges in Duino, Italy.

April 3. The President of India arrived at Gatwick Airport for a State visit. 6. The President of India left Buckingham Palace at the conclusion of his State visit. The Queen and the Duke of Edinburgh attended a concert at the Royal Albert Hall to mark the 50th anniversary of the Battle of Britain. 10. The Queen received the President of Colombia and his wife at Windsor Castle. The Princess Royal gave a speech at the World Ministerial Drug Summit in London. 25. The Queen and the Duke of Edinburgh laid a wreath at the Cenotaph to mark the 75th anniversary of ANZAC Day. The Prince of Wales launched The Volunteers, a national scheme of community service for young people. 28. The Queen unveiled a statue of Field Marshal the Viscount Slim at Whitehall, London.

May 16. The Princess of Wales attended a National Aids Trust conference at the

Commonwealth Institute. **17.** The Prince of Wales opened the Valuing the Rainforest conference at the Royal Geographical Society, London. **18.** The Queen unveiled the Queen Caroline Memorial in Hyde Park, London. The Princess Royal opened the National Garden Festival 1990 in Gateshead. **24.** The Princess Royal left RAF Lyneham for the Soviet Union. **29.** The Queen, with the Duke of Edinburgh and the Queen Mother, visited Eton College to mark the 550th anniversary of its foundation.

June 6. The Queen, accompanied by other members of the Royal Family, visited Epsom Races. The Princess Royal arrived at RAF Lyneham from the Soviet Union. **7.** The Queen attended the annual general meeting of the National Federation of Women's Institutes at the Royal Albert Hall, London. **11.** The Queen Mother opened the Courtauld art galleries at Somerset House, London. **13.** The Queen and the Duke of Edinburgh attended a reception at the Royal Albert Hall to mark the 50th anniversary of General de Gaulle's rallying call to the Free French and the 45th anniversary of the founding of the Association des Francais Libres. **16.** The Queen, accompanied by other members of the Royal Family, was present at the Queen's Birthday Parade on Horse Guards Parade, London. **19.** The Queen, accompanied by other members of the Royal Family, visited Ascot Races. **25.** The Queen and the Duke of Edinburgh left Heathrow Airport on a State visit to Iceland.

July 7. The Princess Royal visited the Cutty Sark Tall Ships Race at Plymouth. The Prince of Wales attended the 50th Anniversary Airborne Forces Pageant of the Parachute Regiment at Rushmoor Arena, Aldershot. **10.** The Princess Royal attended the Hampton Court Palace International Flower Show. **12.** The Queen Mother attended a reception at the Guildhall in London to mark the 50th anniversary of the Battle of Britain. **18.** The Queen and the Duke of Edinburgh attended the 50th anniversary parade of the Dunkirk Veterans' Association at Aldershot. **28.** The Duchess of York opened the 1990 World Stoke Mandeville Wheelchair Games.

Aug. 2. The Duke of Edinburgh left Heathrow Airport for Sweden, to attend the World Equestrian Games. **3.** The Queen opened an exhibition, '90 Memorable Years', in the Guildhall, Windsor, to mark the 90th birthday of the Queen Mother. **5.** The Queen Mother visited the '90 Memorable Years' exhibition at the Guildhall, Windsor. **8.** The Queen embarked in HMY *Britannia* and sailed for Scotland.

BRITISH POLITICS

(1989). Sept. 9. The Prime Minister (Margaret Thatcher) vetoed plans for a government-funded survey of sexual habits in Britain. **10.** The Social and Liberal Democrats conference began in Brighton. On Sept. 12 delegates voted in favour of a defence policy that included the retention of the Trident missile system. **16.** Lord Trafford, the Minister of State for Health, died following a short illness. **21.** The Green Party conference began in Wolverhampton. **24.** The Social Democratic Party conference began in Scarborough. On Sept. 26 the party leader, Dr David Owen, said that the SDP would be willing to enter into a coalition with either major party if the next general election produced a hung parliament. **27.** The Secretary of State for Energy (John Wakeham) announced that the proposed privatization of electricity would include the country's nuclear power stations.

Oct. 1. The Labour Party conference began in Brighton. On Oct. 2 the conference accepted the policy review statement on multilateral nuclear disarmament, but delegates went against the advice of the party leadership by voting for major cuts in defence spending. On Oct. 5 the delegates voted not to adopt proportional representation. **10.** The Conservative Party conference began in Blackpool. On Oct. 12 the Chancellor of the Exchequer (Nigel Lawson) told the conference that there was no alternative to high interest rates in the battle against inflation. **25.** The Foreign Secretary (John Major) announced that the British and Hong Kong Governments had reached agreement on the forcible repatriation of Vietnamese refugees. **26.** Nigel Lawson resigned from office as Chancellor of the Exchequer; he was replaced by John Major. The Home Secretary, Douglas Hurd, moved to the Foreign Office to replace Mr. Major, and the chief whip, David Waddington, moved to the Home Office as Home Secretary.

Nov. 9. The Energy Secretary (John Wakeham) announced that the Government had decided to abandon its plans to privatize the nuclear power industry. **15.** The Chancellor of the Exchequer (John Major) presented his Autumn Statement to the House of Commons. **21.** Proceedings in the House of Commons were televised for the first time. **28.** A Conservative back bench MP, Sir Anthony Meyer, announced that he would stand as a candidate in the annual ballot for the leadership of the Conservative Party.

Dec. 4. Under questioning by the House of Commons Public Accounts committee, the Permanent Secretary at the Department of Trade and Industry (Sir Peter Gregson) admitted that the Government had not revealed the £38 million cash inducement in the sale of the Government-owned Rover Group to British Aerospace due to concern that Britain's relationship with the European Commission would be damaged. The concessions had been made after it became clear that British Aerospace was not prepared to buy the Rover Group under the terms approved by the European Commission. 5. In the ballot for leadership of the Conservative Party, the Prime Minister received 314 votes and Sir Anthony Meyer 33 votes. There were 24 spoilt papers and 3 non-voters. 6. The Government announced the appointment of Robert Reid as the new chairman of British Rail. 17. The Labour Party announced its support for the European Commission's Social Charter. 19. The Government announced that it would pay a total of £150 million in compensation to small investors who lost their savings in the collapse of the Barlow Clowes company. The Conservative MP for Mid-Staffordshire, John Heddle, was found dead in his car near Canterbury.

(1990). Jan. 3. Norman Fowler, the Secretary of State for Employment, resigned from the Cabinet for family reasons. He was replaced as Employment Secretary by Michael Howard, previously Minister of State at the Department of the Environment. 30. The Government published a Public Expenditure White Paper.

Feb. 6. The Government published a White Paper, *Crime, Justice and Protecting the Public.* 13. The Minister of Agriculture, Fisheries and Food (John Gummer) announced that the Government would be increasing the amount of compensation paid to owners of cattle affected by bovine spongiform encephalopathy (BSE), also known as 'mad cow disease'.

March 4. The Secretary of State for Wales (Peter Walker) announced that he would leave the Cabinet in May, and that he would not contest the next general election. 7. The Conservative MP for Winchester, John Browne, was suspended from the House of Commons for four weeks for failing to declare all his business interests. Mr. Browne subsequently announced that he would not stand for election at the next general election. 11. The spring conference of the Social and Liberal Democrat Party began in Cardiff. The conference closed on March 12. 14. Dick Douglas, MP for Dunfermline West, formally resigned the Labour whip. 20. The Chancellor of the Exchequer presented his Budget statement to the House of Commons. 22. The Labour candidate, Sylvia Heal, won the by-election in Mid-Staffordshire, overturning a Conservative majority of 14,654. 27. The actress Glenda Jackson was chosen as the Labour Party candidate for Hampstead and Highgate at the next general election. 28. The secretary-general of the Arts Council, Luke Rittner, resigned over Government plans to devolve many of the Arts Council's responsibilities.

April 3. The Environment Secretary (Chris Patten) announced that 20 local authorities would be charge-capped, i.e. have a limit set by the Government on the community charge they intended to levy. On April 10 Mr Patten added Lambeth Council in London to the list. 4. Fourteen life peerages were conferred by the Queen to increase the number of working peers in the House of Lords. 18. In a statement to the House of Commons the Trade and Industry Secretary (Nicholas Ridley) confirmed the Government's belief that steel cylinders detained by Customs officers on Teesside on April 10 were part of a 'supergun'. Mr. Ridley also confirmed that the DTI had been contacted in 1988 by the two engineering firms that manufactured the cylinders but that it had been decided at the time that export licences were not necessary. 20. The Commons trade and industry select committee announced that it would conduct an inquiry into the affair. 24. MPs voted in the House of Commons against a proposal to reduce the abortion limit to 22 weeks.

May 3. Local elections took place in England, Scotland and Wales. 4. David Hunt took over as Secretary of State for Wales in place of Peter Walker, who had announced his resignation in March. 10. The Scottish Conservative Party conference began in Aberdeen. 18. A by-election in Upper Bann, Northern Ireland, was won by the Official Unionist candidate David Trimble. 24. The Labour party published its policy review document *Looking to the Future,* the result of a process begun at the party's 1987 annual conference. A by-election in Bootle, Merseyside, was won by the Labour candidate, Mike Carr.

June 3. The Social Democratic Party was wound up after its leader, Dr. David Owen, and his two fellow MPs said it was no longer large enough to continue as a national force. 12. The Prime Minister told the House of Commons that the appointment of former Cabinet ministers to posts in companies they had helped to privatize should be left to the discretion of the individuals concerned. 15. The High Court ruled that the government had acted lawfully in community charge capping 21 local authorities in April, and had not acted arbitrarily, as had been claimed by 19 of the councils. 18. The Defence Secretary (Tom King) announced that an order for 33 Tornado jets had been cancelled, a saving of more than £600 million in defence expenditure. 21. The Home Secretary (David

Waddington) accepted the recommendations of the Calcutt committee report into press invasion of privacy. The major recommendation of the report was that the Press Council should be replaced by a non-statutory Press Complaints Commission to adjudicate on complaints from the public and implement a new 18-point code of practice.

July 9. Anthony Everitt was appointed secretary-general of the Arts Council. **12.** The Trade and Industry Secretary, Nicholas Ridley, was censured severely by members of all parties over remarks about Germany that he made in an interview for the *Spectator*. On July 14 Mr. Ridley resigned from the Cabinet. Peter Lilley, Financial Secretary to the Treasury, replaced him as Secretary of State for Trade and Industry. **20.** Mike Carr, elected as Labour MP for Bootle in May, died suddenly. **23.** Mrs. Thatcher announced ministerial changes involving 31 junior ministers. **25.** The Defence Secretary (Tom King) announced that the strength of the three armed services would be cut by 18 per cent and the British Army of the Rhine force halved within five years.

Aug. 6. Patrick Wall, the Labour MP for Bradford North, died after a long illness.

IRELAND

(1989). Sept. 8. The wife of a British soldier, Heidi Hazell, was shot dead in her car in Unna Messen, West Germany. The IRA said that it was responsible for the shooting. **14.** The Royal Ulster Constabulary appointed John Stevens, the deputy chief constable of Cambridgeshire, to investigate the suspected leaking of information by RUC officers. **22.** An IRA bomb attack on a Royal Marines base in Deal, Kent, killed ten people. The base, the home of the Royal Marines School of Music, was serviced by unarmed, private security guards. On Sept. 25 the Prime Minister (Margaret Thatcher) announced a review of security at military establishments.

Oct. 8. Police officers arrested 28 members of the Ulster Defence Regiment as part of their investigation into collusion between security force personnel and loyalist paramilitaries. **12.** The Irish Government announced that no charges were to be brought against Patrick Ryan in connection with allegations of his involvement in acts of terrorism. **13.** The IRA claimed to have obtained documents giving details of British intelligence operations intended to recruit as agents Irish expatriates in Europe. **23.** The West German federal prosecutor announced that he would apply for the extradition of three suspected IRA terrorists held in France. The three, along with two others held in France, had been indicted in West Germany

for terrorist activities. **26.** An RAF corporal, Maheshkuran Islania, and his six-month-old daughter were shot dead near RAF Wildenrath, West Germany. The IRA claimed responsibility.

Nov. 3. The Secretary of State for Northern Ireland (Peter Brooke) said that the IRA looked unbeatable by military means and refused to rule out talks with Sinn Fein if violence were to cease. **14.** An IRA car bomb was discovered in London beneath a car belonging to an airline executive. The police believed that the bomb was planted beneath the wrong vehicle and was aimed at Lt.-Gen. Sir David Ramsbotham who lived nearby. **18.** Three paratroopers were killed in an IRA bomb attack near Mayobridge, Co. Down. A military police sergeant and his wife were injured when an IRA bomb exploded in their car in Colchester, Essex.

Dec. 7. An IRA bomb exploded in Lisburn, Co. Antrim, injuring 20 people. **13.** Two soldiers died and another was seriously injured in a gun and bomb attack on a border checkpoint in Co. Fermanagh. **21.** Police arrested two Irishmen in west Wales and seized a large quantity of Semtex explosive, firearms and bomb-making equipment.

(1990). Jan. 2. A taxi-driver was killed by an IRA car bomb in east Belfast. **8.** Security forces in Belfast arrested more than a dozen people suspected of being members of a loyalist paramilitary organization, the Ulster Defence Association. Daniel McBrearty was cleared by a London court of charges of handling explosives, but was ordered to leave mainland Britain by the Home Secretary (David Waddington) and was excluded from the country for three years under the Prevention of Terrorism Act 1989. **10.** Danny Morrison, vice-president of Sinn Fein, appeared in court in Belfast charged with murder, false imprisonment and membership of the IRA. **13.** Undercover British troops shot dead three unarmed men robbing a betting shop in the Falls Road, west Belfast. **30.** The Government admitted that a policy of spreading disinformation had been carried out in Northern Ireland during the 1970s. **31.** Four members of the Ulster Defence Association were jailed for a total of 36 years for offences including blackmail and intimidation.

Feb. 20. Two army personnel were injured when an IRA bomb blew up a military vehicle in Leicester. **23.** Robert Campbell, an escapee from Crumlin Road jail, Belfast, failed to appear in court in Dublin to face extradition proceedings.

March 6. A cache of bomb-making material was discovered in the Ardoyne area of Belfast. **8.** A part-time member of the Ulster Defence

Regiment was killed in an ambush by IRA gunmen near Donaghmore, Co. Tyrone. **13.** The Irish Supreme Court decided not to extradite two convicted terrorists, Dermot Finucane and James Clarke, to Northern Ireland. **16.** The IRA sent a demand for £2 million to the Bank of Ireland, threatening to attack buildings and personnel. **20.** Two IRA bombs exploded inside the Short's missile factory in Belfast, injuring five workers. **21.** The Home Secretary announced an inquiry into the case of six Irishmen, known as the 'Birmingham Six', convicted of bomb outrages in Birmingham in 1975. **28.** The Irish People's Liberation Organization (IPLO) was proscribed by the Secretary of State for Northern Ireland.

April 6. The Irish Supreme Court decided not to extradite the former Republican MP Owen Carron to Northern Ireland, where he is wanted in connection with arms possession offences. **9.** Four soldiers were killed in an IRA bomb attack near Downpatrick, Co. Down. **27.** The Court of Appeal freed three Irish people, Martina Shanahan, Finbar Cullen and John McCann, who were convicted in 1988 of conspiracy to murder Tom King, who was at that time Secretary of State for Northern Ireland. The Appeal Court judges ruled that comments by Mr King at the time had prevented a fair trial. An Irish businessman, Kenneth Graham, was killed by an IRA car-bomb in Kilkeel, Co. Down.

May 4. An attempt by the IRA to place two bombs at British Army quarters in Hanover, West Germany, was foiled by a civilian guard. **14.** Seven people were injured when an IRA bomb exploded outside an army education office at Eltham, London. **16.** One soldier was killed and another seriously injured when an IRA bomb blew up a minibus outside an army careers information office in Wembley, London. **17.** A report by John Stevens, deputy chief constable of Cambridgeshire, found that some members of the security forces 'gravely abused their positions of trust' by supplying information to loyalist terrorists. **22.** An Irishman was arrested in Wood Green, London, after guns were found in his car. **28.** IRA terrorists killed two London-based Australian lawyers on holiday in Roermond, the Netherlands. The IRA said the men were mistaken for British Army personnel.

June 1. Three off-duty soldiers were shot by two men at Lichfield City station, Staffordshire. One of the soldiers later died. The IRA admitted to the shootings. A British Army officer was shot and killed by the IRA in Dortmund. **4.** Police detained six men under the Prevention of Terrorism Act. **6.** A former RUC reservist was killed by an IRA boobytrap bomb in Belfast. **9.** An IRA bomb exploded at a Territorial Army unit in Islington, London,

injuring 15 people who were attending a dinner. **12.** An IRA bomb damaged the former home at West Green, Hampshire, of Lord McAlpine, a former treasurer of the Conservative Party. No one was injured. **16.** Three suspected IRA members engaged in target practice were discovered by Belgian farmers in woods near the Dutch border. Police arrested one of the suspects, Donna Maguire, but two men escaped. One was later arrested in the Netherlands. **25.** A bomb exploded at the Carlton Club, London, injuring eight people. The IRA admitted responsibility for the attack. **31.** Two policemen were shot dead by IRA gunmen in Belfast.

July 20. An IRA bomb exploded at the Stock Exchange, London, causing extensive damage. **24.** A landmine planted by a road in Co. Armagh killed three policemen and a Roman Catholic nun. **30.** The Conservative MP for Eastbourne, Ian Gow, was killed outside his home in East Sussex by an IRA car bomb.

Aug. 6. An IRA bomb attached to the car of an American businesswoman in London fell off and was found and defused before it could explode. Police believe that IRA terrorists mistook the car for that of Lord Armstrong of Ilminster. **13.** A bomb was defused in the garden of General Sir Anthony Farrar-Hockley, a former army commander in Northern Ireland. **16.** Two men, Terence McGeough and Gerard Hanratty, went on trial in West Germany on charges linked to attacks on British army bases.

ACCIDENTS AND DISASTERS

(1989). Sept. 2. A Boeing 737 disappeared in the Brazilian Amazon region with 54 people on board. On Sept. 5 the aircraft was found with 46 passengers alive. **10.** Following a collision between a Romanian ship and a Bulgarian tugboat on the Danube, 164 people were missing from the Romanian vessel. **12.** Thunderstorms and flash floods hit southern England and one man was killed by lightning. **17.** Two oil tankers collided off the east coast of Britain causing a 20-mile oil slick. The north-east Caribbean was hit by Hurricane Hugo, leaving at least five people dead. **25.** Two people died on a Danish ferry, *Tor Scandinavia*, in a fire on the ship during a voyage to England.

Oct. 18. An earthquake struck San Francisco, USA, killing at least 273 people and injuring 650 others. The earthquake lasted for 15 seconds and measured 6·9 on the Richter scale. On Oct. 21 rescue workers freed a man from the wreckage of a double-decker highway. **22.** Storms in southern England killed at least thirteen people. On Oct. 29 storms in south Wales and the west of England killed eight people.

Nov. 13. Five people were killed and many injured in a series of road accidents caused by dense fog in southern and central England.

Dec. 16. A Scottish fishing boat, *Destiny*, was wrecked during fierce storms and its six-man crew was lost. **18.** Five people were killed when a helicopter crashed shortly after taking off from Biggin Hill airport, Kent.

(1990). Jan. 25. At least 32 people died as hurricane-force winds struck southern Britain. By Jan. 26 the death toll had reached 47. **30.** A Greek cargo ship, *Flag Theofano*, sank off the Isle of Wight with the loss of its crew of nineteen.

Feb. 4. Heavy rain caused flooding in several parts of Britain. **12.** Fire destroyed the Savoy Theatre in the Strand, London. **26.** The town of Towyn, Clwyd, was evacuated after huge waves, driven by heavy winds, breached the sea wall and flooded most of the town.

March 11. Three young boys died in Cleehill, Shropshire, after accidentally locking themselves in a disused freezer. **20.** Six people were injured by an explosion at an oil refinery in Ellesmere Port, Cheshire.

April 2. An earthquake affected large areas of Britain. It was centred on Wrexham, North Wales, and measured 5·2 on the Richter scale. **30.** An RAF Shackleton aircraft crashed into a hillside in South Harris, in the Outer Hebrides, killing all ten crew members.

June 3. A coach carrying British holiday-makers crashed near Joigny in France, killing eleven people and injuring 60 others.

Aug. 1. A commuter train travelling from Tonbridge to Reading crashed into another train at Reading station, injuring 41 people. **22.** Two trains collided head-on near Manchester, injuring 26 people.

CRIMES, TRIALS, ETC.

(1989). Sept. 3. Four people were injured by a bomb outside the Liberty store in London. The bomb was believed to have been planted in protest at the sale of *The Satanic Verses* at a bookshop in the store. **5.** Alison Anders and Royston Allen were each jailed for five years at Aberdeen High Court for attempting to defraud Britoil of £23 million. **14.** Anthony Hughes, wanted for questioning over the murder of a police inspector, shot himself dead at Barnsley. **15.** The defence manufacturers Ferranti called in the accountants Coopers and Lybrand to investigate 'signifi-

cant irregularities' in their accounts. On Sept. 18 the Serious Fraud Office was called in to investigate suspect contracts which may have cost Ferranti up to £200 million.

Oct. 10. Detectives discovered a large quantity of explosives on Hampstead Heath, London. **12.** A police officer, PC Peter Anderson, was jailed for seven years for the rape of a woman in his patrol car. **17.** Paul Downs was convicted of swindling nearly £500,000 from five women and was sentenced to five years imprisonment at Southwark Crown Court.

Nov. 8. Edward Browning was convicted at Shrewsbury Crown Court of the murder of Marie Wilks on the M50 motorway, and was sentenced to life imprisonment. **9.** The City of London Fraud Squad charged with fraud two stockbroking companies, UBS Phillips and Drew Securities, and 11 individuals who work in the City. The charges followed investigations into Blue Arrow's rights issue to finance the takeover of Manpower in 1987. **13.** A gang broke into a Post Office sorting office in East London and stole registered mail estimated to be worth up to £4 million. **16.** Three Chelsea football supporters who were jailed two years ago for plotting violence were cleared by the Court of Appeal after it was revealed that evidence had been falsified.

Dec. 11. At Stafford Crown Court Leslie Wood was jailed for ten years for the sexual abuse of a four-year-old boy. The judge, Mr. Justice McCullough, had delayed sentencing to ensure that his own anger did not affect his decision. **12.** A motorist, Jeremy Smith, was banned from driving for a record 30 years at Leicester Magistrates Court after being convicted of drink-driving offences for the eighth time. **21.** Rene Black, the mastermind behind a conspiracy to import drugs into Britain, was jailed for 15 years at Southwark Crown Court.

(1990). Jan. 9. The Labour MP Ron Brown was found guilty of causing criminal damage to his ex-lover's flat, and was fined £1,000 at Lewes Crown Court. **11.** A 36-hour-old baby girl, Alexandra Griffiths, was kidnapped from St. Thomas's Hospital in London. On Jan. 27 the child was found by police in a Cotswold village and reunited with her parents. A woman was arrested and charged with the abduction. **17.** A Dutchman, Rene Hillebrand, was sentenced to three concurrent life terms at the Central Criminal Court for the murder of his estranged wife and her parents.

Feb. 4. A seven-year-old girl was abducted from near her home in Brighton, sexually assaulted and abandoned on the Sussex Downs. On Feb. 7 a man was charged with the kidnap, indecent assault and attempted murder of the girl. **12.** The trial began at Southwark Crown Court of Ernest Saunders (former chairman and chief executive of the Guinness company), Gerald Ronson (chairman of Heron Corporation), the stockbroker Anthony Parnes and the financier Sir Jack Lyons variously charged on 24 counts with theft, false accounting and breaches of the Companies Act in relation to Guinness' takeover of the Distillers drinks group in 1986. **13.** A 10-year-old girl, Christine Lee, was killed by an unknown abductor in Glasgow. **28.** Victor Castigador was jailed for life at the Central Criminal Court for murdering two guards at a Soho amusement arcade by setting them on fire. Four other people involved in the crime received custodial sentences.

March 12. A police sergeant, Dennis Davies, was sentenced at Shrewsbury Crown Court to six years in prison for the rape of a woman held in a police cell after being arrested on a drink-driving charge. **15.** Criminal charges were dropped against 14 London police officers accused of offences during a demonstration outside the News International plant, Wapping, in 1987. **18.** One man was killed and seven people wounded when a gunman opened fire on a crowd in central Glasgow. **19.** A former Manchester police officer, convicted in 1989 of robbery and firearms offences, was cleared on appeal by the Court of Appeal. Lord Lane referred to the trial of Thomas Corley as a 'travesty of justice'. A multiple rapist, David Lashley, was convicted of the murder in 1977 of Australian heiress Janie Shepherd, and was sentenced to life imprisonment. **23.** The Transport and General Workers Union asked the Metropolitan Police serious crime squad to investigate allegations of ballot irregularities. **30.** Three men who committed a series of offences including violent robbery, burglary, rape and murder, in areas adjacent to the M25 were sentenced at the Central Criminal Court to life imprisonment.

April 1. Prisoners at Strangeways Prison, Manchester, rioted and took over several wings of the prison. Prison officers and police surrounded the prison. Most prisoners left the prison during the following week but a group of about a dozen remained in the prison until captured by prison officers or persuaded to give themselves up. The last prisoners left Strangeways on April 25. In the rioting severe damage was caused to the prison buildings and a number of prisoners and prison officers were injured. A remand prisoner, Derek White, died on April 3 from injuries sustained in the riot. On April 5 the Home Secretary (David Waddington) announced that a judicial inquiry into the riot would be held. There was unrest and rioting at over a dozen other prisons during April. **22.** At Birmingham Crown Court Susan de

Stempel was sentenced to seven years' imprisonment for leading a conspiracy to steal £55,000 from her aunt, the late Lady Illingworth.

May 2. Lou Macari, the former manager of Swindon Town Football Club, Brian Hillier, the club's former chairman, and Vince Farrar, the club's former accountant, were charged with tax-related offences. **15.** At Liverpool Crown Court, John Heeley was sentenced to life imprisonment for the rape and murder of nine-year-old Annette Wade. **23.** In a speech at the Police Federation's annual conference the Home Secretary (David Waddington) ruled out the possibility of creating a direct-entry officer class for the police.

June 4. A police disciplinary tribunal found Detective Chief Superintendent Graham Melvin guilty of one charge of misconduct during his investigation into the murder of PC Keith Blakelock during the Broadwater Farm riot in 1985. **8.** Animal rights activists were blamed for a bomb which exploded under the car of Margaret Baskerville, a vet working at Porton Down. Mrs. Baskerville escaped unhurt through the window of her vehicle. **13.** The parents of Stephanie Charalambous, a two-year-old suffering from leukaemia, took her from the Great Ormond Street Hospital in London and fled to Cyprus in order to prevent her being given a blood transfusion which would have conflicted with their religious views as Jehovah's Witnesses. In Cyprus the child was put in the care of the state social welfare department and given a transfusion on June 15. **20.** Nicholas Bennett, Conservative MP for Pembroke, was sent a letter bomb which was intercepted by a postal worker. Two more letter bombs were sent to Conservative MPs the following day. Police assumed an extreme Welsh nationalist group to be responsible. **26.** Seventeen people were arrested in Merseyside following an investigation into child sex abuse.

July 16. A team of robbers used a three-ton lorry as a battering ram to smash through the front window of Asprey the jewellers in Regent Street, London. They stole a diamond necklace valued at £742,000. **23.** The bodies of two women were found in a car in London. **29.** A gunman held over 100 people hostage in a siege at a London nightclub. Nobody was hurt and the man surrendered after ten hours.

Aug. 10. Robert Black was jailed for life at the High Court in Edinburgh for the abduction and assault of a six-year-old girl. **21.** The jury in the Guinness trial retired to consider their verdict. On Aug. 27 the four defendants, Ernest Saunders, Gerald Ronson, Anthony Parnes and Sir Jack Lyons, were convicted of theft, false accounting and breaches of the

Companies Act. On Aug. 28 sentence was passed. Saunders was sentenced to five years' in prison, Parnes to 2½ years in prison, and Ronson to one year in prison and a fine of £5 million. Sentencing of Sir Jack Lyons was postponed until the end of September as he was due to undergo major surgery. **28.** A London police constable, Laurence Brown, was shot dead in Hackney, London. A man was charged with the murder.

ECCLESIASTICAL

(1989). Sept. 29. The Archbishop of Canterbury (Dr. Robert Runcie) began a visit to Rome. On Sept. 30, during a service presided over by Pope John Paul II, Dr. Runcie called for the unity of Christian churches, led by the Pope.

Nov. 7. The General Synod of the Church of England voted in favour of the ordination of women as priests.

(1990). Jan. 29. A Church of England report on life in urban areas, *Living Faith in the City*, was published.

Feb. 20. The House of Commons voted to allow the ordination as priests of divorcees who had remarried.

March 25. The Archbishop of Canterbury, Dr Robert Runcie, announced that he would retire at the end of January 1991.

May 8. Cardinal Tomás Ó Fiaich, the Roman Catholic Primate of All Ireland, died while on pilgrimage to Lourdes.

June 24. Kathleen Young and Irene Templeton were ordained at St. Anne's Cathedral, Belfast, becoming the first Anglican women priests in the United Kingdom.

July 25. It was announced that Dr. George Carey, the Bishop of Bath and Wells, will succeed Dr. Robert Runcie as Archbishop of Canterbury.

EDUCATION

(1989). Sept. 15. The Government announced the establishment in Brighton of a new city technology college, the Michael Faraday College, which will specialize in environmental issues.

Nov. 6. Research commissioned by the six teachers' unions indicated that teacher shortages in England and Wales were twice as serious as the Government had admitted.

Dec. 20. The major clearing banks refused to administer the Government's student top-up loan scheme. **22.** The Universities Funding Council announced that it was allocating £25 million for the improvement of university buildings.

(1990). Jan. 5. The Secretary of State for Education (John MacGregor) announced a plan to tackle specialist teacher shortages with a two-tier pay arrangement. **16.** Two Muslim girls were sent home from school because they insisted on wearing headscarves in accordance with the requirements of their religion. On Jan. 24 the girls, Alisha and Fatima Alvi, were allowed to return to Altrincham Grammar School for Girls after governors decided to modify the school rules to allow headscarves to be worn.

Feb. 5. In his annual report the Senior Chief Inspector of Schools (Eric Bolton) said that one in three schoolchildren was 'getting a raw deal' from the state education system. **19.** Representatives of Britain's universities, polytechnics and colleges told the Secretary of State for Education that they would refuse to co-operate with Government plans to introduce a top-up loan scheme for students.

April 9. The Secretary of State for Education announced that national testing in all subjects for primary school children was to be abandoned and testing would be only in mathematics, English and science.

June 6. The National Curriculum working group on geography published its report.

July 26. The Education Secretary (John MacGregor) announced greater emphasis on facts and dates in his proposals for the new national curriculum for history.

Aug. 19. The School Examinations and Assessment Council announced that the six GCSE examining groups will be required to phase out awards based 100 per cent on coursework assessment.

ENVIRONMENT AND LOCAL AFFAIRS

(1989). Sept. 12. The Government announced that cut-price shares would be offered to people investing in the water companies serving their area as part of the privatization of the water industry.

Oct. 2. Thames Water Authority was fined £3,000 with £1,000 costs after it admitted discharging virtually raw sewage into a stream at Winterbourne, Berks.

Nov. 6. The Secretary of State for the Environment (Chris Patten) announced that the community charge in England for 1990 would be approximately £278 per person if local authorities adhered to Government spending targets. **8.** The Prime Minister (Margaret Thatcher) announced in a speech to the United Nations that Britain would spend £100 million in helping to preserve tropical rainforests.

Dec. 20. Mr Patten rejected proposals for a new town at Bramshill, Hampshire. **28.** A government-sponsored report for the Intergovernmental Panel on Climate Change said that Britain's energy consumption could be reduced by up to 60 per cent over the next 15 years if the Government gave higher priority to conservation measures. Yorkshire Water was fined £1,000 with £250 costs for polluting a trout stream, Ewden Beck.

(1990). Jan. 14. Five leading conservation groups formed an alliance to contest the Government's proposals to break up and restructure the Nature Conservancy Council and the Countryside Commission.

Feb. 23. Shell UK was fined £1 million for polluting the River Mersey with oil.

March 2. The London Borough of Wandsworth set a community charge of £148, believed to be the lowest in England. **6.** Demonstrations against the community charge took place at town halls across the country as councils met to set the community charge for their area. A number of demonstrations became violent. **15.** The Lord Provost of Edinburgh, Eleanor McLaughlin, had her bank account frozen for refusing to pay her community charge. **30.** A protest march against the community charge in central London ended in violent confrontations between some protesters and the police, and rioting and looting took place in the West End of London. Over 300 people were injured and 308 protesters were arrested.

June 1. A report by the district auditor found that West Wiltshire District Council had acted unlawfully in paying large bonuses and redundancy payments to senior officers. **5.** David Trippier, Minister of State for the Environment, announced that in future English seaside resorts would be expected to indicate publicly whether their bathing waters met or failed EC standards.

July 16. Five banks issued writs against the London Borough of Hammersmith and Fulham and four councillors, to try to recover money that the council had failed to pay in interest on swap contracts.

Aug. 6. Councillors in Lambeth, London, voted for budget cuts totalling £8 million in order to reduce the borough's community charge rate by £26.

FINANCE

(1989). Sept. 8. The General-Electric Company (GEC) and Siemens took control of another electronics company, Plessey, at a cost of £2,000 million.

Oct. 5. The bank base lending rate rose from 14 per cent to 15 per cent.

Dec. 12. Trading started in shares in the privatized water industry. **19.** Over 800 Lloyd's members began legal proceedings against the underwriting agency RHM Outhwaite for alleged negligence.

(1990). Jan. 3. Shares on the London Stock Exchange reached the highest level ever. The FT-SE 100 share index was 2,463·7 at the close of business.

Feb. 14. National Westminster Bank offered to pay £30 million in compensation to people who bought shares in Blue Arrow after the failure of the 1987 rights issue.

March 7. The Department of Trade and Industry published a report on the take-over of Harrods by the Fayed family.

May 9. The Monopolies and Mergers Commission announced an investigation into the pricing of new cars sold in Britain.

June 1. The Rank Organization launched a hostile take-over bid for its rival, Mecca Leisure Group. On June 27 the Mecca board agreed to accept the offer. **7.** Coloroll, the home furnishings group, collapsed after its bank creditors called in the receiver. **15.** Inflation in May reached 9·7 per cent, the highest rate for more than eight years.

July 30. Fujitsu, the Japanese computer company, bought an 80 per cent stake in ICL, Britain's largest computer company, for £743 million.

Aug. 9. The Union of Democratic Mineworkers announced a plan for a management buyout of PowerGen. **15.** The furniture and carpet retailing group Lowndes Queensway went into receivership with debts of £300 million.

LABOUR AND TRADE UNIONS

(1989). Sept. 4. The Trades Union Congress annual conference began in Blackpool. The Congress voted to increase the number of seats reserved for women on the ruling body. On Sept. 7 the TUC voted to drop its commitment to unilateral nuclear disarmament. **13.** Ambulance crews began an overtime ban after management negotiators rejected a request for arbitration on pay awards.

Oct. 9. Journalists at the *Daily Telegraph* and the *Sunday Telegraph* started a 36-hour strike over proposals to make 33 people redundant. **23.** Police vans were used to answer emergency calls in London after ambulance service managers stopped the pay of ambulance crews who were working to rule, declaring them off duty. **30.** Engineering unions began a series of selective strikes as part of a campaign to reduce the working week to 35 hours.

Nov. 7. The Secretary of State for Health (Kenneth Clarke) announced that troops were being drafted in to help run London's ambulance service after regular crew members were suspended from duty.

Dec. 20. The results of a ballot of Ford manual workers showed a 4 to 1 vote in favour of a strike over pay. **21.** The Department of Health rejected a call from the Association of Professional Ambulance Personnel for further talks to end the ambulance dispute.

(1990). Jan. 5. The TUC gave its full support to calls for a nationwide 15-minute stoppage in support of striking ambulance staff. **10.** The Ford Motor Company increased the pay offer to its manual workers to 10·2 per cent in an attempt to avert a threatened strike. On Jan. 15 the Ford factories at Bridgend and Halewood were disrupted by unofficial strikes. On Jan. 24 Ford manual workers agreed to accept the 10·2 per cent pay offer.

Feb. 7. Engineering workers at Ford's Dagenham plant called off a strike after failing to gain support for the stoppage. **23.** Ambulance union leaders reached agreement with the health authorities about the pay increase for ambulance crews, and members were asked to vote for acceptance of the deal. Merseyside ambulance crews voted for an indefinite strike in protest. **26.** The Rover Group agreed a cut in working hours to a 37-hour week for its manual workers.

March 2. Workers at British Aerospace factories in Preston and Chester voted to end a 17-week strike after agreement was reached to reduce the working week to 37 hours. **4.** The National Union of Mineworkers called a special executive meeting to question their president, Arthur Scargill, on the use of Soviet and Libyan aid during the miners' strike of 1984–85. **10.** The NUM executive ordered an independent inquiry into allegations of financial irregularity in the use of strike funds.

April 9. Ford announced that a proposed £225 million investment in its Bridgend

factory would instead be made at its Cologne factory, West Germany. **23.** Rover agreed with unions to cut the working week of its Longbridge Plant workers to 31 hours and to create 1,200 new jobs in a deal that will allow 24-hour production.

May 3. Rover manual workers at Longbridge rejected a deal which union leaders had supported. **16.** British Steel announced that it intended to close the hot strip mill at its Ravenscraig plant in Motherwell.

July 3. The National Union of Mineworkers (NUM) made public the report by Gavin Lightman, QC, following Mr Lightman's inquiry into the existence and use of funds donated to the union during the 1984–85 miners' strike. The union's president, Arthur Scargill, and general secretary, Peter Heathfield, were cleared of using union funds for their own purposes but were censured for failing to inform the union of the existence of the funds and failing to keep proper records of the administration of the money. **19.** The NUM said it would sue Arthur Scargill and Peter Heathfield to recover money supposed to have been donated to the NUM during the miners' strike.

Aug. 8. The North Sea oil and gas industry was hit by its third 24-hour strike in a week due to a dispute over safety and union recognition offshore.

LEGAL

(1989). Sept. 24. The four regional directors of the Crown Prosecution Service were retired and their posts abolished as part of a reorganization of the Service.

Oct. 16. Jones, Alexander and Co., a firm of solicitors from Retford, Notts., were found guilty of negligence on six counts and ordered to pay damages of £425,071 to a woman they represented in a divorce case. **17.** The four people convicted of bombings in Guildford and Woolwich were cleared after an investigation by the Avon and Somerset police. Carole Richardson, Paul Hill, Gerard Conlon and Patrick Armstrong, known as the Guildford Four, had served 14 years of their life sentences. On Oct. 19 Richardson, Conlon and Armstrong were released and the setting up of a judicial inquiry into the case, led by Sir John May, was announced. Hill was released on Oct. 20.

Nov. 1. The High Court ruled that money-market dealings by Hammersmith and Fulham Council were unlawful. **6.** The damages awarded to Mrs. Sonia Sutcliffe against the magazine *Private Eye* for libel were reduced from £600,000 to £60,000 by the Court of Appeal. **30.** Lord Aldington was awarded libel damages of £1·5 million against Count Nikolai Tolstoy and Nigel Watts in the High Court. Allegations that Lord Aldington knowingly sent 70,000 Yugoslavs and Cossacks to their deaths in 1945 were disproved.

Dec. 6. Professor Frederick Hartt was awarded £7,500 costs against the *Independent* in a libel action in the High Court. **22.** A judge of the Court of Session in Scotland, Lord Dervaird, resigned. On **Jan. 17** it emerged that he was one of three Scottish judges who had been interviewed by their senior colleagues concerning allegations of homosexuality.

(1990). Jan. 12. The Home Secretary (David Waddington) announced plans for the long-term reform of prison conditions. **29.** The report of the investigation into the Hillsborough Stadium tragedy by Lord Justice Taylor was published. **30.** Andrew Neil, editor of the *Sunday Times*, was awarded £1,000 libel damages against Peregrine Worsthorne, editor of the *Sunday Telegraph*.

Feb. 28. The athlete Tessa Sanderson won £30,000 libel damages against Mirror Group Newspapers and two journalists over stories alleging that she stole another woman's husband.

March 8. Lord Aldington said that he would be willing to forgo most of the £1·5 million libel damages awarded to him against Count Nikolai Tolstoy. Count Tolstoy turned down the offer. **13.** The athlete Linford Christie was awarded substantial, undisclosed damages against the police for wrongful arrest. **29.** Viscount Linley was awarded damages of £35,000 against *Today* newspaper over allegations about his behaviour. He chose to waive £30,000 of the award.

April 9. Three High Court judges dismissed a plea by Muslims to overturn a magistrate's decision not to issue summonses against Salman Rushdie and his publishers under the blasphemy laws.

May 9. The inquest opened on the 47 passengers who died when a British Midland Boeing 737 crashed on the M1 in 1989. **10.** Relatives of the 11 people killed on the ground in the 1988 Lockerbie air crash, along with others who suffered, reached an out-of-court settlement of compensation with Pan Am. **14.** The inquiry by Lord Justice Woolf, into the Strangeways prison riot, began. **21.** The judicial inquiry by Sir John May into the forensic evidence which convicted the Maguire family ('The Maguire Seven') opened in London.

July 9. The Lord Chancellor announced plans for a network of 'family hearing centres'

or children's courts in England and Wales which will handle children's cases and will be presided over by specially trained judges. **16.** The Department of Trade and Industry began legal action against Midland Bank, which operated accounts on behalf of Barlow Clowes, and several firms of financial advisers in order to recover compensation paid by the DTI to victims of the collapse of the Barlow Clowes companies.

Aug. 17. The ban on the video film *International Guerrillas*, which depicts Salman Rushdie as a drunken murderer, was lifted by the appeals committee of the British Board of Film Censors. **29.** The Home Secretary (David Waddington) ordered the cases of the 'Birmingham Six', six men convicted of killing 21 people in pub bombings in 1974, to be referred back to the Court of Appeal for the second time. The order came after doubt was cast on some of the police evidence at the trial.

SOCIAL

(1989). Sept. 5. St. Bartholomew's Hospital, London, announced that it intended to open a private out-patients clinic in an attempt to generate extra income. **27.** St. Bartholomew's announced the closure of 75 beds in an attempt to cut spending by £1·4 million.

Oct. 15. The British Medical Association warned that many general practitioners would resign rather than accept the new contracts being imposed on them by the Government. **20.** Figures published by the Department of Health showed that National Health waiting lists were at their highest level for six years.

Nov. 21. The Health Education Authority announced that it planned to close its Aids division. **22.** The Government published the National Health Service and Community Care Bill. **23.** The Government announced that an extra £19 million would be made available to help haemophiliacs who contracted the HIV virus after receiving treatment with infected blood. **24.** The Minister of State for Health (Virginia Bottomley) announced that mass anonymous testing of blood for the HIV virus would begin in January 1990.

Dec. 4. Three doctors faced charges of serious professional misconduct at a General Medical Council disciplinary hearing inquiring into their part in cases in which four Turks were paid to donate their kidneys for transplant operations. **28.** Figures released by the Office of Population Censuses and Surveys indicated that 472 people had died in a flu epidemic which reached its peak in December. **28.** St. Mary's Hospital in Manchester became the first NHS hospital to open a human egg donor centre.

(1990). Jan. 3. Cattle infected with bovine spongiform encephalopathy (BSE), or mad cow disease, were found on sale for slaughter in North Yorkshire by trading standards officers. On Jan. 10 the Government announced that it would spend £12 million on research into BSE.

Feb. 14. The French mineral water company Perrier ordered a world-wide withdrawal of its product after traces of benzene were found in bottles on sale in Britain. It was discovered that a faulty warning light at the Perrier plant had been undetected for six months, allowing filters to become clogged. **15.** Research findings were published which suggest a link between the exposure to radiation of workers at the Sellafield nuclear plant and leukaemia in their children. **22.** Police and firemen began clearing canisters of potassium cyanide from beaches along the East Sussex coast. Authorities believed that the canisters were washed overboard from a Qatar-registered ship.

April 1. NHS prescription charges rose from £2·80 to £3·05. **4.** A doctor, Raymond Crockett, who was involved in the sale of kidneys for transplant operations, was ordered to be struck off the medical register. The two surgeons involved in the operations, Michael Bewick and Michael Joyce, were found guilty by the General Medical Council of serious professional misconduct but allowed to continue practising.

June 14. Admissions to the oncology unit at Alder Hey children's hospital, Liverpool, were halted after an outbreak of tuberculosis which killed a four-year-old patient. **22.** Michael Spicer, the Minister of State responsible for housing, announced that the Government was making available £15 million to alleviate the problems of homelessness.

July 2. Three hospitals in the Mersey regional health authority area became the first to apply for self-governing status.

SPORT

(1989). Sept. 15. The St. Leger was postponed when it was discovered that part of the Doncaster race course had subsided. The race was run at Ayr on Sept. 23. **24.** The British Formula 1 racing driver Nigel Mansell was fined $50,000 for failing to respond to a black flag during the Portuguese Grand Prix.

Oct. 5. The Dutch soccer club Ajax was banned from European competition for at least two seasons following crowd trouble

during a match in Amsterdam against Austria-Vienna.

Nov. 6. Arsenal and Norwich football clubs were charged by the Football Association with misconduct and with bringing the game into disrepute following incidents at a match between the clubs. On Nov. 27 the clubs were found guilty and fined £20,000 and £50,000 respectively. **23.** West Ham United and Wimbledon were charged by the Football Association with bringing the game into disrepute following incidents at a match between the clubs the previous day. On Dec. 19 the clubs were fined £20,000 each by the Football Association.

(1990). Jan. 19. A team of English cricketers led by Mike Gatting arrived in South Africa to undertake an unofficial tour. **21.** John McEnroe was disqualified from the Australian Open tennis championships after abusing officials during a match. **24.** The XIVth Commonwealth Games began in Auckland, New Zealand. On Jan. 30 a Welsh weightlifter, Ricky Chaplin, was tested positive for drugs and was stripped of his gold medal. On Jan. 31 a second Welsh weightlifter, Gareth Hives, also failed a drugs test.

Feb. 11. James (Buster) Douglas defeated Mike Tyson in a boxing match in Tokyo to become heavyweight boxing champion of the world. **13.** The unofficial English cricket tour of South Africa was curtailed as cricketing authorities agreed with anti-apartheid campaigners to end the tour on Feb. 22. In March it was announced that the return cricket tour in the winter of 1990–91 had been cancelled. **18.** Lou Macari resigned as manager of West Ham United. Macari was fined £1,000 and censured by the Football Association on Feb. 13 for betting on his team to lose a match when he was manager of Swindon. **20.** The British and United States tennis associations announced that the Wightman Cup for 1990 had been cancelled and that the competition had been suspended pending further study of its future. **28.** The British Amateur Weightlifters Association banned from the sport for life two Welsh weightlifters, Ricky Chaplin and Gareth Hives, who tested positively for drugs at the Commonwealth Games.

April 26. The New York Court of Appeal ruled that San Diego Yacht Club were the winners of the America's Cup 1988 series of races.

May 6. Leeds United followers rioted in Bournemouth where their team were playing. **8.** Following demands from the Home Secretary (David Waddington), the football authorities agreed that the police should have the final say on whether fixtures should go ahead when violence was possible. **24.** Bobby Robson, the England football team manager, announced that he would resign after the World Cup to join the Dutch club PSV Eindhoven.

June 7. Swindon Town Football Club, which won promotion to the first division for the first time in May, was relegated to the third division by a Football League Commission after admitting to 35 charges involving irregular payments to players. **8.** The Football World Cup began in Italy.

July 2. Following Swindon's appeal against the Football League's decision to relegate the club to the third division, the Football Association decided that Swindon would stay in the second division, and that Sunderland would be promoted to the first. **7.** Martina Navratilova won the Wimbledon women's singles competition for a record ninth time. **8.** In the Football World Cup final, West Germany beat Argentina 1–0. **10.** UEFA, Europe's soccer ruling body, lifted the ban on English clubs playing in European competitions, except for Liverpool, which remained suspended for at least another year. **15.** British racing driver Nigel Mansell announced that he would retire from Formula One racing at the end of the current season. Graham Taylor was appointed England's new soccer manager. **31.** Aldershot Football Club was compulsorily wound up in the High Court, with debts of £490,000.

Aug. 2. The chairmen of Football League clubs voted to expand the first division to 22 clubs. **27.** Graham Gooch, the England cricket captain, broke Don Bradman's 60-year-old record for the most runs scored in test matches in a season. Gooch passed Bradman's record of 974 runs during his second innings against India at the Oval. **30.** Peter Elliott, the British runner, was pushed by an opponent and fell in the 1,500m semi-final at the European Championships in Yugoslavia. He did not finish the race. The appeals jury decided to disqualify the althlete who pushed him and to award Elliott a place in the final.

TRANSPORT

(1989). Sept. 14. British Rail announced the final route for the high-speed rail link between London and the Channel Tunnel. **25.** A group of nine environmental organizations published *Roads to Ruin*, their response to the Government's White Paper *Roads for Prosperity* published in May 1989.

Oct. 31. British Rail announced that it would delay plans to build a high-speed Channel Tunnel rail link for at least a year because of the Government's refusal to help finance the project.

Nov. 1. The French national railway service, SNCF, offered to increase British Rail's share of the revenue from the Channel Tunnel in order to revive British Rail's plans for a high-speed rail link.

Dec. 14. The Department of Transport published a discussion document *Traffic in London: A discussion document on initiatives to tackle the problems.* **19.** The Secretary of State for Transport (Cecil Parkinson) announced that subsidies to British Rail would be cut and that the subsidy for Network SouthEast would be removed by 1993.

(1990) Feb. 11. The Department of Transport announced that British Rail would be subject to 'rigorous scrutiny' over the next three years, and would be required to meet performance standards. **20.** A financial crisis threatening to halt work on the Channel Tunnel was averted when Transmanche-Link, the builders, settled differences with Eurotunnel, paving the way for additional funds to be made available by the project's bankers.

March 27. Mr Parkinson announced that he did not plan to proceed with road building plans for London.

April 4. Mr Parkinson announced that three new roads would be built by private companies who will recover their costs by charging tolls.

May 9. British Aerospace and Aerospatiale announced a joint Anglo-French research project aimed at developing a successor to Concorde.

June 12. The Prime Minister told the House of Commons that the Government would not subsidize the Channel Tunnel high-speed rail link. On June 14 the Transport Secretary announced that the Government had decided to shelve plans for the high-speed link.

July 3. Mr Parkinson announced that a 260-mile stretch of the A1 trunk road from London to Newcastle upon Tyne would be upgraded to motorway standard.

AFRICA

(1989). Sept. 6. In a general election the South African National Party retained power, though with a severely reduced majority. An anti-apartheid defiance campaign culminating in a national general strike on Sept. 5–6 resulted in mass arrests and violent clashes between police and demonstrators. **9.** The Algerian Prime Minister, Kasdi Merbah, was dismissed by President Chadli Bendjedid. **10.** Mouloud Hamrouche was named new Prime Minister of Algeria. **14.** Sam Nujoma, president of the South West Africa People's Organization (SWAPO), returned to Namibia after nearly 30 years in exile. **20.** F. W. de Klerk was sworn in as President of South Africa. **27.** The Prime Minister of Tunisia, Hedi Baccouche, was dismissed by President Zine el-Abidine Ben Ali and replaced by Hamed Karoui.

Oct. 15. Walter Sisulu and seven other members of the anti-apartheid movement were released from prison in South Africa on the orders of President de Klerk.

Nov. 7–11. In Namibia, elections leading to independence took place under United Nations supervision. On Nov. 14 the South West Africa People's Organization (SWAPO) was declared the winner with 57·3 per cent of the vote. **16.** The South African Government announced that hitherto segregated bathing beaches would be open to all races, and on Nov. 24 four whites-only residential areas were opened to mixed settlement. **27.** President Ahmed Abdallah Abdermane of the Comoros was assassinated.

Dec. 13. President F. W. de Klerk of South Africa met the jailed ANC leader Nelson Mandela for the first time.

(1990). Jan. 5. Troops loyal to President Samuel Doe of Liberia quashed an attempted coup. **19.** South African police broke up protests against the unofficial cricket tour led by Mike Gatting.

Feb. 2. At the opening of the South African Parliament President de Klerk announced the lifting of restrictions on over 30 organizations (including the African National Congress and the Communist Party), the freeing of political prisoners, the suspension of the death sentence and the abolition of emergency restrictions on the media. The President also announced that Nelson Mandela would be released soon and unconditionally. **11.** Nelson Mandela was released from the Victor Verster prison near Cape Town. **16.** The Kenyan Foreign Minister, Robert Ouko, was murdered near his home at Kisumu. On Feb. 21 the authorities banned demonstrations following protests by students claiming that there was an official cover-up of the circumstances of Mr. Ouko's death, and demanding President Moi's resignation. **23.** In Kenya there were violent clashes at Nairobi and Kisumu between police and mourners of Robert Ouko.

March 2. President Moi of Kenya imposed a permanent ban on demonstrations following anti-government riots. Nelson Mandela was elected deputy president of the African National Congress (ANC) by a national executive committee meeting in Zambia.

5. President Mengistu of Ethiopia announced radical changes to the ruling Workers Party of Ethiopia, and invited dissident groups to take part in national politics. **20.** Following the first free presidential elections in the Comoros since independence in 1975, Said Mohamed Djohar was sworn in as president for a six-year term. **21.** The Republic of Namibia became an independent sovereign state.

April 15. Fighting between black factions in Natal, South Africa, left twenty people dead. **22.** In Nigeria an attempted coup by junior army officers was put down by troops loyal to the government. **23.** A coup attempt alleged to have taken place against the military government in Sudan resulted in the execution of 31 army and police officers.

May 2. The first formal meeting took place between representatives of the South African government and the African National Congress, in preliminary talks about negotiating a post-apartheid constitution. **6.** P. W. Botha, the former South African president, announced his resignation from the ruling National Party. **13.** An attempted coup by armed rebels against the government of Madagascar failed when security forces intervened.

June 7. President F. W. de Klerk announced the end of South Africa's four-year nationwide state of emergency, except in Natal province. **12.** In Algerian local elections, the fundamentalist Islamic Salvation Front won control of a majority of municipal and provincial assemblies. **19.** As part of an economic recovery programme in Zambia, the price of maize meal rose by over 100 per cent. **25.** One person was shot by police when 2,000 students demonstrated in the Zambian capital, Lusaka, protesting against food prices and the government. The ensuing violence culminated in a curfew being imposed, and on June 30 an attempted coup by a small group of army officers was put down by troops loyal to the government.

July 2. Anti-government rebels led by Charles Taylor of the National Patriotic Front launched an attack on the Liberian capital Monrovia, cutting all main land routes out of the city. **7.** Police in Nairobi, Kenya, used clubs and tear gas to disperse a crowd of 10,000 pro-democracy demonstrators. Riots spread, and at least nine people were reported to have died by July 10. **30.** As atrocities escalated in the Liberian civil war, troops loyal to President Doe massacred at least 600 refugees sheltering in a church in the capital, Monrovia.

Aug. 5. The United States sent marines into the besieged Liberian capital of Monrovia to evacuate US citizens. On Aug. 8 West African states decided to send a multi-national military force to Liberia, in an attempt to end the civil war. On Aug. 31 Liberian rebels were reported to have killed over 200 foreigners whose governments were involved in the proposed West African peace force. **8.** Jerry Richardson, one of Winnie Mandela's bodyguards, was sentenced to death for murdering 14-year-old Stompie Mokhetsi Seipei. **20.** Kenya's Labour minister, Peter Habenga Okondo, resigned. **24.** The South African minister of Law and Order, Adriaan Vlok, imposed 'mini states of emergency' on 27 townships in and around Johannesburg following three weeks of violence which had left about 300 people dead. **31.** President de Klerk of South Africa declared that the ruling National Party would in future be open to all races.

THE AMERICAS

(1989). Sept. 1. The United States of America broke off diplomatic relations with Panama in protest at the installation of a government subservient to General Manuel Noriega, who was accused of falsifying the results of the election in May. **4.** In the general election in Belize, the opposition People's Unity Party led by George Price won by a slim majority of seats.

Oct. 3. In Panama an attempted coup against General Noriega failed. In Peru, Guillermo Larco Cox was sworn in as Prime Minister following the resignation of Luis Alberto Sánchez on Sept. 28. **24.** Former television evangelist Jim Bakker was sentenced to 45 years in prison for fraud and fined $500,000.

Nov. 2. The Sandinista government in Nicaragua launched an offensive against the Contra rebels, ending a 19-month ceasefire. **12.** President Cristiani of El Salvador declared a state of siege and curfew as rebel guerrillas won control of parts of the capital, San Salvador. **26.** El Salvador suspended relations with Nicaragua, accusing it of supplying missiles to Salvadorean guerrillas. In the first free presidential elections since 1971, Luis Alberto Lacalle became President-elect of Uruguay.

Dec. 6. A bomb destroyed the headquarters of Colombia's security and intelligence agency in Bogota, killing at least 40 people. **14.** Following the first presidential elections in Chile since a 1973 military coup, Patricio Aylwin was named President-elect. **15.** A leading Colombian drug baron, Gonzalo Rodríguez Gacha, was killed in a shoot-out with anti-narcotics squad police. **19.** Fernando Collor de Mello became President-elect of

Brazil but rejected proposals that he assume office early. **20.** US troops invaded Panama to depose General Manuel Noriega and installed Guillermo Endara Galimany as head of state. General Noriega and several of his associates took sanctuary inside the Vatican diplomatic mission. Ben Jones was appointed Prime Minister of Grenada following the death of Herbert Blaize on Dec. 19.

(1990). Jan. 3. General Noriega gave himself up to US troops in Panama and was flown to Miami to face drug trafficking charges. **18.** The Mayor of Washington DC, Marion Barry, was arrested for possession of the cocaine derivative crack.

Feb. 26. In a general election in Nicaragua, the ruling Sandinista Party was defeated by a coalition led by Señora Violeta Chamorro.

March 11. Patricio Aylwin was sworn in for a four-year term as President of Chile. **13.** Mrs. Ertha Trouillot became President of Haiti. **14.** President Bush lifted the USA's five-year economic embargo against Nicaragua and promised substantial economic aid. **25.** A man was arrested after a fire in a New York dance club killed 87 people. **28.** The Peruvian capital Lima was seriously affected by a strike called by Shining Path guerrillas as part of a campaign to sabotage presidential and congressional elections.

April 25. Violeta Chamorro was sworn in as President of Nicaragua, and promised to end the nine-year war against the Contra rebels.

May 4. At talks between President Chamorro of Nicaragua and a delegation from the Contra rebels it was agreed that the rebels would disarm and that demobilization would be completed by June 10. **8.** Rafael Angel Calderón Fournier was inaugurated as President of Costa Rica for a four-year term. **13.** At least 26 people were killed by car bombs in Bogota and Cali. Colombian police said the bombs were planted by the Medellin drug traffickers. **25.** In Nicaragua, Contra leaders suspended their earlier agreement to disband, claiming insufficient government protection from the troops of the Sandinista People's Army. On May 30 a new agreement was signed, the government having promised to police the five security zones containing an estimated 13,000 Contras. By May 31, around 1,500 Contras were reported to have demobilized. **27.** In Presidential elections in Colombia, César Gaviria emerged as President-elect, due to take office in August. **29.** An earthquake measuring 5·8 on the Richter scale struck northern Peru, killing over 100 people.

June 4. The trial opened of Marion Barry, mayor of Washington DC, accused of cocaine possession and perjury. **11.** Defeating Mario Vargas Uosa in the second round of presidential elections, Alberto Fujimori was elected President of Peru. John Poindexter, US national security adviser to the Reagan administration, was sentenced to six months in prison for his role in the Iran-Contra affair. **18.** A man whose car had been repossessed shot dead seven people in a loan office in Jacksonville, Florida, before killing himself. **23.** The Meech Lake Accord between the Canadian provinces, a package of proposed amendments to the Canadian Constitution, collapsed after three provinces opposed plans to afford Quebec special status if it signed the 1982 Constitution. **26.** President Bush announced that 'tax revenue increases' would be essential to help bridge the federal budget deficit, abandoning his election campaign pledge not to raise taxes. **27.** The 11-year civil war in Nicaragua formally ended when the Contra rebel military chief handed his weapons to UN forces in San Pedro de Lóbago.

July 20. The United States' federal appeal court ordered a re-hearing of the trial of Oliver North, convicted on charges arising from the Iran-Contra affair. **27.** In a coup attempt by Muslim extremists, Trinidad's Prime Minister, Arthur Robinson, was held hostage with explosives strapped to him in the parliament building. On July 31 Mr. Robinson was freed but about 40 others remained as hostages.

Aug. 1. The attempted coup in Trinidad ended when the Muslim rebels released their hostages and unconditionally surrendered to government forces.

ASIA

(1989). Sept. 20. A ceasefire between Indian troops and Tamil guerrillas began in Sri Lanka. **21.** Vietnam began the final withdrawal of its troops from Kampuchea. **27.** The Khmer Rouge launched an attack on the town of Pailin in western Kampuchea.

Nov. 9. Deng Xiaoping resigned from his position as chairman of the Central Military Commission. **26.** The governing Congress (I) party, led by Rajiv Gandhi, suffered severe losses in the Indian general election. On Nov. 29 Mr. Gandhi resigned as Prime Minister.

Dec. 1. A coup attempt against President Corazon Aquino of the Philippines was defeated following the intervention of American forces. **2.** V. P. Singh was sworn in as Prime Minister of India. **12.** The Hong Kong authorities began the involuntary repatriation of Vietnamese boat people. **29.** Several thousand Vietnamese boat people fought with Hong Kong police inside their detention camps.

(1990). Jan. 4. Over 300 people were killed in a train crash in southern Pakistan. **10.** The Chinese premier, Li Peng, lifted martial law in Peking. On Jan. 18 it was announced that 573 people jailed for involvement in the 1989 democracy demonstrations had been released.

Feb. 5. At least three people were killed and 15 injured when Indian border guards opened fire to repel Pakistani demonstrators who had crossed into Indian-administered territory near Jammu, Kashmir. **19.** The ruling Liberal Democratic Party won the general election in Japan.

March 1. Security forces in Kashmir killed at least 29 people when they fired on Muslim protesters. **6.** President Najibullah of Afghanistan said on Kabul Radio that an attempted coup by army officers had been put down.

April 6. Nepalese police killed an estimated 150 people when they opened fire on demonstrators demanding more democratic government in Kathmandu. **8.** King Birendra of Nepal announced that he was lifting a 30-year ban on political parties. More than 200 people were dead or missing after a ferry sank in the Gyaing River in Burma. **19.** A pro-democracy government, led by Krishna Prasad Bhattarai, was installed in Nepal. **30.** China announced that it was lifting martial law in Lhasa, the capital of Tibet. Martial law was imposed in March 1989 after violent demonstrations in favour of Tibetan independence from China.

May 4. In Afghanistan, President Najibullah lifted the national state of emergency which had been in force since the Soviet troop withdrawal in February 1989. Over 180 people were arrested when Hong Kong riot police stormed a camp for Vietnamese refugees in an operation to stop gang violence. A large number of illegal weapons was found. **9.** Anti-government protesters, mostly students, clashed with police on 80 university campuses throughout South Korea. **10.** China announced the release of 211 people who had been detained since anti-government demonstrations were crushed in June 1989. **11.** The Mongolian parliament approved legislation introducing a multi-party system and creating the new post of President. **20.** Lee Teng-hui was sworn in as President of Taiwan. **24.** Kim Il Sung was re-elected President of the Democratic People's Republic of Korea for a fifth consecutive four-year term. **27.** The first multi-party elections in 30 years were held in Myanmar (Burma). On May 28 the ruling military junta conceded that the opposition appeared to have won the elections.

July 2. The final results in Myanmar's elections showed that the opposition National League for Democracy had won, but no date was given by the ruling military junta for a handover of power to a civilian government. **16.** An earthquake in the Philippines, measuring 7·7 on the Richter scale, killed at least 90 people. **19.** Two teenage British girls, Karen Smith and Patricia Cahill, were arrested by police in Bangkok after 67 lb of heroin was found in their luggage.

Aug. 6. The Prime Minister of Pakistan, Miss Benazir Bhutto, and her government were dismissed from office by President Ghulam Ishaq Khan, who accused the administration of corruption, nepotism and political ineptitude. A state of emergency was declared and all fundamental rights suspended. The President dissolved the National Assembly and ordered new elections on Oct. 24. The opposition leader, Mustafa Jatoi, was appointed as caretaker prime minister.

AUSTRALASIA AND THE PACIFIC

(1989). Sept. 4. The Australian Government agreed to pay compensation to Australian servicemen who developed leukaemia or bone marrow cancer after taking part in British nuclear tests in Australia in the 1950s.

Oct. 16. Bikenibeu Paeniu was elected Prime Minister of Tuvalu.

Dec. 28. An earthquake measuring 5·5 on the Richter scale hit New South Wales in Australia, leaving 11 people dead in the city of Newcastle.

(1990). Jan. 5. The remaining army officers with seats in the Fiji cabinet, including Maj.-Gen. Sitiveni Rabuka (Minister of Home Affairs) resigned from office and Fiji returned to full civilian rule.

Feb. 12. Carmen Lawrence became the first woman state premier in Australia when she was elected state premier of Western Australia following the resignation of Peter Dowding.

March 24. A general election was held in Australia. The ruling Labor Party was re-elected to serve for a fourth term.

April. Torrential rains in Australia caused severe flooding; floodwater covered an area of the outback the size of western Europe.

May 17. Secessionist rebels issued a statement declaring the island of Bougainville to be independent from Papua New Guinea. The Prime Minister of Papua New Guinea called the declaration invalid and unlawful.

EUROPE

(1989). Sept. 7. Ruud Lubbers, leader of the Christian Democrat Party, won a third term in office in the general election in the Netherlands. **11.** In a general election in Norway, the governing Labour party failed to gain an overall majority.

Oct. 13. The Norwegian Government led by Mrs. Gro Harlem Brundtland resigned. A centre-right coalition took power. **29.** In a general election in Spain, the ruling Socialist Party retained power but with a much reduced majority. **31.** The Prime Minister of Turkey, Turgut Özal, was elected President of Turkey.

Nov. 7. In the Netherlands, a new centre-left coalition cabinet was sworn in. **9.** Yildirim Akbulut became Prime Minister of Turkey. **13.** Franz Josef II, Prince of Liechtenstein, died. **22.** An interim all-party coalition cabinet was formed in Greece following inconclusive elections on Nov. 5.

Dec. 4. Three elected members of the Basque separatist party Herri Batasuna were expelled from the Spanish Parliament after refusing fully to swear allegiance to the constitution.

(1990). Jan. 14. A fire in a discotheque in Zaragoza, Spain, caused the deaths of 43 people.

Feb. 15. The Social Democratic government in Sweden resigned after losing a vote in Parliament on its economic austerity package. On Feb. 26 the Social Democratic leader, Ingvar Carlsson, was reappointed Prime Minister at the head of a new Social Democratic government.

April 4. King Baudouin of Belgium stepped down from the throne after refusing to sign a new law legalizing abortion. On April 5 the Belgian Parliament voted to restore King Baudouin to the throne. **7.** At least 110 people died when fire broke out aboard a passenger ferry travelling from Oslo, Norway, to Frederikshavn, Denmark. **9.** In a general election in Greece the New Democracy Party won 46·9 per cent of the vote. On April 11 a New Democracy government led by Constantine Mitsotakis was sworn in.

EASTERN EUROPE

(1989). Sept. 11. Hungary opened its border with Austria, and thousands of East Germans who had travelled to Hungary crossed to the West. **12.** The Polish Parliament approved the new Solidarity-dominated Government led by Tadeusz Mazowiecki. **18.** The ruling Hungarian Communist Party signed an accord with the main opposition parties agreeing to transition to Western-style democracy. **20.** Three leading conservatives were dropped from the Soviet Communist Party Politburo.

Oct. 1. In a 'one-off' deal between East and West Germany, some 7,000 East Germans who had taken refuge in West German embassies in the capitals of Czechoslovakia and Poland were allowed to leave for the West. **3.** Another 11,000 East Germans were allowed to leave but the East German Government announced new travel restrictions to stop people crossing into Czechoslovakia and then into the West. **7.** East Germany's 40th anniversary celebrations were followed by mass protest demonstrations throughout the country. **16.** In Leipzig, East Germany, 120,000 people demonstrated in favour of political reforms. **18.** The East German Communist Party leader, Erich Honecker, was replaced by Egon Krenz. The Hungarian Parliament voted to abolish the People's Republic and approved the new constitution of the Hungarian Republic, declaring itself an independent democratic state. **27.** East Germans' freedom to travel to Czechoslovakia was reinstated.

Nov. 4. Frequent nationwide demonstrations and demands for reform in East Germany culminated in a rally of over 500,000 in East Berlin. **7.** The East German Prime Minister and his cabinet resigned, followed the next day by the resignation of the Communist Party Politburo. **8.** Hans Modrow, a moderate, was appointed the new Prime Minister of East Germany. **9.** The East German Government declared that East German citizens could leave the country freely. **10.** East German border guards began to dismantle sections of the Berlin Wall, allowing hundreds of thousands access to the West for the first time. The leader of the Bulgarian Communist Party, Todor Zhivkov, resigned after 35 years in power; on Nov. 17 Petur Mladenov was appointed as the new head of state. Riots in Kishinev, the capital of Soviet Moldavia, left many injured. On Nov. 12 troop reinforcements arrived in an attempt to restore order. **16.** The Moldavian Communist Party leader, Semyon Grossu, was sacked. **17.** East Germany's first coalition government was sworn in, and Parliament accepted plans for democratic elections and economic reform. **24.** The leader of Czechoslovakia's Communist Party, Milos Jakes, and a majority of the party leadership resigned following massive demonstrations against Communist rule. **27.** Millions of people took part in a two-hour general strike in Czechoslovakia in support of the protest movement. **29.** The Czech Federal Assembly voted to end the Communist Party's monopoly of power.

Dec. 1. East Germany's Parliament voted to abolish the Communist Party's constitutionally guaranteed leading role. **3.** The East German central committee of the Communist Party and the newly elected Politburo resigned. Former leader Erich Honecker and several other prominent members of his Politburo were arrested and stripped of party membership following allegations of corruption. On Dec. 6 Egon Krenz, the head of state, resigned his post. **10.** Gustáv Husák resigned as President of Czechoslovakia after swearing in the country's first non-communist majority government for 41 years. On Dec. 28 Alexander Dubcek was elected chairman of the Parliament, and on Dec. 29 Vaclav Havel took office as President of Czechoslovakia. **11.** The Bulgarian head of state, Petur Mladenov, proposed that democratic elections be held by June 1990. **17.** A riot in the Romanian city of Timisoara was put down by troops. However, rioting escalated and spread to other parts of the country. **20.** President Ceausescu declared a state of emergency in Timisoara. The Lithuanian Communist Party declared itself independent of the Soviet Communist Party. **21.** A rally of thousands of people in Bucharest demonstrated against President Ceausescu, and anti-government protests, many of them violent, erupted throughout the country. **22.** President Ceausescu and his wife Elena were captured attempting to flee the country. The army declared its support for the revolution, but a counter-attack was launched by the secret police force, the Securitate. The leaders of East and West Germany, Hans Modrow and Helmut Kohl, met at the opening ceremony of the Brandenburg Gate, symbol of the division of Europe since the building of the Berlin Wall in 1961. **25.** In Romania, Ceausescu and his wife were condemned to death and executed by the army for committing crimes of genocide and corruption. **28.** The provisional government in Romania, the National Salvation Front, announced forthcoming free elections and the abolition of the leading role of the Communist Party. **30.** Poland's formal title was changed from the Polish People's Republic to the Polish Republic.

(1990). Jan. 2. Crowds rioted along an 80 mile stretch of the border between Soviet Azerbaijan and Iran. **7.** Troops were sent to the Soviet republic of Georgia to quell ethnic violence. **13.** Up to 60 people died in continued disputes between Azerbaijan and Armenia over the Nagorno-Karabakh region which escalated into attacks on Armenians in Baku, capital of Azerbaijan. **15.** A state of emergency was declared in and around Nagorno-Karabakh, and in Baku on Jan. 19. **15.** The Bulgarian National Assembly voted to end the Communist Party's monopoly of power. **25.** Limited reforms were announced in Albania.

Feb. 1. The Yugoslav government sent troops to Kosovo province in an attempt to end clashes between ethnic Albanians and the Serbian authorities. On Feb. 21 a state of emergency was imposed throughout the Kosovo province. **7.** The Central Committee of the Soviet Communist Party voted to end the party's monopoly of power, paving the way for multi-party elections. On Feb. 27 the Soviet parliament approved the establishment of the new post of President of the USSR. **12.** A state of emergency and a curfew were imposed in Dushanbe, capital of the Soviet republic of Tadjikistan, following rioting.

March 4. Democratic elections for republican parliaments and local councils took place in several parts of the Soviet Union. **8.** The Lithuanian national movement, Sajudis, voted to declare the republic of Lithuania independent of the Soviet Union. On March 11 independence was declared by the republic's supreme soviet. **9.** Senior officials from East and West Germany met in East Berlin for preliminary talks on reunification. **15.** Mikhail Gorbachov was sworn in as the first executive President of the Soviet Union. **18.** Free elections in East Germany were won by the Alliance for Germany party. **25.** In the first round of parliamentary elections in Hungary, no party won a clear majority. The Hungarian Democratic Forum and the Alliance of Free Democrats were the two leading parties.

April 8. The second round of parliamentary elections in Hungary resulted in victory for the Hungarian Democratic Forum and its allies. **10.** President Gorbachov said that direct presidential rule might be introduced in Lithuania if civil war broke out. On April 13 Lithuania was told to annul the parliament in Vilnius within 48 hours or the Soviet Union would impose economic sanctions. On April 17 the Soviet Union reduced gas supplies to Lithuania and introduced other economic sanctions. **12.** In East Germany, a five-party coalition government aiming to achieve German unity was sworn in. **13.** The Soviet Union admitted that its secret police were responsible for the massacre of nearly 15,000 Polish officers during World War Two, including those killed at Katyn in Byelorussia.

May 1. During the May Day celebrations in Moscow, the traditional May Day parade was followed by a demonstration of opposition groups. President Gorbachov and other members of the state and Communist Party leadership were jeered at and left the balcony of Lenin's mausoleum. **4.** Latvia declared its independence from the Soviet Union, with a 'transition period' for negotiations. **8.** Estonia declared its independence from the Soviet Union, and established a provisional system of government for an unspecified period of transition. **11.** The US ambassador to Romania was recalled by his government

in protest at the pre-election intimidation of opponents by supporters of the ruling National Salvation Front. The British government rebuked the Romanian government over the violence. **20.** In Romania's first free elections since 1937, the ruling National Salvation Front led by Ion Iliescu won a decisive victory. **23.** The Soviet government announced that the country's first referendum would be held, the issue being whether people wanted market reforms and the inevitable price rises these would bring. **27.** Free elections were held at local level in Poland for the first time in over 50 years. **29.** Boris Yeltsin was elected Chairman of the Russian Supreme Soviet, making him *de facto* President of the RSFSR. **30.** An earthquake measuring 6·8 on the Richter scale struck eastern Europe, causing 70 deaths in Romania.

June 10. In Czechoslovakia's first free general election since 1946, the twin citizens' movements Civic Forum (Czech) and Public Against Violence (Slovak) won about half the seats. New federal and republican governments were appointed at the end of June. **12.** The Soviet Union's largest republic, the Russian Soviet Federal Socialist Republic, declared itself a sovereign state. **13.** Armed police cleared a square in central Bucharest, Romania, which had been occupied by anti-communist demonstrators since April 22. On June 14 miners armed with clubs and iron bars travelled to Bucharest, and attacked anyone suspected of opposing the government. **14.** The former ruling Bulgarian Communist Party, renamed the Bulgarian Socialist Party, was declared the winner of the country's first free multi-party elections for over 40 years, held on June 10 and 17. **20.** The Soviet republic of Uzbekistan declared its sovereignty within a 'renewed Soviet federation'. **21.** The parliaments of East and West Germany both approved a treaty on economic union, to take effect on July 1, and a joint declaration on the inviolability of the Polish border. **23.** The Supreme Soviet of the Soviet republic of Moldavia adopted a declaration of sovereignty.

July 2. The Yugoslavian republic of Slovenia adopted a declaration of sovereignty, and Albanian legislators in Kosovo province declared political independence from the republic of Serbia. **3.** Police and soldiers attempted to prevent Albanian people seeking refuge in foreign embassy compounds in the capital, Tirana. On July 9 the first Albanians were allowed to leave the country and on July 13 thousands of Albanians were taken to Italy and France by ferry. **5.** Vaclav Havel was re-elected President of Czechoslovakia by the new parliament six months after he had taken office in the wake of the revolution. **6.** Petur Mladenov, the President of Bulgaria, resigned his post. **16.** The parliament of the Soviet republic of the Ukraine passed a declaration of sovereignty.

Aug. 3. Arpad Goncz was elected President of Hungary. **8.** The East German Parliament voted in favour of unification with West Germany and of federal state elections on October 14. On Aug. 9 the West German Parliament rejected the plan for elections in October and set a date for the elections of December 2. On Aug. 31 East and West Germany signed a treaty agreeing their unification on Oct. 3. **19.** The Social Democrat (SPD) members resigned from East Germany's coalition government a week after the Prime Minister, Lothar de Maiziere, dismissed two SPD ministers. Serbs in the Yugoslav republic of Croatia held a referendum on Serbian autonomy in Croatia. **29.** A state of emergency was declared and a curfew imposed on Yerevan, the capital of the Soviet republic of Armenia.

EUROPEAN COMMUNITY

(1989). Sept. 8. A French member of the European Parliament, Claude Autant-Lara, resigned his seat after being accused of anti-Semitism.

Oct. 3. The EC Parliament voted to increase aid to Poland and Hungary. **17.** In a speech to the College of Europe in Bruges, the president of the European Commission, Jacques Delors, denied that he was trying to build a United States of Europe.

Nov. 18. A summit meeting of the European Community began in Paris to discuss events in Eastern Europe.

Dec. 8. The heads of state of the twelve European Community countries began a summit meeting in Strasbourg. **13.** A report by the EC's Court of Auditors revealed evidence of fraud within the Community. **18.** The EC informed Turkey that negotiation of its membership would be deferred until 1993 at the earliest.

(1990). Jan. 16. Ireland began its six-month presidency of the Economic Community.

Feb. 8. The first meeting took place of a task force set up by the European Commission to study the implications of German reunification.

April 2. European Community moves to agree a common visa and immigration policy failed when Italy vetoed a collective decision by the Community to scrap visas for East Germans. **5.** The European Parliament voted to retain Strasbourg as its primary home.

28. An extraordinary European Community summit meeting of heads of government began in Dublin to discuss the Community's response to the prospect of German unification and to the rapid changes in eastern Europe.

May 7. The EC signed a series of trade agreements with eastern European countries. **31.** France banned all imports from Britain of beef and live cattle because of fears of bovine spongiform encephalopathy (BSE).

June 1. West Germany banned the import of British beef and live cattle because of fears of BSE. Italy followed suit on June 6. **7.** Following an EC emergency council of agriculture ministers, France, Italy and West Germany agreed to lift their bans under certain conditions guaranteeing the safety of British beef. **19.** The European Court of Justice ruled that courts in Britain were empowered to suspend Acts of Parliament on the grounds of incompatability with European Community law. **25.** European Community leaders gathered in Dublin for a summit meeting.

Aug. 21. Jacques Delors, the president of the European Commission, unveiled final plans for monetary union and challenged Britain to say whether it would go the whole way towards economic and monetary union.

MIDDLE EAST

(1989). Sept. 18. The Israeli defence minister, Yitzhak Rabin, arrived in Cairo to discuss an Egyptian plan to resolve the Israeli-Palestinian conflict. **23.** A ceasefire arranged by the Arab League began in Beirut, Lebanon.

Oct. 6. The Israeli cabinet rejected Egypt's proposals for discussions with a Palestinian delegation about elections in the occupied territories. **22.** Lebanon's Christian and Muslim deputies accepted an Arab League plan aimed at bringing lasting peace, but it was rejected by Gen. Michel Aoun, Prime Minister of the Christian military administration in east Beirut.

Nov. 1. Members of the pro-Iranian Islamic Jihad shot dead a Saudi Embassy employee in west Beirut. **5.** Rene Mouawad was elected President of Lebanon; on Nov. 13 Dr Selim al-Hoss was named as Prime Minister. **8.** In elections in Jordan, Muslim fundamentalists won the largest bloc of seats. **22.** President Mouawad of Lebanon was killed in a bomb attack in west Beirut. Elias Hrawi was elected as the new President on Nov. 24.

Dec. 4. Mudar Badran was appointed Prime Minister of Jordan. **10.** The Palestinian *intifada* (uprising) entered its third year. **14.**

Palestinian and Sunni Muslim guerrillas attacked a Syrian post south of Beirut to free Palestinian detainees held by the Syrian Army. Six people were killed and 20 wounded in the attack. **19.** Martial law was lifted in Jordan after 22 years. **26.** Israeli planes destroyed the headquarters of the Lebanese Communist Party in south Lebanon, killing at least three guerrillas. **31.** The Israeli Prime Minister, Yitzhak Shamir, dismissed the Science and Technology minister Ezer Weizman for having contacts with the PLO. Under a compromise reached on Jan. 2, Weizman retained his portfolio but resigned from the inner cabinet.

(1990). Jan. 31. At least 52 people were killed and 190 wounded in tank and artillery battles between the troops of Gen. Michel Aoun and the Phalangist militia in Christian east Beirut.

Feb. 1. A ceasefire was agreed between rival Christian militias in Beirut but the ceasefire collapsed on Feb. 2 when Gen. Aoun's troops laid siege to part of east Beirut. **4.** Eight people were killed and more than 20 were injured when masked gunmen opened fire on an Israeli tourist bus in Egypt travelling from the Gaza strip to Cairo. **12.** The Trade and Industry Minister Ariel Sharon resigned from the Israeli government in protest at the intention of the Prime Minister, Yitzhak Shamir, to hold peace talks with the Palestinians. **24.** A passenger ferry travelling from Cyprus to Lebanon was attacked by a Syrian gunboat. One person was killed and at least 18 were injured.

March 1. A fire in a hotel in Cairo killed at least 16 people. **13.** The Israeli Prime Minister, Yitzhak Shamir, dismissed the Deputy Prime Minister, Shimon Peres, from the cabinet. Other Labour ministers resigned in support of Mr. Peres, ending the Likud-Labour coalition government. On March 15 Mr. Shamir lost a vote of no confidance against his government, which continued in office as an interim government while attempts were made to form a new government. **22.** Two Palestinians were killed by Israeli troops in a new wave of unrest in the occupied territories.

April 2. President Hussein of Iraq said that Iraq possessed advanced chemical weapons and threatened to destroy 'half of Israel' if Israel attacked Iraq. **11.** Three European hostages held in Lebanon by the Libyan-backed Fatah Revolutionary Council were released in west Beirut. The three were Jacqueline Valente, a Frenchwoman, Fernand Houtekins, a Belgian, and their two-year-old daughter Sophie-Liberté, who was born in captivity. Their release occurred a few weeks after France delivered to Libya three Mirage fighter jets impounded since 1986, contravening the 1986 EC embargo on supplying arms to Libya. **18.** Eleven children and four adults died in east Beirut when a school minibus was hit by incendiary gunfire. **22.** Professor Robert Polhill, an American, held captive in Lebanon by pro-Iranian kidnappers for 39 months, was released in Syria. On April 30 another American hostage, Frank Reed, held captive since September 1986, was released in west Beirut.

May 14. Jordanian troops halted an attempt by thousands of pro-Palestinian demonstrators to storm the Allenby Bridge which divides Jordan from the Israeli-occupied West Bank. **20.** An apparently deranged Israeli shot dead seven Palestinians. The attack sparked riots in the occupied territories, and by May 22, 21 Palestinians had been killed by the Israeli Defence Forces. **22.** The Yemen Arab Republic and the People's Democratic Republic of Yemen formally declared the creation of a new unified state, the Republic of Yemen.

June 11. The Israeli parliament approved the new coalition government of Yitzhak Shamir, the Prime Minister, replacing the coalition which collapsed in March. **20.** The USA suspended its 18-month dialogue with the PLO after the PLO failed to condemn a terrorist attack on an Israeli beach in May. **21.** An earthquake measuring 7·7 on the Richter scale struck north-west Iran, killing over 35,000 people. The earthquake was followed by numerous aftershocks and tremors, which hampered rescue attempts.

July 2. Over 1,400 pilgrims died in a crush in a tunnel near the Muslim holy city of Mecca, when heavy congestion led to a frantic bid to escape. **27.** OPEC oil ministers agreed to raise the price of crude oil by $3 a barrel, the first increase announced by the organization in a decade.

Aug. 24. Brian Keenan, the Irish hostage held captive in Beirut for over four years, was released by his captors, Islamic Dawn.

THE GULF CRISIS

(1990). July 17. President Saddam Hussein of Iraq said that the other Arab states of the Gulf were undermining Iraq's foreign exchange earnings by depressing oil prices on the international markets through overproduction. He accused Kuwait and the United Arab Emirates in particular. **18.** Iraq accused Kuwait of violating its southern border and exploiting an Iraqi oilfield, and demanded compensation for the 'stolen' oil.

19. Kuwait refuted Iraq's accusations. Iraqi troops started massing on the disputed border with Kuwait.

Aug. 1. Iraq and Kuwait began talks to try to settle Iraqi territorial and oil claims but the talks collapsed when Kuwait refused to bow to Iraq's demands. 2. Iraqi troops invaded and occupied Kuwait. Iraq said that it had sent troops to support a coup overthrowing the Emir of Kuwait. A pro-Iraqi government was installed in Kuwait and the dismissal of the Emir and the ruling al-Sabah family was announced. The UN Security Council condemned the invasion and demanded the immediate, unconditional withdrawal of Iraq. 4. Iraqi troops started to mass on the border with Saudi Arabia. Thirty-five British servicemen at a military base in Kuwait were seized by Iraqi troops and taken to Baghdad. The European Community countries, the USA and Japan put an embargo on oil imports from Iraq and Kuwait. 6. The UN Security Council voted to impose mandatory economic sanctions on Iraq, including a world-wide ban on oil exports and an arms embargo. The Iraqi foreign ministry confirmed reports that people of certain nationalities were being prevented from leaving Kuwait and were being moved from Kuwait to Iraq. 7. President Bush offered to send American troops to Saudi Arabia to protect the kingdom from the threat of Iraqi attack. King Fahd accepted the offer and American troops, ships and planes began to leave for the Middle East. 8. Iraq announced the annexation of Kuwait. The British government decided to send air and naval forces to join the multi-national effort to defend Saudi Arabia. 10. President Saddam Hussein called for a holy war to drive western forces from the Gulf. Twelve of the 20 nations at a League of Arab Nations summit in Cairo voted to send troops to defend Saudi Arabia. 16. Iraq ordered all Britons and Americans in Kuwait to report to hotels. However, those arriving at the hotels found no one there to direct them and returned home. 18. The UN Security Council adopted resolution 664 calling for the release of foreign nationals held in Iraq and Kuwait. 19. Iraqi troops in Kuwait began house-to-house searches to round up Britons, Americans, French and Germans in Kuwait to be used as a human shield at sites of strategic importance to deter attacks. 20. Foreign embassies in Kuwait were ordered by Iraq to close by Aug. 24 and to transfer staff to Baghdad. 24. Embassies which did not comply with the order to close were surrounded by Iraqi troops and essential services were cut off. 25. The UN Security Council adopted resolution 665, authorizing states with vessels in the Gulf to ensure compliance with the economic sanctions against Iraq. 28. Iraq declared Kuwait the 19th province of Iraq and changed the name of Kuwait City to Khadima. 31. The UN secretary-general,

Javier Perez de Cuéllar, and the Iraqi foreign minister, Tariq Aziz, held talks in Jordan.

INTERNATIONAL RELATIONS

(1989). Sept. 18. Hungary and Israel re-established full diplomatic relations after a break of 22 years. 23. It was announced that a summit meeting between the Soviet Union and the USA would be held in the USA in the spring or summer of 1990. 25. President Bush of the USA proposed that immediate steps should be taken to ensure the elimination of chemical weapons within ten years.

Oct. 1. Pakistan formally re-acceded to the Commonwealth as its 49th member state. 18. The Commonwealth Heads of Government meeting began in Kuala Lumpur, Malaysia. On the first day of the meeting, the heads of government elected Chief Emeka Anyaoku of Nigeria to succeed Sir Shridath Ramphal as Secretary-General of the Commonwealth Secretariat in July 1990. 19. Britain and Argentina formally agreed to end the hostilities begun in 1982 over the Falkland Islands.

Nov. 7. The US Government agreed to repay the greater part of Iranian assets in the USA, which were frozen following the seizure of the US Embassy in Tehran in 1979. 16. The United Nations General Assembly voted to support the Khmer Rouge and their non-communist allies in Kampuchea.

Dec. 1. Pope John Paul II and the Soviet leader, Mikhail Gorbachov, agreed on the resumption of official relations between the Holy See and the USSR. 2. A summit meeting between President Bush of the USA and Mr. Gorbachov began in Malta. 19. The Soviet Foreign Minister, Eduard Shevardnadze, visited the NATO headquarters in Belgium.

(1990). Jan. 29. The USA announced that it was to reduce its military presence in Britain, withdrawing 2,750 troops.

Feb. 1. The British Home Secretary (David Waddington) ordered the deportation of nine Iranians for 'reasons of national security'. 13. The Soviet Union accepted proposals by President Bush for major troop reductions in Europe. 15. Britain and Argentina agreed to restore diplomatic relations. 23. The UN General Assembly declared the period 1991–2000 the UN Decade Against Drug Abuse.

March 8. Farzad Bazoft, an Iranian-born journalist with British residency rights, and a British nurse, Daphne Parish, went on trial in Baghdad accused of espionage. On March 10 Bazoft was sentenced to death and Mrs. Parish to 15 years in prison. President Hussein of Iraq rejected British protests at the sentences and international appeals for clemency, and on March 15 Bazoft was hanged. **27.** Senior officials of the 10 member countries of COMECON agreed to abolish two of the organization's primary functions: multi-lateral co-operation and the co-ordination of economic planning. **28.** A joint British and US customs investigation uncovered a clandestine operation to smuggle nuclear devices from the USA to Iraq via Britain.

April 9. The World Ministerial Drugs summit began in London. Iraq announced that it was expelling an American diplomat in retaliation for the declaration by the US Government that an Iraqi delegate to the United Nations was *persona non grata*. **10.** British customs and excise officers at Teesport detained a consignment of steel cylinders bound for Iraq, which they believed to be part of a huge gun capable of firing nuclear or chemical shells. On April 20 parts for the 'supergun' were seized in Greece and Turkey.

May 31. President Bush of the USA and President Gorbachov of the USSR began a summit meeting in Washington.

June 1. The USA and the USSR signed a preliminary accord on a treaty to reduce long-range nuclear missiles and signed an agreement banning the production of chemical weapons. The newly formed Group of 15 (G-15), formed by 15 non-aligned, industrializing nations, met for its first summit in Kuala Lumpur, Malaysia. **7.** Mrs Thatcher arrived in Moscow for a summit meeting with President Gorbachov.

July 6. After its two-day summit in London, Nato issued a declaration widely regarded as formally ending the Cold War. It outlined unprecedented co-operation with Warsaw Pact countries, and plans for cutting conventional forces in Europe. **16.** The Soviet Union accepted that a united Germany was free to ally itself with Nato, despite initial worries that this would alter the balance of security in Europe. **18.** The USA announced that it would forge new contacts with Vietnam as part of an effort to prevent Khmer Rouge

forces regaining power in Cambodia. Daphne Parish, the British nurse who in March was imprisoned for 15 years in Iraq, was released from prison following the intercession of President Kaunda of Zambia.

Aug. 28. The five permanent members of the UN Security Council reached agreement on a UN peace plan to end the civil war in Cambodia. The proposal is to be discussed by the country's four warring factions at talks in September.

MISCELLANEOUS

(1989). Oct. 12. Archaeologists working on the south bank of the Thames in London discovered the remains of the Globe Theatre.

Nov. 12. Hereford Cathedral's Mappa Mundi was saved from auction and possible export by the provision of £2 million by the National Heritage Memorial Fund and £1 million by John Paul Getty to build and endow a heritage centre to house the map and other historic artefacts. **30.** The Arts Council announced that its grant aid to Kent Opera would not continue.

Dec. 5. A large Roman docks complex was uncovered in the grounds of Guy's Hospital, London.

(1990). Jan. 28. A new Sunday newspaper, the *Independent on Sunday*, was launched.

March 21. The Australian businessman Alan Bond sold the Van Gogh painting *Irises* to the Getty Museum in California for £25 million. Mr. Bond bought the painting in 1987 for £30·2 million, which made it the world's most expensive painting.

May 16. A painting by Van Gogh, *Portrait of Dr. Gachet*, sold for £49·5 million at Christie's in New York.

Aug. 3. This was the hottest day in Britain since records began. A temperature of 37·1°C (98·8°F) was officially recorded at Cheltenham.

OBITUARIES

SEPT. 1, 1989–AUG. 31, 1990

Agnew, Cdr. Sir Peter, Bt., Conservative MP for Camborne 1931–50 and for South Worcestershire 1955–66, *aged* 90—Aug. 26.

Ailey, Alvin, American dancer, choreographer and director, *aged* 58—Dec. 1, 1989.

Allen, Sir George (Gubby), CBE, cricketer, *aged* 87—Nov. 29, 1989.

Allen, Elizabeth, film and stage star and television personality, *aged* 80—July 27.

Ames, Leslie, CBE, cricketer, *aged* 84—Feb. 27.

Arias, Dr. Roberto, Panamanian diplomat and politician, *aged* 71—Nov. 22, 1989.

Bailey, Pearl, entertainer, *aged* 72—Aug. 17.

Barker, Eric, actor and comedian, *aged* 78—June 1.

Barrington, 11th Viscount, *aged* 81—April 6.

Bavadra, Dr. Timoci, Prime Minister of Fiji April–May 1987, *aged* 55—Nov. 3, 1989.

Bawden, Edward, CBE, RA, artist and book illustrator, *aged* 86—Nov. 21, 1989.

Bazoft, Farzad, *Observer* journalist, *aged* 31—*executed* March 15.

Beckett, Samuel, Irish playwright and Nobel laureate, *aged* 83—Dec. 22, 1989.

Berkeley, Sir Lennox, CBE, composer, *aged* 86—Dec. 26, 1989.

Berlin, Irving, American songwriter, *aged* 101—Sept. 22, 1989.

Blaize, Rt. Hon. Herbert, Prime Minister of Grenada since 1984, *aged* 71—Dec. 19, 1989.

Blundy, David, war correspondent for the *Sunday Correspondent*, *aged* 44—Nov. 17, 1989.

Braybrooke, 9th Baron, *aged* 93—Feb. 12.

Bruce-Gardyne, Lord, journalist and former Conservative MP and Minister, *aged* 60—April 15.

Bülbring, Prof. Edith, FRS, Professor of Pharmacology, Oxford University 1967–71, *aged* 86—July 5.

Cameron, Prof. Gordon, Master of Fitzwilliam College, Cambridge, since 1988, *aged* 52—March 14.

Capucine, French actress, *aged* 57—March 17.

Carey Evans, Lady Olwen, DBE, *aged* 97—March 2.

Carr, Michael, MP, Labour MP for Bootle since May 1990 by-election, *aged* 43—July 20.

Ceausescu, Nicolae, President of Romania 1967–89, *aged* 71—*executed* Dec. 25, 1989.

Chancellor, Sir Christopher, CMG, manager of Reuters 1944–59, *aged* 85—Sept. 9, 1989.

Chapman, Graham, actor, *aged* 48—Oct. 4, 1989.

Charleson, Ian, actor, *aged* 40—Jan. 6.

Chesham, 5th Baron, PC, Labour politician, *aged* 73—Dec. 23, 1989.

Cholmondeley, 6th Marquess, GCVO, MC, Lord Great Chamberlain since 1966, *aged* 70—March 13.

Cochrane of Cults, 3rd Baron, *aged* 67—June 15.

Craven, 8th Earl, *aged* 28—Aug. 30.

Cromartie, 4th Earl, MC, TD, *aged* 85—Dec. 13, 1989.

Daresbury, 2nd Baron, *aged* 87—Feb. 15.

Davis, Bette, actress, *aged* 81—Oct. 6, 1989.

Davis, jun., Sammy, American actor and entertainer, *aged* 64—May 16.

Dexter, John, theatre and opera director, *aged* 64—March 23.

Drake, Fabia, OBE, actress, *aged* 86—Feb. 28.

Drogheda, 11th Earl of, KG, KBE, *aged* 79—Dec. 24, 1989.

Duarte, José Napoléon, President of El Salvador 1984–89, *aged* 64—Feb. 23.

Earle, Air Chief Marshal Sir Alfred, GBE, CB, *aged* 82—March 27.

Eastaugh, Rt. Rev. John, Bishop of Hereford since 1974, *aged* 69—Feb. 16.

Edwards, Robert (Bob), Labour MP for Bilston 1955–74 and Wolverhampton South East 1974–87, *aged* 85—June 4.

Elliott, Rev. Keith, VC, *aged* 73—Oct. 7, 1989.

Elwyn-Jones, Lord, CH, PC, Lord Chancellor 1974–79, *aged* 80—Dec. 4, 1989.

Erté (Romain de Tirtoff), Russian-born artist and designer, *aged* 97—April 21.

Esmond, Jill, film and stage actress, *aged* 82—July 28.

Fletcher, Ted, PC, Labour MP for East Islington 1945–70 and Deputy Speaker 1966–68, *aged* 87—June 9.

Fletcher, Sir Alexander, Conservative MP for Edinburgh North 1973–83 and for Edinburgh Central 1983–87, *aged* 60—Sept. 18, 1989.

Forbes, Malcolm, American magazine publisher, *aged* 70—Feb. 24.

Franz Josef II, Prince of Liechtenstein since 1938, *aged* 83—Nov. 13, 1989.

Gammans, Lady (Ann), Conservative MP for Hornsey 1957–66, *aged* 91—Dec. 28, 1989.

Garbo, Greta, Swedish-born film actress, *aged* 84—April 15.

Gardiner, Lord, CH, PC, Lord Chancellor 1964–70, *aged* 89—Jan. 7.

Gardner, Ava, American film actress, *aged* 67—Jan. 25.

Gascoigne, Maj.-Gen. Sir Julian, KCMG, KCVO, CB, DSO, Governor General of Bermuda 1959–64, *aged* 86—Feb. 26.

Gibbons, Stella, author, *aged* 87—Dec. 19, 1989.

Goddard, Paulette, American film actress, *aged* 78—April 23.

Goldfarb, David, Soviet geneticist and dissident, *aged* 71—Feb. 24.

Goodall, Sir Reginald, conductor, *aged* 88—May 5.

Gow, Ian, TD, MP, Conservative MP for Eastbourne since 1974, *aged* 53—July 30.

Graziano, Rocky, boxer, *aged* about 68—May 22.

Greenhill, 2nd Baron, MD, *aged* 72—Sept. 28, 1989.

Gucci, Aldo, Italian fashion accessories designer, *aged* 84—Jan. 20.

Hall, Henry, bandleader, *aged* 91—Oct. 28, 1989.

Halston, American fashion designer, *aged* 57—March.

Hamilton of Dalzell, 3rd Baron, GCVO, MC, *aged* 78—Jan. 31.

Harmsworth, 2nd Baron, artist, *aged* 86—June 1.

Harrison, Sir Rex, actor, *aged* 82—June 2.

Harting, Hans, artist, *aged* 85—Dec. 7, 1989.

Harvie-Watt, Sir George, Bt., Conservative MP for Keighley 1931–35 and Richmond upon Thames 1937–59, *aged* 86—Dec. 18, 1989.

Harwood, Elizabeth, opera and lieder singer, *aged* 52—June 22.

Heddle, John, MP, Conservative MP for Lichfield and Tamworth 1979–83 and for Mid Staffordshire since 1983, *aged* 48—Dec. 19, 1989.

Henson, Jim, creator of the Muppets, *aged* 53—May 16.

Heycock, Lord, CBE, *aged* 84—March 14.

Hiley, Joseph, Conservative MP for Pudsey 1959–74, *aged* 87—Nov. 17, 1989.

Hopkins, Adm. Sir Frank, KCB, DSO, DSC, *aged* 79—April 14.

Hopkinson, Sir Tom, CBE, author and journalist, *aged* 85—June 20.

Horowitz, Vladimir, Russian-born pianist, *aged* 85—Nov. 5, 1989.

Hughes, Sean, MP, Labour MP for Knowsley South since 1983, *aged* 44—June 24.

Hull, Field Marshal Sir Richard, KG, GCB, DSC, *aged* 82—Sept. 17, 1989.

Huntingdon, 15th Earl, *aged* 89—Aug. 24.

Huntley, Raymond, actor, *aged* 86—June 15.

Ibárruri, Dolores (La Pasionaria), Communist leader in Spanish Civil War, *aged* 93—Nov. 12, 1989.

Inchyra, 1st Baron, GCMG, CVO, *aged* 89—Oct. 16, 1989.

Ireland, Jill, film actress, *aged* 54—May 18.

Irving of Dartford, Lord, PC, Labour politician and former MP for Dartford, *aged* 71—Dec. 18, 1989.

Jackson, Gordon, OBE, actor, *aged* 66—Jan. 14.

Jennings, John, Conservative MP for Burton-on-Trent 1955–74, *aged* 87—June 17.

Jessel, 2nd Baron, CBE, *aged* 86—June 13.

Keys, William (Bill), general secretary of SOGAT 1974–85, *aged* 67—May 19.

Kilbrandon, Lord, PC, former Lord of Appeal, *aged* 83—Sept. 10, 1989.

Kintore, 12th Earl, *aged* 81—Oct. 1, 1989.

Kreisky, Dr. Bruno, Federal Chancellor of Austria 1970–83, *aged* 79—July 29.

Lawrence, Ashley, conductor, *aged* 55—May 7.

Lehmann, Rosamond, CBE, novelist, *aged* 89—March 12.

Lewis, Ronald, Labour MP for Carlisle 1964–87, *aged* 80—June 18.

Lockwood, Margaret, CBE, actress, *aged* 73—July 15.

Loss, Joe, LVO, OBE, bandleader, *aged* 80—June 6.

Lungley, Alfred, GC, *aged* 84—Dec. 31, 1989.

McAlpine of Moffat, Lord, *aged* 82—Jan. 7.

McBean, Angus, photographer, *aged* 86—June 9.

McCarthy, Mary, American writer, *aged* 77—Oct. 25, 1989.

MacColl, Ewan, folk singer, songwriter and playwright, *aged* 74—Oct. 22, 1989.

McCusker, Harold, MP, Ulster Unionist MP for Upper Bann since 1983, *aged* 50—Feb. 12.

McLachlan, Charles, CBE, QPM, Inspector of Constabulary since 1987, *aged* 58—April 3.

Maclean, Lord, Bt., KT, GCVO, KBE, Royal Victorian Chain, PC, Lord Chamberlain of HM Household 1971–84, *aged* 73—Feb. 8.

McNeill, Mr Justice (Sir David), High Court judge since 1979, *aged* 67—Feb. 26.

MacPherson, Rt. Rev. Colin, RC Bishop of Argyll and the Isles since 1969, *aged* 72—March.

Marcos, Ferdinand, President of the Philippines 1965–86, *aged* 72—Sept. 28, 1989.

Marley, 2nd Baron, *aged* 76—March 13.

Mawby, Raymond, Conservative MP for Totnes 1955–83, *aged* 68—July.

Mercer, Joe, OBE, football player and manager, *aged* 76—Aug. 9.

Milburn, Colin, cricketer, *aged* 48—Feb. 28.

Molony, Tim, National Hunt jockey and trainer, *aged* 70—Dec. 14, 1989.

Morris of Grasmere, Lord, KCMG, *aged* 92—May 30.

Mumford, Lewis, American writer and social philosopher, *aged* 94—Jan. 26.

Ó Fiaich, Cardinal Tomás, RC Archbishop of Armagh and Primate of All Ireland since 1977, *aged* 66—May 8.

O'Neill of the Maine, Lord, PC(NI), Prime Minister of Northern Ireland 1963–69, *aged* 75—June 12.

Orr, Capt. Lawrence (Willy), Unionist MP for Down South 1950–74, *aged* 71—July 11.

Paget of Northampton, Lord, QC, Labour politician and former MP for Northampton, *aged* 81—Jan. 2.

Palmer, 3rd Baron, OBE, *aged* 74—June 26.

Paradjanov, Sergei, Armenian film director, *aged* 66—July 20.

Parkinson, Norman, CBE, photographer, *aged* 76—Feb. 14.

Pavitt, Laurie, Labour MP for Willesden West (later Brent South) 1959–87, *aged* 75—Dec. 14, 1989.

Pertini, Alessandro (Sandro), President of Italy 1978–85, *aged* 93—Feb. 24.

Phillimore, 3rd Baron, *aged* 50—Feb. 26.

Pimen, Patriarch of Moscow and All Russia since 1971, *aged* 79—May 3.

Ponsonby of Shulbrede, 3rd Baron, Chief Opposition Whip in the House of Lords since 1982, *aged* 59—June 13.

Portland, 9th Duke, CMG, *aged* 93—July 30.

Powell, Michael, film director, *aged* 84—Feb. 19.

Pritchard, Sir John, CBE, conductor, *aged* 68—Dec. 5, 1989.

Puig, Manuel, Argentine novelist, *aged* 57—July 22.

Quayle, Sir Anthony, CBE, actor, *aged* 76—Oct. 21, 1989.

Rajneesh, Bhagwan Shree, guru, *aged* 58—Jan. 19.

Rathcreedan, 2nd Baron, TD, *aged* 84—May 15.

Ray, Johnnie, American singer, *aged* 63—Feb. 24.

Reid, Prof. Gordon, Governor of Western Australia 1984–88, *aged* 66—Oct. 1989.

Reid, Maj. Pat, escape officer at Colditz prisoner-of-war camp 1940–42, *aged* 79—May 22.

Richmond (9th) and Gordon (4th), Duke of, *aged* 85—Nov. 2, 1989.

Roberts, Allan, MP, Labour MP for Bootle since 1979, *aged* 46—March 22.

Rothschild, 3rd Baron, GBE, GM, FRS, scientist and government adviser, *aged* 79—March 20.

Rugby, 2nd Baron, *aged* 76—Jan. 12.

Runciman of Doxford, 2nd Viscount, OBE, AFC, *aged* 89—Sept. 1, 1989.

Sachs, Leonard, actor and *Good Old Days* master of ceremonies, *aged* about 80—June 15.

Saint Brides, Lord, GCMG, CVO, MBE, PC, former diplomat, *aged* 73—Nov. 26, 1989.

Sakharov, Andrei, Soviet nuclear physicist and dissident, *aged* 68—Dec. 14, 1989.

Scott, William, CBE, RA, artist, *aged* 76—Dec. 28, 1989.

Semprini, OBE, pianist, *aged* 81—Jan. 19.

Simenon, Georges, Belgian author, *aged* 86—Sept. 4, 1989.

Smith-Ryland, Sir Charles, KCVO, Lord Lieutenant of Warwickshire since 1968, *aged* 62—Nov. 14, 1989.

Soupault, Philippe, French writer and founder of Surrealism, *aged* 92—March 11.

Spear, Ruskin, CBE, RA, artist, *aged* 78—Jan 17.

Stanwyck, Barbara, American film actress, *aged* 82—Jan. 20.

Starcevich, Leslie, VC, *aged* 71—Nov. 17, 1989.

Stewart of Fulham, Lord, CH, PC, Labour MP 1945–74, Minister 1964–70 and Foreign Secretary 1965–66 and 1968–70, *aged* 83—March 10.

Stollmeyer, Jeffrey, Trinidadian cricketer, *aged* 68—Sept. 1989.

Stratton, Lt.-Gen. Sir William, KCB, CVO, CBE, DSO, *aged* 86—Nov. 25, 1989.

Strong, Patience (Mrs Winifred Cushing), authoress of verses, *aged* 83—Aug. 28.

Sumner, Donald, OBE, QC, former circuit judge and Conservative MP for Orpington 1955–62, *aged* 76—May 12.

Swaythling, 3rd Baron, OBE, *aged* 91—Jan. 5.

Syme, Sir Ronald, OM, historian, *aged* 86—Sept. 4, 1989.

Terry-Thomas, actor, *aged* 78—Jan. 8.

Thomas, Dorothy, GC, SRN, *aged* 84—Nov. 22, 1989.

Thomson, Virgil, American writer, *aged* 92—Sept. 30, 1989.

Tinling, Teddy, fashion designer and tennis official, *aged* 79—May.

Trafford, Lord, Minister of State for Health since July 1989, *aged* 57—Sept. 16, 1989.

Trewin, J. C., critic and author, *aged* 81—Feb. 16.

Turner, Dame Eva, DBE, opera singer, *aged* 98—June 16.

Van Cleef, Lee, American film actor, *aged* 64—Dec. 16, 1989.

van Praagh, Dame Peggy, DBE, ballet dancer and director, *aged* 79—Jan. 15.

Vaughan, Sarah, jazz singer, *aged* 66—April 3.

Wall, Max, actor and comedian, *aged* 82—May 22.

Wall, Pat, MP, Labour MP for Bradford North since 1987, *aged* 57—Aug. 6.

Wallace, Irving, American author, *aged* 74—June 29.

Waters, Elsie, entertainer, *aged* about 95—June 14.

Waverley, 2nd Viscount, *aged* 79—Feb. 21.

Wedemeyer, Gen. Albert, American military strategist, *aged* 92—Dec. 17, 1989.

Wells, William, Labour MP for Walsall 1945–55 and for Walsall North 1955–Feb. 1974, *aged* 81—Jan. 3.

Wilde, Cornel, American film actor and director, *aged* 74—Oct. 16, 1989.

Wright, Peter, VC, *aged* 73—April 5.

Wynne, Greville, businessman and British intelligence agent, *aged* 71—Feb. 28.

Yana, singer, *aged* 57—Nov. 21, 1989.

Zetland, 3rd Marquess, *aged* 80—Oct. 5, 1989.

The Princess Royal visited the Soviet Union in May–June, the first member of the British royal family to do so since the 1917 revolution (*Popperfoto*)

514

[1991]

NEW PRESIDENT OF CZECHOSLOVAKIA

Popular unrest led to constitutional reform in Czechoslovakia and the election of dissident writer Vaclav Havel as President in December 1989 (*Popperfoto*)

Popular unrest in Romania led to the overthrow of the Ceausescu regime in December 1989 (*Popperfoto*)

Popular unrest in East Germany led to the downfall of Communist power, symbolized by the opening of
the Berlin Wall crossing-points in November 1989 (*Popperfoto*)

TREATY ON GERMANY

The USA, Britain, the USSR, France, and East and West Germany signed an agreement in September formally ending the Second World War and permitting German reunification (*Associated Press*)

SOUTH AFRICA

The black nationalist leader Nelson Mandela was released in February after 27 years in prison (*Popperfoto*)

NAMIBIA

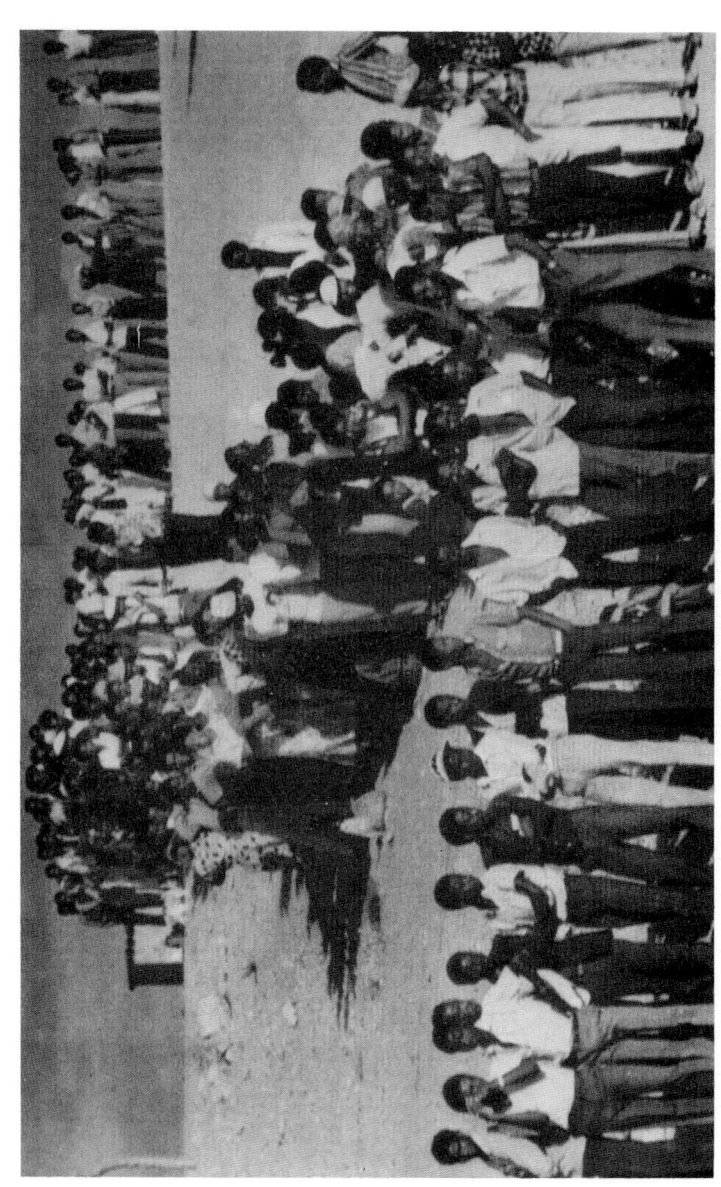

Namibian voters elected a government in November 1989, in preparation for the country's independence in March (*Popperfoto*)

POLL TAX RIOT

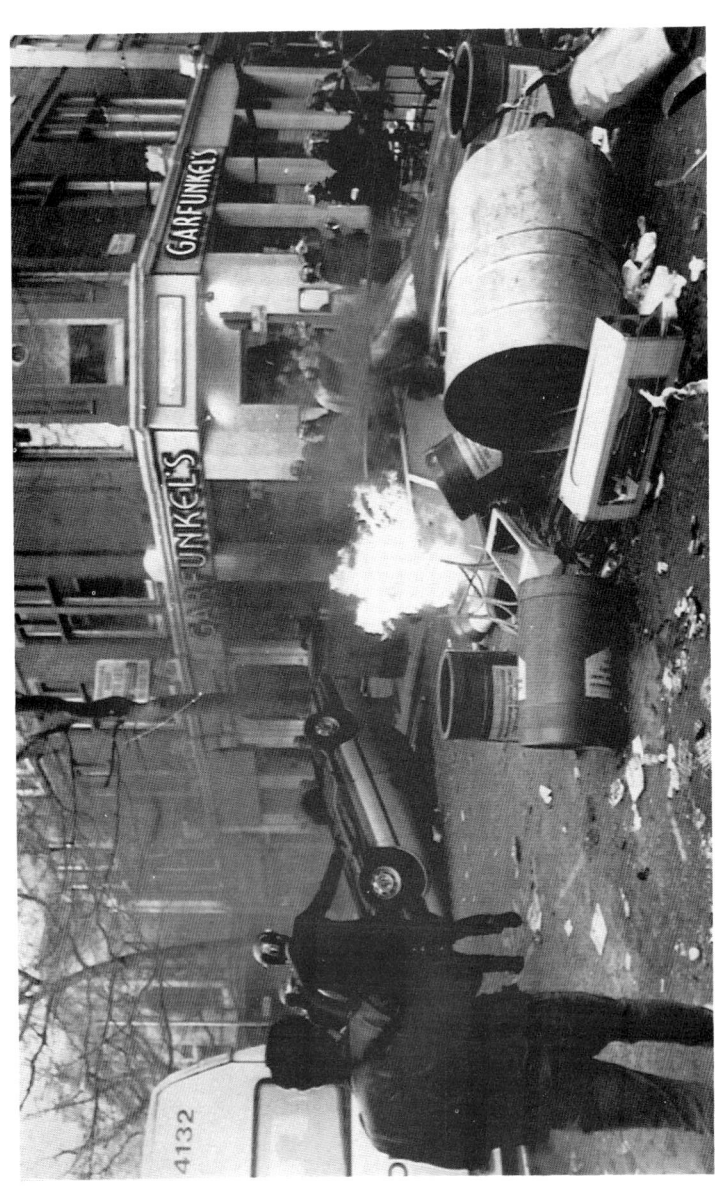

A march to protest against the community charge ended in violence, with rioting and looting in the West End of London, in March (*Press Association*)

STRANGEWAYS SIEGE

After a riot at Strangeways prison, Manchester, in April, prisoners took over and held the prison for 25 days (*Popperfoto*)

KUWAIT

Iraq invaded and occupied Kuwait in August (*Popperfoto*)

WINTER STORMS

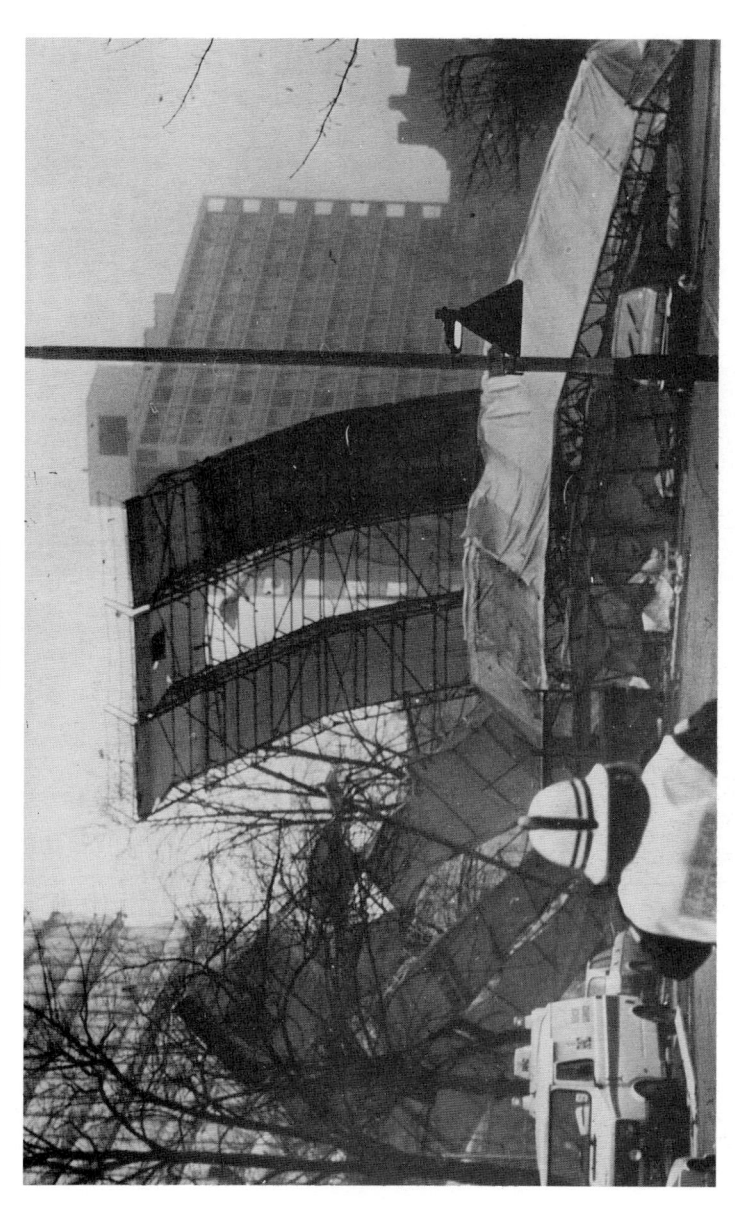

Gales and flooding caused extensive damage nationwide in January (*Popperfoto*)

Andrei Sakharov (*top left*), Vladimir Horowitz (*top right*), Max Wall (*bottom left*), Samuel Beckett.

Greta Garbo (*top left*), Bette Davis (*top right*), Ava Gardner (*bottom left*), Rex Harrison.

WIMBLEDON RECORD

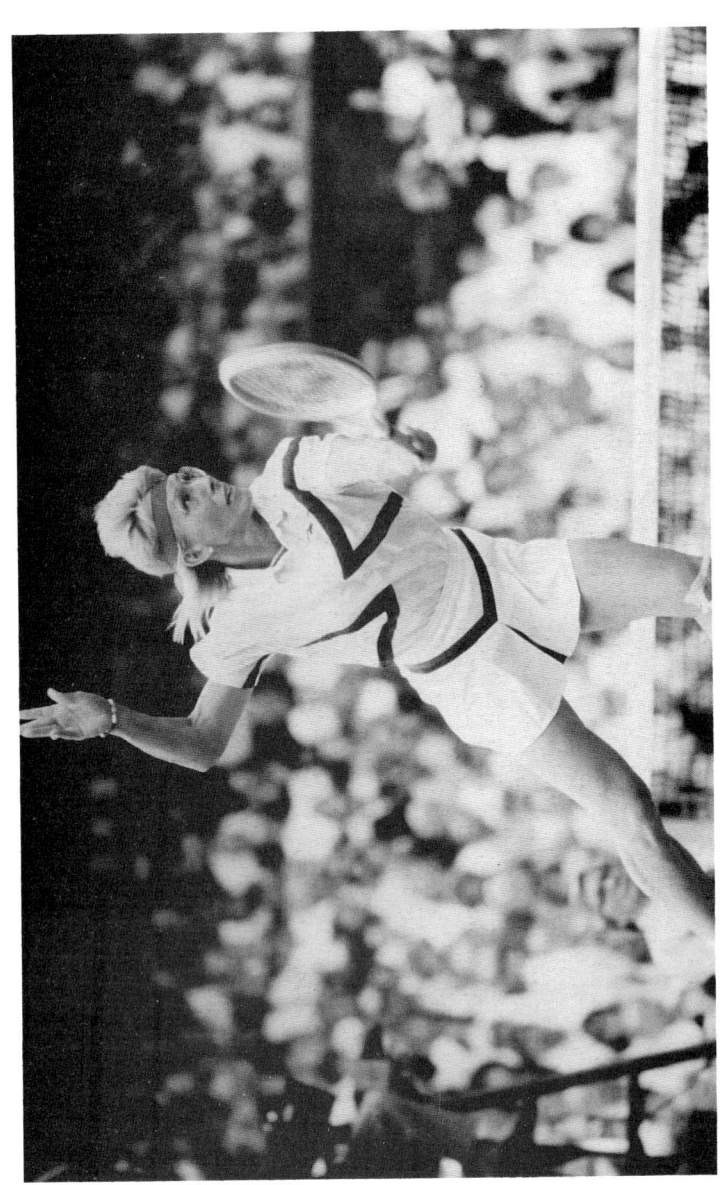

Martina Navratilova won the women's singles title at Wimbledon in July for a record ninth time (*Sporting Pictures*)

GOLFING TRIUMPH

After winning the US Masters in April, Nick Faldo also won the Open at St. Andrews in July (*Press Association*)

Graham Gooch, the England cricket captain, made record scores in the Test series against New Zealand and India in the summer (*Press Association*)

ONE HUNDRED YEARS AGO

Events of 100 Years Ago (1891).—A selection follows of 'Remarkable Occurrences' (as 'Events of the Year' was then called), as printed in the 1892 and 1893 editions of *Whitaker's Almanack* covering the year 1891.

The Prime Minister of the day was the Marquis of Salisbury and George Goschen was Chancellor of the Exchequer. Irish Home Rule agitation continued, but the standing of Charles Stewart Parnell, the movement's most charismatic leader, had been irreparably damaged when he was cited as co-respondent in the O'Shea divorce case in 1890. Parnell died on October 6, 1891.

January

1. Temporary thaw after 21 days' frost.
— Victoria Dock strike renewed.
3. Eviction of Scottish railway strikers commenced at Motherwell.
5. Military called out at Motherwell evictions.
— Frost renewed in London.
7. Conference of Irish members at Boulogne concluded.
— Chilian navy in revolt.
9. Meetings of unemployed in London; great distress reported owing to frost.
13. Parnell presided over meeting of the National League, Dublin.
14. Mrs. Mitchell, baby farmer at Vauxhall, sentenced to 12 months imprisonment.
19. Work by Aristotle discovered at British Museum.
23. Commons: Mr. Channing's motion on Railway Servants' hours lost by 141 to 124.
26. Lords: Smoke Abatement Bill introduced.
27. Commons expunged resolution of June 22, 1880, relating to Mr. Bradlaugh and the Oath.
29. Scottish railway strike compromised.

February

3. Mr. Bradlaugh buried at Woking.
4. Gladstone's Disabilities Removal Bill rejected by 256 to 223.
9. Bill introduced in the House of Lords allowing women to serve on County Councils.
— Lord Mayor's memorial to the Tsar touching Jewish persecutions in Russia returned.
12. Mr. Dillon and Mr. O'Brien arrested at Folkestone.
13. Tenth Whitechapel murder.
— Messrs. Dillon and O'Brien taken to Clonmel Prison.
16. Meeting of Parnellites in Committee Room No. 15, under Parnell, passed resolution of confidence in him.
17. Lords rejected Women's Franchise Bill without division.
20. Commons rejected Morgan's motion for disestablishing the Welsh Church by 235 to 203.
24. Hearing of the will suit O'Shea *v.* Wood commenced before Justice Jeune.
25. Riot at eviction of strikers on Lord Londonderry's Silksworth Collieries, thirty men injured in baton charge.
26. Details received of fall of Iquique—250 women and children killed.

March

2. Wesley's statue in the City Road unveiled and centenary commemorated by Methodists.
3. Commons rejected Mr. Stansfeld's 'One man one vote' resolution by 62 to 39.
9. Mrs. Jackson abducted by her husband.
— Great snowstorm and gale; many ships lost, and many trains snowed up in Devonshire.
13. Mr. Parnell issued manifesto to Irish in America asking for funds.

16. Submarine telephone cable from London to Paris completed.
—Writ of Habeas Corpus compelling Mr. Jackson to produce his wife refused by Justices Cave and Jeune.
17. Alice Reeves, baby farmer, sentenced to 10 years penal servitude.
19. The Lord Chancellor, Master of the Rolls, and Lord Justice Fry, on appeal, order Mrs. Jackson's liberation.
20. Prince Napoleon buried at Turin.
25. Mr. Morley examined as witness at Tipperary riots trial, Cork.
27. Cork courthouse accidentally burned during judge's summing up in Tipperary riots case.
30. News received of the murder of 400 Goorkhas by Manipuris in Assam.

April

1. Prince Victor formally recognized as head of the Bonaparte family.
— Chilian government ship *Florence* destroyed by shell from ironclad *Blanco Encalada*.
3. Australian convention rejected the one man one vote principle.
6. Lieutenant Grant repulsed 3,000 Manipuris at Thobal.
— Information received of rising among Chins in Upper Burmah.
9. Confirmation of murder of British Commissioner in Assam received at India Office.
13. Strike riots at Bradford. Troops called out, many persons injured.
14. Captain Presgrave defeated 300 Manipuris at Paleh.
16. First ballot at Geestemünde results in Prince Bismarck's return.
— Advance of 11,000 men from Kohima to Manipur.
— Appeal Court decided against Miss Cobden's claim to vote as a county councillor.
18. Expeditionary force attacked and routed the Miranzais.
20. Lords passed Electoral Disabilities Removals Bill through committee.
22. Tsar decreed the expulsion of the Jews from Moscow.
23. Mr. Goschen's budget showed surplus of nearly £2,000,000.
25. Severe engagement at Manipur.
27. Information received of the arrival of the British troops at Manipur. City deserted.

May

1. May-Day labour demonstrations, rioting in France and at Rome.
2. Bismarck returned for Geestemünde by large majority over Socialist opponent.
— Monster labour demonstration in Hyde Park.
4. Exciting debate in French Chamber on May-Day riots. Order of the day adopted expressing sympathy with the National Army and the working classes.

11. Attempt on the life of the Tsarevitch at Kioto, Japan.

— Mr. Cunninghame Graham, MP, expelled from France for seditious speeches.

14. Riots at Wuhu, British Consulate wrecked, French Romanist mission burned.

15. Publication of official dispatches on Manipur disaster.

18. Rioting at Belgrade consequent on attempt of Government to forcibly expel Queen Natalie.

19. Queen Natalie left Servia.

21. Four thousand tailors struck in London.

24. Lord Romilly suffocated by upsetting of paraffin lamp.

26. Commons rejected motion in favour of lady county councillors by 78 to 52.

— Lieutenant Grant promoted to major and given Victoria Cross for bravery at Thobal.

June

1. Orient express raided by brigands near Constantinople, five passengers seized, ransomed later.

— Baccarat trial commenced, Sir W. Gordon Cumming denied cheating.

2. Trial of the Regent of Manipur.

— Baccarat case. Prince of Wales examined.

6. Great omnibus strike in London began.

9. Baccarat case resulted in verdict for defendants.

10. Sir W. Gordon Cumming married Miss Garner, an American lady of fortune.

12. End of omnibus strike; directors' terms (reducing working day to twelve hours) accepted.

14. Regent of Manipur condemned to death for treachery.

16. Parliamentary Committee rejected Bill for new line through St. John's Wood.

17. Sentence of high treason passed on M. Turpin, M. Tripone, and two others involved in the Melinite scandals.

19. First section of Manchester Ship Canal opened.

27. Sixty Welsh tinplate works stopped, 25,000 hands thrown out.

July

2. Dr. Jardin, journalist, lost in crater of Mount Vesuvius.

7. Four murderers executed by electricity at Sing Sing prison, New York.

9. Telegram announcing defeat of Balmaceda received at Washington from Iquique.

30. Messrs. Dillon and O'Brien released from Galway Gaol.

— Largest turret ship ever built undocked at Chatham by Viscountess Hood.

August

1. Six hundredth anniversary of Swiss Independence celebrated.

2. Severe storm in London: main sewer burst at Hampstead Heath, carrying away part of L. & N. W. Railway.

10. Manipur massacre: death sentences on Senapati and Tongal General confirmed by Viceroy of India.

11. Export of every kind of grain from Russia prohibited.

16. Socialist congress opened at Brussels; three Anarchists excluded.

19. Cyclone and earthquake at Martinique. All ships in port destroyed; 340 persons killed.

21. Battle of Aconcagua between Balmaceda and Chilian insurgents: heavy losses.

22. Manipur: Viceroy appointed native ruler, the Queen foregoing her rights to annex the State.

23. Further fighting in Chili. Insurgents victorious at Vina del Mar.

26. Further insurgent successes near Valparaiso.

28. Valparaiso captured by insurgents: 5,000 killed and wounded reported. Balmaceda escaped.

29. Sultan consented to throw open Dardanelles to Russian vessels only.

30. Salvationists attacked by a mob at Eastbourne.

31. Santiago captured by insurgents. Order restored at Valparaiso; 200 rioters shot.

September

4. Balmaceda's last warships surrendered.

— Encounter between Parnellites and M'Carthyites at New Tipperary.

5. Chilian Congressionalist army disbanded.

— Mayor of Eastbourne proclaimed Salvationist processions and bands illegal.

12. Sultan received British Ambassador, and is reported to have satisfactorily explained the Dardanelles question.

14. Intelligence of British landing and erecting fortifications in Mitylene, caused great sensation in all European capitals.

16. 'Lohengrin' performed at Paris Opera House; great anti-German demonstration.

— Chilian Provisional Government recognized by France, Germany, and Italy.

17. The Young Ireland League inaugurated at Dublin.

18. Second performance of 'Lohengrin' at Paris: more arrests.

19. Balmaceda committed suicide at Argentine Legation at Santiago.

20. Pope addressed pastoral letter against duelling to German and Austrian Bishops.

— Third representation of 'Lohengrin' passed off quietly.

24. Porte denies that any new measures had been taken with regard to the passage of the Dardanelles.

— Salvationists declared their intention to adhere to musical processions at all risks.

27. Sunday disturbances at Eastbourne renewed.

28. Scottish Eight Hours Legal Day League formed at Glasgow.

30. Boulanger committed suicide.

October

1. Women's Suffrage Bill, Victoria, withdrawn.

2. O'Brien found guilty of libelling Prince George of Wales at Montreal.

6. M. Rochefort's goods confiscated and sold.

7. New King of Würtemberg proclaimed.

10. Funerals of Mr. Parnell at Glasnevin, and of Mr. W. H. Smith at Hambleden.

12. Prayers for Russian Jews offered in London synagogues.

— Heavy destructive gales in the British Isles, lasting three days.

21. Rev. Dr. Clutterbuck, Government Inspector at Workhouse Schools, charged with fraud.

22. Publication of Dr. Koch's new remedy for tuberculosis.

25. 'Jack the Ripper' murder in Berlin.

26. Dynamite outrage in Dublin.

27. Collision between Parnellites and anti-Parnellites at Cork.

29. Terrible Earthquake reported from Yokohama.

November

7. Further deaths reported from earthquake of Oct. 28, making total 6,500.

11. Terrible gales, especially on south coast. Numerous wrecks at Sandgate, Hastings, and Folkestone.

21. Dr. Clutterbuck sentenced to four years' penal servitude.

24. Marshal da Fonseca's Government overthrown in Brazil.

30. News received of massacre of European and native Christians in North China.

December

1. Commencement of the Russell divorce suit.

2. Mr. Goschen addressed special meeting of London Chamber of Commerce concerning £1 notes.

6. Continuation of Salvation Army disturbances at Eastbourne.

7. Her Majesty congratulates the Prince and Princess of Wales on the betrothal of their eldest son, the Duke of Clarence and Avondale, to the Princess Victoria of Teck.

— Relief works opened on large scale in Madras in aid of the famishing population.

11. Judgment given in Russell divorce suit in favour of Earl Russell.

15. Serious election riots at Waterford between Parnellites and Anti-Parnellites.

— Opening of 'Osborne *v.* Hargreaves' slander case, in connection with stolen jewels, the case being known as the 'Pearl Mystery'.

20. Further fighting at Mayun (Upper Burma), 70 of the enemy killed, 120 wounded—complete submission of the Hunzais.

22. In the 'Pearl Mystery' case, 'Osborne *v.* Hargreave', the plaintiff, Mrs. Osborne, consents to a verdict for the defendants.

24. Warrant issued for the apprehension of Mrs. Osborne, the plaintiff in the 'Pearl Mystery' case.

26. Terrible panic in Theatre at Gateshead; 10 persons crushed to death.

28. Rising of Malays at Pahang; several persons wounded.

31. Explosion in Dublin Castle, much damage done.

The 1892 edition of *Whitaker's Almanack* devotes considerable space to describing the passage through Parliament of the Elementary Education Act 1891. This legislation gave parents the right to demand free education for their children. 'Fee-grants' of ten shillings a year were available for each child between the ages of three and fifteen.

The **Scientific and Engineering Summary for 1891** gives details of progress made in the field of aeronautics, where 'the balloon has been to some extent forsaken for the aeroplane, that is to say, the kite. Mr. Maxim, the inventor of the well-known quick-firing gun, has made a steam kite, 13 feet long by 4 feet wide, which is propelled through the air by a light screw, making 2,500 revolutions a minute ... M. Gustave Trouvé has gone a step further, and devised an experimental flying machine, the "aviateur", which is, in fact, a skeleton bird with two wings, which beat up and down ... A small model flew 80 metres'.

Electricity was also the subject of experimentation and development as a source of power. The summary records that the introduction of electric railways and the electric light had 'suffered no abatement during the year'. London in particular had been 'parcelled out with installations, the streets broken up for laying the wires, and a beginning made for the supply of electricity on a great scale'. However, the opening of the electric railway between Monument and Clapham had 'caused a disturbing effect on the magnetic needles of the Greenwich Observatory'.

In March 1891 the first submarine telephone cable was laid between Sangatte, near Calais, and St. Margaret's Bay, near Dover. This cable was part of the new London-Paris telephone line which was opened to the public on April 1. Calls could be made from public call offices at Bath Street and at Threadneedle Street in London. The fee for a three-minute conversation was eight shillings, and *Whitaker's Almanack* draws readers' attention to the fact that the time in Paris was 10 minutes earlier than in London.

Among the financial information, *Whitaker's Almanack* records that in 1891 income tax was sixpence in the pound on an annual income of over £150. If earnings were under £400 a year, the first £120 was tax exempt.

The **Excise, Stamps and Taxes** section lists a number of activities which required licences. Hawkers needed an annual licence (£2), while pedlars paid a police licence of five shillings. The annual licence for armorial bearings was £1.1s (£2.2s if used on any carriage), while employing male servants required an annual licence of 15 shillings per servant. A special marriage licence cost £5, 'not special' 10 shillings.

Another source of revenue for the Government was the trade in opium in India. According to the **British Empire in India** article, by 1891 opium manufacture in British India had been a government monopoly for over one hundred years. Manufacture was strictly confined to the districts of Behar and Benares in Bengal, 'in which however about 500,000 acres in 1890 were under poppy cultivation'. A large quantity of opium was also manufactured in the Native States of Central India and exported from Bombay, in British territory. In 1890-91 the total net revenue from sales of opium at auction and export duties on opium from Bengal and the Native States was Rupees 84,510,000. Nearly all the opium was exported to China. The revenue raised by China from its tax on Indian opium amounted to about £2,000,000.

A range of goods and services are advertised in contemporary editions of *Whitaker's Almanack*. The *Cornhill Magazine*, which was then edited by James Payn, was obtainable monthly for 6d, and a bassinette perambulator with rubber tyres cost £1.15s. A Fitch typewriter cost the princely sum of £12, but the company was 'prepared to afford gratuitous instruction in type-writing to a limited number of pupils—young ladies and youths'. Fares for steamer voyages on the White Star Line from Liverpool to New York varied from £12 to £35. In one advertisement various pharmacists testify to the reliability of Dr. J. Collis Browne's Chlorodyne, which is described as a cure for cholera, dysentery, gout, cancer, toothache and epilepsy.

Among advertisements placed by charities appealing for funds are: the New Hospital for Women, London, revolutionary in that it was run and staffed by women; the Royal Sea-Bathing Infirmary (for the cure of the Scrofulous Poor of all England), which was celebrating its centenary in 1891; the Hospital for Sick Children in Great Ormond Street; and the City of London Truss Society for the Relief of the Ruptured Poor.

THE CENTENARIES OF 1991

1891

Jan. 16	Léo Delibes, French composer, died.
April 2	Max Ernst, German artist, born.
April 7	Phineas T. Barnum, American showman, died.
April 23	Sergei Prokofiev, Russian composer, born.
Aug. 2	Sir Arthur Bliss, composer and Master of the Queen's Music 1953–1975, born.
Aug. 6	Field Marshal Viscount Slim, born.
Sept. 28	Herman Melville, American novelist and poet, died.
Oct. 6	Charles Stewart Parnell, Irish politician, died.
Nov. 10	Arthur Rimbaud, French poet, died.
Dec. 26	Henry Miller, American author, born.

1791

Jan. 28	Louis Hérold, French composer, born.
March 2	John Wesley, founder of Methodism, died.
April 2	Comte de Mirabeau, French statesman, died.
April 27	Samuel Morse, American inventor of the electric telegraph and Morse code, born.

1892

Jan. 3	J. R. R. Tolkien, writer, born.
March 10	Dame Eva Turner, opera singer, born.
March 26	Walt Whitman, American poet, died.
April 13	Marshal of the RAF Sir Arthur ('Bomber') Harris born.
May 7	Marshal Josip Tito, Yugoslav leader, born.
June 21	Prof. Reinhold Niebuhr, American theologian, born.
June 26	Pearl S. Buck, American novelist, born.
Aug. 29	Lady Diana Cooper, society hostess and writer, born.
Sept. 4	Darius Milhaud, French composer, born
Oct. 6	Alfred, Lord Tennyson, poet, died.
Nov. 6	Sir John Alcock, airman, born
Dec. 15	John Paul Getty, American oil tycoon, born.
Dec.25	Dame Rebecca West, novelist and critic, born.

1792

Feb. 23	Sir Joshua Reynolds, portrait painter, died.
Feb. 29	Gioacchino Rossini, Italian composer, born.
March 3	Robert Adam, Scottish architect, died.
March 7	Sir John Frederick Herschel, astronomer, born.

1891 (continued)

May 2	Giacomo Meyerbeer, German composer, died.
Sept. 22	Michael Faraday, physicist and chemist, born.
Dec. 4	First publication of *The Observer*.
Dec. 5	Wolfgang Amadeus Mozart, Austrian composer, died.

1691

Dec. 30	Robert Boyle, chemist and philosopher, died.

1591

Aug. 24	Robert Herrick, poet, baptized.

1491

*	Saint Ignatius Loyola, founder of the Jesuits, born.
June 28	Henry VIII born.

1291

Aug. 1	Swiss Confederation founded.

1191

July 12	Capture of Acre by Crusaders.

THE CENTENARIES OF 1992

April 25	John Keble, churchman and writer, born.
July 10	Capt. Frederick Marryat, naval officer and novelist, born.
Aug. 3	Richard Arkwright, inventor of cotton-spinning machine, died.
Aug. 4	Percy Bysshe Shelley, poet, born.
Aug. 5	Frederick, 8th Lord North, statesman, died.
Aug. 18	John, 1st Earl Russell, statesman, born.
Sept. 20	Battle of Valmy.
Sept. 27	George Cruickshank, caricaturist and illustrator, born.
Oct. 28	John Smeaton, engineer, died.

1692

Feb. 13	Massacre at Glencoe.
Nov. 19	Thomas Shadwell, dramatist, died.

1592

Aug. 20	George, 1st Duke of Buckingham, statesman, born.
Sept. 13	Michel de Montaigne, French essayist, died.

1492

Aug. 3	Columbus set out on his first voyage across the Atlantic.

* Exact date unknown.

PATRON SAINTS

ST. GEORGE
Patron Saint of England

St. George is believed to have been born in Cappadocia, of Christian parents, in the latter part of the 3rd century and to have served with distinction as a soldier under the Emperor Diocletian, including a visit to England on a military mission. When the persecution of Christians was ordered, St. George sought a personal interview to remonstrate with the Emperor and after a profession of faith resigned his military commission. Arrest and torture followed and he was martyred at Nicomedia on April 23, 303, a day ordered to be kept in remembrance as a national festival by the Council of Oxford in 1222, although it was not until the reign of Edward III that he was made patron saint of England.

St. George's connection with a dragon seems to date from the close of the 6th century and to be due to the transfer of his remains from Nicomedia to Lydda, close to the scene of the legendary exploit of Perseus in rescuing Andromeda and slaying the sea monster, credit for which became attached to the Christian martyr.

ST. DAVID
Patron Saint of Wales

St. David is believed to have been born near the beginning and to have died towards the end of the 6th century. St. David was an eloquent preacher, who founded the monastery at Menevia, now St.

David's. He became the patron of Wales, but there is no record of any papal canonization before 1181. His annual festival is observed on March 1.

ST. ANDREW
Patron Saint of Scotland

St. Andrew, one of the Christian Apostles and brother of Simon Peter, was born at Bethsaida on the Sea of Galilee and lived at Capernaum. He preached the Gospel in Asia Minor and in Scythia along the shores of the Black Sea and became the patron saint of Russia. It is believed that he suffered crucifixion at Patras in Achaea, on a *crux decussata* (now known as St. Andrew's Cross) and that his relics were removed from Patras to Constantinople and thence to St. Andrews, probably in the 8th century, since which time he has been the patron saint of Scotland. The festival of St. Andrew is held on November 30.

ST. PATRICK
Patron Saint of Ireland

St. Patrick was born, probably in England, about 389 and was carried off to Ireland as a slave about sixteen years later, escaping to Gaul at the age of 22. He was ordained deacon at Auxerre and having been consecrated Bishop in 432 was despatched to Wicklow to reorganize the Christian communities in Ireland. He founded the see of Armagh and introduced Latin into Ireland as the language of the Church. He died *c.* 461 and his festival is celebrated on March 17.

WEDDING ANNIVERSARIES

First	Cotton		Fourteenth	Ivory
Second	Paper		Fifteenth	Crystal
Third	Leather		Twentieth	China
Fourth	Fruit and Flower		Twenty-fifth	Silver
Fifth	Wood		Thirtieth	Pearl
Sixth	Sugar/Iron		Thirty-fifth	Coral
Seventh	Wool		Fortieth	Ruby
Eighth	Bronze/Electrical appliances		Forty-fifth	Sapphire
Ninth	Copper/Pottery		Fiftieth	Gold
Tenth	Tin		Fifty-fifth	Emerald
Eleventh	Steel		Sixtieth	Diamond
Twelfth	Silk and Fine Linen		Seventieth	Platinum
Thirteenth	Lace			

DUTY AND TAX-FREE ALLOWANCES

You are entitled to the allowances in either of the columns below (but not both) for any category of goods, as represented by the boxes (*see* Notes on Allowances). Passengers under 17 are not, however, entitled to tobacco and drinks allowances.

Column 1 Goods obtained duty and tax free in the EC, or duty and tax free on a ship or aircraft, or goods obtained outside the EC.	Column 2 Goods obtained duty and tax paid in the EC.
Tobacco goods 200 cigarettes or 100 cigarillos or 50 cigars or 250 grammes of tobacco	**Tobacco goods** 300 cigarettes or 150 cigarillos or 75 cigars or 400 grammes of tobacco
Alcoholic drinks 2 litres of still table wine	**Alcoholic drinks** 5 litres of still table wine
plus	plus
1 litre over 22% vol. (e.g. spirits and strong liqueurs) or 2 litres not over 22% vol. (e.g. low strength liqueurs, fortified wine or sparkling wine) or A further 2 litres of still table wine	1·5 litres over 22% vol. (e.g. spirits and strong liqueurs) or 3 litres not over 22% vol. (e.g. low strength liqueurs, fortified wine, or sparkling wine) or A further 3 litres of still table wine
Perfume 50 grammes (60 cc or 2 fl oz)	**Perfume** 75 grammes (90 cc or 3 fl oz)
Toilet water 250 cc (9 fl oz)	**Toilet water** 375 cc (13 fl oz)
Other goods £32 worth	**Other goods** £265 worth

NB. A maximum of 50 litres of beer and 25 lighters may be imported duty-free, subject to the limitations of the 'Other goods' monetary allowance.

If you are visiting the United Kingdom for less than six months, you are also entitled to bring in, free of duty and tax, all personal effects (except tobacco goods, alcoholic drinks and perfume) which you intend to take with you when you leave.

Notes on Allowances

(1) The countries of the European Community are Belgium, Denmark, France, West Germany, Greece, the Irish Republic, Italy, Luxembourg, the Netherlands, Portugal, Spain (but not the Canary Islands), and the United Kingdom (but not the Channel Islands).

(2) The allowances apply only to goods carried and cleared by you at the time of your arrival.

(3) The allowances do not apply to goods brought in for sale or for other commercial purposes.

(4) Reduced allowances apply to certain persons crossing the Irish land boundary and to seamen and aircrew members.

(5) Whisky, gin, rum, brandy, vodka and most liqueurs normally exceed 22% vol. (38.8° proof) but advocaat, cassis, fraise, suze and aperitifs may be less. Fortified wines include port, sherry, vermouth and madeira. Sparkling wines include champagne, perelada, spumante and semi-sparkling wines. Still table wines include claret, Sauterne, Graves and Chianti. Burgundy, Chablis, hock and Moselle may be either sparkling or still, depending on manufacture.

(6) You may not mix goods obtained duty and tax free or outside the EC with goods of the same category (as represented by the boxes) obtained duty and tax paid in the EC to obtain the higher allowance, e.g. you will not get the higher allowance for tobacco goods if any of the items in that category were obtained duty and tax free or outside the EC.

(7) Where there are alternative quantities within a category of goods they may be apportioned. For example, 150 cigarettes (half allowance) plus 75 cigarillos (half allowance).

(8) One litre is approximately 1¾ pints or 35 fl oz.

(9) A cigarillo is a cigar with a maximum weight of 3 grammes.

PROHIBITED AND RESTRICTED GOODS

Customs officers are able to provide full information. This is a list of more frequently met items:

Controlled drugs, such as opium, heroin, morphine, cocaine, cannabis, amphetamines, lysergide (LSD) and barbiturates.

Firearms (including gas pistols, electric shock batons and similar weapons), ammunition and explosives (including fireworks).

Flick knives.

Counterfeit currency.

Horror comics. Indecent or obscene books, magazines, films, video cassettes and other articles.

Radio transmitters (walkie-talkies, Citizen's Band radios, cordless telephones, etc.) not approved for use in the UK.

Meat and poultry, and most of their products, including ham, bacon, sausage, paté, eggs, milk and cream. (Exception : 1 kg per passenger of fully cooked meat or poultrymeat products in cans or other hermetically-sealed containers of glass or foil).

Plants, parts thereof and plant produce, including trees and shrubs, potatoes and certain other vegetables, fruit, bulbs and seeds.

Animals and birds, whether alive or dead (e.g. stuffed), certain fish and fish eggs, whether live or dead, or bees; certain articles derived from rare species including furskins, ivory, reptile leather and goods made from them.

NB. Cats, dogs and other mammals must not be landed unless a British import licence (rabies) has previously been issued.

EXPORT CONTROL

The following are some of the goods subject to export control and should be declared to the customs officer. There are formalities to be completed in respect of these goods prior to your arrival at the port of exportation and further information is available through any local office of Customs and Excise (address in the telephone directory).

● Controlled drugs.
● Firearms and ammunition.
● Photographic material over 60 years old and valued at £400 or more.
● Portraits (including sculptures) of British historical personages which are over 50 years old and valued at £4,000 or more.
● Antiques, collectors' items, etc. (including paintings and other works of art) over 50 years old and valued at £16,000 or more.
● Certain archaeological material.
● Most live animals and birds, and items made from animals occurring wild in the UK.

HM COASTGUARD

Founded in 1822 to guard the coasts against smuggling, HM Coastguard's role today is a very different one—that of complete dedication to the guarding and saving of all life at sea. Administered by the Department of Transport, it is responsible for co-ordinating all civil marine search and rescue operations around the 2,500 mile coastline of Great Britain and Northern Ireland and 1,200 miles into the Atlantic, as well as co-operating with search and rescue organizations of neighbouring countries both in Western Europe and around the Atlantic seaboard. In addition, the Service maintains a 24-hour radar watch on the Dover Strait, providing a Channel Navigation Information Service for all shipping in one of the busiest sea lanes in the world.

Since 1978 HM Coastguard has been organized into six Regions, each with a Regional Controller operating from a Maritime Rescue Co-ordination Centre. Each Region is subdivided into Districts under District Controllers, operating from Maritime Rescue Sub-Centres. In all there are 21 of these centres. They are on 24-hour watch and are fitted with a comprehensive range of communications and rescue equipment. They are supported by some 350 smaller stations manned by Auxiliary Coastguards under the direction of Regulars, each of which keeps its parent centre fully informed of day-to-day casualty risk, particularly on the more remote danger spots around the coast.

Between January 1 and December 31, 1989, the 500 Regular and 7,500 Auxiliary Coastguards co-ordinated 6,753 incidents requiring search and rescue facilities, resulting in assistance being given to 9,500 persons. All distress telephone and radio calls are centralized on the 21 centres, which are on the alert for people or vessels in distress, shipping hazards and oil slicks. Using their modern telecommunications equipment and the facilities provided by British Telecom's Coast Radio Stations, they can alert and co-ordinate the most appropriate rescue facilities: RNLI lifeboats, Royal Navy, RAF or Coastguard helicopters, fixed-wing aircraft, Naval vessels, ships in the vicinity, or Coastguard shore and cliff rescue teams.

For those who regularly sail in local waters or make longer passages, the Coastguard Yacht and Boat Safety Scheme provides a valuable free service. Its aim is to give the Coastguard a record of the details of craft, their normal operating areas and their passage plans. Yacht and Boat Safety Scheme Cards are available from all Coastguard stations, harbourmasters' offices, and most yacht clubs and marinas.

Members of the public who see an accident or a potentially dangerous incident on or around the coast should without hesitation dial 999 and ask for the Coastguard.

DISTANCES FROM LONDON BY AIR

The list of the distances in statute miles from London, Heathrow, to various places abroad has been supplied by the publishers of *IATA/IAL Air Distances Manual*, Southall, Middx.

To	Miles	To	Miles	To	Miles
Abidjan	3,197	Detroit	3,754	Munich	588
Abu Dhabi	3,425	Dhaka	4,976	Nairobi	4,248
Addis Ababa	3,675	Doha	3,253	Naples	1,011
Aden	3,670	Dubai	3,414	Nassau	4,333
Algiers	1,035	Dublin	279	New York (J. F. Kennedy)	3,440
Amman	2,287	Durban	5,937	Nice	645
Amsterdam	230	Düsseldorf	310	Oporto	806
Ankara	1,770	Entebbe	4,033	Oslo (Fornebu)	723
Athens	1,500	Frankfurt	406	Ottawa	3,321
Auckland	11,404	Freetown	3,046	Palma, Majorca	836
Baghdad	2,551	Geneva	468	Paris . . . . 215 (Orly 227)	
Bahrain	3,163	Gibraltar	1,084	Perth, Australia	9,008
Bangkok	5,928	Gothenburg (Landvetter)	664	Port of Spain, Trinidad	4,405
Barbados	4,193	Hamburg	463	Prague	649
Barcelona	712	Harare	5,156	Rangoon	5,582
Basle	447	Havana	4,647	Reykjavik	1,167
Beijing (Peking)	5,063	Helsinki (Vantaa)	1,147	Rhodes	1,743
Beirut	2,161	Hong Kong	5,990	Rio de Janeiro	5,745
Belfast	325	Honolulu	7,220	Riyadh	3,067
Belgrade	1,056	Istanbul	1,560	Rome (Fiumicino)	895
Berlin (Tegel)	588	Jeddah	2,947	Salzburg	651
Bermuda	3,428	Johannesburg	5,634	San Francisco	5,351
Berne	476	Karachi	3,935	Seoul	5,507
Bombay	4,478	Khartoum	3,071	Shannon	369
Brasilia	5,452	Kingston, Jamaica	4,668	Singapore	6,756
Brisbane	10,273	Kuala Lumpur	6,557	Sofia	1,266
Brussels	217	Kuwait	2,903	Stockholm (Arlanda)	908
Bucharest	1,307	Lagos	3,107	Sydney, Australia	10,568
Budapest	923	Larnaca, Cyprus	2,036	Tangier	1,120
Buenos Aires	6,915	Leningrad	1,314	Teheran	2,741
Cairo	2,194	Lima	6,303	Tel Aviv	2,227
Calcutta	4,958	Lisbon	972	Tokyo (Narita)	5,956
Canberra	10,563	Lomé	3,129	Toronto	3,545
Cape Town	6,011	Los Angeles	5,439	Tripoli	1,468
Caracas	4,639	Madrid	773	Tunis	1,137
Casablanca	1,300	Malta	1,305	Turin (Caselle)	570
Chicago (O'Hare)	3,941	Manila	6,685	Valencia	826
Cologne	331	Marseilles	614	Vancouver	4,707
Colombo	5,411	Mauritius	6,075	Venice (Tessera)	715
Copenhagen	608	Mexico City	5,529	Vienna (Schwechat)	790
Dakar	2,706	Milan	609	Warsaw	912
Damascus	2,223	Montego Bay	4,687	Washington	3,665
Dar-es-Salaam	4,662	Montevideo	6,841	Wellington	11,692
Darwin	8,613	Montreal (Mirabel)	3,241	Zagreb	848
Delhi	4,180	Moscow (Sheremetievo)	1,557	Zürich	490

GROSS DOMESTIC PRODUCT BY INDUSTRY

(Before depreciation but after stock appreciation)

£ million

	1982	1983	1984	1985	1986	1987	1988
Agriculture, forestry and fishing...	5,117	4,902	5,892	5,197	5,706	5,791	5,625
Energy and water supply	26,091	30,071	30,026	32,381	23,681	23,981	21,845
Manufacturing	58,658	61,299	65,984	72,226	76,485	83,013	93,433
Construction	14,098	15,647	16,990	17,849	20,309	22,683	25,745
Distribution; hotels and catering; repairs	30,190	33,133	35,960	40,428	44,990	48,610	55,131
Transport and communication.....	17,201	18,243	19,772	21,323	23,323	25,741	28,657
Banking, finance, insurance, business services and leasing	30,949	36,444	40,603	48,511	57,127	65,580	76,922
Ownership of dwellings	15,044	15,944	16,734	17,963	19,170	20,180	21,407
Public administration, national defence and compulsory social security	17,367	18,806	20,175	21,598	23,066	24,795	27,023
Education and health services	21,308	23,305	24,487	26,101	28,928	31,609	35,237
Other services	13,305	15,072	16,463	18,371	20,560	22,872	25,785
Total	249,328	272,866	293,086	321,948	343,345	374,855	416,810
Adjustment for financial services ..	−11,781	−12,208	−14,629	−16,094	−18,845	−19,204	−22,204
Statistical discrepancy (income component)...................	203	−259	926	5	−469	−96	181
Gross domestic product (average estimate)	237,750	260,399	279,383	305,859	324,031	355,555	394,787

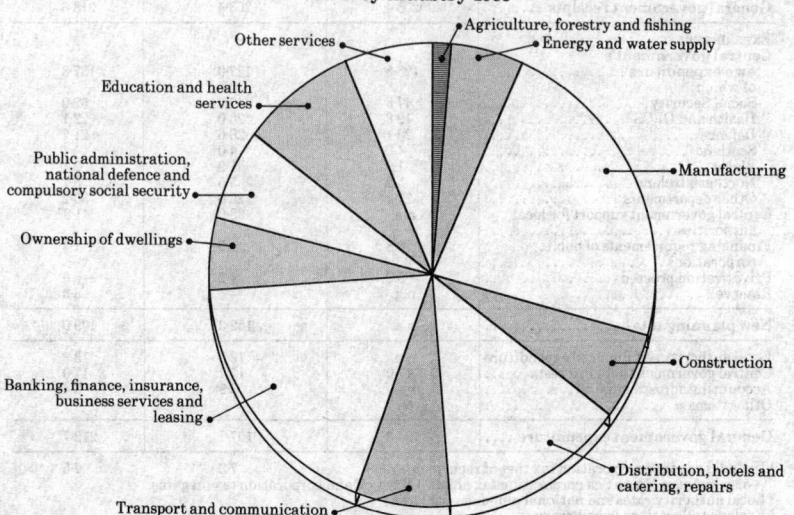

GDP by industry 1988

Other services

Agriculture, forestry and fishing

Energy and water supply

Education and health services

Public administration, national defence and compulsory social security

Manufacturing

Ownership of dwellings

Construction

Banking, finance, insurance, business services and leasing

Distribution, hotels and catering, repairs

Transport and communication

BUDGET 1990 STATISTICS

The Finances of the Public Sector (£ billion)

	1989–90		1990–91 Forecast
	1989 Budget	Latest estimate	
RECEIPTS			
Inland Revenue:			
Income tax	46·9	48·7	55·0
Corporation tax[1]	22·4	21·4	20·7
Petroleum revenue tax	1·4	1·1	1·1
Capital gains tax	2·1	1·9	2·1
Inheritance tax	1·1	1·2	1·2
Stamp duties	2·4	2·1	1·9
Total Inland Revenue	76·3	76·4	81·9
Customs & Excise:			
Value added tax	30·0	29·7	32·1
Petrol, derv duties etc.	8·8	8·8	9·7
Tobacco duties	5·1	5·0	5·4
Alcohol duties	4·7	4·6	4·9
Betting and gaming duties	1·0	1·0	1·0
Car tax	1·4	1·5	1·5
Customs duties	1·8	1·8	1·9
Agricultural levies	0·1	0·1	0·1
Total Customs and Excise	52·9	52·4	56·7
Vehicle excise duties	2·9	2·9	3·0
Oil royalties	0·6	0·6	0·7
Rates[2]	19·7	20·1	12·2
Other taxes and royalties	3·7	4·4	4·4
Total taxes and royalties	156·1	156·8	159·0
National insurance and other contributions	34·3	33·1	35·9
Community charge	0·8	0·8	11·2
Interest and dividends	7·0	7·2	6·4
Gross trading surpluses and rent	3·3	3·0	3·0
Other receipts	4·8	2·5	3·1
General government receipts	206·4	203·4	218·6
EXPENDITURE			
Central government's own expenditure	125·8	127·0	137·8
of which:			
Social Security	47·5	47·0	52·0
Health and OPCS	19·8	20·0	22·1
Defence	20·1	20·6	21·2
Scotland	4·0	4·0	4·4
Wales	1·9	1·9	2·1
Northern Ireland	5·2	5·5	5·7
Other departments	27·4	28·0	30·2
Central government support for local authorities	n.a.	38·0	41·8[3]
Financing requirements of public corporations	0·8	1·6	1·4
Privatization proceeds	−5·0	−4·2	−5·0
Reserve	n.a.	—	3·0
New planning total	n.a.	162·3	179·0
Local authority self financed expenditure	n.a.	13·9	13·3
Central government debt interest	17·0	17·7	17·0
Accounting adjustments	n.a.	3·9	3·4
Other items	55·7		
General government expenditure	194·3	197·7	212·7

[1] Includes advance corporation tax (net of repayments):6·8   7·3   7·5
—also includes North Sea corporation tax after ACT set off and corporation tax on gains.
[2] Local authority rates and national non-domestic rates.
[3] Excludes allocations from Reserve.

Receipts, Expenditure and Debt Repayment (£ billion)

	1989–90		1990–91 Forecast
	1989 Budget	Latest estimate	
General government receipts	206·4	203·4	218·6
General government expenditure	194·3	197·7	212·7
General government debt repayment	12·1	5·7	5·9
Public corporations market and overseas debt repayment	1·7	1·4	1·0
Public sector debt repayment	13·8	7·1	6·9

Public Expenditure (£ billion)

	1988–89 Outturn	1989–90 Estimated outturn	1990–91 Plans	1991–92 Plans	1992–93 Plans
Central government's own expenditure	116·3	127·0	137·8	145·3	152·3
of which:					
Dept. of Social Security	44·5	47·0	52·0	56·2	59·5
Dept. of Health and OPCS	18·4	20·0	22·1	23·4	24·5
Ministry of Defence	19·1	20·6	21·2	22·4	23·4
Scotland	3·8	4·0	4·4	4·7	4·9
Wales	1·7	1·9	2·1	2·2	2·3
Northern Ireland	5·1	5·5	5·7	6·0	6·3
Other departments	23·6	28·0	30·2	30·5	31·5
Central government support for local authorities	36·4	38·0	41·8	43·7	44·8
of which:					
Revenue/Rate Support Grant..........	12·8	13·0	13·1 ⎫	25·9	26·7
Non-domestic rate payments	10·4	11·2	12·1 ⎭		
Current specific grants[1]	8·9	9·9	11·5	12·4	12·8
Capital grants	0·5	0·6	1·3	1·3	1·3
Credit approvals	3·7	3·4	3·8	4·0	4·0
Financing requirements for public corporations........................	−0·1	1·6	1·4	2·3	2·3
Privatization proceeds	−7·1	−4·2	−5·0	−5·0	−5·0
Reserve................................			3·0	6·0	9·0
Planning total	145·5	162·3	179·0	192·3	203·4
Local authority self-financed expenditure[2]	10·1	13·9	13·3	14	15
Central government debt interest[3]	17·5	17·7	17·0	15¼	15
Other adjustments[3]	5·0	3·9	3·4	3½	4½
General government expenditure	178·2	197·7	212·7	225	238

[1] Excludes allocation from the Reserve to meet higher payments of community charge benefit than assumed in previous year.
[2] Local authority self-financed expenditure is the difference between total local authority expenditure and central government support to local authorities.
[3] 1991–92 and 1992–93 figures rounded to nearest £¼ billion.

General Government Expenditure (£ billion)

	1988–89	1989–90	1990–91	1991–92	1992–93
General government expenditure, excluding privatization proceeds:					
cash	185·3	201·9	217·7	230	243
real terms[1,2]........................	185·3	189·9	195·7	198	202
		(189·8)	(192·3)	(194)	(198)
per cent of GDP[1]	38¼	39	39¼	39¼	39¼
		(39)	(39)	(38¼)	(38¼)

[1] The figures in brackets use figures for money GDP and the GDP deflator which adjust for the distortion arising from the abolition of domestic rates.
[2] Base year 1988–89.

Source: Financial Statement and Budget Report 1990–91

HOME FINANCE
Central government funds and accounts transactions £ million

| | Consolidated Fund | | Consolidated Fund surplus/deficit | National Loans Fund | | Borrowing required | Other funds and accounts | Central government borrowing requirement |
	Revenue	Expenditure		Receipts	Payments			
1986	110,867	113,305	−2,438	14,984	20,397	7,851	−555	8,406
1987	119,517	120,729	−1,212	16,353	21,344	6,203	2,142	4,061
1988	129,739	125,865	3,874	17,697	21,532	−39	4,620	−4,659
1989	141,388	134,504	6,884	18,655	22,960	−2,579	2,419	−4,998
Financial years								
1987–88	122,970	120,562	2,408	16,406	20,538	1,724	887	837
1988–89	133,593	128,002	5,591	18,239	22,218	−1,612	5,373	−6,985
1989–90	144,920	141,492	3,428	18,857	20,395	−1,890	3,717	−5,607
1990 1st quarter..	43,716	40,999	2,717	5,476	4,175	−4,018	935	−4,953
2nd quarter .	31,743	40,989	−9,246	3,989	3,959	9,216	4,893	4,323
1989 June	10,565	10,338	227	881	650	−458	−1,545	1,087
July	12,317	9,505	2,812	482	2,728	−566	629	−1,195
August	9,826	12,407	−2,581	3,241	2,353	1,693	155	1,538
September ..	10,392	11,897	−1,505	1,926	1,953	1,532	1,544	−12
October	13,735	12,164	1,571	1,511	1,890	−1,192	904	−2,096
November ..	12,364	11,487	877	1,753	1,800	−830	−1,316	486
December ..	12,050	10,957	1,093	613	620	−1,086	289	−1,375
1990 January ...	17,247	13,349	3,898	2,372	2,680	−3,590	1,786	−5,376
February ...	11,484	10,319	1,165	1,319	94	−2,390	−795	−1,595
March	14,985	17,331	−2,346	1,785	1,401	1,962	−56	2,018
April	12,250	13,738	−1,488	1,407	1,387	1,468	1,071	397
May	10,336	14,103	−3,767	1,740	1,938	3,965	2,254	1,711
June	9,157	13,148	−3,991	842	634	3,783	1,568	2,215

Public sector borrowing requirement £ million

	Total		Contributions by			Financed by			Other private sector	
						Banks and building societies/Overseas sector				
						External finance				
	Not seasonally adjusted	Seasonally adjusted†	Central government*	Local authorities	Public corporations	Borrowing in sterling from banks	Foreign currency borrowing from banks	Other external finance	Notes and coin	Other
1986	2,485	4,166	8,406	5,132	789	−2,713	44	602	745	6,410
1987	−1,434	−1,713	4,061	4,664	831	−1,243	−365	−6,234	709	8,008
1988	−11,598	−11,710	−4,659	4,222	2,717	−687	−571	−721	1,042	−7,187
1989	−9,129	−9,268	−4,998	1,992	2,139	−3,658	203	4,094	907	−10,159
Financial years										
1987–88	−3,404	−3,404	837	2,737	1,504	−932	−1,342	−6,182	1,718	4,443
1988–89	−14,524	−14,524	−6,985	4,602	2,937	−4,003	293	447	414	−7,967
1989–90	−7,897	−7,896	−5,607	963	1,327	−655	117	2,340	880	−10,666
1989 1st quarter	−5,727	−4,367	−4,344	−136	1,519	−4,569	98	289	−285	−1,439
2nd quarter	−20	−1,268	2,000	1,511	509	1,293	35	872	394	2,434
3rd quarter	−437	−1,425	331	676	92	965	−1	1,394	93	−2,852
4th quarter	−2,945	−2,193	−2,985	−59	19	−1,347	71	1,539	705	−3,434
1990 1st quarter	−4,495	−3,010	−4,953	−1,165	707	−1,566	12	−1,465	−312	−1,946
2nd quarter	6,488		4,323	−2,217	52	—	—	—	—	—

†Financial year constrained.　　*An increase in debt is shown positive.

HOUSEHOLDS AND THEIR EXPENDITURE[1]

(United Kingdom)

	1984	1985	1986	1987
Number of households supplying data	7,081	7,012	7,178	7,396
Total number of persons	18,557	18,206	18,330	18,735
Total number of adults[2]	13,618	13,401	13,554	13,902
Household percentage distribution by tenure				
Rented unfurnished	*35·4*	*34·9*	*33·9*	*32·5*
Rented furnished	*2·7*	*2·5*	*3·0*	*3·3*
Rent-free	*1·8*	*2·1*	*2·0*	*2·1*
Owner-occupied	*60·1*	*60·5*	*61·1*	*62·2*
Average number of persons per household				
All persons	2·621	2·596	2·554	2·553
Males	1·266	1·258	1·236	1·223
Females	1·355	1·339	1·317	1·310
Adults[2]	1·923	1·911	1·888	1·880
Persons under 65	1·572	1·552	1·526	1·512
Persons 65 and over	0·351	0·359	0·362	0·368
Children[2]	0·698	0·685	0·665	0·653
Children under 2	0·068	0·077	0·073	0·078
Children 2 and under 5	0·114	0·114	0·118	0·118
Children 5 and under 18	0·516	0·495	0·474	0·457
Persons working	1·179	1·164	1·160	1·161
Persons not working	1·442	1·433	1·394	1·372
Men 65 and over, women 60 and over	0·399	0·407	0·403	0·408
Others	1·043	1·026	0·991	0·965
Average weekly household expenditure on commodities and services (£)				
Housing[3]	24·06	26·63	29·92	34·35
Fuel, light and power	9·42	9·95	10·43	10·55
Food	31·43	32·70	34·97	35·79
Alcoholic drink	7·25	7·95	8·21	8·70
Tobacco	4·37	4·42	4·55	4·67
Clothing and footwear	11·10	11·92	13·46	13·32
Durable household goods	11·57	11·61	13·83	13·48
Household services	—	—	—	8·23
Personal goods and services	—	—	—	7·02
Other goods	11·89	12·59	13·87	—
Transport and vehicles	22·77	24·56	25·43	23·80
Fares and other travel costs	—	—	—	4·60
Services	17·41	19·48	22·67	—
Leisure goods	—	—	—	9·03
Leisure services	—	—	—	18·11
Miscellaneous	0·64	0·68	0·74	0·88
Total	151·92	162·50	178·10	—
Expenditure on commodity or service as a percentage of total expenditure (per cent)				
Housing[3]	*15·8*	*16·4*	*16·8*	—
Fuel, light and power	*6·2*	*6·1*	*5·9*	*5·6*
Food	*20·7*	*20·1*	*19·6*	*19·0*
Alcoholic drink	*4·8*	*4·9*	*4·6*	*4·6*
Tobacco	*2·9*	*2·7*	*2·6*	*2·5*
Clothing and footwear	*7·3*	*7·3*	*7·5*	*7·1*
Durable household goods	*7·6*	*7·2*	*7·8*	*7·1*
Household services	—	—	—	*4·4*
Personal goods and services	—	—	—	*3·7*
Other goods	*7·9*	*7·8*	*7·8*	—
Transport and vehicles	*15·0*	*15·1*	*14·3*	—
Fares and other travel costs	—	—	—	*2·4*
Services	*11·5*	*12·0*	*12·7*	*12·6*
Leisure goods	—	—	—	*4·8*
Leisure services	—	—	—	*9·6*
Miscellaneous	*0·4*	*0·4*	*0·4*	*0·5*
Total	*100·0*	*100·0*	*100·0*	—

Source: HMSO—Annual Abstract of Statistics

[1] Information derived from the Family Expenditure Survey.
[2] Adults = all persons 18 and over and married persons under 18.
  Children = all unmarried persons under 18.
[3] Excludes mortgage payments but includes imputed expenditure (i.e. the weekly equivalent of rateable value).

DEFENCE MANPOWER STRENGTHS

Thousands

	1983	1984	1985	1986	1987	1988	1989
UK SERVICE PERSONNEL							
All services: total	320·6	325·9	326·2	322·5	319·8	316·9	311·6
Female	15·4	16·2	16·4	16·0	16·2	15·9	16·3
Royal Navy: total	64·0	63·7	62·8	60·3	58·7	57·7	57·0
Female	3·9	3·9	3·7	3·4	3·4	3·3	3·5
Royal Marines: total	7·8	7·6	7·6	7·6	7·8	7·8	7·7
Army: total	159·1	161·5	162·4	161·4	159·7	158·1	155·6
Female	6·1	6·6	6·8	6·6	6·5	6·3	6·5
Royal Air Force: total	89·8	93·1	93·4	93·2	93·6	93·3	91·4
Female	5·4	5·7	6·0	6·0	6·3	6·3	6·3
Personnel locally entered overseas:							
total	10·1	10·1	10·2	10·1	9·8	9·4	9·1
Regular Reserves: total	193·4	198·0	205·5	211·4	220·9	230·2	240·4
Royal Navy	23·9	23·5	23·3	24·2	24·5	24·7	25·1
Royal Marines	2·2	2·2	2·2	2·3	2·3	2·4	2·5
Army	138·3	143·2	150·1	153·8	160·4	167·7	175·3
Royal Air Force	28·9	29·0	29·8	31·2	33·7	35·4	37·5
Volunteer Reserves and Auxiliary							
Forces: total	87·5	85·9	88·6	95·4	96·8	92·8	90·4
Royal Navy	5·4	5·2	5·2	5·5	5·7	5·6	5·6
Royal Marines	1·1	1·1	1·1	1·2	1·2	1·3	1·2
Territorial Army	72·8	71·4	73·7	77·7	78·5	74·7	72·5
Ulster Defence Regiment	7·1	6·8	6·4	6·6	6·5	6·4	6·3
Home Service Force	0·3	0·3	0·9	3·0	3·3	3·1	3·0
Royal Air Force	0·8	1·1	1·2	1·4	1·6	1·8	1·7
Cadet Forces: total	149·0	146·5	144·7	143·4	145·7	144·6	139·2
Royal Navy	29·4	28·4	28·4	28·0	27·5	27·1	26·5
Army	74·5	73·8	72·1	70·9	71·2	69·3	65·9
Royal Air Force	45·1	44·3	44·1	44·5	47·0	48·3	46·7
Ministry of Defence civilians:							
total	242·7	232·5	206·5	201·7	196·1	175·1	172·5
UK based	208·9	199·1	174·1	169·4	164·0	143·3	141·3
Non-industrial	105·6	103·2	94·9	93·8	93·3	88·5	88·7
Industrial	103·3	95·9	79·1	75·6	70·7	54·8	52·5
Locally engaged overseas	33·8	33·4	32·4	32·2	32·1	31·8	31·2
Non-industrial	10·5	10·4	10·2	10·3	10·3	10·2	10·2
Industrial	23·3	23·0	22·2	22·0	21·8	21·6	21·1

Recruitment of UK Service Personnel to each Service

Number

	1982–83	1983–84	1984–85	1985–86	1986–87	1987–88	1988–89
All Services: total	21,647	36,991	34,721	32,651	34,049	33,826	33,863
Female	2,305	3,231	2,645	2,244	2,902	2,611	3,001
Royal Navy: total	3,584	4,785	4,582	4,276	5,336	5,181	5,298
Female	506	562	351	289	545	580	700
Royal Marines: total	447	447	954	1,093	1,233	991	937
Army: total	13,071	22,348	22,278	20,268	19,918	21,041	21,348
Female	1,392	1,537	1,364	1,095	1,200	1,146	1,427
Royal Air Force: total	4,545	9,411	6,907	7,014	7,562	6,613	6,280
Female	407	1,132	930	860	1,157	885	874

CIVIL SERVICE STAFF

Analysis by ministerial responsibility at April 1 in each year

† Full-time equivalents (thousands)

	1983	1984	1985	1986	1987	1988	1989
Total civil and defence departments	648·9	624·0	599·0	594·4	597·8	579·6	569·2
of which Non-industrials	518·5	504·3	498·0	498·2	507·5	506·6	499·8
Industrials	130·4	119·7	101·0	96·2	90·3	73·0	69·4
Total civil departments	440·0	424·8	425·0	424·9	433·8	436·2	427·9
Agriculture, Fisheries and Food	12·7	12·1	12·1	11·7	11·3	11·1	10·9
Chancellor of the Exchequer's							
Departments:........................	117·4	112·4	111·9	110·0	110·1	108·6	109·1
Customs and Excise	25·4	25·1	25·4	25·1	25·8	26·3	26·4
Inland Revenue	73·1	69·8	69·8	69·3	67·8	66·6	67·0
Department for National Savings	8·3	8·0	7·8	7·8	7·7	7·4	7·3
Treasury and others..............	10·6	9·5	8·9	8·8	8·8	8·3	8·3
Education and Science................	3·5	2·4	2·4	2·4	2·4	2·5	2·5
Employment	57·9	56·4	54·7	55·7	60·5	58·3	55·0
Energy	1·1	1·1	1·1	1·0	1·0	1·0	1·1
Environment	39·4	36·6	35·8	34·9	34·2	33·0	30·6
Foreign and Commonwealth	11·1	10·0	9·8	9·6	9·5	9·6	9·6
Home	35·1	36·4	36·6	37·5	37·6	39·2	40·8
Industry	7·7	–	–	–	–	–	–
Scotland	13·1	12·8	13·0	12·9	13·0	13·0	12·3
Social Services......................	96·4	92·6	94·9	94·9	97·7	102·3	94·3
Trade	8·9	–	–	–	–	–	–
Trade and Industry..................	–	14·7	14·8	14·8	14·8	14·6	14·7
Transport	13·0	14·2	14·4	14·7	12·3	14·1	14·1
Wales	2·2	2·2	2·3	2·3	2·3	2·2	2·2
Other civil departments..............	20·5	20·9	21·2	21·5	25·1	26·7	30·7
Total Ministry of Defence	208·9	199·2	174·0	169·5	164·0	143·4	141·3

† Part-time employees are counted as half units.

HOUSING

Stock of dwellings (Great Britain)

	1985	1986	1987	1988*
Estimated annual gains and losses (thousands)				
Gains: New construction	195·3	201·7	205·7	215·5
Other	12·8	10·8	10·8	11·2
Losses: Slum clearance	11·0	8·8	8·4	8·6
Other	11·7	9·6	9·8	9·6
Net gain	185·4	194·1	198·3	208·5
Stock at end of year	21,813	22,007	22,205	22,414
Estimated tenure distribution at end of year (percentage)				
Owner occupied	*61·5*	*62·5*	*63·6*	*64·9*
Rented: From local authorities and new towns	*27·1*	*26·5*	*25·8*	*24·7*
From housing associations	*2·5*	*2·5*	*2·6*	*2·7*
From private owners including other tenures	*8·9*	*8·5*	*8·1*	*7·7*

*provisional.

Permanent dwellings completed 1988

	Total	For local housing authorities	For private owners	Housing associations and other
United Kingdom	225,716	20,912	192,211	12,593
England and Wales	195,352	16,470	170,648	10,234
Scotland	18,155	2,730	14,052	1,373
Northern Ireland	10,209	1,712	7,511	986

EMPLOYMENT

Distribution of the workforce

Thousands

At mid-June	1984	1985	1986	1987	1988
United Kingdom					
Workforce[1]	27,265	27,714	27,791	27,979	28,211
Males	16,315	16,484	16,383	16,352	16,363
Females	10,950	11,230	11,408	11,628	11,848
Unemployed[2]	3,030	3,179	3,229	2,905	2,341
Males	2,120	2,197	2,217	2,023	1,632
Females	910	982	1,012	882	709
Workforce in employment[3]	24,235	24,536	24,561	25,074	25,870
Males	14,196	14,288	14,166	14,329	14,731
Females	10,040	10,248	10,396	10,745	11,140
HM Forces	326	326	322	319	316
Males	310	309	305	302	300
Females	16	16	16	16	16
Self-employed persons (with or without employees)[4]	2,496	2,610	2,627	2,860	2,986
Males	1,903	1,975	1,989	2,152	2,257
Females	594	635	637	708	729
Employees in employment	21,238	21,423	21,387	21,584	22,226
Males	11,888	11,903	11,744	11,698	11,970
Females	9,350	9,521	9,644	9,886	10,257
of whom					
Total, production and construction industries	7,062	6,974	6,760	6,669	6,745
Total, all manufacturing industries	5,409	5,362	5,227	5,152	5,215
Work Related Government Training Programmes[5]	175	176	226	311	343
Males	95	100	127	177	205
Females	80	76	99	134	138
Great Britain					
Workforce[1]	26,582	27,021	27,095	27,282	27,516
Males	15,903	16,067	15,966	15,935	15,951
Females	10,679	10,954	11,129	11,347	11,565
Unemployed[2]	2,911	3,057	3,103	2,780	2,225
Males	2,034	2,109	2,126	1,931	1,548
Females	877	948	978	848	677
Workforce in employment[3]	23,671	23,964	23,992	24,502	25,291
Males	13,869	13,958	13,841	14,003	14,403
Females	9,802	10,006	10,151	10,498	10,887
HM Forces	326	326	322	319	316
Males	310	309	305	302	300
Females	16	16	16	16	16
Self-employed persons (with or without employees)[4]	2,435	2,550	2,567	2,801	2,926
Males	1,850	1,923	1,937	2,099	2,205
Females	586	628	630	701	721
Employees in employment	20,741	20,920	20,886	21,080	21,714
Males	11,619	11,632	11,477	11,431	11,699
Females	9,123	9,288	9,409	9,650	10,015
of whom					
Total, production and construction industries	6,919	6,830	6,622	6,531	6,605
Total, all manufacturing industries	5,302	5,254	5,122	5,049	5,110
Work Related Government Training Programmes[5]	168	168	218	303	335
Males	91	94	122	171	199
Females	78	74	96	132	135

Source: HMSO—Annual Abstract of Statistics

[1] The workforce is the workforce in employment plus the claimant unemployed.
[2] From April 1983 the figures of unemployment reflect the effects of the provisions in the Budget for some men aged 60 and over who no longer have to sign on at an unemployment office.
[3] The workforce in employment comprises employees in employment, the self-employed, HM Forces and work-related government training programmes.
[4] Estimates of the self-employed are based on the 1981 census and the results of the Labour Force Surveys.
[5] Includes participants in the Youth Training Scheme except those who have contracts of employment, and participants in the Job Training Scheme. Additionally, for the UK this includes some participants on Northern Ireland schemes: Youth Training Programme (excluding second year trainees in further education colleges); Job Training Programme; and Attachment Training Scheme participants and other management training scheme participants training with an employer.

RATES OF UNEMPLOYMENT[1]

Analysis by standard regions. Seasonally adjusted — Percentages

Annual averages	1983	1984	1985	1986	1987	1988	1989
United Kingdom	10·5	10·7	11·0	11·2	10·1	8·1	6·3
North	14·6	15·3	15·5	15·4	14·3	12·1	10·0
Yorkshire and Humberside	11·4	11·7	12·1	12·6	11·5	9·6	7·7
East Midlands	9·5	9·8	9·9	9·9	9·0	7·2	6·2
East Anglia	8·0	7·9	8·0	8·1	6·8	4·8	4·4
South East	7·5	7·8	8·1	8·3	7·2	5·3	3·9
South West	8·7	9·0	9·3	9·5	8·2	6·3	4·5
West Midlands	12·9	12·7	12·7	12·6	11·1	8·5	6·7
North West	13·4	13·6	13·7	13·8	12·5	10·4	8·4
England	10·0	10·6	11·0	11·3	10·1	8·0	6·2
Wales	12·9	13·2	13·8	13·9	12·5	10·5	7·8
Scotland	12·3	12·6	12·9	13·4	13·1	11·3	9·3
Northern Ireland	15·5	15·9	16·0	17·4	17·2	16·0	15·1

[1] Percentages calculated using mid-year estimates of total employees in employment, unemployed, self-employed and HM Forces, and participants in work-related government training schemes.

Unemployment in the United Kingdom

Thousands

	Not seasonally adjusted		Seasonally adjusted*			
	Total	% rate	Males	Females	Total	% rate
1984...............	3,159·8	11·6	2,058·2	862·4	2,920·6	10·7
1985...............	3,271·2	11·8	2,114·3	921·5	3,035·8	10·9
1986...............	3,292·9	11·8	2,148·3	959·0	3,107·3	11·2
1987...............	2,953·4	10·6	1,971·0	851·3	2,822·3	10·3
1988...............	2,370·4	8·4	1,607·1	686·8	2,293·9	8·3
1989...............	1,798·7	6·3	1,289·6	507·0	1,796·6	6·4
1990 January	1,687·0	5·9	1,180·3	431·8	1,612·1	5·7
February	1,675·7	5·9	1,180·4	430·0	1,610·4	5·6
March	1,646·6	5·8	1,176·3	428·1	1,604·4	5·6
April	1,626·3	5·7	1,176·4	430·2	1,606·6	5·6
May	1,578·5	5·5	1,183·9	427·6	1,611·5	5·7
June	1,555·6	5·5	1,191·4	425·7	1,617·1	5·7

* The seasonally adjusted figures relate only to claimants aged 18 or over, in order to maintain the consistent series, available back to 1971, allowing for the effect of the change in benefit regulations for under 18 year-olds from September 1988.

Industrial Stoppages

Thousands

	Workers beginning involvement in period in any dispute	Total working days lost						
		All industries and services	Coal, coke, mineral oil and natural gas	Metals, engineering and vehicles	Textiles, footwear and clothing	Construction	Transport and communication	All other industries and services
1984...............	1,436	27,135	22,484	2,055	66	334	666	1,530
1985...............	643	6,402	4,143	590	31	50	197	1,391
1986...............	538	1,920	143	895	38	33	190	622
1987...............	884	3,546	217	458	50	22	1,705	1,095
1988...............	759	3,702	222	1,456	90	17	1,490	428
1989...............	727	4,128	52	655	16	128	625	2,652
1990 January	45	443	1	273	1	—	3	165
February	21	508	5	343	1	—	7	151
March ...	16	226	12	104	16	1	25	68
April	48	98	3	50	1	1	6	36
May	19	114	1	67	—	—	24	21

CRIMINAL STATISTICS

ENGLAND AND WALES
Notifiable offences recorded by the police (thousands)

	1984	1985	1986	1987	1988
Total	3,499·1	3,611·9	3,847·4	3,892·2	3,715·8
Violence against the person	114·2	121·7	125·5	141·0	158·2
Sexual offences.............................	20·2	21·5	22·7	25·2	26·5
Burglary	892·9	866·7	931·6	900·1	817·8
Robbery	24·9	27·5	30·0	32·6	31·4
Theft and handling stolen goods	1,808·0	1,884·1	2,003·9	2,052·0	1,931·3
Fraud and forgery..........................	126·1	134·8	133·4	133·0	133·9
Criminal damage	497·8	539·0	583·6	589·0	594·0
Other offences	15·0	16·7	16·7	19·3	22·7

SCOTLAND
Crimes and offences recorded by the police (thousands)

	1984	1985	1986	1987	1988
Total crimes and offences	809·4	800·4	822·4	858·2	855·6
Total crimes	474·9	462·0	463·8	481·2	470·0
Non-sexual crimes of violence against the person	13·7	15·1	15·7	18·4	17·9
Crimes involving indecency	5·7	5·7	5·4	5·3	5·1
Crimes involving dishonesty	359·2	342·3	342·5	356·5	344·5
Fire-raising, malicious and reckless conduct ..	79·1	79·5	78·9	76·4	73·5
Other crimes................................	17·3	19·2	21·4	24·6	29·0
Total offences..............................	334·5	338·4	358·5	377·0	385·6
Miscellaneous offences	114·9	118·1	120·4	127·3	124·9
Motor vehicle offences	219·6	220·3	238·1	249·7	260·7

PRISONS
Receptions into prison: by number of previous convictions (England and Wales)

	1980	1981	1982	1983*†	1984	1985	1986	1987	1988
Number of previous convictions									
Males: total	38,016	43,388	46,779	42,716	39,930	43,626	40,004	41,442	41,385
None	1,731	1,518	1,773	1,848	1,765	1,686	2,004	1,655	2,562
1–2 sentences............	2,685	3,002	3,164	2,969	2,924	3,394	3,165	3,046	2,808
3–5 sentences............	6,092	7,161	7,312	6,104	5,694	6,273	5,727	5,619	4,911
6–10 sentences...........	9,665	11,152	11,845	10,048	9,009	9,861	8,695	8,427	7,977
11 or more sentences	11,905	13,343	14,057	13,632	13,169	13,835	11,855	11,363	10,716
Previous conviction information not recorded	5,938	7,212	8,628	8,115	7,369	8,577	8,558	11,332	12,411
Females: total	2,265	2,533	2,692	2,349	2,388	2,475	2,374	2,388	2,235
None	155	177	176	271	289	208	300	247	324
1–2 sentences............	172	234	261	273	252	241	289	258	217
3–5 sentences............	322	423	445	419	374	347	349	338	344
6–10 sentences...........	331	434	443	401	397	360	327	351	271
11 or more sentences	195	267	322	294	265	261	258	242	261
Previous conviction information not recorded	1,090	998	1,045	691	811	1,058	851	952	818

*From 1983 data are not comparable with previous years because of the Criminal Justice Act 1982.
†Youth custody for offenders aged 15–20 replaced imprisonment on May 24, 1983.

Source: HMSO—Annual Abstract of Statistics

AGRICULTURE

Estimated quantity of crops and grass harvested

Thousand tonnes

	1983	1984	1985	1986	1987	1988
Cereals						
Wheat	10,800	14,970	12,050	13,910	11,940	n/a
Barley	9,980	11,070	9,740	10,010	9,225	n/a
Oats	465	515	615	505	452	n/a
Mixed corn for threshing	35	35	31	29	26	n/a
Rye for threshing	24	28	35	32	32	n/a
Potatoes						
Early crop	322	397	403	363	395	420
Main crop	5,535	7,001	6,489	6,083	6,365	6,479
Fodder crops						
Beans for stockfeeding	105	125	155	230	294	n/a
Turnips and swedes	3,655	3,960	3,300	3,855	3,451	n/a
Fodder beet and mangolds	295	570	815	845	782	n/a
Maize for threshing or stockfeeding	550	580	770	915	782	n/a
Rape, kale, cabbage, savoys and kohlrabi for stockfeeding	1,660	1,805	1,555	1,380	1,320	n/a
Peas harvested dry for stockfeeding	85	170	215	330	310	n/a
Other crops						
Sugar beet	7,495	9,015	7,715	8,120	7,992	n/a
Rape grown for oilseed	565	925	895	965	1,326	n/a
Hops	9	8	6	5	5	5
Hay	6,000	5,700	4,650	4,675	—	n/a
Horticultural crops						
Vegetables grown in the open:						
Brussels sprouts	154	169	152	168	161	170
Cabbage (including savoys and spring greens)	518	670	683	688	692	691
Cauliflowers	298	344	356	360	373	373
Carrots	554	572	600	634	568	663
Parsnips	51	57	62	68	62	66
Turnips and swedes	135	142	140	163	166	177
Beetroot	94	115	114	95	101	96
Onions, dry bulb	175	238	268	247	286	309
Onions, salad	25	22	25	30	31	30
Leeks	44	53	60	71	71	66
Broad beans	17	21	19	14	11	11
Runner beans including French	65	77	65	67	51	48
Peas, green for market	23	27	26	20	12	13
Peas, green for processing	198	241	206	239	182	183
Celery	46	57	53	65	55	59
Lettuce	155	153	166	160	176	204
Rhubarb	29	26	26	28	27	26
Protected crops						
Tomatoes	121	129	125	131	130	135
Cucumbers	61	68	71	76	79	87
Lettuce	49	48	49	50	52	54
Fruit crops						
Total dessert apples	186	184	161	163	165	134
Total culinary apples	126	163	145	139	125	124
Pears	54	48	51	47	66	32
Plums	36	34	24	33	36	24
Cherries	3	5	5	4	4	2
Soft fruit	124	114	111	109	106	105

Cattle, Sheep, Pigs and Poultry on Agricultural Holdings

Thousands

At June each year	1982	1983	1984	1985	1986	1987	1988
Cattle and calves: total	13,244	13,290	13,213	12,911	12,533	12,158	11,872
Dairy herd	3,250	3,333	3,281	3,150	3,138	3,042	2,911
Beef herd.........................	1,389	1,358	1,351	1,333	1,308	1,343	1,373
Heifers in calf (first calf)	851	847	811	874	879	774	834
Bulls for service....................	84	83	80	78	76	74	75
Other cattle:							
Two years old and over	937	904	905	852	769	732	726
One year old and under two	3,057	3,059	3,069	3,012	2,819	2,749	2,669
Six months old and under one year .	1,890	1,924	1,949	1,905	1,876	1,844	1,702
Under six months old	1,786	1,783	1,768	1,707	1,668	1,599	1,581
Sheep and lambs: total..............	33,067	34,069	34,802	35,628	37,016	38,701	40,942
Breeding ewes	12,909	13,310	13,648	13,893	14,252	14,780	15,461
Rams for service	366	383	393	406	419	437	461
Other sheep	3,748	3,764	3,680	3,763	3,961	4,107	4,433
Lambs under one year old	16,044	16,612	17,080	17,566	18,384	19,377	20,587
Pigs: total	8,023	8,174	7,689	7,865	7,937	7,942	7,980
Breeding herd	864	856	800	828	824	820	804
Boars for service	45	45	42	44	44	44	43
Gilts not yet in pig	89	82	77	80	79	81	73
Barren sows for fattening	12	15	12	12	12	11	12
Other pigs:							
110 kg and over	117	100	91	89	80	67	62
80 kg and under 110 kg	630	605	599	589	603	615	621
50 kg and under 80 kg	1,824	1,868	1,787	1,813	1,863	1,890	1,898
20 kg and under 50 kg	2,281	2,362	2,198	2,260	2,270	2,253	2,263
Under 20 kg	2,163	2,241	2,082	2,151	2,163	2,160	2,204
Poultry: total......................	135,363	127,618	127,507	128,968	—	—	—
Fowls: total	126,091	117,854	118,846	119,456	120,740	128,628	130,809
Growing pullets..................	14,766	11,828	12,536	12,503	12,502	12,230	11,236
Laying flock	44,792	41,127	40,573	39,538	38,096	38,498	37,389
Breeding flock	6,457	6,012	6,396	6,104	6,334	7,146	6,879
Table birds	60,075	58,887	59,341	61,311	63,807	70,754	75,305
Ducks*...........................	1,443	1,566	\} 1,566	1,648	1,747	1,744	1,821
Geese*...........................	157	157			—	—	—
Turkeys..........................	7,672	8,198	7,134	7,864	—	—	—

*Excludes Scotland except from 1983 to 1986.

Agricultural land: area

Thousand hectares

	1982	1983	1984	1985	1986	1987	1988
Total tillage	5,127	5,124	5,196	5,265	5,287	5,312	5,311
All grasses under five years old	1,859	1,846	1,794	1,796	1,723	1,691	1,613
Total arable	6,986	6,970	6,990	7,061	7,010	7,003	6,924
All grasses five years old and over	5,097	5,107	5,105	5,019	5,077	5,112	5,161
Total crops and grass	12,083	12,078	12,095	12,080	12,088	12,115	12,085
Rough grazings							
Sole rights........................	4,984	4,927	4,895	4,872	4,829	4,743	4,712
Common (estimated)...............	1,214	1,212	1,212	1,216	1,216	1,214	1,216
Woodland on agricultural holdings	285	292	299	312	316	322	333
All other land on agricultural holdings .	217	227	218	223	227	225	229
Total area of agricultural land	18,783	18,735	18,720	18,703	18,676	18,619	18,575
Total area of the United Kingdom	24,088	24,088	24,088	24,085	24,086	24,086	24,086

Source: HMSO—Annual Abstract of Statistics

FISHERIES

Fishing fleet

Number

At December 31	1982	1983	1984	1985	1986	1987	1988
England and Wales							
Trawlers	1,759	1,757	1,686	1,285	1,561	1,730	1,711
Seine nets	216	195	181	150	83	63	71
Lines	469	499	629	534	802	810	656
Purse seine	3	5	3	2	1	—	—
Other nets	89	111	114	99	257	183	104
Other and unknown	1,692	2,113	2,454	3,311	2,935	2,790	2,891
Scotland							
Total fishing vessels	2,233	2,214	2,180	2,198	2,183	2,263	2,334
Demersal trawl	315	291	244	253	235	253	288
Demersal pair trawl	70	76	104	116	122	132	129
Industrial trawl	19	17	12	10	6	6	6
Seine net	296	302	291	291	283	277	251
Lines	147	112	94	83	70	69	63
Purse seine	45	42	44	45	47	47	46
Pelagic trawl	34	26	23	20	12	7	6
Other nets*	27	43	48	46	43	32	31
Nephrops trawl	302	317	337	335	383	412	446
Other shellfishing†	978	988	983	999	982	1,028	1,068

*Gill and cod nets, drift and ring nets.
†All shellfishing methods except nephrops trawl.

Landings of fish of British taking (Great Britain)

	Landed weight (Thousand tonnes)				Value (£ thousand)			
	1985	1986	1987	1988	1985	1986	1987	1988
Total all fish	762·1	716·9	790·4	742·0	323,825	361,680	435,162	402,893
Total wet fish	687·2	629·3	679·3	645·5	258,904	284,161	339,223	310,412
Demersal: total	402·3	383·2	381·3	366·0	227,175	256,705	304,326	276,948
Catfish	1·4	1·5	1·6	1·6	755	1,035	1,318	1,223
Cod	90·0	76·5	93·4	77·7	69,945	69,140	86,312	74,849
Dogfish	13·8	11·6	13·6	13·0	4,550	6,376	7,201	7,066
Haddock	132·2	131·0	102·4	97·6	67,757	79,019	78,079	68,708
Hake	2·7	3·0	3·3	3·6	3,851	4,549	5,540	6,389
Halibut	0·1	0·1	0·1	0·1	365	372	446	482
Lemon sole	5·7	5·0	5·3	5·4	7,137	8,265	9,018	8,788
Plaice	20·4	21·3	25·7	27·3	13,821	16,048	22,541	22,348
Redfish	0·2	0·1	0·2	0·2	75	56	62	71
Saithe (coalfish)	14·4	17·7	15·2	14·4	3,874	6,361	7,077	5,657
Skate and ray	7·0	6·9	8·6	8·4	2,992	3,908	4,742	4,796
Sole	2·7	3·2	3·1	3·0	9,093	14,500	16,991	14,067
Turbot	0·5	0·6	0·7	0·7	1,976	2,607	3,612	3,690
Whiting	50·2	41·1	51·9	45·6	18,997	18,460	25,198	21,143
Livers	—	—	—	—	1	1	—	—
Roes	0·5	0·5	0·5	0·5	390	348	499	473
Other demersal	60·5	63·1	55·0	66·9	21,596	25,660	35,690	37,198
Pelagic: total	285·0	246·1	298·0	279·5	31,730	27,456	34,897	33,464
Herring	95·4	106·1	100·3	93·2	11,493	11,881	12,213	11,244
Mackerel	174·2	132·1	189·4	176·1	18,694	14,766	21,484	20,791
Other pelagic	15·4	7·9	8·3	10·2	1,543	809	1,200	1,429
Total shellfish	74·8	87·6	111·1	96·5	64,920	77,519	95,939	92,481
Cockles	7·8	19·4	39·0	24·6	476	1,165	4,285	3,276
Crab	13·5	12·6	13·5	15·2	8,557	9,599	11,400	13,908
Lobster	1·1	1·0	1·1	1·3	8,030	7,680	9,346	10,163
Mussels	5·8	6·3	4·9	6·9	467	541	543	906
Nephrop (Norway lobster)	24·8	25·4	24·2	27·4	31,548	39,119	43,007	44,585
Oysters	0·5	0·6	0·1	0·1	734	845	241	225
Shrimps	0·8	1·4	3·3	1·7	711	1,254	2,346	1,785
Whelks	1·6	2·0	2·7	2·0	355	418	665	473
Other shellfish	18·9	18·9	22·3	17·3	14,042	16,898	24,106	17,165

Source: HMSO—Annual Abstract of Statistics

TRANSPORT

Goods transport in Great Britain

	1983	1984	1985	1986	1987	1988
Total tonne kilometres (thousand millions)	182·4	182·7	187·1	187·1	195·2	219·9
Road	95·1	99·4	102·9	105·4	113·3	130·2
Rail (British Rail only)	17·1	12·7	15·4	16·5	17·3	18·0
Water: coastwise oil products*	40·2	41·3	39·5	34·4	31·7	35·7
Water: other*	20·1	18·9	18·1	20·4	22·4	25·2
Pipelines (except gases)	9·9	10·4	11·2	10·4	10·5	10·8
Total (million tonnes)	1,714	1,696	1,797	1,835	1,909	2,145
Road	1,344	1,390	1,445	1,471	1,542	1,758
Rail (British Rail only)	145	78	122	140	141	150
Water: coastwise oil products*	53	53	50	46	43	46
Water: other*	90	87	92	99	100	106
Pipelines (except gases)	82	88	89	79	83	85

*'Coastwise' includes all sea traffic within the UK, Isle of Man and Channel Islands. 'Other' means other coastwise plus inland waterway traffic and one-port traffic.

Seaport traffic of Great Britain

Million gross tonnes

	1983	1984	1985	1986	1987	1988
Foreign traffic						
Imports						
Bulk fuel traffic	42·0	60·0	57·2	61·7	57·3	62·9
Other bulk traffic	34·3	34·6	36·7	37·3	42·0	45·0
Container and roll-on traffic	26·0	28·1	29·8	31·1	34·0	38·0
Semi-bulk traffic	14·6	14·6	14·5	15·8	16·9	18·9
Conventional traffic	2·3	2·3	1·7	1·5	1·6	1·6
All imports	119·1	139·6	139·9	147·4	151·8	166·4
Exports						
Bulk fuel traffic	96·0	97·3	103·1	101·9	100·2	91·1
Other bulk traffic	16·3	18·7	17·7	21·1	20·4	18·5
Container and roll-on traffic	18·6	20·3	21·3	22·1	23·9	26·5
Semi-bulk traffic	3·5	3·6	4·1	4·0	5·1	4·6
Conventional traffic	2·1	1·8	1·6	1·2	1·2	1·0
All exports	136·5	141·7	147·8	150·4	150·7	141·7
Domestic traffic						
Bulk fuel traffic	130·7	123·2	119·9	112·2	108·1	115·3
Other bulk traffic	31·7	31·0	31·7	32·7	34·8	40·4
Container and roll-on traffic	5·4	5·4	5·9	6·2	7·3	7·6
Semi-bulk traffic	0·2	0·4	0·3	0·2	0·2	0·3
Conventional traffic	0·3	0·2	0·3	0·3	0·3	0·3
Non-oil traffic with UK offshore installations	2·2	3·2	3·6	2·9	3·1	3·5
All domestic traffic	170·4	163·5	161·6	154·5	153·8	167·5
Total foreign and domestic traffic	426·0	444·7	449·3	452·3	456·2	475·6

Passenger transport in Great Britain
(Estimated passenger kilometres)

Thousand million passenger kilometres

	1983	1984	1985	1986	1987	1988†
Total	506	527	535	558	595	615
Air	3	3	4	4	4	5
Rail*	34	35	36	37	39	41
Road:						
Public service vehicles	42	42	42	41	41	41
Cars and taxis	412	432	439	463	498	517
Motorcycles	9	9	8	8	7	6
Pedal cycles	6	6	6	5	6	5

*including London Regional Transport and Passenger Transport Executive railway systems.
†provisional.

Source: HMSO—Annual Abstract of Statistics

AIR

Air Traffic Between the United Kingdom and Abroad*

Thousands

	1983	1984	1985	1986	1987	1988
Flights: total	518·5	566·3	579·3	615·8	675·7	735·2
United Kingdom airlines						
Scheduled services	141·9	151·3	170·8	177·5	188·5	216·9
Non-scheduled services	184·9	214·0	196·2	198·8	219·2	225·5
Overseas airlines†						
Scheduled services	155·2	160·9	172·8	195·8	222·8	249·8
Non-scheduled services	36·5	40·2	39·5	43·6	45·2	43·0
Passengers carried: total	46,284·9	51,154·8	52,862·7	51,608·1	66,578·6	71,415·5
United Kingdom airlines						
Scheduled services	12,140·0	13,174·2	14,854·3	15,082·9	17,473·8	19,237·6
Non-scheduled services	14,661·9	16,643·7	15,529·0	12,929·7	22,250·5	23,062·1
Overseas airlines†						
Scheduled services	16,065·6	17,623·0	18,815·6	19,409·5	22,441·5	25,029·3
Non-scheduled services	3,417·4	3,713·9	3,663·8	4,186·0	4,412·8	4,086·5

* Excludes travel to and from the Channel Islands.
† Includes airlines of overseas UK Territories.

Activity at Civil Aerodromes

	1983	1984	1985	1986	1987	1988
Movement of civil aircraft (thousands)	2,238	2,363	2,354	2,439	2,614	2,868
Commercial: total	1,243	1,179	1,205	1,238	1,312	1,402
Transport	1,019	1,079	1,097	1,125	1,193	1,279
Other	224	100	108	113	118	123
Non-commercial	995	1,184	1,149	1,201	1,303	1,466
Passengers handled (thousands): total	62,301	68,830	71,812	76,593	87,517	94,640
Terminal	61,099	67,572	70,434	75,161	86,041	93,162
Transit	1,202	1,258	1,377	1,432	1,476	1,479
Commercial freight handled (tonnes): total	725,897	860,629	850,268	881,202	975,879	1,088,151
Set down	332,162	388,292	377,127	419,275	485,468	572,426
Picked up	393,737	472,335	473,140	461,927	490,412	515,725
Mail handled (tonnes): total	124,080	136,640	145,770	153,467	155,199	153,308
Set down	56,943	61,461	64,138	67,802	67,758	66,978
Picked up	67,138	75,179	81,632	85,665	87,441	86,330

Air Passengers by Type of Operator, 1988

Airport	Total terminal and transit	Scheduled UK and overseas		Charter UK and overseas	
		Terminal	Transit	Terminal	Transit
All UK airports: total	100,553,068	71,194,274	1,258,019	27,703,987	396,788
London area airports: total .	65,679,845	51,932,668	387,738	13,275,644	92,089
Battersea Heliport	8,294	—	—	8,294	—
Gatwick..................	21,258,486	10,929,435	87,983	10,220,146	20,922
Heathrow	39,881,922	39,533,908	292,182	53,873	1,324
London City	216,383	213,573	—	2,810	—
Luton.....................	2,848,244	853,570	486	1,974,168	20,020
Southend.................	99,499	73,124	2	26,302	71
Stansted	1,375,311	329,058	6,450	990,051	49,752
Other UK airports: total	34,864,929	19,261,606	870,281	14,428,343	304,699
Aberdeen.................	1,758,334	970,269	27,661	760,048	356
Barrow-in-Furness	513	—	—	513	—
Belfast	2,164,564	1,750,351	—	407,196	7,017
Belfast City	506,993	506,302	—	691	—
Bembridge................	662	—	—	659	3
Benbecula	32,630	30,395	1,635	597	3
Birmingham	3,431,445	1,734,236	85,013	1,599,240	12,956
Blackpool	133,525	77,435	1,000	54,400	690
Bournemouth..............	131,421	82,603	472	47,786	560
Bristol	869,000	165,936	21,816	671,782	9,466
Cambridge................	25,389	14,209	—	11,180	—
Cardiff	735,715	95,793	21,251	600,538	18,133
Carlisle	2,182	—	—	2,131	51
Coventry	18,288	15,160	—	3,124	4
Dundee	11,270	7,509	2,945	816	—
East Midlands	1,453,985	520,416	394	932,122	1,053
Edinburgh................	2,460,033	2,154,275	90,963	208,516	6,279
Exeter	237,942	118,981	14,339	101,430	3,122
Glasgow	3,959,880	2,657,205	86,293	1,205,076	11,306
Gloucester/Cheltenham.....	5,621	—	—	5,621	—
Hawarden	921	—	—	919	2
Humberside	153,235	86,927	22,850	43,382	76
Inverness	210,750	201,308	5,900	3,473	69
Islay	23,660	22,408	260	992	—
Isle of Man	533,169	501,391	23,323	8,379	76
Isles of Scilly–St. Mary's	113,700	112,174	—	1,526	—
–Tresco	18,176	17,733	379	50	14
Kirkwall	110,932	91,245	14,051	4,662	974
Leeds/Bradford	883,446	616,109	15,811	249,892	1,634
Lerwick (Tingwall).........	15,224	10,066	1,886	3,255	17
Liverpool.................	478,324	432,202	663	44,342	1,117
Londonderry	19,136	15,668	—	988	—
Lydd	2,962	27	—	2,928	7
Manchester................	10,392,733	4,060,285	240,910	5,998,495	93,043
Manston	17,085	247	—	14,633	2,205
Newcastle	1,570,218	685,861	47,756	806,001	30,600
Norwich	225,329	159,527	29,638	36,038	126
Penzance Heliport..........	92,309	92,204	—	105	—
Plymouth	145,090	124,618	17,815	2,657	—
Prestwick	425,589	215,938	44,080	101,106	64,465
Scatsta	17,204	—	—	17,204	—
Shoreham	277	—	—	277	—
Southampton	493,721	473,287	2,620	17,650	164
Stornoway	71,047	69,699	45	1,152	151
Sumburgh	408,948	72,473	632	300,379	35,464
Swansea..................	562	—	—	550	12
Teesside..................	361,595	262,281	26,679	69,742	2,893
Tiree.....................	6,061	5,128	667	266	—
Unst	86,145	2,460	—	83,193	492
Wick	47,989	26,715	20,534	641	99
Channel Is. airports: total ...	2,918,759	2,630,727	93,209	192,703	2,120
Alderney	102,649	102,248	8	393	—
Guernsey.................	925,868	853,339	58,463	14,066	—
Jersey....................	1,890,242	1,675,140	34,738	178,244	2,120

Source: Civil Aviation Authority

AERODROMES AND AIRPORTS

The following aerodromes in Great Britain, Northern Ireland, the Isle of Man and the Channel Islands are either State owned or licensed for use by civil aircraft. A number of unlicensed aerodromes not included in this list are also available for private use by permission of the owner or controlling authority.

Aerodromes designated as Customs airports are printed in **bold** type. Customs facilities are available at certain other aerodromes by special arrangement.

BAA = Owned by BAA PLC.
H = Licensed helicopter aerodrome.
HIAL = Operated by Highland and Islands Airports
    Ltd.

J = Military aerodromes available for civil use by
    prior permission.
M = Owned by the municipal authority.
S = Owned and operated by the Government.

ENGLAND AND WALES

Aberporth, Dyfed. J
Abingdon, Oxon. J
Andrewsfield, Essex.
Barrow (Walney Island), Cumbria.
Bembridge, IOW.
Benson, Oxon. J
Biggin Hill, Kent.
Birmingham, W. Midlands. M
Blackbushe, Hants.
Blackpool, Lancs. M
Bodmin, Cornwall.
Bourn, Cambridge.
Bournemouth, Dorset. M
Bristol, Avon. M
Brize Norton, Oxford. J
Brough, N. Humberside.
Caernarfon, Gwynedd.
Cambridge.
Cardiff, S. Glamorgan. M
Carlisle, Cumbria. M
Chichester (Goodwood), Sussex.
Chivenor, Devon. J
Church Fenton, N. Yorks. J
Clacton, Essex.
Compton Abbas, Dorset.
Cosford, Wolverhampton. J
Coventry, W. Midlands. M
Cranfield, Beds.
Cranwell, Lincs. J
Culdrose, Cornwall. J
Denham, Bucks.
Dishforth, N. Yorks. J
Doncaster, S. Yorks.
Dunkeswell, Devon.
Dunsfold, Surrey. M
Duxford, Cambs. M
Eaglescott, Devon.
Earls Colne, Halstead.
East Midlands, Derbys. M
Elstree, Herts.
Exeter, Devon.
Fairoaks, Surrey.
Farnborough, Hants. S
Fenland, Lincs.
Filton, Bristol.
Finningley, S. Yorks. J
Gloucester/Cheltenham
  (Staverton), Glos. M
Great Yarmouth (North Denes),
  Norfolk.
Halfpenny Green, Staffs.
Halton, Bucks. J
Hatfield, Herts.
Haverfordwest, Dyfed. M
Hawarden, Clywd. J
Hucknall, Notts.
Humberside. M
Ipswich, Suffolk.
Isle of Wight/Sandown.
Kemble, Glos. J
Land's End (St. Just), Cornwall.

Lashenden, Headcorn, Kent.
Leavesden, Herts.
Leeds/Bradford, Yorks. M
Lee-on-Solent, Hants. J
Leicester, Leics.
Linton-on-Ouse, Yorks. J
Liverpool, Merseyside.
Llanbedr, Gwynedd. J.
London/City.
London/Gatwick. BAA
London/Heathrow. BAA
London/Stansted. BAA
London/Westland Heliport. H
Luton, Beds. M
Lydd, Kent.
Lyneham, Wilts. J
Manchester. M
Manchester (Barton).
Manston, Kent. J
Netherthorpe, S. Yorks.
Newcastle, Tyne and Wear. M
Newton, Notts. J
Northampton (Sywell), Northants.
Northolt, Middx. J
Norwich, Norfolk. M
Nottingham, Notts.
Old Sarum, Wilts.
Oxford (Kidlington), Oxfordshire.
Panshanger, Herts.
Penzance, Cornwall. H
Peterborough (Conington).
Peterborough (Sibson), Cambs.
Plymouth (Roborough), Devon.
Portland Naval, Dorset. JH
Redhill, Surrey.
Retford/Gamston, Notts.
Rochester, Kent.
St. Mawgan, Cornwall. J
Sandtoft, Humberside.
Scilly Isles (St. Mary's). M
Seething, Norfolk.
Shawbury, Shropshire. J
Sherburn-in-Elmet, N. Yorks.
Shipdham, Norfolk.
Shobdon, Herefordshire.
Shoreham, W. Sussex. M
Silverstone, Northants.
Skegness (Ingoldmells), Lincs.
Sleap, Shropshire.
Southampton/Eastleigh, Hants.
Southend, Essex. M
Stapleford, Essex.
Sturgate, Lincs.
Swansea, W. Glam. M
Teesside, Cleveland. M
Thruxton, Hants.
Tresco, Isles of Scilly. H
Valley, Gwynedd. J
Warton, Lancs.
Wattisham, Suffolk. J
Wellesbourne Mountford,
  Warwick.
Weston, Avon. H

White Waltham, Berks.
Wickenby, Lincs.
Woodford, Gtr. Manchester.
Woodvale, Merseyside. J
Wycombe Air Park (Booker),
  Bucks.
Yeovil, Somerset.
Yeovilton, Somerset. J

SCOTLAND

Aberdeen (Dyce). BAA
Barra, Hebrides.
Benbecula, Hebrides. HIAL
Cumbernauld, Strathclyde.
Dounreay (Thurso). S
Dundee, Angus. M
Eday. M
Edinburgh. BAA
Fair Isle.
Fife/Glenrothes. M
Flotta, Orkneys.
Glasgow. BAA
Inverness (Dalcross). HIAL
Islay (Port Ellen). HIAL
Isle of Skye. M
Kirkwall. HIAL
Lerwick (Tingwall). M
Machrihanish, Kintyre. J
North Ronaldsay, Orkneys. M
Papa Westray, Orkneys. M
Perth (Scone).
Prestwick. BAA
Sanday, Orkneys. M
Scatsta.
Stornoway, Hebrides. HIAL
Stronsay, Orkneys. M
Sumburgh, Shetlands. HIAL
Tiree. HIAL
Unst, Shetlands. M
West Freugh, Dumfries. S
Westray, Orkneys. M
Whalsay, Shetlands.
Wick. HIAL
Wigtown/Baldoon, Dumfries.

NORTHERN IRELAND

Belfast (Aldergrove). S
Belfast (City).
Enniskillen (St. Angelo). M
Londonderry (Eglinton). M
Newtownards.

ISLE OF MAN

Ronaldsway. S

CHANNEL ISLANDS

Alderney. S
Guernsey. S
Jersey. S

Transport—Shipping

MERCHANT SHIPPING
Principal Merchant Fleets of the World

Flag	1979 No.	1979 Gross Tonnage	1984 No.	1984 Gross Tonnage	1988 No.	1988 Gross Tonnage	1989 No.	1989 Gross Tonnage
Liberia	2,466	81,528,175	1,934	62,024,700	1,507	49,733,615	1,455	47,892,529
Panama	3,803	22,323,931	5,499	37,244,233	5,022	44,604,071	5,121	47,365,362
Japan	9,981	39,992,925	10,425	40,368,749	9,804	32,074,417	9,880	28,030,425
USSR	8,120	22,990,201	7,095	24,492,469	6,741	25,783,969	6,555	25,853,712
Greece	3,827	37,352,597	2,904	35,068,593	1,874	21,978,820	1,839	21,324,340
*USA	5,088	17,542,220	6,441	19,291,868	6,442	20,832,137	6,375	20,587,812
China, People's Republic of	846	6,336,747	1,262	9,300,358	1,841	12,919,876	1,907	13,513,578
China, Republic of (Taiwan)	490	2,011,311	543	3,958,418	617	4,631,474	641	5,169,337
Cyprus	762	2,355,543	737	6,727,887	1,352	18,390,642	1,278	18,134,011
Norway	2,531	22,349,337	2,271	17,662,916	2,078	9,350,303	2,304	15,596,900
Bahamas	91	120,581	163	3,191,971	572	8,962,892	724	11,578,891
Philippines	620	1,606,019	946	3,441,076	1,483	9,311,555	1,424	9,384,757
Korea, South	1,287	3,952,946	1,799	6,771,402	1,930	7,333,704	1,974	7,832,453
United Kingdom	3,211	27,951,342	2,468	15,874,062	2,142	8,260,431	2,053	7,645,750
Italy	1,711	11,694,872	1,590	9,151,867	1,583	7,794,247	1,571	7,602,032
Singapore	1,031	7,869,152	825	6,512,344	715	7,208,974	712	7,272,506
India	601	5,854,285	710	6,414,741	797	6,160,773	834	6,315,135
Hong Kong	177	1,469,623	340	5,784,336	394	7,328,984	366	6,151,261
Brazil	585	4,007,498	706	5,721,821	719	6,122,386	716	6,078,150
Denmark	1,315	5,524,416	1,101	5,211,262	1,240	4,501,727	1,256	4,962,706
Iran	219	1,207,372	306	2,105,549	375	4,336,609	386	4,732,551
France	1,247	11,945,837	1,174	8,945,046	930	4,506,227	921	4,413,464
Bermuda	112	1,726,672	76	822,123	116	3,774,298	107	4,076,093
Germany, Federal Republic of	1,926	8,562,780	1,813	6,242,467	1,233	3,917,257	1,185	3,966,571
Spain	2,773	8,313,658	2,529	7,004,852	2,343	4,415,122	2,341	3,961,941
Romania	286	1,797,108	393	2,666,820	462	3,560,736	468	3,783,444
Yugoslavia	478	2,407,221	480	2,681,879	499	3,476,354	500	3,680,687
Netherlands	1,233	5,403,350	1,337	4,585,991	1,265	3,726,464	1,218	3,654,973
Poland	813	3,580,294	783	3,267,281	714	3,489,449	710	3,416,014
Malta	47	116,299	195	1,366,149	356	2,685,888	410	3,329,120
Turkey	475	1,421,715	776	3,124,784	872	3,281,153	855	3,239,825
Canada	1,290	3,015,752	1,310	3,449,496	1,225	2,902,394	1,227	2,824,852
Gibraltar	5	2,291	54	247,458	107	3,041,811	85	2,611,304
Australia	457	1,651,747	622	2,172,850	709	2,365,923	706	2,494,021
Sweden	697	4,636,662	679	3,520,352	633	2,116,079	644	2,166,918
Saudi Arabia	172	1,442,952	422	3,863,272	320	2,269,398	312	2,119,220
Belgium	276	1,788,538	338	2,406,714	344	2,118,422	333	2,043,594
Indonesia	1,122	1,309,911	1,484	1,856,967	1,736	2,126,016	1,722	2,035,060
Kuwait	270	2,428,200	250	2,551,074	206	735,318	220	1,865,066
Argentina	495	2,343,671	530	2,422,111	451	1,876,673	465	1,832,518
Malaysia	196	620,894	429	1,664,312	499	1,608,155	491	1,668,014
German Democratic Republic	453	1,552,148	409	1,421,714	369	1,442,840	372	1,499,940

* Including ships of the United States Reserve Fleet.
CLASSIFICATION WITH LLOYD'S REGISTER OF SHIPPING.—Ships classed or to be classed with Lloyd's Register at June 30, 1989, totalled 8,509 with an aggregate of almost 90 million gross tonnage.

Source: Lloyd's Register of Shipping

MERCHANT SHIPPING

Merchant Ships Completed in the World During 1989

Country of Build	Total		For Registration in	Total	
	No.	Gross Tonnage		No.	Gross Tonnage
Japan	640	5,364,600	Panama	127	2,795,704
Korea, South	102	3,101,566	Liberia	61	2,567,502
*China, People's Republic of	20	325,719	Japan	464	1,219,385
China, Republic of (Taiwan)	9	404,892	Bahamas	20	662,624
Yugoslavia	26	498,716	USSR	135	531,915
Germany, Federal Republic of	54	430,845	Korea, South	32	468,929
Denmark	33	342,960	Singapore	17	451,505
Italy	35	327,202	Denmark	30	377,618
*Romania	17	307,331	Italy	35	324,602
German Democratic Republic	33	287,185	Romania	12	292,033
Spain	130	230,906	Hong Kong	18	283,377
Poland	44	199,391	Norway	34	267,377
Finland	21	193,970	Germany, Federal Republic of	32	258,964
*USSR	59	174,277	China, People's Republic of	10	150,680
Brazil	11	164,885	China, Republic of (Taiwan)	7	95,854
France	27	159,565	Kuwait	4	202,765
United Kingdom	35	102,393	Australia	16	183,207
Argentina	11	89,759	Brazil	11	168,711
Netherlands	53	88,814	India	30	149,008
India	17	80,349	Sweden	16	134,219
Bulgaria	10	76,603	Finland	12	132,276
Belgium	2	39,438	United Kingdom	41	120,341
Mexico	2	37,973	Czechoslovakia	6	107,904
Canada	13	32,980	Yugoslavia	7	105,611
Norway	35	32,710	Netherlands	36	104,038
Singapore	20	23,638	Vanuatu	7	102,733
Portugal	16	21,430	Bermuda	4	98,759
Turkey	13	14,783	Argentina	11	89,759
Egypt	2	13,300	Poland	13	88,838
Sweden	14	12,983	Greece	7	84,509
Indonesia	3	8,300	Philippines	2	72,987
Other Countries	86	46,706	Other Countries	336	543,115
WORLD TOTAL	1,593	13,236,169	WORLD TOTAL	1,593	13,236,169

* Information incomplete.

Of the steamships and motorships completed in the world during the year 2,959,836 gross tonnage (22·4 per cent) is to be classed with Lloyd's Register.

Source: Lloyd's Register of Shipping

BRITISH RAILWAYS

The British Railways Board was set up by the Transport Act, 1962, and assumed its responsibilities on January 1, 1963. (For members, see **Government and Public Offices**.)

The railway business is broken down into five distinct business sectors each with its own Director. The sectors focus on three passenger businesses of InterCity; Network SouthEast; and Provincial; together with the Railfreight and Parcels businesses. In addition for the purposes of management and operation the railways are divided into Regions. They cover the following areas:

London Midland Region—bounded by a line joining Carlisle, Oldham, Nottingham, Bedford, London, Banbury, Kidderminster and Aberystwyth.

Western Region—west of a line joining Yeovil, Westbury, Reading, London and the southern border of the LM Region.

Southern Region—south of a line joining Dorchester, Salisbury, London and the Thames.

Eastern Region—east of a line joining London, Peterborough, Sheffield, Bradford and Carlisle, but excluding Anglia Region.

Anglia Region—east of a line joining London with Hertford East, Meldreth and Whittlesea.

Scottish Region—north of a line joining Carlisle and Berwick.

Financial Results

The Profit and Loss Account for 1989–90 showed a deficit of £22·6 million, £46·4 million after interest, compared with a surplus of £18·2 million after interest in 1988–89. The railway working deficit was £41·1 million compared with a surplus of £110·5 million for the previous year.

	£ million
Railways	1989–90
Gross receipts:	
Passenger (including grants)	2,626·2
Freight (inc. parcels and mails)	813·7
TOTAL	3,439·9
Working expenses:	
Train services	1,442·7
Terminals	354·8
Miscellaneous traffic expenses	161·4
Track and signalling	715·7
General expenses	411·9
Provision for replacement of assets	174·9
TOTAL	3,261·4
Railway net deficit	(46·4)
Surplus from subsidiaries, operational and non-operational property letting	316·2
GROUP OPERATING SURPLUS	269·8

Staff

On March 31, 1990, British Rail employed 129,696 staff (130,461 at March 31, 1989). Including BR Property Board, Transmark, BR Maintenance Ltd. and BR Pension Trustee Co. Ltd., the group total at March 31, 1990, was 134,361 (135,243 at March 31, 1989).

OPERATING STATISTICS

At March 31, 1990, British Rail had 23,518 miles of standard gauge lines and sidings in use, representing 10,307 miles of route of which 2,825 miles were electrified. Standard rail on main line has a weight of 110 lb. per yard. British Rail had 2,095 locomotives (diesel and diesel electric, 1,835 and electric, 260); 2,134 diesel multiple-unit vehicles, 7,197 electric multiple-unit vehicles and 2,465 locomotive-hauled passenger carriages.

Loaded train miles run in passenger service totalled 213·5m. 746·4m. passenger journeys were made during the year, including 360·1m. made by holders of season tickets. The average distance of each passenger journey on ordinary fare was 36·1 miles; and on season ticket, 18·8 miles. Passenger stations in use in 1990 numbered 2,483 and freight stations 127.

Freight

There were 21,970 freight-vehicles and 1,319 other vehicles in the non-passenger-carrying stock. Train miles run in freight service totalled 30·7m.

Accidents on Railways

	1987	1988
Train accidents: total	1,164	1,130
Persons killed: total	10	40
Passengers	3	34
Railway staff	1	2
Others	6	4
Persons injured: total	396	705
Passengers	310	615
Railway staff	65	68
Others	21	22
Other accidents through movement of railway vehicles		
Persons killed	57	53
Persons injured	2,776	3,010
Other accidents on railway premises		
Persons killed	37	4
Persons injured	6,614	7,351
Trespassers and suicides		
Persons killed	132	324
Persons injured	46	70

ROADS

Highway Authorities

The powers and responsibilities of highway authorities in England and Wales are set out in the Highways Acts 1980: for Scotland there is separate legislation.

Responsibility for trunk road motorways and other trunk roads in Great Britain rests in England with the Secretary of State for Transport, in Scotland with the Secretary of State for Scotland, and in Wales with the Secretary of State for Wales. The costs of construction, improvement and maintenance are paid for by central government. The highway authority for non-trunk roads in England and Wales is, in general, the county council, metropolitan district council or London borough council in whose area the roads lie, and in Scotland the regional or islands council. In Northern Ireland the Northern Ireland Department of the Environment is responsible for public roads and their maintenance and construction.

Expenditure

Transport Supplementary Grant (TSG) is a block grant and was introduced in England and Wales on April 1, 1975, to replace a variety of specific grants paid towards local transport expenditure.

In England grant was paid towards capital and current spending on transport by county councils and the GLC from 1975–76 to 1984–85. From April 1, 1985, TSG has only been paid towards capital spending on highways and the regulation of traffic, current expenditure having been subsumed by Rate Support Grant. With the abolition of the GLC and the metropolitan county councils on April 1, 1986, grant has become payable to London boroughs, the Common Council of the City of London and metropolitan district councils. In Wales, grant was also paid to the Welsh county councils towards current and capital expenditure on transport. Since April 1982, TSG became payable on capital expenditure only; current expenditure having been subsumed into the Rate Support Grant. From April 1, 1990, the grant for Wales has been renamed Transport Grant.

Grant rates are determined by the respective Secretaries of State; at present grant is paid at 50 per cent of expenditure accepted for grant in England and Wales.

For the financial year 1989–90 local authorities in England received £204 million in TSG. Total expenditure on building and maintaining motorways and trunk roads in 1989–90 was £1,316 million in England, of which new construction of national roads accounted for over £1,296 million.

In the financial year 1990–91, local authorities in Wales will receive £26·8 million in TSG. Total expenditure on roads in Wales in 1988–89 was £242 million.

Total expenditure on roads during the financial year 1988–89 was £440 million in Scotland.

Road Lengths (miles)
(at April 1989)

	Public Roads	Trunk Roads (incl. motorways)	*Trunk Motorways
England	168,711	6,687	1,576
Wales	20,640	1,057	74
Scotland ...	32,027	1,999	145
N. Ireland ..	14,909	1,441†	69
UK	236,287	11,184	1,864

*There were in addition 42 miles of local authority motorway in England and 15 miles in Scotland.
†Renamed Class 1 Roads in 1984.

Motorways

The network in England and Wales is based on five main routes—London–Yorkshire (M1), London–South Wales (M4), Birmingham–Bristol–Exeter (M5), Birmingham–Carlisle (M6) and Lancashire–North Humberside (M62).

Other important motorways in use include: Medway Towns (M2); London–Basingstoke (M3); London–Cambridge (M11); Rotherham–Goole (M18); London–Folkestone (M20); London orbital route (M25); London–Oxford (M40); North Cheshire (M56); and South Humberside (M180).

Motorways in use in Scotland include: Edinburgh–Glasgow–Greenock (M8); Edinburgh–Stirling (M9); Maryville–Mollisburn (M73); Millbank–Maryville (M74); Stirling–Haggs (M80); Friarton Bridge–Perth (M85); Inverkeithing–Perth (M90), and (M80)–Kincardine Bridge (M876).

Driving Tests

The number of driving tests conducted in Great Britain in 1989 was 1,995,412, of which 52·34 per cent resulted in a pass. In addition 97,170 HGV/PSV tests were undertaken, of which 53·34 per cent were successful. In 1989 3,003 Part I motorcycle tests were conducted by Departmental examiners (48·75 per cent successful) and 51,287 by approved training bodies (96·5 per cent successful).

Motor Vehicles

The number of vehicles in Great Britain with current licences in 1989 was:

Private and light goods	21,277,000
Motor cycles, scooters, mopeds	876,000
Public transport vehicles	122,000
Heavy goods vehicles	675,000
Agricultural tractors	384,000
Others	77,000
TOTAL	24,196,000

This total includes 785,000 Crown vehicles and vehicles exempt from licensing.

Buses and Coaches 1988–89
(Great Britain)

No. of vehicles (average)	72,400
Vehicle kilometres (millions)	3,781
Passenger journeys (millions)...........	5,810
Passenger receipts (£ million)	2,511

Road Accidents 1988

Road accidents	246,994
Vehicles involved:	
Pedal cycles	26,561
Motor vehicles	404,571
Total casualties	322,305
Pedestrians	58,843
Vehicle users	263,462
Killed*	5,052
Pedestrians	1,753
Pedal cycles	227
All two-wheeled motor vehicles	670
Cars and taxis	2,142
Others	260

*Died within 30 days of accident.

Year	Killed	Injured	Year	Killed	Injured
1965	7,952	389,985	1985	5,165	312,359
1970	7,499	355,869	1986	5,382	316,069
1975	6,366	318,584	1987	5,125	306,348
1980	6,010	323,000	1988	5,052	317,253

VEHICLE LICENCES, ETC.

Since October 1, 1974, registration and first licensing of vehicles has been done through local offices (known as Vehicle Registration Offices) of the Department of Transport's Driver and Vehicle Licensing Centre in Swansea. The records of existing vehicles are held at Swansea. Local facilities for relicensing are available as follows:—

(i) with a licence reminder (form V11) in person at any Post Office which deals with vehicle licensing or post it to the Post Office, shown on the form.

(ii) with a vehicle licence renewal (form V10). You may normally apply in person at any licensing Post Office. You will need to take your vehicle registration document with you: if this is not available you must complete form V62 which is held at Post Offices. Postal applications can be made to the Post Offices shown on form V100, available at any Post Office. This form also provides guidance on registering and licensing vehicles.

Details of the present duties chargeable on motor vehicles are available at Post Offices and Vehicle Registration Offices. The Vehicles (Excise) Act, 1971 provides *inter alia* that any vehicle kept on a public road but not used on roads is chargeable to excise duty as if it were in use.

Rates of duty for motor car and motor cycle licences are shown below.

Type of Vehicle	Exceeding	Not Exceeding	12 Months	6 Months
Motor Cars			£	£
Those first constructed before January 1, 1947....	—	—	60·00	33·00
Other than above	—	—	100·00	55·00
Motor Cycles				
With or without sidecar	—	150 cc	10·00	—
With or without sidecar	150 cc	250 cc	20·00	—
With or without sidecar	250 cc	—	40·00	22·00
If first constructed before January 1, 1933 and weighs not more than 101·6 kgs................	250 cc	—	20·00	—
Three Wheelers				
Other than pedestrian-controlled	—	150 cc	10·00	—
Other than pedestrian-controlled	150 cc	—	40·00	22·00
Hackney Carriages				
Seating less than 9 persons	—	—	100·00	55·00
Seating 9–16 persons............................	—	—	130·00	71·50
Seating 17–35 persons...........................	—	—	200·00	110·00
Seating 36–60 persons...........................	—	—	300·00	165·00
Seating over 60 persons	—	—	450·00	247·50

Driving Licences—Fees

On or after 1.2.90

FULL LICENCE

First full licence	£17·00*
Changing a provisional to a full licence after passing a driving test	free
Renewal of full licence if last full licence was issued after 1·1·76	free
New licence after a period of disqualification	£5·00

PROVISIONAL LICENCE

First provisional licence	£17·00*
First renewal of provisional licence issued before 1.10.82	£17·00
DUPLICATE LICENCE	£5·00
EXCHANGE LICENCE	£5·00

* Once you have paid the life fee for *either* a provisional *or* a full licence all renewals are free except where additional entitlement is required.

The minimum age for driving motor cars, light goods vehicles and motor cycles is 17 (moped, 16).

Driving Test–Fees

For cars	£19·50
For motor cycles, part I	£17·94*
part II	£26·00

*When conducted by the Department of Transport. Appointed motor cycle training organizations, who conduct the majority of part I tests within the framework of their own training courses, are free to set their own fee.

Driving tests for invalid carriages are free.

MoT Testing

Cars, motor cycles, motor caravans, light goods and dual-purpose vehicles more than three years old must be covered by an effective vehicle test certificate (often called the MoT certificate). Copies of the legislation governing MoT testing can be obtained from any bookshop which stocks HMSO publications. The legislation comprises The Road Traffic Act 1978 (Sections 45 and 46), The Motor Vehicles (Test) Regulations 1981, and The Motor Vehicles (Tests) (Extension) Order 1982.

FUEL AND POWER

Coal: supply and demand

Million tonnes

	1983	1984	1985	1986	1987	1988
SUPPLY						
Production of deep-mined coal..................	101·7	35·2	75·2	90·4	85·9	83·5
Production of opencast coal	14·7	14·3	15·6	14·3	15·8	17·9
Recovered slurry, fines, etc.	2·8	1·6	3·3	3·5	2·8	2·4
Imports..	4·5	8·9	12·6	10·6	9·8	12·0
Change in colliery stocks	+1·2	−7·9	−5·3	+0·3	−1·1	+0·7
Change in stocks at opencast sites	+0·8	+4·7	−6·3	−0·8	−1·5	+0·5
Total supply	121·7	63·2	118·2	119·2	116·8	114·6
HOME CONSUMPTION						
Electricity supply industry	81·6	53·4	73·9	82·6	86·2	82·5
Coke ovens.....................................	10·4	8·2	11·1	11·1	10·9	10·9
Low temperature carbonization plants	1·2	1·1	1·4	1·0	1·0	0·8
Manufactured fuel plants	0·9	0·2	0·8	1·0	1·0	1·2
Railways.......................................	—	—	—	—	—	—
Collieries	0·5	0·2	0·3	0·3	0·2	0·2
Industry (disposals to users)...................	7·2	6·1	7·4	8·1	7·9	8·0
Domestic (disposals to users)	8·0	6·5	8·6	8·4	7·2	6·6
Public services.................................	1·4	1·3	1·3	1·3	1·2	1·0
Miscellaneous	0·4	0·5	0·4	0·2	0·2	0·2
Total home consumption	111·4	77·3	105·4	114·2	115·9	111·5
Overseas shipments and bunkers	6·6	2·3	2·4	2·7	2·4	1·8
Total consumption and shipments	+118·0	79·6	107·8	120·9	118·2	113·3
Change in distributed stocks*	+3·5	−17·1	+10·0	+4·0	−2·8	+1·7
Balance†	—	+0·7	+0·5	−1·8	+1·3	−0·4

*Stock change excludes industrial and domestic stocks.
†This is the balance between supply and consumption, shipments and changes in known distributed stocks.

Fuel input and gas output; gas sales

	1983	1984	1985	1986	1987	1988
FUEL INPUT TO GAS INDUSTRY:			million tonnes			
Petroleum..................................	0·1	0·1	0·1	—	—	—
			million therms			
Petroleum gases†	33	30	28	36	6	1
Natural gas	—	—	—	—	—	—
Coke oven gas	—	—	—	—	—	—
Total to gas works	61	56	57	55	20	6
Natural gas for direct supply	17,153	17,739	18,988	19,215	20,198	19,083
Total fuel input.............................	17,214	17,794	19,046	19,270	20,218	19,089
GAS OUTPUT AND SALES			million therms			
Gas output:						
Town gas	23	21	20	18	13	4
Natural gas supplied direct	17,186	17,764	19,017	19,243	20,205	19,083
Gross total available	17,209	17,785	19,038	19,261	20,218	19,087
Own use	−121	−129	−140	−152	−137	−120
Statistical difference*	−244	−354	−508	−585	−708	−328
Total sales	16,844	17,302	18,390	18,524	19,373	18,639
Analysis of gas sales						
Power stations	77	178	197	75	79	83
Final users:						
Iron and steel industry	342	462	464	414	468	449
Other industries	5,295	5,258	5,319	4,677	5,275	4,811
Domestic	8,871	8,931	9,682	10,360	10,255	10,255
Public administration	1,050	1,071	1,183	1,279	1,326	1,242
Miscellaneous	1,210	1,337	1,474	1,652	1,655	1,755

†Butane, propane, ethane and refinery tail gases.
*Supply greater than recorded demand (−). Includes losses in distribution.

THE ELECTRICITY SUPPLY INDUSTRY

Under the Electricity Act 1989 twelve new public electricity supply companies have been formed from the twelve Area Electricity Boards in England and Wales. These companies are due to be floated on the Stock Market in November 1990. Four new companies have been formed from the Central Electricity Generating Board: three new generating companies (National Power PLC, Nuclear Electric PLC and PowerGen PLC) and the National Grid Company PLC. National Power PLC and PowerGen PLC are due to be floated on the Stock Market in early 1991.

In Scotland, there are three new companies: Scottish Power PLC, Scottish Hydro-Electric PLC and Scottish Nuclear Ltd. Flotation of Scottish Power PLC and Scottish Hydro-Electric PLC on the Stock Market is due in summer 1991.

A new trade and representational organization, the Electricity Association, has been created by the newly formed British electricity companies; its trading arm is Electricity Association Services Ltd.

Electricity Association Services Ltd., 30 Millbank, SW1P 4RD. (Tel: 071–834 2333).—*Chief Exec.*, R. Farrance.

CEGB Successor Companies

The National Grid Company PLC, National Grid House, Sumner Street, SE1 9JU. (Tel: 071–620 8000).—*Chief Exec.*, B. Kerss.

National Power PLC, Sudbury House, 15–20 Newgate Street, EC1A 7AU. (Tel: 071–634 5111).—*Chief Exec.*, J. Baker.

Nuclear Electric PLC, Barnett Way, Barnwood, Glos. GL4 7RS. (Tel: 0452–652222).—*Chairman*, J. Collier.

PowerGen PLC, 53 New Broad Street, EC2M 1JJ. (Tel: 071–638 5742.—*Chief Exec.*, E. Walliss.

Regional Electricity Companies

East Midlands Electricity PLC, PO Box 4 North PDO, 398 Coppice Road, Arnold, Nottingham NG5 7HX.

Eastern Electricity PLC, PO Box 40, Wherstead, Ipswich IP2 9AQ.

London Electricity PLC, Templar House, 81–87 High Holborn, WC1V 6NU.

Manweb PLC, Sealand Road, Chester CH1 4LR.

Midlands Electricity PLC, Mucklow Hill, Halesowen, W. Midlands B62 8BP.

Northern Electric PLC, Carliol House, Newcastle upon Tyne NE99 1SE.

Norweb PLC, Talbot Road, Manchester M16 0MQ.

SEEBOARD PLC, Grand Avenue, Hove, E. Sussex BN3 2LS.

South Wales Electricity PLC, St Mellons, Cardiff CF3 9XW.

South Western Electricity PLC, 800 Park Avenue, Aztec West, Almondsbury, Avon BS12 4SE.

Southern Electric PLC, Littlewick Green, Maidenhead, Berks. SL6 3QB.

Yorkshire Electricity Group PLC, Scarcroft, Leeds LS14 3HS.

Scottish Companies

Scottish Hydro-Electric PLC, 16 Rothesay Terrace, Edinburgh EH3 7SE. (Tel: 031–225 1361).—*Chief Exec.*, R. Young.

Scottish Nuclear Ltd., Minto Building, 6 Inverlair Avenue, Glasgow G44 4AD. (Tel: 041–633 1166).—*Chief Exec.*, R. M. Yeoman.

Scottish Power PLC, Cathcart House, Spean Street, Glasgow G44 4BE. (Tel: 041–637 7177).—*Chief Exec.*, Dr. I. Preston.

Electricity: production and fuel used

	1983	1984	1985	1986	1987	1988
Electricity generated: total (GWh*)	261,082	266,645	280,602	282,913	283,320	289,220
England and Wales	226,324	227,010	242,248	246,895	246,521	250,303
S. Scotland Electricity Board	20,332	22,938	25,771	23,748	25,814	23,942
N. Scotland Hydro-Electric Board	8,395	10,451	6,015	5,611	4,204	7,933
Northern Ireland	5,384	5,591	5,938	6,018	6,157	6,366
Railway and transport authorities	647	655	630	641	625	677
Method of generation (GWh*)						
Steam plant, nuclear	45,776	49,498	56,354	54,005	50,282	58,867
Steam plant, other	209,116	209,711	216,830	221,981	226,957	223,527
Gas turbines and oil engines	401	2,012	1,138	609	562	533
Hydro-electric plant other than pumped storage plant	3,892	3,368	3,447	3,925	3,313	3,973
Pumped storage plant	1,897	2,055	2,831	2,394	2,207	2,320
Fuel used (thousand tonnes)						
Coal	81,437	53,411	73,940	82,647	86,177	82,470
Coke and coke breeze	33	19	—	—	—	—
Oil	4,746	21,313	10,638	6,097	4,812	5,391
Natural gas†	311	712	762	285	298	332
Electricity sales total (GWh*)	220,532	224,660	235,570	242,969	250,927	256,317
Domestic and farm premises	84,713	85,667	90,068	93,496	94,927	93,951
Domestic and commercial	1,980	1,987	1,712	1,417	1,408	1,395
Shops, offices, other commercial premises	49,055	51,113	55,459	59,242	62,012	65,164
Factories, other industrial premises	80,034	81,105	83,419	83,870	87,531	90,687
Public lighting	2,261	2,296	2,335	2,316	2,345	2,381
Traction	2,488	2,492	2,577	2,627	2,704	2,739

*GWH = gigawatt-hour. † Expressed in thousand tonnes of coal equivalent.

BRITISH GAS PLC
152 Grosvenor Road, SW1V 3JL
[071–821 1444]

British Gas was privatized following the Gas Act, 1986. Its primary activities are the purchase, distribution and sale of gas. It also explores for and produces hydrocarbons.
Chairman and Chief Executive, R. Evans, CBE

Gas Regions

East Midlands, PO Box 145, De Montfort Street, Leicester LE1 9DB.
Eastern, Star House, Potters Bar, Herts. EN6 2PD.
North Eastern, New York Road, Leeds LS2 7PE.
North Thames, North Thames House, London Road, Staines, Middx. TW18 4AE.
North Western, Welman House, Altrincham, Cheshire WA15 8AE.
Northern, PO Box 1GB, Killingworth, Newcastle upon Tyne NE99 1GB.
Scotland, Granton House, 4 Marine Drive, Edinburgh EH5 1YB.
South Eastern, Katherine Street, Croydon CR9 1JU.
South Western, Riverside, Temple Street, Keynsham, Bristol BS18 1EQ.
Southern, 80 St. Mary's Road, Southampton SO9 5AT.
Wales, Helmont House, Churchill Way, Cardiff CF1 4NB.
West Midlands, Wharf Lane, Solihull, West Midlands B91 2JP.

British Gas PLC Finance (£ million)

	1987	1988
Turnover		
Gas supply	6,967	6,679
Installation and contracting	310	347
Appliance trading	300	307
Exploration subsidiaries	189	224
Other activities	28	27
	7,794	7,584
Less: intra-group sales	(184)	(220)
TOTAL.	7,610	7,364
Operating costs		
Gas prime materials	3,024	2,717
Gas levy	503	469
Salaries, wages, associated costs	1,180	1,139
Cost of sales adjustment.	2	4
Monetary working capital adjustment	(27)	(14)
Current cost depreciation	779	789
Lease rentals	34	27
Exploration expenditure	22	61
Research, testing and development	74	77
Employee profit-sharing scheme	—	38
Auditor's remuneration	0·581	0·635
Current cost pre-tax profit	1,058	1,008
Gearing adjustment	(8)	(23)
Total funds generated from operations	1,492	1,485
New Loans	—	225
Proceeds from disposal of tangible fixed assets	23	51
Total funds generated	1,515	1,761
Taxation paid	410	553
Dividends paid	—	270

BRITISH OIL STATISTICS

(million tonnes)

	1984	1985	1986	1987	1988
Oil production†					
Land	0·3	0·4	0·5	0·6	0·8
Offshore	125·6	127·1	126·5	122·7	113·6
Refinery output	73·2	72·9	74·1	74·7	79·8
Deliveries of petroleum products for inland consumption	81·4	70·1	69·2	67·7	71·6
Exports (including re-exports):					
Crude petroleum	75·9	79·6	82·1	80·6	63·8
Refined petroleum products and process oils	16·4	18·9	20·2	18·5	18·6
Imports:					
Crude petroleum	25·0	26·9	32·6	33·1	32·8
Refined petroleum products and process oils	28·5	25·0	22·9	20·5	21·2

† Crude oil plus condensates and petroleum gases derived at onshore treatment plants.

THE WATER INDUSTRY

ENGLAND AND WALES

In England and Wales the Secretaries of State for the Environment and for Wales, and the Director General of Water Services, are responsible for the general oversight of the industry and for ensuring that the private water companies fulfil their statutory obligation to provide water supply and sewerage services.

The Minister of Agriculture, Fisheries and Food and the Secretary of State for Wales are responsible for policy relating to land drainage, flood protection, sea defences and the protection and development of fisheries.

The National Rivers Authority is responsible for the quality of river, coastal and ground waters and the control of pollution, the management of water resources and nature conservation.

The Water Companies

Until the end of 1989, nine regional water authorities in England and the Welsh Water Authority in Wales were responsible for water supply and the development of water resources, sewerage and sewage disposal, pollution control, freshwater fisheries, flood protection, water recreation, and environmental conservation. The Water Act 1989, which received Royal Assent on July 6, 1989 provided for the creation of a privatized water industry under public regulation.

Of the 99 per cent of the population of England and Wales who are connected to a public water supply, 75 per cent are supplied by the new water companies (through their principal operating subsidiaries, the water service companies), which have replaced the regional water authorities. The remaining 25 per cent are supplied by 29 statutory water companies which were already in the private sector. The statutory water companies bear no responsibility for sewage disposal or land drainage. They may convert to public limited company (PLC) status.

The water service companies are:

ANGLIAN WATER SERVICES LTD, Ambury House, Huntingdon, Cambs. PE18 6NZ.

DWR CYMRU CYFYNGEDIG (WELSH WATER AUTHORITY), Cambrian Way, Brecon, Powys LD3 7HP.

NORTHUMBRIAN WATER LTD, Northumbria House, Regent Centre, Gosforth, Newcastle upon Tyne NE3 3PX.

NORTH WEST WATER LTD, Dawson House, Liverpool Road, Great Sankey, Warrington WA5 3LW.

SEVERN TRENT WATER LTD, Abelson House, 2297 Coventry Road, Sheldon, Birmingham B26 3PU.

SOUTHERN WATER SERVICES LTD, Southern House, Yeoman Road, Worthing, W. Sussex BN13 3NX.

SOUTH WEST WATER SERVICES LTD, Peninsula House, Rydon Lane, Exeter EX2 7HR.

THAMES WATER UTILITIES LTD, Nugent House, Vastern Road, Reading RG1 8DB.

WESSEX WATER SERVICES LTD, Wessex House, Passage Street, Bristol BS2 0JQ.

YORKSHIRE WATER SERVICES LTD, West Riding House, 67 Albion Street, Leeds LS1 5AA.

Regulatory Bodies

A Director General of Water Services has been appointed by the Secretaries of State for the Environment and for Wales. Independent of Ministers and directly accountable to Parliament, his main duties are to ensure that the water companies comply with the terms of their appointments (or licences) and to protect the interests of the consumer. All 39 water companies are subject to a system of price control which sets a limit on the average increase in their prices each year. The Office of Water Services, similar to the Office of Telecommunications and the Office of Gas Supply, has been set up to support the Director General's activities.

An independent national body, the National Rivers Authority (NRA) was established under the Water Act 1989 to take over the regulatory and river management functions of the regional water authorities. Its responsibilities include monitoring the quality of inland, coastal and underground waters and controlling pollution, and the management of water resources, land drainage, flood protection and fisheries.

Methods of charging

In England and Wales, householders have until 1990 paid for domestic water supply and sewage disposal services through charges based on the rateable value of their property (domestic rates). Industrial and most commercial users are charged according to consumption, which is recorded by meter.

The replacement of domestic rates by the community charge in April 1990 necessitates new methods of charging the private consumer for water and sewage services. The Water Act 1989 gives the water companies until the end of the century to decide on and introduce a suitable method of charging. Two options under consideration by the water industry are a flat-rate licence fee and metering. Large-scale trials of domestic metering are currently taking place.

SCOTLAND

Overall responsibility for national water policy in Scotland rests with the Secretary of State for Scotland. Most aspects of water policy are administered through the Scottish Development Department, but fisheries and certain aspects of land drainage are the responsibility of the Department of Agriculture and Fisheries for Scotland. The supply of water and sewerage services and the development of water resources are administered by separate authorities from those responsible for the control of water pollution.

Water supply and sewerage services are local authority responsibilities and are provided by the nine Regional Councils and the three Islands Councils.

Seven river purification boards have the specific duty of restoring and maintaining the quality of water in mainland Scotland's rivers, lochs and coastal waters. The Islands Councils of Orkney, Shetland and the Western Isles are responsible for the prevention of pollution within their own areas.

The Water (Scotland) Act 1967 brought into being a bulk water supply authority, the Central Scotland Water Development Board. The main statutory function of the board is to develop new sources of water supply for the purpose of providing water in bulk to water authorities whose limits of supply are within the board's area, i.e. Central, Fife, Lothian, Strathclyde and Tayside Regional Councils.

The community charge, which was introduced in Scotland in April 1989, includes a community water charge set by each Regional and Islands Council.

CENTRAL SCOTLAND WATER DEVELOPMENT BOARD, Balmore, Torrance, Glasgow G64 4AJ.—*Director*, W. G. Mitchell

NORTHERN IRELAND

In Northern Ireland ministerial responsibility for water services lies with the Secretary of State for Northern Ireland. The Department of the Environment for Northern Ireland, operating through the Water Service, is responsible for policy and co-ordination with regard to supply and distribution of water, and provision and maintenance of sewerage services.

The Water Service is divided into four regions: the Eastern, Northern, Western and Southern Divisions. These are based in Belfast, Ballymena, Londonderry and Craigavon respectively.

On all major policy issues the Department of the Environment for Northern Ireland seeks the views of the Northern Ireland Water Council, a body appointed to advise the Department on the exercise of its water and sewerage functions. The Council includes representatives from agriculture, angling, industry, commerce, tourism, trade unions and local government.

Usually householders do not pay directly for water and sewerage services; the costs of these services are allowed for in the Northern Ireland regional rate. Water consumed by industry, commerce and agriculture in excess of 100 cubic metres (22,000 gallons) per half year is charged through meters.

THE CINQUE PORTS

As their name implies, the Cinque Ports were originally five in number: Hastings, New Romney, Hythe, Dover and Sandwich. They existed before the Norman Conquest and were the Anglo-Saxon successors to the Roman system of coast defence organized from the Wash to Spithead to resist Saxon onslaughts. William the Conqueror reconstituted them and granted peculiar jurisdiction, most of which was abolished in 1855. Only jurisdiction in Admiralty still survives.

At some time after the Conquest the 'antient towns' of Winchelsea and Rye were added with equal privileges. The other members of the Confederation, known as Limbs, are Lydd, Faversham, Folkestone, Deal, Tenterden, Margate and Ramsgate.

The Barons of the Cinque Ports have the ancient privilege of attending the Coronation Ceremony and are allotted special places in Westminster Abbey.

Lord Warden of the Cinque Ports, HM Queen Elizabeth the Queen Mother.
Judge, Court of Admiralty, Gerald Darling, RD, QC.
Registrar, I. G. Gill, PO Box 9, Margate, Kent CT9 1XZ.

Lord Wardens of the Cinque Ports since 1904

Marquess Curzon	1904
The Prince of Wales	1905
Earl Brassey	1908
Earl Beauchamp	1913
Marquess of Reading	1934
Marquess of Willingdon	1936
Sir Winston Churchill	1941
Sir Robert Menzies	1965
HM Queen Elizabeth the Queen Mother	1978

NEW TOWNS IN GREAT BRITAIN

Commission for the New Towns, Glen House, Stag Place, SW1E 5AJ.—The Commission was established under the New Towns Act, 1959. Its remit is to (a) take over and, with a view to its eventual disposal, to hold, manage and turn to account the property of Development Corporations transferred to the Commission and (b) as soon as it considers it expedient to do so, to dispose of property so transferred and any other property held by it. In carrying out its remit the Commission must have due regard to the convenience and welfare of persons residing, working or carrying on business there and, until disposal, the maintenance and enhancement of the value of the land held and return obtained from it.

The Commission has such responsibilities in Basildon, Bracknell, Central Lancashire, Corby, Crawley, Harlow, Hatfield, Hemel Hempstead, Northampton, Peterborough, Redditch, Skelmersdale, Stevenage, Warrington and Runcorn, Washington and Welwyn Garden City. The Commission has minimal responsibilities (principally financial and litigation) in Aycliffe and Peterlee, and Cwmbran following the wind-up of their Development Corporations in 1988.

Chairman, Sir Neil Shields, MC.

Deputy Chairman, Sir Reginald Eyre.

Members, R. B. Caws, CBE; W. J. Mackenzie, OBE; P. M. Vine, CBE; Sir Gordon Roberts, CBE; The Lord Bellwin; B. J. Jenkins; M. H. Mallinson; R. W. P. Luff.

Chief Executive, D. M. Woodhall.

Director of Estates and Technical Services, H. J. M. Thomas.

Director of Finance, Administrative and Legal Services, G. T. C. Probart.

BASILDON, Essex.—*Executive Officer,* H. Bacon. *Offices,* Gifford House, London Road, Bowers Gifford, Basildon SS13 2EX.

BRACKNELL, Berks.—Glen House, SW1E 5AJ.

CENTRAL LANCASHIRE, Lancs.—*Executive Officer,* B. Birtwistle. *Offices,* Cuerden Pavilion, Shady Lane, Bamber Bridge, Preston PR5 6AZ.

CORBY, Northants.—*Executive Officer,* J. G. Lloyd. *Offices,* Chisholm House, 9 Queen's Square, Corby NN17 1PA.

CRAWLEY, Sussex.—Glen House, SW1E 5AJ.

HARLOW, Essex.—Glen House, SW1E 5AJ.

HATFIELD, Herts.—Glen House, SW1E 5AJ.

HEMEL HEMPSTEAD, Herts.—Glen House, SW1E 5AJ.

NORTHAMPTON.—*Executive Officer,* I. McKay. *Offices,* Highfield House, Headless Cross Drive, Redditch B97 5EU.

PETERBOROUGH, Cambs.—*Executive Officer,* P. Way. *Offices,* PO Box 3, Stuart House, City Road, Peterborough PE1 1UJ.

REDDITCH, Worcs.—*Executive Officer,* I. McKay. *Offices,* Highfield House, Headless Cross Drive, Redditch B97 5EU.

SKELMERSDALE, Lancs.—*Executive Officer,* M. V. Anderson. *Offices,* Pennylands, Skelmersdale WN8 8AR.

STEVENAGE, Herts.—Glen House, SW1E 5AJ.

WARRINGTON AND RUNCORN, Cheshire.—*Executive Officer,* J. Leigh. *Offices,* PO Box 49, New Town House, Buttermarket Street, Warrington WA1 2LF.

WASHINGTON, Tyne and Wear.— *Executive Officer,* J. Edwards. *Offices,* 19 Parsons Road, District 2, Washington NE37 1EZ.

WELWYN GARDEN CITY, Herts.—Glen House, SW1E 5AJ.

DEVELOPMENT CORPORATIONS

England and Wales

MILTON KEYNES, Bucks.—Formed 1967. *Chairman,* Lord Chilver, FRS. *General Manager,* F. C. Henshaw. *Offices,* Saxon Court, 502 Avebury Boulevard, Milton Keynes MK9 3HS. Area, 22,000 acres. Population, 150,000. Estimated eventual population, 200,000.

TELFORD, Shropshire.—Formed 1963. *Chairman,* F. J. Jones. *General Manager,* M. D. Morgan. *Offices,* New Town House, Telford Square, Town Centre, Telford, Shropshire TF3 4JS. Area, 19,311 acres. Population, 117,500. Estimated eventual population, 130,000.

DEVELOPMENT BOARD FOR RURAL WALES.—Formed 1977. *Chairman,* G. Davies. *Offices,* Ladywell House, Newtown, Powys SY16 1JB.

Scotland

CUMBERNAULD, Strathclyde.—Formed 1956. *Chairman,* D. W. Mitchell, CBE. *Chief Executive,* D. Millan. *Headquarters,* Cumbernauld House, Cumbernauld G67 3JH. Area, 7,788 acres. Population, 50,100. Estimated eventual population, 55,000.

EAST KILBRIDE, Strathclyde.—Formed 1947. *Chairman,* J. A. Denholm. *Managing Director,* J. C. Shaw. *Offices,* Atholl House, East Kilbride, Glasgow G74 1LU. Area, 10,250 acres. Population, 69,500. Estimated eventual population, 70,000.

GLENROTHES, Fife.—Formed 1948. *Chairman,* Prof. C. Blake. *Chief Executive,* W. M. Cracknell. *Offices,* Unicorn House, Falkland Place, Glenrothes KY7 5PD. Area, 5,760 acres. Population, 38,500. Estimated eventual population, 48,000.

IRVINE, Ayrshire.—Formed, 1966. *Chairman,* A. R. Belch, CBE. *Managing Director,* Brig. R. A. Rickets. *Offices,* Perceton House, Irvine, Ayrshire KA11 2AL. Area, 12,404 acres. Population, 56,000. Estimated eventual population, 65,000.

LIVINGSTON, West Lothian.—Formed 1962. *Chairman,* R. S. Watt, CBE. *Chief Executive,* J. A. Pollock. *Offices,* Sidlaw House, Almondvale, Livingston, West Lothian EH54 6QA. Area, 6,868 acres. Population, 42,430. Estimated eventual population, 70,000.

565

LOCAL GOVERNMENT

ENGLAND AND WALES

The London Government Act, 1963, and the Local Government Acts of 1972 and 1985 have brought about the present system of local government in England and Wales. The system is based on two tiers of local authorities, county and district councils, in the non-metropolitan areas; and a single tier, of metropolitan district and London borough councils, in the six metropolitan areas of England and in London respectively.

Structures and Areas in England

England outside Greater London is divided into counties. Each county is divided into districts. Six *metropolitan counties* cover the main conurbations outside Greater London: Tyne and Wear, West Midlands, Merseyside, Greater Manchester, West Yorkshire and South Yorkshire. They are divided into 36 *metropolitan districts*, most of which have a population of over 200,000. There are 39 *non-metropolitan counties*; each of these is divided into *non-metropolitan districts*, of which there are 296. These districts have populations broadly in the range of 60,000 to 100,000: some however, have larger populations, because of the need to avoid dividing large towns, and some in mainly rural areas have smaller populations. Greater London is divided into 32 *London boroughs*, with populations between 134,000 and 390,000, and the *City*, with a daytime population of 340,000 but only 5,400 by night.

There are also about 10,000 parishes, in 219 of the non-metropolitan and 18 of the metropolitan districts.

A permanent Local Government Boundary Commission keeps the areas and electoral arrangements under review, and makes proposals to the Secretary of State for changes found necessary.

Constitution and Elections

For districts, non-metropolitan counties, London boroughs, the City, and for about 8,000 parishes, there are elected councils, consisting of directly elected councillors. Broadly, county councils range from 60–100 members; metropolitan district councils 50–80 members; non-metropolitan district councils 30–60 members. The councillors elect annually one of their number as chairman.

The general pattern in England is that councillors serve 4 years and there are no elections of district and parish councillors in county elections years. In metropolitan districts one-third of the councillors for each ward are elected each year except in the year of county elections. Non-metropolitan districts can choose whether to have elections by thirds or whole council elections. In the former case, one-third of the council, as nearly as may be, is elected in each year of metropolitan district elections. If whole council elections are chosen, these are held in the year midway between county elections. The London boroughs have whole council elections, in the year immediately following the county council election years. Local elections are normally held on the first Thursday in May.

Generally speaking, all British subjects or citizens of the Republic of Ireland of 18 years or over, resident on the qualifying date in the area for which the election is being held, are entitled to vote at local government elections. A register of electors is prepared and published annually by local electoral registration officers.

A returning officer has the overall responsibility for an election. Voting takes place at polling stations, arranged by the local authority and under the supervision of a presiding officer specially appointed for the purpose. Candidates, who are subject to various statutory qualifications and disqualifications designed to ensure that they are suitable persons to hold office, must be nominated by electors for the electoral area concerned.

Internal Organization

Local authorities increasingly are organized along party political lines and over 80 per cent are now controlled by groups of councillors having allegiance to one of the main political parties. However, the council as a whole is the final decision-making body within any authority. Councils are free to a great extent to make their own internal organizational arrangements. Normally, questions of major policy are settled by the full council, while the administration of the various services is the responsibility of committees of members. Day to day decisions are delegated to the council's officers, who act within the policies laid down by the members.

Functions

Local authorities are empowered or required by various Acts of Parliament to carry out functions in their areas. The legislation concerned comprises public general Acts and 'local' Acts which local authorities have promoted as private bills. In non-metropolitan areas, functions are divided between the districts and counties, those requiring the larger area or population for their efficient performance going to the county. The metropolitan district councils, with the larger population in their areas, already had wider functions than non-metropolitan councils, and following abolition of the metropolitan county councils have now been given most of their functions also. A few functions continue to be exercised over the larger area by joint bodies, made up of councillors from each district.

The allocation of functions is as follows:

county councils: education; strategic planning; traffic, transport and highways; police; fire service; consumer protection; refuse disposal; smallholdings; social services; libraries.

non-metropolitan district councils: local planning; housing; highways (maintenance of certain urban roads and off-street car parks); building regulations; environmental health; refuse collection; cemeteries and crematoria.

metropolitan district and London borough councils: their functions are all those listed above, except that fire, civil defence (and in some cases, refuse disposal) in all areas and police and passenger transport in the metropolitan counties only are exercised by joint bodies.

Functions exercised concurrently by county and district councils and London boroughs: recreation (parks, playing fields, swimming pools); museums; encouragement of the arts, tourism and industry.

The sewerage and sewage disposal functions of local authorities were transferred to nine water authorities in England and the Welsh Water Authority. The water authorities were responsible for water supply and conservation; river pollution control and river management; fisheries; land drainage; and use of water space for recreation and amenity purposes. These functions were transferred in 1989 to the National Rivers Authority (NRA) and privatized public water companies.

The personal health functions of local authorities were transferred in 1977 to area health authorities, whose areas were the same as non-metropolitan and Welsh counties and metropolitan districts. From April 1982 this two-tier structure was replaced by about 199 District Health Authorities. They work in close collaboration with local education, social services and environmental health authorities.

Residuary Bodies

Residuary bodies were set up in 1985 to deal with the business of the Greater London and Metropolitan County Councils which had not already devolved onto other bodies at the time of the Councils' abolition in 1986. They are progressively being wound up. Addresses and details of principal officers are given on page 579 (page 598 for Greater London).

Parishes

Parishes with 200 or more electors must generally have parish councils, and about three-quarters of the parishes have councils. A parish council comprises at least five members, the number being fixed by the district council. Elections are held every four years, in the year in which the local district council is elected. All parishes have parish meetings, comprising the electors of the parish. Where there is no council, the meeting must be held at least twice a year.

Parish council functions include: allotments; encouragement of arts and crafts; community halls, recreational facilities (e.g. open spaces, swimming pools), cemeteries and crematoria; and many minor functions. They must also be given an opportunity to comment on planning applications. They may, like county and district councils, spend limited sums for the general benefit of the parish. They precept on the district councils for their funds.

Civic Dignities

District councils may petition for a Royal Charter granting borough status to the district. In boroughs the chairman of the council is the mayor. The status 'City' and the right to call the mayor 'Lord Mayor' may also be granted by letters patent. Parish councils may call themselves 'town councils', in which case their chairman is the 'town mayor'.

Charter trustees were established for those former boroughs which were too large to have parish councils when local government was reorganised in 1974 and they became part of districts without city or borough status. The charter trustees are the district councillors representing the area of the former borough and they elect a town mayor, continue civic tradition, and look after the charters, insignia and civic plate of the former borough.

Local Commissioners for England and Wales

Commissioners for Local Administration in England and in Wales (*see* page 339) have been appointed with the duty of investigating complaints of maladministration in aspects of local government; they report to the local council concerned.

Wales

Since 1974 Wales, including the former Monmouthshire, has been divided into eight counties: Gwynedd; Clwyd; Powys; Dyfed; West, Mid and South Glamorgan; and Gwent. There are 37 districts in Wales, many of those in the less populated parts reflecting the areas of former Welsh counties.

The arrangements for Welsh counties and districts are generally similar to those for English non-metropolitan counties and districts. There are some differences in functions: Welsh district councils have refuse disposal as well as refuse collection functions and they may provide on-street as well as off-street car parks with the consent of the county council. A few districts have also been designated as library authorities.

In Wales parishes have been replaced by communities. Unlike England, where many areas are not in any parish, communities have been established for the whole of Wales, approximately 1,000 communities in all. Community meetings may be convened as and when desired. Community councils exist in about 770 communities and further councils may be established at the request of a community meeting. Community councils have broadly the same range of powers as English parish councils. Community councillors are elected en bloc on the same basis as parish councillors in England, i.e. at the same time as a district council election and for a term of four years.

Local Government Finance

Local government is financed from various sources.

(1) *Community charges.*—These replaced domestic rates on April 1, 1990 under the provisions of the Local Government Finance Act 1988. They are raised by the charging authorities (district councils and, in London, borough councils and the City Corporation). Liability to pay a community charge arises from an entry in the community charges register which is compiled by the community charges registration officer of each charging authority. Sums required by county and parish councils and joint boards for police, fire and transport are included by the charging authority when calculating its community charge. There are three types of charge: the personal community charge, payable by people aged 18 or over (unless exempt); the collective community charge paid in respect of certain designated buildings whose occupants move frequently and are difficult to register, and who will therefore pay their community charge contributions to the landlord; and the standard community charge which is payable in respect of domestic property which is not occupied.

The personal Community Charge (Relief) (England) Regulations provide for a scheme of transitional relief to ease the effects of the change from domestic rates. In general, relief is payable where one or two assumed community charges exceeds the previous year's rates bill by more than £156. There is additional help for the elderly and disabled who were not ratepayers.

(2) *Non-domestic (business) rates.*—Collected from April 1, 1990 by charging authorities, i.e. by district councils, the Council of the Isles of Scilly and in London by the borough councils and the Common Council of the City of London. The Local Government Finance Act 1988 provides for liability for rates to be assessed on the basis of a poundage (multiplier) tax on the rateable value of property (hereditaments). The multiplier is to be set by central Government and rates collected by the charging authority for the area where a property is located. Rate income collected by charging authorities is paid into a central national non-domestic rating (NNDR) pool and redistributed to individual authorities on the basis of adult resident population. For the years 1990–91 to 1994–95 actual payment of rates in certain cases will be subjected to transitional arrangements, to phase in the larger increases and reductions in rates resulting from the combined effects of the 1990 revaluation and the introduction of a uniform national business rate (UBR).

Rateable values for the rating lists came into force on April 1, 1990. They are derived from the rental value of property as at April 1, 1988 and determined on certain statutory assumptions by valuation officers of the Board of Inland Revenue. New property is added to the list, and significant changes to existing property necessitate amendments to the rateable value, on the same basis. Rating lists remain in force until the next general revaluation, which is scheduled for April 1, 1995.

Certain types of property are exempt from rates, e.g. agricultural land and buildings, and places of public religious worship. Charities and other non-profit-making organizations may receive full or partial relief. Specified classes of empty property are liable to pay rates at 50 per cent.

(3) *Government grants.*—In addition to specific grants in support of revenue expenditure on particular services, central Government pays revenue support grant to local authorities. This grant is paid to each charging authority so that if all authorities in its area spend at a level sufficient to provide a standard level of service, it can set the same community charge before taking account of any transitional arrangements. In 1990–91 there are a number of transitional arrangements in operation to ease the transition to the new system of local authority finance.

The 1990–91 revenue support grant settlement provided for a total of £9,468 million in revenue support grants to be paid to local authorities.

Expenditure 1990–91

Forecasts of local authority net revenue expenditure for 1990–91 in England adopted by the Government for revenue support grant purposes were as follows. The amounts given are at 1990–91 cash prices.

Service	£m
Education	17,023
School catering	386
Libraries, museums and art galleries	626
Personal social services	4,100
Police	4,354
Fire	944
Other Home Office services	613
Local transport	2,329
Local environmental services	4,310
Agricultural services	29
Consumer protection and trading standards	102
Employment	153
Non-Housing Revenue Account housing	262
Housing benefits	1,421
Other	−11
Total current expenditure	36,642
Capital charges	3,621
Capital charged to revenue	459
Other non-current	2,134
Interest receipts	−1,002
Total revenue expenditure	41,854
Specific grants	−6,808
Community charge benefit grant	−1,721
Other	−19
Net revenue expenditure	33,306

Aggregate external finance for 1990–91 was determined at £23,100 million. Of this, specific grants were estimated at £300 million and transitional grants at £200 million. £9,500 million was in respect of revenue

support grant and £10,400 million was support from the national non-domestic rate pool. Total standard spending by local authorities considered for grant purposes was £32,800 million.

Average Community Charges.—The average charges levied in England at April 1, 1990 were: London Boroughs, £368; Metropolitan Districts, £366; Shire Districts, £360. The average charge levied in England was £363.

Non-domestic rates.—National non-domestic rate (or Uniform Business Rate). The rate in England for 1990–91 is £10·7bn. The amount estimated to be raised is £10·7bn. Total rateable value held on local authority lists at December 1, 1989 was £28·6bn.

SCOTLAND

Since 1975, mainland Scotland has been divided for local government purposes into nine regions within which there are 53 districts. Regional and district councils have separate responsibility for specific functions. In the three islands areas, Orkney, Shetland and the Western Isles, there are single tier Islands Councils responsible for most local authority functions.

Local Government Electors.—In 1990 the Register shows 3,936,737 electors in Scotland. Elections took place in 1990 for regional and island councils, and are due in 1992 for district councils.

Functions

Regional Councils are responsible for education; social work; strategic planning; the provision of infrastructure such as roads, water and sewerage; consumer protection; flood prevention; coast protection; and valuation and rating. They also have responsibility for the police and fire services; civil defence; and electoral registration, and in relation to public transport and registration of births, deaths and marriages.

District Councils deal with more local matters such as housing; leisure and recreation, including tourism, parks, libraries, museums and galleries; development control and building control; environmental health, including cleansing, refuse collection and disposal, food hygiene, inspection of shops, offices and factories, clean air, markets and slaughterhouses, burial and cremation; licensing, including liquor, cinemas and theatres, taxis, street traders, betting and gaming, and charitable collections; allotments; public conveniences; the administration of district courts.

Community Councils.—Unlike the parish councils of England or community councils of Wales, Scottish community councils are not local authorities. Their purpose as defined in statute is to ascertain and express the views of the communities which they represent, and to take in the interests of their communities such action as appears to be expedient or practicable. Over 1,000 community councils have been established under schemes drawn up by district and islands councils in Scotland.

Rates and Community Charge

In 1988–89, the final year under the old rating system, a total of £2,299,000,000 was received from the general rates of local government in Scotland and £78,000,000 from domestic water rates. The rateable value on which rates were leviable was £3,220,000,000 on the general rates and £1,358,000,000 on the domestic water rates. The average general rate levied was 78·7p and the domestic water rate levied was 4·9p.

Provisional figures for 1989–90 show total receipts from non-domestic rates of £1,220,000,000 and £1,020,000,000 from the community charge. The average non-domestic rate per £ levied for 1989–90 was 76·6p and the average personal community charge payable in Scotland was £280·00.

Local Commissioner

The Commissioner for Local Administration in Scotland is responsible for investigating complaints from members of the public who claim to have suffered injustice as a consequence of maladministration in local government (*see* page 339).

NORTHERN IRELAND

For the purpose of local government Northern Ireland has a system of 26 single-tier district councils. There are 566 members of the councils, elected for periods of four years at a time on the principle of proportional representation.

The district councils all have the same three main roles. These are:

(a) an executive role in which the councils are responsible for a wide range of local services including the provision of recreational, social, community, and cultural facilities; environmental health; consumer protection; the enforcement of building regulations; the promotion of tourist development schemes; street cleansing; refuse collection and disposal; litter prevention; and miscellaneous licensing and registration provisions, including dog control;

(b) a representative role in which they nominate representatives to sit as members of the various statutory bodies responsible for the administration of regional services such as education and libraries, health and personal social services, drainage, fire and electricity; and

(c) a consultative role in which they act as the media through which the views of local people are expressed on the operation in their area of other regional services, notably planning, roads, and conservation (including water supply and sewerage services) provided by those departments of central government which have an obligation, either statutorily or otherwise, to consult the district councils about proposals affecting their areas.

PARTY REPRESENTATION IN LOCAL GOVERNMENT
(as at end May 1990)

Abbreviations: *A.* = Liberal/SDP Alliance; *C.* = Conservative; *Com.* = Communist; *Dem.* = Democrat; *Grn.* = Green; *Ind.* = Independent; *Ind.C.* = Independent Conservative; *Ind.Lab.* = Independent Labour; *Lab.* = Labour; *Lib.* = Liberal; *Lib.Dem.* = Social and Liberal Democrat; *MK* = Mebyon Kernow; *NP* = Non-Political/Non-Party; *PC* = Plaid Cymru; *RA* = Ratepayers'/Residents' Associations; *SDP* = Social Democratic Party; *SNP* = Scottish National Party.

ENGLAND

County Councils

Avon ....*Lab.* 36, *C.* 33, *Lib. Dem.* 7.
Bedfordshire........*C.* 35, *Lab.* 25, *Lib. Dem.* 11, *Ind. Lab.* 2.
Berkshire ....*C.* 38, *Lab.* 19, *Lib. Dem.* 15, *Ind.* 1, *Ind.C.* 1, *Lib.* 1, *RA* 1.
Buckinghamshire ...*C.* 50, *Lab.* 11, *Lib. Dem.* 6, *Ind.* 2, *Lib.* 1, *SDP* 1.
Cambridgeshire .....*C.* 45, *Lab.* 21, *Lib. Dem.* 9, *Ind.* 1, *Lib.* 1.
Cheshire ....*Lab.* 32, *C.* 29, *Lib. Dem.* 10.
Cleveland ....*Lab.* 48, *C.* 19, *Lib. Dem* 10.
Cornwall ....*Lib. Dem.* 31, *Ind.* 24, *C.* 14, *Lab.* 8, *Lib.* 1, *MK* 1.
Cumbria............*C.* 37, *Lab.* 37, *Lib. Dem.* 6, *Ind.* 3.
Derbyshire ....*Lab.* 52, *C.* 27, *Lib. Dem.* 3, *Ind.* 2.
Devon..............*C.* 56, *Lab.* 13, *Lib. Dem.* 11, *Ind.* 2, *SDP* 2, *Lib.* 1.
Dorset ....*C.* 43, *Lib. Dem.* 22, *Lab.* 6, *Ind.* 5, *Ind. C.* 1.
Durham ....*Lab.* 57, *C.* 7, *Lib. Dem.* 4, *Ind.* 3, *Ind. Lab.* 1.
East Sussex ....*C.* 38, *Lab.* 17, *Lib. Dem.* 15.
Essex ....*C.* 55, *Lab.* 26, *Lib. Dem.* 15, *Ind.* 2.
Gloucestershire .....*C.* 23, *Lib. Dem.* 23, *Lab.* 16, *Others* 1.
Hampshire ....*C.* 57, *Lib. Dem.* 25, *Lab.* 19, *Ind.* 1.
Hereford and
  Worcester ....*C.* 38, *Ind. C.* 22, *Lib. Dem.* 11, *Ind.* 4, *Ind. Lib.* 1.
Hertfordshire ....*C.* 45, *Lab.* 27, *Lib. Dem.* 5.
Humberside ....*Lab.* 42, *C.* 30, *Lib.Dem.* 3.
Isle of Wight ....*Lib. Dem.* 23, *C.* 15, *Ind.* 4, *Com.* 1.

Kent ....*C.* 55, *Lab.* 25, *Lib. Dem.* 18, *SDP* 1.
Lancashire ....*Lab.* 50, *C.* 42, *Lib.Dem.* 7.
Leicestershire ......*C.* 38, *Lab.* 34, *Lib. Dem.* 12, *Ind.* 1.
Lincolnshire........*C.* 40, *Lab.* 19, *Lib.* 13, *Ind.* 4.
Norfolk ....*C.* 47, *Lab.* 28, *Lib. Dem.* 9.
Northamptonshire ..*C.* 33, *Lab.* 31, *Lib. Dem.* 2, *Ind.* 1, (1 Vac.).
Northumberland ....*Lab.* 38, *C.* 17, *Lib. Dem.* 8, *Ind.* 2, *Others* 1.
North Yorkshire ....*C.* 44, *Lab.* 22, *Lib. Dem.* 21, *Ind.* 6, *SDP* 3.
Nottinghamshire....*Lab.* 50, *C.* 33, *Lib. Dem.* 4, *Ind.* 1.
Oxfordshire ....*C.* 33, *Lab.* 23, *Lib. Dem.* 13, *Grn.* 1.
Shropshire ....*C.* 31, *Lab.* 24, *Lib. Dem.* 8, *Ind.* 3.
Somerset ....*C.* 32, *Lib. Dem.* 17, *Lab.* 6, *Ind.* 1, *SDP* 1.
Staffordshire ......*Lab.* 50, *C.* 28, *Lib. Dem.* 2, *RA* 1, (1 Vac.).
Suffolk ....*C.* 45, *Lab.* 27, *Lib. Dem.* 5, *Ind.* 3.
Surrey ....*C.* 54, *Lab.* 9, *Lib. Dem.* 8, *Ind.* 2, *RA* 2, (1 Vac.).
Warwickshire ......*C.* 32, *Lab.* 24, *Lib. Dem.* 4, *Ind.* 1, *RA* 1.
West Sussex ....*C.* 46, *Lib. Dem.* 16, *Lab.* 9.
Wiltshire...........*C.* 35, *Lab.* 18, *Lib. Dem.* 17, *Ind.* 3, *SDP* 2.

Metropolitan District Councils
GREATER MANCHESTER

Bolton ....*Lab.* 43, *C.* 14, *Lib. Dem.* 3.
Bury ....*Lab.* 27, *C.* 21.
Manchester........*Lab.* 78, *C.* 10, *Lib. Dem.* 8, *Ind.* *C.* 2, *Lib.* 1.

Oldham ....*Lab.* 42, *Lib. Dem.* 14, *C.* 4.
Rochdale ....*Lab.* 36, *Lib. Dem.* 13, *C.* 11.
Salford ....*Lab.* 55, *C.* 5.
Stockport ....*Lib. Dem.* 25, *C.* 18, *Lab.* 17, *Ind.* 3.
Tameside ....*Lab.* 49, *C.* 6, *Lib.* 2.
Trafford ....*C.* 37, *Lab.* 24, *Ind. Lab.* 1, *Lib. Dem.* 1.
Wigan ....*Lab.* 63, *Lib. Dem.* 5, *C.* 2, *Ind. Lab.* 1, (1 *Vac.*).

MERSEYSIDE

Knowsley ....*Lab.* 62, *C.* 3, *Ind. Lab.* 1.
Liverpool ....*Lab.* 67, *Lib. Dem.* 28, *C.* 2, *Lib.* 1, *SDP* 1.
St. Helens ....*Lab.* 38, *Lib. Dem.* 10, *C.* 6.
Sefton ....*Lab.* 27, *C.* 24, *Lib. Dem.* 18.
Wirral ....*Lab.* 33, *C.* 23, *Lib. Dem.* 7, *Ind. Lab.* 3.

SOUTH YORKSHIRE

Barnsley ....*Lab.* 62, *C.* 2, *Ind.* 1, *RA* 1.
Doncaster ....*Lab.* 55, *C.* 8.
Rotherham ....*Lab.* 62, *Lib.* 2, *C.* 1, *Ind.* 1.
Sheffield ....*Lab.* 69, *C.* 11, *Lib. Dem.* 7.

TYNE AND WEAR

Gateshead ....*Lab.* 60, *Lib. Dem.* 4, *C.* 2.
Newcastle upon
  Tyne ....*Lab.* 63, *Lib. Dem.* 10, *C.* 4, *SDP* 1.
North Tyneside .....*Lab.* 38, *C.* 15, *Lib.* 5, *SDP* 2.
South Tyneside .....*Lab.* 57, *C.* 2, *Lib. Dem.* 1.
Sunderland ....*Lab.* 64, *C.* 8, *Lib. Dem.* 3.

WEST MIDLANDS

Birmingham ....*Lab.* 68, *C.* 37, *Lib. Dem.* 9, *Ind.* 2, (1 *Vac.*).
Coventry ....*Lab.* 44, *C.* 9, *Lib. Dem.* 1.
Dudley ....*Lab.* 41, *C.* 31.
Sandwell ....*Lab.* 57, *C.* 12, *Lib.* 3.
Solihull ....*C.* 27, *Lab.* 15, *Lib. Dem.* 5, *RA* 4.
Walsall ....*Lab.* 34, *C.* 18, *Lib. Dem.* 7, *Ind. C.* 1.
Wolverhampton .....*Lab.* 31, *C.* 24, *Lib. Dem.* 4, *Lib.* 1.

WEST YORKSHIRE

Bradford ....*Lab.* 47, *C.* 40, *Lib. Dem.* 2, (1 *Vac.*).
Calderdale ....*Lab.* 29, *C.* 20, *Lib. Dem.* 5.
Kirklees ....*Lab.* 45, *C.* 14, *Lib. Dem.* 12, *Ind.* 1.
Leeds ....*Lab.* 66, *C.* 21, *Lib. Dem.* 11, *Ind.* 1.
Wakefield ....*Lab.* 58, *C.* 3, *Ind. Lab.* 1, *Lib. Dem.* 1.

Non-Metropolitan District Councils
(* one-third of councillors of Councils so denoted
retire each year, except in those years when County
Council elections are held)

*Adur..............*Lib. Dem.* 22, *C.* 14, *RA* 2, *Lab.* 1.
Allerdale ....*Lab.* 25, *Ind.* 18, *C.* 12.
Alnwick............*Lib.* 12, *C.* 3, *Ind.* 3, *Lab.* 2, *Ind. A.* 1, *Ind. Lab.* 1, *Others* 7.
*Amber Valley .....*C.* 22, *Lab.* 18, *Ind.* C. 3.
Arun ....*C.* 48, *Lib. Dem.* 7, *Lab.* 1.
Ashfield ....*Ind. Lab.* 27, *C.* 4, *SDP* 2.
Ashford ....*C.* 31, *Lib. Dem.* 9, *Lab.* 7, *Ind.* 1, *Others* 1.
Aylesbury Vale ....*C.* 36, *Lib. Dem.* 10, *Ind.* 7, *Lab.* 3, *SDP* 1, (1 *Vac.*).

Babergh ....*C.* 16, *Ind.* 11, *NP* 7, *Lab.* 4, *Lib. Dem.* 4.
*Barrow-in-Furness .*Lab.* 21, *C.* 15, *Ind.* 2.
*Basildon ....*Lab.* 23, *C.* 14, *Lib. Dem.* 5.
*Basingstoke and
  Deane ....*C.* 31, *Lab.* 15, *Lib. Dem.* 10, *Ind.* 3.
*Bassetlaw ....*Lab.* 29, *C.* 15, *Ind.* 2, *Ind. Lab.* 2, *Lib. Dem.* 1, *Others* 1.
*Bath ....*C.* 24, *Lib. Dem.* 13, *Lab.* 11.
Berwick-upon-
  Tweed ....*Lib. Dem.* 13, *Ind.* 10, *C.* 4, *Lab.* 1.
Beverley ....*C.* 26, *Lib. Dem.* 14, *Ind. C.* 9, *Ind.* 2, *Lab.* 2.
Blaby ....*C.* 32, *Ind.* 3, *Others* 4.
*Blackburn ....*Lab.* 36, *C.* 19, *Lib. Dem.* 5.
Blackpool ....*C.* 22, *Lab.* 15, *Lib. Dem.* 5, *Ind.* 1, *Lib.* 1.
Blyth Valley ....*Lab.* 29, *Lib. Dem.* 15, *SDP* 3.
Bolsover ....*Lab.* 31, *Ind.* 3, *C.* 1, *Lib. Dem.* 1, (1 *Vac.*).
Boothferry ....*C.* 17, *Lab.* 10, *Ind.* 8.
Boston ....*C.* 14, *Ind.* 9, *Lib.* 6, *Lab.* 5.
Bournemouth......*C.* 36, *Lib. Dem.* 12, *Lab.* 5, *Ind.* 3, (1 *Vac.*).
Bracknell Forest ...*C.* 39, *Lab.* 1.
Braintree ....*C.* 29, *Lab.* 16, *Ind.* 6, *Lib. Dem.* 6, *RA* 3.
Breckland ....*C.* 33, *Lab.* 7, *Ind.* 5, *NP* 5, *Lib. Dem.* 1, *SDP* 1, (1 *Vac.*).
*Brentwood ....*C.* 21, *Lib. Dem.* 16, *Lab.* 2.
Bridgnorth ....*Ind.* 16, *C.* 9, *Lab.* 3, *SDP* 3, *Lib.* 2.
*Brighton ....*Lab.* 29, *C.* 17, *Ind. C.* 1, *Lib. Dem.* 1.
*Bristol ....*Lab.* 43, *C.* 21, *Lib. Dem.* 4.
*Broadland ....*C.* 32, *Ind.* 6, *Lab.* 5, *Lib. Dem.* 5, (1 *Vac.*).
Bromsgrove ....*C.* 29, *Lab.* 7, *Lib. Dem.* 4, *RA* 1.
*Broxbourne ....*C.* 35, *Lab.* 6, *Lib. Dem.* 1.
Broxtowe..........*C.* 36, *Lab.* 10, *Lib. Dem.* 2, *Grn.* 1.
*Burnley ....*Lab.* 44, *Lib. Dem.* 5, *C.* 3, *Lib.* 1.
*Cambridge.........*Lab.* 24, *C.* 11, *Lib. Dem.* 7.
*Cannock Chase ....*Lab.* 30, *Lib. Dem.* 8, *C.* 3, *Com.* 1.
Canterbury ....*C.* 33, *Lib. Dem.* 11, *Lab.* 5.
Caradon...........*Ind.* 25, *Lib. Dem.* 8, *C.* 4, *RA* 3, *Lab.* 1.
*Carlisle ....*Lab.* 32, *C.* 17, *Lib. Dem.* 1, *Others* 1.
Carrick ....*Lib. Dem.* 20, *C.* 15, *Ind.* 6, *Lab.* 4.
Castle Morpeth ....*Ind.* 10, *SDP* 10, *Lab.* 5, *C.* 4, *Lib.* 3, *Others* 2.
Castle Point ......*C.* 38, *Lab.* 1.
Charnwood ....*C.* 39, *Lab.* 10, *Lib. Dem.* 2, *Ind.* 1.
Chelmsford ....*Lib. Dem.* 28, *C.* 24, *Ind.* 3, *SDP* 1.
*Cheltenham ....*C.* 15, *Lib. Dem.* 15, *Lab.* 2, *Ind.* 1.
*Cherwell ....*C.* 32, *Lab.* 17, *Lib. Dem.* 2, *Ind.* 1.
*Chester ....*C.* 24, *Lab.* 22, *Lib. Dem.* 13, *Ind.* 1.
Chesterfield ....*Lab.* 35, *Lib. Dem.* 7, *C.* 5.
Chester-le-Street ..*Lab.* 25, *Lib.* 4, *C.* 1, *Ind.* 1, (2 *Vac.*).
Chichester ....*C.* 35, *Lib. Dem.* 12, *Ind.* 2, *RA* 1.
Chiltern...........*C.* 42, *Lib. Dem.* 4, *Lab.* 1, *RA* 1, *SDP* 1, (1 *Vac.*).

Melton .... *C.* 14, *Lib. Dem.* 7, *Ind.* 5.
Mendip............ *Lib. Dem.* 18, *C.* 17, *Ind.* 4, *Lab.* 2, *Ind. SDP.* 1, *Lib.* 1.
Mid Bedfordshire .. *C.* 42, *Ind.* 5, *A.* 3, *Lab.* 3.
Mid Devon .... *Ind.* 28, *A.* 7, *Lib.* 5.
Middlesbrough .... *Lab.* 36, *C.* 12, *Lib. Dem.* 4, *Ind.* 1.
Mid Suffolk .... *C.* 18, *Ind. C.* 11, *Lab.* 5, *Lib. Dem.* 5, (1 Vac.).
*Mid Sussex .... *C.* 37, *Lib. Dem.* 11, *Ind.* 5, (1 Vac.).
*Milton Keynes .... *Lab.* 24, *C.* 13, *Lib. Dem.* 7, *Ind.* 2.
*Mole Valley .... *C.* 14, *Ind.* 13, *Lib. Dem.* 12, *Grn.* 1, *Lab.* 1.
Newark and *C.* 26, *Lab.* 24, *Ind.* 2, *Lib. Dem.* Sherwood .... 2.
Newbury .... *C.* 32, *Lib. Dem.* 12, *Ind.* 1.
*Newcastle under Lyme .... *Lab.* 40, *C.* 9, *Lib. Dem.* 7.
New Forest .... *C.* 33, *Lib. Dem.* 15, *SDP* 1, *Others* 9.
Northampton ..... *C.* 24, *Lab.* 16, *SDP* 2, (1 Vac.).
Northavon .... *C.* 30, *Lib. Dem.* 11, *Lab.* 8, *SDP* 4, *Lib.* 3, *Ind.* 1.
*North Bedfordshire *C.* 24, *Lab.* 14, *Lib. Dem.* 13, *Ind.* 1, (1 Vac.).
North Cornwall .... *Lib. Dem.* 6, *C.* 2, *Lab.* 1, *Others* 29.
North Devon ...... *Ind.* 18, *Lib. Dem.* 18, *C.* 8.
North Dorset ...... *Ind.* 24, *Lib. Dem.* 8, (1 Vac.).
NE Derbyshire ..... *Lab.* 29, *C.* 14, *Ind.* 6, *Lib.* 1, (3 Vac.).
*North Hertfordshire *C.* 29, *Lab.* 15, *RA* 3, *Lib. Dem.* 2, *SDP* 1.
North Kesteven .... *C.* 14, *Ind.* 12, *Lib. Dem.* 5, *Lab.* 3, *Others* 5.
North Norfolk ..... *Ind.* 13, *C.* 10, *Lab.* 4, *Lib. Dem.* 3, *Others* 16.
North Shropshire .. *NP* 32, *C.* 6, *Lab.* 2.
N. Warwickshire ... *Lab.* 20, *C.* 12, *Lib. Dem.* 1, *NP* 1.
NW Leicestershire . *Lab.* 18, *C.* 14, *Lib. Dem.* 3, *Others* 3, (2 Vac.).
North Wiltshire .... *C.* 27, *Lib. Dem.* 23, *Ind.* 1, *Lab.* 1.
*Norwich .... *Lab.* 37, *Lib. Dem.* 8, *C.* 3.
Nottingham .... *C.* 27, *Lab.* 27, *Com.* 1.
*Nuneaton and Bedworth .... *Lab.* 35, *C.* 10.
*Oadby & Wigston .. *C.* 15, *Lib. Dem.* 11.
Oswestry .... *NP* 14, *C.* 7, *Lab.* 5, *Lib. Dem.* 3.
*Oxford .... *Lab.* 30, *C.* 10, *Lib. Dem.* 5.
*Pendle .... *Lib.* 23, *Lab.* 22, *C.* 5, *Others* 1.
*Penwith........... *C.* 13, *Lab.* 10, *Ind.* 7, *Ind. Lab.* 1, *Lib. Dem.* 1, *MK* 1, *SDP* 1.
*Peterborough ...... *Lab.* 23, *C.* 21, *Lib.* 4.
Plymouth .... *C.* 31, *Lab.* 23, *SDP* 5, *Lib. Dem.* 1.
Poole .... *C.* 21, *Lib. Dem.* 13, *SDP* 2.
*Portsmouth........ *C.* 18, *Lab.* 14, *Lib. Dem.* 4, *Grn.* 1, *Ind.* 1, *Ind. C.* 1.
*Preston .... *Lab.* 35, *C.* 16, *Lib. Dem.* 6.
*Purbeck .... *C.* 9, *Ind.* 8, *Lib. Dem.* 3, *Lib.* 2.
*Reading .... *Lab.* 27, *C.* 11, *Lib. Dem.* 5, *Others* 2.
*Redditch .... *Lab.* 21, *C.* 7, *Lib. Dem.* 1.
*Reigate and *C.* 27, *Lab.* 11, *Lib. Dem.* 6, *Ind.* Banstead .... 2, *RA* 2, *SDP* 1.
Restormel .... *Lib. Dem.* 22, *NP* 10, *Ind.* 6, *C.* 5, *Lab.* 1.
Ribble Valley ...... *C.* 32, *Lab.* 4, *Ind.* 2, *Lib. Dem.* 1.
Richmondshire .... *Ind.* 28, *SDP* 3, *A.* 2, *C.* 1.
Rochester upon *C.* 29, *Lab.* 15, *Lib. Dem.* 5, *Ind.* Medway .... 1.

*Rochford .... *C.* 16, *Lib. Dem.* 15, *Lab.* 7, *RA* 2.
*Rossendale .... *Lab.* 24, *C.* 12.
Rother .... *C.* 29, *Ind.* 8, *Lib. Dem.* 6, *Lab.* 2.
*Rugby............. *C.* 22, *Lab.* 16, *RA* 6, *Ind.* 3, *Lib. Dem.* 1.
*Runnymede ...... *C.* 26, *Lab.* 8, *Ind.* 6, *Grn.* 1, *Lib. Dem.* 1.
Rushcliffe .... *C.* 45, *Lib. Dem.* 6, *Lab.* 3.
*Rushmoor .... *C.* 32, *Lib. Dem.* 8, *Lab.* 5.
Rutland .... *Ind.* 9, *C.* 8, *Lib. Dem.* 3.
Ryedale .... *Lib. Dem.* 17, *Ind.* 11, *NP* 9, *C.* 5.
*St. Albans .... *C.* 31, *Lib. Dem.* 17, *Lab.* 8, *Ind.* 1.
St. Edmundsbury ... *C.* 31, *Lab.* 7, *Lib. Dem.* 4, *Ind.* 1, (1 Vac.).
Salisbury .... *C.* 29, *Ind.* 17, *Lib. Dem.* 10, *Others* 2.
Scarborough .... *C.* 21, *Ind.* 13, *Lab.* 8, *Lib. Dem.* 7.
*Scunthorpe .... *Lab.* 32, *C.* 5, *SDP* 3.
Sedgefield .... *Lab.* 36, *Lib. Dem.* 4, *Ind.* 3, *SDP* 3, *C.* 2, *Others* 1.
Sedgemoor .... *C.* 33, *Lib. Dem.* 7, *Lab.* 4, *Ind.* 3, *Ind. Lab.* 1, (1 Vac.).
Selby .... *C.* 24, *Ind.* 12, *Lab.* 10, *Others* 4.
Sevenoaks .... *C.* 35, *Ind.* 7, *Lib. Dem.* 7, *Lab.* 2, *NP* 2.
Shepway .... *C.* 26, *Lib. Dem.* 25, *Ind.* 3, *Ind. C.* 1, *Lab.* 1.
*Shrewsbury and Atcham .... *Lab.* 22, *C.* 18, *Lib. Dem.* 8.
*Slough .... *Lab.* 28, *C.* 6, *Lib.* 5.
*Southampton ...... *Lab.* 25, *C.* 15, *Lib. Dem.* 4, *Ind. Lab.* 1.
*South Bedfordshire. *C.* 37, *Lab.* 9, *Lib. Dem.* 5, *Ind.* 2.
South Bucks. ...... *C.* 32, *RA* 4, *Ind.* 2, *Lib. Dem.* 2, *SDP* 1.
*South *Ind.* 28, *C.* 20, *Lab.* 5, *Lib. Dem.* Cambridgeshire ... 1, (1 Vac.).
South Derbyshire .. *Lab.* 20, *C.* 9, *Ind.* 3, *Ind. C.* 2.
*Southend-on-Sea ... *C.* 23, *Lib. Dem.* 11, *Lab.* 5.
South Hams .... *C.* 27, *Ind.* 5, *Lib.* 2, *Lab.* 1, *Lib. Dem.* 1, *Others* 7, (1 Vac.).
*South Herefordshire *Ind.* 29, *C.* 5, *Lib.* 1.
South Holland ..... *C.* 9, *Lab.* 2, *Ind.* 1, *Others* 26.
South Kesteven ... *C.* 33, *Lab.* 10, *Lib. Dem.* 7, *Ind.* 6, (1 Vac.).
*South Lakeland .... *C.* 21, *Lib. Dem.* 12, *Lab.* 5, *Others* 14.
South Norfolk ..... *C.* 26, *Lib. Dem.* 16, *Ind.* 5.
South Northants. .. *C.* 27, *Ind.* 10, *Lab.* 3.
South Oxfordshire .*C.* 36, *Lab.* 8, *Ind.* 6, *Lib. Dem.* 6.
South Ribble .... *C.* 36, *Lab.* 10, *Lib. Dem.* 7, (1 Vac.).
South Shropshire .. *Lib. Dem.* 6, *C.* 5, *Ind.* 4, *Ind. Lab.* 1, *Others* 24.
South Somerset .... *Lib. Dem.* 35, *C.* 18, *Ind.* 7.
South Staffordshire .*C.* 41, *Lab.* 4, *Ind.* 3, *Lib. Dem.* 3, *Others* 3.
South Wight .... *C.* 13, *Ind.* 5, *Lib. Dem.* 5, *RA* 1.
Spelthorne .... *C.* 38, *Lab.* 2.
Stafford .... *C.* 31, *Lab.* 17, *Lib. Dem.* 12.
Staffordshire Moorlands .... *Ind. C.* 28, *Lab.* 10, *Others* 18.
*Stevenage .... *Lab.* 32, *Lib. Dem.* 6, *C.* 1.
Stockton-on-Tees .. *Lab.* 28, *C.* 18, *Lib. Dem.* 9.
*Stoke-on-Trent .... *Lab.* 55, *C.* 5.
*Stratford-upon- *C.* 31, *Lib. Dem.* 15, *Ind.* 6, *Lab.* Avon .... 2, *Ind. C.* 1.
*Stroud .... *Lab.* 18, *C.* 17, *Lib. Dem.* 10, *Ind.* 7, *Grn.* 4.

Suffolk Coastal .... *C.* 39, *Lib. Dem.* 6, *Ind.* 5, *Lab.* 2, *Others* 3.

Surrey Heath ...... *C.* 35, (1 Vac.).

*Swale .... *C.* 19, *Lab.* 16, *Lib. Dem.* 14.

*Tamworth .... *Lab.* 20, *C.* 10.

*Tandridge .... *C.* 20, *Lib. Dem.* 15, *Lab.* 6, *Ind.* 1.

Taunton Deane .... *C.* 28, *Lab.* 7, *Lib. Dem.* 7, *SDP.* 7, *Ind.* 3, (1 Vac.).

Teesdale............ *Ind.* 22, *Lab.* 6, *C.* 1, *Ind. Lab.* 1, *Lib.* 1.

Teignbridge .... *C.* 27, *Ind.* 24, *A* 3, *Lab.* 3, *Ind. C.* 1.

Tendring .... *C.* 30, *A* 14, *Lab.* 6, *RA* 5, *Ind.* 2, *Ind. C.* 1, *Lib. Dem.* 1, (1 Vac.).

Test Valley .... *Lab.* 26, *Lib. Dem.* 14, *Ind.* 2, *NP* 2.

Tewkesbury .... *Ind.* 20, *C.* 15, *Lib. Dem.* 5, *Lab.* 2, *Others* 3.

*Thamesdown ...... *Lab.* 39, *C.* 10, *Lib. Dem.* 4, *Ind.* 1.

Thanet............. *Ind.* 15, *C.* 14, *Lab.* 10, *Ind. C.* 8, *NP* 7.

*Three Rivers ...... *C.* 19, *Lib. Dem.* 17, *Lab.* 11.

*Thurrock........... *Lab.* 31, *C.* 7, *Ind.* 1.

*Tonbridge and Malling .... *C.* 35, *Lib. Dem.* 11, *Lab.* 6.

*Torbay .... *C.* 17, *Lib. Dem.* 12, *Lab.* 3, *Ind.* 1, *Others* 3.

Torridge .... *NP* 17, *C.* 7, *Ind.* 6, *Lab.* 4, *Lib.* 1, *Lib. Dem.* 1.

*Tunbridge Wells .. *C.* 31, *Lib. Dem.* 12, *Lab.* 4, *Ind.* 1.

Tynedale .... *C.* 16, *Lib. Dem.* 13, *Ind.* 10, *Lab.* 8.

Uttlesford .... *C.* 26, *Lib. Dem.* 8, *Ind.* 7, *Ind. C.* 1.

Vale of White Horse .... *C.* 41, *Lib. Dem.* 7, *Lab.* 2, *Ind.* 1.

Vale Royal .... *C.* 28, *Lab.* 25, *Ind.* 3, *Lib. Dem.* 3, *RA* 1.

Wansbeck .... *Lab.* 39, *Lib.* 7.

Wansdyke .... *C.* 28, *Lab.* 16, *Ind.* 3.

Warrington .... *Lab.* 38, *C.* 14, *Lib. Dem.* 8.

Warwick .... *C.* 29, *Lab.* 7, *Lib. Dem.* 6, *RA* 3.

*Watford .... *Lab.* 20, *C.* 11, *Lib. Dem.* 3, *Ind. Lab.* 2.

*Waveney .... *Lab.* 27, *C.* 16, *Lib. Dem.* 4, *Ind.* 1.

Waverley.......... *C.* 41, *Lib. Dem.* 10, *SDP* 3, *Ind.* 2, *Lab.* 1.

Wealden .... *C.* 46, *Lib. Dem.* 6, *Ind. C.* 3, *RA* 3.

Wear Valley ...... *Lab.* 23, *Ind.* 8, *Lib. Dem.* 6, *C.* 3.

Welling .... *C.* 20, *Lab.* 11, *Ind.* 2, *Lib.* 1.

*Welwyn Hatfield ... *Lab.* 24, *C.* 19.

West Devon .... *C.* 11, *NP* 11, *Ind.* 6, *A.* 1, *Lab.* 1.

West Dorset .... *Ind.* 21, *C.* 15, *A.* 12, *Lab.* 3, *Ind. C.* 2, *Lib.* 1, (1 Vac.).

*West Lancashire .. *C.* 28, *Lab.* 25, *Lib. Dem.* 2.

*West Lindsey ...... *Lib. Dem.* 13, *C.* 10, *Ind.* 9, *Lab.* 5.

*West Oxfordshire . *Ind.* 28, *C.* 9, *Lab.* 6, *Lib. Dem.* 6.

West Somerset ..... *Ind.* 25, *C.* 6, *Lab.* 1.

West Wiltshire..... *C.* 20, *Ind. C.* 7, *Lib. Dem.* 6, *Ind.* 3, *Lab.* 3, *Others* 4.

*Weymouth and Portland .... *C.* 13, *Lab.* 13, *Lib. Dem.* 4, *Ind.* 3, *RA* 1, *Others* 1.

*Winchester .... *C.* 27, *Lib. Dem.* 22, *Lab.* 6.

Windsor and Maidenhead ...... *C.* 41, *Lib. Dem.* 9, *RA* 7, *SDP* 1.

*Woking .... *C.* 16, *Lib. Dem.* 13, *Lab.* 6.

*Wokingham .... *C.* 37, *Lib. Dem.* 14, *Lab.* 3.

Woodspring .... *C.* 45, *Ind.* 4, *Lab.* 4, *Lib. Dem.* 3, *SDP* 2, *Grn.* 1.

*Worcester .... *Lab.* 24, *C.* 11, *Lib. Dem.* 1.

*Worthing .... *C.* 27, *Lib. Dem.* 9.

Wrekin .... *Lab.* 30, *C.* 11, *Ind.* 3, *Lib. Dem.* 2.

Wychavon......... *C.* 35, *Lib. Dem.* 9, *Ind.* 3, *Lab.* 2.

Wycombe.......... *C.* 47, *Lab.* 5, *Lib. Dem.* 3, *Ind.* 2, *Lib.* 1, *RA* 1, *SDP* 1.

Wyre .... *C.* 41, *Lab.* 9, *Lib.* 4, *Ind.* 1, *RA* 1.

*Wyre Forest ...... *Lab.* 16, *Lib. Dem.* 13, *C.* 10, *Ind.* 3.

*York .... *Lab.* 31, *C.* 10, *Lib. Dem.* 4.

Greater London Boroughs

Barking and Dagenham .... *Lab.* 44, *RA* 3, *Lib.* 1.

Barnet .... *C.* 39, *Lab.* 18, *Lib. Dem.* 3.

Bexley .... *C.* 35, *Lab.* 18, *Lib. Dem.* 9.

Brent .... *C.* 31, *Lab.* 29, *Lib. Dem.* 6.

Bromley .... *C.* 43, *Lab.* 11, *Lib. Dem.* 6.

Camden .... *Lab.* 42, *C.* 15, *Lib. Dem.* 2.

City of Westminster . *C.* 45, *Lab.* 15.

Croydon .... *C.* 41, *Lab.* 29.

Ealing .... *C.* 40, *Lab.* 30.

Enfield .... *C.* 34, *Lab.* 32.

Greenwich .... *Lab.* 44, *C.* 12, *SDP* 4, *Lib.* 2.

Hackney .... *Lab.* 48, *Lib. Dem.* 8, *C.* 4.

Hammersmith and Fulham .... *Lab.* 28, *C.* 22.

Haringey .... *Lab.* 42, *C.* 17.

Harrow .... *C.* 36, *Lib.* 13, *Lib. Dem.* 11, *RA* 3.

Havering .... *Lab.* 25, *C.* 19, *RA* 13, *Lib. Dem.* 6.

Hillingdon......... *C.* 35, *Lab.* 34.

Hounslow .... *Lab.* 43, *C.* 15, *Lib. Dem.* 1, (1 Vac.).

Islington .... *Lab.* 49, *Lib. Dem.* 2, *SDP* 1.

Kensington and Chelsea .... *C.* 39, *Lab.* 15.

Kingston upon Thames .... *C.* 25, *Lib. Dem.* 18, *Lab.* 7.

Lambeth .... *Lab.* 40, *C.* 20, *Lib. Dem.* 4.

Lewisham .... *Lab.* 58, *C.* 6, *Lib. Dem.* 3.

Merton............ *Lab.* 29, *C.* 22, *Ind.* 3, *RA* 3.

Newham .... *Lab.* 57, *C.* 2, *Lib. Dem.* 1.

Redbridge .... *C.* 42, *Lab.* 18, *Lib. Dem.* 3.

Richmond upon Thames .... *Lib. Dem.* 48, *C.* 4.

Southwark .... *Lab.* 36, *Lib. Dem.* 21, *C.* 7.

Sutton .... *Lib. Dem.* 32, *C.* 18, *Lab.* 6.

Tower Hamlets..... *Lib. Dem.* 29, *Lab.* 20, (1 Vac.).

Waltham Forest .... *Lab.* 30, *C.* 16, *Lib. Dem.* 11.

Wandsworth........ *C.* 48, *Lab.* 13.

WALES

County Councils

Clwyd .... *Lab.* 34, *Ind.* 16, *C.* 9, *Radical* 7.

Dyfed .... *Ind.* 33, *Lab.* 27, *PC* 4, *Lib. Dem.* 3, *Ind. Lab.* 1, *Lib.* 1, *RA* 1.

Gwent .... *Lab.* 54, *C.* 7, *Ind.* 1, (1 Vac.).

Gwynedd .... *Ind.* 34, *PC* 12, *Lab.* 11, *Lib. Dem.* 4, *C.* 1.

Mid Glamorgan ..... *Lab.* 65, *PC* 5, *Ind.* 2, *Lib. Dem.* 1, *RA* 1.

Powys............. *Ind.* 36, *Lab.* 5, *Lib. Dem.* 3, *SDP* 1, (1 Vac.).

South Glamorgan ...*Lab.* 40, *C.* 13, *Lib. Dem.* 6, *SDP* 2, *PC* 1.
West Glamorgan ....*Lab.* 46, *C.* 6, *Ind.* 6, *Lib. Dem.* 2, *PC* 1.

District Councils

Aberconwy ....*Lib. Dem.* 11, *C.* 8, *Lab.* 5, *Ind.* 5, *PC* 1, *Others* 11.
Alyn & Deeside .....*Lab.* 24, *Ind.* 8, *C.* 6, *Lib. Dem.* 4, *Others* 1.
Arfon ....*Ind.* 17, *Lab.* 11, *PC* 10, *Lib. Dem.* 1.
Blaenau Gwent .....*Lab.* 34, *RA* 5, *C.* 1, *Ind.* 1, *Ind. Lab.* 1, *Lib.* 1, *PC* 1.
Brecknock..........*Ind.* 29, *Lab.* 13, *Lib. Dem.* 2.
Cardiff ....*Lab.* 28, *C.* 23, *Lib. Dem.* 12 (2 Vac.).
Carmarthen ....*Ind.* 29, *Lab.* 4, *RA* 2, *Lib. Dem.* 1, *PC* 1.
Ceredigion ....*Ind.* 23, *Lib.* 9, *SDP* 6, *PC* 4, *Lab.* 2.
Colwyn ....*Lib. Dem.* 14, *Ind.* 10, *Lab.* 5, *C.* 3, *RA.* 2.
Cynon Valley ....*Lab.* 30, *PC* 5, *Com.* 1, *Ind.* 1, *Ind. Lab.* 1.
Delyn ....*Ind.* 19, *Lab.* 10, *Ind. Lab.* 5, *C.* 4, *Lib. Dem.* 4.
Dinefwr ....*Lab.* 17, *Ind.* 11, *PC* 2, *Ind. Lab.* 1, (1 Vac.).
Dwyfor.............*PC* 7, *Others* 22.
Glyndŵr ....*Ind.* 28, *Lab.* 4, *Lib. Dem.* 3.
Islwyn ....*Lab.* 23, *PC* 10, (2 Vac.).
Llanelli ....*Lab.* 26, *Ind.* 2, *Lib. Dem.* 2, *Lib.* 1, *Others* 4.
Lliw Valley ....*Lab.* 25, *Ind.* 5, *PC* 2, *C.* 1.
Meirionnydd ....*PC* 8, *Lab.* 6, *Ind.* 1, *Others* 26.
Merthyr Tydfil ......*Lab.* 22, *Ind.* 5, *RA* 5, *PC* 1.
Monmouth ....*C.* 25, *Lab.* 12, *Ind.* 3.
Montgomeryshire ...*Ind.* 39, *Lib. Dem.* 2, *Lib.* 2, *C.* 1, *Lab.* 1, *PC* 1.
Neath ....*Lab.* 29, *SDP* 2, *Com.* 1, *Ind.* 1, *PC* 1.
Newport ....*Lab.* 40, *C.* 7.
Ogwr ....*Lab.* 32, *C.* 16, *Ind.* 1.
Port Talbot ....*Lab.* 24, *RA* 4, *Ind.* 1, *Lib. Dem.* 1, *SDP* 1.
Preseli
 Pembrokeshire .... *Ind.* 37, *C.* 1, *Lab.* 1, *Lib. Dem.* 1.
Radnor.............*Ind.* 26, *RA* 4, *Lab.* 1, (2 Vac.).
Rhondda ....*Lab.* 29, *PC* 2, *RA* 2.
Rhuddlan ....*Ind.* 18, *C.* 7, *Lab.* 7.
Rhymney Valley ....*Lab.* 33, *PC* 6, *Ind.* 3, *A.* 1, *Ind. Lab.* 1, *RA* 1, *Others* 1.
South Pembrokeshire *NP* 23, *Ind.* 2, *Lab.* 2, *Lib. Dem.* 1, *PC* 1, (1 Vac.).
Swansea............*Lab.* 31, *C.* 9, *Lib. Dem.* 7, *Ind.* 4.
Taff-Ely ....*Lab.* 22, *PC* 11, *MK* 6, *Lib.* 2, *C.* 1, *Lib. Dem.* 1.
Torfaen ....*Lab.* 34, *Ind.* 5, *C.* 1, *Com.* 1, *Ind. Lab.* 1, *Lib. Dem.* 1, *RA* 1.
Vale of Glamorgan ..*C.* 24, *Lab.* 14, *Ind.* 4, *PC* 4.
Wrexham Maelor ...*Lab.* 27, *C.* 9, *Ind.* 6, *Lib.* 2, *Lib. Dem.* 1, *PC* 1.
Ynys Môn ....*Ind.* 30, *PC* 4, *Lab.* 3, *C.* 1, *Ind. Lab.* 1.

SCOTLAND
Regional Councils

Borders ....*Ind.* 13, *SLD* 6, *C.* 2, *SNP* 2.
Central ....*Lab.* 22, *SNP* 6, *C.* 5, *Ind.* 1.
Dumfries &   *Lab.* 10, *SNP* 4, *Lib. Dem.* 2,
 Galloway .... *Ind. Lab.* 1, *Others* 18.

Fife ....*Lab.* 30, *Lib. Dem.* 10, *C.* 2, *SNP* 2, *Com.* 1, *Ind.* 1.
Grampian ....*Lab.* 19, *SNP* 14, *Lib. Dem.* 11, *C.* 10, *Ind.* 3.
Highland ....*NP* 22, *Ind.* 12, *Ind. C.* 10, *Lib.* 2, *SNP* 2, *C.* 1, *Grn.* 1, *Ind. Lib. Dem.* 1, *Lib. Dem.* 1.
Lothian ....*Lab.* 34, *C.* 12, *Lib. Dem.* 2, *SNP* 1.
Orkney ....*Ind.* 23, *Others* 1.
Shetland ....*Ind.* 16, *Lab.* 2, *Others* 7.
Strathclyde.........*Lab.* 90, *C.* 5, *Lib. Dem.* 4, *Ind.* 3, *SNP* 1.
Tayside ....*Lab.* 18, *C.* 14, *SNP* 10, *Lib. Dem.* 2, *Ind.* 1, *Ind. Lab.* 1.
Western Isles ....*Ind.* 29, (1 Vac.).

District Councils

Aberdeen ....*Lab.* 27, *Lib. Dem.* 14, *Ind. C.* 9, *SNP* 2.
Angus..............*SNP* 13, *C.* 6, *Ind.* 1, *Others* 1.
Annandale &
 Eskdale ....*Lib. Dem.* 8, *Ind.* 6, *Lab.* 1, *Lib.* 1.
Argyll & Bute.......*Ind.* 7, *Lib. Dem.* 4, *SNP* 4, *C.* 3, *Lab.* 1, *Others* 7.
Badenoch and
 Strathspey ....*Ind.* 9, *SNP* 1, (1 Vac.).
Banff & Buchan .....*Ind.* 10, *SNP* 8.
Bearsden and
 Milngavie ....*C.* 6, *Lib. Dem.* 2, *Ind.* 1, *Lab.* 1.
Berwickshire ....*C.* 9, *Ind.* 2, *Lib. Dem.* 1.
Caithness ....*Ind.* 13, *Lab.* 2, *Lib.* 1.
Clackmannan ....*Lab.* 10, *C.* 1, *SNP* 1.
Clydebank ....*Lab.* 11, *C.* 1.
Clydesdale..........*Lab.* 9, *SNP* 4, *Ind. C.* 2, *C.* 1.
Cumbernauld
 & Kilsyth.........*Lab.* 6, *SNP* 6.
Cumnock and
 Doon Valley ......*Lab.* 8, *Ind. Lab.* 1, *SDP* 1.
Cunninghame ......*Lab.* 24, *C.* 4, *Ind.* 2.
Dumbarton ....*Lab.* 7, *C.* 4, *SNP* 3, *Ind.* 1, *NP* 1.
Dundee ....*Ind. C.* 29, *C.* 10, *SNP* 5.
Dunfermline........*Lab.* 25, *C.* 3, *Lib. Dem.* 3, *SNP* 3.
East Kilbride ....*Lab.* 14, *C.* 2.
East Lothian........*Lab.* 12, *C.* 4, *SNP* 1.
Eastwood...........*C.* 8, *Ind.* 1, *Lab.* 1, *Lib. Dem.* 1, *RA* 1.
Edinburgh..........*Lab.* 32, *C.* 22, *Lib. Dem.* 5, *SNP* 3.
Ettrick and
 Lauderdale ....*Ind.* 5, *Lab.* 1, *SNP* 1, *Others* 9.
Falkirk ....*Lab.* 20, *SNP* 10, *C.* 3, *Ind.* 2, *Ind. Lab.* 1.
Glasgow ....*Lab.* 59, *C.* 4, *Lib. Dem.* 2, *Ind. Lab.* 1.
Gordon.............*Lib. Dem.* 10, *Ind.* 6.
Hamilton ....*Lab.* 15, *Lib. Dem.* 2, *C.* 1, *Ind. Lab.* 1, *SNP* 1.
Inverclyde..........*Lab.* 12, *Lib. Dem.* 7, *C.* 1.
Inverness ....*Ind.* 14, *Lab.* 12, *Lib.* 1, *Lib. Dem.* 1.
Kilmarnock and
 Loudoun ....*Lab.* 13, *C.* 3, *SNP* 2.
Kincardine and
 Deeside ....*Ind.* 6, *Lib. Dem.* 3, *C.* 2, *SNP* 1.
Kirkcaldy ....*Lab.* 32, *C.* 2, *Ind.* 2, *Lib. Dem.* 2, *SNP* 2.
Kyle and Carrick ....*Lab.* 16, *C.* 7, *Ind. C.* 1, *Ind. Lab.* 1.
Lochaber ....*Ind.* 8, *Lab.* 5, *Ind. Lab.* 2.
Midlothian ....*Lab.* 14, *C.* 1.

Monklands .... *Lab.* 18, *SNP* 2.
Moray .... *SNP* 8, *NP* 5, *Ind.* 3, *Lab.* 2.
Motherwell .... *Lab.* 22, *Ind.* 3, *SNP* 3, *C.* 2.
Nairn .... *Ind. C.* 9, *C.* 1.
Nithsdale .... *Lab.* 12, *Ind.* 6, *SNP* 5, *C.* 4, *Others* 1.
North East Fife ..... *Lib.* 12, *C.* 4, *NP* 2.
Perth and Kinross ... *C.* 11, *SNP* 9, *Lab.* 5, *Ind.* 2, *Lib. Dem.* 2.
Renfrew .... *Lab.* 31, *C.* 6, *SNP* 4, *Lib. Dem.* 2, *Lib.* 1, (1 Vac.).

Ross & Cromarty .... *Ind.* 17, *Lab.* 2, *SNP* 2, *C.* 1.
Roxburgh .... *Ind.* 8, *Lib. Dem.* 3, *NP* 2, *C.* 1, *SNP* 1, *Others* 1.
Skye & Lochalsh .... *Ind.* 10, *Lib. Dem.* 1.
Stewartry .... *Ind.* 2, *Others* 9, (1 Vac.).
Stirling .... *C.* 10, *Lab.* 10.
Strathkelvin .... *Lab.* 12, *C.* 2, *A* 1.
Sutherland .... *Ind.* 14.
Tweeddale .... *Ind.* 7, *C.* 1, *Lab.* 1, *SNP* 1.
West Lothian .... *Lab.* 13, *SNP* 8, *Ind.* 3.
Wigtown .... *NP* 10, *SNP* 3, *Lab.* 1.

THE KINGDOM OF ENGLAND

Position and extent.—The Kingdom of England lies between 55° 46′ and 49° 57′ 30″ N. latitude (from a few miles north of the mouth of the Tweed to the Lizard), and between 1° 46′ E. and 5° 43′ W. (from Lowestoft to Land's End). England is bounded on the north by the Cheviot Hills; on the south by the English Channel; on the east by the Straits of Dover (Pas de Calais) and the North Sea; and on the West by the Atlantic Ocean, Wales and the Irish Sea. It has a total area of 50,363 sq. miles (130,439 sq. km): land 50,070 sq. miles (129,681 sq. km); inland water 293 sq. miles (758 sq. km).

Population.—The population at the 1981 Census was 46,362,836 (males 22,520,723; females 23,842,113). The average density of the population in 1981 was 915 per square mile. The population, mid-1988 estimate, was 47,536,000.

Flag.—The cross of St. George, the patron saint of England (*cross gules in a field argent*), has been used since the 13th century.

Relief.—There is a marked division between the upland and lowland areas of England. In the extreme north the Cheviot Hills (highest point, *The Cheviot*, 2,674 ft) form a natural boundary with the Kingdom of Scotland. Running south from the Cheviots, though divided from them by the Tyne Gap, is the Pennine range (highest point, *Cross Fell*, 2,930 ft), the main orological feature of the country. The Pennines culminate in the Peak District of Derbyshire (*Kinder Scout*, 2,088 ft). West of the Pennines are the Cumbrian mountains, which include *Scafell Pike* (3,210 ft), the highest peak in England, and to the east are the Yorkshire Moors, their highest point being *Urra Moor* (1,490 ft).

In the west, the foothills of the Welsh mountains extend into the bordering English counties of Shropshire (the *Wrekin*, 1,334 ft; *Long Mynd*, 1,694 ft) and Hereford and Worcester (the Malvern Hills—*Worcestershire Beacon*, 1,394 ft). Extensive areas of high land and moorland are also to be found in the south-western peninsula formed by Somerset, Devon and Cornwall: principally Exmoor (*Dunkery Beacon*, 1,704 ft), Dartmoor (*High Willhays*, 2,038 ft) and Bodmin Moor (*Brown Willy*, 1,377 ft). Ranges of low, undulating hills run across the south of the country, including the Cotswolds in the Midlands and south-west, the Chilterns to the north of Greater London, and the North (Kent) and South (Sussex) Downs of the south-east coastal areas.

The lowlands of England lie in the Vale of York, East Anglia and the area around the Wash, the lowest lying being the Cambridgeshire Fens in the valleys of the Great Ouse and the River Nene, which are below sea-level in places; since the 17th century extensive drainage has brought much of the Fens under cultivation. The North Sea coast between the Thames and the Humber, low-lying and formed of sand and shingle for the most part, is subject to erosion and defences against further incursion have been built along many stretches.

Hydrography.—The *Severn* is the longest river in Great Britain, rising in the north-eastern slopes of Plinlimmon (Wales) and entering England in Shropshire with a total length of 220 miles (354 km) from its source to its outflow into the Bristol Channel, where it receives on the east the Bristol Avon, and on the west the Wye, its other tributaries being the Vyrnwy, Tern, Stour, Teme and Upper (or Warwickshire) Avon. The Severn is tidal below Gloucester, and a high bore or tidal wave sometimes reverses the flow as high as Tewkesbury (13½ miles above Gloucester). The scenery of the greater part of the river is very picturesque and beautiful, and the Severn is a noted salmon river, some of its tributaries being

famous for trout. Navigation is assisted by the Gloucester and Berkeley Ship Canal (16½ miles), which admits vessels of 350 tons to Gloucester. The Severn Tunnel was begun in 1873 and completed in 1886 at a cost of £2,000,000 and after many difficulties from flooding. It is 4 miles 628 yards in length (of which 2¼ miles are under the river). The Severn road bridge between Haysgate, Gwent, and Almondsbury, Glos., with a centre span of 3,240 ft, was opened in 1966.

The longest river wholly in England is the *Thames*, with a total length of 215 miles (346 km) from its source in the Cotswold hills to the Nore, and is navigable by ocean-going ships to London Bridge. The Thames is tidal to Teddington (69 miles from its mouth) and forms county boundaries almost throughout its course; on its banks are situated London, Windsor Castle, the home of the Sovereign, Eton College, the first of the public schools, and Oxford, the oldest university in the kingdom.

Of the remaining English rivers those flowing into the North Sea are the Tyne, Wear, Tees, Ouse and Trent from the Pennine Range, the Great Ouse (160 miles), which rises in Northamptonshire, and the Orwell and Stour from the hills of East Anglia. Flowing into the English Channel are the Sussex Ouse from the Weald, the Itchen from the Hampshire Hills, and the Axe, Teign, Dart, Tamar and Exe from the Devonian hills. Flowing into the Irish Sea are the Mersey, Ribble and Eden from the western slopes of the Pennines and the Derwent from the Cumbrian mountains. The English Lakes, noteworthy for their picturesque scenery and poetic associations, lie in Cumbria, the largest being *Windermere* (10 miles long), *Ullswater* and *Derwentwater*.

Islands.—The *Isle of Wight* is separated from Hampshire by the Solent; total area 147 sq. miles, population about 124,600. The climate is mild and healthy, making the island a popular holiday resort. The capital, Newport, stands at the head of the estuary of the Medina, Cowes (at the mouth) being the chief port. Other centres are Ryde, Sandown, Shanklin, Ventnor, Freshwater, Yarmouth, Totland Bay, Seaview and Bembridge.

Lundy (= Puffin Island), 11 miles NW of Hartland Point, Devon, is about 2 miles long and about half a mile broad (average), with a total area of about 1,116 acres, and a population of about 20; it became the property of the National Trust in 1969 and is now principally a bird sanctuary.

(*See also* The Isles of Scilly, p. 619.)

Climate.—England has a generally mild and temperate climate. Because of the prevailing south-westerly winds, the weather day to day is variable, being affected mainly by depressions moving eastwards across the Atlantic Ocean. This maritime influence means that the west of the country tends to experience wetter but also milder weather than the east. Rainfall also increases with altitude, the mountainous areas of the north and west having more rain than the lowlands of the south and east. Rain is fairly well-distributed throughout the year in all areas but, on average, the driest months are March to June, and the wettest September to January.

The mean annual temperature reduced to sea-level varies from 11°C in the south-west to 9°C near Berwick-on-Tweed. In winter, temperatures tend to be higher in the south and west than in the east, while the warmest in summer are the south and inland areas. Latitude for latitude the mean annual temperature is lower in the east; the decrease of mean temperature with height is about 0·6°C per 100 metres.

EARLY INHABITANTS

Prehistoric Man.—Archaeological evidence suggests that England has been inhabited since at least the Palaeolithic period, though the extent of the various Palaeolithic cultures was dependent upon the degree of glaciation. The succeeding Neolithic and Bronze Age cultures have left abundant remains throughout the country, the best-known of these being the henges and stone circles of Stonehenge (10 miles north of Salisbury, Wilts.) and Avebury (Wilts.), both of which are believed to have been of religious significance. In the latter part of the Bronze Age the Goidels, a people of Celtic race, and in the Iron Age other Celtic races of Brythons and Belgae, invaded the country and brought with them Celtic civilization and dialects, place names in England bearing witness to the spread of the invasion over the whole kingdom.

The Roman Conquest.—The Roman conquest of Gaul (57–50 BC) brought Britain into close contact with Roman civilization, but although Julius Caesar raided the south of Britain in 55 BC, and 54 BC, conquest was not undertaken until nearly 100 years later. In AD 43 the Emperor Claudius dispatched Aulus Plautius, with a well-equipped force of 40,000, and himself followed with reinforcements in the same year. Success was delayed by the resistance of Caratacus (Caractacus), the British leader from AD 48–51, who was finally captured and sent to Rome, and by a great revolt in AD 61 led by Boudicca (Boadicea), Queen of the Iceni; but the south of Britain was secured by AD 70, and Wales and the area north to the Tyne by about AD 80.

In AD 122, the Emperor Hadrian visited Britain and built a continuous rampart, since known as Hadrian's Wall, from Wallsend to Bowness (Tyne to Solway). The work was entrusted by the Emperor Hadrian to Aulus Platorius Nepos, legate of Britain from AD 122 to 126, and it was intended to form the northern frontier of the Roman Empire.

The Romans administered Britain as a Province under a Governor, with a well-defined system of local government, each Roman municipality ruling itself and surrounding territory, while London was the centre of the road system and the seat of the financial officials of the Province of Britain. Colchester, Lincoln, York, Gloucester and St. Albans stand on the sites of five Roman municipalities, and Wroxeter, Caerleon, Chester, Lincoln and York were at various times the sites of legionary fortresses. Well-preserved Roman towns have been uncovered at (or near) Silchester (*Calleva Atrebatum*), 10 miles south of Reading, Wroxeter (*Viroconium Cornoviorum*), near Shrewsbury, and St. Albans (*Verulamium*) in Hertfordshire.

Four main groups of roads radiated from London, and a fifth (the Fosse) ran obliquely from Lincoln through Leicester, Cirencester and Bath to Exeter. Of the four groups radiating from London one ran SE to Canterbury and the coast of Kent, a second to Silchester and thence to parts of Western Britain and South Wales, a third (later known as Watling Street) ran through Verulamium to Chester, with various branches, and the fourth reached Colchester, Lincoln, York and the eastern counties.

In the 4th century Britain was subject to raids along the east coast by Saxon pirates, which led to the establishment of a system of coast defence from the Wash to Southampton Water, with forts at Brancaster, Burgh Castle (Yarmouth), Walton (Felixstowe), Bradwell, Reculver, Richborough, Dover, Lympne, Pevensey and Porchester (Portsmouth). The Irish (Scoti) and Picts in the north were also becoming more aggressive; from about AD 350 incursions became more frequent and more formidable. As the Roman Empire came under attack increasingly towards the end of the 4th century, many troops were removed from Britain for service in other parts of the Empire. The island was eventually cut off from Rome by the Teutonic conquest of Gaul, and with the withdrawal of the last Roman garrison early in the 5th century, the Romano-British were left to themselves.

Saxon Settlement.—According to legend, the British King Vortigern called in the Saxons to defend him against the Picts, the Saxon chieftains being Hengist and Horsa, who landed at Ebbsfleet, Kent, and established themselves in the Isle of Thanet; but the events during the one and a half centuries between the final break with Rome and the re-establishment of Christianity are unclear. However, it would appear that in the course of this period the raids turned into large-scale settlement by invaders traditionally known as Angles (England north of the Wash and East Anglia), Saxons (Essex and southern England) and Jutes (Kent and the Weald), which pushed the Romano-British into the mountainous areas of the north and west, Celtic culture outside Wales and Cornwall surviving only in topographical names. Various kingdoms were established at this time which attempted to claim overlordship of the whole country, hegemony finally being achieved by Wessex (capital, Winchester) in the 9th century. This century also saw the beginning of raids by the Vikings (Danes), which were resisted by Alfred the Great (871–899), the greatest of the Wessex kings, who fixed a limit to the advance of Danish settlement by the Treaty of Wedmore (878), giving them the area north and east of Watling Street, on condition they adopt Christianity.

In the 10th century the Kings of Wessex recovered the whole of England from the Danes, but subsequent rulers were unable to resist a second wave of invaders. England paid tribute (*Danegeld*) for many years, and was invaded in 1013 by the Danes and ruled by Danish Kings from 1016 until 1042, when Edward the Confessor was recalled from exile in Normandy. In 1066 Harold Godwinson (brother-in-law of Edward and son of Earl Godwin of Wessex) was chosen King of England. After defeating (at Stamford Bridge, Yorkshire, September 25) an invading army under Harald Hadraada, King of Norway (aided by the outlawed Earl Tostig of Northumbria, Harold's brother), Harold was himself defeated at the Battle of Hastings on October 14, 1066, and the Norman Conquest secured the throne of England for Duke William of Normandy, a cousin of Edward the Confessor.

Christianity reached the Roman province of Britain from Gaul in the 3rd century (or possibly earlier); Alban, traditionally Britain's first martyr, was put to death as a Christian during the persecution of Diocletian (June 22, 303), at his native town Verulamium; and the Bishops of Londinium, Eboracum (York), and Lindum (Lincoln) attended the Council of Arles in 314. However, the Anglo-Saxon invasions submerged the Christian religion in England until the 6th century when conversion was undertaken in the north from 563 by Celtic missionaries from Ireland led by St. Columba, and in the south by a mission sent from Rome in 597 which was led by St. Augustine, who became the first archbishop of Canterbury. England appears to have been converted again by the end of the 7th century and followed, after the Council of Whitby in 663, the practices of the Roman Church, which brought the kingdom into the mainstream of European thought and culture.

ENGLISH COUNTIES AND SHIRES

LORD LIEUTENANTS AND HIGH SHERIFFS

County or Shire	Lord Lieutenant	*High Sheriff, 1990–91
Avon	Sir John Wills, Bt., TD	R. F. Robertson-Glasgow
Bedfordshire............	Lt.-Col. H. C. Hanbury, LVO, MC	R. F. Willmott
Berkshire	J. R. Henderson	Lady Elizabeth Godsal
Buckinghamshire	Cdr. the Hon. J. T. Fremantle	Sir Peter Reynolds, CBE
Cambridgeshire	M. B. M. Bevan	N. S. Elgood
Cheshire	W. A. Bromley-Davenport	D. M. Stern
Cleveland	The Rt. Hon. the Lord Gisborough	Col. R. M. Stewart, OBE, TD
Cornwall	The Rt. Hon. the Viscount Falmouth	J. M. Williams
Cumbria...............	Maj. Sir Charles Graham, Bt.	T. P. Naylor
Derbyshire	Col. P. Hilton, MC	J. K. Bather
Devon.................	Lt.-Col. the Rt. Hon. the Earl of Morley	Maj. G. E. F. North, MC
Dorset	The Rt. Hon. the Lord Digby	P. W. Allsebrook, CBE
Durham	D. J. Grant, CBE	Capt. J. H. McBain
East Sussex	Adm. Sir Lindsay Bryson, KCB	P. H. E. R. Dunn
Essex	Adm. Sir Andrew Lewis, KCB	P. G. Lee
Gloucestershire	Col. M. St. J. V. Gibbs, CB, DSO, TD	Col. J. E. B. Hills
Greater London	Field Marshal the Lord Bramall, GCB, OBE, MC	Mrs. C. R. Scott
Greater Manchester	Col. J. B. Timmins, OBE, TD	N. Quick, CBE
Hampshire	Lt.-Col. Sir James Scott, Bt.	Maj. C. R. Marriott
Hereford and Worcester	Capt. T. R. Dunne	M. A. C. Brinton
Hertfordshire...........	S. A. Bowes Lyon	Capt. C. G. E. Barclay
Humberside	R. A. Bethell	G. A. Marr, CBE
Isle of Wight	The Rt. Hon. the Lord Mottistone, CBE	H. E. C. Noyes
Kent	The Rt. Hon. Robin Leigh-Pemberton	J. St. A. Warde
Lancashire	S. Towneley	P. W. Townsend
Leicestershire	T. G. M. Brooks	Maj. R. D. F. Bream, TD
Lincolnshire............	Capt. H. N. Neville	A. J. L. Worth
Merseyside	H. E. Cotton	Cdr. E. J. Billington
Norfolk	T. J. Colman	A. J. Gurney
Northamptonshire	J. L. Lowther, CBE	W. R. F. Chamberlain
Northumberland	The Rt. Hon. the Viscount Ridley, TD	Lt.-Col. H. Crossman
North Yorkshire	Sir Marcus Worsley, Bt.	Mrs. V. A. Worthington
Nottinghamshire........	Sir Gordon Hobday	Mrs. R. Abel-Smith
Oxfordshire	Sir Ashley Ponsonby, Bt., MC	C. Gascoigne
Shropshire	J. R. S. Dugdale	H. B. Meynell
Somerset	Col. G. W. F. Luttrell, MC	M. H. A. Fraser
South Yorkshire	J. H. Neill, CBE, TD	S. M. Hamilton
Staffordshire	Sir Arthur Bryan	Maj. C. R. M. Boote, TD
Suffolk	Sir Joshua Rowley, Bt.	G. W. Paul
Surrey	R. E. Thornton, OBE	Dr. A. J. Blowers, CBE
Tyne and Wear	Sir Ralph Carr-Ellison, TD	N. Sherlock
Warwickshire	The Rt. Hon. the Viscount Daventry	J. D. S. Ainscow
West Midlands	The Rt. Hon. the Earl of Aylesford	D. L. Burbidge
West Sussex	His Grace the Duke of Richmond and Gordon	D. W. Bowerman
West Yorkshire	The Rt. Hon. the Lord Ingrow, OBE, TD	P. J. D. Marshall
Wiltshire	Field Marshal Sir Roland Gibbs, GCB, CBE, DSO, MC	N. J. M. Anderson, MC

* High Sheriffs are nominated by the Queen on November 12 and come into office after Hilary Term.

ENGLISH COUNTY COUNCILS
AREAS AND POPULATIONS

County Council	Administrative Headquarters	Area (*hectares*)	Estimated Resident Population 1988	Total demand upon collection fund 1990 £
Avon	Avon House North, St. James Barton, Bristol	134,614	954,300	533,700,000
Bedfordshire	*Bedford	123,460	530,800	302,650,000
Berkshire	†Reading	125,890	747,000	410,976,000
Buckinghamshire	*Aylesbury	188,284	627,200	343,500,000
Cambridgeshire	†Cambridge	340,892	651,500	328,000,000
Cheshire	*Chester	232,846	955,800	534,000,000
Cleveland	Municipal Buildings, Middlesbrough	58,308	553,100	372,000,000
Cornwall	*Truro	354,792‡	458,600	250,000,000
Cumbria	The Courts, Carlisle	681,012	489,200	285,434,000
Derbyshire	County Offices, Matlock	263,094	924,200	520,600,000
Devon	*Exeter	671,088	1,021,100	524,132,000
Dorset	*Dorchester	265,375	655,600	302,000,000
Durham	*Durham	243,592	596,800	324,712,584
East Sussex	Pelham House, St. Andrews Lane, Lewes	179,512	708,300	377,077,000
Essex	*Chelmsford	367,192	1,529,500	776,899,000
Gloucestershire	†Gloucester	264,266	527,500	273,940,000
Hampshire	The Castle, Winchester	377,698	1,542,900	770,510,000
Hereford and Worcester	*Worcester	392,650	671,000	320,493,000
Hertfordshire	*Hertford	163,415	986,000	506,910,000
Humberside	*Beverley, N. Humberside	351,212	850,500	520,191,000
Isle of Wight	*Newport, IOW	38,066	129,800	70,493,000
Kent	*Maidstone	373,060	1,520,300	760,000,000
Lancashire	*Preston	306,346	1,382,000	827,759,000
Leicestershire	*Leicester	255,293	885,500	494,968,000
Lincolnshire	County Offices, Lincoln	591,485	582,600	295,220,000
Norfolk	*Norwich	536,776	744,400	369,696,970
Northamptonshire	*Northampton	236,737	570,300	313,829,000
Northumberland	*Morpeth	503,165	301,400	165,000,000
North Yorkshire	*Northallerton	830,865	713,200	345,649,800
Nottinghamshire	*Nottingham	216,365	1,007,000	574,101,000
Oxfordshire	*Oxford	260,782	578,900	291,052,000
Shropshire	The Shirehall, Shrewsbury	349,014	400,800	219,922,000
Somerset	*Taunton	345,094	457,700	249,951,000
Staffordshire	County Buildings, Stafford	271,615	1,032,900	525,924,000
Suffolk	*Ipswich	379,663	638,500	318,704,000
Surrey	*Kingston upon Thames	167,924	999,800	482,000,000
Warwickshire	†Warwick	198,053	484,600	249,762,000
West Sussex	*Chichester	198,935	703,400	312,727,000
Wiltshire	*Trowbridge	348,070	557,000	282,184,000

* County Hall.   † Shire Hall.   ‡ Excluding Isles of Scilly.

CHIEF EXECUTIVES, TREASURERS AND CHAIRMEN

County Council	Chief Executive	County Treasurer	Chairman of County Council
Avon	B. D. Smith	D. G. Morgan	Mrs. B. Perry
Bedfordshire........	V. F. Phillips	B. Phelps	J. P. B. Kinchella
Berkshire	A. J. Allen	D. J. Bowles	W. A. Wiseman
Buckinghamshire ...	C. M. Garrett	H. R. H. Spring-thorpe	Mrs. G. M. M. Miscampbell, OBE
Cambridgeshire	A. G. Lister	D. Prince‡	Mrs. J. M. Brookes
Cheshire	M. E. Pitt	J. E. H. Whiteoak	Mrs. P. W. Hayward
Cleveland	B. Stevenson	P. Riley†	E. Wood
Cornwall	G. K. Burgess	A. L. Wilkes	D. L. C. Roberts
Cumbria	J. R. Ford	R. Wirth	G. Whalley
Derbyshire	J. S. Raine*	R. C. Beard	A. Morris
Devon..............	R. D. Clark	B. J. Weston	E. M. McGahey, OBE
Dorset	K. A. Abel, CBE	D. M. Gasson	Sir Stephen Hammick, Bt.
Durham	K. W. Smith°	J. Kirkby	J. Graham
East Sussex	R. M. Beechey	M. R. Hancock	Mrs. J. M. Mont
Essex	R. W. Adcock	K. D. Neale	P. E. W. White
Gloucestershire	M. G. Bichard	J. R. Cockroft	F. B. Wilton
Hampshire	A. R. Hodgson	J. E. Scotford	C. M. Jones
Hereford and Worcester	G. A. Price	G. A. Price	R. J. Carrington, OBE
Hertfordshire.......	B. Briscoe	K. S. Cliff	R. H. Fielding
Humberside	J. A. Parkes	G. T. Southern‡	E. E. Blackband
Isle of Wight........	J. S. Horsnell	J. B. W. Proctor	B. M. Pratt, OBE
Kent	P. R. Sabin	P. Martin‡	Sir John Grugeon
Lancashire	B. Hill, CBE	D. Morgan	J. Bury
Leicestershire	S. Jones	R. Hale	A. N. Strachan
Lincolnshire........	R. J. D. Procter	D. G. Barrett	D. C. Hoyes
Norfolk	B. J. Capon	C. A. Boar‡	L. J. Potter
Northamptonshire ..	A. J. Greenwell	D. W. Cleggett‡	T. G. Fordyce
Northumberland	T. P. Urwin	K. Morris	S. H. Newton
North Yorkshire	R. A. Leyland	D. Martin	K. Cooper
Nottinghamshire....	M. T. Lyons	G. S. Luff	J. Thierry
Oxfordshire	J. Harwood	J. T. Vokins	B. H. Duggan
Shropshire	M. Suter	M. N. Davis	Mrs. J. A. Hayward
Somerset	B. M. Tanner	(vacant)	H. Hobhouse
Staffordshire	B. A. Price	B. Smith	J. O'Leary
Suffolk	P. F. Bye	P. B. Atkinson	J. P. Patton
Surrey	D. J. Thomas	R. Wolstenholme	A. J. Brigstocke
Warwickshire	I. G. Caulfield	J. P. Hunt	M. M. Gerold
West Sussex	B. Fieldhouse	D. P. Rigg	M. Long
Wiltshire...........	I. A. Browning	A. F. Gould	Mrs. M. E. Salisbury

* County Director.   ° Principal Executive Officer.   ‡Director of Finance.   †County Finance Officer.

Residuary Bodies

GREATER LONDON, (*see* page 598).

GREATER MANCHESTER.—The residuary body was wound up in October 1989.

MERSEYSIDE.—The residuary body was wound up on March 31, 1990.

TYNE AND WEAR.—The residuary body was wound up in October 1988.

WEST MIDLANDS, 1 Lancaster Circus, Queensway, Birmingham B4 7DJ (021–300 5151).
Chairman, T. McDonald.
Chief Executive, R. A. Steer.

SOUTH YORKSHIRE.—The residuary body was wound up in July 1989.

WEST YORKSHIRE, PO Box 22, Pearl Assurance House, Queen Street, Wakefield, WF1 2QN (0924–290662).
Chairman, T. McDonald.
Chief Executive, H. S. Hoare.

METROPOLITAN COUNCILS

A list of Metropolitan Borough and City Councils. Those accorded CITY status are in SMALL CAPITALS.

Metropolitan Boroughs	Estimated Resident Population 1988	Community charge per head 1990 £	Chief Executive	Mayor (a) Lord Mayor 1990–91
Greater Manchester	2,577,700			
Bolton	263,700	344·46	K. P. Bounds	G. Smith
Bury	175,000	373·38	D. J. Burton	M. Adler
MANCHESTER	445,900	425·00	G. Hainsworth	(a) J. Gilmore
Oldham	219,500	365·00	C. Smith	S. G. W. Jacobs
Rochdale	206,900	335·00	J. F. D. Pierce	J. D. Gorman
SALFORD	235,700	396·00	R. C. Rees, OBE	J. W. Smith
Stockport	290,900	399·00	A. L. Wilson	D. West
Tameside	216,900	349·00	M. Greenwood	R. Denyer
Trafford	215,700	298·00	W. A. Lewis	J. R. Haydock
Wigan	307,600	347·60	S. M. Jones	R. McAllister
Merseyside	1,448,100			
Knowsley	158,400	365·00	D. G. Henshaw	D. Smith
LIVERPOOL.............	469,600	449·00	(vacant)	(a) Ms. D. Gavin
St. Helens	187,700	379·35	F. Kendall	K. Cleary
Sefton.................	297,600	373·00	A. G. Corless	Mrs. B. Lamont
Wirral	334,800	341·00	A. White	J. D. Edwards
South Yorkshire	1,292,700			
Barnsley	220,900	270·00	J. A. Edwards	R. Fisher
Doncaster	291,700	298·85	C. B. Jeynes	J. Meredith
Rotherham	251,800	295·00	J. Bell	M. R. Kirk
SHEFFIELD	528,300	355·00	Mrs. P. Gordon	(a) J. A. Moore
Tyne and Wear	1,130,600			
Gateshead	206,200	320·00	L. N. Elton	Mrs. P. Wallace
NEWCASTLE UPON TYNE ..	279,400	390·60	G. N. Cook	(a) C. Stephenson
North Tyneside	192,900	353·73	‡‡E. D. Nixon	M. S. Alderson
South Tyneside	155,700	309·00	S. Clark	W. Pargeter
Sunderland	296,000	310·00	G. P. Key	A. W. Myers
West Midlands	2,617,300			
BIRMINGHAM	993,700	406·10	R. M. W. Taylor	(a) B. Zissman
COVENTRY	306,200	394·00	I. Roxburgh	(a) W. A. Hardy
Dudley	304,300	387·00	A. V. Astling	C. L. Woodall
Sandwell	296,300	423·00	Miss A. C. Griffin	L. C. Taylor
Solihull	205,000	389·00	J. Scampion	I. L. Meeson
Walsall................	262,300	425·00	J. W. Hadley	M. T. Barton
Wolverhampton.........	249,400	418·00	N. H. Perry, PH.D.	J. Geraghty
West Yorkshire	2,056,500			
BRADFORD	464,100	276·00	R. Penn	(a) E. Saville
Calderdale.............	196,000	247·00	M. Ellison	J. Tolan
Kirklees...............	375,300	289·76	R. V. Hughes	T. P. O'Donovan
LEEDS	709,600	348·00	D. A. Ansbro	(a) W. Kilgallon
WAKEFIELD	311,600	305·09	J. G. Stanbury	G. Clarke

‡‡ Director of Administrative Services.

DISTRICT COUNCILS

A list of non-Metropolitan District Councils in England. Those accorded CITY status are in SMALL CAPITALS, those with Borough status are distinguished by having § prefixed.

District	Estimated Resident Population 1988	Community charge per head 1990 £	Chief Executive (*Clerk)	Chairman 1990–91 (a) Mayor (b) Lord Mayor
Adur, West Sussex	56,800	349·55	F. M. G. Staden	Mrs. M. Robinson
Allerdale, Cumbria	96,600	285·42	A. G. Perry	L. Conaway
Alnwick, Northumberland	30,400	354·44	L. St. Ruth	R. Elliott
§Amber Valley, Derbyshire.....	111,900	394·42	A. Dow	R. A. Coates
Arun, West Sussex	130,300	314·39	A. S. Potts	Mrs. M. Gale-Whorlow
Ashfield, Nottinghamshire	107,700	320·00	S. Beedham	D. Hague

District	Estimated Resident Population 1988	Community charge per head 1990 £	Chief Executive (*Clerk)	Chairman 1990–91 (a) Mayor (b) Lord Mayor
§Ashford, Kent................	95,100	297·00	E. H. W. Mexter	(a) B. G. Moorman
Aylesbury Vale, Bucks.	145,500	347·00	B. J. Quoroll	Gp. Capt. J. F. Stewart
Babergh, Suffolk	78,500	321·00	D. C. Bishop	T. M. Bailey-Smith
§Barrow in Furness, Cumbria ..	72,400	328·00	R. H. McCulloch	(a) J. F. Park
Basildon, Essex	157,600	443·00	J. C. Rosser°	D. Marks
§Basingstoke and Deane, Hants.	139,700	319·60	D. W. Pilkington, RD	(a) C. B. Evans
Bassetlaw, Notts..............	104,800	370·00	R. D. Blair	J. H. V. Hall
BATH, Avon	84,800	385·00	N. C. Abbott	(a) J. Higgins
§Berwick-upon-Tweed, Northumberland	26,900	321·38	J. V. Picking	(a) G. M. Elliott
§Beverley, Humberside	114,000	373·00	W. J. H. Thomas	(a) Mrs D. Stephenson
Blaby, Leics.................	84,200	333·14	G. E. Phillips	T. W. Lees
§Blackburn, Lancs.............	134,400	365·00	G. L. Davies	(a) M. T. Doherty
§Blackpool, Lancs.............	143,800	384·00	D. Wardman	(a) A. W. Rhodes
§Blyth Valley, Northumberland	78,500	415·24	D. Crawford	(a) A. J. Duffield
Bolsover, Derbys.............	69,800	297·00	C. A. Tucker	S. Patrick
§Boothferry, Humberside	64,000	313·80	J. W. Barber	(a) Mrs. B. M. Stephenson
§Boston, Lincs................	52,200	280·00	R. E. Coley	(a) A. A. Cutting
§Bournemouth, Dorset.........	154,800	320·00	K. Lomas	(a) W. Coe
§Bracknell Forest, Berks.	98,200	393·50	A. J. Targett	(a) E. Thompson
Braintree, Essex	117,200	343·00	C. R. Daybell	Ms. K. Richards
Breckland, Norfolk	104,200	310·36	J. B. Heath	T. C. Byford
Brentwood, Essex	70,000	375·00	C. P. Sivell	A. Earl
Bridgnorth, Salop	51,000	322·14	A. L. Bain	P. M. Whiteman
§Brighton, East Sussex	144,700	372·50	G. Jones	(a) Mrs. C. J. Simpson
BRISTOL, Avon	377,700	425·30	W. Miller	(b) J. Williams
Broadland, Norfolk	104,400	319·63	J. H. Bryant	D. J. Hastings
Bromsgrove, Hereford and Worcs.................	89,600	337·00	R. P. Bradshaw	A. J. Mace
§Broxbourne, Herts.	82,500	361·04	M. J. Walker	(a) J. G. E. Swannell
§Broxtowe, Notts.	108,300	377·89	M. Brown	(a) W. Shaw
§Burnley, Lancs.	85,300	299·00	B. Whittle	(a) Mrs. P. Bennett
CAMBRIDGE	97,900	428·00	R. Hammond	(a) Dr. G. A. Reid
Cannock Chase, Staffs..........	87,800	354·58	C. E. Evans	M. C. Stretton
CANTERBURY, Kent	131,900	299·50	C. Gay	(b) J. Nock
Caradon, Cornwall	75,000	315·58	J. O. Collins	W. E. Williams
CARLISLE, Cumbria	102,000	365·00	R. S. Brackley	(a) J. L. Amos
Carrick, Cornwall	80,300	317·79	P. M. Talbot	F. J. Warne
§Castle Morpeth, Northumberland	50,400	432·95	M. Cole	(a) C. Temple
Castle Point, Essex	85,400	377·41	B. Rollinson	R. Sweeting
§Charnwood, Leics.............	148,500	359·87	R. M. Holroyd	(a) W. L. McCombe
§Chelmsford, Essex	151,700	392·42	R. M. C. Hartley	(a) Ms. F. Sturt
§Cheltenham, Glos.	86,500	364·42	B. N. Wynn	(a) W. V. P. Bullingham
Cherwell, Oxon...............	122,400	380·00	A. M. Brace	D. E. Jelfs
CHESTER, Cheshire	117,100	399·87	P. F. Durham	(a) J. P. Bramall
§Chesterfield, Derbyshire.......	99,700	412·00	D. R. Shaw	(a) A. Webber
Chester-le-Street, Co. Durham ..	53,100	341·72	J. A. Greensmith	Mrs S. Hubbard
Chichester, West Sussex	105,800	294·49	P. Ryan	H. N. Allen
Chiltern, Bucks.	87,900	390·76	D. G. Sainsbury	M. J. Batt
§Chorley, Lancs...............	96,700	360·55	J. W. Davies	(a) F. Culshaw
§Christchurch, Dorset	40,400	340·00	C. H. Dewsnap	(a) M. C. Kidman
§Cleethorpes, Humberside	68,400	364·00	P. Daniel	(a) A. A. Archer
§Colchester, Essex	150,200	332·50	J. Cobley	(a) K. Cooke
§Congleton, Cheshire	86,600	397·37	D. N. Mills	(a) K. A. Hemsley
§Copeland, Cumbria	71,600	326·00	R. G. Smith	(a) A. Benson
Corby, Northants..............	51,000	350·00	T. J. Simmons	R.W. Hipkiss
Cotswold, Glos.	75,100	379·88	D. A. Sketchley	I. M. Maitland-Hume
Craven, North Yorks	49,600	249·92	A. Howell*	Mrs J. Gott
§Crawley, West Sussex	84,400	345·00	M. D. Sander	(a) Ms. B. Smith
§Crewe and Nantwich, Cheshire	96,800	414·70	R. Mather	(a) A. G. Pheasey
§Dacorum, Herts..............	133,100	398·00	K. Hunt	(a) K. J. Coleman
§Darlington, Co. Durham	99,700	356·00	H. R. C. Owen	(a) E. Roberts
§Dartford, Kent	78,400	324·70	C. R. Shepherd	(a) A. R. Bassam
Daventry, Northants...........	63,000	353·92	R. J. Symons, RD	Dr. R. A. Sladden

° Town Manager.

District	Estimated Resident Population 1988	Community charge per head 1990 £	Chief Executive (*Clerk)	Chairman 1990–91 (a) Mayor (b) Lord Mayor
DERBY	215,300	399·00	R. H. Cowlishaw	(a) B. Chadwick
Derbyshire Dales	66,900	427·00	D. Wheatcroft	Mrs. E. M. Plumbly
Derwentside, Co. Durham	85,900	332·00	N. F. Johnson	Mrs. M. Armstrong
Dover, Kent	106,400	295·00	J. P. Moir, TD	P. A. Watkins
DURHAM	85,900	353·00	C. G. Firmin	(a) W. H. Hartwell
Easington, Co. Durham	94,900	272·00	T. Robinson†	D. Raine
§Eastbourne, East Sussex	80,300	385·00	C. A. Bloor	(a) A. Vickers
East Cambridgeshire	60,600	303·30	T. T. G. Hardy	H. J. Brooks
East Devon	118,100	340·34	F. J. Vallender	W. J. Thorne
East Dorset	79,600	353·00	A. Breakwell	G. W. Ridge
East Hampshire	102,500	362·50	B. P. Roynon	Mrs. E. A. F. Wilson
East Hertfordshire	118,700	370·55	D. J. Anstey	R. A. Martin
§Eastleigh, Hants.	101,000	368·00	M. C. Brainsby	(a) P. F. W. Hoadley
East Lindsey, Lincs.	117,700	272·13	A. W. Silcox-Crowe	R. W. Scott
East Northamptonshire	66,500	294·67	R. K. Heath	Mrs. G. M. Murdin
East Staffordshire	95,800	333·69	F. W. Saunders	P. Haynes
§East Yorkshire, Humberside	84,800	326·00	J. H. Gibson	(a) R. Saul
Eden, Cumbria	46,300	295·00	I. W. Bruce	J. M. Carlyle
§Ellesmere Port and Neston, Cheshire	79,700	406·00	S. Ewbank	(a) C. O'Brien
§Elmbridge, Surrey	107,100	448·00	D. W. L. Jenkins	(a) K. M. N. Robertson
Epping Forest, Essex	111,800	381·03	A. V. Hackman	E. B. Hudspeth
§Epsom and Ewell, Surrey	67,500	452·00	D. J. Smith	(a) R. L. Lewis
§Erewash, Derbyshire.	107,900	419·00	G. A. Pook (*acting*)	(a) J. W. Fildes
EXETER, Devon	99,600	344·00	B. Frowd	(a) G. A. Clark
§Fareham, Hants.	100,300	360·00	O. D. Ellis	(a) E. A. Crouch
Fenland, Cambs.	73,200	291·00	E. S. Thompson	R. C. Lake
Forest Heath, Suffolk	57,600	363·91	J. F. Gale	H. Adam
Forest of Dean, Glos.	78,000	335·20	P. R. Starling	A. C. Cooper
§Fylde, Lancs.	73,200	387·11	J. P. Johnson	(a) Mrs. M. E. Hall
§Gedling, Notts.	110,300	369·00	W. Brown	(a) J. H. Andrews
§Gillingham, Kent.	95,300	284·79	J. A. McBride	(a) K. E. T. Jury
§Glanford, Humberside	72,100	357·00	D. D. H. Cameron	(a) T. E. Atherton
GLOUCESTER	90,500	353·72	G. Garbutt	(a) A. J. Potts
§Gosport, Hants.	76,900	339·80	W. D. Hooper	(a) S. Leyland
§Gravesham, Kent	90,200	293·00	E. V. J. Seager	(a) D. E. Menzies
§Great Grimsby, Humberside	89,100	384·00	R. S. G. Bennett	(a) Mrs. H. Hooton
§Great Yarmouth, Norfolk	88,900	325·00	K. G. Ward	(a) W. Dougal
§Guildford, Surrey	123,300	397·00	D. T. Watts	(a) Mrs. M. Lloyd-Jones
§Halton, Cheshire	124,000	395·00	R. Turton	(a) W. R. Flynn
Hambleton, North Yorks.	77,200	307·81	C. Spencer	Mrs. M. Potter
Harborough, Leics.	66,900	365·00	J. Ballantyne	D. Hobbs
Harlow, Essex	72,000	425·00	D. F. Byrne	S. A. Warner
§Harrogate, North Yorks.	147,000	360·00	J. V. Lovell	(a) E. C. Waight
Hart, Hants.	85,900	380·55	M. W. Tyler	Mrs. A. Abbott
§Hartlepool, Cleveland	88,400	385·00	B. J. Dinsdale	(a) J. Lynch
§Hastings, East Sussex	83,100	380·00	R. A. Carrier	(a) P. Smith
§Havant, Hants.	117,500	338·90	D. E. Ridley	(a) Mrs. B. G. Moss
HEREFORD	49,000	289·00	C. E. S. Willis	(a) Mrs. J. E. Kelly
§Hertsmere, Hertfordshire	88,600	413·74	J. N. Pearson	(a) T. J. Gilligan
§High Peak, Derbyshire.	84,300	388·30	R. P. H. Brady	(a) P. Coackley
§Hinckley and Bosworth, Leics.	96,300	346·83	F. Shaw	(a) R. Watchorn
§Holderness, Humberside	50,500	359·80	A. Johnson	(a) R. Stephenson
Horsham, West Sussex	108,000	297·00	M. J. Pearson	Mrs. M. I. Ward
§Hove, East Sussex	90,700	329·97	J. P. Teasdale	(a) F. E. Dupré
Huntingdonshire, Cambs.	147,700	298·06	T. J. Gee	J. C. Mugglestone
§Hyndburn, Lancs.	78,900	315·00	M. J. Wedgeworth	(a) W. B. Sumner
§Ipswich, Suffolk	114,900	440·00	J. D. Hehir	(a) C. J. West
Kennet, Wilts.	67,700	297·73	P. L. Owens	G. A. Taylor
Kerrier, Cornwall	86,800	325·76	G. G. Cox	H. Eva
§Kettering, Northants.	74,600	323·00	T. P. Williams	(a) A. Gordon
§King's Lynn and W. Norfolk	134,000	281·00	A. E. Pask	(a) Wg. Cdr. V. A. Stapley, OBE
KINGSTON UPON HULL, Humberside	247,000	307·00	A. B. Wood	(b) L. A. Taylor
§Kingswood, Avon	89,700	393·67	A. Smith	(a) G. J. Rogers
LANCASTER, Lancs.	131,200	385·50	W. Pearson	(a) E. Simpson

† Principal Chief Officer.

District	Estimated Resident Population 1988	Community charge per head 1990 £	Chief Executive (*Clerk)	Chairman 1990–91 (a) Mayor (b) Lord Mayor
§Langbaurgh-on-Tees, Cleveland	144,800	420·00	K. Abigail	(a) Mrs. B. Lythgoe
LEICESTER	278,600	405·00	D. Mellor	(b) P. D. Kimberlin
Leominster, Hereford and Worcs.	39,300	275·71	G. R. Chilton	G. B. Bray
Lewes, East Sussex	90,800	351·35	C. W. Mann	Mrs. F. E. Tufnell
Lichfield, Staffs.	93,800	349·24	J. T. Thompson	G. T. Kemp
LINCOLN	80,400	284·00	C. J. Thomas	(a) D. B. Jackson
§Luton, Beds.	167,600	402·80	J. C. Southwell	(a) J. M. Goldsmith
§Macclesfield, Cheshire	152,300	428·12	B. W. Longden	(a) K. Jagger
§Maidstone, Kent	136,100	327·30	J. D. Makepeace	(a) Mrs. M. Black
Maldon, Essex	53,600	339·00	T. K. Griffin	K. S. Munnion
Malvern Hills, Hereford and Worcs.	87,900	331·07	M. J. Jones	W. M. Johns
Mansfield, Notts.	100,000	378·00	R. P. Goad	J. Abell
§Medina, Isle of Wight	73,000	342·00	J. Sprake‡‡	(a) T. P. Cunningham
§Melton, Leics.	43,500	338·39	P. J. G. Herrick°	(a) G. Y.-C. Green
Mendip, Somerset	94,000	360·00	G. Jeffs	Mrs. J. C. Mackereth
Mid Bedfordshire	114,900	396·00	P. A. Freeman	M. J. Randall
Mid Devon	63,300	335·46	R. C. Greensmith	Air Vice-Marshal D. L. Attlee, CB, LVO
§Middlesbrough, Cleveland	143,100	429·00	J. R. Foster	(a) Ms. M. Barker
Mid Suffolk	77,600	332·22	H. McFarlane	B. R. P. Siffleet
Mid Sussex	120,000	317·38	B. J. Grimshaw	Mrs. C. Preston
§Milton Keynes, Bucks.	177,600	398·00	M. J. Murray	(a) Ms. B. C. Hanks
Mole Valley, Surrey	76,100	387·00	A. A. Huggins	R. Tring
Newark and Sherwood, Notts.	103,900	363·99	V. G. Crawley	D. Whicher
Newbury, Berks.	138,600	385·00	P. E. McMahon	W. A. Palmer, CBE
§Newcastle under Lyme, Staffs.	117,500	349·00	E. Wetherell	(a) J. Whalley
New Forest, Hants.	163,200	328·00	P. A. D. Hyde	D. S. Burdle
§Northampton	182,100	349·00	R. J. B. Morris	(a) G. P. Howes
Northavon, Avon	130,800	412·66	F. Maude	Mrs. T. I. Smith
§North Bedfordshire	136,700	397·65	L. W. Gould	(a) R. L. Oliver
North Cornwall	71,700	311·45	D. H. Westwell	H. S. Medland
North Devon	84,300	320·00	R. D. Hall	J. W. J. Milton
North Dorset	54,600	295·00	A. J. Bridgeman	G. A. Pitt-Rivers
North East Derbyshire	96,700	412·00	Mrs. C. A. Gilby	R. W. Brunt
North Hertfordshire	112,300	397·53	K. Sutton	H. Greenfield
North Kesteven, Lincs.	84,000	278·00	S. M. Peatfield	Mrs. M. H. Brighton
North Norfolk	94,700	284·88	T. V. Nolan	C. C. Durrant
North Shropshire	56,200	320·00	K. Flood	D. Evans
§North Warwickshire	59,100	385·23	D. Monks	(a) Mrs. A. Lewis
North West Leicestershire	79,500	363·00	J. E. White	A. Pearson
North Wiltshire	113,300	300·12	H. Miles	N. L. Hills
NORWICH, Norfolk	117,300	365·00	J. R. Packer	(b) B. Smith
NOTTINGHAM	273,500	390·00	E. F. Cantle	(b) C. Gibson
§Nuneaton and Bedworth, Warwickshire	116,000	386·00	J. Walton‡‡	(a) M. J. Jones
§Oadby and Wigston, Leics.	51,500	370·00	J. B. Burton*	(a) J. W. Royce
§Oswestry, Shropshire	32,500	330·29	D. A. Towers	(a) Mrs. B. V. Gull
OXFORD	115,400	489·00	R. S. Block	(b) Mrs. Q. L. Hamilton
§Pendle, Lancs.	84,300	299·00	F. Wood	(a) Mrs. D. J. Allen
Penwith, Cornwall	59,300	312·57	M. J. Furneaux†	J. F. W. Jago
PETERBOROUGH, Cambs.	152,800	360·00	P. B. Sidebottom	(a) A. A. Sapey
PLYMOUTH, Devon	258,100	350·00	M. S. Boxall	(b) J. Finnigan
§Poole, Dorset	130,700	325·00	I. K. D. Andrews*	(a) Mrs. A. M. Stribley
PORTSMOUTH, Hants.	183,800	308·50	R. Trist	(b) S. Rapson
§Preston, Lancs.	128,100	389·00	A. Owens	(a) A. J. Richardson
Purbeck, Dorset	46,200	284·47	P. B. Croft	V. A. Stone
§Reading, Berks.	132,400	447·00	G. Filkin	(a) G. W. Canning
§Redditch, Hereford and Worcs.	77,500	345·46	D. H. Phipps	(a) Mrs. K. J. Tyers
§Reigate and Banstead, Surrey	113,600	446·00	C. T. Pollard	(a) N. C. Smith
§Restormel, Cornwall	85,700	318·72	D. Brown	(a) K. W. Hughes
§Ribble Valley, Lancs.	52,800	355·39	O. Hopkins	(a) R. H. Jones
Richmondshire, North Yorks.	51,600	272·00	M. F. Tooze	Mrs. K. M. Carr
ROCHESTER UPON MEDWAY, Kent	146,700	248·00	R. I. Gregory	(a) Mrs. E. J. Chitty
Rochford, Essex	74,400	383·00	A. G. Cooke	B. Crick

‡‡ Borough General Manager.   ° Borough Secretary.   † Director of Central Services.

District	Estimated Resident Population 1988	Community charge per head 1990 £	Chief Executive (* Clerk)	Chairman 1990–91 (a) Mayor (b) Lord Mayor
§Rossendale, Lancs.	64,600	337·00	J. S. Hartley	(a) J. P. Dunne
Rother, East Sussex	84,700	352·00	D. F. Powell	B. Kentfield
§Rugby, Warwicks.	86,300	346·00	J. S. R. Lawton	(a) Mrs. J. Parsons
§Runnymede, Surrey	71,300	295·00	T. N. Williams	(a) P. Jones
§Rushcliffe, Notts.	99,300	382·21	J. Saxton	(a) P. S. Lawson
§Rushmoor, Hants.	77,000	325·00	D. Hartley	(a) A. M. Ferrier
Rutland, Leics.	36,500	370·00	(vacant)	E. F. Rippington
Ryedale, North Yorks.	90,800	283·15	D. Cudworth	E. Ibbotson
St. Albans, Herts.	128,600	394·00	E. A. Hackford	(a) M. MacMillan
§St. Edmundsbury, Suffolk	92,300	317·71	G. R. N. Toft	(a) R. Self
Salisbury, Wilts.	101,000	312·00	D. R. J. Rawlinson	Mrs. E. M. R. Casley
§Scarborough, North Yorks.	105,500	274·65	J. M. Trebble	(a) C. C. Mann
§Scunthorpe, Humberside	60,500	356·00	I. M. Hutchinson	(a) A. V. Skinner
Sedgefield, Co. Durham	88,400	274·74	A. J. Roberts	V. Robson
Sedgemoor, Somerset	96,400	349·57	D. D. Tremlett	Mrs. J. M. Hooper
Selby, North Yorks.	90,900	277·29	J. C. Edwards	S. Beaumont
Sevenoaks, Kent	107,300	304·38	B. C. Cova, MBE	A. L. Trethowan
Shepway, Kent................	87,600	342·33	R. H. Summers	W. H. Payne
§Shrewsbury and Atcham	90,900	324·51	D. M. Clarke	(a) Mrs. B. J. Coward
§Slough, Berks.	100,300	359·00	A. Bhattacharya*	(a) V. Hills
Southampton, Hants.	196,700	317·00	E. A. Urquhart	(a) Mrs. M. Key
South Bedfordshire...........	111,500	408·02	T. D. Rix	P. G. J. Roberts
South Bucks.	60,000	393·17	S. R. Jobson	Mrs. P. H. Watkins
South Cambridgeshire	119,300	328·29	B. J. Hancock	J. B. H. Impey
South Derbyshire	71,600	438·50	T. Day	J. T. Ford
§Southend-on-Sea, Essex	165,400	378·00	D. Moulson*	(a) D. Ascroft
South Hams, Devon	75,700	327·93	F. G. Palmer	M. Beaumont
South Herefordshire...........	51,100	273·31	A. Hughes	Mrs. A. Carter
South Holland, Lincs.	66,400	281·76	C. J. Simpkins	R. Gaunt
South Kesteven, Lincs.	105,300	278·00	K. R. Cann	Mrs. M. Clark
South Lakeland, Cumbria	100,200	345·55	A. F. Winstanley*	E. Proctor
South Norfolk	100,700	302·46	A. G. T. Kellett	Mrs. V. K. Alexander
South Northamptonshire	66,800	351·04	C. Nye	G. V. Smith
South Oxfordshire	131,100	442·44	J. B. Chirnside	T. C. Lester
§South Ribble, Lancs.	100,200	366·50	J. B. R. Leadbetter	(a) Mrs. E. M. Nicholls
South Shropshire	35,900	305·00	G. C. Biggs	Maj. A. H. Coles, TD
South Somerset	141,800	362·94	D. J. Ashford	Mrs. J. P. Clark
South Staffordshire	108,100	315·60	G. J. Haywood	R. J. Crompton
§South Wight, IOW	56,900	370·00	D. W. Jaggar	(a) Mrs. W. D. Hollis
§Spelthorne, Surrey	85,800	368·00	M. B. Taylor	(a) H. R. Jaffer
§Stafford	117,900	336·00	J. K. M. Krawiec*	(a) M. R. Heenan
Staffordshire Moorlands	97,200	314·35	A. W. Law	M. Ward
§Stevenage, Herts.	73,700	435·00	H. L. Miller	(a) Mrs. J. Lloyd
§Stockton-on-Tees, Cleveland ..	176,800	428·00	F. F. Theobalds*	(a) Mrs. G. Pragnell
Stoke-on-Trent, Staffs.	246,800	313·00	S. W. Titchener	(b) Ms. S. Halfpenny
Stratford-upon-Avon, Warwicks................	106,800	374·85	I. B. Prosser	Sir William Lawrence, Bt.
Stroud, Glos..................	110,500	373·23	R. M. Ollin	G. S. Reeves
Suffolk Coastal	111,300	389·77	D. L. Blay	M. Rowland
§Surrey Heath	83,600	399·00	N. M. Pughe	(a) A. J. Barnett
§Swale, Kent.................	115,300	298·97	W. Croydon, CBE	(a) Mrs. J. M. Newman
§Tamworth, Staffs.	68,100	329·00	G. Morrell	(a) R. Birbeck
Tandridge, Surrey.............	75,700	375·00	C. W. Rockall	A. N. Dumville
§Taunton Deane, Somerset	94,100	349·67	P. F. Berman	(a) P. Lee
Teesdale, Co. Durham..........	24,800	241·54	C. E. Fell	K. Walton
Teignbridge, Devon	107,900	364·64	P. B. Young	A. W. Thompson
Tendring, Essex	129,600	342·00	D. Mitchell-Gears	W. Bleakley
§Test Valley, Hants.	102,300	325·00	G. Blythe	(a) Mrs. P. D. White
§Tewkesbury, Glos.	87,200	355·00	R. A. Wheeler	(a) Mrs. B. E. Evans
§Thamesdown, Wilts.	168,800	328·20	D. M. Kent	(a) D. Montaut
Thanet, Kent	129,700	300·00	I. G. Gill	W. H. Dawson
Three Rivers, Herts.	80,100	419·70	A. Robertson	Mrs. A. Shaw
§Thurrock, Essex	124,400	414·00	K. Barnes	(a) K. Evans
§Tonbridge and Malling, Kent ..	101,200	311·00	T. Thompson	(a) M. Dobson
§Torbay, Devon	119,000	395·00	D. P. Hudson	(a) Mrs. F. Johnson
Torridge, Devon	51,200	284·67	R. K. Brasington	Mrs. M. E. E. Dart
§Tunbridge Wells, Kent........	99,300	315·00	R. J. Stone	(a) P. Holman

District	Esti-mated Resident Popula-tion 1988	Community charge per head 1990 £	Chief Executive (* Clerk)	Chairman 1990–91 (a) Mayor (b) Lord Mayor
Tynedale, Northumberland	56,300	383·23	A. Baty	D. Elwell
Uttlesford, Essex	66,100	348·00	J. F. Vernon	Mrs. D. M. Haggerwood
Vale of White Horse, Oxon......	112,300	413·00	D. J. Heavens°	J. Jones, OBE
§Vale Royal, Cheshire	113,300	385·00	W. R. T. Woods	(a) R. J. Woodier
Wansbeck, Northumberland	59,000	348·00	A. G. White	Mrs. E. Tully
Wansdyke, Avon	82,100	398·50	P. May‡	G. J. Wood
§Warrington, Cheshire	186,100	391·10	M. I. M. Sanders	(a) G. Stokes
Warwick	116,400	386·00	M. J. Ward	G. B. Guest
§Watford, Herts................	75,100	403·58	D. Plank	(a) Ms. V Conlon
Waveney, Suffolk	106,500	349·46	M. Berridge	T. C. Chipperfield
§Waverley, Surrey	109,700	411·00	G. W. Nuttall	(a) Brig. G. E. Dennison, OBE
Wealden, East Sussex	133,900	348·40	D. R. Holness	B. H. F. Trew
Wear Valley, Co. Durham	64,100	308·00	F. A. Dobson†	K. Reed
§Wellingborough, Northants....	66,300	288·00	W. B. Veal	(a) G. A. Willmott
Welwyn Hatfield, Herts.	93,500	433·00	D. Riddle	J. Lonergan
§West Devon....................	43,800	333·55	J. S. Ligo	(a) O. R. Phillips
West Dorset	85,300	301·18	R. C. Rennison	M. J. Pengelly
West Lancashire	105,400	377·01	J. Cowdall	D. S. Elliot
West Lindsey, Lincs.	76,800	285·73	R. W. Nelsey	R. H. P. Ballerini
West Oxfordshire	97,800	412·17	N. J. B. Robson	Mrs. M. I. Frost
West Somerset	31,500	334·65	H. Close	F. J. Hutchings
West Wiltshire................	106,200	334·00	D. G. Latham	A. G. Phillips, OBE
§Weymouth and Portland, Dorset	64,100	335·00	M. N. Ashby	(a) P. J. W. Rendall
WINCHESTER, Hants.	96,000	358·81	D. H. Cowan	(a) Mrs. P. Peskett
§Windsor and Maidenhead, Berks..........................	127,400	449·31	G. B. Blacker	(a) R. Austin
§Woking, Surrey	86,200	358·70	P. Russell	(a) R. H. B. Lofting
Wokingham, Berks.	150,000	434·00	N. B. J. Gurney	Mrs. J. Mayers
Woodspring, Avon	189,000	432·00	C. A. Stephens	W. R. German
WORCESTER	81,200	339·00	R. G. Grant	(a) P. Elkins
§Worthing, West Sussex	98,200	296·00	M. J. Ball	(a) M. Clinch
Wrekin, Shropshire	134,200	382·78	D. G. Hutchinson	G. Bould
Wychavon, Hereford and Worcs.	101,000	315·50	T. Du Sautoy	Mrs. E. Hope
Wycombe, Bucks...............	156,300	400·36	R. J. Cummins	F. V. J. Sweatman
§Wyre, Lancs..................	103,000	375·00	M. Brown	(a) C. R. Ashworth
Wyre Forest, Hereford and Worcs.	94,400	340·58	A. S. Dick	N. L. Broome
YORK, North Yorks.	100,600	264·00	J. Cairns	(b) K. Wood

°Director of Administration.   ‡General Manager.   †Managing Director.

PRINCIPAL ENGLISH CITIES

BIRMINGHAM

BIRMINGHAM (West Midlands) is Britain's second city and the largest metropolitan district in the country. It is a focal point in national communications networks with a rapidly expanding International Airport. The generally accepted derivation of 'Birmingham' is the *ham* or dwelling-place of the *ing* or the family of *Beorma*, presumed to have been a Saxon. During the Industrial Revolution the town grew into a major manufacturing centre. In 1889 Birmingham was granted City status.

Despite the decline in manufacturing, Birmingham is still a major hardware trade and motor component industry centre. Recent development includes the National Exhibition Centre and the Aston Science Park. An Urban Development Agency has been set up.

The principal buildings are the Town Hall, built in 1832–34; the Council House (1879); Victoria Law Courts (1891); the University (1909); the 13th century Church of St. Martin (rebuilt 1873); the Cathedral (formerly St. Philip's Church) (1711) and the Roman Catholic Cathedral of St. Chad (1839–41).

BRADFORD

BRADFORD (West Yorkshire), 192 miles NNW of London, is the administrative centre of the Metropolitan District of Bradford. The District covers an area of 91,444 acres and lies on the southern edge of the Yorkshire Dales National Park, including within its boundaries the village of Haworth, home of the Brontë sisters and Ilkley Moor.

Originally a Saxon township, Bradford received a market charter in 1251 but developed only slowly until the industrialization of the textile industry brought rapid growth during the 19th century. The prosperity of that period is reflected in much of the city's architecture, particularly the public buildings—City Hall (1873), Wool Exchange (1867), St. George's Hall (Concert Hall, 1853), Cartwright Hall

(Art Gallery, 1904) and Technical College (1882). Other chief buildings are the Cathedral (15th century) and Bolling Hall (14th century).

Textiles still play an important part in the city's economy but industry is now more broadly based, including engineering and micro-electronics. The city has a strong banking, insurance and building society sector, and a growing tourism industry.

BRISTOL

BRISTOL (Avon) is the largest non-metropolitan district in population in the country, and lies 119 miles W. of London. The present municipal area is 10,954 hectares.

Bristol's commercial port systems comprise the largest municipally owned port in the country. The Avonmouth dock complex and Royal Portbury Dock handle import and export cargoes. Principal imports include cocoa, timber, metals, animal feeding stuffs, oil products, chemicals, vehicles and molasses. The Royal Portbury Dock, opened in Aug. 1977, is capable of accommodating up to six vessels of 70,000 d.w.t.

The chief buildings include the 12th century Cathedral (with later additions), with Norman chapter house and gateway, the 14th century Church of St. Mary Redcliffe, Wesley's Chapel, Broadmead, the Merchant Venturers' Almshouses, the Council House (1956), Guildhall, Exchange (erected from the designs of John Wood in 1743), Cabot Tower, the University and Clifton College. The Roman Catholic Cathedral at Clifton was opened in 1973.

The Clifton Suspension Bridge, with a span of 702 feet over the Avon, was projected by Brunel in 1836 but was not completed until 1864. Brunel's SS *Great Britain*, the first ocean going propeller driven ship, is now being restored in the City Docks from where she was launched in 1843. The docks themselves have been extensively restored and redeveloped.

Bristol was a Royal Borough before the Norman Conquest. The earliest form of the name is *Bricgstow*. In 1373 it received from Edward III a charter granting it county status.

CAMBRIDGE

CAMBRIDGE, a settlement far older than its ancient University, lies on the Cam or Granta, 51 miles north of London. It has an area of 10,060 acres.

The city is a county town and regional headquarters. Its industries include electronics, flour milling, cement making and the manufacture of scientific instruments. Among its open spaces are Jesus Green, Sheep's Green, Coe Fen, Parker's Piece, Christ's Pieces, the University Botanic Garden, and the Backs, or lawns and gardens through which the Cam winds behind the principal line of college buildings. East of the Cam, King's Parade, upon which stand Great St. Mary's Church, Gibbs' Senate House and King's College Chapel with Wilkins' screen, joins Trumpington Street to form one of the most beautiful thoroughfares in Europe.

University and college buildings provide the outstanding features of Cambridge architecture but several churches (especially St. Benet's, the oldest building in the City, and St. Sepulchre's, the Round Church) also are notable. The modern Guildhall (1939) stands on a site of which at least part has held municipal buildings since 1224.

CANTERBURY

CANTERBURY, the Metropolitan City of the Anglican Communion, has a history going back to prehistoric times. It was the Roman *Durovernum*

Cantiacorum and the Saxon *Cant-wara-byrig* (stronghold of the men of Kent). Here in 597 St. Augustine began the conversion of the English to Christianity, when Ethelbert, King of Kent, was baptized.

Of the Benedictine St. Augustine's Abbey, burial place of the Jutish Kings of Kent (whose capital Canterbury was) only extensive ruins remain. St. Martin's Church, on the eastern outskirts of the City, is stated by Bede to have been the place of worship of Queen Bertha, the Christian wife of King Ethelbert, before the advent of St. Augustine.

In 1170 the rivalry of Church and State culminated in the murder in Canterbury Cathedral, by Henry II's knights, of Archbishop Thomas Becket, whose shrine became a great centre of pilgrimage as described by Chaucer in his *Canterbury Tales*. After the Reformation pilgrimages ceased, but the prosperity of the City was strengthened by an influx of Huguenot refugees, who introduced weaving. The Elizabethan poet and playwright Christopher Marlowe was born and reared in Canterbury, and there are literary associations also with Defoe, Dickens, Joseph Conrad and Somerset Maugham.

The Cathedral, with architecture ranging from the 11th to 15th centuries, is world famous. Modern pilgrims are attracted particularly to the Martyrdom, The Black Prince's Tomb, the Warriors' Chapel and the many examples of medieval stained glass.

The medieval City Walls are built on Roman foundations and the 14th century West Gate is one of the finest buildings of its kind in the country.

The 1,000 seat Marlowe Theatre is the base for the Canterbury International Festival of the Arts each autumn.

CARLISLE

CARLISLE is situated at the confluence of the River Eden and River Caldew, 309 miles north west of London and a few miles from the Scottish border. It has an area of 254,955 acres, and was granted a charter in 1158.

The city stands at the western end of Hadrian's Wall and dates from the original Roman settlement of *Luguvalium*. Granted to Scotland in the 10th century, Carlisle is not included in the Domesday Book. William Rufus reclaimed the area in 1092 and the Castle and city walls were built to guard Carlisle and the western border; the Citadel is a Tudor addition to protect the south of the city. Until the Union of the Crowns in 1603, Carlisle changed hands several times and was frequently besieged. During the Civil War the city remained Royalist; in 1745 it supported the Young Pretender.

The Cathedral, originally a 12th century Augustinian priory, was enlarged in the 13th and 14th centuries after the diocese was created in 1133. To the south is a restored Tithe Barn and nearby the 18th century church of St. Cuthbert, the third to stand on a site dating from the 7th century.

Carlisle is the major shopping, commercial and agricultural centre for the area, and industries include the manufacture of metal goods, biscuits and textiles. However, the largest employer is the services sector, notably in retailing and transport. The city has an important communications position at the centre of a network of major roads, as an important stage on the main west coast rail services, and with its own airport at Crosby.

CHESTER

CHESTER is situated on the River Dee, 189 miles north west of London. The city administers an area of 173 square miles and was granted Borough and City status in 1974.

Chester's recorded history dates from the 1st century when the Romans founded the fortress of *Deva*. The city's name is derived from the Latin *castra* (a camp or encampment). During the Middle Ages, Chester was the principal port of north west England but declined with the silting of the Dee estuary and competition from Liverpool. The city was also an important military centre, notably during Edward I's Welsh campaigns and the Elizabethan Irish campaigns. During the Civil War, Chester supported the King and was besieged from 1643–46. Chester's first charter was granted c. 1175 and the city was incorporated in 1506. The office of Sheriff is the earliest created in the country (c. 1120s), and the Mayor also enjoys the title 'Admiral of the Dee'.

The city's architectural features include the city walls (an almost complete two mile circuit), the unique Rows (covered galleries above the street level shops), the Victorian Gothic Town Hall (1869), the Castle (rebuilt 1788 and 1822) and numerous half-timbered buildings. The Cathedral was a Benedictine abbey until the Dissolution. Remaining monastic buildings include the chapter house, refectory and cloisters and there is a modern free-standing bell tower. The Norman church of St. John the Baptist was a Cathedral church in the early Middle Ages.

Chester is primarily a regional service centre and has considerable tourist appeal. In 1984 the city was awarded Development Area status which has attracted a range of nationally known companies to expand or locate in Chester.

COVENTRY

COVENTRY (West Midlands) is 92 miles NW of London, and an important industrial centre, producing cars, machine tools, agricultural machinery, man-made fibres, composite materials and telecommunications equipment.

The city owes its beginning to Leofric, Earl of Mercia and his wife Godiva who, in 1043, founded a Benedictine monastery. The guildhall of St. Mary dates from the 14th century, three of the city's churches date from the 14th and 15th centuries and 16th century almshouses may still be seen. Coventry's first cathedral was destroyed at the Reformation, its second in the 1940 blitz (its walls and spire remain) and the new cathedral designed by Sir Basil Spence, consecrated in 1962, now draws innumerable visitors.

Coventry is the home of the University of Warwick and its Science Park, the rapidly-expanding Westwood Business Park and the Museum of British Road Transport.

DERBY

DERBY stands on the banks of the River Derwent, 127 miles NNW of London, and covers an area of 30 square miles. The name Derby dates back to 880 when the Danes settled in the locality and changed the original Saxon name of 'Northworthy' to 'Deoraby'.

Derby has a wide range of industries: its products include aero engines, lawn mowers, pipework, specialized mechanical engineering equipment, textiles, chemicals, plastics and the Royal Crown Derby porcelain. The city is an established railway centre, the site of British Rail's Technical Centre with its research laboratories.

Buildings of interest include St Peter's Church and the Old Abbey Building (14th century), the Cathedral (1525), St Mary's Roman Catholic Church (1839) and the Industrial Museum, formerly the Old Silk Mill (1721). The traditional city centre is complemented by the new Eagle Centre and 'out-of-centre' retail developments. In addition to the Derby

Playhouse, the Assembly Rooms are a multi-purpose venue.

The first charter granting a Mayor and Aldermen was that of Charles I in 1637. Previous charters date back to 1154. It was granted City status in 1977.

DURHAM

The city of DURHAM is a district in the county of Durham and covers an area of 73 square miles. The city is a major tourist attraction in the county because of its prominent Norman Cathedral and Castle set high on a wooded peninsula overlooking the River Wear. The Cathedral was founded as a shrine for the body of St. Cuthbert in 995. The present building dates from 1093 and among its many treasures is the tomb of the Venerable Bede (673–735). Durham's Prince Bishops had unique powers up to 1836, being lay rulers as well as religious leaders. As a palatinate Durham could have its own army, nobility, coinage and courts. The Castle was the main seat of the Prince Bishops for nearly 800 years; it is now used as a college by the University.

The University, founded on the initiative of Bishop William Van Mildert, is England's third oldest. Its students live in 14 colleges spread across the city.

Among other buildings of interest is the Guildhall in the Market Place which dates originally from the 14th century. Much work has been carried out to conserve this area, forming part of the city's major contribution to the Council of Europe's Urban Renaissance Campaign. Annual events include Durham's Regatta in June (claimed to be the oldest rowing event in Britain) and the Annual Gala (formerly Durham Miners' Gala) in July.

In the past 20 years the economy of Durham has undergone a significant change with the replacement of mining as the dominant feature by 'white collar' employment. Although still a predominantly rural area, the industrial and commercial sector is growing and a wide range of manufacturing and service industries are based on industrial estates in and around the City area.

EXETER

EXETER lies on the River Exe 170 miles SW of London and 10 miles from the sea. It covers an area of 11,661 acres and was granted a Royal Charter by Henry II.

The Romans founded *Isca Dumnoniorum* in the 1st century AD, and in the 3rd century a stone wall (most of which remains) was built, providing protection against Saxon, and then Danish invasions. After the Conquest, the city led resistance to William in the west, until reduced by siege. The Normans built the motte and bailey castle of Rougemont, the gatehouse and one tower of which remain, although the rest was pulled down in 1784. The first bridge across the Exe was built in the 13th century. The city's role as a port declined due to the silting of the river, but was somewhat restored by the construction in the 1560s of the first ship canal in England. Exeter was the Royalist headquarters in the West during the Civil War.

The diocese of Exeter was established by Edward the Confessor in 1050, although a church existed on the Cathedral site in the early 10th century. A new cathedral was built in the 12th century but the present building was begun c.1275 in the Gothic style, although incorporating the Norman towers, and completed about a century later with the West Front. The Guildhall dates from the 12th century and there are many other medieval buildings in the city, as well as architecture in the Georgian and Regency styles (Custom House, The Quay). Damage suffered by bombing in 1942 led to the redevelopment of the city centre.

Exeter's prosperity from medieval times was based on trade in wool and woollen cloth (commemorated by Tuckers Hall), which remained at its height until the late 18th century when export trade was hit by the French Wars. Subsequently Exeter has developed as an administrative and commercial centre, notably in the distributive trades, light manufacturing industries and tourism.

KINGSTON UPON HULL

HULL (officially 'Kingston upon Hull') lies in the mostly rural County of Humberside, at the junction of the River Hull with the Humber, 22 miles from the North Sea and 205 miles N. of London. The municipal area is 17,535 acres.

Hull is one of the great seaports of the United Kingdom. It has docks covering a water area of 172 acres, equipped to handle cargoes by unit-load techniques, and is a departure point for car ferry services to continental Europe. There is a great variety of industry and service industries, as well as increasing tourism and conference business.

The city, restored after very heavy air raid damage during World War II, has good office and administrative buildings, its municipal centre being the Guildhall, its educational centre the University of Hull and its religious centre the Parish Church of the Holy Trinity. The old Town area is being renovated and includes a new marina and shopping complex. Just west of the city is the Humber Bridge, the world's longest single span suspension bridge, which was officially opened by HM The Queen in July 1981.

Kingston upon Hull was so named by Edward I. City status was accorded in 1897 and the office of Mayor raised to the dignity of Lord Mayor in 1914.

LEEDS

LEEDS (West Yorkshire), a Metropolitan District from April 1, 1974, is a junction for road, rail, canal and air services and an important commercial centre, situated in the lower Aire Valley, 195 miles by road NNW of London. The metropolitan area is 138,915 acres.

The main manufacturing industries are mechanical engineering, printing, publishing and clothing. However, 65 per cent of employment is in services, notably professional and scientific, particularly education and medicine, distributive trades, finance and banking.

The principal buildings are the Civic Hall (1933), the Town Hall (1858), the Municipal Buildings and Art Gallery (1884) with the Henry Moore Gallery (1982), the Corn Exchange (1863) and the University. The Parish Church (St. Peter's) was rebuilt in 1841; the 17th century St. John's Church has a fine interior with a famous English renaissance screen; the last remaining 18th century church is Holy Trinity, Boar Lane (1727). Kirkstall Abbey (about 3 miles from the centre of the city), founded by Henry de Lacy in 1152, is one of the most complete examples of Cistercian houses now remaining. Temple Newsam, birthplace of Lord Darnley, was acquired by the Council in 1922. The present house was largely re-built by Sir Arthur Ingram in about 1620. Adel Church, about 5 miles from the centre of the city, is a fine Norman structure.

Leeds was first incorporated by Charles I in 1626. The earliest forms of the name are *Loidis* or *Ledes*, the origins of which are obscure.

LEICESTER

LEICESTER is situated geographically in the centre of England, 100 miles N. of London. The City dates back to pre-Roman times and was one of the five Danish *Burhs*. In 1589 Queen Elizabeth I granted a Charter to the City and the ancient title was confirmed by Letters Patent in 1919. Under local government reorganization Leicester's area remained unchanged at 18,141 acres, and it retains its designation as a City.

The principal industries of the city are hosiery, knitwear, footwear manufacturing and engineering. The growth of Leicester as a hosiery centre increased rapidly from the introduction there of the first stocking frame in 1670 and today it has some of the largest hosiery factories in the world, with much of the output being exported.

The principal buildings in the city are the Town Hall, the New Walk Centre, the University, Leicester Polytechnic, De Montfort Hall, one of the finest concert halls in the provinces seating over 2,750 persons, and the Granby Halls, a major indoor sports facility. The ancient Churches of St. Martin (now Leicester Cathedral), St. Nicholas, St. Margaret, All Saints, St. Mary de Castro, and buildings such as the Guildhall, the 14th century Newarke Gate, the Castle and the Jewry Wall Roman site still exist. The Haymarket Theatre, an integral part of a large shopping and car-parking complex, was opened in 1973.

LINCOLN

Situated 143 miles N. of London and 40 miles inland on the River Witham, LINCOLN derives its name from a contraction of *Lindum Colonia*, the settlement founded in AD 48 by the Romans to command the crossing of Ermine Street and Fosse Way. Sections of the 3rd century Roman city wall can be seen, including an extant gateway (Newport Arch), and excavations have discovered traces of a sewerage system unique in Britain. The Romans also drained the surrounding fenland and created a canal system, laying the foundations of Lincoln's agricultural prosperity, and also of the city's importance in the medieval wool trade as a port and Staple town. As one of the Five Boroughs of the Danelaw, Lincoln was an important trading centre in the 9th and 10th centuries and medieval prosperity from the wool trade lasted until the 14th century, enabling local merchants to build parish churches (of which three survive), and attracting in the 12th century a Jewish community (Jew's House and Court, Aaron's House). However, the removal of the Staple to Boston in 1369 heralded a decline from which the city only recovered fully in the 19th century when improved fen drainage made Lincoln agriculturally important, and improved canal and rail links led to industrial development, mainly in the manufacture of machinery, components and engineering products.

The Castle was built shortly after the Conquest and is unusual in having two mounds; on one motte stands a Keep (Lucy's Tower) added in the 12th century. The Cathedral was begun *c.*1073 when the first Norman bishop moved the see of Lindsey to Lincoln, but was mostly destroyed by fire and earthquake in the 12th century. Rebuilding was begun by St. Hugh and completed over a century later. The Wren library contains manuscripts including one of the four surviving originals of the Magna Charta. Other notable architectural features of the city are the 12th century High Bridge, the oldest in Britain still to carry buildings, and the Guildhall situated above the 15–16th century Stonebow gateway.

LIVERPOOL

LIVERPOOL (Merseyside) on the right bank of the River Mersey, 3 miles from the Irish Sea and 210 miles NW of London, is the UK's fourth most important port and the foremost for the Atlantic trade. The municipal area of 27,864 acres includes 2,840 acres in the bed of the river Mersey. Tunnels link Liverpool with Birkenhead and Wallasey.

There are 2,100 acres of dockland on both sides of the river and the Gladstone and Royal Seaforth Docks can accommodate the largest vessels afloat. Annual tonnage of cargo handled is approximately 10,500,000 tonnes. The main imports are crude oil, grain, ores, edible oils, timber, containers and break bulk cargo. Liverpool Free Port, Britain's largest, was opened in 1984.

Liverpool was created a free borough in 1207 and a city in 1880. From the early eighteenth century it expanded rapidly with the growth of industrialization and Atlantic trade. Surviving buildings from this date include the Bluecoat Chambers (1717, formerly the Bluecoat School), the Town Hall (1754, rebuilt to the original design 1795), and buildings in Rodney Street, Canning Street and the suburbs. Notable from the 19th and 20th centuries are the Anglican Cathedral, built from the designs of Sir Giles Gilbert Scott (the foundation stone was laid in 1904, and the building was only completed in 1980), the Catholic Metropolitan Cathedral (designed by Sir Frederick Gibberd, consecrated 1967) and St. George's Hall, (1838–54), regarded as one of the finest modern examples of classical architecture. The recently refurbished Albert Dock (designed by Jesse Hartley) contains the Merseyside Maritime Museum and Tate Gallery, Liverpool. In 1852 an Act was obtained for establishing a public library, museum and art gallery: as a result Liverpool had one of the first public libraries in the country. The Brown, Picton and Hornby libraries now form one of the country's major libraries. The Victoria Building of Liverpool University, the Royal Liver, Cunard and Mersey Docks & Harbour Company buildings at the Pier Head, the Municipal Buildings and the Philharmonic Hall are other examples of the City's fine buildings. Britain's first International Garden Festival was held in Liverpool in 1984.

MANCHESTER

MANCHESTER (the *Mamucium* of the Romans, who occupied it in AD 78) is 189 miles NW of London and covers about 43 square miles.

Manchester is a commercial and industrial centre with a population engaged in engineering, chemical, clothing, food processing and textile industries. Banking and insurance are among the prime commercial activities. The city is connected with the sea by the Manchester Ship Canal, opened in 1894, 35½ miles long, and accommodating ships up to 15,000 tons. Manchester Airport handles more than 5 million passengers yearly.

The principal buildings are the Town Hall, erected in 1877 from the designs of Alfred Waterhouse, RA, together with a large extension of 1938; the Royal Exchange (1869, enlarged 1921) the Central Library (1934); Heaton Hall; the 17th century Chetham Library; the Rylands Library (1899), which includes the Althorp collection; the University precinct; the 15th century Cathedral (formerly the parish church) and the Free Trade Hall. Manchester is the home of the Hallé Orchestra, the Royal Northern College of Music, the Royal Exchange Theatre and seven public art galleries.

The town received its first charter of incorporation in 1838 and was created a city in 1853. The title of city was retained under local government reorganization.

NEWCASTLE UPON TYNE

NEWCASTLE UPON TYNE (Tyne and Wear) a Metropolitan District on the north bank of the River Tyne, is 8 miles from the North Sea, 272 miles N. of London and has an area of 27,640 acres. A Cathedral and University City, it is the administrative, commercial and cultural centre for north-east England and the principal port. It is an important manufacturing centre with a wide variety of industries.

The principal buildings include the Castle Keep (12th century), Black Gate (13th century), Blackfriars (13th century), West Walls (13th century), St. Nicholas's Cathedral (15th century, fine lantern tower), St. Andrew's Church (12th–14th century), St. John's (14th–15th century), All Saints (1786 by Stephenson), St. Mary's Roman Catholic Cathedral (1844), Trinity House (17th century), Sandhill (16th century houses), Guildhall (Georgian), Grey Street (1834–39), Central Station (1846–50), Laing Art Gallery (1904), University of Newcastle Physics Building (1962) and Medical Building (1985), Civic Centre (1963), Central Library (1969) and Eldon Square Shopping Development (1976). Open spaces include the Town Moor (927 acres) and Jesmond Dene. Eight bridges span the Tyne at Newcastle.

The City derives its name from the 'new castle' (1080) erected as a defence against the Scots. In 1400 it was made a County, and in 1882 a City.

NORWICH

NORWICH (Norfolk) is an ancient City 110 miles NE of London. It grew from an early Anglo-Saxon settlement near the confluence of the Rivers Yare and Wensum, and now serves as provincial capital for the predominantly agricultural region of East Anglia. The name is thought to relate to the most northerly of a group of Anglo-Saxon villages or 'wics'. The present City has an area of 9,655 acres. The City's first known Charter was granted in 1158 by Henry II.

Norwich serves its surrounding area as a market town and commercial centre, banking and insurance being prominent among the City's businesses. From the 14th century until the Industrial Revolution, Norwich was the regional centre of the woollen industry, but now the biggest single industry is financial services and principal trades are engineering, printing, shoemaking, double glazing, and the production of chemicals, clothing, confectionery and other foodstuffs. Norwich is accessible to seagoing vessels by means of the River Yare, entered at Great Yarmouth, 20 miles to the east.

Among many historic buildings are the Cathedral (completed in the 12th century and surmounted by a 15th century spire 315 feet in height), the Keep of the Norman Castle (now a museum and art gallery), the 15th century flint-walled Guildhall (now a tourist information centre), some thirty medieval parish churches, St. Andrew's and Blackfriars' Halls, the Tudor houses preserved in Elm Hill and the Georgian Assembly House. The University of East Anglia has been established in Norwich on a spacious site at Earlham on the City's western boundary and received its first students in 1963.

NOTTINGHAM

NOTTINGHAM (Nottinghamshire) stands on the River Trent, 124 miles NNW of London in one of the most valuable coalfields of the country connected by canal with the Atlantic and the North Sea. The municipal area is 18,364 acres.

The principal industries are hosiery, lace, bleaching, dyeing and spinning, tanning, engineering and cycle works, brewing and the manufacture of tobacco, chemicals, furniture, typewriters and mechanical products.

The chief buildings are the 17th century Nottingham Castle (restored in 1878, and now the City Museum and Gallery of Art), Wollaton Hall (1580–88) owned by the City Council and now a Natural History Museum, St. Mary's, St. Peter's, and St. Nicholas's Churches, the Roman Catholic Cathedral (Pugin, 1842–44), the Council House (1929), the Guildhall and Court House (1888), Shire Hall, Albert Hall, the University, Trent Polytechnic, Newstead Abbey, home of Lord Byron, the Theatre Royal (1865), the Playhouse (1963) and the Royal Concert Hall (1982).

Snotingaham or *Notingeham*, 'the village or home of the sons of Snot' (the Wise), is the Anglo-Saxon name for the Celtic *Tuigogobauc*, 'Cave Homes'. The City possesses a Charter of Henry II, and was created a City in 1897. Under local government reorganization, the style of City was reaccorded from April, 1974.

OXFORD

OXFORD is a University City, an important industrial centre, and a market town, with an area of 8,785 acres. Industry played a minor part in Oxford until the motor industry was established in 1912.

It is for its architecture that Oxford is of most interest to the visitor, its oldest specimens being the reputed Saxon tower of St. Michael's church, the remains of the Norman castle and city walls and the Norman church at Iffley. It is chiefly famous however for its Gothic buildings, such as the Divinity Schools, the Old Library at Merton College, William of Wykeham's New College, Magdalen College and Christ Church and many other college buildings. Later centuries are represented by the Laudian quadrangle at St. John's College, the Renaissance Sheldonian Theatre by Wren, Trinity College Chapel, and All Saints Church; Hawksmoor's mock-Gothic at All Souls College, and the 18th century Queens' College. In addition to individual buildings, High Street and Radcliffe Square, just off it, both form architectural compositions of great beauty. Most of the Colleges have gardens, those of Magdalen, New College, St. John's (designed by 'Capability' Brown) and Worcester being the largest.

PLYMOUTH

PLYMOUTH is situated on the borders of Devon and Cornwall at the confluence of the Rivers Tamar and Plym, 210 miles from London, with an area of 19,572 acres. The city has a long maritime history; it was the home port of Sir Francis Drake and the starting point for his circumnavigation of the world, as well as the last port of call for the *Mayflower* when the Pilgrim Fathers sailed for the New World in 1620. Today Plymouth is host to many international yacht races. The Barbican harbour area has many Elizabethan buildings, and on Plymouth Hoe stands the first lighthouse to be built on the Eddystone Rocks, some miles offshore.

Following extensive war damage, the city centre, comprising a large shopping centre, municipal offices, law courts and public buildings, has been re-built. The main employment is provided at the Naval Base, though many new industrial firms and service industries have become established in the post-war period and the city is a growing tourism centre. In 1982 the Theatre Royal was opened. In conjunction with the Cornwall County Council, the Tamar Bridge was constructed linking the City by road with Cornwall.

PORTSMOUTH

PORTSMOUTH occupies Portsea Island, Hampshire, with boundaries extending to the mainland. It has an area of 15½ sq. miles and is 70 miles SW of London.

Portsmouth is a centre of industry and commerce, including many high technology and manufacturing industries. It is the UK headquarters of several major international companies. HM Naval Base still has a substantial work force, although this has decreased in recent years. The commercial port and Continental Ferry Port is owned and run by the City Council, and carries passengers and vehicles to France.

A major port since the 16th century, Portsmouth is also a thriving seaside resort catering for thousands of visitors and day-trippers annually. Among many historic attractions are Lord Nelson's flagship, HMS *Victory*, the Tudor warship *Mary Rose*, Britain's first 'ironclad', HMS *Warrior*, the D-Day Museum, Charles Dickens' birthplace at 393 Old Commercial Road, the Royal Naval and Royal Marine museums, Southsea Castle (built by Henry VIII), the Round Tower and Point Battery, which for hundreds of years have guarded the entrance to Portsmouth Harbour, Fort Widley on Portsdown Hill and the Sealife Centre.

ST. ALBANS

Twenty-five miles NW of London and situated on the River Ver, ST. ALBANS' origins stem from the major Roman town of *Verulamium*. Named after the first Christian martyr in Britain, who was executed here, St. Albans has developed around the Norman Abbey and Cathedral Church (consecrated 1115), built partly of materials from the old Roman city. The museums house Iron Age and Roman artefacts and the Roman Theatre, unique in Britain, has a stage as opposed to an amphitheatre. Archaeological excavations in the city centre continue also to reveal evidence of pre-Roman, Saxon and medieval occupation.

The town's significance grew to the extent that it was a signatory and venue for the drafting of the Magna Charta. It was also the scene of major riots during the Peasants' Revolt, the French King John was imprisoned there after the Battle of Poitiers, and heavy fighting took place during the Wars of the Roses.

Previously controlled by the Abbot, the town achieved a Royal Charter in 1553 and City status in 1877. The street market, first established in 1553, is still an important feature of the city, as are many hotels and inns which survive from the days when St. Albans was an important coach stop. Tourist attractions include historic churches and houses, and a 15th century clock tower.

The city now contains a wide range of firms, with special emphasis on micro-technology and electronics, particularly in the medical field. In addition, it is the home of the Royal National Rose Society, and of Rothamsted Park, the agricultural research centre.

In 1974 the City and District of St. Albans was formed, taking in the town of Harpenden and many villages, and it now covers an area of 63 square miles.

SHEFFIELD

SHEFFIELD (South Yorkshire), the centre of the special steel and cutlery trades, is situated 159 miles NNW of London, at the junction of the Sheaf, Porter, Rivelin and Loxley with the River Don.

Sheffield has an area of 91,000 acres (nearly 150 square miles), including 4,619 acres of publicly owned parks and woodland. Though its cutlery, silverware and plate have long been famous, Sheffield has other and now more important industries—special and alloy steels, engineering and tool-making. Research in glass, metallurgy, radiotherapy and other fields is carried on.

The parish church of St. Peter and St. Paul, founded in the 12th century, became the Cathedral Church of the Diocese of Sheffield in 1914. The Roman Catholic Cathedral Church of St. Marie (founded 1847) was created Cathedral for the new diocese of Hallam in 1980. Parts of the present building date from c.1435. The principal buildings are the Town Hall (1897, 1923 and 1977), the Cutlers' Hall (1832), the University (1905 and recent extensions, including 19-storey Arts Tower), City Hall (1932), Graves Art Gallery (1934), Castle Market Building (1959), the retail market (1973), Mappin Art Gallery and the Crucible Theatre.

Sheffield was created a city in 1893 and on April 1, 1974 became a Metropolitan District Council incorporating Stocksbridge and most of the Wortley Rural area, and retained city status.

Master Cutler (1990–91) of the Company of Cutlers in Hallamshire, H. R. Sykes.

SOUTHAMPTON

SOUTHAMPTON is the leading British deep sea port on the Channel and is situated on one of the finest natural harbours in the world. The first Charter was granted by Henry II and Southampton was created a county of itself in 1447. In February 1964, The Queen granted city status by Royal Charter. The city has an area of 12,071 acres excluding tidal waters.

There have been Roman and Saxon settlements on the site of the city, which has been an important port since the time of the Conquest due to its natural deep-water harbour. The oldest church is St. Michael's (1070) which has a black tournai marble font and an unusually tall spire built in the 18th century as a landmark for navigators of Southampton Water. Other buildings and monuments within the city walls are the Tudor House, God's House Tower, Bargate Museum, the Tudor Merchants Hall, the Weighhouse, West Gate, King John's House, Long House, Wool House, the ruins of Holy Rood Church, St. Julien's Church and the Mayflower Memorial. The medieval town walls, built for artillery, are among the most complete in Europe. Public open spaces total over 1,000 acres in extent and comprise 9 per cent of the city's area. The Common covers an area of 328 acres in the central district of the city and is mostly natural parkland.

STOKE-ON-TRENT

STOKE-ON-TRENT (Staffordshire), familiarly known as The Potteries, stands on the River Trent 157 miles N. of London. The present municipal area is 22,916 acres (36 square miles) and the city is the main centre of employment for the population of North Staffordshire. It is the largest clayware producer in the world (china, earthenware, sanitary goods, refractories, bricks and tiles) and has a considerable coal mining output drawn from one of the richest coalfields in Western Europe. The city has steelworks, foundries, chemical works, engineering plants, rubber works, paper mills, and a very wide range of manufactures. Extensive reconstruction has been carried on in recent years.

The City was formed by the federation in 1910 of the separate municipal authorities of Tunstall, Burslem, Hanley, Stoke-upon-Trent, Fenton, and Longton, all of which are now combined in the present City of Stoke-on-Trent.

WINCHESTER

WINCHESTER, the ancient capital of England, is situated on the River Itchen 65 miles SW of London and 12 miles N. of Southampton. Since local government reorganization in 1974, the style of City has been accorded to the whole of the new district of Winchester, which embraces an area of 162,921 acres of mid-Hampshire.

Winchester is rich in architecture of all types but the Cathedral takes pride of place. The longest Gothic cathedral in the world, it was built in 1079–93 and exhibits examples of Norman, Early English and Perpendicular styles. Winchester College, founded in 1382, is one of the most famous public schools, the original building (of 1393) remaining unaltered. St. Cross Hospital, another great medieval foundation, lies 1 mile south of the city. The Almshouses were founded in 1136 by Bishop Henry de Blois, and Cardinal Henry Beaufort added a new Almshouse of 'Noble Poverty' in 1446. The Chapel and dwellings are of great architectural interest, and visitors may still receive the 'Wayfarer's Dole' of bread and ale.

Recent excavations have done much to clarify the origins and development of Winchester. Part of the forum and several of the streets of the Roman town have been discovered; and excavations in the Cathedral Close have uncovered the entire site of the Anglo-Saxon cathedral (known as the Old Minster) and parts of the New Minster, built by Alfred's son Edward the Elder, and the burial place of the Alfredian dynasty. The original burial place of St. Swithun, before his remains were translated to a site in the present cathedral, was also uncovered.

Excavations in other parts of the City have thrown much light on Norman Winchester, notably on the site of the Royal Castle, adjacent to which the new Law Courts have been built, and in the grounds of Wolvesey Castle, where the great house built by Bishops Giffard and Henry de Blois in the 12th century has been uncovered.

YORK

The City of YORK is a District in the County of North Yorkshire, and is an archiepiscopal seat.

The recorded history of York dates from AD 71, when the Roman Ninth Legion established a base under Petilius Cerealis which later became the fortress of *Eburacum*. In Anglo-Saxon times the city was the royal and ecclesiastical centre of Northumbria, and was captured by a Viking army in AD 866, after which it became the capital of the Viking kingdom of Jorvik. By the 14th century the city had become a great mercantile centre, mainly owing to its control of the wool trade, and was used as the chief base against the Scots. Under the Tudors its fortunes declined, though Henry VIII made it the headquarters of the Council of the North. Recent excavations on many sites, including Coppergate, have greatly expanded knowledge of Roman, Viking and medieval urban life.

With its development as a railway centre in the 19th century the commercial life of York expanded. The principal industries are the manufacture of chocolate, railway coaches, scientific instruments, and sugar.

The City is rich in examples of architecture of all periods. The earliest church was built in AD 627 and in the 12th to the 15th centuries, the present Minster was built in a succession of styles. Other examples within the city are the medieval city walls and gateways, churches and guildhalls. Domestic architecture includes the Georgian mansions of The Mount, Micklegate and Bootham. Its museums include the Castle Museum, the National Railway Museum and the Jorvik Viking Centre.

THE CORPORATION OF LONDON

The City of London is the historic centre at the heart of London known as 'the square mile' around which the vast metropolis has grown over the centuries. The City's residential population is 5,300 (1981 Census). The civic government is carried on by the Corporation of the City of London through the Court of Common Council, a body consisting of the Lord Mayor, 24 other Aldermen and 132 Common Councilmen. The legal title of the Corporation is 'the Mayor and Commonalty and Citizens of the City of London'.

The City is the financial and business centre of London and includes the head offices of the principal banks, insurance companies and mercantile houses, in addition to buildings ranging from the historic interest of the Roman Wall and the 15th century Guildhall, to the massive splendour of St. Paul's Cathedral and the architectural beauty of Wren's spires.

The City of London was described by Tacitus in AD 62 as 'a busy emporium for trade and traders'. Under the Romans it became an important administration centre and hub of the road system. Little is known of London in Saxon times when it formed part of the kingdom of the East Saxons. In 886 Alfred recovered London from the Danes and reconstituted it a burgh under his son-in-law. In 1066 the citizens submitted to William the Conqueror who in 1067 granted them a charter, which is still preserved, establishing them in the rights and privileges they had hitherto enjoyed.

The *Mayoralty* was probably established about 1189, the first Mayor being Henry Fitz Ailwyn who filled the office for 23 years and was succeeded by Fitz Alan (1212–14). A new charter was granted by King John in 1215, directing the Mayor to be chosen annually, which has ever since been done, though in early times the same individual often held the office more than once. A familiar instance is that of 'Whittington, thrice Lord Mayor of London' (in reality four times, 1397, 1398, 1406, 1419); and many modern cases have occurred. The earliest instance of the phrase 'Lord Mayor' in English is in 1414. It was used more generally in the latter part of the 15th century and became invariable from 1535 onwards. At Michaelmas the Liverymen in Common Hall choose two Aldermen who have served the office of Sheriff for presentation to the Court of Aldermen, and one is chosen to be Lord Mayor for the ensuing mayoral year.

Lord Mayor's Day.—The Lord Mayor of London was previously elected on the feast of St Simon and St Jude (Oct. 28), and from the time of Edward I, at least, was presented to the King or to the Barons of the Exchequer on the following day, except that day be a Sunday. The day of election was altered to Oct. 16 in 1346, and after some further changes was fixed for Michaelmas Day in 1546, but the ceremonies of admittance and swearing-in of the Lord Mayor continued to take place on Oct. 28 and 29 respectively until 1751. In 1752, at the reform of the Calendar (*see* page 114), the Lord Mayor was continued in office until Nov. 8, the 'New Style' equivalent of Oct. 28. The Lord Mayor is now presented to the Lord Chief Justice at the Royal Courts of Justice on the second Saturday in November to make the final declaration of office, having been sworn in at Guildhall on the preceding day. The procession to the Royal Courts of Justice is popularly known as the Lord Mayor's Show.

Aldermen are mentioned in the 11th century and their office is of Saxon origin. They were elected annually between 1377 and 1394, when an Act of Parliament of Richard II directed them to be chosen for life. The *Common Council*, elected annually on the first Friday in December, was, at an early date, substituted for a popular assembly called the *Folkmote*. At first only two representatives were sent from each ward, but the number has since been greatly increased.

Sheriffs were Saxon officers: their predecessors were the *wic-reeves* and *portreeves* of London and Middlesex. At first they were officers of the Crown, and were named by the Barons of the Exchequer; but Henry I (in 1132) gave the citizens permission to choose their own Sheriffs, and the annual election of Sheriffs became fully operative under King John's charter of 1199. The citizens lost this privilege, as far as the election of Sheriff of Middlesex was concerned, by the Local Government Act, 1888; but the Liverymen continue, as heretofore, to choose two Sheriffs of the City of London, who are appointed on Midsummer Day, and take office at Michaelmas.

Officers.—The Recorder was first appointed in 1298. The office of Chamberlain is an ancient one, the first contemporary record of which is 1237. The Town Clerk (or Common Clerk) is mentioned in 1274 and the Common Serjeant in 1291.

Activities.—The work is assigned to a number of committees which present reports to the Court of Common Council. These Committees are:—City Lands and Bridge House Estates, Policy and Resources, Coal, Corn and Rates Finance, Planning and Communications, Central Markets, Billingsgate and Leadenhall Markets, Spitalfields Market, Police, Port and City of London Health and Social Services, Libraries, Art Galleries and Records, Boards of Governors of Schools, Music (Guildhall School of Music and Drama), Establishment, Housing, Gresham (City side), Hampstead Heath Management, Epping Forest and Open Spaces, West Ham Park, Privileges, Barbican Residential and Barbican Centre (Barbican Arts and Conference Centre).

The City's Estate, in the possession of which the Corporation of London differs from other municipalities, is managed by the City Lands and Bridge House Estates Committee, the Chairmanship of which carries with it the title of 'Chief Commoner'. *Chairman* (1990), G. H. Challis.

The Honourable the Irish Society (The Irish Chamber, Guildhall Yard, London EC2V 5AE. *Sec.,* B. E. Manning), which manages the Corporation's Estates in Ulster, consists of a Governor and five other Aldermen, the Recorder, and 19 Common Councilmen, of whom one is elected Deputy Governor.

The Lord Mayor 1989–90*

The Rt. Hon. the Lord Mayor (1989–90), Sir Hugh Bidwell, GBE, RD.
Secretary, Rear-Adm. A. J. Cook, CB.

The Sheriffs 1990–1

C. R. Walford (*Alderman, Farringdon Within*) and J. A. F. Taylor, TD; *elected,* June 25, 1990; *assumed office,* September 28, 1990.

Officers

Recorder, L. J. Verney, TD, QC (1990).
Chamberlain, B. P. Harty (1983).
Town Clerk, G. W. Rowley, CBE (1982).
Common Serjeant, R. Lymbery, RD, QC (1990).

* The Lord Mayor for 1990–1 was elected on Michaelmas Day. *See* **Occurrences During Printing**.

The Aldermen

Aldermen	Ward	Born	C.C.	Ald.	Shff.	Lord Mayor
Cdr. Sir Robin Gillett, Bt., GBE, RD	Bassishaw	1925	1965	1969	1973	1976
Sir Peter Gadsden, GBE	Farringdon Wt.	1929	1969	1971	1970	1979
Sir Christopher Leaver, GBE	Dowgate	1937	1973	1974	1979	1981
Dame Mary Donaldson, GBE	Coleman St.	1921	1966	1975	1981	1983
Sir Alan Traill, GBE	Langbourn	1935	1970	1975	1982	1984
Sir Allan Davis, GBE	Cripplegate	1921	1971	1976	1982	1985
Sir David Rowe-Ham, GBE	Bridge	1935	....	1976	1984	1986
Sir Greville Spratt, GBE, TD	Castle Baynard	1927	....	1978	1984	1987
Sir Christopher Collett, GBE	Broad Street	1931	1973	1979	1985	1988
Sir Hugh Bidwell, GBE	Billingsgate	1934	....	1979	1986	1989

All the above have passed the Civic Chair

Alexander Michael Graham	Queenhithe	1938	1978	1979	1986	....
Brian Garton Jenkins	Cordwainer	1935	....	1980	1987	....
Francis McWilliams	Aldersgate	1926	1978	1980	1988	....
Paul Henry Newall, TD	Walbrook	1934	1980	1981	1989	....
Christopher Rupert Walford	Farringdon Wn.	1935	....	1982	1990	....
Roderic Neil Young	Bread Street	1933	1980	1982	....	....
Roger William Cork	Tower	1947	1978	1983	....	....
Bryan Edward Toye	Lime Street	1938	....	1983	....	....
Richard Everard Nichols	Candlewick	1938	1983	1984	....	....
Peter Anthony Bull	Cheap	1937	1968	1984	....	....
Sir Peter Keith Levene, KBE	Portsoken	1941	1983	1984	....	....
Leonard John Chalstrey	Vintry	1931	1981	1984	....	....
Clive Haydn Martin, OBE, TD	Aldgate	1935	....	1985	....	....
David Howarth Seymour Howard	Cornhill	1945	1972	1986	....	....
James Michael Yorrick Oliver	Bishopsgate	1940	1980	1987	....	....

The Common Council of London

Deputy.—Each Common Councilman so described serves as Deputy to the Alderman of her/his Ward.

Anstee, N. J. (1987) . . . . Aldersgate
Archibald, W. W. (1986) . . . . Cornhill
Arthur, G. F. (1988) . . . . Farringdon Wt.
Ballard, K. A., MC (1969) . . . . Castle Baynard
Balls, *Deputy* H. D. (1970) . . . . Cripplegate Wt.
Barker, J. A. (1981) . . . . Cripplegate Wt.
Barnes, H. M. F. (1986) . . . . Coleman Street
Beale, M. J. (1979) . . . . Lime Street
Bird, J. L. (1977) . . . . Bridge
Biroum-Smith, P. L. (1988) . . . . Dowgate
Block, S. A. A. (1983) . . . . Cheap
Boreham, B. P. (1986) . . . . Dowgate
Bramwell, F. M. (1983) . . . . Langbourn
Brighton, R. L. (1984) . . . . Portsoken
Brooks, W. I. B. (1988) . . . . Billingsgate
Brown, *Deputy* D. T. (1971) . . . . Walbrook
Cann, T. J. (1988) . . . . Cripplegate Wn.
Cassidy, M. J. (1989) . . . . Coleman Street
Catt, B. F. (1982) . . . . Farringdon Wn.
Challis, G. H. (1978) . . . . Langbourn
Chandler, *Deputy* E. G., CBE (1982) . . . . Cornhill
Clements, *Deputy* G. E. I. (1960) . . . . Farringdon Wt.
Cohen, Mrs. C. M. (1986) . . . . Lime Street
Cole, Lt.-Col. Sir Colin, KCVO, TD
   (1964) . . . . Castle Baynard
Cope, Dr. J. (1963) . . . . Farringdon Wt.
Coven, *Deputy* Mrs. E. O., CBE
   (1972) . . . . Dowgate
Currie, Miss S. E. M. (1985) . . . . Cripplegate Wt.
Daily-Hunt, R. B. (1989) . . . . Cripplegate
David, C. P. (1984) . . . . Aldgate
Delderfield, D. W. (1982) . . . . Aldersgate
de Silva, D., QC (1980) . . . . Farringdon Wt.
Donnelly, T. A., MBE (1982) . . . . Bread Street
Duckworth, *Deputy* H., CBE (1960) . . Lime Street
Dunitz, A. A. (1984) . . . . Portsoken
Durnin, J. C. (1976) . . . . Cordwainer
Edwards, R. D. K. (1978) . . . . Bassishaw
Eskenzi, A. N. (1970) . . . . Farringdon Wn.
Evans, Mrs. J. (1975) . . . . Farringdon Wt.

Eve, R. A. (1980) . . . . Cheap
Everett, K. M. (1984) . . . . Candlewick
Falk, F. A., TD (1984) . . . . Farringdon Wt.
Farrow, M. W. W. (1987) . . . . Bishopsgate
Farthing, R. B. C. (1981) . . . . Aldgate
Fell, J. A. (1982) . . . . Queenhithe
FitzGerald, R. C. A. (1981) . . . . Bread Street
Floyd-Ewin, *Deputy* Sir David,
   LVO, OBE (1963) . . . . Castle Baynard
Frankenberg, P. B. (1989) . . . . Cordwainer
Frappell, C. E. (1973) . . . . Bread Street
Fraser, W. B. (1981) . . . . Vintry
Frazer, C. M. (1986) . . . . Farringdon Wt.
Galloway, A. D. (1981) . . . . Broad Street
Gass, *Deputy* G. J. (1967) . . . . Coleman Street
Gold, R. (1965) . . . . Castle Baynard
Graves, A. C. (1985) . . . . Bishopsgate
Harding, N. H. (1970) . . . . Farringdon Wn.
Hardwick, Dr. P. B. (1987) . . . . Aldgate
Hart, *Deputy* M. G. (1970) . . . . Bridge
Haynes, J. E. H. (1986) . . . . Cornhill
Henderson, *Deputy* J. S., OBE (1975) . Langbourn
Henderson-Begg, M. (1977) . . . . Coleman Street
Holland, *Deputy* J. (1972) . . . . Aldgate
Horlock, *Deputy* H. W. S. (1969) . . . . Farringdon Wn.
Humphrays, Mrs. R. (1976) . . . . Cripplegate Wt.
Ide, W. R. (1972) . . . . Castle Baynard
Jackson, L. St. J. T. (1978) . . . . Bassishaw
Jennings, I. G. (1988) . . . . Cripplegate Wn.
Keep, Mrs. B. (1987) . . . . Cripplegate Wn.
Kellett, Mrs. M. W. F. (1986) . . . . . . Tower
Kemp, D. L. (1984) . . . . Coleman Street
Knowles, S. K. (1984) . . . . Candlewick
Lamport, J. C. (1987) . . . . Cripplegate Wt.
Langman, A. D. G., TD (1982) . . . . . . Tower
Lawrence, D. W. O., TD (1979) . . . . . Bridge
Lawson, G. C. H. (1971) . . . . Portsoken
McAuley, *Deputy* C. (1957) . . . . Bread Street
MacLellan, A. P. W. (1989) . . . . Walbrook
McNeil, I. D. (1977) . . . . Lime Street

Malins, J. H. (1981) .... *Farringdon Wt.*
Martin, R. C. (1986) .... *Queenhithe*
Mayhew, Miss J. (1986) .... *Queenhithe*
Mills, A. P. (1969) .... *Bassishaw*
Minshull-Fogg, J., TD (1986) .... *Walbrook*
Mitchell, C. R. (1971) .... *Castle Baynard*
Mizen, *Deputy* D. H. (1979) .... *Broad Street*
Mobsby, D. J. L. (1985) .... *Billingsgate*
Morgan, *Deputy* B. L., CBE (1963) .... *Bishopsgate*
Moss, A. D. (1989) .... *Tower*
Murkin, *Deputy* C. H., OBE (1969) .... *Vintry*
Nash, *Deputy* Mrs. J. C. (1983) ...... *Aldersgate*
Neary, J. E. (1982) .... *Aldgate*
Newman, Mrs. P. B. (1989) .... *Aldersgate*
Northall-Laurie, P. D. (1975)........ *Walbrook*
Olson, A. H. F. (1972) .... *Dowgate*
Owen, Mrs. J. (1975) .... *Langbourn*
Owen-Ward, J. R. (1983)............ *Bridge*
Packard, Brig. J. J. (1972) .... *Cripplegate Wn.*
Pembroke, *Deputy* Mrs. A. M. F.
   (1978) .... *Cheap*
Ponsonby of Shulbrede, The Lady
   (1981) .... *Farringdon Wt.*
Pulman, G. A. G. (1983) .... *Tower*
Ratner, R. A., TD (1981) .... *Broad Street*
Reed, *Deputy* J. L., MBE (1967)...... *Farringdon Wn.*
Revell-Smith, P. A., CBE (1959) ...... *Vintry*
Rigby, P. P. (1972) .... *Farringdon Wn.*

Robinson, Mrs. D. C. (1989) .... *Bishopsgate*
Rodgers, Miss E. H. L. (1987) .... *Vintry*
Roney, E. P. T., CBE (1974) .... *Bishopsgate*
Samuel, *Deputy* Mrs. I. (1971) ...... *Portsoken*
Saunders, *Deputy* R. (1975) .... *Candlewick*
Savory, M. B. (1980) .... *Broad Street*
Scriven, R. G. (1984) .... *Candlewick*
Scrivener, M. J. H. (1986)........... *Cripplegate Wn.*
Shalit, D. M. (1972) .... *Farringdon Wn.*
Sharp, *Deputy* Mrs. I. M. (1974) .... *Queenhithe*
Shindler, *Deputy* A. B. (1966) ...... *Billingsgate*
Simpson, A. S. J. (1987)............. *Aldersgate*
Smithers, H. J. (1986) .... *Billingsgate*
Snyder, M. J. (1986)................. *Cordwainer*
Spanner, J. H., TD (1984)............ *Broad Street*
Stevenson, J. L. (1970) .... *Coleman Street*
Stitcher, *Deputy* G. M., CBE (1966) ... *Farringdon Wt.*
Swan, N. E. B. (1985) .... *Coleman Street*
Walsh, S. (1989) .... *Farringdon Wt.*
Webb, C. J. (1986)................... *Bishopsgate*
White, J. W. (1986) .... *Cornhill*
Williams, G. M. E. (1985) .... *Aldersgate*
Willoughby, P. J. (1985) .... *Bishopsgate*
Wilmot, *Deputy* R. T. D. (1973) ..... *Cordwainer*
Wilson, A. B., CBE (1984)............ *Cheap*
Wixley, G. R. A., TD (1964) .... *Bassishaw*
Woodward, *Deputy* C. D., OBE (1971) *Cripplegate Wn.*
Wooldridge, F. D. (1988)............ *Farringdon Wn.*

THE CITY GUILDS (LIVERY COMPANIES)

The Livery Companies of the City of London derive their name from the assumption of a distinctive dress or livery by their members in the 14th century. The order of precedence, omitting extinct companies, is given in parentheses after the name of each Company.

Liverymen of the Guilds (23,387 in number) are entitled to vote at elections in Common Hall.

The Twelve Great Companies
(in order of Civic precedence)

MERCERS (*1*). *Hall*, Ironmonger Lane, EC2V 8HE. *Livery*, 250.—*Clerk*, G. M. M. Wakeford; *Master*, J. A. Watney.

GROCERS (2). *Hall*, Princes Street, EC2R 8AD. *Livery*, 335.—*Clerk*, C. G. Mattingley, CBE; *Master*, H. R. D. Billson.

DRAPERS (*3*). *Hall*, Throgmorton Street, EC2N 2DQ. *Livery*, 250.—*Clerk*, R. C. G. Strick; *Master*, J. G. Stitt.

FISHMONGERS (*4*). *Hall*, London Bridge, EC4R 9EL. *Livery*, 361.—*Clerk*, M. R. T. O'Brien; *Prime Warden*, A. J. Butterwick.

GOLDSMITHS (*5*). *Hall*, Foster Lane, EC2V 6BN. *Livery*, 277.—*Clerk*, R. D. Buchanan-Dunlop, CBE; *Prime Warden*, The Lord Adrian, FRS.

MERCHANT TAYLORS (*6*). *Hall*, 30 Threadneedle Street, EC2R 8AY. *Livery* 330.—*Clerk*, Capt. D. A. Wallis, RN; *Master*, J. H. Pascoe, CBE.

SKINNERS (7). *Hall*, 8 Dowgate Hill, EC4R 2SP. *Livery*, 361.—*Clerk*, Capt. D. H. Dyke, CBE, LVO, RN; *Master*, E. St. John Brice.

HABERDASHERS (*8*). *Hall*, Staining Lane, EC2V 7DD. *Livery*, 320.—*Clerk*, Capt. M. E. Barrow, DSO, RN; *Master*, Sir John Welch, Bt.

SALTERS (9). *Hall*, 4 Fore Street, EC2Y 5DE. *Livery*, 150.—*Clerk*, Col. M. P. Barneby; *Master*, Sir Peter Hordern, MP.

IRONMONGERS (*10*). *Hall*, Barbican, EC2Y 8AA. *Livery*, 107.—*Clerk*, J. A. Oliver; *Master*, H. R. C. Matthews.

VINTNERS (*11*). *Hall*, Upper Thames Street, EC4V 3BJ. *Livery*, 326.—*Clerk*, Brig. G. Read, CBE; *Master*, M. J. Langton.

CLOTHWORKERS (*12*). *Hall*, Dunster Court, Mincing Lane, EC3R 7AH. *Livery*, 185.—*Clerk*, C. M. Mowll; *Master*, Lt.-Col. G. R. W. Howell.

Other City Guilds
(in alphabetic order)

ACCOUNTANTS, CHARTERED (*86*). *Livery*, 340.—*Clerk*, G. H. Kingsmill, The Grove, Hinton Parva, Swindon SN4 0DH; *Master*, D. B. Shaw.

ACTUARIES (*91*). *Livery*, 160.—*Clerk*, P. D. Esslemont, 16A Cadogan Square, SW1X 0JU; *Master*, P. J. Turvey.

AIR PILOTS AND AIR NAVIGATORS, GUILD OF (*81*). *Livery*, 400.—*Grand Master*, HRH the Prince Philip, Duke of Edinburgh, KG, KT; *Clerk*, Gp. Capt. J. W. Tritton, 291 Gray's Inn Road, WC1X 8QF; *Master*, Capt. M. Bannister.

APOTHECARIES, SOCIETY OF (*58*). *Hall*, Black Friars Lane, EC4V 6EJ. *Livery*, 1,160.—*Clerk*, Maj. J. C. O'Leary; *Master*, D. G. A. Eadie.

ARBITRATORS (*93*). *Livery*, 190.—*Clerk*, B. W. Vigrass, OBE, VRD, 75 Cannon Street, EC4N 5BH; *Master*, A. B. Shindler.

ARMOURERS AND BRASIERS (*22*). *Hall*, 81 Coleman Street, EC2R 5BJ. *Livery*, 120.—*Clerk*, Lt. Col. R. R. F. Cowe; *Master*, J. H. Hale.

BAKERS (*19*). *Hall*, Harp Lane, Lower Thames Street, EC3R 6DP. *Livery*, 410.—*Clerk*, P. F. Wilson, DFC; *Master*, S. Wise.

BARBERS (*17*). *Hall*, Monkwell Square, EC2Y 5BL. *Livery*, 220.—*Clerk*, Col. A. B. Harfield, CBE; *Master*, A. W. F. Lettin.

BASKETMAKERS (*52*). *Livery*, 500.—*Clerk*, D. J. Farrier, 5 The Spinney, Warren Road, Purley, Surrey CR8 1AB; *Prime Warden*, G. Rowley.

BLACKSMITHS (*40*). *Livery*, 283.—*Clerk*, R. C. Jorden, 27 Cheyne Walk, Grange Park, N21 1DB; *Prime Warden*, G. W. Hughes.

BOWYERS (*38*). *Livery*, 97.—*Clerk*, A. Black, CBE, 2 Serjeants' Inn, Fleet Street, EC4Y 1LL; *Master*, R. Cork.

BREWERS (*14*). *Hall*, Aldermanbury Square, EC2V 7HR. *Livery*, 100.—*Clerk*, Rear-Adm. M. L. T. Wemyss, CB; *Master*, M. N. F. Cottrell.

BRODERERS (*48*). *Livery*, 100.—*Clerk*, P. J. C. Crouch, 11 Bridge Road, East Molesey, Surrey KT8 9EU; *Master*, T. J. T. Metcalf.

BUILDERS MERCHANTS (*88*). *Livery*, 200.—*Clerk*, Ms. S. Robinson, 14 Charterhouse Street, EC1M 6AX; *Master*, C. R. Carr.

BUTCHERS (*24*). *Hall*, 87 Bartholomew Close, EC1A 7EB. *Livery*, 80.—*Clerk*, A. H. Emus; *Master*, G. J. Sharp.

CARMEN (*77*). *Livery*, 482.—*Clerk*, Lt.-Col. G. T. Pearce, MBE, St. Olave's Rectory, 8 Hart Street, EC3R 7NB; *Master*, Sir Robert Reid, CBE.

CARPENTERS (*26*). *Hall*, 1 Throgmorton Avenue, EC2N 2JJ. *Livery*, 150.—*Clerk*, Capt. K. G. Hamon, RN; *Master*, J. G. Ridley.

CHARTERED SECRETARIES AND ADMINISTRATORS (*87*). *Livery*, 230.—*Hon. Clerk*, G. H. Challis, The Irish Chamber, Guildhall Yard, EC2V 5AE; *Master*, D. D. Durban, CBE.

CLOCKMAKERS (*61*). *Livery*, 286. *Hall*, St. Dunstan's House, Carey Lane, EC2V 8AA.—*Clerk*, Air Cdre. B. G. Frow, DSO, DFC; *Master*, A. W. Henn.

COACHMAKERS AND COACH-HARNESS MAKERS (*72*). *Livery*, 430.—*Clerk*, Maj. W. H. Wharfe, 149 Banstead Road, Ewell, Epsom, Surrey KT17 3HL; *Master*, G. Boxall.

COOKS (*35*). *Livery*, 75.—*Clerk*, M. C. Thatcher, 49 Queen Victoria Street, EC4N 4SE; *Master*, R. S. Anderson.

COOPERS (*36*). *Hall*, 13 Devonshire Square, EC2M 4TH. *Livery*, 260.—*Clerk*, J. A. Newton; *Master*, B. M. Taylor.

CORDWAINERS (*27*). *Livery* 143.—*Clerk*, Cdr. C. Shears, CVO, OBE, Eldon Chambers, 30 Fleet Street, EC4Y 1AA; *Master*, J. M. L. Uren.

CURRIERS (*29*). *Livery*, 93.—*Clerk*, Lt.-Col. J. B. Ray, MBE, Hornbeam House, Yew Tree Close, Middle Winterslow, Salisbury SP5 1RT; *Master*, H. R. G. Duckham.

CUTLERS (*18*). *Hall*, Warwick Lane, EC4M 7BR. *Livery*, 100.—*Clerk*, K. S. G. Hinde, TD; *Master*, R. A. Everest.

DISTILLERS (*69*). *Livery*, 280.—*Clerk*, B. Dehn, 71 Lincolns Inn Fields, WC2A 3JF; *Master*, J. M. Broadbent.

DYERS (*13*). *Hall*, Dowgate Hill, EC4R 2ST. *Livery*, 132.—*Clerk*, J. R. Chambers; *Prime Warden*, P. J. Q. Back, DFC.

ENGINEERS (*94*). *Livery*, 299.—*Clerk*, Cdr. B. D. Gibson, 1 Carlton House Terrace, SW1Y 5DB; *Master*, F. McWilliams.

ENVIRONMENTAL CLEANERS (*97*). *Livery*, 192.—*Clerk*, S. J. Holt, Whitethorns, Rannoch Road, Crowborough, E. Sussex TN6 1RA; *Master*, A. R. Barlow.

FAN MAKERS (*76*). *Hall*, St. Botolph's Hall, Bishopsgate, EC2M 3TL. *Livery*, 250.—*Clerk*, Lt.-Col. I. R. P. Green; *Master*, H. D. E. Woods.

FARMERS (*80*). *Hall*, 3 Cloth Street, EC1A 7LD. *Livery*, 300.—*Clerk*, C. M. Taylor; *Master*, R. J. Upton.

FARRIERS (*55*). *Livery*, 375.—*Clerk*, H. W. H. Ellis, 37 The Uplands, Loughton, Essex IG10 1NQ; *Master*, T. P. Neligan.

FELTMAKERS (*63*). *Livery*, 225.—*Clerk*, R. M. Peel, 10 Carteret Street, SW1H 9DR; *Master*, J. Wallworth.

FLETCHERS (*39*). *Hall*, 3 Cloth Street, EC1A 7LD. *Livery*, 114.—*Clerk*, J. R. Garnett; *Master*, J. A. B. Redgrave.

FOUNDERS (*33*). *Hall*, 1 Cloth Fair, EC1A 7HT. *Livery*, 180.—*Clerk*, A. J. Gillett; *Master*, H. H. Draycott.

FRAMEWORK KNITTERS (*64*). *Livery*, 225.—*Clerk*, C. J. Eldridge, Apothecaries' Hall, Black Friars Lane, EC4V 6EL; *Master*, P. Corah.

FRUITERERS (*45*). *Livery*, 240.—*Clerk*, Cdr. M. T. H. Styles, Denmead Cottage, Chawton, Alton, Hants. GU34 1SB; *Master*, D. L. Hounen.

FUELLERS (*95*). *Livery*, 250.—*Clerk*, Wg. Cdr. H. F. C. Squire, OBE, 4 Maycross Avenue, Morden, Surrey SM4 4DA; *Master*, G. McGecham.

FURNITURE MAKERS (*83*). *Livery*, 261.—*Clerk*, Wg. Cdr. G. Acklam, MBE, 30 Harcourt Street, W1H 2AA; *Master*, R. B. C. Waring.

GARDENERS (*66*). *Livery*, 250.—*Clerk*, A. L. McGeachy, 14–15 Craven Street, WC2N 5AD; *Master*, D. H. S. Howard.

GIRDLERS (*23*). *Hall*, Basinghall Avenue, EC2V 5DD. *Livery*, 80.—*Clerk*, T. J. Straker; *Master*, J. S. Maitland.

GLASS-SELLERS (*71*). *Livery*, 180.—*Hon. Clerk*, B. J. Rawles, 43 Aragon Avenue, Thames Ditton, Surrey KT7 0PY; *Master*, O. C. T. R. Normandale.

GLAZIERS AND PAINTERS OF GLASS (*53*). *Hall*, 9 Montague Close, SE1 9DD. *Livery*, 280.—*Clerk*, P. R. Bachelor; *Master*, P. H. Trollope.

GLOVERS (*62*). *Livery*, 300.—*Clerk*, Gp. Capt. D. G. F. Palmer, OBE, Glovers, Tismans Common, Rudgwick, W. Sussex RH12 3DU; *Master*, M. S. Lea.

GOLD AND SILVER WYRE DRAWERS (*74*). *Livery*, 350.—*Clerk*, J. R. Williams, 50 Cheyne Avenue, E18 2DR; *Master*, A. W. H. Clover.

GUNMAKERS (*73*). *Livery*, 140.—*Clerk*, F. B. Brandt, The Proof House, 48–50 Commercial Road, E1 1LP; *Master*, G. A. Brooks.

HORNERS (*54*). *Livery*, 430.—*Clerk*, Dr. E. M. Hunt, 11 Hobart Place, SW1W 0HL; *Master*, N. K. Grant.

INNHOLDERS (*32*). *Hall*, College Street, Dowgate Hill, EC4R 2SY. *Livery*, 120.—*Clerk*, J. R. Edwardes Jones; *Master*, A. J. D. Mathews.

INSURERS (*92*). *Hall*, 20 Aldermanbury, EC2V 7HY. *Livery*, 333.—*Clerk*, V. D. Webb; *Master*, R. K. Bishop.

JOINERS AND CEILERS (*41*). *Livery*, 128.—*Clerk*, D. A. Tate, Parkville House, Bridge Street, Pinner, Middx. HA5 3JD; *Master*, T. F. R. Stockwell.

LAUNDERERS (*89*). *Hall*, 9 Montague Close, SE1 9DD. *Livery*, 204.—*Clerk*, P. E. Coombe; *Master*, F. H. Scott.

LEATHERSELLERS (*15*). *Hall*, 15 St. Helen's Place, EC3A 6DQ. *Livery*, 150.—*Clerk*, Capt. N. MacEacharn, CBE, RN; *Master*, M. J. R. Tusting, OBE.

LIGHTMONGERS (*96*). *Livery*, 119.—*Clerk*, S. H. Birch, 53 Leithcote Gardens, SW16 2UX; *Master*, A. Robertson.

LORINERS (*57*). *Livery*, 350.—*Clerk*, J. R. Williams, 50 Cheyne Avenue, E18 2DR; *Master*, B. Willson-Pemberton.

MARKETORS (*90*). *Livery*, 181.—*Clerk*, B. F. Catt, 42 Tottenham Lane, N8 7EA; *Master*, R. H. Wilson.

MASONS (*30*). *Livery*, 111.—*Clerk*, H. J. Maddocks, 9 New Square, WC2R 3QN; *Master*, R. G. St. J. Rowlandson.

MASTER MARINERS, HONOURABLE COMPANY OF (*78*). HQS *Wellington*, Temple Stairs, WC2R 2PN. *Livery*, 300.—*Clerk*, D. H. W. Field; *Admiral*, HRH the Duke of Edinburgh, KG, KT; *Master*, HRH the Prince of Wales, KG, KT, GCB, PC.

MUSICIANS (*50*). *Livery*, 279.—*Clerk*, M. J. G. Fletcher, 1 The Sanctuary, Westminster, SW1P 3JT; *Master*, M. J. Hubble.

NEEDLEMAKERS (*65*). *Livery*, 250.—*Clerk*, M. G. Cook, 17 Southampton Place, WC1A 2EH; *Master*, P. W. Barrows.

PAINTER STAINERS (28). *Hall*, 9 Little Trinity Lane, EC4V 2AD. *Livery*, 400.—*Clerk*, Wg. Cdr. B. C. Pratt; *Master*, J. F. S. Northcott.

PATTENMAKERS (70). *Livery*, 250.—*Clerk*, P. Merritt, 25 Wellesley Road, W4 4BU; *Master*, D. Gilbert.

PAVIORS (56). *Livery*, 275.—*Clerk*, R. F. Coe, Cutlers' Hall, Warwick Lane, EC4M 7BR; *Master*, A. G. Tate.

PEWTERERS. (16). *Hall*, Oat Lane, EC2V 7DE. *Livery*, 110.—*Clerk*, Maj. J. M. Halford, RM; *Master*, B. J. Fazan.

PLAISTERERS (46). *Hall*, 1 London Wall, EC2Y 5JU. *Livery*, 207.—*Clerk*, H. Mott; *Master*, J. R. Dalrymple.

PLAYING CARDS, MAKERS OF (75). *Livery*, 150.—*Clerk*, M. J. Smyth, 6 The Priory, Godstone, Surrey RH9 8NL; *Master*, J. G. Thorpe.

PLUMBERS (31). *Livery*, 310.—*Clerk*, Col. E. M. P. Hardy, 3rd Floor, 21 Fleet Street, EC4Y 1AA; *Master*, L. Hill.

POULTERS (34). *Hall*, Armourers' Hall, 81 Coleman Street, EC2R 5BJ. *Livery*, 175.—*Clerk*, Lt.-Col. R. R. F. Cowe; *Master*, H. R. Braithwaite.

SADDLERS (25). *Hall*, 40 Gutter Lane, EC2V 6BR. *Livery*, 70.—*Clerk*, Gp. Capt. K. M. Oliver; *Master*, M. W. Goold.

SCIENTIFIC INSTRUMENT MAKERS (84). *Hall*, 9 Montague Close, SE1 9DD. *Livery*, 250.—*Clerk*, F. G. Everard; *Master*, J. E. Herrin, CBE.

SCRIVENERS (44). *Livery*, 202.—*Clerk*, H. J. W. Harman, The Galleria, Station Road, Crawley, W. Sussex RH10 1HY; *Master*, R. S. Kinsey of Kinsey.

SHIPWRIGHTS (59). *Livery*, 500.—*Clerk*, Gp. Capt. R. C. Olding, CBE, DSC, Ironmongers' Hall, Barbican, EC2Y 8AA; *Permanent Master*, HRH the Duke of Edinburgh, KG, KT; *Prime Warden*, Dr. E. C. B. Corlett.

SOLICITORS (79). *Livery*, 411.—*Clerk*, Miss S. H. Robinson, TD, 14 Charterhouse Square, EC1M 6AX; *Master*, D. L. Biddle.

SPECTACLE MAKERS (60). *Livery*, 330.—*Clerk*, C. J. Eldridge, Apothecaries' Hall, Black Friars Lane, EC4V 6EL; *Master*, Mrs. A. C. A. Silk.

STATIONERS AND NEWSPAPER MAKERS (47). *Hall*, Ave Maria Lane, EC4M 7DD. *Livery*, 450.—*Clerk*, Capt. P. Hames, RN; *Master*, T. S. Corrigan.

SURVEYORS, CHARTERED (85). *Livery*, 320.—*Clerk*, Mrs. A. L. Jackson, 16 St. Mary-at-Hill, EC3R 8EE; *Master*, M. G. Clark, TD.

TALLOW CHANDLERS (21). *Hall*, 4 Dowgate Hill, EC4R 2SH. *Livery*, 180.—*Clerk*, Brig. W. K. L. Prosser, CBE; *Master*, P. J. Ensor.

TIN PLATE WORKERS Alias Wire Workers (67). *Livery*, 200.—*Hon. Clerk*, Mrs. A. M. Irving, 14 Talbot House, 98 St. Martin's Lane, WC2N 4AX; *Master*, G. S. Firth.

TOBACCO PIPE MAKERS AND TOBACCO BLENDERS (82). *Livery*, 171.—*Clerk*, I. J. Kimmins, Bouverie House, 154 Fleet Street, EC4A 2HX; *Master*, J. A. Ostick.

TURNERS (51). *Livery*, 165.—*Clerk*, R. G. Woodwark, DSC, 33A Hill Avenue, Amersham, Bucks. HP6 5BX; *Master*, G. A. Todd.

TYLERS AND BRICKLAYERS (37). *Livery*, 130.—*Clerk*, F. A. G. Rider, 6 Martin Lane, Cannon Street, EC4R 0DP; *Master*, M. J. Stokes.

UPHOLDERS (49). *Livery*, 200.—*Clerk*, W. R. Wallis, Charrington House, The Causeway, Bishops Stortford CH23 2EW; *Master*, D. Glatzel.

WAX CHANDLERS (20). *Hall*, Gresham Street, EC2V 7AD. *Livery*, 100.—*Clerk*, T. Wood; *Master*, R. N. P. Griffiths.

WEAVERS (42). *Livery*, 128.—*Clerk*, J. G. Ouvry, 1 The Sanctuary, Westminster, SW1P 3JT; *Upper Bailiff*, N. F. Townsend.

WHEELWRIGHTS (68). *Livery*, 271.—*Clerk*, M. R. Francis, Greenup, Milton Avenue, Gerrards Cross, Bucks. SL9 8QW; *Master*, C. B. Davis.

WOOLMEN (43). *Livery*, 150.—*Clerk*, F. Allen, Kingsmead House, 250 King's Road, SW3 5UE; *Master*, W. B. Dunn, CBE.

PARISH CLERKS (No livery). (Members, 99).—*Clerk*, J. D. Hebblethwaite, General Synod Office, Church House, Great Smith Street, SW1P 3NZ; *Master*, J. H. Gaze.

WATERMEN AND LIGHTERMEN (No livery). (Craft Owning Freemen, 325).—*Hall*, 16 St. Mary-at-Hill, EC3R 8EE.—*Clerk*, W. A. A. Wells, TD; *Master*, H. G. Mack.

NOTE.—In certain companies the election of Master or Prime Warden for the year does not take place till the autumn. In such cases the Master or Prime Warden for 1989-90 is given.

LONDON BOROUGHS

City or Borough (§Inner London Borough)	Municipal Offices	Estimated resident population 1988	Community charge per head 1990 £	Chief Executive (a) Town Clerk (b) Managing Director	Mayor or (a) Lord Mayor
Barking and Dagenham....	°Dagenham, RM10 7BN	147,600	280·00	D. C. J. Farr	F. C. Jones
Barnet	†The Burroughs, Hendon, NW4 4BG	301,400	338·00	M. M. Caller	R. Schutz
Bexley	‡Bexleyheath, Kent DA6 7LB	220,400	280·00	T. Musgrave	G. R. Holland
Brent	†Forty Lane, Wembley, HA9 9HX	257,200	471·00	C. Wood	R. Stone
Bromley........	°Bromley, BR1 3UH	298,200	283·00	N. T. Palk	Mrs. J. Hillier
§Camden	†Euston Road, NW1 2RU	182,500	500·00	J. Smith	N. Roy
§City of Westminster	City Hall, Victoria Street, SW1E 6QP	169,700	195·00	(b) R. W. Phillips	(a) Dr. D. Avery
Croydon........	Taberner House, Park Lane, Croydon CR9 3JS	317,200	287·00	(a) F. S. H. Birch	M. Fowler
Ealing	°Uxbridge Road, W5 2HL	297,300	435·00	Ms. J. Hunt	W. Hill
Enfield	°Enfield, EN1 3XA	260,900	329·00	B. A. McAndrew	J. W. E. Jackson
§Greenwich	†Wellington Street, SE18 6PW	214,500	350·00	C. Roberts	G. Dhillon
§Hackney	†Mare St., E8 1EA	189,000	499·00	J. White	S. Shaikh
§Hammersmith and Fulham ..	†King St., W6 9JU	149,600	320·95	T. Eddison	F. Innis
Haringey.......	°Wood Green, N22 4LE	192,300	508·34	G. Singh	Ms. M. Neuner
Harrow........	°Harrow, HA1 2UH	197,100	322·00	A. G. Redmond	J. Cripps
Havering.......	†Romford, RM1 3BD	235,600	350·00	D. R. Bradley	R. F. Latchford
Hillingdon......	°Uxbridge, UB8 1UW	231,900	289·91	P. Johnson	Mrs. E. G. Boff
Hounslow	°Lampton Rd., Hounslow, TW3 4DN	190,700	396·00	vacant	S. S. Jassar
§Islington	†Upper St., N1 2UD	169,200	481·27	E. W. Dear	Ms. M. Leigh
§Kensington and Chelsea (RB)..	†Hornton St., W8 7NX	125,600	375·00	R. A. Taylor	J. Wheeler
Kingston upon Thames (RB)..	Guildhall, Kingston upon Thames KT1 1EU	134,600	344·95	R. McCloy	Mrs. E. Gray, OBE
§Lambeth	†Brixton Hill, SW2 1RW	239,100	521·00	H. Ousley	G. Huish
§Lewisham	†Catford, SE6 4RU	228,900	297·00	T. Hanafin	J. L. H. Eytle
Merton.........	Crown House, London Rd., Morden, SM4 5DX	164,000	279·00	W. A. McKee	J. Abrams, OBE
Newham	†East Ham, E6 2RP	206,900	449·00	J. Samuel	Ms. S. Murray
Redbridge	†Ilford, IG1 1DD	230,800	290·00	G. U. Price	Mrs. W. J. Roberts
Richmond upon Thames	°York Street, Twickenham, TW1 3BZ	160,800	395·00	R. L. Harbord	Ms. K. Gent
§Southwark	†Peckham Rd., SE5 8UB	216,900	329·00	Ms. A. Whyatt	J. Maurice
Sutton	‡St. Nicholas Way, Sutton, SM1 1EA	168,200	381·00	vacant	J. Brennan
§Tower Hamlets .	†Patriot Square, E2 9LN	161,800	297·00	(acting) K. Ivory, A. Golding	J. Ludlow
Waltham Forest .	†Forest Rd., Walthamstow, E17 4JF	213,300	438·00	A. Tobias	F. E. Georges
§Wandsworth...	†Wandsworth, SW18 2PU	257,000	148·00	G. K. Jones	J. L. Sedgwick

RB Royal Borough.   °Civic Centre.   †Town Hall.   ‡Civic Offices.

GREATER LONDON SERVICES

The abolition of the Greater London Council on April 1, 1986, led to the bulk of its work being passed to the London Boroughs, government departments and Government-appointed bodies, and to joint boards and committees.

The London Residuary Body (LRB) was established by the Local Government Act, 1985, which abolished the GLC. Its brief was to wind up the affairs of the GLC within a maximum life of five years.

With the Government's abolition of the Inner London Education Authority, the London Residuary Body has been given the task of dealing with residual ILEA affairs as it dealt with the GLC. Its reponsibilities include closing ILEA's accounts, disposing of about 200 surplus ILEA pieces of property and land, paying redundancy to ILEA staff and temporarily taking over services such as school transport, adult education, and the payment of grants. This will prolong the life of the LRB for up to three years beyond ILEA's abolition, until March 31, 1993.

The boroughs and successor bodies finance the LRB. In Feb. 1990 the LRB announced a levy of £22 million on London's 12 inner boroughs and the City of London, to pay for the education-related services it took over from ILEA. More than £800 million will have been distributed amongst the boroughs by the end of 1990.

London Residuary Body, Globe House, Temple Place, WC2R 3HP (071-633 5000).
Chairman, Sir Godfrey Taylor.
Director of Administration, J. Howes.
Director of Finance, D. Judd.

Solid waste disposal

Responsibility for the disposal of London's household, commercial and civic amenity refuse lies with 16 waste disposal authorities.

There are four statutory bodies—*West London Waste Authority* (Brent, Ealing, Harrow, Hillingdon, Hounslow, Richmond upon Thames), *North London Waste Authority* (Barnet, Camden, Enfield, Hackney, Haringey, Islington, Waltham Forest), *East London Waste Authority* (Barking and Dagenham, Havering, Newham, Redbridge) and *Western Riverside Waste Authority* (Hammersmith and Fulham, Kensington and Chelsea, Lambeth, Wandsworth).

Twelve boroughs are waste disposal authorities in their own right and eleven of them have come together in voluntary groupings—*Central London Group* (City of London, City of Westminster, Tower Hamlets), *South London Group* (Bromley, Croydon, Kingston upon Thames, Merton, Sutton) and *South East London Group* (Greenwich, Lewisham, Southwark). The twelfth, Bexley, liaises with Kent County Council.

The London Waste Regulation Authority regulates and controls waste management activities in both the public and private sectors.

London Waste Regulation Authority, Hampton House, 20 Albert Embankment, SE1 7TJ (Tel: 071-587 3074).

Fire Service

The authority for London's fire service is the London Fire and Civil Defence Authority (LFCDA). The Fire Brigade is organized into five Area Commands, which coincide with Borough boundaries. The LFCDA's responsibilities also include petroleum licensing.

London Fire and Civil Defence Authority, London Fire Brigade Headquarters, 8 Albert Embankment, SE1 7SD (Tel: 071-582 3811).

ROMAN NAMES OF ENGLISH TOWNS AND CITIES

Bath	*Aquae Sulis*
Canterbury	*Durovernum Cantiacorum*
Carlisle	*Luguvalium*
Chelmsford	*Caesaromagus*
Chester	*Deva*
Chichester	*Noviomagus Regnensium*
Cirencester	*Corinium Dobunnorum*
Colchester	*Camulodunum*
Doncaster	*Danum*
Dorchester	*Durnovaria*
Dover	*Dubris*
Exeter	*Isca Dumnoniorum*
Gloucester	*Glevum*
Leicester	*Ratae Corieltauvorum*
Lincoln	*Lindum*
London	*Londinium*
Manchester	*Mamucium*
Newcastle upon Tyne	*Pons Aelius*
Pevensey	*Anderetium*
Rochester	*Durobrivae*
St. Albans	*Verulamium*
Salisbury (Old Sarum)	*Sorviodunum*
Silchester	*Calleva Atrebatum*
Winchester	*Venta Belgarum*
Wroxeter	*Viroconium Cornoviorum*
York	*Eburacum*

LONDON AND ITS ENVIRONS
(For National Art Galleries and Museums in London, *see* Index.)

Adelphi, Strand, WC2.—Adelphi Terrace and district commemorate the four Adam brothers, James, John, Robert and William, who laid out the district (formerly Durham House) at the close of the 18th century, though few 18th century buildings now remain. Four of the streets were formerly called after the brothers but are now Adam Street, John Adam Street, Robert Street and Durham House Street. In the neighbourhood of the Adelphi was York House, built by the Duke of Buckingham in 1625 (the Water Gate of which still stands in Embankment Gardens), the commemorative streets being Charles Street, Villiers Street, Duke Street, Buckingham Street.

Alexandra Palace and Park, Wood Green, N22 4AY.—Set in 200 acres of parkland. The Victorian Palace was severely damaged by fire in 1980 but has been restored and developed and reopened in January 1988. Alexandra Palace provides modern facilities for exhibitions, sports, conferences and leisure activities. The Palace is a charitable trust administered by the London Borough of Haringey.

Baltic Exchange, St. Mary Axe, EC3.—The world market for the chartering of cargo ships. The present Exchange was built in 1903 and the new wing opened by HM The Queen on Nov. 21, 1956.

Bank of England, Threadneedle Street, EC2. (Not open to the public).—The Bank of England, founded in 1694, has always been closely connected with the Government. The present building, completed in 1940 to the designs of Sir Herbert Baker, incorporates features reminiscent of the earlier architects, Sampson (1734), Sir Robert Taylor (1765) and Sir John Soane (1788).

Bank of England Museum (entrance in Bartholomew Lane).—The Museum charts the Bank's history since the granting of the Royal Charter in 1694. Open Mon.-Fri. 10-6, Sat., Sun. and Bank Hols. 11-5. Admission free.

Banqueting House, Whitehall, SW1P 3EB.—The only important building left of the great Palace of Whitehall. The previous banqueting house was burnt down in 1619, and replaced by the present structure designed by Inigo Jones. In 1635 it was enriched with Rubens' ceiling paintings. Charles I was executed on a scaffold set up just in front of the present entrance. Open Tues.-Sat. 10-5, Sun. 2-5. Closed Mon. Admission (1991) £2·05, concessions £1·65.

Barbican Centre, Silk Street, EC2Y 8DS.—Owned, funded and managed by the Corporation of London, the Barbican Centre was opened on March 3, 1982 by HM The Queen, and is the largest complex of its kind in Western Europe. It houses the 1,166 seat Barbican Theatre, the London base of the Royal Shakespeare Company, along with a smaller 200 seat studio theatre (The Pit), and the 2,026 seat Barbican Hall, the home of the London Symphony Orchestra. There are also three cinemas, an art gallery, a sculpture court, a large lending library, facilities for trade exhibitions and conferences, and bars and restaurants.

Blackheath, SE10.—272 acres of parkland. Morden College, founded in 1695 as a home for 'decayed Turkey merchants', is near the SE corner. The building was designed by Wren and its Chapel doors have carvings attributed to Grinling Gibbons. Not open to the public. Concerts and poetry recitals are held at Rangers House, a villa built *c*.1700 which houses the Suffolk collection of English portraits from Larkin to Lely, and the Dolmetsch Collection of musical instruments. Open daily 10-5 (Nov.-Jan. 10-4). Closed Good Friday, Dec. 24, 25. Admission free.

Bridges.—The bridges over the Thames (from East to West) are: *Tower Bridge* (built by the Corporation of London and opened in 1894), with its bascules, operated now by new electrically-run machinery, walkway, opened to the public in 1982, and museum, opened in 1983; *London Bridge* (opened after rebuilding in 1831 by Rennie; the new London Bridge was completed in 1973 and opened by HM The Queen on March 16, 1973); *Southwark Bridge* (opened in 1819; also by Rennie. Rebuilt by the Corporation of London, 1922); *Blackfriars Bridge* (opened in 1769, rebuilt 1869, and widened by the Corporation of London in 1909); *Waterloo Bridge* (Rennie), opened in 1817, commanding a fine view of western London, rebuilt by LCC and reopened 1944; *Hungerford Bridge*, 1863 (railway bridge with a footbridge); *Westminster Bridge* (built in 1750 and then presenting a view that inspired Wordsworth's sonnet; rebuilt and re-opened in 1862; width, 84 ft.); *Lambeth Bridge* (built 1862, rebuilt 1932) leading from Lambeth Palace to Millbank; *Vauxhall Bridge* (built in 1811-16, rebuilt in 1906), leading to Kennington Oval; *Chelsea Bridge*, leading from Chelsea Hospital to Battersea Park (reconstructed and widened, 1937) and *Albert Bridge* (1873); *Battersea Bridge* (opened in 1890); *Wandsworth Bridge* (opened in 1873; rebuilt and re-opened in 1940); *Putney Bridge* (built 1729, rebuilt 1884, widened in 1933), where the Oxford and Cambridge Boat Race starts for Mortlake; *Hammersmith Bridge* (rebuilt 1887); *Barnes Bridge* (for pedestrians only, 1933); *Chiswick Bridge* (opened in 1933); *King Edward VII Bridge, Kew* (rebuilt in 1902, opened 1903), leading to the Royal Botanic Gardens, Kew; *Twickenham Lock Bridge; Twickenham Bridge* (opened 1933); *Richmond Bridge* (opened in 1777); *Kingston Bridge* (built 1828 and widened 1914) and *Hampton Court Bridge* (rebuilt 1933).

Buckingham Palace, SW1A 1AA. (Not open to the public).—Purchased by King George III in 1762 from the heir of the Duke of Buckingham, the Palace has been the London home of the Sovereign since Queen Victoria's accession in 1837. It was altered by Nash for King George IV, and refronted in stone (part of the Queen Victoria Memorial) by Sir Aston Webb in 1913.

The Queen's Gallery, containing a changing selection of the finest pictures and works of art from all parts of the royal collection, was opened to the public on July 25, 1962. Open Tues.-Sat. and Bank Holidays 10.30-5, Sun. 2-5. Admission charges are payable, entering from Buckingham Palace Road.

The Royal Mews is open to visitors on Wed. and Thurs. throughout the year (except in Ascot Week), 2-4. Admission charges, the net proceeds of which are devoted to charities, are payable at the entrance.

Canonbury Tower, N1.—The largest remaining part of a 16th century house originally built by the Priors of St. Bartholomew, and since 1952 used as the headquarters of a non-professional theatre company. Contains the 'Spencer' and 'Compton' oak-panelled rooms. Other relics of Canonbury House can be seen nearby.

Catholic Central Library, St. Francis Friary, 47 Francis Street, SW1P 1QR.—Founded as a private library in 1914, it was taken over in 1959 by the Franciscan Friars of the Atonement. It is an up-to-date lending and research library of over 55,000 volumes and 150 periodicals, for the general reader, student and ecumenist. Books are sent by post when required. Open Mon.-Fri. 10-5, Sat. 10-1.30.

Cemeteries.—In *Kensal Green Cemetery*, North Kensington, W10 (70 acres), are tombs of Thackeray,

Trollope, Sydney Smith, Wilkie Collins, Tom Hood, George Cruikshank, John Leech, Leigh Hunt, I. K. Brunel and Charles Kemble. In *Highgate Cemetery*, N6, are the tombs of George Eliot, Herbert Spencer, Faraday and Marx. Guided tours only, £2. In *Abney Park Cemetery*, Stoke Newington, N16, the tomb of General Booth, founder of the Salvation Army, and memorials to many Nonconformist Divines are to be found. In the *South Metropolitan Cemetery*, Norwood, SE27, are the tombs of Sir Henry Bessemer, Sir Hiram Maxim, Mrs. Beeton, Sir Henry Tate and Joseph Whitaker, FSA (*Whitaker's Almanack*). In the churchyard of the former *Marylebone Chapel* are buried Charles Wesley and his son Samuel Wesley (musician). The chapel itself was demolished in 1949. Crematoria.—*Ilford* (City of London); *Norwood*; *Hendon*; *Streatham Park*; *Finchley* (St. Marylebone) and *Golders Green* (12 acres), near Hampstead Heath, with 'Garden of Rest' and memorials to famous men and women.

Cenotaph, Whitehall, SW1.—(Literally 'empty tomb'.) Monument erected 'To the Glorious Dead', as a memorial to all ranks of the Sea, Land and Air Forces who gave their lives in the service of the Empire during the First World War. Designed by Sir Edwin Lutyens. Erected as a temporary memorial in 1919 and replaced by a permanent structure in 1920. Unveiled by King George V on Armistice Day, 1920. An additional inscription was added after the Second World War to commemorate those who gave their lives in that conflict.

Charterhouse, Sutton's Hospital, Charterhouse Square, EC1M 6AN.—A Carthusian monastery from 1371–1537, when it came into the possession of Sir Edward (later first Lord) North, who sold it in 1565 to the fourth Duke of Norfolk. After Norfolk's execution in 1572 following the Ridolfi Plot (hatched at Charterhouse), it was eventually granted by Queen Elizabeth I in 1587 to Norfolk's second son, Thomas Howard, later Earl of Suffolk. In 1611 he sold it to Thomas Sutton, who endowed it as a Hospital for aged men 'of gentle birth' and a school for poor scholars (removed to Godalming in 1872). The buildings are partly 15th but mainly 16th and 17th century. Parts of the building were damaged by bombing in 1941 but have been largely restored and now accommodate some 30 pensioners. Roger Williams, founder and governor of Rhode Island, was a scholar on the foundation. Among other famous pupils were John Wesley, Lord Baden-Powell, the poets and writers Crashaw, Lovelace and Thackeray, and more recently Lord Beveridge. Visitors are shown round on Wednesdays at 2.15 (April–July). Admission £1·50.
Master, E. E. Harrison, FSA.
Registrar and Clerk to the Governors, Lt.-Col. I. Macdonald.

Chelsea Physic Garden, 66 Royal Hospital Road, SW3 4HS.—A garden of general botanical research, maintaining a wide range of rare and unusual plants. The garden was established in 1673 by the Society of Apothecaries. Open on Wed. and Sun. p.m. during summer months. All enquiries to the Curator at above address.

City Business Library (Corporation of London), 106 Fenchurch Street, EC3M 5JB. Open Mon.-Fri. 9.30-5.00.

College of Arms or Heralds' College, Queen Victoria Street, EC4V 4BT.—Her Majesty's Officers of Arms (Kings, Heralds and Pursuivants of Arms) were first incorporated by Richard III, and granted Derby House on the site of the present College building by Philip and Mary. The building now in use dates from 1671–88. The powers vested by the

Crown in the Earl Marshal (The Duke of Norfolk) with regard to State ceremonial are largely exercised through the College, which is also the official repository of English pedigrees and all Arms granted to subjects of the Queen, except in Scotland and (since 1988) Canada. Enquiry may be made to the Officer on duty in the Public Office, Mon.-Fri. 10-4.

The Heralds Museum at the Tower of London (admission charge included in the Tower's own charge) aims to explain what heraldry is about and traces its development over the centuries to its application and use in modern times. Open April-Oct.

Commonwealth Institute, Kensington High Street, W8 6NQ.—A cultural and educational centre opened on Nov. 6, 1962, by HM The Queen, replacing the former Imperial Institute opened in 1893 in Kensington. A distinctive feature of the building is its paraboloid copper-sheathed roof. The Institute contains, in 60,000 square feet arranged in three floors of circular galleries, a visual representation of the history, geography and ways of life of the Commonwealth countries and dependencies, as well as educational resource, information and conference centres, and a restaurant and craft/bookshop.
Open Mon.–Sat. 10–5, Sun. 2–5. Admission free. Closed Christmas Eve, Christmas Day, Boxing Day, New Year's Day, Good Friday and May Day.

Courtauld Institute Galleries, Somerset House, Strand, WC2R 0RN.—The galleries of the University of London contain the Lee collection and the Gambier-Parry collections (14th century to 18th century old masters); the important Courtauld collection of Impressionist and Post-Impressionist paintings; the Roger Fry collection and the Witt and Spooner collections (old master drawings and English water-colours). A major new bequest, the Princes Gate collection of old master paintings and drawings, was received in July 1978, and the Alastair Hunter bequest of modern British works was received in 1983. The Galleries moved to Somerset House from Woburn Square in June 1990. Open weekdays 10–6, Sun. 2–6. Admission £2·50, concessions £1·00.

Design Museum, Butlers Wharf, SE1 2YD.—Comprising a study collection, temporary exhibitions, a review of new products, a library and a lecture theatre, the Museum attempts to increase the understanding of design by explaining how mass-produced consumer objects work and why they look as they do. Open Tues.–Sun. and Bank Hols. 11.30–6.30. Admission £2·50, concessions £1·50.

Downing Street.—Number 10 Downing Street, SW1, is the official town residence of the Prime Minister, No. 11 of the Chancellor of the Exchequer and No. 12 is the office of the Government Whips. The street was named after Sir George Downing, Bt., soldier and diplomatist, who was MP for Morpeth from 1660 to 1684.
Chequers, a Tudor mansion in the Chilterns, about three miles from Princes Risborough, was presented together with a maintenance endowment by Lord and Lady Lee of Fareham in 1917 to serve, from Jan. 1, 1921, as a country residence for the Prime Minister of the day, the Chequers estate of 700 acres being added to the gift by Lord Lee in 1921. The mansion contains a famous collection of Cromwellian portraits and relics.

Dulwich, SE21.—Contains *Dulwich College* (founded by Edward Alleyn in 1619) and the *Dulwich Picture Gallery*, built by Sir John Soane to house the collection bequeathed by the artist Sir Francis Bourgeois. The gallery, which is England's oldest public art gallery, was damaged in the Second World

War but rebuilt with the aid of a grant from the Pilgrim Trust and reopened in 1953. Open daily (not Mon.); Sun., afternoons only. *Dulwich Village* retains many of the rural characteristics of the presuburban period.

Eltham, SE9.—Contains remains of 13th–15th century *Eltham Palace,* the birthplace of John of Eltham (1316), son of Edward II. The hall, built by Edward IV, has a hammer-beam roof of chestnut. In the churchyard of St. John the Baptist is the tomb of Thomas Doggett, the comedian and founder of the Thames Watermen's championship (Doggett's Coat and Badge).

Ely Place, Holborn Circus, EC1.—Previously the site of the London house of the Bishop of Ely, Ely Place is a private street (built in 1773) whose affairs are administered by Commissioners under a special Act of Parliament. The 14th century chapel, now St. Etheldreda's (RC) Church, is open daily until dusk.

Fulham Palace, Bishop's Avenue, Fulham, SW6.—The courtyard is 16th century, the remainder 18th and 19th century. Former residence of the Bishop of London.

Geffrye Museum, Kingsland Road, E2 8EA.—The Museum is housed in a building erected originally as almshouses in 1713. The exhibits are displayed in a series of period rooms dating from 1600 to 1939, showing the development of decorative art and design. A display of woodworking tools focuses on furniture-making, and the museum has an interesting picture collection. Events and temporary exhibitions are held. Special arrangements exist for children visiting the Museum in school parties (which must be booked in advance) and in their leisure time. Open on Tues.–Sat. 10–5, Sun. 2–5. Closed on Christmas Eve, Christmas Day, Boxing Day, New Year's Day and Good Friday and on Mondays except Bank Holidays. Admission free.
Director, vacant.

George Inn, Borough High Street, SE1.—Near London Bridge Station. Given to the National Trust in 1937. Last galleried inn in London, built in 1677. Open during licensed hours.

Greenwich, SE10.—*Greenwich Hospital* (since 1873, the Royal Naval College) was built by Charles II, largely from designs by John Webb, and by Queen Anne and William III, from designs by Wren. It stands on the site of an ancient royal palace, and of the more recent *Palace of Placentia,* an enlarged edition of the palace, constructed by Humphrey, Duke of Gloucester (1391–1447), son of Henry IV. Henry VIII, Queen Mary I and Queen Elizabeth I were born in the Royal Palace (which reverted to the Crown in 1447) and King Edward VI died there. In the principal quadrangle is a marble statue of George II by Rysbraeck. (For National Maritime Museum, *see* Index.) *Painted Hall* and *Chapel,* open daily (not Thurs.) 2.30–5. Visitors are also admitted to Sunday Service in the Chapel at 11 a.m., summer and winter, except during College vacations. *Greenwich Park* (196½ acres) was enclosed by Humphrey, Duke of Gloucester, and laid out by Charles II, from the designs of Le Nôtre. *The Queen's House,* begun in 1616, was designed for Anne of Denmark by Inigo Jones. Open Mon.–Sat. 10–6, Sun. 2–6. £6, concs. £3. On a hill in Greenwich Park is the former Royal Observatory (founded 1675). Part of its buildings at Greenwich have been taken over by the Maritime Museum and named *Flamsteed House,* after John Flamsteed (1646–1719), first Astronomer Royal. Astronomical and navigational equipment is exhibited, and the time ball and zero meridian of longitude can also be seen.

The Parish church of Greenwich (*St. Alfege*) was rebuilt by Hawksmoor (Wren's pupil) in 1728, and restored after severe damage during the Second World War. General Wolfe and Thomas Tallis are buried in the church. Henry VIII was christened in the former church. *Charlton House* was built in the early 17th century (1607–1612) for Adam Newton, tutor to Prince Henry, brother to Charles I. It is largely in the Jacobean style of architecture. *Cutty Sark,* the last of the famous tea clippers, which has been preserved as a memorial to ships and men of a past era is fully restored and re-rigged, with a museum of sail on board. Open weekdays 11–5 (summer 11–6), Sundays and Boxing Day 2.30–5. The yacht *Gipsy Moth IV* in which Sir Francis Chichester sailed single-handed round the world, 1966–67, is preserved alongside the *Cutty Sark.*

Guildhall, Gresham Street, City, EC2.—Scene of civic government for the City for more than a thousand years. Built *c.*1440; façade built 1788–9; damaged in the Great Fire, 1666, and by incendiary bombs, 1940. The main hall and crypt (the most extensive medieval crypt in London) have been restored. Events in Guildhall include the annual election of Lord Mayor, election of Sheriffs, receptions in honour of Sovereigns and Heads of State, and the meetings of the Court of Common Council (*see* 'Corporation of London'). Open weekdays and Sun. (May to Sept.) 10–5. Admission free.
Keeper of the Guildhall, J. H. Lucioni.
The *Guildhall Library* (reference) and the Library and Museum of the Clockmakers' Company are housed in new premises. Library open Mon.–Sat. 9.30–5, Museum open Mon.–Fri. 9.30–4.45. Admission free (entrance in Aldermanbury). The Library contains plans of London, 1570; Deed of Sale with Shakespeare's signature; first, second and fourth folios of Shakespeare's plays etc. (*See also* City Business Library.)

Hampton Court Palace, East Molesey, Surrey.—Sixteenth-century palace built by Cardinal Wolsey, with additions by Sir Christopher Wren for William and Mary. Beautiful gardens with maze and grape vine (planted in 1769). State Apartments and collection of pictures. Tennis Court, built by King Henry VIII in 1530. Collection of Mantegna paintings. Gardens open daily until dusk, Maze and Palace open mid March–mid Oct. daily 9.30–6, mid Oct.–March 9.30–4.30. Admission charge for Maze and Palace. Gardens free.

Honourable Artillery Company's Headquarters, City Road, EC1Y 2BQ.—The HAC received its charter of incorporation from Henry VIII in 1537, and has occupied its present ground since 1641. The Armoury House dates from 1735. The present castellated barracks date from 1860. Four of its members who emigrated in the 17th century, founded in 1638 the Ancient and Honorable Artillery Company of Massachusetts. The HAC is the senior regiment of the Territorial Army Volunteer Reserves, and maintains a Headquarters, four squadrons, a gun troop, and two companies of the Home Service Force.
Chief Exec., Capt. G. C. Lloyd, CBE, RN.

Horniman Museum and Library, London Road, Forest Hill, SE23 3PQ.—The Museum was presented in 1901 to the London County Council by F. J. Horniman, MP. With the adjoining Gardens, it is now an independent charitable trust. The Museum has three main departments: ethnography, musical instruments and natural history. In the ethnography department the large collections include exhibits illustrating man's progress in the arts and crafts from prehistoric times. The natural history department includes an aquarium. Reference library (not Mon.). Education Service (adults and schoolchildren). Free

concerts and lectures (autumn and spring). Special exhibitions. Open Mon.–Sat. 10.30–6, Sun. 2–6 (not Christmas). Admission free.
Director, D. M. Boston, OBE.

Horse Guards, Whitehall, SW1.—Archway and offices built about 1753. The mounting of the guard (Life Guards, or the Blues and Royals) at 11 a.m. (10 a.m. on Sundays) and the dismounted inspection at 4 p.m. are picturesque ceremonies. Only those on the Lord Chamberlain's list may drive through the gates and archway into *Horse Guard's Parade* (230,000 sq. ft.), where the Colour is 'trooped' on the Queen's Official Birthday.

The Houses of Parliament, Westminster, SW1.—An ordinance issued in the reign of Richard II stated that 'Parliament shall be holden or kepid wheresoever it pleaseth the King' and to the present day the Sovereign summons Parliament to meet and prescribes the time and place of meeting. The royal palace of Westminster, originally built by Edward the Confessor (Westminster Hall (*q.v.*) being added by William Rufus), was the normal place of Parliament from about 1340. St. Stephen's Chapel was used from about 1550 for the meetings of the House of Commons, which had previously been held in the Chapter House or Refectory of Westminster Abbey. The House of Lords met in an apartment of the royal palace.

The fire of 1834 destroyed much of the palace and the present Houses of Parliament were erected on the site from the designs of Sir Charles Barry and Augustus Welby Pugin between 1840 and 1867. The Chamber of the House of Commons was destroyed by bombing in 1941 and a new Chamber designed by Sir Giles Gilbert Scott was used for the first time on Oct. 26, 1950.

The *Victoria Tower* of the House of Lords is about 330 ft. high, and when Parliament is sitting the Union Flag flies by day from its flagstaff. *The Clock Tower* of the House of Commons is about 320 ft. high and contains 'Big Ben', the hour bell said to be named after Sir Benjamin Hall, First Commissioner of Works when the original bell was cast in 1856. This bell, which weighed 16 tons 11 cwt., was found to be cracked in 1857. The present bell (13½ tons) is a recasting of the original and was first brought into use in July 1859. The dials of the clock are 23 ft. in diameter, the hands being 9 ft. and 14 ft. long (including balance piece). A light is displayed from the Clock Tower at night when Parliament is sitting.

For security reasons tours of the Houses of Parliament are available only to those who have made advance arrangements through a Member or Peer.

Admission to the Strangers' Gallery of the House of Lords is arranged by a Peer or by queue via St. Stephen's Entrance. Admission to the Strangers' Gallery of the House of Commons is by Members' order (Members' orders should be sought several weeks in advance), or by queue via St. Stephen's Entrance. Queues are usually shorter after 6 p.m., Mon.–Thurs. Overseas visitors may obtain cards of introduction from their Embassy or High Commission.

Inns of Court.—The *Inner* and *Middle Temple*, S. of Fleet Street, EC4, and N. of Victoria Embankment, to which the gardens extend, have occupied (since the early 14th century) the site of the buildings of the Order of Knights Templars. *Inner Temple Hall* (rebuilt in 1955 after bomb damage) is open Mon.–Fri. 10.30–11.30 and 3–4 on application to Treasurer's Office during law sittings. *Middle Temple Hall* (1562–70) is open when not in use, Mon.–Fri. 10–12 and 3–4. Closed on Public Holidays. In Middle Temple Gardens (not open to the public) Shakespeare (Henry VI, Part

I) places the incident which led to the 'Wars of the Roses' (1455–85).

Temple Church, EC4, was restored in 1958 after severe damage by bombing. The nave formed one of five remaining round churches in England (the others being at Cambridge, Northampton, Little Maplestead (Essex) and Ludlow Castle). Open weekdays 10–4.—Services: 8.30 and 11.15 a.m. except in August and September. *Master of the Temple*, Rev. Canon J. Robinson.

Lincoln's Inn, from Chancery Lane to Lincoln's Inn Fields, WC2, occupies the site of the palace of a former Bishop of Chichester and of a Black Friars monastery. Records show the Society as being in existence in 1422. The Hall and Library Buildings are of 1845, although the Library is first mentioned in 1474, the old Hall early 16th century and the Chapel was rebuilt *c.*1619–23. Halls open by appointment, Chapel and Gardens, Mon.–Fri. 12–2.30. Tours, weekdays mid March–mid Sept. 9.30–11.30, £2. Chapel services Sun. 11.30 a.m. during Law Terms. *Lincoln's Inn Fields* (7 acres). The Square, laid out by Inigo Jones, contains many fine old houses with handsome interiors.

Gray's Inn, Holborn/Gray's Inn Road, WC1. Early 14th century. Hall (1556–60). Chapel (largely rebuilt after bomb damage in the Second World War). Services 11.15 a.m. (during Law Dining Terms only.) Holy Communion 1st Sunday in every month except Aug.–Sept. Public welcome. Gardens open to the public Mon.–Fri. The Inn has been completely restored to its former beauty with gracious red brick buildings overlooking grass covered squares and gardens. Strong Elizabethan associations.

No other 'Inns' are active, but what remains of *Staple Inn* is worth visiting as a relic of Elizabethan London; though heavy damage was done by a flying-bomb, it retains a picturesque gabled front on Holborn (opposite Gray's Inn Road). *Clement's Inn* (near St. Clement Danes' Church), *Clifford's Inn,* Fleet Street, and *Thavies Inn,* Holborn Circus, are all rebuilt. *Serjeant's Inn,* Fleet Street (damaged by bombing) and another (demolished 1910) of the same name in Chancery Lane, were composed of Serjeants-at-Law, the last of whom died in 1922.

Jewish Museum, Woburn House, Tavistock Square, WC1H 0EP.—Opened in 1932, the Museum contains a rich collection of ceremonial art, portraits and antiquities, illustrating Jewish life, history and religion. Open Tues.–Thurs. and Sun. (and Fri. in summer) 10–4, Fri. in winter 10–12.45. Closed on public and Jewish holidays. Group visits by arrangement with Secretary.

Kensington Palace, W8 4PX.—The original house was bought by William III in 1689 and enlarged by Christoper Wren. The State Apartments contain pictures and furniture from the royal collections. A suite of rooms devoted to the memory of Queen Victoria is also shown and there is a display of royal wedding dresses. The *Court Dress Collection* is also open, and includes three restored rooms: the Red Saloon, the Teck Saloon and the room where Queen Victoria is said to have been born in 1819. Both open weekdays 9–5, Sun. 1–5. Admission £3.50, concessions £2.60, £2.30.

Kenwood, NW3 7JR.—Nearly 200 acres forming the northern part of Hampstead Heath. Open air symphony concerts each summer. The Iveagh Bequest, in an Adam villa, includes valuable paintings and furniture. Recitals and poetry readings in the Orangery. House open daily, except Good Friday and Dec. 24, 25. Times vary seasonally. Admission free.

Kew, Surrey.—A favourite home of the early Hanoverian monarchs. Kew House, the residence of Frederick, Prince of Wales, and later of his son,

George III, was pulled down in 1803, but the earlier Dutch House, now known as *Kew Palace*, survives. It was built in 1631 and acquired by George III as an annexe to Kew House in 1781. Open April–Sept., 11–5.30. The famous Kew Gardens (*see* Index) were originally laid out as a private garden for Kew House for George III's mother in 1759 and were much enlarged in the 19th century, notably by the inclusion of the grounds of the former Richmond Lodge. *Queen Charlotte's Cottage* is also open at the weekends.

Kneller Hall, Twickenham, TW2 7DU.—Royal Military School of Music. A band of up to 120 instrumentalists gives concerts in the grounds on Wednesdays throughout the summer, commencing at 8 p.m. Admission charge. Season tickets and party bookings available.

Lambeth Palace, SE1.—The official residence of the Archbishop of Canterbury, on the south bank of the Thames; the oldest part is 13th century, the house itself being early 19th century. For leave to visit the historical portions, applications should be made by letter to the Archbishop's Chaplain.

Livery Companies' Halls.—The principal Companies (*see* Index) have magnificent halls but admission to view them has generally to be arranged beforehand. The following are among the finest or more interesting. *Goldsmiths' Hall*, Foster Lane. The present hall was completed in 1835, and contains some magnificent rooms. *Fishmongers' Hall*, London Bridge (built 1831–3), restored after severe bomb damage, also contains fine rooms. *Apothecaries' Hall*, Black Friars Lane, was rebuilt in 1670 after the Great Fire, and has library, hall and kitchen which are good examples of this period. *Vintners' Hall*, Upper Thames Street, was also rebuilt after the Great Fire, and its hall has late 17th century panelling. The Watermen and Lightermen's Company is not, strictly speaking, a Livery Company, but its *Hall*, in St. Mary-at-Hill, is a good example of a smaller 18th century building, with pilastered façade. It was completed in 1780. *Stationers' Hall*, in Stationers' Hall Court, behind Ludgate Hill, has a particularly finely carved screen; its façade dates from 1800. *Barbers' Hall*, Monkwell Street, with a Hall attributed to Inigo Jones, was completely destroyed by bombing, but has been rebuilt. The new hall was built some 30 ft. from the old site to enable one of the bastions and part of the wall of the Roman fort to remain exposed to view.

Lloyd's, Lime Street, EC3M 7HA.—Society of private underwriters which evolved during the 18th century from Lloyds Coffee House. Housed in the Royal Exchange for 150 years and in Leadenhall Street and Lime Street from 1928–1986. The present building was opened for business in May 1986, and houses the Lutine Bell. Underwriting is on four floors with a total area of 114,000 sq. ft. A visitors' gallery is open daily and incorporates an exhibition showing the history and operation of the insurance market at Lloyds.

London Planetarium, Marylebone Road, NW1 5LR.—Open daily (except Christmas Day), star shows 11–4.30. Admission charge.

London Transport Museum, Covent Garden, WC2E 7BB.—Housed in the former Flower Market, the Museum contains a collection of buses, trams, trolley-buses, trains, working displays and London Transport paraphernalia. There is a research library and lecture theatre. Open daily 10–6 (except Dec. 24, 25, 26). Admission £2·60, concessions £1·20.

Lord's Cricket Ground, St. John's Wood Road, NW8 8QN.—The headquarters (since 1814) of the Marylebone Cricket Club, the premier cricket club in England (founded 1787). Lord's is the scene of some

of the principal matches of the season and Middlesex County headquarters. Real tennis court and squash courts in building behind members' pavilion.

The MCC Museum is open on match days 10.30–5. Admission £1, concessions 50p. Conducted tours on most days throughout the year can be arranged in advance with the Tours Manager.

Madame Tussaud's Exhibition, Marylebone Road NW1 5LR.—Open daily (except Christmas Day) 10–5.30. Admission charge.

Mansion House, City, EC4.—(Built 1739–53, reconstructed 1930–31.) The official residence of the Lord Mayor; the Egyptian Hall and Ballroom are the chief attractions. Group visits only by arrangement with the Principal's Assistant.

Markets.—The London markets (administered by the Corporation of the City of London) provide foodstuffs for 8,500,000 to 9,000,000 people. *Central Meat, Fish, Fruit, Vegetable, and Poultry Markets*, Smithfield (built 1866) (now moved) the largest meat market in the world and site of St. Bartholomew's Fair from 9th to 19th century; *Leadenhall Market* (meat and poultry), built 1881, part recently demolished; *Billingsgate* (fish), Thames Street, built 1875, part recently demolished, a market site for over 1,000 years (moved to the Isle of Dogs in Jan. 1982); *Spitalfields*, E1 (vegetables, fruit, etc.), enlarged 1928, and opened by Queen Mary (moved to Leyton, Sept. 1990); *London Fruit Exchange*, Brushfield Street, built by Corporation of London 1928–29; *Covent Garden* (vegetables, fruit, flowers, etc.), (now moved to Nine Elms) established under a charter of Charles II, in 1661; *Borough Market*, SE1 (vegetables, fruit, flowers, etc.).

Marlborough House, Pall Mall, SW1A 2AF.—Built by Wren for the first Duke of Marlborough and completed in 1711, the house finally reverted to the Crown in 1835. Prince Leopold lived there until 1831, and Queen Adelaide from 1837 until her death in 1849. In 1863 it became the London house of the Prince of Wales and was the London home of Queen Mary until her death in 1953. The Queen's Chapel, Marlborough Gate, begun in 1623 from the designs of Inigo Jones for the Infanta Maria of Spain, and completed for Queen Henrietta Maria, is open to the public for services on Sundays at 8.30 a.m. and 11.15 a.m. between Easter Day and end July (*see also* St. James's Palace for winter services in The Chapel Royal). In 1959 Marlborough House was given by the Queen as a centre for Commonwealth Government conferences and it was opened as such in March, 1962.

London Monument (commonly called 'The Monument'), Monument Street, EC3.—Built from designs of Wren, 1671–77, to commemorate the Great Fire of London, which broke out in Pudding Lane, Sept. 2, 1666. The fluted Doric column is 120 ft. high (the moulded cylinder above the balcony supporting a flaming vase of gilt bronze is 42 ft. in addition), and is based on a square plinth 40 ft. high, with fine carvings on W. face (making a total height of 202 ft.). Splendid views of London from gallery at top of column (311 steps). Open April–Sept., Mon.–Fri. 9–6, Sat. and Sun. 2–6. Oct.–March, Mon.–Sat. 9–4. Closed Christmas Day, Boxing Day and Good Friday. Admission charge.

Monuments.—*Albert Memorial*, South Kensington; *Royal Air Force*, Victoria Embankment; *Beaconsfield*, Parliament Square; *Beatty, Jellicoe* and *Cunningham*, Trafalgar Square; *Belgian Gratitude* (Reginald Blomfield), Victoria Embankment; *Boadicea* (or 'Boudicca'), Queen of the Iceni (Thomas Thornycroft), Westminster Bridge; *Brunel* (Marochetti), Victoria Embankment; *Burghers of Calais* (Rodin), Victoria Tower Gardens, Westminster;

Burns, Embankment Gardens; *Carlyle* (Boehm), Cheyne Walk, Chelsea; *Cavalry,* Hyde Park; *Edith Cavell* (Frampton), St. Martin's Place; *Cenotaph* (Lutyens), Whitehall; *Charles I,* Trafalgar Square; *Charles II,* inside the Royal Exchange; *Churchill,* Parliament Square; *Cleopatra's Needle* (68½ ft. high, *c.*1500 BC, erected on the Thames Embankment in 1877–8; the Sphinxes are Victorian); *Clive,* Whitehall; *Captain Cook* (Brock), The Mall; *Crimean,* Broad Sanctuary; *Oliver Cromwell* (Thornycroft), outside Westminster Hall; *Lord Dowding* (Faith Winter), between Australia House and St. Clement Danes, Strand; *Duke of Cambridge,* Whitehall; *Duke of York* (124 ft.), Carlton House Terrace; *Edward VII* (Mackennal), Waterloo Place; *Elizabeth I* (1586, oldest outdoor statue in London; from Ludgate), Fleet Street; *Eros* (Shaftesbury Memorial) (Gilbert), Piccadilly Circus; *Marechal Foch,* Grosvenor Gardens; *Charles James Fox,* Bloomsbury Square; *George III,* Cockspur Street; *George IV* (Chantrey), riding without stirrups, Trafalgar Square; *George V,* Old Palace Yard; *George VI,* Carlton Gardens; *Gladstone,* facing Australia House, Strand; *Guards'* (Crimea), Waterloo Place; (Great War), Horse Guards' Parade; *Haig* (Hardiman), Whitehall; *Irving* (Brock), N. side of National Portrait Gallery; *James II,* Trafalgar Square; *Samuel Johnson,* opposite St. Clement Danes; *Kitchener,* Horse Guards' Parade; *Abraham Lincoln,* Parliament Square; *Milton,* St. Giles, Cripplegate; *The Monument* (*see* above); *Mountbatten,* Foreign Office Green; *Nelson* (170 ft. 2 in.), Trafalgar Square, with Landseer's lions (cast from guns recovered from the wreck of the *Royal George*); *Florence Nightingale,* Waterloo Place; *Palmerston,* Parliament Square; *Peel,* Parliament Square; *Pitt* (Chantrey), Hanover Square; *Portal,* Embankment Gardens; *Prince Consort,* Holborn Circus; *Raleigh,* Whitehall; *Richard Coeur de Lion* (Marochetti), Old Palace Yard; *Roberts,* Horse Guards' Parade; *Franklin D. Roosevelt* (Reid Dick), Grosvenor Square; *Royal Artillery* (South Africa), The Mall; (Great War), Hyde Park Corner; *Captain Scott* (Lady Scott), Waterloo Place; *Shackleton,* Kensington Gore; *Shakespeare,* Leicester Square; *Smuts* (Epstein), Parliament Square; *Sullivan,* Victoria Embankment; *Trenchard,* Victoria Embankment; *Victoria Memorial,* in front of Buckingham Palace; *George Washington* (Houdon copy), Trafalgar Square; *Wellington,* Hyde Park Corner; *Wellington* (Chantrey) riding without stirrups, Royal Exchange; *John Wesley,* City Road; *William III,* St. James's Square; *Wolseley,* Horse Guards' Parade.

Percival David Foundation of Chinese Art, 53 Gordon Square, WC1H 0PD.—Set up in 1950, the Foundation contains the collection of Chinese ceramics formed by Sir Percival David and his important library of books on Chinese art. To these was added a gift from the Hon. Mountstuart Elphinstone of part of his collection of Chinese monochrome porcelains. The Foundation is administered on behalf of the University of London by the School of Oriental and African Studies. Galleries, Mon.–Fri. 10.30–5. Closed weekends and Bank Holidays. Library available to ticket holders only; applications in writing to the *Curator,* Miss R. Scott.

Port of London.—The Port of London covers the tidal portion of the River Thames from Teddington to the seaward limit (Tongue light vessel), a distance of 150 km. The governing body is the Port of London Authority (PLA), whose Head Office is at International House, World Trade Centre, E1 9UN.

The enclosed dock at Tilbury is wholly-owned by the PLA and is 40 km. below London Bridge. The docks perform every type of cargo-handling operation. Tilbury is principally used by vessels to and from Australia, North and South America, India,

Middle and Far East, Scandinavia, USSR and continental Europe.

Passenger vessels and cruise liners can be handled at moorings at Greenwich, Tower Bridge and Tilbury Passenger Landing Stage. The latter provides accommodation for liners at all states of the tide.

Prince Henry's Room, 17 Fleet Street, EC4.— Early 17th century timber-framed house containing fine room on first floor with panelling and moulded plaster ceiling. Includes an exhibition on Samuel Pepys and the London in which he lived. Open Mon.– Fri. 1.45–5, Sat 1.45–4.30. Closed Christmas Day, Good Friday and Bank Holidays. Admission free. Available for morning or evening lettings on application to The Town Clerk, Guildhall, EC2.

Richmond, Surrey.—Contains the red brick gateway of *Richmond Palace* (Henry VII, 1485–1509) and buildings of the Jacobean, Queen Anne, and early Georgian periods, including *White Lodge* in Richmond Park, the former home of Queen Mary's mother (the Duke of Windsor was born there, June 23, 1894), and now the home of the Royal Ballet Lower School. The *Star and Garter* Home for Disabled Soldiers, Sailors, and Airmen (the Women's Memorial of the Great War) was opened by Queen Mary in 1924. *Richmond Park* (2,469 acres) contains herds of fallow and red deer.

Roman London.—Although visible remains from this period are few, excavations carried out in the City on sites due for redevelopment often reveal Roman features. Sections of the City Wall are the most striking remains to be seen of Roman *Londinium,* although even these are largely medieval due to the Roman wall being rebuilt during the medieval period. Sections may be seen near the White Tower in the Tower of London; at Tower Hill; at Coopers' Row; at All Hallows, London Wall, its vestry being built on the remains of a semi-circular Roman bastion; at St. Alphage, London Wall, showing a striking succession of building repairs from Roman until the late medieval period, and at St. Giles, Cripplegate. Excavations in the Cripplegate area have revealed that a Roman fort was built there *c.* AD 100–120. It was later incorporated into the city wall when this was built *c.* AD 200.

The administrative centre of the Roman city was the great forum and basilica, more than 165 metres square, sections of which have been encountered during excavations in the area of Leadenhall, Gracechurch Street and Lombard Street. Excavations during the past few years have revealed Roman activity along the river. Traces of a massive riverside wall, built in the late Roman period, have been found and a succession of Roman timber quays have been excavated along Lower and Upper Thames Street helping to prove that Roman London was a thriving commercial centre.

Other major buildings found are the *Provincial Governor's Palace* in Cannon Street; remains of a bath-building, preserved in Lower Thames Street; and the *Temple of Mithras* in Walbrook. The fine sculptures from this temple are displayed in the Museum of London (*see* Index) where many other relics from the Roman City may be seen. There is also an Ordnance Survey map of Roman London.

Royal Albert Hall, Kensington Gore, SW7 2AP.— The elliptical hall, one of the largest in the world, was completed in 1871, and since 1941 has been the venue each summer for the Promenade Concerts founded in 1895 by Sir Henry Wood. Also used for public meetings, concerts, sports and other entertainments. Guided tours are available in the summer months.
Chief Exec., P. Deuchar.

Royal Exchange, EC3V 3LS.—Founded by Sir Thomas Gresham, 1566, opened as 'The Bourse' and proclaimed 'The Royal Exchange' by Queen Elizabeth I, 1571, rebuilt 1667–69 and 1842–44. The building is occupied by Guardian Royal Exchange Assurance and by the London International Financial Futures Exchange. It is administered by the Gresham Committee.
Clerk, Mercers' Hall, Ironmonger Lane, EC2.

Royal Geographical Society, Kensington Gore, SW7 2AR.—Map room open to public, admission free. Advice for scientific expeditions abroad, by appointment only.

Royal Hospital, Chelsea, Royal Hospital Road, Chelsea, SW3 4SL. Founded by Charles II, in 1682, and built by Wren; opened in 1692 for old and disabled soldiers. Great Hall, Chapel and Museum open daily 10–12, 2–4 (Museum closed on Sunday afternoons Oct.–March). The extensive grounds include the former Ranelagh Gardens, and are the venue for the Chelsea Flower Show held each May by the Royal Horticultural Society.
Governor, General Sir Roland Guy, GCB, CBE, DSO.
Lieut.-Governor and Secretary, Maj.-Gen. A. L. Watson, CB.

Royal Opera House, Covent Garden, WC2E 7DD.—Home of The Royal Ballet (1931), The Royal Opera (1946) and the Birmingham Royal Ballet (1990), formerly Sadler's Wells Royal Ballet (1946), the Royal Opera House is the third theatre to be built on the site, opening May 15, 1858: the first was opened Dec. 7, 1732. The season of the resident companies runs mid Sept.–Aug.
General Director, J. Isaacs.

St. James's Palace, in Pall Mall, SW1.—(Closed to the public). Built by Henry VIII; the Gatehouse and Presence Chamber remain; later alterations were made by Wren and Kent. The Chapel Royal is open for services on Sundays at 8.30 a.m. and 11.15 a.m. between beginning October and Good Friday (*see also* **Marlborough House** for summer services in The Queen's Chapel). Representatives of Foreign Powers are still accredited 'to the Court of St. James's'. *Clarence House* (1825) in the palace precinct is the home of HM The Queen Mother.

St. Paul's Cathedral, EC4M 8AD.—Built 1675–1710, cost £747,660. The cross on the dome is 365 ft. above the ground level, the inner cupola 218 ft. above the floor. 'Great Paul' in the south-west tower weighs 17 tons. Organ by Father Smith (enlarged by Willis and rebuilt by Mander) in a case carved by Grinling Gibbons (who also carved the choir stalls). The choir and high altar were restored in 1958 after war damage and the North Transept in 1962. The American War Memorial Chapel was consecrated in November, 1958. The chapel of the Most Excellent Order of the British Empire in the Crypt of the Cathedral was dedicated in 1960. Nave and transepts free. The following parts open weekdays 10–4.15 (Sat. 11–4.15). Admission: Ambulatory, £1; Crypt, Treasury and historical display, £1·50; whispering gallery, stone gallery, £2·50 (Children reduced price.)—Services: Sundays, 8, 10.30, 11.30 and 3.15. Weekdays, 7.30, 8, 12.30 and 5.

Sherlock Holmes Museum, 221B Baker Street, NW1 6XE.—Looks at the 'Life and Times' of Sherlock Holmes as portrayed by Sir Arthur Conan Doyle. Run by the Sherlock Holmes International Society. Open Mon.–Fri., 10–6; weekend by appointment. £5, conc. £3.

Sir John Soane's Museum, 13 Lincoln's Inn Fields, WC2A 3BP.—The house and galleries, built 1812–24, are the work of the founder, Sir John Soane (1753–1837) and contain his collections, arranged as he left them, in pursuance of an Act procured by him in 1833. Exhibits include the Sarcophagus of Seti 1 (*c.*1290 BC), Classical vases and marbles, Hogarth's *Rake's Progress* and *Election* series, paintings by Canaletto, Reynolds, Turner, Lawrence, etc., and sculpture by Chantrey, Flaxman, etc. Soane's library of 8,000 vols, and collection of 40,000 architectural drawings are available for study by appointment. Open Tues.–Sat. 10–5. Closed Bank Holidays. Tours must be booked in advance.
Curator, P. Thornton, FSA.

Somerset House, Strand, WC2, and Victoria Embankment, WC2.—The beautiful river façade (600 ft. long) was built in 1776–86 from the designs of Sir William Chambers; the eastern extension, which houses part of King's College, was built by Smirke in 1829. Somerset House was the property of Lord Protector Somerset, at whose attainder in 1552 the palace passed to the Crown, and it was a royal residence until 1692.

South Bank, SE1.—The arts complex on the south bank of the River Thames includes the South Bank Centre, owned and managed by the South Bank Board, and consisting of the 2,903-seat *Royal Festival Hall* (opened in 1951 for the Festival of Britain), a major venue for concert and ballet seasons, with the adjacent 1,056-seat *Queen Elizabeth Hall* and 368-seat *Purcell Room,* accommodating smaller-scale performances.

The *National Film Theatre* (opened 1958), administered by the British Film Institute, has two auditoria showing films, television and video of outstanding historical, artistic or technical merit. The London Film Festival is held here every November.

The *National Theatre* opened in 1976 and stages classical, modern, new and neglected plays in its three auditoria: the 1,160-seat Olivier theatre (open stage), the 890-seat Lyttelton theatre (proscenium stage) and the experimental Cottesloe theatre (adaptable stage) which seats up to 400.

The *Museum of the Moving Image* charts the history of the moving image in cinema and television from the earliest devices through to disc technology. Open Tues.–Sat. 10–8, Sun. and Bank Holidays 10–6 (Oct.–May), 10–8 (June–Sept.). Admission £3·95, concessions £2·75.

Southwark Cathedral, SE1 9DA.—Mainly 13th century, but the nave is largely rebuilt. The tomb of John Gower (1330–1408) is between the Bunyan and Chaucer memorial windows in the north aisle; Shakespeare's effigy backed by a view of Southwark and the Globe Theatre in the south aisle; the altar screen (erected 1520) has been restored; the tomb of Bishop Andrews (died 1626) is near the screen. The Early English Lady Chapel (behind the choir), restored 1930, was the scene of the Consistory Courts of the reign of Mary (Gardiner and Bonner) and is still used as a Consistory Court. John Harvard, after whom Harvard University is named, was baptized here in 1607, and the Chapel by the North Choir Aisle is his memorial chapel. Open 8.30–6, admission free.—Services: Sundays, 11, 3. Weekdays, 12.30, 12.45, 5.30 (sung on Tuesdays and Fridays), Saturdays, 12 noon.

Stock Exchange, EC2.—The market floor of the new Stock Exchange building in London opened for trading in June, 1973. Since 'Big Bang' in 1986, the floor has been used solely by the London Traded Options Market. A tower, 331 feet high, and the new Market replace the complex of buildings started in 1801 on the same site. The new building is the headquarters of the Stock Exchange, following the amalgamation of all the Stock Exchanges in Great Britain and Ireland on March 25, 1973.

The Visitors Gallery is open Mon.–Fri., 9.30–5. Admission free and without ticket. Film show, advance bookings are advisable via the Public Information Unit (071-588 2355).

Thames Embankments.—The *Victoria Embankment*, on the N. side (from Westminster to Blackfriars), was constructed by Sir Joseph William Bazalgette for the Metropolitan Board of Works, 1864–70 (the seats, of which the supports of some are a kneeling camel, laden with spicery, and of others a winged sphinx, were presented by the Grocers' Company, and by Rt. Hon. W. H. Smith, MP, in 1874); the *Albert Embankment*, on the S. side (from Westminster Bridge to Vauxhall), 1866–69; the *Chelsea Embankment*, 1871–74. The total cost exceeded £2,000,000. Bazalgette (1819–91) also inaugurated the London main drainage system, 1858–65. A medallion has been placed on a pier of the Victoria Embankment to commemorate the engineer of the Thames waterside improvements (*'Flumini vincula posuit'*). County Hall includes an embankment on the Surrey side.

Thames Flood Barrier.—Officially opened in May 1984, though. first used in Feb. 1983, the Barrier consists of ten rising sector gates which span 570 yards from bank to bank of the Thames at Woolwich Reach. When not in use the gates lie horizontally, allowing shipping to navigate the river normally; when the Barrier is closed, the gates turn through 90 degrees to stand vertically more than 50 feet above the river bed. The Barrier took eight years to complete and can be raised within about 30 minutes.

Thames Tunnels.—The *Rotherhithe Tunnel*, opened in 1908 at a cost of £1,506,914, connects Commercial Road, E14, with Lower Road, Rotherhithe; it is 1 mile 332 yards long, of which 474 yards are under the river. The first *Blackwall Tunnel* (vehicles) opened in 1897 at a cost of £1,323,663, connects East India Dock Road, Poplar, with Blackwall Lane, East Greenwich. A second tunnel (for southbound vehicles only) was opened in 1967 at a cost of £9,750,000 and the old tunnel was improved at a cost of £1,350,000 and made one-way northbound. Both tunnels are now for vehicles only. The relative lengths of the tunnels measured from East India Dock Road to the Gate House on the south side are 6,215 ft. (old tunnel) and 6,152 ft. *Greenwich Tunnel* (pedestrians only), opened in 1902 at a cost of £180,000, connects the Isle of Dogs, Poplar, with Greenwich. It is 406 yards long. The *Woolwich Tunnel* (pedestrians only), opened in 1912 at a cost of £86,000, connects North and South Woolwich below the passenger and vehicular ferry from North Woolwich Station, E16, to High Street, Woolwich, SE18. The tunnel is 552 yards long.

Tower Bridge Walkway and Museum, SE1 2UP.—Owned by the Bridge House Trust of the City of London and open daily April–Oct. 10–6·30, Nov.–March 10–4·45. Admission £2·50, concessions £1. Attractions include exhibitions, videos, the observation platform and walkway, engine rooms, working models and souvenir gift shop.

Tower of London, EC3.—Admission to a general view of the Tower, the White Tower, the History, Oriental, Ordnance and 18th–19th century Galleries, the Royal Armouries (National Museum of Arms and Armour), and the Wall Walk Phases I and II.

The White Tower is the oldest and central building of the Royal Palace and Fortress of the Tower of London. It was built at the order of William I and constructed by Gundulph, Bishop of Rochester, in the years 1078–98. The Inner Wall, with thirteen towers, was constructed by Henry III in the 12th century. The Moat was extended and completed by Richard I and the Wharf first mentioned in 1228. The Outer Wall was completed in the reign of Edward I and now incorporates six towers and two bastions. The last Monarch to reside in the Tower of London was James I. The Crown Jewels came to the Tower in the reign of Henry III. All coinage used in Great Britain was minted in the Outer Ward of the Tower of London until 1810 when the Royal Mint was formed. The Tower of London has had a military garrison since 1078. The Chapel Royal of St. John the Evangelist, within the White Tower (1080–1088) is the oldest Norman church in London. The chapel of St. Peter ad Vincula was built in the early 16th century.

Open weekdays March–Oct., 9.30–5.45, Nov.–Feb., 9.30–4.30; Sundays, March–Oct., 2–5.45. Tower closed Christmas Eve, Christmas Day, Boxing Day, New Year's Day and Good Friday. On Sundays throughout the year (except August) the public is admitted to Holy Communion, 9.15 a.m. and Morning Service, 11 a.m. Admission £5·50 (reduced rate when Jewel House closed for cleaning in Feb.); various concessions.

Constable, Field Marshal Sir John Stanier, GCB, MBE. *Lieutenant*, Lt.-Gen. Sir Derek Boorman, KCB. *Resident Governor and Keeper of the Jewel House*, Maj.-Gen. C. Tyler, CB. *Master of the Armouries*, G. Wilson. *Chaplain at the Chapel Royal of St. Peter ad Vincula*, Rev. N. A. Hood.

Waltham Abbey (or Waltham Holy Cross), Essex.—The Abbey ruins, 'Harold's' Bridge (14th century), the Nave of the former cruciform Abbey Church c.1120 and the traditional burial place of King Harold II (1066), and a Guild Chapel of Edward II, with crypt below, which houses a visitors centre with permanent exhibition. New evidence of four former churches on the site, and the shape of the east end of Harold's church, have been revealed in recent excavations. Lee Valley Regional Park Authority has a country centre in the Abbey grounds. At Waltham Cross, one mile from the Abbey, is one of the crosses (partly restored) erected by Edward I to mark a resting place of the corpse of Queen Eleanor on its way to Westminster Abbey. (Ten crosses were erected, but only those at Geddington, Northampton and Waltham survive; 'Charing' Cross originally stood near the spot now occupied by the statue of Charles I at Whitehall.)

Wellington Museum, Apsley House, 149 Piccadilly, at Hyde Park Corner, W1.—Known as 'No. 1 London', Apsley House was designed by Robert Adam for Lord Bathurst and built 1771–78. It was bought in 1817 by the Duke of Wellington, who in 1828–29 employed Benjamin Wyatt to enlarge it, face it with Bath stone and add the Corinthian portico. The museum contains many fine paintings, sculptures, services of porcelain and silver plate and personal relics of the 1st Duke of Wellington (1769–1852). The House was given to the nation by the 7th Duke and was first opened to the public in 1952, under the administration of the Victoria and Albert Museum. Open daily 11–5. Closed Mon., Christmas Eve, Christmas Day, Boxing Day and New Year's Day. Admission £2, concessions £1.

Westminster Abbey, SW1.—Built 1050–1745. Chapel of Henry VII, Chapter House and Cloisters; King Edward the Confessor's shrine, AD 1269, tombs of kings and queens (Henry III, Edward I, Edward III, Henry V, Mary Queen of Scots, Elizabeth I), and many other monuments and objects of interest, including the grave of 'The Unknown Warrior' and Poets' Corner. The Coronation Chair encloses the 'Stone of Scone', which was removed from Scotland by Edward I in 1296. Open on weekdays 9–6 (9–7.45

Wed.). Admission to the Royal Chapels, Poets' Corner, Quire and Statesmen's Aisle £2·20, concessions £1·10/50p. Last admission Mon.–Fri. 4 p.m., Sat. 5 p.m. Wed. 6–8 p.m. free. Nave open on Sundays between services.—Services: Sundays, 8, 10, 11.15, 3, 6.30 (generally preceded by an organ recital). Monday–Friday, 7.30, 8, 12.30 (Wednesdays, Lunch-hour Service), 5. Saturdays, 8, 9.20, 3.

Westminster Cathedral, Ashley Place, SW1P 1QW.—Built 1895–1903 from the designs of J. F. Bentley. The campanile is 283 feet high. Cathedral open 6.45 a.m.–8 p.m.—Masses: Sundays, 7, 8, 9, 10.30 (sung), 12, 5.30 and 7; Solemn Vespers and Benediction 3.30. Monday–Friday, 7, 8, 8.30, 9, 10.30, 12.30, 1.05 and 5.30 (sung). Morning Prayer 7.40, Vespers 5. Saturdays 7, 8, 8.30, 9, 10.30 (sung), 12.30 and 6, Morning Prayer 7.40, Vespers 5.30. Holy days of obligation, Low Masses 7, 8, 8.30, 9, 10.30, 12.30, 1.05, 5.30 (sung) and 7.

Westminster Hall, SW1A 0AA.—The only part of the old Palace of Westminster to survive the fire of 1834, Westminster Hall is adjacent to and incorporated in the Houses of Parliament. Westminster Hall was built by William Rufus from 1097–99 and altered by Richard II, 1394–99. It is about 240 ft. long, 68 ft. wide and 92 ft. high; the hammerbeam roof of carved oak dates from 1396–98. The Hall was the scene of the trial of Charles I. Westminster Hall is included on the route followed by those who have arranged a visit to the Houses of Parliament with their MP.

Whitechapel Art Gallery, Whitechapel High Street, E1 7QX.—Opened in 1901; administered by a charitable trust. There is no permanent collection; temporary exhibitions, mainly of modern art, are presented, and community and educational projects are run. Open Tues.–Sun. 11–5; Wed. 11–8.

Wimbledon Lawn Tennis Museum, SW19 5AE.—Exhibits include fashion, trophies, replicas and memorabilia representing the history of lawn tennis. A theatre shows films of great matches. Open Tues.–Sat. 11–5, Sun. 2–5. Admission £1·50, concessions £1/75p.

Windsor Castle (begun by William the Conqueror, AD 1066–87).—The Castle Precincts are open daily. Admission free. The *State Apartments* of Windsor Castle are open throughout the year unless HM The Queen is in residence. Admission charge. *Queen Mary's Dolls' House* and the *Exhibition of The Queen's Presents and Royal Carriages* can be seen on the same days as the State Apartments; admission charge. When the State Apartments are closed, the other exhibitions remain open to the public. The *Albert Memorial Chapel* is open throughout the year (closed on Sundays). Admission free. A fee is charged to visit *St. George's Chapel.*

The *Royal Mausoleum,* Frogmore Gardens, Home Park, is open annually on two days in early May in conjunction with the opening of Frogmore Gardens in aid of the National Gardens Scheme. Also open on the Wednesday nearest to May 24 (Queen Victoria's birthday). Admission free.

Zoological Gardens, Regent's Park, NW1.— (Opened in 1828). Open daily (except Christmas Day) March–Oct. 9–6 or dusk (Bank Holidays and associated Suns. Easter–Aug. and Suns. July 12–Sept. 13, 9–7). Oct.–March opens 10. Admission £4·70, various concessions. Aquarium and Children's Zoo free.

[London Tourism Board and Convention Bureau.—Tourist Information Centre, Victoria Station Forecourt, SW1V 1JU. (071–730 3488).]

PARKS, SPACES AND GARDENS

The principal Parks and Open Spaces in the Metropolitan area are maintained as under:—

By the Crown

BUSHY PARK (1,099 acres).—Adjoining Hampton Court, contains avenue of horse-chestnuts enclosed in a four-fold avenue of limes planted by William III. 'Chestnut Sunday' (when the trees are in full bloom with their 'candles') is usually about May 1 to 15.

GREEN PARK (49 acres), W1.—Between Piccadilly and St. James's Park with Constitution Hill, leading to Hyde Park Corner.

GREENWICH PARK (196½ acres), SE10.

HAMPTON COURT GARDENS (54 acres).

HAMPTON COURT GREEN (17 acres).

HAMPTON COURT PARK (622 acres).

HYDE PARK (341 acres).—From Park Lane, W1, to Kensington Gardens, W2, containing the Serpentine. Fine gateway at Hyde Park Corner, with Apsley House, the Achilles Statue, Rotten Row and the Ladies' Mile. To the north-east is the Marble Arch, originally erected by George IV at the entrance to Buckingham Palace and re-erected in the present position in 1851.

KENSINGTON GARDENS (275 acres), W2.—From western boundary of Hyde Park to Kensington Palace, containing the Albert Memorial.

KEW, ROYAL BOTANIC GARDENS *see* p. 357.

REGENT'S PARK and PRIMROSE HILL (464 acres), NW1.—From Marylebone Road to Primrose Hill surrounded by the Outer Circle and divided by the Broad Walk leading to the Zoological Gardens.

RICHMOND PARK (2,469 acres).

ST. JAMES'S PARK (93 acres), SW1.—From Whitehall to Buckingham Palace. Ornamental lake of 12 acres. The original suspension bridge built in 1857 was replaced in 1957. The Mall leads from the Admiralty Arch to the Queen Victoria Memorial and Buckingham Palace, Birdcage Walk from Storey's Gate, past Wellington Barracks, to Buckingham Palace.

By the Corporation of London

BURNHAM BEECHES and FLEET WOOD, Bucks. (540 acres).—Purchased by the Corporation for the benefit of the public in 1880, Fleet Wood (65 acres) being presented in 1921.

COULSDON COMMON, Surrey (133 acres).

EPPING FOREST (6,500 acres).—Purchased by the Corporation and thrown open to the public in 1882. The present forest is 12 miles long by 1 to 2 miles wide, about one-tenth of its original area.

FARTHINGDOWN, Surrey (121 acres).

HAMPSTEAD HEATH (789 acres), NW3.—Including Golders Hill (36 acres) and Parliament Hill (271 acres), this was transferred to the Corporation on April 1, 1989.

HIGHGATE WOOD (70 acres).

KENLEY COMMON, Surrey (138 acres).

QUEEN'S PARK, Kilburn (30 acres).

RIDDLESDOWN, Surrey (90 acres).

SPRING PARK, West Wickham (51 acres).

WEST HAM PARK (77 acres).

WEST WICKHAM COMMON, Kent (25 acres).

Also smaller open spaces within the City of London, including FINSBURY CIRCUS GARDENS.

THE PRINCIPALITY OF WALES

Position and extent.—The Principality of Wales (*Cymru*) occupies the extreme west of the central southern portion of the island of Great Britain, with a total area of 8,018 sq. miles (20,768 sq. km): land 7,968 sq. miles (20,638 sq. km); inland water 50 sq. miles (130 sq. km). It is bounded on the N. by the Irish Sea, on the S. by the Bristol Channel, on the E. by the English counties of Cheshire, Shropshire, Hereford and Worcester, and Gloucestershire, and on the W. by St. George's Channel. Across the Menai Straits is the Welsh island of *Ynys Môn* (Anglesey) (276 sq. miles), communication with which is facilitated by the Menai Suspension Bridge (1,000 ft. long) built by Telford in 1826, and by the tubular railway bridge (1,100 ft. long) built by Stephenson in 1850. Holyhead harbour, on Holy Isle (NW of Anglesey), provides accommodation for ferry services to Dublin (70 miles).

Population.—The population at the Census of 1981 was 2,791,851 (males 1,352,639; females 1,439,212). The average density of population in 1981 was 343 per square mile. The population, mid-1988 estimate, was 2,857,000.

Relief.—Wales is a country of extensive tracts of high plateau and shorter stretches of mountain ranges deeply dissected by river valleys. Lower-lying ground is largely confined to the coastal belt and the lower parts of the valleys. The highest mountains are those of Snowdonia in the north-west (*Snowdon*, 3,559 ft), Berwyn (*Aran Fawddwy*, 2,971 ft), Cader Idris (*Pen y Gadair*, 2,928 ft), Dyfed (*Plynlimon*, 2,467 ft), and the Black Mountain, Brecon Beacons and Black Forest ranges in the south-east (*Carmarthen Van*, 2,630 ft, *Pen y Fan*, 2,906 ft, *Waun Fâch*, 2,660 ft).

Hydrography.—The principal river rising in Wales is the *Severn* (*see* p. 575), which flows from the slopes of Plynlimon to the English border. The *Wye* (130 miles) also rises in the slopes of Plynlimon. The *Usk* (56 miles) flows into the Bristol Channel, through Gwent. The *Dee* (70 miles) rises in Bala Lake and flows through the Vale of Llangollen, where an aqueduct (built by Telford in 1805) carries the Pontcysyllte branch of the Shropshire Union Canal across the valley. The estuary of the Dee is the navigable portion, 14 miles in length and about 5 miles in breadth, and the tide rushes in with dangerous speed over the 'Sands of Dee'. The *Towy* (68 miles), *Teifi* (50 miles), *Taff* (40 miles), *Dovey* (30 miles), *Taf* (25 miles), and *Conway* (24 miles), the last named broad and navigable, are wholly Welsh rivers.

The largest natural lake in Wales is *Bala* (Llyn Tegid) in Gwynedd, nearly 4 miles long and about 1 mile wide; *Lake Vyrnwy* is an artificial reservoir, about the size of Bala, and forms the water supply of Liverpool; and Birmingham is supplied from a chain of reservoirs in the Elan and Clærwen valleys.

Welsh language.—According to the 1981 Census results, the percentage of persons of three years and over able to speak Welsh were:

Clwyd	18·7	Powys	20·2
Dyfed	46·3	S. Glamorgan	5·8
Gwent	2·5	W. Glamorgan	16·4
Gwynedd	61·2		
Mid Glamorgan	8·4	**Wales**	18·9

The 1981 figure represents a slight decline from 20·8 per cent in 1971 (1961, 26 per cent; 1951, 28·9 per cent).

Flag.—A red dragon on a green and white field (*per fess argent and vert a dragon passant gules*). The flag was augmented in 1953 by a royal badge on a shield encircled with a riband bearing the words *Ddraig Goch Ddyry Cychwyn* and imperially crowned. Only the unaugmented flag is flown on Government offices in Wales and, where appropriate, in London. Both flags continue to be used elsewhere.

EARLY HISTORY

Celts and Romans.—The earliest inhabitants of whom there is any record appear to have been subdued or exterminated by the Goidels (a people of Celtic race) in the Bronze Age, and a further invasion of Celtic Brythons and Belgae followed in the ensuing Iron Age. The Roman conquest of South Britain and Wales was for some time successfully opposed by Caratacus (Caractacus or Caradog), chieftain of the Catuvellauni and son of Cunobelinus (Cymbeline). South east Wales was subjugated and the legionary fortress at Caerleon-on-Usk established by about AD 75–77: the conquest of Wales was completed by Agricola about AD 78. Communications were opened up by the construction of military roads from Chester to Caerleon-on-Usk and Caerwent, and from Chester to Conway (and thence to Carmarthen and Neath). Christianity was introduced during the Roman occupation, in the 4th century.

The Anglo-Saxon Attacks.—The Anglo-Saxon invaders of South Britain drove the Celts into the mountain stronghold of Wales, and into Strathclyde (Cumberland and SW Scotland) and Cornwall, giving them the name of *Waelisc*, or Welsh (= foreign). The West Saxons' victory of Deorham (AD 577) isolated Wales from Cornwall and the battle of Chester (AD 613) cut off communication with Strathclyde and northern Britain. In the 8th century the boundaries of the Welsh were further restricted by the annexations of Offa, King of Mercia, and counter-attacks were largely prevented by the construction of an artificial boundary from the Dee to the Wye (Offa's Dyke). In the 9th century Rhodri Mawr (784–78) united the country and successfully resisted further incursions of the Saxons by land and raids of Norse and Danish pirates by sea, but at his death his three provinces of Gwynedd (N.), Powys (Mid.) and Deheubarth (S.) were divided among his three sons—Anarawd, Mervyn and Cadell. Cadell's son Hywel Dda ruled a large part of Wales and codified its laws but the provinces were not united again until the rule of Llewelyn ap Seisyllt (husband of the heiress of Gwynedd) from 1018 to 1023.

The Norman Conquest.—After the Norman conquest of England, William I created Palatine counties along the Welsh frontier, and the Norman barons began to make encroachments into Welsh territory. The Welsh princes recovered many of their losses, however, during the civil wars of Stephen's reign and in the early 13th century Owen Gruffydd, prince of Gwynedd, was the dominant figure in Wales. Under Llywelyn ap Iorwerth (1194–1240) the Welsh united in powerful resistance to English incursions and Llywelyn's privileges and *de facto* independence were recognized in Magna Charta. His grandson, Llywelyn ap Gruffydd, was the last native prince; he was killed in 1282 during hostilities between the Welsh and English, allowing Edward I of England to establish his authority over the country. On Feb. 7, 1301, Edward of Caernarvon, son of Edward I, was created Prince of Wales, a title which has subsequently been borne by the eldest son of the sovereign.

Strong Welsh national feeling continued, expressed in the early 15th century in the rising led by Owain Glyndŵr, but the situation was altered by the accession to the English throne in 1485 of Henry VII of the Welsh House of Tudor. Wales was politically assimilated to England under the Act of Union of

1535, which extended English laws to the Principality and gave it parliamentary representation for the first time.

Eisteddfod.—The Welsh are a distinct nationality, with a language and literature of their own, and the national bardic festival (Eisteddfod), instituted by Prince Rhys ap Griffith in 1176, is still held annually (for date, *see* p. 1184). These *Eisteddfodau* (sessions) form part of the *Gorsedd* (assembly), which is believed to date from the time of Prydian, a ruling prince in an age many centuries before the Christian era.

LORD LIEUTENANTS AND HIGH SHERIFFS

County	Lord Lieutenant	High Sheriff, 1990–91
Clwyd	Sir William Gladstone, Bt.	Sir Watkin Williams-Wynn
Dyfed	D. C. Mansel Lewis	Dr. J. H. T. Rees
Gwent	R. Hanbury-Tenison	A. T. Beverley-Jones
Gwynedd	R. E. Meuric Rees, CBE	Mrs. T. G. R. Preece
Mid Glamorgan	M. A. McLaggan	I. T. Rees
Powys....................	M. L. Bourdillon	N. O. Tyler
South Glamorgan	Capt. N. Lloyd-Edwards	B. K. Thomas
West Glamorgan	Lt.-Col. Sir Michael Llewellyn, Bt.	J. B. D. Simpson

WELSH COUNTY COUNCILS

AREAS AND POPULATIONS

County Council	Administrative Headquarters	Area (*hectares*)	Population 1988	Total demand upon collection fund 1990 £
Clwyd	Shire Hall, Mold	242,650	407,000	68,157,000
Dyfed	County Hall, Carmarthen	576,577	348,400	44,977,134
Gwent	County Hall, Cwmbran	137,599	445,400	57,272,865
Gwynedd	County Offices, Caernarfon	386,708	239,000	30,405,000
Mid Glamorgan ...	County Hall, Cathays Park, Cardiff	101,867	535,900	67,530,000
Powys............	County Hall, Llandrindod Wells	507,741	114,900	13,484,223
South Glamorgan .	County Hall, Atlantic Wharf, Cardiff	41,629	403,400	49,552,000
West Glamorgan ..	County Hall, Swansea	81,657	363,000	56,030,000

COUNTY OFFICIALS AND CHAIRMEN

County Council	Chief Executive *County Clerk	County Treasurer	Chairman of County Council
Clwyd............	M. H. Phillips	A. Dalby	W. R. Thomas
Dyfed	D. H. Davies	A. C. Williams	M. Evans
Gwent	M. J. Perry	J. P. Walsh	R. F. Morgan
Gwynedd.........	I. B. Rees	T. D. Heald	M. L. Vaughan
Mid Glamorgan ...	D. H. Thomas*	L. D. Heycock	R. C. Reed
Powys............	A. J. Barnish	A. J. Barnish	H. E. Lewis
South Glamorgan .	M. Boyce	R. G. Tettenborn	W. J. Bowen
West Glamorgan ..	vacant	S. G. Dunster	F. J. Kingdom, CBE

WELSH DISTRICT COUNCILS

Those accorded CITY Status are shown in SMALL CAPITALS; those with Borough Status are distinguished by having § prefixed.

District	Estimated resident population 1988	Community charge per head 1990 £	Chief Executive	Chairman 1990–91 (a) Mayor (b) Lord Mayor
§Aberconwy, Gwynedd	54,200	219·91	J. E. Davies	(a) E. G. Davies
Alyn and Deeside, Clwyd	72,600	262·00	W. E. Rogers	J. F. Jones
§Arfon, Gwynedd	55,100	209·97	D. L. Jones	(a) Mrs. B. H. Williams
§Blaenau Gwent, Gwent	77,300	231·78	R. Leadbeter	(a) J. Taylor
§Brecknock, Powys	41,100	189·58	R. O. Doylend	(a) T. Denzil Griffiths
CARDIFF, South Glamorgan	283,900	253·00	R. E. Paine	(b) F. J. Smith
Carmarthen, Dyfed	55,800	195·97	R. R. Morgan	J. E. O. Jones
Ceredigion, Dyfed	67,000	201·13	D. Morgan	H. M. Jones
§Colwyn, Clwyd	54,800	261·00	W. N. Breeze	(a) M. T. Jones
§Cynon Valley, Mid Glamorgan ..	64,300	217·00	T. B. Roberts	(a) Dr. R. K. J. Grant
§Delyn, Clwyd	65,100	268·00	P. J. McGreevy	(a) N. J. Brackenbury
§Dinefwr, Dyfed	38,900	177·58	E. W. Harries	(a) D. A. James
Dwyfor, Gwynedd	27,000	224·00	E. Davies	T. J. Williams
Glyndŵr, Clwyd	41,500	262·00	J. H. Parry	M. J. White
§Islwyn, Gwent	66,400	218·00	B. Bird	(a) T. J. Williams
§Llanelli, Dyfed	74,100	196·75	A. B. Thomas	(a) L. R. McDonagh
§Lliw Valley, West Glamorgan ...	61,800	216·00	J. C. Howells	(a) J. Martin
Meirionnydd, Gwynedd	31,600	224·00	G. W. Hughes	R. V. Jones
§Merthyr Tydfil, Mid Glamorgan	58,100	211·66	R. V. Morris	(a) D. R. Tovey
§Monmouth, Gwent	81,300	220·00	G. Cummings	(a) K. G. C. Reece
Montgomeryshire, Powys	51,200	165·20	N. J. Bardsley	D. Wyn Jones
§Neath, West Glamorgan........	65,200	249·00	S. Penny	(a) S. M. Tudor
§Newport, Gwent	128,100	238·00	C. Tapp	(a) H. G. Jones
§Ogwr, Mid Glamorgan	137,500	224·00	J. G. Cole	(a) D. H. Davies
§Port Talbot, West Glamorgan ...	49,100	247·00	I. K. Lewis	(a) Mrs. H. Mears
Preseli Pembrokeshire, Dyfed	70,800	189·79	I. W. R. David	W. W. Ladd
Radnor, Powys	22,500	175·00	G. C. Read	J. L. Davies
§Rhondda, Mid Glamorgan	76,500	175·00	G. Evans	(a) Mrs. M. E. Chard
§Rhuddlan, Clwyd	56,100	279·74	E. O. Lake	(a) H. C. Irving
Rhymney Valley, Mid Glamorgan	104,500	228·00	P. A. Bennett	J. R. P. Evans
South Pembrokeshire, Dyfed	41,900	177·96	G. H. James	D. M. Davies
SWANSEA, West Glamorgan	186,900	264·00	A. K. B. Boatswain	(b) C. Hammacott
§Taff-Ely, Mid Glamorgan	94,900	217·00	D. Gethin	(a) G. H. Jury
§Torfaen, Gwent	92,400	213·00	M. B. Mehta	(a) Mrs. S. Richards
§Vale of Glamorgan, South Glamorgan	119,500	211·00	J. R. Gau	(a) H. J. W. James
§Wrexham Maelor, Clwyd	116,900	262·00	R. J. Dutton	(a) M. Williams
§Ynys Môn (Isle of Anglesey), Gwynedd	71,000	241·00	E. L. Gibson	(a) Mrs. M. Brownson

PRINCIPAL WELSH CITIES

CARDIFF

CARDIFF (South Glamorgan), at the mouth of the rivers Taff, Rhymney and Ely, is the capital city of Wales and one of Britain's major administrative, commercial and business centres. It has many industries, including steel and cigars, and is a flourishing port with a substantial and varied trade. There are many fine buildings in the civic centre started early this century which includes the City Hall, the National Museum of Wales, University Buildings, Law Courts, Welsh Office, County Hall, Police Headquarters and the Temple of Peace and Health. Also in the city are Llandaff Cathedral, the Welsh National Folk Museum at St. Fagans, Cardiff Castle, the New Theatre, the Sherman Theatre and the Cardiff College of Music and Drama. New buildings include St. David's Hall, a 2,000-seat concert and conference hall, and the Welsh National Ice Rink.

SWANSEA

SWANSEA (*Abertawe*) is a city and a seaport of West Glamorgan with its own municipal airport. The beautiful Gower Peninsula was brought within the City boundary under a local government reform in 1974. The trade of the port includes coal, patent fuel, ores, and the import and export of oil. The municipal area is 60,511 acres.

The principal buildings are the Norman Castle (rebuilt in 1330), the Royal Institution of South Wales, founded in 1835 (including Library), the University College at Singleton and the Guildhall, containing the Brangwyn panels. New buildings include the Industrial and Maritime Museum, the new Maritime Quarter and Marina and the leisure centre. Swansea was chartered by the Earl of Warwick, c.1158–1184, and further charters were granted by King John, Henry III, Edward II, Edward III and James II, Cromwell (two) and the Marcher Lord William de Breos.

THE KINGDOM OF SCOTLAND

Position and extent.—The Kingdom of Scotland occupies the northern portion of the main island of Great Britain and includes the Inner and Outer Hebrides, and the Orkney, Shetland, and many other islands. The Kingdom lies between 60° 51′ 30″ and 54° 38′ N. latitude and between 1° 45′ 32″ and 6° 14′ W. longitude, its southern neighbour being the Kingdom of England, with the Atlantic Ocean on the N. and W., and the North Sea on the E. The greatest length of the mainland (Cape Wrath to the Mull of Galloway) is 274 miles, and the greatest breadth (Buchan Ness to Applecross) is 154 miles. The customary measurement of the island of Great Britain is from the side of John o' Groats house, near Duncansby Head, Caithness to Land's End, Cornwall, a total distance of 603 miles in a straight line and (approximately) 900 by road. The total area of the Kingdom is 30,414 sq. miles (78,772 sq. km): land 29,761 sq. miles (77,080 sq. km); inland water 653 sq. miles (1,692 sq. km).

Population.—The population (1981 Census) was 5,130,735 (males 2,466,437; females 2,664,298). The average density of the population in 1981 was 168 persons per square mile. The population, mid-1988 estimate, was 5,094,000.

Relief.—There are three natural orographic divisions of Scotland. The Southern Uplands have their highest points in Merrick (2,766 ft), Rhinns of Kells (2,669 ft), and Cairnsmuir of Carsphairn (2,614 ft), in the west; and the Tweedsmuir Hills in the east (*Hartfell* 2,651 ft, *Dollar Law* 2,682 ft, *Broad Law* 2,756 ft). The Central Lowlands, formed by the valleys of the Clyde, Forth and Tay, divide the Southern Uplands from the Northern Highlands, which extend almost from the extreme north of the mainland to the central lowlands, and are divided into a northern and southern system by the *Great Glen*. The Grampian Mountains, which entirely cover the southern Highland area, include in the west *Ben Nevis* (4,406 ft), the highest point in the British Isles, and in the east the Cairngorm Mountains (*Cairn Gorm* 4,084 ft, *Braeriach* 4,248 ft, *Ben Macdui* 4,296 ft). The north-western Highland area contains in the mountains of Wester and Easter Ross *Carn Eige* (3,880 ft) and *Sgurr na Lapaich* (3,775 ft).

Created, like the Central Lowlands, by a major geological fault, the Great Glen (60 miles long) runs between Inverness and Fort William, and contains Loch Ness, Loch Oich and Loch Lochy. These are linked to each other and to the north-east and south-west coasts of Scotland by the Caledonian Canal, providing a navigable passage between the Moray Firth and the Inner Hebrides.

Hydrography.—The western coast of Scotland is fragmented by peninsulas and islands, and indented by fjords (sea-lochs), the longest of which is *Loch Fyne* (42 miles long) in Argyll. Although the east coast tends to be less fractured and lower, there are several great drowned inlets (firths), e.g. Firth of Forth, Firth of Tay, Moray Firth, as well as the Firth of Clyde in the west.

The lochs are the principal hydrographic feature of the Kingdom. The largest in the Kingdom and in Great Britain is *Loch Lomond* (27 square miles), in the Grampian valleys; the longest and deepest is *Loch Ness* (24 miles long and 800 feet deep), in the Great Glen; and Lochs Shin (20 miles long) and Maree in the northern Highlands.

The longest river in Scotland is the *Tay* (117 miles/ 188 km), noted for its salmon. It flows into the North Sea, with Dundee on the estuary, which is spanned by the Tay Bridge (10,289 ft) opened in 1887 and the Tay Road Bridge (7,365 ft) opened in 1966. Other noted salmon rivers are the *Dee* (90 miles) which flows into the North Sea at Aberdeen, and the *Spey*

(110 miles), the swiftest flowing river in the British Isles, which flows into Moray Firth. The *Tweed*, which gave its name to the woollen cloth produced along its banks, marks in the lower stretches of its 96-mile course the border between Scotland and England.

The most important river commercially is the *Clyde* (106 miles), formed by the junction of the Daer and Portrait water, which flows through the city of Glasgow to the Firth of Clyde. During its course it passes over the picturesque Falls of Clyde, *Bonnington Linn* (30 ft), *Corra Linn* (84 ft), *Dundaff Linn* (10 ft) and *Stonebyres Linn* (80 ft), above and below Lanark. The *Forth* (66 miles), upon which stands Edinburgh, the capital, is spanned by the Forth (Railway) Bridge (1890), which is 5,330 feet long, and the Forth (Road) Bridge (1964), which has a total length of 6,156 feet (over water) and a single span of 3,000 feet.

The highest waterfall in Scotland, and the British Isles, is *Eas a'Chùal Aluinn* with a total height of 658 feet (200 m), which falls from Glas Bheinn in Sutherland. The *Falls of Glomach*, on a head-stream of the Elchaig in Wester Ross, have a drop of 370 feet.

Gaelic language.—According to the 1981 Census, 82,620 people, mainly in the Highlands and western coastal regions, were able to speak, read or write the Scottish form of Gaelic.

Flag.—The cross of St. Andrew, the patron saint of Scotland (*saltire argent in a field azure*).

THE SCOTTISH ISLANDS

The Hebrides did not become part of the Kingdom of Scotland until 1266, when they were ceded to Alexander III by Magnus of Norway. Orkney and Shetland fell to the Scottish Crown as a pledge for the unpaid dowry of Margaret of Denmark, wife of James III, in 1468, the Danish claims to suzerainty being relinquished in 1590 when James VI married Anne of Denmark.

Orkney.—The Orkney Islands (total area 375½ sq. miles) lie about six miles north of the mainland, separated from it by the Pentland Firth. Of the 90 islands and islets (holms and skerries) in the group, about one-third are inhabited. The total population at the 1981 Census was 19,040; the 1981 populations of the islands shown here include those of smaller islands forming part of the same civil parish.

Mainland	14,299	Shapinsay	345
Eday	154	South Ronaldsay	1,188
Hoy and Graemsay	80	Stronsay	462
Papa Westray	94	Walls and Flotta	761
Rousay and Egilsay	264	Westray	741
Sanday and North Ronaldsay	652		

The islands are rich in Pictish and Scandinavian remains, the most notable being the Stone Age village of Skara Brae, the burial chamber of Maeshowe, the many brochs (Pictish towers) and St. Magnus Cathedral. Scapa Flow, between the Mainland and Hoy, was the war station of the British Grand Fleet from 1914–19 and the scene of the scuttling of the surrendered German High Seas Fleet (June 21, 1919).

Most of the islands are low-lying and fertile, and farming (principally beef cattle) is the main industry. Flotta, to the south of Scapa Flow, is now the site of the oil terminal for the Piper, Claymore and Tartan fields in the North Sea.

Capital.—Kirkwall (pop. 6,881) on Mainland.

Shetland.—The Shetland Islands (total area 551 sq. miles; population at the 1981 Census 27,271) lie about 50 miles north of the Orkneys, with Fair Isle about half way between the two groups. Out Stack, off Muckle Flugga, one mile north of Unst, is the most northerly part of the British Isles (60° 51′ 30″ N. lat.). There are over 100 islands, of which 16 are inhabited. Populations at the 1981 census were:

Mainland	22,184	Muckle Roe	101
Bressay	335	Out Skerries	79
East and West Burra,		Papa Stour	29
and Trondra	930	Unst	1,206
Fair Isle	69	Whalsay	1,026
Fetlar	102	Yell	1,168
Foula	39		

Shetland's many archaeological sites include Jarlshof, Mousa and Clickhimin, and its long connection with Scandinavia has resulted in a strong Norse influence on its place names and dialect.

Industries include fishing, knitwear and farming. In addition to the fishing fleet there are fish processing factories, while the traditional handknitting of Fair Isle and Unst is supplemented now with machine knitted garments. Farming is mainly crofting, with sheep being raised on the moorland and hills of the islands. Latterly the islands have become an important centre of the North Sea oil industry, with pipelines from the Brent and Ninian fields running to the terminal at Sullom Voe, the largest of its kind in Europe. Lerwick is the main centre for supply services for offshore oil exploration and development.

Capital.—Lerwick (pop. 7,901) on Mainland.

The Hebrides.—Until the closing years of the 13th century the Hebrides included other Scottish islands in the Firth of Clyde, the peninsula of Kintyre (Argyllshire), the Isle of Man, and the (Irish) Isle of Rathlin. The origin of the name is stated to be the Greek *Eboudai*, latinized as *Hebudes* by Pliny, and corrupted to its present form. The Norwegian name *Sudreyjar* (Southern Islands) was latinized as *Sodorenses*, a name that survives in the Anglican bishopric of Sodor and Man.

There are over 500 islands and islets, of which about 100 are inhabited, though mountainous terrain and extensive peat bogs mean that only a fraction of the total area is under cultivation. Stone, Bronze and Iron Age settlement has left many remains, including those at Callanish on Lewis, and Norse colonization has influenced language, customs and place-names. Occupations include farming (mostly crofting and stock-raising), fishing and the manufacture of tweeds and other woollens. Tourism is also an important factor in the economy.

The **Inner Hebrides** lie off the west coast of Scotland and relatively close to the mainland. The largest and best-known is *Skye* (area 643 sq. miles; pop. 8,139; chief town, Portree), which contains the Cuillin Hills (*Sgurr Alasdair* 3,257 ft), the Red Hills (*Beinn na Caillich* 2,403 ft) as well as *Bla Bheinn* (3,046 ft) and *The Storr* (2,358 ft). Skye is also famous as the refuge of the Young Pretender in 1746. Other islands in the Highland Region include *Raasay* (pop. 182) *Rum, Eigg* and *Muck*. Islands in the Strathclyde Region include *Arran* (pop. 4,726) containing *Goat Fell* (2,868 ft); *Coll and Tiree* (pop. 933); *Colonsay and Oronsay* (pop. 137); *Islay* (area 235 sq. miles; pop. 3,997); *Jura* (area 160 sq. miles; pop. 239) with a range of hills culminating in the Paps of Jura (*Beinn-an-Oir*, 2,576 ft, and *Beinn Chaolais*, 2,477 ft); *Mull* (area 367 sq. miles; pop. 2,605; chief town Tobermory) containing *Ben More* (3,171 ft).

The **Outer Hebrides**, separated from the mainland by the Minch, now form the Western Isles Islands Council area (area 1,119 sq. miles; population at the 1981 Census 31,842). The main islands are *Lewis with Harris* (area 770 sq. miles, pop. 23,390), whose chief town, Stornoway (pop. 13,409), is the administrative headquarters; *North Uist* (pop. 1,454); *South Uist*

(pop. 2,223); *Benbecula* (pop. 1,988) and *Barra* (pop. 1,232). Other inhabited islands include *Bernera* (292), *Berneray* (134), *Eriskay* (219), *Grimsay* (206), *Scalpay* (461) and *Vatersay* (108).

EARLY HISTORY

Prehistoric Man.—The Picts, believed to be of non-Aryan origin, seem to have inhabited the whole of North Britain and to have spread over the north of Ireland. Remains are most frequent in Caithness and Sutherland and the Orkney Islands. Celts arrived from Belgic Gaul during the latter part of the Bronze Age and in the early Iron Age, and except in the extreme north of the mainland and in the islands, the civilization and speech of the people were definitely Celtic at the time of the Roman invasion of Britain.

The Roman Invasion.—In AD 79–80 Julius Agricola extended the Roman conquests in Britain by advancing into *Caledonia* and building a line of fortifications across the isthmus between the Forth and Clyde, but after a victory at *Mons Graupius* he was recalled. Hadrian's Wall, mostly complete by AD 130, marked the frontier until about AD 143 when the frontier moved north to the Forth-Clyde isthmus and and was secured by the Antonine Wall. From about AD 155 the Antonine Wall was damaged by frequent attacks and by the end of the second century the northern limit of Roman Britain had receded to Hadrian's Wall.

The Scots.—After the withdrawal (or absorption) of the Roman garrison of Britain there were many years of tribal warfare between the Picts and Scots (the Gaelic tribe then dominant in Ireland), the Brythonic Waelisc (Welsh) of Strathclyde (southwest Scotland and Cumberland), and the Anglo-Saxons of Lothian. The Waelisc were isolated from their kinsmen in Wales by the victory of the West Saxons at Chester (613), and towards the close of the 9th century the Scots under Kenneth Macalpine became the dominant power in Caledonia. In the reign of Malcolm I (943–954) Strathclyde was brought into subjection, and the English lowland kingdom (Lothian) being conquered by Malcolm II (1005–1034). From the late 11th century until the middle of the 16th century there were constant wars between Scotland and England, the outstanding figures in the struggle being William Wallace, who defeated the English at Stirling Bridge (1297) and Robert Bruce, who won the victory of Bannockburn (1314). James IV and many of his nobles fell at the disastrous battle of Flodden (1513).

The Jacobite Revolts.—In 1603 James VI of Scotland succeeded Elizabeth I on the throne of England (his mother, Mary Queen of Scots, was the great-granddaughter of Henry VII), his successors reigning as Sovereigns of Great Britain, although political union of the two countries did not occur until 1707. After the abdication (by flight) in 1688 of James VII and II, the crown devolved upon William III (grandson of Charles I) and Mary (daughter of James VII and II). In 1689 Graham of Claverhouse roused the Highlands on behalf of James VII and II, but died after a military success at Killiecrankie. After the death of Anne (second daughter of James VII and II) the throne devolved upon George I (great-grandson of James VI and I). In 1715, armed risings on behalf of James Stuart (the Old Pretender) led to the indecisive battle of Sheriffmuir, but the Jacobite movement died down until 1745, when Charles Stuart (the Young Pretender) defeated the Royalist troops at Prestonpans and advanced to Derby in England (1746). From Derby, the adherents of 'James VIII and III' (the title claimed for his father by Charles Stuart) fell back on the defensive, and the movement was finally crushed at Culloden (April 16, 1746).

LORD LIEUTENANTS IN SCOTLAND

Region	Title	Name
Borders	Berwickshire	Maj.-Gen. Sir John Swinton, KCVO, OBE
	Roxburgh, Ettrick and Lauderdale	The Duke of Buccleuch and Queensberry, KT, VRD
	Tweeddale	Lt.-Col. A. M. Sprot of Haystoun, MC
Central	Clackmannan	The Earl of Mar and Kellie
	Stirling and Falkirk	Lt.-Col. J. Stirling of Garden, CBE, TD
Dumfries & Galloway	Dumfries	Capt. J. G. M. Home, TD
	The Stewartry of Kirkcudbright	Sir Michael A. R. Y. Herries, OBE, MC
	Wigtown	Maj. E. S. Orr Ewing
Fife	Fife	The Earl of Elgin and Kincardine, KT
Grampian	Aberdeenshire	Capt. C. A. Farquharson
	Banffshire	J. A. S. McPherson, CBE
	Kincardineshire	The Viscount of Arbuthnott, DSC, FRSE
	Morayshire	Capt. Sir Iain Tennant, KT
Highland	Caithness	The Viscount Thurso
	Inverness	Lt.-Cdr, L. R. D. Mackintosh of Mackintosh, OBE
	Nairn	The Earl of Leven and Melville
	Ross and Cromarty	Capt. R. W. K. Stirling of Fairburn, TD
	Sutherland	Col. Sir Allan M. Gilmour, KCVO, OBE, MC
Lothian	East Lothian........................	Sir Hew Hamilton-Dalrymple, Bt., KVCO
	Midlothian	Sir John Dutton Clerk of Penicuik, Bt., CBE, VRD
	West Lothian	The Earl of Morton
Strathclyde	Argyll and Bute	The Marquess of Bute
	Ayr and Arran	Col. Sir Bryce Knox, KCVO, MC, TD
	Dunbartonshire.....................	Brig. D. D. G. Hardie, TD
	Lanarkshire	Col. The Lord Clydesmuir, KT, CB, MBE, TD
	Renfrewshire	Maj. J. D. M. Crichton Maitland
Tayside	Angus...............................	The Earl of Airlie, KT, GCVO, PC
	Perth and Kinross..................	Maj. D. H. Butter, MC
Orkney	Orkney	Brig. M. G. Dennison
Shetland	Shetland	M. M. Shearer
Western Isles	Western Isles	The Earl Granville, MC

NOTE.—The Lord Provosts of the four city districts of Aberdeen, Dundee, Edinburgh and Glasgow are Lord Lieutenants for those districts *ex officio.*

PRECEDENCE IN SCOTLAND

THE SOVEREIGN.

The Prince Philip, Duke of Edinburgh.

The Lord High Commissioner to the General Assembly (while that Assembly is sitting).

The Duke of Rothesay (eldest son of the Sovereign).

The Sovereign's younger sons.

The Sovereign's cousins.

Lords Lieutenant of Counties, Lord Provosts of Counties of Cities, and Sheriffs Principal (successively—within their own localities and during holding of office).

Lord Chancellor of Great Britain.

Moderator of the General Assembly of the Church of Scotland.

The Prime Minister.

Keepers of the Great Seal and of the Privy Seal (successively—if Peers).

Hereditary Lord High Constable of Scotland.

Hereditary Master of the Household.

Dukes (successively) of England, Scotland, Great Britain and United Kingdom (including Ireland since date of Union).

Eldest sons of Dukes of the Blood Royal.

Marquesses, in same order as Dukes.

Dukes' eldest sons.

Earls, in order as Dukes.

Younger sons of Dukes of Blood Royal.

Marquesses' eldest sons.

Dukes' younger sons.

Keepers of the Great Seal and of the Privy Seal (successively if not Peers).

Lord Justice General.

Lord Clerk Register.

Lord Advocate.

Lord Justice Clerk.

Viscounts, in order as Dukes.

Earls' eldest sons.

Marquesses' younger sons.

Lord-Barons, in order as Dukes.

Viscounts' eldest sons.

Earls' younger sons.

Lord-Barons' eldest sons.

Knights of the Garter.

Privy Counsellors.

Senators of College of Justice (Lords of Session).

Viscounts' younger sons.

Lord-Barons' younger sons.

Sons of Life Peers.

Baronets.

Knights of the Thistle.

Knights Grand Cross, Grand Commander, and Knight Commanders, as in England.

Solicitor-General for Scotland.

Lord Lyon King of Arms.

Sheriffs Principal (except as shown in first column).

Knights Bachelor.

Sheriffs.

Companions of Orders, as in England.

Commanders of Royal Victorian and British Empire Orders.

Eldest sons of younger sons of Peers.

Companions of Distinguished Service Order.

Lieutenants of Royal Victorian Order.

Officers of British Empire Order.

Baronets' eldest sons.

Knights' eldest sons successively (from Garter to Bachelor).

Members, Royal Victorian Order.

Members, British Empire Order.

Baronets' younger sons.

Knights' younger sons.

Queen's Counsel.

Barons-feudal.

Esquires.

Gentlemen.

SCOTTISH REGIONAL AND ISLANDS COUNCILS
AREA AND POPULATION

Region	Administrative Headquarters	Area (*hectares*)	Population	Regional community charge per head 1990 £	Community water charge per head 1990 £
Borders	Newtown St. Boswells	467,158	102,592	180·00	28·00
Central	Stirling	263,609	271,526	227·00	15·00
Dumfries and Galloway ..	Dumfries	637,006	147,462	189·00	34·00
Fife	Glenrothes	130,700	344,717	332·00	15·00
Grampian	Aberdeen	870,400	499,580	177·00	32·00
Highland	Inverness	2,539,122	201,900	190·00	26·00
Lothian	Edinburgh	175,509	742,900	311·00	19·00
Orkney	Kirkwall	97,581	19,455	135·00	31·00
Shetland	Lerwick	143,268	22,170	87·26	40·04
Strathclyde.............	Glasgow	1,385,716	2,311,200	225·00	21·00
Tayside	Dundee	750,318	392,500	225·00	21·00
Western Isles	Stornoway, Lewis	7,289,758	31,519	151·00	45·00

CHIEF EXECUTIVES, DIRECTORS OF FINANCE AND CONVENERS

Region	Chief Executive	Director of Finance	Convener
Borders	K. J. Clark, CBE	P. Jeary	The Earl of Minto
Central	D. Sinclair	S. C. Craig	Mrs. A. Wallace
Dumfries and Galloway	N. W. D. McIntosh, CBE	J. C. Stewart	D. R. Robinson
Fife........................	Dr. J. A. Markland	A. E. Taylor	R. Gough, CBE
Grampian	J. D. Macnaughton	A. McLean	B. Middleton
Highland	R. H. Stevenson	J. W. Bremner	D. J. McPherson
Lothian	G. M. Bowie	D. B. Chynoweth	E. Milligan
Orkney	R. H. Gilbert	R. H. Gilbert	J. A. Tait
Shetland	M. A. Gerrard	M. E. Green	E. Thomason, OBE
Strathclyde.................	Sir Robert Calderwood	A. Gillespie	D. Sanderson
Tayside	R. W. Black	I. B. McIver	G. W. Buckman
Western Isles	Dr. G. Macleod	D. G. Macleod	Rev. D. Macaulay, OBE

PRINCIPAL SCOTTISH CITIES

ABERDEEN

ABERDEEN, 130 miles north-east of Edinburgh, received its charter as a Royal Burgh from William the Lion in 1179. Scotland's third largest city, Aberdeen is the second largest Scottish fishing port and the main European centre for offshore oil exploration. It is also an ancient university town and distinguished research centre. Other industries include engineering, shipbuilding, food processing, textiles, paper manufacturing and chemicals. Places of interest: King's College, St. Machar's Cathedral, Brig o' Balgownie, Duthie Park and Winter Gardens, the Kirk of St. Nicholas, Mercat Cross, Marischal College and Museum of Human History, Provost Skene's House, Art Gallery, James Dun's House (children's museum), Satrosphere Hands-On Discovery Centre, and Provost Ross's House (maritime museum).

DUNDEE

DUNDEE, a Royal Burgh, is situated on the north bank of the Tay estuary. The city's port and dock installations are important to the offshore oil industry and the airport also provides servicing facilities. Principal industries include textiles, computers and other electronic industries, lasers, printing, tyre manufacture, food processing, carpets, engineering and clothing manufacture. Six sites have Enterprise Zone status, including the Technology Park, airport and port. The unique City Churches—three churches under one roof, together with the 15th century St. Mary's Tower—are the most prominent architectural feature. RRS *Discovery*, the ship which took Captain Scott to the Antarctic and which was built in Dundee in 1901, is now berthed in Victoria Dock.

EDINBURGH

EDINBURGH is the capital and seat of government in Scotland. The city is built on a group of hills and contains in Princes Street one of the most beautiful thoroughfares in the world. The principal buildings are the Castle, which includes St. Margaret's Chapel, the oldest building in Edinburgh, and near it, the Scottish National War Memorial; the Palace of Holyroodhouse; Parliament House, the present seat of the judicature; two universities (Edinburgh and Heriot-Watt); St. Giles' Cathedral (restored 1879–83); St. Mary's (Scottish Episcopal) Cathedral (Sir Gilbert Scott); the General Register House (Robert Adam): the National and the Signet Libraries; the National Gallery; the Royal Scottish Academy; and the National Portrait Gallery.

GLASGOW

GLASGOW, a Royal Burgh, is the principal commercial and industrial centre in Scotland. The city occupies the north and south banks of the Clyde, formerly one of the chief commercial estuaries in the world. The principal industries include engineering, aero and marine engines, chemicals, and printing. The city has also developed recently as a tourism and conference centre. The chief buildings are the 13th century Gothic Cathedral, the University (Sir Gilbert Scott), the City Chambers, Pollok House, the School of Art (Mackintosh), Kelvingrove Art Galleries, the Burrell Collection museum and the Mitchell Library. The city is home of the Scottish National Orchestra, Scottish Opera and Scottish Ballet.

SCOTTISH DISTRICT COUNCILS

District	Administrative Headquarters	Population	District community charge per head 1990 £	Chief Executive	Chairman (a) Convener (b) Provost (c) Lord Provost
Aberdeen City (5)	Aberdeen	214,100	96·00	J. J. K. Smith‡	(c) R. A. Robertson
Angus (9).............	Forfar	95,080	55·00	P. B. Regan	(b) B. M. C. Milne
Annandale and Eskdale (3).........	Annan	35,911	56·00	J. A. Whitecross	(a) F. Park
Argyll and Bute (8) ...	Lochgilphead	66,360	72·00	M. A. J. Gossip	W. R. Hunter
Badenoch and Strathspey (6)......	Kingussie	10,807	30·00	Mrs. J. M. Fraser	J. A. McCook
Banff and Buchan (5) .	Banff	84,000	61·00	R. M. Blackburn	(a) W. R. Cruick-shank
Bearsden and Milngavie (8)	Bearsden	40,720	75·00	I. C. Laurie	(b) Mrs. J. Cameron
Berwickshire (1)	Duns	18,900	31·00	R. A. Christie	Capt. J. Evans
Caithness (6).........	Wick	27,098	27·00	A. Beattie	(a) J. M. Young
Clackmannan (2)	Alloa	47,200	109·00	I. F. Smith	(a) W. G. Watt
Clydebank (8)	Clydebank	47,180	97·00	J. T. McNally	(b) D. S. Grainger
Clydesdale (8)	Lanark	58,324	82·00	P. W. Daniels	(a) Mrs. E. Logan
Cumbernauld and Kilsyth (8).........	Cumbernauld	62,830	60·00	J. Hutton	(b) Ms. R. McKenna
Cumnock and Doon Valley (8)	Cumnock	43,200	61·00	D. T. Hemmings, OBE	Vacant
Cunninghame (8).....	Irvine	137,900	69·00	B. Devine	(a) J. Carson
Dumbarton (8)	Dumbarton	78,411	108·00	A. Nisbet	(b) W. Petrie
Dundee City (9)	Dundee	172,540	90·00	J. F. Hoey	(c) T. Mitchell
Dunfermline (4)	Dunfermline	129,049	63·00	G. Brown	(b) J. Cameron
East Kilbride (8).....	East Kilbride	81,767	107·00	D. J. Liddell	(b) Ms. H. Biggins
East Lothian (7)	Haddington	82,871	77·00	M. Duncan	G. M. Wanless
Eastwood (8)	Giffnock	58,142	44·00	M. D. Henry	(b) Mrs. J. Y. Macfie
Edinburgh City (7) ...	Edinburgh	433,480	108·00	A. Hepburn	(c) Rt. Hon. Eleanor T. McLaughlin
Ettrick and Lauderdale (1)	Galashiels	33,797	40·00	C. M. Anderson	(b) A. L. Tulley, MBE
Falkirk (2)	Falkirk	143,070	46·00	J. P. H. Paton	(b) D. Goldie
Glasgow City (8)	Glasgow	696,577	92·00	S. F. Hamilton	(c) Rt. Hon. Susan Baird
Gordon (5)	Inverurie	72,850	43·00	M. C. Barron	(b) J. Lawrence
Hamilton (8)	Hamilton	106,997	77·00	A. Baird	(b) R. Gibb
Inverclyde (8)	Greenock	94,370	72·00	I. C. Wilson, OBE	(b) F. A. McGlone
Inverness (6).........	Inverness	62,252	26·00	B. Wilson	(b) A. G. Sellar
Kilmarnock and Loudoun (8)	Kilmarnock	81,743	56·00	R. W. Jenner	(a) J. Mills
Kincardine and Deeside (5).........	Stonehaven	49,820	26·00	T. Hyder	(a) D. J. Mackenzie
Kirkcaldy (4)	Kirkcaldy	147,384	66·00	§{ J. M. Smith H. Wilson	(a) R. King
Kyle and Carrick (8) ..	Ayr	113,290	86·00	I. R. D. Smillie†	(b) D. MacNeill
Lochaber (6)	Fort William	19,561	47·00	D. A. B. Blair	D. P. MacFarlane
Midlothian (7)	Dalkeith	81,335	64·00	T. Muir	(a) D. Lennie
Monklands (8)	Coatbridge	106,100	90·00	M. V. P. Hart	(b) E. Cairns
Moray (5)............	Elgin	85,460	42·00	J. P. C. Bell	(a) E. Aldridge
Motherwell (8)	Motherwell	146,740	70·00	J. Bonomy	(b) J. Armstrong
Nairn (6)	Nairn	10,348	28·00	A. M. Kerr†	(b) S. A. Macarthur
Nithsdale (3)	Dumfries	57,293	50·00	T. Orr	(b) E. D. Gibson
North-East Fife (4) ...	Cupar	66,720	79·00	R. G. Brotherton	Dr. C. R. Sneddon
Perth and Kinross (9) .	Perth	124,671	58·00	J. E. D. Cormie	(b) A. Murray
Renfrew (8)	Paisley	200,409	94·00	A. I. Cowe*	(b) G. Murray
Ross and Cromarty (6)	Dingwall	48,199	49·00	R. Mair	(a) G. D. Finlayson, OBE
Roxburgh (1).........	Hawick	34,890	43·00	K. W. Cramond	G. Yellowlees
Skye and Lochalsh (6).	Portree	11,590	27·00	D. H. Noble	J. F. Munro
Stewartry (3)	Kirkcudbright	23,374	39·00	J. C. Howie	(a) J. Nelson
Stirling (2)	Stirling	81,160	115·00	G. Bonner	(a) J. Hendry
Strathkelvin (8)......	Kirkintilloch	89,475	89·00	C. Mallon	(b) R. M. Coyle
Sutherland (6)	Golspie	12,960	16·00	J. Allison†	D. I. MacRae
Tweeddale (1)	Peebles	14,608	42·00	G. H. T. Garvie	M. A. R. Maher
West Lothian (7)	Bathgate	144,800	57·00	A. M. Linkston	(a) D. McCauley
Wigtown (3)	Stranraer	30,430	40·00	A. Geddes	J. Brown

‡ Town Clerk.   § Joint Chief Officers.   † Director of Administration.   * Managing Director.

REGIONS.—(1) Borders; (2) Central; (3) Dumfries and Galloway; (4) Fife; (5) Grampian; (6) Highland; (7) Lothian; (8) Strathclyde; (9) Tayside.

NORTHERN IRELAND

(For geographical and historical notes on Ireland, *see* Index)

The usually resident population of Northern Ireland, as revised at the 1981 Census was 1,556,039 (males, 761,882; females, 794,157) compared with a total population of 1,536,065 at the Census of 1971. (NB. This revised figure takes account of the population effect of non-enumerated households, estimated at 74,000 persons.) In 1981 the number of persons in the various religious denominations (expressed as percentages of the total usually resident population) were: Roman Catholic, 28·0; Presbyterian, 22·9; Church of Ireland, 19·0; Methodist, 4·0; others 7·6; not stated, 18·5.

Northern Ireland has a total area of 5,452 sq. miles (14,121 sq. km): land, 5,206 sq. miles (13,483 sq. km); inland water and tideways, 246 sq. miles (638 sq. km). There was a density of population of 282 persons per sq. mile in 1981. The population, mid-1988 estimate, was 1,578,100.

CONSTITUTION AND GOVERNMENT

A separate parliament and executive Government was established for Northern Ireland in 1921 by the Government of Ireland Act. The Northern Ireland Constitution Act, 1973, abolished the post of Governor and the Parliament of Northern Ireland and provided for the transfer of certain legislative functions to a Northern Ireland Assembly and Executive. Devolved government came into operation with effect from January 1, 1974 but when the Executive collapsed the Northern Ireland Assembly was prorogued on May 29, 1974. The Northern Ireland Act, 1974, which became law in July 1974, made provision for temporary arrangements for the government of Northern Ireland by the Secretary of State for Northern Ireland and also provided for the holding of elections and a constitutional convention. Direct rule continues in being under the terms of the Northern Ireland Act 1974.

Attempts have been made by successive governments to find a way of restoring devolved government to Northern Ireland. The most recent attempt failed when the Northern Ireland Assembly (elected on October 20, 1982) was dissolved on June 23, 1986.

FLAG.—The white star in the centre of the flag of Northern Ireland (*cross gules in a field argent*) has six points representing the counties of Northern Ireland. It encloses a red hand and stands below a crown.

THE PRIVY COUNCIL

R. J. Bailie (1971); D. W. Bleakley (1971); R. H. Bradford (1969); W. Craig (1963); J. Dobson (1969); W. K. Fitzsimmons (1965); Lt.-Col. the Lord Glentoran (1953); Sir Edward Jones (1965); Mr. Justice Kelly (1969); H. V. Kirk (1962); Capt. W. J. Long (1966); Lord Lowry (1971); R. W. B. McConnell (1964); W. B. McIvor (1971); W. J. Morgan (1961); The Lord Moyola (1966); Sir Ivan Neill (1950); Sir Robert Porter, QC (1969); Lord Rathcavan (1969); R. Simpson (1969); J. D. Taylor (1970); H. W. West (1960).

FINANCE

Taxation in Northern Ireland is largely imposed and collected by the United Kingdom Government. After deducting the cost of collections and of Northern Ireland's contributions to the European Economic Community the balance, known as the Attributed Share of Taxation, is paid over to the Northern Ireland Consolidated Fund. Northern Ireland's revenue is insufficient to meet its expenditure and is supplemented by a grant in aid.

	1989–90*	1990–91**
	£	£
Public income.....	4,473,122,225	4,595,404,000
Public expenditure	4,473,048,509	4,595,304,000
* Outturn	** Estimate	

PRODUCTION

Industries.—The products of the engineering, shipbuilding and aircraft industries, which employed 28,600 persons in 1985, were valued at £856 million. The textile industries, employing about 10,500 per-

sons, produced products valued at approximately £273 million. The food and drink industry, employing about 20,000 persons, produced goods valued at £2,575 million.

Minerals.—1,308 persons were employed in mining and quarrying operations in Northern Ireland in 1989 and the minerals raised (19,239,24 tonnes) were valued at £34,260,152.

COMMUNICATIONS

Seaports.—The total tonnage handled by N. Irish ports in 1988 was 14·1m. Regular ferry, freight and container services operate to ports in Great Britain and Europe from Belfast, Larne, Londonderry and Warrenpoint.

Road and rail transport.—The Northern Ireland Transport Holding Company is largely responsible for the supervision of the subsidiary companies, Ulsterbus and Citybus (which operate the public road passenger services) and Northern Ireland Railways. Road freight services are also provided by a large number of hauliers operating competitively under licence.

Air transport.—Belfast International Airport is run by Northern Ireland Airports Ltd., a subsidiary of the Northern Ireland Transport Holding Company and provides scheduled and chartered services on domestic and international routes.

Scheduled services also operate from Belfast Harbour Airport to eleven British destinations and from Eglinton, Co. Londonderry, to Blackpool, Glasgow and Dublin.

BELFAST

BELFAST, the administrative centre of Northern Ireland, is situated at the mouth of the River Lagan at its entrance to Belfast Lough. The city grew, owing to its easy access by sea to Scottish coal and iron, to be a great industrial centre.

The principal buildings are of a relatively recent date and include the Parliament Buildings at Stormont, the City Hall, the Law Courts, the Public Library and the Museum and Art Gallery.

Belfast received its first charter of incorporation in 1613 and was created a city in 1888; the title of Lord Mayor was conferred in 1892.

LONDONDERRY

LONDONDERRY, situated on the River Foyle, was reputedly founded in 546 by St. Columba. Londonderry (formerly *Derry*) has important associations with the City of London. The Irish Society, under its royal charter of 1613, fortified the city and was for long closely associated with its administration.

The city is famous for the great siege of 1688–9, when for 105 days the town held out against the forces of James II until relieved by sea. The city walls are still intact and form a circuit of almost a mile around the old city. Interesting buildings are the Protestant Cathedral of St. Columb's (1633) and the Guildhall, reconstructed in 1912 and containing a number of beautiful stained glass windows, many of which were presented by the livery companies of London.

COUNTIES OF NORTHERN IRELAND

Counties and ‡County Boroughs	Area* sq. miles	Lord Lieutenant	High Sheriff, 1990
Antrim	1,093	Capt. R. A. F. Dobbs	The Lord O'Neill
Belfast City‡	25	Sir Robin Kinahan, ERD	T. J. Kirkpatrick
Armagh	484	The Earl of Caledon	A. J. Whitten
Down	945	Col. W. S. Brownlow	Dr. S. Kingan
Fermanagh	647	The Earl of Erne	Lord Anthony Hamilton
Londonderry†	798	Col. M. W. McCorkell, OBE, TD	T. B. F. Thompson
Londonderry City‡	3·4	J. T. Eaton, TD	W. Ferris, MBE
Tyrone	1,211	The Duke of Abercorn	J. E. Herdman

† Excluding the City of Londonderry.   * Excluding inland waters and tideways.

MUNICIPAL DIRECTORY OF NORTHERN IRELAND

District and §Borough Councils	Population (June 30, 1988)	Net Annual Value £	Council Clerk	Mayor (†) or Chairman 1990
§Antrim, Co. Antrim	48,100	6,570,755	S. J. Magee	†J. Graham
§Ards, Co. Down	64,500	7,321,190	D. J. Fallows	†R. Gibson
Armagh, Co. Armagh	49,000	4,747,395	D. R. D. Mitchell	W. G. Macartney
§Ballymena, Co. Antrim	57,200	7,684,498	R. Mathers	†A. Spence, MBE
§Ballymoney, Co. Antrim	23,900	2,427,267	W. J. Williamson, MBE	†J. A. Gaston
Banbridge, Co. Down	31,900	3,390,459	R. Gilmore	W. J. Martin
Belfast, Co. Antrim and Co. Down	296,900	51,732,828	S. McDowell	F. Cobain (Lord Mayor)
§Carrickfergus, Co. Antrim	30,400	4,684,614	R. Boyd	†C. Johnston
§Castlereagh, Co. Down	58,000	7,649,732	A. D. Nicol	†A. S. Carson
§Coleraine, Co. Londonderry	48,500	7,385,174	W. E. Andrews	†Mrs. E. T. Black
Cookstown, Co. Tyrone	27,600	2,905,501	(vacant)	A. Kane
§Craigavon, Co. Armagh	77,700	10,035,007	E. A. McKinley	†S. J. McCammick
Derry, Co. Londonderry	99,500	11,126,709	C. M. Geary	†D. G. Davis
Down, Co. Down	57,200	5,588,768	S. Byrne	W. Brown
Dungannon, Co. Tyrone	43,700	4,240,870	W. J. Beattie	M. McLoughlin
Fermanagh, Co. Fermanagh	50,400	4,938,799	G. Burns, MBE	C. McClaughrey
§Larne, Co. Antrim	29,100	3,815,754	G. McKinley	†Mrs. R. G. Armstrong
§Limavady, Co. Londonderry	29,800	2,661,796	J. K. Stevenson	†J. Dolan
§Lisburn, Co. Antrim and Co. Down	97,400	12,422,095	M. S. Fielding	†W. J. McAllister
Magherafelt, Co. Londonderry	32,900	3,243,890	W. R. S. McMaster	P. A. Kirkpatrick
Moyle, Co. Antrim	15,100	1,381,285	J. O'Kane	A. G. Kane
Newry and Mourne, Co. Down and Co. Armagh	88,900	7,673,345	K. O'Neill	A. Ruddy
§Newtownabbey, Co. Antrim	72,900	10,585,369	J. Campbell	†W. A. F. Agnew
§North Down, Co. Down	71,900	8,835,188	J. McKimm	†G. M. Dunne
Omagh, Co. Tyrone	44,900	4,121,208	J. P. McKinney	L. McQuaid
Strabane, Co. Tyrone	35,600	2,978,889	J. T. Keanie	E. Turner
Northern Ireland	1,583,000	200,148,385		

NOTE.—Since the reorganization of local government, rates in Northern Ireland are collected by the Department of the Environment and consist of two rates, a regional rate made by the Department of Finance and a district rate made by individual District Councils.

THE ISLE OF MAN
(ELLAN VANNIN)

The Isle of Man is an island situated in the Irish Sea, in lat. 54° 3′–54° 25′ N. and long. 4° 18′–4° 47′ W., nearly equidistant from England, Scotland, and Ireland. Although the early inhabitants were of Celtic origin, the Isle of Man was part of the Norwegian Kingdom of the Hebrides until 1266, when this was ceded to Scotland. Subsequently granted to the Stanleys (Earls of Derby) in the 15th century and later to the Dukes of Atholl, it was brought under the direct administration of the Crown in 1765. The island forms the bishopric of Sodor and Man.

The total land area is 141,263 acres (221 sq. miles). The report on the 1986 Census showed a resident population of 64,282 (males, 30,782; females, 33,500). In 1988 births numbered 781 and deaths 993. The main language in use is English. There are no remaining native speakers of Manx Gaelic but around 200 people are able to speak the language.

CAPITAL, ΨDouglas. Population (1986), 20,368; ΨCastletown (3,019) is the ancient capital; the other towns are ΨPeel (3,660), and ΨRamsey (5,778).

FLAG.—Three legs in white and gold armed conjoined on a red ground.

TYNWALD DAY.—July 5.

LEGISLATURE AND GOVERNMENT

The Isle of Man is a self-governing Crown dependency, having its own parliamentary, legal and administrative system; the Crown is responsible for international relations and defence. The Lieutenant-Governor is the Queen's personal representative in the Island.

The legislature, Tynwald, is the oldest parliament in the world in continuous existence. It has two branches—the Legislative Council and the House of Keys. The Council consists of the Bishop of Sodor and Man, the Attorney-General (who does not have a vote) and eight members chosen by the House of Keys. The House of Keys consists of 24 members, elected by universal adult suffrage. The branches sit separately to consider legislation and sit together, as Tynwald Court, for other parliamentary purposes.

The presiding officer in Tynwald Court is the President of Tynwald, elected by the members, who also presides over sittings of the Legislative Council. The presiding officer of the House of Keys is Mr. Speaker, who is elected by members of the House.

The principal members of the Manx Government are the Chief Minister and nine departmental ministers, who comprise the Council of Ministers.

ECONOMY

Most of the income generated in the island is earned in the services sector with financial and business services being considerably larger than the traditional industry of tourism. Manufacturing industry is also a major generator of income whilst the island's other traditional industries of agriculture and fishing now play a smaller role in the economy.

Under the terms of the island's special relationship with the European Community the Island has free access to EC markets.

A twenty-acre Freeport has been developed adjacent to the main airport at Ronaldsway.

The island's unemployment rate is approximately 1 per cent and price inflation is around 7 per cent per annum.

FINANCE

The island's Budget for 1989–90 provided for gross expenditure of £230,005,590. The principal sources of Government revenue are taxes on income and expenditure. Income tax is payable at a rate of 15 per cent. on the first £26,000 of taxable income of resident individuals and 20 per cent on the balance. The rate of income tax is 20 per cent on the whole taxable income of non-residents and companies. By agreement with the United Kingdom Government, the island keeps most of its rates of indirect taxation (Value Added Tax and duties) the same as those in the United Kingdom, but this agreement may be terminated by either party. A reciprocal agreement on national insurance benefits and pensions exists between the Governments of the Isle of Man and the United Kingdom. Taxes are also charged on property (rates), but these are comparatively small.

The major Government expenditure items are health, social security and education, which account for 53 per cent of the Government budget. The island makes a voluntary annual contribution to the United Kingdom for defence and other external services.

Although the island has a special relationship with the European Community it neither contributes money to nor receives funds from the EC Budget.

Lieutenant-Governor, His Excellency Air Marshal Sir Laurence Jones, KCB, AFC.
 ADC to the Lieutenant-Governor, Capt. C. P. Dawson.
President of Tynwald, The Hon. Sir Charles Kerruish, OBE.
Speaker, House of Keys, The Hon. G. V. H. Kneale, CBE (*acting*).
His Honour the First Deemster and Clerk of the Rolls, J. W. Corrin.
Clerk of Tynwald, Secretary to the House of Keys, and Counsel to the Speaker, Prof. T. St. J. N. Bates.
Attorney-General, T. W. Cain, QC.
Chief Minister, The Hon. M. R. Walker.
Chief Secretary, J. F. Kissack.
Chief Financial Officer, W. Dawson.

THE CHANNEL ISLANDS

The Channel Islands, situated off the north-west coast of France (at distances of from ten to thirty miles), are the only portions of the Dukedom of Normandy now belonging to the Crown, to which they have been attached ever since the Conquest. They consist of Jersey (28,717 acres), Guernsey (15,654 acres), and the dependencies of Guernsey—Alderney (1,962 acres), Brechou (74), Great Sark (1,035), Little Sark (239), Herm (320), Jethou (44) and Lihou (38)—a total of 48,083 acres, or 75 square miles. In 1986 the population of Jersey was 80,212; and of Guernsey, 54,380; Alderney, 2,000 and Sark, 604.

GOVERNMENT

The islands are Crown dependencies with their own legislative assemblies (the States in Jersey, Guernsey and Alderney, and the Court of Chief Pleas in Sark), and systems of local administration and of law, and their own courts. Acts passed by the States require the sanction of The Queen-in-Council. The British Government is responsible for defence and international relations.

In both Bailiwicks the Lieutenant-Governor and

Commander-in-Chief, who is appointed by the Crown, is the personal representative of the Queen and is the channel of communication between the Crown (via the Privy Council) and the insular government. The Bailiffs of Jersey and Guernsey, also appointed by the Crown, are President of the States and of the Royal Courts of their respective islands. The government of each Bailiwick is conducted by committees appointed by the States. Justice is administered by the Royal Courts of Jersey and Guernsey, each consisting of the Bailiff and 12 elected Jurats.

Each Bailiwick constitutes a deanery under the jurisdiction of the Bishop of Winchester (*see* Index).

ECONOMY

A mild climate and good soil have led to the development of intensive systems of agriculture and horticulture, which form a significant part of the economy of the Channel Islands. Equally important are invisible earnings, principally from the tourist trade and from banking and finance, the low rate of income tax (20p in the £ in Jersey and Guernsey; no tax of any kind in Sark) and the absence of super-tax and death duties making the Channel Islands a popular tax-haven. Principal exports are agricultural produce and flowers; imports are chiefly machinery, manufactured goods, food, fuel and chemicals. Trade with the UK is regarded as internal trade.

British currency is legal tender in the Channel Islands but each Bailiwick issues its own coins, and some notes, of the same values as those of the UK. They also issue their own postage stamps; UK stamps are not valid.

LANGUAGE

The official languages are English and French, but French is gradually being supplanted by English, which is the language in daily use. In country districts of Jersey and Guernsey and throughout Sark a Norman-French *patois* is also in use, though to a declining extent.

CHIEF TOWNS.—ΨSt. Helier on the south coast of Jersey; ΨSt. Peter Port, on the east coast of Guernsey, and St. Anne on Alderney.

JERSEY

Lieutenant-Governor and Commander-in-Chief of Jersey, His Excellency Air Marshal Sir John Sutton, KCB (1990).

Secretary and ADC, Cdr. D. M. L. Braybrooke, LVO.
Bailiff of Jersey, Sir Peter Crill, CBE.
Deputy Bailiff, V. A. Tomes.
Attorney-General and Receiver-General, P. M. Bailhache, QC.
Solicitor-General, T. C. Sowden, QC.
Greffier of the States, E. J. M. Potter.
States Treasurer, L. May.

Year to Dec. 31:	1988	1989
Revenue	£258,281,219	£295,967,172
Revenue Expenditure	201,673,508	228,530,891
Capital Expenditure ..	38,022,000	38,675,000
Public Debt	−1,166,690	−1,166,690

FLAG.—A white field charged with a red saltire, and coat of arms.

GUERNSEY AND DEPENDENCIES

Lieutenant-Governor and Commander-in-Chief of the Bailiwick of Guernsey and its Dependencies, His Excellency Lt.-Gen. Sir Michael Wilkins, KCB, OBE (1990).
Secretary and ADC, Capt. D. P. L. Hodgetts.
Bailiff of Guernsey, Sir Charles Frossard.
Deputy Bailiff, G. M. Dorey.
HM Procureur and Receiver-General, de V. G. Carey, QC.
HM Comptroller, A. C. K. Day, QC.
States Supervisor, F. N. Le Cheminant.

Year to Dec. 31:	1988	1989
Revenue	£117,243,209	£129,639,543
Expenditure	97,645,270	112,025,191

FLAG.—White, bearing a red cross of St. George, with an argent a cross gules superimposed on the cross.

Alderney

President of the States, J. Kay-Mouat.
Clerk of the States, D. V. Jenkins.
Clerk of the Court, P. Beer.

Sark

Le Seigneur of Sark, J. M. Beaumont.
The Seneschal, L. P. de Carteret.
The Greffier, J. P. Hamon.

Brechou, Lihou and Jethou are leased by the Crown. Herm is leased by the States of Guernsey.

THE ISLES OF SCILLY

There are about 140 islands and skerries in the Scillies group (total area, 6 square miles) situated 28 miles south-west of Land's End, of which only five are inhabited: St. Mary's, St. Agnes, Bryher, Tresco and St. Martin's. The population is 1,978. The entire group has been designated a Conservation Area, a Heritage Coast, and an Area of Outstanding Natural Beauty, and has been given National Nature Reserve status by the Nature Conservancy Council because of its unique flora and fauna. Tourism and the winter/spring flower trade for the home market form the basis of the economy of the Isles. The island group is a recognized rural development area.

The islands are administered by the Council of the Isles of Scilly, a 21-member non-political body, which combines the powers and duties of a County Council and a District Council under the Local Government

Act 1972 and the Isles of Scilly Orders 1978. Legislation is specifically applied to the Isles of Scilly by Special Order. The Council is responsible for education, fire services, highways, planning and social services, and Cornwall County Council provides other services on an agency basis; the police service is administered by the Devon and Cornwall Police Authority, of which the Council is a member. The Isles are part of the St. Ives electoral division.

Administrative Headquarters, Town Hall, St. Mary's, Isles of Scilly, TR21 0LW.
Chairman of the Council, H. R. Duncan.
Clerk, Chief Executive and Chief Financial Officer, L. W. Michell.
Chief Technical Officer, B. M. Lowen.

COUNTRIES OF THE WORLD

No complete survey of many countries has yet been achieved and consequently accurate area figures are not always available. Similarly, many countries have not recently, or have never, taken a census. The areas of countries given below are derived from estimated figures published by the United Nations. The conversion factors used are: (i) to convert square miles to square km—multiply by 2·589988; (ii) to convert square km to square miles—multiply by 0·3861022.

Population figures for countries are derived from the most recent estimates available. Accurate and up-to-date data for the populations of capital cities are scarce, and definitions of cities' extent differ. The figures given below are the latest estimates available, and where it is known that the figure applies to an urban agglomeration this is indicated.

AFRICA

COUNTRY	AREA		POPULATION	CAPITAL	POPULATION OF CAPITAL
	Sq. miles	Sq. km			
Algeria.............	919,595	2,381,741	23,841,000	Ψ Algiers	3,250,000
Angola..............	481,354	1,246,700	9,767,000	Ψ Luanda	2,000,000
Benin	43,484	112,622	4,444,000	Ψ Porto Novo.......	208,258
Botswana	224,607	581,730	1,300,000	Gaborone	125,000
Burkina............	105,869	274,200	8,509,000	Ouagadougou	400,000
Burundi............	10,747	27,834	5,149,000	Bujumbura	150,000
Cameroon	183,569	475,442	10,166,000	Yaoundé	635,670
Cape Verde Islands	1,557	4,033	358,000	Ψ Praia	57,748
Central African Rep. ..	240,535	622,984	2,771,000	Bangui	473,817
Chad................	495,755	1,284,000	5,401,000	Ndjaména........	402,000
Comoros.............	838	2,171	488,000	Moroni	17,267
Congo...............	132,047	342,000	1,888,000	Brazzaville	600,000
Côte d'Ivoire.........	124,503	322,463	11,613,000	Ψ Abidjan	3,500,000
Djibouti	8,494	22,000	383,000	Ψ Djibouti..........	200,000
Egypt	386,662	1,001,449	51,897,000	Cairo	14,000,000
Equatorial Guinea	10,830	28,051	420,000	Ψ Malabo	34,980
Ethiopia	471,778	1,221,900	47,882,000	Addis Ababa.....	1,464,901
Gabon..............	103,347	267,667	1,095,000	Ψ Libreville	251,000
Gambia	4,361	11,295	800,200	Ψ Banjul (u.a.).....	44,536*
Ghana	92,100	238,537	14,131,000	Ψ Accra (u.a.)	1,420,066*
Guinea..............	94,926	245,857	5,071,000	Ψ Conakry	763,000
Guinea-Bissau	13,948	36,125	945,000	Ψ Bissau	109,486*
Kenya	224,961	582,646	23,883,000	Nairobi	1,103,554
Lesotho	11,720	30,355	1,676,000	Maseru	288,951*
Liberia	43,000	111,369	2,429,000	Ψ Monrovia	425,000
Libya	679,362	1,759,540	4,232,000	Ψ Tripoli...........	1,000,000
Madagascar	226,669	587,041	11,238,000	Antananarivo	1,000,000
Malawi.............	45,747	118,484	7,982,607*	Lilongwe........	175,000*
Mali	478,791	1,240,000	8,918,000	Bamako	600,000
Mauritania..........	397,955	1,030,700	1,916,000	Nouakchott	500,000
Mauritius	790	2,045	1,047,532	Ψ Port Louis	138,272
Mayotte	144	372	67,000	Mamoundzou	12,000
Morocco.............	172,414	446,550	27,575,000	Ψ Rabat...........	1,123,000
Western Sahara	102,703	266,000	163,868*	Laayoune	96,784*
Mozambique	309,495	801,590	15,200,000	Ψ Maputo	1,150,000
Namibia.............	318,261	824,292	1,184,000	Windhoek........	110,000
Niger	489,191	1,267,080	6,688,000	Niamey	410,000
Nigeria.............	356,669	923,768	105,472,000	Ψ Lagos	3,000,000
Réunion	969	2,510	565,000	St. Denis	109,072
Rwanda	10,169	26,338	6,755,000	Kigali	156,000
St. Helena	47	122	5,544	Ψ Jamestown	1,330
Ascension I.	34	88	1,029	Ψ Georgetown	..
Tristan da Cunha ...	38	98	306	Ψ Edinburgh	..
Sao Tomé & Principé ..	372	964	106,000	Ψ São Tomé	25,000
Senegal	75,750	196,192	7,113,000	Ψ Dakar	1,000,000
Seychelles	108	280	66,745	Ψ Victoria	24,733
Sierra Leone..........	27,699	71,740	3,946,000	Ψ Freetown	470,000*
Somalia	246,201	637,657	7,107,000	Ψ Mogadishu	1,000,000
South Africa........	471,445	1,221,031	33,748,000	{ Pretoria (u.a.) ..	822,925
				{ Ψ Cape Town (u.a.)..	1,911,521
Sudan................	967,500	2,505,813	23,798,000	Khartoum (u.a.) ..	3,000,000
Swaziland	6,704	17,363	737,000	Mbabane	30,000
Tanzania	364,900	945,087	23,174,336*	Ψ Dar es Salaam	1,096,000
Togo	21,925	56,785	3,247,000	Ψ Lomé	366,476
Tunisia	63,170	163,610	7,809,000	Ψ Tunis	1,394,749
Uganda	91,259	236,036	17,500,000	Kampala (u.a.)....	750,000
Zaire...............	905,567	2,345,409	33,458,000	Kinshasa	2,778,281*
Zambia	290,586	752,614	7,531,000	Lusaka (u.a.)	1,000,000
Zimbabwe	150,804	390,580	9,000,000	Harare...........	658,364

*latest census result   Ψ seaport   u.a. urban agglomeration

AMERICA

COUNTRY	AREA Sq. miles	AREA Sq. km	POPULATION	CAPITAL	POPULATION OF CAPITAL
North America					
Canada.............	3,849,646	9,970,537	25,309,330*	Ottawa (u.a.)	819,263*
Greenland............	840,004	2,175,600	52,940	Ψ Godthab	..
Mexico...............	761,605	1,972,547	82,734,000	Mexico City (u.a.) .	18,748,000
St. Pierre and Miquelon	93	242	6,500	Ψ St. Pierre	..
United States	3,618,787	9,372,614	226,545,805*	Washington, DC ..	617,000
Central America and the West Indies					
Anguilla	35	91	8,000	The Valley	500
Antigua and Barbuda..	170	440	85,000	Ψ St. John's	30,000
Aruba................	75	193	62,500	Ψ Oranjestad	20,000
Bahamas	5,380	13,935	245,000	Ψ Nassau...........	153,620
Barbados	166	431	254,000	Ψ Bridgetown	7,466
Belize	8,867	22,965	175,000	Belmopan	2,935
Bermuda	20	53	60,000	Ψ Hamilton	2,000
Cayman Islands	100	259	25,535*	Ψ George Town	12,972*
Costa Rica	19,575	50,700	2,922,372	San José (u.a.)	1,068,206
Cuba.................	42,804	110,861	10,468,661	Ψ Havana	2,100,000
Dominica	290	751	81,300	Ψ Roseau...........	11,000
Dominican Republic ...	18,816	48,734	6,867,000	Ψ Santo Domingo (u.a.)	1,313,172*
Grenada.............	133	344	100,000	Ψ St. George's	10,000
Guadeloupe...........	687	1,779	337,000	Ψ Basse-Terre	15,778
Guatemala	42,042	108,889	8,681,000	Guatemala City ...	1,300,000
Haiti................	10,714	27,750	5,523,000	Ψ Port au Prince	1,000,000
Honduras	43,277	112,088	4,443,721	Tegucigalpa	640,900
Jamaica	4,244	10,991	2,392,300	Ψ Kingston (u.a.) ...	696,300
Martinique...........	425	1,102	334,000	Ψ Fort de France....	100,576
Montserrat	38	98	12,000	Ψ Plymouth	3,000
Netherlands Antilles ..	371	961	188,000	Ψ Willemstad	50,000
Nicaragua	50,193	130,000	3,622,000	Managua	615,000
Panama	29,762	77,082	2,314,391*	Ψ Panama City	1,063,565
Puerto Rico..........	3,435	8,897	3,346,000	Ψ San Juan (u.a.) ...	1,816,300
St. Christopher and Nevis	101	261	45,100	Ψ Basseterre	15,000
St. Lucia	238	616	133,000	Ψ Castries	55,000
St. Vincent and the Grenadines	150	388	108,000	Ψ Kingstown	33,694
El Salvador	8,124	21,041	5,500,000	San Salvador (u.a.)	2,000,000
Trinidad and Tobago ..	1,981	5,130	1,243,000	Ψ Port of Spain	59,649
Turks and Caicos Is. ...	166	430	14,000	Ψ Grand Turk	4,500
Virgin Islands:—					
British	59	153	10,985*	Ψ Road Town	2,479
US.................	132	342	106,000	Ψ Charlotte Amalie .	11,756
South America					
Argentina	1,068,302	2,766,889	31,963,000	Ψ Buenos Aires (u.a.)	3,323,000
Bolivia	424,165	1,098,581	6,993,000	La Paz	1,000,000
Brazil	3,286,488	8,511,965	144,428,000	Brasilia	1,576,657
Chile.................	292,258	756,945	12,748,000	Santiago	4,132,293
Colombia	439,737	1,138,914	30,241,000	Bogotá	3,967,988*
Ecuador	109,484	283,561	10,157,000	Quito	1,200,000
Falkland Islands	4,700	12,173	1,916	Ψ Stanley	1,231
French Guiana........	35,135	91,000	89,000	Ψ Cayenne	38,135
Guyana	83,000	214,969	799,000	Ψ Georgetown	185,000
Paraguay.............	157,048	406,752	4,157,287	Asunción (u.a.) ...	729,307*
Peru	496,225	1,285,216	22,332,100	Lima (u.a.)	6,415,000
South Georgia	1,580	4,092	..	..	..
Suriname.............	63,037	163,265	410,000	Ψ Paramaribo	110,000
Uruguay	68,037	176,215	3,060,000	Ψ Montevideo	1,355,312
Venezuela	352,144	912,050	18,757,000	Caracas	4,000,000

*latest census result   Ψ seaport   *u.a.* urban agglomeration

ASIA

COUNTRY	AREA Sq. miles	AREA Sq. km	POPULATION	CAPITAL	POPULATION OF CAPITAL
Afghanistan	250,000	647,497	15,513,000	Kabul............	2,000,000
Bahrain	240	622	503,000	Ψ Manama	121,986*
Bangladesh	55,598	143,998	104,532,000	Dhaka	3,458,602
Bhutan	18,147	47,000	1,451,000	Thimphu	15,000
Brunei	2,226	5,765	241,000	Bandar Seri Begawan	58,000
Cambodia	69,898	181,035	7,870,000	Ψ Phnom Penh	500,000
China[1]	3,705,408	9,596,961	1,160,000,000	Beijing (Peking) ..	10,810,000
Taiwan	13,800	35,742	19,954,397	Taipei	2,888,326
Hong Kong	416	1,074	5,812,300	Ψ Victoria	..
India................	1,269,346	3,287,590	797,000,000	Delhi	6,220,000*
Indonesia	735,358	1,904,569	174,951,000	Ψ Jakarta	6,503,449
Iran	636,296	1,648,000	55,000,000	Tehran	10,000,000
Iraq.................	167,925	434,924	17,657,000	Baghdad	3,205,645*
Israel	8,019	20,770	4,437,000	Jerusalem	506,200
Japan	145,834	377,708	121,870,000	Tokyo (*u.a.*)	11,718,720
Jordan	37,738	97,740	2,910,000	Amman	1,100,000
Korea DPR (North)....	46,540	120,538	21,902,000	Pyongyang	1,500,000
Korea Rep. of (South) ..	38,025	98,484	41,975,000	Seoul	9,991,089
Kuwait	6,880	17,818	1,958,000	Ψ Kuwait (city)	400,000
Laos	91,429	231,800	3,875,000	Vientiane	120,000
Lebanon.............	4,015	10,400	2,828,000	Ψ Beirut	702,000
Macao	6	16	439,000	Ψ Macao	..
Malaysia	127,317	329,749	16,921,300*	Kuala Lumpur....	1,103,200
Maldives	115	298	202,000	Ψ Malé............	46,334
Mongolia	604,250	1,565,000	2,000,000	Ulan Bator	530,000
Myanmar (Burma)	261,218	676,552	39,966,000	Ψ Rangoon (*u.a.*) ..	3,973,872
Nepal	54,342	140,747	18,000,000	Kathmandu	235,000
Oman	82,030	212,457	1,378,000	Ψ Muscat	400,000
Pakistan	307,374	746,045	105,409,000	Islamabad (*u.a.*) ...	350,000
Philippines	115,831	300,000	58,721,000	Ψ Manila	1,630,485
Qatar	4,247	11,000	341,000	Ψ Doha	220,000
Saudi Arabia	830,000	2,149,640	14,016,000	Riyadh	1,500,000
Singapore	241	626	2,703,500	..	..
Sri Lanka	25,332	65,610	16,587,000	Ψ Colombo	643,000
Syria................	71,498	185,180	11,338,000	Damascus	1,168,000
Thailand	198,457	514,000	55,888,393	Ψ Bangkok	5,400,000
Turkey (in Asia)	292,261	756,953	44,485,734*	Ankara	3,196,460
USSR (in Asia)........	6,498,486	16,831,000	63,070,000	..	..
United Arab Emirates .	32,278	83,600	1,501,000	..	..
Vietnam	127,242	329,556	64,412,000	Hanoi............	1,089,000
Yemen	203,850	527,696	12,500,000	Sana'a	427,150

*latest census result   Ψ seaport   *u.a.* urban agglomeration

[1] Including Tibet.

THE LARGEST CITIES OF THE WORLD*

	Population		Population
MEXICO CITY, Mexico	18,748,000	São Paulo, Brazil	8,490,763
CAIRO, Egypt	14,000,000	Ψ Bombay, India	8,202,000
Ψ Shanghai, China	12,620,000	Ψ New York, USA	7,352,700
TOKYO, Japan	11,718,720	Ψ LONDON, UK	6,735,400
BEIJING, China	10,810,000	Manila, Philippines.................	6,720,050
SEOUL, South Korea	9,991,089	Ψ JAKARTA, Indonesia	6,503,449
Ψ Calcutta, India	9,166,000	Karachi, Pakistan	6,500,000
Moscow, USSR	8,879,000	DELHI, India	6,220,000
PARIS, France	8,706,963	TEHRAN, Iran	6,000,000

* In most cases figures refer to urban agglomerations.

EUROPE

COUNTRY	AREA		POPULATION	CAPITAL	POPULATION OF CAPITAL
	Sq. miles	Sq. km			
Albania	11,099	28,748	3,410,000	Tirana	210,757
Andorra	175	453	49,000	Andorra La Vella .	16,000
Austria	32,374	83,849	7,595,000	Vienna	1,531,346
Belgium	11,781	30,513	9,925,000	Brussels (*u.a.*)	976,536
Bulgaria	42,823	110,912	8,995,000	Sofia	1,136,875
Cyprus	3,572	9,251	698,300	Nicosia	166,900
Czechoslovakia	49,370	127,869	15,608,000	Prague...........	1,190,576
Denmark	16,629	43,069	5,130,000	Ψ Copenhagen (*u.a.*).	1,495,736
Faroe Is.	540	1,399	46,000	Ψ Thorshavn	..
Finland	137,851	337,032	4,954,484	Ψ Helsinki	485,626
France	211,208	547,026	55,873,000	Paris (*u.a.*)	8,706,963*
German DR (East)	41,768	108,178	16,674,632	East Berlin	1,284,535
Germany, FR (West)[1] ..	95,976	248,577	61,999,000	Bonn	276,500
Gibraltar	2	6	30,689	Ψ Gibraltar	..
Greece	50,944	131,944	10,013,000	Athens (*u.a.*)	3,027,331*
Hungary	35,919	93,030	10,560,000	Budapest..........	2,072,000
Iceland..............	39,768	103,000	253,482	Ψ Reykjavik (*u.a.*) ..	95,811
Ireland, Republic of	27,136	70,283	3,515,000	Ψ Dublin	502,749*
Italy	116,304	301,225	57,441,000	Rome (*u.a.*)	2,821,420
Liechtenstein.........	61	157	28,181	Vaduz	4,919
Luxembourg	998	2,586	377,100	Luxembourg	77,500
Malta and Gozo	122	316	349,014	Ψ Valletta	9,239*
Monaco	0·4	1	27,063	Monaco-Ville.....	1,234
Netherlands	15,770	40,844	14,891,000	Ψ Amsterdam (*u.a.*) .	1,031,000
Norway[2]	125,181	324,219	4,224,606	Ψ Oslo	450,808
Poland	120,725	312,677	37,862,000	Warsaw	1,644,626
Portugal[3]	35,553	92,082	10,408,000	Ψ Lisbon	2,128,000
Romania	91,699	237,500	23,112,000	Bucharest........	1,961,189
San Marino..........	23	61	23,000	San Marino	..
Spain[4]	194,897	504,782	39,054,000	Madrid (*u.a.*)	4,731,224
Sweden	173,732	449,964	8,462,00	Ψ Stockholm (*u.a.*) ..	1,435,474
Switzerland	15,943	41,293	6,620,000	Berne	135,000
Turkey (in Europe)	9,121	23,623	6,942,780*		..
United Kingdom[5]	94,227	244,046	57,065,000	Ψ London (*u.a.*)	6,735,400
England.............	50,363	130,439	47,536,000		..
Wales	8,018	20,768	2,857,000	Ψ Cardiff	283,900
Scotland	30,414	78,772	5,094,000	Ψ Edinburgh	433,480
Northern Ireland	5,452	14,121	1,578,000	Ψ Belfast.........	296,900
USSR (in Europe)	2,150,975	5,571,000	218,607,000	Moscow	8,879,000
Vatican City State	0·2	0·44	1,000	Vatican City	..
Yugoslavia	98,766	255,804	23,559,000	Belgrade	1,455,000

*latest census result   Ψ seaport   *u.a.* urban agglomeration

[1] Data include West Berlin.

[2] Excludes Svalbard and Jan Mayen Is. (approx. 24,101 sq. miles (62,422 sq. km.) and 3,000 population).

[3] Includes Madeira (314 sq. miles) and the Azores (922 sq. miles).

[4] Includes Balearic Is., Canary Is., Ceuta and Melilla.

[5] Includes Isle of Man (227 sq. miles (588 sq. km.), 64,282 population), and Channel Is. (75 sq. miles (195 sq. km.), 137,196 population).

OCEANIA

COUNTRY	AREA		POPULATION	CAPITAL	POPULATION OF CAPITAL
	Sq. miles	Sq. km			
Australia............	2,967,909	7,686,848	16,806,700	Canberra........	297,300
Norfolk Island	14	36	1,977*	Ψ Kingston.........	..
Fiji	7,055	18,274	727,000	Ψ Suva.............	75,000
French Polynesia	1,544	4,000	189,000	Ψ Papeete	22,967
Guam	212	549	138,089	Agaña	..
Kiribati	281	728	67,000	Tarawa	17,921
Marshall Is............	70	181	43,000	Majuro	20,000
Micronesia, Fed. States					
of.	271	701	100,000	Kolonia	6,000
Nauru	8	21	9,000	Ψ Nauru	..
New Caledonia........	7,358	19,058	146,000	Ψ Noumea..........	60,112
New Zealand..........	103,736	268,676	3,307,084*	Ψ Wellington (u.a.)..	324,600
Cook Islands	91	236	17,185*	Avarua	..
Niue	100	259	2,531*	Alofi.............	..
Ross Dependency†...	286,696	750,310	..	..	..
Northern Mariana Is ..	184	476	21,777	Saipan	19,156
Palau	192	497	14,000	Koror...........	8,100
Papua New Guinea	178,260	461,691	3,562,000	Ψ Port Moresby	139,300
Pitcairn Islands	1·9	5	65	..	..
Samoa, Eastern (US)...	76	197	38,200	Ψ Pago Pago........	..
Samoa, Western	1,097	2,842	167,000	Ψ Apia............	33,100*
Solomon Islands.......	10,983	28,446	285,176	Ψ Honiara..........	30,499*
Tonga...............	270	699	116,000	Ψ Nuku'alofa	30,000
Tuvalu	10	25	8,229	Ψ Funafuti	2,856
Vanuatu	4,706	12,190	142,630*	Ψ Vila	19,400
Wallis and Futuna Is...	106	274	12,000	Ψ Mata-Utu	..

*latest census result   Ψ seaport   u.a. urban agglomeration
† Includes permanent shelf ice.

WORLD POPULATION

The total population of the world in mid-1985, was estimated at 4,837,500,000, compared with 3,003,000,000 in 1960 and 2,070,000,000 in 1930.

Continent, etc	Area		Estimated population, mid-1985
	Sq. miles '000	Sq. km '000	
Africa.........	11,704	30,313	555,000,000
North America[1]	8,311	21,525	264,000,000
Latin America[2]	7,933	20,547	405,000,000
Asia[3].........	10,637	27,549	2,813,000,000
Europe[4]	1,915	4,961	497,000,000
USSR	8,649	22,402	279,000,000
Oceania[5]	3,286	8,510	24,500,000
Total	52,435	135,807	4,837,500,000

[1] Includes Greenland and Hawaii.
[2] Mexico and the remainder of the Americas south of the USA.
[3] Includes Asiatic Turkey, excludes USSR.
[4] Includes European Turkey, excludes USSR.
[5] Includes Australia, New Zealand and the islands inhabited by Micronesian, Melanesian and Polynesian peoples.
Source: *UN Demographic Yearbook 1985 (pub. 1987).*

A United Nations report (*The Future Growth of World Population*) in 1958, pointed out that the population of the world had increased since the beginning of the 20th century at an unprecedented rate: in 1850 it was estimated at 1,094,000,000 and in 1900 at 1,500,000,000, an increase of 42 per cent in 50 years. By 1925 it had risen to 1,907,000,000—23 per cent in 25 years—and by 1950 it had reached 2,500,000,000, an increase of 31 per cent in 25 years. Levels of population and the trend in distribution of the population by continents as forecast for the year 2000 were:—

Continents, etc.	2000	
	Estimated population	per cent
Africa.....................	517,000,000	8·2
North America............	312,000,000	5·0
Latin America†	592,000,000	9·4
Asia (excluding USSR).....	3,870,000,000	61·8
Europe (including USSR) ..	947,000,000	15·1
Oceania	29,000,000	0·5
World	6,267,000,000	100

† Mexico and the remainder of the Americas south of USA.

THE COMMONWEALTH

The Commonwealth is a free association of the 50 sovereign independent states listed below together with their associated states and dependencies.

ANTIGUA AND BARBUDA
AUSTRALIA
BAHAMAS
BANGLADESH
BARBADOS
BELIZE
BOTSWANA
BRUNEI
CANADA
CYPRUS
DOMINICA
GAMBIA, THE
GHANA
GRENADA
GUYANA
INDIA
JAMAICA
KENYA
KIRIBATI
LESOTHO
MALAWI
MALAYSIA
MALDIVES
MALTA
MAURITIUS
NAMIBIA

NAURU
NEW ZEALAND
NIGERIA
PAKISTAN
PAPUA NEW GUINEA
SAINT CHRISTOPHER
    AND NEVIS
SAINT LUCIA
SAINT VINCENT AND THE
    GRENADINES
SEYCHELLES
SIERRA LEONE
SINGAPORE
SOLOMON ISLANDS
SRI LANKA
SWAZILAND
TANZANIA
TONGA
TRINIDAD AND TOBAGO
TUVALU
UGANDA
UNITED KINGDOM
VANUATU
WESTERN SAMOA
ZAMBIA
ZIMBABWE

Area and Population.—The total surface area of the independent Commonwealth is estimated at 29,369,202 sq. km (11,339,513 sq. miles) (UN estimate 1988), about a quarter of the world total. The total population of the Commonwealth is estimated to be about one quarter of the world total. In 1988 this amounted to 1,384,631,000 (UN estimate). Details of the areas and populations of the Member States and dependencies appear in the following pages.

History and Government.—The status and relationship of member nations was first defined by the Inter-Imperial Relations Committee of the 1926 Imperial Conference, under the chairmanship of Lord Balfour, in what came to be known as the Balfour Declaration: 'They are autonomous communities . . . equal in status, in no way subordinate one to another in any aspect of their domestic or external affairs, though united by a common allegiance to the Crown and freely associated as members of the British Commonwealth of Nations.' This formula was given legal substance by the Statute of Westminster 1931.

The concept of a group of countries owing allegiance to a single Crown changed in 1949 when India decided to become a republic, and her continued membership of the Commonwealth was agreed by the other members on the basis of her 'acceptance of the King as the symbol of the free association of its independent member nations and as such the Head of the Commonwealth'. Member nations agreed at the time of the accession of Queen Elizabeth II to recognize Her Majesty as the new Head of the Commonwealth. The position is not vested in the British Crown.

Most members of the Commonwealth are parliamentary democracies.

Queen Elizabeth II is Head of State of 17 member countries of the Commonwealth: Antigua and Barbuda, Australia, the Bahamas, Barbados, Belize, Britain, Canada, Grenada, Jamaica, Mauritius, New Zealand, Papua New Guinea, St. Christopher and Nevis, Saint Lucia, Saint Vincent and the Grenadines, Solomon Islands and Tuvalu. In each of these countries (except Britain) The Queen is personally represented by a Governor-General, who holds in all essential respects the same position in relation to the administration of public affairs in the realm as is held by Her Majesty in Britain (with the exception of certain constitutional functions which are performed by The Queen personally). The Governor-General is appointed by The Queen on the advice of the Government of the country concerned.

Twenty-seven member countries are republics: Bangladesh, Botswana, Cyprus, Dominica, The Gambia, Ghana, Guyana, India, Kenya, Kiribati, Malawi, The Maldives, Malta, Namibia, Nauru, Nigeria, Pakistan, Seychelles, Sierra Leone, Singapore, Sri Lanka, Tanzania, Trinidad & Tobago, Uganda, Vanuatu, Zambia and Zimbabwe. In Malaysia, the Head of State is elected from among the nine hereditary Malay rulers and holds office for five years. Brunei, Lesotho, Tonga, and Swaziland have their own monarchs. Western Samoa has a Head of State whose functions are analogous to those of a constitutional monarch.

Membership of the Commonwealth is subject only to the approval of existing members. Two countries, Nauru and Tuvalu, are special members, with the right to participate in all functional Commonwealth meetings and activities, but not to attend Meetings of Commonwealth Heads of Government.

Consultation.—Commonwealth Heads of Government meet every two years to discuss international developments and to consider co-operation among members. These meetings, the successors to the pre-war Imperial Conferences, have grown in importance as they are the only regular forum of leaders from both developed and developing countries, constituting a broad sample of the world community. Decisions are reached by consensus, and the views of the meeting are set out in a communiqué.

In addition, there are annual meetings of Finance Ministers, and frequent meetings of Ministers and officials in the fields of trade, education, health, law, science, agriculture, labour and employment, and youth affairs.

Defence.—The Commonwealth is not a military alliance and members make their own defence arrangements in the light of their particular requirements. Some are parties to multi-lateral treaties, for example ANZUS and NATO. Various members of the Commonwealth co-operate with each other in combined exercises, joint research organizations and exchanges of personnel and training facilities.

Law.—English common law forms the basis of the legal system in many Commonwealth countries, although in most cases it has been adapted by local statute to suit individual needs and circumstances. There are countries where other systems have been adopted—for example, the law of Quebec Province and of Mauritius is founded on that of France, and Roman Dutch law forms the basis in Sri Lanka and Lesotho.

The Judicial Committee of the Privy Council sitting in London hears appeals from a number of territories of which The Queen is Head of State including Antigua and Barbuda, the Bahamas, Barbados, Belize, Jamaica, Mauritius, New Zealand, St. Christopher and Nevis, St. Lucia, St. Vincent and the Grenadines, Tuvalu, the Channel Islands, the Isle of Man and the dependent territories. Appeals from Brunei are referred by the Sultan to the Judicial Committee and the Committee also hears appeals from five republics in the Commonwealth: Dominica, The Gambia, Kiribati, Singapore, and Trinidad and Tobago.

Citizenship and Nationality.—Each member of the Commonwealth defines the citizenship and nationality of its own people and determines the status of other Commonwealth nationals within its own boundaries. Members of the Commonwealth differentiate, to a greater or lesser degree, as regards the grant of privileges, between citizens of the Commonwealth and aliens. The Republic of Ireland, which in 1949 ceased to be a member of the Commonwealth, is not regarded by the other Commonwealth nations as a foreign country nor her citizens as foreigners.

Finance and Development.—Complete financial autonomy is enjoyed by all members of the Commonwealth. In some countries, customs tariffs are lower for merchandise of Commonwealth origin than for imports from foreign countries. Developing countries, including those in the Commonwealth, obtain preference for exports of industrial goods and some agricultural exports from the developed countries under the Generalised Scheme of Preferences (GSP). Many smaller Commonwealth countries are also party to the Lomé Convention which accords preferential access to the European Community. Many former Commonwealth preferences have been replaced by these arrangements.

British aid for the development needs of the Commonwealth countries and dependent territories are dealt with under the provisions of the Overseas Aid Act 1966, administered by the Overseas Development Administration. This Act succeeds the former Colonial Development and Welfare Acts. Those countries which are party to the Lomé Convention also receive aid under that Convention from the European Community.

Commonwealth Secretariat. Marlborough House, Pall Mall, SW1Y 5HX (Tel: 071 839 3411).— This was established by decision of Commonwealth Heads of Government in 1965, and is the main agency for multi-lateral communication between Commonwealth Governments on issues relating to the Commonwealth as a whole. It promotes consultation and disseminates information on matters of common concern, organizes meetings and conferences, co-ordinates Commonwealth activities and provides technical assistance for economic and social development through the Commonwealth Fund for Technical Cooperation.

Secretary General, Chief Emeka Anyaoku.

Commonwealth Institute.—See p. 600.

Dependent Territories and Associated States. —Britain, Australia and New Zealand have a number of dependent territories. New Zealand also has two associated states: Cook Islands (since 1965) and Niue (since 1974).

Member States of the Commonwealth
(with dates of independence)

1867* Canada
1901* Australia
1907* New Zealand
1947 India (Republic, 1950)
     Pakistan (Republic, 1956)
1948 Sri Lanka (Republic, 1972)
1957 Ghana (Republic, 1960)
     Federation of Malaya (Federation of Malaysia since 1963—indigenous monarchy)
1960 Cyprus (Republic on independence; joined Commonwealth 1961)
     Nigeria (Republic, 1963)
1961 Sierra Leone (Republic, 1971)
     Tanganyika (Republic, 1962; united 1964 with Zanzibar as Tanzania)
1962 Western Samoa (Republic on independence; joined Commonwealth 1970)

Jamaica
     Trinidad and Tobago (Republic, 1976)
     Uganda (Republic, 1967)
1963 Kenya (Republic, 1964)
     Singapore (as State in Federation of Malaysia; seceded as Republic, 1965)
1964 Malawi (Republic, 1966)
     Malta (Republic, 1974)
     Zambia (Republic on independence)
1965 The Gambia (Republic, 1970)
     Maldives (Republic, 1968; joined Commonwealth as a Special Member 1982; full member 1985)
1966 Guyana (Republic, 1970)
     Botswana (Republic on independence)
     Lesotho (indigenous monarchy)
     Barbados
1968 Mauritius
     Nauru (Republic on independence—Special Member)
     Swaziland (indigenous monarchy)
1970 Tonga (indigenous monarchy)
1971 Bangladesh (Republic on independence; joined Commonwealth 1972)
1973 Bahamas
1974 Grenada
1975 Papua New Guinea
1976 Seychelles (Republic on independence)
1978 Solomon Islands
     Tuvalu (Special Member)
     Dominica (Republic on independence)
1979 Saint Lucia
     Kiribati (Republic on independence)
     Saint Vincent and the Grenadines (Joined as a Special Member; became a full member 1985)
1980 Zimbabwe (Republic on independence)
     Vanuatu (Republic on independence)
1981 Belize
     Antigua and Barbuda
1983 Saint Christopher and Nevis
1984 Brunei (indigenous monarchy)
1990 Namibia (Republic on independence)

* These are the effective dates of independence, given legal effect by the Statute of Westminster 1931.

(The above member states are Realms of Queen Elizabeth II unless otherwise stated.)

Associated States

The Cook Islands and Niue are self-governing states in association with New Zealand, which likewise remains responsible for their external affairs and defence.

Countries which have left the Commonwealth

1949 Republic of Ireland
1961 South Africa
1972 Pakistan (rejoined 1989)
1987 Fiji

ANTIGUA AND BARBUDA
(State of Antigua and Barbuda)

AREA, POPULATION, ETC.—Antigua and Barbuda comprises the islands of Antigua (108 sq. miles (279 sq. km)), Barbuda (62 sq. miles (160 sq. km)) 25 miles north of Antigua, and Redonda (½ square mile; 1·2 sq. km) 25 miles south-west of Antigua. Antigua is part of the Leeward Islands in the Eastern Caribbean and lies 17° 3′ N. and 61° 48′ W. It is distinguished from the rest of the Leeward group by its absence of high hills and forest, and a drier climate than most of the

W. Indies. Barbuda, formerly a possession of the Codrington family, is very flat, mainly scrub-covered, with a large lagoon. Antigua was first settled by the English in 1632, and was granted to Lord Willoughby by Charles II. The total population (UN estimate 1988) is 85,000. In a 1985 estimate Antigua had a population of 80,000, Barbuda 1,500, and Redonda was uninhabited.

CAPITAL.—ΨSt. John's. Population, 30,000. The town of Barbuda is Codrington.

CURRENCY.—East Caribbean dollar (EC$) of 100 cents.

FLAG.—Inverted triangle (centred on a red field) divided horizontally into three bands of black over blue over white; rising sun device in gold on black band.

NATIONAL ANTHEM.—Fair Antigua and Barbuda.
NATIONAL DAY.—November 1 (Independence Day).

GOVERNMENT

Antigua became internally self-governing in 1967 and fully independent on November 1, 1981, as a constitutional monarchy with HM The Queen as Head of State, represented by the Governor-General. There is a Senate of 17 appointed members and a House of Representatives elected every 5 years. The Attorney-General may be appointed.

The Antigua Labour party led by Mr. Vere Bird won the general election of March 9, 1989 and a fourth successive term of office.

Governor-General, Sir Wilfred Ebenezer Jacobs, GCMG, GCVO, OBE, QC.

Cabinet
(as at June 30, 1990)

Prime Minister, Defence, and Information, Rt. Hon. Vere C. Bird, sen.
Deputy PM and Minister for Foreign Affairs, Economic Development, Tourism and Energy, Hon. Lester Bird.
Public Utilities and Aviation, Hon. Robin Yearwood.
Finance, Hon. John E. St. Luce.
Education, Culture and Youth Affairs and Sport, Hon. Reuben H. Harris.
Labour and Health, Hon. Adolphus Freeland.
Home Affairs, Hon. Christopher M. O'Mard.
Agriculture, Fisheries and Lands, Housing, Hon. Hilroy Humphreys.

Attorney General (apptd), Hon. Keith Ford.
Public Works, and Communications, Hon. Eustace Cochrane.
Trade, Industry and Commerce, Hon. Hugh Marshall.
Ministers within a Ministry:
Foreign Affairs, Economic Development, Tourism and Energy, Hon. Molwyn Joseph.
Finance and Port Authority, Hon. Henderson St. Clair Simon.
Prime Minister's Office, Senator Hon. Bernard Percival.

HIGH COMMISSION FOR
ANTIGUA AND BARBUDA
15 Thayer Street, W1M 5LD
[071–486 7073]

High Commissioner, His Excellency James Thomas (1987).

ECONOMY

Tourism is the main feature of the economy, with several hotels (and a number under construction) to take advantage of the many white sand beaches which made Antigua one of the first Caribbean islands to attract tourists.

For many years sugar was the dominant crop but is now produced only for local consumption. Areas of agricultural development include livestock, sea island cotton, corn (for cornmeal production) and improved vegetable and fruit production.

FINANCE

	1989*	1990*
Revenue	EC$236,720,991	EC$249,560,916
Expenditure (recurrent) ...	263,579,351	271,730,204
*estimated		

Trade with UK

	1988	1989
Imports from UK	£20,755,000	£23,954,000
Exports to UK	10,845,000	3,447,000

BRITISH HIGH COMMISSION
38 St. Mary's Street (PO 483), St. John's
[St. John's 462 0008/9]

High Commissioner, (resides at Bridgetown, Barbados).
Resident Representative, I. D. Marsh (*First Secretary*).

THE COMMONWEALTH OF AUSTRALIA
AREA AND POPULATION

States	Estimated Area (sq. km)	Estimated Resident Population		
		June 30, 1981 (a)	June 30, 1986 (a)	June 30, 1989p
States				
New South Wales (NSW)	801,600	5,234,900	5,531,500	5,761,900
Queensland (Qld.)	1,727,200	2,345,200	2,624,600	2,830,200
South Australia (SA)	984,000	1,318,800	1,382,600	1,423,300
Tasmania (Tas.)	67,800	427,200	446,500	451,000
Victoria (Vic.)	227,600	3,946,900	4,160,900	4,315,200
Western Australia (WA)	2,525,500	1,300,100	1,459,000	1,591,100
Territories				
Australian Capital Territory (ACT)	2,400	227,600	258,900	277,900
Northern Territory (NT)	1,346,200	122,600	154,400	156,100
Total........................	7,682,300	14,923,300	16,018,400	16,806,700

p preliminary

Inter-Censal Increases, 1961–1986

Year of Census	Population at Census			Inter-Censal Increase	Net Immigration during Period	
	Males	Females	Total			
1961	5,333,185	5,215,082	10,548,267	(b) 1,521,656	1954–1961 ..	584,754
1966	5,841,588	5,757,910	11,599,498	1,051,231	1961–1966 ..	395,485
1971 (a)	6,567,936	6,499,329	13,067,265	(c) 1,156,140	1966–1971 ..	521,139
1976 (a)	7,032,034	7,001,049	14,033,083	965,818	1971–1976 ..	281,074
1981 (a)	7,448,267	7,474,993	14,923,260	890,177	1976–1981 ..	370,865
1986 (a)	8,000,187	8,018,163	16,018,350	1,095,090	1981–1986 ..	449,960

(a) Based on Census counts, place of usual residence, adjusted for under-enumeration, and including an estimate of Australian residents temporarily overseas on Census night.
(b) Excludes full-blood Aboriginals.
(c) Based on 1971 Census figure as enumerated.

Population of Aboriginal and Torres Strait Islander Origin

	June 1986	
	Number	Percentage of State Population
States		
New South Wales ...	59,011	1·1
Queensland.........	61,268	2·4
South Australia	14,291	1·1
Tasmania...........	6,716	1·5
Victoria............	12,611	0·3
Western Australia ..	37,789	2·7
Territories		
Australian Capital Territory.........	1,220	0·5
Northern Territory .	34,739	22·4
Total.......	227,645	1·5

Births, Deaths, Marriages and Divorces
(Year ended June 30)

	1987	1988	1989*
Births......	242,797	246,200	250,444
Deaths	116,139	120,463	118,988
Marriages ..	110,690	114,350	120,121
Divorces† ..	39,725	41,007	n/a

*provisional   †year ended December 31

Migration
(Year ended June 30)

	1987	1988	1989
Permanent arrivals ..	113,540	143,470	145,320
Permanent departures	19,930	20,470	21,650

PHYSICAL FEATURES

Australia, including Tasmania, comprises a land area of 7,682,300 square kilometres lying between latitudes 10°41′S (Cape York) and 43°39′S (South East Cape, Tasmania) and longitudes 113°09′E (Steep Point) and 153°39′E (Cape Byron). The latitudinal distance between Cape York and South East Cape is about 3,680 kilometres and the longitudinal distance between Steep Point and Cape Byron is about 4,000 kilometres. (The latitudinal distance between Cape York and the most southerly point on the mainland South Point, Wilson's Promontory, is about 3,180 kilometres.)

Australia has three major landforms: the western plateau, the interior lowlands and the eastern uplands. The western half of the continent consists mainly of a great plateau of altitude 300–600 metres. The interior lowland includes the channel country of south-west Queensland (drainage to Lake Eyre) and the Murray-Darling river system to the south. The eastern uplands consist of a broad belt of varied width extending from north Queensland to Tasmania and composed largely of tablelands, ranges and ridges with only limited mountain areas above 1,000 metres. The highest point is Mt. Kosciusko (2,228 m) and the lowest, Lake Eyre (−15 m).

Australia's large area and latitudinal range have resulted in climatic conditions ranging from the alpine to the tropical. Two-thirds of the continent is arid or semi-arid although good rainfalls (over 800 mm annually) occur in the northern monsoonal belt under the influence of the Australian Asian Monsoon and along the eastern and southern highland regions under the influence of the great atmospheric depressions of the Southern Ocean. The effectiveness of the rainfall is greatly reduced by marked alternations of wet and dry seasons, unreliability from year to year, high temperatures and high potential evaporation.

Fifty per cent of the area of Australia has a medium rainfall of less than 300 mm per year and 80 per cent has less than 600 mm. Extreme minimum temperatures are not as low as those recorded in other continents because of the absence of extensive mountain masses and because of the expanse of ocean to the south. However, extreme maxima are comparatively high, reaching 50°C over the inland, mainly due to the great east–west extent of the continent in the vicinity of the Tropic of Capricorn.

Only one-third of the Australian land mass drains directly to the ocean, mainly on the coastal side of the Main Divide and inland with the Murray-Darling system. With the exception of the Murray-Darling system, most rivers draining to the ocean are comparatively short and account for the majority of the country's average annual discharge.

GOVERNMENT

The Commonwealth of Australia was constituted by an Act of the Imperial Parliament dated July 9, 1900, and was inaugurated Jan. 1, 1901. The Government is that of a Federal Commonwealth within the British Commonwealth of Nations, the executive power being vested in the Sovereign (through the Governor-General), assisted by a Federal Ministry of Ministers of State. Under the Constitution the Federal Government has acquired and may acquire certain defined powers as surrendered by the States, residuary legislative power remaining with the States. The right of a State to legislate on any matter is not abrogated except in connection with matters exclusively under Federal control, but where a State law is inconsistent with a law of the Commonwealth the latter prevails to the extent of the inconsistency.

CURRENCY.—Australian dollar ($A) of 100 cents.

FLAG.—The British Blue Ensign, consisting of a blue flag, with the Union Flag occupying the upper quarter next the staff, differenced by a large white star (representing the six States of Australia and the Territories of the Commonwealth) in the centre of the lower quarter next the staff and pointing direct to the centre of the St. George's Cross in the Union Flag and five white stars, representing the Southern Cross, in the fly.

NATIONAL ANTHEM.—Advance Australia Fair.

NATIONAL DAY.—January 26 (Australia Day).

Governor-General and Staff

Governor-General, His Excellency the Hon. Bill Hayden, AC, *born* January 23, 1933; *assumed office,* February 16, 1989.

Official Secretary, R. D. Sturkey.

Deputy Official Secretary, Mrs L. Lawless.

Cabinet
(as at June 30, 1990)

Prime Minister, Hon. Robert Hawke, AC.

Deputy PM and Treasurer, Hon. Paul Keating.

Immigration, Local Government and Ethnic Affairs, Hon. Gerry Hand.

Attorney-General, Hon. Michael Duffy.

Defence, Senator Hon. Robert Ray.

Industrial Relations, Senator Hon. Peter Cook.

Transport and Communications, Hon. Kim Beazley.

Finance, Hon. Ralph Willis.

Foreign Affairs and Trade, Senator Hon. Gareth Evans.

Administrative Services, Senator Hon. Nick Bolkus.

Industry, Technology and Commerce, Senator Hon. John Button.

Primary Industries and Energy, Hon. John Kerin.

Social Security, Senator Hon. Graham Richardson.

Employment, Education and Training, Hon. John Dawkins.

Arts, Sport, the Environment, Tourism and Territories, Hon. Roslyn Kelly.

Community Services and Health, Hon. Brian Howe.

Trade Negotiations, Hon. Neal Blewett.

Junior Ministers

Land Transport, Hon. Robert Brown.

Justice and Consumer Affairs, Senator Hon. Michael Tate.

Small Business and Customs, Hon. David Beddall.

Veterans' Affairs, Hon. Benjamin Humphreys.

Aboriginal Affairs, Hon. Robert Tickner.

Shipping and Aviation Support, Senator Hon. Bob Collins.

Aged, Family and Health Services, Hon. Peter Staples.

Higher Education and Employment Services, Hon. Peter Baldwin.

Defence Science and Personnel, Hon. Gordon Bilney.

Local Government, Hon. Wendy Fatin.

Resources, Hon. Alan Griffiths.
Arts, Tourism and Territories, Hon. David Simmons.
Science and Technology, Hon. Simon Crean.

AUSTRALIAN HIGH COMMISSION
Australia House, Strand, London, WC2B 4LA
[071–379 4334]

High Commissioner, His Excellency The Hon. Douglas McClelland.
Deputy High Commissioner, D. W. Evans.
Official Secretary, D. Connors.
Ministers, Ms. K. Campbell (*Political*); R. K. H. Lim (*Commercial*); E. F. Delofski (*Economic*).
Defence Adviser and Head of Defence Staff, Air Cdre. B. Lane.

BRITISH HIGH COMMISSION
Commonwealth Avenue, Canberra
[Canberra (06) 270 6666]

High Commissioner, His Excellency Sir John Coles, KCMG (1988).
Deputy High Commissioner, Head of Chancery, I. Mackley.
Defence and Naval Adviser and Head of British Defence Liaison Staff, Cdre. A. C. G. Wolstenholme.
Counsellor, D. P. R. MacKilligin (*Economic and Commercial*).
First Secretaries, D. Moorhouse (*Management*); D. Blunt, LVO; G. Minter (*Commercial, Agriculture*); W. C. Patey; M. R. Eastburn (*Information*); M. R. Maiden (*Defence Exports*); G. Burrows (*Defence Research*); K. Harding.
Military Adviser, Col. C. D. McCarthy.
Air Adviser, Gp. Capt. J. G. Sheldon.
Consuls-General, B. S. Jones (*Brisbane*); S. D. R. Brown (*Melbourne*); L. W. Boyes (*Perth*); C. Wilson (*Sydney*).
Cultural Adviser and British Council Representative, M. C. Foot, OBE, Edgecliff Centre, 203–233 New South Head Road (PO Box 88), Edgecliff, Sydney 2027.

THE LEGISLATURE

Parliament consists of The Queen, the Senate and the House of Representatives. The Constitution provides that the number of members of the House of Representatives shall be, as nearly as practicable, twice the number of Senators. Members of the Senate are elected for six years by universal suffrage, half the members retiring every third year. Each of the six States returns an equal number of 10 Senators, and the Australian Capital Territory and the Northern Territory two each. The House of Representatives, similarly elected for a maximum of three years, contains members proportionate to the population, with a minimum of five members for each State. There are now 148 members in the House of Representatives, including one member for the Northern Territory and two for the Australian Capital Territory.
President of the Senate, Senator Hon. Kerry Sibraa.
Speaker, House of Representatives, Hon. Leo McLeay.

THE JUDICATURE
HIGH COURT OF AUSTRALIA
(as at May 31, 1990)

Chief Justice, Hon. Sir Anthony Frank Mason, KBE.
Justices, Hons. Sir Gerard Brennan, KBE; Sir William Deane, KBE; Sir Daryl Dawson, KBE, CB; John Toohey; Mary Gaudron; Michael McHugh.
Registrar, F. W. D. Jones.

FEDERAL COURT OF AUSTRALIA
(as at May 31, 1989)

Chief Justice, Hon. Sir Nigel Bowen, AC, KBE.
Judges, Hons. C. A. Sweeney, CBE; Sir Edward Woodward, OBE; R. M. Northrop; J. A. Keely; F. R. Fisher; J. F. Gallop; J. D. Davies; J. S. Lockhart; I. F. Sheppard; J. J. A. Kelly; T. R. Morling; K. J. Jenkinson; A. R. Neaves; B. A. Beaumont; M. R. Wilcox; J. E. J. Spender; P. R. A. Gray; C. W. Pincus; J. C. S. Burchett; J. A. Miles; D. M. Ryan; W. M. C. Gummow; R. S. French; M. R. Einfeld; T. R. Hartigan; M. L. Foster; A. B. Nicholson; M. C. Lee; H. W. Olney; J. W. von Doussa; D. G. Hill.
Registrar, J. T. Howard, RFD, ED.

SUPREME COURT OF THE AUSTRALIAN CAPITAL TERRITORY
(as at May 31, 1989)

Judges, Hons. J. A. Miles (*Chief Judge*); J. J. A. Kelly; J. F. Gallop (*Resident Judges*); Sir Edward Woodward, OBE; R. M. Northrop; J. D. Davies; J. S. Lockhart; I. F. Sheppard; T. R. Morling; K. J. Jenkinson; B. A. Beaumont; M. R. Wilcox; J. E. J. Spender; C. W. Pincus; M. L. Foster; D. M. Ryan; J. W. von Doussa (*Additional Judges*).
Registrar, P. G. Dingwall.

SUPREME COURT OF THE NORTHERN TERRITORY
(as at May 31, 1990)

Chief Justice, Hon. K. J. A. Asche.
Judges, Hons. J. A. Nader; Sir William Kearney; P. J. Rice; B. J. Martin; D. N. Angel.
Master, P. G. Lefevre.

DEFENCE

A single Department of Defence was created in 1973, following the abolition of the Departments of the Navy, Army and Air, though the separate identities of the three services have been retained. The defence research and development elements of the former Department of Supply, along with other research groups on the three services, were incorporated in 1978 into the Defence, Science and Technology Organization. The Chief of Defence Force Staff is responsible for command of the Defence Force through the three Service Chiefs of Staff and is also the principal military adviser to the Minister.

The Secretary to the Department of Defence is responsible to the Minister for Defence for advice on policy, resources and organization.

Total defence expenditure was $A 8,170,924,000 in 1988–89.

The personnel strengths of the Permanent Defence Force at June 30, 1989 were:—

	Males	Females
Navy	13,957	1,793
Army	28,671	2,581
Air Force	19,519	3,108
Total	62,147	7,482

FINANCE
COMMONWEALTH GOVERNMENT FINANCE

Outlays and revenue of the Commonwealth Government were ($Amillion):

	1988–89*	1989–90†
Current outlays	77,828	83,455
Capital outlays	4,083	3,463
Revenue and grants received	88,317	96,130
Financing transactions	−6,405	−9,213

*preliminary †estimate

State Government Finance 1988–89*
($A million)

State	Outlay (current and capital)	Revenue and grants received	Financing trans-actions
NSW..........	18,570	17,991	579
Victoria......	15,498	12,934	2,564
Queensland....	8,625	9,001	−376
S. Australia....	5,065	4,647	418
W. Australia...	6,410	5,580	830
Tasmania......	2,136	1,666	470
NT	1,290	1,215	76
Total..........	57,594	53,034	4,561

* preliminary

BANKING

In June 1988 the trading banks had total liabilities of $A120,770 million including total deposits of $A61,434 million; and total assets of $A145,758 million, including $A13,870 million of public sector securities.

PRODUCTION AND INDUSTRY

In 1985, 63·6 per cent of the Australian land area consisted of agricultural establishments, with the remainder being urban areas, State forests, mining leases and unoccupied land. Crop-growing areas constituted up to 4·32 per cent of the total agricultural establishments, emphasizing the relative importance of the livestock industries in Australia (sheep in the warm, temperate, semi-arid lands and beef cattle in the tropics).

The wide range of climatic and soil conditions over the agricultural regions of Australia has resulted in a diversity of crops being grown throughout the country. Generally, cereal crops (excluding rice and sorghum) are grown in all States over wide areas, while other crops are confined to specific locations in a few States. However, scanty or erratic rainfall, limited potential for irrigation and unsuitable soils or topography have restricted intensive agriculture.

Mines and Minerals.—Significant mineral resources comprise bauxite, coal, copper, crude petroleum, gems, gold, ilmenite, iron ore, lead, limestone, manganese, nickel, rutile, salt, silver, tin, tungsten, uranium, zinc and zircon. Recently, geological exploration has significantly increased the mineral resources of the nation and a number of oilfields are in production.

In 1987–88, value added by the mining industry was $A13,605·8m. Mine production of black coal was 167,761,000 tonnes, crude oil (including condensate) was 31,297 megalitres and natural gas 14,751 gigalitres. Production of principal metals was:—

Iron ore	102,202,000 tonnes
Copper	241,706* ,,
Lead-Zinc concentrate	178,694 ,,
Gold	64,780* kg

*1985–86 figures

Gross Value of Agricultural Commodities 1988–89p
($A million)

	NSW	Qld.	SA	Tas.	Vic.	WA	ACT	NT	Total
Crops	2,587·5	2,286·1	1,052·2	232·3	1,511·1	1,739·3	1·4	16·2	9,426·0
Livestock slaughter-ings and other disposals	1,519·5	1,497·1	418·0	121·1	1,141·6	424·4	2·0	70·3	5,194·0
Livestock products ..	2,512·4	713·0	714·3	247·6	2,205·7	1,506·4	16·7	n/a	7,916·2
Wool	2,110·0	455·1	594·0	154·7	1,205·3	1,406·6	n/a		5,925·7
Total agriculture ..	6,619·4	4,496·2	2,184·5	601·0	4,858·3	3,670·2	20·1	96·8	22,546·5

p preliminary

Livestock Numbers at March 31, 1988
(Thousands)

	NSW	Qld.	SA	Tas.	Vic.	WA	ACT	NT	Total
Cattle	4,962	8,825	947	542	3,474	1,705	11	1,385	21,851
Sheep	54,932	14,367	17,352	4,746	26,997	33,951	97	—	152,443
Pigs...............	853	617	441	48	437	307	—	3	2,706
Poultry	31,867	9,893	4,500	1,030	13,904	5,156	226	238	66,813

Gross Value of Crops 1988–89p

	NSW	Qld.	SA	Tas.	Vic.	WA	ACT	NT	Total
Cereals for grain	1,256·7	592·7	478·7	8·7	476·4	1,252·1	—	1·4	4,066·6
Cotton	433·7	94·7	—	—	—	—	—	—	528·4
Crops for hay	15·9	2·8	17·1	1·8	18·6	45·3	—	0·2	101·8
Fruit and nuts	387·8	259·3	280·2	40·5	302·5	67·2	n/a	2·9	1,340·4
Legumes for grain	38·9	27·8	49·9	0·7	87·4	166·5	—	0·1	371·2
Nursery production	94·7	68·1	31·0	19·1	98·0	46·5	n/a	2·6	359·9
Oilseeds	37·2	61·0	3·5	—	18·6	1·1	—	0·2	121·7
Peanuts	0·8	26·5	—	—	—	—	—	—	27·5
Sugar cane for crushing......	40·4	730·4	—	—	—	—	—	—	770·7
Tobacco	3·2	41·8	—	—	23·4	—	—	—	68·4
Vegetables.................	168·3	325·0	147·2	101·6	236·5	106·3	n/a	8·0	1,092·8
Pastures and grasses.........	99·9	40·0	39·6	42·6	209·1	53·9	0·1	0·7	486·0
Total crops	2,587·5	2,286·1	1,052·2	232·3	1,511·1	1,739·3	1·4	16·2	9,426·0

p preliminary

Manufactures.—In 1987–88 there were in Australia 31,606 industrial establishments, employing 1,064,000 persons; wages paid amounted to $A23,950m; and turnover $A133,820m.

TRADE

	1987–88	1988–89
Imports	$A40,596,569,000	$A47,064,168,000
Exports	41,077,819,000	43,462,242,000

Of Australia's total exports in the year 1988–89, the largest category was metalliferous ores and metal scrap, worth $A6,345m. This was followed by textile fibres and their wastes, $A6,254m; coal, coke and briquettes, $A4,744m; and non-ferrous metals, $A4,163m. Cereals and cereal preparations to the value of $A2,742m were exported, and meat and meat preparations worth $A2,249m.

The largest category of Australia's imports was road vehicles, worth $A4,807m. This was followed by office and automatic data processing machines, $A3,326m; miscellaneous manufactured articles, $A2,883m; general industrial machinery and equipment, $A2,523m; specialized machinery for particular industries, $A2,360m; and electrical machinery, $A2,359m.

MAIN TRADING PARTNERS

In 1988–89, 27·2 per cent of Australia's total exports went to Japan. The USA received 10·2 per cent, New Zealand 5·1, Republic of Korea 5·0, Hong Kong 4·3, Taiwan 3·6, UK 3·5 and Singapore 3·4.

Of Australia's total imports in 1988–89, 21·5 per cent came from the USA, 20·8 from Japan, 7·3 UK, 6·3 West Germany, 4·2 New Zealand, 4·1 Taiwan, 2·9 Italy and 2·7 France.

Trade with UK

	1988	1989
Imports from UK	£1,377,997,000	£1,711,241,000
Exports to UK ..	745,570,000	864,965,000

Food Exports to UK 1988–89

Meat and meat preparations	$A65,575,000
Vegetables and fruit	47,874,000
Sugar, sugar preparations and honey ..	13,226,000
Dairy products and birds' eggs	8,749,000
Fish, crustaceans etc.	1,693,000

COMMUNICATIONS

Railways.—There are six government owned railways systems, operated by the State Rail Authority of NSW, Victorian Railways, Queensland Government Railways, Western Australian Government Railways, the State Transport Authority of Southern Australia, and the Australian National Railways Commission. The ANRC incorporates the former Commonwealth Railways system, and the Tasmanian and non-metropolitan South Australian railways (urban rail services in Southern Australia remain the responsibility of the State Transport Authority). In 1987 there were 38,393 route-kilometres open.

Gross earnings 1986–87 were:	$A million
New South Wales	1,121·2
Victoria	481·3
Queensland	1,028·9
South Australia*	14·4
Western Australia	258·2
ANRC	283·3
Total	3,187·3

*Includes urban rail operations only.

In 1986–87 there were 388,634,000 rail passenger journeys on government railways and 174,530,000 tonnes of goods and livestock carried.

Shipping.—Total arrivals and departures of vessels engaged in overseas trade at the various Australian ports in 1988–89 were: arrivals 12,153 (465,978,000 deadweight tonnes); departures 12,029 (458,595,000 deadweight tonnes).

Broadcasting and Television.—On June 30, 1984, the Australian Broadcasting Corporation operated 144 stations. Privately owned commercial broadcasting stations totalled 137. On June 30, 1984, 276 national and 152 commercial television and translator stations were in operation.

Motor Vehicles.—At June 30, 1988, there were 9,221,200 motor vehicles registered in Australia and 323,300 motor cycles.

Civil Aviation.—Figures for domestic and overseas services in 1986–87 are as follows:

	Domestic	Overseas
Paying passengers ...	12,509,000	3,052,000
Freight (tonnes)	137,627	110,389
Mail (tonnes)	18,761	5,327

FEDERAL CAPITAL

CANBERRA is the capital of Australia. It is situated in the Australian Capital Territory which has an area of 939 sq. miles (2,395 sq. km) and was acquired from New South Wales in 1911. Canberra, which is the seat of the federal government, had a population (estimated) at June 30, 1988, of 297,300. Apart from Parliament House, the city also contains other national institutions, such as the Australian War Memorial, National Library, Royal Australian Mint and the Australian National University. Most Government departments have their headquarters in Canberra. An artificial lake is a central feature of this planned city, based on Walter Burley Griffin's design.

THE NORTHERN TERRITORY

The Northern Territory has a total area of 519,770 sq. miles (1,346,200 sq. km), and lies between 129°–138° east longitude and 11°–26° south latitude. The estimated population in the Northern Territory at June 30, 1989 was 159,100, of which about a quarter are Aboriginals.

The administration was taken over by the Commonwealth on January 1, 1911 from the government of the State of South Australia.

The Northern Territory (Self-Government) Act 1978 established the Northern Territory as a body politic as from July 1, 1978, with Ministers having control over and responsibility for Territory finances and the administration of the functions of government as specified by the Federal Government by regulations made pursuant to the Act. Proposed laws passed by the Legislative Assembly in relation to a transferred function require the assent of the Administrator. Proposed laws in all other cases may be assented to by the Administrator or reserved by the Administrator for the Governor General's pleasure. The Governor General may disallow any laws assented to by the Administrator within six months of the Administrator's assent.

The Northern Territory has federal representation electing one member to the House of Representatives and two members to the Senate.

Seat of Administration.—Darwin.

Administrator, His Honour the Honourable J. H. Muirhead, QC.

THE MINISTRY
(as at June 30, 1990)

Chief Minister, Treasurer, Minister for Police, Fire and Emergency Services, Hon. Marshall Perron.

Deputy Chief Minister, Minister for Mines and Energy, Industries and Development, Hon. Barry Coulter.

Attorney-General, Minister for Lands and Housing, Hon. Daryl Manzie.

Education, Arts and Cultural Affairs, Hon. Tom Harris.

Health and Community Services, Conservation, Hon. Steve Hatton.

Transport and Works, Racing and Gaming, Hon. Fred Finch.

Labour, Administrative Services, Local Government Minister assisting on Aboriginal Affairs, Hon. Terry McCarthy.

Primary Industry and Fisheries, Correctional Services, Hon. Mike Reed.

Tourism, Youth, Sport, Recreation and Ethnic Affairs, Minister assisting on Central Australian Affairs, Hon. Roger Vale.

Various Aboriginal Land Trusts hold title to land previously called Reserves, totalling about one-fifth of the Northern Territory.

The Aboriginal Land Rights (NT) Act of 1976 provides for the investigation and determination of Aboriginal traditional claims to vacant Crown land or land already owned by or on behalf of Aboriginals. Successful land claims to date have increased Aboriginal ownership to 34 per cent of the Northern Territory whilst a further 13 per cent is the subject of claims.

A number of major Aboriginal communities previously administered by Church Mission Societies and the Federal Government are now controlled by the Aboriginal people themselves, through local Aboriginal Councils. A recent phenomenon is the voluntary movement of some Aboriginals to their traditional homeland areas where they feel that their culture will be better preserved.

ECONOMY

Northern Territory's economy is based on the exploitation of its natural resources of minerals, land, fisheries and tourist attractions. Following the introduction of a number of government measures designed to expand and diversify primary production, the Territory's agricultural and horticultural industries are also beginning to contribute an increasing amount to Territory rural output. The beef cattle industry continues to be the major user of pastoral lands.

Mining has played a major part in the development of the Northern Territory and in 1989 total value of production was $A1·5 billion. The Territory is a leading uranium producer, extracting 3,290,069 kg of uranium oxide in 1989 with a value of $A291 million. In 1989 more than 2·1 million tonnes of manganese was sold, with a total value of about $A199 million. Gold production for 1989 was estimated at $A275 million. The value of oil and gas production for 1990 is estimated to be $A850 million.

Tourism is of importance to the Territory's economy. It is a major growth industry and generates over $A400 million annually.

COMMUNICATIONS

The Northern Territory has three main ports—Darwin, managed by the Darwin Port Authority, and the private mining ports of Gove and Groote Eylandt.

The standard gauge rail link between Southern Australia and Alice Springs was officially opened in October 1980. The link between Alice Springs and Darwin is provided by a fully co-ordinated rail-road service.

The main population centres are linked by the Stuart Highway, which connects Alice Springs to Darwin via Tennant Creek and Katherine. Of special interest to the Northern Territory is the operation of 'road trains'. These are basically massive trucks hauling two or three trailers, having a net capacity of about 100 tonnes and measuring up to 45 metres in length.

AUSTRALIAN EXTERNAL TERRITORIES

ASHMORE AND CARTIER ISLANDS

Ashmore Islands (known as Middle, East and West Islands) and Cartier Island are situated in the Indian Ocean some 850 km and 790 km west of Darwin respectively. The islands lie at the outer edge of the continental shelf. They are small and low and are composed of coral and sand. Vegetation consists mainly of grass. Turtles are plentiful at certain times of the year and beche-de-mer is abundant. The islands are uninhabited.

Great Britain took formal possession of the Ashmores in 1878 and Cartier was annexed in 1909. By Imperial Order in Council of July 23, 1931 the islands were placed under the authority of the Commonwealth of Australia, and were accepted in 1933 under the name of the Territory of Ashmore and Cartier Islands. The territory was annexed to the Northern Territory of Australia. With the granting of self-government to the Northern Territory on July 1, 1978 responsibility for the administration of Ashmore and Cartier Islands became a direct responsibility of the Commonwealth Government. In 1983 Ashmore Reef was declared a national nature reserve.

In accordance with an agreement between the governments of Indonesia and Australia, Indonesian fishermen who have traditionally plied the area may engage in limited fishing activity within the territory but are prohibited from taking any products from the nature reserve. They can land to collect water at certain locations.

THE AUSTRALIAN ANTARCTIC TERRITORY

The Australian Antarctic Territory was established by an Order in Council, dated February 7, 1933, which placed under the government of the Commonwealth of Australia all the islands and territories, other than Adélie Land, which are situated south of the latitude 60° S. and lying between 160° E. longitude and 45° E. longitude. The Order came into force on August 24, 1936, after the passage of the Australian Antarctic Territory Acceptance Act 1933. The boundaries of Terre Adélie were definitely fixed by a French Decree of April 1, 1938, as the islands and territories south of 60° S. latitude lying between 136° E. longitude and 142° E. longitude. The Australian Antarctic Territory Act 1954 declared that the laws in force in the Australian Capital Territory are, so far as they are applicable, in force in the Australian Antarctic Territory. The territory is administered by the Antarctic Division of the Department of Science, which, since its inception in 1947, has organized yearly expeditions to Antarctica, known as Australian National Antarctic Research Expeditions (ANARE).

On February 13, 1954 ANARE opened Mawson Station in Mac-Robertson Land at latitude 67° 36′ S. and longitude 62° 53′ E. Scientific research conducted at Mawson includes upper atmosphere physics, cosmic ray physics, meteorology, earth sciences, biology and medical science. Mawson is also a centre for coastal and inland exploration.

Davis Station was opened on the coast of Princess Elizabeth Land on January 13, 1957, at latitude 68° 35′ S. and longitude 77° 58′ E. Scientific programmes carried out at Davis include meteorology, biology, upper atmosphere physics, with field investigations in biology.

In February 1959 the Australian Government accepted from the US Government custody of Wilkes Station on the Budd Coast, Wilkes Land. The station was closed in February 1969, and activities were transferred to the nearby Casey Station at 66° 17′ S., 110° 32′ E. Scientific programmes carried out there include geophysics, meteorology with field programmes in glaciology, geology, etc.

Each of the stations on continental Antarctica are being replaced by new station buildings of advanced design, in a building programme which is expected to be completed in 1998.

Since 1948 ANARE has operated a station on Macquarie Island, a dependency of Tasmania, situated at 54° 30′ S. and 158° 57′ E., about 900 miles north of the Antarctic Continent.

Summer stations have been established in the Bunger Hills, 200 miles west of Casey, at Cape Denison in Commonwealth Bay, in the Larsemann Hills and on Heard Island.

CHRISTMAS ISLAND

Until the end of 1957 a part of the then Colony of Singapore, Christmas Island was administered as a separate colony until October 1, 1958, when it became an Australian territory. It is situated in the Indian Ocean about 1,408 km NW of North West Cape in Western Australia, and has an area of 135 sq. km. Population (estimated, June 30, 1990) is 1,300, consisting of former employees of the Phosphate Mining Corporation, and present employees of the Christmas Island Administration, the Christmas Island Services Corporation, and their families. There is no indigenous population.

The island is densely wooded and had extensive deposits of phosphates, the extraction of which has traditionally been the major economic activity. An Australian Government company, the Phosphate Mining Corporation of Christmas Island, which carried out the mining operation ceased operating in 1987. Extensive deposits of low grade phosphate ore still remain but alternative economic development is being encouraged. The principal current development is a hotel complex.

The Administrator is responsible to the Australian Minister for Arts, Sport, the Environment, Tourism and Territories in Canberra. The Christmas Island Local Assembly is presently chaired by the Administrator and has nine elected members. The Assembly is responsible for directing the operations of the Christmas Islands Services Corporation, which was established in 1984 to provide municipal functions and services.

Administrator, Hon. W. McKenzie, OA.

COCOS (KEELING) ISLANDS

The Cocos (Keeling) Islands were declared a British possession in 1857. All land in the islands was granted to George Clunies-Ross and his heirs by Queen Victoria in 1886. In 1955 the islands, which had been governed through the British colonies of Ceylon (from 1878), the Straits Settlements (1886) and Singapore (1903), were accepted as a Territory of Australia.

In 1978 the Australian Government purchased all Clunies-Ross land and property interests except for the family home and grounds. In 1979 ownership of the kampong area of Home Island was transferred to the Cocos (Keeling) Islands Council, the local government body established in 1979. Title to most of the remaining land purchased from Clunies-Ross in 1978 was transferred to the Council in 1984.

The Cocos (Keeling) Islands Act, 1955, provides the legal framework for the present political and administrative arrangements in the territory. On April 6, 1984, the Cocos community, in a UN supervised Act of Self-Determination, chose to integrate with Australia. The Government's major commitment was that living standards would reach comparable mainland levels by 1994. The Commonwealth Grants Commission monitors the progress.

The islands are two separate atolls (North Keeling Island and, 24 km to the south, the main atoll) comprising some 27 small coral islands with a total area of about 14 sq. km, situated in the Indian Ocean in latitude 12° 5′ South and longitude 96° 53′ East. The main islands of the southern atoll are West Island (the largest, about 9 km from north to south) on which are the administrative centre, the aerodrome, and the Australian-based employees of government departments; Home Island, where the Cocos Malay community and the Clunies-Ross family live; Direction Island, Horsburgh and South Island.

The territory has no viable economic base at present. In 1986–87 the copra industry suffered severe losses and in 1987 ceased production. Tourism is being developed as a likely successor to the copra industry.

The climate is equable and pleasant, being usually under the influence of the south-east trade winds for about three-quarters of the year. A weekly air charter service operates between Perth, the Cocos (Keeling) Islands and Christmas Island. Population (June 30, 1989), 667. The islands are administered by the Australian Government through the Department of the Arts, Sport, the Environment, Tourism and Territories in Canberra. All proposed Ordinances, Regulations and By-laws for the islands must be submitted to the Islands Council (est. 1979) for its consideration.

Administrator, Ms. D. Lawrie.

CORAL SEA ISLANDS TERRITORY

The Coral Sea Islands Territory lies east of Queensland between the Great Barrier Reef and longitude 156° 06′ E., and between latitudes 12° and 24° S. It comprises scattered islands, often little more than sandbanks, spread over a sea area of 780,000 sq. km. The islands are formed mainly of coral and sand. Some have grass or scrub cover but most are extremely small, with no permanent fresh water.

There is a manned metereological station in the Willis Group but the remaining islands are uninhabited. Large populations of sea birds nest and breed in the area, and two national nature reserves were designated in the Territory in 1982.

The Australian Government bases its claim to the islands on numerous acts of sovereignty since early this century and enacted the Coral Sea Islands Act 1969 which declares the islands a territory of the Commonwealth of Australia. The Department of the Arts, Sport, the Environment, Tourism and Territories, Canberra, is responsible for the administration of the territory.

HEARD ISLAND AND McDONALD ISLANDS

The Heard and McDonald islands, about 4,100 km south-west of Fremantle, comprise all the islands and rocks lying between 52° 30′ and 53° 30′ S. latitude and 72° and 74° 30′ E. longitude. Sovereignty over the islands was transferred by the UK to the Commonwealth of Australia in 1947. The Heard Island and McDonald Islands Act 1953 provides for the government of the islands as one territory. Under this Act the law operating there is that of the Australian Capital Territory. The islands are administered by the Department of the Arts, Sport, the Environment, Tourism and Territories. Under the Environment Protection and Management Ordinance 1987, a permit system regulates entry to the territory and a range of activities there.

NORFOLK ISLAND

Norfolk Island is situated in the South Pacific Ocean at latitude 29° 02′ S. and longitude 167° 57′ E., being about 1,676 km NE of Sydney and 1,063 km north of Auckland. It is about 8 km long by 5 km wide, with an area of 3,455 hectares. The climate is mild and sub tropical. Resident population at the 1986 Census was 1,977.

The island, discovered by Capt. Cook in 1774, served as a penal colony from 1788 to 1814 and 1825 to 1855. In 1856, 194 descendants of the *Bounty* mutineers accepted an invitation to leave Pitcairn and settle on Norfolk Island, which led to Norfolk Island becoming a separate settlement under the jurisdiction of the Governor of NSW. In 1897 Norfolk Island became a dependency of NSW, and in 1914, pursuant to the Norfolk Island Act 1913, a territory of Australia. From that date, Norfolk Island has been regarded as an integral part of Australia.

In 1979 Norfolk Island gained a substantial degree of self-government, enabling the island to run its affairs to the greatest practical extent. Wide powers are exercised by a nine-member Legislative Assembly. The Act preserves the Commonwealth's responsibility for Norfolk Island as a territory under its authority, with the Minister for the Arts, Sport, the Environment, Tourism and Territories as the responsible Minister.

The island is a popular tourist resort, and a large proportion of the population depends on tourism and its ancillaries for employment. In 1988–89 there were 28,891 tourist arrivals on the Island. Regular air services operate from mainland Australia and New Zealand.

The seat of government and administration offices are in Kingston.

Administrator, H. B. MacDonald.

STATES OF THE COMMONWEALTH OF AUSTRALIA

NEW SOUTH WALES

The State of New South Wales is situated entirely between the 28th and 38th parallels of S. lat. and 141st and 154th meridians of E. long., and comprises an area of 309,433 sq. miles (801,427 sq. km) (exclusive of 939 sq. miles of Australian Capital Territory which lies within its borders).

POPULATION.—Preliminary estimated resident population at June 30, 1989 was 5,761,900.

Births, deaths and marriages of usually resident population were:

	1988	1989p
Births	85,901	87,274
Deaths	44,067	42,695
Marriages	38,810	44,379

p preliminary

Annual rate per 1,000 of estimated resident population in 1988:—Births 14·8; Deaths 7·8; Marriages 7·2. Deaths under 1 year per 1,000 live births, 9·0.

Religions

The members of the Roman Catholic Church in New South Wales, according to the Census of 1986, numbered 1,529,176, Anglican Church 1,519,806, Uniting (including Methodist) 327,360, Presbyterian 227,663, Orthodox 165,659, Baptist 67,187, Lutheran 31,890, other Christian 288,865, Muslim 57,551, Hebrew 28,236 and other religions 57,079. The religion of 1,101,409 persons was either not stated in the census schedules or was stated as 'none'.

PHYSIOGRAPHY

Natural features divide the State into four main zones extending from north to south: the Coastal Districts; the Tablelands, which form the Great Dividing Range between the coastal districts and the plains; the Western Slopes of the Dividing Range; and the Western Plains. The highest points are Mounts Kosciusko, 7,314 ft., and Townsend, 7,251 ft. The western portion of the State is watered by the rivers of the Murray-Darling system. The Darling, the major part of whose 1,712 miles is in NSW, and the Murrumbidgee, 981 miles, are both tributaries of the Murray, part of which forms the boundary between the States of New South Wales and Victoria.

Climate.—New South Wales is situated entirely in the temperate zone. At Sydney the average mean shade temperature is 18° C. Rainfall varies widely over the State diminishing from an annual average of about 2,000 mm in parts of the north coast to about 200 mm in the far north-west.

GOVERNMENT

New South Wales was first colonized as a British possession in 1788, and after progressive settlement a partly elective legislature was established in 1843. In 1855 responsible government was granted, the present Constitution being founded on the Constitution Act of 1902. New South Wales federated with the other States of Australia in 1901. The executive authority of the State is vested in a Governor (appointed by the Crown), assisted by a Council of Ministers.

GOVERNOR

Governor of New South Wales, His Excellency Rear-Adm. Peter Sinclair, AO, RAN, *assumed office* August 1990.

Lt. Governor and Chief Justice of NSW, The Hon. Mr. Justice Gleeson, AO.

THE MINISTRY
(as at June 30, 1990)

Premier, Treasurer, and Minister for Ethnic Affairs, Hon. N. F. Greiner, MP.

Deputy Premier, Minister for State Development, and Public Works, Hon. W. T. J. Murray, MP.

Health, and Arts, Hon. P. E. J. Collins, MP.

Agriculture and Rural Affairs, Hon. I. M. Armstrong, OBE, MP.

Attorney General, Hon. J. R. A. Dowd, MP.

Housing, Hon. J. J. Schipp, MP.

Environment, Hon. T. J. Moore, MP.

Chief Secretary, and Minister for Tourism, Hon. G. B. West, MP.

Police and Emergency Services, Vice-President of Executive Council, Hon. E. P. Pickering, MLC.

Sport and Recreation, and Racing, and Assistant Minister for Transport, Hon. R. B. Rowland Smith, MLC.

Family and Community Services, Hon. Virginia Chadwick, MLC.

Education and Youth Affairs, Hon. T. A. Metherell, MP.

Transport, Hon. B. G. Baird, MP.

Business and Consumer Affairs, Hon. G. B. P. Peacocke, MP.

Minerals and Energy, Hon. N. E. W. Pickard, MP.

Industrial Relations and Employment, and Minister Assisting the Premier, Hon. J. J. Fahey, MP.

Natural Resources, Hon. I. R. Causley, MP.

Local Government, and Planning, Hon. D. A. Hay, MP.

Corrective Services, Hon. M. R. Yabsley, MP.

Administrative Services, and Assistant Minister for Transport, Hon. R. J. Webster, MP.

AGENT-GENERAL IN LONDON

Agent-General, N. K. Brunsdon, 75 King William Street, EC4N 7HA.

THE LEGISLATURE

The Legislative Council consists of 45 members, elected by popular vote and the Legislative Assembly consists of 109 members elected for a maximum period of four years. Party representation in the Council at June 8, 1988 was; Labor 21, Liberal 12, National 7, Australian Democrat 2, and Independent 3. Party representation in the Assembly at June 8, 1988 was: Liberal-National coalition 59 (Liberal 39, National 20), Labor 43, and Independent 7.

President of the Legislative Council, Hon. J. R. Johnson, MLC.

Speaker, Legislative Assembly, Hon. K. R. Rozzoli, MP.

THE JUDICATURE

The judicial system includes a Supreme Court, Industrial Commission, District Court, Land and Environment Court, Compensation Court, and Local Courts (Magistrates).

Chief Justice, Supreme Court, The Hon. Mr. Justice Gleeson, AO.

President, Court of Appeal, Hon. Mr. Justice Kirby, CMG.

EDUCATION

Education.—Education is compulsory between the ages of 6 and 15 years. It is non-sectarian and free at all government schools. The enrolment in July 1988 in 2,204 government and 856 non-government schools was 1,038,600. The six universities had an enrolment of 71,902 students at April 30, 1988. In addition, there were 61,077 students enrolled in advanced education courses (predominantly in colleges of advanced education) in 1988. Students enrolled in technical and further education colleges in 1988 numbered 474,051.

PRODUCTION AND INDUSTRY

Livestock and Livestock Products.—A large area is suitable for sheep-raising, the principal breed of sheep being the merino, which was introduced in 1797.

Mining Industry.—The principal minerals are coal, lead, zinc, gold, rutile, copper and zircon. The total value of minerals extracted in 1987–88 was $A3,222 million. The average number of persons employed in the mining industry during 1987–88 was 22,761. In 1987–88, 76,268,000 tonnes of coal were produced.

Manufacturing Industry.—In 1987–88 there were 15,906 manufacturing establishments (employing four or more persons). The number of persons employed at June 30, 1988 was 379,000. Production of raw steel in 1989–89 was 5,259,000 tonnes.

TOWNS

ΨSydney, the State capital and the largest city in Australia, stands on the shores of Port Jackson. Sydney Harbour extends inland for 21 km; the total area of water is about 55 sq. km.

The preliminary estimated resident population at June 30, 1988 of the Sydney Statistical Division was 3,596,000. The Newcastle and Wollongong Statistical subdivisions contain populations of 422,100 and 235,300 respectively.

The populations of principal municipalities located outside the boundaries of these statistical areas are: Albury 39,610, Dubbo 31,290, Greater Taree 36,960, Hastings 42,220, Lismore 38,130, Orange 32,520, Shoalhaven 59,470, Tamworth 33,830, Wagga Wagga 50,930.

LORD HOWE ISLAND

Lord Howe Island, which is part of New South Wales, is situated 702 kilometres north-east of Sydney. Lat. 31° 33′ 4″ S., Long. 159° 4′ 26″ E. Area 6·37 sq. miles (16·5 sq. km.). Population, June 30, 1987, 290. The island is of volcanic origin with Mount Gower reaching an altitude of 866 m. The affairs of the Island are administered by the Lord Howe Island Board.

QUEENSLAND

This State, situated in lat. 9° 14′–29° S. and long. 138°–153° 30′ E., comprises the whole north-eastern portion of the Australian continent.

Queensland possesses an area of 666,798 sq. miles (1,727,000 sq. km).

POPULATION.—At June 30, 1989 the estimated resident population numbered 2,830,200.

Births, Deaths and Marriages were:

	1988	1989p
Births.................	39,280	40,793
Deaths	19,206	18,913
Marriages	18,746	19,007

p preliminary

Annual rate per 1,000 of estimated resident population in 1988 was:—Births 14·7; Deaths 6·9; Marriages 6·9. Deaths under 1 year per 1,000 live births, 8·4.

Religions

At the Census of 1986, there were 640,867 Anglican, 628,906 Catholics, 255,287 Uniting Church, 120,239 Presbyterians, 56,910 Lutherans, 30,089 Baptists, and 211,316 other Christians.

PHYSIOGRAPHY

The Great Dividing Range on the eastern coast of the continent produces a similar formation to that of New South Wales, the eastern side having a narrow slope to the coast and the western a long and gradual slope to the central plains, where the Selwyn Range divides the land into a northern and southern watershed.

GOVERNMENT

Queensland was constituted a separate colony with responsible government in 1859, having previously formed part of New South Wales. The executive authority is vested in a Governor (appointed by the Crown), aided by an Executive Council of 18 members.

GOVERNOR

Governor of Queensland, His Excellency Hon. Sir Walter Benjamin Campbell, AC, QC.

EXECUTIVE COUNCIL
(HE the Governor presides)
(as at June 30, 1990)

Premier, Minister for Economic and Trade Development, and the Arts, Hon. W. K. Goss.

Deputy Premier, Minister for Housing and Local Government, Hon. T. J. Burns.

Police and Emergency Services, Hon. T. M. Mackenroth.

Treasurer and Minister for Regional Development, Hon. K. E. De Lacy.

Tourism, Sport and Racing, Hon. R. J. Gibbs.

Transport, Minister Assisting the Premier on Economic and Trade Development, Hon. D. J. Hamill.

Employment, Training and Industrial Relations, Hon. N. G. Warburton.

Resource Industries, Hon. K. H. Vaughan.

Primary Industries, Hon. E. D. Casey.

Health, Hon. K. V. McElligott.

Education, Hon. P. J. Braddy.

Environment and Heritage, Hon. P. Comben.
Attorney-General, Hon. D. M. Wells.
Family Services and Aboriginal and Islander Affairs, Hon. A. M. Warner.
Justice and Corrective Services, Hon. G. R. Milliner.
Administrative Services, Hon. R. T. McLean.
Manufacturing and Commerce, Hon. G. N. Smith.
Land Management, Hon. A. G. Eaton.

AGENT-GENERAL IN LONDON

Agent-General, D. T. McVeigh, 392–393 Strand, WC2R 0LT.

THE LEGISLATURE

Parliament consists of a Legislative Assembly of 89 members, elected by all persons aged 18 years and over. The Assembly, as at June 30, 1990, was composed of: Australian Labor Party, 54; National Party of Australia, 26; Liberal Party of Australia, 9.
Speaker, Hon. D. Fouras.
Chairman of Committees, C. B. Campbell.
Leader of the Opposition, T. R. Cooper.

THE JUDICATURE

There are a Supreme Court; District Courts; Children's Courts; an Industrial Court; a Land Court and a Medical Assessment Tribunal; a Local Government Court; the Industrial Conciliation and Arbitration Commission; Inferior Courts at all the principal towns, presided over by Stipendiary Magistrates; a Small Claims Tribunal; Small Debts Court; a Licensing Court and a Mining Warden's Court.
Chief Justice, Supreme Court, Hon. J. M. Macrossan.

EDUCATION

Primary education is compulsory, secular and free between the ages of 6 and 15. At July 15, 1988, there were 2,010 government primary schools, 134 primary–70 primary/secondary, and 170 secondary schools with 245,726 primary students, and 141,712 secondary students.

Post-secondary education involves technical and further education (TAFE) and higher education. During 1988, 118,785 students were enrolled in TAFE courses, excluding 71,502 enrolled in adult education courses. At April 30, 1989, there were 38,962 full-time, 16,007 part-time, and 11,218 external students enrolled in higher education courses.

PRODUCTION AND INDUSTRY

Forestry.—Total Australian grown timber processed in 1988–89 amounted to 1,568,528 cubic metres (gross volume measure).

Minerals.—There are rich deposits of both metallic and non-metallic minerals. Coal is mined extensively in Central Queensland and on a lesser scale in the Ipswich district.

Manufacturing.—In 1987–88 there were 4,624 establishments with four or more workers, employing 127,544 persons, and producing goods and services worth $A17,255 million. Much of the production was the processing of foodstuffs, minerals and chemical, petroleum and coal products. Included in other factory production were the products from engineering, transport equipment, timber, basic and fabricated metal, cement, paper and textile mills and oil refineries.

CAPITAL.—ΨBrisbane, is situated on the Brisbane River, which is navigable by large vessels to the city, over 23 kilometres from Moreton Bay. The estimated resident population of the Brisbane Statistical Division at June 30, 1989 was 1,272,378. This area includes the cities of Brisbane (744,557), Ipswich (75,293), Logan (142,025) and Redcliffe (48,025).

Other cities with population over 30,000 at June 30, 1989, are: ΨTownsville 83,241; Gold Coast 135,163; Toowoomba 80,953; ΨRockhampton 58,880; ΨCairns 42,755; ΨCaloundra 44,893; ΨThuringowa 36,048; Ψ Bundaberg 32,990.

SOUTH AUSTRALIA

The State of South Australia is situated between 26° and 38° S. lat. and 129° and 141° E. long., the total area being 380,070 sq. miles (984,376 sq. km).

POPULATION.—At June 30, 1989, the resident population was estimated to be 1,423,300.

Births, deaths and marriages were:

	1988	1989
Births	19,155	19,675
Deaths	10,690	11,364
Marriages	11,128	9,769

Annual rate per 1,000 of estimated resident population in 1988 was:—Births 13·7; Deaths 7·6; Marriages 7·2. Deaths under 1 year per 1,000 live births, 8·1.

Religions

Religion is free and receives no State aid. At the Census, 1986, the persons belonging to the principal religious denominations were as follows: Catholic 267,137; Anglican 242,722; Uniting Church 176,980; Lutheran 64,851; Orthodox 37,149; Baptist 21,415; Presbyterian 18,566; Church of Christ 16,629; and Pentecostal 14,997.

PHYSIOGRAPHY

The most important physical features of South Australia are broad plains, divided longitudinally by four great secondary features, which form barriers to east-west movement, and which have thus largely determined the direction of roads and railways, the sites of towns and villages and the manner of distribution of the population. These four barriers are Spencer Gulf, Gulf St. Vincent, the Mt. Lofty-Flinders Ranges and the River Murray.

The north-western portion of the State is mostly desert, while north of latitude 32° S. the country is unpromising by comparison with the fertile land which surrounds the hill country of the east. The Murray, which flows for some 400 miles through the south-eastern corner, is the only river of importance.

The lack of rivers and fresh-water lakes in the settled areas has necessitated the building of a number of reservoirs, which are supplemented by pipelines from the River Murray.

Climate.—The mean annual temperature at Adelaide is 17·1°C, the winter temperature (June-August) averaging 11·9°C, and the summer (Nov.-March) 22·3°C. During the summer months the maximum temperature at times exceeds 40°C, but is associated with a relatively low humidity. The average annual rainfall at Adelaide is 21 inches.

GOVERNMENT

South Australia was proclaimed a British Province in 1836, and in 1851 a partially elective legislature was established. The present Constitution rests upon a Law of Oct. 24, 1856, the executive authority being vested in a Governor appointed by the Crown, aided by a Council of 13 Ministers.

GOVERNOR

Governor of South Australia, His Excellency Lt. Gen. Sir Donald B. Dunstan, KBE, CB (1982).
Lt. Governor, The Hon. Sir Condor Laucke, KCMG (1982).

THE MINISTRY
(as at May 31, 1990)

Premier, Treasurer, and Minister of State Development, Hon. John Bannon.

Deputy Premier, Minister of Family and Community Services, the Aged, Hon. Donald Hopgood.

Attorney General, Minister of Crime Prevention, Corporate Affairs, Hon. Christopher Sumner.

Industry, Trade and Technology, Agriculture, Fisheries and Ethnic Affairs, Hon. Lynn Arnold.

Education and Children's Services, Hon. Gregory Crafter.

Transport, Finance and Correctional Services, Hon. Frank Blevins.

Tourism and Consumer Affairs/Small Business, Hon. Barbara Wiese.

Housing and Construction, Public Works, Recreation and Sport, Hon. Kym Mayes.

Environment and Planning, Water Resources and Lands, Hon. S. Lenehan.

Emergency Services, Mines, Energy and Forests, Hon. J. Klunder.

Labour, Occupational Health and Safety, Marine, Hon. R. Gregory.

Local Government, State Services and the Arts, Hon. J. Levy.

Employment and Further Education, Youth Affairs, Aboriginal Affairs, and assisting Ethnic Affairs, Hon. M. Rann.

AGENT-GENERAL IN LONDON

Agent-General, G. Walls, South Australia House, 50 Strand, WC2N 5LW.

THE LEGISLATURE

Parliament consists of a Legislative Council of 22 members elected for 8 years, one-half retiring every 4 years; and a House of Assembly of 47 members, elected for a maximum duration of 4 years. Election is by ballot, with universal adult suffrage for both the Legislative Council and the House of Assembly.

The representation in the House of Assembly is 22 Labor, 22 Liberals, 1 National Party and 2 Independent.

President of the Legislative Council, Hon. G. L. Bruce.
Speaker of the House of Assembly, Hon. N. T. Peterson.

THE JUDICATURE

Law and Justice.—The Supreme Court is presided over by the Chief Justice and 13 Puisne Judges.

EDUCATION

Education at the primary and secondary level is available at Government schools controlled by the Education Department and at non-government schools, most of which are denominational. In 1989 there were 708 government schools with 185,769 students, and 183 independent schools with 56,363 students. Tertiary education is available through universities, colleges of advanced education, and technical and further education.

The two universities had, in 1989, a total enrolment of 16,069 full-time students.

CAPITAL.—ΨAdelaide, the chief city and capital, estimated resident population on June 30, 1989, 1,036,747 inclusive of suburbs. Other centres (with 1989 populations) are: ΨWhyalla (26,706); ΨMt. Gambier (22,194); ΨPort Pirie (15,210); ΨPort Augusta (15,752); and ΨPort Lincoln (12,941).

TASMANIA

Tasmania is an island state of Australia situated in the Southern ocean off the south-eastern extremity of the mainland. It is separated from the Australian mainland by Bass Strait and incorporates King Island and the Furneaux group of islands which are in the Strait. It lies between 40° 38′–43° 39′ S. lat. and 144° 36′–148° 23′ E. long., and contains an area of 26,383 sq. miles (68,331 sq. km). Macquarie Island, situated at 54° 30′ S. and 158° 57′ E., about 900 miles north of the Antarctic Continent, is a dependency of Tasmania.

POPULATION.—The estimated resident population at June 30, 1989 was 451,000.

Births, deaths and marriages were:

	1988	1989p
Births	6,669	6,866
Deaths	3,614	3,641
Marriages	3,309	3,140

p preliminary

Annual rate per 1,000 of estimated resident population in 1988 was:—Births 15·0; Deaths 7·8; Marriages 6·8. Deaths under 1 year per 1,000 live births, 8·9.

Religions

In 1986 there were 154,748 members of the Anglican Church of Australia, 80,479 Catholics, 36,724 Uniting Church of Australia, 12,084 Presbyterians and 8,092 Baptists.

PHYSIOGRAPHY

The surface of the country is generally hilly and wooded, with mountains from 1,500 to 5,300 ft. in height, and expanses of level, open plains. There are numerous rivers, the South Esk, Gordon, Derwent and Huon being the largest. At Hobart the mean maximum temperature ranges from about 12°C in winter to 21°C in summer, the mean minimum from 5°C to 11°C. The western side of the island is very wet, the eastern side being much drier.

GOVERNMENT

The island was first settled by a British party from New South Wales in 1803, becoming a separate colony in 1825. In 1851 a partly elective legislature was inaugurated, and in 1856 responsible government was established. In 1901 Tasmania became a State of the Australian Commonwealth. The State executive authority is vested in a Governor (appointed by the Crown), but is exercised by Cabinet Ministers responsible to the Legislature, of which they are members.

GOVERNOR

Governor of Tasmania, His Excellency Gen. Sir Phillip Bennett, AC, KBE, DSO.

THE MINISTRY
(as at May 31, 1990)

Premier, Treasurer, Minister for State Development, Finance, Hon. M. W. Field.

Deputy Premier, Attorney-General, Minister for Justice, Education and the Arts, Hon. P. J. Patmore.

Environment and Planning, Employment, Industrial Relations and Training, and Minister assisting the Premier on Youth Affairs, Hon. M. A. Aird.

Administrative Services and Consumer Affairs, and Minister assisting the Premier on the Status of Women, Hon. F. M. Bladel.

Tourism, Sport and Recreation, Hon. H. N. Holgate.

Community Services, Parks, Wildlife and Heritage, Hon. J. L. Jackson.

Primary Industry, Forests, Hon. D. E. Llewellyn.

Resources and Energy, Construction, Hon. M. W. Weldon.

Health, Minister assisting the Premier on Multicultural Affairs, and on Aboriginal Affairs, Hon. J. C. White.

Roads and Transport, Police and Emergency Services, Hon. K. S. Wriedt.

THE LEGISLATURE

Parliament consists of two Houses, a Legislative Council of 19 members, elected for six years (3 retiring annually, in rotation, except in every sixth year, when four retire) and a House of Assembly of 35 members, elected by proportional representation for four years in five 7-member constituencies, the electors for both Houses being all Tasmanians of 18 years and over who have resided continuously in the State for at least 6 months. Elections for the Assembly are held every four years.

The election of May 13, 1989 resulted in a 'hung parliament' with 17 Liberal, 13 Labor and 5 Independent members. The Government was formed by the Labor Party in alliance with the Independents. The state of the parties in the Legislative Council following the election was Independent 18, Labor 1.
Speaker of the House of Assembly, Hon. M. R. Polley.
President of the Legislative Council, Hon. G. A. Shaw.

THE JUDICATURE

The Supreme Court of Tasmania, with civil, criminal ecclesiastical, admiralty and matrimonial jurisdiction, was established by Royal Charter on October 13, 1823.

Local Courts are held before Commissioners who are legal practitioners. Courts of General Sessions, constituted by a chairman who is a Justice of the Peace and at least one other Justice, are established in the municipalities and Courts of Petty Sessions are constituted by Magistrates sitting alone, or by two or more justices. A single justice may hear and determine certain matters.
Chief Justice, Supreme Court, Hon. Sir Guy Green, KBE.

EDUCATION

Government schools are of three main types: primary, secondary and secondary colleges. On July 1, 1989 there were 64,977 students enrolled in 254 government schools. There were also 66 independent schools with an enrolment of 18,394. The University of Tasmania at Hobart, established 1890, had 3,999 full-time students and 1,619 part-time (including external) students in 1989. The Tasmanian State Institute of Technology, offering degree and diploma courses, was established in 1972. In 1989 3,392 students were enrolled.

PRODUCTION AND INDUSTRY

Electrical Energy.—Tasmania, the smallest Australian state, ranks fourth as a producer of electrical energy—most of it derived from water power, with a total installed generator capacity of 2,315,000 kW at June 30, 1988. By reason of its low-cost electrical energy, Tasmania has large plants producing ferro-manganese and newsprint. A large aluminium plant is situated at Bell Bay and Tasmania is the source of the bulk of Australian requirements of zinc and fine papers. The Hydro-Electric Commission has completed a network of 26 stations including a dual machine oil fired station at Bell Bay. Work is continuing on three hydro-electric developments in the remote western region of the State, which will increase the installed generator capacity to 2·54 million kW.

Forestry.—The quantity of timber (excluding firewood) of various species cut in 1988–89 was 5,071,200 cubic metres, including 4,149,400 cubic metres for woodchip and wood-pulp.

Minerals.—The chief ores mined are those containing copper, tin, iron, silver, zinc and lead.

Manufactures.—The chief manufactures for export are refined metals, preserved fruit and vegetables, butter, cheese, textiles, paper, confectionery, wood chips and sawn timber. In 1987–88, 686 manufacturing establishments employed 24,828 persons, including working proprietors.

CAPITAL.—ΨHobart, founded 1804. Population (June 30, 1989), 181,210. Other towns (with population at June 30, 1989) are ΨLaunceston (63,150), ΨDevonport (25,370), Burnie-Somerset (21,110), Ulverstone (14,490).

VICTORIA

The State of Victoria comprises the south-east corner of Australia, at the part where its mainland territory projects farthest into the southern latitudes; it lies between 34°–39° S. latitude and 141°–150° E. longitude. Its extreme length from east to west is about 493 miles, its greatest breadth is about 290 miles, and its extent of coast-line is about 1,043 geographical miles, including the length around Port Phillip Bay, Western Port and Corner Inlet, the entire area being 87,876 sq. miles (227,597 sq. km).

Population.—The estimated resident population at June 30, 1989 was 4,315,200.

Births, deaths and marriages were:

	1988	1989p
Births	62,404	63,327
Deaths	31,598	31,385
Marriages	30,533	30,670
p preliminary		

Annual rate per 1,000 of estimated resident population in 1988 was:—Births 14·6; Deaths 7·2; Marriages 7·2. Deaths under 1 year per 1,000 live births, 7·9.

Religions

At the Census in 1986, members of the Catholic Church numbered 1,104,044, Anglican 715,414, Uniting (union of Presbyterian, Congregationalist and Methodist) 280,262, Presbyterian 138,000, Orthodox 177,565, and Baptist 39,784. The number of persons who did not state their religion was 589,132.

PHYSIOGRAPHY

The Australian Alps and the Great Dividing Range pass through the centre of the State, and divide it into a northern and southern watershed, the latter sloping down to the ocean and containing, especially in the south-east, well-wooded valleys. The length of the Murray River, which forms part of the northern boundary of Victoria, is about 1,196 miles along the Victorian bank. Melbourne, the capital city, stands upon the Yarra River, which rises in the southern slopes of the Dividing Range.

GOVERNMENT

Victoria was originally known as the Port Phillip District of New South Wales and was created a separate colony in 1851, with a partially elective legislature. In 1855 Responsible Government was conferred. The executive authority is vested in a Governor, appointed by the Crown, aided by an Executive Council of Ministers.

The Legislative Assembly (elected October 2, 1988) consists of Australian Labor Party 46, Liberal Party 33, and National Party 9.
Governor of Victoria, His Excellency Rev. Dr. John Davis McCaughey, *assumed office* Feb. 18, 1986.
Lt. Governor, The Hon. Sir John McIntosh Young, KCMG (1974).

THE MINISTRY
(as at May 31, 1990)

Premier, Minister for Ethnic Affairs, and responsible for Women's Affairs, Hon. John Cain.
Deputy Premier, Minister for Education, Hon. Joan Kirner.
Conservation and Environment, Tourism, Hon. S. Crabb.
Health, Hon. C. Hogg.
Attorney-General, Hon. J. Kennan.
Local Government, the Aged, Hon. M. Lyster.
Planning and Urban Growth, Arts, Hon. A. McCutcheon.
Consumer Affairs, Prices, and responsible for Aboriginal Affairs, Hon. B. Mier.

Labour, and responsible for Youth Affairs, Hon. N. Pope.

Housing and Construction, Hon. B. Pullen.

Treasurer, Hon. T. Roper.

Agricultural and Rural Affairs, Hon. B. Rowe.

Police and Emergency Services, Corrections, Hon. M. Sandon.

Community Services, Hon. K. Setches.

Transport, Hon. P. Spyker.

Sport and Recreation, and responsible for the Olympic Games, Hon. N. Trezise.

Property and Services, and assisting the Minister for Labour, Hon. R. Walsh.

Industry and Economic Planning, Major Projects, Hon. D. White.

AGENT-GENERAL IN LONDON

Agent-General, L. T. Baldock, Victoria House, Melbourne Place, Strand, WC2B 4LG.

THE LEGISLATURE

Parliament consists of a Legislative Council of 44 members, elected for the 22 Provinces for two terms of the Legislative Assembly, one-half retiring every 4 years at a General Election; and a Legislative Assembly of 88 members, elected for a maximum duration of four years. Voting is compulsory.

President of the Legislative Council, Hon. A. J. Hunt.

Speaker of the Legislative Assembly, Hon. Dr. K. A. Coghill.

THE JUDICATURE

There is a Supreme Court with a Chief Justice and 21 Puisne Judges, a County Court and Magistrates' Courts.

Chief Justice, Supreme Court, Hon. Sir John Young, KCMG.

Chief Judge, County Court, Hon. G. R. D. Waldron.

EDUCATION

Primary education is compulsory, secular and free between the ages of 6 and 15. At July 15, 1988, there were 2,010 government primary schools, 134 primary–secondary schools and 510 secondary schools attended by 419,371 primary students and 363,173 secondary students. In addition there are technical and further education institutions and colleges of advanced education.

At July 15, 1988, 256,712 pupils attended non-government schools, 69 per cent of which were Roman Catholic.

There are four state-aided Universities.

PRODUCTION AND INDUSTRY

Minerals.—Minerals raised include oil and natural gas, brown coal, limestone, clays and stone for construction material. Production of brown coal in 1988–89 was valued at $A1,144,834,000.

Crude Oil and Natural Gas.—In 1965 natural gas was first discovered in commercial quantities in the offshore waters of the Gippsland Basin in eastern Victoria and in 1966–67, three more valuable oilfields were located in the same general area. These fields are still the largest yet found in Australia. Production from Victorian natural gas and crude oil fields during 1989 was 5,244,959 Mg. litres.

Secondary Industry.—At June 30, 1988 there were 9,858 manufacturing establishments in which total employees numbered 364,788.

CAPITAL.—ΨMelbourne had a resident population at June 30, 1989, estimated at 3,039,100. Other urban centres are ΨGeelong 148,980; Ballarat 80,090; Bendigo 67,920; Shepparton-Mooroopna 39,700; ΨWarrnambool 24,480; Wodonga 25,800.

WESTERN AUSTRALIA

Includes all that portion of the continent west of 129° E. long., the most westerly point being in 113° 9′ E. long. and from 13° 44′ to 35° 8′ S. lat. Its extreme length is 1,480 miles, and 1,000 miles from east to west; total area 975,920 sq. miles (2,527,621 sq. km).

POPULATION.—At June 30 1989 the estimated resident population was 1,591,100.

Births, deaths and marriages were:

	1988	1989p
Births	24,309	24,806
Deaths	9,184	9,579
Marriages	10,385	10,499

p preliminary

Annual rate per 1,000 of estimated resident population in 1988 was:—Births 16·3; Deaths 6·2; Marriages 6·6. Deaths under 1 year per 1,000 live births, 8·4.

Religions

Census of 1986—Anglican Church 371,302, Roman Catholics 347,695, Uniting Church 82,876, and Presbyterians 31,641.

PHYSIOGRAPHY

Large areas of the State, for some hundreds of miles inland, are hilly and even mountainous, although the altitude, so far as ascertained, rises nowhere above that of Mount Meharry (4,097 ft.) in the north-west division or that of Bluff Knoll (3,640 ft.) in the Stirling Range in the south-west. The Darling and Hamersley ranges of the west have a seaward slope to the Indian Ocean, into which flow many streams, notably the Preston, Collie, Murray, Swan, Murchison, Gascoyne, Ashburton, Fortescue and De Grey. In the north the Fitzroy flows from the King Leopold ranges into the Indian Ocean, and the Drysdale and Ord into the Timor Sea. The greater portion of the State may be described as an immense tableland, with an average elevation of 1,000 to 1,500 ft. above sea-level. The climate is one of the most temperate in the world. Of the total area two-thirds is suitable for pastoral purposes.

GOVERNMENT

Western Australia was first settled by the British in 1829, and in 1870 it was granted a partially elective legislature. In 1890 responsible government was granted, and the administration vested in a Governor, a Legislative Council, and a Legislative Assembly. The present constitution rests upon the Constitution Act, 1889, the Constitution Acts Amendment Act, 1899, and amending Acts. The Executive is vested in a Governor appointed by the Crown and aided by a Council of responsible Ministers.

Governor of Western Australia, His Excellency the Hon. Sir Francis Burt, AC, KCMG.

Lt. Governor and Administrator, Hon. D. K. Malcolm.

THE MINISTRY
(as at May 31, 1990)

Premier, Treasurer, Minister for Public Sector Management, the Family, Aboriginal Affairs, Multicultural and Ethnic Affairs, Women's Interests, Hon. Dr. Carmen M. Lawrence.

Deputy Premier, Minister for Finance and Economic Development, Trade, Goldfields, Hon. I. F. Taylor.

Attorney General, Minister for Resources, Corrective Services, Leader of the Government in the Legislative Council, Hon. J. M. Berinson, QC.

Planning, Lands, Heritage, the Arts, Hon. E. K. Hallahan.

Mines, Fuel and Energy, Mid-West, Small Business, Hon. J. P. Carr.

Environment, Leader of the House in the Legislative Assembly, Hon. R. J. Pearce.

Health, Hon. K. J. Wilson.

Productivity and Labour Relations, Hon. G. J. Troy.

Transport, Racing and Gaming, Tourism, Hon. P. A. Beggs.

Agriculture, Water Resources, North-West, Hon. E. F. Bridge.

Local Government, Fisheries, Sport and Recreation, Youth, Hon. G. L. Hill.

Police, Emergency Services, the Aged, Hon. G. J. Edwards.

Housing, Consumer Affairs, Hon. Y. D. Henderson.

Community Services, Justice, the South-West, Hon. D. L. Smith.

Works, Services, Regional Development, Hon. P. A. Buchanan.

Education, Parliamentary and Electoral Reform, Hon. G. I. Gallop.

Parliamentary Secretary of the Cabinet, W. I. Thomas.

AGENT-GENERAL IN LONDON

Agent-General, R. Davies, Western Australia House, 115 Strand, WC2R 0AJ.

THE LEGISLATURE

Parliament consists of a Legislative Council and a Legislative Assembly, elected by adult suffrage subject to qualifications of residence and registration. The qualifying age for electors for both the Legislative Council and Legislative Assembly is 18 years. There are 34 members in the Legislative Council elected for a period of 4 years. The Legislative Assembly has 57 members, who are elected for a term of 4 years. The Legislative Assembly (elected February 4, 1989) is composed of Australian Labor Party 31, Liberal Party 20, National Party of Australia 6.

President of the Legislative Council, Hon. C. E. Griffiths.

Speaker of the Legislative Assembly, Hon. M. Barnett.

THE JUDICATURE

Chief Justice, Hon. D. K. Malcolm.

Senior Puisne Judge, Hon. A. R. A. Wallace.

Puisne Judges, Hons. P. F. Brinsden; G. A. Kennedy; W. P. Pidgeon; B. W. Rowland; E. M. Franklyn; P. L. Seaman; R. D. Nicolson; T. A. Walsh; D. A. Ipp; H. A. Wallwork; M. J. Murray.

EDUCATION

In 1989 there were 751 government and 241 non-government primary and secondary school campuses with 212,444 and 67,503 full-time students respectively. The total recurrent and capital outlay expended on education (by State authorities) during the year ended June 30, 1989 was $A1,352,951,000. The principal higher education institutions are the University of Western Australia (10,423 enrolments in 1989), Murdoch University (6,267), Curtin University (14,944) and the Western Australian College of Advanced Education (14,108).

PRODUCTION AND INDUSTRY

Manufacturing Industries.—There were 4,164 manufacturing establishments operating in the State at June 30, 1988. The total number of persons employed (including working proprietors) by these establishments at the end of June 1988 was 76,303.

Forestry.—The forests contain some of the finest hardwoods in the world. The total quantity of sawn timber produced during 1988–89 was 335,191 cubic metres.

Minerals.—The State has large deposits of a wide range of minerals, many of which are being mined or are under development for production. The ex-mine

value of all minerals produced during 1987–88 was $A5,935,544,000.

CAPITAL.—ψPerth, on the right bank of the Swan River estuary, 12 miles from Fremantle. Estimated resident population (June 30, 1989) of Perth Statistical Division, including the port of ψFremantle, 1,158,387.

THE BAHAMAS
(The Commonwealth of The Bahamas)

AREA, POPULATION, ETC.—The Bahama Islands are an archipelago lying in the North Atlantic Ocean between 20° 55′–25° 22′ N. lat. and 72° 35′–79° 35′ W. long. They extend from the coast of Florida on the north-west almost to Haiti on the south-east. The group consists of 700 islands, of which 30 are inhabited and 2,400 cays comprising an area of more than 5,380 sq. miles, (19,935 sq. km). The population (UN estimate 1988) is 245,000. The principal islands include: Abaco, Acklins, Andros, Berry Islands, Bimini, Cat Island, Crooked Island, Eleuthera, Exumas, Grand Bahama, Harbour Island, Inagua, Long Island, Mayaguana, New Providence (on which is located the capital, Nassau), Ragged Island, Rum Cay, San Salvador and Spanish Wells. San Salvador was the first landfall in the New World of Christopher Columbus on October 12, 1492.

The Bahamas were settled by British subjects when the islands were deserted. The ownership of The Bahamas was taken over in 1782 by the Spanish, but the Treaty of Versailles in 1783 restored them to the British.

CAPITAL.—ψNassau, population (UN estimate) 153,620.

CURRENCY.—Bahamian dollar (B$) of 100 cents.

FLAG.—Horizontal stripes of aquamarine, gold and aquamarine, with a black equilateral triangle on the hoist.

NATIONAL ANTHEM.—March on, Bahamaland.

NATIONAL DAY.—July 10 (Independence Day).

GOVERNMENT

The Bahamas gained independence on July 10, 1973. The Head of State is HM Queen Elizabeth II, represented in the islands by a Governor General. There is a Senate of 16 members and an elected House of Assembly of 49 members.

Acting Governor General, His Excellency Sir Henry Milton Taylor (1988).

Cabinet
(as at Oct. 1, 1990)

Prime Minister and Minister of Tourism, Rt. Hon. Sir Lynden Pindling, KCMG.

Deputy PM, Minister of Foreign Affairs and of Public Personnel, Hon. Sir Clement Maynard.

National Security and Government Leader in the House of Assembly, Hon. Darrell Rolle.

Finance, Hon. Paul L. Adderley.

Works and Lands, Hon. Philip M. Bethel.

Employment and Immigration, Hon. Alfred T. Maycock.

Transport, Hon. Peter J. Bethell.

Housing and National Insurance, Hon. George W. Mackey.

Agriculture, Trade and Industry, Hon. Perry Christie.

Health, Hon. E. Charles Carter.

Education, Hon. Dr. Bernard J. Nottage.

Youth, Sports and Community Affairs, Hon. Dr. Norman Gay.

Consumer Affairs, Hon. Vincent A. Peet.

Local Government, Hon. Marvin B. Pinder.

Attorney General, Senator Hon. Sean G. McWeeney.

President of the Court of Appeal, Kenneth Henry.
Chief Justice, J. C. Gonsalves-Sabola.

BAHAMAS HIGH COMMISSION
Bahamas House, 10 Chesterfield Street, W1X 8AH
[071–408 4488]

High Commissioner, Her Excellency Dr. Patricia
Rodgers (1988).

ECONOMY

Tourism is the economic mainstay of The Bahamas,
employing about two-thirds of the labour force. It
provides about two-thirds of Government revenue
and about half the country's foreign exchange
earnings. The second main industry is international
banking and trust business. The Bahamas' absence
of any direct taxation and internal stability have
enabled the country to become one of the world's
leading financial centres.

Agricultural production is mainly of fresh vegetables, fruit, meat and eggs for the domestic market,
and crawfish, mostly for export. There are large
reserves of aragonite, and reserves of limestone and
salt, all of which are being commercially exploited.
Freeport is the country's leading industrial centre,
with a pharmaceutical and chemicals plant, an oil
trans-shipment and storage terminal, and port and
bunkering facilities. There are also a brewery and a
rum distillery on New Providence.

EDUCATION

Education is compulsory between the ages of 5 and
14. More than 62,000 students are enrolled in
Ministry of Education and independent schools in
New Providence and the Family Islands.

COMMUNICATIONS

The main ports are Nassau (New Providence),
Freeport (Grand Bahama), Mathew Town (Inagua).
International air services are operated from Abaco,
Bimini, Eleuthera, Exuma, Grand Bahama and New
Providence. About 50 smaller airports and landing
strips facilitate services between the islands, the
services being mainly provided by Bahamasair, the
national carrier. There are roads on the larger
islands, and roads are under construction on the
smaller islands. There are no railways. Wireless and
telephone services are in operation to all parts of the
world.

FINANCE AND TRADE

	1988	1989p
Public revenue......	B$432·6m	B$448·1m
Expenditure........	505·1m	561·6m
p provisional		

Trade with UK

	1988	1989
Imports from UK.......	£20,708,000	£22,543,000
Exports to UK.........	24,781,000	17,681,000

The imports are chiefly foodstuffs, manufactured
articles, building materials, vehicles and machinery,
chemicals and petroleum. The chief exports are rum,
petroleum, hormones, salt, crawfish and aragonite.

BRITISH HIGH COMMISSION
PO Box N-7516, Nassau
[Nassau 325-7471]

High Commissioner, His Excellency Colin Garth
Mays, CMG (1986).
Deputy High Commissioner, P. A. Connolly *(Head of
Chancery).*

BANGLADESH
(Ghana Praja Tantri Bangladesh)

AREA, POPULATION, CLIMATE, ETC.—The People's
Republic of Bangladesh consists of the territory
which was formerly East Pakistan (the old province
of East Bengal and the Sylhet district of Assam),
covering an area of 55,598 sq. miles (143,998 sq. km)
in the region of the Gangetic delta, and has a
population (UN estimate 1988) of 104,532,000.

The country is crossed by a network of navigable
rivers, including the eastern arms of the Ganges, the
Jamuna (Brahmaputra) and the Meghna, flowing
into the Bay of Bengal. The climate is tropical and
monsoon: hot and extremely humid during the
summer, and mild and dry during the short winter.
The rainfall is heavy, varying from 50 inches to 135
inches in different districts and the bulk of it falls
during monsoon season from June to September.

CAPITAL.—Dhaka, population (UN estimate)
3,458,602.

CURRENCY.—Taka (Tk) of 100 poisha.

FLAG.—Red circle on a bottle-green ground.

NATIONAL ANTHEM.—Amar Sonar Bangla.

NATIONAL DAY.—March 26 (Independence Day).

GOVERNMENT

Prior to becoming East Pakistan, the territory had
been part of British India. It acceded to Pakistan in
October 1947, which became a Republic on March 23,
1956.

By a proclamation of March 26, 1971, Bangladesh
purported to secede from the central government,
and a government-in-exile was set up which formally
declared independence on April 17. Bangladesh
achieved its independence on December 16, 1971,
following the conclusion of the Indo-Pakistan war.
Pakistan and Bangladesh accorded one another
mutual recognition in February 1974.

From 1975 a non-political administration ran the
country under martial law. A Presidential election
was held in June 1978 and President Zia was elected.
Martial law was subsequently lifted. Zia was assassinated in May 1981 in an unsuccessful coup. In 1982
General Ershad, then the Chief of Army Staff, took
over responsibility for running the country. Following elections in May 1986 a civilian Cabinet was
appointed and Gen. Ershad was elected President in
October 1986. Martial law was lifted and the 1972
Constitution fully restored. A constitutional amendment passed in July 1989 created an elected post of
Vice President and limited the President's tenure of
office to two elected five-year terms.

The most recent parliamentary elections were held
on March 3, 1988. In the new Parliament which
convened on April 25, the Jatiya Party of President
Ershad had a two-thirds majority.

President, Hussain Muhammad Ershad.
Vice President, and Minister for Industries, Moudud
Ahmed.

Council of Ministers
(as at May 31, 1990)

Prime Minister, and Minister for Education, Kazi
Zafar Ahmed.
Deputy Prime Minister, and Minister for Food, Shah
Moazzem Hossain.
Finance and Planning, Maj.-Gen. M. A. Munim
(ret'd).
Home Affairs, Maj.-Gen. M. Mahmudul Hasan (ret'd).
Commerce, Maj.-Gen. Shamsul Huq (ret'd).
Law and Justice, Justice Habibul Islam Bhuiyan.
Foreign Affairs, Anisul Islam Mahmood.
Ports, Shipping and Inland Water Transport, Korban
Ali.

Labour and Manpower, Serajul Hossain Khan.
Communications, Amwar Hossain.
Jute, Sheikh Shahidul Islam.
Irrigation, Water Development and Flood Control, A. B. M. Ghulam Mostafa.
Fisheries and Livestock, A. Sattar.
Works, Mustafa Jamal Haider.
Social Affairs, Rezwanul Haq Chowdhury.
Women Affairs, Mrs. Razia Faiz.
Relief, Mahmudur Rahman Chowdhury.
Energy and Mineral Resources, Ziauddin Ahmed.
Textiles, A. B. M. Ruhul Amin Howlader.
Civil Aviation and Tourism, Lt.-Col. H. M. A. Gaffar.
Forest and Environment, Zafar Imam.
Local Government, Rural Development and Co-operatives, Mohammad Naziur Rahman.
Post and Telecommunications, Kazi Firoz Rashid.
Health and Family Planning, Dr. Azizur Rahman.
Agriculture, Sardar Amzad Hossain.
Information, Dr. Mizanur Rahman Shelley.
Land, Tajul Islam Chowdhury.

BANGLADESH HIGH COMMISSION
28 Queen's Gate, SW7 5JA
[071–584 0081]

High Commissioner, His Excellency Maj.-Gen. K. M. Safiullah (1987).

RELIGION

The faith of over 90 per cent of the population is Islam. Islam has been constitutionally declared the state religion of Bangladesh.

LANGUAGE

The state language is Bengali. Use of Bengali is compulsory in all government departments. English, however, is understood and is used widely as an unofficial second language.

EDUCATION

Primary education is free and planned to be universal by the year 2000. There are about 4,393 primary schools, mostly managed by the Government. There are about 8,983 secondary schools and 947 colleges offering general and technical education. There are seven universities including one for engineering and technology, one for agriculture and another for islamic education and research. In 1990 the literacy rate was estimated to be 24 per cent (of which 31 per cent male and 16 per cent female).

TRANSPORT AND COMMUNICATIONS

Principal seaports are Chittagong and Mongla. The Bangladesh Shipping Corporation has been set up by the Government to operate the Bangladesh merchant fleet. The principal airports are Dhaka (Zia International) and Chittagong. The international airline, Bangladesh Biman, serves Europe, the Middle East, South and South-East Asia, and an internal network.

There are about 6,880 miles of roads in Bangladesh; 4,724 miles are metalled. There are 2,798 miles of railway track.

Radio Bangladesh is the main national broadcasting service. A television service was introduced in 1965 and colour transmissions began in 1981.

ECONOMY

Bangladesh is a principal producer of raw jute. Other agricultural products are rice, tea, oil seeds, pulses and sugar cane. The chief industries are jute, cotton, tea, leather, pharmaceuticals, fertilizer, sugar, prawn fishing, natural gas and garment manufacture. Remittances sent home by Bangladeshi workers abroad have been of considerable support to the economy in recent years.

Aid

Bangladesh is a major recipient of bilateral and multilateral development aid. The total annual development plan for 1990–91 is budgeted at US$1,624 million of which US$1,467 million will be financed from external sources.

Trade with UK

	1988	1989
Imports from UK	£64,018,000	£78,270,000
Exports to UK	50,249,000	52,527,000

BRITISH HIGH COMMISSION
Abu Bakr House, Plot 7, Road 84, Gulshan Dhaka, PO Box 6079
[Dhaka 600133/7]

High Commissioner, His Excellency Colin Henry Imray, CMG (1989).
Deputy High Commissioner, J. F. Holding.

British Council Representative, G. Ness, 5 Fuller Road (PO Box 161), Dhaka 2.

BARBADOS

AREA, ETC.—Barbados, the most easterly of the Caribbean islands, is situated in latitude 13° 14′ N. and longitude 59° 37′ W. The island has a total area of 166 sq. miles, (430 sq. km), the land rising in a series of tablelands marked by terraces to the highest point, Mt. Hillaby (1,116 ft.). It is nearly 21 miles long by 14 miles broad. The climate is equable with annual average temperature 26·6°C (79·8°F) and rainfall varying from a yearly average of 75 inches in the high central district to 50 inches in some of the low-lying coastal areas.

POPULATION.—The population of Barbados (1988 UN estimate) was 254,000. There are eleven administrative areas (parishes): St. Michael, Christ Church, St. Andrews, St. George, St. James, St. John, St. Joseph, St. Lucy, St. Peter, St. Philip and St. Thomas.

CAPITAL.—ΨBridgetown (population, estimated April, 1980, 7,466) in the parish of St. Michael. There are three other towns, Oistins in Christ Church, Holetown in St. James and Speightstown in St. Peter.

CURRENCY.—Barbados dollar (BD$) of 100 cents.

FLAG.—Three vertical stripes, dark blue, gold and dark blue, with a trident head on gold stripe.

NATIONAL ANTHEM.—In Plenty and in Time of Need.

NATIONAL DAY.—November 30 (Independence Day).

GOVERNMENT

The first inhabitants of Barbados were Arawak Indians but the island was uninhabited when first settled by the British in 1627. It was a Crown Colony from 1652 until it became an independent state within the Commonwealth on November 30, 1966. The Legislature consists of the Governor General, a Senate and a House of Assembly. The Senate comprises 21 Senators appointed by the Governor General, of whom 12 are appointed on the advice of the Prime Minister, two on the advice of the Leader of the Opposition and seven by the Governor General at his discretion to represent religious, economic or social interests in the Island or such other interests as the Governor General considers ought to be represented. The House of Assembly comprises 27 members elected every five years by adult suffrage. The last General Election took place on May 28, 1986 and, as a result, seats in the House of Assembly were distributed as follows: Democratic Labour Party 24, Barbados Labour Party 3.

Governor General, Dame Nita Barrow, GCMG, DA (1990).

Cabinet
(as at June 30, 1990)

Prime Minister, Minister of Economic Affairs and Finance, Civil Service, Rt. Hon. L. Erskine Sandiford.
Deputy PM, Minister of International Transport, Telecommunications, and Immigration, Hon. Philip M. Greaves, QC.
Attorney General and Minister of Legal Affairs, Foreign Affairs, Hon. Maurice A. King, QC.
Agriculture, Food and Fisheries, Hon. Warwick O. Franklin.
Employment, Labour Relations and Community Development, Hon. N. Keith Simmons.
Trade, Industry and Commerce, Hon. E. Evelyn Greaves.
Health, Hon. Branford M. Taitt.
Housing and Lands, Hon. Harold A. Blackman.
Transport and Works, Telecommunications, Hon. Dr. Donald G. Blackman.
Tourism and Sport, Hon. Wesley W. Hall.
Education and Culture, Hon. Cyril V. Walker.
Minister of State, Finance and Economic Affairs, Senator Hon. Dr. Carl Clarke.
Minister of State for the Civil Service, and to the Ministry of Agriculture, Minister of State in the PM's office and Leader of Government Business in the Senate, Senator Hon. L. V. Harcourt Lewis.
President of the Senate, Senator Hon. Sir Frank Walcott, KA, OBE.
Speaker, House of Assembly, Hon. Lawson Weekes.

BARBADOS HIGH COMMISSION
1 Great Russell Street, WC1B 3NH
[071–631 4975]

High Commissioner, His Excellency Sir Roy Marshall, CBE (1989).

JUDICATURE

There is a Supreme Court of Judicature consisting of a High Court and a Court of Appeal. In certain cases a further appeal lies to the Judicial Committee of the Privy Council. The Chief Justice and Puisne Judges are appointed by the Governor-General on the recommendation of the Prime Minister and after consultation with the Leader of the Opposition.
Chief Justice, The Hon. Sir Denys Ambrose Williams.

EDUCATION

Primary and secondary education is free in Government schools. There are 105 primary schools, 21 Government secondary schools and 15 approved Government secondary schools.

COMMUNICATIONS

Barbados has some 965 miles of roads, of which about 917 miles are asphalted. The Grantley Adams International airport is situated at Seawell, 12 miles from Bridgetown, and frequent scheduled services connect Barbados with the major world air routes. Bridgetown, the only port of entry, has a deep-water harbour with berths for 8 ships, but oil is pumped ashore at Spring Gardens and at an Esso installation

on the West Coast. Barbados has a colour television service, three radio broadcasting services, and a wired broadcasting service.

FINANCE

	1987–88*
Current revenue	BD$698,071,077
Current expenditure	711,636,404
Capital expenditure	176,518,229

* estimated.

ECONOMY

The economy of the island is based on tourism, sugar and light manufacturing. In 1986, 369,770 tourists visited Barbados and 145,335 cruise ship passengers. Chief exports are, electrical components (52·1 per cent of exports in 1986), sugar and its by-products (15·7 per cent) and clothing (8·4 per cent).

Trade with UK

	1988	1989
Imports from UK	£32,061,000	£38,136,000
Exports to UK	19,487,000	22,304,000

BRITISH HIGH COMMISSION
Lower Collymore Rock, PO Box 676,
Bridgetown
[Bridgetown 436 6694]

High Commissioner, His Excellency Kevin Francis Xavier Burns, CMG (1986).

BELIZE

AREA, ETC.—Belize lies on the east coast of Central America, bounded on the north and north-west by Mexico, and on the west and south by Guatemala. The total area (including offshore islands) is about 8,867 sq. miles (22,965 sq. km.), with a length and breadth of 174 miles and 68 miles respectively. The climate is sub-tropical, with a mean annual temperature of 20°C, but is tempered by sea breezes. There are two dry seasons, the main one from March to May and the other (the Maugre season) from August to September. The country is occasionally affected by hurricanes.

The coastal areas are mostly flat and swampy but the country rises gradually towards the interior. The northern and western districts are hilly, and in the south the Maya Mountains and the Cockscombs form the backbone of the country, reaching a height of 3,800 feet at Victoria Peak.

POPULATION.—The population is 175,000 (1988 UN estimate), of which the main racial groups are Creole, Mestizo (Maya-Spanish) and Carib, plus a number of East Indian and Spanish descent. The races are now heavily inter-mixed. The majority of the population is Christian, about 60 per cent Catholic and most of the remainder Protestant.

CAPITAL.—Belmopan (estimated population, 1980, 2,935). The largest city and the former capital is ΨBelize City (population, 1980 census, 39,771). Other towns are Corozal (6,899), San Ignacio (5,616), Dangriga (6,661), Orange Walk (8,439), Punta Gorda (2,396).

CURRENCY.—Belize dollar (BZ$) of 100 cents. The Belize dollar is tied to the US dollar—BZ$2 = US$1.

FLAG.—Blue ground with red band along top and bottom edges, and in centre a white disc containing the coat of arms surrounded by a green garland.

NATIONAL ANTHEM.—Land of the Gods.

NATIONAL DAY.—September 21 (Independence Day).

GOVERNMENT

The early history of Belize is little known, although the numerous ruins in the area indicate that it was heavily populated by the Maya Indians. The first British settlement was established in 1638 but was subject to repeated attacks by the Spanish, who claimed sovereignty over the area, until the decline of Spanish power in the Americas in the 19th century. In 1862 the area was recognized by Britain as a colony and called British Honduras. On June 1, 1973 the colony was officially renamed Belize, and was granted independence on September 21, 1981. The long-standing territorial dispute with Guatemala, which had delayed independence earlier, remains unresolved despite efforts to reach a settlement.

The Queen is Head of State, represented in Belize by a Governor General, who is a citizen of the country, appointed in consultation with the Prime Minister of Belize. There is a National Assembly, comprising a House of Representatives (28 members elected for 5 years) and a Senate (8 members appointed by the Governor General). Executive power is vested in the Cabinet, which is responsible to the National Assembly.

Governor General, Her Excellency Dame Minita Elmira Gordon, GCMG, GCVO.

The Cabinet
(as at May 31, 1990)

Prime Minister and Minister of Finance, Home Affairs and Defence, Trade and Commerce, Rt. Hon. George Price.
Deputy PM and Minister of Industry and Natural Resources, Hon. Florencio Marin.
Foreign Affairs, Economic Development, Education, Hon. Said Musa.
Housing, Co-operatives, Hon. Valdemar Castillo.
Works, Hon. Leopoldo Briceño.
Health, Urban Development, Hon. Dr. Theodore Aranda.
Attorney General, Minister of Tourism and the Environment, Hon. Glenn Godfrey.
Social Services, Community Development, Hon. Remijio Montejo.
Agriculture and Fisheries, Hon. Michael Espat.
Labour, Public Service and Local Government, Hon. Samuel Waight.
Energy and Communications, Hon. Carlos Diaz.
Ministers of State, Finance, Home Affairs and Defence, Trade and Commerce, Hon. Ralph Fonseca, Hon. Daniel Silva.
Minister of State, Foreign Affairs, Economic Development, Education, Hon. Vildo Marin.
Minister of State, Industry and Natural Resources, Hon. Guadalupe Pech.
Minister of State, Energy and Communications, Hon. Miguel Ruiz.

BELIZE HIGH COMMISSION
200 Sutherland Avenue,
W9 1RX
[071-266 3485]

High Commissioner, His Excellency Sir Edney Cain, OBE.

ECONOMY

About 42 per cent of the population is engaged in agriculture. Corn (maize), rice, red kidney beans, root crops and fruit are the main food crops, although main agricultural exports are sugar, bananas and citrus products. The country is more or less self-sufficient in fresh beef, pork and poultry, but processed meat and dairy products are imported. About 25 per cent of timber production (mostly mahogany) is exported, and there is a large US market for lobster, conch and scale fish. Tourism is also a valuable source of income.

FINANCE

	1987–88	1988–89p
Revenue	BZ $114·2 m	BZ$132·2 m
Expenditure	134·6 m	131·3 m
Deficit	− 20·4 m	0·9 m
p = provisional		

TRADE

	1986	1987
Total imports	BZ $243·9 m	BZ$285·9 m
Total exports	185·2 m	205·7 m

Trade with UK

	1988	1989
Imports from UK	£12,064,000	£11,842,000
Exports to UK	22,461,000	24,272,000

EDUCATION

Education is compulsory from 5 to 14 years of age. In 1985 primary education was provided by 225 schools, most of which are government aided. Enrolment totalled 38,512. Secondary education is provided by 29 secondary and post-secondary institutions with an enrolment of 7,441. Plans are underway for Ferris State College of Michigan, USA, to establish an affiliate university in Belize. The Government also offers scholarships for students to go abroad. There is an extra-mural faculty of the University of the West Indies, with a resident tutor.

COMMUNICATIONS

There is a Government-operated radio service but no official television service in the country. An automatic telephone service operated by Belize Telecommunications Ltd. covers the whole country.

The principal airport is at Belize City and various airlines operate international flights to US and other Central American states. The main port is also Belize City, where construction of deep water quays was recently completed. There are 1,865 miles of road, including four main highways, but there is no railway system.

BRITISH HIGH COMMISSION
PO Box 91, Belmopan
[Belmopan 2146/7]

High Commissioner, His Excellency Peter Alexander Bremner Thomson, CVO (1987).
Deputy High Commissioner, J. Bentley.

BOTSWANA
(The Republic of Botswana)

AREA, ETC.—Botswana (formerly the British Protectorate of Bechuanaland) lies between latitudes 18° and 26° S. and longitudes 20° and 28° W. and is bounded by the Cape and Transvaal Provinces of South Africa on the south and east, by Zimbabwe, the Zambezi and Chobe (Linyanti) Rivers on the north and north-east and by Namibia on the west. Botswana has a total area of 224,607 sq. miles (581,730 sq. km). The climate of the country is generally subtropical, but varies considerably with latitude and altitude. A plateau at a height of about 4,000 feet divides Botswana into two main topographical regions. To the east of the plateau streams flow into the Marico, Notwani and Limpopo Rivers; to the west lies a flat region comprising the Kgalagadi Desert, the Okavango Swamps and the Northern State Lands area. Large areas of the country support only herds of game. Elephant numbers have been estimated at 15–30,000.

POPULATION.—Botswana has an estimated population (1990) of 1,300,000. The eight principal Botswana tribes are Bakgatla, Bakwena, Bangwaketse, Bamalete, Bamangwato, Barolong, Batawana and Batlokwa. The principal languages in use in Botswana are Setswana and English.

CAPITAL.—Gaborone, estimated population 125,000. Other centres are Francistown (60,000), Lobatse (25,000), and Selebi-Phikwe (46,000).

CURRENCY.—Pula (P) of 100 thebe.

FLAG.—Horizontal bands of blue, white, blue, with a black stripe on the white band.

NATIONAL ANTHEM.—Fatshe La Rona.

NATIONAL DAY.—September 30.

GOVERNMENT

On September 30, 1966, Bechuanaland became a Republic within the Commonwealth under the name Botswana. The President of Botswana is Head of State and appoints as Vice President a member of the National Assembly who is his principal assistant and leader of Government business in the National Assembly. The Assembly consists of the President, 34 members elected on a basis of universal adult suffrage, 4 specially elected members, the Attorney-General (non-voting) and the Speaker. Presidential and legislative elections are held every five years. There is also a House of Chiefs.

President, His Excellency Dr. Q. K. J. Masire, *sworn in* October 10, 1989 for a third five-year term.

Cabinet
(as at May 31, 1990)

Vice President, Local Government and Lands, Peter Mmusi.
Presidential Affairs, Public Administration, Lt.-Gen. Mompati Merafhe.
Finance and Development Planning, Festus Mogae.
External Affairs, Dr. Gaositwe Chiepe.
Mineral Resources and Water, Archibald Mogwe.
Commerce and Industry, Ponatshego Kedikilwe.
Agriculture, Daniel Kwelagobe.
Works and Communications, Chapson Butale.
Health, Kebatlemang Morake.
Education, Ray Molomo.
Home Affairs, Patrick Balopi.
Assistant Minister of Finance, David Magang.
Local Government and Lands, Ronald Sebego, Michael Tshipinare.
Agriculture, Geoffrey Oteng.

BOTSWANA HIGH COMMISSION
6 Stratford Place, W1N 9AE
[071–499 0031]

High Commissioner, Her Excellency Mrs. Margaret Nasha (1989).

ECONOMY

Botswana is predominantly a pastoral country. The national herd is normally around 3 million cattle and 1 million sheep and goats but drought conditions during the past 6 years have reduced the number of cattle to around 2·5 million.

Cattle rearing accounts for about 85 per cent of agricultural output and livestock products, particularly beef, are a major source of foreign exchange earnings. The Government has a number of programmes to improve land use and cattle and crop production, and schemes to provide financial assistance for farmers.

Mineral extraction and processing is now the major source of income for the country following the opening of large mines for diamonds and copper-nickel. Botswana is one of the largest producers of diamonds in the world. Large deposits of coal have been discovered and are being mined on a small scale. Much of the country has yet to be fully prospected. Manufacturing industry is growing and will continue to do so as communications improve but it is still a small sector of the economy.

EDUCATION

There are over 500 primary schools (enrolment approx. 248,800), 81 community junior secondary schools (enrolment approx. 33,400) and 24 government and government-aided senior secondary schools (enrolment 7,000). The government embarked on a massive expansion of secondary education in January 1984 aimed at providing universal access to junior secondary education; over 50 more schools were to be opened by 1990. There are 5 teacher training establishments (total enrolment 1,540) including one for secondary teachers (enrolment 340), one polytechnic with 770 students and the University of Botswana with 2,300 undergraduates. Further expansion of the technical education system is planned via a network of vocational training centres.

COMMUNICATIONS

The railway from Cape Town to Zimbabwe passes through eastern Botswana. The main roads in the country are the north–south road, which closely follows the railway, and the road running east–west that links Francistown and Maun. A new road from Nata to Kazungula provides a direct link to Zambia from Botswana. Air services are provided on a scheduled basis between the main towns.

FINANCE

	1987–88	1988–89
Actual Revenue ...... (Recurrent and		
development)	P2,226 m	P2,556 m
Actual Expenditure ..	1,312 m	1,788 m

TRADE

Principal exports are diamonds, copper-nickel matte, and beef and beef products.

	1988	1989p
Imports	P1,851 m	P2,136 m
Exports	2,703 m	3,613 m
p preliminary		

Trade with UK

	1988	1989
Imports from UK	£26,763,000	£34,682,000
Exports to UK	6,942,000	13,135,000

BRITISH HIGH COMMISSION
Private Bag 0023, Gaborone
[Gaborone 352841]

High Commissioner, His Excellency Brian Smith, OBE (1989).
British Council Representative, T. A. Jones, MBE.

BRUNEI
(Negara Brunei Darussalam)

Brunei is situated on the north-west coast of the island of Borneo, total area of 2,226 sq. miles (5,765 sq. km), population (UN estimate 1988) 241,000 of whom 68 per cent are of Malay, 18 per cent Chinese and 5 per cent other indigenous races. The country has a humid tropical climate.

CAPITAL.—Bandar Seri Begawan, with a population of 58,000 (1981).

CURRENCY.—Brunei dollar (B$) of 100 sen. It is fully interchangeable with the currency of Singapore.

FLAG.—Yellow, with diagonal bands of white over narrow black band (from top by staff), with red device on diagonal bands.

NATIONAL ANTHEM.—Ya Allah Lanjutkan Lah Usia Duli Tuanku (O God, long live our Majesty the Sultan).

NATIONAL DAY.—February 23.

GOVERNMENT

In 1959, the Sultan of Brunei promulgated the first written Constitution, which provides for a Privy Council, a Council of Ministers and a Legislative Council. On January 1, 1984 Brunei resumed full independence. A ministerial system of government was established at independence, the seven Ministers being appointed by the Sultan and responsible to him. The Sultan presides over the Privy Council and the Council of Ministers. The Legislative Council was disbanded in February 1984.

Sultan, HM Sultan Haji Hassanal Bolkiah Mu'izzaddin Waddaulah, Sultan and Yang Di-Pertuan, *acceded* 1967, *crowned* Aug. 1, 1968.

The Council of Ministers
(as at May 31, 1990)

Prime Minister, Minister of Defence, HM The Sultan.
Foreign Affairs, HRH Prince Mohammed.
Finance, HRH Prince Jefri.

Special Adviser to the Sultan and Minister for Home Affairs, Pehin Dato Haji Isa.
Education, Pehin Dato Abdul Aziz.
Law, Pengiran Bahrin.
Industry and Primary Resources, Pehin Dato Abdul Rahman.
Religious Affairs, Pehin Dato Mohammed Zain.
Development, Pengiran Dato Dr. Ismail.
Culture, Youth and Sports, Pehin Dato Haji Hussein.
Health, Dato Dr. Johar.
Communications, Dato Haji Zakaria.

BRUNEI DARUSSALAM HIGH COMMISSION
49 Cromwell Road, SW7 2ED
[071–581 0521]

High Commissioner, (new appointment awaited).

FINANCE

	1988
Revenue	B$2,487 m
Expenditure	2,721 m

Trade with UK

	1988	1989
Imports from UK	£171,556,000	£264,371,000
Exports to UK	142,461,000	186,110,000

BRITISH HIGH COMMISSION
Hong Kong and Shanghai Bank Building (3rd floor)
Bandar Seri Begawan
[Bandar Seri Begawan 22231]

High Commissioner, His Excellency Roger Westbrook, CMG (1986).

British Council Representative, J. Dobson, PO Box 3049, Bandar Seri Begawan 1930.

CANADA
AREA AND POPULATION

Provinces or Territories (with official contractions)	Area (Sq. Miles) Land and Water	Population	
		Census 1981	Census 1986
Alberta (Alta.)	255,285	2,237,724	2,365,825*
British Columbia (BC)	365,944	2,744,467	2,883,365*
Manitoba (Man.)	250,945	1,026,241	1,063,015*
New Brunswick (NB)	28,355	696,403	709,440*
Newfoundland and Labrador (Nfld.)	156,648	567,681	568,350
Nova Scotia (NS)	21,425	847,442	873,175*
Ontario (Ont.)	412,578	8,625,107	9,101,690*
Prince Edward Island (PEI)	2,185	122,506	126,645
Quebec (Que.)	594,855	6,438,403	6,532,460*
Saskatchewan (Sask.)	251,864	968,313	1,009,615*
Yukon Territory (YT)	186,660	23,153	23,505
Northwest Territories (NWT)	1,322,900	45,741	52,240
Total	3,849,646	24,343,181	25,309,330*

*Excludes 1986 Census data for one or more incompletely enumerated Indian reserves or Indian settlements.
Of the total immigration of 191,545 in 1989, 10,880 were from the Caribbean, 9,743 from the United Kingdom and Ireland, and 6,916 from the United States of America.

PHYSIOGRAPHY

Canada was originally discovered by Cabot in 1497, but its history dates only from 1534, when the French took possession of the country. The first permanent settlement at Port Royal (now Annapolis), Nova Scotia, was founded in 1605, and Quebec was founded in 1608. In 1759 Quebec was captured by the British forces under General Wolfe, and in 1763 the whole territory of Canada became a possession of Great Britain by the Treaty of Paris of that year. Nova Scotia was ceded in 1713 by the Treaty of Utrecht, the Provinces of New Brunswick and Prince Edward Island being subsequently formed out of it. British Columbia was formed into a Crown colony in 1858, having previously been a part of the Hudson Bay

Mother Tongues of the Population

	1981	1986
Single Responses		
English	14,684,365	15,334,085
French	6,127,530	6,159,740
Non-Official Languages	2,933,305	2,860,570
Cree	60,845	57,645
Inuktitut	18,650	21,050
Ojibway	17,605	16,380
Multiple Responses		
English and French	208,245	332,610
English and non-official language(s)	325,530	525,720
French and non-official language(s)	22,255	36,310
English, French and non-official language(s)	29,475	46,585
Non-official languages	12,485	13,715
Total Population	24,343,180	25,309,330

Territory, and was united to Vancouver Island in 1866.

Canada occupies the whole of the northern part of the North American Continent (with the exception of Alaska), from 49° North latitude to the North Pole, and from the Pacific to the Atlantic Ocean. In Eastern Canada, the southernmost point is Middle Island in Lake Erie, at 41° 41′.

Relief.—The relief of Canada is dominated by the mountain ranges running north and south on the west side of the Continent, by the pre-Cambrian shield on the east, with, in between, the northern extension of the North American Plain. From the physiographic point of view Canada has six main divisions. These are: (1) Appalachian-Acadian Region, (2) the Canadian Shield, (3) the St. Lawrence-Great Lakes Lowland, (4) the Interior Plains, (5) the Cordilleran Region and (6) the Arctic Archipelago. The first region occupies all that part of Canada lying south-east of the St. Lawrence. In general, the relief is an alternation of highlands and lowlands and is hilly rather than mountainous. The great Canadian Shield comprises more than half the area. The interior as a whole is an undulating, low plateau (general level 1,000 to 1,500 feet), with the more rugged relief lying along the border between Northern Quebec and Labrador. Throughout the whole area water or muskeg-filled depressions separate irregular hills and ridges, 150 to 200 feet in elevation. Newfoundland, an outlying portion of the shield, consists of glaciated, low rolling terrain broken here and there by mountains.

The flat relief of the St. Lawrence-Great Lakes lowland varies from 500 feet in the east to 1,700 feet south of Georgian Bay. The most striking relief is provided by the eastward facing scarp of the Niagara escarpment (elevation 250 to 300 feet). The interior plains, comprising the Pacific Provinces, slope eastward and northward a few feet per mile. The descent from west to east is made from 5,000 feet to less than 1,000 feet in three distinct levels, with each new level being marked by an eastward facing conteau or scarp. Five fairly well-developed topographic divisions mark out the Cordilleran region of western Canada. These are: (1) coastal ranges, largely above 5,000 feet with deep fjords and glaciated valleys, (2) the interior plateau, around 3,500 feet and comparatively level, (3) the Selkirk ranges, largely above 5,000 feet, (4) the Rocky Mountains with their chain of 10,000 to 12,000 feet peaks, and (5) the Peace River or Tramontane region with its rolling diversified country.

The Arctic Archipelago, with its plateau-like character has an elevation between 500 and 1,000 feet, though in Baffin Land and Ellesmere Island the mountain ranges rise to 8,500 and 9,500 feet. Two tremendous waterway systems, the St. Lawrence and the Mackenzie, providing thousands of miles of water highway, occupy a broad area of lowland with their dominant axis following the edge of the shield.

Climate.—The climate of the eastern and central portions presents greater extremes than in corresponding latitudes in Europe, but in the southwestern portion of the Prairie Region and the southern portions of the Pacific slope the climate is milder. Spring, summer and autumn are of about seven to eight months' duration, and the winter four to five months.

GOVERNMENT

The Constitution of Canada had its source in the British North America Act of 1867 which formed a Dominion, under the name of Canada, of the four provinces: Ontario, Quebec, New Brunswick and Nova Scotia; to this Federation the other Provinces have subsequently been admitted. Under this Act Canada came into being on July 1, 1867, and under the Statute of Westminster, which received the royal assent on December 11, 1931, Canada and the Provinces were exempted (in common with other self-governing Dominions of the Commonwealth of Nations) from the operation of the Colonial Laws Validity Act, the Statute of Westminster having removed all limitations with regard to the legislative autonomy of the Dominions, except that the British North America Act could be amended in important respects only by Acts of the British Parliament.

Provinces admitted since 1867 are: Manitoba (1870), British Columbia (1871), Prince Edward Island (1873), Alberta and Saskatchewan (1905) and Newfoundland (1949).

Agreement was reached in November 1981 between the Federal and Provincial Governments (except Quebec) to patriate the Constitution so that it was amendable only in Canada. The inclusion in the Constitution of a Charter of Rights was also agreed. At the request of the Canadian Parliament, legislation was passed at Westminster and the Constitution formally patriated on April 17, 1982.

The Executive power is vested in a Governor-General appointed by the Sovereign on the advice of the Canadian Ministry, and aided by a Privy Council.

CURRENCY.—Canadian dollar (C$) of 100 cents.

FLAG.—Red maple leaf with 11 points on white square, flanked by vertical red bars one half the width of the square.

NATIONAL ANTHEM.—O Canada.

NATIONAL DAY.—July 1 (Dominion Day).

Governor General

Governor General and Commander-in-Chief, His Excellency the Rt. Hon. Ramon John Hnatyshyn, PC, CC, CMM, CD, QC.

Secretary to the Governor General, L. Amyot.

The Cabinet
(as at June 30, 1990)

Prime Minister, Rt. Hon. M. Brian Mulroney.

Secretary of State for External Affairs, Rt. Hon. C. Joseph Clark.

International Trade, Hon. John C. Crosbie.

Deputy PM, President of the Queen's Privy Council for Canada and Minister of Agriculture, Hon. Donald F. Mazankowski.

Public Works and Minister for the purposes of the Atlantic Canada Opportunities Agency Act, Hon. Elmer M. MacKay.

Energy, Mines and Resources, Hon. A. Jacob Epp.

President of the Treasury Board, Acting Minister of the Environment, Hon. Robert R. de Cotret.

National Health and Welfare, Hon. H. Perrin Beatty.

Finance, Hon. Michael H. Wilson.

Minister of State and Leader of the Government in the House of Commons, Hon. Harvie Andre.

National Revenue, Hon. Otto J. Jelinek.

Indian Affairs and Northern Development, Hon. Thomas E. Siddon.

Western Economic Diversification and Minister of State for Grains and Oilseeds, Hon. Charles J. Mayer.

National Defence, Hon. William H. McKnight.

Industry, Science and Technology, Hon. Benoit Bouchard.

Communications, Hon. Marcel Masse.

Employment and Immigration, Hon. Barbara J. McDougall.

Veterans' Affairs, Hon. Gerald S. Merrithew.

Minister of State for Employment and Immigration, and for Seniors, Hon. Monique Vézina.

Forestry, Hon. Frank Oberle.

Leader of the Government in the Senate and Minister of State for Federal-Provincial Relations, Hon. Lowell Murray.

Supply and Services, Hon. Paul W. Dick.

Solicitor General, Hon. Pierre H. Cadieux.

Minister of State for Small Businesses and Tourism, Hon. Thomas Hockin.

External Relations, Hon. Monique Landry.

Fisheries and Oceans, Hon. Bernard Valcourt.

Secretary of State of Canada and Minister of State for Multiculturalism and Citizenship, Hon. Gerry Weiner.

Transport, Hon. Douglas G. Lewis.

Consumer and Corporate Affairs, Minister of State for Agriculture, Hon. Pierre Blais.

Minister of State for Privatization and Regulatory Affairs, Hon. John Horton McDermid.

Minister of State for Indian Affairs and Northern Development, Hon. Shirley Martin.

Associate Minister of National Defence and Minister Responsible for the Status of Women, Hon. Mary Collins.

Minister of State for Housing, Hon. Alan Redway.

Science, Hon. William Charles Winegard.

Justice, and Attorney General, Hon. Kim Campbell.

Labour, and Minister of State for Transport, Hon. Jean Corbeil.

Minister of State for Finance, Hon. Gilles Loiselle.

Minister of State for Youth, and Fitness and Amateur Sport, Deputy Leader of the Government in the House of Commons, Hon. Marcel Danis.

CANADIAN HIGH COMMISSION

Macdonald House, 1 Grosvenor Square, W1X 0AB
[071–629 9492]

High Commissioner, His Excellency Donald Macdonald (1988).

Deputy High Commissioner, Gaétan Lavertu.

Ministers, J. T. Boehm (*Political and Public Affairs*); R. J. L. Berlet (*Commercial/Economic*).

Minister-Counsellor, R. Girard (*Immigration*).

BRITISH HIGH COMMISSION

80 Elgin Street, Ottawa K1P 5K7
[Ottawa 237 1530]

High Commissioner, His Excellency Brian James Proetel Fall, CMG.

Deputy High Commissioner, P. M. Newton.

Counsellor, R. T. Fell (*Economic and Commercial*).

Defence and Military Adviser, Brig. F. R. Maynard.

Naval Adviser, Cdr. J. J. Howard, MBE.

Air Adviser, Gp. Capt. M. A. Radforth.

First Secretaries, V. Welborn (*Administration*); A. Jordan; I. D. Kydd (*Commercial*); N. Penrhys-Evans; M. D'Ath (*Information*).

Cultural Affairs and British Council Representative, M. Evans.

British Council Representative in Quebec, S. Dawbarn, c/o British Consulate General, 1155 University Street, Montreal, Quebec H3B 3A7.

THE LEGISLATURE

Parliament consists of a Senate and a House of Commons. The Senate consists of 104 members, nominated by the Governor General (age limit 75). They are distributed between the various provinces thus: 24 each for Ontario and Quebec, 10 each for Nova Scotia and New Brunswick, 6 each for Newfoundland, British Columbia, Manitoba, Alberta and Saskatchewan, and 4 for Prince Edward Island, 1 for Northwest Territories and 1 for Yukon. Each Senator must be at least thirty years old, a resident in the province for which he is appointed, a natural-born or naturalized subject of the Queen, and the owner of a property qualification amounting to $4,000. The Speaker of the Senate is chosen by the Government of the day.

The House of Commons has 295 members and is elected every five years at longest. Representation by provinces is at present as follows: Newfoundland 7, Prince Edward Island 4, Nova Scotia 11, New Brunswick 10, Quebec 75, Ontario 99, Manitoba 14, Saskatchewan 14, Alberta 26, British Columbia 32, Yukon 1, Northwest Territories 2.

THE SENATE

The state of the parties in the Senate as at April 24, 1990 was Liberals 53, Progressive Conservatives 34, Independent 4, Independent Liberal 1, Vacant 12.

Speaker of the Senate, Hon. Guy Charbonneau, QC.

Clerk of the Senate and Clerk of the Parliaments, Gordon Barnhart.

THE HOUSE OF COMMONS

The state of parties in the House of Commons as at July 9, 1990, was Progressive Conservatives 158, Liberals 79, New Democratic Party 43, Independent 8, Reform Party 1, Vacant 3.

Speaker of the House of Commons, Hon. John A. Fraser.

Deputy Speaker, Andrée Champagne.

Clerk of the House of Commons, Robert Marleau.

THE JUDICATURE

The Judicature is administered by judges following the Civil Law in Quebec Province and Common Law in other Provinces. Each Province has its Court of Appeal. All Superior, County and District Court Judges are appointed by the Governor General, the others by the Lieutenant Governors of the Provinces.

The highest federal court is the Supreme Court of Canada, composed of a Chief Justice and eight puisne judges, which exercises general appellate jurisdiction throughout Canada in civil and criminal cases, and which usually holds three sessions each year. There is one other federally constituted Court, the Federal

Court of Canada, which has jurisdiction on appeals from its Trial Division, from Federal Tribunals and reviews of decisions and references by Federal Boards and Commissions. The Trial Division has jurisdiction in claims by or against the Crown, its officers or servants or Federal bodies. It also deals with inter-Provincial and Federal-Provincial disputes.

SUPREME COURT OF CANADA

Chief Justice of Canada, Rt. Hon. A. Lamer, PC.
Puisne Judges, Hons. Bertha Wilson; G. V. LaForest; Claire L'Heureux-Dube; J. Sopinka; C. Gonthier; P. Cory; Beverley McLachlin.

FEDERAL COURT OF CANADA

Chief Justice, Hon. F. Iacobucci.
Associate Chief Justice, Hon. J. A. Jerome.
Appeal Division Judges, Hons. L. Pratte; D. V. Heald; J. J. Urie; P. M. Mahoney, PC; L. Marceau; J. K. Hugesson; A. J. Stone; M. MacGuigan; Alice Desjardins; R. Décary; A. M. Linden.
Trial Division Judges, Hons. G. A. Addy; J.-E. Dubé; P. U. C. Rouleau; F. C. Muldoon; B. L. Strayer; J. C. McNair; Barbara J. Reed; P. Denault; Y. Pinard; L. M. Joyal; B. Cullen; L. A. Martin; M. A. Teitelbaum; F. U. Collier; W. A. MacKay.

VITAL STATISTICS

BIRTHS, DEATHS AND MARRIAGES 1988

Province	Births	Deaths	Marriages
Alberta	42,055	13,894	19,272
British Columbia .	42,930	22,546	24,461
Manitoba........	17,030	9,100	7,908
New Brunswick ..	9,617	5,450	5,292
Newfoundland ...	7,487	3,591	3,686
Nova Scotia	12,182	7,412	6,894
Ontario	138,066	70,679	78,533
PEI	1,977	1,112	965
Quebec...........	86,612	47,771	33,519
Saskatchewan ...	16,763	8,100	6,767
Yukon	521	136	209
NW Territories	1,555	220	222
Total......	376,795	190,011	187,728

Canada's birth rate per 1,000 population (1988) 14·5; Death Rate 7·3; Marriage Rate 7·2. Divorces 90,985 in 1987.

FINANCE

Federal Government gross general revenue and expenditure was:—

	1988–89	1989–90*
Total Revenue	C$117,988 m	C$118,896 m
Total Expenditure.....	144,752 m	149,320 m
*preliminary		

DEBT

	1987–88	1988–89
Gross Public Debt	C$342,025 m	C$373,290 m
Net Public Debt	289,046 m	318,022 m

Banking.—There were 67 chartered banks on Dec. 31, 1989, with assets of C$441,163 m (booked in Canada). Deposits were C$331,055 m. of which C$188,828 m. were personal savings.

NATIONAL DEFENCE

The Minister of National Defence has the control and management of the Canadian Armed Forces and all matters relating to National Defence establishments and works for the defence of Canada.

The Canadian Forces are organized on a functional basis to reflect the major commitments assigned by the government and are formed into National Defence Headquarters and five major Commands reporting to the Chief of the Defence Staff. The roles of the five Commands are: *Mobile Command*—Provision of ground forces for the protection of Canadian territory, combat forces in Canada for support of overseas commitments, and forces for support of United Nations or other peace-keeping operations. *Maritime Command*—Provision of sea forces for the defence of Canada, anti-submarine defence in support of NATO. Maritime Command also has operational control of Maritime aircraft. *Air Command*—Provision of operationally ready air forces to national, continental and international commitments. *Canadian Forces Communications Command*—Manages, operates and maintains strategic communications for the Canadian Forces. *Canadian Forces Europe*—Canadian Forces allocated to support NATO in Europe consisting of land and air elements.

National Defence expenditure for the fiscal year 1989–90 was estimated at C$11,340 million. Canadian Armed Forces strength at May 1990: 87,976 authorized force.

EDUCATION

Education is under the control of the Provincial Governments, the cost of the publicly controlled schools being met by local taxation, aided by provincial grants. In 1989–90 there were 15,410 publicly controlled elementary and secondary schools with 5,074,300 pupils. Of these, 1,380 were private schools with 236,500 pupils; 399 federal schools with 50,200 pupils and 21 special schools for the blind and deaf with 2,500 pupils.

In 1989–90 there were 70 degree-granting universities with a full-time enrolment of 513,900, as well as 315,150 students in 198 other post-secondary, non-university institutions.

PRODUCTION

Agriculture.—About 7 per cent of the total land area of Canada is classified as farm land and approximately half of this is under cultivation, the remainder being woodland or suitable only for grazing purposes. More than three-quarters of the land now cultivated is found in the prairie region of Western Canada. Farm cash receipts from the sale of farm products in 1989 were C$22,415,599,000. Livestock and animal products contributed C$10,778,072,000; field crops C$8,397,607,000.

Grain crop production ('000 tonnes):

	1988	1989
Wheat	15,996·1	24,382·9
Oats	2,993·1	3,548·9
Barley	10,212·3	11,672·4
Rye	267·9	835·4
Flaxseed	372·9	530·6
Canola	4,311·0	3,057·6
Total...............	34,153·3	44,027·8

Livestock.—In July 1989 the livestock included 22,199,100 cattle, 10,763,000 pigs, 728,900 sheep and lambs and 21,940,000 chickens (layers).

Fur Production.—Canada in 1988–89 produced pelts valued at C$75,821,116. Wild life pelts made up 44·9 per cent of the total, with a value of C$34,045,682.

Fisheries.—The marketed value of catches in 1988 was C$3,202,927,000 (revised).

Forestry.—About 43 per cent of the total land area

is considered as inventoried forest area. The value of shipments from forestry related industries in 1987 was: logging $6,668,140,000; sawmill and planing mill products $8,862,110,000; shingle and shake $226,780,000; veneer and plywood $1,147,402,000; pulp and paper $18,384,814,000; paper and allied products $23,993,462,000.

Minerals.—In 1988, Canada was the world's largest producer of zinc and uranium, and the second largest of asbestos, potash, gypsum and titanium concentrate. The country is also rich in many other minerals, including gold, silver, copper, cobalt, lead, molybdenum, platinum group metals, elemental sulphur and titanium concentrates.

	1988	1989
	('000 tonnes)	
Copper	758·5	706·1
Nickel	198·7	196·1
Lead	351·1	275·8
Molybdenum........	13·5	13·7
Zinc	1,370·0	1,315·2
Iron Ore.............	39,934·0	40,773·0
Asbestos............	710·0	619·0
Gypsum	9,512·0	8,457·0
Cement	12,350·0	12,550·0
Lime	2,518·0	2,616·0
Salt	10,687·0	11,350·0
Potash	8,154·0	7,036·0

Production of gold was 158,440,000 grams in 1989 and of silver 1,262,000 kg. Uranium production in 1989 was 11,564,000 kilograms.

TRADE

Merchandise imports into Canada in 1989 were valued at C$135,033 million and merchandise exports (including re-exports) at C$138,339 million. The main exports in 1989 were passenger automobiles and chassis, motor vehicle parts (except engines), trucks, truck tractors and chassis, wood pulp and similar pulp, newsprint paper, softwood lumber, crude petroleum and aluminium (including alloys). Trade with the USA accounts for about 69·9 per cent of total trade in merchandise, although efforts are being made to develop alternative markets. Value of trade with Canada's largest trading partners in 1989 was as follows (C$'000):

Country	Imports	Domestic Exports*
United States	87,914,306	97,930,009
Japan	9,549,626	8,749,572
United Kingdom	4,566,034	3,422,828
Germany, Fed. Rep. of .	3,704,270	1,800,099
Korea, Rep. of	2,440,953	1,592,343
France	2,019,868	1,266,985

*Excluding re-exports

Trade with UK

	1988	1989
Imports from UK	£2,038,433,000	£2,165,731,000
Exports to UK	2,038,245,000	2,174,334,000

COMMUNICATIONS

Railways.—The total track of railways in operation on Dec. 31, 1988, was 91,365 km. In 1988 freight transportation was 271,044,894,000 tonne-kilometres, and the balance of property accounts at end 1988 was C$18,187,658 million.

Shipping.—The registered shipping on Jan. 1, 1988 including inland vessels, was 39,699 vessels with gross tonnage 5,221,481. The volume of international shipping handled at Canadian ports in 1988 was 171,064,410 metric tonnes loaded and 78,911,838 metric tonnes unloaded.

Canals.—The bulk of canal shipping in Canada is handled through the two sections of the St. Lawrence Seaway, which provide access to the Great Lakes for ocean-going ships. In 1989, transits on the Montreal-Lake Ontario section numbered 2,768 for a total of 37,070,370 cargo tonnes; transits in the Welland Canal section numbered 3,598 for a total of 39,909,450 cargo tonnes. Principal commodities carried were iron ore, wheat, corn, barley, soybeans, fuel oil, manufactured iron and steel, coal and coke.

Civil Aviation.—The number of passengers carried in 1988 (all major Canadian carriers) was 36,014,000; 1,600,522,000 tonne-km of freight was carried in 1988.

Motor Vehicles.—Total motor vehicle registrations numbered 16,336,261 in 1988.

Post.—Post office revenue in the fiscal year 1988–89 was C$3,411 m.; total expenditure C$3,313 m.

FEDERAL CAPITAL

OTTAWA, the federal capital, 111 miles west of Montreal and 247 miles north-east of Toronto, is a city on the south bank of the Ottawa river. The city was chosen as the capital of the Province of Canada in 1857 and was later selected as the site of the Dominion capital. Ottawa contains the Parliamentary Buildings, the Public Archives, Royal Mint, several national museums, the National Art Gallery and the Dominion Observatory.

Manufacturing is also carried on, medical advancement, high technology (communications, defence), printing and publishing being of greatest importance. Ottawa is connected with Lake Ontario by the Rideau Canal. The City population was 300,763 at the Census of 1986; and Metropolitan Ottawa 819,263.

YUKON TERRITORY

The area of the Territory is 186,660 sq. miles (483,450 sq. km), with a population (1989 preliminary estimate) of 29,154. Minerals and tourism are the chief industries, followed closely by transportation, communications and other utilities industry.

Seat of Government, Whitehorse, population (1989 preliminary estimate) 20,298.

The Yukon Act, 1970, as amended, provides for the administration of the Territory by a Commissioner acting under instructions from time to time given by the Governor-in-Council or the Minister of Indian Affairs and Northern Development. Legislative powers, analogous to those of a provincial government, are exercised by a Legislative Assembly of 16 members elected from electoral districts in the Territory. The Executive Council of the Assembly consists of the government leader as chairman and four elected members.

Commissioner, J. K. McKinnon.

EXECUTIVE COUNCIL
(as at June 30, 1990)

Government Leader, Minister of the Executive Council Office, Health and Human Resources, Minister responsible for the Yukon Development Corporation, Hon. Tony Penikett.

House Leader, Minister of Education, Finance, Economic Development, Mines and Small Business, Hon. Piers McDonald.

Justice, Minister responsible for the Public Service Commission, the Workers' Compensation Board, the Women's Directorate, Hon. Margaret Joe.

Renewable Resources, Tourism, and the Yukon Liquor Corporation, Hon. Art Webster.

Community and Transportation Services, Yukon Housing Corporation, Hon. Maurice Byblow.

NORTHWEST TERRITORIES

The area of the Northwest Territories is 1,322,900 sq. miles (3,426,320 sq. km), with a population (1989 preliminary estimate) of 53,326. The chief industry is mining, with a total value of $956,897,000 in 1988. Lead, zinc, gold, silver, oil exploration and natural gas contributed about 36 per cent of the 1988 GDP of the Northwest Territories.

The Northwest Territories are subdivided into the districts of Mackenzie, Keewatin and Franklin.

Seat of Government, Yellowknife, population (1989 preliminary estimate) 13,511.

The Northwest Territories Act 1979, as amended, provides for a Legislative Assembly of 24 elected members, of which the Executive Council under the chairmanship of the government leader is the senior decision-making body of the government in the Territory.

Commissioner, D. L. Norris.

EXECUTIVE COUNCIL
(as at June 30, 1990)

Government Leader, Minister responsible for the Executive, for the NWT Science Institute, the Devolution Office and Minister of Intergovernmental Affairs, Hon. Dennis Patterson.

Culture and Communications, Renewable Resources, Associate Minister of Aboriginal Rights and Constitutional Development, Hon. Titus Allooloo.

House Leader, Minister of Finance, Justice and Public Utilities Board, Hon. Michael Ballantyne.

Health, Energy, Mines and Petroleum Resources, Public Works and Highways, Hon. Nellie Cournoyee.

Education, Aboriginal Rights and Constitutional Development, Safety and Public Services, Minister responsible for Workers' Compensation Board, Hon. Stephen Kakfwi.

Social Services, Personnel, Equal Employment Directorate, Women's Secretariat, and the Highway Transport Board, Hon. Jeannie Marie-Jewell.

Government Services, and the NWT Housing Corporation, Hon. Tom Butters.

Municipal and Community Affairs, Economic Development and Tourism, Transportation, Hon. Gordon Wray.

PROVINCES OF CANADA

ALBERTA

Area and Population.—The Province of Alberta has an area of 661,185 sq. km (255,285 sq. miles), including about 6,485 sq. miles of water (16,796 sq. km), with a population (April 1990) of 2,458,600.

Government.—The Government is vested in a Lieutenant Governor and Legislative Assembly composed of 83 members, elected for five years, representing 83 electoral districts in the Province. At a provincial election held on March 20, 1989, the Progressive Conservative Party took 59 seats, the New Democratic Party 16 seats and the Liberal Party 8 seats.

Lt. Governor, Her Honour Helen Hunley.

EXECUTIVE
(as at June 30, 1990)

Premier, President of Executive Council, Hon. Don Getty

Deputy Premier and Minister of Federal and Intergovernmental Affairs, Government House Leader, Hon. Jim Horsman.

Provincial Treasurer, Hon. Dick Johnston.

Transportation and Utilities, Hon. Al Adair.

Forestry, Lands and Wildlife, Hon. LeRoy Fjordbotten.

Economic Development and Trade, Hon. Peter Elzinga.

Energy, Hon. Rick Orman.

Agriculture, Hon. Ernie Isley.

Health, Hon. Nancy Betkowski.

Attorney General, Hon. Ken Rostad.

Technology, Research and Telecommunications, Hon. Fred Stewart.

Public Works, Supply and Services, Hon. Ken Kowalski.

Career Development and Employment, Hon. Norm Weiss.

Education, Hon. Jim Dinning.

Tourism, Hon. Don Sparrow.

Labour, Hon. Elaine McCoy.

Consumer and Corporate Affairs, Hon. Dennis Anderson.

Family and Social Services, Hon. John Oldring.

Associate Minister of Family and Social Services, Hon. R. Brassard.

Occupational Health and Safety, Workers' Compensation Board, Hon. Peter Trynchy.

Advanced Education and Deputy House Leader, Hon. John Gogo.

Recreation and Parks, Hon. Steve West.

Associate Minister of Agriculture, Hon. Shirley McClellan.

Municipal Affairs, Hon. Ray Speaker.

Environment, Hon. Ralph Klein.

Solicitor General, Hon. Dick Fowler.

Culture and Multiculturalism, Hon. Doug Main.

Agent-General in London, Mary LeMessurier, Alberta House, 1 Mount Street, W1Y 5AA.

THE JUDICATURE

Court of Appeal of Alberta, Chief Justice, Hon. J. H. Laycraft.

Court of Queen's Bench of Alberta, Chief Justice, Hon. W. K. Moore.

Associate Chief Justice, Hon. T. H. Miller.

ECONOMY

The total GDP at factor cost in 1988 (preliminary figures) amounted to C$61,411 million. Preliminary estimates for mineral production in 1988 came to C$14,906,395,000. Of this total, crude oil amounted to C$7,724,165,000, and natural gas and its by-products to C$5,974,265,000.

Manufacturing.—The total value of manufacturing shipments (1988) was C$17,924,824,000. Number of industrial establishments 2,747 (1986), total employees 53,268 (1986). The leading industrial products are refined petroleum and coal products, meat and meat products, chemicals and chemical products, fabricated metal products, non-metallic mineral products and primary metals.

GOVERNMENT FINANCE
Budgetary Estimates

	1988–89	1989–90
Revenue	C$9,129 m	C$10,181 m
Expenditure	10,867 m	11,674 m
Deficit	1,738 m	1,493 m

NOTE: The Budgetary revenue figure does not include funds allocated to the Alberta Heritage Savings Trust Fund.

CAPITAL.—Edmonton—city population (1988) 576,249, metropolitan area, 783,909. Other centres are Calgary (657,118), Lethbridge (66,610), Red Deer (54,839), Medicine Hat (42,290), St. Albert (38,318), Fort McMurray (34,949).

BRITISH COLUMBIA

Area and Population.—British Columbia has a total area estimated at 947,790 sq. km (365,944 sq. miles), with a population of 3,053,300 (June 1989).

Government.—The Government consists of a Lieutenant Governor and an Executive Council together with a Legislative Assembly of 57 members.

The Social Credit Party formed a government after a General Election on October 22, 1986. The present standing in the Assembly is Social Credit Party 34, New Democratic Party 22, Independent 1.

Lt. Governor, His Honour Dr. David See-Chai Lam.

EXECUTIVE COUNCIL
(as at May 31, 1990)

Premier and President of the Council, Hon. William N. Vander Zalm.
Regional and Economic Development, Hon. Stanley Hagen.
Attorney-General, Hon. Stuart D. Smith, QC.
Forests, Hon. Claude H. Richmond.
Finance and Corporate Relations, Hon. Melville B. Couvelier.
Agriculture and Fisheries, Hon. John Savage.
Energy, Mines and Petroleum Resources, Hon. John Davis, PC.
Education, Hon. Anthony J. Brummet.
Labour and Consumer Services, Hon. Norman Jacobsen.
Municipal Affairs, Recreation and Culture, Hon. Lyall Hanson.
Health, Hon. John Jansen.
Social Services and Housing, Hon. Peter H. Dueck.
Transportation and Highways, Hon. Rita M. Johnston.
Environment, Hon. John Reynolds.
Parks, Hon. Ivan Messmer.
Crown Lands, Hon. David F. H. Parker.
Native Affairs, Hon. Jack Weisgerber.
International Business and Immigration, Hon. Elwood Veitch.
Government Management Services and Minister responsible for Women's Programs, Hon. Carol Gran.
Solicitor General, Hon. Russ Fraser.
Tourism, Hon. Cliff Michael.
Provincial Secretary, Hon. Howard Dirks.
Speaker, Legislative Assembly, Hon. John D. Reynolds

Agent-General in London, G. Gardom, QC; British Columbia House, 1 Regent Street, SW1 4NR.

THE JUDICATURE

Court of Appeal, Chief Justice of British Columbia, Hon. A. McEachern.
Supreme Court, Chief Justice, Hon. W. A. Esson.
Associate Chief Justice, Hon. D. H. Campbell.

FINANCE

	1989–90	1990–91
Estimated Revenue	C$13,502·0 m	C$15,260·0 m
Estimated Expenditure	13,362·0 m	15,260·0 m
Net Guaranteed Debt ..	7,247·9 m	6,965·1 m

ECONOMY

Production and Industry.—Manufacturing activity is based largely on the processing of the output of the logging, mineral, fishing and agriculture industries. The principal manufacturing centres are

Vancouver, New Westminster, Victoria, North Vancouver, Kelowna and Prince George. Forestry and forest-based industries form the most important economic activity, accounting for approximately 40 per cent of total production. British Columbia is the leading province of Canada in the quantity and value of its timber and sawmill products. Mining, the second most important non-service economic activity, is based on copper, zinc, lead, iron concentrates, molybdenum, coal, natural gas, crude petroleum, asbestos, gold and silver. Molybdenum production is approximately 99 per cent of the Canadian total.

The production levels for important industries were estimated for 1989 as follows:—

Lumber	35,951,600 cu. metres
Paper	2,851,600 tonnes
Pulp	6,990,400 tonnes
Coal	24,281,800 tonnes
Natural Gas	12,816,800,000 cu. metres

Mineral production for 1989 was valued at C$4,162·6 million.

The most important agricultural products are livestock, eggs and poultry, fruits and dairy products. Salmon accounts for approximately 60 per cent of the value of fisheries. Other species include halibut, herring, sole, cod, flounder, perch, tuna and shellfish. In 1989 farm cash receipts were valued at C$1,152·8 million.

The economy is dependent upon markets outside the province for the disposal of most of the products of industry. An estimated 55–60 per cent of production is exported to foreign markets. Manufacturing shipments in 1989 were valued at C$25,854·3 million.

Transport.—The Province has deep water harbours which are well serviced by railways and modern highways. Vancouver is the base for regular scheduled air routes to other parts of Canada, the United States, Europe, Mexico, South America, Hawaii, Fiji, Australia, Japan, Hong Kong and the Middle East.

CAPITAL.—ΨVictoria, metropolitan population (1989) 273,242. ΨVancouver, metropolitan population (1989) 1,498,980, possesses one of the finest natural harbours in the world, servicing a variety of vessels, including large bulk cargo carriers. Other principal cities are Prince George, Kamloops, Kelowna and Nanaimo.

MANITOBA

Area and Population.—Manitoba, originally the Red River settlement, is the central province of Canada. The Province has a considerable area of prairie land but is also a land of wide diversity combining 645 kilometres (401 miles) of coastline on Hudson Bay, large lakes and rivers covering an area of 101,592 sq. km (39,225 sq. miles) and pre-cambrian rock which covers about three-fifths of the Province. The total area is 649,947 sq. km (250,946 sq. miles), with a population (1987 estimate) of 1,082,800.

Government.—The Lieutenant Governor is The Queen's personal representative in Manitoba. There is a Legislative Assembly of 57 members, of which the Executive Council of Ministers are all members.

The Progressive Conservatives formed a minority government after a General Election held on April 26, 1988. The standing in the House at July 7, 1989 was: Progressive Conservatives 24, Liberal 21, New Democratic Party 12.

Lt. Governor, His Honour George Johnson.

EXECUTIVE COUNCIL
(as at May 31, 1990)

Premier, President of the Executive Council and Minister of Federal-Provincial Relations, Hon. Gary A. Filmon.
Natural Resources, Hon. Harry J. Enns.

Northern and Native Affairs and Seniors, Hon. James E. Downey.
Health, Hon. Donald W. Orchard.
Highways and Transportation, and Government Services, Hon. Albert Driedger.
Finance, Hon. Clayton S. Manness.
Family Services, Hon. Charlotte L. Oleson.
Environment, Hon. James G. Cummings.
Attorney-General, Minister for Constitutional Affairs and Corrections, Hon. James C. McCrae.
Co-operative, Consumer and Corporate Affairs, Hon. Edward J. Connery.
Industry, Trade and Tourism, Hon. James A. Ernst.
Agriculture, Hon. Glen M. Findlay.
Education and Training, Hon. Leonard Derkach.
Urban Affairs and Housing, Hon. Gerald Ducharme.
Culture, Heritage and Recreation, Hon. Bonnie E. Mitchelson.
Rural Development, Hon. John Penner.
Energy and Mines, Hon. Harold J. Neufeld.
Labour, the Status of Women, Hon. Gerrie Hammond.

THE JUDICATURE

Court of Appeal, Chief Justice, vacant.
Queen's Bench Division, Chief Justice, Hon. B. Hewak.
Associate Chief Justices, Hon. R. J. Scott (*QBD*), Hon. A. C. Hamilton (*Family Division*).

ECONOMY

Finance.—The projected revenue for the province in the fiscal year 1989–90 was C$4,679 million while expenditures were forecast at C$4,766 million.

Agriculture.—The total land area in Manitoba is 135,342,565 acres, of which 19,126,517 acres are in occupied farms. The gross value of agriculture production in 1988 was estimated at C$1,800 million.

Manufactures.—Manufacturing enterprises employed about 63,000 persons on average in 1988. The chief manufacturing centres are Winnipeg, Brandon, Selkirk and Portage la Prairie. The largest manufacturing industry is the food and beverage industry, followed by the machinery and metal fabricating industries.

CAPITAL.—Winnipeg, population 614,400 (1987 estimate). Other cities are Brandon (38,708), Thompson (14,701), Portage la Prairie (13,198) and Flin Flon (7,243).

NEW BRUNSWICK

Area and Population.—New Brunswick is situated between 45°–48° N. lat. and 63° 47′–69° W. long. and comprises an area of 73,439 sq. km (28,355 sq. miles), with a population (June 1989) of 718,600. It was first colonized by British subjects in 1761, and in 1783 by inhabitants of New England, who had been dispossessed of their property in consequence of their loyalty to the British Crown. New Brunswick entered Confederation in 1867.

Government.—Government is administered by a Lieutenant Governor, an Executive Council, and a Legislative Assembly of 58 members elected by the people. The present Legislative Assembly of the Province was elected on Oct. 13, 1987 and has 58 members, all of whom are from the Liberal Party.
Lt. Governor, His Honour Gilbert Finn.

EXECUTIVE
(as at June 30, 1990)

Premier, Hon. Frank McKenna.
Justice, Hon. James Lockyer.
Transportation, Hon. Sheldon Lee.
Agriculture, Hon. Alan Graham.
Commerce and Technology, Hon. Al Lacey.

Health and Community Services, Hon. Raymond Frenette.
Minister of State for Child Services, Hon. Jane Barry.
Education, Hon. Shirley Dysart.
Advanced Education and Training, Hon. Russell King.
Labour, Hon. Michael McKee.
Finance, Hon. Allan Maher.
Environment, Hon. Vaughn Blaney.
Municipal Affairs, Hon. Hubert Seamans.
Fisheries and Aquaculture, Hon. Denis Losier.
Tourism, Recreation and Heritage, Hon. Roland Beaulieu.
Chairman, Board of Management, Hon. Gérald Clavette.
Supply and Services, Hon. Bruce Smith.
Natural Resources and Energy, Hon. Morris Green.
Minister of State for Mines, Hon. Edmond Blanchard.
Income Assistance, Hon. Laureen Jarrett.
Housing, Hon. Peter Trites.
Minister responsible for Intergovernmental Affairs, Hon Aldéa Landry.
Speaker of the House, Hon. Frank Branch.
Solicitor General, Hon. Joseph-Conrad Landry.
Chairman, NB Electric Power Commission, Hon. Rayburn Doucett.

THE JUDICATURE

Court of Appeal, Chief Justice, Hon. S. G. Stratton.
Queen's Bench Division, Chief Justice, Hon. G. A. Richard.

ECONOMY

Finance.—The estimated revenue for the year ending March 31, 1989, was C$3,264,094,800 and ordinary expenditure, $3,297,778,113.

Manufactures.—New Brunswick's largest manufacturing group, in terms of shipments, is the paper and allied industries, followed by the food and wood industries. Together these industries accounted in 1989 for 57·3 per cent of the total value of manufacturing shipments of C$6,152 million. Saint John has a major ice-free port and is the principal manufacturing centre of the Province.

Agriculture.—Total land area 27,633 sq. miles; farms numbered 3,554 and averaged 284 acres each in 1986. Dairy products and potatoes are the leading agricultural products. Both industries together accounted for 49·3 per cent of total farm cash receipts in 1989. Farm cash receipts in 1989 totalled C$272,059,000.

Fisheries.—Fishing is an important industry, employing about 7,900 fishermen. The chief commercial fish are lobsters, herring, tuna, crab and cod. Landings reached 150,846 tonnes valued at C$87,728,000 in 1989.

Minerals.—Extensive zinc, lead and copper deposits are now being mined in the north-eastern part of the province with New Brunswick being the third largest producer of zinc in Canada. A lead smelter, fertilizer plant and port facilities have been constructed at Belledune. Canada's only primary antimony producer is located at Lake George. There is exploration and development near Sussex and Salt Springs, where potash production continues to escalate. A potash terminal has been built at the port of St. John. Coal is mined at Grand Lake and exploration for other deposits is being undertaken. Total mineral production was valued at C$909,547,000 in 1989.

Tourism.—Tourism is of increasing value to the economy.

CAPITAL.—Fredericton, population (1986), 65,768. Other cities are ΨSaint John (121,265); Moncton (102,084); Bathurst (34,895); Edmundston (22,614); Campbellton (17,418).

NEWFOUNDLAND AND LABRADOR

Area and Population.—The Island of Newfoundland is situated between 46° 37′–51° 37′ N. latitude and 52° 44′–59° 30′ W. longitude, on the north-east side of the Gulf of St. Lawrence, and is separated from the North American continent by the Straits of Belle Isle on the NW and by Cabot Strait on the SW. The island is about 510 km long and 508 km broad and is triangular in shape. It comprises an area of 111,390 sq. km (43,008 sq. miles), with a population (1986 Census) (inclusive of Labrador) of 568,349.

Labrador forms the most easterly part of the North American continent, and extends from Point St. Charles, at the north-east entrance to the Straits of Belle Isle, on the south, to Cape Chidley, at the eastern entrance to Hudson's Straits on the north. It has an area of 294,328 sq. km (113,641 sq. miles), with a population (1986 Census) of 28,741. Labrador is noted for its cod fisheries and also possesses valuable salmon, herring, trout and seal fisheries.

Government.—On March 31, 1949 Newfoundland became the 10th Province of the Dominion of Canada. The Government is administered by a Lieutenant Governor, aided by an Executive Council and a Legislative Assembly of 52 members elected for a term of five years. A General Election was held on April 20, 1989. The standings in the current House of Assembly are : Liberals 32 ; Progressive Conservatives 20.

Lt. Governor, His Honour James A. McGrath.

EXECUTIVE
(as at June 30, 1990)

Premier, Hon. Clyde Wells.
Treasury Board President, Hon. Winston Baker.
Fisheries, Hon. Walter Carter.
Employment, Hon. Patt Cowan.
Health, Hon. Chris Decker.
Justice, Hon. Paul Dicks.
Social Services, Hon. John Efford.
Forestry, Hon. Graham Flight.
Development, Hon. Chuck Furey.
Mines and Energy, Hon. Rex Gibbons.
Works, Services and Transportation, Hon. Dave Gilbert.
Municipal and Provincial Affairs, Hon. Eric Gullage.
Environment and Lands, Hon. Jim Kelland.
Finance, Hon. Hubert Kitchen.
Education, Hon. Philip Warren.
Speaker of the House of Assembly, Hon. Thomas Lush.
Clerk of the Executive Council, H. H. Stanley.

THE JUDICATURE

Court of Appeal, Chief Justice, Hon. Noel H. A. Goodridge.
Trial Division, Chief Justice, Hon. T. A. Hickman.

ECONOMY

Finance.—The estimated gross capital and current account revenues for 1990–91 are C$2,962,081,000 and the gross current and capital account expenditures C$3,319,357,400.

Production and Industry.—The main primary industries are fishing, forestry and mining. In 1985 shipments of fish products were valued at C$465 million. In 1989 newsprint shipments from the three pulp and paper mills were valued at C$496 million, mining plus structural materials shipments were estimated at C$959 million, of which C$788 million was from the two iron ore mines in Labrador. Total manufacturing shipments were valued at C$1,510 million in 1989. The hydro-electric plant on the Churchill river is the largest underground plant in the world, with a capacity of 5,225,000 Kw.

Petroleum and Natural Gas.—Over 138 wells have been drilled off Newfoundland since 1965. Discovery of oil was made in 1979 on the Grand Banks. Oil production is expected to begin in the 1990s, with a peak production of 110,000 barrels of oil a day. In 1989 offshore exploration expenditure was approximately C$54 million

Transport.—The Province is connected to mainland Canada by a ferry service from North Sydney, Nova Scotia to Port aux Basques and Argentina. An official agreement on June 20, 1988 signified the end of the railway in Newfoundland. Transport between various points on the island is by highway but the south coast and Labrador still rely on the coastal boat service.

CAPITAL.—ꟼSt. John's (population 1986 Census, Greater St. John's 161,901) is North America's oldest city, and thus of historical interest and is the seat of the provincial legislature, the site of most provincial and federal government offices and the principal port for the island of Newfoundland. Newfoundland's second city of Corner Brook (population 1986 Census, 22,719) is situated on the west coast, its principal industry being its pulp and paper mill.

NOVA SCOTIA

Area and Population.—Nova Scotia is a peninsula between 43° 25′–47° N. lat. and 59° 40′–66° 25′ W. long., and is connected to New Brunswick by a low fertile isthmus about 28 km wide. It comprises an area of 55,490 sq. km (21,425 sq. miles), including 2,650 sq. km of lakes and rivers and 10,424 km of shoreline. No place is more than 56 km from the Atlantic Ocean. Population (April 1990 estimate) 886,800.

Government.—The Government consists of a Lieutenant Governor and a 52-member elected Legislative Assembly, from which the Executive Council is selected. The state of the parties in June 1990 was Conservatives 28, Liberals 21, New Democratic Party 2 and 1 vacant.

The Lieutenant Governor represents the Queen and is appointed by the Governor-in-Council.

Lt. Governor, His Honour Lloyd R. Crouse, PC.

EXECUTIVE COUNCIL
(as at June 30, 1990)

Premier, Hon. John M. Buchanan, PC, QC.
Deputy Premier and Minister for Housing, Hon. Roger S. Bacon.
Mines and Energy, Hon. John A. MacIssac.
Tourism and Culture, Hon. Roland J. Thornhill.
Industry, Trade and Technology, Hon. Donald W. Cameron.
Small Business Development, Hon. Kenneth Streatch.
Education, Hon. Ronald C. Giffin, QC.
Management Board, Government Services, Hon. Terence R. B. Donahoe, QC.
Attorney General, Hon. Thomas J. McInnis.
Advanced Education and Job Training, Hon. Joel R. Matheson, QC.
Labour, Hon. Ronald S. Russell.
Finance, Hon. Greg Kerr.
Environment, Hon. John G. Leefe.
Transportation and Communications, Hon. George C. Moody.
Health and Fitness, Hon. David Nantes.
Community Services, Hon. Guy J. LeBlanc.
Municipal Affairs, Hon. Brian A. Young.
Fisheries, Hon. Donald P. McInnes.
Consumer Affairs, Hon. Colin D. Stewart.
Agriculture and Marketing, Hon. George Archibald.
Lands and Forests, Hon. Charles W. MacNeil.
Solicitor General and Provincial Secretary, Hon. Neil J. LeBlanc.

Speaker of the House of Assembly, Hon. Arthur R. Donahoe, QC.

Clerk of the Executive Council, H. F. G. Stevens, QC.

Agent-General in London, Donald M. Smith, 14 Pall Mall, SW1Y 5LU.

THE JUDICATURE

Supreme Court, Appeal Division, Chief Justice, Hon. L. O. Clarke.

Trial Division, Chief Justice, Hon. Constance R. Glube.

ECONOMY

Finance.—The revenue for the fiscal year ending March 31, 1989 was C$3,411,924 and expenditure was C$3,526,635.

Manufacturing.—Manufacturing constitutes the most important goods producing sector of the economy. Manufacturing plants provide employment for 12.3 per cent of the labour force.

Utilities.—Electric power in Nova Scotia is supplied by the Nova Scotia Power Corporation, a Crown corporation. The Corporation's generating stations, which are predominantly coal fired have a nameplate capacity of 1,964,305 kilowatts.

Petroleum Activity.—By mid-1988 a total of 125 wells had been completed off-shore since drilling began in 1967, the drilling being done by five major operations. There was one well drilled onshore in 1989–90.

Mining.—The total value of mineral production in 1989 (preliminary) was estimated at C$499 million. Dollar value of coal production was C$200 million, and salt production C$63,176,000.

Agriculture.—About 3 per cent of the total area, or 390,000 acres, is classified as farm land. Ranch-raised fur and frozen blueberries are the largest foreign exports.

Fishing.—A total of 580,000 tonnes of fish and shellfish was harvested in 1989 for a landed value of C$427 million.

Forestry.—Forest lands total 10,000,000 acres or 73 per cent of the land area. About 71 per cent of forest land is privately owned. Forest based industries employed an average of 9,000 in 1989.

Tourism.—Between May 15 and October 31, 1989, about 1·2 million visitors spent about C$260 million in the Province.

CAPITAL.—ΨHalifax, including the neighbouring city of Dartmouth, has a population of 178,820. The harbour, ice-free all year round, is the main Atlantic winter port of Canada. Other cities and towns include ΨSydney (27,754), ΨGlace Bay (20,467), Amherst (9,671) and New Glasgow (10,022).

Cape Breton Island

This has been part of Nova Scotia since 1819. It is the centre of the steel manufacturing and coal mining industries, and is also noted for its lakes and coastal scenery, making it a tourist attraction in Canada.

ONTARIO

Area and Population.—The Province of Ontario contains a total area of 1,068,572 sq. km (412,578 sq. miles), with a population (1986 Census) of 9,113,515.

Government.—The Government is vested in a Lieutenant Governor and a Legislative Assembly of 125 members elected for five years.

After the last election on September 10, 1987, there were 95 Liberals, 19 New Democrats and 16 Progressive Conservatives.

Lt. Governor, His Honour Lincoln Alexander, PC, QC.

EXECUTIVE COUNCIL
(as at June 30, 1990)

Premier, President of the Council and Minister of Intergovernmental Affairs, Hon David Peterson.

Deputy Premier, Treasurer, Minister of Economics, Hon. Robert Nixon.

Minister of Education, Colleges and Universities and Skills Development, Hon. Sean Conway.

Environment, Hon. James Bradley.

Attorney General and Minister responsible for Native Affairs, Hon. Ian Scott.

Mines, Culture and Communications, Hon. Hugh O'Neil.

Housing and Municipal Affairs, Hon. John Sweeney.

Chairman of Management Board, Chairman of Cabinet, Minister of Financial Institutions, Hon. Murray Elston.

Transportation, Hon. William Wyre.

Industry, Trade and Technology, Hon. Monte Kwinter.

Consumer and Commercial Relations, Hon. Gregory Sorbara.

Health, Hon. Elinor Caplan.

Northern Development, Hon. Rene Fontaine.

Agriculture and Food, Hon. David Ramsay.

Government Services and House Leader, Hon. Christopher Ward.

Energy and Natural Resources, Hon. Lyn McLeod.

Correctional Services, Hon. Richard Patten.

Labour, Hon. Gerry Phillips.

Citizenship, responsible for Race Relations, Multiculturalism and Human Rights, Hon. Robert Wong.

Revenue, Hon. Remo Mancini.

Minister without Portfolio, responsible for Women's Affairs, Hon. Mavis Wilson.

Solicitor General, Hon. Steven Offer.

Community and Social Services, Minister responsible for Francophone Affairs, Hon. Charles Beer.

Tourism and Recreation, Minister responsible for Provincial Anti-Drug Strategy, Hon. Kenneth Black.

Minister without Portfolio, responsible for Senior Citizens' Affairs, Hon. Gilles Morin.

Minister without Portfolio, responsible for Disabled Persons, Hon. Shirley Collins.

Agent-General in London, T. Wells, 21 Knightsbridge, SW1X 7LY.

THE JUDICATURE

Chief Justice of Ontario, Hon. C. L. Dubin.

Chief Justice of the High Court, Hon. F. W. Callaghan.

ECONOMY

Agriculture.—Ontario has the highest total of agricultural production in Canada with a gross value of C$5,520 million and a total net farm income of C$5,460 million in 1986.

Forestry.—Productive forested lands cover 377,000 sq. km or 35·3 per cent of the land area of the Province. Paper and allied industries are by far the most important sector of Ontario's forest industry.

Minerals.—Ontario's natural resources include 15 basic minerals, such as copper, iron ore, zinc, sulphur, gold and platinum. The province has half the world's supply of nickel and the largest amount of uranium in the western world. Total value of the mineral production in 1986 was estimated at C$4,800 million.

Energy.—Total electrical energy generated in Ontario in 1985 was 121,000 million kWh (34 per cent hydro, 40 per cent nuclear and 26 per cent other conventional fossil fuels).

Manufacture.—Ontario is the chief manufacturing province in Canada, producing 50 per cent of all manufactured goods. During 1985 Ontario's exports totalled C$59,000 million, an increase in value of

C\$4,000 million over 1984. A C\$4,200 million growth in the value of end products—the sector which contains the bulk of Ontario's manufactured exports—was also achieved.

CAPITAL.—ΨToronto (metropolitan population 1986, 2,192,721) has a wide range of manufacturing and service industries and is a centre of education, business and finance. Other major urban areas are: Ottawa, the national capital (300,763); ΨHamilton (306,140), with iron and steel industry, metal fabrication, machinery, electrical and chemical industries; London (269,140), a business and manufacturing centre; ΨWindsor (193,111); Kitchener (150,604) and Sudbury (88,717).

PRINCE EDWARD ISLAND

Area and Population.—Prince Edward Island lies in the southern part of the Gulf of St. Lawrence, between 46°–47° N. lat. and 62°–64° 30′ W. long. It is about 225 km in length, and from 6 to 64 km in breadth; its area is 5,659 sq. km (2,185 sq. miles), and its population (1989) 130,000.

Government.—The Government is vested in a Lieutenant Governor, an Executive Council, and Legislative Assembly of 32 members elected for a term of up to 5 years, 16 as Councillors and 16 as Assemblymen. After the election of May 29, 1989 there were 30 Liberals and 2 Progressive Conservatives.

Lt. Governor, His Honour Lloyd G. MacPhail.

EXECUTIVE COUNCIL
(as at June 30, 1990)

Premier, President of the Executive Council, Minister of Justice and Attorney General, Hon. Joseph A. Ghiz, QC.

Finance, Environment, Hon. Gilbert R. Clements.

Community and Cultural Affairs, Fisheries and Aquaculture, Hon. Leonce Bernard.

Industry, Hon. Robert Morrissey.

Health and Social Services, Hon. Wayne Cheverie, QC.

Transportation and Public Works, Hon. Gordon MacInnis.

Agriculture, Hon. Keith Milligan.

Education, Hon. Paul Connolly.

Energy and Forestry, Hon. Barry Hicken.

Tourism and Parks, Hon. Nancy Guptill.

Labour, Hon. Roberta Hubley.

Speaker of the Legislative Assembly, Hon. Edward W. Clark.

THE JUDICATURE

Appeal Division, Chief Justice, Hon. Norman H. Carruthers.

Trial Division, Chief Justice, Hon. K. R. MacDonald.

ECONOMY

Finance.—The ordinary revenue of the Province in 1989–90 was C\$656·6 million and the expenditure C\$654·3 million.

Agriculture.—Approximately 48 per cent of the total area of the Province is farmland. The value of farm cash receipts in 1989 was C\$253.8 million, of which 46·9 per cent was from the sale of potatoes. Dairy, beef and hogs are also important agriculture products.

Fisheries.—Fish landings were valued at C\$72.4 million in 1989 of which 63·7 per cent was of lobster.

Manufacturing.—The total value of manufacturing shipments was C\$366.1 million in 1989, of which 69·4 per cent was in the food products industries and 21·4 per cent in the fish products industries.

Tourism.—A major summer economic activity is tourism. Non-resident tourists spent C\$98.3 million in the Province in 1989.

Education.—A university and a college of applied arts and technology were established in 1969, estimated full- and part-time enrolment for 1989–90 being 3,181 (University of Prince Edward Island), and 912 for the college of applied arts and technology (Holland College).

CAPITAL.—ΨCharlottetown (population July 1986 Census, 15,776), on the shore of Hillsborough Bay, which forms a good harbour.

QUEBEC

Area and Population.—The Province of Quebec contains an area estimated at 1,540,667 sq. km (594,855 sq. miles) with a population (June 1989 estimate) of 6,688,700.

Government.—The Government of the Province is vested in a Lieutenant Governor, a Council of ministers and a National Assembly of 125 members elected for five years. At September 1989, there were 92 Liberals, 29 Parti Quebecois, and 4 Equality members.

Lt. Governor, His Honour Gilles Lamontagne.

EXECUTIVE
(as at June 30, 1990)

Prime Minister, Hon. Robert Bourassa.

Deputy Premier, Energy and Resources, Regional Development, Hon. Lise Bacon.

Recreation, Fish and Game, Hon. Gaston Blackburn.

Manpower, Income Security, Hon. André Bourbeau.

Jun. minister for Cultural Communities, Hon. Normand Cherry.

International Affairs, Native Affairs, Hon. John Ciaccia.

Forests, Hon. Albert Côté.

Health and Social Services, Electoral Reform, Hon. Marc-Yvan Côté.

Supply and Services, Hon. Robert Dutil.

Transport, Public Security, Hon. Sam Elkas.

Communications, Hon. Liza Frulla-Hébert.

Cultural Communities and Immigration, Hon. Monique Gagnon-Tremblay.

Treasury Board, Hon. Daniel Johnson.

Finance, Hon. Gérard D. Levesque.

Jun. minister for Agriculture, Hon. Robert Middlemiss.

Agriculture, Fisheries and Food, House Leader, Hon. Michel Pagé.

Environment, Hon. Pierre Paradis.

Municipal Affairs, responsible for Housing, Hon. Yvon Picotte.

Justice, Intergovernmental Affairs, Hon. Gil Rémillard.

Responsible for La Francophonie, Hon. Guy Rivard.

Jun. minister for Finance, Hon. Louise Robic.

Cultural Affairs, Hon. Lucienne Robillard.

Education, Higher Education and Science, Hon. Claude Ryan.

Jun. minister for Mines and for Regional Development, Hon. Raymond Savoie.

Revenue, Labour, Hon. Yves Séguin.

Jun. minister for Health and Social Services, Hon. Christos Sirros.

Industry, Trade and Technology, Hon. Gérald Tremblay.

Jun. minister for the Status of Women and for the Family, Hon. Violette Trépanier.

Tourism, Hon. André Vallerand.

Jun. minister for Transport, Hon. Yvon Vallières.

Agent-General in London, Reed Scowen, 59 Pall Mall, SW1Y 5JH.

THE JUDICATURE

Court of Appeal, Chief Justice of Quebec, Hon. Claude Bisson.

Superior Court, Chief Justice of Quebec (Montreal), Hon. Pierre F. Coté.

Finance.—The revenue for the year 1987–88 was C\$28,363,891,000; expenditure amounted to C\$30,738,141,000.

Production and Industry.—The principal manufacturing centres are Montreal, Montreal East, Quebec, Trois-Rivières, Sherbrooke, Shawinigan Drummondville and Lachine. Forest lands cover 779,256 sq. km, of which 556,044 sq. km are productive.

Total estimated value of shipments in the manufacturing industries in 1989 was C\$73,994 million. Value of 1989 shipments in the chief industries was accounted for by food, C\$9,239 million; paper and allied industries, C\$8,032 m; primary metal industries, C\$7,131 m, and transport equipment, C\$6,866 m.

Agriculture and Fisheries.—In 1989 total farm receipts were:

Crops .... C\$679,360,000
Livestock and livestock products..... 2,484,134,000
Other farm receipts................. 509,675,000

In 1989 79,101 tonnes of fish, to the value of C\$79,467,000 were landed.

Mineral Production.—Minerals to the value of C\$2,721,380,000 were mined in 1988. This included copper, \$145,127,000; asbestos, C\$190,285,000; and gold, C\$562,868,000.

CAPITAL.—ΨQuebec. Population (Census 1986) 164,580; historic city visited annually by thousands of tourists, and one of the great seaport towns of Canada. ΨMontreal (1,015,420) is the commercial metropolis. Other important cities are Laval (284,164); Verdun (60,246), Sherbrooke (74,438), Montreal-Nord (90,303) and La Salle (75,621).

SASKATCHEWAN

Area and Population.—The Province of Saskatchewan lies between Manitoba to the east and Alberta to the west and has an area of 652,324 sq. km (251,864 sq. miles) (of which the land area is 570,269 sq. km, or 220,182 sq. miles), with a population (estimated 1988) of 1,012,800. Saskatchewan extends along the Canada–USA boundary for 632 km (393 miles) and northwards for 1,224 km (761 miles). Its northern width is 440 km (276 miles).

Government.—The Government is vested in the Lieutenant Governor, with a Legislative Assembly of 64 members. There is an Executive Council of 18 members. The Legislative Assembly is elected for 5 years and the state of the parties in June 1990 was: Progressive Conservative 36; New Democratic Party 26; vacancies 2.

Lt. Governor, Her Honour Sylvia O. Fedoruk.

EXECUTIVE COUNCIL
(as at May 31, 1990)

Premier, President of the Council, Minister of Agriculture and Food, Hon. Grant Devine.
Deputy Premier, Urban Affairs, and interim Minister of Culture, Multiculturalism and Recreation, Hon. Pat Smith.
Agriculture and Food, Hon. Harold Martens (*associate minister*).
Attorney General, Minister of Justice, Telephones, Provincial Secretary, Hon. Gary Lane.
Consumer and Commercial Affairs, Hon. Jack Klein.
Economic Diversification and Trade, Human Resources, Labour and Employment, Hon. Grant Schmidt.
Economic Diversification and Trade, Hon. John Gerich (*associate minister*).
Education, Hon. Ray Meiklejohn.
Energy and Mines, Hon. Rick Swenson.
Environment and Public Safety, Hon. Grant Hodgins.
Finance, Hon. Lorne Hepworth.
Health, Hon. George McLeod.

Health, Hon. Jack Wolfe (*associate minister*).
Highways and Transportation, Hon. Sherwin Petersen.
Ministry of the Family, Hon. Beattie Martin.
Parks and Renewable Resources, Hon. Lorne Kopelchuk.
Rural Development, Hon. Neal Hardy.
Social Services, Hon. Bill Neudorf.

THE JUDICATURE

Court of Appeal, Chief Justice, Hon. E. D. Bayda.
Queen's Bench, Chief Justice, Hon. D. K. MacPherson.
Provincial Court, Chief Judge, Hon. B. P. Carey.

Agent-General in London.—P. Rousseau, 16 Berkeley Street, W1X 5AE.

Finance.—Consolidated Fund and Heritage combined revenue for year ending March 1991 is C\$4,278,200,000 and combined expenditure C\$4,641,345,000.

CAPITAL.—Regina. Population (1989 estimate), 178,348. Other cities: Saskatoon (183,896), Moose Jaw (35,074); Prince Albert (34,015) and Yorkton (16,000).

CYPRUS
(Kypriaki Dimokratia/Kibris Cumhuriyeti)

AREA AND CLIMATE.—Cyprus with an area of 3,572 sq. miles (9,251 sq. km), is the third largest island in the Mediterranean Sea. Its greatest length is 140 miles and greatest breadth 60 miles, situated at latitude 35°N. and longitude 33° 30′E. It is about 40 miles distant from the nearest point of Asia Minor, 60 miles from Syria and 240 miles from Port Said.

Cyprus has a Mediterranean climate with a hot dry summer and a variable warm winter, while the intermediate seasons are short and transitional.

POPULATION.—In 1989 the population (estimate) was 698,300. There are two major communities, Greek Cypriots (80·1 per cent) and Turkish Cypriots (18·6 per cent); and minorities of Armenians, Maronites and others.

CAPITAL.—Nicosia, near the centre of the island, with a population of 166,900 (in the Government controlled area); the other principal towns are ΨLimassol, ΨFamagusta, ΨLarnaca, Paphos and Kyrenia.

CURRENCY.—Cyprus pound (C£) of 100 cents.
FLAG.—Gold map of Cyprus on a white ground, surmounting crossed olive branches (green).
NATIONAL ANTHEM.—Ode to Freedom.
NATIONAL DAY.—October 1 (Independence Day).

GOVERNMENT

Cyprus passed under British administration from 1878. Cyprus was formally annexed to Great Britain in November 1914, on the outbreak of war with Turkey. From 1925 to 1960 it was a Crown Colony administered by a Governor, assisted by an Executive Council and also for a time by a partly-elected Legislative Council. Following the launching in April 1955 of an armed campaign by EOKA in support of union with Greece, a state of emergency was declared in November 1955, which lasted for four years. After a meeting at Zürich between the Prime Ministers of Greece and Turkey, a conference was held in London and an agreement was signed on February 19, 1959 between the United Kingdom, Greece, Turkey and the Greek and Turkish Cypriots which provided that Cyprus would be an independent Republic.

Under the Cyprus Act, 1960, the island became an independent sovereign republic on August 16, 1960. The constitution provided for a Greek Cypriot

President and a Turkish Cypriot Vice-President elected for a five-year term by the Greek and Turkish communities respectively. The House of Representatives, elected for five years by universal suffrage of each community separately, was to consist of 35 Greek and 15 Turkish members. The 1960 Constitution proved unworkable in practice and led to intercommunal troubles. The UN Peace Keeping Force in Cyprus (UNFICYP) was set up in March 1964; its mandate was last renewed on June 15, 1990.

In July 1974, mainland Greek officers of the Greek Cypriot National Guard launched a coup d'état against President Makarios and installed a former EOKA member, Nikos Sampson, in his place. Turkey reserved to itself the right to maintain constitutional order and the independence and territorial integrity of the island, invaded Northern Cyprus and occupied over a third of the island. In February 1975 a 'Turkish Federated State of Cyprus' under Mr. Rauf Denktash was declared in this area, its constitution being approved by referendum in July 1975. In November 1983 a 'Declaration of Statehood' was issued which purported to establish the 'Turkish Republic of Northern Cyprus'. The declaration was condemned by the UN Security Council and only Turkey has recognized the new 'state'. In May 1985 a referendum in the north of Cyprus approved a constitution for the 'Turkish Republic of Northern Cyprus': in June 1985 Mr. Denktash was elected President of the 'state' and a General Election was held. Mr. Denktash was re-elected in April 1990, and a General Election was held in May 1990.

Since 1974 attempts to reach a settlement have focused on intercommunal talks under the auspices of the UN. The latest talks began in August 1988.

A general election was held for the Greek House of Representatives on December 8, 1985, resulting in the parties gaining the following number of seats: Democratic Rally (Right Wing) 19; Democratic Party (Centre) 16; AKEL (Communist) 15; EDEK (Socialist) 6. In April 1990 5 AKEL members broke away and formed a separate party, ADESOC. They continue to hold their seats in Parliament.

President, George Vassiliou, *elected* February 21, 1988.

Council of Ministers
(as at May 31, 1990)

Foreign Affairs, George Iacovou.
Interior, Christodoulos Veniamin.
Finance, George Syrimis.
Education, Christophoros Christofides.
Justice, Nicos Papaioannou.
Defence, Andreas Aloneftis.
Communications and Works, Pavlos Savvides.
Health, Panicos Papageorghiou.
Commerce and Industry, Takis Nemitsas.
Labour and Social Insurance, Iacovus Aristidou.
Agriculture and Natural Resources, Andreas Gavrielides.

CYPRUS HIGH COMMISSION
93 Park Street, W1Y 4ET
[071-499 2810]

High Commissioner, His Excellency Tasos Panayides, Hon. GCVO (1979).

ECONOMY

Although agriculture still occupies a prime position in the Cyprus economy it is unlikely to expand further. Main products are citrus fruits, grapes and vine products, potatoes and other vegetables. Manufacturing, construction, distribution and other service industries are other major employers. Tourism is the main growth industry with over 1·2 million long-

stay tourists producing C£490 million in foreign exchange earnings in 1989. Over 5,000 foreign firms and individuals have registered as offshore companies in Cyprus, which supports Cyprus' claim to be a centre for Middle East trade.

Britain continues to be the country's most important trading partner, taking some 23·4 per cent of its exports in 1989 and supplying 11·4 per cent of its imports. Cyprus is seeking to diversify its export markets and until recently sold almost half its exports to the Middle East. However, these traditional markets are now drying up, and Cyprus is looking more towards Europe. A Customs Union between Cyprus and the EC came into force in January 1988.

There is a large visible trade deficit (C£737·2 million in 1989), which is offset by invisible earnings, particularly from tourism. The current account in 1989 showed a deficit of C£72·8 m, which includes the cost of one aircraft amounting to C£80·7 m.

FINANCE

	1988	1989
Total Revenue	C£535·0 m	C£632·7 m
Ordinary Expenditure ...	598·4 m	663·8 m

TRADE

	1988	1989
Imports	C£866·8 m	C£1,130·3 m
Exports (including re-exports)..........	330·9 m	393·0 m

Trade with UK

	1988	1989
Imports from UK	C£159,788,000	C£173,092,000
Exports to UK	121,828,000	145,047,000

BRITISH HIGH COMMISSION
Alexander Pallis Street (PO Box 1978)
Nicosia
[Nicosia 02-473131]

High Commissioner, His Excellency David John Michael Dain (1990).

British Council Representative, C. Mogford, PO Box 5654, 3 Museum Street, Nicosia.

BRITISH SOVEREIGN AREAS

The United Kingdom retained full sovereignty and jurisdiction over two areas of 99 square miles in all—Akrotiri–Episkopi–Paramali and Dhekelia–Pergamos–Ayios Nicolaos–Xylophagou—and use of roads and other facilities. The British Administrator of these areas is appointed by the Queen and is responsible to the Secretary of State for Defence.

Administrator of the British Sovereign Areas, Air Vice-Marshal A. F. C. Hunter, CBE, AFC.

DOMINICA
(The Commonwealth of Dominica)

AREA, POPULATION, ETC.—Dominica, the loftiest of the Lesser Antilles, lies in the Windward Group, between 15° 12′ and 15° 39′ N. lat. and 61° 14′ and 61° 29′ W. long., 95 miles S. of Antigua. It is about 29 miles long and 16 broad comprising an area of 289 sq. miles (748·5 sq. km). The island is of volcanic origin and very mountainous, and the soil is very fertile. The temperature varies, according to the altitude, from 13°–29°C. The climate is healthy. The population is 81,300 (1988 estimate).

CAPITAL.—ΨRoseau, on the south-west coast, population 11,000. The other principal town is Portsmouth, population 2,220.

CURRENCY.—East Caribbean dollar (EC$) of 100 cents.

FLAG.—Green ground with a cross overall of yellow, white and black stripes, and in the centre a red disc charged with a Sisserou parrot in natural colours within a ring of 10 green stars.

NATIONAL ANTHEM.—Dominica Day Song.

NATIONAL DAY.—November 3 (Independence Day).

GOVERNMENT

The island was discovered by Columbus in 1493, when it was a stronghold of the Caribs, who remained virtually the sole inhabitants until the French established settlements in the 18th century. It was captured by the British in 1759 but passed back and forth between France and Britain until 1805, after which British possession was not challenged. From 1871–1939 Dominica was part of the Leeward Islands Colony, then from 1940 the island was a unit of the Windward Islands group. Internal self-government from 1967 was followed on November 3, 1978 by independence as a republic with the name The Commonwealth of Dominica. Executive authority is vested in the President, who is elected by the House of Assembly for not more than two terms of five years. Parliament consists of the President and the House of Assembly (representatives elected by universal adult suffrage) and nine Senators, who may be appointed by the President or elected. Parliament has a life of five years.

At the general election of May 1990, the Dominica Freedom Party won 11 seats, the Dominica United Workers' Party 6, and the Labour Party of Dominica the remaining 4.

President, His Excellency Sir Clarence Seignoret, GCB, OBE.

Cabinet
(as at May 31, 1990)

Prime Minister, Minister for Finance and Economic Affairs, Hon. M. Eugenia Charles.

Legal Affairs, Information and Public Relations, Hon. Jenner Armour.

External Affairs and OECS Unity, Hon. Brian Alleyne.

Agriculture, Trade, Industry and Tourism, Hon. Charles Maynard.

Education and Sports, Hon. Rupert Sorhaindo sen.

Community Development and Social Affairs, Hon. Henry George.

Health and Social Security, Hon. Allan Guye.

Labour and Immigration, Hon. Heskeith Alexander.

Communications, Works and Housing, Hon. Alleyne Carbon.

Minister without Portfolio, Ministry of Agriculture, Trade, Industry and Tourism, Hon. Maynard Joseph.

Minister without Portfolio, Prime Minister's Office, Hon. Dermott Southwell sen.

Parliamentary Secretary in the Ministry of Agriculture, Trade, Industry and Tourism, Hon. Ossie Walsh.

Parliamentary Secretary in the Ministry of Communications, Works and Housing, Hon. Clem Shillingford.

HIGH COMMISSION FOR THE COMMONWEALTH OF DOMINICA
1 Collingham Gardens, SW5 0HW
[071–370 5194/5]

High Commissioner, His Excellency Franklin A. Baron (1986) (resident in Roseau).

Minister Counsellor (London), Ashworth Elwin.

FINANCE

	1985–86 revised	1986–87 estimated
Recurrent Revenue ...	EC$83·6 m	EC$88·2 m
Recurrent Expenditure	81·1 m	91·6 m
Capital Revenue	37·9 m	49·3 m
Capital Expenditure ...	45·3 m	57·2 m

ECONOMY

Agriculture is the principal occupation, with tropical and citrus fruits the main crops. Products for export are bananas, lime juice, lime oil, bay oil, copra and rum. Forestry and fisheries are being encouraged. The only commercially exploitable mineral is pumice, used chiefly for building purposes. Manufacturing consists largely of the processing of agricultural products.

TRADE

	1988
Imports	US$87·55 m
Exports	55·55 m

Trade with UK

	1988	1989
Imports from UK	£8,416,000	£8,727,000
Exports to UK	32,423,000	23,709,000

BRITISH HIGH COMMISSION

High Commissioner, (resides at Bridgetown, Barbados).

THE GAMBIA
(The Republic of the Gambia)

AREA, POPULATION, ETC.—The Gambia takes its name from the Gambia River, which it straddles for over 200 miles inland from the west coast of Africa. It is a narrow strip, surrounded by the Republic of Senegal, except at the coast, lying between 13° 10′–13° 45′ N. and 13° 90′–16° 50′ W. The area is 4,361 sq. miles (11,295 sq. km), of which one-fifth is the river. The climate is typically Sahelian, with a dry season between October and May and heavy rainfall during the months of July and August (32–40 inches a year).

The population comprises mainly Wolof, Mandinka and Fula peoples who originally migrated there from the north and east. Population (1988 estimate) was 800,300.

The Gambia River basin was part of the region dominated in the 10th–16th centuries by the strong Songhai and Mali kingdoms centred on the upper Niger. The first recorded Europeans to reach the Gambia River were the Portuguese in 1447. In 1588 Queen Elizabeth I gave the first charter to English merchants to trade along the river. Merchants from France, Courland (now part of Latvia) and the Netherlands also established trading posts there. The English presence was strongly challenged by the French, who were dominant further north up the coast, but in 1783 the Treaty of Versailles acknowledged English rights. In 1816, after the Napoleonic Wars, and in order to enforce abolition of the slave trade, the British stationed a garrison on a low sandy island called Banjul at the river mouth. Renamed Bathurst, this became the capital of a small British-administered colony, initially under the Governor of Sierra Leone. Negotiations with France continued sporadically until 1889 when it was agreed that the British rights along the upper river should extend 10 km on either bank. British administration was extended from the Colony to this Protectorate. The Gambia became independent within the Commonwealth on February 18, 1965, and a Republic on April 24, 1970.

The Gambia's relationship with Senegal has always been an important factor in political and economic policy. Moves towards a closer association were accelerated after an abortive coup in The Gambia in July 1981 was put down with the help of Senegalese troops. In February 1982 the Senegambia Confederation was formally instituted based on certain joint institutions and integration of policies, with each country remaining sovereign and independent. However, following disagreements it was decided to dissolve the confederation, and formal dissolution took place on December 31, 1989.

CAPITAL.—ΨBanjul. Population (1983 Census) of the island of Banjul was 44,536, and of adjacent Kombo St. Mary district 102,858. Total population of Banjul/Kombo St. Mary, 147,394.

CURRENCY.—Dalasi (D) of 100 butut.

FLAG.—Horizontal stripes of red, blue and green, separated by narrow white stripes.

NATIONAL ANTHEM.—For The Gambia, Our Homeland.

NATIONAL DAY.—February 18 (Independence Day).

GOVERNMENT

The constitution is democratic and Parliamentary, with an executive President elected for five years. The House of Representatives has 35 elected members, 5 elected Chiefs Representatives and up to 8 nominated members plus the Attorney-General (ex-officio). The Vice-President and other Ministers are appointed by the President. Parliament must be dissolved after five years. The last general elections were held in March 1987. The present state of the parties for elected members is PPP (People's Progressive Party) 31; NCP (National Convention Party) 5.

President and Cabinet
(as at May 31, 1990)

President and Minister of Defence, His Excellency Alhaji Sir Dawda Kairaba Jawara, GCMG.

Vice-President and Minister of Education, Youth, Sports and Culture, Hon. Bakary Bunja Darbo.

Attorney-General and Minister of Justice, Hon. Hassan B. Jallow.

Finance and Trade, Hon. Saihou Sabally.

External Affairs, Hon. Alhaji Omar Sey.

Interior, Hon. Lamin Kiti Jabang.

Agriculture and Natural Resources, Hon. Omar A. Jallow.

Local Government and Lands, Hon. Landing Jallow Sonko.

Water Resources, Forestry and Fisheries, Hon. Sarjo Touray.

Health, Environment, Labour and Social Welfare, Hon. Mrs. Louise A. N'Jie.

Works and Communications, Hon. Matthew Yaya Baldeh.

Economic Planning and Industrial Development, Hon. Mbemba Jatta.

Information and Tourism, Hon. Alkali James Gaye.

Chief Justice, Hon. E. Olayinka Ayoola.

Speaker, Alhaji Hon. M. B. N'Jie.

GAMBIA HIGH COMMISSION
57 Kensington Court, W8 5DG
[071-937 6316]

High Commissioner, His Excellency Horace R. Monday, jun. (1987).

COMMUNICATIONS

There is an international airport at Yundum, 17 miles from Banjul, with scheduled services flying to other West African states and to the UK and Belgium. Banjul is the main port. Internal communication is by road and river. There is no railway system. There are two broadcasting stations and a UHF telephone service linking Banjul with the principal towns in the provinces. There is no television service.

EDUCATION

There are 24 secondary schools (eight high and 16 technical) with a total enrolment of 15,635 students. Two High Schools provide A-level education. Gambia College provides post-secondary courses in education, agriculture, public health and nursing. There are seven vocational training institutions with a total enrolment of 1,400. Higher education and advanced training courses are taken outside The Gambia, currently by over 200 students.

PRODUCTION

Seventy-five per cent of the population depend for their livelihood on agriculture (40 per cent of GDP). The chief product, groundnuts, is also the most important export item, forming over 80 per cent of all domestic exports. Other crops are rice, millet, sorghum, maize and cotton. Fishing and livestock industries are being developed. Thirty per cent of the country's basic food requirements are imported. There are no significant deposits of minerals. Manufactures are limited to groundnut processing, minor metal fabrications, paints, furniture, soap and bottling. Tourism is developing quickly, with 98,248 visitors in 1987–88. The entrepôt trade through The Gambia, re-exporting imported goods to neighbouring countries, is an important element in the national economy.

FINANCE

	1984–85	1985–86
Recurrent Revenue ...	D172,600,000	D218,000,000
Recurrent Expenditure	180,900,000	203,100,000

Over 80 per cent of capital expenditure comes from external aid grants and loans. In 1987–88 there was a GDP growth rate of 5·4 per cent.

TRADE

	1987–88	1988–89
Total imports	D844,900,000	D940,000,000
Total exports	576,600,000	311,400,000

Trade with UK

	1988	1989
Imports from UK	£19,236,000	£16,583,000
Exports to UK	2,927,000	2,340,000

BRITISH HIGH COMMISSION
48 Atlantic Road, Fajara (PO Box 507), Banjul
[Banjul 95133]

High Commissioner, His Excellency Alec Ibbott, CBE (1988).

GHANA
(The Republic of Ghana)

AREA.—Ghana (formerly known as the Gold Coast) is situated on the Gulf of Guinea, between 3° 07′ W. long. and 1° 14′ E. long. (about 334 miles), and extends 441 miles north from Cape Three Points (4° 45′ N.) to 11° 11′ N. It is bounded on the north by Burkina, on the west by the Côte d'Ivoire, on the east by Togo, and on the south by the Atlantic Ocean. Although a tropical country, Ghana is cooler than many countries within similar latitudes. Ghana has a total area of 92,099 sq. miles (238,537 sq. km).

POPULATION.—The population at the Census of 1984 was 12,205,574. A 1988 UN estimate gave a figure of 14,131,000. Almost all Ghanaians are Sudanese Negroes, although Hamitic strains are common in Northern Ghana. The official language is English. The principal indigenous language group is Akan, of which Twi and Fanti are the most commonly used. Ga, Ewe and languages of the Mole–Dagbani group are common in certain regions.

CAPITAL.—ΨAccra. Population of the Greater Accra Region (including Tema) was (1984 Census) 1,420,066. Other towns are Kumasi, Tamale, ΨSekondi-Takoradi, ΨCape Coast, Sunyani, Ho, Koforidua, Tarkwa and ΨWinneba.

CURRENCY.—Cedi of 100 pesewas.

FLAG.—Equal horizontal bands of red over yellow over green; five-point black star on gold stripe.

NATIONAL ANTHEM.—Hail the Name of Ghana.

NATIONAL DAY.—March 6 (Independence Day).

GOVERNMENT

There is no recorded history of the Gold Coast region before the coming of Europeans in the fifteenth century. The constituent parts of the State came under British administration at various times, the original Gold Coast Colony (the coastal and Southern areas) being first constituted in 1874; Ashanti in 1901; and the Northern Territories Protectorate in 1901. The territory of Trans-Volta-Togoland, part of the former German colony of Togo, was mandated to Britain by the League of Nations after the First World War, and remained under British administration as a United Nations Trusteeship after the Second World War. After a plebiscite in May 1956, under the auspices of the United Nations, the territory was integrated with the Gold Coast Colony.

The former Gold Coast Colony and associated territories became the independent state of Ghana and a member of the British Commonwealth on March 6, 1957 and adopted a Republican constitution on July 1, 1960. A coup in June 1979 led to the formation of an Armed Forces Revolutionary Council chaired by Flt.-Lt. Jerry Rawlings. Civilian rule was restored in September 1979 but overthrown on December 31, 1981, when another coup brought back into power Flt.-Lt. Rawlings.

Provisional National Defence Council

Chairman, Flt.-Lt. Jerry J. Rawlings.
Vice-Chairman, Justice Daniel Annan.
Members, Dr. Mary Grant; Ebo Tawiah; Alhaji Mahama Iddrisu; P. V. Obeng; Capt. Kojo Tsikata (retd); Lt.-Gen. Arnold Quainoo; Maj.-Gen. W. M. Mensa-Wood.

PNDC Secretaries
(as at May 31, 1990)

Foreign Affairs, Obed Y. Asamoah.
Internal Affairs, Nii Okaija Adamafio.
Finance and Economic Planning, Dr. Kwesi Botchwey.
Defence, Alhaji Mahama Iddrisu.
Fuel and Power, Ato Ahwoi.
Trade and Tourism, Huudu Yahaya.
Local Government, K. Ahwoi.
Education and Culture, K. B. Asante.
Youth and Sports, K. Saarah-Mensah.
Transport and Communications, J. A. Danso.
Works and Housing, Capt. K. A. Buta.
Industries, Science and Technology, Col. R. Commey.
Justice and Attorney-General, E. G. Tanoh.

Agriculture, Cdre. Steve Obimpeh.
Information, Kofi Totobi Quakyi.
Lands and Natural Resources, Kwame Peprah.
Roads and Highways, Lt.-Col. Mensah Gbedemah.
Committee for the Defence of the Revolution, W. H. Yeboah.
Health, Nana A. Sarpong.
Mobilization and Productivity, D. S. Boateng.

GHANA HIGH COMMISSION
13 Belgrave Square, SW1X 8PR
[071-235 4142]

High Commissioner, His Excellency K. B. Asante (1990).

PRODUCTION, ETC.

Agriculture.—Agriculture forms the basis of Ghana's economy, employing 70 per cent of the working population. Crops of the Forest Zone include cocoa, which is the largest single source of revenue, rice and a variety of other foodstuff crops grown on mixed-crop farms. Fruits such as avocado pears, oranges and pineapples are grown. Cassava is the most important crop of the Coastal Savannas Zone, of the lower Volta area. Production of pulses such as groundnuts is widespread. Near the Togo border oil palms, yams, maize, cassava, fruit and vegetables are produced. Livestock is raised in the uncultivated areas. The Northern Savanna Zone is Ghana's principal cattle rearing area and other livestock production there is important for home consumption. Corn and millet crops are produced in the far north and maize, yams, rice and groundnut crops in more southerly parts of the Zone.

Attempts are being made to diversify agricultural production, with cash crops being extensively cultivated for export and to provide raw materials for local industry.

Fisheries.—Fishing is important in coastal areas and in the Volta itself. However production cannot meet demand and there are considerable imports of fish products. About 80 per cent of home supply is obtained from sea fisheries, but production from the Volta Lake and other inland fisheries is increasing.

Mineral Production.—The area within a 60 mile radius of Dunkwa produces 90 per cent of Ghana's mineral exports. Manganese production from Nsuta ranks among the world's highest and gold, industrial diamonds and bauxite are also produced. Some 30,000 persons are employed by the mining companies.

Manufactures.—Examples of the small-scale traditional industries are tailoring, goldsmithing and carpentry. Priority has been given in recent years to the establishment of a number of 'Pioneer Industries' including timber products, vehicle and refrigerator assembly, cigarettes, boatbuilding, food processing, cotton textiles, clothing, footwear, printing and other light industries. A modern industrial complex is growing in the Accra-Tema area.

Volta River Project.—Since 1966 the Volta Dam at Akosombo has generated hydro-electric power for the processing of bauxite and fed a power transmission network for the Accra-Kumasi-Takoradi area. Electricity is now also sent to Togo and Benin.

COMMUNICATIONS

Accra Airport is an international airport and Ghana Airways Corporation is the national airline. There are also internal airports at Takoradi, Kumasi and Tamale.

There are 20,000 miles of motorable roads, of which 2,335 miles are bitumenized. There are 600 miles of railway, linking Accra and the principal ports of Takoradi and Tema with their hinterlands, and with each other.

Takoradi Harbour consists of seven quay berths—one is leased specially for manganese exports. Tema Harbour has 10 berths for larger ocean going vessels and the largest dry dock on the West African coast. An oil berth has also been built to serve the Ghaip refinery which has been constructed at Tema.

Trade with UK

	1988	1989
Imports from UK	£126,148,000	£121,076,000
Exports to UK	106,314,000	92,208,000

Principal exports are cocoa, timber and gold. Principal imports are road vehicles, manufacturing equipment, petroleum and raw materials.

BRITISH HIGH COMMISSION
PO Box 296, Osu Link, Accra
[Accra 221665]

High Commissioner, His Excellency Anthony Michael Goodenough, CMG (1989).

British Council Representative, J. M. Day, Liberia Road (PO Box 771), Accra, and an office in *Kumasi*.

GRENADA
(The State of Grenada)

AREA, POPULATION, ETC.—Grenada is situated between the parallels of 12° 13′–11° 58′ N. lat. and 61° 20′–61° 35′ W. long., and is about 80 miles north of Trinidad, 68 miles SSW of St. Vincent, and about 120 miles SW of Barbados. The island is about 21 miles in length and 12 miles in breadth, with an area of 133 sq. miles (344 sq. km). Also included in the territory of Grenada are some of the Grenadines islets, the largest of which is Carriacou, 13 square miles in area. The population is estimated at 100,000 (1988 UN estimate). The country is mountainous and very picturesque, and the climate is healthy.

CAPITAL.—ΨSt. George's (population 10,000) lies on the south-west coast, and possesses a good harbour.

CURRENCY.—East Caribbean dollar (EC$) of 100 cents.

FLAG.—Rectangle formed of yellow triangles top and bottom, and green triangles at side, with yellow five-pointed star on red circle in centre, and a nutmeg in green triangle nearest the fly; all on a red ground with three yellow five-pointed stars at top and bottom.

NATIONAL DAY.—February 7 (Independence Day).

GOVERNMENT

Grenada was discovered by Columbus in 1498, and named Conception. It was originally colonized by the French, and was ceded to Great Britain by the Treaty of Versailles in 1783. It became an Associated State in 1967 and an independent nation within the Commonwealth on February 7, 1974.

The government of Sir Eric Gairy was overthrown on March 13, 1979 by the New Jewel Movement and a People's Revolutionary Government was set up. Disagreements within the PRG led, in October 1983, to violence and the death of the Prime Minister, whose government was replaced by a Revolutionary Military Council. These events prompted the intervention of Caribbean and US forces. The Governor General installed an advisory council to act as an interim government until a General Election was held, on December 3, 1984. A phased withdrawal of US forces was completed by June 1985.

The Queen is Head of State and is represented by a Governor General. Legislative power is vested in a bicameral parliament consisting of an elected House of Representatives and a 13-member Senate. The

most recent General Election was held in March 1990. Nicholas Brathwaite of the National Democratic Congress was sworn in as Prime Minister on March 16, 1990.

Governor General, Sir Paul Scoon, GCMG, GCVO, OBE (1978).

Cabinet
(as at May 31, 1990)

Prime Minister, Minister of External Affairs and Home Affairs, Nicholas Brathwaite.
Finance, Trade and Industry, George Brizan.
Attorney General, Minister of Legal Affairs and Local Government, Francis Alexis.
Public Works, Phinsley St. Louis.
Tourism, Aviation and Women's Affairs, Joan Purcell.
Health and Community Development, Kenny Lalsingh.
Agriculture, Ben Jones.
Education, Culture, Youth Affairs, Sport and Social Affairs, Carlyle Glean.
Labour, Social Security, Housing, Michael Andrew.
Minister of State, Ministry of Works, Edzel Thomas.

GRENADA HIGH COMMISSION
1 Collingham Gardens, SW5 0HW
[071–373 7808]

High Commissioner, (new appointment awaited).

ECONOMY

The economy is principally agrarian, with cocoa, nutmegs and bananas the major crops. Fruit and vegetables are grown and a little livestock raised for domestic consumption. The fishing industry is being developed. Manufacturing is mostly confined to processing agricultural products.

Tourism has prospered since the opening in 1984 of the Point Salines International Airport. British Airways began regular weekly flights in April 1987. A hotel expansion programme is planned. The number of cruise ships visiting Grenada in 1988 was 234.

Total value of imports in 1988 was EC$248·6 million. Principal domestic exports for 1988 were nutmeg (EC$31·3m), cocoa (EC$8·75m), mace (EC$7·3m) and fruit (EC$3·8m).

Trade with UK

	1988	1989
Imports from UK	£7,162,000	£9,058,000
Exports to UK	6,115,000	5,924,000

BRITISH HIGH COMMISSION
14 Church Street, St. George's
[St. George's 440-3222]

High Commissioner, (resides at Bridgetown, Barbados).

Resident Representative, G. Roberts (*First Secretary*).

GUYANA
(The Co-operative Republic of Guyana)

AREA, POPULATION, ETC.—Guyana, the former colony of British Guiana, which includes the Counties of Demerara, Essequibo and Berbice, is situated on the north-east coast of South America, bordering on Venezuela, Brazil and Suriname. It has a total area of 83,000 sq. miles (214,969 sq. km), and a population estimate (1988) of 799,000. There are three distinct areas. (1) A narrow alluvial coastal belt 10 to 40 miles deep, the eastern part of which is intensively cultivated and contains some 90 per cent of the population. Much of this is below the level of the sea and is drained and irrigated by an intricate system of canals constructed by the Dutch. (2) A mountainous area of dense rain forest behind the coastland, still partly unexplored, which reaches its highest point at Mount Roraima (9,000 ft.) on the junction of the Guyana–Brazil–Venezuela borders. (3) The open savanna country of the Rupununi in the south-west where cattle ranching is practised and oil deposits have been discovered.

The entire country is intersected by numerous large rivers, though these are of limited navigational use because of rapids and waterfalls, the most notable of which are the Kaieteur Fall on the Potaro River with a sheer drop of 741 ft., the Horse Shoe Falls on the Essequibo and the Marina Fall on the Ipobe River.

Climate.—The two dry seasons normally last from mid February to end April, and from mid August to end November. In the August–October period it is hot. The mean temperature is 27°C, the usual extremes being 21°C and 32°C. In the interior the mean temperature is higher: 28°C, its extremes ranging from 19°C to 40°C. The yearly rainfall is subject to marked variation, its mean on the coast lands averaging about 90 inches with an average of 58 inches on the savannas.

CAPITAL.—ΨGeorgetown. Estimated population, including environs, 185,000. Other towns are: Linden (29,000); ΨNew Amsterdam (23,000); Corriverton (17,000).

CURRENCY.—Guyana dollar (G$) of 100 cents.

FLAG.—Red triangle with black border, pointing from hoist to fly, on a yellow triangle with white border, all on a green field.

NATIONAL ANTHEM.—Dear Land of Guyana.

NATIONAL DAYS.—May 26 (Independence Day); February 23 (Republic Day).

GOVERNMENT

Guyana became independent on May 26, 1966, with a Governor General appointed by The Queen. It became a Co-operative Republic on February 23, 1970. Under the Independence Constitution the Prime Minister and Cabinet were responsible to a National Assembly elected by secret ballot every 5 years. The last election under this Constitution was in 1973 and the term of that Assembly was later extended to October 1980.

A new Constitution was passed into law in February 1980 and promulgated in October 1980. It provides for an Executive President, a National Assembly of 65 members, and also for a National Congress of Local Democratic Organs responsible for local government. The Supreme Congress of the People consists of all members of these two assemblies.

The electoral system is a proportional representation or 'single list' system, each voter casting his vote for a party list of candidates. The voting age is 18.

Executive President, H. Desmond Hoyte, *took office* Aug. 1985, *sworn in* Dec. 12, 1985 for five-year term.

Cabinet
(as at May 31, 1990)

Executive President (with responsibility for Home Affairs, Co-operatives, Regional Development), H. D. Hoyte.

First Vice President and Prime Minister (Youth and Sports, Housing, Health), Hamilton Green.

Vice President (Culture and Social Development) and Deputy PM, Mrs. Viola Burnham.

Attorney-General and Minister for Justice, Keith Massiah.

Deputy PM (Planning and Development), William H. Parris.

Deputy PM (Public Utilities), Robert H. O. Corbin.

SENIOR MINISTERS

Agriculture, Patrick McKenzie.
Finance, Carl Greenidge.
Foreign Affairs, Rashleigh Jackson.
Trade and Tourism, Winston Murray.
Planning and Development, Seeram Prashad.
Regional Development, Jeffrey Thomas.
Senior Minister in the President's Office, Yvonne Harewood-Benn.
Education, Deryck Bernhard.

GUYANA HIGH COMMISSION
3 Palace Court, Bayswater Road, W2 4LP
[071-229 7684]

High Commissioner, His Excellency Cecil Stanley Pilgrim (1986).

JUDICATURE

The Supreme Court of Judicature consists of a Court of Appeal and a High Court. There are also Courts of Summary Jurisdiction. The Court of Appeal consists of the Chancellor as President, the Chief Justice and such number of Justices of Appeal as may be prescribed by Parliament.

The High Court consists of the Chief Justice, as President, and nine Puisne Judges. It is a court with unlimited jurisdiction in civil matters and exercises exclusive jurisdiction in probate, divorce and admiralty, and certain other matters.

Chancellor, K. M. George.
Chief Justice, R. Harper.

PRODUCTION, ETC.

The economy is based almost entirely on the main export items of sugar, rice, bauxite and alumina. Diamonds and gold are also mined, timber and rum are produced and there is some cattle ranching. The fishing industry is being expanded. Industry is fairly small-scale.

COMMUNICATIONS

Georgetown and New Amsterdam are the principal ports, though bauxite ships also sail to Linden, on the River Demerara, and Everton, on the River Berbice. There are no public railways and the few roads are confined mainly to the coastal areas. Air transport is the easiest form of communication between the coast and the interior. There is a state-owned radio broadcasting station which operates two channels and a fledgling television service.

EDUCATION

The Government assumed total control of the education system in September 1976 and made education free from nursery to university level. The Government trains teachers for primary and secondary schools at its own institutions.

Approximately 1,800 students were enrolled at the University of Guyana in degree programmes and certificate and diploma courses in 1986.

There are several technical and vocational institutions, as well as some 30 adult education schools (with an enrolment of 13,500). There are also a number of technical and vocational institutions not under the aegis of the Ministry of Education.

Trade with UK

	1988	1989
Imports from UK	£10,590,000	£13,216,000
Exports to UK	43,518,000	54,523,000

BRITISH HIGH COMMISSION
44 Main Street (PO Box 10849),
Georgetown
[Georgetown 65881/4]

High Commissioner, His Excellency David Purvis Small, CMG, MBE (1987) (also Ambassador to Suriname).

INDIA
(The Republic of India)

AREA AND CLIMATE.—The Republic of India has an area of 1,269,346 sq. miles (3,287,590 sq. km), composed of three well-defined regions: the mountain range of the Himalayas, the Indo–Gangetic plain, and the Southern Peninsula. The main mountain ranges are the Himalayas in the north (over 29,000 feet) and the Western and Eastern Ghats (over 8,000 feet). Major rivers include the Ganges, Indus, Krishna, Godavari and Mahanadi.

There are four seasons: the cold season (December–March); the hot season (April–May); the rainy season (June–September); and the season of the retreating SW monsoon (October–November). Temperatures vary over the whole country, between averages of about 10°C and 33°C, reaching over 38°C in some parts during the hot season. There are similar variations in rainfall, from only a few inches a year falling in the western Thar Desert to over 400 inches in Meghalaya.

POPULATION.—India is the second most populous country in the world. The population at the 1981 Census was 685,184,692, of which slightly more than 20 per cent was urban. A 1988 UN estimate gave a figure of 797 million. The majority of the population is Hindu (82 per cent), the rest being Muslim (11 per cent), Christian (2·5 per cent), Sikh (1·8 per cent), Buddhist (0·7 per cent) and Jain (0·5 per cent). The official languages are Hindi in the Devanagari script and English, though 14 regional languages also are recognized for adoption as official State languages.

HISTORY.—The Indus civilization was fully developed by *c*2500 BC but collapsed *c*1750 BC, subsequently being replaced by an Aryan civilization spread from the west. The first Arab invasions of the north-west began in the seventh century and Muslim, Hindu and Buddhist states developed until the establishment of the Mogul dynasty in 1526. The British East India Company established settlements throughout the 17th century; clashes with the French and native princes led to the British government taking control of the company in 1784. The separate dominions of India and Pakistan became independent within the Commonwealth in 1947 and India became a Republic in 1950.

CAPITAL.—Delhi (population in 1981 was 6,220,000). Populations of other principal cities (1981 figures) were Ahmedabad 2,124,000; Bangalore 2,914,000; ΨBombay (Mumbai) 8,202,000; ΨCalcutta 9,166,000; Hyderabad 2,566,000; Kanpur 1,685,000; Lucknow 1,007,000; ΨMadras 4,277,000; Pune 1,685,000.

CURRENCY.—Indian rupee (Rs) of 100 paisa.

FLAG.—The National Flag is a horizontal tricolour with bands of deep saffron, white and dark green in equal proportions. In the centre of the white band appears an Asoka wheel in navy blue.

NATIONAL ANTHEM.—Jana-gana-mana.

NATIONAL DAY.—January 26 (Republic Day).

STATES AND TERRITORIES OF THE UNION

There are 25 States and seven Union Territories. Each State is governed by a Governor appointed by the President who holds office for five years, and a Council of Ministers. All States have a Legislative Assembly, and some have also a Legislative Council, elected directly by adult suffrage for a maximum period of five years. The judges of the High Court of a State are appointed by the President.

The Union Territories are administered, except where otherwise provided by Parliament, by the President acting through an Administrator or Lieutenant Governor, or other authority appointed by him.

GOVERNMENT

The Constitution of India came into force in 1950. Executive power is vested in the President, who is elected for a five year term by an electoral college consisting of the elected members of the Union and State Legislatures. He appoints the Prime Minister and, on the latter's advice, the Ministers, and can dismiss them. The Council of Ministers is collectively responsible to the *Lok Sabha* (Lower House). The Vice-President is ex-officio chairman of the *Rajya Sabha* (Upper House).

Legislative power rests with the President, the Rajya Sabha (which has up to 250 members) and the Lok Sabha (which has up to 544 members). Twelve members of the Rajya Sabha are nominated by the President, the rest are indirectly elected representatives of the State and Union Territories. They hold office for six years. The 525 members of the Lok Sabha representing the States are directly elected by universal adult franchise, and 17 representatives of the Union Territories are chosen, for a maximum term of five years. Subject to the provisions of the Constitution, the Union Parliament can make laws for the whole of India and the State legislatures for their respective units.

The Supreme Court consists of the Chief Justice and not more than 17 other judges, appointed by the President. It is the highest court in respect of all constitutional matters and the final Court of Appeal.

President of the Republic of India, Ramaswami Venkataraman, *elected* July 16, 1987.

Vice-President, Shankar Dayal Sharma.

Cabinet
(as at Aug. 1990)

Prime Minister, Minister of Defence, Personnel, Public Grievances and Pensions, Science and Technology, Atomic Energy, Electronics, Space, Vishwanath Pratap Singh.

Deputy Prime Minister, Agriculture, vacant.

Finance, Prof. Madhu Dandavate.

Railways, George Fernandes.

Industry, Ajit Singh.

Textiles, Food Processing Industries, Sharad Yadav.

Home Affairs, Mufti Mohammad Sayeed.

Commerce, Tourism, Arun Kumar Nehru.

Energy, Civil Aviation, Arif Mohammad Khan.

Labour and Welfare, Ram Vilas Paswan.

Environment and Forests, Nilamani Routray.

External Affairs, I. K. Gujral.

Petroleum and Chemicals, M. S. Gurupadaswamy.

Information and Broadcasting, Parliamentary Affairs, P. Upendra.

Surface Transport, K. P. Unnikrishnan.

Steel and Mines, Law and Justice, Dinesh Goswami.

Urban Development, Murasoli Maran.

Food and Civil Supplies, Nathu Ram Mirdha.

MINISTERS OF STATE (INDEPENDENT CHARGE)

Water Resources, Manobhai Kotadia.

Health and Family Welfare, Rashid Mashood.

Communications, Janeshwar Mishra.

In addition there are a number of junior ministers, making a total of 40 in the Council of Ministers.

States and Territories (Capitals)	Area (sq. km)	Population (1981 Census)	Governor	Chief Minister
States				
Andhra Pradesh (Hyderabad) ..	275,100p	53,549,673	K. Kant	Marri Chenna Reddy
Arunachal Pradesh (Itanagar) .	83,700p	631,839	D. D. Thakur	Gegong Apang
Assam (Dispur)	78,400	19,896,843†	D. D. Thakur	P. K. Mahanta
Bihar (Patna).................	173,900p	69,914,734	Y. Salim	L. P. Yadav
Goa (Panaji)..................	3,701	1,000,000†	K. A. Khan	C. Alemao
Gujurat (Gandhinagar)........	196,000p	34,085,799	M. Shastri	Chimanbhai Patel
Haryana (Chandigarh) .	44,200p	12,922,618	D. L. Mandal	Banarasi Das Gupta
Himachal Pradesh (Shimla)	55,700	4,280,818	B. Rachaiah	Shanta Kumar
Jammu and Kashmir* (Srinagar/Jammu)	222,200p	5,987,389	Girish Chandra Saxena	(Governor's rule)
Karnataka (Bangalore)	191,800	37,135,714	B. P. Singh	Veerendra Patil
Kerala (Trivandrum)	38,900p	25,453,680	Dr. S. Singh	E. K. Nayanar
Madhya Pradesh (Bhopal)	443,500p	52,178,844	K. M. Ali	Sunderlal Patwa
Maharashtra (Bombay-Mumbai)	307,700p	62,784,171	C. Subramaniam	Sharad Pawar
Manipur (Imphal)	22,300	1,420,953	C. Panigrahi	R. K. Ranbir Singh
Meghalaya (Shillong)..........	22,400p	1,335,819	M. Dighe	B. B. Lyngdoh
Mizoram (Aizawl)	21,100	493,757	S. Kaushal	Lal Thanhawla
Nagaland (Kohima)	16,600	774,930	M. M. Thomas	Vamuzo
Orissa (Bhubaneswar)	155,700	26,370,271	Y. D. Sharma	J. B. Patnaik
Punjab (Chandigarh)..........	50,400	16,788,915	Virendra Verma	(President's rule)
Rajasthan (Jaipur)	342,200	34,261,862	D. P. Chattopa- dhyaya	Bhairon Singh Shek- hawat
Sikkim (Gangtok)	7,100	316,385	Adm. R. H. Tahiliani	N. B. Bhandari
Tamil Nadu (Madras)..........	130,100p	48,408,077	Surjit Singh Barnala	M. Karunanidhi
Tripura (Agartala)	10,500	2,053,058	R. Reddy	S. R. Majumdar
Uttar Pradesh (Lucknow)......	294,400p	110,862,013	S. S. N. Reddy	Mulayem Singh Yadav
West Bengal (Calcutta)	88,800p	54,580,647	Prof. N. Hasan	Jyoti Basu
Union Territories			*Lt. Governor*	
Andaman and Nicobar Is. (Port Blair).................	8,200	188,741	Lt.-Gen. R. S. Dyal	
Chandigarh	100	451,610	V. Verma	
Dadra and Nagar Haveli (Silvassa)	500	103,676	K. A. Khan	
Daman and Diu	112	51,602†	K. A. Khan	
Delhi	1,500	6,220,406	Air Chief Marshal Ar- jan Singh	
Lakshadweep (Kavaratti)......	30	40,249	W. Habibullah	
Pondicherry..................	500	604,471	Mrs. Chandrawati	

p provisional figure   † estimated figure

* Jammu and Kashmir is an area disputed between India, Pakistan and China, all three controlling a part of the territory. The area figure includes those parts occupied by Pakistan and China, which are claimed by India, but the population figure excludes the population of these areas, where the census was not taken. The state's capital is at Srinagar in summer and Jammu in winter.

INDIAN HIGH COMMISSION
India House, Aldwych, WC2B 4NA
[071–836 8484]

High Commissioner, His Excellency Kuldip Nayar (1990).
Deputy High Commissioner, S. Haider.

DEFENCE

The supreme command of the armed forces is vested in the President. Administrative and operational control resides in the Army, Navy and Air Headquarters under the supervision of the Ministry of Defence.

The Army has five Commands, Southern, Eastern, Northern, Western and Central.

The Indian Navy consists of two aircraft-carriers, a number of frigate squadrons, including some of the latest type of anti-submarine and anti-aircraft frigates, a squadron of anti-submarine patrol vessels, minesweeping squadrons, conventional type submarines and a submarine depot ship. A Naval aviation wing and a hydrographic office have also been set up. India has started building her own naval craft.

The Indian Air Force is organized in seven major formations, the Western, Eastern, Central, Southern and South Western Air Commands, and the Training and Maintenance Commands. Aircraft in use include SU-7, Hunter, Gnat, MiG 21 and MiG 23, Canberra bomber, Jaguar and Mirage-2000, helicopter and training planes.

PRODUCTION

Agriculture.—Agriculture is the chief industry, supporting about 70 per cent of the population, and providing nearly 40 per cent of the Gross Domestic

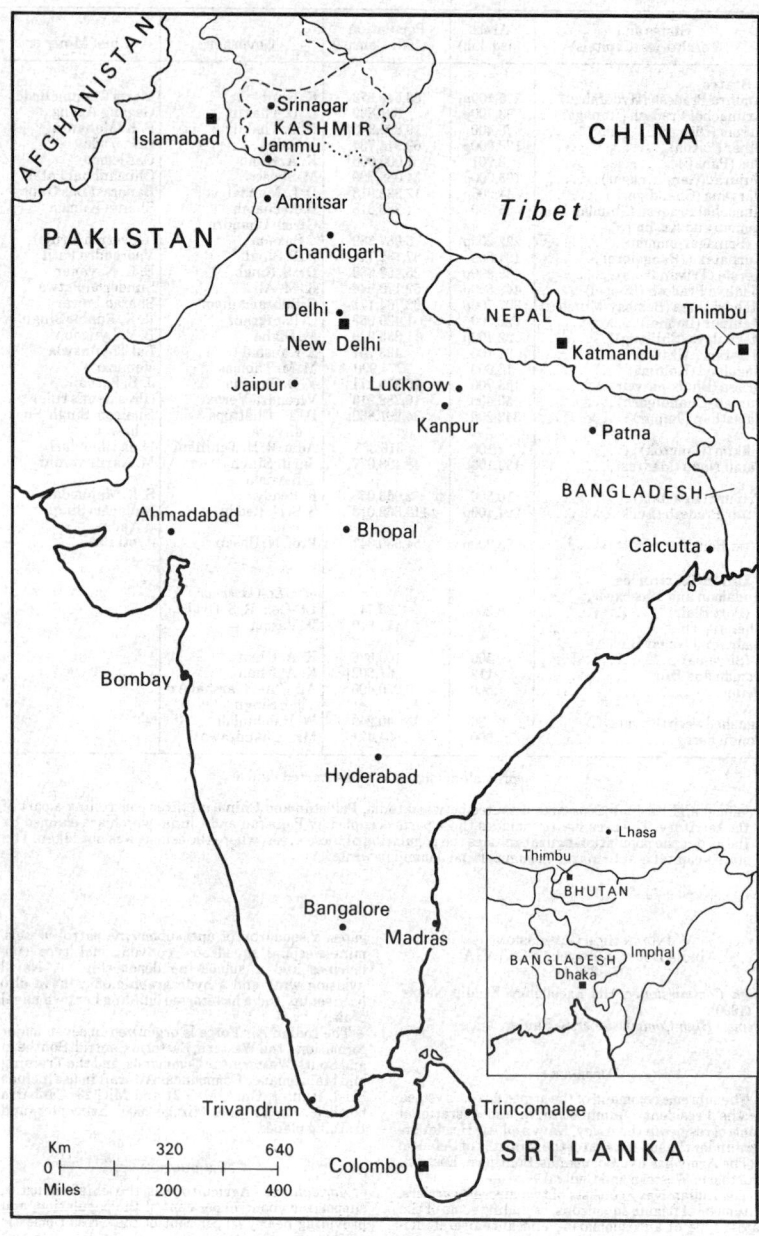

Product. The area under cultivation has been increased by irrigation schemes, but most holdings are less than five acres. Production has grown by three per cent each year since 1951, remaining slightly ahead of the two per cent increase necessary to keep pace with the rising population. Food crops occupy three-quarters of the total cropped area and production of food grains amounted to 143 million tonnes in 1986–87 but declined to 138 million tonnes in 1987–88 owing to severe drought. In 1988–89 foodgrains production was expected to reach about 169 million tonnes following good rains. The main food crops are rice, cereals (principally wheat) and pulses. The major cash crops include sugar cane, jute, cotton and tea. Other products include oil seeds, spices, groundnuts, tobacco, rubber and coffee. Livestock is raised, principally for dairy purposes or for the hides: cattle (an estimated 181 million), goats (71 million), sheep (41 million) and pigs (9·9 million).

Industry.—India's major industries are based on the exploitation and processing of her mineral resources, principally coal, oil and iron. The coal industry, nationalized in the early 1970s, reached an output in 1988–89 of 195 million tonnes. Production of crude oil, from the main fields in Assam and from offshore drilling was about 32·2 million tonnes in 1988–89. Steel production is mainly in the hands of the public sector, with five public and one private sector integrated steel plants producing 12·4 million tonnes of ingot steel in 1986–87. The engineering industry, heavy and light, is also primarily in the hands of the public sector. The manufacture of chemicals, fertilizers, petrochemicals, motor vehicles and commercial vehicles has been expanded.

Other principal manufactures are those derived from agricultural products, textiles, jute goods, sugar, leather, which along with tea, fish, and iron ore and concentrates, are India's major exports.

FINANCE

The budget estimates for 1989–90, placed current expenditure (on revenue account) at Rs.596,420 million. Current revenue (excluding States' shares) was estimated at Rs.518,950 million.

Trade with UK

	1988	1989
Imports from UK	£1,110,740,000	£1,382,436,000
Exports to UK	559,684,000	701,985,000

COMMUNICATIONS

Civil Aviation.—Four international airports—Palam (Delhi), Sahar (Bombay), Dum Dum (Calcutta), Meenambakkam (Madras)—are managed by the International Airports Authority. The other 87 aerodromes are controlled and operated by the Civil Aviation Department of the Government. The national airlines are Indian Airlines (internal) and Air India (international).

Railways.—The railways are grouped into nine administrative zones, Southern, Central, Western, Northern, North-Eastern, North-East Frontier, Eastern, South-Eastern and South-Central.

Gross traffic receipts (1989–90), crores of rupees, 10,633. Working expenses, 9,788. Net railway revenues, 945.

Ports.—The chief seaports are Bombay (Mumbai), Calcutta, Haldia, Madras, Mormugao, Cochin, Visakhapatnam, Kandla, Paradip, Mangalore and Tuticorin. There are 139 minor working ports with varying capacity.

Shipping.—On November 30, 1988, 377 ships totalling 5,590,752 gross tons were on the Indian Register.

BRITISH HIGH COMMISSION
Chanakyapuri, New Delhi, 21, 1100–21.
[New Delhi 601371]

High Commissioner, His Excellency Sir David Goodall, KCMG (1987).

Minister for Cultural Affairs and British Council Representative in India, R. Arbuthnott. Offices also at *Bombay, Calcutta* and *Madras.* There are British Council libraries at these four centres and British libraries at *Ahmedabad, Bangalore, Bhopal, Hyderabad, Lucknow, Patna, Pune, Ranchi* and *Trivandrum.*

JAMAICA

AREA, POPULATION, ETC.—Jamaica is situated in the Caribbean Sea south of the eastern extremity of Cuba and lies between latitudes 17° 43′ and 18° 32′ North, and longitude 76° 11′ and 78° 21′ West. Jamaica is 4,244 sq. miles (10,991 sq. km) in area and is divided into three counties (Surrey, Middlesex and Cornwall) and 14 parishes. The greatest length from east to west (Morant Point to Negril Point) is 146 miles and the extreme breadth 51 miles.

The topography consists mainly of coastal plains, divided by the Blue Mountain Range in the east, and the hills and limestone plateaux which occupy the central and western areas of the interior. The central chain of high peaks of the Blue Mountains is over 6,000 feet above sea level, and the Blue Mountain Peak, the highest of these, reaches an elevation of 7,402 feet.

At December 31, 1989 Jamaica's population was estimated to be 2,392,300.

CAPITAL.—The seat of government is ΨKingston, the largest town and seaport (estimated population of the Corporate area of Kingston and St. Andrew in 1982, 696,300). Other main towns are ΨMontego Bay, Ocho Rios, Spanish Town, Mandeville and May Pen.

CURRENCY.—Jamaican dollar (J$) of 100 cents.

FLAG.—Gold diagonal cross forming triangles of green at top and bottom, triangles of black at hoist and in fly.

NATIONAL ANTHEM.—Jamaica, Land We Love.

NATIONAL DAY.—First Monday in August (Independence Day).

GOVERNMENT

The island was discovered by Columbus on May 4, 1494, and occupied by the Spanish from 1509 until 1655 when a British expedition, sent out by Oliver Cromwell, under Admiral Penn and General Venables, attacked the island, which capitulated after a token resistance. In 1670 it was formally ceded to England by the Treaty of Madrid.

Jamaica became an independent state within the Commonwealth on August 6, 1962. The Legislature consists of a Senate of 21 nominated members and a House of Representatives consisting of 60 members elected by universal adult suffrage. The Constitution provides for a Leader of the Opposition.

At the General Election of February 9, 1989, the People's National Party won 45 seats and the Jamaica Labour Party won 15.

Governor General, His Excellency Sir Florizel Glasspole, GCMG, GCVO.

Cabinet
(as at June 30, 1990)

Prime Minister, Rt. Hon. Michael Manley.
Deputy Prime Minister, Hon. P. J. Patterson, QC.
Finance and the Public Service, Hon. Seymour Mullings.

Foreign Affairs and Foreign Trade, Senator the Hon.
David Coore, QC.
Information, Senator Dr. the Hon. Paul D. Robertson.
Minister without Portfolio and Leader of Parliamentary Affairs, Hon. Dr. Kenneth McNeil.
Minister for Justice and Attorney General, Senator
the Hon. Carl Rattray, QC.
Agriculture, Hon. Horace Clarke.
Labour, Welfare and Sport, Hon. Portia Simpson.
Construction, Hon. O. D. Ramtallie.
Public Utilities and Transport, Hon. Robert Pickersgill.
Education, Senator the Hon. Carlyle Dunkley.
Local Government, Hon. Ralph Brown.
Mining and Energy, Hon. Hugh Small, QC.
National Security, Hon. K. D. Knight, QC.
Health, Hon. Easton Douglas.
Youth, Culture and Community Development, Dr. the
Hon. Douglas Manley.
Tourism, Senator the Hon. Frank Pringle.

JAMAICAN HIGH COMMISSION
1–2 Prince Consort Road, SW7 2BZ
[071–823 9911]

High Commissioner, Her Excellency Mrs. Ellen Gray
Bogle (1989).

JUDICATURE

Chief Justice and Keeper of Records, Hon. E. Zacca.
Judges of the Court of Appeal, Hon. I. D. Rowe
(*President*); Hons. J. S. Kerr, H. D. Carberry, R. O.
C. White, J. Campbell, M. L. Wright.

COMMUNICATIONS

There are several excellent harbours, Kingston
being the principal port. The island has 2,944 miles
of main roads and over 7,000 miles of subsidiary roads.

There are two international airports capable of
handling the largest civil jet aircraft, the Norman
Manley International Airport on the south coast
serving Kingston, and Sangster Airport on the north
coast serving the major tourist areas. In addition
there are licensed aerodromes at Port Antonio, Ocho
Rios, Mandeville and Negril. There are 16 privately
owned, seven public and two military airstrips.

Air Jamaica, the national airline, operates international services; Trans-Jamaica Airlines operates
scheduled internal services.

ECONOMY

Jamaica is a popular tourist resort, attracting
1,163,326 visitors during 1989. Actual foreign exchange receipts from tourism amounted to
US$457·76m in 1989.

Alumina, bananas, bauxite and sugar, the four
major categories of Jamaica's traditional exports,
accounted for 94·2 per cent of the total value of
exports in 1989. The export of alumina amounted to
2,145,400 tonnes. Earnings from sugar in 1989
amounted to US$66·3m, rum US$16·1m, and bananas
US$19·3m. Less traditional exports include garments,
processed food products, limestone and ornamental
horticultural products. The 1988 hurricane adversely affected the export of coffee, citrus and other
tree crops.

FINANCE

	1988	1989
Revenue	US$2,037·8m	US$2,083·0m
Expenditure	2,219·7m	2,610·3m

TRADE

	1988	1989
Total imports	US$1,449·4m	US$1,826·3m
Total exports	834·4m	970·3m

Trade with UK

	1988	1989
Imports from UK	£48,855,000	£61,355,000
Exports to UK	89,693,000	95,516,000

BRITISH HIGH COMMISSION
PO Box 575, Trafalgar Road, Kingston 10
[Kingston 926 9050]

High Commissioner, His Excellency Derek Francis
Milton, CMG (1989).

British Council Representative in the Caribbean,
Gillian Roche, 3rd Floor, First Life Building, 64
Knutsford Boulevard, Kingston 5.

KENYA
(Jamhuri ya Kenya)

AREA, POPULATION, ETC.—Kenya is bisected by the
equator and extends approximately from latitude
4° N. to latitude 4° S. and from longitude 34° E. to
41° E. From the coast of the Indian Ocean in the east,
the borders of Kenya are with Somalia in the east
and Ethiopia and Sudan in the north and north-west.
To the west lie Uganda and Lake Victoria. On the
south is Tanzania. The total area is 224,961 sq. miles
(582,646 sq. km), including 5,171 square miles of water.
The country is divided into 8 provinces (Central,
Coast, Eastern, Nairobi, Nyanza, North Eastern, Rift
Valley, Western). The population is 23,883,000 (1988
UN estimate). The main tribal groups are the Kikuyu,
Luhya, Luo, Kamba, Kalenjin and Masai. The official
languages are Swahili, which is generally understood
throughout Kenya, and English; numerous indigenous languages are also spoken.

CAPITAL.—Nairobi, population 1,103,554 (1984 estimate).

CURRENCY.—Kenya shilling (Ksh) of 100 cents.

FLAG.—Three equal horizontal bands of black over
red over green; red and white spears and shield
device in centre.

NATIONAL ANTHEM.—Kenya, Land of the Lion.

NATIONAL DAY.—December 12 (Independence
Day).

GOVERNMENT

Kenya became an independent state and a member
of the British Commonwealth on December 12, 1963,
after six months of internal self-government. Kenya
became a Republic on December 12, 1964. In 1982 the
Government introduced amendments to the constitution and election law, making the country a one-party state. The Kenya African National Union
(KANU) is the sole legal political organization. There
is a uni-cameral National Assembly of 202 members.

President and C.-in-C. Armed Forces, Hon. Daniel T.
arap Moi, *took office*, October 14, 1978, returned for
a third five-year term on February 29, 1988.

Cabinet
(as at May 31, 1990)

Vice-President and Minister for Finance, Hon. Prof.
George Saitoti.
Environment and Natural Resources, Hon. Jeremiah
Nyagah.
Lands, Housing and Physical Planning, Hon. Darius
Mbele.

Water Development, Hon. John Okwanyo.
Home Affairs and National Heritage, Hon. Davidson Kuguru.
Planning and National Development, Hon. Dr. Z. Onyonka.
Transport and Communications, Hon. J. J. Kamotho.
Energy, Hon. N. K. Biwott.
Local Government, Hon. William ole Ntimama.
Foreign Affairs and International Co-operation, Hon. Wilson Ndolo Ayah.
Commerce, Hon. Arthur K. Magugu.
Tourism and Wildlife, Hon. Katana Ngala.
Culture and Social Services, Hon. James Njiru.
Agriculture, Hon. Maina Wanjigi.
Health, Hon. Mwai Kibaki.
Public Works, Hon. Timothy Mibei.
Co-operative Development, Hon. John Cheruiyot.
Labour, Hon. Peter Habenga Okondo.*
Education, Hon. Peter Oloo Aringo.
Information and Broadcasting, Hon. Nahashon Kanyi.
Livestock Development, Hon. Elijah W. Mwangale.
Industry, Hon. Dalmas Anyango Otieno.
Research, Science and Technology, Hon. George Muhoho.
Supplies and Marketing, Hon. Wycliffe Musalia Mudavadi.
Technical Training and Applied Technology, Hon. Prof. Sam K. Ongeri.
Manpower Development and Employment, Hon. Paul Ngei.
Reclamation and Development of Arid, Semi-Arid and Waste Land, Hon. George Ndoto.
Regional Development, Hon. Onyango Midika.
Attorney General, Hon. Justice Mathew Muli.
* Resigned Aug. 1990.

KENYA HIGH COMMISSION
45 Portland Place, W1N 4AS
[071-636 2371]

High Commissioner, Her Excellency Dr. Sally Kosgei (1987).

PRODUCTION

Agriculture provides about 52 per cent of total export earnings (excluding processed oil products). The great variation in altitude and ecology provide conditions under which a wide range of crops can be grown. These include wheat, barley, pyrethrum, coffee, tea, sisal, coconuts, cashew nuts, cotton, maize and a wide variety of tropical and temperate fruits and vegetables. The total area of well-farmed land on which concentrated mixed farming can be practised is small and the remainder is arid or semi-arid country but population pressure and the need to increase agricultural production for export has led to attempts to develop such areas.

Prospecting and mining are carried on in some parts of the country, the principal minerals produced being soda ash, salt and limestone.

Hydro-electric power has been developed, particularly on the Upper Tana River. Kenya is now almost self-sufficient in electric power generation but the connection with Owen Falls in Uganda is still in being.

There has been considerable industrial development over the last 15 years and Kenya has a wide variety of industries processing agricultural produce and manufacturing an increasing range of products from local and imported raw materials. New industries have recently come into being such as steel, textile mills, dehydrated vegetable processing and motor tyre manufacture as well as many smaller schemes which have added to the country's already considerable consumer goods. There is an oil refinery in Mombasa supplying both Kenya and Uganda, and a fuel pipeline now connects Mombasa and Nairobi.

COMMUNICATIONS

The Kenya Railways Corporation has 1,300 miles of railway open to traffic. There are also 31,000 miles of road, of which 2,700 are bitumen surfaced. Trans-border links with Tanzania were re-opened in 1985 with rail services for freight and steamer services for passengers and freight.

The principal port is Mombasa, operated by the Kenya Ports Authority.

International air services operate from airports at Nairobi and Mombasa.

TRADE

Principal exports are coffee and tea, which account for 33 per cent of total export earnings. Also exported are fruit, vegetables, and crude animal and vegetable material. Petroleum products account for about 37 per cent of imports; other imports are manufactured goods, particularly machinery, transport equipment, metals, pharmaceuticals and chemicals.

Trade with UK

	1988	1989
Imports from UK	£202,094,000	£208,464,000
Exports to UK	142,455,000	154,313,000

BRITISH HIGH COMMISSION
Bruce House, Standard Street, PO Box 30465
Nairobi
[Nairobi 335944]

High Commissioner, His Excellency Roger Tomkys (1990).

British Council Representative, T. Edmundson, (PO Box 40751) ICEA Building, Kenyatta Avenue, Nairobi. There are offices at *Kisumu* and *Mombasa*.

KIRIBATI
(Ribaberikin Kiribati)

AREA, POPULATION, ETC.—Kiribati, the former Gilbert Islands, became an independent Republic in 1979. Kiribati comprises 36 islands—the Gilberts Group (17) including Banaba, formerly Ocean Island; the Phoenix Islands (8); and the Line Islands (11) — situated in the south west central Pacific around the point at which the International Date Line cuts the Equator. The total land area of 281 sq. miles (728 sq. km) is spread over some 2 million square miles of ocean. Few of the atolls are more than half a mile in width or more than 12 feet high. The vegetation consists mainly of coconut palms, breadfruit trees and pandanus. The population (UN estimate 1988) is 67,000, and predominantly Christian.

CAPITAL.—Tarawa, population estimated at 17,921).

CURRENCY.—Kiribati uses the Australian dollar ($A) of 100 cents.

FLAG.—Red, with blue and white wavy lines in base, and in the centre a gold rising sun and a flying frigate bird.

NATIONAL ANTHEM.—Teirake Kain Kiribati (Stand Kiribati).

NATIONAL DAY.—July 12 (Independence Day).

GOVERNMENT

The President is Head of State as well as Head of Government and is elected nationally. There is an elected House of Assembly (41 members); executive authority is vested in the Cabinet.

Cabinet
(as at May 31, 1990)

President and Minister of Foreign Affairs, Hon.
Ieremia Tabai, GCMG.
Vice-President and Minister of Finance, Hon. Teatao
Teannaki.
Works and Energy, Hon. Baitika Toum.
Natural Resources Development, Hon. Taomati T.
Iuta.
Home Affairs and Decentralization, Hon. Babera
Kirata, OBE.
The Line and Phoenix Islands, Hon. Tekinaiti
Kaiteie.
Trade, Industry and Labour, Hon. Raion Bataroma.
Transport and Communications, Hon. Uera Rabaua.
Health and Family Planning, Hon. Rotaria Ataia.
Education, Hon. Ataraoti Bwebwenibure.
Attorney-General, Hon. Michael N. Takabwebwe.
Chief Justice, vacant.

HONORARY CONSULATE

c/o Faith House, 7 Tufton Street, SW1P 3QN
Honorary Consul, Hon. Maurice Chandler, CBE.

ECONOMY

Most people still practise a semi-subsistence economy, the main staples of their diet being coconuts
and fish.
Estimated recurrent revenue for 1988 is $A24·9m.
The principal imports are foodstuffs, consumer goods,
machinery and transport equipment. The principal
exports are copra, which earned $A4,203,000, and
fish, income from which was around $A1,606,000 in
1988. Total value of exports in 1988 was $A6,670,000.

COMMUNICATIONS

Air communication exists between most of the
islands, and is operated by Air Tungaru, a statutory
corporation. Air Marshall Islands operate a weekly
service between Majuro, Tarawa, Funafuti and
Nandi, and Air Nauru between Tarawa, Nauru and
Nandi. Inter-island shipping is operated by a statutory corporation, the Shipping Corporation of Kiribati.

SOCIAL WELFARE

The Government maintains a teacher training
college and a secondary school. Four junior secondary schools are maintained by missions. Throughout
the Republic there are about a hundred primary
schools. The total enrolment of children of school
age is about 16,000. The Marine Training School at
Tarawa trains seamen for service with overseas
shipping lines. There is a general hospital at Tarawa.
The other inhabited islands have dispensaries.

Trade with UK

	1988	1989
Imports from UK .	£522,000	£378,000
Exports to UK . .	128,000	26,000

BRITISH HIGH COMMISSION
PO Box 61, Bairiki, Tarawa
[Bairiki 21327]

High Commissioner, His Excellency Derek White
(1990).

LESOTHO
('Muso oa Lesotho)

Lesotho is a landlocked mountainous state entirely
surrounded by the Republic of South Africa. Of the
total area of 11,720 sq. miles (30,355 sq. km), a belt
between 20 and 40 miles in width lying across the
western and southern boundaries and comprising
about one-third of the total is classed as lowlands,
being between 5,000 and 6,000 ft. above sea level. The
remaining two-thirds are classed as foothills and
highlands, rising to 11,425 ft. The population (UN
estimate 1988) is 1,676,000.

CAPITAL.—Maseru, population (1986 Census)
288,951.
CURRENCY.—Loti (M) of 100 lisente.
FLAG.—Diagonally white over blue over green
with the white of double width, and an assegai and
knobkerrie on a Basotho shield in brown in the upper
hoist.
NATIONAL ANTHEM.—Pina ea Sechaba.
NATIONAL DAY.—October 4 (Independence Day).

GOVERNMENT

Lesotho (formerly Basutoland) became a constitutional monarchy within the Commonwealth on
October 4, 1966. The independence constitution was
suspended in January 1970, when the country was
governed by a Council of Ministers, until the
establishment of a nominated National Assembly in
April 1974. The Government was overthrown in
January 1986, and executive and legislative powers
were conferred upon the King, to be advised by the
Military Council and Council of Ministers. In March
1990 the King's powers were formally revoked and
vested in the Chairman of the Council of Ministers.
An eight-member 'task force for democratization'
was formed, due to re-instate civilian rule in June
1992.
The country is divided into ten administrative
districts. In each district there is a District Secretary
who co-ordinates all Government activity in the
area, working in co-operation with hereditary chiefs.

Head of State, HM King Moshoeshoe II.

Military Council

Chairman, Maj.-Gen. Justin Metsing Lekhanya.
Members, Col. Elias P. Ramaema; Brig. B. M.
Berotholi; Col. Michael N. Ts'otetsi; Col. J. M.
Jane; Lt.-Col. E. M. Mokete.

Council of Ministers
(as at February 19, 1990)*

Chairman, Minister of Defence and Internal Security,
HE Maj.-Gen. Justin Metsing Lekhanya.
Foreign Affairs, Hon. M. T. Thabane.
*Law, Public Service, Constitutional and Parliamen-
tary Affairs*, Hon. B. M. Khaketla (*acting*).
*Finance, Planning and Economic Manpower Devel-
opment, Agriculture, Co-operatives and Marketing*,
Hon. E. R. Sekhonyana.
Works, Transport and Communications, Lt.-Col. M.
V. Mokone.
Justice and Prisons, Hon. K. A. Maope.
Employment, Social Welfare and Pensions, Lt. T. P.
Molapo.
Tourism, Sports and Culture, Hon. M. L. Mathealire.
Water, Energy and Mining, Hon. Col. A. L. Jane.
Highlands, Water and Energy Affairs, Maj. R. Habi.
*Interior and Chieftainship Affairs and Rural Devel-
opment*, Hon. P. J. Molapo.
Education, Hon. Prof. L. B. B. J. Machobane.
Trade and Industry, Hon. M. Mokoroane
Health, Hon. A. L. Thoahlane.

*At the time of going to press, a recent government
list was not available.

JUDICIARY

The Lesotho Courts of Law consist of the Court of Appeal, the High Court, Magistrates' Courts, Judicial Commissioners' Court, Central and local Courts. Magistrates' and higher courts administer the laws of Lesotho. They also adjudicate appeals from the Judicial Commissioner's and Subordinate Courts.

Chief Justice, Hon. B. P. Cullinan.

LESOTHO HIGH COMMISSION
10 Collingham Road, SW5 0NR
[071–373 8581]

High Commissioner, His Excellency M. K. Tsekoa (1989).

EDUCATION

Most schools are mission-controlled, the Government providing grants for salaries and buildings. There are over 1,000 primary and over 100 secondary schools; few areas lack a school and there is a high literacy rate of about 70 per cent. Increasing emphasis is being laid on agricultural and vocational education. The National University of Lesotho at Roma was established in 1975.

COMMUNICATIONS

A tarred road of 110 miles links Maseru to several of the main lowland towns, and this is being extended in the south of the country. The mountainous areas are linked by 1,300 miles of gravelled and earth roads and tracks. Roads link border towns in South Africa with the main towns in Lesotho. Maseru is connected by rail with the main Bloemfontein–Natal line of the South African Railways. Scheduled international air services are operated daily between Maseru and Johannesburg and other scheduled international flights are to Gaborone, Harare, Manzini and Maputo. There are around 30 airstrips. Internal scheduled services are operated by the Lesotho Airways Corporation.

The telephone network is fully automated in all urban centres. Radio telephone communication is used extensively in the remote rural areas.

PRODUCTION

The economy of Lesotho is based on agriculture and animal husbandry, and the adverse balance of trade (mainly consumer and capital goods) is offset by the earnings of the large numbers of the population who work in South Africa. Apart from some diamonds, Lesotho has few natural resources and only small-scale industrial development. The Lesotho National Development Corporation was set up to promote the development of industry, mining, trade and tourism. Work has commenced on the Highlands Water Scheme designed to provide water for the Vaal industrial zone in South Africa and hydro-electricity for Lesotho. Drilling is being carried out for oil. A National Park has been established at Sehlabathebe in the Maluti mountains. A number of light manufacturing and processing industries have recently been established.

FINANCE AND TRADE

The main sources of revenue are customs and excise duty. Estimates of expenditure and revenue (1986) are recurrent revenue M241·2 million; recurrent expenditure M265·3 million; capital revenue M144 million; capital expenditure M198 million.

Trade with UK

	1988	1989
Imports from UK	£1,260,000	£795,000
Exports to UK	977,000	734,000

BRITISH HIGH COMMISSION
PO Box 521, Maseru
[Maseru 313961]

High Commissioner, His Excellency John Coates Edwards, CMG (1988).

British Council Representative, D. Bates, Hobson's Square, PO Box 429, Maseru 100.

MALAWI
(Mfuko La Malawi)

AREA, POPULATION, ETC.—Malawi comprises Lake Malawi (formerly Lake Nyasa) and its western shore, with the high tableland separating it from the basin of the Luangwa River, the watershed forming the western frontier with Zambia; south of the lake, Malawi reaches almost to the Zambezi and is surrounded by Mozambique, the frontier lying on the west on the watershed of the Zambezi and Shire Rivers, and to the east on the Ruo, a tributary of the Shire, and Lakes Chiuta and Chirwa. This boundary reaches the eastern shore of Lake Malawi and extends up to the mid-point of the lake for about half its length where it returns to the eastern and northern shores to form a frontier with Tanzania. Malawi has a total area of 45,747 sq. miles (118,484 sq. km). The population according to the Census held in 1987 was 7,982,607. The official languages are Chichewa and English.

CAPITAL.—Lilongwe, population (1987) 175,000. The city of Blantyre in the Southern Region, incorporating Blantyre and Limbe (population (1987) 289,000), is the major commercial and industrial centre. Other main centres are: Mzuzu, Thyolo, Mulanje, Mangochi, Salima, Dedza and Zomba, the former capital.

CURRENCY.—Kwacha (K) of 100 tambala.

FLAG.—Horizontal stripes of black, red and green, with rising sun in the centre of the black stripe.

NATIONAL ANTHEM.—O God Bless Our Land of Malawi.

NATIONAL DAY.—July 6 (Independence Day).

GOVERNMENT

Malawi (formerly Nyasaland) became a republic on July 6, 1966, having assumed internal self-government on February 1, 1963, and achieved independence on July 6, 1964. There is a Cabinet consisting of the Life President and other Ministers. The Parliament consists of 112 members, each elected by universal suffrage. Under the 1981 Amendment to the Constitution, the Life President has the power to nominate as many Members of Parliament as he wishes. Being a one-party State (the Malawi Congress Party), all elected members are required to be members of the Party. The Parliament, which usually meets three times a year, is presided over by a Speaker.

President, Minister of External Affairs, Agriculture, Justice, Works, Supplies, Dr. H. Kamuzu Banda, *elected* 1966, *sworn in as President for Life,* July 6, 1971.

Cabinet
(as at May 31, 1990)

Trade, Industry and Tourism, Hon. Robson Chirwa.
Transport and Communications, Hon. Dalton Katopola.
Health, Hon. E. C. Katola Phiri.
Finance, Hon. Louis Chimango.
Labour, Hon. Wadson Bini Deleza.
Education and Culture, Hon. Michael Mlambala.

Community Services, Hon. M. M. Mwakikunga.
Forestry and Natural Resources, Local Government, Hon. Stanford Demba.
Minister without Portfolio, Hon. Maxwell Pashane.

JUDICIARY

Chief Justice, Hon. F. L. Makuta.

MALAWI HIGH COMMISSION
33 Grosvenor Street, W1X 0DE
[071–491 4172]

High Commissioner, A. A. D. Khauyeza (acting).

EDUCATION

Primary education is the responsibility of local authorities in both urban and rural areas, although policy, curricula and inspection are the responsibility of the Ministry of Education and Culture. The Ministry is also responsible for secondary schools, technical education and primary teacher training. Religious bodies, with Government assistance, still play an important part in these fields. The University of Malawi was opened in 1965 and has four constituent colleges. The total number of students in 1988–89 was 1·2 million in primary schools, 28,000 in secondary schools and 2,330 at university.

COMMUNICATIONS

A single-track railway runs from Mchinji on the Zambian border, through Lilongwe and Salima on Lake Malawi (itself served by two passenger and a number of cargo boats) through to Blantyre. The route south to the Mozambique port of Beira is severed at the Zambesi, but the route to Nacala in Mozambique has recently re-opened. There are 12,215 km of roads in Malawi of which about 21·8 per cent are bituminised.

There is an international airport 26 km from Lilongwe, which handles regional and inter-continental flights.

FINANCE
(excluding Development Account)

	1987–88	1988–89
Revenue	K583m	K752m
Expenditure	823m	1071m

ECONOMY

The economy is largely agricultural, with maize the main subsistence crop. Tobacco, sugar, tea, groundnuts and cotton are the main cash crops and principal exports. There are two sugar mills and total production in 1989 was 157m kg. A number of light manufacturing industries have been established, mainly in agricultural processing, clothing/textiles and building materials.

TRADE

	1987	1988
Imports	K654m	K1080m
Exports	602m	742m

Trade with UK

	1988	1989
Imports from UK	£27,618,000	£30,604,000
Exports to UK	30,183,000	27,890,000

BRITISH HIGH COMMISSION
Lingadzi House (PO Box 30042),
Lilongwe 3
[Lilongwe 731544]

High Commissioner, His Excellency Nigel Wenban Smith (1990).

Deputy High Commissioner and Head of Chancery, J. Wilde.

British Council Representative, S. Newton, PO Box 30222, Lilongwe 3. There is also a library at Blantyre.

MALAYSIA
(Persekutuan Tanah Malaysia)

AREA, POPULATION, ETC.—Malaysia, comprising the 11 states of peninsular Malaya plus Sabah and Sarawak, forms a crescent well over 1,000 miles long between latitudes 1° and 7° N. and longitudes 100° and 119° E. It occupies two distinct regions—the Malay peninsula which extends from the isthmus of Kra to the Singapore Strait and the north-west coastal area of the island of Borneo. Each is separated from the other by 400 miles of the South China Sea. The total area of Malaysia, including the Federal Territories of Kuala Lumpur and Labuan, is about 127,317 sq. miles, (329,749 sq. km), with a population of 16,921,300 (1988 Census).

The principal racial groups are the Malays, the Chinese and those of Indian and Sri Lankan origin, as well as the indigenous races of Sarawak and Sabah. Bahasa Malaysia (Malay) is the sole official language, but English, various dialects of Chinese, and Tamil are also widely spoken. There are a few indigenous languages widely spoken in Sabah and Sarawak.

RELIGION.—Islam is the official religion of Malaysia, each Ruler being the head of religion in his State, though the Heads of State of Sabah and Sarawak are not heads of the Muslim religion in their States. The Yang di-Pertuan Agung is the head of religion in Melaka and Penang. The Constitution guarantees religious freedom.

CLIMATE.—The year is commonly divided into the south-west and north-west monsoon seasons. Rainfall averages about 100 inches throughout the year. The average daily temperature throughout Malaysia varies from 21° C to 32° C, though in higher areas temperatures are lower and vary widely.

CAPITAL.—Kuala Lumpur was proclaimed Federal Territory on February 1, 1974. Its population (1985) is 1,103,200.

CURRENCY.—Malaysian dollar (ringgit) (M$) of 100 sen.

FLAG.—Equal horizontal stripes of red (7) and white (7); 14 point yellow star and crescent in blue canton.

NATIONAL ANTHEM.—Negara-Ku.

NATIONAL DAY.—August 31 (Hari Kebangsaan).

STATES OF THE FEDERATION

The 13 States of the Federation of Malaysia (State capitals in brackets) and their populations at the 1988 Census are:

ΨJohore (Johore Bahru)	2,007,300
Kedah (Alor Setar)	1,353,500
Kelantan (Kota Bahru)	1,150,400
ΨMelaka (Melaka)	560,700
Negri Sembilan (Seremban)	694,100
ΨPahang (Kuantan)	1,001,200
ΨPenang (Georgetown)	1,103,200
Perak (Ipoh)	2,143,200
Perlis (Kangar)	179,700
ΨSabah (Kota Kinabalu)	1,371,000
ΨSarawak (Kuching)	1,591,000
ΨSelangor (Shah Alam)	1,878,300
ΨTerengganu (Kuala Terengganu)	705,200

FEDERAL TERRITORIES

The two Federal Territories and their population at the 1988 Census are:

Kuala Lumpur . . . . } 1,182,700
Labuan . . . .

GOVERNMENT

The Federation of Malaya became an independent country within the Commonwealth on August 31, 1957, as a result of an agreement between HM the Queen and the Rulers of the Malay States. On September 16, 1963 the Federation was enlarged by the accession of the states of Singapore, Sabah (formerly British North Borneo) and Sarawak, and the name of Malaysia was adopted from that date. On August 9, 1965 Singapore seceded from the Federation.

The Constitution was designed to ensure the existence of a strong Federal Government and also a measure of autonomy for the State Governments. It provides for a constitutional Supreme Head of the Federation (HM the *Yang di-Pertuan Agung*) to be elected for a term of five years by the Rulers from among their number, and for a Deputy Supreme Head (HRH *Timbalan Yang di-Pertuan Agung*) to be similarly elected. The Malay Rulers are either chosen or succeed to their position in accordance with the custom of the particular state. In other states of Malaysia choice of the Head of State is at the discretion of the Yang di-Pertuan Agung after consultation with the Chief Minister of the State.

The Federal Parliament consists of two houses, the Senate and the House of Representatives. The Senate (*Dewan Negara*) consists of 68 members, under a President (*Yang di-Pertua Dewan Negara*), 26 elected by the Legislative Assemblies of the States (two from each) and 42 appointed by the Yang di-Pertuan Agung. The House of Representatives (*Dewan Rakyat*), consists of 177 members (Peninsular Malaysia 134; Sarawak 24; and Sabah 20). Members are elected on the principle of universal adult suffrage with a common electoral roll.

The Constitution provides that each State shall have its own Constitution not inconsistent with the Federal Constitution, with the Ruler or Governor acting on the advice of an Executive Council appointed on the advice of the Chief Minister and a single chamber Legislative Assembly. The State Secretary, the State Legal Adviser and the State Financial Officer sit in the Executive Council as *ex-officio* members. The Legislative Assemblies are fully elected on the same basis as the Federal Parliament.

Supreme Head of State, HM Sultan Azlan Muhibuddin Shah Ibni-Almarhum Sultan Yusuff Izzuddin Ghafarullahu-Lahu Shah (Sultan of Perak), sworn in April 26, 1989.

Deputy Supreme Head of State, HRH Tuanku Jaafar Ibni Al-Marhum Tuanku Abdul Rahman (Yang Dipertuan Besar of Negeri Sembilan).

Ministry
(as at May 31, 1990)

Prime Minister and Minister of Home Affairs, Datuk Seri Dr. Mahathir Muhammad.
Deputy PM and Minister of National and Rural Development, Ghafar Baba.
Labour, Datuk Lim Ah Lek.
Welfare Services, Datuk Mustaffa Muhammad.
Youth and Sports, Datuk Najib Tun Razak.
Land and Regional Development, Datuk Kasitah Gadam.
Works, Datuk Leo Moggie.
Health, Datuk Ng Cheng Kiat.
Finance, Datu Paduka Daim Zainuddin.

Foreign Affairs, Datuk Haji Abu Hassan Omar.
Education, Anwar Ibrahim.
Information, Datuk Muhammad Rahmat.
Transport, Datuk Seri Ling Liong Sik.
Trade and Industry, Datuk Seri Rafidah Aziz.
Defence, Tengku Ahmad Rithaudden.
Agriculture, Datuk Seri Sanusi Junid.
Public Enterprises, Datuk Napsiah Omar.
Primary Industries, Datuk Seri Lim Kheng Yaik.
Science, Technology and Environment, Datuk Amar Stephen Yong.
Energy, Telecommunications and Posts, Datuk Seri S. Sammy Vellu.
Housing and Local Government, Lee Kim Sai.
Culture and Tourism, Datuk Hj Sabaruddin Chik.
Ministers in Prime Minister's Department, Datuk Dr. Sulaiman Daud (*Justice Minister*); Datuk Dr. Yusoff Noor.

NOTE.—The words 'Tunku/Tengku', 'Tun', 'Tan Sri', and 'Datuk' are titles. The word 'Tunku/Tengku' is equivalent to 'Prince'. 'Tun' denotes membership of a high Order of Malaysian Chivalry and 'Tan Sri' and 'Datuk' ('Datuk Seri' in Perak and 'Datu' in Sabah) are each the equivalent of a knighthood. The wife of a 'Tun' is styled 'Toh Puan', that of a 'Tan Sri' is styled 'Puan Sri' and of a 'Datuk' 'Datin'. The honorific 'Tuan' or 'Encik' is equivalent to 'Mr.' and the honorific 'Puan' is equivalent to 'Mrs.'. The words 'Al-Haj' or 'Haji' indicate that the person so named has made the pilgrimage to Mecca.

MALAYSIAN HIGH COMMISSION
45 Belgrave Square, SW1X 8QT
[071–235 8033]

High Commissioner, His Excellency Dato Wan Sidek (1990).

JUDICATURE

The Judicial System consists of a Supreme Court and two High Courts, one in Peninsular Malaysia and one for Sabah and Sarawak (sitting alternately in Kota Kinabalu and Kuching).

The Supreme Court comprises a President, the two Chief Justices of the High Courts and other judges. It possesses appellate, original and advisory jurisdiction.

Each of the High Courts consists of a Chief Justice and not less than four other judges. The Federal Constitution allows for a maximum of twelve such judges for Malaya and eight for Borneo. In Peninsular Malaysia the Subordinate Courts consist of the Sessions Courts and the Magistrates' Courts. In Sabah/Sarawak the Magistrates' Courts constitute the Subordinate Courts.

DEFENCE

The Malaysian Armed Forces consist of the Army, Navy and Air Force, together with volunteer forces for each arm. The defence of the country is largely borne by the army in its role of providing defence against external threat and counter-insurgency operations and also to assist the police in the performance of public order duties. The Royal Malaysian Navy (RMN) has the responsibility of defending the 3,000 miles of the country's coastline and maintaining constant patrol of 500 miles of the high seas that separate Sabah and Sarawak from the mainland. The Royal Malaysian Air Force (RMAF) is capable of providing close strategic and tactical support to the army and police in the defence and internal security of the country.

FINANCE

	1988	1989
Revenue	M$22·0 billion	M$24·7 billion
Expenditure	25·9 billion	29·7 billion

PRODUCTION AND TRADE

Malaysia is the largest exporter of natural rubber, tin, palm oil and tropical hardwoods. Other major export commodities are manufactured and processed products, petroleum, oil, and other minerals, palm kernel oil, tea and pepper.

Manufacturing has overtaken agriculture as the largest single contributor to the economy.

Exports of major commodities were (percentage of total exports):

	1988	1989
Manufactured goods	48·5	54·1
Agriculture	33·4	28·3
Minerals	16·7	16·9

Another commodity which is produced throughout Malaysia is rice, the staple food, and efforts are being made to achieve self-sufficiency.

Imports consist mainly of machinery and transport equipment, manufactured goods, foods, mineral fuels, chemicals and inedible crude materials.

	1988	1989
Imports	M$42·8 billion	M$60·9 billion
Exports	54·4 billion	67·8 billion

Trade with UK

	1988	1989
Imports from UK	£310,462,000	£441,762,000
Exports to UK	525,017,000	676,258,000

BRITISH HIGH COMMISSION
185 JLN Ampang
(PO Box 11030), 50732 Kuala Lumpur
[Kuala Lumpur 03–2482122]

High Commissioner, His Excellency Sir John Nicholas Teague Spreckley, KCVO, CMG (1986).

British Council Representative, A. Johnson, CBE, PO Box 10539, Jalan Bukit Aman, Kuala Lumpur 50916; offices at *Kota Kinabalu* (Sabah) and *Kuching* (Sarawak), and a library in *Penang*.

THE MALDIVES
(Divehi Jumhuriya)

AREA, POPULATION, ETC.—The Maldives are a chain of coral atolls, some 400 miles to the south-west of Sri Lanka, stretching from just south of the equator for about 600 miles to the north. There are about 20 coral atolls comprising over 1,200 islands, 202 of which are inhabited. Total area of the islands is 115 sq. miles (298 sq. km). No point in the entire chain of islands is more than 8 feet above sea-level. The population of the islands (UN estimate 1988) is 202,000. The people are Sunni Muslims and the Maldivian (Dhivehi) language is akin to Elu or old Sinhalese.

CAPITAL.—ΨMalé, population (1985) 46,334. There is an international airport at Malé.

CURRENCY.—Rufiyaa of 100 laaris.

FLAG.—Green field bearing a white crescent, with wide red border.

NATIONAL ANTHEM.—Qawmee Salaam.

NATIONAL DAY.—July 26.

GOVERNMENT

Until 1952 the islands were a Sultanate under the protection of the British Crown. Internal self-government was achieved in 1948 and full independence in 1965. In 1982 the Republic of The Maldives became a special member of the Commonwealth, and a full member in 1985.

The Maldives form a Republic which is elective. There is a Parliament (the *Citizens' Majlis*) with representatives elected from all the atolls. The life of

the Majlis is 5 years. The Government consists of a Cabinet, which is responsible to the Majlis.

President, His Excellency Maumoon Abdul Gayoom, *elected* 1978, 1983, *re-elected* September 1989 (also *Minister of Defence and National Security, and Minister of Finance*).

Cabinet
(as at June 30, 1990)

Foreign Affairs, Hon. Fathulla Jameel.
Justice, Hon. Mohamed Rasheed Ibrahim.
Home Affairs and Sports, Hon. Umar Zahir.
Education, Hon. Abdulla Hameed.
Health and Welfare, Hon. Abdul Sattar Moosa Didi.
Fisheries and Agriculture, Hon. Abbas Ibrahim.
Atolls Administration, Hon. Abdulla Jameel.
Trade and Industries, Hon. Ahmed Mujuthaba.
Tourism, Hon. Ismail Shafeeu.
Public Works and Labour, Hon. Abdulla Kamaludeen.
Speaker of the Citizens' Majlis, Hon. Ahmed Zaki.
Attorney General, Hon. Ahmed Zahir.
Chief Justice, Hon. Moosa Fathy.
Transport and Shipping, vacant.
Minister at the President's Office, Hon. Mohamed Zahir Hussain.

PRODUCTION

The vegetation of the islands is coconut palms with some scrub. Hardly any cultivation of crops is possible and nearly all food to supplement the basic fish diet has to be imported. The principal industry is fishing and considerable quantities of fish are exported to Japan. Dried fish is exported to Sri Lanka, where it is a delicacy. The tourist industry is expanding rapidly (131,000 visitors in 1987). Maldives Shipping Ltd. has a fleet of some 30 merchant ships.

Trade with UK

	1988	1989
Imports from UK	£1,689,000	£3,412,000
Exports to UK	1,859,000	5,224,000

BRITISH HIGH COMMISSION
High Commissioner, (resides at Colombo, Sri Lanka).

MALTA
(Repubblika Ta'Malta)

AREA, POPULATION, ETC.—Malta lies in the Mediterranean Sea, 58 miles from Sicily and about 180 miles from the African coast, about 17 miles in length and 9 in breadth, and having an area of 94·9 square miles. Malta includes also the adjoining islands of Gozo (area 25·9 sq. miles), Comino and minor islets. The estimated population at 1988 was 349,014. The Maltese are mainly Roman Catholic.

The Maltese language is of Semitic origin and held by some to be derived from the Carthaginian and Phoenician tongues. Maltese and English are the official languages of administration and Maltese is ordinarily the official language in all the courts of law and the language of general use in the islands.

Malta was in turn held by the Phoenicians, Greeks, Carthaginians, Romans and Arabs. In 1090 it was conquered by Count Roger of Normandy. In 1530 it was handed over to the Knights of St. John, who made it a stronghold of Christianity. In 1565 it sustained the famous siege, when the last great effort of the Turks was successfully withstood by Grandmaster La Valette. The Knights expended large sums in fortifying the island and carrying out many magnificent works, until they were expelled by Napoleon in 1798. The Maltese rose against the French garrison soon afterwards, and the island was subsequently blockaded by the British fleet. The Maltese people freely requested the protection of the British Crown in 1802 on condition that their rights and privileges would be preserved and respected. The islands were finally annexed to the British Crown by the Treaty of Paris in 1814.

Malta was again closely besieged in the last war. From June 1940, to the end of the war, 432 members of the garrison and 1,540 civilians were killed by enemy aircraft, and about 35,000 houses were destroyed or damaged. The island was awarded the George Cross in 1942.

CAPITAL.—ΨValletta. Population (Census 1985), 9,239. Valletta Grand Harbour is very deep and large vessels can anchor alongside the shore. It is an important port of call and ship repairing centre for vessels, being half-way between Gibraltar and Port Said.

CURRENCY.— Maltese lira (LM) of 100 cents and 1,000 mils.

FLAG.—Two equal vertical stripes, white at the hoists and red at the fly. A representation of the George Cross is carried edged in red in the top corner of the white stripe.

NATIONAL ANTHEM.—Lil Din I-Art Helwa.

NATIONAL DAY.—September 21 (Independence Day).

GOVERNMENT

On September 21, 1964, under the Malta Independence Order 1964, Malta became an independent state within the Commonwealth; on December 13, 1974, Malta became a republic within the Commonwealth.

Elections are held every five years by a system of proportional representation. Seats are obtained by the highest number of votes in the respective districts. The party with the highest number of votes forms the government, with extra members being co-opted if necessary.

President.—Dr. Vincent Tabone, *took office* April 4, 1989.

Cabinet
(as at May 31, 1990)

Prime Minister, Hon. Dr. Edward Fenech Adami.
Deputy PM and Minister of Foreign Affairs and Justice, Hon. Dr. Guido De Marco.
Education and the Interior, Hon. Dr. Ugo Mifsud Bonnici.
Environment, Hon. Dr. Stanley Zammit.
Youth, Culture, Consumer Protection, Hon. Dr. Michael Frendo.
Social Policy, Hon. Dr. Louis Galea.
Health, Hon. Dr. George Hyzler.
Elderly, Hon. Prof. John Rizzo Naudi.
Housing, Hon. Dr. Joe Cassar.
Finance, Hon. Dr. G. Bonello Du Puis.
Infrastructure Development, Hon. Michael Falzon.
Water and Energy, Hon. Dr. Ninu Zammit.
Transport and Communications, Hon. Dr. Francis Zammit Dimech.
Agriculture and Fisheries, Hon. Lawrence Gatt.
Tertiary Sector Development, Hon. Dr. Emmanuel Bonnici.
Tourism, Hon. Dr. Michael Refalo.
Maritime and Offshore Activities, Hon. Dr. Joe Fenech.
Gozo, Hon. Anton Tabone.
Economic Affairs, Hon. John Dalli.

MALTA HIGH COMMISSION
16 Kensington Square, W8 5HH
[071–938 1712]

High Commissioner, His Excellency John A. Manduca (1987).

EDUCATION

In June 1988 there were 91 government primary schools with 26,399 pupils and 40 secondary schools and new lyceums, with a total of 15,536 pupils.

The government also runs 26 technical/trade schools (with an enrolment of 6,465 students). Schools of art, music, secretarial studies, catering, nursing and dramatic art are sponsored by the government. Tertiary education is available at the University of Malta, which had 1,447 students in 1988.

A number of private schools offer more or less the same facilities that exist in Government schools. All state education is free.

AGRICULTURE

Agriculture plays a significant role in the economy. There are 3,090 full time farmers and about 12,400 part time farmers. Crop production consists mainly of tomatoes, potatoes, onions, cabbages and cauliflowers, and fruit. Grape is the largest fruit crop. Flowers and cuttings are produced for export markets.

INDUSTRY

The island's leading industry is the state-owned Malta Drydocks, employing about 5,000 people. The main port of Grand Harbour handled traffic (excluding mineral oils) of 1,989,673 tonnes in 1988.

At the end of 1989 manufacturing firms employed some 28,800 people. The wide range of produce includes food processing, textiles and clothing, plastics and chemical products, electronic equipment and components. The gross output of the manufacturing industry in 1988 was LM388·3 million, of which LM214·5 million were export sales.

Tourism has assumed primary importance, with over 783,846 tourists visiting the island in 1988, and Marsamxett Harbour is being further developed by the extension of a yacht centre. Gross income from this industry stood at LM132·4 million.

FINANCE

	1988	1989
Revenue	LM304,225,000	LM291,779,000
Expenditure	270,786,000	320,744,000

TRADE

The principal imports for home consumption are foodstuffs (mainly wheat, meat and bullocks, milk and fruit), fodder, beverages and tobacco, fuels, chemicals, textiles and machinery (industrial, agricultural and transport). The chief domestic exports are processed food, electronics, textiles, and other manufactures.

	1988	1989
Imports	LM447,100,000	LM515,000,000
Exports	235,700,000	294,200,000

Trade with UK

	1988	1989
Imports from UK	£121,696,000	£132,287,000
Exports to UK	40,189,000	42,194,000

BRITISH HIGH COMMISSION
7 St. Anne Street, Floriana
[233134/8]

High Commissioner, His Excellency Brian Hitch, CMG, CVO (1988).

British Council Representative, G. Graves, 89 Archbishop Street, Valletta.

MAURITIUS

AREA, POPULATION, ETC.—Mauritius is an island group lying in the Indian Ocean, 550 miles east of Madagascar, between 57° 17′–57° 46′ E. long. and 19° 58′–20° 33′ S. lat., and comprising with its dependencies an area of 790 square miles (2,045 sq. km). The population (December 1989 estimate, excluding Rodrigues and the outer islands) was 1,047,532, made up of Asiatic races (Hindus 52·6 per cent, Muslims 16·5 per cent), and persons of European (mainly French) extraction, mixed and African descent (28·3 per cent).

English is the official language but French may be used in the Legislative Assembly and lower law courts. However, Creole is the mostly commonly used language.

CLIMATE.—Mauritius enjoys a sub-tropical maritime climate, with a wide range of rainfall and temperature resulting from the mountainous nature of the island. Humidity is rather high throughout the year and rainfall is sufficient to maintain a green cover of vegetation, except for a brief period in the driest districts.

CAPITAL.—ΨPort Louis, population (1985) 138,272; other centres are Beau Bassin-Rose Hill (93,059); Curepipe (64,072); Vacoas-Phoenix (55,330) and Quatre Bornes (65,405).

CURRENCY.—Mauritius rupee of 100 cents.

FLAG.—Red, blue, yellow and green horizontal stripes.

NATIONAL ANTHEM.—Glory to the Motherland.

NATIONAL DAY.—March 12.

GOVERNMENT

Mauritius was discovered in 1511 by the Portuguese; the Dutch visited it in 1598 and named it Mauritius, after Prince Maurice of Nassau. From 1638 to 1710 it was held as a small Dutch colony and in 1715 the French took possession but did not settle it until 1721. Mauritius was taken by a British Force in 1810. A British garrison remained on the island until June 1960. The French language and French law were preserved under British rule.

A Crown Colony for 158 years, Mauritius became an independent state within the Commonwealth on March 12, 1968. The Constitution defined by Order in Council in 1964 was slightly altered in 1966 on the recommendation of the Banwell Commission, the effect being to increase the membership of the Legislative Assembly to 70, 62 elected by block voting in multi-member constituencies (including two members for Rodrigues) and eight specially-elected members. Of the latter, four seats go to the 'best loser' of whichever communities in the island are underrepresented in the Assembly after the General Election and the four remaining seats are allocated on the basis of both party and community. The Constitution provides for the appointment of a Governor General who acts on the advice of the Council of Ministers, collectively responsible to the Legislative Assembly.

In the August 1987 General Election, the Mouvement Socialiste Mauricien (MSM), allied with the Labour Party (MLP), the Parti Mauricien Social Democrate and the Organisation du Peuple Rodriguais (OPR), defeated the Mouvement Militant Mauricien and formed the Government, with a majority of 22 seats. The Parti Mauricien Social Democrate left the alliance in August 1988.

Governor General, His Excellency Sir Veerasamy Ringadoo, GCMG, QC.

Council of Ministers
(as at May 31, 1990)

Prime Minister, Minister of Defence and Internal Security, Information, Internal and External Com- munications and the Outer Islands, Rt. Hon. Sir Anerood Jugnauth, KCMG, QC (MSM).

Deputy PM, Attorney General and Minister of Justice, External Affairs and Emigration, Hon. Sir Satcam Boolell, QC (MLP).

Deputy PM and Minister of Finance, Hon. Seetanah Lutchmeenaraidoo (MSM).

Deputy PM and Minister of Economic Planning and Development, Dr. the Hon. Beergoonath Ghurburrun (MSM).

Education, Arts and Culture, Hon. Armoogum Parsuramen (MSM).

Trade and Shipping, Hon. Dwarkanath Gungah (MSM).

Energy, Water Resources and Postal Services, Hon. Mahyendrah Utchanah (MSM).

Social Security, National Solidarity, and Reform Institutions, Dr. the Hon. Dineshwar Ramjuttun (MSM).

Housing, Lands and the Environment, Hon. Sir Ramesh Jeewoolall (MLP).

Labour and Industrial Relations, Women's Rights and Family Welfare, Hon. Mrs. Sheilabai Bappoo (MSM).

Youth, Sports and Tourism, Hon. Michael Glover (MSM).

Rodrigues, Hon. Serge Clair (OPR).

Co-operatives, Hon. Vishwanath Sajadah (MLP).

Health, Hon. Jagdishwar Goburdhun (MSM).

Agriculture, Fisheries and Natural Resources, Hon. Murlidas Dulloo (MSM).

Industry, Hon. Clarel Malherbe (MLP).

Works, Hon. Ramduthsing Jaddoo (MSM).

Local Government, Hon. Regis Finnette (MSM).

Civil Service Affairs and Employment, Hon. Mrs. France Roussety (MLP).

MAURITIUS HIGH COMMISSION
32–33 Elvaston Place, SW7 5NW
[071–581 0294]

High Commissioner, His Excellency Dr. Boodhun Teelock (1989).

EDUCATION

Primary education is free and in 1987 was provided for 137,935 children at 273 primary schools. Although education is not compulsory it is estimated that about 90 per cent of children of primary age attend school. At post-primary level there were a total of 69,825 students attending secondary schools; fees and teachers' salaries in the private secondary schools are paid by government. There are a number of training facilities offering training in engineering and mechanical trades, nursing, building, seamanship, hotel and catering etc. The College of Education trains primary school teachers. The Institute of Education is responsible for training secondary school teachers and for curriculum development. The University of Mauritius consists of Schools of Agriculture, Administration, Law and Industrial Technology. Estimated expenditure on education in 1989–90 was Rs.1,054,800,000.

COMMUNICATIONS

Port Louis, on the NW coast, handles the bulk of the island's external trade. A bulk sugar terminal capable of handling the total crop began operating in 1980. The international airport is located at Plaisance in the south-east of the island about 5 miles from Mahébourg. There are six daily newspapers and five weeklies, mostly in French, and two Chinese daily papers and one weekly paper. The Mauritius Broadcasting Corporation has a monopoly of radio broadcasting in the country; television was introduced in 1965. There is a satellite communications ground station near Port Louis.

PRODUCTION

In September 1989 the manufacturing sector employed 107,758, while the sugar industry employed 42,099.

About 55 per cent of the total sugar crop is produced on a plantation scale, while smaller owners (cultivating less than 10 acres) cultivate about 24 per cent of the land under cane. Tea and tobacco are also grown commercially but on a smaller scale than sugar.

	1988	1989
	tonnes	
Sugar	634,224	568,301
Tea (manufactured)	6,857	5,500
Tobacco (leaves)............	970	1,058

In 1989 production of molasses, mainly for export, was 177,000 tonnes. Other products include alcohol, rum, denatured spirits, perfumed spirits and vinegar.

The bulk of the island's requirements in manufactured products still has to be imported. However, the Mauritius Export Processing Zone (MEPZ) scheme, introduced in 1971, has attracted investment from overseas and the number of export-orientated enterprises has risen from ten in 1971 to 563 at the end of 1989, employing 88,650 people. The biggest firms are in clothing manufacture, particularly woollen knitwear, but the range of goods produced includes toys, plastic products, leather goods, diamond cutting and polishing, watches, television sets and telephones.

Tourism is a major source of income for Mauritius, with an estimated 265,300 tourists in 1989. Earnings from tourism in 1989 are estimated to be Rs2,830 million. The neighbouring French island of Réunion is the most important source of tourists, followed closely by mainland France.

FINANCE

The main sources of Government revenue are private and company income tax, customs and excise duties, mainly on imports, but also on sugar exports.

	1988–89	1989–90*
Public revenue	Rs.7,193m	Rs.8,283m
Public expenditure (recurrent)	7,655m	8,290m
* estimate		

TRADE

Most foodstuffs and raw materials have to be imported from abroad. Apart from local consumption (about 36,500 tonnes per annum), the sugar produced is exported, mainly to Britain.

	1988	1989
Total imports	Rs.17,460m	Rs.20,217m
Total exports	13,854m	15,517m

Trade with UK

	1988	1989
Imports from UK	£38,553,000	£43,528,000
Exports to UK	186,240,000	216,190,000

BRITISH HIGH COMMISSION
King George V Avenue, Floreal
[Floreal 6865795/9]

High Commissioner, His Excellency Michael Edward Howell, CMG, OBE.

British Council Representative, J. Edmundson, PO Box 111, Foondun Building, 2nd Floor, Royal Road, Rose Hill.

RODRIGUES AND DEPENDENCIES OF MAURITIUS

Rodrigues, formerly a dependency but now part of Mauritius, is about 350 miles east of Mauritius, with an area of 40 square miles. Population (1989) 37,538.

Cattle, salt fish, sheep, goats, pigs, maize and onions are the principal exports. The island is administered by an Island Commissioner.

Island Commissioner, Claude Wong So.

The islands of Agalega and St. Brandon are dependencies of Mauritius. Total population (1989) 500. Other small islands, formerly Mauritian dependencies, have since 1965 constituted the British Indian Ocean Territory (*see* p. 706).

NAMIBIA
(The Republic of Namibia)

AREA, POPULATION, ETC.—Namibia stretches from the southern border of Angola (lat. 17° 23′ S.) to the northern (Orange River) and north-western borders of the Cape Province of the Republic of South Africa; and from the Atlantic Ocean in the west to Botswana in the east. The average rainfall over 70 per cent of the country is below 400 mm per annum.

Namibia has an area of 318,261 sq. miles (824,292 sq. km), including the area of Walvis Bay (434 sq. miles) which is claimed by Namibia but remains under South African sovereignty. The population was estimated at 1,184,000 in 1986 and the main population groups are: Ovambo (587,000), Kavango (110,000), Damara (89,000), Herero (89,000), Whites (78,000), Nama (57,000), Coloured (48,000), Caprivians (44,000), Bushmen (34,000), Rehoboth Baster (29,000), Tswana (7,000).

CAPITAL.—Windhoek (population, 1987 estimate, 110,000). The only port of any size is ΨWalvis Bay.

CURRENCY.—South African rand (R) of 100 cents is legal tender.

FLAG.—Blue (above) and green; divided by diagonal red stripe bordered by white; golden sun on blue band near staff.

NATIONAL DAY.—March 21 (Independence Day).

GOVERNMENT

A German protectorate from 1880 to 1915, Namibia, as South West Africa, was administered until the end of 1920 by the Union of South Africa. Under the terms of the Treaty of Versailles, the territory was entrusted to South Africa with full powers of administration and legislation over the territory. After the dissolution of the League of Nations and in the absence of a trusteeship agreement, South Africa informed the United Nations that it would continue to administer South West Africa.

On June 21, 1971 the International Court of Justice at The Hague delivered an advisory opinion as requested by the UN Security Council on the legal consequences for states of the continued presence of South Africa in Namibia (South West Africa). It was the Court's majority opinion that the continued presence of South Africa was illegal, and that it was to withdraw its administration from Namibia immediately, putting an end to its occupation of the territory. The South African Government rejected this opinion, but accepted the principle that the territory should attain independence.

Following the failure of constitutional talks (known as the Turnhalle Conference) begun in 1975, the five Western members of the UN Security Council in 1977 drew up a plan, later incorporated into Security Council Resolution 435, for a peaceful settlement.

After a series of talks between Cuba, Angola, South Africa and the USA, agreement was reached in December 1988 for the withdrawal over 27 months of Cuban troops in Angola in exchange for South African withdrawal from Namibia leading to Namibian independence under UN Security Council

Resolution 435. Implementation of Resolution 435 began on April 1, 1989. The UN Secretary General sent his Special Representative to Namibia to oversee the seven-month run-up to elections and a 4,500 strong United Nations Transition Assistance Group (UNTAG) was deployed to monitor South African troop withdrawal and the conduct of the parties.

Elections for 72 seats in Namibia's first nationally elected body took place under UN supervision on November 7–11, 1989. Of voters registered, 95·9 per cent took part. Seats were allocated to parties according to the percentage of the vote won. The South West Africa People's Organization (SWAPO) won 41 seats with 57·32 per cent of the vote, the Democratic Turnhalle Alliance won 21 seats with 28·55 per cent, the United Democratic Front won 4 seats, Action Christian National 3, Namibia Patriotic Front 1, Federal Convention of Namibia 1, and Namibia National Front 1.

The National Assembly met for the first time on November 21, 1989 at the legislative building in Windhoek (the Tintenpalast). The Independence Constitution was adopted unanimously on February 9, 1990, and independence was declared on March 21, 1990. Namibia joined the Commonwealth upon independence.

Now constitutionally defined as a multiparty, secular, democratic republic, Namibia has an executive President as Head of State who exercises the functions of government with the assistance of a Cabinet headed by a Prime Minister. Legislative authority lies with the National Assembly, which is the lower house of a bicameral parliamentary structure; an upper house (National Council) representing Regional Councils is to be created in 1992. The main function of the National Council will be to review and consider legislation from the National Assembly. Under a system of proportional representation, elections to the National Assembly are to take place every five years, or earlier if decided by the President. Members of the National Council will hold their seats for six years.

President, Sam Nujoma.

Cabinet
(as at June 30, 1990)

Prime Minister, Hage Geingob.
Home Affairs, Hifikepunye Pohamba.
Foreign Affairs, Theo-Ben Gurirab.
Defence, Peter Mueshihange.
Finance, Otto Herrigel.
Education, Culture and Sport, Nahas Angula.
Information and Broadcasting, Hidipo Hamutenya.
Health and Social Services, Dr. Nicky Iyambo.
Labour, Public Service and Manpower Development, Hendrik Witbooi.
Mines and Energy, Andimba Toivo Ya Toivo.
Justice, Ngarikutuke Tjiriange.
Local Government and Housing, Dr Libertine Amathila.
Agriculture, Fisheries, Water and Rural Development, Gert Hanekom.
Trade and Industry, Ben Amathila.
Wildlife and Conservation, and Tourism, Nico Bessinger.
Works, Transport, and Communication, Richard Kapelwa.
Lands Resettlement and Rehabilitation, Marco Hausiku.

ECONOMY

Mining (mainly diamonds and uranium), agriculture and fisheries account for over 40 per cent of Namibia's GDP. Most of the labour force is employed in the agricultural sector.

Trade with UK

	1988	1989
Imports from UK	£3,259,000	£4,264,000
Exports to UK	10,729,000	4,568,000

BRITISH HIGH COMMISSION
116A Leutwein Street, Windhoek
[Windhoek 223022]

High Commissioner, Francis Neville Richards (1990).

British Council Representative, J. Uttley, PO Box 24224, 14 Van Rhijn Street, Windhoek 9000.

REPUBLIC OF NAURU

The Republic of Nauru is an island of 8·2 sq. miles (21 sq. km) in size, situated in 166° 55′ E. longitude and 0° 32′ S. of the Equator. It had a population (Census May 1983) of 8,042 (Nauruans 4,964; other Pacific Islanders 2,134; Asians 682; Caucasians 262). The UN estimated a total population of 9,000 in 1988. About 43 per cent of Nauruans are adherents of the Nauruan Protestant Church and there is a Roman Catholic Mission on the island. The main languages are English and Nauruan.

CURRENCY.—Nauru uses the Australian dollar ($A) of 100 cents as legal tender.

FLAG.—Twelve-point star (representing the 12 original Nauruan tribes) below a gold bar (representing the Equator), all on a blue ground.

NATIONAL DAY.—January 31 (Independence Day).

GOVERNMENT

From 1888 until the First World War Nauru was administered by Germany, in 1920 becoming a British mandated territory under the League of Nations administered by Australia. A Trusteeship superseding the Mandate was approved in 1947 by the UN and Nauru continued to be administered by Australia until it became independent on February 1, 1968. It was announced in November 1968 that a limited form of membership of the Commonwealth had been devised for Nauru at the request of its Government.

Parliament has eighteen members including the Cabinet and Speaker. Voting is compulsory for all Nauruans over 20 years of age, except in certain specified instances. Elections are held every three years. The Cabinet is chosen by the President and comprises not fewer than five nor more than six members including the President.

President and Minister for External Affairs, Internal Affairs, Island Development and Industry, Civil Aviation Authority and the Public Service, His Excellency Hon. Bernard Dowiyogo.

Cabinet
(as at June 30, 1990)

Works and Community Services and Minister Assisting the President, Hon. Vinson Detenamo.
Finance, Hon. Kinza Clodumar.
Health and Education, Hon. Vinci Clodumar.
Justice, Hon. Nimes Ekwona.

JUDICIARY

A Supreme Court of Nauru is presided over by the Chief Justice. The District Court, which is subordinate to the Supreme Court, is presided over by a Resident Magistrate. Both the Supreme Court and the District Court are Courts of Record. The Supreme Court exercises both original and appellate jurisdiction.

EDUCATION AND WELFARE

Nauru has a hospital service and other medical and dental services. There is also a maternity and child welfare service. Education is available in 9 primary and 2 secondary schools on the island with a total enrolment of about 1,600 pupils receiving primary education and 500 secondary education.

PRODUCTION, ETC.

The only fertile areas are the narrow coastal belt and local requirements of fruit and vegetables are mostly met by imports. The economy is heavily dependent on the extraction of phosphate, of which the island has one of the world's richest deposits. About 1·5 million tonnes of phosphate are mined each year, providing employment for over 1,000 people. The industry has been run since 1970 by the Nauru Phosphate Corporation. Considerable investments have been made abroad with the royalties on phosphate exports to provide for a time when production declines.

The Nauru Pacific Line owns six ships; the Government-owned Air Nauru normally operates air services throughout the Pacific region and to Australia, New Zealand, Japan, Singapore and the Philippines.

Trade with UK

	1988	1989
Imports from UK	£759,000	£549,000
Exports to UK	642,000	662,000

BRITISH HIGH COMMMISSION
British High Commissioner, (resides at Suva, Fiji).

NEW ZEALAND

AREA AND POPULATION

Islands	Area (Sq. miles)	Population at Census March 4, 1986†
(a) Exclusive of Island Territory		
North Island	44,281	2,441,615
South Island	58,093	865,469
Stewart Island	670	531*
Chatham Islands	372	755*
Minor Islands		
Inhabited—		
Kermadec Islands .	13	5(d)
Campbell Island ...	44	10(d)
Uninhabited—		
Three Kings	3	..
Snares	1	..
Solander	½	..
Antipodes	24	..
Bounty...........	½	..
Auckland	234	..
Total...............	103,736	3,307,084
(b) Island Territory		
Tokelau	5	1,690 (e)
(c) Niue¶.............	100	2,531 (f)
Cook Islands¶.....	93	17,185 (g)
Ross Dependency ..	175,000	..

* Included in North Island and South Island totals.
† Excluding members of the Armed Forces overseas—979 in 1981; 1,247 in 1986.
¶ The Cook Islands have had complete internal self-government since August 4, 1965, as has Niue since October 19, 1974, but Cook Islanders and Niueans remain New Zealand citizens.
(a) November 2, 1981. (b) January 1, 1981. (c) December 1, 1981. (d) March 31, 1983. (e) October 10, 1986. (f) September 29, 1986. (g) December 1, 1986.

Vital Statistics

	1988	1989
Births...........................	57,546	58,091
Deaths	27,408	27,042
Marriages	23,485	22,733

Infant mortality per 1,000 live births in 1989, 10·77.

Races

	1981	1986
European...............	2,696,568	2,612,958
Maori	279,084	294,201
Chinese	18,480	19,206
Polynesian (other than NZ Maori)	88,827	90,612

Religions

	1981 per cent	1986 per cent
Church of England	25·7	24·0
Presbyterian.............	16·7	18·0
Roman Catholic.........	14·3	15·2
Methodist	4·7	4·7
Baptist	1·6	2·1

PHYSIOGRAPHY

New Zealand consists of a number of islands of varying size in the South Pacific Ocean, and has also administrative responsibility for the Ross Dependency in Antarctica. The two larger and most important islands, the North and South Islands of

New Zealand, are separated by only a relatively narrow strait. The remaining islands are very much smaller and, in general, are widely dispersed over a considerable expanse of ocean. The boundaries, inclusive of the most outlying islands and dependencies, range from 33° to 53° South latitude, and from 162° East longitude to 173° West longitude.

Geographical features.—The two principal islands have a total length of 1,040 miles, and a combined area of 102,344 sq. miles (265,069 sq. km). A large proportion of the surface is mountainous in character. The principal range is the Southern Alps, extending over the entire length of the South Island and having its culminating point in Mount Cook (12,349 ft). The North Island mountains include several volcanoes, two of which are active, others being dormant or extinct. Mt. Ruapehu (9,175 ft) and Mt. Ngauruhoe (7,515 ft) are the most important. Of the numerous glaciers in the South Island, the Tasman (18 miles long by 1¼ wide), the Franz Josef and the Fox are the best known. The North Island is noted for its hot springs and geysers. For the most part the rivers are too short and rapid for navigation. The more important include the Waikato (270 miles in length), Wanganui (180), and Clutha (210). Lakes (Taupo, 234 sq. miles in area; Wakatipu, 113; and Te Anau, 133) are abundant.

In addition to North and South Islands:—

Chatham Islands, comprising Chatham, Pitt, South East Islands and some rocky islets, in 44°S. lat. and 176° 20′ W. long., have a combined area of 965 sq. km (373 sq. miles). They lie 700 km SE of Wellington, and are largely uninhabited.

Stewart Island, largely uninhabited, lies 30 km S. of South Island and has an area of 1,746 sq. km (674 sq. miles).

The Kermadec Group (population normally 9 or 10) between 29° 10′ to 31° 30′ S. lat., and 177° 45′ to 179° W. long., includes Raoul or Sunday, Macaulay, Curtis Islands, L'Esperance, and some islets. All the inhabitants are government employees at a meteorological station. Campbell Island (used as a weather station).

The Three Kings (discovered by Tasman on the Feast of the Epiphany), in 34° 9′ S. lat. and 172° 8′ 8″ E. long. Auckland Islands, about 290 miles south of Bluff Harbour, in 50° 32′ S. lat. and 166° 13′ E. long. Antipodes Group, 40° 41′ 15″ S. lat. and 178° 43′ E. long. Bounty Islands, 47° 4′ 43″ S. lat., 170° 0′ 30″ E. long. Snares Islands and Solander. All these islands are uninhabited.

Climate.—New Zealand has a moist-temperate marine climate, but with abundant sunshine. A very important feature is the small annual range of temperature which permits some growth of vegetation, including pasture, all the year round. Very little snow falls on the low levels even in the South Island. The mean temperature ranges from 15° C in the North to about 9° C in the South. Rainfall over the more settled areas in the North Island ranges from 35 to 70 inches and in the South Island from 25 to 45 inches. The total range is from approximately 13 to over 250 inches.

CAPITAL.—ψWellington, in the North Island (estimated population March 1989, Wellington urban area, 324,600.

Other large urban areas; ψAuckland 850,900; ψChristchurch 301,500; ψDunedin 106,400; Hamilton 104,100; ψ Napier-Hastings 107,700.

CURRENCY.—New Zealand dollar (NZ$) of 100 cents.

FLAG.—Blue ground, with Union Flag in top left quarter, four five-pointed red stars with white borders on the fly. On June 20, 1968, a naval ensign bearing the Southern Cross was adopted, replacing the British white ensign.

NATIONAL ANTHEM.—God Save The Queen/God Defend New Zealand.

NATIONAL DAY.—February 6 (Waitangi Day).

GOVERNMENT

The discoverers and first colonists of New Zealand were Polynesian people, ancestors of the Maori of today. Whether there was a single colonization, several, or many, is not known but the 9th century is generally considered to be the date of the first settlement. By the 13th or 14th century early exploration was over and there were well established Maori settlements.

The first European to discover New Zealand was a Dutch navigator, Abel Tasman, who sighted the coast on December 13, 1642 but did not land. It was the British explorer James Cook who circumnavigated New Zealand and landed in 1769. Traders, whalers and sealers made up the majority of Europeans in New Zealand from the end of the 18th century until the late 1830s, when the proportion of permanent European settlers became significant.

Largely as a result of increased British emigration, the country was annexed by the British Government in 1840. The British Lieutenant Governor, William Hobson, RN, proclaimed sovereignty over the North Island by virtue of the Treaty of Waitangi, signed by him and many Maori chiefs, and over the South Island and Stewart Island by right of discovery.

On May 3, 1841 New Zealand was, by letters patent, created a separate colony distinct from New South Wales. Organized colonization on a large scale commenced in 1840 with the New Zealand company's settlement at Wellington. On September 26, 1907 the designation was changed to 'The Dominion of New Zealand'. The Constitution rests upon the Constitution Act of 1852, and other Imperial statutes such as the Bill of Rights. A 1986 Constitution Act brought a number of statutory constitutional provisions. The Statute of Westminster was formally adopted by New Zealand in 1947. The executive authority is entrusted to a Governor General appointed by the Crown and aided by an Executive Council, within a Legislature consisting of one chamber, the House of Representatives.

Governor General

Governor General and Commander-in-Chief of New Zealand, Her Excellency Dame Catherine (Anne) Tizard, DBE, *sworn in,* November 1990.

The Executive Council
(as at June 30, 1990)
The Governor General

Prime Minister, Minister for the Environment, Rt. Hon. Geoffrey Palmer.

Deputy Prime Minister, Minister for Health, Labour, Rt. Hon. Helen Clark.

External Relations and Trade, Foreign Affairs, Overseas Trade and Marketing, Rt. Hon. M. K. Moore.

Finance, Hon. D. F. Caygill.

State Owned Enterprises, Police, Railways, Pacific Island Affairs, Hon. R. W. Prebble.

Maori Affairs, Hon. K. T. Wetere.

Social Welfare, Hon. Dr. Michael Cullen.

Education, Hon. P. B. Goff.

Housing, Communications, Broadcasting, Rt. Hon. J. L. Hunt.

Justice, Transport, Civil Aviation and Meteorological Services, Hon. W. P. Jeffries.

Consumer Affairs, Statistics, Women's Affairs, Hon. Margaret Shields.

Defence, Lands, Hon. P. Tapsell.

Commerce, Energy, Hon. D. Butcher.

Employment, Immigration, Youth Affairs, Hon. Annette King.

Disarmament and Arms Control, Tourism, Hon. Fran Wilde.

Attorney-General, Minister of State, Rt. Hon. D. R. Lange.

Recreation and Sport, Hon. Noel Scott.
Regional Development, Hon. P. F. Dunne.
Ministers without Portfolio, Hon. F. M. Gerbic, Hon. Ralph Maxwell.
Fisheries, Hon. Ken Shirley.

NEW ZEALAND HIGH COMMISSION
New Zealand House, Haymarket, SW1Y 4TQ
[071–930 8422]

High Commissioner, His Excellency Bryce Harland (1985).
Deputy High Commissioner, J. P. Larkindale.
Minister, D. Walker (*Commercial*).
Head, Defence Liaison Staff, Cdre. J. G. Leonard.

LEGISLATURE

Parliament consists of a House of Representatives consisting of 97 members elected for three years. There are four Maori electorates. Women have been entitled to vote since 1893, and to be elected Members of the House of Representatives since the passing of the Women's Parliamentary Rights Act 1919. Following the General Election of August 15, 1987, the state of the parties in Parliament was Labour 57 and National Party 40. A general election is constitutionally due to take place by October 1990.
Speaker of the House of Representatives, Hon. Sir (Thomas) Kerry Burke.

JUDICATURE

The judicial system comprises a High Court and a Court of Appeal; also District Courts having both civil and criminal jurisdiction.
Chief Justice, Rt. Hon. Sir Thomas Eichelbaum, GBE, PC.
President, Court of Appeal, Rt. Hon. Sir Robin Cooke, KBE.
Judges, Rt. Hons. Sir Ivor Richardson; Sir Duncan McMullin; Sir Edward Somers; M. E. Casey; G. E. Bisson.
High Court Puisne Judges, Hons. M. F. Chilwell; J. F. Jeffries; R. I. Barker; J. B. Sinclair; A. D. Holland; T. M. Thorp; L. M. Greig; M. Hardie-Boys; J. H. Wallace; P. G. Hillyer; R. G. Gallen; D. L. Tompkins; J. S. Henry; R. A. Heron; N. W. Williamson; A. A. T. Ellis; R. P. Smellie; R. E. Wylie; R. A. McGechan; J. A. Doogue; A. P. C. Tipping; N. C. Anderson; T. M. Gault; J. B. Robertson.
High Court Administrative Divn., Rt. Hon. Sir Ronald Davison (*Chief Justice*); Hons. M. F. Chilwell; J. F. Jeffries; A. D. Holland; L. M. Greig; D. L. Tompkins.
Chief Judge, Labour Court, J. R. P. Horn.

POLICE

On March 31, 1989 the strength of the New Zealand Police Force was 5,328 of all ranks, equivalent to 1 for every 625 of the population. Total police expenditure for the year 1988–89 was NZ$484,940,000.

DEFENCE

The Governor-General, representing the Crown, is Commander-in-Chief of the armed forces. Executive power, however, is vested in the Cabinet. The Chief of Defence Staff (CDS) heads the New Zealand Defence Force (NZDF). The Chief of Naval Staff, Chief of General Staff and Chief of Air Staff are directly responsible to the CDS. The Secretary of Defence is the chief executive of the Defence Office, and the CDS and the Secretary of Defence are both directly responsible to the Minister of Defence.
Annual defence expenditure for the year 1989–90 was about 5 per cent of total net government

expenditure. At August 31, 1989 the total number of armed forces personnel was 12,397.

FINANCE

Into the Consolidated Account (New Zealand's main public account) are paid the proceeds of income tax, goods and services tax, customs and excise duties and other taxes, also interest, profits from trading undertakings, and departmental receipts. Revenue from taxation is also paid into the National Roads Fund principally from a tax on motor spirits and registration and licence fees for motor vehicles.
Revenue and expenditure including the National Roads Fund for year ended March 31:

	1988	1989
Revenue	NZ$29,871·7m	NZ$32,150·6m
Expenditure (net) ...	30,476·8m	32,151·2m

Taxation receipts in 1988–89 for all purposes amounted to NZ$22, 863·9 million (an average of NZ$6,807 per head of population).

Gross expenditure includes:

	1988	1989
Debt services	NZ$6,945·7m	NZ$4,883·6m
Education	3,179·3m	3,637·9m
Health	3,397·1m	3,652·6m
Social welfare	7,190·8m	8,234·4m
Defence	1,278·5m	1,390·8m
Other	8,485·4m	10,351·9m
Total...............	30,476·8m	32,151·2m

BANKING

The New Zealand financial system comprises a central bank (the Reserve Bank of New Zealand), registered banks and a range of other financial institutions. The number of registered banks is presently 20.
The Reserve Bank is the sole issuer of notes and coin.

EDUCATION

Schools are free and attendance is compulsory between the ages of 6 and 15. At July 1988 there were 398,189 pupils attending public primary schools, and 12,053 pupils attending registered private primary schools. The secondary education of boys and girls is carried on in 315 state secondary schools, 35 area high schools and 18 registered private secondary schools. The total number of pupils receiving full-time secondary education in July 1988 was 233,603 and in addition there were 103,646 students attending technical classes. Almost all the students attending technical classes are part-time. There are seven universities with a total of 72,313 students in 1988. The university system is co-ordinated by the University Grants Committee.

PRODUCTION AND INDUSTRY

Agricultural Production

	Year ended March	
	1986–87	1987–88
	NZ$(million)	
Gross output	6,902	7,352
Sheep....................	646	690
Wool	1,215	1,373
Cattle	974	935
Dairy products	1,130	1,294
Fruit, nuts, oilseeds	531	578
Agricultural services.....	474	538
Sales of live animals	607	590

Agricultural and Pastoral Production

	1988	1989
*Wheat, metric tons	206,000	135,000
*Wool, metric tons	346,000	341,000
†Butter, metric tons	242,000	246,000
†Cheese, metric tons.....	128,000	128,000
‡Stock Slaughtered—		
Lambs................	30,414,000	30,302,000
Sheep	7,927,000	9,757,000
Cattle	2,222,000	2,289,000
Calves	981,000	876,000
Pigs..................	782,000	781,000

* Year ended June 30
† Year ended May 31
‡ Year ended September 30

Forestry.—The output of sawn timber for 1989 was 1,877,000 cubic metres, of which 1,802,000 cubic metres represented exotic varieties, mainly radiata pine.

Livestock.—Livestock on farms at June 30, 1989, included 3,302,377 dairy cattle, 4,526,056 beef cattle and 411,334 pigs. Sheep numbered 60,568,653.

Minerals.—Non-metallic minerals such as coal, clay, limestone and dolomite are both economically and industrially more important than metallic ones. Coal output in 1988 was 2,400,000 tonnes (provisional). Of the metals, the most important is ironsand. Natural gas deposits in Taranaki are being used for electricity generation and as a premium fuel, piped to all the major North Island centres.

TRADE

	1987–88	1988–89
Imports (v.f.d.)	NZ$10,625·1m	NZ$11,401·7m
Exports (f.o.b.)	12,451·5m	14,905·4m

Trade with UK

	1988	1989
Imports from UK ..	£300,016,000	£399,295,000
Exports to UK	443,081,000	436,772,000

New Zealand produce exported to the UK in the 12 months ending June 1989, included butter and cheese, valued at NZ$292,702,000; wool NZ$133,280,000; lamb NZ$272,262,000; hides, skins and leather NZ$55,224,000.

COMMUNICATIONS

Railways.—The national railway system is owned and operated by the New Zealand Railways Corporation. In March 1989, there were 4,776 route km of Government railway in operation.

Motor Vehicles.—At March 31, 1988 there were 2,217,259 licensed motor vehicles.

Shipping.—During 1989 the vessels entered from overseas ports numbered 3,741 (gross tonnage 30,940,000) and those cleared for overseas 3,730 (gross tonnage 30,190,000).

Civil Aviation—Domestic flights in 1988 carried 4,125,000 passengers and 39,300 tonnes of freight. International flights carried 3,340,000 passengers, 127,981 tonnes of freight and 4,529 tonnes of mail.

BRITISH HIGH COMMISSION
Reserve Bank of New Zealand Building,
2 The Terrace (PO Box 1812), Wellington, 1
[Wellington 726-049]

High Commissioner, His Excellency David Joseph Moss, CMG (1990).
Deputy High Commissioner, I. C. Orr.
Defence Adviser, Capt. M. Matthews, RN.
First Secretaries, Mrs. E. Blackwell (*Agriculture and Food*); P. Rogan (*Commercial*); J. R. Setterfield (*Chancery, Information*).

Second Secretaries, R. Leadbeater (*Consular and Management*); T. A. Torlot (*Chancery*).
Attaché, Mrs. J. Harris (*Consular*).

British Council Representative, D. J. F. King.

BRITISH CHAMBER OF COMMERCE FOR AUSTRALIA AND NEW ZEALAND, PO Box 141, Manuka, ACT 2603, Australia; UK OFFICE, Suite 615, 6th Floor The Linen Hall, 162–168 Regent Street, W1R 5TB.

TERRITORIES

TOKELAU (OR UNION ISLANDS)
A group of atolls (Fakaofo, Nukunonu and Atafu) (population 1,690 at October 10, 1986), proclaimed part of New Zealand as from January 1, 1948.

THE ROSS DEPENDENCY
The Ross Dependency, placed under the jurisdiction of New Zealand by Order in Council dated July 30, 1923, is defined as all the islands and territories between 160° E. and 150° W. longitude which are situated south of the 60° S. parallel. The Ross Dependency includes Edward VII Land and portions of Victoria Land. Since 1957 a number of research stations have been established in the Dependency.

ASSOCIATED STATES

COOK ISLANDS
Included in the boundaries of New Zealand since June 1901, the group consists of the islands of Rarotonga, Aitutaki, Mangaia, Atiu, Mauke, Mitiaro, Manuae, Takutea, Palmerston, Penrhyn or Tongareva, Manihiki, Rakahanga, Suwarrow, Pukapuka or Danger and Nassau. The total population of the group was 17,185 at December 1, 1986. The chief industries of the Cook Islands are tourism, financial services and the production of fruit juice, clothing, copra, bananas, citrus fruit and pulp, and pearl shell. The trade is chiefly with New Zealand, Australia, Japan, the UK and the USA. The New Zealand Government continues to give financial aid to the Cook Islands.

The Queen has a representative on the islands, as does the New Zealand government. Since August 4, 1965, the islands have enjoyed complete internal self-government, executive power being in the hands of a Cabinet consisting of the Premier and five other ministers. The new Constitution Act was passed by the New Zealand Parliament in November 1964, but did not come into force until it had been endorsed by the 22-member Legislative Assembly of the Cook Islands, elected in April 1965.

The New Zealand citizenship of the Cook Islanders is embodied in the Constitution, and assurances have been given that the changed status of the islands will in no way affect the consideration of subsidies or the right of free entry into New Zealand for exports from the group.

HM Representative, Sir Tangaroa Tangaroa, KBE.
New Zealand Representative, A. Simcock.

NIUE
The population of Niue was estimated at 2,155 at March 31, 1989.

A New Zealand Representative is stationed at Niue, which since October 1974 has been self-governing in free association with New Zealand, which is responsible for external affairs and defence, and continues to give financial aid. Executive power is in the hands of a Premier and a Cabinet of three drawn from the Assembly of 20 members.

New Zealand Representative, M. J. Taylor.

NIGERIA
(Federal Republic of Nigeria)

AREA, POPULATION, ETC.—The Republic of Nigeria is situated on the west coast of Africa. It is bounded on the south by the Gulf of Guinea, on the west by the Republic of Benin, on the north by Niger and on the east by Cameroon. It has an area of 356,669 sq. miles (923,768 sq. km), with a population (UN estimate 1988) of 105,472,000. The population is almost entirely African. The main ethnic groups are Hausa/Fulani, Yoruba and Ibo, and the principal languages are English, Hausa, Yoruba and Ibo. Over half the population are Muslim, these being concentrated in the north and west. In the southern areas in particular there are many Christians.

A belt of mangrove swamp forest 10–60 miles in width lies along the entire coastline. North of this there is a zone 50–100 miles wide of tropical rain forest and oil-palms. North of this the country rises and the vegetation changes to open woodland and savanna. In the extreme north the country is semi-desert. There are few mountains, but in Northern Nigeria the central plateau rises to an average level of 4,000 feet. The Niger, Benue, and Cross are the main rivers.

The climate varies with the types of country described above, but Nigeria lies entirely within the tropics and temperatures are high. The rainy season is from about April to October; rainfall varies from under 25 inches a year in the extreme north to 172 inches on the coast line. During the dry season the *harmattan* wind blows from the desert; it is cool and laden with fine particles of dust.

CAPITAL.—ΨLagos, estimated population, 3,000,000. Other important towns are Ibadan, Kaduna, Kano, Benin City, Enugu and ΨPort Harcourt. Movement of Federal Ministries to a new capital at Abuja has begun.

CURRENCY.—Naira (N) of 100 kobo.

FLAG.—Three equal vertical bands, green, white and green.

NATIONAL ANTHEM.—Arise, O Compatriots.

NATIONAL DAY.—October 1 (Republic Day).

GOVERNMENT

The Federation of Nigeria attained independence as a member of the Commonwealth on October 1, 1960 and became a republic in 1963. On January 15, 1966 the military took power, suspended the Constitution and dissolved the legislature. In 1979 civil rule was restored under a new constitution similar to that of the United States after elections at National and State level. After similar elections in 1983 the new administration was removed by the military on December 31, this regime itself being overthrown in August 1985. A 28-member Armed Forces Ruling Council (AFRC) was sworn in on August 30. It is the country's most senior decision-making body. The Council of Ministers is the third most senior body after the AFRC and the National Council of States, which comprises the 21 State Governors.

Originally regional in structure, the Federation was divided into 12 states in 1967. It was divided again into 19 states in 1976, and a further two states were created in 1987.

On May 3, 1989 Gen. Babangida promulgated the new draft constitution paving the way for a return to civilian rule by 1992. He also announced that a ban on political parties was to be lifted, leading to the formation in October 1989 of two new parties, the Social Democratic Party and the National Republican Convention.

Head of State, Commander-in-Chief of the Armed Forces, Chairman of the Armed Forces Ruling Council, Maj.-Gen. Ibrahim Babangida.

Armed Forces Ruling Council

Chairman, General Ibrahim Badamasi Babangida.
Members, Vice-Adm. A. Aikhomu; Lt.-Gen. D. Y. Bali; Lt.-Gen. S. Abacha; Vice-Adm. P. S. Koshoni; Air Marshal I. Alfa; A. M. A. Gambo; Maj.-Gen. M. G. Nasko; Maj.-Gen. P. Omu; Air Vice-Marshal M. Yahaya; Maj.-Gen. P. Adomokhai; Maj.-Gen. D. O. Ajayi; Maj.-Gen. A. B. Mamman; Maj.-Gen. S. O. Ifere; Maj.-Gen. G. Duba; Brig. O. Diya; Brig. J. N. Dogonyaro; Cdre. M. A. B. Elegbede; Cdre. N. Kanu; Cdre. S. Aluko; Rear-Adm. A. Nyako; Air Vice-Marshal N. Yusuf; Air Cdre. L. Koinyan; Air Vice-Marshal N. M. Imam; Col. J. N. Shagaya; Col. H. Akilu; Col. D. Mark; Maj.-Gen. Y. Y. Kure; Maj.-Gen. S. Sami.

Council of Ministers
(as at May 31, 1990)

Agriculture and Natural Resources, Sumaila Mamman.
Aviation, T. O. Graham-Douglas.
Budget and Planning, Abubakar Alhaji.
Communications, Col. David Mark.
Culture and Social Welfare, Mamman Anka.
Education, Babs Fafunwa.
Employment, Labour and Productivity, Abubakar Umar.
External Affairs, Rilwanu Lukman.
Federal Capital Territory, Maj.-Gen. M. Gado Nasko.
Finance and Economic Planning, Olu Falae.
Health, Koye Ransome Kuti.
Industry, Air Vice-Marshal Mohammed Yahaya.
Information, Prince Tony Momoh.
Internal Affairs, Commodore Lamba Dung Gwom.
Justice; Attorney-General, Prince Bola Ajibola.
Mines, Power and Steel, Air Vice-Marshal Nura Imam.
Petroleum Resources, Jibril Aminu.
Youth and Sports, Air Cmdre. Anthony Ikazobor.
Science and Technology, Gordian Ezekwe.
Trade, S. J. Ukpanah.
Transport, Lt.-Gen. Alani Akinrinade (retd).
Works and Housing, Brig. M. T. Kontagora.
Special Duties, Air Vice-Marshal Hamza Abdullahi (retd).
Water Resources, Bonu Shariff Musa.
Minister of State for External Affairs, Eyoma Ita Eyoma.

NIGERIA HIGH COMMISSION
56–57 Fleet Street, EC4Y 1JU
[071–353 3776]

High Commissioner, His Excellency Mr. George Dove-Edwin (1986).

EDUCATION

A programme was introduced in September 1976 intended to achieve universal primary education. Numbers of pupils in 1982–83 were: 15·4 million in primary schools, 3·5 million in secondary schools, 53,766 in polytechnics and 88,636 in universities. There are 24 universities.

COMMUNICATIONS

The Nigerian railway system, which is controlled by the Nigerian Railway Corporation, is the most extensive in West Africa. There are 2,178 route miles of lines. The principal international airlines operating from Lagos, Kano and Port Harcourt bring Nigeria within about six hours of the Western European capitals. There are also services to other parts of Africa and to the United States. A network of internal air services connects the main centres. The principal seaports are served by a number of shipping lines, including the Nigerian National Line. A nationwide television and radio network is being developed, with each State eventually having its own television and radio station. There is a network of meteorological reporting stations.

PRODUCTION AND INDUSTRY

Nigeria was a predominantly agricultural country until the early 1970s with agriculture contributing over 60 per cent of export revenue and 45 per cent of GNP. Tin and calumbite mining on the Jos plateau, textiles and coal mining were also important. The major exports were ground nuts, palm products, tin, cocoa, rubber and timber. Recently oil has provided over 90 per cent of exports revenue and agricultural exports were greatly declined. Though agriculture still employs half the labour force it contributes only 20 per cent of GNP, exceeded by trading and oil. The construction sector is twice as large as the manufacturing sector and industries dependent on imported raw materials such as vehicle assembly have faltered recently. Three oil refineries are in operation at Port Harcourt, Warri and Kaduna. A steel plant has been opened near Warri and a larger one is being completed at Ajaokuta. Other projects include natural gas liquifaction, petro-chemicals, fertilizers and several power stations plus the Abuja Federal Capital. Several large irrigation schemes have been completed and more are planned.

TRADE

Oil revenues have been falling since 1981 and are now restricted by an OPEC production quota and lower prices to half their peak level. In March 1982 imports curbs and payments restrictions were introduced but exchange reserves fell and debts increased. Austerity measures were introduced, and continue, while the present Government attempts to stimulate greater self-reliance in the economy by encouraging non-oil exports and the use of local rather than imported raw materials.

Trade with UK

	1988	1989
Imports from UK	£390,476,000	£388,777,000
Exports to UK	128,123,000	129,406,000

BRITISH HIGH COMMISSION
11 Eleke Crescent, Victoria Island, Lagos
[Lagos 619531]

High Commissioner, His Excellency Brian Leon Barder (1988).

British Council Representative, Jim Whittell, OBE, 11 Kingsway Road, Ikoyi (PO Box 3702), Lagos. Branch offices at *Enugu, Kaduna* and *Kano City.*

PAKISTAN
(Islami Jamhuriya-e-Pakistan)

AREA, POPULATION, ETC.—The Islamic Republic of Pakistan consists of country situated to the north-west of the Indian sub-continent, bordered by Iran, Afghanistan, the disputed territory of Kashmir, and India. It covers a total area of 307,374 sq. miles (746,045 sq. km). Running through Pakistan are five great rivers, the Indus, Jhelum, Chenab, Ravi and Sutlej. The upper reaches of these rivers are in Kashmir, and their sources in the Himalayas.

The Government of Pakistan Census in 1981 showed a population figure of 83,780,000 (1988 UN estimate, 105,409,000). Of these, about 95 per cent are

Muslims, about 1 per cent Hindus, 3·5 per cent Christians, and 0·5 per cent Buddhists.

CAPITAL.—Islamabad, population 350,000. ΨKarachi (estimated population 6,500,000) is the largest city and seaport; Lahore has a population of about 3,500,000.

CURRENCY.—Pakistan rupee of 100 paisa.

FLAG.—Dark green ground, with white vertical stripes at the mast, the green portion bearing a white crescent in the centre and a five-pointed heraldic star.

NATIONAL ANTHEM.—Quami Tarana.

NATIONAL DAYS.—March 23 (Pakistan Day), August 14 (Independence Day).

GOVERNMENT

Pakistan was constituted as a Dominion under the Indian Independence Act 1947, which received Royal Assent on July 18, 1947. In terms of the Act the Dominion of Pakistan consisted of former territories of British India. The States of Bahawalpur and Khairpur (in Punjab and Sind), with a Muslim population of almost 80 per cent and with Muslim rulers, acceded to Pakistan in October, 1947. The following States also acceded to Pakistan: the Baluchistan States of Kalat, Mekran, Las Bela and Kharan, and the North-West Frontier States of Amb, Chitral, Dir and Swat. (The States of Junagadh and Manavadar which had acceded to Pakistan were occupied by India on November 8, 1947.) Boundaries of the Provinces of East Bengal and of Punjab (West Punjab) were defined by a Boundary Commission. Thus, until 1972 when East Pakistan seceded, Pakistan consisted of two geographical units, West and East Pakistan, which were separated by about 1,100 miles of Indian territory.

Pakistan became a Republic on March 23, 1956, when a Parliamentary Constitution came into force. On October 7, 1958, however, this Constitution was abrogated and Pakistan came under martial law.

The first general elections held in Pakistan on a basis of 'one man, one vote', were held in December 1970 and January 1971. The Awami League in East Pakistan, led by Sheikh Mujibur Rahman, and the Pakistan People's Party in West Pakistan, led by Zulfikar Ali Bhutto, won large majorities. Following the elections there was total disagreement between the two main parties on the question of a new Constitution for Pakistan, Sheikh Mujibur insisting on complete autonomy for East Pakistan. The proposed opening of the National Assembly at Dacca on March 25, 1971, was postponed and civil war broke out. East Pakistan seceded by unilateral declaration the following day. Fighting continued until December 1971 when a ceasefire was arranged, and 'The Democratic Government of Bangladesh' was formally proclaimed on April 17, 1972.

Following general elections in March 1977 and allegations of vote-rigging, the armed forces under Gen. Zia-ul-Haq assumed power on July 5, 1977 and imposed martial law throughout the country. The military government scheduled new general elections for October 1977, but these were postponed. Gen. Zia declared himself President on September 16, 1978. In December 1984 Gen. Zia got a five-year mandate as a civilian President through a national referendum. Martial law was lifted on December 30, 1985. On May 29, 1988, Zia dissolved the National Assembly and the Cabinet and announced fresh elections. A caretaker cabinet was announced on June 9. Zia was killed in a plane crash on August 17, 1988, and the Senate Chairman, Ghulam Ishaq Khan, assumed the office of President. The Pakistan People's Party won the election to the National Assembly and Benazir Bhutto became Prime Minister on December 2, 1988. The legislature then elected President Ghulam Ishaq Khan as a constitutional President.

Pakistan left the Commonwealth in 1972, but formally re-acceded on October 1, 1989.

President, Ghulam Ishaq Khan, *elected* December 12, 1988 *for a four-year term.*

Prime Minister, Defence, Finance, Economic Affairs, Planning and Development, Ms. Benazir Bhutto, *sworn in* December 2, 1988.

Ministers
(as at June 30, 1990)

Senior Minister without Portfolio, Begum Nusrat Bhutto.
Labour, Mukhtar Ahmed Awan.
Interior, Aitzaz Ahsan.
Communications, Makhdoom Amin Faheem.
Culture, Agha Tariq Khan.
Food, Agriculture and Co-operatives, Rao Sikander Iqbal.
Commerce, Local Government and Rural Development, Syed Faisal Saleh Hayat.
Health, Special Education and Social Welfare, Syed Amir Haider Kazmi.
Petroleum and Natural Resources, Jehangir Badar.
Foreign Affairs, Sahabzada Yaqub Khan.
States and Frontier Regions, Kashmir Affairs, Mohammad Hanif Khan.
Water and Power, Sardar Farooq Ahmed Khan Leghari.
Law and Justice, Syed Iftikhar Hussain Gillani.
Environment and Urban Affairs, Mir Baz Mohammad Khan Khatran.
Parliamentary Affairs, Khawaja Ahmed Tariq Rahim.
Religious Affairs, Khan Bahadur Khan.
Education, Syed Ghulam Mustafa Shah.
Railways, Zafar Leghari.
Industries, Ali Nawaz Shah.
Youth, Parvez Ali Shah.
Housing and Works, Yousaf Raza Gillani.
Manpower and Overseas Pakistanis, Mian Ghulam Mohammad Ahmad Khan Maneka.
Women's Division, Begum Rahana Sarwar.

In addition there are 19 Ministers of State and 2 Advisers to the Prime Minister.

HIGH COMMISSION FOR PAKISTAN
35 Lowndes Square, SW1X 9JN
[071–235 2044]

High Commissioner, His Excellency Shaharyar M. Khan (1987).

EDUCATION

Formal education in Pakistan is organized into five stages. These are five years of primary education (5–9 years), three years of middle or lower secondary (general or vocational), two years of upper secondary, two years of higher secondary (intermediate) and two to five years of higher education in colleges and universities. Education is free to upper secondary level. It was expected that primary education would become universal for boys by mid-1985 and for girls by mid-1988.

At primary level enrolment had increased to 6·5 million in 1984–85, and the number of schools to 75,000. At the middle level enrolment had increased to 1·7 million in 1984–85, and the number of schools to 6,200. At the upper secondary level enrolment increased to 570,000 in 1984–85.

Provincial Governments are responsible for the total financial support of the government institutions and for grants to non-government institutions. But policy making is authorized by the national Government, which makes annual grants. In 1986, 24 per cent of adults were estimated as being literate.

COMMUNICATIONS

The main seaport is Karachi. The main airport at Karachi occupies an important position on international trunk routes and is equipped with modern facilities and equipment. Pakistan International Airlines operates air services between the principal cities within the country as well as abroad.

Post and telegraph facilities are available to every country in the world.

FINANCE

The 1989–90 Budget anticipated net federal revenues of Rs.127,407·4 million and current expenditure (excluding development expenditure) of some Rs.124,878·5 million.

PRODUCTION

Pakistan's economy is chiefly based on agriculture. The principal crops are cotton, rice, wheat, sugar cane, maize and tobacco. There are large deposits of rock salt. Pakistan has one of the longest irrigation systems in the world. The total area irrigated is 33 million acres.

Pakistan also produces hides and skins, leather, wool, fertilizers, paints and varnishes, soda ash, paper, cement, fish, carpets, sports goods, surgical appliances and engineering goods, including switchgear, transformers, cables and wires.

TRADE

Pakistan imported manufactured goods and raw materials to the value of US$5,792 million in 1986–87 and exported mainly agricultural products valued at US$3,498 million. Principal imports are petroleum products, machinery, fertilizers, transport equipment, edible oils, chemicals and ferrous metals. Principal exports are raw cotton, cotton yarn and cloth, carpets, rice, petroleum products, synthetic textiles, leather, and fish.

Trade with UK

	1988	1989
Imports from UK	£263,300,000	£233,532,000
Exports to UK	175,337,000	216,110,000

BRITISH HIGH COMMISSION
Diplomatic Enclave, Ramna 5,
PO Box 1122, Islamabad
[Islamabad 822131/5]

High Commissioner, His Excellency Sir Nicholas Barrington, KCMG, CVO (1987).

There is a British Consulate-General at *Karachi* and a Consulate at *Lahore.*

British Council Representative, L. Phillips, PO Box 1135, Islamabad. There are offices at *Karachi, Lahore* and *Peshawar.*

PAPUA NEW GUINEA

AREA, POPULATION, ETC.—Papua New Guinea extends from the equator to Cape Baganowa in the Louisiade Archipelago at 11° S. latitude and from the border with Irian Jaya to 160° E. longitude. The total area of Papua New Guinea is 178,260 sq. miles, (461,691 sq. km), of which approximately 152,420 sq. miles form the mainland, on the island of New Guinea. The country has many island groups, principally the Bismarck Archipelago, a portion of the Solomon Islands, the Trobriands, the D'Entrecasteaux Islands and the Louisade Archipelago. The main islands of the Bismarck Archipelago are New Britain, New Ireland and Manus. Bougainville is the largest of the Solomon Islands within Papua New Guinea.

Papua New Guinea lies within the tropics and has a typically monsoonal climate. Temperature and humidity are uniformly high throughout the year. The average rainfall is about 80 inches per year but there are wide variations—from 47 inches at Port Moresby to over 200 inches in mountainous western areas.

The estimated population in 1988 was 3,562,000.

CAPITAL.—ψPort Moresby. Estimated population (1985), 139,300. Other major towns are Lae, Rabaul, Madang, Wewak, Goroka and Mount Hagen.

CURRENCY.—Kina (K) of 100 toea.

FLAG.—A rectangle divided diagonally from the top of the hoist to the bottom of the fly, the upper segment scarlet and containing a soaring yellow bird of paradise. The lower segment is black charged with five white five-pointed stars representing the Southern Cross.

NATIONAL ANTHEM.—Arise All You Sons.

NATIONAL DAY.—September 16 (Independence Day).

GOVERNMENT

New Guinea was sighted by Portuguese and Spanish navigators in the early sixteenth century, but remained largely isolated from the rest of the world. In 1884 a British Protectorate was proclaimed over the southern coast of New Guinea (Papua) and the adjacent islands. British New Guinea, as the Protectorate was called, was annexed outright in 1888. In 1906 the Territory of British New Guinea was placed under the authority of the Commonwealth of Australia. Also in 1884 Germany had formally taken possession of certain northern areas, which later came to be known as the Trust Territory of New Guinea. In 1914 the German areas were occupied by Australian troops and remained under military administration until 1921, when the League of Nations conferred on Australia a mandate for their government.

New Guinea was administered under the Mandate and Papua under the Papua Act until the invasion by the Japanese in 1942 when the civil administration was suspended until the surrender of the Japanese in 1945.

The first House of Assembly for the whole country met in 1964 and included an elected majority and ten nominated official members. After 1970 there was a gradual assumption of powers by the Papua New Guinea Government, culminating in formal self-government in December 1973. Final reserve powers held by Australia over defence and foreign relations were relinquished to Papua New Guinea in March 1975, and Papua New Guinea achieved full independence on September 16, 1975.

Elections are held every five years. The Parliament comprises 109 elected Members, 20 from Regional electorates, the remainder from Open electorates. There are 19 provinces, which have their own provincial governments with certain legislative and administrative powers.

Governor General, His Excellency Sir Serei Eri, GCMG.

National Executive Council
(as at May 31, 1990)

Prime Minister, Rt. Hon. Rabbie Namaliu.
Deputy PM and Minister for Public Service, Ted Diro.
Public Service, Finance and Planning, Paul Pora.
Civil Aviation, Bernard Vogae.
Communications, Brown Sinamoi.
Labour and Employment, Peter Garong.
Justice, Bernard Narokobi.
Lands and Physical Planning, Kala Swokin.
Police, Mathias Ijape.
Provincial Affairs, John Momis.
Administrative Services, William Ank.
Education, Jack Genia.

Environment and Conservation, Jim Yer Waim.
Foreign Affairs, Rt. Hon. Sir Michael Somare, CH.
Forests, Karl Stack.
Health, Gerald Beona.
Home Affairs, Timothy Bonga.
Defence, Benais Sabumei.
Culture and Tourism, Aruru Matiabe.
Trade and Industry, John Giheno.
Minister for State, Akoka Doi.
Housing, Michael Singan.
Minerals and Energy, Patterson Lowa.
Correctional Institution Service, Melchior Pep.
Transport, Anthony Temu.
Works, Paul Wanjik.
Fisheries, Allen Ebu.
Agriculture and Livestock, Galen Lang.

PAPUA NEW GUINEA HIGH COMMISSION
3rd Floor, 14 Waterloo Place, SW1Y 4AR
[071–930 0922/6]

High Commissioner, His Excellency Philip Bouraga (1989).

COMMUNICATIONS

Road communications are very limited, the most important road being that linking Lae with the populous highlands.

Air Niugini (the national airline) and Qantas operate regular air services between Port Moresby and Australia. Air Niugini also operates services to Manila (Philippines), Honiara (Solomon Islands), Jayapura (Indonesia), Honolulu and Singapore. Internal air services are operated by Air Niugini, Douglas Airways, and Talair.

Several shipping companies operate cargo services between Papua New Guinea and Australia, Europe, the Far East and USA. There are very limited cargo and passenger services between Papua New Guinea main ports, outports, plantations and missions.

Papua New Guinea is linked by international cable to Australia, Guam, Hong Kong, Kota Kinabalu, the Far East and USA. Telecommunications are widely available.

ECONOMY

Until the 1970s the Papua New Guinea economy was based almost entirely on agriculture. At the beginning of the 20th century copra plantations formed the basis of the cash economy. Further crops which have been introduced over the years are cocoa, tea, coffee, palm oil, rubber, groundnuts, spices and timber. A variety of commercial agricultural developments now co-exist with the traditional informal rural economy. Government expenditure is still reliant on Australian budgetary support, to the extent of just under 30 per cent in 1983.

In 1972, Bougainville Copper Pty Ltd (BCL) began mining in the North Solomons Province, producing copper, silver and gold. However, the Bougainville Copper Mine closed indefinitely in May 1989. There are extensive mineral deposits throughout Papua New Guinea, including nickel, chromite, bauxite and possibly commercial deposits of oil and gas. The most important new development is the exploitation of large copper and gold deposits on the Ok Tedi, in the Western Province.

In 1984 the Papua New Guinea economy was influenced by good prices for agricultural commodities, offset by low prices for copper and gold. New developments to promote export crops and increase employment, typically involving foreign investment, are planned for the future.

Industry includes processing of primary products, and brewing, bottling and packaging, paint, plywood, and metal manufacturing and the construction industries.

Although the formal economy is still dominated by non-Papua New Guineans, the participation of Papua New Guineans is increasing.

Trade with UK

	1988	1989
Imports from UK	£20,520,683	£15,822,000
Exports to UK	44,291,211	47,839,000

BRITISH HIGH COMMISSION
PO Box 4778, Boroko, Port Moresby
[Port Moresby 212500]

High Commissioner, His Excellency Edward John Sharland (1989).

ST. CHRISTOPHER AND NEVIS
(The Federation of St. Christopher and Nevis)

The State of St. Christopher and Nevis is located at the northern end of the Eastern Caribbean. It comprises the islands of St. Christopher (St. Kitts) (65 sq. miles: 168 sq. km; population about 35,700) and Nevis (36 sq. miles: 93·2 sq. km; population about 9,400).

St. Christopher, lat. 17° 18' N. and long. 62° 48' W. was the first island in the British West Indies to be colonized (1623). The central area of the island is forest-clad and mountainous, rising to the 3,792 ft. Mount Liamuiga.

Nevis, lat. 17° 10' N. and long. 62° 35' W. is separated from the southern tip of St. Christopher by a strait two miles wide and is dominated by the central Nevis Peak, 3,232 ft.

CAPITAL.—ΨBasseterre (estimated population, 15,000). Chief town of Nevis is ΨCharlestown (population 1,200), which is a port of entry.

CURRENCY.—East Caribbean dollar (EC$) of 100 cents.

FLAG.—Three diagonal bands, green, black and red; each colour separated by a stripe of yellow. Two white stars on the black band.

NATIONAL ANTHEM.—Our Land of Beauty.

NATIONAL DAY.—September 19 (Independence Day).

GOVERNMENT

The Territory of St. Christopher and Nevis became a State in Association with Britain on February 27, 1967. The State of St. Christopher and Nevis became an independent nation on September 19, 1983, with a new constitution under which Great Britain relinquished its responsibility for defence and external affairs. Under the new Constitution, The Queen is Head of State, represented in the islands by the Governor General. There is a central Cabinet Government with a Ministerial system, the Head of which is the Prime Minister of St. Christopher and Nevis, and a National Assembly located on St. Christopher. On Nevis there is a Nevis Island Administration, the Head being styled Premier of Nevis, and a Nevis Island Assembly.

Governor General, His Excellency Sir Clement Athelston Arrindell, GCMG, GCVO, QC (1983).

Cabinet
(as at May 31, 1990)

Prime Minister and Minister of Finance, Home Affairs and Foreign Affairs, Rt. Hon. Dr. Kennedy A. Simmonds.

Deputy P.M. and Minister of Labour and Tourism, Hon. Michael O. Powell.

Education, Youth and Community Affairs, Commu-

nications, Works and Public Utilities, Hon. Sydney E. Morris.

Agriculture, Lands, Housing and Development, Hon. Hugh C. Heyliger.

Health and Women's Affairs, Hon. Constance Mitcham.

Trade and Industry, Hon. Fitzroy P. Jones.

In Ministry of Finance, Hon. Richard L. Caines.

Attorney-General, Hon. S. W. Tapley Seaton, CVO.

Cabinet Secretary, C. Farier.

ST. KITTS HIGH COMMISSION
10 Kensington Court, W8 5DL
[071-937 9522]

High Commissioner for the Eastern Caribbean States,
His Excellency Richard Gunn (1987).

FINANCE

	1988	1989
Revenue	EC$79,275,862	EC$91,508,604
Expenditure	78,453,932	84,427,961

ECONOMY

The economy of the islands has been based on sugar for over three centuries. Tourism and light industry are now being developed. The economy of Nevis centres on small peasant farmers, but a sea-island cotton industry is being developed for export.

COMMUNICATIONS

Basseterre is a port of registry and has deep water harbour facilities. Golden Rock airport, on St. Kitts, can take most large jet aircraft; Newcastle airstrip on Nevis can take small aircraft and has night landing facilities.

The sea ferry route from Basseterre to Charlestown is 11 miles.

Trade with UK

	1988	1989
Imports from UK	£8,025,000	£5,887,000
Exports to UK	4,271,000	4,866,000

British Representative, (resides at Antigua), Ian Marsh.

ST. LUCIA

St. Lucia, the second largest of the Windward group, situated in 13° 54' N. lat. and 60° 50' W. long., at a distance of about 21 miles N. of St. Vincent, and 24 miles S. of Martinique, is 27 miles in length, with an extreme breadth of 14 miles. It comprises an area of 238 sq. miles (616 sq. km), with an estimated population (1988) of 133,000. It possesses perhaps the most interesting history of all the smaller islands. Fights raged hotly around it, and it constantly changed hands between the English and the French. It is mountainous, its highest point being Mt. Gimie (3,145 ft) and for the most part it is covered with forest and tropical vegetation.

CAPITAL.—ΨCastries (estimated population 1988, 55,000) is recognized as being one of the finest ports in the West Indies on account of its reputation as a safe anchorage in the hurricane season.

CURRENCY.—East Caribbean dollar (EC$) of 100 cents.

FLAG.—Blue, bearing in centre a device of yellow over black over white triangles having a common base.

NATIONAL ANTHEM.—Sons and Daughters of Saint Lucia.

NATIONAL DAY.—February 22 (Independence Day).

GOVERNMENT

St. Lucia became independent within the Commonwealth on February 22, 1979. The Head of State is The Queen, represented in the island by a St. Lucian Governor General, and there is a bicameral legislature. The Senate has 11 members, 6 appointed by the ruling party, 3 by the Opposition and 2 by the Governor General. The House of Assembly, which has a life of five years, has 17 elected Members and a Speaker, who may be elected from outside the House.

Acting Governor General, His Excellency Stanislaus James, CMG, OBE.

Cabinet
(as at June 30, 1990)

Prime Minister, Minister of Finance, Foreign Affairs, Development and Home Affairs, Rt. Hon. John G. M. Compton.
Deputy PM and Minister of Trade, Industry and Tourism, Hon. George Mallet.
Communications, Works and Transport, Hon. Gregory Avril.
Health, Housing, Information and Broadcasting, Hon. Romanus Lansiquot.
Youth, Community Development, Social Affairs, Sport, Hon. Stephenson King.
Attorney General and Minister for Legal Affairs, Hon. Senator Parry Husbands.
Agriculture, Lands, Fisheries and Co-operatives, Hon. Ferdinand Henry.
Education and Culture, Hon. Louis George.

ST. LUCIA HIGH COMMISSION
10 Kensington Court, W8 5DL
[071–937 9522]

High Commissioner for the Eastern Caribbean States, His Excellency Richard Gunn (1987).

ECONOMY

The economy is mainly agrarian, with manufacturing based on the processing of agricultural products. Principal crops are bananas, coconuts, cocoa, mangoes, avocado pears, breadfruit, spices, root crops such as cassava and yams, and citrus fruit. Attempts are being made to diversify the economy, in particular through greater industrialization; tourism is also of increasing importance, with 204,000 visitors to the island in 1989.

The principal exports are bananas, coconut products (copra, edible oils, soap), cardboard boxes, beer, and textile manufactures. The chief imports are flour, meat, machinery, building materials, motor vehicles, cotton piece goods, petroleum and fertilizers.

Trade with UK

	1988	1989
Imports from UK	£19,750,000	£19,601,000
Exports to UK	58,385,000	48,746,000

OFFICE OF THE BRITISH HIGH COMMISSION
Columbus Square, PO Box 227, Castries
[Castries 22484]

High Commissioner, (resides at Bridgetown, Barbados).
Resident Representative, P. T. Rouse, MBE.

ST. VINCENT AND THE GRENADINES

The territory of the State of St. Vincent includes certain of the Grenadines, a chain of small islands stretching 40 miles across the Caribbean Sea between Grenada and St. Vincent, some of the larger of which

are Bequia, Canouan, Mayreau, Mustique, Union Island, Petit St. Vincent and Prune Island. The whole territory extends 150 sq. miles (388 sq. km).

The main island, St. Vincent, is situated between 13° 6′ and 14° 35′ N. latitude and 61° 6′ and 61° 20′ W. longitude, approximately 21 miles south-west of St. Lucia and 100 miles west of Barbados. The island is 18 miles long and 11 miles wide at its extremities comprising an area of 133 sq. miles (344 sq. km), and a population (1988 UN estimate) of 108,000.

CAPITAL.—ΨKingstown, estimated population 33,694.

CURRENCY.—East Caribbean dollar (EC$) of 100 cents.

FLAG.—Three vertical bands, of blue, yellow and green, with three green diamonds in the shape of a 'V' mounted on the yellow band.

NATIONAL ANTHEM.—St. Vincent, Land So Beautiful.

NATIONAL DAY.—October 27 (Independence Day).

GOVERNMENT

St. Vincent was discovered by Christopher Columbus in 1498. It was granted by Charles I to the Earl of Carlisle in 1627 and after subsequent grants and a series of occupations alternately by the French and English, it was finally restored to Britain in 1783.

St. Vincent achieved full independence within the Commonwealth as St. Vincent and the Grenadines on October 27, 1979.

St. Vincent has a constitution under which there is a Governor General who is Her Majesty's Representative. Except where otherwise provided, the Governor General is required to act in accordance with the advice of the Prime Minister.

The House of Assembly consists of 15 elected members and four Senators appointed by the Government and two by the Opposition. It is presided over by a Speaker elected by the House from within or without it. All 15 seats were won by the governing New Democratic Party at the election held on May 16, 1989.

Governor General, His Excellency David Jack, *sworn in* September 20, 1989.

Cabinet
(as at June 30, 1990)

Prime Minister, Minister of Finance and Foreign Affairs, Rt. Hon. James Mitchell.
Attorney General and Minister of Justice, Information and Culture, Hon. Parnell Campbell, CVO.
Education, Youth and Women's Affairs, Hon. John Horne.
Agriculture, Industry and Labour, Hon. Allan Cruickshank.
Trade and Tourism, Hon. Herbert Young.
Health and the Environment, Hon. Burton Williams.
Housing, Local Government, Community Development and Social Welfare, Hon. Louis Jones.
Communications and Works, Hon. Jeremiah Scott.
Ministers of State, Hon. Mrs. Yvonne Gibson (*Education, Youth and Women's Affairs*); Hon. Jonathan Peters (*Trade and Tourism*).

ST. VINCENT AND THE GRENADINES
HIGH COMMISSION
10 Kensington Court, W8 5DL
[071–937 9522]

High Commissioner for the Eastern Caribbean States, His Excellency Richard Gunn (1987).

ECONOMY

This is based mainly on agriculture but the tourist and manufacturing industries have been expanding.

The main products are bananas, arrowroot, coconuts, cocoa, spices and various kinds of food crops. The main imports are foodstuffs (meat, rice, beverages), textiles, lumber, cement and other building materials, fertilizers, motor vehicles and fuel.

Trade with UK

	1988	1989
Imports from UK	£8,011,000	£11,075,000
Exports to UK	29,709,000	31,570,000

OFFICE OF THE BRITISH HIGH COMMISSION
Granby Street (PO Box 132), Kingstown
[St Vincent 71701]

High Commissioner, (resides at Bridgetown, Barbados).
Resident Representative, G. Greaves.

SEYCHELLES
(The Republic of Seychelles)

The Republic of Seychelles, in the Indian Ocean, consists of 115 islands with a total land area of 108 sq. miles (280 sq. km), spread over 400,000 square miles of ocean. There is a relatively compact granitic group, 32 islands in all, with high hills and mountains (highest point about 2,990 ft.), of which Mahé is the largest and most populated (90 per cent of the population live on Mahé); and the outlying coralline group, for the most part only a little above sea-level. Although only 4° S. of the Equator, the climate is pleasant though tropical. The population was estimated (mid 1988) to be 66,745.

CAPITAL.—ΨVictoria (population, 1982, 24,733), on the north-east side of Mahé.

CURRENCY.—Seychelles rupee (Rs) of 100 cents.

FLAG.—Red over green, divided by wavy white band.

NATIONAL ANTHEM.—Fyer Seselwa (Proud Seychellois).

NATIONAL DAY.—June 5.

GOVERNMENT

Proclaimed as French territory in 1756, the Mahé group began to be settled as a dependency of Mauritius from 1770, was captured by a British ship in 1794, changed hands several times between 1803 and 1814, when it was finally assigned to Great Britain. By Letters Patent of September, 1903, these islands, together with the coralline group, were formed into a separate Colony. On June 29, 1976, the islands became an independent republic within the Commonwealth. A coup d'état took place on June 5, 1977.

A new constitution making Seychelles a one-party state came into force in June 1979. The executive power lies with the President, who is elected by universal suffrage for a five year term. Legislative power lies with the President and the People's Assembly which has 23 elected members and two nominated by the President.

President, France Albert René, *assumed office* June 5, 1977; *elected* June 26, 1979; *re-elected* June 18, 1984, and June 12, 1989.

Council of Ministers
(as at June 30, 1990)

Defence, Environment, Legal Affairs, Industry, The President.
Finance, James Michel.
Tourism and Transport, Jacques Hodoul.
Administration and Manpower, Joseph Belmont.
Community Development, Esme Jumeau.
Foreign Relations, Danielle de St. Jorre.

Health, Ralph Adam.
Agriculture and Fisheries, Jeremie Bonnelame.
Employment and Social Affairs, William Herminie.
Education, Simone Testa.
Information and Culture, Sylvette Frichot.

SEYCHELLES HIGH COMMISSION
Box No. 4PE, 111 Baker Street, 2nd Floor, Eros House, W1M 1FE
[071–224 1660]

Acting High Commissioner, Sylvester Radegonde.

ECONOMY

The economy is based on tourism, fishing, small-scale agriculture and manufacturing, and the re-export of fuel for aircraft and ships.

Deep sea tuna fishing by foreign fleets under licence, improved trans-shipment and other port facilities at Victoria, exports from a tuna canning factory opened in 1987 and the export of fresh and frozen fish, attract growing revenues.

TRADE

	1988	1989
Imports	Rs.856,000,000	Rs.925,771,000
Exports	75,980,000	67,789,000
Re-exports......	95,628,000	109,407,000

The principal imports are foodstuffs, beverages, tobacco, mineral fuels, manufactured items, building materials, machinery and transport equipment.

Trade with UK

	1988	1989
Imports from UK	£10,478,000	£10,741,000
Exports to UK	1,297,000	993,000

BRITISH HIGH COMMISSION
Victoria House, PO Box 161,
Victoria, Mahé
[Victoria 23055]

High Commissioner, His Excellency Guy William Pulbrook Hart, OBE (1989).

SIERRA LEONE
(The Republic of Sierra Leone)

AREA, POPULATION, ETC.—Sierra Leone, with a total land area of 27,699 sq. miles (71,740 sq. km.), is on the west coast of Africa, between Guinea and Liberia. A Census of December 1985 put the population at 3,700,000. The 1988 UN estimate was 3,946,000. The southern half of Sierra Leone is inhabited by peoples whose languages fall into the Mende group; the northern half by the Temne, and smaller groups such as the Limba, Loko, Koranko and Susu.

CAPITAL.—ΨFreetown (population at 1985 Census, 470,000).

CURRENCY.—Leone (Le) of 100 cents.

FLAG.—Three horizontal stripes of leaf green, white and cobalt blue.

NATIONAL ANTHEM.—High We Exalt Thee, Realm of the Free.

NATIONAL DAY.—April 27 (Independence Day).

GOVERNMENT

The origins of the country date back to the late 18th century when a project was begun to settle destitute Africans from England on Freetown peninsula. In 1808 the settlement was declared a Crown Colony and became the main base in West Africa for enforcing the 1807 Act outlawing the slave trade. The Colony was also used as a settlement for Africans from North America and the West Indies, and great numbers of Africans rescued from slave ships also settled there.

In 1896 a Protectorate was declared over the hinterland. In 1951 a new Constitution was set up that united the colony of Freetown and the Protectorate and on April 27, 1961 Sierra Leone became a fully independent state within the Commonwealth. On April 19, 1971 a Republican Constitution was adopted and Dr. Siaka Stevens became the first Executive President. In June 1978 Sierra Leone became a one-party state, following approval by Parliament and a Referendum. The first General Election under the one party system was held on May 1, 1982. The Parliament now comprises 85 elected members and 12 Paramount Chiefs, plus nine nominated members, two of whom are the Army Commander and the Inspector General of Police.

President, His Excellency Maj.-Gen. Joseph Saidu Momoh, *sworn in* November 28, 1985.

Cabinet
(as at June 30, 1990)

President and Minister of Defence with responsibility for Public Services, His Excellency Maj.-Gen. J. S. Momoh.
First Vice-President, Hon. Abu Bakarr Kamara.
Second Vice-President, Hon. Salia Jusu Sheriff.
Finance, Hon. Tommy Taylor-Morgan.
Attorney-General and Minister of Justice, Hon. Dr. Abdulai Conteh.
Foreign Affairs, Hon. Abdul Karim Koroma.
Economic Planning and National Development, Hon. Dr. Sheka Kanu.
Agriculture, Natural Resources and Forestry, Hon. M. O. Bash-Taqi.
Trade, Hon. Joseph Bandabla Dauda.
Education, Cultural Affairs and Sports, Hon. Dr. Moses Dumbuya.
Transport and Communications, Hon. Philipson Kamara.
Mines, Hon. Birch Conteh.
Health, Hon. Dr. Wiltshire Johnson.
Works, Hon. J. E. Laverse.
Energy and Power, Hon. Dr. Shekou Sesay.
Information and Broadcasting, Hon. V. J. V. Mambu.
Tourism, Hon. Abdul Iscandari.
Internal Affairs, Hon. Ahmed Sesay.
Rural Development, Social Services and Youth, Hon. Alhaji Musa Kabia.
Industry and State Enterprises, Hon. Ben Kanu.
Labour, Hon. M. L. Sidique.
Lands, Housing and Environment, Hon. Dominic Musa.
Ministers of State, Hon. E. R. Ndomahina (*Leader of the House*); Hon. Maj.-Gen. M. Sheku Tarawallie (*Force Cdr.*); Hon. James Bambay Kamara (*Inspector General of Police*); Hon. E. T. Kamara (*Party Affairs*).

SIERRA LEONE HIGH COMMISSION
33 Portland Place, W1N 3AG
[071–636 6483]

High Commissioner, His Excellency Caleb B. Aubee (1987).

COMMUNICATIONS

Since the phasing out of the railway system in 1974 the road network has been developed considerably and there are now 5,000 miles of roads in the country, over 2,000 miles being surfaced. A bridge has been constructed over the Mano River linking Sierra Leone and Liberia.

The Freetown international airport is situated at Lungi, across the Sierra Leone River from Freetown. The main port is Freetown, which has one of the largest natural harbours in the world, and where there is a deep water quay providing about six berths for medium sized ships. There are smaller ports at Pepel, Bonthe and Niti.

Radio is operated by the Department of Broadcasting of the Sierra Leone Government. There are two shortwave transmitting and receiving stations in Freetown. Broadcasts are made in several of the more important indigenous languages in addition to English. There is also a weekly broadcast in French.

EDUCATION

In 1989 there were 2,554 primary schools in Sierra Leone and 201 secondary schools. Technical education is provided in the two Government Technical Institutes, situated in Freetown and Kenema, in two Trade Centres and in the technical training establishments of the mining companies. Teacher training is carried out at the university, six colleges in the Provinces and in the Milton Margai Training College near Freetown. The University of Sierra Leone (1967), consists of Fourah Bay College (1827), the Institute of Public Administration and Management (1980), the College of Medicine and Allied Health Sciences (1988) and Njala University College (1964).

PRODUCTION AND TRADE

On the Freetown peninsula, farming is largely confined to the production of cassava and garden crops, such as maize and vegetables, for local consumption. In the hinterland, the principal agricultural product is rice, which is the staple food of the country, and cash crops such as cocoa, coffee, palm kernels, and ginger.

The economy depends largely on mineral exports; mainly diamonds, gold, bauxite and rutile. Diamond exports provided Le1,254·5m in 1989. Total imports for 1989 were to the value of Le10,901·8m and exports were Le8,269·5m.

Trade with UK

	1988	1989
Imports from UK	£14,256,000	£20,402,000
Exports to UK	14,462,000	15,899,000

BRITISH HIGH COMMISSION
Standard Bank of Sierra Leone Building
Lightfoot Boston Street, Freetown
[Freetown 23961]

High Commissioner, His Excellency Derek William Partridge, CMG (1986).

British Council Representative, Theresa Harvey, PO Box 124, Tower Hill, Freetown.

SINGAPORE

AREA, POPULATION, ETC.—The Republic of Singapore consists of the island of Singapore and 58 islets, covering a total area of 625·6 sq. km (241·5 sq. miles). Singapore island is 26 miles long and 14 miles in breadth and is situated just north of the Equator off the southern extremity of the Malay Peninsula, from which it is separated by the Straits of Johore. A causeway, carrying a road, railway and a water pipeline, crosses the three-quarters of a mile to the mainland. The highest point of the island is 581 feet above sea level. The climate is hot and humid and there are no clearly defined seasons. Rainfall averages 240 cm a year and temperature ranges from 24°–32° C (76°–89° F).

In December 1989, the population was 2,703,500, which comprised 2,049,500 Chinese, 413,200 Malays, 175,700 Indians (including those of Pakistani, Bangladeshi and Sri Lankan origin) and 65,100 from other ethnic groups. Malay, Mandarin, Tamil and English are the official languages. At least 8 Chinese dialects are used.

CURRENCY.—Singapore dollar (S$) of 100 cents.

FLAG.—Horizontal bands of red over white; crescent with five five-point stars on red band near staff.

NATIONAL ANTHEM.—Majulah Singapura.

NATIONAL DAY.—August 9.

GOVERNMENT

Singapore, where Sir Stamford Raffles had first established a trading post under the East India Company in 1819, was incorporated with Penang and Malacca to form the Straits Settlements in 1826. The Straits Settlements became a Crown Colony in 1867. Singapore fell into Japanese hands in 1942 and civil government was not restored until 1946, when it became a separate colony. Internal self-government and the title 'State of Singapore' were introduced in 1959. Singapore became a state of Malaysia when the Federation was enlarged in September 1963, but left Malaysia and became an independent sovereign state within the Commonwealth on August 9, 1965. Singapore adopted a Republican constitution from that date, the Yang di-Pertuan Negara being re-styled President. There is a Cabinet collectively responsible to a fully-elected Parliament of 81 members.

After the General Election of September 3, 1988 the People's Action Party (PAP) had 80 seats in Parliament. The other seat was taken by the Singapore Democratic Party (SDP).

President (Head of State), Wee Kim Wee, *re-elected* August 1989 for a second five-year term.

Cabinet
(as at June 30, 1990)*

Prime Minister, Lee Kuan Yew, GCMG, CH.

First Deputy PM and Minister for Defence, Goh Chok Tong.

Second Deputy PM, Ong Teng Cheong.

National Development, S. Dhanabalan.

Education, Dr. Tony Tan Keng Yam.

Environment, Dr. Ahmad Mattar.

Communications and Information, Dr. Yeo Ning Hong.

Law and Home Affairs, Prof. S. Jayakumar.

Finance, Dr. Richard Hu Tsu Tau.

Labour, Lee Yock Suan.

Foreign Affairs and Community Development, Wong Kan Seng.

Trade and Industry, Lee Hsien Loong.

Health (acting), Yeo Cheow Tong.

*Lee Kuan Yew is to retire as PM by the end of 1990.

Speaker of Parliament, Tan Soo Khoon.

SINGAPORE HIGH COMMISSION
2 Wilton Crescent, SW1X 8RW
[071–235 8315]

High Commissioner, His Excellency Abdul Aziz Mahmood (1988).

COMMUNICATIONS

Singapore is one of the largest and busiest seaports in the world, with deep water wharves and ship repairing facilities. Ships also anchor in the roads, unloading into lighters. In 1988, 90,600,000 freight tonnes of seaborne cargo was discharged and 64,100,000 freight tonnes loaded. More than 500 shipping lines use the port, with 35,966 ship arrivals in 1988. The international airport is at Changi, in the east of the island. There are 25·75 km of metric gauge railway connected to the Malaysian rail system by the causeway across the Straits of Johore, and 2,760 km of roads. There are both wireless and wired

broadcasting services carrying commercial advertising. There are three television channels. The Singapore Broadcasting Authority Corporation was established in February 1980.

ECONOMY

Historically Singapore's economy was largely based on the sale and distribution of raw materials from surrounding countries and on entrepot trade in finished products. However, new manufacturing industries have been successfully introduced, including ship building and repairing, iron and steel, textiles, footwear, wood products, micro-electronics, scientific instruments, detergents, confectionery, pharmaceuticals, petroleum products, etc. Singapore has also become a financial centre with 137 commercial banks and 63 merchant banks established in the Republic, and an oil-refining centre.

In September 1988 it was announced that Singapore had been promoted by the World Bank to the 'high income' bracket of countries earning at least US$6,000 per capita annually.

Finance (estimates)

	1988–89	1989–90
Revenue	S$11,560·0m	S$13,274·3m
Expenditure	12,470·0m	12,634·9m

Trade

	1987	1988
Total imports	S$68,415·2m	S$88,226·7m
Total exports	60,265·7m	79,051·3m

Trade with UK.

	1988	1989
Imports from UK	£632,452,000	£773,866,000
Exports to UK	579,368,000	903,248,000

BRITISH HIGH COMMISSION
Tanglin Road, Singapore 1024
[Singapore 4739333]

High Commissioner, His Excellency Sir Michael Pike, KCVO, CMG (1987).

British Council Representative, A. Webster, 30 Napier Road, Singapore 1025.

SOLOMON ISLANDS

Forming a scattered archipelago of mountainous islands and low-lying coral atolls, the Solomon Islands stretches about 900 miles in a south-easterly direction from Bougainville, in Papua New Guinea, to the Santa Cruz islands. The archipelago covers an area of about 249,000 square nautical miles while the land area is 10,938 sq. miles (28,446 sq. km). Solomon Islands lies between the east longitudes 155° 30′ and 170° 30′ and between south latitudes 5° 10′ and 12° 45′. The six biggest islands are: Choiseul, New Georgia, Santa Isabel, Guadalcanal, Malaita and Makira. They are characterized by precipitous, thickly-forested mountain ranges intersected by deep, narrow valleys, and vary between 90 to 120 miles in length and between 20 to 30 miles in width.

Distribution of the total population of 285,176 at the Census of 1986 was: Melanesian 268,536; Polynesian 10,661; Micronesian 3,929; European 1,107; Chinese 379; Others 564. English is the official language; there are over 80 local languages.

CAPITAL.—ΨHoniara, population (1986), 30,499.

CURRENCY.—Solomon Islands dollar (SI$) of 100 cents.

FLAG.—Blue over green divided by a diagonal yellow band, with five white stars in the top left quarter.

NATIONAL ANTHEM.—God Bless our Solomon Islands.

NATIONAL DAY.—July 7 (Independence Day).

GOVERNMENT

The origin of the present Melanesian inhabitants is uncertain. European discovery of the islands began in the mid-16th century and continued intermittently for about 300 years, when the inauguration of sugar plantations in Queensland and Fiji (which created a need for labour) and the arrival of missionaries and traders led to increased European interest in the region. Great Britain declared a Protectorate in 1893 over the Southern Solomons, adding the Santa Cruz group in 1898 and 1899. The islands of the Shortland groups were transferred by treaty from Germany to Great Britain in 1900.

The Solomon Islands achieved internal self-government in 1976, and became independent in July 1978. The Solomon Islands is a constitutional monarchy, The Queen being represented locally by the Governor General. Legislative power is vested in a unicameral National Parliament of 38 members, elected for a four-year term. The executive authority is exercised by the Cabinet.

The present government was elected in February 1989.

Governor General, His Excellency Sir George Lepping, GCMG, MBE.

Cabinet
(as at June 30, 1990)

Prime Minister, Hon. Solomon Mamaloni.
Deputy PM and Minister for Home Affairs, Danny Philip.
Agriculture and Lands, Abraham Kapei.
Education and Human Resources Development, Albert Laore.
Finance and Economic Planning, Christopher Columbus Abe.
Foreign Affairs and Trade Relations, Sir Baddeley Devesi, GCMG, GCVO.
Health and Medical Services, Nathaniel Supa.
Housing and Government Services, Allan Qurusu.
Natural Resources, Allen Paul.
Police and Justice, Allen Kemakeza.
Post and Communications, Ben Gale.
Provincial Government, Nathaniel Waena.
Tourism and Aviation, Victor Ngele.
Transport, Works and Utilities, Michael Maena.
Commerce and Primary Industries, Edmund Andressen.

HONORARY CONSULATE
19 Springfield Road, SW19 7AL
[081–946 1744]

Honorary Consul, E. E. Nielsen.

JUDICIARY

The High Court of Solomon Islands, constituted by the Solomon Islands Independence Order, consists of a Chief Justice and not fewer than two nor more than three Puisne Judges. The Court of Appeal Act was enacted on May 8, 1978.

COMMUNICATIONS

A new international air service was started by Solomon Airlines in June 1990. Services are operated from Honiara to Brisbane, Sydney, Auckland, Port Moresby, Vila and Nadi (Fiji). In addition there is a weekly Qantas flight Brisbane–Honiara–Brisbane and Air Niugini flight Port Moresby–Honiara–Port Moresby.

There are about 52 miles of secondary and minor roads in the urban areas of Honiara, Auki and Gizo. About 18 miles of road in and around Honiara and one mile in Gizo are bitumen sealed, the remainder being coral or gravel surfaced. In the rural areas there are some 800 miles of road, including those in private plantations, forestry areas and roads built and maintained by councils.

Telekom, a company jointly owned by Cable and Wireless Limited and Solomon Islands Government, operates the international and domestic telephone circuits from a ground station in Honiara via the Intelsat Pacific Ocean communication satellite.

FINANCE AND TRADE

The main imports are foodstuffs, consumer goods, machinery and transport materials. Principal exports are timber, fish, copra, and palm oil. Fisheries exports for 1989 totalled SI$65·3m, timber SI$41·3m and copra SI$21m. Other exports include cocoa and marine shells.

Trade with UK

	1988	1989
Imports from UK	£2,576,000	£1,088,000
Exports to UK	5,153,000	6,404,000

BRITISH HIGH COMMISSION
Telekom House, Mendana Avenue, (PO Box 676), Honiara
[Honiara 21705]

High Commissioner, His Excellency (David) Junor Young (1988).

SRI LANKA
(Sri Lanka Prajatantrika Samajawadi Janarajaya)

AREA, CLIMATE, ETC.—Sri Lanka (formerly Ceylon) is an island in the Indian Ocean, off the southern tip of the peninsula of India and separated from it by a narrow strip of shallow water, the Palk Strait. Situated between 5° 55′–9° 50′ N. latitude and 79° 42′–81° 52′ E. longitude, it has an area of 25,332 sq. miles (65,610 sq. km), including 33 square miles of inland water. Its greatest length is from north to south, 270 miles; and its greatest width 140 miles, no point in Sri Lanka being more than 80 miles from the sea.

Forests, jungle and scrub cover the greater part of the island, often being intermingled. In areas over 2,000 feet above sea level grasslands (*patanas* or *talawas*) are found. One of the highest peaks in the central massif is Adam's Peak (7,360 ft), a place of pilgrimage for Buddhists, Hindus and Muslims.

The climate of Sri Lanka is warm throughout the year, with a high relative humidity. In the hills the climate is more temperate. Rainfall is generally heavy, with marked regional variations. The two main monsoon seasons are mid-May to September (south-west) and November to March (north-east).

POPULATION.—The population at the 1981 census was 14,800,001. (A 1988 UN estimate gave a figure of 16,587,000.) Of these 74 per cent were Sinhalese, 12·6 per cent Sri Lankan Tamils, 5·6 per cent Indian Tamils, 7·1 per cent Sri Lankan Moors and 0·7 per cent Burghers, Malays and others. The religion of the great majority of inhabitants is Buddhism, introduced from India, according to ancient Sinhalese chronicles, in 247 BC After Buddhism (69·3 per cent), Hinduism has the largest following (15·5 per cent); 7·6 per cent of the population are Muslims and 7·5 per cent Christians. The national languages are Sinhalese, Tamil and English.

CAPITAL.—ΨColombo, population (1981) 585,776.

1984 estimate 643,000. Other principal towns are Ψ Jaffna (118,215), Kandy (101,281), Ψ Galle (77,183), Ψ Negombo (51,376) and Ψ Trincomalee (44,913).

CURRENCY.—Sri Lankan rupee (Rs) of 100 cents.

FLAG.—On a dark red field, within a golden border, a golden lion passant holding a sword in its right paw, and a representation of a *bo*-leaf, issuing from each corner; and to its right, two vertical stripes of saffron and green also placed within a golden border, to represent the minorities of the country.

NATIONAL ANTHEM.—Namo Namo Matha (We all stand together).

NATIONAL DAY.—February 4 (Independence Commemoration Day).

GOVERNMENT

Early in the sixteenth century the Portuguese landed in Ceylon and founded settlements, eventually conquering much of the country. Portuguese rule in Ceylon lasted 150 years, but in 1658, following a twenty-year period of decline, Portuguese rule gave way to that of the Dutch East India Company which was to exploit Ceylon with varying fortunes until 1796.

The Maritime Provinces of Ceylon were ceded by the Dutch to the British on February 16, 1798, becoming a British Crown Colony in 1802 under the terms of the Treaty of Amiens. With the annexation of the Kingdom of Kandy in 1815, all Ceylon came under British rule.

On February 4, 1948 Ceylon became a self-governing state and a member of the British Commonwealth of Nations. A republican Constitution was adopted on May 22, 1972, providing for a unicameral legislature, the National State Assembly, which has a six year term, and the country was renamed the Republic of Sri Lanka (meaning 'Resplendent Island'). On September 5, 1978 a new Constitution introduced the title the Democratic Socialist Republic of Sri Lanka and a system of proportional representation. Legislative power is exercised by Parliament, the executive power being exercised by the President.

A Bill providing for the holding of the Provincial Council elections was passed on January 22, 1988. President Jayewardene issued a proclamation on September 8, 1988, merging the Northern and Eastern Provinces, as envisaged under the Indo-Sri Lanka Agreement. The Eelam People's Revolutionary Liberation Front (EPRLF) gained a clear majority in the Northern-Eastern Provincial Council, while the ruling United National Party (UNP) gained an absolute majority in elections to the seven other newly formed Provincial Councils.

In the General Election of February 15, 1989 the United National Party gained a decisive victory. The results were as follows: United National Party 125 seats, Sri Lanka Freedom Party 67, Independent Tamils 14, Tamil United Liberation Front 10, Sri Lanka Muslim Congress 3, United Socialist Alliance 3, Mahajana Eksath Peramuna 3.

President, His Excellency Ranasinghe Premadasa, *elected* Dec. 20, 1988, *sworn in* Jan. 2, 1989 (*also Minister of Buddha Sasana, Policy Planning and Implementation, and Defence*).

Cabinet
(as at June 30, 1990)

Prime Minister and Minister of Finance, Hon. D. B. Wijetunge.
Transport and Highways, Hon. Wijayapala Mendis.
Justice, Hon. A. C. S. Hameed.
Environment and Parliamentary Affairs, Hon. M. Vincent Perera.
Education and Higher Education, Hon. Lalith Athulathmudali.
Public Administration, Provincial Councils and Home Affairs, Hon. Festus Perera.
Tourism and Rural Industrial Development, Hon. S. Thondaman.
Industries, Science and Technology, Hon. Ranil Wickramasinghe.
Lands, Irrigation and Mahaweli Development, Hon. P. Dayaratne.
Fisheries and Aquatic Resources, Hon. Joseph Michael Perera.
Cultural Affairs and Information, Hon. W. J. M. Lokubandara.
Posts and Telecommunications, Hon. Alick Aluvihare.
Youth Affairs and Sports, Hon. C. Nanda Mathew.
Trade and Commerce, Hon. A. R. Munsoor.
Handlooms and Textile Industries, Hon. U. B. Wijekoon.
Health and Women's Affairs, Hon. Renuka Herath.
Reconstruction, Rehabilitation and Social Welfare, Hon. A. M. S. Adikari.
Housing and Construction, Hon. B. Sirisena Cooray.
Plantation Industries, Hon. Ranjan Wijeratne.
Foreign Affairs, Hon. Harold Herat.
Food and Co-operatives, Hon. Weerasinghe Mallimarachchi.
Agricultural Development and Research, Hon. Dharmadasa Banda.
Power and Energy, Hon. K. D. M. Chandra Bandara.
Ports and Shipping, Hon. Rupa Karunatilleke.
Labour and Vocational Training, Hon. G. M. Premachandra.

HIGH COMMISSION FOR THE DEMOCRATIC SOCIALIST REPUBLIC OF SRI LANKA
13 Hyde Park Gardens, W2 2LU
[071–262 1841]

High Commissioner, His Excellency Gen. D. S. Attygalle (1990).

THE JUDICATURE

The Judicial System provides for a Supreme Court, a Court of Appeal, a High Court and other Courts of First Instance.

COMMUNICATIONS

There are over 15,660 miles of motorable roads in Sri Lanka and a government-run railway system with 984 miles of lines.

There is a satellite earth station at Padukka, in south-west Sri Lanka, which provides telecommunication links via satellite with any part of the globe.

The principal airports are at Katunayake, 19 miles north of Colombo, and Ratmalana, nine miles south of the capital. Air Lanka operates on 76 flights weekly to the Gulf States, the Maldives, Western Europe and throughout the Far East.

PRODUCTION

Agriculture.—The staple products of the island are tea, rubber, copra, spices and gems. There is increasing emphasis on local production of food, especially rice, and plans for the large-scale production of sugar cane, cotton and citrus fruits.

Industry.—Factories are established for the manufacture or processing of ceramic ware, vegetable oils and by-products, paper, tobacco, tanning and leather goods, plywood, cement, chemicals, sugar, flour, salt, textiles, ilmenite, tiles, tyres, fertilizers, clothing, jewellery and hardware and there is a petroleum refinery.

Trade with UK

	1988	1989
Imports from UK	£92,528,000	£92,465,000
Exports to UK	56,661,000	63,527,000

BRITISH HIGH COMMISSION
Galle Road, Kollupitiya (PO Box 1433),
Colombo 3
[Colombo 27611/9]

High Commissioner, His Excellency David Arthur
Steuart Gladstone, CMG (1987).

British Council Representative, Dr. N. R. Kemp, OBE,
49 Alfred House Gardens, Colombo 3. Library also
in *Kandy*.

SWAZILAND
(Umbuso we Swatini)

AREA, POPULATION, ETC.—Surrounded by South
Africa on its northern, western and southern borders
and by Mozambique to the east, this small land-locked
country is geographically and climatically divided
into three principal areas. The broken mountainous
Highveld along the western border with an average
altitude of 4,000 feet is densely forested mainly with
conifers and eucalyptus; the Middleveld, averaging
about 2,000 feet, is a mixed farming area including
cotton and pineapples; and the Lowveld in the east,
which was mainly scrubland until the introduction
of large sugar cane plantations west of the Lubombo
mountain range and the Mozambique border. Four
rivers, the Komati, Usutu, Mbuluzi and Ngwavuma,
flow from west to east. The total area of Swaziland is
6,704 sq. miles (17,363 sq. km), and the population (UN
estimate 1988) is 737,000.

CAPITAL.—Mbabane (estimated population,
30,000), the headquarters of the Government, is
situated at an average altitude of 3,800 ft. Other
main townships are: Manzini (estimated population,
30,000), Big Bend, Mhlambanyati, Mhlume, Nhlan-
gano, Pigg's Peak and Simunye.

CURRENCY.—Lilangeni (E) of 100 cents. South
African currency is also in circulation. Swaziland is
a member of the Common Monetary Area and its unit
of currency *Emalangeni* (singular *Lilangeni*) has a
par value with the South African Rand.

FLAG.—Five horizontal bands, crimson, bearing
shield and spears device, bordered by narrow yellow
bands; blue bands at top and foot.

NATIONAL ANTHEM.—Elwatini.

NATIONAL DAY.—September 6 (Independence Day).

GOVERNMENT

The Kingdom of Swaziland came into being on
April 25, 1967, under a new internal self-government
constitution and became an independent kingdom,
headed by HM Sobhuza II, in membership of the
Commonwealth on September 6, 1968.

A new Constitution was introduced in 1978, under
which the King, assisted by his appointed Cabinet,
holds considerable executive, legislative and judicial
authority. In addition, there is a bicameral legislative
body comprising a Senate and a House of
Assembly. Each of the 40 traditional Tinkhundla
(chieftaincies) elects two members to the electoral
college who elect 40 members to the House of
Assembly. The King appoints ten members to the
House of Assembly, making 50 in all, who then elect
ten members (not of their own number) to the Senate.
To these are added ten senators appointed by the
King, bringing the full membership of the Senate to
20. All political parties are banned under the 1978
Constitution.

Head of State, HM King Mswati III, *inaugurated*
April 25, 1986.

Cabinet
(as at June 30, 1990)

Acting Prime Minister, Hon. Obed Dlamini.
Labour and Public Service, Hon. Sen. Ben Sibandze.
Commerce, Industry and Tourism, Hon. Sen. Douglas
 Ntiwane.
Natural Resources, Prince Nqaba.
Foreign Affairs, Hon. Sen. George M. Mamba.
Justice, Hon. Sen. Reginald Dladla.
Education, Hon. Chief Sipho Shongwe.
Health, Dr. Fanny Friedman.
Works and Communications, Hon. Sen. Wilson
 Mkhonta.
Finance, Hon. Sibusiso Dlamini.
Interior and Immigration, Hon. Sen. Senzenjani
 Shabalala.
Agriculture, Hon. Sipho Mamba.

KINGDOM OF SWAZILAND HIGH COMMISSION
58 Pont Street, SW1X 0AE
[071–581 4976/8]

High Commissioner, His Excellency Mboni N. Dlamini (1988).

COMMUNICATIONS

Swaziland's railway is about 150 miles long and
runs from Ngwenya in the west to the Mozambique
border near Goba in the east, and thence to the
Mozambique port of Maputo. A southern link from
Phuzumoya in central Swaziland joins up with the
South African railway network to Richards Bay. A
rail link from Mpaka in central Swaziland to the
north-west border opened in 1986 and provides a link
to Komatipoort.

Most passenger and goods traffic is carried by
privately-owned motor transport services. There are
daily scheduled air services by Royal Swazi National
Airways to Johannesburg and scheduled routes to
Durban, Harare, Lusaka, Gaborone, Nairobi and
Dar es Salaam. International telecommunications
and television services are provided through a
satellite earth station opened in 1983. There is also a
national telephone network through a series of
microwave links.

FINANCE

In the 1989–90 budget, total expenditure, including
debt repayment, was projected at E447,000,000. A
surplus of E12,500,000 was predicted due to increase
in revenue.

Manufacturing was announced to have replaced
agriculture as the dominant sector in 1988.

Trade with UK

	1988	1989
Imports from UK	£1,564,000	£1,358,000
Exports to UK	27,973,000	31,368,000

BRITISH HIGH COMMISSION
Allister Miller Street, Mbabane
[Mbabane 42581]

High Commissioner, His Excellency Brian Watkins
(1990).

TANZANIA
(Jamhuri ya Mwungano wa Tanzania)

AREA, ETC.—Tanganyika, the mainland part of the
United Republic of Tanzania (Tanganyika and Zan-

zibar), occupies the east-central portion of the African continent, between 1°–11° 45′ S. lat. and 29° 20′–40° 38′ E. long. It is bounded on the N. by Kenya and Uganda; on the SW by Lake Malawi, Malawi and Zambia; on the S. by Mozambique; on the W. it is bounded by Rwanda, Burundi and Zaire; on the E. the boundary is the Indian Ocean. Tanzania has an area of 364,900 sq. miles (945,087 sq. km). The greater part of the country is occupied by the Central African plateau from which rise, among others, Mt. Kilimanjaro (19,340 ft), the highest point on the continent of Africa, and Mt. Meru (14,974 ft). The Serengeti National Park, which covers an area of 6,000 sq. miles in the Arusha, Mwanza and Mara Regions, is famous for its variety and number of species of game.

POPULATION.— The total population of Tanzania at the Census held in 1988 was 23,174,336 (preliminary figures). Africans form a large majority, while Europeans, Asians, and other non-Africans form the minority. The African population consists mostly of tribes of mixed Bantu race. Swahili is the national and official language. The use of English is widespread both for educational and government purposes.

Zanzibar.—Formerly ruled by the Sultan of Zanzibar, and a British Protectorate until December 10, 1963. Zanzibar consists of the islands of Zanzibar, Pemba and Latham. The surface area is 2,461 sq. km, and the population (UN estimate 1988), is 625,000. ΨZanzibar (population, 110,669) is the chief town and seaport of the island.

CAPITAL.—ΨDar es Salaam (population 1,096,000 1985 estimate). Other towns (1978 population) are ΨTanga (103,409), Mwanza (110,611), Arusha (55,281), Moshi (52,223), Morogoro (61,890), Dodoma (45,703), Tabora (67,392) and ΨMtwara (48,510).

CURRENCY.—Tanzanian shilling of 100 cents.

FLAG.—Green (above) and blue; divided by diagonal black stripe bordered by gold, running from bottom (next staff) to top (in fly).

NATIONAL ANTHEM.—Mungu Ibariki Afrika (God Bless Africa).

NATIONAL DAY.—April 26 (Union Day).

GOVERNMENT

Tanganyika became an independent state and a member of the British Commonwealth on December 9, 1961, and a Republic, within the Commonwealth, on December 9, 1962, with an executive President, elected by universal suffrage as the Head of State and Head of the Government. On December 10, 1963, Zanzibar became an independent state within the Commonwealth and on April 26, 1964, Tanganyika united with Zanzibar to form the United Republic of Tanzania.

Tanzania became a one-party state on July 10, 1965 but with the Tanganyika African National Union (TANU) and the Afro-Shirazi Party (ASP) remaining the ruling parties in Tanganyika and Zanzibar respectively. On February 5, 1977 these two parties merged to form the Chama Cha Mapinduzi (CCM) (Revolutionary Party).

A new constitution was introduced on April 26, 1977 and revised in October 1984. There is a President and two Vice-Presidents, one the President of Zanzibar and the other the Prime Minister. The President may only serve two five year terms and if he comes from Zanzibar the Prime Minister will be the First Vice-President and must come from Tanganyika. If the President comes from Tanganyika the President of Zanzibar will be the First Vice President. In a presidential election a single presidential candidate nominated by the CCM must to obtain an affirmative majority of the votes cast, failing which a fresh candidate must be nominated. The National Assembly contains 243 members, of whom 118 are elected

from mainland constituencies and 50 from Zanzibar, 25 are ex-officio, 15 nominated and 35 indirectly elected. The Speaker may either be elected from among the members or be an additional member. Constituency members are elected by popular vote at a general election held at a maximum of five-yearly intervals in which the CCM nominates two candidates to contest each seat.

A new constitution was also approved in 1984 for Zanzibar providing for an elected President and House of Representatives. Although Zanzibar has its own government and Chief Minister, Tanganyika is governed by the government of the Union. Overall policy is decided by the CCM whose chairman, Julius Nyerere, was re-elected in 1987 by the Party National Conference for a 5 year term.

President of the United Republic, HE Hon. Ali Hassan Mwinyi, b. 1925; *elected* Oct. 27, 1985; *sworn in* Nov. 5, 1985.
First Vice-President of the United Republic and Prime Minister, Hon. Joseph Sinde Warioba.
Second Vice-President of the United Republic and President of Zanzibar, HE Idris Abdul Wakil.

Cabinet
(as at June 30, 1990)

Defence and National Service, HE Hon. Ali Hassan Mwinyi.
Without Portfolio, Hon. Rashidi Kawawa.
Foreign Affairs, Hon. Benjamin Mkapa.
Finance, Economic Affairs and Planning, Hon. Stephen Kibona.
Communications and Works, Hon. Dr. Pius Ng'wandu.
Local Government, Community Development, Co-operatives and Marketing, Hon. Anna Abdallah.
Agriculture and Livestock Development, Hon. Stephen Wassira.
Labour, Culture and Social Welfare, Hon. Joseph Rwegasira.
Home Affairs, Hon. Nalaila Kiula.
Energy, Minerals and Water, Hon. Jakaya Kikwete.
Lands, Natural Resources and Tourism, Hon. Marcel Komanya.
Industry and Trade, Hon. Cleopa Msuya.
Education, Hon. Amran Mayagilo.
Health, Hon. Charles Kabeho.
Justice, Hon. Damian Lubuva.
Information, Hassan Diria.

TANZANIA HIGH COMMISSION
43 Hertford Street, W1Y 7TF
[071–499 8951]

High Commissioner, His Excellency John S. Malecela (1989).

EDUCATION

All Tanzanian secondary schools are expected to include practical subjects in the basic course. All who receive secondary (or equivalent) education are called up for a period of National Service. The school system is administered in Swahili but the Government is making efforts to improve English standards for the purposes of secondary and higher education. For higher education Tanzanian students go to the University of Dar es Salaam, Sokoine University of Agriculture in Morogoro, other East African universities, or to universities and colleges outside East Africa, including Britain.

COMMUNICATIONS

The main port is Dar es Salaam, and there are other ports on the coast at Tanga, Mtwara, Zanzibar, Mkoani and Wete, in addition to Mwanza, Musoma and Bukoba on Lake Victoria and Kigoma on Lake Tanganyika. Coastal shipping services connect the mainland to Zanzibar, and lake services are operated on Lake Tanganyika and Lake Malawi with neighbouring countries.

The principal international airports are Dar es Salaam and Kilimanjaro. Other airports include Zanzibar, Arusha, Mwanza and Tanga.

There are two railway systems: one connecting Dar es Salaam to Zambia, and the second having two main lines running from Dar es Salaam, one to northern Tanzania and Kenya and the other to Lake Tanganyika and Victoria.

PRODUCTION AND TRADE

The economy is based mainly on the production and export of primary produce and the growing of foodstuffs for local consumption. The islands of Zanzibar and Pemba produce a large part of the world's supply of cloves and clove oil; and coconuts, coconut oil and copra are also produced. The mainland's chief export crops are coffee, cotton, sisal, tea, tobacco, cashew nuts and diamonds. The most important minerals are diamonds. Hides and skins are another valuable export. Industry is at present largely concerned with the processing of raw material for either export or local consumption. There are also secondary manufacturing industries, including factories for the manufacture of leather and rubber footwear, knitwear, razor blades, cigarettes and textiles, and a wheat flour mill.

Trade with UK

	1988	1989
Imports from UK	£88,686,000	£93,036,000
Exports to UK	26,386,000	22,641,000

BRITISH HIGH COMMISSION
Hifadhi House, Samora Avenue (PO Box 9200),
Dar es Salaam
[Dar es Salaam 29601]

High Commissioner, His Excellency John Thorold Masefield, CMG. (1989).

British Council Representative, J. Mayatt, OBE, Ohio Samora Avenue, (PO Box 9100), Dar es Salaam.

TONGA
(Kingdom of Tonga)

Tonga, or the Friendly Islands, comprises a group of islands situated in the Southern Pacific some 450 miles to the ESE of Fiji, with an area of 270 sq. miles (699 sq. km), and population (1988 UN estimate) of 116,000. The largest island, Tongatapu, was discovered by Tasman in 1643. Most of the islands are of coral formation, but some are volcanic (Tofua, Kao and Niuafoou or 'Tin Can' Island). The limits of the group are between 15° and 23° 30′ S., and 173° and 177° W.

CAPITAL.—ΨNuku'alofa (population estimate 30,000), on Tongatapu.

CURRENCY.—Pa'anga (T$) of 100 seniti.

FLAG.—Truncated red cross on rectangular white ground (next staff) on a red field.

NATIONAL ANTHEM.—E, 'Otua Mafimafi (Oh, Almighty God Above).

NATIONAL DAY.—June 4 (Independence Day).

GOVERNMENT

The Kingdom of Tonga is an independent constitutional monarchy within the Commonwealth. Prior to June 4, 1970 it had been a British-protected state for 70 years. The constitution provides for a Government consisting of the Sovereign, a privy council which functions as a cabinet, a legislative assembly and a judiciary. The legislative assembly includes the King, privy council, nine hereditary nobles and nine popularly elected representatives (who hold office for three years). The most recent election took place on February 15, 1990.

Head of State, HM King Taufa'ahau Tupou IV, GCMG, GCVO, KBE, *acceded* Dec. 16, 1965.

Heir, HRH Crown Prince Tupouto'a.

Cabinet
(as at June 30, 1990)

Prime Minister, Minister of Agriculture, Fisheries, Forests, and Marine, HRH Prince Fatafehi Tu'ipelehake, KBE.

Acting Deputy Prime Minister, Minister of Labour, Commerce and Industries, Baron Vaea of Houma.

Education, Works, Civil Aviation, Hon. Hu'akavameiliku.

Police, Prisons and Fire Services, Hon. 'Akau'ola.

Health, Hon. Dr. S. Tapa.

Foreign Affairs and Defence, HRH Crown Prince Tupouto'a.

Finance, Hon. J. Cecil Cocker.

Attorney General, Minister of Justice, Hon. Tevita P. Tupou.

Minister without Portfolio, Hon. Ma'afu Tuku'i'aulahi.

Acting Minister of Lands, Survey, and Natural Resources, Hon. Dr. S. Ma'afu Tupou.

Governor of Ha'apai, Hon. Fakafanua.

Acting Governor of Vava'u, Hon. Tu'i'afitu.

TONGA HIGH COMMISSION
New Zealand House, Haymarket, SW1Y 4TE
[071–839 3287]

High Commissioner, His Excellency S. M. Tuita (1989).

ECONOMY

The economy is primarily agricultural; the main crops are coconuts, bananas, vanilla, yams, taro, cassava, groundnuts and other fruits. Fish is an important staple food though recent shortfalls have led to canned fish being imported. Industry is based on the processing of agricultural produce, and the manufacture of foodstuffs, clothing and sports equipment. The principal exports are copra, other coconut products, tropical root crops, bananas, knitwear, leather goods and fibreglass boats.

TRADE

	1985	1989
Total imports	T$58,900,000	T$68,334,194
Total exports	7,700,000	11,517,597

Trade with UK

	1988	1989
Imports from UK	£856,000	£831,000
Exports to UK	145,000	28,000

BRITISH HIGH COMMISSION
PO Box 56, Nuku'alofa
[Nuku'alofa 21020]

High Commissioner, His Excellency William Lawson Cordiner (1990).

TRINIDAD AND TOBAGO
(The Republic of Trinidad and Tobago)

AREA, POPULATION, ETC.—Trinidad, the most southerly of the West Indian islands, lies close to the north coast of S. America, the nearest point being Venezuela, 7 miles distant. The island is situated between 10° 2′–11° 12′ N. lat. and 60° 30′–61° 56′ W. long., and is about 50 miles in length by 37 miles in width, with an area of 1,864 sq. miles (4,827 sq. km). Two mountain systems, the Northern and Southern Ranges, stretch across almost its entire width and a third, the Central Range, lies diagonally across its middle portion; otherwise the island is mostly flat. The climate is tropical with temperatures averaging 82° F (27·8° C) by day and 74° F (23·3° C) by night, and a rainfall averaging 82 inches a year. There is a well-marked dry season from January to May, and a wet season from June to December broken by a short dry season (the *Petite Careme*) in September and October.

Tobago (population *c.*45,200) lies between 11° 9′ and 11° 21′ N. lat. and between 60° 30′ and 60° 50′ W. long., 19 miles north-east of Trinidad. The island is 32 miles long at its widest point, and 11 wide, and has an area of 116 sq. miles (300 sq. km). It is a popular tourist resort. It was ceded to the British Crown in 1814 and amalgamated with Trinidad in 1888.

In 1988 the population of Trinidad and Tobago was estimated by the UN to be 1,243,000.

Other Islands.—Corozal Point and Icacos Point, the NW and SW extremities of Trinidad, enclose the Gulf of Paria. West of Corozal Point lie several islands, of which Chacachacare, Huevos, Monos and Gaspar Grande are the most important.

CAPITAL.—ΨPort of Spain (population approximately 59,649 in 1985) is the administrative centre of the islands. About 33 miles south of the capital is San Fernando (population approximately 34,300 in 1985), a town of growing importance which is emerging as the industrial centre of Trinidad, and which is in close proximity to a number of large industrial plants. The main town of Tobago is ΨScarborough.

CURRENCY.—Trinidad and Tobago dollar (TT$) of 100 cents.

FLAG.—Black diagonal stripe bordered with white stripes, running from top to staff, all on a red field.

NATIONAL DAYS.—August 31 (Independence Day); September 24 (Republic Day).

GOVERNMENT

Trinidad was discovered by Columbus in 1498, was colonized in 1532 by the Spaniards, capitulated to the British under Abercromby in 1797, and was ceded to Britain under the Treaty of Amiens (March 25, 1802).

Tobago was discovered by Columbus in 1498. Dutch colonists arrived in 1632; Tobago subsequently changed hands numerous times until it was ceded to the British Crown by France in 1814 and amalgamated with Trinidad in 1888.

The Territory of Trinidad and Tobago became an independent state and a member of the British Commonwealth on August 31, 1962, and a Republic in 1976. The President is elected for five years by all members of the Senate and the House of Representatives. The House of Representatives has 36 members, elected by universal adult suffrage, and the Senate has 31, of whom 16 are appointed on the advice of the Prime Minister, six on the advice of the Leader of the Opposition and nine at the discretion of the President. Legislation was passed in Sept. 1980 which afforded Tobago a degree of self-administration through the 12-member Tobago House of Assembly.

President, His Excellency Noor Mohammed Hassan-ali.

Cabinet
(as at June 30, 1990)

Prime Minister and Minister for Finance and the Economy, Hon. Arthur Robinson.
Finance, Hon. Selby Wilson.
Justice and National Security, Hon. Selwyn Richardson.
Environment and National Service, Hon. Lincoln Myers.
Education, Hon. Clive Pantin.
External Affairs and International Trade, Hon. Sahadeo Basdeo.
Health, Hon. Emmanuel Hosein.
Industry, Enterprise, and Tourism, Hon. Dr. Bhoendradatt Tewarie.
Labour, Employment and Manpower Resources, Hon. Albert Richards.
Energy, Hon. Herbert Atwell.
Planning and Mobilization, Hon. Winston Dookeran.
Youth, Sports, Culture and Creative Arts, Hon. Jennifer Johnson.
Works, Infrastructure and Decentralization, Hon. Carson Charles.
Attorney General, Hon. Anthony Smart.
Social Development and Family Services, Hon. Gloria Henry.
Settlements and Public Utilities, Hon. Pamela Nicholson.
Food Production and Marine Exploitation, Hon. Brinsley Samaroo.

HIGH COMMISSION OF THE REPUBLIC OF TRINIDAD AND TOBAGO
42 Belgrave Square, SW1X 8NT
[071–245 9351]

High Commissioner, His Excellency Mr. Justice Ulric Cross (1990).

EDUCATION

The education system provides for free education at all state-owned and government-assisted denominational schools and certain faculties at the University of the West Indies. In addition there are various private teaching establishments. Attendance is compulsory for children aged 6–12 years, after which attendance at free secondary schools is determined by success in the common entrance examination at 11 years. There are three technical institutes, two teachers' training colleges, and one of the three branches of the University of the West Indies is located in Trinidad, at the St. Augustine campus. A medical teaching complex was built at Mt. Hope, and operates in collaboration with the University of the West Indies.

COMMUNICATIONS

There are some 6,436 km of all-weather roads in Trinidad and Tobago. The only general cargo port is Port of Spain but there are specialized port facilities elsewhere for landing crude oil, loading refinery products and sugar, and for storing and transmitting bauxite and cement. Regular shipping services call here and many inter-island craft use the port. Another rapidly growing port is at Port Lisas where new industries powered by local natural gas are located.

International scheduled airlines, including the national airline, Trinidad and Tobago Airways (BWIA) Corporation, use Piarco International Airport outside Port of Spain. The airline also flies between Piarco and Crown Point Airport in Tobago.

Two commercial broadcasting stations and one commercial television station operate in Trinidad and Tobago. The internal telephone system and the external telephone and telegraph connections are operated by part-state-owned companies.

PRODUCTION

Trinidad and Tobago's main source of revenue is from oil. Production of domestic crude was 8·6 m cubic metres in 1989. Daily average throughput from the two oil refineries was 70,360 barrels per day. Trinidad has large reserves of natural gas, and reserves are estimated to be in the region of 100 years at the current rates of production. An integrated steel plant, an anhydrous ammonia plant and a methanol plant have been constructed at Point Lisas.

Fertilizers, tyres, clothing, soap, furniture and foodstuffs are manufactured locally while motor vehicles, radios, TV sets, and electro-domestic equipment are assembled from parts, mainly from Japan.

Finance

	1988	1989
Revenue	TT$4,947·6m	TT$4,977·5m
Expenditure	5,931·4m	5,687·1m
Gross public debt	11,516·8m	11,623·1m

TRADE

	1988	1989
Imports	TT$4,310·3m	TT$5,167·2m
Exports	5,424·2m	6,679·5m

Trade with UK

	1988	1989
Imports from UK	£39,868,000	£45,881,000
Exports to UK	35,728,000	37,426,000

BRITISH HIGH COMMISSION
Furness House, 90 Independence Square
(PO Box 778) Port of Spain
[Port of Spain 62528616]

High Commissioner, His Excellency Sir Martin Berthoud, KCVO, CMG.

TUVALU

Tuvalu comprises nine coral atolls situated in the South West Pacific around the point at which the International Date Line cuts the Equator. The total land area is about 10 sq. miles. Few of the atolls are more than 12 ft above sea level or more than half a mile in width. The vegetation consists mainly of coconut palms. The resident population in 1985 was 8,229, but it is estimated that about 1,500 Tuvaluans work overseas, mostly in Nauru, or as seamen. The people are almost entirely Polynesian. The principal languages are Tuvaluan and English. The entire population is Christian and is predominantly Protestant.

CAPITAL.—ΨFunafuti, estimated population 2,856. The capital has a grass strip airfield from which a service operates regularly to Fiji and Kiribati, and is also the only port.

CURRENCY.—Tuvalu uses the Australian dollar ($A) of 100 cents as legal tender. In addition there are Tuvalu dollar and cent coins in circulation.

FLAG.—Blue ground with Union Flag in top left quarter and nine five-pointed gold stars in the fly.

NATIONAL ANTHEM.—Tuvalu Mo Te Atua (Tuvalu for the Almighty).

NATIONAL DAY.—October 1 (Independence Day).

GOVERNMENT

Tuvalu, formerly the Ellice Islands, formed part of the Gilbert and Ellice Islands Colony until October 1,

1975, when separate constitutions came into force. Separation from the Gilbert Islands was implemented on January 1, 1976.

On October 1, 1978 Tuvalu became fully independent as a sovereign state within the Commonwealth. The Constitution provides for a Prime Minister and four other Ministers who must be members of the 12-member elected Parliament. The Prime Minister presides at meetings of the Cabinet, which consists of the five Ministers, and is attended by the Attorney General. Local Government services are provided by elected Island Councils.

Governor General, His Excellency Sir Tupua Leupena, GCMG, MBE, *sworn in* March 1, 1986.

Cabinet
(as at June 30, 1990)

Prime Minister, Rt. Hon. Bikenibeu Paeniu.
Minister for Finance and Commerce, Hon. Dr. Alesana Seluka.
Natural Resources and Home Affairs, Hon. Tomu Sione, OBE.
Works and Communications, Hon. Ionatana Ionatana, CVO, OBE.
Health, Education and Community Affairs, Hon. Naama Latasi.
Secretary to Government, Tauaasa Taafaki.
Attorney-General, David Ballantyne.

EDUCATION AND WELFARE

There are eight primary schools in Tuvalu and a church secondary school run jointly with the Government. A Maritime Training School started in 1979 now caters for 60 boys per annum.

There is a 30-bed hospital at Funafuti. All islands are served by a dispensary and a primary school.

ECONOMY

Most people still practise a subsistence economy, the main staples of their diet being coconuts and fish. The main imports are foodstuffs, consumer goods and building materials. The only export is copra, but philatelic sales provide a major source of revenue and handicraft sales are increasing.

Trade with UK

	1988	1989
Imports from UK	£105,000	£162,000
Exports to UK	1,000	—

BRITISH HIGH COMMISSION
British High Commissioner, (resides at Suva, Fiji).

UGANDA
(Republic of Uganda)

AREA, POPULATION, ETC.—Situated in Eastern Africa, Uganda is flanked by Zaire, Sudan, Kenya and on the south by Tanzania and Rwanda. Large parts of Lakes Victoria, Edward and Albert (Mobuto) are within its boundaries, as are Lakes Kyoga, Kwania, George and Bisina (formerly Salisbury) and the course of the River Nile from its outlet from Lake Victoria to the Sudan frontier post at Nimule. Uganda has an area of 91,259 sq. miles (236,036 sq. km) (water and swamp 16,400 sq. miles) and population (1990 estimate) of 17,500,000. The official language is English. The main local vernaculars are of Bantu, Nilotic and Hamitic origins. Ki-Swahili is generally understood in trading centres.

Despite its tropical location, the climate is tempered by its situation some 3,000 ft. above sea level, and well over that altitude in the highlands of the Western and Eastern Regions. In South Uganda, temperatures seldom rise above 85° F (29° C) or fall below 60° F (15° C). The rainfall averages about 50 inches a year. Uganda has three National Parks and a fourth (Lake Mburo) has been designated.

CAPITAL.—Kampala (estimated population of Greater Kampala, 1990, 750,000). Other principal towns are Jinja (45,000), Mbale (28,000) and Masaka (29,000).

CURRENCY.—Uganda shilling of 100 cents.

FLAG.—Six horizontal stripes of black, yellow and red (repeated) with a crested crane emblem on a white orb in the centre.

NATIONAL ANTHEM.—Oh Uganda.

NATIONAL DAY.—October 9 (Independence Day).

GOVERNMENT

Uganda became an independent state and a member of the Commonwealth on October 9, 1962, after some 70 years of British rule. A Republic was instituted on September 8, 1967, under an executive President, assisted by a Cabinet of Ministers.

Early in 1971 an army coup took place and Maj.-Gen. Idi Amin, the Army Commander, proclaimed himself Head of State. In 1979, following risings and military intervention by Tanzania, President Amin was overthrown. Following elections in 1980, Dr. Milton Obote became President. A military coup on July 27, 1985 ousted Dr. Obote and installed a military council which attempted to negotiate a power-sharing agreement with the National Resistance Movement led by Yoweri Museveni. However, the National Resistance Army captured Kampala in late January 1986, securing control of the rest of the country in the following few months. Yoweri Museveni was sworn in as President in January 1986; subsequently the Prime Minister and a National Resistance Council (NRC) were appointed. The NRC acts as a legislative body with an interim mandate to form a constitution. Since the most recent elections in February 1989 it consists of 210 elected and 68 presidentially appointed members. In October 1989 the NRC voted to extend its term of office by five years from January 26, 1990.

President, Yoweri Museveni, *sworn in* Jan. 29, 1986.

Cabinet
(as at June 30, 1990)

President and Minister of Defence, Lt.-Gen. Yoweri Museveni.

Prime Minister, Dr. Samson Kisseka.

1st Deputy PM, Eriya Kategaya.

2nd Deputy PM and Minister for Foreign Affairs, Paul Ssemogerere.

3rd Deputy PM, Abu Bakar Mayanja.

Internal Affairs, Ibrahim Mukiibi.

Finance, Dr. Crispus Kiyonga.

Planning and Economic Development, Joshua Mayanja-Nkangi.

Agriculture and Forestry, Mrs. Victoria Ssekitoleko.

Industry and Technology, E. T. S. Adriko.

Commerce, Paul Etiang.

Local Government, Jaberi Bidandi-Ssali.

Animal Industries and Fisheries, Prof. George Mondo Kagonyera.

Youth, Culture and Sports, vacant.

Public Services and Cabinet Affairs, Tom Rubale.

Regional Co-operation, Joseph Mulenga.

Information and Broadcasting, Kintu Musoke.

Education, Amanya Mushega.

Land and Surveys, Ben Okello Luwum.

Water and Mineral Development, Henry Kajura.

Justice and Attorney General, George Kanyeihamba.

Constitutional Affairs, Sam Njuba.

Co-operatives and Marketing, James Wapakabulo.

Labour, Stanislaus Okurut.

Transport and Communications, Dr. Ruhakana-Rugunda.

Energy, Richard Kaijuka.

Tourism and Wildlife, Samuel Sebageraka.

Works, Daniel Serwano Kigozi.

Health, Zak Kaberu.

Housing and Urban Development, John Ssebana-Kizito.

Environmental Protection, Moses Kintu.

Relief and Social Rehabilitation, Adoko Nekyon.

Minister without Portfolio, David Kibirango.

UGANDA HIGH COMMISSION
Uganda House, 58–59 Trafalgar Square, WC2N 5DX
[071–839 5783]

High Commissioner, His Excellency Prof. George Kilya (1990).

EDUCATION

Education is a joint undertaking by the Government, local authorities and, to some extent, voluntary agencies. In 1988 it was estimated that Uganda had 7,905 primary schools with an enrolment of 2,638,100 children. Secondary schools numbered 774 with 240,834 students enrolled; and 7,291 students in various technical training institutions.

The national university is Makerere University, Kampala, founded as a trade school in 1921 and becoming an independent university in 1970. In 1989 a University of Science and Technology was opened at Mbarara.

COMMUNICATIONS

There is an international airport at Entebbe, with direct flights to destinations in Africa and Europe. There are eight other airfields in Uganda. Having no sea coast, Uganda is heavily dependent upon rail and road links to Mombasa and Dar es Salaam for its trade. Many rural areas remain cut off, but over 5,000 km of the country's dilapidated roads are currently being rehabilitated. A railway network joins the capital to the western, eastern and northern centres.

TRADE, ETC.

The principal export earner is coffee (over 90 per cent of all exports), which earned US$264 million in 1988. Attempts are being made to increase production of cotton and tea for export. Hydro-electricity is produced from the Owen Falls power station which generated 564 kW in 1988, 110 kW of which was exported to Kenya. The principal food crops are plantains, bananas, cassava, sweet potatoes, potatoes, maize and sorghum.

Trade with UK

	1988	1989
Imports from UK	£35,340,000	£39,218,000
Exports to UK	30,487,000	20,985,000

BRITISH HIGH COMMISSION
10–12 Parliament Avenue, PO Box 7070, Kampala
[Kampala 257054/9]

High Commissioner, His Excellency Charles A. K. Cullimore (1989).

British Council Representative, Lloyd Mullen.

VANUATU
(Ripablik Blong Vanuatu)

AREA, POPULATION, ETC.—Vanuatu, the former Anglo-French Condominium of the New Hebrides, is situated in the South Pacific Ocean, between 13° and 21° S. and 166° and 170° E. It includes 13 large and some 70 small islands, of coral and volcanic origin, including the Banks and Torres Islands in the North, and has a total land area of 4,706 sq. miles (12,190 sq. km). The principal islands are Vanua Lava, Espiritu Santo, Maewo, Pentecost, Aoba, Malekula, Ambrym, Epi, Efate, Erromango, Tanna and Aneityum. Most islands are mountainous and there are active volcanoes on several. The climate is oceanic tropical, moderated by the south-east trade winds which blow between May and October. At other times winds are variable and cyclones may occur. Temperatures range between 17° C and 28° C, with annual rainfall averaging 90 in. to the south and 155 in. to the north.

Provisional results of a national census which took place in May 1989 show a population of 142,630. About 95 per cent of the population are Melanesian, the rest being made up largely of Micronesians, Polynesians and Europeans. The national language is Bislama, but English and French are also official languages.

SEAT OF ADMINISTRATION—ΨVila, Efate, population (1989) 19,400. The only other town is Luganville (population, 1989, 6,900), on Espiritu Santo.

CURRENCY.—Vatu of 100 centimes.

FLAG.—Red over green with a black triangle in the hoist, the three parts being divided by fimbriations of black and yellow, and in the centre of the black triangle a boar's tusk overlaid by two crossed fern leaves.

NATIONAL ANTHEM.—Nasinal sing sing long Vanuatu.

NATIONAL DAY.—July 30 (Independence Day).

GOVERNMENT

The Condominium of the New Hebrides became an independent republic within the Commonwealth under the name of Vanuatu on July 30, 1980.

Parliament consists of 46 members elected for a term of four years. A Council of Chiefs advises on matters of custom. Executive power is held by the Prime Minister (elected from and by parliament) and a Council of Ministers who are responsible to parliament. The President is elected for a five-year term by the presidents of the 11 regional councils and the members of parliament.

President, His Excellency Frederick Karlomuana Timakata, *elected* 1989.

Council of Ministers
(as at May 31, 1990)

Prime Minister and Minister of Planning, Hon. Father Walter Lini, CBE.

Education, Hon. S. J. Regenvanu.

Finance and Housing, Hon. S. Molisa.

Lands, Minerals and Rural Water Supply, Hon. W. Mahit.

Foreign Affairs and Judicial Services, Hon. D. Kalpokas.

Health, Hon. J. M. Chilia.

Agriculture, Forestry and Fisheries, Hon. J. Hopa.

Home Affairs, Hon. I. Abbil.

Trade, Commerce, Industry, Co-operatives and Energy, Hon. H. Qualao.

Transport, Public Works and Tourism, Hon. E. Natapei.

Chief Justice, Hon. Mr. Justice F. G. Cooke.

Attorney-General, S. Hakwa.

ECONOMY

Most of the population is employed on plantations or in subsistence agriculture. Subsistence crops include yams, taro, manioc, sweet potato and breadfruit; principal cash crops are copra, cocoa and coffee. Large numbers of cattle are kept on the plantations and beef is the second largest export after copra.

Principal exports are copra, meat (frozen, tinned and chilled), timber and cocoa.

Tourism is an important revenue earner, and the absence of direct taxation has led to growth in the finance and associated industries.

Trade with UK

	1988	1989
Imports from UK	£991,000	£363,000
Exports to UK	5,000	52,000

BRITISH HIGH COMMISSION
Melitco House, Rue Pasteur, Vila
[Vila 3100]

High Commissioner, His Excellency John Thompson, MBE (1988).

WESTERN SAMOA
(Malututo'atasi o Samoa i Sisifo)

AREA, ETC.—Western Samoa lies in the south Pacific Ocean between latitudes 13° and 15° S. and longitudes 171° and 173° W. It consists of the islands of Savai'i (662 sq. miles) and of Upolu, which, with seven other islands (Apolima, Manono, Fanuatapu, Namua, Nuutele, Nuulua and Nuusafee) has an area of 435 sq. miles (1,714 sq. km). All the islands are mountainous. Upolu, the most fertile, contains the harbours of ΨApia and ΨSaluafata, and Savai'i the harbour of ΨAsau.

POPULATION.—The population at the 1981 census was 158,130, the largest numbers being on Upolu (114,980) and Savai'i (43,150); a 1988 UN estimate put the figure at 167,000. The Samoans are a Polynesian people, though the population also includes other Pacific Islanders, Euronesians, Chinese and Europeans. The main languages spoken are Samoan and English. The islanders are Christians of different denominations.

CAPITAL.—ΨApia, on Upolu (population, 1981 census, 33,100). Robert Louis Stevenson died and was buried at Apia in 1894.

CURRENCY.—Tala (WS$) of 100 sene.

FLAG.—Five white stars (depicting the Southern Cross) on a quarter royal blue at top next staff, and three quarters red.

NATIONAL ANTHEM.—The Banner of Freedom.

NATIONAL DAY.—January 1 (Independence Day).

GOVERNMENT

Formerly administered by New Zealand (latterly with internal self-government), Western Samoa became, on January 1, 1962 the first fully-independent Polynesian State. The State was treated as a member country of the Commonwealth until its formal admission on August 28, 1970.

The 1962 Constitution provides for a Head of State to be elected by the Legislative Assembly for a five year term. However, it was decided that initially two of the four Paramount chiefs should jointly hold the office of Head of State for life. When one of the chiefs died in April 1963, Malietoa Tanumafili II became the holder of the office of Head of State for life. The Head of State's functions are analogous to those of a constitutional monarch. Executive government is carried out by a Cabinet of Ministers.

Head of State, HH Malietoa Tanumafili II, GCMG, CBE (April 15, 1963).
Deputy Head of State, Hon. Mataafa Faasuamaleaui Puela.

Cabinet
(as at May 31, 1990)

Prime Minister and Minister of Foreign Affairs, Hon. Tofilau Eti Alesana.
Finance, Hon. Tuilaepa Sailele.
Agriculture, Hon. Pule Lameko.
Economic Development, Hon. Tanuvasa Livi.
Lands and Survey, Hon. Sifuiva Sione.
Education, Hon. Patu Afaese.
Health, Hon. Polataivao Fosi.
Justice and Post Office, Hon. Leiataua Vaiao.
Public Works, Transport and Civil Aviation, Hon. Jack Netzler.

ECONOMY

Agriculture is the basis of Western Samoa's economy, the principal cash crops (and exports) being coconuts (copra), cocoa and bananas. Other agricultural exports include coffee, timber, tropical fruits and seeds. Efforts are being made to develop fishing on a commercial scale. Manufacturing is very small in scope and concerned largely with processing agricultural products, but is being encouraged by the Government. Tourism is increasing rapidly.

Trade with UK

	1988	1989
Imports from UK	£757,000	£296,000
Exports to UK	1,323,000	1,376,000

BRITISH HIGH COMMISSION
High Commissioner, (resides at Wellington, New Zealand).

ZAMBIA
(Republic of Zambia)

AREA, POPULATION, ETC.—The Republic of Zambia lies on the plateau of Central Africa between the longitudes 22° E. and 33° 33′ E. and between the latitudes 8° 15′ S. and 18° S. It has an area of 290,586 sq. miles (752,614 sq. km) within boundaries 3,515 miles in length and a population (UN estimate, 1988) of 7,531,000.

With the exception of the valleys of the Zambezi, the Luapula, the Kafue and the Luangwa Rivers, and the Luano valley, elevations vary from 3,000 to 5,000 feet above sea level, but in the north-east the plateau rises to occasional altitudes of over 6,000 feet.

Although Zambia lies within the tropics, and fairly centrally in the African land mass, its elevation relieves it from extremely high temperatures and humidity.

CAPITAL.—Lusaka, situated in the Central Province. Population (1989 estimate) 1 million. Other centres are Livingstone, Kabwe, Chipata, Mazabuka, Mbala, Kasama, Solwezi, Mongu, Mansa, Ndola, Luanshya, Mufulira, Chingola, Chililabombwe, Kalulushi and Kitwe, the last six towns being the main centres on the Copperbelt.

CURRENCY.—Kwacha (K) of 100 ngwee.

FLAG.—Green with three small vertical stripes, red, black and orange (next fly); eagle device on green above stripes.

NATIONAL ANTHEM.—Stand and Sing of Zambia, Proud and Free.
NATIONAL DAY.—October 24 (Independence Day).

GOVERNMENT

At the dissolution of the Federation of Rhodesia and Nyasaland, on December 31, 1963, Northern Rhodesia (as Zambia was then known) achieved internal self-government under a new constitution. Zambia became an independent republic within the Commonwealth on October 24, 1964, 75 years after coming under British rule and nine months after achieving internal self-government.

In July 1973, a new Constitution was introduced, making the United National Independence Party (UNIP) the only party. In July 1990 it was announced that a referendum on introducing a multi-party system would be held in August 1991.

President, Dr. Kenneth David Kaunda, *assumed office* Oct. 24, 1964; *re-elected,* Dec. 1973, Dec. 1978, Oct. 1983 and Oct. 1988.

Cabinet
(as at June 30, 1990)

Prime Minister and Minister for Co-operatives, Gen. Hon. Malimba Masheke.
UNIP Secretary General, Hon. A. Grey Zulu.
Secretary of State for Defence and Security, Hon. Alex K. Shapi.
Defence, Hon. Frederick Hapunda.
Home Affairs, Gen. the Hon. Kingsley Chinkuli.
Agriculture, Hon. Justin J. Mukando.
Water, Lands and Natural Resources, Hon. Paul Malukutila.
Foreign Affairs, Hon. Luke J. Mwananshiku.
Attorney General and Minister for Legal Affairs, Hon. Frederick M. Chomba.
Information and Broadcasting Services, Hon. Arnold Simuchimba.
Commerce and Industry, Hon. Rabson Chongo.
Finance, Hon. Gibson G. Chigaga.
Mines, Hon. Bernard N. Fumbelo.
Power, Transport and Communications, Brig. Gen. the Hon. Enos Haimbe.
Tourism, Hon. Pickson Chitambala.
Higher Education, Science and Technology, Prof. the Hon. Lameck K. H. Goma.
General Education, Youth and Sport, Dr. the Hon. Eli Mwanang'onze.
Health, Hon. Mavis Muyunda.
Labour, Social Development and Culture, Hon. Lavu Mulimba.
Works and Supply, Hon. Haswell Mwale.

ZAMBIA HIGH COMMISSION
2 Palace Gate, W8 5NG
[071–589 6655]

High Commissioner, His Excellency Edward Lubinda (1989).

JUDICATURE

There is a Chief Justice appointed by the President, all other judges being appointed on the recommendation of the Judicial Service Commission consisting of the Chief Justice, the chairman of the Public Service Commission, a senior Justice of Appeal and one Presidential nominee.

PRODUCTION

Principal products are maize, sugar, groundnuts, cotton, livestock, vegetables and tobacco.

Mineral production was valued at K8,390,765,000

in 1987, of which copper production (of 483,100 tonnes) accounted for K6,870,386,000.

FINANCE AND TRADE

Gross Domestic Product (current prices) was K18,079·8m in 1987. GDP per capita (current prices) was K2,486·9.

	1986	1987
Imports	K4,447,687	K6,627,473
Exports	3,074,357	8,058,595

Trade with UK

	1988	1989
Imports from UK	£85,746,000	£119,057,000
Exports to UK	24,882,000	21,565,000

BRITISH HIGH COMMISSION
Independence Avenue (PO Box 50050), Lusaka [Lusaka 228955]

High Commissioner, His Excellency Peter Hinchcliffe, CMG (1990).

British Council Representative, J. Mulholland, OBE, Heroes Place, Cairo Road, (PO Box 34571), Lusaka. There is also a library in *Ndola.*

ZIMBABWE
(Republic of Zimbabwe)

AREA, POPULATION, ETC.—Zimbabwe, the former Southern Rhodesia (named after Cecil Rhodes) comprising eight provinces (Manicaland, Masvingo, Matabeleland North, Matabeleland South, Midlands, Mashonaland West, Central and East), lies south of the Zambezi river. The political neighbours are Zambia and Mozambique on the N., South Africa and Botswana on the S. and W., and Mozambique on the E. It has a total area of 150,804 sq. miles (390,580 sq. km), and a population (estimated 1989) of 9,000,000.

CAPITAL.—Harare (formerly Salisbury) situated on the Mashonaland plateau, population (August 1982) 658,364. Bulawayo—the largest town in Matabeleland, population (August 1982) 495,317. Other centres are, Chitungwiza, Mutare, Gweru, Kadoma, Kwe Kwe, Masvingo and Hwange.

CURRENCY.—Zimbabwe dollar (Z$) of 100 cents.

FLAG.—Seven horizontal stripes (green, gold, red, black, red, gold, green) with white triangle at the hoist containing the Zimbabwe bird superimposed on red five-point star.

NATIONAL ANTHEM.—Ishe Komborerai Africa.

NATIONAL DAY.—April 18 (Independence Day).

GOVERNMENT

Southern Rhodesia was granted responsible government in 1923. An illegal declaration of independence on November 11, 1965 was finally terminated on December 12, 1979. Following elections in February 1980 the country obtained independence on April 18, 1980 as the Republic of Zimbabwe, a member of the British Commonwealth.

A Constitutional Amendment Bill designed to replace the 20 reserved white seats with nominated members from any race, was approved in September 1987. On October 30, 1987 a Constitutional Amendment Bill was passed providing for the creation of an executive presidency. On December 30, 1987 Robert Mugabe was elected by MPs and Senators as the first President. The Bill provides for a President to be popularly elected every six years. The President has the power to appoint a Cabinet and to veto parliamentary bills.

A merger agreement between the ZANU (PF) and ZAPU parties was signed on December 22, 1987 with a view to the eventual creation of a one-party state. The new party is known as ZANU-PF.

The latest general election was held in March 1990. ZANU-PF won 116 of the 120 elective seats, and the legislature became unicameral, comprising a House of Assembly of 160 members.

Executive President, Hon. Robert Gabriel Mugabe, *elected* Dec. 30, 1987, re-elected March 1990.

Cabinet
(as at April 30, 1990)

President, Robert Mugabe.
Senior Minister in the President's Office, Joshua Nkomo.
Senior Minister, Political Affairs, Didymus Mutasa.
Senior Minister, Finance, Economic Planning and Development, Dr. Bernard Chidzero.
Foreign Affairs, Dr. Nathan Shamuyarira.
Justice, Legal and Parliamentary Affairs, Emmerson Munangagwa.
Defence, Richard Hove.
Higher Education, David Karimanzima.
Education and Culture, Fay Chung.
Home Affairs, Moven Mahachi.
Local Government, Rural and Urban Development, Joseph Msika.
Construction and National Housing, Enos Chikowore.
Lands, Agriculture and Rural Settlement, Dr. Witness Mangwende.
Information, Posts and Telecommunications, Victoria Chitepo.
Labour, Manpower Planning and Social Welfare, John Nkomo.
Industry and Commerce, Kumbirai Kangai.
Energy, Water Resources and Development, Herbert Ushewokunze.
Mines, Chris Anderson.
Transport and National Supplies, Dennis Norman.
Health, Timothy Stamps.
Community Development and Co-operatives, Joyce Mujuru.
Environment and Tourism, Herbert Murerwa.

In addition, there are eight Ministers of State.

HIGH COMMISSION OF THE REPUBLIC OF ZIMBABWE
Zimbabwe House, 429 Strand, WC2R 0SA
[071-836 7755]

Acting High Commissioner, Dr. E. Sakupwanya.

EDUCATION

Since independence, a policy of free primary education and accelerated expansion at secondary level has resulted in rapidly expanding enrolment. In 1986 there were 2,260,367 primary school and 545,841 secondary school pupils in both Government and Government aid schools. Over 80 per cent of schools are government aided schools. The University of Zimbabwe was founded in 1955.

ECONOMY

The country is endowed with minerals, water, forests, wildlife and other resources. The agricultural sector is well developed with both commercial and communal farmers. Tobacco remains the most important crop in terms of export and maize the most important for domestic consumption. Other crops include wheat, cotton, and sugar. Beef is exported to the EC. Production can be severely affected by drought.

The manufacturing sector has a high degree of inter-dependency and many industries depend on the agricultural sector for their raw materials. Industry is dependent on vital imports e.g. fuel oil, steel products and chemicals, as well as heavy machinery and items of transport. The mining sector, although contributing a relatively small portion to GDP (7·6 per cent in 1984) is important to the economy as a foreign exchange earner (26 per cent of total in 1984). Almost all mineral production is exported. Gold is the most important mineral, others are asbestos, silver, nickel, copper, chrome ore, tin, iron ore and cobalt. There is a successful ferro-chrome industry and a substantial steel works which has been heavily subsidized by Government.

A high domestic budget deficit combining with a high external debt service ratio has put the economy into decline. The 1986–87 drought made this worse.

GOVERNMENT FINANCE

	1984–85	1985–86
Revenue	Z$2,212·3m	Z$2,616·2m
Expenditure	2,923·0m	3,307·8m

Trade with UK

	1988	1989
Imports from UK	£58,077,000	£87,013,000
Exports to UK	86,268,000	85,792,000

BRITISH HIGH COMMISSION
Stanley House, Jason Moyo Avenue,
(PO Box 4490), Harare
[Harare 793781]

High Commissioner, His Excellency Kieran Prendergast, CMG (1989).

British Council Representative, N. M. Ross, 23 Jason Moyo Avenue, (PO Box 664), Harare.

British Dependent Territories, etc.

ANGUILLA

Anguilla is a flat coralline island, about 16 miles in length, 3½ miles in breadth at its widest point and its area is about 35 sq. miles (91 sq. km). It lies approximately 18° N. latitude and 63° W longitude, to the north of the Leeward Islands group.

The island is covered with low scrub and fringed with some of the finest white coral-sand beaches in the Caribbean. The climate is pleasant and healthy with temperatures in the range of 24-30°C throughout the year. The population (UN estimate 1988) is about 8,000.

CAPITAL.—The Valley (population 500).

CURRENCY.—East Caribbean dollar (EC$) of 100 cents.

GOVERNMENT

Anguilla has been a British colony since 1650. For most of its history it has been linked administratively with St. Christopher, but three months after the Associated State of Saint Christopher (St. Kitts)-Nevis-Anguilla came into being in 1967 the Anguillans repudiated government from St. Kitts. A Commissioner was installed in 1969 and in 1976 Anguilla was given a new status and separate constitution. Final separation from St. Kitts and Nevis was effected on December 19, 1980 and Anguilla reverted to a British Dependency. A new Constitution was introduced in 1982, providing for a Governor, an Executive Council comprising four elected Ministers and two ex-officio members (Attorney General and Permanent Secretary, Finance), and an 11-member legislative House of Assembly presided over by a Speaker.

The 1982 Constitution (Amendment) Order 1990 came into operation on May 30, 1990. Among the new constitutional provisions are a Deputy Governor (who replaces the Permanent Secretary (Finance) in the Executive Council and the Legislature), a Parliamentary Secretary, Leader of Opposition and Deputy Speaker.

Governor, His Excellency B. G. J. Canty, OBE (1989).
Deputy Governor, Hon. Alan N. Hoole (1990).

Executive Council
(as at June 30, 1990)

Chief Minister and Minister of Home Affairs, Tourism and Agriculture, Hon. Emile Gumbs.

Social Services and Lands, Hon. Eric Reid.
Communications, Public Utilities and Works, Hon. Kenneth Harrigan.
Finance, Economic Development, Hon. Osbourne Fleming.
Attorney-General, (acting), Hon. Kurt De Freitas.

ECONOMY

Low rainfall limits agricultural output and export earnings are mainly from sales of lobsters. Tourism has developed rapidly in recent years and accounts for most of the island's economic activity. In 1989 there were 28,761 tourists and a further 43,044 day visitors.

FINANCE

	1988	1989
Revenue	EC$27,602,700	EC$32,530,300
Expenditure	23,046,900	28,725,600

Trade with UK

	1988	1989
Imports from UK	£1,372,000	£1,962,000
Exports to UK	68,000	1,402,000

ASCENSION
See St. Helena

BERMUDA

The Bermudas, or Somers Islands, are a cluster of about 100 small islands (about 20 of which are inhabited) situated in the west of the Atlantic Ocean, in 32° 18′ N. lat. and 64° 46′ W. long., the nearest point of the mainland being Cape Hatteras in North Carolina, about 570 miles distant. The colony derives its name from Juan Bermudez, a Spaniard, who sighted it before 1515, but no settlement was made until 1609 when Sir George Somers, who was shipwrecked there on his way to Virginia, colonized the islands.

The total area is approximately 20·59 sq. miles (53 sq. km), which includes 2·3 sq. miles leased to the USA. The civil population is approximately 60,000 (1989 estimate).

CAPITAL.—ΨHamilton (population 1989, 2,000).
CURRENCY.—Bermuda dollar of 100 cents.

GOVERNMENT

Internal self-government was introduced on June 8, 1968. There is a Senate of 11 members and an elected House of Assembly of 40 members. The Governor retains responsibility for external affairs, defence, internal security and the police, although administrative matters for the Police Service have been delegated to the Minister of Home Affairs.

At the General Election of February 9, 1989 the United Bermuda Party gained 23 seats, the Progressive Labour Party 15, National Liberal Party 1, and Independent Environmentalist 1.

Governor and Commander-in-Chief, His Excellency Sir Desmond Langley, KCVO, MBE (1988).
Deputy Governor, John Kelly, MBE.

Cabinet
(as at May 31, 1990)

Premier, Hon. Sir John W. Swan, KBE.
Minister of Delegated and Legislative Affairs, Hon. Sir John Sharpe.
Health, Social Services and Housing, Hon. Quinton Edness.
Telecommunications, Hon. Sir Charles T. M. Collis.
Labour and Home Affairs, Hon. J. Irving Pearman.
Education and Culture, Hon. Gerald D. E. Simons.
Deputy Premier and Minister of the Environment, Hon. A. F. Cartwright DeCouto.
Works and Engineering, Dr. the Hon. Clarence Terceira.
Youth, Sport and Recreation, Hon. Harry W. Soares.
Community Affairs, Hon. Leonard O. Gibbons.
Tourism, Hon. C. V. Jim Woolridge.
Transport, Hon. Ralph Marshall.
Finance, Dr. the Hon. David Saul.
Management and Information Services, Hon. Michael Winfield.

President of the Senate, Hon. A. S. Jackson, MBE.
Speaker of the House of Assembly, Hon. D. Wilkinson.
Chief Justice, Hon. Sir James R. Astwood.
Puisne Judges, Hon. L. Austin Ward, QC; Hon. M. Ward; Hon. D. Hull.

ECONOMY

Locally manufactured concentrates, perfumes, cut flowers and pharmaceuticals are now the colony's leading exports. Little food is produced except vegetables and fish, other foodstuffs being imported.

The islands' economic structure is based on tourism, the major industry, and international company business, attracted by the low level of taxation and sophisticated telecommunications system. In 1989 a total of 549,624 visitors arrived by air and cruise ship. Cruise ships dock at Hamilton, Somerset and St. George's.

EDUCATION

Free elementary education was introduced in 1949. Free secondary education was introduced in 1965 for those children who were below the upper limit of the statutory school age of 16 (from 1969 onwards).

FINANCE

	1988–89	1989–90
Public revenue	$279,639,200	$307,439,000
Public expenditure	245,542,700	274,738,000

Trade with UK

	1988	1989
Imports from UK	£24,995,000	£77,122,000
Exports to UK	8,767,000	4,517,000

THE BRITISH ANTARCTIC TERRITORY

The British Antarctic Territory was designated in 1962 and consists of the areas south of 60°S. latitude which were previously included in the Falkland Islands Dependencies. The territory lies between longitudes 20° and 80°W., south of latitude 60°S. and includes the South Orkney Islands, the South Shetland Islands, the mountainous Antarctic Peninsula (highest point Mount Jackson, 13,620ft, in Palmer Land) and all adjacent islands, and the land mass extending to the South Pole. The territory has no indigenous inhabitants and the British population consists of the scientists and technicians who man the British Antarctic Survey stations. The number averages about 60 to 70 in winter, but increases considerably in the summer months with the arrival of field workers. Argentina, Brazil, Chile, China, Poland, USA, USSR and Uruguay also have scientific stations in the territory.

The first two British Antarctic Survey stations were established in the South Shetland Islands in 1944, and by 1956 the number of stations had risen to twelve. Due to the completion of field work in some areas and increased mobility, the number has now been reduced to five. These are Signy (Signy Island, S. Orkney Islands), Faraday (Argentine Islands, Graham Coast), Rothera (Adelaide Island), Halley (Caird Coast) and, in summer only, Fossil Bluff (George VI Sound). Fifteen other stations have been established but are at present unoccupied.

The territory is administered by a High Commissioner, resident in the Falkland Islands.

High Commissioner, His Excellency William Hugh Fullerton, CMG (1988).

THE BRITISH INDIAN OCEAN TERRITORY

The British Indian Ocean Territory was established by an Order in Council in 1965 and included islands formerly administered from Mauritius and the Seychelles. After the independence of both, the territory was redefined in 1976 as comprising only the islands of the Chagos Archipelago.

The Chagos Archipelago consists of six main groups of islands situated on the Great Chagos Bank and covering some 21,000 sq. miles (54,389 sq. km). The largest and most southerly of the Chagos Islands is Diego Garcia, a sand cay with a land area of about 17 square miles approximately 1,100 miles east of Mahé, used as a joint naval support facility by Britain and USA.

The other main island groups of the archipelago, Peros Banhos (29 islands with a total land area of 4 sq. miles) and Salomon (11 islands with a total land area of 2 sq. miles) are uninhabited. The islands have a typical tropical maritime climate, with average temperatures between 25° C and 29° C in Diego Garcia, and rainfall in the whole archipelago of 90–100 inches a year.

Trade with UK

	1988	1989
Imports from UK	£2,302,000	£2,246,000
Exports to UK	460,000	506,000

Commissioner and Administrator, R. Edis.

THE BRITISH VIRGIN ISLANDS

The Virgin Islands are a group of islands at the eastern extremity of the Greater Antilles, divided between Great Britain and the USA. Those of the group which are British number 46, of which 11 are inhabited, and have a total area of about 59 sq. miles, (153 sq. km). The principal are Tortola, the largest (situated in 18° 27′ N. lat. and 64° 40′ W. long., area, 21 sq. miles), Virgin Gorda (8¼ sq. miles), Anegada (15 sq.miles) and Jost Van Dyke (3⅓ sq. miles). The 1980 Census showed a total population of 10,985: Tortola (9,119); Virgin Gorda (1,443); Anegada (169); Jost Van Dyke (136); and other islands (82). A 1988 UN estimate gave a total figure of 14,000. Apart from Anegada, which is a flat coral island, the British Virgin Islands are hilly, being an extension of the Puerto Rico and the US Virgin Islands archipelago. The highest point is Sage Mountain on Tortola which rises to a height of 1,780 feet.

The islands lie within the trade winds belt and possess a pleasant and healthy sub-tropical climate. The average temperature varies from 22°–28° C in winter and 26°–31° C in summer. The summer heat is tempered by sea breezes and the temperature usually falls by about 6° C at night. Average rainfall is 53 inches.

CAPITAL.—ΨRoad Town, on the south-east of Tortola. Population 2,479.

CURRENCY.—The US dollar (US$) of 100 cents is legal tender.

GOVERNMENT

Under the 1977 Constitution the Governor, appointed by the Crown, remains responsible for defence and internal security, external affairs and the civil service but in other matters acts in accordance with the advice of the Executive Council. The Executive Council consists of the Governor as Chairman, one ex officio member (the Attorney-General), the Chief Minister and three other ministers. The Legislative Council consists of a Speaker chosen from outside the Council, one ex officio member (the Attorney-General), and nine elected members returned from nine one-member electoral districts.

Governor, His Excellency (John) Mark (Ambrose) Herdman, CBE, LVO (1986).
Deputy Governor, E. Georges, OBE.
Financial Secretary, R. Mathavious.

The Executive Council
(as at June 30, 1990)

Chairman, The Governor.
Chief Minister and Minister of Finance, Hon. H. Lavity Stoutt.
Natural Resources and Labour, Hon. Ralph O'Neal, OBE.
Communications and Works, Hon. Oliver Cills.
Health, Education and Welfare, Hon. Louis Walters, MBE.
Attorney-General, Hon. Karl S. Atterbury.

Puisne Judge (resident), Justice Lloyd J. Williams.

COMMUNICATIONS

The principal airport is on Beef Island, linked by bridge to Tortola, and an extended runway of 3,600 ft enables larger aircraft to call. There is a second airfield on Virgin Gorda and a third on Anegada. There are direct shipping services to the United Kingdom and the United States and fast passenger services connect the main islands by ferry.

FINANCE

	1988	1989
Revenue	US$32,629,000	US$41,400,000
Expenditure	31,038,000	40,600,000

ECONOMY

Tourism is the main industry but the financial centre is growing steadily in importance. Other industries include a rum distillery, three stone-crushing plants and factories manufacturing concrete blocks and paint. The major export items are fresh fish, gravel, sand, fruit and vegetables: exports are largely confined to the US Virgin Islands. Chief imports are building materials, machinery, cars and beverages.

Trade with UK

	1988	1989
Imports from UK	£7,108,000	£6,727,000
Exports to UK	4,030,000	1,170,000

THE CAYMAN ISLANDS

The Cayman Islands, between 79° 44′ and 81° 26′ W. and 19° 15′ and 19° 46′ N., consist of three islands, Grand Cayman, Cayman Brac, and Little Cayman, with a total area of 100 sq. miles (259 sq. km). About 150 miles south of Cuba, the islands are divided from Jamaica, 180 miles to the south-east, by the Cayman Trench, the deepest part of the Caribbean. The nearest point on the US mainland is Miami in Florida, 450 miles to the north. Cooled by trade winds, the annual average temperature and rainfall is 27.2° C and 50.7 inches, respectively.

The colony derives its name from the Carib word for the crocodile, 'Caymanas', which appeared in the log of the first English visitor to the Cayman Islands, Sir Francis Drake. Although tradition has it that the first settlers arrived in 1658, the first recorded settlers arrived in 1666–71. The first recorded permanent settlers followed the first land grant by Britain in 1734. The islands were placed under direct control of Jamaica in 1863. When Jamaica became independent in 1962, the islands opted to remain under the British Crown.

Population (Census 1989) 25,535 (excludes an estimated undercount of 400), of which 23,881 are on Grand Cayman, 1,441 on Cayman Brac and 33 on Little Cayman.

CAPITAL.—ΨGeorge Town, in Grand Cayman, population (1989) 12,972.

CURRENCY.—Cayman Islands dollar (CI$) of 100 cents, which is fixed at CI$ = US$1·20.

GOVERNMENT

The constitution provides for a Governor, a Legislative Assembly and an Executive Council, and effectively allows a large measure of self-government. Unless there are exceptional reasons, the Governor accepts the advice of the Executive Council, which comprises three official members and four others elected from the 12 elected members of the Assembly. The Governor has responsibility for the police, civil service, defence and external affairs. He presides over the Assembly, in which the three official members also sit, though there is provision for the appointment of a Speaker if the members request it. The normal life of the Assembly is four years, with a general election next due in November 1992.

Governor, His Excellency Alan James Scott, CVO, CBE (1987).

Executive Council
(as at June 30, 1990)

President, The Governor.
Financial Secretary, Hon. T. C. Jefferson, OBE.
Attorney-General, Hon. R. W. Ground, QC.
Administrative Secretary, Hon. J. L. Hurlston, MBE.
Member for Tourism, Aviation and Trade, Hon. W. N. Bodden, OBE.

Member for Education, Environment, Recreation and Culture, Hon. B. O. Ebanks, OBE.
Member for Health and Social Services, Hon. D. E. Miller.
Member for Communications, Works and Agriculture, Hon. L. Pierson.

LONDON OFFICE
Cayman Islands Government Office,
100 Brompton Road, SW3 1EX
[071–581 9418]
Government Representative, T. Russell, CMG, CBE.

ECONOMY

Based on a complete absence of direct taxation, the Cayman Islands have been successfully promoted over the past 25 years as an offshore financial centre. With representation from 60 countries, there were, at the end of 1989, 538 banks and trust companies, of which local offices were maintained by 71. In addition, there were 357 licensed insurance companies and over 20,000 registered companies at the end of 1989.

Promotion of tourism, with an emphasis on scuba diving, has also been successful. There were 213,878 visitors by air and 403,891 cruise ship callers in 1989.

The two industries support a heavy imbalance in trade resulting from the need to import most of what is consumed and used on the islands, and have created a thriving local economy in which the GNP reached US$480m (US$18,750 per capita) in 1988. Import duty and fees from financial centre operations have provided revenue enabling the government to undertake heavy investment in education (which is provided free to all 4–16 year olds), health and other social programmes.

FINANCE

	1989	1990*
Revenue	CI$100·4m	CI$102·8m
Expenditure	97·9m	110·8m
*estimated		

TRADE

	1987	1988
Total imports	CI$162·6m	CI$192·6m
Total exports	1·8m	1·9m

Trade with UK

	1988	1989
Imports from UK	£5,051,000	£5,174,000
Exports to UK	9,858,000	8,693,000

FALKLAND ISLANDS

The Falkland Islands, the only considerable group in the South Atlantic, lie about 300 miles east of the Straits of Magellan, between 52° 15′–53° S. lat. and 57° 40′–62° W. long. They consist of East Falkland (area 2,610 sq. miles; 6,759 sq. km), West Falkland (2,090 sq. miles; 5,413 sq. km) and upwards of 100 small islands in the aggregate. Mount Usborne (E. Falkland), the loftiest peak, rises 2,312 feet above the level of the sea.

The climate is cool. At Stanley the mean monthly temperature varies between 9° C in January and 2° C in July. The islands are chiefly moorland.

The Falklands were sighted first by Davis in 1592, and by Hawkins in 1594; the first known landing was by Strong in 1690. A settlement was made by France in 1764; this was subsequently sold to Spain, but the latter country recognized Great Britain's title to a part at least of the group in 1771. After Argentina declared independence from Spain, the Argentine government in 1820 proclaimed its sovereignty over the Falklands and a settlement was founded in 1826. The settlement was destroyed by the Americans in 1831. In 1833 occupation was resumed by the British for the protection of the seal-fisheries, and the islands were permanently colonized as the most southerly organized colony of the British Empire. Argentina continued to claim sovereignty over the islands (known to them as las Islas Malvinas), and in pursuance of this claim invaded the islands on April 2, 1982 and also occupied South Georgia. A Task Force despatched from Great Britain recaptured South Georgia on April 25, and after landing at San Carlos Bay on May 21, recaptured the islands from the Argentines, who surrendered on June 14, 1982. A British naval and military presence remains in the area.

The population was 1,916 at December 31, 1986 and is almost totally British.

CHIEF TOWN.—ᵠStanley, population 1,231 (1986). Stanley is distant from England about 8,103 miles.

CURRENCY.—Falkland pound of 100 pence.

GOVERNMENT

Under the 1985 Constitution, the Governor is advised by an Executive Council consisting of three elected members of the Legislative Council and two ex-officio members, the Chief Executive and the Financial Secretary. The Legislative Council consists of eight elected members and the same two ex-officio members.

Governor and Chairman of the Executive Council, His Excellency William Hugh Fullerton, CMG (1988).
Chief Executive, R. Sampson.
Financial Secretary, J. Buckland-James.
Commander, British Forces, Falkland Islands, Maj.-Gen. M. P. J. Hunt.
Attorney General, D. G. Lang, QC.

LONDON OFFICE
Falkland Islands Government Office,
Falkland House, 14 Broadway, SW1H 0BH
[071-222 2542]
Government Representative, Miss S. Cameron.

FINANCE

	1987–88*	1988–89*
Public Revenue	£39,762,000	£35,761,000
Expenditure	24,592,000	28,646,000
*estimated		

ECONOMY

The economy was formerly based solely on agriculture, principally sheep-farming with a little dairy farming for domestic requirements and crops for winter fodder. Since the establishment of an interim conservation and management zone around the islands and the consequent introduction on February 1, 1987 of a licensing regime for vessels fishing within the zone the economy has diversified and income from the associated fishing activities is now the largest source of revenue. Chief imports are provisions, alcoholic beverages, timber, clothing and hardware.

Trade with UK

	1988	1989
Imports from UK	£9,037,000	£10,200,000
Exports to UK	4,209,000	5,375,000

GIBRALTAR

Gibraltar is a rocky promontory, 2¾ miles in length, three-quarters of a mile in breadth and 1,396 ft. high at its greatest elevation, near the southern extremity of Spain, with which it is connected by a low isthmus. It is about 14 miles distant from the opposite coast of Africa. The town stands at the foot of the promontory on the W. side. In a total area of 2¼ sq. miles (6 sq. km), the population at the end of 1989 stood at 30,689.

CURRENCY.—Gibraltar pound of 100 pence.

GOVERNMENT

Gibraltar was captured in 1704, during the war of the Spanish Succession, by a combined Dutch and English force, under Sir George Rooke, and was ceded to Great Britain by the Treaty of Utrecht, 1713. Several attempts have been made to retake it, the most celebrated being the great siege, 1779–83, when General Eliott, afterwards Lord Heathfield, held it for three years and seven months against a combined French and Spanish force.

The Constitution of Gibraltar, approved in 1969, made formal provision for certain domestic matters to devolve on Ministers appointed from among elected members of the House of Assembly then set up to replace the former Legislative Council. The House of Assembly consists of an independent Speaker, 15 elected members, the Attorney-General and the Financial and Development Secretary.

Governor and Commander-in-Chief, His Excellency Admiral Sir Derek Reffell, KCB.
Flag Officer, Gibraltar, and Admiral Supr., HM Naval Base, Gibraltar, Rear-Adm. G. W. R. Biggs.
Deputy Governor, W. E. Quantrill £37,600
Financial and Development Secretary, B. Traynor £36,818
Attorney-General, K. Harris £36,818
Chief Justice, A. Kneller £37,600

Chief Minister, J. Bossano.
Speaker, Mayor R. J. Peliza, OBE.

ECONOMY

Gibraltar enjoys the advantages of an extensive shipping trade and is a popular shopping centre. The chief sources of revenue are the port dues, the rent of the Crown estate in the town, and duties on consumer items. The free port tradition of Gibraltar is still reflected in the low rates of import duty. The gradual change from a fortress city to a holiday centre has led to a flourishing tourist trade.

A total of 3,445 merchant ships (36,179,242 gross registered tons aggregate) entered the port during 1989. Of these 1,932 were deep-sea ships (35,790,002 gross registered tons aggregate). In addition 4,972 yachts (146,170 gross registered tons) called at the port. There are 26·75 miles of roads.

EDUCATION

Education is compulsory and free for children between the ages of 4 and 15 whose parents are ordinarily resident in Gibraltar. Scholarships are available for higher education in Britain. The total enrolment in Government schools was 4,621 in December 1989.

FINANCE AND TRADE

	1987–88	1988–89
Revenue	£76,553,000	£82,124,000
Expenditure	78,216,000	81,904,000

	1988	1989
Total imports	£144,717,000	£165,500,000
Total exports	46,093,000	42,100,000

Trade with UK

	1988	1989
Imports from UK	£67,944,000	£69,350,000
Exports to UK	4,537,000	4,560,000

HONG KONG

Hong Kong, consisting of a number of islands and of a portion of the mainland (Kowloon and the New Territories), on the south-eastern coast of China, is situated at the eastern side of the mouth of the Pearl River, between 22° 9′ and 22° 37′ N. lat. and 113° 52′–114° 30′ E. long. The total area of the territory (including recent reclamation) is 416 sq. miles (1,074 sq. km) with a population which at the end of 1989 was 5,812,300.

The island of Hong Kong is about 11 miles long and from two to five miles broad, with a total area of 29 sq. miles; at the eastern entrance to the harbour it is separated from the mainland by a narrow strait.

CLIMATE.—Hong Kong's climate is sub-tropical, tending towards the temperate for nearly half the year. The mean monthly temperature ranges from 16° C to 29° C. The average annual rainfall is 2,225 mm, of which nearly 80 per cent falls between May and September. Tropical cyclones passing at various distances from Hong Kong occur between June and October, causing high winds and heavy rain.

CAPITAL.—Ψ Victoria, situated on the island of Hong Kong, is about 81 miles SE of Canton and 40 miles E. of the Portuguese province of Macao at the other side of the Pearl River. It lies along the northern shore of the island and faces the mainland; the harbour (23 sq. miles water area) lies between the city and the mainland.

CURRENCY.—Hong Kong dollar (HK$) of 100 cents.

GOVERNMENT

The island was first occupied by Great Britain in January, 1841, and formally ceded by the Treaty of Nanking in 1842. Kowloon was subsequently acquired by the Peking Convention of 1860, and the New Territories, consisting of a peninsula in the southern part of the Guangdong province together with adjacent islands, by a 99-year lease signed June 9, 1898.

Hong Kong is administered by the Hong Kong Government, at the head of which is the Governor, and its administration has developed from the basic pattern applied to all British-governed territories overseas. Under the terms of the Joint Declaration of the British and Chinese Governments, which entered into force on May 27, 1985, Hong Kong will become with effect from July 1, 1997, a Special Administrative Region of the People's Republic of China. However, the social and economic systems in the SAR will remain unchanged for 50 years.

The Governor governs aided by an Executive Council, consisting of four ex-officio and ten appointed members, and a Legislative Council, which consists of three ex-officio and seven official members, 20 appointed members, 12 elected by the Electoral College and 14 by the functional constituencies.

There is also an Urban Council which provides services relating to public health and sanitation, culture and recreation in the urban area. A Regional Council was also set up in 1986 to provide similar services in the New Territories. Both Councils are financially autonomous.

Governor, His Excellency Sir David Wilson, KCMG (1987).
Chief Justice, The Hon. Sir Ti Liang Yang.
Chief Secretary, Hon. Sir David Ford, KBE, LVO.

Commander, British Forces, Maj.-Gen. P. R. Duffell, CBE, MC.
Financial Secretary, Hon. Sir Piers Jacobs, KBE.
Attorney-General, Hon. J. F. Mathews, CMG
Secretary for the Civil Service, Hon. E. B. Wiggham.
Planning, Environment and Lands, Hon. G. Barnes, CBE.
Transport, Hon. Michael M. K. Leung.
Education and Manpower, Hon. K. Y. Yeung.
Economic Services, Hon. Mrs. Anson Chan.
Home Affairs, Hon. Peter K. W. Tsao, CBE, CPM.
Health and Welfare, Hon. Mrs. Elizabeth C. L. Wong, ISO.
Security, Hon. A. P. Asprey, OBE, AE.
Monetary Affairs, D. A. C. Nendick, CBE.
Recreation and Culture, Augustine K. Chui.
Treasury, N. W. H. Macleod.
Trade and Industry John C. C. Chan, LVO, OBE.
Constitutional Affairs, Michael M. Y. Suen.
Works, Kenneth W. K. Kwok, OBE.

British Council Representative, J. Davey, Easey Commercial Building, 225 Hennessy Road, Wanchai, Hong Kong.

LONDON OFFICE
Hong Kong Government Office
6 Grafton Street, W1X 3LB
[071-499 9821]

Commissioner, John Yaxley, CBE (1989).

COMMUNICATIONS

Hong Kong, one of the world's finest natural harbours, possesses excellent wharves. The Kwai Chung container terminal has 11 berths. A pier at the Ocean Terminal can accommodate large liners and cargo vessels up to 290 metres length and 10 metres draught. Mooring buoys in the harbour are available to vessels of up to 12 metres draught. Available dockyard facilities include six floating drydocks, the largest being capable of docking vessels up to 150,000 tonnes deadweight. In 1989 some 18,999 ocean-going vessels and 94,472 river-trade vessels called at Hong Kong and loaded and discharged more than 85 million tonnes of cargo.

Hong Kong International Airport, Kai Tak, situated to the east of the Kowloon peninsula, is regularly used by over 42 international airlines, providing some 1,700 frequent scheduled passenger and cargo services each week. During 1989, over 94,300 aircraft on international flights arrived and departed, carrying 16·5 million passengers and 740,081 tonnes of freight.

EDUCATION

In September 1989 there were 2,096 day schools with 1,218,153 pupils. Free education for children up to the age of 15 was made compulsory in 1979. Postsecondary education is provided by two universities, two polytechnics, the Hong Kong Baptist College and two approved post-secondary colleges. The Hong Kong Polytechnic and City Polytechnic of Hong Kong have about 11,350 and 5,000 full-time students respectively. There are also eight technical institutes and four teacher-training colleges.

FINANCE

	1987–88	1988–89
Public revenue	HK$60,875m	HK$72,600m
Public expenditure	48,375m	64,800m

TRADE AND INDUSTRY

The manufacturing sector is the mainstay of Hong Kong's economy, contributing about 20 per cent to the GDP and accounting for about 32 per cent of total employment. Up to 90 per cent of Hong Kong's manufacturing output is eventually exported.

Hong Kong's manufacturing industries produce light consumer goods, such as electronics, plastics, electrical products, watches and clocks, which accounted for 37 per cent of Hong Kong's total domestic exports in 1989. The corresponding share of textiles and clothing, Hong Kong's traditional leading industries, was 40 per cent in 1989.

Diversification in terms of products and markets continues to be the main feature of recent industrial development, as are industrial partnerships with overseas companies. The economy of Hong Kong is based on export rather than the domestic market. In 1989, the total value of visible trade (including domestic exports, re-exports and imports) amounted to 231 per cent of the GDP. Hong Kong's visible trade account attained in 1989 a surplus of HK$7,728 million. Taking visible and invisible trade together, there was a combined surplus of HK$41,291 million, compared with HK$24,486 million in 1988. In 1989, Hong Kong's principal customers for its domestic products, in order of value of trade, were USA, China, the Federal Republic of Germany, the United Kingdom, Japan, Canada and Singapore. China was its principal supplier.

	1988	1989
Total Exports	HK$493,069m	HK$570,509m
Total Imports	498,798m	562,781m

Trade with UK

	1988	1989
Imports from UK	£1,030,725,000	£1,111,517,000
Exports to UK	1,788,631,000	2,036,976,000

MONTSERRAT

Situated in 16° 45′ N. lat. and 61° 15′ W. long., 27 miles SW of Antigua, the island is about 11 miles long and seven wide, with an area of 38 sq. miles (98 sq. km), and a population (UN estimate 1988), of 12,000. Discovered by Columbus in 1493, it was settled by Irishmen in 1632, conquered and held by the French for some time, and finally assigned to Great Britain in 1783. Fertile and green, it is volcanic with several hot springs. About two-thirds of the island is mountainous, the rest capable of cultivation.

CHIEF TOWN.—ΨPlymouth, population 3,000.
CURRENCY.—East Caribbean dollar (EC$) of 100 cents.

GOVERNMENT

A Ministerial system was introduced in Montserrat in 1960. The Executive Council is presided over by the Governor and is composed of four elected members (the Chief and three other Ministers) and two ex-officio members (the Attorney-General and the Financial Secretary). The four Ministers are appointed from the members of the political party holding the majority in the Legislative Council. The Legislative Council consists of the Speaker, two ex-officio members (the Attorney General and the Financial Secretary), two nominated unofficial members and seven elected members.

Governor, His Excellency David Taylor (1990).

Executive Council
(as at May 31, 1990)

President, The Governor.
Chief Minister and Minister of Finance, Hon. J. A. Osborne.
Communications and Works, Hon. J. B. Chalmers.

Education, Health and Community Services, Hon. V.
K. Jeffers.
Agriculture, Trade, Lands and Housing, Hon. N.
Tuitt.
Attorney-General, Hon. O. Adams.
Financial Secretary, C. T. John.

Speaker of the Legislative Council, Dr. the Hon. H. A.
Fergus, OBE.

ECONOMY

The economy is dominated by tourism, related
construction activities, offshore business services
and specializations in telecommunications and media
services. The chief export in 1988 was light fixtures
assembled on the island, but increased efforts are
directed at the expansion of the sea-island cotton
market, upgrading agriculture and agro-processing,
and some data processing.

FINANCE

	1988	1989
Revenue	EC$32,118,491	EC$35,049,330
Expenditure	30,059,525	34,308,150

Trade with UK

	1988	1989
Imports from UK	£2,524,000	£3,092,000
Exports to UK	125,000	494,000

PITCAIRN ISLANDS

Pitcairn, a small volcanic island, 1·9 sq. miles (5 sq.
km), in area, is the chief of a group of islands situated
about midway between New Zealand and Panama in
the South Pacific Ocean at longitude 130° 06′ W. and
latitude 25° 04′ S.
The island rises in cliffs to a height of 1,100 feet and
access from the sea is possible only at Bounty Bay, a
small rocky cove, and then only by surf boats. Mean
monthly temperatures vary between 66°F (19°C) in
August and 75°F (24°C) in February and the average
annual rainfall is 80 inches. With an equable climate,
the island is very fertile and produces both tropical
and sub-tropical trees and crops.
The small community, numbering 65 (April 1990),
are descendants of the Bounty mutineers and their
Tahitian companions who did not wish to remain on
Norfolk Island when the entire community was
transferred there in 1856, and returned to Pitcairn
three years later.
Pitcairn became a British Settlement under the
British Settlement Act, 1887, and was administered
by the Governor of Fiji from 1952 until 1970, when
the administration was transferred to the British
High Commission in New Zealand and the British
High Commissioner was appointed Governor. The
local Government Ordinance of 1964 provides for a
Council of ten members of whom six are elected.

*Governor of Pitcairn, Henderson, Ducie and Oeno
Islands,* His Excellency David Joseph Moss, CMG
(British High Commissioner to New Zealand).
Island Magistrate and Chairman of Island Council,
B. Young.
Education Officer and Government Adviser, L. Buck-
ley.

The islanders live by subsistence gardening and
fishing, and their limited monetary needs are satisfied
by the manufacture of wood carvings and other
handicrafts which are sold to passing ships and to a
few overseas customers. Other than small fees
charged for gun and driving licences there are no
taxes and Government revenue is derived almost

solely from the sale of postage stamps. Communication with the outside world is maintained by cargo
vessels travelling between New Zealand and Panama
which call at irregular intervals; and by means of
telephone telegraphic links with New Zealand.
The New Zealand Education Department provides
assistance in recruiting a teacher for the sole-charge
school. Education is compulsory between the ages of
five and fifteen. Secondary education in New Zealand
is encouraged by the Administration which provides
scholarships and bursaries for the purpose. Medical
care is provided by a registered nurse when a doctor
is not present. Since 1887 the islanders have all been
adherents of the Seventh Day Adventist Church.
The other three islands of the group (Henderson
lying 105 miles ENE of Pitcairn, Oeno lying 75 miles
NW and Ducie lying 293 miles E.) are all uninhabited.
Henderson Island is occasionally visited by the
Pitcairn Islanders to obtain supplies of 'miro' wood
which is used for their carvings. Oeno is visited for
excursions of about a week's duration every two
years or so.

ST. HELENA

Probably the best known of all the solitary islands
in the world, St. Helena is situated in the South
Atlantic Ocean, 955 miles S. of the Equator, 702 SE of
Ascension, 1,140 from the nearest point of the African
Continent, 1,800 from the coast of South America,
1,694 from Cape Town (transit 5 days), in 15° 55′ S.
lat. and 5° 42′ W. longitude. It is 10½ miles long, 6½
broad, and encloses an area of 47 sq. miles (122 sq.
km), with a population of 5,544 (1987).
St. Helena is of volcanic origin, and consists of
numerous rugged mountains, the highest rising to
2,700 feet, interspersed with picturesque ravines.
Although within the tropics, the south-east 'trades'
keep the temperature mild and equable. St. Helena
was discovered by the Portuguese navigator, Juan
da Nova Castella, in 1502 (probably on St. Helena's
Day) and remained unknown to other European
nations until 1588. It was used as a port of call for
vessels of all nations trading to the East until it was
annexed by the Dutch in 1633. It was never occupied
by them, however, and the English East India
Company seized it in 1659. In 1834 it was ceded to the
Crown. During the period 1815 to 1821 the island was
lent to the British Government as a place of exile for
the Emperor Napoleon Bonaparte who died in St.
Helena on May 5, 1821. It was formerly an important
station on the route to India, but its prosperity
decreased after the construction of the Suez Canal.
Since the collapse of the New Zealand flax industry
in 1965, there have been no significant exports. ΨSt.
James's Bay, on the north-west of the island, possesses
a good anchorage. There is as yet no airport or
airstrip.
CAPITAL.—ΨJamestown. Population (1987) 1,330.
CURRENCY.—St. Helena pound (£) of 100 pence.

GOVERNMENT

The government of St. Helena is administered by a
Governor, with the aid of a Legislative Council,
consisting of a Speaker, three ex-officio members
(Chief Secretary, Financial Secretary and Attorney
General) and twelve elected members. Five committees of the Legislative Council are responsible for
general oversight of the activities of government
departments and have in addition a wide range of
statutory and administrative functions. The Governor is also assisted by an Executive Council of the
three ex-officio members and the Chairmen of the
Council committees.

Governor, His Excellency Robert F. Stimson (1988).
Chief Secretary, vacant.
Financial Secretary, M. Rosling.
Attorney General, D. Jeremiah.
Chief Medical Officer, Dr. R. Grant.
Director of Agriculture and Natural Resources, V. Hart.
Chief Education Officer, B. George.
Director of Works, A. Rennie.
Chief Social Services and Employment Officer, I. Ellick.

FINANCE AND TRADE

	1986–87	1987–88
Local revenue	£2,205,400	£2,866,300
Budgetary	3,650,000	3,015,200
Recurrent expenditure ..	5,563,200	5,734,900
Development aid	2,081,700	2,595,300
Total imports	5,049,000	5,656,000
Total exports	73,000	100,000

Trade with UK

	1988	1989
Imports from UK	£6,103,000	£7,208,000
Exports to UK	205,000	504,000

ASCENSION

The small island of Ascension lies in the South Atlantic (7° 56′ S., 14° 22′ W.) some 700 miles north-west of the island of St. Helena. It is a rocky peak of purely volcanic origin, the highest point (Green Mountain) some 2,817 ft. is covered with lush vegetation. Ascension Island Services operate a farm of some 10 acres on the mountain, producing vegetables and livestock. The island is famous for turtles, which land on the beaches from January to May to lay their eggs. It is also a breeding area for the sooty tern, or wideawake, large numbers of which settle on the south-western coastal section every eighth month to hatch their eggs. Other wildlife on the island includes feral donkeys and cats, rabbits and francolin partridge. All wildlife except rabbits and cats is protected by law. The ocean surrounding the island contains shark, barracuda, tuna, bonito and many other fish.

Ascension is said to have been discovered by Juan da Nova Castella, on Ascension Day, 1501, and two years later was visited by Alphonse d'Albuquerque, who gave the island its present name. It was uninhabited until the arrival of Napoleon in St. Helena in 1815 when a small British naval garrison was stationed on the island. It remained under the supervision of the Board of Admiralty until 1922, when it was made a dependency of St. Helena by Royal Letters Patent.

The British Foreign Secretary appoints the Administrator who is responsible to the Governor resident in St. Helena. There is a small Police Force and Post Office. The British organizations through Ascension Island Services (AIS) provide and operate various common services for the island (school, hospital, public works etc).

Ascension Island is a main relay point of the coaxial submarine cable system laid between South Africa, Portugal and the United Kingdom, which is operated by the South Atlantic Cable Company. Cable & Wireless PLC operates the international telephone and cable services and maintains an internal telephone service. The BBC opened its Atlantic relay station broadcasting to Africa and South America in 1967.

The resident population in March 1990 totalled 1,029, of whom 728 were from St. Helena, 184 from the UK, 112 from the USA and 5 from the Republic of South Africa. The residents consist of the employees and families of the British organizations, of the

contractors of the US Air Force (Computer Sciences Raytheon) and of the St. Helena Government.

British forces returned to the island in April 1982 in support of operations in the Falkland Islands. At present there are over100 RAF/PSA personnel on the island supporting the air link to the Falklands.
CAPITAL.—Georgetown.

Administrator, J. J. Beale.

TRISTAN DA CUNHA

Tristan da Cunha is the chief of a group of islands of volcanic origin lying in lat. 37° 6′ S. and long. 12° 2′ W., discovered in 1506 by a Portuguese admiral (Tristão da Cunha), after whom they are named. They have a total area of 38 sq. miles (98 sq. km). Population (1990) 290 islanders. The main island, with a peak rising to 6,760 ft., is about 1,500 miles W. of the Cape of Good Hope, 3,600 miles NE of Cape Horn, and about 1,320 miles SSW of St. Helena. It was the resort of British and American sealers from the middle of the 18th century, and in 1760 a British naval officer visited the group and gave his name to Nightingale Island. On August 14, 1816 the group was annexed to the British Crown and a garrison was placed on Tristan da Cunha, but this force was withdrawn in 1817. William Glass, a corporal of artillery (died 1853), remained at his own request with his wife and two children. This party, with five others, formed a settlement. In 1827 five women from St. Helena, and afterwards others from Cape Colony, joined the party.

The islands form a dependency of St. Helena, being administered by the Foreign and Commonwealth Office through a resident Administrator, with headquarters at the settlement of Edinburgh. Under a new constitution introduced in 1969, he is advised by an elected Island Council of eight members of whom one must be a woman, and three appointed members, with universal suffrage at 18.

In October, 1961 a volcano, believed to have been extinct for thousands of years, erupted and the danger of further volcanic activity led to the evacuation of inhabitants to the United Kingdom. An advance party returned to Tristan da Cunha in the spring of 1963, and subsequently the main body of the islanders returned to the island.

A boat harbour was completed in 1967. The first freezing factory was re-established in 1966. There are no taxes on Tristan, income being derived from royalties paid by the fishing company and from the sale of stamps and handicrafts. The Camogli Hospital was opened early in 1971 and a new school in 1975.
CAPITAL.—Edinburgh.

Administrator, Bernard Pauncefort, OBE.

INACCESSIBLE ISLAND is a lofty mass of rock with sides two miles in length; the island is the resort of penguins and sea-fowl. Cultivation was started in 1937, but has been abandoned.

THE NIGHTINGALE ISLANDS are three in number, of which the largest is 1 mile long and ¼ mile wide, and rises in two peaks, 960 and 1,105 ft. above sea-level respectively. The smaller islands, Stoltenhoff and Middle Isle, are little more than huge rocks. Seals, innumerable penguins, and vast numbers of sea-fowl visit these islands.

GOUGH ISLAND (or Diego Alvarez), in 40° 20′ S. and 9° 44′ W., lies about 250 miles SSE of Tristan da Cunha. The island is about 8 miles long and 4 miles broad, with a total area of 40 square miles, and has been a British possession since 1816. The island is the resort of penguins and sea-elephants and has valuable guano deposits. There is no permanent population, but there is a meteorological station maintained on the island by the South African Government and manned by South Africans.

SOUTH GEORGIA AND THE SOUTH SANDWICH ISLANDS

South Georgia is an island 800 miles east-south-east of the Falkland group, with an area of 1,450 sq. miles. The population comprises an army unit at King Edward Point, and staff of the British Antarctic Survey at Bird Island, in the north-west of S. Georgia.

The South Sandwich Islands lie some 470 miles SE of South Georgia. The group is a chain of uninhabited, actively volcanic islands about 150 miles long, with a wholly Antarctic climate.

The present constitution came into effect on October 3, 1985. It provides for a Commissioner who, for the time being, shall be the officer administering the Government of the Falkland Islands.

Commissioner for South Georgia and the South Sandwich Islands, William Hugh Fullerton, CMG (1988).

TURKS AND CAICOS ISLANDS

The Turks and Caicos Islands are situated between 21° and 22° N. latitude and 71° and 72° W. longitude, about 100 miles north of the Dominican Republic and 50 miles south-east of the Bahamas of which they are geographically an extension. There are over 30 islands of which eight are inhabited covering an estimated area of 166 sq. miles (430 sq. km). The principal is Grand Turk. The population in 1988 was estimated to be 14,000 (Grand Turk 4,500).

The Islands lie in the trade wind belt. The average temperature varies from 24°–27° C in the winter and 29°–32° C in the summer and humidity is generally low. Average rainfall is 21 inches per annum.

GOVERNMENT

A new Constitution was introduced in 1988, providing for an enlarged Executive Council and Legislative Council. The Executive Council is presided over by the Governor and comprises the Chief Minister and four elected Ministers, together with the Chief Secretary, the Attorney General and the Financial Secretary ex-officio.

At the General Election of March 3, 1988, the People's Democratic Movement won 11 seats and the People's National Party 2 seats in the Legislative Council.

Governor, His Excellency Michael John Bradley, CMG, QC (1987).

Executive Council
(as at May 31, 1990)

President, The Governor.
Chief Secretary, Hon. M. Cox, MVO.
Attorney-General, Hon. I. S. Lamb.
Financial Secretary, Hon. A. Robinson, MBE.
Members, Hon. O. O. Skippings (*Chief Minister*); Hon. L. N. A. Handfield; Hon. W. L. Swann; Hon. S. I. Harvey; Hon. D. H. Taylor.

The principal airports are on the islands of Grand Turk, Providenciales and South Caicos. There are direct shipping services to the USA (Miami). There is an air service between Miami, Providenciales and Grand Turk, and between South Caicos and the Bahamas. An internal air service provides a twice daily service between the principal islands. A comprehensive telephone and telex service is provided by Cable and Wireless (WI) Ltd.

The most important industries are fishing, tourism and offshore finance.

FINANCE		
	1988–89	1989–90*
Local Revenue	US$17,222,903	US$21,095,740
Expenditure	16,843,099	20,763,035
Budgetary Aid	237,000	Nil
*estimate		

Trade with UK		
	1988	1989
Imports from UK	£710,000	£731,000
Exports to UK	66,000	74,000

BRITISH PASSPORT REGULATIONS

Applications for United Kingdom Passports must be made on the forms obtainable at any of the Passport Offices (addresses given below) or at any main Post Office (except in Northern Ireland).

London.—Clive House, 70–78 Petty France, SW1H 9HD.

Liverpool.—India Buildings, Water Street, Liverpool L2 0QZ.

Newport.—Olympia House, Upper Dock Street, Newport, Gwent NP9 1XA.

Peterborough.—Passport Office, Aragon Court, Northminster Road, Peterborough PE1 1QG.

Glasgow.—3 Northgate, 96 Milton Street, Cowcaddens, Glasgow G4 0BT.

Belfast.—Passport Office, Hampton House, 47–53 High Street, Belfast BT1 2QS.

Hours. The above offices are open Mon.-Fri. 9 a.m. to 4.30 p.m. (9 a.m.–4 p.m. in London). The Passport Office, London, is also open for cases of special emergency (e.g. death or serious illness) arising outside normal office hours between 4.00 p.m. and 6.00 p.m. and on Saturdays between 10 a.m. and noon.

Completed forms of application should be sent to one of the six Passport Offices, with photographs, supporting documents and the fee of £15, in the form of a cheque or postal order which should be crossed and made payable to the Passport Office.

A passport cannot be issued or extended on behalf of a person already abroad; such person should apply to the nearest British High Commission or Consulate.

United Kingdom Passports are granted to:—
 (i) British Citizens.
 (ii) British Dependent Territories Citizens.
 (iii) British Nationals (Overseas).
 (iv) British Overseas Citizens.
 (v) British Subjects.
 (vi) British Protected Persons.

A passport granted to a child under 16 will normally be valid for an initial period of five years, after which it may be extended for a further five years with no extra charge. Children who have reached the age of sixteen years require separate passports. Their applications must be signed by one of their parents.

A passport granted to a person over 16 will normally be valid for 10 years and will not be renewable. Thereafter, or if at any time the passport contains no further space for visas, a new passport must be obtained.

The issue of passports including details of the holder's spouse has been discontinued, but existing family passports may be used until expiry.

A passport including particulars of the holder's spouse is not available for his/her use when he/she is travelling alone.

Completed passport applications should be countersigned by a Member of Parliament, Justice of the Peace, Minister of Religion, a professionally qualified person (e.g. doctor, engineer, lawyer, teacher), bank officer, established Civil Servant, police officer or a person of similar standing who has personally known the applicant for at least two years, and who is either a British Citizen, a British Dependent Territories Citizen, British Overseas Citizen, a British subject or a citizen of a Commonwealth country. A relative must not countersign the application. The applicant's birth certificate or previous British passport, and other evidence in support of the statements made in the application must be produced.

In the case of children under the age of 16 requiring a separate passport, an application should be made by one of the parents on Form B.

If the applicant for a passport is a British national by naturalization or registration, the certificate of naturalization or registration must be produced with the application, unless the applicant holds a previous United Kingdom Passport issued after registration or naturalization.

United Kingdom Passports are generally available for travel to all countries. The possession of a passport does not, however, exempt the holder from compliance with any immigration regulations in force in British or foreign countries, or from the necessity of obtaining a visa where required.

Photographs

Duplicate unmounted photographs of the applicant must be sent. These photographs should be printed on normal thin photographic paper. They should measure 45 mm by 35 mm (1·77 in. by 1·38 in.) and should be taken full face without a hat. One photograph should be certified as a true likeness of the applicant by the person who countersigns the application form.

Extension of Passports

Applications for the extension of United Kingdom passports which have been valid for less than ten years must be made on Form D.

94-Page Passports

In 1973, a new type of passport became available. Intended to meet the needs of frequent travellers who fill standard passports well before the ten-year validity has expired, it contains 94 pages, is valid for ten years and costs £30.

British Visitor's Passports

A simplified form of travel document is available for British Citizens, British Dependent Territories Citizens or British Overseas Citizens wishing to pay short visits (not exceeding three months) to the following countries:

Andorra; Austria; Belgium; Bermuda; Denmark; Finland; France (including Corsica); Greece (and the Greek islands); W. Germany (including West Berlin by air only); Gibraltar; Iceland; Italy; Liechtenstein; Luxembourg; Malta; Monaco; Netherlands; Norway; Portugal (including Madeira and the Azores); San Marino; Spain (including Balearic and the Canary Islands); Sweden; Switzerland; Tunisia; Turkey; Yugoslavia.

A fee of £7·50 (£11·25 if particulars of spouse included) is charged for the issue of a British Visitor's Passport, which is valid for 12 months, cannot be amended and is not renewable. On expiry, application should be made for a new passport if required. Particulars of an applicant's spouse and/or children under 16 years can be included at the time of issue only. A child of 8 years of age and over is eligible to hold a British Visitor's Passport. Applications for, or including, a person under 18 years of age (unless married or serving in HM Forces) must be countersigned by the legal guardian.

British Visitor's Passports are obtainable by application on Form VP (from any main Post Office except in Northern Ireland). Applicants in England, Scotland and Wales should take the completed form in person to any main Post Office which will normally issue the passport without further delay; applicants in Northern Ireland to the Passport Office, Belfast, from whom application forms may also be obtained. British Visitor's Passports are not obtainable from Passport Offices other than Belfast.

Two recent passport photographs will be required of the applicant; photographs of his/her spouse and children included on the British Visitor's Passport are not required. Size of photographs must be 50 mm by 38 mm (2 in. × 1½ in.). They should be unmounted and must be printed on normal thin photographic paper. No visas are required on British Visitor's Passports.   Applicants must also produce for the purpose of identification the documents listed on the application form.

VISAS

The visa requirements of a country may vary depending upon the purpose or the length of the visit. Visa regulations are also liable to change, sometimes at short notice, and enquiries should always be made at the Consulate or Embassy concerned (addresses and telephone numbers are given in the **Commonwealth** and **Foreign Countries** sections).

For entry for tourist purposes into the following countries a visa or permit may be required: Afghanistan; Albania; Algeria; Angola; Australia; Benin; Bhutan; Bulgaria; Burkina; Burundi; Cameroon Republic; Cape Verde; Central African Republic; Chad; China; Congo; Czechoslovakia; Djibouti; Egypt; Equatorial Guinea; Ethiopia; Gabon; Ghana; Guatemala; Guinea; Guinea Bissau; Guyana; Haiti; Hong Kong; Hungary; India; Indonesia; Iran; Iraq; Jordan; Kuwait; Laos; Lebanon; Liberia; Libya; Madagascar; Mali; Mauritania; Mongolia; Mozambique; Myanmar; Nepal; Nigeria; Oman; Pakistan; Papua New Guinea; Philippines; Poland; Romania; Rwanda; Saudi Arabia; Senegal; Sierra Leone; Somali Democratic Republic; Sudan; Syria; Turkey; USSR; Vietnam; Yemeni Republic; Zaire.

WORK AND BUSINESS OVERSEAS

A passport issued after December 31, 1982 showing the holder's national status as British citizen will secure for the holder the right to take employment or to establish himself in business or other self-employed activity in another member state of the European Community (except Spain and Portugal). A passport bearing the endorsement 'holder has the right of abode in the United Kingdom' where the holder so qualifies will also secure the same right. Employment permits are required in most other countries, even for casual labour. The nearest representative of the country concerned should be consulted. Local Employment Offices have a booklet entitled *Working abroad*.

Those planning to travel abroad on export business are advised to contact the Department of Trade and Industry–British Overseas Trade Board, 1 Victoria Street, London SW1H 0ET or its Regional Offices in London, Birmingham, Bristol, Cambridge, Leeds, Manchester, Newcastle upon Tyne and Nottingham. In Wales, contact the Welsh Office Industry Division, Cathays Park, Cardiff CF1 3NQ; in Scotland, the Scottish Office Industry Department, Alhambra House, 45 Waterloo Street, Glasgow G2 6AT; in Northern Ireland, the Industrial Development Board for Northern Ireland, Department of Economic Development, Netherleigh, Massey Avenue, Belfast BT4 2JP. These offices will send advance notification of visits to the Commercial Section of the relevant Consulate or Embassy, and can offer advice and information about the markets to be visited.

VACCINATION

In very general terms vaccination for protection against cholera, typhoid and polio are recommended for all countries outside Europe, except North America, Australia and New Zealand. Protection, in the form of tablets, is advised for malaria similarly.

Vaccination against yellow fever is essential for entry into Benin, Burkina, Cameroon, Central African Republic, Chad, Congo, Côte d'Ivoire, French Guiana, The Gambia, Ghana, Liberia, Mali, Mauritania, Niger, Panama, Rwanda, São Tomé and Príncipé, Senegal, Sierra Leone, Sudan, Tanzania, Togo and Uganda, and is recommended for most other African and South American countries. Fuller details are set out in Department of Health leaflet SA 40 *The Traveller's Guide to Health*. For up-to-date information about vaccination requirements, contact one of the following health departments: *England*—Communicable Disease Surveillance Centre, 61 Colindale Avenue, London NW9 5EQ (081-200 4400); *Wales*—Welsh Office, Cathays Park, Cardiff CF1 3NQ (0222-825111); *Scotland*—Scottish Home and Health Department, St. Andrew's House, Edinburgh EH1 3DE (031-556 8501) or the Communicable Diseases (Scotland) Unit, Ruchill Hospital, Bilsland Drive, Glasgow G20 9NB (041-946 7120); *Northern Ireland*—DHSS, Dundonald House, Upper Newtownards Road, Belfast BT4 3SF (0232-63939).

Your doctor should be consulted at least eight weeks before departure, and will advise you and arrange vaccinations. If children will be travelling outside Europe, North America, Australia and New Zealand the doctor should be informed, especially if they have not completed their full course of childhood immunization.

Details of free or reduced cost emergency medical treatment when visiting other European countries, Australia, British Dependent Territories, Hong Kong or New Zealand are set out in leaflet T1, available from some travel agents, local post offices or the Health Publications Unit, No. 2 Site, Manchester Road, Heywood, Lancs. OL10 2PZ.

THE ANTARCTIC

THE ANTARCTIC is generally defined as the area lying within the Antarctic Convergence—the zone where cold northward-flowing Antarctic sea water sinks below warmer southward-flowing water. This zone is at about lat. 50° S. in the Atlantic Ocean and lat. 55°–62° S. in the Pacific Ocean. The continent itself lies almost entirely within the Antarctic Circle, an area of about 5·5 million square miles, 99 per cent of which is permanently ice-covered. The average thickness of the ice is 7,100 ft. but in places exceeds 14,500 ft., submerging entire mountain ranges; some mountains protrude—the highest being Vinson Massif, 16,067 ft. The ice amounts to some 7·2 million cubic miles and represents more than 90 per cent of the world's fresh water.

Along one-third of the Antarctic coastline, land-ice flowing outwards forms extensive ice shelves, fragments of which break off to form tabular icebergs, leaving ice cliffs up to 150 ft. high. Much of the sea freezes in winter, forming fast ice which breaks up in summer and drifts north as pack ice. The presence of ice and continuous darkness in winter restrict access to the coastline by sea to the summer months.

The most conspicuous physical features of the continent are its high inland plateau (much of it over 10,000 ft.), the Transantarctic Mountains (which together with the large embayments of the Weddell Sea and Ross Sea mark the approximate boundary between Greater and Lesser Antarctica), and the mountainous Antarctic Peninsula and off-lying islands (which extend northwards towards South America). The continental shelf averages about 20 miles in width (half the global mean, and in places it is non-existent) and reaches exceptional depths (1,300–2,600 ft., which is 3–6 times the global mean).

Climate.—On land, summer temperatures range from just below freezing around the coast to −34° C (about −30° F) on the plateau, and in winter −20° C (about −4° F) on the coast to −65° C (about −85° F) inland. Over a large area the maxima do not exceed −15° C (+5° F).

Precipitation is scanty over the plateau but amounts to 25–76 cms (10–30 ins) (water equivalent) along the coast and some scientific stations are permanently buried by snow. Some rain falls over the more northerly areas in summer. Gravity winds on the plateau slopes and cyclonic storms further north can both exceed 100 m.p.h. and gusts have been known to reach 150 m.p.h. Visibility can be reduced to zero in blizzards.

Flora and Fauna.—Although a small number of flowering plants, ferns and clubmosses occur on the sub-Antarctic islands, only two (a grass and a pearlwort) extend south of 60° S. Antarctic vegetation is dominated by lichens and mosses, with a few liverworts, algae, and fungi. Most of these occur around the coast or on islands, but lichens and some mosses also occur inland.

The only land animals are tiny insects and mites with nematodes, rotifers, and tardigrades in the mosses, but large numbers of seals, penguins, and other sea-birds go ashore to breed in the summer. The emperor penguin is the only species which breeds ashore throughout the winter. In contrast, the Antarctic seas abound with life—a wide variety of invertebrates (including krill) and fish providing food for the seals, penguins, and other birds and a residual population of whales.

Exploration and Antarctic Treaty.—In the 180 years from Captain James Cook's circumnavigation of the Antarctic in 1772–75 to the mid-1950's, about half of all expeditions to the Antarctic were British and a number of these made major contributions to geographical and scientific knowledge of the area. Notable were the expeditions of Sir James Clark Ross, Captain Robert Scott, and Sir Ernest Shackleton.

Apart from four years during World War II, British Antarctic research has been continuous since 1925, and most of it is now organized and carried out by the British Antarctic Survey (a component of the Natural Environment Research Council).

The world-wide International Geophysical Year, 1957–58, gave great impetus to Antarctic research. Prior to the mid-1950's, only 17 stations were operated in the Antarctic by four nations and vast areas of the continent were still unknown. By 1957, 44 stations had been established by 12 nations. The co-operative scientific effort proved so fruitful that the 12 nations involved pledged themselves to continue to promote scientific and technical co-operation unhampered by politics (territorial claims being left in abeyance) and agreed that the continent should be used for peaceful purposes only. These aims were embodied in the Antarctic Treaty (covering the area south of lat. 60° S., excluding the high seas but including the ice shelves), which came into force in 1961. It has since been signed by a further 25 acceding nations, seven of which are active in the Antarctic and have therefore been accorded consultative status.

Potential resources.—Increasing pressure on the world's food and mineral supplies has stimulated the search for new sources even in the extremely hostile polar environment. Minerals have been found in great variety but not in commercially exploitable concentrations in accessible localities. (For example, coal seams occur in the Theron Mountains and Horlick Mountains.)

There are indications that off-shore hydrocarbons could be present but mostly below great depths of stormy, ice-infested seas. However, the Antarctic Treaty nations and their scientific advisors are already considering the environmental implications of possible mineral exploration and exploitation.

Currently, the chief interest is in marine protein, including the shrimp-like krill already fished commercially by Japan, Poland and the USSR. Research to ensure rational management of stocks of this organism is being continued by international groups, but it is estimated that they could sustain a yield equal to the present total annual world fish catch.

Scientific research.—At present, six British stations are maintained in the British Antarctic Territory and at South Georgia. Two are biological stations, two geophysical observatories, one is the centre for airborne earth sciences and one is the meteorological station.

There are another 44 permanently occupied stations operated by the following nations: Argentina (6), Australia (4), Brazil (1), Chile (3), China (2), East Germany (1), France (4), India (1), Japan (2), New Zealand (2), Poland (1), South Africa (3), South Korea (1), Uruguay (1), USA (3, including one at the South Pole), USSR (8), West Germany (1). There is also a station operated by Greenpeace.

The staff of these stations and summer field-workers are the only people present on the continent and off-lying islands. There are no indigenous inhabitants.

(British Antarctic Survey, *see* entry on p. 973).

FOREIGN COUNTRIES

The following articles have been revised under the direction of the various Governments or of the British Representatives at foreign capitals and by the Foreign and Commonwealth Office in London, whom the Editor warmly thanks. The Editor is also greatly indebted to the Embassies and Consulates-General in London for various corrections and additions.

AFGHANISTAN
(Da Afghanistan Jamhuriat)

President of the Republic of Afghanistan, Najibollah.
Vice Presidents, Abdul Rahim Hatif, Col.-Gen. Mohammad Rafie, Abdul Hamid Mohtat, Abdul Wahed Sorabi.

COUNCIL OF MINISTERS
(as at July 1990)

Prime Minister, Fazal Hag Khaleqiar.
Deputy Prime Ministers, Mahmud Barialay, Dr. Abdol Wahed Sorabi (*and Minister for Planning*); Dr. Nehmat Ullah Pazhwak, Abdol Qayum Nurzay, Sarwar Mangal, Mahbobullah Koshani.
Education and Training, Masoma Esmati Wardak.
Justice, Prof. Gholam Mahaynodin Darez.
Public Health, Prof. Mehr Mohammad Ejazi.
Foreign Affairs, Abdul Wakil.
Internal Affairs, Dr. Raz Mohammad Paktin.
Social Security, Saleha Faruq Etemadi.
Finance, Mohammad Hakim.
Defence, Mohammad Aslam Watanjar.
State Security, Gholam Faruq Yaqubi.
Islamic Affairs and Endowments, Mohammad Sediq Saylani.
Central Statistics, Gholam Mahaynodin Shabaz.
Border Affairs, Sarjang Zazai.
Agriculture (*and Land Reform*), Mohammad Ghofran.
Light Industries and Foodstuffs, Dr. Mohammad Anwar Dost.
Construction Affairs, Dr. Faqir Mohammad Nekzad.
Mines and Industries, Abdol Samad Jalah.
Civil Aviation, Hamidollah Tarzi.
Communications, Sayed Nasem Ulowi.
Water and Electricity, Mir Abdul Gaafur Rahim.
Information and Culture, Abdol Bashir Roygar.
Higher and Vocational Education, Dr. Prof. Mohammad Anwar Shamas.
Returnees Affairs, Fateh Mohammad Tarin.
Rehabilitation and Rural Development, Hayatollah Azizi.
Transport, Lt.-Gen. Khalilollah.
Ministers without Portfolio, Nur Ahmed Berits, Dr. Faqir Mohammad Yaqubi, Dr. Shah Wali, Sayed Ekram Paygir.
Chairman of National Assembly, Khalil Ahmad Abawi.
Chairman of Senate, Mahmoud Habibi.

Hezb-e-Watan
(Homeland Party)

Chairman, Mohammad Najibollah.
Vice Chairmen, Solayman Laeq, Farid Ahmad Mazdak, Najmuddin Kawiani, Nazar Mohammad.
Executive Board of the Central Council, Raz Mohammad Paktin, Soltan Ali Keshtmand, Solayman Laeq, Abdul Wakil, Gholam Faruq Yaqubi, Farid Ahmad Mazdak, Mohammad Aslam Watanjar, Mohammad Rafi, Mahmud Barialay, Majmoddin Kawiani, Nazar Mohammad, Nur Ahmad Nur (*Full Members*); Sayed Ekram Paygir, Abdol Qudus Ghorbandi (*Candidate Members*).

EMBASSY OF THE REPUBLIC OF AFGHANISTAN
31 Prince's Gate, SW7 1QQ
[071–589 8891]

Minister-Counsellor and Chargé d'Affaires, Taza Khan Wial.

Afghanistan lies to the N. and W. of Pakistan. Its ancient name was Aryana, by which title it is referred to by Strabo, the Greek geographer who lived in the 1st century BC. The estimated area is 250,000 sq. miles (647,497 sq. km), and the population 15,513,000 (1988 UN estimate). It is estimated that over four million have become refugees in Pakistan and over one million in Iran since the Soviet invasion. The population is very mixed. The most numerous race is the Pushtuns who predominate in the south and west, the Tadjiks, a Persian-speaking people, Uzbeks and Turkomans in the north, Hazaras in the centre, Baluchis in the south-west and Nuristanis, who live near the Chitral border. All are Sunni Muslims, except the Hazaras and Kizilbashes, who belong to the Shia sect.

Afghanistan is bounded on the W. by Iran, on the S. by Pakistan, on the N. by the USSR, and on the E. by Pakistan and China.

Mountains, chief among which are the Hindu Kush, cover three-quarters of the country, the elevation being generally over 4,000 feet. There are three great river basins, the Oxus, Helmand, and Kabul. The climate is dry, with extreme temperatures.

Government.—The constitutional monarchy, introduced by the 1964 Constitution, was overthrown by a coup on July 17, 1973. The country was ruled by Presidential decree until February 1977 when a constitution was approved by a Loya Jirgah (Grand Assembly). Mohammad Daoud was elected President of the Republic but was overthrown on April 27, 1978 by the Armed Forces and power was handed to the People's Democratic Party of Afghanistan (PDPA). In December 1979 Soviet troops invaded Afghanistan and installed Babrak Karmal as Secretary General of the PDPA, President of the Revolutionary Council and Head of State. Karmal was replaced as Secretary General of the PDPA by Najibollah in May 1986. A peace agreement in April 1988 led to the withdrawal of Soviet troops which was completed by February 1989. A new Constitution, approved in November 1987, provides for a President, a Council of Ministers, a national Assembly and a Senate.

President Najibollah declared a State of Emergency on February 19, 1989 and the Supreme Council for the Defence of the Homeland was established to take control of the country's affairs. The State of Emergency was lifted and the Supreme Council disbanded on May 4, 1990. A new Prime Minister and Cabinet were appointed, and changes to the 1987 Constitution were ratified by a *Loya Jerga* (Grand Tribal Council).

Following a Second Party Congress in late June 1990, the PDPA was renamed Hezb-e-Watan (Homeland Party) and its Politburo and Central Committee were abolished and replaced by an Executive Board and Central Council. Najibollah was elected Chairman of the Party for a four-year term.

Seghbatullah Mujjaddedi was elected President of an interim government-in-exile on February 23, 1989.

Afghanistan is divided into 30 provinces each under a centrally appointed governor.

Judiciary.—The Constitution introduced in 1965 provided for the creation of a legal code, and for a new structure of courts, consisting of a lower court in each *woleswali* (sub province), and a court of appeal in each province, with a Supreme Court in Kabul. The complete separation of executive and judiciary in this constitution was abolished by Presidential Decree in July 1973. In late 1976 and early 1977 new Penal and Civil Codes were published. The 1987 Constitution and recent amendments leave the judicial system largely untouched.

Defence.—The Army, which numbered about 80,000 before the Soviet invasion, has been greatly depleted by desertions. Men between the ages of 18 and 40 are liable to four years' military service. A military academy and military colleges are located in Kabul; some regular officers are trained in the USSR. A small Air Force is maintained. All military and air force equipment is now of Russian pattern.

Production.—Agriculture and sheep raising are the principal industries. There are generally two crops a year, one of wheat (the staple food), barley, or lentils, the other of rice, millet, maize, and dal. Sugar beet and cotton are grown. Afghanistan is rich in fruits. Sheep, including the Karakuli, and transport animals are bred. Silk, woollen and hair cloths and carpets are manufactured. Salt, silver, copper, coal, iron, lead, rubies, lapis lazuli, gold, chrome, barite, uranium, and talc are found.

Main roads run from Kabul to Kandahar, Herat, Maimana via Mazari-Sharif and Faizabad via Khanabad. The road from Kabul to the north was shortened by the completion in 1964 of the Salang pass. Roads cross the border with Pakistan at Chaman and via the Khyber Pass, and there are roads from Herat to the Russian and Iranian borders. A network of minor roads fit for motor traffic in fine weather links up all important towns and districts.

In 1982 the Afghan and Soviet shores of the River Oxus were linked by a road and rail bridge which joins the Afghan port of Hairatan and the Soviet port of Termez. A network of internal air services operates between the main towns.

Language and Literature.—The principal languages of the country are Dari (a form of Persian) and Pushtu, although a number of minority languages are also spoken in various provinces. All schoolchildren learn both Persian and Pushtu. Education is free and nominally compulsory, elementary schools having been established in most centres; there are secondary schools in large urban areas and two universities, one in Kabul (established 1932) and one in Jalalabad (established early 1970s).

Trade.—Exports are mainly Persian lambskins (Karakul), dried fruits, nuts, cotton, raw wool, carpets, spice and natural gas, while the imports are chiefly oil, cotton yarn and piece goods, tea, sugar, machinery and transport equipment.

Trade with UK

	1988	1989
Imports from UK	£12,109,000	£5,376,000
Exports to UK	11,501,000	4,813,000

CAPITAL.—Kabul (about 2,000,000). The chief commercial centres are Kabul and Kandahar (185,000). Other provincial capitals are Herat (145,000), Mazar-i-Sharif (105,000), Jalalabad (55,000).

CURRENCY.—Afghani (Af) of 100 puls.

FLAG.—Black, red and green horizontal stripes with a device in top left-hand corner.

NATIONAL ANTHEM.—Soroud-e-Melli.

NATIONAL DAY.—April 27.

BRITISH EMBASSY
Karte Parwan, Kabul
[Kabul 30511/3]

Staff were temporarily withdrawn from post in February 1989.

ALBANIA
(Republika Popullore Socialiste e Shqipërisë)

Chairman of the Presidium of the People's Assembly (*Head of State*), Ramiz Alia, *assumed office*, Nov. 22, 1982; *re-elected*, Feb. 19, 1987.

Deputy Chairmen, Rita Marko, Xhafer Spahiu, Emine Guri.

Secretary, Sihat Tozaj.

COUNCIL OF MINISTERS
(as at June 30, 1990)

Prime Minister, Adil Çarçani.

Deputy Prime Ministers, Pali Miska, Hekuran Isai.

Agriculture, Pali Miska.

Communal Economy, Xhemal Tafaj.

Construction, Ismail Ahmeti.

Education, Skender Gjinush.

Energy, Industry and Mining, Besnik Bekteshi.

Finance, Andrea Nako.

Food Industry, Ylli Bufi.

Foreign Affairs, Reiz Malile.

Foreign Trade, Shane Korbeci.

Internal Affairs, Hekuran Isai.

Internal Trade, Pajtim Ajazi.

Justice, Enver Halili.

Light Industry, Bashkim Sykaj.

People's Defence, Kico Mustaqi.

Public Health, Ahmet Kamberi.

Transportation, Hajredin Celiku.

Minister to the Presidium of the Council of Ministers, Farudin Hoxha.

Minister Secretary General of the Council of Ministers, Niko Gjyzari.

Chairman of State Planning Commission, Bujar Kolaneci.

Chairman of State Control Commission, Simon Stefani.

Albanian Workers' Party (AWP)

Politbureau of the Central Committee, R. Alia; M. Asllani; B. Bekteshi; F. Cami; A. Çarçani; H. Celiku; V. Cerrava; Ms. L. Cuko; H. Isai; X. Gjoni; P. Miska; K. Mustaqi; S. Stefani (*full members*); X. Dymylja; L. Gegprifti; N. Gjyzari; P. Kondi; Q. Mihali; (*candidate members*).

Secretariat of the Central Committee, R. Alia (*First Secretary*); A. Backa; F. Çami; X. Gjoni.

Chairman of the Party Control Commission, P. Peristeri.

Situated on the Adriatic Sea, Albania is bounded on the north and east by Yugoslavia and on the south by Greece. The area of the Republic is estimated at 11,099 sq. miles (28,748 sq. km), with a population (1988 estimate) of 3,410,000.

Albania was under Turkish suzerainty from 1468 until 1912, when independence was declared. After a period of unrest, a republic was declared in 1925, and in 1928 a monarchy. The King went into exile in 1939 when the country was occupied by the Italians; Albania was liberated in November 1944. Elections in 1945 resulted in a Communist-controlled Assembly; the King was deposed in absentia and a republic declared in January 1946.

Much of the country is mountainous and nearly a half is covered by forest. There are fertile areas along the Adriatic coast and the Koritza Basin and there have been land reclamation and irrigation programmes. The main crops are wheat, maize, sugar-beet, potatoes and fruit.

All industry is nationalized. The principal industries are agricultural product processing, textiles, oil products and cement. Output is small at present but the chemical and engineering industries are being built up and the country's considerable mineral resources are being increasingly exploited.

Exports include crude oil, minerals (bitumen, chrome, nickel, copper), tobacco, fruit and vegetables.

Trade with UK

	1988	1989
Imports from UK	£1,126,000	£1,957,000
Exports to UK	2,764,000	605,000

CAPITAL.—Tirana, population (1984) 210,757.
CURRENCY.—Lek (Lk) of 100 qindarka.
FLAG.—Black two-headed eagle surmounted by yellow outline star, all on a red field.
NATIONAL DAY.—January 11.

At present the United Kingdom has no diplomatic relations with Albania.

ALGERIA
(Al-Jumhuriya al-Jazairiya ad-Dimuqratiya ash-Shabiya)

President of State, Secretary-General of the Party, Chadli Bendjedid, *elected,* Feb. 1979, *re-elected,* Jan. 1984 and Dec. 1988.

GOVERNMENT
(as at June 30, 1990)

Prime Minister, Mouloud Hamrouche.
Foreign Affairs, Sid Ahmed Ghozali.
Justice, Ali Benflis.
Religious Affairs, Dr. Said Chibane.
Interior, Mohamed Salih Mohammedi.
Education, Mohamed El Mili Brahimi.
Youth, Dr. Abdelkader Boudjemaa.
Economy, Ghazi Hidouci.
Social Affairs, Mohamed Ghrib.
Agriculture, Abdelkader Bendaoud.
Industry, Hacene Kahlouche.
Equipment, Cherif Rahmani.
Mines, Saddek Boussena.
Transport, El-Hadi Khediri.
Posts and Telecommunications, Hamid Sidi Said.
Health, Dr. Akli Kheddis.
Secretary of State for Maghreb Affairs, Abdelaziz Khellef.
Secretary-General of the Government, Ahmed Medjhouda.
Deputy Ministers, Benali Henni (*Local Government*), Dr. Abdesselam Ali-Rachedi (*Universities*), Abdenour Keramane (*Professional Training*), Smail Goumeziane (*Organization and Trade*), Mohamed Kara-Amar (*Employment*).

ALGERIAN EMBASSY
54 Holland Park, W11 3RS
[071–221 7800]

Ambassador Extraordinary and Plenipotentiary, His Excellency Abdelkrim Gheraieb (1989).

Algeria lies between 8° 45′ W. to 12° E. longitude 27° 6′ N. to a southern limit about 19° N. and has an area of 919,595 sq. miles (2,381,741 sq. km). The population (1987 Census) was 22,971,558. A 1988 UN estimate gives a figure of 23,841,000.

Government.—Algiers surrendered to a French force on July 5, 1830, and Algeria was annexed to France in 1842. From 1881 the three northern departments of Algiers, Oran and Constantine formed an integral part of France. The Southern Territories of the Sahara, formerly a separate colony, became an integral part of Algeria on the attainment of independence. An armed rebellion led by the Muslim Front de Liberation Nationale (FLN) against French rule broke out on November 1, 1954. French control of Algeria came to an end when President de

Gaulle declared Algeria independent on July 3, 1962; by October 1963 all agricultural land held by foreigners had been expropriated and by 1965 more than 80 per cent of the French population had left Algeria.

Ben Bella was elected President of the Republic in September 1963, but was deposed; a Council of the Revolution presided over by Col. Boumediène assumed power on June 19, 1965. A new constitution was established by referendum on November 19, 1976, and in December 1976 President Boumediène was elected for a six-year term of office. Elections for a national popular assembly were held in February 1977. Following President Boumediène's death in December 1978, Chadli Bendjedid was elected President in February 1979. A new Constitution was agreed by referendum in February 1989 which moves Algeria away from a one-party socialist system to a more pluralist political system.

Development in Algeria is regulated by a series of national development plans. The 1970–73 Plan placed emphasis on industrial development, and the 1974–77 Plan on infrastructure development and social services. The 1980–84 Plan concentrated on housing, water supply and agriculture. The 1985–89 Plan continued with these objectives and also included food and processing industries. Agrarian reform started in 1987. The 4,000 state farms have been broken up into 23,000 units. Following riots in October 1988, economic reform was speeded up and now endorses the industrial and financial sectors. The aim is to decentralize planning and devolve management. The private sector is also receiving official encouragement.

Algeria's main industry is the hydrocarbons industry. Oil and natural gas are pumped from the Sahara to terminals on the coast before being exported; the gas is first liquefied at liquefaction plants at Skikda and Arzew, although pipelines serve Libya and Italy direct.

Other major industries being developed include a steel industry, motor vehicles, building materials, paper making, chemical products and metal manufactures. Most major industrial enterprises are still under State control.

Trade with UK

	1988	1989
Imports from UK	£86,615,000	£74,368,000
Exports to UK	159,748,000	177,546,000

Algeria's main exports are crude oil and liquefied natural gas. Principal imports from the United

Kingdom are capital plant, equipment for industrial use and foodstuffs.

Algeria has a rapidly expanding network of roads and railways. Considerable sums are also being spent on the development of the State airline, the national shipping company and telecommunications.

CAPITAL.—ΨAlgiers, population 3,250,000 (approx). It is one of the principal ports of the Mediterranean as well as an important industrial centre. Other towns include ΨOran; Constantine; ΨAnnaba; Blida; Setif; Sidi-Bel-Abbès; Tlemcen; ΨMostaganem; ΨSkikda; ΨBejaia and Tizi Ouzou.

CURRENCY.—Algerian dinar (DA) of 100 centimes.

FLAG.—Red crescent and star on vertically divided green and white background.

NATIONAL ANTHEM.—Qassaman.

NATIONAL DAY.—November 1.

BRITISH EMBASSY
7 Chemin Capitaine Slimane Hocine,
El-Mouradia, Algiers
[Algiers 605601]

Ambassador Extraordinary and Plenipotentiary, His Excellency Christopher Charles Richard Battis-combe (1990).

Counsellor, Head of Chancery and Consul General, J. Illman.

Cultural Attaché, British Council Representative, W. M. Jefferson, OBE, 6 Avenue Souidani Boudje-maa, Algiers.

ANDORRA
(Principat d'Andorra)

Viguier Français, Louis Deblé.
Viguier Episcopal, Francesc Badia.
Head of Government, Oscar Ribas Reig.

A small, neutral principality (formed by a treaty in 1278), situated on the southern slopes of the Pyrenees between Spain and France, with an approximate area of 175 sq. miles (453 sq. km), and population (UN estimate 1988) of 49,000, less than one-fifth of whom are native Andorrans. It is surrounded by mountains of 6,500 to 10,000 feet. Andorra is divided into seven Parishes, each of which has four Councillors elected by vote to the Valleys of Andorra Council of twenty-eight. The Council appoints the head of the executive government, who designates the members of his government. Constitutionally, the sovereignty of Andorra is vested in two co-Princes, the President of the French Republic and the Spanish Bishop of Urgel. These two co-princes can veto certain decisions of the Council of the Valleys but cannot impose their own decisions without the consent of the Council. They are represented by Permanent Delegates of whom one is the French Prefect of the Pyrenees Orientales Department at Perpignan and the other is the Spanish Vicar-General of the Diocese of Urgel. They are in turn represented in Andorra la Vella by two resident Viguiers known as the Viguier Français and the Viguier Episcopal, who have a joint responsibility for law and order and overall adminis-tration policy, together with judicial powers as members of the Supreme Court.

The language of the country is Catalan, but French and Spanish (Castilian) are also spoken. The Budget is expressed in pesetas. The estimated national revenue (1988) was US$754 million, with a per capita income of US$15,403. The climate is cold for six months, but mild in spring and summer. Potatoes are produced in the highlands and tobacco in the valleys. The mountain slopes have been developed for skiing, and it is estimated that 10,000,000 tourists visit the Valleys during the year. The economy is largely

based on tourism, commerce, tobacco, construction and forestry; a third of the country is classified as forest in which pine, fir, oak, birch and box-tree predominate. Andorra has negotiated a commercial agreement with the European Community which will regulate future trade with and through neigh-bouring countries.

A good road into the Valleys from Spain is open all year round, and that from France is closed only occasionally in winter. An airport at Seo d'Urgell just outside Andorra provides very limited air connections. There are two radio stations in An-dorra, one privately-owned and one operated by a French Government corporation. Both pay dues to the Council of the Valleys.

Trade with UK

	1988	1989
Imports from UK	£10,780,000	£10,493,000
Exports to UK	46,000	236,000

CAPITAL.—Andorra la Vella (population 16,000).

CURRENCY.—French francs and Spanish pesetas are both in use.

FLAG.—Three vertical bands, blue, yellow, red; Andorran coat of arms frequently imposed on central (yellow) band but not essential.

NATIONAL DAY.—September 8.

HM Consul-General, D. Joy, CBE (resident in Barce-lona, Spain) (Tel. 3–322 2151).

ANGOLA
(República Popular de Angola)

President, Jose Eduardo Dos Santos.

COUNCIL OF MINISTERS
(as at June 30, 1990)

Interior, Lt.-Gen. Francisco Magalhaes Paiva.
State Security, Kundi Paihama.
Defence, Col.-Gen. Pedro Tonha.
Foreign Affairs, Col. Pedro de Castro Van-Dunem.
Planning, Fernando José Franca van Dunem.
Trade and Industry, Dumilde das Chagas Simoes Rangel.
Justice, vacant.
Petroleum and Energy, Zeferino Cassa Yombo.
Health, Flavio Joao Fernandes.
Labour and Social Security, Diogo Jorge de Jesus.
Construction, Vitoriano Ferreira Nicolau.
Fisheries, Francisco Jose Ramos Da Cruz.
Agriculture, Fernando Faustino Muteka.
Transport and Communications, Col. Antonio Paulo Kassoma.
Education, Augusto Teixeira.
Finance, Aguinaldo Jaime.
Youth and Sport, Marcolino Jose Carlos Moco.

EMBASSY OF THE PEOPLE'S REPUBLIC OF ANGOLA
87 Jermyn Street, SW1Y 6JD
[071–839 5743]

Ambassador Extraordinary and Plenipotentiary, His Excellency Luis Antonio Neto Kiambata (1989).

Angola, which has an area of 481,354 sq. miles (1,246,700 sq. km), lies on the western coast of Africa; its population in 1990 was estimated at 9,767,000.

After a Portuguese presence of five centuries, and an anti-colonial war since 1961, Angola became independent on November 11, 1975 in the midst of civil war. Soviet-Cuban military assistance to the Popular Movement for the Liberation of Angola (MPLA) enabled it to defeat its rivals early in 1976. However, the MPLA government remains under pressure from the UNITA guerrilla movement (led by Dr. Jonas Savimbi) which now controls up to one-third of the country and operates freely in all other provinces. On August 8, 1988 it was announced that a ceasefire between South African, Cuban and Angolan forces had taken place pending talks on withdrawal of South African troops from Angola. The ceasefire agreement was signed, and came into effect, on August 22. In December 1988 an agreement providing for the withdrawal of the 50,000 Cuban troops by July 1991 was signed in New York.

The MPLA, a Marxist-Leninist party, is the sole legal party. The Constitution provides for a President, who appoints a Council of Ministers to assist him, and a National People's Assembly.

Angola has valuable oil and diamond deposits and exports of these two commodities account for over 90 per cent of total exports.

Principal agricultural crops are cassava, maize, bananas, coffee, palm oil and kernels, cotton and sisal. Coffee, sisal, maize and palm oil are exported; exports also include mahogany and other hardwoods from the tropical rain forests in the north of the country.

Trade with UK

	1988	1989
Imports from UK	£26,154,000	£24,785,000
Exports to UK	10,036,000	1,286,000

CAPITAL.—ΨLuanda, population estimate 1990, 2 million.

CURRENCY.—Kwanza (Kz) of 100 lwei.

FLAG.—Red and black with a yellow star, machete and cog-wheel.

NATIONAL ANTHEM.—Angola Avante.

NATIONAL DAY.—November 11 (Independence Day).

BRITISH EMBASSY
Rua Diogo Caõ 4 (Caixa Postal 1244), Luanda
[Luanda 334582/3]

Ambassador Extraordinary and Plenipotentiary, His Excellency John Gerard Flynn (1990).

ARGENTINA
(República Argentina)

President, Dr. Carlos Saúl Menem, *took office* July 8, 1989.

Vice President, Dr. Eduardo Alberto Dunalde.

CABINET
(as at July 5, 1990)

Interior, José Mera Figueroa.
Foreign Affairs, Dr. Domingo Cavallo.
Labour, Sr. Jorge Triaca.
Economy, Antonio Erman González.
Education and Justice, Dr. Antonio Salonia.
Defence, Humberto Romero.
Health and Social Welfare, Eduardo Bauzá.
Public Works, Sr. Roberto Dromi.

EMBASSY FOR ARGENTINA
53 Hans Place, SW1X 0LA
[071-584 6494]

Ambassador Extraordinary and Plenipotentiary, His Excellency Mario Cámpora (1990).

Argentina occupies the greater portion of the southern part of the South American Continent, and extends from Bolivia to Cape Horn, a total distance of nearly 2,300 miles; its greatest breadth is about 930 miles. It is bounded on the north by Bolivia, on the north-east by Paraguay, Brazil and Uruguay, on the south-east and south by the Atlantic, and on the west

by Chile, from which it is separated by the Cordillera de los Andes. On the west the mountainous Cordilleras, with their plateaux, extend from the northern to the southern boundaries; on the east are the great plains.

The Republic consists of 23 provinces and one federal district (Buenos Aires), comprising in all an area of 1,068,302 sq. miles (2,766,889 sq. km.), with a population (UN estimate 1988) of 31,963,000.

Government.—The estuary of La Plata was discovered in 1515 by Juan Díaz de Solís, but it was not until 1534 that Pedro de Mendoza founded Buenos Aires. This city was abandoned and later re-founded by Don Juan de Garay in 1580. In 1810 Spanish rule was defied, and in 1816, after a long campaign of liberation conducted by General José de San Martín, the independence of Argentina was declared by the Congress of Tucumán.

In 1946 Juan Domingo Perón became President until overthrown in 1955. There followed eighteen years of political and economic instability, and eventually in 1973, Perón was recalled from exile. Elected President he died within a year and was succeeded by his widow, Vice President María Estela Martínez de Perón. However, warring factions in the Perónist movement and increasing terrorist activity eventually led to a coup by the armed forces on March 24, 1976. A Junta, consisting of the three commanders of the Armed Forces, was established with one of their number as President. Following the Falkland Islands defeat in 1982 the President, Gen. Galtieri, resigned and the Army appointed Gen. Bignone as President. The Navy and Air Force withdrew from the Junta but this was reconstituted shortly afterwards. Elections for a civilian government to replace the military one were held on October 30, 1983 and the Radical Party's candidate, Raúl Alfonsín, was elected President. Presidential elections in May 1989 were won by the Peronist candidate Carlos Menem.

Agriculture.—Of a total land area of approximately 700 million acres, farms occupy about 425 million. About 60 per cent of the farmland is pasture, 10 per cent annual crops, 5 per cent permanent crops and the remaining 25 per cent forest and wasteland. A large proportion of the land is still held in large estates devoted to cattle raising but the number of small farms is increasing. The principal crops are wheat, maize, oats, barley, rye, linseed, sunflower seed, alfalfa, sugar, fruit and cotton. Argentina is pre-eminent in the production of beef, mutton and wool, and pastoral and agricultural products provide about 85 per cent of Argentina's exports.

Mineral Production.—Oil is found in various parts of the Republic and the production of oil is of first importance to Argentina's industries and, to some extent, to its economic and financial development. Total petroleum output for 1986 was 450,000 b.p.d. There is a refinery in San Lorenzo (Santa Fé province). Natural gas is also produced in a number of provinces.

Coal, lead, zinc, tungsten, iron ore, sulphur, mica and salt are the other chief minerals being exploited. There are small worked deposits of beryllium, manganese, bismuth, uranium, antimony, copper, kaolin, arsenate, gold, silver and tin. Coal is produced at the Rio Turbio mine in the province of Santa Cruz. The output of other materials is not large but greater attention is now being paid to the development of these natural resources, especially copper for which the Government and private companies are carrying out exploration.

Industries.—Meat-packing is one of the principal industries; flour-milling, sugar-refining, and the wine industry are also important. In recent years progress has been made by the textile, plastic and machine tool industries and engineering, especially in the production of motor vehicles and steel manufactures.

Communications.—There are 25,386 miles of railways, which are State property. Plans are in hand for complete re-organization of the railways in order to improve their operating efficiency and reduce a very large financial deficit. The combined national and provincial road network totals approximately 137,000 miles of which 23,180 miles are surfaced. There are air services between Argentina and all the neighbouring republics, Europe, Asia, Canada, the USA and South Africa.

Defence.—The Army consists of four corps organized into 12 brigades, including mountain, jungle, airborne and armoured troops. It numbers about 47,000, consisting of 20,000 officers and NCOs and 27,000 conscripts who serve for between 6 months and 1 year.

The Navy consists of 1 aircraft carrier, 6 destroyers, 6 corvettes, 4 submarines, 6 minesweepers and ancillary craft. Strength is about 27,000, consisting of 19,500 officers and NCOs and 7,500 conscripts.

The Air Force consists of 9 brigades and a training force, with a strength of 12,000, consisting of 6,900 officers and NCOs and 5,100 conscripts.

Education.—Education is compulsory for the 7 grades of primary school (6 to 13). Secondary schools (14 to 17+) are available in and around Buenos Aires and in most of the important towns in the interior of the country. Most secondary schools are administered by the Central Ministry of Education in Buenos Aires, while primary schools are administered by the Central Ministry or by Provincial Ministries of Education. Private schools, of which there are many, are also loosely controlled by the Central Ministry. The total number of universities is over 50 with 24 national, 25 private and a small number of provincial universities.

Language and Literature.—Spanish is the language of the Republic and the literature of Spain is accepted as an inheritance by the people. There is little indigenous literature before the break from Spain, but all branches have flourished since the latter half of the nineteenth century. About 450 daily newspapers are published in Argentina, including 7 major ones in the city of Buenos Aires. The English language newspaper is the *Buenos Aires Herald* (daily). There are several other foreign language newspapers.

Trade with UK

	1988	1989
Imports from UK	£12,991,000	£13,585,000
Exports to UK	66,281,000	98,490,000

CAPITAL.—ΨBuenos Aires, population (1988), metropolitan area 3,323,000; with suburbs, 9,677,200. Other large towns are: ΨRosario de Santa Fé (798,292), Córdoba (798,663), ΨLa Plata (408,300), Ψ Mar del Plata (317,444), San Miguel de Tucumán (326,000), ΨSanta Fé (312,427) and Mendoza (118,568).

CURRENCY.—Austral (A) of 100 centavos or 1,000 pesos.

FLAG.—Horizontal bands of blue, white, blue; gold sun in centre of white band.

NATIONAL ANTHEM.—Oid Mortales! El Grito Sagrado, Libertad (Hear, oh mortals! The sacred cry, freedom).

NATIONAL DAY.—May 25.

BRITISH EMBASSY
Dr. Luis Agote 2412 52, 1425 Buenos Aires

Ambassador Extraordinary and Plenipotentiary, His Excellency Hon. Humphrey Maud, CMG (1990).

BRITISH CHAMBER OF COMMERCE, Av. Corrientes 457, 10 piso, 1043 Buenos Aires.

AUSTRIA
(Republik Österreich)

President of the Republic of Austria, Dr. Kurt Waldheim, *born* 1918; *elected* June 8, 1986.

CABINET
(as at May 31, 1990)

Chancellor, Dr. Franz Vranitzky (SPÖ).
Vice-Chancellor and Minister for the Constitution and Federalism, Josef Riegler (ÖVP).
Foreign Affairs, Alois Mock (ÖVP).
Interior, Franz Löschnak (SPÖ).
Justice, Dr. Egmont Foregger (Ind.).
Finance, Ferdinand Lacina (SPÖ).
Nationalized Industries and Transport, Dr. Rudolf Streicher (SPÖ).
Agriculture and Forestry, Franz Fischler (ÖVP).
Defence, Dr. Robert Lichal (ÖVP).
Science and Research, Dr. Erhard Busek (ÖVP).
Employment and Social Affairs, Walter Geppert (SPÖ).
Education, Arts and Sports, Dr. Hilde Hawlicek (SPÖ).
Economic Affairs, Wolfgang Schüssel (ÖVP).
Environment, Youth and Family, Dr. Marilies Flemming (ÖVP).
Ministers at Federal Chancellery, Harald Ettl (SPÖ) *(Civil Servants and Health)*; Günter Stummvoll (ÖVP) *(Finance)*; Johanna Dohnal (SPÖ) *(Women's Affairs)*.

SPÖ: Socialists; ÖVP: People's Party (Conservatives).

AUSTRIAN EMBASSY
18 Belgrave Mews West, SW1X 8HU
[071–235 3731]

Ambassador Extraordinary and Plenipotentiary, His Excellency Dr. Walter F. Magrutsch (1987).

Austria is a country of Central Europe bounded on the north by Czechoslovakia, on the south by Italy and Yugoslavia, on the east by Hungary, on the north-west by the Federal Republic of Germany and on the west by Switzerland and Liechtenstein. Its area is 32,374 sq. miles (83,849, sq. km), and its population is 7,595,000 (UN estimate 1988).

Government.—The Republic of Austria comprises nine provinces (Vienna, Lower Austria, Upper Austria, Salzburg, Tyrol, Vorarlberg, Carinthia, Styria and Burgenland) and was established in 1918 on the break-up of the Austro-Hungarian Empire. On March 13, 1938, as a result of the *Anschluss*, Austria (*Österreich*) was incorporated into the *Deutsches Reich* under the name *Ostmark*. After the liberation of Vienna in 1945, the Republic of Austria was reconstituted within the frontiers of 1937 and a freely-elected Government took office on December 20, 1945. The country was divided at this time into four zones occupied respectively by the UK, USA, USSR and France, while Vienna was jointly occupied by the four Powers. On May 15, 1955 the Austrian State Treaty was signed in Vienna by the Foreign Ministers of the four Powers and of Austria. This Treaty recognized the re-establishment of Austria as a sovereign, independent and democratic state, having the same frontiers as on January 1, 1938.

There is a national assembly of 183 Deputies. After the elections of November 1986, the Socialists formed a coalition with the People's Party. The state of the parties in the Nationalrat (Lower House) was:

Socialist Party (Social Democrat)	80
People's Party (Conservative)	77
Freedom Party (Liberal)	18
Green Party	8

In the Bundesrat (Upper House) in March 1990 the People's Party held 30 seats, the Socialist Party 29 and the Liberal Party 5.

Religion and Education.—The predominant religion is Roman Catholic. Education is free and compulsory between the ages of 6 and 15 and there are good facilities for secondary, technical and professional education. There are 12 state-maintained universities and six colleges of art.

Language and Literature.—The language of Austria is German, but the rights of the Slovene- and Croat-speaking minorities in Carinthia, Styria and Burgenland are protected. The press is free.

Communications.—Internal communications in Austria are partly restricted because of the mountainous nature of the country, although there has been an extensive programme to increase the number of motorways (*Autobahn*), many of which are tunnelled through the mountains. There were, in 1990, 115,799 km of roads, including a network of *Autobahn* between major cities which also links up with the West German and Italian networks. The railways in Austria (ÖBB) are state-owned and in 1988 had 5,630 km of track, 3,186 km of which is electrified. Of the 425 km of waterways, 355 km. are navigable and there is considerable trade through the Danube ports by both local and foreign shipping. There are six commercial airports catering for 6,629,262 passengers in 1989.

Tourism.—In 1989, 18,201,763 tourists visited Austria. Foreign exchange receipts from tourism were Schilling 123,257 billion—a major contribution to the balance of payments.

PRODUCTION AND INDUSTRY

The origin of Gross Domestic Product in 1988 was as follows (in per cent):

Agriculture and forestry	4·7
Manufacturing and mining	30·4
Energy and water supply	3·2
Construction	6·2
Commerce, hotels, restaurants	16·4
Transport and communications	6·4
Asset management	12·6
Other services and producers	16·7
Import duties and other items	2·9

The value of GDP in 1988 was Schilling 133·9 billion (real).

The following table gives an indication of the relative importance of different industries (1988 figures):

Industry	Approx. number of employees	Value of output (million Schilling)
Mining	9,295	8,771
Oil (petroleum)	6,204	19,468
Iron	24,755	29,662
Other metallurgical	7,615	19,237
Stone, ceramics	21,860	26,355
Glass	7,479	7,190
Chemicals	55,802	86,925
Paper-making and processing . . .	21,635	47,654
Timber processing	24,949	23,421
Food and tobacco	42,599	87,429
Leather-making and processing .	10,119	7,884
Textiles	31,791	28,636
Clothing	25,183	14,642
Foundries	8,138	7,136
Mechanical engineering	73,104	70,409
Vehicle production	30,103	36,535
Iron and metal goods	51,210	45,893
Electrical engineering	72,504	60,415

Agriculture.—The arable land produces wheat, rye, barley, oats, maize, potatoes, sugar beet, turnips, and miscellaneous crops. Many varieties of fruit trees flourish and the vineyards produce excellent wine. The pastures support horses, cattle and pigs. Timber forms a valuable source of Austria's indigenous wealth, about 40·7 per cent of the total land area consisting of forest areas. Coniferous species predominate (75 per cent of afforested area).

FINANCE

	1987	1988
	Schilling, million	
Federal Budget:		
Revenue	409,556	399,905
Expenditure	514,461	517,466
Gross Budget Deficit . . .	104,905	117,561

TRADE

Main exports are processed goods (iron and steel, textiles, paper and cardboard products), machinery and transport equipment, other finished goods (including clothing), raw materials and foodstuffs. Main imports are machinery and transport equipment, processed goods, chemical products, foodstuffs, fuel and energy.

	1987	1988
	Schilling, million	
Imports	411,859	451,441
Exports	342,433	383,212

Over 80 per cent of all trade is with other European countries, EC countries accounting for about 60 per cent, Eastern Europe for about 9 per cent and EFTA members for 9 per cent.

Trade with UK

	1988	1989
Imports from UK	£509,991,000	£598,099,000
Exports to UK	874,430,000	933,971,000

CAPITAL.—Vienna, on the Danube, population 1,531,346. Other larger towns are Graz (243,166), Linz (199,910), Innsbruck (117,287), Salzburg (139,426), and Klagenfurt (87,321).

CURRENCY.—Schilling of 100 Groschen.

FLAG.—Horizontal stripes of red, white, red, with eagle crest on white stripe.

NATIONAL ANTHEM.—Land der Berge, Land am Strome (Land of mountains, land on the river).

NATIONAL DAY.—October 26.

BRITISH EMBASSY
Jauresgasse 12, 1030 Vienna
[Vienna 7131575]

Ambassador Extraordinary and Plenipotentiary, His Excellency Brian Lee Crowe, CMG (1989).

Counsellor, Consul General and Head of Chancery, R. P. Nash, LVO.

Counsellors, D. H. Cecil; P. A. S. Wise.

First Secretaries, S. J. O'Flaherty; S. G. Ratcliffe (*Commercial*); J. Moorby, MBE (*HM Consul*); A. N. King, LVO (*Administration*); M. G. Dalton (*Economic*); R. Dear (*Chancery/Information*); S. G. Barnes.

Defence Attaché, Lt.-Col. J. M. Craster.

There is a British Consular Office at *Vienna,* and Honorary Consulates at *Bregenz, Graz, Innsbruck* and *Salzburg.*

British Council Representative, John Green, OBE, Schenkenstrasse 4, A-1010 Vienna.

BAHRAIN
(Dawlet al-Bahrein)

Amir, HH Shaikh Isa bin Sulman Al Khalifa, GCMG, *born* 1932; *acceded* Dec. 16, 1961.

Crown Prince and C.-in-C., Bahrain Defence Force, HE Shaikh Hamad bin Isa Al Khalifa, KCMG.

CABINET
(as at May 31, 1990)

Prime Minister, HE Shaikh Khalifa bin Sulman Al Khalifa.

Foreign Affairs, Shaikh Mohammed bin Mubarak Al Khalifa.

Defence, Maj.-Gen. Shaikh Khalifa bin Ahmed Al Khalifa.

Justice and Islamic Affairs, Shaikh Abdullah bin Khalid Al Khalifa.

Development and Industry, and Cabinet Affairs, Yusuf Ahmad Shirawi.

Education, Dr. Ali Fakhro.

Health, Jawad Salim Al-Arayyed.

Transportation, Ibrahim Mohammed Humaidan.

Interior, Shaikh Mohammed bin Khalifa Al Khalifa.

Information, Tariq Abdulrahman Al Moayed.

Labour and Social Affairs, Shaikh Khalifa bin Sulman bin Mohammed Al Khalifa.

Works, Power and Water, Majid Jawad Al-Jishi.

Housing, Shaikh Khalid bin Abdullah Al Khalifa.

Finance and National Economy, Ibrahim Abdul Karim.

Commerce and Agriculture, Habib Ahmed Kassim.

Minister of State, Legal Affairs, Dr. Hussain Al-Baharna.

EMBASSY OF THE STATE OF BAHRAIN
98 Gloucester Road, SW7 4AU
[071–370 5132]

Ambassador Extraordinary and Plenipotentiary, His Excellency Karim Ebrahim Alshakar (1990).

Area and Population.—Bahrain consists of a group of low-lying islands situated about half-way down the Gulf, some 20 miles off the east coast of Arabia. The largest of these, Bahrain island itself, is about 30 miles long and 10 miles wide at its broadest. The capital, Manama, is situated on the north shore of this island. The next largest, Muharraq, with the town and Bahrain International Airport, is connected to Manama by a causeway 1½ miles long.

The population (1990 estimate) is 503,000, of whom 68·4 per cent are Bahraini. About 35 per cent of the Bahrainis are Sunni Muslims, the remaining 65 per cent being Shias; the ruling family and many of the most prominent merchants are Sunnis.

Climate.—The climate is humid all the year round, with rainfall of about 3 in. concentrated in the mild winter months, December to March; in summer, May to October, temperatures can exceed 110° F (44°C).

Government.—Bahrain has been a fully independent state since 1971. Government takes the form of a constitutional monarchy, in which traditional consultative procedures continue to play an important role.

Economy.—The largest sources of revenue are oil production and refining. The Bahrain field, discovered in 1932, is wholly owned by the Bahrain National Oil Co. Production in 1988 stood at about 42,000 b.p.d. The Sitra refinery derives about 70 per cent of its crude oil by submarine pipeline from Saudi Arabia. Bahrain also has a half share with Saudi Arabia in the profits of the offshore Abu Sa'afa field. A reservoir of unassociated gas has recently been developed on Bahrain island.

Heavy industry is currently limited to the Aluminium Bahrain (ALBA) smelter, producing 183,000 tonnes in 1988; the Gulf Petrochemical Industries Co. (GPIC) producing 375,000 tonnes of ammonia and 395,000 tonnes of methanol in 1988, the Gulf Aluminium Rolling Mill (GARMCO), and the Arab Shipbuilding and Repair Yard (ASRY), operating dry dock facilities up to 500,000 tons.

There are a number of small to medium sized industrial units.

The state has developed as a financial centre. Apart from commercial banks, led by the National Bank of Bahrain, the Standard Chartered Bank, the British Bank of the Middle East and the Bank of Bahrain and Kuwait, many international banks have been licensed as offshore banking units; there are also money brokers and merchant banks.

Trade with UK

	1988	1989
Imports from UK	£138,150,000	£138,529,000
Exports to UK	75,786,000	61,018,000

Communications.—Bahrain International airport is one of the main air traffic centres of the Gulf; it is the headquarters of Gulf Air, and a stopping point on routes between Europe and Australia and the Far East for other airlines. A causeway linking Bahrain to Saudi Arabia was opened in November 1986.

A world-wide telephone and telex service, by satellite and cable, is operated by Bahrain Telecommunications Company.

CAPITAL.—ΨManama, population (1981 Census) 121,986. In 1990, it was estimated that 32 per cent of Bahrain's population lives in Manama.

CURRENCY.—Bahrain dinar (BD) of 1,000 fils.

FLAG.—Red, with vertical serrated white bar next to staff.

NATIONAL DAY.—December 16.

BRITISH EMBASSY
21 Government Avenue,
Manama 306, PO Box 114
[Manama 534404]

Ambassador Extraordinary and Plenipotentiary, His Excellency John Alan Shepherd, CMG (1988).

First Secretaries, W. I. Rae, MBE (*Commercial and Head of Chancery and Consul*); J. C. A. Rundall.
Second Secretary, D. Leith (*Commercial*).
Third Secretary, S. Harrison.

British Council Representative, J. Wright, 21 Government Avenue (PO Box 452), Manama 306.

BELGIUM
(Royaume de Belgique)

King of the Belgians, HM King Baudouin, KG, *born* Sept. 7, 1930; *succeeded* July 17, 1951, on the abdication of his father, King Leopold III, after having acted as Head of the State since August 11, 1950; *married* Dec. 15, 1960, Doña Fabiola de Mora y Aragòn.
Heir Presumptive, HRH Prince Albert, *born* June 6, 1934, *brother* of the King; *married* July 2, 1959, Donna Paola Ruffo di Calabria, and has *issue* Prince Philippe Léopold Louis Marie, *b.* April 15, 1960; Princess Astrid Josephine-Charlotte Fabrizia Elisabeth Paola Marie, *b.* June 5, 1962; Prince Laurent, *b.* Oct. 20, 1963.

CABINET
(as at June 30, 1990)

Prime Minister, Dr. Wilfried Martens (CVP).
Deputy PM and Minister for the Brussels Region, and Institutional Reform (French sector), Philippe Moureaux (PS).
Deputy PM and Minister for Economic Affairs and Planning, and National Education (Flemish sector), Willy Claes (SP).
Deputy PM and Minister of Communications, and Institutional Reform (Dutch sector), Jean-Luc Dehaene (CVP).
Deputy PM and Minister of Justice, and the Middle Classes, Melchior Wathelet (PSC).
Deputy PM and Minister for the Budget and Scientific Policy, Hugo Schiltz (VU).
Foreign Affairs, Mark Eyskens (CVP).
Finance, Philippe Maystadt (PSC).
Foreign Trade, Robert Urbain (PS).
Posts and Telecommunications, Marcel Colla (SP).
Social Affairs, Philippe Busquin (PS).
Defence, Guy Coëme (PS).
Interior, Modernization of Public Services and National Scientific and Cultural Institutions, Louis Tobback (SP).
Co-operation and Development, André Geens (VU).
Pensions, Gilbert Moltard (PS).
Employment and Work, Luc Vanden Brande (CVP).
Civil Service, Raymond Langendries (PSC).

CVP—Christian Social Party (Flemish); PS—Socialist Party (Francophone); SP—Socialist Party (Flemish); PSC—Christian Social Party (Francophone); VU—Flemish Peoples' Union.

BELGIAN EMBASSY
103 Eaton Square, SW1V 9AB
[071–235 5422]

Ambassador Extraordinary and Plenipotentiary, His Excellency Jean-Paul van Bellinghen (1984).
Minister Counsellor, L. Willems.
Minister Counsellor (Economic), J. Maricou.
Military, Naval and Air Attaché, Capt. G. H. A. Busard.

A Kingdom of Western Europe, with a total area of 11,781 sq. miles (30,513 sq. km), and a population (1986) of 9,858,895 (Greater Brussels 976,536; Flanders 5,676,194; Wallonia 3,206,165, of whom 66,445 are German-speaking). A 1988 UN estimate gives a total figure of 9,925,000. The majority of Belgians are Roman Catholics. The Kingdom of Belgium is bounded on the N. by the Netherlands, on the S. by France, on the E. by the Federal Republic of Germany and Luxembourg, and on the W. by the North Sea.

Belgium has a frontier of 898 miles, and a seaboard of 41 miles. The Meuse and its tributary, the Sambre, divide it into two distinct regions, that in the west being generally level and fertile, while the table-land of the Ardennes, in the east, has for the most part a poor soil. The polders near the coast, which are protected by dykes against floods, cover an area of 193 sq. miles. The highest hill, Signal de Botranges, rises to a height of 2,276 feet, but the mean elevation of the whole country does not exceed 526 feet. The principal rivers are the Scheldt and the Meuse.

Government.—The kingdom formed part of the Low Countries (Netherlands) from 1815 until October 14, 1830, when a National Congress proclaimed its independence, and on June 4, 1831, Prince Leopold of Coburg was chosen hereditary king. The separation from the Netherlands and the neutrality and inviolability of Belgium were guaranteed by a Conference of the European Powers, and by the Treaty of London (April 19, 1839), the famous 'Scrap of Paper,' signed by Austria, France, Great Britain, Prussia, The Netherlands, and Russia. On August 4, 1914 the Germans invaded Belgium, in violation of the terms of the treaty. The kingdom was again invaded by Germany on May 10, 1940. The whole kingdom eventually fell and was occupied by Nazi troops until liberated by the Allies in September 1944.

According to the Constitution of 1831 the form of government is a constitutional representative and hereditary monarchy with a bicameral legislature, consisting of the King, the Senate and the Chamber of Deputies. The parliamentary term is four years.

The last general election was held on December 13, 1987. The results were as follows (seats):

Chamber of Deputies: CVP 43; PS 40; SP 32; PVV (Flemish Freedom and Progress Party) 25; PRL (Liberal Reform Party (Francophone)) 23; PSC 18; VU 16; Agalev (Flemish Environmental Party) 6; Ecolo (Francophone Ecology Party) 3; FDF (Francophone Democratic Front) 3; Vlaams Blok (Flemish Nationalist Party) 2.

Senate: CVP 22; PS 20; SP 17; PRL 12; PVV 11; PSC 9; VU 8; Ecologists 5; FDF 1; Vlaams Blok 1.

Besides these directly elected representatives the Senate also includes 51 members who are elected by the Provincial Councils and 26 who are co-opted in the proportions of the directly elected seats. HRH Prince Albert is a *sénateur de droit.*

Regional Governments.—The 1980 regionalization law made provision for the establishment of three Regional Community Parliaments (Assemblies) with executive councils which were set up in November 1981 and became effective in January 1982. The executives are autonomous from the central government, and their members are elected by the members of the Assemblies to whom they are responsible. They prepare Bills within the limits of their regional/community competences, and once these Bills have been passed by the regional assembly and published in the *Moniteur Belge*, they have the force of law.

The Flemish Community Assembly (186 members) and Executive (a President and 8 Regional Ministers) covers the provinces of Antwerp, East and West Flanders, Limbourg and the Flemish *arrondissements* (Halle, Vilvoorde, Leuven) in the province of Brabant, and is also responsible for the Flemish population of Brussels. The Walloon Regional Assembly (104 members) and Executive (a President and 6 Regional Ministers) covers the provinces of Hainaut, Liège, Luxembourg and Namur, and the *arrondissement* of Nivelles in the province of Brabant. The French Community Assembly (132 members) and Executive (a President and 3 Community Ministers) has no fixed territory but is responsible for the Francophone population of Brussels and, in concert with the Walloon Regional Assembly, deals with certain Walloon regional affairs. The German-speaking community (about 66,000) also has an Assembly, which gained autonomy in 1984. It is based in Eupen.

Since June 1989 there has been a 75-member Brussels Regional Council with a 5-member Executive: 2 Flemings, 2 Francophones and a President.

An Arbitration Court was set up in 1984 to resolve conflicts between laws made by the various legislative bodies.

Language and Literature.—Belgium is divided between those who speak Dutch (the Flemings) and those who speak French (the Walloons). Dutch is spoken in the provinces of West Flanders, East Flanders, Antwerp, Limburg, and the northern half of Brabant, and French in the provinces of Hainault, Namur, Luxembourg, Liège and the southern half of Brabant. Dutch is recognized as the official language in the northern areas and French in the southern (Walloon) area and there are guarantees for the respective linguistic minorities. Brussels is officially bi-lingual. There is a small German-speaking area (Eupen and Malmedy) along the German border, east of Liège.

The literature of France and the Netherlands is supplemented by an indigenous Belgian literary activity, in both French and Dutch. Maurice Maeterlinck (1862–1949) was awarded the Nobel Prize for Literature in 1911. Emile Verhaeren (1855–1916) was a poet of international standing. Of contemporary Belgian writers, perhaps the most celebrated was Georges Simenon (1903–89). There are 39 daily newspapers in Belgium (23 in French, 15 in Dutch and 1 in German).

Education.—The nursery schools provide free education for the 2½ to 6 age group. There are over 8,000 primary schools (6 to 12 years) of which approximately 5,000 are administered by the local Communities, on authority delegated to them by the State. The remainder are free institutions (predominantly Roman Catholic). There are more than 1,100 secondary schools offering a general academic education slightly over half of which are free institutions (predominantly Roman Catholic but subsidized by the State) and the remainder official institutions. The official school leaving age is 18.

Production.—Belgium is a manufacturing country. With no natural resources except coal, annual production of which was approximately 6 million tonnes in 1986, industry is based largely on the processing for re-export of imported raw materials. Gross National Product per capita in 1988 was BFr.520,600. Principal industries are steel and metal products, chemicals and petrochemicals, textiles, glass, and foodstuffs.

Budget	1988	1989
Revenue	BFr.1,505,500m	BFr.1,037,000m
Expenditure	1,901,600m	1,409,600m

TRADE

External trade figures relate to Luxembourg as well as Belgium since the two countries formed an Economic Union in 1921.

	1987	1988
Total Imports	US$83,523m	US$92,250m
Total Exports	83,288m	92,103m

Trade with UK (Belgium and Luxembourg)

	1988	1989
Imports from UK	£9,835,241,000	£4,872,641,000
Exports to UK	13,235,784,000	5,700,534,000

Communications.—In 1983, there were 3,920 kilometres of normal gauge railways operated by the Belgian National Railways, of which 1,763 kilometres were electrified. The Belgian National Light Railways (SNCV) also operated 27,671 kilometres of regular bus routes.

Ship canals include Ghent-Terneuzen (18 miles, of which half is in Belgium and half in the Netherlands) which permits the passage to Ghent of ships up to 60,000 tons; the Canal of Willebroek Rupel-Brussels (20 miles, by which ships drawing 18 ft reach Brussels from the sea; opened in 1922); and Bruges (from Zeebrugge on the North Sea to Bruges, 6¼ miles). The Albert Canal (79 miles), links Liège with Antwerp; it was completed in 1939 and accommodates barges up to 1,350 tons. The modernization of the port of Antwerp is well advanced. Inland waterway approaches to Antwerp are also to be improved. The river Meuse from the Dutch to the French frontiers, the river Sambre between Namur and Monceau, the river Scheldt from Antwerp to Ghent and the Brussels-Charleroi Canal are being widened or deepened to take barges up to 1,350 tons. Most of the maritime trade of Belgium is carried in foreign shipping.

In 1986 there were 14,260 km of trunk roads of which about 1,550 km were motorways.

The Belgian National Airline Sabena operates regular services between Brussels and London, and many continental centres, as well as overseas services to Northern and Central America, Africa, Middle East, Far East, etc. Many foreign airlines call at Brussels.

CAPITAL.—Brussels, has a population (1986) of 976,536. Other towns are ΨAntwerp, the chief port (918,963); ΨGhent (484,295); Liège (592,732); Charleroi (430,767); Bruges (258,917); ΨOstend (134,215); Malines (293,050).

CURRENCY.—Belgian franc of 100 centimes (centiemen).

FLAG.—Three vertical bands, black, yellow, red.

NATIONAL ANTHEM.—La Brabançonne.

NATIONAL DAY.—July 21 (Accession of King Leopold I, 1831).

BRITISH EMBASSY
Britannia House, 28 rue Joseph II,
1040 Brussels
[Brussels 2179000]

Ambassador Extraordinary and Plenipotentiary, His Excellency Robert (Robin) James O'Neill, CMG (1989).

Counsellors, N. M. McCarthy, OBE (*Head of Chancery*); B. Attewell (*Commercial*).
Defence and Military Attaché, Col. K. Woodrow.
Naval and Air Attaché, Wing Cdr. B. A. Horton.

There are British Consular Offices at *Brussels, Antwerp* and *Liège*.

British Council Representative to Belgium and Luxembourg, K. McGuinness.
BRITISH CHAMBER OF COMMERCE FOR BELGIUM AND LUXEMBOURG (INC.), 30 rue Joseph II, 1040 Brussels.

BENIN
(République du Benin)

President and Head of the Armed Forces, Mathieu Kerekou.

CABINET
(as at March 31, 1990)

Prime Minister, Defence, Nicéphore Soglo.
Internal Affairs, Public Security and Territorial Administration), Florentin Feliho.
Foreign Affairs and Co-operation, Théophile Nata.
Planning and Statistics, Paul Dossou.
Finance, Idelphonse Lemon.
National Education, Paulin Hountondji.
Culture, Youth and Sports, Dramane Karim.
Justice and Legislation, Yves Yehouessi.
Rural Development and Co-operatives, Adamou N'diaye.
Equipment and Transport, Eustache Sarre.
Public Health, Véronique Lawson.
Information and Communications, Toussaint Tchitchi.
Labour and Social Affairs, Véronique Ahoyo.
Industry, Energy and Public Enterprises, Fatiou Adekounte.
Trade, Arts, Crafts and Tourism, Richard Adjaho.

A republic situated in West Africa, between 2° and 3° W. and 6° and 12° N., Benin (formerly known as Dahomey) has a short coastline of 78 miles on the Gulf of Guinea but extends northwards inland for 437 miles. It is flanked on the west by Togo, on the north by Burkina and Niger and on the east by Nigeria. It is divided into four main regions running horizontally: a narrow sandy coastal strip, a succession of inter-communicating lagoons, a clay belt and a sandy plateau in the north. It has an area of 43,484 sq. miles (122,622 sq. km), and a population of 4,444,000 (1988 estimate). The official language is French. Although poor in resources, Benin is one of the most heavily populated areas in West Africa, with a high standard of education.

Government.—The first treaty with France was signed by one of the kings of Abomey in 1851 but the country was not placed under French administration until 1892. Benin became an independent republic within the French Community in December 1958; full independence outside the Community was proclaimed on August 1, 1960. In October 1963 a popular revolution led to the fall of the government and the Army held power until a civilian government was formed. The government's life was very short, however, and in the subsequent nine years successive governments were overthrown by the military after only a short term in office until a coup d'état of October 26, 1972 brought to power a Military Revolutionary Government, Marxist-Leninist in ideology, headed by Lt.-Col. Kerekou.
In response to mounting unrest, the government agreed to drop Marxism-Leninism as the official ideology in December 1989. Following a 'National Conference of Active Forces of the Nation,' the

Constitution was revoked on March 1, 1990 and the country's official name was changed from the People's Republic of Benin to the Republic of Benin. The Revolutionary National Assembly (legislature) was dissolved and replaced by a High Council of the Republic (HCR). This, in conjunction with a new 15-member civilian government, is implementing a political transition programme; a new Constitution, new electoral laws and the free formation of political parties are to lead to legislative and presidential elections in February and March 1991.

Trade.—The principal exports are cotton, palm products, ground nuts, shea-nuts, and coffee. Small deposits of gold, iron and chrome have been found; oil production started in 1983.

Trade with UK

	1988	1989
Imports from UK	£8,169,000	£7,294,000
Exports to UK	2,450,000	356,000

CAPITAL.—ΨPorto Novo, population (1982 estimate) 208,258. Political capital and principal commercial town and port, ΨCotonou (487,020).
CURRENCY.—Franc CFA of 100 centimes.
FLAG.—Green, with five-pointed red star in the top left corner.
NATIONAL DAY.—November 30.

British Ambassador (resident in Lagos, Nigeria).

BHUTAN
(Druk-yul)

King of Bhutan, HM Jigme Singye Wangchuk, *born* Nov. 11, 1955; *succeeded his father*, July 1972; *crowned*, June 2, 1974.
Heir, Crown Prince Jigme Gesar Namgyal Wangchuk, *designated*, Oct. 31, 1988.

COUNCIL OF MINISTERS
(as at June 30, 1990)

Chairman of Council of Ministers, HM The King.
HM Representative in Ministry of Finance, HRH Ashi Sonam Chhoden Wangchuk.
HM Representative in Ministry of Agriculture, HRH Ashi Dichen W. Wangchuk.
Home Affairs, HRH Namgyel Wangchuk.
Finance, Dorji Tshering.
Foreign Affairs, Dawa Tshering.
Communications, Social Services and Tourism, Dr. T. Tobgyal.
Trade and Industries, Om Pradhan.
Deputy Minister of Defence, Chief Operations Officer of Royal Bhutan Army, Maj.-Gen. Lam Dorji.
Speaker of the National Assembly, Chief Justice, Sangye Penjor.

Bhutan is a small Himalayan Kingdom situated between Tibet (to the north) and India (to the west, south and east). The total area is about 18,147 sq. miles (47,000 sq. km), with a mountainous northern region which is infertile and sparsely populated, a central zone of upland valleys where most of the population and cultivated land is found, and in the south the densely forested foothills of the Himalayas, which are mainly inhabited by Nepalese settlers and indigenous tribespeople.
The population of Bhutan is estimated at 1,451,000 (UN estimate 1988), about three-quarters of whom are Buddhists. The remainder (mostly the Nepali Bhutanese) are Hindu. The official language, for administrative and religious purposes, is Dzongkha, a variant of Tibetan, which functions as a lingua franca amongst a variety of languages and dialects. It is government policy to make the study of

Dzongkha compulsory in schools, although English is the medium of instruction and has become widely used within the administration.

In 1949 a treaty was concluded with the Government of India under which the Kingdom of Bhutan agreed to be guided by the advice of the Government of India in regard to its external relations. It has its own diplomatic representatives and is a member of the UN and other international and regional organizations. It also receives from the Government of India an annual payment of Rs500,000 as compensation for portions of its territory annexed by the British Government in India in 1864.

Government.—Bhutan has a 150-member National Assembly which meets twice a year. The ten-member Royal Advisory Council, nominated by the King and the National Assembly, acts as a consultative body when the National Assembly is not in session. The King is also assisted by a Council of Ministers. There are no political parties.

Economy.—The sixth 5-year Plan (1987–92) has a projected expenditure of Nu9,485m. Economic emphasis is on the infrastructure, especially roads and telecommunications. The economy is based on agriculture and animal husbandry, which engage over 90 per cent of the workforce in what is largely a self-sufficient rural society. The principal food crops are rice, wheat, maize and barley. Vegetables and fruit are also produced. Bhutan is the world's largest producer of cardamom, which forms its principal export to countries other than India. Mineral resources include dolomite and small amounts of coal, which are exported to India. A modest industrial base is being developed. A distillery and cement, chemicals and food processing plants are in production; a forestry industries complex is being expanded. Tourism and postage stamps are increasingly important sources of foreign exchange. Over 90 per cent of foreign trade is with India. Principal exports are agricultural products, timber, cement and coal; main imports are textiles, cereals and consumer goods. Bhutan's airline, Druk Air, flies between Paro and Calcutta.

Trade with UK

	1988	1989
Imports from UK	£12,464,000	£363,000
Exports to UK	175,000	328,000

CAPITAL.—Thimphu, population estimate (1987) 15,000.

CURRENCY.—Ngultrum of 100 chetrums. Indian currency is also legal tender.

FLAG.—Saffron yellow and orange-red divided diagonally, with dragon device in centre.

NATIONAL DAY.—December 17.

BOLIVIA
(República de Bolivia)

President of the Republic, Jaime Paz Zamora, *inaugurated,* August 6, 1989.
Vice President, Luis Ossio Sanjines.

CABINET
(as at July 31, 1990)

Foreign Affairs, Carlos Iturralde Ballivián.
Interior, Guillermo Capobianco Rivera.
Secretary General, Gustavo Fernández Saavedra.
Defence, Héctor Ormachea Peñaranda.
Finance, David Blanco Zavala.
Planning, Enrique García Rodríguez.
Education, Mariano Baptista Gumucio.
Transport, Willy Vargas Vacaflor.
Industry and Commerce, Guido Céspedes Argandoña.
Labour, Oscar Zamora Medinacelli.

Health, Mario Paz Zamora.
Mining, Walter Soriano Lea-Plaza.
Agriculture, Mauro Bertero Gutiérrez.
Energy and Hydrocarbons, Angel Zannier Claros.
Urban Development, Enrique Prada Abasto.

BOLIVIAN EMBASSY
106 Eaton Square, SW1W 9AD
[071–235 2257/4248]

Ambassador Extraordinary and Plenipotentiary, His Excellency Gen. Gary Prado Salmon (1990).
First Secretary, Marta Bosacoma Bonel.
Second Secretary, Patricia Quintanilla.
Trade Attaché, J. M. Bueno.

The land-locked Republic of Bolivia extends between lat. 10° and 23° S. and long. 57° 30' and 69° 45' W. It has an area estimated at 424,165 sq. miles (1,098,581 sq. km), with a population (UN estimate 1988) of 6,993,000. The Republic derives its name from its liberator, Simon Bolivar (1783–1830).

The chief topographical feature is the great central plateau (65,000 square miles) over 500 miles in length, at an average altitude of 12,500 feet above sea level, between the two great chains of the Andes, which traverse the country from south to north. The total length of the navigable streams is about 12,000 miles, the principal rivers being the Itenez, Beni, Mamore and Madre de Dios.

Language and Literature.—The official language of the country is Spanish, but many of the Indian inhabitants (about two-thirds of the population) speak Quechua or Aymará, the two linguistic groups being more or less equal in numbers.

The Roman Catholic religion was disestablished in 1961. Elementary education is compulsory and free and there are secondary schools in urban centres. Provision is also made for higher education; in addition to St. Francisco Xavier's University at Sucre, founded in 1624, there are six other universities, the largest being the University of San Andres at La Paz. There are nine principal daily newspapers in Bolivia.

Production.—Mining, natural gas, petroleum and agriculture are the principal industries. The ancient silver mines of Potosí are now worked chiefly for tin, but gold, partly dug and partly washed, is obtained on the Eastern Cordillera of the Andes; the tin output is one of the largest in the world, and together with other minerals (copper, antimony, lead, zinc, asbestos, wolfram, bismuth salt and sulphur), provides over half of Bolivia's exports.

In 1982 Bolivia produced 1·4 million cubic metres of oil, sufficient for internal consumption. Gas (currently providing about a quarter of Bolivia's export income) is piped to Argentina and there are plans to build a pipeline to São Paulo, Brazil. Bolivia's agricultural produce consists chiefly of rice, barley, oats, wheat, sugar-cane, maize, cotton, indigo, rubber, cacao, potatoes, cinchona bark, medicinal herbs, brazil nuts etc.

Transport and Communications.—There are 2,200 miles of railways in operation including the lines from Corumbá to Santa Cruz (312 miles). There are about 10,950 miles of telegraphs, and microwave telephone communications between La Paz, Santa Cruz, Cochabamba, Oruro and Sucre. Most other towns have radio/telephone communication with the main cities. There is direct railway communication to the sea at Antofagasta (32 hours), Arica (10 hours), and Mollendo (2 days), and also to Buenos Aires (3½ days). Communication with Peru is by road from La Paz via Copacabana and thence to the railhead at Puno.

Commercial aviation in Bolivia is conducted by the national airline, Lloyd Aereo Boliviano and

Transporte Aereo Militar between the major towns, and Lloyd Aereo Boliviano and a number of foreign airlines provide international flights to the USA, South and Central America and Europe.

Bolivia is without a coastline, having been deprived of the ports of Tocopilla, Cobija, Mejillones and Antofagasta by the Pacific War of 1879–1884.

FINANCE

The economy has deteriorated since 1977, with disappointing petroleum reserves, a large external debt, and the collapse of world tin prices in 1985. Tin prices began to increase once more from April 1989. The peso was replaced in January 1987 with the Boliviano of 1,000,000 old pesos in an effort to stem inflation. The inflation rate at the end of 1988 was about 20 per cent. Gross Domestic Product in 1987 was US$4,640 m.

Trade with UK

	1988	1989
Imports from UK	£6,029,000	£6,148,000
Exports to UK	13,224,000	17,666,000

Mineral exports represent about 94 per cent of these totals. A large part of Bolivia's minerals were shipped to UK for smelting and re-export, but Bolivia is now developing her own smelters and will in future be exporting metals. The chief imports are wheat and flour, iron and steel products, machinery, vehicles and textiles.

CAPITAL.—La Paz (Population, 1,000,000). Other large centres are Cochabamba (250,000), Oruro (180,000), Santa Cruz (380,000), Potosí (90,000), Sucre, the legal capital and seat of the judiciary (80,000) and Tarija (45,000).

CURRENCY.—Boliviano ($b) of 100 centavos.

FLAG.—Three horizontal bands; red, yellow, green.

NATIONAL ANTHEM.—Bolivianos, El Hado Propicio (Oh Bolivia, our long-felt desires).

NATIONAL DAY.—August 6 (Independence Day).

BRITISH EMBASSY
Avenida Arce 2732–2754,
(Casilla 694) La Paz
[La Paz 329401/4]

Ambassador Extraordinary and Plenipotentiary, His Excellency Michael Francis Daly, CMG (1989).
First Secretary, A. W. Shave (*Commercial and Head of Chancery*).

There is a British Consulate at *Santa Cruz.*

BRAZIL
(República Federativa do Brasil)

President, Fernando Collor de Mello, *inaugurated* March 15, 1990.
Vice President, Itamar Franco.

CABINET
(as at June 30, 1990)

Labour, Antonio Rogério Magri.
Social Action, Margarida Procópio.
Education, Carlos Chíarelli.
Justice, Bernardo Cabral.
Air Force, Brig. Sócrates de Costa Monteiro.
Army, Gen. Carlos Tinoco Ribeiro Gomes.
Navy, Adm. Mário Cesar Flores.
Infrastructure, Ozires Silva.
Economy, Zélia Cardoso de Mello.
Foreign Affairs, Jose Francisco Rezek.
Agriculture, vacant.
Health, Dr. Alceni Guerra.

Environmental Secretariat, Jose Lutzenberger.
Internal Revenue, Federal Police, Romeu Tuma.
Governor of Central Bank, Ibrahim Eris.
Government Leader in Chamber of Deputies, Renan Calheiros.

BRAZILIAN EMBASSY
32 Green Street, W1Y 4AT
[071–499 0877]

Ambassador Extraordinary and Plenipotentiary, His Excellency Paulo-Tarso Flecha de Lima (1990).

There is also a Brazilian Consulate-General in *London* and honorary consular offices at *Cardiff* and *Glasgow*.

Area and Population.—Brazil, discovered in 1500 by Portuguese navigator Pedro Alvares Cabral, is bounded on the north by the Atlantic Ocean, the Guianas, Colombia and Venezuela; on the west by Peru, Bolivia, Paraguay, and Argentina; on the south by Uruguay; and on the east by the Atlantic Ocean. Brazil extends between lat. 5° 16′ N. and 33° 45′ S. and long. 34° 45′ and 73° 59′22″ W. The Republic comprises an area of 3,286,488 sq. miles (8,511,965 sq. km), with a population (UN estimate 1988) of 144,428,000.

The northern States of Amazonas and Pará are mainly wide, low-lying, forest-clad plains. The central states of Mato Grosso are principally plateau land and the eastern and southern States are traversed by successive mountain ranges interspersed with fertile valleys. The principal ranges are Serra do Mar, the Serra da Mantiqueira and the Serra do Espinhaco along the east coast. The River Amazon with a total length of some 4,000 miles has tributaries which are themselves great rivers, and flows from the Peruvian Andes to the Atlantic. Its principal northern tributaries are the Rio Branco, Rio Negro, and Japurá; its southern tributaries are the Juruá, Purus, Madeira and Tapajós, while the Xingú meets it within 200 miles of its outflow into the Atlantic. The Tocantins and Araguaia flow northwards from Mato Grosso and Goiás to the Gulf of Pará. The Parnaiba flows from Piaui into the Atlantic. The São Francisco rises in the South of Minas Gerais and flows to the eastern coast. The Paraguai, rising in the south-west of Mato Grosso, flows through Paraguay to its confluence with the Paraná, which rises in the mountains of that name and divides Brazil from Paraguay.

Government.—Brazil was colonized by Portugal in the early part of the sixteenth century, and in 1822 became an independent empire under Dom Pedro, son of the refugee King Joao VI of Portugal. On November 15, 1889, Dom Pedro II, second of the line, was dethroned and a republic was proclaimed.

The Federative Republic of Brazil is made up of the Federal District and 24 States. The two territories of Amapá and Roraima are due to become states following gubernatorial elections in October 1990.

The constitution of October 1988 draws on the same conceptual basis as that of the United States, and envisages an equal distribution of power between the executive, the legislature and the judiciary. Under the existing constitutional provisions the President, who heads the executive, is directly elected for a five-year term.

The Congress consists of a Senate (3 Senators per State elected for an 8-year term) and a Chamber of Deputies which is elected every 4 years. (The number of Deputies per State depends upon the State's population). Each State has a Governor, and a Legislative Assembly with a 4-year term.

Production.—There are large and valuable mineral deposits including iron ore (hematite), manganese, bauxite, beryllium, chrome, nickel, tungsten, cassiterite, lead, gold, monazite (containing rare earths and thorium) and zirconium. Diamonds and precious and semi-precious stones are also found. The mineral wealth is being exploited to an increasing extent. The iron ore deposits of Minas Gerais are exceeded by those of the Amazon region, principally in the Carajás areas where deposits are estimated at 35,000 million tonnes. Mining operations began in February 1985.

Electric power production in 1987 was 202,287 Gwh. In the same year, the total output of steel was 22,227 million tonnes. Production of oil was 566,000 b.p.d. Of these 487,000 b.p.d. were produced from offshore fields.

Agriculture production was (tonnes):

	1986	1987
Black Beans	2,221,000	2,019,000
Cassava	25,542,000	23,399,000
Cocoa	459,000	337,000
Coffee	2,007,000	4,220,000
Cotton	2,314,000	1,672,000
Maize	20,510,000	26,787,000
Peanuts	216,000	196,000
Potatoes	1,834,000	2,343,000
Rice	10,399,000	10,422,000
Soya	13,335,000	16,814,000
Tobacco	386,000	398,000
Wheat	5,433,000	5,889,000

Defence.—The peace-time strength of the Army is 192,000. The strength of the Navy is 49,000. The Air Force has a strength of 45,000.

Education.—Primary education is compulsory and is the responsibility of State governments and municipalities. At this level approximately 10 per cent attend private schools. Secondary education is largely the responsibility of State and municipal governments, although a small number of very old foundations (the Pedro II Schools) remain under direct federal control. Over 50 per cent of all pupils at this level attend private schools. Higher education is available in Federal, State, municipal and private universities and faculties.

Language and Literature.—Portuguese is the language of the country, but Italian, Spanish, German, Japanese and Arabic are also spoken by minorities, and newspapers of considerable circulation are produced in those languages.

Public libraries have been established in urban centres and there is a flourishing national press with widely circulated daily and weekly newspapers.

Communications.—In 1983 there were 1,552,463 km of highways. The route-length of railways in 1980 was 35,100 km. Internal air services are highly developed. There are 21,944 miles of navigable inland waterways. During 1982, 9,574 vessels entered Rio de Janeiro and Santos, the two leading ports.

FINANCE

	1987	1988
	Cruzados	
Revenue	1,203,001m	10,519m
Expenditure	1,392,120m	15,511m

In 1989 Brazil's total external public debt stood at U.S.$112,000 million.

TRADE

Principal imports are fuel and lubricants, machinery, chemicals, wheat, metals and metal manufactures. Principal exports are coffee, iron ore, soya, meat, steel and orange juice. In 1987 the Brazilian automobile industry produced 920,300 vehicles. Of these, 339,900 vehicles were exported.

	1987	1988
Total imports	US$26,224m	US$33,784m
Total exports	15,052m	14,688m

Trade with UK

	1988	1989
Imports from UK	£304,735,000	£338,634,000
Exports to UK	742,145,000	817,545,000

CAPITAL.—Brasilia (inaugurated on April 21, 1960). Population (1985 estimate) 1,576,657. Other important centres (1980 Census) are São Paulo (8,490,763); the former capital ψRio de Janeiro (5,094,396); Belo Horizonte (1,774,712); ψRecife (1,204,794); ψSalvador (1,017,591); ψPorto Alegre (1,125,091); ψFortaleza (1,308,859); and Belem (934,330).

CURRENCY.—Cruzeiro (BRC) of 100 centavos.

FLAG.—Green, with yellow lozenge in centre; blue sphere with white band and stars in centre of lozenge.

NATIONAL ANTHEM.—Ouviram do Ipirangas Margens (From peaceful Ypiranga's banks).

NATIONAL DAY.—September 7 (Independence Day).

BRITISH EMBASSY

Setor de Embaixadus Sul, Quadra 801, Conjunto K, 70.408 Brasilia DF
[Brasilia 225–2710]

Ambassador Extraordinary and Plenipotentiary, His Excellency Michael John Newington, CMG (1987).

There are British Consulates-General at *Rio de Janeiro* and *São Paulo*.

British Council Representative, John Lawrence, OBE, SCRN, 708/9-BLF Nos 1/3 (Caixa Postal 6104), 70.740 Brasilia DF. Regional Directors in *Recife, Rio de Janeiro* and *São Paulo*.

BRITISH AND COMMONWEALTH CHAMBER OF COMMERCE IN SÃO PAULO, Rua Barão de Itapetininga 275, 7th Floor, 01042, São Paulo (*Postal Address*, PO Box 1621, 01000 São Paulo) and Rua Real Grandeza 99, 22281 Rio de Janeiro.

BULGARIA
(Narodna Republika Bulgaria)

COUNCIL OF STATE

Head of State, Zhelyu Zhelev, *elected* August 1, 1990.

COUNCIL OF MINISTERS
(as at July 31, 1989)

Chairman (Prime Minister), Georgi Atanasov.
Deputy Chairman, Grigor Stoichkov.
Culture, Science and Education, Georgi Yordanov.
Economy and Planning, Stoyan Ovcharov.
Agriculture and Forests, Georgi Menov.
Foreign Economic Relations, Andrei Lukanov.
Foreign Affairs, Petur Mladenov.

Internal Affairs, Georgi Tanev.
Justice, Mrs. Svetla Daskalova.
National Defence, Gen. Dobri Dzhurov.
Public Health and Social Welfare, Mincho Peychev.
Transport, Trifon Pashov.
Minister, Ambassador to the USSR, Georgi Pankov.
Chairman, Committee on State and People's Control, Georgi Georgiev.

A new government was formed in late September 1990 but no details were available at time of going to press.

EMBASSY OF THE PEOPLE'S REPUBLIC OF BULGARIA
186–188 Queen's Gate, SW7 5HL
[071–584 9400/9433]

Ambassador Extraordinary and Plenipotentiary, new appointment awaited.

The Republic of Bulgaria is bounded on the north by Romania, on the west by Yugoslavia, on the east by the Black Sea, and on the south by Greece and Turkey. The total area is 42,823 sq. miles (110,912 sq. km), with a population of 8,948,388 at the 1985 Census. A 1988 UN estimate gives a figure of 8,995,000. The largest religion of the Bulgarians is the Bulgarian Orthodox Church.

A Principality of Bulgaria was created by the Treaty of Berlin (July 13, 1878) and in 1885 Eastern Roumelia was added to the newly-created principality. In 1908 the country was declared to be an independent kingdom. In 1912–13 a successful war of the Balkan League against Turkey increased the size of the kingdom, but in August 1913, a short campaign against the remaining members of the League reduced the acquired area, and led to the surrender of Southern Dobrudja to Romania. In October 1915, Bulgaria entered the War on the side of the Central Powers by declaring war on Serbia. Involved in the defeats of 1918, Bulgaria made an unconditional surrender to the Allied Powers in September 1918, and in November 1919, signed the Treaty of Neuilly, which ceded to the Allies the Thracian territories (later handed over to Greece) and some territory on the western frontier to Yugoslavia.

Nazi troops entered the country on March 3, 1941, and occupied Black Sea ports, but Bulgaria was not at war with the Soviet Union. On August 26, 1944, the government declared Bulgaria to be neutral in the Russo-German war and sought terms of peace from Great Britain and the United States. The Soviet Union refused to recognize the so-called neutrality and called upon Bulgaria to declare war against Germany, and no satisfactory reply being received on September 5 1944, the USSR declared war on Bulgaria. Bulgaria then asked for an armistice and on September 7 declared war on Germany, hostilities with USSR ending on September 10. The armistice with the Allies was signed in Moscow, October 28, 1944. The Peace Treaty with Bulgaria was signed on February 22, 1947, and came into force on September 15, 1947. It recognized the return of Southern Dobrudja to Bulgaria.

On September 9, 1944 a coup d'état gave power to the Fatherland Front, a coalition of Communists, Agrarians, Social Democrats and officers and intellectuals. In August 1945, the main body of Agrarians and Social Democrats left the Government. On September 8, 1946 a referendum was held, which led to the abolition of the monarchy and the setting up of a Republic.

The post-war political scene was dominated by the Communist Party (BCP), led since 1954 by Todor Zhivkov. After he was forced to resign in November 1989, further leadership changes and reforms culminated, in January 1990, in the National Assembly voting to abolish the BCP's constitutional guarantee of power. Multi-party elections to a 400-seat Grand National Assembly (parliament), due to draw up a new Constitution by the end of 1991, were held in June 1990. The BCP, renamed the Bulgarian Socialist Party in April, emerged as the majority party.

Production.—Until 1939 Bulgaria was a predominantly agricultural country, but has since pursued an elaborate programme of industrialization. About 90 per cent of the country's agriculture has been turned over to co-operatives, and a smaller proportion mechanized. The principal crops are wheat, maize, beet, tomatoes, tobacco, oleaginous seeds, fruit, vegetables and cotton. The livestock includes cattle, sheep, goats, pigs, horses, asses, mules and water buffaloes.

There is now a substantial engineering industry which accounts for about two-thirds of Bulgaria's exports; and considerable production of ferrous and non-ferrous metals. In 1988 production of electricity was 4,500 million kilowatt-hours, of steel 2,875,000 tons and of coal 35,800,000 tons.

There are mineral deposits of varying importance. Bulgaria's heavy industry includes the Kremikovtsi Steel Plant near Sofia and the Lenin steel mill at Pernik, the chemical complex at Devnia, the petrochemical plant at Bourgas and various other chemical and metallurgical works situated around the country. The Soviet-designed nuclear power station at Kozlodui has four reactors, each with a capability of producing 800 million kilowatt-hours.

Defence.—Under the Peace Treaty signed between Bulgaria and the Allies, the Bulgarian Army is limited to 55,000 men, but the peacetime strength of the ground forces is at present estimated to be 100,000.

Education.—Free basic education is compulsory for children from 7 to 15 years inclusive. The Bulgarian educational system was reorganized on Soviet lines in September 1950, providing kindergartens and educational establishments for primary and secondary education including vocational, technical and other specialized schools for secondary age pupils. There are three universities (at Sofia, Plovdiv and Veliko Turnovo) and 21 higher educational establishments.

Language and Literature.—Bulgarian is a Southern Slavonic tongue, closely allied to Serbo-Croat and Russian with local admixtures of modern Greek, Albanian and Turkish words. The alphabet is Cyrillic.

Finance.—Planned public expenditure for 1990 was 25,851 million leva, while the internal budget deficit was expected to reach 1,200 m leva.

TRADE

The principal imports are industrial and agricultural machinery, industrial raw materials and fuels, machine tools, chemicals, dyestuffs, pharmaceuticals, rubber, paper. The principal exports are non-ferrous metals, electric trucks and motors, pumps, ships, accumulators and machine tools, cereals, tobacco, fruit, vegetables, oil seeds, fats, textiles, eggs, chemicals and oils including attar of roses. In 1988, 79 per cent of Bulgaria's foreign trade was within the CMEA, including approximately 57 per cent with the Soviet Union.

Trade with UK

	1988	1989
Imports from UK	£82,156,000	£86,209,000
Exports to UK	28,068,000	34,272,000

CAPITAL.—Sofia, population (1988), 1,136,875, at the foot of the Vitosha Range, the capital and commercial centre is on the main railway line to Istanbul, 338 miles from the Black Sea port of ΨVarna (306,300) and 125 miles from Lom (32,121), on the Danube; ΨBourgas (200,464) is also a Black Sea port.

Other important trading and industrial centres are Plovdiv (364,162), Rousse (190,720), Pleven (136,287), Stara Zagora (158,150), Pernik (97,930), Sliven (109,432), Yambol (97,414), Khaskovo (93,609) and Tolbukhin (112,582).

CURRENCY.—Lev of 100 stotinki.

FLAG.—3 horizontal bands, white, green, red; national emblem on white stripe near hoist.

NATIONAL DAY.—March 3.

BRITISH EMBASSY
Boulevard Marshal Tolbukhin 65–67, Sofia
[Sofia 885361/2]

Ambassador Extraordinary and Plenipotentiary, His Excellency Richard Thomas, CMG (1989).

First Secretaries, M. E. Frost, LVO (*Deputy Head of Mission, Consul*), K. I. Malin (*Political/Economical Press*), Miss C. M. Laidlaw (*Commercial*).

Cultural Attaché and British Council Representative, Peter Lyner.

BURKINA
(République Démocratique Populaire de Burkina Faso)

President of the Popular Front, Head of State, Minister of Defence and Security, Capt. Blaise Compaoré, *assumed office*, October 1987.

COUNCIL OF MINISTERS
(as at May 10, 1990)

Rural Co-operatives, Capt. Laurent Sedgo.
Environment and Tourism, Maurice Dieudonne Bonnane.
Health and Social Action, Kanidoua Naboho.
Information and Culture, Beatrice Damiba.
Foreign Relations, Prosper Vokouma.
Sports, Capt. Theodore Kilmite Hien.
Labour, Social Security and Civil Service, Salif Sampebgo.
Regional Administration, Jean Leonard Compaore.
Finance, Bintou Sanogoh.
Economic Promotion, Thomas Sanon.
Planning and Foreign Aid Relations, Pascal Zagre.
Trade and Supply, Frederic Assomption Korsaga.
Agriculture, Albert Djigma.
Public Works, Comm. Daprou Kambou.
Transport and Communications, Jacques Ouedraogo.
Primary Education and Literacy, Alice Tiendrebeogo.
Secondary and Higher Education, Scientific Research, Mouhoussine Nacro.
Justice, Guardian of the Seals, Sambo Antoine Komi.
Water, Sabane Koanda.
Secretaries of State, Salif Diallo (*at the Presidency*), Tiraogo Celestin Tiendrebeogo (*Finance, responsible for Budget*), Joseph Kabore (*Housing, Town Planning*), Alimata Salembere (*Culture*), Elie Sarre (*Social Action*), Amadou Maurice Guiao (*Livestock*), Aboubacar Yahya Diallo (*Mineral Resources*).
Secretary General of the Government and of the Council of Ministers, Alfred Nombre.

Secretary responsible for Political Affairs of the Executive Committee of the Popular Front, Roch Marc Christian Kabore.

Burkina (formerly Upper Volta) is an inland savanna state in West Africa, situated between 9° and 15°N. and 2°E. and 5°W. with an area of 105,869 sq. miles (274,200 sq. km), and a population of 8,509,000 (UN estimate 1988). It has common boundaries with Mali on the west, Niger and Benin on the east and Togo, Ghana and the Côte d'Ivoire on the south. The largest tribe is the Mossi whose king, the Moro Naba, still wields a certain moral influence.

Burkina was annexed by France in 1896 and between 1932 and 1947 was administered as part of the Colony of the Ivory Coast. It decided on December 11, 1958 to remain an autonomous republic within the French Community; full independence outside the Community was proclaimed on August 5, 1960. The official language is French.

The 1960 constitution provided for a presidential form of government with a single chamber National Assembly, but in January 1966 the Army assumed power. A new constitution allowing for a partial return to civilian rule but with the Army still in effective control was adopted in 1970, but in 1974 this was suspended. Full legislative and presidential elections were held again in 1978. Following a number of military coups, Capt. Blaise Compaoré took power in October 1987, also by coup. The present government, a broad-based coalition (the Popular Front), held a congress in March 1990 which decided to appoint a committee to draft a 'Constitution leading to democratization'. This is to be put to referendum by November 1990, following which legislative and presidential elections are to take place in 1991.

Trade.—The 1988 Budget totalled Franc CFA 90,300 million.

The principal industry is the rearing of cattle and sheep and the chief exports are livestock, groundnuts, millet and sorghum. Small deposits of gold, manganese, copper, bauxite and graphite have been found. Trade in 1987 was valued at imports, CFA 130,527 m, exports, CFA 46,593 m.

Trade with UK

	1988	1989
Imports from UK	£3,732,000	£4,647,000
Exports to UK	546,000	954,000

CAPITAL.—Ouagadougou (400,000). Other principal towns; Bobo-Dioulasso (211,538) and Koudougou (30,000).

CURRENCY.—Franc CFA.

FLAG.—Equal bands of red over green, with a yellow star in centre.

NATIONAL DAY.—August 4.

BRITISH REPRESENTATION

British Ambassador (resident in Abidjan, Côte d'Ivoire).

BURUNDI
(République de Burundi)

President and Minister for National Defence, Major Pierre Buyoya, *elected* Sept. 9, 1987, *sworn in* Oct. 2, 1987.

COUNCIL OF MINISTERS
(as at November 30, 1989)

Prime Minister, Adrien Sibomana.
Foreign Affairs and Co-operation, Cyprien Mbonimpa.
Agriculture and Animal Husbandry, Jumiane Hussein.
Finance, Gerard Niyibigira.
Rural Development and Handicrafts, Gabriel Toyi.
Justice, Evariste Niyonkuru.
Interior, Aloys Kadoyi.
Commerce and Industry, Bonaventure Kidwingira.
Transport, Posts and Telecommunications, Maj. Simon Rusuku.
Public Works and Urban Development, Evariste Simbarakiye.
Energy and Mines, Gilbert Midende.
Public Health, Norbert Ngendabanyikwa.
Civil Service, Didace Rudargi.
Labour and Professional Training, Charles Karikurubu.

Family and Women's Affairs, Pia Ndayiragije.
Social Affairs, Julie Ngiriye.
Information, Frederick Ngenzebuhoro.
Youth, Sport and Culture, Adolphe Nahayo.
Tourism, Land Use and Development, Basile Sindaharaye.
Higher Education and Scientific Research, Nicholas Mayugi.
Primary and Secretary Education, Gamariel Ndaruzaniye.
Secretaries of State, Fridolin Hatungimana (*Economic Co-operation*), Salvator Sahinguvu (*Planning*).

Formerly a Belgian trusteeship under the United Nations, Burundi was proclaimed independent on July 1, 1962. Situated on the east side of Lake Tanganyika, the State has an area of 10,747 sq. miles (27,834 sq. km) and a population (UN estimate 1988) of 5,149,000. The majority of the population are of the Bahutu ethnic group, but power rests in the hands of the minority Batutsi ethnic group.

Burundi became independent as a constitutional monarchy but this was overthrown on November 28, 1966 and the country became a republic. On Nov. 1, 1976, the government of President Micombero was overthrown and a Supreme Revolutionary Council led by Col. Jean-Baptiste Bagaza took power. In 1980 the SRC was replaced by a political bureau and central committee as part of a process of political normalization, which continued with elections to the National Assembly, a 65-member legislature. In September 1987 the government of President Bagaza was overthrown by a Military Committee of National Redemption led by Major Pierre Buyoya.

The chief crop is coffee, representing about 80 per cent of Burundi's export earnings. Cotton is the second most important crop. Mineral, tea, hide and skin exports are also important.

Trade with UK

	1988	1989
Imports from UK	£2,922,000	£2,738,000
Exports to UK	1,807,000	1,974,000

CAPITAL.—Bujumbura (formerly Usumbura), with about 150,000 inhabitants. Kitega (18,000 inhabitants) is the only other sizeable town. Official languages are Kirundi, a Bantu language, and French. Kiswahili is also used.

CURRENCY.—Burundi franc of 100 centimes.

FLAG.—White diagonal cross on green and red quarters, with a circular white panel in the centre.

NATIONAL DAY.—July 1.

British Ambassador (resident in Kinshasa, Zaire).

CAMBODIA

NATIONAL GOVERNMENT OF CAMBODIA
(**formerly Coalition Government of Democratic Kampuchea**)

President, Prince Norodom Sihanouk, *resigned* July 1988 *and again in* Aug. 1989 *after previously resuming the Presidency in* Feb. 1989.
Vice-President responsible for Foreign Affairs, Khieu Samphan.
Prime Minister, Son Sann.

STATE OF CAMBODIA
(**formerly People's Republic of Kampuchea**)

Head of State, Heng Samrin.
Chairman of Council of Ministers and Foreign Minister, Hun Sen.

Area and Population.—Situated between Thailand and the south of Vietnam and extending from the border with Laos on the north to the Gulf of Thailand, Cambodia covers an area of 69,898 sq. miles, (181,035 sq. km). It has a population (UN estimate 1988) of 7,870,000. The climate is tropical monsoon with a rainy season from May to October.

Fifty per cent of the total land area is forest or jungle. Around the Tonlé Sap lake in the centre of the country and along the Mekong river, which traverses the country, there is ample fertile land for the support of the population in times of peace.

History.—Once a powerful kingdom, which, as the Khmer Empire, flourished between the tenth and fourteenth centuries, Cambodia became a French protectorate in 1863 and was granted independence within the French Union as an Associate State in 1949. Full independence was proclaimed on November 9, 1953 and the process was completed when, in January 1955, the Kingdom of Cambodia became financially and economically independent not only of France but also of Laos and Vietnam. For the next fifteen years the political life of the country was dominated by Prince Norodom Sihanouk, first as King, then as Head of Government after he had abdicated in favour of his father and finally (following his father's death in 1960) as Head of State.

On March 18, 1970, during his absence from the country, Prince Sihanouk was deposed as Head of State by a vote of the National Assembly. A Republic was declared on October 9, 1970 and the name of the country changed to the Khmer Republic.

In April 1970 widespread fighting developed between communist insurgents and government forces which gradually developed into a general civil war. In April 1975 Phnom Penh fell to the North Vietnamese-backed Khmer Rouge. Prince Sihanouk returned to Cambodia on September 9, as nominal Head of State. However, a new Constitution was promulgated in 1976 and elections to a People's Representative Assembly were held in March. Prince Sihanouk resigned as Head of State in April, and Khieu Samphan was elected President of the State Presidium. A Government led by Pol Pot, the leader of the Khmer Rouge (Communist) party, was appointed and the state was renamed Democratic Kampuchea. During the years of Khmer Rouge rule thousands of Cambodians died or fled into exile. Relations between the Khmer Rouge regime and their Vietnamese backers deteriorated sharply, and in December 1978 Vietnamese troops invaded Cambodia in support of an uprising. The Cambodian capital, Phnom Penh, fell on January 7, 1979. The following day the Cambodian National United Front for National Salvation established a People's Revolutionary Council, recognized by Vietnam, USSR and by other, chiefly Soviet-aligned, countries. The state was renamed The People's Republic of Kampuchea (PRK).

With strong support from the Vietnamese army the PRK gained control of most of the country, containing the challenge from the resistance guerrilla forces of the Coalition Government of Democratic Kampuchea (CGDK), which was formed in June 1982 by the Khmer Rouge and two non-communist groups. Following the final withdrawal of Vietnam's main fighting units in September 1989, the resistance forces have regained ground inside Cambodia, posing a growing threat to the State of Cambodia (SOC) (the name adopted by the PRK in 1989 in a package of measures aimed at attracting non-communist support). Encouraged by the five permanent members of the UN Security Council and other interested parties, the four Cambodian factions have agreed to the general principles of a peace settlement, including the ending of external military support and the holding of free and fair elections under international supervision, but there are still major differences between the SOC and the National Government of Cambodia (NGC) (the name adopted by the CGDK in February 1990) on the method of implementation.

The NGC continues to occupy Cambodia's seat at the UN.

Economy.—Cambodia has an economy based on agriculture, fishing and forestry, the bulk of its people being rice-growing farmers. In addition to rice, which is the staple crop, the major products are rubber, livestock, maize, timber, pepper, palm sugar, fresh and dried fish, kapok, beans, soya and tobacco. Rice and rubber used to be the main exports though production was brought to a standstill by the hostilities. Following the Khmer Rouge victory, the populations of Phnom Penh and other towns were forcibly evacuated to the country to work on the land, and re-establish the plantations producing such crops as cotton, rubber and bananas. Following the Vietnamese invasion of 1978 the towns were repopulated and commerce revived; currency was reintroduced. Factories, in particular textile mills, iron smelting works and cement works were put back in production.

Trade with UK

	1988	1989
Imports from UK	£322,000	£530,000
Exports to UK	55,000	219,000

Communications.—The country had over 5,000 kilometres of roads, of which nearly half were hardsurfaced and passable in the rainy season, although now in a state of disrepair. There are two railways, one from Phnom Penh to the Thai border; the other from Phnom Penh to Kampot and Kompong Som, but operations and repairs are hindered by the continuing fighting. Phnom Penh is on a river capable of receiving ships of up to 2,500 tons all the year round. The deep water port at Kompong Som on the Gulf of Thailand can receive ships up to 10,000 tons. The port is linked to Phnom Penh by a modern highway.

Religion and Education.—The state religion was Buddhism of the 'Little Vehicle'. The constitution guaranteed religious freedom, but in practice Buddhism was suppressed by the Khmer Rouge. There has been some revival recently and Buddhism has been re-established as the state religion. There were also small Muslim and Christian communities, but many members of them died or fled the country during Khmer Rouge rule. The national language is Khmer. In the years preceding the civil war considerable efforts were devoted to the development of education and new schools, colleges and technical institutes had been established. Until April 1975 there was a Buddhist University in Phnom Penh, and several residential teachers' training colleges were in operation. However, most of the country's educated elite died under the Khmer Rouge regime, which closed all institutions of higher education. The university was re-opened in 1988.

CAPITAL.—Phnom Penh, population 500,000 (1983 estimate).

CURRENCY.—Riel of 100 sen.

FLAG.—(NGC) Horizontal stripes of blue, wide red stripe bearing emblem (Temple of Angkor Wat in white), and blue.

NATIONAL DAY.—(NGC) April 17; (SOC) January 7.

CAMEROON
(République Unie du Cameroun)

President, Head of State, Government and Commander in Chief of the Armed Forces, His Excellency Paul Biya, *acceded* Nov. 6, 1982, *elected* Jan. 14, 1984, *re-elected* April 24, 1988, *sworn in* May 13, 1988.

MINISTRY
(as at June 30, 1990)

At the Presidency, Edouard Akame Mfoumou (*Secretary General*); Michel Meva'a M'Eboutou (*Minister Delegate for Defence*); Prof. Titus Edzoa (*Special Adviser*); Laurent Esso (*Dir. of Civil Cabinet*); Ogork Ebot Ntui (*Special Missions*).
Ministers:
Territorial Administration, Ibrahim Mbombo Njoya.
Women's Affairs and Social Welfare, Aissatou Yaou.
Agriculture, John Niba Ngu.
Industrial and Commercial Development, Joseph Tsanga Abanda.
National Education, Prof. Joseph Mboui.
Animal Husbandry, Fisheries and Animal Industries, Hamadjoda Adjoudji.
Higher Education, Scientific Research, Public Contracts, and Computer Services, Abdoulaye Babale.
Finance, Sadou Hayatou.
Public Service and State Control, Prof. Joseph Owono.
Information and Culture, Henri Bandolo.
Youth and Sports, Dr. Joseph Fofe.
Justice, Adolphe Moudiki.
Lands, Water and Energy, Francis Wainchom Nkwain.
Planning and Territorial Development, Elisabeth Tankeu.
Posts and Telecommunications, Sanda Oumarou.
External Relations, Jacques Roger Booh Booh.
Public Health, Prof. Joseph Mbede.
Public Works and Transport, Paul Tessa.
Labour and Social Welfare, Jean Baptiste Bokam.
Town Planning and Housing, Ferdinand Leopold Oyono.
Tourism, Benjamin Itoe.

EMBASSY OF THE REPUBLIC OF CAMEROON
84 Holland Park, W11 3SB
[071–727 0771]

Ambassador Extraordinary and Plenipotentiary, His Excellency Dr. Gibering Bol-Alima (1987).

The Republic of Cameroon lies on the Gulf of Guinea between Nigeria to the west, Chad and the Central African Republic to the east and Congo and Gabon and Equatorial Guinea to the south. It has an area of 183,569 sq. miles, (475,442 sq. km) and a population of 10,166,000 (UN estimate 1988).
The whole territory was administered by Germany from 1884 to 1916. From 1916 to 1959, the former East Cameroon was administered by France as a League of Nations (later UN) trusteeship. On January 1, 1960 it became independent as the Republic of Cameroon. The Republic was joined on October 1, 1961 by the former British administered trust territory of the Southern Cameroons, after a plebiscite held under United Nations auspices. Cameroon became a Federal Republic with separate East and West Cameroon state governments. Subsequently, after a plebiscite held in May 1972, Cameroon became a United Republic.
Cameroon is the only country in Africa where French and English are both official languages enjoying equal status, and the government's declared long-term objective is to achieve complete bilingualism and biculturalism.
The main economic emphasis is on agricultural development, both through encouraging small-scale peasant agriculture, and through the development of large-scale agro-industrial complexes, with the aim of making the country agriculturally self-sufficient and a major food exporter.
Principal products are cocoa, coffee, bananas, cotton, timber, ground-nuts, aluminium, rubber and palm products. There is an aluminium smelting plant at Edéa with an annual capacity of 50,000 tons. Oil is now also one of Cameroon's principal products with an estimated production of 7·31 m. tonnes during 1989.

TRADE

	1987	1988
	CFA million	
Total imports	526,186	378,726
Total exports	487,849	468,683

Trade with UK

	1988	1989
Imports from UK	£20,472,000	£24,838,000
Exports to UK	16,180,000	11,362,000

CAPITAL.—Yaoundé, population estimate (1986) 653,670. Ψ Douala (1,029,736) is the commercial centre.
CURRENCY.—Franc CFA of 100 centimes.
FLAG.—Vertical stripes of green, red and yellow with single five-pointed yellow star in centre of red stripe.
NATIONAL ANTHEM.—O Cameroun, Berceau de Nos Ancêtres (O Cameroon, cradle of our forefathers).
NATIONAL DAY.—May 20.

BRITISH EMBASSY
Avenue Winston Churchill, BP 547
Yaoundé
[Yaoundé 220545]

Ambassador Extraordinary and Plenipotentiary, His Excellency Martin Reith (1987).
First Secretary, B. Donaldson (*Head of Chancery and Commercial*).
Second Secretary, R. W. Hyde, MBE (*Aid/Vice Consul*).
British Council Representative, Harley Brookes, Immeuble Christo, Rue Charles de Gaulle (BP 818), Yaoundé.

CAPE VERDE
(República de Cabo Verde)

President, Aristides Pereira, *born* 1924, *assumed office,* July 5, 1975, *re-elected,* Jan. 13, 1986.

COUNCIL OF MINISTERS
(as at June 30, 1990)

Prime Minister, Finance, Planning and Co-operation, Gen. Pedro Verona Rodrigues Pires.
Foreign Affairs, Col. Silvino Manuel da Luz.
Transport, Trade and Tourism, Maj. Osvaldo Lopes da Silva.
Armed Forces and Security, Maj. Julio de Carvalho.
Agriculture and Fisheries, Maj. João Pereira Silva.
Local Government and Town Planning, Tito Santos de Oliveira Ramos.
Health, Labour and Social Welfare, Ireneu Gomes.
Industry and Energy, Adão Silva Rocha.
Deputy Minister to the PM and of Co-operation and Planning, Maj. Herculano Adelaide Vieira.
Deputy Minister of Finance, Arnaldo Vasconcellos Franca.
Information, Culture and Sport, David Hopffer Cordeiro Almada.
Education, André Corsino Tolentino.
Justice, Corsino Fortes.
Interior, Cortino Cortes.
Public Works, Adriano de Oliveira Lima.

Cape Verde, off the west coast of Africa, consists of two groups of islands, Windward (Santo Antão, São Vicente, Santa Luzia, São Nicolau, Boa Vista and Sal) and Leeward (Maio, São Tiago, Fogo and Brava) with a total area of 1,557 sq. miles (4,033 sq. km). The population (UN estimate 1988) was 358,000, the majority of whom are Roman Catholic.

The islands, colonized c.1460, achieved independence from Portugal on July 5, 1975 under the nationalist party of Guinea Bissau and Cape Verde. A federation of the islands with Guinea Bissau was planned (till 1879 Guinea-Bissau and the islands were a single administrative unit) but this was dropped following the 1980 coup in Guinea Bissau.

The Republic is a one-party (the PAICV) state with a President elected by the National Assembly. He has a mandate of five years, as do Assembly deputies, who are elected by universal adult suffrage. The introduction of a multi-party state has been agreed in principal. An extraordinary congress of the PAICV and legislative elections are scheduled for late 1990.

The islands have had little rain since 1969, and agriculture is mostly confined to irrigated inland valleys, the chief products being bananas and coffee (for export), maize, sugarcane and nuts. Fish and shellfish are important exports. Salt is obtained on Sal, Boa Vista and Maio; volcanic rock is also mined for export. The main ports are Praia and Mindelo, and there is an international airport on Sal.

Trade with UK

	1988	1989
Imports from UK	£1,812,000	£2,301,000
Exports to UK	132,000	178,000

CAPITAL.—ΨPraia, population (1980) 57,748.

CURRENCY.—Escudo Caboverdiano of 100 centavos.

FLAG.—Horizontal band of yellow over green, with a vertical red band in the hoist charged with a black star over a garland of maize sheaves, two corn cobs and a clam shell.

NATIONAL DAY.—July 5 (Independence Day).

British Ambassador (resident in Dakar, Senegal).

CENTRAL AFRICAN REPUBLIC
(République Centrafricaine)

President and General of the Armed Forces, Gen. André Kolingba, *assumed office* Sept. 1, 1981, *re-elected* Nov. 21, 1986.

COUNCIL OF MINISTERS
(June 5, 1990)

Minister in Charge of the Cabinet Secretariat, Edouard Frank.

Economy, Finance, Planning and International Co-operation, Dieudonné Wazoua.

Defence, Christophe Grelombe.

Social Security and Territorial Administration, Thomas Mapouka.

Foreign Affairs, Laurent Gomina-Pampali.

Justice and Bearer of the Seals, Hugues Dobozendi.

Primary, Secondary and Technical Education, Joseph Mabingui.

Higher Education, Jean-Marie Bassia.

Transport and Civil Aviation, Pierre Gonifei-Gaibon-anou.

Civil Service, Labour, Social Security and Professional Training, Gaston Azibolo.

Public Health and Social Affairs, Genevieve Lombilo.

Rural Development, Casimir Amakpio.

Posts and Telecommunications, Jean Tchombego.

Public Works and Territorial Development, Dieudonne Nana.

Energy, Mines, Geology and Water Resources, Dieudonne Padoundji Yadjoua.

Water, Forests, Fish, Wildlife and Tourism, Raymond Mbitikon.

Trade, Industry and Small and Medium Enterprises, Thimothée Marboua.

Communications, Arts and Culture, Tony Da Sylva.

Secretaries of State, Patrice Endjingboma (*Economy and Finance, in charge of Budget and Debt Management*); Thierry Bingaba (*Planning, Statistics and International Co-operation*); Augustin Mbanda (*Social Security and Territorial Administration*); Octave Cossi Houdegbe (*Energy, Mines, Geology and Water Resources*); Jules Kouale Yaboro (*Foreign Affairs*); Christian Yamale (*for the Cabinet Secretariat*); Antoinette Teguedere (*Social Affairs*).

The Republic lies just north of the Equator between the Cameroon Republic, the Republic of Chad, the southern part of Sudan and Zaire. The Republic has an area of 240,535 sq. miles (622,984 sq. km), and a population (UN estimate 1988) of 2,771,000.

On December 1, 1958 the French colony of Ubanghi Shari elected to remain within the French Community and adopted the title of the Central African Republic. It became fully independent on August 17, 1960. The first President of the Central African Republic, David Dacko, held office from 1960 until January 1, 1966, when he was replaced by the then Col. Bokassa after a coup d'état. On Dec. 4, 1976, President Bokassa proclaimed himself Emperor and a new constitution was introduced, the country being known as the Central African Empire. On Sept. 20, 1979 Emperor Bokassa was deposed by David Dacko in a bloodless coup and the country reverted to a republic. President Dacko surrendered power on September 1, 1981 to army commander Gen. André Kolingba in a bloodless coup. In September 1985 President Kolingba dissolved the Military Committee for National Recovery (CMRN) and appointed a civilian-dominated cabinet. Moves towards democratization have been made and in November 1986, a referendum was held whereby voters approved a new Constitution and the establishment of a one-party state.

Economy.—In an effort to revive an ailing economy, the Government launched a structured adjustment programme in 1986, streamlining the civil service, increasing tax revenues, and reducing price controls. Cotton, diamonds, coffee and timber are the major exports.

Trade with UK

	1988	1989
Imports from UK	£733,000	£1,630,000
Exports to UK	195,000	418,000

CAPITAL.—Bangui, near the border with Zaire, population (1984 estimate) 473,817.

CURRENCY.—Franc CFA of 100 centimes.

FLAG.—Four horizontal stripes, blue, white, green, yellow, crossed by central vertical red stripe with a yellow five-pointed star in top left-hand corner.

NATIONAL DAY.—December 1.

British Ambassador, (resident in Yaoundé, Cameroon).

CHAD REPUBLIC
(Republique du Tchad)

Head of State, Hissène Habré, *took office* June 1982.

COUNCIL OF MINISTERS
(as at June 30, 1990)

President and Minister of Defence, Veterans and War Victims, Hissène Habré.

Minister of State, Djidingar Dono Ngardoum.

Foreign Affairs, Acheikh Ibn Oumar.

Territorial Administration, Djime Toga.

Justice, Wadal Abdelkader Kamougue.

National Education, Mahamat Senoussir.
Finance and Data Processing, Mbailim Bana Ngarnayal.
Transport and Civil Aviation, Djibril Negue Djogo.
Civil Service, Oudalbaye Naham.
Livestock, Animal Resources and Rural Hydraulics, Mahamat Nour Mallaye.
Agriculture, Gouara Lassou.
Mines, Petroleum and Energy, Mahamat Senoussi Khatir.
Public Health, Alphonse Kotiga Guerina.
Public Works, Abdoulaye Douto.
Social Affairs and Women's Advancement, Ruth Yeneko Romba.
Labour and Employment, Capt. Routouang Yoma Galom.
Food, Security and Afflicted Groups, Seid Bauche.
Post and Telecommunications, Kassire Delwa Koumakoye.
Planning and Co-operation, Ibn Omar Mahqmat.
Culture, Youth and Sport, Djibrine Grinky.
Trade and Industry, Moussa Raouiengar.
Presidential Adviser, Ouangmoutching Homsala.
Information and Civil Orientation, Adoum Moussa Seif.
Higher Education and Scientific Research, Youssouf Mbodou Mbami.
National Education, Assilek Hazlata.
Territorial Development, Town Planning and Housing, Blial Soubiane.
Minister Delegate to the Presidency, Inspector General and Comptroller of State, Korom Ahmed.

Situated in north-central Africa, the Chad Republic extends from 23° N. latitude to 7° N. latitude and is flanked by the Republics of Niger and Cameroon on the west, by Libya on the north, by the Sudan on the east and by the Central African Republic on the south. It has an area of 495,755 sq. miles (1,284,000 sq. km) and a population (UN estimate 1988) of 5,401,000.

Chad became a member state of the French Community on November 28, 1958, and was proclaimed fully independent on August 11, 1960. On April 14, 1962, a new Constitution was adopted involving a presidential-type regime. This was suspended on April 13, 1975 when President Tombalbaye was killed in a military coup. The country was run by a Supreme Military Council, under General Felix Malloum until his overthrow in February 1979. A Transitional Government of National Unity, headed by Goukouni Oueddei, was replaced in June 1982 by the government of Hissène Habre. A ceasefire between Chad and Libya was agreed in Sept. 1987. In May 1988, Libya formally recognized the government of Habré and offered to help in the reconstruction of northern Chad. The war was formally ended on Oct. 3, 1988.

About 90 per cent of the workforce is occupied in agriculture, fishing and forestry. There is an oilfield in Kanem and salt is mined around Lake Chad, but the most important activities are cotton growing (mostly in the south) and animal husbandry (in central areas). Raw cotton and meat are the main exports.

Trade with UK

	1988	1989
Imports from UK	£639,000	£3,463,000
Exports to UK	1,764,000	822,000

CAPITAL.—Ndjaména (formerly known as Fort Lamy) south of Lake Chad (402,000).
CURRENCY.—Franc CFA of 100 centimes.
FLAG.—Vertical stripes, blue, yellow and red.
NATIONAL DAY.— April 13.

British Ambassador (resident in London).

CHILE
(República de Chile)

President of the Republic, Patricio Aylwin Azócar, assumed office March 11, 1990.

CABINET
(as at July 31, 1990)

Interior, Enrique Krauss.
Foreign Affairs, Enrique Silva Cimma.
Defence, Patricio Rojas.
Trade and Industry, Carlos Ominami.
Finance, Alejandro Foxley.
Education, Ricardo Lagos.
Justice, Francisco Cumplido.
Public Works, Carlos Hurtado.
Agriculture, Juan Agustin Figueroa.
National Properties, Luis Alvarado.
Labour, Rene Cortazar.
Public Health, Jorge Jimenez.
Mining, Juan Hamilton.
Housing, Alberto Etchegaray.
Transport, German Correa.
General Secretary of Government, Enrique Correa.
General Secretary of Presidency, Edgardo Boeninger.
Central Planning, Sergio Molina.
National Commission for Energy, Jaime Toha.
Corporation for Promotion of Production (CORFO), Rene Abeliuk.

EMBASSY OF CHILE
12 Devonshire Street, W1N 2DS
[071–580 6392/7]

Ambassador Extraordinary and Plenipotentiary, His Excellency German Riesco (1990).

A state of South America lying between the Andes and the shores of the South Pacific, Chile extends coastwise from just north of Arica to Cape Horn south, between lat. 17° 15′ and 55° 59′ S. and long. 66° 30′ and 75° 48′ W. Extreme length of the country is about 2,800 miles, with an average breadth, north of 41°, of 100 miles. The great chain of the Andes runs along its eastern limit, with a general elevation of 5,000 to 15,000 feet above sea level; but numerous summits attain a greater height. The chain lowers considerably towards its southern extremity. The Andes form a boundary with Argentina, and at the head of the pass where the international road from Chile to Argentina crosses the frontier, has been erected a statue of Christ the Redeemer, 26 feet high, made of bronze from old cannon, to commemorate the peaceful settlement of a boundary dispute in 1902. There are no rivers of great size, and none of them is of much service as a navigable highway. In the north the country is arid. The total area of the Republic is 292,258 sq. miles (756,945 sq. km), with a population (UN estimate 1988) of 12,748,000.

Among the island possessions of Chile are the Juan Fernandez group (three islands) about 360 miles distant from Valparaiso. One of these islands is the reputed scene of Alexander Selkirk's (Robinson Crusoe) shipwreck. Easter Island (27° 8′ S. and 109° 28′ W.), about 2,000 miles distant in the South Pacific Ocean, contains stone platforms and hundreds of stone figures, the origin of which has not yet been determined. The area of the island is about 45 sq. miles (116·5 sq. km).

Chile is divided into 12 regions and the Metropolitan Area. The disputed boundary with Argentina in the Beagle Channel was settled by a treaty ratified in May 1985.

The Chilean population has four main sources: indigenous Araucanian Indians, Fuegians, and Changos; Spanish settlers and their descendants; mixed Spanish Indians; and European immigrants. Only the few remaining indigenous Indians and some originally Bolivian Indians in the north are racially separate. Following extensive intermarriage there is no effective distinction among the remainder.

Government.—Chile was discovered by Spanish adventurers in the 16th century and remained under Spanish rule until 1810, when a revolutionary war, culminating in the Battle of Maipu (April 5, 1818), achieved the independence of the nation.

At a general election held in September 1970, the Marxist candidate Dr. Allende was elected President by a narrow margin. After severe industrial unrest and widespread violent incidents, Allende was overthrown on September 11, 1973 in a coup carried out by leaders of the Armed Forces and National Police.

After a national plebiscite, the Constitution of 1925 was replaced early in 1981 and General Pinochet was sworn in as President, to serve until 1989. Pinochet was defeated in a plebiscite of October 5, 1988 regarding his term of office being extended for a further eight years. He resisted calls for his resignation. Another plebiscite on July 30, 1989 was held on changes to the 1980 Constitution. Presidential and Congressional elections were held in December 1989. Patricio Aylwin was elected President of the Republic for four years, thus beginning a gradual transition to full democracy.

Executive power is held by the President, legislative power is exercised by a Parliament which comprises an Upper Chamber of 47 Senators and a Lower Chamber of 120 Deputies.

Production.—Cereals, legumes, sugar beet, vegetables, fruit, tobacco, hemp and vines are grown extensively (especially in the central zone) and livestock accounts for nearly 40 per cent of agricultural production. Sheep farming predominates in the extreme south. There are large timber tracts in the central and southern zones of Chile, some types of which are exported, along with wood derivatives such as cellulose and pulp. Industrial-scale fishing, which exceeded 6·5 million tonnes in 1989, makes Chile the fifth largest nation in terms of catch. The principal end product is fish meal.

The mineral wealth is considerable, the country being particularly rich in copper-ore, iron-ore and nitrates. Chile also produces iodine, manganese ore, coal, mercury, molybdenum, zinc, lead and a small quantity of gold. Uranium is also said to have been discovered in small quantities. The rainless north is the scene of the only commercial production of nitrate of soda (Chile saltpetre) from natural resources in the world. The country has also large deposits of high grade sulphur, but mostly around high extinct volcanoes in the Andes Cordillera, difficult of access. Oil was struck in Magallanes (Tierra del Fuego) in 1945, and oil and natural gas are produced in the Magallanes area from on- and off-shore wells. This domestic production, now declining, covers approximately 30 per cent of total oil requirement, and imported crude oil is refined at Concon and San Vicente in the central part of the country. There is a steel plant at Huachipato, near Concepción.

Production figures for 1989 were:

Coal (tonnes)	2,100,419
Copper (tonnes)	1,620,910
Crude oil (cu. metres)	1,282,200
Natural gas (cu. metres)	4,236,100,000
Steel ingots (tonnes)	760,100

Industry is based on the processing of mineral, forestry, fish and agricultural products, and the manufacture of consumer goods.

Communications.—Chilean ships have a virtual monopoly in the coastwide trade, though, with the improvement of the roads, an increasing share of internal transportation is moving by road and rail.

The Chilean mercantile marine numbers 77 vessels (of over 100 tons gross) with a total deadweight tonnage of 1,016,282 (1989).

There are 6,575 miles of railway track. A metre-gauge line (the Longitudinál) runs from La Calera, just north of Santiago, to Iquique; however, road transport has caused considerable reduction in rail traffic along this route. The wide gauge railway runs from Valparaiso through La Calera, 60 miles inland, and after passing through Santiago ends at Puerto Montt.

With the completion of a section of 435 miles from Corumba, Brazil, to Santa Cruz, Bolivia, the Trans-Continental Line will link the Chilean Pacific port of Arica with Rio de Janeiro on the Atlantic. Another line from Antofagasta to Salta (Argentina) was opened in 1948.

Chile is served by over 20 international airlines. Domestic traffic is carried by Linea Aerea Nacional (LAN) and LADECO, which also operate internationally, and smaller regional carriers.

Chile's road system is about 65,000 kilometres in length.

Defence.—Military service is compulsory, but not all those who are liable are required. Recruitment for the Navy is mostly voluntary, but there are some conscripts. The Navy consists of 1 cruiser, 10 destroyers, frigates and escorts, 6 patrol vessels and FPBs and 4 submarines. There is a support force of transports, tankers, 1 submarine depot ship and ancillary small craft. The strength of the Navy is 28,000 (3,000 conscripts) including men of the Marine Force. The Army's total strength is 53,000, which includes 3,000 officers and 30,000 conscripts (2 years). In addition there is a police force of Carabineros of 28,000 officers and men. The Air Force total strength is 15,000 with a strength of 120 aircraft.

Education.—Elementary education is free, and has been compulsory since 1920. There are eight universities (three in Santiago, two in Valparaiso, one each in Antofagasta, Concepción and Valdivia). The religion is Roman Catholic.

Language and Literature.—Spanish is the language of the country, with admixtures of local words of Indian origin. Recent efforts have reduced illiteracy and have thus afforded access to the literature of Spain, to supplement the vigorous national output. The Nobel Prize for Literature was awarded in 1945 to Señorita Gabriela Mistral, for Chilean verse and prose, and in 1971 to the poet Pablo Neruda. There are over 100 newspapers and a large number of periodicals.

FINANCE

	1987	1988
Total revenue	US$8,469·8 m	US$8,967·1 m
Total expenditure	8,421·6 m	9,452·4 m

Foreign debt at December 31, 1989 was US$17,518 million, including Central Bank obligations with the IMF of US$1,268 million.

TRADE

	1988	1989
Total imports	US$4,924·0 m	US$6,734·2 m
Total exports	7,048·3 m	8,190·4 m

Trade with UK

	1988	1989
Imports from UK	£80,901,000	£96,003,000
Exports to UK	179,628,000	193,280,000

The principal exports are metallic and non-metallic minerals (copper represented 50 per cent of total export earnings in 1989), sawn timber, cellulose and other wood derivatives, some metal products, fish products, vegetables, fruit and wool. The principal imports are sugar and other food products, industrial raw materials, machinery, equipment and spares, oil fuels, lubricants and transportation equipment.

CAPITAL.—Santiago, population 4,132,293 (Greater Santiago). Other large towns are:—ΨValparaiso (500,000), Concepción (170,000), Temuco (110,000), Ψ Antofagasta (110,000), Chillán (79,461), ΨTalcahuano (75,643), Talca (75,354); ΨValdivia (70,000), ΨIquique (50,000), ΨPunta Arenas (50,000). Punta Arenas on the Straits of Magellan, is the southernmost city in the world.

CURRENCY.—Chilean peso of 100 centavos.

FLAG.—Two horizontal bands, white, red; in top sixth a white star on blue square, next staff.

NATIONAL ANTHEM.—Canción Nacional de Chile.

NATIONAL DAY.—September 18 (National Anniversary).

BRITISH EMBASSY

Avenida La Concepción 177, Santiago 9
(Casilla 72-D)
[Santiago 2239166]

Ambassador Extraordinary and Plenipotentiary, His Excellency Richard A. Nielson, CMG, LVO (1990).

Counsellor, Head of Chancery and Consul-General, R. Lavers.

Defence Attaché, Capt. J. Finnigan, RN.

Air Attaché, Gp. Capt. B. Hall.

BRITISH CONSULAR OFFICES

There are British Consular Offices at *Arica, Concepción, Santiago, Punta Arenas, Valparaiso.*

BRITISH COUNCIL

Cultural Attaché and British Council Representative, W. Campbell, Eliodoro Yañez 832, Santiago, Casilla 15-T Tajamar. The Council supplies books to the libraries of the Instituto Chileno-Britanico in *Santiago, Viña del Mar/Valparaiso* and *Concepción.*

BRITISH-CHILEAN CHAMBER OF COMMERCE

Av. Suecia 155-C, Casilla 536, Santiago

CHINA
(Zhonghua Renmin Gongheguo—
The People's Republic of China)

President of the People's Republic of China, Yang Shangkun, *elected* April 1988.

Vice President, Wang Zhen.

Chairman of the Standing Committee of the Seventh National People's Congress, Wan Li.

Chairman of the Central Military Commission, Jiang Zemin.

STATE COUNCIL
(as at July 15, 1990)

Premier, Li Peng.

Vice-Premiers, Yao Yilin; Tian Jiyun; Wu Xueqian.

State Councillors, Li Tieying; Qin Jiwei; Wang Bingqian; Song Jian; Wang Fang; Zou Jiahua; Li Guixian; Chen Xitong; Chen Junsheng.

Ministers:

Aeronautics and Astronautics Industry, Lin Zongtang.

Agriculture, Liu Zhongyi.

Chemical Industry, Gu Xiulian.

Civil Affairs, Cui Naifu.

Commerce, Hu Ping.

Communications, Qian Yongchang.

Construction, Lin Hanxiong.

Culture, He Jingzhi.

Energy Resources, Huang Yicheng.

Finance, Wang Bingqian.

Foreign Affairs, Qian Qichen.

Foreign Economic Relations and Trade, Zheng Tuobin.

Forestry, Gao Dezhan.

Geology and Mineral Resources, Zhu Xun.

Justice, Cai Cheng.

Labour, Ruan Chongwu.

Light Industry, Zeng Xianlin.

Machine Building and Electronics Industry, He Guangyuan.

Materials, Liu Suinian.

Metallurgical Industry, Qi Yuanjing.

National Defence, Qin Jiwei.

Personnel, Zhao Dongwan.

Posts and Telecommunications, Yang Taifang.

Public Health, Chen Minzhang.

Public Security, Wang Fang.

Radio, Film and Television, Ai Zhisheng.

Railways, Li Senmao.

State Security, Jia Chunwang.

Supervision, Wei Jianxing.

Textile Industry, Wu Wenying.

Water Resources, Yang Zhenhuai.

MINISTERS IN CHARGE OF STATE COMMISSIONS

Education, Li Tieying.

Family Planning, Peng Peiyun.

Nationalities Affairs, Ismail Amat.

Physical Culture and Sports, Wu Shaozu.

Planning, Zou Jiahua.

Restructuring Economy, Li Peng.

Science, Technology and Industry for National Defence, Ding Henggao.

Science and Technology, Song Jian.

Auditor General, Lu Peijian.

Secretary General, Luo Gan.

President of the People's Bank of China, Li Guixian.

THE CHINESE COMMUNIST PARTY

General Secretary, Jiang Zemin.

The Politburo Standing Committee, Jiang Zemin; Li Peng; Qiao Shi; Yao Yilin; Li Ruihuan; Song Ping.

The Politburo of the Central Committee, Wan Li; Tian Jiyun; Qiao Shi; Jiang Zemin; Li Tieying; Li Ruihuan; Li Ximing; Yang Rudai; Yang Shangkun; Wu Xueqian; Song Ping; Hu Qili; Yao Yilin; Qin Jiwei; Li Peng (*full members*); Ding Guangen (*alternate member*).

The Secretariat of the Central Committee, Li Ruihuan; Ding Guan'Gen; Qiao Shi; Yang Baibing (*full members*); Wen Jiabao (*alternate member*).

The Advisory Commission, Chen Yun (*Chairman*); Bo Yibo; Song Renqiong (*Vice Chairmen*).

The Discipline Inspection Commission, Secretary, Qiao Shi; *Deputy Secretaries*, Chen Zuolin; Li Zhengting; Xiao Hongda.

Membership, 48,000,000 (1989).

EMBASSY OF THE PEOPLE'S REPUBLIC OF CHINA

49–51 Portland Place, W1N 3AH
[071–636 9375]

Ambassador Extraordinary and Plenipotentiary, His Excellency Ji Chaozhu (1987).

Area and Population.—The area of China is 3,705,408 sq. miles, (9,596,961 sq. km). A nationwide census (the third) was held in July 1982, which recorded a total population of 1,008,175,288. According to the PRC State Statistical Bureau, the population at the beginning of 1989 was 1,160,000,000. Results of a new census will be published in 1991.

China is anxious to control the growth of the population and has introduced stringent policies intended to result in a population of 1,200 million by the year 2000. About 6 per cent of the population belong to around 55 ethnic minorities. Among the largest are the Zhuang of Guangxi, the Uygurs of Xinjiang, the Tibetans and the Mongols.

THE PROVINCES OF CHINA
(1988 estimated population figures)

Anhui	53,770,000
Beijing	10,810,000
Fujian	28,450,000
Gansu	21,360,000
Guangdong	59,280,000
Guangxi Zhuang Autonomous Region	40,880,000
Guizhou	31,270,000
Hainan	6,280,000
Hebei	57,950,000
Heilongjiang	34,660,000
Henan	80,940,000
Hubei	51,850,000
Hunan	58,900,000
Jiangsu	64,380,000
Jiangxi	36,090,000
Jilin	23,730,000
Liaoning	38,200,000
Nei Monggol Autonomous Region	20,940,000
Ningxia Hui Autonomous Region	4,450,000
Qinghai	4,340,000
Shaanxi	31,350,000
Shandong	80,610,000
Shanghai	12,620,000
Shanxi	27,550,000
Sichuan	105,760,000
Tianjin	8,430,000
Tibet Autonomous Region	2,120,000
Xinjiang Uygur Autonomous Region	14,260,000
Yunnan	35,940,000
Zhejiang	41,700,000
Armed Forces	4,238,210

Government.—On October 10, 1911, the party of reform forced the Imperial dynasty to a 'voluntary' abdication, and a Republic was proclaimed at Wuchang.

On September 30, 1949 the Chinese People's Political Consultative Conference (CPPCC) met in Beijing (Peking) and appointed the National People's Government Council under the Chairmanship of Mao Zedong (Mao Tse-tung). On October 1, Mao proclaimed the inauguration of the Chinese People's Republic.

The regime was recognized by all the Communist bloc countries in quick succession, and soon after by the Asian countries of the Commonwealth, the United Kingdom and by a number of other countries. Others, led by the United States, continued to recognize the Chiang Kai-shek regime of Taiwan as the rightful Government of China. In 1971 the People's Republic won acceptance into the United Nations on the expulsion of Taiwan. Since then many more countries have accorded recognition.

A new Constitution was adopted in December 1982, under which the National People's Congress is the highest organ of state power. It is elected for a term of five years and is supposed to hold one session a year. It is empowered to amend the Constitution, make laws, select the President and Vice-President and other leading officials of the state, approve the national economic plan, the state budget and the final state accounts, and to decide on questions of war and peace. The State Council is the highest organ of the state administration. It is composed of the Premier, the Vice Premiers, the State Councillors, heads of Ministries and Commissions, the Auditor General and the Secretary General. Command over the armed forces is vested in the Central Military Commission, of which Jiang Zemin is the Chairman.

Deputies to congresses at the primary level are 'directly elected' by the voters 'through a secret ballot after democratic consultation'. This is now extended to county level. These Congresses elect the Deputies to the Congress at the next higher level.

Deputies to the National People's Congress are elected by the People's Congresses of the provinces, autonomous regions and municipalities directly under the Central Government, and by the armed forces.

Local government is conducted through People's Governments at provincial, municipal and county levels. Autonomous regions, prefectures and counties exist for national minorities and are described as self-governing. The system prevailing is that found elsewhere, i.e. People's Congresses and People's Governments. Beijing, Shanghai and Tianjin continue to come directly under the central government.

Following the deaths of Mao Zedong and Zhou Enlai in 1976, the disgraced Vice-Premier Deng Xiaoping was recalled. At the 11th Party Congress in 1977 Deng was elected Vice-Chairman and has since become the dominant force within the Party by eliminating leftist influence, rehabilitating fallen leaders and adjusting Maoist policies to permit economic liberalization. Deng's policies were reaffirmed at the 12th Congress in 1982. The Congress also elected a new Party leadership dominated by Deng and his supporters. The post of Chairman of the Party was abolished. The Party leader now holds the post of General Secretary. The 13th Party Congress in 1987 reaffirmed open-door policies. Most of the old revolutionary generation were removed, in elections, from the top posts.

Student-led pro-democracy demonstrations throughout April and May ended on June 3–4, 1989 when the People's Liberation Army took control of Beijing, killing thousands of protesters.

Armed Forces.—All three military arms in China are parts of the People's Liberation Army (PLA) The size of this body has not been formally given, but it is estimated that China has approximately 3·5 million men under arms, with a further 12 million (or perhaps many more) reserves who take part in militia activities. In June 1985 a planned reduction of over 1 million in the course of a year was officially announced. In 1955 compulsory military service was introduced for all men between the ages of 18 and 40. This service was on a selective basis. The present length of service for those conscripted is three years in the Army, four years in the Air Force and five years in the Navy. The rank structure, abolished in 1965, was reinstated in 1988.

Religion.—The indigenous religions of China are Confucianism (which includes ancestor worship), Taoism (originally a philosophy rather than a religion) and, since its introduction in the first century of the Christian era, Buddhism. There are also Chinese Muslims (officially estimated at about 12 million) and Christians (unofficially estimated at about 50 million). Religious freedoms, severely curtailed during the Cultural Revolution, are reviving slightly under more liberal policies. Ethnic unrest in Buddhist Tibet and Muslim Xinjiang could threaten such liberalization.

Education.—The Cultural Revolution caused considerable disruption to the educational system and since 1976 attempts have been made to raise academic standards. Primary education now lasts five years, and enrolment (1988) was 143,903,000 including kindergarten. Secondary education lasts five years (three years in junior middle school and two years in senior middle school). There were 47,600,000 middle school pupils in 1988. There are 220 million illiterates; efforts are being made to expand secondary education, particularly in the rural areas. Particular attention is being paid to higher education where there are over 1,000 universities, colleges and institutes with an enrolment (1988) of 2 million students. In May 1985 the Central Committee of the Party announced the abolition of free higher education except for teacher training, and the aim of providing all children with junior secondary education within 10 years.

Language and Literature.—The Chinese language has many dialects, notably Cantonese, Hakka, Amoy, Foochow, Changsha, Nanchang, Wu (Shanghai) and the northern dialect. The Common Speech or *Putonghua* (often referred to as Mandarin) which is being taught throughout the country is based on the northern dialect. The Communists have promoted it as the national language and made intensive efforts to propagate it throughout the country. Since the most important aspect of this policy is the use of the spoken language in writing, the old literary style and ideographic form of writing has fallen into disuse.

In 1956, after some 4 years of study, the Government decided to introduce 230 simplified characters with a view to making reading and writing easier. The list was enlarged and there are now over 2,000 simplified characters in use. In January 1956 all Chinese newspapers and most books began to appear with the characters printed horizontally from left to right, instead of vertically reading from right to left, as previously.

In February 1958 the National People's Congress adopted a system of romanization, known as pinyin, using 25 of the letters of the Latin alphabet (not v). This has been used within the country largely for assisting schoolchildren and others to learn the pronunciation of characters in Putonghua, and is now used for Chinese names in foreign-language publications.

Chinese literature is one of the richest in the world. Paper has been employed for writing and printing for nearly 2,000 years. The Confucian classics which formed the basis of the traditional Chinese culture date from the Warring States period (4th–3rd centuries BC) as do the earliest texts of the rival tradition, Taoism. Histories, philosophical and scientific works, poetry, literary and art criticism, novels and romances survive from most periods. Many have been translated into English. In the past all this considerable literature was available only to a very small class of literati, but with the spread of literacy in the 20th century, a process which has received enormous impetus since the Communists took over in 1950, the old traditional literature has been largely superseded by modern works of a popular kind and by the classics of Marxism and modern developments from them.

The most important among the newspapers and magazines are the *People's Daily* and the twice-monthly *Qiushi*, which replaced *Red Flag* as the CCP's mouthpiece in August 1989.

Production and Industry.—China is essentially an agricultural and pastoral country: peasants constitute about 80 per cent of the population. People's communes gave way to townships as the basic level of State administration in rural districts under the 1982 Constitution.

New agricultural policies, designed to give greater incentives to the rural population, have meant that the responsibility for agricultural production has been devolved down to individual households, whereas previously work was generally assigned on a collective basis.

Wheat, barley, maize, millet and other cereals, with peas and beans, are grown in the northern provinces, and rice and sugar in the south. Rice is the staple food of the inhabitants. Cotton (mostly in valleys of the Yangtze and Yellow Rivers), tea (in the west and south), with hemp, jute and flax, are the most important crops.

Livestock is raised in large numbers. Silkworm culture is one of the oldest industries. Cottons, woollens and silks are manufactured in large quantities. The mineral wealth of the country is great. Coal, iron ore, tin, antimony, wolfram, bismuth and molybdenum are abundant. Oil is produced in several northern provinces, particularly in Heilongjiang and

Shandong, and off-shore deposits are being sought in co-operation with Western and Japanese companies.

The Chinese State Statistical Bureau issues production figures annually. The following are of note for 1989:

Grain (tons)	407,450,000
Pork, beef, mutton (tons)	23,280,000
Tea (tons)	540,000
Cotton (tons)	3,790,000
Timber (cu. metres)	61,000,000
Crude oil (tons)	137,000,000
Steel (tons)	61,240,000
Electric power (kWh)	582 billion
Machine tools	165,300
Motor vehicles	573,700

The State Statistical Bureau valued the national income for 1989 at Yuan 1,300 billion, an increase of 3·7 per cent over 1988. The Gross National Product in 1989 was Yuan 1,567·7 billion, a 3·9 per cent increase over 1988. The total value of agricultural output rose by 3·3 per cent over the 1988 figure to Yuan 655 billion. The total value of industrial output rose by 8·3 per cent to Yuan 2,188 billion in 1989.

In 1982 China set itself the aim of quadrupling the 1980 gross agricultural and industrial output value by the year 2000. The focus of its reform programme was switched to industry in 1984. Wide-ranging reforms have been introduced to make the industrial sector more efficient by narrowing the scope of central planning and broadening enterprise decision-making, material incentives and the role of the market.

Foreign trade and external economic relations have expanded quickly since the open-door policy, adopted in the late 1970s. The principal articles of export are animals and animal products, oil, textiles, ores, metals, tea and manufactured goods. The principal imports are motor vehicles, machinery, chemical fertilizer plants, aircraft, books, paper and paper-making materials, chemicals, metals and ores, and dyes.

Trade with UK

	1988	1989
Imports from UK	£411,563,000	£417,911,000
Exports to UK	443,698,000	530,720,000

Communications.—Of the total area of China over half consists of tableland and mountainous areas where communications and travel are generally difficult. The country has more than 52,000 kilometres of railway trunk and branch lines and some 995,600 kilometres of highway (1988). In addition, internal civil aviation has been developed, with routes now totalling more than 373,800 kilometres. As a result the communications network now covers most of the country.

In the past where roads did not exist the principal means of communication east to west was provided by the rivers, the most important of which are the Yangtze (Changjiang) (3,400 miles long), the Yellow River (Huanghe) (2,600 miles long) and the West River (Xihe) (1,650 miles). These, together with the network of canals connecting them are still much used, but their overall importance is less than it was. Coastal port facilities are being improved and the merchant fleet expanded. In the past 10 years great progress has been made in developing postal services and telecommunications. It is claimed that 95 per cent of all rural townships are on the telephone and that postal routes reach practically every production brigade headquarters.

CAPITAL.—Beijing (Peking), population (1988) 10,810,000.

Population of major cities in 1988:

ΨShanghai	12,620,000	Harbin	2,930,000
Tianjin	5,620,000	Chengdu	2,740,000
Shenyang	4,440,000	Xian	2,650,000
Wuhan	3,640,000	Nanjing	2,433,000
Guangzhou		Taiyuan	2,010,000
(Canton)	3,490,000	Kunming	1,480,000
Chongqing	2,750,000	Lanzhou	1,450,000

CURRENCY.—The currency is called Renminbi (RMB). The unit of currency is the yuan of 10 jiao or 100 fen.

FLAG.—Red, with large gold five-point star and four small gold stars in crescent, all in upper quarter next staff.

NATIONAL ANTHEM.—March of the Volunteers.

NATIONAL DAY.—October 1 (Founding of People's Republic).

BRITISH EMBASSY
11 Guang Hua Lu,
Jian Guo Men Wai, Beijing
[Beijing 521961/5]

Ambassador, His Excellency Sir Alan Ewen Donald, KCMG (1988).

Counsellors, D. Coates; J. K. Chapman (*Commercial*); D. Marler, OBE (*Cultural, and British Council Representative*).

Defence, Military and Air Attaché, Col. C. A. Lees.

First Secretaries, Dr. J. E. Hoare (*Head of Chancery and Consul General*); G. R. Duff (*Administration and Consul*); P. Davies (*Consul*); P. Clark (*Chancery*); S. Prince (*Commercial*); C. O. Piggott (*Chancery*); S. S. Calder (*Energy*); I. A. Seaton (*Cultural ELO*); Dr. J. P. Eyres (*Cultural/Science*).

There is also a Consulate-General in *Shanghai*.

TIBET

Tibet is a plateau seldom lower than 10,000 feet, which forms the northern frontier of India (boundary imperfectly demarcated), from Kashmir to Burma, but is separated therefrom by the Himalayas. The area is estimated at 463,000 square miles with a population of 2,120,000 in 1988.

From 1911 to 1950, Tibet was virtually an independent country though its status was never officially so recognized. In October 1950, Chinese Communist forces invaded Eastern Tibet. On May 23, 1951 an agreement was reached whereby the Chinese army was allowed entry into Tibet. A Communist military and administrative headquarters was set up. In 1954 the Government of India recognized that Tibet was an integral part of China, in return for the right to maintain trade and consular representation there.

A series of revolts against Chinese rule over several years culminated on March 17, 1959 in a rising in Lhasa. Heavy fighting continued for several days before the rebellion was suppressed by Chinese troops and military rule imposed. The Dalai Lama fled to India where he and his followers were granted political asylum. On March 28, 1959 the Chinese Premier issued an order dissolving the Tibetan Government. In its place the 16-member Preparatory Committee for the Tibetan Autonomous Region, originally set up in 1955 with the Dalai Lama as Chairman, was to administer Tibet under the State Council. The Preparatory Committee was to have the Panchen Lama as Acting Chairman and also to include 4 Chinese Officials. Elections were held to choose local People's Congresses in Tibet, thus indicating that the government organization there no longer differed significantly from that of any ordinary province in China.

In December 1964 the Dalai Lama was declared to be a traitor, and both he and the Panchen Lama were dismissed. The position of Acting Chairman of the Preparatory Committee was assumed by Ngapoi Ngawang Jigmi, who had long been the most prominent secular figure in Tibet. This move marked the end of the period of co-operation by the Chinese Government with the traditional religious authorities, and the eclipse of the latter. The Preparatory Committee completed its work with the setting up of Tibet as an Autonomous Region of China on Sept. 9, 1965. The Panchen Lama was rehabilitated as an official of the CPPCC, but died in 1989. The Chinese have invited the Dalai Lama to return from exile, but suggested negotiations between the Chinese and the Dalai Lama have failed to materialize. Sporadic outbursts of unrest continue in Tibet.

TAIWAN (REPUBLIC OF CHINA)
(Chung-hua Min-kuo)

President, Lee Teng-hui, *elected*, Jan. 13, 1988, re-elected May 20, 1990.

Vice-President, Li Yuan-zu.

Premier, Hau Pei-tsun.

An island of some 13,800 sq. miles, (35,742 sq. km), in the China Sea, Taiwan, formerly Formosa, lies 90 miles east of the Chinese mainland in latitude 21° 45′N.–25° 56′N. The population (19,954,397 in 1988), is almost entirely Chinese in origin. About 2,000,000 mainlanders came to the island with Chiang Kai-shek in 1947–49.

The territories administered by the Chinese Nationalists include the Pescadores Islands (50 sq. miles), some 35 miles west of Taiwan, as well as Quemoy (68 sq. miles) and Matsu (11 sq. miles) which are only a few miles from the mainland. Settled for centuries by the Chinese, the island was administered by Japan from 1895 to 1945. General Chiang Kai-shek withdrew to Taiwan in 1949, towards the end of the war against the Communist regime, accompanied by 500,000 Nationalist troops, after which the territory continued under his presidency until his death on April 5, 1975. A mutual defence treaty between the United States and Taiwan Governments was signed in 1954 but this was terminated when the United States recognized the People's Republic of China on January 1, 1979. Martial law was lifted in July 1987, after 38 years. Chiang Kai-shek's son Chiang Ching-kuo died in January 1988 and was succeeded by Vice-President Lee Teng-hui, a native Taiwanese.

The eastern part of the main island is mountainous and forest covered. Mt. Morrison (Yu Shan) (13,035 ft.) and Mt. Sylvia (Tz'ukaoshan) (12,972 ft.) are the highest peaks. The western plains are watered by many rivers and the soil is very fertile, producing sugar, rice, sweet potatoes, tea, bananas, pineapples and tobacco. Mineral resources are meagre. Taiwan produces one tenth of its coal needs and some natural gas. There are important fisheries. The principal seaports Ψ Keelung and Ψ Kaohsiung are situated in the northern and southern sections of the island.

Trade with UK

	1988	1989
Imports from UK	£355,786,000	£407,432,000
Exports to UK	1,150,392,000	1,351,695,000

CAPITAL.—Taipei, population (1988), 2,888,326. Other towns are Ψ Kaohsiung (1,095,330); Tainan (667,622); Taichung (730,376); and Ψ Keelung (348,672).

CURRENCY.—New Taiwan dollar (NT$) of 100 cents.

FLAG.—Red, with blue quarter at top next staff, bearing a twelve-point white sun.

NATIONAL DAY.—October 10.

COLOMBIA
(República de Colombia)

President, César Gaviria Trujillo, *assumed office,* August 7, 1990.

CABINET
(as at August 7, 1990)

Interior, Julio César Sanchez.
Foreign Affairs, Luis Fernando Jaramillo.
Justice, Jaime Giraldo Angel.
Finance and Public Credit, Rudolph Hommes Rodriguez.
Defence, Gen. Oscar Botero.
Agriculture, María Sintes de Restrepo.
Economic Development, Ernesto Samper Pizano.
Mines and Energy, Luis Fernando Vergara.
Education, Alfonso Valdivieso.
Labour and Social Security, Francisco Posada de la Peña.
Health, Antonio Navorro Wolf.
Communications, Alberto Casas Santamaría.
Public Works and Transport, Juan Felipe Gavira.

COLOMBIAN EMBASSY
3 Hans Crescent, SW1X 0LR
[071–589 9177]

Ambassador Extraordinary and Plenipotentiary, His Excellency Dr. Virgilio Barco Vargas (1990).

The Republic of Colombia lies in the extreme northwest of South America, having a coastline on both the Caribbean Sea and Pacific Ocean. It is situated between 4° 13′ S. to 12° 30′ N. lat. and 68° to 79° W. long., with an area of 439,737 sq. miles (1,138,914 sq. km), and a population (UN estimate 1988) of 30,241,000.

The country is divided into a narrow coastal strip in the west and extensive plains in the east by the Cordillera de los Andes. The Eastern Cordillera consists of a series of vast tablelands. This temperate region is the most densely peopled portion of the Republic. The principal rivers are the Magdalena, Guaviare, Cauca, Atrato, Caquetá, Putumayo and Patia.

Government.—The Colombian coast was visited in 1502 by Christopher Columbus, and in 1536 a Spanish expedition under Jiménez de Quesada penetrated to the interior and established on the site of the present capital a government which continued under Spanish rule until the revolt of the Spanish–American colonies of 1811–1824. In 1819 Simón Bolívar (1783–1831) established the Republic of Colombia, consisting of the territories now known as Colombia, Panama, Venezuela and Ecuador. In 1829–1830 Venezuela and Ecuador withdrew from the association of provinces, and in 1831 the remaining territories were formed into the Republic of New Granada. In 1858 the name was changed to the Granadine Confederation and in 1861 to the United States of Colombia. In 1866 the present title was adopted. In 1903 Panama seceded from Colombia, and became a separate Republic.

During the early 1950s Colombia suffered a period of virtual civil war between the supporters of the traditional political parties, the Conservatives and the Liberals. From 1957–1974 the country was governed under the 'National Front' agreement with the presidency alternating between the two parties every four years and ministerial posts being shared equally by the parties. The alternation of the presidency was ended in 1974 and parity in appointments in 1978. Thereafter, the constitution lays down that Government portfolios and administrative appointments shall be divided among the two majority parties in Congress in an adequate and equitable

manner. However, after a General Election in 1986, the Liberal Party won a large majority. The Liberals are now known as the majority and the Conservatives, the Opposition.

Defence.—The Army peace effective strength is 60,000; war effective, approx. 400,000. The Navy, with 9,000 personnel including approximately 5,000 marines, has four corvettes, one destroyer, one frigate, one sail training ship, two submarines and a number of patrol boats. The Air Force, with 6,000 personnel, is equipped with Mirage fighters, 837B's, C47's and a number of support helicopters.

Production.—Much of Colombia's natural resources in coal, natural gas and hydro-electricity remain largely unexploited. Development of coal is being given priority but no new hydro projects are likely to be started for the next 4–5 years. Annual coal production is increasing from the recent peak of 5·5 million tonnes now that the Cerrejón Norte coalfield is being fully worked. This is essentially for export. Proven coal reserves stand at 16,000 million tonnes. Estimated natural gas reserves are 3,788,000 million cu. ft., with daily use at 381,772 million B.t.u. Proven crude oil reserves stand at 1,300 million barrels. Colombia is again a net exporter of oil. In 1987 exports averaged 152,000 b.p.d. and are expected to rise to 282,000 b.p.d. by 1989.

The hydrocarbon sector accounts for over half of the mining output with precious metals (gold, platinum and silver) and iron ore accounting for the remainder. Other mineral deposits include nickel (a processing plant started operating in 1982), bauxite, copper, gypsum, limestone, phosphates, sulphur and uranium. Colombia is also the world's largest producer of emeralds and has deposits of other precious and semi-precious stones.

Because of the range of climate, a wide variety of crops can be grown, and the country is close to self-suffiency in food. The principal agriculture products are coffee (Colombia is second only to Brazil as the world's largest coffee producer) and other major cash crops are sugar, bananas, cut flowers and cotton. Cattle are raised in large numbers, and meat and cured skins and hides are also exported.

Industry.—The Government has encouraged diversification to reduce dependence on coffee as the major export and this has led to the growth of new export-orientated industries, particularly textiles, paper products and leather goods. Stimulus to the economy has been provided by large loans from the World Bank and IADB for project development, particularly in the power sector (in which hydroelectric projects have predominated) and for telecommunications.

Communications.—The massive ranges of the Andes make surface transport difficult therefore air transport is used extensively. There are daily passenger and cargo air services between Bogotá and all the principal towns, as well as daily services to the USA, frequent services to other countries in South America, and to Europe. The 'Atlantic Railway' links the departmental lines running down to the river, and completes the connection between Bogotá and Santa Marta. Although the railways generally are in a poor state there are about 2,600 miles of rail in use at present. The total road network (1985) consists of 105,201 km of roads of all types, of which 21,800 km are classified as main trunk and transversal roads.

Large appropriations have been made for modernization of the country's telecommunication system. There are 485 radio stations (1983) and two national television channels with several regional ones.

Language and Literature.—Spanish is the language of the country and education has been free since 1870. Great efforts have been made in reducing illiteracy and estimates (1980) put the literacy rate at 77·6 per cent of those over 10 years of age. In addition to the National University with headquarters at Bogotá there are 26 other universities. There is a flourishing press in urban areas and a national literature supplements the rich inheritance from the time of Spanish rule.

Roman Catholicism is the established religion.

TRADE

Colombia's principal export is still coffee although other products, principally bananas, cut flowers, clothing and textiles, ferro-nickel and coal are important exports. Principal trading partners are USA, the EC and Latin America.

Trade with UK

	1988	1989
Imports from UK	£53,132,000	£61,733,000
Exports to UK	61,835,000	70,715,000

CAPITAL.—Bogotá, population (1985 census) 3,967,988. Bogotá is an inland city in the Eastern Cordilleras, at an elevation of 8,600 to 9,000 ft. above sea level. Other centres are Medellin (1,500,000); Cali (1,350,000); ΨBarranquilla (900,000); ΨCartagena (530,000); Bucaramanga (350,000); ΨBuenaventura (130,000) is the country's major port.

CURRENCY.—Colombian peso of 100 centavos.

FLAG.—Broad yellow band in upper half, surmounting equal bands of blue and red.

NATIONAL ANTHEM.—Oh gloria inmarcesible.

NATIONAL DAY.—July 20 (National Independence Day).

BRITISH EMBASSY
Torre Propaganda Sancho, Calle 98 No. 9–03 Piso 4, Bogotá
[Bogota 2185111]

Ambassador Extraordinary and Plenipotentiary, His Excellency Keith E. H. Morris, CMG, (1990).

There are British Consular Offices at *Barranquilla, Bogotá, Cali* and *Medellin*.

British Council Representative, J. Coope, Calle 87 No. 12–79, Bogotá DE.

COLOMBO-BRITISH CHAMBER OF COMMERCE, Apartado Aereo 054 728, CVA 13 No. 82-20, Bogotá DE.

THE COMOROS
(Republique Fédérale Islamique des Comores)

Head of State, President Said Mohamed Djohar, *sworn in* March 20, 1990.

COUNCIL OF GOVERNMENT
(as at March 1990)

Ministers of State:
Economy and Commerce, Said Ali Kemal.
Transport, Tourism and Immigration, Said Ali Youssouf.
Ministers:
Production, Industry, Ali Mroudjae.
Foreign Affairs and Co-operation, Dr. Mtara Maecha.
Finance, Tadjiddine Ben Said Massonde.
Environment, Post and Telecommunications, Said Hassane Said Hachim.
Health and Population, Mohamed Taki Mboreha.
Justice, Said Attoumane.
Interior, Ibrahim Halidi.
Education and Culture, Arbabidine Mohamed.

Secretaries of State:
Information, Youth and Sport, Mouhtare Rachid.
Islamic Affairs, Daoud Attoumane.

The Comoro archipelago includes the islands of Great Comoro, Anjouan, Mayotte and Moheli and certain islets in the Indian Ocean with an area of 838 sq. miles (2,171 sq. km) and a population (UN estimate 1988) of 488,000, most of whom are Muslim. The islanders voted for independence from France in December 1974 and three islands became independent on July 6, 1975. (The island of Mayotte was against independence and has remained under French administration.)

On October 1, 1978 the three islands voted in a referendum to adopt a new Constitution which provides for a President, directly elected for a six year term. The Council of Government, consisting of a Prime Minister and up to nine other Ministers, is appointed by the President. There is a 39-member Federal Assembly elected for 5 years. Each island is administered by a Governor, assisted by up to four Commissioners whom he appoints, and has an elected Legislative Council. The latest elections took place in March 1990, following the assassination of the former President, Ahmed Abdallah Abderrahman, in December 1989.

The most important products are vanilla, copra, cloves and essential oils, which are the principal exports; cacao, sisal and coffee are also cultivated. Great Comoro is well forested and produces some timber.

Trade with UK

	1988	1989
Imports from UK	£333,000	£419,000
Exports to UK	33,000	60,000

CAPITAL.—Moroni, on Great Comoro (pop. 17,267).

CURRENCY.—Comorian franc of 100 centimes. The Comoros also use the Franc CFA of 100 centimes.

FLAG.—Green ground with a crescent and four stars all in white in the half by the hoist.

NATIONAL DAY.—July 6 (Independence Day).

British Ambassador, (resident in Mauritius).

CONGO
(République Populaire du Congo)

President, Gen. Denis Sassou-Nguesso, *appointed* 1979, *re-elected*, July 30, 1984 *and* July 30, 1989 (also holds *Defence and Security Portfolios*).

COUNCIL OF MINISTERS
(as at May 31, 1990)

Prime Minister, A. Poaty-Souchlaty.
Planning, Economy, P. Moussa.
Youth and Rural Development, G. Oba-Apounou.
Forestry, R. D. Ngollo.
Foreign Affairs and Co-operation, A. Ndinga Oba.
Information, P. Ngatse Obala.
Culture and the Arts, J. B. Tati Loutard.
Territorial Administration and Local Government, C. Goma Foutou.
Trade, Small and Medium Enterprises, A. Bouda Nesa.
Industry, Fisheries and Crafts, H. Babassana.
Mines and Energy, Posts and Telecommunications, A. E. Yoka.
Public Works, Col. F. Ntsiba.
Primary Education and Literacy, P. D. Boussoukou Boumba.
Labour, Social Security and Justice, J. Dambenzet.
Secondary and Higher Education, Scientific Research, R. Adada.
Health and Social Affairs, Ossebi Douniam.
Sport and Recreation, J. C. Ganga.

Finance, Budget, E. Gakosso.
Justice, A. Nzoungou.
Transport and Civil Aviation, F. Bita.
Secretary of State for Foreign Affairs and Co-operation, P. Gayama.

The Republic lies on the Equator between Gabon on the west and Zaire on the east, the River Congo and its tributary the Ubangui forming most of the eastern boundary of the state. The Congo has a short Atlantic coastline. The area of the Republic of Congo is 132,047 sq. miles (342,000 sq. km), with a population of 1,888,000 (UN estimate 1988). Formerly the French colony of Middle Congo, it became a member state of the French Community on November 28, 1958, and was proclaimed fully independent on August 17, 1960.

In 1968, conduct of affairs was assumed by a National Council of Army officers. The Parti Congolais du Travail (PCT) was created by the Congress of December 29–31, 1969 and the People's Republic of the Congo was established. Under the present Constitution, approved by referendum in 1979, executive power is vested in the President, who is elected by the Congress of the PCT, the only legal party. The Council of Ministers is appointed and led by the President.

Congo has its own oil deposits, producing about 8 million tonnes annually. It also produces lead, zinc and gold. The principal agricultural products are timber, cassava, sugar cane and yams. Imports are mainly of machinery.

Trade with UK

	1988	1989
Imports from UK	£8,521,000	£8,258,000
Exports to UK	2,018,000	3,442,000

CAPITAL.—Brazzaville (600,000); Ψ Pointe Noire (350,000).
CURRENCY.—Franc CFA of 100 centimes.
FLAG.—Red, with hammer and hoe in wreath of leaves in top corner.
NATIONAL DAY.—August 15.

BRITISH EMBASSY
Ave. General de Gaulle (BP 1038), Brazzaville
[Brazzaville 834944]

Ambassador Extraordinary and Plenipotentiary, His Excellency Peter Chandley, MVO (1990).

COSTA RICA
(República de Costa Rica)

President, Rafael Angel Calderón Fournier, *took office*, May 8, 1990.

MINISTERS
(as at May 8, 1990)

Vice Presidents, G. Serrano Pinto; A. López Echandi.
Minister for the Presidency, R. Méndez Mata.
Foreign Affairs and Worship, B. Niehaus Quesada.
Interior and Police, L. Fishman Zonzinski.
Justice, Elizabeth Odio Benito.
Public Security, V. E. Herrera Algaro.
Finance, T. Vargas Madrigal.
Agriculture, J. R. Lizano Sáenz.
Economy, Industry and Commerce, G. Fajardo Salas.
Natural Resources, Energy and Mines, H. Bravo Trejos.
Public Works and Transport, G. Madriz de Mezerville.
Education, H. Herrera Araja.
Health, C. Castro Charpentier.
Culture, Youth and Sports, Aida de Fishman.
Labour and Social Security, E. Thompson Piñeres.
Planning, H. Fallas Venegas.

Housing and Urban Development, C. Zawadzki Wojtasiak.
Foreign Trade, R. Rojas López.
Science and Technology, O. Morales Matamores.

COSTA RICAN EMBASSY
Flat 1, 14 Lancaster Gate, W2 3LH
[071–723 1772/9630]

Ambassador Extraordinary and Plenipotentiary, new appointment awaited.

The Republic of Costa Rica in Central America extends across the isthmus between 8° 17′ and 11° 10′ N. lat. and from 82° 30′ to 85° 45′ W. long., has an area of 19,575 sq. miles (50,700 sq. km), and a population (1989 estimate) of 2,992,372. The population is basically of European stock, in which Costa Rica differs from most Latin American countries. The Republic lies between Nicaragua and Panama and between the Caribbean Sea and the Pacific Ocean. The coastal lowlands by the Caribbean Sea and Pacific have a tropical climate but the interior plateau, with a mean elevation of 4,000 feet, enjoys a temperate climate.

For nearly three centuries (1530–1821) Costa Rica formed part of the Spanish American dominions, the seat of government being at Cartago. In 1821 the country obtained its independence, although from 1824 to 1839 it was one of the United States of Central America.

On December 1, 1948, the Army was abolished, the President declaring it unnecessary, as the country loved peace.

Economy.—Agriculture is the chief industry and the principal products are coffee, bananas, sugar and cattle (for meat), all of which are important exports. Other crops are cocoa, rice, maize, potatoes and hemp. Industrial activity is principally in the manufacturing sector and manufactured goods are the largest category of exports. The main goods are foodstuffs, textiles and clothing, plastic goods, pharmaceuticals, fertilizers and electrical equipment.

Communications.—The chief ports are Limón, on the Atlantic coast, through which passes most of the coffee exported, and Caldera on the Pacific coast, currently under construction with Japanese aid. The railway system is nationalized. About 500 miles of railroad are open. LACSA is the national airline, operating flights throughout Central and South America, the Caribbean and USA, besides internal flights to local airports by SANSA.

Language, etc.—Spanish is the language of the country. Education is compulsory and free. The literacy rate is the highest in Latin America.

FINANCE

	1988
Revenue	₡54,200·0m
Expenditure	58,790·3m

TRADE

The chief exports are manufactured goods and other products, coffee, bananas, cocoa and sugar. The chief imports are machinery, including transport equipment, manufactures, chemicals, fuel and mineral oils and foodstuffs.

	1988*	1989*
Total imports ...	US$1,404,368,879	US$1,742,979,673
Total exports ...	1,245,671,652	1,403,874,048

* preliminary

Trade with UK

	1988	1989
Imports from UK	£11,390,000	£12,780,000
Exports to UK	16,902,000	24,113,000

CAPITAL.—San José, population (estimate 1989) 1,068,206; Alajuela (519,351); Cartago (328,259); Heredia (235,700); Guanacaste (234,962); ΨPuntarenas (326,163); ΨLimón (209,731). (Populations shown are of provinces, cantons and districts.)

CURRENCY.—Costa Rican colón (₡) of 100 céntimos.

FLAG.—Five horizontal bands, blue, white, red, white, blue (the red band twice the width of the others with emblem near staff).

NATIONAL ANTHEM.—Himno Nacional de Costa Rica.

NATIONAL DAY.—September 15.

BRITISH EMBASSY
Apartado 815, Edificio Centro Colon 1007, San José
[San José 215566]

Ambassador Extraordinary and Plenipotentiary and Consul-General, His Excellency William Marsden (1989).

CÔTE D'IVOIRE
(République de Côte d'Ivoire)

President, Félix Houphouët-Boigny, *elected* for five years in 1960; *re-elected* 1965, 1970, 1975, 1980 and 1985.

CABINET
(as at May 31, 1990)

Ministers of State:
August Denise; Mathieu Ekra; Emile Kei Boguinard; Paul Gui Dibo; Balla Keita; Guy Alain Gauze.
Ministers:
Defence, Jean Konan Banny.
Foreign Affairs, Siméon Aké.
Interior, Léon Konan Koffi.
Fight Against Drugs, Internal Security, Issouf Koné.
Economy and Finance, Moise Koumoue Koffi.
Technical Education and Vocational Training, A. F. Barry-Battesti.
Construction, Town Planning, Public Works and Transport, Bamba Vamoussa.
Justice, Noël Nemin.
Communication, Auguste Miremont.
Labour, Albert Vanié Bi Tra.
Health and Population, Frederic Alain Ekra.
Women's Affairs, Hortense Aka Anghui.
Commerce, Angba Nicolas Kouandi.

Public Service, Jean-Jacques Béchio.
Youth, Sport and Social Affairs, Yaya Ouattara.
Plan and Industry, Oumar Diarra.
Scientific Research, Alhassane N'Diaye.
Budget, Moïse Koumoué Koffi.
Pre-School and Primary Education, Odette Kouamé N'Guessan.
Mines, Yed Esaïe Angoran.
Posts and Telecommunications, Vincent Tieko Djedje.
Animal Production, Christophe Gboho.
Agriculture, Water Resources and Forests, Vincent-Pierre Lokrou.
Tourism, Jean-Claude Delafosse.
President of the National Assembly, Henri Konan Bédie.
President of the Economic and Social Council, Philippe Yacé.

EMBASSY OF THE REPUBLIC OF CÔTE D'IVOIRE
2 Upper Belgrave Street, SW1X 8BJ
[071–235 6991]

Ambassador Extraordinary and Plenipotentiary, His Excellency Yao Gervais Attoungbre (1989).
First Counsellor, G. G. Ballou.

Côte d'Ivoire is situated on the Gulf of Guinea between 5° and 10° N. and 3° and 8° W. and is flanked on the west by Guinea and Liberia, on the north by Mali and Burkina and on the east by Ghana. It has an area of 124,503 sq. miles (322,463 sq. km)—tropical rain forest in the southern half and savanna in the northern—and a population of 11,613,000 (UN estimate, 1988) divided into a large number of ethnic and tribal groups.

Although French contact was made in the first half of the 19th century, Côte d'Ivoire became a colony only in 1893 and was finally pacified in 1912. It decided on December 5, 1958 to remain an autonomous republic within the French Community; full independence outside the Community was proclaimed on August 7, 1960. Special agreements with France, covering financial and cultural matters, technical assistance, defence, etc., were signed in Paris on April 24, 1961. The official language is French.

Côte d'Ivoire has a presidential system of government modelled on that of the United States and the French Fifth Republic. The single Chamber National Assembly of 175 members was elected in 1985. The defence of the Constitution which was promulgated in November 1960 is vested in a Supreme Court. Although the Constitution provides for a multi-party system, it was not until May 1990 that any party other than the ruling PDCI party was authorized. Multi-party elections are scheduled for October and November 1990.

BUDGET

	1990
Current Expenditure	CFA609,400 billion
Investment and Equipment...	129,600 billion

Trade.—The principal exports are coffee, cocoa, timber, palm oil, pineapples, bananas, and cotton. There are a few deposits of diamonds and minerals including manganese and iron.

TRADE

	1988	1989
Imports	US$1,907m	US$1,781m
Exports	2,354m	2,588m

Trade with UK

	1988	1989
Imports from UK ..	£31,172,000	£29,434,000
Exports to UK	64,041,000	65,943,000

CAPITAL.—ΨAbidjan (population, 3,500,000) which is also the main port. In March 1983 the National Assembly ratified a decision to transfer the political and administrative capital from Abidjan to Yamoussoukro.

CURRENCY.—Franc CFA of 100 centimes.

FLAG.—Three vertical stripes, orange, white and green.

NATIONAL ANTHEM.—L'Abidjanaise.

NATIONAL DAY.—December 7.

BRITISH EMBASSY
Immeuble Les Harmonies, 01 BP 2581,
Abidjan 01
[Abidjan 226850]

Ambassador Extraordinary and Plenipotentiary, new appointment awaited.
Head of Chancery and Consul, D. Flanagan.
First Secretary (Education) and British Council Representative, C. Stevenson.

CUBA
(Republica de Cuba)

President of Council of State and Head of Government, Dr. Fidel Castro Ruz, *appointed* November 2, 1976.

COUNCIL OF STATE
(as at June 30, 1990)

President, Dr. Fidel Castro Ruz.
First Vice-President, Raúl Castro Ruz.
Vice-Presidents, Juan Almeida Bosque; Osmany Cienfuegos Gorriarán; José Ramón Machado Ventura; Pedro Miret Prieto; Carlos Rafael Rodríguez.
Secretary, José M. Miyar Barrueco.

COUNCIL OF MINISTERS

President, Dr. Fidel Castro Ruz.
First Vice-President, Raúl Castro Ruz.
Vice-Presidents, Dr. Carlos Rafael Rodríguez; Pedro Miret Prieto; José Ramón Fernández Alvarez; Osmany Cienfuegos Gorriarán; Antonio Esquivel Yedra; Joel Domenech Benítez; Antonio Rodriguez Maurell; Jaime Crombet Hernández-Baquero; Aldofo Diaz Suárez; Lionel Soto Prieto.
Secretary, Osmany Cienfuegos Gorriarán.
Presidents of State Committees: Antonio Rodriquez Maurell (*Central Planning Board*); Hector Rodri-

guez Llompart (*National Bank*); Ernesto Melendez Bachs (*Economic Co-operation*); Rodrigo J. Garcia Leon (*Finance*); Francisco Linares Calvo (*Labour and Social Security*); Sonia Rodriguez Cardona (*Material and Technical Supply*); Arturo Guzman Pascual (*Prices*); Ramón Darias Rodés (*Standardization*); Fidel Emilio Vasco Gonzalez (*Statistics*).
Ministers, Carlos Pérez León (*Agriculture*); Marcos J. Portal Leon (*Basic Industry*); Manuel Castillo Rabasa (*Communications*); Homero Crabb (*Construction*); José M. Cañete Alvarez (*Construction Materials Industry*); Armando Enrique Hart Davalos (*Culture*); Manuel Vila Sosa (*Domestic Trade*); José Ramon Fernandez Alvarez (*Education*); Jorge A. Fernandez Cuervo-Vinent (*Fishing*); Alejandro Roca Iglesias (*Food Industry*); Isidoro Octavio Malmierca Peoli (*Foreign Relations*); Ricardo Cabrisas Ruiz (*Foreign Trade*); Fernando Vecino Alegret (*Higher Education*); Gen. Abelardo Colomé Ibarra (*Interior*); Juan Escalona Reguera (*Justice*); Antonio Esquivel Yedra (*Light Industry*); Julio Jesus Teja Pérez (*Public Health*); Raul Castro Ruz (*Revolutionary Armed Forces*); Marcos Lage Coello (*Steel Industry*); Juan Ramon Herrera Machado (*Sugar Industry*); Gen. Senén Casas Regueiro (*Transport*); Jose Alberto Naranjo Morales; Joaqin Benavides Rodrioguez (*Ministers without Portfolio*).

EMBASSY OF THE REPUBLIC OF CUBA
167 High Holborn, WC1V 6PA
[071–240 2488]

Ambassador Extraordinary and Plenipotentiary, Her Excellency Maria A. Flores (1990).
Councillor, M Martinez-Moles Cifrian.

Cuba, the largest island in the Caribbean, lies between 74° and 85° W. long., and 19° and 23° N. lat., with a total area of 42,804 sq. miles (110,861 sq. km). The country is divided into 14 provinces. The population in December 1988 was 10,468,661.

The island of Cuba was visited by Christopher Columbus during his first voyage, on Oct. 27, 1492, and was then believed to be part of the western mainland of India. Early in the 16th century the island was conquered by the Spanish, to be used later as a base of operations for the conquest of Mexico and Central America, and for almost four centuries Cuba remained under a Spanish Captain-General. (The island was under British rule for one year, 1762–1763, when it was returned to Spain in exchange for Florida.) Separatist agitation culminated in the closing years of the 19th century in open warfare. In 1898 the government of the United States intervened and on April 20, 1898, demanded the evacuation of Cuba by the Spanish forces. A short Spanish–American war led to the abandonment of the island, which was occupied by US troops. Cuba was under US military rule from January 1, 1899 until May 20, 1902, when an autonomous government was inaugurated with an elected President, and a legislature of two houses. The island was, however, again the prey of revolution from August to September 1906, when the US Government resumed control. On January 28, 1909 a republican government was again inaugurated.

A revolution led by Dr. Fidel Castro overthrew the Government of General Batista on January 1, 1959. In October 1965 the Communist Party of Cuba was formed to succeed the United Party of the Socialist Revolution. It is the only authorized political party. The new Socialist Constitution came into force on February 24, 1976 and indirect elections to the National Assembly of People's Power were subsequently held.

Production.—The Government has carried out programmes of land and urban reform and of nationalization; by March 1968, virtually all industrial and commercial enterprises were nationalized. About 85 per cent of the cultivated land is in state farms or state-controlled co-operatives. Private smallholders, who own the remainder, have to sell all their produce to the state.

Although efforts are being made to diversify the economy, sugar is still its mainstay and principal source of foreign exchange. In 1989–90 the harvest was 8·04 million tons. Cuba's other main exports are oil, nickel, seafood, citrus fruits, tobacco and rum.

Despite increased trade with Western Europe and Japan, COMECON member countries, particularly the Soviet Union, form Cuba's main trading partners, covering about 86 per cent of imports and exports. In addition, the USSR offers aid through a system of subsidies.

There are 12,700 km of railway track, of which 5,000 km are in public service. In 1986 there were 13,247 km of road. At present scheduled international air services run to North, Central and South American countries and Europe.

Language and Literature.—Spanish is the language of the island. English, formerly widely understood, is now spoken less. Education is compulsory and free. In 1964 illiteracy was officially declared to be completely eliminated. The press and broadcasting and television are under the control of the Government.

	1987	1988
	Pesos million	
Imports	7,611·5	7,579·4
Exports	5,401·0	5,518·3

Trade with UK

	1988	1989
Imports from UK	£31,162,000	£53,255,000
Exports to UK	28,489,000	34,388,000

CAPITAL.—ΨHavana, population estimate (1986) 2,100,000; other towns are ΨSantiago (429,800), Santa Clara (198,800), Camagüey (279,800), Holguín (254,300), and ΨCienfuegos (124,600).

CURRENCY.—Cuban peso of 100 centavos.

FLAG.—Five horizontal bands, blue and white (blue at top and bottom) with red triangle, close to staff, charged with 5-point star.

NATIONAL ANTHEM.—Al Combate, Corred Bayameses (To battle, men of Bayamo).

NATIONAL DAY.—January 1 (Day of Liberation).

BRITISH EMBASSY
Edificio Bolívar, Cárcel 101–103,
e Morro y Prado, Apartado 1069, Havana.
[Havana 623071]

Ambassador Extraordinary and Plenipotentiary, His Excellency (Anthony) David Brighty, CMG, CVO (1989).

Counsellor, N. R. Jarrold (*Deputy Head of Mission*).

First Secretary, R. Daly (*Commercial and HM Consul*).

CZECHOSLOVAKIA
(Čescá a Slovenská Federativní Republika)

President, Václav Havel, *elected* December 29, 1989, *re-elected* July 7, 1990.

Federal Government
(as at August 1, 1990)

Prime Minister, Marián Čalfa.
Deputy Prime Ministers, Jiří Dienstbier (*also Minister for Foreign Affairs*); Jozef Mikloško; Pavel Rychetsky; Václav Valeš.

Transport, Jiří Nezval.
Finance, Václav Klaus.
Defence, Miroslav Vacek.
Labour and Social Affairs, Petr Miller.
Telecommunications, Theodor Petrik.
Interior, Ján Langoš.
Foreign Trade, Slavomír Stračár.
Economy, Vladimír Dlouhý.
Environment, Josef Vavroušek.
Strategic Planning, Pavel Hoffmann.
Inspection, Květoslava Kořínková.

EMBASSY OF THE CZECH AND SLOVAK
FEDERATIVE REPUBLIC
25 Kensington Palace Gardens, W8 4QY
[071–229 1255]

Ambassador Extraordinary and Plenipotentiary, His Excellency Dr. Karel Duda (1990).
Counsellor-Minister, J. Přibyl.
Commercial Counsellor, S. Žiak.
Military and Air Attaché, Col. J. Puchner.
Commercial Attachés, J. Slánský; J. Navara.

Area and Population.—Czechoslovakia, formerly part of the Austro-Hungarian Empire, declared its independence on October 28, 1918 (Czechoslovak Independence Day). It has an area of 49,370 sq. miles (127,869 sq. km). The population (UN estimate 1988) is 15,608,000.

Government.—The Communist Party came to power in Czechoslovakia in February 1948, and remained in power until December 1989.

In 1968 the Czechoslovak Communist Party, under the then General Secretary Alexander Dubček, embarked on a reform programme leading to proposals for economic reform, the democratization of the country's political life, greater guarantees of fundamental liberties and the establishment of a federal system.

The implications for the internal development of the other communist regimes in Eastern Europe and the Soviet Union alarmed the Soviet Union. On the night of August 20, Czechoslovakia was invaded by Soviet, Polish, East German, Hungarian and Bulgarian troops, the capital and all major towns being occupied. The Czechoslovak leadership was forced to modify its policies and to legalize the presence of Soviet troops on Czechoslovak territory. With the exception of the federal system of government, the reforms of 1968 were abandoned when Gustáv Husák became leader of the Communist party in April 1969 (President 1987–9).

Opposition to Communist Party rule gathered pace in the late 1980s encouraged by the political and economic reforms taking place in the Soviet Union and other Eastern bloc countries. An upsurge in mass street protests in November 1989 led to the resignation of the Communist Party Central Committee. The Communist Party was forced to concede its monopoly of power and on December 10 a new government was appointed in which only half the Ministers were Communist Party members. Gustáv Husák resigned as President and was replaced by Václav Havel.

Free elections were held in June 1990 in which the Civic Forum movement and its Slovak sister movement, Public Against Violence, obtained over 50 per cent of the vote. The new government, appointed in June 1990, comprises a coalition of Civic Forum/ Public Against Violence and the Christian Democratic Movement. Its two main tasks are to produce a programme of economic reform and to draw up a new Constitution.

Under the present constitution, Czechoslovakia (renamed the Czech and Slovak Federative Republic in April 1990) consists of the Czech Republic and the Slovak Republic, each of which has its own government responsible to its legislative body—the National Council. Areas such as the constitution, defence, foreign affairs and currency are the responsibility of the federal administration. The Federal Government is responsible to the Federal Assembly, which is composed of two Chambers, the Chamber of the People, whose deputies are elected throughout the federation, and the Chamber of the Nations, consisting of an equal number of Czech and Slovak deputies.

The Economic System.—Under Communist rule industry was state-owned and nearly all agricultural land was cultivated by state or co-operative farms. An economic reform programme was begun in 1990 aimed at producing a free-market economy in Czechoslovakia. New laws passed in the spring of 1990 provided a legal basis for private enterprise, joint ventures and foreign investment.

Production.—Czechoslovakia is not rich in minerals, although significant quantities of coal and lignite are mined. Principal agricultural products are sugar-beet, potatoes and cereal crops; the timber industry is also very important. The country has long been highly industrialized, and machinery, industrial consumer goods and raw materials are major exports.

Language and Literature.—Czech and Slovak are the official languages, each having its own literature. The Reformation gave a wide-spread impulse to Czech literature, the writings of Jan Hus (martyred in 1415 as a religious and social reformer) familiarizing the people with Wyclif's teaching. This impulse endured to the close of the 17th century when Jan Amos Komensky or Comenius (1592–1670) was expelled from the country. Under Austrian rule and with the persistent pursuit of Germanization, there was a period of stagnation until the national revival in the first half of the 19th century. Authors of international reputation include Jaroslav Hašek (1883–1923), Jaroslav Seifert (1901–1986, Nobel Prize for Literature, 1985), Václav Havel (b. 1936) and Milan Kundera (b. 1929).

Education.—Education is compulsory and free for all children from the ages of 6 to 16. There are five universities in Czechoslovakia of which the most famous is Charles University in Prague (founded 1348), the others being situated at Bratislava, Brno, Olomouc and Košice. In addition there are a considerable number of other institutions of university standing, technical colleges, agricultural colleges, etc.

Trade with UK

	1988	1989
Imports from UK	£130,420,000	£131,418,000
Exports to UK	148,248,000	156,649,000

CAPITAL.—Prague (Praha), on the Vltava (Moldau), the former capital of Bohemia with a population (1985) of 1,190,576. Other towns are Brno (Brünn), capital of Moravia (381,000), Bratislava (Pressburg), capital of Slovakia (401,000), Ostrava (324,000), Košice (214,000) and Plzen (Pilsen) (174,000).

CURRENCY.—Koruna (Kčs) or Czechoslovak crown of 100 Haléřu (Heller).

FLAG.—Two equal horizontal stripes, white (above) and red; a blue triangle next to staff.

NATIONAL ANTHEM.—Kde Domov Můj (Where is my Motherland) (Czech); Nad Tatrom sa blýska (Storm over the Tatras) (Slovak).

NATIONAL DAY.—May 9, October 28.

BRITISH EMBASSY
Thunovská 14, 11800 Prague 1
[Prague 533347]

Ambassador Extraordinary and Plenipotentiary, His Excellency (Peter) Laurence O'Keeffe, CMG, CVO (1988).

Counsellor, J. M. Macgregor (*Head of Chancery*).
Defence and Military Attaché, Col. R. J. M. Drummond, OBE.
Air Attaché, Wing Cdr. B. Blackford.
Cultural Attaché, J. R. Potts (*British Council Representative*).

DENMARK
(Kongeriget Danmark)

Queen, Margrethe II, eldest daughter of King Frederik IX, *born* April 16, 1940, *succeeded* Jan. 14, 1972, *married* June 10, 1967, Count Henri de Monpezat (Prince Henrik of Denmark) and *has issue* Crown Prince Frederik *born* May 26, 1968; and Prince Joachim, *born* June 7, 1969.

CABINET
(as at July 31, 1990)

Prime Minister, Poul Schlüter (C).
Foreign Affairs, Uffe Ellemann-Jensen (V).
Finance, Henning Dyremose (C).
Economic Affairs, Niels Helveg Petersen (RL).
Fiscal Affairs, Anders Fogh Rasmussen (V).
Defence, Knud Enggaard (V).
Education and Research, Bertel Haarder (V).
Justice, Hans Engel (C).
Interior and Nordic Affairs, Thor Pedersen (V).
Housing, Agnete Laustsen (C).
Agriculture, Laurits Toernæs (V).
Energy, Jens Bilgrav-Nielsen (RL).
Culture, Ole Vig Jensen (RL).
Environment, Lone Dybkjær (RL).
Social Affairs, Aase Olesen (RL).
Ecclesiastical Affairs and Communications, Torben Rechendorff (C).
Transport, Knud Østergaard (C).
Fisheries, Kent Kirk (C).
Labour, Knud Erik Kirkegaard (C).
Industry, Anne Birgitte Lundholt (C).
Health, Ester Larsen (V).

C: Conservative Party; V: Venstre (Liberals); RL: Radical Liberal Party.

ROYAL DANISH EMBASSY
55 Sloane Street, SW1X 9SR
[071–235 1255]

Ambassador Extraordinary and Plenipotentiary, His Excellency R. A. Thorning-Petersen (1989).
Minister Counsellors, H. M. Kofoed-Hansen; P. Essemann (*Commercial*); F. A. Axmark (*Press and Culture*); C. Søndergaard (*Economic and Consular Affairs*).
Defence Attaché, Capt. E. Fage-Pedersen.

Area and Population.—A Kingdom of Northern Europe, consisting of the islands of Zeeland, Funen, Lolland, etc., the peninsula of Jutland, and the outlying island of Bornholm in the Baltic, the Faröes and Greenland. Denmark is situated between 54° 34′ and 57° 45′ N. lat., 8° 5′–15° E. 12′ long., with an area of 16,629 sq. miles (43,069 sq. km), and a population (UN estimate 1988) of 5,130,000.

Government.—Under the Constitution of the Kingdom of Denmark Act of June 5, 1953, the legislature consists of one chamber, the *Folketing*, of not more than 179 members, including 2 for the Faröes and 2 for Greenland. The voting age is 18.

The coalition government of Poul Schlüter was formed in June 1988 after the General Election on May 10.

Education is free and compulsory. Special schools are numerous, commercial, technical and agricultural predominating. There are universities at Copenhagen (founded in 1479), Aarhus (1933), Odense (1966), Roskilde (1972) and Aalborg (1974). A further university at Esbjerg is planned.

Language and Literature.—The Danish language is akin to Swedish and Norwegian. Danish literature, ancient and modern, embraces all forms of expression, familiar names being Hans Christian Andersen (1805–1875), Søren Kierkegaard (1813–1855) and Karen Blixen (1885–1962). Some 48 newspapers are published in Denmark; two daily papers are published in Copenhagen.

Production and Industry.—Of the labour force, in 1988, 1·8 per cent was engaged in agriculture, fishing, forestry, etc.; 27·5 per cent in manufacturing, building and construction; 15·4 per cent in commerce, 0·2 per cent in liberal professions and 53·2 per cent in administration, transport and the financial services. The chief agricultural products are pigs, cattle, dairy products, poultry and eggs, seeds, cereals and sugar beet; manufactures are mostly based on imported raw materials but there are also considerable imports of finished goods.

Communications.—Mercantile marine (ships above 100 gross tonnage) at beginning of 1988, totalled 618 ships. In 1985 there was 2,471 km of state-owned railway and 494 km of privately-owned railway systems.

FINANCE (BUDGET ESTIMATES)

	1988	1989
Revenue	Kr201,280m	Kr221,008m
Expenditure	212,823m	222,179m

Denmark's balance of payments on current account showed a deficit for 1988 of Kr12,200 million (1987, Kr20,700 million).

TRADE

The principal imports are industrial raw materials, consumer goods, construction inputs, machinery, raw materials, vehicles and textile products. The chief exports are miscellaneous manufactured articles, agricultural and dairy products.

	1987	1988
Total Imports	Kr174,066m	Kr178,269m
Total Exports	175,302m	187,381m

Trade with UK

	1988	1989
Imports from UK	£1,170,853,000	£1,209,220,000
Exports to UK	2,028,089,000	2,229,340,000

CAPITAL.—ΨCopenhagen, population (1988) 467,850; Greater Copenhagen 1,495,736. Ψ Aarhus 259,493; Ψ Odense 174,948; Ψ Aalborg 154,547; Ψ Esbjerg 81,480; Ψ Randers 61,094; Ψ Kolding 57,128; Ψ Helsingør 56,754; Ψ Horsens 54,940; Ψ Vejle 50,879; Roskilde 48,996; Ψ Fredericia 45,992.

CURRENCY.—Danish krone (Kr) of 100 øre.

FLAG.—Red, with white cross.

NATIONAL ANTHEM.—Kong Kristian.

NATIONAL DAY.—April 16 (The Queen's Birthday).

BRITISH EMBASSY
36–40 Kastelsvej, DK-2100 Copenhagen
[Copenhagen 264600]

Ambassador Extraordinary and Plenipotentiary, His Excellency Nigel Christopher Ransome Williams, CMG (1989).

Counsellors, J. W. Hodge (*Head of Chancery*); P. Longworth (*Commercial*).

Defence Attaché, Cmdr. R. Woolgar, RN.

There are Consulates at *Aabenraa, Aalborg, Aarhus, Esbjerg, Fredericia, Herning, Odense, Rønne* (Bornholm) and at *Tórshavn* (Faröe Islands).

British Council Representative, Michael Holcroft, Møntergade 1, 1116 Copenhagen K.

Outlying Parts of the Kingdom

THE FARÖES, or Sheep Islands (540 sq. miles; 1,399 sq. km; pop. (1985) 46,000), capital, Tórshavn, are governed by a *Lagting* of 26 members, a *Landsstyre* of four members which deals with special Faröes affairs, and send two representatives to the *Folketing* at Copenhagen. On Sept. 14, 1946 the Lagting, with the consent of the Danish Government, for its own guidance held a plebiscite on the Faröes. About one-third of the electors did not, however, take part in the voting; of the rest a little more than half the votes cast were in favour of separation from Denmark and the establishment of a republic. At the subsequent general election for the Lagting a great majority voted in favour of remaining part of the Kingdom of Denmark with a certain measure of home rule and in 1948 the Faröes received this. The Faröes are not part of the EC.

Prime Minister, Jogvan Sundstein.

Trade with UK

	1988	1989
Imports from UK	£4,445,000	£6,353,000
Exports to UK	23,141,000	31,042,000

GREENLAND (total area 2,175,600 sq. km, of which approx. 16 per cent is ice-free) with a population (1985) of 52,940, is divided into three provinces (West, North and East). Greenland (capital, Nuuk (Godthåb)) has a *Landsraad* of 17 members and sends two representatives to the *Folketing* at Copenhagen. Greenland attained a status of internal autonomy on May 1, 1979. The trade of Greenland is mainly under the management of the Royal Greenland Trade Department. Following a plebiscite Greenland negotiated its withdrawal from the EC, but without discontinuing relations with Denmark, and left on February 1, 1985.

Mineral and oil prospecting revealed deposits of lead, zinc, iron ore, oil, gas and uranium. Commercial exploitation of these resources has already begun. The United States of America has acquired certain rights to maintain air bases in Greenland.

Premier, Jonathan Motzfeldt.

Trade with UK

	1988	1989
Imports from UK	£1,151,000	£1,487,000
Exports to UK	1,430,000	3,793,000

DJIBOUTI
(Jumhouriyya Djibouti)

President, Hassan Gouled Aptidon, *elected* 1977, re-elected 1981 and 1987.

CABINET
(as at May 31, 1990)

Prime Minister and Minister for Port Affairs, Barkat Gourad Hamadou.
Justice, M. Alaf Orbis.
Foreign Affairs and Co-operation, Moumin Bahdon Farah.
Interior, Posts and Telecommunications, Khaireh Allaleh Robleh.
Defence, M. Houssein Barkat.
Finance, Mohamed Djama Elabeh.
Commerce, Transport and Tourism, Moussa Bouraleh Robleh.
Education, Youth and Sports, Omar Chirdon Abbas.
Public Health, Hassan Ougoreh.
Labour, Ahmed Ibrahim Aidi.
Civil Service and Administrative Reform, Ismail Ali Youssouf.
Public Works, Town Planning and Housing, Ahmed Aden Youssouf.
Industry, Salem Abdou Yaya.
Rural Development, Mohamed Moussa Chehem.

Formerly known as French Somaliland and then the French Territory of the Afars and the Issas, the Republic of Djibouti became independent on June 27, 1977. Djibouti is situated on the north-east coast of Africa (i.e. the Horn of Africa) and has an area of 8,494 sq. miles (22,000 sq. km.). It has a population (UN estimate 1988) of 383,000. The climate is harsh and much of the country is semi-arid desert. The most recent elections to the 65-member Chamber of Deputies took place in April 1987. The sole legal party is *Rassemblement Populaire pour le Progrès* (RPP—the Popular Rally for Progress). The French continue to maintain army, navy and air force bases. Djibouti has an excellent port, international airport and a railway line runs to Addis Ababa.

Trade with UK

	1988	1989
Imports from UK	£8,479,000	£10,656,000
Exports to UK	169,000	489,000

CAPITAL.—Ψ Djibouti, population (1985) 200,000.
CURRENCY.—Djibouti franc of 100 centimes.
FLAG.—Blue over green with white triangle in the hoist containing a red star.
NATIONAL DAY.—June 27 (Independence Day).

BRITISH CONSULATE
PO Box 81, 9–11 Rue de Geneve, Djibouti
Honorary Consul, E. Vandendriessche.

DOMINICAN REPUBLIC
(República Dominicana)

President, Dr. Joaquin Balaguer, *took office*, Aug. 16. 1986, *re-elected* May 16, 1990.
Vice-President, Carlos Morales Troncoso.

CABINET
(as at August 31, 1989)*

Presidency, Rafael Bello Andino.
Finance, Guillermo Caram.
Foreign Affairs, Joaquín Ricardo.
Education and Culture , Nicolas Almanzar.
Agriculture, Manual de Jesus Pina Cacarels.
Labour, Rafael Emiliano Agramonte.
Public Health and Social Welfare, Rafael Gautreaux.
Public Works and Commmunications, Marcos Subero Sajuin.
Industry and Trade, Julio Valerio Sánchez.
Sports, Physical Education and Recreation, Temistocles Metz.

Tourism, Fernando Rainieri Marrancini.
Defence; Interior and Police, Manuel Estrada Medina.
Without Portfolio, Manuel Guaroa Liranzo; Simón Tomás Fernández.
Administrative Secretary to Presidency, Luis Toral.
Technical Secretary to Presidency, Roberto Martínez Villanueva.
Governor of Central Bank, Luis Julián Pérez.
Secretaries of State Without Portfolio, Donald Reid Cabral; Juan Rafael Peralta Pérez.

* At time of going to press, it was not known whether cabinet changes would follow President Balaguer's re-election.

HONORARY CONSULATE GENERAL
539 Martins Building, Water Street,
Liverpool L2 3TE
[051–236 0722]

Honorary Consul-General, T. V. Anthony.
Honorary Vice-Consul, Mrs. Hilary Gatenby.

There are also Consular Offices at *Birmingham, Cardiff, Grimsby, London* (6 Queen's Mansions, Brook Green, W6 7EB), and *Plymouth*.

The Dominican Republic, formerly the Spanish portion of the island of Hispaniola, is the oldest settlement of European origin in America. The western part of the island forms the Republic of Haiti. The island lies between Cuba on the west and Puerto Rico on the east and the Republic covers an area of 18,816 sq. miles (48,734 sq. km), with a population (1984 Census) of 6,416,000. A 1988 UN estimate gives a figure of 6,867,000. The climate is tropical in the lowlands and semi-tropical to temperate in the higher altitudes.

Spanish is the language of the Republic.

Government.—Santo Domingo was discovered by Christopher Columbus in December 1492, and remained a Spanish colony until 1821. In 1822 it was subjugated by the neighbouring Haitians who remained in control until 1844 when the Dominican Republic was proclaimed. The country was occupied by American marines from 1916 until the adoption of a new Constitution in 1924. From 1930 until May 30, 1961 (when he was assassinated) Generalissimo Rafael Trujillo ruled the country.

President Juan Bosch held office from December 1962 to September 1963, when he was deposed by a military junta. A revolt in favour of ex-President Bosch in April 1965 developed into civil war lasting until September the same year when a provisional President was elected. On June 1, 1966 Dr. Joaquin Balaguer was elected President and in November 1966 a new Constitution was introduced.

Executive power is vested in the President, who is elected by direct vote and serves for four years. The President forms his cabinet without reference to the Congress.

Legislative power is exercised by the Congress, which has a term of four years concurrent with the Presidency. The Upper Chamber is the Senate of 27 senators, one for each province and one for Santo Domingo. The lower is the Chamber of Deputies which has 120 members, one for each 50,000 inhabitants in each province, with the provision that no province has less than two members. Judicial power is exercised by the Supreme Court of Justice.

Communications.—According to local classification there are 2,932 miles of first class and 1,392 miles of second class and inter-communal roads in the Republic. There is a direct road from Santo Domingo to Port-au-Prince, the capital of Haiti, but that part of it in the border area has fallen into disuse. The frontier has been closed since September 1967, except for that section crossed by the main road linking the two capitals. A telephone system connects practically all the principal towns of the republic and there is a telegraph service with all parts of the world. There are more than 90 commercial broadcasting stations and six television stations.

The Republic is served by two national and six foreign airlines, and an international airport 18 miles to the east of the capital is in operation. Another has been built near Puerto Plata on the north coast.

Economy.—Sugar, coffee, cocoa, and tobacco are the most important crops. Other products are peanuts, maize, rice, bananas, molasses, salt, cement, ferro-nickel, gold, silver, cattle, sisal products, honey and chocolate. There is a growing number of light industries producing beer, tinned foodstuffs, glass products, textiles, soap, cigarettes, construction materials, plastic articles, shoes, papers, paint, rum, matches, peanut oil and other products.

FINANCE

	1986
Expenditure	RD$2,251m
Revenue	2,113m

TRADE

The chief imports are machinery, food stuffs, iron and steel, cotton textiles and yarns, mineral oils (including petrol), cars and other motor vehicles, chemical and pharmaceutical products, electrical equipment and accessories, construction material, paper and paper products, and rubber and rubber products. The chief exports are sugar, coffee, cocoa, tobacco, chocolate, molasses, bauxite, ferro-nickel and gold. Tobacco and tobacco manufactures are the principal exports to the UK.

	1984	1985
Imports	RD$1,459,000,000	RD$1,285,900,000
Exports	1,211,100,000	739,300,000

Trade with UK

	1988	1989
Imports from UK	£17,235,000	£25,519,000
Exports to UK	8,523,000	11,223,000

CAPITAL.—Ψ Santo Domingo, population of the Capital District (1981 census) 1,313,172. Other centres, with populations (1981 census): Santiago de los Caballeros (550,372); La Vega (385,043); San Francisco De Macoris (235,544); San Juan (239,957); San Cristóbal (446,132).

CURRENCY.—Dominican Republic peso (RD$) of 100 centavos.

FLAG.—Red and blue, with white cross bearing an emblem at centre.

NATIONAL ANTHEM.—Quisqueyanos Valientes, Alcemos (Brave men of Quisqueya, let's raise our song).

NATIONAL DAY.—February 27 (Independence Day, 1844).

British Ambassador, (resident in Caracas, Venezuela).

ECUADOR
(Republica del Ecuador)

President, Rodrigo Borja Cevallos, *took office* Aug. 10, 1988.
Vice President, Luis Parodi.

CABINET
(as at July 31, 1990)

Interior and Police, César Verduga.
Foreign Affairs, Diego Cordovéz.
Education and Culture, Alfredo Vera Arrata.
Social Welfare, Raul Baca Carbo.
Health, Plutarco Naranjo.

Agriculture and Livestock, Enrique Delgado.
Public Works, Juan Neira.
Finance, Jorge Gallardo Zavala.
Industry and Commerce, Jacinto Jouvin Marquez.
Energy and Mines, Diego Tamariz.
Employment, César Verduga.
Defence, Gen. Jorge Félix.
Labour, Roberto Gomez.

EMBASSY OF ECUADOR
Flat 3B, 3 Hans Crescent, SW1X 0LS
[071-584 1367/2648]

Ambassador Extraordinary and Plenipotentiary, His Excellency Jose Antonio Correa (1989).

Area and Population.—Ecuador is an equatorial state of South America, the mainland extending from lat. 1° 38′ N. to 4° 50′ S., and between 75° 20′ and 81° W. long., comprising an area reduced by boundary settlements with Peru (January 1942) to about 109,484 sq. miles (283,561 sq. km).

The Republic of Ecuador is divided into 20 provinces. It has a population (1988) of 10,157,000, mostly descendants of the Spanish, aboriginal Indians, and Mestizoes. The territory of the Republic extends across the Western Andes, the highest peaks in Ecuador being Chimborazo (20,408 ft.) and Ilinza (17,405 ft.) in the Western Cordillera; and Cotopaxi (19,612 ft.) and Cayambe (19,160 ft.) in the Eastern Cordillera. Ecuador is watered by the Upper Amazon, and by the rivers Guayas, Mira, Santiago, Chone, and Esmeraldas on the Pacific coast. There are extensive forests.

Government.—The former Kingdom of Quito was conquered by the Incas of Peru in the latter part of the 15th century. Early in the 16th century Pizarro's conquests led to the inclusion of the present territory of Ecuador in the Spanish Vice-royalty of Peru. The independence of the country was achieved in a revolutionary war which culminated in the battle of Mount Pichincha (May 24, 1822).

After seven years of military rule, Ecuador returned to democracy in 1979. The present constitution, introduced in 1978, provides for an elected President and Vice-President who serve for a four year term. Neither may stand for re-election. There is a Chamber of Representatives with 71 members elected every four years, 12 of whom are elected on a national basis and the rest by the provinces. The Chamber meets for two months every year (Aug.-Oct.) but can be convoked at any time for extraordinary sessions. Four Legislative Commissions meet through the year.

Voting is compulsory for all literate and (since 1980) voluntary for all illiterate citizens over the age of 18. Sixteen political parties took part in the 1988 elections.

Agriculture and Industry.—Agriculture is the most important sector of the economy, supporting nearly 50 per cent of the population (particularly the poorest) and contributing 14·5 per cent of the Gross Domestic Product and 19·5 per cent of exports. The main products for export are fish (mainly shrimps, tuna and sardines), which had become the largest agricultural export by early 1982; bananas, which provide a third of agricultural exports; cocoa and coffee. Other important crops are sugar, corn, soya, rice, cotton, African palm (for oil), vegetables, fruit and timber, the temperate crops being produced mostly in the highlands.

The economy was transformed by the discovery in 1972 of major oil fields in the Oriente area, and oil accounted for two-thirds of 1981 export earnings. The economy grew rapidly in the 1970s but is now faced with reduced growth, due mainly to the fall in the price of oil. The oil deposits in the Oriente are estimated at between 10,000 and 15,000 million barrels, and further exploration and development is taking place. The oil is evacuated by a trans-Andean pipeline to the port of Balao (near Esmeraldas).

Communications.—There are 23,256 km of permanent roads and 5,044 km of roads which are only open during the dry season. There are about 750 miles of railway, including the railway from Quito to Guayaquil. Ten commercial airlines operate international flights, linking Ecuador with major foreign cities and there are internal services between all important towns.

Defence.—The standing Army has a strength of about 38,000. There is an Air Force of some 120 aircraft of various kinds and 4,800 personnel. The Navy is 4,500 strong.

Language, etc.—Spanish is the principal language of the country but Quechua is also a recognized language and is spoken by the majority of the Indian population. As a result of an intensive national education programme more than 75 per cent of the population are now literate. Elementary education is free and compulsory. There are nine universities (two at Quito, three at Guayaquil, and one each at Cuenca, Machala, Loja and Portoviejo), polytechnic schools at Quito and Guayaquil and eight technical colleges in other provincial capitals. Two daily newspapers are published at Quito and four at Guayaquil.

Finance.—The estimated government budget in 1986 was: revenue 186,824 million sucres; expenditure 216,466 million sucres.

TRADE

Import licences are required for all merchandise and these are issued by the Central Bank of Ecuador. Manufactured goods and machinery are the main imports.

	1987	1988
Imports	US$2,229·0m.	US$1,713·5m.
Exports	1,998·6m.	2,192·9m.

Trade with UK

	1988	1989
Imports from UK	£50,417,000	£29,410,000
Exports to UK	13,120,000	19,319,000

CAPITAL.—Quito, population (1988 estimate) 1,200,000; Ψ Guayaquil (1,600,000) is the chief port; Cuenca (151,000).

CURRENCY.—Sucre of 100 centavos.

FLAG.—Three horizontal bands, yellow, blue and red (the yellow band twice the width of the others); emblem in centre.

NATIONAL DAY.—August 10 (Independence Day).

BRITISH EMBASSY
Calle Gonzalez Suarez, 111 (Casilla 314),
Quito
[Quito 560669]

Ambassador Extraordinary and Plenipotentiary, His Excellency Frank Basil Wheeler, CMG (1989).

There are British Consular Offices at *Cuenca* and *Guayaquil*.

British Council Representative, Gillian Marsh, Av. Amazonas 1646 (Casilla 8829), Quito.

The GALÁPAGOS (Giant Tortoise) ISLANDS forming the province of the Archipelago de Colón, were annexed by Ecuador in 1832. The archipelago lies in the Pacific, about 500 miles from Saint Elena peninsula, the most westerly point of the mainland. There are 12 large and several hundred smaller islands with a total area of about 3,000 sq. miles and an estimated population (1982) of 6,119. The capital is San Cristobal, on Chatham Island. Although the archipelago lies on the equator, the temperature of the surrounding water is well below equatorial average owing to the Antarctic Humboldt Current. The province consists for the most part of National Park Territory, where unique marine birds, iguanas, and the giant tortoises are conserved. There is some local subsistence farming; the main industry, apart from tourism, is tuna and lobster fishing.

EGYPT
(Al-Jumhuriyal Misr al-Arabiya)

President, Muhammad Hosni Mubarak, *elected*, Oct. 13, 1981, *re-elected* 1987.

COUNCIL OF MINISTERS
(as at June 30, 1990)

Prime Minister, Dr. Atef Muhammad Naguib Sidqi.
Presidential Assistant, Muhammad Abdul Halim Abu Ghazala.
Defence and Military Production, Gen. Youssef Sabri Abu Taleb.
Deputy PM and Foreign Minister, Dr. Ahmed Ismat Abdul Magid.
Deputy PM and Minister of Planning and International Co-operation, Dr. Kamal Ahmed al-Ganzuri.
Deputy PM and Minister of Agriculture and Land Reclamation, Dr. Yussif Amin Wali.
Economy and Foreign Trade, Dr. Yussri Ali Mustafa.
Finance, Dr. Muhammad Ahmed el-Razzaz.
Interior, Maj.-Gen. Mohammed Abdul Halim Mousa.
Oil and Mineral Wealth, Abdul-Hadi Muhammad Qandil.
Tourism and Civil Aviation, Fouad Abdul Latif Sultan.
Justice, Farouq Saif al-Nasr.
Culture, Farouq Hosni.
Industry, Muhammad Mahmoud Abdul Wahhab.
Parliamentary and Shura Council Affairs, Dr. Ahmed Salama.
Supply and Internal Trade, Dr. Mohammed Galaleddin Abdul-Dahab.
Public Works and Water Resources, 'Issam Abdul Hamid Radi.
Manpower and Vocational Training, Assem Abdul Haq.
Education, Dr. Ahmed Fathi Sorour.
Transport, Communications and Marine Transport, Suliman Metwalli Suliman.
Scientific Research, Dr. Adel Abul-Hamid 'Ezz.
Health, Dr. Mohammed Ragheb Dawidar.
Information, Muhammad Safwat al-Sharif.
Cabinet Affairs and Administrative Development, Dr. 'Atif Mohammad 'Ebeid.
Religious Affairs (Waqfs), Dr. Muhammad Ali Mahgoub.
Social Affairs and Social Insurance, Dr. Amal Abdul Rahim Osman.
Electricity and Energy, Mohammad Mahir Osman Abaza.
Housing, New Communities and Public Utilities, Hasaballah Mohammad al-Kafrawi.
Ministers of State, Dr. Boutros Yussef Boutros-Ghali (*Foreign Affairs*); Gamal al-Sayyid Ibrahim (*Military Production*); Dr. Fouad Iskander (*Immigration and Egyptians living abroad*); Dr. Mouris Makramallah (*International Co-operation*).

EMBASSY OF THE ARAB REPUBLIC OF EGYPT
26 South Street, W1Y 8EL
[071–499 2401]

Ambassador Extraordinary and Plenipotentiary, His Excellency Mohamed I. Shaker (1988).

Area and Population.—The total area of Egypt is 386,662 sq. miles (1,001,449 sq. km), only three per cent of which is cultivated land, with a population (UN estimate 1988) of 51,897,000.

There are three distinct elements in the native population. The largest, or 'Egyptian' element, is a Hamito-Semite race, known in the rural districts as *Fellahin* (*fellâh*—ploughman, or tiller of the soil). A second element is the *Bedouin*, or nomadic Arabs of the Western and Arabian deserts, of whom about one-seventh are real nomads, and the remainder semi-sedentary tent-dwellers on the outskirts of the cultivated end of the Nile Valley and the Fayûm. The third element is the *Nubian* of the Nile Valley between Aswân and Wadi-Halfa of mixed Arab and Negro blood. Over 90 per cent of the population are Muslims of the Sunni denomination, and most of the rest Coptic Christians.

The territory of Egypt comprises (1) Egypt Proper, forming the N.E. corner of the African continent, divisible into (a) the valley and delta of the Nile, (b) the Western Desert, and (c) the Arabian or Eastern Desert; (2) The Peninsula of Sinai, forming part of the continent of Asia; and (3) a number of islands in the Gulf of Suez and Red Sea, of which the principal are Jubal, Shadwan, Gafatin and Zeberged (or St. John's Island). This territory lies between 22° and 32° N. lat. and 24° and 37° E. long. The northern boundary is the Mediterranean, and in the south Egypt is conterminous with the Sudan. The western boundary runs from a point on the coast 10 kilometres N.W. of Sollûm to the latitude of Siwa and thence due S. along the 25th meridian. The E. boundary follows a line drawn from Rafa on the Mediterranean (34° 15' E. long.) to the head of the Gulf of 'Aqaba.

Physical Features.—The country is mainly flat but there are mountainous areas in the south-west, along the Red Sea coast and in the south of the Sinai peninsula, rising in some places to peaks of over 6,000 ft. The highest mountain in Egypt is Mt. Catherina (8,668 ft). Most of the land is desert but the Nile valley and delta are covered by silt 20–30 feet deep, and areas of desert are increasingly being reclaimed by irrigation and fertilization.

The Nile has a total length of 4,145 miles. In the 960 miles of its course through Egypt it receives not a single tributary stream. The river formerly had a regular yearly rise and fall of about 13 feet at Cairo, but since the completion of the Aswan High Dam in 1965 (about a mile upstream from the smaller Aswan Dam, built around the turn of the century), there has been no flood downstream of the dam and the water

level remains almost constant throughout the year. The area of fertile land, a 5–15 mile wide strip in the Nile valley and some 6,000 square miles of the Nile delta, has been increased by the opening of the Aswan Dam. This has allowed the reclamation of about 1,300,000 acres, and a further 700,000 acres have been converted from basin to perennial irrigation. Westward from the Nile Valley stretches the Western desert, containing some depressions, whose springs irrigate small areas known as Oases, of which the principal, from SE to N.W., are known as Kharga, Dakhla, Farafra, Baharia and Siwa.

In the Eastern Desert between the Nile and the mountains along the Red Sea coast, are plateaux of sandstones and limestones, dissected by wadis (dry water-courses), often of great length and depth, with some wild vegetation and occasional wells and springs.

History.—The unification of the Kingdoms of Lower and Upper Egypt under the Pharaohs c. 3100 BC marked the establishment of the Egyptian state, with Memphis as its capital. Egypt was ruled for nearly 2,800 years by a succession of Pharaonic dynasties (31 in all), which built the pyramids at Gizeh. The oldest of these is that of Zoser, built c. 2700 BC, and the highest the Great Pyramid of Cheops, at 451 feet; nearby is the Sphinx, 189 feet long. A period of Hellenic rule began in 332 BC, after the conquest of Egypt by Alexander the Great, followed by a period of rule by Rome (30 BC to AD 324) and then by the Byzantine Empire. In AD 640 Egypt was subjugated by Arab Muslim invaders, becoming a province of the Eastern Caliphate. In 1517 the country was incorporated in the Ottoman Empire under which it remained until early in the 19th century.

A British Protectorate over Egypt declared on Dec. 18, 1914, lasted until Feb. 28, 1922, when Sultan Ahmed Fuad was proclaimed King of Egypt. In July 1952, following a military coup d'état, King Farouk abdicated in favour of his infant son, who became King Ahmed Fuad II. In June 1953 however, Gen. Neguib's military council deposed the young king, and Egypt became a Republic.

In 1956, as a result of Egypt's trade agreements with Communist countries, Britain and USA withdrew offers of financial aid and in retaliation President Nasser seized the assets of the Suez Canal Company. An Egyptian invasion of the Canal Zone while repulsing an Israeli attack provoked military action by Britain and France in support of their Suez Canal Company interests. A ceasefire and Anglo-French withdrawal were negotiated by the UN.

The Israeli invasion of 1956 overran the Sinai peninsula but six months later Israel withdrew and a UN peace-keeping force was established in the area. However, mounting tension culminated in a second invasion of Sinai (the Six Day War of June 1967) and occupation of the peninsula by Israel. Egypt's attempt to recapture the territory (the Yom Kippur War of October 1973) was unsuccessful but Sinai was returned to Egypt in April 1982, under the treaty of 1979 which resulted from the Camp David talks between President Sadat and the Israeli Prime Minister Menachem Begin and formally terminated a 31-year old state of war between the two countries. President Mubarak came to power on October 13, 1981 after the assassination of President Sadat by Muslim fundamentalists.

Government.—The Constitution of 1971 provides for an executive President who appoints Ministers to the Cabinet. The President determines policy which the Cabinet implements and Ministers are responsible to him. The Legislature consists of the People's Assembly (458 members, 448 of whom are elected, the remaining 10 nominated by the President); the Shura Council, or Consultative Assembly (258 members) has an advisory role. The Constitution also guarantees the independence of the Judiciary. Religious courts were abolished in 1956 and their functions transferred to the national court system. Freedom of the press is guaranteed under the Constitution.

Agriculture.—Despite increasing industrialization, agriculture remains the most important economic activity, employing over 45 per cent of the labour force and contributing to 17 per cent of the country's exports. Agricultural output has been increased as a result of land reclamation programmes and the introduction of more efficient methods, e.g. the change from basin to perennial irrigation which yields 2–3 crops per year instead of one, the pivotal sprinkling irrigation system which uses water more efficiently, and the increasing mechanization and use of fertilizers. Egypt is still a net importer of foodstuffs, especially grain, and a food security programme has been set up with the aim of achieving self-sufficiency through the use of more advanced technology. Estimates suggest that an additional 3 million acres of land could be reclaimed by the end of the century.

The main cash crop is cotton, of which Egypt is one of the world's main producers. Production in 1986 was 403,000 tons. Other important summer crops are maize, rice and sugar cane. Important winter crops are wheat and beans. Citrus fruit and other fruits and vegetables are also grown.

Energy.—With its considerable reserves of petroleum and natural gas in Sinai, the Nile Delta and the Western Desert, and the hydro-electric power produced by the Aswan and High Dams, Egypt is self-sufficient in energy. Electricity has been provided to almost all of the country and there are plans to extend the natural gas network to all major cities.

Industry.—The production of petroleum provides Egypt with its major export (60–65 per cent of total exports), and supports a growing refining industry. Steel production is another important heavy industry. The major manufacturing industries are in food processing, motor cars and electrical goods, chemical products and yarns and textiles.

FINANCE

	1986–87	1987–88
Estimated revenue	£E12·4m	£E14·2m
Total expenditure	19·9m	21·7m

TRADE

The main imports are wheat and flour, wood and trucks. The main exports are crude petroleum, cotton, cotton yarn, oranges, rice and cotton textiles.

	1986–87
Imports	£E7·8m
Exports	2·6m

Trade with UK

	1988	1989
Imports from UK	£289,309,000	£296,272,000
Exports to UK	163,038,000	212,727,000

Communications.—The road and rail networks link the Nile Valley and Delta with the main development areas to east and west of the river.

The Suez Canal was re-opened in 1975 and a two-stage development project begun to widen and deepen the canal to allow the passage of larger shipping and to permit two-way traffic. Port Said and Suez have been reconstructed and the port of Alexandria is being improved.

CAPITAL.—Cairo (population, estimated in 1986 at 14,000,000), stands on the E. bank of the Nile, about 14 miles from the head of the Delta. Its oldest part is the fortress of Babylon in old Cairo, with its Roman bastions and Coptic churches. The earliest Arab building is the Mosque of 'Amr, dating from AD 643,

and the most conspicuous is the Citadel, built by Saladin towards the end of the 12th century and containing in its walls the Mosque of Mohamed Ali built in the 19th century.

ΨAlexandria (estimated population in 1986 of 5,000,000), founded 332 BC by Alexander the Great, was for over 1,000 years the capital of Egypt and a centre of Hellenic culture which vied with Athens herself. Its great *pharos* (lighthouse), 480 feet high, with a lantern burning resinous wood, was one of the Seven Wonders of the World. Other towns are: Ismailia (400,000); ΨPort Said (285,000); Mansura (120,000); Asyût (300,000); Faiyûm (180,000); Tanta (150,000); Mahalla el Kubra (130,000); ΨSuez; ΨDamietta (100,000).

CURRENCY.—Egyptian pound (£E) of 100 piastres and 1,000 millièmes.

FLAG.—Horizontal bands of red, white and black, with an eagle in the centre of the white band.

NATIONAL DAY.—July 23 (Anniversary of Revolution in 1952).

BRITISH EMBASSY
Ahmed Ragheb Street, Garden City, Cairo
[Cairo 354–0850]

Ambassador Extraordinary and Plenipotentiary, His Excellency (William) James Adams, CMG (1987).

British Council Representative, J. Barnett, OBE, 192 Sharia el Nil, Agouza, Cairo. There is also a library in *Alexandria*.

EQUATORIAL GUINEA
(República de Guinea Ecuatorial)

President of the Supreme Military Council and Minister of Defence, Brig.-Gen. Teodoro Obiang Nguema Mbasogo, *took office*, Aug. 1979, *re-elected* June 1989.

MINISTERS
(as at May 31, 1990)

Prime Minister, Cristino Seriche Bioko.

Deputy PM, Education, Youth and Sport, Isidoro Eyi Monsuy Andeme.

Minister of State, Minister Secretary-General to the Presidency, Marcelino Nguemo Ongueme.

Ministers of State at the Presidency, Eloy Elo Nve Mbengono; Alejandro Evuna Asangono.

Minister Deputy Secretary-General to the Presidency, Martin Nka Esono Nsing.

Justice, Silvestre Siale Sale Bileka.

Public Works, Urban Development and Transport, Alejandro Envoro Ovono.

Agriculture, Fishing and Forestry, Anatolio Nolong Mba.

Industry and Energy, Francisco Pascual Obama Asue.

Labour and Social Development, Antonio Pascual Oko Ebobo.

Ministers Delegate:

Economic and Financial Affairs, Antonio Fernando Nve Ngu.

Mines and Hydrocarbons, Juan Olo Mba Nseng.

Culture, Tourism and Handicrafts, Leandro Mbomio Nsue.

Foreign Affairs and Co-operation, Santiago Eneme Ovono.

National Defence, Melanio Ebendeng Nsomo.

Economy, Commerce and Planning, Casto Nvono Akhele.

Territorial Administration and Communications, Segundo Munoz Italo.

Health, Alejandro Masoko Bengono.

Women's Development, Purificaçion Angue Ondo.

Equatorial Guinea (formerly Spanish Guinea) consists of the island of Biogo (formerly Macias Nguema), in the Bight of Biafra about 20 miles from the west coast of Africa, Pagalu Island (formerly Annobon) in the Gulf of Guinea, the Corisco Islands (Corisco, Elobey Grande and Elobey Chico) and Rio Muni, a mainland area between Cameroon and Gabon. It has a total area of 10,830 sq. miles (28,051 sq. km), and a population (UN estimate 1988) of 420,000.

Government.—Formerly colonies of Spain, the territories now forming the Republic of Equatorial Guinea were constituted as two provinces of Metropolitan Spain in 1960, became autonomous in 1964 and fully independent in 1968. Serious disorders in Rio Muni early in 1969 caused many of the Spanish community to leave.

In August 1979, President Macias was deposed by a revolutionary military council headed by his nephew Col. T. Obiang Nguema. The first parliamentary elections since 1968 were held in August 1983, under a new constitution approved by a referendum in August 1982. The most recent elections to the 41-member National Assembly took place in July 1988. All candidates were nominated by the President and elected unopposed for a five-year term.

Economy.—The chief products are cocoa, coffee and wood (which is exported almost entirely from Rio Muni). Production has declined and except for cocoa, there is little commercial agriculture and the economy is now heavily dependent on outside aid, principally from Spain. Equatorial Guinea entered the 'Franc zone' in 1985.

Trade with UK

	1988	1989
Imports from UK	£1,029,000	£640,000
Exports to UK	—	2,000

CAPITAL.—ΨMalabo on the island of Bioco, population (1983 estimate) 34,980. ΨBata is the principal town and port of Rio Muni.

CURRENCY.— Franc CFA of 100 centimes.

FLAG.—Three horizontal bands, green over white over red; blue triangle next staff; coat of arms in centre of white band.

NATIONAL DAY.—October 12.

British Ambassador, (resident in Yaoundé, Cameroon).

BRITISH CONSULATE
World Bank Compound, Apartado 801, Malabo
[Tel. Malabo 2400]

Honorary Consul, George Pudney, OBE.

ETHIOPIA
(Hebretesebawit Ityopia)

President of the People's Democratic Republic, Lt.-Col. Mengistu Haile Mariam, *elected* Sept. 10, 1987.
Vice President of the Republic, Fisseha Desta.
Vice Presidents of the State Council, Amanual Ande Michael (*Legal and Foreign Relations*); Lemma Sutema; Yusuf Ahmed (*Planning, Finance, Economy*); Berhana Bayih.

COUNCIL OF MINISTERS
(as at May 31, 1990)

Deputy Prime Minister (Acting PM), Hailu Yemanu.
Deputy PM in charge of Economic Affairs, Walle Chekol.
Deputy PM in charge of Social Affairs, Ashagre Yigletu.
Agriculture, Geremew Debele.

Coffee and Tea Development, Hambissa Wakoya.
Construction, Kassa Gebre.
Culture and Sports, Maj. Girma Yilma.
Defence, vacant.
Domestic Trade, Mersha Wodajo.
Education, Dr. Yayeh-Yirad Kitaw.
Finance, Tekola Dejene.
Foreign Affairs, Tesfaye Dinka.
Foreign Trade, Getachew Habte Selasie.
Health, Dr. Gizaw Tsehay.
Work—Industry, Tadeos Hagere.
Information and National Guidance, Abdulhafes Yusuf.
Internal Affairs, Col. Tesfaye Wolde Selasie.
Labour and Social Affairs, Shimelis Adugna.
Law and Justice, Wondayen Mehretu.
Mines, Energy and Water Resources, Tekeze Shewa Aytenfisu.
State Farms, Yoseph Muleta.
Transport and Communications, Asegid Wolde Amanuel.
Urban Development and Housing, Tadesse Kidone-Mariam.
Ministers in President's Office, Dr. Feleke Gedle-Giorgis (*Foreign Relations*); Maj.-Gen. Kefelegn Yibza (*Chief Inspector of Military Affairs*); Neguse Wolde Mikael (*Chief Inspector of Economic, Social and Administrative Affairs*); Maj.-Gen. Seyoum Mekonen (*Chief of Defence and Security*).

EMBASSY OF THE PEOPLE'S DEMOCRATIC
REPUBLIC OF ETHIOPIA
17 Prince's Gate, SW7 1PZ
[071–589 7212]

Ambassador Extraordinary and Plenipotentiary, His Excellency Ato Teferra Haile-Selassie (1985).

Area and Population.—Ethiopia is in North-Eastern Africa, bounded on the north-west by the Sudan, on the south by Kenya, on the east by Djibouti and the Republic of Somalia, and on the north-east by the Red Sea. The area is 471,778 sq. miles (1,221,900 sq. km), with a population (UN estimate 1988) of 47,882,000. About one-third are of the dominant race of Semitic origin (Amharas and Tigreans) and the remainder mainly Gallas (about 40 per cent of the population), Somalis and Afar.

Ethiopia has a large central plateau (average height, 6,000–7,000 ft.) which rises to nearly 15,000 ft. at Ras Dashan in the north. The plateau drops to the Nile basin in the west and the Red Sea in the east. To the north (Eritrea) and east (Ogaden) the land is mostly desert. The chief river is the Blue Nile, issuing from Lake Tana; the Atbara and many other tributaries of the Nile also rise in the Ethiopian highlands.

Those of Semitic origin (Amharas and Tigreans), and many of the Gallas, are Christians of the Ethiopian Orthodox Church, which was formerly led by the head of the Coptic Church, the Patriarch at Alexandria. Since 1959, however, the Ethiopian Church has been autocephalous and the new Patriarch, Abuna Markarious, was enthroned in Sept. 1988. The Afar people, who inhabit lowland Eritrea, Wollo, Hararghe and Bale provinces, and the Somalis, in the south-east, are Muslim. The Falashas, to be found principally in Gandar and Tigre provinces, practise Judaism. Between autumn 1984 and February 1985 a secret airlift (Operation Moses) took 7,000 of the estimated 25,000 Falashas to Israel, via Sudan.

History.—The basic Hamitic culture was heavily influenced by Semitic immigration from Arabia in the centuries about the time of Christ. Christianity was introduced in the 4th century. The empire expanded sporadically, attaining a zenith in the 6th century under the Axum rulers, but subsequently checked by Islamic expansion from the east. Modern Ethiopia dates from 1855 when Theodore succeeded in establishing supremacy over the various tribes. The last Emperor was Haile Selassie who reigned from 1930, though in exile from 1936–1941 during the Italian occupation. After considerable military and civil unrest the armed forces assumed power in September 1972 and deposed the Emperor. A Workers' Party on the Soviet model was formed in September 1984, with Mengistu as General Secretary.

In July 1977, Somalia, claiming the Ogaden region of Ethiopia in support of Western Somalia Liberation Front guerrillas, invaded the region. Ethiopia, with Soviet arms, and the aid of Cuban troops, was able to defeat the Somalis. In April 1988 both governments agreed to re-establish diplomatic relations and to withdraw troops from their common border.

The civilian government of the People's Democratic Republic of Ethiopia was established in Sept. 1987 with Lt.-Col. Mengistu being elected the first President. A new constitution was established and provides for the *Shengo* (National Assembly) of 835 seats. The Shengo votes on the membership of the 24-member State Council. One of the first acts of the Shengo was to endorse the government's proposed new internal boundaries which created 24 administrative and 5 autonomous regions out of the 14 existing provinces. The Eritrean People's Liberation Front (EPLF) and the Tigre People's Liberation Front (TPLF) oppose these boundaries.

Eritrea was administered by Great Britain from the end of the Second World War until September 15, 1952, when it was federated with Ethiopia. It was incorporated as a province of Ethiopia in 1962. An armed campaign for independence started in 1962 and has intensified since the early 1970s.

The Tigrean province, which lies south of Eritrea, seeks to establish greater autonomy; the activities of the TPLF have escalated since the early 1980s, and it now claims to control and administer the province.

Production and Industry.—The principal pursuit is agriculture, which accounts for approximately 40 per cent of GDP, 85 per cent of exports and 80 per cent of total employment. Land was nationalized in 1975 and tenants given rights of use to the land they had tilled; large private holdings became state farms. The major food crops are teff, maize, barley, sorghum, wheat, pulses and oil seeds. Coffee, the principal export crop, generates over 50 per cent of the country's export earnings.

Famine conditions, which attracted world attention in 1984–85, again prevail in 1990. As before, the situation is exacerbated by guerrilla activity.

Manufacturing industry accounts for less than 9 per cent of GDP and is heavily dependent on agriculture. Ethiopia's known, but as yet largely unexploited, natural resources include gold, platinum, copper and potash. Traces of oil and natural gas have been found.

Communications.—With the aid of loans from the IBRD, China and the African Development Bank, a network of roads has been built in rural areas and link the major cities with each other, and with the Sudanese and Kenyan borders and the Red Sea coast. Transport links have suffered during the secessionist wars and under the heavy burden of famine relief traffic. The two roads to the north are usable only under heavy military escort in Tigre and Eritrea. There is a railway link from Addis Ababa to Djibouti although this is vulnerable to guerrilla activity. The narrow gauge line in Eritrea has been closed by conflict. Ethiopian Airlines maintains regular services from Addis Ababa to many provincial towns. External services are operated throughout Africa and to Europe.

Defence.—Under the Ministry of Defence the armed forces comprise the Army, the Air Force and the Navy. The Army strength (1990) totals 313,000 personnel (including a People's Militia) divided into 28 divisions.

The Air Force comprises a transport squadron, a reconnaissance squadron, five fighter squadrons, a training squadron, and two helicopter squadrons. There are 150 fighter planes, all of Russian manufacture. The Air Force headquarters is situated at Debre Zeit.

National Military Service was introduced in January 1984.

Education.—Elementary education is provided without religious discrimination by Government schools in the main centres of population; there are also Mission schools, and cadet-schools for the Army, Navy, Air Force and Police. Government secondary schools are found mainly in Addis Ababa, but also in most of the provincial capitals. The National University (founded 1961) co-ordinates the institutions of higher education (University College, Engineering, Building and Theological Colleges in Addis Ababa, Agricultural College at Alemaya, near Harar, and Public Health Centre in Gondar, etc.). It is intended to develop the provincial colleges to university level and status.

Amharic is the official language of instruction, with English as the first foreign language and main language of instruction from secondary level upwards. Arabic is taught in Koran Schools; and Ge'ez (the ancient Ethiopic) in Christian Church Schools, which abound.

FINANCE

	1987–88
Revenue	US$1,709·5m
Expenditure	2,226·4m

TRADE

The chief imports by value are machinery and transport equipment, manufactured goods and chemicals (from UK); the principal exports by value being coffee, oilseeds, hides and skins, and pulses.

	1987–88
Total Imports	US$1,083·6m
Total Exports	393·7m

Trade with UK

	1988	1989
Imports from UK	£47,661,000	£44,148,000
Exports to UK	8,451,000	12,772,000

CAPITAL.— Addis Ababa (population, 1985 estimate, 1,464,901), also capital of the province of Shoa;

Asmara (population 275,000) is the capital of the Province of Eritrea. Dire Dawa is the most important commercial centre after Addis Ababa and Asmara, ΨMassawa and ΨAssab are the two main ports. There are ancient architectural remains at Aksum, Gondar, Lalibela and elsewhere.

CURRENCY.—Ethiopian birr (EB) of 100 cents.
FLAG.—Three horizontal bands: green, yellow, red.
NATIONAL ANTHEM.—Ityopya, Ityopya Kidemi.
NATIONAL DAY.—September 12 (People's Revolution Day).

BRITISH EMBASSY
Fikre Mariam Abatechan Street (PO Box 858)
Addis Ababa
[Addis Ababa 612354]

Ambassador Extraordinary and Plenipotentiary, His Excellency Michael John Carlisle Glaze, CMG (1990).

There is a British Consular Office at *Addis Ababa.*

British Council Representative, B. Nightingale, Artistic Building, Adwa Avenue (PO Box 1043), Addis Ababa. There is also a library in *Asmara.*

FIJI
(Matanitu Ko Fiti—Republic of Fiji)

President, Ratu Sir Penaia Ganilau, GCMG, KCVO, KBE, DSO, *appointed* Dec. 5, 1987.

CABINET
(as at July 11, 1990)

Prime Minister, Home Affairs and Foreign Affairs, Ratu Sir Kamisese Mara, GCMG, KBE.
Fijian Affairs and Rural Development, Col. Vatiliai Navunisaravi.
Finance and Economic Planning, Josefata Kamikamica.
Education, Youth and Sport, Filipe Bole, CBE.
Primary Industries and Co-operatives, Viliame Gonelevu.
Trade and Commerce, Berenado Vunibobo.
Health, Apenisa Kurisaqila.
Infrastructure and Public Utilities, Apisai Tora.
Attorney-General and Justice, Sailosi Kepa.
Tourism, Civil Aviation and Energy, David Pickering, CBE.
Indian Affairs, Mrs. Irene Jai Narayan.
Forests, Ratu Ovini Bokini.
Employment and Industrial Relations, Taniela Veitata.
Women and Social Welfare, Adi Finau Tabakaucoro.
Housing and Urban Development, Tomasi Vakatora.
Lands and Mineral Resources, Ratu William Toganivalu.
Information, Broadcasting, Television and Telecommunications, Ratu Inoke Kubuabola.

EMBASSY OF FIJI
34 Hyde Park Gate, SW7 5BN
[071-584 3661/2]

Ambassador Extraordinary and Plenipotentiary, His Excellency Brig.-Gen. Ratu Epeli Nailatikau, LVO, OBE (1988).

Area, Population, etc.—Fiji is made up of about 332 islands and over 500 islets (including numerous atolls and reefs) in the South Pacific Ocean, about 1,100 miles north of New Zealand. About 100 islands are permanently inhabited. The gross area of the group, which extends 300 miles from east to west, and 300 north to south, between 15° 45'—21° 10' S. lat. and 176° E.—178° W. long. is 7,055 sq. miles (18,274 sq. km). The International Date Line has been diverted to the east of the island group. The largest islands are Viti Levu and Vanua Levu. The main groups of islands

are Lomaiviti, Lau and Yasawas. Most of the larger islands are mountainous with sharp peaks and crags, but also have conspicuous areas of flat land and many of the rivers have built extensive deltas. The climate is tropical, without extremes of heat and temperatures rarely exceed 32°C and seldom fall below 15°C.

The population (Census 1986) was 715,373, comprising 48·6 per cent Indians, 46·2 per cent Fijians, and 5·2 per cent other races. A UN estimate (1988) gives a total figure of 727,000.

Government.—Fiji was a British colony from 1874 until October 10, 1970 when it became an independent state and a member of the Commonwealth.

A coalition of the left under Dr. Timoci Bavadra defeated the Alliance Party of Ratu Sir Kamisese Mara in a General Election on April 12, 1987. The new Government, drawing its support mainly from the Indian population, was overthrown in a military coup on May 14 by Lt.-Col. Sitiveni Rabuka. In the wake of the constitutional crisis an Advisory Council of 19 members was set up by the Governor General as an interim government to consider constitutional reform.

A second coup occurred on September 25, 1987. On October 7 Rabuka declared Fiji to be a republic; the Governor General resigned on October 15 and Fiji's Commonwealth membership lapsed. An Executive Council of Ministers, with Rabuka at its head, assumed control until December 5 when Ratu Sir Penaia Ganilau was appointed President. The President called upon Ratu Sir Kamisese Mara to form another interim administration to work for a resolution to the political crisis.

In June 1990 the Great Council of Chiefs approved a new Constitution for promulgation later in the year.

FINANCE

	1987	1988
Public Income	F$342m	F$358m
Public Expenditure	416m	399m

Economy.—The economy is primarily agrarian, with about 600,000 acres under cultivation. The principal cash crop is sugar cane, which is the main export, followed by coconuts, ginger and copra. A variety of other fruit, vegetables and root crops are also grown, and self-sufficiency in rice is a major aim. Forestry, fishing and beef production are being encouraged in order to diversify the economy. The processing of agricultural, marine and timber products are the main industries, along with gold mining. A policy of tax concessions for export-oriented manufacturing has encouraged expansion of the garment industry.

Tourism is also a major factor in the economy, second only to sugar as a money-earner.

TRADE

	1988	1989
Total Imports	F$570,700,000	F$961,870,139
Total Exports	493,800,000	598,201,244

Trade with UK

	1988	1989
Imports from UK	£6,358,000	£10,221,000
Exports to UK	65,273,000	69,558,000

The chief imports are foodstuffs, machinery, mineral fuels, chemicals, beverages, tobacco and manufactured articles. Chief exports are sugar, coconut oil, gold, lumber, garments, molasses, ginger and canned fish.

Communications.—Fiji is one of the main aerial crossroads in the Pacific, providing services to New Zealand, Australia, Tonga, Western Samoa, Vanuatu, the Solomon Islands, Kiribati, Tuvalu, New Caledonia and American Samoa.

Fiji has three ports of entry, at Suva, Lautoka and Levuka.

CAPITAL.—ΨSuva, on the island of Viti Levu. Population (1985) 75,000.

CURRENCY.—Fiji dollar (F$) of 100 cents.

FLAG.—Light blue ground with Union flag in top left quarter and the shield of Fiji in the fly.

NATIONAL ANTHEM.—Hail to Fiji.

NATIONAL DAY.—October 10 (Fiji Day).

BRITISH EMBASSY
Victoria House, 47 Gladstone Road,
PO Box 1355, Suva
[Suva 311033]

Ambassador Extraordinary and Plenipotentiary, His Excellency (Alexander Basil) Peter Smart, CMG (1989).

FINLAND
(Suomen Tasavalta)

President, Dr. Mauno Koivisto, *born*, 1923, *elected*, Jan 26, 1982, *re-elected*, March 1, 1988.

CABINET
(as at May 31, 1990)

Prime Minister, Harri Holkeri (NCP).
Foreign Affairs, Pertti Paasio (SDP).
Cabinet, Ilkka Kanerva (NCP).
Foreign Trade, Pertti Salolainen (NCP).
Justice, Tarja Halonen (SDP).
Interior, Jarmo Rantanen (SDP).
Defence, Ole Norrback (SPP).
Finance, Matti Louekoski (SDP).
Deputy Minister of Finance, Ulla Puolanne (NCP).
Education, Christoffer Taxell (SPP).
Deputy Minister of Education, Anna-Liisa Kasurinen (SDP).
Agriculture and Forestry, Toivo T. Pohjola (NCP).
Transport and Communications, Raimo Vistbacka (FRP).
Trade and Industry, Ilkka Suominen (NCP).
Social Affairs and Health, Helena Pesola (NCP).
Deputy Minister of Social Affairs and Health, Tuulikki Hämäläinen (SDP).
Labour, Matti Puhakka (SDP).
Environment, Kaj Bärlund (SDP).

NCP: National Coalition Party, SDP: Social Democratic Party, SPP: Swedish People's Party of Finland, FRP: Finnish Rural Party.

FINNISH EMBASSY AND CONSULATE
38 Chesham Place, SW1X 8HW
[071–235 9531]

Ambassador Extraordinary and Plenipotentiary, His Excellency Ilkka Pastinen, KCMG (1983).

Minister Counsellor, J. Leino.

Counsellors, Dr. H. Markala; J. Muttonen; T. Airaksinen.

Defence Attaché, Col. T. Aaltonen.

Area and Population.—A country situated on the Gulfs of Finland and Bothnia, with a total area of 137,851 sq. miles (337,032 sq. km), of which 65 per cent is forest, 8 per cent cultivated land and 9 per cent lakes. The population (1989) is 4,954,484; population density is 16 inhabitants per square km. The population is predominantly Lutheran.

The Aland Archipelago (Ahvenanmaa), a group of small islands at the entrance to the Gulf of Bothnia, covers about 572 square miles, with a population (December 1985) of 23,600 (95·2 per cent Swedish-speaking). The islands have a semi-autonomous status.

Government.—Under the Constitution there is a single Chamber (*Eduskunta*) composed of 200 members, elected by universal suffrage. The legislative power is vested in the Chamber and the President. The highest executive power is held by the President who is elected for a period of 6 years.

The present government came into office on April 30, 1987. The four parties in the coalition are the National Coalition Party (conservative), the Social Democratic Party, the Swedish People's Party of Finland, and the Finnish Rural Party.

Defence.—By the terms of the Peace Treaty (February 10, 1947) with UK and USSR, the Army is limited to a force not exceeding 34,400. The Navy is limited to a total of 10,000 tons displacement with personnel not exceeding 4,500. The Air Force, including naval air arm, is limited to 60 machines with a personnel not exceeding 3,000. Bombers or aircraft with bomb-carrying facilities are expressly forbidden. The Defence Forces contain a cadre of regular officers and NCO's, but their bulk is provided by conscripts who serve for 8–11 months. Total strength of trained and equipped reserves is over 700,000, 16,500 of whom have served in the UN peacekeeping force.

Education.—Primary education (co-educational comprehensive school) is compulsory for children from 7 to 16 years, and free of charge. In the autumn of 1986, there were 678,463 in comprehensive schools and 113,117 in vocational institutions of senior level. There are 21 universities or other schools of academic level, and enrolment was (1985) 92,230.

Language and Literature.—There are two official languages in Finland. 93·6 per cent of the population speak Finnish as their first language, 6·2 Swedish (1986). The remaining 0·2 per cent speak other languages (mainly Lapps who number about 2,500 and live in the far north). Both Finnish and Swedish are used for administration and education; newspapers, books, plays and films appear in both languages.There is a vigorous modern literature. F. E. Sillanpää, who died in 1964, was awarded the Nobel prize for Literature in 1939. In 1988 there were 103 daily newspapers (12 Swedish).

Production and Industry.—Finland is a highly industrialized country producing a wide range of capital and consumer goods. Timber and the products of the forest-based industries remain the backbone of the economy, but the importance of the metal-working, shipbuilding and engineering industries has been growing. The textile industry is well developed and Finland's glass, ceramics and furniture industries enjoy international reputations. Other important industries are rubber, plastics, chemicals and pharmaceuticals, footwear, foodstuffs and electronic equipment.

Communications.—There are 9,000 kilometres of railroad, a railway connection with Sweden and USSR, passenger boat connection with Sweden, Federal Republic of Germany, Poland and USSR. Vessels on the London to Leningrad route call at Helsinki. There are also passenger/cargo services between Britain and Helsinki, Kotka and other Finnish ports. External civil air services are maintained by most European airlines. The merchant fleet at the end of 1986 totalled 1,900,000 tons gross.

TRADE

The principal imports are raw materials, machinery and manufactured goods. In 1988 more than half of all industrial production was exported. The value of exports was broken down as follows: paper 33·4 per cent, wood 8·2 per cent, metal and engineering products 31 per cent, basic metal industry 8·3 per cent, chemicals 9 per cent, textiles and clothing 4·6 per cent.

	1987	1988
Total Imports	Mk86,696m	Mk88,192m
Total Exports	87,564m	90,861m

Trade with UK

	1988	1989
Imports from UK	£824,951,000	£925,784,000
Exports to UK	1,813,549,000	1,893,163,000

CAPITAL.—ΨHelsinki (Helsingfors), population (1986) 485,626; other towns are Tampere (Tammerfors), 169,153; ΨTurku (Åbo), 161,508; Espoo (Esbo), 156,851; Vantaa (Vanda), 143,986; ΨOulu (Oleåborg), 97,329; Lahti (Lahtis), 94,467; ΨPori (Björneborg), 78,365.

CURRENCY.—Markka (Mk) of 100 penniä.

FLAG.—White with blue cross.

NATIONAL DAY.—December 6 (Independence Day).

BRITISH EMBASSY
Itäinen Puistotie 17, 00140 Helsinki
[Helsinki 661293]

Ambassador Extraordinary and Plenipotentiary, His Excellency Neil Smith (1989).

Counsellor (Commercial), J. Noss.

First Secretaries, G. S. Hand (*Head of Chancery*); R. M. F. Kelly, W. Hamilton.

Defence, Naval, Military and Air Attaché, Lt.-Col. J. M. F. Thomson.

There are British Consular offices at *Helsinki, Jyväskylä, Kotka, Kuopio, Oulu, Pori, Tampere, Turku* and *Vaasa.*

British Council Representative, G. Coe, Erottajankatu 7B, 00130 Helsinki 13.

FRANCE
(La République Française)

President of the French Republic, François Mitterrand, *elected* May 10, 1981, *re-elected* May 8, 1988.

COUNCIL OF MINISTERS
(as at July 31, 1990)

Prime Minister, Michel Rocard (PS).
National Education, Youth and Sport, Lionel Jospin (PS).
Economy, Finance and Budget, Pierre Bérégovoy (PS).
Civil Service and Administrative Reform, Michel Durafour (UDF).
Foreign Affairs, Roland Dumas (PS).
Justice, Pierre Arpaillange (NP).
Defence, Jean-Pierre Chevènement (PS).
Interior, Pierre Joxe (PS).
European Affairs, Edith Cresson (PS).
Equipment and Housing, Transport, Sea, Michel Delebarre (PS).
Labour and Employment, Jean-Pierre Soisson (UDF).
Co-operation and Overseas Development, Jacques Pelletier (UDF).
Culture and Communications, Major Public Works, Jack Lang (PS).
Overseas Departments and Territories, Government Spokesman, Louis Le Pensec (PS).
Agriculture and Forestry, Henri Nallet (PS).
Posts and Telecommunications, and Space, Paul Quilès (PS).
Relations with Parliament, Jean Poperen (PS).
Solidarity, Health, Social Protection, Claude Evin (PS).
Research and Technology, Hubert Curien (PS).
Foreign Trade, Jean-Marie Rausch (UDF).
Industry and Local Planning, Roger Fauroux (NP).

PS: Parti socialiste; UDF: Union pour la démocratie française; NP: Non-party.

FRENCH EMBASSY
58 Knightsbridge, SW1X 7JT
[071–235 8080].

Ambassador Extraordinary and Plenipotentiary, His Excellency Vicomte Luc de La Barre de Nanteuil (1986).

Area and Population.—France extends from 42° 20′ to 51° 5′ N. lat., and from 7° 85′ E. to 4° 45′ W. long. Its area is estimated at 211,208 sq. miles (547,026 sq. km), divided into 95 departments, including the island of Corsica, in the Mediterranean, off the west coast of Italy. The population (UN estimate 1988) is 55,873,000.

POPULATION OF THE REGIONS 1987
(Names of Departments in brackets)

Alsace (Bas-Rhin, Haut-Rhin)	1,605,000
Aquitaine (Dordogne, Gironde, Landes, Lot-et-Garonne, Pyrénées-Atlantiques)	2,708,000
Auvergne (Allier, Cantal, Haute-Loire, Puy-de-Dôme)	1,329,000
Basse-Normandie (Calvados, Manche, Orne)	1,374,000
Bourgogne (Côte-d'Or, Nièvre, Saône-et-Loire, Yonne)	1,604,000
Bretagne (Côtes-du-Nord, Finistère, Ille-et-Vilaine, Morbihan)	2,767,000
Centre (Cher, Eure-et-Loir, Indre, Indre-et-Loire, Loir-et-Cher, Loiret)	2,333,000
Champagne-Ardenne (Ardennes, Aube, Marne, Haute-Marne)	1,359,000
Corse (Corse-du-Sud, Haute-Corse)	243,000
Franche-Comté (Doubs, Haute-Saône, Jura, Territoire-de-Belfort)	1,099,000
Haute-Normandie (Eure, Seine-Maritime)	1,685,000
Île-de-France (Essonne, Hauts-de-Seine, Seine-et-Marne, Seine-St-Denis, Val-de-Marne, Val-d'Oise, Ville de Paris, Yvelines)	10,290,000
Languedoc-Roussillon (Aude, Gard, Hérault, Lozère, Pyrénées-Orientales)	2,072,000
Limousin (Corrèze, Creuse, Haute-Vienne)	735,000
Lorraine (Meurthe-et-Moselle, Meuse, Moselle, Vosges)	2,320,000

Midi-Pyrénées (Ariège, Aveyron, Haute-Garonne, Gers, Lot, Hautes-Pyrénées, Tarn, Tarn-et-Garonne)	2,370,000
Nord-Pas-de-Calais (Nord, Pas-de-Calais)	3,923,000
Pays de la Loire (Loire-Atlantique, Maine-et-Loire, Mayenne, Sarthe, Vendée)	3,013,000
Picardie (Aisne, Oise, Somme)	1,787,000
Poitou-Charentes (Charente, Charente-Maritime, Deux-Sèvres, Vienne)	1,601,000
Provence-Alpes-Côte d'Azur (Alpes-de-Haute-Provence, Alpes-Maritime, Bouches-du-Rhône, Haute-Alpes, Var, Vaucluse)	4,116,000
Rhône-Alpes (Ain, Ardèche, Drôme, Isère, Loire, Rhône, Savoie, Haute-Savoie)	5,177,000

Archaeology, etc.—There are dolmens and menhirs in Brittany, prehistoric remains and cave drawings in Dordogne and Ariège, and throughout France various megalithic monuments erected by primitive tribes, predecessors of Iberian invaders from Spain (now represented by the Basques), Ligurians from northern Italy and Celts or Gauls from the valley of the Danube. Julius Caesar found Gaul 'divided into three parts' and described three political groups—Aquitanians south of the Garonne, Celts between the Garonne and the Seine and Marne, and Belgae from the Seine to the Rhine. Roman remains are plentiful throughout France in the form of aqueducts, arenas, triumphal arches, etc., and the celebrated Norman and Gothic Cathedrals, including Notre Dame in Paris, and those of Chartres, Reims,

Amiens (where Peter the Hermit preached the First Crusade for the recovery of the Holy Sepulchre), Bourges, Beauvais, Rouen, etc., have survived invasions and bombardments with only partial damage, and many of the renaissance and the seventeenth and eighteenth century chateaux survived the French Revolution.

Language and Literature.—French is the official language. The work of the French Academy, founded by Richelieu in 1635, has established *le bon usage*, equivalent to 'The Queen's English' in Great Britain. French authors have been awarded the Nobel Prize for Literature on twelve occasions, including R. F. A. Sully-Prudhomme (1901), Anatole France (1921), André Gide (1947), François Mauriac (1952), Albert Camus (1957), Jean Paul Sartre (1964) and Claude Simon (1985).

GOVERNMENT

Parliament consists of the National Assembly of 577 deputies (555 for Metropolitan France and 22 for the overseas departments and territories) and the Senate composed of 319 Senators (296 for Metropolitan France; 13 for the overseas departments and territories and 10 for French dependencies). The normal session of Parliament is confined to 5½ months each year and it may also meet in extraordinary session for 12 days at the request of the Prime Minister or a majority of the Assembly.

The Prime Minister is appointed by the President,

as is the Cabinet on the Prime Minister's recommendation. They are responsible to Parliament, but as the executive is constitutionally separate from the legislature Ministers may not sit in Parliament.

A Constitutional Council is responsible for supervising all elections and referenda and must be consulted on all constitutional matters and before the President of the Republic assumes emergency powers.

DEFENCE

The personnel of the Defence Forces in 1988 totalled 442,400. National nuclear forces include medium-range ballistic missiles, submarine-launched ballistic missiles and *Mirage* IV medium bombers. The Army has a variety of new French-made equipment in service, including medium tanks, field and anti-aircraft SP guns, trucks and radio equipment.

EDUCATION

The educational system is highly centralized and is administered by the Ministry of National Education. Local administration comprises 25 Territorial Academies, with inspecting staff for all grades, and Departmental Councils presided over by the *Préfet*, and charged especially with primary education.

Primary and secondary education are compulsory, free and secular, the school age being from 6 to 16. Schools may be single-sex or co-educational. Primary education is given in nursery schools, primary schools and *collèges d'enseignement général* (4-year secondary modern course); secondary education in *collèges d'enseignement technique*, *collèges d'enseignement secondaire* and *lycées* (7-year course leading to one of the five *baccalauréats*). Special schools are numerous.

There are many *Grandes Ecoles* in France which award diplomas in many subjects not taught at university, especially applied science and engineering. Most of these are state institutions but have a competitive system of entry, unlike the universities. There are universities in twenty-four towns in France, two or three in some major provincial towns, and thirteen in Paris and the immediate surrounding district.

In 1987–88 enrolment in public primary schools was 5,739,016; in secondary schools 4,235,757, and in post-secondary education 1,139,018 (of which university students accounted for 972,700).

COMMUNICATIONS

Roads.—The length of roads in use at the end of 1987 was 805,000 km of which 6,400 km were motorways.

Railways.—The system of railroads in France is very extensive. The length of lines open for traffic at the end of 1986 was 34,640 km, of which 11,584 km were electrified.

Shipping.—The French mercantile marine consisted in 1989 of 241 ships of over 100 tons gross, of which 25 were passenger vessels (167,000 tons gross), 58 tankers (2,269,000 tons gross) and 158 cargo vessels (1,693,000 tons gross). The principal rivers of France are the Seine, Loire, Garonne, and Rhône.

ECONOMY

Budget.—Government expenditure (ordinary and capital) by function, as provided for in the 1989 general Budget, was:

	F million
Agriculture and Forestry	36,238
Co-operation and Development	6,978
Culture and Communications	9,959
Defence	221,807
Economy, Finance and Budget	263,240
Education	209,208
Equipment and Housing	64,357
Foreign Affairs	10,828
Industry, Local Planning and Tourism	20,071
Interior	61,944
Justice	15,729
Labour and Employment	86,686
Overseas Departments	1,993
Prime Ministerial	3,887
Research and Technology	23,146
Solidarity, Health, Social Protection	35,802
Transport and the Sea	51,809
Veterans	26,317
Youth and Sports	2,323
Total	1,152,322

PRODUCTION

Agriculture.—Approximately 31,389,000 hectares of land is used for agricultural purposes, 14,620,000 hectares is forested. Production in 1987 included wheat, 27,414,700 tonnes; sugar-beet, 25,739,160 tonnes; maize, 12,040,300 tonnes; barley, 10,489,020 tonnes; and potatoes 6,719,970 tonnes.

The vine is extensively cultivated, regions famous for their wines including Bordeaux, Burgundy and Champagne. Production of wine in 1988 was 72,488,400 hectolitres. Cognac, liqueurs and cider are also important products.

Energy.—France produces its own oil, the greater part coming from fields in the Landes area, but is a net importer of crude oil, for processing by its important oil-refining industry. Natural gas is produced in the foothills of the Pyrenees. Electricity production was 372,400 kW in 1988.

Industry.—France's heavy industries include oil-refining and the production of iron and steel, and aluminium. In 1987 production of steel was 16,500,000 tonnes, cement 23,600,000 tonnes and paper products 5,700,000 tonnes. Other important industries produce chemicals, tyres, aluminium, textiles, and processed food. Engineering products include motor vehicles, and television and radio sets.

TRADE

The principal imports are raw materials for the heavy and manufacturing industries (e.g. oil, minerals, chemicals), machinery and precision instruments, agricultural products and vehicles. Raw materials, semi-manufactured and manufactured goods are also France's principal exports. Other member countries of the EC are France's main trading partners.

TOTAL TRADE

	1987	1988
Imports	F1,093,900	F1,208,500
Exports	1,104,300	1,217,000

Trade with UK

	1988	1989
Imports from UK	£8,270,408,000	£9,461,648,000
Exports to UK	9,390,207,000	10,785,429,000

CAPITAL.—Paris, on the Seine. Population (census 1982) 2,176,243 (town); 8,706,963 (incl. suburbs).

The largest conurbations (populations 1982) are ΨMarseilles (1,111,000); Lyons (1,221,000); Toulouse (541,000); Lille (936,000) and ΨBordeaux (640,000).

The chief towns of Corsica are ΨAjaccio (55,279) and ΨBastia (45,081).

CURRENCY.—French franc of 100 centimes.
FLAG.—The tricolour, three vertical bands, blue, white, red (blue next to flagstaff).
NATIONAL ANTHEM.—La Marseillaise.
NATIONAL DAY.—July 14 (Bastille Day, 1789).

BRITISH EMBASSY

35 rue du Faubourg St. Honoré, 75383 Paris Cedex 08
[Paris 42 66 91 42]

Ambassador Extraordinary and Plenipotentiary, His Excellency Sir Ewen Alastair John Fergusson, KCMG (1987).
Minister, M. J. Llewellyn Smith, CMG.
Defence and Air Attaché, Air Cdre. C. R. Adams, AFC.
Counsellor and Head of Chancery, J. M. Macgregor.
Consul-General, J. Daly.

BRITISH CONSULAR OFFICES

There are British Consulates-General in Metropolitan France at *Bordeaux, Lille, Lyons, Marseilles* and *Paris.*

BRITISH COUNCIL

Representative in Paris, P. J. Prescott, 9 rue de Constantine, 75007 Paris.

FRANCO-BRITISH CHAMBER OF COMMERCE

8 rue Cimarosa, 75116 Paris

President, R. Lyon.
Vice-President, B. Cordery, OBE.

OVERSEAS DEPARTMENTS

Legislation passed in December 1982 by the French Parliament granted greater powers of self-government to four of the five overseas departments—French Guiana, Guadeloupe, Martinique and Réunion. These former colonies had enjoyed departmental status since 1947 and the status of regions of France since 1974. Elections to their new directly-elected Assemblies were held in each department in 1983 and the Assemblies will operate in parallel with the existing, indirectly constituted Regional Councils. The French government is represented by a Commissioner (a Prefect in French Guiana).

French Guiana.—Situated on the north-eastern coast of South America, French Guiana is flanked by Suriname on the west and by Brazil on the south and east. Area, 34,749 sq. miles (90,000 sq. km). Population (1987 estimate) 89,000. Capital, ΨCayenne (38,135). Under the administration of French Guiana is a group of islands (St. Joseph, Ile Royal and Ile du Diable), known as Iles du Salut. On Devil's Isle, Captain Dreyfus was imprisoned from 1894 to 1899.
Prefect, J.-P. Lacroix.

Guadeloupe.—A number of islands in the Leeward Islands group of the West Indies, consisting of the two main islands of Guadeloupe (or Basse-Terre) and Grande-Terre, with the adjacent islands of Marie-Galante, La Désirade and Iles des Saintes, and the islands of St. Martin and St. Barthélemy over 150 miles to the north-west. Area, 687 sq. miles (1,779 sq. km). Population (1987 estimate) 337,000. Capital ΨBasse Terre (15,778) in Guadeloupe. Other towns are ΨPointe à Pitre (23,889) on Grande-Terre and ΨGrand Bourg (6,611) in Marie Galante.
Commissioner, Y. Bonnet.

Martinique.—An island situated in the Windward Islands group of the West Indies, between Dominica in the north and St. Lucia in the south. Area, 425 sq. miles (1,102 sq. km). Population (1987) 334,000. Capital ΨFort de France (100,576). Other towns are ΨTrinité (11,214) and ΨMarin (6,104).
Commissioner, J.-C. Roure.

Réunion.—Réunion, which became a French possession in 1638, lies in the Indian Ocean, about 569 miles east of Madagascar and 110 miles S.W. of

Mauritius. Area, 969 sq. miles (2,510 sq. km). Population (1987 estimate) 565,000. Capital, St. Denis (109,072).
Commissioner, J. Anciaux.

Also lying in the Indian Ocean adjacent to Madagascar are the smaller, uninhabited islands of Bassas da India, Europa, Iles Glorieuses, Juan de Nova and Tromelin, which are administered from Réunion.

TERRITORIAL COLLECTIVITÉS

Mayotte.—Area, 144 sq. miles (372 sq. km). Population (1987 estimate) 67,000. Capital, Mamoundzou (12,000). Part of the Comoros Islands group, Mayotte remained a French dependency when the other three islands became independent as the Comoros Republic in 1975. Since 1976 the island has been a *collectivité territoriale,* an intermediate status between Overseas Department and Overseas Territory.
Commissioner, A. Khider.

St. Pierre and Miquelon—Area 93 sq. miles (242 sq. km). Population (1987) 6,500. Two small groups of islands off the coast of Newfoundland. Became a *collectivité territoriale* in June 1985.
Commissioner, J.-P. Marquie.

OVERSEAS TERRITORIES

French Polynesia.—Five archipelagos in the south Pacific, comprising the Society Islands (Windward Islands group includes Tahiti, Moorea, Makatea, Mehetia, Tetiaoro, Tubuai Manu, etc; Leeward Islands group includes Huahine, Raiatea, Tahaa, Bora-Bora, Maupiti, etc.), the Tuamotu Islands (Rangiroa, Hao, Turéia, etc.), the Gambier Islands (Mangareva, etc.), the Tubuai Islands (Rimatara, Rurutu, Tubuai, Raivavae, Rapa, etc.) and the Marquesas Islands (Nuku-Hiva, Hiva-Oa, Fatu-Hiva, Tahuata, Ua Huka, etc.). Area, 1,544 sq. miles (4,000 sq. km). Population (1987 estimate) 189,000. Capital, ΨPapeete (22,967) in Tahiti. Economy based on tourism and exports of copra, coffee, vanilla, citrus fruits and cultured pearls.
High Commissioner, J. Montpezat.

New Caledonia.—A large island in the Western Pacific, 700 miles E. of Queensland. Dependencies are the Isles of Pines, the Loyalty Islands (Mahé, Lifou, Urea, etc.), the Bélep Archipelago, the Chesterfield Islands, the Huon Islands and Walpole. New Caledonia was discovered in 1774 and annexed by France in 1854; from 1871 to 1896 it was a convict settlement. A referendum in 1987 on the question of independence for New Caledonia was boycotted by the indigenous Kanaks, and New Caledonia therefore voted to remain French. However, a new independence referendum has been promised for 1998. Area, 7,358 sq. miles (19,058 sq. km). Population (1987 estimate) 146,000. Capital ΨNoumea (60,112). It is one of the world's largest producers of nickel.
High Commissioner, B. Grasset.

Southern and Antarctic Territories.—Created in 1955 from the former Réunion dependencies, the territory comprises the islands of Amsterdam (25 sq. miles) and St. Paul (2·7 sq. miles), the Kerguelen Islands (2,700 sq. miles) and Crozet Islands (116 sq. miles) archipelagos and Adélie Land (116,800 sq. miles) in the Antarctic continent. The only population are members of staff of the scientific stations.

Wallis and Futuna Islands.—Two groups of islands (the Wallis Archipelago and the Iles de Hooru) in the central Pacific, N.E. of Fiji. Area, 106 sq. miles (274 sq. km). Population (1987 estimate) 12,000. Capital, Mata-Utu on Uvea, the main island of the Wallis group.

THE FRENCH COMMUNITY

The Constitution of the fifth French Republic promulgated on Oct. 6, 1958, envisaged the establishment of a French Community of States. A number of the former French states in Africa have seceded from the Community but for all practical purposes continue to enjoy the same close links with France as those that remain formally members of the French Community. With the exception of Guinea, all the former French African colonies are closely linked to France by a series of financial, technical and economic agreements.

FRANCOPHONE COUNTRIES

In the following countries French is either the official or national language or the language of instruction; where there is another national language the name of it is shown after the name of the country:—Algeria (*Arabic*); Belgium (*Flemish*); Benin; Burkina; Burundi (*Kirundi*); Cambodia (*Khmer*); Cameroon (*English*); parts of Canada (in Quebec, parts of Ontario and New Brunswick) (*English*); Central African Republic (*Sangho*); Chad; Congo; Côte d'Ivoire; France; Gabon; Guinea; Haiti (*Creole*); Laos (*Laotian*); Lebanon (*Arabic*); Luxembourg (*German and Letzeburgesch*); Madagascar (*Malagasy*); Mali; Morocco (*Arabic*); Mauritania (*Arabic*); Niger; Rwanda (*Kinyarwanda*); Senegal; Switzerland (1,000,000 French speaking); Togo; Tunisia (*Arabic*); Vietnam (*Vietnamese*); Zaire. French is also spoken in the Overseas Departments (*see* above).

GABON
(République Gabonaise)

President, El Hadj Omar Bongo, *assumed office*, Dec. 1967, *re-elected*, Feb. 1973, Dec. 1979 and Nov. 1986.

COUNCIL OF MINISTERS
(as at April 30, 1990)

Prime Minister, Casimir Oyé Mba.
Public Works, Construction and Territorial Administration, Zacharie Myboto.
Justice, Keeper of the Seals, Paul Mba-Abessole.
Foreign Affairs and Co-operation, Ali Bongo.
Commerce, Consumption and Industry, Relations with Parliament, Jules Bourdes Ogouliguendé.
Town Planning, Housing, Henri Minko.
National Defence, War Veterans, Public Security and Immigration, Martin Fidèle Magnaga.
Territorial Administration and Local Collectives, Antoine Mboumbou-Miyakou.
Civil Service and Administrative Reform, Paulette Moussavou.
Finance, Budget and State Holdings, Paul Toungui.
Planning and Economic Development, Marcel Doupamby-Matoka.
Information, Posts and Telecommunications, and Government Spokesman, Jean Rémy Pendy-Bouyiki.
Mines, Hydrocarbons, Energy and Hydraulic Resources, Jean Ping.
National Education, Higher Education and Scientific Research, Michel Anchouey.
Public Health, Population, Social Affairs and National Solidarity, Serge Mba.
Employment, Human Resources and Professional Training, Thierry Moussavou.
Agriculture, Livestock and Rural Economy, André Mba-Obame.
Water, Forests and Environment, Jean Robert Goulongana.
Youth, Sports, Culture and Popular Education, in charge of Francophone Affairs, Pierre Claver Nzeng.

Transport, Pierre Nziengui Mabila.
State Control and Para-Public Sector Reform, Pépin Mongokodji.
Tourism, National Parks and Leisure, Thomas Dydime Nzé-Emane.
Small and Medium-Sized Enterprises and Handicrafts, Jeanne Thérèse Mboumba-Rekoula.
Minister-Delegate in Prime Minister's Office in charge of Decentralization, Simon Oyono-Aba'a.
Ministers of State, François Engongah-Owono, Jean-Pierre Madoungou-Boudianga, Eugène Kakou-Mayaza, Patrice Nziengui, Charles Mefane.

EMBASSY OF THE REPUBLIC OF GABON
27 Elvaston Place, SW7 5NL
[071–937 5285]

Ambassador Extraordinary and Plenipotentiary, new appointment awaited.
Chargé d'Affaires, Pierre Claver Nze-Obame.

Gabon lies on the Atlantic coast of Africa at the Equator and is flanked on the north by Equatorial Guinea and Cameroon and on the east and south by the People's Republic of Congo. It has an area of 103,347 sq. miles (267,667 sq. km) and a population (UN estimate 1988) of 1,095,000.

Gabon elected on November 28, 1958 to remain an autonomous republic within the French Community and was proclaimed fully independent on August 17, 1960. The Constitution provides for an Executive President directly elected for a seven-year term, who appoints the Council of Ministers. There is a unicameral National Assembly comprising 120 members of whom 111 are directly elected for a five-year term and nine members are nominated by the President. A multi-party system was adopted in April 1990.

Gabon's economy remains heavily dependent on oil, and, to a much lesser extent, other mineral resources, including manganese and uranium. Gabon has considerable timber reserves (particularly Okoumé) although production in this industry has stagnated in recent years.

The economy, which experienced considerable growth in real terms from the mid-1970s onwards, had since 1986 been adversely affected by the fall in oil prices. Revenue is expected to increase in the 1990s following major oil exploitation at Rabi-Kounga.

Gabon is a full member of OPEC.

Trade with UK

	1988	1989
Imports from UK	£18,808,000	£14,945,000
Exports to UK	5,091,000	2,389,000

CAPITAL.—ΨLibreville (251,000).
CURRENCY.—Franc CFA of 100 centimes.
FLAG.—Horizontal bands, green, yellow and blue.
NATIONAL ANTHEM.—La Concorde.
NATIONAL DAY.—August 17.

BRITISH EMBASSY
BP 476, Libreville
[Libreville 74 31 83]

Ambassador Extraordinary and Plenipotentiary, His Excellency Mark Aubrey Goodfellow (1986).
Second Secretary, D. A. Pearce.

GERMANY
* Deutsches Reich (German Realm)

The term 'deutsch' (German) probably began to be used in the 8th century and initially described the

---

* Nazi historians referred to the National Socialist regime as *Drittes Reich*.

language spoken in the eastern part of the Frankish realm which reached its apogee in Charlemagne's reign, subsequently being divided into an eastern and western realm whose political and linguistic borders coincided. Then the term was transferred from the language to its speakers, and ultimately to the region they lived in. The first German realm was the Holy Roman Empire, established in AD 962 when Otto I of Saxony was crowned Emperor. The Empire endured until 1806, but from as early as the 12th century the achievement of a national state was prevented by territorial fragmentation into small principalities and dukedoms, the gradually increasing autonomy of their rulers weakening the central power.

The Holy Roman Empire was replaced by a loose association of the individual sovereign states known as the German Confederation, which survived until 1866 when it was dissolved and replaced by the Prussian-dominated North German Federation. Prussia, directed by its Prime Minister (later Chancellor) Otto von Bismarck, had translated its earlier economic predominance amongst the German states into political hegemony by the annexation of the duchies of Schleswig and Holstein from Denmark in 1864 and a decisive defeat of Austria in 1866 (the Seven Weeks' War) which ended Austrian influence over German politics. After the Franco-Prussian War of 1870–71 resulted in the defeat of France and the cession of Alsace and Lorraine, the south German principalities united with the northern federation to form a second German Empire, the King of Prussia being proclaimed Emperor at Versailles on January 18, 1871.

Germany's defeat in the 1914–18 War led to the abdication of the Emperor and the princes, and the country became a Republic. The 1919 Treaty of Versailles returned Alsace and Lorraine to France, large areas in the east of the country were lost to the newly created state of Poland, and all German colonies placed under the administration of other countries. The world economic crisis of 1929 led to the collapse of the Weimar Republic and the subsequent rise to power of the National Socialist movement of Adolf Hitler, who became Chancellor in 1933.

After concluding a Treaty of Non-Aggression with Soviet Russia in August 1939, Germany invaded Poland (Sept. 1, 1939), thus precipitating World War II, which lasted until 1945. Hitler committed suicide on April 30, 1945. On May 8, 1945, the unconditional surrender of all German forces was accepted by representatives of the Western Allied and Soviet Supreme Commanders.

THE POST WAR PERIOD.—After the surrender the Allied Powers exercised supreme authority in Germany on lines laid down in the Potsdam agreement (August 1945) between the UK, USA and USSR. Germany was divided into American, British and Soviet occupation zones. Two French zones were later formed from parts of the American and British zones. Power was exercised by the Commanders-in-Chief, each in his own zone of occupation and jointly in matters affecting Germany as a whole through a Control Council. Berlin, some hundred miles within the Soviet zone, was governed jointly by the four occupying powers.

No central German government was permitted but several German central administrations were established as support organs for the Control Council. The Potsdam agreement was to have been confirmed or revised by a peace treaty but no treaty was ever drawn up. Differences in interpretation of the Potsdam agreement among the Allies made it impossible to implement in full and the system of quadripartite control broke down when the Russians withdrew from the Control Council in March 1948.

The Federal Republic of Germany (FRG) grew out of the fusion of the three western zones. In 1952 a contractual agreement was signed between the Federal Republic and the western Allies, whereby the Republic regained virtual sovereignty in May 1955. The conversion of the Soviet (eastern) zone of occupation into a separate state, the German Democratic Republic (GDR), also occurred in 1955.

In August 1961 the Soviet zone was sealed off, and the Berlin Wall was built along the zonal boundary, partitioning the western sectors of the city from the eastern. While the GDR viewed the two Germanies as completely separate nations, in terms of international law the FRG never recognized the GDR as a foreign country, though conceding its autonomy and independence.

Mounting unrest and subsequent reforms in the GDR in 1989 culminated in the opening of the Berlin Wall in November. The popular wish in both German states for unification soon became apparent. Bilateral talks, and negotiations in such fora as the EC, NATO and the 'Two-plus-four' (established in February 1990, comprising the two German states plus the four wartime allies) got under way. Contacts between the two German states led to agreement that elections for a new all-German Parliament would be held on December 2, 1990, linked to the establishment of unity and the restoration of full German sovereignty. Monetary, economic and social union took place in July 1990. (*See also* **Occurrences during printing**.)

FEDERAL REPUBLIC OF GERMANY
(Bundesrepublik Deutschland)

Federal President, Dr. Richard von Weizsäcker, *born* 1920, *elected* May 22, 1984, *re-elected* May 23, 1989, *sworn in*, July 1, 1989, *for five years.*

CABINET
(as at July 31, 1990)*

Federal Chancellor, Dr. Helmut Kohl (CDU).
Foreign Minister and Vice-Chancellor, Hans Dietrich Genscher (FDP).
Interior, Wolfgang Schäuble (CDU).
Justice, Hans Engelhard (FDP).
Finance, Theodor Waigel (CSU).
Economics, Helmut Haussmann (FDP).
Food, Agriculture and Forestry, Ignaz Kiechle (CSU).
Intra-German Relations, Dr. Dorothee Wilms (CDU).
Labour and Social Affairs, Dr. Norbert Blüm (CDU).
Defence, Dr. Gerhard Stoltenberg (CDU).
Youth, Family Affairs, Women and Health, Prof. Dr. Ursula Lehr (CDU).
Transport, Dr. Friedrich Zimmermann (CSU).
Environment, Nature Conservation and Reactor Safety, Prof. Klaus Töpfer (CDU).
Posts and Telecommunications, Dr. Christian Schwarz-Schilling (CDU).
Regional Planning, Building and Urban Development, Gerda Hasselfeldt (CSU).
Research and Technology, Dr. Heinz Riesenhuber (CDU).
Education and Science, Jürgen Möllemann (FDP).
Economic Co-operation, Dr. Jürgen Warnke (CSU).
Federal Minister at the Chancellery, Rudolf Seiters (CDU)
Federal Minister and Government Spokesman, Dr. Hans Klein (CSU).

CDU: Christian Democratic Union; CSU: Christian Social Union; FDP: Free Democratic Party.

* West and East Germany reunited on October 3, 1990. Elections for a new all-German Parliament are to be held on December 2, 1990.

EMBASSY OF THE FEDERAL REPUBLIC OF GERMANY
23 Belgrave Square, SW1X 8PZ
[071–235 5033]

Ambassador Extraordinary and Plenipotentiary, His Excellency Baron Hermann von Richthofen (1988).
Minister Plenipotentiary, Helmut Wegner.
Minister-Counsellor, Dr.Klaus-Peter Klaiber, CMG.
First Counsellors, B. Weber (*Head of Press Dept.*); Dr. R. Huber (*Head of Economic Dept.*); E.-O. Bitzegeio (*Defence Research*); D. Greineder (*Scientific Affairs*); Dr. R. Peters (*Agriculture*).

NOTE.—Except where otherwise indicated statistical data on the Federal Republic of Germany include Berlin (West).

Area and Population.—The area of the Federal Republic is approximately 95,976 sq. miles (248,577 sq. km). Estimated population of the Federal Republic mid 1989 was 61,999,000. Distribution of the population among the *Länder* at end 1987 was:

Baden-Württemberg	9,327,000
Bavaria	11,026,000
Berlin (West)	1,879,000
Bremen	654,000
Hamburg	1,571,000
Hesse	5,544,000
Lower Saxony	7,196,000
North Rhine Westphalia	16,677,000
Rhineland Palatinate	3,611,000
Saarland	1,042,000
Schleswig-Holstein	2,613,000

Vital Statistics.—There were 11·0 live births per 1,000 inhabitants in the Federal Republic in 1989.

Government.—The Basic Law provides for a President, elected for a five-year term, a Lower House (*Bundestag*), with a four-year term of office, elected by direct universal suffrage, and an Upper House (*Bundesrat*) composed of 45 delegates of the *Länder*, without a fixed term of office.

The results of the elections held for the Bundestag on Jan. 25, 1987, were as follows:

Party	Numbers
Social Democrats	186
Christian Democratic Union	174
Christian Social Union	49
Free Democrats	46
The Greens	42

with an additional 22 representatives of Berlin elected by the House of Representatives of Berlin (CDU 11; SPD 7; FDP 2; Alternative Liste 2).

The Prime Ministers of the *Länder* governments in July 1990, were:

Ministers-President

Baden-Württemberg.—Lothar Späth (CDU).
Bavaria.—Max Streibl (CSU).
Berlin.—Walter Momper (*Governing Mayor*) (SPD).
Bremen.—Klaus Wedemeier (*Mayor*) SPD.
Hamburg.—Henning Voscherau (*First Mayor*) (SPD).
Hesse.—Dr. Walter Wallmann (CDU).
Lower Saxony.—Gerhard Schröder (SPD).
North Rhine-Westphalia.—Johannes Rau (SPD).
Rhineland-Palatinate.—Ludwig Wagner (CDU).
Saarland.—Oskar Lafontaine (SPD).
Schleswig-Holstein.—Björn Engholm (SPD).

Law and Justice.—Judicial authority is exercised by the Federal Constitutional Court, the Federal courts provided for in the Basic Law and the courts of the Länder.

The death sentence has been abolished.

ECONOMY

Despite the difficulties arising from the division of Germany, which cut off from the Federal Republic the main food-producing areas of Eastern Germany and some of the principal centres of light industry, Germany regained her position as the main industrial power on the Continent, and is the most economically powerful member of the European Community. The Gross National Product at current prices in 1989 was estimated at DM2,260,400 million, an increase of 6·5 per cent in nominal terms over 1988. In real terms GNP grew by 4 per cent, after a 3·6 per cent growth in 1988.

Industrial Production.—The Federal Republic has a predominantly industrial economy. Principal industries are coal mining, iron and steel production, machine construction, the electrical industry, the manufacture of steel and metal products, chemicals and textiles, and the processing of foodstuffs. The index of industrial net production adjusted for irregularities of the calendar (1985 = 100) is as follows:

	1988	1989
Mining	87·4	85·9
Manufacturing industry	106·8	112·4
(i) Basic materials	105·6	108·9
(ii) Capital goods	108·4	116·2
(iii) Consumer goods	106·2	110·5
(iv) Foodstuffs	102·3	105·4
Power (electricity and gas)	105·2	108·6
Construction	110·6	118·2
Total industry	106·3	111·7

Annual production figures were:

	1988	1989
	Tonnes '000	
Hard coal	73,304	71,428
Brown coal	108,563	109,811
Crude petroleum	3,937	3,772
Pig iron	31,388	31,360
Raw steel	40,668	40,700
Rolled steel	30,385	31,697
Fuel oils	34,332	29,370
Petrol	19,662	20,068
Chemical fibres	996	1,018
Cement	26,412	28,494
	Number	
Passenger cars	3,978,000	4,113,000
Colour televisions	3,706,000	3,253,000

Agriculture.—In 1988 total area of farmland was 11,915,000 hectares, of which 7,261,000 hectares were arable land. Forest areas cover 7,360,000 hectares.

Crop yields were (tonnes):

	1987	1988
Rye	1,599,000	1,579,000
Wheat	9,931,600	11,922,200
Maslin	45,700	54,400
Barley	8,571,300	9,587,200
Oats	2,008,000	2,038,500
Potatoes	6,836,100	7,433,700
Sugar beet	19,049,000	18,590,000
Colza and rape	1,264,600	1,216,100

Milk production in 1988 was 23,974,000 tonnes. Total yield of fisheries was 142,207 tonnes, valued at DM213,004,000.

Labour.—Labour figures, in annual averages, were:

	1988	1989
Employment	27,354,000	27,729,000
Unemployed	2,242,000	2,038,000
Men	1,199,000	1,070,000
Youths under 20	106,000	78,000
Foreign workers	1,577,000	1,690,000

FINANCE

	1990	1991
Expenditure	DM311·80 billion	DM324·00 billion
Revenue	280·79 billion	292·66 billion

The 1990 plan included expenditure of DM92·1 m on social welfare, DM53·7 m on defence, DM25·7 m on transport and DM10 m on agriculture.

TRADE

	1988	1989
	DM million	
Total imports	439,609·4	506,647·6
Total exports	567,654·0	641,341·7

Of 1988 imports, 12·1 per cent were foodstuffs and 6·3 per cent industrial raw materials. Main trading partners in 1989 were (figures shown as percentage of total trade):

	Imports	Exports
France	11·9	13·2
Netherlands	10·3	8·5
Italy	8·9	9·3
USA	7·6	7·3
Belg./Lux.	6·9	7·2
UK	6·8	9·3
Japan	6·4	2·4

Trade with UK

	1988	1989
Imports from UK	£9,521,851,000	£11,110,623,000
Exports to UK	17,667,097,000	20,005,276,000

Communications.—At the end of 1987 the state-owned railways of the Federal Republic (*Deutsche Bundesbahn*) measured 27,431 kilometres of which 11,493 kilometres were electrified, and the privately owned railways 2,904 kilometres, a total of 30,335 kilometres. Railway rolling stock included, in 1987, 2,584 electric locomotives, 4,064 diesel locomotives and 238,748 goods waggons; in 1987 the railways handled 306·9 million tonnes of goods. Classified roads measured 173,590 kilometres in 1988, of which motorways were 8,618 kilometres. The total number of motor vehicles registered at the beginning of 1990 was 34 million. Ocean-going shipping under the German flag in Dec. 1987, amounted to 4,072,000 tons gross. Inland waterways handled 220,998,000 tonnes of goods in 1987.

Social Welfare.—There is compulsory insurance against sickness, accident, old age and unemployment. Children's allowances, child rearing benefits and parental leave of absence are available in respect of all children. Pension schemes for widows and orphans of public servants are in operation. Public assistance is given to persons unable to earn their living, or with insufficient income to maintain a decent standard of living.

Education.—School attendance is compulsory for all children and juveniles between the ages of 6 and 18 and comprises nine years full-time compulsory education at primary and main schools (*Grund-und Hauptschulen*) and three years of compulsory vocational education on a part-time basis. In autumn 1987, there were in the Federal Republic 21,072 primary and main schools (*Grund-und Hauptschulen*) with 3,660,741 pupils. Secondary modern schools (*Realschulen*) numbered 2,593 with 915,253 pupils. There were 2,820 other general secondary schools (*Gymnasien* including *Gesamtschulen*) with 1,840,342 pupils.

There were also 2,816 special schools (*Sonderschulen*) for physically and mentally handicapped and socially maladjusted children in the Federal Republic with 254,163 pupils.

The secondary school leaving examination (*Abitur*) entitles the holder to a place of study at a university or another institution of higher education.

Children below the age of 18 who are not attending a general secondary or a full-time vocational school have compulsory day-release at a vocational school. In autumn 1987, there were 2,761 full and part-time vocational schools (*Berufsschulen*) with 1,885,375 pupils and 289 vocational extension schools (*Berufsaufbauschulen*) with 9,657 pupils, 2,335 full-time vocational schools (*Berufsfachschulen*) with 301,837 pupils, 977 schools for secondary technical studies (*Fachoberschulen/Fachgymnasien*) with 198,796 students.

Results for the winter term 1988–89 show a total of 1,470,738 students at institutions of higher education, of whom 989,805 were attending universities. The largest universities are in Munich, Berlin, Hamburg, Bonn and Cologne.

Language and Literature.—Modern (or New High) German has developed from the time of the Reformation to the present day, with differences of dialect in Austria and Alsace and in the German-speaking cantons of Switzerland. The literary language is usually regarded as having become fixed by Luther and Zwingli at the Reformation, since which time many great names occur in all branches, notably philosophy, from Leibnitz (1646–1716) to Kant (1724–1804), Fichte (1762–1814), Schelling (1775–1854) and Hegel (1770–1831); the drama from Goethe (1749–1832) and Schiller (1759–1805) to Gerhart Hauptmann (1862–1946); and in poetry, Heine (1797–1856). German authors have received the Nobel Prize for Literature on seven occasions—Theodor Mommsen (1902), R. Eucken (1908), P. Heyse (1909), Gerhart Hauptmann (1912), Thomas Mann (1929), N. Sachs (1966) and Heinrich Böll (1972). In 1988 there were 388 daily papers.

Religion.—In 1987 there were 25,412,600 Protestants in the Federal Republic, 26,232,000 Roman Catholics, and 1,651,000 belonging to the Islamic religious community. The number of Jews is estimated to be around 30,000.

Capital.—Bonn, in North Rhine Westphalia, 15 miles distant from Cologne. Population (June 1987) 276,500.

The population of the principal cities and towns in the Federal Republic at June 1987 was:

Berlin (West)	2,016,100	Dortmund ...	583,600
ΨHamburg...	1,593,600	Düsseldorf ...	563,400
Munich	1,188,800	Stuttgart....	552,300
Cologne	927,500	ΨBremen	533,400
Essen	623,000	Duisburg	525,200
Frankfurt am		Hanover	495,300
Main......	618,500	Nuremberg ..	471,800

Currency.—Deutsche Mark (DM) of 100 Pfennig.

Flag.—Horizontal bars of black, red and gold.

National Anthem.—Einigkeit und Recht und Freiheit (Unity and right and freedom).

National Day.—May 23.

BRITISH EMBASSY
Friedrich-Ebert-Allee 77, 5300 Bonn 1
[Bonn 23 40 61]

Ambassador Extraordinary and Plenipotentiary, His Excellency Sir Christopher Leslie George Mallaby, KCMG (1988).
Minister, Miss L. P. Neville Jones, CMG.
Counsellors, C. Budd (*Head of Chancery*); B. H. Dinwiddy; Miss A. Walker (*Defence Supply*); D. S. Broucher (*Economic*); R. F. Escritt (*Science and Technology*); P. V. Rollitt (*Management*); J. Franklin (*Labour*).
First Secretaries, J. I. Link; R. E. Brinkley; R. W. Barnett; V. Evans; D. J. Grieg; E. Jenkinson; P. Cunningham; D. A. Drake; S. Wordsworth.
Legal Adviser, J. O. Hill.
Defence and Military Attaché, Brig. A. P. Sims.
Asst. Military Attaché, Lt.-Col. J. D. Colson.
Naval Attaché, Capt. J. McLees.
Asst. Naval Attaché, Lt.-Cdr. J. Apps.
Air Attaché, Air Cdre. B. T. Sills.
Head of Visa Section (*Düsseldorf*), M. Carbine.
Chaplain, Rev. J. Newsome.

There are British Consulates-General at *Berlin, Düsseldorf, Frankfurt, Hamburg, Munich* and *Stuttgart*.

BRITISH COUNCIL
Representative, N. Ward, Hahnenstrasse 6, 5000 Cologne 1. Offices at *Berlin, Hamburg* and *Munich* and British Council libraries at all four centres.

BRITISH CHAMBER OF COMMERCE
Neumarkt 14, D-5000 Köln 1
Director, Herr Heumann.

BERLIN
Commandant and GOC British Sector, Maj.-Gen. R. J. S. Corbett.
Minister and Deputy Commandant, M. St. E. Burton, CMG, CVO.
Counsellor, O. Lamont (*Political Adviser*).

GERMAN DEMOCRATIC REPUBLIC
(Deutsche Demokratische Republik)

President of the Volkskammer and Acting Head of State, Dr. Sabine Bergmann-Pohl, *elected* April, 1990.
Deputy President of the Volkskammer, Dr. Reinhard Höppner.

COUNCIL OF MINISTERS
(as at April 12, 1990)*

Minister-President, Chairman of the Council, Lothar de Mazière.
Minister in the Office of the Minister-President, Klaus Reichenbach.
Deputy Minister-President, Internal Affairs, Dr. Peter-Michael Diestel.
Foreign Affairs, Markus Meckel.
Regional and Local Affairs, Dr. Manfred Preiss.
Economics, Dr. Gerhard Pohl.
Finance, Dr. Walter Romberg.
Trade and Tourism, Sybille Reider.
Justice, Prof. Dr. Kurt Wünsche.
Food, Agriculture and Forestry, Dr. Peter Pollack.
Labour and Social Affairs, Dr. Regine Hildebrandt.

Disarmament and Defence, Rainer Eppelmann.
Youth and Sport, Cordula Schubert.
Family and Women's Affairs, Dr. Christa Schmidt.
Health, Prof. Dr. Jürgen Kleditzsch.
Transport, Horst Gibtner.
Environment, Nature Protection, Energy and Reactor Safety, Prof. Dr. Karl-Hermann Steinberg.
Post and Telecommunications, Dr. Emil Schnell.
Construction, Town Planning and Housing Economy, Dr. Axel Viehweger.
Research and Technology, Prof. Dr. Frank Terpe.
Education and Science, Prof. Dr. Hans-Joachim Meier.
Culture, Herbert Schirmer.
Media Policy, Dr. Gottfried Müller.
Economic Co-operation, Hans-Wilhelm Ebeling.
Goverment Spokesman, Matthias Gehler.
Parliamentary State Secretary to the Minister-President, Dr. Günter Krause.

*Changes to the Cabinet in August 1990 could not be confirmed at time of going to press.

On August 23, 1990 the East German parliament voted to unite with West Germany on October 3, 1990. Elections for a new all-German parliament are to be held on December 2, 1990.

EMBASSY OF THE GDR
34 Belgrave Square, SW1X 8QB
[071–235 9941]

Chargé d'Affaires, Siegfried Reichel.
Counsellors, H. Vorpahl (*Commercial*); M. Rudolph.
First Secretaries, J. Döring; P. Husung.

Area and Population.—The German Democratic Republic comprises the five former German *Länder* of Brandenburg, Mecklenburg, Saxony, Saxony-Anhalt and Thuringia (an area of 41,768 sq. miles; 108,178 sq. km). The seat of Government is in the eastern part of Berlin (156 sq. miles). The population of the Republic (end of 1988) was 16,674,632. In 1952 the former *Länder* were replaced by fourteen *Bezirke* (regions): Potsdam, Cottbus and Frankfurt (formerly Brandenburg); Rostock, Schwerin and Neubrandenburg (formerly Mecklenburg); Karl-Marx-Stadt, Dresden and Leipzig (formerly Saxony); Halle and Magdeburg (formerly Saxony-Anhalt); Erfurt, Gera and Suhl (formerly Thuringia.)

Government.—Following the collapse of the Communist-dominated government in January 1990, a general election held in March resulted in the formation of a broad coalition government including Christian Democrats, Social Democrats and Liberals. According to the new Constitution, the GDR became a 'free, democratic, federative, social and ecological state based on the rule of law'. The new government aimed to 'achieve the unity of Germany swiftly and responsibly', and in August 1990 parliament voted to merge with West Germany on October 2, 1990.

ECONOMY

The GDR economy is at present in a state of rapid transition. Central economic planning, which characterized the post-war period, has been abandoned in favour of market-orientated reform. A State Treaty signed by the FRG and GDR finance ministers introduced economic, monetary and social union from July 1, 1990. The Treaty extends FRG monetary and commercial legislation to the GDR as well as laws governing pensions, social insurance, the budget, employment and taxes. The Deutsche Mark has replaced the Ostmark as the currency in the GDR.

Agriculture.—Land has been cultivated mostly on state or collective farms, though some has been cultivated independently. Crop yields in 1988 were: potatoes 11,546,395 tonnes; sugar-beet 4,625,433

tonnes; corn (green and silage) 16,650,605 tonnes; grain 9,839,645 tonnes, and oilseeds 435,319 tonnes.

Industry.—The GDR is the leading world producer of lignite: production in 1987 was 310,314,000 tonnes. The iron and steel industry is also important. Other highly developed industries include basic chemicals and petro-chemicals, machine tools and industrial plant, ship-building and transport equipment, electronic and engineering equipment, printing machinery, precision tools and optical instruments.

Trade with UK

	1988	1989
Imports from UK	£113,239,000	£106,455,000
Exports to UK	152,977,000	168,742,000

Principal cities and towns (population, end of 1988): East Berlin (1,284,535); Leipzig (545,307); Dresden (518,057); Chemnitz (Karl-Marx-Stadt) (311,765); Magdeburg (290,579); Rostock (253,990); Halle (Saale) (236,044); Erfurt (220,016); Potsdam (142,862).

CURRENCY.—Deutsche Mark (DM) of 100 Pfennig.
FLAG.—Horizontal bands of black, red, gold; hammer, compasses and corn device at centre.
NATIONAL ANTHEM.—Auferstanden aus Ruinen (Risen from ruins).
NATIONAL DAY.—October 7.

BRITISH EMBASSY
108 Berlin, Unter den Linden 32–34
[Berlin 220 2431]

Ambassador Extraordinary and Plenipotentiary, His Excellency Patrick Howard Caines Eyers, CMG, LVO (1990).
Counsellor and Deputy Head of Mission, Sir John Ramsden, Bt.
First Secretaries, R. M. Sands (*Head of Political Section*); G. Deane (*Chancery*); D. J. Peate, OBE (*Commercial*).
Second Secretaries, A. R. Weeks (*Management and Consul*); R. Healy; Dr. C. M. Sweeney.
Third Secretaries, R. C. Morton; Miss J. Wigzell.
Cultural Attaché, I. G. Frater (*British Council Representative*).

GREECE
(Elliniki Dimokratia)

President of the Hellenic Republic, Constantine Karamanlis, *elected* May 4, 1990.

CABINET
(as at July 31, 1990)

Prime Minister, Merchant Marine, Constantine Mitsotakis.
Deputy PM, Culture, Tzannis Tzannetakis.
Deputy PM, Justice, Athanasios Kanellopoulos.
Minister to the Prime Minister, Miltiades Evert.
Foreign Affairs, Antonios Samaras.
Interior, Sotirios Kouvelas.
National Defence, Ioannis Varvitsiotis.
National Economy, Tourism, George Souflias.
Finance, Ioannis Palaiokrassas.
Agriculture, Michael Papakonstantinou.
Labour, Aristides Kalantzakos.
Health and Welfare, Marietta Yannakou-Koutisikou.
Education and Religion, Vassilios Kontoyannopoulos.
Public Order, Ioannis Vassiliadis.
Macedonia and Thrace, George Tzitzikostas.
Aegean, George Missailidis.
Environment, Regional Planning and Public Works, Stefanos Manos.
Industry, Energy and Technology, Stavros Dimas.
Commerce, Athanasios Xarchas.

Transport and Communications, Nikolaos Gelestathis.
Minister without Portfolio, Mikis Theodorakis.

EMBASSY OF GREECE
1A Holland Park, W11 3TP
[071–727 8040]

Ambassador Extraordinary and Plenipotentiary, His Excellency George D. Papoulias (1990).
Defence Attaché, Capt. S. Gouleas.

There are Honorary Consulates at *Belfast, Birmingham, Edinburgh, Falmouth, Glasgow, Leeds* and *Southampton.*

A maritime state in the south-east of Europe, bounded on the N. by Albania, Yugoslavia and Bulgaria, on the S. and W. by the Ionian and Mediterranean seas, and on the E. by Turkey, with an estimated area of 50,944 sq. miles (131,944 sq. km). Population (UN estimate 1988) is 10,013,000.

The main areas of Greece are: *Macedonia* (which includes Mt. Athos and the island of Thasos), *Thrace* (including the island of Samothrace), *Epirus, Thessaly, Continental Greece* (which includes the island of Euboea and the Sporades or 'scattered islands' of which the largest is Skyros), the *Peloponnese* (or *Morea*), the *Dodecanese* or *Southern Sporades* (12 islands occupied by Italy in 1911 during the Italo-Turkish War and ceded to Greece by Italy in 1947) consisting of Rhodes, Astypalaia, Karpathos, Kassos, Nisyros, Kalymnos, Leros, Patmos, Kos, Symi, Khalki and Tilos, the *Cyclades* (a circular group numbering about 200, with a total area of 923 sq. miles; the chief islands are Syros, Andros, Tinos, Naxos, Paros, Santorini, Milos and Serifos), the *Ionian Islands* (Corfu, Paxos, Levkas, Ithaca, Cephalonia, Zante and Cerigo), the *Aegean Islands* (Chios, Lesbos, Limnos and Samos). In *Crete* there was for over 1,500 years (3000 to 1400 BC) a flourishing civilization which spread its influence far and wide throughout the Aegean, and the ruins of the palace of Minos at Knossos afford evidence of astonishing comfort and luxury. Greek civilization emerged about 1300 BC and the poems of Homer, the blind poet of Chios, which were probably current about 800 BC, record the 10-year struggle between the Achaeans of Greece and the Phrygians of Troy (1194–1184 BC).

Language and Literature.—The spoken language of modern Greece is descended by a process of natural development from the Common Greek of Alexander's empire. *Katharevousa,* a conservative literary dialect evolved by Adamantios Corais (Diamant Coray), who lived and died in Paris (1748–1833) and used for official and technical matters, is to be phased out over the next few years. Novels and poetry are mostly composed in *dimotiki,* a progressive literary dialect which owes much to John Psycharis (1854–1929). The poets Solomos, Palamas, Cavafis, Sikelianos, Seferis and Elytis have won a European reputation.

Religion.—Over 97 per cent of the people are adherents of the Greek Orthodox Church, which is the State religion, all others being tolerated and free from interference. The Church of Greece recognizes the spiritual primacy of the Œcumenical Patriarch of Constantinople, but is otherwise a self-governing body administered by the Holy Synod under the Presidency of the Archbishop of Athens and All Greece. It has no jurisdiction over the Church of Crete, which has a degree of autonomy under the Œcumenical Patriarch, nor over the Monastic Community of Mount Athos and the Church in the Dodecanese, both of which come directly under the Œcumenical Patriarch.

Government.—A military coup on April 21, 1967, suspended parliamentary government and, following an unsuccessful royal counter-coup on December 13, 1967, King Constantine went into voluntary exile in Rome. On June 1, 1973 the monarchy was abolished and a republic established under the Presidency of George Papadopoulos.

The overthrow of Archbishop Makarios, President of Cyprus, on July 15, 1974, by a military coup led by Greek officers of the Cypriot National Guard caused an international crisis, in the wake of which the heads of the Greek armed forces decided, on July 23, to relinquish power. Konstantinos Karamanlis, Prime Minister between 1955 and 1963, returned from his self-imposed exile in Paris to form a provisional Government, and the first elections for ten years were held on November 17, 1974.

The constitutional position of the King, who was still in exile, remained unsettled until December 8, when by a referendum, the Greek people rejected 'crowned democracy' by 69·2 per cent to 30·8 per cent and Greece became a republic. A new constitution came into force on June 11, 1975.

The unicameral 300-member Chamber of Deputies is elected for a four-year term by universal adult suffrage under a system of proportional representation. The most recent general election was held on April 8, 1990.

Defence.—The strength of the Army is 130,000 backed up by some 50,000 in the National Guard. The Navy consists of 19,500 men and is equipped with a fleet of destroyers, submarines, patrol boats and amphibious warfare vessels, mostly of US, French, Dutch and German origin. The Air Force consists of 25,000 men and is equipped with aircraft disposed in 14 combat squadrons supported by the necessary transport, training, helicopter and reconnaissance squadrons. National service is 2 years on average.

Communications.—The 2,650 kilometres of Greek railways are state-owned with the exception of the Athens–Piraeus Electric Railway. Greek roads total somewhat over 35,500 kilometres, of which about 25 per cent are classified as national highways and just under 30,000 km are classified as provincial roads. The road connection with Albania was reopened in 1985.

On Dec. 31, 1986 the Greek mercantile fleet numbered 2,138 ships with a total tonnage of 24,792,516 tons gross. On the same day Greek-owned ships over 100 tons gross and registered under foreign flags numbered 276 with a total tonnage of 5,176,347 tons gross. Athens has direct airline links with Australasia, North America, most countries in Europe, Africa and the Middle East.

Education is free and compulsory from the age of 6 to 15 and is maintained by state grants. There are six universities, Athens, Salonika, Patras, Thrace, Ioannina and Crete. There are several other institutes of higher learning, mostly in Athens.

Production.—Though there has in recent years been a substantial measure of industrialization, agriculture still employs about a quarter of the working population. The most important agricultural products are tobacco, wheat, cotton, sugar and rice. The most important of the fruit trees are the olive, peach, vine, orange, lemon, fig, almond and currant-vine, and now exports of Greek fresh fruit and vegetables have established themselves as an important contributor to the economy and have considerable growth potential. Currants, grown mainly around Patras, remain one of Greece's main exports, the United Kingdom being the principal purchaser.

The principal minerals mined in Greece are nickel, bauxite, iron ore, iron pyrites, manganese magnesite, chrome, lead, zinc and emery, and prospecting for petroleum is being carried on. Oil refineries are in operation near Athens and at Salonika, where there is also a petro-chemical plant. The chief industries are textiles (cotton, woollen and synthetics), chemical, cement, glass, metallurgy, shipbuilding, domestic electrical equipment and footwear. In recent years new factories have been opened for the production of aluminium, nickel, iron and steel products, tyres, chemicals, fertilizers and sugar (from locally-grown beet). Food processing and ancillary industries have also grown up throughout the country. The development of the country's electric power resources, irrigation and land reclamation schemes and the exploitation of Greece's lignite resources for fuel and industrial purposes are also being carried out. Tourism has developed rapidly, but is now slowing down.

TRADE

	1986	1987
Total imports ...	Drs1,587,214·0m	Drs1,758,951·1m
Total exports ...	789,994·6m	880,958·2m

Trade with UK

	1988	1989
Imports from UK	£468,032,000	£571,409,000
Exports to UK	356,974,000	395,086,000

CAPITAL.—Athens, population (including ΨPiraeus and suburbs), 3,027,331 (1981 Census). Other large towns are ΨSalonika (706,180); ΨPatras (154,596); ΨVolos (107,407); Larissa (102,426); and ΨKavalla (56,705).

Larger towns in the islands are: in Crete—ΨHeraklion or Candia (102,398), ΨCanea (47,451), and ΨRethymnon (18,190); in the Ionian Islands—ΨCorfu (36,901); in the Dodecanese—ΨRhodes (41,425); in the Cyclades—ΨSyros Hermoupolis (13,877); in Lesbos—ΨMytilene (24,991); in Chios—ΨChios (24,070).

CURRENCY.—Drachma of 100 leptae.

FLAG.—Blue and white stripes with a white cross on a blue field in the canton.

NATIONAL ANTHEM.—Imnos Eis Tin Eleftherian (Hymn to Freedom).

NATIONAL DAY.—March 25 (Independence Day).

BRITISH EMBASSY
1 Ploutarchou Street, 10675 Athens
[Athens 7236–211/9]

Ambassador Extraordinary and Plenipotentiary, His Excellency Sir David Miers, KBE, CMG (1989).

Counsellors, J. B. Donnelly (*Political and Consul-General*); B. S. T. Eastwood (*Economic and Commercial*); W. V. Fell; Dr. R. T. Taylor (*Cultural Affairs*).

Defence and Military Attaché, Brig. G. R. A. Evans.
Naval and Air Attaché, Capt. R. Evans, LVO.
Hon. Attaché, Elizabeth Bayard French (*Director, British School of Archaeology*).

BRITISH CONSULAR OFFICES

There are British Consular Offices at *Athens, Corfu, Samos, Rhodes, Salonika, Heraklion* (Crete), *Syros, Volos* and *Patras*.

BRITISH COUNCIL
17 Plateia Philikis Etairias (PO Box 3488)
Kolonaki Square, Athens 10210

Representative, Dr. R. T. Taylor, CBE.
There is also an office at *Salonika* and British Council libraries at both centres.

BRITISH-HELLENIC CHAMBER OF COMMERCE
25 Vas. Sofias Avenue, GR-106 74 Athens
[72 10 361]

GUATEMALA
(República de Guatemala)

Head of State, President Marco Vinicio Cerezo Arévalo, *inaugurated*, Jan. 14, 1986.

CABINET
(as at July 31, 1990)

Vice President, Roberto Carpio Nicolle.
Minister of Government, Carlos Morales Villatoro.
Foreign Affairs, Ariel Rivera.
National Defence, Gen. Juan Leonel Bolaños Chavez.
Finance, Francisco Pinto Casarola.
Communications, Sigfrido Mendizabal Garcia.
Education, Eduardo Meyev Maldonado.
Agriculture, Rodolfo Augusto Estrada.
Economy, Lizardo Arturo Sosa Lopez.
Public Health and Social Welfare, Carlos Gehelert Matta.
Labour and Social Insurance, Rodolfo Maldonado.
Energy and Mines, Raul Castañeda.
Special Affairs, Carlos Enrique Soto Menegazzo.
Urban and Rural Development, Rene Armando De-Léon Schlotter.
Culture and Sport, Marta Regina de Fahsen.

EMBASSY OF GUATEMALA
13 Fawcett Street, SW10 9HN
[071–351 3042]

Ambassador Extraordinary and Plenipotentiary, His Excellency Dr. Erwin Blandon (1987).

Guatemala, in Central America, is situated in N. lat. from 13° 45′ to 17° 49′, and in W. long. from 88° 12′ 49″ to 92°13′ 43″, and has an area of 42,042 sq. miles (108,889 sq. km.), and a population (UN estimate 1988) of 8,681,000.

The Republic is divided into 22 departments, and is traversed from W. to E. by an elevated mountain chain, containing several volcanic summits rising to 13,000 feet above sea level; earthquakes are frequent. The country is well watered by numerous rivers; the climate is hot and malarial near the coast, temperate in the higher regions. The rainfall in the capital averages 57 in. per annum. The chief seaports are San José de Guatemala and Champerico on the Pacific and Santo Tomás de Castilla and Puerto Barrios on the Atlantic side.

Language and Literature.—Spanish is the language of the country, but 40 per cent of the population speak an Indian language. Since the establishment of the university in the capital, education has received a marked impulse and the high figure of illiteracy is being reduced. The National library contains about 80,000 volumes in Spanish.

Government.—The constitutionally elected president, Gen. Miguel Ydigoras Fuentes, was overthrown on March 31, 1963 by the Army, which handed executive and legislative powers to the Minister of Defence, Col. Enrique Peralta Azurdia. Elections for a new Congress and for President and Vice-President took place on March 6, 1966. The constitution was suspended 'for as long as the situation demands' following a military coup in March 1982. An amnesty for guerrillas was unsuccessful and the Army was fully occupied dealing with the proliferating subversive groups throughout the country.

Elections for a Constituent Assembly were held on July 1, 1984, as promised by Gen. Ríos Montt in 1983. The Assembly drew up a new Constitution, promulgated in June 1985, and a new electoral law, paving the way for presidential, governmental and municipal elections which took place on Nov. 3 and Dec. 8, 1985. The elections were won by the Christian Democratic party and Vinicio Cerezo Arévalo was elected President. The next presidential elections are due in November 1990.

Finance.—The Central Government revenue in 1988 was Quetzales 2,500 million, and expenditure Quetzales 3,000 million.

TRADE

	1988
Imports (c.i.f.)	US$1,557·0 m
Exports (f.o.b.)	1,033·8 m

Trade with UK

	1988	1989
Imports from UK	£15,387,000	£52,324,000
Exports to UK	10,678,000	6,950,000

The principal export is coffee, other articles being manufactured goods, sugar, bananas, cotton, beef and essential oils. The chief imports are petroleum, vehicles, machinery and foodstuffs.

CAPITAL.—Guatemala City, population estimate, 1,300,000. Quezaltenango has a population of over 100,000. Other towns are ΨPuerto Barrios (23,000), Mazatenango (21,000), and Antigua (30,000).

CURRENCY.—Quetzal (Q) of 100 centavos.

FLAG.—Three vertical bands, blue, white, blue; coat of arms on white stripe.

NATIONAL ANTHEM.—Guatemala Feliz (Guatemala be praised).

NATIONAL DAY.—September 15.

BRITISH EMBASSY
Centro Financiero Torre II (7th Floor), Seventh Avenue 5–10 Zone 4, Guatemala City
[Guatemala City 321601]

Ambassador Extraordinary and Plenipotentiary, His Excellency Bernard Everett.

GUINEA
(République de Guinée)

President, Gen. Lansana Conté, *took power*, April 3, 1984.

COUNCIL OF MINISTERS
(as at March 7, 1990)

Regional Ministers, Cmdt. Abou Camara (*Maritime Guinea*); Cmdt. Alpha Oumar Barou Diallo (*Upper Guinea*); Lt.-Col. Sory Doumbouya (*Middle Guinea*); Cmdt. Alhoussény Fofana (*Forest Region*).
Permanent Secretary to CMRN, Cmdt. Babacar Ndiaye.
Foreign Affairs, Cmdt. Jean Toure.

Ministers of the Presidency, Cmdt. Henri Tofani (*National Defence and Security*); Hervé Vincent Bangoura (*Information, Culture and Tourism*); Cmdt. Henri Foulah (*Economy and Finance*); Réné Alsény Gomez (*Secretary General*).
Planning and International Co-operation, Ibrahima Sylla.
Economy and Finance, Edouard Benjamin.
Administrative Reform and the Civil Service, Mamouna Bangoura.
Interior and Decentralization, Cmdt. Mamadou Baldet.
Agriculture and Animal Resources, Capt. Abdourahmane Diallo.
Natural Resources and the Environment, Cmdt. Mohamed Lamine Traore.
Post and Telecommunications, Lamine Bolivogui.
Town Planning and Housing, Bahna Sidibe.
Public Health and Population, Dr. Madigbé Fofana.
Transport and Public Works, Cmdt. Facinet Toure.
Industry, Trade and Handicrafts, Ousmane Sylla.
National Education, Higher Education and Scientific Research, Lt.-Col. Jean Kolipé Lama.
Justice, Bassirou Barry.
Social Affairs and Employment, Saliou Coumbassa.
Youth and Sports, Capt. Joseph Gbago Zoumanigui.

In addition, there are 5 Ministers of State.

Formerly part of French West Africa, Guinea has a coastline on the Atlantic Ocean between Guinea-Bissau and Sierra Leone and in the interior is adjacent to Senegal, Mali, Côte d'Ivoire, Liberia and Sierra Leone. Area, 94,926 sq. miles (245,857 sq. km). The population (UN estimate 1988) is 5,071,000, mostly the Fullah, Malinké and Soussou tribes.

Government.—Guinea was separated from Senegal in 1891 and administered by France as a separate colony until 1958. In a referendum held in Sept. 1958, Guinea rejected the new French Constitution and on October 2, 1958 became an independent republic governed by a Constituent Assembly. M. Sékou Touré, Prime Minister in the Territorial Assembly, assumed office as head of the new Government, and was elected President in 1961.

Under a provisional constitution, adopted in November 1958, powers of government are exercised by a president assisted by the Cabinet. The President, eligible for a term of seven years and for re-election, is head of state and of the armed forces. President Sékou Touré died in March 1984; a few days later there was a military coup. Guinea is now ruled by a military government, which is directed by a Military Committee for National Recovery (CMRN). The country's foreign policy is one of non-alignment.

Guinea withdrew from the Franc Zone on March 1, 1960, and established its own currency. Guinea is in receipt of economic aid and technical assistance from a number of countries, including the United States, Canada, Federal Republic of Germany, Yugoslavia, the Soviet Union and China.

Production, etc.—The principal products of Guinea are bauxite, alumina, iron-ore, palm kernels, millet, rice, coffee, bananas, pineapples and rubber. At Sangaredi in the mountainous hinterland, where the rivers Senegal, Gambia and Niger have their sources, large deposits of bauxite are mined. Deposits of iron ore, gold, diamonds and uranium have also been discovered. Principal imports are cotton goods, manufactured goods, tobacco, petroleum products, sugar, rice, flour and salt; exports, bauxite, alumina, iron-ore, diamonds, coffee, hides, bananas, palm kernels and pineapples.

Trade with UK

	1988	1989
Imports from UK	£10,106,000	£20,402,000
Exports to UK	7,582,000	15,899,000

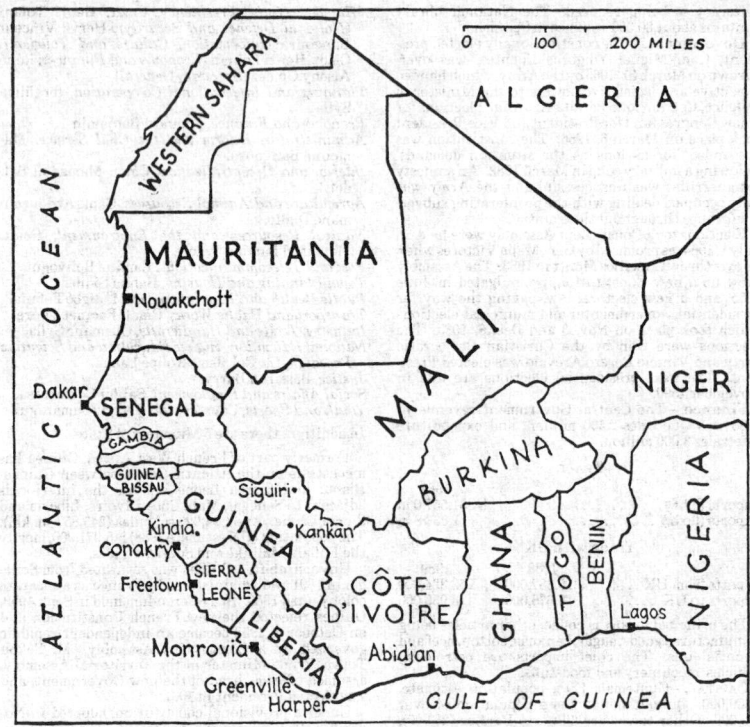

Kankan, which is connected with Conakry by a railway, Kindia, N'Zérékoré, Mamou, Siguiri and Labé.

CURRENCY.—Guinea franc of 100 centimes.

FLAG.—Three vertical stripes of red, yellow and green.

NATIONAL DAY.—October 2 (Anniversary of Proclamation of Independence).

British Ambassador (resident in Dakar, Senegal).

GUINEA-BISSAU
(República da Guiné-Bissau)

President of the Council of State (Head of State), Brig.-Gen. João Bernardo Vieira, *took power,* Nov. 1980; *elected for a five-year term,* June 1989.

COUNCIL OF MINISTERS
(as at March 8, 1990)

First Vice President, Minister of State for the Armed Forces, Col. Iafai Camara.

Second Vice President, Vasco Cabral.

Minister of State for Rural Development and Agriculture, Carlos Correia.

Minister of State for Social Affairs, Carmen Pereira.

Minister of State for Economy and Finance, Manuel Santos.

Minister of State at the Presidency, Fidelis Cabral de Almada.

Interior, Jose Pereira.

Women's Affairs, Francisca Pereira.

Justice, Mario Cabral.

Natural Resources and Industry, Filinto de Barros.

Foreign Affairs, Julio Semedo.

Civil Service, Labour, Alexandre Nunes Correia.

Commerce and Tourism, Luis Oliveira Sanca.

Fisheries, Freire Monteiro.

International Co-operation, Bernardino Cardoso.

Public Health, Henriqueta Godinho Gomes.

Transport, Avito Jose da Silva.

Public Works, Construction and Town Planning, Alberto Antonio Voss Lima Gomes.

Information and Telecommunications, Mussa Djassi.

Regional Ministers, Mario Mendes (*Eastern Province*); Nicandro Pereira Barreto (*Southern Province*); Zeca Martins (*Northern Province*).

Minister-Governor of the Central Bank, Pedro Godinho Gomes.

Education, Manuel Rambout Barcelos.

In addition, there are 16 Secretaries of State.

Guinea-Bissau, formerly Portuguese Guinea, lies in Western Africa, between Senegal and Guinea; it has an area of 13,948 sq. miles (36,125 sq. km), and has a population (UN estimate 1988) of 945,000. The main ethnic groups are the Balante, Malinké, Fulani, Mandjako and Pepel.

Guinea-Bissau achieved independence on September 10, 1974. Luis Cabral was ousted in a coup led by Maj. (now Brig.-Gen.) Vieira in November, 1980. Following the coup the Assembly was suspended, and a Revolutionary Council was established. Under a new constitution adopted in April 1984 the Revolutionary Council became a 15-member Council of State, and a parliament was set up. An attempted coup to overthrow President Vieira was defeated in November 1985.

Economy.—The country produces rice, coconuts, ground-nuts and palm oil products. Cattle are raised, and there are bauxite deposits in the south.

Trade with UK

	1988	1989
Imports from UK	£925,000	£1,185,000
Exports to UK	22,000	29,000

CAPITAL.—ΨBissau, population (Census 1979), 109,486 is also the chief port.

CURRENCY.—Guinea-Bissau peso of 100 centavos.

FLAG.—Horizontal bands of yellow over green with vertical red band in the hoist charged with a black star.

NATIONAL DAY.—September 24 (Independence Day).

British Ambassador, (resident in Dakar, Senegal).

HAITI
(République d'Haïti)

Interim President, Ertha Pascal-Trouillot, *sworn in* March 13, 1990.

CABINET
(as at March 18, 1990)*

Interior, Joseph Maxi.
National Defence, Jean Thomas.
Justice, Pierre Labissiere.
Foreign Affairs and Worship, Kesner Clermont.
Economy and Finance, Pierre Louis.
National Education, Youth and Sports, Charles Tardieu.
Information and Co-ordination, Carlo Desinor.
Public Health and Population, Serge Fils-Aime.
Agriculture, National Resources and Rural Development, Lyonel Richard.
Social Affairs, Claudette Werleigh.
Public Works, Transport and Communications, Jean-Pierre Moise Pierre-Louis.
Planning, External Co-operation and Civil Service, Ludovic Pierre.
Commerce and Industry, Maurice Lafortune.

* Presidential and legislative elections are scheduled for November 1990.

The London Embassy of the Republic of Haiti closed on March 30, 1987.

The Republic of Haiti occupies the western third of the island of Hispaniola, which, after Cuba, is the largest island in the West Indies.

The area of the Republic, including off-shore islands, is 10,714 sq. miles (27,750 sq. km) (of which about three-quarters is mountainous), with a population (UN estimate 1988) of 5,523,000.

Climate.—The climate is tropical with comparatively little difference in the temperatures between the summer (March–Oct.) and the winter (Nov.–Feb.). Humidity is high, especially in the autumn.

Language.—Following the new constitution of March 1987 both French and Creole are regarded as the official languages of Haiti. French is the language of the government and the press, but it is only spoken by the educated minority. The usual language of the people is Creole.

Government.—Haiti was a French colony under the name of Saint-Domingue from 1697. The slave population, estimated at 500,000, revolted in 1791 under the leadership of Toussaint L'Ouverture, who was born a slave and made himself Governor General of the colony. He capitulated to the French in 1802 and died in captivity in 1803. Resistance was continued by Jean Jacques Dessalines, also a former negro slave, who, on January 1, 1804, declared the former French colony to be an independent state. It was at this time that the name Haiti, an aboriginal word meaning mountainous, was adopted. Dessalines became Emperor of Haiti, but was assassinated in 1806. In 1915, following a period of political upheaval, the country was occupied by a force of US marines. The occupation came to an end in 1934, and US control of the revenue of Haiti officially ended on October 1, 1947.

Dr. Duvalier was installed as President in 1957 and held the position until his death in 1971. He was succeeded as President for life on the same day by his son, Jean Claude Duvalier, whom he had nominated as his successor. President Duvalier fled to France in February 1986 in the face of sustained popular unrest, and a council headed by Gen. Henri Namphy assumed power. In March 1987, by popular referendum, a new Constitution was agreed and Presidential elections scheduled for November; these were aborted following violence in the capital. The elections held in January 1988 were boycotted by a number of leading candidates but Leslie Manigat eventually won after a very low turnout. President Manigat was inaugurated in February 1988, but he and his government were ousted on June 19 by Gen. Henri Namphy. Manigat was deported to the Dominican Republic and Namphy set up a military government until he in turn was replaced in a coup by Lt.-Gen. Prosper Avril on September 18, 1988. Following growing government opposition in 1990, Prosper Avril resigned on March 10. The presidency devolved upon Ertha Pascal-Trouillot, to be advised by a 19-member Council of State until democratic elections later in the year. An interim Cabinet was announced on March 18, 1990.

Production.—In recent years measures for agricultural rehabilitation have been taken with the aim of a gradual restoration of productivity, which had declined after the ending of the colonial plantation system. The main project is a scheme for the irrigation of more than 70,000 acres of the Artibonite valley.

Coffee accounts for about 32 per cent of total exports, worth approximately US$55 million in 1986. Cocoa is the second largest export earner at US$4·5 million. Corn, 110,000 tonnes (1985), sorghum, 108,000 tonnes (1985), and rice are also grown. Increased production of tropical fruits and vegetables is being encouraged.

Industry.—Export assembly industries account for about 30 per cent of the total manufacturing industry in Haiti, employing an estimated 40,000 people. Items such as leather goods, textiles, electronic components and sports equipment are manufactured, using imported raw materials, for re-export, primarily to the USA Principal imports are raw materials for the export assembly sector, foodstuffs, machinery, vehicles, mineral oils and textiles.

Communications.—The main roads are asphalted and secondary roads are fair. Internal air services are maintained between the capital and the principal provincial towns. International air-services connect Port-au-Prince with the USA and other Caribbean and South American cities. The principal towns and villages are connected by telephone and/or telegraph. The telephone company is state owned (51 per cent) and the service both in Port-au-Prince and Interurban has been greatly improved. External telegraph, telephone and postal services are normal. There are several commercial radio stations and two television stations at Port-au-Prince.

Regular passenger liner services to New York have ceased, but cruise ships call occasionally. Freight sailings are frequent for the USA, Canada, Europe, Latin America (except Cuba) and the main Caribbean ports.

Education.—Education is free but estimates of illiteracy are as high as 85 per cent.

Trade with UK

	1988	1989
Imports from UK	£6,760,000	£6,566,000
Exports to UK	844,000	803,000

CAPITAL.—Ψ Port-au-Prince. Population estimated at about 1 million. Other centres are: Ψ Cap Haitien (54,691); Gonaives (36,736); Les Cayes (27,222); Jérémie (25,117); St. Marc (20,504); Jacmel (16,449); Ψ Port de Paix (21,733).

CURRENCY.—Gourde of 100 centimes.

FLAG.—Horizontal blue over red with national arms on a white square in the centre.

NATIONAL ANTHEM.—La Dessalinienne.

NATIONAL DAY.—January 1.

British Ambassador, (resident in Kingston, Jamaica).

HOLY SEE
see, VATICAN CITY STATE

HONDURAS
(Republica de Honduras)

President of the Republic, Rafael Leonardo Callejas, *assumed office*, January 27, 1990.

CABINET
(as at May 31, 1990)

Interior and Justice, Francisco Cardona Arguelles.
Foreign Affairs, Mario Carias Zapata.
Defence, Col. Francisco Zepeda Andino.

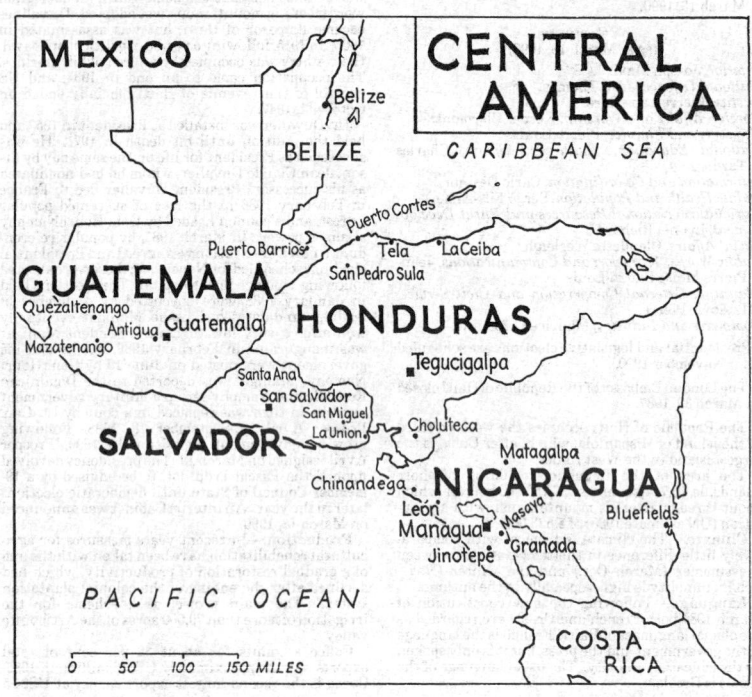

Education, Jaime Martinez Guzman.
Finance, Benjamin Villanueva.
Economy, Ramon Medina Luna.
Communications, Public Works and Transport, Maur-
icio Membreno.
Health, Dr. Cesar Castellanos.
Labour and Social Security, Rodolfo Rosales Abella.
Natural Resources, Mario Nufio Gamero.
Culture and Tourism, Sonia Canales De Mendieta.
Economic Planning, Manlio Martinez Cantor.
Director of National Agrarian Institute, Juan Ramon
Martinez.

EMBASSY OF HONDURAS
115 Gloucester Place, W1H 3PJ
[071–486 4880]

Ambassador Extraordinary and Plenipotentiary, His
Excellency Max Velásquez-Diaz (1984).

Honduras, in Central America, lies between lat. 13°
and 16° 30′ N. and long. 83° and 89° 41′ W. with a
seaboard of about 375 miles on the Caribbean Sea and
an outlet, consisting of a small strip of coast 63 miles
in length on the Pacific. Its frontiers are contiguous
with those of Guatemala, Nicaragua and El Salvador.

The Republic contains a total area of approximately
43,277 sq. miles (112,088 sq. km) and is very mountainous, being traversed by the Cordilleras, with peaks
rising to 1,500 and 2,400 metres above sea level. Most
of the soil is poor and acidic, except for the coastal
plains of the north and some areas of the interior.
Rainfall is seasonal, May to October being wet and
November to April dry. Three-quarters of the territory is covered by pine forests which contribute to
much of the country's wealth in natural resources.
The population of 4,443,721 (1988) is of mixed Spanish
and Indian blood. Garifunas in Northern Honduras
are of West Indian origin.

The language of the country is Spanish, although
English is the first language of many in the islands
and on the north coast. Primary and secondary
education is free, primary education being compulsory, and the Government has launched a campaign
to eradicate illiteracy.

Government.—Originally discovered and settled
by the Spanish at the beginning of the sixteenth
century Honduras formed part of the Spanish American Dominions for nearly three centuries until 1821
when independence was proclaimed. Under military
government from 1972–81, and after two terms of
Liberal administration, the most recent legislative
election in November 1989 was won by the Partido
Nacional (National Party). The new Government
took office in January 1990.

The Republic is divided into 18 departments, the
newest of which, Gracias a Dios, formed in 1957, is
now the home of thousands of Miskito Indian refugees
from Nicaragua.

Production.—Agriculture is mainly confined to
the large and fertile valleys on the wide Caribbean
plain, and the extensive valleys found in the Comay-
agua and Olancho regions of the interior. Reaching
inland from the Caribbean towards the eastern border
with Nicaragua a vast tropical forest area called the
Mosquitia provides valuable reserves of timber. Lead,
zinc and silver are mined on a small scale.

The chief exports are coffee, bananas and timber,
the most important woods being pine, mahogany and
cedar. Cattle raising and the exporting of frozen
meat is an important industry, and exports of shrimps
and lobsters are increasing. Other products are
tobacco, beans, maize, rice, cotton, palm oil, sugar
cane, cement and tropical fruits. There are large
tracts of uncultivated land.

Communications.—There are about 1,004 km of
railway in operation, chiefly to serve the banana
plantations and the Caribbean ports. There are

17,947 km of roads, of which 2,173 are paved, excluding
some 250 km of new major highways recently inaugurated. Improvements are being made and new
roads built. There are 33 smaller airstrips and three
international airports, Tegucigalpa, San Pedro Sula
and La Ceiba.

Ψ The chief ports are Puerto Cortes, Tela and La
Ceiba on the north coast, through which passes the
bulk of the trade with the United States and Europe.
Puerto Castilla is being developed as a deep-water
container port, and San Lorenzo is also experiencing
rapid growth.

TRADE

	1987	1988
	Lempiras	
Imports	2,646·1m	2,786·2m
Exports	1,986·9m	2,057·5m

Trade with UK

	1988	1989
Imports from UK	£7,891,000	£5,518,000
Exports to UK	8,295,000	12,121,000

CAPITAL.—Tegucigalpa, population (1987 estimate)
640,900; other towns are San Pedro Sula (429,300),
ΨLa Ceiba (66,000), ΨPuerto Cortes (42,100), Cholu-
teca (64,500) and ΨTela (27,800).

CURRENCY.—Lempira of 100 centavos.

FLAG.—Three horizontal bands, blue, white, blue
(with five blue stars on white band).

NATIONAL ANTHEM.—Tu Bandera Es Un Lampo De
Cielo (Your flag is a heavenly light).

NATIONAL DAY.—September 15.

BRITISH EMBASSY
Apartado Postal 290, Tegucigalpa
[Honduras 32–0612/18]

Ambassador Extraordinary and Plenipotentiary, His
Excellency Peter John Streams, CMG (1989).

HUNGARY
(Magyar Köztársaság)

President, Arpad Göncz, *sworn in* August 3, 1990.

CABINET
(as at May 31, 1990)

Prime Minister, Dr. Jozsef Antall.
Interior, Dr. Balazs Horvath.
Agriculture, Ferenc Jozsef Nagy.
Justice, Dr. Istvan Balsai.
Industry and Commerce, Dr. Peter Bod.
Environmental Protection, Sandor Keresztes.
Transport and Communications, Csaba Siklos.
Foreign Affairs, Geza Jeszenszky.
Defence, Lajos Fur.
Labour, Dr. Sandor Gyorivanyi.
Education and Culture, Dr. Bertalan Andrasfalvy.
Public Welfare, Laszlo Surjan.
International Economic Relations, Bela Kadar.
Finance, Ferenc Rabar.
Ministers without Portfolio, Ferenc Madl, Dr. Gyula
Kiss, Jeno Gerbovits.
State Secretaries:
International Economic Relations, Laszlo Bogar.
Finance, Katalin Botos.
PM's Office, Geza Entz, Gyorgy Matolcsi, Dr. Miklos
Palos.
Justice, Dr. Tamas Isepy.
Foreign Affairs, Tamas Katona.
Social Welfare, Dr. Andras Keleman.
Transport, Telecommunications, Zsolt Rajkai.
Agriculture, Laszlo Sarossy.
Labour, Tamas Szabo.
Environment, Mrs. Laszlo Tarjan.

EMBASSY OF THE REPUBLIC OF HUNGARY
35 Eaton Place, SW1X 8BY
[071–235 4048/7191]

Ambassador Extraordinary and Plenipotentiary, new appointment awaited.

Counsellors, Dr. P. Kallós (*Consul*); B. Juszel (*Press*); T Antalpéter (*Commercial*).

Defence, Military and Air Attaché, Col. P. Szücs.

Area and Population.—The area of Hungary is 35,919 sq. miles (93,030 sq. km) with a population (1990) of 10,560,000.

Government.—Hungary, reconstituted a kingdom in 1920 after having been declared a republic on November 17, 1918, joined the Anti-Comintern Pact in February 1939 and entered the 1939–45 War on the side of Germany in 1941. On January 20, 1945 a Hungarian provisional government of liberation, which had been set up during the preceding December, signed an armistice under the terms of which the frontiers of Hungary were withdrawn to the limits existing in 1937.

After the liberation, a coalition of the Smallholder, National Peasant, Social Democrat and Communist parties carried out major land reform and mines, heavy industry, banks and schools were nationalized. By 1949 the Communists had succeeded in gaining a monopoly of power. A campaign was opened to collectivize agriculture and by 1952 practically the entire economy had been 'socialized'. The Party formulated policy and the function of the Government was mainly executive.

The period from July 1956 to the outbreak of the national revolution on October 23 was marked by growing ferment in intellectual circles and increased discord within the Party. The withdrawal of Soviet troops from the country and free elections were among the demands put forward. Fighting broke out on the night of October 23 between demonstrators, who had been joined by large numbers of factory workers, and the State Security Police. Soviet forces intervened in strength early the next morning. By October 30 Soviet troops had withdrawn from Budapest and on November 3 an all-party coalition government under Imre Nagy was formed. This government was overthrown and the revolution suppressed as the result of a renewed attack by Soviet forces on Budapest in the early hours of November 4. The formation of a new Hungarian Revolutionary Worker Peasant Government under the leadership of Mr. Kádár was announced.

This government gradually introduced economic reforms and some political liberalization. Kádár was forced to resign in May 1989. In October 1989 the National Assembly (*Országgyülés*) approved an amended Constitution which described Hungary as an independent, democratic state. Multi-party elections took place in March and April 1990. The majority of seats were won by the Hungarian Democratic Forum, followed by the Alliance of Free Democrats. In May 1990 a coalition government was installed. The former ruling Communist Party, reconstituted as the Hungarian Socialist Party, is now in opposition.

Economy.—Since 1968 the Hungarian economy had been run according to a system which allowed more decentralized decision-making than in some other Eastern European countries, although central control in vital areas such as the allocation of fuels and raw materials remained. Privatization and the return of private land-ownership are now among the expected changes.

Industrialization has made considerable progress in the last decade and now produces 68 per cent of national income. Industry is mainly based on imported raw materials but Hungary has its own coal (mostly brown), bauxite, considerable deposits of natural gas (some not yet under full exploitation), some iron ore and oil. Output figures in 1985 (1,000 tons): coal 24,042; bauxite 2,815; rolled steel 2,860; crude oil 2,000; cement 3,678. Natural gas production totalled 7,441 million cubic metres.

Agriculture still occupies an important place in the Hungarian economy. Ten and a half per cent of the entire land area is owned by state farms and a further 63·8 per cent is within co-operative farms. Co-operative farms will remain a feature of Hungarian agriculture. Production in 1989 was (tons):

Maize	6,700,000
Wheat	6,500,000
Sugar beet	5,300,000
Barley	854,000
Rye	261,000
Oats	145,000

Although there was a 1·8 per cent drop in GDP in 1989, per capita real income increased by about 2 per cent.

Religion and Education.—About two-thirds of the population are Roman Catholics, and the remainder mostly Calvinist. There are five types of schools under the Ministry of Education: kindergartens 3–6, general schools 6–14 (compulsory), vocational schools (15–18), secondary schools (15–18), universities and adult training schools (over 18).

Language and Literature.—Magyar, or Hungarian, is one of the Finno-Ugrian languages. Hungarian literature began to flourish in the second half of the sixteenth century. Among the greatest writers of the nineteenth and twentieth centuries are Mihály Vörösmarty (1800–1855), Sándor Petőfi (1823–1849), János Arany (1817–1882), Imre Madach (1823–1864), Kálmán Miksxáth (1847–1910), Endre Ady (1877–1918), Attila József (1905–1937), Mihály Babits (1883–1941) and Dezső Kosztolányi (1885–1936).

TRADE

	1986	1987
		Forints
Imports	439,700m	463,100m
Exports	420,300m	450,100m

Trade with UK

	1987	1988
Imports from UK	£131,212,000	£117,947,000
Exports to UK	98,288,000	105,221,000

CAPITAL.—Budapest, on the Danube; population (1985) 2,072,000. Other large towns are: Miskolc (212,000); Debrecen (210,000); Szeged (181,000) and Pecs (175,000).

CURRENCY.—Forint of 100 fillér.

FLAG.—Red, white, green (horizontally).

NATIONAL ANTHEM.—Isten Aldd Meg A Magyart (God Bless the Hungarians).

NATIONAL DAY.—October 23.

BRITISH EMBASSY
Harmincad Utca 6, Budapest V
[Budapest 118–2888]

Ambassador Extraordinary and Plenipotentiary, His Excellency John Allan Birch, CMG (1989).

Counsellor, P. G. Harborne (*Head of Chancery*).

Defence and Military Attaché, Col. F. N. J. Davies.

Air Attaché, Wg.-Cdr. O. J. A. Knight.

First Secretary and British Council Representative, D. J. Harvey.

Consul, F. A. Blogg.

ICELAND
(Island)

President, Vigdís Finnbogadóttir, *born* 1930, *elected* June 29, 1980, *re-elected*, July 1984 and June 1988.

CABINET
(as at May 31,1990)

Prime Minister, Steingrímur Hermannsson (Pr).
Foreign Affairs and Trade, Jón Baldvin Hannibalsson (SDP).
Finance, Ulafur Ragnar Grímsson (PA).
Fisheries, Halldór Asgrímsson. (Pr).
Education and Culture, Svavar Gestsson (PA).
Social Affairs, Jóhanna Sigurthardóttir (SDP).
Health and Social Security, Guthmundur Bjarnason (Pr).
Commerce, Industry and Nordic Co-operation, Jón Sigurthsson (SDP).
Agriculture and Communications, Steingrímur Sigfusson (PA).
Justice and Ecclesiastical Affairs, Óli Th. Gudbjartsson (CP).
Environmental Affairs, Julius Solnes (CP).

Pr: Progressive Party; SDP: Social Democrat Party; PA: People's Alliance; CP: Citizens' Party.

EMBASSY OF ICELAND
1 Eaton Terrace, SW1W 8EY
[071–730 5131]

Ambassador Extraordinary and Plenipotentiary, His Excellency Helgie Agústsson (1989).
Minister Counsellor, T. Karlsson.

Iceland is a large volcanic island in the North Atlantic Ocean, extending from 63° 23′ to 66° 33′ N. lat., and from 13° 22′ to 24° 35′ W. long., with an estimated area of 39,768 sq. miles (103,000 sq. km). The population was 253,482 on December 1, 1989.

Iceland was uninhabited before the ninth century, when settlers came from Norway. For several centuries a form of republican government prevailed, with an annual assembly of leading men called the *Althing*, but in 1241 Iceland became subject to Norway, and later to Denmark. During the colonial period, Iceland maintained its cultural integrity but a deterioration in the climate, together with frequent volcanic eruptions and outbreaks of disease, led to a serious fall in the standard of living and to a decline in the population to little more than 40,000. In the nineteenth century a struggle for independence began which led first to home rule for Iceland under the Danish Crown (1918), and later to complete independence under a republican form of rule in 1944.

Government.—The parliamentary (*Althing*) elections in April 1987 gave the Independence Party 18 seats, Progressives 13, Social Democratic Party 10,

People's Alliance 8, Citizens' Party 7, Women's Alliance 6 and Independent 1. The coalition government resigned on September 18, 1988 and on September 28 Steingrímur Hermannsson formed a new government. The coalition was extended in September 1989 to include the Citizens' Party.

Language and Literature.—The ancient Norraena (or Northern tongue) presents close affinities to Anglo-Saxon and as spoken and written in Iceland today differs little from that introduced into the island in the ninth century. There is a rich literature with two distinct periods of development, from the mid-11th to the late 13th century and from the early 19th century to the present.

Production.—Iceland has considerable resources of hydro-electric and geothermal energy. It is estimated that exploited water power (4,000 Gigawatt hours/a) represents only about 9 per cent of that economically exploitable, whereas only 5 per cent of the estimated 80,000 Gigawatt hours/a of available geothermal power has so far been harnessed. Energy-intensive heavy industry includes an aluminium smelter, a nitrogen fertilizer factory, a diatomite plant and a ferro-silicone plant.

The principal exports are frozen fish fillets, salt fish, stock fish, fresh fish on ice, frozen scampi, fishmeal and oil, skins and aluminium; the imports consist of almost all the necessities of life, the chief items being petroleum products, transport equipment, textiles, foodstuffs, animal feeds, timber, and alumina.

At January 1, 1990, the mercantile marine consisted of 622 vessels of under 100 gross tons and 345 ships of 100 gross tons and over; a total of 967 vessels (178,314 gross tons), of which 842 (116,011 gross tons) are decked fishing vessels. There are regular shipping services between Reykjavík and Felixstowe, Humber ports and the Continent.

A regular air service is maintained between Glasgow and London and Reykjavík. There are also air services from the island to Scandinavia, USA, Germany, France and Luxembourg.

Road communications are adequate in summer but greatly restricted by snow in winter. Only roads in town centres and key highways are metalled, the rest being of gravel, sand and lava dust. The climate and terrain make first-class surfaces for highways out of the question. There are no railways.

FINANCE

	1988	1989
Revenue	Kr63,091m	Kr77,100m
Expenditure	55,198m	67,651m

TRADE

	1988	1989
Exports	Kr61,674m	Kr80,072m
Imports	68,971m	80,250m

Trade with UK

	1988	1989
Imports from UK	£87,100,000	£69,497,000
Exports to UK	198,365,000	196,678,000

CAPITAL.—ΨReykjavík, population (Dec. 1, 1989), 95,811.
Other centres in approximate order of importance are ΨAkureyri, Kópavogur, ΨHafnarfjördur, Keflavík, Westmann Islands, Akranes, Isafjördur and ΨSiglufjördur.
CURRENCY.—Icelandic króna (Kr) of 100 aurar.
FLAG.—Blue, with white-bordered red cross.
NATIONAL ANTHEM.—O Gud Vors Lands (Our Country's God).
NATIONAL DAY.—June 17.

BRITISH EMBASSY
Laufásvegur 49, Reykjavik
[Reykjavik 15883/4]

Ambassador Extraordinary and Plenipotentiary and Consul-General, His Excellency Sir Richard Radford Best, KCVO, CBE (1989).
Deputy Head of Mission, Second Secretary and Consul, A. Mehmet, MVO.

BRITISH CONSULAR OFFICES

There are Consular Offices at *Akureyri* and *Reykjavík.*

INDONESIA
(Republik Indonesia)

President, General Suharto, *born* June 9, 1921. *Acting President,* March 12, 1967; *confirmed as President,* March 28, 1968, *re-elected for a term of 5 years,* March 1973, March 1978, March 1983 and March 1988.
Vice-President, Lt.-Gen. Sudharmono, *elected* March 1988.

CABINET
(as at June 30, 1990)

Co-ordinating Ministers, Adm. Sudomo (*Political and Security Affairs*); Dr. Radius Prawiro (*Economy, Finance, Industry and Development Supervision*); Gen. Supardjo Rustam (*Public Welfare*).
Ministers, Gen. Rudini (*Internal Affairs*); Ali Alatas (*Foreign Affairs*); Gen. L. B. Murdani (*Defence and Security*); Lt.-Gen. Ismail Saleh (*Justice*); Mr.

Harmoko (*Information*); Dr. J. B. Sumarlin (*Finance*); Dr. Arifin Siregar (*Trade*); Mr. Hartarto (*Industry*); Mr. Wardoyo (*Agriculture*); Air Vice Marshal Ginandjar Kartasasmita (*Mines and Energy*); Radinal Mochtar (*Public Works*); Maj.-Gen. Azwar Anas (*Communications*); Maj.-Gen. Bustanil Arifin (*Co-operatives*); Cosmas Batubara (*Manpower*); Lt.-Gen. Sugiarto (*Transmigration*); Gen. Susilo Sudarman (*Tourism, Posts and Telecommunications*); Prof. Fuad Hassan (*Education and Culture*); Dr. Adhyatma (*Health*); Haji Munawir Sjadzali (*Religious Affairs*); Prof. Haryati Subadio (*Social Affairs*); Hasjrul Harahap (*Forestry*).
Ministers of State, Maj.-Gen. Murdiono (*State Secretary*); Dr. Saleh Afif (*National Development Planning*); Siswono Judo Husodo (*Housing*); Prof. Emil Salim (*Population and Environment*); Sarwono Kusumaatmadja (*Administrative Reform*); Prof. B. J. Habibie (*Research and Technology*); Mrs. A. Sulasikin Murpratomo (*Women's Affairs*); Akbar Tandjung (*Sport and Youth Affairs*).

INDONESIAN EMBASSY
38 Grosvenor Square, W1X 9AD
[071–499 7661]

Ambassador Extraordinary and Plenipotentiary, His Excellency Teuku Mohammad Hadi Thayeb (1990).
Minister, Hidayat Soemo (*Deputy Chief of Mission*).

Situated between latitudes 6° North and 11° South and between longitudes 95° and 141° East, Indonesia comprises the islands of Java, Madura, and Sumatra, the Riouw-Lingga Archipelago (which with Karimon, Anambas, Natuna Islands, Tambelan, and part of Sumatra, forms the province of Riau), the islands of Bangka and Billiton, part of the island of Borneo (Kalimantan), Sulawesi (formerly Celebes) Island, the Molucca Islands (Ternate, Tidore, Halmahera, Buru, Seram, Banda, Timor-Laut, Larat, Bachiam, Obi, Kei, Aru, Babar, Leti and Wetar), the island of Bali and the islands of Lombok, Sumbawa, Sumba, Flores, Timor and others comprising the provinces of East and West Nusa Tenggara and the western half of the island of New Guinea (Irian Jaya), with a total area of 735,358 sq. miles (1,904,569 sq. km), and a population (UN estimate 1988) of 174,951,000.

From the early part of the 17th century much of the Indonesian Archipelago was under Netherlands rule. Following the World War 1939–45, during which the Archipelago was occupied by the Japanese, a strong nationalistic movement manifested itself and after sporadic fighting the formal transfer of sovereignty by the Netherlands of all the former Dutch East Indies except western New Guinea took place on December 27, 1949.

Western New Guinea became part of Indonesia in 1963 under the name West Irian (now Irian Jaya), this interpretation being confirmed in an 'Act of Free Choice' in July 1969, of which the United Nations took note in November 1969. Following a unilateral declaration of independence by the Fretilin, Indonesia took over the former Portuguese colony of East Timor, which in July 1976 was declared the 27th province of Indonesia.

Following a three-week period of unrest and violent student demonstrations the Minister of the Army, General Suharto, took over effective political power in March 1966.

General Suharto was made Acting President with full powers, on March 11, 1967, and on March 28, 1968 appointed full President for a period of five years.

In the general election of April 1987, Golkar obtained 299 seats, the Muslim United Development Party 61 seats and the Indonesian Democratic Party 40 seats. President Suharto was subsequently re-elected in March 1988.

Production.—Nearly 70 per cent of the population of Indonesia is engaged in agriculture and related production. Copra, kapok, nutmeg, pepper and cloves are produced, mainly by smallholders; palm oil, sugar, fibres and cinchona are produced by large estates. Rubber, tea, coffee and tobacco are also produced by both in large quantities. Rice is a traditional staple food for the people of Indonesia and the islands of Java, Sulawesi and Sumatra are important producers. Production has risen rapidly in recent years to 25 million tons and the country is now self sufficient.

Oil and liquefied natural gas are the most important assets, the export of which in 1985–86 earned about US $11,000 million (around 80 per cent of Indonesia's exports), but more recent developments have underscored the vulnerability of the economy to depressed international markets and weak oil prices. Timber is the second largest foreign exchange earner after oil. Strenuous efforts have been made to develop non-oil exports, and these have now reached about 50 per cent of total exports.

Indonesia is rich in minerals, particularly tin, of which the country is the world's third biggest producer; petroleum, coal, nickel and bauxite are the other principal products; there are also considerable deposits of gold, silver, manganese phosphates and sulphur. Aid to Indonesia is channelled through the Inter-Governmental Group on Indonesia (IGGI). Indonesia received about US$4·6 billion in 1990.

Indonesia's Fifth Development Programme started in 1984 and its main objectives are the diversification of the economy to reduce dependence on crude oil, with particular emphasis on agriculture and manufacturing.

Trade with UK

	1988	1989
Imports from UK	£203,275,000	£184,032,000
Exports to UK	233,807,000	273,102,000

Principal exports to the United Kingdom are rubber, timber, non-ferrous metals, clothing, tea, coffee, spices, vegetable oils and fats, and crude oil for refinement. Imports from the United Kingdom are mainly of machinery, transport equipment, electrical equipment and chemicals.

Transport.—In Java a main railway line connects Jakarta with Surabaya in the east of Java and there are several branches. In Sumatra the important towns of Medan, Padang and Palembang are the centres of short railway systems.

Sea communications in the archipelago are maintained by the state-run shipping companies Djakarta-Lloyd (ocean-going) and Pelni (coastal and inter-island) and other small concerns. Transport by small craft on the rivers of the larger islands plays an important part in trade. Air services in Indonesia are operated by Garuda Indonesian Airways and other local airlines, and Jakarta is served by various international services. There are approximately 50,000 miles of roads.

CAPITAL.—ΨJakarta (population 6,503,449). Other important centres are: (Java) ΨSurabaya (2,027,913), ΨSemarang (1,026,671), Bandung (1,462,637); (Sumatra) Palembang (787,187), Medan (1,378,955); (Sulawesi), ΨUjung Pandang (formerly *Makassar*) (709,038); (Kalimantan) Banjarmasin (381,286), ΨPontianak (304,778), ΨBalikpapan (280,675); (Moluccas) Ambon (208,898); (Bali) Denpasar, Singaraja (for whole island 2,174,105); (Nusa Tenggara) Kupang (329,371); (Irian Jaya) Jayapura (107,164).

CURRENCY.—Rupiah (Rp) of 100 sen.

FLAG.—Equal bands of red over white.

NATIONAL ANTHEM.—Indonesia Raya (Great Indonesia).

NATIONAL DAY.—August 17 (Anniversary of Proclamation of Independence).

BRITISH EMBASSY
Jalan M. H. Thamrin 75, Jakarta 10310
[Jakarta 330904]

Ambassador Extraordinary and Plenipotentiary, His Excellency Roger Carrick, CMG, LVO (1990).

BRITISH CONSULAR OFFICES

There are British Consular Offices at *Jakarta, Medan* and *Surabaya.*

British Council Representative, Howard Thompson, OBE, S Widjojo Centre, Jalan Jenderal Sudirman, 71, Jakarta 12190. There are also libraries at *Bandung* and *Medan.*

INDONESIA BRITAIN ASSOCIATION

c/o Mr. R. A. M. Ramsay, Sarinah Building, 13th Floor, J1. M. H. Thamrin 11, Jakarta.

IRAN
(Jomhori-e-Islami-e-Iran)

Leader of the Islamic Republic, Ayatollah Seyed Ali Khamenei, *appointed* June 1989.
President, Hojjatoleslam Ali Akbar Hashemi Rafsanjani, *elected* July 28, 1989.

CABINET
(as at May 31, 1990)

Agriculture, Issa Kalantari.
Commerce, Abdol-Hossein Vahaji.
Construction Crusade, Gholamreza Forouzesh.

Higher Education, Mostafa Moin.
Defence and Armed Forces Logistics, Akbar Torkan.
Economy and Finance, Mohsen Nourbakhsh.
Education, Mohammad Ali Najafi.
Energy, Bizhan Namdar Zanganeh.
Islamic Guidance, Mohammad Khatami.
Foreign Affairs, Ali Akbar Velayati.
Health, Iraj Fazel.
Heavy Industries, Mohammad Hadi Nezhad-Hossein-
   ian.
Housing and Urban Development, Serajuddin Kazer-
   ouni.
Industries, Mohammad Reza Nematzadeh.
Intelligence, Ali Fallahian.
Interior, Abdollah Nouri.
Justice, Esmail Shoushtari.
Labour and Social Affairs, Hossein Kamali.
Mines and Metals, Mohammad Hossein Mahloujchi.
Oil, Gholamreza Aghazadeh.
Posts, Telephones and Telegraphs, Mohammad Ghar-
   razi.
Roads and Transport, Mohammad Saidi-Kia.

DIPLOMATIC REPRESENTATION

Following the breaking off of diplomatic relations
with Iran on March 7, 1989, an Iranian Interests
section has been set up at the Embassy of Pakistan.

Area and Population.—Iran has an area of
636,296 sq. miles (1,648,000 sq. km), with a population
of around 55 million. It is mostly an arid table-land,
encircled, except in the east, by mountains, the
highest in the north rising to 18,934 ft. The central
and eastern portion is a vast salt desert.

The Iranians are mostly Shi'ah Muslims but among
them are Zoroastrians, Bahais, Sunni Muslims and
Armenian and Assyrian Christians. Emigration has
much reduced the once substantial Jewish community.

Language and Literature.—Persian, or Farsi,
the language of Iran, and of some other areas formerly
under Persian rule, is an Indo-European tongue with
many Arabic elements added; the alphabet is mainly
Arabic, with writing from right to left. Among the
great names in Persian literature are those of Abu'l
Kásim Mansúr, of Firdausi (AD 939–1020), Omar
Khayyám, the astronomer-poet (died AD 1122), Mus-
lihu'd-Din, known as Sa'di (born AD 1184) and Shems-
ed-Din Muhammad, or Hafiz (died AD 1389).

Government.—Iran was ruled from the end of the
18th century by Shahs of the Qajar Dynasty. A
nationalist movement became active in December
1905, and in August 1906, the Shah, Muzaffer-ud-Din,
granted a Constitution. After the war of 1914–18, the
subsequent troubles and the signature of the Soviet-
Iranian Treaty of 1921, a vigorous Prime Minister,
Reza Khan, re-established general order. On Oct. 31,
1925, the last representative of the Qajar Dynasty,
Sultan Ahmed Shah was deposed in his absence by
the National Assembly, which handed over the
government to the Prime Minister, Reza Khan, who
was elected Shah on Dec. 13, 1925 by the Constituent
Assembly, and took the title Reza Shah Pahlavi. On
September 16, 1941 Reza Shah abdicated in favour of
the Crown Prince, who ascended the throne under
the title of Mohammed Reza Shah Pahlavi.

Following widespread and persistent opposition to
his regime, the Shah departed from Iran in January
1979. Ayatollah Khomeini, the main spiritual leader
of the Shi'ah Muslims, returned to Iran from exile on
February 1. Following a national referendum, Iran
was declared an Islamic Republic on April 1, 1979. A
new constitution, providing for a President, Prime
Minister and Consultative Assembly, and also for
overall leadership by Ayatollah Khomeini, was approved by referendum in December 1979. The government's severe measures suppressed violent
opposition. In June 1989 Khomeini died and Presi-

dent Khamenei was appointed Leader of the Islamic
Republic. Rafsanjani was elected President in July
1989.

Iran was at war with Iraq following the Iraqi
invasion of Iran in September 1980. International
efforts to end the fighting focused on United Nations
Security Council Resolution 598 of July 1987, and a
ceasefire came into effect on August 20, 1988. In
August 1990 Iraq accepted all of Iran's conditions for
a peace treaty, thus formally ending the war.

Defence.—The Army has a strength of about
150,000 men, in 4 armoured divisions, 4 infantry
divisions and one airborne division. The Air Force
has a strength of about 35,000, with some 70 combat
aircraft. The Navy has a strength of about 20,000 and
consists of 3 destroyers, 3 frigates, 4 corvettes, 5
minesweepers, and patrol boats, support ships, landing craft and hovercraft. The Islamic Revolutionary
Guards Corps numbers about 500,000 men. Total
armed forces personnel including paramilitary forces
number over one million.

Education.—Since 1943 primary education has
been compulsory and free, but there is large scale
absenteeism, particularly outside the towns. There
are 22 universities in Iran (eight in Tehran, 14 in the
provinces). The educational system has been reformed following the revolution.

Agriculture.—While petroleum is the principal
product and by far the greatest export, Iran is
otherwise largely an agricultural and pastoral country. After the 1979 revolution the Government
announced its intention of giving greater emphasis
to the development of agriculture with a view to
reducing Iran's dependence on food imports, but it
has so far had only limited success. Some re-
distribution of land has taken place, but no basic land
reform.

Wheat is the principal crop; other important crops
are barley, rice, cotton, sugar beet, fruit, nuts and
vegetables. Wool is also a major product. There are
extensive forests in the north and west, the conservation of which is a continuing problem.

Industry.—Apart from oil, the principal industrial
products are carpets, textiles, sugar, cement and
other construction materials, ginned cotton, vegetable oil and other food products, leather and shoes,
metal manufactures, pharmaceuticals, motor vehicles, fertilizers and plastics. Industrial output was
severely curtailed by the 1979 revolution, as a result
of which many industrialists left the country. In

July 1979 the Government nationalized a wide range of major industrial concerns, having nationalized the banks and the insurance companies the previous month. Foreign trade is controlled by the state, but the private sector plays an increasingly important role.

Energy.—The oilfields, which lie in south-western Iran, were nationalized in 1951. From 1957 until the 1979 revolution a consortium of eight oil companies (one British, one French, one Dutch, and five US) was responsible for the production, refining and sale of oil. In July 1979 the National Iranian Oil Company assumed full control of the oil industry. In addition to that extracted from the onshore wells, oil is also produced from a number of off-shore oilfields. Oil production is approximately 3 million b.p.d., of which some 2·3 million b.p.d. is exported. Iran is a member of OPEC.

Communications.—Tehran is at the centre of a network of highways linking the capital with other major towns, the ports and the frontiers with Turkey, USSR, Afghanistan and Pakistan, and with the Caspian Sea. The Trans-Iranian Railway runs from Bandar Turcoman, on the Caspian Sea, via Tehran to Bandar Khomeini, on the Persian Gulf. Other lines link Tehran with Tabriz and with Mashad. There are also railways from Tabriz to Julfa and from Zahedan to Quetta, and a branch line from Ahwaz to Khorramshahr. An extension from Qom to Kerman is now in operation, as is one from Bandar Turcoman to Gorgan. The Iranian rail system is linked to the Turkish system via Van. There is an international airport at Tehran (Mehrabad), and airports at all the major provincial centres. The national airline, Iranair, is government-owned and operates international and domestic routes.

FINANCE

	1990
Revenue	Rials 4,009,700m
Expenditure	5,595,800m

TRADE

Imports to Iran declined dramatically at the beginning of 1979 as a result of the economic disruption caused by the revolution. Iran's aggressive oil sales policy during 1982 enabled foreign exchange reserves to recover from the 1981 low level and made possible increased imports. However, the drop in world oil prices in 1986 again affected Iran's foreign exchange earnings, and the level of imports declined.

Imports into Iran consist mainly of industrial and agricultural machinery, motor vehicles and motor vehicle components for assembly, iron and steel (including manufactures), electrical machinery and goods, meat, various other foods, and certain textile fabrics and yarns. The principal exports, apart from oil, are cotton, carpets, dried fruit, nuts, hides and skins, mineral ores, wool, gums, caviare, cumin seed and spices. Federal Republic of Germany and Japan are Iran's leading suppliers.

Trade with UK

	1988	1989
Imports from UK ...	£247,768,000	£257,149,000
Exports to UK	140,207,000	250,548,000

CAPITAL.—Tehran, population (1989 estimate) 10 million. Other large towns are Tabriz, Isfahan, Meshed, Shiraz, Resht, Kerman, Hamadan, Yazd, Kermanshah and Ahwaz.

CURRENCY.—Rial of 100 dinars.

FLAG.—Equal horizontal bands of green, white and red; with an emblem of the Islamic Republic.

NATIONAL ANTHEM.—Sorood-e Jomhoori-e Eslami.

NATIONAL DAY.—February 11.

BRITISH DIPLOMATIC REPRESENTATION

Diplomatic relations were broken off by Iran in March 1989, and British interests are handled by the Swedish Embassy.

IRAQ
(Al-Jumhouriya al-'Iraqia)

President, Prime Minister, Chairman of the Revolutionary Command Council, Saddam Hussein, *assumed Office* July 16, 1979.

CABINET
(as at April 30, 1990)

First Deputy PM, Taha Yasin Ramadhan.
Deputy PM, Foreign Affairs, Tariq Aziz.
Deputy PM, Sa'adoun Hammadi.
Defence, Gen. Abdel-Jabbar Khalil Shanshal.
Agriculture and Irrigation, Abdul Wahab Mahmoud al-Sabbagh.
Waqfs (Religious Endowments) and Religious Affairs, Abdullah Fadil Abbas.
Information and Culture, Latif Naseef al-Jasim.
Education, Abdul Qadir Izz ad-Din.
Health, Abdel-Salem Mohammed Saeed.
Higher Education and Scientific Research, Mundhir Ibrahim.
Housing and Construction, Taher Mohammed Hassoun al-Marzouk.
Industry and Minerals; Military Industries, Brig.-Gen. Hussein Kamil.
Interior, Samir Muhammad Abdul Wahhab.
Justice, Akram Abdel-Qader Ali.
Labour and Social Affairs, Umeed Madhat Mubarak.
Local Government, Ali Hasan al-Majid.
Oil, Issam Abdel Rahim al Chalabi.
Planning, Samal Majid Faraj.
Trade, Finance (acting), Mohammad Mehdi Saleh.
Transport and Communications, Mohammad Hamza al Zubaidi.
Youth Affairs, Abdel-Fattah Mohammad Amin.
Minister of State, Arshad Ahmed az-Zibari.
Minister of State at the President's Office, Hashim Subhi.
Director of the Presidential Office, Ahmed Hussein as-Samarra'i.

EMBASSY OF THE REPUBLIC OF IRAQ
21 Queen's Gate, SW7 5JG
[071–584 7141/6]

Ambassador Extraordinary and Plenipotentiary, His Excellency Dr. Azmi M. Shafeeq Al-Salihi (1989).

Area, etc.—Traversed by the Rivers Euphrates and Tigris, Iraq extends from Turkey on N. and N.E. to the Gulf on the S. and SE and from Iran on E. to Syria and Arabian Desert on W., the approximate position being between 37¼° to 48¼° E. long., and 37¼° to 30° N. lat. (*see* MAP, p. 782). The area of Iraq is 167,925 sq. miles (434,924 sq. km), of which 37 per cent is desert land. About 35 to 40 per cent of the remainder is potentially cultivable either by rainfall or by irrigation.

The Euphrates (which has a total length of 1,700 miles from its source to its outflow in the Persian Gulf) is formed by two arms, of which the Murad Su (415 miles) rises in eastern Erzurum and flows westwards to a junction with the Kara Su, or Frat Su (275 miles); the other arm rises in the north-west of Erzurum in the Dumlu Dagh. The River Tigris has a total length of 1,150 miles from its source to its junction with the Euphrates at Qurna, 70 miles from the Gulf, and rises in two arms south of the Taurus mountains, in Kurdistan, uniting at Til, where the boundaries of the districts of Diarbekir, Van and Bitlis conjoin.

Population.—At the Census of October 1987 Iraq had a total population of 16,278,316. A 1988 UN estimate gives a figure of 17,657,000.

Language.—The official language is Arabic. Minority languages include Kurdish (about 15 per cent), Turkic and Aramaic.

Antiquities.—In 1944 excavations at Tell Hassuna, near Shura (on the Tigris in north Iraq) unearthed abundant traces of culture dating back to 5000 BC. Excavations in 1948 at Tel Abu Shahrain, south of 'Ur of the Chaldees,' confirm Eridu's claim to be the most ancient city of the Sumerian world. Hillah, the ancient city on the left bank of the Shatt el Hillah, a branch of the Euphrates, about 70 miles south of Baghdad, is near the site of Babylon and of the 'house of the lofty-head' or 'gate of the god' (Tower of Babel). Mosul Governorate covers a great part of the ancient kingdom of Assyria, the ruins of Ninevah, the Assyrian capital, being visible on the banks of the Tigris, opposite Mosul. Qurna, at the junction of the Tigris and Euphrates, is traditionally supposed to be the site of the Garden of Eden.

Government.—Under the Treaty of Lausanne (1923), Turkey renounced sovereignty over Mesopotamia. A provisional Arab Government was set up in November 1920, and in August 1921 the Emir Faisal was elected King of Iraq. The country was a monarchy until July, 1958, when King Faisal II was assassinated. From 1958 Iraq has been under Presidential rule.

According to the Constitution, the highest state authority is the Revolutionary Command Council (RCC), which elects the President from among its own members. The President appoints the Council of Ministers. Legislative authority is shared by the RCC and the 250-member National Assembly, which is elected every four years by universal adult suffrage. Following general elections in April 1989 the Arab Ba'ath Socialist Party holds the majority of the Assembly seats, the remainder being held by the state-sponsored National Progressive Patriotic Front.

Iraq invaded Kuwait on August 2 1990. The subsequent announcement of annexation was declared void by the UN Security Council. In August 1990 Iraq accepted Iran's conditions for a peace treaty, thus formally ending hostilities in which the two states had been involved since September 1980.

Communications and Trade.—New roads are being rapidly built, and communications between Baghdad and the provincial capitals are being improved and secured. Facilities at the port of Basra have been improved but the port has not been used since the outbreak of hostilities with Iran in September 1980. Continuous dredging of the Shatt-al-Arab has also been suspended by hostilities and the channel has seriously silted. The port of Um Qasr near the Kuwaiti border has been developed for freight and sulphur handling and a container terminal is ready for operation but not in use due to the port's proximity to the war zone. Road routes from Turkey and the Mediterranean are well used, and carry through traffic to Kuwait and the south. The border between Syria and Iraq was closed in late 1977, reopened in November, 1978 and closed again in April 1982.

There is an international airport at Baghdad. Iraqi Airways provide flights between Baghdad and London, and other international airlines operate to Europe. Iraqi Republican Railways provide regular passenger and goods services between Basra, Baghdad and Mosul, and links up through Syria and Turkey with the Mediterranean and the Bosphorus, though no through traffic has used the line since the Syrian

government cut the rail link in April 1982. There is also a metre gauge line connecting Baghdad with Khanaqin, Kirkuk and Arbil. Iraq sealed its borders in August 1990, following the invasion of Kuwait.

Agriculture and Industry.—Apart from the valuable revenues to be derived from oil, agricultural development makes a valuable contribution to the wealth of the country and two harvests can usually be gathered in the year. Production fluctuates from year to year according to rainfall. The Government's concern with agricultural development is shown in the large financial allocations made to the sector. Salinity and soil erosion, caused by a high water table, inadequate irrigation and drainage and traditional farming methods, are the major problems now being addressed by development planners.

Increasing industrialization is taking place. Since 1987 the Government has been encouraging increased private and mixed sector involvement in the economy. Priority is being given to petro-chemicals, food industries, construction industries and engineering. Existing industries include cement, building materials, steel fabrications, food processing and the manufacture of consumer goods, as well as the development of mineral resources.

Iraq's major industry is oil production. It was nationalized on June 1, 1972 and accounts for approximately 98 per cent of the total government revenue and 45 per cent of the Gross National Product. Production was some 3·5 million barrels per day in 1979 but the effects of war damage on the Basra terminals and the closure of the trans-Syria pipeline reduced production until new pipelines were built via Turkey and Saudi Arabia. Total revenues from oil are estimated at \$11,000–14,000 million in 1988, although they are difficult to calculate due to fluctuations in price.

In August 1990, the UN imposed mandatory economic sanctions on Iraq, including a world-wide ban on its oil exports.

Trade with UK

	1988	1989
Imports from UK	£412,091,000	£450,495,000
Exports to UK	43,406,000	55,175,000

The principal imports are iron and steel, cement and other building materials, mechanical and electrical machinery, motor vehicles, textiles and clothing, essential foodstuffs, grain, tinned foods and raw industrial materials. The chief exports are crude petroleum, dates, raw wool, raw hides and skins and raw cotton.

CAPITAL.—Baghdad. Population of the governorate (Census 1977) 3,205,645. Other towns of importance are Ψ Basra, Mosul and Kirkuk.

CURRENCY.—Iraqi dinar (ID) of 1,000 fils.

FLAG.—Horizontal stripes of red, white and black, with three green stars on the white stripe.

NATIONAL DAY.—July 17 (Revolution Day).

BRITISH EMBASSY
Zukaq 12, Mahala 218,
Hai Al Kheloud, Baghdad
[Baghdad 5372121/5]

Ambassador Extraordinary and Plenipotentiary, His Excellency Harold Berners Walker, CMG (1989).

Counsellor, R. A. Kealy (*Head of Chancery and Consul General*).

First Secretary, A. R. Brown, MVO (*Commercial*).

Defence Attaché, Col. J. C. Cochrane, OBE.

British Council Representative, P. Elborn, OBE, Waziriya 301, Street 3, (PO Box 298), Baghdad.

IRELAND

Position and Extent.—Ireland lies in the Atlantic Ocean, to the W. of Great Britain, and is separated from Scotland by the North Channel and from Wales by the Irish Sea and St. George's Channel. The area of the island is 32,588 sq. miles (84,402 sq. km), and its geographical position between 51° 26′ and 55° 21′ N. latitude and from 5° 25′ to 10° 30′ W. longitude. The greatest length of the island, from N.E. to S.W. (Torr Head to Mizen Head), is 302 miles, and the greatest breadth, from E. to W. (Dundrum Bay to Annagh Head), is 174 miles. On the N. Coast of Achill Island (Co. Mayo) are the highest cliffs in the British Isles, 2,000 feet sheer above the sea. Ireland is occupied for the greater part of its area by the Central Plain, with an elevation 50 to 350 ft. above mean sea level, with isolated mountain ranges near the coastline. The principal mountains, with their highest points, are the Sperrin Mountains (Sawel 2,240 ft.) of County Tyrone; the Mountains of Mourne (Slieve Donard 2,796 ft.) of County Down, and the Wicklow Mountains (Lugnaquilla 3,039 ft.); the Derryveagh Mountains (Errigal 2,466 ft.) of County Donegal; the Connemara Mountains (Twelve Pins 2,695 ft.) of County Galway; Macgillicuddy's Reeks (Carrantuohill 3,414 ft., the highest point in Ireland); and the Galtee Mountains (3,018 ft.) of County Tipperary, and the Knockmealdown (2,609 ft.) and Comeragh Mountains (2,470 ft.) of County Waterford. The principal river of Ireland (and the longest in the British Isles) is the Shannon (240 miles), rising in County Cavan and draining the central plain; the Shannon flows through a chain of loughs to the city of Limerick, and thence to an estuary on the western Atlantic seaboard. The Slaney flows into Wexford Harbour, the Liffey to Dublin Bay, the Boyne to Drogheda, the Lee to Cork Harbour, the Blackwater to Youghal Harbour, and the Suir, Barrow and Nore, to Waterford Harbour. As in Scotland, the principal hydrographic feature is the Loughs, of which Lough Neagh (150 sq. miles) in the north-east is the largest in Ireland and the British Isles, others being the Shannon Chain of Allen, Boderg, Forbes, Ree and Derg, and the Erne Chain of Gowna, Oughter, Lower Erne, and Erne; Melvin, Gill, Gara and Conn in the north-west; and Corrib and Mask (joined by a hidden channel) in the west. In County Kerry, to the east of Macgillicuddy's Reeks, are the famous lakes of Killarney.

Primitive Man.—Although little is known concerning the earliest inhabitants of Ireland, there are many traces of neolithic man throughout the island; a grave containing a polished stone axehead assigned to 2,500 BC was found at Linkardstown, Co. Carlow, in 1944, and the use of bronze implements appears to have become known about the middle of the 17th century BC. In the later Bronze Age a Celtic race of Goidels appears to have invaded the island, and in the early Iron Age Brythons from South Britain are believed to have effected settlements in the south-east, while Picts from North Britain established similar settlements in the north. Towards the close of the Roman occupation of Britain, the dominant tribe in the island was that of the Scoti, who afterwards established themselves in Scotland.

History.—According to Irish legends, the island of Ierne was settled by a Milesian race, who came from Scythia by way of Spain, and established the Kingdom of Tara, about 500 BC. The supremacy of the Ardri (high king) of Tara was acknowledged by eight lesser kingdoms (Munster, Connaught, Ailech, Oriel, Ulidia, Meath, Leinster and Ossory) ruled by descendants of the eight sons of Miled. The basalt columns on the coast of Antrim, eight miles from Portrush, known as the Giant's Causeway, are connected with the legendary history of Ireland as the remnants of a bridge built in the time of Finn M'Coul (Fingal) to connect Antrim with Scotland (Staffa).

Hibernia was visited by Roman merchants but never by Roman legions, and little is known of the history of the country until the invasions of *Northmen* (Norwegians and Danes) towards the close of the 8th century AD. The Norwegians were distinguished as Findgaill (White Strangers) and the Danes as Dubgaill (Black Strangers), names which survive in Fingall, MacDougall and MacDowell, while the name of the island itself is held to be derived from the Scandinavian *Ira-land* (land of the Irish), the names of the Provinces being survivals of Norse dialect forms (Ulaids-tir, Laiginstir, Mumans-tir and Kunnak-tir). The outstanding events in the encounters with the Northmen are the *Battle of Tara* (980), at which the Hy Neill king Maelsechlainn II defeated the Scandinavians of Dublin and the Hebrides under the king Amlaib Cuarán; and the *Battle of Clontarf* (1014) by which the Scandinavian power was completely broken. After Clontarf the supreme power was disputed by the O'Briens of Munster, the O'Neills of Ulster, and the O'Connors of Connaught, with varying fortunes. In 1152 Dermod MacMurrough (Diarmit MacMurchada), the deposed king of Leinster, sought assistance in his struggle with Rauidhri O'Connor (the high king of Ireland), and visited Henry II, the Norman king of England. Henry authorized him to obtain armed support in England for the recovery of his kingdom, and Dermod enlisted the services of Richard de Clare, the Norman Earl of Pembroke, afterwards known as *Strongbow*, who landed at Waterford (Aug. 23, 1170) with 200 knights and 1,000 other troops for the reconquest of Leinster, where he eventually settled, after marriage with Dermod's daughter. In 1172 (Oct. 18) Henry II himself landed in Ireland. He received homage from the Irish kings and established his capital at Dublin. The invaders subsequently conquered most of the island and a feudal government was created. In the 14th and 15th centuries, the Irish recovered most of their lands, while many Anglo-Irish lords became virtually independent, royal authority being confined to the Pale, a small district round Dublin. Though, under Henry VII, Sir Edward Poynings, as Lord Deputy, had passed at the *Parliament of Drogheda* (1494) the act later known as *Poynings' Law*, subordinating the Irish Legislature to the Crown, the Earls of Kildare retained effective power until, in 1534, Henry VIII began the reconquest of Ireland. Parliament in 1541 recognized him as King of Ireland and by 1603 English authority was supreme.

REPUBLIC OF IRELAND
(Poblacht Na hEireann)

President, Patrick J. Hillery, *born* 1923, *assumed office*, Dec. 3, 1976, *sworn in for 2nd term*, Dec. 3, 1983.

CABINET
(as at July 15, 1990)

Taoiseach and Minister for the Gaeltacht, Charles J. Haughey (FF).

Tánaiste and Minister for Defence, Brian Lenihan (FF).

Foreign Affairs, Gerry Collins (FF).

Finance, Albert Reynolds (FF).

Industry and Commerce, Des O'Malley (PD).

Labour, Bertie Ahern (FF).

Justice and Communications, Ray Burke (FF).

Energy, Bobby Molloy (PD).

Marine, John Wilson (FF).

Agriculture and Food, Michael O'Kennedy (FF).

Social Welfare, Michael Woods (FF).
Environment, Padraig Flynn (FF).
Health, Rory O'Hanlon (FF).
Education, Mrs. Mary O'Rourke (FF).
Attorney General, John Murray (FF).
Tourism and Transport, Seamus Brennan (FF).

The present coalition Government was formed by the Fianna Fail Party (FF) and the Progressive Democrat Party (PD) following a general election on June 15, 1989.

IRISH EMBASSY
17 Grosvenor Place, SW1X 7HR
[071-235 2171]

Ambassador Extraordinary and Plenipotentiary, His Excellency Andrew O'Rourke (1987).

Area and Population.—The Republic has a land area of 27,136 sq. miles (70,283 sq. km), divided into the four Provinces of *Leinster* (Carlow, Dublin, Kildare, Kilkenny, Laoighis, Longford, Louth, Meath, Offaly, Westmeath, Wexford and Wicklow); *Munster* (Clare, Cork, Kerry, Limerick, Tipperary and Waterford); *Connacht* (Galway, Leitrim, Mayo, Roscommon and Sligo); and part of *Ulster* (Cavan, Donegal and Monaghan).

The estimated population of the Republic in 1989 was 3,515,000. Figures also showed 51,659 births, 17,769 marriages and 31,103 deaths in the year 1989 (provisional).

GOVERNMENT

The Constitution.—The constitution, approved by a plebiscite on July 1, 1937, came into operation on December 29, 1937. The Constitution declares the national territory to be the whole island of Ireland, its islands and the territorial seas. Pending the reintegration of the national territory, and without prejudice to the right of the Parliament and the Government established by the Constitution to exercise jurisdiction over the whole of the national territory, the laws enacted by that Parliament shall have the like area and extent of application as those of the Irish Free State, which did not include the six counties of Northern Ireland.

The Irish language, being the national language, is the first official language. The English language is recognized as a second official language.

The President (*Uachtarán na hEireann*) is elected by direct vote of the people for a period of seven years. A former or retiring President is eligible for a second term. The President summons and dissolves Dáil Éireann on the advice of the Head of the Government (*Taoiseach*). He signs and promulgates laws. The supreme command of the Defence forces is vested in him, its exercise being regulated by law. He has the power of pardon. The President, in the exercise and performance of certain of his constitutional powers and functions, is aided and advised by a Council of State.

The National Parliament (*Oireachtas*) consists of the President and two Houses: a House of Representatives (*Dáil Éireann*) and a Senate (*Seanad Éireann*).

Dáil Éireann is composed of 166 members elected by adult suffrage on a basis of proportional representation by means of the single transferable vote. All citizens, and such other persons in the state as may be determined by law, who have reached the age of 18 years and are not disqualified by law have the right to vote. Each Dáil may continue for a period not exceeding five years from the date of election.

Seanad Éireann is composed of 60 members, of whom 11 are nominated by the Taoiseach and 49 are elected; six by institutions of higher education, and 43 from panels of candidates, established on a vocational basis.

Members of Dáil are paid an allowance of IR£26,559 per annum (and members of Seanad IR£15,258). They are allowed travelling facilities between Dublin and their constituencies and are, subject to certain restrictions, granted free telephone and postal facilities from Leinster House and allowances for overnight stays in Dublin.

The executive authority is exercised by the Government subject to the Constitution. The Government is responsible to the Dáil, meets and acts as a collective authority, and is collectively responsible for the Departments of State administered by the Ministers.

The Taoiseach is appointed by the President on the nomination of the Dáil. The other members of the government are appointed by the President on the nomination of the Taoiseach with the previous approval of the Dáil. The Taoiseach appoints a member of the Government to be the *Tánaiste*, who acts for all purposes in the place of the Taoiseach in the event of the death, permanent incapacitation, or temporary absence of the Taoiseach. The Taoiseach, the Tánaiste and the Minister for Finance must be members of the Dáil. The other members of the Government must be members of the Dáil or the Seanad, but not more than two may be members of the Seanad.

The result of the general election on June 15, 1989 was as follows: Fianna Fáil 77; Fine Gael 55; Labour 15; Workers' Party 7; Progressive Democrats 6; Independent 6. Total membership including the *Ceann Comhairle* (Chairman), 166.

JUDICIAL SYSTEM

The judicial system comprises Courts of First Instance and a Court of Final Appeal called the Supreme Court (*Cúirt Uachtarach*). The Courts of First Instance include a High Court (*Ard-Chúirt*) and Courts of local and limited jurisdiction, with a right of appeal as determined by law. The High Court alone has original jurisdiction to consider the question of the validity of any law having regard to the provisions of the Constitution. The Supreme Court has appellate jurisdiction from all decisions of the High Court, with such exceptions and subject to such regulations as may be prescribed by law.

Chief Justice, Hon. Thomas A. Finlay .... IR£69,767
President of the High Court, Hon. Liam
 Hamilton .... IR£62,040
Judges, Supreme Court, Hons. Francis
 Griffin; Anthony Hederman; Niall J.
 McCarthy; Hugh O'Flaherty .... IR£59,235
Judges, High Court, Hons. John M. Gannon; Rory O'Hanlon; Declan Costello;
 Ronan Keane; Mella Carroll; Henry D.
 Barron; Francis D. Murphy; Kevin
 Lynch; Seamus Egan; Robert Barr;
 Gerard Lardner; John J. Blayney; John
 P. McKenzie; Richard Johnson; Vivian
 Lavan. .... IR£54,513
Attorney-General, John Murray.

RELIGION
(Census of 1981)

Catholic	3,204,476
Church of Ireland	95,366
Presbyterians	14,255
Methodists	5,790
Others	123,518
Total	3,443,405

DEFENCE

Establishments provide at present for a Permanent Defence Force of approximately 17,980 all ranks, including the Air Corps and the Naval Service. Recruitment is on a voluntary basis. Minimum term of enlistment is three years in the Permanent Defence Force followed by six years in the Reserve Defence Force. Establishments also provide for a Reserve Defence Force of 22,110 all ranks. Recruitment is also on a voluntary basis; minimum term of enlistment is three years. The Defence Estimate for the year ending December 31, 1989 provides for an expenditure of IR£292,393,000.

FINANCE

	1989*	1990†
Total Current Revenue	IR£7,756m	IR£8,130m
Total Current Expenditure.	8,019m	8,387m
Current Revenue		
Customs	132m	147m
Excise Duties	1,638m	1,684m
Capital Taxes	60m	64m
Stamp Duties	279m	286m
Income Tax	2,810m	2,920m
Income Levy	—	—
Corporation Tax	303m	338m
Value-Added Tax	1,943m	2,015m
Agricultural Levies (EC) .	13m	13m
Motor Vehicle Duties	148m	149m
Employment and Training Levy	117m	124m
Total Tax Revenue	7,443m	7,740m
Non-Tax Revenue	313m	390m

*Provisional out-turn
†Post-Budget estimate

	1989*	1990†
Current Expenditure		
Debt Service	IR£2,141m	IR£2,310m
Industry and Labour	199m	214m
Agriculture	260m	233m
Fisheries	15m	16m
Forestry	13m	8m
Tourism	24m	25m
Roads and Transport	15m	21m
Sanitary Services	3m	3m
Health	1,069m	1,148m
Education	1,146m	1,138m
Social Welfare	1,585m	1,551m
Housing	24m	20m
Subsidies	167m	168m
Defence	302m	330m
Garda	275m	299m
Prisons.................	55m	62m
Legal, etc.	44m	51m
Other	713m	815m
Total (excluding Local Loans Fund Subsidies)	8,050m	8,412m
Add back: Local Loans Fund Subsidies	—	—
Total (including Local Loans Fund Subsidies)	8,050m	8,412m

*Provisional out-turn
†Post-Budget estimate
Note: The figures do not take account of Departmental balances.
The Gross Debt at end 1987 was IR£23,690,800,000.

EDUCATION

Primary education is directed by the state, with the exception of 63 private primary schools with an enrolment of 8,041 in 1988–89.
There were 3,364 state-aided primary schools with an enrolment of 560,021.

In 1988-89 there were 496 recognized secondary schools with 213,640 pupils under private management (mainly religious orders), and 251 vocational schools with 84,442 pupils. Vocational schools are controlled by 38 statutory local Vocational Education Committees. There were 16 state comprehensive schools in 1988–89 with a total enrolment of 8,837 students, and 47 community schools with an enrolment of 31,651 students. There were also other miscellaneous second-level schools and the total full-time enrolment at second-level for 1988–89 was 341,831.

Third-level education is catered for by seven University Colleges, and also by third-level courses offered by the Technical Colleges and Regional Technical Colleges and other miscellaneous third-level institutions. There were 62,982 full-time third-level students in 1988–89, of whom 33,811 were attending university courses.

The estimated state expenditure on education in 1990, excluding administration and inspection, is first-level education IR£463,487,000; second-level education IR£450,167,000. The vote for third-level education amounted to IR£207,808,000.

MINERALS AND FISHERIES

Minerals.—About 200 persons were employed in the coal mines in 1989 and 42,900 tons of coal were produced.
Sea Fisheries.—An estimated 7,750 persons were employed in the fisheries in 1987. Total value of all fish landed in 1988 was IR£86·6 million.

COMMUNICATIONS

Railways.—In the year ended December 31, 1988, there were 1,944 km of railway; 24,043,000 passengers and 3,010,000 tonnes of merchandise were conveyed; the receipts were IR£134,220,000 and expenditure IR£127,329,000. These figures are in respect of railway working by *Iarnród Eireann.*
Road Motor Services.—In 1988 road motor vehicles carried 225,577,221 passengers, the gross receipts being IR£126,867,672.
Shipping.—In 1988 the number of ships with cargo which arrived at Irish ports was 12,526 (25,630,000 net registered tons); of these 2,805 (6,208,000 net registered tons) were of Irish nationality.

CIVIL AVIATION

Shannon Airport, 15 miles W. of Limerick, is on the main transatlantic air route. In 1989 the airport handled 1,469,095 passengers.
Dublin Airport, 6 miles N. of Dublin, serves the cross-channel and European services operated by the Irish national airline Aer Lingus and other airlines. In 1989 the airport handled 5,099,253 passengers.
Cork Airport, 5 miles S. of Cork serves the cross Channel and European services operated by Aer Lingus and other airlines. In 1989 the airport handled 627,032 passengers.

Trade with UK

	1988	1989
Imports from UK	£4,057,046,000	£4,714,780,000
Exports to UK	3,876,630,000	4,279,202,000

OVERSEAS TRADE

	1988	1989
Imports	IR£10,213,064,564	IR£12,287,833,068
Exports	12,300,705,135	14,569,912,275
Trade balance .	2,087,640,571	2,309,079,207

PRINCIPAL ARTICLES

Principal imports 1989

	IR£
Live animals	81,131,000
Food, drink and tobacco	1,212,238,000
Petrol and petroleum products	493,888,000
Chemicals	1,524,802,000
Machinery	3,757,343,000
Transport equipment	892,486,000
Metal and manufactures	757,525,000
Textiles and clothing	919,965,000
Paper, paperboard and manufactures	382,597,000
Professional, scientific etc. goods	272,528,000

Principal exports 1989

	IR£
Live animals	194,948,000
Meat and meat preparations	888,493,000
Other food, drink and tobacco	2,423,361,000
Machinery and transport equipment	4,652,376,000
Clothing, headgear and footwear	259,023,000
Textiles	441,745,000
Metal ores and scrap	319,549,000
Metal and manufactures	368,725,000
Non-metallic mineral manufactures	199,843,000
Chemicals	2,084,847,000
Professional, scientific etc., goods	522,785,000

CAPITAL.—ΨDublin (*Baile Atha Cliath*) is a City and County Borough on the River Liffey at the head of Dublin Bay. In April 1986 the population (1986 Census) was 502,749.

Other cities and towns with their populations at the Census of 1986 are ΨCork (133,271); ΨLimerick (56,279); ΨDun Laoghaire (54,715); ΨWaterford (39,529); Ψ Galway (47,104); and ΨDundalk (26,669).

CURRENCY.—Punt (IR£) of 100 pence.

FLAG.—Equal vertical stripes of green, white and orange.

NATIONAL ANTHEM.—Amhrán na BhFiann (The Soldier's Song).

NATIONAL DAY.—March 17 (St. Patrick's Day).

BRITISH EMBASSY
31 Merrion Road, Dublin 4
[Dublin 695211]

Ambassador Extraordinary and Plenipotentiary, His Excellency Sir Nicholas Maxted Fenn, KCMG (1986).

Counsellor and Head of Chancery, J. Thorp.

First Secretaries, D. F. B. Edye (*Commercial*); W. M. L. Dickinson; G. M. Johnston; G. Fergusson; D. Harris; A. Cobden.

British Council Representative, Dr. Ken Churchill.

ISRAEL
(Medinat Israel)

President of Israel, Chaim Herzog, *born* 1918, *elected* 1983, *re-elected* Feb. 20, 1988, *inaugurated*, May 8, 1988.

CABINET
(as at June 30, 1990)

Prime Minister and acting Minister for Labour, Social Affairs, Environment, Yitzhak Shamir.
Deputy PM, Foreign Affairs, David Levy.
Deputy PM, Industry and Trade, Moshe Nissim.
Defence, Moshe Arens.
Interior, Arye Der'i.
Agriculture, Rafael Eitan.
Education and Culture, Zevulun Hammer.
Transport, Moshe Katsav.
Economy and Planning, David Magen.
Justice, Dan Meridor.
Police, Ronni Milo.

Finance, Yitzhak Moda'i.
Science and Technology, Energy and Infrastructure, Yuval Ne'eman.
Health, Ehud Olmert.
Tourism, Gideon Patt.
Immigrant Absorption, Yitzhak Haim Peretz.
Communications, Raphael Pinchasi.
Religious Affairs, Avner Hai Shaki.
Construction and Housing, Ariel Sharon.

EMBASSY OF ISRAEL
2 Palace Green, Kensington, W8 4QB
[071–937 8050]

Ambassador Extraordinary and Plenipotentiary, His Excellency Yoav Biran (1988).

Area and Population.—Israel lies on the western edge of the continent of Asia at the eastern extremity of the Mediterranean Sea, between lat. 29° 30'–33° 15' N. and longitude 34° 15'–35° 40' E. Its political neighbours are Lebanon on the North, Syria on the North and East, Jordan on the East and the Egyptian province of Sinai on the South West.

The area is estimated at 8,019 sq. miles (20,770 sq. km). The population (UN estimate 1988) is 4,437,000. During the upheavals of 1948–49 a large number of Arabs left the country as refugees and settled in neighbouring countries.

Hebrew and Arabic are the official languages of Israel. Arabs are entitled to transact all official business with Government Departments in Arabic, and provision is made in the *Knesset* for the simultaneous translation of all speeches into Arabic.

Physical Features.—Israel comprises four main regions: (*a*) the hill country of Galilee and Judea and Samaria, rising in places to heights of nearly 4,000 ft.; (*b*) the coastal plain from the Gaza strip to North of Acre, including the plain of Esdraelon running from Haifa Bay to the south-east, and cutting in two the hill region; (*c*) the Negev, a semi-desert triangular-shaped region, extending from a base south of Beersheba, to an apex at the head of the Gulf of 'Aqaba; and (*d*) parts of the Jordan valley, including the Hula Region, Tiberias and the south-western extremity of the Dead Sea. The principal river is the Jordan, which rises from three main sources in Israel, the Lebanon and Syria, and flows through the Hula valley and the canals which have replaced Lake Hula, drained in 1958. Between Hulata and Tiberias (Sea of Galilee) the river falls 926 ft. in 11 miles and becomes a turbulent stream. Lake Tiberias is 696 ft. below sea-level and liable to sudden storms. Between it and the Dead Sea the Jordan falls 591 ft. The other principal rivers are the Yarkon and Kishon. The largest lake is the Dead Sea (shared between Israel and Jordan); area 393 sq. miles, 1,286 feet below sea-level, 51·5 miles long, with a maximum width of 11 miles and a maximum depth of 1,309 ft.; it receives the waters of the Jordan and of six other streams, and has no outlet, the surplus being carried off by evaporation. The water contains an extraordinarily high concentration of mineral substances. The highest mountain peak is Mount Meron, 3,962 ft. above sea-level, near Safad, Upper Galilee.

Climate.—The climate is variable, similar to that of Lower Egypt, but modified by altitude and distance from the sea. The summer is hot but tempered in most parts by daily winds from the Mediterranean. The winter is the rainy season lasting from November to April, the period of maximum rainfall being January and February.

Antiquities.—The following are among the principal historic sites in Israel: *Jerusalem*: the Church of the Holy Sepulchre: the Al Aqsa Mosque and Dome of the Rock, standing on the remains of the Temple Mount of Herod the Great, of which the Western (wailing) Wall is a fragment; the Church of the

Dormition and the Coenaculum on Mount Zion; Ein Karem: Church of the Visitation, Church of St. John the Baptist. *Galilee*: The Sea; Church and Mount of the Beatitudes, ruins of Capernaum and other sites connected with the life of Christ. *Mount Tabor*: Church of the Transfiguration. *Nazareth*: Church of the Annunciation and other Christian shrines associated with the childhood of Christ. There are also numerous sites dating from biblical and medieval days, such as Ascalon, Caesarea, Atlit, Massada, Megiddo and Hazor. Other antiquities in the West Bank of Jordan and the Golan Heights at present occupied by Israel can now be visited from Israel. In accordance with the terms of the peace treaty signed between Egypt and Israel on March 26, 1979, Israel withdrew in April 1982 to the pre-1967 boundary, returning the Sinai area to Egyptian sovereignty.

Government.—There is a Cabinet and a single-chamber Parliament (*Knesset*) of 120 members. A general election is held at least once every four years. The last General Election, held in November 1988, resulted in the formation of a 'national unity' coalition government. Disputes between Labour and Likud, the two main partners, led to the collapse of the coalition in March 1990. The present cabinet, announced on June 11, 1990, represents a new coalition between Likud, three religious parties and three right-wing nationalist parties.

Immigration.—The Declaration of Independence of May 14, 1948, laid down that 'the State of Israel will be open to the immigration of Jews from all countries of their dispersion.' The Law of Return, passed by the *Knesset* on July 5, 1950, provides that an immigrant visa shall be granted to every Jew who expresses his desire to settle in Israel. From the establishment of the State until 1988, about 1·8 million immigrants had entered Israel from over 100 different countries.

Education.—Elementary education for all children from 5 to 15 years is free, though secondary education is not compulsory. The law also provides for working youth, age 15–18 who for some reason has not completed their primary education, to be exempted from work in order to do so.

In 1985–86 enrolment in all educational establishments was 1,383,838: kindergartens 277,200; elementary education 622,056; secondary education 348,262; post-secondary 98,420.

Finance.—Government expenditure in 1986 was 25,399,234,000 new Shekels at market prices. GNP at market prices was 40,354,955,000 new Shekels.

COMMUNICATIONS

Railways and Roads.—Israel State Railways started operating in August 1949. Towns now served are Haifa, Tel Aviv, Jerusalem, Lod, Nahariya, Beersheba, Dimona, Ashdod and intermediate stations. In 1986 the total railway network amounted to 528 km. There were 12,823 km of paved road and in 1986 819,102 licensed vehicles.

Shipping.—Israel's merchant marine had reached a total of 2,805,000 tons deadweight by December 1985.

The chief ports are Haifa, a modern harbour, with a depth of 30 ft. alongside the main quay; the harbour on the Red Sea at Eilat, inaugurated in September 1965, has a capacity of 10,000 tons a day; Acre has an anchorage for small vessels; the deep-water port at Ashdod, 20 miles south of Tel Aviv, which started operations at the end of 1965, handled 8,006,000 tons of cargo in 1986. In the same year Israel's three main ports handled 17,048,000 tons of cargo.

Civil Aviation.—In 1986, 3,098,000 passengers passed through Ben Gurion airport, of which 230,146 arrived by charter flight.

PRODUCTION AND INDUSTRY

Agriculture.—The country is generally fertile and climatic conditions vary so widely that a large variety of crops can be grown, ranging from temperate crops, such as wheat and cherries, to subtropical crops such as sorghum, millet and mangoes. The famous 'Jaffa' orange is produced in large quantities mostly in the coastal plain for export; high-profit export crops such as strawberries and cut flowers are increasingly important. The citrus yield during the 1985–86 season was 1,308,700 tons. Specialized glasshouse crops for export, such as flowers, tomatoes and strawberries, are becoming increasingly popular and exports of flowers in 1985 earned US$75,454,000. Olives are cultivated, mainly for the production of oil used for edible purposes and for the manufacture of soap. The main winter crops are wheat and barley and various kinds of pulses, while in summer sorghum, millet, maize, sesame and summer pulses are grown. Large areas of seasonal vegetables are planted. Beef, cattle and poultry farming have been developed and the production of mixed vegetables and dairy produce has greatly increased. Tobacco and medium staple cotton are now grown. Fishing production (mostly from fish farms) was 14,958 tons in 1985–86. All kinds of summer fruits such as figs, grapes, plums and apples are produced in increasing quantities for local consumption. Water supply for irrigation is the principal limiting factor to greater production. The area under cultivation is 4,370,000 dunams, of which 2,370,000 is under irrigation. The Israel land measure is the *dunam*, equivalent to 1,000 square metres (approximately a quarter of an acre).

Industry.—In value polished diamonds account for about one quarter of Israel's total exports. Amongst the most important exporting industries are textiles, foodstuffs, chemicals (mainly fertilizers and pharmaceuticals). Metal-working and science-based industries are highly sophisticated and technologically advanced. These include the aircraft and military industries. Other important manufacturing industries include plastics, rubber, cement, glass, paper and oil refining.

TRADE

The principal imports are foodstuffs, crude oil, machinery and vehicles, iron, steel and manufactures thereof, and chemicals. The principal exports are citrus fruits and by-products, polished diamonds, plywood, cement, tyres, minerals, finished and semi-finished textiles.

	1986	1987
Imports	US$9,275·4m	US$11,451·0m
Exports	6,914·2m	8,222·4m

Trade with UK

	1988	1989
Imports from UK	£487,255,000	£502,411,000
Exports to UK	460,289,000	479,840,000

CAPITAL.—Most of the Government departments are in Jerusalem, population (1984) 506,200. A resolution proclaiming Jerusalem as the capital of Israel was adopted by the *Knesset* on January 23, 1950. It is not, however, recognized as the capital by the United Nations. Other principal towns (1986) were ΨTel Aviv and district (1,624,100); ΨHaifa and district (393,000) and Beersheba and district (115,000).

CURRENCY.—Shekel of 100 agora.

FLAG.—White, with two horizontal blue stripes, the Shield of David in the centre.

NATIONAL ANTHEM.—Hatikvah (The Hope).

JERUSALEM

Until 1967 Jerusalem was divided between Israel and Jordan, two of the 36 recognized Christian Holy Places (in the New City) being under Jewish administration, the remainder under Arab administration in the Old City. At the conclusion of hostilities between Israel and the surrounding Arab countries in 1967 the entire city was under Israeli control.

BRITISH EMBASSY
192 Hayarkon Street, Tel Aviv
[Tel Aviv 249171/8]

Ambassador Extraordinary and Plenipotentiary, His Excellency Mark Elliott, CMG (1988).

Counsellor, T. R. V. Phillips (*Head of Chancery, Consul-General and Counsellor*).

Defence and Military Attaché, Col. E. C. Loden, MC.

British Council Representative, P. Sandiford, 140 Hayarkon Street, Tel Aviv 61032.

There is a library in *Tel Aviv* and in *West Jerusalem.*

ISRAEL-BRITISH CHAMBER OF COMMERCE, 76 IBN Guirol Street, Tel Aviv 64162.

ITALY
(Repubblica Italiana)

President of the Italian Republic, Francesco Cossiga, *born* 1928, *sworn in,* July 3, 1985.

COUNCIL OF MINISTERS
(as at July 31, 1990)

Prime Minister, Giulio Andreotti (DC).
Deputy PM, Claudio Martelli (PSI).
Foreign Affairs, Gianni de Michelis (PSI).
Interior, Antonio Gava (DC).
Justice, Prof. Giuliano Vassalli (PSI).
Treasury, Sen. Guido Carli (DC).
Budget, Cirino Pomicino (DC).
Finance, Rino Formica (PSI).
Defence, Virginio Rognoni (DC).
Education, Gerardo Bianco (DC).
Public Works, Gianni Prandini (DC).
Agriculture, Prof. Vito Saccomandi (DC).
Transport, Prof. Carlo Bernini (DC).
Posts and Telecommunications, Oscar Mammi (PRI).
Industry, Adolfo Battaglia (PRI).
Labour, Carlo Donat-Cattin (DC).
Foreign Trade, Amb. Renato Ruggiero (PSI).
Merchant Marine, Sen. Carlo Vizzini (PSDI).
State Participation, Prof. Franco Piga (DC).
Health, Francesco de Lorenzo (PLI).
Tourism, Carlo Tognoli (PSI).
Culture, Ferdinand Facchiano (PSDI).
Environment, Sen. Giorgio Ruffolo (PSI).
South (Mezzogiorno), Prof. Giovanni Morongiu (DC).
Civil Protection, Vito Lattanzio (DC).
Social Affairs, Sen. Rosa Jervolino Russo (DC).
Relations with Parliament, Egidio Sterpa (PLI).
Urban Areas, Carmelo Conti (PSI).
Community Affairs, Pier Luigi Romita (PSDI).
Scientific Research, Prof. Antonio Ruberti (PSI).
Regional Affairs and Institutional Reforms, Dr. Antonio Maccanico (PRI).
Public Administration, Remo Gaspari (DC).

DC: Christian Democrat Party; PSI: Socialist Party; PLI: Liberal Party; PSDI: Social Democratic Party; PRI: Republican Party.

ITALIAN EMBASSY
14 Three Kings Yard, Davies Street, W1Y 2EH
[071–629 8200]

Ambassador Extraordinary and Plenipotentiary, His
Excellency Boris Biancheri (1987).
Minister-Counsellor, Livio Muzi-Falconi.
First Counsellors, A. V. de Mohr; F. Pigliapoco; N.
Cappello; L. Visconti di Modrone; S. Ronca.

There are also consular offices in *Bedford, Edinburgh* and *Manchester.*

Italy is a Republic in the south of Europe, consisting
of a peninsula, the large islands of Sicily and Sardinia,
the island of Elba and about 70 other small islands.
Italy is bounded on the N. by Switzerland and
Austria, on the S. by the Mediterranean, on the E. by
the Adriatic and Yugoslavia, and on the W. by France
and the Ligurian and Tyrrhenian Seas. The total
area is about 116,304 sq. miles (301,225 sq. km).

The peninsula is for the most part mountainous,
but between the Apennines, which form its spine,
and the east coastline are two large fertile plains:
Emilia/Romagna in the north and Apulia in the
south. The Alps form the northern limit of Italy,
dividing it from France, Switzerland, Austria and
Yugoslavia. Mont Blanc (15,771 ft.), the highest peak,
is in the French Pennine Alps, but partly within the
Italian borders are Monte Rosa (15,217 ft.), Matterhorn (14,780 ft.) and several peaks from 12,000 to
14,000 ft.

The chief rivers are the Po (405 miles), which flows
through Piedmont, Lombardy and the Veneto, and
the Adige (Trentino and Veneto) in the north, the
Arno (Florentine Plain) and the Tiber (flowing
through Rome to Ostia). The Rubicon, a small stream
flowing into the Adriatic near Rimini, formed the
boundary between Italy and Cisalpine Gaul: 'crossing
the Rubicon' (as Caesar did in 49 BC, thus invading
Italy in arms) is used to indicate definite committal
to some course of action.

Population.—In February 1986 Italy's population
was 57,193,708. A 1988 UN estimate gives a figure of
57,441,000.

Government.—Italian unity was accomplished
under the House of Savoy, after a struggle from 1848
to 1870, in which Mazzini (1805–72), Garibaldi (1807–
82) and Cavour (1810–61) were the principal figures.
It was completed when Lombardy was ceded by
Austria in 1859 and Venice in 1866, and through the
evacuation of Rome by the French in 1870. In 1871

the King of Italy entered Rome, and that city was declared to be the capital.

Benito Mussolini, known as *Il Duce* (The Leader) was continuously in office as Prime Minister from October 30, 1922 until July 25, 1943, when the Fascist regime was abolished. He was captured by Italian partisans while attempting to escape across the Swiss frontier and killed on April 28, 1945.

In fulfilment of a promise given in April 1944 that he would retire when the Allies entered Rome, a decree was signed on June 5, 1944, by King Victor Emmanuel III under which Prince Umberto, the King's son, became Lieutenant General of the Realm. The King remained head of the House of Savoy and retained the title King of Italy until his abdication on May 9, 1946, when he was succeeded by the Crown Prince.

A general election was held on June 2, 1946, together with a referendum on the future of the monarchy. The result showed a majority in favour of replacing the monarchy with a Republic. The Royal Family left the country on June 13, and on June 28, 1946, a provisional President was elected.

Constitution.—The constitution of the Republic of Italy, approved by the Constituent Assembly on December 22, 1947, provides for the election of the President by an electoral college which consists of the two Houses of Parliament (the Chamber of Deputies and the Senate) sitting in joint session together with three delegates from each region (one in the case of the Valle d'Aosta). The President, who must be over 50 years of age, holds office for 7 years. He has numerous carefully defined powers, the main one of which is the right to dissolve one or both Houses of Parliament, after consultation with the Speakers.

Defence.—The Army has around 265,000 men, of whom 215,000 are conscripts. In addition, the para-military *Carabinieri* force, which is part of the Army, has around 105,000 men. The Army, which has three Corps concentrated in the north, is equipped with Leopard 1 and M60 tanks and M113 armoured personnel carriers. There is also a parachute brigade, five alpine brigades, a missile brigade, and a Light Aviation Arm with over 300 helicopters. The Navy consists of one helicopter carrier, 3 cruisers, 4 destroyers, 9 submarines, 24 frigates and corvettes and 24 mine warfare ships. Manpower strength is around 45,000. The Air Force has 73,000 men and 400 combat aircraft. It is largely a tactical air force, equipped with Tornado, F104 and G91 aircraft, but also has transport, anti-submarine and helicopter search and rescue units. There is a large Reserve Force of ex-conscripts under the age of 35.

REGIONS OF ITALY

Rome and Central Italy.—Rome was founded, according to legend, by Romulus in the year now known as 753 BC. It was the focal point of Latin civilization and dominion under the Republic and afterwards under the Roman Empire, and became the capital of Italy when the Kingdom was established in 1871. The capital is concerned mainly with tourism and government, but its importance as a business centre is steadily increasing, and it is reportedly the third largest industrial centre in the country.

Lombardy and Milan.—In the Lombardy region are to be found some 15·7 per cent of Italy's commercial and banking services and some 21·9 per cent of the manufacturing industry. The whole range of Italian industry is represented, most important being the steel, machine tool and motor car factories.

Turin and Piedmont.—Turin between 1861 and 1865 was Italy's first capital as the home of the Piedmontese Royal Family. Now it is the headquarters of Europe's largest manufacturer of motor cars, produces 75 per cent of Italy's motor vehicles and

over 80 per cent of its roller bearings. Turin is also Italy's second largest steel producing city. Piedmont is the centre of the Italian textile industry based mainly on Biella.

Genoa and the Ligurian Riviera.—Genoa has been one of Europe's major ports since the Middle Ages, and handles one-third of Italy's foreign trade. About 80 per cent of the goods handled are imports.

Venice and the North-East.—Venice is primarily a tourist attraction of unique beauty. It was founded in the middle of the 5th century by refugees from the mainland fleeing attacks, and by the 16th century it was one of the strongest and richest states of Europe, dominating Eastern Mediterranean trade. It lost its independence in 1797 when Napoleon handed it over to Austria. Industry (paper and stationery, mechanical equipment, consumer goods, electrical appliances, woollens) is now developing in the Venice area, particularly on the autostrada linking Venice with Verona, Vicenza, Padua and in the areas around Treviso and Pordenone. Near Trieste, is the modern Monfalcone shipyard.

Tuscany, Emilia and Romagna.—Florence, the capital of Tuscany, was one of the greatest cities in Europe from the 11th to the 16th centuries, and the cradle of the Renaissance. Under the Medici family in the 15th century flourished many of the greatest names in Italian art, including Filippo Lippi, Botticelli, Donatello and Brunelleschi and in the 16th century great Florentine artists like Michelangelo and Leonardo da Vinci. These regions were the agricultural centre of Italy but the post-war period has seen the development of large industrial centres at Bologna, Florence, Modena, Pistoia and Ravenna. The footwear industry is based in Florence, textiles in Prato, reproduction furniture at Cascina and Poggibonsi, ceramics at Sassuolo, and glass and pottery at Empoli and Montelupo. Bologna is an important centre for the food industry.

Naples and the toe of Italy.—Naples, formerly the capital and administrative centre of the Kingdom of Naples and Sicily, remains the dominant city in the area, but it is beset with great problems of unemployment and the need for modernization. Around it, however, helped by Government incentives, industry is slowly developing, northwards to Caserta, southwards to Salerno and eastwards to Benevento.

Puglia.—Bari has always been a commercial centre and now industrial development is also taking place in the areas of Taranto, Brindisi and Foggia. At Taranto there are a highly-mechanized steel-works and a modern oil refinery. The Bari industrial zone has factories producing electronic and pneumatic valves, specialized vehicle bodies and tyres, etc. The main industry of Brindisi is a petro-chemical plant. At Foggia there is a textile factory.

Sicily.—The main source of income is agriculture, particularly citrus fruits, almonds and tomatoes. Oil in small quantities has been found off the southern shore of the island and drilling continues, while onshore there are growing oil-refining, natural gas and petrochemical industries. Small and medium sized industries, benefiting from the Government's incentives, are developing, and tourism is bringing an increasing amount of revenue to the island.

Sardinia.—Sardinia is an autonomous region, with its capital at Cagliari. Six main industrial development areas have been officially designated. The major industries are aluminium production (there is a smelting plant at Porto Vesme), petrochemicals, lead and zinc mining; and the tourist industry is flourishing.

ECONOMY

Italian gross domestic product in 1989 was US$859,996 million. The economy has recovered from the setbacks of the early seventies, reversing the balance of payments and halving inflation, but this was accompanied by stagnation and increasing unemployment. The rate of inflation in 1989 was 6·5 per cent.

Industry.—The general index of industrial production (1980=100) stood at +2·7 per cent in 1985–86. The state-owned sector of Italian industry is important, dominated by the holding companies IRI (mechanical, steel, airlines), ENI (petro-chemicals) and ENEL (electricity).

Mineral Production.—Italy is generally poor in mineral resources but since the war deposits of natural methane gas and small deposits of oil have been discovered and rapidly exploited. Production of lignite has also increased. Other minerals produced in significant quantities include iron ores and pyrites, mercury (over one-quarter of the world production), lead, zinc and aluminium. Marble is a traditional product of the Massa Carrara district.

Agriculture.—Agriculture accounted for 5·2 per cent of gross domestic product in 1984. The agricultural labour force was 2,242,000 in 1986.

Tourist Traffic.—In 1987 an estimated 52 million foreign tourists visited Italy, spending an estimated L15,782,808 million.

Communications.—The main railway system is state-run by the *Ferrovia dello Stato.* A network of motorways (*autostrade*) covers the country, built and operated mainly by the IRI state-holding company and ANAS the state highway authority. Alitalia, the principal international and domestic airline, is also state-controlled by the IRI group. Other smaller companies, including ATI (an Alitalia subsidiary) and Air Mediterranea operate on domestic routes. The Italian mercantile marine totalled 7,587,117 tons in December 1985.

FOREIGN TRADE

The balance of trade in 1987 showed a deficit of 11,138 billion lira, compared with 3,722 billion lira in 1986.

The main markets for Italian exports in 1987 were the OECD countries, which accounted for almost 80 per cent of the total, and the EC markets with 56 per cent of the total. Imports came principally from the Federal Republic of Germany, France and the USA.

Trade with UK

	1988	1989
Imports from UK ..	£4,057,046,000	£4,630,896,000
Exports to UK	3,878,530,000	6,701,683,000

Language and Literature.—Italian is a Romance language derived from Latin. It is spoken in its purest form in Tuscany, but there are numerous dialects, showing variously French, German, Spanish and Arabic influences. Sard, the dialect of Sardinia, is accorded by some authorities the status of a distinct Romance language. Italian literature (in addition to Latin literature, which is the common inheritance of Western Europe) is one of the richest in Europe, particularly in its golden age (Dante, 1265–1321; Petrarch, 1304–1374; Boccaccio, 1313–1375) and in the renaissance (Ariosto, 1474–1533; Machiavelli, 1469–1527; Tasso, 1544–1595). Modern Italian literature has many noted names in prose and verse, notably Manzoni (1785–1873), Carducci (1835–1907) and Gabriele d'Annunzio (1864–1938). The Nobel Prize for Literature has been awarded to Italian authors on five occasions—G. Carducci (1906), Signora G. Deledda (1926), Luigi Pirandello (1934), Salvatore Quasimodo (1959) and Eugenio Montale (1975). In 1987, there were 72 daily newspapers published in Italy, of which 14 were published in Rome and seven in Milan.

Education.—Education is free and compulsory between the ages of 6 and 14; this comprises five years at primary school and three in the 'middle school', of which there are about 8,000. Pupils who obtain the middle school certificate may seek admission to any 'senior secondary school', which may be a lyceum with a classical or scientific or artistic bias, or an institute directed at technology (of which there are eight different types), trade or industry (including vocational schools), or teacher-training. Courses at the lyceums and technical institutes usually last for five years and success in the final examination qualifies for admission to university. There are 35 state and 14 private universities, some of ancient foundation; those at Bologna, Modena, Parma and Padua were started in the 12th century. University education is not free, but entrants with higher qualifications are charged reduced fees according to a sliding scale. In general, schools, lyceums and universities are financed by local taxation and central government grants.

ISLANDS.—*Pantelleria Island* (part of Trapani Province) in the Sicilian Narrows, has an area of 31 sq. miles and a population of 9,601. The *Pelagian Islands* (Lampedusa, Linosa and Lampione) are part of the Province of Agrigento and have an area of 8 sq. miles, pop. 4,811. The Tuscan Archipelago (including Elba), area 293 sq. km, pop. 31,861; Pontine Archipelago (including Ponza, area 10 sq. km, pop. 2,515); Flegrean Islands (including Ischia, area 60 sq. km, pop. 51,883); Capri; Eolian Islands (including Lipari, area 116 sq. km, pop. 18,636); Tremiti Islands (area 3 sq. km, pop. 426).

CAPITAL.—Rome. Population of the commune (1986) 2,821,420.

1986 estimates of the population of the communes of the principal cities and towns are Milan 1,511,193; Ψ Naples 1,204,959; Turin 1,034,007; Ψ Genoa 733,990; Bologna 436,570; Florence 429,865; *Sicily,* Ψ Palermo 719,960; *Sardinia,* Ψ Cagliari 223,021.

CURRENCY.—Lira of 100 centesimi.

FLAG.—Vertical stripes of green, white and red.

NATIONAL ANTHEM.—Inno di Mameli.

NATIONAL DAY.—June 2.

BRITISH EMBASSY
Via XX Settembre 80A, 00187 Rome
[Rome 482–5441]

Ambassador Extraordinary and Plenipotentiary, His Excellency Sir Stephen Egerton, KCMG (1989).

Ministers, T. C. Wood, CMG; J. R. Goldsack, MBE (*FAO*).

Defence and Military Attaché, Brig. A. R. Jones.

Naval Attaché, Capt. W. C. McKnight.

Air Attaché, Group-Capt. A. R. Tolcher, RAF.

Counsellors, J. P. Watson (*Political*); G. M. Gowlland, LVO (*Political/Management*); C. R. L. de Chassiron (*Commercial/Economic*).

First Secretaries, N. E. Cole, OBE (*Management*); D. J. Hollamby (*Social Affairs*); N. K. Darroch(*Economic*); G. Roberts (*Consul*); H. Kershaw (*Commercial*); D. B. A. Evans (*Agriculture*); Miss K. Coombs (*Information*); N. J. L. Martin (*Political*); J. A. Towner (*Economic*); J. Ashton (*Political*).

Second Secretaries, J. M. Moodey (*Political/Information*); C. J. Ley (*Management*).

There are British Consular Offices at *Milan, Rome, Naples, Genoa, Florence, Venice, Trieste, Cagliari, Bari* and *Turin.*

British Council Representative, Keith Hunter, OBE, Palazzo del Drago, Via Quattro Fontane 20, 00184 Rome.

There are *British Council Offices* at *Milan* and *Naples,* each with a library.

BRITISH CHAMBER OF COMMERCE, Via San Paolo 7, 20121 Milan.

JAPAN
(Nihon Koku—Land of the Rising Sun)

Emperor of Japan, His Imperial Majesty the Emperor Akihito, *born* December 23, 1933; *succeeded* January 8, 1989; *enthroned* November 12, 1990; *married* April 10, 1959, Miss Michiko Shoda, and has *issue* Prince Naruhito Hironomiya (*Crown Prince*), *born* February 23, 1960, Prince Akishino, *born* November 30, 1965, and Princess Sayako, *born* April 18, 1969.

CABINET
(as at June 30, 1990)

Prime Minister, Toshiki Kaifu.
Justice, Shin Hasegawa.
Foreign Affairs, Taro Nakayama.
Finance, Ryutaro Hashimoto.
Education, Kosuke Hori.
Health and Welfare, Yuji Tsushima.
Agriculture, Forestry, Fisheries, Tomio Yamamoto.
International Trade and Industry, Kabun Moto.
Transport, Akira Ono.
Posts and Telecommunications, Takashi Fukaya.
Labour, Shunpei Tsukahara.
Construction, Tamisuke Watanuki.
Home Affairs, Keiwa Okuda.

In addition, there are eight State Ministers.

EMBASSY OF JAPAN
101–104 Piccadilly, W1V 9FN
[071-465 6500]

Ambassador Extraordinary and Plenipotentiary, His Excellency Kazuo Chiba (1988).
Ministers, Hiroshi Hashimoto; Shotaro Miyake (*Financial*); Hikoharu Kure (*Commercial*).
Counsellors, Yukio Takeuchi; Hiroyasu Ando (*Information and Cultural*); Wataru Hayashi (*Economic*); Sakura Shiga (*Financial*); Shoji Miyamoto (*Agricultural*); Dr. Niro Tode (*Medical Attaché*); Satoru Kanazawa (*Transport*); Makoto Mizutani (*Political*).
Defence Attaché, Capt. Isamu Kyoda.

Area and Population.—Japan consists of four large islands: *Honshū* (or Mainland), 230,448 sq. km (88,839 sq. m), *Shikoku*, 18,757 sq. km (7,231 sq. m), *Kyūshū*, 42,079 sq. km (16,170 sq. m), *Hokkaido*, 78,508 sq. km (30,265 sq. m), and many small islands situated in the North Pacific Ocean between longitude 128° 6′ East and 145° 49′ East and between latitude 26° 59′ and 45° 31′ N., with a total area of 145,834 sq. miles (377,708 sq. km), and a population (1988) of 121,870,000. In 1988 the birth rate was 10·8 per 1,000, and the death rate 6·5 per 1,000.

Physiography.—The coastline exceeds 17,000 miles and is deeply indented, so that few places are far from the sea. The interior is very mountainous, and crossing the mainland from the Sea of Japan to the Pacific is a group of volcanoes, mainly extinct or dormant. Mount Fuji, the loftiest and most sacred mountain of Japan, about 60 miles from Tokyo, is 12,370 ft. high and has been dormant since 1707, but there are other volcanoes which are active, including Mount Aso in Kyūshū. There are frequent earthquakes, mainly along the Pacific coast near the Bay of Tokyo. Japan proper extends from sub-tropical in the south to cool temperate in the north. Heavy snowfalls are frequent on the western slopes of Hokkaidō and Honshū, but the Pacific coasts are warmed by the Japan current. There is a plentiful rainfall and the rivers are short and swift-flowing offering abundant opportunities for the supply of hydro-electric power.

Government.—According to Japanese tradition, Jimmu, the first Emperor of Japan, ascended the throne on February 11, 660 BC. Under the *Meiji* constitution of February 11, 1889, the monarchy was hereditary in the male heirs of the Imperial house.

After the unconditional surrender to the Allied Nations (August 14, 1945), Japan was occupied by Allied forces under General MacArthur (September 15, 1945). A Japanese peace treaty conference held in San Francisco in September 1951[1] led to 48 nations signing the treaty, which became effective on April 28, 1952. Japan then resumed her status as an independent power.

A new constitution came into force on May 3, 1947. Legislative authority rests with the Diet, which is bicameral, consisting of a House of Representatives and a House of Councillors, both Houses being composed of elected members. Executive authority is vested in the Cabinet which is responsible to the Legislature.

The conservatives have governed Japan almost without interruption since World War II. Since 1955, when it was formed, the Liberal Democratic Party has maintained an absolute majority in the House of Representatives. In June 1990 the strength of the Parties was: Liberal Democratic Party 285; Japan Socialist Party 139; Komeito 46; Japan Communist Party 16; Democratic Socialist 14; Independents, 7; others 5.

The House of Councillors, whose powers are subordinate to the House of Representatives, re-elects half of its members every three years. In June 1990 the strength of the Parties was: Liberal Democratic Party 110; Japan Socialist Party 73; Komeito 21; Japan Communist Party 14; Democratic Socialist, Sports and People Alliance 10; San'in Club 4; Taxpayers' and Peace Association 4; Independent 4.

Agriculture and Livestock.—Owing to the mountainous nature of the country not more than one-sixth of its area is available for cultivation. The forest land includes Cryptomeria japonica, Pinus massoniana, Zeikowaskeaki, and Paulownia imperialis, in addition to camphor trees, mulberry, vegetable wax tree and a lacquer tree which furnishes the celebrated lacquer of Japan. The soil is only moderately fertile, but intensive cultivation secures good crops. Tobacco, tea, potato, rice, wheat and other cereals are all cultivated; rice is the staple food of the people, about 10,627,000 tonnes being produced in 1987. Fruit is abundant, including the mandarin, persimmon, loquat and peach; European fruits such as apples, strawberries, pears, grapes and figs are also produced. There is a small-scale beef industry and pigs and chickens are widely reared.

Minerals.—The country has mineral resources, including gold and silver, and copper, lead, zinc, iron chromite, white arsenic, coal, sulphur, petroleum, salt and uranium, but iron ore, coal and crude oil are among the principal post-war imports to supply deficiencies at home.

Industry.—Japan is the most highly industrialized nation in the Far East, with the whole range of modern light and heavy industries, including motor vehicles, electronics, metals, machinery, chemicals, textiles (cotton, silk, wool and synthetics), cement, pottery, glass, rubber, lumber, paper, oil refining and shipbuilding. The labour force of Japan in 1988 (average) was 61,700,000, of which around 2·5 per cent were unemployed. Of the total labour force, over 15 per cent are over 65 and this rate is increasing. Industrial, manufacturing and services workers numbered 53,430,000 and agricultural, forestries and fisheries workers 5,090,000 in 1985.

Communications.—There were 1,120,051 km of road and 44,297 km of rail road (steam and electric) in 1984. Also new Shinkansen (bullet train) tracks are currently being expanded. Japan National Railways was privatized on April 1, 1987 and is known as Japan Railways (JR). There are six regional companies and one goods company. The merchant fleet had a shipping capacity of 38·5 million gross tons in 1986. The opening in 1988 of the Seikan rail tunnel and the Seto Ohashi rail bridge means that the four major islands are now linked for the first time.

Armed Forces.—After the unconditional surrender of August, 1945 the Imperial Army and Navy were disarmed and disbanded.

Although the Constitution of Japan prohibits the maintenance of armed forces, internal security forces came into being in 1950, and 1952. In July 1954, the mission of the forces was extended to include the defence of Japan against direct and indirect aggression.

The defence budget allocated for the fiscal year 1986–87 amounted to Yen 3,343,549 million, equivalent to 6·18 per cent of the General Account budget. The authorized uniformed strength was: Ground Self-Defence Force (GSDF) 180,000 (Reserve 43,000); Maritime Self-Defence Force (MSDF) 43,897 (Reserve 600); Air Self-Defence Force (ASDF) 46,204. Actual strengths of all three services are slightly below their authorized figure.

The GSDF is organized into five regional Armies, totalling thirteen Divisions, one of which is an Armoured Division. Major equipment includes tanks, APCs, towed and SP guns and rocket launchers, Hawk AA missiles, and 425 aircraft. Equipment is now largely manufactured in Japan.

The MSDF has 164 warships and auxiliaries including four DDH, four TARTAR-equipped GMDs, 42 destroyers, 14 submarines and 99 others, 205 fixed-wing aircraft and 97 helicopters.

The ASDF has 820 aircraft including 375 trainers; 43 transports and 75 support aircraft (including helicopters). There are 6 groups of Nike SAM missiles and one training unit of Patriot.

Religion.—All religions are tolerated. The principal religions of Japan are Mahayana Buddhism and Shinto. About 1 per cent of Japanese are Christians.

Education.—Under the Education Law of 1947, education at elementary (six year course) and lower secondary (three year course) schools is free, compulsory and co-educational. The (three year) upper secondary schools are attended by 94 per cent of the age group. They have courses in general, agricultural, commercial, technical, mercantile marine, radio-communication and home-economics education, etc. Of the population aged between 18 and 21, 33 per cent were enrolled in higher education in 1984. There are two- or three-year junior colleges and four-year universities. Some of the universities have graduate schools. In 1987 there were 1,003 universities and junior colleges, the vast majority of which are privately maintained. The most prominent universities are the seven state universities of Tokyo, Kyoto, Tohoku (Sendai), Hokkaido (Sapporo), Kyushu (Fukuoka), Osaka and Nagoya, and the two private universities, Keio and Waseda.

Language and Literature.—Japanese is said to be one of the Uro-Altaic group of languages and remained a spoken tongue until the fifth–seventh centuries AD, when Chinese characters came into use. Japanese who have received school education (99·8 per cent of the population) can read and write the Chinese characters in current use (about 1,800 characters) and also the syllabary characters called Kana. English is the best known foreign language. It is taught in all middle and high schools and universities. There are 125 daily newspapers in Japan.

FINANCE

The Budget for the financial year 1990 for revenue and expenditure on the general account was Yen 66,236,700 million.

PRODUCTION AND TRADE

Being deficient in natural resources, Japan has had to develop a complex foreign trade. Principal imports in 1988 consisted of mineral oils (20·5 per cent), raw materials (8·7 per cent) e.g. metal ores and scrap, 4·5 per cent, timber, 3·8 per cent, foodstuffs (15·5 per cent) (e.g. wheat and sugar), machinery (14·2 per cent), chemicals (7·9 per cent) and textiles (5·7 per cent).

Principal exports consist of non-electric machinery (21·2 per cent), motor vehicles (18·4 per cent), electric machinery and appliances (18·4 per cent), steel (5·8 per cent), chemicals (4·5 per cent), textile goods (2·6 per cent) and ships (1·5 per cent).

FOREIGN TRADE

	1987	1988
	(US$'000)	
Total imports	149,515,113	187,353,686
Total exports	229,221,230	264,916,803

Trade with UK

	1988	1989
Imports from UK ..	£1,742,747,000	£2,259,823,000
Exports to UK	6,509,137,000	7,108,441,000

CAPITAL.—Tokyo, population (December 1989) 11,718,720. The other chief cities had the following populations:

ΨOsaka (2,633,000); ΨNagoya (2,152,000); ΨYokohama (3,197,000); Kyoto, the ancient capital (1,471,000); ΨKobé (1,464,000); Kita-Kyushu (1,034,000); Sapporo (1,652,000); ΨKawasaki (1,159,000); ΨFukuoka (1,220,000).

CURRENCY.—Yen of 100 sen.

FLAG.—White, charged with sun (red).

NATIONAL ANTHEM.—Kimigayo.

NATIONAL DAY.—December 23 (the Emperor's Birthday).

BRITISH EMBASSY

No. 1 Ichiban-cho, Chiyoda-ku, Tokyo 102
[Tokyo 265–5511]

Ambassador Extraordinary and Plenipotentiary, His Excellency Sir John Stainton Whitehead, KCMG, CVO (1986).

Minister, E. J. Field.

Counsellors, P. Dimond (*Commercial*); C. Humfrey (*Economic*); G. H. Fry (*Head of Chancery*); Dr. R. Hinder (*Science and Technology*); C. Loughlin (*Atomic Energy*); R. Seeley (*Chancery*); J. Kirby (*Financial*); D. Pragnell (*Management*); J. A. Barnett (*Cultural*).

First Secretaries, N. Hook, S. Plater (*Commercial*); D. H. Powell, P. Sprunt, P. Bateman (*Chancery*); J. Alderson, P. Madden, S. McNeil-Ritchie (*Economic*); T. Salusbury (*Science and Technology*); A.

T. MacDermott (*Information*); Mrs. S. Hogwood (*Consul*).

Defence and Air Attaché, Gp. Capt. A. Terrett.

Naval Attaché, Capt. C. Crawford.

There is a British Consulate-General at *Osaka* and Honorary Consulates at *Fukuoka* and *Hiroshima*.

British Council Representative, J. A. Barnett, CBE, 2 Kagurazaka 1-Chome, Shinjuku-ku, Tokyo 162. There is also an office and library in *Kyoto*.

BRITISH CHAMBER OF COMMERCE

No. 16 Kowa Building, 1–9–20 Akasaka, Minato-ku, Tokyo 107.

JORDAN
(Al-Mamlaka al Urduniya al-Hashemiyah)

King of the Jordan, Hussein, GCVO, *born* November 14, 1935, *succeeded* on the deposition of his father, King Talal, Aug. 11, 1952, *assumed constitutional powers*, May 2, 1953, on coming of age.

Crown Prince, Prince Hassan, third son of King Talal of Jordan, *born* 1948, *appointed Crown Prince*, April 1, 1965.

CABINET
(as at June 30, 1990)

Prime Minister and Minister of Defence, Mudar Badran.

Deputy PM and Minister of Interior, Salem Masa'deh.

Deputy PM and Minister for Foreign Affairs, Marwan Al Qasem.

Social Development, Abdul Majid Shreideh.

Health, Dr. Addoub Al Zaben.

Public Works and Housing, Abdul Raouf Al-Rawabdeh.

Telecommunications, Transport, Ibrahim Ayyoub.

Planning, Awni Al Masri.

Information, Ibrahim Izzedine.

Finance, Basil Jardaneh.

Industry and Trade, Dr. Ziyad Fariz.

Minister of State for Parliamentary Affairs, Abdul Baqi Gammo.

Education, Dr. Mohammad Hamdan.

Water and Irrigation, Daoud Khalaf.

Supply, Nabil Abul Huda.

Justice, Yousef Mbeideen.

Energy and Mineral Resources, Thabet Al Taher.

Agriculture, Dr. Suleiman Arabiyat.

Culture, Dr. Khaled Al Karaki.

Awqaf and Islamic Affairs, Dr. Ali Faqir.

Labour, Dr. Qassem Obeidat.

Youth, Ibrahim Ghababsheh.

Tourism and Antiquities, Abdul Karim Kabarity.

Municipal and Rural Affairs, Environment, Abdul Karim Al Dughmi.

EMBASSY OF THE HASHEMITE KINGDOM OF JORDAN

6 Upper Phillimore Gardens, W8 7HB
[071-937 3685/7]

Ambassador Extraordinary and Plenipotentiary, His Excellency Dr. Albert Butros.

Minister Counsellor, Dr. Abdulla Madadha.

Defence Attaché, Col. I. Al-Khatib.

Service Office: 16 Upper Phillimore Gardens, W8. (071-937-9611).

Area and Population.—The Hashemite Kingdom of the Jordan, which covers 37,738 sq. miles (97,740 sq. km), is bounded on the north by Syria, on the west by Israel, on the south by Saudi Arabia and on the east by Iraq. Since the hostilities of June 1967, that part of the country lying to the west of the Jordan River has been under Israeli occupation. The majority of the population are Sunni Muslims and Islam is the religion of the State; freedom of belief is, however, guaranteed by the Constitution. Total population on the East Bank of the Jordan was estimated (1988) to be 2,910,000.

History.—After the defeat of Turkey in the First World War the Amirate of Transjordan was established in the area east of the River Jordan as a state under British mandate. The mandate was terminated after the Second World War and the Amirate, still ruled by its founder, the Amir Abdullah, became the Hashemite Kingdom of Jordan. Following the 1948 war between Israel and the Arab States, that part of Palestine remaining in Arab hands (but excluding Gaza) was incorporated into the Hashemite Kingdom. King Abdullah was assassinated in 1951; his son Talal ruled briefly but abdicated in favour of the present King, Hussein, in 1952.

All of Jordan west of the River has been under Israeli occupation since 1967. In 1988 Jordan severed its legal and administrative ties with the occupied West Bank, but did not formally renounce sovereignty over the area. As a result of the wars of 1948 and 1967 there are about 991,000 refugees and displaced persons living in East Jordan, about 200,000 of whom live in refugee and displaced persons camps established by the UN Relief and Works Agency (UNRWA). In addition there are some 300,000 entirely self-supporting Palestinian members of the East Jordanian community.

Government.—The present constitution of the Kingdom came into force in 1952. It provides for a senate of 40 members (all appointed by the King) and an elected House of Representatives. Until 1988, the House of Representatives had 60 members representing both the East and West Banks. Legislation passed in 1989 stipulated that in future elections, seats would be contested on the East Bank only. The first parliamentary elections since 1967 to the new 80-member House of Representatives took place in November 1989.

The King appoints the members of the Council of Ministers. Crown Prince Hassan normally acts as Regent when King Hussein is away from Jordan.

Production and Industry.—The main agricultural areas are the Jordan Valley, the hills overlooking the valley and the flatter country to the south of Amman and around Madaba and Irbid, though several large farms, which depend for irrigation on water pumped from deep aquifers, have been established in the Southern desert area. The rest of the country is desert and semi-desert. The principal crops are wheat, barley, vegetables, olives and fruit (mainly grapes and citrus fruits). Agricultural production has increased considerably in recent years due to improvements in production and irrigation techniques, and exports to Europe and elsewhere are increasing.

Important industrial products are raw phosphates (1988: 5·6 million tons) and potash (1988: 1·3 million tons), most of which is exported. The Trans-Arabian oil pipeline (Tapline) runs through North Jordan on its way from the eastern province of Saudi Arabia to the Lebanese port of Sidon. A branch pipeline, together with oil trucked by road from Iraq, feeds a refinery at Zerqa (production 1988: 2·3 million tons) which meets most of Jordan's requirements for refined petroleum products. Sufficient reserves of natural gas have been discovered in the north-east to produce electricity for the national grid (generators were commissioned in May 1989). Despite extensive efforts no significant reserves of oil have been found.

Tourism has steadily developed. International-class hotels cater for businessmen and tourists in Amman and Aqaba. A spa hotel has been opened by hot springs close to the Dead Sea and a hotel complex is planned at the Dead Sea.

Communications.—The trunk road system is good. Amman is linked to Aqaba, Damascus, Baghdad and Jeddah by roads which are of considerable importance in the overland trade of the Middle East. The former Hejaz Railway enters Jordan from Syria east of Ramtha and runs through Zerqa and Amman to Ma'an with a spur to the top of the Ras al-Naqb escarpment. It is little used, mainly for freight between Amman and Damascus. The Aqaba railway carries phosphate rock from the mines of al Hasa and al Abiad to Aqaba. A total of 2,583 vessels called at Aqaba in 1988, and 20,096,200 tons of cargo were handled. The Royal Jordanian Airline operates from Amman to Aqaba and has an extensive network of routes to the Middle East, Europe, North America and the Far East.

FINANCE

	1987	1988
	(JD'000)	
Revenue	869,969	917,562
Expenditure	965,808	1,045,680
Surplus/Deficit............	−95,839	−128,118

Trade with UK

	1988	1989
Imports from UK	£183,555,000	£110,684,000
Exports to UK	21,310,000	18,462,000

CAPITAL.—Amman, population (1988 estimate) 1,100,000.

CURRENCY.—Jordanian dinar (JD) of 1,000 fils.

FLAG.—Black, white and green horizontal stripes, surcharged with white seven-point star on red triangle.

NATIONAL ANTHEM.—Long Live the King.

NATIONAL DAY.—May 25 (Independence Day).

BRITISH EMBASSY
Abdoun (PO Box 87),
Amman
[Amman 823100]

Ambassador Extraordinary and Plenipotentiary, His Excellency Anthony Reeve, CMG (1988).

Counsellors, H. G. Hogger (*Deputy Head of Mission and Consul-General*); M. S. Allen.

Defence Attaché, Col. P. A. Goddard.

Air Attaché, Wing-Cdr. P. W. Mayes.

First Secretaries, M. J. H. Tobin (*Consul and Management*); M. S. Thomas (*Commercial*).

Second Secretary, M. A. Ives (*Development*).

British Council Representative, M. Roddis, Rainbow Street, (PO Box 634), Jebel Amman, Amman.

KOREA

Korea is situated between 124° 11″ and 130° 57′ E. long., and between 33° 7′ and 43° 1″ N. lat. It has an area of 84,565 sq. miles (219,022 sq. km), with a population (UN estimate 1988) of 63,877,000, of whom about 42 million live south of the present dividing line. The southern and western coasts are fringed with innumerable islands, of which the largest, forming a province of its own, is Cheju.

History.—The last native dynasty (Yi) ruled from 1392 until 1910, in which year Japan formally annexed Korea. The country remained an integral part of the Japanese Empire until the defeat of Japan in 1945, when it was occupied by troops of the USA and the USSR, the 38th parallel being fixed as the boundary between the two zones of occupation. The US Government endeavoured to reach agreement with the Soviet Government for the creation of a Korean Government for the whole country and the withdrawal of all Russian and American troops. These efforts met with no success, and in September 1947 the US Government laid the whole question of the future of Korea before the General Assembly of the United Nations. The Assembly in November 1947 resolved that elections should be held in Korea for a National Assembly under the supervision of a temporary Commission formed for that purpose by the United Nations and that the National Assembly when elected should set up a Government. The Soviet Government refused to allow the Commission to visit the Russian Occupied Zone and in consequence it was only able to discharge its function in that part of Korea which lies to the south of the 38th parallel.

A general election was held on May 10, 1948, and the first National Assembly met in Seoul on May 31. The Assembly passed a constitution on July 12, and on August 15, 1948 the Republic was formally inaugurated and American Military Government came to an end.

Meanwhile in the Russian-occupied zone north of the 38th parallel the Democratic People's Republic had been set up with its capital at Pyongyang; a Supreme People's Soviet was elected in September 1948, and a Soviet-style Constitution adopted.

The Korean War.—The country remained effectively divided into two along the line of the 38th parallel until June 1950, when the North Korean forces invaded South Korea. In response to Security Council recommendations that United Nations members should furnish assistance to repel the attack, 16 nations, including the USA and the UK, came to the aid of the Republic of Korea. China entered the war on the side of North Korea in November, 1950. The fighting was ended by an Armistice Agreement signed on July 27, 1953. By this Agreement (which was not signed by the representatives of the Republic of Korea) the line of division between North and South Korea remained in the neighbourhood of the 38th parallel. Talks between North and South Korea on the reunification of the country have taken place intermittently.

Language and Literature.—Despite the great cultural influence of the Chinese, Koreans have developed and preserved their own cultural heritage. The Korean language is of the Ural-Altaic Group. Its script, Hangul, was invented in the 15th century; prior to this Chinese characters alone were used. Also invented around this time was the first metal movable printing type.

REPUBLIC OF KOREA
(Daehanminkuk)

President, Roh Tae Woo, *took office* February 24, 1988.

CABINET
(as at June 30, 1990)

Prime Minister, Kang Young Hoon.
Deputy PM and Head of the Economic Planning Board, Lee Seung Yun.
Foreign Affairs, Choi Ho Joong.
Home Affairs, Ahn Eung Mo.
Finance, Chung Yong Euy.
Justice, Lee Chong Nam.
Defence, Lee Sang Hoon.
Education, Chong Won Shik.
Sports, Chung Dong Sung.
Agriculture and Fisheries, Kang Bo Seung.
Energy and Resources, Lee Hee Il.
Environment, Cho Kyung Shik.
Trade and Industry, Park Pil Soo.
Construction, Kwon Young Gack.
Health and Social Affairs, Kim Jeung Soo.
Labour, Choi Young Choul.
Transport, Kim Chang Shik.
Communication, Lee Woo Jae.

Culture, Lee O. Young.
Government Administration, Lee Yon Tack.
Science and Technology, Chung Kun Mo.
Unification, Hong Sung Chol.
Political Affairs I, Kim Yoon Hwan.
Political Affairs II, Mrs. Lee Kye Soon.
Legal Affairs, Choi Sang Yop.
Veterans' Affairs, Lee Sang Yeon.
Dir. of National Security Planning Agency, Chang Se Tong.

KOREAN EMBASSY
4 Palace Gate, W8 5NF
[071–581 0247]

Ambassador Extraordinary and Plenipotentiary, His Excellency Jay Hee Oh (1987).
Minister, Keun Bae Choi.

The Republic of Korea has been officially recognized by the Governments of the United States, France, United Kingdom, and most other countries but, until recently, not by any Communist bloc country. Since 1989 diplomatic relations have been established with all eastern European countries except Albania.

Government.—Following extensive political unrest in 1987, a new Constitution was adopted in February 1988. The President, who is Head of State, Chief of the Executive and Commander-in-Chief of the Armed Forces, is directly elected for a single term of five years. He appoints the Prime Minister with the consent of the National Assembly, and members of the State Council (Cabinet) on the recommendation of the Prime Minister. The President is also empowered to take wide-ranging measures in an emergency, including the declaration of martial law, but must obtain the agreement of the National Assembly. The National Assembly of 299 members is directly elected for a four-year term.

The most recent elections to the National Assembly were held in April 1989. The Democratic Justice Party (DJP) failed to achieve an overall majority despite emerging as the largest single party. In February 1990 the DJP merged with two opposition parties to form the Democratic Liberal Party, which now holds the majority.

Armed Forces.—The Republic of Korea has an army of about 550,000, a small navy mostly for coastal patrol and protection duties, an air force with over 500 combat aircraft and a marine corps which is incorporated in the navy. About five per cent of the nation's GNP is currently spent on defence.

Education and Religion.—Primary education is compulsory for six years from the age of seven. Secondary and higher education is extensive. The national illiteracy rate is among the lowest in Asia.

There is freedom of religion. Buddhism has the most followers (13 million) followed by Protestantism (8 million) and Confucianism (4·7 million). Catholics number 2·2 million.

Agriculture and Fisheries.—The soil is fertile but the arable land is limited by the mountainous nature of the country. Staple agricultural products are rice, barley and other cereals, beans, tobacco and hemp. Fruit growing and sericulture are also practised. Ginseng, a medicinal root much used by both the Chinese and Koreans, forms a useful source of revenue. The Korean fishing industry is a major contributor to both food supply and exports.

Minerals.—The Republic of Korea is deficient in mineral resources, except for deposits of coal on the east coast and tungsten. There are some prospects of discovering oil in the sea between Korea and Japan.

Finance.—The budget for 1990 totals Won 22,689,000. Since the beginning of 1962 a series of successful five-year plans resulted in real economic growth averaging around 10 per cent a year. The sixth economic development plan (1987–91) envisages a growth rate of 7·5 per cent. Annual per capita GNP is US$4,045 (1988).

Trade and Industry.—Since the 1960s the Republic of Korea has industrialized rapidly on the basis of greatly expanded exports. Important exports include cars, electrical and electronic equipment, footwear, ships, railway rolling stock and iron and steel products.

TRADE

	1988	1989
Imports	US$48,105m	US$56,775m
Exports	59,666m	61,290m

Trade with UK

	1988	1989
Imports from UK	£450,924,000	£493,945,000
Exports to UK	1,135,107,000	1,164,723,000

Communications and Transport.—In 1980 there were 15,599 km of paved road. Seoul has a subway system and there are national railway and airline systems. Korean Air operates regular flights to Europe, the United States, the Middle East and South East Asia. Pusan and Inchon are the major ports with Pusan serving the industrial areas of the southeast. Inchon, 28 miles from Seoul, serves the capital, but development and operation at Inchon are hampered by a tidal variation of 9–10 metres.

CAPITAL.—Seoul, population (Nov. 1987) 9,991,089. Other main centres are ΨPusan (3,654,097), Taegu (2,165,954) and ΨInchon (1,526,435).

CURRENCY.—Won of 100 jeon.

FLAG.—White, with red over blue device in centre, three black parallel bars, some broken, in each quarter.

NATIONAL ANTHEM.—Aegukka.

NATIONAL DAY.—August 15 (Independence Day).

BRITISH EMBASSY
No. 4, Chung-Dong, Chung-Ku, Seoul 100
[Seoul 735–7341/3]

Ambassador Extraordinary and Plenipotentiary, His Excellency David John Wright (1990).

Counsellor, R. M. Jackson, CVO (*Commercial*).

Defence and Military Attaché, Brig. D. S. Williams.

First Secretaries, W. Morris (*Head of Chancery and Consul*); A. V. Hill (*Commercial/Information*).
There is an Honorary British Consul at *Pusan*.

British Council Representative, T. White, Anglican Church Annex, 3–7 Chung Dong, Choong-ku, Seoul.

BRITISH CHAMBER OF COMMERCE, c/o Chartered Bank, 1st and 2nd Floors, Samsung Building, 50, 1-Ka Ulchi Ro, Chung-Ku, Seoul.

DEMOCRATIC PEOPLE'S REPUBLIC OF KOREA
(Chosun Minchu-chui Inmin Kongwa-guk)

Politburo of the Central Committee, Kim Il-sung; Kim Chong-il; O Chin-u (*full members and members of the presidium*); Yi Chong-ok; Pak Song-chol; So Chol; Kim Yong-nam; Yon Hyong-muk; Kye Ung-tae; Kang Song-san; So Yun-sok; Ho Tam; Chon Pyong-ho; Choe Kwang; Han Song-yong (*full members*). Cho Se-ung; Chong Chun-ki; Hyon Mukwang; Yi Son-sil; Kang Hui-won; Kim Pok-sin; Hong Si-hak; Hong Song-nam; Choe Tae Pok; Kim Chol-man; Choe Yong-nim (*alternate members*).

Secretariat of the Central Committee, Kim Il-sung (*General Secretary*); Kim Chong-il; Hwang Changyop; Ho Chong-suk; So Kwan-hui; Pak Nam-ki; Kim Chung-nin; Kye Ung-tae; Chon Pyong-ho; Choe Tae-pok; Han Song-yong; Yun Ki-pok; Kim Yong-sun.

The area of North Korea is 46,540 sq. miles (120,538 sq. km), with a population of 21,902,000 (UN estimate 1988). North Korea is rich in minerals and industry has been developed, but the economy has stagnated in recent years because of poor planning and a shortage of foreign exchange. The armed forces are believed to number about 840,000 men.

Government.—The Constitution of the Democratic People's Republic of Korea provides for a Supreme People's Assembly, presently consisting of 687 deputies, which is elected every four years by universal suffrage. The Assembly elects a President, and the Central People's Committee. In turn, the Central People's Committee directs the Administrative Council which implements the policy formulated by the Committee. The Administrative Council (48 members), formally the government of North Korea, includes the Prime Minister and various ministers. In practice however, the country is ruled by the Communist Party which elects a Central Committee; this in turn appoints a Politburo. The senior ministers of the Administrative Council are all members of the Communist Central Committee and the majority are also members of the Politburo. Kim Il-sung was elected President for a fifth four-year term on May 24, 1990.

Trade with UK

	1988	1989
Imports from UK	£3,125,000	£3,087,000
Exports to UK	824,000	1,095,000

CAPITAL.—Pyongyang, approximate population, 1,500,000.

CURRENCY.—Won of 100 chon.

FLAG.—Broad red horizontal band bordered by white lines bearing a five-point red star on a white disc in centre; blue horizontal bands at top and bottom.

NATIONAL DAY.—September 8.

NATIONAL ANTHEM.—A Chi Mun Bin No Ra I Gang San (Shine bright, oh dawn, on this land so fair).

KUWAIT
(Dowlat al- Kuwait)

Amir, HH Sheikh Jaber Al Ahmad Al Sabah, *born* 1928; acceded Jan. 1, 1978.

CABINET
(as at June 30, 1990)*

Prime Minister, HH Crown Prince Sheikh Saad Al-Abdullah.

Deputy Premier and Minister of Foreign Affairs, Sheikh Sabah Al-Ahmed Al Jaber.

Affairs of National Council, Badr Jasim al Yaqub.

Information, Sheikh Jabir Mubarak al Hamad.

Social Affairs and Labour, Jabir al Abdullah al Jabir.

Public Works, Jasim Mohammed al Musa.

Communications, Habib Jawhar Hayat.

Electricity and Water, Hamud Abdullah al Raqabah.

Oil, Rashid Salim al Amiri.

Interior, Sheikh Salim as Sabah as Salim.

Planning, Sulayman Abdullah al Razzaq al Muttawa.

Justice and Legal Affairs, Dari Abdullah al Uthman.

Cabinet Affairs, Abdel-Rahman Abdullah al Awadi.

Education, Abdel Yusuf al Ghunaym.

Public Health, Abdel al Wahab Sulayman al Fawzan.

Finance, Sheikh Ali al Khalifah al Adhibi.

Higher Education, Anwar Abdullah al Nuri.

Municipal Affairs, Fahd Abdullah al Hassawi.

Waqfs and Islamic Affairs, Mohammed Nasir al Hamdan.

Commerce and Industry, Nasir Abdel Allah al Rawdan.

Defence, Sheikh Nawaf al Ahmad al Jabir.
Housing, Yahya Fahd al Sumayt.

*Following Iraq's invasion and subsequent annex-
ation of Kuwait in August 1990, the government
went into exile.

EMBASSY OF THE STATE OF KUWAIT
45–46 Queen's Gate, SW7 5JN.
[071–589 4533]

Ambassador Extraordinary and Plenipotentiary, His
Excellency Ghazi M. A. Al-Rayes (1980).

Area and Population.—Kuwait extends along
the shore of the Persian Gulf from Iraq to Saudi
Arabia, with an area of 6,880 sq. miles (17,818 sq. km).
Kuwait has a dry, desert climate with a summer
season extending from April to September. The mean
temperature varies between 29–45°C in summer, and
8–18°C in winter. Humidity rarely exceeds 60 per
cent except in July and August. At the 1985 census
the population was 1,695,128, of which about 42 per
cent were Kuwaiti citizens, the remainder being
other Arabs, Iranians, Indians and Pakistanis. The
total European and American population was about
12,500. The gross population growth rate is 6·4 per
cent, a growth rate of 3·5 per cent for Kuwaiti
citizens. A 1988 UN estimate gives a total population
figure of 1,958,000.

The official language is Arabic, and English is
widely spoken as a second language. Islam is the
official religion, though religious freedom is constitutionally guaranteed.

Government.—Although Kuwait had been independent for some years, the 'exclusive agreement' of
1899 between the Sheikh of Kuwait and the British
Government was formally abrogated by an exchange
of letters dated June 19, 1961. This exchange was
immediately followed by Iraqi claims to sovereignty
over Kuwait but in October 1963 Iraq recognized
Kuwait's independence, although the Kuwait-Iraqi
border has not yet been determined formally.

Under the Constitution legislative power is vested
in the Amir and the 50-member National Assembly,
and executive power in the Amir and the Cabinet.
The sixth National Assembly was dissolved in July
1986. Elections to a new National Assembly took
place in June 1990.

Education, etc.—As a result of considerable oil
revenues, the Kuwait Government embarked on a
large scale development scheme and plans for social
services. Education and medical treatment are free.
New hospitals and schools continue to be built.
Kuwait University was opened in 1966, and in 1987–
88 had 15,602 students. In 1987–88 there were over
489,000 pupils at government and private schools.

Public Utilities.—Kuwait has a domestic water
supply from water distillation plants which operate
on natural gas from the oil fields. These plants can
produce over 118,000,000 gallons of fresh water daily.
Total water storage capacity, in reservoirs and water
towers, amounts to over 1,201 million gallons. A
natural source of fresh water, discovered at Raudha-
tain in the north of the State, has been developed to
produce up to 3,000,000 gallons per day for at least 20
years and a pipeline has been built to carry the water
to Kuwait town.

Electricity is produced by six power stations in
Kuwait. Production in 1987 was 18,092 million Kwh.

Communications.—Ships of British, Dutch, Kuwaiti and other lines make regular calls at Kuwait.
Several international and Middle Eastern airlines
operate regular air services, and other companies
make non-scheduled flights to Kuwait under charter.
There is a network of dual-carriageway roads and
more are under construction. Telecommunications
and postal services are conducted by the Kuwait
Government, which has built an earth satellite
station.

Finance.—Expected revenue for the financial year
1989–90 was KD2,230·5 m and expenditure
KD3,549·1 m. Oil revenues constitute about 90 per
cent of total revenue. There are a large number of
investment banks in some of which the Government
holds equity. The banking system is controlled by
the Central Bank of Kuwait.

Production.—The GDP of Kuwait in 1987 was
estimated at KD5,444·5 million.

Despite the desert terrain, 8·4 per cent of land is
under cultivation, fruit and vegetables being the
main crops. Shrimp fishing is becoming important.

The government of Kuwait began to participate in
the ownership of the British- and American-owned
Kuwait Oil Company in 1974 and an agreement was
signed in November 1975 which brought 100 per cent
government ownership. After a reorganization of
the national oil industry in 1980, all the business was
taken over by the Kuwait Petroleum Corporation.

The centre of Kuwait oil production is at Burgan,
south of Kuwait City. Oil is also lifted in the Kuwait/
Saudi Arabia Partitioned Zone (Wafra) south of the
state. Oil is exported through a specially constructed
port at Mina al Ahmadi. Production of crude oil in
1987 was approximately 1·2 million barrels per day.
About 3,000 people are employed, including Kuwaitis,
British, Americans, Indians, Pakistanis and citizens
of other Arab countries.

Trade.—Oil exports constitute about 88 per cent
of Kuwait's total exports. Non-oil exports include
chemical fertilizers, ammonia and other chemicals,
metal pipes, shrimps and building materials; re-
exports accounted for 73 per cent of non-oil exports
in 1982. Major trading partners are Asian countries,
followed by EC countries and Arab states.

Trade with UK

	1988	1989
Imports from UK	£237,515,000	£228,711,000
Exports to UK	72,318,000	150,364,000

CAPITAL.— Ψ Kuwait, population (excluding suburbs) 400,000.

CURRENCY.—Kuwaiti dinar (KD) of 1,000 fils.

FLAG.—Three horizontal stripes of green, white
and red, with black trapezoid next to staff.

NATIONAL DAY.—February 25.

BRITISH EMBASSY
PO Box Safat 2,
Arabian Gulf Street, Kuwait
[Kuwait 2432046/9]

Ambassador Extraordinary and Plenipotentiary, His
Excellency Michael Weston, CVO (1990).
Counsellor, I. L. Blackley.
First Secretaries, T. Millson (*Head of Chancery*); L.
Banks (*Consul*); A. J. Paice (*Chancery*); D. A. R
Macauley (*Commercial*); J. Brand; A. Young.

British Council Representative, Dr. F. Frankel, 2 al
Arabi Street, (PO Box 345), Mansouriyah.

LAOS
(Sathalamalid Pasathu' Paait)

President, Phoumi Vongvichit (*acting*).
President of the Supreme People's Assembly, Nouhak
Phoumsavan (*acting*).
Deputy President, Khamsouk Keola.

COUNCIL OF MINISTERS
(as at June 30, 1989)

Prime Minister, Kaysone Phomvihan.
First Deputy PM, Nouhak Phoumsavan (*responsibility for Economic Matters*).

Deputy PMs, Phoumi Vongvichit (*responsibility for Education, Culture, Health and Justice*); Phoun Sipaseut (*Minister, Foreign Affairs*); Khamtai Siphandone (*Minister of Defence*); Sali Vongkhamsao (*Minister of Economics, Planning and Finance*).

Ministers attached to the PM's Office, Ma Khaykhamphithoune (*Special Affairs*); Souli Nanthavong (*Chairman, State Commission for Science and Technology*); Thongchan Ouplavan (*Prices*); Soth Phetrasi (*Mapping and Frontiers*).

Agriculture, Forestry, Irrigation and Co-operatives, Inkong Mahavong.

Construction, Khemphon Phouipaseut.

Culture, Thongsing Thammavong.

Education, Bounthiam Phitsamai.

Finance, Yao Phonvantha.

Public Health, Khamlieng Pholsena.

Industry and Handicrafts, Soulivang Daravong.

Chairman, Committee for Economic Relations with Foreign Countries and State Commerce, Phao Bounnaphon.

Interior, Sisavath Keobounphan.

Chairman, Information, Press, Radio and Television Committee, Son Khamvanvongsa.

Justice, Kou Souvannamethi.

Chairman, State Bank, Nouphan Sitprasai.

Chairman, Nationalities Committee, Nhiaveu Lobliayao.

Chairman, Social Welfare and Veterans Committee, Khambou Sounisai.

Trade, Vanthong Sengmuong.

Transport, Posts and Construction, Oudom Khattigna.

Position and Extent.—The People's Democratic Republic of Laos is in the northerly part of Indo-China, lying between China and Vietnam, on the north and east, and Myanmar (Burma) and Thailand on the west. Laos has a common boundary with Cambodia to the south. The area of the country is 91,429 sq. miles (231,800 sq. km), with a population (UN estimate 1988) of 3,875,000.

Government.—The Kingdom of Lane Xang, the Land of a Million Elephants, was founded in the 14th century, but broke up at the beginning of the 15th century into the separate kingdoms of Luang Prabang and Vientiane and the Principality of Champassac, which together came under French protection in 1893. In 1945 the Japanese executed a coup and suppressed the French administration. Under a Constitution of 1947 Laos became a constitutional monarchy under King Sisvang Vong of the House of Luang Prabang, and an independent sovereign state in 1949. The next twenty-five years in Laos were marked by power struggles and civil war.

The Lao People's Democratic Republic was proclaimed in December 1975 following victory by the communist Lao Patriotic Front and the abdication of the King. A President and Council of Ministers were installed, and a 45-member Supreme People's Council was appointed to draft a Constitution. The first draft text was published in June 1990. The Lao People's Revolutionary Party (LPRP) is the sole legal political organization.

Economy.—There is no significant industrial base in Laos, an estimated 85 per cent of the work force being engaged in agriculture, largely concerned with rice cultivation. Rice production in 1984 amounted to 1·3 million tonnes, thus rendering the country theoretically self-sufficient in this staple food.

In 1984, exports amounted to US$36·2m and imports to US$98·4m. Hydro-electric power was 88·3 per cent of exports, timber 8·5 per cent and coffee 1·2 per cent. Clearing agreements have been signed with certain socialist countries and the trade gap is largely financed by foreign aid, of which some 60 per cent is provided by socialist countries.

Laos' economic performance so far has been poor and shows no signs of early recovery, the free market rate for the dollar is much higher than the official rate and prices of consumer items continue to increase.

Trade with UK

	1988	1989
Imports from UK	£1,332,000	£908,000
Exports to UK	2,000	1,369,000

CAPITAL.—Vientiane, population (estimated 1984) 120,000.

CURRENCY.—Kip (K) of 100 at.

FLAG.—Blue background with a central white circle, framed by two horizontal red stripes.

NATIONAL DAY.—December 2.

British Ambassador, resident in Bangkok, Thailand.

LEBANON
(Al-Jumhouriya al-Lubnaniya)

President of the Republic of Lebanon, Elias Hrawi, November 25, 1989.

CABINET
(as at June 30, 1990)

Prime Minister and Foreign Minister, Selim al-Hoss.

Deputy PM and Minister of Labour, Michel Sassin.

Posts and Telecommunications, George Sa'adah.

Economy and Trade, Dr. Nazih Bizri.

Finance, Ali al-Khalil.

Justice and Information, Edmond Rizq.

Industry and Oil, Souren Khanamirian.

Health and Tourism, Abdallah Rassi.

Housing, Hydro-electric Resources, Nabih Berri.

Public Works, Walid Jumblatt.

Defence, Albert Mansur.

Interior, Elias al-Khazen.

Education, Omar Karame.

Agriculture, Mohsen Dallul.

LEBANESE EMBASSY IN LONDON
21 Kensington Palace Gardens, W8 4QM
[071–229 7265/6]

Ambassador Extraordinary and Plenipotentiary, His Excellency Mahmoud Hammoud (1990).

First Secretaries, Michel El-Khoury; Mohammed Dib.

Consular Section, 15 Palace Gardens Mews, W8 (071–727 6696)

Area and Population.—Lebanon forms a strip about 120 miles in length and varying in width from 30 to 35 miles, along the Mediterranean littoral, and extending from the Israel frontier on the south to the Nahr al Kebir (15 miles north of Tripoli) on the north; its eastern boundary runs down the Anti-Lebanon range and then down the Great Central depression, the *Beqaa,* from which flow the rivers Orontes and Litani. It is divided into five districts, North Lebanon, Mount Lebanon, Beirut, South Lebanon and Beqaa. The seaward slopes of the mountains have a Mediterranean climate and vegetation. The inland range of Anti-Lebanon has the characteristics of steppe country. There is a mixed Arabic-speaking population of Christians, Muslims and Druses. The total area of Lebanon is 4,015 sq. miles, (10,400 sq. km), population (UN estimate 1988) 2,828,000.

Government.—Lebanon became an independent state in September 1920, administered under French mandate until November 22, 1943. Powers were transferred to the Lebanese Government from January 1944, and French troops were withdrawn in 1946.

In April 1975, serious fighting broke out in Beirut between members of the predominantly Christian

Phalangist Party and mainly Muslim militias later supported by Palestinian guerrillas based in Lebanon. The fighting continued and increased throughout 1975 and 1976. In the autumn of 1976 the Arab Deterrent Forces, composed mainly of Syrian troops, imposed an effective ceasefire. In March 1978 Israeli forces invaded but withdrew some months later, handing over their positions, except for a belt in the south, to the UN Interim Force in Lebanon (UNIFIL). Major outbreaks of fighting took place in October 1978 and April/May 1981, interspersed with regular clashes on a smaller scale. In the summer of 1982 Israeli forces again invaded the country, penetrating as far as Beirut. Following negotiations, Palestine Liberation Organization guerrillas left Beirut for various Arab countries. Although the bulk of Israeli troops withdrew from southern Lebanon in 1985, a buffer zone controlled by Israeli-backed Christian militias has been established along the Israeli-Lebanon border. Syrian forces are deployed in west Beirut and in the north and the east of the country.

In September 1988 outgoing President Gemayel appointed a transitional Christian-led military government under Gen. Michel Aoun to replace the Muslim-led government of Selim al-Hoss. Each party claimed to represent the constitutional government of Lebanon, and refused to accept the other's authority.

An 'accord for national conciliation', drawn up by an Arab League-appointed committee, gained the approval of a majority of Lebanese MPs in October 1989, but was rejected by Michel Aoun, who insisted on an immediate Syrian troop withdrawal. The present government was formed in November 1989. International peace initiatives are continuing, and a ceasefire was declared in March 1990.

Production.—Fruits are the most important products and include citrus fruit, apples, grapes, bananas and olives. There is some light industry, mostly for the production of consumer goods, but most factories have been adversely affected by the instability of the past fifteen years. Heavy intra-Christian fighting in the early months of 1990 seriously damaged what remained of Lebanon's industrial and commercial infrastructure.

Communications.—The railways are not functioning as a result of the civil war. There is an international airport at Beirut, served by the national carrier MEA and a few others from east Europe. An internal service operates from Beirut to Tripoli. Operations can be disrupted by fighting in the city. A ferry service links Jounieh in east Beirut with Larnaca, Cyprus.

Archaeology, etc.—Lebanon has some important historical remains, notably Baalbek (Heliopolis) which contains the ruins of first to third century Roman temples and Jubail (Biblos), one of the oldest continuously inhabited towns in the world, and ancient Tyre.

Language and Literature.—Arabic is the official language, and French and English are also widely used.

Education.—There are six universities in Beirut, the American and the French Universities established in the last century, and the Lebanese National University, the Beirut University College, the Kasik Saint Esprit University and the Arab University which are recent foundations in the early stages of development. There are several institutions for vocational training, and there is a good provision throughout the country of primary and secondary schools, among which are a great number of private schools. Education at all levels has been severely disrupted by the civil war.

Finance.—No reliable statistics have been published for some time. The country is known to have a deficit, and the Lebanese pound has lost much of its value against foreign currencies. At its May 1990 summit meeting, the Arab League agreed to set up an international fund for Lebanon's reconstruction.

Trade.—Principal imports are gold and precious metals, machinery and electrical equipment, textiles and yarns, vegetable products, iron and steel goods, and motor vehicles. There has been a gradual decline in the overall amount of imports, as a result of continued instability.

Principal exports include gold and precious metals, fruits and vegetables, textiles, building materials, furniture, plastic goods, foodstuffs, tobacco and wine.

At one time there was a considerable transit trade through Beirut into the Arab hinterland. Lebanon is the terminal for two oil pipe lines, one formerly belonging to the Iraq Petroleum Company, debouching at Tripoli, the other belonging to the Trans Arabian Pipeline Company, at Sidon. These lines have not functioned for some years.

Trade with UK

	1988	1989
Imports from UK	£55,675,000	£48,474,000
Exports to UK	14,172,000	11,054,000

CAPITAL.— ΨBeirut (population 702,000). Other towns are ΨTripoli (175,000), Zahlé (46,800), ΨSidon (24,740), ΨTyre (14,000).

CURRENCY.—Lebanese pound (£L) of 100 piastres.

FLAG.—Horizontal bands of red, white and red with a green cedar of Lebanon in the centre of the white band.

NATIONAL ANTHEM.—Kulluna Lil Watan Lil'ula Lil'alam (We all belong to the homeland).

NATIONAL DAY.—November 22.

BRITISH EMBASSY
Shamma Building, Raouché, Ras Beirut, Beirut
[Beirut 417007]

Ambassador Extraordinary and Plenipotentiary, His Excellency David Tatham (1989).

LIBERIA
(Republic of Liberia)

President and Commander-in-Chief, Dr. Samuel Kanyon Doe, *assumed power* April 1980*.

CABINET
(as at May 31, 1989)*

Defence, Maj. Gen. Gray D. Allison.
Finance, David Farhat.
Justice, Jenkins Scott.
Internal Affairs, Edward Sackor.
Public Works, Yudu Gray.
Posts and Telecommunications, Morris Dukuly.
Planning and Economic Affairs, Dr. Elijah Taylor.
Agriculture, Scott Gblorzuo Toweh.
Health and Social Welfare, Martha Sendolo Belleh.
Commerce and Industry, Wisseh McClain.
Lands, Mines and Energy, William Freeman.
Minister of State for Presidential Affairs, Alvin Jones.
Rural Development, Samuel Brownell.
Youth and Sports, Haven Grigsby.
Education, Othello Gongar.
Foreign Affairs, Rudolph Johnson.
Information, Culture and Tourism, Emmanuel Bowier.
Labour, Peter Naigow.
National Security, Patrick Minikon.
Transport, Macleod Darpoh.
Minister of State without Portfolio, John Beh.
Director General of the Cabinet, Momolu Getaweh.

*A rebellion launched in December 1989 by the National Patriotic Front of Liberia has developed into full-scale civil war. By July 1990 most members of the government had left the country.

EMBASSY OF THE REPUBLIC OF LIBERIA
2 Pembridge Place, W2 4XB
[071–221 1036]

Ambassador Extraordinary and Plenipotentiary, His Excellency Willie A. Givens (1985).

An independent republic of West Africa, occupying that part of the coast between Sierra Leone and the Côte d'Ivoire, which is between the rivers Mano in the N.W. and Cavalla in the SE, a distance of about 350 miles, with an area of about 43,000 sq. miles (111,369 sq. km), and extending to the interior to latitude 8° 50', a distance of 150 miles from the seaboard. It was founded by the American Colonization Society in 1822 as a colony for freed American slaves, and has been recognized since 1847 as an independent state. The population at the Census of 1974 was 1,481,524; a 1988 UN estimate put the figure at 2,429,000. The official language is English. Over 16 ethnic languages are spoken.

William V. S. Tubman, President of Liberia since 1944, died in 1971 and was succeeded by Dr. Tolbert. The Constitution was suspended following a military coup on April 12, 1980 led by M/Sgt. Samuel K. Doe, who then became Head of State. Executive power is now vested in the Head of State assisted by an appointed Cabinet. A new Constitution was endorsed by a referendum on July 3, 1984 and on July 22 the People's Redemptive Council was dissolved and replaced by an interim National Assembly, comprising the Council and 35 civilian members, which was to oversee the country's return to civilian rule. Presidential and legislative elections were held in October 1985; and in January 1986 the Interim Assembly was dissolved and replaced by a Legislative Assembly.

The Army of Liberia consists of one division of two brigades of militia, three regular infantry battalions, one engineer battalion and a small coastguard.

The artificial harbour and free port of Monrovia was opened on July 26, 1948. There are nine ports of entry, including three river ports. International and African airlines call at Robertsfield, 35 miles from Monrovia. Spriggs Payne airfield, on the outskirts of Monrovia, is used for internal flights.

Liberia is receiving assistance from a number of countries, including the United Kingdom, and from the EC and various international agencies. This aid is mainly directed towards the implementation of Liberia's National Socio-Economic Development Plan.

FINANCE

	1987	1988
Revenue	US$183,800,000	US$207,100,000
Expenditure	345,740,000	356,084,000

TRADE

The principal exports are iron ore, crude rubber, timber, uncut diamonds, palm kernels, cocoa and coffee. The chief imports are manufactured goods of all kinds, transport and iron-ore mining equipment and foodstuffs.

	1987	1988
Imports	US$307,600,000	US$282,530,000
Exports	382,200,000	416,920,000

Trade with UK

	1988	1989
Imports from UK	£11,684,000	£15,148,000
Exports to UK	9,574,000	12,776,000

CAPITAL, ΨMonrovia, population estimate (1984) 425,000. Other ports are ΨBuchanan, ΨGreenville (Sinoe) and ΨHarper (Cape Palmas).

CURRENCY.—Liberian dollar (L$) of 100 cents.

FLAG.—Alternate horizontal stripes (5 white, 6 red), with 5-pointed white star on blue field in upper corner next to flagstaff.

NATIONAL ANTHEM.—All Hail, Liberia, Hail.

NATIONAL DAY.—July 26.

BRITISH EMBASSY
PO Box 10-0120, 1000 Monrovia 10
[Monrovia 221055]

Ambassador Extraordinary and Plenipotentiary, and Consul-General, His Excellency Michael Edward John Gore (1988).

Consul and Head of Chancery, S. J. Seaman.

LIBYA
(Al-Jamahiriya Al-Arabiya
Al-Libya Al-Shabiya Al-Ishtirakiya)

Leader of the Revolution and Supreme Commander of the Armed Forces, Col. Muammar al-Gadaffi.

SECRETARIAT OF THE GENERAL PEOPLE'S CONGRESS
(as at June 30, 1990)

Secretary, Dr. Miftah al Usta Umar.
Asstistant Secretaries, Ibrahim Abu Khizam; Salmin Ali al Uraybi.
Secretary (Affairs of People's Congresses), Umar Ishkal.
Secretary (Affairs of People's Committees), Sulayman Sasi al-Shuhumi.
Secretary (Affairs of Professional Congresses), Bashir Huwayj Humaydi.

GENERAL PEOPLE'S COMMITTEE

Secretary-General, Umar Mustafa al-Muntasir.
Foreign Liaison, Jadallah Azzuz al-Talhi.
Petroleum, Fawzi al-Shakshuki.
Communications and Maritime Transport, Mubarak al-Shamikh.
Higher Education, Ahmad Muhammad Ibrahim.
Economy and Foreign Trade, Dr. Farhat Sharnanah.
Planning, Dr. Muhammad Lutfi Farhat.
Health, Dr. Mustafa Muhammad al-Zaydi.
Strategic Industries, Dr. Fathi Ahmad bin Shatwan.
Treasury, Muhammad al Madani al Bukhari.
Information and Culture, Dr. Rajab Miftah Abu Dabbus.
Marine Wealth, Miftah Muhammad Ku'aybah.
Vocational Training, Ma'tuq Muhammad Ma'tuq.
Mass Mobilization and Revolutionary Guidance, Ali al Sha'iri.
Scientific Research, Nuri al-Fayturi al Madani.
Agrarian Reform and Land Reclamation, Abd al-Majid al-Qa'ud.
Justice, Izz al-Din al Hinshiri.
Education, Fatimah Abd al-Hafiz Muktar.
Light Industries, Amin Halimi Othman Kamil.

LIBYAN DIPLOMATIC MISSION IN LONDON

Following the break of diplomatic relations with Libya in April 1984, the Royal Embassy of Saudi Arabia has handled Libyan interests in Britain.

Libya, on the Mediterranean coast of Africa, is bounded on the East by Egypt and Sudan, on the South by the Republics of Chad and Niger, and on the West by Algeria and Tunisia. It consists of the three former provinces of Tripolitania, Cyrenaica and the Fezzan, with a combined area of 679,362 sq. miles (1,759,540 sq. km) and a population (UN estimate 1988) of 4,232,000. The people of Libya are principally Arab with some Berbers in the west and aboriginal tribes in the Fezzan. Islam is the official religion of

Libya, but other religions are tolerated. The official language is Arabic.

Vast lands and rock deserts, almost completely barren, occupy the greater part of Libya. The southern part of the country lies within the Sahara Desert. There are no rivers and as rainfall is irregular, good harvests are rare. The ancient ruins in Cyrenaica, at Cyrene, Ptolemais (Tolmeta) and Apollonia, are outstanding, as are those at Leptis Magna near Homs, 70 miles from Tripoli and at Sabratha, 40 miles west of Tripoli. An Italian expedition found in the SW of the Fezzan a series of rock-paintings more than 5,000 years old.

Government.—Libya was occupied by Italy in 1911–12 in the course of the Italo-Turkish War, and under the Treaty of Ouchy (October 1912) the sovereignty of the province was transferred by Turkey to Italy. In 1939 the four Provinces of Libya (Tripoli, Misurata, Benghazi and Derna) were incorporated in the national territory of Italy as *Libia Italiana*. After the Second World War Tripolitania and Cyrenaica were placed provisionally under British and the Fezzan under French administration, and in conformity with a resolution of the UN General Assembly in November 1949, Libya became on December 24, 1951 the first independent state to be created by the United Nations. The monarchy was overthrown by a revolution in September 1969, and the country was declared a republic. It was ruled by the Revolutionary Command Council (RCC) under the leadership of Colonel Muammar Gadaffi.

In March 1977 a new form of direct democracy, the 'Jamahiriya' (state of the masses) was promulgated and the official name of the country was changed to Socialist People's Libyan Arab Jamahiriya. At local level authority is now vested in about 1,500 Basic and 14 Municipal People's Congresses which appoint Popular Committees to execute policy. Officials of these congresses and committees, together with representatives from unions and other organizations, form the General People's Congress, which normally meets for about a week early each year. This is the highest policy-making body in the country. The General People's Congress appoints its own General Secretariat and the General People's Committee, whose members head the 13 government departments which execute policy at national level. The Secretary of the General People's Committee has functions similar to those of a Prime Minister.

Since a reorganization in March 1979 neither Col. Gadaffi nor his former RCC colleagues have held formal posts in the administration. Gadaffi continues to hold the ceremonial title 'Leader of the Revolution'.

Communications.—Besides the coastal road running from the Tunisian frontier through Tripoli to Benghazi, Tobruk and the Egyptian border, which serves the main population centres, main roads now link the provincial centres, and the oil-producing areas of the south with the coastal towns. There are airports at Tripoli and Benghazi (Benina), Tobruk, Mersa Brega, Sebha, Ghadames and Kufra regularly used by commercial airlines, and military airfields near Tobruk, near Tripoli and at Al Watiya, south of Zuara.

Production and Industry.—Agriculture is confined mainly to the coastal areas of Tripolitania and Cyrenaica, where barley, wheat, olives, almonds, citrus fruits and dates are produced, and to the areas of the oases, many of which are well supplied with springs supporting small fertile areas. Among the important oases are Jaghbub, Ghadames, Jofra, Sebha, Murzuq, Brak, Ghat, Jalo and the Kufra group in the South-East. The main industry is oil and gas production. There are pipelines from Zelten to the terminal at Mersa Brega, from Dahra to Ras-es-Sider, from Amal to Ras Lanuf and from the Intisar field to

Zuetina. Since 1984 average production of crude oil has been about 1 million barrels per day. A major petrochemical complex is under construction at Ras Lanuf where a refinery and ethylene plant began operations in early 1985. The construction of an iron and steel plant at Misurata is under way, though its completion has been slower than expected. Economic constraints have delayed some projects, particularly since Libya decided in 1983 to go ahead with a major irrigation scheme, the 'Great Man-Made River'.

Exports from Libya are dominated by crude oil, but some wool, cattle, sheep and horses, olive oil, and hides and skins are also exported. Principal imports are foodstuffs, including sugar, tea and coffee, and most constructional materials and consumer goods. In recent years the private sector has been virtually eliminated and Libya is now a state trading country with imports controlled by state monopolies. In early 1988, however, reforms were proposed which will allow a small private sector to be re-established.

Libya has technical assistance agreements with a number of countries, and also employs large numbers of foreign labourers and experts.

Trade with UK

	1988	1989
Imports from UK	£235,957,000	£239,191,000
Exports to UK	111,812,000	104,546,000

CAPITAL.—ΨTripoli, population estimate (1989) 1,000,000. The principal towns are: ΨBenghazi (500,000); ΨMisurata (200,000); Sirte (100,000).

CURRENCY.—Libyan dinar (LD) of 1,000 dirhams.

FLAG.—Libya uses a plain emerald green flag.

NATIONAL DAY.—September 1.

BRITISH EMBASSY

Diplomatic relations between the UK and Libya were broken in April 1984. British interests are currently handled by a section at the Italian Embassy, Sharia Uahram 1, (PO Box 4206), Tripoli.

LIECHTENSTEIN
(Fürstentum Liechtenstein)

Prince, Hans Adam II, *born* Feb. 14, 1945; *succeeded* November 13, 1989; *married* July 30, 1967, Countess Marie Kinsky; and has *issue*, Prince Alois, *b.* June 11, 1968; Prince Maximilian, *b.* May 16, 1969; Prince Constantin, *b.* March 15, 1972; Princess Tatjana, *b.* April 10, 1973.

MINISTRY
(as at June 30, 1990)

Prime Minister, Hans Brunhart (*Head of Government 'Presidium', Foreign Affairs, Education, Finance, Construction*).

Deputy PM, Dr. Herbert Wille (*Interior, Agriculture, Forestry and Environment, Culture, Youth and Sport, Justice*).

Government Councillors, René Ritter (*Economy*), Dr. Peter Wolff (*Social and Health Services*), Wilfried Büchel (*Communications*).

DIPLOMATIC REPRESENTATION

Liechtenstein is represented in diplomatic and consular matters in the United Kingdom by the Swiss Embassy.

Liechtenstein is a principality on the Upper Rhine, between Vorarlberg (Austria) and Switzerland, with an area of 61 sq. miles (158 sq. km), and a population in 1988 of 28,181. The language of the principality is German.

At the General Election on March 5, 1989 the Patriotic Union Party won 13 seats and Progressive Citizens' Party 12.

The main industries are high and ultra-high vacuum engineering, semi-conductor industry, roller bearings, fastenings and securing systems, artificial teeth, heating and hot water equipment, synthetic fibres, woollen and homespun fabrics.

FINANCE

	1987	1988
Revenue	F318,401,301	F319,016,168
Expenditure	308,306,099	321,229,914

(F = Swiss francs)

CAPITAL.—Vaduz, population (1988) 4,919.

CURRENCY.—Swiss franc of 100 rappen (or centimes).

FLAG.—Equal horizontal bands of blue over red; gold crown on blue band near staff.

NATIONAL ANTHEM.—Oben am Jungen Rhein (High on the Rhine).

NATIONAL DAY.—August 15.

British Consul General, Anthony Hugh Morgan (*office* at Dufourstrasse 56, 8008 Zürich).

LUXEMBOURG
(Grand-Duché de Luxembourg)

Grand Duke, HRH Jean, *born* Jan. 5, 1921, *married,* April 9, 1953, Princess Joséphine-Charlotte of Belgium, and has *issue,* three sons and two daughters; *succeeded* (on the abdication of his mother) Nov. 12, 1964.

Heir Apparent, Prince Henri, *born* April 16, 1955, *married* February 14, 1981, Maria Teresa Mestre, and has *issue,* Prince Guillaume, *b.* Nov. 11, 1981; Prince Felix, *b.* June 3, 1984; Prince Louis, *b.* Aug. 3, 1986.

CABINET
(as at June 30, 1990)

Christian Socialists:

Minister of State, President of the Government, Minister of the Treasury and Cultural Affairs, Jacques Santer.

Interior, Jean Spautz.

The Family, Social Solidarity, Women's Affairs and the Retired, Fernand Boden.

Budget, Finance and Labour, Jean-Claude Juncker.

Education, Justice and the Civil Service, Marc Fischbach.

Agriculture and Viticulture, Rural Development and Scientific Research, Rene Steichen.

Socialists:

Vice-President of the Government, Minister of Foreign Affairs, Foreign Trade and Aid, and Defence, Jacques Poos.

Public Health and Social Security, Physical Education and Sports, and Youth Affairs, Johny Lahure.

Economy, Transport and Public Works, Robert Goebbels.

Environment, Regional Development, Posts and Telecommunications, Energy and Information Technology, Alex Bodry.

State Secretary for Social Security, Health, Sports and Youth Affairs, Mady Delvaux-Stehres.

State Secretary for Foreign Affairs, Overseas Trade, Aid and Defence, Georges Wohlfart.

EMBASSY OF LUXEMBOURG
27 Wilton Crescent, SW1X 8SD
[071–235 6961]

Ambassador Extraordinary and Plenipotentiary, His Excellency Edouard Molitor (1989).

Luxembourg is a Grand Duchy in western Europe, bounded by the Federal Republic of Germany, Belgium, and France. The area is 998 sq. miles (2,586 sq. km), the population (December 1989) 377,100, nearly all Roman Catholics. The country is well wooded, with many deer and wild boar. The language is Letzeburgesch but French is the official language; most speak German.

Established as an independent state under the sovereignty of the King of the Netherlands as Grand Duke by the Congress of Vienna in 1815, Luxembourg formed part of the Germanic Confederation 1815–66, and was included in the German 'Zollverein'. In 1867 the Treaty of London declared it a neutral territory. On the death of the King of the Netherlands in 1890 it passed to the Duke of Nassau. The territory was invaded and overrun by the Germans at the beginning of the war in 1914, but was liberated in 1918. By the Treaty of Versailles, 1919, Germany renounced its former agreements with Luxembourg and in 1921 an economic union was made with Belgium. The Grand Duchy was again invaded and occupied by Germany on May 10, 1940. The constitution of the Grand Duchy was modified on April 28, 1948, and the stipulation of permanent neutrality was then abandoned. Luxembourg is now a signatory of the Brussels and North Atlantic Treaties, and also a member of the European Communities. Luxembourg is a member of the Belgium-Netherlands-Luxembourg Customs Union (Benelux 1960).

The Court of the European Communities has its seat in Luxembourg, as does the Secretariat of the European Parliament, the European Investment Bank, the European Audit Court and the European Monetary Co-operation Fund.

There is a Chamber of 64 Deputies, elected by universal suffrage for 5 years. Legislation is submitted to the Council of State.

The Grand Duchy possesses an important iron and steel industry with an annual productive capacity over 5,700,000 tons. Government revenue for 1989 was estimated at LF 89,600 million, expenditure LF 88,900 million. The Luxembourg franc has at present the same value as the Belgian franc.

There are 170 miles of railway.

Trade with UK (Belgium and Luxembourg)

	1988	1989
Imports from UK	£4,251,961,000	£4,872,641,000
Exports to UK	4,956,037,000	5,700,534,000

CAPITAL.—Luxembourg, population (1987) 77,500, is a dismantled fortress.

CURRENCY.—Luxembourg franc (LF) of 100 centimes. Belgian currency is also legal tender.

FLAG.—Three horizontal bands, red, white and blue.

NATIONAL ANTHEM.—Ons Hémécht (Our homeland).

NATIONAL DAY.—June 23.

BRITISH EMBASSY
14 Boulevard F. D. Roosevelt, L-2450 Luxembourg
[Luxembourg 29864]

Ambassador Extraordinary and Plenipotentiary, Her Excellency Juliet Jeanne Campbell, CMG (1988).

MADAGASCAR
(Repoblika Demokratika n'i Madagaskar)

President, Didier Ratsiraka, *took office* 1975, *re-elected* 1982 and March 12, 1989 for a seven-year term.

COUNCIL OF MINISTERS
(as at June 30, 1990)

Prime Minister, Lt.-Col. Victor Ramahatra.

Finance and State Budget, Léon Rajaobelina.

Agricultural Production, Jose Michel Andrianoelison.

Animal Production, Water and Forests, Maxime Pascal Zafera.
Trade, Georges Solofoson.
Industry, Energy and Mines, Jose Rakotomavo.
Population and Social Condition, Youth and Sports, Badhroudine.
Revolutionary Art and Culture, Gisèle Rabesahala.
Posts and Telecommunications, Simon Pierre.
Justice, Joseph Bedo.
Transport, Meteorology and Tourism, Lucien Zasy.
Civil Service and Labour, Georges Ruphin.
Defence, Gen. Mahasampa Raveloson.
Health, Dr. Jean-Jacques Séraphin.
Interior, Ampy Portos.
Primary and Secondary Education, Aristide Velompanay.
Higher Education, Ignace Rakoto.
Scientific Research, Antoine Zafera.
Information, Jean Claude Rahaga.
Foreign Affairs, Jean Bemananjara.
Public Works, Cmdt. Jean Emile Tsaranazy.

HONORARY CONSULATE OF THE DEMOCRATIC REPUBLIC OF MADAGASCAR
16 Lanark Mansions, Pennard Road, W12 8DT
[081-746 0133]
Honorary Consul, Stephen Hobbs.

Madagascar lies 240 miles off the east coast of Africa and is the fourth largest island in the world. It has an area of 226,669 sq. miles (587,041 sq. km), and a population (UN estimate 1988) of 11,238,000. The people are of mixed Polynesian, Arab and African origin. The official languages are Malagasy and French. There are sizeable French, Chinese and Indian communities.

Government.—Madagascar (known from 1958 to 1975 as the Malagasy Republic) became a French protectorate in 1895, and a French colony in 1896 when the former queen was exiled. Republican status was adopted on October 14, 1958, and independence was proclaimed on June 26, 1960.

The post-independence civilian government was replaced by a military government in January 1975 and the following month martial law was declared. A Supreme Council of the Revolution of 18 members under Capitaine de Frégate (now Admiral) Didier Ratsiraka was established on June 15, 1975.

In December 1975 a new constitution was approved in a referendum, which vested executive power in the President. He appoints a Council of Ministers to assist him, with the guidance of the Revolutionary Supreme Council. There is a 137-member National People's Assembly elected for a five-year term by universal suffrage,

Revised agreements with France, signed on June 4, 1973, provided for the withdrawal of the French forces stationed in the country after independence. The French naval base at Diégo Suarez (now called Antsiranana) was turned into a civilian ship repair yard. Madagascar also withdrew from the Franc Zone and announced a claim to the islands of Juan de Nova, Glorieuses, Isle de l'Europe, Bassa da India and Tromelin which had remained integral parts of the French Republic after independence.

Economy.—The island's economy is still largely based on agriculture, which accounts for three-quarters of its exports. Development plans have placed emphasis on increasing agricultural and livestock production, the improvement of communications, the exploitation of mineral deposits and the creation of small industries.

TRADE

	1985	1986
Imports	US$ 400·54m	US$ 441·54m
Exports	274·23m	351·18m

Trade with UK

	1988	1989
Imports from UK	£4,747,000	£3,352,000
Exports to UK	7,154,000	5,866,000

CAPITAL.—Antananarivo, population estimate 1,000,000. Other main towns are the chief port ΨToamasina (55,000); ΨMahajanga (50,000); Fianarantsoa (47,000); ΨAntsiranana (41,000).
CURRENCY.—Franc Malgache (Malagasy franc) (FMG) of 100 centimes.
FLAG.—Equal horizontal bands of red (above) and green, with vertical white band by staff.
NATIONAL DAY.—June 26 (Independence Day).

BRITISH EMBASSY
BP 167, Antananarivo
[Antananarivo 277 49]

Ambassador Extraordinary and Plenipotentiary, His Excellency Dennis Oldgrieve Amy, OBE (1990).
Second Secretary, J. J. Macadie.

MALI
(République du Mali)

Secretary-General of the UDPM, President of the Government, and Minister of Defence, Gen. Moussa Traoré, *born* 1937, *assumed office* Nov. 20, 1968, *elected* June 19, 1979, *re-elected* June 9, 1985.

GOVERNMENT MINISTERS
(as at June 30, 1990)

Secretary General to the Presidency, Diango Cissoko.
National Education, Gen. Sékou Ly.
Territorial Administration and Basic Development, Col. Issa Ongoiba.
Sports, Art and Culture, Bakary Traoré.
Public Works, Urbanism and Construction, Cheikh Oumar Doumbia.
Agriculture, Moulaye Mohamed Haidara.
Finance and Commerce, Tiéna Coulibaly.
Environment and Livestock, Morifing Kone.
Employment and the Civil Service, Mme. Diallo Lalla Sy.
Foreign Affairs and International Co-operation, Dr. N'Golo Traoré.
Transport and Tourism, Zeini Moulaye.
Information and Telecommunications, Naimanto Diarra.
Planning, Souleymane Dembele.
Justice, Mamadou Sissoko.
Industry, Hydraulics and Energy, Amadou Deme.
Public Health and Social Affairs, Dr. Abdoulaye Diallo.
Minister delegate to the Ministry of Defence, Gen. Abdoulaye Ouologuem.

The Republic of Mali, an inland state in north-west Africa, has an area of 478,791 sq. miles (1,240,000 sq. km), and a population (UN estimate 1988) of 8,918,000. The principal rivers are the Niger and the Senegal.

Formerly the French colony of Soudan, the territory elected on November 24, 1958 to remain as an autonomous republic within the French Community. It associated with Senegal in the Federation of Mali which was granted full independence on June 20, 1960. The Federation was effectively dissolved on August 22 by the secession of Senegal. The title of the Republic of Mali was adopted in September 1960.

Government.—The regime of Modibo Keita was overthrown on Nov. 19, 1968 by a group of Army officers who formed a National Liberation Committee and appointed a Prime Minister. Moussa Traoré assumed the functions of Head of State. A new civil constitution came into being in 1979. The new government formed on May 4, 1978 contained a majority of civilians. On June 19, 1979, elections were held for an 82-member National Assembly. Presidential elections held on the same day confirmed Traoré as President. The sole legal political party is the Mali People's Democratic Union (UDPM).

Economy.—Mali's principal exports are ground-nuts (raw and processed), cotton fibres, meat and dried fish. The Republic rejoined the CFA Franc Zone on June 1, 1984.

Trade with UK

	1988	1989
Imports from UK	£12,732,000	£7,102,000
Exports to UK	2,240,000	2,305,000

CAPITAL.—Bamako (600,000). Other towns are Gao, Kayes, Mopti, Sikasso, Segou and Timbuktu (all regional capitals).

CURRENCY.—Franc CFA of 100 centimes.

FLAG.—Vertical stripes of green (by staff), yellow and red.

NATIONAL DAY.—September 22.

British Ambassador, resident in Dakar, Senegal.

MAURITANIA
(République Islamique de Mauritanie)

President, Prime Minister, Minister of Defence, Col. Maaouya Ould Sid' Ahmed Taya, *took power* Dec. 12, 1984.

GOVERNMENT MINISTERS
(as at April 30, 1990)

Interior, Posts and Telecommunications, Cmdt. Cheikh Sidy Ahmed Oud Baba.

Equipment and Transport, Cmdt. Diang Oumar Arouna.

Foreign Affairs and Co-operation, Hosny Oud Didy.

Justice, Sow Samba Sow.

Planning and Employment, Moustapha Ould Obeyd Rahmane.

Finance, Muhammad Ould Maychel.

Culture and Islamization, Didy Ould Bou Naamah.

Industry and Mining, Blahy Ould Maaghaya.

Health and Social Affairs, Mohamed Abdou-Rahaman Ould Amin.

Fisheries and Maritime Economy, Ahmed Ould Khalifa Ould Dyidou.

Information, Muhammad Lamine Ould Ahmed.

Civil Service, Sports, Muhammad Ould Al-Haymir.

Trade and Tourism, Khadydia Minte Ahmed.

National Education, Al-Moukhtar Oud Haye.

Rural Development, Hamoud Aud A-Abou.

Mauritania lies on the north-west coast of Africa immediately to the north of Senegal. It is bounded on the east by the Republic of Mali. To the north it is bounded by Morocco and the Western Sahara. Area 397,955 sq. miles (1,030,700 sq. km). The population (UN estimate 1988) is 1,916,000. The official languages are French and Arabic.

The Republic of Mauritania declared on November 28, 1958 to remain within the French Community as an autonomous republic. It became fully independent on November 28, 1960. In 1972 Mauritania broke with the Franc Zone.

Mauritania and Morocco took possession of the Western Sahara territory in February 1976 when Spain formally relinquished all right to it and in April 1976 agreed on a new frontier dividing the territory between them. In August 1979, Mauritania relinquished all claim to the southern sector of the Western Sahara after a three-year war against the Polisario front guerrilla army.

Since a military coup deposed the first President in 1978, Mauritania has been ruled by a Military Committee for National Salvation (CMSN).

Mauritania's main source of potential wealth lies in rich deposits of iron ore around Zouérate, in the north of the country. Exports began in 1963, via a railway laid for the purpose from the mine to the port of Nouadhibou. The deposits are being exploited under the aegis of the *Société Nationale Industrielle Minière* following the nationalization in 1974 of the internationally based company MIFERMA. There are copper deposits at Akjoujt which are being exploited by SOMIMA, a company nationalized in February 1975; the mine was closed in 1978, but re-opened in 1981.

Trade with UK

	1988	1989
Imports from UK	£3,048,000	£7,102,000
Exports to UK	7,259,000	15,387,000

CAPITAL.—Nouakchott (500,000).

CURRENCY.—Ouguiya of 5 khoums.

FLAG.—Yellow star and crescent on green ground.

NATIONAL DAY.—November 28.

British Ambassador, resident in Rabat, Morocco. All staff resident in Dakar, Senegal.

MEXICO
(Estados Unidos Mexicanos)

President (1988–94), Lic. Carlos Salinas de Gortari, *elected*, June 4, 1988, *took office*, Dec. 1, 1988.

THE CABINET
(as at May 31, 1990)

Interior, Lic. Fernando Gutiérrez Barrios.

Foreign Affairs, Lic. Fernando Solana Morales.

Finance and Public Credit, Dr. Pedro Aspe Armella.

Defence, Gral de División D.E.M. Antonio Riviello Bazán.

Navy, E. M. N. Mauricio Shleskes Sanchez.

Budget and Planning, Dr. Ernesto Zedillo Ponce de León.

Energy, Mines and Parastatal Industries, Ing. Fernando Hiriart Balderrama.

Trade and Industrial Development, Dr. Jaime Serra Puche.

Agriculture and Water Resources, Lic. Carlos Hank González.

Communications and Transport, Lic. Andrés Caso Lombardo.

Education, Lic. Manuel Bartlett Díaz.

Urban Development and Ecology, Lic. Patricio Chirinos C.

Health, Dr. Jesús Kumate Rodríguez.

Labour and Social Security, Lic. Arsenio Farell Cubillas.

Agrarian Reform, Victor Cervera Pacheco.

Tourism, Lic. Pedro Joaquin Coldwell.

Fisheries, Lic. María de los Angeles Moreno.

Attorney-General, Dr. Enrique Alvarez del Castillo.

Attorney-General of Federal District, Lic. Ignacio Morales Lechuga.

Comptroller-General, Lic. María Elena Vazquez Nava.

Mayor of Mexico City, Lic. Manuel Camacho Solís.

MEXICAN EMBASSY
8 Halkin Street, SW1X 7DW
[071–235 6393/6]

Ambassador Extraordinary and Plenipotentiary, His Excellency Bernardo Sepulveda (1989).

Area and Population.—Mexico occupies the southern part of the continent of North America, with an extensive seaboard to both the Atlantic and Pacific Oceans, extending from 14° 33′ to 32° 43′ N. lat. and 86° 46′ to 117° 08′ W. long., and comprising one of the most varied zones in the world. It contains

31 states and the federal district of Mexico, making in all 32 political divisions, covering an area of 761,605 sq. miles (1,972,547 sq. km). At the 1980 Mexican General Census, the total population was 67,383,000; a 1988 UN estimate gives a figure of 82,734,000.

The two great ranges of North America, the Sierra Nevada and Rocky Mountains, are prolonged from the north to a convergence towards the narrowing isthmus of Tehuantepec, their course being parallel to the west and east coasts. The surface of the interior consists of an elevated plateau between the two ranges, with steep slopes both to the Pacific and Atlantic (Gulf of Mexico). In the west is the peninsula of Lower California, with a mountainous surface, separated from the mainland by the Gulf of California. The Sierra Nevada, known in Mexico as the Sierra Madre, terminates in a transverse series of volcanic peaks, from Colima on the west to Citlaltepetl (El Pico de Orizaba) on the east. The low-lying lands of the coasts form the *Tierra Caliente*, or tropical regions (below 3,000 ft.), the higher levels form the *Tierra Templada*, or temperate region (from 3,000 to 6,000 ft.), and the summit of the plateau with its peaks is known as *Tierra Fría*, or cold region (above 6,000 ft.). The main rivers are the Rio Grande del Norte which forms part of the northern boundary, and is navigable for about 70 miles from its mouth in the Gulf of Mexico, and the Rio Grande de Santiago, the Rio Balsas and Rio Papaloapan. The largest fresh-water lakes are Chapala (70 miles long and 20 miles wide), and Pátzcuaro.

History and Archaeology.—The present Mexico and Guatemala were once the centre of a remarkable indigenous civilization, which flowered in the periods from AD 500 to 1100 and AD 1300 to 1500 and collapsed before the little army of Spanish adventurers under Hernán Cortés in the years following 1519. Pre-Columbian Mexico was divided between different but connected Indian cultures, each of which has left distinctive archaeological remains: the best-known of these are Chichén Itzá, Uxmal, Bonampak and Palenque, in Yucatán and Chiapas (Maya); Teotihuacon, renowned for the Pyramid of the Sun (216 feet high) in the Valley of Mexico (Teotihuacáno); Monte Albán and Mitla, near Oaxaca (Zapotec); El Tajín in the state of Veracruz (Totonac); and Tula in the state of Hidalgo (Toltec). The last and most famous Indian culture of all, the Aztec, based on Tenochitlán, suffered more than the others from the Spanish and very few Aztec monuments remain.

A few years after the conquest, the Spanish built Mexico City on the ruins of Tenochitlán, and appointed a Viceroy to rule their new dominions, which they called New Spain. The country was largely converted to Christianity, and a distinctive colonial civilization, representing a marriage of Indian and Spanish traditions, developed and flourished, notably in architecture and sculpture. In 1810 a revolt began against Spanish rule. This was finally successful in 1821, when a precarious independence was proclaimed. Friction with the United States in Texas led to the war of 1845–48, at the end of which Mexico was forced to cede the northern provinces of Texas, California and New Mexico. In 1862 Mexican insolvency led to invasion by French forces which installed Archduke Maximilian of Austria as Emperor. The empire collapsed with the execution of the Emperor in 1867 and the austere reformer, Juárez, restored the republic. Juárez's death was followed by the dictatorship of Porfirio Diaz, which saw an enormous increase of foreign, particularly British and United States, investment in the country. In 1910 began the Mexican Revolution which reformed the social structure and the land system, curbed the power of foreign companies and ushered in the independent industrial Mexico of today.

Government.—Under the Constitution of 1917 (as subsequently amended), Congress consists of a Senate of 64 members, elected for six years, and of a Chamber of Deputies, at present numbering 400, elected for three years. Presidents, who wield full executive powers, are elected for six years; they cannot be re-elected.

There are nine political parties registered in Mexico, of which the largest and most influential is the Partido Revolucionario Institucional (PRI) which has for many years constituted the governing party. The Mexican Communists allied with several like-minded smaller parties to form the Mexican United Socialist Party (PSUM) in 1982.

Communications.—Veracruz, Tampico and Coatzacoalcos are the chief ports of the Atlantic, and Guaymas, Mazatlán, Puerto Lázaro Cárdenas, Acapulco, Salina Cruz and Puerto Madero on the Pacific. Work is proceeding on the reorganization and re-equipment of the whole system; help in this has been forthcoming from the World Bank, the Export-Import Bank and private sources in the United States. The railways were completely nationalized in 1970.

Mexico City may be reached by at least three highways from the United States, and work is complete on roads southward from Mexico City to Yucatán as well as on two principal highways to the Guatemalan border.

International telegraph services to the United States frontier are provided by the government-owned Mexican Telegraph Company and then through the United States to Canada and Europe.

Teléfonos de México, a state-controlled company, controls about 98 per cent of all telephone services. Satélite Latinoamericano (SATELAT) is a joint government/private sector venture disseminating television programmes to Latin America through Intelsat IV satellite facilities leased by the Mexican Government.

There are 1,113 airports and landing fields in Mexico, of which eighteen are equipped to handle long-distance flights. There are 166 airline companies, including two of the major national airlines—Mexicana de Aviación and Aeroméxico. Passenger traffic is growing by about 14 per cent yearly, while cargo is increasing by a similar percentage.

Production.—The principal agricultural crops are maize, beans, rice, wheat, sugar cane, coffee, cotton, tomatoes, chili, tobacco, chick-peas, groundnuts, sesame, alfalfa, vanilla, cocoa and many kinds of fruit, both tropical and temperate. The maguey, or Mexican cactus, yields several fermented drinks, mezcal and tequila (distilled) and pulque (undistilled). Another species of the same plant supplies sisal-hemp (henequen). The forests contain mahogany, rosewood, ebony and chicle trees. Agriculture employs an estimated 30 per cent of the working population.

The principal industries are mining and petroleum, although there has been considerable expansion of both light and heavy industries. Exports of manufactured goods now average about 20 per cent of total exports. The steel industry expanded steadily until recently and current production is around 6·5m tons. The mineral wealth is great, and principal minerals are gold, silver, copper, lead, zinc, quicksilver, iron and sulphur. Substantial reserves of uranium have been found. In the non-metals sector, Mexico continues to produce 25 per cent of the world's supply of fluorspar.

The total proven petroleum reserves were 72 billion barrels in 1983. Daily production of natural gas is approximately 3 billion cubic feet. Oil reserves have increased substantially due to important discoveries in the Gulf of Campeche. A new refinery at Tula, State of Hidalgo, is the nation's largest; and new refineries in Monterrey, State of Nuevo Leon, and Salina Cruz, State of Oaxaca, are under construction.

Textile production is led by the artificial fibres sector, which comprised 66 per cent of the industry's output in 1983.

Defence.—Supreme command is vested in the President, exercised through the Ministries of Defence (for Army and Air Force) and Marine.

The country is divided into 36 zones in which the regular army (106,000) and part-time conscripts (250,000) are trained. The Army in 1985 had three HQ Brigades, five Artillery Regiments, 26 mechanized and one Horse Cavalry Regiments, Transport, Engineering and Signals Regiments, and 78 Infantry Battalions. In addition, there is a Rural Defence Militia of some 12,000 men.

The Navy has a strength of about 38,500 officers and men including the Naval Air Force and Marines. The Marine Infantry has 10 battalions (4,300 officers and men). The Naval Air Force consists of four squadrons and 49 aircraft.

The Air Force has an approximate strength of 5,500 officers and men and 298 aircraft. There is a Parachute Brigade consisting of three Parachute battalions (approx. 2,000 men).

Language and Literature.—Spanish is the official language of Mexico and is spoken by about 95 per cent of the population. In addition to Spanish, there are five basic groups of Indian languages spoken in Mexico. The 1970 Census showed that of the 3,111,415 inhabitants speaking an Indian language, 25·7 per cent spoke Náhuatl; 14·6 per cent Maya; 9·1 per cent Zapotec; 7·1 per cent Otomi; 7·5 per cent Mixtec and 36 per cent one or other of the 59 dialects derived from these basic languages.

Education.—Education is divided into primary, secondary, preparatory and university. Primary education is free, secular and nominally compulsory.

Trade with UK

	1988	1989
Imports from UK	£190,011,000	£205,130,000
Exports to UK	144,947,000	165,295,000

Imports consist largely of transport, sound-recording and power-generating equipment, chemicals, industrial machinery, pharmaceuticals and specialized appliances. Principal exports are oil, fertilizers, minerals, metallic ores and scrap, sugar, honey, textiles and power-generating equipment.

CAPITAL.—Mexico City, estimated population of metropolitan area (1986) 18,748,000. Other cities (with 1986 population estimates) are:

Guadalajara	2,587,000	Puebla	1,217,600
Monterrey	2,335,000	León	946,800
Torréon	729,800	Ciudad	
San Luis		Juarez	595,700
Potosì	601,900	Mérida	580,300

CURRENCY.—Peso of 100 centavos.

FLAG.—Three vertical bands in green, white, red, with the Mexican emblem (an eagle on a cactus devouring a snake) in the centre.

NATIONAL ANTHEM.—Mexicanos, Al Grito De Guerra (Mexicans, to the war cry).

NATIONAL DAY.—September 16 (Proclamation of Independence).

BRITISH EMBASSY
Calle Río Lerma 71, Colonia Cuauhtémoc,
06500 Mexico City, DF
[Mexico City 207 20 89]

Ambassador Extraordinary and Plenipotentiary, His Excellency Michael Keith Orlebar Simpson-Orlebar, CMG (1989).

There are British Consular Offices at *Mexico City, Acapulco, Guadalajara, Mérida, Monterrey, Tampico* and *Cuidad Juarez.*

British Council Representative.—Dr. Brian Havercombe, Maestro Antonio Caso 127, Col. San Rafael (PO Box 30-588), Mexico 06470 DF.

BRITISH CHAMBER OF COMMERCE, British Trade Centre, Rio de la Plata 30, Col. Cuauhtemoc, CP 06500, Mexico City DF.—*Manager*, Ing. Carlos J. Espinoza.

MONACO
(Principauté de Monaco)

Sovereign Prince, HSH Rainier III Louis-Henri-Maxence Bertrand, *born* May 31, 1923, *succeeded* May 9, 1949; *married* April 19, 1956, Miss Grace Patricia Kelly (died Sept. 14, 1982) and *has issue* Prince Albert Alexandre Louis Pierre, *born* March 14, 1958, Princess Caroline Louise Marguerite, *born* January 23, 1957; and Princess Stephanie Marie Elisabeth, *born* Feb. 1, 1965.

President of the Crown Council, Jean-Charles Marquet.

President of the National Council, Jean-Charles Rey.

Minister of State, Jean Ausseil, *appointed* 1985.

CONSULATE GENERAL OF MONACO
4 Audley Square, W1Y 5DR
[071–629 0734]

Consul-General, I. B. Ivanovic.

A small principality on the Mediterranean, with land frontiers joining France at every point, Monaco is divided into the districts of Monaco-Ville, La Condamine, Fontvielle and Monte Carlo. The principality comprises a narrow strip of country about 2 miles long (area approx. 195 hectares), with approximately 27,063 inhabitants (1989) and a yearly average of over 250,000 visitors.

The principality, ruled by the Grimaldi family since the late 13th century, was abolished during the French Revolution and re-established in 1815 under the protection of the Kingdom of Sardinia. In 1861 Monaco came under French protection. The 1962 Constitution, which can be modified only with the approval of the National Council, maintains the traditional hereditary monarchy and guarantees freedom of association, trade union freedom and the right to strike. Legislative power is held jointly by the Prince and a uni-cameral, 18 member National Council elected by universal suffrage. Executive power is exercised by the Prince and a four-member Council of Government, headed by a Minister of State. The judicial code is based on that of France.

The whole available ground is built over, so that there is no cultivation, though there are some notable public and private gardens. Monaco has a small harbour (30 ft. alongside quay) and the import duties are the same as in France.

CAPITAL.—Monaco-Ville, population (1982) 1,234.

CURRENCY.—Monaco uses the French franc of 100 centimes as legal tender.

FLAG.—Two equal horizontal stripes, red over white.

NATIONAL ANTHEM.—Hymne Monegasque.

NATIONAL DAY.—November 19.

HM Consul-General, John Illman (1990), resident in Marseilles, France.

MONGOLIA
(Mongolian People's Republic— Bugd Nairamdakh Mongol Ard Uls)

Chairman of the Presidium of the Great People's Hural (Head of State), Punsalmaagiyn Ochirbat, *elected* March 1990.

Chairman of Council of Ministers, Sharavyn Gungaadorj.

First Deputy Chairman, B. Byambasuren.

Deputy Chairman, B. Sharavsambuu, K. Zardykhan, Ch. Purevdorj.

EMBASSY OF THE MONGOLIAN PEOPLE'S REPUBLIC
7 Kensington Court, W8 5DL
[071–937 0150]

Ambassador Extraordinary and Plenipotentiary, His Excellency Ishetsogyin Ochirbal (1987).

Third Secretary, L. Davaadelger.

Attachés, N. Batsaikhan, B. Bazarkhand.

Area and Population.—The Mongolian People's Republic is a large and sparsely populated country to the north of China. Its area is 604,250 sq. miles (1,565,000 sq. km). Its population (July 1988) is about 2,000,000. However, this total constitutes only part of the Mongolians of Asia, a number of whom are to be found in China and in the neighbouring regions of the Soviet Union (especially the Mongolian Buryat Autonomous Region).

Mongolia, which is almost nowhere below 1,000 metres above sea level, forms part of the Central Asiatic Plateau and rises towards the west in the high mountains of the Mongolian Altai and Khanggai Ranges. The Khentai Mountain Range, situated to the north-east of the capital Ulan Bator, is less high. The Gobi region covers much of the southern half of the country. It contains some sand deserts, but between these less hospitable areas there is semidesert which provides pasture for great numbers of sheep, goats, camels and horses (the latter is still the characteristic means of transport for the rural population) and some cattle. In the steppe areas to the north pasturage is better and livestock more abundant. Even further north, in the better watered provinces, grain, fodder and vegetable crops are increasingly grown. There are several long rivers and many lakes, but good water is scarce since much of the lake water is salty. The climate is harsh, with a short mild summer giving way to a long winter when temperatures can drop as low as minus 50°C.

Government.—Mongolia, under Genghis Khan the conqueror of China and much of Asia, was for many years a buffer state between Tsarist Russia and China, although it was under general Chinese suzerainty. The outbreak of the Chinese Revolution in 1911 led to a declaration of autonomy under Chinese suzerainty which was confirmed by the Sino-Russian Treaty of Kiakhta (1915), but cancelled by a unilateral Chinese declaration in 1919. Later the country became a battleground of the Russian civil war, and Soviet and Mongolian troops occupied Ulan Bator in 1921; this was followed by another declara-

tion of independence. However, in 1924 the Soviet Union in a Treaty with China again recognized the latter's sovereignty over Mongolia; but this was never properly exercised because of China's pre-occupation with internal affairs, and later by the war with Japan.

The Mongolian People's Republic was formally established in 1924. Under the Yalta Agreement, Chiang Kai-shek agreed to a plebiscite, held in 1945, in which the Mongolians declared their desire for independence and this was formally recognized by Nationalist China. The country entered the United Nations in 1961. The heroes of Mongolian history during the earlier part of the century were Sukhebator, who died in 1923, and the Communist Choibalsan (died 1952), who carried out a systematic destruction of the power of the Lamas and the old princely houses which had previously been the dominant force in both economy and government.

The Mongolian People's Revolutionary Party (MPRP) has been the ruling party since 1924. A series of demonstrations in favour of political and economic reform began in December 1989 and led to changes in the MPRP leadership in March 1990. The MPRP's constitutionally guaranteed monopoly of power was subsequently relinquished, and the introduction of a multi-party system was approved by the Great People's Hural. In May 1990 the formation of a Small Hural was approved. While the Great Hural is still the supreme body (and has a large MPRP majority), the Small Hural is now the permanent legislative body. Some 40 per cent of its members are from opposition parties. The first multi-party elections took place in July and August 1990.

Production, etc.—The total of Mongolia's livestock was 23 million in 1988. Traditionally the Mongolians lead a nomadic life tending flocks of sheep, goats and horses, cows and camels. With the coming of the Communist regime and especially since 1952, great efforts have been made to settle the population, but a large proportion still live nomadically or semi-nomadically in the traditional *ger* (circular tent). The pastoral population was collectivized at the end of the 1950s into huge *negdels* (co-operatives) and state farms which have hastened the process of settlement, but within these the herdsmen and their families still move with their *gers* from pasture to pasture as the seasons change. The country, and three city districts (Ulan Bator, Darkhan and Erdenet), is today divided into 18 *aimaks* (provinces) and beneath these into 258 *somons* (districts), and these form the basis of the State organization of the country.

Membership of the Communist bloc has brought Mongolia considerable quantities of aid from other Socialist countries, especially Czech, Polish and East German aid to supplement the massive assistance from the Soviet Union. Soviet and Bloc aid is hastening the process of industrialization; for although the economy remains predominantly based on the herds of animals, and the principal exports of the country are still animal by-products (especially wool, hides and furs) and cattle, factories serving the needs of the country have been started up and the coal and electricity industries are being developed to provide an industrial base. A joint Mongolian/Soviet enterprise for copper and molybdenum mining was opened in 1978 at Erdenet in northern Mongolia. It is now in full production and processes 16 million tonnes of ore annually. A major geological survey is being carried out by the CMEA countries, in order to prepare for the extraction of the considerable mineral deposits known to exist in Mongolia. Coal production in 1980 was 4·5 million tons and was expected to rise to 6·8 million tons by 1985.

Ulan Bator, which contains over a quarter of the country's population, is the main seat of industry.

The second largest industrial centre is at Darkhan, north of the capital, near the Soviet frontier. Its industries include lime, cement and building materials, a flour mill and a power station. Choibalsan, in the east, is also being developed industrially. Agriculture, formerly little practised, is now being extended. Average cereal production for 1976–80 was 347,000 tons, but by 1983 had risen to 800,000 tonnes. Communication is still difficult in the country as there are very few tarmac roads. The trans-Mongolian railway, following the line of the old north-south trade route, was opened in 1955 and links Mongolia with both China and Russia. Mongolia's fundamental difficulty is its very small population and labour force.

Foreign trade is dominated by the Soviet Union, with the eastern European countries taking most of what is left. Trade with western countries and Japan is increasing as Mongolia embarks on its own version of perestroika.

Trade with UK

	1988	1989
Imports from UK	£1,637,000	£979,000
Exports to UK	1,857,000	405,000

CAPITAL.—Ulan Bator, population (1989) 530,000.
CURRENCY.—Tugrik of 100 möngö.
FLAG.—Vertical tri-colour red, blue, red and in the hoist the traditional Soyombo symbol in gold.
NATIONAL DAY.—July 11 (Anniversary of the Mongolian People's Republic).

BRITISH EMBASSY
30 Enkh Taivny Gudamzh (PO Box 703),
Ulan Bator 13
[Ulan Bator 51033/4]

Ambassador Extraordinary and Plenipotentiary, His Excellency David Keith Sprague, MVO (1989).
Second Secretary, J. L. Hartley (*Head of Chancery*).
Attachés, R. Townsend; C. G. Bain.

MOROCCO
(Al-Mamlaka Al-Maghrebia)

King, HM King Hassan II (Moulay Hassan Ben Mohammed), *born* July 9, 1929; *acceded* February 26, 1961.
Heir, Crown Prince Sidi Mohamed, *b.* August 21, 1963.

MINISTERS
(as at May 31, 1990)

Prime Minister, Azeddine Laraki
Ministers of State, Hadj M'hamid Bahnini; Moulay Ahmed Alaoui.
Justice, Moulay Mustapha Belarbi Alaoui.
Interior and Information, Driss Basri.
Foreign Affairs and Co-operation, Abdellatif Filali.
National Education, Prof. Taieb Chkili.
Health, Tayeb Bencheikh.
Religious Endowments and Islamic Affairs, Abdelkebir Alaoui M'Daghri.
Equipment, Training of Cadres and Professional Training, Mohamed Kabbaj.
Finance, Mohamed Berrada.
Tourism, Moussa Saadi.
Traditional Industry and Social Affairs, Mohamed Abied.
Transport, Mohamed Bouamoud.
Energy and Mines, Mohamed Fettah.
Youth and Sport, Abdellatif Semlali.
Fisheries and Merchant Shipping, Bensalem Smili.
Secretary General of the Government, Abbès Kaissi.
Culture, Mohamed Benaissa.
Environment, Abderrahmane Boufettass.

Posts and Telecommunications, Mohamed Laensar.
Agriculture and Agricultural Reform, Othman Demnati.
Trade and Industry, Abdellah Al Azmani.
Employment, Hassan Abbadi.
Overseas Trade, Hassan Abouyoub.
Prime Minister's Office, Moulay Zine Zahidi (*Economic Affairs*); Khali Hanna Ould Errachid (*Development of the Sahara Provinces*); Rachidi Ghazouani (*the Plan*); Abdeslem Baraka (*Relations with Parliament*); Abderrahim Ben Abdeljalil (*Administrative Affairs*).

EMBASSY OF THE KINGDOM OF MOROCCO
49 Queen's Gate Gardens, SW7 5NE
[071–581 5001/4]

Ambassador Extraordinary and Plenipotentiary, His Excellency Abdeslam Zenined, GCVO (1987).
Military, Naval and Air Attaché, Col. M. Jabrane.

Area and Population.—Morocco is situated in the north-western corner of the African continent between latitude 27° 40′–36° N. and longitude 1°–13° W. with an area estimated at 172,414 sq. miles (446,550 sq. km), and a population (1990 estimate) of 27,575,000. It is traversed in the north by the Rif mountains and in a general SW to NE direction, by the Middle Atlas, the High Atlas, the Anti-Atlas and the Sarrho ranges. The northern flanks of the Middle and High Atlas mountains are well wooded but their southern slopes, exposed to the dry desert winds, are generally arid and desolate. The north-westerly point of Morocco is the peninsula of Tangier which is separated from the continent of Europe by the narrow strait of Gibraltar. The Jebel Mousa dominates the promontory and, with the rocky eminence of Gibraltar, was known to the ancients as the Pillars of Hercules, the western gateway of the Mediterranean.

Western Sahara.—Formerly the Spanish Sahara, the territory was split between Morocco and Mauritania in 1976 after Spain withdrew in Dec. 1975. In 1979 Mauritania renounced its claim to its share of the territory, which was added by Morocco to its area. Morocco's annexation has been opposed by Polisario guerrillas, who want the territory to become an independent state. On August 30, 1988, Morocco and the Polisario Front accepted a UN peace plan. Under the plan a ceasefire is to come into effect, and a referendum to determine the future of the area will be held.

Climate.—The climate of Morocco is generally good and healthy, especially on the Atlantic coast (where a high degree of humidity is, however, prevalent), the country being partially sheltered by the Atlas mountains from the hot winds of the Sahara. The rainy season may last from November to April. The plains of the interior are intensely hot in summer. Average summer and winter temperatures for Rabat are 27°C and 7°C.

Government.—Morocco became an independent sovereign state in 1956, following joint declarations made with France on March 2, 1956, and with Spain on April 7, 1956. The Sultan of Morocco, Sidi Mohammad ben Youssef, adopted the title of King Mohammad V.

Following serious disturbances in Casablanca in March 1965, attempts were made by King Hassan, in consultation with all political parties, to form a government of national union. These efforts were unsuccessful and on June 7, 1965 the King proclaimed a 'state of exception' and suspended Parliament. Assuming himself the office of Prime Minister, he announced the formation of a new government and indicated that constitutional changes were to follow. A revised constitution was approved by a national referendum on July 24, 1970 and brought into effect soon after. It was superseded by another constitution, also approved by a national referendum, on March 1, 1972. This provides that not only political parties, but trade unions, chambers of commerce and professional bodies will participate in the organization of the state and representation of the people; specifies that the King is the supreme representative of the people; makes changes in the composition of the Regency Council and the Sovereign's rights and establishes a unicameral legislature. The Chamber has 306 members, 204 elected by direct universal suffrage (including 5 representing overseas workers) and 102 members elected by electoral colleges representing local government, industry, agriculture and working class groups. There were elections in September 1984 and the new Parliament began its six year term on October 12. A new government was named in April 1985 which included members of three political parties, though over half the portfolios went to non-political appointees. The term of the current Chamber of Representatives has been extended by two years, following a referendum held in December 1989.

Defence.—The Moroccan army, formed in 1956, is about 200,000 strong. A Moroccan air force was formed in 1959 and a navy in 1960. Their strengths are about 13,500 and 8,000 respectively. The armed forces possess quantities of French, Spanish and American equipment, including aircraft, as well as a little Soviet-supplied hardware.

Production and Trade.—Morocco's main sources of wealth are agricultural and mineral. The Five Year Plan (1981–85) for economic development placed particular emphasis on social improvement. Other priority sectors were industrial development, fisheries, agriculture and tourism. The next development plan (1987 onwards) is similar to the last. The world recession and high energy prices, coupled with a fall in the price of phosphates and poor harvests due to low rainfall have created problems for the economy since the end of the 1970s. However, rains in the winter of 1985–86 ended the long drought and the 1986 harvest was good. Similarly the fall in oil prices, the value of the dollar and interest rates have helped.

Agriculture employs more than 40 per cent of the working population and accounts for about 36 per cent of Morocco's exports. The main agricultural exports are fruit and vegetables. Cork and wood-pulp are the most important commercial forest products. Esparto grass is also produced. There is a fishing industry and substantial quantities of canned fish, mainly sardines and fishmeal, are exported. Manufacturing industries are centred in Casablanca, Fez, Tangier and Safi.

Morocco's mineral exports are phosphates, fluorite, barite, manganese, iron ore, lead, zinc, cobalt, copper and antimony. Morocco possesses nearly three-quarters of the world's estimated reserves of phosphates. There are oil refineries at Mohammedia and Sidi Kacem handling about four million tonnes of crude oil per year, but no significant quantities of hydrocarbons have been found.

Tourism is of increasing importance to the Moroccan economy with development concentrated in Agadir and Marrakesh.

Morocco's main import requirements are petroleum products, motor vehicles, building materials, agricultural and other machinery, chemical products, sugar, green tea and other foodstuffs.

	1987	1988
Imports	DH 1,066,711,000	DH 1,154,867,000
Exports	627,664,000	870,246,000

Trade with UK

	1988	1989
Imports from UK	£79,017,000	£84,475,000
Exports to UK	78,896,000	96,138,000

Communications.—The railway runs south from Tangier to Sidi Kacem. From this junction, one line runs eastwards through Fez to Oujda, and another continues southwards, through Rabat and Casablanca, to Marrakesh. A line running due south from Oujda skirts the Morocco-Algeria frontier and reaches Bouarfa. Moroccan railroads cover 1,250 miles and traction is electric or diesel. An extensive network of well-surfaced roads covers all the main towns in the kingdom.

There are air services between Casablanca, Tangier, Agadir (seasonal), Marrakesh and London, and also between Tangier and Gibraltar connecting with London. Royal-Air-Maroc operates internal services.

Language.—Arabic is the official language. Berber is the vernacular mainly in the mountain regions. French and Spanish are also spoken mainly in the towns. In 1984 there were seven Arabic and five French daily newspapers.

Education.—There are government primary, secondary and technical schools. At Fez there is a theological university of great repute in the Muslim world. There is a secular university at Rabat. Schools for special denominations, Jewish and Catholic, are permitted and may receive government grants. American schools operate in Rabat and Casablanca.

CAPITAL.—ΨRabat population (including Salé) 1,123,000. Regional capitals, with municipal population figures as at 1989, are: ΨCasablanca (2,904,000); Marrakesh (1,425,000); Fez (933,000); Oujda (895,000); Meknes (1,425,000); Ψ Agadir (700,000). The towns of Fez, Marrakesh and Meknes were capitals at various times in Morocco's history.

CURRENCY.—Dirham (DH) of 100 centimes.

FLAG.—Red, with green pentagram (the Seal of Solomon).

NATIONAL DAY.—March 3 (Anniversary of the Throne).

BRITISH EMBASSY
17 Boulevard de la Tour Hassan (BP 45), Rabat
[Rabat 20905]

Ambassador Extraordinary and Plenipotentiary, His Excellency John Esmond Campbell Macrae, CMG (1990).

First Secretary, S. R. H. Pease (*Head of Chancery/Commercial, and Consul*).

Defence Attaché, Lt.-Col. R. Chetwyn-Stapylton.

Vice Consul (Tangier), W. A. T. Pulleyblank, OBE.

There is a British Consulate/Commercial Office at *Casablanca* and an Honorary Consul at *Agadir*.

British Council Representative, P. Taylor, CBE BP 427), 22 Avenue Moulay Youssef, Rabat.

BRITISH CHAMBER OF COMMERCE, 291 Boulevard Mohamed V, Casablanca (Tel: 30 37 60).

MOZAMBIQUE
(República Popular de Moçambique)

President, Joaquim Alberto Chissano, *sworn in,* November 1986.

COUNCIL OF MINISTERS
(as at June 30, 1990)

Prime Minister, Mario da Graca Machungo.
Foreign Affairs, Pascoal Mocumbi.
National Defence, Alberto Joaquim Chipande.
Chief of Staff of the Armed Forces, Lt.-Gen. Antonio Hama Thai.
Co-operation, Jacinto Veloso.
Minister in the Presidency, Feliciano Gundana.
State Administration, Jose Oscar Monteiro.
Education, Aniceto dos Muchangos.
Interior, Manuel Antonio.

Security, Mariano de Araujo Matsinha.
Transport and Communications, Armando Emilio Guebuza.
Finance, Abdul Magid Osman.
Health, Dr. Leonardo Simao.
Information, Teodato Hunguana.
Construction and Water, Joao Salomao.
Trade, Gabriel Tembe.
Agriculture, Alexandre Jose Zandamela.
Industry and Energy, Antonio Branco.
Mineral Resources, John Kachamila.
Justice, Ossumane Ali Dauto.

EMBASSY OF THE PEOPLE'S REPUBLIC OF MOZAMBIQUE
21 Fitzroy Square, W1P 5HJ
[071–383 3800]

Ambassador Extraordinary and Plenipotentiary, His Excellency Armando Alexandre Panguene (1988).

Area and Population.—The People's Republic of Mozambique lies on the east coast of Africa, and is bounded by Swaziland in the south, South Africa in the south and west, Zimbabwe in the west, Zambia and Malawi in the north-west and Tanzania in the north. It has an area of 309,495 sq. miles (801,590 sq. km), with a population estimated at 15,200,000 (1989). The official language is Portuguese.

Government.—Mozambique, discovered by Vasco de Gama in 1498, and colonized by Portugal, achieved complete independence from Portugal on June 25, 1975. The date had been agreed in September 1974 by Portugal and Frelimo (Frente de Libertação de Moçambique), the Marxist liberation movement.

The country is governed by a Council of Ministers and by the Permanent Political Committee of the Frelimo Party; membership of these two bodies virtually overlaps. No other political parties are permitted. The principal legislative body, the People's Assembly, consists of 216 members nominated by Frelimo.

In August 1990 President Chissano announced government plans to adopt a multi-party system. Free general elections are to be held in 1991.

The basis of the economy is subsistence agriculture, but there is an industrial sector based mainly in Beira and Maputo. After giving priority to the development of collective farms and state enterprises in all sectors, the government is now encouraging the private sector and foreign investment, particularly in agriculture and consumer goods production. Main exports are sugar, cashew nuts, copra, cotton, tea and sisal. There are substantial coal deposits in Tete province. Mozambique has a range of aid and co-operation agreements with a number of countries in eastern Europe and in the West. An agreement of non-aggression and good neighbourliness with South Africa was signed on March 16, 1984 (the Nkomati Accord).

Trade with UK

	1988	1989
Imports from UK	£24,200,000	£20,268,000
Exports to UK	5,600,000	14,582,000

CAPITAL.—Ψ Maputo, estimated population (1990), 1,150,000. Other main ports are Ψ Beira and Ψ Nacala.
CURRENCY.—Metical (MT) of 100 centavos.
FLAG.—From top, three lateral bands of green, black and yellow separated by white stripes, and red half diamond pointing to centre of flag over which is superimposed a yellow star, book, and crossed rifle and hoe.
NATIONAL DAY.—June 25 (Independence Day).

BRITISH EMBASSY
Av. Vladimir I Lenine 310, CP 55, Maputo
[Maputo 420111/2/5/6/7]

Ambassador Extraordinary and Plenipotentiary, Her Excellency Maeve Geraldine Fort, CMG (1989).

First Secretary, D. S. Gordon-MacLeod (*Head of Chancery and Consul*); J. M. Winter (*Aid/Commercial*); C. A. Pagett, OBE (*Chancery*).
Second Secretary, J. Fielder.

British Council Representative, C. ffrench Blake.

MYANMAR (BURMA)
(Pyidaungsu Myanma Naingngandaw)

STATE LAW AND ORDER RESTORATION COUNCIL
(SLORC)
(as at June 30, 1990)

Chairman of SLORC, Prime Minister and Minister for Defence and Foreign Affairs, Gen. Saw Maung.
Vice-Chairman of SLORC, Gen. Than Shwe.
Energy and Mines, Vice-Adm. Maung Maung Khin.
Transport and Communications, Social Welfare and Labour, Lt.-Gen. Tin Tun.
Home and Religious Affairs, Information and Culture, Lt.-Gen. Phone Myint.
Construction, Co-operatives, Lt.-Gen. Aung Ye Kyaw.
Industry, Lt.-Gen. Sein Aung.
Livestock and Fisheries, Agriculture and Forests, Lt.-Gen. Chit Swe.
Trade and Planning, Finance, Brig. Abel.
Health and Education, Col. Pe Thein.
Secretaries, Maj.-Gen. Khin Nyunt, Maj.-Gen. Tin Oo.

EMBASSY OF THE UNION OF MYANMAR
19A Charles Street, Berkeley Square, W1X 8ER
[071–499 8841]

Ambassador Extraordinary and Plenipotentiary, His Excellency U Tin Hlaing (1989).

Area and Population.—The Union of Myanmar (Burma) forms the western portion of the Indo-Chinese district of the continent of Asia, lying between 9° 58′ and 28° N. latitude and 92° 11′ and 101° 9′ E. longitude, with an extreme length of approximately 1,200 miles and an extreme width of 575 miles. It has a sea coast on the Bay of Bengal to the south and west and a frontier with Bangladesh along the Naaf River (defined in 1964) and India to the north-west (defined in 1967). In the north and east the frontier with China was determined by a treaty with the People's Republic in October 1960, and has since been demarcated; there is a short frontier with Laos in the east, while the long finger of Tenasserim stretches southward along the west coast of the Malay Peninsula, forming a frontier with Thailand to the east. The total area of the Union is 261,218 sq. miles (676,552 sq. km), with a population (UN estimate 1988) of 39,966,000.

Physical Features.—There are four natural divisions. Arakan (with the Chin Hills region), the Irrawaddy basin, Tenasserim, including the Salween basin and extending southwards to the Myanmar-Thailand peninsula, and the elevated plateau on the east. Mountains enclose the Union on three sides, the highest point being Hka-kabo Razi (19,296 ft.) in the northern Kachin hills. Mt. Popa, 4,981 ft., in the Myingyan district is an extinct volcano and a well-known landmark in central Myanmar. The principal river systems are the Kaladan-Lemro in Arakan, the Irrawaddy-Chindwin and the Sittang in central Myanmar, and the Salween which flows through the Shan Plateau.

Races, Language and Religions.—The indigenous inhabitants who entered the country from the north and east are of similar racial types and speak languages of the Tibeto-Burman, Mon-Khmer and Thai groups. The three important non-indigenous elements are Indians, Chinese and those from the former East Pakistan. Burmese is the official language, but minority languages include Shan, Karen,

Chin, Kayah and the various Kachin dialects. English is spoken in educated circles. Buddhism is the religion of 85 per cent of the people, with 5 per cent Animists, 4 per cent Muslims, 4 per cent Hindus and less than 3 per cent Christians.

Government.—The Union of Burma (the name was officially changed to the Union of Myanmar in June 1989) became an independent republic outside the British Commonwealth on January 4, 1948 and remained a parliamentary democracy for 14 years. On March 2, 1962 the army took power and suspended the parliamentary Constitution. A Revolutionary Council of senior officers under General Ne Win took measures to create a Socialist State.

In January 1974 a new Constitution was adopted under which the highest authority was the People's Assembly with a Council of State, the senior executive body being the Council of Ministers.

After months of popular demonstrations and rioting and a series of Presidents throughout the summer of 1988, Gen. Saw Maung, leader of the armed forces, assumed power in September 1988. The People's Assembly, the Council of State and the Council of Ministers were abolished and replaced by the State Law and Order Restoration Council (SLORC) headed by Gen. Saw Maung as Prime Minister. The Constitution was effectively abrogated.

A People's Assembly Election Law was published in March 1989 committing the SLORC to hold multi-party elections. These were held on May 27 1990, resulting in a majority for the National League for Democracy. No date has yet been given for the transfer of power from the military to a new civilian government.

Political Divisions.—Myanmar is comprised of seven states (Chin, Kachin, Karen, Kayah, Mon, Rakhine, Shan) and seven divisions (Irrawaddy, Magwe, Mandalay, Pegu, Rangoon, Sagaing, Tenasserim).

Education.—The literacy rate is high compared to other Asian countries, there is no caste system and women engage freely in social intercourse and play an important part in agriculture and retail trade.

Most children attend primary school, and about four million are currently enrolled; in middle and high schools, 11 million. There are three universities, at Rangoon, Mandalay and Moulmein, and in 1986–87 the numbers graduating were 9,981. A number of autonomous institutes of university standard award their own degrees. Under the universities are three affiliated Degree Colleges and the Workers' College, Rangoon. There are also 14 two-year colleges affiliated to the universities, spread throughout the country. All higher educational establishments have been closed since June 1988.

There are three teachers' training institutes for middle and primary schools, and 13 teachers' training schools for primary only. Seven government technical institutes offer post-secondary technical training courses and 14 technical high schools train semi-skilled tradesmen. Six agricultural institutes offer training courses in agriculture and veterinary science; nine agricultural high schools train semi-skilled agriculturists. There are 34 vocational schools for weaving, handicrafts, etc.

Finance.—The chief sources of revenue are profits on state trading, income-tax, customs duties, commercial taxes and excise duties; the chief heads of expenditure are defence, education and police. The budget estimates for 1990–91 were: Revenue K38,270 million; Expenditure, K48,670 million.

Production, Industry and Commerce.—Three-quarters of the population depend on agriculture; the chief products are rice, oilseeds (sesamum and groundnut), maize, millet, cotton, beans, wheat, grain, tea, sugarcane, tobacco, jute and rubber. Rice was for many years the mainstay of the economy, but in 1985 teak overtook rice. The quantity of teak available for export in 1989 was 180,000 tons; the quantity of rice and by-products available for export was 160,000 tons.

Myanmar is rich in minerals, including petroleum, lead, silver, tungsten, zinc, tin, wolfram and gemstones. Of these, petroleum products are the most important. Oil is now being produced from oilfields in Myanaung, Prome and Shwepyitha and at Chauk, Yenangyaung, Mann, and Letpando. Production of crude oil in 1986–87 totalled 10,103,000 US barrels. There is a refinery at the main oilfield, Chauk, another at Syriam near Rangoon and a third at Mann. There has been a steady decline in Burma's oil production in recent years and the country is no longer self-sufficient. Onshore exploration continues. There has also been some offshore oil exploration on a small scale. Major reserves of natural gas have been discovered in the Martaban Gulf, which Myanmar is hoping to develop.

All industrial activity of any size is in the public sector. Under development plans, projects completed or under construction with overseas financial and technical assistance include the production of cement, bricks and tiles, sheet glass, steel sections, jute bags and twine, cotton yarns, cotton and cotton mixture cloth, pharmaceuticals, sugar, paper, plywood, urea fertilizers, soda ash, tractors and tyres; also a hydro-electric scheme and various irrigation works.

Faced with a serious foreign exchange shortage, Myanmar was included in the UN's list of Least Developed Countries in December 1987.

Trade with UK

	1988	1989
Imports from UK	£11,685,000	£12,217,000
Exports to UK	4,427,000	3,484,000

Communications.—The Irrawaddy and its chief tributary, the Chindwin, form important waterways, the main stream being navigable beyond Bhamo (900 miles from its mouth) and carrying much traffic.

The chief seaports are Rangoon, Moulmein, Akyab and Bassein.

The railway network covers 2,764 route miles, extending to Myitkyina, on the Upper Irrawaddy. There were 2,452 miles of Union highways and 11,767 miles of other main roads in 1982–83. The airport at Mingaladon, about 13 miles north of Rangoon, only handles limited international air traffic.

CAPITAL.—The chief city of lower Myanmar and the seat of the government of the Union is ψRangoon (Yangon), on the left bank of the Rangoon river, about 21 miles from the sea. The city contains the Shwe Dagon pagoda, much venerated by Buddhists. Population (1983): Rangoon District 3,973,872; city population 2,458,712.

Mandalay is the chief city of upper Myanmar, population (1983): Mandalay district 4,580,923; city 532,985; Moulmein of 219,991 and Bassein of 144,092. Pagan, on the Irrawaddy, SW of Mandalay, contains many sacred buildings.

CURRENCY.—Kyat (K) of 100 pyas.

FLAG.—The Union flag is red, with a canton of dark blue, inside which are a cogwheel and two rice ears surrounded by 14 white stars.

NATIONAL DAY.—January 4.

BRITISH EMBASSY
80 Strand Road (Box No. 638), Rangoon
[Rangoon 81700]

Ambassador Extraordinary and Plenipotentiary, His Excellency Julian Hartland-Swann (1990).

Deputy Head of Mission, First Secretary (Commercial) and Consul, C. S. M. Shelton.

Cultural Attaché and British Council Representative, Ralph Isaacs, MBE.

NEPAL

Sovereign, HM King Birendra Bir Bikram Shah Dev, *born* Dec. 28, 1945; *succeeded* Jan. 31, 1972; *crowned* Feb. 24, 1975; *married,* Feb. 1970, HM Queen Aishwara Rajya Laxmi Devi Shah.

Heir, HRH Crown Prince Dipendra Bir Bikram Shah Dev, *born* June 27, 1971.

COUNCIL OF MINISTERS
(as at May 31, 1990)

Prime Minister, Royal Palace, Defence and Foreign Affairs, Rt. Hon. Krishna Prasad Bhattarai.

Industry and Commerce, Rt. Hon. Sahana Pradhan.

Education and Culture, General Administration, Rt. Hon. Dr. Keshar Jung Rayamajhi.

Housing and Physical Planning, Rt. Hon. Achyut Raj Regmi.

Water Resources and Local Development, Rt. Hon. Mahendra Narayan Nidhi.

Home and Communications, Rt. Hon. Yog Prasad Upadhyaya.

Law and Justice, Labour and Social Welfare, Tourism, Rt. Hon. Nilambar Acharya.

Supply, Works and Transport, Rt. Hon. Marshal Julum Shakya.

Agriculture, Land Reforms and Management, Forest and Soil Conservation, Rt. Hon. Jhal Nath Khanal.

Finance, Rt. Hon. Dr. Devendra Raj Pandey.

Health, Rt. Hon. Dr. Mathura Prasad Shrestha.

ROYAL NEPALESE EMBASSY
12A Kensington Palace Gardens, W8 4QU
[071–229 1594/6231]

Ambassador Extraordinary and Plenipotentiary, His Excellency Maj.-Gen. Bharat Kesher Simha (1988).
First Secretary, Badri Prasad Khanal.

Area and Population.—Nepal lies between India and the Tibet Autonomous Region of China on the slopes of the Himalayas, and includes Mount Everest (29,078 ft). It has a total area of 54,342 sq. miles (140,747 sq. km), and a population estimated (1988) at about 18 million. The country comprises three distinct horizontal formations. In the south, joining the Indian plains, is the Terai, a fair proportion of which was covered with jungle. It has recently been more widely cultivated but wild life is preserved in parts. The region represents 23 per cent of the total land area and nearly 44 per cent of the population live there. The central belt of the country is hilly, but with many fertile valleys, leading up to the snowline at about 14,000 feet. The hills account for 42 per cent of the area of the country and about 48 per cent of the population. The remainder of the country, the Himalayan region, consists of high mountains which are sparsely inhabited. The country is drained by three great river systems rising within and beyond the Himalayan mountain ranges and eventually flowing into the Ganges in India.

The inhabitants are of mixed stock, with Mongolian characteristics prevailing in the north and Indian in the south. The official religion is Hinduism: 89·5 per cent of the population are Hindus and 6 per cent are Buddhist. Gautama Buddha was born in Nepal.

History and Government.—The country was originally divided into numerous hill clans and petty principalities, but Nepal emerged as a nation in the middle of the 18th century when its component parts were unified by the warrior Raja of Gorkha, Prithvi Narayan Shah, who founded the present Nepalese dynasty. In 1846 power was seized by Jung Bahadur Rana after a massacre of nobles, and he was the first of a line of hereditary Rana Prime Ministers who ruled Nepal for 104 years. During this time the role of the monarchs was mainly ceremonial.

In 1950–51 a revolutionary movement achieved its aim of breaking the hereditary power of the Ranas and restoring the monarchy to its former position. After ten years, during which various parties and individuals tried their hand at government, King Mahendra proscribed all political parties and assumed direct powers on December 16, 1960, with the object of leading a united country to democracy. In 1962 he introduced a new Constitution embodying a tiered, partyless system of panchayat (council) democracy, under which there were elected councils at village level which in turn elect members to district council and thence to zonal councils; a referendum in May 1980 decided in favour of retaining the panchayat system, with some reforms. Mass agitation for political reform led in April 1990 to the lifting of the ban of political parties and the abolition of the Panchyat system. An interim government was appointed. Elections are expected to be held in 1991.

Economy.—Nepal exports carpets, jute, handicrafts, garments, hides and skins, medicinal herbs, cardamom, pulses etc., and imports textiles, machinery and parts, transport equipment, medicine, construction materials etc. Tourism is the single largest commercial earner of foreign exchange (US$55·9 million in 1986–87).

The budget for the fiscal year 1988–89 was estimated at NRs. 19,520·2 million, of which NRs. 6,152,139 million was allocated to regular and NRs. 13,368,061 million to development expenditures. Revenue was estimated at NRs. 9,300 million, foreign aid and grants NRs. 8,890·2 million, and domestic borrowing NRs. 1,330 million.

Trade with UK

	1988	1989
Imports from UK	£4,968,000	£7,802,000
Exports to UK	9,384,000	8,306,000

A State Bank was inaugurated on April 26, 1956 to issue bank notes, regulate the Nepalese currency, fix foreign exchange rates and help in the preparation of a national budget. There are three commercial banks with branches throughout Nepal and three further banks, based only in Kathmandu, established since 1984 with approximately 49 per cent foreign bank participation.

Communications.—Kathmandu is connected with India by a road, the mountain section of which was built by India under the Colombo Plan, and to Tibet by a road to Kodari on the border which was built by the Chinese and opened on May 26, 1967. The Indian-aided Sunauli-Pokhara road (128 miles) was inaugurated in April 1972, and a road between Pokhara and Kathmandu, constructed by the Chinese, was opened in 1973. A link road between Mugling and Naryanghat, completed by the Chinese in 1981, has further improved communications between Kathmandu and the Terai. The East–West Highway (Mahendra Raj Marg) running along the entire length of the country is complete except for the Kohalpur-Mahahali section. The total length of roads in Nepal in 1987–88 was 6,525 km. British assistance has included major road projects, agriculture, education and forestry.

Telecommunication services, both domestic and international, are available from the Central Telegraph Office or hotels. There are international subscriber dialling facilities from Nepal to 35 countries. Nepal television was introduced in 1984.

Royal Nepal Airlines operates an extensive network of domestic flights, and there are international flights to India, Pakistan, Bangladesh, Myanmar, Singapore, Thailand, West Germany, and the Middle East.

CAPITAL.—Kathmandu, population (1981) 235,000. Other towns of importance are Biratnagar (94,000),

Lalitpur (81,000) and Bhaktapur (50,500) and Pokhara (48,500).

CURRENCY.—Nepalese rupee of 100 paisa.

FLAG.—Double pennant of crimson with blue border on peaks; white moon with rays in centre of top peak; white quarter sun, recumbent in centre of bottom peak.

NATIONAL ANTHEM.—May Glory Crown Our Illustrious Sovereign.

NATIONAL DAY.—February 18 (National Democracy Day).

BRITISH EMBASSY
Lainchaur Kathmandu, PO Box 106
[Kathmandu 411583]

Ambassador Extraordinary and Plenipotentiary, His Excellency Timothy George (1990).

First Secretary, A. Maclean (*Head of Chancery and Consul*).

Defence and Military Attaché, Col. M. G. Allen.
Vice-Consul, B. Mason.

British Council Representative, P. Moss, (PO Box 640), Kantipath, Kathmandu.

THE NETHERLANDS
(Koninkrijk der Nederlanden)

Queen of the Netherlands, Her Majesty Queen Beatrix Wilhelmina Armgard, KG, GCVO, *born* Jan. 31, 1938; *succeeded,* April 30, 1980, upon the abdication of her mother Queen Juliana; *married* March 10, 1966, HRH Prince Claus George Willem Otto Frederik Geert of the Netherlands, Jonkheer van Amsberg; and has *issue,* Prince Willem Alexander, *b.* April 27, 1967; Prince Johan Friso, *b.* Sept, 25, 1968; Prince Constantijn Christof, *b.* Oct. 11, 1969.

CABINET
(as at July 31, 1990)

Prime Minister, Ruud F. M. Lubbers (CDA).
Minister of General Affairs, Deputy PM and Minister of Finance, W. Kok (PvdA).
Home Affairs, Mrs. C. J. Dales (PvdA).
Foreign Affairs, H. van der Broek (CDA).
Development Co-operation, J. Pronk (PvdA).
Defence, A. L. ter Beek (PvdA).
Economic Affairs, Dr. J. E. Andriessen (CDA).
Justice, Prof. E. H. M. Hirsch Ballin (PvdA).
Agriculture and Fisheries, G. Braks (CDA).
Education and Science, Prof. Dr. J. M. M. Ritzen (PvdA).
Social Affairs and Employment, Antillian Affairs, Dr. B. de Vries (CDA).
Transport and Public Works, Mrs. H. May-Weggen (CDA).
Housing, Physical Planning and Environment, J. G. M. Alders (PvdA).
Welfare, Health and Culture, Mrs. H. d'Acona (PvdA).

CDA: Christian Democratic Appeal; PvdA: Labour Party.

ROYAL NETHERLANDS EMBASSY
38 Hyde Park Gate, SW7 5DP
[071–584 5040]

Ambassador Extraordinary and Plenipotentiary, His Excellency Johan Bernard Hoekman (1990).

Ministers Plenipotentiary, E. J. P. Roberts; R. R. Smit.
Counsellors, H. W. de Boer; P. A. Hamoen; A. E. Moses; A. Verduyn.
First Secretaries, M. R. O. Baron Bentinck; A. C. Brouwer; R. G. de Vos.
Defence, Naval and Air Attaché, Capt. A. H. A. G. Remmen.
Military Attaché, Col. J. Smit.

Area and Population.—The Kingdom of the Netherlands is a maritime country of western Europe, situated on the North Sea, in lat. 50° 46′–53° 34′ N. and long. 3° 22′–7° 14′ E., consisting of 12 provinces (Eastern and Southern Flevoland being amalgamated to form the twelfth province) and containing a total area of 15,770 sq. miles (40,844 sq. km). The population (1989 estimate) is 14,891,000. The live birth rate in 1988 was 187 per 1,000 of the population, and the death-rate was 124.

The land is generally flat and low, intersected by numerous canals and connecting rivers. The principal rivers are the Rhine, Maas, Yssel and Scheldt.

Language and Literature.—Dutch is a West-Germanic language of Saxon origin, closely akin to Old English and Low German. It is spoken in the Netherlands and the northern part of Belgium. It is also used in the Netherlands Antilles. Afrikaans, one of the two South African languages, has Dutch as its origin, but differs from it in grammar and pronunciation. There are six national papers, four of which are morning papers, and there are many regional daily papers.

Government.—In 1815 the Netherlands became a constitutional Kingdom under King William I, a Prince of Orange-Nassau, a descendant of the house which had taken a leading part in the destiny of the nation since the 16th century. The States-General consists of the *Eerste Kamer* (First Chamber) of 75 members, elected for four years by the Provincial Council; and the *Tweede Kamer* (Second Chamber) of 150 members, elected for four years by voters of 18 years and upwards. Members of the *Tweede Kamer* are paid. The most recent election to the Second Chamber was held in September 1989, and resulted in the formation of a centre-left coalition.

Production.—The chief agricultural products are potatoes, wheat, rye, barley, sugar beet, cattle, pigs, milk and milk products, cheese, butter, poultry, eggs, beans, peas, vegetables, fruit, flower bulbs, plants and cut flowers and there is an important fishing industry. Among the principal industries are engineering, both mechanical and electrical, electronics, nuclear energy, petro-chemicals and plastics, road vehicles, aircraft and defence equipment, shipbuilding repair, steel, textiles of all types, electrical appliances, metal ware, furniture, paper, cigars, sugar, liqueurs, beer, clothing etc.

Of a total GDP of US$213·2 billion in 1987, industry accounted for 20 per cent, agriculture for 4·3 per cent and mining 3·8 per cent.

Defence.—The armed forces are almost entirely committed to NATO. All ground and air units are assigned to the NATO Central Region, and naval forces to the Atlantic and Channel commands. Total armed forces number 106,183, which includes 48,720 conscripts and 1,495 women. In addition there are over 176,000 reservists. There is compulsory military service of 14–17 months.

Education.—Primary and secondary education is given in both denominational and state schools, the denominational schools being eligible for state assistance on equal terms with the state schools. Attendance at primary school is compulsory. The principal universities are at Leiden, Utrecht, Groningen, Amsterdam (2), Nijmegen and Rotterdam, and there are technical universities at Delft (polytechnic); Eindhoven (polytechnic), Enschede (polytechnic) and Wageningen (agriculture). Illiteracy is practically non-existent.

Communications.—The total extent of navigable rivers including canals, was 4,845 km at Jan. 1, 1985, and of metalled roads 97,189 km. In 1985 the total length of the railway system amounted to 2,867 km, of which 1,810 km were electrified. The mercantile marine in January 1985 consisted of 550 ships of total 3,461,000 gross registered tons. The total length of air routes covered by KLM (Royal Dutch Airlines) in 1985 was 370,640 km.

FINANCE

	1989
Budget Revenue	Guilders 147,000m
Budget Expenditure	170,000m

TRADE

The Dutch are traditionally a trading nation. Entrepot trade, banking and shipping are of particular importance to the economy. The geographical position of the Netherlands, at the mouths of the Rhine, Meuse and Scheldt, brings a large volume of transit trade to and from the interior of Europe to Dutch ports.

Principal trading partners are the Federal Republic of Germany and Belgium/Luxembourg. UK supplied 9·2 per cent of Netherlands imports in 1988 and took 7·7 per cent of Netherlands exports.

Excluding the construction industry, the index of industrial production in the Netherlands (1980 = 100) was 106 in 1988 and the index of industrial production per worker (1980 = 100) was 129 in 1988.

	1987	1988
	Guilders	
Imports	184,500m	196,300m
Exports	187,600m	203,700m

Trade with UK

	1987	1988
Imports from UK	£5,856,164,000	£6,515,325,000
Exports to UK	7,148,036,000	9,585,699,000

CAPITAL.—ΨAmsterdam, population 1,031,000 (urban agglomeration).

SEAT OF GOVERNMENT, The Hague (Den Haag or, in full, 's-Gravenhage), population 443,456.

Other principal cities ΨRotterdam 571,081; Utrecht, 229,969; Eindhoven, 191,675; Haarlem 151,025; Groningen 168,119; Tilburg 153,812.

CURRENCY.—Netherlands guilder or florin of 100 cents.

FLAG.—Three horizontal bands of red, white and blue.

NATIONAL ANTHEM.—Wilhelmus.

BRITISH EMBASSY
Lange Voorhout 10, The Hague, 2514 ED
[The Hague 364 5800]

Ambassador Extraordinary and Plenipotentiary, His Excellency Sir Michael Romilly Heald Jenkins, KCMG (1988).

Counsellors, R. P. Flower; A. D. Sprake (*Commercial/Agriculture*).

Defence and Naval Attaché, Capt. M. Bickley, RN.

Military and Air Attaché, Lt.-Col. P. Cook.

First Secretary and Head of Chancery, P. J. Sullivan.

British Council Representative, J. Andrews, Keizersgracht 343, 1016 EH Amsterdam.

NETHERLANDS-BRITISH CHAMBER OF COMMERCE, The Dutch House, 307–308 High Holborn, WC1V 7LS.

UK OFFICE IN THE HAGUE, Holland Trade House, Bezuidenhoutseweg 181, 2594 AH The Hague.

OVERSEAS TERRITORIES

ARUBA covers an area of 75 sq. miles (193 sq. km) with a population (1988 estimate) of 62,500. The island of Aruba was from 1828 part of the Dutch West Indies and from 1845 part of the Netherlands Antilles. On January 1, 1986 it became a separate territory within the Kingdom of the Netherlands. The 1983 Constitutional Conference agreed that Aruba's separate status would last for ten years from 1986, after which the island would become fully independent.

The economy of Aruba is based largely on tourism. In 1986 there were over 180,000 tourists.

Governor, F. B. Tromp.

Prime Minister, Nelson Oduber.

Trade with UK

	1988	1989
Imports from UK	£7,315,000	£12,751,000
Exports to UK	133,000	653,000

CAPITAL.—ΨOranjestad (population 20,000); and Sint Nicolaas (17,000).

CURRENCY.—Aruban florin.

NETHERLANDS ANTILLES comprise certain islands in the West Indies (Curaçao, Bonaire, part of St. Martin, St. Eustatius, and Saba). The islands cover an area of 308 sq. miles (800 sq. km) with a population (1986 estimate) of 188,000. The Netherlands Antilles (which have a federal parliament) are largely self-governing under the terms of the Realm Statute which took effect on December 29, 1954.

The economy of the Netherlands Antilles is based on small manufacturing industries. The soil is too poor to permit large-scale agriculture and most products for consumption, and industrial raw materials must be imported.

Governor, Dr. R. A. Römer (1983).

Prime Minister, Mrs. Maria Liberia Peters.

Trade with UK

	1988	1989*
Imports from UK	£20,089,000	£19,396,000
Exports to UK	7,823,000	5,115,000
*Curaçao		

CAPITAL.—ΨWillemstad (on Curaçao) (pop. 50,000).

CURRENCY.—Netherlands Antilles guilder of 100 cents.

NICARAGUA
(República de Nicaragua)

President, Minister of Defence, Violeta Barrios de Chamorro, *inaugurated* April 25, 1990.
Vice-President, Virgilio Godoy.

COUNCIL OF MINISTERS
(as at May 31, 1990)

Minister to the Presidency, Antonio Lacayo.
External Relations and Co-operation, Enrique Dreyfus.
Interior, Carlos Hurtado.
Finance, Silvio de Franco.
Secretariat of Planning and Budget, Erwin Krugger.
Construction and Transport, Gilberto Cuadra.
Health, Ernesto Salmerón.
Agriculture, Jaime Cuadra.
Labour, Francisco Rosales.
Education, Sofonias Cisneros.

EMBASSY OF NICARAGUA
8 Gloucester Road, SW7 4PP
[071–584 4365]

Ambassador Extraordinary and Plenipotentiary, new appointment awaited.

Nicaragua is the largest state of Central America, with a long seaboard on both the Atlantic and Pacific Oceans, situated between 10° 45'–15° N. lat. and 83° 40'–87° 38' W. long., containing an area of 50,193 sq. miles (130,000 sq. km). It has a population (UN estimate 1988) of 3,622,000 of whom about three-quarters are of mixed blood. Another 15 per cent are white, mostly of pure Spanish descent and the remaining 10 per cent are West Indians or Indians. The latter group includes the Mosquitos, who live on the Atlantic coast and were formerly under British protection.

Government.—The eastern coast of Nicaragua was touched by Columbus in 1502, and in 1518 was overrun by Spanish forces under Davila, and formed part of the Spanish Captaincy-General of Guatemala until 1821, when its independence was secured. In 1927 Augusto Cesar Sandino began a guerrilla war against the occupation of Nicaragua by US Marines, which continued until they were expelled in 1933. Sandino was assassinated by Anastasio Somoza, Director of the National Guard, and in 1936 Somoza assumed the Presidency. He was succeeded in power by his sons Luis and Anastasio Somoza, until 1979 when the family and the National Guard were overthrown by guerrillas of the Sandinista National Liberation Front. A Junta of National Reconstruction subsequently took power. Elections for President, Vice-President and a National Assembly were held in November 1984, and in January 1985 they replaced the Junta and the Council of State.

After ten years in power, the Sandinistas lost their parliamentary majority in elections held in February 1990. A coalition of former opposition parties, Unión Nacional de Opositora (UNO) now holds the majority.

Agriculture and Industry.—The country is mainly agricultural. The major crops are cotton, coffee (30 per cent of total export earnings), sugar cane, tobacco, sesame and bananas. Beans, rice, maize and ipecacuanha, livestock and timber production are also important. However, fishing, forestry, grain and cattle production have been hit by the civil war in the main growing areas. Nicaragua possesses deposits of gold and silver.

Communications.—There are 252 miles of railway, all on the Pacific side and approximately 5,500 miles of telegraph. There are 51 radio stations and two television stations in Managua. An automatic telephone system has been installed in the capital and extended to all major cities. A ground station

for satellite communication was inaugurated in 1973. Transport except on the Pacific slope, is still attended with difficulty but many new roads have either been opened or are under construction. The Inter-American Highway runs from the Honduras frontier in the north to the Costa Rican border in the south; the inter-oceanic highway runs from the Corinto on the Pacific coast via Managua to Rama, where there is a natural waterway to Bluefields on the Atlantic. The country's main airport is at Managua. The chief port is Corinto on the Pacific.

Language and Literature.—The official language of the country is Spanish and the majority profess Catholicism, although the English language and the Moravian Church are widespread on the Atlantic coast. There are three daily newspapers published at Managua, apart from the official Gazette (*La Gaceta*). A national literacy campaign in 1980 has reduced illiteracy to 12 per cent. There are universities at León and Managua.

Trade with UK

	1988	1989
Imports from UK	£6,856,000	£6,985,000
Exports to UK	725,000	918,000

Considerable quantities of foodstuffs are imported as well as cotton goods, jute, iron and steel, machinery and petroleum products. The chief exports are cotton, coffee, beef, gold, sugar, cottonseed and bananas.

CAPITAL.—Managua, population 615,000. The centre was almost totally destroyed in the earthquake of December 1972. León, 158,577; Granada, 72,640; Masaya, 78,308; Chinandega, 144,291.

CURRENCY.—Córdoba (C$) of 100 centavos.

FLAG.—Horizontal stripes of blue, white and blue, with the Nicaraguan coat of arms in the centre of the white stripe.

NATIONAL DAY.—September 15.

NATIONAL ANTHEM.—Salve A Ti Nicaragua (Hail, Nicaragua).

BRITISH EMBASSY
El Reparto 'Los Robles', Primera Etapa, Entrada Principal de la Carretera de Masaya, Managua, Nicaragua.
[Managua 70034]

British Ambassador and Consul-General, (resident in San José, Costa Rica).

NIGER
(République du Niger)

President, Minister of Defence, Brig.-Gen. Ali Saibou.

MINISTERS
(as at May 31, 1990)

Prime Minister, Aliou Mahamidou.
Foreign Affairs and Co-operation, Mahamane Sani Bako.
Social and Women's Affairs, Moumouni Aissata.
Youth, Sport and Culture, Capt. Abdoulrahamane Seydou..
Interior, Lt.-Col. Tanja Mamadou.
Education, Lt.-Col. Issa Amsa.
Health, Lt.-Col. Ousmane Gazere.
Equipment, Maj. Issaka Ousmane.
Transport and Tourism, Cmdt. Hamadou Moussa Gros.
Agriculture and Livestock, Adamou Souna.
Finance, Wassalke Boukari.
Planning, Almoustapha Soumaila.
Mining and Energy, Abdou Insa.
Water and the Environment, Karadji Ayarga.

Minister-Delegate to the Presidency in charge of Administrative Reform, Mamane Boukari.
Justice, Keeper of the Seals, Ali Bandiere.
Civil Service and Employment, Dagra Mamadou.
Communication, Khamed Abdoulaye.
Economic Promotion, Nassirou Sabo.
Higher Education, Research and Technology, Aboubacar Adamou.

Situated in west central Africa, between 12° and 24° N. and 0° and 16° E., Niger has common boundaries with Algeria and Libya in the north, Chad, Nigeria, Benin, Mali and Burkina.

It has an area of about 489,191 sq. miles (1,267,000 sq. km), with a population (UN estimate, 1988) of 6,688,000. Apart from a small region along the Niger Valley in the south-west near the capital the country is entirely savanna or desert. The main ethnic groups are the Hausa (54 per cent) in the south, the Songhai and Djerma in the south-west, the Fulani, the Beriberi–Manga, and the nomadic Tuareg in the north. The official language is French.

The first French expedition arrived in 1891 and the country was fully occupied by 1914. It decided on December 18, 1958 to remain an autonomous republic within the French Community; full independence outside the Community was proclaimed on August 3, 1960. Special agreements with France, covering financial and cultural matters, technical assistance, defence, etc., were signed in Paris on April 24, 1961. These are now being revised.

The constitution of Niger, adopted on November 8, 1960, provided for a presidential system of government, modelled on that of the United States and the French Fifth Republic, and a single Chamber National Assembly. In April 1974 Lt.-Col. Seyni Kountché seized power, suspended the Constitution, dissolved the National Assembly, and suppressed all political organizations. He then set up a Supreme Military Council with himself as President. President Kountché died on November 10, 1987 and was succeeded peacefully by his cousin, Col. Ali Saibou.

Since coming to power, Ali Saibou has restored a measure of normal political life. There is a single political party, the Mouvement National de la Société de Developpement (MNSD). A new constitution was adopted by referendum in September 1989; President Saibou was re-elected in December 1989.

Finance.—The 1989 General Budget allocation was CFA 220,100 million.

Trade.—The cultivation of ground-nuts and the production of livestock are the main industries and provide two of the main exports. A company formed by the Government, the French Atomic Energy Authority and private interests is exploiting uranium deposits at Arlit, and this is the main export. There is also some oil exploration.

Trade with UK

	1988	1989
Imports from UK	£7,562,000	£6,862,000
Exports to UK	1,359,000	1,472,000

CAPITAL.—Niamey, population 410,000.
CURRENCY.—Franc CFA of 100 centimes.
FLAG.—Three horizontal stripes, orange, white and green with an orange disc in the middle of the white stripe.
NATIONAL DAY.—December 18.

British Ambassador, (resident in Abidjan, Côte d'Ivoire).

NORWAY
(Kongeriket Norge)

King, HM Olav V, KG, KT, GCB, GCVO, *b.* July 2, 1903; *succeeded*, Sept. 21, 1957, on death of his father

King Haakon VII; *married* March 21, 1929, Princess Märtha of Sweden (1901–54); having *issue*, Prince Harald (*see below*), Princess Ragnhild (*b.* 1930), and Princess Astrid (*b.* 1932).

Heir-Apparent, HRH Prince Harald, GCVO, *b.* Feb. 21, 1937; *m.* Aug. 29, 1968, Sonja Haraldsen, and has *issue* Princess Märtha Louise, *b.* Sept. 22, 1971; and Prince Haakon Magnus, *b.* July 20, 1973.

CABINET
(as at June 30, 1990)

Prime Minister, Jan P. Syse (H).
Foreign Affairs, Kjell Magne Bondevik (KrF).
Local Government, Johan J. Jakobsen (SP).
Health and Social Affairs, Wenche Frogn Sellæg (H).
Finance, Arne Skauge (H).
Industry, Petter Thomassen (H).
Petroleum and Energy, Eivind Reiten (SP).
Church and Cultural Affairs, Eleonore Bjartveit (KrF).
Defence, Per Ditlev-Simonsen (H).
Agriculture, Anne Vik (SP).
Development Co-operation, Tom Vraalsen (SP).
Transport and Communications, Lars Gunnar Lie (KrF).
Family and Consumer Affairs, Solveig Sollie (KrF).
Education and Research, Einar Steensnæs (KrF).
Justice and the Police, Else Bugge Fougner (H).
Environment, Kristin Hille Valla (SP).
Fisheries, Svein Munkejord (H).
Trade and Shipping, Kaci Kullmann Five (H).
Labour and Government Administration, Kristin Clemet (H).

SP: Senterpartiet (Centre Party); H: Höyre (Conservative Party); KrF: Kristelig Folkeparti (Christian People's Party).

ROYAL NORWEGIAN EMBASSY
25 Belgrave Square, SW1X 8QD
[071–235 7151]

Ambassador Extraordinary and Plenipotentiary, His Excellency Kjell Eliassen (1989).
Minister-Counsellor, vacant.
Counsellors, Paul Moe (*Press and Cultural*); Marius Hauge (*Fisheries*); Eva Bugge (*Economic*); Viggo Smestad (*Commercial*).
First Secretaries, R. Aasheim (*Political*); T. S. Kijewski (*Consul*); L. Engesaeth (*Economic*).
Second Secretaries, Katja Nordgaard (*Press, Information and Cultural*).

Area and Population.—Norway is a kingdom in the northern and western portion of the Scandinavian peninsula, and was founded in AD 872. It is 1,752 km in length, its greatest width about 430 km. The length of the coastline is 2,542 km, and the frontier between Norway and the neighbouring countries is 2,542 km (Sweden 1,619 km, Finland 727 km and USSR 196 km). It is divided into 19 counties (*fylker*) and comprises an area of 149,282 sq. miles (386,638 sq. km), of which Svalbard and Jan Mayen have a combined area of 24,101 sq. km, with a total population (April 1989) of 4,224,606.

The Norwegian coastline is extensive, deeply indented with numerous fjords, and fringed with an immense number of rocky islands. The surface is mountainous, consisting of elevated and barren tablelands, separated by deep and narrow valleys. At the North Cape the sun does not appear to set from the second week in May to the last week in July, causing the phenomenon known as the Midnight Sun; conversely, there is no apparent sunrise from about November 18 to January 23. During the long winter nights are seen the multiple coloured Northern Lights or Aurora Borealis, which have a maximum intensity in a line crossing North America from

Alaska to Labrador and Northern Europe to the Arctic coast and Siberia.

Language and Literature.—Old Norse literature is among the most ancient and richest in Europe. Norwegian in both its present forms is closely related to other Scandinavian languages. Independence from Denmark (1814) and resurgent nationalism led to the development of 'new Norwegian' based on dialects, which now has equal official standing with 'bokmål', in which Danish influence is more obvious. This was formed in the time of the Reformation, and Ludvig Holberg (1684–1754) is regarded as the father of Norwegian literature, though the modern period begins with the patriotic and romantic writings of Henrik Wergeland (1808–1845). Some of the famous names are Henrik Ibsen (1828–1906), Bjørnstjerne Bjørnson (1832–1910), Nobel Prizewinner in 1903, and the novelists Jonas Lie (1833–1908), Alexander Kielland (1849–1906), Knut Hamsun (1859–1952) and Sigrid Undset (1882–1949), the latter two also Nobel Prizewinners. In 1990 there were 155 daily newspapers.

Government.—From 1397 to 1814 Norway was united with Denmark, and from November 4, 1814 with Sweden, under a personal union which was dissolved on June 7, 1905, when Norway regained complete independence. Under the constitution of May 17, 1814, the *Storting* (Parliament) itself elects one-quarter of its members to constitute the *Lagting* (Upper Chamber), the other three-quarters forming the *Odelsting* (Lower Chamber). Legislative questions alone are dealt with by both parts in separate sittings.

A three-party coalition government with a Conservative Prime Minister replaced the previous Labour government in October 1986.

Production.—The cultivated area is about 8,636 sq. km (2·3 per cent of total surface area); forests cover nearly 25 per cent; the rest consists of highland pastures or uninhabitable mountains.

The Gulf Stream pours from 140 to 170 million cubic feet of warm water per second into the sea around Norway and causes the temperature to be higher than the average for the latitude. It brings shoals of herring and cod into the fishing grounds and causes a warm current of air over the west coast, making it possible to cultivate potatoes and barley in latitudes which in other countries are perpetually frozen. In normal years the quantity of fish caught by Norwegian fishing vessels is greater than that of any other European country except USSR. In 1987 the total catch amounted to 1,867,720 tonnes.

The chief industries are manufactures, agriculture and forestry, fisheries, mining, production of metals and ferro-alloys and shipping. Also in recent years industries providing both manufactured products and services for the development of North Sea oil and gas resources have assumed growing importance. In 1988, the total workforce was 2,163,000 of which 324,000 persons were employed in Norwegian industry. Manufactures are aided by great resources of hydro-electric power. Actual production in 1988 amounted to 110,063 Gwh.

Defence.—Norway is a member of the North Atlantic Treaty Organization, and the Headquarters of Allied Forces, Northern Europe, is situated near Oslo. The period of compulsory national service is 15 months (without refresher training) in the Navy and Air Force, and 12 months (with refresher training) in the Army.

Education from 7 to 16 is free and compulsory in the 'basic schools' maintained by the municipalities with state grants-in-aid. The majority of the pupils receive post-compulsory schooling at 'upper secondary' schools, colleges of education (19), regional colleges akin to polytechnics (12), universities (4) and other university-level specialist institutions.

Communications.—The total length of railways open at the end of 1988 was 4,070 km, excluding private lines. There are 87,603 km of public roads in Norway (including urban streets). At the end of 1988, 2,893,639 road motor vehicles were registered.

Scheduled internal air services are operated by Scandinavian Airlines System (SAS) on behalf of Det Norske Luftfartselskap (DNL), by Braathens South American and Far East Airtransport (SAFE), and by Widerøes Flyveselskap AS.

The Mercantile Marine, 1988, consisted of 1,532 vessels of 12,921,932 gross tons (vessels above 100 gross tons, excluding fishing boats, floating whaling factories, tugs, salvage vessels, icebreakers and similar types of vessel).

FINANCE

	1987	1988
Total Revenue	K321,677,000	K342,900,000
Total Expenditure	282,648,000	309,717,000

TRADE

	1987	1988
Total imports	K211,794m	K217,455m
Total exports	199,731m	213,117m

Trade with UK

	1988	1989
Imports from UK	£1,053,613,000	£1,056,506,000
Exports to UK	3,074,312,000	3,637,119,000

The chief imports are raw materials, motor vehicles, chemicals, motor spirit, fuel and other oils; coal, ships and machinery; together with manufactures of silk, cotton and wool. The exports consist chiefly of crude oil and gas, manufactured goods, fish and products of fish (as canned fish, whale oils), pulp, paper, iron ore and pyrites, nitrate of lime, stone, calcium carbide, aluminium, ferro-alloys, zinc, nickel, cyanamides, etc.

CAPITAL.—ΨOslo (including Aker), population (Jan. 1987) 450,808. Other towns are ΨTrondheim

135,542; ΨBergen 209,912; ΨStavanger 96,316;
ΨKristiansand 63,637; ΨDrammen 51,807; ΨTromsø
49,358.

CURRENCY.—Krone of 100 øre.

FLAG.—Red, with white-bordered blue cross.

NATIONAL ANTHEM.—Ja, Vi Elsker Dette Landet
(Yes, we love this country).

NATIONAL DAY.—May 17 (Constitution Day).

BRITISH EMBASSY
Thomas Heftyesgate 8, 0244 Oslo 2
[Oslo 55 24 00]

Ambassador Extraordinary and Plenipotentiary, His
Excellency David John Edward Ratford, CMG
(1990).

Counsellors, R. G. Short, MVO (*Head of Chancery and
Consul General*); Dr. C. P. Burdess, LVO (*Economic
and Commercial*).

First Secretaries, J. Venning; A. L. Wotton (*Economic
and Commercial*); R. H. Tonkin (*Management*).

Defence and Air Attaché, Wg. Cdr. S. A. Wrigley.

Naval Attaché, Cdr. H. L. Foxworthy.

Military Attaché, Lt.-Col. W. R. de W. Lash.

BRITISH CONSULAR OFFICES

There is a British Consular Office at *Oslo* and
Honorary Consulates at *Bergen, Tromsø, Alesund,
Kristiansund, Stavanger, Trondheim, Kristiansand,
Haugesund* and *Harstad*.

British Council Representative, D. N. Constable,
Fridtjof Nansens Plass 5,0160, Oslo 1.

TERRITORIES

SVALBARD. The Svalbard Archipelago lies between
74°–81° N. lat. and between 10°–35° E. long., with an
estimated area of 24,295 square miles. The archipelago consists of a main island, known as Spitsbergen
(15,200 sq. miles); North East Land, closely adjoining
and separated by Hinlopen Strait; the Wiche Islands,
separated from the mainland by Olga Strait; Barents
and Edge Islands, separated from the mainland by
Stor Fjord (or Wybe Jansz Water); Prince Charles
Foreland, to the W.; Hope Island, to the SE; Bear
Island (68 square miles) 127 miles to the S.; with many
similar islands in the neighbourhood of the main
group.

By Treaty (Feb. 9, 1920) the sovereignty of Norway
over the Spitsbergen (Pointed Mountain) Archipelago was recognized by other nations, and on August
14, 1925 Norway assumed sovereignty. In September
1941 Allied forces (British, Canadian and Norwegian)
landed on the main island. After destruction of the
accumulated stocks of coal and dismantling of mining
machinery and the wireless installation, the Norwegian inhabitants (about 600) were evacuated to a
British port and the Russians (about 1,500) to the
USSR. After the war the Norwegian mining plants
were rebuilt. In addition to those engaged in coal-
mining, the archipelago is also visited by hunters for
seals, foxes and polar bears.

South Cape is 355 miles from the Norwegian coast.
Ice Fjord is 520 miles from Tromsø, 650 miles from
Murmansk, and 1,300 miles from Aberdeen. Transit
from Tromsø to Green Harbour takes 2–3 days; from
Aberdeen 5–6 days.

JAN MAYEN, an island in the Arctic Ocean (70° 49′–
71° 9′ N. lat. and 7° 53′–9° 5′ W. long.) was joined to
Norway by law of February 27, 1930.

Norwegian Antarctic Territories

BOUVET ISLAND (54° 26′ S. lat. and 3° 24′ E. long.)
was declared a dependency of Norway by law of Feb.
27, 1930.

PETER THE FIRST ISLAND (68° 48′ S. lat. and 90° 35′
W. long.), was declared a dependency of Norway by
resolution of Government, May 1, 1931.

PRINCESS RAGNHILD LAND (from 70° 30′ to 68° 40′ S.
lat. and 24° 15′ to 33° 30′ E. long.) has been claimed as
Norwegian since February 17, 1931.

QUEEN MAUD LAND.—On January 14, 1939 the
Norwegian Government declared the area between
20° W. and 45° E., adjacent to Australian Antarctica,
to be Norwegian territory.

OMAN
(The Sultanate of Oman)

*Sultan, Prime Minister, Minister of Foreign Affairs,
Defence and Finance*, HM Qaboos Bin-Said, *suc-
ceeded* on deposition of Sultan Said bin Taimur,
July 23, 1970.

COUNCIL OF MINISTERS
(as at June 30, 1990)

Personal Representative of HM The Sultan, HH
Sayyid Thuwaini bin Shihab Al Said.

Agriculture and Fisheries, HE Muhammad bin Abdullah bin Zahir al Hinai.

Civil Service, HE Ahmad Bin Abdul Nabi Macki.

Commerce and Industry, HE Col. Salim bin Abdullah
al Ghazali.

Communications, HE Hamoud bin Abdullah al Har-
thi.

Deputy PM, Security and Defence, HH Sayyid Fahr
bin Taimur Al Said.

Diwan of Royal Court Affairs, HE Sayyid Saif bin
Hamad bin Saud.

Education and Youth Affairs, HE Yahya bin Mahfuth
al Manthari.

Electricity and Water, HE Sheikh Mohammed bin Ali
al Qatabi.

Environment, HH Sayyid Shabib bin Taimur Al Said.

Deputy PM, Financial and Economic Affairs, HE Qais
bin Abdul Munim al Zawawi.

Minister of State for Foreign Affairs, HE Yusuf bin
Alawi bin Abdullah.

Health, HE Dr. Ali bin Muhammad bin Musa.

Housing, HE Malik bin Sulaiman al Ma'mari.

Information, HE Abdul Aziz bin Muhammad al Rowas.

Interior, HE Sayyid Badr bin Saud bin Harib al Bu
Saidi.

Justice, Awqaf and Islamic Affairs, HE Sayyid Hilal
Bin Saud bin Hamad Al Bu Saidi.

Labour and Vocational Training, HE Sayyid al
Mutassim bin Hamoud al bu Saidi.

Deputy Prime Minister for Legal Affairs, HH Sayyid
Fahd bin Mahmoud Al Said.

National Heritage and Culture, HH Sayyid Faisal bin
Ali Al Said.

Palace Office Affairs, HE Lt.-Gen. Ali bin Majid al
Maamari.

Petroleum and Minerals, HE Said bin Ahmad bin
Said al Shanfari.

Posts, Telegraphs and Telephones, HE Ahmad bin
Suwaidan al Balushi.

Regional Municipalities, HE Sheikh Amor bin Shu-
wain al Hosni.

Social Affairs, HE Sheikh Mustahail bin Ahmad al
Mashani.

Water Resources, HE Khalfan bin Nasr al Waihibi.

Minister of State and Wali of Dhofar, HE Sayyid
Musallim Bin Ali Al Bu Saidi.

Secretary General of the Development Council, HE
Muhammed bin Musa al Yousef.

President, Consultative Council of the State, HE
Sheikh Abdullah Bin Ali Bin Muhammad Al Qutbi.

Secretary to the Council of Ministers, HE Sayyid
Hamoud bin Faisal Al Bu Saidi.

EMBASSY OF THE SULTANATE OF OMAN
44A/B Montpelier Square, SW7 1JJ
[071–584 6782/3/4]

Ambassador Extraordinary and Plenipotentiary, His
Excellency Abdulla Mohammed Al-Dhahab (1990).

The independent Sultanate of Oman lies at the
eastern corner of the Arabian Peninsula. Its seaboard
is nearly 1,000 miles long and extends from near Tibat
on the west coast of the Musandam Peninsula round
to Ras Darbat Ali, with the exception of the stretch
between Dibba and Kalba on the east coast which
belongs to Sharjah and Fujairah of the United Arab
Emirates. Ras Darbat Ali marks the boundary
between the Sultanate and the southern border of
the Republic of Yemen. The Sultanate extends inland
to the borders of the Rub al Khali, or Empty Quarter
of the Arabian Desert.

The area of Oman has been estimated at 82,030 sq.
miles (212,457 sq. km), and the population (UN
estimate 1988) is 1,378,000. The inhabitants of the
north are for the most part Arab but there are large
communities of Hindus, Khojas and Baluch, in
addition to Omanis of Zanzibari origin. In Dhofar
there is also a large proportion of Omanis of Zanzibari
origin around Salalah, but in the mountains the
inhabitants are either of pure Arab descent or belong
to tribes of pre-Arab origin, the Qarra and Mahra,
who speak their own dialects of semitic origin.

Physically and historically modern Oman can be
split into two main parts, the north and the south,
divided by a large tract of desert. Northern Oman
has three main sections. The Batinah, the coastal
plain, varies in width from 30 miles in the neighbourhood of Suwaiq to almost nothing at Muscat where
the mountains descend abruptly to the sea. The plain
is fertile, with date gardens extending over its full
length of 150 miles. The Hajjar is a mountain spine
running from north-west to south-east, reaching
nearly 10,000 feet in height on Jabal Akhdar. For the
most part the mountains are barren, but numerous
valleys penetrate the central massif of Jabal Akhdar
and in these there is considerable cultivation irrigated by wells or a system of underground canals
called *falajs* which tap the water table. The two
plateaus leading from the western slopes of the
mountains, the Dhahirah in the north and the
Sharqia in the south-east, also have centres of
settlements and cultivation. They fall from an
average height of 1,000 feet into the sands of the
Empty Quarter. The north is separated from the
south by nearly 400 miles of inhospitable country
crossed by one trunk road, the only land link. Dhofar,
the southern province, is the only part of the Arabian
Peninsula to be touched by the south-west monsoon.
Temperatures are more moderate than in the north
and sugar cane and coconuts are grown on the coastal
plain, while cattle are bred on the mountains.

Government.—A Consultative Council for the
State was established by Sultanic decree on October
18, 1981. The Council is a nominated body consisting
of 55 members (36 representing the public and 19
representing the government). The Council's jurisdiction is confined to economic affairs and social
development.

Commerce and Trade.—Trade is mainly with the
UAE, UK, Japan, the Netherlands, USA, Federal
Republic of Germany, France and India. Total
imports for the year 1988 were OR846,430,275. Chief
imports were machinery, cars, building materials,
food and telecommunications equipment.

Trade with UK

	1988	1989
Imports from UK	£344,875,000	£298,974,000
Exports to UK	146,751,000	84,009,000

Production.—Petroleum Development (Oman)
Ltd. (owned 60 per cent by Oman Government and 34
per cent by Shell) began exporting oil in 1967.
Concessions (off and on shore) are held by several
major international companies. The current level of
oil production is about 650,000 barrels per day,
planned to increase to 700,000.

Development.—For many years the Sultanate
was a poor country with a total annual income of less
than £1,000,000. The advent of oil revenues since
1967 and the change of regime in 1970 led to the
initiation of a wide-ranging development programme,
especially concerned with health, education and
communications. New hospitals have been completed
in the main provincial centres and there are now
nearly 50 hospitals with around 3,400 beds; 759
schools, with 327,131 pupils, were in operation in
1989. A gas turbine power station operates at Rusail,
where there is also a 200 plot industrial estate. There
is a power station and a desalination plant near
Muscat and flour, animal feed, cement and copper
production facilities.

Communications.—Since 1972 ships have been
using Port Qaboos at Matrah, where eight deep water
berths have been constructed as part of the new
harbour facilities.

A modern telecommunications service to the main
population centres and an international service are
operated by the General Telecommunications Organization. There are good tarmac roads linking most
main population centres of the country with the
coast and with the towns of the UAE. There is now
over 4,000 km of asphalted road in the Sultanate.

CAPITAL.—Ψ Muscat, estimated population
400,000. The commercial centre has grown around
Mutrah, 3 miles away and the main port, and Ruwi.
The main towns on the northern coast are ΨSur,
ΨBarka and ΨSohar. The main town of Dhofar is
Salalah.

CURRENCY.—Rial Omani (OR) of 1,000 baiza.

FLAG.—Red, green and white with crossed daggers
in red sector.

NATIONAL DAY.—November 18.

BRITISH EMBASSY
PO Box 300, Muscat
[Muscat 738501/5]

Ambassador Extraordinary and Plenipotentiary, His
Excellency Terence Joseph Clark, CMG, CVO (1990).
Counsellor, A. M. Layden (*Deputy Head of Mission*).
Defence Attaché, Brig. M. J. Smith.
Naval and Air Attaché, Cdr. K. Harris, OBE, R.N
First Secretaries, B. Baldwin; N. H. Bates.

British Council Representative, R. A. Steedman, PO
Box 7090, Mutrah, Oman.

PANAMA
(República de Panama)

President, Guillermo Endara Galimany, *sworn in*
December 27, 1989.
*First Vice-President and Minister of Government and
Justice*, Dr. Ricardo Arias Calderon.
*Second Vice-President and Minister of Planning and
Political Economy*, Guillermo Ford Boyd.

CABINET
(as at May 31, 1990)

Foreign Affairs, Dr. Julio Linares.
Treasury and Finance, Dr. Mario Galindo.
Agricultural Development, Dr. Ezequiel Rodriguez.
Commerce and Industry, Juan Chevalier.
Labour and Social Welfare, Jorge Rosas.
Health, Dr. Jose Castillero.
Housing, Raul Figueroa.

Education, Prof. Ada de Gordon.
Presidency, Julio Harris.
Public Works, Rene Orillac.

EMBASSY OF THE REPUBLIC OF PANAMA
119 Crawford Street, W1H 1AF
[071–487 5633]

Ambassador Extraordinary and Plenipotentiary, His
Excellency Teodoro F. Franco (1990).
Minister-Counsellor, Elena Barletta de Nottebohm.

There are also Consular Offices at *Liverpool* and
London (24 Tudor Street, EC4Y 0JD).

Panama lies on the isthmus of that name which
connects N. and S. America. The area of the Republic
is 29,762 sq. miles (77,082 sq. km), the population
(preliminary Census result 1990) 2,314,391. Spanish
is the official language.

Government.—After a revolt in November 1903,
Panama declared its independence from Colombia
and established a separate Government. After 1968
control of Panama was increasingly taken over by
Gen. Omar Torrijos, Commander of the National
Guard, following a military coup. In 1972 General
Torrijos was designated as 'Leader of the Revolution'
with wide overriding powers. In October 1978 he
withdrew from the government, and Dr. Aristides
Royo was elected President by the Assembly of
Representatives. In a Presidential election in May
1984, Dr. Nicolas Barletta was elected president. He
resigned in September 1985 after disagreements with
military leaders and was succeeded by his Vice-
President, Eric Arturo Delvalle. An attempt in
February 1988 by President Delvalle to remove Gen.
Noriega as Commander of the Defence Forces failed.
Noriega ousted Delvalle and replaced him with
Manuel Solis Palma. Presidential elections were held
in May 1989, but Noriega annulled the results, which
had appeared to give victory to the opposition. A US
military invasion on December 20, 1990 followed
Noriega's formal assumption of power as Head of
State on December 15. Guillermo Endara, believed to
have won the May elections, was installed as
President following the ousting of General Noriega.

Legislative power is vested in a unicameral Legislative Assembly of 67 members; executive power is
held by the President, assisted by two elected Vice-
Presidents and an appointed Cabinet. Elections are
held every five years under a system of universal and
compulsory adult suffrage.

Economy.—The soil is moderately fertile, but
nearly one-half of the land is uncultivated. The chief
crops are bananas, sugar, coconuts, cacao, coffee and
cereals. The shrimping industry plays an important
role in the Panamanian economy. A railway 47 miles
in length joins the Atlantic and Pacific oceans.
Education is compulsory and free from 7 to 15
years.

TRADE

Imports are mostly manufactured goods, machinery, lubricants, chemicals and foodstuffs; exports are
bananas, petroleum products, shrimps, sugar, meat
and fishmeal.

Republic of Panama	1988	1989
Imports	US$712·3m	US$796·0m
Exports	283·0m	297·3m
Colon Free Zone		
Imports	US$1,843m	US$243·8m
Exports	2,119m	249·9m

Trade with UK†

	1988	1989
Imports from UK	£32,497,000	£32,875,000
Exports to UK	12,230,000	6,818,000

† Including Colon Free Zone.

The Panama Canal Zone.—With effect from Oct.
1, 1979 the Canal Zone (647 sq. miles) was disestablished, with all areas of land and water within the
Zone reverting to Panama. By the 1977 treaty with
the USA, the USA is allowed the use of operating
bases for the Panama Canal, together with several
military bases, but the Republic of Panama is
sovereign in all such areas. Control of the Canal will
revert to Panama in the year 2000.

CAPITAL.—ΨPanama City, population estimate
(1990) 1,063,565.

CURRENCY.—Balboa of 100 centésimos. US$ notes
are also in circulation.

FLAG.—Four quarters; white with blue star (top,
next staff), red (in fly), blue (below, next staff) and
white with red star.

NATIONAL ANTHEM.—Alcanzamos Por Fin La Victoria (Victory is ours at last).

NATIONAL DAY.—November 3.

Dependencies of Panama.—Taboga Island (area
4 sq. miles) is a popular tourist resort some 12 miles
from the Pacific entrance to the Panama Canal.
Tourist facilities have also been developed in the Las
Perlas Archipelago in the Gulf of Panama, particularly on the island of Contadora. There is a penal
settlement at Guardia on the island of Coiba (area 19
sq. miles) in the Gulf of Chiriqui.

BRITISH EMBASSY
Torre Swiss Bank, Calle 53 (Apartado 889 Zona 1),
Panama City, Panama 1
[Panama City 69–0866]

Ambassador Extraordinary and Plenipotentiary, His
Excellency John Grant MacDonald, CBE (1990).
Second Secretary and Deputy Head of Mission, T. A.
Walford.
Defence, Naval, Military and Air Attaché, Lt.-Col. R.
J. Lawson.

There is a British consular office at *Panama City.*

PARAGUAY
(República del Paraguay)

President, General Andrés Rodriguez, *elected* May 1,
1989.

CABINET MINISTERS
(as at June 30, 1990)

Foreign Affairs, Dr. Luis Maria Argaña.
Interior, Gen. Orlando Machuca Vargas.
Finance, Enzo Debernardi.
Education and Worship, Prof. Dr. Dionisio González
Torres.
Agriculture and Livestock, Hernando Bertoni.
Public Works and Communications, Gen. Porfirio
Pereira Ruiz Diaz.
Defence, Gen. Angel Juan Souto.
Public Health and Social Welfare, Dra. Cynthia
Prieto.
Justice and Labour, Dr. Alexis Frutos Vaesken.
Industry and Commerce, Sr. Pedro Antonio Zuccol-
illo.
Without portfolio, Dr. Juan Ramón Cháves.
President of the Central Bank, Dr. Crispiniano
Sandoval.

EMBASSY OF PARAGUAY
Braemar Lodge, Cornwall Gardens, SW7 4AQ
[071–937 1253]

Ambassador Extraordinary and Plenipotentiary, new
appointment awaited.
Chargé d'Affaires, Graciela Scorza de Jauregui.

Area and Population.—Paraguay is an inland subtropical state of South America, situated between Argentina, Bolivia and Brazil.

The area is estimated at 157,048 sq. miles (406,752 sq. km), with a population (1990 estimate) of 4,157,287.

Paraguay is a country of grassy plains and dense forest, the soil being marshy in many parts and liable to floods; while the hills are covered for the most part with immense forests. The streams flowing into the Alto Paraná descend precipitously into that river. In the angle formed by the Paraná-Paraguay confluence are extensive marshes, one of which, known as Neembucú, or endless, is drained by Lake Ypoa, a large lagoon, south-east of the capital. The Chaco, lying between the rivers Paraguay and Pilcomayo and bounded on the north by Bolivia, formed the subject of a long-standing dispute with that country and led to war between Paraguay and Bolivia from 1932 to 1935. The Chaco is a flat plain, rising uniformly towards its western boundary to a height of 1,140 feet; it suffers much from floods and still more from drought, but the building of dams and reservoirs has converted part of it into good pasture for cattle raising.

Government.—In 1535 Paraguay was settled as a Spanish possession. In 1811 it declared its independence of Spain.

The constitution provides for a two-chamber parliament consisting of a 36-member Senate and a 72-member Chamber of Deputies. Two-thirds of the seats in each chamber are allocated to the majority party and the remaining one-third shared among the minority parties in proportion to the votes cast. Voting is compulsory for all citizens over 18.

The President is elected for five years and may be re-elected for a further term. He appoints the Cabinet, which exercises all the functions of government. During parliamentary recess it can govern by decree through the Council of State, the members of which are representative of the Government, the armed forces and various other bodies.

Production.—About three-quarters of the population are engaged in agriculture and cattle raising. Cassava, sugar cane, soya, corn, cotton and wheat are the main agricultural products. The forests contain many varieties of timber which find a good market abroad. Paraguay's hydroelectric power station at Acaray produced 1,118 kWh in 1985 of which a surplus was exported to Argentina and Brazil.

At Itaipú the largest hydroelectric dam in the world, a joint project by Paraguay and Brazil, was inaugurated in 1982. It is expected to be completed in 1991 when it will have a capacity of over 12 million kW. Work is also under way on a hydroelectric project with Argentina at Yacyretá which it is hoped will be in operation by the end of the decade.

Communications.—A railway, 985 miles in length, connects Asunción with Buenos Aires. The journey takes 55 hours. Train ferries enable the run to be accomplished without break of bulk. River steamers also connect Buenos Aires and Asunción (3–5 days). This service is liable to cancellation without warning when the river is low or in flood. There are direct shipping services to Asunción from Britain, Western Europe and the USA. Eight airlines operate services from Asunción.

There are 1,176 km of asphalted roads in Paraguay, connecting Asunción with São Paulo (26 hrs) via the Bridge of Friendship and Foz de Yguazú and with Buenos Aires (24 hrs) via Puerto Pilcomayo, and about 4,050 miles of earth roads in fairly good condition, but liable to be closed or to become impassable in wet weather. A 1,000 km road, of which 300 km are paved, links Asunción with the Bolivian border. There are services to Buenos Aires, São Paulo and Paranagua, a port on the Brazilian coast.

Defence.—There is a permanent military force of about 25,000 all ranks, most of whom are conscripts doing their military service; and about 6,500 armed police (again mostly conscripts). Three gunboats and a number of small armed launches patrol inland waters.

Language and Literature.—Spanish is the official language of the country but outside the larger towns Guarani, the language of the largest single unit of original Indian inhabitants, is widely spoken. One daily and five weekly newspapers are published in Asunción.

Education.—Education is free and compulsory. In 1984 there were 3,209 government primary schools and 587 private schools with 559,080 pupils and 22,091 teachers. There were 713 secondary schools with 149,019 pupils and 2,448 teachers. The National University in Asunción had 20,343 students in 1984. The Catholic University had 10,971 students.

BUDGET 1990

	Central Government	Decentralized Bodies
Expenditure	Gs815·6m	Gs1,600·5m

Trade.—Total value of imports in 1989 was US$660,778,000. The chief imports were machinery (US$211·6m); fuels and lubricants (US$115·0m); transport and accessories (US$61·7m); and drinks and tobacco (US$45·5m). Total value of exports in 1989 was US$660,778,000. The chief exports were soya bean (US$382·9m); cotton fibres (US$306·9m); meat (US$96·1m); and coffee (US$40·3m).

Trade with UK

	1988	1989
Imports from UK	£22,024,000	£19,282,000
Exports to UK	1,950,000	8,898,000

CAPITAL.—Asunción, about 1,000 miles up the River Paraguay from Buenos Aires. Population (1985 census) 729,307; other centres are Ciudad del Este (98,491); Encarnación (31,445); Concepción (25,607); P. Juan Caballero (41,475).

CURRENCY.—Guaraní (Gs) of 100 céntimos.

FLAG.—Three horizontal bands, red, white, blue with the National seal on the obverse white band and the Treasury seal on the reverse white band.

NATIONAL ANTHEM.—Paraguayos, Republica O Muerte (Paraguayans, republic or death).

NATIONAL DAY.—May 14.

BRITISH EMBASSY
Calle Presidente Franco 706,
(PO Box 404), Asunción
[Asuncion 444472]

Ambassador Extraordinary and Plenipotentiary and Consul-General, His Excellency Terence Harry Steggle, CMG (1989).

PERU
(República del Peru)

President of the Republic, Alberto Fujimori, *assumed office* July 28, 1990.

First Vice-President and President of the Senate, Máximo San Román.

Second Vice-President, Carlos García.

CABINET
(as at July 31, 1990)

President of the House of Deputies, Victor Paredes.

President of the Council of Ministers and Minister of Economy and Finance, Juan Carlos Hurtado.

Agriculture, Carlos Amat y León.

Defence, Jorge Torres.

Education, Gloria Helfer.
Energy and Mines, Fernando Sánchez.
Fisheries, Raúl Sánchez.
Foreign Affairs, Luis Marchand.
Health, Dr. Carlos Vidal.
Housing and Construction, Guillermo del Solar.
Industry, Domestic Trade, Tourism and Integration,
Dr. Guido Pennano.
Interior, Adolfo Alvarado.
Justice, Dr. Augusto Antoniolli.
Labour and Social Development, Carlos Torres.
Transport and Communications, Eduardo Toledo.

PERUVIAN EMBASSY
52 Sloane Street, SW1X 9SP
[071–235 1917/2545]

Ambassador Extraordinary and Plenipotentiary,
Felipe Valdivieso-Belaúnde (1989).
Minister, Gilbert Chauny.
Counsellor, Julio Florián.

Area and Population.—Peru is a maritime Republic of South America, situated between 0° 00′ 48″ and 18° 21′ 00″ S. latitude and between 68° 39′ 27″ and 81° 20′ 13″ W. longitude. The area of the Republic is 496,225 sq. miles (1,285,216 sq. km), with a population (1990 estimate) of 22,332,100.

Physical Features.—The country is traversed throughout its length by the Andes, running parallel to the Pacific coast, the highest points in Peru being Huascaran (22,211 ft), Huandoy (20,855 ft), Ausangate (20,235 feet), Misti volcano (18,364 ft), Hualcan (20,000 ft), Chachani (19,037 ft), Antajasha (18,020 ft), Pichupichu (17,724 ft), and Mount Meiggs (17,583 ft).

There are three main regions, the *Costa*, west of the Andes, the *Sierra* or mountain ranges of the Andes, which include the Punas or mountainous wastes below the region of perpetual snow and the *Montaña*, or *Selva*, which is the vast area of jungle stretching from the eastern foothills of the Andes to the eastern frontiers of Peru. The coastal area, lying upon and near the Pacific, is not tropical, though close to the Equator, being cooled by the Humboldt Current.

In the mountains, where most of the Indians live, are to be found minerals in great richness and variety, and cattle, sheep, llamas and alpacas are bred there.

Language.—Spanish, the language of the original Spanish stock from which the governing and professional classes are mainly recruited, was formerly the only official language of the country. However, in May 1975, Quechua was declared the second official language. Quechua and Aymará are widely spoken by more than half the population of the country.

Government.—Peru was conquered in the early 16th century by Francisco Pizarro (1478–1541). He subjugated the Incas (the ruling caste of the Quechua Indians), who had started their rise to power some 500 years earlier, and for nearly three centuries Peru remained under Spanish rule. A revolutionary war of 1821–1824 established its independence, declared on July 28, 1821. The constitution rests upon the fundamental law of October 18, 1856 and is that of a democratic Republic. The current constitution was drawn up and approved in July 1979.

Production.—The chief products of the coastal belt are cotton, sugar and petroleum. There are large tracts of land suitable for cultivation and stock raising on the eastern slopes of the Andes, and in the mountain valleys maize, potatoes and wheat are grown. The jungle area is a source of timber and petroleum. Other major crops are fruit, vegetables, rice, barley, grapes and coffee. Mineral exports include lead, zinc, copper, iron ore and silver. Peru is normally the world's largest exporter of fishmeal.

Communications.—In recent years the coastal and sierra zones have been opened up by means of roads and air routes and there is air communication, as well as communication by protracted land routes, with the tropical and little known eastern zones which lie east of the Andes towards the borders of Brazil. The completion in 1944 of the trunk road of the Andean Highway from the Pacific port of Callao, via Lima to Pucallpa, the river port on the Ucayali, forms a link between the Pacific, the Amazon and the Atlantic. The Panamerican Highway runs along the Peruvian coast connecting it with Ecuador and Chile. The Inter-Ocean Corridor linking the port of Matarani and Buenos Aires will be opened soon.

The first railway was opened in 1850 and the 2,400 miles of track are now administered by the Government. There is also steam navigation on the Ucayali and Huallaga, and in the south on Lake Titicaca. Air services are maintained throughout Peru, and many international services call at Lima.

Defence.—The Army is recruited by voluntary enlistment, supplemented by conscription (two years), and numbers about 45,000 of all ranks. Armoured units are equipped with American, Soviet and French vehicles. Engineer units are employed on the construction of roadways in Peru using American equipment. The main naval base is in Callao and supports all ships of the Fleet. There are training establishments in Callao and La Punta. The Naval Air Arm consists of US and French helicopters; US anti-submarine aircraft and DC3's. The Air Force is equipped with British, Soviet, US and French aircraft and Soviet, US and French helicopters. There are military airfields at Talara, Piura, Chiclayo, Lima, Pisco, Joya, Iquitos and Arequipa plus a seaplane base at Iquitos. The National Police is made up of the Security Police, General Police and Technical Police.

Education.—Education is compulsory and free for both sexes between the ages of 5 and 16.

Trade.—Import trade of Peru in 1989 totalled US$2,370 million and exports US$1,159 million.

Trade with UK

	1988	1989
Imports from UK	£31,384,000	£29,707,000
Exports to UK	90,844,000	125,538,000

The principal imports are machinery and chemicals and pharmaceutical products. The chief exports are minerals and metals, fishmeal, sugar, cotton and coffee.

CAPITAL.—Metropolitan Lima (including ΨCallao), population estimate (1990) 6,415,000. Other major cities are: Arequipa (712,279) and Lambayeque (625,553).

CURRENCY.—Inti of 100 céntimos.

FLAG.—Three vertical bands, red, white, red; coat of arms on white band.

NATIONAL ANTHEM.—Somos Libres, Seámoslo Siempre (We are free, let us remain so forever).

NATIONAL DAY.—July 28 (Anniversary of Independence).

BRITISH EMBASSY

Natalio Sánchez 125 Piso 12, Santa Beatriz
(PO Box 854), Lima 1.
[Lima 334738]

Ambassador Extraordinary and Plenipotentiary, His Excellency Keith Haskell, CVO (1990).

First Secretaries, B. B. Low (*Deputy Head of Mission and Consul*); M. J. Pawley (*Commercial*).

Defence Attaché, Col. C. H. Van der Noot, MBE.

There is a British Consular Office at *Lima* and Honorary Consulates in *Arequipa, Piura* and *Trujillo*.

British Council Representative, A. Moore, PO Box No. 14-0114, Calle Alberto Lynch 110, San Isidro, Lima 27.

THE PHILIPPINES
(República ng Pilipinas)

President, Corazon C. Aquino, *assumed office* February 25, 1986.

CABINET SECRETARIES
(as at June 30, 1990)

Foreign Affairs, Raul Manglapus.
Finance, Vicente Jayme.
Justice, Franklin Drilon.
Agriculture, Senen Bacani.
Public Works and Highways, Fiorello Estuar.
Education, Culture and Sports, Isidro Cariño.
Labour, Ruben Torres.
Health, Alfredo Bengzon.
Trade and Industry, Jose Concepcion.
Social Services and Development, Mita Pardo de Tavera.
Economic Planning, Cayetano Paderanga.
Agrarian Reform, Benjamin Leung.
Local Government, Luis Santos.
Tourism, Pedro Garrucho.
Natural Resources, Fulgenio Factóran.
Budget, Guillermo Carague.
Transport and Communications, Oscar Orbos.
National Defence, Fidel Ramos.
Executive Secretary, Catalino Macaraig Jr.
Muslim Affairs and Cultural Communities, Dimas Pundato.
Chairman, Presidential Commission on Good Government, Mateo Caparas.
Science and Technology, Ceferino Follosco.
Presidential Spokesman and Chief Presidential Legal Counsel, Adolfo Azcuna.
Presidential Adviser on National Security, Rafael Illeto.
Cabinet Secretary, Aniceto Sobrepeña.
Press Secretary, Tomas Gomez.

EMBASSY OF THE PHILIPPINES

9A Palace Green, W8 4QE
[071–937 1600/9]

Ambassador Extraordinary and Plenipotentiary, His Excellency Tomas T. Syquia (1989).

Deputy Chief of Mission and Consul General, Edmundo Libid.

Commercial Counsellor, S. Ileto.

Area and Population.—The Philippines are situated between 21° 20′–4° 30′ N. Lat. and 116° 55′–126° 36′ E. long., and are distant about 500 miles from the south-east coast of the continent of Asia. (For MAP, see p. 780).

The total land area of the country is 115,831 sq. miles (300,000 sq. km). There are eleven larger islands and 7,079 smaller islands.

The principal islands are:—

	sq. miles		sq. miles
Luzon	40,422	Mindoro	3,759
Mindanao	36,538	Leyte	2,786
Samar	5,050	Cebu	1,703
Negros	4,906	Bohol	1,492
Palawan	4,550	Masbate	1,262
Panay	4,446		

Other groups in the Republic are the Sulu islands (capital, Jolo), Babuyanes and Batanes; the Catanduanes; and Culion Islands.

The population of the Philippines (UN estimate 1988) is 58,721,000.

The inhabitants, known as Filipinos, are basically of Malay stock, with a considerable admixture of Spanish and Chinese blood in many localities, and about 90 per cent of them are Christians, predominantly Roman Catholics. Most of the remainder are Muslims, in the south, and Animists and pagans, mainly in the north. There is a Chinese minority estimated at 500,000, and other much smaller foreign communities, notably Spanish, American and Indian.

Government.—The Portuguese navigator Magellan came to the Philippines in 1521 and was slain by the natives of Mactan, a small island near Cebu. In 1565 Spain undertook the conquest of the country which was named Filipinas, after the son of the King of Spain, and in 1571 the city of Manila was founded by the conquistador Legaspi, who subdued the inhabitants of almost all the islands, their conversion being undertaken by the Augustinian friars in Legaspi's train. In 1762 Manila was occupied by a British force, but in 1764 it was restored to Spain. In the Spanish–American War of 1898, Manila was captured by American troops with the help of Filipinos and the Islands were ceded to the United States by the Treaty of Paris of December 10, 1898. Despite a rebellion against the US government between 1899 and 1902, the Americans remained in control of the country until 1946.

The Republic of the Philippines came into existence on July 4, 1946 with a presidential form of government based on the American system.

Ferdinand Marcos was President from 1965 to 1986. Although he gained a majority of votes in the official count of a Presidential election in February 1986, the election was marred by widespread electoral abuse and his rival, Mrs Corazon Aquino, launched a series of non-violent civil disturbance actions which gained wide support. On February 25, Marcos, his family and aides left for Hawaii. Mrs Aquino took over as President.

A new Constitution was approved by referendum in February 1987. Legislative authority is vested in a bicameral elected Congress comprising a House of Representatives of up to 250 members and a 24-member Senate. Elections to the Congress were held in May and the new Constitution came into force on July 27, 1987.

There is unrest in many of the islands due to insurgency. Muslim insurgents, the Moro National Liberation Front, operate in western Mindanao and the Sula archipelago. Most of the current activity is due to the Communist New People's Army, which is strongest in eastern Mindanao, Negros, Samar, Bicol, the mountains of northern Luzon, and Bataan. As of June 1987 the ceasefire agreed between the Government and the Moro National Liberation Front was still holding, unlike the ceasefire with the Communists which ended in February 1987.

Language and Literature.—The official languages are Filipino and English. Filipino, the national language, is based on Tagalog, one of the Malay–Polynesian languages and the language of the part of Luzon surrounding Metro Manila. Filipino is spoken by 29·66 per cent of the total number of households, but local languages and dialects are strong and Cebuano is spoken by 24·20 per cent of total households. English, which is the language of government and of instruction in secondary and university education, is spoken by at least 44 per cent of the population. Spanish, which ceased to be an official language in 1973, is now spoken by a very small minority; 89 per cent of the population are literate.

Education.—Secondary and higher education is extensive and there are 37 private universities recognized by the Government, including the Dominican University of Santo Tomas (founded in 1611); there are also 296 state-supported colleges and universities, including the University of the Philippines, founded 1908.

Roads and Railways.—The highway system covered 161,709 kilometres in 1985 and there was a total of 1,120,172 registered road vehicles. The Philippine National Railway operates 740 km of track on Luzon Island.

Shipping.—There are 94 ports of entry in the Philippines and 164,404 vessels of various types totalling 50,467,000 tons, are engaged in inter-island traffic.

Civil Aviation.—There 82 national airports and 137 privately operated airports. Philippine Air Lines have regular flights throughout the Far East, to the USA and Europe, in addition to inter-island services.

TRADE

	1987	1988
Total imports .	US$6,736,969,000	US$8,159,378,000
Total exports .	5,720,238,000	6,994,425,000

Trade with UK

	1988	1989
Imports from UK	£175,685,000	£137,367,000
Exports to UK	328,013,000	233,128,000

The Philippines is a predominantly agricultural country, the chief products being rice, coconuts, maize, sugar-cane, abaca (manila hemp), fruits, tobacco and lumber. There is, however, an increasing number of manufacturing industries and it is the policy of the Government to diversify its economy.

Principal exports are sugar, coconut oil, copper concentrate, lumber and copra.

CAPITAL.—Ψ Manila, on the island of Luzon, population (1980): City area 1,630,485; Manila with suburbs (incl. Quezon City, Pasay City, Caloocan City, Makati, Parañaque, San Juan Mandaluyong and Navotas) 6,720,050. The next largest cities are Ψ Cebu (490,281), Ψ Davao (610,375), Ψ Iloilo (244,027), Ψ Zamboanga (343,722), and Bacolod (262,415).

CURRENCY.—Philippine peso (P) of 100 centavos.

FLAG.—Equal horizontal bands of blue (above) and red; gold sun with three stars on a white triangle next staff.

NATIONAL ANTHEM.—Pambansang Awit.
NATIONAL DAY.—June 12 (Independence Day).

BRITISH EMBASSY
Locsin Building, 6752 Ayala Avenue,
Corner Makati Avenue, Makati, Metro Manila
(PO Box 1970)
[Manila 816-7116]

Ambassador Extraordinary and Plenipotentiary, His Excellency Keith Gordon MacInnes, CMG (1987).
Counsellor, A. Collins.
Defence Attaché, Col. J. P. Clough.
First Secretary, P. R. Nelson.
Second Secretaries, D. Curran; A. E. Conroy; R. Cork (*Commercial*); J. Fulton (*Consul*); H. C. Brown (*Management*).
Cultural Attaché, N. Bisset (*British Council Representative.*

POLAND
(Rzeczpospolita Polska)

President, Gen. Wojciech Jaruzelski, *elected* July 20, 1989 *for a six-year term.*

COUNCIL OF MINISTERS
(as at July 31, 1990)

Chairman, Tadeusz Mazowiecki (S).
Deputy Chairman, Finance, Leszek Balcerowicz (S)
Deputy Chairman, Agriculture, Forestry and Food Economy, Artur Balazs (RS).
Deputy Chairman, Science and Technology, Jan Stanislaw Janowski (DP).
Deputy Chairman, Internal Affairs, Krzysztof Kozlowski.
Council of Ministers, Jacek Ambroziak (S).
Justice, Aleksander Bentkowski (UPP).
Culture and Arts, Izabella Cywinska (S).
Environmental Protection and Natural Resources, Bronislaw Kaminski (UPP).
Health and Social Welfare, Andrzej Kosiniak-Kamysz (UPP).
Labour and Social Policy, Jacek Kuron (S).
Domestic Market, Aleksander Mackiewicz (DP).
Housing and Construction, Aleksander Paszynski (S).
National Education, Henryk Samsonowicz (S).
National Defence, Adm. Piotr Kolodziejczyk.
Foreign Affairs, Krzysztof Skubiszewski (SDU).
Foreign Economic Co-operation, Marcin Swiecicki.
Industry, Tadeusz Syryjczyk (S).
Transport, Shipping and Communications, Ewaryst Waligorski.
Central Planning Office, Jerzy Osiatynski (S).
Without Portfolio, Aleksander Hall (S), Witold Trzeciakowski (S).

S: Solidarity; RS: Rural Solidarity; DP: Democratic Party; UPP: United Peasants' Party; SDU: Social Democratic Union.

EMBASSY OF THE REPUBLIC OF POLAND
47 Portland Place, W1N 3AG
[071–580 4324]

Ambassador Extraordinary and Plenipotentiary, His Excellency Tadeusz de Virion (1990).

Area and Population.—Poland adjoins East Germany in the west, the boundary being formed by the rivers Oder and Neisse, Czechoslavakia in the south, and the USSR in the east. (The present frontiers were established at the end of the Second World War.) To the north is the Baltic Sea. The country has an area of 120,725 sq. miles (312,677 sq. km), and a population (UN estimate 1988) of 37,862,000. Roman Catholicism, the religion of 95 per cent of the inhabitants, was legalized in May 1989.

Government.—The Polish Commonwealth ceased to exist in 1795 after three successive partitions in 1772, 1793 and 1795, in which Prussia, Russia and Austria shared. The Republic of Poland (reconstituted within the limits of the old Polish Commonwealth) was proclaimed at Warsaw in November, 1918, and its independence guaranteed by the signatories of the Treaty of Versailles.

German forces invaded Poland on September 1, 1939; on September 17, Russian forces invaded eastern Poland, and on September 21, 1939 Poland was declared by Germany and Russia to have ceased to exist. A line of demarcation was established between the areas occupied by German and Russian forces. At the end of the war a Coalition Government was formed in which the Polish Workers' Party played a large part. In December 1948, the Polish Workers' Party and the Polish Socialist Party fused in the new Polish United Workers' Party (PUWP). A new Constitution modelled on the Soviet Constitution of 1936 was adopted in July 1952, and was modified in February 1976. It changed the title of the country to the Polish People's Republic (*Polska Rzeczpospolita Ludowa*). It made no provision for a President of the Republic, whose functions were to be jointly exercised by a Council of State. Private ownership of land and freedom of religion were recognized. Church and State were to be separate.

In July 1980 steep rises in food prices but static wages led to widespread strikes. The strikes continued throughout August, obliging the government to agree to allow independent trade unions, the right to strike, the easing of censorship and other political and economic demands. The independent trade union movement, Solidarity, led by Lech Walesa, became a powerful force but many of its leaders, including Walesa, were detained and union activity suspended when martial law was declared in December 1981. Initially there was some passive resistance to martial law, which was suspended in December 1982 and finally lifted in July 1983.

Solidarity continued as an underground movement until 1988 when a wave of strikes and the call for the legalization of Solidarity resulted in talks between Walesa and the PUWP early in 1989. By April plans for political and economic reforms had been drawn up. These included the restoration of the legal status of Solidarity (April 17); the introduction of a bi-cameral parliamentary system comprising an upper house (Senate) and lower house (Sejm), and an Executive Presidency; multi-party parliamentary elections were held in the summer of 1989.

General Jaruzelski was elected President by Poland's MPs on July 20, and on August 20, 1989 Tadeusz Mazowiecki became the first non-communist Prime Minister since 1945. Under the new constitution the Prime Minister can appoint all members of the Council of Ministers.

In December 1989 Poland's official title was changed from the Polish People's Republic to the Republic of Poland. The PUWP, since August 1989 no longer the ruling party, disbanded in January 1990. Fresh parliamentary elections are expected in spring 1991.

Education.—Elementary education (ages 7–15) is compulsory and free. Secondary education is optional and free. There are universities at Kraków, Warsaw, Poznan, Lódź, Wroclaw, Lublin and Toruń and a considerable number of other towns.

Language and Literature.—Polish is a western Slavonic tongue (*see* USSR), the Latin alphabet being used. Polish literature developed rapidly after the foundation of the University of Kraków (a printing press was established there in 1474 and there Copernicus died in 1543). A national school of poetry and drama survived the dismemberment and the former era of romanticism, whose chief Polish exponent was Adam Mickiewicz, was followed by realistic and historical fiction, including the works of Henryk Sienkiewicz (1846–1916), Nobel Prize-winner for Literature in 1905; Boleslaw Prus (1847–1912); and Stanislaw Reymont (1868–1925), Nobel Prize-winner in 1924.

Production and Industry.—On January 3, 1946, a decree was issued to provide for the nationalization of mines, petroleum resources, water, gas and electricity services, banks, textile factories and large retail stores. Until recently over 99 per cent of Polish industry was stated to be 'socialized', but 68 per cent of agricultural land was privately farmed. Legislation passed in July 1990 provides a framework for 80 per cent of the economy to be transferred from the state to the private sector.

Trade with UK

	1988	1989
Imports from UK	£175,685,000	£196,446,000
Exports to UK	328,013,000	330,163,000

CAPITAL.—Warsaw, on the Vistula, population (1984) 1,644,626. Other large towns are Lódź (849,000); Kraków (735,000); Wroclaw (632,000); Poznan (571,000); Gdansk (464,000); Szczecin (389,000); Katowice (361,000); Bydgoszcz (358,000).

CURRENCY.—Zloty of 100 groszy.

FLAG.—Equal horizontal stripes of white (above) and red.

NATIONAL ANTHEM.—Jeszcze Polska Nie Zginela (Poland has not yet been destroyed).

NATIONAL DAY.—May 3.

BRITISH EMBASSY
No. 1 Aleja Róz, 00-556 Warsaw
[Warsaw 281001]

Ambassador Extraordinary and Plenipotentiary, His Excellency Stephen Jeremy Barrett, CMG (1988).
Counsellor, G. G. Wetherell (*Head of Chancery*).
Defence and Air Attaché, Gp. Capt. A. Harris.
Naval and Military Attaché, Lt.-Col. A. Cumings.

British Council Representative, Charles Chadwick, OBE, Al. Jerozolimskie 59, 00–697 Warsaw.

PORTUGAL
(República Portuguesa)

President of the Republic, Dr. Mario A. Nobre Lopes Soares, *elected,* February 16, 1986.

<small>MINISTERS</small>
(as at June 30, 1990)

Prime Minister, Prof. Anibal Cavaco Silva.
Minister at the PM's office, Defence, Dr. Joaquim Fernando Nogueira.
Justice, Dr. Alvaro Laborinho Lucio.
Parliamentary Affairs, Dr. Manuel Joaquim Dias Loureiro.
Finance, Dr. Miguel Beleza.
Planning and Territorial Administration, Prof. Luis Valente de Oliveira.
Internal Administration, Dr. Manuel Pereira.
Foreign, Prof. João de Deus Pinheiro.
Agriculture, Fisheries and Food, Arlindo Marques da Cunha.
Industry and Energy, Luis Mira Amaral.
Education, Dr. Roberto Carneiro.
Public Works, Transport and Communications, Joaquim Ferreira do Amaral.
Health, Dr. Arlindo Gomes de Carvalho.
Employment and Social Security, Dr. José Silva Peneda.
Trade and Tourism, Fernando Faria de Oliveira.
Youth, Albino Couto dos Santos.
Environment and Natural Resources, Prof. Dr. Fernando Ferreira Real.

<small>PORTUGUESE EMBASSY</small>
11 Belgrave Square, SW1X 8PP
[071–235 5331]

Ambassador Extraordinary and Plenipotentiary, His Excellency Antonio Vaz-Pereira (1989).
Minister Counsellor, Francisco Seixas-da-Costa.
First Secretary, Graça Andresen-Guimarães.

Area and Population.—Continental Portugal occupies the western part of the Iberian Peninsula, covering an area of 34,317 sq. miles (88,880 sq. km). It lies between 36° 58'–42° 12" N. lat. and 6° 11' 48"–9° 29' 45" W. long., being 362 miles in length from N. to S., and averaging about 117 in breadth from E. to W. The population (UN estimate 1988) is 10,408,000 (including the Azores and Madeira).

Language and Literature.—Portuguese is a Romance language with admixtures of Arabic and other idioms. It is the language of Portugal and Brazil, and is the *lingua franca* of Angola, Mozambique and Guinea-Bissau. Portuguese language and literature reached the culminating point of their development in the *Lusiadas* (dealing with the voyage of Vasco da Gama) and other works of Camoens (Camões) (1524–80). There are four morning and three evening daily newspapers in Lisbon and three morning papers in Oporto, and six main weekly newspapers.

Government.—From the eleventh century until 1910 the government of Portugal was a monarchy, and for many centuries included the Vice-Royalty of Brazil, which declared its independence in 1822. In 1910 an armed rising in Lisbon drove King Manuel II and the royal family into exile, and the National Assembly of August 21, 1911 sanctioned a republican form of government. A period of great political instability ensued until eventually the military stepped in. The Constitution of 1933 gave formal expression to the corporative 'Estado Novo' (New State) which was personified by Dr. Salazar, Prime Minister 1932–68. Dr. Caetano succeeded Salazar as Prime Minister in 1968 but his failure to liberalize the regime or to conclude the wars in the African colonies resulted in his government's overthrow by a military coup on April 25, 1974. The next two years were characterized by great political turmoil with no fewer than six provisional governments between April 1974 and July 1976 but with the failure of an attempted coup by the extreme left in November 1975 the situation began to become more stable.

Constitutional reforms introduced in 1982 have reduced the President's scope for day-to-day intervention in government but the decision to dissolve the Assembly is still largely the President's. The revisions also ended the military's capacity for political interference, and created two new organs of state, the Constitutional Tribunal and the Council of State, to advise the President. Further constitutional reforms were made in 1989. The President, elected for a five-year term by universal adult suffrage, appoints the Prime Minister. Legislative authority is vested in the 250-member Assembly of the Republic, elected by a system of proportional representation for a term of up to four years.

In the General Election held on July 19, 1987, the Social Democratic Party (PSD) won 148 of the 250 seats; the Socialist Party (PS) 60 seats; the Communist Party (PCP) 31 seats, the Democratic Renewal Party (PRD) 7 seats and the Christian Democrats (CDS) 4 seats.

Defence.—Most physically fit males are liable for military service but conscription is becoming increasingly selective as the armed forces were greatly reduced following the end of the colonial wars, and reorganized and re-equipped for a conventional national defence role. The present strength of the Army is about 43,000. One brigade is earmarked for NATO service. The Navy consists of about 14,800 officers and men, including 2,500 marines, manning about 60 craft of various types. The present serving strength of the Air Force is about 12,600, (including 2,200 paratroops) and about 80 combat aircraft plus helicopters and transport and training aircraft. Changes to the size and structure of the armed forces are expected to take place in 1991–92.

Education is free and compulsory for nine years from the age of 6. Secondary education is mainly conducted in state lyceums, commercial and industrial schools, but there are also private schools. There are also military, naval, technical, polytechnic and other special schools. There are old established universities at Coimbra (founded in 1290), Oporto and Lisbon. New universities have been established at Lisbon, Braga, Aveiro and in the Azores.

Communications.—There is an international airport at Portela, about 5 miles from Lisbon, and the airport of Pedras Rubras near Oporto is also used for scheduled international services. There are direct flights between London and Faro in the Algarve.

Agriculture.—The chief agricultural products are cork, cereals, rice, vegetables, olives, figs, citrus fruits, almonds, timber, port wine and table wines. There are extensive forests of pine, cork, eucalyptus and chestnut covering about 20 per cent of the total area of the country.

Minerals.—The principal mineral products are pyrites, wolfram, tin, iron ores, copper and sodium and calcium minerals.

Industry.—The country is so far only moderately industrialized, but is fairly rapidly extending its industries. The principal manufactures are textiles, clothing and footwear, machinery (including electric machinery and transport equipment), foodstuffs (tomato concentrates and canned fish), chemicals, fertilizers, wood, cork, furniture, cement, glassware and pottery. There is a modern steelworks, and two modern and very large shipbuilding and repair yards at Lisbon and Setúbal working mainly for foreign ship-owners. There are several hydro-electric power stations and a new thermal power station.

Finance.—Portugal is a member of the European Monetary Agreement, the World Bank, the International Monetary Fund and the International Finance Corporation. The country has substantial gold and foreign exchange reserves.

Trade.—The principal imports are cereals, meat, raw and semi-manufactured iron and steel, industrial machinery, chemicals, crude oil, motor vehicles and raw materials for textiles.

The principal exports are textiles, footwear, timber, cork, electrical and other machinery, and chemicals.

	1988	1989
Total imports	£6,164,627m	£11,535,432m
Total exports	4,230,727m	7,738,209m

Trade with UK

	1988	1989
Imports from UK ..	£810,537,000	£915,682,000
Exports to UK	928,015,000	1,040,706,000

The British share of the Portuguese market was 7·4 per cent in 1989 and the UK was the third largest market for Portuguese exports.

CAPITAL.—ΨLisbon, population estimate (1989) 2,128,000. ΨOporto 1,683,000.

CURRENCY.—Escudo (Esc) of 100 centavos.

FLAG.—Vertical band of green (next staff) and square of red, bearing arms of the Republic, framed.

NATIONAL ANTHEM.—A Portuguesa.

NATIONAL DAY.—June 10.

BRITISH EMBASSY
35–37 Rua de S. Domingos à Lapa,
1200 Lisbon
[Lisbon 3961191]

Ambassador Extraordinary and Plenipotentiary, His Excellency Hugh James Arbuthnott, CMG (1989)

There are British Consulates in *Oporto*, *Portimão*, *Funchal* (Madeira) and *Ponta Delgada* (Azores).

British Council Representative, J. Mallon, OBE, Rua de Sao Marçal 174, 1294 Lisbon.

BRITISH PORTUGUESE CHAMBER OF COMMERCE, Rua da Estrela 8, 1200 Lisbon and Rua Sa de Bandeira 784–20E, Frente, 4000 Oporto.

MADEIRA AND THE AZORES

Madeira and The Azores are two administratively autonomous regions of Portugal, having locally elected Assemblies and Governments.

MADEIRA is a group of islands in the Atlantic Ocean about 520 miles south-west of Lisbon, and consists of Madeira, Porto, Santo and three uninhabited islands (Desertas). The total area is 314 sq. miles (813 sq. km), with a population of 271,400 (1989). ΨFunchal in Madeira, the largest island (270 square miles), is the capital, with a population of 44,111; Machico (10,905).

THE AZORES are a group of nine islands (Flores, Corvo, Terceira, São Jorge, Pico, Faial, Graciosa, São Miguel and Santa Maria) in the Atlantic Ocean, with a total area of 922 sq. miles (2,387 sq. km), and a population of 255,100 (1989). ΨPonta Delgada, on São Miguel, is the capital of the group; population is 137,700. Other ports are ΨAngra, in Terceira (55,900) and ΨHorta (16,300).

MACAO

Macao, situated at the mouth of the Pearl River, comprises a peninsula and the islands of Coloane and Taipa, having an area of six sq. miles (15·5 sq. km), with a population (UN estimate 1988) of 439,000. Portuguese trade with China began early in the 16th century and Macao became a Portuguese colony in 1557; in a Sino-Portuguese treaty of 1887 China recognized Portugal's sovereignty over, and government of, Macao. In 1974 Portugal changed Macao's status from that of an Overseas Province to 'a territory under Portuguese administration'. Following the Sino-British Joint Declaration on Hong Kong in 1984, Sino-Portuguese negotiations on the transfer of administration began on June 30, 1986. The agreement on the transfer of the administration of Macao to the Chinese authorities was signed on April 13, 1987. Macao will become a 'special administrative region' of China when transferred on December 20, 1999.

Macao is subject to Portuguese constitutional law but otherwise enjoys administrative, economic and financial autonomy. The Governor is appointed by the Portuguese President and since 1976 there has been a 17-member legislative assembly, which has a three-year term. The assembly comprises 12 elected deputies appointed by the Governor. A new electoral system which came into effect February 28, 1984 gave equal voting rights to all residents, thus enfranchising the Chinese population.

Macao's major industry is textile manufacturing which accounts for 62 per cent of all exports. Port Macao is served by British, Portuguese and Dutch shipping lines and has regular services to Hong Kong, some 35 miles away.

Governor, Carlos Melancia.

Trade with UK

	1988	1989
Imports from UK	£4,348,000	£7,498,000
Exports to UK	41,116,000	45,299,000

QATAR
(Dawlat Qatar)

Head of State, HH Sheikh Khalifa bin Hamad Al Thani, GCMG, GCB, the Amir of Qatar, *assumed power* February 22, 1972.

Heir Apparent, Minister of Defence and Commander-in-Chief of Armed Forces, HH Sheikh Hamad bin Khalifa Al Thani, KCMG.

COUNCIL OF MINISTERS
(as at May 31, 1990)

Interior, HE Sheikh Abdullah bin Khalifa Al Thani.

Finance and Petroleum, HE Sheikh Abdulaziz bin Khalifa Al Thani.

Foreign Affairs, HE Mubarak Ali Al Khater.

Education, HE Abdulaziz Abdullah Turki.

Justice, HE Sheikh Ahmed bin Saif Al Thani.

Economy and Commerce HE Sheikh Hamad bin Jassim bin Hamad Al Thani.

Electricity and Water, vacant.

Industry and Public Works, HE Ahmed Mohamed Ali Al Subai.

Municipal Affairs and Agriculture, temporary Minister for Electricity and Water, HE Sheikh Hamad bin Jassim bin Jabor Al Thani.

Labour, Social Affairs and Housing, HE Abdulrahman Saad Al Derham.

Communications and Transport, HE Abdulla bin Saleh Al Mana.

Public Health, HE Sheikh Khaled bin Mohamed bin Ali Al Thani.

Information and Culture, HE Sheikh Hamad bin Suhaim Al Thani.

Amiri Diwan Affairs, HE Dr. Issa Ghanim Al Kuwari.

EMBASSY OF THE STATE OF QATAR
27 Chesham Place, SW1X 8HG
[071–235 0851/4]

Ambassador Extraordinary and Plenipotentiary, His Excellency Abdul Rahman Abdulla Al-Wohaibi (1989).

The state of Qatar covers the peninsula of Qatar from approximately the northern shore of Khor al

Odaid to the eastern shore of Khor al Salwa. The area is about 4,247 sq. miles (11,000 sq. km), with a population (UN estimate 1988) of 341,000. The great majority of the population is concentrated in the urban district of the capital Doha. Only a small minority still pursue the traditional life of the semi-nomadic tribesmen and fisherfolk.

Until 1971, Qatar was one of the nine independent Emirates in the Arabian Gulf in special treaty relations with the UK. In that year, with the withdrawal of British forces from the area, these special treaty relations were terminated. On April 2, 1970 a provisional constitution for Qatar was proclaimed, providing for the establishment of a Council of Ministers and for the formation of a Consultative Council to assist the Council of Ministers in running the affairs of the State. There are no political parties or legislature. Qatar is a member of the Arab League as well as of the United Nations.

Production.—Although Qatar is a desert country, there are gardens and smallholdings near Doha and to the north and encouragement is being given to the development of agriculture.

The Qatar General Petroleum Corporation is the state-owned company controlling Qatar's interests in oil, gas and petrochemicals. The corporation is responsible for Qatar's oil production onshore and offshore. The production level for Qatar agreed in OPEC is currently 371,000 b.p.d. Explorations continue for further oil. The large reserves of natural gas in the North Field are expected to come into production by 1991. A 50,000 b.p.d. oil refinery was commissioned in 1984 to increase domestic refinery capacity.

Current industries include a steel mill, a fertilizer plant, a cement factory, a petrochemical complex and two natural gas liquids plants. With the exception of the cement works, which is at Umm Bab, all these industries are at Umm Said, about 30 miles south of Doha. There are tentative plans for new industry, including an aluminium smelter, a second ammonia plant and a methanol plant, downstream of the North Field. Qatar is also expanding its infrastructure including electrical generation and water distillation, roads, houses, and government buildings, although reduced demand for crude oil in international markets has led to a downturn in the economy and a slower rate of development than hitherto.

Communications.—Regular air services connect Qatar with Bahrain and the United Arab Emirates, Kuwait, Muscat, Saudi Arabia, Jordan, Syria, Lebanon, Egypt, the Indian sub-continent, Africa and Europe. The Qatar Broadcasting Service transmits on medium, shortwave, and VHF. Regular television transmissions in colour began in 1974 and a second channel opened in 1982.

Trade with UK

	1988	1989
Imports from UK	£88,920,000	£89,256,000
Exports to UK	3,888,000	4,342,000

CAPITAL.—ΨDoha, population (estimated) 220,000. Other towns include Khor, Dukhan, Wakra and ΨUmm Said.

CURRENCY.—Qatar riyal of 100 dirhams.

FLAG.—White and maroon, white portion nearer the mast; vertical indented line comprising 17 angles divides the colours.

NATIONAL DAY.—September 3.

BRITISH EMBASSY
PO Box 3, Doha
[Doha 421991]

Ambassador Extraordinary and Plenipotentiary, His Excellency Graham Boyce (1990).

First Secretary, J. G. Rice (*Commercial*).

Second Secretary, G. D. Cole (*Consul and Administration*).

Attaché, P. D. G. Cook (*Commercial*).

Vice Consul, R. J. Clark.

British Council Representative, Richard Long, Ras Abu Aboud Road (PO Box 2992), Doha.

ROMANIA
(România)

President of the Republic, Ion Iliescu, *elected*, May 20, 1990.

COUNCIL OF MINISTERS
(as at June 30, 1990)

Prime Minister, Petre Roman.

Minister of State responsible for Industrial and Commercial Activity, Anton Vatasescu.

Minister of State responsible for Quality of Life and Social Security, Ion Aurel Stoica.

Minister of State responsible for Economic Orientation, Eugen Dijmarescu.

Deputy PM, Reform and Relations with Parliament, Adrian Severin.

Foreign Affairs, Adrian Nastase.

National Defence, Victor Stanculescu.

Finance, Theodor Stolojan.

Interior, Doru Viorel Ursu.

Justice, Victor Babiuc.

Resources and Industry, Mihai Zisu.

Trade and Tourism, Constantin Fota.

Agriculture and Food Industry, Ioan Tipu.

Communications, Andrei Chirica.

Public Works, Transport and Territorial Planning, Doru Pana.

Education and Science, Stefan Gheorghe.

Environment, Valeriu Eugen Pop.

Culture, Andrei Gabriel Plesu.

Health, Bogdan Marinescu.

Labour and Social Security, Catalin Zamfir.

Youth and Sports, Bogdan Nicolae Niculescu Duvaz.

Secretaries of State, Romolus Neagu (*Foreign Affairs*), Andrei Tugulea (*Education and Science*).

EMBASSY OF ROMANIA
4 Palace Green, W8 4QD
[071–937 3902]

Ambassador Extraordinary and Plenipotentiary, new appointment awaited.

Chargé d'Affaires, Nicu Bujlr.

Area and Population.—Romania is a republic of south-eastern Europe, formerly the classical *Dacia* and *Scythia Pontica*, having its origin in the union of the Danubian principalities of Wallachia and Moldavia under the Treaty of Paris (April 1856). The area of Romania is 91,699 sq. miles (237,500 sq. km) and the population (1988 estimate) is 23,112,000.

Government.—The principalities remained separate entities under Turkish suzerainty until 1859, when Prince Alexandru Ion Cuza was elected Prince of both, still under the suzerainty of Turkey. Prince Cuza abdicated in 1866 and was succeeded by Prince Charles of Hohenzollern-Sigmaringen, in whose successors the crown was vested. By the Treaty of Berlin (July 13, 1878) the principality was recognized as an independent state, and part of the Dobrudja (which had been occupied by the Romanians) was incorporated. On March 27, 1881 it was recognized as a Kingdom.

The outcome of the War of 1914–18 added Bessarabia, the Bukovina, Transylvania, the Banat and Crisana-Maramures, these additions of territory being confirmed in the Treaty of St. Germain, 1919, and the Treaty of Petit Trianon, 1920.

On June 27, 1940, in compliance with an ultimatum from USSR, Bessarabia and Northern Bukovina were ceded to the Soviet Government, and in August 1940 Romania ceded to Bulgaria the portion of southern Dobrudja taken from Bulgaria in 1913.

Romania became 'The Romanian People's Republic' in December 1947, on the abdication of King Michael. A new Constitution, modelled on the Soviet Constitution of 1936, was adopted unanimously on September 24, 1952, by the Grand National Assembly. A new Constitution was approved by the Grand National Assembly in 1965 when the name of the state was changed to the Socialist Republic of Romania. The Constitution stated that the leading political force of society was the Romanian Communist Party.

A revolution in December 1989 led to the overthrow of Nicolae Ceauşescu, President since 1967, and the collapse of his government. A provisional government was formed which abolished the leading role of the Communist Party, promised free elections and changed the country's name to Romania. In May 1990 presidential and parliamentary elections took place under a system of universal adult suffrage and proportional representation. The National Salvation Front won 66 per cent of the vote. There is a Senate of 119 members and a 387-member Assembly of Deputies. A new government was formed in June 1990.

Agriculture.—Wallachia, Moldavia and Transylvania are potentially among the most fertile areas in Europe, and agriculture and sheep and cattle raising are the principal industries of Romania, although extreme weather conditions can have adverse effects on crops. These are principally cereal crops, legumes and other vegetables, flax and hemp. Vines and fruits are also grown. The forests of the mountainous regions are extensive, and the timber industry is important.

Socialization of agriculture was completed when collectivization was achieved in the spring of 1962. Since December 1989 agricultural workers have been allocated plots of land and are allowed to sell their produce on the open market. One third of the arable land is now farmed independently. Of the remaining 6 million hectares, one third belongs to state farms and two-thirds to co-operative farms.

Natural Resources and Industry.—Before the war petroleum and agriculture were the backbone of the Romanian economy but rapid industrialization since 1948 has meant that they no longer hold the same dominant position. There are plentiful supplies of natural gas, together with various mineral deposits including coal, iron ore, bauxite, lead, zinc, copper and uranium in quantities which allow a substantial part of the requirements of industry to be met from local resources. Production of crude oil was put at about 9,400,000 tonnes in 1988.

The economy has faced increasing problems since the late 1970s, the result of over investment in energy-intensive heavy industry and neglect of agriculture, which has led to food shortages. The effects of these policies were aggravated by the international recession and by high interest rates, and Romania was severely in debt by the early 1980s. The government has sought to alleviate the situation by reducing borrowing and cutting imports. The formerly centrally-planned economy is expected to be quickly transformed into a market economy under the new government.

Language and Religion.—Romanian is a Romance language with many archaic forms and with admixtures of Slavonic, Turkish, Magyar and French words. There is wealth of folk-songs and folklore, transmitted orally through many centuries and collected in the 19th century. The leading religion is that of the Romanian Orthodox Church; the Roman Catholics and some Protestant denominations are of importance numerically. There is a Hungarian minority of around 2·5 million, and a dwindling German minority of around 150,000.

Education is free and nominally compulsory. There are universities at Bucharest, Iasi, Cluj, Timişoara, Craiova and Braşov, polytechnics at Bucharest, Timişoara, Cluj, Braşov, Galati and Iasi, two commercial academies at Bucharest and Braşov, and agricultural colleges at Bucharest, Iasi, Cluj, Craiova and Timişoara.

Communications.—In 1979 there were 11,113 km of railway open for traffic. The mercantile marine had a gross tonnage of 13,220,000 tons in 1979. The principal ports are Constanta (on the Black Sea), Sulina (on the Danube Estuary), Galati, Braila, Giurgiu and Turnu Severin. The Danube and the Black Sea are linked by a canal completed in 1984. Romania is a member of the Danube Commission whose seat is at Budapest.

TRADE

In 1988 combined imports and exports totalled Lei 329,500 million. Imports are chiefly semi-manufactured goods, raw materials, machinery and metals; export consists principally of maize, wheat, barley, oats, petroleum, timber, cattle, meat, machines and industrial equipment.

Trade with UK

	1988	1989
Imports from UK	£50,111,000	£38,141,000
Exports to UK	100,906,000	117,685,000

CAPITAL.—Bucharest, on the Dimbovita, population 1,961,189. Other large towns are:

Braşov	290,722	Ψ Galati........	254,636
Constanţa	284,801	Craiova	243,117
Cluj-Napoca ...	270,820	Ploieşti.......	215,500
Iasi	265,176	Ψ Brăila	214,561
Timişoara	261,950		

CURRENCY.—Leu (*plural* Lei) of 100 bani.
FLAG.—Three vertical bands, blue, yellow, red.
NATIONAL ANTHEM.—Trei Culori (Three colours).
NATIONAL DAY.—August 23 (Liberation Day, 1944).

BRITISH EMBASSY
24 Strada Jules Michelet, Bucharest
[Bucharest 111634/6]

Ambassador Extraordinary and Plenipotentiary, His Excellency Michael William Atkinson, CMG, MBE (1989).
Counsellor, Deputy Head of Mission, A. Godson.
Defence, Naval and Military Attaché, Lt.-Col. P. A. Crocker.
Cultural Attaché and British Council Representative, A. Pattison, OBE.

RWANDA
(Republika y'u Rwanda)

President, Minister of Defence, Maj.-Gen. Juvénal Habyarimana, *assumed office*, July 5, 1973, *elected*, Dec. 24, 1978, *re-elected*, Dec. 19, 1983 and Dec. 17, 1988.

MINISTERS
(as at May 31, 1990)

Agriculture, Livestock and Forests, Anastase Ntezir-yayo.
Economy and Consumption, Juvénal Uwilingiyimana.
Finance, Benoît Ntigulirwa.
Industry and Crafts, Col. Aloys Nsekalije.
Public Works, Energy and Water, Joseph Nzirorera.
Transport and Communications, André Ntagerura.
Health and Social Affairs, Dr. Placidé Ngendahayo.

Primary and Secondary Education, Daniel Mban-gura.
Higher Education and Scientific Research, Charles Nyandwi.
Youth, Sports and Co-operative Societies, Maj. Augustin Ndindiliyimana.
Interior and Community Development, Jean-Marie Vianey Mugemana.
Civil Service and Labour, François Habiyakare.
Justice, Théoneste Muryanama.
Institutional Relations, Antoine Ntashamaje.
Planning, Callixte Nzabonimana.
Foreign Affairs and International Co-operation, Dr. Casimir Bizimungu.
Minister at the Presidency, Siméon Nteziryayo.

Rwanda, formerly part of the Belgian-administered trusteeship of Ruanda-Urundi, has an area of 10,169 sq. miles (26,338 sq. km), and a population (UN estimate 1988) of 6,755,000, mainly of the Bahutu tribe, with Batutsi and Batwa minorities.

A referendum held in September 1961 showed the majority of the population were opposed to the retention of the monarchy which was accordingly abolished on October 2, 1961. Rwanda became an independent Republic on July 1, 1962, with Gregoire Kayibanda as Head of State and Head of the Government. He was deposed in 1973, and replaced by a military government under Maj.-Gen. Juvénal Habyarimana. The sole legal political party is the Mouvement Révolutionnaire National pour le Developpement (MRND). Presidential and legislative elections to the 70-member National Development Council were last held in December 1988.

Coffee (accounting for 90 per cent of Rwanda's export earnings in 1989), tea and sugar are grown. Tin, hides, bark of quinine and extract of pyrethrum flowers are also exported.

The National University of Rwanda is situated at two campuses, Butare and Ruhengeri.

In 1987 total imports were valued at US$351·7m; total exports, US$112·3m.

Trade with UK

	1988	1989
Imports from UK	£1,636,000	£1,790,000
Exports to UK	8,434,000	2,991,000

CAPITAL.—Kigali (156,000).
CURRENCY.—Rwanda franc of 100 centimes.
FLAG.—Three vertical bands, red, yellow and green with letter R on yellow band.
NATIONAL DAY.—July 1.

British Ambassador (resident in Kinshasa, Zaire).

EL SALVADOR
(República de El Salvador)

President, Alfredo Felix Cristiani Burkard, *elected* March 19, 1989, *assumed office* June 1, 1989.
Vice-President, Francisco Merino.

CABINET
(as at May 31, 1990)

Minister of the Presidency, vacant.
Foreign Affairs, Dr. Manuel Pacas Castro.
Planning, Mirna Lievano de Márquez.
Interior, Juan Antonio Martínez Varela.
Justice, Dr. Oscar Santamaria.
Finance, Dr. Rafael Alvarado Cano.
Economy, Arturo Zablah.
Education, Dr. René Hernández Valiente.

Defence, Humberto Larios.
Labour, Mauricio González.
Agriculture, Antonio Cabrales.
Public Health, Dr. Lisandro Vásquez Sosa.
Public Works, Mauricio Stubig.
Secretary of Information, Mauricio Sandoval.

In addition there are ten Vice-Ministers.

EMBASSY OF EL SALVADOR
9 Welbeck House, 62 Welbeck Street, W1M 7HB
[071-486 8182]

Ambassador Extraordinary and Plenipotentiary, His Excellency Dr. Maurico Rosales-Rivera (1986).
First Secretary and Consul General, Carolina Calderón.

Area and Population.—The Republic of El Salvador extends along the Pacific coast of Central America for 160 miles with a general breadth of about 50 miles, and contains an area of 8,124 sq. miles (21,041 sq. km), with a population (1989 estimate) of 5,500,000. The population density is one of the highest in the world with 253 inhabitants per square km. It is divided into 14 Departments.

The surface of the country is very mountainous, many of the peaks being extinct volcanoes. The highest are the Santa Ana volcano (7,700 ft.) and the San Vicente volcano (7,200 ft.). Much of the interior has an average altitude of 2,000 feet. The climate varies from tropical to temperate. The lowlands along the coast are generally hot, but towards the interior the altitude tempers the severity of the heat. There is a wet season from May to October, and a dry season from November to April. Earthquakes have been frequent in the history of El Salvador, the most recent being that of October 10, 1986, when considerable damage was done to San Salvador.

The principal river is the Rio Lempa. There is a large volcanic lake (Ilopango) a few miles to the east of the capital, while farther away and to the west lies the smaller lake of Coatepeque, which appears to have been formed in a vast crater flanked by the Santa Ana volcano.

Government.—El Salvador was conquered in 1526 by Pedro de Alvarado, and formed part of the Spanish vice-royalty of Guatemala until 1821.

After two years of government by a junta headed by José Napoleon Duarte, elections for a Constituent Assembly were held in March 1982, ending decades of military rule. Presidential elections, although boycotted by the guerrilla movement (Farabundo Martí National Liberation Front (FMLN)), were held in March 1984 and in the run-off between the two largest parties, Duarte, the Christian Democrat leader, won with a 54 per cent majority over the Nationalist Republican Alliance (ARENA) candidate. Alfredo Cristiani (ARENA) won the presidential elections in March 1989 with 54 per cent of the vote. The FMLN guerrillas again boycotted the elections. ARENA also overturned a Christian Democrat majority in the National Assembly and since the March 1988 elections has held 32 of the 60 seats, with 22 seats held by the Christian Democratic Party (PDC) and the remaining 6 seats held by the National Conciliation Party (PCN).

Agriculture.—The principal cash crops are coffee, which is grown principally on the slopes of the volcanoes, cotton, which is cultivated on the coastal plains, and sugarcane and shrimps. (However, cotton and sugar production have decreased as a result of the civil war.) Also cultivated are maize, sesame, indigo, rice, balsam, etc. In the lower altitudes towards the east, sisal is produced and used in the manufacture of coffee and cereal bags. Land reforms, announced in March 1980, have largely been implemented. The Salvadorean Coffee Company, sugar exports and the banking system are nationalized but

President Cristiani is in the process of privatizing these industries and introducing competition.

Industry.—Existing factories make textiles, clothing, constructional steel, furniture, cement and household items. In 1989 GDP amounted to US$4,808 million (US$874 per capita). El Salvador is a member of the Central American Common Market. The first trade zone was inaugurated in November 1974 and others are planned.

Education.—The illiteracy rate has risen to 68·1 per cent (1985) since 1980 when the figure was 30·5 per cent. Primary education is nominally compulsory, but the number of schools and teachers available is too small to enable education to be given to all children of school age.

Language and Literature.—The language of the country is Spanish. There are five daily newspapers published at the capital, and four in the provinces.

Communications.—The Executive Autonomous Port Commission (CEPA) administers the port of Cutuco, at La Union and the principal port of Acajutla, and the railways through FENADESAL. There is a railway line between San Salvador and Guatemala City and Puerto Barrios on the Caribbean coast but it is subject to interruption. The roads are paved and in good condition but some bridges are temporary structures following guerrilla action. There are good roads between Acajutla and the capital (60 miles), and between the capital and Guatemala City. The Pan-American Highway from the Guatemalan frontier follows this route and continues to the Honduran frontier. The El Salvador international airport can receive jet aircraft with daily flights to other Central American capitals, Mexico, and five US cities.

There are post and telegraph offices throughout the country. There are 100 broadcasting stations and six television stations.

BUDGET

	1988
Revenue	₡2,843·8m
Expenditure	₡3,042·2m

Trade with UK

	1988	1989
Imports from UK	£8,186,000	£9,594,000
Exports to UK	2,961,000	2,133,000

There is foreign exchange control. There is also a parallel market in US dollars.

Chief exports are coffee, cotton, sugar, shrimps, sisal (in the form of bags used for exporting coffee, sugar, etc.), balsam, meat, towels, hides and skins. The chief imports are chemicals, fertilizers, pharmaceutical goods, petroleum, manufactured goods, industrial and electronic machinery and equipment, vehicles and consumer goods.

CAPITAL.—San Salvador. Estimated population of metropolitan area, 2,000,000. Other towns are Santa Ana (417,000), San Miguel (157,838), ψ La Union (Cutuco), ψ La Libertad and ψ Acajutia.

CURRENCY.—El Salvador colón (₡) of 100 centavos.

FLAG.—Three horizontal bands, light blue, white, light blue; coat of arms on white band.

NATIONAL ANTHEM.—Saludemos La Patria Orgullosos (Let us proudly hail the Fatherland).

NATIONAL DAY.—September 15.

BRITISH EMBASSY
PO Box 1591, San Salvador

British Ambassador, (resident in Tegucigalpa, Honduras).

Chargé d'affaires a.i., I. R. Murray (*First Secretary*).

SAN MARINO
(Repubblica di San Marino)

Regents, Two 'Capitani Reggenti'.

CONSULATE GENERAL IN LONDON
166 High Holborn, WC1V 6TT
[071–836 7744]

Consul-General, The Lord Forte.

A small Republic in the hills near Rimini, on the Adriatic, founded, it is stated, by a pious stonecutter of Dalmatia in the 4th century. The Republic resisted Papal claims and those of neighbouring dukedoms during the 15th–18th centuries, and its integrity and sovereignty is recognized and respected by Italy. The area is approximately 23 sq. miles (61 sq. km.), population (UN estimate 1988) is 23,000.

The Republic is governed by a State Congress of ten members, under the presidency of two Heads of State, who are elected at six-monthly intervals. The Great and General Council, a legislative body of 60 members, is elected by universal suffrage for a term of five years. A Council of Twelve forms in certain cases a Supreme Court of Justice. A coalition government of the Communist Party and the Christian Democratic Party was returned to power in the general election of May 1988.

The city of San Marino, on the slope of Monte Titano, has three towers, a fine church and Government palace, a theatre and museums. The principal products are wine; cereals, and cattle, and the main industries are tourism, ceramics, lime, concrete, cotton yarns, colour and paints.

CURRENCY.—Italian currency is in circulation.

FLAG.—Two horizontal bands, white, blue (with coat of arms of the Republic in centre).

NATIONAL DAY.—September 3.

British Consul-General, Miss M. L. Croll (resident in Florence, Italy).

SÃO TOMÉ AND PRÍNCIPE
(República Democrática de São Tomé e Príncipe)

President, Dr. Manuel Pinto da Costa.

COUNCIL OF MINISTERS
(as at May 31, 1990)

Prime Minister, Celestino Rocha da Costa.
Defence and Internal Security, Raul Braganca Neto.
Foreign Affairs, Carlos da Graca.
Justice and Public Affairs, Francesco Fortunato Pires.
Economy and Finance, Agapito Mendes Dias.
Agriculture and Fisheries, Oscar Aguiar Sacramento e Sousa.
Co-operation, Guillermo Posser da Costa.
Education and Culture, Ligia do Espirito Santo Costa.
Health, Labour and Social Security, Armindo Vaz de Almeida.
Equipment, Environment, Transport and Communications, Carlos Ferreira.
Ministers Delegate, Manuel Quaresma Costa (*Principe Islands*); Manuel Vaz Alfonso Fernades (*Secretary General*).

The islands of São Tomé and Príncipe are situated in the gulf of Guinea, off the west coast of Africa. They have an area of 372 sq. miles (964 sq. km), and a population (UN estimate 1988) of 106,000.

Following Portugal's decision to grant independence, a transitional government was installed in December 1974, and the islands became an independent democratic republic on July 12, 1975.

Cacao is the main product.

Trade with UK

	1988	1989
Imports from UK	£416,000	£819,000
Exports to UK	20,000	4,000

CAPITAL.—ΨSão Tomé (25,000).

CURRENCY.—Dobra of 100 centavos.

FLAG.—Horizontal stripes of green, yellow, green, the yellow of double width and bearing two black stars; and a red triangle in the hoist.

NATIONAL DAY.—July 12 (Independence Day).

British Ambassador (resident in Luanda, Angola).

SAUDI ARABIA
(Al Mamlaka al Arabiya as-Sa'udiyya)

Custodian of the Two Holy Mosques and King of Saudi Arabia, HM King Fahd bin Abdul Aziz, *born,* 1921, *ascended the throne* June 1, 1982.

Crown Prince, HRH Amir Abdullah bin Abdul Aziz.

COUNCIL OF MINISTERS
(as at June 30, 1990)

Prime Minister, HM King Fahd bin Abdul Aziz.

First Deputy Prime Minister and Commander of the National Guard, HRH Prince Abdullh bin Abdul Aziz.

Second Deputy Prime Minister, Defence and Aviation, HRH Prince Sultan bin Abdul Aziz.

Public Works and Housing, HRH Prince Mit'ab bin Abdul Aziz.

Interior, HRH Prince Naif bin Abdul Aziz.

Foreign Affairs, HRH Prince Saud al-Faisal bin Abdul Aziz.

Finance and National Economy, Muhammad Aba al-Khail.

Agriculture and Water, Dr. Abdul Rahman bin Abdul Aziz bin Hassan Al al-Shaikh.

Municipal and Rural Affairs, Dr. Khalid bin Mohammed al Angari.

Justice, Sheikh Mohammed bin Ibrahim al Jubeir.

Commerce, Dr Sulaiman al-Solaim.

Communications, Dr. Hussain Mansouri.

Petroleum and Mineral Resources, Hisham Nazer *(and acting Minister of Planning).*

Labour and Social Affairs, Dr. Mohamed Ali al-Faiz.

Information, Ali Sha'er.

Health, Faisal bin Abdul Aziz al Hejailan.

Pilgrimage and Endowments, Abdul Wahhab Ahmed Abdul Wasi.

Education, Dr. Abdul Aziz Al-Abdullah al-Khuwaiter *(and acting Minister of Higher Education).*

Posts, Telegraphs and Telephones, Dr. Alawi Darwish Kayyal.

Industry and Electricity, Abdul Aziz al-Zamil.

Ministers of State, Muhammad Ibrahim Mas'oud; Dr. Muhammad Abdul Latif al-Melhem; Omar Abdul Qader Faqih; Dr. Fayez Ibrahim Badr; Turki bin Khalid Al Sudairi; Mohammed bin Abdulaziz Bin Zar'a; Ibrahim bin Abdullah al Angari; Sheikh Abdulaziz bin Mohammed bin Ibrahim Al al-Shaikh.

ROYAL EMBASSY OF SAUDI ARABIA
30 Belgrave Square, SW1X 8QB
[071–235 0831]

Ambassador Extraordinary and Plenipotentiary, His Excellency Sheikh Nasser Almanqour, GCVO (1980).

Ministers Plenipotentiary, Ibrahim M. Mosly; Saud Ahmed M. Alyahya, LVO; Abdullah O. Barry, LVO.

The Kingdom of Saudi Arabia is a personal union of two countries, the Sultan of Nejd becoming also King of the Hejaz. Great Britain recognized Abdul Aziz Ibn Saud as an independent ruler, King of the Hejaz and of Nejd and its Dependencies, by the Treaty

of Jeddah (May 20, 1927). The name was changed to the Kingdom of Saudi Arabia in September 1932.

The total area of the Kingdom is about 830,000 sq. miles (2,149,640 sq. km), with a population (UN estimate 1988) of 14,016,000. Islam is the established and only permitted religion.

In the 18th century Nejd was an independent state governed from Diriya (now in ruins, 25 km from Riyadh) and the stronghold of the Wahhabis, a puritanical Islamic sect. It subsequently fell under Turkish rule; in 1913 Abdul Aziz Ibn Saud threw off Turkish rule and captured the Turkish province of Al Hasa. In 1920 he captured the Asir, and in 1921, by force of arms, he added to his dominions the Jebel Shammar territory of the Rashid family. In 1925 he completed the conquest of the Hejaz.

Saudi Arabia comprises almost the whole of the Arabian peninsula, with the exception of the Republic of Yemen in the extreme south, Oman and the UAE in the south-east and Qatar in the east. In the north-west it borders Jordan and in the north-east Iraq and Kuwait, while to the west lies the Red Sea and to the east the Gulf. The Nejd ('Plateau'), now the Central Province, extends over the centre of the peninsula, including the Nafud and Dahna deserts. The Hejaz ('the Boundary'), now the Western Province, extends along the Red Sea coast to Asir and contains the holy towns of Mecca and Medina. The former, about 60 km east of Jeddah, is the birthplace of the Prophet Mohammed, and contains the Great Mosque, within which is the Kaaba or sacred shrine of the Muslim religion. This is the focus of the annual Hajj ('Pilgrimage'), performed by 1·4 million in 1990. Medina Al Munawwarah ('The City of Light'), some 300 km north of Mecca, is celebrated as the first city to embrace Islam and as the Prophet Mohammed's burial place (he died there on Rabia 12, AH 11, corresponding to June 7, AD 632).

Asir ('Inaccessible') is named for its mountainous terrain, and, with the coastal plain of the Tihama, lies along the southern Red Sea coast from Hejaz to the border with Yemen. It is the only region to enjoy substantial rainfall. Water supplies are, however, supplemented by dams and irrigation. The east and south-east of the country are lower-lying and largely desert. Outside the manufacturing centres which have grown up around some of the towns, most of the population are engaged in agriculture. The productivity of traditional dryland farming is increasingly supplemented by irrigation.

Industry.—Oil was first found in commercial quantities in Dhahran, near Dammam, in 1938. Total production of crude oil peaked at 9·9 million b.p.d. in 1980, and in 1986 was 4·8 million b.p.d. About 97 per cent of the total is extracted by the Arabian-American Oil Company. Recoverable reserves stood at about 167 billion barrels at the end of 1986, equivalent to about 95 years' production at the 1986 rate. Aramco's 66-year lease will terminate in 1999 but the company was effectively nationalized in 1980.

The government actively encourages the establishment of manufacturing industries in the country. Industries have developed in the fields of construction materials, metal fabrication, simple machinery and electrical equipment, food and beverages, chemicals and plastics. Investment in industrial gases, intermediate petrochemicals, light engineering and machinery is encouraged. Two industrial poles have been established at Jubail and Yanbu, financed by the state agency Saudi Arabian Basic Industries Corporation. Linked by gas and oil pipelines, both are to have petrochemical complexes producing, initially, ethylene and methanol; six of the seven plants now on-stream are joint ventures with American and Japanese companies. Complete new cities are being built at each pole: Jubail will eventually house 300,000 and Yanbu 190,000. The state agency Petromin operates three domestic refineries and two lubricant plants and the last of three joint-venture export refineries came on-stream in 1986. Total refining capacity is now approximately 1,950,000 b.p.d.

Communications.—The railway from the port of Dammam to the oilfields at Abqaiq and through Hofuf to Riyadh was opened in 1951, and a direct Dammam-Riyadh line opened in 1985. An extension to Jeddah via Medina and the reopening of the Hejaz railway are planned. Metalled roads connect all the cities and main towns; the network consisted of 28,500 km in 1985. The principal port of the Gulf is Dammam which has 39 berths and an annual capacity of 9·1 million tons. Jeddah is the centre of commercial traffic on the Red Sea and has 51 piers, giving an annual capacity of 17 million tons. The government-owned Saudi Arabian Airlines (Saudia) operate scheduled services to 19 domestic airports. There are international airports at Dhahran, Jeddah and Riyadh. Work on the new King Fahd International Airport in Eastern Province was due to be completed in 1990. Saudia have an extensive overseas operation, and a large number of international airlines operate into the country. Telecommunications are being rapidly expanded. The government is a major participant in the Arab Satellite Communications Organization.

Education.—With the exception of a few schools for expatriate children, all schools are government supervised and segregated for boys and girls. By mid-1985 there were a total of 1,692,300 schoolchildren in 5,323 primary and 1,219 intermediate and 418 secondary schools. There are universities in Jeddah, Mecca, Riyadh (branches in Abha and Qassim), Dammam (branch at Hofuf) and Dhahran, and there are Islamic universities in Medina and Riyadh. In addition there is great emphasis on vocational training, provided at 24 literacy and artisan skill training centres and 21 more advanced industrial, commercial and agricultural education institutes. Education in government-owned institutes is free at all levels.

Finance and Trade.—Oil remains the main source of receipts in the balance of payments. As a result, government revenues are markedly affected by oil prices and volume of production. The 1990 budget provided for expenditure of SR143,000 million (36 per cent on defence), and a revenue of SR25,000 million.

The leading suppliers of imports are USA, Japan, West Germany, the UK, Italy and France and the chief customers for exports are Japan, France, USA and Singapore. There is a total ban on the importa-

tion of alcohol, pork products, firearms and items regarded as non-Islamic or pornographic.

	1988	1989
Total imports	SR81,582m	SR79,219m
Total exports	88,896m	103,892m

Trade with UK

	1988	1989
Imports from UK	£1,713,423,000	£2,432,941,000
Exports to UK	614,144,000	502,416,000

CAPITAL.—Riyadh, population (1990) about 1·5 million. Other major centres are Jeddah (estimated population 1 million), Buraydah, Dammam, Hofuf, Mecca, Medina and Tabuk.

CURRENCY.—Saudi riyal (SR) of 20 qursh or 100 halala.

FLAG.—Green oblong, white Arabic device in centre: 'There is no God but God and Muhammad is the Prophet of God,' and a white scimitar beneath the lettering.

NATIONAL ANTHEM.—Long live our beloved King.

BRITISH EMBASSY
PO Box 94351, Riyadh 11693
[Riyadh 488 0077]

Ambassador Extraordinary and Plenipotentiary, His Excellency Sir Alan Gordon Munro, KCMG (1989).
Counsellors, D. J. Plumbly (*Head of Chancery and Consul-General*); C. Wilton (*Commercial*).
Defence and Military Attaché, Brig. P. Sincock, MBE.
Air Attaché, Wing Cdr. J. Ambler.
Naval Attaché, Cdr. N. Kerr.
First Secretaries, M. D. K. Halsey (*Chancery*); P. O. Gooderham (*Economic*); H. Formstone (*Commercial*); C. H. Woodland (*Consul General*); D. G. Lloyd (*Commercial*).

Consul General, Jeddah, H. J. Tunnell, PO Box 393, Jeddah 21411.

British Council Representative, Clive Smith, OBE, Olaya Main Road, Al Mousa Centre, Tower B (PO Box 58012), Riyadh 11594. There is also an office in *Jeddah*.

SENEGAL
(République du Sénégal)

President and Head of Government, Abdou Diouf, installed, Jan. 1, 1981, *elected for a second five-year term*, Feb. 28, 1988.

MINISTERS
(as at May 31, 1990)

Armed Forces, Médoune Fall.
Justice, Guardian of the Seals, Serigne Lamine Diop.
Minister, Secretary-General at the Presidency, André Sonko.
Minister, Special Adviser to the President, Seydou Madani Sy.
Foreign Affairs, Seydina Oumar Sy.
Interior, Famara Ibrahima Sagna.
Economy and Finance, Moussa Toure.
National Education, Djibo Ka.
Public Works, Transport and Housing, Robert Sagna.
Rural Development and Water Resources, Cheikh Abdoul Khadre Cissokho.
Industry and Handicrafts, Alassane Dialy Ndiaye.
Tourism and Environmental Protection, Jacques Baudin.
Health and Social Development, Assane Diop.
Culture and Communication, Moustapha Ka.
Labour and Professional Training, Moctar Kebe.
Youth and Sports, Abdoulaye Makhtar Diop.
Animal Resources, Mbaye Diouf.

Ministers-Delegate, Cheikh Amidou Kane (*African Economic Integration*); Ndioro Ndiaye (*Women and Child Welfare*); Coumba Ndoffène Bouna Diouf (*Parliamentary Relations*); Mata Sy Diallo (*Emigration*).

EMBASSY OF THE REPUBLIC OF SENEGAL
11 Phillimore Gardens, W8 7QG
[071–937 0925/6]

Ambassador Extraordinary and Plenipotentiary, His Excellency Gen. Idrissa Fall, GCVO, MBE (1984).

Senegal lies on the west coast of Africa between Mauritania in the north, Mali in the east, and Guinea-Bissau and Guinea in the south. The Gambia lies entirely within Senegal, except for its sea-coast. (For MAP, *see* p. 774.) Senegal has an area of 75,750 sq. miles (196,192 sq. km), and a population (UN estimate 1988) of 7,113,000.

Formerly a French colony, Senegal elected in November 1958 to remain within the French Community as an autonomous republic. In March 1963 (after an attempted coup d'état by the then Prime Minister in the previous December) a new constitution was approved giving executive powers to the President, on the lines of the present French constitution. The process of political liberalization continued; there are now 16 political parties officially recognized. Six parties contested the General Election in February 1988. The Parti Socialiste (PS) took 103 seats and the Parti Démocratique Sénégalais (PDS) 17.

In 1982, after an attempted coup in The Gambia in July 1981 had been put down with the aid of Senegalese troops, the Senegambia Confederation was established, based on certain joint institutions and the integration of defence, security and some other matters. Each country remains sovereign and independent. The President of Senegal is President of the Confederation and the President of The Gambia is Confederal Vice-President.

Senegal's principal exports are groundnuts (raw and processed) and phosphates. Tourism is also of growing importance as a revenue earner.

Trade with UK

	1988	1989
Imports from UK	£14,840,000	£13,448,000
Exports to UK	11,284,000	6,820,000

CAPITAL—Ψ Dakar (1,000,000).
CURRENCY.—Franc CFA of 100 centimes.
FLAG.—Three vertical bands, green, yellow and red; a green star on the yellow band.
NATIONAL DAY.—April 4.

BRITISH EMBASSY
BP 6025, Dakar
[Dakar 237392]

Ambassador Extraordinary and Plenipotentiary, His Excellency Roger Campbell Beetham, LVO (1990).
First Secretary, R. S. Dewar (*Head of Chancery and Consul*).
Second Secretary, Miss J. M. Pearce.
Third Secretary, N. J. Enescott (*Vice Consul*).

British Council Representative, Dr. M. Cooper, 34–36 Blvd. de la Republique, Immeuble Sonatel, BP 6232, Dakar.

SOMALIA
(Jamhuuriyadda Diimoqraadiga ee Soomaaliya)

President and Secretary General of the Somali Revolutionary Socialist Party, Maj.-Gen. Mohamed Siad Barre, *assumed office* Oct. 21, 1969.

COUNCIL OF MINISTERS*
(as at June 30, 1990)

Prime Minister, Lt.-Gen. Mohamed Ali Samantar.
Planning, Juba Valley Development, Mohamed Godah Barre.
Interior, Abdulkadir Haji Mohamed.
Industry and Commerce, Bashir Farah Kahiye.
Defence, Dr. Hussein Abdirahman Mattan.
Foreign Affairs, Ahmed Jama Abdulle (Jengeli).
Finance and Revenues, Mohamed Gheile Yusuf.
Agriculture, Mohamud Mohamed Ulussow.
Education and Culture, A. M. Mireh.
Livestock, Forestry and Range, Abdurahman Jama Mohamed.
Information and Tourism, Dahir Farah Afey.
Land and Air Transport, Mohamed Sheikh Osman (Jawari).
Mineral and Water Resources, Abdirazak Ali Elmi.
Health, Dr. M. A. Munassar.
Posts and Telecommunications, Abukar Hassan Wehliye.
Public Works and Housing, Mohamed Sa'id Hirsi (Morgan).
Labour and Sports, Col. Abdi Warsameh Issak.
Fishing, Marine Transport and Ports, Mohamed Saeed Mohamed Ghes.
Justice and Religious Affairs, Sheikh Mohamed Gulaid.

* In early September 1990 it was reported that Samantar's government was sacked by President Barre, and Mohamed Madar was installed as Prime Minister.

Chairman, People's Assembly, Maj.-Gen. Hussein Kulmie Afrah.

EMBASSY OF THE SOMALI DEMOCRATIC REPUBLIC
60 Portland Place, W1N 3DG
[01–580 7148]

Ambassador Extraordinary and Plenipotentiary, new appointment awaited.
Chargé d'Affaires, Dool Abdullahi Mohamed.

The Somali Democratic Republic occupies part of the north-east horn of Africa, with a coast-line on the Indian Ocean extending from the boundary with Kenya (2° South latitude) to Cape Guardafui (12° N.); and on the Gulf of Aden to the boundary with Djibouti. Somalia is bounded on the west by Djibouti, Ethiopia and Kenya and covers an area of approximately 246,201 sq. miles (637,657 sq. km). The population, of which a large proportion is nomadic, is 7,107,000 (UN estimate 1988).

Government.—The Somali Democratic Republic, consisting of the former British Somaliland Protectorate and the former Italian trust territory of Somalia, was established on July 1, 1960. British rule in Somaliland lasted from 1887 until 1960 except for a short period in 1940–41 when the Protectorate was occupied by Italian forces. Somalia, formerly an Italian colony, was occupied by British forces in 1941. In 1950 it was placed under Italian administration by a resolution of the UN; this trusteeship lasted until independence. Following the assassination of President Shermake on October 15, 1969, the armed forces, assisted by the police, took over the Government without resistance and a Revolutionary Council under Siad Barre assumed control of the country. A new constitution was introduced following a referendum in 1979. This provides for an elected People's Assembly of 171 seats. The Assembly met for the first time in January 1980. In July 1990 it was announced that a referendum on a new Constitution in October 1990 would be followed by multi-party elections in February 1991.

Following a dispute with Ethiopia over territory, which lasted many years, a peace agreement between the two countries was signed on April 3, 1988 in Mogadishu.

Civil war broke out in May 1988 between the Government and the opposition Somali National Movement. The situation is still confused but there was great damage to property and a significant number of casualties. There are now 400,000 refugees in Ethiopia. Most of southern Somalia is now under de facto military rule.

Economy.—Livestock raising is the main occupation in Somalia and there is a modest export trade in livestock on the hoof, skins and hides. Italy, the Gulf States and Saudi Arabia import the bulk of the banana crop, the second biggest export.

Trade with UK

	1988	1989
Imports from UK	£10,379,000	£10,508,000
Exports to UK	1,151,000	508,000

CAPITAL.—ΨMogadishu, population (estimated 1987), 1,000,000. Other towns are Hargeisa (20,000), Boroma (65,000), ΨKisimayu (60,000), ΨBerbera (15,000) and Burao (15,000).

CURRENCY.—Somali shilling of 100 cents.

FLAG.—Five-pointed white star on blue ground.

NATIONAL DAY.—October 21.

BRITISH EMBASSY
(PO Box No. 1036) Mogadishu
[Mogadishu 20288/9]

Ambassador Extraordinary and Plenipotentiary, His Excellency Ian McCluney, CMG (1989).

Second Secretary and Consul, D. P. Gething.

SOUTH AFRICA
(Republiek van Suid-Afrika)

State President, Frederick Willem de Klerk, *sworn in* September 20, 1989.

CABINET
(as at June 30, 1990)

Foreign Affairs, Pik Botha.

Constitutional Development and National Education, Gerrit Viljoen.

Defence, Magnus Malan.

Mineral and Energy Affairs and Public Enterprises, Dawie de Villiers.

Justice, Kobie Coetsee.

Finance, Barend du Plessis.

Manpower, Eli Louw.

Law and Order, Adriaan Vlok.

Environment and Water Affairs, Gert Kotze.

Education and Development Aid, Stoffel van der Merwe.

Home Affairs, Gene Louw.

Trade, Industry and Tourism, Kent Durr.

Transport, George Bartlett.

Planning and Provisional Affairs, Hernus Kriel.

Health and Population Development, Rina Venter.

Agriculture, Jacob de Villiers.

Administration and Privatization, Wim de Villiers.

President's Council, Willie van Niekerk.

EMBASSY OF THE REPUBLIC OF SOUTH AFRICA
South Africa House, Trafalgar Square, WC2N 5DP
[071–930 4488]

Ambassador Extraordinary and Plenipotentiary, His Excellency P. R. (Rae) Killen (1987).

Minister, J. De Goede.

Counsellor (Press and Information), R. Ballard-Tremeer.

Minister (Trade), J. H. C. Engelbrecht.

There is a Consulate-General at Golden Cross House, 8 Duncannon Street, WC2N 4JF.

Area and Population.—The Republic, comprising the Provinces of the Cape of Good Hope, Natal, the Transvaal and the Orange Free State, occupies the southernmost part of the African continent from the courses of the Limpopo, Molopo and Orange Rivers (34° 50′ 22″ S.) to the Cape of Good Hope, with the exception of Lesotho, Botswana and Swaziland, and part of Mozambique. It has a total area of 471,445 sq. miles (1,221,031 sq. km) and a total population (UN estimate 1988) of 33,748,000. Approximately 18 per cent of the population is white (1985).

The southernmost province contains many parallel ranges, which rise in steps towards the interior. The south-western peninsula contains the famous Table Mountain (3,582 ft.), while the Great Swartberg and Langeberg run in parallel lines from west to east of the Cape Province. Between these two ranges and the Roggeveld and Nuweveld ranges to the north is the Great Karoo Plateau, which is bounded on the east by the Sneeuberg, containing the highest summit in the province (Kompasberg, 7,800 ft.). In the east are ranges which join the Drakensberg (11,000 ft.) between Natal and the Orange Free State.

The Orange Free State presents a succession of undulating grassy plains with occasional hills or kopjes. The Transvaal is also mainly an elevated plateau with parallel ridges in the Magaliesberg and Waterberg ranges of no great height. The eastern province of Natal has pastoral lowlands and rich agriculture land between the slopes of the Drakensberg and the coast, the interior rising in terraces as in the southern provinces. The Orange, with its tributary the Vaal, is the principal river of the south, rising in the Drakensberg and flowing into the Atlantic between Namibia and the Cape Province. The Limpopo, or Crocodile River, in the north, rises in the Transvaal and flows into the Indian Ocean through Mozambique. Most of the remaining rivers are furious torrents after rain, with partially dry beds at other seasons.

Government.—The self-governing colonies of the Cape of Good Hope, Natal, the Transvaal and the Orange River Colony became united on May 31, 1910 under the South Africa Act 1909, in a legislative union under the name of the Union of South Africa, the four colonies becoming provinces of the Union. The Union of South Africa continued as a member of the British Commonwealth until 1961. After a referendum held among white voters on October 5, 1960, the Union of South Africa became a republic on May 31, 1961, and withdrew from the Commonwealth.

Since 1948, South Africa's social and political structure has been based on a policy of racial segregation (apartheid). A new Constitution came into effect in September 1984 which provided for an executive President and a three-chamber Parliament: the House of Assembly (178 members) representing Whites, the House of Representatives (85 members) representing Coloureds, and the House of Delegates (45 members) representing Indians. The majority black population has no representation. There is joint parliamentary responsibility for 'general' affairs (foreign policy, defence, finance, law and order, justice, transport, manpower, commerce and industry, agriculture), and each chamber has separate responsibility for the 'own' affairs of the population group it represents (housing, social welfare, health, education, local government and some aspects of agriculture). Disputes between the chambers may be referred by the President to the President's Council (60 members—20 White, 10 Coloured, 5 Indian elected by their respective chambers, 15 nominated by the President, 10 nominated by Opposition parties).

The President is chosen by an 88-member electoral college (in the proportion 4 White : 2 Coloured : 1 Indian) of the majority parties of the three chambers. The President appoints the Cabinet from all three communities, and also appoints each community's ministerial council for 'own' affairs.

The promulgation of the new Constitution in 1984 coincided with rioting in the black townships and the continuing unrest led to the declaration on July 20, 1985 of a State of Emergency in 36 districts. A nationwide State of Emergency was declared on June 12, 1986; it was renewed annually until it was finally lifted in the Cape, Transvaal and Orange Free State provinces in June 1990. It remains in force in Natal.

Elections to the House of Assembly took place on September 6, 1989 and the National Party retained its majority with 93 seats; the Conservative Party won 39; the Democratic Party 33. In elections to the House of Representatives and House of Delegates, the Coloured Labour Party (led by the Rev. H. J. Hendrickse) and the Indian National Peoples Party (led by Mr. A. Rajbansi) won the majority of seats respectively.

In the face of continuing internal unrest and external condemnation, the government is beginning to introduce some reforms. Negotiations with black political activists are under way.

The Black Homelands.—The homelands are areas set aside for occupation by blacks. Six areas (Gazankulu, Lebowa, KwaNdbele, KaNgwane, Qwaqwa and KwaZulu) are designated self-governing national states. A further four areas (Bophuthatswana, Ciskei, Transkei and Venda) are regarded as independent republics by the South African government but they are not recognized as such by the United Nations.

Education.—The Provinces have been relieved of all vocational education (technical and industrial). The Department of National Education under the minister is concerned with universities, technical colleges, schools of industries, reformatories and state technical, housecraft and commercial high schools, state-aided vocational schools and state and state-aided special schools for the physically handicapped.

Communications.—The previously state-owned and controlled South African Transport Services has been privatized. Independent companies now operate the national railway system, the principal harbours, most long-distance passenger and freight road transport services, the South African Airways airline and a network of pipelines for petroleum products.

There are international airports at Johannesburg (Jan Smuts), Durban (Louis Botha) and Cape Town (D. F. Malan), with another under construction at La Mercy, Natal. South African Airways operates international services to Europe, South America, the Far East and the Middle East, as well as to neighbouring countries, and it is the principal operator of domestic flights.

The largest sea-port is Durban, Natal. Other major ports are Cape Town, Port Elizabeth, East London, Saldanha Bay and Mossel Bay in Cape Province and Richards Bay, Natal.

Production.—Mining is of great importance to the South African economy. Minerals to the value of R29,240·1 million were sold in 1986. Principal minerals produced are: gold, coal, diamonds, copper, iron ore, manganese, lime and limestone, and chrome ore. South Africa is the world's largest producer of gold.

Agriculture, forestry and fishing account for about 6 per cent of GDP. Over 50 per cent of land is pasture so livestock farming is widespread with meat and wool important products. Principal crops are maize, sugar-cane, fruits and vegetables, wheat, sorghum, sunflower seed and groundnuts. Cotton is widely grown because of its suitability to the climate, and viticulture is also widespread.

Industries, concentrated most heavily around Johannesburg, Pretoria and the major ports, process foodstuffs, metals and non-metallic mineral products, and also produce beverages and tobacco, motor vehicles, chemicals and chemical products, machinery, textiles and clothing, and paper and paper products.

Trade.—Principal exports are: gold, base metals and metal products, diamonds, food (especially fruit), chemicals, machinery and transport equipment, and wool. Principal imports are: machinery, chemicals, motor vehicles, metals and metal products, food, inedible raw materials and textiles.

Trade with UK

	1988	1989
Imports from UK	£1,074,826,000	£1,038,242,000
Exports to UK	807,669,000	884,607,000

Finance.—Estimated revenue for 1988–89 was R47,460 million, and estimated expenditure was R56,556 million.

CAPITAL.—The administrative seat of the Government is Pretoria, Transvaal; population (1985 estimate) 822,925; the seat of the legislature is ΨCape Town, population (1985) 1,911,521. Other large towns (1985 figures) are Johannesburg, Transvaal (1,609,408); ΨDurban, Natal, the largest seaport (634,301); ΨPort Elizabeth, Cape (651,993); Bloemfontein, capital of Orange Free State (232,984); ΨEast London, Cape (167,992); and Pietermaritzburg, capital of Natal (192,417).

CURRENCY.—Rand (R) of 100 cents.

FLAG.—Three horizontal stripes of equal width; from top to bottom, orange, white, blue; in the centre of the white stripe, the old Orange Free State flag hanging vertical, towards the pole the Union Flag horizontal, away from the pole the old Transvaal Vierkleur, all spread full.

NATIONAL ANTHEM.—Die Stem Van Suid-Afrika (The Call of South Africa).

NATIONAL DAY.—May 31.

BRITISH EMBASSY
255 Hill Street, Pretoria
[Pretoria 433121]
91 Parliament Street, Cape Town (Jan.–June)
[Cape Town 4617220]

Ambassador Extraordinary and Plenipotentiary, His Excellency Sir Robin (William) Renwick, KCMG (1987).
Counsellor, Deputy Head of Mission, J. Poston.
First Secretaries, R. J. Sawers; C. G. Crawford; P. Haggie; A. E. Gay (*Administration*).

Cultural Attaché and British Council Representative, W. L. Radford, 19 Juta Street, (PO Box 30637), Braamfontein 2017, Johannesburg (Tel. 339 3715).

There are British Consular Offices at *Cape Town*, *Johannesburg* and *Durban*; and Honorary Consuls at *Port Elizabeth* and *East London*.

SPAIN
(España)

Head of the Spanish State, King Juan Carlos I de Borbón y Borbón, KG, *born* Jan. 5, 1938, *acceded to the throne*, Nov. 22, 1975, *married* May 14, 1962, Princess Sophie of Greece *and has issue*, Infante Felipe Juan Pablo Alfonso y Todos los Santos (Prince of Asturias, *and heir to the throne*), *born* Jan. 30, 1968; Infanta Elena Maria Isabel Dominga, *born* Dec. 20, 1963; and Infanta Cristina Federica Victoria Antonia, *born* June 13, 1965.

CABINET
(as at June 30, 1990)

Prime Minister, Felipe González.
Deputy PM, Alfonso Guerra.
Foreign Affairs, Francisco Fernández Ordóñez.
Justice, Enrique Múgica.
Defence, Narcis Serra Serra.
Economy and Finance, Carlos Solchaga.
Interior, José Luis Corcuera.
Transport, Tourism and Communications, José Barrionuevo.
Public Works and Urban Planning, Javier Sáenz de Coscullela.
Education and Science, Javier Solana.
Labour and Social Security, Luis Martínez Noval.
Industry and Energy, José Claudio Aránzadi.
Agriculture, Fisheries and Food, Carlos Romero Herrera.
Public Administration, Joaquín Almunia.
Culture, Jorge Semprún.
Health and Consumer Affairs, Julián García Vargas.
Cabinet Secretary and Parliamentary Relations, Virgilio Zapatero.
Social Welfare, Matilde Fernández.
Chief Government Spokeswoman, Rosa Conde.

SPANISH EMBASSY
24 Belgrave Square, SW1X 8QA
[071-235 5555]

Ambassador Extraordinary and Plenipotentiary, His Excellency Felipe de la Morena (1990).
Minister-Counsellor, Vicente Blanco.

Area and Population.—Situated in the south-west of Europe, between 36°–43° 45′ N. lat. and 4° 25′ E.–9° 20′ W. long., Spain is bounded on the south and east by the Mediterranean, on the west by the Atlantic and Portugal, and on the north by the Bay of Biscay and France, from which it is separated by the Pyrenees. Continental Spain occupies about eleven-thirteenths of the Iberian peninsula, the remaining portion forming the Republic of Portugal. Its coast-line extends 1,317 miles, 712 formed by the Mediterranean and 605 by the Atlantic, and it comprises a total area of 194,897 sq. miles (504,782 sq. km), with a population (UN estimate 1988) of 39,054,000.

Physical Features.—The interior of the Iberian Peninsula consists of an elevated tableland surrounded and traversed by mountain ranges—the Pyrenees, the Cantabrian Mountains, the Sierra Guadarrama, Sierra Morena, Sierra Nevada, Montes de Toledo, etc. The principal rivers are the Duero, the Tajo, the Guadiana, the Guadalquivir, the Ebro and the Miño.

Government.—Spain was a monarchy until April 1931, when King Alfonso XIII left the country and a Republic was proclaimed. A Provisional Government, drawn from the various Republican and Socialist parties, was formed. On July 18, 1936 a counter-revolution broke out in many military garrisons in Spanish Morocco and spread rapidly throughout Spain. The principal leader was General Francisco Franco Bahamonde, leader of the Military-Fascist fusion, or *Falange*. On March 29, 1939 the Civil War was declared to have ended, the Popular Front Governments in Madrid and Barcelona surrendering to the Nationalists (as General Franco's followers were then named). On June 5, 1939 the Grand Council of the *Falange Española Tradicionalista y de las Juntas Ofensivas Nacional-Sindicalistas*, met at Burgos to legislate for the reorganization of the country under the presidency of General Franco.

On July 22, 1969, General Franco nominated Prince Juan Carlos (Alfonso) of Bourbon (grandson of the late King Alfonso XIII) to succeed him as head of state at his death or retirement. The nomination was approved in the *Cortes* by a large majority. Following the death of General Franco on November 20, 1975, Juan Carlos acceded to the throne.

Under the Constitution drawn up in 1977–78 there is a bicameral *Cortes* comprising a 350-member Congress of Deputies elected for four years by universal adult suffrage, and a Senate consisting of directly elected representatives of the provinces, islands, autonomous regions, and Ceuta and Melilla. At the General Election on October 29, 1989, PSOE (Spanish Socialist Workers' Party) won 175 seats, and the PP (Popular Party) 107.

Regions.—Since the promulgation of the 1978 Constitution, 17 autonomous regions have been established, with their own parliaments and governments. These are Andalucia, Aragon, Asturias, Balearics, the Basque country, Canaries, Castilla-La Mancha, Castilla-Leon, Cantabria, Cataluña, Extremadura, Galicia, Madrid, Murcia, Navarre, La Rioja and Valencia.

Defence.—Army: There are in Spain 1 armoured, 1 mechanized, 1 motorized and 2 mountain divisions; 1 artillery brigade, 2 cavalry brigades, 1 air-transportable brigade, 1 helicopter brigade, 1 coastal artillery brigade. The *Guardia Civil* operates as a gendarmerie in the rural areas under the control of the Ministry of Defence.

The active Spanish Navy consists of 1 aircraft

carrier, 9 destroyers, 12 frigates and corvettes, 12 minesweepers, 6 major amphibious vessels, 8 submarines, 12 fast patrol craft, 6 hydrographic vessels, 1 tanker, and many smaller patrol craft and auxiliaries. The Navy also has 50 helicopters and 10 Harrier aircraft.

The Air Force is divided geographically into three regions covering Spain, plus an Air Zone for the Canaries. There are also functional Combat, Tactical and Transport Commands. The Air Force consists of 2 attack squadrons, 9 air defence squadrons, 1 maritime squadron, 7 transport squadrons, 3 search and rescue squadrons, 9 training squadrons and 1 fire-fighting squadron.

Spain became a member of NATO in May 1982. Continued membership (linked to non-military integration) was confirmed in a referendum in March 1986. The present government has initiated reorganization of the military structure.

Education.—Education is free for all those aged 6–18, and compulsory up to the age of 14. Under the 1985 Education Law, private schools (30 per cent of primary and 60 per cent of secondary schools) will have to fulfill certain criteria to receive government maintenance grants.

There are 33 public sector universities, the oldest of which, Salamanca, was founded in 1218. Other ancient foundations are Valladolid (1346), Barcelona (1430), Zaragoza (1474), Santiago (1495), Valencia (1500), Seville (1505), Madrid (1508), Granada (1531), Oveido (1604). Private universities are Deusto in Bilbao, Navarra in Pamplona, one in Madrid and one in Salamanca. Student numbers in the universities in 1989–90 totalled 1,067,874.

Language and Literature.—Castilian is the language of more than three-quarters of the population of Spain. Basque, reported to have been the original language of Iberia, is spoken in Vizcaya, Guipuzcoa and Alava. Catalan is spoken in Provençal Spain, and Galician, spoken in the north-western provinces, is akin to Portuguese; the governments of these regions actively encourage use of their local languages.

The literature of Spain is one of the oldest and richest in the world, the *Poem of the Cid*, the earliest of the heroic songs of Spain, having been written about AD 1140. The outstanding writings of its golden age are those of Miguel de Cervantes Saavedra (1547–1616), Lope Felix de Vega Carpio (1562–1635) and Pedro Calderón de la Barca (1600–1681). The Nobel Prize for Literature has five times been awarded to Spanish authors—J. Echegaray (1904), J. Benavente (1922), Juan Ramón Jimenez (1956), Vicente Aleixandre (1977) and Camilo José Cela (1989).

Production and Industry.—The expansion of the Spanish economy and accession to the EC have led to changes in Spanish agriculture. It accounts for over 5 per cent of GDP and employs over 13 per cent of the working population (down from 28 per cent in 1970). Between 1970 and 1985 the net value of agricultural production increased by 56 per cent in real terms.

The country is generally fertile, and well adapted to agriculture and the cultivation of heat-loving fruits—olives, oranges, lemons, almonds, pomegranates, bananas, apricots, tomatoes, peppers, cucumbers and grapes. The agricultural products include wheat, barley, oats, rice, hemp and flax. The orange crop is exported mainly to Germany, France and the United Kingdom. The vine is cultivated widely; in the southwest, Jerez, the well-known sherry and tent wines are produced. The fishing industry is important.

Spain's mineral resources of coal, iron, wolfram, copper, zinc, lead and iron ores are variously exploited. Output of coal in 1988 was 15·5 million tonnes; output of steel (1988) 11·9 million tonnes.

The principal goods produced are cars, steel, ships, manufactured goods, textiles, chemical products,

footwear and other leather goods. In 1988 an estimated 54,172,000 tourists visited Spain.

TRADE

	1988	1989
	million pesetas	
Imports	7,039,516	8,458,300
Exports	4,686,376	5,257,600

The balance of payments on current account showed a deficit of US$10,410 million in 1989 and reserves stood at US$44,697 million.

Trade with UK†

	1988	1989
Imports from UK	£2,691,662,000	£3,227,793,000
Exports to UK	2,482,360,000	2,846,543,000

† Including Canary Islands.

The principal imports are cotton, tobacco, cellulose, timber, coffee and cocoa, food products, fertilizers, dyes, machinery, motor vehicles and agricultural tractors, wool and petroleum products. The principal exports include cars, petroleum products, iron ore, cork, salt, vegetables, fruits, wines, olive oil, potash, mercury, pyrites, tinned fruit and fish, tomatoes and footwear.

CAPITAL.—Madrid, population (1986) 4,731,224. Other large cities are ΨBarcelona (4,597,429), ΨValencia (2,078,812), Seville (1,594,250), Zaragoza (824,781), ΨMálaga (1,137,782), Bilbao (1,179,148); Murcia (1,006,788).

CURRENCY.—Peseta of 100 céntimos.

FLAG.—Three horizontal bands, red, yellow and red, with coat of arms on yellow band.

NATIONAL ANTHEM.—Marcha Real Española.

NATIONAL DAY.—October 12.

BRITISH EMBASSY
Calle Fernando el Santo, 16, Madrid 4
[Madrid 419 0200]

Ambassador Extraordinary and Plenipotentiary, His Excellency Robin Fearn, CMG (1989).

Minister, I. V. Roberts.

Counsellor, D. R. Christopher (*Commercial*).

Defence and Naval Attaché, Capt. S. N. G. Sloot, LVO, RN.

Head of Political Section, G. C. Gillham.

There are Consulates General in *Barcelona, Bilbao;* Consulates in *Tenerife, Alicante, Seville, Malaga, Palma de Mallorca, Las Palmas, Santander, Tarragona, Vigo* and *Lanzarote,* and Vice Consulates in *Algeciras, Ibiza* and *Minorca.*

British Council Representative, R. T. Joscelyne, Calle Almagro 5, 28010 Madrid. There is a branch library in *Barcelona.*

BRITISH CHAMBER OF COMMERCE, Plaza de Santa Barbara 10, 1st Floor, 28004 Madrid, also Paseo de Gracia 11, Barcelona 7 and Alameda de Mazarredo 5, Bilbao 1.

The BALEARIC ISLES form an archipelago off the east coast of Spain. There are four large islands (Majorca, Minorca, Ibiza and Formentera), and seven smaller (Aire, Aucanada, Botafoch, Cabrera, Dragonera, Pinto and El Rey). The islands were occupied by the Romans after the destruction of Carthage and provided contingents of the celebrated Balearic slingers. The total area is 1,935 sq. miles (5,011 sq. km), with a population of 685,088. The archipelago forms a province of Spain, the capital being ΨPalma in Majorca, pop. 304,422; ΨMahon (Minorca), pop. 22,926.

The CANARY ISLANDS are an archipelago in the Atlantic, off the African coast, consisting of seven islands and six mostly uninhabited islets. The total area is 2,807 sq. miles (7,270 sq. km), with a population of 1,444,626. The Canary Islands form two Provinces of Spain.—*Las Palmas* (Gran Canaria, Lanzarote (38,500), Fuerteventura (19,500) and the islets of Alegranza, Roque del Este, Roque del Oeste, Graciosa, Montaña Clara and Lobos), with seat of administration at ΨLas Palmas (366,454) in Gran Canaria, where major oil companies have installations for re-fuelling shipping; and *Santa Cruz de Tenerife* (Tenerife, La Palma (76,000), Gomera (31,829), and Hierro (10,000)), with seat of administration at ΨSanta Cruz in Tenerife, population estimate 190,784.

ISLA DE FAISANES is an uninhabited Franco-Spanish condominium, at the mouth of the Bidassoa in La Higuera bay.

ΨCEUTA is a fortified post on the Moroccan coast, opposite Gibraltar. The total area is 5 sq. miles (13 sq. km), with a population of 70,864.

ΨMELILLA is a town on a rocky promontory of the Rif coast, connected with the mainland by a narrow isthmus. Melilla has been in Spanish possession since 1492. Population 58,449. Ceuta and Melilla are parts of Metropolitan Spain.

OVERSEAS TERRITORIES

Spanish settlements on the Moroccan seaboard are:—

Peñon de Alhucemas, the bay of that name includes six islands: population 366.

Peñon de la Gomera (or *Peñon de Velez*) is a fortified rocky islet about 40 miles west of Alhucemas Bay; population 450.

The *Chaffarinas* (or Zaffarines) are a group of three islands near the Algerian frontier, about two miles north of Cape del Agua; population 610.

The protectorate of Spanish Morocco was incorporated in Morocco on the latter's independence in 1956. Ifni, the former enclave in Morocco, was incorporated by treaty on June 30, 1969, and the Spanish Sahara came under joint Moroccan and Mauritanian control in November 1975.

SUDAN
(Al-Jamhuryat es-Sudan Al-Democratia)

CABINET
(as at May 31, 1990)

Prime Minister and Minister for Defence, Lt.-Gen. Omar Hassan Ahmad al-Bashir.
Deputy PM, Maj.-Gen. Zubir Mohammed Saleh.
Presidential Affairs, Lt.-Col. Tayib Ibrahim Mohammed Khayr.
Foreign Affairs, Ali Sahlul.
Interior, Maj.-Gen. Faisal Ali Abu Salih.
Justice and Attorney General, Hassan Ismail al-Billi.
Culture and Information, Mohammed Khogali Saliheen.
Finance and National Economic Planning, Abdel Rahim Mahmoud Hamdi.
Agriculture and Natural Resources, Ahmad Ali al-Genief.
National Guidance and Orientation, Abdella Deng Danyal.
Local Government and Co-ordination of Provincial Affairs, Natali Yanku Ambu.
Irrigation, Yacoub Abu Shura Musa.
Energy and Mining, Abdel Munim Khujali.
Industry, Mohammed Omar Abdullah.
Education, Abdallah Mohammed Ahmed.
Housing, Construction and Public Utilities, Hussein Suleiman Abu Saleh.
Relief and Refugee Affairs, Peter Arat Ador.
Transport and Communications, Ali Ahmad Ibrahim.
Labour and Social Security, George Kinga.

Commerce, Co-operation and Supply, Faruq al-Bushra.
Health and Social Welfare, Shakir al-Sarraj.

EMBASSY OF THE REPUBLIC OF THE SUDAN
3 Cleveland Row, SW1A 1DD
[071-839 8080]

Ambassador Extraordinary and Plenipotentiary, His Excellency El Rasheed Abushama (1989).

Area and Population.—Sudan extends from the southern boundary of Egypt, 22° N. lat., to the northern boundary of Uganda, 3° 36′ N. lat., and reaches from the Republic of Chad about 21° 49′ E. (at 12° 45′ N.) to the north-west boundary of Ethiopia in 38° 35′ E. (at 18° N.). On the east lie the Red Sea and Ethiopia; on the south lie Kenya, Uganda and Zaire; and on the west the Central African Republic, Chad, and Libya. The greatest length from north to south is approximately 1,300 miles, and east to west 950 miles.

The White Nile enters from Uganda at Nimule as the Bahr el Jebel, and leaves Sudan at Wadi Halfa. The Blue Nile flows from Lake Tana on the Ethiopian Plateau. Its course in Sudan is nearly 500 miles long, before it joins the White Nile at Khartoum. The next confluence of importance is at Atbara where the main Nile is joined by the River Atbara. Between Khartoum and Wadi Halfa lie five of the six cataracts.

The estimated area is about 967,500 sq. miles (2,505,813 sq. km), with a population of 23,798,000 (UN estimate 1988). Arab and Nubian peoples populate the northern and central two-thirds of Sudan, Nilotic and Negro peoples the southern third. Arabic is the official language and Islam the state religion, although the Nilotics of the Bahr el Ghazal and Upper Nile Valleys are generally Animists or Christians.

Government.—The Anglo-Egyptian Condominium over Sudan which had been established in 1899 ended when the Sudan House of Representatives, on December 19, 1955, voted unanimously a declaration that Sudan was a fully independent sovereign state. A Republic was proclaimed on January 1, 1956, and was recognized by Great Britain and Egypt, a Supreme Commission being sworn in to take over sovereignty. Sudan was under military rule from November 1958 until 1964 when a new civilian Cabinet was appointed. Government of the country was taken over on May 25, 1969 by a ten-man revolutionary council headed by Col. Gaafar

Mohamed El Nimeri. In February 1972 an agreement was signed at Addis Ababa which brought to an end nearly 17 years of insurrection and civil war in the six southern provinces, and which recognized southern regional autonomy within a unified Sudanese State. Insurrection broke out again in 1983. In April 1985 the Army command assumed power after popular demonstrations, deposed Nimeri and appointed a transitional government. In May 1986 power was transferred to a civilian regime following multi-party elections.

The third military coup since Sudan's independence took place on June 30, 1989 when the government of Sadiq al Mahdi was overthrown by Brig.-Gen. Omar Hassan Ahmad al-Bashir. The Constitution was suspended and parliament was replaced by a 15-member ruling junta who have de facto control over a cabinet of 21 ministers.

Education.—School education is free for most children, but not compulsory, beginning with six years primary education, followed by three years secondary education at general secondary schools, the more academic higher secondary schools or vocational schools. The medium of instruction is Arabic. English is taught as the principal foreign language in all schools.

Khartoum University has ten faculties. There is a branch of Cairo University in Khartoum, an Islamic University at Omdurman and universities at Wad Medani and Juba.

In addition to the universities there are various technical post-secondary institutes as well as professional and vocational training establishments.

Production.—The principal grain crops are *dura* (great millet) and wheat, the staple food of the people in Sudan. Sesame and ground-nuts are other important food crops, which also yield an exportable surplus and a promising start has been made with castor seed. The principal export crop is cotton. Traditionally a major producer of long-staple cotton, Sudan has in recent years grown more short and medium-staple cotton. These grades now account for more than half total production. Production in 1987–88 is estimated to have been around 837,000 bales. Sudan also produces the bulk of the world's supply of gum arabic. Sugar is an increasingly important crop, although Sudan still has to achieve self sufficiency in its production. Livestock is the mainstay of the nomadic Arab tribes of the desert and the Negro tribes of the swamp and wooded grassland country in the south. Production has, however, been affected by drought, famine and flooding.

Sudan's agriculture production provided employment for over 60 per cent of the labour force and contributed 37 per cent to GDP in 1986–87. It is based on large and medium sized public sector irrigation projects with small scale private irrigation schemes providing mostly fruit and vegetables. Mechanized and traditional agriculture is practised in areas of sufficient rainfall.

The manufacturing sector contributed less than 8 per cent to GDP in 1986–87 and provided employment for 4 per cent of the work force. The main manufacturing enterprises are concentrated in the areas of food processing, textiles, shoes, cigarettes and batteries.

Communications.—The railway system, adversely affected by the civil war, has a route length of about 3,200 miles, linking Khartoum with Wadi Halfa, Karima, Port Sudan, Wad Medani, Sennar, El Damazin, Kosti, El Obeid and Nyala. Nile river services between Khartoum and Juba have been interrupted by the southern insurrection. Port Sudan is a well-equipped modern seaport. Sudan Airways fly services from Khartoum to many parts of the Sudan and to other African states, Europe and the Middle East.

FINANCE

	[1986–87]
Revenue	£S2,741·1m
Expenditure	6,100·7m
Deficit	2,527·6m
Deficit financing	2,527·6m

TRADE

	1985–86*	1986-87*
Total imports ...	US$1,055·2m	US$832·3m
Total exports ...	497·2m	481·6m
*estimates		

Trade with UK

	1988	1989
Imports from UK	£86,480,000	£60,602,000
Exports to UK	9,910,000	9,532,000

The principal exports are cotton, livestock, gum arabic and other agricultural produce. The chief imports are petroleum goods and other raw materials, machinery and equipment, transport and equipment, medicines and chemicals.

CAPITAL.—Khartoum. The town contains many mosques, a Catholic cathedral and an Anglican cathedral, and the university with extensive government buildings. The combined population of Khartoum, Khartoum North and Omdurman (excluding refugees and displaced people) is estimated at 3,000,000.

CURRENCY.—Sudanese pound (£S) of 100 piastres and 1,000 millièmes.

FLAG.—Three horizontal stripes of red, white and black with a green triangle next to the hoist.

NATIONAL ANTHEM.—Nahnu Djundullah (We are the army of God).

NATIONAL DAY.—January 1 (Independence Day).

BRITISH EMBASSY
(PO Box 801)
Khartoum
[Khartoum 70760/7]

Ambassador Extraordinary and Plenipotentiary, His Excellency Alan John Ramsay, CMG (1990).
Counsellor, Head of Chancery and Consul General, F. X. Gallagher.
Defence and Military Attaché, Col. R. J. M. Carson, OBE.

British Council Representative, P. B. M. Early, 14 Abu Sinn Street (PO Box 1253), Khartoum.

SURINAME
(Nieuwe Republick van Suriname)

President, Head of State, Government and the Armed Forces, Ramsewak Shankar, *sworn in* Jan. 25, 1988.
Head of the National Military Council, Lt.-Col. Desi Bouterse.

COUNCIL OF MINISTERS
(as at May 31, 1990)

Vice President, Chairman of Council of Ministers, Henk A. E. Arron.
Foreign Affairs, Dr. A. Sedoc.
Finance and Planning, Subhes Chandra Mungra.
Natural Resources and Energy, Pretaapnarian Radhakishun.
Home Affairs, District Administration and Mobilization, Evelyn Alexander-Vanenburg.
Public Works, Telecommunications and Construction, H. Jankipersadsing.
Health, Henk Ali Mahumed.
Education, Science, Culture, Sport and Youth Affairs, Roland Venetiann.
Transport, Trade and Industry, W. Grep.

Labour, Romeo Van Russel.
Agriculture, Livestock, Fisheries and Forestry, S. Redjosenpono.
Housing and Social Affairs, Willy Soemita.
Justice and Police, J. Adjodhia.
Army, Maj. A. Sheikkariem.

Suriname is situated on the north coast of South America and is bounded by French Guiana in the east, Brazil in the south and Guyana in the west. It has an area of 63,037 sq. miles (163,265 sq. km), with a population (1988 estimate) of 410,000.

Formerly known as Dutch Guiana, Suriname remained part of the Netherlands West Indies until November 25, 1975, when it achieved complete independence. Suriname had received autonomy in domestic affairs under the Realm Statute which took effect on December 29, 1954. The civilian government was ousted in February 1980 by the military who appointed a predominantly civilian Cabinet in 1982.

According to the Constitution approved by referendum in September 1987, a National Assembly of 51 members elects the President. The Army remains the 'vanguard of the people'. Elections to the National Assembly were held on November 25, 1987. The Front for Democracy and Development, a coalition comprising three former opposition parties, won 40 of the 51 seats. President Shankar and Vice-President Arron were sworn in on January 25, 1988, and a new Council of Ministers was installed on January 26.

Suriname has large timber resources. Rice and sugar cane are the main crops. Bauxite is mined, and is the principal export. In 1987, GDP amounted to US$1,080 million. Principal trading partners are the Netherlands, USA and Norway.

TRADE

	1985
Imports	US$359·5m
Exports	337·3m

Trade with UK

	1988	1989
Imports from UK	£6,107,000	£6,777,000
Exports to UK	11,256,000	16,366,000

CAPITAL.—ΨParamaribo, population (1971) 110,000.

CURRENCY.—Suriname guilder of 100 cents.

FLAG.—Horizontal stripes of green, white, red, white, green, with a five-pointed yellow star in the centre.

NATIONAL DAY.—November 25.

British Ambassador (resident in Georgetown, Guyana).

British Consulate, c/o VSH United Buildings, Van't Hogerhuystraat, PO Box 1300, Paramaribo.

Honorary Consul, J. J. Healy, MBE.

SWEDEN
(Konungariket Sverige)

King of Sweden, HM Carl XVI Gustaf, *born* April 30, 1946, *succeeded* September 15, 1973, *married* June 19, 1976 Fräulein Silvia Renate Sommerlath and has *issue,* Crown Princess Victoria Ingrid Alice Désirée, Duchess of Västergötland, *born* July 14, 1977; Prince Carl Philip Edmund Bertil, Duke of Värmland, *born* May 13, 1979; Princess Madeleine Thérèse Amelie Josephine, Duchess of Hälsingland and Gästrikland, *born* June 10, 1982.

COUNCIL OF MINISTERS
(as at June 30, 1990)

Prime Minister, Ingvar Carlsson.
Justice, Laila Freivalds.

Foreign Affairs, Sten Andersson.
Agriculture, Mats Hellström.
Finance, Allan Larsson.
Housing, Ulf Lönnqvist.
Labour, Mona Sahlin.
Education and Culture, Bengt Göransson.
Industry and Energy, Rune Molin.
Health and Social Affairs, Ingela Thalén.
Equality and Immigration, Majlis Lööw.
Environment, Birgitta Dahl.
Public Sector, and Wages and Salaries, Bengt K. A. Johansson.
Foreign Trade, Anita Gradin.
Defence, Roine Carlsson.
Health and Social Affairs (Deputy Minister), Bengt Lindqvist.
Communications, Georg Andersson.
Aid, Lena Hjelm-Wallén.
Sport, Youth and Tourism, Margot Wallström.
Education (Deputy Minister), Göran Persson.
Finance (Deputy Minister), Erik Åsbrink.

SWEDISH EMBASSY
11 Montagu Place, W1H 2AL
[071-724 2101]

Ambassador Extraordinary and Plenipotentiary, His Excellency Leif Leifland, GCVO (1982).
Minister Plenipotentiary, P. O. Jödahl.
Counsellors, A. Alsterdal (*Press*); P. Bruce (*Commodities*); P. Järborg (*Consular and Administration*); N. Daag (*Political*).
Defence and Naval Attaché, Cmdr. J. Bring.
Military and Air Attaché, Col. E. J. Hjelm.
Trade Commissioner, M. Nilsson (73 Welbeck Street, W1M 8AN.).

Area and Population.—Sweden occupies the eastern area of the Scandinavian peninsula in NW Europe and comprises 24 local government districts, (*Län*), with a total area of 173,732 sq. miles (449,964 sq. km), and population at December 31, 1988 of 8,462,000. In 1986 the birth rate was 12·2 per 1,000 inhabitants, the death rate 11·1 per 1,000 inhabitants and infant mortality rate was 6·8 per 1,000 live births.

Government.—Sweden is a constitutional monarchy, with the monarch retaining purely ceremonial functions as Head of State. Under the Act of Succession of June 6, 1809 (with amendments) the throne is hereditary in the House of Bernadotte. (A 1979 amendment vested the succession in the monarch's eldest child, irrespective of sex.) Jean-Baptiste Jules Bernadotte, Prince of Ponte Corvo, a Marshal of France, was invited to accept the title of Crown Prince, with succession to the throne. He succeeded Charles XIII in 1818.

There is a unicameral Diet (*Riksdag*) of 349 members elected by universal suffrage for three years. The Council of Ministers (*Statsråd*) is responsible to the *Riksdag*. In the General Election held in September 1988, the following seats were won: Social Democrats 156; Moderates 66; Liberals 44; Centre 42; Communists 21; Green Party 20.

Production and Industry.—The country's industrial prosperity is based on an abundance of natural resources in the form of forests, mineral deposits and water power. The forests are extensive, covering about half the total land surface, and sustain flourishing timber, pulp and paper milling industries. The mineral resources include iron ore, lead, zinc, sulphur, granite, marble, precious and heavy metals (the latter not exploited) and extensive deposits of low grade uranium ore. Industries based on mining, principally iron and steel, aluminium and copper are important but it is the general engineering industry that provides the basis of Sweden's exports. Growth areas are largely in the specialized machinery and systems and chemical industries. The relative importance of agriculture has declined and in 1988 only 4 per cent of the population was engaged in farming.

Apart from water power Sweden has no significant indigenous resources of conventional hydrocarbon fuels and relies to a high degree upon imported oil. Much of Sweden's electricity is generated by nuclear power but as a result of a referendum in 1980 the nuclear programme is to be discontinued by 2010. Small supplies of natural gas are imported from Denmark into southern Sweden, with the pipeline being extended to Gothenburg.

Communications.—The total length of Swedish railroads is 11,745 km. The road network is over 400,000 km in length.

The mercantile marine amounted on December 31, 1985 to 2,619,625 gross tonnage. The Board of Civil Aviation under the control of the Ministry of Communications handles civil aviation matters. Regular domestic air traffic is maintained by the Scandinavian Airlines System and by Linjeflyg. Regular European and inter-continental air traffic is maintained by the Scandinavian Airlines System.

Defence.—Based on the policy of non-alignment in peace leading to neutrality in war Sweden maintains a 'total defence' intended to make any attack on her costly. Total defence includes peacetime organizations for civil, economic and psychological defence as well as universal conscription of men aged 18–47. Some 50,000 national servicemen are called up for 5–15 months training each year and most are recalled every fourth year for refresher training. On mobilization the Army strength totals 4 armoured brigades, 1 mechanized brigade and 16 infantry and winter warfare brigades. The Navy has 12 submarines, 30 fast attack craft, a number of minor craft and auxiliaries and 5 coast artillery units. The Air Force has modern supersonic aircraft of Swedish manufacture forming a standing force of 200 air defence, 100 attack and 55 reconnaissance with support aircraft and a modern air defence radar system. Facilities exist for rapid dispersal from main bases in war.

Religion.—The state religion is Lutheran Protestant, to which over 95 per cent of the people officially adhere.

Language and Literature.—Swedish belongs, with Danish and Norwegian, to the North Germanic language group. Swedish literature dates back to King Magnus Eriksson, who codified the old Swedish provincial laws in 1350. With his translation of the Bible, Olaus Petri (1493–1552) formed the basis for the modern Swedish language. Literature flourished during the reign of Gustavus III, who founded the Swedish Academy in 1786. Notable Swedish writers include Almquist (1795–1866), Strindberg (1849–1912) and Lagerlöf (1858–1940), Nobel Prize Winner in 1909. Contemporary authors include Lagerquist (1891–1974), Nobel Laureate in 1951, Martinson (1904–78) and Johnson (1900–76), Nobel Laureates jointly in 1974. The Swedish scientist Alfred Nobel (1833–96) founded the Nobel Prizes for literature, science and peace.

Education.—Tuition within the state system, which is maintained by the state and by local taxation, is free. It provides 9 years' compulsory schooling from the age of 7 to 16 in the comprehensive elementary schools; further education of 2–4 years' duration in the upper secondary schools; a unified higher education system administered in six regional areas containing one of the universities—Uppsala (founded 1477); Lund (1668); Stockholm (1878); Gothenburg (1887); Umeå (1963) and Linköping (1967). At present there are 33 institutions of higher education including three technical universities in Stockholm, Gothenburg and Luleå, and the Karolinska Institute in Stockholm, which specializes in medicine and dentistry.

FINANCE

	1990–91 Kronor
Revenue	407,900m
Expenditure	408,200m

TRADE

	1988	1989
	Kronor	
Imports	280,649·5m	315,061·0m
Exports	305,055·9m	332,144·9m

Trade with UK

	1988	1989
Imports from UK	£2,195,032,000	£2,350,122,000
Exports to UK	3,366,524,000	3,747,600,000

Sweden's main imports from Britain, accounting for 8·6 per cent of total imports in 1988, are engineering products, semi-manufactures and chemical products. Britain's main imports from Sweden are paper and board, road vehicles, machinery, wood, steel and pulp.

CAPITAL.—ΨStockholm. Population (1985): City 659,030; Greater Stockholm, 1,435,474; ΨGothenburg (Göteborg) (425,495); ΨMalmö (229,936); Uppsala (154,859)

CURRENCY.—Swedish krona of 100 øre.

FLAG.—Yellow cross on a blue ground.

NATIONAL ANTHEM.—Du Gamla, Du Fria (Thou ancient, thou freeborn).

NATIONAL DAY.—June 6 (Day of the Swedish Flag).

BRITISH EMBASSY
Skarpögatan 6–8, 115 27 Stockholm
[Stockholm 6670140]

Ambassador Extraordinary and Plenipotentiary, His Excellency Sir John Ure, KCMG, LVO (1987).
British Council Representative, Dr. S. M. Lewis.

There is a British Consular Office at *Stockholm*.

BRITISH-SWEDISH CHAMBER OF COMMERCE, Grevgatan 34, 11453 Stockholm.

SWITZERLAND
(Schweizerische Eidgenossenschaft—
Confédération Suisse—Confederazione
Svizzera.)

FEDERAL COUNCIL

President of the Swiss Confederation (1990) *and Head of Justice and Police*, Arnold Koller.
Vice President (1990) *and Head of Home Affairs (Interior)*, Flavio Cotti.
Military, Kaspar Villiger.
Transport, Energy and Communications, Adolf Ogi.
Foreign Affairs, René Felber.
Public Economy, Jean-Pascal Delamuraz.
Finance, Otto Stich.

EMBASSY OF SWITZERLAND
16–18 Montagu Place, W1H 2BQ
[071–723 0701]

Ambassador Extraordinary and Plenipotentiary, His Excellency Franz E. Muheim (1989).
Minister, C. M. W. Faessler.
Counsellors, J. Bucher (*Economic and Financial*); H. Hofer (*Commodities and Agriculture*).
Defence, Military, Naval and Air Attaché, Maj.-Gen. G. de Loës.
Consul General and Head of Administration, A. Mehr.

There is a Swiss Consulate-General in *Manchester*.

Area and Population.—Switzerland, the Helvetia of the Romans, is a federal republic of central Europe, situated between 45° 50′–47° 48′ N. lat. and 5° 58′–10° 3′ E. long. It is composed of 23 Cantons, three subdivided, making 26 in all, and comprises a total area of 15,943 sq. miles (41,293 sq. km), with a population (December 31, 1988) of 6,620,000. In 1988 there were 80,300 live births, 60,600 deaths and 45,700 marriages. Of the total population in 1980, 44·3 per cent was Protestant, 47·6 per cent Roman Catholic and 0·3 per cent Jewish.

Physical Features.—Switzerland is the most mountainous country in Europe. The Alps, covered with perennial snow and from 5,000 to 15,217 feet in height, occupy its southern and eastern frontiers, and the chief part of its interior; the Jura mountains rise in the north-west. The Alps occupy 61 per cent, and the Jura mountains 12 per cent of the country. The Alps are a crescent-shaped mountain system situated in France, Italy, Switzerland, Bavaria and Austria, covering an area of 80,000 square miles from the Mediterranean to the Danube (600 miles). The highest peak, Mont Blanc, Pennine Alps (15,782 ft.) is partly in France and Italy; Monte Rosa (15,217 ft.) and Matterhorn (14,780 ft.) are partly in Switzerland and partly in Italy. The highest wholly Swiss peaks are Dufourspitze (15,203 ft.), Finsteraarhorn (14,026), Aletschhorn (13,711), Jungfrau (13,671), Mönch (13,456), Eiger (13,040), Schreckhorn (13,385), and Wetterhorn (12,150) in the Bernese Alps, and Dom (14,918), Weisshorn (14,803) and Breithorn (13,685).

The Swiss lakes are famous for their beauty and include Lakes Maggiore, Zürich, Lucerne, Neuchâtel, Geneva, Constance, Thun, Zug, Lugano, Brienz and the Walensee. There are also many artificial lakes.

Government.—The legislative power is vested in a Parliament consisting of two Chambers, a National Council (*Nationalrat*) of 200 members, and a States Council (*Ständerat*) of 46 members; both Chambers united are called the Federal Assembly. Members of the National Council are elected for four years, elections taking place in October. The executive power is in the hands of a Federal Council (*Bundesrat*) of seven members, elected for four years by the Federal Assembly and presided over by the President of the Confederation. Each year the Federal Assembly elects from the Federal Council the President and the Vice-President. Not more than one of the same canton may be elected member of the Federal Council; on the other hand, there is a tradition that Italian and French-speaking areas should between them be

represented on the Federal Council by at least two members.

Defence.—All Swiss males must undertake military service in the Army or the Air Force, which is part of the Army. Swiss Army equipment includes some British items, such as Centurion tanks, Bloodhound missiles, Vampire and Hunter aircraft, the Medium Girder Bridge, the Rapier guided missile, the Hawk aircraft plus 3 watchman radars and the IMFS trunk communication system.

Production and Industry.—Agriculture is followed chiefly in the valleys and all over the Mittelland, where cereals, flax, hemp, and tobacco are produced, and nearly all temperate zone fruits and vegetables as well as grapes are grown. Dairying and stock-raising are the principal industries, about 3,000,000 acres being under grass for hay and 2,000,000 acres pasturage. The forests cover about one-quarter of the whole surface. The chief manufacturing industries comprise engineering and electrical engineering, metal-working, chemicals and pharmaceuticals, textiles, watchmaking, woodworking, foodstuffs and footwear. Banking, insurance and tourism are major industries.

Communications.—There are 5,020 km of railway tracks (Swiss Federal Railways, 2,990 km; Swiss privately owned railways, 2,030 km). At the end of 1988 the number of telephones amounted to 5,879,200 and the network was fully automatic throughout the country. At the same time there were 2,590,200 licensed radio receivers and 2,338,300 television receivers.

At the end of 1987 the total length of motorways was 1,451 km. The number of motor vehicles licensed in 1987 was 3,593,474.

A merchant marine, established in 1941, consisted at June 1990 of 20 vessels with a total gross tonnage of 287,487 tonnes. In 1989, goods handled at Basle Rhine ports amounted to 8,845,162 tonnes. In 1987, 163 lake and river vessels (excluding the Rhine) transported 10,608,200 passengers and 500 tonnes of freight. Swiss airlines have a network covering 310,729 km (1988) and in 1988 carried 8,402,718 passengers. Swissair, the state airline, flies to and from the airports at Zürich, Geneva and Basle.

Education.—Education is controlled by cantonal and communal authorities: there is no central organization. Illiteracy is practically unknown. Primary education is free and compulsory. School age varies, generally 7 to 14. Secondary education, age 12–15 for boys and girls. Schools numerous and well-attended, and there are many private institutions. Special schools make a feature of commercial and technical instruction. Universities are Basle (founded 1460), Berne (1834), Fribourg (1889), Geneva (1873), Lausanne (1890), Zürich (1832), and Neuchâtel (1909), and the technical universities of Lausanne and Zürich and commercial university of St. Gall.

Language and Literature.—There are four official languages: French, German, Italian and Romansch. German is the dominating language in 19 of the 26 cantons; French in Fribourg, Jura, Geneva, Neuchâtel, Valais and Vaud; Italian in Ticino, and Romansch in parts of the Grisons.

Many modern authors, alike in the German school and in the Suisse Romande, have achieved international fame. Karl Spitteler (1845–1924) and Hermann Hesse (1877–1962) were awarded the Nobel Prize for Literature, the former in 1919, the latter in 1946.

FINANCE

	1988	1989*
Revenue	SFr27,219m	SFr28,031m
Expenditure	26,000m	27,555m

*estimate

TRADE

The principal imports are machinery, electrical and electronic equipment, textiles, motor vehicles, non-ferrous metals, chemical elements, clothing, food, medicinal and pharmaceutical products. The principal exports are machinery, chemical elements, non-ferrous metals, watches, electrical and electronic equipment, textiles, dyeing, tanning and colouring equipment. Switzerland is a member of EFTA.

	1987	1988
Total Imports	SFr75,171m	SFr82,398,669
Total Exports	67,477m	74,063,586

Trade with UK†

	1988	1989
Imports from UK	£1,854,918,000	£2,245,354,000
Exports to UK	3,840,643,000	4,125,731,000

†(Including Liechtenstein)

CAPITAL.—Berne, population 135,000 (city). Other large towns are Zürich (359,084), Basle (173,147), Geneva (160,668), Lausanne (127,839), Winterthur (86,992), St. Gallen (70,817), Lucerne (62,400).

CURRENCY.—Swiss franc of 100 centimes or rappen.

FLAG.—Red, with white cross.

NATIONAL ANTHEM.—Trittst im Morgenrot Daher (Radiant in the morning sky).

NATIONAL DAY.—August 1.

BRITISH EMBASSY
Thunstrasse 50, 3000 Berne 15
[Berne 445021]

Ambassador Extraordinary and Plenipotentiary, His Excellency Christopher William Long, CMG (1988).

Counsellors, C. C. Bright; C. W. Wainwright.

First Secretary, I. N. Hughes.

Second Secretaries, A. M. M. McDermott; P. Cole.

Defence, Naval and Military Attaché, Lt.-Col. J. Bolton-Clark.

Air Attaché, Wing. Cdr. J. L. Bishop.

Attaché, P. C. Albrecht (*Commercial*).

BRITISH CONSULAR OFFICES

There is a Consular Section at the Embassy in Berne; Consulates-General at *Zürich* and *Geneva* and Consular offices at *Lugano* and *Montreux*. The Directorate of British Export Promotion in Switzerland is in the Consulate-General Office in *Zürich*.

BRITISH-SWISS CHAMBER OF COMMERCE, Freiestrasse 155, 8032 Zürich.

SWISS-BRITISH SOCIETIES:

Berne.—*President*, Dr. H. Beriger.

Zürich.—*President*, J.-P. Müller.

Basle.—*President*, G. Simons.

SYRIA

(Al-Jamhouriya Al-Arabia as-Souriya)

President, Lt.-Gen. Hafez el Assad, *b.* 1930, *assumed office* March 14, 1971, *re-elected*, Feb. 1978, March 13, 1985.

Vice-Presidents, Abdul Halim Khaddam, Rifaat Al Assad, Zuhair Mashariqa.

MINISTERS
(as at May 31, 1990)

Prime Minister, Mahmoud Al Zubi.

Deputy Prime Minister and Minister for Defence, Gen. Mustafa Tlass.

Deputy Prime Minister for Public Services, Mahmoud Qaddur.

Deputy Prime Minister for Economic Affairs, Dr. Salim Yassin.

Education, Ghassan Halabi.

Higher Education, Kamal Sharaf.

Interior, Mohammad Harbah.

Transport, Yusuf al-Ahmed.

Information, Mohammad Salman.

Local Administration, Ahmed Diab.

Supply and Internal Trade, Hassan Saqqa.

Economy and Foreign Trade, Mohammad al-Imadi.

Culture, Najah al-Attar.

Foreign Affairs, Farooq ash-Shar'.

Tourism, Adnan Quli.

Health, Iyad al-Shatti.

Waqfs (Religious Endowments), Abdel-Majid Tarabulsi.

Irrigation, Abd ar-Rahman Madani.

Electricity, Kamil al-Baba.

Oil and Mineral Resources, Antonios Habib.

Construction, Marwan Farra.

Housing and Utilities, Mohammad Nur Antabi.

Agriculture and Agrarian Reform, Mohammad Ghabbash.

Finance, Khaled al-Mahayni.

Industry, Antoine Jubran.

Communications, Murad Quwatli.

Justice, Khalid Ansari.

Presidential Affairs, Wahib Fadil.

Labour and Social Affairs, Haydar Buzu.

SYRIAN EMBASSY IN LONDON

The Syrian Embassy has been closed since October 31, 1986, when Syria and the UK broke off diplomatic relations. The Lebanese Embassy represents Syrian interests in the UK.

Area and Population.—Syria is in the Levant, covering a portion of the former Ottoman Empire. Bounded by the Mediterranean and Lebanon on the W., Israel and Jordan on the SW, Iraq on the E. and Turkey on the N., it has an estimated area of 71,498 sq. miles (185,180 sq. km), and a population (January 1988) of 11,338,000, most of whom are Arabic-speaking and Muslim. The Orontes flows northwards from the Lebanon range across the northern boundary to Antakya (Antioch, Turkey). The Euphrates crosses the northern boundary near Jerablus and flows through north-eastern Syria to the boundary of Iraq.

Archaeology, etc.—The region is rich in historical remains. Damascus (Dimishq ash-Sham) is said to be the oldest continuously inhabited city in the world (although Aleppo disputes this claim), having existed as a city for over 4,000 years. It is situated on the river Barada, in an oasis at the eastern foot of the Anti-Lebanon, and at the edge of the wide sandy desert which stretches to the Euphrates. The city contains the Omayed Mosque, the Tomb of Saladin, and the 'street which is called Straight' (Acts 9:11), while to the north-east is the Roman outpost of Dmeir and further east is Palmyra.

On the Mediterranean coast at Amrit are ruins of the Phoenician town of Marath, where the well has been found and is being excavated and also ruins of Crusaders' fortresses at Markab, Sahyoun, and Krak des Chevaliers. At Tartous (also on the coast) the cathedral of Our Lady of Syria, built by the Knights Templars in the 12th and 13th centuries has been restored as a museum. One of the oldest alphabets in the world has been discovered at Ugarit (Ras Shamra), a Phoenician village near the port of Latakia.

Hittite cities dating from 2000 to 1500 BC, have recently been explored on the west bank of the Euphrates at Jerablus and Kadesh.

Government.—Syria, which had been under French mandate since the 1914–18 war, became an independent republic during the 1939–45 war. The first independently elected Parliament met on August 17, 1943, but foreign troops were in part occupation until April 1946. Syria remained an independent republic until February 1958, when it became part of the United Arab Republic. It seceded from the United Arab Republic on September 28, 1961.

A new Constitution was promulgated in March 1973: this declared that Syria is a 'democratic, popular socialist State', and that the Arab Socialist Renaissance (Ba'ath) Party, which has been the ruling party since 1963, is 'the leading party in the State and society'. Elections to the expanded 250-seat Peoples' Council in May 1990 resulted in a large majority for the Ba'ath Party, which won 134 seats; its National Progressive Front allies (Arab Socialist Union, Socialist Unionist Movement, Arab Socialist Party, Syrian Communist Party) together won 32 seats. The Independents won 84.

Production and Industry.—Agriculture is the principal source of production; wheat and barley are the main cereal crops, but the cotton crop is the highest in value. Tobacco is grown in the maritime plain in Sahel, the Sahyoun and the Djebleh district of Latakia. Large new areas are coming under irrigation and cultivation in the north-east of the country as a result of the Thawra dam. Skins and hides, leather goods, wool and silk, textiles, cement, vegetable oil, glass, soap, sugar, plastics and copper and brass utensils are produced. There are an increasing number of light assembly plants as Syria's industrialization programme develops. Oil has been found at Karachuk and other parts in the north-eastern corner of the country and production of high quality reserves is proceeding in the region of Deir ez Zor. Syria produces nearly 400,000 barrels of oil per day at present. A pipeline has been built to the Mediterranean port of Banias, via Homs. Two oil refineries are in production at Homs and Banias. Syria also has deposits of phosphate and rock salt, and produces asphalt.

Language and Literature.—Arabic is the principal language, but Kurdish, Turkish and Armenian are spoken among significant minorities and a few villages still speak Aramaic, the language spoken by Christ and the Apostles. There are three daily newspapers and several periodicals in Arabic published in Damascus, and also a daily newspaper in English. English has taken over from French as the main foreign language, especially among the young.

Education.—Education in Syria is under state control and, although a few of the schools are privately owned, they all follow a common system and syllabus. Elementary education is free at state schools, and is compulsory from the age of seven. Secondary education is not compulsory and is free only at the state schools. Because of the shortage of places, entry to these state schools is competitive. Damascus University, founded in 1924, has nine faculties and a Higher Teachers' Training College. The number of students has risen to over 60,000. There are also about 20,000 students at Aleppo University (founded 1961), over 10,000 at Tishrin University, Latakia (founded 1975) and 6,000 at Ba'ath University, Homs. Approximately 10 per cent of all students receive scholarships, and at the present time Palestinian refugees are admitted free. The rest pay fees.

Communications.—Although railway lines run from Damascus to both Beirut and Amman, train services go only to Amman, as much of the Lebanese line has been dismantled. A track has been opened connecting Homs with Damascus. A track links Homs, Hamah, Aleppo, Deir ez Zor and Qamishliye to the Iraq frontier. Branch lines connect the ports of Tartous and Latakia to the system and another line runs from Aleppo down Euphrates valley to Deir ez Zor and thence north to Qamishliye, with a branch going to the Euphrates Dam. All the principal towns in the country are connected by roads which vary from modern dual carriageways to narrow country lanes. An internal air service operates between all major towns. The main international airport is at Damascus and there are also flights to Eastern Europe, Turkey, Greece and Armenia from Aleppo.

Trade.—The principal imports are foodstuffs (fruit, vegetables, cereals, meat and dairy products, tea, coffee and sugar), mineral and petroleum products, yarn and textiles, iron and steel manufactures, machinery, chemicals, pharmaceuticals, fertilizers and timber. Exports include raw cotton, oil, cereals, fruit, phosphates, cement, livestock and dairy products, other foodstuffs, textiles and raw wool.

Trade with UK

	1988	1989
Imports from UK	£24,647,000	£38,537,000
Exports to UK	36,100,000	65,256,000

CAPITAL.—Damascus, population (estimated) 1,168,000. Other important towns are Aleppo, Homs and Hama, and the principal port is ΨLatakia.

CURRENCY.—Syrian pound (S£) of 100 piastres.

FLAG.—Red over white over black horizontal bands, with two green stars on central white band.

NATIONAL DAY.—April 17.

BRITISH INTERESTS SECTION
Quartier Malki, 11 rue Mohammad Kurd Ali,
Imm. Kotob, Damascus
[Damascus 712561]

Following the break in diplomatic relations with Syria in October 1986, Australia has been representing British interests in Syria.

THAILAND
(Prathes Thai)

King, HM Bhumibol Adulyadej, *born* 1927; *succeeded his brother* June 9, 1946; *married* Princess Sirikit Kitiyakara, April 28, 1950; *crowned* May 5, 1950; and has *issue*, Princess Ubolratana, *born* April 6, 1951; Crown Prince Vajiralongkorn, *born* July 28, 1952; Princess Sirindhorn, *born* April 2, 1955; Princess Chulabhorn *born* July 4, 1957.

CABINET
(as at August 31, 1990)

Prime Minister, Minister of Defence, Gen. Chatichai Choonhavan (CTP).

Deputy Prime Ministers, Pramual Sabhavasu (CTP); Thongyod Chittavira (SAP); Maj.-Gen. Sanan Khajornprasat (DP); Gen. Mana Ratanakoses (RP); Gen. Arthit Kamlang-Ek (TPP).

Finance, Virabongsa Ramangura.

Foreign Affairs, Dr. Subin Pinkayan (SAP).

Agriculture and Co-operatives, Chuan Leekpai (DP).

Transport and Communications, Montree Pongpanit (SAP).

Commerce, Amaret Sila-on (SAP).

Interior, Banharn Silpa-archa (CTP).

Justice, Pol. Lt.-Gen. Chamras Mangklarat (CTP).

Science, Technology and Energy, Prachuab Chaiyasan (DP).

Education, Gen. Tienchai Sirisumpan (RP).

Public Health, Marut Bunnag (DP).

Industry, Pol. Gen. Pramarn Adireksarn (CTP).

University Affairs, Anuwat Wattanapongsiri (CTP).

CTP: Chart Thai Party; SAP: Social Action Party; DP: Democrat Party; RP: Rassadon Party; TPP: Thai People's Party.

ROYAL THAI EMBASSY IN LONDON
29–30 Queen's Gate, SW7 5JB
[071–589 0173]

Ambassador Extraordinary and Plenipotentiary, His Excellency Sudhee Prasasvinitchai (1986).

Area and Population.—The Kingdom of Thailand, formerly known as Siam, has an area of 198,457 sq. miles (514,000 sq. km), with a population (1989) of 55,888,393. The population growth rate averages 2·4 per cent per year. Thailand has a common boundary with Malaysia in the south, is bounded on the west by Myanmar (Burma) and on the north-east and east by Laos and Cambodia. Although there is no common boundary between Thailand and China, the Chinese province of Yunnan is separated from the Thai northern border only by a narrow stretch of Burmese and Laotian territory.

Thailand is divided geographically into four regions: central, north-eastern, northern and southern. The capital, Bangkok, is situated in the south of the central plain area. To the north-east there is a plateau area and to the north-west mountains. The south of Thailand consists of a narrow mountainous peninsula. The principal rivers are the Chao Phraya in the central plains, and the Mekong on the northern and north-eastern borders.

Language and Religion.—Thai is basically a monosyllabic, tonal language, a branch of the Indo-Chinese linguistic family, but its vocabulary has been strongly influenced by Sanskrit and Pali. It is written in an alphabetic script derived from ancient Indian scripts. The principal religion is Buddhism. In 1988 94·37 per cent of the population were Buddhists, 3·95 per cent Muslims, 0·53 per cent Christians and 1·15 per cent other religions.

Government.—Thailand became a Constitutional Monarchy in 1932. The Constitution promulgated in December 1978 provides for a National Assembly consisting of a 261-member Senate appointed by the monarch and 347-member House of Representatives elected by universal adult suffrage for a term of four years. Martial law was declared in 1976.

A General Election was held on July 24, 1988. The results were: Chart Thai 87; Social Action 54; Democrat 48; Ruam Thai 35; Prachakorn Thai 31; Rassadorn 21; Prachachon 19; Puangchon Chao Thai 17; Palang Dharma 14; Community Action 9; Progressive 8; Muan Chon 5; United Democratic 5; Liberal 3; Others 1. A coalition government was appointed in August 1988.

Education.—Primary education is compulsory and free and secondary education in government schools is free. In 1988 there were 37,696 schools and training colleges, with a total of 10,699,132 pupils and 562,028 teachers. Private universities and colleges are playing an increasing role in higher education. In 1984 the government agreed to upgrade four private colleges to universities. Out of 43 universities and other similar higher institutes of learning, 21 are private and attended by some 53,708 students. In 1986 their total enrolment was 171,438 students.

Agriculture and Industry.—The agricultural sector provides just under half the national income and employs 67·5 per cent of the labour force, which in 1985 was estimated at 26·8 million. Rice remains the most important crop, accounting for 60 per cent of the area planted. After rice the main crops are sugar, maize, rubber, tobacco, kenaf and jute. In recent years the production of livestock and poultry, especially pigs and chickens for export, has gained importance. There is a large fishing industry with more than 20,000 vessels registered. Fish farming is popular in many inland areas. A ban on hardwood export has resulted in the decline of the forestry industry.

The discovery of onshore oil and offshore gas in the late 1970s ushered in a new economic era. Crude oil production which began in 1983 stood at around 1·85 million tonnes in 1989, or about 15 per cent of the country's needs. In 1988, 212,641 million cubic feet of natural gas was produced. The predicted surplus of natural gas has led the Government to designate an area on the east coast as the future centre of the petrochemical industry. Another energy resource becoming more important is lignite which is found mainly in the north and is being used increasingly for electricity production.

Mineral resources are mainly tin, tungsten, lead, antimony and iron. Among these, tin is the most important. In addition, about 60,000 tons of zinc ingots a year are expected to be produced by a zinc refinery which was opened in early 1984.

Industry is divided into two main categories: service and manufacturing. Since 1982 tourism has replaced rice as the country's top foreign exchange earner. There were 4,231,000 overseas visitors in 1988, generating an estimated 31,768 million baht for the country. The banking system is large and contributes much to the economy, especially employment. There are over 1,800 bank branches in the country employing some 72,000 workers.

Since 1960 the government has actively promoted industrial investments by means of tax relief and other incentives to local and foreign investors; in 1985, 74·6 per cent of this investment was in Thai projects. Most of the industries established under this scheme in early years were import-substituting. However, there has been an increasing shift to export-oriented industries, taking advantages of low-wage labour and available domestic resources. Manufacturing now accounts for about 21·8 per cent of the national income. Crops contribute 12·1 per cent of GDP.

Communications.—The importance of rivers and canals as the traditional mode of transportation has been replaced by highways and roads. The existing road and highway network, totalling 34,701 kilometres in 1984, reaches all parts of the country. Most of the smaller towns and bigger villages are now served by paved roads.

Navigable waterways have a length of about 1,100 km in the dry season and 1,600 km in the wet season. About 3,825 km of state-owned railways were open to traffic in 1984. Main lines run from Bangkok to Aranya Prathet on the Cambodian border via Korat to Ubon and to Nong Khai, the ferry terminal on the River Mekong opposite Vientiane, capital of Laos; to Chiang Mai and to Hat Yai, whence lines go down the eastern and western sides of the Malay peninsula, via Sungei Galok and Penang respectively, to Singapore. A new line to Sattahip on the east coast is being constructed.

Bangkok is an important international air centre and has direct flights to most of the world's major cities. The airports at Chiang Mai, Phuket and Hat Yai also receive international flights. Most major provincial towns have airports. Thai International and Thai Airways merged in April 1988. Now named THAI, the airline is state-owned.

Thailand has an extensive network of telecommunications services, and the telephone service though still poor is being improved. All major cities and towns are linked by direct long-distance calls. Thailand has two mobile telephone networks, AMPS (urban), and NMT (rural) presently covering only the central area but expanding rapidly.

There are two important ports in the country. Bangkok, which is a river port, can serve vessels up to 27 ft. draught. The deep-sea port at Sattahip caters for larger vessels. Phuket and Songkhla deep water ports have already been completed and are the first to be managed privately under a ten-year concession. Construction of Laem Chabang deep water port started in 1988.

TRADE

Thailand's main exports are rice, tapioca and tapioca products, garments, rubber, integrated circuit boards, precious stones, pearls and other ornaments, maize, canned sea food, fabrics, sugar and tin. Main imports are crude oil, chemicals and pharmaceuticals, electrical and non-electrical machinery and spare parts, industrial machinery, iron and steel, diesel oil and other fuel oil, vehicle and transport equipment.

	1988	1989
Total imports	Baht 501·4m	Baht 646·1m
Total exports	399·2m	509·6m

Trade with UK

	1988	1989
Imports from UK	£279,717,000	£427,484,000
Exports to UK	321,241,000	443,144,000

CAPITAL.—ΨBangkok, at the mouth of the River Chao Phraya, population (1985) 5,400,000. Other centres are Chiang Mai, Phitsanuloke, Chon Buri, Korat, Khon Kaen, Surat Thani, Hat Yai and ΨPhuket but none approaches Bangkok in size or importance.

CURRENCY.—Baht of 100 satang.

FLAG.—Five horizontal bands, red, white, dark blue, white, red (the blue band twice the width of the others).

NATIONAL ANTHEM.—Sanrasern Pra Barami.

NATIONAL DAY.—December 5 (The King's Birthday).

Wireless Road, Bangkok 10330
[Bangkok 253 0191]

Ambassador Extraordinary and Plenipotentiary, His Excellency Michael Ramsay Melhuish, CMG (1985).

British Council Representative, E. C. Pugh, 428 Rama 1 Road, Siam Square Soi, Pathumwan, Bangkok 10330.

BRITISH CHAMBER OF COMMERCE,
302 Silom Road, Bangkok 10500

TOGO
(République Togolaise)

President and Minister of Defence, Gen. Gnassingbé Eyadéma, *born* 1937, *assumed office*, April 14, 1967; *re-elected for seven-year term*, Dec. 23, 1986.

CABINET
(as at June 30, 1990)

Interior and Security, Gen. Yao Mawulikplimi Amegi.
Justice, Yagninim Bitoktipou.
Planning and Mines, Barry Moussa Barque.
Rural Development, Koudjolou Dogoh.
Minister Delegate to the Presidency (Information), Gbegnon Amegboh.
Equipment, Posts and Telecommunications, Souleymane Galo.
National Education and Scientific Research, Tchaa-Kozah Tchalim.
Public Health, Aissah Agbetra.
Youth, Sports and Culture, Mensah Agbeyomé Kodjo.
Foreign Affairs and Co-operation, Yaovi Adodo.
Industry and State Enterprises, Koffi Djondo.
Technical Instruction and Professional Training, Koffi Edoh.
Economy and Finance, Komla Alipui.
Labour and Civil Service, Dahuku Pere.

EMBASSY OF TOGO
30 Sloane Street, SW1X 9NE.
[071–235 0147/9]

Ambassador Extraordinary and Plenipotentiary, new appointment awaited.
Chargé d'Affaires, Djibril Akanga.

The Republic is situated in West Africa between 0°–2° W. and 6°–11° N., with a coastline 35 miles long on the Gulf of Guinea, and extends northward inland for 350 miles. It is flanked on the west by Ghana, on the north by Burkina and in the east by Benin. It has an area of 21,925 sq. miles (56,785 sq. km), and a population (UN estimate 1988) of 3,247,000, including people of several African races. The official language is French; Ewe is spoken by about 47 per cent.

The first President of Togo, Sylvanus Olympio, assassinated on January 13, 1963, was succeeded by Nicolas Grunitzky, who was himself overthrown by an army coup d'état on January 13, 1967. On April 14, 1967, the Commander-in-Chief of the Togolese army, Lt. Col. (later promoted General) Eyadéma named himself President.

Production and Trade.—Although the economy of Togo remains largely agricultural, exports of phosphates have superseded agricultural products as the main source of export earnings. Other exports include palm kernels, copra and manioc. The production of phosphates entirely for export was taken over completely by the government in February 1974.

Trade with UK

	1988	1989
Imports from UK	£22,231,000	£15,009,000
Exports to UK	690,000	2,022,000

CAPITAL.—ΨLomé, population (1983) 366,476.

CURRENCY.—Franc CFA of 100 centimes.

FLAG.—Five alternating green and yellow horizontal stripes; a quarter in red at top next staff bearing a white star.

NATIONAL DAY.—January 13 (National Liberation Day).

BRITISH EMBASSY
British Ambassador (resident in Accra, Ghana).

TUNISIA
(Al-Djoumhouria Attunusia)

President, Zine el-Abidine Ben Ali *took office* Nov. 7, 1987, *re-elected* April 2, 1989.

CABINET
(as at May 31, 1990)

Prime Minister, Hamed Karoui.
Justice, Chedli Neffati.
Minister Director of the President's Cabinet, Mohammed El Jeri.
Minister Special Councillor to the President, Habib Boulares.
Foreign Affairs, Ismael Khelil.
National Defence, Abdallah Kallel.
Interior, Abdel Hamid Escheikh.
Economy and Finance, Mohammed Ghannouchi.
Planning and Regional Development, Mustapha Nabli.
Agriculture, Nouri Zorgati.
State Properties, Mustapha Bouaziz.
Equipment and Housing, Ahmed Friaa.
Transport, Ahmed Smaoui.
Tourism and Handicrafts, Mohamed Jegham.
Communications, Sadok Rabah.
Education, Higher Education and Scientific Research, Mohamed Charfi.
Culture and Information, Ahmed Khaled.
Public Health, Daly Jazi.
Social Affairs, Moncer Rouissi.
Vocational Training and Employment, Tahar Azaiez.
Youth and Childhood, Hammouda Ben Slama.
Secretary General for the Government, Taoufik Cheikhrouhou.

TUNISIAN EMBASSY
29 Prince's Gate, SW7 1QG
[071–584 8117]

Ambassador Extraordinary and Plenipotentiary, His Excellency Abdelwaheb Abdallah (1988).

Area and Population.—Tunisia lies between Algeria and Libya and extends southwards to the Sahara Desert, with a total area of 63,170 sq. miles (163,610 sq. km), and a population (UN estimate 1988) of 7,809,000.

Government.—A French Protectorate from 1881 to 1956, Tunisia became an independent sovereign state with the signing on March 20, 1956 of an agreement whereby France recognized Tunisia's independence and right to conduct its own foreign policy and to form an army.

Following a first general election held on March 25, 1956, a Constituent Assembly met for the first time on April 8. On July 25, 1957 the Constituent Assembly abolished the monarchy and elected M. Bourguiba first President of the Republic. On June 1, 1959 the Constitution was promulgated and on December 7, 1959 the National Assembly held its first session. In March 1975 the National Assembly proclaimed M. Bourguiba as President for life. On November 7, 1987 M. Bourguiba was deposed and succeeded by President Zine el-Abidine Ben Ali. Presidential and legislative elections were held in April 1989. The RCD (Rassemblement Constitutionnel Democratique) won all 141 seats in the National Assembly. Seven political parties contested the election. President Ben Ali was re-elected with 99 per cent of the vote.

The country is divided into 22 regions (*gouvernorats*) each administered by a governor.

Production, Trade, etc.—The valleys of the northern region support large flocks and herds, and contain rich agricultural areas, in which wheat, barley, and oats are grown. Vines and olives are extensively cultivated.

The chief exports are crude oil, phosphates, olive oil, finished textiles, and fruit. The chief imports are machinery and equipment, foodstuffs, petroleum products, and textiles. Some oil has been discovered and crude oil production in 1989 was 4·8 million tons. Gas has also been discovered off the east coast but exploitation is not viable at present. Tourists numbered almost 3 million in 1989.

	1988	1989
Total Imports	TD3,167,000	TD4,150,000
Total Exports	2,055,000	2,762,000

France remains the main trading partner, supplying 27·6 per cent of the country's imports and purchasing 22·9 per cent of Tunisia's exports.

Trade with UK

	1988	1989
Imports from UK	£30,780,000	£31,148,000
Exports to UK	36,062,000	43,266,000

Tunisia became an associate member of the EC early in 1969, and signed a new agreement with the EC in 1976. In 1977 the introduction of import quota measures by the EC on some textile goods resulted in a reduction of growth in this important sector of the Tunisian market. The quotas for some textile products was renegotiated and increased in 1982, and textile exports are now the main foreign exchange earner after tourism.

CAPITAL.—Ψ Tunis, connected by canal with La Goulette on the coast, head a population (1984) of 1,394,749. The ruins of ancient Carthage lie a few miles from the city. Other towns of importance are: Ψ Sfax (577,992); Ψ Sousse (322,491); Ψ Bizerta (394,670); Kairouan; Gabes; Menzel Bourguiba.

CURRENCY.—Tunisian dinar of 1,000 millimes.

FLAG.—Red crescent and star in a white orb, all on a red ground.
NATIONAL ANTHEM.—Himat Al Hima.
NATIONAL DAY.—March 20.

BRITISH EMBASSY
5 Place de la Victoire, Tunis 1015 RP
[Tunis 245100]

Ambassador Extraordinary and Plenipotentiary and Consul-General, His Excellency Stephen Peter Day, CMG (1987).

First Secretary, S. P. Collis (*Head of Chancery*).
Second Secretary, C. Innes-Hopkins (*Commercial and Consul*).
British Council Representative, D. Handforth.

TURKEY
(Türkiye Cumhuriyeti)

President, Turgut Özal, *elected for a seven-year term*, October 31, 1989.

GOVERNMENT
(as at May 31, 1990)

Prime Minister, Yildirim Akbulut.
Deputy PM, vacant.
Ministers of State, Mehmet Kececiler, Husnu Dogan, Günes Taner, Cemil Cicek, Isin Celebi, Vehbi Dincerler, Mehmet Yazar, Ismet Özarslan, Ercüment Konukman, Ibrahim Ozdemir, Mustafa Tasar, Kemal Akkaya, Husamettin Oruc, Kamran Inan.
Justice, Oltan Sungurlu.
National Defence, Safa Giray.
Interior, Abdulkadir Aksu.
Foreign, Ali Bozer.
Finance and Customs, Adnan Kahveci.
Education, Avni Akyol.
Public Works and Housing, Cengiz Altinkaya.
Health, Halil Sivgin.
Transport, Cengiz Tuncer.
Agriculture, Lütfullah Kayalar.
Labour and Social Security, Imren Aykut.
Industry and Commerce, Sükrü Yürür.
Energy and Natural Resources, Fahrettin Kurt.
Culture, Namik Kemal Zeybek.
Tourism, Ilhan Aküzüm.

TURKISH EMBASSY
43 Belgrave Square, SW1X 8PA
[071–235 5252]

Ambassador Extraordinary and Plenipotentiary, His Excellency Nurver Nures (1989).

Area and Population.—People of Turkic stock are to be found scattered throughout a wide belt extending from China through the Soviet Union, Afghanistan and Iran to Turkey, and into Bulgaria.

Turkey itself extends from Edirne (Adrianople) to Transcaucasia and Iran, and from the Black Sea to the Mediterranean, Syria and Iraq. Total population at the Census of 1985 was 51,428,514, of which 6,942,780 were in Europe and 44,485,734 in Asia. A 1988 UN estimate gives a total figure of 52,422,000.

Turkey in Europe consists of Eastern Thrace, including the cities of Istanbul and Edirne, and is separated from Asia by the Bosporus at Istanbul and by the Dardanelles—about 40 miles in length with a width varying from 1 to 4 miles—the political neighbours being Greece and Bulgaria on the west.

Turkey in Asia comprises the whole of Asia Minor or Anatolia and extends from the Aegean Sea to the western boundaries of Georgia, Soviet Armenia and Iran, and from the Black Sea to the Mediterranean and the northern boundaries of Syria and Iraq.

Government.—On October 29, 1923 the National Assembly declared Turkey a Republic and elected

Gazi Mustafa Kemal (later known as Kemal Ataturk) President. In 1945 a multi-party system was introduced but in 1960 the government was overthrown by the Turkish Armed Forces. A new Constitution was adopted in July 1961 and, after a general election, a civilian government took office. Civilian governments remained in power until September 1980 when mounting problems with the economy and terrorism led the military to assume legislative powers. A civilian technocratic government was appointed later that month.

A new Constitution, extending the powers of the President, was approved by a referendum on November 7, 1982. It provided for the separation of powers between the legislature, executive and judiciary, and the holding of free elections to the unicameral Grand National Assembly, which has 450 members elected every five years. Following the General Election in November 1983 the military leadership handed over power to a newly elected civilian government.

Party representation at June 1990 was: Motherland Party 282; Social Democratic Populist Party 81; Correct Way Party 57; Independent 25; Vacant 5.

Turkey is divided for administrative purposes into 73 *il* with subdivisions into *ilçe* and *nahiye*. Each *il* has a governor (*vali*) and elective council.

Religion and Education.—Islam ceased to be the state religion in 1928. However, 98·99 per cent of the population are Muslim. The main religious minorities, which are concentrated in Istanbul and on the Syrian frontier, are Greek Orthodox, Armenian, Syriani Christian, and Jewish. Education is free, secular and compulsory at primary level. There are elementary, secondary and vocational schools.

There are 27 universities in Turkey, including four in Istanbul, four in Ankara, two in Izmir, and one each in Erzurum and Trabzon.

The expenditure allocated to education in the 5th Five Year Plan (1985–89) was TL326,500,000, compared with TL76,000,000,000 in the 4th Five Year Plan (1979–83).

Language and Literature.—Until 1926, Turkish was written in Arabic script, but in that year the Roman alphabet was substituted for use in official correspondence and in 1928 for universal use, with Arabic numerals as used throughout Europe. The revolution of 1908 led to the introduction of native literature free from foreign influences and adapted to the understanding of the people. The leading Turkish newspapers are centred in Istanbul and Ankara, although most provincial towns have their own daily papers. There are foreign language papers in French, Greek, Armenian and English and numerous magazines and weeklies.

Agricultural Production.—In 1985 agricultural production accounted for some 16 per cent of the gross domestic product at constant factor prices. About 50 per cent of the working population are in the rural sector. Estimated production figures for the principal crops in 1989 were ('000 tons):

Wheat	16,200	Olives	650
Barley	4,500	Tea (wet leaves)	660
Rice	183	Hazelnuts	471
Tobacco	253	Citrus fruit	1,388
Sugar beet	11,000	Grapes and figs	3,638

With the important exception of wheat, which is mostly grown on the arid central Anatolian plateau, most of the crops are grown on the fertile littoral. Tobacco, sultana and fig cultivation is centred around Izmir, where substantial quantities of cotton are also grown. The main cotton area is in the Cukurova plain around Adana. The forests which lie between the littoral plain and the Anatolian plateau contain beech, pine, oak, elm, chestnut, lime, plane, alder, box, poplar and maple. In 1987 26 per cent of the land area was forest.

Industry.—After agriculture, Turkey's most important industry is based on the considerable mineral wealth which is, however, comparatively unexploited. The main export minerals are chromite and boron. Production in 1989 was (tons):

Coal	6,259,000
Lignite	50,926,000
Crude petroleum	2,868,000
Crude iron	3,523,000
Boron minerals	1,884,000

The bulk of the country's requirements in sugar, cotton, woollen and silk textiles, and cement, is produced locally, while other industries contributing substantially to local needs include vehicle assembly, paper, glass and glassware, iron and steel, leather and leather goods, sulphur refining, canning and rubber goods, soaps and cosmetics, pharmaceutical products, prepared foodstuffs and a host of minor industries.

Steep rises in oil prices from 1973 onwards led to a succession of economic crises culminating in January 1980 in the introduction of an economic stability programme. Exports have since risen dramatically, topping US$11,846 million in 1988. Inflation, however, remains high (68 per cent in 1989). GNP growth for 1989 was about 3·4 per cent and unemployment remains high.

COMMUNICATIONS

Railways.—The complete network became the property of the State Railways Administration in 1948. The total length of lines in operation (1989) is 10,369 km.

Roads.—At the end of 1988 there were 58,712 km of roads (31,048 of which were national).

The Bosporus is spanned by two bridges; plans are being drawn up for a third fixed link between the two continents.

Shipping.—By the end of 1988 the number of ships over 18 gross tons was 3,805.

Civil Aviation.—The state airline (THY) operates all internal services and has services to Europe and the Middle East. Most of the leading European airlines operate services to Istanbul and some also to Ankara.

FINANCE

	1990
Estimated expenditure	TL64,400·4 billion
Estimated revenue	53,860·0 billion

TRADE

	1988	1989
Total imports ...	US$14,339·7m	US$15,762·6m
Total exports ...	11,662·1m	11,627·3m

The main imports are machinery, crude oil and petroleum products, iron and steel, vehicles, medicines and dyes, chemicals, fertilizers and electrical appliances. Agricultural commodities (cotton, tobacco, fruits, nuts, livestock) represent 47 per cent of total exports. Other exports are minerals, textiles, glass and cement.

Trade with UK

	1988	1989
Imports from UK	£477,539,000	£434,562,000
Exports to UK	509,636,000	533,769,000

CAPITAL.—Ankara (Angora), an inland town of Asia Minor, about 275 miles ESE of Istanbul, with a population (1980) of 3,196,460. Ankara (or Ancyra) was the capital of the Roman Province of *Galatia Prima*, and a marble temple (now in ruins), dedicated to Augustus, contains the *Monumentum* (*Marmor*) *Ancyranum*, inscribed with a record of the reign of Augustus Caesar.

Ψ Istanbul (4,870,747), the former capital, was the Roman city of Byzantium. It was selected by Constantine the Great as the capital of the Roman Empire about AD 328 and renamed Constantinople. Istanbul contains the celebrated church of St. Sophia, which, after becoming a mosque, was made a museum in 1934. It also contains Topkapi, former Palace of the Ottoman Sultans, which is also a museum.

Other cities are ΨIzmir (1,968,614); Adana (1,467,346); Bursa (1,161,553); Gaziantep (387,093); and Eskişehir (543,733).

CURRENCY.—Turkish lira (TL) of 100 kurus.

FLAG.—Red, with white crescent and star.

NATIONAL ANTHEM.—Istikâl Marşi (The Independence March).

NATIONAL DAY.—October 29 (Republic Day).

BRITISH EMBASSY
Sehit Ersan Caddesi 46/A, Cankaya, Ankara
[Ankara 274310/4]

Ambassador Extraordinary and Plenipotentiary, His Excellency Sir Timothy Lewis Achilles Daunt, KCMG (1986).

Counsellor, Deputy Head of Mission, W. B. McCleary.

First Secretaries, S. N. Evans (*Political*); R. H. J. Ashton (*Chancery*); L. E. Walker LVO, OBE (*Commercial*); J. M. Brown (*Management*); C. P. M. Harrison, A. J. Mounford, Ms. R. L. Varley (*Cultural Affairs*).

Defence and Military Attaché, Brig. R. D. H. H. Greenwood.

Naval and Air Attaché, Wing Cdr. A. Campbell.

BRITISH CONSULAR OFFICES

There is a British Consulate-General at *Istanbul,* Vice-Consulates at *Izmir* and *Mersin,* and Honorary British Consulates at *Antaly, Bodrun, Iskenderun* and *Marmaris.*

British Council Representative, Colin Perchard, OBE, Kirklangic Sokak 9, Gazi Osman Pasa, Ankara 06700. There is also a centre and library at *Istanbul.*

BRITISH CHAMBER OF COMMERCE OF TURKEY INC., Mesrutiyet Caddessi No. 34, Tepebasi Beyoğlu, Istanbul (Postal Address, PO Box 190 Karaköy, Istanbul).

UNION OF SOVIET SOCIALIST REPUBLICS
(Soyuz Sovetskikh Sotsialisticheskikh Respublik)

President of the USSR, Mikhail Sergevich Gorbachov, elected March 15, 1990.

The Supreme Soviet of the USSR

Chairman, A. I. Lukyanov.
Chairman of the Council of the Union, I. D. Laptev.
Chairman of the Council of Nationalities, R. Nishanov.

The Presidential Council

Members, Ch. Aitmatov; V. V. Bakatin, V. I. Boldin; A. E. Kauls, V. A. Kryuchkov; Yu. D. Maslyukov; V. A. Medvedev; Yu. A. Osipyan; E. M. Primakov; V. G. Rasputin; G. I. Revenko; N. I. Ryzhkov (*ex officio*); S. S. Shatalin; E. A. Shevardnadze; A. N. Yakovlev; V. A. Yarin; D. T. Yazov.

Council of the Federation

Head: M. S. Gorbachov. The Council comprises the highest state officials of the republics.

The Council of Ministers of the USSR
(The Government)

Chairman, N. I. Ryzhkov.

FIRST DEPUTY CHAIRMEN OF THE COUNCIL OF MINISTERS

Chairman of Gosplan, Yu. D. Maslyukov.
General Responsibilities, L. A. Voronin.
Chairman, State Commission for Food and Procurements, vacant.

DEPUTY CHAIRMEN OF THE COUNCIL OF MINISTERS

Head, Economic Reform Commission, L. I. Abalkin.
Head, Commission for Military Industrial Questions, I. S. Belousov.
Head, Buro for Social Development, A. P. Biryukova.
Head, Emergency Commission, V. K. Doguzhiev.
Head, Buro for the Chemical-Timber Complex, V. K. Gusev.
Chairman, State Committee for Science and Technology, N. P. Laverov.
Chairman, State Committee for Material and Technical Supplies, P. I. Mostovoi.
Head, Buro for the Fuel and Energy Complex, L. D. Ryabev.
Head, Buro for the Machine Building Complex, I. S. Silaev.
Chairman, State Foreign Economic Relations Commission, S. A. Sitaryan.

ALL-UNION MINISTRIES

Aviation Industry, A. S. Systsov.
Automobile and Agricultural Machine Building, N. A. Pugin.
Atomic Energy and Industry, V. F. Konovalov.
External Economic Relations, K. F. Katushev.
Water Management Construction, (vacant).
Geology, G. A. Gabrielyants.
Civil Aviation, B. E. Panyukov.
Medical Industry, V. A. Bykov.
Metallurgy, S. V. Kolpakov.
Maritime Fleet, Yu. M. Volmer.
Oil and Gas Industry, L. I. Filimonov.
Defence Industry, B. M. Belousov.
Defence, D. T. Yazov.
General Machine Building, O. N. Shishkin.
Railways, N. S. Konarev.
Radio Industry, V. I. Shimko.
Fish Industry, N. I. Kotlyar.
Tool Building and Instrument Industry, N. A. Panichev.
Construction of Oil and Gas Industry Enterprises, V. G. Chirskov.
Ship Building Industry, I. V. Koksanov.
Transport Construction, V. A. Brezhnev.
Heavy Machine Building, V. M. Velichko.
Coal Industry, M. I. Shchadov.
Chemical and Oil Refining Industry, N. V. Lemayev.
Electronics Industry, V. G. Kolesnikov.
Electrotechnical Industry and Equipment Building, O. G. Anfimov.

UNION REPUBLICAN MINISTRIES

Internal Affairs, V. V. Bakatin.
Health, I. N. Denisov.
Foreign Affairs, E. A. Shevardnadze.
Culture, N. N. Gubenko.
Timber Industry, V. I. Melnikov.
Assembly and Special Building Work, A. I. Mikhalchenko.
Communications, E. K. Pervyshin.
Trade, K. Z. Terekh.
Finance, V. S. Pavlov.
Energy and Electrification, Yu. K. Semenov.
Justice, V. F. Yakovlev.

ALL-UNION STATE COMMITTEES

Science and Technology (GKNT), N. P. Laverov.
Quality Control and Standards, V. V. Sychev.
Computer and Information Technology, B. L. Tolstykh.
Hydrometeorology, Yu. A. Izrael.

UNION REPUBLICAN STATE COMMITTEES

State Planning Committee (Gosplan), Yu. D. Maslyukov.
Material Technical Supply (Gossnab), P. I. Mostovoi.
State Building Committee (Gosstroi), V. M. Serov.
Labour and Social Questions (Goskomtrud), V. I. Shcherbakov.
State Price Committee (Goskomtsen), V. K. Senchagov.
Statistics, V. N. Kirichenko.
Education, G. A. Yagodin.
Television and Radio (Gostelradio), M. F. Nenashev.
Cinematography, A. I. Kamshalov.
The Press, N. I. Efimov.
Forestry, A. S. Isaev.
Nature Conservation (Goskompriroda), N. N. Vorontsov.
Physical Culture and Sport (Goskomsport), N. I. Rusak.
State Security Committee, V. A. Kryuchkov.
National Questions, (vacant).
Supervision of Safe Work in Atomic Energy, V. M. Malyshev.

OTHER POSTS

Chairman, USSR State Bank (Gosbank), V. V. Gerashchenko.
Council of Ministers' Business Manager, M. S. Shkabardnya.
Chairman of Committee for Light Industry attached to Gosplan, L. E. Davletova.
First Deputy Chairman of Gosplan, V. A. Durasov.
Chairman of People's Control Committee, G. V. Kolbin.

Ministries.—There are three groups of departmental ministries, with a total of 57 ministers—26 All Union Ministries, i.e. federal ministries, 11 Union Republican Ministries (co-ordinating ministries of individual republics) and 20 State Committees whose Chairmen rank as Ministers. The Prime Ministers of the 15 constituent republics belong to the Council of Ministers ex officio.

The Communist Party of the Soviet Union
(KPSS—Kommunisticheskaya Partiya Sovetskogo Soyuza)

Politburo, M. S. Gorbachov; M. M. Burokevicius; G. G. Gumbaridze; S. I. Gurenko; A. S. Dzasokhov; V. A. Ivashko; I. A. Karimov; P. K. Luchinsky; A. M. Masaliev; K. Makhkamov; V. M. Movsisyan; A. N. Mutalibov; N. A. Nazarbaev; S. A. Niyazov; I. K. Polozkov; Yu. A. Prokofiev; A. P. Rubiks; G. V. Semenova; E.-A. A. Sillari, E. E. Sokolov; E. S. Stroev; I. T. Frolov; O. S. Shenin; G. I. Yanaev.
Secretaries, M. S. Gorbachov (General Secretary since March 11, 1985); V. A. Ivashko (*Deputy General Secretary since July 11, 1990*); O. D. Baklanov; B. V. Gidaspov; A. N. Girenko; A. S. Dzasokhov; V. A. Kuptsov; Yu. A. Manaenkov; G. V. Semenova; E. S. Stroev; V. M. Falin; O. S. Shenin; G. I. Yanaev.
Members of Secretariat, V. V. Aniskin; V. A. Gaivoronsky; I. I. Melnikov; A. I. Teplenichev; G. Turgunova.
Komsomol (Young Communist League), V. Zyukin.

EMBASSY OF THE USSR
13 Kensington Palace Gardens, W8 4QX
[071–229 3628]

Ambassador Extraordinary and Plenipotentiary, His Excellency Leonid M. Zamyatin (1986).

AREA AND POPULATION

The total area of the USSR is 8,649,461 sq. miles (22,402,000 sq. km); the total population (January 1, 1989) 286,700,000. The proportion of women to men is 53 to 47. In 1987 the birth-rate was 19·0 and the mortality rate, 10·2. In 1987, 66 per cent of the population lived in urban areas.

Area and population (January 1987) of the constituent Republics of the USSR with their date of incorporation into the Union:

Republic	Sq. miles	Population
Armenia (1936)......	11,306	3,412,000
Azerbaijan (1936)....	33,436	6,811,000
Belorussia (1922)	80,300	10,078,000
Estonia (1940)	17,413	1,556,000
Georgia (1936)	26,911	5,266,000
Kazakhstan (1936)...	1,049,155	16,244,000
Kirghizia (1936)	76,642	4,143,000
Latvia (1940)........	24,695	2,647,000
Lithuania (1940)	26,173	3,641,000
Moldavia (1940)	13,912	4,185,000
RSFSR (1922)	6,593,391	145,300,000
Tadjikistan (1929) ...	54,019	4,807,000
Turkmenistan (1924)	188,417	3,361,000
Ukraine (1922)	252,046	51,200,000
Uzbekistan (1924) ...	172,742	19,026,000

Before the outbreak of the Second World War (1941–45 in USSR), the USSR consisted of 11 Republics. In August 1940, the major part of Bessarabia ceded by Romania in June was joined to the Moldavian ASSR to form a Moldavian SSR. The same month, the three independent Baltic States, Estonia, Latvia and Lithuania, were forcibly incorporated into the Soviet Union. In October 1944 Tannu-Tuva, until the Second World War a nominally independent state lying to the north-west of Outer Mongolia, became the autonomous province of Tuva and in 1961, the Autonomous Republic of Tuva, within the RSFSR.

In July 1956 the Karelo-Finnish Republic (formed in 1940 from the Karelian ASSR and land ceded by Finland) reverted to the status of an Autonomous (*Karelian*) Republic within the RSFSR.

Main Nationalities
(1979 Census)

The most numerous national groups of USSR are: Russian, 137 million and Ukrainian, 42 million. There are between 6 and 12 million Kazakhs, Tatars, Belorussians, and Uzbeks. Azerbaidjani, Armenians and Georgians number between 3·5 and 5·5 million each group. There are some 1·9 to 2·9 million Lithuanians, Kirghizians, Turkomans, Germans, Moldavians and Tadjiks. In each of the following nationality groups the population numbers between 1·02 and 1·8 millions: Chuvashes, Latvians, Poles, Mordovians, Bashkirs, Estonians, Dagestanis and Jews.

The 1979 census revealed a marked difference between the growth rates of individual nationalities; while the Slav nations showed an annual increase of under one per cent, certain Central Asian and Caucasian (mostly Muslim) nations recorded an annual net growth of 2·5 to 3·5 per cent.

Chronological System.—On February 14, 1918 the Soviet government adopted the Gregorian calendar. In 1981 Summer Time was introduced between April 1 and October 1, but there are some geographical anomalies in its application. The country is divided into 10 time zones.

LANGUAGE, LITERATURE AND ARTS

Russian is a branch of the Slavonic family of languages which is divided into the following groups: *eastern*, including Russian, Ukrainian and White

Russian; *western*, including Polish, Czech, Slovak and Sorbish (or Lusatian Wendish); and *southern*, including Serbo-Croat, Slovene, Macedonian and Bulgarian. The western group and part of the southern group are written in the Latin alphabet, the others in the Cyrillic, said to have been instituted by SS. Cyril and Methodius in the ninth century and largely based on the Greek alphabet. Before the westernization of Russia under Peter the Great (1682–1725), Russian literature consisted mainly of folk ballads (*byliny*), epic songs, chronicles and works of moral theology. The eighteenth and particularly the nineteenth centuries saw a brilliant development of Russian poetry and fiction. Romantic poetry reached its zenith with Alexander Pushkin (1799–1837) and Mikhail Lermontov (1814–41). The 20th century produced great poets like Alexander Blok (1880–1921), the 1958 Nobel Prize laureate Boris Pasternak (1890–1960), Vladimir Mayakovsky (1893–1930) and Anna Akhmatova (1888–1966). Realistic fiction is associated with the names of Nikolai Gogol (1809–52), Ivan Turgenev (1818–83), Fedor Dostoyevsky (1821–81) and Leo Tolstoy (1828–1910), and later with Anton Chekhov (1860–1904), Maxim Gorky (1868–1936), Ivan Bunin (1870–1953) and Alexander Solzhenitsyn (*b.* 1918).

Great names in music include Glinka (1804–57), Borodin (1833–87), Mussorgsky (1839–81), Rimsky-Korsakov (1844–1908), Rubinstein (1829–94), Tchaikovsky (1840–93), Rakhmaninov (1873–1943), Skriabin (1872–1915), Prokofiev (1891–1953), Stravinsky (1882–1971) and Shostakovich (1906–75).

GOVERNMENT

On October 7, 1977 a new Constitution was adopted to replace the 1936 Constitution. Amendments to the 1977 Constitution were adopted on December 1, 1988, creating a new parliamentary structure and amending electoral procedures.

A new supreme representative body, a 2,250-member Congress of People's Deputies, held its inaugural session in May 1989. Partly superseding the former USSR Supreme Soviet, the Congress is to convene once or twice a year to decide on constitutional, political and socio-economic questions. Elections to the Congress are to be held every five years. The reorganized bicameral 542-member Supreme Soviet is responsible for all legislative and administrative matters. Its members are elected by and from the Congress of People's Deputies.

The Congress on March 13, 1990 approved the creation of the post of President of the USSR. M. S. Gorbachov was elected on March 15 for a five-year term. Thereafter, Presidents are to be elected by universal direct suffrage by secret ballot. The President's executive powers include the appointment of the Chairman and members of the Council of Ministers (subject to ratification by Congress), declaring war in the event of an attack on the USSR, imposing temporary presidential rule with the agreement of a union republic, and issuing decrees which are binding throughout the USSR.

A Presidential Council, subordinate to and appointed by the President, acts as an advisory body on the main aspects of domestic, foreign and security policy. A Council of the Federation, comprising the highest state officials of the union republics, advises on nationalities questions.

In March 1990 the Congress of People's Deputies abolished the Communist Party's guaranteed monopoly of power. The Constitution has been amended to provide for the emergence of a multi-party system. Although there is now the right to form political organizations, the KPSS remains the sole political party operating nationwide.

DEFENCE

Defence expenditure in the USSR for 1988 was set officially at 20,244 million roubles (or 4·6 per cent of total budget). It was later admitted that this covered only manpower costs, not weapon procurement, etc. The overall defence budget for 1989 was officially stated to be 77,300 million roubles (15·6 per cent of the total Soviet budget). For 1990 the official budget was 70,975 million roubles (14·5 per cent of the total budget). A further reduction is promised for 1991.

The basic military service is two years in the Army or Air Force or three years in the Navy.

The total size of the Soviet regular forces was estimated at the beginning of 1989 to be about 5,130,000, excluding some 1,135,000 Border Guard, internal security, railway and construction troops (mainly uniformed civilians), but including some 1,500,000 command and general support troops not otherwise listed. Individual force levels are constantly changing.

Late in 1988 it was announced that within the next two years there would be unilateral cuts in Soviet conventional forces of 500,000 men and 10,000 tanks. Withdrawals of Soviet forces from Hungary, Czechoslovakia, the GDR and Mongolia are under way. All Soviet forces in Czechoslovakia and Hungary are scheduled to have left by July 1991. The position, before Soviet unilateral cuts and withdrawals began, was as follows:

Operational ICBMs, i.e. Inter-Continental Ballistic Missiles, totalled about 1,450. SLBMs numbered 978. The number of MRBMs and IRBMs deployed was 383. The operational personnel of the Strategic Rocket Forces totalled 287,000 (not including 123,500 assigned from Air and Navy).

The total strength of all Soviet air elements (including helicopters) was some 19,500. Of these, 10,000 can be classified as combat aircraft. The total strength of the Air Forces, excluding the Naval Air Force (68,000) and the bomber forces of the Aviation Armies (108,000), was about 450,000. The total personnel of the separate Air Defence Command, now merged with the Air Defence Troops of the Ground Forces, was estimated at 630,000.

The total size of the Soviet Ground Forces was estimated at 1,596,000.

The total personnel strength of the Soviet Navy and Naval Air Force was 437,000. In total tonnage, it is the second largest navy in the world, and its main strength lies in the submarine fleet. In mid-1989 there were 69 strategic nuclear and 280 tactical/attack submarines, with a further 19 converting to other roles including SSN, and 55 attack submarines in reserve.

The Soviet Navy has 264 major surface combat vessels, including five aircraft carriers, 37 cruisers and 52 destroyers and some 171 frigates, with 24 varied destroyers and 23 frigates in store. The landbased Naval Air Force comprised about 1,040 combat aircraft, including 355 bombers, and some 300 helicopters.

The para-military forces numbered 570,000, including 230,000 border troops of the KGB and 340,000 internal security troops. There are also DOSAAF members (claimed active membership, 80 million) who participate in such activities as athletics, flight training, shooting, parachuting and pre-military training.

Minister of Defence, Marshal D. T. Yazov.
Chief of General Staff, Army Gen. M. A. Moiseev.
Chief, Political Administration, Soviet Army and Navy, Army Gen. A. D. Lizichev.

On May 14, 1955 a Treaty of Friendship, Mutual Assistance and Co-operation was signed in Warsaw between the Soviet Union and its European associates

(Bulgaria, East Germany, Hungary, Poland, Romania, and Czechoslovakia) (and Albania which left the Pact in September 1968) to serve as a counterpoise to NATO. A united military command was set up in Moscow. The Treaty (Warsaw Pact), due to have expired in June 1985, was extended by Protocol in its existing form for a further 20 years at a meeting of Pact leaders in Warsaw on April 26, 1985. The Pact came into force on May 31, 1985.

In the wake of East–West detente and the recent political changes in Eastern Europe, including the election of democratic governments and the prospect of German unification, the Pact's role as a military organization was recognized to be virtually over. A summit of the seven member countries' leaders in June 1990 undertook to review urgently the Pact's nature and functions, and to seek co-operation with NATO.

The present *C.-in-C.* is Army Gen. P. G. Lushev; *Chief of Staff*, Army Gen. V. N. Lobov.

INDUSTRY AND AGRICULTURE

One of the most remarkable aspects of the Soviet economy has been the transformation of an essentially agricultural country into the second-strongest industrial power in the world. The 1988 output amounted to 163 million tonnes of steel, 116 million tonnes of rolled metal, 772 million tonnes of coal, 624 million tonnes of crude oil, 139 million tonnes of cement, 1,705,000 million kW/h of electricity and 1,300,000 cars.

Agricultural development has been slower, mainly owing to lack of incentives among peasants organized in collective farms. Repeated droughts, such as in 1980-81, were a contributing factor to a shortage of grain. The 1988 harvest was 195 million tonnes. Stock breeding has also suffered from the general mismanagement of farming, and from shortages of fodder in recent years. The livestock at January 1, 1989 included 41,800,000 cows, 78,100,000 pigs and 147,500,000 sheep and goats. Besides *kolkhozy* (collective farms) and *sovkhozy* (state farms) a significant contribution to agricultural production is made by the private plots cultivated by individual peasants. The cultivation of these plots is encouraged by the Soviet authorities. The level of productivity remains very low. Forests cover nearly 40 per cent of the whole area of the Union and form a considerable source of wealth.

Trade with UK

	1988	1989
Imports from UK	£511,653,000	£681,599,000
Exports to UK	732,115,000	833,369,000

COMMUNICATIONS

European Russia is relatively well served by railways, Leningrad and Moscow being the two main focal points of rail routes. The centre and south have a good system of north-south and east-west lines, but the eastern part (the Volga lands), traversed as it is by trunk lines between Europe and Asia which enter Siberia via Sverdlovsk, Chelyabinsk, Magnitogorsk and Ufa, lacks north-south routes. In Asia, there are still large areas of the USSR, notably in the far north and Siberia, with few or no railways. Railways built since 1928 include the Turkestan-Siberian line (*Turksib*) which has made possible a large-scale industrial exploitation of Kazakhstan, a number of lines within the system of the Trans-Siberian Railway (Magnitogorsk-Kartaly-Troitsk, Sverdlovsk-Kurgan, Novosibirsk-Proyektnaya, etc.), which are of great importance for the industrial development in the east, the Petropavlovsk-Karaganda-Balkhash line which has made possible the development of the Karaganda coal basin and of the Balkhash copper mines, and the Moscow-Donbass trunk line. In the

northern part of European Russia, the North Pechora Railway has been completed, while in the Far East a recently completed second Trans-Siberian line (the Baikal-Amur Railway) is partially in use; it follows a more northerly alignment than the earlier Trans-Siberian and terminates in the Pacific port of Sovetskaya Gavan.

Sea Ports and Inland Waterways.—The most important ports (Odessa, Nikolayev, Batumi, Taganrog, Rostov, Kerch, Sevastopol and Novorossiisk) lie around the Black Sea and the Sea of Azov. The northern ports (Leningrad, Murmansk and Archangel) are, with the exception of Murmansk, icebound during winter. Several ports have been built along the Arctic Sea route between Murmansk and Vladivostok and are in regular use every summer. The far eastern port of Vladivostok, the Pacific naval base of the USSR, is kept open by icebreakers all the year round. Inland waterways, both natural and artificial, are of great importance in the country, although some of them are icebound in winter (from 2½ months in the south to 6 months in the north). The great rivers of European Russia flow outwards from the centre, linking all parts of the plain with the chief ports, an immense system of navigable waterways which carried about 690 million tons of freight in 1988. They are supplemented by a system of canals which provide a through traffic between the White, Baltic, Black and Caspian Seas. The most notable are the White Sea-Baltic Canal, the Moscow-Volga Canal and the Volga-Don Canal linking the Baltic and the White Seas in the north to the Caspian, the Black Sea and the Sea of Azov in the south.

CURRENCY.—Rouble of 100 kopeks.

FLAG.—Red, with five-pointed star above hammer and sickle.

NATIONAL DAY.—November 7 (commemorating the October Bolshevik Revolution of 1917).

NATIONAL ANTHEM.—Soyuz Nerushimy Respublik Svobodnykh (Indissoluble union of free republics).

BRITISH EMBASSY
Naberezhnaya Morisa Toreza 14, Moscow 72
[Moscow 2318511]

Ambassador Extraordinary and Plenipotentiary, His Excellency Sir Rodric Braithwaite, KCMG (1988).
Minister and Deputy Head of Mission, D. B. C. Logan.

There is a Consular Section attached to the Embassy.

UNION REPUBLICS

In its Constitution, the USSR is described as a 'unitary federal multi-national state, formed as a result of the free self-determination of nations and the voluntary union of equal Soviet Socialist Republics'. Each union republic has a Constitution and state structure modelled broadly on that of the central administration and, in theory, has always had the freedom to secede.

In April 1990 a law passed by the Supreme Soviet of the USSR outlined 'procedures for resolving matters connected with a union republic's secession from the USSR'. A republic might secede subject to a referendum called by the republic's Supreme Soviet either on its own initiative or in response to a petition signed by at least 10 per cent of USSR citizens permanently resident in that republic. A majority vote of two-thirds of the total electorate would be required, followed by a transitional period of up to five years during which issues arising from secession would be resolved, including the status of any territories ceded to the republic after its original accession to the Soviet Union. A repeat referendum to confirm the decision might be called in the final year of the transitional period, again requiring a two-thirds majority. Completion of the secession process would be subject to ratification by the USSR Congress of People's Deputies.

Almost all the union republics have taken steps towards greater autonomy since 1989.

ARMENIA

Chairman of the Supreme Soviet, L. Ter-Petrosyan.
First Secretary of the Communist Party Central Committee, V. M. Movsisyan.
Chairman of the Council of Ministers, V. Manukyan.

The Armenian SSR occupies the south-western part of Transcaucasia; it was formed in 1920. In 1922 it joined the Transcaucasian Federation, and on its liquidation in 1936 became a Union Republic. In the south it borders on Turkey. It is a mountainous country consisting of several vast tablelands surrounded by ridges. The population and the economic life are concentrated in the low-lying part of Armenia, the Aras valley and the Erevan hollow; the climate is continental, dry and cold, but the Araks valley has a long, hot and dry summer. Irrigation is essential for agriculture. Industrial and fruit crops are grown in the low-lying districts, grain in the hills. Armenia is traditionally noted for its wine. There are large copper ore and molybdenum deposits and other minerals. The Armenian Church centred in Etchmiadzin is the oldest established Christian Church, Christianity having been recognized as the State religion in AD 300.

Nearly 90 per cent of the population is Armenian.

Armenia's Supreme Soviet passed a declaration of independence in August 1990.

CAPITAL.—Erevan. Population, 1,186,000 (1988).

AZERBAIJAN

President of the Republic, First Secretary of the Communist Party Central Committee, A. N. Mutalibov.
Chair of the Supreme Soviet, E. M. Kafarova.
Chairman of the Council of Ministers, G. A. Gasanov.

The Azerbaijan SSR occupies the eastern part of Transcaucasia, on the shore of the Caspian Sea, and borders on Iran. It was formed in 1920. Between 1922 and 1936 it formed part of the Transcaucasian Federation. In 1936 it became a Union Republic. It includes the Nakhichevan Autonomous Republic and the Nagorno-Karabakh Autonomous Province.

The north-eastern part of the Republic is taken up by the south-eastern end of the main Caucasus ridge, its south-western part by the smaller Caucasus hills, and its south-eastern corner by the spurs of the Talysh Ridge. Its central part is a depression irrigated by the Kura and by the lower reaches of its tributary Araks. Sheltered by the mountains from the humid west winds blowing from the Black Sea, Azerbaijan has a continental climate. The land requires artificial irrigation. Industry is dominated by oil and natural gas extraction and related chemical and engineering industries centred in Baku and Sumgait. A large power station on the Araks was completed in 1969, in conjunction with Iran. Azerbaijan is also important as a cotton growing area. The Azerbaijani (Turkic) make up more than three-quarters of the population of the Republic, Armenians about 8 per cent, and Russians 8 per cent.

CAPITAL.—Ψ Baku. Population 1,772,000 (1988).

BELORUSSIA

Chairman of the Supreme Soviet, N. I. Dementei.
First Secretary of the Communist Party Central Committee, E. E. Sokolov.
Chairman of the Council of Ministers (Prime Minister), V. F. Kebich.

The Belorussian SSR, lying in the western part of the European area of the USSR, was formed early in 1919. It now consists of six provinces (Brest, Gomel, Grodno, Minsk, Mogilev and Vitebsk). Belorussians make up four-fifths of the population, with Russians and Poles coming next. It is largely a plain with many lakes, swamps and marshy land. Since the revolution of 1917 agriculture has been greatly developed, thanks to draining of swamps. Most of the Republic's industry is also of recent growth. Woodworking is of great importance, but engineering has been greatly extended with several major plants built in Gomel and Minsk.

The main rivers are the upper reaches of the Dnieper, of the Niemen and of the Western Dvina.

The Belorussian Supreme Soviet declared its sovereignty in July 1990.

CAPITAL.—Minsk. Population 1,583,000 (1988).

ESTONIA

Chairman of the Supreme Soviet, A. F. Ryuitel.
Chairman of the Communist Party, V. Valyas.
Prime Minister, E. E. Savisaar.

Estonia, formerly a Baltic province of the Russian Empire, was proclaimed an independent republic in 1918. In 1940, it was forcibly incorporated into the USSR. It lies on the shores of the Baltic and of the Finnish Gulf in the north and of the Gulf of Riga in the south-west. Some 800 islands, among them Dagö and Ösel, form part of Estonian territory.

The country forms a low-lying plain with many lakes, among them the Chud (or Pskov) Lake, on the border with the RSFSR. Forests take up about one-fifth of the territory. Agriculture and dairy-farming are the chief industries, rye, oats, barley, flax and potatoes being the chief crops, and butter, bacon and eggs the chief products of dairy farming. There are important manufactures, including textiles, engineering, shipbuilding, woodworking etc.

The population consists of Estonians (64·7 per cent) and Russians (27·9 per cent).

In November 1989 the Estonian Supreme Soviet declared Estonia's 1940 annexation illegal. In February 1990 the guaranteed leading role of the Communist Party was abolished, and in May 1990, following multi-party elections to the Supreme Soviet in March, the formal title 'Republic of Estonia' was reinstated. A law was passed establishing a provisional system of government for the period of transition to independence.

CAPITAL.—Ψ Tallinn (formerly Reval). Population, 484,000 (1988).

GEORGIA

Chairman of the Supreme Soviet, First Secretary of the Communist Party Central Committee, G. G. Gumbaridze.
Chairman of the Council of Ministers, N. A. Chitanava.

Georgia, occupying the north-western part of Transcaucasia, lies on the shore of the Black Sea and borders in the south-east on Turkey. It was formed in 1921; in 1922 it joined the Transcaucasian Federation which, in its turn, adhered to the USSR in the same year. After the liquidation of the Transcaucasian SFSR in 1936 Georgia became a Union Republic. It contains two Autonomous Republics (Abkhazia and Adjaria) and the South Osetian Autonomous Province. Georgia is a country of mountains, with the Greater Caucasus in the north and the Lesser Caucasus in the south. A relatively low-lying land between these two ridges is divided into two parts by the Surz Ridge: Western Georgia with a mild and damp climate and Eastern Georgia with a more continental and dry climate. The Black Sea shore and the Rioni lowland are subtropical in their climatic character. The most important mineral deposits are manganese (Chiatura), coal (Tkibuli and Tkvarcheli) and oil (Kakhetia). Georgia is a leading producer of manganese in the USSR. There are also many oil refineries. Viniculture, tea and tobacco-growing are the three main agricultural industries. The Black Sea harbours many famous holiday resorts. Georgians make up 68·8 per cent of the population, the remainder being largely composed of Armenians (9 per cent), Russians, Azerbaijanis and Osetians.

In March 1990 the Georgian Supreme Soviet declared illegal the treaties of 1921–22 by which Georgia had joined the Soviet Union. The republic's Constitution was amended to abolish the Communist Party's guaranteed monopoly of power. Multi-party elections to the Supreme Soviet were scheduled for the end of 1990.

CAPITAL.—Tbilisi (Tiflis), population 1,211,000 (1987).

KAZAKHSTAN

Chairman of the Supreme Soviet, E. M. Asanbaev.
President, First Secretary of the Communist Party Central Committee, N. A. Nazarbaev.
Chairman of the Council of Ministers, U. K. Karamanov.

The Kazakh SSR, the second-largest Union Republic, stretching from the lower reaches of the Volga and the Caspian in the west to the Altai and Tienshan in the east, and bordering on China, was formed in 1920 as an autonomous republic (under the name of the Kazakh ASSR) within the RSFSR., and was constituted a Union Republic in 1936. It consists of 17 Provinces: Aktyubinsk, Alma-Ata, Chimkent, Dzhambul, Dzhezkazgan, East-Kazakhstan, Guryev, Karaganda, Kokchetav, Kustanay, Kzyl-Orda, North-Kazakhstan, Pavlodar, Semipalatinsk, Taldy-Kurgan, Tselinograd and Uralsk.

Kazakhstan is a country of arid steppes and semi-deserts, flat in the west, hilly in the east and mountainous in the south-east (Southern Altai and Tienshan). The climate is continental and very dry. The main rivers are the (Upper) Irtysh, the Ural, the Syr-Darya and the Ili. Kazakhstan is very rich in minerals: copper in Kounrad and Dzhezkazgan, lead and zinc in the Altai and Karatau mountains, iron ore in Radryg and Lisakovsk, coal in Ekibastuz and Karaganda and oil and natural gas in the Mangyshlak peninsula. Major centres of metal industry exist in the Altai Mountains, in Chimkent, north of the Balkhash Lake and in Central Kazakhstan. Stock-raising is highly developed, particularly in the central and south-western parts of the Republic. Grain is grown in the north and north-east and cotton in the south and south-east.

The Kazakhs (a Turkic people) are in a minority in the Republic named after them; they constitute only 36 per cent of its population, Russian settlers make up 41 per cent and Ukrainians 6 per cent.

CAPITAL.—Alma-Ata (formerly Verny). Population 1,134,000 (1988). Karaganda, a major mining centre, had a population (1987) of 633,000.

KIRGHIZIA

Chairman of the Supreme Soviet, First Secretary of the Communist Party Central Committee, A. M. Masaliev.
Chairman of the Council of Ministers, A. Dzhumagulov.

The Kirghiz SSR occupies the north-eastern part of Soviet Central Asia and borders in the south-east on China. In 1924 a Kara-Kirghiz Autonomous Province was formed within the RSFSR. In 1926 it became a Kirghiz Autonomous Republic, and in 1936 a Union Republic. It contains two provinces, Issyk-Kul and Osh. The Kirghiz Republic is a mountainous country, the major part being covered by the ridge of the Central Tienshan, while mountains of the Pamir-Altai system occupy its southern part. There are a number of spacious mountain valleys, the Alai, Susamyr, the Issyk-Kul lake and others. The majority of the population is concentrated in plains, lying at the foot of mountains—Chu, Talass, part of the Ferghana Valley where agriculture prospers. Crops include sugar beet and cotton, and sheep are important in the mountains. Industry is being developed and some mining is done. The Kirghiz constitute 47·9 per cent of the population, the Russians 25·9 per cent. The Uzbeks (in Eastern Ferghana) amount to 12·1 per cent.

CAPITAL.—Frunze (formerly Pishpek). Population 646,000 (1988).

LATVIA

Chairman of the Supreme Soviet, A. V. Gorbunov.
First Secretary of the Communist Party Central Committee, A. P. Rubiks.
Chairman of the Independent Communist Party of Latvia, I. Ya. Kezbers.
Chairman of the Council of Ministers, I. T. Godmanis.

Latvia, lying on the shores of the Baltic and of the Gulf of Riga, was formerly a Baltic Province of the Russian Empire. It was proclaimed an independent state in 1918 and was forcibly incorporated into the USSR in August 1940.

The surface of the country is generally flat, interspersed by occasional chains of hills. The climate is moderately continental. The main rivers are the lower reaches of the Western Dvina and its tributaries. Forests occupy 20 per cent of the total territory.

The Latvians make up 53·7 per cent of the Republic's population, Russians 32·8 per cent.

Latvian industry was always highly developed, with shipbuilding, engineering, chemical industry, textile industry, wood-working and dairying being the chief occupations. Both Riga and Liepaja (Libava, Libau) are important sea-ports.

In January 1990 the Latvian Supreme Soviet amended the Constitution to abolish the Communist Party's guaranteed leading role. In May 1990, following multi-party elections to the Supreme Soviet in March, a resolution was passed proclaiming Latvia's independence from the Soviet Union. A transitional period for negotiations on independence has been declared. The formal title, Republic of Latvia, was reinstated.

CAPITAL.—Ψ Riga. Population, 913,000 (1988).

LITHUANIA

Chairman of Supreme Council, and of the Council of the Seimas of Sajudis, V. V. Landsbergis.
First Secretary of the Communist Party Central Committee, A.-M. K. Brazauskas.
First Secretary of the Central Committee of the Communist Party of Lithuania (KPSS), M. M. Burokyavichyus.
Prime Minister, K.-D. Prunskene.

Lithuania, formerly a Baltic Province of the Russian Empire, was declared an independent republic at Vilna in 1918 and was forcibly incorporated into the USSR in August 1940. The Republic forms a plain with a large number of lakes and swamps. The forests occupy 19 per cent of the whole area. The main river is the Niemen with its tributaries.

The chief industries are agriculture and forestry, the chief products being rye, oats, wheat, barley, flax, sugar-beet and potatoes.

The Lithuanians make up four-fifths of the population, Russians and Poles, 7–9 per cent each.

Following the abolition in December 1989 of the Communist Party's constitutionally guaranteed monopoly of power in Lithuania, multi-party elections to the Supreme Soviet (subsequently renamed the Supreme Council) were held in February and March 1990. A majority of seats were won by candidates affiliated to the nationalist Sajudis (Popular Front for Perestroika) movement.

On March 11, 1990 Lithuania became the first union republic to declare unilaterally its independence from the Soviet Union.

CAPITAL.—Vilnius (Vilna). Population 579,000 (1988).

MOLDOVA

Chairman of the Supreme Soviet, M. I. Snegur.
First Secretary of the Communist Party Central Committee, P. K. Luchinski.
Prime Minister, M. G. Druk.

Moldova (formerly Moldavia), occupying the south-western corner of the USSR, borders in the west on Romania with the Pruth forming the frontier. In 1918, Romania seized the Russian Province of Bessarabia, but in 1940 the USSR forced Romania to give back Bessarabia, the major part of which was merged with the Moldavian ASSR (formed in 1924) to create the Moldavian SSR. In June 1990 the republic's Supreme Soviet voted to change the name to the SSR Moldova.

The northern part of the Republic consists of flat steppe lands, now all under plough. Some forests skirt the Dniester. Further south, around Kishinev, there are woody hills and further south again, low-lying steppe lands. The climate is moderate. The main river is the Dniester, navigable along the whole course.

The main industry is agriculture (viniculture, fruit-growing and market-gardening). Industry is insignificant in both parts of Moldova, but the Republic has the densest population in the USSR. Moldavians make up 64 per cent of the population, with Ukrainians (14·2 per cent), and Russians (12·8 per cent) next.

On June 23, 1990 the Supreme Soviet adopted a declaration of sovereignty.

CAPITAL.—Kishinev (Chisinau). Population 684,000 (1988).

RSFSR

(The Russian Soviet Federal Socialist Republic)

Chairman of the Supreme Soviet, B. N. Yeltsin.
Chairman of the Council of Ministers, I. S. Silaev.
First Secretary of the Central Committee of the Communist Party of the RSFSR, I. K. Polozkov.

The RSFSR, the largest and the most powerful of the Republics, occupies the major half of the European part of the USSR and the major northern portion of its Asiatic part and makes up 77 per cent of the total territory of the USSR with 53 per cent of the total population. (About 83 per cent of the population are Russians.)

The RSFSR comprises 16 Autonomous Republics (the Bashkir, Buryat, Checheno-Ingush, Chuvash, Daghestan, Kabardin-Balkar, Kalmyk, Karelian, Komi, Mari, Mordovian, North Osetian, Tatar, Tuva, Udmurt and Yakut, ASSRs); 6 regions (Altai, Khabarovsk, Krasnodar, Krasnoyarsk, Maritime and Stavropol) containing in their turn 5 autonomous provinces; 49 provinces (Amur, Archangel, Astrakhan, Belgorod, Bryansk, Chelyabinsk, Chita, Gorky, Irkutsk, Ivanovo, Kalinin, Kaliningrad, Kaluga, Kamchatka, Kemerovo, Kirov, Kostroma, Kuibyshev, Kurgan, Kursk, Leningrad, Lipetsk, Magadan, Moscow, Murmansk, Novgorod, Novosibirsk, Omsk, Orel, Orenburg, Penza, Perm, Pskov, Rostov, Ryazan, Sakhalin, Saratov, Smolensk, Sverdlovsk, Tambov, Tomsk, Tula, Tyumen, Ulyanovsk, Vladimir, Volgograd, Vologda, Voronezh and Yaroslavl).

There are three principal geographic areas: a low-lying flat Western part stretching eastwards up to the Yenisei and divided in two by the Ural ridge; an eastern part, between the Yenisei and the Pacific, consisting of a number of tablelands and ridges, and a southern mountainous part. Climatically, the RSFSR extends from Arctic and tundra belts to the sub-tropical in the south. It has a very long coast-line, including the longest Arctic coastline in the world (about 17,000 miles). The most important rivers are the Volga, the Northern Dvina and the Pechora, the Neva, the Don and the Kuban in the European part, and in the Asiatic part, the Ob, the Irtysh, the Yenisei, the Lena and the Amur, and, further north, Khatanga, Olenek, Yana, Indigirka, Kolyma and Anadyr. Lakes are abundant, particularly in the north-west. The huge Baikal Lake in Eastern Siberia is the deepest lake in the world. There are also two large artificial water reservoirs within the Greater Volga canal system, the Moscow and Rybinsk 'Seas'.

Government.—As reforms to the Soviet Constitution in 1988 made possible, the RSFSR has adopted a two-tier legislative structure comprising its own Congress of People's Deputies as well as a bicameral Supreme Soviet, whose chairman and members are to be elected by Congress. The RSFSR's Congress of People's Deputies, convened in May 1990, issued a declaration of sovereignty on June 12, 1990.

Minerals.—The Republic has some of the richest mineral deposits in the world. Coal is mined in the Kuznetsk area, in the Urals, south of Moscow, in the Donets basin (its Eastern part lies in the RSFSR) and in the Pechora area in the North. Oil is produced in the Northern Caucasus, in the area between the Volga and the Ural and in Western Siberia, which also has large deposits of natural gas. Coal and gas deposits in Siberia and the Far East (especially Yakutia) are currently being developed, now that some deposits in the western parts of the USSR are approaching exhaustion. The Ural mountains contain a unique assortment of minerals—high-quality iron ore, manganese, copper, aluminium, gold, platinum, precious stones, salt, asbestos, pyrites, coal, oil, etc. Iron ore is also mined near Kursk, Tula, Lipetsk, in several areas in Siberia and in the Kola Peninsula. Non-ferrous metals are found in the Altai, in Eastern Siberia, in the Northern Caucasus, in the Kuznetsk-Basin, in the far east and in the far north. Nine-tenths of all USSR forests are located in the RSFSR.

Production and Industry.—The vast area of the Republic and the great variety in climatic conditions cause great differences in the structure of agriculture from north to south and from west to east. In the far north reindeer breeding, hunting and fishing are predominant. Further south, timber industry is combined with grain growing. In the southern half of the forest zone and in the adjacent forest-steppe zone, the acreage under grain crops is far larger and the structure of agriculture more complex. An extensive programme of land improvement mainly involving this zone aims to double its total agricultural output by 1990. In the eastern part of this zone, between the Volga and the Urals, cericulture is predominant (particularly summer wheat), followed by cattle breeding. Beyond the Urals is another important grain-growing and stock-breeding area in the southern part of the Western-Siberian plain. The southern steppe zone is the main wheat granary of the USSR, containing also large acreages under barley, maize and sunflower. In the extreme south cotton is now cultivated. Vine, tobacco and other southern crops are grown on the Black Sea shore of the Caucasus.

Industrially, the RSFSR occupies the first place among the Soviet Republics. Moscow and Leningrad are still the two largest industrial centres in the country, but new industrial areas are being developed in the Urals, the Kuznetsk basin, and more recently in Siberia and the Far East. Most of the oil produced in the USSR now comes from the RSFSR, half annual output comes from Tyumen Oblast in Western Siberia. All industries are represented in the RSFSR, including iron and steel and engineering.

CAPITAL.—Moscow. Population 8,879,000 (1988). Moscow, founded about AD 1147 by Yuri Dolgoruki, became first the centre of the rising Moscow principality and in the 15th century, the capital of the whole of Russia (Muscovy). In 1325 it became the seat of the Metropolitan of Russia. In 1703 Peter the Great transferred the capital to the newly-built St. Petersburg, but on March 14, 1918, Moscow was again designated as the capital. ΨLeningrad (before the First World War St. Petersburg and from 1914–1924 Petrograd) has a population of 4,948,000 (January 1, 1987).

Other towns with populations (January 1, 1987) exceeding 1,000,000 are:—

Gorky (Nizhny-Novogorod)	1,425,000
Novosibirsk (Novonikolayevsk)	1,423,000
Sverdlovsk (Yekaterinburg)	1,331,000
Kuibyshev (Samara)	1,280,000
Omsk	1,134,000
Chelyabinsk	1,119,000
Ufa	1,092,000
Perm (Molotov)	1,075,000
Kazan	1,068,000
Rostov-on-Don	1,004,000

TADJIKISTAN

Chairman of the Supreme Soviet, First Secretary of the Communist Party Central Committee, K. Makhkamov.

Chairman of the Council of Ministers, I. Khaeev.

The Tadjik SSR lies in the extreme south-east of Soviet Central Asia and borders in the south on Afghanistan and in the east on China. It was originally formed in 1924 as an Autonomous Republic within the Uzbek SSR and became a Union Republic in 1929. It includes the Gorno-Badakhshan Autonomous Province and the Kulyab Kurgan-Tyubinsk and Leninabad Provinces.

The country is mountainous; in the east lie the Pamir highlands with the highest point in the USSR, Pik Kommunizma (24,590 feet), in the centre the high ridges of the Pamir-Altai system. Plains are formed by wide stretches of the Syr-Darya valley in the north and of the Amu-Darya in the south.

Like the other Central Asiatic Republics, Tadjikistan is a cotton-growing country. Its climatic conditions favour the cultivation of Egyptian cotton. Irrigation is of great importance. Of the population 58·8 per cent are Tadjiks (linguistically and culturally akin to the Persians), 23 per cent Uzbeks, the rest Russians and others.

In August 1990 it was reported that the Supreme Soviet of Tadjikistan had issued a declaration of sovereignty.

CAPITAL.—Dushanbe (formerly Stalinabad; Dyushambe). Population, 596,000 (1988).

TURKMENISTAN

First Secretary of the Communist Party Central Committee, Chairman of the Supreme Soviet, S. A. Niyazov.

Chairman of the Council of Ministers, Kh. Akhemedov.

Turkmenia occupies the extreme south of Soviet Central Asia, between the Caspian and the Amu-Darya, and borders in the south on Iran and Afghanistan. It was formed in 1924 and contains five Provinces: Ashkhabad, Chardjou, Krasnovodsk, Mary and Tashauz. The country is a low-lying plain, fringed by hills in the south. Ninety per cent of the plain is taken up by the arid Kara-Kum desert. Of all Central-Asiatic Republics, Turkmenia is the lowest and driest. The cultivation of cotton, stock-raising and mineral extraction are the principal industries. The republic produces about 16 per cent of the Soviet Union's natural gas, as well as astrakhan furs and carpets. Most of the arable land is artificially irrigated. The oil and silk industries are of old standing. There are also some fisheries in the Caspian.

Turkomans make up 68·4 per cent of the population, Russians 12·6 per cent, and Uzbeks 8·5 per cent.

In August 1990 it was reported that Turkmenia had declared itself a sovereign national state.

CAPITAL.—Ashkhabad (formerly Askhabad, Poltoratsk). Population 390,000 (1988).

UKRAINE

First Secretary of the Communist Party Central Committee, S. I. Gurenko.

Chairman of the Supreme Soviet, vacant.

Chairman of the Council of Ministers, V. A. Masol.

This Republic, second largest in population, lying in the south-western part of the European half of the USSR, was formed in December 1917. Ukrainians make up nearly 75 per cent of the population, with 21 per cent Russians. It consists of 25 provinces—Cherkassy, Chernigov, Chernovtsy, Crimea, Dnepropetrovsk, Donetsk, Ivano-Frankovsk, Kharkov, Kherson, Khmelnitsky, Kiev, Kirovograd, Lugansk, Lvov, Nikolayev, Odessa, Poltava, Rovno, Sumy, Ternopol, Transcarpathia, Vinnitsa, Volhynia, Zaporozhye and Zhitomir.

Physical Features.—The larger part of the Ukraine forms a plain with small elevations. The Carpathian mountains lie in the south-western part of the Republic. The climate is moderate, with relatively mild winters (particularly in the southwest) and hot summers. The main rivers are the Dnieper with its tributaries, the Southern Bug and the Northern Donets (a tributary of the Don).

Production and Industry.—The main centre of Soviet coal mining and iron and steel industry is situated in the southern part of the Ukraine. In 1980, the Ukraine provided 36 per cent of the total Soviet steel, 51 per cent of iron ore and 27 per cent of coal. The engineering and chemical industries are also of importance. The central forest-steppe region (mainly on the right bank of the Dnieper) is the greatest sugar-producing area in the USSR. The Ukraine also leads in grain-growing and stock-raising.

There are large deposits of coal and salt in the Donets Basin, of iron ore in Krivoy Rog and near Kerch in the Crimea, of manganese in Nikopol, and of quicksilver in Nikitovka.

In July 1990 the Ukrainian Supreme Soviet issued a declaration of sovereignty, stating its intention to become a neutral state, but making no mention of secession from the Soviet Union.

CAPITAL (since 1934).—Kiev, one of the oldest cities in the USSR, founded in the 6th–7th century AD, was the capital of the Russian State from 865 to 1240. Population (1988) 2,577,000. Other towns are:—

Kharkov 1,587,000
Dnepropetrovsk (Yekaterinoslav)........ 1,182,000
Ψ Odessa 1,141,000
Donetsk (Stalino; Yuzovka, i.e.
  Hughesovka) 1,090,000

UZBEKISTAN

First Secretary of the Communist Party Central Committee and President of Uzbekistan, I. A. Karimov.
Chairman of the Supreme Soviet, M. I. Ibragimov.
Chairman of the Council of Ministers, Sh. R. Mirsaidov.

The Uzbek SSR was formed in 1924 and consists of the Kara-Kalpak ASSR and of 12 provinces (Andizhan, Bokhara, Dzhizak, Ferghana, Kashka-darya, Khorezm, Namangan, Navoi, Samarkand, Surkhandarya, Syr-darya and Tashkent). It lies between the high Tienshan Mountains and the Pamir highlands in the east and south-east and sandy lowlands in the west and north-west. The major part of the territory is a plain with huge waterless deserts and several large oases, which form the main centres of population and economic life. The largest is the Ferghana valley, watered by the Syr-darya. Other oases include Tashkent, Samarkand, Bokhara and Khorezm. The climate is continental and dry. Minerals include gold, natural gas, oil, copper, lead, zinc and coal.

The Uzbeks, a Turkic people, make up 68·7 per cent of the population, the Russians 10·8 per cent, Tatars 4·2 per cent and Kazakhs 4 per cent.

There are major agricultural and textile machinery plants and several chemical combines. Uzbekistan is the main cotton-growing area of the USSR producing more than 60 per cent of all Soviet cotton. Irrigation has always been of decisive importance in this area, and the Soviet Government has done much in this field, including the construction of the Great Ferghana Canal (230 miles).

In June 1990 the Supreme Soviet of Uzbekistan adopted a declaration of sovereignty within 'a renewed Soviet federation'.

CAPITAL.—Tashkent. Population 2,210,000 (1988). Samarkand (population (1987) 388,000) contains the Gur-Emir (Tamerlane's Mausoleum), completed AD 1400 by Ulugbek, Tamerlane's astronomer-grandson, and a 15th-century observatory.

UNITED ARAB EMIRATES
(Al-Imarat Al-Arabiya Al-Muttahida)

President, Shaikh Zayed bin Sultan al Nahyan (*Abu Dhabi*).
Vice-President, Shaikh Rashid bin Said al Maktoum (*Dubai*).

COUNCIL OF MINISTERS
(as at June 30, 1990)

Prime Minister, the Vice-President.
Deputy Prime Minister, Shaikh Maktoum bin Rashid al Maktoum.
Interior, Shaikh Mubarak bin Muhammad al Nahyan.
Finance and Industry, Shaikh Hamdan bin Rashid al Maktoum.
Defence, Shaikh Muhammad bin Rashid al Maktoum.
Minister of State for Foreign Affairs, Sayyid Rashid Abdullah al Nu'aimi.
Petroleum and Mineral Resources, Dr. Mana Said al Otaiba.
Economy and Commerce, Sayyid Saif al Jarwan.

Information and Culture, Shaikh Ahmad bin Hamid bin Butti.
Communications, Sayyid Muhammad Said al Mulla.
Public Works and Housing, Sayyid Muhammad Khalifa al Kindi.
Education, Sayyid Faraj Fadel al Mazroui.
Planning, Shaikh Humaid bin Ahmad al Mulla.
Justice, Islamic Affairs and Awqaf, Shaikh Mohammad bin Hassan al Khazraji.
Agriculture and Fisheries, Sayyid Said al Raqabani.
Water and Electricity, Sayyid Humaid bin Nasser al Owais.
Labour and Social Affairs, Sayyid Khalfan al Roumi.
Health, Sayyid Hamad Abdul Rahman al Madfa.
Minister of State for Cabinet Affairs, Sayyid Al Ghaith.
Minister of State for Supreme Council Affairs, Sayyid Ghobash.

EMBASSY OF THE UNITED ARAB EMIRATES
30 Prince's Gate, SW7 1PT
[071–581 1281]

Ambassador Extraordinary and Plenipotentiary, Dr. Khaifa Mohamed Sulaiman (1988).

Area and Population.—The approximate area of the UAE is 32,278 sq. miles (83,600 sq. km), and the population (UN estimate 1988) is 1,501,000.

The United Arab Emirates (formerly the Trucial States) is composed of seven Emirates (Abu Dhabi, Ajman, Dubai, Fujeirah, Ras al Khaimah, Sharjah and Umm al Qaiwain) which came together as an independent state on December 2, 1971 when they ended their individual special treaty relationships with the British Government (Ras al Khaimah joined the other six on February 10, 1972). Six of the Emirates lie on the shore of the Gulf between the Musandam peninsula in the east and the Qatar peninsula in the west while the seventh, Fujeirah, lies on the gulf of Oman.

Government.—The British Government, by virtue of a treaty made in 1892, had been responsible for the external affairs of the states through the British Political Resident in the Persian Gulf and the British Political Agents in each state, but on independence the Union Government assumed full responsibility for all internal and external affairs apart from some internal matters that remained the prerogative of the individual Emirates. Overall authority lies with the Supreme Council of the seven Emirate rulers, each of whom is an absolute monarch in his own state. The President and Vice-President are elected by the Supreme Council from among its members. The President appoints the Council of Ministers.

Security in the area is maintained by the UAE Armed Forces. The Ministry of Defence is located in Dubai with a general headquarters in Abu Dhabi. Most of the separate police forces have also been merged.

Revenue is chiefly derived from oil, re-exports and customs dues on imports.

Trade with UK

	1988	1989
Imports from UK	£463,344,000	£571,421,000
Exports to UK	84,217,000	165,003,000

CURRENCY.—UAE dirham of 100 fils.
FLAG.—Horizontal stripes of green over white over black with vertical red stripe in the hoist.
NATIONAL DAY.—December 2.

Abu Dhabi

Abu Dhabi is the largest Emirate of the UAE in area, stretching from Khor al Odaid in the west to the borders with Dubai in the Jebel Ali area. It includes six villages in the Buraimi oasis, the other three being part of the Sultanate of Oman, and a number of settlements in the Liwa Oasis system. Following negotiations with Saudi Arabia, some adjustment of the border has now been made in the Khor al Odaid region, but the agreement has not yet been ratified. The population of the Emirate is now about 670,000

The Abu Dhabi government controls oil, gas and petrochemical operations in the Emirate through the Supreme Petroleum Council. This body in turn issues instructions to the Abu Dhabi National Oil Company (ADNOC) which has majority shareholdings in the several oil operating and gas treatment companies. ADNOC also has majority shareholdings in oil industry-related companies covering drilling, refining, distribution, chemical manufacture and investment. Offshore production began in 1962, the most important fields being Umm Shaif and Lower Zakum, near Das Island, site of a large associated gas liquefaction plant. The Upper Zakum field came on stream in late 1982, and four other offshore fields are being developed, one near Abu Dhabi city and three near Delma. Production of oil onshore began in 1963 from the Murban field. A large onshore associated gas liquefaction project based at Ruwais started production in 1981. Other large natural gas finds in recent years will consolidate Abu Dhabi's position as a holder of some of the largest reserves of natural gas in the world. Abu Dhabi's crude oil production in 1989 was approximately 1·47 million barrels per day.

With its oil wealth the Emirate has seen a decade of growth (which is currently slowing down), not only at Abu Dhabi, now a modern city of about 450,000 people, but also at Al Ain in the Buraimi Oasis and at the new petro-chemical city at Ruwais. An international airport opened in 1982 at Abu Dhabi and another is under construction at Al Ain. There are airfields at Das Island and Jebel Dhanna. The port and harbour on Abu Dhabi island are now completed and there are port facilities at Ruwais.

Ajman and Umm al Qaiwain

Ajman and Umm al Qaiwain are the smallest Emirates, having populations of around 64,000 and 29,000 respectively. Both lie on the Gulf coast although Ajman has two inland enclaves at Manama and Masfut. Exploration work continues in both Emirates for oil and gas but so far only Umm Al Qaiwain has experienced any success, with the offshore discovery of natural gas, but the field has yet to be commercially developed. The discovery of onshore gas in nearby Sharjah has increased hopes of similar discoveries in both Ajman and Umm Al Qaiwain.

Dubai

Dubai is the second largest Emirate both in size and in population, which is about 419,000. The town of Dubai is the main port for the import of goods into the UAE and has a wide re-export trade to the other Gulf States. Dubai's prosperity was established by this trade long before the discovery of oil. Oil was discovered in 1966 and production began in September 1969. The producer in Dubai's offshore oilfields is Dubai Petroleum Company, operated by CONOCO. Production is in excess of 350,000 b.p.d. In 1982 an ARCO-Britoil joint venture discovered an extensive gas and condensate field onshore. A small amount of condensate is produced from the onshore Margam field.

Oil income has been used to finance Dubai's infrastructure, and major construction projects include an international airport, a dry dock complex and an international trade and exhibition centre. There is also a 66 berth port at Jebel Ali, forming the heart of an industrial complex which includes an aluminium smelter with an associated de-salination plant and a gas processing plant. The port and its immediate area is a free trade zone which is expected to attract more industry.

Fujeirah

Fujeirah, with a population of 40,000, is the most remote of the seven Emirates lying on the Gulf of Oman coast, and only connected by a metal road to the rest of the country since the end of 1975. Largely agricultural, its population is spread between the slopes of the inland Hajar mountain range and the town of Fujeirah itself, together with a number of smaller settlements on the comparatively fertile plain on the coast. Although exploration work continues, there have been no hydrocarbon discoveries in the Emirate. However, there are some chrome and other mineral deposits. Fujeirah has a new general cargo port.

Ras al Khaimah

Ras al Khaimah has a population of 116,000 of whom more than half live in the town. An ancient sea-port, near to which archaeological remains have been found, Ras al Khaimah is developing as the most agricultural of the Emirates, producing vegetables, dates, fruit and tobacco. In 1982 Ras al Khaimah announced the discovery of oil and gas offshore and this field currently produces approximately 5,000 b.p.d. An industrial area has been developed to the north of the Emirate, which includes two cement works. Ras al-Khaimah has an international airport and has also expanded its port. A new international airport is nearing completion. A new trade centre has been completed and it is hoped that more industry will be attracted to the Emirate.

Sharjah

Sharjah, with a population of approximately 269,000, has declined from its former position as principal town in the area. It became the third oil producing Emirate in the summer of 1974, following the discovery of oil offshore. The field declined over the years and by 1982 was yielding less than 6,000 b.p.d. However, new oil and gas discoveries were made in 1982 in the northern emirates and production now stands at about 50,000 b.p.d. Sharjah is well connected by metalled roads to all the other northern Emirates. It experienced a construction boom in the mid-1970s including an ambitious layout of roads and flyovers within the town. A new container port has been constructed on the Gulf of Oman at Khor Fakkan. The international airport was officially opened in 1979.

BRITISH EMBASSIES
PO Box 248, Abu Dhabi
[Abu Dhabi 326600]

Ambassador Extraordinary and Plenipotentiary, His Excellency Graham Stuart Burton, CMG (1990).
British Council Representative, Dr. P. Clark.

PO Box 65, Dubai
[Dubai 521070]

Counsellor and Consul General, R. A. M. Hendrie.

British Council Representative, A. Swales, PO Box 1636, Dubai.

UNITED STATES OF AMERICA

Physiography

The conterminous States of the Republic occupy nearly all that portion of the North American Continent between the Atlantic and Pacific Oceans, in latitude 25° 07′–49° 23′ North and longitude 66° 57′–124° 44′ West, its northern boundary being Canada and the southern boundary Mexico. The separate State of Alaska reaches a latitude of 71° 23′ N., at Point Barrow (2,502 miles from the US geographic centre).

The general coastline of the 50 States has a length of about 2,069 miles on the Atlantic, 7,623 miles on the Pacific, 1,060 miles on the Arctic, and 1,631 miles on the Gulf of Mexico.

The principal river is the mighty Mississippi-Missouri-Red, traversing the whole country from north to south, and having a course of 3,710 miles to its mouth in the Gulf of Mexico, with many large affluents, the chief of which are the Yellowstone, Platte, Arkansas, and Ohio rivers. The rivers flowing into the Atlantic and Pacific Oceans are comparatively small; among the former may be noticed the Hudson, Delaware, Susquehanna, Potomac, James, Roanoke and Savannah; of the latter, the Columbia-Snake, Sacramento, and Colorado. The Nueces, Brazos, Trinity, Pearl, Mobile-Tombigbee-Alabama, Apalachicola-Chattahoochee, Suwannee and Colorado of Texas fall into the Gulf of Mexico, also the Rio Grande, a long river partly forming the boundary with Mexico. The areas of the water-basins have

been estimated as follows:—Rivers flowing to the Pacific, 647,300 square miles; to the Atlantic, 488,877; and to the Gulf of Mexico, 1,683,325 square miles, of which 1,234,600 are drained by the Mississippi-Missouri-Red. The chain of the Rocky Mountains separates the western portion of the country from the remainder, communications being carried on over certain elevated passes, several of which are now traversed by railroads and major highways; west of these, bordering the Pacific coast, the Cascade Mountains and Sierra Nevada form the outer edge of a high tableland, consisting in part of stony and sandy desert and partly of grazing land and forested mountains, and including the Great Salt Lake, which extends to the Rocky Mountains. In the Eastern States (which form the more settled and most thickly inhabited portion of the country) large forests of valuable timber, as beech, birch, maple, oak, pine, spruce, elm, ash, walnut; and in the south, live oak, water-oak, magnolia, palmetto, pine, tulip-tree, cypress, etc., still exist, the remnants of the forests which formerly extended over all the Atlantic slope, but into which great inroads have been made by the advance of civilization. The mineral kingdom produces ore of iron, copper, lead, zinc, and aluminium, the non-metallic minerals include large quantities of coal, petroleum, stone, phosphate rock, and salt. The highest point is Mount McKinley (Alaska), 20,320 ft. above sea level and the lowest point of dry land is in Death Valley (Inyo, California), 282 ft. below sea-level.

AREA AND POPULATION

	Area 1980 (sq. miles)		Population	
	Total	Land	Census 1970	Census 1980
The United States (a)	3,618,770	3,539,289	203,302,031*	226,545,805
Puerto Rico........................	3,515	3,459	2,712,033	3,196,520
Outlying areas under US jurisdiction .	1,176	1,176	314,657*	368,856
Territories	459	459	179,519**	235,927
Guam	209	209	84,996	105,979
Virgin Islands of US	132	132	62,468	96,569
American Samoa	77	77	27,159	32,297
Midway Islands	2	2	2,220	453
Wake Island	3	3	1,647	302
Canton Island and Enderbury Island	27	27	—	—
Johnston Atoll (b)	0·5	0·5	1,007	327
Other (c)	9	9	—	—
Pacific Islands Trust Territory (excluding N. Mariana Is.)........	533	533	81,300	116,149
Northern Mariana Islands	184	184	9,640	16,780
Population abroad (d)			1,737,836†	995,546
Armed Forces.....................			1,057,776	515,408
Total	3,543,924	3,623,461	208,066,557	231,106,727

(a) The 50 States and the Federal District of Columbia.

(b) Formerly listed as Johnston and Sand Island. Sand Island uninhabited at time of enumeration.

(c) Navassa, Baker, Howland and Jarvis Islands, Kingman Reef, and Palmyra Atoll.

(d) Excludes US citizens temporarily abroad on private business.

* Includes population of Swan Islands (22) and Panama Canal Zone (44,198). Jurisdiction over the Swan Islands was transferrred to Honduras in 1972. Due to the 1978 Treaty, the Census is no longer conducted in the Canal Zone.

** Includes population of Swan Islands (22).

† Includes US citizens abroad for long periods who were not connected with the US government (236,336) and crews of US merchant vessels (15,910).

Immigrants by Place of Birth, 1951–89

(1951–76, year ends June 30; from 1977, year ends September 30)

Place of Birth	1951–60	1961–70	1971–80	1988	1989*
Europe	1,492,200	1,238,600	801,300	64,797	82,891
Asia	159,000	445,300	1,633,800	264,465	312,149
North America	769,200	1,351,100	1,645,000	250,009	607,398
Canada	274,900	286,700	114,800	11,783	12,151
Mexico	319,300	443,300	637,200	95,039	405,172
West Indies	122,900	519,600	759,800	112,357	88,932
Central America	44,600	97,700	132,400	30,715	101,034
South America	72,200	228,300	284,400	41,007	58,926
Africa	14,800	39,300	91,500	18,882	25,166
Australia	4,600	9,800	14,300	1,356	1,546
New Zealand	1,700	3,700	5,300	668	789
Other countries	1,800	5,500	17,700	2,841	2,059
TOTAL	3,277,200	3,321,700	4,493,300	643,025	1,090,924

From 1820 to 1988, 54,366,541 immigrants were admitted to the United States.

* Figures for 1989 include 478,814 formerly illegal residents, admitted under the Immigration and Control Act, 1986.

Resident Population by Race 1980
(in thousands)

White	188,372
Black	26,495
American Indian*	1,420·4
Chinese	806
Filipino	774·7
Japanese	701
Asian Indian	361·5
Korean	354·6
Vietnamese	261·7
Spanish origin**	14,609
Cuban	803
Mexican	8,740
Puerto Rican	2,014
Other Spanish	3,051
All other races	6,999·2
TOTAL	226,546

*Includes Eskimo and Aleut.

**Persons of Spanish origin may be of any race.

Largest Cities 1988 (estimated populations)

Ψ New York, NY	7,353,000
Ψ Los Angeles, California	3,353,000
Ψ Chicago, Illinois	2,978,000
Ψ Houston, Texas	1,698,000
Ψ Philadelphia, Pennsylvania	1,647,000
Ψ San Diego, California	1,070,000
Ψ Detroit, Michigan	1,036,000
Dallas, Texas	987,000
San Antonio, Texas	941,000
Phoenix, Arizona	924,000
Ψ Baltimore, Maryland	751,000
San Jose, California	738,000
Ψ San Francisco, California	732,000
Ψ Indianapolis, Indiana	727,000
Memphis, Tennessee	645,000
Jacksonville, Florida	635,000
Washington, DC	617,000
Ψ Milwaukee, Wisconsin	599,000
Ψ Boston, Massachusetts	578,000
Columbus, Ohio	570,000
Ψ New Orleans, Louisiana	532,000
Ψ Cleveland, Ohio	521,000
El Paso, Texas	511,000
Ψ Seattle, Washington	502,000
Denver, Colorado	492,000

Ψ Seaport

Registered Births and Deaths

Cal-endar Year	Live Births Number	Live Births Rate per 1,000	Deaths Number	Deaths Rate per 1,000
1983	3,638,933	15·5	2,019,201	8·6
1984	3,669,141	15·5	2,039,369	8·6
1985	3,760,561	15·8	2,086,440	8·7
1986	3,756,547	15·6	2,105,361	8·7
1987	3,809,394	15·7	2,123,323	8·7
1988*	3,913,000	15·9	2,171,000	8·8
1989*	4,021,000	16·2	2,155,000	8·7

For 1983–84 births based on 100 per cent sample in most states and 50 per cent sample in remaining states. Beginning with 1985 sample base was 100 per cent.

Note.—Figures tabulated are for the United States. Deaths exclude foetal deaths. Rates are based on the population as estimated on July 1.

* Provisional.

Marriage and Divorce

Laws of marriage and of divorce are within the exclusive jurisdiction of each State. Each State legislature enacts its own laws prescribing rules and qualifications pertaining to marriage and its dissolution.

Year	Marriages	Per 1,000 Pop.§	Estimated Divorces	Per 1,000 Pop.§
1983	2,445,604	10·5	1,158,000	4·9
1984	2,477,192	10·5	1,169,000	5·0
1985	2,412,625	10·1	1,190,000	5·0
1986	2,407,099	10·0	1,178,000	4·9
1987	2,403,378	9·9	1,116,000	4·8
1988*	2,389,000	9·7	1,183,000	4·8
1989*	2,404,000	9·7	1,163,000	4·7

§ Population as estimated on July 1.

* Provisional.

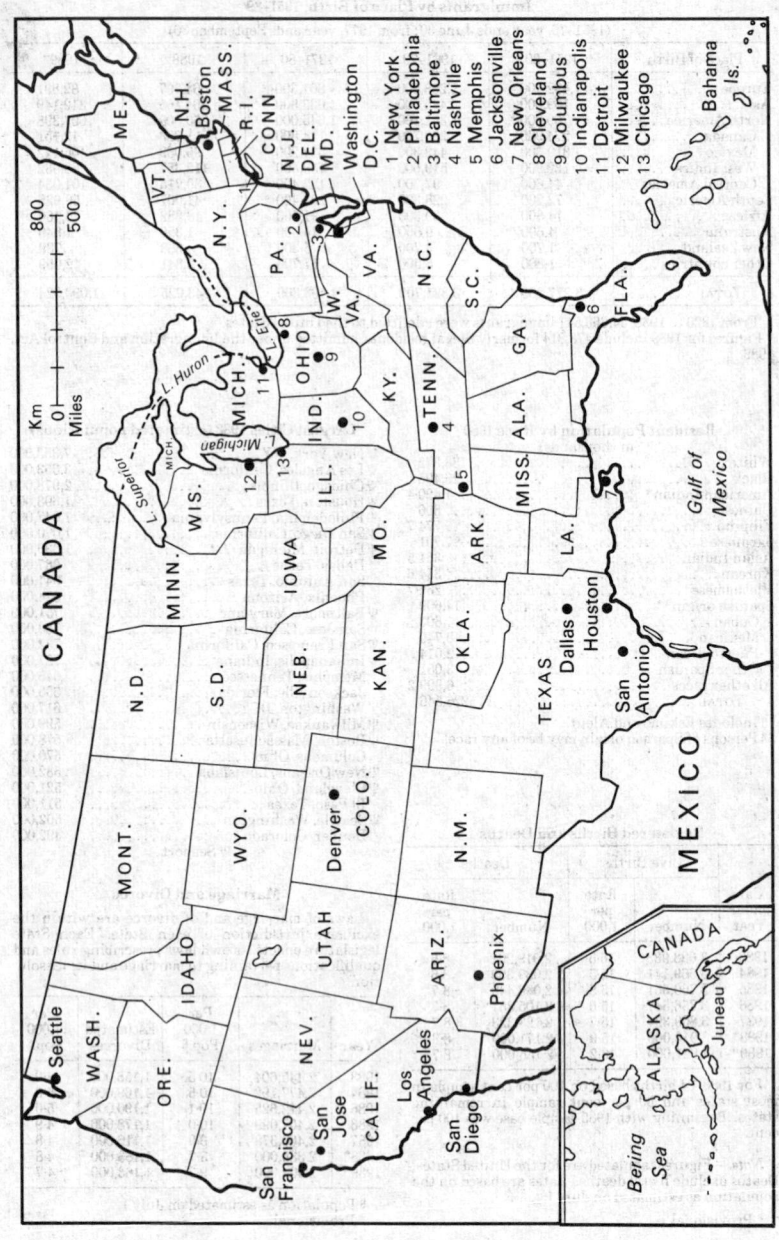

THE UNITED STATES

State (with date and *order* of admission)	Land area sq. m.	Population, (1986 estimates)	Capital	Governor (term of office in years, and expiry year)
Alabama (Ala.) (1819) (*22*)	50,767	3,893,888	Montgomery..	Harold G. Hunt (*R*) (4—1991)
Alaska (1959) (*49*)	570,833	401,851	Juneau	Steven Cowper (*D*) (4—1990)
Arizona (Ariz.) (1912) (*48*)	113,508	2,718,215	Phoenix	Rose Mofford (*D*)* (4—1991)
Arkansas (Ark.) (1836) (*25*)	52,078	2,286,435	Little Rock ..	Bill Clinton (*D*) (4—1991)
California (Calif.) (1850) (*31*)	156,299	23,667,902	Sacramento ..	George Deukmejian (*R*) .. (4—1991)
Colorado (Colo.) (1876) (*38*)	103,595	2,889,964	Denver	Roy Romer (*D*) (4—1991)
Connecticut (Conn.)§(1788) (*5*) .	4,872	3,107,576	Hartford	William O'Neill (*D*) (4—1991)
Delaware (Del.) § (1787) (*1*)	1,932	594,338	Dover	Michael N. Castle (*R*) (4—1993)
Florida (Fla.) (1845) (*27*)	54,153	9,746,324	Tallahassee ..	Bob Martinez (*R*) (4—1991)
Georgia (Ga.) § (1788) (*4*)	58,056	5,463,105	Atlanta	Joe F. Harris (*D*) (4—1991)
Hawaii (1959) (*50*)	6,425	964,691	Honolulu	John D. Waihee III (*D*).. (4—1990)
Idaho (1890) (*43*)	82,412	943,935	Boise	Cecil D. Andrus (*D*) (4—1991)
Illinois (Ill.) (1818) (*21*)	55,645	11,426,518	Springfield ...	James R. Thompson (*R*) . (4—1991)
Indiana (Ind.) (1816) (*19*)	35,932	5,490,224	Indianapolis ..	Evan Bayh (*D*) (4—1993)
Iowa (1846) (*29*)	55,965	2,913,808	Des Moines ...	Terry Branstad (*R*) (4—1991)
Kansas (Kan.) (1861) (*34*)	81,778	2,363,679	Topeka	Mike Hayden (*R*) (4—1991)
Kentucky (Ky.) (1792) (*15*)	39,669	3,660,777	Frankfort	Wallace G. Wilkinson (*D*) (4—1992)
Louisiana (La.) (1812) (*18*)	44,521	4,205,900	Baton Rouge..	Buddy Roemer (*D*) (4—1992)
Maine (Me.) (1820) (*23*)	30,995	1,124,660	Augusta	John R. McKernan, Jr.(*R*) (4—1991)
Maryland (Md.)§ (1788) (*7*)	9,837	4,216,975	Annapolis	William D. Schaefer (*D*) . (4—1991)
Massachusetts (Mass.)§(1788) (*6*)	7,824	5,737,037	Boston	Michael S. Dukakis (*D*) .. (4—1991)
Michigan (Mich.) (1837) (*26*)	56,954	9,262,078	Lansing	James J. Blanchard (*D*) .. (4—1991)
Minnesota (Minn.) (1858) (*32*) ..	79,548	4,075,970	St. Paul	Rudy Perpich (*DFL*) (4—1991)
Mississippi (Miss.) (1817) (*20*)...	47,233	2,520,638	Jackson	Ray Mabus (*D*) (4—1992)
Missouri (Mo.) (1821) (*24*)	68,945	4,916,686	Jefferson City.	John Ashcroft (*R*) (4—1993)
Montana (Mont.) (1889) (*41*)	145,388	786,690	Helena	Stan Stephens (*R*) (4—1993)
Nebraska (Neb.) (1867) (*37*)	76,644	1,569,825	Lincoln	Kay A. Orr (*R*) (4—1991)
Nevada (Nev.) (1864) (*36*)	109,894	800,493	Carson City ..	Robert J. Miller (*D*)**
New Hampshire (NH)§ (1788) (*9*)	8,993	920,610	Concord	Judd Gregg (*R*) (2—1991)
New Jersey (NJ)§ (1787) (*3*)	7,468	7,364,823	Trenton	James S. Florio (*D*) (4—1994)
New Mexico (NM) (1912) (*47*)...	121,335	1,302,894	Santa Fé	Garry E. Carruthers (*R*) . (4—1991)
New York (NY)§ (1788) (*11*)	47,377	17,558,072	Albany	Mario M. Cuomo (*D*) (4—1991)
North Carolina (NC)§ (1789) (*12*)	48,843	5,881,766	Raleigh	James G. Martin (*R*) (4—1993)
North Dakota (ND) (1889) (*39*)	69,300	652,717	Bismarck	George A. Sinner (*D*) (4—1993)
Ohio (1803) (*17*)	41,004	10,797,630	Columbus	Richard F. Celeste (*D*) ... (4—1991)
Oklahoma (Okla.) (1907) (*46*)	68,655	3,025,290	Oklahoma City	Henry Bellmon (*R*) (4—1991)
Oregon (Ore.) (1859) (*33*)	96,184	2,632,105	Salem	Neil Goldschmidt (*D*) .... (4—1991)
Pennsylvania (Pa.)§ (1787) (*2*) ..	44,888	11,863,895	Harrisburg ...	Robert P. Casey (*D*) (4—1991)
Rhode Island (RI)§ (1790) (*13*) .	1,055	947,154	Providence	Edward D. Di Prete (*R*) . (2—1991)
South Carolina (SC)§ (1788) (*8*) .	30,203	3,121,820	Columbia	Carroll A. Campbell, Jr.(*R*) (4—1991)
South Dakota (SD) (1889) (*40*) ..	75,952	690,768	Pierre	George S. Mickelson (*R*).. (4—1991)
Tennessee (Tenn.) (1796) (*16*)...	41,155	4,591,120	Nashville	Ned R. McWherter (*D*)... (4—1991)
Texas (1845) (*28*)	262,017	14,229,191	Austin	William P. Clements, Jr. (*R*) (4—1991)
Utah (1896) (*45*)	82,073	1,461,037	Salt Lake City	Norman H. Bangerter (*R*) (4—1993)
Vermont (Vt.) (1791) (*14*)	9,273	511,456	Montpelier ...	Madeleine M. Kunin (*D*) . (2—1991)
Virginia (Va.)§ (1788) (*10*)	39,704	5,346,818	Richmond	L. Douglas Wilder (*D*) .... (4—1994)
Washington (Wash.) (1889) (*42*)	66,511	4,132,156	Olympia	Booth Gardner (*D*) (4—1993)
West Virginia (W. Va.) (1863)(*35*)	24,119	1,949,644	Charleston ...	Gaston Caperton (*D*) (4—1993)
Wisconsin (Wis.) (1848) (*30*)	54,426	4,705,767	Madison	Tommy Thompson (*R*) ... (4—1991)
Wyoming (Wyo.) (1890) (*44*)	96,989	469,557	Cheyenne	Michael Sullivan (*D*) (4—1991)
Dist. of Columbia (DC) (1791)...	63	638,333	..	†

OUTLYING TERRITORIES AND POSSESSIONS

American Samoa	76	32,395	Pago Pago	Peter Tali Coleman (*D*) .. (4—1993)
Guam	209	105,816	Agaña	Joseph Ada (*R*) (4—1991)
Marshall Is.	70	31,042	Majuro	..
Fed. States of Micronesia	271	73,160	Kolonia	..
Northern Mariana Is.	184	16,780	Saipan	Lorenzo I. DeLeon Guerrero (*R*) (4—1994)
Palau	192	12,177	Koror	..
Puerto Rico	3,421	3,187,570	San Juan	R. Hernandez-Colon (*PDP*)(4—1993)
Virgin Is.	132	95,591	Charlotte Amalie	Alexander Farrelly (*D*) .. (4—1991)

§ The 13 Original States.   *D.*—Democratic Party.   *DFL.*—Democrat-Farmer-Labor.   *I.*—Independent.   *PDP.*—Popular Democratic party.   *R.*—Republican Party.
† The capital territory is governed by Congress through a Commissioner and City Council.
* Succeeded to governor's office April 1988, after her predecessor's impeachment.
** Acting Governor until previous governor's term expires in 1991. (Former Gov. Bryan was elected to the US Senate.)

THE PRESIDENTS OF THE UNITED STATES OF AMERICA

Name (*with Native State*)	Party	Born	Inaug.	Died	Age
George Washington, *Va.*	Fed.	1732, Feb. 22	1789	1799, Dec. 14	67
John Adams, *Mass.*	,,	1735, Oct. 30	1797	1826, July 4	90
Thomas Jefferson, *Va.*	Rep.	1743, April 13	1801	1826, July 4	83
James Madison, *Va.*	,,	1751, Mar. 16	1809	1836, June 28	85
James Monroe, *Va.*	,,	1758, April 28	1817	1831, July 4	73
John Quincy Adams, *Mass.*	,,	1767, July 11	1825	1848, Feb 23	80
Andrew Jackson, *SC*	Dem.	1767, Mar. 15	1829	1845, June 8	78
Martin Van Buren, *NY*	,,	1782, Dec. 5	1837	1862, July 24	79
William Henry Harrison†, *Va.*	Whig	1773, Feb. 9	1841	1841, April 4	68
John Tyler (*a*), *Va.*	,,	1790, Mar. 29	1841	1862, Jan. 17	71
James Knox Polk, *NC*	Dem.	1795, Nov. 2	1845	1849, June 15	53
Zachary Taylor†, *Va.*	Whig	1784, Nov. 24	1849	1850, July 9	65
Millard Fillmore (*a*), *NY*	,,	1800, Jan. 7	1850	1874, Mar. 8	74
Franklin Pierce, *NH*	Dem.	1804, Nov. 23	1853	1869, Oct. 8	64
James Buchanan, *Pa.*	,,	1791, April 23	1857	1868, June 1	77
Abraham Lincoln†§, *Ky.*	Rep.	1809, Feb. 12	1861	1865, April 15	56
Andrew Johnson (*a*), *NC*	,,	1808, Dec. 29	1865	1875, July 31	66
Ulysses Simpson Grant, *Ohio*	,,	1822, April 27	1869	1885, July 23	63
Rutherford Birchard Hayes, *Ohio*	,,	1822, Oct. 4	1877	1893, Jan. 17	70
James Abram Garfield†§, *Ohio*	,,	1831, Nov. 19	1881	1881, Sept. 19	49
Chester Alan Arthur (*a*), *Vt.*	,,	1830, Oct. 5	1881	1886, Nov. 18	56
Grover Cleveland, *NJ*	Dem.	1837, Mar. 18	1885	1908, June 24	71
Benjamin Harrison, *Ohio*	Rep.	1833, Aug. 20	1889	1901, Mar. 13	67
Grover Cleveland, *NJ*	Dem.	1837, Mar. 18	1893	1908, June 24	71
William McKinley†§, *Ohio*	Rep.	1843, Jan. 29	1897	1901, Sept. 14	58
Theodore Roosevelt (*a*), *NY*	,,	1858, Oct. 27	1901	1919, Jan. 6	60
William Howard Taft, *Ohio*	,,	1857, Sept. 15	1909	1930, Mar. 8	72
Woodrow Wilson, *Va.*	Dem.	1856, Dec. 28	1913	1924, Feb. 3	67
Warren Gamaliel Harding†, *Ohio*	Rep.	1865, Nov. 2	1921	1923, Aug. 2	57
Calvin Coolidge (*a*), *Vt.*	,,	1872, July 4	1923	1933, Jan. 5	60
Herbert Clark Hoover, *Iowa.*	,,	1874, Aug. 10	1929	1964, Oct. 20	90
Franklin Delano Roosevelt†‡, *NY*	Dem.	1882, Jan. 30	1933	1945, April 12	63
Harry S. Truman (*a*), *Missouri*	,,	1884, May 8	1945	1972, Dec. 26	88
Dwight David Eisenhower, *Texas*	Rep.	1890, Oct. 14	1953	1969, Mar. 28	78
John Fitzgerald Kennedy, *Mass.*†§	Dem.	1917, May 29	1961	1963, Nov. 22	46
Lyndon Baines Johnson (*a*), *Texas*	,,	1908, Aug. 27	1963	1973, Jan. 22	64
Richard Milhous Nixon, *California*	Rep.	1913, Jan. 9	1969	..	..
Gerald Rudolph Ford (*b*), *Nebraska*	,,	1913, July 14	1974	..	..
James Earl Carter, *Georgia*	Dem.	1924, Oct. 1	1977	..	..
Ronald Wilson Reagan, *Illinois*	Rep.	1911, Feb. 6	1981	..	..
George Herbert Walker Bush, *Mass.*	,,	1924, June 12	1989	..	..

† Died in office.   (*a*) Elected as Vice-President.   § Assassinated.
‡ Re-elected Nov. 5, 1940, the first case of a third term; re-elected for a fourth term Nov. 7. 1944.
(*b*) Appointed under the provisions of the 25th Amendment.

CAPITAL

In 1790 Congress ratified the cession of 100 sq. miles by the States of Maryland and Virginia as a site for a Federal City to be the national capital of the United States. In 1791 it was decided to name the capital Washington and in 1793 the foundation-stone of the Capitol building was laid. In 1800 the seat of Government was removed to Washington, which was chartered as a city in 1802. In 1846 the Virginia portion was retroceded and the present area of the District of Columbia (with which the City of Washington is considered co-extensive) is 63 sq. miles, with a resident population (mid-1989 estimate) of 604,000.

The District of Columbia is governed by an elected mayor and City Council.

The City of Washington is situated on the west central edge of Maryland, opposite the State of Virginia, on the left bank of the Potomac at its confluence with the Anacostia. The population of the metropolitan area in 1988 was estimated at 3,734,200.

GOVERNMENT

The United States of America is a Federal Republic consisting of 50 States and one Federal District (of which 13 are original states, seven were admitted without previous organization as territories, and 30 were admitted after such organization), and of organized Territories. Hawaii formally entered the Union as the 50th State on August 21, 1959, from which date the flag of the United States has 13 stripes and 50 stars in 9 horizontal rows of six and five alternately.

NATIONAL ANTHEM.—The Star-Spangled Banner.
NATIONAL DAY.—July 4 (Independence Day).
THE CONSTITUTION.—By the Constitution of Sept. 17, 1787 (to which ten amendments were added on Dec. 15, 1791 and eleventh to twenty-sixth, Jan. 8, 1798, Sept. 25, 1804, Dec. 18, 1865, July 28, 1868, March 30, 1870, Feb. 25, 1913, May 31, 1913, Jan. 16, 1920, Aug. 26, 1920, Feb. 6, 1933, Dec. 5, 1933, Feb. 26, 1951, March 29, 1961, Jan. 23, 1964, Feb. 10, 1967 and June 30, 1971), the government of the United States is entrusted to three separate authorities—the Executive, the Legislative, and the Judicial.

THE EXECUTIVE

THE executive power is vested in a President, who is elected every four years. The mode of electing the President is as follows:—Each State elects (on the first Tuesday after the first Monday in November of the year preceding the year in which the Presidential term expires), a number of electors, equal to the whole number of Senators and Representatives to which the State may be entitled in the Congress; but no Senator or Representative, or anyone holding office under Government, shall be appointed an elector. The electors for each State meet in their respective States on the first Monday after the second Wednesday in December following, and there vote for a President by ballot. The ballots are then sent to Washington, and opened on the sixth day of January by the President of Senate in presence of Congress, and the candidate who has received a majority of the whole number of electoral votes cast is declared President for the ensuing term. If no one has a majority, then from the highest on the list (not exceeding three) the House of Representatives elects a President, the votes being taken by States, the representation from each State having one vote. There is also a Vice-President, who, on the death of the President, becomes President for the remainder of the term. Under the XXth Amendment to the Constitution the terms of the President and Vice-President end at noon on the 20th day of January of the years in which such terms would have ended if the Amendment had not been ratified, and the terms of their successors then begin. In case of the removal or death of both President and Vice-President, a statute provides for the succession. Under the XXIInd Amendment to the Constitution, the tenure of the Presidency is limited to two terms.

Executive duties:—(1) He is Commander-in-Chief of the Army and of the Navy (and of the Militias when they are in Federal service), and he commissions all officers therein. (2) With the consent of the Senate, he appoints the Cabinet officers and all the chief (and many minor) officials. (3) He exercises a general supervision over the whole Federal Administration and sees that the Federal Laws are duly carried out. Should disorder arise in any state which the authorities thereof are unable to suppress, the aid of the President is invoked. (4) He conducts the foreign policy of the Republic, and has power, 'by and with the Advice and Consent of the Senate, to make Treaties, provided two-thirds of the senators present concur.' The declaration of war rests with Congress. (5) He makes recommendation of a general nature to Congress, and when laws are passed by Congress he may return them to Congress with a veto. But if a measure so vetoed is again passed by both Houses of Congress by two-thirds majority in each House, it becomes law, notwithstanding the objection of the President. The President must be at least 35 years of age and a native citizen of the United States.

President of the United States, GEORGE HERBERT WALKER BUSH, *born* June 12, 1924, *sworn in* January 20, 1989. Republican.

Vice-President, DAN QUAYLE, *born* Feb. 4, 1947, *sworn in* Jan. 20, 1989.

THE CABINET

Secretary of State, James Baker.
Secretary of the Treasury, Nicholas Brady.
Secretary of Defence, Richard Cheney.
Attorney General, Richard Thornburgh.
Secretary of the Interior, Manuel Lujan.
Secretary of Agriculture, Clayton Yeutter.
Secretary of Commerce, Robert Mosbacher.
Secretary of Labour, Elizabeth Dole.
Secretary of Health and Human Services, Dr. Louis Sullivan.
Secretary of Housing and Urban Development, Jack Kemp.
Secretary of Transportation, Samuel Skinner.
Secretary of Energy, James Watkins.
Secretary of Education, Dr. Lauro Cavazos.
Secretary of Veterans' Affairs, Edward Derwinski.

Other senior positions:
Director of CIA, William Webster.
Director, Office of National Drug Control Policy, William Bennett.
White House Chief of Staff, John Sununu.
National Security Adviser, Brent Scowcroft.
Director, Office of Management and Budget, Richard Darman.

UNITED STATES EMBASSY
24 Grosvenor Square W1A 1AE
[071-499 9000]

Ambassador Extraordinary and Plenipotentiary, The Honourable Henry E. Catto (1989).
Minister, Hon. Ronald Woods.
Minister for Economic Affairs, Mrs. Ann R. Berry.
Minister Counsellors, Norbert J. Krieg (*Consular Affairs*); John Condayan (*Administrative Affairs*); James Blow (*Commercial Affairs*); James P. Rudbeck (*Agricultural Affairs*); Bruce G. Burton (*Political Affairs*); Charles E. Courtney (*Public Affairs*); Lester P. Slezak (*Political/Labour Affairs*); James B. Devine (*Scientific and Technical Affairs*).
Defence and Naval Attaché, Capt. Joseph R. McCleary.
Army Attaché, Col. David Smith.
Air Attaché, Col. Chester Garrison.

THE CONGRESS

The Legislative power is vested in two Houses, the Senate and the House of Representatives, the President having a veto power, which may be overcome by a two-thirds vote of each House. The Senate is composed of two Senators from each State, elected by the people thereof for the term of six years, and each Senator has one vote. Representatives are chosen in each State, by popular vote, for two years. The average number of persons represented by each Congressman is 1 for 550,000. The Senate consists of 100 members. The House of Representatives consists of 435 Representatives, a resident commissioner from Puerto Rico and a delegate from American Samoa, the District of Columbia, Guam and the Virgin Islands. By the XIXth Amendment, sex is no disqualification for the franchise. The Bureau of the Census estimated that there were 182,628,000 persons of voting age, excluding members of the armed forces overseas as of November 1988.

THE 101ST CONGRESS

President of the Senate, Dan Quayle (*Vice President of the United States*).
Speaker of the House of Representatives, Thomas S. Foley, *Washington*.
Secretary of the Senate, Walter J. Stewart, *District of Columbia*.
Clerk of the House of Representatives, Donnald K. Anderson, *California*.

Members of the 101st Congress were elected on November 8, 1988. The 101st Congress is constituted as follows:
Senate.—Democrats 55; Republicans 45; Total 100.
House of Representatives.—Democrats 257; Republicans 175; Vacancies 3. Total 435 (July 1, 1989).

THE JUDICATURE

The Federal Judiciary consists of three sets of Federal Courts: (1) The Supreme Court at Washington, DC, consisting of a Chief Justice and eight Associate Justices, with original jurisdiction in cases affecting Ambassadors, etc., or where a State is a party to the suit, and with appellate jurisdiction from inferior Federal Courts and from the judgments of the highest Courts of the States. (2) The United States Courts of Appeals, dealing with appeals from District Courts and from certain federal administrative agencies, and consisting of 168 Circuit Judges within 13 circuits. (3) The 94 United States District Courts served by 575 District Court Judges.

The Supreme Court
US Supreme Court Building, Washington DC, 20543

Chief Justice, William H. Rehnquist, *Ariz., born* Oct. 1, 1924, *appointed* 1986.

ASSOCIATE JUSTICES

Name	Born	Apptd
Byron R. White, *Colo.*	1917	1962
Thurgood Marshall, *NY*	1908	1967
Harry Blackmun, *Minn.*	1908	1970
John Paul Stevens, *Ill.*	1920	1975
Sandra Day O'Connor, *Ariz.*	1930	1981
Antonin Scalia, *Va.*	1936	1986
Anthony M. Kennedy, *Calif.*	1936	1988

Clerk of the Supreme Court, Joseph F. Spaniol, Jr.

CRIMINAL STATISTICS
(Number of offences)

	1988	1989
Murder and Non-negligent Manslaughter	20,675	21,500
Forcible Rape	92,486	94,504
Robbery	542,968	578,326
Aggravated Assault	910,092	951,707
Burglary	3,218,077	3,168,170
Larceny—Theft	7,705,872	7,872,442
Thefts of Motor Vehicles	1,432,916	1,564,800
Total	13,923,086	14,251,449

DEFENCE

Department of Defence

Secretary of Defence (*in the Cabinet*), Richard B. Cheney.
Secretary of the Army, Michael P. W. Stone.
Secretary of the Navy, H. L. Garrett.
Secretary of the Air Force, D. B. Rice.
Chairman, Joint Chiefs of Staff, Gen. Colin Powell.
Vice Chairman, Adm. David E. Jeremiah.

The Department of Defence includes the Secretary of Defence as its head, the Deputy Secretary of Defence, the Defence staff offices, the Joint Chiefs of Staff and the Joint Staff, the three military departments and the military services within those departments, the unified and specified commands, and other Department of Defence agencies as the Secretary of Defence establishes to meet specific requirements. The Defence staff offices and the joint Chiefs of Staff, although separately organized, function in full co-ordination and co-operation. They include the offices of the Director of Defence Research and Engineering, the Assistant Secretaries of Defence, the General Counsel of the Department of Defence and such other staff offices as the Secretary of Defence may establish. The Joint Chiefs of Staff, as a group, are directly responsible to the Secretary of Defence for the functions assigned to them. Each member of the Joint Chiefs of Staff, other than the Chairman and Vice Chairman, is responsible for keeping the Secretary of his military department fully informed on matters considered or acted upon by the Joint Chiefs of Staff.

Each military department is separately organized under its own Secretary and functions under the direction, authority and control of the Secretary of Defence.

Commanders of unified and specified commands are responsible to the President and the Secretary of Defence for the accomplishment of military missions assigned to them.

Unified Defence Commands

COMMANDERS-IN-CHIEF

US European Command, Brussels.—Gen. Crosbie Saint (*US Army*).
US Southern Command, Quarry Heights, Panama Canal Zone.—Gen. Maxwell R. Thurman.
US Atlantic Command, Norfolk, Virginia.—Adm. Leon Edney (*US Navy*).
US Pacific Command, Hawaii.—Adm. Huntington Hardisty (*US Navy*).
US Space Command, Gen. John L. Piotrowski (*USAF*).
**Strategic Air Command,* Omaha.—Gen. John T. Chain (*USAF*).
**US Transportation Command,* Gen. Hansford T. Johnson (*USAF*).
US Special Operations Command, Florida.—Gen. James J. Lindsay (*US Army*).
US Central Command, Gen. H. Norman Schwarzkopf (*US Army*).
* A specified command.

Army.—The US Army had a strength on April 30, 1990, of 745,763.
Chief of the Staff of the Army, Gen. Carl E. Vuono.
Navy.—The strength of the Navy on April 30, 1990 was 580,682 active duty personnel.
Chief of Naval Operations, Adm. Frank B. Kelso II.
Marine Corps.—Established 1775. Strength on April 30, 1990 was 195,384 active duty personnel.
Commandant, Gen. Alfred M. Gray.
Air.—The United States Air Force was established as a separate organization on September 18, 1947. In March 1961 the Air Force was assigned primary responsibility for the Department of Defence space development programmes and projects. On April 30, 1990, there were 541,071 officers and airmen on active duty.
Chief of Staff of the US Air Force, Gen. Michael J. Dugan.

FINANCE

The Budget
(US$ billions)

Receipts by Source	1989 (actual)	1990 (estimated)
Individual income taxes	445·7	489·4
Corporation income taxes	103·6	112·0
Social insurance taxes and contributions	359·4	385·4
Excise taxes	34·1	36·2
Estate and gift taxes	8·7	9·3
Customs duties	16·3	16·8
Miscellaneous	22·8	24·4
TOTAL	990·7	1,073·5
Outlays by Function		
National defence	303·6	296·3
International affairs	9·6	14·6
Income security	136·0	146·6
Health	48·4	57·8
Medicare	85·0	96·6
Social security	232·5	248·5
Veterans' benefits and services	30·1	28·9
Education, training, employment and social services	36·7	37·7

Commerce and housing credit	27·7	22·7
Transportation	27·6	29·2
Natural resources and environment	16·2	17·5
Energy	3·7	3·2
Community and regional development	5·4	8·8
Agriculture	16·9	14·6
Net interest	169·1	175·6
General science, space and technology	12·8	14·1
General government	9·1	10·6
Administration of justice	9·4	10·5
Undistributed offsetting receipts	−37·2	−36·5
TOTAL	1,142·6	1,197·2

Social Welfare Expenditure

Total expenditure by programme was (US$ millions):

	1986	1987
Social insurance	390,769	415,023
Education	189,276	204,541
Public aid	104,602	110,695
Health and medical	44,497	47,619
Veterans' programmes	27,445	28,051
Other social welfare	14,161	15,278
Housing	12,037	13,240
TOTAL	782,787	834,447

Expenditure per capita was:

Social insurance	US$1,588	US$1,671
Education	772	826
Public aid	427	447
Health and medical	182	192
Veterans' programmes	111	112
Other social welfare	58	62
Housing	49	53
TOTAL	3,187	3,364

Public Debt

At the end of September 1989 the total gross federal debt of the United States stood at US$2,881,112 million.

Cost of Living in USA

The Consumer Price Index for all urban consumers (CPI-U) with prices collected in 91 areas across the USA was measured for the year 1989 at 124·0 (1982–84 = 100), versus 118·3 for 1988.

National Income

National income without capital consumption adjustment was (US$ millions):

Domestic industries	4,236,800
Private industries	3,630,500
Agriculture, forestry, fisheries	97,900
Mining	37,600
Construction	224,000
Manufacturing	818,700
Durable goods	467,200
Nondurable goods	351,500
Transportation and public utilities	320,800
Transportation	140,600
Communication	89,000
Electric, gas, and sanitary services	91,100
Wholesale trade	255,100
Retail trade	357,000
Finance, insurance, and real estate	631,200
Services	888,300
Government and government enterprises	606,300
Rest of the world	35,600
TOTAL national income without capital consumption adjustment	4,272,500

GNP, national and personal income in 1989 were (US$ million):—

Gross national product	5,234,000
Net national product	4,681,700
National income	4,266,500
Personal income	4,427,300
Disposable personal income	3,778,800
Personal saving	204,400

Personal consumption expenditure in 1989 was US$3,471,100 million, of which durable goods accounted for US$473,200 million, non-durable goods US$1,123,400 million and services US$1,874,400 million. Gross private domestic investment in 1986 was US$773,400 million.

Stock of Currency and Coin

The US unit of currency is the dollar ($) of 100 cents.
US stock of currency and coin at March 31, 1988 was:—

	US$ million
Gold	11,062·5
Dollars	340·1
Subsidiary Coin	93·8
Minor Coin	20·7
Silver Certificates	198·8
US Notes	322·5
Federal Reserve Notes	255,200·3
TOTAL	267,238·5

AGRICULTURE AND LIVESTOCK

The total number of farms in 1988 was 2,158,800, with a total area of land in farms of 998,692,000 acres, and an average acreage per farm of 463 acres. The total number of people employed on farms during the week of April 9–15, 1989 was 2,805,000, of whom 1,777,000 were unpaid workers, 830,000 hired workers and 198,000 agricultural service workers.

Principal crops are corn for grain, soybeans, wheat hay, cotton, tobacco, grain sorghums, potatoes, oranges and barley.

Livestock on farms on Jan. 1, 1987 and 1988 was:—

	1987	1988
All cattle	102,000,000	98,994,000
Milk cows	10,502,000	10,307,000
Sheep and lambs	10,334,000	10,774,000
Hogs and pigs	50,920,000	53,795,000
Chickens	369,131,000	377,516,000

Gross income from farming in 1987 was US$169,765 million, of which cash receipts from marketing were US$138,094 million and government payments US$16,747 million. Cash income from all crops in 1987 was US$61,876 million and from livestock and livestock products US$76,218 million.

NONFUEL MINERALS

The value of nonfuel raw mineral production in the United States in 1988 totalled an estimated US$30,002 million compared with US$26,317 million in 1987.

Trading Figures

	1987	1988
Imports	US$28,534m	US$33,904m
Exports	13,426m	19,597m

Production Figures

('000 tonnes)

	1988	1989p
Aluminium	3,944	4,000
Iron Ore†	57,500	58,700
Phosphate rock*	45,389	51,000
Zinc Ore	244	325
Refined Copper	1,857	1,980
Refined Lead	1,062	1,110

p=preliminary
† measured in long tons
* marketable production

ENERGY

Energy Overview

(Quadrillion (10^{15}) Btu)

	1988	1989p
Production	65·97	65·71
Coal	20·74	21·23
Natural Gas	17·49	17·53
Crude Oil	17·28	16·15
Consumption	80·20	81·23
Petroleum	34·23	34·02
Coal	18·85	18·92
Natural Gas	18·55	19·50
Imports	17·56	18·74
Crude Oil	11·03	12·51
Petroleum	4·72	4·47
Exports	4·41	4·72
Coal	2·50	2·65

p=preliminary

LABOUR

Employment and Unemployment.—The civilian labour force was 125,004,000 in May 1990. The number of employed persons was 118,350,000. This includes self-employed, wage and salary-earners, and unpaid family workers. Unemployment was estimated at 6,653,000 in May 1990 (5·3 per cent) (it was 5·2 per cent in May 1989).

Wages.—In March 1990, gross average weekly earnings in industry ranged from US$812·59 per week in malt beverage industry (43·2 hours and US$18·81 average hourly earnings) to US$122·00 in eating and drinking places (25·0 hours and US$4·88 average hourly earnings). The average for all manufacturing was US$436·71 compared with US$426·81 in March 1989.

On April 1, 1990, the minimum wage set by federal law became US$3·80 an hour. The law requires at least time and a half of an employee's regular rate of pay for all hours over 40 a week for most covered workers.

EXTERNAL TRADE

	1986	1987
	US$ million	
General imports:		
c.i.f. value	387,082·0	424,082·3
customs value	369,961·0	405,900·6
Exports and re-exports:		
f.a.s. value†	217,292·0	252,852·7
Trade balance:		
f.a.s. exports: c.i.f.		
imports	−169,790·0	−171,229·6
f.a.s. exports: customs		
imports	−152,669·0	−153,048·0

† Excluding military aid.

Exports by Principal Commodities of Domestic Origin, 1987

Commodity	Value
	US$ million
Food and live animals	19,178·9
Grain and cereal preparations	8,058·1

Beverages and tobacco	3,666·7
Crude materials (inedible) except fuel	20,416·3
Mineral fuels, lubricants, etc.	7,713·1
Oils and fats (animal and vegetable)	961·4
Chemicals and products	26,380·9
Machinery and transport equipment	108,596·0
Other manufactured goods	19,409·0
Unclassified commodities	20,380·7

US Imports by Principal Commodities, 1987

Commodity	Value
	US$ million
Food and live animals	20,547·1
Fish and fish preparations	5,590·0
Vegetables and fruit	4,475·9
Coffee–crude	2,705·8
Beverages and tobacco	4,104·9
Crude materials (inedible), except fuels	11,525·7
Mineral fuels, lubricants, etc.	64,219·5
Oils and fats (animal and vegetable)	568·1
Chemicals and products	16,213·4
Machinery and transport equipment	177,808·7
Other manufactured goods	66,183·1
Unclassified commodities	12,373·4

US Foreign Trade by Principal Areas and Countries, 1987

Area/Country	Exports and Re-exports to	General Imports from
	US$ million	
Africa	6,283	11,939
Asia	73,268	174,452
Japan	28,249	84,575
Taiwan	7,418	24,622
Korea, Rep. of	8,099	16,987
Oceania	6,526	4,136
Australia	5,495	3,007
Europe	71,917	97,419
EC	60,575	81,188
N. & Central America	81,758	97,591
Canada	59,814	71,085
Mexico	14,582	20,271
S. America	13,036	20,363

Trade with UK

	1988	1989
Imports from UK	£10,544,077,000	£12,098,549,000
Exports to UK	10,767,750,000	12,888,890,000

COMMUNICATIONS

Railways

Data on Class I line-haul railroads (US$ thousands)

	1987	1988
Operating Revenues	26,662,482	27,999,839
Freight	25,797,002	27,154,961
Passenger	93,559	84,677
Total operating expenses	23,878,116	24,889,015
Net working capital	34,081	−217,182
Average number of employees	248,526	236,891

Roads

In 1988 there were 3·87 million miles of public roads and streets in the United States, of which 3·13 million miles were in rural areas and 739,474 miles were in urban areas. Surfaced roads and streets account for 90·2 per cent of the total.

An estimated total of US$66,044 million was spent

in 1988 for roads and streets in the United States. Capital outlay accounts for 49·9 per cent of the total expenditure; 28·7 per cent was spent for maintenance, and 7·8 per cent for administration; 9·3 per cent for highway police and safety; and 4·3 per cent for interest on highway funds.

Motor Vehicles and Taxation.—The number of motor vehicles registered in 1988 in the United States was 184,396,732, an increase of 3·0 per cent over the 1987 total.

Accidents.—In 1988 there were 47,093 deaths caused by motor vehicle accidents. The death rate per 100,000,000 vehicle-miles of travel was 2·32 in 1988 compared with 2·41 in 1987.

Shipping

The ocean-going Merchant Marine of the US on April 1, 1990 consisted of 634 vessels of 1,000 gross tons and over, of which 402 were privately owned and 232 were government-owned ships. There were 212 ships in the National Defence Reserve Fleet of inactive government-owned vessels.

Air Transport

United States domestic and international scheduled airlines in 1984 carried 344,460,600 passengers over 304,987,288,000 revenue passenger miles. Cargo revenue ton-miles totalled 8,200,000,000, an increase of 8·0 per cent over 1983. Air cargo ton-miles were distributed as follows: freight 6,500,000,000 (up 7·7 per cent); express 64,400,000 (up 2·8 per cent); and air mail 1,600,000,000 (up 9·3 per cent).

Total operating revenues of all US scheduled airlines were US$43,800,000,000 in 1984, an increase of 13·5 per cent from 1983.

Total operating expenses rose to US$41,700,000,000 in 1984, a 9·0 per cent increase over 1983. Scheduled operations showed a net operating profit of US$2,100,000,000 in 1984, compared with a net operating profit of US$361,700,000 in 1983.

US SCHEDULED AIRLINE INDUSTRY STATISTICS 1984 (Thousands)

	Majors	Nationals	Regionals	System
Revenue Passenger Carried	250,150	80,337	13,974	344,461
Revenue Passengers Miles	252,295,400	43,820,182	8,871,706	304,987,288
Air Mail Ton Miles	1,402,063	199,028	15,841	1,616,932
Express Ton Miles	60,255	2,024	131	62,410
Freight Ton Miles	3,905,550	2,445,897	145,714	6,497,161
Revenue Ton Miles	30,597,429	7,028,968	1,048,857	38,675,254
Revenue Plane Miles	2,391,806	579,533	159,890	3,131,229

EDUCATION

State School Systems

All the 50 States and the District of Columbia have compulsory school attendance laws. In general, children are obliged to attend school from 7 to 16 years of age. Officers of local administrative units, usually known as truant or attendance officers, are charged with enforcing the compulsory attendance laws.

In the autumn of 1988, 45,433,000 children were enrolled in regular elementary and secondary day schools in the United States, of whom 5·2 million or 11·5 per cent attended private schools.

The following percentages of the school-age population were estimated to be enrolled in school in the autumn of 1988: 95 per cent of 5- and 6-year-olds; 99 per cent of 7- to 13-year-olds; 95 per cent of 14- to 17-year-olds, and 34 per cent of 18- to 24-year-olds.

During the 1987–88 school year, the average daily attendance in regular public elementary and secondary day schools was 37,050,707. In the 1988–89 school year 2,495,965 students graduated from regular public high schools, 291,000 graduated from private high school. In addition some 25,000 graduated from evening schools and adult education programmes, and an estimated 357,000 received high school equivalency certificates. Public school teachers numbered 2,316,428, with an average salary of US$29,547.

Most of the revenue for public elementary and secondary school purposes comes from Federal, State, and local governments. Less than 0·5 per cent comes from gifts from tuition and transportation fees. Estimated revenue receipts during 1987–88 amounted to US$169,650,907,000; 6·3 per cent from the Federal Government, 49·5 per cent from State governments, and 44·1 per cent from local sources. Estimated current expenditure in the 1987–88 school year was US$157,222 million; for sites, buildings, furniture and equipment expenditures, US$10,680 million; for interest in school debt US$2,938 million.

Institutions of Higher Education

In the autumn of 1988, total enrolment in universities, colleges, professional schools, and two-year schools numbered 13,043,118.

Degrees conferred during the academic years 1986–87 and 1987–88 were:—

Degree	1986–87	1987–88
Bachelor's	991,339	993,362
First-Professional	72,750	70,415
Master's...................	289,557	298,733
Doctorates	34,120	34,839

During 1987–88 the major fields for bachelor's degrees were business and management (243,344), social sciences (100,270), education (91,013) and engineering (88,791). First-profession degrees in law (35,469) and medicine (15,091) predominated. Master's degrees were heavily concentrated in education (77,704) and business and management (69,630). The most popular fields of study for doctorates were education (6,544) and life sciences (3,804).

During the 1987–88 academic year, the 3,587 colleges and universities employed about 680,000 (full-time equivalent) instructional faculty. Total expenditures for colleges and universities during the 1987–88 academic year were US$125,700 million.

Particulars of some of the universities (with opening autumn enrolment figures, 1988) are: *Harvard* (24,194 students, including 13,227 women), founded at Cambridge, Mass. on Oct. 28, 1636, and named after John Harvard of Emmanuel College, Cambridge, England, who bequeathed to it his library and a sum of money in 1638; *Yale* (10,893 students, including 6,038 women), founded at New Haven, Connecticut, in 1701; *Bowdoin*, Brunswick, Me. (founded 1794; 1,426 students including 776 women); *Brown*, Providence, RI (founded 1764; 7,612 students, including 4,097 women); *Columbia*, New York, NY (founded 1754; 17,296 students, including 9,484 women); *Cornell* (founded at Ithaca, NY, 1865; 11,525 students, including 7,434 women); *Dartmouth*, Hanover, NH (founded 1769, 4,777 students, including 2,865 women); *Georgetown*, Washington, DC (founded 1789; 11,516 students, including 6,025 women); *North Carolina*, Chapel Hill, NC (founded in 1789; 23,626 students, including 10,211 women); *Pennsylvania*, Philadelphia, Pa. (founded 1740; 37,269 students, including 21,051 women); *Princeton*, NJ (founded 1746; 6,338 students and 3,994 women); and *William and Mary*, Williamsburg, Va. (founded 1693; 7,372 students, including 3,477 women).

WEIGHTS AND MEASURES

The weights and measures in common use in the United States are of British origin, and date back to the American Revolution when practically all the standards were intended to be equivalent to those used in England at that period. Divergencies in these weights and measures were, however, quite common, due no doubt to the fact that the system of weights and measures in England was not itself well established, and hence the copies brought to the United States were often adjusted to different standards.

Because of these discrepancies, the system of weights and measures in the United States (US inch-pound system) is not identical with the British system.

The US ton (short) = 2,000 pounds (British Imperial ton = 2,240 pounds, or 1 US long ton). The US gallon = 231 cubic inches (277·42 cubic inches in UK) or 128 fluid ounces (160 fluid ounces in UK). In the British system the units of dry measure are the same as those of liquid measure. In the United States these two are not the same, the gallon and its subdivisions being used in the measurement of liquids, while the bushel, with its subdivisions, is used in the measurement of certain dry commodities. The US gallon is divided into 4 liquid quarts and the US bushel into 32 dry quarts.

In 1971, a study recommended a concerted, coordinated, but voluntary national effort to make the International System of Units (SI) the predominant form of measurement in the United States. In December 1975, legislation was passed which established the United States Metric Board to co-ordinate voluntary conversion to the metric system. Since 1982 this function has been assumed by the Office of Metric Programmes of the US Department of Commerce.

TERRITORIES, ETC. OF THE UNITED STATES

The territories and the principal islands and island groups under the sovereignty of the United States of America comprise the Commonwealth of Puerto Rico, the Commonwealth of the Northern Mariana Islands, and the following territories: Guam, American Samoa, US Virgin Islands, Johnston Atoll, Midway Islands, Wake Islands.

Johnston Atoll (formerly Johnston and Sand Islands) comprises two small islands, less than 1 sq. mile in area, to the south-west of Hawaii which are administered by the US Air Force. The two Midway Islands (area, 3 sq. miles), at the western end of the Hawaiian chain, are administered by the US Navy. The Wake Islands have an area of about 3 sq. miles and an average elevation of less than 3 metres. They lie about 2,300 miles west of Hawaii and are administered by the US Air Force.

Under the terms of a Treaty of Friendship between the United States and Kiribati, signed in 1979 and subsequently ratified by the US Senate, the United States renounced its claim to Canton and Enderbury Islands.

There are certain small guano islands, rocks, or keys which, in pursuance of action taken under the Act of Congress, August 18, 1856, subsequently embodied in Sections 5570–5578 of the Revised Statutes are considered as appertaining to the United States. Responsibility for territorial affairs generally is centred in the Office of the Assistant Secretary, Territorial and International Affairs, Dept. of the Interior, Washington DC. Puerto Rico was removed from the Department of the Interior's administrative jurisdiction with the acquisition of Commonwealth status in 1952.

THE COMMONWEALTH OF PUERTO RICO

Puerto Rico (Rich Port) is an island of the Greater Antilles group in the West Indies, and lies between 17° 50′–18° 30′ N. lat. and 65° 30′–67° 15′ W. long., with a total area of 3,421 sq. miles (8,860 sq. km), and an estimated population (1987) of 3,346,000. The majority of the inhabitants are of Spanish descent and Spanish is the official language. The island is about 111 miles from west to east, and 36 miles from north to south. The capital is 1,600 miles distant from New York, and 1,000 miles from Miami.

Puerto Rico was discovered in 1493 by Christopher Columbus and explored by Ponce de Léon in 1508. It continued as a Spanish possession until October 18, 1898, when the United States took formal possession as a result of the Spanish-American War. It was ceded by Spain to the United States by the Treaty ratified on April 11, 1899.

The Constitution approved by the Congress and the President of the United States, which came into force on July 25, 1952, establishes the Commonwealth of Puerto Rico with full powers of local government. Legislative functions are vested in the Legislative Assembly, which consists of two elected houses; the Senate of 27 members (two from each of eight senatorial districts and 11 at large) and the House of Representatives of 51 members (one from each of 40 representative districts and 11 at large). Membership of each house may be increased slightly to accommodate minority representatives. The term of the Legislative Assembly is four years. The selection of the Secretary of State must be approved also by the House of Representatives.

The Governor is popularly elected for a term of four years. A Supreme Court of seven members is appointed by the Governor, with the advice and consent of the Senate. The Governor appoints all Judges. Residents of Puerto Rico are US citizens. Puerto Rico is represented in Congress by a Resident Commissioner, elected for a term of four years, who has a seat in the House of Representatives, but not a vote, although he has a right to vote on those committees of which he is a member.

Preliminary 1983 figures for the Commonwealth Government's budget were Receipts, US$4,948 million (of which US$1,180 million were transfers from the Federal Government) and Expenditures, US$4,111 million (including payments of US$135 million to the Federal Government). Manufacturing added US$5,765 million to net Commonwealth income in 1983 (preliminary figures), trade US$1,743 million, finance, insurance and real estate US$1,841 million and agriculture US$435 million. Principal crops are sugar cane, coffee, vegetables, fruits and tobacco. Most valuable areas of manufacturing are chemicals and allied products, metal products and machinery. Public and private schools are established throughout—enrolment in 1985–86 was 686,914. Enrolment in private colleges and universities for 1985–86 was 98,402.

CAPITAL.—ΨSan Juan, population of the municipality (1984), 1,816,300; Other major towns are: ΨPonce (234,500); ΨMayagüez (209,800); and ΨArecibo (163,300).

Governor, Rafael Hernández Colón.
Secretary of State, Hector Luis Acevedo.
Resident Commissioner, Jaime Fuster.
Chief Justice, Victor Pons.

TRADE

	1985	1986
Total Imports	US$10,113 m	US$10,108 m
Total Exports	10,543 m	11,588 m

Trade with UK

	1988	1989
Imports from UK	£38,877,000	£79,851,000
Exports to UK	91,909,000	117,628,000

GUAM

Guam, the largest of the Ladrone or Mariana Islands in the North Pacific Ocean, lies in 13° 26' N. lat. and 144° 39' E. long., at a distance of about 1,506 miles east of Manila. The area of the island is estimated at 209 sq. miles (541 sq. km), with an estimated population (1989) of 138,089.

The Guamanians are of Chamorro stock mingled with Filipino and Spanish blood. The Chamorro language belongs to the Malayo-Polynesian family, but has had considerable admixture of Spanish. Chamorro and English are the official languages and most residents are bilingual.

Guam was occupied by the Japanese in December 1941 but was recaptured and occupied throughout by US forces before the end of July, 1944. Under the Organic Act of Guam of August 1, 1950 (Public Law 630 of the 81st Congress), Guam has statutory powers of self-government, and Guamanians are United States citizens. A 21-member unicameral legislature is elected biennially. The Governor and Lieutenant Governor are popularly elected. A non-voting Delegate is elected to serve in the US House of Representatives. There is also a District Court of Guam, with original jurisdiction in cases under federal law.

Guam's two main sources of revenue are tourism and US military spending.

CAPITAL.—Agaña. Port of entry, ΨApra.

Governor, Joseph F. Ada.
Lt. Governor, Frank Blas.

AMERICAN SAMOA

American Samoa consists of the island of Tutuila, Anu'u, Ofu, Olesega, Ta'u, Rose and Swains Islands, with a total area of 76 sq. miles (197 sq. km) and an estimated population of 38,200 in 1989.

Tutuila, the largest of the group, has an area of 52 square miles and contains a magnificent harbour at ΨPago Pago, the capital. The remaining islands have an area of about 24 square miles. Tuna and copra are the chief exports.

American Samoans are US nationals, but some have acquired citizenship through service in the United States armed forces or other naturalization procedure.

The 1960 Constitution grants American Samoa a measure of self-government, with certain powers reserved to the US Secretary of the Interior. There is a bicameral legislature with popularly elected Representatives and Governors, and a popularly-elected Governor. A non-voting Delegate is elected to serve in the US House of Representatives.

The constitution of American Samoa designates the village of Fagatogo as the seat of government.

Governor, Peter Tali Coleman.
Lt. Governor, Galea'i Poumele.

VIRGIN ISLANDS

Purchased by the United States from Denmark for the sum of US$25 million, and proclaimed January 25, 1917. The total area of the islands is 132 sq. miles (342 sq. km), with an estimated population (1988) of 106,000. There are three main islands, St. Thomas (28 sq. miles), St. Croix (84 sq. miles), St. John (20 sq. miles) and about 50 small islets or cays, mostly uninhabited.

The government of the Virgin Islands is organized under the provisions of the Revised Organic Act of the Virgin Islands, enacted by the Congress of the United States on July 22, 1954. Legislative power is vested in the Legislature of the Virgin Islands, a unicameral body composed of 15 senators popularly elected for two-year terms. Virgin Islanders are citizens of the United States. From the elections of November 1970, the Governor has been popularly elected. A non-voting Delegate is elected to serve in the US House of Representatives. A referendum is to take place in June 1991 to determine the future political status of the islands.

The Virgin Islands are now a favourite tourist area in the Caribbean.

CAPITAL.—ΨCharlotte Amalie on St. Thomas. Population (1980) 11,756.

Governor, Alexander Farrelly.
Lt. Governor, Derek M. Hodge.

NORTHERN MARIANA ISLANDS

The land area of the Northern Mariana Islands is 184 sq. miles (476 sq. km) with an estimated population (1988) of 21,777. Saipan, the government seat and commerce centre, has an estimated population of 19,156 (1988).

A law enacted by Congress on March 24, 1976 provides a Covenant to establish a Commonwealth of the Northern Mariana Islands. The provisions of the Covenant became fully effective upon termination of the Trusteeship Agreement on November 3, 1986. Most of the residents became US citizens. There is a popularly elected bicameral legislature and a popularly elected Governor.

Governor, Lorenzo D. L. Guerrero.
Lt. Governor, Benjamin M. Manglona.

MARSHALL ISLANDS

The land area of the Marshall Islands is 70 sq. miles (181 sq. km), with an estimated population of 43,000.

In May 1979 Constitutional Government was installed in the Marshall Islands which provides for a bicameral legislature comprising a Senate and a House of Assembly. A Compact of Free Association with the United States was signed on June 25, 1983, becoming law on January 14, 1986. This allows the Marshall Islands self government and vests in the United States full responsibility for the defence of the Marshall Islands for 15 years.

CAPITAL.—Majuro, population 20,000.

President, Amata Kabua.

FEDERATED STATES OF MICRONESIA

The Federated States of Micronesia comprise the four states of Kosrae, Ponape, Truk and Yap, which have a combined area of 271 sq. miles (701 sq. km) and an estimated population of 100,000 in 1988.

Constitutional government was installed in the Federated States of Micronesia in May 1979 and provides for a unicameral 14-member National Congress comprising members from the four states. Each state also elects its own Governor and legislature.

A Compact of Free Association with the United States was signed in October 1982, becoming law on

January 14, 1986. The Federated States enjoy full self-government and the responsibility for their defence is vested fully in the United States for 15 years.

CAPITAL.—Kolonia, on Ponape. Estimated population 6,000.

President of the Federated States of Micronesia, John R. Haglelgam.
Vice President, Hiroshi Ismael.

REPUBLIC OF PALAU

Palau consists of more than 200 Pacific Ocean islands of which eight are permanently inhabited. The Palau archipelago stretches over 400 miles. The land area is 191 sq. miles (494 sq. km), with an estimated population of 14,000. The major island is Koror with a population of 8,100.

Palau and the USA signed a Compact of Free Association in August 1982, which, when approved by a two-thirds majority of the voters of Palau, will recognize the Republic of Palau to be a self-governing state. The USA is responsible for financial support, and for the defence of Palau for 50 years.

Constitutional government was installed in Palau in January 1981 and provides for a bicameral legislature. The President and Vice President are directly elected.

President, Ngiratkel Etpison.
Vice President, Kuniwo Nakamura.

THE PANAMA CANAL

As a result of the Panama Canal Treaty, 1977, the Canal Zone was disestablished, with all areas of land and water within the former Canal Zone reverting to Panama with effect from October 1, 1979. Under the treaty, the United States is allowed the use of operating areas for the Panama Canal, together with several military bases, although the Republic of Panama is sovereign in all such areas. The Panama Canal Commission, an arm of the US Government, will continue to operate the canal until the year 2000.

TOTAL OCEAN GOING COMMERCIAL TRAFFIC

Fiscal Year	No. of Transits	Canal, Net Tons	Cargo Tons
1981	13,884	188,718,328	171,221,762
1982	14,009	202,956,182	185,452,332
1983	11,707	169,577,417	145,590,759
1984	11,230	162,399,908	140,470,818
1985	11,515	168,990,073	138,643,243
1986	11,925	182,791,695	139,945,181
1987	12,230	186,488,707	148,690,380
1988	12,234	191,566,065	156,482,641
1989	11,989	185,825,532	151,636,113

The canal is fifty statute miles long (44·08 nautical miles), and the channel is from 500 to 1,000 feet wide at the bottom. It contains 12 locks in twin flights; three steps at Gatun on the Atlantic side, one step at Pedro Miguel and two at Miraflores on the Pacific side. Each lock chamber is 1,000 feet long and 110 feet wide. Transit from sea to sea takes on average 8 to 10 hours. The least width is in Gaillard Cut, and the greatest in Gatun Lake.

BRITISH EMBASSY

3100 Massachusetts Avenue NW
Washington DC 20008
[Washington DC 462 1340]

Ambassador Extraordinary and Plenipotentiary, His Excellency Sir Antony Acland, GCMG, KCVO, (1986).

Ministers, D. Peretz (*Economic*); C. V. Balmer (*Defence Equipment*); C. J. R. Meyer, CMG (*Commercial*); A. M. Wood, CMG; P. Lo.
Head of British Defence Staff and Defence Attaché, Maj.-Gen. E. H. A. Beckett, CB, MBE.
Naval Attaché, Rear-Adm. A. P. Hoddinott.
Military Attaché, Brig. E. F. G. Burton.
Air Attaché, Air Cdre. S. A. Baldwin.
Counsellors, R. Ralph (*Head of Chancery*); A. F. Smith (*Admin. and HM Consul-General*); R. C. Pratt (*Economic*); D. J. Hall (*Commercial*); R. M. Graham-Harrison (*Overseas Development*); Miss S. A. Luke (*Hong Kong Commercial Affairs*); R. J. Griffin (*Civil Aviation and Shipping*); A. W. R. Allcock (*Science, Technology and Energy*); R. F. Cornish, LVO (*Information*); P. D. Little; J. D. Hansen; J. D. N. R. Clibborn; B. J. Limbert (*Defence Supply*); K. R. Tebbit; Mrs. C. J. Valentine.
Cultural Attaché and British Council Representative, G. Tindale.

There are British Consulates General in *Atlanta*, *Boston*, *Chicago*, *Houston*, *Los Angeles*, *New York* and *San Francisco*.

There are British Consulates in *Anchorage*, *Cleveland*, *Dallas*, *Kansas City*, *Miami*, *New Orleans*, *Philadelphia*, *Portland*, *St. Louis*, *Seattle* and *Puerto Rico*.

BRITISH-AMERICAN CHAMBER OF COMMERCE, 275 Madison Avenue, New York 10016; UK OFFICE, Suite 201, High Holborn, WC1V 6RR.

URUGUAY
(República Oriental del Uruguay)

President, Dr. Luis Alberto Lacalle, *took office* March 1, 1990.
Vice President, Dr. Gonzalo Aguirre Ramírez.

CABINET
(as at June 30, 1990)

Interior, Dr. Juan Andrés Ramírez.
Foreign Affairs, Dr. Héctor Gros Espiell.
Economy and Finance, Enrique Braga.
Transport and Public Works, Wilson Elso Goñi.
Public Health, Dr. Alfredo Solari.
Labour and Social Security, Carlos Cat.
Livestock, Agriculture and Fisheries, Alvaro Ramos.
Education and Culture, Dr. Guillermo García Costa.
National Defence, Dr. Mariano R. Brito.
Industry and Energy, Dr. Augusto Montesdeoca.
Tourism, José Villar.
Housing, Territorial Regulation and Environment, Raul Lago.
Planning and Budget Office, Conrado Hughes Alvarez.

EMBASSY OF THE ORIENTAL REPUBLIC OF URUGUAY
48 Lennox Gardens, SW1X 0DL
[071–589 8835; *Consulate* 071–589 8735]

Ambassador Extraordinary and Plenipotentiary, His Excellency Dr. Luis Alberto Solé-Romeo (1987).

Area and Population.—The smallest Republic in South America, on the east coast of the Rio de la Plata situated in lat. 30°–35° S. and long. 53° 15'–57° 42' W., with an area of 68,037 sq. miles (176,215 sq. km), and a population (UN estimate 1988) of 3,060,000, almost entirely white and predominantly of Spanish and Italian descent. Many Uruguayans are Roman Catholics. There is complete freedom of religion and no church is established by the state.

Physical Features.—The country consists mainly of undulating grassy plains. The principal chains of hills are the Cuchilla del Haedo, which cross the

Brazilian boundary and extend southwards to the Cuchilla Grande of the south and east. In no case do the peaks exceed 2,000 feet.

The principal river is the Rio Negro (with its tributary the Yi), flowing from north-east to south-west into the Rio Uruguay. The boundary river Uruguay is navigable from its estuary to Salto, about 200 miles north, and the Negro is also navigable for a considerable distance. Smaller rivers are the Cuareim, Yaguaron, Santa Lucia, Queguay and the Cebollati.

The summer is warm, but the heat is often tempered by the breezes of the Atlantic. The winter is, on the whole, mild, but cold spells, characterized by winds from the South Polar regions, are experienced in June, July and August. Rainfall is regular throughout the year, but there are occasional droughts. Floods also occur.

Government.—Uruguay—or the *Banda Oriental*, as the territory lying on the eastern bank of the Uruguay River was then called—resisted all attempted invasions of the Portuguese and Spanish until the beginning of the 17th century, and 100 years later the Portuguese settlements were captured by the Spanish. From 1726 to 1814 the country formed part of Spanish South America and underwent many vicissitudes during the wars of independence. In 1814 the armies of the Argentine Confederation captured the capital and annexed the province, and it was afterwards annexed by Portugal and became a province of Brazil. In 1825, the country threw off Brazilian rule. This action led to war between Argentina and Brazil which was settled by the mediation of the United Kingdom, Uruguay being declared an independent state in 1828. In 1830 a Republic was inaugurated.

According to the Constitution the President appoints a council of 11 ministers and a Secretary (Planning and Budget Office), and the Vice-President presides over Congress. The legislature consists of a Chamber of 99 deputies and a Senate of 30 members (plus the Vice-President), elected for five years by a system of proportional representation. General elections held in November 1984 marked the return to civilian rule after 11 years of presidential rule with military support. The first fully free presidential and legislative elections since 1971 were held in November 1989, and were won by the Partido Nacional Blanco.

The Republic is divided into 19 Departments each with a chief of police and a Departmental Council.

Production and Industry.—Wheat, barley, maize, linseed, sunflower seed and rice are cultivated. The wealth of the country is obtained from its pasturage, which supports large herds of cattle and sheep. There are just over 9 million cattle and just under 24 million sheep. In addition to wool, meat packing, other foodstuffs (citrus, wine, beer), fishing and textile industries are of importance.

The development of local industry continues and, in addition to the greatly augmented textile industry, marked expansion in local production is notable in respect of tyres, sheet-glass, three-ply wood, cement, leather-curing, beet-sugar, plastics, household consumer goods, edible oils and the refining of petroleum and petroleum products.

Mineral Deposits.—There are some ferrous minerals, not extracted at present. Non-ferrous exploited minerals include clinker, dolomite, marble and granite.

Communications.—There are about 9,899 km of national highways, and about 12,083 km of telegraph and 48,375 miles of telephone communications.

There are about 2,987 km of standard gauge railway in use in Uruguay. Passenger rail services were cancelled in January 1988. Services are now limited to cargo transport. A State Autonomous Entity was formed to administer the railway systems purchased

by the Government from four British companies in 1948.

An airline, PLUNA, which is owned by the state, runs daily services to southern Brazil, Paraguay and Argentina, and two flights a week to Spain. The principal capitals of the interior and a limited freight service are connected to Montevideo by TAMU, another state-owned airline, using principally military aircraft and personnel. International passenger and freight services are maintained by American, South American and European airlines. The international airport of Carrasco lies 12 miles outside Montevideo.

Education.—Primary education is compulsory and free, and technical and trade schools and evening courses for adult education are state controlled. There are about 322,053 pupils in the 2,362 state schools. The university at Montevideo (founded in 1849) has about 18,000 students enrolled in its ten faculties.

Language and Literature.—Spanish is the language of the Republic. Five daily newspapers are published in Montevideo with an estimated total circulation of 150,000. Most of them are distributed throughout the country.

FINANCE

	1988	1989
	pesos	
Revenue	456,675·2 m	753,573 m
Expenditure	510,651·4 m	918,442 m

The external debt at June 1990 was US$6,117·3 million. Central Bank reserves (December 1989) were US$1,017 million.

TRADE

	1988	1989
Total exports	US$1,404,527 m	US$1,598,800 m
Total imports	1,176,945 m	1,195,900 m

The major exports are meat and by-products, wool and by-products, hides and bristle and agricultural products. The principal imports are raw materials, construction materials, oils and lubricants, automotive vehicles, kits and machinery. Principal trading partners are Brazil, USA and Argentina.

Trade with UK

	1988	1989
Imports from UK	£34,999,000	£26,119,000
Exports to UK	35,410,000	52,185,000

The principal export items to the UK are wool and beef, the main imports are chemicals, machinery, raw materials, metals and beverages.

CAPITAL.—ΨMontevideo, population (1984) 1,355,312. Other centres are Salto, ΨPaysandu, Mercedes, Minas, Melo, and Rivera.

CURRENCY.—New Uruguayan peso of 100 centésimos.

FLAG.—Four blue and five white horizontal stripes surcharged with sun on a white ground in the top corner, next flagstaff.

NATIONAL ANTHEM.—Orientales, La Patria O La Tumba (Uruguayans, the fatherland or death).

NATIONAL DAY.—August 25 (Declaration of Independence, 1825).

BRITISH EMBASSY
Calle Marco Bruto 1073, Montevideo 11300
[Montevideo 623650]

Ambassador Extraordinary and Plenipotentiary, His Excellency Colum John Sharkey, C.M.G., M.B.E. (1989)

First Secretary, A. T. Lovelock (*Head of Chancery and Consul*).

Second Secretaries, B. McIntyre (*Commercial*); W. A. Allan; R. Graham; R. S. Dillow.
Defence Attaché, Capt. J. W. Porter.

There is a British Consular Office at *Montevideo*.

ANGLO-URUGUAYAN CULTURAL INSTITUTE, San José 1426, Montevideo. There are branch Institutes throughout Uruguay.

BRITISH-URUGUAYAN CHAMBER OF COMMERCE, Avenida Labertador Brig. Gen., Lavalleja 1641, P2-OF 201, Montevideo.

VATICAN CITY STATE
(Stato della Città del Vaticano)

Sovereign Pontiff, His Holiness Pope John Paul II (Karol Wojtyla), *born* at Wadowice (Krakow, Poland), May 18, 1920, *elected* Pope (in succession to Pope John Paul I), Oct. 16, 1978.
Secretary of State, Cardinal Agostino Casaroli, *appointed* April, 1979.

APOSTOLIC NUNCIATURE
54 Parkside, SW19 5NF
[081–946 1410]

Apostolic Pro Nuncio, His Excellency Archbishop Luigi Barbarito (1986).
Counsellor, Mons. Abraham Kattumana.

The office of the ecclesiastical head of the Roman Catholic Church (Holy See) is vested in the Pope, the Sovereign Pontiff. For many centuries the Sovereign Pontiff exercised temporal power, but by 1870 the Papal States had become part of unified Italy. The temporal power of the Pope was in suspense until the treaty of February 11, 1929, which recognized the full and independent sovereignty of the Holy See in the City of the Vatican. The area of the Vatican City is 108 acres and its population in 1989 was about 1,000.

Trade with UK

	1988	1989
Imports from UK	£447,000	£955,000
Exports to UK	111,000	24,000

CURRENCY.—Italian currency is legal tender.
FLAG.—Square flag; equal vertical bands of yellow (next staff) and white; crossed keys and triple crown device on white band.
NATIONAL DAY.—October 22 (Inauguration of present Pontiff).

BRITISH EMBASSY TO THE HOLY SEE
91 Via Condotti, 00187 Rome
[Rome 678 9462]

Ambassador Extraordinary and Plenipotentiary, His Excellency John Kenneth Elliott Broadley, CMG (1988).
First Secretary, P. J. McCormick.

VENEZUELA
(La Republica de Venezuela)

President, Carlos Andrés Pérez, *elected* Dec. 4, 1988, *inaugurated*, Feb. 2, 1989.

COUNCIL OF MINISTERS
(as at July 30, 1990)

Interior, Alejandro Izaguirre.
Foreign Affairs, Reinaldo Figueredo Planchart.
Finance, Roberto Pocaterra.
Defence, Gen. Italo de Valle Alliegro.
Transport and Communications, Roberto Smith.
Urban Development, Luis Penzini Fleuri.
Energy and Mines, Celestino Armas.
Development, Moises Naim.

Environment and Natural Resources, Enrique Colmenares Finol.
Health and Social Welfare, Manuel Adrianza.
Agriculture and Livestock, Jonathan Coles.
Education, Gustavo Rossen.
Labour, German Lairet.
The Family, Marisela Padron.
Justice, Jesus Moreno Guacaron.
Presidential Secretariat, Armando Duran.
Science and Technology, Dulce Arnao.
Culture, Jose Antonio Abreu.
Co-ordination and Planning, Miguel Rodriguez.
Guyana Development, Leopoldo Sucre Figarella.
Congressional Relations, Jesus Ramon Carmona.
Tourism, Vladimir Gessen.
Minister, President of the Venezuelan Investment Fund, Gerver Torres.
Fight against Drugs, Regulo Villegas.

VENEZUELAN EMBASSY
1 Cromwell Road, SW7 2HW
[071–584 4206/7]

Ambassador Extraordinary and Plenipotentiary, His Excellency Dr. Francisco Kerdel-Vegas, CBE (1988).
Minister Counsellor, Jocelyn Henríquez-King.

There is also a Consulate-General at *Liverpool*.

Area and Population.—A South American Republic, situated approximately between 0° 45′ S. lat. and 12° 12′ N. lat. and 59° 45′–73° 09′ W. long., Venezuela consists of one Federal District, 20 states and two territories. It has a total area of 352,144 sq. miles (912, 050 sq. km) and a population (UN estimate 1988) of 18,757,000.

Venezuela lies on the north of the South American continent, and is bounded on the north by the Caribbean Sea, west by the Republic of Colombia, east by Guyana, and south by Brazil. Included in the area of the Republic are 72 islands off the coast, with a total area of about 14,650 square miles, the largest being Margarita, which is politically associated with Tortuga, Cubagua and Coche to form the state of Nueva Esparta. Margarita has an area of about 400 square miles.

Physical Features.—The Eastern Andes from the south-west cross the border and reach to the Caribbean coast, where they are prolonged by the Maritime Andes of Venezuela to the Gulf of Paria on the north-east. The main range is known as the Sierra Nevada de Merida, and contains the highest peaks in the country in Pico Bolivar (16,411 feet) and Picacho de la Sierra (15,420 feet). Near the Brazilian border the Sierras Parima and Pacaraima, and on the eastern border the Sierras de Rincote and de Usupamo, enclose the republic with parallel northward spurs, between which are valleys of the Orinoco tributaries. The slopes of the mountains and foothills are covered with dense forests, but the basin of the Orinoco is mainly llanos, or level stretches of open prairie, with occasional woods.

The principal river is the Orinoco, with innumerable affluents, the main river exceeding 1,600 miles in length from its rise in the southern highlands of the republic to its outflow in the deltaic region of the north-east. The Orinoco is navigable for large steamers from its mouth for 700 miles, and by smaller vessels as far as the Maipures cataract, some 200 miles farther up-stream. Dredging operations have opened the Orinoco to ocean-going ships, of up to 40 ft. draft, as far as Ciudad Guayana (about 150 miles up-stream). The upper waters of the Orinoco are united with those of the Rio Negro (a Brazilian tributary of the Amazon) by a natural river or canal, known as the Casiquiare.

The coastal regions of Venezuela are much indented and contain many lagoons and lakes, of which Maracaibo, with an area of 8,296 square miles, is the largest lake in South America. Other lakes are Zulia (290 square miles), south-west of Maracaibo, and Valencia (216 square miles) about 1,400 ft. above sea-level in the Maritime Andes.

The climate is tropical and, except where modified by altitude or tempered by sea breezes, is unhealthy, particularly in the coastal regions and in the neighbourhood of lowland streams and lagoons. The hot, wet season lasts from April to October, the dry, cooler season from November to March.

Government.—The Republic of Venezuela gained independence from Spain in 1830. According to the 1961 Constitution, executive power is held by the President, who also appoints the Council of Ministers. Legislative power is exercised by a bicameral National Congress, comprising a 196-member Chamber of Deputies and a Senate of 49 elected members plus the former Presidents of constitutional governments as life members. The President and National Congress are directly elected for concurrent five-year terms. The most recent elections were held in December 1988.

Language and Literature.—Spanish is the language of the country. There are 61 daily newspapers in Venezuela, of which ten are published in Caracas, and about 60 to 70 weekly news magazines. There is also a large number of fortnightly, monthly and quarterly publications.

Education is free and compulsory between the ages of 7 and 13. There are ten universities in Venezuela, five in Caracas and the others in Maracaibo, Mérida, Valencia, Cumaná and Barquisimeto.

Production and Industry.—Products of the tropical forest region include orchids, wild rubber, timber, mangrove bark, balata gum and tonka beans; of agricultural areas, cocoa beans, coffee, cotton, rice, maize, sugar, sesame, groundnuts, potatoes, tomatoes, other vegetables, sisal and tobacco. There is an extensive beef and dairy farming industry. Despite substantial improvements in agriculture, Venezuela is heavily reliant upon food imports, which constitute about 60 per cent of total consumption.

The principal industry is that of petroleum, which in 1986 contributed 83 per cent of Venezuela's foreign exchange income. Daily production in the oilfields (nationalized 1976) has steadily declined since 1973 in line with Venezuela's conservation policies, reaching 1·7m b.p.d. in 1986 (compared with 3·366m in 1973).

There are refineries at Punta Cardon, Amuay, Caripitó, San Lorenzo, Puerto La Cruz, Tucupeido, El Chaure and El Palito. Development of the Orinoco heavy oil belt is now moving ahead with the inauguration of the Lagovén continuous steam injection pilot plant at El Jobo in southern Monagas. It has been estimated conservatively that there might exist recoverable resources of 70,000 million barrels in the Orinoco region.

Aluminium is the second highest source of foreign exchange after petroleum. The Venezuelan state now holds the majority stake in both the principal producing companies, Venalum and Alcasa, and is moving towards a consolidation of the aluminium industry, with both companies sharing their resources and adopting general policies of marketing and procurement of supplies.

Rich iron ore deposits in eastern Venezuela have been developed. Secondary processes for pelletizing and briqueting ore for export have been installed. The government-owned steel mill at Matanzas in the Guayana uses local iron ore and obtains its electric power from hydro-electric installations on the Caroni River. It produces seamless steel tubes, billets, wire and profiles. A mill at Ciudad Guayana for the production of centrifugally-cast iron pipe came into operation at the end of 1970, with an annual capacity of 30,000 tons.

Other industries include petrochemicals, gold, diamonds and asbestos; textiles, clothing and footwear; plastics; manufacture or preparation of foodstuffs, alcoholic and non-alcoholic beverages; manufacture of paper, cement, glass, tyres, cigarettes, soap, animal feeding concentrates, simple steel products, tins, jewellery, rope, furniture, sacks, paint and motor-vehicle assembly; preparation of pharmaceutical goods; pearl fishing, sanitary ware, electric home appliances, pumps, toys, agricultural machinery, bicycles, electronic components, cosmetics and many others.

Communications.—There are about 62,449 km of roads, 22,975 km of them paved. The state has now acquired all but a very few of the railway lines, whose total length is only some 372 kilometres. Road and river communications have made railways of negligibile importance in Venezuela except for carrying iron ore in the south-east. However, the government is restoring the Puerto Cabello-Barquisimeto line and expanding it to Turén in the agricultural heartland of Venezuela. A new line connecting Caracas with La Guaira and the Litoral is planned, and in 1983 the Caracas Metro came into operation. British, US and European airlines provide Venezuela with a wide range of services. There are three Venezuelan airlines (two of them state-owned) which between them have a comprehensive network of internal lines and also connect Caracas with the United States, Central and South America, the Caribbean and Europe. Foreign vessels are not permitted to engage in the coast trade. The telegraph, radio-telegraph and radio-telephone services are state-owned. There are four television stations in Venezuela, all in Caracas. Two are government controlled.

TRADE

	1987	1988
Total imports	US$8,711 m	US$10,472 m
Total exports	10,843 m	10,365 m

Trade with UK

	1988	1989
Imports from UK	£177,787,000	£124,672,000
Exports to UK	76,563,000	111,072,000

CAPITAL.—Caracas, population around 4,000,000. Other principal towns are Ψ Maracaibo (1·7 m), Barquisimeto (504,000), Valencia (495,000), Maracay

INDO-
CHINA

(322,000), San Cristobal (230,000), Cumaná (155,000) and Ciudad Guayana (250,000).

CURRENCY.—Bolivar (BS) of 100 céntimos.

FLAG.—Three horizontal bands, yellow, blue, red (with seven white stars on blue band and coat of arms next staff on yellow band).

NATIONAL ANTHEM.—Gloria Al Bravo Pueblo (Glory to the brave people).

NATIONAL DAY.—July 5.

BRITISH EMBASSY
Apartado 1246, Caracas 1010-A
[Caracas 911255]

Ambassador Extraordinary and Plenipotentiary, His Excellency Giles Eden FitzHerbert, CMG (1987).
Counsellor, A. R. Murray. *(Head of Chancery)*.
Defence Attaché, Capt. C. R. Pack, RN.
British Council Representative, Dr. V. A. Atkinson.

There are British Consular Offices at *Caracas, Maracaibo, Puerto La Cruz* and *Valencia*.

BRITISH-VENEZUELAN CHAMBER OF COMMERCE, Apartado 5713 Edificio Blandin, Piso I Oficina I-C, Plaza Chacaito, Caracas.

VIETNAM
(Công Hòa Xã Hôi Chu Nghĩa Viêt Nam)

COUNCIL OF STATE
(as at May 31, 1990)

Chairman, Vo Chi Cong.
Deputy Chairmen, Nguyen Huu Tho; Huynh Tan Phat; Le Quang Dao; Nguyen Quyet; Dam Quang Trung; Mrs. Nguyen Thi Dinh.

General Secretary, Nguyen Viet Dung.
Members, Y-Ngong Nie-kdam; Pham The Duyet; Tran Do; Nguyen Xuan Huu; Vu Mao; Hoang Bich Son; Nguyen Dinh Tu.

COUNCIL OF MINISTERS

Chairman, Do Muoi.
First Vice-Chairman, Senior Gen. Vo Van Kiet.
Vice Chairmen, Nguyen Co Thach (Foreign Affairs); Dong Sy Nguyen; Vo Nguyen Giap; Nguyen Khanh (*General Secretary*); Tran Duc Luong.
Members, all Ministers, and Chairmen of most State Committees (around 35 in all).

VIETNAMESE COMMUNIST PARTY

Politburo of the Central Committee, Nguyen Van Linh (*General Secretary*); Vo Chi Cong; Do Muoi; Vo Van Kiet; Le Duc Anh; Nguyen Duc Tam; Nguyen Co Thach; Dong Sy Nguyen; Nguyen Thanh Binh; Doan Khue; Mai Chi Tho; Dao Duy Tung (*full members*).

EMBASSY OF THE SOCIALIST REPUBLIC OF VIETNAM
12–14 Victoria Road, W8 5RD
[071–937 1912]

Ambassador Extraordinary and Plenipotentiary, His Excellency Chau Phong (1990).
Second Secretaries, Bui Xuan Khoa; Nguyen Thi Yen.

Vietnam, with an area of 127,242 sq. miles (329,556 sq. km), and an estimated population (1989) of 64,412,000, is bordered on the north by China and the west by Laos and Cambodia.

Government.—Following the end of the war in Vietnam in 1975, and the establishment of a Provisional Revolutionary Government to administer South Vietnam, a National Assembly representing the whole of Vietnam was elected on April 25, 1976. The Assembly met in Hanoi on June 24, and on July 2 approved the reunification of North and South Vietnam under the name of the Socialist Republic of Vietnam. The national flag, anthem and capital of North Vietnam were unanimously adopted for the Socialist Republic, and Saigon was renamed Ho Chi Minh City.

Effective power lies with the ruling party, the Vietnamese Communist Party (VCP), its highest executive body being the Central Committee, elected by a Party Congress on a national basis.

The Sixth Party Congress of the VCP in December 1986 elected a new Central Committee. It is the Politburo and the Secretariat of the Central Committee which exercises real power and rules Vietnam. A Seventh Party Congress will take place in 1991.

Economy.—During the last ten years, Vietnam's economy has faced considerable problems. These include serious agricultural losses because of adverse weather, major reductions in Western aid (as a result of Vietnam's invasion and occupation of neighbouring Cambodia), border hostilities with China, and the continued allocation of resources to military expenditure. Efforts to integrate the economies of the north and south have not been very successful.

Although food production has substantially increased (over 19 million tonnes of grain in 1988) as has GDP in general, Vietnam's overall economic position at the end of 1989 was not good. There was little foreign exchange because of minimal exports to hard currency areas. Vietnam was in default of repayments to the international banking world from the IMF to major commercial and merchant banks and therefore received very few long term credits. Some attempted reforms of the economic system in 1985, including devaluation and a currency change, had adverse effects and inflation increased rapidly in late 1985 and early 1986. Despite assistance from the Soviet Union (estimated at US$2·3 billion p.a. in 1987) and other member countries of CMEA (of which Vietnam is a member), Vietnam's economy continued to decline. Economic reforms were instituted in the wake of the Sixth Party Congress and have begun to take effect. Inflation is down to single figures per month; the exchange rate has been rationalized, subsidies removed and much greater economic activity allowed. Foreign investment is being actively encouraged and is beginning to have effect.

Trade with UK

	1988	1989
Imports from UK	£2,213,000	£4,108,000
Exports to UK	492,000	1,711,000

CAPITAL.—Hanoi, population (1989) 1,089,000. Other cities are Ho Chi Minh City (3,169,000) and Hai Phong (456,000).
CURRENCY.—Dông of 10 hao or 100 xu.
FLAG.—Red, with yellow five-point star in centre.
NATIONAL ANTHEM.—Tien Quan Ca (The troops are advancing).
NATIONAL DAY.—September 2.

BRITISH EMBASSY
16 Pho Ly Thuong Kiet, Hanoi
[Hanoi 52349]

Ambassador Extraordinary and Plenipotentiary, His Excellency Peter Keegan Williams (1990).
Deputy Head of Mission, A. J. J. Cantor.
First Secretary, A. J. Dean.

REPUBLIC OF YEMEN
(Al-Jamhuriya Al-Yamaniya)

President, Col. Ali Abdullah Saleh, *appointed* May 22, 1990.
Vice President, Ali Salim al-Bid.
Members of Presidential Council, Qadi Abdel-Karim al-Arashi; Abdel Aziz Abdel Ghani; Salim Salih Mohammed.

COUNCIL OF MINISTERS
(as at May 31, 1990)

Prime Minister, Haider Abu Bakr al-Attas.
First Deputy PM, Dr. Hassan Mohammed Makki.
Deputy PM, Minister for Internal Affairs, Brig.-Gen. Mujahid Yahya Abu Shawarib
Deputy PM, Security and Defence, Brig.-Gen. Salih Ubayd Ahmed.
Deputy PM, Development of Manpower and Administrative Reform, Hohammed Haider Masdus.
Construction, Abdullah Hussayn al-Kurshumi.
Foreign Affairs, Abdullah Ali al-Karim al-Iryani.
Expatriates' Affairs, Brig.-Gen. Salih Munassar as-Siyayli.
Industry, Mohammed Said al-Attar.
Oil and Mineral Resources, Salih Abu Bakr Bin Hussain.
Supply and Trade, Fadl Mohsin Abdullah.
Legal Administration, Mohammed Said Abdullah Muhsin.
Electricity and Water, Abdul-Wahhab Mahmud Abdul-Hamid.
Civil Service and Administrative Reform, Mohammed al-Khadim al-Wajih.
Planning and Development, Faraj Bin Ghanim.
Telecommunications, Ahmad Mohammed al-Unsi.
Legal Affairs, Ismail Ahmad al-Wazir.
Waqfs (Religious Affairs) and Guidance, Muhsin Mohammed al-Ulufi.
Securities and Social Affairs, Ahmad Mohammed Luqman.
Culture, Hasan Ahmad al-Lawzi.
Youth and Sports, Mohammed Ahmad al-Kabab.

Education, Mahammed Abdullah al-Jayfi.
Justice, Abdul Wasi Ahmed Sallam.
Information, Mohammed Ahmed Jirghum.
Transport, Salih Abdullah Muthanna.
Fisheries, Salim Muhammad Jubran.
Housing and Urban Planning, Abdul Qawi Muthena Hadi.
Finance, Alawi Salih al-Salami.
Public Health, Mohammed Ali Muqbil.
Agriculture and Water Resources, Sadiq Amin Abu Ras.
Tourism, Mohammed Abdullah al-Arashi.
Interior and Security, Col. Ghalib Motahar al-Qomesh.
Defence, Brig.-Gen. Haytham Qasim Tahir.
Labour and Vocational Training, Abdul Rahman Dhiban.
Higher Education and Scientific Research, Ahmad Salim al-Qadi.

In addition there are four Ministers of State.

EMBASSY OF THE REPUBLIC OF YEMEN
41 South Street, W1Y 5PD
[071–629 9905]

Ambassador Extraordinary and Plenipotentiary, His Excellency Ahmed Abdo Rageh (1987).

Area and Population.—The Republic of Yemen comprises that area of the Arabian peninsula formerly occupied by the Yemen Arab republic (North Yemen) and the People's Democratic Republic of Yemen (South Yemen). Bounded on the west by the Red Sea, on the north by Saudi Arabia, on the east by Oman and on the south by the Gulf of Aden, Yemen has an estimated area of 203,850 sq. miles (527,969 sq. km) and an estimated combined population (1990) of 12,500,000. Included in the state are the offshore islands of Perim and Kamaran in the Red Sea, and Socotra in the Gulf of Aden.

The highlands and central plateau, and the highest portions of the maritime range of what was South Yemen, form the most fertile part of Arabia, with abundant but irregular rainfall. The area of North Yemen is largely composed of mountains and desert, and rainfall is generally scarce.

Government.—Turkish occupation of North Yemen (1872–1918) was followed by the rule of the Hamid al-Din dynasty until a revolution in 1962 overthrew the monarchy and the Yemen Arab Republic was declared. The People's Republic of South Yemen was set up in November 1967 when the British government ceded power to the National Liberation Front, thus bringing to an end 129 years of British rule in Aden and some years of protectorate status in the hinterland. The name was changed to the People's Democratic Republic of Yemen in November 1970. Negotiations towards merging the two states began in 1979.

A draft joint Constitution, proposing the establishment of a unified multi-party state, was published by the leaders of North and South Yemen in December 1989. Unification was proclaimed on May 22, 1990 following ratification the previous day by both parliaments. Elections are to be held at the end of 1992.

A five-member Presidential Council comprising former senior government figures of the separate states was formed for the period of transition. The former President of North Yemen was declared President of the unified state, with the former President of South Yemen becoming Prime Minister. The parliament of the unified state, the House of Representatives, comprises 270 members, 159 of which were former members of North Yemen's government, and 111 of South Yemen's.

Economy and Production.—*North Yemen*: The main exports are cotton, coffee, hides and skins. Oil

has been produced at Marib since December 1987; production averages 175,000 b.p.d.

South Yemen: Agriculture is the main occupation of the inhabitants outside Aden. This is largely of a subsistence nature, sorghum, sesame and millets being the chief crops, with wheat and barley widely grown at the higher elevations. Significant traces of hydrocarbons were found during exploration activities offshore in 1982. The Aden Refinery Company has a refining capacity of 8 million tons per annum but for a number of years output has not exceeded a rate equivalent to 5m tons annually. Several Western companies are now involved in oil exploration. The exact reserves and estimated production levels are unknown.

Trade with U.K.
(North Yemen)

	1988	1989
Imports from UK	£42,564,000	£41,653,000
Exports to UK	1,532,000	1,598,000

(South Yemen)

	1988	1989
Imports from UK	£20,862,000	£17,246,000
Exports to UK	1,827,000	5,029,000

CAPITAL.—Sana'a, population (1986) 427,150.
CURRENCY.—Yemeni dinar (YD) of 1,000 fils and Riyals of 100 fils are both legal tender (1 Dinar = 26 Riyals).
FLAG.—Horizontal bands of red, white and black.
NATIONAL DAYS.—September 26, October 14.

BRITISH EMBASSY
PO Box 1287, Sana'a
[Sana'a 215630/3]

Ambassador Extraordinary and Plenipotentiary, His Excellency Mark Anthony Marshall (1987).
First Secretaries, G. Kirby (*Head of Chancery and Aid*); R. Kay, MBE (*Commercial*).

There is a British Consulate at *Aden*

British Council Representative, J. McGrath, Beit Al-Mottahar, Al-Bonia Street, Harat Handhal (PO Box 2157), Sana'a.

YUGOSLAVIA
(Socijalistička Federativna Republika Jugoslavije)

THE PRESIDENCY

President of the Presidency (1990–91), Borisav Jović (*Serbia*).
Vice-President of the Presidency (1990–91), Stipe Šuvar (*Croatia*).
Members of the Presidency, Janez Drnovšek (*Slovenia*); Borisav Jović (*Serbia*); Stipe Šuvar (*Croatia*); Nenad Bućin (*Montenegro*); Dragutin Zelenović (*Vojvodina*); Riza Sapunxhiu (*Kosovo*); Vasil Tupurkovski (*Macedonia*); Bogić Bogičević (*Bosnia and Hercegovina*).

FEDERAL EXECUTIVE COUNCIL
(as at May 31, 1990)

President (Federal Prime Minister), Ante Markovic.
Vice-Presidents, Aleksandar Mitrovic; Zivko Pregl.
Foreign Affairs, Budimir Lončar.
National Defence, Veljko Kadijević.
Internal Affairs, Petar Gracanin.
Finance, Branko Zekan.
Foreign Trade, Franc Horvat.
Trade and General Economic Affairs, Nazmi Mustafa.
Justice and Organization of Federal Administration, Vlado Kambovski.
Agriculture, Stevo Mirjanic.

Transport and Communications, Joze Slokar.
Labour, Health and Social Security, Questions concerning War Veterans and Disabled Veterans, Radisa Gacic.
Energy and Industry, Stevan Santo.

President of the SFRY Assembly, Gligorijević.
President of the Socialist Alliance of the Working People, Josip Hrvatin.

EMBASSY OF THE SOCIALIST FEDERAL
REPUBLIC OF YUGOSLAVIA
5–7 Lexham Gardens, W8 5JU
[071–370 6105]

Ambassador Extraordinary and Plenipotentiary, Svetozar Rikanovic (1989).
Minister Counsellors, Branko Brankovic; Dr. Milisav Stanković *(Economic)*.
Counsellor, Nikola Mišljenović *(Press and Culture)*.
Defence Attaché, Comm. (SG) Zlatko Jazbinsek.

Area and Population.—The area of Yugoslavia is estimated at 98,766 sq. miles (255,804 sq. km). The population (UN estimate 1988) is 23,559,000; the latest Census (April 1981) broke down the population into 8,140,000 Serbs, 4,430,000 Croats, 1,750,000 Slovenes, 1,730,000 Albanians, 1,341,000 Macedonians and 1,220,000 'Yugoslavs', as well as a variety of other minorities.

Government.—Yugoslavia is a federation comprising the Socialist Republics of Serbia, Bosnia and Hercegovina, Croatia, Montenegro, and Macedonia, and the Republic of Slovenia (which dropped 'Socialist' from its formal name in March 1990). Serbia includes the Socialist Autonomous Provinces of Vojvodina and Kosovo. On November 29, 1945, the Constituent Assembly of Yugoslavia at a joint session of the Skupština and the House of Nationalities, proclaimed Yugoslavia a Republic. The official name of the country, 'The Socialist Federal Republic of Yugoslavia', was adopted by the 1963 Constitution.

Several amendments to the Constitution were made in 1971. The most important formed a new ruling body called the Presidency, which has eight members, one from each Republic and Autonomous Province. Since the death of President Tito in May 1980, its members take it in turns according to a fixed order of succession to become President of the Presidency of the Republic for a period of 12 months each.

A new Constitution was proclaimed in 1974 followed by the reconstitution of the Federal Assembly into two chambers consisting of the Federal Chamber (220 delegates) and the Republican/Provincial Chamber (88 delegates). A new Federal Executive Council (i.e. government) was also formed. The current Council was elected in March 1989. The first election of the SFRY Presidency since President Tito's death occurred in May 1984; each new member has a five-year mandate.

Yugoslavia which has been a communist state since 1946, is gradually being transformed into a multi-party state. Multi-party political systems have already been introduced by constitutional changes in Slovenia and Croatia; democratic elections are expected to have taken place in all republics by federal level by the end of 1990.

Political and economic decisions on many issues are devolved from federal to republican/provincial level. Yugoslavia has a 'self-management' form of industrial organization under which the workforce have the constitutional right to own and control their own enterprises. This is, however, under review, and likely to be abolished in some parts of the country.

Defence.—The Army, Navy and Air Force on a peace footing consist of 250,000 officers and men.

Religion and Education.—The three main religions are the Orthodox, Catholic and Islamic, and freedom to practice is constitutionally guaranteed.

Education.—Eight years' elementary education is compulsory and all education is free. There are 18 universities.

Language and Literature.—The language mainly used throughout Yugoslavia and in the Federal Government is Serbo-Croat but Slovenian and Macedonian (also South Slav tongues) and Albanian, Bulgarian, Romanian, Italian, Slovak, Ruthenian, Hungarian and Turkish are also spoken in certain areas. There is, however, no official language since all are constitutionally equal, except in the Armed Forces where Serbo-Croat is obligatory. In Serbia, Macedonia and Montenegro, the Cyrillic script is used and in the rest of the country the Latin. There are four Serbian daily newspapers in Belgrade, two Slovene dailies in Ljubljana, two Croat dailies in Zagreb, and many other dailies published in other towns. There are also many local newspapers and radio programmes in the different 'minority' languages.

Production and Industry.—The share of industry in Gross Domestic Product (average annual rate in real terms of 6·5 per cent in 1981) is now 40 per cent, while agriculture is 14 per cent. In industry the high level of investment of recent years is being cut back and present efforts are directed towards development of high priority areas such as mining, energy resources and transport and communications. Agricultural policy is directed towards substantially increased production, to make the country self-sufficient and to provide significant exports of foodstuffs. Some 80 per cent of land is still privately owned.

The main crops are wheat, maize, sugar beet, sunflower and soya. Yields in 1988 were (tons): wheat 6·3m; maize 7·7m; sugar beet 4·6m. According to Yugoslav official estimates, the livestock population in 1988 was approximately as follows: 4,881,000 cattle; 7,824,000 sheep; 8,323,000 pigs; 78,589,000 poultry.

Minerals are an important source of wealth particularly in the central and south-eastern regions. Production in 1988 included the following (tons):—

Coal	72,590,000
Coke	3,208,000
Iron ore	5,545,000
Pig iron	2,916,000
Steel	4,485,000
Crude oil	3,681,000

Smaller quantities of copper, zinc and mercury are produced.

Communications.—In 1984 there were 9,279 km of standard and narrow gauge railway and approximately 116,600 km of classified roads. In 1987 there were 3,909,000 telephones in use in the country. The principal ports on the long Adriatic seaboard of Yugoslavia are Rijeka, Bakar, Šibenik, Split, Zadar, Kardeljeva (formerly Ploče), Dubrovnik, Bar, Kotor (Cattaro) and Koper. The Danube forms a great commercial highway and the tributary rivers Sava and Tisa provide other shipping routes.

FINANCE

	1987	1988
Revenue	US$20,451m	US$22,953m
Expenditure	US$19,203m	20,466m

The rate of exchange is variable. On June 6, 1980 the dinar was devalued against all convertible currencies and there have been numerous devaluations since then.

Trade with UK

	1988	1989
Imports from UK	£203,066,000	£219,866,000
Exports to UK	197,254,000	202,450,000

CAPITAL.—Belgrade, population (1981) 1,455,000.
Other towns are Zagreb (763,000); Skopje (503,000);
Ljubljana (253,000); Sarajevo (447,000); Novi Sad
(169,000); Priština (1971) (153,000); Ψ Split (152,000);
Ψ Rijeka (133,000); Titograd (95,000).

CURRENCY.—Yugoslav dinar of 100 paras.

FLAG.—Five-point red star outlined by narrow
yellow stripe, on a ground of three horizontal bars,
blue, white and red.

NATIONAL ANTHEM.—Hej, Slaveni, Jošte Živi Reč
Naših Dedova (Oh! Slavs, our ancestors' words still
live).

NATIONAL DAY.—November 29.

BRITISH EMBASSY
General Ždanova 46, Belgrade
[Belgrade 645055]

Ambassador Extraordinary and Plenipotentiary, His
Excellency Peter E. Hall, CMG, (1989).

Counsellor, M. McGlashan.

Defence and Military Attaché, Col. E. D. Powell-
Jones.

Naval and Air Attaché, Wg. Cdr. M. B. M. Canavan.

First Secretaries, W. Jackson-Houlston (*Economic*);
H. D. Marcelin (*Admin. and Consular*); J. D. Clark
(*Commercial*).

Second Secretary, R. J. A. Huxter (*Chancery and
Information*).

There are British Consular Offices at *Belgrade,
Dubrovnik, Split* and *Zagreb*.

British Council Representative, J. Acton, Generala
Zdanove 34-Mezanin, (Post Fah 248), 11001 Belgrade.

ZAIRE
(République du Zaïre)

President of the Republic and National Security,
Marshal Mobutu Sésé Séko, *born* Oct. 30, 1930;
assumed office November 25, 1965; *elected* Nov. 5,
1970; *re-elected for third term*, July 28, 1984.

EXECUTIVE COUNCIL
(as at Aug. 31, 1990)

First State Commissioner (Prime Minister), Lunda
Bululu.

*Deputy First State Commissioner, Territorial Admin-
istration and Decentralization*, Engulu Baanga
Mpongo Bakokele Lokonga.

*Deputy First State Commissioner, Industry, Com-
merce and Crafts*, Nzanda Buana Kalemba.

Foreign Affairs, Mushobekwa Kalimba Wa Katana.

*National Defence, Territorial Security and Veterans'
Affairs*, Adm. Mavua Mudima.

Justice, Muyabo Nkulu.

Citizens' Rights, Sabi Ngampoub Mubiem.

Information, Arts and Culture, Ngongo Kamanda.

Relations with Parliament, Banza Mukalay Nsungu.

Planning, Ilunga Ilukamba.

International Co-operation, Buketi Bukayi.

Finance, Bompito Botomba.

Budget, Mananga Ma Pholo.

Agriculture, Rural Affairs, Community Development,
Onyembe Pene Mbutu.

Mines and Energy, Mboso Nkodia Puanga.

Public Works, Town Planning and Housing, Bangila
Basila.

Transport and Communications, Kimasi Matuika
Basaula.

*Further and Higher Education and Scientific Re-
search*, Kambayi Bwatshia.

Primary, Secondary and Professional Education, Koli
Elombe Motokoa.

Social Affairs, Ishibangu Muyembe Kanza.

Environment and Nature Conservation, Diur Katond.

Labour and Social Security, Muduka Inyanza.

Family and Women's Affairs, Mitheo Lola Mara
Tumba.

Civil Service, Bashala Kantu Wa Milandu.

Posts and Telecommunications, Boshua Bokwete.

Youth, Sports and Leisure, Nyamwisi Muvingi.

Land Affairs, Okitakula Djambokota.

Health, Lengelo Muyangandu.

Arts and Culture, and Tourism, Agbiano Biamba
Gambe.

EMBASSY OF THE REPUBLIC OF ZAIRE
26 Chesham Place, SW1X 8HG
[071–235 6137]

Ambassador Extraordinary and Plenipotentiary, new
appointment awaited.

Situated between long. 12°–31° E. and lat. 5° N.–13°
S., the Republic of Zaire comprises an area of 905,567
sq. miles (2,345,409 sq. km), with a population (1985
Census) of 34,671,607. A 1988 UN estimate gives a
figure of 33,458,000.

Climate.—Apart from the coastal district in the
west which is fairly dry, the rainfall averages between
60 and 80 inches. The average temperature is about
27°C, but in the south the winter temperature can
fall nearly to freezing point. Extensive forest covers
the central districts.

Government.—The State of the Congo, founded
in 1885, became a Belgian Colony in November 1908,
and was administered by Belgium until independence
in 1960, when it became the Democratic Republic of
the Congo. In October 1971 the name changed to the
Republic of Zaire.

Mobutu Sésé Seko, formerly Commander-in-Chief
of the Congolese National Army, came to power in a
coup in 1965, and was elected President in 1970.
Legislative power was vested in a unicameral National
Legislative Council, elected for a five-year term by
compulsory, direct and universal suffrage. All candidates are proposed by the sole legal political party,
Mouvement Populaire de la Révolution (MPR). In
1980 a MPR central committee was formed with
powers to overrule the National Legislative Council.

Following mounting social tension, political reforms were announced in April 1990. They include
the separation of the roles of head of state and head
of government, and the gradual introduction of a
three-party system. A transitional government was
appointed in May, and a commission is to be set up to
draft a new constitution. Elections at all levels,
including Presidential, are to be held in 1991.

Provinces.—There are 11 regions, each under a
Governor and provincial administration (names of
capitals in brackets) Bas-Zaire (Matadi); Bandundu
(Bandundu); Equateur (Mbandaka); Haut-Zaire (Kis-
angani); Kinshasa (Kinshasa); Maniema (Kindu);
Nord-Kivu (Goma); Sud-Kivu (Bukavu); Shaba, for-
merly Katanga (Lubumbashi); East Kasai (Mbuji-
Mayi); West Kasai (Kananga).

Language, Religion and Education.—The population is composed almost entirely of Bantu groups,
divided into semi-autonomous tribes, each speaking
a Bantu tongue. Minorities include Sudanese, Nil-
otes, Pygmies and Hamites, as well as around 300,000
refugees from Angola.

Swahili, a Bantu dialect with an admixture of
Arabic, is the nearest approach to a common language
in the east and south, while Lingala is the language
of a large area along the river and in the north, and
Kikongo of the region between Kinshasa and the sea.
French is the language of administration.

The National University of Zaire has campuses in Kinshasa, Kisangani and Lubumbashi.

Production.—The cultivation of oil palms is widespread, palm oil being the most important agricultural cash product though it is no longer exported. Coffee, rubber, cocoa and timber are the most important agricultural exports. The production of cotton, pyrethrum and copal fell sharply on independence but is now increasing. The country is rich in minerals, particularly Shaba (ex-Katanga) province. Copper is widely exploited, and industrial diamonds and cobalt are also produced. Oil deposits are exploited off the Zaire estuary and reef-gold is mined in the north-east of the country.

There is a wide variety of small secondary industries, the main products being foodstuffs, beverages, tobacco, textiles, leather, wood products, cement and building materials, matallurgy, small river craft and bicycles. There are large reserves of hydro-electric power and the huge Inga dam on the river Zaire supplies electricity to Matadi, Kinshasa and Shaba.

The chief exports are copper, crude oil, coffee, diamonds, rubber, cobalt, gold, cassiterite, zinc and other metals.

Communications. There are approximately 20,500 km of roads (earth-surfaced) of national importance, and 6,000 km of railways. The country has four international and 40 principal airports.

Trade with UK

	1988	1989
Imports from UK	£26,132,000	£28,419,000
Exports to UK	7,542,000	9,069,000

CAPITAL.—Kinshasa (formerly Leopoldville), population (1985 Census) 2,778,281. Principal towns, Lubumbashi (formerly Elisabethville) (403,623); Kisangani (formerly Stanleyville) (310,705); Likasi (146,394); Kananga (601,239); Ψ Matadi (143,598); and Mbandaka (134,495).

CURRENCY.—Zaïre of 100 makuta.

FLAG.—Dark brown hand and torch with red flame in yellow roundel on green background.

NATIONAL DAY.—November 24.

BRITISH EMBASSY
191 Avenue de l'Equateur (5th Floor), BP 8049,
Kinshasa
[Kinshasa 21327]

Ambassador Extraordinary and Plenipotentiary, His Excellency Robert Linklater Burke Cormack, CMG (1987).

First Secretaries, K. W. Oliver (*Consul and Deputy Head of Mission*); F. G. Geere (*Commercial*).

There are British Consulates at *Lubumbashi, Goma* and *Kisangani*.

MIGRATION TO THE UK
Acceptances for settlement in the UK by nationality

Geographical region and nationality	Number of persons			Geographical region and nationality	Number of persons		
	1986	1987	1988		1986	1987	1988
Belgium	110	60	90	Sierra Leone	90	100	110
Denmark	140	110	110	Somalia	70	70	60
France	490	420	430	South Africa	780	1,020	870
Germany (Federal				Sudan	50	70	80
Republic)	550	450	480	Tanzania	250	210	230
Greece	230	240	220	Tunisia	50	30	60
Italy	400	260	300	Uganda	90	90	120
Luxembourg	—	—	—	Zambia	120	150	180
Netherlands	410	280	220	Zimbabwe	280	350	440
Portugal	210	230	250				
Spain	360	370	370	**Africa: total**	4,130	5,150	5,840
European Community	**2,900**	**2,430**	**2,470**				
				Bangladesh	4,760	3,080	2,890
				India	4,210	4,610	5,020
Austria	80	100	90	Pakistan	5,580	3,930	4,280
Cyprus	370	380	350				
Finland	110	140	130	**Indian sub-continent**	**14,550**	**11,620**	**12,180**
Malta	160	120	100				
Norway	170	180	160				
Sweden	350	490	520	Iran	1,770	1,450	1,500
Switzerland	160	130	170	Iraq	460	450	450
Turkey	420	460	600	Israel	340	300	240
Yugoslavia	130	170	190	Jordan	140	130	120
				Kuwait	10	10	20
Other Western Europe	**1,950**	**2,160**	**2,310**	Lebanon	190	220	330
				Saudi Arabia	40	30	20
				Syria	80	100	120
Bulgaria	20	10	30				
Czechoslovakia	20	40	20	**Middle East**	**3,030**	**2,690**	**2,810**
German Democratic							
Republic	—	—	10				
Hungary	40	50	40	China	100	120	160
Poland	250	270	650	Indonesia	60	60	70
Romania	20	20	30	Japan	1,060	1,300	1,340
USSR	40	70	60	Malaysia	580	630	740
				Philippines	990	1,240	1,140
Eastern Europe	**390**	**470**	**830**	Singapore	110	140	180
				Sri Lanka	840	720	860
Europe: total	**5,240**	**5,060**	**5,620**	Thailand	410	470	390
Argentina	50	40	50	BDTC Hong Kong*	880	920	1,150
Barbados	40	60	50				
Brazil	160	160	190	**Remainder of Asia**	**5,030**	**5,600**	**6,020**
Canada	1,220	1,180	1,190				
Chile	40	40	60				
Colombia	140	160	220	**Asia: total**	**22,610**	**19,920**	**21,010**
Cuba	—	—	—				
Guyana	140	180	200	Australia	2,870	3,020	3,520
Jamaica	490	510	620	New Zealand	2,510	2,690	2,680
Mexico	60	80	60				
Peru	50	50	60	**Australasia: total**	**5,380**	**5,710**	**6,190**
Trinidad and Tobago	160	140	160				
USA	3,790	3,710	3,750				
Uruguay	—	—	10	British Overseas Citizens	1,680	1,860	1,910
Venezuela	40	40	40	Other countries not else-			
				where specified	750	890	960
Americas: total	**6,380**	**6,350**	**6,480**	Stateless†	1,550	1,040	1,270
				All nationalities	**47,720**	**45,980**	**49,280**
Algeria	60	80	100				
Egypt	260	250	300	Foreign	23,950	22,160	23,370
Ethiopia	50	60	50	Commonwealth	23,830	23,810	25,900
Ghana	520	920	1,180				
Kenya	350	400	440	Old Commonwealth	6,610	6,900	7,380
Libya	130	100	110	New Commonwealth and			
Mauritius	270	300	280	Pakistan	22,660	20,850	22,800
Morocco	140	170	270	Foreign excluding			
Nigeria	570	780	970	Pakistan	18,520	18,230	19,100

*British Dependent Territories Citizens.　　†Includes refugees from south-east Asia.

CURRENCIES OF THE WORLD
and Exchange Rates against £ sterling

NOTE:—Franc CFA = Franc de la Communauté financière africaine; Franc CFP = Franc des Comptoirs français du Pacifique.

Country	Monetary Unit	Average Rate to £ September 4, 1989	Average Rate to £ September 3, 1990
Afghanistan	Afghani (Af) of 100 puls	Af 99·25	Af 99·25
Albania	Lek (Lk) of 100 qindarka	Lk 9·7912	Lk 9·9194
Algeria	Algerian dinar (DA) of 100 centimes	DA 11.90276	DA 16·4868
Andorra	French and Spanish currencies are both in use		
Angola	Kwanza (Kz) of 100 lwei	Kz 47·786	Kz 58·403
Antigua and Barbuda	East Caribbean dollar (EC$) of 100 cents	EC$ 4·19445	EC$ 5·0584
Argentina	Austral (A) of 100 centavos or 1,000 pesos	A 1014·98	A 11749·95
Aruba	Aruban florin	Florins 2·78077	Florins 3·3536
Australia	Australian dollar ($A) of 100 cents	$A 2·0388	$A 2·30125
Austria	Schilling of 100 Groschen	Schilling 21·635	Schilling 20·825
Azores	Currency is that of Portugal	Esc 256$80	Esc 261$30
Bahamas	Bahamian dollar (B$) of 100 cents	B$ 1·5540	B$ 1·8730
Bahrain	Bahrain dinar (BD) of 1,000 fils	BD 0·5845	BD 0·7067
Balearic Isles	Currency is that of Spain	Pesetas 191·90	Pesetas 184·75
Bangladesh	Taka (Tk) of 100 poisha	Tk 48·40	Tk 65·00
Barbados	Barbados dollar (BD$) of 100 cents	BD$ 3·1246	BD$ 3·7682
Belgium	Belgian franc (or frank) of 100 centimes (centiemen)	Francs 64·25	Francs 60·85
Belize	Belize dollar (BZ$) of 100 cents	BZ$ 3·107	BZ$ 3.747
Benin	Franc CFA	Francs 518·5	Francs 497·25
Bermuda	Bermuda dollar of 100 cents	$ 1·5540	$ 1·8730
Bhutan	Ngultrum of 100 chetrum (Indian currency is also legal tender)	Ngultrum 25·60	Ngultrum 33·00
Bolivia	Boliviano ($b) of 100 centavos	$b 4·2954	$b 6·0139
Botswana	Pula (P) of 100 thebe	P 3·21	P 3·4750
Brazil	Cruzeiro (BRC) of 100 centavos	CZ$ 4·3478	BRC 134·023
British Virgin Islands	US dollar (US$) (£ sterling and EC$ also circulate)	US$ 1·5540	US$ 1·8730
Brunei	Brunei dollar of 100 sen (fully interchangeable with Singapore currency)	$ 3·0665	$ 3·3085
Bulgaria	Lev of 100 stotinki	Leva 1·4344	Leva 5·5416
Burkina	Franc CFA	Francs 518·5	Francs 497·25
Burundi	Burundi franc of 100 centimes	Francs 252·7475	Francs 325·20
Cambodia	Riel of 100 sen	Riel 115·40	Riel 861·58
Cameroon	Franc CFA	Francs 518·5	Francs 497·25
Canada	Canadian dollar (C$) of 100 cents	C$ 1·8350	C$ 2·1585
Canary Islands	Currency is that of Spain	Pesetas 191·90	Pesetas 184·75
Cape Verde	Escudo Caboverdiano of 100 centavos	Esc 119$627	Esc 128$71
Cayman Islands	Cayman Islands dollar (CI$) of 100 cents	CI$ 1·2894	CI$ 1·5550
Central African Republic	Franc CFA	Francs 518·5	Francs 497·25
Chad	Franc CFA	Francs 518·5	Francs 497·25
Chile	Chilean peso of 100 centavos	Pesos 413·9255	Pesos 561·44
China	Yuan of 10 jiao or 100 fen	Yuan 5·8381	Yuan 8·9023
Colombia	Colombian peso of 100 centavos	Pesos 618·19	Pesos 975·68
Comoros	Comorian franc of 100 centimes (Franc CFA also in circulation)	Francs 518·5	Francs 497·25
Congo	Franc CFA	Francs 518·5	Francs 497·25
Costa Rica	Costa Rican colón (₡) of 100 céntimos	₡ 122·9595	₡ 176·17
Côte d'Ivoire	Franc CFA	Francs 518·5	Francs 497·25
Cuba	Cuban peso of 100 centavos	Pesos 1·183	Pesos 1·4922
Cyprus	Cyprus pound (C£) of 100 cents	C£ 0·791	C£ 0·8401
Czechoslovakia	Koruna (Kčs) of 100 haléru	Kčs 24·22	Kčs 30·32
Denmark	Danish krone of 100 øre	Kroner 11·92	Kroner 11·3500
Djibouti	Djibouti franc of 100 centimes	Francs 274·97	Francs 325·00
Dominica	East Caribbean dollar (EC$) of 100 cents	EC$ 4·19445	EC$ 5·0584
Dominican Republic	Dominican Republic peso (RD$) of 100 centavos	RD$ 9·9579	RD$ 20·4039
Ecuador	Sucre of 100 centavos	Sucres 835·81	Sucres 1636·43

Country	Monetary Unit	Average Rate to £ September 4, 1989	Average Rate to £ September 3, 1990
Egypt	Egyptian pound (£E) of 100 piastres or 1,000 millièmes	£E 3·984	£E 5·105
Equatorial Guinea	Franc CFA	Francs 518·5	Francs 497·25
Ethiopia	Ethiopian birr (EB) of 100 cents	EB 3·19145	EB 3·8510
Falkland Islands	Falkland pound of 100 pence	(at parity with £ sterling)	
Faroe Islands	Currency is that of Denmark	Kroner 11·92	Kroner 11·3500
Fiji	Fiji dollar (F$) of 100 cents	F$ 2·3607	F$ 2·6941
Finland	Markka (Mk) of 100 penniä	Mk 6·9503	Mk 6·9712
France	Franc of 100 centimes	Francs 10·37	Francs 9·9450
French Guiana........	Currency is that of France	Francs 10·37	Francs 9·9450
French Polynesia	Franc CFP	Francs 187·54	Francs 177·00
Gabon................	Franc CFA	Francs 518·5	Francs 497·25
Gambia	Dalasi (D) of 100 butut	D 9·554	D 15·8048
Germany, East	Deutsche Mark (DM) of 100 Pfennig	M 3·075	DM 2·9675
Germany, West	Deutsche Mark (DM) of 100 Pfennig	DM 3·075	DM 2·9675
Ghana	Cedi of 100 pesewas	Cedi 431·3170	Cedi 629·516
Gibraltar	Gibraltar pound of 100 pence	(at parity with £ sterling)	
Greece	Drachma of 100 leptae	Drachmae 264·40	Drachmae 292·75
Greenland	Currency is that of Denmark	Kroner 11·92	Kroner 11·3500
Grenada..............	East Caribbean dollar (EC$) of 100 cents	EC$ 4·19445	EC$ 5·0584
Guadeloupe...........	Currency is that of France	Francs 10·37	Francs 9·9450
Guam	Currency is that of USA	US$ 1·5540	US$ 1·8730
Guatemala	Quetzal (Q) of 100 centavos	Q 4·4318	Q 8·4714
Guinea	Guinea franc of 100 centimes	Francs 466·05	Francs 562·05
Guinea-Bissau	Guinea-Bissau peso of 100 centavos	Pesos 1009·775	Pesos 1217·77
Guyana	Guyana dollar (G$) of 100 cents	G$ 46·635	G$ 83·39
Haiti	Gourde of 100 centimes	Gourdes 7·7675	Gourdes 9·3675
Honduras	Lempira of 100 centavos	Lempiras 3·11	Lempiras 9·1817
Hong Kong	Hong Kong dollar (HK$) of 100 cents	HK$ 12·1398	HK$ 14·5452
Hungary	Forint of 100 fillér	Forints 95·8284	Forints 120·6295
Iceland	Icelandic króna (Kr) of 100 aurar	Kr 95·85	Kr 108·80
India................	Indian rupee (Rs) of 100 paisa	Rs 25·60	Rs 33·00
Indonesia	Rupiah (Rp) of 100 sen	Rp 2787·485	Rp 3522·10
Iran	Rial of 100 dinars	Rials 116·30	Rials 126·50
Iraq.................	Iraqi dinar (ID) of 1,000 fils	ID 0·4843	ID 0·6060
Ireland, Republic of....	Punt (IR£) of 100 pence	IR£ 1·1510	IR£ 1·1060
Israel	Shekel of 100 agora	Shekels 3·115	Shekels 3·877
Italy	Lira of 100 centesimi	Lire 2202·00	Lire 2207·25
Jamaica	Jamaican dollar (J$) of 100 cents	J$ 8·4720	J$ 12·8125
Japan	Yen of 100 sen	Yen 226·75	Yen 268·75
Jordan	Jordanian dinar (JD) of 1,000 fils	JD 1·0081	JD 1·2302
Kenya	Kenya shilling (Ksh) of 100 cents	Ksh 33·30	Ksh 43·68
Kiribati	Australian dollar ($A) of 100 cents	$A 2·0388	$A 2·30125
Korea, North	Won of 100 jun	Won 1·5069	Won 1·8173
Korea, South	Won of 100 jeon	Won 1041·72	Won 1348·15
Kuwait	Kuwaiti dinar (KD) of 1,000 fils	KD 0·46550	n/a
Laos	Kip (K) of 100 at	K 887·049	K 1330·18
Lebanon..............	Lebanese pound (L£) of 100 piastres	L£ 838·89	L£ 2009·7
Lesotho	Loti (M) of 100 lisente	M 4·3330	M 4·8312
Liberia	Liberian dollar (L$) of 100 cents	L$ 1·5540	L$ 1·8730
Libya	Libyan dinar (LD) of 1,000 dirhams	LD 0·4715	LD 0·5193
Liechtenstein.........	Swiss franc of 100 Rappen (or centimes)	Francs 2·6575	Francs 2·4650
Luxembourg	Luxembourg franc (LF) of 100 centimes (Belgian currency is also legal tender)	LF 64·25	LF 60·85
Macao	Pataca of 100 avos	Pataca 12·5265	Pataca 15·0221
Madagascar	Franc malgache (FMG) of 100 centimes	FMG 2384·75	FMG 2265·75
Madeira..............	Currency is that of Portugal	Esc 256$80	Esc 261$30
Malawi...............	Kwacha (K) of 100 tambala	K 4·4120	K 5·0175
Malaysia	Malaysian dollar (ringgit) (M$) of 100 sen	M$ 4·1958	M$ 5·0357
Maldives	Rufiyaa of 100 laaris	Rufiyaa 13·0649	Rufiyaa 17·9912
Mali	Franc CFA	Francs 518·5	Francs 497·25
Malta	Maltese lira (LM) of 100 cents or 1,000 mils	LM 0·5620	LM 0·5770
Martinique	Currency is that of France	Francs 10·37	Francs 9·9450
Mauritania	Ouguiya (UM) of 5 khoums	UM 133·756	UM 154·5263
Mauritius	Mauritius rupee of 100 cents	Rs 24·56	Rs 26·85
Mayotte..............	Currency is that of France	Francs 10·37	Francs 9·9450

Country	Monetary Unit	Average Rate to £ September 4, 1989	Average Rate to £ September 3, 1990
Mexico	Peso of 100 centavos	Pesos 3897·73	Pesos 5414·49
Monaco	French franc of 100 centimes	Francs 10·37	Francs 9·9450
Mongolia	Tugrik of 100 möngö	Tugriks 5·2128	Tugriks 6·2865
Montserrat	East Caribbean dollar (EC$) of 100 cents	EC$ 4·19445	EC$ 5·0584
Morocco	Dirham (DH) of 100 centimes	DH 13·36	DH 15·4294
Mozambique	Metical (MT) of 100 centavos	1186 MT 24	1722 MT 19
Myanmar (Burma)	Kyat (K) of 100 pyas	K 10·7780	K 11·5102
Namibia	South African rand (R) of 100 cents	R 4·3330	R 4·8312
Nauru	Australian dollar ($A) of 100 cents	$A 2·0388	$A 2·30125
Nepal	Nepalese rupee of 100 paisa	Rs 37·284	Rs 54·9479
Netherlands	Gulden (guilder) or florin of 100 cents	Guilders 3·465	Guilders 3·3425
Netherlands Antilles	Netherlands Antilles guilder of 100 cents	Guilders 2·7963	Guilders 3·3536
New Caledonia	Franc CFP	CFP 187·54	Francs 177·00
New Zealand	New Zealand dollar (NZ$) of 100 cents	NZ$ 2·6255	NZ$ 3·0425
Nicaragua	Córdoba (C$) of 100 centavos	C$ 33121·50	C$ 1798560
Niger	Franc CFA	Francs 518·5	Francs 497·25
Nigeria	Naira (N) of 100 kobo	N 11·1428	N 14·80
Norway	Krone of 100 øre	Kroner 11·1775	Kroner 11·4575
Oman	Rial Omani (OR) of 1,000 baiza	OR 0·5969	OR 0·7217
Pakistan	Pakistan rupee of 100 paisa	Rs 32·00	Rs 41·00
Panama	Balboa of 100 centésimos (US notes are also in circulation)	Balboa 1·5540	Balboa 1·8730
Papua New Guinea	Kina (K) of 100 toea	K 1·3547	K 1·7625
Paraguay	Guaraní (Gs) of 100 céntimos	Gs 1963·96	Gs 2244·71
Peru	Inti of 100 céntimos	Inti 5667·97	Inti 72835·55
Philippines	Philippine peso (P) of 100 centavos	P 32·50	P 46·00
Poland	Złoty of 100 groszy	Złotys 1726·00	Złotys 18537·00
Portugal	Escudo (Esc) of 100 centavos	Esc 256·80	Esc 261·30
Puerto Rico	Currency is that of USA	US$ 1·5540	US$ 1·8730
Qatar	Qatar riyal of 100 dirhams	Riyals 5·6471	Riyals 6·8252
Réunion	Currency is that of France	Francs 10·37	Francs 9·9450
Romania	Leu (Lei) of 100 bani	Lei 14·78	Lei 37·02
Rwanda	Rwanda franc of 100 centimes	Francs 127·706	Francs 143·82
St. Christopher and Nevis	East Caribbean dollar (EC$) of 100 cents	EC$ 4·19445	EC$ 5·0584
St. Helena	St. Helena pound (£) of 100 pence	At parity with £ sterling	
St. Lucia	East Caribbean dollar (EC$) of 100 cents	EC$ 4·19445	EC$ 5·0584
St. Pierre and Miquelon	Currency is that of France	Francs 10·37	Francs 9·9450
St. Vincent and the Grenadines	East Caribbean dollar (EC$) of 100 cents	EC$ 4·19445	EC$ 5·0584
El Salvador	El Salvador colón (₡) of 100 centavos	₡ 7·775	₡ 11·9058
San Marino	Italian currency is in circulation	Lire 2202·00	Lire 2207·25
São Tomé and Príncipe	Dobra of 100 centavos	Dobra 167·042	Dobra 188·3484
Saudi Arabia	Saudi riyal (SR) of 20 qursh or 100 halala	SR 5·1890	SR 7·0247
Senegal	Franc CFA	Francs 518·5	Francs 497·25
Seychelles	Seychelles rupee of 100 cents	Rs 8·89	Rs 9·71
Sierra Leone	Leone (Le) of 100 cents	Le 98·30	Le 298·00
Singapore	Singapore dollar (S$) of 100 cents	S$ 3·0665	S$ 3·3085
Solomon Islands	Solomon Islands dollar (SI$) of 100 cents	SI$ 3·7155	SI$ 4·7575
Somalia	Somali shilling of 100 cents	Shillings 636·935	Shillings 768·135
South Africa	Rand (R) of 100 cents	R 4·3330	R 4·8312
Spain	Peseta of 100 céntimos	Pesetas 191·90	Pesetas 184·75
Sri Lanka	Sri Lankan rupee of 100 cents	Rs 58·50	Rs 75·00
Sudan	Sudanese pound (£S) of 100 piastres or 1,000 millièmes	£S 6·99075	£S 21·4516
Suriname	Suriname guilder of 100 cents	Guilders 2·77299	Guilders 3·3442
Swaziland	Lilangeni (E) of 100 cents (South African currency also in circulation)	E 4·3330	E 4·8312
Sweden	Swedish krona of 100 öre	Kronor 10·36	Kronor 10·8825
Switzerland	Swiss franc of 100 Rappen (or centimes)	Francs 2·6575	Francs 2·4650
Syria	Syrian pound (S$) of 100 piastres	S£ 32·6235	S£ 39·3435

Country	Monetary Unit	Average Rate to £ September 4, 1989	Average Rate to £ September 3, 1990
Taiwan	New Taiwan dollar (NT$) of 100 cents	NT$ 41·45	NT$ 51·05
Tanzania	Tanzanian shilling of 100 cents	Shillings 224·30	Shillings 369·40
Thailand	Baht of 100 satang	Baht 40·00	Baht 48·00
Togo	Franc CFA	Francs 518·5	Francs 497·25
Tonga	Pa'anga (T$) of 100 seniti	T$ 2·0388	T$ 2·30125
Trinidad and Tobago ..	Trinidad and Tobago dollar (TT$) of 100 cents	TT$ 6·602375	TT$ 7·9624
Tunisia	Tunisian dinar of 1,000 millimes	Dinars 1·51255	Dinars 1·6440
Turkey...............	Turkish lira (TL) of 100 kurus	TL 3484·89	TL 5240·17
Tuvalu	Australian dollar ($A) of 100 cents	$A 2·0388	$A 2·30125
Uganda	Uganda shilling of 100 cents	Shillings 310·743	Shillings 849·777
Union of Soviet Socialist Republics	Rouble of 100 kopeks	Roubles 1·0082	Roubles 1·1018
United Arab Emirates .	UAE dirham of 100 fils	Dirham 5·6978	Dirham 6·8772
United Kingdom	Pound sterling (£) of 100 pence	£ 1·00	£ 1·00
United States of America............	US dollar (US$) of 100 cents	US$ 1·5540	US$ 1·8730
Uruguay	New Uruguayan peso of 100 centésimos	Pesos 1014·63	Pesos 2348·74
Vanuatu	Vatu of 100 centimes	Vatu 185·00	Vatu 210·50
Vatican City State	Italian currency is legal tender	Lire 2202·00	Lire 2207·25
Venezuela	Bolívar (Bs) of 100 céntimos	Bs 59·09	Bs 91·0539
Vietnam	Dông of 10 hâo or 100 xu	Dông 6990·75	Dông 8430·75
Virgin Islands (US)....	Currency is that of USA	US$ 1·5540	US$ 1·8730
Western Samoa	Tala (WS$) of 100 sene	WS$ 3·64	WS$ 4·3917
Republic of Yemen	{ Yemeni dinar (YD) of 1,000 fils	YD 0·53285	YD 0·8646
	{ Riyal of 100 fils	Riyals 15·12	Riyals 22·482
Yugoslavia	Dinar of 100 paras	Dinars 42456·56	Dinars 20·9218
Zaire.................	Zaïre of 100 makuta	Zaïre 652·68	Zaïre 1266·04
Zambia	Kwacha (K) of 100 ngwee	K 24·20	K 75·7063
Zimbabwe	Zimbabwe dollar (Z$) of 100 cents	Z$ 3·4650	Z$ 4·6975

BALANCE OF PAYMENTS OF THE UNITED KINGDOM (£ million)

	1983	1984	1985	1986	1987	1988
Current account						
Visible trade						
Exports (fob)	60,698	70,263	77,988	72,656	79,421	80,602
Imports (fob)	62,207	75,432	81,120	82,020	90,350	101,428
Visible balance	−1,509	−5,169	−3,132	−9,364	−10,929	−20,826
Invisibles						
Credits	65,887	77,665	80,583	77,421	80,037	87,233
Debits	60,619	70,611	74,248	67,991	72,779	81,024
Invisibles balance	5,267	7,054	6,335	9,430	7,258	6,209
of which:						
Services balance	*3,995*	*4,339*	*6,606*	*6,247*	*5,682*	*4,165*
Interest, profits and dividends balance	*2,857*	*4,449*	*2,763*	*5,364*	*4,987*	*5,619*
Transfers balance	*−1,585*	*−1,734*	*−3,034*	*−2,181*	*−3,411*	*−3,575*
Current balance	3,758	1,885	3,203	66	−3,671	−14,617
Transactions in external assets and liabilities*						
Investment overseas by UK residents						
Direct	−5,417	−6,033	−8,799	−11,304	−18,615	−15,219
Portfolio	−7,194	−9,870	−19,435	−23,068	2,702	−9,718
Total UK investment overseas	−12,612	−15,903	−28,234	−34,379	−15,913	−24,937
Investment in the UK by overseas residents						
Direct	3,386	−181	3,784	4,846	8,108	7,346
Portfolio	1,888	1,419	7,121	8,135	10,440	4,639
Total overseas investment in UK	5,274	1,238	10,905	12,981	18,548	11,985
Foreign currency lending abroad by UK banks	−16,162	−9,439	−20,200	−47,885	−45,684	−14,692
Foreign currency borrowing abroad by UK banks	17,192	18,648	25,306	58,361	44,283	20,300
Net foreign currency transactions of UK banks	1,030	9,209	5,106	10,476	−1,401	5,608
Sterling lending abroad by UK banks	−2,232	−4,933	−1,635	−5,955	−4,638	−4,569
Sterling borrowing and deposit liabilities abroad of UK banks	3,945	6,149	4,155	5,605	8,547	13,556
Net sterling transactions of UK banks	1,713	1,216	2,520	−350	3,909	8,987
Deposits with and lending to banks abroad by UK non-bank private sector	863	−3,239	−1,253	−2,782	−5,311	−3,035
Borrowing from banks abroad by:						
UK non-bank private sector	73	−2,176	2,598	3,735	2,069	3,830
Public corporations	−35	−47	64	−31	−166	−253
General government	78	49	87	100	104	−10
Official reserves (additions to − drawings on +)	607	908	−1,758	−2,891	−12,012	−2,761
Other external assets of:						
UK non-bank private sector and public corporations	−161	1,281	533	1,933	433	812
General government	−478	−743	−730	−509	−796	−891
Other external liabilities of:						
UK non-bank private sector and public corporations	−55	517	728	539	1,402	2,089
General government	−661	−89	−64	78	1,466	912
Net transactions in assets and liabilities	−4,366	−7,780	−9,497	−11,091	−7,667	2,334
Balancing item	608	5,895	6,294	11,025	11,338	12,283

Source: HMSO—Annual Abstract of Statistics

* Assets: increase −/decrease +. Liabilities: increase +/decrease −.

VALUE OF UNITED KINGDOM IMPORTS (cif)
Analysis by sections and divisions (£ million)

	1985	1986	1987	1988*
Total UK imports	85,027·0	86,175·5	94,026·2	106,412·9
Food and live animals chiefly for food	8,106·5	8,718·6	8,723·9	9,064·3
Live animals chiefly for food	238·3	293·4	236·4	287·1
Meat and meat preparations	1,400·9	1,465·3	1,562·2	1,646·3
Dairy products and birds' eggs	606·3	653·2	617·8	761·2
Fish, crustaceans and molluscs, and preparations thereof	600·4	747·8	759·1	785·8
Cereals and cereal preparations	713·2	769·3	740·8	751·3
Vegetables and fruit	2,037·1	2,184·4	2,394·0	2,462·4
Sugar, sugar preparations and honey	508·1	530·3	521·2	556·9
Coffee, tea, cocoa, spices, and manufactures thereof	1,205·7	1,220·6	997·2	932·0
Feeding-stuff for animals (not including un-milled cereals)	487·4	527·3	506·5	557·7
Miscellaneous edible products and preparations	309·0	326·9	388·5	323·7
Beverages and tobacco	1,230·8	1,346·7	1,433·2	1,521·9
Beverages	843·6	1,007·9	1,105·4	1,196·3
Tobacco and tobacco manufactures	387·2	338·7	327·9	325·7
Crude materials, inedible, except fuels	4,856·8	4,622·4	5,183·9	5,619·7
Hides, skins and furskins, raw	238·9	216·4	264·1	194·2
Oil seeds and oleaginous fruit	238·8	271·3	255·0	227·5
Crude rubber (including synthetic and reclaimed)	228·3	203·5	227·1	236·3
Cork and wood	895·3	1,000·3	1,198·6	1,355·9
Pulp and waste paper	505·9	523·3	657·2	725·3
Textile fibres (other than wool tops) and their wastes (not manufactured into yarn or fabric)	662·8	546·9	633·5	686·4
Crude fertilizers and crude minerals (excluding coal, petroleum and precious stones)	354·1	317·1	286·6	354·0
Metalliferous ores and metal scrap	1,371·8	1,139·5	1,223·1	1,372·9
Crude animal and vegetable materials	361·0	404·1	438·6	465·2
Mineral fuels, lubricants and related materials	10,663·6	6,400·4	6,117·0	5,058·3
Petroleum, petroleum products and related materials	8,316·2	4,461·3	4,493·3	3,495·2
Coal, coke, gas and electric current	2,347·4	1,939·1	1,623·7	1,563·1
Animal and vegetable oils, fats and waxes ..	531·5	365·1	427·0	372·2
Total manufactured goods	58,312·2	62,825·3	70,995·1	83,364·1
Chemicals and related products	6,900·8	7,345·3	8,329·8	9,312·7
Organic chemicals	1,893·8	1,830·7	2,025·7	2,352·9
Inorganic chemicals	897·0	951·4	987·3	910·8
Dyeing, tanning and colouring materials	310·9	396·5	448·1	543·5
Medicinal and pharmaceutical products	590·4	679·7	786·3	875·9
Essential oils and perfume materials; toilet, polishing and cleansing materials	443·3	480·3	554·5	615·1
Fertilizers, manufactured	217·3	213·2	210·6	203·6
Explosives and pyrotechnic products	20·0	22·0	24·1	1,935·3
Artificial resins and plastic materials, and cellu-lose esters and ethers	1,763·5	1,985·2	2,415·6	910·7
Chemical materials and products, not elsewhere specified	764·6	786·4	877·5	964·9

* provisional.

Value of United Kingdom Imports (cif) (£ million)—*Continued*

	1985	1986	1987	1988*
Total UK imports	85,027·0	86,175·5	94,026·2	106,412·9
Manufactured goods classified chiefly by material	14,342·3	15,328·1	16,968·7	19,586·1
Leather, leather manufactures, nes, and dressed furskins	250·3	247·9	299·4	245·3
Rubber manufactures, nes	527·4	589·2	682·4	798·8
Cork and wood manufactures (excluding furniture)	632·0	687·8	784·6	964·7
Paper, paperboard, and articles of paper pulp, of paper or of paperboard	2,532·0	2,702·8	3,237·8	3,622·7
Textile yarn, fabrics, made-up articles, nes, and related products	3,032·0	3,162·4	3,497·3	3,635·6
Non-metallic mineral manufactures, nes	2,242·6	2,661·7	2,747·4	3,301·0
Iron and steel	1,715·5	1,796·2	1,889·9	2,367·4
Non-ferrous metals	1,903·4	1,835·7	1,942·3	2,504·2
Manufactures of metal, nes	1,507·2	1,644·5	1,887·5	2,146·4
Machinery and transport equipment	26,937·5	28,765·7	32,808·9	40,043·1
Power generating machinery and equipment	1,997·5	2,237·3	2,513·3	3,047·0
Machinery specialized for particular industries	2,327·3	2,362·7	2,856·2	3,476·1
Metalworking machinery	525·1	645·7	567·7	800·8
General industrial machinery and equipment, nes, and machine parts, nes	2,603·9	2,757·2	3,014·2	3,544·9
Office machines and automatic data processing equipment	4,510·0	4,542·1	5,431·1	6,278·6
Telecommunications, sound recording and re-producing apparatus and equipment	2,130·6	2,401·6	2,800·8	3,176·7
Electrical machinery, apparatus and appliances, nes, and electrical parts thereof (including non-electrical counterparts, nes, of electrical household type equipment)	4,276·9	4,445·9	5,051·7	5,813·5
Road vehicles (including air cushion vehicles)	6,800·6	7,938·8	8,807·4	11,247·9
Other transport equipment	1,765·6	1,434·5	1,766·4	2,657·7
Miscellaneous manufactured articles	10,131·6	11,386·1	12,887·8	14,422·2
Sanitary, plumbing, heating and lighting fix-tures and fittings, nes	177·2	216·6	254·5	336·2
Furniture and parts thereof	662·8	776·0	877·7	988·9
Travel goods, handbags and similar containers	174·9	199·9	230·9	250·7
Articles of apparel and clothing accessories	2,090·1	2,386·1	2,777·7	3,108·1
Footwear	671·1	734·4	799·3	907·7
Professional, scientific and controlling instru-ments and apparatus, nes	1,761·5	1,790·0	1,903·2	2,024·6
Photographic apparatus, equipment and sup-plies and optical goods, nes, watches and clocks	1,173·0	1,285·6	1,357·4	1,465·1
Miscellaneous manufactured articles, nes	3,420·9	3,997·5	4,687·2	5,340·9
Commodities and transactions not classi-fied elsewhere	1,325·7	1,897·0	1,146·2	1,412·3

Source: HMSO—Annual Abstract of Statistics

nes   not elsewhere specified.   * provisional.

VALUE OF UNITED KINGDOM EXPORTS (fob)
Analysis by sections and divisions (£ million)

	1985	1986	1987	1988*
Total UK exports	78,391·8	72,987·7	79,848·7	81,476·2
Food and live animals chiefly for food	3,252·4	3,745·8	3,730·3	3,461·4
Live animals chiefly for food	262·0	299·9	325·8	254·8
Meat and meat preparations	497·4	521·9	625·9	590·4
Dairy products and birds' eggs	281·3	331·5	314·1	389·6
Fish, crustaceans and molluscs, and prepara- tions thereof	260·3	328·9	407·2	384·4
Cereals and cereal preparations	833·0	1,177·5	831·2	676·7
Vegetables and fruit	205·3	251·7	300·3	222·3
Sugar, sugar preparations and honey	220·8	170·4	218·6	196·4
Coffee, tea, cocoa, spices and manufactures thereof	390·8	364·0	377·5	363·4
Feeding-stuff for animals (not including un- milled cereals)	121·8	139·3	155·8	176·4
Miscellaneous edible products and preparations	179·7	160·6	173·9	207·1
Beverages and tobacco	1,719·1	1,737·9	1,861·4	2,075·5
Beverages	1,253·7	1,331·6	1,411·6	1,575·5
Tobacco and tobacco manufactures	465·4	406·3	449·8	500·0
Crude materials, inedible, except fuels	2,032·1	1,940·9	1,926·4	2,032·0
Hides, skins and furskins, raw	288·5	260·2	311·5	254·8
Oil seeds and oleaginous fruit	90·4	155·5	86·2	41·7
Crude rubber (including synthetic and reclaimed)	173·9	183·0	180·0	193·0
Cork and wood	25·7	22·9	26·0	26·2
Pulp and waste paper	24·7	25·0	33·9	46·4
Textile fibres (other than wool tops) and their wastes (not manufactured into yarn or fabric)	419·4	373·0	397·0	439·5
Crude fertilizers and crude minerals (excluding coal, petroleum and precious stones)........	269·2	271·9	340·6	339·3
Metalliferous ores and metal scrap	645·8	538·9	451·6	593·4
Crude animal and vegetable materials	94·3	110·4	99·7	97·6
Mineral fuels, lubricants and related mater- ials	16,795·5	8,671·9	8,769·0	5,817·8
Petroleum, petroleum products and related materials	16,133·9	8,207·9	8,465·8	5,575·9
Coal, coke, gas and electric current	661·6	464·0	303·1	241·9
Animal and vegetable oils, fats and waxes ..	95·9	105·3	263·5	88·7
Total manufactured goods	52,506·1	54,580·5	61,036·8	66,035·3
Chemicals and related products	9,411·7	9,676·8	10,518·6	11,332·7
Organic chemicals	2,742·8	2,571·0	2,830·6	3,138·3
Inorganic chemicals	976·6	1,123·3	1,099·6	1,105·6
Dyeing, tanning and colouring materials	692·0	763·2	878·9	938·8
Medicinal and pharmaceutical products	1,427·0	1,532·7	1,620·7	1,735·3
Essential oils and perfume materials; toilet, polishing and cleansing materials	767·9	807·7	886·4	943·5
Fertilizers, manufactured	74·8	67·4	85·4	90·0
Explosives and pyrotechnic products	45·7	42·8	45·7	1,113·9
Artificial resins and plastic materials, and cellu- lose esters and ethers	1,330·7	1,401·1	1,553·1	616·1
Chemical materials and products, not elsewhere specified	1,351·3	1,367·5	1,518·1	1,651·1

* provisional.

Value of United Kingdom Exports (fob) (£ million)—*Continued*

	1985	1986	1987	1988*
Total UK exports	78,391·8	72,987·7	79,848·7	81,476·2
Manufactured goods classified chiefly by material......	10,430·2	10,977·8	11,875·8	12,708·6
Leather, leather manufactures, nes, and dressed furskins..............	295·2	321·5	372·9	311·4
Rubber manufactures, nes................	554·4	611·8	678·0	715·5
Cork and wood manufactures (excluding furniture).............	84·1	77·2	85·6	82·7
Paper, paperboard, and articles of paper pulp, of paper or of paperboard	767·6	824·3	971·2	1,093·7
Textile yarn, fabrics, made-up articles, nes, and related products.................	1,709·1	1,711·5	1,886·2	1,934·9
Non-metallic mineral manufactures, nes........	2,164·5	2,549·3	2,654·3	2,971·1
Iron and steel	1,856·2	1,866·5	2,185·8	2,391·2
Non-ferrous metals	1,379·6	1,551·3	1,502·2	1,648·6
Manufactures of metal, nes	1,619·6	1,464·5	1,539·7	1,559·6
Machinery and transport equipment	24,667·5	25,351·2	28,802·8	31,886·4
Power generating machinery and equipment...	3,061·3	3,251·1	3,241·5	3,884·8
Machinery specialized for particular industries	3,077·6	3,101·1	3,300·5	3,288·4
Metalworking machinery	521·1	581·2	691·1	780·1
General industrial machinery and equipment, nes, and machine parts, nes................	2,937·5	3,037·2	3,097·5	3,577·5
Office machines and automatic data processing equipment...............	3,746·7	3,561·9	4,483·2	5,296·6
Telecommunications and sound recording and reproducing apparatus and equipment.......	1,295·1	1,401·6	1,567·6	1,758·3
Electrical machinery, apparatus and appliances, nes, and electrical parts thereof (including non-electrical counterparts, nes, of electrical household type equipment)	3,380·1	3,382·6	3,785·7	4,343·4
Road vehicles (including air cushion vehicles)..	3,910·6	3,953·5	4,876·8	4,992·3
Other transport equipment...................	2,737·4	3,080·9	3,758·9	3,964·9
Miscellaneous manufactured articles	7,996·8	8,574·7	9,839·6	10,107·6
Sanitary, plumbing, heating and lighting fixtures and fittings, nes......................	135·0	126·3	133·0	199·4
Furniture and parts thereof	357·7	356·3	394·7	377·6
Travel goods, handbags and similar containers .	29·4	30·6	34·8	43·9
Articles of apparel and clothing accessories	1,171·7	1,228·2	1,428·7	1,414·3
Footwear..............................	159·2	167·2	186·6	210·4
Professional, scientific and controlling instruments and apparatus, nes	2,151·7	2,283·7	2,328·5	2,531·6
Photographic apparatus, equipment and supplies and optical goods, nes, watches and clocks.......................	817·3	843·3	976·2	1,004·1
Miscellaneous manufactured articles, nes	3,174·9	3,539·2	4,357·1	4,326·2
Commodities and transactions not classified elsewhere	1,990·7	2,205·5	2,261·3	1,965·5

Source: HMSO—Annual Abstract of Statistics

nes .not elsewhere specified.   * provisional.

INTERNATIONAL ORGANIZATIONS

THE UNITED NATIONS

The foundations of the Charter of the United Nations were laid at the Conference of Foreign Ministers in Moscow in 1943, and upon those foundations a structure was built at the meetings at Dumbarton Oaks, Washington, DC, from Aug. 21 to Oct. 7, 1944. The design was discussed and criticized at San Francisco from April 25 to June 26, 1945, on which date representatives of 50 Allied Nations appended their signatures to the Charter.

The United Nations formally came into existence on October 24, 1945. It was later decided that its seat should be in the United States. Permanent headquarters have been erected at Manhattan, New York. October 24 has been designated United Nations Day.

The following 159 states are members of the United Nations:—

Afghanistan
Albania
Algeria
Angola
Antigua and Barbuda
*Argentina
*Australia
Austria
Bahamas
Bahrain
Bangladesh
Barbados
*Belgium
Belize
Benin
Bhutan
*Bolivia
Botswana
*Brazil
Brunei
Bulgaria
Burkina
Burundi
*Byelorussian SSR
Cameroon
*Canada
Cape Verde
Central African Rep.
Chad
*Chile
*China
*Colombia
Comoros
Congo
*Costa Rica
Côte d'Ivoire
*Cuba
Cyprus
*Czechoslovakia
*Denmark
Djibouti
Dominica
*Dominican Rep.
*Ecuador
*Egypt
Equatorial Guinea
*Ethiopia
Fiji
Finland
*France
Gabon
Gambia
German Democratic Rep.
Germany, Federal Rep. of
Ghana
*Greece
Grenada

*Guatemala
Guinea
Guinea-Bissau
Guyana
*Haiti
*Honduras
Hungary
Iceland
*India
Indonesia
*Iran
*Iraq
Ireland, Rep. of
Israel
Italy
Jamaica
Japan
Jordan
Kampuchea (Cambodia)
Kenya
Kuwait
Laos
*Lebanon
Lesotho
*Liberia
Libya
*Luxembourg
Madagascar
Malawi
Malaysia
Maldives
Mali
Malta
Mauritania
Mauritius
Myanmar (Burma)
*Mexico
Mongolia
Morocco
Mozambique
Namibia
Nepal
*Netherlands
*New Zealand
*Nicaragua
Niger
Nigeria
*Norway
Oman
Pakistan
*Panama
Papua New Guinea
*Paraguay
*Peru
*Philippines
*Poland
Portugal
Qatar
Romania

Rwanda
St. Christopher and Nevis
St. Lucia
St. Vincent and the Grenadines
*El Salvador
São Tomé and Príncipe
*Saudi Arabia
Senegal
Seychelles
Sierra Leone
Singapore
Solomon Is.
Somalia
*South Africa
Spain
Sri Lanka
Sudan
Suriname
Swaziland
Sweden
*Syria
Tanzania

Thailand
Togo
Trinidad and Tobago
Tunisia
*Turkey
Uganda
*Ukrainian SSR
*Union of Soviet Socialist Republics
United Arab Emirates
*United Kingdom
*United States of America
*Uruguay
Vanuatu
*Venezuela
Vietnam
Western Samoa
Yemen
*Yugoslavia
Zaire
Zambia
Zimbabwe

*Original member (i.e. from 1945). (From October 25, 1971 'China' was taken to mean the People's Republic of China.)

The principal organs of the United Nations are:— The General Assembly; The Security Council; The Economic and Social Council; The Trusteeship Council; The International Court of Justice; The Secretariat.

The General Assembly

The General Assembly consists of all the members of the United Nations. Each member is entitled to be represented at its meetings by five representatives, but has only one vote. The General Assembly meets once a year in regular session beginning on the third Tuesday in September. A new President is elected by the General Assembly at the start of every annual session. Special Sessions may also be held.

The work of the General Assembly is divided among seven main committees, on each of which every member has the right to be represented:—(1) Disarmament and related security questions; (2) Economic and Financial; (3) Social, Humanitarian and Cultural; (4) Decolonization (including Non-Self Governing Territories); (5) Administrative and Budgetary; (6) Legal. There is also a Special Political Committee, to relieve the burden on the first Committee.

The main committees consider items referred to them by the General Assembly and recommend draft resolutions for submission to the Assembly's plenary meetings.

The Assembly has two procedural committees—a General Committee and a Credentials Committee; and three standing committees—an Advisory Committee on Administrative and Budgetary Questions, a Committee on Contributions and a Disarmament Commission.

The General Assembly appoints such *ad hoc* committees as may be required from time to time for special purposes. The Assembly is also assisted in its work by subsidiary bodies such as the Board of Auditors, the Committee on Conferences, the International Law Commission, etc. In 1964 the General Assembly set up the United Nations Conference on Trade and Development (UNCTAD) as a permanent body.

The United Nations Industrial Development Organization was set up on January 1, 1967, to promote industrialization and co-ordinate United Nations activities in this field.

President of the United Nations General Assembly, Peter Florin (*GDR*) (1987).

The Security Council

The Security Council consists of fifteen members, each of which has one representative and one vote. There are five permanent members and ten non-permanent members elected for a two-year term.

The Security Council bears the primary responsibility for the maintenance of peace and security. Decisions on procedural questions are made by an affirmative vote of nine members. On all other matters the affirmative vote of nine members must include the concurring votes of the permanent members, and it is this clause which makes the Veto possible.

The General Assembly, any member of the United Nations, or the Secretary-General, can bring to the Council's attention any matter considered to threaten international peace and security. A non-member State can bring a dispute before the Council provided it accepts in advance the UN Charter obligations for peaceful settlement.

The Security Council also establishes *ad hoc* committees and commissions which may be required from time to time for special purposes.

The five permanent members are China, France, UK, USA, and USSR. The ten non-permanent members in 1990 are: Canada, Colombia, Ethiopia, Finland and Malaysia (*term expires Dec. 31, 1990*), Cote d'Ivoire, Cuba, Romania, Yemen and Zaire (*term expires Dec. 31, 1991*).

The Economic and Social Council

This body is responsible under the General Assembly for carrying out the functions of the United Nations with regard to international economic, social, cultural, educational, health and related matters.

The Council has 54 members who are elected for three-year terms by the General Assembly.

It has established the following Commissions: Statistical, Human Rights, Social Development, Status of Women, Narcotic Drugs, Population, Regional Economic Commissions for Europe, Asia and the Pacific, Western Asia, Latin America and Africa. The Council also makes recommendations for the co-ordination of the policies and activities of 15 specialized agencies and other organizations in the UN system.

Trusteeship Council

The Trusteeship Council now consists of five members: the USA (administering authority of Micronesia, the only remaining trust territory of the original 11), and the other four permanent members of the Security Council, China, France, UK and USSR. China does not participate in the Trusteeship Council's work

The Trusteeship Council considers reports from administering authorities; examines petitions in consultation with the administering authority; makes periodic inspection visits; and checks conditions with an annual questionnaire on the political, economic, social, and educational advancement of the inhabitants of trust territories.

International Court of Justice

The International Court of Justice is the principal judicial organ of the United Nations. The Statute of the court is an integral part of the Charter and all members of the United Nations are *ipso facto* parties to it. The Court is composed of 15 judges, elected by both the General Assembly and the Security Council. Judges hold nine-year terms, which end on February 5 of the year indicated below. The Court is based at The Hague.

If any party to a case fails to adhere to the judgment of the Court, the other party may have recourse to the Security Council.

President, Jose Maria Ruda (*Argentina*) (1991).

Vice-President, K. Mbaye (*Senegal*) (1991).

Judges, M. Lachs (*Poland*) (1994); T. O. Elias (*Nigeria*) (1994); S. Oda (*Japan*) (1994); R. Ago (*Italy*) (1997); M. Shahabuddeen (*Guyana*) (1997); S. Schwebel (*USA*) (1997); Sir Robert Jennings (*UK*) (1991); M. Bedjaoui (*Algeria*) (1997); Ni Zhengyu (*China*) (1994); J. Evensen (*Norway*) (1994); N. K. Tarassov (*USSR*) (1997); G. Guillaume (*France*) (1991); R. S. Pathak (*India*) (1991).

(The judges are listed in order of precedence.)

The Secretariat

Secretary General, Javier Pérez de Cuellar (*Peru*).

Director General, Development and International Economic Co-operation, Antoine Blanca (*France*).

UN Office and Information Centre, Ship House, 20 Buckingham Gate, SW1E 6LB (Tel: 071-630 1981).

OTHER ORGANS

The UN Centre for Human Settlements (Habitat), Nairobi; UN Children's Fund (UNICEF), New York; UN Conference on Trade and Development (UNCTAD), Geneva; UN Development Programme (UNDP), New York; UN Disaster Relief Office (UNDRO), Geneva; UN Environment Programme (UNEP), Nairobi; UN Fund for Population Activities (UNFPA), New York; UN High Commissioner for Refugees (UNHCR), Geneva; UN Institute for Training and Research (UNITAR), New York; International Research and Training Institute for the Advancement of Women (INSTRAW); UN Relief and Works Agency for Palestine Refugees in the Near East (UNRWA), Vienna; UN University (UNU), Tokyo; World Food Council (WFC), Rome; World Food Programme (WFP), Rome.

These programmes are supported by voluntary contributions from governments, non-governmental organizations and individuals. The UN programmes receiving the largest total contributions in 1983 were: the UN Development Programme (UNDP.—US$714m); the UN Children's Fund (UNICEF.—US$297m), and the UN Fund for Population Activities (UNFPA.—US$310m). The World Food Programme (WFP), jointly administered by the UN and FAO, provided aid worth US$900m in 1983.

BUDGET OF THE UNITED NATIONS

The budget proposed at the 44th session for the biennium 1990–91 was US$1,983 million. The scale of assessment contributions of 77 UN members is set at 0·01 per cent, that of a further 10 at 0·02 per cent, and a further six at 0·03 per cent. The ten largest assessments are as follows: USA, 25 per cent.; USSR, 11·37 per cent; Japan, 11·4 per cent; West Germany, 8·08 per cent; France, 6·25 per cent; UK, 4·86 per cent; Italy, 3·99 per cent; Canada, 3·09 per cent; Spain, 1·95 per cent and Netherlands, 1·65 per cent

UK MISSION TO THE UNITED NATIONS
845 Third Avenue, New York, NY 10022, USA

Permanent Representative to the United Nations and Representative on the Security Council, Sir David Hannay, KCMG (1990).
Deputy Permanent Representative, T. L. Richardson.
Counsellors, C. O. Hum (*Head of Chancery*); A. I. Aust (*Legal Adviser*); J. F. R. Martin (*Economic and Social Affairs*); R. A. Fulton; R. Kinchen, MVO; I. C. Sloane (*Management*).

UK MISSION TO THE UN AND OTHER INTERNATIONAL ORGANIZATIONS IN GENEVA
37–39 rue de Vermont, 1211 Geneva 20, Switzerland

Permanent UK Representative, Martin Robert Morland, CMG (1990).
Deputy Permanent Representatives, G. W. Hewitt (*Head of Chancery*); P. W. M. Vereker (*Economic Affairs*).

SPECIALIZED AGENCIES

Sixteen other independent international organizations, each with its own membership, budget and headquarters, carry out their responsibilities in co-ordination with the UN under agreements made with the Economic and Social Council. These agencies set standards and provide technical assistance in economic, social and cultural and technical fields.

Food and Agriculture Organization of the United Nations (FAO), Via delle Terme di Caracalla, 00100 Rome, Italy.—Established on October 16, 1945, to raise levels of nutrition and standards of living, to secure improvements in the efficiency of the production and distribution of all food and agricultural products and to better the condition of rural populations, thus contributing to the expansion of world economy and ensuring man's freedom from hunger.

In addition to serving as an agricultural information centre, international forum and technical assistance agency, FAO plays a government advisory role, assisting in national agricultural policy and planning. The Organization also helps countries to prepare viable investment projects that will attract external financing for development schemes.

FAO's regular programme is financed by its 158 member nations according to a scale of contributions set by the biennial Conference. Consisting of all FAO member nations, the Conference is a self-governing body which approves the Organization's programme of work and budget for the following biennium. The Conference also elects a 49-member Council which serves as an interim governing body between its biennial sessions. The 1989 Conference set funding for the 1990–91 biennium at US$568·8 million.

Improving and strengthening crop production continues to be the most important priority of FAO's field programme (accounting for about 25 per cent of technical assistance spending). Other important activities are rural development (allocated about 16 per cent of field programme resources) and livestock development (11 per cent). During 1989, FAO carried out 1,984 field projects funded by extra-budgetary sources to a value of US$220.3 million. Extra-budgetary financing is provided by the UN Development Fund (UNDP) and trust funds made available mainly by donor countries and international financing agencies. In addition, 599 projects involving expenditure of US$76 million were implemented under FAO's Technical Cooperation Programme (TCP), financed from the Organization's own regular programme budget.
Director General, Edouard Saouma (*Lebanon*).
Permanent UK Representative, J. Goldsack.

International Bank for Reconstruction and Development (IBRD), Washington DC 20433, USA; *European office*, 66 Ave. d'Iéna, 75116 Paris, France; *Tokyo office*, Kokusai Building 1–1, Marunouchi 3-Chome, Chiyoda-ku, Tokyo 100, Japan.—(Together with IDA known as the World Bank). Established on December 27, 1945, to help raise standards of living in developing countries by the provision of financial resources through loans made for productive purposes to a government, or guaranteed by the government concerned. Loans are directed towards developing countries at more advanced stages of economic and social growth.

The Bank, which is owned by the governments of 152 countries and whose capital is subscribed by its member countries, finances its lending operations primarily from its own borrowing in the world capital markets, and derives a substantial contribution to its resources from its retained earnings and the repayment of loans. The interest rate on its loans is calculated in relation to its cost of borrowing; loans generally have a grace period of five years and are repayable over 20 years or less. The loans made by the Bank since its inception to June 30, 1989, totalled US$171,482 million to 108 countries. Subscribed capital, US$115,668,095 million.

The Board of Governors consists of one Governor and one alternate appointed by each of the member countries. Twenty-two Executive Directors exercise all powers of the Bank except those reserved to the Board of Governors. The President, selected by the Executive Directors, conducts the business of the Bank, with the assistance of an international staff.
President, B. B. Conable (*USA*).
UK Executive Director, F. Cassell.

International Civil Aviation Organization (ICAO), 1000 Sherbrooke Street West, Montreal, Quebec, Canada H3A 2R2.—ICAO was established on April 4, 1947, to study problems of international civil aviation, to establish international standards and recommended practices for civil aviation in areas such as airworthiness, personnel licensing, aeronautical charts, rules of the air, etc. ICAO encourages the use of safety measures, uniform regulations or operation, and simpler procedures at international airports. It promotes the use of new technical methods and equipment. With the co-operation of members, it has evolved a pattern for meteorological services, traffic control, telecommunications, search and rescue organization, and other facilities required for safe international flight. It has secured much simplification of government customs, immigration, and public health regulations as they apply to international air transport. ICAO has 163 member states.

An Assembly of delegates from member states meets at least once every three years. A Council of 33 members is elected by the Assembly, taking into account the countries of chief importance in air transport: countries which make the largest contribution to the provision of facilities for international civil air transport and those ensuring representation of the main geographical areas of the world. The Council is the executive body, working through subsidiary committees.
President of Council, Dr. Assad Kotaite (*Lebanon*).
Secretary General, Dr. Shivinder Singh Sidhu (*India*).

International Development Association (IDA), Washington DC 20433, USA; *European office*, 66 Ave. d'Iéna, 75116 Paris, France; *Tokyo office*, Kokusai

Building 1-1, Marunouchi 3-Chome, Chiyoda-ku, Tokyo 100, Japan.—The IDA is an affiliate of the IBRD (the two together comprising the World Bank) and was established in September 1960 to provide assistance for the same purposes as the IBRD but primarily in the poorer developing countries and on terms that bear less heavily on their balance of payments than IBRD loans. Assistance is concentrated on the very poor countries, i.e. those with an annual per capita GNP of less than US$1,070 (in 1988 dollars); more than 50 countries are eligible.

Membership is open to all members of IBRD and 137 have joined to date. Funds, called credits to distinguish them from IBRD loans, come mostly in the form of subscriptions and contributions by IDA's richer members, and transfers from the net earnings of the IBRD. The term of IDA credits, which are made to governments only, are ten-year grace periods, 35 or 40 year maturities, and no interest. By June 30, 1989, IDA had extended development credits totalling US$48,665 million in 90 countries.

Although legally and financially distinct from the IBRD, IDA is administered by the same staff, and the Board of Governors and Executive Directors are the same as those holding equivalent positions in the IBRD.

International Finance Corporation (IFC), 1818 H Street, Washington DC 20433, USA; *European Representative,* New Zealand House, Haymarket, SW1Y 4TQ.—The IFC was established in 1956 as an affiliate of the World Bank to assist developing member countries by promoting the growth of the private sector of their economies and helping to mobilize domestic and foreign capital for this purpose. Membership of the IBRD is a prerequisite for membership in the IFC, which has 133 members. Legally and financially the IFC and IBRD are separate entities, the Corporation has its own operating and legal staff, but draws upon the Bank for administrative and other services. IFC's subscribed share capital was US$1,300 million at June 30, 1988, and it is also empowered to borrow up to four times the amount of its unimpaired subscribed capital and accumulated earnings for use in its lending programme. At the end of June 1988, IFC had made approved investments totalling more than US$10,500 million in over 90 countries.
President, B. B. Conable (*USA*).

International Fund for Agricultural Development (IFAD), 107 Via del Serafico, 00142 Rome, Italy.—The establishment of the Fund was proposed by the 1974 World Food Conference and it began operations in December 1977. The Fund's purpose is to mobilize additional funds for agricultural and rural development in developing countries through projects and programmes directly benefiting the poorest rural populations.

All powers of the Fund are vested in the Governing Council, which is made up of the 145 member states. IFAD's operations are directed by the 18-member Executive Board. Its governing structure provides for equal voting rights among the three groups of member countries, namely, the developed countries, the oil-exporting developing countries and other developing countries.
President, Idriss Jazairy (*Algeria*).

International Labour Organization (ILO), Geneva, Switzerland; *London Branch Office,* Vincent House, Vincent Square, SW1P 2NB.—Established with the League of Nations in 1919 under the Treaty of Versailles, the ILO became in 1946 the first specialized agency associated with the United Nations. In May 1990 the Organization had 149 member states. The aim of the ILO is to promote lasting peace

through social justice, and to this end it works for better economic and social conditions everywhere. It was awarded the Nobel Peace Prize in 1969.

The ILO establishes international labour standards, which set guidelines for improving working conditions and protecting basic human rights; runs a world-wide programme of technical assistance to developing countries; conducts research and disseminates information on the human aspects of economic activity, with a view to improving social and economic well-being. Through its World Employment Programme, the ILO is attempting to reduce unemployment and its associated ills by aiding national and international efforts to provide productive work for the world's fast-growing population. It is also developing an international programme for the improvement of working conditions and the working environment.

The ILO is financed by contributions from its member states. A proportion of its budget is devoted to its technical assistance programme, but this is financed mainly by funds from UNDP and other sources. The estimated ILO budget for 1990–91 amounted to US$330,440,000.

The International Labour Conference, composed of national delegations of two government delegates, one worker delegate and one employer delegate, meets annually. It formulates international labour standards and broad policies of the Organization, provides a forum for discussion of world labour and social problems, and approves the ILO's work programme and budget, which is financed by member States.

A 56-member Governing Body, composed of 28 government members, 14 worker members and 14 employer members, acts as the Organization's executive council. Ten governments hold seats on the Governing Body because of their industrial importance.

The International Labour Office, the secretariat of the Organization, collects and distributes information, assists governments on request in drafting legislation on the basis of international labour standards, directs technical co-operation activities, and issues publications.
Director General, Michel Hansenne (*Belgium*).

International Maritime Organization (IMO), Albert Embankment, London SE1 7SR, UK.—A United Nations Specialized Agency established on March 17, 1958, to provide means for co-operation and exchange of information among governments on technical matters related to international shipping, especially with regard to safety at sea and preventing marine pollution caused by ships. IMO is responsible for calling maritime conferences and drafting maritime agreements. It has produced numerous technical codes relating to the carriage of various types of cargo such as chemicals, ores, and dangerous goods and to the construction and equipment of ships, e.g., gas and chemical carriers. In June 1990, 134 nations were in membership. Budget, 1990–91, £24,906,600. (The Organization changed its name from the Inter-Governmental Maritime Consultative Organization (IMCO) on May 22, 1982.)
Secretary General, William A. O'Neil (*Canada*).

International Monetary Fund (IMF), 700 19th Street NW, Washington DC 20431, USA.—Established on December 27, 1945, the Fund exists to promote international monetary co-operation and the expansion of international trade; to promote exchange stability, maintain orderly exchange arrangements and avoid competitive exchange depreciations; and to assist in the establishment of a multilateral system of payments in respect of current transactions between members and in the elimination of foreign exchange restrictions which hamper world trade. In June 1988, 151 countries were in membership of the Fund.

The Fund's financial assistance takes the form of a foreign exchange transaction. The member pays to the Fund an amount of its own money equivalent to the amount of foreign currency it wishes to purchase. The member is expected to 'repurchase' its own currency from the Fund, usually within three to five years, with a payment of SDRs (Special Drawing Rights) or dollars or usable currency acceptable to the Fund. These arrangements are subject to certain charges.

Currencies drawn from the Fund may be used in a flexible way to relieve the member's payments difficulty, and usually the member is expected to undertake policy changes, where needed, to correct the payment imbalance.

Each member of the Fund is assigned a quota which determines its voting power and the amount of resources that it may draw from the Fund. The subscription of each member is equal to its quota, and is payable in the member's own currency and SDRs.
Managing Director, Michel Camdessus (*France*).
UK Executive Director, F. Cassell.

International Telecommunication Union (ITU), Place des Nations, 1211 Geneva 20, Switzerland.—Founded at Paris in 1865 as the International Telegraph Union, ITU became a UN Specialized Agency in 1947. ITU's aims are to promote international co-operation and the development of technical facilities for the improvement of telecommunications of all kinds, as well as to provide technical assistance to developing countries.

The Union effects allocation of the radio frequency spectrum and registration of radio frequency assignments in order to avoid harmful interference between radio stations of different countries; fosters international co-operation in the delivery of technical assistance to the developing countries and the development of telecommunication equipment and networks in developing countries; fosters collaboration among members in order to establish the lowest possible charges; promotes the adoption of measures for ensuring the safety of life through the co-operation of telecommunication services; and undertakes studies, makes regulations, adopts resolutions, formulates recommendations and opinions, and collects and publishes information concerning telecommunication matters. The Budget for 1990 was SFr127,106,000.
Secretary General, Dr. P. Tarjanne (*Finland*).

United Nations Educational, Scientific and Cultural Organization (UNESCO), 7 Place de Fontenoy, Paris 75700, France.—Under its constitution, the Organization makes its contribution to peace and security by promoting collaboration among its member states in the fields of education, science, culture and communication. It aims at furthering a universal respect for justice, for the rule of law and for human rights, without distinction of race, sex, language or religion, in accordance with the Charter of the United Nations.

The Organization is composed of three organs: (i) the General Conference, consisting of representatives of member states, which meets biennially to decide the programme and budget; (ii) the Executive Board, composed of 51 members elected by the General Conference to supervise the execution of the approved programme; and (iii) the Secretariat, which is responsible for Unesco's day-to-day functioning and the execution of the programme. In most member states National Commissions serve as a link with Unesco and help to carry out the programme. Member states in June 1990, 161 and three Associate Members

(Aruba, Netherlands Antilles and the British Virgin Islands).

The UK withdrew from Unesco in 1985. At its 124th session in May 1986, the Executive Board of Unesco decided to grant to the UK observer facilities.
Director General, Federico Mayor Zaragoza (*Spain*).

United Nations Industrial Development Organization (UNIDO), Wagramerstrasse 5, PO Box 300, 1400 Vienna, Austria.—Established as an organ of the UN General Assembly in 1966, as an action-orientated body, replacing the Centre for Industrial Development. It became a UN specialized agency on January 1, 1986, with the aim of promoting the industrialization of developing countries, with special emphasis upon the mobilization of the manufacturing sector. UNIDO provides help on formulation of planning policies, and technical advice and assistance to developing countries. UNIDO's principal policy-making body is the Industrial Development Board, with 53 members each serving a four year term.
Director General, Domingo Siazon (*Philippines*).

Universal Postal Union (UPU), Weltpoststrasse 4, 3000 Berne 15, Switzerland.—Established on October 9, 1874 by the postal Convention of Berne and in operation from July 1, 1875, UPU exists to form a single postal territory of all the countries, members of the Union, for the reciprocal exchange of correspondence in order to secure the organization and improvement of the various postal services and to promote in this sphere the development of international collaboration. Every member agrees to transmit the mail of all other members by the best means used for its own mail. The Union includes almost all the countries of the world. Budget, 1990, SFr24,389,550. A Universal Postal Congress meets at five-yearly intervals. The last was held in Washington in late 1989, and the next is scheduled to take place in the autumn of 1994.
Director General, A.C. Botto de Barros (*Brazil*).

World Bank, *see* International Bank for Reconstruction and Development *and* International Development Association.

World Health Organization (WHO), 1211 Geneva 27, Switzerland.—Established on April 7, 1948, the aim of the World Health Organization is the attainment by all peoples of the highest possible level of health. It co-operates with its member governments in their efforts to develop health manpower, streamline health services, control communicable diseases, promote family health—including mother and child care, family planning, nutrition and health education—and strengthen environmental health. It promotes biomedical and health services research through some 850 collaborating research centres in different parts of the world. Its other services include the International Pharmacopoeia, drug evaluation and monitoring, biological standardization, epidemiological surveillance and scientific publications. Approved budget for 1990 and 1991, US$654 million. Membership (May 1990), 167.

Organs are a World Health Assembly meeting annually to frame policy, an Executive Board (31 members), meeting at least twice a year, and a Secretariat.
Director General, Dr. H. Nakajima (*Japan*).

World Intellectual Property Organization (WIPO), 34 chemin des Colombettes, 1211 Geneva 20, Switzerland.—Established by a 1967 convention to succeed the United International Bureau for the Protection of Intellectual Property, WIPO became a specialized agency of the United Nations in 1974, and has 125 members. The World Intellectual Property Organization is the United Nations specialized agency for intergovernmental co-operation in 'industrial property' (patents and other rights in technological inventions, rights in trademarks, industrial designs, appellations of origin, etc.) and 'copyright and neighbouring rights' (in literary, musical and artistic works, in films, performances of performing artists, phonograms, etc.). WIPO carries out a substantial programme of activities to promote creative intellectual activity and to facilitate the transfer of technology, especially to and among developing countries.

The Conference and the General Assembly control the International Bureau (or secretariat). The Bureau provides the necessary documentation and other services for meetings and carries out projects for the promotion of increased international co-operation among member states.

Director General: Arpad Bogsch (*USA*).

World Meteorological Organization (WMO),
41 Giuseppe-Motta, PO Box 2300, 1211 Geneva 2, Switzerland.—Came into existence in 1951. The present membership is 156 states and 5 territories. WMO exists to facilitate world-wide co-operation in establishing networks of stations making observations related to meteorology and hydrology, and to promote the establishment and maintenance of centres providing meteorological and related services; to promote the establishment of systems for the rapid exchange of weather information; to promote standardization of meteorological observations and to ensure their uniform publication; to further the application of meteorology to aviation, shipping, water problems, agriculture, and other human activities; to promote activities in operational hydrology and to further close co-operation between meteorological and hydrological services; to encourage research and training in meteorology and to co-ordinate their international aspects. Budget (1988–91), SFr170m. A World Meteorological Congress meets at least once every four years. An Executive Council (36 members), meeting at least annually, carries out the resolutions of the Congress, initiates studies and makes recommendations on matters requiring international action. Other organs are six Regional Meteorological Associations (Africa, Asia, South America, North and Central America, Europe and South-West Pacific), eight technical commissions and a Secretariat.

Secretary General, G. O. P. Obasi (*Nigeria*).

RELATED ORGANIZATIONS

International Atomic Energy Agency, Wagramerstrasse 5, PO Box 100, A–1400 Vienna, Austria.— Set up on July 29, 1957, to accelerate and enlarge the contribution of atomic energy to peace, health and prosperity throughout the world and to ensure that assistance provided by it or under its supervision is not used to further any military purpose. Agreements have been reached concerning the Agency's working relationship with the United Nations and some of the specialized agencies. In June, 1990, 113 states were members.

A General Conference of all members meets in regular annual session and in such special session as may be necessary. A Board of Governors (35 members) carries out the functions of the Agency and meets usually four times a year. The regular budget for 1990 amounted to US$162,800,000.

Director General, Hans Blix (*Sweden*).

Permanent UK Representative, G. E. Clark.

General Agreement on Tariffs and Trade (GATT), Centre William Rappard, Rue de Lausanne 154, 1211 Geneva 21, Switzerland.—A multilateral treaty, in operation since 1948, to which 96 countries are party, and one acceded provisionally; a further 28 countries apply GATT *de facto.* Its rules thus govern nearly 90 per cent of world trade. Objectives of GATT are to expand international trade and promote economic development. GATT provides a permanent forum for discussion and solution of particular international trade problems, and for multilateral negotiations to reduce tariffs and other obstacles to the expansion of international trade. Special attention is given to trade problems of developing countries. An International Trade Centre, set up by GATT in 1964 to aid developing countries in export promotion, is now operated jointly by GATT and UNCTAD.

The Uruguay Round of trade negotiations was launched in October 1986 and is scheduled to finish in December 1990. The 105 governments participating in this eighth GATT Round are conducting negotiations (covering market access and new trade rules) regarding tariffs, non-tariff measures, tropical products, textiles, agriculture, subsidies, etc. In addition, and for the first time, negotiations are being conducted to create new multilateral rules for trade in services, trade-related intellectual property rights, and trade-related investment measures. Institutional changes to GATT are also being considered, including new procedures for a streamlined dispute settlement system and increased surveillance of national trade policies.

Director General, A. Dunkel (*Switzerland*).

EUROPEAN COMMUNITY

The twelve member states: Belgium, Denmark, France, Federal Republic of Germany, Greece, Republic of Ireland, Italy, Luxembourg, The Netherlands, Portugal, Spain, the United Kingdom.

The beginnings of the European Community date from May 9, 1950, when Robert Schuman, France's Foreign Minister, proposed that France and Germany should pool their coal and steel industries under an independent (supranational) high authority, in a Community open to the membership of any other European country wishing to join. Not only West Germany, but also Italy, Belgium, the Netherlands, and Luxembourg accepted this invitation.

The Coal and Steel Community (ECSC), European Economic Community and Euratom share a single institutional framework: a Commission, Council of Ministers, Parliament and Court of Justice. The core

of the Community policymaking process is the dialogue between the Commission, which initiates and implements policy, and the Council of Ministers, which takes major policy decisions. The beginnings of democratic control are exercised by the European Parliament, while the Court of Justice ensures the rule of law and is the final arbiter in all matters arising from the Community Treaties.

Since the start of the European Economic Community and Euratom in 1958, the Parliament and Court of Justice have been common to all three Communities. Up to July 1967, each Community had its own executive body (the EEC and Euratom Commissions, and the ECSC High Authority) and its own Council of Ministers.

In April 1965 the Six signed a treaty providing for the merger of the three executive bodies in a single Commission and the three Councils in a single Council, with a view to the eventual merger of the three Communities themselves. The merger treaty came into force on July 1, 1967; the single Commission and single Council then took office. They enjoy the same powers under the three Community Treaties as did their predecessors.

On December 1 and 2, 1969, the Heads of State or Government of the Six met at the Hague and decided on the completion, strengthening and, provided that other European countries wished to accept the Treaties of Rome, enlargement of the Community. They instructed the Commission to draw up a plan for economic and monetary union, and the foreign ministers to report by the end of July on possible moves towards political unification. They also resolved to intensify the co-ordination of research and development programmes.

In accordance with the Hague decisions the Council of Ministers agreed in April, 1970, that as from 1975 the Community would have its own revenue, independent of national contributions. The foreign ministers agreed to hold formal political consultations twice a year.

In June 1970 the Six invited Britain, the Republic of Ireland, Denmark and Norway to open negotiations on their applications to join the Community. On January 22, 1972, the four applicant countries signed the Treaty of Accession in Brussels. Norway conducted a referendum on its Common Market entry and as a result withdrew its application. The enlarged Community of the Nine came into existence on January 1, 1973.

With the advent of a Labour Government in the UK in 1974, there followed a period of renegotiation of the terms of Britain's entry into the Community, culminating in a referendum on June 5, 1975, as to whether or not the country should remain a member of the EC. The result of the referendum showed two to one in favour of staying in. British Labour Party representatives who had hitherto boycotted the European Parliament then took up their 18 allotted seats.

Negotiations with Greece were concluded and the Treaty of Accession signed on May 28, 1979. Greece became the tenth member of the Community on January 1, 1981. Portugal and Spain applied to join the Community and became the eleventh and twelfth members on January 1, 1986.

Following a plebiscite, Greenland negotiated its withdrawal from the EC (but without discontinuing relations with Denmark) and formally left on February 1, 1986.

The European Council, an addition to the institutionalized meetings provided under the Treaties, evolved from the summit conference of December 1974, when the Heads of Government decided to meet at least three times a year in order to discuss Community problems and matters requiring political co-operation.

OFFICE OF THE UNITED KINGDOM PERMANENT
REPRESENTATIVE TO THE EUROPEAN COMMUNITIES
Rond-point Robert Schuman 6, 1040 Brussels, Belgium.

Ambassador and UK Permanent Representative, John Kerr, KCMG (1990).

Commission of the European Communities
200 Rue de la Loi, 1049 Brussels, Belgium

There are 17 Commissioners, two each from the United Kingdom, France, Germany, Italy and Spain, and one each for the other members.

The members of the Commission are appointed by agreement among the twelve member governments for a four-year renewable term; the president and vice-presidents are appointed from among the members for a two-year term, also renewable.

The members of the Commission are pledged to independence of the governments and of national or other particular interests. They accept joint responsibility for their decisions, which are taken by majority vote.

In addition to being the initiator of Community action and having specific powers, the Commission acts as a mediator between the member governments in Community affairs and is the guardian of the Community Treaties.

Commissioners

President

Jacques Delors (France) (*Secretariat General; Legal Services; Monetary Affairs; Spokesman's Service; Joint Interpreting and Conference Service; Think Tank; Security Office*).

Vice-Presidents

Frans Andriessen (Netherlands) (*External Relations and Trade Policy; Co-operation with other European Countries*).

Henning Christophersen (Denmark) (*Economic and Financial Affairs; Co-ordination of Structural Instruments; Statistical Office*).

Manuel Marin (Spain) (*Co-operation and Development; Fisheries*).

Filippo Maria Pandolfi (Italy) (*Research and Science; Telecommunications; Information Technology and Innovation; Joint Research Centre*).

Martin Bangemann (Fed. Rep. of Germany) (*Internal Market and Industrial Affairs; Relations with the European Parliament*).

Sir Leon Brittan (UK) (*Competition Policy; Financial Institutions*).

Members

Carlo Ripa Di Meana (Italy) (*Environment; Nuclear Safety; Civil Protection*).

Antonio Cardoso E. Cunha (Portugal) (*Personnel and Administration; Energy; Euratom Supply Agency; Policy on Small and Medium Sized Enterprises; Tourism; Social Economy*).

Abel Matutes (Spain) (*Mediterranean Policy; Relations with Latin America; North-South Relations*).

Peter Schmidhuber (Fed. Rep. of Germany) (*Budget; Financial Control*).

Christiane Scrivener (France) (*Taxation; Customs Union; Questions relating to Obligatory Levies*).

Bruce Millan (UK) (*Regional Policy*).

Jean Dondelinger (Luxembourg) (*Audio-Visual Policy; Cultural Affairs; Information and Communication Policy; Citizens' Europe; Office for Official Publications*).

Ray MacSharry (Rep. of Ireland) (*Agriculture, Rural Development*).

Karel Van Miert (Belgium) (*Transport; Credit, Investments and Financial Instruments; Consumer Protection*).

Vasso Papandreou (Greece) (*Social Affairs and Employment; Education and Training; Human Resources*).

Secretary General, D. Williamson (UK).

The Commission maintains information offices in London (8 Storey's Gate, SWIP 3AT. Tel: 071-222 8122), Edinburgh (7 Alva Street EH2 4PH), Cardiff (4 Cathedral Road), Belfast (Windsor House, 9–15 Bedford Street), Dublin (39 Molesworth Street), Washington (2100 M Street, NW (Suite 707), Washington DC 20037), New York (1 Dag Hammarskjöld Plaza, 245 East 47th Street, New York, NY 10017), Ottawa (Inn of the Provinces, Office Tower (Suite 1110), 350 Sparks Street, Ontario, KIR 7S8), and other cities.

The Council of the European Communities
170 Rue de la Loi, 1048 Brussels, Belgium

This consists of ministers from the governments of each of the twelve member states, the ministers concerned depending on the subject under discussion. A single Council exists for the three European Communities. It is the main decision-taking body within the Community legislative process. The Council acts, in almost all cases, on the basis of proposals submitted by the Commission, which is present at Council sessions to participate in the shaping of the measures taken. Before examining Commission proposals the Council normally obtains the opinions of the European Parliament and the Economic and Social Committee on them.

As prescribed by the EC treaty, under which the great majority of the Council's business falls, decisions are taken by majority vote, qualified majority vote (a system in which the members' votes are weighted) or by unanimity. The Council acts under the EC treaty by issuing (a) regulations, which are binding in their entirety and directly applicable in all member states; (b) directives, which are binding as to the result to be achieved but leave open to national governments the method of attaining this result; (c) decisions, which bind those addressed; (d) recommendations; and (e) opinions, which have no binding force. The Euratom treaty has the same system of voting and taking action; the ECSC system differs in certain respects.

The presidency of the Council is held in rotation for periods of six months. The sessions of the Council are prepared by a Committee of Permanent Representatives of the member states. The Council and its committees are serviced by a general secretariat.

European Parliament

Secretariat, Centre Européen, Kirchberg, Luxembourg.
UK Information Office, 2 Queen Anne's Gate, SW1H 9AA (Tel: 071-222 0411).

The first direct elections to the European Parliament were held in mid-1979, the second in 1984 and the latest in June 1989. Of 518 seats, the United Kingdom, France, Germany and Italy have 81 each, Spain 60, the Netherlands 25, Belgium, Greece, and Portugal 24, Denmark 16, Ireland 15 and Luxembourg 6. The Parliament meets in Strasbourg and its Committees in Brussels.

Set up in 1952 under the European Coal and Steel Community Treaty of 1951, the Parliament's authority was extended by the 1957 Convention on Common Institutions to cover the European Economic Community and Euratom. It must be consulted on all major issues and has the right to dismiss the Commission by a vote of censure.

On the bulk of legislation concerning the European Single Market due to be completed by the end of 1992, the Parliament enjoys additional powers under the co-operation procedure introduced by the Single European Act in July 1987. Apart from general powers of supervision and consultation, it questions the Commission and the Council of Ministers and has a measure of control over the Community's annual budget including its final adoption. It can reject the budget as a whole and can amend items of non-obligatory expenditure (i.e. expenditure not specified in the original treaties or derived legislation—amounting to some 27 per cent of the total budget).

The Members of the Parliament serve on 18 specialized committees and sit in political groupings as follows: Socialists 180; European People's Party, 121 Liberal Democratic Reformist 49; European Democratic Group 34; Green 29; European United Left 28; European Democratic Alliance 22; European Right 17; Coalition Left 14; Rainbow Group 14; Independent 10.
President, Enrique Baron Crespo (*Spain*).

European Court of Justice
L–2925 Luxembourg

The European Court superseded the Court of Justice of ECSC and is common to the three European Communities. It exists to safeguard the law in the interpretation and application of the Community treaties, to decide on the legality of decisions of the Council of Ministers or the Commission, and to determine violations of the Treaties. Cases may be brought to it by the member States, the Community institutions, firms or individuals. Its decisions are directly binding in the member countries. The thirteen judges and six advocates-general of the Court are appointed for renewable six-year terms by the member Governments in concert. During 1989, 385 new cases were lodged at the court and 188 judgments were delivered.

Composition of the Court in order of precedence, with effect from March 29, 1990:
O. Due (*President*); Sir Gordon Slynn (*President of the 1st and 5th Chambers*); C. N. Kakouris (*President of the 4th and 6th Chambers*); F. A. Schockweiler (*President of the 2nd Chamber*); M. Zuleeg (*President of the 3rd Chamber*); W. Van Gerven (*1st Advocate-General*); G. F. Mancini; C. O. Lenz (*Advocate-General*); M. Darmon (*Advocate-General*); R. Joliet; T. F. O'Higgins; J. Mischo (*Advocate-General*); J. C. Moitinho de Almeida; G. C. Rodriguez Iglesias; F. Grevisse; M. Diez de Velasco; F. G. Jacobs (*Advocate-General*); G. Tesauro (*Advocate-General*); P. J. G. Kapteyn; J.-G. Giraud (*Clerk of the Court*).

COURT OF FIRST INSTANCE
L–2529 Luxembourg

Established by a Council decision of October 24, 1988, exercising powers conferred by the Single European Act, the Court of First Instance took up its duties in 1989 and started to exercise its functions at the end of October. It has jurisdiction to hear and determine certain categories of cases brought by natural or legal persons, in particular cases brought by European Community officials, or cases on competion law.

Composition of the Court in order of precedence, with effect from October 7, 1989:
J. L. da Cruz Vilaca (*President*); D. P. M. Barrington (*President of the 2nd Chamber*); A. Saggio (*President of the 3rd Chamber*); D. A. O. Edward (*President of the 4th Chamber*); H. Kirschner (*President of the 5th Chamber*); C. Yeraris; R. Schintgen; C. P. Briett; B. Vesterdorf; R. Garcia-Valdecasas Y Fernandez; J. Biancarelli; K. Lenaerts; H. Jung (*Registrar*).

The European Investment Bank
100 Boulevard Konrad Adenauer
L–2950 Luxembourg

The European Investment Bank (EIB) was set up in 1958 under the terms of the Treaty of Rome to finance capital investment projects promoting the balanced development of the European Community.

It grants long-term loans to private enterprises, public authorities and financial institutions, to finance projects which further: the economic development of less advanced regions (Assisted Areas); improve communication systems between member states; environmental protection; attainment of the Communities energy policy objectives; modernization of enterprises, co-operation between undertakings in the different member states, and the activities of small and medium sized enterprises.

EIB activities have also been extended outside member countries as part of the Community's development co-operation policy, under the terms of different association or co-operation agreements with twelve countries in the Mediterranean region and, under the Lomé Conventions, 70 in Africa, the Caribbean, the Pacific, Poland and Hungary.

The Bank's total financing operations in 1989 amounted to 12,246 million ECU,* of which 11,634 million were for investments in the European Community and 611 million for outside the Community. Between 1973 and 1988 the EIB had made available a total of £7,460 million ECU for investment in the UK.

The members of the European Investment Bank are the twelve member states of the Community, who have all subscribed to the Bank's capital, of 28,000 million ECU (of which 2,596 ECU is the paid in or due to be paid in portion). The bulk of the funds required by the Bank to carry out its tasks are borrowed on the capital markets of the Community and non-member countries, and on the international market.

As it operates on a non-profit-making basis, the interest rates charged by the EIB reflect the cost of the Bank's borrowings and closely follow conditions on world capital markets.

The Board of Governors of the European Investment Bank consists of one government minister nominated by each of the member countries, usually the finance minister, who lay down general directives on the policy of the Bank and appoint members to the Board of Directors (21 nominated by the member states, one by the Commission of the European Communities), which takes decisions on the granting and raising of loans and the fixing of interest rates. A Management Committee, also appointed by the Board of Governors, is responsible for the day-to-day operations of the Bank.

President, Ernst-Günther Bröder.
Vice-Presidents, Lucio Izzo; Alain Prate; Miguel A. Arnedo Orbañanos; Ludovicus Meulemans; Roger Lavelle; Hans Duborg.

(The President and Vice-Presidents also preside as Chairman and Vice-Chairmen at meetings of the Board of Directors.)
UK Office: 68 Pall Mall, SW1Y 5ES (Tel: 071-839 3351).

EUROPEAN COAL AND STEEL COMMUNITY

This, the first of the European Communities, was established in 1952. Since then, for coal, iron ore and scrap, it has abolished customs duties, quantitative restrictions, the dual pricing system whereby prices charged on exported coal or steel differed from those charged to home consumers, currency restrictions and discrimination in transport rates based on the nationality of customers and the special frontier

---

* The financial statements of the European Investment Bank are drawn up in European currency unit (ECU) which at June 30, 1990 equalled ± £0·71, US$1·23.

charges which made international transport of these goods within the Community dearer than transport within national frontiers. It has applied rules for fair competition and a harmonized external tariff for the whole Community.

THE TREATY OF ROME

Discussions were held at Messina, Sicily, in 1955 between the foreign ministers of the six member states of ECSC (Belgium, France, Federal Republic of Germany, Italy, Luxembourg and The Netherlands) on proposals for further advances towards economic integration in Europe, and after intensive study of these proposals, a treaty was signed at Rome on March 25, 1957, setting up the European Economic Community.

The Treaty aimed to lay the foundations of an enduring and closer union between the European peoples by gradually removing the economic effects of their political frontiers. The Treaty provides for the elimination of customs duties and quotas in trade between member states; the establishment of a common customs tariff and a common trade policy towards third countries; the abolition of the obstacles to free movement of persons, services and capital between member states; the inauguration of common policies for agriculture and transport; the establishment of a system ensuring that competition shall not be distorted in the Common Market; the co-ordination of economic policies; the harmonization of social and economic legislation to the extent necessary in order to enable the Common Market to work; the creation of a European Social Fund in order to improve the possibilities of employment for workers and to contribute to the raising of their standard of living; the establishment of an Economic and Social Committee which must be consulted on major proposals, consisting of representatives of employers, workers, consumers and other groups; the establishment of a European Investment Bank intended to aid investment in underdeveloped areas and help to finance modernization; and the association of overseas countries and territories with the Community with a view to increasing trade and to pursuing jointly their effort towards economic and social development.

EUROPEAN ATOMIC ENERGY COMMUNITY (EURATOM)

A second treaty, arising from the Messina discussions between the ECSC powers on additional means of co-operation, was signed in Rome on March 25, 1957, setting up the European Atomic Energy Community. The task of Euratom, defined in detail in the Treaty, is to create within a short period the technical and industrial conditions necessary to utilize nuclear discoveries and especially to produce nuclear energy on a large scale. The United Kingdom, Denmark and Ireland joined Euratom in 1973, Greece in 1981, and Spain and Portugal in 1986.

OTHER INTERNATIONAL ORGANIZATIONS

ASIAN DEVELOPMENT BANK
2330 Roxas Boulevard, 1300 Metropolitan Manila
Philippines

The Asian Development Bank began operations in December 1966. It has 49 member countries, 34 countries from the Asia–Pacific region and 15 from Europe and North America.

The aim of the Bank is to promote the economic and social progress of its developing member coun-

tries. It makes loans and equity investments; provides technical assistance for development programmes and advisory services; promotes public and private investment in development schemes; and co-ordinates development plans and policies.

The Bank's highest policy-making body is the board of Governors, which meets annually. Each member country appoints one governor and one alternate governor. The President, who is elected by the Board of Governors for a term of five years, acts as the

Chairman of the Board of Directors. The twelve-man Board of Directors is responsible for the direction of the Bank's operations.
President, Kimimasa Tarumizu *(Japan).*

ASSOCIATION OF SOUTH EAST ASIAN NATIONS
70 A. Jl. Sisingamangaraja Kebayoran Baru, Jakarta, Indonesia

Formed in 1967, the main aims of the Association of South East Asian Nations (ASEAN) are the acceleration of economic growth, social progress and cultural development, the promotion of collaboration and mutual assistance in matters of common interest, and the continuing stability of the South East Asian region.

The Heads of Government of the member countries are the highest authority and give directions to ASEAN as and when necessary. The main policy-making body is the annual meeting of foreign ministers of the member countries. The members of the Association are Brunei, Indonesia, Malaysia, the Philippines, Singapore and Thailand.
Sec. Gen., Rusli Noor *(Indonesia).*

BANK FOR INTERNATIONAL SETTLEMENTS
Centralbahnplatz 2, 4051 Basle, Switzerland

The objectives of the Bank for International Settlements (founded in 1930) are to promote the co-operation of central banks; to provide facilities for international financial operations; and to act as trustee or agent in international financial settlements entrusted to it. The London agent is the Bank of England, and the Governor of the Bank of England is a member of the Board of Directors, in which administrative control is vested.
Chairman of the Board of Directors and President of the Bank for International Settlements, Dr. W. F. Duisenberg *(Netherlands)* (1988).

CAB INTERNATIONAL
Wallingford, Oxon. OX10 8DE
[0491-32111]

CAB International (formerly the Commonwealth Agricultural Bureaux) was founded in 1929. It consists of four Institutes and eleven Bureaux under the control of an Executive Council comprising representatives of the countries which contribute to its funds. The functions of CABI are to provide a scientific information service, identification of pests, biological control services and mutual assistance. Each Institute and Bureau acts as an effective clearing house for the collection, collation and dissemination of information in its particular branch of agricultural science.
Director General, D. Mentz.

CARIBBEAN COMMUNITY AND COMMON MARKET
PO Box 10827, Georgetown, Guyana

The Caribbean Community and Common Market (Caricom) was established in 1973 with three objectives: economic co-operation through the Caribbean Common Market; the co-ordination of foreign policy among the independent member states; the provision of common services and co-operation in functional matters such as health, education and culture, communications and industrial relations. The principal organs are the Conference of Heads of Government, which determines policy, and the Common Market Council of Ministers, consisting of ministers of government (usually ministers of trade)

designated by each member state, which is responsible for the development and smooth running of the Common Market and for the settlement of any problems arising out of its functioning. The principal administrative arm is the Secretariat, based in Guyana.

The 13 member states are Antigua and Barbuda, The Bahamas (which is not a member of the Common Market), Barbados, Belize, Dominica, Grenada, Guyana, Jamaica, Montserrat, St. Christopher and Nevis, St. Lucia, St. Vincent and the Grenadines and Trinidad and Tobago. The Dominican Republic, Suriname and Haiti have observer status.
Sec. Gen., Roderick Rainford *(Jamaica).*

CONFERENCE ON DISARMAMENT
Palais des Nations, 1211 Geneva 10, Switzerland

The Conference on Disarmament (CD) was constituted in its original form as the 18-nation Committee on Disarmament in 1962. The present title of the organization was adopted in 1984. The membership stood at 40 nations in June 1990.

The Conference holds two regular sessions per year, February–April and June–August. The work of the Conference is conducted both in plenary meetings and in *ad hoc* committees set up with the consent of all members to deal with specific items of the agenda. Currently on the agenda are, *inter alia,* negotiations towards a global ban on chemical weapons.

The Conference on Disarmament is regarded by the UN as the single multilateral disarmament negotiating forum.
Secretary General, His Excellency Miljan Komatina.
UK Delegation to the Conference on Disarmament, 37–39 rue de Vermont, 1211 Geneva 20, Switzerland.—*Leader of UK Delegation,* Miss T. A. H. Solesby, CMG.

CONFERENCE ON SECURITY AND CO-OPERATION IN EUROPE

Following a series a conferences, the Conference on Security and Co-operation in Europe (CSCE) was launched in 1975 under the Helsinki Final Act. The 35 signatories were all the European countries (except Albania), Canada and the USA; they represented the entire membership of NATO, the Warsaw Pact, and the non-aligned (NNA) countries (Austria, Cyprus, Finland, the Vatican, Ireland, Liechtenstein, Malta, Monaco, San Marino, Sweden, Switzerland and Yugoslavia). Until recently CSCE consisted of episodic summits, but a permanent secretariat is expected to be established after the next summit in autumn 1990.

COUNCIL FOR MUTUAL ECONOMIC ASSISTANCE
56 Kalinin Avenue, Moscow G–205, USSR

Established in 1949, the aim of the Council for Mutual Economic Assistance (CMEA or Comecon) is to promote the development of the national economies of the member states and the development of socialist economic integration, through the co-operation of members in the most rational use of resources and the acceleration of economic and technical progress, industrialisation and productivity. The highest body is the Session of the Council, which consists of delegations from all member states, usually led by the heads of government. The Executive Committee consists of representatives of member states at the level of deputy heads of government, and is responsible for the implementation of the tasks set by the Session of the Council and for directing the work of the Committees, Standing Commissions, Secretariat and other bodies. In 1988 the CMEA established official relations with the EC.

In 1989 the member countries were Bulgaria, Cuba, Czechoslovakia, German Democratic Republic, Hungary, Mongolia, Poland, Romania, USSR and Vietnam. Yugoslavia participated in the work of some CMEA bodies. There were also co-operation agreements with Afghanistan, Angola, Ethiopia, Finland, Iraq, Mexico, Mozambique, Nicaragua, the People's Democratic Republic of Yemen, and Yugoslavia.

Following the revolutions in Eastern Europe, the Council has at present virtually ceased to function. Radical restructuring is under consideration.

Secretary, V. Sytchev (USSR).

THE COUNCIL OF EUROPE
67006 Strasbourg, France

The Council of Europe was founded in 1949. Its aim is to achieve greater unity between its members to safeguard their European heritage and to facilitate their economic and social progress through discussion and common action in economic, social, cultural, educational, scientific, legal and administrative matters and in the maintenance and furtherance of human rights and fundamental freedoms.

The 23 members are Austria, Belgium, Cyprus, Denmark, Finland, France, the Federal Republic of Germany, Greece, Iceland, the Republic of Ireland, Italy, Liechtenstein, Luxembourg, Malta, Netherlands, Norway, Portugal, San Marino, Spain, Sweden, Switzerland, Turkey and the UK. 'Special guest status' was granted to Hungary, Poland, USSR and Yugoslavia in June 1989.

The organs are the Committee of Ministers, consisting of the foreign ministers of member countries, who meet twice yearly, and the Parliamentary Assembly of 177 members, elected or chosen by the national parliaments of member countries in proportion to the relative strength of political parties. There is also a Joint Committee of Ministers and Representatives of the Parliamentary Assembly.

The Committee of Ministers is the executive organ of the Council. The majority of its conclusions take the form of international agreements (known as European Conventions) or recommendations to governments. Decisions of the Ministers may also be embodied in partial agreements to which a limited number of member governments are party. Member governments accredit Permanent Representatives to the Council in Strasbourg, who are also the Ministers' Deputies. The Committee of Deputies meets every month to transact business and to take decisions on behalf of Ministers.

The Parliamentary Assembly holds three week-long sessions a year. It debates reports on, *inter alia*, political, economic, agricultural, social, educational, legal and regional planning affairs, and also reports received annually from the OECD, other European organizations and certain specialized agencies of the United Nations. Its 13 permanent committees meet, normally in private, once or twice between each public plenary session of the Assembly. The Standing Conference of Local and Regional Authorities of Europe each year brings together mayors and municipal councillors in the same numbers as the members of the Parliamentary Assembly.

One of the principal achievements of the Council of Europe is the European Convention of Human Rights (1950) under which was established the European Commission and the European Court of Human Rights. Among the 131 other conventions and agreements which have been concluded are the European Social Charter, the European Social Security Code, and conventions on extradition, the legal status of migrant workers, conservation, and the transfer of sentenced prisoners.

Non-member states take part in certain Council of Europe activities on a regular or *ad hoc* basis; thus the Holy See and Yugoslavia participate in all the educational, cultural and sports activities. The European Youth Foundation funds events in both Eastern and Western European countries and in some outside Europe, while nationals of these countries attend courses and seminars at the European Youth Centre.

Secretary General, Catherine Lalumière (*France*).
Permanent UK Representative, His Excellency Noël Marshall, CMG (1990).

EUROPEAN FREE TRADE ASSOCIATION
9–11 rue de Varembé, 1211 Geneva 20, Switzerland

The members of the European Free Trade Association (EFTA), which was established on May 3, 1960, are Austria, Finland, Iceland, Norway, Sweden and Switzerland.

In 1973 all the EFTA member states entered into a new relationship with the EC. Two—Denmark and the United Kingdom—withdrew from EFTA at the end of December 1972 to become members of the EC on January 1, 1973. Agreements establishing industrial free trade between most of the other EFTA member states and the enlarged EC came into force on that same date. Similar agreements with Norway and Finland came into force on July 1, 1973, and January 1, 1974, respectively. In 1986 Portugal became a member of the EC. The free trade agreements therefore now apply to trade between the six countries remaining in EFTA and Portugal.

EFTA's first objective was free trade between its original members and this was realized at the end of 1966. Its second objective was the creation of a single market to include all Western European countries, achieved through the free trade agreements.

The final abolition of tariffs on EFTA–EC trade was marked by a meeting in Luxembourg in April 1984 when ministers from all EFTA and EC countries met. They agreed on general guidelines for greatly increased co-operation between their countries. The main preoccupation of EFTA now is its commitment to work together with the EC to create the European Economic Space (EES). The aim is to have the EES Treaty enter into force by January 1, 1993 to coincide with the completion of the EC's internal market.

All EFTA and EC countries have co-operated in a successful attempt to simplify border formalities for trade in goods in Western Europe; multilateral conventions now provide for the use of a single administrative document for customs purposes and for the introduction of a common transit procedure.

The Council of EFTA meets every week at the level of the heads of the permanent national delegations to EFTA and usually twice a year at the level of ministers. Each state has a single vote and recommendations must normally be unanimous. Decisions of the Council are binding on member countries.

Secretary General, Georg Reisch (*Austria*).

EUROPEAN ORGANIZATION FOR NUCLEAR RESEARCH (CERN)
1211 Geneva 23, Switzerland

The Convention establishing the European Organization for Research (CERN) came into force in 1954. The Organization promotes European collaboration in high energy physics of a purely scientific nature. It is not concerned with research of a military nature.

The member countries are Austria, Belgium, Denmark, France, Federal Republic of Germany, Greece,

Italy, Netherlands, Norway, Portugal, Spain, Sweden, Switzerland and the UK. The following have observer status: Poland, Turkey, Yugoslavia, the EC Commission and UNESCO.

The Council is the highest policy-making body and is made up of two delegates from each member state. There is also a Committee of the Council comprising a single delegate from each member state (who is also a Council member) and the chairmen of the scientific policy and finance advisory committees. The Council is chaired by a President who is elected by the Council in Session. The Council also elects the Director General, the person responsible for the internal organization of CERN. The Director General heads a workforce of approximately 3,500, including physicists, craftsmen, technicians and administrative staff. At present over 5,000 physicists use CERN's facilities.

The member countries contribute to the budget directly in proportion to their net national revenue. The 1990 budget was SFr 840 million.

President of the Council, J. Rembser (*Federal Republic of Germany*).

Director General, C. Rubbia (1989–1993).

EUROPEAN SPACE AGENCY
8–10 rue Mario Nikis, 75738 Paris, France

The European Space Agency (ESA) was set up on May 31, 1975. It was formed from two earlier space organizations—the European Space Research Organization (ESRO) and the European Launcher Development Organization (ELDO). Its aims include the advancement of space research and technology, the implementation of a long-term European space policy and the co-ordination of national space programmes.

The member countries are Austria, Belgium, Denmark, France, Federal Republic of Germany, Republic of Ireland, Italy, Netherlands, Norway, Spain, Sweden, Switzerland and the United Kingdom. Finland is an associate member and Canada a co-operating state.

The agency is directed by a Council composed of the representatives of the member states, and its chief officer is the Director General.

Director General, John-Marie Luton (1990).

INTERNATIONAL CONFEDERATION OF FREE TRADE UNIONS
37–41 rue Montagne aux Herbes Potageres, 1000 Brussels, Belgium

Formed in 1949 the International Confederation of Free Trade Unions (ICFTU) was created to promote free trade unionism worldwide. It aims to establish, maintain and promote free trade unions, and to promote peace with economic security and social justice.

Affiliated to the ICFTU are 144 individual unions and representative bodies in 101 countries and territories. On May 11, 1990 there were over 99 million members.

The supreme authority of the organization is the Congress which convenes at least every four years. It is composed of delegates from the affiliated trade union organizations. The Congress elects an Executive Board of 35 members which meets at least twice a year. The Board establishes the budget and receives suggestions and proposals from affiliates as well as acting on behalf of the Confederation. The Congress also elects the General Secretary.

General Secretary, John Vanderveken.

UK Affiliate, TUC, Congress House, 23–28 Great Russell Street, WC1B 3LS.

INTERNATIONAL CRIMINAL POLICE ORGANIZATION
50 Quai Achille Lignon, BP 6041, 69411 Lyon, France

The International Criminal Police Commission (Interpol) was set up in 1923 to establish an international criminal records office and to harmonize extradition procedures. In 1956 a revised Constitution was adopted and the organization adopted its present name. On August 1, 1990 the organization comprised 146 member states.

Interpol's aims are to ensure and promote mutual assistance between all criminal police authorities, and to support government agencies concerned with combating crime, whilst respecting the national sovereignty of members. Interpol is financed by annual contributions from the governments of member states.

Interpol's policy is decided by the General Assembly which meets annually; it is composed of delegates appointed by the member states. The 13-member Executive Committee is elected by the General Assembly from among the member states' delegates, and is chaired by the President, who has a four-year term of office. The permanent administrative organ is the General Secretariat, headed by the Secretary General, who is appointed by the General Assembly.

President, Ivan Barbot.

UK Office, Criminal Investigation Department, New Scotland Yard, SW1H 0BG.—*UK Representative*, J. A. Smith, QPM.

INTERNATIONAL ENERGY AGENCY
Chateau de la Muette, 2 rue Andre-Pascal, 75775 Paris, France

The International Energy Agency (IEA), founded in November 1974, is an autonomous agency within the framework of the Organization for Economic Co-operation and Development (OECD). The IEA had 21 member countries at June 1990.

The IEA's objectives include improvement of energy supply and demand worldwide, increased efficiency, development of alternative energy sources and the promotion of relations between oil producing and oil consuming countries. The IEA also maintains an emergency system to alleviate the effects of severe oil supply disruptions.

The main decision-making body is the Governing Board composed of senior energy officials from member countries. Various standing groups and special committees exist to facilitate the work of the Board. The IEA Secretariat, with a staff of energy experts, carries out the work of the Governing Board and its subordinate bodies. The Executive Director is appointed by the Board.

Executive Director, Mrs. Helga Steeg (*Federal Rep. of Germany*).

INTERNATIONAL MARITIME SATELLITE ORGANIZATION
40 Melton Street, London NW1 2EQ

The International Maritime Satellite Organization (Inmarsat) was founded in July 1978 and began operations on February 1, 1982. Inmarsat operates a system of satellites to provide telephone, telex, data and facsimile transmission, as well as distress and safety communication services to the world's shipping, aviation and offshore industries.

Inmarsat comprises three bodies: the Assembly the Council and the Directorate. The Assembly is composed of representatives of all member countries, each with one vote. It meets every two years to review activities and objectives, to make recommendations to the Council. The Council is the main decision-making body and consists of representatives of the 18 members with the largest investment shares. Four others who represent the interests of developing countries are elected to the Council on the basis of geographical representation. The Council meets at least three times a year and oversees the activities of the Directorate, the permanent staff of Inmarsat.

As at May 1990 there were 59 member countries.
Director General, Olof Lundberg.

INTERNATIONAL RED CROSS AND RED CRESCENT MOVEMENT
17 avenue de la Paix, 1211 Geneva, Switzerland

The International Red Cross and Red Crescent Movement is composed of three elements. The International Committee of the Red Cross (ICRC) is the founding body of the Red Cross and was formed in 1863. It is a neutral intermediary negotiating between warring factions, working throughout the world to protect and assist victims of armed conflict. It also ensures the application of the Geneva Conventions with regard to prisoners of war and detainees.

The League of Red Cross and Red Crescent Societies, founded in 1919, is the international federation which exists to contribute to the development of the humanitarian activities of National Societies, to co-ordinate their relief operations for victims of natural disasters, and to care for refugees outside areas of conflict. There are national Red Cross and Red Crescent Societies in 149 countries with a global membership of 250 million.

The International Conference of the Red Cross and Red Crescent meets every four years, bringing together delegates of the ICRC, the League and the National Societies, as well as representatives of nations bound by the Geneva Conventions.
President of the ICRC, Cornelio Sommaruga.
British Red Cross Society, 9 Grosvenor Crescent, SW1X 7EJ.—*Acting Director-General*, Lt.-Gen. Sir Cameron Moffat, KBE.

INTERNATIONAL TELECOMMUNICATIONS SATELLITE ORGANIZATION
3400 International Drive NW, Washington DC 20008–3098, USA

Formed in 1964, the International Telecommunications Satellite Organization (Intelsat) owns and operates the world-wide commercial communications satellite system. The system is composed of a network of thirteen satellites and more than 800 antennas which link together over 700 member and non-member users.

Intelsat provides an international telephony service; an international television service; the Intelsat Business Service (IBS); Intelnet (a digital service designed for data collection and distribution); domestic telecommunications services and the Vista service providing telecommunications to remote communities.

Each of the 117 national signatories contributes to the capital costs of the organization in proportion to its investment share. The investment share is based on the relative usage of the system by member countries.

There is a four-tier hierarchy. The Assembly of Parties to the agreement meets every two years to consider long-term objectives and is composed of representatives of the member governments. The Meeting of Signatories annually considers the financial, technical and operational aspects of the system. The Board of Governors has 28 members; the Executive Organ is the permanent staff of Intelsat and is headed by a Director General who reports to the Board of Governors.

LEAGUE OF ARAB STATES
Maidane Al-Tahrir, Nile Cornish, Cairo, Egypt

The purpose of the League of Arab States (founded 1945) is to ensure co-operation among member states and protect their independence and sovereignty, to supervise the affairs and interests of Arab countries and to control the execution of agreements concluded among the member states. The League considers itself a regional organization and is an observer at the United Nations.

Member states are Algeria, Bahrain, Djibouti, Egypt, Iraq, Jordan, Kuwait, Lebanon, Libya, Mauritania, Morocco, Oman, Palestine, Qatar, Saudi Arabia, Somalia, Sudan, Syria, Tunisia, United Arab Emirates and the Republic of Yemen.
Secretary General, Chedli Klibi (*Tunisia*).
UK Office— 52 Green Street, WIY 3RH. *Head of Mission in London*, Assaad Moukaddem.

NORTH ATLANTIC TREATY ORGANIZATION
Brussels 1110, Belgium

The North Atlantic Treaty was signed on April 4, 1949, by the foreign ministers of twelve nations: Belgium, Canada, Denmark, France, Iceland, Italy, Luxembourg, the Netherlands, Norway, Portugal, the UK and USA. Greece and Turkey acceded to the Treaty in 1952, the Federal Republic of Germany in 1955, and Spain in 1982.

The North Atlantic Council, chaired by the Secretary General, is the highest authority of the Alliance and is composed of permanent representatives of the sixteen member countries. It meets at ministerial level (foreign ministers) at least twice a year. The permanent representatives (Ambassadors) head national delegations of advisers and experts.

Defence matters are dealt with in the Defence Planning Committee (DPC), composed of representatives of all member countries, except France. Within the specialized field of defence, the DPC has the same functions and authority as the Council. Like the Council it meets regularly at ambassador level and twice a year in ministerial sessions, when the nations are represented by their defence ministers.

The Council/DPC, as a forum for confidential and constant inter-governmental consultation and as the main decision-making body within the North Atlantic Alliance, is assisted by an International Staff, divided into five divisions: Political Affairs; Defence Planning and Policy; Defence Support; Infrastructure, Logistics and Civil Emergency Planning; Scientific Affairs.
UK Permanent Representative, His Excellency Sir Michael Alexander KCMG.

The senior military authority in NATO, under the Council and DPC, is the Military Committee composed of the Chief of Defence of each member country except France and Iceland. The Military Committee, which is assisted by an international military staff, also meets in permanent session with permanent military representatives and is responsible for making recommendations to the Council and Defence Planning Committee on measures considered necessary for the common defence of the NATO area and for supplying guidance on military matters to the Major NATO Commanders.
Chairman of the Military Committee, Gen. Vigleik Eide (*Norway*).

The strategic area covered by the North Atlantic Treaty is divided among three Commands (European, Atlantic and Channel) and a Regional Planning Group (Canada and the United States).

The Major NATO Commanders are responsible for the development of defence plans for their respective areas, for the determination of force requirements and for the deployment and exercise of the forces under their command. The Major NATO Commanders report to the Military Committee.

The three Major NATO Commanders are:

Supreme Allied Commander, Europe, Gen. John R. Galvin (*US*).

Supreme Allied Commander, Atlantic, Adm. Leon A. Edney (*US*).

Commander-in-Chief, Channel, Adm. Sir Benjamin Bathurst, KCB (*UK*).

Secretary General, Manfred Wörner (*Federal Rep. of Germany*).

ORGANIZATION FOR ECONOMIC CO-OPERATION AND DEVELOPMENT
2 rue André-Pascal, 75116 Paris

Formed on September 30, 1961, the Organization for Economic Co-operation and Development (OECD) replaced the Organization for European Economic Co-operation. The OECD is the instrument for international co-operation among industrialized member countries on economic and social policies. Its objectives are to assist its member governments in the formulation and co-ordination of policies designed to achieve high, sustained economic growth while maintaining financial stability, to contribute to world trade on a multilateral basis and to stimulate members' aid to developing countries.

The following countries belong to the OECD: Australia, Austria, Belgium, Canada, Denmark, Federal Republic of Germany, Finland, France, Greece, Iceland, Republic of Ireland, Italy, Japan, Luxembourg, the Netherlands, New Zealand, Norway, Portugal, Spain, Sweden, Switzerland, Turkey, UK and USA (Yugoslavia participates with a special status).

The Council is the supreme body of the Organization. Composed of one representative for each member country, it meets at permanent representative level under the Chairmanship of the Secretary General, or at ministerial level (usually once a year) under the Chairmanship of a minister elected annually. Decisions and recommendations are adopted by mutual agreement of all members of the Council. Fourteen members of the Council are chosen annually to form an Executive Committee to assist the Council. However, most of the OECD's work is undertaken in over 200 specialized committees and working parties. Five autonomous or semi-autonomous bodies are related in varying degrees to the Organization: the Nuclear Energy Agency, the International Energy Agency, the Development Centre, the Centre for Educational Research and Innovation, and the European Conference of Ministers of Transport. These bodies, the committees and the Council are serviced by an international Secretariat headed by the Secretary General of the Organization.

Secretary General, Jean-Claude Paye (*France*).

UK Permanent Representative, John Walton David Gray, CMG, 19 rue de Franqueville, Paris 75116.

ORGANIZATION OF AFRICAN UNITY
PO Box 3243, Addis Ababa, Ethiopia

The Organization of African Unity (OAU) was established in 1963 and has 50 members. It aims to further African unity and solidarity, to co-ordinate political, economic, social and defence policies, and to eliminate colonialism in Africa.

The chief organs are the Assembly of heads of state or government and the Council of foreign ministers. The main administrative body is the Secretariat, based in Addis Ababa.

Sec. Gen., Salim Ahmed Salim (*Tanzania*).

ORGANIZATION OF AMERICAN STATES
17th Street and Constitution Ave. NW, Washington DC 20006, USA

Originally founded in 1890 for largely commercial purposes, the Organization of American States (OAS) adopted its present name and charter in 1948. Its aims are to strengthen the peace and security of the continent; to prevent possible causes of difficulties and to ensure the pacific settlement of disputes that may arise among the member states; to provide for common action on the part of those states in the event of aggression; to seek the solution of political, judicial and economic problems that may arise among them; and to promote, by co-operative action, their economic, social and cultural development. The OAS is a regional organization within the United Nations.

Policy is determined by the annual General Assembly. Meetings of Ministers of Foreign Affairs consider urgent problems, and advise in cases of armed attack and threats to peace.

The 33 member states are Antigua and Barbuda, Argentina, Bahamas, Barbados, Bolivia, Brazil, Canada, Chile, Colombia, Costa Rica, Cuba, Dominica, Dominican Republic, Ecuador, Grenada, Guatemala, Haiti, Honduras, Jamaica, Mexico, Nicaragua, Panama, Paraguay, Peru, St. Christopher and Nevis, St. Lucia, St. Vincent and the Grenadines, El Salvador, Suriname, Trinidad and Tobago, USA, Uruguay and Venezuela.

Secretary General, João Clemente Baena Soares (*Brazil*).

ORGANIZATION OF ARAB PETROLEUM EXPORTING COUNTRIES
PO Box 20501 Safat, 13066 Kuwait

The Organization of Arab Petroleum and Exporting Countries (OAPEC) was founded in 1968. The objectives of the organization are to promote co-operation in economic activities; to safeguard members' interests; to unite efforts to ensure the flow of oil to consumer markets; and to create a favourable climate for the investment of capital and expertise.

The Ministerial Council is composed of oil ministers from the member countries and meets twice a year to determine policy, to direct activities and to approve the budgets and accounts of the General Secretariat and the Judicial Tribunal. The Judicial Tribunal is composed of nine part-time judges who rule on disputes between member nations and disputes between nations and oil companies. The executive organ of OAPEC is the General Secretariat.

The member countries of OAPEC are Algeria, Bahrain, Egypt, Iraq, Kuwait, Libya, Qatar, Saudi Arabia, Syria and the United Arab Emirates. (Tunisia's membership has been inactive since 1987).

Acting Secretary General, Abdelaziz Alwattari.

ORGANIZATION OF THE PETROLEUM EXPORTING COUNTRIES
Obere Donaustrasse 93, 1020 Vienna, Austria

The Organization of the Petroleum Exporting Countries (OPEC) was created in 1960 as a permanent intergovernmental organization with the aims of unifying and co-ordinating the pertroleum policies of members and determining the best means of protecting their interests, individually and collectively.

The supreme authority is the Conference of Ministers of Oil, Mines and Energy of member countries which meets at least twice a year and formulates policy. The Board of Governors, nominated by member countries, directs the management of OPEC and implements Conference resolutions. The Secretariat, based in Vienna, carries out executive functions under the direction of the Board of Governors.

The 13 member countries are Algeria, Ecuador, Gabon, Indonesia, Iran, Iraq, Kuwait, Libya, Nigeria, Qatar, Saudi Arabia, UAE and Venezuela.

Secretary General, Dr. Subrota (*Indonesia*).

SOUTH PACIFIC COMMISSION
Anse Vata, Noumea, New Caledonia

The South Pacific Commission is a technical assistance agency with an advisory and consultative role in such fields as marine resources, rural management and technology, and community and education services. The management committee is involved with the day-to-day running of the organization and is headed by the Secretary General. The other members are the Director and the Deputy Director of Programmes.

The South Pacific Commission was established in February 1947 following the signing of the Canberra Agreement by the governments of Australia, France, the Netherlands, New Zealand, the UK and the USA. The aim was to promote the economic and social stability of the islands in the region.

In 1983, the South Pacific Conference adopted a resolution that the Conference's 27 governments and administrations should have full and equal membership. Since 1967 the Conference has met annually to discuss the future policy of the Commission, to adopt the budget and to nominate the officers of the Commission.

Secretary General, Atanraoi Baiteke (*Kiribati*).

Director of Programmes, Hélène Courte (*New Caledonia*).

Deputy Director of Programmes, Vaasatia Poloma Komiti (*Western Samoa*).

THE WORLD COUNCIL OF CHURCHES
PO Box 2100, 1211 Geneva 2
Switzerland

The World Council of Churches (WCC) was constituted in Amsterdam in 1948 to promote unity among the many different Christian churches. The 311 member churches of the WCC have adherents in more than 100 countries. With the exception of Roman Catholicism, virtually all Christian traditions are included in the WCC membership.

The policies of the Council are determined by delegates of the member churches meeting in Assembly, about every eight years, the next Assembly being in Canberra, Australia, in February 1991. More detailed decisions are taken by a 150-member Central Committee which is elected by the Assembly and meets, with the seven WCC Presidents, annually. The Central Committee in turn appoints a smaller Executive Committee and also nominates commissions and working groups, to guide the various programmes.

General Secretary, Dr. Emilio Castro (*Uruguay*).

British Council of Churches, 35–41 Lower Marsh, SE1 7RL.

WORLD FEDERATION OF TRADE UNIONS
Vinohradska 10, 12147 Prague 2, Czechoslovakia

The World Federation of Trade Unions (WFTU) was founded in October 1945. In 1949 a number of members withdrew and founded the International Confederation of Free Trade Unions. The WFTU now has 94 affiliated federations with 214 million members, mainly in Eastern Europe and the developing nations.

The Congress, which is comprised of delegates from member nations, meets every four years to review WFTU's work and to elect the General Council and Bureau. The General Council is elected from members of national federations and meets once a year. Each affiliated organization has one member and one deputy. The Bureau of 40 members is elected by the General Council and carries out the executive work of the WFTU

General Secretary, Ibrahim Zakaria (*Sudan*).

BROADCASTING

BRITISH BROADCASTING CORPORATION
(see also entry on page 303)

Radio

BBC Radio broadcasts five national services to the United Kingdom, Isle of Man and the Channel Islands plus a sixth tier consisting of national regional services in Wales, Scotland and Northern Ireland and local radio services in England and the Channel Islands. In Wales there are two regional services based on the Welsh and English languages respectively.

The five national services are:

Radio 1: (Pop and rock music network)—5 a.m.–2 a.m. daily. Frequencies: VHF-FM 98–99 MHz, coverage 86%; MW 1053 kHz/285m and 1089 kHz/275m, plus two local fillers giving population coverage 96% (day) and 57% (night).

Radio 2: (Light music, entertainment and sport)—24 hours a day. Frequency: VHF-FM 88–90·2 MHz, coverage 98%.

Radio 3: (Serious music, drama and documentaries, poetry, and cricket in season)—6.55 a.m.–12 midnight daily. Frequencies: VHF-FM 90·2–92·4 MHz, population coverage 98%; MW (main centres of population only), 1215 kHz/247m, plus four local fillers on 1197 kHz/251m, coverage 87% (day) and 38% (night).

Radio 4: (News, documentaries, drama and entertainment)—5.50 a.m. to 12.45 a.m. daily. Frequencies: VHF-FM England, CI and IOM plus part of Wales, Scotland and N. Ireland 92·4–95·8 MHz, coverage 92%; LW 198kHz/1515m, plus eight local fillers on MW giving population coverage 98% (day) and 91% (night).

Radio 5: (Speech radio for the family, with sport, education, children and youth programmes and elements of World Service)—6a.m.–12 midnight daily. Frequencies: MW 693 kHz/433m and 909 kHz/330m, plus three local fillers giving population coverage 98% (day) and 65% (night).

The national regional services are:

Radio Scotland: Frequencies: MW 810 kHz/370m plus two local fillers, coverage 95% (day) and 87% (night); VHF-FM 92–95 MHz, coverage 94%.
   Local programmes on VHF-FM 92–95 MHz: *Radio Aberdeen* (also MW 990 kHz/303m); *Radio Highland; Radio nan Eilean; Radio nan Gaidheal; Radio Orkney; Radio Shetland; Radio Solway* (also MW 585 kHz/513m); *Radio Tweed.*

Radio Ulster: Frequencies: MW 1341 kHz/224m, plus one local filler, coverage 96% (day) and 80% (night); VHF-FM 92–95 MHz, coverage 97%.
   Radio Foyle: Frequencies: MW 792 kHz/379m; VHF-FM 92–95 MHz.

Radio Wales: Frequency: MW 882 kHz/340m and 1125 kHz plus two local fillers giving coverage 96% (day) and 63% (night).
   Radio Clwyd: Frequency: MW 657 kHz/457m.

Radio Cymru (Welsh-language): Frequencies: VHF-FM 92–95 MHz, coverage 91%.

Local Radio: There are 38 local stations serving England and the Channel Islands (*see* below).

Television

The BBC's experiments in television broadcasting started in 1929 and in 1936 the BBC began the world's first public service of high-definition television from Alexandra Palace.
   The BBC broadcasts two national television services, BBC 1 (BBC Wales in Wales, BBC Scotland in

Scotland, BBC Northern Ireland in Northern Ireland) and BBC 2. These are broadcast in colour on 625-lines and UHF from a network of transmitting stations planned and built jointly with the Independent Broadcasting Authority. All stations (with a few exceptions) carry four channels including the two IBA channels.
   Transmissions from 50 main stations and more than 800 relays are available to more than 99 per cent of the population.

World Service

The World Service broadcasts 780 hours of programmes a week in 38 languages including the English Service. Ninety-five transmitters are used, 44 of them in the UK and 51 at relay stations overseas. In addition the World Service supplies many recorded programmes to other radio stations.

World Service in English, 24 hours a day, directed to all parts of the world, and with additional streams of programmes specially designated for audiences in Africa and South Asia at appropriate peak listening times.

African Service, which broadcasts in Swahili, Somali and Hausa.

Arabic Service, on the air for 9 hours a day to Middle East and North Africa.

Central European Service, in Czech and Slovak, Hungarian, Polish and Finnish.

Eastern Service, which broadcasts in Bengali, Burmese, Hindi, Nepali, Pashto, Persian, Sinhalese, Tamil and Urdu.

Far Eastern Service, in Chinese (Cantonese and Mandarin), Indonesian, Japanese, Malay, Thai and Vietnamese.

French and Portuguese Service, directed to Europe and Africa.

German Service, directed to Germany, Austria, and German-speaking Switzerland.

Latin American Service, in Spanish and Portuguese.

Russian Service, on the air for 6¼ hours a day in Russian to the USSR.

South-East European Service, in Bulgarian, Romanian, Serbo-Croat, Slovene, Greek and Turkish.

BBC English by Radio and Television teaches English to learners outside Britain through radio, television and a wide range of published courses.

Monitoring Service provides regional summaries and a teleprinted news service from the output of overseas radio stations.

Topical Tapes provides a variety of programmes on tape for overseas radio stations and produces the twice-weekly 'Calling the Falklands' programme.

Transcription Service produces and sells to overseas radio stations recorded programmes drawn from the whole range of BBC Radio.

BBC Local Radio Stations

BEDFORDSHIRE, PO Box 476, Hastings Street, Luton LU1 5BA. (Tel: 0582-459111). *Wavelengths*: 258/476m, 1161/630 kHz, 95·5/103·8/104·5 VHF-FM.

BERKSHIRE/SURREY, BBC Berkshire, Portman Road, Reading; BBC Surrey, University of Surrey Campus, Guildford GU2 5XH. Broadcasting from 1991. *Wavelengths:* 94·6/95·4/104·1/104·4/104·6 VHF-FM.

BRISTOL, 3 Tyndalls Park Road, Bristol BS8 1PP. (Tel: 0272-741111). *Wavelengths:* 194/227m, 1548/1323 kHz, 94·9/95·5/104·6 VHF-FM.

CAMBRIDGESHIRE, Broadcasting House, 104 Hills Road, Cambridge CB2 1LD. (Tel: 0223-315970). *Wavelengths*: 207/292m, 1449/1026 kHz, 96·0/95·7 VHF-FM.

CLEVELAND, PO Box 1548, Broadcasting House, Newport Road, Middlesbrough, Cleveland TS1 5DG. (Tel: 0642-225211). *Wavelengths*: 194m, 1548 kHz, 95·0/95·8 VHF-FM.

CORNWALL, Phoenix Wharf, Truro, Cornwall TR1 1UA. (Tel: 0872-75421). *Wavelengths*: 476/457m, 630/657 kHz, 95·2/96·0/103·9 VHF-FM.

CUMBRIA, Hilltop Heights, London Road, Carlisle CA1 2NA. (Tel: 0228-31661). *Wavelengths*: 397/206/ 358m, 756/1458/837 kHz, 95·2/95·6/96·1/104·2 VHF-FM.

CWR (COVENTRY AND WARWICKSHIRE RADIO), 25 Warwick Road, Coventry CV1 2FA. (Tel: 0203-525341). *Wavelengths*: 94·8/103·7 VHF-FM.

DERBY, 56 St. Helen's Street, Derby DE1 3HT. (Tel: 0332-361111). *Wavelengths*: 269m, 1116 kHz, 104·5/ 94·2/95·3 VHF-FM.

DEVON, PO Box 100, St. David's Hill, Exeter EX4 4DB. (Tel: 0392-215651). *Wavelengths*: 351/303/206/375m, 855/990/1458/801 kHz, 103·4/96·0/95·8/94·8 VHF-FM.

ESSEX, 198 New London Road, Chelmsford CM2 9AB. (Tel: 0245-262393). *Wavelengths*: 392/196/412m, 765/ 729/1530 kHz, 103·5/95·3 VHF-FM.

GLOUCESTERSHIRE, London Road, Gloucester GL1 1SW. (Tel: 0452-308585). *Wavelengths*: 498m, 603 kHz, 95·0/104·7 VHF-FM.

GLR (GREATER LONDON RADIO), 35A Marylebone High Street, W1A 4LG. (Tel: 071-224 2424). *Wavelengths*: 206m, 1458 kHz, 94·9 VHF-FM.

GMR (GREATER MANCHESTER RADIO), PO Box 90, New Broadcasting House, Oxford Road, Manchester M60 1SJ. (Tel: 061-228 3434). *Wavelengths*: 206m, 1458 kHz, 95·1 VHF-FM.

HEREFORD AND WORCESTER, 43 Broad Street, Hereford HR4 9HH; and Hylton Road, Worcester WR2 5WW. (Tel: 0905-748485). *Wavelengths*: 819 kHz (Hereford); 738 kHz (Worcester); 104·0/ 94·7/104·6 VHF-FM.

HUMBERSIDE, 63 Jameson Street, Hull HU1 3NU. (Tel: 0482-23232). *Wavelengths*: 202m, 1485 kHz, 95·9 VHF-FM.

KENT, Sun Pier, Chatham, Kent ME4 4EZ. (Tel: 0634-830505). *Wavelengths*: 290/388/187m, 1035/774/1602 kHz, 96·7/104·2 VHF-FM.

LANCASHIRE, 20–26 Darwen Street, Blackburn BB2 2EA. (Tel: 0254-62411). *Wavelengths*: 351/193m, 855/ 1557 kHz, 95·5/104·5/103·9 VHF-FM.

LEEDS, Broadcasting House, Woodhouse Lane, Leeds LS2 9PN. (Tel: 0532-442131). *Wavelengths*: 388m, 774 kHz, 92·4/95·3 VHF-FM.

LEICESTER, Epic House, Charles Street, Leicester LE1 3SH. (Tel: 0533-516688). *Wavelengths*: 358m, 837 kHz, 104·9/95·1 VHF-FM.

LINCOLNSHIRE, Radio Buildings, PO Box 219, Newport, Lincoln LN1 3EU. (Tel: 0522-511411). *Wavelengths*: 219m, 1368 kHz, 94·9 VHF-FM.

MERSEYSIDE, 55 Paradise Street, Liverpool L1 3BP. (Tel: 051-708 5500). *Wavelengths*: 202m, 1485 kHz, 95·8 VHF-FM.

NEWCASTLE, Broadcasting Centre, Barrack Road, Fenham, Newcastle upon Tyne NE99 1RN. (Tel: 091-232 4141). *Wavelengths*: 206m, 1458 kHz, 95·4/ 104·4/96·0 VHF-FM.

NORFOLK, Norfolk Tower, Surrey Street, Norwich NR1 3PA. (Tel: 0603-617411). *Wavelengths*: 351/ 344m, 855/873 kHz, 95·1/104·4 VHF-FM.

NORTHAMPTON, PO Box 1107, Abington Street, Northampton NN1 2BE. (Tel: 0604-239100). *Wavelengths*: 271m, 1107 kHz, 104·2/103·6 VHF-FM.

NOTTINGHAM, York House, Mansfield Road, Nottingham NG13JA. (Tel: 0602-415161). *Wavelengths*: 197/189m, 1521/1584 kHz, 103·8/95·5 VHF-FM.

OXFORD, 269 Banbury Road, Oxford OX2 7DW. (Tel:

0865-311444). *Wavelengths*: 202m, 1485 kHz, 95·2 VHF-FM.

SHEFFIELD, Ashdell Grove, 60 Westbourne Road, Sheffield S10 2QU. (Tel: 0742-686185). *Wavelengths*: 290m, 1035 kHz, 104·1/88·6 VHF-FM.

SHROPSHIRE, 2–4 Boscobel Drive, Shrewsbury SY1 3TT. (Tel: 0743-248484). *Wavelengths*: 189/397m, 1584/756 kHz, 95·0/96·0 VHF-FM.

SOLENT, South Western House, Canute Road, Southampton SO9 4PJ. (Tel: 0703-631311). *Wavelengths*: 300m, 999 kHz, 96·1 VHF-FM, 221m, 1359 kHz.

STOKE-ON-TRENT, Conway House, Cheapside, Hanley, Stoke-on-Trent ST1 1JJ. (Tel: 0782-208080). *Wavelengths*: 200m, 1503 kHz, 94·6 VHF-FM.

SUFFOLK, Broadcasting House, St. Matthew's Street, Ipswich IP1 3EP. (Tel: 0473-250000). *Wavelengths*: 103·9/104·6 VHF-FM.

SUSSEX, Marlborough Place, Brighton BN1 1TU (Tel: 0273-680231). *Wavelengths*: 202/258/219m, 1485/ 1161/1368 kHz, 95·3/104·5/104·0/95·1 VHF-FM.

WILTSHIRE SOUND, Broadcasting House, 56–58 Prospect Place, Swindon SN1 3RW. (Tel: 0793-513626). *Wavelengths*: 1332/1368 kHz, 103·6/104·3/103·5 VHF-FM.

WM (WEST MIDLANDS), PO Box 206, Pebble Mill Road, Birmingham B5 7SD. (Tel: 021-414 8484). *Wavelengths*: 206/362m, 1458/828 kHz, 95·6 VHF-FM.

YORK, 20 Bootham Row, York YO3 7BR. (Tel: 0904-641351). *Wavelengths*: 450/238m, 666/1260 kHz, 103·7/104·3/95·5 VHF-FM.

Stations outside the UK:—

GUERNSEY, Commerce House, Les Banques, St. Peter Port, Guernsey. (Tel: 0481-28977). *Wavelengths*: 269m, 1116 kHz, 93·2 VHF-FM.

JERSEY, Broadcasting House, Rouge Bouillon, St. Helier, Jersey. (Tel: 0534-70000). *Wavelengths*: 292m, 1026 kHz, 88·8 VHF-FM.

INDEPENDENT BROADCASTING AUTHORITY
(*see also* entry on pages 332)

Independent Television Companies

(Only one address is given for each company)

ANGLIA TELEVISION (*East of England*), Anglia House, Norwich. (Tel: 0603-615151).

BORDER TELEVISION (*The Borders*), Television Centre, Carlisle. (Tel: 0228-25101).

CENTRAL INDEPENDENT TELEVISION (*East and West Midlands*), Central House, Broad Street, Birmingham. (Tel: 021-643 9898).

CHANNEL FOUR TELEVISION COMPANY LTD, 60 Charlotte Street, W1. (Tel: 071-631 4444).

CHANNEL TELEVISION (*Channel Islands*), The Television Centre, St. Helier, Jersey. (Tel: 0534-73999).

GRAMPIAN TELEVISION (*North Scotland*), Queen's Cross, Aberdeen. (Tel: 0224-646464).

GRANADA TELEVISION (*North-West England*), Granada TV Centre, Manchester. (Tel: 061-832 7211).

HTV (*Wales and West of England*), HTV Wales, Television Centre, Cardiff CF5 6XJ. (Tel: 0222-590590).

INDEPENDENT TELEVISION COMPANIES ASSOCIATION LTD., Knighton House, 56 Mortimer Street, W1. (Tel: 071-636 6866).

INDEPENDENT TELEVISION NEWS LTD., ITN House, 48 Wells Street, W1. (Tel: 071-637 2424).

LONDON WEEKEND TELEVISION (*London* (*weekends*)), South Bank Television Centre, SE1 9LT. (Tel: 071-620 1620).

ORACLE TELETEXT LTD., Craven House, 25–32 Marshall Street, W1. (Tel: 071-434 3121).

SCOTTISH TELEVISION (*Central Scotland*), Cowcaddens, Glasgow. (Tel: 041-332 9999).

THAMES TELEVISION (*London* (*weekdays*)), Thames Television House, 306–316 Euston Road, NW1. (Tel: 071-387 9494).

TSW (TELEVISION SOUTH WEST) (*South-West England*), Derry's Cross, Plymouth. (Tel: 0752-663322).

TV-AM, Hawley Crescent, NW1. (Tel: 071-267 4300).

TVS (TELEVISION SOUTH) (*South and South-East England*), Television Centre, Southampton. (Tel: 0703-34211).

TYNE TEES TELEVISION (*North-East England*), The Television Centre, City Road, Newcastle upon Tyne. (Tel: 091-261 0181).

ULSTER TELEVISION (*Northern Ireland*), Havelock House, Ormeau Road, Belfast. (Tel: 0232-228122).

WELSH FOURTH CHANNEL AUTHORITY (Sianel Pedwar Cymru), Sophia Close, Cardiff CF1 9XY. (Tel: 0222-43421).

YORKSHIRE TELEVISION (*Yorkshire*), The Television Centre, Leeds. (Tel: 0532-438283).

Independent Local Radio Stations

BEACON RADIO (Beacon Broadcasting Ltd.), PO Box 303, 267 Tettenhall Road, Wolverhampton. (Tel: 0902-757211). *Wavelengths*: 303m, 990 kHz, 97·2 VHF-FM.

BRMB RADIO, (Birmingham Broadcasting Ltd.), PO Box 555, Radio House, Aston Road North, Aston, Birmingham. (Tel: 021-359 4481/9). *Wavelengths*: 261m, 1152 kHz, 96·4 VHF-FM.

CAPITAL RADIO PLC, Euston Tower, NW1. (Tel: 01-388 1288). *Wavelengths*: 194m, 1548 kHz, 95·8 VHF-FM.

CHILTERN RADIO PLC, Chiltern Radio, Dunstable, Bedfordshire. (Tel: 0582-666001). *Wavelengths*: 362m, 828 kHz, 97·6 VHF-FM (Luton), 379m, 792 kHz, 96·9 VHF-FM (Bedford).

COUNTY SOUND PLC, The Friary, Guildford. (Tel: 0483-505566). *Wavelengths*: 203m, 1476 kHz, 96·4 VHF-FM.

DEVONAIR RADIO, The Studio Centre, 35–37 St. David's Hill, Exeter EX4 4DA. (Tel: 0392-430703). *Wavelengths*: 666 kHz, VHF-FM 97·0 (Exeter); 954 kHz, VHF-FM 96·4 (Torbay); VHF-FM 103 (Opt-out service for East Devon, West Dorset and South Somerset).

DOWNTOWN RADIO (Community Radio Services Ltd.), PO Box 293, Kiltonga Industrial Estate, Newtownards, Northern Ireland. (Tel: 0247-815555). *Wavelengths*: 293m, 1026 kHz, 97·4 VHF-FM.

ESSEX RADIO PLC, Radio House, Clifftown Road, Southend-on-Sea. (Tel: 0702-333711). *Wavelengths*: 210m, 1431 kHz, 96·3 VHF-FM (Southend), 220m, 1359 kHz, 102·6 VHF-FM (Chelmsford).

GWR RADIO WEST PLC, PO Box 963, Watershed, Canons Road, Bristol. (Tel: 0272-279900). *Wavelengths*: 238m, 1260 kHz, 96·3 VHF-FM.

GWR (Wiltshire Radio) PLC, Old Lime Kiln, High Street, Wootton Bassett, Swindon. (Tel: 0793-853222). *Wavelengths*: 258m, 1161 kHz, 97·2 VHF-FM (Swindon), 321m, 936 kHz, 102·6 VHF-FM (West Wiltshire).

HEREWARD RADIO LTD., PO Box 225, 114 Bridge Street, Peterborough. (Tel: 0733-46225). *Wavelengths*: 225m, 1332 kHz, 102·7 VHF-FM.

INVICTA RADIO PLC (incorporating Northdown Radio), 15 Station Road East, Canterbury, Kent. (Tel: 0227-58761). *Wavelengths*: 242m, 1242 kHz, 103·1 VHF-FM.

INVICTA RADIO PLC (incorporating Network East Kent), 15 Station Road East, Canterbury, Kent. (Tel: 0227-58761). *Wavelengths*: 497m, 603 kHz, 97·0 VHF-FM (Dover), 95·9 VHF-FM (Thanet), 102·8 VHF-FM (Canterbury), 96·1 MHz (Ashford).

JAZZ FM, 26–27 Castlereagh Street, W1H 5YR. (Tel: 071-706 4100). *Wavelength*: VHF 102·2 MHz.

LBC (London Broadcasting Company Ltd.), Crown House, 72 Hammersmith Road, W14 8YE. (Tel: 071-371 1515). *Wavelengths*: 261m, 1152 kHz, 97·3 VHF-FM.

LEICESTER SOUND, Granville House, Granville Road, Leicester LE1 7RW. (Tel: 0533 551616). *Wavelengths*: 238m, VHF-FM 103·2 MHz.

MARCHER SOUND/SAIN-Y-GORORAU, The Studios, Mold Road, Gwersyllt, Wrexham, Clwyd. (Tel: 0978-752202). *Wavelengths*: 238m, 1260 kHz, 95·4 VHF-FM.

MELODY RADIO, 180 Brompton Road, SW3 1HF. (Tel: 071-584 1049). *Wavelength*: VHF 104·9 MHz.

MERCIA SOUND (Midland Community Radio Ltd.), Hertford Place, Coventry. (Tel: 0203-28451). *Wavelengths*: 220m, 1359 kHz, 95·9 VHF-FM.

METRO RADIO (North East Broadcasting Company Ltd.), Radio House, Long Rigg, Swalwell, Newcastle upon Tyne. (Tel: 091-488 3131). *Wavelengths*: 261m, 1152 kHz, 97·1 VHF-FM.

MORAY FIRTH RADIO LTD., PO Box 271, Inverness. (Tel: 0463-224433). *Wavelengths*: 271m, 1107 kHz, 97·4 VHF-FM.

NORTHANTS 96 (Hereward Radio) PLC, PO Box 193, 73 Abington Street, Northampton. (Tel: 0733-46225). *Wavelengths*: 193m, 1557 kHz, 96·6 VHF-FM.

NORTH SOUND (North of Scotland Radio Ltd.), 45 Kings Gate, Aberdeen. (Tel: 0224-632234). *Wavelengths*: 290m, 1035 kHz, 96·9 VHF-FM.

OCEAN SOUND LTD., 43–44 Bedford Place, Southampton. *Wavelengths*: 257m, 1170 kHz, 103·2 VHF-FM (Southampton), 97·5 VHF-FM (Portsmouth).

PENNINE RADIO, (Bradford Community Radio Ltd.), PO Box 235, Pennine House, Forster Square, Bradford. (Tel: 0274-390417). *Wavelengths*: 235/196m, 1278/1530 kHz, 97·5 VHF-FM (Bradford, Huddersfield, Halifax), 102·5 VHF-FM.

PICCADILLY RADIO LTD., 127-131 The Piazza, Piccadilly Plaza, Manchester. (Tel: 061-236 9913). *Wavelengths*: 261m, 1152 kHz, 103·0 VHF-FM.

PLYMOUTH SOUND LTD., Earl's Acre, Alma Road, Plymouth. (Tel: 0752-27272). *Wavelengths*: 261m, 1152 kHz, 96·0 VHF-FM.

RADIO AIRE (West Yorkshire Broadcasting PLC), PO Box 362, 51 Burley Road, Leeds. (Tel: 0532-452299). *Wavelengths*: 362m, 828 kHz, 96·3 VHF-FM.

RADIO BROADLAND, PO Box 260, Norwich. (Tel: 0603-660926). *Wavelengths*: 260m, 1152 kHz, 97·6 MHz.

RADIO CITY (Sound of Merseyside Ltd.), PO Box 194, 8–10 Stanley Street, Liverpool. (Tel: 051-227 5100). *Wavelengths*: 194m, 1548 kHz, 96·7 VHF-FM.

RADIO CLYDE LTD., Clydebank Business Park, Clydebank, Glasgow. (Tel: 041-941 1111). *Wavelengths*: 261m, 1152 kHz, 95·1 VHF-FM.

RADIO FORTH LTD., Forth House, Forth Street, Edinburgh. (Tel: 031-556 9255). *Wavelengths*: 194m, 1548 kHz, 97·3 VHF-FM.

RADIO HALLAM LTD., PO Box 194, Hartshead, Sheffield. (Tel: 0742-71188). *Wavelengths*: 194m, 1548 kHz, 96·1 VHF-FM (Rotherham), 97·4 VHF-FM (Sheffield), 302m, 990 kHz, 103·4 VHF-FM (Doncaster).

RADIO MERCURY, Broadfield House, Brighton Road, Crawley, W. Sussex. (Tel: 0293-519161). *Wavelengths*: 197m, 1521 kHz, 102·7, 97·5 VHF-FM (Horsham).

RADIO ORWELL LTD., Electric House, Lloyds Avenue, Ipswich. (Tel: 0473-216971). *Wavelengths*: 257m, 1170 kHz, 97·1 VHF-FM.

RADIO TAY (Tay Sound Broadcasting Ltd.), PO Box 123, Dundee. (Tel: 0382-29551). *Wavelengths*: 258m, 1161 kHz, 95·8 VHF-FM (Dundee); 189m, 1584 kHz, 96·4 VHF-FM (Perth).

RADIO TFM (Sound Broadcasting (Teesside) Ltd.), 74 Dovecot Street, Stockton-on-Tees, Cleveland. (Tel: 0642-615111). *Wavelengths*: 257m, 1170 kHz, 96·6 VHF-FM.

RADIO TRENT LTD., 29–31 Castle Gate, Nottingham. (Tel: 0602-581731). *Wavelengths*: 301m, 999 kHz, 96·2 VHF-FM.

RADIO 210 THAMES VALLEY (Thames Valley Broadcasting Ltd.), PO Box 210, Reading, Berkshire. (Tel: 0734-413131). *Wavelengths*: 210m, 1431 kHz, 97·0 VHF-FM.

RADIO WYVERN PLC, 5–6 Barbourne Terrace, Worcester. (Tel: 0905-612212). *Wavelengths*: 314m, 954 kHz, 97·6 VHF-FM (Hereford), 196m, 1530 kHz, 102·8 VHF-FM (Worcester).

RED DRAGON RADIO, Radio House, West Canal Wharf, Cardiff. (Tel: 0222-384041). *Wavelengths*: 230m, 1305 kHz, 97·4 VHF-FM.

RED ROSE RADIO PLC, PO Box 301, St. Paul's Square, Preston, Lancashire. (Tel: 0772-556301). *Wavelengths*: 301m, 999 kHz, 97·3 VHF-FM.

SAXON RADIO LTD. IN ASSOCIATION WITH RADIO ORWELL LTD., Long Brackland, Bury St. Edmunds, Suffolk. (Tel: 0284-701511). *Wavelengths*: 240m, 1251 kHz, 96·4 VHF-FM.

SEVERN SOUND (Gloucestershire Broadcasting Company Ltd.), PO Box 388, Old Talbot House, 67 Southgate Street, Gloucester. (Tel: 0452-423791). *Wavelengths*: 388m, 774 kHz, 102·4 VHF-FM.

SIGNAL RADIO, 67–73 Stoke Road, Stoke-on-Trent. (Tel: 0782-417111). *Wavelengths*: 257m, 1170 kHz, 102·6 VHF-FM.

SOUTHERN SOUND PLC, Radio House, Franklin Road, Portslade. (Tel: 0273-422288). *Wavelengths*: 225m, 1332 kHz, 103·4 MHz.

SWANSEA SOUND LTD., Victoria Road, Gowerton, Swansea. (Tel: 0792-893751). *Wavelengths*: 257m, 1170 kHz, 95·1 VHF-FM.

TWO COUNTIES RADIO LTD., 5–7 Southcote Road, Bournemouth. (Tel: 0202-294881). *Wavelengths*: 362m, 828 kHz, 97·2 VHF-FM.

VIKING RADIO LTD., Commercial Road, Hull. (Tel: 0482-25141). *Wavelengths*: 258m, 1161 kHz, 96·9 VHF-FM.

WEST SOUND (Radio Ayrshire Ltd.), Radio House, 54 Holmston Road, Ayr. (Tel: 0292-283662). *Wavelengths*: 290m, 1035 kHz, 96·7 VHF-FM (Ayr), 97·1/ 97·5 VHF-FM (Girvan).

DIRECT BROADCASTING BY SATELLITE TELEVISION STATIONS

BRITISH SATELLITE BROADCASTING, The Marco Polo Building, Queenstown Road, SW8 4NQ. (Tel: 071-978 2222). Broadcasts five channels (*Sport, Power Station, Galaxy, Now* and *Movie Channel*).

SKY TELEVISION, 6 Centaurs Business Park, Grant Way, Isleworth, Middx. TW7 5QD. (Tel: 071-782 3000). Broadcasts four channels (*Sky 1, Sky News, Eurosport* and *Sky Movies*).

SERVICES SOUND AND VISION CORPORATION
(Incorporating BFBS)

Chalfont Grove, Gerrards Cross, Bucks. SL9 8TN
[02407–4461]

The Services Sound and Vision Corporation (SSVC) is the official organization providing the Ministry of Defence, HM Forces and their families with radio and television broadcasting, audio-visual and electronic training and educational support, training film production, and entertainment. The SSVC is a private limited company and registered charity with 1,100 employees and an annual turnover approaching £40 million; financial surpluses are donated to Services' welfare.

The Corporation's radio arm (British Forces Broadcasting Service) operates stations in London, Germany, Gibraltar, Cyprus, the Falklands, Hong Kong, Brunei and Belize. BFBS provides programmes from London for inclusion with local input by its overseas staff, and broadcasts to overseas stations by satellite throughout the year. Cassettes are provided for HM Ships at sea.

SSVC television broadcasts its own, BBC and ITV programmes in Germany, Cyprus and the Falkland Islands. Up to 60 isolated detachments of HM Forces (including ships at sea and the Service Children's Education Authority schools overseas), receive daily TV programmes on cassette.

In-flight films on RAF long-haul passenger services are organized by SSVC and Combined Services Entertainment provides stage shows to such isolated garrisons and units as the Falklands and Ascension Islands. SSVC also operates cinemas around the world.

Audio-visual rentals and sales are provided through SSVC's Sound and Vision Centre shops in Germany and at home.

Training films for the three Armed Services are produced, distributed to units and sold to other governments by SSVC, which has its own crews and studios. Audio-visual and electronic training and educational equipment is assessed, issued to British Forces' units, and maintained by SSVC staff.

All SSVC services are available to other organizations and are provided to overseas governments and many UK companies.

Managing Director, SSVC, A. Protheroe, MBE, TD.

THE BROADCASTING COMPLAINTS COMMISSION
Grosvenor Gardens House, 35–37 Grosvenor Gardens, SW1W 0BS
[071–630 1966]

The Broadcasting Complaints Commission's function and authority derive from the Broadcasting Act 1981 and the Cable and Broadcasting Act 1984. Their task is to consider and adjudicate upon complaints of unjust or unfair treatment in sound or television programmes broadcast by the BBC or the IBA on or after June 1, 1981; or upon complaints of unjust or unfair treatment in programmes included in a licensed cable programme service on or after January 1, 1985 otherwise than by the reception and immediate re-transmission of broadcasts made by a broadcasting body; or upon complaints of unwarranted infringement of privacy in, or in connection with the obtaining of material included in such programmes. This function extends to all sound, television and cable programmes, including advertisements and teletext transmissions and programmes broadcast by the BBC's World Services.

The Members of the Commission are appointed by the Home Secretary.

Chairman, Lady Anglesey, DBE.
Members, D. Allen; T. Christopher, CBE; D. Holmes; H. M. Johnston, CB; Mrs. B. Wells.
Legal Adviser, Sir Basil Hall, KCB, MC, TD.
Secretary, R. D. Hewlett.

PRINCIPAL NEWSPAPERS

DAILY NEWSPAPERS

National

Daily Express, Ludgate House, 245 Blackfriars Road, SE1 9UX.

Daily Mail, Northcliffe House, 2 Derry Street, W8 5TT.

Daily Mirror, Holborn Circus, EC1P 1DQ.

Daily Sport, 3rd Floor, Marten House, 39–47 East Road, N1 6AH

Daily Telegraph, Peterborough Court at South Quay, 181 Marsh Wall, E14 9SR.

Financial Times, 1 Southwark Bridge, SE1 9HL.

The Guardian, 119 Farringdon Road, EC1R 3ER.

The Independent, 40 City Road, EC1Y 2DB.

Morning Star, 74 Luke Street, EC2A 4PY.

Racing Post, 112–120 Coombe Lane, SW20 0BA.

The Sporting Life, Orbit House, 1 New Fetter Lane, EC4A 1AR.

The Star, Ludgate House, 245 Blackfriars Road, SE1 9UX.

The Sun, Virginia Street, E1 9BD.

The Times, 1 Pennington Street, E1 9XN.

Today, 70 Vauxhall Bridge Road, SW1V 2RP.

Regional

ABERDEEN—Press and Journal, and Evening Express, PO Box 43, Lang Stracht, Mastrick, AB9 8AF.

BARROW-IN-FURNESS—North-West Evening Mail, Newspaper House, Abbey Road, LA14 5QS.

BATH—Bath Evening Chronicle, 33–34 Westgate Street, BA1 1EW.

BELFAST—Belfast Telegraph, 124–144 Royal Avenue, BT1 1EB; Irish News and Belfast Morning News, 113–117 Donegall Street, BT1 2GE; News Letter, 51–59 Donegall Street, BT1 2GB.

BIRMINGHAM—The Birmingham Post, and Birmingham Evening Mail, PO Box 18, 28 Colmore Circus, Queensway, B4 6AX (Birmingham Evening Mail B4 6AY).

BLACKBURN—Lancashire Evening Telegraph, Telegraph House, High Street, BB1 1HT.

BLACKPOOL—West Lancashire Evening Gazette, PO Box 20, FY4 4AU.

BOLTON—Bolton Evening News, Newspaper House, Churchgate, BL1 1DE.

BOURNEMOUTH—Evening Echo, Richmond Hill, BH2 6HH.

BRADFORD—Telegraph and Argus, PO Box 234, Hall Ings, BD1 1JR.

BRIGHTON—Evening Argus, Argus House, 89 North Road, BN1 4AU.

BRISTOL—Bristol Evening Post, and Western Daily Press, Temple Way, BS99 7HD.

BURTON-ON-TRENT—Burton Mail, 65–68 High Street, DE14 1LE.

CAMBRIDGE—Cambridge Evening News, 51 Newmarket Road, CB5 8EJ.

CARDIFF—South Wales Echo, and Western Mail, Thomson House, Havelock Street, CF1 1WR.

CHELTENHAM—Gloucestershire Echo, 1 Clarence Parade, GL50 3NZ.

COLCHESTER—Evening Gazette, Oriel House, 43–44 North Hill, CO1 1TZ.

COVENTRY—Coventry Evening Telegraph, Corporation Street, CV1 1FP.

DARLINGTON—Northern Echo, Priestgate, DL1 1NP.

DERBY—Derby Evening Telegraph, Northcliffe House, Meadow Road, DE1 2DW.

DUNDEE—Courier and Advertiser, and Evening Telegraph and Post, 7 Bank Street, DD1 9HU.

EDINBURGH—The Scotsman, and Evening News, 20 North Bridge, EH1 1YT.

EXETER—Express and Echo, Sidwell House, Sidwell Street, EX4 6RS.

GLASGOW—Daily Record, 40 Anderston Quay, G3 8DA; Glasgow Herald, and Evening Times, 195 Albion Street, G1 1QP.

GLOUCESTER—The Gloucestershire Citizen, St. John's Lane, GL1 2AY.

GREENOCK—Greenock Telegraph, 2 Crawfurd Street, PA15 1LH.

GRIMSBY—Grimsby Evening Telegraph, 80 Cleethorpe Road, DN31 3EH.

GUERNSEY—Guernsey Evening Press and Star, PO Box 57, Braye Road, Vale.

HALIFAX—Evening Courier, PO Box 19, Courier Buildings, HX1 2SF.

HARTLEPOOL—Hartlepool Mail, Clarence Road, TS24 8BU.

HUDDERSFIELD—Huddersfield Daily Examiner, Ramsden Street, HD1 2TD.

HULL—Hull Daily Mail, Blundell's Corner, Beverley Road, HU3 1XS.

IPSWICH—East Anglian Daily Times, and Evening Star, 30 Lower Brook Street, IP4 1AN.

JERSEY—Jersey Evening Post, PO Box 582, Five Oaks, St. Saviour.

KETTERING—Northamptonshire Evening Telegraph, Northfield Avenue, NN16 9JN.

LEAMINGTON SPA—Leamington & District Morning News, PO Box 45, Tachbrook Road, CV31 3EP.

LEEDS—Yorkshire Evening Post, and Yorkshire Post, Wellington Street, LS1 1RF.

LEICESTER—Leicester Mercury, St. George Street, LE1 9FQ.

LINCOLN—Lincolnshire Echo, Brayford Wharf East, LN5 7AT.

LIVERPOOL—Daily Post, and Liverpool Echo, PO Box 48, Old Hall Street, L69 3EB.

LONDON—The London Evening Standard, Northcliffe House, 2 Derry Street, W8 5HY.

MAIDSTONE—Kent Evening Post, New Hythe Lane, Larkfield, ME20 6SG.

MANCHESTER—Manchester Evening News, 164 Deansgate, M60 2RD.

MIDDLESBROUGH—Evening Gazette, Gazette Building, Borough Road, TS1 3AZ.

NEWCASTLE UPON TYNE—Evening Chronicle, and The Journal, Thomson House, Groat Market, NE1 1ED.

NEWPORT—South Wales Argus, Cardiff Road, Maesglas, NP9 1QW.

NORTHAMPTON—Chronicle and Echo, Upper Mounts, NN1 3HR.

NORWICH—Eastern Daily Press, and Eastern Evening News, Prospect House, Rouen Road, NR1 1RE.

NOTTINGHAM—Evening Post, Forman Street, NG1 4AB.

NUNEATON—Nuneaton Evening Tribune, Watling House, Whitacre Road, CV11 6BJ.

OLDHAM—Evening Chronicle, 172 Union Street, OL1 1EQ.

OXFORD—Oxford Mail, Newspaper House, Osney Mead, OX2 0EJ.

PAISLEY—Paisley Daily Express, Hellenic House, 87–97 Bath Street, Glasgow, G2 2DZ.

PETERBOROUGH—Peterborough Evening Telegraph, Telegraph House, Priestgate, PE1 1JW.

PLYMOUTH—Western Morning News, and Evening Herald, 65 New George Street, PL1 1RE.

PORTSMOUTH—The News, The News Centre, Hilsea, PO2 9SX.

PRESTON—Lancashire Evening Post, 127 Fishergate, PR1 2DN.

READING—Evening Post, 8 Tessa Road, RG1 8NS.

SCARBOROUGH—Scarborough Evening News, 17–23 Aberdeen Walk, YO11 1BB.

SCUNTHORPE—Scunthorpe Evening Telegraph, Telegraph House, Doncaster Road, DN15 7RE.

SHEFFIELD—The Star, York Street, S1 1PU.

SOUTH SHIELDS—Shields Gazette, Chapter Row, NE33 1BL.

SOUTHAMPTON—Southern Evening Echo, 45 Above Bar, SO9 7BA.

STOKE-ON-TRENT—Evening Sentinel, Sentinel House, Etruria, ST1 5SS.

SUNDERLAND—Sunderland Echo, Pennywell Industrial Estate, SR4 9ER.

SWANSEA—South Wales Evening Post, Adelaide Street, SA1 1QT.

SWINDON—Evening Advertiser, Newspaper House, 100 Victoria Road, SN1 3BE.

TELFORD—Shropshire Star, Ketley, TF1 4HU.

TORQUAY—Herald Express, Harmsworth House, Barton Hill Road, TQ2 8JN.

WEYMOUTH—Dorset Evening Echo, 57 St. Thomas Street, DT4 8EU.

WOLVERHAMPTON—Express and Star, 51–53 Queen Street, WV1 3BU.

WORCESTER—Evening News, St. John's House, St. John's Road, Stourbridge, DY8 1EH.

YORK—Yorkshire Evening Press, PO Box 29, 76–78 Walmgate, YO1 1YN.

WEEKLY NEWSPAPERS

The European—Orbit House, 5 New Fetter Lane, EC4A 1AR.

The Independent on Sunday—40 City Road, EC1Y 2DB.

The Mail on Sunday—Northcliffe House, 2 Derry Street, W8 5TT.

News of the World—Virginia Street, E1 9XR.

The Observer—Chelsea Bridge House, Queenstown Road, SW8 4NN.

The People—Holborn Circus, EC1P 1DQ.

Scotland on Sunday—20 North Bridge, Edinburgh EH1 1YT.

Sunday Correspondent—19–21 Clerkenwell Close, EC1R 0AA.

Sunday Express—Ludgate House, 245 Blackfriars Road, SE1 9UX.

Sunday Mail—40 Anderston Quay, Glasgow G3 8DA.

Sunday Mirror—Holborn Circus, EC1P 1DQ.

Sunday News—51–59 Donegall Street, Belfast BT1 2GB.

Sunday Post—Courier Place, Dundee DD1 9QJ.

Sunday Sport—3rd Floor, Marten House, 39–47 East Road, N1 6AH.

Sunday Telegraph—Peterborough Court at South Quay, 181 Marsh Wall, E14 9SR.

The Sunday Times—1 Pennington Street, E1 9XW.

RELIGIOUS PAPERS

Alt. = Alternate; *M.* = Monthly; *W.* = Weekly

Baptist Times—4 Southampton Row, WC1B 4AB. *W.*

Catholic Herald—Herald House, Lambs Passage, Bunhill Row, EC1Y 8TQ. *W.*

Challenge: the Good News Paper—Revenue Buildings, Chapel Road, Worthing, W. Sussex BN11 1BQ. *M.*

Christian Herald—Herald House, Dominion Road, Worthing, W. Sussex BN14 8JP. *W.*

Christian Week—11 Carteret Street, SW1H 9DJ. *W.*

Church of England Newspaper—11 Carteret Street, SW1H 9DJ. *W.*

Church of Ireland Gazette—48 Bachelor's Walk, Lisburn, Co. Antrim, BT28 1XN. *W.*

Church Times—33 Upper Street, N1 0PW. *W.*

English Churchman—Mill Lane House, Margate, Kent CT9 1ND. *Alt. W.*

The Friend—Drayton House, 30 Gordon Street, WC1H 0BQ. *W.*

The Inquirer—1–6 Essex Street, WC2R 3HY. *Alt. W.*

Jewish Chronicle—25 Furnival Street, EC4A 1JT. *W.*

Jewish Gazette—27 Bury Old Road, Prestwich, Manchester M25 8EY. *W.*

Jewish Telegraph—Telegraph House, 11 Park Hill, Bury Old Road, Prestwich, Manchester M25 8HH. *W.*

Leadership Today—37 Elm Road, New Malden, Surrey KT3 3HB. *M.*

Life and Work—Church of Scotland, 121 George Street, Edinburgh EH2 4QS. *M.*

Methodist Recorder—122 Golden Lane, EC1Y 0TL. *W.*

Orthodox News—64 Prebend Gardens, W6 0XU. *M.*

Reform—86 Tavistock Place, WC1H 9RT. *M.*

The Tablet—48 Great Peter Street, SW1P 2HB. *W.*

The Universe—33–39 Bowling Green Lane, EC1R 0AB. *W.*

The War Cry—101 Queen Victoria Street, EC4P 4EP. *W.*

PERIODICALS, MAGAZINES AND REVIEWS

Alt. = Alternate; *M.* = Monthly; *Q.* = Quarterly; *W.* = Weekly

Amateur Gardening—Westover House, West Quay Road, Poole, Dorset BH15 1JG. *W.*

Amateur Photographer—Prospect House, 9–13 Ewell Road, Cheam, Surrey SM1 4QQ. *W.*

Angler's Mail—King's Reach Tower, Stamford Street, SE1 9LS. *W.*

Antiquaries Journal—Oxford University Press, Pinkhill House, Southfield Road, Eynsham, Oxford OX8 1JJ. *Three times a year.*

The Antique Collector—National Magazine House, 72 Broadwick Street, W1V 2BP. *M.*

Apollo Magazine—22 Davies Street, W1Y 1LH. *M.*

Arena—The Old Laundry, Ossington Buildings, Moxon Street, W1M 3JD. *Alt. M.*

The Artist—Caxton House, 63–65 High Street, Tenterden, Kent TN30 6BD. *M.*

Autocar and Motor—38–42 Hampton Road, Teddington, Middx. TW11 0JE. *W.*

Bella—2nd Floor, Shirley House, 25–27 Camden Road, NW1 9LL. *W.*

Best—10th Floor, Portland House, Stag Place, SW1E 5AU. *W.*

Blitz—40–42 Newman Street, W1P 3PA. *M.*

Boxing News—PO Box 94, W4 2ER. *W.*

Brain—Oxford University Press, Pinkhill House, Southfield Road, Eynsham, Oxford OX8 1JJ. *Alt. M.*

Brides & Setting up Home—Vogue House, Hanover Square, W1R 0AD. *Alt. M.*

British Birds—Fountains, Park Lane, Blunham, Bedford MK44 3NJ. *M.*

British Book News—The British Council, 65 Davies Street, W1Y 2AA. *M.*

The Burlington Magazine—6 Bloomsbury Square, WC1A 2LP. *M.*

Buses—Terminal House, Station Approach, Shepperton, Middx. TW17 8AS. *M.*

Cage and Aviary Birds—Prospect House, 9–13 Ewell Road, Cheam, Surrey SM1 4QQ. *W.*

Camping & Caravanning—11 Lower Grosvenor Place, SW1W 0EY. *M.*

Caravan Magazine—Link House, Dingwall Avenue, Croydon CR9 2TA. *M.*

Chat—King's Reach Tower, Stamford Street, SE1 9LS. *W.*

Classical Quarterly—Oxford University Press, Pinkhill House, Southfield Road, Eynsham, Oxford OX8 1JJ. *Twice a Year.*

Classical Review—Oxford University Press, Pinkhill House, Southfield Road, Eynsham, Oxford OX8 1JJ. *Twice a Year.*

Coal News—Hobart House, Grosvenor Place, SW1X 7AE. *M.*

Coin Monthly—Sovereign House, Brentwood, Essex CM14 4SE. *M.*

Coin News—Crossways Road, Grayshott, Hindhead, Surrey GU26 6HF. *M.*

Company—72 Broadwick Street, W1V 2BP. *M.*

Contemporary Review—61 Carey Street, WC2A 2JG. *M.*

Cosmopolitan—72 Broadwick Street, W1V 2BP. *M.*

Country Homes and Interiors—King's Reach Tower, Stamford Street, SE1 9LS. *M.*

Country Life—King's Reach Tower, Stamford Street, SE1 9LS. *W.*

Country Living—72 Broadwick Street, W1V 2BP. *Alt. M.*

The Countryman—23–27 Tudor Street, EC4Y 0HR. *Q.*

Cricketer International—Beech Hanger, Ashurst, Tunbridge Wells, Kent TN3 9ST. *M.*

Criminologist—Little London, Chichester, W. Sussex PO19 1PG. *Q.*

Cycling Weekly—Prospect House, 9–13 Ewell Road, Cheam, Surrey SM1 4QQ. *W.*

Daltons Weekly—CI Tower, St. George's Square, New Malden, Surrey KT3 4JA. *W.*

Dance and Dancers—248 High Street, Croydon CR0 1NF. *M.*

Dancing Times—Clerkenwell House, 45–47 Clerkenwell Green, EC1R 0BE. *M.*

Dog World—9 Tufton Street, Ashford, Kent TN23 1QN. *W.*

Do It Yourself—Link House, Dingwall Avenue, Croydon CR9 2TA. *M.*

Drama—British Theatre Association, Regent's College, Inner Circle, Regent's Park, NW1 4NW. *Q.*

Economic Journal—108 Cowley Road, Oxford OX4 1JF. *Q.*

Economica—108 Cowley Road, Oxford OX4 1JF. *Q.*

The Economist—25 St. James's Street, SW1A 1HG. *W.*

Edinburgh Gazette (*Official*)—HMSO, PO Box 276, London SW8 5DT. *Alt. W.*

Elle—Rex House, 4–12 Lower Regent Street, SW1Y 4PE. *M.*

Encounter—44 Great Windmill Street, W1V 7PA. *Ten times a year.*

The English Historical Review—Longman House, Burnt Mill, Harlow, Essex CM20 2JE. *Q.*

Essentials—Garden House, 57–59 Long Acre, WC2E 9JL. *M.*

Everywoman—34 Islington Green, N1 8DU. *M.*

Exchange and Mart—25 West Street, Poole, Dorset BH15 1LL. *W.*

The Face—The Old Laundry, Ossington Buildings, Moxon Street, W1M 3HX. *M.*

Family Circle—King's Reach Tower, Stamford Street, SE1 9LS. *Thirteen times a year.*

The Field—10 Sheet Street, Windsor, Berks. SL4 1BG. *W.*

Garden News—Bushfield House, Orton Centre, Peterborough PE2 0UW. *W.*

Geographical Magazine—27 Kensington Court, W8 5DN. *M.*

Golf Illustrated Weekly—37 Mill Harbour, E14 9TX. *Alt. W.*

Golf Monthly—Hamilton House, 3–4 Claremont Terrace, Glasgow G3 7XR. *M.*

Good Housekeeping—72 Broadwick Street, W1V 2BP. *M.*

Good Motoring—352 Lewisham High Street, SE13 6LE. *Alt. M.*

Gramophone—177–179 Kenton Road, Harrow, Middx. HA3 0HA. *M.*

Granta—44A Hobson Street, Cambridge CB1 1NL. *Q.*

Greece and Rome—Oxford University Press, Pinkhill House, Southfield Road, Eynsham, Oxford OX8 1JJ. *Twice a year.*

Guiding—17–19 Buckingham Palace Road, SW1W 0PT. *M.*

Hansard—*see* Parliamentary Debates.

Harpers and Queen—72 Broadwick Street, W1V 2BP. *M.*

Hello—44A Floral Street, WC2E 9DE. *W.*

High Magazine—164 Barker Road, Leicester LE2 2LD. *M.*

History—108 Cowley Road, Oxford OX4 1JF. *Three times a year.*

History Today—83–84 Berwick Street, W1V 3PJ. *M.*

Homes and Gardens—King's Reach Tower, Stamford Street, SE1 9LS. *M.*

Homoeopathy—27A Devonshire Street, W1N 1RJ. *Alt. M.*

Horse and Hound—King's Reach Tower, Stamford Street, SE1 9LS. *W.*

House and Garden—Vogue House, Hanover Square, W1R 0AD. *M.*

I-D Magazine—27–29 Macklin Street, WC2B 5LX. *M.*

Ideal Home—King's Reach Tower, Stamford Street, SE1 9LS. *M.*

Illustrated London News—Laurence House, 91–93 Southwark Street, SE1 0HX. *Q.*

In Britain—BTA, Thames Tower, Black's Road, W6 9EL. *M.*

International Affairs—Cambridge University Press, The Edinburgh Building, Shaftesbury Road, Cambridge CB2 2RU. *Q.*

Irish Post—Lex House, 77 South Road, Southall, Middx. UB1 1SQ. *W.*

Jazz Journal International—113–117 Farringdon Road, EC1R 3BT. *M.*

Just Seventeen—52–55 Carnaby Street, W1V 1PF. *W.*

Kennel Gazette—1 Clarges Street, W1Y 8AB. *M.*

Labour Research— 78 Blackfriars Road, SE1 8HF. *M.*

The Lady—39–40 Bedford Street, WC2E 9ER. *W.*

Land and Liberty—177 Vauxhall Bridge Road, SW1V 1EU. *Alt. M.*

Light—College of Psychic Studies, 16 Queensberry Place, SW7 2EB. *Three times a year.*

The Listener—199 Old Marylebone Road, NW1 5QS. *W.*

Literary Review—51 Beak Street, W1R 3LF. *M.*

Living—King's Reach Tower, Stamford Street, SE1 9LS. *Thirteen times a year.*

Local Government Chronicle—122 Minories, EC3N 1NT. *W.*

London Gazette (*Official*)—HMSO, PO Box 276, SW8 5DT. *Four times a week.*

London Review of Books—Tavistock House South, Tavistock Square, WC1H 9JZ. *Alt. W.*

London Weekly Diary of Social Events—25 Park Row, SE10 9NL. *W.*

Majesty—80 Highgate Road, NW5 1PB. *M.*

Marie Claire—2 Hatfields, SE1 9PG. *M.*

Melody Maker (MM)—King's Reach Tower, Stamford Street, SE1 9LS. *W.*

Meteorological Magazine—HMSO, PO Box 276, SW8 5DT. *M.*

Mind—Oxford University Press, Pinkhill House, Southfield Road, Eynsham, Oxford OX8 1JJ. *Q.*

Model Boats—Argus House, Boundary Way, Hemel Hempstead, Herts. HP2 7ST. *M.*

Model Railways—Argus House, Boundary Way, Hemel Hempstead, Herts. HP2 7ST. *M.*

Modern Languages—10 Holt Park Way, Leeds LS16 7QR. *Q.*

Month—114 Mount Street, W1Y 6AH. *M.*

Monthly Digest of Statistics (*Official*)—HMSO, PO Box 276, SW8 5DT. *M.*

Mother—Victory House, 14 Leicester Place, WC2H 7NB. *M.*

Motor Cycle News—PO Box 11, Huxloe Place, High Street, Kettering, Northants. NN16 8SS. *W.*

Municipal Review and AMA News—35 Great Smith Street, SW1P 3BJ. *Ten times a year.*

Museums Journal—34 Bloomsbury Way, WC1A 2SF. *Q.*

Music and Letters—Oxford University Press, Pinkhill House, Southfield Road, Eynsham, Oxford OX8 1JJ. *Q.*

My Weekly—80 Kingsway East, Dundee DD4 8SL. *W.*

Nature—4 Little Essex Street, WC2R 3LF. *W.*

Nautical Magazine—4–10 Darnley Street, Glasgow G41 2SD. *M.*

Navy International—Hunters Moon, Hogspudding Lane, Newdigate, Dorking, Surrey RH5 5DS. *Eleven times a year.*

NME—King's Reach Tower, Stamford Street, SE1 9LS. *W.*

New Scientist—Commonwealth House, 1–19 New Oxford Street, WC1A 1NG. *W.*

New Statesman and Society—Foundation House, Perseverance Works, 38 Kingsland Road, E2 8DQ. *W.*

19—King's Reach Tower, Stamford Street, SE1 9LS. *M.*

Notes and Queries—Oxford University Press, Pinkhill House, Southfield Road, Eynsham, Oxford OX8 1JJ. *Q.*

Nursery World—Unit 8, The Schoolhouse Workshop, 51 Calthorpe Street, WC1X 0HH. *Alt. W.*

Opera—1A Mountgrove Road, N5 2LU. *M.*

Options—King's Reach Tower, Stamford Street, SE1 9LS. *M.*

Our Dogs—5 Oxford Road, Station Approach, Manchester M60 1SX. *W.*

Parents—Victory House, 14 Leicester Place, WC2H 7NB. *M.*

Parliamentary Debates (Commons) (Hansard)— HMSO, PO Box 276, SW8 5DT. *Daily or weekly during Session.*

Parliamentary Debates (Lords) (Hansard)—HMSO, PO Box 276, SW8 5DT. *Daily or weekly during Session.*

People's Friend—80 Kingsway East, Dundee DD4 8SL. *W.*

Philosophy—Cambridge University Press, The Edinburgh Building, Shaftesbury Road, Cambridge CB2 2RU. *Q.*

Pins and Needles—4th Floor, 4 Brandon Road, N7 9TP. *M.*

Plays and Players—Media House, 55 Lower Addiscombe, Croydon CR0 6TQ. *M.*

Poetry Review—21 Earl's Court Square, SW5 9DE. *Q.*

Political Quarterly—108 Cowley Road, Oxford OX4 1JF. *Q.*

Pony—296 Ewell Road, Surbiton, Surrey KT6 7AQ. *M.*

Poultry World—Greenfield House, 69–73 Manor Road, Wallington, Surrey SM6 0DE. *M.*

Practical Boat Owner—Westover House, West Quay Road, Poole, Dorset BH15 1JG. *M.*

Practical Caravan—38–42 Hampton Road, Teddington, Middx. TW11 0JE. *M.*

Practical Gardening—Bushfield House, Orton Centre, Peterborough PE2 0UW. *M.*

Practical Householder—Greater London House, Hampstead Road, NW1 7QQ. *M.*

Practical Photography—Bushfield House, Orton Centre, Peterborough PE2 0UW. *M.*

Prima—Portland House, Stag Place, SW1E 5AU. *M.*

Private Eye—6 Carlisle Street, W1V 5RG. *Alt. W.*

Progress (*Braille type*)—338–346 Goswell Road, EC1V 7JE. *M.*

Punch—Ludgate House, 245 Blackfriars Road, SE1 9UZ. *W.*

Racing Calendar—The Jockey Club, Weatherbys, Sanders Road, Wellingborough, Northants. NN8 4BX. *W.*

Radio Control Models and Electronics—Argus House, Boundary Way, Hemel Hempstead, Herts. HP2 7ST. *M.*

Radio Times—35 Marylebone High Street, W1M 4AA. *W.*

Railway Magazine—Prospect House, 9–13 Ewell Road, Cheam, Surrey SM1 4QQ. *M.*

Railway World—Terminal House, Station Approach, Shepperton, Middx. TW17 8AS. *M.*

Reader's Digest—Berkeley Square House, Berkeley Square, W1X 6AB. *M.*

Riding—Corner House, Foston, Grantham, Lincs. NG32 2JU. *M.*

Ritz Newspaper—21 Jerdan Place, SW6 1BE. *M.*

Scots Independent—51 Cowans Street, Stirling FK8 1JW. *M.*

Scottish Field—7th Floor, The Plaza Tower, East Kilbride, Glasgow G74 1LW. *M.*

Scouting—Baden-Powell House, Queen's Gate, SW7 5JS. *M.*

The Seafarer—202 Lambeth Road, SE1 7JW. *Q.*

She—72 Broadwick Street, W1V 2BP. *M.*

Shoot—King's Reach Tower, Stamford Street, SE1 9LS. *W.*

Shooting Times and Country Magazine—10 Sheet Street, Windsor, Berks. SL4 1BG. *W.*

Slimming Magazine—Victory House, 14 Leicester Place, WC2H 7NB. *Alt. M.*

The Social and Liberal Democrats News—4 Cowley Street, SW1P 3NB. *W.*

Sociological Review—11 New Fetter Lane, EC4P 4EE. *Q.*

Spare Rib—27 Clerkenwell Close, EC1R 0AT. *M.*

The Spectator—56 Doughty Street, WC1N 2LL. *W.*

The Strad—4th Floor, Centro House, Mandela Street, NW1 0DU. *M.*

Studio International—Tower House, Southampton Street, WC2E 7LS. *Q.*

Tatler—Vogue House, Hanover Square, W1R 0AD. *M.*

Tennis World—Chiltern House, 184 High Street, Berkhamsted, Herts. HP4 3AP. *M.*

This England—Alma House, Rodney Road, Cheltenham, Glos. GL50 1YQ. *Q.*

Time—Time and Life Building, New Bond Street, W1Y 0AA. *W.*

The Times Educational Supplement—Priory House, St. John's Lane, EC1M 4BX. *W.*

The Times Higher Education Supplement—Priory House, St. John's Lane, EC1M 4BX. *W.*

The Times Literary Supplement—Priory House, St. John's Lane, EC1M 4BX. *W.*

Tribune—308 Gray's Inn Road, WC1X 8DY. *W.*

Trout and Salmon—Bretton Court, Bretton, Peterborough PE3 8DZ. *M.*

True Romances—159–161 Camden High Street, NW1 7JY. *M.*

True Story—159–161 Camden High Street, NW1 7JY. *M.*

TV Times—247 Tottenham Court Road, W1P 0AU. *W.*

Vacher's Parliamentary Companion—113 High Street, Berkhamsted, Herts. HP4 2DJ. *Q.*

Vogue—Vogue House, Hanover Square, W1R 0AD. *M.*

Weather—James Glaisher House, Grenville Place, Bracknell, Berks. RG12 1BX. *M.*

Welsh Nation—51 Cathedral Road, Cardiff CF1 9HD. *M.*

West Africa—43–45 Coldharbour Lane, SE5 9NR. *W.*

Which?—2 Marylebone Road, NW1 4DX. *M.*

Woman—King's Reach Tower, Stamford Street, SE1 9LS. *W.*

Woman and Home—King's Reach Tower, Stamford Street, SE1 9LS. *M.*

Woman's Journal—King's Reach Tower, Stamford Street, SE1 9LS. *M.*

Woman's Own—King's Reach Tower, Stamford Street, SE1 9LS. *W.*

Woman's Realm—King's Reach Tower, Stamford Street, SE1 9LS. *W.*

Woman's Weekly—King's Reach Tower, Stamford Street, SE1 9LS. *W.*

Woman's World—King's Reach Tower, Stamford Street, SE1 9LS. *M.*

The World Today—Chatham House, 10 St. James's Square, SW1Y 4LE. *M.*

Yachting Monthly—King's Reach Tower, Stamford Street, SE1 9LS. *M.*

Yachting World—Prospect House, 9–13 Ewell Road, Cheam, Surrey SM1 4QQ. *M.*

Yachts and Yachting—196 Eastern Esplanade, Southend-on-Sea, Essex SS1 3AB. *Alt. W.*

TRADE, PROFESSIONAL AND BUSINESS JOURNALS

Alt. = Alternate; *M.* = Monthly; *Q.* = Quarterly; *W.* = Weekly

Accountancy—40 Bernard Street, WC1N 1LD. *M.*

The Accountant—Axe & Bottle Court, 70 Newcomen Street, SE1 1YT. *M.*

Accountants' Magazine—27 Queen Street, Edinburgh EH2 1LA. *M.*

Administrator—38 St. John's Street, EC1M 4AY. *M.*

Agriculture International—Yew Tree House, Horne, Horley, Surrey RH6 9JP. *M.*

Antique Dealer and Collectors' Guide—King's Reach Tower, Stamford Street, SE1 9LS. *M.*

Antiques Trade Gazette—17 Whitcomb Street, WC2H 7PL. *W.*

Architects' Journal—9 Queen Anne's Gate, SW1H 9BY. *W.*

Architectural Review—9 Queen Anne's Gate, SW1H 9BY. *M.*

The Author—84 Drayton Gardens, SW10 9SB. *Q.*

Bakers' Review—Turret House, 171 High Street, Rickmansworth, Herts. WD3 1SN. *M.*

The Banker—102–108 Clerkenwell Road, EC1M 5SA. *M.*

Banking World—Headway House, 66–73 Shoe Lane, EC4P 4AB. *M.*

The Bookseller—12 Dyott Street, WC1A 1DF. *W.*

Brewers' Guardian—209 Central Markets, Smithfield, EC1A 9LH. *M.*

British Baker—PO Box 109, Maclaren House, 19 Scarbrook Road, Croydon CR9 1QH. *W.*

British Clothing Manufacturer—100 Avenue Road, NW3 3TP. *Q.*

British Dental Journal—BMA House, Tavistock Square, WC1H 9JR. *Alt. W.*

British Food Journal—MCB University Press Ltd., 62 Toller Lane, Bradford BD8 9BY. *Alt. M.*

British Jeweller—Equity and Law House, 11–19 Priestgate, Peterborough PE1 1EL. *M.*

British Journal for the Philosophy of Science—Oxford University Press, Pinkhill House, Southfield Road, Eynsham, Oxford OX8 1JJ. *Q.*

British Journal of Photography—244–249 Temple Chambers, Temple Avenue, EC4Y 0DT. *W.*

British Medical Journal—BMA House, Tavistock Square, WC1H 9JR. *W.*

British Printer—Maclean Hunter House, Chalk Lane, Cockfosters Road, Barnet, Herts. EN4 0BU. *M.*

British Sugar Beet Review—PO Box 26, Oundle Road, Peterborough PE2 9QU. *Q.*

British Tax Review—8th Floor, South Quay Plaza, 183 Marsh Wall, E14 9FT. *Alt. M.*

British Veterinary Journal—24–28 Oval Road, NW1 7DX. *Alt. M.*

Building Trade & Industry—Industry House, 74 West Street, Bedminster, Bristol BS3 3LL. *M.*

Building Trade News—100 Avenue Road, NW3 3TP. *Q.*

Business Connections—Node Court, Drivers End, Codicote, Hitchin, Herts. SG4 8TR. *Alt. M.*

Cabinet Maker—Sovereign Way, Tonbridge, Kent TN9 1RW. *W.*

Campaign—22 Lancaster Gate, W2 3LY. *W.*

Carpet and Floorcoverings Review—Sovereign Way, Tonbridge, Kent TN9 1RW. *Alt. W.*

Caterer and Hotelkeeper—Quadrant House, The Quadrant, Sutton, Surrey SM2 5AS. *W.*

Chemist and Druggist—Sovereign Way, Tonbridge, Kent TN9 1RW. *W.*

Chemistry and Industry—14 Belgrave Square, SW1X 8PS. *Alt. M.*

Chemistry in Britain—Burlington House, Piccadilly, W1V 0BN. *M.*

Child Education—Marlborough House, Holly Walk, Leamington Spa, Warks. CV32 4LS. *M.*

Chiropodist—53 Welbeck Street, W1M 7HE. *M.*

Club Mirror—29–31 Lower Coombe Street, Croydon CR9 1LX. *M.*

Colliery Guardian—Queensway House, 2 Queensway, Redhill, Surrey RH1 1QS. *M.*

Commercial Motor—Quadrant House, The Quadrant, Sutton, Surrey SM2 5AS. *W.*

Computer Survey—33–35 Bowling Green Lane, EC1R 0DA. *Alt. M.*

Computing—VNU House, 32–34 Broadwick Street, W1A 2HG. *W.*

Concrete—Thomas Telford House, 1 Heron Quay, E14 9XF. *M.*

Construction Weekly—Morgan-Grampian House, Calderwood Street, SE18 6QH. *W.*

Containerisation International—72 Broadwick Street, W1V 2BP. *M.*

Contract Journal—Carew House, Wallington, Surrey SM6 0DX. *W.*

Control and Instrumentation—Morgan-Grampian House, 30 Calderwood Street, SE18 6QH. *M.*

CSE News—Camping and Sports Equipment Ltd., Exhibition House, 4 Spring Street, W2 3RB. *M.*

Dairy Farmer—Wharfedale Road, Ipswich IP1 4LG. *M.*

Dairy Industries International—33–35 Bowling Green Lane, EC1R 0DA. *M.*

Design—The Design Centre, 28 Haymarket, SW1Y 4SU. *M.*

Director—Mountbarrow House, Elizabeth Street, SW1W 9RB. *M.*

Dock and Harbour Authority—20 Harcourt Street, W1H 2AX. *M.*

DR The Fashion Business—100 Avenue Road, NW3 3TP. *W.*

Education—21–27 Lamb's Conduit Street, WC1N 3NJ. *W.*

Education Equipment—Sovereign Way, Tonbridge, Kent TN9 1RW. *Eleven times a year.*

Electrical and Radio Trading—Quadrant House, The Quadrant, Sutton, Surrey SM2 5AS. *M.*

Electrical Review—Quadrant House, The Quadrant, Sutton, Surrey SM2 5AS. *W.*

Electrical Times—Quadrant House, The Quadrant, Sutton, Surrey SM2 5AS. *M.*

Electronic Engineering—Morgan-Grampian House, 30 Calderwood Street, SE18 6QH. *M.*

Electronics Weekly—Quadrant House, The Quadrant, Sutton, Surrey SM2 5AS. *W.*

Embroidery—PO Box 42B, East Molesey, Surrey KT8 9BB. *Q.*

The Engineer—Morgan-Grampian House, 30 Calderwood Street, SE18 6QH. *W.*

Engineering—28 Haymarket, SW1Y 4SU. *M.*

Engineer's Digest—Convex House, 43 Dudley Road, Tunbridge Wells, Kent TN1 1LE. *Ten times a year.*

Estates Gazette—151 Wardour Street, W1V 4BN. *W.*

Fairplay International Shipping Weekly—20 Ullswater Crescent, Coulsdon, Surrey CR3 2HR. *W.*

Farmers Weekly—Greenfield House, 69–73 Manor Road, Wallington, Surrey SM6 0DE. *W.*

Fire—Queensway House, 2 Queensway, Redhill, Surrey RH1 1QS. *M.*

Fire and Security Protection—Stanley House, 9 West Street, Epsom, Surrey KT18 7RL. *M.*

Fish Friers Review—289 Dewsbury Road, Leeds LS11 5HW. *M.*

Fish Trader—Queensway House, 2 Queensway, Redhill, Surrey RH1 1QS. *W.*

Flight International—Quadrant House, The Quadrant, Sutton, Surrey SM2 5AS. *W.*

Food Trade Review—Station House, Hortons Way, Westerham, Kent TN16 1BZ. *M.*

Forestry and British Timber—Sovereign Way, Tonbridge, Kent TN9 1RW. *M.*

Foundry Trade Journal—Queensway House, 2 Queensway, Redhill, Surrey RH1 1QS. *Alt. W.*

Frozen and Chilled Foods—Queensway House, 2 Queensway, Redhill, Surrey RH1 1QS. *M.*

Fuel—PO Box 63, Westbury House, Bury Street, Guildford GU2 5BH. *M.*

Funeral Service Journal—43 Stockens Green, Knebworth, Herts. SG3 6DQ. *M.*

Fur Weekly News—4 Great Saint Thomas Apostle, EC4V 2BH. *W.*

Gas Marketing—Sovereign Way, Tonbridge, Kent TN9 1RW. *M.*

Gas World—Sovereign Way, Tonbridge, Kent TN9 1RW. *M.*

Gifts International—Sovereign Way, Tonbridge, Kent TN9 1RW. *M.*

Glass—Queensway House, 2 Queensway, Redhill, Surrey RH1 1QS. *M.*

The Grocer—5–7 Southwark Street, SE1 1RQ. *W.*

The Grower—50 Doughty Street, WC1N 2LS. *W.*

Hair and Beauty—Quadrant House, The Quadrant, Sutton, Surrey SM2 5AS. *M.*

Hairdressers' Journal International—Quadrant House, The Quadrant, Sutton, Surrey SM2 5AS. *W.*

Handy Shipping Guide—230–234 Long Lane, SE1 4QE. *W.*

Hardware Today—20 Harborne Road, Edgbaston, Birmingham B15 3AB. *M.*

Harpers Sports & Leisure—Unit 2, Mill Hill Industrial Estate, Flower Lane, NW7 2HU. *Every three weeks.*

Harpers Wine and Spirit Gazette—Harling House, 47–51 Great Suffolk Street, SE1 0BS. *W.*

The Health Service Journal—4 Little Essex Street, WC2R 3LF. *W.*

Health Visitor—BMA House, Tavistock Square, WC1H 9JR. *M.*

Heating and Ventilating Engineer—177 Hagden Lane, Watford, Herts. WD1 8LW. *Alt. M.*

Ice Cream and Frozen Confectionery—90–94 Gray's Inn Road, WC1X 8AH. *M.*

Investors Chronicle—Greystoke Place, Fetter Lane, EC4A 1ND. *W.*

Journal of The Chemical Society—Thomas Graham House, Science Park, Milton Road, Cambridge CB4 4WF. *Five parts each M.*

The Journalist—Acorn House, 314 Gray's Inn Rd., WC1X 8DP. *M.*

Justice of the Peace—East Row, Little London, Chichester, W. Sussex PO19 1PG. *W.*

Knitting and Haberdashery Review—Marshall's Chambers, 80A South Street, Romford RM1 1RX. *Alt. M.*

The Lancet—46 Bedford Square, WC1B 3SL. *W.*

Law Quarterly Review—8th Floor, South Quay Plaza, 183 Marsh Wall, E14 9FT. *Q.*

The Law Reports—3 Stone Buildings, Lincoln's Inn, WC2A 3XN. *W.*

Law Society's Gazette—50 Chancery Lane, WC2A 1SX. *W.*

Leather—Sovereign Way, Tonbridge, Kent TN9 1RW. *M.*

The Legal Executive Journal—Silbury Court, 356 Silbury Boulevard, Milton Keynes, Bucks. MK9 2LR. *M.*

Library Review—62 Toller Lane, Bradford BD8 9BY. *Q.*

Litho Week—38–42 Hampton Road, Teddington, Middx. TW11 0JE. *W.*

Lloyd's Loading List—Sheepen Place, Colchester, Essex CO3 3LP. *W.*

Lloyd's Shipping Index—Sheepen Place, Colchester, Essex CO3 3LP. *Daily.*

Locomotive Journal—9 Arkwright Road, NW3 6AA. *M.*

London Corn Circular—54 Wentworth Crescent, Ash Vale, Aldershot, Hants. GU12 5LF. *W.*

Machinery and Production Engineering—Franks Hall, Franks Lane, Horton Kirby, Dartford, Kent DA4 9LL. *Alt. W.*

Machinery Market—6 Blyth Road, Bromley, Kent BR1 3RX. *W.*

Management Accounting—29 Princes Street, W1R 7RG. *M.*

Management Decision—62 Toller Lane, Bradford BD8 9BY. *Alt. M.*

Management Today—22 Lancaster Gate, W2 3LY. *M.*

Manufacturing Chemist—Morgan-Grampian House, 30 Calderwood Street, SE18 6QH. *M.*

Marketing—22 Lancaster Gate, W2 3LY. *W.*

Materials Reclamation Weekly—PO Box 109, Maclaren House, 19 Scarbrook Road, Croydon CR9 1QH. *W.*

Meat Trades' Journal—100 Avenue Road, NW3 3TP. *W.*

Medico-Legal Journal—5 New Square, Lincoln's Inn, WC2A 3RJ. *Q.*

Men's Wear—100 Avenue Road, NW3 3TP. *W.*

Metal Bulletin—Park House, Park Terrace, Worcester Park, Surrey KT4 7HY. *Twice a week.*

Metallurgia—Queensway House, 2 Queensway, Redhill, Surrey RH1 1QS. *M.*

Milk Industry—37 Spearpoint Gardens, Aldborough Road North, Newbury Park, Ilford, Essex IG2 7SX. *M.*

Mining Journal—60 Worship Street, EC2A 2HD. *W.*

Mining Magazine—60 Worship Street, EC2A 2HD. *M.*

Model Engineer—Argus House, Boundary Way, Hemel Hempstead, Herts. HP2 7ST. *Alt. W.*

Modern Railways—Terminal House, Station Approach, Shepperton, Middx. TW17 8AS. *M.*

Motor Boat and Yachting—Prospect House, 9–13 Ewell Road, Cheam, Surrey SM1 4QQ. *M.*

Motor Trader—Quadrant House, The Quadrant, Sutton, Surrey SM2 5AS. *W.*

Motor Transport—Quadrant House, The Quadrant, Sutton, Surrey SM2 5AS. *W.*

The Musical Times—4th Floor, Centro House, Mandela Street, NW1 0DU. *M.*

National Builder—82 New Cavendish Street, W1M 8AD. *M.*

Natural Gas—Sovereign Way, Tonbridge, Kent TN9 1RW. *Alt. M.*

New Law Journal—9–12 Bell Yard, WC2A 2JR. *W.*

Nuclear Engineering International—Quadrant House, The Quadrant, Sutton, Surrey SM2 5AS. *M.*

Nurseryman & Garden Centre—Heath Road, Boughton Monchelsea, Maidstone, Kent ME17 4JD. *Alt. W.*

Nursing Times & Nursing Mirror—4 Little Essex Street, WC2R 3LF. *W.*

Off-Licence News—5–7 Southwark Street, SE1 1RQ. *W.*

Optician—Quadrant House, The Quadrant, Sutton, Surrey SM2 5AS. *W.*

Optometry Today—Bridge House, 233–234 Blackfriars Road, SE1 8NW. *Alt. W.*

Packaging—Turret House, 171 High Street, Rickmansworth, Herts. WD3 1SN. *M.*

Packaging Week—Sovereign Way, Tonbridge, Kent TN9 1RW. *W.*

Paint & Resin—Turret House, 171 High Street, Rickmansworth, Herts. WD3 1SN. *Alt. M.*

Paper—Sovereign Way, Tonbridge, Kent TN9 1RW. *Alt. W.*

Personnel Management—57 Mortimer Street, W1N 7TD. *M.*

Pharmaceutical Journal—1 Lambeth High Street, SE1 7JN. *W.*

The Photographer—Fox Talbot House, Anwell End, Ware, Herts. SG12 9HN. *M.*

Physics Education—Techno House, Redcliffe Way, Bristol BS1 6NX. *Alt. M.*

Physics in Technology—Techno House, Redcliffe Way, Bristol BS1 6NX. *Alt. M.*

Physics World—Techno House, Redcliffe Way, Bristol BS1 6NX. *M.*

Plumbing and Heating Equipment News—Peterson House, Northbank, Berryhill Industrial Estate, Droitwich, Worcs. WR9 9BL. *M.*

Police Review—14 St. Cross Street, EC1N 8FE. *W.*

Power Farming—Greenfield House, 69–73 Manor Road, Wallington, Surrey SM6 0DE. *M.*

Practical Wireless—Enefco House, The Quay, Poole, Dorset B15 1PP. *M.*

Practical Woodworking—King's Reach Tower, Stamford Street, SE1 9LS. *M.*

The Practitioner—Morgan-Grampian House, 30 Calderwood Street, SE18 6QH. *M.*

Precision Toolmaker—Queensway House, 2 Queensway, Redhill, Surrey RH1 1QS. *Q.*

Printing World—Sovereign Way, Tonbridge, Kent TN9 1RW. *W.*

Product Finishing—127 Stanstead Road, SE23 1JE. *M.*

Public Law—8th Floor, South Quay Plaza, 183 Marsh Wall, E14 9FT. *Q.*

Public Service—1 Mabledon Place, WC1H 9AJ. *M.*

Quarry Management—7 Regent Street, Nottingham NG1 5BY. *M.*

Quarterly Journal of Medicine—Oxford University Press, Pinkhill House, Southfield Road, Eynsham, Oxford OX8 1JJ. *M.*

Railway Gazette International—Quadrant House, The Quadrant, Sutton, Surrey SM2 5AS. *M.*

Rating & Valuation Reporter—2 Paper Buildings, Temple, EC4Y 7ET. *M.*

Resale Weekly—1–23 Queen's Road West, E13 0PE. *W.*

Retail Jeweller—100 Avenue Road, NW3 3TP. *Alt. W.*

Retail Newsagent Tobacconist Confectioner—60–66 Saffron Hill, EC1N 8QX. *W.*

The Review: Worldwide Reinsurance—33–35 Bowling Green Lane, EC1R 0DA. *Alt. W.*

Review of English Studies—Oxford University Press, Pinkhill House, Southfield Road, Eynsham, Oxford OX8 1JJ. *Q.*

Safety at Sea—Queensway House, 2 Queensway, Redhill, Surrey RH1 1QS. *M.*

The Scottish Farmer—7th Floor, The Plaza Tower, East Kilbride, Glasgow G74 1LW. *W.*

Scottish Grocer—10 Park Circus, Glasgow G3 6AX. *M.*

Service Station—Suite D, Overcliffe House, 55 New Road, Gravesend, Kent DA11 0AD. *M.*

Sheet Metal Industries—Queensway House, 2 Queensway, Redhill, Surrey RH1 1QS. *M.*

Shipping World & Shipbuilder—4 Hubbard Road, Houndsmill, Basingstoke, Hants. RG21 2UH. *M.*

Shoe & Leather News—100 Avenue Road, NW3 3TP. *W.*

Soap, Perfumery and Cosmetics—33–35 Bowling Green Lane, EC1R 0DA. *M.*

Solicitors' Journal—21–27 Lamb's Conduit Street, WC1N 3NJ. *W.*

Sports Retailing—Sovereign Way, Tonbridge, Kent TN9 1RW. *Alt. W.*

The Stage and Television Today—47 Bermondsey Street, SE1 3XT. *W.*

Structural Engineer—11 Upper Belgrave Street, SW1X 8BH. *M. (Part A), Q. (Part B).*

Surveyor—Carew House, Wallington, Surrey SM6 0DX. *W.*

Tableware International—Queensway House, 2 Queensway, Redhill, Surrey RH1 1QS. *M.*

Taxation—Tolley House, 2 Addiscombe Road, Croydon, Surrey CR9 5AF. *W.*

The Teacher—Derbyshire House, Lower Street, Kettering, Northants. NN16 8BB. *W.*

Teaching History—108 Cowley Road, Oxford OX4 1JF. *Three times a year.*

Television—King's Reach Tower, Stamford Street, SE1 9LS. *M.*

Textile Horizons—10 Blackfriars Street, Manchester M3 5DR. *M.*

Textile Month—Caidan House, Canal Road, Timperley, Altrincham, Cheshire WA14 1TD. *M.*

Timber Trades Journal & Wood Processing—Sovereign Way, Tonbridge, Kent TN9 1RW. *W.*

Tobacco—Queensway House, 2 Queensway, Redhill, Surrey RH1 1QS. *M.*

Town and Country Planning—17 Carlton House Terrace, SW1Y 5AH. *M.*

Town Planning Review—Liverpool University Press, PO Box 147, Liverpool L69 3BX. *Q.*

Toy Trader—177 Hagden Lane, Watford, Herts. WD1 8LN. *M.*

Trade Marks Journal—25 Southampton Buildings, WC2A 1AY. *W.*

Traffic Engineering and Control—29 Newman Street, W1P 3PE. *M.*

UK Press Gazette—244–249 Temple Chambers, Temple Avenue, EC4Y 0DT. *W.*

Ultrasonics—PO Box 63, Westbury House, Bury Street, Guildford, Surrey GU2 5BH. *Alt. M.*

Weekly Law Reports—3 Stone Buildings, Lincoln's Inn, WC2A 3XN. *W.*

Welding and Metal Fabrication—Queensway House, 2 Queensway, Redhill, Surrey RH1 1QS. *Ten times a year.*

Whitaker's Books of the Month and Books to Come—12 Dyott Street, WC1A 1DF. *M.*

Whitaker's Classified Monthly Book List—12 Dyott Street, WC1A 1DF. *M.*

Wire Industry—110–112 Station Road East, Oxted, Surrey RH8 0QA. *M.*

Woodworker—Argus House, Boundary Way, Hemel Hempstead, Herts. HP2 7ST. *M.*

World's Fair—2 Daltry Street, Oldham OL1 4BB. *W.*

REPORTING AND NEWS AGENCIES IN LONDON

THE ASSOCIATED PRESS LTD.—12 Norwich Street, EC4A 4BP. (071–353 1515).

BRENARD PRESS LTD.—Building 221, Heathrow Airport, Hounslow, Middx. TW6 2BU. (081–759 1235).

CENTRAL PRESS FEATURES LTD.—131 Aldersgate Street, Barbican, EC1A 4JA. (071–600 4502).

THE EXCHANGE TELEGRAPH CO. LTD.—Extel House, 298 Regent's Park Road, N3 2LZ. (071–353 1080).

HAYTERS.—4–5 Gough Square, EC4A 3DE. (071–353 0971).

PARLIAMENTARY AND EEC NEWS SERVICE.—29 Tufton Street, SW1P 3QL. (071–399 2049).

PRESS ASSOCIATION LTD.—85 Fleet Street, EC4P 4BE. (071–353 7440).

REUTERS LTD.—85 Fleet Street, EC4P 4AJ. (071–250 1122).

UNITED PRESS INTERNATIONAL (UK) LTD.—8 Bouverie Street, EC4Y 8BB. (071–353 2282).

UNIVERSAL NEWS SERVICE LTD.—Communications House, Gough Square, Fleet Street, EC4 4DP. (071–353 5200).

THE PRESS COUNCIL
1 Salisbury Square, EC4Y 8AE
[071–353 1248]

The Press Council was set up in 1953. The objects of the Council are: to preserve the established freedom of the British Press; to maintain the character of the British Press in accordance with the highest professional and commercial standards; to consider complaints about the conduct of the Press or the conduct of persons and organizations towards the Press; to deal with these complaints in whatever manner might seem practical and appropriate and record resultant action; to keep under review developments likely to restrict the supply of information of public interest and importance; to report publicly on developments that may tend towards greater concentration or monopoly in the Press (including changes in ownership, control and growth of Press undertakings) and to publish statistical information relating thereto; to make representations on appropriate occasions to the Government, organs of the United Nations and Press organizations abroad; and to publish periodical reports recording the Council's work and to review, from time to time, developments in the Press and the factors affecting them.

In March 1990 the Press Council adopted and published a code of practice agreed by most newspaper editors. The code of practice covers the obligation on journalists to report accurately; to provide an opportunity to reply; to respect privacy; to distinguish between comment and fact; to avoid subterfuge in obtaining information or pictures; to observe the Press Council's guidelines on payment for articles; to avoid intruding on grief; to exercise discretion before identifying relatives of persons convicted or accused of crime; to identify themselves when making enquiries at hospitals and similar institutions; and to protect confidential sources of information. The code also covers the interviewing of children, the identification of children in sex cases and of rape victims, financial probity in financial journalism, the use of pictures which might cause distress, and references to race and colour in news reports.

The constitution of the Council provides for 18 Press members who are editorial and managerial nominees of The Newspaper Publishers Association Ltd. (3), The Newspaper Society (3), The Periodical Publishers Association Ltd. (2), The Scottish Daily Newspaper Society (1), Scottish Newspaper Proprietors' Association (1), The Guild of British Newspaper Editors (2), The National Union of Journalists (4), The Institute of Journalists (2) plus 18 public members appointed by the Press Council Appointments Commission. In addition each constituent body nominates one official as a non-voting member. In June 1990 the Committee on Privacy and Related Matters appointed by the government recommended replacing the Press Council by a Press Complaints Commission, which would initially also be a voluntary body but could become a statutory body in certain circumstances. It suggested that the Press Complaints Commission, unlike the Press Council, should not be responsible for defending press freedom, but only for dealing with complaints against the Press.

Chairman, L. Blom-Cooper, QC.
Director, K. Morgan, OBE.

PRINCIPAL BOOK PUBLISHERS AND THEIR ADDRESSES

More than 12,000 firms, individuals and societies have published one or more books in recent years. The list which follows is a selective one comprising, in the main, those firms whose names are most familiar to the general public. An interleaved list, *Publishers in the United Kingdom and Their Addresses*, containing some 2,000 names and addresses is published annually in April by the publishers of *Whitaker's Almanack*.

Abelard-Schumann, 7 Leicester Place, WC2H 7BP.

Allan (Ian), Terminal House, Station Approach, Shepperton, Middx. TW17 8AS.

Allen (J. A.), 1 Lower Grosvenor Place, SW1W 0EL.

Allen (W. H.), 26 Grand Union Centre, 338 Ladbroke Grove, W10 5AH.

Anaya Publishers, 49 Neal Street, WC2H 9PJ.

Angus & Robertson, 16 Golden Square, W1R 4BN.

Apple Press, 6 Blundell Street, N7 9BH.

Argus Books, Argus House, Boundary Way, Hemel Hempstead, Herts. HP2 7ST.

Arlington Books, 38 Bury Street, SW1Y 6AU.

Armada Books, 77 Fulham Palace Road, W6 8JB.

Arms & Armour Press, 41 Strand, WC2N 5JE.

Arnold (Edward), Mill Road, Dunton Green, Sevenoaks TN13 2YA.

Arrow Books, 20 Vauxhall Bridge Road, SW1V 2SA.

Athlone Press, 1 Park Drive, NW11 7SG.

Aurum Press, 33 Museum Street, WC1A 1LD.

B.B.C. Books, 80 Wood Lane, W12 0TT.

Baillière, Tindall, 24 Oval Road, NW1 7DX.

Bantam Books., 61 Uxbridge Road, W5 5SA.

Barker (Arthur), 91 Clapham High Street, SW4 9TA.

Barrie & Jenkins, 20 Vauxhall Bridge Road, SW1V 2SA.

Bartholomew (John) & Son, 12 Duncan Street, Edinburgh EH9 1TA.

Batsford (B. T.), 4 Fitzhardinge Street, W1H 0AH.

Benn (Ernest), 35 Bedford Row, WC1R 4JH.

Bingley (Clive), 7 Ridgmount Street, WC1E 7AE.

Black (A. & C.), 35 Bedford Row, WC1R 4JH.

Blackie & Son, Wester Cleddens Road, Bishopbriggs, Glasgow G64 2NZ.

Blackwell (Basil), 108 Cowley Rd., Oxford OX4 1JF.

Blandford Press, 41 Strand, WC2N 5JE.

Bloomsbury Publishing, 2 Soho Square, W1V 5DE.

Bodley Head, 20 Vauxhall Bridge Road, SW1V 2SA.

Boxtree, 36 Tavistock Street, WC2E 7PB.

Boyars (Marion), 24 Lacy Road, SW15 1NL.

Bracken Books, 50 Eastcastle Street, W1N 7AP.

British Museum Publications, 46 Bloomsbury Street, WC1B 3QQ.

Brown, Son & Ferguson, 4 Darnley Street, Glasgow G41 2SD.

Butterworth & Co., Borough Green, Sevenoaks TN15 8PH.

Calder (John), 9/15 Neal Street, WC2H 9TU.

Cambridge University Press, Shaftesbury Road, Cambridge CB2 2RU.

Cape (Jonathan), 20 Vauxhall Bridge Road, SW1V 2SA.

Cassell, 41 Strand, WC2N 5JE.

Centaur Press, Fontwell, Arundel, Sussex BN18 0TA.

Century Publishing Co., *see* Random Century Group.

Chambers (W. & R.), 43 Annandale Street, Edinburgh EH7 4AZ.

Chapman & Hall, 2 Boundary Row, SE1 8HN.

Chapman (Geoffrey), 41 Strand, WC2N 5JE.

Chatto & Windus, 20 Vauxhall Bridge Road, SW1V 2SA.

Chivers Press, Windsor Bridge Road, Bath BA2 3AX.

Church House Publishing, Church House, Great Smith Street, SW1P 3NZ.

Churchill Livingstone, 1–3 Baxter's Place, Leith Walk, Edinburgh EH1 3AF.

Collins (William), 77 Fulham Palace Road, W6 8JB.

Constable & Co., 3 The Lanchesters, 162 Fulham Palace Road, W6 9ER.

Consumers' Association, 2 Marylebone Road, NW1 4DX.

Corgi Books, 61 Uxbridge Road, W5 5SA.

Darton, Longman & Todd, 89 Lillie Road, SW6 1UD.

David & Charles, Brunel House, Newton Abbot, Devon TQ12 4PU.

Dean & Son, *see* Hamlyn.

Dent (J. M.) & Sons, 91 Clapham High Street, SW4 9TA.

Deutsch (Andre), 105 Great Russell Street, WC1B 3LJ.

Dorling Kindersley, 9 Henrietta Street, WC2E 8PS.

Doubleday, 61 Uxbridge Road, W5 5SA.

Duckworth & Co., 43 Gloucester Crescent, NW1 7DY.

Elliot Right Way Books, Kingswood Building, Kingswood, Tadworth, Surrey KT20 6TD.

Encyclopaedia Britannica, Carew House, Station Approach, Wallington, Surrey SM6 0DA.

Epworth Press, Welsey Methodist Church, Christ's Pieces, Cambridge CB1 1LB.

Evans Bros., 2A Portman Mansions, Chiltern Street, W1M 1LE.

Faber & Faber, 3 Queen Square, WC1N 3AU.

Fontana, 77 Fulham Palace Road, W6 8JB.

Foulis (G. T.), Sparkford, Yeovil, Somerset BA22 7JJ.

Foulsham (W.) & Co., Yeovil Road, Slough SL1 4JH.

Fountain Press, 2 Claremont Road, Surbiton KT6 4QU.

French (Samuel), 52 Fitzroy Street, W1P 6JR.

Futura, *see* Macdonald & Co.

Gee & Co., 183 Marsh Wall, W14 9FS.

Geographia, 12 Duncan Street, Edinburgh EH9 1TA.

Gibbons (Stanley), 5 Parkside, Christchurch Road, Ringwood, Hants. BH24 3SH.

Gibson (Robert), 17 Fitzroy Place, Glasgow G3 7SF.

Ginn & Co., Prebendal House, Parson's Fee, Aylesbury, Bucks. HP20 2QZ.

Glasgow (Mary), 131 Holland Park Avenue, W11 4UT.

Gollancz (Victor), 14 Henrietta Street, WC2E 8QJ.

Gower Publishing Co., Croft Road, Aldershot, Hants. GU11 3HR

Grafton Books, 77 Fulham Palace Road, W6 8JB.

Graham (Frank), 10 Blythswood North, Osborne Road, Jesmond, Newcastle NE2 2AZ.

Green (W.), 2 St. Giles Street, Edinburgh EH1 1PU.

Guinness Publishing, 33 London Road, Enfield, Middx. EN2 6DJ.

Hale (Robert), 45 Clerkenwell Green, EC1R 0HT.

Hamilton (Hamish), 27 Wright's Lane, W8 5TZ.

Hamlyn Publishing Group, 81 Fulham Road, SW3 6RB.

Harcourt Brace Jovanovich, 24 Oval Road, NW1 7DX.

Harlequin, 18 Paradise Road, Richmond, Surrey TW9 1SR.

Harper & Row, 34 Cleveland Street, W1P 5FB.

Harrap, 26 Market Square, Bromley BR1 1NA.

Hart-Davis, 77 Fulham Palace Road, W6 8JB.

Harvester Wheatsheaf, Wolsey House, Wolsey Road, Hemel Hempstead HP2 4SS.

Haynes (J. H.), Sparkford, Yeovil, Somerset BA22 7TJ.

Headline Book Publishing, 79 Great Titchfield Street, W1P 7FN.

Heinemann (William), 81 Fulham Road, SW3 6RB.

Her Majesty's Stationery Office, 51 Nine Elms Lane, SW8 5DR.

Hodder & Stoughton, 47 Bedford Square, WC1B 3DP.

Hogarth Press, 20 Vauxhall Bridge Road, SW1V 2SA.

Holmes McDougall, 137 Leith Walk, Edinburgh EH6 8NS.

Hutchinson, 20 Vauxhall Bridge Road, SW1V 2SA.

Jane's Information Group, 163 Brighton Road, Coulsdon CR3 2NX.

Jarrold Publishing, Barrack Street, Norwich
NR3 1TR.

Johnston & Bacon, PO Box 1, Stirling.

Jordan & Sons, 21 St. Thomas Street, Bristol BS1 6JS.

Joseph (Michael), 27 Wright's Lane, W8 5TZ.

Kaye & Ward, 38 Hans Crescent, SW1X 0LZ.

Kegan Paul International, PO Box 256, WC1B 3SW.

Kelly's Directories, East Grinstead House, East
Grinstead, Sussex RH19 1XB.

Kimber (William), 77 Fulham Palace Road, W6 8JB.

Kimpton Medical, 205 Great Portland Street,
W1N 6LR.

Kingsway Publications, 1 St. Anne's Road, Eastbourne, E. Sussex BN21 3UN.

Kogan Page, 120 Pentonville Road, N1 9JN.

Ladybird Books, Beeches Road, Loughborough
LE11 2NQ.

Lawrence & Wishart, 144A Old South Lambeth Road,
SW8 1XX.

Letts (Charles), 77 Borough Road, SE1 1DW.

Lion Publishing, Peter's Way, Littlemore, Oxford
OX4 5HG.

Longman Group, Burnt Mill, Harlow, Essex
CM20 2JE.

Lund Humphries, 16 Pembridge Road, W11 3HL.

Lutterworth Press, PO Box 60, Cambridge CB1 2NT.

Macdonald & Co., 1 New Fetter Lane, EC4A 1AR.

Macdonald & Evans, 128 Long Acre, WC2E 9AN.

McGraw-Hill, Shoppenhangers Road, Maidenhead,
Berks. SL6 2QL.

Macmillan Publishers, 4 Little Essex Street,
WC2R 3LF.

Mandarin, 81 Fulham Road, SW3 6RB.

Marshall Cavendish, 58 Old Compton Street,
W1V 5PA.

Marshall Pickering, 34 Cleveland Street, W1P 5FB.

Mayflower, 77 Fulham Palace Road, W6 8JB.

Methodist Publishing, 20 Ivatt Way, Peterborough
PE3 7PG.

Methuen London, 81 Fulham Road, SW3 6RB.

Mills & Boon, 18 Paradise Road, Richmond, Surrey
TW9 1SR.

Mitchell Beazley, 14 Manette Street, W1V 5LB.

Mowbray, 41 Strand, WC2N 5JE.

Muller (Frederick), 20 Vauxhall Bridge Road,
SW1V 2SA.

Murray (John), 50 Albemarle Street, W1X 4BD.

National Christian Education Council, Robert Denholm House, Nutfield, Redhill RH1 4HW.

Nelson (Thomas), Mayfield Road, Walton-on-Thames
KT12 5PL.

New English Library, 47 Bedford Square, WC1B 3DP.

Nisbet & Co., 78 Tilehouse St., Hitchin, Herts.
SG5 2DY.

Novello & Co., 8 Lower James Street, W1R 3PL.

Octopus Books, 81 Fulham Road, SW3 6RB.

Oliver & Boyd, Longman House, Burnt Mill, Harlow,
Essex CM20 2JE.

O'Mara (Michael) Books, 9 Lion Yard, 11 Tremadoc
Road, SW4 7NF.

Owen (Peter), 73 Kenway Road, SW5 0RE.

Oxford University Press, Walton Street, Oxford
OX2 6DP.

Paladin Books, 77 Fulham Palace Road, W6 8JB.

Pan Books, 18 Cavaye Place, SW10 9PG.

Panther, 77 Fulham Palace Road, W6 8JB.

Paul (Stanley), 20 Vauxhall Bridge Road, SW1V 2SA.

Pelham Books, 27 Wright's Lane, W8 5TZ.

Penguin Books, Harmondsworth, Middx. UB7 0DA.

Pergamon Press, Headington Hill Hall, Oxford
OX3 0BW.

Phaidon Press, Musterlin House, Jordan Hill Road,
Oxford OX2 8DP.

Pharmaceutical Press, 1 Lambeth High Street,
SE1 7JN.

Philip (George), 59 Grosvenor Street, W1X 9DA.

Piatkus Books, 5 Windmill Street, W1P 1HF.

Piccadilly Press, 5 Castle Road, NW1 8PR.

Pitkin Pictorials, North Way, Andover, Hants.
SP10 5BE.

Pitman Publishing, 128 Long Acre, WC2E 9AN.

Putnam & Co., 24 Bride Lane, EC4Y 8DR.

Quartet Books, 27 Goodge Street, W1P 1FD.

Quiller Press, 46 Lillie Road, SW6 1TN.

Random Century Group, 20 Vauxhall Bridge Road,
SW1V 2SA.

Ravette Books, 3 Glenside Estate, Star Road, Partridge Green, Horsham, W. Sussex RH13 8RA.

Reader's Digest, 25 Berkeley Square, W1X 6AB.

Religious & Moral Education Press, Hennock Road,
Exeter EX2 8RP.

Rider & Co., 20 Vauxhall Bridge Road, SW1V 2SA.

Routledge, 11 New Fetter Lane, EC4P 4EE.

SCM Press, 26 Tottenham Road, N1 4BZ.

SPCK, Holy Trinity Church, Marylebone Road,
NW1 4DU.

St. Andrew Press, 121 George Street, Edinburgh
EH2 4YN.

Scripture Union, 130 City Road, EC1V 2NJ.

Secker & Warburg, 81 Fulham Road, SW3 6RB.

Severn House, 35 Manor Road, Wallington, Surrey
SM6 0BW.

Sheed & Ward, 2 Creechurch Lane, EC3A 5AQ.

Sheldon Press, Holy Trinity Church, Marylebone
Road, NW1 4DU.

Sidgwick & Jackson, 1 Tavistock Chambers,
WC1A 2SG.

Simon & Schuster, Wolsey House, Wolsey Road,
Hemel Hempstead HP2 4SS.

Smythe (Colin), PO Box 6, Gerrards Cross, Bucks.
SL9 8XA.

Souvenir Press, 43 Great Russell Street, WC1B 3PA.

Sphere Books, 27 Wright's Lane, W8 5TZ.

Spon (E. & F. N.), 11 New Fetter Lane, EC4P 4EE.

Stephens (Patrick), 77 Fulham Palace Road, W6 8JB.

Stevens & Sons, 183 Marsh Wall, E14 9FT.

Sweet & Maxwell, 183 Marsh Wall, E14 9FT.

Thames & Hudson, 30 Bloomsbury Street, WC1B 3QP.

Thorsons Publishers, 77 Fulham Palace Road,
W6 8JB.

Times Books, 16 Golden Square, W1R 4BN.

Turnstone Books, 77 Fulham Palace Road, W6 8JB.

University of Wales Press, Gwennyth Street, Cardiff
CF2 4YD.

Unwin Hyman, 77 Fulham Palace Road, W6 8JB.

Vallentine Mitchell, 11 Gainsborough Road, E11 1RS.

Viking, 27 Wright's Lane, W8 5TZ.

Virago Press, 20–23 Mandela Street, NW1 0HQ.

Walker Books, 87 Vauxhall Walk, SE11 5HJ.

Ward Lock, 41 Strand, WC2N 5JE.

Ward Lock Educational Co., TR House, Christopher
Road, East Grinstead, W. Sussex, RH19 3BT.

Warne (Frederick), 27 Wright's Lane, W8 5TZ.

Webb & Bower, 5 Cathedral Close, Exeter EX1 1EZ.

Weidenfeld & Nicolson, 91 Clapham High Street,
SW4 9TA.

Wheaton (A.), Hennock Road, Exeter EX2 8RP.

Whitaker (J.), 12 Dyott Street, WC1A 1DF.

Wildwood House, Gower House, Croft Road, Aldershot, Hants. GU11 3HR.

Wisden (John), 25 Market Street, Guildford
GU1 4LB.

Witherby (H. F. & G.), 14 Henrietta Street,
WC2E 8QJ.

Wolfe Publishing, 2 Torrington Place, WC1E 7LT.

World's Work, *see* Heinemann (William).

Wright (John), PO Box 63, Guildford GU2 5BH.

Zomba Books, 165 High Road, NW10 2SG.

ANNUAL REFERENCE BOOKS

Advertiser's Annual.—East Grinstead House, East Grinstead, W. Sussex RH19 1XE. £55·00.

Allied Dunbar Investment Guide.—Fourth Avenue, Harlow, Essex CM19 5AA. £15·99.

Allied Dunbar Tax Guide.—Fourth Avenue, Harlow, Essex CM19 5AA. £15·99.

Annual Register of World Events.—Fourth Avenue, Harlow, Essex, CM19 5AA. £69·00.

Antique Shops of Britain, Guide to the.—5 Church Street, Woodbridge, Suffolk IP12 1DS. £12·95.

Art Sales Index.—1 Thames Street, Weybridge, Surrey KT1 8JG. £90·00.

Association of Consulting Engineers Who's Who & Year Book.—178–202 Great Portland Street, W1N 6NH. £34·00.

Astronomical Almanac.—HMSO, PO Box 276, SW8 5DT. (Aug.) £14·50.

Automobile Year.—Unit 6, Pilton Estate, Croydon, Surrey CR0 3RY. £24·95.

Baily's Hunting Directory.—1 Lower Grosvenor Place, SW1W 0EL. (Oct.) £25·00.

Banker's Almanac & Year Book.—East Grinstead House, East Grinstead, W. Sussex RH19 1XE. (Feb.) 2 v. £150·00.

Benedictine Year Book.—Ampleforth Abbey, York YO6 4EN. £1·00.

Benn's Direct Marketing Services.—PO Box 20, Sovereign Way, Tonbridge, Kent TN9 1RQ. £75·00.

Benn's Hardware & Do-it-Yourself Buyer's Guide.—PO Box 20, Sovereign Way, Tonbridge, Kent TN9 1RQ. £32·00.

Benn's Media Directory.—PO Box 20, Sovereign Way, Tonbridge, Kent TN9 1RQ. 2v. each £75·00.

Birmingham Post & Mail Year Book & Who's Who.—Colmore Circus, Birmingham B4 6AX. (July) £13·25.

Britain: An Official Handbook.—HMSO, PO Box 276, SW8 5DT. (Jan.) £14·50.

Britannica Book of the Year.—Carew House, Station Approach, Wallington, Surrey SM6 0DA. (Apr.) £44·00.

British Clothing Industry Year Book.—Westbury House, 701–705 Warwick Road, Solihull B91 3DA. £40·00.

British Music Year Book.—241 Shaftesbury Avenue, WC2H 8EH. £10·95.

British Plastics & Rubber Directory.—Catalyst House, 159 Clapham High Street, SW4 7SS. £10·00.

Brown's Nautical Almanack Daily Tide Tables.—4–10 Darnley Street, Glasgow G41 2SD. (Sept.) £26·00.

Building Societies Year Book.—7 Swallow Place, W1R 8AB. £37·00.

Buses Yearbook.—Coombelands House, Addlestone, Weybridge, Surrey KT15 1HY. £8·95.

Carpet Annual.—PO Box 20, Sovereign Way, Tonbridge, Kent TN9 1RQ. £58·00.

Catholic Directory of England and Wales.—18 Crosby Road North, Liverpool L22 4QF. £17·50.

Charities Digest.—501–505 Kingsland Road, E8 4AU. £9·95.

Chemical Industry Directory.—PO Box 20, Sovereign Way, Tonbridge, Kent TN9 1RQ. £72·00.

Chemist & Druggist Directory.—PO Box 20, Sovereign Way, Tonbridge, Kent TN9 1RQ. £65·00.

Christies' Review of the Season.—Musterlin House, Jordan Hill Road, Oxford OX2 8DP. (Dec.) £30·00.

Church of England Year Book.—Church House, Dean's Yard, Westminster, SW1P 3NZ. (Jan.) £14·50.

Church of Scotland Year Book.—121 George Street, Edinburgh EH2 4YN. (Apr.) £9·50.

City of London Directory & Livery Companies Guide.—Fairfax House, Causton Road, Colchester CO1 1RJ. £15·50.

Civil Aviation Review.—Coombelands House, Addlestone, Weybridge, Surrey KT15 1HY. £8·95.

Civil Service Year Book.—HMSO, PO Box 276, SW8 5DT. (Feb.) £15·95.

Commonwealth Universities Year Book.—36 Gordon Square, WC1H 0PF. (Sept.) £102·00.

Commonwealth Year Book.—HMSO, PO Box 276, SW8 5DT. (May) £18·50.

Computer Users' Year Book.—32–34 Broadwick Street, W1A 2HG. £95·00.

Concrete Year Book.—Thomas Telford House, 1 Heron Quay, E14 9XF. £45·00.

Coventry Evening Telegraph Year Book and Who's Who.—Coventry Newspapers Ltd., Corporation Street, Coventry CV1 1FP. (Nov.) £9·75.

Current Law Year Book.—11 New Fetter Lane, EC4P 4EE. £60·00.

Daily Mail Year Book.—New Carmelite House, Fleet Street, EC4Y 0JA. (Dec.) £3·95.

Diplomatic Service List.—HMSO, PO Box 276, SW8 5DT. (April) £17·50.

Directory of Directors.—East Grinstead House, East Grinstead, W. Sussex RH19 1XE. (Apr.) £110·00.

Directory of Official Architecture & Planning.—Fourth Avenue, Harlow, Essex CM19 5AA. £47·50.

Directory of Opportunities for Graduates.—Newpoint House, St. James's Lane, N10 3DF. 7v. each £9·95.

Dod's Parliamentary Companion.—Hurst Green, Etchingham, E. Sussex TN19 7PX. £56·00.

Education Authorities' Directory and Annual.—Derby House, Bletchingley Road, Merstham, Surrey RH1 3DN. (Jan.) £45·00.

Education Year Book.—Fourth Avenue, Harlow, Essex CM19 5AA. £52·50.

Electrical & Electronics Trades Directory.—Michael Faraday House, Six Hills Way, Stevenage, Herts. SG1 2AY. (Feb.) £53·00.

Electricity Supply Handbook.—Quadrant House, The Quadrant, Sutton, Surrey SM2 5AS. (Feb.) £17·50.

Engineer Buyers' Guide.—40 Beresford Street, SE18 6BQ. £40·00.

Europa World Year Book.—18 Bedford Square, WC1B 3JN. 2 v. £210·00.

European Food Trades Directory.—48 Poland Street, W1V 4PP. £89·00.

European Glass Directory & Buyer's Guide.—2 Queensway, Redhill, Surrey RH1 1QS. £43·00.

Fairplay World Shipping Directory.—PO Box 96, Coulsdon, Surrey CR3 2TE. £45·00.

Farm and Garden Equipment Data Book.—63 Ulcombe Gardens, Canterbury, Kent CT2 7QZ. £10·95.

Flight International Directory of British Aviation.—PO Box 1315, Potters Bar, Herts. EN6 1PU. £28·00.

Frozen & Chilled Foods Year Book.—2 Queensway, Redhill, Surrey RH1 1QS. £36·50.

Furnishing Trade, Directory to the.—PO Box 20, Sovereign Way, Tonbridge, Kent TN9 1RQ. £70·00.

Gas Industry Directory.—PO Box 20, Sovereign Way, Tonbridge, Kent TN9 1RQ. (Jan.) £55·00.

Gibbons' Stamps of the World Catalogue.—5 Parkside, Christchurch Road, Ringwood, Hants. BH24 3SH. (Oct.) 2v. each £15·50.

Good Food Guide.—PO Box 6, Mill Road, Dunton Green, Sevenoaks, Kent TN13 2XX. £12·95.

Good Hotel Guide.—PO Box 6, Mill Road, Dunton Green, Sevenoaks, Kent TN13 2XX. £10·99.

Government & Municipal Contractors Register.—55 High Street, Epsom, Surrey KT19 8DW. (Jan.) £40·00.

Guinness Book of Answers.—33 London Road, Enfield EN2 6DJ. £9·95.

Guinness Book of Records.—33 London Road, Enfield EN2 6DJ. (Oct.) £11·95.

Historic Houses, Castles and Gardens in Great Britain and Ireland.—East Grinstead House, East Grinstead, W. Sussex RH19 1XA. (Jan.) £4·95.

Hollis Press and PR Annual.—Contact House, Lower Hampton Road, Sunbury-on-Thames, TW16 5HG. (Oct.) £69·50.

Hospitals & Health Services Yearbook & Directory of Hospital Suppliers.—75 Portland Place, W1N 4AN. £55·00.

Hotel, Restaurant & Catering Supplies.—55 High Street, Epsom, Surrey KT19 8DW. £40·00.

Hutchins' Priced Schedules.—33 Station Road, Bexhill-on-Sea, E. Sussex TN40 1RG. £26·00.

Independent Schools Year Book.—35 Bedford Row, WC1R 4JH. 2v. £14·95, £9·95.

International Paper Directory, Philips'.—PO Box 20, Sovereign Way, Tonbridge, Kent TN9 1RQ. £80·00.

International Yearbook & Statesman's Who's Who.—East Grinstead House, East Grinstead, W. Sussex RH19 1XE. (Apr.) £105·00.

Jane's All The World's Aircraft.—Sentinel House, 163 Brighton Road, Coulsdon, Surrey CR3 2NX. (Oct.) £110·00.

Jane's Armour & Artillery.—Sentinel House, 163 Brighton Road, Coulsdon, Surrey CR3 2NX. (Nov.) £100·00.

Jane's Containerization Direct.—Sentinel House, 163 Brighton Road, Coulsdon, Surrey CR3 2NX. (Nov.) £110·00.

Jane's Fighting Ships.—Sentinel House, 163 Brighton Road, Coulsdon, Surrey CR3 2NX. £110·00.

Jane's High Speed Marine Craft & Air Cushion Vehicles.—Sentinel House, 163 Brighton Road, Coulsdon, Surrey CR3 2NX. £105·00.

Jane's Infantry Weapons.—Sentinel House, 163 Brighton Road, Coulsdon, Surrey CR3 2NX. (Aug.) £110·00.

Jane's Weapon Systems.—Sentinel House, 163 Brighton Road, Coulsdon, Surrey CR3 2NX. £100·00.

Jane's World Railways.—Sentinel House, 163 Brighton Road, Coulsdon, Surrey CR3 2NX. £115·00.

Jewish Year Book.—25 Furnival Street, EC4A 1JT. (Jan.) £12·00.

Kelly's Business Directory.—East Grinstead House, East Grinstead, W. Sussex RH19 1XB. £110·00.

Kelly's Post Office London Business Directory.—East Grinstead House, East Grinstead, W. Sussex RH19 1XB. 2v, £135·00.

Kelly's UK Exports.—East Grinstead House, East Grinstead, W. Sussex RH19 1XB. £50·00.

Kempe's Engineers Year Book.—40 Beresford Street, SE18 6BQ. £85·00.

Kemp's International Film & TV Year Book.—Westbury House, 701–705 Warwick Road, Solihull B91 3DA. (May) £40·00.

Kemp's International Music & Recording Industry Year Book.—Westbury House, 701–705 Warwick Road, Solihull B91 3DA. £25·00.

Kime's International Law Directory.—PO Box 67, Carlisle CA4 9DE. (June) £24·00.

Laxton's National Building Price Book.—East Grinstead House, East Grinstead, W. Sussex RH19 1XE. £61·00.

Library Association Yearbook.—7 Ridgmount Street, WC1E 7AE. (May) £27·50.

Lloyd's List of Shipowners.—71 Fenchurch Street, EC3M 4BS. (Sept.) £70·00.

Lloyd's Maritime Directory.—Sheepen Place, Colchester CO3 3LP. (Jan.) £105·00.

Lloyd's Nautical Year Book.—Sheepen Place, Colchester CO3 3LP. (Sept.) £25·00.

Lloyd's Register of Ships.—71 Fenchurch Street, EC3M 4BS. (July) £275·00.

London Trade Directory.—3rd Floor, Albany House, Hurst Street, Birmingham B5 4BD. (Sept.) £75·00.

Lyle's Official Antiques Review.—Glenmayne, Galashiels TD1 3NR. £14·95.

Lyle's Official Arts Review.—Glenmayne, Galashiels TD1 3NR. £14·95.

Macmillan & Silk Cut Nautical Almanack.—Little Essex Street, WC2R 3LF. £17·95.

Magistrates' Court Guide.—Borough Green, Sevenoaks, Kent TN15 8PH. £16·95.

Medical Annual.—PO Box 63, Westbury House, Bury Street, Guildford, Surrey GU2 5BH. (July). £29·50.

Medical Directory.—Fourth Avenue, Harlow, Essex CM19 5AA. (Apr.) 2v, £115·00.

Medical Register.—44 Hallam Street, W1N 6AE. (Mar.) 3v. £65·00.

Middle East & North Africa.—18 Bedford Square, WC1B 3JN. (Oct.) £95·00.

Miller's Antiques Price Guide.—Sissinghurst Court, Sissinghurst, Kent TN17 2JA. £17·95.

Mining Annual Review.—PO Box 10, Edenbridge, Kent TN8 5NE. £35·00.

Mining International Year Book.—Fourth Avenue, Harlow, Essex CM19 5AA. (June) £90·00.

Motor Industry of Great Britain World Automotive Statistics.—Forbes House, Halkin Street, SW1X 7DS. (Oct.) £60·00.

Municipal Yearbook & Public Services Directory, 178 Great Portland Street, W1N 6NH. (Dec.) 2v. £75·00.

Museums and Galleries in Great Britain and Ireland.—East Grinstead House, East Grinstead, W. Sussex RH19 1XA. (Nov.) £3·95.

Nautical Almanac.—HMSO, PO Box 276, SW8 5DT. (Oct.) £12·50.

Old Moore's Almanac.—Yeovil Road, Slough, Bucks. SL1 4JH. (July) £0·65.

Owen's Africa Business Directory.—18 Farndon Road, Oxford OX6 2RT. £80·00.

Owen's Gulf Directory.—18 Farndon Road, Oxford OX6 2RT. £80·00.

Packaging Industry Directory.—PO Box 20, Sovereign Way, Tonbridge, Kent TN9 1RQ. £49·00.

Pears Cyclopedia.—27 Wright's Lane, W8 5TZ. £12·99.

Photography Year Book.—45 The Broadway, Tolworth, Surbiton, Surrey KT6 7DW. £16·95.

Polymers, Paint & Colour Year Book.—2 Queensway, Redhill, Surrey RH1 1QS. £40·00.

Ports of the World.—Sheepen Place, Colchester, Essex CO3 3LP. £95·00.

Printers' Year Book.—11 Bedford Row, WC1R 4DX. £40·00.

Printing Trades Directory.—PO Box 20, Sovereign Way, Tonbridge, Kent TN9 1RQ. £72·00.

Publishing, Directory of.—Artillery House, Artillery Row, SW1P 1RT. (Oct.) £27·50.

RAC Continental Hotel Guide.—PO Box 100, RAC House, Lansdowne Road, Croydon CR9 2JA. (Jan.) £6·95.

RAC Hotel Guide.—PO Box 100, RAC House, Lansdowne Road, Croydon CR9 2JA. (Apr.) £9·95.

RUSI & Brassey's Defence Year Book.—Headington Hill Hall, Oxford OX3 0BW. £35·00.

Railway Directory & Year Book.—Quadrant House, The Quadrant, Sutton, Surrey SM2 5AS. (Dec.) £36·00.

Railway World Year Book.—Coombelands House, Addlestone, Weybridge, Surrey KT15 1HY. £8·95.

Reed's Nautical Almanac & Tide Tables.—80 Coombe Road, New Malden, Surrey KT3 4QS. (Oct.) £15·95.

Retail Directory of the United Kingdom.—48 Poland Street, W1V 4PP. £96·00.

RIBA Directory of Practices.—Royal Institute of British Architects, 39 Moreland Street, EC1V 8BB. (Oct.) £38·00.

Rothmans Football Year Book.—Headway House, 66–73 Shoe Lane, EC4P 4AB. (Aug.) £16·95; £12·95.

Royal Society Year Book.—6 Carlton House Terrace, SW1Y 5AG. (Feb.) £12·50.

Ruff's Guide to the Turf & Sporting Life Annual.—PO Box 54, Desborough, Northants. NN14 2LU. (Dec.) £50·00.

Salvation Army Year Book.—117–121 Judd Street, WC1H 9NN. (Apr.) £7·95, £3·99.

Scottish Current Law Year Book.—2 St. Giles Street, Edinburgh EH1 1PU. £115·00.

Scottish Law Directory.—59 George Street, Edinburgh EH2 2LQ. £27·00.

Screen International Film & Television Year Book.—6 Great Chapel Street, W1V 3AG. £31·00.

Screen World.—Brookmount House, 62–65 Chandos Place, WC1N 4NW. £16·95.

Sell's Aerospace Europe.—55 High Street, Epsom, Surrey KT19 8DW. £45·00.

Sell's British Exporters.—55 High Street, Epsom, Surrey KT19 8DW. £40·00.

Sell's Building Index.—55 High Street, Epsom, Surrey KT19 8DW. £40·00.

Sell's Directory of Products and Services.—55 High Street, Epsom, Surrey KT19 8DW. (July) £50·00.

Sell's Health Service Buyers Guide.—55 High Street, Epsom, Surrey KT19 8DW. £40·00.

Sheet Metal Industries Year Book.—2 Queensway, Redhill, Surrey RH1 1QS. £39·00.

Shipowners, Shipbuilders & Marine Engineers, Directory of.—Quadrant House, The Quadrant, Sutton, Surrey SM2 5AS. £50·00.

Solicitors & Barristers Directory.—Paulton House, 8 Shepherdess Walk, N1 7LB. £38·00.

Specification.—9–13 Queen Anne's Gate, SW1H 9BY. (May) 6v. £52·00.

Spon's Architects' & Builders' Price Book.—11 New Fetter Lane, EC4P 4EE. £49·50.

Spon's Mechanical & Electrical Services Prices Book.—11 New Fetter Lane, EC4P 4EE. £52·50.

Statesman's Yearbook.—4 Little Essex Street, WC2R 3LF. (Aug.) £32·50.

Stock Exchange Official Year Book.—4 Little Essex Street, WC2R 3LF. £135·00.

Stone's Justices' Manual.—Borough Green, Sevenoaks, Kent TN15 8PH. 3v. (May) £130·00.

Tanker Register.—12 Camomile Street, EC3A 7BP. (May) £110·00.

Timber Trades Journal Telephone Address Book.—Sovereign Way, Tonbridge, Kent TN9 1RQ. £37·00.

Training Directory.—120 Pentonville Road, N1 9JN. £20·00.

Travel Trade Directory.—40 Beresford Street, SE18 6BQ. (July) £40·00.

UK Kompass Register.—East Grinstead House, East Grinstead, W. Sussex RH19 1XD. v. 1–3, £285·00, v. 4, £138·00.

United Kingdom Minerals Yearbook.—Keyworth, Nottingham NG12 5GG. £25·00.

Unit Trust Year Book.—7th Floor, 50–64 Broadway, SW1H 0DB. (Mar.) £45·00.

United Reformed Church Year Book.—86 Tavistock Place, WC1H 9RT. (Sept.) £7·00.

Veterinary Annual.—Borough Green, Sevenoaks, Kent TN15 8PH. £45·00.

Water Services Year Book.—2 Queensway, Redhill, Surrey RH1 1QS. (Oct.) £33·00.

Whitaker's Almanack.—12 Dyott Street, WC1A 1DF. (Nov.) £32·50; £19·95; £10·50.

Whitaker's Books in Print.—12 Dyott Street, WC1A 1DF. (Sept.) £148·00.

Whitaker's Publishers in the United Kingdom and their Addresses.—12 Dyott Street, WC1A 1DF. (Mar.) £4·75.

Who Owns Whom?—Holmers Farm Way, High Wycombe, Bucks. HP12 4UL. 2v. £220·00.

Who's Who.—35 Bedford Row, WC1R 4JH. £65·00.

Who's Who, International.—18 Bedford Square, WC1R 4JH. (Sept.) £95·00.

Willing's Press Guide.—East Grinstead House, East Grinstead, W. Sussex RH19 1XE. (Feb.) £62·00.

Wisden Cricketers' Almanack.—13–14 Eldon Way, Lineside Estate, Littlehampton, W. Sussex BN17 7HE. £18·50; £15·50.

World Advertising Review.—Artillery House, Artillery Row, SW1P 1RT. £40·00.

World Hotel Directory.—Fourth Avenue, Harlow, Essex CM19 5AA. £60·00.

World Insurance.—Fourth Avenue, Harlow, Essex CM19 5AA. £95·00.

World of Learning.—18 Bedford Square, WC1B 3JN. (Jan.) 2v. £130·00.

Writers' & Artists' Year Book.—35 Bedford Row, WC1R 4JH. (Jan.) £7·95.

SYMBOLS FOR CORRECTING PROOFS

Supplied by WILLIAM CLOWES LTD, Beccles, Suffolk, printers of '*Whitaker's Almanack*'

Letter(s) or word(s) requiring alteration should be struck through IN INK in the text and the substitution should be written in the nearest margin followed by / (the symbol used to denote that the marginal mark is concluded). Insertions should be indicated by / or ∧ at the conclusion of the marginal mark *and* at the desired place in the text.

Alteration required	Mark in margin	Mark in text	Alteration required	Mark in margin	Mark in text
Delete (take out)	ϑ or ϑ/	/ or Vertical stroke to delete one or two letters; horizontal line to delete more	Take letter(s) or word(s) from beginning of one line to end of preceding line	*back* or *take back*	⌐
Delete and close up	ϑ or ϑ/ (with close up marks)	Strike out letter(s) not required and add 'close up' mark above and below	Begin a new paragraph	*n.p.*	⌐ before first word of new paragraph
Close up: delete space between letters	⌒	⌒ linking letters or words	No new para. here or run on previous matter with later matter	*run on*	between paras. or other matter
Use ligature (fi, fl, ffl, etc.) or diphthong (æ, œ)	⌒ *enclosing ligature or diphthong required*	⌒ enclosing letters to be altered	Spell out in full the abbreviation, contraction, or figure	*spell out*	Encircle, words, etc., or figures concerned
Insert space between letters or words	#∧	∧	Insert omitted portion of copy	*out - see copy*	∧ Attach the relevant copy to the proof, indicating omitted portion
Leave as printed (i.e. a cancellation of previous marking)	*stet*	.... under letter(s) or word(s) crossed out but to be retained	Inserted or substituted letter(s), figure(s), or sign(s) under which this is placed to be superscript (i.e. high alignment)[1]	⌐ (*see footnote*)	∧ for insertions For substitutions encircle letter(s). figure(s). or sign(s) to be altered
Invert type (of letter(s) upside down)	↻	Encircle letter(s) to be altered	Inserted or substituted letter(s), figure(s), or sign(s) over which this is placed to be subscript (low alignment)[2]	⌐ (*see footnote*)	∧ for insertions For substitutions encircle letter(s), figure(s), etc., to be altered
'Battered' letter(s) to be replaced by similar but undamaged characters	✕	Encircle letter(s) or word(s) to be replaced and write the correct letter(s) in the margin	Change to lower case	*l.c.*	Encircle letter(s) to be altered
Push down space or 'high' letter(s) or word(s)	�	Encircle space, letter(s), or word(s) affected	Replace 'wrong fount' by letter(s) of correct fount	*w.f.*	Encircle letter(s) or word(s) to be altered
Transpose	*tr.* or *trs.*	⌐⌐ between letters or words, numbered when necessary	Change to capital letters	*caps.*	≡ under letter(s) or word(s) to be altered
Take letter(s) or word(s) from end of one line to beginning of next line	*take over* or *over*	⌐	Change to small capitals	*s.c.*	═ under letter(s) or word(s) to be altered

ᒕ indicates a superior (superscript) figure one   ᒣ[2] indicates an inferior (subscript) figure two

Alteration required	Mark in margin	Mark in text	Alteration required	Mark in margin	Mark in text
Use capital letters for initial letter(s) (as desired) and small capitals for rest of word(s)	*caps* & *s.c.*	under initial letter(s) and under the remainder of the word(s)	Move lines to the left		at right side of group of lines to be moved (indicating approx. position)
Change to bold type	*bold*	Draw wavy line under letter(s) or word(s) to be altered	Move portion of matter so that it is positioned as indicated	[ ]	at limits of required position
Change to roman type	*rom.*	Encircle letter(s) or word(s) to be altered	Raise lines	*raise*	over lines to be raised
Change to italic type	*italic*	Draw this straight line under letter(s) or word(s) to be altered	Lower lines	*lower*	under lines to be lowered
Letter(s) or word(s) to be underlined	*underline*	under letter(s), word(s), etc. to be underlined	Correct the vertical alignment	‖	‖
Equalize space between words	*eq. #*	between words	Straighten lines	=	through lines to be straightened
Reduce space	*less #*	between words	Insert parentheses (round-shaped brackets)	(/) or c/)l	
Space to be inserted between lines or paragraphs	#>	*Amount of space should be indicated*	Insert [square] brackets	[/] or c/]l	
To be placed in centre of line, etc.	*centre*	Position to be indicated by	Insert hyphen	-/	
Indent one en (approx. space occupied by n of type in use)	en	indicating approximate position	Insert en (= half-em) rule (*see above*)	en/	
Indent one em (approx. space occupied by M of type in use)	em	Ditto	Insert one-em rule (*see above*)	em/	
Indent two ems (approx. space occupied by MM of type in use)		Ditto	Insert two-em rule (*see above*)	2em/	
Move to the left		Ditto	Insert apostrophe	'/	
Move to the right		Ditto	Insert single quotation marks	' '	
			Insert double quotation marks	'' ''	
Move lines to the right		at left side of group of lines to be moved (indicating approx. position)	Insert ellipsis	.../	
			Insert leader (*visual guide to alignment in contents pages, etc.*)	••• •• •	(*three, two, or one dot*)
			Insert oblique stroke	(/)	
Punctuation		,/ ;/ ./ ; / ⊙ ⊙ ?/ ?/ !/ !/			

PRINCIPAL LONDON CLUBS

ALPINE (1857), 118 Eaton Square, SW1W 9AF. (Tel: 071-259 5591).—*Hon. Sec.*, Dr. M. J. Esten.

ANGLO-BELGIAN (1955), 60 Knightsbridge, SW1X 7LF. (Tel: 071-235 2121).—*Sec.*, Lt.-Col. T. C. Morris, LVO.

ARMY AND NAVY (1837), 36–39 Pall Mall, SW1Y 5JN. (Tel: 071-930 9721).—*Sec.*, Col. D. O. O'Reilly.

ARTS (1863), 40 Dover Street, W1X 3RB.—*Sec.*, Lt.-Col. C. Miers.

ARTS THEATRE (1927), 7 Great Newport Street, WC2.—*Sec.*, Miss C. Dowling.

THE ATHENAEUM (1824), 107 Pall Mall, SW1Y 5ER. (Tel: 071-930 4843).—*Sec.*, R. R. T. Smith.

AUTHORS' (1892), 40 Dover Street, W1X 3RB. (Tel: 071-499 8581).—*Sec.*, Mrs. H. Ridgway.

BEEFSTEAK (1876), 9 Irving Street, WC2H 7AT. (Tel: 071-930 5722).—*Sec.*, E. Pool, MC.

BOODLE'S (1762), 28 St. James's Street, SW1A 1HJ. (Tel: 071-930 7166).—*Sec.*, R. J. Edmonds.

BROOKS'S (1764), St. James's Street, SW1A 1LN. (Tel: 071-493 4411).—*Sec.*, M. A. Roberts.

BUCK'S (1919), 18 Clifford Street, W1X 1RG. (Tel: 071-734 2337).—*Sec.*, Miss J. Turner.

CALEDONIAN (1891), 9 Halkin Street, SW1X 7DR. (Tel: 071-235 5162).—*Sec.*, P. J. Varney.

CANNING (1910), 42 Half Moon Street, W1Y 8DS. (Tel: 071-499 5163).—*Sec.*, T. M. Harrington.

CARLTON (1832), 69 St. James's Street, SW1A 1PJ. (Tel: 071-493 1164).—*Sec.*, R. N. Linsley.

CAVALRY AND GUARDS (1893), 127 Piccadilly, W1V 0PX. (Tel: 071-499 1261).—*Sec.*, L. D. de Pinna.

CHALLONER (1949), 59–61 Pont Street, SW1 0BG—*Gen. Manager*, G. W. Jago.

CHELSEA ARTS (1891), 143 Old Church Street, SW3 6EB.—*Sec.*, Hon. D. Winterbottom.

CITY LIVERY (1914), Sion College, Victoria Embankment, EC4Y 0DN. (Tel: 071-353 2431).—*Hon. Sec.*, B. L. Morgan, CBE.

CITY OF LONDON (1832), 19 Old Broad Street, EC2N 1DS. (Tel: 071-588 7991).—*Sec.*, G. S. Chisholm.

CITY UNIVERSITY (1895), 50 Cornhill, EC3V 3PD.—*Sec.*, Miss R. C. Graham.

EAST INDIA (1849), 16 St. James's Square, SW1Y 4LH.—*Sec.*, J. G. F. Stoy.

FARMERS (1842), 3 Whitehall Court, SW1A 2EL. (Tel: 071-930 3751).—*Sec.*, Lt.-Col. G. B. Murray.

FLYFISHERS' (1884), 24a Old Burlington Street, W1X 1RG. (Tel: 071-734 9229).—*Sec.*, Cdr. N. T. Fuller (*retd.*).

GARRICK (1831), 15 Garrick Street, WC2E 9AY. (Tel: 071-379 6478).—*Sec.*, M. J. Harvey.

GREEN ROOM (1877), 9 Adam Street, WC2N 6AA.—*Sec.*, J. Booth.

GRESHAM (1843), 15 Abchurch Lane, EC4N 7BB.—*Sec.*, Mrs. J. S. Downing.

GROUCHO (1985), 45 Dean Street, W1V 5AP. (Tel: 071-439 4685).—*Company Sec.*, Ms. A. Howarth.

HURLINGHAM (1869), Ranelagh Gardens, SW6 3PR. (Tel: 071-736 8411).—*Sec.*, P. H. Covell.

KEMPTON PARK (1878), Kempton Park Racecourse, Sunbury-on-Thames, Middx., TW16 5AQ. (Tel: 0932-782292).—*Sec.*, Mrs C. Milburn-Lee.

KENNEL (1873), 1 Clarges Street, W1Y 8AB. (Tel: 071-493 6651).—*Sec.*, Maj.-Gen. M. H. Sinnatt, CB.

LANSDOWNE (1934), 9 Fitzmaurice Place, W1X 6JD.—*Sec.*, Lt.-Cdr. T. P. Havers (*retd.*).

LONDON ROWING (1856), Embankment, Putney, SW15 1LB. (Tel: 081-788 0666).—*Hon. Sec.*, N. A. Smith.

LONDON THAMES FENCING (1848), 83 Perham Road, W14 9SY.—*Hon. Sec.*, G. Morrison.

MCC (MARYLEBONE CRICKET CLUB) (1787), Lord's Cricket Ground, NW8 8QN. (Tel: 071-289 1611).—*Sec.*, Lt.-Col. J. R. Stephenson, OBE.

MINING (1910), 3 London Wall Buildings, EC2.—*Sec.*, Miss P. Warner.

NATIONAL (1845), c/o Carlton Club (*q.v.*).—*Sec.*, I. E. Nash.

NATIONAL LIBERAL (1882), Whitehall Place, SW1A 2HE. (Tel: 071-930 9871).—*Sec.*, G. Snell.

NAVAL (1946), 38 Hill Street, W1X 8DP.—*Gen. Sec.*, Cdr. C. R. Parkes, RD.

NAVAL AND MILITARY (1862), 94 Piccadilly, W1V 0BP. (Tel: 071-499 5163).—*Sec.*, A. Hickey.

NEW CAVENDISH (1984), (formerly VAD), 44 Great Cumberland Place, W1H 8BS.—*Sec.*, Miss H. Bateman.

ORIENTAL (1824), Stratford House, Stratford Place, W1N 0ES. (Tel: 071-629 5126).—*Sec.*, S. C. Doble.

PORTLAND (1816), 42 Half Moon Street, W1Y 7RD. (Tel: 071-499 1523).—*Sec.*, R. B. Little.

PRATT'S (1841), 14 Park Place, SW1A 1LP. (Tel: 071-493 0397).—*Sec.*, Capt. P. W. E. Parry, MBE.

QUEEN'S (1886), Palliser Road, W14 9EQ.—*Sec.*, J. A. S. Edwardes.

RAILWAY (1899), Keen House, 4 Calshot Street, N1 9DA.—*Hon. Sec.*, A. G. Wells.

REFORM (1836), 104–105 Pall Mall, SW1Y 5EW. (Tel: 071-930 9374).—*Sec.*, R. A. M. Forrest.

ROEHAMPTON (1901), Roehampton Lane, SW15 5LR. (Tel: 081-876 5505).—*Chief Exec.*, M. Yates.

ROYAL AIR FORCE (1918), 128 Piccadilly, W1V 0PY. (Tel: 071-499 3456).—*Sec.*, Sqn. Ldr. J. Swaffield.

ROYAL AUTOMOBILE (1897), 89–91 Pall Mall, SW1Y 5HS.—*Sec.*, J. N. Cranfield.

ROYAL OCEAN RACING (1925), 20 St. James's Place, SW1A 1NN. (Tel: 071-493 2248).—*Dir.*, E. A. Green.

ROYAL OVER-SEAS LEAGUE (1910), Over-Seas House, Park Place, St. James's Street, SW1A 1LR. (Tel: 071-408 0214).—*Gen. Manager*, Capt. J. Rumble.

ROYAL THAMES YACHT (1775), 60 Knightsbridge, SW1X 7LF. (Tel: 071-235 2121).—*Sec.*, Capt. A. R. Ward, CBE, RN.

ST. STEPHEN'S CONSTITUTIONAL (1870), 34 Queen Anne's Gate, SW1H 9AB. (Tel: 071-222 1382).—*Sec.*, L. D. Mawby.

SAVAGE (1857), 9 Fitzmaurice Place, W1X 5DE.—*Hon. Sec.*, D. Coomber, OBE.

SAVILE (1868), 69 Brook Street, W1Y 2ER. (Tel: 071-629 5462).—*Sec.*, P. Aldersley.

SKI CLUB OF GREAT BRITAIN (1903), 118 Eaton Square, SW1W 9AF. (Tel: 071-245 1033).—*Sec.*, Air Vice-Marshal J. M. Jones, CB (*retd.*).

THAMES ROWING (1860), Embankment, Putney, SW15 1LB. (Tel: 081-788 0676).—*Hon. Sec.*, M. J. S. Levy.

TRAVELLERS' (1819), 106 Pall Mall, SW1Y 5EP.—*Sec.*, M. S. Allcock.

TURF (1868), 5 Carlton House Terrace, SW1Y 5AQ. (Tel: 071-930 8555).—*Sec.*, Col. J. G. B. Rigby, OBE.

UNITED NURSING SERVICES (1921), 40 South Street, W1.—*Sec.*, W. Oakes.

UNITED OXFORD AND CAMBRIDGE UNIVERSITY (1972), 71 Pall Mall, SW1Y 5HD. (Tel: 071-930 5151).—*Gen. Secs.*, D. McDougall; D. Gwynne.

UNIVERSITY WOMEN'S (1886), 2 Audley Square, W1Y 6DB.—*Sec.*, Mrs. P. J. Gray.

VICTORIA (1863), 1 North Court, Great Peter Street, SW1P 3LL.—*Sec.*, Ms. H. David.

VICTORY SERVICES (1907), 63–79 Seymour Street, W2 2HL.—*Gen. Manager*, Capt. G. F. Taylor.

WHITE'S (1693), 37–38 St. James's Street, SW1A 1JG. (Tel: 071-493 6671).—*Sec.*, W. H. West.

WIG AND PEN (1908), 229–230 Strand, WC2R 1BA. (Tel: 071-583 7255).—*Sec.*, J. Reynolds.

PRINCIPAL CLUBS OUTSIDE LONDON

Aldershot.—ROYAL ALDERSHOT OFFICERS CLUB (1856), Farnborough Road, Aldershot, Hants. (Tel: 0252-24036).—*Sec.*, Lt.-Col. A. F. J. Channon, MBE (*retd.*).

Bath.—BATH AND COUNTY CLUB (1865), Queens Parade, Bath, BA1 2NJ. (Tel: 0225-423732).—*Sec.*, Mrs. G. M. Jones.

Birmingham.—BIRMINGHAM CLUB (1872), Winston Churchill House, 8 Ethel Street, Birmingham B2 4BG. (Tel: 021-643 3357).—*Hon. Sec.*, T. R. Pepper.

ST. PAUL'S CLUB (1859), 34 St. Paul's Square, Birmingham B3 1QZ. (Tel: 021-236 1950).—*Hon. Sec.*, J. S. Scott, TD.

Bishop Auckland.—THE CLUB (1868), 1 Victoria Avenue, Bishop Auckland, Co. Durham DL14 7JH. (Tel: 0388-603219).—*Hon. Sec.*, L. Cooke.

CLIFTON CLUB (1882), 22 The Mall, Clifton, Bristol BS8 4DS. (Tel: 0272-735527).—*Sec.*, H. B. Peckham.

Cambridge.—AMATEUR DRAMATIC CLUB (1855), ADC Theatre, Park Street, Cambridge CB5 9AS. (Tel: 0223-359547).—*Sec.*, Ms. G. Jordan.

HAWKS CLUB (1874).—*Pres.*, M. Risman, Emmanuel College, Cambridge.

THE UNION (1815), Bridge Street, Cambridge CB2 1UB. (Tel: 0223-61521).—*Chief Clerk*, B. Thoday.

UNIVERSITY PITT CLUB (1835), Jesus Lane, Cambridge CB5 8BA. (Tel: 0223-35844).—*Hon. Sec.*, S. d'O. Duckworth.

Canterbury.—KENT AND CANTERBURY CLUB (1868), 17 Old Dover Road, Canterbury CT1 3JB.—*Sec.*, F. T. Bedingham.

Cheltenham.—NEW CLUB (1874), Montpellier Parade, Cheltenham GL50 1UD. (Tel: 0242-523285).—*Hon. Sec.*, J. A. Warhurst, OBE.

Chester.—CITY CLUB (1807), St. Peter's Churchyard, Chester CH1 2AG.—*Sec.*, C. Hodkinson.

Chichester.—WEST SUSSEX COUNTY CLUB (1872), 5 Stirling Road, Chichester, W. Sussex PO19 2EW.—*Sec.*, Mrs. P. Green.

Colchester.—THE CLUB (1874), 3–5 Culver Street West, Colchester, Essex.—*Sec.*, N. Duncan.

Devizes.—DEVIZES AND DISTRICT CLUB (1932), 27 St. John Street, Devizes, Wilts. SN10 1BN.—*Sec.*, D. J. J. Cox.

Durham.—COUNTY CLUB (1890), 52 Old Elvet, Durham.—*Sec.*, Mrs. C. Arnot.

DURHAM UNION SOCIETY (1842), North Bailey Club, 24 North Bailey, Durham DH1 3EP. (Tel: 091-384 3724).—*Sec.*, Mrs. E. M. Hardcastle.

Eastbourne.—DEVONSHIRE CLUB (1872), Hartington Place, Eastbourne, Sussex BN21 3RN.—*Hon. Sec.*, D. G. Matthews.

Exeter.—EXETER AND COUNTY CLUB (1871), 5 Cathedral Close, Exeter EX1 1EZ.—*Sec.*, Miss M. J. Toogood.

Guildford.—COUNTY CLUB, 158 High Street, Guildford GU1 3HF. (Tel: 0483-575370).—*Hon. Sec.*, R. W. D. Hemingway.

Harrogate.—THE CLUB (1857), 36 Victoria Avenue, Harrogate, N. Yorks.—*Hon. Sec.*, C. L. Leslie.

Henley-on-Thames.—LEANDER CLUB (1818), Henley-on-Thames, Oxon. RG9 2LP.—*Hon. Sec.*, K. Hylton-Smith.

PHYLLIS COURT CLUB (1906), Marlow Road, Henley, Oxon. RG9 2HT.—*Sec.*, R. I. Bulloch.

Hove.—HOVE CLUB (1882), 28 Fourth Avenue, Hove, E. Sussex BN3 2PJ. (Tel: 0273-730872).—*Sec.*, Sqn. Ldr. G. A. Inverarity, DFC.

Leamington.—TENNIS COURT CLUB (1846), 50 Bedford Street, Leamington, Warks. CV32 5DT. (Tel: 0926-424977).—*Hon. Sec.*, O. D. R. Dixon.

Leeds.—LEEDS CLUB (1850), 3 Albion Place, Leeds LS1 6JL.—*Administrator*, Mrs. D. Kavanagh.

Leicester.—LEICESTERSHIRE CLUB (1873), 9 Welford Place, Leicester LE1 6ZH.—*Manager*, J. A. Evans.

Liverpool.—THE ATHENAEUM (1797), Church Alley, Liverpool L1 3DD. (Tel: 051-709 7700).—*Hon. Sec.*, R. B. Brown.

Macclesfield.—OLD BOYS' AND PARK GREEN CLUB, 7 Churchside, Macclesfield, Cheshire SK10 1HG. (Tel: 0625-23292).—*Hon. Sec.*, N. C. Rowcliffe.

Manchester.—ST. JAMES'S CLUB, St. James's House, Charlotte Street, Manchester M1 4DZ. (Tel: 061-236 2235).—*Hon. Sec.*, C. R. I. Estridge.

Newcastle upon Tyne.—NORTHERN CONSTITUTIONAL CLUB (1882), 37 Pilgrim Street, Newcastle upon Tyne NE1 6QE. (Tel: 091-232 0884).—*Hon. Sec.*, J. L. Browne.

Northampton.—NORTHAMPTON AND COUNTY CLUB (1873), George Row, Northampton NN1 1DF. (Tel: 0604-32962).—*Sec.*, Maj. G. D. Denholm, BEM(*retd.*).

Norwich.—NORFOLK CLUB (1770), 17 Upper King Street, Norwich NR3 1RB. (Tel: 0603-610652).—*Sec.*, A. J. M. Williamson.

Nottingham.—NOTTINGHAM AND NOTTS. UNITED SERVICES CLUB (1920), Newdigate House, Castle Gate, Nottingham NG1 6AF.—*Hon. Sec.*, A. C. Ready.

Oxford.—FREWEN CLUB (1869), 98 St. Aldate's, Oxford OX1 1BT. (Tel: 0865-243816).—*Hon. Sec.*, W. H. Miller, BEM.

OXFORD UNION SOCIETY (1823), Frewin Court, Oxford OX1 3JB.—*Sec.*, S. Green.

VINCENT'S CLUB (1863), 1A King Edward Street, Oxford OX1 4HS. (Tel: 0865-722984).—*Sec.*, J. I. Ferguson.

Paignton.—PAIGNTON CLUB (1882), The Esplanade, Paignton, Devon TQ4 6ED. (Tel: 0803-559682).—*Hon. Sec.* P. Grafton.

Peterborough.—CITY AND COUNTIES CLUB (1867), Priestgate, Peterborough PE6 7LT.—*Sec.*, J. R. Fillingham.

Reading.—BERKSHIRE ATHENAEUM CLUB (1972), 53 Blagrave Street, Reading, Berks.—*Hon. Sec.*, W. J. Stuck.

Rye.—DORMY HOUSE CLUB (1896), Rye, E. Sussex TN31 7LD.—*Hon. Sec.*, M. J. O'Brien.

Shrewsbury.—SALOP CLUB (1974), The Old House, Dogpole, Shrewsbury SY1 1EP. (Tel: 0743-362182).—*Hon. Sec.*, T. P. Roberts.

Teddington.—ROYAL CANOE CLUB (1866), Trowlock Island, Teddington, Middx. TW11 9QZ. (Tel: 081-977 5269).—*Hon. Sec.*, Mrs. J. S. Evans.

Worcester.—UNION AND COUNTY CLUB (1861), 40 Foregate Street, Worcester.—*Sec.*, M. G. Maton.

York.—YORKSHIRE CLUB (1839), 17 Museum Street, York YO1 2DW. (Tel: 0904-624116).—*Hon. Sec.*, D. E. Gabbitas.

Wales

Cardiff.—CARDIFF AND COUNTY CLUB (1866), Westgate Street, Cardiff CF1 1DA. (Tel: 0222-220846).—*Hon. Sec.*, A. G. Robertson.

Scotland

Ayr.—COUNTY CLUB (1872), Savoy Park Hotel, Ayr KA7 2XA.—*Hon. Sec.*, J. K. Templeton.

Edinburgh.—CALEDONIAN CLUB (1825), 32 Abercromby Place, Edinburgh EH3 6QE.—*Sec.*, I. Harvey.

NEW CLUB (1787), 86 Princes Street, Edinburgh EH2 2BB. (Tel: 031-226 4881).—*Sec.*, A. D. Orr Ewing.

Glasgow.—GLASGOW ART CLUB (1867), 185 Bath Street, Glasgow G2 4HU.—*Sec.*, L. J. McIntyre.

ROYAL SCOTTISH AUTOMOBILE CLUB (1899), 11 Blythswood Square, Glasgow G2 4AG. (Tel: 041-221 3850).—*Sec.*, H. Dewar.

WESTERN CLUB (1825), 32 Royal Exchange Square, Glasgow G1 3AB.—*Sec.*, D. H. Gifford.

Northern Ireland

Belfast.—ULSTER REFORM CLUB (1885), 4 Royal Avenue, Belfast BT1 1DA. (Tel: 0232-323411).—*Secs.*, Miss M. P. Mackintosh; N. H. Caters.

Enniskillen.—FERMANAGH COUNTY CLUB (1883), 20 Church Street, Enniskillen, N. Ireland BT74 6DF.—*Hon. Sec.*, P. Little.

Channel Islands

Jersey.—VICTORIA CLUB (1853), Beresford Street, St. Helier, Jersey. (Tel: 0534-23381).—*Sec.*, Gp. Capt. J. W. E. Holmes, DFC, AFC.

YACHT CLUBS

Bembridge.—BEMBRIDGE SAILING CLUB (1886), Embankment Road, Bembridge, IOW, PO35 5NR. (Tel: 0983-873087).—*Hon. Sec.*, B. J. B. Sloley.

Birkenhead.—ROYAL MERSEY YACHT CLUB (1844), Bedford Road East, Rock Ferry, Birkenhead, Merseyside L42 1LS. (Tel: 051-645 3204).—*Hon. Sec.*, C. P. Broad.

Bridlington.—ROYAL YORKSHIRE YACHT CLUB (1847), 1 Windsor Crescent, Bridlington, N. Humberside YO15 3HX. (Tel: 0262-678319).—*Sec.*, I. Harness.

Burnham-on-Crouch.—ROYAL CORINTHIAN YACHT CLUB (1872), Burnham-on-Crouch, Essex CM0 8AX. (Tel: 0621-78210).—*Hon. Sec.*, K. W. Bushell.

Cowes.—ROYAL YACHT SQUADRON (1815), The Castle, Cowes, IOW, PO31 7QT. (Tel: 0983-292191).—*Sec.*, Maj. R. P. Rising, RM.

ROYAL LONDON YACHT CLUB (1838), The Parade, Cowes, IOW, PO31 7QS. (Tel: 0983-299727).—*Sec.*, M. White.

Dover.—ROYAL CINQUE PORTS YACHT CLUB (1872), 5 Waterloo Crescent, Dover, Kent CT16 1LA. (Tel: 0304-206262).—*Sec.*, T. V. Taylor.

Fishbourne.—ROYAL VICTORIA YACHT CLUB (1844), Fishbourne Lane, Ryde, IOW, PO33 4EU. (Tel: 0983-882325).—*Hon. Sec.*, Ms. H. Vrba.

Fowey.—ROYAL FOWEY YACHT CLUB (1881), Fowey, Cornwall PL23 1BH. (Tel: 0726-833573).—*Hon. Sec.*, E. P. Warren.

Harwich.—ROYAL HARWICH YACHT CLUB (1843), Woolverstone, Ipswich IP9 1AT.—*Sec.*, D. E. Gooch.

Kingswear.—ROYAL DART YACHT CLUB (1866), Priory Street, Kingswear, Dartmouth, Devon TQ6 0AB. (Tel: 080 425-272).—*Hon. Sec.*, Mrs. B. Locke.

Leigh-on-Sea.—ESSEX YACHT CLUB (1890), HQS Bembridge, Foreshore, Leigh-on-Sea, Essex SS9 1BD. (Tel: 0702-78404).—*Hon. Sec.*, A. Manning.

London.—THE CRUISING ASSOCIATION (1908), Ivory House, St. Katharine Dock, E1 9AT.—*Gen. Sec.*, Mrs. L. Hammett.

ROYAL CRUISING CLUB (1880), c/o Naval and Military Club, 42 Half Moon Street, W1Y 8DS.—*Hon. Sec.*, C. Buckley.

Lowestoft.—ROYAL NORFOLK AND SUFFOLK YACHT CLUB (1859), Royal Plain, Lowestoft, Suffolk NR33 0AQ. (Tel: 0502-566726).—*Sec.*, vacant.

Lymington.—ROYAL LYMINGTON YACHT CLUB (1922), Bath Road, Lymington, Hants. SO41 9SE. (Tel: 0590-672677).—*Sec.*, Gp. Capt. J. D. Hutchinson *(retd.)*.

Plymouth.—ROYAL WESTERN YACHT CLUB (1827), Queen Anne's Battery, Plymouth PL4 0TW. (Tel: 0752-660077).—*Sec.*, Cdr. R. J. Harvey.

ROYAL PLYMOUTH CORINTHIAN YACHT CLUB (1877), Madeira Road, Plymouth PL1 2NY. (Tel: 0752-664327).—*Hon. Sec.*, V. J. de Boo.

Poole.—EAST DORSET SAILING CLUB (1875), 352 Sandbanks Road, Poole, Dorset BH14 8HY.—*Hon. Sec.*, K. H. Okey.

PARKSTONE YACHT CLUB (1895), Pearce Avenue, Parkstone, Poole, Dorset BH14 8EH.—*Sec.*, J. Shore.

POOLE HARBOUR YACHT CLUB (1949), 38 Salterns Way, Lilliput, Poole, Dorset BH14 8JR. (Tel: 0202-707321).—*Sec.*, J. N. J. Smith.

POOLE YACHT CLUB (1865), New Harbour Road West, Hamworthy, Poole, Dorset BH15 4AQ. (Tel: 0202-672687).—*Sec.*, Miss L. Clark.

Portsmouth.—ROYAL NAVAL CLUB AND ROYAL ALBERT YACHT CLUB (1867), 17 Pembroke Road, Portsmouth PO1 2NT. (Tel: 0705-824491).—*Sec.*, Cdr. T. C. C. Greaves, OBE *(retd.)*.

Ramsgate.—ROYAL TEMPLE YACHT CLUB (1857), 6 Westcliff Mansions, Ramsgate, Kent CT11 9HY. (Tel: 0843-591766).—*Hon. Sec.*, G. F. Randell.

Southampton.—ROYAL AIR FORCE YACHT CLUB (1932), Riverside House, Rope Walk, Hamble, Southampton SO3 5HD. (Tel : 0703-452208).—*Sec.*, Miss R. M. Clements.

ROYAL SOUTHAMPTON YACHT CLUB, 1 Channel Way, Ocean Village, Southampton SO1 1XE. (Tel : 0703-223352).—Mrs. J. Cox.

ROYAL SOUTHERN YACHT CLUB (1837), Hamble, Southampton SO3 5HB. (Tel: 0703-453271).—*Sec.*, M. Pringle.

Southend.—ALEXANDRA YACHT CLUB (1873), Clifton Terrace, Southend-on-Sea SS1 1DT.—*Hon. Sec.*, D. C. Osborn.

Westcliff-on-Sea.—THAMES ESTUARY YACHT CLUB (1895), 3 The Leas, Westcliff-on-Sea, Essex SS0 7ST.—*Hon. Sec.*, J. G. Davison (until Dec. 1989).

Weymouth.—ROYAL DORSET YACHT CLUB (1875), 11 Custom House Quay, Weymouth, Dorset DT4 8BG. (Tel: 0305-771155).—*Sec.*, Mrs. J. B. Cannon.

Windermere.—ROYAL WINDERMERE YACHT CLUB (1860), Fallbarrow Road, Bowness-on-Windermere, Cumbria LA23 3DJ.—*Hon. Sec.*, M. C. Bentley.

Yarmouth.—ROYAL SOLENT YACHT CLUB (1878), Yarmouth, IOW, PO41 0NS. (Tel: 0983-760256).—*Sec.*, Mrs. S. Tribe.

Wales

Beaumaris.—ROYAL ANGLESEY YACHT CLUB (1802), 6–7 Green Edge, Beaumaris, Gwynedd LL58 8AL. (Tel: 0248-810295).—*Hon. Sec.*, V. G. Keep.

Caernarvon.—ROYAL WELSH YACHT CLUB (1847), Porth-Yr-Aur, Caernarvon, Gwynedd LL55 1SW. —*Hon. Sec.*, J. N. L. Thomas.

Penarth.—PENARTH YACHT CLUB (1880). The Esplanade, Penarth, S. Glamorgan CF6 2AU. (Tel: 0222-708196).—*Hon. Sec.*, R. S. McGregor.

Swansea.—BRISTOL CHANNEL YACHT CLUB (1875), 744 Mumbles Road, Mumbles, Swansea SA3 4EL. (Tel : 0792-366000).—*Hon. Sec.*, B. G. T. Rees.

Scotland

Dundee.—ROYAL TAY YACHT CLUB (1885), 34 Dundee Road, Broughty Ferry, Dundee DD5 1LX.—*Hon. Sec.*, T. Black.

Edinburgh.—ROYAL FORTH YACHT CLUB (1868), Middle Pier, Granton Harbour, Edinburgh, EH5 1HF.—*Hon. Sec.*, A. R. Woods.

Glasgow.—ROYAL WESTERN YACHT CLUB (1875).—*Hon. Sec.*, D. G. M. Watson, Lochaber, 20 Barclay Drive, Helensburgh, Dunbartonshire G84 9RB.

Oban.—ROYAL HIGHLAND YACHT CLUB (1881).—*Sec.*, M. Bolton. Whins, 8 Grianach Gardens, Oban, Argyll PA34 4LZ.

Rhu.—ROYAL NORTHERN AND CLYDE YACHT CLUB (1978), Rhu, Helensburgh, Dunbartonshire G84 8NG. (Tel : 0436-820322).—*Hon. Sec.*, J. S. Holgate.

Northern Ireland

Bangor.—ROYAL ULSTER YACHT CLUB (1866), 101 Clifton Road, Bangor, Co. Down BT20 5HY. (Tel: 0247-270568).—*Hon. Sec.*, T. O'Hara.

Channel Islands

Jersey.—ROYAL CHANNEL ISLANDS YACHT CLUB (1862), Le Boulevard, Bulwarks, St. Aubin, Jersey.—*Hon. Sec.*, A. K. Jackson.

PRINCIPAL BRITISH SOCIETIES AND INSTITUTIONS

THE ROYAL ACADEMY OF ARTS (1768), Burlington House, W1V 0DS—*President*, Roger de Grey, PRA, (1984); *Keeper*, Prof. N. Adams, RA; *Treas.*, Sir Philip Powell, CH, OBE, RA; *Sec.* P. Rodgers.

Royal Academicians

1972 Adams, Norman	1984 Hogarth, Paul
1988*Agar, Eileen	1986 Jones, Allen
1988 Aitchison, Craigie	1986 Kenny, Michael
1976 Blackadder, Elizabeth, OBE	1988 King, Phillip, CBE
	1974 Kneale, Bryan
1981 Blake, Peter, CBE	1986*Lessore, Helen
1975 Blamey, Norman	1986 Levene, Ben
1978 Blow, Sandra	1989*Lubetkin, Berthold
1975 Bowey, Olwyn	1956*Machin, Arnold, OBE
1981 Bowyer, William	
1971 Bratby, John	1989*McWilliam, F. E., CBE
1972 Brown, Ralph	
1972 Butler, James	1979 Manasseh, Leonard, OBE
1975*Cadbury-Brown, H. T., OBE	
	1985*Martin, Sir Leslie
1984 Camp, Jeffery	1985*Medley, Robert
1970*Casson, Sir Hugh, CH, KCVO	1979*Moynihan, Rodrigo, CBE
1989 Christopher, Ann	1979 Paolozzi, Sir Eduardo, CBE
1976 Clarke, Geoffrey	
1973 Clatworthy, Robert	1988 Partridge, John, CBE
1972 Coker, Peter	1983*Pasmore, Victor, CH, CBE
1972 Cooke, Jean	
1974 Cuming, Frederick	1981 Philipson, Sir Robin
1983 Dannatt, Trevor	1989 Phillips, Tom
1969 de Grey, Roger	1977 Powell, Sir Philip, CH, OBE
1976 Dickson, Jennifer	
1985 Dowson, Sir Philip, CBE	1973*Roberts-Jones, Ivor, CBE
1955*Dring, William	1984 Rogers, Richard
1968 Dunstan, Bernard	1969*Rosoman, Leonard, OBE
1953*Eurich, Richard, OBE	1983*Rothenstein, Michael
1986 Eyton, Anthony	
1985 Fraser, Donald Hamilton	1961*Sanders, Christopher
1977 Frink, Dame Elisabeth, DBE	1989 Sandle, Michael
1972*Gore, Frederick, CBE	1969*Soukop, Willi
	1986 Stephenson, Ian
1989 Gowing, Sir Lawrence, CBE	1988 Sutton, Philip
	1979 Tindle, David
1977 Green, Anthony	1965 Ward, John, CBE
1960*Greenham, Peter, CBE	1965*Weight, Carel, CBE
1981 Harpley, Sydney	1989 Whishaw, Anthony
1970 Hayes, Colin	1974 Williams, Kyffin, OBE
1961*Hepple, Norman	
1990*Herman, Josef	

Associates

1989 Abrahams, Ivor	1985 Hockney, David
1988 Ackroyd, Norman	1983 Howard, Ken
1989 Armfield, Diana	1983 Hoyland, John
1982 Ayres, Gillian, OBE	1987 Huxley, Paul
	1989 Jacklin, Bill
	1989 Kiff, Ken
1986 Bellany, John	1984 Kitaj, R. B.
1982 Crosby, Theo	1986 Koralek, Paul, CBE
1989 Cullinan, Edward	1982 Lawson, Sonia
1990 Draper, Kenneth	1987 McComb, Leonard
1987 Flanagan, Barry	1987 Nolan, Sir Sidney
1983 Foster, Norman	1990 Rooney, Michael
1990 Freeth, Peter	1985 Stirling, James

1983 Symons, Patrick	1990 Wilson, Colin St. John	
1985 Tilson, Joe		
1986 Titchell, John	1983 Wragg, John	

* Senior.

Former Presidents of the Royal Academy

Sir J. Reynolds, 1768	Sir F. Dicksee, 1924
Benjamin West, 1792	Sir W. Llewellyn, 1928
James Wyatt, 1805	Sir E. Lutyens, 1938
Benjamin West, 1806	Sir A. J. Munnings, 1944
Sir T. Lawrence, 1820	
Sir M. A. Shee, 1830	Sir G. F. Kelly, 1949
Sir C. Eastlake, 1850	Sir A. E. Richardson, 1954
Sir F. Grant, 1866	
Lord Leighton, 1878	Sir C. Wheeler, 1956
Sir J. Millais, 1896	Sir T. Monnington, 1966
Sir E. Poynter, 1896	
Sir A. Webb, 1919	Sir Hugh Casson, 1976

THE ROYAL CAMBRIAN ACADEMY OF ART (1882), Plas Mawr, High Street, Conwy, Gwynedd LL32 8DE—*Pres.*, R. Fields; *Hon. Sec.*, Ms. A. Hind; *Curator and Sec.*, L. H. S. Mercer.

THE ROYAL SCOTTISH ACADEMY (1826), Princes Street, Edinburgh EH2 2EL—*Pres.*, Sir Anthony Wheeler, OBE, RSA; *Sec.*, R. R. Steedman, RSA; *Treas.*, W. J. L. Baillie, RSA; *Librarian*, P. Collins, RSA; *Admin. Sec.*, W. T. Meikle.

Senior Academicians

1958 Armour, Mrs. M.	1967 Lorimer, Hew
1974 Crosbie, William	1977 Whiston, Peter
1956 Fleming, Ian	1957 Patrick, J. McIntosh
1981 Glover, J. Hardie, OBE	1966 Peploe, Denis
1967 Gordon, Esmé	1986 Reiach, Alan
1966 Johnston, Ninian	1977 Robertson, R. Ross

Royal Scottish Academicians

1979 Baillie, W. J. L.	1990 Metzstein, Isi
1972 Blackadder, Elizabeth, OBE	1972 Michie, David
	1963 Morocco, Alberto
1986 Bushe, Fred	1989 Morris, James
1977 Butler, Vincent	1990 Pelly, Frances
1971 Cameron, Gordon	1962 Philipson, Sir Robin
1981 Campbell, Alex	
1974 Collins, Peter	1976 Reeves, Philip
1970 Cumming, James	1989 Richards, John, CBE
1962 Donaldson, David	
1989 Evans, David	1989 Robertson, James
1989 Fraser, Alexander	1984 Scott, Bill
1989 Harvey, Jake	1990 Shanks, Duncan
1972 Houston, John	1987 Smith, Ian McKenzie
1979 Knox, John	
1973 Littlejohn, W.	1985 Snowden, Michael (*elect.*)
1971 McClure, David	
1990 MacMillan, Andrew	1979 Steedman, R. R.
	1975 Wheeler, Sir Anthony, OBE
1976 Malcolm, Ellen	1982 Walker, Frances

Associates

Arnott, Ian	Bryce, Gordon
Balmer, Barbara	Buchan, Dennis
Black, Robert	Busby, John
Boys, John	Cairns, Joyce
Brotherston, William	Campbell, A. Buchanan
Brown, Neil Dallas	Clarke, Derek

Clifford, J. G.
Cocker, Douglas
Crowe, Victoria
Dean, Fiona
Docherty, Michael
Donald, George
Fairgrieve, James
Fisher, Beth
Gasson, Barry
The Earl Haig
Howard, Ian
Johnstone, John
Law, Graham
Low, Bet
McCulloch, Ian
McIntosh, Iain
Maclean, William

MacPherson, George
Main, Kirkland
Merrylees, Andrew
Mooney, John
Morrison, James
Onwin, Glen
Pottinger, Frank
Rae, Barbara
Renton, James, OBE
Rodger, Willie
Ross, Alastair
Smart, Alastair
Squire, Geoffrey
Stenhouse, Andrew
Stiven, Fred
Watson, Arthur
Wedgwood, Roland
Wyllie, George

Non-Resident Associates, Charles Pulsford, Peter Womersley, Leon Morrocco.

ROYAL IRISH ACADEMY (1786), 19 Dawson Street, Dublin 2.—*Pres.,* Prof. A. Clarke; *Treas.,* Prof. A. F. Hegarty; *Sec.,* Prof. G. Watson.

ABBEYFIELD SOCIETY, 186–192 Darkes Lane, Potters Bar, Herts. EN6 1AB.—*Housing for elderly people. 1,000 houses nationwide.—Chief Exec.,* B. Palmer.

ACCOUNTANTS, INSTITUTE OF CHARTERED, IN ENG-LAND AND WALES (1880), PO Box 433, Chartered Accountants' Hall, Moorgate Place, EC2P 2BJ.—*Sec.,* A. J. Colquhoun.

ACCOUNTANTS, CHARTERED ASSOCIATION OF CERTI-FIED (1904), 29 Lincoln's Inn Fields, WC2A 3EE.—*Sec.,* A. W. Sansom.

ACCOUNTANTS OF SCOTLAND, THE INSTITUTE OF CHARTERED (1854), 27 Queen Street, Edinburgh EH2 1LA.—*Chief Exec.,* P. W. Johnston.

ACCOUNTANTS IN IRELAND, INSTITUTE OF CHARTERED (1888), Chartered Accountants House, 87–89 Pem-broke Road, Dublin 4.—*Dir.,* R. F. Hussey.

ACCOUNTANTS, INSTITUTE OF COMPANY (1974), 40 Tyndalls Park Road, Bristol BS8 1PL.—*Sec. Gen.,* B. T. Banks.

ACCOUNTING TECHNICIANS, ASSOCIATION OF (1980), 154 Clerkenwell Road, EC1R 5AD.—*Sec.,* J. Han-son.

ACTION RESEARCH FOR THE CRIPPLED CHILD (1952), Vincent House, North Parade, Horsham, W. Sussex RH12 2DA.—*Dir. Gen.,* Col. A. N. Brearley-Smith, OBE.

ACTORS' BENEVOLENT FUND (1882), 6 Adam Street, WC2N 6AA.—*Gen. Sec.,* Mrs. R. Stevens.

ACTORS' CHARITABLE TRUST (1896), 19–20 Euston Centre, NW1 3JH.—*Gen. Sec.,* Ms. A. Stewart.

ACTORS' CHURCH UNION (1899), St. Paul's Church, Bedford Street, WC2E 9ED.—*Senior Chaplain,* Canon W. Hall.

ACTUARIES IN SCOTLAND, THE FACULTY OF (1856), 23 St. Andrew Square, Edinburgh EH2 1AQ.—*Sec.,* W. W. Mair.

ACTUARIES, INSTITUTE OF (1848), Staple Inn Hall, High Holborn, WC1V 7QJ.—*Sec. Gen.,* C. D. A. Mackie.

ADMINISTRATIVE MANAGEMENT, INSTITUTE OF (1915), 40 Chatsworth Parade, Orpington, Kent BR5 1RW.—*Chief Exec.,* M. J. Ainsworth.

ADULT SCHOOL ORGANIZATION, NATIONAL (1899), Masu Centre, Gaywood Croft, Cregoe Street, Birmingham B15 2ED.—*Gen. Sec.,* W. J. Scarle.

ADVERTISING BENEVOLENT SOCIETY, NATIONAL (1913), 3 Crawford Place, W1H 1JB.—*Dir.,* Mrs. D. Larkin.

ADVERTISING, INSTITUTE OF PRACTITIONERS IN (1927), 44 Belgrave Square, SW1X 8QS.—*Dir. Gen.,* N. Phillips.

ADVERTISING STANDARDS AUTHORITY (1962), Brook House, 2–16 Torrington Place, WC1E 7HN.—*Dir. Gen.,* Mrs. M. Alderson.

AERONAUTICAL SOCIETY, ROYAL (1866), 4 Hamilton Place, W1V 0BQ.—*Sec.,* R. J. Kennett.

AFRICAN INSTITUTE, INTERNATIONAL (1926), Lionel Robbins Building, 10 Portugal Street, WC2A 2HD.—*Dir.,* Prof. P. Lloyd.

AFRICAN MEDICAL AND RESEARCH FOUNDATION, 11 Waterloo Street, Clifton, Bristol BS8 4BT.—*Exec. Dir.,* Mrs. E. Young.

AGE CONCERN ENGLAND (1940), Astral House, 1268 London Road, SW16 4EJ.—*Dir.,* Ms. S. Greengross.

AGE CONCERN NORTHERN IRELAND (1976), 6 Lower Crescent, Belfast, BT2 7BG.—*Chief Exec.,* J. A. O'Neill.

AGE CONCERN SCOTLAND (1943), 54A Fountainbridge, Edinburgh EH3 9PT.—*Dir.,* M. Cairns.

AGE CONCERN WALES, 4th Floor, 1 Cathedral Road, Cardiff, CF1 9SD.—*Chief Officer,* D. Haydn Thomas.

AGED POOR SOCIETY (1708), St. Joseph's House, 42 Brook Green, W6 7BW.—*Sec.,* Flt. Lt. W. Watson.

AGEING, CENTRE FOR POLICY ON (1947), 25–31 Iron-monger Row, EC1V 3QP.—*Dir.,* E. Midwinter, D.Phil.

AGEING, RESEARCH INTO (1978), 49 Queen Victoria Street, EC4N 4SA.—*Dir.,* R. Bowen.

AGRICULTURAL BENEVOLENT INSTITUTION, ROYAL (1860), Shaw House, 27 West Way, Oxford OX2 0QH.—*Chief Exec.,* Maj. Gen. P. L. Spurgeon, CB.

AGRICULTURAL BENEVOLENT INSTITUTION, ROYAL SCOTTISH (1897), Ingliston, Edinburgh, EH28 8NB.—*Organizing Sec.,* I. G. Cumming, TD.

AGRICULTURAL ENGINEERS ASSOCIATION (1875), Sam-uelson House, Paxton Road, Orton Centre, Peter-borough PE2 0LT.—*Dir. Gen.,* J. Vowles.

AGRICULTURAL SOCIETY, EAST OF ENGLAND, East of England Showground, Peterborough PE2 0XE.—*Chief Exec.,* R. W. Bird, MBE.

AGRICULTURAL SOCIETY OF ENGLAND, ROYAL (1838), National Agricultural Centre, Stoneleigh, Kenil-worth, Warks. CV8 2LZ.—*Chief Exec.,* R. E.Hicks.

AGRICULTURAL SOCIETY OF THE COMMONWEALTH, ROYAL (1957), 55 Sleaford Street, SW8 5AB.—*Hon. Sec.,* F. R. Francis, LVO, MBE.

AGRICULTURAL SOCIETY, ROYAL ULSTER (1826), The King's Hall, Balmoral Show Grounds, Belfast BT9 6GW.—*Chief Exec.,* W. H. Yarr.

AGRICULTURE, ASSOCIATION OF (1947), Victoria Cham-bers, 16–20 Strutton Ground, SW1P 2HP.—*Dir.,* C. Flint.

AIR LEAGUE, THE (1909), 4 Hamilton Place, W1V 0BQ.— *Sec. Gen.,* Air Cdre. J. C. Atkinson, CBE.

ALCOHOLICS ANONYMOUS (1947), PO Box 1, Stonebow House, Stonebow, York YO1 2NJ.—*Gen. Sec.,* J. Gow.

ALEXANDRA ROSE DAY COMMITTEE (1912), 1 Castel-nau, Barnes, SW13 9RP.—*Nat. Organizing Sec.,* Mrs. G. Greenwood.

ALLOTMENT AND LEISURE GARDENERS LIMITED, NA-TIONAL SOCIETY OF (1930), Hunters Road, Corby, Northants. NN17 1JE.—*Nat. Sec.,* G. W. Stokes.

ALMSHOUSES, NATIONAL ASSOCIATION OF (1946), Billingbear Lodge, Wokingham, Berks. RG11 5RU.—*Dir.*, D. M. Scott.

AMNESTY INTERNATIONAL (1961), International Secretariat, 1 Easton Street, WC1X 8DJ.—*Sec. Gen.*, I. Martin.

ANAESTHETISTS OF GREAT BRITAIN AND IRELAND, ASSOCIATION OF (1932), 9 Bedford Square, WC1B 3RA.—*Hon. Sec.*, Dr. W. L. M. Baird.

ANCIENT BUILDINGS, SOCIETY FOR THE PROTECTION OF (1877), 37 Spital Square, E1 6DY.—*Sec.*, P. Venning.

ANCIENT MONUMENTS SOCIETY (1924), St. Andrew-by-the-Wardrobe, Queen Victoria Street, EC4V 5DE.—*Sec.*, M. Saunders.

ANGLO-ARAB ASSOCIATION (1961), The Arab British Centre, 21 Collingham Road, SW5 0NU.—*Exec. Dir.*, A. Lee.

ANGLO-BELGIAN SOCIETY (1982).—*Hon. Sec.*, Mrs. S. G. Ault, 46 Belgrave Manor, Brooklyn Road, Woking, Surrey GU22 7TW.

ANGLO-BRAZILIAN SOCIETY (1943), 32 Green Street, W1Y 3FD.—*Sec.*, Mrs. M. J. Fyfe.

ANGLO-DANISH SOCIETY (1924), 25 New Street Square, EC4A 3LN.—*Chairman*, Sir Andrew Stark, KCMG, CVO.

ANGLO-NORSE SOCIETY (1918), 25 Belgrave Square, SW1X 8QD.—*Chairman*, Mrs. A. Dixon.

ANGLO-POLISH SOCIETY (1832), London HQ, c/o SPCK, 238–246 King Street, W6 0RF.—*Hon. Sec.*, Mrs. K. Szymaniak.

ANGLO-THAI SOCIETY (1962).—*Hon. Sec.*, J. A. Bradstreet, 500 Grovely Lane, Birmingham B45 8PD.

ANIMAL CONCERN (SCOTLAND) (1988), 62 Old Dumbarton Road, Glasgow G3 8RE.—*Organizing Sec.*, J. F. Robins.

ANIMAL HEALTH TRUST (1942), PO Box 5, Newmarket, Suffolk CB8 7DW.—*Dir.*, A. J. Higgins, PH.D.

ANTHROPOLOGICAL INSTITUTE, ROYAL (1843), 50 Fitzroy Street, W1P 5HS.—*Dir.*, J. C. M. Benthall.

ANTHROPOSOPHICAL SOCIETY IN GREAT BRITAIN (1923), Rudolf Steiner House, 35 Park Road, NW1 6XT.—*Gen. Sec.*, N. C. Thomas.

ANTIQUARIES, SOCIETY OF (1717), Burlington House, Piccadilly, W1V 0HS.—*Dir.*, Dr Helen Clarke.

ANTIQUARIES OF SCOTLAND, SOCIETY OF (1780), Royal Museum of Scotland, Queen Street, Edinburgh EH2 1JD.—*Sec.*, Miss C. R. Wickham-Jones.

ANTI-SLAVERY SOCIETY FOR THE PROTECTION OF HUMAN RIGHTS (1839), 180 Brixton Road, SW9 6AT.—*Dir.*, Miss L. Roberts.

ANTI-VIVISECTION: BRITISH UNION FOR THE ABOLITION OF VIVISECTION (1898), 16A Crane Grove, N7 8LB.—*Gen. Sec.*, C. Fisher.

ANTI-VIVISECTION SOCIETY, THE NATIONAL (1875), 51 Harley Street, W1N 1DD.—*Gen. Sec.*, Ms. J. Creamer.

APOSTLESHIP OF THE SEA (1920), Stella Maris, 66 Dock Road, Tilbury, Essex RM18 7BX.—For active and retired seafarers. *Nat. Dir.*, Rev. J. Maguire.

APOTHECARIES OF LONDON, SOCIETY OF (1617), Black Friars Lane, EC4V 6EJ.—*Clerk*, Maj. J. C. O'Leary; *Registrar*, D. H. C. Barrie.

ARBITRATORS, THE CHARTERED INSTITUTE OF (1915), 75 Cannon Street, EC4N 5BH.—*Sec.*, K. R. K. Harding.

ARCHAEOLOGICAL ASSOCIATION, BRITISH (1843), 24 Lower Street, Harnham, Salisbury SP2 8EY.—*Asst. Sec.*, M. Cowan.

ARCHAEOLOGICAL ASSOCIATION, CAMBRIAN (1846).—*Gen. Sec.*, R. S. Kelly, Arlwyn, 52 Upper Garth Road, Bangor, Gwynedd LL57 2SS.

ARCHAEOLOGICAL INSTITUTE, ROYAL (1843), c/o Society of Antiquaries of London, Burlington House, Piccadilly, W1V 0HS.—*Sec.*, J. G. Coad.

ARCHAEOLOGY, COUNCIL FOR BRITISH (1944), 112 Kennington Road, SE11 6RE.—*Dir.*, Dr. H. F. Cleere.

ARCHITECTS, THE ROYAL INSTITUTE OF BRITISH (1834), 66 Portland Place, W1N 4AD.—*Pres.*, M. Hutchinson; *Dir. Gen.*, The Rt. Hon. W. Rodgers.

ARCHITECTS AND SURVEYORS, INCORPORATED ASSOCIATION OF (1925), Jubilee House, Billing Brook Road, Weston Favell, Northampton NN3 4NW.—*Administrator*, B. D. Hughes.

ARCHITECTS AND SURVEYORS INSTITUTE, 15 St. Mary Street, Chippenham, Wilts. SN15 3JN.—*Chief Exec.*, B. A. Hunt.

ARCHITECTS BENEVOLENT SOCIETY (1850), 66 Portland Place, W1N 4AD.—*Hon. Sec.*, R. J. Double.

ARCHITECTS IN SCOTLAND, ROYAL INCORPORATION OF (1922), 15 Rutland Square, Edinburgh EH1 2BE.—*Sec.*, C. A. McKean, FRSA.

ARCHITECTS REGISTRATION COUNCIL OF THE UNITED KINGDOM (1931), 73 Hallam Street, W1N 6EE.—*Registrar*, D. W. G. Smart.

ARCHITECTURAL ASSOCIATION (INC.) (1847), 34–36 Bedford Square, WC1B 3EG.—*Sec.*, E. Le Maistre.

ARCHITECTURAL HERITAGE FUND, THE (1976), 17 Carlton House Terrace, SW1Y 5AW.—*Sec.*, Lady Weir.

ARCHIVISTS, SOCIETY OF (1947).—*Hon. Sec.*, Ms. M. Turner, West Yorks. Archive Service, Registry of Deeds, Newstead Road, Wakefield WF1 2DE.

ARK ENVIRONMENTAL FOUNDATION, THE (1988), 498 Harrow Road, W9 3QA.—*Chairman*, R. Boorer.

ARMY BENEVOLENT FUND (1944), 41 Queen's Gate, SW7 5HR.—*Controller*, Maj.-Gen. G. M. G. Swindells, CB.

ARMY CADET FORCE ASSOCIATION (1930), E Block, Duke of York's HQ, SW3 4RR.—*Gen. Sec.*, Brig. R. B. MacGregor-Oakford, CBE, MC.

ART COLLECTIONS FUND, NATIONAL (1903), 20 John Islip Street, SW1P 4JX.—*Dir.*, Sir Peter Wakefield, KBE, CMG.

ARTHRITIS AND RHEUMATISM COUNCIL (1936), 41 Eagle Street, WC1R 4AR.—*Gen. Sec.*, J. Norton.

ARTHRITIS CARE (1949), 5 Grosvenor Crescent, SW1X 7ER.—*Sec.*, J. R. Collins.

ARTISTS, FEDERATION OF BRITISH, 17 Carlton House Terrace, SW1Y 5BD.—*Chief Exec.*, O. Warman.

ARTISTS' GENERAL BENEVOLENT INSTITUTION (1814) AND ARTISTS' ORPHAN FUND (1871), Burlington House, Piccadilly, W1V 0DJ.—*Sec.*, Mrs. C. M. Rees.

ARTISTS, ROYAL SOCIETY OF BRITISH, 17 Carlton House Terrace, SW1Y 5BD.— *Sec.*, R. Morgan.

ART LIBRARIES SOCIETY (ARLIS) (1969).—*Sec.*, Ms. E. Howlett, 32 Eland Road, SW11 5JY.

ART WORKERS' GUILD (1884), 6 Queen Square, WC1N 3AR.—*Sec.*, H. Krall.

ASLIB (The Association for Information Management) (1924), Information House, 20–24 Old Street, EC1V 9AP.—*Chief Exec.*, R. Bowes.

ASSISTANT MASTERS AND MISTRESSES ASSOCIATION (1978), 7 Northumberland Street, WC2N 5DA.—*Gen. Sec.*, P. Smith.

ASTHMA CAMPAIGN, NATIONAL (1927), 300 Upper Street, N1 2XX.—*Chairman*, Sir Peter Emery, MP.

ASTRONOMICAL ASSOCIATION, BRITISH (1890), Burlington House, Piccadilly, W1V 9AG. Meetings at 23 Savile Row, W1X 1AB.— *Asst. Sec.*, Miss P. M. Barber.

ASTRONOMICAL SOCIETY, ROYAL (1820), Burlington House, Piccadilly, W1V 0NL.—*Pres.*, Prof. K. A. Pounds, FRS; *Exec. Sec.*, J. A. Steff-Langston.

ATS and WRAC BENEVOLENT FUNDS (1964), Queen Elizabeth Park, Guildford, Surrey GU2 6QH.— *Sec.*, Mrs. A. H. S. Matthews.

AUDIT BUREAU OF CIRCULATIONS LTD. (1931), 13 Wimpole Street, W1M 7AB.—*Dir.*, J. G. Holmes.

AUTHORS, THE SOCIETY OF (1884), 84 Drayton Gardens, SW10 9SB.—*Gen. Sec.*, M. Le Fanu.

AUTOMOBILE ASSOCIATION (1905), Fanum House, Basingstoke, Hants. RG21 2EA.—*Dir. Gen.*, S. Dyer.

AVICULTURAL SOCIETY (1894), c/o Bristol Zoological Gardens, Clifton, Bristol BS8 3HA.—*Hon. Sec.*, G. R. Greed.

AYRSHIRE CATTLE SOCIETY OF GREAT BRITAIN AND IRELAND (1877), PO Box 8, 1 Racecourse Road, Ayr KA7 2DE.—*Gen. Sec.*, S. J. Thomson.

BALTIC AIR CHARTER ASSOCIATION (1949), The Baltic Exchange, St. Mary Axe, EC3A 8BU.—*Hon. Exec.*, D. Shepherd.

BALTIC EXCHANGE LTD. (1903), 14–20 St. Mary Axe, EC3A 8BU.—*Sec.*, D. J. Walker.

BALTIC EXCHANGE CHARITABLE SOCIETY (1978), 14–20 St. Mary Axe, EC3A 8BU.—*Sec.*, R. T. Wheelans.

BALZAN FOUNDATION, INTERNATIONAL (1956), Piazzetta U. Giordano 4, Milan 20122, Italy. Awards prizes for Literature, Moral Sciences and the Arts, Physical, Mathematical and Natural Sciences, Medicine, Humanity, Peace and Brotherhood.— *Sec. Gen.*, Dr. F. M. Tedeschi.

BANKERS, THE CHARTERED INSTITUTE OF (1879), 10 Lombard Street, EC3V 9AS.—*Sec. Gen.*, E. Glover.

BANKERS IN SCOTLAND, THE INSTITUTE OF (1875), 19 Rutland Square, Edinburgh EH1 2DE.—*Sec.*, Dr. C. W. Munn.

BAPTIST MISSIONARY SOCIETY (1792), Baptist House, 129 Broadway, Didcot, Oxon. OX11 8RT.—*Gen. Sec.*, Rev. R. G. S. Harvey.

BAR ASSOCIATION FOR LOCAL GOVERNMENT AND THE PUBLIC SERVICE (1945).—*Chairman*, P. G. Stivadoros, 23 Wentworth Way, Bletchley, Milton Keynes MK3 7RW.

BARNARDO'S (1866), Tanners Lane, Barkingside, Ilford, Essex IG6 1QG. Helps over 18,000 children and young people each year who face disadvantage or disability in the United Kingdom, Australia and New Zealand.—*Senior Dir.*, R. Singleton.

BARONETAGE, STANDING COUNCIL OF THE (1898).— *Hon. Sec.*, Sir Tobias Clarke, Bt., The Church House, Bibury, Cirencester, Glos. GL7 5NR.

BARRISTERS' BENEVOLENT ASSOCIATION, THE (1873), 14 Gray's Inn Square, WC1R 5JP.—*Sec.*, Miss K. M. Hopper.

BEECHAM TRUST, SIR THOMAS (1946), Denton House, Denton, Harleston, Norfolk IP20 0AA.—*Sec.*, Shirley, Lady Beecham.

BEE-KEEPERS' ASSOCIATION, BRITISH (1874), National Agricultural Centre, Stoneleigh, Kenilworth, Warks. CV8 2LZ.—*Gen. Sec.*, vacant.

BIBLE CHURCHMEN'S MISSIONARY SOCIETY (1922), 251 Lewisham Way, SE4 1XF.—*Gen. Sec.*, Rev. Canon J. M. Ball.

BIBLE SOCIETY, BRITISH AND FOREIGN (1804), Stonehill Green, Westlea, Swindon SN5 7DG.—*Exec. Dir.*, R. Worthing-Davies.

BIBLIOGRAPHICAL SOCIETY (1892), British Library, Humanities and Social Sciences, Great Russell Street, WC1B 3DG.—*Hon. Sec.*, Dr. M. M. Foot.

BIBLIOGRAPHICAL SOCIETY, EDINBURGH (1890), c/o New College Library, Mound Place, Edinburgh EH1 2LU.—*Hon. Sec.*, Dr. M. C. T. Simpson.

BIOCHEMICAL SOCIETY (1911), 59 Portland Place, W1N 3AJ.—*Exec. Sec.*, G. D. Jones.

BIOLOGICAL COUNCIL, THE (1945), c/o Institute of Biology, 20 Queensberry Place, SW7 2DZ.—*Hon. Sec.*, Prof. M. Sandler.

BIOLOGICAL ENGINEERING SOCIETY (1960), Royal College of Surgeons, Lincoln's Inn Fields, WC2A 3PN.—*Hon. Sec.*, Dr. R. E. Trotman.

BIOLOGY, THE INSTITUTE OF (1950), 20 Queensberry Place, SW7 2DZ.—*Gen. Sec.*, Dr. R. H. Priestley.

BIRD PRESERVATION, INTERNATIONAL COUNCIL FOR (BRITISH SECTION) (1922), c/o Flora and Fauna Preservation Society, 79–83 North Street, Brighton BN1 12A.—*Exec. Sec.*, J. R. Wilson.

BIRMINGHAM AND MIDLAND INSTITUTE (1854) and PRIESTLEY LIBRARY (1779), Margaret Street, Birmingham B3 3BS.—*Admin.* J. Hunt.

BIRTHDAY TRUST FUND, NATIONAL (1928), 27 Sussex Place, NW1 4RG. For extension of maternity services.—*Sec.*, Mrs. M. C. Matthews.

BLIND, GUIDE DOGS FOR THE, *see* GUIDE DOGS FOR THE BLIND ASSOCIATION.

BLIND, INCORPORATED ASSOCIATION FOR PROMOTING THE GENERAL WELFARE OF THE (1854), 37–55 Ashburton Grove, N7 7DW.—*Chief Exec.*, G. P. Robinson.

BLIND, LONDON ASSOCIATION FOR THE (1857), 14–16 Verney Road, SE16 3DZ.—*Dir.*, A. Kent.

BLIND, NATIONAL LIBRARY FOR THE (1882), Cromwell Road, Bredbury, Stockport, Cheshire SK6 2SG. Over 400,000 volumes available.—*Dir. Gen.*, A. Leach.

BLIND, ROYAL LONDON SOCIETY FOR THE (1838), 105–109 Salusbury Road, NW6 6RH.—*Chief Exec.*, R. J. Pocock.

BLIND, ROYAL NATIONAL COLLEGE FOR THE (1872), College Road, Hereford HR1 1EB.—*Principal*, L. Marshall.

BLIND, ROYAL NATIONAL INSTITUTE FOR THE (1868), 224 Great Portland Street, W1N 6AA.—*Dir. Gen.*, I. Bruce.

BLIND, ROYAL SCHOOL FOR THE (1799), Leatherhead, Surrey KT22 8NR.—*Dir.*, Rev. B. A. E. Coote.

BLOOD TRANSFUSION ASSOCIATION, SCOTTISH NATIONAL (1940), 29 Abercromby Place, Edinburgh EH3 6UE.—*Sec.*, P. C. Taylor.

BLOOD TRANSFUSION SERVICE, NATIONAL (1948), National Directorate, North Western Regional Health Authority, Gateway House, Piccadilly South, Manchester M60 7LP.—*Nat. Dir.*, Dr. H. H. Gunson.

BLUE CROSS ANIMALS' HOSPITAL (1897), Hugh Street, SW1V 1QQ.—*Sec.*, A. Kennard, MBE.

BODLEIAN, FRIENDS OF THE (1925), Bodleian Library, Oxford OX1 3BG.—*Sec.*, G. Groom.

BOOKSELLERS ASSOCIATION OF GREAT BRITAIN AND IRELAND (1895), 272–274 Vauxhall Bridge Road, SW1V 1BA.—*Dir.*, T. E. Godfray.

BOOK TRADE BENEVOLENT SOCIETY (1967), Dillon Lodge, The Retreat, Kings Langley, Herts. WD4 8LT.—*Exec. Sec.*, Mrs. A. R. Brown.

BOOK TRUST (1986), Book House, 45 East Hill, SW18 2QZ.—*Chief Exec.*, K. McWilliams.

BOTANICAL SOCIETY OF THE BRITISH ISLES (1836), Dept. of Botany, The Natural History Museum, Cromwell Road, SW7 5BD.—*Hon. Gen. Sec.*, Mrs. M. Briggs, MBE.

BOTANICAL SOCIETY OF EDINBURGH, Royal Botanic Garden, Inverleith Row, Edinburgh EH3 5LR.—*Hon. Gen. Sec.*, Dr. I. Edwards.

BOY SCOUTS ASSOCIATION, *see* SCOUT ASSOCIATION, THE.

BOYS' BRIGADE, THE (1883), 1 Galena Road, W6 0LT. Membership worldwide: 400,000 in 60 countries.—*Brigade Sec.*, S. Jones.

BOYS' CLUBS, NATIONAL ASSOCIATION OF (1925), 369 Kennington Lane, SE11 5QY. Has affiliated to it 2,000 clubs.—*Nat. Dir.*, D. P. Harris.

BOYS' CLUBS, NORTHERN IRELAND ASSOCIATION OF (1940), Bryson House, 28 Bedford Street, Belfast BT2 7FE.—*Gen. Sec.*, K. Culbert

BREWING, INSTITUTE OF (1886), 33 Clarges Street, W1Y 8EE.—*Chief Exec.*, P. W. E. Istead.

BRIDEWELL ROYAL HOSPITAL (1553), Witley, Surrey GU8 5SG.—*Clerk to the Governors*, G. Wilson.

BRITAIN-NEPAL SOCIETY (1960).—*Hon. Sec.*, Mrs. C. Brown, 1 Allen Mansions, Allen Street, W8 6UY.

BRITISH ACADEMY, THE (1901), 20–21 Cornwall Terrace, NW1 4QP.—*Pres.*, Dr. A. J. P. Kenny; *Sec.*, P. W. H. Brown.

BRITISH AND FOREIGN SCHOOL SOCIETY (1808), Richard Mayo Hall, Eden Street, Kingston upon Thames, Surrey KT1 1HZ.—*Sec.*, S. M. A. Banister.

BRITISH ATLANTIC COMMITTEE (1952), 5 St. James's Place, SW1A 1NP.—*Dir.*, Maj.-Gen. C. J. Popham, CB.

BRITISH INSTITUTE IN EASTERN AFRICA (1959), 1 Kensington Gore, SW7 2AR.—*London Sec.*, Mrs. J. Moyo.

BRITISH INSTITUTE OF ARCHAEOLOGY AT ANKARA (1948), 28 Ladbroke Grove, W11 3BQ.—*London Sec.*, Ms. F. Chapman-Purchas.

BRITISH INSTITUTE OF PERSIAN STUDIES (1961), 13 Cambrian Road, Richmond, Surrey TW10 6JQ.—*Sec.*, Mrs. M. E. Gueritz, MBE.

BRITISH INTERPLANETARY SOCIETY (1933), 27–29 South Lambeth Road, SW8 1SZ.—*Exec. Sec.*, L. J. Carter.

BRITISH ISRAEL WORLD FEDERATION (1919), 8 Blades Court, Deodar Road, SW15 2NU.—*Sec.*, A. E. Gibb.

BRITISH LEGION, ROYAL (1921), 48 Pall Mall, SW1Y 5JY.—*Gen. Sec.*, Lt.-Col. P. C. E. Creasy.

BRITISH LEGION SCOTLAND, ROYAL (1921), New Haig House, Logie Green Road, Edinburgh EH7 4HR.—*Gen. Sec.*, Brig. R. W. Riddle, OBE.

BRITISH MEDICAL ASSOCIATION (1832), BMA House, Tavistock Square, WC1H 9JP.—*Pres.*, Dame Rosemary Rue, DBE; *Sec.*, Dr. I. T. Field.

BRITISH RED CROSS SOCIETY (1870), 9 Grosvenor Crescent, SW1X 7EJ.—*Dir. Gen.*, Lt.-Gen. Sir Cameron Moffat, KBE (acting).

BRITISH SCHOOL OF ARCHAEOLOGY IN JERUSALEM (1919), The British Academy, 20 Cornwall Terrace, NW1 4QP.—*Pres.*, The Rev. Prof. H. Chadwick, KBE, FBA; *Dir.*, Dr. R. P. Harper.

BRUSH MANUFACTURERS' ASSOCIATION, BRITISH (1908), 35 Billing Road, Northampton NN1 5DD.—*Sec.*, A. N. Nisbet.

BTVC (BRITISH TRUST FOR CONSERVATION VOLUNTEERS) (1970), 36 St. Mary's Street, Wallingford, Oxon. OX10 0EU.—*Chief Exec.*, R. Morley.

BUDDHIST SOCIETY, THE (1924), 58 Eccleston Square, SW1V 1PH.—*Gen. Sec.*, R. C. Maddox.

BUDGERIGAR SOCIETY, THE (1925), 49–53 Hazelwood Road, Northampton NN1 1LG.—*Gen. Sec.*, A. C. Crook.

BUILDING, CHARTERED INSTITUTE OF (1834), Englemere, Kings Ride, Ascot, Berks. SL5 8BJ.—*Chief Exec.*, K. Banbury.

BUILDING SERVICES ENGINEERS, CHARTERED INSTITUTION OF (1897), Delta House, 222 Balham High Road, SW12 9BS.—*Sec.*, A. V. Ramsay.

BUILDING SOCIETIES ASSOCIATION (1936), 3 Savile Row, W1X 1AF.—*Dir. Gen.*, M. J. Boléat.

BUSINESS AND PROFESSIONAL WOMEN, UNITED KINGDOM FEDERATION OF (1938), 23 Ansdell Street, W8 5BN.—*Sec.*, Mrs. R. Bangle.

BUSINESS ARCHIVES COUNCIL (1934), 185 Tower Bridge Road, SE1 2UF.—*Sec. Gen.*, vacant.

BUSINESS EDUCATION, THE FACULTY OF (1872), 1 The Old School, Pant Glas, Oswestry SY10 7HS.—*Gen. Sec.*, L. Garner.

BUTCHERS' AND DROVERS' CHARITABLE INSTITUTION (1828), 61 West Smithfield, EC1A 9EA.—*Sec.*, J. A. Fordyce.

CADET FORCE ASSOCIATION, COMBINED (1952), 'E' Block, The Duke of York's HQ, SW3 4RR.—*Sec.*, Brig. R. B. MacGregor-Oakford, CBE, MC.

CALOUSTE GULBENKIAN FOUNDATION (1956), 98 Portland Place, W1N 4ET.—*Dir.*, B. Whitaker.

CAMBRIDGE PRESERVATION SOCIETY (1929), Wandlebury Ring, Gog Magog Hills, Babraham, Cambridge CB2 4AE.—*Sec.*, G. Brewster.

CAMERA CLUB, THE (1885), 8 Great Newport Street, WC2H 7JA.—*Sec.*, D. Pincham.

CAMERON FUND, THE (1971), Tavistock House North, Tavistock Square, WC1H 9JP.—*Sec.*, Mrs. J. Martin.

CAMPAIGN FOR NUCLEAR DISARMAMENT (CND) (1958), 162 Holloway Road, N7 8DQ.—*Gen. Sec.*, Ms. M. Beresford.

CANCER RELIEF MACMILLAN FUND (1911), Anchor House, 15–19 Britten Street, SW3 3TZ.—*Dir.*, D. Scott.

CANCER RESEARCH CAMPAIGN, 2 Carlton House Terrace, SW1Y 5AR.—*Dir. Gen.*, D. de Peyer.

CANCER RESEARCH FUND, IMPERIAL (1902), PO Box 123, Lincoln's Inn Fields, WC2A 3PX.—*Sec.*, Maj.-Gen. A. W. Dennis, CB, OBE.

CANCER RESEARCH, THE INSTITUTE OF, Royal Cancer Hospital, 17A Onslow Gardens, SW7 3AL.—*Sec.*, J. Kipling.

CANCER UNITED PATIENTS, BRITISH ASSOCIATION OF (BACUP) (1985), 121–123 Charterhouse Street, EC1M 6AA.—*Chairman*, M. Slevin.

CAREER TEACHERS, ASSOCIATION OF (1975), Hillsboro., Castledine Street, Loughborough, Leics. LE11 2DX.—*Gen. Sec.*, Miss P. Yaffé.

CARERS NATIONAL ASSOCIATION (1988), 29 Chilworth Mews, W2 3RG.—*Dir.*, Ms. J. Pitkeathley.

CARNEGIE DUNFERMLINE TRUST (1903), Abbey Park House, Dunfermline KY12 7PB. Social and cultural purposes in Dunfermline.—*Sec.*, F. Mann.

CARNEGIE HERO FUND TRUST (1908). Abbey Park House, Dunfermline KY12 7PB. Makes grants and allowances to people injured or the dependants of people killed in saving human life within the British Isles and territorial waters.— *Sec.*, F. Mann.

CARNEGIE UNITED KINGDOM TRUST (1913), Comely Park House, Dunfermline, KY12 7EJ.—*Sec.*, G. Lord, OBE.

CATHEDRALS ADVISORY COMMISSION FOR ENGLAND (1949), 83 London Wall, EC2M 5NA.—*Sec.*, Dr. R. Gem.

CATHOLIC FUND FOR OVERSEAS DEVELOPMENT (CAFOD) (1962), 2 Romero Close, Stockwell Road, SW9 9TY.—*Dir.* J. Filochowski.

CATHOLIC MARRIAGE ADVISORY COUNCIL (1946), Clitherow House, 1 Blythe Mews, Blythe Road, W14 0NW.—*Chief Exec.*, Mrs. J. C. Judge.

CATHOLIC RECORD SOCIETY (1904).—*Hon. Sec.*, Miss R. Rendel, 43 Lansdowne Road, W11 2LQ.

CATHOLIC TRUTH SOCIETY (1868), 38–40 Eccleston Square, SW1V 1PD.—*Gen. Sec.*, D. Murphy.

CATHOLIC UNION OF GREAT BRITAIN (1872), St. Maximilian Kolbe House, 63 Jeddo Road, W12 9EE.—*Pres.*, The Duke of Norfolk, KG, GCVO, CB, CBE, MC; *Hon. Sec.*, Mrs. J. Stuyt, MBE.

CATTLE BREEDERS' ASSOCIATION, NATIONAL, 24 Courtenay Park, Newton Abbot, Devon TQ12 2HB.—*Sec.*, J. H. Pappin.

CATTLE BREEDER'S CLUB, LTD. (1945), Lavenders, Isfield, Uckfield, E. Sussex TN22 5TX.—*Sec.*, C. R. Stains.

CECIL HOUSES (Inc.) (1926), 2 Priory Road, Kew, Richmond, Surrey TW9 3DG. (Housing Association).—*Sec.*, D. S. Cottrell.

CENTRAL BUREAU (for educational visits and exchanges) (1948), Seymour Mews House, Seymour Mews, W1H 9PE.—*Dir.* A. H. Male.

CERAMICS, INSTITUTE OF (1955), Shelton House, Stoke Road, Shelton, Stoke-on-Trent ST4 2DR.—*Pres.*, Dr. D. W. F. James.

CHADWICK TRUST (1895), Department of Civil Engineering, University College London, Gower Street, WC1E 6BT. For the promotion of health and prevention of disease.—*Sec to the Trustees*, I. K. Orchardson PH.D.

CHANTREY BEQUEST (1875), Royal Academy of Arts, Burlington House, Piccadilly, W1V 0DS.—*Sec.*, P. Rodgers.

CHARTERED SECRETARIES AND ADMINISTRATORS, INSTITUTE OF (1891), 16 Park Crescent, W1N 4AH.—*Sec.*, M. J. Ainsworth.

CHEMICAL ENGINEERS, INSTITUTION OF (1922), George E. Davis Building, 165–171 Railway Terrace, Rugby, Warks. CV21 3HQ.—*Gen. Sec.*, Dr. T. J. Evans.

CHEMISTRY, THE ROYAL SOCIETY OF, Burlington House, Piccadilly, W1V 0BN.—*Pres.*, Sir Rex Richards, FRS; *Sec. Gen.*, Dr. J. S. Gow, FRSE.

CHESHIRE (LEONARD) FOUNDATION, *see* LEONARD CHESHIRE FOUNDATION.

CHESS FEDERATION, BRITISH (1904), 9A Grand Parade, St. Leonards-on-Sea, E. Sussex TN38 0DD.—*Gen. Sec.*, Ms. G. White.

CHEST, HEART AND STROKE ASSOCIATION (1899), Tavistock House North, Tavistock Square, WC1H 9JE.—*Dir. Gen.*, Sir David Atkinson, KBE.

CHILDBIRTH TRUST, NATIONAL (1956), Alexandra House, Oldham Terrace W3 6NH.—*Nat. Sec.*, Ms. M. Newburn.

CHILDMINDING ASSOCIATION, NATIONAL (1977), 8 Masons Hill, Bromley, Kent BR2 9EY.—*Gen. Sec.*, Mrs. J. Burnell.

CHILDREN'S HOME, NATIONAL (1869), 85 Highbury Park, N5 1UD. Supports over 10,000 disadvantaged and disabled children and their parents annually in Great Britain and the Third World.—*Principal*, T. White, CBE.

CHILDREN'S SOCIETY, THE (1881), Edward Rudolf House, Margery Street, WC1X 0JL.—*Dir.*, I. Sparks.

CHINA ASSOCIATION (1889), Swire House, 59 Buckingham Gate, SW1E 6AJ.—*Exec. Dir.*, Brig. B. G. Hickey, OBE, MC.

CHIROPODISTS, SOCIETY OF (1945), 53 Welbeck Street, W1M 7HE.—*Gen. Sec.*, J. G. C. Trouncer.

CHOIRS SCHOOLS ASSOCIATION (1921), King's School, College Green, Worcester WR1 2LH.—*Hon. Sec.*, Dr. J. M. Moore.

CHRISTIAN ACTION, St. Peter's House, 308 Kennington Lane, SE11 5HY.—*Hon. Dir.*, Rev. Canon E. James.

CHRISTIAN AID (1945), PO Box 100, SE1 7RT.—*Dir.*, Rev. M. H. Taylor.

CHRISTIAN EDUCATION COUNCIL, NATIONAL (1809), Robert Denholm House, Nutfield, Redhill RH1 4HW.—*Head of Publishing*, D. Trenaman.

CHRISTIAN EDUCATION MOVEMENT (1965), Royal Buildings, Victoria Street, Derby DE1 1GW.—*Gen. Sec.*, Rev. Dr. S. Orchard.

CHRISTIAN EVIDENCE SOCIETY (1870), St. Stephen's House, St. Stephen's Crescent, Brentwood, Essex CM13 2AT.—*Hon. Sec.*, Mrs. G. M. Ryeland.

CHRISTIAN KNOWLEDGE, SOCIETY FOR PROMOTING (SPCK) (1698), Holy Trinity Church, Marylebone Road, NW1 4DU.—*Gen. Sec.*, P. N. G. Gilbert.

CHRISTIANS AND JEWS, COUNCIL OF (1942), 1 Dennington Park Road, NW6 1AX.—*Exec. Dir.*, Rev. Canon J. Richardson.

CHURCH ARMY (1882), Independents Road, SE3 9LG.—*Chief Sec.*, Capt. P. Johanson.

CHURCH BUILDING SOCIETY, INCORPORATED (1818), Fulham Palace, SW6 6EA.—*Sec.*, vacant.

CHURCH EDUCATION CORPORATION, Bedgebury School, Goudhurst, Cranbrook, Kent TN17 2SH.—*Sec.*, R. P. Gilbert.

CHURCH HOUSE, THE CORPORATION OF (1888), Dean's Yard, SW1P 3NZ.—*Sec.*, Capt. P. W. E. Parry, MBE.

CHURCH LADS' AND CHURCH GIRLS' BRIGADE (1891), 2 Barnsley Road, Wath upon Dearne, Rotherham, S. Yorks. S63 6PY.—*Gen. Sec.*, Wg. Cdr. J. S. Cresswell (retd.).

CHURCH MISSIONARY SOCIETY (1799), 157 Waterloo Road, SE1 8UU.—*Sec.*, Ms. S. Parks.

CHURCH MUSIC, ROYAL SCHOOL OF (1927), Addington Palace, Croydon CR9 5AD.—*Sec.*, R. Lawrence.

CHURCH OF ENGLAND PENSIONS BOARD (1926), 7 Little College Street, SW1P 3SF.—*Sec.*, R. G. Radford.

CHURCH OF ENGLAND SOLDIERS', SAILORS' AND AIRMEN'S CLUBS (1891), 1 Shakespeare Terrace, 126 High Street, Portsmouth PO1 2RH.—*Chairman*, Rear-Adm. A. G. Watson, CB.

CHURCH UNION (1859), Faith House, 7 Tufton Street, SW1P 3QN.—*Gen. Sec.*, A. Leggatt.

CHURCHES, COUNCIL FOR THE CARE OF (1921), 83 London Wall, EC2M 5NA.—*Sec.*, Dr. T. Cocke.

CHURCHES FOR BRITAIN AND IRELAND, COUNCIL OF (1942), Inter-Church House, 35–41 Lower Marsh, SE1 7RL.—*Gen. Sec.*, Rev. J. P. Reardon.

CHURCHES, FRIENDS OF FRIENDLESS (1957), 12 Edwardes Square, W8 6HG.—*Hon. Sec.*, L. E. Jones.

CHURCHES MAIN COMMITTEE (1941), Fielden House, Little College Street, SW1P 3JZ.—*Sec.*, B. M. Thimont, CB.

CITIZENS' ADVICE BUREAUX, NATIONAL ASSOCIATION OF (1931), Myddelton House, 115–123 Pentonville Road, N1 9LZ.—*Chief Exec. (acting)*, R. Cattle.

CITY PAROCHIAL FOUNDATION (1891), 10 Fleet Street, EC4Y 1AU.—*Clerk*, T. Cook.

CIVIC TRUST, THE (1957), 17 Carlton House Terrace, SW1Y 5AW.—*Dir.*, M. C. Bradshaw.

CIVIL DEFENCE, INSTITUTE OF (1938), Bell Court House, 11 Blomfield Street, EC2M 7AY.—*Hon. Gen. Sec.*, T. B. Schofield.

CIVIL ENGINEERS, INSTITUTION OF (1818), Great George Street, SW1P 3AA.—*Sec.*, J. C. McKenzie.

CIVIL LIBERTIES, NATIONAL COUNCIL FOR (1934), 21 Tabard Street, SE1 4LA.—*Gen. Sec.*, A. Puddephatt.

CLASSICAL ASSOCIATION (1903).—*Hon. Treas.*, R. Wallace, Dept. of Classics, University of Keele, Keele, Newcastle, Staffs. ST5 5BG.

CLASSICAL TEACHERS, JOINT ASSOCIATION OF (1962), 31–34 Gordon Square, WC1H 0PY.—*Exec. Sec.*, Mrs. L. Kellett.

CLEAN AIR AND ENVIRONMENTAL PROTECTION, NATIONAL SOCIETY FOR (1899), 136 North Street, Brighton BN1 1RG.—*Sec. Gen.*, J. Langston, CBE.

CLERGY ORPHAN CORPORATION (1749), 57B Tufton Street, SW1P 3QL.—*Sec.*, Miss J. Buncher.

CLERKS OF WORKS OF GREAT BRITAIN INC., INSTITUTE OF (1882), 41 The Mall, Ealing, W5 3TJ.—*Sec.*, A. P. Macnamara.

COACHING CLUB (1871), 8 Parthenia Road, SW6 4BD.—*Sec.*, D. H. Clarke.

COMMERCE, ASSOCIATION OF BRITISH CHAMBERS OF (1860), Sovereign House, 212 Shaftesbury Avenue, WC2H 8EW.—*Dir. Gen.*, R. G. Taylor, CBE.

COMMERCE, ASSOCIATION OF SCOTTISH CHAMBERS OF, 30 George Square, Glasgow G2 1EQ.—*Sec.*, E. Marwick.

COMMERCE AND INDUSTRY, LONDON CHAMBER OF (1881), 69 Cannon Street, EC4N 5AB.—*Chief Exec.*, A. M. W. Platt.

COMMERCE AND MANUFACTURERS, EDINBURGH CHAMBER OF (1786), 3 Randolph Crescent, Edinburgh EH3 7UD.—*Chief Exec.*, D. M. Mowat.

COMMERCE AND MANUFACTURERS, GLASGOW CHAMBER OF (1783), 30 George Square, Glasgow G2 1EQ.—*Sec.*, E. Marwick.

COMMERCE, CANADA UNITED KINGDOM CHAMBER OF (1921), 3 Regent Street, SW1Y 4NZ.—*Exec. Dir.*, G. F. Bacon.

COMMERCIAL AND INDUSTRIAL EDUCATION, BRITISH ASSOCIATION FOR (BACIE) (1919), 16 Park Crescent, W1N 4AP.—*Dir.*, B. V. Murphy.

COMMERCIAL TRAVELLERS' BENEVOLENT INSTITUTION (1849).—*Sec.*, M. N. Bown, Gable End, Mill Hill Road, Arnesby, Leics. LE8 3WG.

COMMISSIONAIRES, THE CORPS OF (1859), provides employment for ex-members of HM forces and ex-police, fire service and merchant navy men and prison officers. *Headquarters*, 76 Bedford Court Mansions, Bedford Avenue, WC1B 3AE. Divisions in Belfast, Birmingham, Bristol, Edinburgh, Glasgow, Leeds, Liverpool, London, Manchester, Newcastle upon Tyne. Total strength, 3,200.—*Commandant*, Col. R. B. Robertson.

COMMONWEALTH TRUST (linking the Royal Commonwealth Society and the Victoria League for Commonwealth Friendship), Commonwealth House, 18 Northumberland Avenue, WC2N 5BJ.—*Dir. Gen.*, Sir David Thorne.

COMPLEMENTARY AND ALTERNATIVE MEDICINE, COUNCIL FOR (1985), 19A Cavendish Square, W1M 9AD.—*Sec.*, Ms. C. Daglish.

COMPLEMENTARY MEDICINE, INSTITUTE FOR (1856), 21 Portland Place, W1N 3AF.—*Dir.*, A. Baird.

COMPOSERS' GUILD OF GREAT BRITAIN (1945), 34 Hanway Street, W1P 9DE.—*Gen. Sec.*, Ms. E. Yeoman.

COMPUTER SOCIETY, BRITISH (1957), 13 Mansfield Street, W1M 0BP.—*Chief Exec.*, J. R. Brookes.

CONSERVATION OF HISTORIC AND ARTISTIC WORKS, INTERNATIONAL INSTITUTE FOR (1950), 6 Buckingham Street, WC2N 6BA.—*Sec. Gen.*, Prof. H. W. M. Hodges.

CONSULTING ECONOMISTS' ASSOCIATION, INTERNATIONAL (1986), 16A Barnes High Street, SW13 9LW.—*Chairman*, J. T. Winpenny.

CONSULTING ENGINEERS, ASSOCIATION OF (1913), Alliance House, 12 Caxton Street, SW1H 0QL.—*Sec.*, Brig. H. Woodrow.

CONSULTING SCIENTISTS, ASSOCIATION OF (1958), 11 Rosemont Road, NW3 6NG.—*Hon. Sec.*, W. G. Simpson.

CONSUMERS' ASSOCIATION (1957), 2 Marylebone Road, NW1 4DX.—*Dir.*, J. Beishon.

CONTEMPORARY APPLIED ARTS (1948), 43 Earlham Street, WC2H 9LD.—*Dir.*, Ms. T. Peters.

CONVEYANCERS, COUNCIL FOR LICENSED (1986), Golden Cross House, Duncannon Street, WC2N 4JF.—*Sec.*, N. R. Osner.

CO-OPERATIVE SOCIETIES AND ASSOCIATIONS:—

Co-operative Party, 342 Hoe Street, E17 9PX.—*Sec.*, D. Wise, OBE.

Co-operative Union Ltd. (1869), Holyoake House, Hanover Street, Manchester M60 0AS.—*Chief Exec. and Gen. Sec.*, D. L. Wilkinson.

Co-operative Wholesale Society Ltd. (CWS) (1863), PO Box 53, New Century House, Manchester M60 4ES.—*Chief Exec.*, Sir Dennis Landau.

Co-operative Women's Guild (1883), 342 Hoe Street, E17 9PX.—*Nat. Pres.*, Ms J. Motyka.

Plunkett Foundation for Co-operative Studies (1919), 23 Hanborough Business Park, Long Hanborough, Oxford OX7 2LH.—*Dir.*, E. Parnell.

COPYRIGHT COUNCIL, BRITISH (1953), 29–33 Berners Street, W1P 4AA.—*Sec.*, G. V. Adams.

CORONERS' SOCIETY OF ENGLAND AND WALES (1846).—*Hon. Sec.*, Dr. J. D. K. Burton, CBE, 7 Orchard Rise, Richmond, Surrey TW10 5BX.

CORPORATE TREASURERS, ASSOCIATION OF (1979), 12 Devereux Court, WC2R 3JJ.—*Sec.*, Ms. G. Pierpoint.

CORPORATE TRUSTEES, ASSOCIATION OF (1974), 2 Withdean Rise, Brighton BN1 6YN.—*Sec.*, L. C. Howes.

CORRESPONDENCE COLLEGES, ASSOCIATION OF BRITISH (1955), 6 Francis Grove, SW19 4DT.—*Sec.*, Mrs. M. Coren.

COTTON GROWING ASSOCIATION, BRITISH (1904), 13 Upper High Street, Thame, Oxon. OX9 3HL.—*Managing Dir.*, M. Maynard.

COUNCIL FOR THE PROTECTION OF RURAL ENGLAND (CPRE), *see* RURAL.

COUNSEL AND CARE FOR THE ELDERLY (1954), Twyman House, 16 Bonny Street, NW1 9LR.—*Gen. Sec.*, J. Smith.

COUNTRY HOUSES ASSOCIATION LTD. (1955), 41 Kingsway, WC2B 6UB.—*Chief Exec.*, R. D. Bratby.

COUNTRY LANDOWNERS' ASSOCIATION (1907), 16 Belgrave Square, SW1X 8PQ.—*Dir. Gen.*, J. Anderson.

County Chief Executives, Association of (1974).— *Hon. Sec.,* I. G. Caulfield, Shire Hall, Warwick CV34 4RR.

County Councils, Association of (1890), Eaton House, 66A Eaton Square, SW1W 9BH.—*Sec.,* R. G. Wendt.

County Emergency Planning Officers' Society (1966).—*Hon. Sec.,* N. B. Knocker, OBE, Emergency Planning Dept., Wiltshire County Council, County Hall, Trowbridge, Wilts. BA14 8JE.

County Secretaries, Society of (1974).—*Hon. Sec.,* A. Fraser, County Secretary, The Courts, Carlisle CA3 8LZ.

County Surveyors' Society (1884).—*Hon. Sec.,* J. J. Stansfield, Suffolk County Council, St. Edmunds House, Rope Walk, Ipswich IP4 1LZ.

County Treasurers, Society of (1903).— *Hon. Sec.,* B. Smith, County Buildings, Eastgate Street, Stafford ST16 2NF.

Cruel Sports, the League Against (1924), 83 Union Street, SE1 1SG.—*Exec. Dir.,* J. Barrington.

Cruelty to Animals, Society for the Prevention of, *see* Royal and Scottish.

Cruelty to Children, Society for the Prevention of, *see* National and Royal Scottish.

Cruse—Bereavement Care (1959), 126 Sheen Road, Richmond, Surrey TW9 1UR.—*Dir.,* A. Sandison.

Cultural Exchange, Association for (1958), Babraham, Cambridge CB2 4AP.—*Gen. Sec.,* P. B. Barnes.

Curwen Institute (1875), 17 Primrose Avenue, Chadwell Heath, Romford RM6 4QB.—*Gen. Sec.,* H. Jones.

Cwmni Urdd Gobaith Cymru (1922), Swyddfa'r Urdd, Aberystwyth, Dyfed SY23 1EN.—*Dir.,* J. E. Williams.

Cyclists' Touring Club (1878), Cotterell House, 69 Meadrow, Godalming, Surrey GU7 3HS.—*Dir.,* A. Harlow.

Cymmrodorion, The Honourable Society of (1751), 30 Eastcastle Street, W1N 7PD.—*Hon. Sec.,* Dr. T. Wyn Jones.

Cystic Fibrosis Research Trust (1964), Alexandra House, 5 Blyth Road, Bromley BR1 3RS.—*Dir.,* Mrs. B. Bentley.

Dairy Association, United Kingdom (1950), Giggs Hill Green, Thames Ditton, Surrey KT7 0EL.—*Sec.,* Mrs. J. M. Newton.

Dairy Farmers, Royal Association of British (1876), 55 Sleaford Street, SW8 5AB.—*Chief Exec.,* P. M. Gilbert.

Dairy Technology, Society of (1943), 72 Ermine Street, Huntingdon, Cambs. PE18 6EZ.—*Nat. Sec.,* Mrs. R. Gale.

DATA (Design and Technology Association), Smallpiece House, 27 Newbold Terrace East, Leamington Spa, Warks. CV32 4ES.—*Dir.,* G. Warren.

D-Day and Normandy Fellowship (1968).—*Hon. Sec.,* Mrs. L. R. Reed, 9 South Parade, Southsea, Hants. PO5 2JB.

Deaf Association, British (1890 *formerly* British Deaf and Dumb Association), 38 Victoria Place, Carlisle CA1 1HU.—*Chief Exec.,* Ms. E. Wincott.

Deaf Children, Royal School for (1792), Victoria Road, Margate, Kent CT9 1NB.—*Sec.,* D. E. Downs.

Deaf, Commonwealth Society for the (1959), Dilke House, Malet Street, WC1E 7JA.—*Chairman,* C. Holborow, OBE, TD, MD.

Deaf, Royal National Institute for the (1911), 105 Gower Street, WC1E 6AH.—*Chief Exec.,* M. Whitlam.

Deaf People, Foley House Residential Home for (1851), Foley House, 115 High Garrett, Braintree, Essex CM7 5NU.—*Dir.,* Mrs. N. Hartard.

Deaf People, Royal Association in Aid of (1841), 27 Old Oak Road, W3 7HN.—*Chief Exec.,* Ms. R. Brotherwood.

Deer Management Societies, The Federation of (1975).—*Chairman.,* J. Hotchkis, Stede Court, Biddenden, Ashford, Kent TN27 8JG.

Defence Studies, Royal United Services Institute for (1831), Whitehall, SW1A 2ET.—*Dir.,* Gp. Capt. D. Bolton.

Dental Association, British (1880), 64 Wimpole Street, W1M 8AL.—*Sec.,* N. H. Whitehouse.

Dental Council, General (1956), 37 Wimpole Street, W1M 8DQ.—*Registrar,* N. T. Davies, MBE.

Dental Hospitals of the United Kingdom, Association of (1942).—*Hon. Sec.,* Mrs. P. Harrington, Birmingham Dental Hospital, St. Chad's Queensway, Birmingham B4 6NN.

Design and Industries Association (1915).—*Dir.,* R. Moxley, 17 Lawn Crescent, Kew Gardens, Surrey TW9 3NR.

Designers for Industry, Faculty of Royal (1936), RSA, 8 John Adam Street, WC2N 6EZ.—*Sec.,* C. Lucas.

Designers, The Chartered Society of (1930), 29 Bedford Square, WC1B 3EG.—*Dir.,* B. Lymbery.

Diabetic Association, British (1934), 10 Queen Anne Street, W1M 0BD.—*Sec. Gen.,* Capt. D. G. Armytage, CBE, RN.

Dickens Fellowship (1902), Dickens House, 48 Doughty Street, WC1N 2LF.—*Hon. Gen. Sec.,* A. S. Watts.

Directors of Public Health, Association of (1982).—*Hon. Sec.,* Dr. J. A. Sorrell, Burton District Hospital Centre, Belvedere Road, Burton upon Trent, Staffs. DE13 0RB.

Directors, Institute of (1903), 116 Pall Mall, SW1Y 5ED.—*Dir. Gen.,* P. Morgan.

Disability and Rehabilitation, Royal Association for, *see* RADAR.

Dispensing Opticians, Association of British (1925), 6 Hurlingham Business Park, Sulivan Road, SW6 3DU.—*Registrar,* D. S. Baker.

Distressed Gentlefolks' Aid Association (1897), Vicarage Gate House, Vicarage Gate, W8 4AQ.—*Gen. Sec.,* N. B. M. Clack.

District Councils, Association of (1974), 26 Chapter Street, SW1P 4ND.—*Sec.,* G. McCartney.

District Secretaries, Association of (1974), 9 Margaret Road, Bishopsworth, Bristol BS13 9DQ.—*Hon. Sec.,* D. C. Lunn.

Ditchley Foundation, Ditchley Park, Enstone, Oxford OX7 4ER.—*Dir.,* Sir John Graham, Bt., GCMG.

Dockland Settlements (1895), Rotherhithe Street, SE16 1LJ.—*Chief Exec.,* J. B. Faul.

Domestic Servants' Benevolent Institution (1846), Royal Bank of Scotland PLC, 7 Burlington Gardens, W1A 3DD.—*Sec.,* A. J. Gibson.

Dowsers, British Society of (1933).—*Sec.,* M. D. Rust, Sycamore Cottage, Tamley Lane, Hastingleigh, Ashford, Kent TN25 5HW.

Drainage Authorities, Association of (1937).— *Sec.,* D. Noble, The Mews, 3 Royal Oak Passage, High Street, Huntingdon, Cambs. PE18 6EA.

DRINKING FOUNTAIN AND CATTLE TROUGH ASSOCIATION, METROPOLITAN (1859).—*Sec.* D. R. W. Randall, 105 Wansunt Road, Bexley, Kent DA5 2DN.

DRIVING SOCIETY, BRITISH (1957), 27 Dugard Place, Barford, Warwick CV35 8DX.—*Sec.*, Mrs. J. M. Dillon.

DRUG DEPENDENCE, INSTITUTE FOR THE STUDY OF (1968), 1–4 Hatton Place, EC1N 8ND.—*Dir.*, J. Woodcock, OBE.

DUKE OF EDINBURGH'S AWARD SCHEME (1956), 5 Prince of Wales Terrace, W8 5PG. 61,455 awards gained world-wide.—*Dir.*, P. Aindow.

DYERS AND COLOURISTS, SOCIETY OF (1884), Perkin House, PO Box 244, 82 Grattan Road, Bradford BD1 2JB.—*Gen. Sec.*, M. Tordoff, PH.D.

EARL HAIG'S (BRITISH LEGION) APPEAL FUND, *see* BRITISH LEGION, ROYAL.

EARLY CHILDHOOD EDUCATION, BRITISH ASSOCIATION FOR (1923), 111 City View House, 463 Bethnal Green Road, E2 9QY.— *Sec.*, Mrs. B. Boon.

ECCLESIASTICAL HISTORY SOCIETY (1961).—*Sec.*, Dr. V. G. Davies, Dept. of History, Queen Mary and Westfield College, Kidderpore Avenue, NW3 7ST.

ECCLESIOLOGICAL SOCIETY (1839).—*Hon. Sec.*, S. C. Humphrey, 1 Cornish House, Otto Street, SE17 3PE.

EDUCATION IN ART AND DESIGN, NATIONAL SOCIETY FOR (1888), 7A High Street, Corsham, Wilts. SN13 0ES.—*Gen. Sec.*, J. Steers.

EDUCATION OFFICERS, SOCIETY OF (1971), 21–27 Lambs Conduit Street, WC1N 3NJ.—*Gen. Sec.*, D. J. Hatfield, CBE.

EDUCATION OFFICERS' SOCIETY, COUNTY (1889).—*Hon. Sec.*, Ms. J. Wisker, Education Dept., County Hall, Taunton TA1 4DY.

EDUCATIONAL CENTRES ASSOCIATION (1921), Chequer Centre, Chequer Street, EC1Y 8PL.—*Gen. Sec.*, D. Delahunt.

EDUCATIONAL RESEARCH IN ENGLAND AND WALES, NATIONAL FOUNDATION FOR (1946), The Mere, Upton Park, Slough SL1 2DQ.—*Dir.*, Ms. C. Burstall, PH.D., D.SC.

EGYPT EXPLORATION SOCIETY (1882), 3 Doughty Mews, WC1N 2PG.—*Sec.*, Dr. P. A. Spencer.

ELECTORAL REFORM SOCIETY OF GREAT BRITAIN AND IRELAND, 6 Chancel Street, SE1 0UU.—*Pres.*, Lord Blake, FBA.

ELECTRICAL ENGINEERS, INSTITUTION OF (1871), Savoy Place, WC2R 0BL.—*Sec.*, J. C. Williams, PH.D.

ELECTRICITY CONSUMERS' COUNCIL, Brook House, 2–16 Torrington Place, WC1E 7LL.—*Dir.*, T. Boorman.

ELGAR FOUNDATION (1973).— *Sec. to the Trustees*, B. Edgington, Nether End, 18 Town Close, Dartmouth, Devon TQ6 9ES.

ELGAR SOCIETY (1951).—*Sec.*, Mrs. C. Holt, 20 Geraldine Road, Malvern, Worcs. WR14 3PA.

ENERGY, INSTITUTE OF (1927), 18 Devonshire Street, W1N 2AU.—*Sec.*, C. Rigg, TD.

ENGINEERING COUNCIL, THE (1981), 10 Maltravers Street, WC2R 3ER.—*Sec.*, L. Chelton.

ENGINEERING DESIGNERS, INSTITUTE OF (1945), Courtleigh, Westbury Leigh, Westbury, Wilts. BA13 3TA.—*Sec.*, M. J. Osborne.

ENGINEERING, FELLOWSHIP OF (1976), 2 Little Smith Street, SW1P 3DL.—*Exec. Sec.*, G. Atkinson.

ENGINEERING INDUSTRIES ASSOCIATION (1941), 16 Dartmouth Street, SW1H 9BL.—*Dir. Gen.*, Col. W. T. Williams.

ENGINEERS AND SHIPBUILDERS, NE COAST INSTITUTION OF (1884), Great North House, Sandyford Road, Newcastle upon Tyne NE1 8ND.—*Sec.*, Mrs. A. J. Rainsford.

ENGINEERS, INSTITUTION OF BRITISH (1928), Royal Liver Building, 6 Hampton Place, Brighton BN1 3DD.—*Sec.*, Mrs. D. Henry.

ENGINEERS, SOCIETY OF (INCORPORATED) (1854), Parsifal College, 527 Finchley Road, NW3 7BG.—*Sec.*, P. A. Lancaster.

ENGLISH ASSOCIATION, THE (1906), The Vicarage, Priory Gardens, W4 1TT.—*Sec.*, Dr. R. Fairbanks-Joseph.

ENGLISH FOLK DANCE AND SONG SOCIETY (1932), Cecil Sharp House, 2 Regent's Park Road, NW1 7AY.—*Chairman*, vacant.

ENGLISH PLACE-NAME SOCIETY (1923).—*Hon. Dir.* Prof. K. Cameron, CBE, FBA, Dept. of English, The University, Nottingham NG7 2RD.

ENGLISH-SPEAKING UNION OF THE COMMONWEALTH (1918), 37 Charles Street, W1X 8AB.—*Dir. Gen.*, D. Hicks, MBE.

ENTOMOLOGICAL SOCIETY OF LONDON, ROYAL (1833), 41 Queen's Gate, SW7 5HU.—*Registrar*, G. G. Bentley.

ENVIRONMENTAL HEALTH OFFICERS, INSTITUTION OF (1883), Chadwick House, Rushworth Street, SE1 0QT.—*Sec.*, A. M. Tanner.

ENVIRONMENT COUNCIL (1969), 80 York Way, N1 9AG.—*Chief Exec.*, S. Robinson.

EPILEPSY ASSOCIATION, BRITISH (1949), Anstey House, 40 Hanover Square, Leeds LS3 1BE.—*Chief Exec.*, T. J. O'Leary.

EPILEPSY, THE NATIONAL SOCIETY FOR (1892), Chalfont Centre for Epilepsy, Chalfont St. Peter, Gerrards Cross, Bucks. SL9 0RJ.—*Chief Exec.*, Col. D. W. Eking.

EQUESTRIAN FEDERATION, BRITISH (1972), British Equestrian Centre, Kenilworth, Warks. CV8 2LR.—*Dir. Gen.*, Maj. M. Wallace.

ESPERANTO ASSOCIATION OF BRITAIN (1977), 140 Holland Park Avenue, W11 4UF—.*Hon. Sec.*, W. Green.

ESTATE AGENTS, NATIONAL ASSOCIATION OF (1962), Arbon House, 21 Jury Street, Warwick CV34 4EH.—*Gen. Sec.*, A. B. Clark.

EUGENICS SOCIETY *see* GALTON INSTITUTE.

EVANGELICAL ALLIANCE (1846), Whitefield House, 186 Kennington Park Road, SE11 4BT.—*Gen. Dir.*, Rev. C. R. Calver.

EVANGELICAL LIBRARY, THE (1928), 78A Chiltern Street, W1M 2HB.—*Librarian*, Miss F. S. Wright.

EXAMINERS UNDER SOLICITORS (SCOTLAND) ACT (1980), Law Society's Hall, 26 Drumsheugh Gardens, Edinburgh EH3 7YR.—*Sec.*, K. W. Pritchard.

EXECUTIVES ASSOCIATION OF GREAT BRITAIN LTD. (1929), Suite 87–89, The Hop Exchange, 24 Southwark Street, SE1 1TY.—*Sec.*, Lt.-Col. J. J. Langdon-Mudge.

EXPORT, INSTITUTE OF, Export House, 64 Clifton Street, EC2A 4HB.—*Sec.*, D. J. Langham.

EX-SERVICES LEAGUE, BRITISH COMMONWEALTH (1921), 48 Pall Mall, SW1Y 5JG.—*Sec. Gen.*, Brig. M. J. Doyle, MBE.

EX-SERVICES MENTAL WELFARE SOCIETY (1919), Broadway House, The Broadway, SW19 1RL.—*Gen. Sec.*, Brig. A. K. Dixon.

FABIAN SOCIETY (1884), 11 Dartmouth Street, SW1H 9BN.—*Gen. Sec.*, S. Crine.

FAIR ISLE BIRD OBSERVATORY TRUST (1948), 21 Regent Terrace, Edinburgh EH7 5BT.—*Hon. Sec.*, Miss V. M. Thom.

FAMILY CONCILIATION COUNCIL, NATIONAL (1982), Shaftesbury Centre, Percy Street, Swindon SN2 2AZ.—*Chairman*, Prof. B. Hoggett.

FAMILY HISTORY SOCIETIES, FEDERATION OF (1974).—*Administrator*, Mrs. P. A. Saul, c/o The Benson Room, Birmingham and Midland Institute, Margaret Street, Birmingham B3 3BS.

FAMILY PLANNING ASSOCIATION (1939), 27–35 Mortimer Street, W1N 7RJ.—*Dir.*, Ms D. E. Massey.

FAMILY WELFARE ASSOCIATION (1869), 501–505 Kingsland Road, E8 4AU.—*Dir.*, R. E. Morley.

FAUNA AND FLORA PRESERVATION SOCIETY (1903), 79–83 North Street, Brighton BN1 1ZA.—*Administrator*, Miss A. Hillier.

FELLOWSHIP HOUSES TRUST (1937), Clock House, Byfleet, Weybridge, Surrey KT14 7RN.—*Sec.*, L. P. Leech.

FIELD ARCHAEOLOGISTS, INSTITUTE OF (1982), Minerals Engineering Building, University of Birmingham, PO Box 363, Birmingham B15 2TT.—*Chairman*, Dr. T. Darvill.

FIELD SPORTS SOCIETY, BRITISH (1930), 59 Kennington Road, SE1 7PZ.—*Dir.*, Maj.-Gen. J. Hopkinson, CB.

FIELD STUDIES COUNCIL (1943), Preston Montford, Montford Bridge, Shrewsbury SY4 1HW.—*Dir.*, A. D. Thomas.

FILM CLASSIFICATION, BRITISH BOARD OF (1912), 3 Soho Square, W1V 5DE.—*Dir.*, J. Ferman.

FILM INSTITUTE, BRITISH (1933), 21 Stephen Street, W1P 1PL.—*Dir.*, W. Stevenson.

FINANCIAL ACCOUNTANTS, INSTITUTE OF (1916), Burford House, 44 London Road, Sevenoaks, Kent TN13 1AS.—*Chief Exec.*, D. Gurney.

FIRE ENGINEERS, INSTITUTION OF (1918), 148 New Walk, Leicester LE1 7QB.—*Gen. Sec.*, Mrs. C. E. Mackwood.

FIRE PROTECTION ASSOCIATION (1946), 140 Aldersgate Street, EC1A 4HX.—*Dir.*, A. S. Kidd.

FIRE SERVICES ASSOCIATION, BRITISH (1949), 86 London Road, Leicester LE2 0QR.—*Gen. Sec.*, T. A. Plummer.

FIRE SERVICES NATIONAL BENEVOLENT FUND (1943), Marine Court, Fitzalan Road, Littlehampton, W. Sussex BN17 5NF.—*Gen. Manager*, R. A. Spackman.

FLEET AIR ARM OFFICERS ASSOCIATION (1957), 94 Piccadilly, W1V 0BP.—*Chairman*, W. J. Hanks.

FOLKLORE SOCIETY, c/o University College London, Gower Street, WC1E 6BT.—*Hon. Sec.*, A. R. Vickery.

FOOD FROM BRITAIN (1983), 301–344 Market Towers, New Covent Garden Market, SW8 5NQ.—*Chairman*, P. R. Judge.

FOOD SCIENCE AND TECHNOLOGY, INSTITUTE OF (1964), 5 Cambridge Court, 210 Shepherd's Bush Road, W6 7NL.—*Exec. Sec.*, Ms. H. G. Wild.

FORCES HELP SOCIETY AND LORD ROBERTS WORKSHOPS (1899), 122 Brompton Road, SW3 1JE.—*Comptroller and Sec.*, Col. A. W. Davis, MBE.

FOREIGN PRESS ASSOCIATION IN LONDON (1888), 11 Carlton House Terrace, SW1Y 5AJ.—*Sec.* Mrs D. Crole.

FORENSIC SCIENCES, BRITISH ACADEMY OF (1959).—*Sec. Gen.*, Dr. P. J. Flynn, Anaesthetic Unit, The London Hospital Medical College, Turner Street, E1 2AD.

FORESTERS, INSTITUTE OF CHARTERED (1982), 22 Walker Street, Edinburgh EH3 7HR.—*Sec.*, Mrs. M. W. Dick.

FORESTRY ASSOCIATION, COMMONWEALTH (1921), c/o Oxford Forestry Institute, South Parks Road, Oxford OX1 3RB.—*Sec.*, M. T. Rogers.

FORESTRY SOCIETY OF ENGLAND, WALES AND NORTHERN IRELAND, ROYAL (1882), 102 High Street, Tring, Herts. HP23 4AF.—*Dir.*, J. E. Jackson, PH.D.

FORESTRY SOCIETY, ROYAL SCOTTISH (1854), 11 Atholl Crescent, Edinburgh EH3 8HE.—*Sec.* W. B. C. Walker.

FOUNDRYMEN, INSTITUTE OF BRITISH (1904), 3rd Floor, Bridge House, 121 Smallbrook Queensway, Birmingham B5 4JP.—*Sec.*, G. A. Schofield.

FRANCO-BRITISH SOCIETY (1924), Room 636, Linen Hall, 162–168 Regent Street, W1R 5TB.—*Exec. Sec.*, Mrs. M. Clarke.

FREE CHURCH FEDERAL COUNCIL (1940), 27 Tavistock Square, WC1H 9HH.—*Gen. Sec.*, Rev. D. Staple.

FREEDOM ASSOCIATION (1975), 35 Westminster Bridge Road, SE1 7JB.—*Chairman*, N. D. McWhirter, CBE.

FREEMASONS, GRAND LODGE OF ANTIENT FREE AND ACCEPTED MASONS OF SCOTLAND (1736), Freemasons' Hall, 96 George Street, Edinburgh EH2 3DH.—*Grand Master Mason of Scotland*, Brig. Sir Gregor MacGregor of MacGregor, Bt.; *Grand Sec.*, A. O. Hazel.

FREEMASONS, UNITED GRAND LODGE OF ENGLAND (1717), Freemasons' Hall, Great Queen Street, WC2B 5AZ.—*Grand Master*, HRH the Duke of Kent, KG, GCMG, GCVO; *Grand Sec.*, Cdr. M. B. S. Higham.

FREEMEN OF ENGLAND (1966).—*Sec.*, H. B. Pate, 611 Old Chester Road, Rock Ferry, Birkenhead, Merseyside L42 4NN.

FREEMEN'S GUILDS:—

Freemen's Guild of Berwick-upon-Tweed, 9 Church Street, Berwick-upon-Tweed TD15 1EF.—*Clerk*, J. R. Reay.

Freemen and Guilds of the City of Chester.—The Guildhall, Chester.

City of Coventry Freemen's Guild (1946).—*Hon. Clerk*, H. J. McCranor, 89 Brinklow Road, Binley, Coventry CV3 2JB.

Guild of Freemen of the City of London (1908), PO Box 153, 40A Ludgate Hill, EC4M 7DE.—*Clerk*, Col. D. Ivy.

Gild of Freemen of the City of Newcastle upon Tyne.—*Hon. Sec.*, F. P. M. Cook, 79 Holly Avenue, Jesmond, Newcastle upon Tyne NE2 7QB.

Gild of Freemen of the City of York (1953).—*Hon. Clerk*, R. Lee, 29 Albemarle Road, York YO2 1EW.

FRIENDLY SOCIETIES, NATIONAL CONFERENCE OF (1887), Room 313, Victoria House, Vernon Place, WC1B 4DP.—*Sec.*, P. M. Madders.

FRIENDS OF CATHEDRAL MUSIC (1956), c/o Addington Palace, Croydon, Surrey CR9 5AD.—*Hon. Gen. Sec.*, N. T. Barnes (*to May 1991*).

FRIENDS OF THE CLERGY CORPORATION, THE (1972), 27 Medway Street, SW1P 2BD.—*Sec.*, J. M. Greany.

FRIENDS OF THE EARTH (1971), 26–28 Underwood Street, N1 7JQ.—*Dir.*, D. Gee.

FRIENDS OF THE ELDERLY AND GENTLEFOLK'S HELP (1905), 42 Ebury Street, SW1W 0LZ.—*Gen. Sec.*, Rev. J. Schofield.

FRIENDS OF THE NATIONAL LIBRARIES (1931), The British Library, WC1B 3DG.—*Hon. Sec.*, J. F. Fuggles.

FURNITURE HISTORY SOCIETY (1964), c/o Dept. of Furniture and Interior Design, Victoria and Albert Museum, SW7 2RL.—*Hon. Sec.*, Miss S. Medlam.

GALLIPOLI ASSOCIATION (1915).—*Hon. Sec.*, J. C. Watson Smith, Berry Cottage, Nuptown, Bracknell, Berks. RG12 6HP.

GALTON INSTITUTE, THE (*formerly* The Eugenics Society) (1907), 19 Northfields Prospect, SW18 1PE.—*Gen. Sec.*, Mrs. L. Brooks.

GAME CONSERVANCY, THE (1969), Fordingbridge, Hants. SP6 1EF.—*Dir.*, R. M. Van Oss.

GARDEN HISTORY SOCIETY (1965), 5 The Knoll, Hereford HR1 1RU.—*Hon. Membership Sec.*, Mrs. A. Richards.

GARDENERS' ASSOCIATION, THE GOOD (1968), Two Mile Lane, Higham, Glos. GL2 8DW.—*Hon. Dir.*, J. D. Wilkin.

GARDENERS' ROYAL BENEVOLENT SOCIETY (1839), Bridge House, 139 Kingston Road, Leatherhead, Surrey KT22 7NT.—*Sec.-Administrator*, C. R. C. Bunce.

GAS CONSUMERS COUNCIL (1986), 6th Floor, Abford House, 15 Wilton Road, SW1V 1LT.—*Dir.*, I. W. Powe.

GAS ENGINEERS, INSTITUTION OF (1863), 17 Grosvenor Crescent, SW1X 7ES.—*Sec.*, D. J. Chapman.

GEMMOLOGICAL ASSOCIATION OF GREAT BRITAIN (1931), 1st Floor, 27 Greville Street, EC1N 8SU.—*Sec.*, Dr. R. R. Harding.

GENEALOGICAL RESEARCH SOCIETY, IRISH (1936).—*Hon. Sec.*, Miss R. McCutcheon, c/o The Challoner Club, 61 Pont Street, SW1X 0BG.

GENEALOGISTS AND RECORD AGENTS, ASSOCIATION OF (1968), 1 Woodside Close, Caterham, Surrey CR3 6AU.—*Sec.*, Mrs. J. Tooke.

GENEALOGISTS, SOCIETY OF (1911), 14 Charterhouse Buildings, Goswell Road, EC1M 7BA.—*Dir.*, A. J. Camp.

GENERAL PRACTITIONERS, ROYAL COLLEGE OF (1952), 14 Princes Gate, Hyde Park, SW7 1PU.—*Gen. Administrator*, Mrs. S. Irvine.

GENTLEPEOPLE, GUILD OF AID FOR (1904), 10 St. Christopher's Place, W1M 6HY.—*Sec.*, Mrs. G. A. Burgess.

GEOGRAPHICAL ASSOCIATION, 343 Fulwood Road, Sheffield S10 3BP.—*Sen. Administrator*, Miss F. Soar.

GEOGRAPHICAL SOCIETY, ROYAL (1830), 1 Kensington Gore, SW7 2AR.—*Pres.*, Sir Crispin Tickell, GCMG, KCVO.

GEOGRAPHICAL SOCIETY, ROYAL SCOTTISH (1884), 10 Randolph Crescent, Edinburgh EH3 7TU.—*Sec.*, A. B. Cruickshank.

GEOLOGICAL SOCIETY (1807), Burlington House, Piccadilly, W1V 0JU.—*Pres.*, Prof. A. L. Harris; *Exec. Sec.*, R. M. Bateman.

GEOLOGISTS' ASSOCIATION (1858), Burlington House, Piccadilly, W1V 9AG.—*Hon. Gen. Sec.*, Mrs. S. M. Dellow.

GEOLOGISTS, THE INSTITUTION OF (1977), Burlington House, Piccadilly, W1V 9AG.—*Sec.*, Dr. J. A. Seymour.

GEORGIAN GROUP (1937), 37 Spital Square, E1 6DY.—*Sec.*, R. White.

GIFTED CHILDREN, NATIONAL ASSOCIATION FOR (1966), 1 South Audley Street, W1Y 5DQ.—*Dir.*, Ms. P. G. Miles (*acting*).

GILBERT AND SULLIVAN SOCIETY (1924).—*Hon. Sec.*, Miss B. Dove, 31A Kenmere Gardens, Wembley, Middx. HA0 1TD.

GINGERBREAD ASSOCIATION FOR ONE PARENT FAMILIES (1970), 35 Wellington Street, WC2E 7BN.—*Chief Exec.*, Ms. R. Robson.

GIRL GUIDES ASSOCIATION (1910), 17–19 Buckingham Palace Road, SW1W 0PT. In 1989 the total membership in the United Kingdom was 735,297.—*Chief Commissioner*, Mrs. A. F. Garside; *Gen. Sec.*, Miss M. W. Hayter.

GIRLS' BRIGADE, THE, Girls' Brigade House, 62 Foxhall Road, Didcot, Oxon. OX11 7BQ.—*Brigade Sec. for England and Wales*, Miss D. M. Cosser.

GIRLS' FRIENDLY SOCIETY AND TOWNSEND FELLOWSHIP (1875), 126 Queens Gate, SW7 5LQ.—*Gen. Sec.*, Miss H. G. Smith.

GIRLS' VENTURE CORPS AIR CADETS (1964), Redhill Aerodrome, Kings Mill Lane, South Nutfield, Redhill RH1 5JY.—*Sec. Gen.*, Miss H. P. Prosper.

GLASS ENGRAVERS, THE GUILD OF (1975).—*Sec.*, Mrs. K. Coleman, 49 Crediton Hill, NW6 1HS.

GLASS TECHNOLOGY, SOCIETY OF (1916), Thornton, 20 Hallam Gate Road, Sheffield S10 5BT.—*Hon. Sec.*, W. Simpson.

GLIDING ASSOCIATION, BRITISH (1930), Kimberley House, Vaughan Way, Leicester LE1 4SE.—*Gen. Sec.*, B. Rolfe.

GOAT SOCIETY, BRITISH (1879), 34–36 Fore Street, Bovey Tracey, Newton Abbot, Devon TQ13 9AD.—*Sec.*, Mrs. S. Knowles.

GRAPHIC FINE ART, SOCIETY OF (1919), 9 Newburgh Street, W1V 1LH.—*Sec.*, Maj. R. W. Neve (retd.).

GRAPHOLOGISTS, THE BRITISH INSTITUTE OF (1983), 4th Floor, Bell Court House, 11 Blomfield Street, EC2M 7AY.—*Chairman*, J. E. Blomfield.

GREEK INSTITUTE (1969), 34 Bush Hill Road, N21 2DS.—*Dir.*, Dr. K. Tofallis.

GREEN PARTY, THE (1973), 10 Station Parade, Balham High Road, SW12 9AZ.—*Office Manager*, J. Bishop.

GREENPEACE (1971), 30 Islington Green, N1 8XE.—*Exec. Dir.*, Lord Melchett.

GROCERS ASSOCIATION, BRITISH INDEPENDENT (1890), Federation House, 17 Farnborough Street, Farnborough, Hants. GU14 8AG.—*Nat. Sec.*, A. Taylor.

GUIDE DOGS FOR THE BLIND ASSOCIATION (1931), Alexandra House, Park Street, Windsor, Berks. SL4 1JR.—*Dir. Gen.*, J. C. Oxley.

GULBENKIAN FOUNDATION, *see* CALOUSTE GULBENKIAN FOUNDATION.

HAEMOPHILIA SOCIETY, THE (1950), 123 Westminster Bridge Road, SE1 7HR.—*Sec.*, D. G. Watters.

HAKLUYT SOCIETY (1846), c/o Map Library, The British Library, Great Russell Street, WC1B 3DG.—*Joint Hon. Secs.*, Dr. T. E. Armstrong; Mrs. S. Tyacke.

HANSARD SOCIETY FOR PARLIAMENTARY GOVERNMENT, THE (1944), 16 Gower Street, WC1E 6DP.—*Dir.*, D. Harris.

HARD OF HEARING, BRITISH ASSOCIATION OF THE (1948), 7–11 Armstrong Road, W3 7JL.—*Chairman*, P. J. Phillips.

HARVEIAN SOCIETY OF EDINBURGH (1782), Dept. of Medicine, The Royal Infirmary, Edinburgh EH3 9YW.—*Joint Secs.*, Dr. A. D. Toft; A. B. MacGregor.

HARVEIAN SOCIETY OF LONDON (1831), 11 Chandos Street, W1M 0EB.—*Exec. Sec.*, Maj. T. Tudor-Williams.

HEAD TEACHERS, NATIONAL ASSOCIATION OF (1897).—*Gen. Sec.*, D. M. Hart, OBE, 1 Heath Square, Boltro Road, Haywards Heath, W. Sussex RH16 1BL.

HEALTH AUTHORITIES AND TRUSTS, NATIONAL ASSOCIATION OF (1974), Birmingham Research Park, Vincent Drive, Birmingham B15 2SQ.—*Dir.*, P. Hunt.

HEALTH CARE ASSOCIATION, BRITISH (1931), The Courtyard, Allerton Park, Knaresborough, Harrogate HG5 0SE.—*Nat. Sec.*, G. K. Waite.

HEALTH EDUCATION, INSTITUTE OF (1962).—*Hon. Sec.*, Prof. L. Baric, Ph.D., 14 High Elm Road, Hale Barns, Altrincham, Cheshire WA15 0HS.

HEALTH, GUILD OF (1904), Edward Wilson House, 26 Queen Anne Street, W1M 9LB.—*Nat. Dir.*, W. R. Booth.

HEALTH SERVICES MANAGEMENT, INSTITUTE OF (1902), 75 Portland Place, W1N 4AN.—*Dir.*, Ms. M. Dixon, Ph.D.

HEART FOUNDATION, BRITISH (1963), 14 Fitzhardinge Street, W1H 9PL.—*Dir. Gen.*, Maj.-Gen. L. F. H. Busk, CB.

HEDGEHOG PRESERVATION SOCIETY, BRITISH (1982), Knowbury House, Knowbury, Ludlow, Salop. SY8 3LQ.—*Sec.*, A. H. Coles.

HELLENIC STUDIES, SOCIETY FOR THE PROMOTION OF (1879), 31–34 Gordon Square, WC1H 0PP.—*Hon. Sec.*, Dr. H. W. Catling.

HELP THE AGED (1960), St. James's Walk, EC1R 0BE.—*Dir. Gen.*, Col. J. Mayo, OBE.

HERALDIC AND GENEALOGICAL STUDIES, INSTITUTE OF (1961), 79–82 Northgate, Canterbury, Kent CT1 1BA.—*Registrar.*, Ms. J. Carter.

HERALDRY SOCIETY, THE (1947), 44–45 Museum Street, WC1A 1LY.—*Sec.*, Mrs. M. Miles, MBE.

HERALDRY SOCIETY OF SCOTLAND (1977).—*Sec.*, Dr. M. Tod, Carnethy, Seafield, Roslin, Midlothian EH25 9RQ.

HERPETOLOGICAL SOCIETY, BRITISH (1947), c/o Zoological Society of London, Regent's Park, NW1 4RY.—*Sec.*, Mrs. M. Green.

HIGHWAYS AND TRANSPORTATION, INSTITUTION OF (1930), 3 Lygon Place, Ebury Street, SW1W 0JS.—*Sec.*, Miss P. A. Steel.

HISPANIC AND LUSO BRAZILIAN COUNCIL (1943), Canning House, 2 Belgrave Square, SW1X 8PJ.—*Dir. Gen.*, Sir Kenneth James, KCMG.

HISTORICAL ASSOCIATION, THE (1906), 59A Kennington Park Road, SE11 4JH.—*Sec.*, Mrs. M. Stiles.

HISTORICAL SOCIETY, ROYAL (1868), University College London, Gower Street, WC1E 6BT.—*Pres.*, Prof. F. M. L. Thompson; *Exec. Sec.*, Mrs. J. N. McCarthy.

HOMEOPATHIC ASSOCIATION, BRITISH (1902), 27A Devonshire Street, W1N 1RJ.—*Gen. Sec.*, Mrs. E. Segall.

HONG KONG ASSOCIATION (1961), Swire House, 59 Buckingham Gate, SW1E 6AJ.—*Exec. Dir.*, Brig. B. G. Hickey, OBE, MC.

HOROLOGICAL INSTITUTE, BRITISH (1858), Upton Hall, Upton, Newark, Notts. NG23 5TE.—*Sec.*, W. M. G. Evans.

HOROLOGICAL SOCIETY, ANTIQUARIAN (1953), New House, High Street, Ticehurst, Wadhurst, E. Sussex TN5 7AL.—*Sec.*, Mrs. M. R. Janes.

HORSE SOCIETY, BRITISH (1947) (incorporating The Pony Club), British Equestrian Centre, Kenilworth, Warks. CV8 2LR.—*Chief Exec.*, Col. T. Eastwood.

HOSPITAL FEDERATION, INTERNATIONAL (1947), 2 St. Andrew's Place, NW1 4LB.—*Dir. Gen.*, Dr. E. N. Pickering.

HOSPITAL SATURDAY FUND, THE (1873), 192–198 Vauxhall Bridge Road, SW1V 1EE.—*Chief Exec.*, K. R. Bradley.

HOSPITAL SAVING ASSOCIATION, THE, Hambleden House, Andover, Hants. SP10 1LQ.—*Gen. Sec.*, J. A. Young.

HOTEL, CATERING AND INSTITUTIONAL MANAGEMENT ASSOCIATION (1971), 191 Trinity Road, SW17 7HN.—*Dir.*, Miss E. Gadsby.

HOTELS, RESTAURANTS AND CATERERS ASSOCIATION, BRITISH (1907), 40 Duke Street, W1M 6HR.—*Chief Exec.*, R. Lees, CB, MBE.

HOUSE OF ST. BARNABAS-IN-SOHO (1846), 1 Greek Street, W1V 6NQ. For homeless women in London.—*Dir.*, D. G. Saunders.

HOUSING, INSTITUTE OF, 9 White Lion Street, N1 9XJ.—*Dir.*, P. McGurk.

HOUSING AID SOCIETY, CATHOLIC (1956), 189A Old Brompton Road, SW5 0AR.—*Dir.*, Ms. R. Rafferty.

HOUSING AND TOWN PLANNING COUNCIL, NATIONAL (1900), 14–18 Old Street, EC1V 9AB.—*Dir.*, R. Walker.

HOUSING ASSOCIATION FOR OFFICERS' FAMILIES (1916), Alban Dobson House, Green Lane, Morden, Surrey SM4 5NS.—*Gen. Sec.*, J. B. Holt.

HOVERCRAFT SOCIETY, THE (1971), 24 Jellicoe Avenue, Alverstoke, Gosport, Hants. PO12 2PE.—*Chairman*, B. J. Russell.

HOWARD LEAGUE FOR PENAL REFORM, THE (1866), 708 Holloway Road, N19 3NL.—*Dir.*, Ms. F. Crook.

HUGUENOT SOCIETY OF GREAT BRITAIN AND IRELAND (1885), The Huguenot Library, University College, Gower Street, WC1E 6BT.—*Sec.*, Mrs. M. Bayliss.

HUMANE RESEARCH TRUST, (1974), Brook House, 29 Bramhall Lane South, Bramhall, Stockport, Cheshire SK7 2DN.—*Chairman*, R. MacAlastair Brown.

HYDROGRAPHIC SOCIETY (1972), c/o Polytechnic of East London, Longbridge Road, Dagenham, Essex RM8 2AS.—*Hon. Sec.*, V. J. Abbott.

HYMN SOCIETY OF GREAT BRITAIN AND IRELAND (1936).—*Sec.*, Rev. M. Garland, St. Nicholas Rectory, Glebe Fields, Curdworth, Sutton Coldfield, W. Midlands B76 9ES.

INDEPENDENT BRITAIN, CAMPAIGN FOR AN (1976), 81 Ashmole Street, SW8 1NF.—*Hon. Sec.*, Sir Robin Williams, Bt.

INDEPENDENT SCHOOL BURSARS' ASSOCIATION (1933).—*Sec.*, D. J. Bird, Woodlands, Closewood Road, Denmead, Portsmouth PO7 6JD.

INDEPENDENT SCHOOLS CAREERS ORGANIZATION (1942), 12A–18A Princess Way, Camberley, Surrey GU15 3SP.—*Dir.* G. W. Searle.

INDEPENDENT SCHOOLS INFORMATION SERVICE (ISIS) (1972), 56 Buckingham Gate, SW1E 6AG.—*Dir.*, D. J. Woodhead.

INDEPENDENT SCHOOLS JOINT COUNCIL (1974), 25 Victoria Street, SW1H 0EX.—*Gen. Sec.*, Dr. A. G. Hearnden.

INDEXERS, SOCIETY OF (1957).—*Sec.*, Mrs. C. Troughton, 16 Green Road, Birchington, Kent CT7 9JZ.

INDUSTRIAL CHRISTIAN FELLOWSHIP (1877).—*Nat. Sec.*, D. Arthur, Dukes Meadow, 1 One Tree Lane, Beaconsfield, Bucks. HP9 2BU.

INDUSTRIAL MANAGERS, INSTITUTION OF (1931), Rochester House, 66 Little Ealing Lane, W5 4XX.—*Chief Exec.*, G. J. Rawlings, OBE.

INDUSTRIAL MARKETING RESEARCH ASSOCIATION (IMRA) (1963), 11 Bird Street, Lichfield, Staffs. WS13 6PW.—*Exec. Officer*, M. Berry.

INDUSTRIAL SOCIETY, THE (1918), Robert Hyde House, 48 Bryanston Square, W1H 7LN.—*Dir.*, A. Graham.

INDUSTRY AND PARLIAMENT TRUST, 1 Buckingham Place, SW1E 6HR. Aims to bridge the gap in understanding between industry and parliament.—*Dir.*, F. R. Hyde-Chambers.

INDUSTRY TRAINING ORGANIZATIONS, NATIONAL COUNCIL OF (1988), 7 Huttles Green, Shepreth, Nr. Royston, Herts. SG8 6PR.—*Administrator*, Mrs. D. Wilson.

INFANT DEATHS, THE FOUNDATION FOR THE STUDY OF (1971), 15 Belgrave Square, SW1X 8PS.—*Chief Exec.*,Ms. E. De'Ath.

INFORMATION SCIENTISTS, INSTITUTE OF (1958), 44–45 Museum Street, WC1A 1LY.—*Exec. Sec.*, Mrs. S. A. Carter.

INNER WHEEL CLUBS IN GREAT BRITAIN AND IRELAND, ASSOCIATION OF (1934), 51 Warwick Square, SW1V 2AT.—*Gen. Sec.*, Miss J. Dobson.

INSURANCE AND INVESTMENT BROKERS' ASSOCIATION, BRITISH, BIIBA House, 14 Bevis Marks, EC3A 7NT.—*Dir. Gen.*, J. C. T. Hackett.

INSURANCE BROKERS REGISTRATION COUNCIL, 15 St. Helen's Place, EC3A 6DS.—*Registrar*, Miss E. J. Rees.

INSURANCE INSTITUTE, CHARTERED (1897), 20 Aldermanbury, EC2V 7HY.—*Dir. Gen.*, Dr. D. E. Bland.

INSURERS, ASSOCIATION OF BRITISH (1985), Aldermary House, 10–15 Queen Street, EC4N 1TT.—*Chief Exec.*, M. A. Jones.

INTERCON (INTERCONTINENTAL CHURCH SOCIETY) (1823), 175 Tower Bridge Road, SE1 2AQ.—*Gen. Sec.*, Rev. Canon D. R. Irving.

INTERNATIONAL AFFAIRS, ROYAL INSTITUTE OF (1920), Chatham House, 10 St. James's Square, SW1Y 4LE.—*Dir.*, Adm. Sir James Eberle, GCB (*to Dec. 1990*); Prof. L. Martin (*from Jan. 1991*).

INTERNATIONAL FRIENDSHIP LEAGUE (1931), 3 Creswick Road, W3 9HE.—*Sec.*, Mrs. B. Macdonald.

INTERNATIONAL LAW ASSOCIATION (1873), Charles Clore House, 17 Russell Square, WC1B 5DR.—*Hon. Sec. Gen.*, B. Mauleverer, QC.

INTERNATIONAL POLICE ASSOCIATION (British Section) (1950), 1 Fox Road, West Bridgford, Nottingham NG2 6AJ.—*Chief Exec. Officer*, K. H. Robinson.

INTERNATIONAL SHIPPING FEDERATION (1909), 30–32 St. Mary Axe, EC3A 8ET.—*Sec.*, D. A. Dearsley.

INTERNATIONAL STUDENTS HOUSE (1962), 229 Great Portland Street, W1N 5HD.—*Sec.*, W. R. Murray.

INTERNATIONAL TIN RESEARCH INSTITUTE (1932), Kingston Lane, Uxbridge, Middx. UB8 3PJ.—*Dir.*, Dr. B. T. K. Barry.

INTERNATIONAL VOLUNTARY SERVICE (1920), 162 Upper New Walk, Leicester LE1 7QA.—*Gen. Secs.*, P. Ticher; D. T. Huggins.

INTERSERVE (*formerly* BMMF) (1852), Whitefield House, 186 Kennington Park Road, SE11 4BT.—*Gen. Dir.*, A. M. S. Pont.

INTER VARSITY CLUBS, ASSOCIATION OF (1946), 26 Chesswood Road, Worthing, W. Sussex BN11 2AD.—*Sec.*, M. A. Rooke-Matthews.

INVALID CHILDREN'S AID NATIONWIDE (I CAN) (1888), Allen Graham House, 198 City Road, EC1V 2PH.—*Dir.*, B. J. Jones.

INVALIDS-AT-HOME (1966).—*Hon. Sec.*, Mrs. E. Pierce, 23 Farm Avenue, NW2 2BJ. Helps seriously disabled people living at home.

INVISIBLE EXPORTS COUNCIL, BRITISH (1983), Windsor House, 39 King Street, EC2V 8DQ.—*Dir. Gen.*, D. P. Thomson.

INVOLVEMENT AND PARTICIPATION ASSOCIATION (1884), 85–95 Tooley Street, SE1 2RA.—*Sec.*, B. C. Stevens.

IRAN SOCIETY (1936), 2 Belgrave Square, SW1X 8PJ.—*Hon. Sec.*, J. R. H. James, OBE.

JAPAN ASSOCIATION (1950), Swire House, 59 Buckingham Gate, SW1E 6AJ.—*Exec. Dir.*, Brig. B. G. Hickey, OBE, MC.

JERUSALEM AND THE MIDDLE EAST CHURCH ASSOCIATION, THE (1887), The Old Gatehouse, Castle Hill, Farnham, Surrey GU9 0AE—*Sec.*, Mrs. V. Wells.

JEWISH HISTORICAL SOCIETY OF ENGLAND (1893), 33 Seymour Place, W1H 5AP.—*Hon. Sec.*, C. M. Drukker.

JEWISH WELFARE BOARD (1859).—*Exec. Dir.*, M. I. Carlowe, 221 Golders Green Road, NW11 9DW.

JEWISH YOUTH, ASSOCIATION FOR (1899), A.J.Y. House, 50 Lindley Street, E1 3AX.—*Exec. Dir.*, M. Shaw.

JEWS, CHURCH'S MINISTRY AMONG THE (1809), 30c Clarence Road, St. Albans, Herts. AL1 4JJ.—*Gen. Dir.*, Rev. J. M. V. Drummond.

JOHN INNES INSTITUTE (1910), Colney Lane, Norwich NR4 7UH.—*Dir.*, Prof. R. B. Flavell, PH.D.

JOURNALISTS, THE INSTITUTE OF (1883), Suite 2, Dock Offices, Surrey Quays, Lower Road, SE16 2XL.—*Joint Gen. Secs.*, C. Underwood; W. Tadd.

JUSTICE (British Section of the International Commission of Jurists) (1957), 95A Chancery Lane, WC2A 1DT.—*Dir.*, Ms. L. Levin.

JUSTICES' CLERKS' SOCIETY (1839), The Court House, Homer Road, Solihull, W. Midlands B91 3RD.—*Hon. Sec.*, A. R. Heath.

KING EDWARD'S HOSPITAL FUND FOR LONDON (THE KING'S FUND) (1897), 14 Palace Court, W2 4HT.—Makes grants to hospitals and related organizations both within and outside the NHS in the Greater London area.—*Sec.*, R. J. Maxwell, PH.D.

KING GEORGE'S FUND FOR SAILORS (1917), 1 Chesham Street, SW1X 8NF. Supports all seafarers or their dependants in need. Distributes over £1,400,000 in grants annually.—*Dir. Gen.*, Hon. H. Lawson.

KIPLING SOCIETY, THE (1927), 18 Northumberland Avenue, WC2N 5BJ.—*Hon. Sec.*, N. Entract.

LADIES IN REDUCED CIRCUMSTANCES, SOCIETY FOR THE ASSISTANCE OF (1886), Lancaster House, 25 Hornyold Road, Malvern, Worcs. WR14 1QQ.—*Sec.*, Miss H. C. Grahamslaw.

LANDSCAPE INSTITUTE (1929), 6–7 Barnard Mews, SW11 1QU.—*Registrar*, P. R. Broadbent, OBE.

LAND VALUE TAXATION AND FREE TRADE, INTERNATIONAL UNION FOR, 177 Vauxhall Bridge Road, SW1V 1EU.—*Sec.*, Mrs. B. Sobrielo.

LAND-VALUE TAXATION LEAGUE, 177 Vauxhall Bridge Road, SW1V 1EU.—*Pres.*, V. G. Saldji.

LANGUAGE LEARNING, ASSOCIATION FOR (1990), 16 Regent Place, Rugby CV21 2PN.—*Gen. Sec.*, Mrs. C. Wilding.

LAW REPORTING FOR ENGLAND AND WALES, INCORPORATED COUNCIL OF (1865), 3 Stone Buildings, Lincoln's Inn, WC2A 3XN.—*Sec.*, B. Symondson.

LEAGUE OF THE HELPING HAND (1908), Baileys, Church Street, Charlbury, Oxford OX7 3PR.—*Sec.*, Mrs. D. R. Colvin.

LEAGUE OF WELLDOERS (1893), 119–121 Limekiln Lane, Liverpool L5 8SN.—*Warden and Sec.*, K. H. Stanton.

LEATHER AND HIDE TRADES' BENEVOLENT INSTITUTION (1860), 60 Wickham Hill, Hurstpierpoint,

Hassocks, W. Sussex BN6 9NP.—*Sec.*, Mrs. G. M. Stapleton, MBE.

LEGAL EXECUTIVES, INSTITUTE OF (1892), Kempston Manor, Kempston, Bedford MK42 7AB.—*Sec. Gen.*, L. A. Evans.

LEONARD CHESHIRE FOUNDATION (1955), Leonard Cheshire House, 26–29 Maunsel Street, SW1P 2QN. 83 residential care and nursing homes and 28 family support services in the UK and affiliated to a further 186 homes worldwide.—*Dir.*, A. L. Bennett.

LEPROSY MISSION, THE (England and Wales) (1874), Goldhay Way, Orton Goldhay, Peterborough, PE2 0GZ.—*Chairman*, Dr. D. Moore.

LEUKAEMIA RESEARCH FUND (1962), 43 Great Ormond Street, WC1N 3JJ.—*Dir.*, G. J. Piller, OBE.

LIBRARY ASSOCIATION (1877), 7 Ridgmount Street, WC1E 7AE.—*Chief Exec.*, G. Cunningham.

LIFEBOATS, *see* ROYAL NATIONAL LIFEBOAT INSTITUTION.

LIGHT HORSE BREEDING SOCIETY, NATIONAL (1885), 96 High Street, Edenbridge, Kent TN8 5AR.—*Sec.*, G. W. Evans.

LINGUISTS, INSTITUTE OF (1910), 24A Highbury Grove, N5 2EA.—*Gen. Sec.*, vacant.

LINNAEAN SOCIETY OF LONDON (1788), Burlington House, Piccadilly, W1V 0LQ.—*Pres.*, Prof. M. F. Claridge.

LIONS CLUBS INTERNATIONAL (British Isles & Ireland) (1949), 5 Vine Terrace, The Square, Harborne, Birmingham B17 9PU.—*Gen. Sec.*, P. Jay.

LLOYD'S, Lime Street, EC3M 7HL.—*Chief Exec.*, A. Lord, CB.

LLOYD'S PATRIOTIC FUND (1803), Lloyd's, Lime Street, EC3M 7HA.—*Sec.*, Mrs. J. H. Bright.

LLOYD'S REGISTER OF SHIPPING (1760), 71 Fenchurch Street, EC3M 4BS.—*Sec.*, W. T. Leadbetter.

LOCAL AUTHORITIES, INTERNATIONAL UNION OF (British Section) (1913), *also* COUNCIL OF EUROPEAN MUNICIPALITIES AND REGIONS (British Section) (1951), 35 Great Smith Street, SW1P 3BJ.—*Sec. Gen.*, P. N. Bongers.

LOCAL AUTHORITY CHIEF EXECUTIVES, SOCIETY OF (1974).—*Hon. Sec.*, S. Jones, County Hall, Glenfield, Leicester LE3 8RA.

LOCAL COUNCILS, NATIONAL ASSOCIATION OF (1947), 108 Great Russell Street, WC1B 3LD.—*Sec.*, J. Clark.

LONDON APPRECIATION SOCIETY (1932), 17 Manson Mews, SW7 5AF.—*Hon. Sec.*, H. L. B. Peers, PH.D.

LONDON BOROUGHS ASSOCIATION (1964), 23 Buckingham Gate, SW1E 6LB.—*Sec.*, J. Hall.

LONDON CITY MISSION (1835), 175 Tower Bridge Road, SE1 2AH.—*Gen. Sec.*, Rev. D. M. Whyte.

LONDON COURT OF INTERNATIONAL ARBITRATION (1892), 75 Cannon Street, EC4N 5BH.—*Pres.*, The Rt. Hon. Sir Michael Kerr; *Registrar*, B. W. Vigrass, OBE, VRD.

LONDON FLOTILLA (1937). (Association of Reserve and Retired Officers of The Royal Navy).—*Hon. Sec.*, Lt. Cdr. P. A. G. Norman RD, RNR, Marden Rise, 81 Lower Road, Fetcham, Leatherhead, Surrey KT22 9HG.

LONDON LIBRARY, THE (1841), 14 St. James's Square, SW1Y 4LG.—*Librarian*, D. Matthews.

LONDON MAGISTRATES' CLERKS' ASSOCIATION (1889).—*Hon. Sec.*, J. V. Mulreany, c/o Marylebone Magistrates Court, 181–183 Marylebone Road, NW1 5QJ.

LONDON PLAYING FIELDS SOCIETY, THE (1890) (incorporating GREATER LONDON PLAYING FIELDS ASSOCIATION), Boston Manor Playing Field, Boston Gardens, Brentford, Middx. TW8 9LR.—*Sec.*, T. W. Syms.

LONDON SOCIETY, THE (1912), Room U722, The City University, Northampton Square, EC1V 0HB.—*Hon. Sec.*, Mrs. B. Jones.

LORD'S DAY OBSERVANCE SOCIETY (1831), 120 Wandle Road, Morden, Surrey SM4 6AE.—*Gen. Sec.*, J. G. Roberts.

LORD'S TAVERNERS, THE (1950), 1 Chester Street, SW1X 7HP.—*Dir.*, Capt. J. A. R. Swainson, OBE, RN.

LOTTERIES COUNCIL, THE (1979), 81 Mansel Street, Swansea SA1 5TT.—*Hon. Sec.* J. H. Solly.

MAGISTRATES' ASSOCIATION, THE (1920), 28 Fitzroy Square, W1P 6DD.—*Sec.*, T. R. P. Rudin.

MAIL USERS' ASSOCIATION (1976), 3 Pavement House, The Pavement, Hay-on-Wye HR3 5BU.—*Chairman*, J. Blackwell.

MALAYSIAN RUBBER PRODUCERS' RESEARCH ASSOCIATION (1938), Tun Abdul Razak Laboratory, Brickendonbury, Hertford SG13 8NL.—*Dir.*, Dr. C. S. L. Baker.

MALCOLM SARGENT CANCER FUND FOR CHILDREN (1968).—*Gen. Administrator*, Miss S. Darley, OBE, 14 Abingdon Road, W8 6AF.

MALONE SOCIETY (for the publication of scholarly editions and facsimiles of early English dramatic texts).—*Exec. Sec.*, Prof. J. Creaser, Royal Holloway and Bedford New College, Egham Hill, Egham, Surrey TW20 0EX.

MANAGEMENT, BRITISH INSTITUTE OF (1947), 64–78 Kingsway, WC2B 6BL.—*Dir. Gen.*, P. Benton.

MANAGEMENT AND PROFESSIONAL STAFFS, ASSOCIATION OF (1972), Parkgates, Bury New Road, Prestwich, Manchester M25 8JX.—*Exec. Sec.*, Mr. A. J. Casey.

MANAGEMENT SERVICES, INSTITUTE OF, 1 Cecil Court, London Road, Enfield, Middx. EN2 6DD.—*Dir. and Gen. Sec.*, E. A. King.

MANORIAL SOCIETY OF GREAT BRITAIN (1906), 104 Kennington Road, SE11 6RE.—*Hon. Chairman*, R. A. Smith.

MANPOWER SOCIETY (1969).—*Administrator*, Mrs. M. P. Bradney, Old Rickyard, School Lane, Newton Burgoland, Leics. LE6 1SL.

MARIE CURIE MEMORIAL FOUNDATION (1948), 28 Belgrave Square, SW1X 8QG.—*Dir. Gen.*, Maj. Gen. M. E. Carleton-Smith, CBE. *Scottish Office*, 21 Rutland Street, Edinburgh EH1 2AH.

MARINE ARTISTS, ROYAL SOCIETY OF (1939), 17 Carlton House Terrace, SW1V 4DG.—*Sec.*, M. Myers.

MARINE BIOLOGICAL ASSOCIATION OF THE UK (1884), Citadel Hill, Plymouth PL1 2PB.—*Sec.*, Dr. M. Whitfield.

MARINE BIOLOGICAL ASSOCIATION, SCOTTISH (1914), PO Box 3, Oban, Argyll PA34 4AD.—*Dir.*, Prof. J. B. L. Matthews.

MARINE ENGINEERS, THE INSTITUTE OF (1889), The Memorial Building, 76 Mark Lane, EC3R 7JN.—*Sec.*, J. E. Sloggett.

MARINE SOCIETY, THE (1756), 202 Lambeth Road, SE1 7JW. Works for the professionalism and welfare of British seafarers.—*Gen. Sec.*, Lt. Cdr. R. M. Frampton.

MARIO LANZA EDUCATIONAL FOUNDATION (for singers) (1976),—*Hon. Sec.*, Miss P. Barron, 7 Lionfields Avenue, Allesley Village, Coventry CV5 9GN.

MARKET AUTHORITIES, NATIONAL ASSOCIATION OF BRITISH (1948).—*Sec.*, B. Ormshaw, 19 Derwent Avenue, Milnrow, Rochdale, Lancs. OL16 3UD.

MARKETING, CHARTERED INSTITUTE OF (1911), Moor Hall, Cookham, Maidenhead, Berks. SL6 9QH.—*Dir. Gen.*, T. J. Nash.

MARKET TRADERS' FEDERATION, NATIONAL (1899), Hampton House, Hawshaw Lane, Hoyland, Barnsley S74 0HA.—*Gen. Sec.*, R. J. Toller.

MARK MASTER MASONS, GRAND LODGE OF (1856), Mark Masons' Hall, 86 St. James's Street, SW1A 1PL.—*Grand Master*, HRH Prince Michael of Kent; *Grand Sec.*, P. G. Williams.

MARRIAGE GUIDANCE, *see* RELATE.

MASONIC BENEVOLENT INSTITUTION, ROYAL (1842), 20 Great Queen Street, WC2B 5BG.—*Sec.*, N. A. Grout.

MASONIC BENEVOLENT INSTITUTIONS IN IRELAND, 17–19 Molesworth Street, Dublin 2.—*Sec.*, M. R. McWilliam.

MASONIC TRUST FOR GIRLS AND BOYS (1985), 31 Great Queen Street, WC2B 5AG.—*Sec.*, Col. R. K. Hind.

MASTER BUILDERS, FEDERATION OF (1941), Gordon Fisher House, 14–15 Great James Street, WC1N 3DP.—*Dir. Gen.*, W. S. Hilton.

MASTERS OF FOXHOUNDS ASSOCIATION (1881).—*Sec.*, A. H. B. Hart, Parsloes Cottage, Bagendon, Cirencester, Glos. GL7 7DU.

MASTERS OF WINE, THE INSTITUTE OF (1955), Five Kings House, 1 Queen Street Place, EC4R 1QS.—*Exec. Dir.*, D. F. Stevens.

MATERNAL AND CHILD WELFARE, NATIONAL ASSOCIATION FOR (1911), 1 South Audley Street, W1Y 6JS.—*Gen. Sec.*, W. H. L. Hedley.

MATERNITY ALLIANCE, THE (1980), 15 Britannia Street, WC1X 9JP.—*Sec.*, Ms. A. Sedley.

MATHEMATICAL ASSOCIATION (1871), 259 London Road, Leicester LE2 3BE.—*Exec. Sec.*, Ms. H. Whitby.

MATHEMATICS AND ITS APPLICATIONS, INSTITUTE OF (1964), 16 Nelson Street, Southend-on-Sea SS1 1EF.—*Registrar*, Miss C. M. Richards.

MECHANICAL ENGINEERS, INSTITUTION OF (1847), 1 Birdcage Walk, SW1H 9JJ.—*Sec.*, R. W. Mellor, CBE.

MEDIC-ALERT FOUNDATION, 17 Bridge Wharf, 156 Caledonian Road, N1 9UU. For the protection, in emergencies, of those with a hidden medical condition or allergy.—*Sec. Gen.*, Mrs. M. L. Stanton.

MEDICAL COUNCIL, GENERAL (1858), 44 Hallam Street, W1N 6AE.—*Registrar*, P. L. Towers.

MEDICAL SOCIETY OF LONDON (1773), 11 Chandos Street, W1M 0EB.—*Registrar*, Maj. T. Tudor-Williams.

MEDICAL WOMEN'S FEDERATION (1917), Tavistock House North, Tavistock Square, WC1H 9HX.—*Hon. Sec.*, Dr. P. Price (*to May 1991*).

MEDIEVAL ARCHAEOLOGY, SOCIETY FOR (1957).—*Hon. Sec.*, A. Vince, PH.D., CLAU, The Lawn, Union Road, Lincoln LN1 3BG.

MEN OF THE TREES (1922), Sandy Lane, Crawley Down, Crawley, W. Sussex RH10 4HS.—*Exec. Sec.*, Mrs. E. Sandwell.

MENTAL AFTER CARE ASSOCIATION (1879), Bainbridge House, Bainbridge Street, WC1A 1HP.—*Dir.*, B. G. Garner.

MENTAL HEALTH FOUNDATION, THE (1949), 8 Hallam Street, W1N 6DH.—*Dir. Gen.*, P. Searle.

MERCHANT NAVY WELFARE BOARD (1948), 19–21 Lancaster Gate, W2 3LN.—*Gen. Sec.*, J. I. K. Walker.

METALS, THE INSTITUTE OF (1985), 1 Carlton House Terrace, SW1Y 5DB.—*Sec.*, Dr. J. A. Catterall.

METAL TRADES BENEVOLENT SOCIETY, ROYAL (1843), Kelvin House, 1 Totteridge Avenue, High Wycombe, Bucks. HP13 6XG.—*Gen. Sec.*, A Whittle, MBE.

METEOROLOGICAL SOCIETY, ROYAL (1850), 104 Oxford Road, Reading, Berks. RG1 7LJ.—*Exec. Sec.*, R. P. C. Swash.

METROPOLITAN AND CITY POLICE ORPHANS FUND (1870), 30 Hazlewell Road, SW15 6LH.—*Sec.*, R. Duff-Cole, BEM.

METROPOLITAN AUTHORITIES, ASSOCIATION OF (1974), 35 Great Smith Street, SW1P 3BJ.—*Sec.*, R. Brooke.

METROPOLITAN HOSPITAL-SUNDAY FUND (1872), 40 High Street, Teddington, Middx. TW11 8EW. In 1989, £31,500 was distributed to NHS hospitals. £362,265 was distributed to hospitals outside the NHS, and £24,100 to other medical charities.—*Sec.*, D. A. B. Lynch.

MIDDLE EAST ASSOCIATION, THE (1961), Bury House, 33 Bury Street, SW1Y 6AX.—*Dir.-Gen.*, Sir James Craig, GCMG.

MIDWIVES, ROYAL COLLEGE OF (1881), 15 Mansfield Street, W1M 0BE.—*Gen. Sec.*, Miss R. M. Ashton.

MIGRAINE ASSOCIATION, BRITISH (1958), 178A High Road, Byfleet, Weybridge, Surrey KT14 7ED.—*Hon. Sec.*, Mrs. J. Liddell.

MIGRAINE TRUST (1965), 45 Great Ormond Street, WC1N 3HD.—*Dir.*, P. Hodgkins.

MILITARY HISTORICAL SOCIETY, National Army Museum, Royal Hospital Road, SW3 4HT.—*Hon. Sec.*, J. Gaylor.

MIND (National Association for Mental Health), 22 Harley Street, W1N 2ED.—*Dir.*, Ms. R. Hepplewhite.

MINERALOGICAL SOCIETY (1876), 41 Queen's Gate, SW7 5HR.—*Hon. Gen. Sec.*, Dr. M. G. Bown.

MINES OF GREAT BRITAIN, FEDERATION OF SMALL, 13A King Street, Newcastle under Lyme, Staffs. ST5 1ER.—*Sec.*, R. W. Bladen.

MINIATURE PAINTERS, SCULPTORS AND GRAVERS, ROYAL SOCIETY OF (1895).—*Exec. Sec.*, Mrs. S. M. Burton, Burwood House, 15 Union Street, Wells, Somerset BA5 2PU.

MINIATURISTS, SOCIETY OF (1895), Castle Gallery, Castle Hill, Ilkley, W. Yorks. LS29 9DT.—*Dir.*, L. Simpson.

MINING INSTITUTE OF SCOTLAND, 14 Pendreich Grove, Bonnyrigg, Midlothian EH19 2EH.—*Sec.*, E. R. Rodger.

MISSION TO DEEP SEA FISHERMEN, ROYAL NATIONAL (1881), 43 Nottingham Place, W1M 4BX.—*Chief Exec.*, A. D. Marsden.

MISSIONS TO SEAMEN, THE (1856), St. Michael Paternoster Royal, College Hill, EC4R 2RL.—*Gen. Sec.*, Rev. Canon G. Jones.

MODERN CHURCHPEOPLE'S UNION (1898). For the advancement of liberal religious thought.—*Hon. Sec.*, Rev. R. C. Truss, The Rectory, Church Square, Shepperton, Middx. TW17 9JY.

MONUMENTAL BRASS SOCIETY (1887).—*Hon. Sec.*, W. Mendelsson, 57 Leeside Crescent, NW11 0HA.

MORAVIAN MISSIONS, LONDON ASSOCIATION IN AID OF (1817), Moravian Church House, 5–7 Muswell Hill, N10 3TJ.—*Sec.*, Rev. F. J. C. Smith.

MOTHERS' UNION, THE (1876), Mary Sumner House, 24 Tufton Street, SW1P 3RB.—*Central Sec.*, Mrs. M. Chapman.

MOTOR INDUSTRY, THE INSTITUTE OF THE, Fanshaws, Brickendon, Hertford SG13 8PQ.—*Sec.*, F. W. Janes.

MOUNTBATTEN MEMORIAL TRUST (1979), 1 Grosvenor Crescent, SW1X 7EF.—*Dir.*, J. Boyd-Brent.

MOUNTBATTEN TRUST, THE EDWINA (1960), 1 Grosvenor Crescent, SW1X 7EF.—*Sec.*, J. Boyd-Brent.

MULTIPLE SCLEROSIS SOCIETY (1953), 25 Effie Road, SW6 1EE.—*Gen. Sec.*, J. Walford.

MUNICIPAL ENGINEERS, ASSOCIATION OF, 1–7 Great George Street, SW1P 3AA.—*Dir.*, K. J. Marchant.

MUSEUMS ASSOCIATION (1889), 34 Bloomsbury Way, WC1A 2SF.—*Dir.*, M. Taylor.

MUSIC HALL SOCIETY, BRITISH (1963), Brodie and Middleton Ltd., 68 Drury Lane, WC2B 5SP.—*Hon. Sec.*, Mrs. J. D. Masterton.

MUSICIANS BENEVOLENT FUND (1921), 16 Ogle Street, W1P 7LG.—*Sec.*, M. B. M. Williams.

MUSICIANS, INCORPORATED SOCIETY OF (1882), 10 Stratford Place, W1N 9AE.—*Chief Exec.*, N. Hoyle.

MUSICIANS OF GREAT BRITAIN, ROYAL SOCIETY OF (1738), 10 Stratford Place, W1N 9AE.—*Sec.*, Mrs. M. E. Gleed, MBE.

MUSIC INFORMATION CENTRE, BRITISH (1967), 10 Stratford Place, W1N 9AE.—*Administrator*, Ms. E. Yeoman.

MUSIC SOCIETIES, NATIONAL FEDERATION OF (1935), Francis House, Francis Street, SW1P 1DE.—*Administrator*, C. Mowat.

MYALGIC ENCEPHALOMYELITIS ASSOCIATION (1976), 4A Corringham Road, Stanford-le-Hope, Essex SS17 0AU.—*Dir.*, S. Powell.

NATIONAL AND UNIVERSITY LIBRARIES, STANDING CONFERENCE OF (SCONUL) (1950), 102 Euston Street, NW1 2HA.—*Sec.*, Miss G. M. Pentelow.

NATIONAL BENEVOLENT INSTITUTION (1812), 61 Bayswater Road, W2 3PG.—*Sec.*, Gp. Capt. D. St. J. Homer.

NATIONAL COUNCIL FOR VOLUNTARY ORGANIZATIONS (1919), 26 Bedford Square, WC1B 3HU.—*Dir.*, Ms. U. Prashar.

NATIONAL COUNCIL OF WOMEN OF GREAT BRITAIN (1895), 36 Danbury Street, N1 8JU.—*Pres.*, Mrs. E. Bavidge.

NATIONAL LISTENING LIBRARY, *see* TALKING BOOKS.

NATIONAL SOCIETY, THE, (1811), Church House, Great Smith Street, SW1P 3NZ. For promoting religious education.—*Gen. Sec.*, G. Duncan.

NATIONAL SOCIETY FOR THE PREVENTION OF CRUELTY TO CHILDREN (NSPCC) (1884), 67 Saffron Hill, EC1N 8RS.—*Dir.*, C. Brown.

NATIONAL TRUST, THE (1895), 36 Queen Anne's Gate, SW1H 9AS.—*Chairman*, Dame Jennifer Jenkins; *Dir. Gen.*, A. Stirling.

NATIONAL TRUST FOR SCOTLAND (1931), 5 Charlotte Square, Edinburgh EH2 4DU.—*Dir.*, L. Borley.

NATIONAL UNION OF STUDENTS (1922), Nelson Mandela House, 461 Holloway Road, N7 6LJ.—*Nat. Pres.*, S. Twigg.

NATIONAL VIEWERS' AND LISTENERS' ASSOCIATION (1964).—*Pres.*, Mrs. M. Whitehouse, CBE, Ardleigh, Colchester CO7 7RH.

NATIONAL WOMEN'S REGISTER (1960), 9 Bank Plain, Norwich, Norfolk NR2 4SL.—*Nat. Organizer*, Ms. J. Cooke.

NATION'S FUND FOR NURSES (1917), 3 Albemarle Way, EC1V 4JB.—*Administrator*, Mrs. S. D. Andrews.

NATURALISTS' ASSOCIATION, BRITISH (1905).— *Hon. Mem. Sec.*, 23 Oak Hill Close, Woodford Green, Essex IG8 9PH.

NATURE CONSERVATION, ROYAL SOCIETY FOR (1912), The Green, Witham Park, Lincoln LN5 7JR.—*Chief Exec.*, T. S. Cordy.

NAUTICAL RESEARCH, SOCIETY FOR (1911), c/o National Maritime Museum, Greenwich, SE10 9NF.—*Hon. Sec.*, Mrs. A. Shirley.

NAVAL, MILITARY AND AIR FORCE BIBLE SOCIETY (1780), Radstock House, Eccleston Street, SW1W 9LZ.—*Gen. Sec.*, R. Kennedy.

NAVAL ARCHITECTS, ROYAL INSTITUTION OF (1860), 10 Upper Belgrave Street, SW1X 8BQ.—*Sec.*, J. Rosewarn.

NAVIGATION, ROYAL INSTITUTE OF (1947), 1 Kensington Gore, SW7 2AT.—*Dir.*, Rear-Adm. R. M. Burgoyne, CB.

NAVY RECORDS SOCIETY (1893), c/o Barclays Bank PLC, Murray House, 1 Royal Mint Court, EC3N 4HH.—*Hon. Sec.*, A. J. McMillan.

NEEDLEWORK, ROYAL SCHOOL OF (1872).—*Principal*, Mrs. E. Elvin, Apt. 38, Hampton Court Palace, West Molesey, Surrey KT8 9AU.

NEWCOMEN SOCIETY (1920), Science Museum, SW7 2DD. For the study of the history of engineering and technology.—*Exec. Sec.*, A. Smith.

NEW ENGLISH ART CLUB (1886), 17 Carlton House Terrace, SW1Y 5BD.—*Sec.*, W. Bowyer, RA.

NEWSPAPER EDITORS, GUILD OF BRITISH (1946), Bloomsbury House, Bloomsbury Square, 74–77 Great Russell Street, WC1B 3DA.—*Sec.*, J. K. Bradbury.

NEWSPAPER PRESS FUND (1864), Dickens House, 35 Wathen Road, Dorking, Surrey RH4 1JY.—*Dir.*, P. W. Evans.

NEWSPAPER SOCIETY (1836), Bloomsbury House, Bloomsbury Square, 74–77 Great Russell Street, WC1B 3DA.—*Dir.*, D. Nisbet-Smith.

NEWSVENDORS' BENEVOLENT INSTITUTION (1839), PO Box 306, Dunmow, Essex CM6 1HY.—*Dir.*, C. S. Jones.

NOISE ABATEMENT SOCIETY (1959), PO Box 8, Bromley BR2 0UH.—*Chairman*, J. Connell.

NON-SMOKERS, NATIONAL SOCIETY OF , *see* QUIT.

NORWOOD CHILD CARE (1795), Stuart Young House, 221 Golders Green Road, NW11 9DL. Jewish welfare organization for Jewish children.—*Exec. Dir.*, S. Brier.

NOTARIES' SOCIETY (1907), 7 Lower Brook Street, Ipswich, Suffolk IP4 1AF.—*Sec.*, A. G. Dunford.

NUCLEAR ENERGY SOCIETY, BRITISH (1962), 1–7 Great George Street, SW1P 3AA.—*Exec. Officer*, P. Bacos.

NUFFIELD FOUNDATION (1943), 28 Bedford Square, WC1B 3EG.—*Dir.*, R. Hazell.

NUFFIELD PROVINCIAL HOSPITALS TRUST (1939), 3 Prince Albert Road, NW1 7SP.—*Sec.*, Dr. M. Ashley-Miller.

NUMISMATIC SOCIETY, BRITISH (1903).—*Hon. Sec.*, W. Slayter, 63 West Way, Edgware, Middx. HA8 9LA.

NUMISMATIC SOCIETY, ROYAL (1836), c/o Dept. of Coins and Medals, The British Museum, Great Russell Street, WC1B 3DG.—*Hon. Secs.*, J. E. Cribb; R. G. Bland.

NURSES ASSOCIATION, ROYAL BRITISH (1887), 94 Upper Tollington Park, N4 4NB.—*Hon. Sec.*, Mrs. H. M. Vorstermans, MBE.

NURSES', RETIRED, NATIONAL HOME (1934), Riverside Avenue, Bournemouth BH7 7EE.—*Chairman*, E. V. Cornell.

NURSES, ROYAL NATIONAL PENSION FUND FOR, Burdett House, 15 Buckingham Street, WC2N 6ED.—*Gen. Manager*, V. G. West.

NURSING, MIDWIFERY AND HEALTH VISITING, UK CENTRAL COUNCIL FOR, 23 Portland Place, W1N 3AF.—*Registrar and Chief Exec.*, C. Ralph.

England.—Victory House, 170 Tottenham Court Road, W1P 0HA.

Wales.—Floor 13, Pearl Assurance House, Greyfriars Road, Cardiff CF1 3AG.

Scotland.—22 Queen Street, Edinburgh EH2 1JX.

N.Ireland.—RAC House, 79 Chichester Street, Belfast BT1 4JE.

NURSING, ROYAL COLLEGE OF, 20 Cavendish Square, W1M 0AB.

NUTRITION FOUNDATION, BRITISH (1967), 15 Belgrave Square, SW1X 8PG.—*Dir. Gen.* Prof. D. M. Conning.

NUTRITION SOCIETY (1941), Grosvenor Gardens House, 35–37 Grosvenor Gardens, SW1W 0BS.—*Hon. Sec.*, Dr. R. F. Grimble.

OBSTETRICIANS AND GYNAECOLOGISTS, ROYAL COLLEGE OF (1929), 27 Sussex Place, NW1 4RG.—*Pres.*, S. Simmons; *Sec.*, P. A. Barnett.

OCCUPATIONAL SAFETY AND HEALTH, INSTITUTION OF (1946), 222 Uppingham Road, Leicester LE5 0QG.—*Sec.*, J. R. Barrell.

OFFICERS' ASSOCIATION, THE (1920), 48 Pall Mall, SW1Y 5JY. Assists former officers of the Armed Forces, their widows and dependants.—*Gen. Sec.*, Brig. P. D. Johnson.

OFFICERS' FAMILIES FUND (1899), 48 Pall Mall, SW1Y 5JY.—*Sec.*, Mrs. I. C. Riley.

OFFICERS' PENSIONS SOCIETY LTD. (1946), 15 Buckingham Gate, SW1E 6NS.—*Gen. Sec.*, Maj.-Gen. Sir Laurence New, CB, CBE.

OIL PAINTERS, ROYAL INSTITUTE OF (1883).—*Sec.*, Mrs. J. Easterling, 76 Coniston Road, Bromley BR1 4JB.

OILSEED, OIL AND FEEDINGSTUFFS TRADES BENEVOLENT ASSOCIATION, 14–20 St. Mary Axe, EC3A 8BU.—*Sec.*, R. T. Wheelans.

ONE PARENT FAMILIES, NATIONAL COUNCIL FOR, 255 Kentish Town Road, NW5 2LX.—*Dir.*, Miss S. Slipman.

OPEN-AIR MISSION, THE (1853), 19 John Street, WC1N 2DL.—*Sec.*, A. J. Greenbank.

OPEN SPACES SOCIETY (1865). Commons, open spaces and footpaths preservation society. 25A Bell Street, Henley-on-Thames, Oxon. RG9 2BA.—*Gen. Sec.*, Miss K. Ashbrook.

OPERATIC AND DRAMATIC ASSOCIATION, NATIONAL (1899), NODA House, 1 Crestfield Street, WC1H 8AU.—*Gen. Administrator*, B. Clarke.

OPTICAL COUNCIL, GENERAL (1958), 41 Harley Street, W1N 2DJ.—*Registrar*, R. Wilshin.

OPTOMETRISTS, BRITISH COLLEGE OF, 10 Knaresborough Place, SW5 0TG.—*Gen. Sec.*, T. H. Collingridge.

ORDERS AND MEDALS RESEARCH SOCIETY (1942).—*Gen. Sec.*, N. G. Gooding, 123 Turnpike Link, Croydon CR0 5NU.

ORIENTAL CERAMIC SOCIETY (1921), 31B Torrington Square, WC1E 7LJ.—*Sec.*, Vice-Adm. Sir John Gray, KBE, CB.

ORNITHOLOGISTS' CLUB, SCOTTISH (1936), 21 Regent Terrace, Edinburgh EH7 5BT.—*Sec.*, Ms. S. Laing.

ORNITHOLOGISTS' UNION, BRITISH (1858), c/o British Museum (Natural History), Sub-dept. of Ornithology, Tring, Herts. HP23 6AP.—*Hon. Sec.*, Mrs. G. Bonham.

ORNITHOLOGY, BRITISH TRUST FOR (1932), Beech Grove, Tring, Herts. HP23 5NR.—*Dir. of Services*, A. Elvin.

ORTHOPAEDIC ASSOCIATION, BRITISH (1918), The Royal College of Surgeons, 35–43 Lincoln's Inn Fields, WC2A 3PN.—*Hon. Sec.*, M. A. Edgar.

OSTEOPATHIC MEDICINE, LONDON COLLEGE OF, 8–10 Boston Place, NW1 6QH.

OUTWARD BOUND TRUST LTD. (1941), Chestnut Field, Regent Place, Rugby, Warks. CV21 2PJ.—*Dir.*, I. L. Fothergill.

OVERSEAS DEVELOPMENT INSTITUTE (1960), Regent's College, Inner Circle, Regent's Park, NW1 4NS.—*Dir.*, Dr. J. Howell.

OVERSEAS SERVICE PENSIONERS' ASSOCIATION (1960), 63 Church Road, Hove, E. Sussex BN3 2BD.—*Sec.*, C. D. Stenton.

OVERSEAS SETTLEMENT, CHURCH OF ENGLAND BOARD FOR SOCIAL RESPONSIBILITY (1925), Great Smith Street, SW1P 3NZ.—*Admin. Sec.*, Miss P. J. Hallett.

OXFAM (1942), 274 Banbury Road, Oxford OX2 7DZ.—*Dir.*, F. Judd.

OXFORD PRESERVATION TRUST (1927), 10 Turn Again Lane, St. Ebbes, Oxford OX1 1QL.—*Sec.*, Mrs. M. Haynes.

OXFORD SOCIETY (1932), 8 Wellington Square, Oxford OX1 2HY.—*Sec.*, Dr. H. A. Hurren.

PAEDIATRIC ASSOCIATION, BRITISH (1928), 5 St. Andrew's Place, NW1 4LB.—*Hon. Sec.*, Dr. R. MacFaul.

PAINTER-PRINTMAKERS, ROYAL SOCIETY OF (1880), Bankside Gallery, 48 Hopton Street, SE1 9JH.—*Sec.*, J. Winkelman.

PAINTERS IN WATER COLOURS, ROYAL INSTITUTE OF (1831), 17 Carlton House Terrace, SW1Y 5BD.—*Sec.*, R. Spurrier.

PALAEONTOGRAPHICAL SOCIETY (1847) c/o British Geological Survey, Keyworth, Nottingham NG12 5GG.—*Sec.*, S. P. Tunnicliff.

PALAEONTOLOGICAL ASSOCIATION (1957).—*Sec.*, Dr. J. A. Crame, c/o British Antarctic Survey, High Cross, Madingley Road, Cambridge CB3 0ET.

PARKINSON'S DISEASE SOCIETY (1969), 36 Portland Place, W1N 3DG.—*Exec. Dir.*, C. A. A. Kilmister.

PARLIAMENTARY AND SCIENTIFIC COMMITTEE (1939), 16 Great College Street, SW1P 3RX.—*Sec.*, A. Butler.

PASTORAL PSYCHOLOGY, GUILD OF (1936).—*Hon. Sec.*, Miss J. Whale, 5 Kilmeny House, 36 Arterberry Road, SW20 8AQ.

PATENT AGENTS, CHARTERED INSTITUTE OF (1882), Staple Inn Buildings, High Holborn, WC1V 7PZ.—*Sec.*, Miss M. E. Poole.

PATENTEES AND INVENTORS, INSTITUTE OF (1919), Triumph House, 189 Regent Street, W1R 7WF.—*Sec.*, J. R. Kay.

PATHOLOGISTS, ROYAL COLLEGE OF, 2 Carlton House Terrace, SW1Y 5AF.—*Sec.*, K. Lockyer.

PATIENTS ASSOCIATION (1963), 18 Victoria Park Square, E2 9PF.— *Chairman*, Rabbi Julia Neuberger.

PEACE COUNCIL, NATIONAL (1908), 29 Great James Street, WC1N 3ES.—*Co-ordinators*, A. L. McLeod; L. Peck.

PEAK AND NORTHERN FOOTPATHS SOCIETY (1894).—*Hon. Gen. Sec.*, D. Taylor, 15 Parkfield Drive, Tyldesley, Manchester M29 8NR.

PEARSON'S HOLIDAY FUND, 2A Amity Grove, Raynes Park, SW20 0LH.—*Gen. Sec.*, G. P. Holloway.

PEDESTRIANS ASSOCIATION (1929), 1 Wandsworth Road, SW8 2XX.—*Chairman*, C. Myerscough.

PEN, INTERNATIONAL (1921), 38 King Street, WC2E 8JT. World association of writers.—*International Sec.*, A. Blokh.

PENSION FUNDS LTD., NATIONAL ASSOCIATION OF (1923), 12–18 Grosvenor Gardens, SW1W 0DH.—*Dir. Gen.*, M. A. Elton.

PEOPLE'S DISPENSARY FOR SICK ANIMALS (1917), Whitechapel Way, Priorslee, Telford, Shropshire TF2 9PQ.—*Gen. Sec.*, M. R. Curtis, MBE.

PERFORMING RIGHT SOCIETY LTD. (1914), 29–33 Berners Street, W1P 4AA.—*Chief Exec.*, M. J. Freegard.

PERIODICAL PUBLISHERS ASSOCATION LTD. (1913), Imperial House, 15–19 Kingsway, WC2B 6UN.—*Chief Exec.*, I. Locks.

PESTALOZZI CHILDREN'S VILLAGE TRUST (1959), Sedlescombe, Battle, E. Sussex TN33 0RR.—*Dir.*, C. C. Wagstaff.

PETROLEUM, INSTITUTE OF (1913), 61 New Cavendish Street, W1M 8AR.—*Dir. Gen.*, A. E. H. Williams.

PHARMACEUTICAL SOCIETY OF GREAT BRITAIN, ROYAL (1841), 1 Lambeth High Street, SE1 7JN.—*Sec. and Registrar*, J. Ferguson.

PHARMACOLOGICAL SOCIETY, BRITISH (1931).—*Hon. Gen. Sec.*, Dr. A. R. Green, Astra Neuroscience Research Unit, 1 Wakefield Street, WC1N 1PJ.

PHILOLOGICAL SOCIETY (1842).—*Hon. Sec.*, Prof. T. Bynon, School of Oriental and African Studies, University of London, Thornhaugh Street, WC1H 0XG.

PHILOSOPHY, ROYAL INSTITUTE OF (1925), 14 Gordon Square, WC1H 0AG.—*Dir.*, Prof. A. Phillips Griffiths.

PHOTOGRAMMETRIC SOCIETY (1952).—*Hon. Sec.*, Dr. A. S. Walker, Kern Instruments Ltd., Revenge Road, Lordswood, Chatham, Kent ME5 8TE.

PHOTOGRAPHY, BRITISH INSTITUTE OF PROFESSIONAL (1901), Fox Talbot House, Amwell End, Ware, Herts. SG12 9HN.—*Chief Exec.*, A. M. Berkeley.

PHYSICAL RECREATION, CENTRAL COUNCIL OF (1935), Francis House, Francis Street, SW1P 1DE.—*Gen. Sec.*, P. Lawson.

PHYSICIANS, ROYAL COLLEGE OF (1518), 11 St. Andrew's Place, NW1 4LE.—*Registrar*, D. A. Pyke, CBE, MD.

PHYSICIANS AND SURGEONS, ROYAL COLLEGE OF (Glasgow) (1599), 234–242 St. Vincent Street, Glasgow G2 5RJ.—*Pres.*, J. McArthur; *Hon. Sec.*, Dr. A. D. Beattie.

PHYSICIANS OF EDINBURGH, ROYAL COLLEGE OF (1681), 9 Queen Street, Edinburgh EH2 1JQ.—*Pres.*, Dr. J. Richmond; *Sec.*, Dr. J. L. Anderton.

PHYSICS, INSTITUTE OF (1874), 47 Belgrave Square, SW1X 8QX.—*Chief Exec.*, Dr. A. Jones.

PHYSIOLOGICAL SOCIETY (1876).—*Hon. Sec.*, Prof. R. A. Chapman, Dept. of Physiology, School of Veterinary Science, Park Row, Bristol BS1 5LS.

PHYSIOTHERAPY, THE CHARTERED SOCIETY OF (1894), 14 Bedford Row, WC1R 4ED.—*Sec.*, T. Simon.

PIG BREEDERS' ASSOCIATION, NATIONAL (1884), 7 Rickmansworth Road, Watford, Herts. WD1 7HE.—*Chief Exec.*, G. E. Welsh.

PILGRIM TRUST, THE (1930), Fielden House, Little College Street, SW1P 3SH.—*Sec.*, Hon. A. H. Millar.

PILGRIMS OF GREAT BRITAIN, THE (1902), Savoy Hotel, WC2R 0EU.—*Hon. Sec.*, Lt. Col. S. W. Chant-Sempill, OBE, MC.

PLANT ENGINEERS, INSTITUTION OF, 138 Buckingham Palace Road, SW1W 9SG.—*Sec. Gen.*, R. S. Pratt.

PLASTICS AND RUBBER INSTITUTE, THE (1921), 11 Hobart Place, SW1W 0HL.—*Sec. Gen.* G. W. Stockdale.

PLAYING CARD SOCIETY, THE INTERNATIONAL (1972), 188 Sheen Lane, SW14 8LF.—*Sec.*, C. C. Rayner.

PLAYING FIELDS ASSOCIATION, NATIONAL (1925), 25 Ovington Square, SW3 1LQ.—*Gen. Sec.*, Mrs. H. Hayes.

POETRY SOCIETY (1909), 21 Earl's Court Square, SW5 9DE.—*Dir. and Gen. Sec.*, C. Green.

POLICY STUDIES INSTITUTE (1978), 100 Park Village East, NW1 3SR—*Dir.*, W. W. Daniel.

POLIO FELLOWSHIP, BRITISH (1939), Bell Close, West End Road, Ruislip, Middx. HA4 6LP.—*Gen. Sec.*, L. P. Jackson.

POLYTECHNIC AND COLLEGE TEACHERS, ASSOCIATION OF (1973), 104 Albert Road, Southsea, Hants. PO5 2SN.—*Chief Exec.*, Ms. C. Cheesman.

POLYTECHNICS, COMMITTEE OF DIRECTORS OF (1970), Kirkman House, 12–14 Whitfield Street, W1P 6AX.—*Chairman*, Prof. G. T. Fowler; *Sec.*, Dr. M. S. Lewis.

PORTRAIT PAINTERS, ROYAL SOCIETY OF (1891), 17 Carlton House Terrace, SW1Y 5BD.—*Pres.*, D. Poole.

POST OFFICE USERS' NATIONAL COUNCIL (1970), Waterloo Bridge House, Waterloo Road, SE1 8UA.—*Sec.*, B. R. Jones.

POULTRY CLUB OF GREAT BRITAIN, THE (1877).—*Gen. Sec.*, Mrs. E. A. Aubrey-Fletcher, Cliveden, Sandy Bank Farm, Chipping, Preston, Lancs. PR3 2GA.

PRAYER BOOK SOCIETY, THE (1975), St. James Garlickhythe, Garlick Hill, EC4 2AL.—*Hon. Sec.*, Mrs. M. Thompson.

PRECEPTORS, COLLEGE OF, (1846), Coppice Row, Theydon Bois, Epping, Essex CM16 7DN. Membership is open to practising educationists, both teachers and administrators.—*Membership Officer*, N. Matthews.

PREPARATORY SCHOOLS, INCORPORATED ASSOCIATION OF, 138 Kensington Church Street, W8 4BN.—*Sec.*, J. M. C. Coates.

PRE-SCHOOL PLAYGROUPS ASSOCIATION, 61–63 Kings Cross Road, WC1X 9LL.—*Nat. Administrator*, Ms. M. Lochrie.

PRESS ASSOCIATION (1868), 85 Fleet Street, EC4P 4BE.—*Sec.*, R. C. Henry.

PRESS UNION, COMMONWEALTH (1909), Studio House, 184 Fleet Street, EC4A 2DU.—*Dir.*, J. Rajepakse.

PREVENTION OF ACCIDENTS, ROYAL SOCIETY FOR THE (1916), Cannon House, Priory Queensway, Birmingham B4 6BS.—*Dir. Gen.*, J. Wethered.

PRINCESS LOUISE SCOTTISH HOSPITAL (Erskine Hospital) (1916), Bishopton, Renfrewshire PA7 5PU. For disabled ex-servicemen and women.—*Commandant*, Col. W. K. Shepherd.

PRINTERS' CHARITABLE CORPORATION (1827), Victoria House, Harestone Valley Road, Caterham, Surrey CR3 6HY—*Deputy Dir.*, H. J. Court.

PRINTING HISTORICAL SOCIETY (1964), St. Bride Institute, Bride Lane, EC4Y 8EE.—*Hon. Sec.*, S. Tuohy.

PRINTING, INSTITUTE OF (1961), 8 Lonsdale Gardens, Tunbridge Wells, Kent TN1 1NU.—*Sec.*, C. F. Partridge.

PRISON VISITORS, NATIONAL ASSOCIATION OF (1922), 46B Hartington Street, Bedford MK41 7RP.—*Gen. Sec.*, Mrs. A. G. McKenna.

PRIVATE LIBRARIES ASSOCIATION (1957).—*Hon. Sec.*, F. Broomhead, Ravelston, South View Road, Pinner, Middx. HA5 3YD.

PROCURATORS IN GLASGOW, ROYAL FACULTY OF (1600), 12 Nelson Mandela Place, Glasgow G2 1BT.—*Clerk*, J. H. Sinclair.

PRODUCTION CONTROL, INSTITUTE OF, Elmcroft House, Tiddington Road, Tiddington, Stratford-upon-Avon, Warks. CV37 7AQ.—*Gen. Sec.*, K. Roberts.

PRODUCTION ENGINEERS, INSTITUTION OF, Rochester House, 66 Little Ealing Lane, W5 4XX.—*Sec.*, Brig. P. V. Crooks.

PROFESSIONAL CLASSES AID COUNCIL (1921), 10 St. Christopher's Place, W1M 6HY.—*Sec.*, Mrs. G. A. Burgess.

PROFESSIONAL ENGINEERS, UK ASSOCIATION OF (1969), Hayes Court, West Common Road, Bromley BR2 7AU.—*Sec.*, C. K. Hickling.

PROFESSIONAL FOOTBALLERS' ASSOCIATION, 2 Oxford Court, Bishopsgate, Manchester M2 3WQ.—*Sec.*, G. Taylor.

PROFESSIONS SUPPLEMENTARY TO MEDICINE, COUNCIL FOR, Park House, 184 Kennington Park Road, SE11 4BU.—*Registrar*, R. Pickis.

PROTESTANT ALLIANCE, THE (1845), 112 Colin Gardens, NW9 6ER.—*Gen. Sec.*, Rev. A. G. Ashdown.

PSORIASIS ASSOCIATION (1968), 7 Milton Street, Northampton NN2 7JG.—*Nat. Sec.*, Mrs. L. Henley.

PSYCHIATRISTS, ROYAL COLLEGE OF (1971), 17 Belgrave Square, SW1X 8PG—*Sec.*, Mrs. V. Cameron.

PSYCHICAL RESEARCH, SOCIETY FOR (1882), 1 Adam and Eve Mews, W8 6UG.—*Pres.*, Dr. A. Gauld.

PSYCHOLOGICAL SOCIETY, THE BRITISH (1901), St. Andrews House, 48 Princess Road East, Leicester LE1 7DR.—*Exec. Sec.*, C. V. Newman, PH.D.

PUBLIC ADMINISTRATION, ROYAL INSTITUTE OF (1922), 3 Birdcage Walk, SW1H 9JH.—*Dir. Gen.*, D. Falcon.

PUBLIC FINANCE AND ACCOUNTANCY, CHARTERED INSTITUTE OF (1885), 3 Robert Street, WC2N 6BH.—*Dir.*, N. P. Hepworth, OBE.

PUBLIC HEALTH AND HYGIENE, THE ROYAL INSTITUTE OF (1937), 28 Portland Place, W1N 4DE.—*Sec.*, Gp. Capt. R. A. Smith (retd.).

PUBLIC HEALTH ENGINEERS, INSTITUTION OF, *see* WATER AND ENVIRONMENTAL MANAGEMENT.

PUBLIC RELATIONS, THE INSTITUTE OF (1948), The Old Trading House, 15 Northburgh Street, EC1V 0PR.—*Exec. Dir.*, J. B. Lavelle.

PUBLIC TEACHERS OF LAW, SOCIETY OF (1908).—*Hon. Sec.*, Prof. D. B. Casson, University of Buckingham, MK18 1EG.

PURCHASING AND SUPPLY, INSTITUTE OF (1967), Easton House, Easton on the Hill, Stamford, Lincs. PE9 3NZ.—*Dir. Gen.*, P. Thomson.

PURE WATER ASSOCIATION, NATIONAL (1960).—*Sec.*, N. Brugge, Meridan, Cae Goody Lane, Ellesmere, Salop. SY12 9DW.

QUALITY ASSURANCE, INSTITUTE OF, 10 Grosvenor Gardens, SW1 0DQ.—*Sec. Gen.*, Dr. J. Davies.

QUARRIER'S HOMES (1871), Bridge of Weir, Renfrewshire PA11 3SA.—*Chief Exec.*, Dr. J. R. Minto, OBE.

QUARRYING, INSTITUTE OF (1917), 7 Regent Street, Nottingham NG1 5BY.—*Sec.*, M. J. Arthur.

QUEEN ELIZABETH'S FOUNDATION FOR THE DISABLED (1967), Leatherhead, Surrey KT22 0BN.—*Dir.*, M. B. Clark, PH.D.

QUEEN VICTORIA CLERGY FUND (1897), Church House, Dean's Yard, SW1P 3NZ—*Sec.*, Capt. P. W. E. Parry, MBE.

QUEEN VICTORIA SCHOOL (1908), Dunblane, Perthshire FK15 0JY.—*Headmaster*, J. D. Hankinson.

QUEEN'S ENGLISH SOCIETY, THE (1972).—*Hon. Sec.*, D. J. Ellis, Fernwood, Nightingales, West Chiltington, Pulborough, W. Sussex RH20 2QT.

QUEEN'S NURSING INSTITUTE (1887), 3 Albemarle Way, EC1V 4JB.—*Dir.*, Mrs. S. Andrews.

QUEKETT MICROSCOPICAL CLUB (1865).—*Hon. Business Sec.*, A. V. Dodge, 61 Pewley Way, Guildford GU1 3PZ.

QUIT (National Society of Non-Smokers) (1926), Latimer House, 40–48 Hanson Street, W1P 7DE.—*Hon. Sec.*, T.W. Hurst.

RADAR (THE ROYAL ASSOCIATION FOR DISABILITY AND REHABILITATION) (1977), 25 Mortimer Street, W1N 8AB.—*Dir.* B. Massie, OBE.

RADIOLOGISTS, ROYAL COLLEGE OF (1934), 38 Portland Place, W1N 3DG.—*Sec.*, A. J. Cowles.

RADIOLOGY, BRITISH INSTITUTE OF (1897), 36 Portland Place, W1N 4AT.—*Gen. Sec.*, Ms. M-A. Piggott.

RAILWAY AND CANAL HISTORICAL SOCIETY.—*Hon. Sec.*, G. H. R. Gwatkin, 17 Clumber Crescent North, The Park, Nottingham NG7 1EY.

RAILWAY BENEVOLENT INSTITUTION (1858), 67 Ashbourne Road, Derby DE3 3FY.—*Exec. Officer and Gen. Sec.*, W. W. K. Humphreys.

RAINER FOUNDATION (1876), 227–239 Tooley Street, SE1 2JX. Helps young people at risk or in need; administers the Intermediate Treatment Fund on behalf of the government.—*Dir.*, R. Kay.

RAMBLERS' ASSOCIATION (1935), 1–5 Wandsworth Road, SW8 2XX.—*Dir.*, A. Mattingly.

RANFURLY LIBRARY SERVICE (1954), 2 Coldharbour Place, 39–41 Coldharbour Lane, SE5 9NR.—*Dir.*, Mrs. S. Harrity.

RARE BREEDS SURVIVAL TRUST LTD. (1973), National Agricultural Centre, Kenilworth, Warks. CV8 2LG.—*Chief Exec.*, A. J. Dymond.

RATEPAYERS' ASSOCIATIONS, NATIONAL UNION OF (1921).—*Hon. Gen. Sec.*, Maj. H. Haydon, Westerlands, 116 Sandy Lane South, Wallington, Surrey SM6 9NR.

RATHBONE SOCIETY, THE (1919), 1st Floor, Princess House, 105–107 Princess Street, Manchester M1 6DD.—*Chief Exec.*, Ms. A. Weinstock.

RATING AND VALUATION ASSOCIATION (1882), 41 Doughty Street, WC1N 2LF.—*Dir.*, C. Farrington.

RECORD SOCIETY, SCOTTISH (1897), Dept. of Scottish History, University of Glasgow, Glasgow G12 8QQ.—*Hon. Sec.*, Dr. J. Kirk.

RECORDS ASSOCIATION, BRITISH (1932), 18 Padbury Court, E2 7EH.—*Hon. Sec.*, J. Davies.

RED CROSS SOCIETY, BRITISH, *see* BRITISH RED CROSS SOCIETY.

RED POLL CATTLE SOCIETY (1888), 6 Church Street, Woodbridge, Suffolk IP12 1DH.—*Sec.*, P. Ryder-Davies.

REFRIGERATION, INSTITUTE OF (1899), Kelvin House, 76 Mill Lane, Carshalton, Surrey SM5 2JR.—*Sec.*, M. J. Horlick.

REFUGEE COUNCIL, BRITISH (1981), Bondway House, 3–9 Bondway, SW8 1SJ.—*Dir.*, A. Dubs.

REGIONAL STUDIES ASSOCIATION (1965), Wharfdale Projects, 15 Micawber Street, N1 17TB.—*Dir.*, Mrs. S. Hardy.

REGULAR FORCES EMPLOYMENT ASSOCIATION (1885), 25 Bloomsbury Square, WC1A 2LN. Finds employment for non-commissioned ex-Regulars.—*Gen. Manager*, Maj.-Gen. D. T. Crabtree, CB.

RELATE: NATIONAL MARRIAGE GUIDANCE (1938), Herbert Gray College, Little Church Street, Rugby, Warks. CV21 3AP.—*Dir.*, D. French.

RENT OFFICERS, INSTITUTE OF (1966).—*Hon. Sec.*, M. R. Webber, Musgrave House, Musgrave Row, Exeter EX4 3TW.

RESEARCH DEFENCE SOCIETY (1908), Grosvenor Gardens House, Grosvenor Gardens, SW1W 0BS.—*Exec. Dir.*, Dr. M. Matfield.

RETAIL BOOK, STATIONERY AND ALLIED TRADES EMPLOYEES' ASSOCIATION (1919), 8–9 Commercial Road, Swindon SN1 5RB.—*Gen. Sec.*, J. Windust.

RETIREMENT PENSIONS ASSOCIATIONS, NATIONAL FEDERATION OF (1938), 14 St. Peter Street, Blackburn BB2 2HD.—*Gen. Sec.*, R. Stansfield.

RICHARD III SOCIETY (1924), 4 Oakley Street, SW3 5NN.—*Sec.*, Miss E. M. Nokes.

ROAD SAFETY OFFICERS, INSTITUTE OF (1971).—*Sec.*, E. M. Marsh, 31 Dyers Close, West Buckland, Wellington, Somerset TA21 9JU.

ROAD TRANSPORT ENGINEERS, INSTITUTE OF (1945), 1 Cromwell Place, SW7 2JF.—*Exec. Sec.*, A. F. Stroud.

ROMAN STUDIES, SOCIETY FOR PROMOTION OF (1910), 31–34 Gordon Square, WC1H 0PP.—*Sec.*, Dr. H. M. Cockle.

ROTARY INTERNATIONAL IN GREAT BRITAIN AND IRELAND (1914), Kinwarton Road, Alcester, Warks. B49 6BP.—*Sec.*, G. S. Large.

ROUND TABLES OF GREAT BRITAIN AND IRELAND, NATIONAL ASSOCIATION OF (1927), Marchesi House, 4 Embassy Drive, Calthorpe Road, Edgbaston, Birmingham B15 1TP.—*Gen. Sec.*, R. H. Renold.

ROYAL AFRICAN SOCIETY (1901), 18 Northumberland Avenue, WC2N 5BJ.—*Sec.*, Mrs. L. Allan.

ROYAL AIR FORCE BENEVOLENT FUND (1919), 67 Portland Place, W1N 4AR.—*Controller*, Air Chief Marshal Sir Thomas Kennedy, GCB, AFC.

ROYAL AIR FORCES ASSOCIATION (1943), 43 Grove Park Road, W4 3RX.—*Sec. Gen.*, M. G. Tomkins, MBE.

ROYAL ALEXANDRA AND ALBERT SCHOOL (1758), Gatton Park, Reigate, Surrey RH2 0TW.—*Sec.*, Capt. A. J. Walsh, RN.

ROYAL ALFRED SEAFARERS' SOCIETY (1865), Weston Acres, Woodmansterne Lane, Banstead, Surrey SM7 3HB.—*Gen. Sec.*, J. H. Moore.

ROYAL ARMOURED CORPS WAR MEMORIAL BENEVOLENT FUND (1946), c/o RHQ RTR, Bovington, Dorset BH20 6JA.—*Sec.*, Maj. R. Clooney.

ROYAL ARTILLERY ASSOCIATION, Artillery House, Connaught Barracks, Grand Depot Road, SE18 6SL.—*Gen. Sec.*, Lt.-Col. M.J. Darmody.

ROYAL ASIATIC SOCIETY (1823), 60 Queen's Gardens, W2 3AF.—*Sec.*, Miss L. Collins.

ROYAL CALEDONIAN SCHOOLS (1815), Aldenham Road, Bushey, Herts. WD2 3TS.—*Master*, Capt. D. F. Watts, RN.

ROYAL CELTIC SOCIETY (1820), 23 Rutland Street, Edinburgh EH1 2RN.—*Sec.*, J. G. Cameron.

ROYAL CHORAL SOCIETY (1871), International House, 2–4 Wendell Road, W12 9RT.—*Gen. Manager*, M. Heyland.

ROYAL ENGINEERS ASSOCIATION, RHQ Royal Engineers, Brompton Barracks, Chatham, Kent ME4 4UG.—*Controller*, Maj. C. F. Cooper, MBE.

ROYAL ENGINEERS, THE INSTITUTION OF (1875), Brompton Barracks, Chatham, Kent ME4 4UG.—*Sec.*, Lt. Col. F. R. Beringer.

ROYAL HIGHLAND AND AGRICULTURAL SOCIETY OF SCOTLAND (1784), Edinburgh Exhibition and Trade Centre, Ingliston, Edinburgh EH28 8NF.—*Sec.*, J. R. Good.

ROYAL HORTICULTURAL SOCIETY (1804), PO Box 313, SW1P 2PE.—*Sec.*, D. P. Hearn.

ROYAL HOSPITAL AND HOME, PUTNEY (1854), West Hill, SW15 3SW.—*Chief Exec.*, Col. B. E. Blunt.

ROYAL HUMANE SOCIETY (1774), Brettenham House, Lancaster Place, WC2E 7EP. Gives bravery awards for saving and attempting to save human life.—*Sec.*, Maj. A. J. Dickinson.

ROYAL INSTITUTION, THE (1799), 21 Albemarle Street, W1X 4BS.—*Pres.*, HRH The Duke of Kent, KG, GCMG, GCVO; *Dir.*, Prof. J. M. Thomas, FRS; *Sec.*, Prof. D. C. Bradley, FRS.

ROYAL LIFE SAVING SOCIETY, UK (1891), Mountbatten House, Studley, Warks. B80 7NN.—*Dir.*, Ms. C. J. Godsall.

ROYAL LITERARY FUND (1790), 144 Temple Chambers, Temple Avenue, EC4Y 0DT. Gives grants to necessitous authors of some published work of approved literary merit or to their immediate dependants.—*Sec.*, Mrs. F. M. Clark.

ROYAL MEDICAL BENEVOLENT FUND (1836), 24 King's Road, SW19 8QN.—*Sec.*, Mrs. G. A. R. Wells.

ROYAL MEDICAL SOCIETY (1737), Students Centre, 5-5 Bristo Square, Edinburgh EH8 9AL.—*Sec.*, S. Blake.

ROYAL MICROSCOPICAL SOCIETY (1839), 37–38 St. Clements, Oxford OX4 1AJ.—*Administrator*, P. B. Hirst.

ROYAL MUSICAL ASSOCIATION (1874).—*Sec.*, P. Owens, 135 Purves Road, NW10 5TH.

ROYAL NATIONAL LIFEBOAT INSTITUTION, (1824), West Quay Road, Poole, Dorset BH15 1HZ.—259 lifeboats are maintained on the coasts of Great Britain and Ireland. In 1989 the lifeboats launched 4,422 times and saved 1,478 lives. The net cost of running the RNLI in 1990 is over £37m.—*Chairman*, M. Vernon.

ROYAL NAVAL AND ROYAL MARINES CHILDREN'S TRUST (1834), HMS *Nelson*, Portsmouth, PO1 3HH.—*Sec.*, Mrs. M. Bateman.

ROYAL NAVAL ASSOCIATION (1950), 82 Chelsea Manor Street, SW3 5QJ.—*Gen. Sec.*, Capt. J. W. Rayner.

ROYAL NAVAL BENEVOLENT SOCIETY (1739), 1 Fleet Street, EC4Y 1BD.—*Sec.*, Capt. M. Murray, RN (retd.).

ROYAL NAVAL BENEVOLENT TRUST (1922), 1 High Street, Brompton, Gillingham, Kent ME7 5QZ.—*Gen. Sec.*, Lt.-Cdr. D. C. Lawrence (retd.).

ROYAL NAVY OFFICERS, ASSOCIATION OF (1920), 70 Porchester Terrace, W2 3TP.—*Sec.*, Lt.-Cdr. I. M. P. Coombes, RN.

ROYAL OVER-SEAS LEAGUE (1910), Over-Seas House, Park Place, St. James's Street, SW1A 1LR.—*Dir. Gen.*, Capt. J. B. Rumble, RN.

ROYAL PATRIOTIC FUND CORPORATION (1854), Golden Cross House, Duncannon Street, WC2 4JR. Administers funds for the benefit of widows, children and other dependants of deceased officers and servicemen of the Armed Forces.—*Sec.*, Brig. T. G. Williams, CBE.

ROYAL PHOTOGRAPHIC SOCIETY (1853), The Octagon, Milsom Street, Bath BA1 1DN.—*Sec.*, Ms. A. Nevill.

ROYAL PINNER SCHOOL FOUNDATION, 110 Old Brompton Road, SW7 3RB. Assists in the education of children of sales representatives where families have suffered adversity.—*Sec.*, S. Thurtell.

ROYAL SAILORS' RESTS (1876), 2A South Street, Gosport, Hants. PO12 1ES.—*Sec.*, A. A. Lockwood.

ROYAL SCOTTISH SOCIETY FOR PREVENTION OF CRUELTY TO CHILDREN (1884), Melville House, 41 Polwarth Terrace, Edinburgh EH11 1NU.—*Gen. Sec.*, A. M. M. Wood, OBE.

ROYAL SIGNALS INSTITUTION (1950), 56 Regency Street, SW1P 4AD.—*Sec.*, Col. A. N. de Bretton-Gordon.

ROYAL SOCIETY, THE (1660), 6 Carlton House Terrace, SW1Y 5AG.—*Pres.*, The Lord Porter of Luddenham, OM; *Treas. and Vice-Pres.*, Prof. R. W. K. Honeycombe; *Secs. and Vice-Presidents*, Prof. R. J. Elliott, Prof. B. K. Follett, Prof. M. A. Epstein; *Exec. Sec.*, Dr. P. T. Warren.

ROYAL SOCIETY FOR ASIAN AFFAIRS (1901), 2 Belgrave Square, SW1X 8PJ.—*Sec.*, Miss M. FitzSimons.

ROYAL SOCIETY FOR THE ENCOURAGEMENT OF ARTS, MANUFACTURES AND COMMERCE (RSA) (1754), 8 John Adam Street, WC2N 6EZ.—*Chief Exec.*, C. Lucas.

ROYAL SOCIETY FOR THE PREVENTION OF CRUELTY TO ANIMALS (1824), Causeway, Horsham, W. Sussex RH12 1HG.—*Chief Exec.*, A. J. Richmond, CB.

ROYAL SOCIETY FOR THE PROTECTION OF BIRDS (1889), The Lodge, Sandy, Beds. SG19 2DL.—*Dir. Gen.*, I. Prestt, CBE.

ROYAL SOCIETY OF EDINBURGH (1783), 22–24 George Street, Edinburgh EH2 2PQ.—*Pres.*, Prof. C. Kemball; *Hon. Gen. Sec.*, Dr. C. D. Waterston; *Exec. Sec.*, Dr. W. Duncan.

ROYAL SOCIETY OF HEALTH, THE (1876), RSH House, 38A St. George's Drive, SW1V 4BH.—*Sec.*, D. Goad.

ROYAL SOCIETY OF LITERATURE (1823), 1 Hyde Park Gardens, W2 2LT.—*Sec.*, Mrs. P. M. Schute.

ROYAL SOCIETY OF MEDICINE (1805), 1 Wimpole Street, W1M 8AE.—*Exec. Dir.*, R. N. Thomson.

ROYAL SOCIETY OF ST. GEORGE, (1894), Dartmouth House, 37 Charles Street, W1X 8AB.—*Chairman*, J. Minshull-Fogg.

ROYAL STAR AND GARTER HOME FOR DISABLED SAILORS, SOLDIERS AND AIRMEN (1916), Richmond, Surrey TW10 6RR.—*Commandant*, Col. R. N. Harris, MBE.

ROYAL STATISTICAL SOCIETY (1834), 25 Enford Street, W1H 2BH.—*Exec. Sec.*, D. W. Harding.

ROYAL TANK REGIMENT BENEVOLENT FUND (1919), RHQ RTR Centre, Bovington, Dorset BH20 6JA.—*Regimental Sec.*, Maj. R. Clooney.

ROYAL TELEVISION SOCIETY (1927), Tavistock House East, Tavistock Square, WC1H 9HR.—*Hon. Sec.*, A. Pilgrim.

ROYAL UNITED KINGDOM BENEFICENT ASSOCIATION (1863), 6 Avonmore Road, W14 8RL.—*Dir.*, W. Rathbone.

RURAL ENGLAND, COUNCIL FOR THE PROTECTION OF (CPRE) (1926), Warwick House, 25–27 Buckingham Palace Road, SW1W 0PP.—*Dir.*, A. Purkis.

RURAL SCOTLAND, ASSOCIATION FOR THE PROTECTION OF (1926), 14A Napier Road, Edinburgh EH10 5AY.—*Dir.*, R. L. Smith, OBE.

RURAL WALES, COUNCIL FOR THE PROTECTION OF (1928), Tŷ Gwyn, 31 High Street, Welshpool, Powys SY21 7JP.—*Dir.*, Dr. N. Caldwell.

SAILORS' CHILDREN'S SOCIETY, THE (1821), Newland, Hull HU6 7RJ. Cares for seafarers' dependants.—*Gen. Sec.*, Lt.-Cdr. C. G. R. Streatfeild-James.

SAILORS' SOCIETY, BRITISH (1818), 406–410 Eastern Avenue, Ilford, Essex, IG2 6NG.—*Gen. Sec.*, G. Chambers.

ST. DEINIOL'S LIBRARY (1902), Hawarden, Deeside, Clwyd CH5 3DF.—*Warden and Chief Librarian*, Rev. Dr. P. J. Jagger.

ST. DUNSTAN'S, PO Box 4XB, 12–14 Harcourt Street, W1A 4XB. For men and women blinded on war service.—*Sec.*, W. C. Weisblatt.

ST. JOHN AMBULANCE (1887), 1 Grosvenor Crescent, SW1X 7EF. Voluntary unpaid body providing first-aid cover at public events and first aid training for industry and the public. *Brigade Strength* (UK 1989), 80,000.—*Dir. of Public Affairs*, Lt.-Col. J. Mills, MBE.

SALES AND MARKETING MANAGEMENT, INSTITUTE OF (1966), Georgian House, 31 Upper George Street, Luton. LU1 2RD.—*Dir. Gen.*, K. Williams.

SALMON AND TROUT ASSOCIATION (1903), Fishmongers' Hall, London Bridge, EC4R 9EL.—*Dir.*, Col. J. Ferguson.

SALTIRE SOCIETY (1936), 9 Fountain Close, High Street, Edinburgh EH1 1TF.—*Sec.*, Miss K. Austin.

SAMARITANS, THE (1953), 17 Uxbridge Road, Slough, Berks. SL1 1SN. Help for the suicidal and despairing. Tel. numbers in local telephone directories.—*Chief Exec.*, S. Armson.

SAMUEL PEPYS CLUB (1903).—*Sec.*, P. L. Gray, 26 Gloucester Street, Faringdon, Oxon. SN7 7HY.

SAVE BRITAIN'S HERITAGE (1975), 68 Battersea High Street, SW11 3HX.—*Pres.*, M. Binney, OBE; *Sec.*, Ms. M. Watson-Smyth.

SAVE THE CHILDREN FUND, THE (1919), Mary Datchelor House, 17 Grove Lane, SE5 8RD.—*Dir. Gen.*, N. J. Hinton, CBE.

SCHIZOPHRENIA FELLOWSHIP, NATIONAL (1970), 28 Castle Street, Kingston upon Thames, Surrey KT1 1SS.—*Dir.*, Ms. J. Weleminsky.

SCHOOL LIBRARY ASSOCIATION (1937), Liden Library, Barrington Close, Liden, Swindon SN3 6HF.—*Exec. Sec.*, Ms. V. Fea.

SCHOOL NATURAL SCIENCE SOCIETY (1903).—*Hon. Gen. Sec.*, Miss D. S. Jackson, 153 Fernside Avenue, Hanworth, Middx. TW13 7BQ.

SCHOOLMASTERS, SOCIETY OF (1798). For the relief of necessitous schoolmasters and their dependants.—*Sec.*, Mrs. M. S. Freeburn, 29 Corrib Court, Fox Lane, N13 4BG.

SCHOOLMISTRESSES AND GOVERNESSES BENEVOLENT INSTITUTION (1843), Queen Mary House, Manor Park Road, Chislehurst, Kent BR7 5PY.—*Dir.*, R. W. Hayward.

SCIENCE, BRITISH ASSOCIATION FOR THE ADVANCEMENT OF (1831), Fortress House, 23 Savile Row, W1X 1AB.—*Exec. Sec.*, Dr. P. Briggs.

SCIENCE AND LEARNING, SOCIETY FOR THE PROTECTION OF (1933), 20–21 Compton Terrace, N1 2UN.—*Sec.*, Ms. E. Fraser.

SCIENCE EDUCATION, ASSOCIATION FOR (1963), College Lane, Hatfield, Herts. AL10 9AA.—*Gen. Sec.*, Dr. D. S. Moore.

SCOTCH WHISKY ASSOCIATION, THE (1919), 20 Atholl Crescent, Edinburgh EH3 8HF.—*Dir. Gen.*, Col. H. F. O. Bewsher, OBE.

SCOTTISH CHURCH HISTORY SOCIETY (1922).—*Hon. Sec.*, Rev. C. G. F. Brockie, Grange Manse, 51 Portland Road, Kilmarnock, Ayrshire KA1 2EQ.

SCOTTISH CORPORATION, THE ROYAL (1611), 37 King Street, WC2E 8JS.—*Chief Exec.*, Wg. Cdr. A. Robertson.

SCOTTISH COUNTRY DANCE SOCIETY, ROYAL (1923), 12 Coates Crescent, Edinburgh EH3 7AF.—*Sec.*, Mrs. J. A. Moore.

SCOTTISH GENEALOGY SOCIETY (1953).—*Hon. Sec.*, Miss J. P. S. Ferguson, 21 Howard Place, Edinburgh EH3 5JY.

SCOTTISH HISTORY SOCIETY (1886).—*Hon. Sec.*, Dr. N. MacDougall, Dept. of Scottish History, St. Salvator's College, University of St. Andrews, Fife KY16 9AJ.

SCOTTISH LANDOWNERS' FEDERATION (1906).—*Dir.*, S. Fraser, 25 Maritime Street, Edinburgh EH6 5PW.

SCOTTISH LAW AGENTS SOCIETY.—*Sec.*, R. M. Sinclair, 3 Albyn Place, Edinburgh EH2 4NQ.

SCOTTISH LIFE OFFICES, ASSOCIATED (1841), 23 St. Andrew Square, Edinburgh EH2 1AQ.—*Sec.*, W. W. Mair.

SCOTTISH NATIONAL INSTITUTION FOR THE WAR BLINDED (1915), Gillespie Crescent, Edinburgh EH10 4HZ.—*Sec.*, J. B. M. Munro.

SCOTTISH NATIONAL WAR MEMORIAL (1927), The Castle, Edinburgh EH1 2YT.—*Sec.*, T. C. Barker.

SCOTTISH SECONDARY TEACHERS' ASSOCIATION (1946), 15 Dundas Street, Edinburgh EH3 6QG.—*Gen. Sec.*, A. A. Stanley.

SCOTTISH SOCIETY FOR THE PREVENTION OF CRUELTY TO ANIMALS (1950), 19 Melville Street, Edinburgh EH3 7PL.—*Chief Exec.*, Sir Cameron Rusby, KCB, LVO.

SCOTTISH SOCIETY FOR THE PROTECTION OF WILD BIRDS (1927), Foremount House, Kilbarchan, Renfrewshire PA10 2EZ.—*Sec.*, Dr. J. A. Gibson.

SCOTTISH WILDLIFE TRUST (1964), 25 Johnston Terrace, Edinburgh EH1 2NH.—*Chief Exec.*, D. J. Hughes Hallett.

SCOUT ASSOCIATION, THE (1907), Baden-Powell House, Queen's Gate, SW7 5JS. Membership in UK (1989), 647,727; World Membership over 16,000,000 in over 150 countries.—*Chief Scout*, W. G. Morrison; *Chief Exec. Commissioner*, A. E. N. Black, OBE.

SCRIBES AND ILLUMINATORS, THE SOCIETY OF (1921).—*Hon. Sec.*, Mrs. S. Cavendish, 54 Boileau Road, SW13 9BL.

SCRIPTURE GIFT MISSION INCORPORATED (1888), Radstock House, 3 Eccleston Street, SW1W 9LZ.—*Gen. Sec.*, R. Kennedy.

SCRIPTURE UNION (1867), 130 City Road, EC1V 2NJ.—*Gen. Dir.*, Rev. D. M. S. Cohen.

SCULPTORS, ROYAL SOCIETY OF BRITISH (1904), 108 Old Brompton Road, SW7 3RA.—*Pres.*, Ms. P. Davidson Davis.

SEA CADETS, (1895), 202 Lambeth Road, SE1 7JF.—*Gen. Sec.*, Cdr. P. J. Everett, OBE.

SEAMEN'S BOYS' HOME, BRITISH (1863), Berry Head Road, Brixham, Devon TQ5 9AE.—*Sec.*, Capt. E. M. Marks, RD, RNR.

SEAMEN'S CHRISTIAN FRIEND SOCIETY (1846), PO Box 60, Wilmslow, Cheshire SK9 1QX.—*Administrator*, M. J. Wilson.

SEAMEN'S PENSION FUND, ROYAL (1919), 65 High Street, Ewell, Epsom, Surrey KT17 1RX.—*Sec.*, D. Barker.

SECONDARY HEADS ASSOCIATION (1978), 130 Regent Road, Leicester LE1 7PG.—*Gen. Sec.*, J. Sutton.

SECULAR SOCIETY LTD., NATIONAL (1866), 702 Holloway Road, N19 3NL.—*Gen. Sec.*, T. Mullins.

SELDEN SOCIETY (1887), Faculty of Laws, Queen Mary and Westfield College, Mile End Road, E1 4NS. To encourage the study and advance the knowledge of the history of English Law.—*Sec.*, V. Tunkel.

SELF EMPLOYED AND SMALL BUSINESSES, NATIONAL FEDERATION OF (1974), Parliamentary Office, 140 Lower Marsh, SE1 7AE.—*Nat. Chairman*, W. Knox.

SENSE (The National Deaf-Blind and Rubella Association) (1955), 311 Grays Inn Road, WC1X 8AT.—*Chairman*, Mrs. J. Hills.

SHAFTESBURY HOMES AND *Arethusa* (1843), 3 Rectory Grove, SW4 0EG.—*Dir.*, Capt. N. C. Baird-Murray, CBE, RN.

SHAFTESBURY SOCIETY, THE (1844), 2A Amity Grove, Raynes Park, SW20 0LH. Cares for physically and mentally handicapped, the elderly and socially deprived.—*Chief Exec.*, G. Holloway.

SHELLFISH ASSOCIATION OF GREAT BRITAIN (1904), Fishmongers' Hall, London Bridge, EC4R 9EL.—*Dir.*, E. Edwards, PH.D.

SHELTER (1966), 88 Old Street, EC1V 9HU.—*Dir.*, Ms. S. McKechnie.

SHERLOCK HOLMES SOCIETY OF LONDON (1951).—*Hon. Sec.*, Cdr. G. S. Stavert, MBE, 3 Outram Road, Southsea, Hants. PO5 1QP.

SHIPBROKERS, INSTITUTE OF CHARTERED (1911), 24 St. Mary Axe, EC3A 8DE.—*Sec.*, J. H. Parker.

SHIRE HORSE SOCIETY (1878), East of England Showground, Peterborough PE2 0XE.—*Sec.*, R. W. Bird, MBE.

SHRIEVALTY ASSOCIATION (1971), 14 Clumber Street, Nottingham NG1 3DS.—*Sec.*, R. Bullock.

SIGHT SAVERS (Royal Commonwealth Society for the Blind) (1950), PO Box 191, Haywards Heath, W. Sussex RH16 1FN.—*Exec. Dir.*, A. W. Johns, CMG, OBE.

SIMPLIFIED SPELLING SOCIETY (1908).—*Chairman*, C. J. H. Jolly, Clare Hall, Chapel Lane, Chigwell, Essex IG7 6JJ.

SIR OSWALD STOLL FOUNDATION (1916), 446 Fulham Road, SW6 1DT.—*Dir.*, R. C. Brunwin.

SMALL FARMERS' ASSOCIATION, THE (1979), PO Box 6, Ludlow, Salop SY8 1ZZ.—*Hon. Sec.*, Miss V. Minet.

SOCIALIST PARTY OF GREAT BRITAIN (1904), 52 Clapham High Street, SW4 7UN.—*Gen. Sec.*, P. Hope.

SOCIAL RESPONSIBILITY AND EDUCATION, QUAKER, Friends House, Euston Road, NW1 2BJ.—*Gen. Sec.*, Ms. B. Smith.

SOCIAL WORKERS, BRITISH ASSOCIATION OF (1970), 16 Kent Street, Birmingham B5 6RD.—*Gen. Sec.*, D. N. Jones.

SOLDIERS' AND AIRMEN'S SCRIPTURE READERS ASSOCIATION, THE (1838), Havelock House, Barrack Road, Aldershot, Hants. GU11 3NP.—*Gen. Sec.*, Lt. Col. K. W. Sear.

SOLDIERS', SAILORS' AND AIRMEN'S FAMILIES ASSOCIATION (1885), 19 Queen Elizabeth Street, SE1 2LP.—*Chairman*, Adm. Sir Peter Herbert, KCB, OBE; *Controller*, Maj.-Gen. C. R. Grey, CBE; *Sec.*, Mrs. B. R. Best, OBE.

SOLDIERS, SAILORS AND AIRMEN'S HELP SOCIETY, *see* FORCES HELP SOCIETY.

SOLDIERS' WIDOWS, ROYAL CAMBRIDGE HOME FOR (1851), 82–84 Hurst Road, East Molesey, Surrey KT8 9AH.—*Superintendent*, Mrs. A. M. Webb.

SOLICITORS BENEVOLENT ASSOCIATION (1858), Lonsdale Chambers, 27 Chancery Lane, WC2A 1NF.—*Sec.*, Lt.-Col. D. G. Martin, OBE.

SOLICITORS IN THE SUPREME COURTS OF SCOTLAND, SOCIETY OF (1784).—*Sec.*, A. R. Brownlie, OBE, 2 Abercromby Place, Edinburgh EH3 6JZ.

SOROPTIMIST INTERNATIONAL OF GREAT BRITAIN AND IRELAND (1923), 127 Wellington Road South, Stockport SK1 3TS.—*Admin. Officer*, Ms. K. Hindley.

SOS SOCIETY, THE, *see* 2CARE.

SOUTH AMERICAN MISSIONARY SOCIETY (1844), Allen Gardiner House, Pembury Road, Tunbridge Wells, Kent TN2 3QU.—*Gen. Sec.*, Rt. Rev. J. W. H. Flagg.

SOUTH WALES INSTITUTE OF ENGINEERS (1857), Empire House, Mount Stuart Square, Cardiff CF1 6DN.—*Hon. Sec.*, R. E. Lindsay.

SPASTICS SOCIETY, THE (1952), 12 Park Crescent, W1N 4EQ.—*Chief Exec.*, K. Young.

SPEAKERS CLUBS, THE ASSOCIATION OF (1971).—*Nat. Sec.*, F. W. P. Dawkins, 3 Leawood Croft, Holloway, Matlock DE4 5BD.

SPINA BIFIDA AND HYDROCEPHALUS, ASSOCIATION FOR (ASBAH), 42 Park Road, Peterborough PE1 2UQ.—*Exec. Dir.*, Miss M. P. Gilbertson.

SPORTS MEDICINE, INSTITUTE OF (1963), Burlington House, Piccadilly, W1V 0LQ.—*Hon. Sec.*, Dr. W. T. Orton.

SPURGEON'S CHILD CARE (1867), 30 Mill Street, Bedford MK40 3HD.—*Dir.*, D. C. Culwick.

STATISTICIANS, INSTITUTE OF (1948), 43 St. Peters Square, Preston PR1 7BX.—*Sec.*, D. A. Holland.

STATUTE LAW SOCIETY (1968), 186 City Road, EC1V 2NU.—*Hon. Sec.*, N. Frudd.

STEWART SOCIETY (1899), 48 Castle Street, Edinburgh EH2 3LX.—*Hon. Sec.*, Mrs. M. Walker.

STRATEGIC PLANNING SOCIETY, THE (1967), 17 Portland Place, W1N 3AF.—*Exec. Sec.*, Miss C. E. Langan.

STRATEGIC STUDIES, THE INTERNATIONAL INSTITUTE FOR (1958), 23 Tavistock Street, WC2E 7NQ.—*Dir.*, F. Heisbourg.

STRUCTURAL ENGINEERS, INSTITUTION OF (1908), 11 Upper Belgrave Street, SW1X 8BH.—*Sec.*, D. J. Clark.

STUDENT CHRISTIAN MOVEMENT (1889), 186 St. Paul's Road, Balsall Heath, Birmingham B12 8LZ.—*Gen. Sec.*, Rev. T. E. McClure.

SUFFOLK HORSE SOCIETY (1878), 6 Church Street, Woodbridge, Suffolk IP12 1DH.—*Sec.*, P. Ryder-Davies.

SURGEONS OF EDINBURGH, ROYAL COLLEGE OF (1505), Nicolson Street, Edinburgh EH8 9DW.—*Pres.*, Prof. G. D. Chisholm; *Sec.*, Prof. A. G. D. Maran.

SURGEONS OF ENGLAND, ROYAL COLLEGE OF (1800), 35–43 Lincoln's Inn Fields, WC2A 3PN.—*Pres.*, T. A. H. English; *Sec.*, R. H. E. Duffett.

SURVEYORS, ROYAL INSTITUTION OF CHARTERED (incorporating the Institute of Quantity Surveyors) (1868), 12 Great George Street, SW1P 3AD.—*Sec. Gen.*, M. Pattison.

SUSSEX CATTLE SOCIETY (1887), Station Road, Robertsbridge, E. Sussex TN32 5DG.—*Manager*, Miss S. G. Kennedy.

SWEDENBORG SOCIETY (1810), 20–21 Bloomsbury Way, WC1A 2TH.—*Sec.*, Ms. M. G. Waters.

TALKING BOOKS FOR THE HANDICAPPED AND HOSPITAL PATIENTS (National Listening Library), 12 Lant Street, SE1 1QH.—*Dir.*, D. J Roskilly.

TAVISTOCK INSTITUTE OF HUMAN RELATIONS (1947), The Tavistock Centre, Belsize Lane, NW3 5BA.—*Sec.*, N. Barnes.

TAXATION, INSTITUTE OF (1930), 12 Upper Belgrave Street, SW1X 8BB.—*Sec.*, R. J. Ison.

TAX PAYERS' SOCIETY (1921), 22 Wheatsheaf House, 4 Carmelite Street, EC4Y 0BN.—*Dir.*, D. J. Bryant.

TEACHERS OF HOME ECONOMICS, NATIONAL ASSOCIATION OF (1896), Hamilton House, Mabledon Place, WC1H 9BJ.—*Gen. Manager*, P. G. Higgins.

TEACHERS OF MATHEMATICS, ASSOCIATION OF (1952), 7 Shaftesbury Street, Derby DE3 8YB—*Hon. Sec.*, Ms. C. Hopkins.

TEACHERS OF THE DEAF, BRITISH ASSOCIATION OF (1977).—*Hon. Sec.*, Ms. S. Dowe, Icknield High School HIU, Riddy Lane, Luton LU3 2AH.

TEACHERS' UNION, ULSTER (1919), 94 Malone Road, Belfast BT9 5HP.—*Gen. Sec.*, D. Allen.

TELECOMMUNICATIONS USERS' ASSOCIATION (1965), 48 Percy Road, N12 8BU.—*Chief Exec.*, Ms. V. Peters.

TEMPERANCE SOCIETIES:—

British National Temperance League (1834), Room 4, Shirley House, 31 Psalter Lane, Sheffield S11 8YL.—*Sec.*, L. Swales.

British Women's Temperance Association (1876), 8 North Bank Street, Edinburgh EH1 2LP.—*Hon. Sec.*, Miss J. E. H. Gillon.

Church of England National Council for Social Aid, 38 Ebury Street, SW1W 0LU.—*Gen. Sec.*, Rev. E. W. F. Agar.

Division of Social Responsibility of the Methodist Church (1932), 1 Central Buildings, Westminster, SW1H 9NH.—*Gen. Sec.*, Rev. B. Duckworth.

National United Temperance Council (1880), 123 Regent Street, W1R 7HA—*Gen. Sec.*, Rev. B. Kinman.

Order of the Sons of Temperance (1855), 5 Ashbourne Road, Derby, DE3 3FQ.—*Sec.*, D. Newbury.

Royal Naval Temperance Society (1876) (auxiliary of Royal Sailors' Rests), 2A South Street, Gosport, Hants. PO12 1ES.—*Sec.*, A. A. Lockwood.

Social Responsibility Dept., General Assembly of Unitarian and Free Christian Churches, Essex Hall, 1–6 Essex Street, WC2R 3HY.—*Hon. Sec.*, Rev. B. Packer.

United Kingdom Alliance (1863), New Gallery, 123 Regent Street, W1R 7HA.—*Gen. Sec.*, Rev. B. Kinman.

TEMPLETON FOUNDATION (1973), 16 Kingfisher Lane, Turners Hill, Crawley, W. Sussex RH10 4QP.—*UK Rep.*, Mrs. N. Pearse.

TERRENCE HIGGINS TRUST (1982), 52–54 Grays Inn Road, WC1X 8JU.—*Chairman*, D. Campbell.

TERRITORIAL, AUXILIARY AND VOLUNTEER RESERVE ASSOCIATIONS, COUNCIL OF (1908), The Chapel, Duke of York's HQ, SW3 4SG.—*Sec.*, Maj.-Gen. M. Matthews, CB.

TEXTILE INSTITUTE, THE (1910), International HQ, 10 Blackfriars Street, Manchester M3 5DR.—*Gen. Sec.*, R. G. Denyer.

THEATRE ASSOCIATION, BRITISH (1919), Cranbourn Mansions, Cranbourn Street, WC2H 7AG.—*Administrator*, R. Haddon.

THEATRE RESEARCH, SOCIETY FOR (1948), c/o The Theatre Museum, 1E Tavistock Street, WC2E 7PA.—*Joint Hon. Secs.*, Ms. E. Cottis; Ms. F. Dann.

THEATRES TRUST, THE (1976), 10 St. Martin's Court, St. Martin's Lane, WC2N 4AJ.—*Chairman*, Sir David Crouch; *Dir.*, J. Earl.

THEATRICAL FUND, ROYAL (1839), 11 Garrick Street, WC2E 9AR.—*Sec.*, J. Berkeley.

THEATRICAL LADIES' GUILD OF CHARITY (1892), 49 Endell Street, WC2H 9AJ.—*Admin. Sec.*, Mrs. K. Nichols.

THEOSOPHICAL SOCIETY IN ENGLAND (1875), 50 Gloucester Place, W1H 3HJ.—*Gen. Sec.*, Miss I. H. Hoskins.

THISTLE FOUNDATION, THE (1945), 27A Walker Street, Edinburgh EH3 7HX.—*Dir.*, P. Croft.

THOMAS CORAM FOUNDATION FOR CHILDREN (formerly The Foundling Hospital) (1739), 40 Brunswick Square, WC1N 1AZ.—*Dir. and Sec.*, C. P. Masters.

TIDY BRITAIN GROUP (1953), The Pier, Wigan WN3 4EX.—*Dir. Gen.*, Prof. G. Ashworth, CBE.

TOC H (1915), Headquarters, 1 Forest Close, Wendover, Aylesbury, Bucks. HP22 6BT.—*Gen. Sec.*, Dr. J. M. A. Kilburn.

TOURIST BOARD, ENGLISH, Thames Tower, Black's Road, W6 9EL.—*Chief Exec.*, M. Medlicott.

TOURIST BOARD, NORTHERN IRELAND, River House, 48 High Street, Belfast BT1 2DS.—*Chief Exec.*, S. B. Belford.

TOURIST BOARD, SCOTTISH (1969), 23 Ravelston Terrace, Edinburgh EH4 3EU.—*Chief Exec.*, T. M. Band.

TOURIST BOARD, WALES, Brunel House, 2 Fitzalan Road, Cardiff CF2 1UY.—*Chief Exec.*, P. Loveluck.

TOWN AND COUNTRY PLANNING ASSOCIATION (1899), 17 Carlton House Terrace, SW1Y 5AS.—*Dir.*, D. Hall.

TOWN PLANNING INSTITUTE, ROYAL (1914), 26 Portland Place, W1N 4BE.—*Sec. Gen.*, D. Fryer.

TOWNSWOMEN'S GUILDS, (1929), Chamber of Commerce House, 75 Harborne Road, Birmingham B15 3DA.—*Nat. Sec.*, Mrs. J. R. Campbell-Tanner.

TOYNBEE HALL, The Universities' Settlement in East London (1884), 28 Commercial Street, E1 6LS.— *Warden and Chief Exec.*, A. L. Williams, MBE.

TRADE, NATIONAL CHAMBER OF (1897), Enterprise House, 59 Castle Street, Reading, Berks. RG1 7SN.—*Chief Exec.*, B. Tennant.

TRADE MARK AGENTS, INSTITUTE OF (1934), 4th Floor, Canterbury House, 2–6 Sydenham Road, Croydon CR0 9XE.—*Sec.*, Mrs. M. J. Tyler.

TRADING STANDARDS ADMINISTRATION, THE INSTITUTE OF (1881), 4–5 Hadleigh Business Centre, 351 London Road, Hadleigh, Essex SS7 2BT.—*Dir. of Admin. and PR*, Mrs. G. Jordan.

TRANSLATION AND INTERPRETING, INSTITUTE OF (1986), 318A Finchley Road, NW3 5HT.—*Chairman*, Dr. J. Sykes.

TRANSPORT ADMINISTRATION, INSTITUTE OF (1944), 32 Palmerston Road, Southampton SO1 1LL.—*Dir.*, Wg. Cdr. P. F. Green.

TRANSPORT, CHARTERED INSTITUTE OF (1919), 80 Portland Place, W1N 4DP.—*Dir. Gen.*, R. P. Botwood.

TRANSPORT CONSULTATIVE COMMITTEE, CENTRAL (1948), 1st Floor, Golden Cross House, Duncannon Street, WC2N 4JF.—*Sec.*, M. Patterson.

TRAVEL AGENTS, ASSOCIATION OF BRITISH (ABTA) (1950), 55–57 Newman Street, W1P 4AH.—*Dir. Gen.*, D. L. Epstein.

TROPICAL MEDICINE AND HYGIENE, ROYAL SOCIETY OF (1907), Manson House, 26 Portland Place, W1N 4EY.

TURNER SOCIETY (1975), BCM Box Turner, WC1N 3XX.— *Chairman*, E. Shanes.

2CARE (FORMERLY THE SOS SOCIETY) (1929), 13 Harwood Road, SW6 4QP. Residential homes for the elderly (3), psychiatric rehabilitation centres (4).—*Chief Exec.*, Col. M. T. O. Lloyd, OBE.

UFAW (Universities Federation for Animal Welfare) (1926), 8 Hamilton Close, South Mimms, Potters Bar, Herts. EN6 3QD.—*Sec.*, Lt.-Col. T. J. Reynolds.

UNIT TRUST ASSOCIATION (1959), 65 Kingsway, WC2B 6TD.—*Chief Exec.*, A. C. Smith.

UNITED NATIONS ASSOCIATION OF GREAT BRITAIN AND NORTHERN IRELAND (1945), 3 Whitehall Court, SW1A 2EL.—*Dir.*, M. C. Harper.

UNITED REFORMED CHURCH HISTORY SOCIETY (1972), 86 Tavistock Place, WC1H 9RT.—*Hon. Sec.*, Rev. Dr. C. Orchard.

UNITED SOCIETY FOR CHRISTIAN LITERATURE (1799), Robertson House, Leas Road, Guildford, Surrey GU14 4QW.—*Gen. Sec.*, Rev. A. Gilmore.

UNITED SOCIETY FOR THE PROPAGATION OF THE GOSPEL (USPG) (1701), Partnership House, 157 Waterloo Road, SE1 8XA.—*Sec.*, Rev. Canon H. V. Taylor.

UNIVERSITIES CENTRAL COUNCIL ON ADMISSIONS (1961), PO Box 28, Cheltenham, Glos. GL50 3SA.— *Gen. Sec.*, P. A. Oakley, MBE.

UNIVERSITIES OF THE UNITED KINGDOM, COMMITTEE OF VICE-CHANCELLORS AND PRINCIPALS OF THE (1918), 29 Tavistock Square, WC1H 9EZ.—*Sec.*, T. U. Burgner.

UNIVERSITY WOMEN, BRITISH FEDERATION OF (1907), Crosby Hall, Cheyne Walk, SW3 5BA.—*Sec.*, Ms. E. Menzies.

VALUERS AND AUCTIONEERS, INCORPORATED SOCIETY OF, 3 Cadogan Gate, SW1X 0AS.—*Sec.*, M. Astbury.

VEGAN SOCIETY, THE (1944), 7 Battle Road, St. Leonards-on-Sea, E. Sussex TN37 7AA.—*Gen. Sec.*, R. Farhall.

VEGETARIAN SOCIETY OF THE UNITED KINGDOM LTD., Parkdale, Dunham Road, Altrincham, Cheshire WA14 4QG.—*Gen. Manager*, Ms. P. McGlashan.

VENEREAL DISEASES, MEDICAL SOCIETY FOR THE STUDY OF (1922).—*Hon. Sec.*, Dr. M. J. Godley, Florey Unit, Royal Berkshire Hospital, Reading RG1 5AN.

VERNACULAR ARCHITECTURE GROUP (1953).—*Hon. Sec.*, R. Meeson, 16 Falna Crescent, Coton Green, Tamworth, Staffs. B79 8JS.

VETERINARY ASSOCIATION, BRITISH (1881), 7 Mansfield Street, W1M 0AT.—*Chief Exec.*, J. H. Baird.

VETERINARY SURGEONS, ROYAL COLLEGE OF, 32 Belgrave Square, SW1X 8QP (1844).—*Pres.*, H. E. Carter; *Registrar*, A. R. W. Porter, CBE.

VICTIM SUPPORT (1979), Cranmer House, 39 Brixton Road, SW9 6DZ.—*Dir.*, Ms. H. Reeves, OBE.

VICTORIA CROSS AND GEORGE CROSS ASSOCIATION, Room 04, Archway Block South, Old Admiralty Building, SW1A 2BE.—*Chairman*, Rear-Adm. B. C. G. Place, VC, CB, DSC.

VICTORIA INSTITUTE, THE (Philosophical Society of Great Britain), PO Box 216, Welling, Kent DA16 2ED.—*Hon. Treas.*, B. H. T. Weller.

VICTORIAN SOCIETY (1958), 1 Priory Gardens, Bedford Park, W4 1TT.—*Sec.*, Ms. T. Sladen.

VICTORY (SERVICES) ASSOCIATION LTD. AND CLUB (1907), 63–79 Seymour Street, W2 2HF.—*Gen. Manager*, G. F. Taylor.

VIKING SOCIETY FOR NORTHERN RESEARCH (1892), University College London, Gower Street, WC1E 6BT.—*Joint Hon. Secs.*, Ms. U. Dronke; Prof. M. P. Barnes.

VITREOUS ENAMELLERS, INSTITUTE OF (1935), Ripley, Derby DE5 3EB.—*Sec.*, J. D. Gardom.

VSO (Voluntary Service Overseas) (1958), 317 Putney Bridge Road, SW15 2PN.—*Dir.*, N. McIntosh.

WATER AND ENVIRONMENTAL MANAGEMENT, INSTITUTION OF (1987), 15 John Street, WC1N 2EB.—*Exec. Dir.*, H. R. Evans.

WATERCOLOUR SOCIETY, ROYAL (1804), Bankside Gallery, 48 Hopton Street, SE1 9JH.—*Pres.*, C. Bartlett; *Sec.*, M. Spender.

WELDING INSTITUTE, THE, Abington Hall, Cambridge CB1 6AL.—*Chief Exec.*, A. B. M. Braithwaite.

WELFARE OFFICERS, INSTITUTE OF (1945), 254 The Corn Exchange, Hanging Ditch, Manchester M4 3ES.—*Sec.*, Mrs. M. Maclean-Ives.

WELLCOME TRUST (1936), 1 Park Square West, NW1 4LJ.—*Dir.*, Dr. P. O. Williams.

WELLS, H. G., SOCIETY (1961), Polytechnic of North London, Prince of Wales Road, NW5 3LB.—*Sec.*, C. Rolfe.

WESLEY HISTORICAL SOCIETY (1893).—*Gen. Sec.*, Dr. E. D. Graham, 34 Spiceland Road, Northfield, Birmingham B31 1NJ.

WEST INDIA COMMITTEE (1750), Commonwealth House, 18 Northumberland Avenue, WC2N 5RA.—*Dir.*, D. A. Jessop.

WEST LONDON MISSION (1887), 19 Thayer Street, W1M 5LJ.—*Supt.*, Rev. L. J. Griffiths, PH.D.

WILDFOWL AND WETLANDS TRUST (1946), The New Ground, Slimbridge, Gloucester GL2 7BT.—*Dir. Gen.*, Dr. B. Bertram.

WILDLIFE ARTISTS, SOCIETY OF (1962), 17 Carlton House Terrace, SW1Y 5AH.—*Hon. Sec.*, K. J. Wood.

WILLIAM MORRIS SOCIETY AND KELMSCOTT FELLOWSHIP (1918), Kelmscott House, 26 Upper Mall, W6 9TA.—*Hon. Sec.*, J. Purkis.

WINE AND SPIRIT ASSOCIATION OF GREAT BRITAIN AND NORTHERN IRELAND (*c.* 1825), Five Kings House, Upper Thames Street, Kennett Wharf Lane, EC4V 3BH.—*Dir.*, R. H. Insoll.

WOMEN, CAREERS FOR (1933), 4th Floor, 2 Valentine Place, SE1 8QH.—*Dir.*, Miss K. M. Menon.

WOMEN, SOCIETY FOR PROMOTING THE TRAINING OF (1859). Loan fund for women in higher and further education.—*Sec.*, Rev. B. Harris, The Rectory, Bent Lane, Warburton, Lymm, Cheshire WA13 9TQ.

WOMEN ARTISTS, SOCIETY OF (1855), Westminster Gallery, Westminster Central Hall, Storey's Gate, SW1H 9NU.—*Pres.*, Ms. B. Tate.

WOMEN'S ENGINEERING SOCIETY (1920), Imperial College of Science and Technology, Dept. of Civil Engineering, Imperial College Road, SW7 2BU.—*Sec.*, Ms. G. Maxwell.

WOMEN'S INSTITUTES, NATIONAL FEDERATION OF (1915), 104 New Kings Road, SW6 4LY.—*Gen. Sec.*, Mrs. A. Ballard.

WOMEN'S INSTITUTES OF NORTHERN IRELAND, FEDERATION OF (1932), 209–211 Upper Lisburn Road, Belfast BT10 0LL.—*Gen. Sec.*, Mrs. I. A. Sproule.

WOMEN'S INTERNATIONAL LEAGUE FOR PEACE AND FREEDOM (British Section) (1915), 157 Lyndhurst Road, Worthing, W. Sussex BN11 2DG.—*Chair*, Ms. M. Miller.

WOMEN'S NATIONAL CANCER CONTROL CAMPAIGN (1964), 1 South Audley Street, W1Y 5DQ.—*Administrator*, Ms. J. Harding.

WOMEN'S ROYAL NAVAL SERVICE BENEVOLENT TRUST (1942), 1A Chesham Street, SW1X 8NL.—*Gen. Sec.*, Mrs. J. Y. Ellis.

WOMEN'S ROYAL VOLUNTARY SERVICE (WRVS) (1938), 234–244 Stockwell Road, SW9 9SP.—*National Chairman*, Hon. Mrs. M. Corsar.

WOMEN'S RURAL INSTITUTES, SCOTTISH (1917), 42 Heriot Row, Edinburgh EH3 6ES.—*Gen. Sec.*, Mrs. E. Nicol.

WOMEN'S TRANSPORT SERVICE (1907), FANY HQ (E Block), Duke of York's HQ, SW3 4SJ.—*Corps Commander*, Mrs. S. Y. Parkinson, OBE.

WOODLAND TRUST, THE (1972), Autumn Park, Dysart Road, Grantham, Lincs. NG31 6LL.—*Exec. Dir.*, J. D. James.

WOOD PRESERVING ASSOCIATION, BRITISH (1930), 6 The Office Village, 4 Romford Road, E15 4EA.—*Dir.*, J. Lefley.

WORKERS' EDUCATIONAL ASSOCIATION, Temple House, 9 Upper Berkeley Street, W1H 8BY.—*Gen. Sec.*, R. Lochrie.

WORKING MOTHERS ASSOCIATION, THE (1985), 77 Holloway Road, N7 8JZ.—*Dir.*, Ms. L. Daniels.

WORLD EDUCATION FELLOWSHIP (1921), 33 Kinnaird Avenue, W4 3SH.—*Gen. Sec.*, Mrs. R. Crommelin.

WORLD ENERGY COUNCIL (1924), 34 St. James's Street, SW1A 1HD.—*Sec. Gen.*, I. D. Lindsay.

WORLD MISSION, COUNCIL FOR (1977), Livingstone House, 11 Carteret Street, SW1H 9DL.—*Gen. Sec.*, vacant.

WORLD SHIP SOCIETY (1946).—*Sec.*, S. J. F. Miller, 35 Wickham Way, Haywards Heath, W. Sussex RH16 1UJ.

WORLD SOCIETY FOR THE PROTECTION OF ANIMALS (1981), 106 Jermyn Street, SW1Y 6EE.—*Dir. Gen.*, G. Walwyn, CVO.

WORLD-WIDE EDUCATION SERVICE (1888), 10 Barley Mow Passage, W4 4PH.—*Asst. Dir.*, Mrs. T. Mulder-Reynolds.

WORLD WIDE FUND FOR NATURE—UK (1961), Panda House, Weyside Park, Godalming, Surrey GU7 1XR.—*Dir.*, G. J. Medley, OBE.

WRITERS TO HM SIGNET, SOCIETY OF (1532), 16 Hill Street, Edinburgh EH2 3LD.—*Clerk*, A. M. Kerr.

YEOMANRY BENEVOLENT FUND (1902), 10 Stone Buildings, Lincoln's Inn, WC2A 3TG.—*Sec.*, Mrs. C. W. Chrystie.

YORKSHIRE AGRICULTURAL SOCIETY (1837), Great Yorkshire Showground, Hookstone Oval, Harrogate HG2 8PW.—*Sec.-Gen.*, Lt.-Col. M. G. A. Young.

YORKSHIRE SOCIETY, THE (1812), 27 Kensington Park, Milford-on-Sea, Hants. SO41 0WD. Educational trust making grants to students of all ages.—*Sec.*, G. G. Prince, TD.

YOUNG FARMERS' CLUBS, NATIONAL FEDERATION OF, The YFC Centre, National Agricultural Centre, Kenilworth, Warks. CV8 2LG.—*Sec.*, F. E. Shields, MBE.

YOUNG MEN'S CHRISTIAN ASSOCIATION (YMCA) (1844), National Council of YMCAs, 640 Forest Road, E17 3DZ.—*Nat. Sec.*, C. J. Naylor.

YOUNG WOMEN'S CHRISTIAN ASSOCIATION OF GREAT BRITAIN (YWCA) (1855), 52 Cornmarket Street, Oxford OX1 3EJ.—*Exec. Dir.*, Miss F. E. Sharples.

YOUTH CLUBS, NORTHERN IRELAND ASSOCIATION OF (1944), Hampton, Glenmachan Park, Belfast BT4 2PJ.—*Dir.*, G. Johnston.

YOUTH CLUBS UK (1911), Keswick House, 30 Peacock Lane, Leicester LE1 5NY.—*Chief Exec.*, D. Stickels.

YOUTH HOSTELS ASSOCIATION (ENGLAND AND WALES) (1930), Trevelyan House, 8 St. Stephens Hill, St.

Albans, Herts. AL1 2DY.—*Chief Exec.*, A. G. F. Chinneck.

YOUTH HOSTELS ASSOCIATION OF NORTHERN IRELAND (1931), Bradbury Buildings, 56 Bradbury Place, Belfast BT7 1RU.—*Hon. Sec.*, E. R. Henderson.

YOUTH HOSTELS ASSOCIATION, SCOTTISH (1931), 7 Glebe Crescent, Stirling FK8 2JA.—*Gen. Sec.*, J. Martin.

ZOO CHECK (1984), Cherry Tree Cottage, Coldharbour, Dorking, Surrey RH5 6HA.—*Chairman*, W. Travers.

ZOOLOGICAL SOCIETY OF LONDON (1826), Regent's Park, NW1 4RY. Attendances (1989), Regent's Park 1,162,915; Whipsnade 392,330.—*Pres.*, Prof. A. Mitchison, FRS; *Managing Dir.*, A. Y. Grant.

ZOOLOGICAL SOCIETY OF SCOTLAND, ROYAL (1913), Scottish National Zoological Park, Murrayfield, Edinburgh EH12 6TS.—*Dir.*, R. J. Wheater, FRSE.

LOCAL HISTORY AND ARCHAEOLOGICAL SOCIETIES

England

Bedfordshire.—SOUTH BEDFORDSHIRE ARCHAEOLOGICAL SOCIETY. *Hon. Sec.* D. H. Kennett, 27 Lords Lane, Bradwell, Great Yarmouth, Norfolk NR31 8NY.

Berkshire.—BERKSHIRE ARCHAEOLOGICAL SOCIETY. *Hon. Sec.*, L. J. Over, 43 Laburnham Road, Maidenhead, Berks. SL6 4DE.

    NEWBURY DISTRICT FIELD CLUB. *Hon. Sec.*, Mrs. P. M. Jermyn, 30 Butson Close, Newbury, Berks. RG14 5JQ.

Buckinghamshire.—BUCKINGHAMSHIRE ARCHAEOLOGICAL SOCIETY. *Hon. Sec.*, Dr. R. P. Hagerty, County Museum, Church Street, Aylesbury, Bucks. HP20 2QP.

Cambridgeshire.—CAMBRIDGE ANTIQUARIAN SOCIETY. *Hon. Sec.*, Dr. A. S. Bendall, Emmanuel College, Cambridge CB2 3AP.

Cheshire.—CHESTER ARCHAEOLOGICAL SOCIETY. *Sec.*, G. R. Coppack, Bryn Gwyn, Ffordd Nant, Rhuddlan, Rhyl, Clwyd LL18 2SW. *See also* under Lancashire.

Cornwall.—CORNWALL ARCHAEOLOGICAL SOCIETY. *Hon. Sec.*, Mrs. A. Cooke, Pentrelew, Flushing, Falmouth, Cornwall TR11 5UD.

Cumberland and Westmorland.—CUMBERLAND AND WESTMORLAND ANTIQUARIAN AND ARCHAEOLOGICAL SOCIETY. *Hon. Sec.*, R. Hall, 2 High Tenterfell, Kendal, Cumbria LA9 4PG.

Derbyshire.—DERBYSHIRE ARCHAEOLOGICAL SOCIETY. *Hon. Sec.*, M. E. Burrows, 12 Wilne Road, Draycott, Derby DE7 3NG.

Devonshire.—DEVON ARCHAEOLOGICAL SOCIETY, Royal Albert Memorial Museum, Queen Street, Exeter EX4 3RX.

Dorset.—DORSET NATURAL HISTORY AND ARCHAEOLOGICAL SOCIETY, Dorset County Museum, Dorchester DT1 1XA. *Sec.*, R. N. R. Peers.

Durham.—DURHAM AND NORTHUMBERLAND ARCHITECTURAL AND ARCHAEOLOGICAL SOCIETY. *Hon. Sec.*, R. Daniels, 56 Welldeck Road, Hartlepool, Cleveland TS26 8JS.

Essex.—ESSEX SOCIETY FOR ARCHAEOLOGY AND HISTORY, Hollytrees Museum, High Street, Colchester CO1 1UG. *Sec.*, N. P. Wickenden.

Gloucestershire.—BRISTOL AND GLOUCESTERSHIRE ARCHAEOLOGICAL SOCIETY. *Hon. Sec.*, D. J. H. Smith, 22 Beaumont Road, Gloucester GL2 0EJ.

Hampshire.—HAMPSHIRE FIELD CLUB AND ARCHAEOLOGICAL SOCIETY. *Hon. Sec.*, Dr. M. A. Hicks, King Alfred's College, Winchester, Hants. SO22 4NR.

Herefordshire.—WOOLHOPE NATURALISTS' FIELD CLUB. *Hon. Sec.*, J. W. Tonkin, FSA, Chy an Whyloryon, Wigmore, Leominster, Herefordshire HR6 9UD.

Hertfordshire.—EAST HERTFORDSHIRE ARCHAEOLOGICAL SOCIETY. *Hon. Sec.*, Mrs. M. C. Readman, 1 Marsh Lane, Stanstead Abbots, Ware, Herts. SG12 8HH.

    ST. ALBANS AND HERTFORDSHIRE ARCHITECTURAL AND ARCHAEOLOGICAL SOCIETY. *Hon. Sec.*, B. E. Moody, 24 Rose Walk, St. Albans, Herts. AL4 9AF.

Isle of Wight.—ISLE OF WIGHT NATURAL HISTORY AND ARCHAEOLOGICAL SOCIETY. *Hon. Sec.*, Mrs. T. Goodley, Ivy Cottage, New Barn Lane, Shorwell, Newport, IOW, PO30 3JQ.

Kent.—KENT ARCHAEOLOGICAL SOCIETY. *Hon. Gen. Sec.*, A. C. Harrison, FSA, Prings Cottage, Pilgrims Road, Upper Halling, Rochester ME2 1HR.

Lancashire.— HISTORIC SOCIETY OF LANCASHIRE AND CHESHIRE. *Hon. Sec.*, Mrs. G. M. Wyatt, 302 Prescot Road, Aughton, Ormskirk, Lancs. L39 6RR.

Leicestershire.—LEICESTERSHIRE ARCHAEOLOGICAL AND HISTORICAL SOCIETY, The Guildhall, Leicester LE1 5FQ. *Hon. Sec.*, Dr. A. D. McWhirr.

London and Middlesex.—CITY OF LONDON ARCHAEOLOGICAL SOCIETY. *Hon. Sec.*, Ms. M. Andrews, 19 Hawes Road, Bromley, Kent BR1 3JS.

    LONDON AND MIDDLESEX ARCHAEOLOGICAL SOCIETY. *Hon. Sec.*, Miss J. Macdonald, 3 Cedar Drive, Pinner, Middx. HA5 4DD.

Norfolk.—NORFOLK AND NORWICH ARCHAEOLOGICAL SOCIETY. *Hon. Gen. Sec.*, R. Bellinger, 30 Brettingham Avenue, Norwich NR4 6XG.

Northumberland and Tyne and Wear.—SOCIETY OF ANTIQUARIES OF NEWCASTLE UPON TYNE, Black Gate, Castle Garth, Newcastle upon Tyne NE1 1RQ. *Secs.*, D. Cutts; Dr. C. M. Fraser.

    SUNDERLAND ANTIQUARIAN SOCIETY. *Hon. Sec.*, Mrs. V. M. Stevens, 16 Grizedale Court, Seaburn Dene, Sunderland SR6 8JP.

Oxfordshire.—OXFORDSHIRE ARCHITECTURAL AND HISTORICAL SOCIETY, Ashmolean Museum, Oxford OX1 2PH. *Hon. Sec.*, D. Dawson.

Shropshire.—SHROPSHIRE ARCHAEOLOGICAL AND HISTORICAL SOCIETY. *Chairman*, J. B. Lawson, Westcott Farm, Pontesbury, Shrewsbury SY5 0SQ.

Somerset.—SOMERSET ARCHAEOLOGICAL AND NATURAL HISTORY SOCIETY, Taunton Castle, Taunton, Somerset TA1 4AD. *Hon. Sec.*, B. Watkin.

Staffordshire.—CITY OF STOKE-ON-TRENT MUSEUM ARCHAEOLOGICAL SOCIETY, City Museum and Art Gallery, Hanley, Stoke-on-Trent. *Chairman*, E. E. Royle.

Suffolk.—SUFFOLK INSTITUTE OF ARCHAEOLOGY AND HISTORY. *Hon. Sec.*, E. A. Martin, Oak Tree Farm, Finborough Road, Hitcham, Ipswich IP7 7LS.

Surrey.—SURREY ARCHAEOLOGICAL SOCIETY, Castle Arch, Guildford, Surrey GU1 3SX. *Hon. Secs.*, Mr. and Mrs. K. D. Graham.

Sussex.—SUSSEX ARCHAEOLOGICAL SOCIETY, Barbican House, High Street, Lewes, E. Sussex BN7 1YE. *Exec. Sec.*, D. P. White.

Warwickshire.—BIRMINGHAM AND WARWICKSHIRE ARCHAEOLOGICAL SOCIETY, c/o Birmingham and Midland Institute, Margaret Street, Birmingham B3 3BS. *Hon. Sec.*, A. J. Wilson.

Wiltshire.—WILTSHIRE ARCHAEOLOGICAL AND NATURAL HISTORY SOCIETY, The Museum, 41 Long Street, Devizes SN10 1NS. *Sec.*, G. G. Brown.

Worcestershire.—WORCESTERSHIRE ARCHAEOLOGICAL SOCIETY. *Hon. Sec.*, Mrs. G. Grice, 91 Hallow Road, Worcester WR2 6DF.

Yorkshire.—YORKSHIRE ARCHAEOLOGICAL SOCIETY. *Hon. Sec.*, P. B. Davidson, Claremont, 23 Clarendon Road, Leeds LS2 9NZ.

    HALIFAX ANTIQUARIAN SOCIETY. *Hon. Sec.*, J. A. Hargreaves, 7 Hyde Park Gardens, Haugh Shaw Road, Halifax, W. Yorks. HX1 3AH.

    THORESBY SOCIETY. *Hon. Sec.*, D. M. Watson. Claremont, 23 Clarendon Road, Leeds LS2 9NZ.

Channel Islands

SOCIETE JERSIAISE, Archaeological Section, La Hougue Bie Museum, Grouville, Jersey. *Hon. Sec.*, Ms. J. D. Aubin.

Scotland

AYRSHIRE ARCHAEOLOGICAL AND NATURAL HISTORY SOCIETY. *Hon. Sec.*, Dr. T. Mathews, 10 Longlands Park, Ayr KA7 4RJ.

DUMFRIESSHIRE AND GALLOWAY NATURAL HISTORY AND ANTIQUARIAN SOCIETY. *Hon. Sec.*, 13 Douglas Terrace, Lockerbie, Dumfriesshire DG11 2DZ.

HAWICK ARCHAEOLOGICAL SOCIETY. *Hon. Sec.*, I. W. Landles, Orrock House, Stirches Road, Hawick, Roxburghshire TD9 7HF.

INVERNESS FIELD CLUB. *Hon. Sec.*, Miss I. McLean, 6 Drumblair Crescent, Inverness IV2 4RG.

Wales

Dyfed.—CEREDIGION ANTIQUARIAN SOCIETY. *Hon. Sec.*, I. M. Jones, Dolau-gwyn, Dole, Bow Street, Dyfed SY24 5AE.

Gwynedd.—ANGLESEY ANTIQUARIAN SOCIETY. *Hon. Sec.*, S. C. G. Caffell, 1 Fronheulog Sling, Tregarth, Bangor LL57 4RD.

Powys.—POWYSLAND CLUB. *Hon. Sec.*, W. G. J. Hughes, Library, Brook Street, Welshpool, Powys SY21 7PH.

    RADNORSHIRE SOCIETY. *Hon. Sec.*, Coley Powys, Llandrindod Wells, Powys LD1 5ES.

PRINCIPAL CHARITABLE BEQUESTS OF THE YEAR

The alphabetical list below represents some of the principal charitable bequests from Wills published since the last edition. The exact amounts available for charities are not known, as prior bequests, testamentary expenses and inheritance tax are all deductible from the net figures given, and, in a few cases, there are prior life interests in the income from estates.

This year the highest estate shown is £6·6 million, though more than 40 estates have a net value of over £1 million. One of the largest single charitable bequests this year was the bulk of the £3·8 million estate of Violet Abbott, which was left to the Marie Curie Memorial Foundation. It is understood that the bequest will be sufficient to build and equip a new home for the Foundation. The Foundation also shared some of the residue of the £4·1 million estate of Grace Anderson with the Imperial Cancer Research Fund, British Heart Foundation and the Sussex Stroke and Circulation Fund at Brighton. She first left a sufficient sum to the RNLI to build and equip a lifeboat in her name. Dora Foster also left the residue of her £990,054 estate to the RNLI for a lifeboat to be known as *RNLI Dora Foster McDougall*, and Ruby Clery left the residue of her £878,913 estate to the RNLI, stating that 'I have a personal feeling for this fine institution as it was founded by my great-great-grandfather'. (She did not give his name.)

The National Trust received several large bequests. Sarah Atkinson left them the residue of her £1·2 million estate, with £4,000 to be spent in the Lake District National Park. Helena Levy left seven eighths of the residue of her £6·6 million estate to the National Trust, and Dorothy Long left all her £750,797 estate to the Trust. Two others in the list who also left their entire estates for charity were Henry Bright, who left £1·2 million to be shared between the Imperial Cancer Research Fund, Guide Dogs for the Blind Association, Spastics Society and the Multiple Sclerosis Society, and Ralph Sperring, who left £2·4 million to such charities as his trustees decide.

The Marchioness of Willingdon left most of her £2·5 million estate variously to a number of charities, including the Dartmoor Pony Society, Ponies of Britian Club, National Pony Society, Arab Horse Society, Home of Rest for Horses at Aylesbury and 'Equine Research at Newmarket'. Dame Frances Qvist, the cardiologist and former Dean and President of the Medical School of the Royal Free Hospital, London, left the bulk of her £1·6 million estate between that Medical School and the Royal College of Surgeons. The Save the Children Fund received the residue of the £581,860 estate of Anita Ryan, a well-known Silk at the Family Bar, who appeared in many leading cases concerning children.

Eleanor Long left the residue of her £1·1 million estate to Fight for Sight, 'in appreciation of the great help Sir Stewart Duke-Elder gave to me thereby saving my sight'. After a personal legacy of £500, Marion Lovell left the rest of her £493,083 estate to the RSPCA. This was probably the longest-standing charitable gift of all time, since she made it in a Will in 1935, never afterwards updated.

Other notable charitable bequests not appearing in the list include those made by Sir George (Gubby) Allen, former president of the MCC, who left 15 per cent of the residue of his £928,987 estate to the MCC, part for encouraging youth cricket and part for helping old cricketers and their families in distress. He also left 8 per cent of the residue to Middlesex County Cricket Club Centenary Youth Trust and 2 per cent to the Association of Cricket Umpires. Mabel Pickles left the residue of her £295,798 estate to the School for Spastics named after her famous brother

Wilfred. Lady Dorothy Foot, widow of Sir Dingle Foot, the former solicitor-general and Ipswich MP, left one quarter of the residue of her £307,220 estate to the Honourable Society of Gray's Inn, and the rest among a number of other charities, including several in Ipswich. Lastly the RNIB received nearly all the £132,364 estate of Anna Melandri. They will have to wait a while for this bequest, however, as she first left the entire income for the upkeep for life of her cat Whisky.

Miss Violet Alice **Abbott**, of Erdington, Birmingham £3,896,806
(The residue to the Marie Curie Memorial Foundation)

Bridget Holmes **A'Court**, of Henstridge, Somerset £640,000
(The residue to the Injured Jockeys Fund)

Diane Dando **Allen**, of Tettenhall, West Midlands £910,266
(£5,000 and one eighth of the residue each to the PDSA (Wolverhampton Branch), International League for the Protection of Horses, National Anti-Vivisection Society, National Animal Rescue Kennels, Donkey Sanctuary, Sidmouth, and the Seal Preservation Action Group)

Rt. Hon. Anne Lorina, Baroness **Allerton**, of Loddington, Leics £5,968,201
(The residue, on the death of her husband, for such charities as her executors appoint, otherwise to the Anne Allerton Fund)

Mrs Esme Grace **Anderson**, of Grosvenor Square, London W1 .... £4,101,137
(Half the residue as to a sufficient sum to the RNLI to build and equip a lifeboat, and the remainder equally between the Marie Curie Memorial Foundation, Imperial Cancer Research Fund, British Heart Foundation and Sussex Stroke and Circulation Fund, Brighton)

Ada **Appleton**, of Breaston, Derbyshire ... £652,062
(The residue equally between the RNLI, Leukaemia Research Fund, and Kidney Research Aid Fund, London)

Elizabeth **Arrand**, of Birmingham £1,210,381
(The residue equally between St. Mary's Parish Church, Handsworth, City of Birmingham Symphony Orchestra Endowment Fund, Birmingham Eye Foundation for the Prevention of Blindness, Moorfields Eye Hospital, London, and Guide Dogs for the Blind Association)

Miss Sarah Muriel **Atkinson**, of Ulverston, Cumbria £1,242,319
(The residue to the National Trust)

Mrs. Mary Drucilla Helena Margaret Vere **Bamber**, of Fairhaven, Lancs £962,367
(One seventh of the residue each to St. Cuthbert's Church, Lytham, the RSPCA, PDSA, RNLI, RAF Benevolent Fund, Guide Dogs for the Blind Association and the RNIB Sunshine Homes)

Moira Morrison **Barrie**, of Broadway, Worcs. £2,356,397
(Two elevenths of the residue to the RNLI, and one eleventh of the residue each to the National Trust, Guide Dogs for the Blind Association, British Red Cross Society, Cancer Research Campaign, St. Dunstan's, Animal Welfare Trust, Royal College of Surgeons, World Wildlife Fund and RUKBA)

Judith Amelia **Bartram**, of Felmingham, Norfolk £1,875,325
(£10,000 and one third of the residue to St. James Church, Southrepps, and £5,000 and one third of the residue each to St. Mary's Church, Antingham, and St. Andrew's Church, Felmingham)

Maurice Eric Fitzhardinge Murray **Berkeley**, of North Bovey, Devon £564,553
(The residue equally between Exeter Cathedral Preservation Trust and the National Trust)

Doris **Bleasdale**, of Lancaster £1,161,568
(The residue equally between the RSPCA, partly for the Lancaster Branch, and the RNLI)

John **Boddy**, of Bridlington, North Humberside £761,036
(The residue equally between Bridlington Priory Church Restoration Fund, RNLI, Bridlington, St. Catherine's Hospice, Scarborough, Arthritis and Rheumatism Council, Barnardo's, Sue Ryder Foundation, Parkinson's Disease Society, Guide Dogs for the Blind Association and Royal Society for Mentally Handicapped Children and Adults)

Lady Charlotte Helen **Bonham-Carter**, of Alton, Hants. £4,904,151
(The residue to the Charlotte Bonham-Carter Charitable Trust)

Leslie **Boothman**, of Scarborough, North Yorks. £705,498
(15 per cent of the residue to the York Civic Trust, and 85 per cent of the residue equally between the Salvation Army, for work in Scarborough, St. Dunstan's and Distressed Gentlefolk's Aid Association)

James Jerram **Briggs**, of Palace Gate, London W8 .... £944,442
(One third of the residue for such charitable purposes as his Trustees determine within two years of his death)

Henry **Bright**, of Lupus Street, London SW1 .... £1,275,672
(His entire estate equally between the Imperial Cancer Research Fund, Guide Dogs for the Blind Association, Spastics Society and Multiple Sclerosis Society)

John Henshaw **Britton**, CBE, of Pucklechurch, Avon. £1,939,197
(One third of the residue to the J. & M. Britton Charitable Trust)

Mrs Ruth Evelyn **Campbell**, of Kew, Surrey £606,706
(The residue to the Imperial Cancer Research Fund)

Henry Holmes **Candy**, of Southampton .. £1,686,786
(The residue equally between the RSPCA, World Wildlife Fund and RSPB)

Roy Leonard **Cann**, of Sheffield, South Yorks. £927,617
(The residue for such charitable purposes as his Trustees select)

Eva **Chayton**, of Wentworth, Surrey £1,227,684
(The residue for such charitable purposes as her Trustees think fit)

Ruby Alexandra **Clery**, of Eamont Street, London NW8 .... £878,913
(The residue to the RNLI)

Lore Leni **Cowan**, of Bushey Heath, Herts. £1,455,871
(The residue to Help the Aged)

Dorothy **Creery**, of Nant Road, London NW2 .... £755,054
(The residue equally between the Marie Curie Memorial Foundation, Spastics Society, RNLI and British Wireless for the Blind Fund)

Ronald Henry **Cross**, of Bournemouth, Dorset £3,273,187
(The residue equally between Age Concern England, Oxfam, Children's Society, British Heart Foundation and British Red Cross Society)

Mrs Phyllis Mary **Currie**, of Great Leighs, Essex £6,021,983
(£5,000, some land and one fifteenth of the residue to the Essex Naturalists Trust, and one fifteenth of the residue each to the PDSA, World

Wildlife Fund, National Canine Defence League, Animal Health Trust, Home of Rest For Horses, Aylesbury, Wildfowl Trust, Imperial Cancer Research Fund, RSPB, RNIB, British Deaf Association, Battersea Dogs Home, Donkey Sanctuary, Sidmouth, British Field Sports Society and the Chelmsford Hospice)

Harold Hibbert **Dale**, of Buxton, Derbyshire £678,039
(The residue to the Population Services Family Planning Programme, London)

Marguerite **Dane**, of Cambridge £496,892
(Half the residue to Barnardo's, and one quarter of the residue each to the National Children's Home and Royal London Society for the Blind)

Mrs Kathleen Ann **Davies**, of Canford Cliffs, Dorset £1,382,108
(One quarter of the residue for such charitable purposes as her Trustees select)

Nansi Gwyneth **Davies**, of Sidmouth, Devon £994,326
(The residue equally between the Salvation Army and Barnardo's)

Miss Mary Esther **Dean**, of Park Road, London NW1 .... £1,050,529
(The residue equally between the Tavistock Clinic, London, the Maudsley Hospital, London, the Melanie Klein Trust, London, the Westminster Society for Mentally Handicapped Children and Adults, RSPCA, Donkey Sanctuary, Sidmouth, National Trust, and Great Ormond Street Children's Hospital, London)

Robert Nicholson **Elmhirst**, of Frinton-on-Sea, Essex £1,119,129
(Half the residue equally between the Ernest Luff Home, Frinton-on-Sea, Ex-Services Mental Welfare Society, Marie Curie Memorial Foundation, RNLI, Pestalozzi Children's Village Trust, RUKBA, Salvation Army, Age Concern England, St. Joseph's Hospice, London, NSPCC, Royal Commonwealth Society for the Blind, London City Mission, the John A. Thompson Memorial Trust, Southsea, Hants., and the Evangelism Centre, Bedworth, Warwickshire)

Hon. Sylvia May **Fletcher-Moulton**, CBE, of Barcombe, East Sussex £1,185,353
(One eighth of the residue to the RSPB, and one sixteenth of the residue each to the Salvation Army, Severn Wildfowl Trust, British Red Cross Society and Guide Dogs for the Blind Association)

Dora **Foster**, of Bowdon, Greater Manchester £990,054
(The residue to the RNLI, for the provision of a lifeboat)

Ann Darwin **Fox**, of Southwold, Suffolk ... £799,180
(The residue to the A. D. B. Fox Charitable Settlement)

Miss Grace Hilary **Goodwin**, of Gillingham, Kent £859,847
(12 properties in Gillingham to Help the Aged, and the residue equally between the International League for Protection of Horses, Women's Holiday Fund, London, Distressed Gentlefolk's Aid Association, Hostel of God, London, Brooke Hospital for Animals, London, RNIB, Universities Federation for Animal Welfare, SPANA, Anglo-Italian Society for Protection of Animals, Greek Animal Welfare Fund, Winged Fellowship Trust, Invalid Children's Aid Association, Ex-Services Mental Welfare Society and Marie Curie Memorial Foundation)

Mrs Edith Winifred **Griffiths**, of Leamington Spa, Warwickshire £1,267,726
(The residue equally between the Spastics Society, Birmingham, Royal Midland Counties Home for the Disabled, Leamington Spa, Guide Dogs

for the Blind Association, Leamington Spa, and the Multiple Sclerosis Society, for use in Leamington Spa)

Elsa Grunberg, of Hendon Lane, London N3...£702,171
(The residue equally between the JNF Charitable Trust and the Central British Fund for World Jewish Relief)

Sheila Alma Halliday, of Sutton Scotney, Hants. £846,991
(The residue equally between the Church Army, Imperial Cancer Research Fund, Distressed Gentlefolk's Aid Association, and the Langley House Trust, Compton, Winchester)

Mrs. Dorothy Cynthia Hayward, of Kelmarsh, Northants. £980,608
(The residue to any charitable settlement made by her in her lifetime, otherwise to the one which founded the British Veterinary Association Animal Welfare Foundation)

Helen Elizabeth Blakey Higinbotham, of Gerrards Cross, Bucks. £1,621,304
(Half the residue to the Imperial Cancer Research Fund, one quarter of the residue to the RNLI, and one eighth of the residue each to the Methodist Homes for the Aged and the Royal College of Obstetricians and Gynaecologists)

Mrs Elizabeth Marian Greenway Hocken, of Welshpool, Powys £639,728
(The residue equally between St. Asaph Diocesan Clergy Widows, Orphans and Dependants Fund, Bangor Diocesan Clergy Widows, Orphans and Dependants Society, USPG, and St. Luke's Hostel, London)

Mary Josephine Hodgson, of Torquay, Devon...£851,951
(Four fifths of the residue to Lady Margaret Hall, Oxford, and one fifth of the residue to Age Concern England)

Godfrey William Iredell, of Braithwaite, Keswick, Cumbria..£640,126
(The residue to Lancaster University, to form the Barbara Dorothy Iredell Trust, to advance the study of law and/or history there)

David Gersom Higgs Jarman, of Llanidloes, Powys..£1,345,992
(The residue equally between the Cheshire Foundation, Barnardo's, Save the Children Fund, Christian Aid, Oxfam, War on Want, Help the Aged, Insitute of Cancer Research, LEPRA, British Home and Hospital for Incurables, London, Marie Curie Memorial Foundation, British Red Cross Society and Voluntary Service Overseas)

James Howard Jellyman, of Lancaster....£603,731
(The residue equally between the RNLI, St. Dunstan's, John Groom's and Barnardo's)

Ada Madeline Johns, of West Wickham, Kent...£1,040,144
(The residue for such charitable purposes as her Trustees think fit)

Dr. Edmund Dugdale Jones, of Winchelsea, E. Sussex £1,447,954
(The residue equally between the Friends of Winchelsea Church, British Heart Foundation and Arthritis and Rheumatism Council)

Mrs. Janet Spalding Kay, of Garstang, Lancs..£1,032,207
(The residue equally between St. John's Hospice, Lancaster, Cancer Research Campaign, Abbeyfield Society, Lancaster, Salvation Army, the Lancaster Charity, Barnardo's, Order of St. John, Guide Dogs for the Blind Association, Association for All Speech Impaired Children, Help the Aged, Save the Children Fund and the Ulverscroft Foundation)

Eric James Keeble, of York £962,092
(Half the residue for such charities for the relief of persons suffering from mental disorder and half the residue for such charities for servicemen and servicewomen and ex-servicemen and ex-servicewomen, in each case as his Trustees select)

Marjorie Logan Johnstone Kirke, of Middle Coombe, Dorset £753,747
(The residue equally between the Distressed Gentlefolk's Aid Association, RNID, Glasgow, National Trust for Scotland, the Scottish National Institute for War Blinded, and the Rehabilitation Centre for Scottish War Wounded, Erskine)

Mrs Reize Last, of Bancroft Avenue, London N2...£1,817,428
(The residue for such charities for the relief of elderly Jewish people of limited means as her Trustees decide)

Victor Morley Lawson, of Queens Gate Gardens, London SW7..£3,153,083
(The residue to the Central British Fund for World Jewish Relief)

Mrs Helena Katherine Greville Levy, of Cadogan Square, London SW1 ....£6,676,431
(Seven eighths of the residue to the National Trust and one eighth of the residue to the Historic Churches Preservation Trust)

Mrs Jeanne Delphine Liwski, of Wolverhampton, West Midlands £1,123,855
(One fifth of her estate equally between the Guide Dogs for the Blind Association, Cheshire Foundation, the Birmingham Diocesan Rescue Society, the Maison Français de Retraite et de Convalescence, Brighton, Barnardo's, Distressed Gentlefolk's Aid Association, Marie Curie Memorial Foundation, Salvation Army, British Red Cross Society, and the Abbeyfield Society, for the home at Tettenhall)

Mrs Dorothy Annie Long, of Milton Ernest, Beds...£750,797
(Her entire estate to the National Trust)

Mrs Eleanor Long, of Hyde Park Square, London W2 ....£1,197,647
(The residue to Fight for Sight, London)

Marion Constance Lovell, of Northampton £493,083
(The residue to the RSPCA)

Charlotte Marx, of Wellington Road, London NW6...£901,428
(Three twenty-fifths of the residue to the British Committee of the General Israel Orphans Home for Girls, Jerusalem, and one twenty-fifth of the residue each to the Weizmann Institute Foundation, London, Leo Baeck Women's Lodge, London, Israel Cancer Association, AJR Charitable Trust Fund, and the Belsize Square Synagogue Welfare Fund, London)

Oscar William Orlando May, of Faversham, Kent...£916,234
(The residue for such charitable purposes in the UK as two nominees select)

Hedley Jack Meek, of Beaconsfield, Bucks...£3,913,707
(Half the residue to the British and Foreign Bible Society, one fifth of the residue to the Billy Graham Evangelist Association, and one tenth of the residue each to the Encounters Ministries Trust, Worldwide Evangelization Crusade, and Westminster Chapel, London)

Bertha Susanna Michael, of Legbourne, Louth, Lincs...£1,010,069
(The residue equally between the Cancer Research Campaign and RNIB)

Eileen Spencer Morris, of George Street, London W1 ....£904,890
(Half the residue to the USPG, and one quarter

of the residue each to the Notting Hill Housing Trust and Church Army)

Mrs Gweneth **Moxon**, of Sidmouth, Devon . £722,643
(The residue to the Mrs Gweneth Moxon Charitable Trust)

John Frank **Musson**, of Bradford, West Yorks £596,770
(The residue to the W.Riding Masonic Charities)

Wilfred **Noble**, of Oakerthorpe, Derbyshire £783,250
(The residue equally between Derbyshire Royal Infirmary, Imperial Cancer Research Fund, RNIB and British Heart Foundation)

Edna **Orford**, of Cooden, East Sussex £1,057,748
(The residue to the Bernard Sunley Charitable Foundation, to build homes for the elderly in or near Truro, Cornwall)

Miss Betty **Phillips**, of Clevedon, Avon. ... £762,294
(The residue to the Clifton Charitable Trust, Bristol)

Mary Florence Robertine **Pitt**, of Walton on Thames, Surrey £1,183,368
(The residue equally between the Royal Medical Benevolent Fund, RNLI and Help the Aged)

Dame Frances Violet **Qvist**, DBE, MD, FRCP, of Fitzroy Park, London N6 .... £1,628,076
(£100,000 and half the residue to the Royal Free Hospital School of Medicine, London, and £50,000, certain royalties and half the residue to the Royal College of Surgeons)

Walter Edward Metcalfe **Radbill**, of Menston, Ilkley, West Yorks £608,327
(The residue equally between St. Gemma's Hospice, Leeds, Yorkshire Cancer Research Campaign, Arthritis and Rheumatism Council and British Heart Foundation)

Mrs Jessie Margaret Isabel **Reglar**, of Kingston, Sturminster Newton, Dorset £540,071
(The residue equally between the Multiple Sclerosis Society, and 'Home for Incurables', SW16)

Avis Ursula **Rekstin**, of Westcott, Dorking, Surrey £1,444,495
(Half her estate equally between the First Church of Christ Scientist, Dorking, the Second Church of Christ Scientist, London W8, and Camphill Village Trust)

Elizabeth Florence Theodosia **Royds**, of Sandbach, Cheshire £3,393,511
(The residue equally between PDSA, RSPCA, Langley House Trust, Compton, Winchester, Leprosy Mission, Save the Children Fund, Oxfam, Christian Aid, and NSPCC, N. Staffs. Branch)

Miss Carrie Brenda Muriel **Rudolf**, of Dean Road, London NW2 .... £1,007,383
(The residue for such charitable purposes as her Trustees think fit)

Miss Anita Mary **Ryan**, QC, of Orme Court Mews, London W2 .... £581,860
(The residue to the Save the Children Fund)

Mrs Gladys Maud **Sherman**, of Rustington, West Sussex £1,090,940
(The residue for charities for the protection and benefit of animals and birds, as Trustees select)

Miss Anna **Simons**, of Hove, East Sussex .. £635,279
(The residue equally between the Jewish Blind and Physically Handicapped Society, Cancer Research Campaign, Brighton and Hove Branch, Salvation Army, and St. Christopher's School, Bristol)

Ralph Dunford **Sperring**, of Midsomer Norton, Avon £2,454,896
(His entire estate for such charities as his Trustees decide)

Minnie Kathleen **Sturdy**, of York £1,808,900
(The residue equally between the Wilberforce Home for the Multiple Handicapped Blind, York, St. Leonard's Hospice, York, Cancer Research

Campaign, British Heart Foundation, London Association for the Blind, World Wildlife Fund and British Red Cross Society)

Ronald Ernest **Summerfield**, of Cheltenham, Glos. £3,964,358
(The residue to the Summerfield Charitable Trust)

Mrs Anne Guild Craig **Sutermeister**, of Eaton Mews North, London SW1 .... £625,522
(The residue equally between the Wood Green Animal Shelter, PDSA, Scottish Society for the Prevention of Vivisection, International League for Protection of Horses, RNIB, SSAFA and World Wildlife Fund)

Miss Mary **Taylor**, of Louth, Lincs. £1,108,937
(The residue equally between the Imperial Cancer Research Fund, British Heart Foundation and Arthritis and Rheumatism Council)

Mrs Audrey Stanley **Thornley**, of Rhosneigr, Anglesey, Gwynedd £1,548,606
(The residue equally between the Imperial Cancer Research Fund, RNLI, Save the Children Fund and Guide Dogs for the Blind Association)

Henry Russ **Thornton**, of Oakham, Leics... £606,513
(The residue to the Arthritis and Rheumatism Council)

Nicholas Alfred **Tooth**, of St. John's Wood Court, London NW8 .... £631,132
(The residue to the Terrence Higgins Trust)

Miss Thelma Louise **Verley**, of The Grampions, London W6 .... £503,433
(The residue to the Verley Home for Gentlewomen, Kingston, Jamaica)

Mrs Marjorie Elizabeth **White**, of Angmering-on-Sea, West Sussex £607,561
(The residue equally between RNLI, Marie Curie Memorial Foundation, Burma Star Association)

The Most Hon. Daphne, Marchioness of **Willingdon**, of Winkfield Row, Berks. £2,586,970
(The sale proceeds of some land and one fifteenth of residue to the World Wildlife Fund, £50,000 and one fifteenth of residue to the Fauna Preservation Society, £5,000, a statue and one fifteenth of residue to the Dartmoor Pony Society, £5,000 and one fifteenth of residue each to Cranbourne Church, Windsor Forest, the Ponies of Britain Club, Ascot, Berkshire Council of the Order of St. John, Arab Horse Society, 'Equine Research at Newmarket', Marie Curie Memorial Foundation, National Pony Society, Cancer Research Campaign, Home of Rest for Horses, Aylesbury, RNIB and SOS Society, some pictures and one fifteenth of residue to the Indian Museum at the Royal Military College, Sandhurst)

Gwendolen Eva **Willis**, of Branksome Park, Dorset £2,303,219
(The residue for such charitable institutions as her Trustee thinks fit)

Joan Mary **Young**, of Hove, East Sussex ... £641,693
(£6,000 and one seventeenth of residue to the RAF Benevolent Fund, £3,000 and one seventeenth of residue to the RAF Association, and one seventeenth of residue each to the Imperial Cancer Research Fund, Royal Commonwealth Society for the Blind, Crusade of Rescue and Homes for Destitute Catholic Children, Cheshire Foundation, Co-Workers of Mother Teresa, the Sisters of Grace and Compassion, Cross in Hand, East Sussex, House of Studies for Late Vocations, Osterley, Middx., Carmelite Priory, Aylesford, Kent, RNLI, British Red Cross Society, St. John Ambulance Service, British Heart Foundation, National Trust, Arthritis and Rheumatism Council, and the Trustees for Roman Catholic Purposes, for mission work outside Europe)

CONFEDERATION OF BRITISH INDUSTRY

Centre Point, 103 New Oxford Street, WC1A 1DU
[01-379 7400]

The Confederation of British Industry was founded in August 1965 and is an independent non-party political body financed by industry and commerce. It exists primarily to ensure that the Government understands the intentions, needs and problems of British business. It is the recognized spokesman for the business viewpoint and is consulted as such by the Government.

The CBI represents, directly and indirectly, some 250,000 companies. All the major nationalized industries are in membership and thereby able to work with the CBI on problems that are the concern of all management.

The governing body of the CBI is the 400-strong Council, which meets monthly in London under the chairmanship of the President. It is assisted by some 27 expert standing committees which advise on the main aspects of policy. There are 13 Regional Councils and offices covering the administrative regions of England, Wales, Scotland and Northern Ireland. There is also an office in Brussels.

President, Sir Brian Corby.
Director-General, J. Banham.
Secretary, M. W. Hunt.

NATIONAL ASSOCIATION OF INDUSTRIES FOR THE BLIND AND DISABLED INC.

Triton House, 43A High Street South,
Dunstable, Beds. LU6 3RZ
[0582-606796]

The National Association of Industries for the Blind and Disabled Inc. was established in 1929 and incorporated in 1936; it is registered as a charity.

The Association acts in the nature of a trade association providing facilities for consultation and co-operation between its members who operate workshops employing blind and disabled people. It represents their interests in discussions with, and

representations to, other organizations (e.g. government departments and local authorities) concerned with sheltered employment. It does not own or operate any of the workshops, which are run by local authorities or voluntary organizations acting as their agents.

Chairman (1990–91), J. J. Williams.
Hon. Secretary, G. J. Entwistle.

EMPLOYERS' AND TRADE BODIES

ADVERTISING ASSOCIATION, Abford House, 15 Wilton Road, SW1V 1NJ. (Tel: 071-828 2771).—*Dir. Gen.,* R. L. Wade.

AEROSPACE COMPANIES LTD., SOCIETY OF BRITISH, 29 King Street, SW1Y 6RD. (Tel: 071-839 3231).— *Dir.,* Sir Barry Duxbury, KCB, CBE.

BAKERS, FEDERATION OF, 20 Bedford Square, WC1B 3HF.—*Dir.,* A. Casdagli, CBE.

BANKERS' ASSOCIATION, BRITISH, 10 Lombard Street, EC3V 9EL. (Tel: 071-623 4001).—*Sec.-Gen.,* Lord Inchyra.

BREWERS' SOCIETY, 42 Portman Square, W1H 0BB. (Tel: 071-486 4831).—*Dir.,* Maj. Gen. W. D. Mangham, CB.

BUILDING EMPLOYERS' CONFEDERATION, 82 New Cavendish Street, W1M 8AD. (Tel: 071-580 5588).— *Dir. Gen.,* J. Owens.

BUILDING MATERIAL PRODUCERS, NATIONAL COUNCIL OF, 26 Store Street, WC1E 7BT. (Tel: 071-323 3770).—*Dir. Gen.,* N. M. Chaldecott, OBE.

BUS AND COACH COUNCIL, Sardinia House, 52 Lincoln's Inn Fields, WC2A 3LZ. (Tel: 071-831 7546).— *Dir. Gen.,* Mrs. A. V. M. Palmer, MBE.

CHEMICAL INDUSTRIES ASSOCIATION LTD., Kings Buildings, Smith Square, SW1P 3JJ. (Tel: 071-834 3399).—*Dir. Gen.,* J. C. L. Cox.

CLOTHING INDUSTRY ASSOCIATION LTD., BRITISH, British Apparel Centre, 7 Swallow Place, W1R 7AA.—*Dir.* J. R. Wilson.

DAIRY TRADE FEDERATION, 19 Cornwall Terrace, NW1 4QP. (Tel: 071-486 7244).—*Dir. Gen.,* J. P. Price.

ELECTROTECHNICAL AND ALLIED MANUFACTURERS' ASSOCIATIONS, FEDERATION OF BRITISH (BEAMA), Leicester House, 8 Leicester Street, WC2H 7BN.— *Dir. Gen.,* J. G. Gaddes.

ENGINEERING EMPLOYERS' FEDERATION, Broadway House, Tothill Street, SW1H 9NQ. (Tel: 071-222 7777).—*Dir. Gen.,* P. Brighton.

FARMERS' UNION, NATIONAL (NFU), Agriculture House, Knightsbridge, SW1X 7NJ. (Tel: 071-235 5077).—*Dir. Gen.,* D. Evans.

FARMERS' UNION OF SCOTLAND, NATIONAL, 17 Grosvenor Crescent, Edinburgh EH12 5EN. (Tel: 031-337 4333).—*Chief Exec.,* D. S. Johnston, OBE.

FARMERS' UNION, ULSTER, Dunedin, 475-477 Antrim Road, Belfast BT15 3DA. (Tel: 0232-370222).—*Gen. Sec.,* J. V. Smyth.

FINANCE HOUSES ASSOCIATION, 18 Upper Grosvenor Street, W1X 9PB. (Tel: 071-491 2783).—*Dir.,* N. A. D. Grant, CBE.

FOOD AND DRINK FEDERATION, 6 Catherine Street, WC2B 5JJ.—*Dir. Gen.,* M. P. Mackenzie.

FREIGHT TRANSPORT ASSOCIATION LTD., Hermes House, 157 St. John's Road, Tunbridge Wells, Kent TN4 9UZ. (Tel: 0892-26171).—*Dir.-Gen.,* G. Turvey.

INSURERS, ASSOCIATION OF BRITISH, Aldermary House, 10-15 Queen Street, EC4N 1TT. (Tel: 071-248 4477).—*Chief Exec.,* M. A. Jones.

KNITTING INDUSTRIES FEDERATION LTD., 7 Gregory Boulevard, Nottingham NG7 6NB.—*Dir.*, J. P. Harrison.

LEATHER CONFEDERATION, BRITISH, Leather Trade House, Kings Park Road, Moulton Park, Northampton NN3 1JD. (Tel: 0604–494131).—*Dir.*, R. L. Sykes, OBE, Ph.D.

LEATHER PRODUCERS' ASSOCIATION, Leather Trade House, Kings Park Road, Moulton Park, Northampton NN3 1JD. (Tel: 0604–494131).—*Nat. Sec.*, J. Purvis.

MANAGEMENT CONSULTANCIES ASSOCIATION, 11 West Halkin Street, SW1X 8JL. (Tel: 071–235 3897).— *Exec. Dir.*, B. O'Rorke.

MAN-MADE FIBRES FEDERATION, BRITISH, British Apparel and Textiles Centre, 7 Swallow Place, W1R 7AA. (Tel: 071–491 9704).—*Dir.*, G. D. Myers.

MARINE INDUSTRIES FEDERATION, BRITISH, Boating Industry House, Vale Road, Oatlands Park, Weybridge, Surrey KT13 9NS.—*Chief Exec.*, P. V. Wagstaffe.

MOTOR MANUFACTURERS AND TRADERS LTD., SOCIETY OF, Forbes House, Halkin Street, SW1X 7DS.—*Dir.*, S. R. Foster.

NEWSPAPER PUBLISHERS ASSOCIATION LTD., 34 Southwark Bridge Road, SE1 9EU. (Tel: 071–928 6928).— *Dir.*, J. E. Lepage.

OFFICE SYSTEMS AND STATIONERY FEDERATION, BRITISH, 6 Wimpole Street, W1M 8AS.—*Dir.*, D. F. Hall.

PAPER AND BOARD INDUSTRY FEDERATION, BRITISH, Papermakers House, Rivenhall Road, Westlea, Swindon SN5 7BE. (Tel: 0793–886086).—*Dir. Gen.*, W. J. Bartlett.

PLASTICS FEDERATION, BRITISH, 5 Belgrave Square, SW1X 8PD.—*Dir.*, D. R. Jones.

PORTS FEDERATION, BRITISH, Victoria House, Vernon Place, WC1B 4LL. (Tel: 071–242 1200).—*Managing Dir.* J. Sharples.

PRINTING INDUSTRIES FEDERATION, BRITISH, 11 Bedford Row, WC1R 4DX. (Tel: 071–242 6904).—*Dir. Gen.*, C. Stanley.

PUBLISHERS ASSOCIATION, 19 Bedford Square, WC1B 3HJ. (Tel: 071–580 6321).—*Chief Exec.*, C. Bradley.

RADIO CONTRACTORS LTD., ASSOCIATION OF INDEPENDENT, Radio House, 46 Westbourne Grove, W2 5SH. (Tel: 071–727 2646).—*Chief Exec.*, B. West.

RETAIL CONSORTIUM, Bedford House, 69–79 Fulham High Street, SW6 3JW. (Tel: 071–371 5177).—*Dir. Gen.*, J. N. W. May.

RETAIL NEWSAGENTS, NATIONAL FEDERATION OF, Yeoman House, Sekforde Street, EC1R 0HD. (Tel: 071–253 4225).—*Chief Exec.*, K. E. J. Peters.

ROAD FEDERATION LTD., BRITISH, Pillar House, 194– 202 Old Kent Road, SE1 5TG. (Tel: 071–703 9769).— *Dir.*, P. J. Witt.

ROAD HAULAGE ASSOCIATION LTD., Roadway House, 35 Monument Hill, Weybridge, Surrey KT13 8RN. (Tel: 0932–841515).—*Dir. Gen.*, D. B. H. Colley, CB, CBE.

RUBBER MANUFACTURERS' ASSOCIATION LTD., BRITISH, 90–91 Tottenham Court Road, W1P 0BR.— *Dir.*, G. C. Gullan.

SHIPPING, GENERAL COUNCIL OF BRITISH, 30–32 St. Mary Axe, EC3A 8ET. (Tel: 071–283 2922).—*Dir. Gen.*, P. Le Cheminant, CB.

SPORTS AND ALLIED INDUSTRIES FEDERATION LTD., BRITISH, 23 Brighton Road, Croydon CR2 4EA.— *Chief Exec.*, L. F. Standen.

TELEVISION ASSOCIATION, INDEPENDENT, Knighton House, 56 Mortimer Street, W1N 8AN. (Tel: 071– 636 6866).—*Dir.*, D. Shaw.

TEXTILE CONFEDERATION, BRITISH, British Apparel and Textiles Centre, 7 Swallow Place, W1R 7AA. (Tel: 071–491 9702).—*Dir.*, C. M. Purvis.

TIMBER GROWERS' UNITED KINGDOM, Admel House, 24 High Street, SW19 5DX. (Tel: 081–944 6340).— *Chief Exec.*, A. R. Williams.

TIMBER MERCHANTS' ASSOCIATION, BRITISH, Stocking Lane, Hughenden Valley, High Wycombe, Bucks. HP14 4JZ. (Tel: 024 024–3602).—*Sec.*, R. T. Allcorn.

TIMBER TRADE FEDERATION, Clareville House, 26–27 Oxendon Street, SW1Y 4EL. (Tel: 071–839 1891).— *Dir. Gen.*, A. A. Lockyer, LVO.

UK OFFSHORE OPERATORS ASSOCIATION LTD., 3 Hans Crescent, SW1X 0LN. (Tel: 071–589 5255).—*Dir. Gen.*, Dr. H. W. D. Hughes, OBE.

UK PETROLEUM INDUSTRY ASSOCIATION LTD., 9 Kingsway, WC2B 6XH.—*Dir. Gen.*, Dr. I. D. G. Berwick.

WHOLESALE AND INDUSTRIAL DISTRIBUTORS, FEDERATION OF, The Old Post Office, Dunchideock, Exeter EX2 9TU.—*Dir.*, J. Hussey.

TRADES UNION CONGRESS (TUC)
Congress House, 23–28 Great Russell Street, WC1B 3LS
[071–636 4030]

The Trades Union Congress, founded in 1868, is a voluntary association of trade unions, the representatives of which meet annually to consider matters of common concern to their members. The Congress has met annually since 1871 and in recent years has met normally on the first Monday in September, its sessions extending through the succeeding four days. Congress is constituted by delegates of the affiliated unions on the basis of one delegate for every 5,000 members, or fraction thereof, on whose behalf affiliation fees are paid. Affiliated unions (in 1989–90) totalled 78 with an aggregate membership of 8,405,143 (women's membership, 2,861,143).

The main business of the annual Congress is to consider the report of its General Council dealing with the activities of the Congress year, along with motions from affiliated societies on questions of policy and organization.

The standing committees of the General Council are serviced by a full time staff appointed by the General Secretary, who is himself elected by Congress and who remains in office until the age of 65, subject to decision of Congress or the General Council.

Through the General Council and its committees the trade union movement maintains systematic relations with the Government and government departments, with the Confederation of British Industry and with a large number of other bodies. It is represented on the National Economic Development Council, the Health and Safety Commission, the council of the Advisory Conciliation and Arbitration Service and a number of other bodies.

Among powers vested in the General Council by consent of the unions in Congress is the responsibility of intervening in disputes and differences between affiliated organizations; if possible this is done through informal conciliation meetings under TUC auspices but where necessary a Disputes Committee is formed consisting of one member of the General Council and two senior officials of unions not involved in the dispute. This investigates the matter concerned and issues its findings.

Unions retain full control of their own affairs and the only sanctions which Congress can apply are suspension or exclusion from membership.

Chairman (1990–91), A. R. Smith (*National Union of Tailors and Garment Workers*).
General Secretary, N. D. Willis.

SCOTTISH TRADES UNION CONGRESS
16 Woodlands Terrace, Glasgow G3 6DF
[041–332 4946]

The Congress was formed in 1897 and acts as a national centre for the trade union movement in Scotland. In 1990 it consisted of 57 unions with a membership of 854,940 and 49 directly affiliated Trades Councils. The majority of the unions organize throughout Britain and affiliate on their membership in Scotland.

The Annual Congress in April elects a 35-member General Council on the basis of 7 industrial sections.

Chairperson, J. C. Lewis.
General Secretary, C. Christie.

TRADES UNIONS AFFILIATED TO TUC

A list of the trades unions affiliated to the Trades Union Congress at September 1, 1990. The number of members of each union is shown in parenthesis.

AMALGAMATED ASSOCIATION OF BEAMERS, TWISTERS AND DRAWERS (HAND AND MACHINE), THE (470), 27 Every Street, Nelson, Lancs. BB9 7NE. (Tel: 0282–64181).—*Gen. Sec.*, A. H. Edmondson.

AMALGAMATED ENGINEERING UNION (AEU) (741,647), 110 Peckham Road, SE15 5EL. (Tel: 071–703 4231).—*Gen. Sec.*, G. H. Laird, CBE.

AMALGAMATED SOCIETY OF TEXTILE WORKERS AND KINDRED TRADES (2,613), Foxlowe, Market Place, Leek, Staffs. ST13 6AD. (Tel: 0538–382068).—*Gen. Sec.*, A. Hitchmough.

ASSOCIATED SOCIETY OF LOCOMOTIVE ENGINEERS AND FIREMEN (ASLEF) (18,685), 9 Arkwright Road, NW3 6AB. (Tel: 071–431 0275).—*Sec.*, D. Fullick.

ASSOCIATION OF CINEMATOGRAPH, TELEVISION AND ALLIED TECHNICIANS (29,976), 111 Wardour Street, W1V 4AY. (Tel: 071–437 8506).—*Gen. Sec.*, A. Sapper.

ASSOCIATION OF FIRST DIVISION CIVIL SERVANTS (10,411), 2 Caxton Street, SW1H 0QH. (Tel: 071–222 6242).—*Gen. Sec.*, Ms. E. Symons.

ASSOCIATION OF PROFESSIONAL, EXECUTIVE, CLERICAL AND COMPUTER STAFF (APEX) (amalgamated with GMB since Dec. 1988).

ASSOCIATION OF SCIENTIFIC, TECHNICAL AND MANAGERIAL STAFFS (ASTMS) (amalgamated with TASS to form Manufacturing, Science and Finance Union).

ASSOCIATION OF UNIVERSITY TEACHERS (31,000), United House, 1 Pembridge Road, W11 3JY. (Tel: 071–221 4370).—*Gen. Sec.*, Ms. D. Warwick.

BAKERS, FOOD AND ALLIED WORKERS' UNION (34,379), Stanborough House, Great North Road, Stanborough, Welwyn Garden City, Herts. AL8 7TA. (Tel: 0707–260150).—*Gen. Sec.*, J. R. Marino.

BANKING, INSURANCE AND FINANCE UNION (170,481), Sheffield House, 1B Amity Grove, SW20 0LG. (Tel: 081–946 9151).—*Gen. Sec.*, L. A. Mills.

BRITISH ACTORS' EQUITY ASSOCIATION (44,269), 8 Harley Street, W1N 2AB. (Tel: 071–637 9311).—*Gen. Sec.*, P. Plouviez.

BRITISH AIR LINE PILOTS ASSOCIATION, THE (6,680), 81 New Road, Harlington, Hayes, Middx. UB3 5BG. (Tel: 081–759 9331).—*Gen. Sec.*, M. Young.

BRITISH ASSOCIATION OF COLLIERY MANAGEMENT, THE (8,436), BACM House, 317 Nottingham Road, Old Basford, Nottingham NG7 7DP. (Tel: 0602–785819).—*Gen. Sec.*, J. D. Meads.

BROADCASTING AND ENTERTAINMENT TRADES ALLIANCE (31,719), 181–185 Wardour Street, W1V 4BE. (Tel: 071–439 7585).—*Gen. Sec.*, D. A. Hearn.

CARD SETTING MACHINE TENTERS' SOCIETY (92), 36 Greenton Avenue, Scholes, Cleckheaton, W. Yorks. BD19 6DT. (Tel: 0274–670022).—*Sec.*, G. Priestley.

CERAMIC AND ALLIED TRADES UNION, THE (29,872), Hillcrest House, Garth Street, Stoke-on-Trent ST1 2AB. (Tel: 0782–272755).—*Gen. Sec.*, A. W. Clowes.

CIVIL AND PUBLIC SERVICES ASSOCIATION, THE (127,976), 160 Falcon Road, SW11 2LN. (Tel: 071–924 2727).—*Gen. Sec.*, J. N. Ellis.

COMMUNICATION MANAGERS' ASSOCIATION (19,229), Hughes House, Ruscombe Road, Twyford, Reading RG10 9JD. (Tel: 0734–342300).—*Gen. Sec.*, T. L. Deegan.

CONFEDERATION OF HEALTH SERVICE EMPLOYEES (COHSE) (220,000), Glen House, High Street, Banstead, Surrey SM7 2LH. (Tel: 0737–353322).—*Gen. Sec.*, H. MacKenzie. (Have voted to merge with NALGO and NUPE).

EDUCATIONAL INSTITUTE OF SCOTLAND, THE (45,000), 46 Moray Place, Edinburgh EH3 6BH. (Tel: 031–225 6244).—*Gen. Sec.*, J. B. Martin.

ENGINEERING AND FASTENERS TRADE UNION (400), 434 Bearwood Road, Smethwick, Warley, W. Midlands B66 4EY. (Tel: 021–434 3092).—*Gen. Sec.*, W. J. Redmond.

ENGINEERS' AND MANAGERS' ASSOCIATION (41,000), Station House, Fox Lane North, Chertsey, Surrey KT16 9HW. (Tel: 0932–564131).—*Gen. Sec.*, J. Lyons, CBE.

FILM ARTISTES' ASSOCIATION (2,114), 61 Marloes Road, W8 6LE. (Tel: 071–937 4567).—*Sec.*, M. Reynel.

FIRE BRIGADES UNION, THE (46,878), Bradley House, 68 Coombe Road, Kingston upon Thames, Surrey KT2 7AE. (Tel: 081–541 1765).—*Gen. Sec.*, K. Cameron.

FURNITURE, TIMBER AND ALLIED TRADES UNION (42,900), Fairfields, Roe Green, NW9 0PT. (Tel: 081–204 0273).—*Gen. Sec.*, C. A. Christopher.

GENERAL UNION OF ASSOCIATIONS OF LOOM OVERLOOKERS, THE (698), Overlookers Institute, 9 Wellington Street, St. Johns, Blackburn, Lancs. BB1 8AF. (Tel: 0254–51760).—*Pres.*, E. Macro.

GMB (formerly GENERAL, MUNICIPAL, BOILERMAKERS AND ALLIED TRADES UNION (850,000), 22–24 Worple Road, SW19 4DF. (Tel: 081–947 3131).—*Gen. Sec.*, J. Edmonds.

HEALTH VISITORS' ASSOCIATION (17,000), 50 Southwark Street, SE1 1UN. (Tel: 071–378 7255).—*Gen. Sec.*, Ms C. Burns. (Have voted to merge with MSF).

HOSPITAL CONSULTANTS AND SPECIALISTS ASSOCIATION, THE (2,360), The Old Court House, London Road, Ascot, Berks. SL5 7EN. (Tel: 0990–25052).—*Chief Exec.*, S. J. Charkham.

INLAND REVENUE STAFF FEDERATION (51,310), Douglas Houghton House, 231 Vauxhall Bridge Road, SW1V 1EH. (Tel: 071–834 8254).—*Gen. Sec.*, C. Brooke.

INSTITUTION OF PROFESSIONALS, MANAGERS AND SPECIALISTS (90,341), 75–79 York Road, SE1 7AQ. (Tel: 071–928 9951).—*Gen. Sec.*, W. Brett.

IRON AND STEEL TRADES CONFEDERATION, THE (56,000), Swinton House, 324 Gray's Inn Road, WC1X 8DD. (Tel: 071–837 6691).—*Gen. Sec.*, R. L. Evans.

MANUFACTURING, SCIENCE AND FINANCE UNION (MSF) (653,000), 79 Camden Road, NW1 9ES. (Tel: 071–267 4422).—*Gen. Sec.*, K. Gill.

MILITARY AND ORCHESTRAL MUSICAL INSTRUMENT MAKERS' TRADE SOCIETY (35), 2 Whitehouse Avenue, Boreham Wood, Herts. WD6 1HD.—*Gen. Sec.*, F. McKenzie.

MUSICIANS' UNION (40,050), 60–62 Clapham Road, SW9 0JJ. (Tel: 071–582 5566).—*Gen. Sec.*, D. Scard.

NATIONAL AND LOCAL GOVERNMENT OFFICERS' ASSOCIATION (NALGO) (750,000), 1 Mabledon Place, WC1H 9AJ. (Tel: 071–388 2366).—*Gen. Sec.*, A. Jinkinson. (Have voted to merge with COHSE and NUPE).

NATIONAL ASSOCIATION OF COLLIERY OVERMEN, DEPUTIES AND SHOTFIRERS (6,395), Simpson House, 48 Nether Hall Road, Doncaster DN1 2PZ. (Tel: 0302–368015).—*Sec.*, P. McNestry.

NATIONAL ASSOCIATION OF CO-OPERATIVE OFFICIALS (4,427), Coronation House, Arndale Centre, Manchester M4 2HW. (Tel: 061–834 6029).—*Gen. Sec.*, L. W. Ewing.

NATIONAL ASSOCIATION OF LICENSED HOUSE MANAGERS (12,000), 9 Coombe Lane, SW20 8NE. (Tel: 081–947 3080).—*Gen. Sec.*, J. Madden.

NATIONAL ASSOCIATION OF PROBATION OFFICERS (6,714), 3–4 Chivalry Road, SW11 1HT. (Tel: 071–223 4887).—*Sec.*, W. L. Beaumont.

NATIONAL ASSOCIATION OF SCHOOLMASTERS/UNION OF WOMEN TEACHERS (NAS/UWT) (159,000), Hillscourt Education Centre, Rose Hill, Rednal, Birmingham B45 8RS. (Tel: 021–453 6150).—*Gen. Sec.*, N. De Gruchy.

NATIONAL ASSOCIATION OF TEACHERS IN FURTHER AND HIGHER EDUCATION (80,000), 27 Britannia Street, WC1X 9JP. (Tel: 071–837 3636).—*Gen. Sec.*, G. Woolf.

NATIONAL COMMUNICATIONS UNION (151,523), Greystoke House, 150 Brunswick Road, W5 1AW. (Tel: 081–998 2981).—*Gen. Sec.*, A. I. Young.

NATIONAL GRAPHICAL ASSOCIATION 1982 (NGA '82) (130,000), Graphic House, 63–67 Bromham Road, Bedford MK40 2AG. (Tel: 0234–51521).—*Sec.*, A. D. Dubbins.

NATIONAL LEAGUE OF THE BLIND AND DISABLED, THE (2,783), 2 Tenterden Road, N17 8BE. (Tel: 081–808 6030).—*Sec.*, M. A. Barrett.

NATIONAL UNION OF CIVIL AND PUBLIC SERVANTS (NUCPS) (113,211), 124–130 Southwark Street, SE1 0TU. (Tel: 071–928 9671).—*Gen. Sec.*, L. Christie.

NATIONAL UNION OF DOMESTIC APPLIANCES AND GENERAL OPERATIVES, THE (3,100), 6–8 Imperial Buildings, Corporation Street, Rotherham, S. Yorks. S60 1PB. (Tel: 0709–382820).—*Gen. Sec.*, A. McCarthy.

NATIONAL UNION OF HOSIERY AND KNITWEAR WORKERS, THE (38,681), 55 New Walk, Leicester LE1 7EB. (Tel: 0533–556703).—*Gen. Sec.*, Mrs. H. F. McGrath.

NATIONAL UNION OF INSURANCE WORKERS (18,057), 27 Old Gloucester Street, WC1N 3AF. (Tel: 071–405 6798).—*Gen. Sec.*, K. Perry.

NATIONAL UNION OF JOURNALISTS (NUJ) (32,206), Acorn House, 314–320 Gray's Inn Road, WC1X 8DP. (Tel: 071–278 7916).—*Gen. Sec.*, S. Turner.

NATIONAL UNION OF LOCK AND METAL WORKERS (5,149), Bellamy House, Wilkes Street, Willenhall, W. Midlands WV13 2BS. (Tel: 0902–366651).—*Gen. Sec.*, M. Bradley.

NATIONAL UNION OF MARINE, AVIATION AND SHIPPING TRANSPORT OFFICERS, THE (19,345), Oceanair House, 750–760 High Road, E11 3BB. (Tel: 081–989 6677).—*Gen. Sec.*, J. Newman.

NATIONAL UNION OF MINEWORKERS (NUM) (58,861), Holly Street, Sheffield S1 2GT. (Tel: 0742–766900).—*Sec.*, P. E. Heathfield.

NATIONAL UNION OF PUBLIC EMPLOYEES (NUPE) (604,912), Civic House, 20 Grand Depot Road, SE18 6SF. (Tel: 081–854 2244).—*Sec.*, R. K. Bickerstaffe. (Have voted to merge with COHSE and NALGO).

NATIONAL UNION OF RAILWAYMEN (NUR) (110,000), Unity House, Euston Road, NW1 2BL. (Tel: 071–387 4771).—*Gen. Sec.*, J. Knapp. (Have voted to merge with NUS).

NATIONAL UNION OF SCALEMAKERS (822), Queensway House, 57 Livery Street, Birmingham B3 1HA. (Tel: 021–236 8998).—*Gen. Sec.*, A. F. Smith.

NATIONAL UNION OF SEAMEN (NUS) (20,308), Maritime House, Old Town, SW4 0JP. (Tel: 071–622 5581).—*Gen. Sec.*, S. J. McCluskie. (Have voted to merge with NUR).

NATIONAL UNION OF TAILORS AND GARMENT WORKERS (73,122), 16 Charles Square, N1 6HP. (Tel: 071–251 9406).—*Gen. Sec.*, A. Smith.

NATIONAL UNION OF TEACHERS (NUT) (190,000), Hamilton House, Mabledon Place, WC1H 9BD. (Tel: 071–388 6191).—*Gen. Sec.*, D. McAvoy.

NATIONAL UNION OF THE FOOTWEAR, LEATHER AND ALLIED TRADES (29,368), The Grange, 108 Northampton Road, Earls Barton, Northampton NN6 0JH. (Tel: 0604–810326).—*Gen. Sec.*, G. F. Browett.

NORTHERN CARPET TRADES' UNION (899), 22 Clare Road, Halifax HX1 2HX. (Tel: 0422–360492).—*Gen. Sec.*, K. Edmondson.

POWER LOOM CARPET WEAVERS' AND TEXTILE WORKERS' UNION, THE (3,500), Carpet Weavers Hall, Callows Lane, Kidderminster, Worcs. DY10 2JG. (Tel: 0562–823192).—*Gen. Sec.*, R. White.

PRISON OFFICERS' ASSOCIATION, THE (24,251), Cronin House, 245 Church Street, N9 9HW. (Tel: 081–803 0255).—*Gen. Sec.*, D. Evans.

ROSSENDALE UNION OF BOOT, SHOE AND SLIPPER OPERATIVES, THE (2,498), Taylor House, 7 Tenterfield Street, Waterfoot, Rossendale, Lancs. BB4 7BA. (Tel: 0706–215657).—*Gen. Sec.*, M. Murray.

SCOTTISH PRISON OFFICERS' ASSOCIATION (3,710), 21 Calder Road, Edinburgh EH11 3PF. (Tel: 031–443 8105).—*Gen. Sec.*, W. Goodall.

SCOTTISH UNION OF POWER-LOOM OVERLOOKERS (70), 3 Napier Terrace, Dundee DD2 2SL. (Tel: 0382–612196).—*Sec.*, K. Reilly.

SCREW, NUT, BOLT AND RIVET TRADE UNION (now called Engineering and Fasteners Trade Union).

SHEFFIELD WOOL SHEAR WORKERS' UNION (15), 50 Bankfield Road, Malin Bridge, Sheffield S9 4RD.—*Sec.*, J. H. R. Cutler.

SOCIETY OF GRAPHICAL AND ALLIED TRADES 1982 (SOGAT '82) (180,000), Sogat House, 274–288 London Road, Hadleigh, Benfleet, Essex SS7 2DE. (Tel: 0702–554111).—*Gen. Sec.*, Ms. B. Dean.

SOCIETY OF SHUTTLEMAKERS (30), 211 Burnley Road, Colne, Lancs. BB8 8JD. (Tel: 0282–866716).—*Gen. Sec.*, L. Illingworth.

SOCIETY OF TELECOM EXECUTIVES (29,961), 1 Park Road, Teddington, Middx. TW11 0AR. (Tel: 081–943 5181).—*Gen. Sec.*, S. Petch.

TECHNICAL, ADMINISTRATIVE AND SUPERVISORY SECTION (TASS) (amalgamated with ASTMS to form Manufacturing, Science and Finance Union).

TRANSPORT AND GENERAL WORKERS' UNION (TGWU) (1,270,776), Transport House, Smith Square, SW1P 3JB. (Tel: 071–828 7788).—*Gen. Sec.*, R. Todd.

TRANSPORT SALARIED STAFFS' ASSOCIATION (38,435), Walkden House, 10 Melton Street, NW1 2EJ. (Tel: 071–387 2101).—*Gen. Sec.*, R. A. Rosser.

UNION OF COMMUNICATION WORKERS, THE (202,500), UCW House, Crescent Lane, SW4 9RN. (Tel: 071–622 9977).—*Gen. Sec.*, A. D. Tuffin.

UNION OF CONSTRUCTION, ALLIED TRADES AND TECHNICIANS (UCATT) (258,616), UCATT House, 177 Abbeville Road, SW4 9RL. (Tel: 071–622 2442).—*Sec.*, A. Williams.

UNION OF SHOP, DISTRIBUTIVE AND ALLIED WORKERS (USDAW) (375,891), Oakley, 188 Wilmslow Road, Fallowfield, Manchester M14 6LJ. (Tel: 061–224 2804).—*Sec.*, D. G. Davies.

UNITED ROAD TRANSPORT UNION (20,372), 76 High Lane, Chorlton, Manchester M21 1FD. (Tel: 061–881 6245).—*Gen. Sec.*, F. Griffin.

WIRE WORKERS' UNION (5,143), Prospect House, Alma Street, Sheffield S3 8SA. (Tel: 0742–721674).—*Gen. Sec.*, A. M. Ardron.

WRITERS' GUILD OF GREAT BRITAIN, THE (1,601), 430 Edgware Road, W2 1EH. (Tel: 071–723 8074).—*Gen. Sec.*, W. J. Jeffrey.

YORKSHIRE ASSOCIATION OF POWER LOOM OVERLOOKERS (524), 20 Hallfield Road, Bradford BD1 3RQ. (Tel: 0274–727966).—*Gen. Sec.*, A. D. Barrow.

Expelled from the TUC Sept. 1988:

ELECTRICAL, ELECTRONIC, TELECOMMUNICATION AND PLUMBING UNION (EETPU) (360,000), Hayes Court, West Common Road, Bromley BR2 7AU. (Tel: 081–462 7755).—*Gen. Sec.*, E. A. B. Hammond, OBE.

THE RESEARCH COUNCILS

The Government funds basic and applied civil science research mostly through the five research councils, which are supported by the Department of Education and Science. The councils conduct research through their own establishments (listed below) and by supporting selected research, study and training in universities and other higher education establishments. They also receive income for research commissioned by government departments and the private sector.

AGRICULTURAL AND FOOD RESEARCH COUNCIL

AFRC Institute for Animal Health
Director of Research: Prof. F. J. Bourne, Ph.D., Compton, Newbury, Berks. RG16 0NN.

Compton Laboratory, Compton, Nr. Newbury, Berks. RG16 0NN.—*Head of Lab. (acting)*, B. Freeman, D.SC.

Houghton Laboratory, Houghton, Huntingdon, Cambs. PE17 2DA.—*Head of Lab. (acting)*, L. N. Payne, D.SC.

Pirbright Laboratory, Ash Road, Woking, Surrey GU24 0NF.—*Head of Lab. (acting)*, C. J. Bostock, Ph.D.

AFRC and MRC Neuropathogenesis Unit, Ogston Building, West Mains Road, Edinburgh EH9 3JF.—*Director (acting)*, J. Hope, Ph.D.

AFRC Institute of Animal Physiology and Genetics Research
Director of Research, R. B. Heap, Ph.D., SC.D., FRS, Babraham Hall, Babraham, Cambridge CB2 4AT.

Cambridge Research Station, Babraham, Cambridge CB2 4AT.—*Head of Station*, Dr. R. G. Dyer.

Edinburgh Research Station, Roslin, Midlothian EH25 9PS.—*Head of Station*, G. Bulfield, Ph.D.

AFRC Institute of Arable Crops Research
Director of Research (acting), Prof. T. Lewis, Rothamsted Experimental Station, Harpenden, Herts. AL5 2JQ.

Long Ashton Research Station, Long Ashton, Bristol BS18 9AF.—*Director*, Prof. P. R. Shewry.

Rothamsted Experimental Station, Harpenden, Herts. AL5 2JQ.—*Head of Station*, Prof. T. Lewis, Ph.D., D.SC.

Broom's Barn Experimental Station, Higham, Bury St. Edmunds, Suffolk IP28 6NP.—*Head of Station*, T. H. Thomas, Ph.D., D.SC.

AFRC Institute of Engineering Research
Director of Research, Dr. B. J. Legg, Wrest Park, Silsoe, Bedford MK45 4HS.

AFRC Institute of Food Research
Director of Research, D. L. Georgala, CBE, Ph.D., Shinfield, Reading RG2 9AT.

Norwich Laboratory, Colney Lane, Norwich NR4 7UA.—*Head of Lab.*, Prof. P. Richmond, D.SC.

Reading Laboratory, Shinfield, Reading RG2 9AT.—*Head of Lab.*, Prof. B. E. B. Moseley, Ph.D.

AFRC Institute of Grassland Environmental Research
Director of Research, Prof. J. L. Stoddart, Ph.D., D.SC., Plas Gogerddan, Aberystwyth, Dyfed SY23 3EB.

Plant Science and Plant Breeding Division:
Welsh Plant Breeding Station, Plas Gogerddan, Aberystwyth, Dyfed SY23 3EB.—*Director and Head of Division*, D. Wilson, Ph.D.

Grassland and Ruminant Division:
Hurley Research Station, Maidenhead, Berks. SL6 5LR.—*Head of Division*, R. J. Wilkins, Ph.D.

North Wyke Research Station, Okehampton, Devon EX20 2SB.—*Officer in Charge*, R. D. Sheldrick, OBE.

AFRC Institute of Plant Science Research
Director of Research, Prof. R. B. Flavell, John Innes Institute, Colney Lane, Norwich NR4 7UH.

John Innes Institute, Colney Lane, Norwich NR4 7UH.—*Director*, Prof. R. B. Flavell.

IPSR Cambridge Laboratory, Colney Lane, Norwich NR4 7UH.—*Head*, C. N. Law, Ph.D.

IPSR Nitrogen Fixation Laboratory, University of Sussex, Brighton BN1 9RQ.—*Head*, Prof. B. E. Smith, Ph.D.

AFRC Computing Division, West Common, Harpenden, Herts. AL5 2JE.—*Head of Division*, A. Windram.

SCOTTISH AGRICULTURAL RESEARCH INSTITUTES

Hannah Research Institute, Ayr KA6 5HL.—*Director,* Prof. M. Peaker.

Macaulay Land Use Research Institute, Craigiebuckler, Aberdeen AB9 2QJ; Bush Estate, Penicuik, Midlothian EH26 0PY.—*Director*, Prof. T. J. Maxwell, Ph.D.

Moredun Research Institute, 408 Gilmerton Road, Edinburgh EH17 7JH.—*Director*, I. D. Aitken, Ph.D.

Rowett Research Institute, Greenburn Road, Bucksburn, Aberdeen AB2 9SB.—*Director*, Prof. W. P. T. James.

Scottish Crop Research Institute, Invergowrie, Dundee DD2 5DA; Pentlandfield, Roslin, Midlothian EH25 9RF.—*Director*, Prof. J. Hillman, Ph.D., FLS, FRSE.

Scottish Agricultural Statistics Service, University of Edinburgh, James Clerk Maxwell Building, The King's Buildings, Mayfield Road, Edinburgh EH9 3JZ.—*Director*, R. A. Kempton.

ECONOMIC AND SOCIAL RESEARCH COUNCIL

Cambridge Group for the History of Population and Social Structure, 27 Trumpington Street, Cambridge CB2 1QA.—*Director*, Dr. R. Schofield.

Centre for Economic Performance, London School of Economics, Houghton Street, London WC2A 2AE.—*Director*, Prof. R. Layard.

Centre for Educational Sociology, 7 Buccleuch Place, Edinburgh EH8 9LW.—*Director*, Prof. D. Raffe.

Centre for Health Economics, University of York, Heslington, York YO2 5DD.—*Director*, Prof. A. Maynard.

Centre for Housing Research, 25 Bute Gardens, Hillhead, The University, Glasgow G12 8LE.—*Director*, Dr. D. MacLennan.

Centre for Research in Ethnic Relations, University of Warwick, Coventry CV4 7AL.—*Director*, Dr. M. Anwar.

Centre for Science Technology and Energy Policy, Science Policy Research Unit, University of Sussex, Mantell Building, Falmer, Brighton BN1 9RF.—*Director,* Prof. G. Oldham.

Centre for Social Work Research, University of Stirling, Stirling FK9 4LA.—*Director,* Prof. Juliet Cheetham.

Centre for Socio-legal Studies, Wolfson College, University of Oxford, Oxford OX2 6UD.—*Director,* D. Harris.

ESRC Data Archive, University of Essex, Colchester, Essex CO4 3SQ.—*Director,* vacant.

Industrial Relations Research Unit, School of Industrial Business Studies, University of Warwick, Coventry CV4 7AL.—*Director,* Prof. K. Sisson.

MRC/ESRC Social and Applied Psychology Unit, Department of Psychology, University of Sheffield, Sheffield S10 2TN.—*Director,* Prof. P. Warr.

Northern Ireland Economic Research Centre, 46–48 University Road, Belfast BT7 1NJ.—*Director,* Dr. G. Gudgin.

Research Centre in Human Communication, University of Edinburgh, 2 Buccleuch Place, Edinburgh EH8 9LW.—*Director,* Prof. K. Stenning.

Research Centre in Micro-Social Change, University of Essex, Colchester, Essex CO4 3SQ.—*Director,* Prof. A. Coxon.

Research Unit in Health and Behavioural Change, University of Edinburgh, 17 Teviot Place, Edinburgh EH1 2QR.—*Director,* Dr. D. McQueen.

MEDICAL RESEARCH COUNCIL

National Institute for Medical Research, Mill Hill, NW7.—*Director,* J. Skehel, Ph.D., FRS.

Clinical Research Centre, Watford Road, Harrow, Middlesex.—*Director,* Dr. K. E. Kirkham.

Research Units

Anatomical Neuropharmacology Unit, Dept. of Pharmacology, University of Oxford, South Park Road, Oxford OX1 3QT.—*Director,* Prof. A. D. Smith, D.Phil.

Applied Psychology Unit, 15 Chaucer Road, Cambridge CB2 2EF.—*Director,* A. D. Baddeley, Ph.D.

MRC Biochemical and Clinical Magnetic Resonance Unit, University Dept. of Biochemistry, South Parks Road, Oxford OX1 3QU.—*Director,* Prof. G. K. Radda, D.Phil., FRS.

Biostatistics Unit, 5 Shaftesbury Road, Cambridge CB2 2BW.—*Director,* N. E. Day, Ph.D.

Blood Group Unit, University College, London, Wolfson House, 4 Stephenson Way, NW1 2EH.—*Director,* Patricia Tippett, Ph.D.

Blood Pressure Unit, Western Infirmary, Glasgow G11 6NT.—*Director,* A. F. Lever, FRCP, FRSE.

Brain Metabolism Unit, University Dept. of Pharmacology, 1 George Square, Edinburgh EH8 9JZ.—*Director,* G. Fink, MD, D.Phil.

Cell Biophysics Unit, Dept. of Biophysics, King's College, 26–29 Drury Lane, WC2.—*Director,* Prof. B. B. Boycott, FRS.

Cell Mutation Unit, University of Sussex, Falmer, Brighton BN1 9RR.—*Director,* Prof. B. A. Bridges, Ph.D.

Cellular Immunology Unit, Sir William Dunn School of Pathology, Oxford OX1 3RE.—*Director,* Dr. A. F. Williams, Ph.D.

Child Psychiatry Unit, Institute of Psychiatry, De Crespigny Park, Denmark Hill, SE5 8AF.—*Director,* Prof. M. Rutter, CBE, MD, FRCP.

Clinical Oncology and Radiotherapeutics Unit, MRC Centre, Hills Road, Cambridge CB2 2QH.—*Hon. Director,* Prof. N. M. Bleehen, FRCP, FRCR.

Clinical Pharmacology Unit, University Department of Clinical Pharmacology, Radcliffe Infirmary, Woodstock Road, Oxford OX2 6HE.—*Hon. Director,* Prof. D. G. Grahame-Smith, Ph.D, FRCP.

Cognitive Development Unit, 17 Gordon Street, WC1.—*Director,* Prof. J. Morton, Ph.D.

MRC Collaborative Centre, 1–3 Burtonhole Lane, Mill Hill, NW7 1AD.—*Director,* C. C. G. Hentschel, Ph.D.

Cyclotron Unit, Hammersmith Hospital, Du Cane Road, W12.—*Director,* K. I. Gibson, Ph.D.

Dental Research Unit, London Hospital Medical College, 30–32 Newark Street, E1 2AA.—*Director,* Prof. N. W. Johnson, Ph.D.

Dunn Nutrition Unit, Downhams Lane, Milton Road, Cambridge.—*Director,* R. G. Whitehead, Ph.D.

Environmental Epidemiology Unit, Southampton General Hospital, Southampton SO9 4XY.—*Director,* Prof. D. J. P. Barker, MD, Ph.D, FRCP.

Epidemiology and Medical Care Unit, Northwick Park Hospital, Watford Road, Harrow, Middx.—*Director,* T. W. Meade, DM, FRCP.

Epidemiology Unit (South Wales), 4 Richmond Road, Cardiff.—*Director,* P. C. Elwood, MD, FRCP.

Experimental Embryology and Teratology Unit, St. George's Hospital Medical School, Cranmer Terrace, SW17 0RE.—*Director,* D. G. Whittingham, D.SC.

Human Biochemical Genetics Unit, Galton Laboratory, University College London, Wolfson House, 4 Stephenson Way, NW1.—*Hon. Director,* D. A. Hopkinson, MD.

Human Genetics Unit, Western General Hospital, Crewe Road, Edinburgh EH4 2XU.—*Director,* Prof. H. J. Evans, Ph.D, FRSE.

MRC Human Movement and Balance Unit, Institute of Neurology, National Hospital, Queens Square, WC1.—*Director,* Prof. C. D. Marsden, FRS.

Immunochemistry Unit, University Department of Biochemistry, South Parks Road, Oxford OX1 3QU.—*Director,* K. B. M. Reid, Ph.D.

Institute of Hearing Research, University of Nottingham, Nottingham NG7 2RD.—*Director,* M. P. Haggard, Ph.D.

MRC Laboratories, The Gambia, Fajara, near Banjul, The Gambia.—*Director,* B. M. Greenwood, CBE, MD, FRCP.

MRC Laboratories, Jamaica, University of the West Indies, Mona, Kingston, Jamaica.—*Director,* Prof. G. R. Serjeant, CMG, MD, FRCP.

Leukaemia Unit, Royal Postgraduate Medical School, Du Cane Road, W12 0HS.—*Hon. Director,* Prof. L. Luzzatto, MD, FRCP.

Mammalian Development Unit, University College London, Wolfson House, 4 Stephenson Way, NW1.—*Director,* Anne McLaren, D.Phil., FRS.

Medical Sociology Unit, 6, Lilybank Gardens, Glasgow, G12 8QQ.—*Director,* Sally Macintyre, Ph.D.

Laboratory of Molecular Biology, Hills Road, Cambridge CB2 2QH.—*Director,* Sir Aaron Klug, Ph.D., FRS.

Molecular Genetics Unit, MRC Centre, Hills Road, Cambridge CB2 2QH.—*Director,* S. Brenner, D.Phil., D.SC., FRCP, FRS.

Molecular Haematology Unit, John Radcliffe Hospital, Headington, Oxford OX3 9DU.—*Director,* Prof. D. J. Weatherall, MD, FRCP, FRS.

MRC Molecular Immunopathology Unit, University Medical School, Hills Road, Cambridge CB2 2QH.—*Director,* Prof. P. J. Lachmann, SC.D., FRCP, FRS.

Molecular Neurobiology Unit, University Medical School, Hills Road, Cambridge CB2 2QH.—*Director,* Prof. E. A. Barnard.

Neurochemical Pathology Unit, Newcastle General

Hospital, Westgate Road, Newcastle upon Tyne NE4 6BE.—*Director*, Prof. J. A. Edwardson, Ph.D.

Neurological Prostheses Unit, Institute of Psychiatry, De Crespigny Park, Denmark Hill, SE5.—*Hon. Director*, Prof. G. S. Brindley, MD, FRCP, FRS.

AFRC/MRC Neuropathogenesis Unit, Ogston Building, West Mains Road, Edinburgh.—*Director*, J. Hope, Ph.D.

MRC Protein Function and Design Unit, Dept. of Chemistry, University of Cambridge, Lensfield Road, Cambridge CB2 1EW.—*Director*, A. R. Fersht, Ph.D., FRS.

Radiobiology Unit, Chilton, Didcot, Oxon. OX11 0RD—*Director*, Prof. G. E. Adams, Ph.D., D.SC.

Reproductive Biology Unit, Centre for Reproductive Biology, 37 Chalmers Street, Edinburgh EH3 9EW.—*Director*, D. W. Lincoln, D.SC.

Social and Applied Psychology Unit, Dept. of Psychology, University of Sheffield S10 2TN.—*Director*, P. B. Warr, Ph.D.

Social (and Community) Psychiatry Unit, Institute of Psychiatry, De Crespigny Park, Denmark Hill, SE5.—*Director*, Prof. J. P. Leff, MD, FRCPsych.

Toxicology Unit, MRC Laboratories, Woodmansterne Road, Carshalton, Surrey SM5 4EF.—*Director*, T. A. Connors, D.SC., Ph.D.

Tuberculosis and Related Infections Unit, Hammersmith Hospital, Du Cane Road, W12 0HS.—*Director*, Dr. J. Ivanyi, MD, Ph.D.

Virology Unit, Institute of Virology, Church Street, Glasgow G11 5JR.—*Hon. Director*, Prof. J. H. Subak-Sharpe, Ph.D, FRSE.

Plymouth Marine Laboratory, Prospect Place, The Hoe, Plymouth PL1 3DH; Citadel Hill, Plymouth PL1 2PB. (Tel: 0752–222772).—*Director*, B. L. Bayne, Ph.D.; *Assistant Director*, Dr. P. N. Claridge.

Proudman Oceanographic Laboratory, Bidston, Birkenhead L43 7RA. (Tel: 051–653 8633).—*Director*, B. S. McCartney, Ph.D.

Sea Mammal Research Unit, c/o British Antarctic Survey. (Tel: 0223–311354).—*Head of Unit*, J. Harwood, Ph.D.

Institute of Hydrology, Maclean Building, Crowmarsh Gifford, Wallingford, Oxon. OX10 8BB. (Tel: 0491–38800).—*Director*, Prof. M. B. Wilkinson.

Institute of Terrestrial Ecology (North), Bush Estate, Penicuik, Midlothian EH26 0QB. (Tel: 031–445 4343).—*Director*, Prof. O. W. Heal, Ph.D.

Institute of Terrestrial Ecology (South), Monks Wood Experimental Station, Abbots Ripton, Huntingdon PE17 2LS. (Tel: 04873–381/8).—*Director*, Dr. T. M. Roberts.

Institute of Virology and Environmental Microbiology, Mansfield Road, Oxford OX1 3SR. (Tel: 0865–512361).—*Director*, Prof. D. H. L. Bishop, Ph.D.

Grant-Aided Institutes

Institute of Freshwater Ecology, The Ferry House, Far Sawrey, Ambleside, Cumbria LA22 0LP. (Tel: 09662–2468/9).—*Director*, Prof. J. G. Jones, Ph.D.

Dunstaffnage Marine Laboratory, PO Box 3, Oban, Argyll PA34 4AD. (Tel: 0631–62244).—*Director*, Prof. J. B. L. Matthews.

Unit of Comparative Plant Ecology, Dept. of Plant Sciences, Sheffield University, Sheffield S10 2TN. (Tel: 0742–768555).—*Head of Unit*, J. P. Grime.

NATURAL ENVIRONMENT RESEARCH COUNCIL

Research Institutes

British Antarctic Survey, Madingley Road, Cambridge CB3 0ET. (Tel: 0223–61188).—*Director*, Dr. D. J. Drewry, Ph.D.

British Geological Survey, Nicker Hill, Keyworth, Nottingham NG12 5GG. (Tel: 06077–6111).—*Director*, Dr. P. Cook.

Institute of Oceanographic Sciences, Deacon Laboratory, Wormley, nr. Godalming GU8 5UB. (Tel: 042879–4141).—*Director*, Dr. C. Summerhayes.

SCIENCE AND ENGINEERING RESEARCH COUNCIL

Research Establishments

Daresbury Nuclear Physics Laboratory, Keckwick Lane, Daresbury, Warrington WA4 4AD.

Royal Greenwich Observatory, Madingley Road, Cambridge CB3 0EZ.—*Director*, A. Boksenberg, FRS.

Royal Observatory, Edinburgh, Blackford Hill, Edinburgh EH9 3HJ.—*Director*, Prof. M. S. Longair.

Rutherford Appleton Nuclear Physics Laboratory, Chilton, Oxon.

INDUSTRIAL AND TECHNOLOGICAL RESEARCH ASSOCIATIONS

The following are members of the Association of Independent Research and Technology Organizations (AIRTO), PO Box 330, Cambridge CB5 8DU.

Aircraft Research Association Ltd., Manton Lane, Bedford MK41 7PF.

Advanced Manufacturing Technology Research Institute, Hulley Road, Macclesfield, Cheshire SK10 2NE.

BCIRA International Centre for Cast Metals Technology, Alvechurch, Birmingham B48 7QB.

BHRA, The Fluid Engineering Centre, Wharley End, Cranfield, Bedford MK43 0AJ.

BICERI—The British Internal Combustion Engine Research Institute Ltd., 111–112 Buckingham Avenue, Slough SL1 4PH.

BNF Metals Technology Centre, Wantage Business Park, Denchworth Road, Wantage, Oxon. OX12 9BJ.

British Ceramic Research Ltd., Queen's Road, Penkhull, Stoke-on-Trent ST4 7LQ.

British Glass, Northumberland Road, Sheffield S10 2UA.

British Leather Confederation, Leather Trade House, Kings Park Road, Moulton Park, Northants. NN3 1JD.

British Maritime Technology Ltd., Orlando House, 1 Waldegrave Road, Teddington, Middx. TW11 8LZ.

British Textile Technology Group, Shirley Towers, Didsbury, Manchester M20 8RX; Wira House, West Park Ring Road, Leeds LS16 6QL.

Building Services Research and Information Association, Old Bracknell Lane West, Bracknell, Berks. RG12 4AH.

Cambridge Consultants Ltd. (*Product and process development of technology applications in business*), Science Park, Milton Road, Cambridge CB4 4DW.

Campden Food and Drink Research Association, Chipping Campden, Glos. GL55 6LD.

CIRIA (The Construction Industry Research and Information Association), 6 Storey's Gate, SW1P 3AU.

Cutlery and Allied Trades Research Association, Henry Street, Sheffield S3 7EQ.

ERA Technology Ltd. (*Electronic and electrical engineering*), Cleeve Road, Leatherhead, Surrey KT22 7SA.

Fulmer Ltd. (*Technological product design and process development*), Hollybush Hill, Stoke Poges, Slough SL2 4QD.

Furniture Industry Research Association, Maxwell Road, Stevenage, Herts. SG1 2EW.

Hazleton UK (*Agro-chemical, chemical and pharmaceutical product development and safety evaluation*), Otley Road, Harrogate, N. Yorks. HG3 1PY.

Hydraulics Research Ltd., Wallingford, Oxon. OX10 8BA.

Inveresk Research International Ltd. (*Pharmaceutical, veterinary, agricultural and chemical product evaluation*), Musselburgh, Midlothian EH21 7UB.

Lambeg Industrial Research Association (*Textiles*), Lambeg, Lisburn, Co. Antrim, N. Ireland BT27 4RJ.

Leatherhead Food Research Association, Randalls Road, Leatherhead, Surrey KT22 7RY.

Life Science Research Ltd., Eye, Suffolk IP23 7PX.

Motor Industry Research Association, Watling Street, Nuneaton, Warks. CV10 0TU.

The National Computing Centre Ltd., Oxford Road, Manchester M1 7ED.

NEI International Research and Development Company Ltd. (*Electronics and mechanical and electrical engineering*), Fossway, Newcastle upon Tyne NE6 2YD.

Paint Research Association, 8 Waldegrave Road, Teddington, Middx. TW11 8LD.

PERA (*Multi-disciplinary research, design, development and consultancy*), Melton Mowbray, Leics. LE13 0PB.

PIRA (*Paper and board, printing, publishing and packaging*), Randalls Road, Leatherhead, Surrey KT22 7RU.

RAPRA Technology Ltd. (*Polymer materials*), Shawbury, Shrewsbury SY4 4NR.

Ricardo Group PLC (*Consulting engineers*), Bridge Works, Shoreham-by-Sea, W. Sussex BN43 5FG.

SATRA Footwear Technology Centre, Satra House, Rockingham Road, Kettering, Northants. NN16 9JH.

Shipowners Refrigerated Cargo Research Association, 140 Newmarket Road, Cambridge CB5 8HE.

SIRA Ltd. (*Instrumentation and systems technology*), South Hill, Chislehurst, Kent BR7 5EH.

Smith Associates Ltd. (*System engineering consultancy*), Surrey Research Park, Guildford, Surrey GU2 5YP.

Spring Research and Manufacturers' Association, Henry Street, Sheffield S3 7EQ.

Steel Castings Research and Trade Association, East Bank Road, Sheffield S2 3PT.

Timber Research and Development Association, Stocking Lane, Hughenden Valley, High Wycombe, Bucks. HP14 4ND.

Toxicol Laboratories Ltd. (*Toxicology*), Bromyard Road, Ledbury, Herts. HR8 1LG.

Water Research Centre, PLC, Henley Road, Medmenham, PO Box 16, Marlow, Bucks. SL7 2HD.

The Welding Institute, Abington Hall, Abington, Cambridge CB1 6AL.

CAB INTERNATIONAL

CAB International (formerly the Commonwealth Agricultural Bureaux International) is an intergovernmental organization that provides information, scientific and development services to agriculture throughout the world. These services provide both developed and developing countries with ready access to scientific information and research back-up and assistance in pest identification and control.

Institutes

CABI Institute of Entomology, 56 Queen's Gate, SW7. *Director,* K. M. Harris, PH.D.

CABI Mycological Institute, Ferry Lane, Kew, Richmond, Surrey. *Director,* D. L. Hawksworth, PH.D.

CABI Institute of Biological Control, Silwood Park, Buckhurst Road, Ascot, Berks. SL5 7TA. *Director,* D. J. Greathead, PH.D.

CABI Institute of Parasitology, 395A Hatfield Road, St. Albans, Herts. *Director,* R. L. J. Muller, PH.D.

CAB International Bureaux
Wallingford, Oxon. OX10 8DE.

Agricultural Economics Bureau.
Animal Breeding and Genetics Bureau.
Animal Health Bureau.
Crop Protection Bureau.
Dairy Science and Technology Bureau.
Forestry Bureau.
Horticulture and Plantation Crops Bureau.
Nutrition Bureau.
Pastures and Field Crops Bureau.
Plant Breeding and Genetics Bureau.
Soils Bureau.

THE QUEEN'S AWARDS FOR EXPORT AND TECHNOLOGY

The Queen's Award for Export Achievement and The Queen's Award for Technological Achievement were instituted by Royal Warrant in 1976. The two separate Awards took the place of The Queen's Award to Industry which had been instituted in 1965.

The Awards are designed to recognize and encourage outstanding achievements in exporting goods or services from the United Kingdom and in advancing process or product technology. They differ from a personal Royal honour in that they are given to a unit as a whole—management and employees working as a team.

They may be applied for by any organization within the United Kingdom, the Channel Islands or the Isle of Man producing goods or services which meet the criteria for the Awards. Eligibility is not influenced in any way by the particular activities of the unit applying, its location, or size. Units or agencies of central and local government with industrial functions, as well as research associations, educational institutions and bodies of a similar character, are also eligible, provided that they can show they have contributed to industrial efficiency.

The criteria on which recommendations for the Awards are based are:

1. Export Achievement

A substantial and sustained increase in export earnings to a level which is outstanding for the products or services concerned and for the size of the applicant unit's operations. Account will be taken of any special market factors described in the application. Applicants for the Award will be expected to explain the basis of the achievement (e.g. improved marketing organization or new initiative to cater for export markets) and this will be taken into consideration. Export earnings considered will include receipts by the applicant unit in this country from the export of goods produced in this country, and the provision of services to non-residents. Account will be taken of the overseas expenses incurred other than marketing expenses. Income from profits (after overseas tax) remitted to this country from the applicant unit's direct investments in its overseas branches, subsidiaries or associates in the same general line of business will be taken into account, but not receipts from profits on other overseas investments or by interest on overseas loans or credits.

2. Technological Achievement

A significant advance, leading to increased efficiency, in the application of technology to a production or development process in British industry or the production for sale of goods which incorporate new and advanced technological qualities.

Each award is formally conferred by a Grant of Appointment and is symbolized by a representation of its emblem cast in stainless steel and encapsulated in a transparent acrylic block.

Awards are held for five years and holders are entitled to fly the appropriate Award flag and to display the emblem on the packaging of goods produced in this country, on the goods themselves, on the unit's stationery, in advertising and on certain articles used by employees. Units may also display the emblem of any previous current Awards during the five years.

Awards are announced on April 21 (the actual birthday of The Queen) and published formally in a special supplement to the London Gazette. All enquiries about the scheme and requests for application forms (completed forms must be returned by October 31) should be made to: The Secretary, The Queen's Awards Office, Dean Bradley House, 52 Horseferry Road, London SW1P 2AG. Telephone: 071-222 2277.

Awards for Export Achievement

In 1990, the Queen's Award for Export Achievement was conferred on the following concerns:

Advisory Services Holdings Ltd. Group of Companies, London W1.

AgriSense-BCS Ltd., Pontypridd, Mid Glam.

Align-Rite Ltd., Bridgend, Mid Glam.

Apollo Fire Detectors Ltd., Havant, Hants.

Aquascutum Group PLC, London W1.

Armabord Ltd., Burnley, Lancs.

Industrial Clutch Division of Automotive Products PLC, Leamington Spa, Warks.

Baker & McKenzie, London WC2.

Bermans & Nathans Ltd., London NW1.

Biomet Ltd., Bridgend, Mid Glam.

The Body Shop International PLC, Littlehampton, W. Sussex.

Bonas Machine Company Ltd., Gateshead, Tyne and Wear.

Border Holdings (UK) Ltd., Clun, Shrops.

British Ceramic Service Company Ltd., Newcastle under Lyme, Staffs.

British Replin Ltd., Ayr, Ayrshire.

British Sidac Ltd., Wigton, Cumbria.

British Steel Stainless, Sheffield.

Butterley Brick Ltd., Ripley, Derbyshire.

C & S Antennas Ltd., Rochester.

C. B. Brook & Company Ltd., Bradford.

Caledonian Airmotive Ltd., Prestwick, Ayrshire.

Cambridge Research Biochemicals Ltd., Cambridge.

Chaucer Foods Ltd., Ashford, Kent.

Chivas Brothers Ltd., Paisley, Renfrewshire.

The College of Petroleum Studies, Oxford.

Courtaulds Speciality Plastics, Derby.

Crabtree of Gateshead Ltd., Gateshead, Tyne and Wear.

Crockett & Jones Ltd., Northampton.

Crosrol Ltd., Halifax.

Crosslee PLC, Hipperholme, Halifax.

Crystalox Ltd., Wantage, Oxon.

Datapaq Ltd., Cambridge.

Dent Instrumentation Ltd., Colne, Lancs.

Douglas Laing & Company Ltd., Glasgow.

Dunhill Scotch Whisky Sales Ltd., London NW1.

Dunkirk Metals Ltd., Nottingham.

Eclipse Blinds Ltd., Glasgow.

Edgeworth Electronics Ltd., Darlington.

The Floor Care Division of Electrolux Ltd., Luton, Beds.

Ethicon Ltd., Edinburgh.

Fairbank Brearley, Bingley, W. Yorkshire.

Fairey Industrial Ceramics Ltd., Stone, Staffs.

Filtermist International Ltd., Bridgnorth, Shrops.

Glaxo Holdings PLC, London W1.

Gloster Leisure Furniture Ltd., Bristol.

Gluck Engineering Company Ltd., London SE15.

Hazleton Laboratories Europe Ltd., Harrogate.

Hepco Slide Systems Ltd., Greenford, Middx.

Heraeus Noblelight Ltd., Cambridge.

History Craft Ltd., Cirencester, Glos.

HMB Subwork Ltd., Great Yarmouth, Norfolk.

Hunt & Moscrop Ltd., Middleton, Manchester.

ICI Agrochemicals, Fernhurst, Surrey.

Imperial College of Science, Technology & Medicine, London SW7.

IOP Publishing Ltd., Bristol.

John Brown Engineering Ltd., Clydebank, Dunbartonshire.

John Guest Ltd., West Drayton, Middx.

Kodak Ltd., Hemel Hempstead, Herts.

Kvaerner (UK) Ltd., South Shields, Tyne and Wear.

The Hilton UK Hotels Division of Ladbroke Group PLC, Watford, Herts.

Laidlaw Drew Ltd., Livingston, Scotland.

Land Rover Commercial Division of Rover Group Ltd., Solihull, W. Midlands.

The Special Products Division of Leslie Hartridge Ltd., Buckingham.

The London School of Economics and Political Science, London WC2.

Lowe Refrigeration Company, Carryduff, Co. Down.

LWT (Holdings) Ltd., London SE1.

MF Industrial Ltd., Stretford, Gtr. Manchester.

The Pedigree Petfoods Division of Mars GB Ltd., Melton Mowbray, Leics.

McLellan & Partners Ltd., West Byfleet, Surrey.

Metrotect Ltd., Cleckheaton, W. Yorkshire.

Mordaunt-Short Ltd., Petersfield, Hants.

Morning Foods Ltd., Crewe.

MTM PLC, Yarm, Cleveland.

Murray Allan of Innerleithen Ltd., Innerleithen, Peeblesshire.

Neve Electronics International PLC, Melbourn, Herts.

Norbrook Laboratories Ltd., Newry, Co. Down.

Orthotech (UK) Ltd., Maltby, S. Yorkshire.

Oyster Marine Ltd., Ipswich.

Pains-Wessex Ltd., Salisbury.

Parker Bath Developments Ltd., New Milton, Hants.

Pendle & Rivett Ltd., t/a Fintex of London, London W1.

Phil Ayliff Products Ltd., Nuneaton, Warks.

Pobjoy Mint Ltd., Sutton, Surrey.

Portmeirion Potteries Ltd., Stoke-on-Trent.

Premier Biscuits Division of Premier Brands UK Ltd., Birmingham.

Psion PLC, London W1.

Purolite International Ltd., Pontycrin, Mid Glam.

QDF Components Ltd., Derby.

Quayle Dental Manufacturing Co. Ltd., Worthing, W. Sussex.

R. Mears & Co. Ltd., London EC3.

Radiodetection Ltd., Bristol.

Randox Laboratories Ltd., Crumlin, Co. Antrim.

Rediffusion Simulation Ltd., Crawley, W. Sussex.

Redwood International Ltd., Hemel Hempstead, Herts.

Reediehill Deer Farm, Cupar, Fife.

Reynard Racing Cars Ltd., Bicester, Oxon.

Reynolds & Kent Ltd., Westbury, Wilts.

Ronacrete Ltd., Dagenham, Essex.

The Automotive Electronics Division of Salford Electrical Instruments Ltd., Heywood, Lancs.

Sandon Flexographic Printing Rollers Ltd., Runcorn, Cheshire.

Serif Cowells PLC, Ipswich.

Serono Diagnostics Ltd., Woking, Surrey.

Sharp Manufacturing Company of UK, Wrexham, Clwyd.

Snell & Wilcox Ltd., Portsmouth.

Sony Manufacturing Company UK, Bridgend, Mid Glam.

Sperrin Metal Products Ltd., Draperstown, Co. Londonderry.

Springpart Manufacturing Ltd., Redditch, Worcs.

Stirling Aquaculture, Stirling, Scotland.

Sunset & Vine PLC, London W1.

Supertrack Ltd., Banbury, Oxon.

TBS Engineering, Cheltenham.

Tankard Carpets Ltd., Bradford.

Technophone Ltd., Camberley, Surrey.

Tiphook Group PLC, Bromley, Kent.

Trusthouse Forte PLC, London WC1.

Unipath Ltd., Bedford.

Vascutek Ltd., Inchinnan, Renfrewshire.

Vico Sutures Ltd., Bidford-on-Avon, Warks.

Vitramon Ltd., High Wycombe, Bucks.

W. Harold John (Metals) Ltd., Crindau, Gwent.

Walker Filtration Ltd., Washington, Tyne and Wear.

Wellman Process Engineering Ltd., Smethwick, W. Midlands.

White & Company (Earls Barton) Ltd., Earls Barton, Northants.

Willan-Wogen Alloys Ltd., Rotherham, S. Yorkshire.

Wolfe Publishing Ltd., London WC1.

Yale Materials Handling Ltd., Wolverhampton.

Awards for Technological Achievement

In 1990 the Queen's Award for Technological Achievement was conferred on the following concerns:

The Paper Division of Allied Colloids Ltd., Bradford (*High quality paper and board*).

The Research Department of Allied Colloids Ltd., Bradford (*Process for production of vynilamino esters*).

Clinical Reagents Division of Amersham International PLC, Little Chalfont, Bucks. (*Amerlite laboratory diagnostic system (jointly with the Wolfson Research Laboratories of the Department of Clinical Medicine of the University of Birmingham)*).

The Implant Division of Applied Materials, Horsham, W. Sussex (*Implantation equipment for semiconductor manufacture*).

Applied Video Systems Ltd., t/a AVS Ltd., Chessington, Surrey (*Conversion of TV signals between incompatible TV systems*).

Bonas Machine Company Ltd., Gateshead, Tyne and Wear (*High speed electronic jaquard for broadcloth weaving*).

Main Optical Networks Division (RT45) British Telecom, Research & Technology, Ipswich (*Optical receivers for undersea cable applications*).

Chas. A. Blatchford & Sons Ltd., Basingstoke, Hants. (*Lightweight lower extremity artificial limbs*).

Croda Application Chemicals Ltd., Goole, N. Humberside (*Dicrol CPS rolling oil*).

Dowty Maritime Ocean Systems, part of Dowty Maritime Ltd., Weymouth, Dorset (*Thermal line-scan recorders*).

Elcometer Instruments Ltd., Droylsden, Manchester (*Microprocessor for controlling thickness gauges*).

EM Electronics, Brockenhurst, Hants. (*Ultra low-level DC voltage measurement*).

Epichem Ltd., Wirral, Merseyside (*Metal organic

precursors for semiconductor materials (jointly with the Electronic Materials Division of The Royal Signals and Radar Establishment)).

Gems of Cambridge Ltd., Cambridge (*Gemsys image processing system*).

Glaxo Group Research Ltd., Greenford, Middx. (*Ceftazidime—an antibiotic*).

Glencast Ltd., Leven, Fife (*The Replicast process of producing high-quality castings (jointly with Steel Castings Research and Trade Association)*).

GPT Telecommunications Systems Group (Switching Networks), Liverpool (*System X telecommunication switching system*).

The Technical Department of Gullick Dobson Ltd., Wigan, Gtr. Manchester (*Automated mine roof support system*).

ICI Cellmark Diagnostics, Abingdon, Oxon. (*DNA fingerprinting (jointly with the Lister Institute of Preventive Medicine)*).

The Electrochemical Technology Business of ICI Chemicals & Polymers Ltd., Runcorn, Cheshire (*Membrane electrolyser for large scale production of chemicals*).

ICI Colours & Fine Chemicals, Blackley, Manchester (*Benzodifuranone-based dyes*).

ICL Retail Systems, Bracknell, Berks. (*Point of sale checkout scanning system*).

The Product Development Division of INMOS Ltd., Almondsbury, Bristol (*Design of parallel microprocessors (jointly with Oxford University Computing Laboratory)*).

J. McIntyre (Non Ferrous) Ltd., Dunkirk, Nottingham (*Energy-saving unit for recycling aluminium scrap and waste*).

The Lister Institute of Preventive Medicine, Stanmore, Middx. (*DNA fingerprinting (jointly with ICI Cellmark Diagnostics)*).

Actuation Division of Lucas Aerospace Ltd., Wolverhampton, W. Midlands (*Geared rotary actuators for aircraft flap systems*).

Lumonics Ltd., Rugby, Warks. (*JK 700 Series industrial laser system*).

Micro Focus Group PLC, Newbury, Berks. (*COBOL/2 work bench*).

Mineral Industries Computing Ltd., London W1 (*Software for mineral deposit evaluation*).

NEI International Combustion Ltd., Derby (*Low NOx combustion in power station boilers*).

The NERC ICP-MS Facility, Egham, Surrey (*Inductively coupled plasma mass spectrometry system (jointly with VG Elemental Ltd.)*).

Oxford University Computing Laboratory, Oxford (*Design of parallel microprocessors (jointly with the Product Development Division of INMOS Ltd.)*).

Pearpoint Ltd., Bordon, Hants. (*Solid state mono and colour CCD cameras*).

Perkins Engines Group, Peterborough, Cambs. (*Prima direct injection high speed diesel engine for cars and vans*).

Philips Components Ltd. Washington, Washington, Tyne and Wear (*Advanced manufacturing techniques for TV deflection units*).

Pilkington PE Ltd., St. Asaph, Clwyd (*Production process for fabrication of holographic optical elements*).

Renishaw Metrology Ltd., Wooton-under-Edge, Glos. (*Motorised probe heads incorporating patented kinematic location system*).

The Design Engineering Group of Rolls-Royce PLC, London SW1 (*Aircraft engine noise reduction technology (jointly with the Propulsion Department of The Royal Aerospace Establishment)*).

The Propulsion Department of The Royal Aerospace Establishment, Farnborough, Hants. (*Aircraft engine noise reduction technology (jointly with the Design Engineering Group of Rolls-Royce PLC)*).

The Electronic Materials Division of The Royal Signals and Radar Establishment, Malvern, Worcs. (*Metal organic precursors for semiconductor materials (jointly with Epichem Ltd.)*).

Sericol Group Ltd., Broadstairs, Kent (*Photo stencil emulsions for screen printing*).

The Flight Deck Display Systems Unit of the Cheltenham Division of Smiths Industries Aerospace and Defence Systems, Cheltenham (*Advanced lightemiting diode display systems for commercial jet aircraft*).

STC Submarine Systems, Greenwich, London SE10 (*NL 420 mbit/s submarine cable systems*).

STC Technology Ltd., Harlow, Essex (*Bipolar and complementary metal oxide semiconductor devices in the same integrated circuit*).

Steel Castings Research and Trade Association, Sheffield (*The Replicast process for producing high quality castings (jointly with Glencast Ltd.)*).

The Wolfson Research Laboratories of the Department of Clinical Medicine of the University of Birmingham, Birmingham (*Amerlite laboratory diagnostic system (jointly with Clinical Reagents Division of Amersham International PLC)*).

VG Elemental Ltd., Winsford, Cheshire (*Inductively coupled plasma mass spectrometry system (jointly with the NERC ICP-MS Facility)*).

The Wellcome Research Laboratories of the Wellcome Foundation Ltd., Beckenham, Kent (*Retrovir for the treatment of HIV infection*).

Yarrow Shipbuilders Ltd., Scotstoun, Glasgow (*Type 23 frigate*).

BRITISH MONETARY UNITS

COIN

Gold Coins	Nickel-Brass Coins
†One hundred pounds £100	Two pounds £2
†Fifty pounds £50	One pound £1
†Twenty-five pounds £25	
†Ten pounds £10	**Cupro-Nickel Coins**
Five pounds £5	Crown £5 (1990)
Two pounds £2	50 pence 50p
Sovereign £1	Crown 25p
Half-Sovereign 50p	20 pence 20p
	10 pence 10p
Silver Coins	5 pence 5p (Old)
‡*Maundy Money*	5 pence 5p (New)
Fourpence 4p	
Threepence 3p	**Bronze Coins**
Twopence 2p	2 pence 2p
Penny 1p	1 penny 1p

†Britannia gold bullion coins, introduced in October 1987.

‡Gifts of special money distributed by the Sovereign annually on Maundy Thursday to the number of aged poor men and women corresponding to the Sovereign's own age.

Gold Coin.—Gold ceased to circulate during the First World War. An Order of April 27, 1966, made it illegal for UK residents to continue holding more than four gold coins minted after 1837, or to acquire such coins unless they had been licensed as genuine collectors by the Bank of England. This Order was revoked on April 1, 1971, by the Exchange Control (Gold Coins Exemption) Order, 1971, whereby residents of the United Kingdom, Channel Islands and the Isle of Man may freely buy and sell and hold gold coins.

The 1971 Order was revoked on April 15, 1975, by the Exchange Control (Gold Coins Exemption) Order, 1975. Under this Order, Section 1 of the Exchange Control Act 1947 (which prohibits dealings in gold or foreign currency except with Treasury permission) was exempted for gold coins minted in or before 1837. The import of gold coins minted after 1837 was prohibited except by authorized dealers in gold with individual import licences from the Department of Trade and Industry, and dealing between other UK residents was restricted to coins already held in the UK.

Under an amendment, dated December 16, 1977, the exemptions contained in the 1975 Order were extended to cover gold coins minted in or before 1937.

The 1975 controls over the import of and dealing in gold coins were abolished on June 13, 1979 under the Exchange Control (Gold Coins Exemption) Order 1979, and gold coins, with certain exceptions,* may now be imported and exported without restriction.

On April 1, 1982 the Government introduced VAT (currently 15 per cent) on sales of all gold coin.

Silver Coin.—Prior to 1920 silver coins were struck from sterling silver, an alloy of which 925 parts in 1,000 were silver. In 1920 the proportion of silver was reduced to 500 parts. From January 1, 1947 all 'silver' coins, except Maundy money, have been struck from cupro-nickel, an alloy of copper 75 parts and nickel 25 parts, except for the 20p, composed of copper 84 parts, nickel 16 parts. Maundy coins continue to be struck from sterling silver.

Bronze Coin.—Bronze, introduced in 1860 to replace copper, is currently an alloy of copper 97 parts, zinc 2½ parts and tin ½ part. These proportions have been subject to slight variations in the past.

The 'remedy' is the amount of variation from standard permitted in weight and fineness of coins when first issued from the Mint.

Legal tender of coin.—Gold, dated 1838 onwards, if not below least current weight, is legal tender to any amount. £5 (Crown 1990), £2 and £1 coins are legal tender to any amount. 50p and 20p coins are legal tender up to £10; 10p and 5p coins are legal tender up to £5 and bronze coins are legal tender for amounts up to 20p. Farthings ceased to be legal tender on December 31, 1960, the halfpenny on August 1, 1969, the halfcrown on January 1, 1970, the threepence and penny on August 31, 1971, the sixpence on June 30, 1980 and the decimal halfpenny on December 31, 1984. Also, the old 5p ceases to be legal tender after December 31, 1990.

The decimal system was introduced on February 15, 1971. Since 1982 the word 'new' in 'new pence' displayed on decimal coins has been dropped.

The Channel Islands and the Isle of Man issue their own coinage, which are legal tender only in the island of issue. (For denominations, *see* p. 979.)

---

*Gold coins which are more than fifty years old and valued at a sum in excess of £8,000 cannot be exported without specific authorization from the Department of Trade and Industry.

BANKNOTES

Bank of England notes are currently issued in denominations of £5, £10, £20 and £50 for the amount of the Fiduciary Note Issue, and are legal tender in England and Wales.

The old white notes for £10, £20, £50, £100, £500 and £1,000, which were issued until April 22, 1943, ceased to be legal tender in May 1945, and the old white £5 note in March 1946.

Denomination	Metal	Standard weight (g)	Standard diameter (cm)
Penny	bronze	3·56400	2·0320
2 pence	bronze	7·12800	2·5910
5p (New)	cupro-nickel	3.25	1.80
5 pence (Old)	cupro-nickel	5·65518	2·3595
10 pence	cupro-nickel	11·31036	2·8500
20 pence	cupro-nickel	5·0	2·14
25p Crown	cupro-nickel	28·27590	3·8608
50 pence	cupro-nickel	13·5	3·0
£1	copper/nickel/zinc	9·5	2·25
£2	copper/nickel/zinc	15·98	2·84
£5 Crown	cupro-nickel	28·28	3·861

The white £5 note issued between October 1945 and September 1956, the £5 notes issued between 1957 and 1963, bearing a portrait of Britannia and the first series to bear a portrait of the Queen, issued between 1963 and 1971, ceased to be legal tender on March 14, 1961, June 27, 1967 and September 1, 1973 respectively. The series of £1 notes issued during the years 1928 to 1960 and the 10s. notes of the same type issued from 1928 to 1961—those without the royal portrait—ceased to be legal tender on May 29 and October 30, 1962 respectively. The £1 note first issued in March 1960 (bearing on the back a representation of Britannia) and the £10 note first issued in February 1964 (bearing a lion on the back) both bearing a portrait of the Queen on the front ceased to be legal tender on June 1, 1979. The 10s. note was replaced by the 50p coin in October 1969, and ceased to be legal tender on November 21, 1970. Bank notes which are no longer legal tender are payable when presented at the Head Office of the Bank of England in London.

The first of the current series of Bank notes was a £20 note issued on July 9, 1970. This was followed by the £5 note on November 11, 1971, £10 note on February 20, 1975, £1 note on February 9, 1978 and £50 note on March 20, 1981. The £1 coin was introduced on April 21, 1983 and the £1 denomination note ceased to be legal tender on March 11, 1988. The predominant identifying feature of each note is the portrayal on the back of a prominent figure from Britain's history namely:

£5	The Duke of Wellington
£10	Florence Nightingale
£20	William Shakespeare
£50	Sir Christopher Wren

The new series £5 note was issued on June 7, 1990 and features George Stephenson on the back. This series will replace series D over the next few years.

Note Circulation.—Note circulation is highest at the two peak spending periods of the year—around Christmas and during the summer holiday period. A peak of £17,564 million was reached immediately prior to Christmas 1989, a 6·1 per cent increase on the previous year.

The proportion of the total value of notes in circulation of £1 and £5 notes at end February 1990 compared with the previous year, fell from 0·7 per cent and 11·7 per cent to 0·4 per cent and 10·2 per cent respectively. £10 notes fell from 41·1 per cent to 39·1 per cent. However, £20 notes increased from 25·9 per cent to 29·2 per cent, as did £50 notes, from 14·6 per cent to 15·3 per cent.

On February 28, 1990 the values of notes in circulation were:

£1	£62,186,089
£5	£1,539,118,595
£10	£5,866,006,400
£20	£4,379,298,780
£50	£2,292,251,100

OTHER BANK NOTES

Scotland.—Bank notes are issued by three Scottish banks. The Royal Bank of Scotland and the Bank of Scotland issue notes for £5, £10, £20 and £100. The Royal Bank of Scotland also issues £1 notes. The Clydesdale Bank issues notes for £5, £10, £20, £50, £100. Scottish notes are not legal tender, but in Scotland they enjoy a status equal to that of the Bank of England note.

Northern Ireland.—Bank notes are issued by four banks in Northern Ireland. The Northern Bank and the Ulster Bank issue notes for £5, £10, £20, £50 and £100. The Allied Irish Bank and the Bank of Ireland issue notes for £5, £10, £20 and £100. Northern Irish notes are not legal tender but in Northern Ireland they circulate widely and enjoy a status comparable to that of Bank of England notes.

Channel Islands.—The States of Jersey issues its own currency notes and coinage. The note denominations are for £1, £5, £10, £20 and £50. Seven denominations of coins are issued: 1p, 2p, 5p, 10p, 20p, 50p and £1. The States of Guernsey issues its own currency notes and coinage. The notes are for £1, £5, £10 and £20. The denomination of coins are 1p, 2p, 5p, 10p, 20p, 50p and £1.

The Isle of Man.—The Isle of Man Government issues notes for £1, £5, £10, £20 and £50. Although these notes are only legal tender in the Isle of Man they are accepted at face value in branches of the clearing banks in the United Kingdom. The Isle of Man issues coins for 1p, 2p, 5p, 10p, 20p, 50p, £1, £2 and £5.

Although none of the series of notes specified above is legal tender in the United Kingdom they are generally accepted by the banks irrespective of their place of issue. At one time the banks made a commission charge for handling Scottish and Irish notes but this was abolished some years ago.

SLANG TERMS FOR MONEY
(Reproduced from *Whitaker's Almanack* 1891)

In addition to the ordinary terms there are others which, although puzzling to a foreigner, are tolerably well understood in this country. In Scotland, a man who flies 'kites' may not be worth a 'bodle', and in England not worth a 'mag'—coins which no one ever saw. Such a man will toss you for a 'bob'. He, of course, would be shunned by the lady who lost a 'pony' on last year's 'Oaks', and by her husband who lost a 'monkey' on the 'Derby' at Epsom a day or two previously. A gentleman who is worth a 'plum' (£100,000) need never be short of 'tin'; while the outcast who begs a few 'coppers' in order to procure a bed generally has no 'blunt'. The following words are commonly in use:

A Joey = 4d.	A Pony = £25.
A Tanner = 6d.	A Monkey = £500.
A Bob = 1s.	A Kite = An accommodation Bill.
Half a Bull = 2s. 6d.	Browns = Copper or bronze.
A Bull = 5s.	Tin = Money generally.
A Quid = £1.	Blunt = Silver, or money in general.

THE INTERNATIONAL STOCK EXCHANGE

The International Stock Exchange of the United Kingdom and Republic of Ireland Ltd. serves the needs of government, industry and investors by providing facilities for raising capital and a central market place for securities trading. There are over 7,000 securities listed on the International Stock Exchange (ISE), which have a value of approximately £2,106,145·6 million. In 1989 securities worth some £1,662,255·4 million changed hands. This central market place covers not only government stocks (called gilts) and UK and overseas company shares (called equities and fixed interest stocks) but other investment instruments such as traded options on equities and indices.

Big Bang

During 1986 the International Stock Exchange went through the greatest period of change in its two hundred year history. In March 1986 it opened its doors for the first time to overseas and corporate membership of the Exchange, allowing banks, insurance companies and overseas securities houses to become members of the Exchange and to buy existing member firms. On October 27, 1986, three major reforms took place, changes which became known as 'Big Bang':

(1) abolition of scales of minimum commissions, allowing clients to negotiate freely with their brokers about the charge for their services

(2) abolition of the separation of member firms into brokers and jobbers. Under the new system, firms are broker/dealers, able to act as agents on behalf of clients; to act as principals buying and selling shares for their own account; and to become registered market makers, making continuous buying and selling prices in specific securities

(3) the introduction of the Stock Exchange Automated Quotations (SEAQ) system. Market makers input their buying and selling prices into SEAQ, which displays the competing quotations on a composite page onscreen. For the largest and most frequently traded company shares ('Alpha'), e.g. Marks and Spencer or BP, the volume of shares traded is also updated continuously throughout the day.

Of all these changes, the implementation of SEAQ has had perhaps the most visible effect. Dealing in stocks and shares now takes place via the telephone in the Firms' own dealing rooms, rather than face to face on the floor of the Exchange. The new systems also provide increased investor protection. All deals taking place via the Exchange's SEAQ system are recorded on a database which can be used to resolve disputes or to carry out investigations.

Members of the International Stock Exchange buy and sell shares on behalf of the public, as well as institutions such as pension funds or insurance companies. In return for transacting the deal, the broker will charge a commission, which is usually based upon the value of the transaction. The market makers, or wholesalers, in each security do not charge a commission for their services, but will quote the broker two prices, a price at which they will buy and a price at which they will sell. It is the middle of these two prices which is published in lists of Stock Exchange prices in newspapers.

Regulatory Bodies

On November 12, 1986 members of the Exchange agreed to merge with members of the international broking community in London, based outside the Exchange, in order to form two new bodies—the International Stock Exchange of the United Kingdom and Republic of Ireland Ltd. and the Securities Association Ltd. These two regulatory bodies have been formed under the provisions of the Financial Services Act 1986, which requires investment businesses to be authorized and regulated by a Self Regulating Organization (SRO) of which the Securities Association is one. The Act also requires business to be conducted through a Registered Investment Exchange (RIE). The International Stock Exchange is an RIE, regulating four main markets: UK equities, international equities, gilts and options.

Primary Markets

The Exchange serves the needs of industry by providing a mechanism where they can raise capital for development and growth through the issue of listed securities. For a company entering the market for the first time there are two possible Stock Exchange markets, depending upon the size, history and requirements of the company. The first is the listed market, which exists for well-established companies which must comply with stringent criteria relating to all aspects of their operations. At present, companies coming to this market require a three-year trading record with a minimum of 25 per cent of the shares held in public hands. The Unlisted Securities Market was established in 1980 with less rigorous entry requirements designed with the smaller and newer company in mind. Companies at present are required to provide a two-year trading record and a minimum of 10 per cent of the shares must be in public hands.

Following a review of the Markets structure, the Third Market, which was launched in January 1987 for smaller companies with a one-year trading record or in certain cases no trading record at all, will be phased out by 1 January 1991.

Once admitted to the Exchange, all companies are obliged to keep their shareholders informed of their progress, making announcements of a price-sensitive nature through the Exchange's company announcements department.

The International Stock Exchange has its headquarters in London, and administrative centres around the UK and the Republic of Ireland. At present there are some 5,100 individual members and about 400 member firms.

The Governing Council

The interests of the membership of the International Stock Exchange are reflected in the governing Council, whose members are the directors under the Companies Act and are responsible for overall policy and the strategic direction of the Exchange. The Council delegates comprehensive powers and responsibilities, coupled with full accountability to the Executive Board and, through the Board, to three strategic business units; Primary Markets (responsible for the Exchange's functions as competent authority for listing in the UK), Trading Markets (responsible for the Exchange's functions as a recognized investment exchange for a variety of trading markets), and Settlement Services (responsible for the Exchange's clearing house functions). The Council consists of 32 members: 25 elected representatives, five lay members, the Chief Executive of the Exchange and the Government Broker.

Chairman, A. C. Hugh Smith.
Deputy Chairman, H. Post; I. G. Salter.
Chief Executive of ISE, P. J. Rawlins.

LIFE AND GENERAL INSURANCE

Authorization of Insurance Companies

Section Three of the Insurance Companies Act 1982 empowers the Department of Trade and Industry (Insurance Division, 10–18 Victoria Street, SW1H 0NN) to authorize corporate bodies to transact insurance in the United Kingdom provided they comply with the financial and other regulations detailed in the Act.

At the end of 1989 there were 838 insurance companies with authorization to transact one or more classes of insurance business in the UK.

Regulation of Insurance Companies

Under the Financial Services Act 1986, the Securities and Investments Board (SIB) is empowered to make, monitor and enforce rules about the conduct of investment business.

The SIB has, in turn, set up a number of Self-Regulating Organizations dealing with different sectors of the investment market. Insurance com-panies offering long-term contracts like life insurance, pensions, unit trusts and annuities can either obtain authorization directly from SIB or from the main SRO dealing with the marketing of life insurance and pensions, the Life And Unit Trust Regulatory Organization (LAUTRO), Centre Point, 103 New Oxford Street, WC1A 1QH. It is possible that insurers may also need authorization from other SROs, for example, the Investment Management Regulatory Organization (IMRO), Centre Point, 103 New Oxford Street, WC1A 1QH.

Association of British Insurers

Ninety per cent of the world-wide business of insurance companies is transacted by the 450 members of the Association of British Insurers. This trade association has represented both life and general insurers since 1985 when it replaced the British Insurance Association, the Life Offices Association and other such organizations.

BRITISH INSURANCE COMPANIES IN 1989

The following insurance company figures refer to members of the Association of British Insurers, and also to certain non-members.

World-wide General Business Trading Result

	1987 £m	1988 £m	1989 £m
Net written premiums	19,709	21,902	24,988
Underwriting profit/loss for one year account business			
Motor	−477	−374	−770
Fire and Accident	−479	−116	−715
Transfer to profit and loss account for other business			
Marine, Aviation, Transport	+52	+29	−170
Other	−228	−106	−366
Total underwriting result	−1,133	−568	−2,022
Investment income	2,631	2,918	3,535
Overall trading profit	1,498	2,350	1,513
Profit as a % of premium income	+7·6	+10·7	+6·1

World-wide General Business Underwriting Result

	1988				1989			
	UK	USA	Other	Total	UK	USA	Other	Total
Fire and Accident								
Premiums (£m)	7,053	1,792	2,407	11,251	7,947	1,997	3,011	12,954
Profit/loss (£m)	+334·0	−299·6	−105·6	−71·3	−19·4	−363·8	−331·9	−715·1
% of premiums	+4·7	−16·7	−4·4	−0·6	−0·2	−18·2	−11·0	−5·5
Motor								
Premiums (£m)	4,017	1,212	1,760	6,989	4,539	1,369	2,323	8,231
Profit/loss (£m)	−152·9	−53·9	−170·8	−377·7	−276·7	−170·5	−322·9	−770·1
% of premiums	−3·8	−4·5	−9·7	−5·4	−6·1	−12·5	−13·9	−9·4

Net Premium Income by Territory 1989

	UK £m	Other EC countries £m	USA £m	Other overseas £m	Total (world-wide) £m
Fire and Accident (non-motor)	8,593 (+13·3%)	1,146 (+19·3%)	2,083 (+11·9%)	3,229 (+10·3%)	15,051 (+12·9%)
Motor...............................	4,589 (+13·3%)	975 (+33·2%)	1,370 (+12·9%)	1,368 (+31·3%)	8,302 (+18·0%)
Marine, Aviation and Transport	1,193 (+6·4%)	155 (+13·5%)	151 (+15·7%)	136 (−5·7%)	1,635 (+6·7%)
Total general business	14,375 (+12·7%)	2,276 (+24·4%)	3,604 (+12·5%)	4,733 (+15·0%)	24,988 (+14·1%)
Ordinary long-term	28,136 (+34·9%)	1,780 (+29·8%)	1,572 (+19·9%)	2,937 (+35·8%)	34,425 (+33·9%)
Industrial long-term................	1,353 (+0·2%)	—	—	—	1,353 (+0·2%)
Total long-term business	29,489 (+32·8%)	1,780 (+29·8%)	1,572 (+19·9%)	2,937 (+35·8%)	35,778 (+32·2%)
Total............................	43,864 (+25·5%)	4,056 (+26·7%)	5,176 (+14·6%)	7,670 (+22·2%)	60,766 (+24·1%)

(Percentages shown are increases of 1989 figures over those for 1988).

Claims Statistics

	1988	1989
Fire claims		
Commercial fires	£475·0 m	£591·5 m (+24·5%)
Domestic fires....................................	£170·9 m	£200·9 m (+17·55%)
Theft claims		
Commercial theft (inc. money)	£134·7 m	£167·9 m (+24·6%)
Domestic theft	£285·9 m	£276·4 m (−3·3%)

LLOYD'S OF LONDON

Lloyd's of London is an incorporated society of private underwriters who provide an international market for almost any type of insurance. Ships, aircraft, oil rigs, cargo of all descriptions, motor cars, civil engineering projects, fire, personal accident and third party liability are a few random examples of the everyday risks placed at Lloyd's which currently earn a premium income of over £6,000 million for underwriters each year. Three-quarters of this business comes from outside Britain and makes a valuable contribution to the country's balance of payments.

A policy is subscribed at Lloyd's by private individuals with unlimited liability. A specialist underwriter accepts risks at Lloyd's on behalf of members (often referred to as 'names') grouped in a syndicate. There are currently over 28,000 members in some 401 syndicates of varying sizes, some with over two thousand names and each managed by an underwriting agent approved by the Council of Lloyd's.

Lloyd's membership today is drawn from many sources. Industry, commerce and the professions are strongly represented while many members work at Lloyd's either for brokerage firms or for underwriting agencies.

Underwriting membership of Lloyd's is open to men and women of any nationality provided that they meet the stringent financial requirements of the Society, or Corporation, of Lloyd's. Assets of up to £250,000 have to be shown and a deposit lodged with the Corporation as security for underwriting liabilities. This deposit, which must be in the form of approved securities, is determined at 30 per cent of the member's annual premium income.

Lloyd's is incorporated by Act of Parliament and governed by a Council of 28 members, twelve of whom are elected from and by underwriting members working at Lloyd's and eight from and by the external membership. Eight Council members are nominated by the Council subject to confirmation by the Governor of the Bank of England.

The Council is a legislative body responsible for deciding on major policy matters, for regulating the Lloyd's market, for the election of new underwriting members, and for establishing the requirements of membership and the rules governing the financial security to be provided by those doing business at Lloyd's.

The Council's 'working' members form the Committee of Lloyd's, an executive body which is responsible for putting the Council's directives into effect, managing the Society's affairs, and administering the Lloyd's market on a day-to-day basis.

The Corporation is a non-profit-making body chiefly financed by its members' subscriptions. It provides the premises, administrative staff and services enabling Lloyd's underwriting syndicates to conduct their business. It does not, however, assume corporate liability for the risks accepted by its members, who remain responsible to the full extent of their personal means for their underwriting affairs.

Lloyd's syndicates have no direct contact with the public. All business is transacted through some 260 firms of insurance brokers accredited by the Corporation of Lloyd's. In addition, non-Lloyd's brokers in the UK when guaranteed by Lloyd's brokers, are able to deal directly with Lloyd's motor syndicates, a facility which has made the Lloyd's market more accessible to the insuring public.

Lloyd's also provides the most comprehensive shipping intelligence service available in the world. Shipping and other information received from Lloyd's agents, shipowners, news agencies and other sources throughout the world, is collated and distributed to newspapers, radio and television services, as well as to maritime and commercial interests in general. This information is published by Lloyd's of London Press Ltd. and distributed worldwide. *Lloyd's List* is London's oldest daily newspaper and contains news of general commercial interest as well as shipping information. *Lloyd's Shipping Index*, also published daily, lists some 25,000 ocean-going vessels in alphabetical order and gives the latest known report of each.

Lloyd's Membership Syndicates and Brokers 1982–1989

	1982	1983	1984	1985	1986	1987	1988	1989
Membership	20,145	21,601	23,438	26,050	28,944	31,484	33,532	28,770
Of which Brokers	266	272	265	261	258	258	275	260

Lloyd's Results 1987

Year of Account	Marine		Non-Marine		Aviation		Motor	
	1986	1987	1986	1987	1986	1987	1986	1987
	£m	£m	£m	£m	£m	£m	£m	£m
Net premiums	1,466·9	1,316·6	1,820·4	1,622·1	428·3	368·8	479·3	404·4
Underwriting result	146·9	260·0	8·7	218·3	176·0	229·3	80·1	37·0
Gross investment return	228·7	166·8	428·4	290·5	91·4	61·2	47·1	31·2
Closed year of account profit	291·9	352·1	281·9	385·6	246·2	266·3	60·8	9·3

Lloyd's Global Accounts
(as at December 31, 1989)

Year of account	1986 £'000	1987 £'000
Gross premiums	5,235,313	6,154,604
Premiums in respect of reinsurance ceded	1,523,399	1,959,696
Net premiums	3,711,914	4,194,908
Reinsurance premiums received from previous accounts	3,666,113	4,656,086
	7,378,027	8,850,994
Gross claims	3,767,819	5,617,587
Reinsurance recoveries	1,455,912	2,718,352
Net claims	2,311,907	2,899,235
Reinsurance premiums paid to close the accounts	4,321,569	5,540,054
	6,633,476	8,439,289
Underwriting result	744,551	411,705
Gross investment income	428,805	607,536
Gross investment appreciation	120,915	188,063

Lloyd's Global Accounts (cont.)

Year of account	1986 £'000	1987 £'000
Gross investment return	549,720	795,599
Profit/(Loss) on currency exchange	(1,636)	14,532
	548,084	810,131
Result before syndicate expenses	1,292,635	1,221,836
Syndicate expenses	279,310	341,055
Closed year of account profit	1,013,325	880,781
Names' personal expenses	363,868	371,618
Profit available to Names before tax	649,457	509,163

INSURANCE BROKERS

The Insurance Brokers Registration Act 1977 empowers the Insurance Brokers Registration Council (15 St. Helens Place, EC3A 6DS) as the statutory body responsible for the registration of insurance brokers. The Council is responsible for the registration and training of insurance brokers, conduct of business, and discipline, and it lays down rules relating to such matters as accounting practice, staff qualifications, advertising, etc.

It is possible to act as an insurance intermediary without being registered with the IBRC but unregistered intermediaries are forbidden to use the words 'Insurance Broker' as a title.

IBRC Registered Brokers

	1990
Registered individuals	14,657
Limited Companies registered	3,187
Sole traders and partnerships...........	1,503
(containing 2,309 partners and directors)	

THE EUROPEAN COMMUNITY AND 1992

In 1986 the European Community's Heads of Government signed the Single European Act, which set out a programme of over 300 EC Directives which are intended to achieve the removal of barriers to a free market within the community.

Progress on the establishment of a single European insurance market was very slow. Sir Leon Brittan, the EC Commissioner responsible for financial services and competition, outlined in November 1989 plans to introduce a number of Directives which will help insurance catch up with other financial sectors in the preparation for a single European market.

Sir Leon's proposals included a 'single passport' system for authorization of insurance companies along the lines of those for banks. These proposals will be outlined in draft life and non-life 'framework' directives to be published during 1990. UK insurers will examine the wording of these directives carefully as the liberal regime in the UK for investment contrasts sharply with those in some other EC countries. This could mean that proposals which have the effect of liberalizing other countries might actually restrict investment by fund managers in the UK.

In the run-up to 1992 UK insurers are concerned not so much by the competition presented by insurers in other EC countries but by their vulnerability to take-overs. In several of the EC countries one insurer dominates the market. This is not the case in the UK where the business is much more widely spread between a much larger number of insurers. As a result the largest of the UK insurers are smaller than some of their European competitors. Some commentators believe that buying into the UK market might be viewed as an easier option than establishing a UK operation or operating entirely from abroad.

INVISIBLE EARNINGS OF INSURANCE

	1987	1988
Insurance	£4,834 m	£3,772 m

LIFE INSURANCE AND PENSIONS

Personal Pensions

The cut-off date for qualifying for the full 2 per cent incentive bonus from the Department of Social Security by contracting out of the State Earnings Related Pension Scheme (SERPS) was April 6, 1989. The weeks leading up to the deadline saw an enormous demand for personal pension contracts, which almost proved to be too great for the insurance companies, who are the providers of the majority of these pensions. In some cases, the sheer weight of demand meant long delays in processing documentation and, in the case of at least one company, the taking of the unprecedented step of refusing to take on any further new business in order to maintain their level of service to existing clients.

Banks and building societies are also providing deposit-based personal pensions but these have proved to be only a fraction of the contracts sold.

Most insurance companies expected demand to tail-off during the rest of 1989 but personal pensions continued to sell well. The premium income they generated proved an excellent buffer for insurance companies against the fall in demand for some types of life insurance policies brought about by the depressed housing market.

Individual Pensions—New Business 1988–89

Personal (or self-employed) pensions	New annual premiums £m			New single premiums £m			DSS rebates* £m	
	Non-Linked	Linked	Total	Non-Linked	Linked	Total	Non-Linked	Linked
1988								
1st quarter	86	78	165	167	68	236	—	—
2nd quarter	135	138	273	244	101	345	—	—
3rd quarter	107	97	204	108	46	155	131	95
4th quarter	122	128	250	118	65	183	141	114
1989								
1st quarter	119	127	246	193	113	306	236	220
2nd quarter	165	191	356	281	236	516	318	300
3rd quarter	100	125	225	260	228	488	80	143
4th quarter	96	122	218	415	286	701	80	116
12 months to:								
December 1988	450	441	892	637	280	919	272	209
December 1989	480	565	1,045	1,149	863	2,011	714	779

The figures given for total years are taken from the annual returns which are completed in the following year and therefore are more accurate than the total of the four quarters.

NB: The figures up to the second quarter of 1988 are in respect of 'self-employed' pension policies. Although 'self-employed' pension policies were not available after June 30, 1988, delays mean that business was still being reported during subsequent quarters; these are included in the table above, as are incremental or additional single premiums paid on 'self-employed' contracts. The single premium figures for previous years have been revised to coincide with the current practice of including incremental payments as new premiums.

* The figures shown here are the best estimate of the current year's DSS rebates and incentives to be received under policies effected in the quarter, whether received or not.

Premium Income for World-wide Long-Term Insurance Business

	1987 £m	1988 £m	1989 £m
Ordinary Branch:			
Yearly premiums for life insurances, annuities and pensions in the UK	10,525	12,585	15,094 (+19·9%)
Single premiums for life insurances, annuities and pensions in the UK	9,446	8,044	12,772 (+58·8%)
Premiums for permanent health and other long-term insurances in the UK	201	226	270 (+19·5%)
Overseas premium income.................................	3,996	4,845	6,289 (+29·8%)
Industrial Branch:			
Premium Income (UK only)	1,301	1,351	1,353 (+0·2%)

(Percentages shown are increases of 1989 figures over those for 1988).

World-wide Long-Term Insurance Business—Outgo

	1987 £m	1988 £m	1989 £m
Ordinary Branch:			
Total payments made to UK policyholders	13,376	13,998	15,984 (+14·2%)
Total payments made to overseas policyholders...............	1,895	2,213	3,308 (+49·5%)
Industrial Branch:			
Total payments made to UK policyholders	1,287	1,435	1,687 (+17·6%)

NB: Payments to policyholders includes death claims, maturities, annuities, surrenders (including planned cashing-in of linked and other similar savings policies and surrenders of bonus and bonuses in cash), refunds under pension schemes and payments under PHI and other long-term contracts.

Investments of insurance companies

In 1989, as in most other years, the underwriting loss of the insurance companies was more than offset by their investment income. Below is a table of the types of investments of the insurance companies.

Investment of funds	Long-term business		General business	
	1988 £m	1989 £m	1988 £m	1989 £m
Index-linked British Government securities ...	3,607	4,220	540	134
British Government authority securities (excluding those in line 1)	30,002	29,086	5,642	5,665
Other government, provincial and municipal stocks	6,494	6,706	7,384	7,043
Debentures, loan stocks, preference and guaranteed stocks and shares	15,473	22,913	5,630	8,753
Ordinary stocks and shares..................	102,456	145,226	11,921	16,184
Mortgages..................................	10,866	13,738	1,688	1,988
Real property and ground rents	35,893	42,585	3,533	4,324
Other invested assets	11,207	13,824	6,391	7,219
'Net current assets'..........................	95	144	4,228	5,904
Total net assets	216,093	277,442	46,957	57,214
Gross income for year on investment holdings (gross of tax and interest paid)	12,418	15,415	3,139	3,893
Interest payable in year	312	447	221	358

DIRECTORY OF INSURANCE COMPANIES

The class of Insurance undertaken is shown in the second column as follows: A—Accident (which includes Motor, Employers' Liability, etc.); F—Fire (including Burglary); L—Life; M—Marine; and Re—Reinsurance.

A number of offices are now included in a Group—the initials of which appear after the name. The main Groups are as follows—ES—Eagle Star; CU—Commercial Union; GRE—Guardian Royal Exchange; GA—General Accident; NU—Norwich Union; R—Royal; SA—Sun Alliance & London.

Est.	Nature of Business	Name of Company	Address
1961	L	Abbey Life.....................	80 Holdenhurst Road, Bournemouth BH8 8AL
1951	AFM Re	Albion	9–13 Fenchurch Buildings, EC3M 5HR
1824	AFM	Alliance...................SA	1 Bartholomew Lane, EC2
1965	L	Allied Dunbar	Allied Dunbar Centre, Swindon
1921	L	American Life	2–8 Altyre Road, Croydon
1960	AF	Ansvar.......................	31 St. Leonards Road, Eastbourne BN21 3UR
1808	AFM	Atlas...................GRE	Royal Exchange, EC3
1849	L	Australian Mutual Provident ..	A.M.P. House, Dingwall Rd., Croydon CR9 2AD
1925	AFL Re	Avon	Tiddington Road, Stratford-upon-Avon
1905	AFM	Baptist.......................	4 Southampton Row, WC1
1965	L	Barclays	94 St Paul's Churchyard, EC4
1894	AFM	Bedford General	Zurich House, Stanhope Road, Portsmouth
1925	AFLM Re	Black Sea and Baltic..........	65 Fenchurch Street, EC3M 4EV
1959	AFLM	Bradford	North Park, Halifax HX1 2TU
	L	Britannia Life	190 West George Street, Glasgow
1866	AFL	Britannic	Moor Green, Moseley, Birmingham B13 8QF
1863	M	British & Foreign Marine .... R	New Hall Place, Liverpool
1878	Engineering	British Engine .... R	Longridge House, Manchester M60 4DT
1854	AFLM	British Equitable......... GRE	Royal Exchange, EC3
1896	L	British Life	Reliance House, Mt. Ephraim, Tunbridge Wells, Kent
1908	AFM	British Oak .... GRE	Royal Exchange, EC3
1881	A	Builders' Accident	31 & 32 Bedford Street, Strand, WC2
1805	L	Caledonian .... GRE	Royal Exchange, EC3
1934	AFM	Cambrian .... GRE	Royal Exchange, EC3
1847	L	Canada Life	Canada Life House, Potters Bar, Herts. EN6 5BA
1963	L	Cannon Lincoln..............	1 Olympic Way, Wembley HA9 0NB
1903	AFM	Car & General .... GRE	Royal Exchange, EC3
1885	AFM	Century ....SA	1 Bartholomew Lane, EC2
1922	AFMex-motor	Chemists' Mutual	321 Chase Road, Southgate, N14
1920	L	Citicorp British National	Perrymount Road, Haywards Heath, W. Sussex
1862	L	City of Glasgow Friendly......	200 Bath Street, Glasgow G2 4HJ
1824	L	Clerical, Medical Group........	10–14 John Adams Street, WC2N 6HA
1873	L	Colonial Mutual	24 Ludgate Hill, EC4P 4BD
1861	AFLM	Commercial Union	St. Helen's, 1 Undershaft, EC3

Est'd.	Nature of Business	Name of Company	Address
1871	L	Confederation	Lytton Way, Stevenage, Herts
1891	AF Re	Congregational	Currer House, Currer Street, Bradford BD1 5BA
1867	AFLM	Co-operative	Miller Street, Manchester M60 0AL
1905	AFLM Re	Cornhill	32 Cornhill, EC3V 3LJ
1900	L	Crown Financial Management .	Crown House, Crown Square, Woking, Surrey
1899	A	Crusader	Woodhatch, Reigate, Surrey RH2 8BL
1908	AF	Dominion	92–94 Gracechurch Street, EC3
1904	AFLM Re	Eagle Star	60 St. Mary Axe, EC3A 8JQ
1887	AFL	Ecclesiastical	Beaufort House, Brunswick Road, Gloucester
1901	AFL	Economic....................	Economic House, London Road, Sittingbourne
1880	AFM	Employers' Liability ...... CU	St. Helen's, 1 Undershaft, EC3
1932	Animal Ins.	Equine and Livestock.........	610–616 Chiswick High Road, W4
1762	L	Equitable Life................	4 Coleman Street, EC2R 5AP
1844	L	Equity & Law	Amersham Road, High Wycombe, Bucks
1802	AF	Essex & Suffolk .... GRE	Royal Exchange, EC3
1894	AFM	Excess	13 Fenchurch Avenue, EC3
1925	AFL	Federation Mutual	29 Linkfield Lane, Redhill, Surrey
1890	AF	Fine Art & General .... CU	St. Helen's, 1 Undershaft, EC3
1832	L	Friends' Provident	Pixham End, Dorking, Surrey
1899	L	FS Assurance	190 West George Street, Glasgow
1885	AFM Re	General Accident	Pitheavlis, Perth, Scotland
1837	L	General Accident Life	2 Rougier Street, York YO1 1HR
1848	L	Gresham Life	2–6 Prince of Wales Road, Bournemouth
1910	AFM	Gresham Fire & Accident	11 Queen Victoria Street, EC4
1840	AFM	Guarantee Society .... GA	36–37 Old Jewry, EC2
1821	ALFM Re	Guardian Assurance ..... GRE	Royal Exchange, EC3
1821	ALFM Re	Guardian Royal Exch. .... GRE	Royal Exchange, EC3
1908	AFM	Hibernian	Haddington Road, Dublin 4
1960	L	Hill Samuel	NLA Tower, Addiscombe Road, Croydon
1932	FL	Ideal	Pitmaston, Birmingham, 13
1935	L	Insurance Corporation of Ireland (Life)	Burlington Road, Dublin 4
1939	L	Irish Life	Lr. Abbey Street, Dublin 2
1880	AF	Iron Trades	Iron Trades House, 21–24 Grosvenor Place, SW1V 7JA
1838	L	LAS Group	10 George Street, Edinburgh EH2 2YH
1896	L	Laurentian Life..............	Laurentian House, Barnwood, Glos GL4 7RZ
1836	AFLM Re	Legal and General	Temple Court, 11 Queen Victoria Street, EC4
1970	L	Liberty Life	Liberty House, Station Road, New Barnet
1890	AFLM	Licenses & General .... GRE	Royal Exchange, EC3
1918	AFM	Liverpool Marine & General....	4–5 King William Street, EC4
1843	L	Liverpool Victoria Friendly	Victoria House, Southampton Row, WC1B 4DB
1890	AFM	Local Government Guarantee .. GRE	Royal Exchange, EC3
1836	AFM Re	Lombard Continental Insurance	77 Gracechurch Street, EC3
1869	AFM Re	London Guar. & Reinsurance...	4 Colston Avenue, Bristol
1919	AFM	London & Lancashire.........	New Hall Place, Liverpool
1806	L	London Life	100 Temple Street, Bristol
1869	L	London & Manchester	Winslade Park, Exeter, Devon
1860	AFM	London & Provincial Marine ... GA	Lloyd's Building, Lime Street, EC3
1862	AFM	London & Scottish .... CU	St. Helen's, 1 Undershaft, EC3
1961	L	M & G Assurance	M & G House, Victoria Road, Chelmsford
1887	L	Manufacturers Life	St. George's Way, Stevenage
1836	M	Marine...................... R	34–36 Lime Street, EC3
1852	L	Marine & General	MGM House, Heene Road, Worthing
1864	M	Maritime .... NU	Surrey Street, Norwich
1884	L	Med., Sickness, Ann. and Life...	7–10 Chandos Street, Cavendish Square, W1
1907	Re	Mercantile & General.........	Moorfields House, Moorfields, EC2
1970	L	Merchant Investors MI Group .	91 Wimpole Street, W1M 7DA
1871	M	Merchants' Marine .... CU	St. Helen's, 1 Undershaft, EC3
1872	AF	Methodist	Brazennose House, Brazennose Street, Manchester
1940	AFM	Minster	Minster House, Arthur Street, EC4
1906	AFM	Motor Union .... GRE	Royal Exchange, EC3
1903	AFL	Municipal Mutual	25–27 Old Queen Street, Westminster, SW1
1890	FL	Nalgo Insurance Association ...	1 Mabledon Place, WC1H 9AJ
1935	L	NEL Britannia................	Milton Court, Dorking, Surrey
1914	AF	NEM Insurance	Station Road, Swindon, Wilts. SN1 1DF
1910	AFL	NFU Mutual..................	Tiddington Road, Stratford-upon-Avon
1863	Fidelity Guar.	Natl. Guaran. & Suretyship CU	St. Helen's, 1 Undershaft, EC3
1894	AF	National Ins. & Guarantee Cor..	Heron House, 145 City Road, EC1

Est.	Nature of Business	Name of Company	Address
1830	L	National Mutual Life	The Priory, Priory Park, Hitchin, Herts.
1835	L	National Provident Institution .	N.P. House, Tunbridge Wells, Kent
1864	Machinery	National Vulcan Eng. Ins. Group................... SA	Empire House, St. Martin's-le-Grand, EC1
1921	Naval Officers' risks, etc.	Navigators & General ...... ES	113 Queens Road, Brighton
1869	L	N.M. Financial Management ...	N.M. House, Seldown, Poole, Dorset
1809	AFLM	North British & Mercantile CU	St. Helen's, 1 Undershaft, EC3
1836	AFLM	Northern................ CU	St. Helen's, 1 Undershaft, EC3
1797	AFM Re	Norwich Union Fire..........	Surrey Street, Norwich
1808	L	Norwich Union Life..........	Surrey Street, Norwich
1871	AFM	Ocean Accident .... CU	St. Helen's, 1 Undershaft, EC3
1859	M	Ocean Marine .... CU	St. Helens, Undershaft, EC3
1931	AFM Aviation	Orion	Orion House, Bouverie Road West, Folkestone, Kent
1886	AFM Re	Palatine.....................	77 Leadenhall Street, EC3
1864	AFLM Re	Pearl.........................	Pearl House, Thorpe Wood, Peterborough
1958	Sickness A	Permanent	7–10 Chandos Street, Cavendish Square, W1
1782	AFLM	Phoenix .... SA	1 Bartholomew Lane, EC2
1891	L	Pioneer Mutual	16 Crosby Road North, Liverpool L69
1987	L	Prolific Life and Pensions	Stramongate, Kendal, Cumbria
1969	L	Property Growth..............	Leon House, High Street, Croydon
1877	L	Provident Life Association	Provident Way, Basingstoke, Hampshire
1840	L	Provident Mutual Life	25–31 Moorgate, EC2R 6BA
1903	AF	Provincial....................	Stramongate, Kendal, Cumbria
1848	AFLM Re	Prudential....................	1 Stephen Street, W1
1986	L	Prudential Holborn	30 Old Burlington Street, W1
1849	AF	Railway Passengers .... CU	St. Helen's, 1 Undershaft, EC3
1864	AFL	Refuge	Refuge House, Alderley Road, Wilmslow, Cheshire SK9 1PF
1911	L	Reliance Mutual	Reliance House, Tunbridge Wells, Kent
1906	AF	Reliance Fire & Accident	Reliance House, Tunbridge Wells, Kent
1881	AF	Reliance Marine .... GRE	Royal Exchange, EC3
1918	AF	Road Transport & General GA	Pitheavlis, Perth
1845	L	Royal Life	New Hall Place, Liverpool
1720	AFM	Royal Exchange..............	Royal Exchange, EC3
1971	L	Royal Heritage Life	Bretton Way, Peterborough
1850	L	Royal Liver Friendly	Royal Liver Building, Pier Head, Liverpool 3
1861	AFL	Royal London.................	Royal London House, Middleborough, Colchester
1887	L	Royal Nat. Pension Fund for Nurses	Burdett House, 15 Buckingham Street, WC2
1909	F	Salvation Army	117–121 Judd Street, WC1
1963	L	Save and Prosper	1 Finsbury Avenue, EC2
1826	L	Scottish Amicable	150 St. Vincent Street, Glasgow
1881	Engineering	Scottish Boiler .... GA	Pitheavlis, Perth, Scotland
1831	L	Scottish Equitable............	28 St. Andrew Square, Edinburgh
1919	AFM	Scottish General .... GA	100 West Nile Street, Glasgow G2
1852	L	Scottish Legal	95 Bothwell Street, Glasgow G2
1881	L	Scottish Life	19 St. Andrew Square, Edinburgh 2
1883	L	Scottish Mutual	109 St. Vincent Street, Glasgow G2
1837	L	Scottish Provident Institution .	6 St. Andrew Square, Edinburgh
1824	AFLM	Scottish Union & National NU	Surrey Street, Norwich
1815	L	Scottish Widows'.............	15 Dalkeith Road, Edinburgh
1875	AFM	Sea .... SA	1 Bartholomew Lane, EC2
1904	L	Sentinel Life.................	2 Eyre Street Hill, EC1
1964	L	Stalwart Assurance	Stalwart House, 142 South Street, Dorking
1825	L	Standard Life	3 George Street, Edinburgh
1891	AFM	State.................... GRE	Royal Exchange, EC3
1710	AFM	Sun .... SA	1 Bartholomew Lane, EC2
*	AFLM	Sun Alliance & London and Phoenix.....................	1 Bartholomew Lane, EC2
1810	L	Sun Life Assurance Group	107 Cheapside, EC2
1865	L Re	Sun Life of Canada	Basing View, Basingstoke, Hants.
1936	FL	Teacher's Assurance	12 Christchurch Road, Bournemouth
1869	L	Tunstall & District	Station Chambers, Tunstall, Stoke-on-Trent
1867	M	Ulster Marine .... GA	Pitheavlis, Perth
1714	AFM	Union Assurance.......... CU	St. Helen's, 1 Undershaft, EC3
1835	AFM	Union Ins. Soc. of Canton GRE	Royal Exchange, EC3
1863	M	Union Marine	4–5 King William Street, EC4
1908	AFL	United Friendly..............	42 Southwark Bridge Road, SE1
1963	L	UK Life Assurance	U.K. House, Worthing Road, Horsham

Est.	Nature of Business	Name of Company	Address
1825	L	University	4 Coleman Street, EC2
1919	Re	Victory Reinsurance	Castle Hill Avenue, Folkestone, Kent
1911	AF	Welsh Insurance Corp'n.... CU	St. Helen's, 1 Undershaft, EC3
1841	AFL	Wesleyan & General	150–158 Corporation Street, Birmingham 4
1886	AF	West of Scotland .... CU	26 George Street, Edinburgh 2
1912	AFLM	Western Australian	Swan Court, Mansel Road, Wimbledon, SW19
1865	AF	White Cross .... CU	St. Helen's, 1 Undershaft, EC3
1963	L	Windsor Life	Windsor House, Telford, Salop.
1894	AFM	World Marine & General ... CU	Dunster House, Mark Lane, EC3
1872	AFM Re	Zurich	Zurich House, Stanhope Road, Portsmouth

* Sun Alliance & London—Incorporating Funds established 1710, 1720, 1782 and 1824.

EXPECTATION OF LIFE

(Interim figures)

	England and Wales		Scotland		Northern Ireland	
	Life Table, 1985–87		Life Table, 1985–87		Life Table, 1985–87	
Age	Males	Females	Males	Females	Males	Females
0.............	72·1	77·8	70·2	76·2	70·4	76·6
5.............	68·0	73·6	66·0	71·9	66·3	72·5
10.............	63·1	68·6	61·1	67·0	61·4	67·5
15.............	58·2	63·7	56·2	62·0	56·4	62·6
20.............	53·4	58·8	51·4	57·1	51·6	57·7
25.............	48·6	53·9	46·7	52·2	46·9	52·8
30.............	43·8	49·0	41·9	47·3	42·2	47·9
35.............	38·9	44·1	37·1	42·4	37·4	43·0
40.............	34·2	39·3	32·4	37·7	32·7	38·2
45.............	29·5	34·5	27·9	33·0	28·1	33·5
50.............	25·0	29·9	23·5	28·4	23·7	28·9
55.............	20·8	25·5	19·5	24·1	19·7	24·5
60.............	16·9	21·3	15·8	20·0	16·0	20·3
65.............	13·5	17·4	12·6	16·3	12·7	16·5
70.............	10·5	13·8	9·9	13·0	9·9	12·9
75.............	8·0	10·6	7·6	10·0	7·6	9·8
80.............	6·0	7·8	5·7	7·4	5·6	7·1
85.............	4·5	5·6	4·3	5·3	4·0	5·0

Source: HMSO—Annual Abstract of Statistics

FRIENDLY SOCIETIES—GREAT BRITAIN

Friendly societies are voluntary mutual organizations, the main purposes of which are the provision of relief or maintenance during sickness, unemployment or retirement, and the provision of life assurance. Many of the older traditional societies complement their business activities by social activity and a general care for individual members in ways normally outside the scope of a purely commercial organization. There are three main categories of friendly societies—societies with separately registered branches, commonly called orders, centralized societies, which conduct business directly with members (having no separately registered branches), and collecting societies. Collecting societies conduct industrial assurance business and are subject to the requirements of the Industrial Assurance Acts in addition to the Friendly Societies Acts. Industrial assurance is life assurance, the premiums in respect of which are payable at intervals of less than two months and are received by means of collectors who make house-to-house visits for the purpose.

Long before the term 'friendly society' came into use, the seeds of voluntary mutual insurance had been sown in the ancient religious and trade guilds. As is evident from the many extant parchment returns detailing their rules and possessions under a decree of Richard II, guilds had become widespread in Britain by the 14th century. By then, the purely charitable character of the original guilds had largely changed with the emergence of numerous small institutions adopting primitive mutual insurance methods of a regular flat rate contribution to insure relief when sick or in old age and a payment to the widow in the event of death.

The present register of friendly societies includes several societies which have been in existence for upwards of 200 years, the oldest, operating in Scotland, being the Incorporation of Carters in Leith, established as long ago as 1555.

The first Act for the encouragement and protection of friendly societies in this country was not passed until 1793, but various amending Acts were passed during the next century as the result of the recommendations of successive Select Committees (including a Royal Commission in 1871). For example, it was not until the 1829 Act that all registered friendly societies were required to keep proper records of individual sickness and mortality amongst their members, which data enabled the construction of standard actuarial tables showing the expected (average) duration of sickness at successive ages, and also (with data from the Census) the corresponding mortality rates.

The rules and other documents of societies deposited with local justices passed into the custody of the Registrar of Friendly Societies following the Act of 1846 and are of considerable interest to social historians. Those relating to some societies no longer on the register have been transferred to the Public Record Office for permanent preservation.

The Friendly Societies Act 1974, which came into force in April, 1975, consolidated the nine Acts which comprised the Friendly Societies Acts 1896 to 1971 and a few other minor enactments relating to societies to which those Acts applied. The Act allows other specific classes (described below) to be registered thereunder, but tax exemption is enjoyed only by registered friendly societies. The £750 sum assured limit for tax exempt business was replaced in 1987 by a more flexible limit applied to premiums—up to £100 per annum.

The Friendly Societies (Long Term Insurance Business) Regulations 1987, implementing the European Community Life Directive for friendly societies, came into force on January 1, 1988, bringing with them a more stringent regulatory regime for the largest societies. The Life Directive affects both insurance companies and friendly societies with an annual contribution income in excess of 500,000 ECUs, the sterling equivalent of which was £345,308 in 1988. Thirty-seven friendly societies have been formally authorized under the Regulations. These societies are required to meet solvency requirements similar to those applied to insurance companies.

In addition to friendly societies there are three other main classes of society which may be registered under the Friendly Societies Act 1974: benevolent societies, working men's clubs and specially authorized societies. Benevolent societies are established for any charitable or benevolent purpose, to provide the same type of benefits as would be permissible for a friendly society, but in contrast the benefits must be for persons who are not members instead of, or in addition to, members. Working men's clubs provide social and recreational facilities for members. Specially authorized societies are registered for any purpose authorized by the Treasury as a purpose to which some or all of the provisions of the 1974 Act ought to be extended. Examples are societies for the promotion of science, literature and the fine arts, or to enable members to pursue an interest in sports and games.

The principal statistics at the end of 1988 are given in the table below.

	Orders and branches	Collecting societies	Other centralized societies	Benevolent societies	Working men's clubs	Specially authorized societies		Other
						Loan	Others	
Number of societies	2,546 (a)	32	412	85	2,406	9	142	1
Number of members 000's	452 (b)	15,081 (c)	2,633	289	2,078 (d)	14	112	—
Total benefits paid £000's	6,941 (b)	160,724	143,194	5,225	Not applicable	Not applicable	34	—
Total funds £000's	161,828 (b)	1,877,956	1,787,899	20,377	141,877 (d)	490	14,616	6

(a) 22 orders, 2,796 branches   (b) 1987 figures   (c) Assurances   (d) 1985 figures

INDUSTRIAL AND PROVIDENT SOCIETIES—GREAT BRITAIN

The familiar 'Co-op' societies are amongst the wide variety which are registered under the Industrial and Provident Societies Act 1965. This consolidating Act which, like the Friendly and the Building Societies Acts, is administered by the Chief Registrar of Friendly Societies, provides for the registration of societies and lays down the broad framework within which they must operate. Internal relations of societies are governed by their registered rules.

Registration under the Act confers upon a society corporate status by its registered name with perpetual succession and a common seal, and limited liability. A society qualifies for registration if it is carrying on an industry, business or trade, and it satisfies the Registrar either (a) that it is a bona fide co-operative society or (b) that in view of the fact that its business is being, or is intended to be, conducted for the benefit of the community there are special reasons why it

should be registered under the Act rather than as a company under the Companies Act.

The Credit Unions Act 1979 added a new class of society registerable under the 1965 Act. The Act also lays down provision for supervision of these savings and loan bodies. A similar framework of law for credit unions has existed in Northern Ireland since 1969.

During 1988 the number of registered societies increased by 385 to 10,871. The largest single group was the 4,164 housing societies. The largest group in terms of turnover was that consisting of the retail societies, which includes those trading under the familiar 'Co-op' sign, with sales (in 1988) of £4,070 million. Sales of wholesale and productive societies amounted to £3,314 million in 1988. The principal statistics at the end of 1988 are given in the table below.

	Retail	Wholesale and productive	Agricultural	Fishing	Social and recreational clubs	General service	Housing	Credit unions	Total
Number of societies	200	246	1,102	104	3,780	1,129	4,164	146	10,871
Number of members 000's	7,464	666	445	8	2,948	500	596	32	12,659
Funds of members £000's	924,910	488,834	230,487	4,726	171,866	4,066,161	7,603,029	8,814	13,498,827
Total assets £000's	1,735,730	1,091,904	545,520	12,526	344,260	4,361,505	11,958,148	9,364	19,811,840

BUILDING SOCIETIES—UNITED KINGDOM

The most significant event for the building societies in recent times was the passage of the Building Societies Act 1986, which received the Royal Assent on July 25, 1986. Most of the provisions of the Act came into effect on January 1, 1987. The Act gave building societies a completely new legal framework, the first since the initial comprehensive building society legislation in 1874. The new Act replaced both the 1962 Act and the 1967 Act covering Northern Ireland, and therefore applies to societies based throughout the United Kingdom.

The 1986 Act made provision for a Building Societies Commission to promote the protection of shareholders and depositors, the financial stability of societies, and to administer the system of regulation of building societies provided under the Act. Much of the Act is concerned with the powers of control of the Commission and provision in relation to the management of societies, accounts, audit and so on. But the greatest impact, and the most visible changes so far as the general public is concerned, flowed from the new powers which societies could adopt, leading

to an increased range of services which they might provide. There were also some interesting changes in relation to members' rights.

Under the 1962 Act, raising funds to make loans was the only purpose for which a building society could exist. Under the 1986 Act that has only to be its principal purpose. The constitutional provisions include the right of members to have access to the register of members, entitlement to have notices of meetings and to vote, and the right of members to have a resolution circulated.

In addition to traditional mortgage business, the power of societies to lend in respect of shared ownership, index-linked and equity-linked schemes is given. Societies may also lend the deposit, lend on registered land before the borrower is registered as the owner and on other equitable interests. Provision is also made for societies to make advances secured on land outside the United Kingdom. Larger societies were able, for the first time, to make unsecured loans, and make loans on mobile homes.

Under the 1962 Act building societies could only

BUILDING SOCIETIES, 1978–1989

Year	Number of societies	Number of share holders 000's	Number of depositors 000's	Number of borrowers 000's	Share balances £m	Deposit balances £m
1979	287	27,878	797	5,251	42,023	1,281
1980	273	30,636	915	5,383	48,915	1,742
1981	253	33,388	995	5,490	55,463	2,539
1982	227	36,609	1,094	5,643	64,977	3,447
1983	206	37,713	1,202	5,928	75,180	5,610
1984	190	39,385	1,550	6,317	88,078	8,426
1985	167	39,997	2,150	6,659	102,331	10,751
1986	151	40,563	2,850	7,025	115,538	16,864
1987	138	41,953	3,648	7,182	129,948	20,575
1988	131	43,816	4,306	7,369	149,791	26,529
1989	126	36,805	4,490	6,699	143,359	30,533

Year	Mortgage balances £m	Total assets £m	Advances during year		Average mortgage rate %	Average share rate %
			Number 000's	Amount £m		
1979	36,801	45,789	1,040	9,002	11·94	8·45
1980	42,437	53,793	936	9,503	14·92	10·34
1981	48,875	61,815	1,096	12,005	14·01	9·19
1982	56,691	73,033	1,320	14,971	13·32	8·77
1983	67,490	85,868	1,513	19,357	11·05	7·26
1984	81,879	102,688	1,657	23,767	11·83	7·71
1985	96,751	120,764	1,678	26,508	13·46	8·65
1986	115,644	140,603	2,058	35,885	12·07	7·75
1987	130,905	160,098	1,889	35,848	11·64	7·42
1988	153,015	188,844	2,080	47,375	11·25	7·04
1989	151,492	187,012	1,585	42,032	13·65	9·32

hold land for the purposes of running their business. Section 17 of the 1986 Act gave building societies power to hold and develop land as a commercial asset. However, the land has to be primarily for residential purposes, or adjoining land, or for purposes incidental to the holding of residential land.

Detailed provisions were contained in the Act for an investor protection scheme similar to those in the Banking Act of 1979. The level of protection given is 90 per cent of accounts up to £10,000.

Societies were also empowered to offer for the first time the following services:—

(a) Money transmission services
(b) Foreign exchange services
(c) Making or receiving of payments as agents
(d) Management, as agents, of mortgage investments
(e) Management, as agents, of land (larger societies only)
(f) Arranging for the provision of services relating to the acquisition or disposal of investments for individuals.
(g) Establishment and management of personal equity plans.
(h) Arranging for the provision of credit to individuals.
(i) Establishment and management of unit trust schemes for the provision of pensions (through a subsidiary).
(j) Establishment and administration of pension schemes.
(k) Arranging for the provision of insurance of any description.
(l) Giving advice on insurance of any description.
(m) Estate agency service (through a subsidiary).
(n) Surveys and valuations of land.
(o) Conveyancing services.

There emerged a number of technical problems in relation to these services and in June 1988 Parliament made Orders which allowed societies to have the power to own up to 100 per cent of a life assurance company, 15 per cent of a general insurance company, 100 per cent of a stockbroking company and to offer an additional range of financial services including executorship and trusteeship, hire purchase and leasing and safe deposit facilities. The Orders also included an increase in the limit on unsecured personal loans from £5,000 to £10,000.

Societies must belong to an ombudsman scheme for the investigation of complaints. Matters to be covered by the scheme include operation of share and deposit accounts, loans (but not the making of new loans), money transmission services, foreign exchange services, agency payments and receipts, and the provision of credit. Grounds for complaint include breach of the Act or contract, unfair treatment or maladministration, and where the complainant has suffered pecuniary loss or expense or inconvenience. A society must agree to be bound by decisions of the adjudicator unless it agrees to give notice to its members and the public of its reasons for not doing so. For address of the Building Societies Ombudsman scheme, *see* Index.

On mergers, the main difference is that borrowers have a vote. For a merger to be approved at least 50 per cent of borrowers who exercise their right to vote must vote in favour, as well as 75 per cent of qualifying share investors who vote. Provision is also made for a society to convert to company status. During 1989 the Abbey National became the first building society to complete the process of conversion to a company. It can no longer use the term 'Building Society' and now falls to be supervised as a bank under the Banking Act 1987.

SOCIETIES WITH TOTAL ASSETS EXCEEDING £1 MILLION AT END OF
FINANCIAL YEAR 1989

Year Established	* Name of Society (abbreviated) and Head Office	Share investors	Total assets £'000
1985	Alliance and Leicester, 49 Park Lane, London W1Y 4EQ	2,542,294	13,552,630
1853	Barnsley, Regent Street, Barnsley, South Yorks S70 2EH	25,848	128,847
1953	Bath Investment and Bldg. Soc., 20 Charles Street, Bath BA1 1HY	11,811	34,940
1879	Bedford, 65 Midland Road, Bedford MK40 1PR	9,264	51,072
1881	Bedford Crown, 117 Midland Road, Bedford MK40 1DE	3,387	12,880
1866	Beverley, 57 Market Place, Beverley, N. Humberside, HU17 8AA	5,648	21,917
1914	Bexhill-on-Sea, 2 Devonshire Square, Bexhill-on-Sea, Sussex TN40 1AE	2,776	13,926
1889	Birmingham Midshires, PO Box 81, 35–49 Lichfield Street, Wolverhampton WV1 1EL	669,108	3,160,482
1851	Bradford and Bingley, PO Box 2, Bingley, West Yorks. BD16 2LW	2,003,118	7,155,797
1850	Bristol and West, Broad Quay, Bristol BS99 7AX	799,328	4,682,623
1856	Britannia, Newton House, Cheadle Road, Leek, Staffs. ST13 5RG	1,134,586	6,298,238
1907	Buckinghamshire, High Street, Chalfont St. Giles, Bucks. HP8 4QB	6,003	32,252
1850	Cambridge, 32 St. Andrew's Street, Cambridge CB2 3AR	35,833	208,704
1960	Catholic, 7 Strutton Ground, London SW1P 2HY	3,196	17,002
1899	Century, 23 Albany Street, Edinburgh EH1 3QW	1,167	8,382
1875	Chelsea, Thirlestaine Hall, Thirlestaine Road, Cheltenham, Glos. GL53 7AL	192,915	1,820,292
1850	Cheltenham and Gloucester, Barnett Way, Gloucester GL4 7RL	925,419	7,270,300
1845	Chesham, 12 Market Square, Chesham, Bucks. HP5 1ER	8,157	45,664
1870	Cheshire, Castle Street, Macclesfield, Chesire SK11 6AH	207,343	694,724
1861	Cheshunt, 100 Crossbrook Street, Waltham Cross, Herts. EN8 8JJ	55,718	360,393
1859	Chorley and District, 49–51 St. Thomas's Road, Chorley, Lancs. PR7 1JL	6,402	36,879
1946	City and Metropolitan, 219 High Street, Bromley, Kent BR1 1PR	10,355	71,333
1859	Clay Cross Benefit, 42 Thanet Street, Clay Cross, Chesterfield S45 9JT	3,148	10,683
1884	Coventry, PO Box 9, High Street, Coventry CV1 5QN	380,569	1,645,946
1850	Cumberland, 38 Fisher Street, Carlisle CA3 8RQ	122,033	350,153
1946	Darlington, Tubwell Row, Darlington, Co. Durham DL1 1NX	38,052	187,554
1859	Derbyshire, Duffield Hall, Duffield, Derby DE5 1AG	277,352	1,043,180
1858	Dudley, Dudley House, Stone Street, Dudley DY1 1NP	14,048	51,528
1869	Dunfermline, 12 East Port, Dunfermline, Fife KY12 7LD	106,824	474,393
1857	Earl Shilton, 22 The Hollow, Earl Shilton, Leicester LE9 7NB	9,103	39,636
1877	Eastbourne Mutual, 22 Gildredge Road, Eastbourne BN3 3NT	52,363	267,890
1980	Ecology, 18 Station Road, Cross Hills, Keighley, West Yorks BD20 7EH	1,839	4,478
1860	Frome Selwood P., 3 Market Place, Frome, Somerset BA11 1DQ	14,227	47,827
1865	Furness, 51–55 Duke Street, Barrow-in-Furness LA14 1RT	61,508	241,477
1911	Gainsborough, 26 Lord Street, Gainsborough, Lincs. DN21 2DB	3,468	15,102
1852	Greenwich, 279–283 Greenwich High Road, London SE10 8NL	29,108	128,931
1871	Guardian, Guardian House, 120 High Holborn, London WC1V 6RH	71,186	1,215,274
1853	Halifax, Trinity Road, Halifax, West Yorks HX1 2RG	8,569,723	47,920,800
1866	Hampshire, Anchor House, Kingston Crescent, Portsmouth, Hants. PO2 8BX	14,801	93,634
1854	Hanley Economic, 42 Cheapside, Hanley, Stoke-on-Trent, Staffs. ST1 1EX	28,953	122,033
1953	Harpenden, 14 Station Road, Harpenden, Herts. AL5 4SE	7,649	32,173
1890	Haywards Heath, 33 Boltro Road, Haywards Heath, West Sussex RH16 1BQ	19,459	105,933
1863	Heart of England, 20–26 Jury Street, Warwick CV34 4ET	174,635	765,986
1926	Hendon, 9 Central Circus, Hendon, London NW4 3JS	3,428	27,847
1865	Hinckley and Rugby, Upper Bond Street, Hinckley, Leics. LE10 1DG	39,482	186,557
1855	Holmesdale B., 43 Church Street, Reigate, Surrey RH2 0AE	6,871	45,619
1853	Ilkeston P., 24–26 South Street, Ilkeston, Derby DE2 5HQ	4,044	12,751
1849	Ipswich, 44 Upper Brook Street, Ipswich IP4 1DP	28,381	126,129
1888	Kent Reliance, Reliance House, Manor Road, Chatham, Kent ME4 6AF	45,366	190,631
1852	Lambeth, 118–120 Westminster Bridge Road, London SE1 7AX	43,068	432,157
1872	Lancastrian, Sadler Street, Middleton, Manchester M24 3UJ	46,839	235,578
1853	Leamington Spa, Leamington House, Milverton Hill, Leamington Spa, Warks. CV32 5FE	117,549	1,180,683
1875	Leeds and Holbeck, 105 Albion Street, Leeds LS1 5AS	242,209	1,489,225
1848	Leeds P., Permanent House, The Headrow, Leeds LS1 1NS	3,308,463	12,920,600

* P. = Permanent; B. = Benefit. The words 'Building Society' are the last words in every society's name.

Year Estab- lished	Name of Society (abbreviated) and Head Office	Share investors	Total assets £'000
1863	Leek United and Midlands, 50 St. Edward Street, Leek, Staffs. ST13 5DH ..	45,027	211,152
1876	Londonderry Provident, 7 Castle Street, Londonderry BT48 6HQ	976	3,733
1867	Loughborough P., 6 High Street, Loughborough, Leics. LE11 2PY	11,256	60,510
1877	Louth, Mablethorpe and Sutton P.B., 3 Eastgate, Louth, Lincs. LN11 9NA	1,489	6,719
1922	Manchester, 18–20 Bridge Street, Manchester M3 3BU	5,977	46,155
1870	Mansfield, Regent House, Regent Street, Mansfield, Notts. NG18 1SS	15,957	72,404
1870	Market Harborough, Welland House, The Square, Market Harborough, Leics. LE16 7PD	24,542	148,947
1860	Marsden, 6–20 Russell Street, Nelson, Lancs. BB9 7NJ	35,400	174,926
1874	Melton Mowbray, 39 Nottingham Street, Melton Mowbray, Leics. LE13 1NR	28,691	139,898
1966	Mercantile, 75 Howard Street, North Shields, Tyne and Wear NE30 1AQ..	18,128	92,742
1880	Mid-Sussex, Mid-Sussex House, 66 Church Road, Burgess Hill, Sussex RH15 9AU	5,653	22,632
1869	Monmouthshire, John Frost Square, Newport, Gwent NP9 1PX	14,500	93,578
1866	Mornington, 158 Kentish Town Road, London NW5 2BT	19,206	188,522
1869	National and Provincial, Provincial House, Bradford BD1 1NL	1,616,646	8,465,142
1896	National Counties, Waterloo House, 147–153 High Street, Epsom, Surrey KT19 8EN	20,376	273,800
1884	Nationwide Anglia, Chesterfield House, Bloomsbury Way, London WC1V 6PW	5,818,374	26,647,194
1856	Newbury, 17–20 Bartholomew Street, Newbury, Berks. RG14 5LY	27,252	153,944
1863	Newcastle, Grainger Chambers, Hood Street, Newcastle upon Tyne NE1 6JP	120,311	731,844
1877	North of England, 57 Fawcett Street, Sunderland SR1 1SA	215,214	759,557
1850	Northern Rock, Northern Rock House, Gosforth, Newcastle upon Tyne NE3 4PL	607,066	2,794,619
1852	Norwich and Peterborough, Peterborough Business Park, Lynchwood, Peterborough PE2 0FZ	188,845	1,017,962
1850	Nottingham, 5–13 Upper Parliament Street, Nottingham NG1 2BX	127,807	427,728
1935	Nottingham Imperial, Imperial Building, 29 Bridgeford Road, West Bridgeford, Nottingham NG2 6AU	6,068	24,621
1879	Peckham Graylaw House, 1 Copers Cope Road, Beckenham, Kent BR3 1NB	12,964	67,244
1877	Penrith, 7 King Street, Penrith, Cumbria CA11 7AR	7,203	35,490
1881	Portman Wessex, 40 Portman Square, London W1H 9FH	198,587	962,458
1896	Portsmouth, Churchill House, Winston Churchill Avenue, Portsmouth PO1 2EP	83,537	760,800
1860	Principality, Principality Buildings, Queen Street, Cardiff CF1 1UA	216,628	769,195
1914	Progressive, 33–37 Wellington Place, Belfast BT1 6HH	30,627	165,813
1872	Regency and West of England, 25, High Street, Marlborough, Wilts. SN8 1GF	234,618	1,254,742
1849	Saffron Walden, Herts. and Essex, 1A Market Street, Saffron Walden, Essex CB10 1HX	29,895	163,642
1937	St. Pancras, 200 Finchley Road, London NW3 6DA	9,722	83,166
1846	Scarborough, Prospect House, 442/444 Scalby Road, Scarborough, Yorks. YO12 6EE	49,494	276,510
1848	Scottish, 23 Manor Place, Edinburgh EH3 7XE	15,618	76,004
1935	Sheffield, 66 Campo Lane, Sheffield, Yorks. S1 2EG	4,253	17,235
1879	Shepshed, Bull Ring, Shepshed, Loughborough, Leics. LE12 9QD	6,308	23,955
1853	Skipton, 59 High Street, Skipton, Yorks. BD23 1DN	198,902	1,662,259
1877	Stafford Railway, 4 Market Square, Stafford ST16 2JH	7,540	32,575
1902	Staffordshire, Jubilee House, PO Box 66, 84 Salop Street, Wolverhampton WV3 0SA	162,402	650,655
1875	Standard, 64 Church Way, North Shields, Tyne and Wear NE29 0AF	2,203	12,070
1850	Stroud and Swindon, 7 Russell Street, Stroud, Glos. GL5 3BG	66,012	339,976
1903	Surrey, Sentinel House, 10–12 Massetts Road, Horley, Surrey RH6 7DE ...	9,308	69,076
1870	Sussex County, 40/42 Friars Walk, Lewes, East Sussex BN7 2LW	88,845	483,182
1923	Swansea, 11 Cradock Street, Swansea SA1 3EW	3,131	18,021
1966	Teachers, Allenview House, Wimborne, Dorset BH21 1AG	9,053	86,809
1901	Tipton and Coseley, 57–60 High Street, Tipton, West Midlands DY4 8HG..	14,943	55,364
1853	Town and Country, 215 Strand, London WC2R 1AY	220,512	2,154,988
1855	Tynemouth, 53–55 Howard Street, North Shields, Tyne and Wear NE30 1AF	6,167	35,188
1863	Universal, 41 Pilgrim Street, Newcastle upon Tyne NE1 6BT	25,821	124,361
1924	Vernon, 19 St. Petersgate, Stockport, Cheshire SK1 1HF	18,835	76,796
1877	Walthamstow, 869 Forest Road, Walthamstow, London E17 4BB	46,000	351,354
1849	West Bromwich, 374 High Street, West Bromwich, West Midlands B70 8LR	276,404	873,711
1882	West Cumbria, Cumbria House, Murray Road, Workington CA14 2AD.....	6,372	26,455
1847	Woolwich Corporate Headquarters, Watling Street, Bexley Heath, Kent DA6 7RR	2,800,000	15,111,200
1885	Yorkshire, Yorkshire House, Westgate, Bradford BD1 2AU	655,145	3,063,455

THE COST OF LIVING

The first cost-of-living index to be calculated in Great Britain was the one which took July 1914 as 100 and was based on the pattern of expenditure of working class families in 1904. Since 1947 the Index of Retail Prices has superseded the cost-of-living index, although the older term is still often popularly applied to it. This index is designed to reflect the month-by-month changes in the average level of retail prices of goods and services purchased by the 'majority' of households in the United Kingdom, including practically all wage-earners and most small and medium salary-earners. For spending coming within the scope of the index, a representative list of items is selected and the prices actually charged for these items are collected at regular intervals. In working out the index figure, the price changes are 'weighted'—that is, given different degrees of importance—in accordance with the pattern of consumption of the average family.

A more widely used guide when considering changes in the average level of prices of all consumer goods and services, particularly over a number of years, is the consumer price index, now renamed the consumers' expenditure deflator. This index, which has been calculated back to 1938, covers the expenditure of all consumers as defined for national income purposes, and compares the price of goods and services actually purchased in a given year with the prices of the same goods and services in a base year.

During 1973 the Central Statistical Office constructed an annual index of prices of consumer goods and services over the period 1914 to 1972. This index has been constructed by linking together the pre-war cost of living index for the period 1914–1938, the consumers' expenditure deflator for the period 1938 and 1946–62* and the General Index of Retail Prices for the period 1962–1972.

In August 1979, the tax and price index (TPI) was introduced in order to provide a statistic which incorporates the effects of direct and indirect taxation, as well as prices, on taxpayers. The TPI is not directly concerned with the purchasing power of money, however, but with the purchasing power of pre-tax income. The General Index of Retail Prices thus retains its function of measuring the changes in the prices of goods and services purchased by households (from their post-tax income), and therefore as an indicator of the purchasing power of money.

* There are no official figures for 1939–45.

	Long Term Index of Consumer Goods and Services Jan. 1987 = 100	Comparable Purchasing Power of £1 in 1989
1914	2·8	41·14
1915	3·5	32·91
1920	7·0	16·46
1925	5·0	23·04
1930	4·5	25·60
1935	4·0	28·80
1938	4·4	26·18
1946	7·4	15·57
1950	9·0	12·80
1955	11·2	10·29
1960	12·6	9·14
1965	14·8	7·78
1970	18·5	6·23
1971	20·3	5·67
1972	21·7	5·31
1973	23·7	4·86
1974	27·5	4·18
1975	34·2	3·37
1976	39·8	2·89
1977	46·1	2·49
1978	50·0	2·30
1979	56·6	2·03
1980	66·8	1·72
1981	74·8	1·54
1982	81·2	1·42
1983	84·9	1·36
1984	89·2	1·29
1985	94·6	1·21
1986	97·8	1·18
1987	101·9	1·13
1988	106·9	1·08
1989	115·2	1·00

By employing this table an annual purchasing power of the pound index may be derived by taking the inverse of the price index. So, for example, if the purchasing power of the pound is taken to be 100p in 1972, then its comparable purchasing power in 1989 would be:

$$100 \times \frac{21·7}{115·2} = 18·9p$$

It should be noted that these figures can only be approximate.

INTEREST RATES – MORTGAGE AND SHARE

The interest rates prevailing on mortgage lending and share investment vary to a degree from society to society and in relation to the type or amount of loan or investment. The system whereby the Building Societies Association advised specific rates ceased in November 1984 and in April 1986 collective discussion, leading to a statement that a reduction or increase of a certain order was appropriate, was discontinued. General rate changes, however, continue in response to market conditions and the predominant rates in recent years, with the dates of change, are given below.

	Nov. 1986	May 1987	Jan. 1988	May 1988	Aug. 1988	Oct. 1988	Jan. 1989	Feb. 1990	April 1990
Mortgages %	12·25–12·375	11·25	10·00–10·30	9·50–9·80	11·50	12·75	13·50	14·50	15·40
Ordinary shares %	6·00	5·00	4·00	3·50	4·75	5·65	6·15	6·75	7·00

BANKING IN BRITAIN

The main institutions within the British banking system are the Bank of England (the central bank, see p. 302), the clearing banks (the major retail banks), the merchant banks, the overseas banks and the discount houses.

The clearing banks are Bank of Scotland, Barclays, Clydesdale, Co-operative, Coutts, Girobank, Lloyds, Midland, National Westminster, The Royal Bank of Scotland Group, the TSB and the Yorkshire Bank.

Deposit-taking institutions may be broadly divided into the monetary sector which is predominantly banks and is supervised by the Bank of England, and those institutions outside the monetary sector of which the most important are the building societies and the National Savings Bank. The Banking Act 1987 established a single category of authorized institutions eligible to carry out banking business.

There follows a list of authorized institutions as at August 24, 1990.

Authorized Institutions

UK—INCORPORATED
(Including partnerships formed under the law of any part of the UK)

ANZ Grindlays Bank PLC
ANZ Merchant Bank Ltd.
Abbey National PLC
Abbey National Treasury Services PLC
Adam & Company PLC
Afghan National Credit & Finance Ltd.
Airdrie Savings Bank
Aitken Hume Bank PLC
Ak International Bank Ltd.
Albaraka International Bank Ltd.
Alexanders Discount PLC
Alliance Trust (Finance) Ltd.
Allied Trust Bank Ltd.
Anglo Irish BankCorp (UK) PLC
Anglo-Romanian Bank Ltd.
Anglo Yugoslav Bank Ltd.
Henry Ansbacher & Co. Ltd.
Arbuthnot Latham Bank Ltd.
Argonaut Securities Ltd.
Assemblies of God Property Trust
Associates Capital Corporation Ltd.
Atlanta Trust Ltd.
Authority Bank Ltd.
Avco Trust Ltd.

BNL Investment Bank PLC
Banca Novara (UK) Ltd.
Banco Hispano Americano Ltd.
Bank in Liechtenstein (UK) Ltd.
Bank Leumi (UK) PLC
Bank of America International Ltd.
Bank of Boston Ltd.
Bank of Cyprus (London) Ltd.
Bank of Scotland
Bank of Tokyo International Ltd.
Bank of Wales PLC
Bankers Trust International Ltd.
Banque Belge Ltd.
Banque de la Méditerranée (UK) Ltd.
Banque Nationale de Paris PLC
The Baptist Union Corporation Ltd.
Barclays Bank PLC
Barclays Bank Trust Company Ltd.
Barclays de Zoete Wedd Ltd.
Baring Brothers & Co. Ltd.
Belmont Bank Ltd.
Benchmark Bank PLC
Beneficial Bank PLC
Birmingham Capital Trust PLC
Boston Safe Deposit and Trust Company (UK) Ltd.
British and Commonwealth Merchant Bank PLC
The British Bank of the Middle East
British Credit Trust Ltd.
The British Linen Bank Ltd.
British Railways Savings Company Ltd.
Brown, Shipley & Co. Ltd.
Bunge Finance Ltd.
Burns-Anderson Trust Company Ltd.

Caledonian Bank PLC
Cater Allen Ltd.
Chancery PLC
The Charities Aid Foundation Money Management Company Ltd.
Chartered Trust PLC
Chartered WestLB Ltd.
Charterhouse Bank Ltd.
Chase Investment Bank Ltd.
Chesterfield Street Trust Ltd.
Citibank Trust Ltd.
Citicorp Investment Bank Ltd.
City Merchants Bank Ltd.
City Trust Ltd.
Clive Discount Company Ltd.
Close Brothers Ltd.
Clydesdale Bank PLC
Clydesdale Bank Finance Corporation Ltd.
Combined Capital Ltd.
Commerical Bank (Cheshire) Ltd.
Commercial Bank of London PLC
Confederation Bank Ltd.
Consolidated Credits Bank Ltd.
Co-operative Bank PLC
Coutts & Co.
Craneheath Securities Ltd.
Credito Italiano International Ltd.
Credit Suisse Financial Products
Credit Suisse First Boston Ltd.

DG Investment Bank Ltd.
Daiwa Europe PLC
Dalbeattie Finance Co. Ltd.
Darlington Merchant Credits Ltd.
Dartington & Co. Ltd.
Deacon Hoare & Co. Ltd.
Den norske Bank PLC
The Dorset, Somerset & Wilts. Investment Society Ltd.
Dryfield Finance Ltd.
Dunbar Bank PLC
Duncan Lawrie Ltd.

East Trust Ltd.
Eccles Savings and Loans Ltd.
Edington PLC
English Trust Company Ltd.
Enskilda Securities-Skandinaviska Enskilda Ltd.
Equatorial Bank PLC
Euro-Latinamerican Bank PLC
Everett Chettle Associates
Exeter Trust Ltd.

FIBI Bank (UK) Ltd.
Fairmount Trust Ltd.
Family Finance Ltd.
Federated Trust Corporation Ltd.
FennoScandia Bank Ltd.
Financial & General Bank PLC

James Finlay Bank Ltd.
First Interstate Capital Markets Ltd.
First National Bank PLC
First National Commerical Bank PLC
The First Personal Bank PLC
Robert Fleming & Co. Ltd.
Ford Motor Credit Co. Ltd.
Foreign & Colonial Management Ltd.
Forward Trust Ltd.
Robert Fraser & Partners Ltd.
Frizzell Banking Services Ltd.

Gartmore Money Management Ltd.
Gerrard & National Ltd.
Girobank PLC
Goldman Sachs Ltd.
Goode Durrant Bank PLC
Granville Trust Ltd.
Gresham Trust PLC
Greyhound Bank PLC
Guinness Mahon & Co. Ltd.

HFC Bank PLC
Habibsons Bank Ltd.
Hambros Bank Ltd.
Hampshire Trust PLC
The Hardware Federation Finance Co. Ltd.
Harrods Bank Ltd.
Harton Securities Ltd.
Havana International Bank Ltd.
The Heritable & General Investment Bank Ltd.
Hill Samuel Bank Ltd.
Hill Samuel Personal Finance Ltd.
C. Hoare & Co.
Julian Hodge Bank Ltd.
Holdenhurst Securities PLC
Hongkong Bank London Ltd.
Humberclyde Finance Group Ltd.
Hungarian International Bank Ltd.

3i PLC
3i Group PLC
IBJ International Ltd.
International Mexican Bank Ltd.
Iran Overseas Investment Bank Ltd.
Italian International Bank PLC

Jabac Finances Ltd.
Japan International Bank Ltd.
Jordan International Bank PLC
Leopold Joseph & Sons Ltd.

King & Shaxson Ltd.
Kleinwort Benson Ltd.
Kleinwort Benson Investment Management Ltd.

Lazard Brothers & Co. Ltd.
Libra Bank PLC
Little Lakes Finance Ltd.
Lloyds Bank PLC
Lloyds Bank (BLSA) Ltd.
Lloyds Bank (France) Ltd.
Lloyds Bowmaker Ltd.
Lloyds Merchant Bank Ltd.
Lombard Bank Ltd.
Lombard & Ulster Ltd.
Lombard North Central PLC
London Arab Investment Bank Ltd.
London Italian Bank Ltd.
London Scottish Bank PLC
Lordsvale Finance PLC

McDonnell Douglas Bank Ltd.
McNeill Pearson Ltd.
Manchester Exchange and Investment Bank Ltd.
W.M. Mann & Co. (Investments) Ltd.
Manufacturers Hanover Ltd.
Marks and Spencer Financial Services Ltd.
Mase Westpac Ltd.
Matheson Bank Ltd.

Matlock Bank Ltd.
Meghraj Bank Ltd.
Mercantile Credit Company Ltd.
Mercury Provident PLC
Merrill Lynch International Bank Ltd.
The Methodist Chapel Aid Association Ltd.
Midland Bank PLC
Midland Bank Finance Corporation Ltd.
Midland Bank Trust Company Ltd.
Minories Finance Ltd.
Minster Trust Ltd.
Moneycare Ltd.
Samuel Montagu & Co. Ltd.
Moorgate Mercantile Holdings PLC
Morgan Grenfell & Co. Ltd.
Moscow Narodny Bank Ltd.
Mount Banking Corporation Ltd.
Municipal Mutual Bank PLC
Mutual Trust and Savings Ltd.
Mynshul Bank Ltd.

NIIB Group Ltd.
NWS Bank PLC
National Guardian Mortgage Corporation Ltd.
The National Mortgage Bank PLC
National Westminster Bank PLC
NatWest Investment Bank Ltd.
The Nikko Bank (UK) PLC
Noble Grossart Ltd.
Nomura Bank International PLC
Northern Bank Ltd.
Northern Bank Executor & Trustee Company Ltd.
Norwich General Trust Ltd.
Nykredit Mortgage Bank PLC

Omega Trust Co. Ltd.

PaineWebber International Bank Ltd.
Panmure Gordon Bankers Ltd.
The People's Bank Ltd.
Philadelphia National Ltd.
Pointon York Ltd.
The Private Bank and Trust Company Ltd.
Property Lending Bank PLC
Provincial Bank Ltd.

Ralli Investment Company Ltd.
R. Raphael & Sons PLC
Rathbone Bros. & Co. Ltd.
Rea Brothers Ltd.
Reliance Bank Ltd.
Riggs AP Bank Ltd.
N. M. Rothschild & Sons Ltd.
Roxburghe Bank Ltd.
Royal Bank of Canada Europe Ltd.
The Royal Bank of Scotland PLC
Royal Trust Bank
RoyScot Trust PLC

SP Finance Ltd.
Sanwa International PLC
Saudi International Bank (Al-Bank Al-Saudi Al-Alami Ltd.)
Scandinavian Bank Group PLC
Schroder Leasing Ltd.
J. Henry Schroder Wagg & Co. Ltd.
Scotiabank (UK) Ltd.
Scottish Amicable Money Managers Ltd.
Seccombe Marshall & Campion PLC
Secure Homes Ltd.
Security Pacific Trust Ltd.
Shire Trust Ltd.
Singer & Friedlander Ltd.
Smith & Williamson Securities
Société Générale Merchant Bank PLC
Southsea Mortgage & Investment Co. Ltd.
Standard Chartered Bank
Standard Chartered Bank Africa PLC

Sterling Bank & Trust Ltd.
Svenska International PLC

TSB Bank PLC
TSB Bank Northern Ireland PLC
TSB Bank Scotland PLC
Treloan Ltd.
Tyndall & Co. Ltd.

UBAF Bank Ltd.
UCB Bank PLC
ULC Trust Ltd.
Ulster Bank Ltd.
Unibank PLC
Unidanmark Holding PLC
Union Discount Company Ltd.

The United Bank of Kuwait PLC
United Dominions Trust Ltd.
Unity Trust Bank PLC

Wagon Finance Ltd.
Wallace, Smith Trust Co. Ltd.
S. G. Warburg & Co. Ltd.
S. G. Warburg Discount Ltd.
Western Trust & Savings Ltd.
Whiteaway Laidlaw Bank Ltd.
Wimbledon & South West Finance Co. Ltd.
Wintrust Securities Ltd.

Yamaichi Bank (UK) PLC
Yorkshire Bank PLC
H.F. Young & Co. Ltd.

INCORPORATED OUTSIDE THE UK

(Including partnerships or other unincorporated associations formed under the law of any member State of the European Community other than the UK)

AIB Capital Markets PLC
AIB Finance Ltd.
ASLK—CGER Bank
African Continental Bank Ltd.
Algemene Bank Nederland NV
Allied Bank of Pakistan Ltd.
Allied Banking Corporation
Allied Irish Banks PLC
American Express Bank Ltd.
Amsterdam-Rotterdam Bank NV
Arab African International Bank
Arab Bank PLC
Arab Banking Corporation BSC
Australia & New Zealand Banking Group Ltd.

BSI—Banca della Svizzera Italiana
Banca Commerciale Italiana
Banca Nazionale dell'Agricoltura SpA.
Banca Nazionale del Lavoro
Banca Popolare di Milano
Banca Serfin SNC
Banco Bilbao–Vizcaya
Banco Central, SA
Banco de la Nación Argentina
Banco de Sabadell
Banco di Napoli
Banco di Roma SpA.
Banco di Santo Spirito
Banco di Sicilia
Banco do Brasil SA
Banco do Estado de São Paulo SA
Banco Español de Crédito SA
Banco Espirito Santo e Comercial de Lisboa
Banco Exterior—UK SA
Banco Mercantil de São Paulo SA
Banco Nacional de México SNC
Banco Português do Atlântico
Banco Real SA
Banco Santander
Banco Totta & Açores SA
Bancomer SNC
Bangkok Bank Ltd.
Bank Julius Baer & Co. Ltd.
Bank Bumiputra Malaysia Berhad
Bank für Gemeinwirtschaft AG
Bank Handlowy w Warszawie SA
Bank Hapoalim BM
Bank Mees & Hope NV
Bank Mellat
Bank Melli Iran
Bank Negara Indonesia 1946
Bank of America NT & SA
Bank of Baroda
The Bank of California NA
Bank of Ceylon

Bank of China
Bank of Credit and Commerce International SA
The Bank of East Asia Ltd.
Bank of India
The Bank of Ireland
Bank of Montreal
Bank of New England NA
The Bank of New York
Bank of New Zealand
The Bank of Nova Scotia
Bank of Oman Ltd.
Bank of Seoul
The Bank of Tokyo Ltd.
The Bank of Yokohama Ltd.
Bank Saderat Iran
Bank Sepah-Iran
Bank Tejarat
Bankers Trust Company
Bankorp Ltd.
Banque Arabe et Internationale d'Investissement
Banque Belgo-Zairoise SA
Banque Bruxelles Lambert SA
Banque de l'Orient Arabe et d'Outre-Mer
Banque Française de l'Orient
Banque Française du Commerce Extérieur
Banque Indosuez
Banque Internationale à Luxembourg SA
Banque Internationale pour L'Afrique Occidentale SA
Banque Nationale de Paris
Banque Paribas
Banque Worms
Bayerische Hypotheken-und Wechsel-Bank AG
Bayerische Landesbank Girozentrale
Bayerische Vereinsbank AG
Beirut Riyad Bank SAL
Berliner Bank AG
Berliner Handels-und Frankfurter Bank
Byblos Bank SAL

CIC-Union Européenne, International et Cie
Caisse Nationale de Crédit Agricole
Canadian Imperial Bank of Commerce
Canara Bank
Cassa di Risparmio delle Provincie Lombarde
The Chase Manhattan Bank NA
Chemical Bank
Cho Hung Bank
Christiania Bank og Kreditkasse
The Chuo Trust & Banking Co. Ltd.
Citibank NA
Commercial Bank of Korea Ltd.
Commerzbank AG
Commonwealth Bank of Australia
Confederacion Española de Cajas de Ahorros

Continental Bank, National Association
Crédit Commercial de France
Crédit du Nord
Crédit Lyonnais
Crédit Lyonnais Bank Nederland NV
Crédit Suisse
Creditanstalt-Bankverein
Credito Italiano
Cyprus Credit Bank Ltd.
The Cyprus Popular Bank

The Dai-Ichi Kangyo Bank Ltd.
The Daiwa Bank Ltd.
Den Danske Bank Aktieselskab
Den norske Bank A/S
Deutsche Bank AG
Deutsche Genossenschaftsbank
The Development Bank of Singapore Ltd.
Discount Bank and Trust Company
Dresdner Bank AG

Fidelity Bank NA
First Bank National Association
First Bank of Nigeria Ltd.
First City, Texas–Houston NA
First Commercial Bank
First Interstate Bank of California
The First National Bank of Boston
The First National Bank of Chicago
Fleet National Bank
French Bank of Southern Africa Ltd.
The Fuji Bank Ltd.

Generale Bank
Ghana Commercial Bank
Girozentrale und Bank der österreichischen Sparkassen AG
Götabanken
Gulf International Bank BSC

Habib Bank AG Zurich
Habib Bank Ltd.
Hamburgische Landesbank Girozentrale
Hanil Bank
Harris Trust and Savings Bank
Hessische Landesbank-Girozentrale
The Hokkaido Takushoku Bank Ltd.
The Hokuriku Bank Ltd.
The Hongkong and Shanghai Banking Corporation Ltd.

The Industrial Bank of Japan Ltd.
The Investment Bank of Ireland Ltd.
Istituto Bancario San Paolo di Torino

Jyske Bank

Kansallis-Osake-Pankki
Keesler Federal Credit Union
Korea Exchange Bank
Korea First Bank
Kredietbank NV
The Kyowa Bank Ltd.

The Long-Term Credit Bank of Japan Ltd.

Malayan Banking Berhad
Manufacturers Hanover Trust Company
Mellon Bank NA
Merchants National Bank & Trust Company of Indianapolis
Middle East Bank Ltd.
The Mitsubishi Bank Ltd.
The Mitsubishi Trust and Banking Corporation
The Mitsui Taiyo Kobe Bank Ltd.
The Mitsui Trust & Banking Co. Ltd.
Monte dei Paschi di Siena
Morgan Guaranty Trust Company of New York
Multibanco Comermex SNC

NBD Bank NA

NCNB National Bank of North Carolina
NCNB Texas National Bank
NMB Postbank Groep NV
National Australia Bank Ltd.
National Bank of Abu Dhabi
National Bank of Canada
The National Bank of Dubai Ltd.
National Bank of Egypt
National Bank of Greece SA
The National Bank of Kuwait SAK
The National Bank of New Zealand Ltd.
The National Commercial Bank
National Bank of Pakistan
NedPerm Bank Ltd.
The Nippon Credit Bank Ltd.
Norddeutsche Landesbank Girozentrale
The Northern Trust Company

Österreichische Länderbank AG
Oversea-Chinese Banking Corporation Ltd.
Overseas Trust Bank Ltd.
Overseas Union Bank Ltd.

Philadelphia National Bank
Philippine National Bank
Postipankki Ltd.

Qatar National Bank SAQ

Rabobank Nederland (Coöperatieve Centrale Raiffeisen-Boerenleenbank BA)
Rafidain Bank
Raiffeisen Zentralbank Osterreich AG
Republic National Bank of New York
Reserve Bank of Australia
The Riggs National Bank of Washington DC
Riyad Bank
The Royal Bank of Canada
The Rural and Industries Bank of Western Australia

The Saitama Bank Ltd.
The Sanwa Bank Ltd.
Saudi American Bank
Security Pacific National Bank
Shanghai Commercial Bank Ltd.
The Siam Commercial Bank Ltd.
Skandinaviska Enskilda Banken
Société Générale
Sonali Bank
State Bank of India
State Bank of New South Wales Ltd.
State Bank of South Australia
State Bank of Victoria
State Street Bank and Trust Company
Südwestdeutsche Landesbank Girozentrale
The Sumitomo Bank Ltd.
The Sumitomo Trust & Banking Co. Ltd.
Svenska Handelsbanken
Swiss Bank Corporation
Swiss Cantobank (International)
Swiss Volksbank
Syndicate Bank

TC Ziraat Bankasi
The Thai Farmers Bank Ltd.
The Tokai Bank, Ltd.
The Toronto-Dominion Bank
The Toyo Trust & Banking Company Ltd.
Turkish Bank Ltd.
Türkiye Iş Bankasi AS

Uco Bank
Ulster Investment Bank Ltd.
Union Bank of Finland Ltd.
Union Bank of Nigeria Ltd.
Union Bank of Norway
Union Bank of Switzerland

United Bank Ltd.
United Mizrahi Bank Ltd.
United Overseas Bank (Banque Unie pour les Pays d'Outre Mer)
United Overseas Bank Ltd.

Volkskas Bank Ltd.

Westdeutsche Landesbank Girozentrale
Westpac Banking Corporation

The Yasuda Trust & Banking Co. Ltd.

Zambia National Commerical Bank Ltd.
Zivnostenská Banka National Corporation

BANKING HOURS

Weekdays
England and Wales.—Monday–Friday 9.30–3.30*; *City of London town clearers*, 9.30–3.00.
Scotland.—Banking hours in Scotland are: Monday–Wednesday, Friday, 9.15–4.45; Thursday, 9.15–5.30.
Northern Ireland.—Monday–Friday 10.00–3.30; Open 9.30 two mornings per week. Open until 5.00 one summer evening per week.

Saturdays
England and Wales.—(Selected branches open): *Barclays* 9.30–12.00; *Lloyds* 9.30–12.30; *Midland* 9.30–3.30; *National Westminster* 9.30–12.30; *TSB* 9.30–12.30.
Scotland.—Closed.
Northern Ireland.—Closed.

* Still the minimum banking hours but many banks are experimenting with longer hours (usually 9.15–4.30).

FINANCIAL FIGURES, ETC. FOR CLEARING BANKS, 1989

Bank Group	Profit/loss before taxation £m	Profit/loss after taxation £m	Total assets £m	Number of UK branches
†Bank of Scotland	193·5	117·5	18,394·5	500
Barclays	692	477	127,616	2,800
Clydesdale	58·6	36·4	4,315	354
Co-operative	18·68	10·89	2·70	110
Coutts & Co.	15	9·8	3,513·5	19
Lloyds	− 715	− 499	57,542	2,187
Midland	− 261	− 204	62,479	1,980
National Westminster	404	198	116,200	3,116
The Royal Bank of Scotland Group	228·6	147·1	27,435,700	850
Yorkshire Bank	113·1	70·7	4,055·9	251

† 1990 figures

BANKING SERVICES

Association for Payment Clearing Services (APACS)
Mercury House, Triton Court, 14 Finsbury Square, EC2A 1BR.

APACS was set up by the banks in 1985 to manage the payment clearing systems and oversee money transmission in the UK.

Three operational clearing companies operate under the aegis of APACS. They are:

BACS LTD., De Havilland Road, Edgware, Middx. HA8 5QA.—Provides an automated service for inter-bank clearing of payment and collection transactions in the UK (e.g. standing orders, direct debits). *Chief Exec.*, A. E. Robinson.

CHEQUE AND CREDIT CLEARING CO. LTD., Mercury House, Triton Court, 14 Finsbury Square, EC2A 1BR.—Operates bulk clearing systems for inter-bank cheques and paper credit items. *Chief Inspector*, E. W. Stubbs.

CHAPS AND TOWN CLEARING CO. LTD., Mercury House, Triton Court, 14 Finsbury Square, EC2A 1BR.—Provides same-day clearing for high value cheques and electronic funds transfer. *Chief Inspector*, E. W. Stubbs.

APACS also oversees the London Dollar Clearing, the London Currency Settlement Scheme and the Cheque Card and eurocheque schemes in the UK.

Membership of APACS and the operational clearing companies is open to any appropriately regulated financial institution providing payment services and meeting the relevant membership criteria.
Chief Executive, R. I. L. Allen.

Committee of London and Scottish Bankers
10 Lombard Street, EC3V 9AP
[071-283 8866]

The Committee is the successor to the Committee of London Clearing Bankers. It consists of the Chairmen of Barclays, Lloyds, Midland, National Westminster, Standard Chartered, Bank of Scotland, Royal Bank of Scotland and the TSB Group, and meets regularly to discuss matters of common interest. It is the body through which the Bank of England communicates official policy to the banks and through which the banks may present their views to the Bank of England and the Treasury.
Secretary-General, The Lord Inchyra.

FINANCIAL OMBUDSMEN

The following Ombudsmen schemes are non-statutory.

The Office of the Banking Ombudsman
Citadel House, 5–11 Fetter Lane, EC4A 1BR
[071-583 1395]

The purpose of the Banking Ombudsman Scheme is to investigate complaints from bank customers dissatisfied with the banking services of member banks. The Scheme was set up in 1985 and became operational on Jan. 1, 1986. The Scheme has 20 member Banks who fund it and in addition there are 21 designated associates. There is a eight-member Council who appoint the Ombudsman, give guidance on the performance of his duties, monitor his terms of reference, prepare the budget and approve the annual report. The Ombudsman and his staff are responsible to the Council.
The Banking Ombudsman, L. Shurman.

The Office of the Building Societies Ombudsman
Grosvenor Gardens House, 35–37 Grosvenor Gardens, SW1X 7AW
[071-931 0044]

The purpose of the Building Societies Ombudsman Scheme, which came into operation on July 1, 1987, is to investigate complaints from building society customers about the services of building societies belonging to the Scheme. All building societies belong to the Scheme and it is funded by contributions from the members. The Ombudsman is appointed by and responsible to an independent Ombudsman Council.
The Building Society Ombudsman, S. Edell.

The Insurance Ombudsman Bureau
31 Southampton Row, WC1B 5HJ
[071-242 8613]

The purpose of the Insurance Ombudsman Scheme is to settle disputes between insurance policyholders and member insurance companies. The Scheme came into operation in March 1981 and is funded by contributions from the member companies. Over 300 companies are members of the Scheme. An independent Council appoints and supervises the work of the Ombudsman.

The Insurance Ombudsman Bureau also runs the Unit Trust Ombudsman Scheme, the purpose of which is to settle disputes between personal unit trust holders and member unit trust management companies. The Unit Trusts Ombudsman scheme came into operation in October 1988.
The Insurance Ombudsman, Dr. J. T. Farrand.
The Unit Trust Ombudsman, C. A. H. Parsons.

THE NATIONAL DEBT

Net central government borrowing each year represents an addition to the National Debt. At the end of March 1989 the National Debt amounted to some £197,300 million of which about £5,300 million was in currencies other than sterling. Of the £192,000 million sterling debt, £141,000 million consisted of gilt-edged stock; of this, 30 per cent had a maturity of up to five years, 44 per cent a maturity of over five years and up to 15 years and 26 per cent a maturity of over 15 years or undated. The remaining sterling debt was made up mainly of national savings (£30,000 million), certificates of tax deposits, Treasury bills, and Ways and Means advances (very short-term internal government borrowing).

The sizable Trust Funds have been established over the past fifty years for the purpose of reducing the National Debt. The National Fund was established in 1927 with an original gift of £499,878. At March 31, 1987 it was valued at £55,628,556; it is administered by Baring Brothers & Co. Ltd. The Elsie Mackay Fund was established in 1929 with an original gift of £527,809 to run for 45–50 years. It was wound up on January 19, 1979, when it was valued at £4,902,864. The John Buchanan Fund was established in 1932 with gifts totalling £36,702 to run for 50 years. It was wound up on February 28, 1982, when it was valued at £204,138.

NATIONAL SAVINGS

Ordinary and Investment Accounts

National Savings Bank.—On May 31, 1990, there were about 15,751,000 active accounts with the sum of approximately £1,542 million due to depositors in Ordinary accounts and about 4,715,000 active accounts with the sum of approximately £8,154 million due to depositors in Investment accounts.

Interest is earned at 5 per cent per year on each Ordinary account for every complete calendar month in which the balance is £500 or more, provided the account is kept open for the whole of 1990 (December 31, 1989—January 1, 1991); and at 2·5 per cent per year for other months or for accounts opened or closed during 1990. The minimum deposit is £5; maximum balance £10,000 plus interest credited. On May 31, 1990 the average amount held in Ordinary accounts was approximately £85.

The Investment account pays a higher rate of interest (the current rate can be found at any post office). The minimum deposit is £5; maximum balance £25,000 plus interest credited. On May 31, 1990 the average amount held in Investment accounts was approximately £1,729.

Premium Bonds

Premium Bonds are a Government security which were first introduced on November 1, 1956. Premium Bonds enable savers to enter a regular draw for tax-free prizes, whilst retaining the right to get their money back. A sum equivalent to interest on each bond is put into a prize fund and distributed by weekly and monthly prize draws. (The rate of interest is 6·5 per cent. a year from July 1, 1988). The prizes are drawn by ERNIE (electronic random number indicator equipment) and are free of all UK income tax and capital gains tax.

Bonds are in units of £1, with a minimum purchase of £100; above this, purchases must be in multiples of £10, up to a maximum holding limit of £10,000 per person. The exception to this is that the minimum purchase by parents, guardians and grandparents for children under 16 is £10. Bonds can only be held in the name of an individual and not by organizations.

Bonds become eligible for prizes once they have been held for three clear calendar months following the month of purchase. Each £1 unit can win only one prize per draw, but it will be awarded the highest for which it is drawn. Bonds remain eligible for prizes until they are repaid. When a holder dies, bonds remain eligible for prizes up to and including the twelfth monthly draw after the month in which the holder dies.

By April 1990 bonds to the value of £4,760 million had been sold. Of these £2,428 million had been cashed, leaving £2,332 million still invested. By the April 1990 prize draw, 34·8 million prizes totalling £2,030 million had been distributed since the first prize draw in June 1957.

Income Bonds

National Savings Income Bonds were introduced in 1982. They are particularly suitable for those who want to receive regular monthly payments of interest while preserving the full cash value of their capital. The Bonds are sold in multiples of £1,000. The minimum holding is £2,000 and the maximum £25,000.

Interest is calculated on a day-to-day basis and paid monthly. Interest is taxable, but is paid without deduction of tax at source. The Bonds have a guaranteed life of ten years, but may be repaid at par before maturity on giving three months' notice. If repayment of a bond is made within the first year of purchase, interest from the date of purchase to the

date of repayment is earned at half rate. If the sole or sole surviving holder dies, however, no formal period of notice is required and there is no loss of interest for repayment made within the first year.

Net investment in National Savings Income Bonds was £8,393,900,000 at the end of April 1990.

Indexed Income Bonds

Indexed Income Bonds were withdrawn from sale on August 28, 1987. Existing holders will continue to receive monthly income in accordance with the prospectus.

Capital Bonds

National Savings Capital Bonds (Series A) were introduced in January 1989, and replaced by Series B in July 1990. For personal savers Capital Bonds offer capital growth over five years with guaranteed returns at fixed rates. The interest is taxable each year (for those who pay income tax) but is not deducted at source. The minimum purchase is £100, with larger purchases in multiples of £100. There is a maximum holding limit of £100,000 for Series B bonds.

Capital Bonds will be repaid in full with all interest gained at the end of five years. Early repayment may be obtained at three months notice. No interest is earned on Bonds repaid in the first year.

Deposit Bonds

National Savings Deposit Bonds were withdrawn from sale on November 19, 1988. All Deposit Bonds purchased on or before that date may continue to be held until the tenth anniversary of purchase. They will continue to earn interest until then.

Yearly Plan

The National Savings Yearly Plan was introduced on July 2, 1984. It offers a guaranteed tax-free return. Applicants agree to make 12 monthly payments, leading to the issue of a Yearly Plan Certificate. The maximum guaranteed rate of interest is earned if the Certificate is held for a full four years. Applications may be made by any individuals aged 7 or over; in the name of children under 7; and by not more than two trustees for a sole beneficiary.

Payments must be made on the same date every month by standing order from a bank or other acceptable account. Only one payment may be made in any one month and must be in multiples of £5. Minimum monthly contribution is £20, maximum £200. Net investment in National Savings Yearly Plan was £566,700,000 at May 31, 1990.

Gilts on the National Savings Stock Register

Government Stock or 'Gilts' are stock Exchange Securities issued by the Government. They usually have a life of between 5 and 20 years and most pay a guaranteed fixed rate of interest twice a year throughout this period. When they reach the end of this period they are 'redeemed' (which means repaid) at their face value.

The National Savings Stock Register enables investors to buy and sell Gilts by post. It is now possible to have most new issues of Gilts registered on the National Savings Stock Register. Interest on Gilts held on the National Savings Stock Register, although taxable, is paid in full without deduction of tax at source.

National Savings Certificates

The amount, including accrued interest, index-linked increase or bonus remaining to the credit of investors in National Savings Certificates on March 31, 1990 was approximately £12,748·8 million. In 1989–90, approx. £1,267·2 million was subscribed and £2,892·6 million (excluding interest, index-linked increase or bonus) was repaid. Interest, index-linked increase, bonus or other sum payable is free of UK income tax (including investment income surcharge) and capital gains tax. The 1st–14th and 16th issues continue to attract interest.

Issue and maximum holding (in units)	Unit cost £	Value after		Interest per unit
		Years	£ p	
Index-Linked Retirement Issue (June 2, 1975–Nov. 15, 1980) (120)	10			Unlike conventional issues where interest is accrued periodically, the repayment value of Index-Linked Certificates, subject to their being held a year, is related to the movement of the UK General Index of Retail Prices.** N.B. Certificates of the Retirement Issue were on sale only to men aged 65 years and over and women aged 60 years and over, but may now be transferred to anyone.
2nd Index-Linked Issue (Nov. 17, 1980–June 29, 1985) (1,000)	10			The repayment value, subject to their being held a year, is related to the movement of the UK General Index of Retail Prices.** N.B. Certificates of the 2nd Index-Linked Issue were made available to anyone, regardless of age, from September 7, 1981.
Twenty-seventh .... (April 5, 1984–Aug. 7, 1984) (200)	25	5	35·48	After 1 year, £1·32 is added, during 2nd year, 41p per completed 3 months, during 3rd year, 50p per completed 3 months, during 4th year, 62p per completed 3 months and during 5th year 76p per completed 3 months.†
Twenty-eighth ...... (Aug. 8, 1984–Sept. 11, 1984) (200)	25	5	38·47	After 1 year, £1·63 is added, during 2nd year, 51p per completed 3 months, during 3rd year, 64p per completed 3 months, during 4th year, 80p per completed 3 months and during 5th year £1·01 per completed 3 months.*
Twenty-ninth........ (Oct. 15, 1984–Feb. 12, 1985) (200)	25	5	36·74	After 1 year, £1·50 is added, during 2nd year, 46p per completed 3 months, during 3rd year, 56p per completed 3 months, during 4th year, 69p per completed 3 months and during 5th year 85p per completed 3 months.*
Thirtieth .... (Feb. 13, 1985–Sept. 9, 1985) (200)	25	5	38·21	After 1 year, £1·69 is added, during 2nd year, 50p per completed 3 months, during 3rd year, 62p per completed 3 months, during 4th year, 78p per completed 3 months and during 5th year 98p per completed 3 months.*
3rd Index-Linked Issue (July 1, 1985–July 31, (1986) (200)	25			The repayment value, subject to their being held for one year, is related to the movement of the UK General Index of Retail Prices.** In addition, there is guaranteed extra interest of 2·5 per cent for the 1st year, 2·75 per cent for the 2nd year, 3·25 per cent for the 3rd year, 4·0 per cent for the 4th year and 5·25 per cent for the 5th year. This interest is worth 3·54 per cent compound over a full five years.
Thirty-first .... (Sept. 26, 1985–Nov. 11, 1986) (200)	25	5	36·48	After 1 year, £1·44 is added, during 2nd year, 44p per completed 3 months, during 3rd year, 55p per completed 3 months, during 4th year, 68p per completed 3 months and during 5th year, 84p per completed 3 months.*
4th Index-Linked Issue (Aug. 1, 1986–June 30, 1990) (200)	25			The repayment value, subject to their being held for one year, is related to the movement of the UK General Index of Retail Prices.** In addition, there is guaranteed extra interest of 3·0 per cent for the 1st year, 3·25 per cent for the 2nd year, 3·5 per cent for the 3rd year, 4·5 per cent for the 4th year, and 6·0 per cent for the 5th year. This interest is worth 4·04 per cent compound over a full five years.
Thirty-second....... (Nov. 12, 1986–March 10, 1987) (200)	25	5	38·03	After 1 year, £1·63 is added, during 2nd year, 50p per completed 3 months, during 3rd year, 62p per completed 3 months, during 4th year, 77p per completed 3 months and during 5th year 96p per completed 3 months.*
Thirty-third .... (May 1, 1987–July 21, 1988) (40, plus special facilities to hold up to a further 200)	25	5	35·06	After 1 year, the repayment value increases by 5·5 per cent for ordinarily held 33rd Issue. However, 33rd Reinvestment Certificates earn interest during the 1st year at the rate of 5·5 per cent per annum for each 3 month period. Thereafter all 33rd Issue earn 5·75 per cent after 2 years, 6·0 per cent after 3 years, 6·5 per cent after 4 years and 7·0 per cent after 5 years.*

Issue and maximum holding (in units)	Unit cost £	Value after		Interest per unit
		Years	£ p	
Thirty-fourth . . . . (July 22, 1988–June 16, 1990) (40, plus special facilities to hold up to a further 400.)	25	5	35·89	After 1 year, the repayment value increases by 6·0 per cent for ordinarily held 34th Issue. However, 34th Reinvestment certificates earn interest during the 1st year at the rate of 6·0 per cent per annum for each 3 month period. Thereafter, all 34th Issue earn 6·25 per cent after two years, 6·5 per cent after 3 years, 7·0 per cent after 4 years, and 7·5 per cent after 5 years.*
Thirty-fifth . . . . (June 18, 1990–) (40, plus special facilities to hold up to a further 400)	25	5	39·36	After 1 year, the repayment value increases by 6·5 per cent for ordinarily held 35th Issue. However, 35th Issue Reinvestment Certificates earn interest during the first year at the rate of 6·5 per cent per annum. Thereafter, all 35th Issue earn 7 per cent after two years; 7·75 per cent after three years; 8·5 per cent after four years and 9·5 per cent after five years.
5th Index-linked Issue (July 2, 1990–) (200, plus special facilities to hold up to a further 400)	25			The repayment value, subject to their being held for one year, is related to the movement of the UK General Index of Retail Prices. In addition there is guaranteed extra interest which is paid from the date of purchase for each full year the certificates are held. For the first year the return is the Retail Price Index (RPI) only. For the second, RPI plus 0·5 per cent; for the third RPI plus 1 per cent; for the fourth RPI plus 2·0 per cent and at the fifth anniversary RPI plus 4·5 per cent.

*As announced by the Treasury.

†From June 1982, savings certificates of the 7th to 14th, 16th, 18th, 19th, 21st, 23rd to 31st Issues will be extended on General Extension Rates as they reach the end of their existing extension periods. The percentage interest rate is determined by the Treasury and any change in this General Extension Rate will be applicable from the 1st of the month following its announcement.

Under the new system, a certificate earns interest for each complete period of three months beyond the expiry of the previous extension terms. Within each three-month period interest is calculated separately for each month at the rate applicable from the beginning of that month. The interest for each month is one twelfth of the annual rate (i.e. it does not vary with the number of days in the month) and is capitalized annually on the anniversary of the date of purchase. The current rate of interest under the General Extension Rate is displayed on special posters at most post offices.

**Index-linked certificates of the 1st and 2nd Issues were eligible for an annual supplement of 1·5 per cent for the year to August 1, 1989. There have been six previous annual supplements of 2·4 per cent for 1982–83 and 1983–84 and 3 per cent for 1984–85, 1985–86, 4 per cent for 1986–87 and 3 per cent for 1987–88. No further bonuses will be payable. At the 5th anniversary there is a bonus of 4 per cent of the purchase price and at the 10th anniversary there is a second bonus of 4 per cent of the full 5th anniversary value. All supplements and bonuses are fully index-linked once earned.

TAXATION

INCOME TAX

Income tax is charged on the total income of individuals for a year of assessment commencing on April 6 and ending on the following April 5. The rates of tax and the calculation of liability will frequently differ, sometimes substantially, as between one year of assessment and another. The following information is confined to the year of assessment 1990–91, ending on April 5, 1991.

Liability to income tax is determined by establishing the taxable income for a year of assessment. The income will be reduced by an individual's personal allowances and other reliefs. The first £20,700 of taxable income remaining is assessable to income tax at the basic rate of 25 per cent, with any excess over this amount taxable at the higher rate of 40 per cent.

The two rates apply to the assessment of both earned and investment income. Indeed there is little distinction between the two classes, although the receipt of earned income may produce an entitlement to some allowances not available against investment income.

The tables on the following two pages show the income tax payable for 1990–91 by an individual on the amount of income specified, after deducting the personal allowance and married couple's allowance also, where appropriate. Elderly persons over the age of 74 years may suffer less tax. The taxpayer may also be entitled to transitional allowances and other reliefs which reduce the tax payable below the amount shown by the tables.

Trustees administering settled property are chargeable to income tax at the basic rate of 25 per cent. Where the trustees retain discretionary powers, or income is accumulated, there will also be liability to the additional rate of 10 per cent. Companies residing in the United Kingdom are not liable to income tax but suffer corporation tax on income, profits and gains.

The charge to income tax broadly arises on all taxable income accruing from sources in the United Kingdom. Individuals who are resident in this territory may also become liable on income arising overseas. An individual is resident in the United Kingdom if he or she normally resides here. Persons not normally residing in the United Kingdom may become resident if they visit this territory for periods which average three months or more throughout a period of years, or are present for at least 183 days in a particular year. The existence of a place of abode in the United Kingdom may be sufficient to indicate residence if visits of any duration are made during the year of assessment.

Income arising overseas will often incur liability to foreign taxation. If that income is also chargeable to United Kingdom income tax, excessive liability may well arise. The United Kingdom has concluded double taxation agreements with many overseas territories and these ensure that the same slice of income is not doubly assessed. In the absence of such an agreement, foreign tax suffered can usually be relieved under the domestic code when calculating liability to United Kingdom income tax.

INDEPENDENT TAXATION

For many years the income of a married woman 'living with' her husband was treated as that of the husband for income tax purposes. This did not generally apply in the year of marriage and it remained possible for the couple to exercise the right of separate assesment or for the wife to be separately assessed as a single person on her earned income. However, the husband was usually responsible for submitting income tax returns, for discharging income tax on the combined incomes and dealing generally with taxation matters.

This practice ceased to apply on April 6, 1990, with the introduction of independent taxation. From this date a husband and wife are independently taxed, with each entitled to a personal allowance. In most situations any unused personal allowance available to one spouse cannot be transferred to the other. A married man 'living with' his wife can obtain a married couple's allowance. This allowance must, if possible, be set against the husband's income but where that income is insufficient any balance of the married couple's allowance may be transferred to the wife.

Each spouse may obtain other allowances and reliefs where the underlying conditions are satisfied. Income must be accurately allocated between a husband and wife by reference to the individual beneficially entitled to that income. Where income arises from jointly-held assets this must be apportioned equally between husband and wife. However, in those cases where the beneficial interests in jointly-held assets are not equal, a special declaration can be made to apportion income by reference to the actual interests in that income.

INCOME TAXABLE

Income tax is assessed and collected under several Schedules. Each Schedule determines the extent of liability and establishes the amount to be included in taxable income. In some instances the actual income arising in a year of assessment will be charged to income tax for that year. A different basis of assessment may arise for income taxable under Cases I to V of Schedule D. Frequently, income assessable under these Cases will be that arising in a previous year or period but there are special rules where a new source is acquired or an existing source discontinued.

Following the withdrawal of income tax liability for most commercial woodlands in the United Kingdom, Schedule B ceased to apply from April 6, 1988. The contents of the remaining schedules are shown below.

Schedule A.—Tax is charged on annual profits arising from the ownership or occupation of land in the United Kingdom. This will include rents, ground rents and other income from land. Expenditure incurred by the landlord on maintenance, repairs, insurance and management can be subtracted from the annual profits. This Schedule does not include profits from farming, market gardening or woodlands, nor does it extend to mineral rents and royalties. Premiums arising on the grant of a lease for a period not exceeding fifty years are assessed to income tax as rent. However, the amount of the taxable premium may be reduced by 2 per cent for each complete year, after the first year, of the leasing period. Income from furnished lettings is assessable under Case VI of Schedule D, unless an option is exercised for such income to be assessed under Schedule A. Where income arises from furnished holiday lettings, additional expenditure may be included in calculating income chargeable to tax. Income from furnished holiday lettings is treated as earned income.

Schedule C.—This Schedule is confined to interest or dividends on Government or public authority

Single Persons and Married Women

Income	Persons under 65		Persons 65 or over*	
	Income tax	Average rate	Income tax	Average rate
£	£	per cent	£	per cent
3,500	124	3·5	—	—
4,000	249	6·2	83	2·1
5,000	499	10·0	333	6·7
6,000	749	12·5	583	9·7
7,000	999	14·3	833	11·9
8,000	1,249	15·6	1,083	13·5
9,000	1,499	16·7	1,333	14·8
10,000	1,749	17·5	1,583	15·8
12,000	2,249	18·7	2,083	17·4
14,000	2,749	19·6	2,749	19·6
16,000	3,249	20·3	3,249	20·3
18,000	3,749	20·8	3,749	20·8
20,000	4,249	21·2	4,249	21·2
25,000	5,693	22·8	5,693	22·8
30,000	7,693	25·6	7,693	25·6
40,000	11,693	29·2	11,693	29·2
50,000	15,693	31·4	15,693	31·4
100,000	35,693	35·7	35,693	35·7

* Persons aged 75 or over suffer rather less tax on income falling below £14,000 on this table.

funds and certain payments made out of the public revenues of overseas countries.

Schedule D.—This Schedule is divided into six Cases, as follows:

Cases I and II.—Profits arising from trades, professions and vocations, including farming and market gardening. Capital expenditure incurred on assets used for business purposes will often produce an entitlement to capital allowances which reduce the profits chargeable. These profits may also be reduced following the submission of claims for loss relief and other matters.

Case III.—Interest on Government Stocks not taxed at source (e.g. War Loan and British Savings Bonds), interest on National Savings Bank deposits and discounts. Interest up to £70 on ordinary National Savings Bank deposits is exempt from income tax. The exemption applies to both husband and wife separately. Interest on National Savings Bank Special Investment Accounts is not exempt.

Cases IV and V.—Interest from overseas securities, rents, dividends and all other income accruing outside the United Kingdom. Assessment is based on the full amount of income arising, whether remitted to the United Kingdom or retained overseas, but individuals who are either not domiciled in the United Kingdom or who are ordinarily resident overseas may be taxed on a remittance basis. Overseas pensions are taxable but the amount arising may be reduced by 10 per cent for assessment purposes.

Case VI.—Sundry profits and annual receipts not assessed under any other Case or Schedule. These may include insurance commissions, post-cessation receipts and numerous other receipts specifically charged under Case VI.

Schedule E.—All emoluments from an office or employment are assessable under this Schedule. There are three Cases, as follows:

Case I.—This applies to all emoluments of an individual resident and ordinarily resident in the United Kingdom.

Case II.—Of application where the individual is not resident or not ordinarily resident and extends to emoluments for duties undertaken in the United Kingdom.

Case III.—Applies in rare situations to other emoluments remitted to the United Kingdom.

Although earnings for overseas duties may be assessable under Case I where the employee is resident and ordinarily resident in the United Kingdom, a deduction of 100 per cent may be available, which reduces the overseas assessable earnings to nil. This deduction can be obtained where duties are performed overseas for a continuous period reaching or exceeding 365 days and is confined to earnings from the overseas activity.

For years up to and including that ending on April 5, 1989, alternative methods could be used to calculate the emoluments for a year of assessment. However, these methods ceased to apply from April 6, 1989 and were replaced by a new 'receipts' basis. Liability is now governed by the date of receipt.

Where emoluments are assessable under Case I or Case II, the date of receipt, and therefore the year of assessment into which the receipt falls, will comprise the earlier of:

(a) the date of payment;
(b) the date entitlement arises.

In the case of company directors it is the earliest of the two dates given above with the addition of the following three which establish the time of receipt:

(c) the date emoluments are credited in the company's books;
(d) where emoluments for a period are determined after the end of that period—the date of determination;
(e) where emoluments for a period are determined in that period—the last day of that period.

In those cases where emoluments for an earlier year were received after April 5, 1989, it was possible to submit an election removing liability for the earlier year and confining liability to the year of receipt.

The emoluments assessable under Schedule E include all salaries, wages, director's fees and other money sums. In addition, there are a wide range of benefits which must be added to taxable emoluments. These include the provision of living accommodation on advantageous terms and advantages arising from the use of vouchers.

Married Men

Income	Couples under 65		Couples 65 or over*	
	Income tax	Average rate	Income tax	Average rate
£	£	per cent	£	per cent
5,000	69	1·4	—	—
6,000	319	5·3	46	0·8
7,000	569	8·1	296	4·2
8,000	819	10·2	546	6·8
9,000	1,069	11·9	796	8·8
10,000	1,319	13·2	1,046	10·5
12,000	1,819	15·2	1,546	12·9
14,000	2,319	16·6	2,259	16·1
16,000	2,819	17·6	2,819	17·6
18,000	3,319	18·4	3,319	18·4
20,000	3,819	19·1	3,818	19·1
25,000	5,069	20·3	5,069	20·3
30,000	7,005	23·4	7,005	23·4
40,000	11,005	27·5	11,005	27·5
50,000	15,005	30·0	15,005	30·0
100,000	35,005	35·0	35,005	35·0

* Persons aged 75 or over suffer rather less tax on income falling below £16,000 on this table.

Further taxable benefits accrue to directors and employees receiving emoluments of £8,500 or more in the year of assessment. These benefits include the reimbursement of expenses, the availability of motor cars for private motoring, the provision of petrol or other fuel for private motoring, the provision of interest free loans, and other benefits provided at the employer's expense. The cost of providing a limited range of child care facilities may be excluded.

In arriving at the amount to be assessed under Schedule E all expenses incurred wholly, exclusively and necessarily in the performance of the duties may be deducted. This includes fees and subscriptions paid to certain professional bodies and learned societies. Fees paid to managers by entertainers, actors and others assessable under Schedule E may be deducted, up to a maximum of 17·5 per cent of earnings.

Compensation for loss of office and other sums received on the termination of an office or employment are assessable to tax. However, the first £30,000 may be excluded and only the balance remains chargeable.

A part, not exceeding one half, of earnings received from an approved profit-related pay scheme is exempt from income tax.

Schedule F.—This Schedule is concerned with company dividends and distributions. A United Kingdom resident company paying a dividend or distribution must account to the Inland Revenue for advance corporation tax at the rate equal to one third of the sum paid to shareholders in 1990–91. A shareholder residing in the United Kingdom receives the dividend or distribution, together with a tax credit equal to the amount of advance corporation tax. The dividend or distribution is regarded as having suffered income tax, equal to the tax credit, at the basic rate, and where the shareholder is not liable, or not fully liable, at this rate a repayment can be obtained. Individuals liable at the higher rate of 40 per cent will incur further liability. Some payments made by an unquoted trading company to redeem or purchase its own shares will not be treated as distributions.

Building society interest and bank interest.— For many years a special composite rate tax scheme has applied to payments of building society interest and most payments of bank interest made to individuals. Interest of this nature incurs no liability to basic rate income tax in the hands of the depositor, nor can tax be recovered by a depositor not liable to income tax. The actual interest received must be 'grossed up' at the rate of one third to establish the amount of total income received by a depositor liable at the higher rate of 40 per cent.

A composite rate scheme is not compatible with a system of independent taxation as a spouse entitled to a personal allowance, but with little income, cannot obtain repayment of composite rate tax. Therefore the composite tax scheme will cease to apply on April 6, 1991. From this date most payments of building society and bank interest will be received after the deduction of income tax at the basic rate.

INCOME NOT TAXABLE

This includes interest on National Savings Certificates, most scholarship income, bounty payments to members of the armed services and annuities payable to the holders of certain awards. Dividend income arising from investments in personal equity plans may be exempt from tax. Income received under most maintenance agreements and court orders made after June 30, 1988 will not be liable to tax. Nor will payments made under many deeds of covenant executed after March 14, 1988 be recognized for tax purposes, unless the recipient is a charity. Interest arising after December 31, 1990 on a Tax Exempt Special Savings Account (TESSA) opened with a building society or bank will be exempt from tax.

SOCIAL SECURITY BENEFITS

Many Social Security benefits are not liable to income tax. These include family income supplement, long-term sickness benefit, child benefit, war widow's pension, mobility allowance and numerous others. Among the limited range of benefits which are taxable is the retirement pension, widow's allowance, widowed mother's allowance, and unemployment benefits. Short-term sickness benefit and maternity pay payable by an employer is also chargeable to tax.

PAY AS YOU EARN

The Pay As You Earn system is not an independent form of taxation but has been designed to collect income tax by deduction from most emoluments. When paying emoluments to employees an employer is usually required to deduct income tax and account for that tax to the Inland Revenue. In many cases this deduction procedure will fully exhaust the individual's liability to income tax, unless there is other income. From the end of July 1989 the date of 'receipt' for assessment purposes (*see* above) will also identify the date of 'payment' when establishing liability for PAYE.

ALLOWANCES

The previous system of conferring personal and other allowances was substantially amended for 1990–91 and future years by the introduction of independent taxation. The available allowances for 1990–91 are outlined below.

Personal allowance.—Each individual receives a basic personal allowance of £3,005. This is increased to £3,670 for individuals over the age of 64 on April 5, 1991, and further increased to £3,820 for those over the age of 74 on the same date. The increased allowance is available for those who died during the year of assessment but would otherwise have achieved the appropriate age not later than April 5, 1991.

The amount of the increased personal allowance for older taxpayers will be reduced by one-half of total income in excess of £12,300. This reduction in the allowance will continue until it has been reduced to the basic personal allowance of £3,005.

Apart from limited transitional matters mentioned below, any unused part of the personal allowance of one spouse cannot be transferred to the other.

Married couple's allowance.—A married man who was 'living with' his wife at any time in the year ending on April 5, 1991, is entitled to a married couple's allowance. The basic allowance is £1,720. This may be increased to £2,145 if either the husband or the wife is 65 years or over at any time in the year ending on April 5, 1991. A further increase to £2,185 can be obtained where either party to the marriage was 75 or over on April 5, 1991. Where an individual would otherwise have reached either age by April 5, 1991, but who died earlier in the year, the increased allowance is given.

The amount of the increased married couple's allowance may be reduced where the income of the husband (excluding the income of the wife) exceeds £12,300. The reduction will comprise:

(a) one-half of the husband's total income in excess of £12,300, less

(b) the amount of any reduction made when calculating the husband's increased personal allowance.

This reduction in the married couple's allowance cannot reduce that allowance below the basic amount of £1,720.

If husband and wife were married during 1990–91 the married couple's allowance of £1,720, or any increased sum, must be reduced by one-twelfth for each complete month commencing on April 6, 1990, and preceding the date of marriage.

Where a husband cannot utilize all or any part of the married couple's allowance due to an absence of income, he may transfer the unused portion to his wife. The decision whether or not to transfer remains with the husband and he cannot be compelled to act.

Additional personal allowance.—An allowance of £1,720 is available to a single person who has a qualifying child resident with him or her in 1990–91.

The allowance can also be obtained by a married man whose wife is totally incapacitated by physical or mental infirmity throughout the year.

A 'qualifying child' for 1990–91 must be born during the year, be under the age of 16 years at the commencement of the year, or be over the age of 16 at the commencement of the year and either receiving full-time instruction at a university, college, school or other educational establishment or undergoing training for a trade, profession or vocation throughout a minimum period of two years. It is also necessary that the child is the claimant's own or, if not such a child, was either born during 1990–91 or under the age of 18 at the commencement of the year and maintained by the claimant at his or her own expense during the whole of the succeeding twelve-month period.

Only one additional personal allowance of £1,720 can be obtained by an individual notwithstanding the number of children involved. Where an unmarried couple are living together as husband and wife it is not possible for both to obtain the additional personal allowance.

Widow's bereavement allowance.—For the year of assessment in which a husband dies his surviving widow may obtain a widow's bereavement allowance which is £1,720 for 1990–91. It is a requirement that the parties were 'living together' immediately before the husband's death. A similar allowance will be available in the year following death, unless the widow remarried in the year of death. No widow's bereavement allowance can be obtained for future years.

Blind person's allowance.—An allowance of £1,080 is available to an individual if at any time during the year ending on April 5, 1991, he or she was registered as blind on a register maintained by a local authority. If the individual is 'living with' a wife or husband any unused part of the blind person's allowance can be transferred to the other spouse.

Transitional allowances.—There are three limited transitional allowances which are intended to ensure that the introduction of independent taxation does not increase liability to income tax. These allowances comprise:

(a) an increased personal allowance available to a wife where the husband cannot fully use that allowance in 1990–91;

(b) a special personal allowance available to a husband where his wife falls into a higher age group, namely over 64 or over 74;

(c) a married couple's allowance available to a separated husband not 'living with' his wife if the separation occurred before April 6, 1990.

LIFE ASSURANCE RELIEF

Life assurance deduction relief is limited to premiums paid on policies made before March 14, 1984. No relief is available for policies issued after this date. Where the terms of a policy made before March 14, 1984 are subsequently varied or extended to produce increased benefits, future premiums paid may no longer qualify for relief.

When paying premiums under a qualifying policy made before March 14, 1984 the payer will deduct and retain income tax at the rate of 12·5 per cent (15 per cent before April 6, 1989). The ability to retain deductions made in this manner is not affected by the payer's liability to income tax on taxable income. No restriction to the deduction procedure arises if aggregate premiums paid during a year of assessment do not exceed £1,500 (calculated before deducting tax). Should premiums exceed this amount, relief will be confined to £1,500 or one-sixth of total income, whichever is the greater. Where sums deducted exceed the maximum limit, the excess must be accounted for to the Inland Revenue.

OTHER DEDUCTIONS

In addition to personal and other allowances, which reduce taxable income, further deductions may be available to an individual. These include payments of interest.

In some instances interest paid by a business proprietor may be included when calculating profits chargeable to income tax under Case I or Case II of Schedule D. Many private individuals cannot obtain relief in this manner and must satisfy stringent requirements before relief will be forthcoming. In general terms, before interest can qualify for relief it must be annual, as opposed to short, interest or paid to a bank, stockbroker or discount house. Relief will not be available to the extent that interest exceeds a reasonable commercial rate and no relief is forthcoming for interest on an overdraft.

For 1990–91 relief will be available on the following payments:

(a) Interest on a loan to purchase, develop or improve an interest in land owned by the individual and used as the only or main residence of that individual. 'Land' includes large houseboats and also caravans used for a similar purpose. No relief is available for interest on loans applied after April 5, 1988 for the development or improvement of land, unless the work involves the construction of a new building. Relief is available for interest paid on a loan applied to acquire a property which is the only or main residence of a dependent relative, a separated spouse or a divorced former spouse, but only where that person occupied the property before April 6, 1988. Relief may also be forthcoming for interest on a loan used to acquire some other property, perhaps to be used as the only or main residence on retirement, by an individual who is compelled to occupy property by reason of his or her work. If the loan, or aggregate of several loans, exceeds £30,000 relief is restricted to interest on that amount. Where two or more persons apply loans after July 31, 1988 to acquire interests in a single building, those persons cannot, collectively, obtain relief for interest on more than £30,000 in relation to that building.

(b) Interest on a loan to purchase or improve an interest in land which is let or available for letting at a commercial rent. This interest is only capable of being deducted from rental income.

(c) Interest on a loan made to acquire an interest in a close company or in a partnership, or to advance money to such a person.

(d) Interest on a loan to a member of a partnership to acquire machinery or plant for use in the partnership business.

(e) Interest on a loan to an employed person to acquire machinery or plant for the purposes of his employment.

(f) Interest on a loan made for the purpose of contributing capital to an industrial co-operative.

(g) Interest on a loan applied for investment in an employee-controlled company.

(h) Interest on a loan made to elderly persons for the purchase of an annuity where the loan is secured on land. If the loan exceeds £30,000 relief is limited to interest on this amount.

(i) Interest on a loan to personal representatives to provide funds for the payment of capital transfer tax or inheritance tax.

Relief for many payments of mortgage interest is obtained through a special scheme known as MIRAS (mortgage interest relief at source). This applies to interest paid to a building society, bank, insurance company and certain other persons. When making payments of this nature the payer will deduct and retain income tax at the basic rate. This will provide the payer with full relief at the basic rate and no other relief will be necessary, unless the payer is liable at the higher rate of 40 per cent. Qualifying payments of interest outside the MIRAS scheme continue to produce relief by deduction from income chargeable to income tax. Where mortgage interest is payable by a husband and/or his wife 'living together', the parties may allocate the interest payment between themselves in whatever manner is most tax efficient.

Many employees pay contributions to an approved occupational pension scheme. The amount of their contributions may be deducted when establishing emoluments assessable under Schedule E. Relief should also be available for any additional voluntary contributions paid.

Self-employed individuals and those receiving earnings not covered by an occupational pension scheme may contribute under personal pension scheme arrangements. These individials may also pay premiums under retirement annuity schemes, if the arrangements were concluded before July 1, 1988. Contributions paid under both headings may obtain income tax relief, subject to maximum limits.

Subject to a maximum of £40,000 in any one year the cost of subscribing for shares in an unquoted company may qualify as a deduction from taxable income under the Business Expansion Scheme. Many requirements must be satisfied before this relief can be obtained, but for 1990–91 and future years husband and wife may each take advantage of the £40,000 annual maximum.

CAPITAL GAINS TAX

A person is chargeable to capital gains tax on chargeable gains which accrue to him or her during a year of assessment ending on April 5. The application of the tax has been amended substantially in recent years and the following information is confined to the year of assessment 1990–91, ending on April 5 1991.

Liability extends to persons who are either resident or ordinarily resident for the year but special rules apply where a person permanently leaves the United Kingdom or comes to this territory for the purpose of acquiring residence. Non-residents are not liable to capital gains tax unless, exceptionally, they carry on a business in the United Kingdom through a branch or agency.

Chargeable gains accruing to companies are assessable to corporation tax and not to capital gains tax.

Capital gains tax is chargeable on the total of chargeable gains which accrue to a person in a year of assessment, after subtracting allowable losses arising in the same year. Unused allowable losses brought forward from some earlier year may be offset against current chargeable gains but in the case of individuals this must not reduce the net chargeable gains for 1990–91 below £5,000.

RATE OF TAX

Where the net chargeable gains accruing to an individual during 1990–91 do not exceed £5,000 there will be no liability to capital gains tax. If the net gains exceed £5,000 the excess is chargeable at the taxpayers marginal rate of income tax. This is achieved by adding to the amount of income chargeable to income tax the net chargeable gains. The rate attributable to this top slice will disclose the rate of capital gains tax payable, which may be at 25 per cent, 40 per cent or a combination of the two. Although income tax rates are used, capital gains tax remains a separate tax.

Capital gains tax for 1990–91 normally falls due for payment on or before December 1, 1991. If the return or other information recording chargeable gains is delayed, interest may become chargeable.

HUSBAND AND WIFE

For 1989–90 and earlier years only one aggregate annual exemption (£5,000 for 1989–90) was available for a husband and wife 'living together'. In addition, apart from the year of marriage, chargeable gains of a married woman 'living with' her husband were assessed and charged on the husband, unless an election for separate assessment was made. This election did not reduce the aggregate tax payable but merely apportioned liability between the spouses on an equitable basis.

This treatment of a married woman's gains ceased to apply on April 6, 1990. For the future, each spouse is independently assessed on his or her gains, with each being separately entitled to the annual exemption of £5,000 for 1990–91.

No liability to capital gains tax arises from the transfer of assets between spouses 'living together'.

DISPOSAL OF ASSETS

Before liability to capital gains tax can arise a disposal, or deemed disposal, of an asset must take place. This occurs not only where assets are sold or exchanged but applies on the making of a gift. There is also a disposal of assets where any capital sum is derived from assets, for example, where compensation is received for loss or damage to an asset.

The date on which a disposal must be treated as having taken place will determine the year of assessment into which the chargeable gain or allowable loss falls. In those cases where a disposal is made under an unconditional contract, the time of disposal will be that when the contract was entered into and not the subsequent date of conveyance or transfer. A disposal under a conditional contract or option is treated as taking place when the contract becomes unconditional or the option is exercised. Disposals by way of gift are undertaken when the gift becomes effective.

VALUATION OF ASSETS

The amount actually received as consideration for the disposal of an asset will be the sum from which

very limited outgoings must be deducted for the purpose of establishing the gain or loss. In some cases, however, the consideration passing will not accurately reflect the value of the asset and a different basis must be used. This applies, in particular, where an asset is transferred by way of gift or otherwise than by a bargain made at arm's length. Such transactions are deemed to take place for a consideration representing market value, which will determine both the disposal proceeds accruing to the transferor and the cost of acquisition to the transferee.

Market value represents the price which an asset might reasonably be expected to fetch on a sale in the open market. In the case of unquoted shares or securities it is to be assumed that the hypothetical purchaser in the open market would have available all the information which a prudent prospective purchaser of shares or securities might reasonably require if he were proposing to purchase them from a willing vendor by private treaty and at arm's length. This is an important consideration as the amount of information deemed to be available to a hypothetical purchaser may materially affect the price 'reasonably' offered in an open market situation. The market value of unquoted shares or securities will usually be established following negotiations with the Shares Valuation Division of the Capital Taxes Office.

Special rules apply to determine the market value of shares quoted on the Stock Exchange.

DEDUCTION FOR OUTGOINGS

Once the actual or notional disposal proceeds have been determined it only remains to subtract eligible outgoings for the purpose of computing the gain or loss. There is the general rule that any outgoings deducted, or which are available to be deducted, when calculating income tax liability must be ignored. Subject to this, deductions will usually be limited to:

(a) the cost of acquiring the asset, together with incidental costs wholly and exclusively incurred in connection with the acquisition;
(b) expenditure incurred wholly and exclusively on the asset in enhancing its value, being expenditure reflected in the state or nature of the asset at the time of the disposal, and any other expenditure wholly and exclusively incurred in establishing, preserving or defending title to, or a right over, the asset; and
(c) the incidental costs of making the disposal.

Where the disposal concerns a leasehold interest having less than 50 years to run, any expenditure falling under (a) and (b) must be written off throughout the duration of the lease. This recognizes that a lease is a wasting asset which, at the termination of the leasing period, will retain no value.

ASSETS HELD ON MARCH 31, 1982

Where the disposal of assets held on March 31, 1982, takes place after April 5, 1988, the actual cost of acquisition will not usually enter into the calculation of gain. It is to be assumed that such assets were acquired on March 31, 1982, for a consideration representing market value on that date. The increase in value, if any, occurring before March 31, 1982, will not be assessable to capital gains tax.

INDEXATION ALLOWANCE

An indexation allowance will be available when calculating the chargeable gain or allowable loss. This allowance is based on percentage increases in the retail prices index between the month of March 1982, or if later the month in which expenditure is incurred, and the month of disposal. The increase is applied to the items of expenditure in (a) and (b) above to determine the amount of the indexation allowance. However, if the asset was acquired before March 31, 1982 and the disposal occurs after April 5, 1988, the allowance will be based on market value at March 31, 1982.

The amount of the indexation allowance will be subtracted from the gain, or added to the loss, to calculate the chargeable gain or allowable loss arising on disposal.

EXEMPTIONS

There is a general exemption from liability to capital gains tax where the net gains of an individual for 1990–91 do not exceed £5,000. From April 6, 1990, this exemption limit applies separately to a husband and to his wife where the parties are 'living together'.

The disposal of many assets will not give rise to chargeable gains or allowable losses and these include:

(a) private motor cars;
(b) Government securities;
(c) Loan stock and other securities (but not shares);
(d) Options and contracts relating to securities within (b) and (c);
(e) National Savings Certificates, Premium Bonds, Defence Bonds and National Development Bonds;
(f) currency of any description acquired for personal expenditure outside the United Kingdom;
(g) decorations awarded for valour;
(h) betting wins and pools, lottery or games prizes;
(i) compensation or damages for any wrong or injury suffered by an individual in his person or in his profession or vocation;
(j) life assurance and deferred annuity contracts where the person making the disposal is the original beneficial owner;
(k) dwelling-houses and land enjoyed with the residence which is an individual's only or main residence;
(l) tangible movable property, the consideration for the disposal of which does not exceed £6,000;
(m) certain tangible movable property which is a wasting asset having a life not exceeding 50 years;
(n) assets transferred to charities and other bodies;
(o) works of art, historic buildings and similar assets;
(p) assets used to provide maintenance funds for historic buildings;
(q) assets transferred to trustees for the benefit of employees.

DWELLING-HOUSES

Exemption from capital gains tax will usually be available for any gain which accrues to an individual from the disposal of, or of an interest in, a dwelling-house or part of a dwelling-house which has been his only or main residence. The exemption extends to land which has been occupied and enjoyed with the residence as its garden or grounds. Some restriction may be necessary where the land exceeds one acre.

The gain will not be chargeable to capital gains tax if the dwelling-house, or part, has been the individu-al's only or main residence throughout the period of ownership, or throughout the entire period except for all or any part of the last two years. A proportionate part of the gain will be exempt if the dwelling-house has been the individual's only or main residence for part only of the period of ownership. In the case of property acquired before March 31, 1982, the period of ownership is treated as commencing on this date.

Where part of the dwelling-house has been used exclusively for business purposes, part of the gain attributable to business use will not be exempt. It will be comparatively unusual for any part to be used exclusively for such a purpose, except perhaps in the case of doctors' or dentists' surgeries.

In those cases where part of a qualifying dwelling-house has been used to provide rented residential accommodation this non-personal use may frequently be ignored when calculating exemption from capital gains tax, unless relatively substantial sums are involved.

Dwellings occupied by dependent relatives or separated or divorced former spouses, may also qualify for the exemption, but only where occupation commenced before April 6, 1988.

ROLL-OVER RELIEF

Persons carrying on business will often undertake the disposal of an asset and use the proceeds to finance the acquisition of a replacement asset. Where this situation arises a claim for roll-over relief may be available. The broad effect of such a claim is that all or part of the gain arising on the disposal of the old asset may be disregarded. The gain or part is then subtracted from the cost of acquiring the replacement asset. As this cost is reduced, any gain arising from the future disposal of the replacement asset will be correspondingly increased, unless of course a further roll-over situation then develops.

It remains a requirement that both the old and the replacement asset must be used for the purpose of the taxpayer's business. Relief will only be available if the acquisition of the replacement asset takes place within a period commencing twelve months before, and ending three years after, the disposal of the old asset, although the Board of Inland Revenue retain a discretion to extend this period where the circumstances were such that it was impossible for the taxpayer to acquire the replacement asset before the expiration of the normal time limit.

Whilst many business assets qualify for roll-over relief there are exceptions.

GIFTS

The gift of an asset is treated as a disposal made for a consideration equal to market value, with a corresponding acquisition by the transferee at an identical value. For gifts made by individuals and trustees before March 14, 1989, a wide-ranging claim for hold-over relief was available where the transferee was resident in the United Kingdom.

In the case of gifts made on or after this date, hold-over relief is limited to the transfer of certain assets only. The more important of these comprise:

(a) assets used for the purposes of a trade or similar activity carried on by the transferor or his family company;
(b) shares or securities of a trading company which is neither quoted on a stock exchange nor dealt in on the Unlisted Securities Market;
(c) shares or securities of a trading company which

is quoted or listed but which is the transferor's family company;

(d) many interests in agricultural property qualifying for 50 per cent or 30 per cent inheritance tax relief;

(e) transactions which are lifetime transfers for inheritance tax purposes, other than potentially exempt transfers.

The effect of the claim is similar to that following a claim for roll-over relief, but adjustments will be necessary where some consideration is given for the transfer, the asset has not been used for business purposes throughout the period of ownership, or not all assets of a company are used for business purposes.

RETIREMENT RELIEF

Retirement relief is available to an individual who disposes by way of sale or gift of the whole or part of a business. It does not necessarily follow that the isolated disposal of assets will represent the disposal of the whole or part of a business. The main condition for granting this relief is that throughout a period of at least one year the business has been owned either by the individual or by a trading company in which the individual retained a sufficient shareholding interest. The relief extends also to cases where an individual disposes by way of sale or gift of shares or securities of a company. It must be demonstrated that the company was a trading company, the individual retained a sufficient shareholding interest, and he was engaged as a full-time working director.

An individual who has attained the age of 60 years at the time of a disposal may obtain maximum retirement relief exceeding £300,000 for disposals taking place after April 5, 1988. The amount of this relief must be reduced if the conditions have not been satisfied throughout a ten year period. With a single exception no retirement relief can be obtained if the disposal occurs before the individual's 60th birthday. This exception arises where an individual is compelled to retire early on the grounds of ill-health. The normal retirement relief may then be obtained. Any retirement relief must be subtracted from the net gains arising on disposal, leaving the balance remaining, if any, chargeable to capital gains tax in the normal manner.

DEATH

No capital gains tax is chargeable on the value of assets retained at the time of death. However, the personal representatives administering the deceased's estate are deemed to acquire those assets for a consideration representing market value on death. This ensures that any increase in value occurring before the date of death will not be chargeable to capital gains tax. If a legatee or other person acquires an asset under a will or intestacy no chargeable gain will accrue to the personal representatives, and the person taking the asset will also be treated as having acquired it at the time of death for its then market value.

INHERITANCE TAX

Throughout a period of some 90 years estate duty was payable on the value of an individual's estate at the time of death. Liability did not extend to lifetime gifts other than those made shortly before death and a limited range of further gifts where the donor continued to retain some benefit from the assets gifted. Estate duty ceased to apply for deaths occurring after March 12, 1975 following the introduction of capital transfer tax. This tax was not limited to the value of an estate at the time of death but applied to many gifts made during lifetime. Although the broad framework of capital transfer tax remains, very substantial changes were introduced for events occurring after March 17, 1986. In recognition of these changes the tax was renamed inheritance tax and now bears many characteristics of the former estate duty.

The nature and scope of inheritance tax is outlined below, but the comments made have little application to events occurring before 18 March 1986 when capital transfer tax applied.

Liability to inheritance tax may arise on a limited range of lifetime gifts and other dispositions and also on the value of assets retained, or deemed to be retained, at the time of death. An individual's domicile at the time of any gift or on death is an important matter. Domicile will generally be determined by applying normal rules, but special considerations may be necessary where an individual was previously domiciled in the United Kingdom but subsequently acquired a domicile of choice overseas. Where a person was domiciled in the United Kingdom at the time of a disposition or on death the location of assets is immaterial and full liability to inheritance tax arises. Individuals domiciled outside the United Kindom are, however, chargeable to inheritance tax only on transactions affecting assets located in the United Kingdom.

The assets of husband and wife are not merged for inheritance tax purposes. Each spouse is treated as a separate individual entitled to receive the benefit of his or her exemptions, reliefs and rates of tax. Where husband and wife retain similar assets, special 'related property' provisions may require the merger of those assets for valuation purposes only.

LIFETIME GIFTS AND DISPOSITIONS

Gifts and dispositions made during lifetime fall under four broad headings, namely:

(a) dispositions which are not transfers of value;
(b) exempt transfers;
(c) potentially exempt transfers; and
(d) chargeable transfers.

Dispositions which are not transfers of value.—Several lifetime transactions are not treated as transfers of value and may be entirely disregarded for inheritance tax purposes. These include transactions not intended to confer gratuitous benefit, the provision of family maintenance, the waiver of the right to receive remuneration or dividends, and the grant of agricultural tenancies for full consideration.

Exempt transfers.—Certain other transfers are treated as exempt transfers and incur no liability to inheritance tax. The main exempt transfers are listed below:

Transfers between spouses.—Transfers between husband and wife are usually exempt. However, if the transferor is, but the transferee spouse is not, domiciled in the United Kingdom transfers will be exempt only to the extent that the total does not exceed £55,000. Unlike the requirement used for income tax and capital gains tax purposes, it is immaterial whether husband and wife are living together.

Annual exemption.—The first £3,000 of gifts and other dispositions made in a year ending on April 5 is exempt. If the exemption is not used, or not wholly used, in any year the balance may be carried forward to the following year only. The annual exemption will only be available for a potentially exempt transfer (*see* below) if that transfer subsequently becomes chargeable by reason of the donor's death.

Small gifts.—Outright gifts of £250 or less to any person in one year ending April 5 are exempt.

Normal expenditure.—A transfer made during lifetime and comprising normal expenditure is exempt. To obtain this exemption it must be shown that:

    (a) the transfer was made as part of the normal expenditure of the transferor;

    (b) taking one year with another, the transfer was made out of income; and

    (c) after allowing for all transfers of value forming part of normal expenditure the transferor was left with sufficient income to maintain his or her usual standard of living.

Gifts in consideration of marriage.—These are exempt if they satisfy certain requirements. The amount allowed will be governed by the relationship between the donor and a party to the marriage. The allowable amounts comprise:

    (a) gifts by a parent—£5,000

    (b) gifts by a grandparent—£2,500

    (c) gifts by a party to the marriage—£2,500

    (d) gifts by other persons—£1,000

Gifts to charities.—Gifts to charities are exempt from liability.

Gifts to political parties.—Gifts to political parties which satisfy certain requirements are generally exempt.

Gifts for national purposes.—Gifts made to an extensive list of bodies are exempt from liability. These include, among others:

    (a) The National Gallery;

    (b) The British Museum;

    (c) The National Trust;

    (d) The National Art Collections Fund;

    (e) The Nature Conservancy Council;

    (f) The Historic Buildings and Monuments Commission for England;

    (g) Any local authority;

    (h) Any university or university college in the United Kingdom.

A number of other gifts made for the public benefit are also exempt.

Potentially exempt transfers.—Lifetime gifts and dispositions which are neither to be ignored nor comprise exempt transfers incur possible liability to inheritance tax. However, relief is available for a range of potentially exempt transfers. These comprise gifts made by an individual to:

    (a) a second individual;

    (b) trustees administering an accumulation and maintenance trust; or

    (c) trustees administering a disabled person's trust.

The accumulation and maintenance trust mentioned in (b) must provide that on reaching a specified age, not exceeding twenty-five years, a beneficiary will become absolutely entitled to trust assets or obtain an interest in possession in the income of those assets.

Further additions were made to the list of potentially exempt transfers for transactions taking place after March 16, 1987. These affect settled property administered by trustees where an individual, or individuals, retain an interest in possession. The transfer of assets to, the removal of assets from, or

the rearrangement of interests in such property comprise potentially exempt transfers if the person transferring an interest and the person benefiting from the transfer are both individuals.

No immediate liability to inheritance tax will arise on the making of a potentially exempt transfer. Should the donor survive for a period of seven years, immunity from liability will be confirmed. However, the donor's death within the seven-year *inter vivos* period produces liability, as explained later, if the amounts involved are sufficiently substantial.

Chargeable transfers.—Any remaining lifetime gifts or dispositions which are neither to be ignored, represent exempt transfers or potentially exempt transfers, incur liability to inheritance tax. The range of such chargeable transfers is severely limited and is broadly confined to transfers made to or affecting certain trusts, transfers to non-individuals and transfers involving companies.

GIFTS WITH RESERVATION

A lifetime gift of assets made at any time after March 17, 1986, may incur additional liability to inheritance tax if the donor retains some interest in the subject matter of the gift. This may arise, for example, where a parent transfers a dwelling-house to a son or daughter and continues to occupy the property or to enjoy some benefit from that property. The retention of a benefit may be ignored where it is enjoyed in return for full consideration, perhaps a commercial rent, or the benefit arises from changed circumstances which could not have been foreseen at the time of the original gift. The gift with reservation provisions will not usually apply to most exempt transfers.

There are three possibilities which may arise where the donor reserves or enjoys some benefit from the subject matter of a previous gift and subsequently dies, namely:

    (a) If no benefit is enjoyed within a period of seven years before death there can be no further liability.

    (b) If the benefit ceased to be enjoyed within a period of seven years before the date of death the original donor is deemed to have made a potentially exempt transfer representing the value of the asset at the time of cessation.

    (c) If the benefit is enjoyed at the time of death the value of the asset must be included in the value of the deceased's estate on death.

It must be emphasised that the existence of a benefit enjoyed at any time within a period of seven years before death will establish liability on gifts with reservation, notwithstanding that the gift may have been made many years earlier, providing it was undertaken after March 17, 1986.

DEATH

Immediately before the time of death an individual is deemed to make a transfer of value. This transfer will comprise the value of assets forming part of the deceased's estate after subtracting most liabilities. Any exempt transfers may, however, be excluded. These include transfers for the benefit of a surviving spouse, a charity and a qualifying political party together with bequests to approved bodies and for national purposes.

Death may also trigger three additional liabilities, namely:

    (a) A potentially exempt transfer made within the period of seven years ending on death loses its potential status and becomes chargeable to inheritance tax.

(b) The value of gifts made with reservation may incur liability if any benefit was enjoyed within a period of seven years preceding death.

(c) Additional tax may become payable for chargeable lifetime transfers made within seven years before death.

VALUATIONS

The valuation of assets is an important matter as this will establish the value transferred for lifetime dispositions and also the value of a person's estate at the time of death. The value of property will represent the price which might reasonably be expected from a sale in the open market. This price cannot be reduced on the grounds that the whole property is placed on the market simultaneously and may therefore depress values.

In some cases it may be necessary to incorporate the value of 'related property'. This will include property comprised in the estate of the transferor's spouse and certain property previously transferred to charities. The purpose of the related property valuation rules is not to add the value of the property to the estate of the transferor. Related property must be merged to establish the aggregate value of the respective interests and this value is then apportioned, usually on a *pro rata* basis, to the separate interests.

The value of shares and securities quoted on the Stock Exchange will be determined by extracting figures from the daily list of official prices.

Where quoted shares and securities are sold within a period of twelve months following the date of death a claim may be made to substitute the proceeds for the value on death. This claim will only be beneficial if the gross proceeds realized are lower than market value on death. A similar claim may be available for interests in land sold within a period of three years following death.

RELIEF FOR ASSETS

Special relief is made available for certain assets, notably woodlands, agricultural property and business property. The effect of this relief is summarized below:

Woodlands.—Where woodlands pass on death the value will usually be included in the deceased's estate. However, an election may be made in respect of land in the United Kingdom on which trees or underwood is growing to delete the value of those assets. Relief is confined to the value of trees or underwood and does not extend to the land on which they are growing. Liability to inheritance tax will arise if and when the trees or underwood are sold on a future occasion.

Agricultural property.—Relief is available for the agricultural value of agricultural property. Such property must be occupied and used for agricultural purposes and relief is confined to the agricultural value.

The value transferred, either on a lifetime gift or on death, must be determined. This value may then be reduced by a percentage. A higher 50 per cent deduction will be available if the transferor retained vacant possession or could have obtained that possession within a period of twelve months following the transfer. The increased deduction of 50 per cent may also be available for certain agricultural property held on March 9, 1981. In other cases, notably including land let to tenants, a lower deduction of 30 per cent is available.

It remains a requirement that the agricultural property was either occupied by the transferor for the purposes of agriculture throughout a two-year period ending on the date of the transfer, or was owned by him throughout a period of seven years ending on that date and occupied for agricultural purposes.

Business property.—Where value transferred is attributable to relevant business property, that value may be reduced by a percentage. The reduction in value applies to:

(a) property consisting of a business or an interest in a business;

(b) shares or securities of a company, whether quoted or unquoted, which provided the transferor with control of the company immediately before the transfer. Control for this purpose may include that created by related property;

(c) unquoted shares or securities not falling within (b) which provided the transferor with more than 25 per cent of voting rights;

(d) other unquoted shares or securities not falling within (c);

(e) any land, building, machinery or plant which, immediately before the transfer, was used wholly or mainly for the purposes of a business carried on by a company of which the transferor had control;

(f) any land, building, machinery or plant which, immediately before the transfer, was used wholly or mainly for the purposes of a business carried on by a partnership of which the transferor was a partner; and

(g) any land, building, machinery or plant which, immediately before the transfer, was used wholly or mainly for the purposes of a business carried on by the transferor and was then settled property in which he retained an interest in possession.

For property falling within (a) or (b) the deduction is 50 per cent. A similar deduction is available for property in (c), if the event occurs after March 16, 1987. A reduced deduction of 30 per cent applies to property in (d) to (g).

It is a general requirement that the property must have been retained for a period of two years before the transfer or death and restrictions may be necessary if the property has not been used wholly for business purposes. The same slice of property cannot obtain both business property relief and the relief available for agricultural property.

CALCULATION OF TAX PAYABLE

The calculation of inheritance tax payable adopts the use of a cumulative total. Each chargeable lifetime transfer is added to the total with a final addition made on death. The top slice added to the total for the current event determines the rate at which inheritance tax must be paid. However, the cumulative total will only include transfers made within a period of seven years before the current event and those undertaken outside this period must be excluded. Although inheritance tax was only introduced on March 18, 1986, the seven-year cumulative total will include chargeable lifetime gifts made before that date, subject to the seven-year limitation.

Lifetime transfers.—The limited range of lifetime transfers must be added to the seven-year cumulative total to calculate the amount of inheritance tax due. The tax is imposed at one-half of the rate shown below. However, if the donor dies within a period of seven years from the date of the chargeable lifetime transfer, additional tax may be due. This is calculated by applying tax at the full rate (in substitution for the one-half rate previously used). The amount of tax is then reduced to a percentage by applying tapering relief. This percentage is governed by the number of years from the date of the lifetime gift to the date of death and is as follows:

Period of years before death	Percentage
Not more than 3	100
More than 3 but not more than 4	80
More than 4 but not more than 5	60
More than 5 but not more than 6	40
More than 6 but not more than 7	20

Should this exercise produce liability greater than that previously paid at the one-half rate on the lifetime transfer, additional tax, representing the difference, must be paid. Where the calculation shows an amount falling below tax paid on the lifetime transfer, no additional liability can arise nor will the deficiency become repayable.

Potentially exempt transfers.—Where a potentially exempt transfer loses immunity from liability, due to the donor's death within the seven-year *inter vivos* period, the value transferred becomes liable to inheritance tax. Liability is calculated by applying the full rate shown below, reduced to the percentage governed by tapering relief if the original transfer occurred more than three years before death.

Death.—The final addition to the seven-year cumulative total will comprise the value of an estate on death. Inheritance tax will be calculated by applying the full rate shown below. No tapering relief can be obtained.

RATES OF TAX

In earlier times there were several rates of inheritance tax which progressively increased as the value transferred grew in size. However, for events taking place after March 14, 1988, a nil rate applies to the first £110,000 of value. This is increased to £118,000 for events after April 5, 1989 and further increased to £128,000 for events occurring after April 5, 1990. Any excess is charged at the single positive rate of 40 per cent.

Only one-half of the 40 per cent rate (namely 20 per cent) will be applicable for chargeable lifetime transfers.

It must be anticipated that the above rate and rateband will be amended on future occasions.

PAYMENT OF TAX

Inheritance tax usually falls due for payment six months after the end of the month in which the chargeable transaction takes place. Where a transfer, other than that made on death, occurs after April 5 and before the following October 1, tax falls due on the following April 30, although there are some exceptions to this general rule.

Inheritance tax attributable to the transfer of certain land, controlling shareholding interests, unquoted shares, businesses and interests in businesses, together with agricultural property, may usually be satisfied by instalments spread over ten years. No liability to interest arises where tax is paid on the due date. In other cases, delay in the payment of tax may incur liability to interest.

SETTLED PROPERTY

Complex rules apply to establish inheritance tax liability on settled property. Where a person is beneficially entitled to an interest in possession, that person is effectively deemed to own the property in which the interest subsists. It follows that where the interest comes to an end during the beneficiary's lifetime and some other person becomes entitled to the property or interest, the beneficiary is treated as having made a transfer of value. However, for events taking place after March 16, 1987 this will usually comprise a potentially exempt transfer. No liability will arise where the property vests in the absolute ownership of the previous beneficiary. The death of a person entitled to an interest in possession will require the value of the underlying property to be added to the value of the deceased's estate.

In the case of other settled property where there is no interest in possession (e.g. discretionary trusts), liability to tax will arise on each ten-year anniversary of the trust. There will also be liability if property ceases to be held on discretionary trusts before the first ten-year anniversary date is reached or between anniversaries. The rate of tax suffered will be governed by several considerations, including previous dispositions made by the settlor, transactions concluded by the trustees, and the period throughout which property has been held in trust.

Accumulation and maintenance settlements which require assets to be distributed not later than a beneficiary's twenty-fifth birthday may be exempt from any liability to inheritance tax.

CORPORATION TAX

Profits, gains and income accruing to companies resident in the United Kingdom incur liability to corporation tax. Non-resident companies are immune from this tax unless they carry on a trade in the United Kingdom through a permanent establishment, branch or office. Companies residing outside the United Kingdom may be liable to income tax at the basic rate on other income arising in the United Kingdom, perhaps from letting property. The following comments are confined to companies resident in the United Kingdom and have little application to those residing overseas.

Liability to corporation tax is governed by the profits, gains or income for an accounting period. This is usually the period for which financial accounts are made up, and in the case of companies preparing accounts to the same accounting date annually will comprise successive periods of twelve months.

RATE OF TAX

The amount of profits or income for an accounting period must be determined on normal taxation principles. The special rules which apply to individuals where a source of income is acquired or discontinued are ignored and consideration is confined to the actual profits or income for an accounting period.

The rate of corporation tax is fixed for a financial year ending on March 31. Where the accounting period of a company overlaps this date and there is a change in the rate of corporation tax, profits and income must be apportioned.

For earlier years the full rate of corporation tax was 52 per cent but this rate was progressively reduced as follows:

Financial year		Per cent
12 months ending March 31, 1984		50
,,	March 31, 1985	45
,,	March 31, 1986	40
,,	March 31, 1987, 1988, 1989, 1990 and 1991	35

The progressive reduction in the rate of corporation tax was made to compensate companies for the loss of stock relief and the withdrawal of certain allowances for capital expenditure which increased the amount of profits and income chargeable to that tax.

SMALL COMPANIES RATE

Where the profits of a company do not exceed stated limits, corporation tax becomes payable at the small companies rate. It is the amount of profits and not the size of the company which governs the application of this rate.

The level of profits which a company may derive without losing the benefit of the small companies rate has been frequently changed. In recent years the following small companies rate applies where profits do not exceed £200,000 for the year ending March 31, 1991, £150,000 for the year ending March 31, 1990 or £100,000 for earlier years:

Financial year		Per cent
12 months ending March 31, 1984		38
,,	March 31, 1985 and 1986	30
,,	March 31, 1987	29
,,	March 31, 1988	27
,,	March 31, 1989, 1990 and 1991	25

If profits do exceed £200,000 (or £150,000 or £100,000) but fall between £1,000,000 (or £750,000 or £500,000 respectively), marginal small companies rate relief applies. The broad effect of marginal relief is that the first £200,000 (or £150,000 or £100,000) of profits is taxed at the appropriate small companies rate. Profits falling in the margin then incur liability at the following marginal rates:

Financial year	Per cent
12 months ending March 31, 1984	55
,, March 31, 1985	48·75
,, March 31, 1986	42·5
,, March 31, 1987	36·5
,, March 31, 1988	37
,, March 31, 1989	37·5
,, March 31, 1990	37·5
,, March 31, 1991	37·5

If the accounting period of a company overlaps March 31, profits must be apportioned to establish the appropriate rate for each part of those profits.

The lower limit of £200,000 (or £150,000 or £100,000) and the upper limit of £1,000,000 (or £750,000 or £500,000) applies for a period of twelve months in duration and must be proportionately reduced for shorter periods. Some restriction in the small companies rate and the marginal rate may be necessary if there are two or more associated companies, namely companies under common control.

For accounting periods commencing after March 31, 1989, the small companies rate is not available for close investment-holding companies. These are mainly investment companies, other than those receiving most of their income from letting land and property.

CAPITAL GAINS

Chargeable gains arising to a company are calculated in a manner similar to that used for individuals. However, companies cannot obtain the annual exemption of £5,000, nor are they assessed to capital gains tax. In place of this tax companies suffer liability to corporation tax on chargeable gains.

For disposals taking place before March 17, 1987 only a fraction of the chargeable gain was assessable to corporation tax at the full rate. The fraction selected ensured that companies effectively suffered corporation tax at the rate of 30 per cent on the full chargeable gain. A different approach is adopted for disposals taking place after this date. The full chargeable gain, and not a fraction, is assessable to corporation tax. However, unlike the previous system, the chargeable gain is treated as ordinary profit, thereby obtaining the benefit of the small companies rate where figures are sufficiently low.

DISTRIBUTIONS

Dividends and other qualifying distributions made by a United Kingdom resident company are not satisfied after deduction of income tax. However, when making a distribution a company is required to account to the Inland Revenue for an amount of advance corporation tax. For distributions made in the year ending April 5, 1991, the amount of advance corporation tax will represent one-third of the distribution. Thus a cash dividend of £75 paid to a shareholder will also require satisfaction of advance corporation tax amounting to £25.

Advance corporation tax accounted for in this manner for distributions made in an accounting period may usually be set against a company's corporation tax liability for the same period. Some restrictions are imposed on the amount which can be offset but any surplus can be carried forward, or carried backwards, and set against corporation tax due for other accounting periods.

A United Kingdom resident shareholder receiving a qualifying distribution also obtains a tax credit, which for the year ending April 5, 1991, is equal to one-third of the distribution made. Therefore the total income of the individual comprises the aggregate of the distribution and the tax credit. If the individual is not liable, or not fully liable, to income tax at the basic rate, all or part of the tax credit can be refunded by the Inland Revenue. Individuals with substantial income incur liability to income tax at the higher rate of 40 per cent on the aggregate of the distribution and the tax credit.

PAYMENT OF TAX

Corporation tax, less any relief for advance corporation tax, usually falls due for payment nine months following the end of the accounting period to which the tax relates. Companies which were carrying on business before 1966 may have a later due and payable date, but this is gradually being amended to achieve a common nine month period for all companies.

INTEREST

On making many payments of interest a company is required to deduct income tax at the basic rate and account for the tax deducted to the Inland Revenue. The gross amount of interest paid will usually comprise a charge on income to be offset against profits on which corporation tax becomes payable.

GROUPS OF COMPANIES

Each company within a group is separately charged to corporation tax on profits, gains and income. However, where one group member realizes a loss, other than a capital loss, a claim may be made to offset the deficiency against profits of some other member of the same group.

Claims are also available to avoid the payment of advance corporation tax on distributions, or the deduction of income tax on the payment of interest, for transactions between members of a group of companies. The transfer of capital assets from one member of a group to a fellow member will incur no liability to tax on chargeable gains.

VALUE ADDED TAX

Unlike income tax, capital gains tax, inheritance tax and corporation tax, which are collected and administered by the Inland Revenue, value added tax is the responsibility of Customs and Excise. Value added tax is charged on the value of supplies made in the United Kingdom by a registered trader and extends both to the supply of goods and to the supply of services. Liability also arises on the value of goods imported into the United Kingdom.

REGISTRATION

All traders, including professional men and women, together with companies, making taxable supplies of a value exceeding stated limits are required to register for value added tax purposes. Taxable supplies represent the supply of goods and services potentially chargeable with value added tax. The limits which govern mandatory registration are amended annually but from March 21, 1990, an unregistered trader must register:

(a) at any time, if there are reasonable grounds for believing that the value of taxable supplies in the next 30 days will exceed £25,400; or

(b) at the end of any month if the value of taxable supplies in the last 12 months then ending has exceeded £25,400.

Liability to register under (b) may be avoided if it can be shown that the value of supplies in the period of 12 months then beginning will not exceed £24,400. There may, however, be liability to register immediately where a business is taken over from another trader as a 'going concern'.

Where the limits governing mandatory registration have been exceeded it is necessary for the trader to notify Customs and Excise. Failure to provide prompt notification may have unfortunate results as the person concerned will be required to account for value added tax from the proper registration date. In some situations a trader whose taxable supplies do not reach the mandatory registration limits may apply for voluntary registration.

A registered trader may submit an application for de-registration if the value of taxable supplies subsequently falls. From June 1, 1990, an application for de-registration can be made if the value of taxable supplies for the year beginning on the application date is not expected to exceed £24,400.

INPUT TAX

A registered trader will both suffer tax (input tax) when obtaining goods or services for the purposes of his business and also become liable to account for tax (output tax) on the value of goods and services which he supplies. Relief can usually be obtained for input tax suffered, either by setting that tax against output tax due or by repayment. Most items of input tax can be relieved in this manner but there are exceptions including the prohibition of relief for the cost of business entertaining. Where a registered trader makes both exempt supplies and also taxable supplies to his customers or clients there may be some restriction in the amount of input tax which can be recovered.

OUTPUT TAX

When making a taxable supply of goods or services a registered trader must account for output tax, if any, on the value of the supply. Usually the price charged by the registered trader will be increased by adding value added tax but failure to make the required addition will not remove liability to account for output tax.

EXEMPT SUPPLIES

No value added tax is chargeable on the supply of goods or services which are treated as exempt supplies. These include the provision of burial and cremation facilities, insurance, finance and education. The granting of a lease to occupy land or the sale of land will usually comprise an exempt supply, but there are numerous exceptions. In particular, the sale of new non-domestic buildings or certain buildings used by charities, constructed after April 1, 1989, can no longer be treated as exempt supplies.

From August 1, 1989 a taxable person may elect to tax rents and other supplies of buildings and agricultural land not used for residential or charitable purposes.

Exempt supplies do not enter into the calculation of taxable supplies which governs liability to mandatory registration. Such supplies made by a registered trader may however limit the amount of input tax which can be relieved. It is for this reason that the election available from August 1, 1989 may be useful.

RATES OF TAX

Two rates of value added tax have applied since June 18, 1979, namely:

(a) a zero, or nil, rate; and

(b) a standard rate of 15 per cent.

Although no tax is due on a zero-rated supply, this does comprise a taxable supply which must be included in the calculation governing liability to register.

ZERO-RATING

A large number of supplies are zero-rated, including, among others:

(a) the supply of many items of food and drink for human consumption. This does not include ice creams, chocolates, sweets, potato crisps and alcoholic drinks. Nor does it extend to supplies made in the course of catering, for example, at a wedding reception or other social function, or to items supplied for consumption in a restaurant or cafe. Whilst the supply of cold items, for example sandwiches, for consumption away from the supplier's premises, is zero rated, the supply of hot food, for example fish and chips, is not;

(b) animal feeding stuffs;

(c) sewerage and water, unless supplied for industrial purposes after June 30, 1990;

(d) books, brochures, pamphlets, leaflets, newspapers, maps and charts;

(e) talking books for the blind and handicapped and wireless sets for the blind;

(f) electricity, gas and coal, but supplies are limited to domestic use after June 30, 1990;

(g) supplies of services, other than professional services, when constructing a new domestic building or a building to be used by a charity. The supply of materials for such a building is also zero-rated, together with the sale or the grant of a long lease for these buildings. Before April 1, 1989 this applied to most new buildings but subsequently it is limited to domestic buildings and buildings used by charities. Alterations to some protected buildings are also zero-rated;

(h) the transportation of persons in a vehicle, ship

or aircraft designed to carry not less than twelve persons;

(i) supplies of drugs, medicines and other aids for the handicapped;

(j) supplies of clothing and footwear for young persons;

(k) exports.

This list is not exhaustive but indicates the wide range of supplies which may be zero-rated.

COLLECTION OF TAX

Registered traders submit value added tax returns for accounting periods. Each accounting period is three months in duration but arrangements can be made to submit returns on a monthly basis. The return will show both the output tax due for supplies made by the trader in the accounting period and also the input tax for which relief is claimed. If the output tax exceeds input tax the balance must be remitted with the value added tax return. Where input tax suffered exceeds the output tax due the registered trader may claim recovery of the excess from Customs and Excise.

This basis for collecting tax explains the structure of value added tax. Where supplies are made between registered traders the supplier will account for an amount of tax which will usually be identical to the tax recovered by the person to whom the supply is made. However, where the supply is made to a person who is not a registered trader there can be no recovery of input tax and it is on this person that the final burden of value added tax eventually falls.

Tax on imports into the United Kingdom must be satisfied at the time of importation or perhaps later where special arrangements have been agreed.

An optional scheme will be made available for registered traders having an annual turnover of taxable supplies not exceeding £250,000. Such traders may, if they wish, render returns annually. Nine equal payments of value added tax will be paid on account, with a final balancing payment accompanying submission of the return.

BAD DEBTS

Many retailers operate special retail schemes for calculating the amount of value added tax due. These schemes are, broadly, based on the volume of consideration received in an accounting period. Should a customer fail to pay for goods or services supplied, there will be no consideration on which value added tax falls to be calculated.

To avoid the problem of bad debts incurred by traders not operating a special retail scheme, an optional system of cash accounting is available. This scheme, confined to traders with annual taxable supplies not exceeding £250,000, enables returns to be made on a cash basis, in substitution for the normal supply basis. Traders using such a scheme will not, of course, include bad debts in the calculation of cash receipts.

Where neither the cash accounting arrangements nor the special retail scheme applies, output tax falls due on the value of the supply and liability is not affected by failure to receive consideration. For some time limited relief has been available for bad debts where a trader becomes insolvent. In future, however, where a debt is more than two years old and is written off in the supplier's books, relief for bad debts will be forthcoming. This first applies to supplies made after April 1, 1989.

OTHER SPECIAL SCHEMES

In addition to the schemes for retailers, there are several special schemes applied to calculate the amount of value added tax due and which also limit the ability to recover input tax. These schemes apply to the supply of second-hand motor cars, motor cycles, caravans, boats, electronic organs, aircraft and firearms, together with works of art, antiques and collectors' pieces.

STAMP DUTIES

The Commissioners as a general rule allow deeds, etc., to be stamped after execution:—

Without Penalty, on Payment of Duty only.
Deeds and instruments not otherwise excepted, within 30 days of first execution.
NB. Where wholly executed abroad, the period begins to run from the date of arrival here.

Penalties Enforceable on Stamping in Addition to Duty:—Instruments presented after the proper time (subject to special provisions in some cases and subject to the Commissioner's power to mitigate) a penalty equal to the duty £10

Agreement for Lease, *see* **Leases.**

Agreement for Sale of Property.—Charged with *ad valorem* duty as if an actual conveyance on sale, with certain exceptions, e.g. agreements for the sale of land, stocks and shares, goods, wares or merchandise, or a ship (*see* S. 59 (1), Stamp Act 1891). If *ad valorem* duty is paid on an agreement in accordance with this provision, the subsequent conveyance or transfer is not chargeable with any *ad valorem* duty and the Commissioners will upon application either place a denoting stamp on such conveyance or transfer or will transfer the *ad valorem* duty thereto. Further, if such an agreement is rescinded, not performed, etc., the Commissioners will return the *ad valorem* duty paid.

Agreement under seal, subject to exemptions 50p

Assignment:
By way of sale—*see* **Conveyance.**
By way of gift—*see* **Voluntary Disposition.**

Assurance—*see* **Insurance Policies.**

Bearer Instrument:
Inland bearer instrument, i.e. share warrant, stock certificate to bearer or any other instrument to bearer by which stock can be transferred, issued by a company or body formed or established in UK .... 1·5%.
Overseas bearer instrument, i.e. such an instrument issued in Great Britain by a company formed out of the UK .... 1·5%.

Bill of sale, Absolute, *see* **Conveyance on Sale.**

Capital Duty.—This was charged at 1 per cent on every £100 or fraction of £100 of the actual value of assets contributed by the members of a company provided the place of effective management of the company was in Great Britain, or its registered office was in Great Britain but the place of its effective management was outside the EC (Finance Act 1973).
The tax was abolished by the Finance Act 1988 in respect of transactions entered into on or after March 16, 1988.

Contract, *see* **Agreement.**

Contract or Grant for Payment of a Superannuation Annuity.—For every £10 or fractional part of £10 .... 5p

Conveyance or Transfer on Sale (in the case of a Voluntary Disposition, *see* below) of any property (except stock or marketable securities), where the Conveyance or Transfer contains a certificate of value certifying that the transaction does not form part of a larger transaction or a series of transactions in respect of which the aggregate amount or value of the consideration exceeds £30,000 . *nil*
Exceeds £30,000 (for every £100 or fraction of £100) £1
If the Conveyance or Transfer on Sale does not contain the appropriate statement, duty at the full rate of £1 for every £100 or fraction of £100 will be payable whatever the amount of the consideration.
However, if the consideration does not exceed £500, and the instrument does not contain a certificate of value, there are graduated duties ranging from 50p to £5.
Conveyances to charities are exempt from duty under this head provided the instrument is stamped with a denoting stamp.

Conveyance or Transfer of any other kind.—Fixed duty 50p
However, under the Stamp Duty (Exempt Instruments) Regulations 1987, instruments which would otherwise fall under this head are exempt from stamp duty provided that the document is duly certified. The certificate must contain a sufficient description of the category into which the instrument falls, and must be signed by the transferor, his solicitor or agent. 'I/We hereby certify that this instrument falls within category ... in the Schedule to the Stamp Duty (Exempt Instruments) Regulations 1987.'

Covenant.—For original creation and sale of any annuity, *see* **Conveyance.**

Declaration of Trust, not being a Will or Settlement 50p

Demise, *see* **Lease**

Duplicate or Counterpart.—Same duty as original, but not to exceed 50p

Gift, *see* **Voluntary Disposition.**

Guarantee.—If under seal 50p

Insurance Policies, Life.—
Exceeding £50 and not exceeding £1,000, for every £100 or part of £100 .... 5p
Exceeding £1,000, for every £1,000 or any fractional part of £1,000 .... 50p
Made after August 1, 1966 for period not exceeding 2 years....................... 5p

The Finance Act 1989 abolished this charge for policies made after December 31, 1989.

Leases.—
Lease or tack for any definite term less than a year of any furnished dwelling-house or apartments where the rent for such term exceeds £500 .... £1

Of any lands, tenements, etc., in consideration of any rent, according to the following table:

Annual rent not exceeding	*Term not exceeding			Term exceeding 100 years
	7 years	35 years	100 years	
£	£ p	£ p	£ p	£ p
5	Nil	0·10	0·60	1·20
10	Nil	0·20	1·20	2·40
15	Nil	0·30	1·80	3·60
20	Nil	0·40	2·40	4·80
25	Nil	0·50	3·00	6·00
50	Nil	1·00	6·00	12·00
75	Nil	1·50	9·00	18·00
100	Nil	2·00	12·00	24·00
150	Nil	3·00	18·00	36·00
200	Nil	4·00	24·00	48·00
250	Nil	5·00	30·00	60·00
300	Nil	6·00	36·00	72·00
350	Nil	7·00	42·00	84·00
400	Nil	8·00	48·00	96·00
450	Nil	9·00	54·00	108·00
500	Nil	10·00	60·00	120·00
Exceeding £500, for every £50 or fraction of £50	0·50	1·00	6·00	12·00

*If the term is indefinite the same duty is payable as if the term did not exceed 7 years.

Agreement for Lease.—Same as actual lease.

Where a consideration other than rent is payable, the same rule applies where the consideration does not exceed £30,000 as under Conveyance or Transfer on Sale (except stock or marketable securities), provided that any rent payable does not exceed £300 a year and a certificate of value is included in the Conveyance or Transfer.

Leases to charities are exempt from duty under this head provided the instrument is stamped with a denoting stamp.

Mortgages.—Exempt.

Receipts for Salaries, Wages and Superannuation, and other like allowances.—Exempt.

Transfer of Stock and Shares by sale ..... 0·5%

Unit Trust Instrument.—Any trust instrument of a unit trust scheme, for every £100 or fraction of £100, of the amount or value of the property subject to the trusts created or recorded by the instrument 25p

By the Finance Act 1989, the transfer of units in certain authorized unit trusts are no longer subject to duty.

Voluntary Disposition *inter vivos:*—....... 50p

LEGAL NOTES

IMPORTANT

The purpose of these notes is to outline some of the more common parts of the law as they may affect the average person. They are believed to be correct at the time of going to press. However, the law is constantly developing and changing, and it is always best to take expert advice. Anyone who does not have a solicitor already, and is unable to find one through the recommendation of a friend, can contact the Citizens' Advice Bureau (whose address can be obtained from the telephone directory or from any post office or town hall). Each CAB has a list of solicitors in the area who deal with particular types of problem. Alternatively, assistance can be sought from The Law Society, 113 Chancery Lane, London, WC2A 1PL or The Law Society of Scotland, 26 Drumsheugh Gardens, Edinburgh, EH3 7YR.

The Legal Aid and Legal Advice and Assistance schemes exist to make the help of the trained lawyer available to everyone whatever their means. The best policy is to go to a solicitor without delay—timely advice will set your mind at rest but sitting on your rights can mean that you lose them.

It is not necessary for a dispute to have arisen before advice is sought from a solicitor; the Legal Advice and Assistance Scheme enables a solicitor to advise you on your rights, for instance under a tenancy agreement, the estate of a deceased person or in connection with matrimonial and consumer matters, and to write letters or take other steps on your behalf. Your entitlement to take advantage of the scheme depends on your means (*see* p. 1041) but a solicitor or Citizens' Advice Bureau will be able to advise about entitlement.

BRITISH CITIZENSHIP

There are three types of citizenship: British Citizenship; Citizenship of the British Dependent Territories; and British Overseas Citizenship.

Acquisition of citizenship on change of law.—The British Nationality Act 1981 which came into force on January 1, 1983 made substantial changes to the law of citizenship, which before that date did not distinguish between the three types of citizenship referred to above. Almost all persons who were then both citizens of the UK and Colonies and who had a right of abode in the UK became British Citizens when the Act came into force. Most UK and Colonies Citizens who did not have a right of abode in the UK became Citizens of the British Dependent Territories. This type of citizenship was, broadly speaking, conferred on citizens of the UK and Colonies by birth, naturalization or registration in dependent territories. Dependent territories include Hong Kong, Gibraltar, the Falkland Islands, and St. Helena and its dependencies. Any UK and Colonies Citizen who, on January 1, 1983, did not acquire either British or British Dependent Territories' Citizenship became a British Overseas Citizen.

Later acquisition of British Citizenship.—British Citizenship is acquired automatically by those born in the UK (including, for this purpose, the Channel Islands and the Isle of Man) who have a parent who is a British Citizen or a parent who is settled in the UK. Certain other categories of children born in the UK also acquire this type of citizenship, i.e. foundlings, those whose parents subsequently settle in the UK, those who live in the UK for ten years from birth and those adopted in the UK.

A person born outside the UK may acquire British Citizenship in the following ways:—

(a) if one of his/her parents is a British Citizen otherwise than by descent (e.g. parent was born in the UK).

(b) if one of his/her parents is a British Citizen serving the Crown overseas.

(c) if the Secretary of State consents to his/her registration while he/she is a minor.

(d) if he/she is a Citizen of the British Dependent Territories, a British Overseas Citizen, a British Subject or a British Protected Person (these last two are residual categories of people who have not acquired one of the three new types of citizenship) and has been lawfully resident in the UK for five years without any time restriction.

(e) if he/she is a British Dependent Territories Citizen who is a national of the UK for the purposes of the EC (i.e. a Gibraltarian).

(f) if he/she is naturalized. Naturalization may be applied for only by adults and the Secretary of State has a discretion whether to permit it. The basic requirements are five years' residence, good character, sufficient knowledge of the English or Welsh language, and an intention to reside in the UK permanently. The requirements are somewhat less restrictive in the case of an applicant who is married to a British Citizen.

Acquisition of British Dependent Territories and British Overseas Citizenship after the Act.—These citizenships are intended for persons connected with certain Commonwealth countries other than the UK. In the case of dependent territories the rules are very similar to those for acquiring British Citizenship except that the connection is with the dependent territory rather than with the UK. British Overseas Citizenship may be acquired by the minor children and wives of British Overseas Citizens in certain circumstances.

Retention of nationality by persons born in or who are citizens of the Republic of Ireland.—By the Ireland Act 1949, a person who was born before December 6, 1922, in what is now the Republic of Ireland (Eire) and was a British subject immediately before January 1, 1949, is not deemed to have ceased to be a British subject unless either he/she (a) was domiciled in the Irish Free State on December 6, 1922 or (b) was on or after April 10, 1935, and before January 1, 1949, permanently resident there, or (c) had before January 1, 1949, been registered as a citizen of Eire under the laws of that country.

In addition, by the British Nationality Act 1948, any citizen of Eire who immediately before January 1, 1949, was also a British subject can retain that status by submitting at any time a claim to the Home Secretary on any of the following grounds:

(a) he/she has been in the service of the United Kingdom Government;

(b) he/she holds a British passport issued in the United Kingdom or in any colony, protectorate, United Kingdom mandated or trust territory;

(c) he/she has associations by way of descent, residence or otherwise with any such place; or on complying with similar legislation in any of the 'dominions'.

The British Nationality Act 1981 provides that persons who have made a claim may continue to be British subjects. Any citizen of Eire who was a

British subject before January 1, 1949, who has not yet made a claim may do so provided that:

(a) he/she is or has been in Crown Service under the government of the United Kingdom; or
(b) he/she has associations by way of descent, residence or otherwise with the United Kingdom or any dependent territory.

Renunciation and Resumption.—A person may cease to be a British Citizen by renouncing his citizenship (with the consent of the Secretary of State in wartime). The renunciation is required to be registered with the Secretary of State and will be revoked if no new citizenship or nationality is acquired within six months. Once renounced, citizenship may be reacquired if the renunciation was necessary to retain or acquire some other citizenship or nationality. Similar rules as to renunciation and reacquisition apply in the case of British Dependent Territories Citizenships and of renunciation (but not reacquisition) in the case of British Overseas Citizenship.

Status of Aliens.—Property may be held by an alien in the same manner as by a natural-born British subject, but he/she may not hold public office, exercise the franchise or own a British ship or aircraft. The Republic of Ireland Act 1949 declares that the Republic, though not part of HM Dominions, is not a foreign country, and any reference in an Act of Parliament to foreigners, aliens, foreign countries, etc., shall be construed accordingly.

CONSUMER LAW

The Supply of Goods and Services

(1) The Sale of Goods Act 1979 provides protection to the purchaser of goods, by implying certain terms into every contract for the Sale of Goods. These implied terms are:

(a) A condition that the seller will pass good title to the buyer (unless the seller agrees to transfer only such title as he or his principal has) and warranties that the goods will be free from undisclosed encumbrances, and that the buyer will enjoy quiet possession of the goods.

(b) Where there is a sale of goods by description, a condition that the goods will correspond with that description, and where the sale is by sample and description, a condition that the bulk of the goods shall correspond with both sample and description.

(c) Where the seller sells goods in the course of a business, a condition that the goods will be of merchantable quality, unless before the contract is made, the buyer has examined the goods and ought to have noticed the defect, bearing in mind the purchaser's knowledge of the goods and the extent of the examination, or the seller has specifically drawn the attention of the buyer to the defect. Merchantable quality means fit for the purpose for which goods of the kind are commonly bought, taking into account any description applied to them, the price and other relevant circumstances.

(d) A condition that where the seller sells goods in the course of a business, the goods are reasonably fit for any purpose made known to the seller by the buyer, unless the buyer does not rely on the seller's skill and judgment, or it would be unreasonable for him to do so.

(e) Where there is a sale of goods by sample, conditions that the bulk of the goods shall correspond with the sample in quality, that the buyer will have a reasonable opportunity of comparing the bulk with the sample, and that the goods are free from any defect rendering them unmerchantable, which would not be apparent from the sample.

For these purposes, the broad difference between a condition and a warranty is that the remedy for a breach of an implied condition may enable the buyer to reject the goods and recover damages if he has suffered loss whereas the remedy for a breach of warranty will only enable the buyer to recover damages.

It is possible for a seller to exclude some of the above terms from a contract, subject to restrictions imposed by the Unfair Contract Terms Act 1977 as given below. These restrictions give more protection ... where the buyer 'deals as consumer'. In a contract of sale of goods, a buyer 'deals as consumer' where there is ... a sale by a seller in the course of a business, the goods are of a type ordinarily bought for private use or consumption, and are sold to a person who does not buy or hold himself out as buying them in the course of a business. A buyer in a sale by auction or competitive tender never 'deals as consumer'.

The 1977 Act prohibits the exclusion of the implied terms given in (b) to (e) above, where the buyer 'deals as consumer'. In sales where the buyer does not 'deal as consumer', terms purporting to exclude these implied terms may be relied upon only to the extent that it would be reasonable to allow reliance. The Act provides guidelines for determining whether it would be reasonable to allow reliance. The implied terms in (a) above cannot be excluded whether the buyer 'deals as consumer' or not.

(2) Similar terms to those implied in contracts of sale of goods are implied into contracts of hire-purchase by the Supply of Goods (Implied Terms) Act 1973, and the 1977 Act limits the exclusion of these implied terms in a similar manner.

(3) Under the Supply of Goods and Services Act 1982, terms similar to those in the Sale of Goods Act relating to quiet possession, compliance with description, merchantable quality, fitness for purpose and correspondence with sample are implied into other types of contract under which ownership of goods passes (e.g. a contract for 'work and materials' such as a supply of new parts during the servicing of a motor car) and also into contracts for the hire of goods. In the case of contracts under which ownership of goods is to pass, there is also an implied condition as to title.

The 1977 Act limits the exclusion of these implied terms in a similar manner to the implied terms in the Sale of Goods Act.

(4) The Supply of Goods and Services Act 1982 also implies into a contract for the supply of services terms that the supplier will use reasonable care and skill, carry out the service within a reasonable time (unless the time is agreed) and make a reasonable charge (unless the charge is agreed).

(5) The Trade Descriptions Act 1968 provides that it is a criminal offence for a trader or businessman to apply a false trade description to any goods, or to supply or offer to supply any goods to which a false trade description has been applied. A trade description includes a description as to quantity, size, method, place and date of manufacture, other history, composition, other physical characteristics, fitness for purpose, behaviour or accuracy, testing or approval. It is also an offence to give a false indication as to the price of goods. Prosecutions are brought by trading standards inspectors.

(6) The Fair Trading Act 1973 is also designed to

protect the consumer. It provides for the appointment of a Director General of Fair Trading, whose duties include keeping under review commercial activities in the UK relating to the supply of goods or services to consumers, and to collect information to discover practices that may adversely affect the economic interests of the consumer. He may refer certain consumer trade practices to the Consumer Protection Advisory Committee, or of his own initiative take proceedings against firms that are trading unfairly. He may also publish information and advice to consumers. Examples of practices which have been prohibited by virtue of references made under this Act, include the use of certain void exclusion clauses in contracts for the sale of goods and hire-purchase, and advertisements by traders appearing to sell as private persons.

(7) The Consumer Protection Act 1987 makes the producer of a product liable for any damage exceeding £275 caused by a defect in that product, subject to certain defences.

(8) The Consumer Protection (Cancellation of Contracts Concluded away from Business Premises) Regulations 1987 allow consumers a seven-day period in which to cancel most contracts for supply of goods or services exceeding £35 in cost, where these contracts have been made following an unsolicited visit to the consumer's home or workplace.

Scotland

The Sale of Goods Act 1979, a consolidating Act, applies with some modification to Scotland. For example, it is not necessary in Scotland to distinguish between the words condition and warranty. The remedies of the buyer in both cases are the same, i.e. the buyer can either within a reasonable time reject the goods and treat the contract as repudiated, or retain the goods and treat the failure to perform such material part as a breach which may give rise to a claim for compensation or damages.

Consumer Credit

The Consumer Credit Act 1974 provides a system for the protection of the consumer, of licensing and control of all matters relating to the provision of credit, or the supply of goods on hire or hire-purchase, administered by the Director-General of Fair Trading. A licence is required to carry on a consumer credit or consumer hire business, or to deal in credit brokerage, debt adjusting, counselling or collecting, for which group licences are available. Any 'fit' person may apply to the Director of Fair Trading for a licence which is normally renewable after ten years. A licence is not necessary if such types of business are only transacted 'occasionally' or if exempt agreements only are involved.

For the Act's provisions to apply the agreement must be 'regulated', i.e. be to individuals or partnerships only; must not be exempt, e.g. certain loans by local authorities or building societies; and the total credit must not exceed £15,000. The terms of a regulated agreement can be varied by the creditor, but only if the agreement gives him the right to do so, and the debtor receives notice in the prescribed form.

To be enforceable the agreement must be properly executed, and the specified information must be given during the antecedent negotiations for the contract. These are conducted by the creditor, credit broker or supplier (these being the creditor's agents) and begin when the parties first begin discussions.

The agreement must state certain information such as the amount of credit, the annual percentage rate of interest and the amount and timing of repayments.

An agreement is cancellable under the Act if oral representations were made in the debtor's presence during antecedent negotiations and the debtor signed the agreement other than at the creditor's (or credit-broker's or negotiator's) place of business. Time for cancellation expires five clear days after the debtor receives a second copy of the agreement. The agreement must inform the debtor of his right to cancel and how to cancel.

Where there are arrangements or connections between the creditor and supplier the former is generally liable for any misrepresentation or breach of contract by the latter, and will thus be liable to indemnify the debtor.

If the debtor is in arrears or is otherwise in breach of the agreement, the creditor may not enforce the agreement, e.g. by repossessing goods, without serving a default notice on the debtor. This notice will give the debtor a chance to remedy the default. Even if the default is not remedied by the debtor, if the agreement is a hire-purchase or conditional sale agreement, the creditor cannot repossess the goods without an order of the court, if the debtor has paid one-third of the total price of the goods.

Where the agreement requires the debtor to make grossly exorbitant payments or is contrary to the ordinary principles of fair dealing the Court can reopen it either at the debtor's request or during enforcement proceedings and (inter alia) alter the terms of the contract or set aside any obligations it imposes so as to do justice between the parties. Whether an agreement is such an extortionate credit bargain is decided by reference (inter alia) to interest rates prevailing at the date of agreement, the pressure for finance the debtor was under, etc.

If a credit reference agency was used to check the debtor's financial standing the creditor must give the agency's name to the debtor who is entitled to see the agency's file on him on payment of a fee of £1.

Scotland

The Consumer Credit Act also extends to Scotland and goes far in assimilating the Scots law on this topic with English law. The Supply of Goods (Implied Terms) Act 1973 also applies to Scotland. Parts II and III only of the Unfair Contract Terms Act 1977 apply to Scotland. The Sale of Goods Act 1979, applies with some modification to Scotland.

Receipts

The law on receipts in Scotland is governed by the Prescription and Limitations (Scotland) Act 1973, which for this purpose came into force on July 25, 1976. Now, receipts need only be kept for a period of five years and if a creditor does not make a relevant claim within that period no action can be raised.

THE CROWN—PROCEEDINGS AGAINST

Before 1947 proceedings against the Crown were generally possible only by a procedure known as a petition of right, which placed the litigant at a considerable disadvantage. However, by the Crown Proceedings Act 1947, which came into operation on January 1, 1948, the Crown, in its public capacity, is largely placed in the same position as a subject, although some procedural disadvantages remain, for example, the enforcement of judgments against the Crown.

Scotland.—The Act as amended extends to Scotland and has the effect of bringing the practice of the two countries as closely together as the different legal systems will permit. While formerly actions against the Crown, when permissible, were confined to the Court of Session, proceedings may now be brought in the Sheriff Court.

The Act lays down that arrestment of money in the

hands of the Crown or of a Government department is competent in any case where arrestment in the hands of a subject would have been competent, but an exception is made in respect of National Savings Bank deposits. Section 2 (1) of the Law Reform (Miscellaneous Provisions) (Scotland) Act 1966 removes the privilege whereby the wages of Crown servants, other than serving members of the armed forces, are exempt from arrestment in execution.

DEATHS
Registration
(For Certificates, *see* under **Family Law— Certificates**)

England and Wales.—When a death takes place, information of it must be given in person to the local Registrar of Births and Deaths, and the register signed in his/her presence, by a relative of the deceased present at the death, or in attendance during the last illness; or by some other relative of the deceased; in default of any relatives by (a) a person present at the death, or the occupier of the house in which the death happened; or (b) an inmate of the house. A person (other than a relative) registering the death must be causing the disposal of the body.

The registration must be made within five days of the death, or within the same time written notice of the death must be sent to the Registrar. If the deceased was attended during his last illness by a registered medical practitioner, a certificate of cause of death must be sent by the doctor to the Registrar. The doctor must give to the informant of the death a written notice of the signing of the certificate, which must be delivered to the Registrar. It is essential that a certificate for disposal should be obtained from the Registrar before the funeral and delivered to the clergyman or other person in charge of the churchyard or cemetery. No fee is chargeable for this certificate.

If the death is not registered within five days (or fourteen days if written notice of the occurrence of the death is sent to him) the Registrar may require any one of the above-mentioned persons to attend to register at a stated time and place. Failure to comply involves a penalty. The registration of a death is free of charge. After twelve months no death can be registered without the Registrar General's consent.

Whenever the death of a child is registered, particulars of the name and occupation of the mother are to be entered in the register.

A body must not be disposed of until: either the Registrar has given a certificate to the effect that he/she has registered or received notice of the death; or until the Coroner has made a disposal order (Births and Deaths Registration Act 1926, s. 1).

A person disposing of a body must within ninety-six hours deliver to the Registrar a notification as to the date, place, and means of the disposal of the body (*ib.*, s. 3).

Still births.—*See* **Births (Registration)**.

Death at Sea.—The master of a British ship must record any death on board and send particulars to the Registrar General of Shipping.

Death Abroad.—Consular Officers are authorized to register deaths of British subjects occurring abroad. Certificates are obtainable at the Registrar General's Office, London. If the deceased was of Scottish domicile, particulars are sent to the Registrar General for Scotland.

With regard to the registration of deaths of members of the armed forces, and deaths occurring on HM ships and aircraft, *see* the Registration of Births, etc. Act 1957.

Scotland.—The Registration of Births, Deaths and Marriages (Scotland) Act 1965 supersedes provisions in former Acts.

Personal notification within eight days must be given to the Registrar of either the registration district in which the death took place, or any registration district in which the deceased was ordinarily resident immediately before his death. When a body is found and the place of death is not known, notification must be given to the Registrar of either the registration district in which the body was found or any other registration district appropriate by virtue of the preceding sentence. When a person dies (in or out of Scotland) in a ship, aircraft or land vehicle during a journey and the body is conveyed therein to any place in Scotland the death shall, unless the Registrar General otherwise directs, be deemed to have occurred at that place.

The register must be signed in the presence of the Registrar by one of the following: (a) any relative of the deceased; (b) any person present at the death; (c) the deceased's executor or other legal representative; (d) the occupier, at the time of the death, of the premises where the death took place; (e) if these fail, any other person having knowledge of the particulars to be registered. Failure to comply involves a penalty.

The medical practitioner who attended the deceased during the last illness must sign a certificate of the cause of death within seven days. If there is no such medical practitioner, any medical practitioner who is able to do so, may sign the certificate. At the time of registering the death the Registrar shall, without charge, give the informant a certificate of registration, and the person to whom the certificate is given must hand it to the undertaker previous to cremation. A body may, however, be interred before the death is registered, in which case the undertaker must deliver a certificate of burial to the Registrar within three days.

Burial
The duty of burial is incumbent on the deceased person's executors (if any appointed); it is also a recognized obligation of the husband of a woman, and the parent of a child, also of a householder where the body lies. Funeral expenses of a reasonable amount will be repayable out of the deceased's estate in priority to any other claims. Directions as to place and mode of burial are frequently contained in the deceased's will or in some memorandum placed with private papers, or may have been communicated verbally to a relative. Consequently, steps should immediately be taken to ascertain the deceased's wishes from the above sources. If the wishes are considered objectionable, they are not necessarily enforceable; legal advice should be taken. A person may legally leave directions for the anatomical examination of his/her body. As to the place of burial—unless closed by Order in Council—the parish churchyard is the normal burying place for parishioners, or any person dying in the parish, but nowadays this will apply only in villages and smaller towns. In populous districts cemeteries and crematoria have been established, either by the local council or a private company, and burials will take place there in accordance with the regulations. For an exclusive right to a burial space in the churchyard a faculty is required from the Ecclesiastical Court. Poor persons may be buried at the public expense by the local authority. As to the necessity for obtaining a Registrar's certificate or authority from the Coroner for disposal, *see* above.

Cremation

Under the Cremation Acts 1902 and 1952, regulations are made by the Home Secretary dealing fully with the cremation of a body, disposal of ashes, etc., and containing numerous essential safeguards.

If cremation is desired it is advisable for instructions to be left in writing to that effect. However, in Scotland, even if the deceased wished his body to be cremated or anatomically dissected, relatives can still veto his or her wishes.

To arrange for cremation, the executor or near relative should instruct the undertaker to that effect and obtain from him the forms required by statute.

INTESTACY

ENGLAND AND WALES

As regards deaths on or after March 15, 1977, the position is governed by the Administration of Estates Act 1925, as amended by the Intestates' Estates Act 1952, the Family Provision Act 1966 and Orders made thereunder. If the intestate leaves a spouse and issue, the spouse takes: (a) the 'personal chattels'; (b) £75,000 with interest at six per cent from death until payment; and (c) a life interest in half of the rest of the estate. This life interest can be capitalized at the option of the spouse. Personal chattels are articles of household use or ornament (including motor-cars), not used for business purposes. The rest of the estate goes to the issue. If the intestate leaves a spouse and no issue, but leaves a parent or brother or sister of the whole blood or issue of such brothers and sisters the spouse takes: (a) the 'personal chattels'; (b) £125,000 with interest at six per cent from death until payment; and (c) half of the rest of the estate absolutely. The other half of the rest of the estate goes to the parents, equally if more than one, or, if none, to the brothers and sisters of the whole blood or issue of such brothers and sisters. If the intestate leaves a spouse, but no issue, no parents and no brothers or sisters of the whole blood or their issue, the spouse takes the whole estate absolutely.

If resident therein at the intestate's death, the surviving spouse may generally require the personal representatives to appropriate the interest of the intestate in the matrimonial home in or towards satisfaction of any absolute interest of the spouse, including the capitalized value of a life interest. In certain cases, leave of Court is required. On a partial intestacy any benefit (other than personal chattels specifically bequeathed) received by the surviving spouse under the will must be brought into account against the statutory legacy of £75,000 or £125,000, as the case may be. If there is no surviving spouse, the estate is distributed among those who survive the intestate in the following order (those entitled under earlier numbers taking to the exclusion of those entitled under later numbers):—(1) children; (2) father or mother (equally, if both alive); (3) brothers and sisters of the whole blood; (4) brothers and sisters of the half blood; (5) grandparents (equally, if more than one alive); (6) uncles and aunts of the whole blood; (7) uncles and aunts of the half blood; (8) the Crown.

In cases (1), (3), (4), (6) and (7) the persons entitled lose their interests unless they or their issue not only survive the intestate, but also attain eighteen or marry under that age, their shares going to the persons (if any) within the same group who do attain eighteen or marry. Moreover, in the same cases, succession is not *per capita*, but *per stirpes*, i.e. by stocks or families. Thus, if the intestate leaves one child and two grandchildren, being the children of a child of the intestate who pre-deceased the intestate,

the two grandchildren represent their deceased parent and take between them one-half of the issue's share, the remaining half going to the surviving child. Similarly, nephews and nieces represent a deceased brother, and so on.

When the deceased died partially intestate (i.e. leaving a will which disposed of only part of his property), the above rules apply to the intestate part.

Children must bring into account (hotchpot) any substantial advances received from the intestate during his lifetime before claiming any further share under the intestacy. Special hotchpot provisions apply to partial intestacy.

In respect of deaths occurring on or after April 4, 1988, Section 18 of the Family Law Reform Act 1987 provides that references to any relationship between two persons shall, unless the contrary intention appears, be construed without regard to whether or not the father and mother of either of them, or the father and mother of any person through whom the relationship is deduced, have or had been married to each other at any time.

In respect of deaths after March 1976 the provisions of the Inheritance (Provision for Family and Dependants) Act 1975 may allow other persons to claim provision out of the estate. *See* Wills.

For personal application for letters of administration, *see* below.

SCOTLAND

The Succession (Scotland) Act 1964, provides that the whole estate of any person dying intestate shall devolve without distinction between heritable and moveable property. By that Act the surviving spouse of an intestate may, as a prior right (in addition to legal rights, *see* below), claim the matrimonial home to a maximum of £65,000, or a choice of one matrimonial home if more than one (or in certain circumstances the value thereof), with its furniture and plenishings not exceeding £12,000 in value, plus the sum of £21,000 if the deceased left issue, or, if no issue, the sum of £35,000. These figures apply from May 1, 1988 and may be increased from time to time by order of the Secretary of State.

The fact that a person was born illegitimate no longer has any effect in their rights of succession as against a legitimate child, by virtue of the Law Reform (Parent and Child) (Scotland) Act 1986.

Legal rights, referred to above, are:—

Jus relicti(ae): the right of a surviving spouse to one half of the deceased's net moveable estate after satisfaction of prior rights if there are no surviving children, or to one third if there are any surviving children.

Legitim: the right of surviving children to one-half of the net moveable estate of deceased parents if no surviving spouse, or one-third of the net moveable estate of deceased parents after satisfaction of prior rights where there is a surviving spouse.

There are no legal rights in heritage.

In general, the lines of succession are: (1) descendants; (2) collaterals; (3) ascendants and their collaterals, and so on in the ascending scale. The Crown is *ultimus haeres.* The right of representation, i.e. the right of the issue of a person who would have succeeded if he/she had survived the intestate, is open to any line of succession where previously it was limited to apply only when there were next of kin or the issue of predeceasing next of kin. The surviving mother of an intestate now has equal rights of succession with the surviving father, where formerly these were restricted. The intestate's maternal relations, who prior to the Act had no rights of succession, are now on an equal footing with the paternal relations. Where the intestate is survived only by parents and by brothers and sisters (collaterals), half of the estate is taken by the parents and the other half by the brothers and sisters, those of the whole blood being preferred to those of the half blood. Where, however, succession opens to collaterals (which expression can include the brothers and sisters of an ancestor of the intestate) of the half blood, they shall rank equally amongst themselves, whether related to the intestate (or his/her ancestor) through their father or their mother.

WILLS

The following notes and those on Intestacy must be read subject to the provisions of the Inheritance (Provision for Family and Dependants) Act 1975 which can affect the estate of anyone dying domiciled in England and Wales after March 1976. Very broadly, a spouse, former spouse who has not remarried, a child of the deceased or one treated by the deceased as a child of his/her family, or any person maintained by him/her at his/her death may apply to the Court under the Act. If the Court thinks that the will or the law of intestacy or both do not make reasonable provision for the applicant it may order payment out of the net estate of maintenance or a lump sum. It may also order the transfer of property, or vary certain trusts and the powers can affect property disposed of by the deceased in his lifetime intending to defeat the Act. It is up to the applicant to take the initiative, and the application must generally be made within six months of the grant of probate or letters of administration.

Making a Will

Every person over the age of 18 should make a will. However small the estate, the rules of Intestacy (*see* above) may not reflect a person's wishes as to his/her property; in any case a will can do more than just deal with property. It can in particular appoint executors, give directions as to the disposal of the body and appoint guardians to take care of children in the event of the parents' death. For the wealthier person an appropriately drawn will can operate to reduce the burden of inheritance tax.

It is considered desirable for a will to be properly drawn up by a solicitor. Although normally the making of a will is not one of the services which can be provided under the Legal Advice and Assistance Scheme, it can be provided for certain special categories of person such as the aged and infirm (*see* below).

In no circumstances should one person prepare a will for another person where the former is to take any benefit under it; this can easily lead to a suggestion of undue influence which may cause the will to be held bad.

Assuming a lawyer is not employed, a person having resolved to make a will must remember that it is only after a person is dead, and cannot explain his/her meaning, that his/her will can be open to dispute. It is the more necessary, therefore, to express what is meant in language of the utmost clarity, avoiding the use of any word or expression that admits of another meaning than the one intended. Avoid the use of legal terms, such as heirs and issue, when the same thing may be expressed in plain language. If in writing the will a mistake be made, it is better to rewrite the whole. Before a will is executed (*see* below) an alteration may be made by striking through the words with a pen, but opposite

to such alteration the testator and witnesses should write their names or place their initials. Never scratch out a word with a knife or other instrument, and no alteration of any kind whatever must be made after the will is executed. If the testator afterwards wishes to change the disposition of his/her estate, it is best to make a new will, revoking the old one. The use of codicils should be left to the lawyer.

A will should be written in ink and very legibly, on a single sheet of paper. Although, of course, forms of wills must vary to suit different cases, the following forms may be found useful to those who, in cases of emergency, are called upon to draw up wills, either for themselves or others. Nothing more complicated should be attempted. The forms should be studied in conjunction with the notes following.

This is the last will and testament of me [*Thomas Smith*] of [*Vine Cottage, Silver Street, Reading, Berks.*] which I make this [*thirteenth*] day of [*February, 1990*] and whereby I revoke all previous wills and testamentary dispositions.

1. I hereby appoint [*John Green of —— and Richard Brown of ——*] to be the executor(s) of this my will.

2. I give all my property real and personal to [*my wife Mary* or *my sons Raymond and David equally* or as the case may be].

Signed by the testator in the presence of us both present at the same time who, at his request, in his presence and in the presence of each other have hereunto set our names as witnesses.

        Thomas Smith
        Signature of
        Testator;

William Jones (*signed*) of Green Gables, South Street, Reading, tailor.

Henry Morgan (*signed*) of 16 North Street, Reading, butcher.

Should it be desired to give legacies and/or gifts of specific property, instead of giving the whole estate to one or more persons, the form above should be used with the substitution for clause 2 of the following clauses:—

2. I give to —— of —— the sum of £—— and to —— of —— the sum of £—— and to —— of —— all my books [*or as the case may require*].

3. All the residue of my property real and personal I give to —— of ——.

Terms.—Real property includes freehold land and houses, while personal property includes debts due, arrears of rents, money, leasehold property, house furniture, goods, assurance policies, stocks and shares in companies, and the like. The words 'my money', apart from the context, will normally only include actual real money. The expression 'goods and chattels' should not be used. In giving particular property, ordinary language is sufficient, e.g., 'my house, Vine Cottage, Silver Street, Reading, Berks.'. Such specific gifts fail if not owned by the testator at his death.

Residuary Legatees.—It is well in all cases where legacies or specific gifts are made, to leave to some person or persons 'the residue of my property', although it may be thought that the whole of the property has been disposed of in legacies, etc., already mentioned in the will. It should be remembered that a will operates on property owned at the time of death.

Execution of a Will, and Witnesses.—The testator should sign his name at the foot or end of the will, in the presence of two witnesses, who will immediately afterwards sign their names in his and in each other's presence. A person who has been left any gift or share of residue in the will, or whose wife or husband has been left such a gift, should not be an attesting witness. Their attestation would be good, but they would forfeit the gift. It is better that a person named as executor should not be a witness. Husband and wife may both be witnesses, provided neither is a legatee. If a solicitor be appointed executor, it is lawful to direct that his/her ordinary fees and charges shall be paid; but in this case the solicitor (as an interested party) must not be a witness to the will.

It is desirable that the witnesses should be fully described, as they may possibly be wanted at some future time. If the testator should be too ill to sign, even by a mark, another person may sign the testator's name to the will for him, in his presence and by his direction, and in this case it should be shown that the testator knew the contents of the document. The attestation clause should therefore be worded: 'Signed by Thomas Brown, by the direction and in the presence of the testator, Thomas Smith, in the joint presence of us, who thereupon signed our names in his presence and in the presence of each other, the will having been first read over to the testator, who appeared fully to understand the same.'

Where there is any suspicion that the testator is not, by reason of age or infirmity, fully in command of his faculties it is desirable to ask his doctor to act as a witness (*see* Testamentary capacity below).

A blind person may make a will in Braille. If the testator be blind the will should be read aloud to him in the presence of the witnesses, and the fact mentioned in the attestation clause. A blind person cannot witness a will.

If by inadvertence the testator should have signed his will without the witnesses being present, then the attestation should be:—'The testator acknowledged his signature already made as his signature to his last will and testament, in the joint presence,' etc. Any omission in the observance of these details may invalidate the will. The stringency of the law as to signature and witnessing of a will is only relaxed in favour of soldiers, sailors and airmen in certain circumstances.

Executors.—It is usual to appoint two executors, although one is sufficient; any number up to and including four may be appointed. The name and address of each executor should be given in full. An executor may be a legatee. Thus a child of full age or wife to whom the whole or a portion of the estate is left may be appointed sole executor, or one of two executors. The addresses of the executors are not essential, but it is desirable here as elsewhere, to avoid ambiguity or vagueness.

Lapsed Legacies.—If a legatee dies in the lifetime of the testator, the legacy generally lapses and falls into the residue. Where a residuary legatee predeceases the testator, his share of the residuary estate will not generally pass to the other residuary legatees, but will pass to the persons entitled on the deceased's intestacy. In all such cases it is desirable to make a new will.

An important exception to the general rule of lapse stated above is contained in the Administration of Justice Act 1982, where there is a gift to a child or remoter issue of the testator who dies before the testator leaving issue who survive the testator. In such a case the gift will pass to the issue of the deceased child.

Testamentary Capacity.—A person under the age of 18 cannot make a will (except for soldiers, sailors and airmen and then only in exceptional circumstances).

So far as mental capacity is concerned the testator must be able to understand and appreciate the nature and effect of making a will, the property of which he can dispose and the claims to which he ought to give effect. If a person is not mentally able to make a will, provision exists (under the Mental Health Act 1983) for the Court to do this for him.

Revocation

A later will revokes an earlier will if it expressly says so, or is completely inconsistent with it. Otherwise the earlier one is only revoked insofar as it is inconsistent with the later one. A will may also be revoked by burning, tearing or otherwise destroying the will with the intention of revoking it. Such destruction must either be by the testator or by some other person in the testator's presence and at his/her direction. It is not sufficient to obliterate the will with a pen. Marriage in every case acts as the revocation of a will, except that under the Administration of Justice Act 1982, there is a provision to the effect that if it appears from a will that at the time it was made the testator was expecting to be married to a particular person and that he/she intended that the will (or a disposition in the will) should not be revoked by the marriage to that person, the will will not be revoked by marriage to that person. The Act also provides that where after a testator has made a will the testator's marriage is terminated by a decree of divorce or nullity, any gift to a spouse shall lapse and any appointment of the spouse as executor shall be omitted from the will unless the will shows a contrary intention.

Probate or Letters of Administration

Application for probate or for letters of administration may be made in person at the Personal Application Department of the Principal Registry of the Family Division, a district probate registry or sub-registry, or a probate office, by the executors or persons entitled to a grant of administration. Applicants should bring (a) the will, if any; (b) a certificate of death; (c) particulars of all property and assets left by the deceased; and (d) a list of debts and funeral expenses.

Intending applicants, before attending at a registry or probate office, should write or telephone to the nearest probate registry or sub-registry for the necessary forms. Postal or telephone applications cannot be dealt with at the local probate offices, which are part-time only.

Certain property can be disposed of on death without a grant of probate or administration, or in pursuance of a nomination made by the deceased, provided the amount involved does not exceed £5,000. *See* The Administration of Estates (Small Payments) Act 1965.

Where to Find a Proved Will

A will proved since 1858 must have been proved either at the Principal Registry at Somerset House, or a District Registry. In the former case the original will itself is preserved at St. Catherine's House, the copy of which probate has been granted is in the hands of the executors who proved the will, and another copy for Parliament is bound up in a folio volume of wills made by testators of that initial and date. The indices to these volumes may be examined at St. Catherine's House and a copy of any will read. In the latter case, the original will proved in the District Registry is kept there, and may be seen or a copy obtained, but a copy is sent to and filed at St. Catherine's House, where also it may be seen. A general index of grants, both probates and administrations, is prepared and printed annually in lexicographical form, and may be seen at either the

Principal or a District Registry. This index is usually ready by about October of the following year.

Recent Deaths.—A system introduced in 1975 enables a person to discover when a grant of probate or letters of administration is made which may be invaluable to a creditor of the deceased or applicant under the Inheritance (Provision for Family and Dependants) Act 1975 (*see* above). A standing search may be made by sending a request in the form set out below to the Record Keeper at the Principal Registry of the Family Division with a small fee. The searcher will receive particulars of any grant made in the previous twelve months or the following six months, including names and addresses of the executors or administrators and the Registry in which the grant was made.

Form of Search

In the High Court of Justice
Family Division
The Principal Registry (Probate)
I/We apply for the entry of a standing search so that there shall be sent to me/us an office copy of every grant of representation in England and Wales in the estate of:—
Full name of deceased:
Alternative or alias name
Full address
Exact date of death

Which either has issued not more than twelve months before the entry of this application or issues within six months hereafter
Signed.—(full address).

SCOTLAND

A domiciled Scotsman, unlike a domiciled Englishman, cannot in certain circumstances dispose effectively of the entirety of his estate. If he leave a widow and children, the widow is entitled to a one-third share in the whole of the moveable estate (her *jus relictae*), and the children are entitled to another one-third share equally between them (their *legitim*). If he leave a widow but no children, or children but no widow, the *jus relictae* or *legitim* is increased to a one-half share of the net moveable estate. The remaining portion is known as the dead's part. A surviving husband and children have comparable rights (*jus relicti* and *legitim*) in the wife's estate. The dead's part is the only portion of which the testator can freely dispose. Legacies and bequests are payable only out of the dead's part. All debts are payable out of the whole estate before any division.

Pupils, i.e. a girl up to the age of twelve or a boy up to the age of fourteen, cannot make wills. Formerly a minor could dispose only of movables but since the passing of the Succession (Scotland) Act 1964, a minor has a like capacity to test on heritable property.

A will must be in writing and may be typewritten or even in pencil. A will may be either: (a) holograph, i.e. written, dated and subscribed by the testator himself/herself, in which case no witnesses are necessary; a printed form filled up by the testator or a typewritten document is not necessarily a holograph but may become so if the testator writes, in hand, at the foot of the form or document the words 'adopted as holograph' followed by his/her signature and the date. Words written on erasure or marginal additions or interlineations in holograph writings, if proved to be in the handwriting of the maker of the deed, are valid; (b) attested, i.e. signed in presence of two witnesses. It is not necessary that these witnesses should sign in the presence of one another, or even that they should see the testator signing so long as the testator acknowledges his signature to the witnesses.

The Conveyancing and Feudal Reform (Scotland) Act 1970, whilst altering generally the rules for the subscription of deeds, specifically (s. 44 (2)) makes no change in the rules applying to wills, which must still be signed by the testator on every page. If the testator cannot write, or is blind, his will may be authenticated by a law agent, notary public or justice of the peace and two witnesses. It is better that the will be not witnessed by a beneficiary thereunder, although this circumstance will not invalidate the attestation of the will or (as it would in England) the gift. A parish minister may act as a notary public for the purpose of subscribing a will in his own parish.

Wills may be registered in the Books of the Sheriffdom in which the deceased died domiciled, or in the Books of Council and Session, HM General Register House, Edinburgh. The original deed may be inspected on payment of a small fee and a certified official copy may be obtained. A Scottish will is not revoked by the subsequent marriage of the testator. The subsequent birth of a child for whom no testamentary provision has been made may revoke a will. A will may be revoked by a subsequent will, either expressly or by implication; but in so far as the two can be read together both wills have effect. If a subsequent will is revoked, the earlier will is revived.

Confirmation

Confirmation, the Scottish equivalent of probate, is obtained in the Sheriff Court of the Sheriffdom in which the deceased was domiciled at the date of his/her death or, where the deceased had no fixed domicile or died abroad, in the commissariat of Edinburgh. Executors are either 'nominate' or 'dative'. An executor nominate is one nominated by the deceased in his will or, where such person has predeceased the testator, by the residuary beneficiary. An executor dative is one appointed by the Court in the case of intestacy or where the deceased had failed to name an executor in his will and there is no residuary beneficiary. In the former case the deceased's next-of-kin are all entitled to be declared executors dative. An inventory of the deceased's estate and a schedule of debts, together with an affidavit, must first be given up. In estates under £17,000 gross, confirmation is obtained under a simplified procedure at reduced fees.

Presumption of Survivorship

The Succession (Scotland) Act 1964 provides, by s. 31, that where two persons die in circumstances indicating that they died simultaneously or if it is uncertain which was the survivor, the younger will be deemed to have survived the elder unless the elder person left testamentary provision in favour of the younger, whom failing in favour of a third person, the younger person having died intestate (partially or wholly); but if the persons so dying were husband and wife, neither shall be presumed to have survived the other.

EMPLOYMENT

Wages and Sick Pay

Under the Wages Act 1986, subject to certain exceptions, employers may not make deductions from an employee's wages unless authorized by statute or contract or with the employee's prior written consent. There is an upper limit of one-tenth of gross pay for deductions from retail workers' wages on account of cash or stock shortages.

Under the Social Security and Housing Benefits Act 1982 as amended, an employee absent from work due to illness or injury is entitled to receive Statutory Sick Pay from the employer for a maximum period of 28 weeks in any period of three years. No payment is made for the first three days of any period of illness. The employer can recoup the payments from his National Insurance contributions.

The Equal Pay Act 1970, which extends to Scotland, prevents discrimination, as regards terms and conditions of employment, between men and women employed on like work in the same employment.

Particulars of Terms of Employment

Under the Employment Protection (Consolidation) Act 1978, an employer must give each full-time employee within 13 weeks of the beginning of the employment a written statement containing the following particulars of the contract between them:

(a) the date when the employment began (when continuous employment began if previous work counts as continuous with this job);
(b) the rate of remuneration (or how it is calculated);
(c) the intervals at which wages are paid;
(d) the hours of work;
(e) the employee's entitlement to holidays (including public holidays) and holiday pay;
(f) the title of the employee's job;
(g) terms relating to sickness, injury and sick pay;
(h) details of any pension scheme;
(i) the length of notice which the employee should give and receive in order to terminate the contract.

In addition, the written particulars must specify any disciplinary rules; and also must identify the person to whom the employee can apply if he is dissatisfied with any disciplinary decision or to seek redress of any grievance and what further steps may ensue.

Termination of Employment

An employee may be dismissed without notice if he is guilty of gross breach of contract, such as disobedience to a lawful order or dishonesty. The employee is then only entitled to wages accrued due at the date of dismissal.

In other cases, the employee is entitled to reasonable notice which, under the Employment Protection (Consolidation) Act 1978, must not be less than one week if he has been continuously employed for four weeks, but less than two years; after two years it is two weeks' notice increasing by one week's notice for each further full year worked up to a maximum of twelve weeks' notice after twelve years' service.

An employer who wrongfully dismisses an employee (i.e. with less than the length of notice to which he is entitled) is generally liable to pay wages for the period of proper notice.

An employee who has a fixed term contract has no claim against his employer for wrongful dismissal if his contract is not renewed when it expires. He may, however, have a claim for a redundancy payment or compensation for unfair dismissal. If he is wrongfully dismissed before his contract expires, he is generally entitled to remuneration payable over the full period of the contract.

An employee may be entitled to a redundancy payment or to compensation for unfair dismissal if the employment has been terminated by the employer (with or without proper notice) or he has a fixed term contract which expires without being renewed or the employment has been terminated by the employee by reason of the employer's breach of contract.

Under the Employment Protection (Consolidation) Act 1978, an employee who satisfies the foregoing conditions and has been continuously employed for two years and who is dismissed by reason of redundancy may be entitled to a redundancy payment calculated by reference to his/her age, pay and length of service.

The Employment Protection (Consolidation) Act 1978 also enables an employee who is unfairly dismissed to complain to an Industrial Tribunal (generally within three months of dismissal). The onus will then be on the employer to prove that the dismissal was due to capability, conduct, redundancy, illegality or some other substantial reason justifying dismissal. The tribunal must then decide whether the employer acted reasonably in dismissing the employee. If the employer fails to prove that the dismissal was due to one or more of the above five reasons, or the tribunal decides that the employer did not act reasonably in dismissing the employee, the dismissal will be unfair, in which case the tribunal can:

(a) order re-engagement or reinstatement; or
(b) award compensation consisting of a basic and a compensatory award.

For an employee to bring himself/herself within the unfair dismissal provisions, he/she must have been continuously employed for a period of two years.

All complaints of unfair dismissal are referred to a conciliation officer or the Department of Employment and a very high proportion of complaints are disposed of in this way.

FAMILY LAW
ADOPTION OF CHILDREN

In England and Wales the adoption of children is now mainly governed by the Children Act 1975 and the Adoption Act 1976. A court order is necessary to legalize the adoption, which, when completed, has the effect of making the adopted child the child of the adopter as if he or she had been born to the adopter in lawful wedlock, and the original rights and duties of the natural parents are thereby cut. The adopter has full rights as to custody, education etc. and the child is treated as his/hers for the purpose of any devolution of property on an intestacy occurring or under any disposition made after the adoption order. The application may be made to the High Court (Family Division) or to a County Court or Magistrates' Court.

Orders may be made in favour of married couples, single, widowed or divorced persons, but not of one party to a marriage alone unless the other spouse cannot be found, is physically or mentally incapable of making an application, or they are separated in circumstances likely to be permanent. A person aged under 21 cannot adopt.

The child's parents or guardians must consent unconditionally to the making of the order unless the court dispenses with the consent, which it may do if the parent cannot be found or is incapable of giving consent, is withholding consent unreasonably, or has neglected or ill-treated the child.

Restrictions are placed on societies which may arrange adoptions.

An adopted person aged over 18 may apply to the Registrar General for information to enable him/her to obtain a full certificate of his/her birth, but before being supplied with the information he/she will be informed that counselling services are available to him/her.

An adopter and the adopted child are within the prohibited degrees for the purposes of marriage to one another.

All adoptions in Great Britain are registered in the Registers of Adopted Children kept by the Registrars General in London and Edinburgh respectively. Certificates from these registers, including short certificates which contain no reference to adoptions, can be obtained on conditions similar to those relating to birth certificates, (*see* below.)

SCOTLAND

The law is consolidated in the Adoption (Scotland) Act 1978 as amended by the Children Act 1989. The law relating to fostering is consolidated in the Foster Children (Scotland) Act 1984. A petition for adoption is presented either to the Sheriff Court or the Court of Session. As in England the petitioner(s) must be 21 or over and may be a married couple or one person who, if married, is living apart permanently from his or her spouse. The consent of the child's natural parents/guardians is required unless dispensed with, or the child is already free for adoption.

The Succession (Scotland) Act 1964 gives the adopted child the same rights of succession as a child born to the adopter in wedlock but deprives him of any such rights in the estates of his natural parents.

BIRTHS (REGISTRATION)

When a birth takes place, personal information of it must be given to the Registrar of Births and Deaths for the sub-district in which the birth occurred, and the register signed in his/her presence by the father or mother of the child; or, if they fail, by (a) the occupier of the house in which the birth happened; (b) a person present at the birth; or (c) the person having charge of the child. The duty of attending to the registration therefore rests firstly on the parents. The mother is responsible for the registration of the birth of an illegitimate child.

The registration is required to be made within 42 days of the birth. Failure to do this, without reasonable cause, involves liability to a penalty. The registration of a birth is free. In England or Wales, the informant, instead of attending before the registrar of the sub-district where the birth occurred, may make a declaration of the particulars required to be registered in the presence of any Registrar. Under the National Health Service Act 1977, notice of every birth must be given by the father, or person in attendance on the mother, to the district medical officer of health by post within 36 hours of the birth. This is in addition to the registration already mentioned.

A still birth must be registered and a certificate signed by the doctor or midwife who was present at the birth or who has examined the body of the child must be produced to the registrar. The certificate must, where possible, state the cause of death and the estimated duration of the pregnancy. A stillbirth may only be registered within three months of the birth.

Re-registration.—The re-registration of the birth of a person legitimated by the subsequent marriage of the parents is provided for in the Births and Deaths Registration Act 1953, as amended by the Family Law Reform Act 1987. Special provisions apply to the registration and re-registration of births of abandoned children, and the re-registration of births of illegitimate children showing the father's name; the mother must normally be party to the latter application.

Birth at Sea.—The master of a British ship must record any birth on board and send particulars to the Registrar General of Shipping.

Birth Abroad.—Consular Officers are authorized to register births of British subjects occurring abroad. Certificates are procurable in due course at Registrar General's Office, London.

The registration of births occurring out of the United Kingdom among members of the armed forces, or occurring on board HM ships and aircraft, is provided for by the Registration of Births, Deaths and Marriages (Special Provisions) Act 1957, applicable also to Scotland.

SCOTLAND

The Registration of Births, Deaths and Marriages (Scotland) Act 1965 supersedes former Acts. Personal notification within 21 days of any birth must be given to the registrar of either the registration district in which the birth took place, or any registration district in which the mother of the child was ordinarily resident at the time of the birth. In the case of a foundling child, dead or alive, when the place of birth is not known, notification must be given to the registrar of the registration district in which the child, or the body, was found, within two months from the date on which the child was found. When a child is born (in or out of Scotland) in a ship, aircraft or land vehicle during a journey and the child is conveyed therein to any place in Scotland, the birth shall, unless the Registrar General otherwise directs, be deemed to have occurred at that place.

The register must be signed in the presence of the registrar by the father or mother of the child, or if they fail, by one of the following: (a) any relative of either parent who has knowledge of the birth; (b) the occupier of the premises in which the child was, to the knowledge of that occupier, born; (c) any person present at the birth; (d) any person having charge of the child. Failure without reasonable cause involves a penalty.

The name of the father of a child born out of wedlock may be entered in the register of births at the time of registration if jointly requested by the mother and father, and the latter's name may also be recorded at a later date on declaration by both parents. A free abbreviated certificate of birth will be issued to the informant at the time of registration.

A still birth must be registered and a certificate, signed by the doctor or certified midwife present at the birth or who has examined the body of the child, must be produced.

Re-registration.—Provision is made for the re-registration of the birth of a person made legitimate by the subsequent marriage of the parents or whose birth entry is affected by any matter respecting status or paternity, or has been so made as to imply that he/she is a foundling.

CERTIFICATES OF BIRTHS, MARRIAGES, OR DEATHS

Certificates of Births, Deaths, or Marriages in England and Wales can be obtained at the Office of Population Censuses and Surveys, St. Catherine's House, 10 Kingsway, WC2B 6JP or from the Superintendent Registrar having the legal custody of the register containing the entry of which a certificate is required. Certificates of marriage can also be obtained from the incumbent of the church in which the marriage took place, or from the Nonconformist minister (or other authorized person) where the marriage takes place in a registered building (*see* **Marriage**).

It is considered desirable when a certificate is required to consult the nearest Register Office who, if told the exact or approximate date and place of registration, will be able to advise on the best way of obtaining it, and any fees payable, which vary according to the type of certificate required and other factors.

Records of births, deaths and marriages registered in England and Wales since 1837 are kept at the Office of Population Censuses and Surveys, St. Catherine's House, 10 Kingsway, WC2B 6JP. The Society of Genealogists, 14 Charterhouse Buildings, Goswell Road, EC1M 7BA, possesses many records of baptisms, marriages and deaths prior to 1837, including copies, in whole or in part of about 4,000 parish registers.

SCOTLAND

Certificates of births, deaths or marriages registered from 1855 (when compulsory registration commenced in Scotland) can be obtained personally at the General Register Office, New Register House, Edinburgh EH1 3YT, or from the appropriate local Registrar, on payment of the fee of £7·00 for a full extract entry of birth, death, or marriage (£9·00 by post), and £6·00 for an abbreviated certificate of birth (£8·00 by post). An abbreviated certificate of registration of deaths is issued free of charge for National Insurance purposes in certain cases. A Register of Divorces (which includes decrees of declaration of nullity of marriage) is kept by the Registrar General at the General Register Office. The fee for an extract decree is £7·00 (£9·00 by post).

There are also available at the General Register Office old parish registers of the date prior to 1855, which were formerly kept under the administration of the established Church of Scotland. An extract of an entry in these registers may be obtained on payment of the appropriate fee. A fee of £13·00 per day is payable for a general search of all the Scottish registers.

Registration of Presumed Deaths (Prescription of Particulars)(Scotland) Regulations 1978 as read with Presumption of Death (Scotland) Act 1977 prescribe the particulars to be notified by the Clerk of Court to the Registrar General after a decree or variation order has been granted in an action of declarator of death of a missing person.

DIVORCE, SEPARATION AND ANCILLARY MATTERS

Matrimonial suits may be conveniently divided into two classes: those in which it is sought to annul the marriage because of some defect; and those in which, the marriage being admitted, it is sought to end the marriage or the duties arising from it. By virtue of the Matrimonial and Family Proceedings Act 1984, all matrimonial causes are commenced in one of the divorce county courts designated by the Lord Chancellor or in the Divorce Registry in London. If the suit becomes defended, it may be transferred to the High Court.

Nullity of Marriage

This is now mainly governed as to England and Wales by the Matrimonial Causes Act 1973. A marriage is void *ab initio* if the parties were within the prohibited degrees of affinity, or were not male and female, or if it was bigamous or if one of the parties was under the age of consent, i.e. 16, or in the case of a polygamous marriage entered into outside England and Wales, if either party was at the time of the marriage domiciled in England and Wales. Where the formalities of the marriage were defective, the marriage is generally void if both parties knew of the defect (e.g. where marriage took place otherwise than in an authorized building). However, absence of the consent of parents or guardians (or of the Court or

other authority, in lieu thereof) in the case of minors does not invalidate the marriage.

A marriage is voidable (i.e. a decree of nullity may be obtained but until such time the marriage remains valid) on the following grounds:

(a) incapacity of either party to consummate;
(b) respondent's wilful refusal to consummate;
(c) that either party did not validly consent to the marriage, whether in consequence of duress, mistake, unsoundness of mind or otherwise;
(d) that either party at the time of marriage was a mentally disordered person;
(e) that at the time of marriage the respondent was suffering from communicable venereal disease;
(f) that at the time of the marriage the respondent was pregnant by another man.

In cases (e) and (f) the petitioner must have been ignorant of the grounds at the date of the marriage, and in (c), (d), (e) and (f) proceedings must be instituted within three years of the marriage, although leave may be obtained to petition outside this period in the case of certain persons suffering from mental illness. In all cases the court shall not grant a decree where the petitioner has led the respondent to believe that he/she would not seek a decree and it would be unjust for it to be granted.

The 1973 Act provides that a decree of nullity in a voidable marriage only annuls the marriage from the date of the decree. The marriage remains valid until the decree, and any children of the marriage are legitimate. Children of a void marriage are illegitimate unless the father was domiciled in England and Wales at the child's birth (or father's death, if earlier), and at the time of conception (or marriage if later) both or either of the parents reasonably believed the marriage was valid.

A spouse's insistence upon the use of contraceptives will not constitute wilful refusal to consummate within (b) above, even though there has been no normal intercourse, but it may in certain circumstances constitute unreasonable behaviour for the purpose of divorce (*see* below). Further, it has been allowed as a defence to a charge of desertion against the aggrieved party.

Judicial Separation and Divorce

The second class of suit includes a suit for judicial separation (which does not dissolve a marriage) and a suit for divorce (which, if successful, dissolves the marriage altogether and leaves the parties at liberty to marry again). Either spouse may petition for judicial separation. It is not necessary to prove that the marriage has broken down irretrievably and the five facts listed under **Divorce** below are grounds for judicial separation.

Divorce

The sole ground on which a divorce is obtained by either husband or wife is the irretrievable breakdown of the marriage. However, the court is precluded from holding that a marriage has irretrievably broken down unless it is satisfied of one or more of the following facts:

(a) that the respondent has committed adultery since the marriage and the petitioner finds it intolerable to live with the respondent;
(b) that the respondent has behaved in such a way that the petitioner cannot reasonably be expected to continue cohabitation;
(c) desertion by the respondent for two years immediately before the petition;
(d) five years separation immediately before the petition (but only two years where the respond-

ent consents to the decree). Matrimonial Causes Act 1973.

The foregoing is subject to a clause prohibiting any petition for divorce (but not for judicial separation) before the lapse of one year from the date of the marriage.

Desertion may be defined as a voluntary withdrawal from cohabitation by one spouse without just cause and against the wishes of the other. Where one spouse is guilty of conduct of a serious nature which forces the other to leave, the party at fault is said to be guilty of constructive desertion.

Encouragement of reconciliation.—The 1973 Act requires the solicitor for the petitioner to certify whether the possibility of a reconciliation has been discussed with the petitioner and whether or not the solicitor has given the petitioner the names and addresses of persons qualified to help effect a reconciliation.

A total period of less than six months during which the parties have resumed living together is to be disregarded in determining whether the prescribed period of desertion or separation has been continuous. Similar provision for effecting a reconciliation exists in relation to the other proofs of breakdown, but a petitioner cannot rely on an act of adultery by the other party if they have lived together for more than six months after discovery of that act of adultery.

Obtaining the Decree Nisi.—Where the suit is defended, i.e. the respondent opposes the dissolution or the fact/ground on which the petitioner seeks it, the petition will be heard by a Judge in open court, the parties giving oral evidence. Where the suit is undefended, the evidence will normally take the form of a sworn written statement made by the petitioner which will be sent to the Court and read over by the Registrar. If the Registrar is satisfied that the petitioner has proved the contents of the petition, he will simply fix a date for a Judge to pronounce the decree nisi, it being unnecessary for either party to attend. Only if the Registrar is not satisfied as above will he order that the petition be heard formally by the Judge.

Children.—Subject to exceptions, the decree nisi cannot be made absolute unless a Judge by order declares that he is satisfied with the proposed arrangements for the welfare of any child of the family who is under 16, or under 18 and receiving education or vocational training. If there is no dispute as to the children between the parties and the proposed arrangements for residence, education etc. are specific, an appointment will be made for the Judge to interview one or both parents informally and if satisfied he will make an order to that effect. (This will usually be on the same day as the decree nisi is pronounced.) If not, the Registrar may inform the parties that it is up to them to seek a hearing before the Judge to resolve the matters in dispute.

Decree Absolute.—Every decree of divorce or nullity is in the first instance a decree nisi, and the marriage subsists until the decree is made absolute, usually six weeks after decree nisi on the petitioner's application. After the decree absolute either party is free to remarry.

Maintenance, etc.—The court has wide powers to order either party to the marriage to make financial provision (e.g. periodical payments, a lump sum, the transfer of property) for the other party or any child of the family, having regard to the party's means, the recipient's needs and all the important aspects of the case. These so-called ancillary matters often present more difficulty than the divorce itself, especially affecting the home, and may go on long after the

marriage is dissolved. There is, however, nothing to stop financial matters being negotiated by the parties through their solicitors before the divorce goes through.

The court may, where the husband has wilfully neglected to provide reasonable maintenance for the wife or children, order the husband to make provision for them, even though no matrimonial suit is pending between the parties to the marriage, and while such an order is in force the court may also deal with custody of and access to the children.

Custody of Children, etc.

The Court may make orders in respect of access to and the custody, maintenance and education of children in connection with a suit for divorce, nullity or judicial separation (above), or with an application to the magistrates (below) whether the suit succeeds or not. In addition, if there is no other matrimonial suit involved a parent may apply for custody under the Guardianship of Minors Acts 1971, and any person interested may apply to the High Court for the child to be made a ward of court.

In all cases the welfare of the child is the first and paramount consideration. The categories of child who may be covered by any particular type of proceedings differ according to the nature of those proceedings and to the nature of the particular relief sought, but it should be borne in mind that in connection with divorce, nullity and judicial separation a child which has been treated by the spouses as a child of the family may be included as a 'child of the family' as well as the children of the spouses themselves. This also applies to most maintenance cases in the magistrates' court (*see* below).

Under the Children Act 1975 a new procedure called Custodianship has been introduced, allowing, for instance, long term foster parents to apply for custody of the foster child.

Any dispute relating to the above matters should be placed in the hands of a solicitor without delay and in particular it should be borne in mind that where there is financial need (because of continuing education or disability, for instance) maintenance may be ordered for children even beyond the age of majority.

The above provisions will be changed by the implementation of the Children Act 1989, which is not yet fully in force.

Separation by Agreement

Husband and wife may enter into an agreement to separate and live apart, but the agreement, to be valid, must be followed by an immediate separation. It is most desirable to consult a solicitor in every such case, who will often advise obtaining a court order by consent.

Magistrates' Custody and Maintenance Orders

For many years the law relating to domestic proceedings in magistrates' courts was out of line with the divorce law which was reformed in 1969. The Domestic Proceedings and Magistrates' Courts Act 1978 took effect in early 1981 and now contains the relevant law.

A husband or wife can apply to a magistrates' court for a matrimonial order on the grounds that the other spouse: (a) has failed to pay reasonable maintenance for the applicant; (b) has failed to make a proper contribution towards the reasonable maintenance of a child of the family; (c) has deserted the applicant; or (d) has behaved in such a way that the applicant cannot reasonably be expected to live with the respondent.

If the case is proved the court can order: (a) periodical payments for the applicant; (b) periodical payments for a child of the family; or (c) a lump sum (not exceeding £1,000) for the benefit of the applicant and for any child of the family.

In deciding what orders (if any) to make the magistrates must consider a number of guidelines which are similar to those governing financial orders on divorce. There are also special provisions relating to consent orders and separation by agreement. The court also has powers to make orders relating to the legal custody of a child of the family and these orders together with orders for child maintenance can be made even though the court makes no order for spouse maintenance. Legal custody can only be granted to one person but the court may order that the other party shall retain certain parental rights and exercise them jointly with the person who is awarded legal custody. Other provisions of the Act relate to access by grandparents, interim orders, and variation, discharge and revival of orders. An order may be enforceable even though the parties are living together, but in some cases it will cease to have effect if they continue to do so for six months. The hearing of matrimonial disputes is separate from ordinary court business, and the public are not admitted.

Domestic Violence

The Domestic Violence and Matrimonial Proceedings Act 1976, the Domestic Proceedings and Magistrates' Courts Act 1978 (the former not being applicable to Scotland and the latter only to a limited extent; *see* below) and the Matrimonial Homes Act 1983 have made it easier for one spouse who has been subjected to violence by the other to obtain an order to restrain further violence and if need be to have the other excluded from the home. Such orders can be obtained very quickly, and a person disobeying them is liable to be imprisoned for contempt of court. There are some differences of detail between the three Acts; in particular the 1976 Act also applies to unmarried couples. Such orders may also be obtained in the course of suits for divorce and judicial separation.

SCOTLAND

Nullity of Marriage

A declaration of nullity of marriage may be obtained on the ground of any impediment, viz., consanguinity and affinity, subsistence of a previous marriage, nonage of one of the parties, incapacity or insanity of one of the parties, or by the absence of genuine consent. The financial provisions on divorce contained in the Family Law (Scotland) Act 1985 also apply to an action for declaration of nullity of marriage.

Judicial Separation

Under the Divorce (Scotland) Act 1976, a decree of judicial separation can be obtained by proof of the same facts necessary to obtain decree of divorce, except that for the principle of irretrievable breakdown there is substituted that of grounds justifying separation. This type of action is competent in both the Court of Session and the Sheriff Court.

Divorce

Actions of divorce could formerly only be raised in the Court of Session, having jurisdiction to entertain such actions only if either of the parties to the marriage in question: is domiciled in Scotland on the date when the action is begun; or was habitually resident in Scotland throughout the period of one year ending with that date. As from May 1, 1984, however, when the Divorce Jurisdiction, Court Fees and Legal Aid (Scotland) Act 1983 came into force, actions of divorce may also be raised in the Sheriff Courts provided the above conditions are complied with, and provided either party to the marriage was resident in the Sheriffdom for a period of forty days ending with the date the action was begun, or was resident in the Sheriffdom for a period of not less than forty days ending not more than forty days before the date the action was begun.

The Scots law of divorce is now governed by the Divorce (Scotland) Act 1976, which for the purposes of divorce came into force on January 1, 1977. The sole ground of divorce is now irretrievable breakdown of the marriage. This can only be established in one of the following ways:

(a) The defending spouse has committed adultery since the date of the marriage. Here it is not necessary for the pursuing spouse to prove that the fact of adultery made it intolerable to live with the defending spouse.

(b) The defending spouse has behaved in such a way that the pursuing spouse cannot reasonably be expected to cohabit with him or her. It is immaterial whether or not the conduct founded upon is active or passive.

(c) The defending spouse has deserted the pursuing spouse for a continuous period of two years. There must be no question of the pursuing spouse having refused a genuine and reasonable offer to adhere. Nor is irretrievable breakdown established if cohabitation is resumed for a period of more than three months, after the two-year period has expired.

(d) There has been no cohabitation at any time during a continuous period of two years immediately preceding the action between the parties to the action, and the defending spouse consents to the divorce being granted.

(e) There has been no cohabitation at any time during a continuous period of five years, as in (d), except that on the expiry of the five-year period, the consent of the defending spouse is not required.

The facts of desertion and separation are not interrupted by the parties cohabiting for a period or periods not exceeding six months. However, such a period or periods of cohabitation would not be included in the calculation of the two-year or five-year periods.

Encouragement of reconciliation.—The burden of promoting a reconciliation between spouses in a divorce action in Scotland falls upon the Court by virtue of the 1976 Act. Where an action of divorce has been raised, it may be postponed by the Court to enable the parties to seek to effect a reconciliation, if the Court feels that there may be a reasonable prospect of such reconciliation. If the parties do cohabit during such postponement, no account shall be taken of such cohabitation if the action later proceeds.

Maintenance, etc.—The 1976 Act also provides that either party to a marriage can apply to the Court at any time prior to decree being granted for: (a) an order for interim custody of all or some of the children of the marriage under 16 years of age; (b) an order for access to all or some of the children of the marriage under 16 years of age in the custody of the other party.

The financial provisions on divorce in the 1976 Act have been superseded by the Family Law (Scotland) Act 1985 which allows either party to the marriage to apply to the court for an order for payment of a capital sum or for a periodical allowance or for an incidental order. The Act sets out principles to be applied by the Court, one of these being that the financial provisions awarded to a party who has been dependent for financial support on the other party should be given over a period of not more than three years.

The Act also defines the rights and obligations of aliment between parents and children, thereby excluding aliment between grandparents and grandchildren and of children to parents, and provides that a child is entitled to aliment up to the age of eighteen or to twenty five if in full-time further education, and for the claiming of aliment whether in connection with an action of divorce etc. or independently.

Procedure.—Appearance in Court at a Proof in an undefended divorce action has been rendered unnecessary since April 1978. A full Proof is still necessary if the action is defended in any respect. In place of court appearance, affidavits (statements sworn before a Notary Public) by the pursuer and any witnesses are lodged in the Court together with a Minute by the solicitor craving decree.

A new simplified procedure for 'do-it-yourself' divorce was introduced in January 1983 for certain divorces. Thus, if the action is based on (d) or (e) above and will not be opposed, there are no children under 16 and no financial claims, then the applicant can write directly to the Court of Session, Divorce Section (SP), Parliament House, Edinburgh or the local Sheriff Court for the appropriate forms to enable him or her to proceed. The fee is £40 unless the applicant receives Income Support, Family Credit or legal advice and assistance, in which case there is no fee.

Custody of Children

In actions for divorce and separation, the Court has a discretion in awarding the custody of the children of the parties. The welfare of the children is the paramount consideration, and the mere fact that a spouse, by reason of his or her behaviour, brought about the breakdown of the marriage does not of itself preclude him or her from being awarded custody. The Children Act 1975, as amended, also applies to Scotland.

Domestic Violence

The Matrimonial Homes (Family Protection) (Scotland) Act 1981, as amended, provides that one spouse, whether or not he or she has title to the matrimonial home, can obtain an exclusion order suspending the other spouse's occupancy rights in the matrimonial home. The Court (either Court of Session or Sheriff Court) is empowered to make such an order if satisfied that it is necessary to protect the applicant or any child of the family from any conduct, actual or threatened or reasonably apprehended of the other spouse which would be injurious to the physical or mental health of the applicant or child. In making the order the Court may include a warrant for the summary ejection of the non-applicant spouse from the matrimonial home and for an interdict prohibiting him/her from entering it.

ILLEGITIMACY AND LEGITIMATION

ENGLAND AND WALES

The former provisions of the Affiliation Proceedings Act 1957, under which a man could be summoned to petty sessions on the application of the mother of an illegitimate child, or by the Supplementary Benefits Commission where benefit has been paid for the requirements of the child, and under which the Justices, on his being proved to be the father of the child, could make an order requiring him to pay for its maintenance and education a sum in their

discretion, have been replaced by extensive provisions relating to parental rights and duties in Part II of the Family Law Reform Act 1987. *Prima facie* every child born of a married woman during a marriage is legitimate; and this presumption can only be rebutted by strong evidence. However, under the Family Law Reform Act 1969, any presumption of law as to the legitimacy (or illegitimacy) of any person may in civil proceedings be rebutted by evidence showing that it is more probable than not that the person is illegitimate (or legitimate) and in any proceedings where paternity is in question, blood tests may be ordered. If however the husband and wife are separated under an Order of the Court, a child conceived by the wife during such separation is presumed not to be the husband's child.

Legitimation

The Legitimacy Act 1976 consolidates earlier legislation dating back to January 1, 1927. Where the parents of an illegitimate person marry, or have married, whether before or after that date, the marriage, if the father is at the date thereof domiciled in England or Wales, renders that person, if living, legitimate as from Jan. 1, 1927, or from the date of the marriage, whichever last happens. Marriage legitimates a person even though the father or mother was married to a third person at the time when the illegitimate person was born. It is the duty of the parents to supply to the Registrar General information for re-registration of the birth of a legitimate child.

Declarations of Legitimacy.—A person claiming that he, his parents, or any remoter ancestor has become legitimated, may petition the High Court or the County Court for the necessary declaration.

Rights and Duties of Legitimated Persons.—A legitimated person, his/her spouse or children may take property under an intestacy occurring after the date of legitimation, or under any disposition (e.g. a will) coming into operation after such date, as if he/she had been legitimate. He/she must maintain all persons whom he/she would be bound to maintain had he/she been born legitimate, and he/she is entitled to the benefit of any Act of Parliament which confers rights on legitimate persons to recover damages or compensation. The Act specially provides that nothing therein contained is to render any person capable of succeeding to or transmitting a right to any dignity or title.

Property Rights of Illegitimate Children

By the Family Law Reform Act 1969 the rights of an illegitimate child on an intestacy were broadly equated with those of a legitimate child, and in any disposition made after December 31, 1969, any reference to children or other relatives was, unless the contrary intention appears, to be construed as including any person who is illegitimate or who is related through another person who is illegitimate. However, these provisions of the 1969 Act have been replaced by the general provision of the Family Law Reform Act 1987 (*see* p. 1025).

Scotland

The Law Reform (Parent & Child) Scotland Act 1986 implements the Scottish Law Commission's report on illegitimacy. The Act contains a general provision granting equality status to all persons whatever the marital status of their parents. The mother of an illegitimate child may raise an action of affiliation and aliment against the father, either in the Court of Session or, more usually, in the Sheriff Court. Where in any such action the Court finds that the defender is the father of the child, the Court shall, in awarding inlying expenses, or aliment, have regard to the means of the parties, and the whole circumstances of the case. The Court may, upon application by the mother or by the father of any illegitimate child, or in any action for aliment for an illegitimate child, make such order as it may think fit regarding the custody of such child and the right of access thereto of either parent, having regard to the welfare of the child and to the conduct of the parents and to the wishes as well of the mother as of the father and may on the application of either parent recall or vary such order. The obligation of the mother and of the father of an illegitimate child to provide aliment for such child shall (without prejudice to any obligation attaching at common law) endure until the child attains the age of sixteen.

Legitimation

By Scots law an illegitimate child is legitimated by and on the date of the subsequent marriage of its parents and there is no objection to there having been an impediment to the marriage of the parents at the time of the child's conception—*see* the Legitimation (Scotland) Act 1968, which came into operation on June 8, 1968, on which date thousands of existing illegitimate children were regarded as legitimated. By the Registration of Births, Deaths and Marriages (Scotland) Act 1965, a child so legitimated, who has already been registered as illegitimate, may be re-registered as legitimate. The consent of the father of an illegitimate child to its adoption is not required unless he has been awarded parental rights by the court.

MARRIAGE

Marriage According to Rites of the Church of England

MARRIAGE BY BANNS

The Marriage Act 1949 prescribes audible publication according to the rubric, on three Sundays preceding the ceremony during morning service or, if there is no morning service on a Sunday on which the banns are to be published, during evening service. Where the parties reside in different parishes, the banns must be published in both. Under the Act, banns may be published and the marriage solemnized in the parish church, which is the usual place of worship of the persons to be married or either of them, although neither of such persons dwells in such parish; but this publication of banns is in addition to any other publication required by law and does not apply if the church or the residence of either party is in Wales. The Act provides specially for the case where one of the parties resides in Scotland and the other in England, the publication being then in the parish in England in which one party resides, and, according to the law and custom in Scotland, in the place where the other party resides. After the lapse of three months from the last time of publication, the banns become useless, and the parties must either obtain a licence (*see* below), or submit to the republication of banns.

MARRIAGE BY LICENCE

Marriage licences are of two kinds:—

Common Licence.—A common licence, dispensing with the necessity for banns, is granted by the Archbishops and Bishops through their surrogates, for marriages in any church or chapel duly licensed for marriages. A common licence can be obtained in London by application at the Faculty Office (1 The Sanctuary, Westminster, SW1) and (for marriages in London) at the Bishop of London's Diocesan Registry (1 The Sanctuary, SW1), by one of the parties about to be married. In the country they may be obtained

at the offices of the Bishop's Registrars, but licences obtained at the Bishop's Diocesan Registry only enable the parties to be married in the diocese in which they are issued; those procured at the Faculty Office are available for all England and Wales. No instructions, either verbal or in writing, can be received, except from one of the parties. Affidavits are prepared from the personal instructions of one of the parties about to be married, and the licence is delivered to the party upon payment of a fee (*see* page 1037). Before a licence can be granted one of the parties must make an affidavit that there is no legal impediment to the intended marriage; and also that one of such parties has had his or her usual place of abode for the space of fifteen days immediately preceding the issuing of the licence within the parish or ecclesiastical district of the church in which the marriage is to be solemnized, or the church in which the marriage is to be solemnized is the usual place of worship of the parties or one of them. In the country there may generally be found a parochial clergyman (surrogate) before whom the affidavit may be taken, and whose office it is to deliver the licence personally to the applicant. (In some dioceses it is necessary for the surrogate to procure the licence from the Bishop's Registry.) The licence continues in force for three months from its date.

Special Licence.—A special licence is granted by the Archbishop of Canterbury, under special circumstances, for marriage at any place with or without previous residence in the district, or at any time, etc.; but the reasons assigned must meet with the Archbishop's approval. Application must be made to the Faculty Office. (For fee, *see* page 1037).

MARRIAGE UNDER SUPERINTENDENT REGISTRAR'S CERTIFICATE

A marriage may be performed in church on the Superintendent Registrar's Certificate (*see* below) without banns, provided that the incumbent's consent is obtained. One of the parties must be resident within the ecclesiastical parish of the church in which the marriage is to take place unless the church is the usual place of worship of the parties or one of them.

Marriage under Superintendent Registrar's Certificate

The following marriages may be solemnized on the authority of a Superintendent Registrar's certificate (either with or without a licence):—

(a) A marriage in a registered building (e.g. a nonconformist church registered for the solemnization of marriages therein).

(b) A marriage in a register office.

(c) A marriage according to the usages of the Society of Friends (commonly called Quakers).

(d) A marriage between two persons professing the Jewish religion according to the usages of the Jews.

(e) A marriage according to the rites of the Church of England (*see* above—in this case the marriage can only be without licence).

(f) A marriage of a person who is housebound or is detained at the place where he or she normally resides (*see* p. 1037).

Notice of the intended marriage must be given as follows:—

Marriage by certificate (without licence).—If both parties reside in the same registration district, they must both have resided there for seven days before the notice can be given. It may then be given by either party. If the parties reside in different registration districts, notice must be given by each to the Superintendent Registrar of the district in which he or she resides, and the preliminary residential qualification of seven days must be fulfilled by each before either notice can be given.

Marriage by certificate (with licence).—One notice only is necessary, whether the parties live in the same or in different registration districts. Either party may give the notice, which must be given to the Superintendent Registrar of any registration district in which one of the parties has resided for the period of fifteen days immediately preceding the giving of notice, but both parties must be resident in England or Wales on the day notice is given.

The notice (in either case) must be in the prescribed form and must contain particulars as to names, marital status, occupation, residence, length of residence, and the building in which the marriage is to take place. The notice must also contain or have added at the foot thereof a solemn declaration that there is no legal impediment to the marriage, and, in the case of minors, that the consent of the person whose consent to the marriage is required by law (*see Minors,* p. 1037) has been duly given, and that the residential qualifications mentioned above have been complied with. A person making a false declaration renders himself or herself liable to prosecution for perjury. The notice is entered in the marriage notice book.

ISSUE OF CERTIFICATE

Without licence.—The notice (or an exact copy thereof) is affixed in some conspicuous place in the Superintendent Registrar's office for 21 days next after the notice was entered in the marriage notice book. After the lapse of this period the Superintendent Registrar may, provided no impediment is shown, issue his certificate for the marriage which can then take place at any time within three months from the date of the entry of the notice.

With licence.—The notice in this case is not affixed in the office of the Superintendent Registrar. After the lapse of one whole day (other than a Sunday, Christmas Day or Good Friday) from the date of entry of the notice, the Superintendent Registrar may, provided no impediment is shown, issue his certificate and licence for the marriage, which can then take place on any day within three months from the date of entry of the notice.

SOLEMNIZATION OF THE MARRIAGE

In a Registered Building.—The marriage must generally take place at a building within the district of residence of one of the parties, but if the usual place of worship of either is outside the district of his or her residence, it may take place in such usual place of worship. Further, if there is not within the district of residence of one of the parties a registered building within which marriages are solemnized according to the rites and ceremonies which the parties desire to adopt in solemnizing their marriage, it may take place in an appropriate registered building in the nearest district.

The presence of a Registrar of Marriages is not necessary at marriages at registered buildings which have adopted the provisions of section 43 of the Marriage Act 1949. This section provides for the appointment of an authorized person (a person, usually the minister or an official of the building, certified by the trustees or governing body as having been duly authorized for the purpose) who must be present and must register the marriage.

The marriage must be solemnized between the hours of 8 a.m. and 6 p.m., with open doors in the presence of two or more witnesses. The parties must

at some time during the ceremony make the following declaration: 'I do solemnly declare that I know not of any lawful impediment why I, A. B., may not be joined in matrimony to C. D.' Also each of the parties must say to the other: 'I call upon these persons here present to witness that I, A. B., do take thee, C. D., to be my lawful wedded wife [or husband],' *or,* if the marriage is solemnized in the presence of an authorized person without the presence of a Registrar, each party may say in lieu thereof: 'I, A. B., do take thee, C. D., to be my wedded wife [or husband].'

In a Register Office.—The marriage may be solemnized in the office of the Superintendent Registrar to whom notice of the marriage has been given. The marriage must be solemnized between the hours of 8 a.m. and 6 p.m., with open doors in the presence of the Superintendent Registrar or a Registrar of the registration district of that Superintendent Registrar, and in the presence of two witnesses. The parties must make the following declaration: 'I do solemnly declare that I know not of any lawful impediment why I, A. B., may not be joined in matrimony to C. D.,' and each party must say to the other: 'I call upon these persons here present to witness that I, A. B., do take thee, C. D., to be my lawful wedded wife [or husband].' No religious ceremony may take place in the Register Office, though the parties may, on production of their marriage certificate, go through a subsequent religious ceremony in any church or persuasion of which they are members.

Other Cases.—If both parties are members of the Society of Friends (Quakers), or if, not being in membership, they have been authorized by the Society of Friends to solemnize their marriage in accordance with its usages, they may be married in a Friends' meeting-house. The marriage must be registered by the registering officer of the Society appointed to act for the district in which the meeting house is situated. The presence of a Registrar of Marriages is not necessary.

If both parties are Jews they may marry according to their usages in a synagogue which has a certified marriage secretary, or in a private dwelling-house at any hour; the building may be situated within or without the district of residence. The marriage must be registered by the secretary of the synagogue of which the man is a member. The presence of a Registrar of Marriages is not necessary.

Marriage under Registrar General's Licence

The main purpose of the Marriage (Registrar General's Licence) Act 1970, which came into force on January 1, 1971, is to enable non-Anglicans to be married in unregistered premises where one of the persons to be married is seriously ill, is not expected to recover and cannot be moved to registered premises.

Detained and Housebound Persons

The Marriage Act 1983 (which does not extend to Scotland) enables marriages of detained persons and housebound persons to be solemnized at their place of residence . The Act came into operation on May 1, 1984.

Marriage in England or Wales when one party lives in Scotland or Northern Ireland

Notice for a marriage by a Superintendent Registrar's certificate in a register office or registered building may be given in the usual way by the party resident in England. As regards Scotland, the party there should give notice of intention to marry to the Registrar. As regards Northern Ireland, the party there, after a residence of seven days, must give notice to the District Registrar of Marriages. Notice cannot be given for such marriages to take place by Certificate with licence of the Superintendent Registrar.

Marriage of such parties may take place in a church of the Church of England after the publication of banns, or by Ecclesiastical licence.

Civil Fees
(from April 1, 1990)

Marriage by Superintendent Registrar's certificate:

If both parties live in same district
In register office........................£27·50
In a registered building when presence of Registrar is required .... £38·00
If the parties live in different districts
In register office........................£40·50
In a registered building when presence of Registrar is required .... £51·00
Marriage by Superintendent Registrar's licence:

In register office.........................£65·50
In a registered building when presence of Registrar is required...........................£76·00
Total fees for the preliminaries to marriage by Registrar General's licence...............£15·00
Marriage of a housebound or detained person:
For attendance of Superintendent Registrar at residence of housebound or detained person to attest notice of marriage ....£27·00
For attendance of Superintendent Registrar at residence of housebound or detained person ....£27·00
For attendance of Registrar at residence of housebound or detained person ....£25·00
In the case of a registered building, further fees may be payable to the Minister or the authorities of the building.

Ecclesiastical Fees
(from April 1, 1990)

Marriage after Banns
Parties residing in same parish .... £48·50
Parties residing in different parishes ...... £57·00
Marriages by Common Licence
Fee for licence (varies, but usually)........£33·00
Fee to Church authorities for ceremony ... £43·00
Marriage on the authority of the Superintendent Registrar's certificate
Parties residing in same registration district
£56·00
Parties residing in different districts ...... £69·00
Marriage by special licence
Fee payable at Faculty office ....£75·00
Marriage of a housebound or detained person
For attendance of a Superintendent Registrar at residence of a housebound or detained person to attest marriage ....£27·00
For entering notice of marriage*..........£13·00
*Two notices are required to be given if the parties reside in different registration districts
Further fees may be payable for additional facilities at the marriage, e.g. the organist's fee.
Some of the above fees may not apply to the Church in Wales.

Miscellaneous Notes

Consanguinity and Affinity.—A marriage between persons within the prohibited degrees of consanguinity or affinity is void. Relaxations have, however, been made by various statutes which have now been replaced by the Marriage Act 1949 (see 1st Schedule

to the Act) and the Marriage (Enabling) Act 1960. It is now permitted to contract a marriage with:—

(a) Sister, aunt or niece of a former wife (whether living or not).
(b) Former wife of brother, uncle or nephew (whether living or not).
No clergyman can be compelled to solemnize any of the foregoing marriages, but he may allow his church to be used for the purpose by another minister.

The Marriage (Prohibited Degrees of Relationship) Act 1986 makes further provision with regard to the marriage of persons related by affinity e.g. after section 1 of the Act comes into force, a marriage between a man and the daughter or grand-daughter of his former wife will not be void by reason only of that relationship if both parties have attained 21 at the time of the marriage and the younger party has not at any time before attaining 18 been a child of the family in relation to the other party.

Minors.—Persons under 18 years of age are generally required to obtain the consent of certain persons (*see* Marriage Act 1949, section 3 and 2nd Schedule as amended by the Family Law Reform Act 1969). Where both parents are living, both must consent. Where one is dead, the survivor, or, if there is a guardian appointed by the deceased parent, the guardian and the survivor must consent. (For the position where the parents of the child were not married to each other at the time of the birth, see section 9 of the Family Law Reform Act 1987.) No consent is required in the case of an infant's second marriage. In certain exceptional cases consent may be dispensed with, e.g. the insanity of a parent.

If consent is refused the Court may, on application being made, consent to the marriage; application can be made for this purpose to the High Court, the County Court, or a court of summary jurisdiction. The Act prohibits any marriage where either party is under 16 years of age.

MARRIAGES IN SCOTLAND

According to the law of Scotland, marriage is a contract which is completed by the mutual consent of parties. The Marriage (Scotland) Act 1977, which came into force on January 1, 1978, states or restates the law in convenient form. References in this section are to that Act.

Impediments to Marriage

These are: (a) nonage, i.e., where either party is under the age of 16; (b) forbidden degrees of relationship (Section 2) as amended by the Marriage Prohibited Degrees of Relationship Act 1986; (c) subsisting previous marriage; (d) incapacity to understand the nature of the contract; (e) both parties of the same sex; (f) non-residence, i.e. if the requirements of prior residence of one or other of the parties in Scotland have not been complied with.
The Act also states the grounds on which certain marriages may be declared void but this is amended by the Law Reform (Miscellaneous Provisions) (Scotland) Act 1980 which prevents a marriage being rendered void solely due to the failure to comply with certain formalities, provided the particulars of that marriage are entered in a register of marriages by or at the behest of an appropriate registrar.

Marriages may be regular or irregular, thus:—

Regular Marriages

A regular marriage is one which is celebrated by a minister of religion or authorized registrar or other celebrant specified in the Act. The parties must submit to the District Registrar a statutory notice of intention to marry, the fee for which is £6·50 each. The Registrar will then enter the parties' names and particulars in the marriage notice book which must also show the intended date of the marriage. The Registrar must then display the notice of intention to marry in a prominent public place until the intended date, and any person claiming an interest may lodge written objections thereto with the Registrar (Section 5). The Registrar, after fourteen days of receipt of the marriage notice and on being satisfied that there are no legal impediments to the marriage, will issue to either or both parties a marriage schedule. The fourteen-day period may be shortened under exceptional circumstances. The marriage schedule must be produced to the celebrant of the marriage. The fee for the solemnization ceremony in a registry office is £15. After the ceremony the marriage must be registered within three days with the Registrar General for inclusion in the Register of Births, Deaths and Marriages. Within one month of the ceremony, the fee for an extract marriage certificate is £4·00; thereafter it is £7·00.

Irregular Marriages

Since the Marriage (Scotland) Act 1939 the only form of irregular marriage to be recognized by law, marriage by habit and repute, remains competent under the 1977 Act. If the parties live together constantly as husband and wife and are held to be such by the general repute of the neighbourhood and among their friends and relations, then there may arise a presumption from which marriage can be inferred. Before such a marriage can be registered, however, a decree of declarator of marriage must be obtained from the Deputy Principal Clerk of the Court of Session. It is the duty of the Deputy Principal Clerk to register the decree as soon as it is granted.

JURY SERVICE

Every local or parliamentary elector between the ages of 18 and 70 who has resided in the United Kingdom, Channel Islands or Isle of Man for at least five years since he/she attained the age of 13 will be qualified to serve on a jury unless he/she is ineligible or disqualified.

Ineligible persons include those who have at any time been judges, magistrates and certain senior court officials, those who within the previous ten years have been concerned with the law (such as barristers and solicitors and their clerks, court officers, coroners, police, prison and probation officers); priests of any religion and vowed members of religious communities; and certain sufferers from mental illness.

Disqualified persons are those who have at any time been sentenced by a Court in the United Kingdom, Channel Islands or Isle of Man, to a term of imprisonment of five years or more, or a person who in the last ten years has (a) served any part of a sentence of imprisonment, youth custody or detention; (b) been detained in a Borstal institution; (c) had passed on him/her or made in respect of him/her a suspended sentence of imprisonment or order for detention; or (d) had made in respect of him/her a community service order. A person who at any time in the last five years has been placed on probation is also disqualified.

Some others are excusable as of right. These include persons over 65, members and officers of the Houses of Parliament, full-time serving members of the forces, registered and practising members of the medical, dental, nursing, veterinary and pharmaceutical professions, and any person who has served on a jury in the two years before he/she is summoned. In other cases the court may excuse a juror at its discretion, e.g. where the service would be a hardship to the juror.

If a person serves on a jury knowing himself/herself to be disqualified or ineligible, he/she is liable to be fined up to £2,000 or £400 respectively.

A juror is entitled to subsistence and travelling expenses, compensation for other expenses incurred in consequence of attendance for jury service, loss of earnings and loss of national insurance benefits, but certain maximum figures (which are revised from time to time) are laid down.

A verdict of a jury must normally be unanimous but after two hours' consideration (or such longer period as the Court thinks reasonable), a majority verdict is acceptable if ten jurors agree to it (or nine if the size of the jury has been reduced to ten, e.g. by illness during the trial).

Jury trial is now very unusual in civil cases but a person charged with any but the least serious crimes is entitled to be tried by a jury. The defendant may object to any juror if he can show that that juror ought not to be on the jury, e.g. because he is ineligible or is biased against him.

The Coroners' Juries Act 1983 (which does not extend to Scotland) makes new provision in relation to qualification to serve on coroners' juries.

SCOTLAND

It is the duty of the sheriff principal of each sheriffdom, in respect of each sheriff court district in his sheriffdom, to maintain a book (the general jury book) containing the names and designations of persons within the district who are qualified and liable to serve as jurors. The book, which is compiled from information which every householder is required to provide, is kept open for the inspection by any person, upon payment of a nominal fee, at the sheriff clerk's office for the district.

Under s.1 of the Law Reform (Miscellaneous Provisions) (Scotland) Act 1980, every man or woman between the ages of 18 and 65 who is for the time being registered as a parliamentary or local government elector and who has been ordinarily resident in the United Kingdom, the Channel Islands or the Isle of Man for any period of at least five years since attaining the age of 13 years, is qualified to serve on a jury.

Ineligible persons include those who at any time within the past ten years have been judges of the supreme courts, sheriffs and certain other senior court officials, those who at any time within the past five years have been concerned with the administration of justice (such as advocates and their clerks, solicitors, court staff, police officers, prison officers, sheriff officers, procurator fiscals, and members of parole boards and children's panels), and certain sufferers from mental illness.

The same rules for disqualified persons operate in Scotland as in England. Those excusable as of right are members and officers of the Houses of Parliament, full-time serving members of the forces, registered and practising members of the medical, dental, nursing, veterinary and pharmaceutical professions, ministers of religion and other persons in holy orders, and any person who has attended for jury service in the past five years.

If a person serves on a jury knowing himself/herself to be disqualified or ineligible, he/she is liable to be fined up to £2,000 or £400 respectively. Jurors failing to attend without good cause are liable to a maximum fine of £400.

Part II of the Juries Act 1949 (amended by regulations following thereon and by the Law Reform (Miscellaneous Provisions) (Scotland) Act 1980) applies only to Scotland and provides, *inter alia*, for the payment of travelling expenses and subsistence allowances to jurors and for loss of earnings.

The number of a jury in a civil cause in the Court of Session is twelve and in the Sheriff Court seven. In a criminal trial the number is fifteen.

LANDLORD AND TENANT

Although basically the relationship between the parties to a lease is governed by the lease itself, the position is complicated by numerous statutory provisions. The few points dealt with may show the desirability of seeking professional assistance in these matters. Important provisions include:—

(1) The Agricultural Holdings Act 1986, among other things, regulates the length of notice necessary to determine an agricultural tenancy, the tenant's right to remove fixtures on the land, his right to compensation for damage done by game, for improvements and for disturbance, and his right to require the consent of the Agricultural Land Tribunal to the operation of a notice to quit.

(2) The Landlord and Tenant Acts 1927 and 1954, as amended. Part II of the 1954 Act gives security of tenure to the tenant of most business premises, and in effect the tenant can only be ousted on one or more of the seven grounds set out in the Act. In some cases, where the landlord can resume possession, the tenant is entitled to compensation.

(3) The complicated mass of legislation regarding dwelling-houses is embodied in the Rent Act 1977 and the Housing Act 1988.

If a tenancy of a house is within the Rent Act, the tenant has a personal right to reside there, and may only be ousted on certain grounds. Tenancies with full Rent Act protection are known as regulated tenancies. The maximum rent recoverable under such a tenancy is the rent agreed between the landlord and tenant, unless a fair rent has been registered, in which case that is the maximum. Application for the registration of a fair rent may be made by either the landlord or tenant, to the Local Rent Officer, and appeal against his decision lies to the Rent Assessment Committee.

Since the Housing Act 1988 came into force on January 15, 1989, it has not generally been possible to create a new regulated tenancy, although the above protection remains for existing regulated tenancies. Tenancies granted on or after January 15, 1989 are known as assured tenancies provided they satisfy certain conditions, which are broadly the same as those for regulated tenancies under the 1977 Act. However, the rent payable by an assured tenant is either that agreed with the landlord or the open market rent fixed by the Rent Assessment Committee.

(4) The Rent Act 1974 gave tenants of dwellings let furnished the same security of tenure as those of unfurnished dwellings unless the landlord lived in part of the house. In the latter case, and in the case of a tenancy of a dwelling granted by a resident landlord after August 13, 1974, the tenancy will usually be outside full Rent Act protection, but may fall within the restricted contract provisions of the Rent Act 1977. In this event, the landlord or the tenant may apply to the Rent Tribunal for a reasonable rent to be registered and once registered, this is the maximum rent recoverable. No new restricted contracts can be created on or after January 15, 1989.

(5) The Protection from Eviction Act 1977, as amended by the Housing Act 1988, provides that if any person with intent to cause the residential occupier of any premises to give up the occupation thereof does any act calculated to interfere with the peace or comfort of the residential occupier or members of the household, that person shall be guilty of an offence. A further provision prevents a landlord enforcing a right to possession against a tenant who is not protected by any security of tenure legislation without a court order, and there are special rules in such cases relating to agricultural employees.

(6) A notice to quit any dwelling-house must be given at least four weeks before it is to take effect, and must be in writing and in the prescribed statutory form.

(7) Part I of the Landlord and Tenant Act 1954 applies to most tenancies of houses for over twenty-one years at a ground rent. Where it applies, the contractual tenancy is continued until brought to an end in the manner prescribed by the Act, and in effect the landlord can only get possession on limited grounds.

Further, under the Leasehold Reform Act 1967, tenants of houses under leases for over twenty-one years at a rent less than two-thirds of the rateable value of the house are in most cases given a right to purchase the freehold or to take an extended lease for a term of fifty years, provided the tenant at the time when he/she seeks to exercise the right has been occupying the house as his/her residence for the last three years or for periods amounting to three years in the last ten years.

(8) Full Rent Act or Housing Act protection is available only if a house is let on a tenancy. If the occupier of a house has a mere licence to occupy, he/she does not have protection. Further, even if he/she has a tenancy, he/she will not be protected if the rent payable is less than two-thirds of the rateable value of the house. For these reasons, many occupants of houses owned by farmers and occupied by farm workers did not enjoy full security of tenure. The Rent (Agriculture) Act 1976 contains detailed provisions conferring security of tenure on certain agricultural workers housed by their employers and on their successors on death.

(9) Under the Landlord and Tenant Act 1985 (which does not extend to Scotland), in a lease of a dwelling-house granted for a term of less than seven years, there is implied a covenant by the landlord (a) to keep in repair the structure and exterior of the house and (b) to keep in repair and proper working order the installations in the house for the supply of water, gas and electricity, for sanitation, and for space heating or heating water.

(10) The Housing Act 1985 gives security of tenure to many tenants of local authorities and certain other bodies. Further, and subject to certain conditions, such tenants may have the right to purchase their houses or to take a long lease of their flats.

(11) Tenants of flats and other dwellings are given a number of special rights by the Landlord and Tenant Act 1987, as amended by the Housing Act 1988.

SCOTLAND

A lease is a contract, the relationship of the parties being governed by the terms thereof. As is also the case in England, legislation has played an important part in regulating that relationship. Thus, what at common law was an agreement binding only the parties to the deed, becomes in virtue of the Leases Act 1449, a contract binding the landlord's successors, as purchasers or creditors, provided the following four conditions are observed: (a) the lease, if for more than one year, must be in writing; (b) there must be a rent; (c) there must be a term of expiry; and (d) the tenant must have entered into possession.

It would be impracticable to enter here upon a general discussion of this branch of the law. A few important provisions include:

(1) The Agricultural Holdings (Scotland) Act 1949 (amended by the Agriculture Act 1958), is a consolidating Act applicable to Scotland. It contains provisions similar to those in the English Act, alluded to in the preceding section.

The Small Landholders Act 1911 provided for the setting up of the Land Court, which has jurisdiction over a large proportion of agricultural and pastoral land in Scotland.

(2) In Scotland business premises are not controlled by statute to so great an extent as in England, but the Tenancy of Shops (Scotland) Act 1949 gives a measure of security to tenants of shops. This Act enables the tenant of a shop who is threatened with eviction to apply to the Sheriff for a renewal of the tenancy. If the landlord has offered to sell the subjects to the tenant at an agreed price the application for a renewal of the tenancy may be dismissed. Reference should be made to Section 1 (3) of the 1949 Act for particulars of other circumstances under which the Sheriff has a discretion to dismiss an application. The Act extends to premises held by the Crown or Government departments, either as landlord or tenant.

(3) The Housing (Scotland) Act 1987 consolidates previous legislation in regard to the extensive powers and duties to local authorities in relation to housing. Included therein is the general provision regarding the rights of public sector tenants to purchase the houses which they occupy and the restrictions regarding this right in certain circumstances where the house has been designed or adapted for occupation by the elderly. This Act also makes provision for secure tenancies for public sector tenants.

(4) The Housing (Scotland) Act 1988 creates, with certain exceptions, two new forms of tenancy for tenancies created after January 2, 1989: assured tenancies and short assured tenancies. The assured tenancy significantly reduces the concept of security of tenure and abolishes any method of regulating rent other than market forces. The short assured tenancy lasts for at least six months and if properly constituted will allow the landlord to recover possession on its expiry. Provision is made for a tenant to apply to the Rent Assessment Committee to fix a rent based on the rent a landlord might reasonably expect for a short assured tenancy of the property.

(5) For most tenancies created before January 2, 1989, the Rent (Scotland) Act 1984 will continue to apply. It defines regulated tenancies, which may be either furnished or unfurnished, and lays down the system by which a landlord or tenant may obtain from the Rent Office registration of a fair rent. The Act gives to tenants of either furnished or unfurnished lets a substantial degree of security of tenure. There are, however, certain exceptions: they do not apply to tenancies where the interest belongs to the

Crown or to a Government department or to a local authority, a development corporation of a new town or a housing corporation. There must be a true tenancy for the Act to apply. It does not apply to licencees such as lodgers or persons allowed to occupy houses on a grace and favour basis or to services occupiers.

The Act regulates the short tenancy, a category of let under which, on compliance with certain conditions, the landlord can be assured of recovering possession on the expiry of the stipulated period of let. The Act defines the circumstances under which generally a landlord may apply for increased rent as a consequence of having carried out improvements to his property and also lays down the system of phasing such rent increases. On the death of a statutory successor to a tenancy, the tenancy may pass for a second time to a member of the family or a relative who has been in residence of the house for a period of at least six months. The Act further lays down the duties and functions of Rent Officers and Rent Assessment Committees with regard to unfurnished accommodation and of rent tribunals for furnished accommodation.

The Secretary of State for Scotland is given power in the 1988 Act to repeal or amend those sections of the 1984 Act relating to the phasing of rent increases. The other major features of the 1988 Act are to establish Scottish Homes, and to permit public sector properties to be transferred to Scottish Homes or a landlord approved by Scottish Homes.

LEGAL AID

The Legal Aid Act 1988 (as amended) is designed to make legal aid and advice more readily available for persons of small and moderate means. The main structure of the service is contained in the Act itself and the Regulations made thereunder, administered by the Legal Aid Board.

Civil Proceedings

Legal aid is available for proceedings (including matrimonial causes) in the House of Lords, Court of Appeal, High Court, County Courts, Lands Tribunal, Restrictive Practices Court, before the Commons Commissioners, and civil proceedings in magistrates' courts. In any event, an application for legal aid will not be approved if it appears that the applicant would gain only a trivial advantage from the proceedings. Further, proceedings wholly or partly in respect of defamation are excepted from the scheme, as are also relator actions and election petitions. It is generally not available for obtaining the decree in undefended divorce and judicial separation, although the Legal Advice and Assistance Scheme (see below) is, and legal aid is still available to deal with property, custody disputes, etc., arising in the suit.

Where a person is concerned in proceedings only in a representative, fiduciary or official capacity, his/her personal resources are not to be taken into account in considering eligibility for legal aid. Apart from this, eligibility in civil proceedings depends upon an applicant's disposable income and disposable capital. The figures change frequently; particulars can be obtained from a solicitor, the Law Society or a Citizens' Advice Bureau. Disposable income is calculated by making deductions from gross income in respect of certain matters such as dependants, interest on loans, income tax, rates, rent and other matters for which the applicant must or reasonably may provide. Disposable capital is calculated by excluding from gross capital part of the value of the house in which the applicant resides, of furniture and household possessions; allowances are made in respect of dependants. Except in cases where the spouses are living apart, or have a contrary interest, any resources of a person's wife or husband are to be treated as that person's resources. These figures will be assessed by the Department of Social Security and will be referred to the Legal Aid Board, who will determine whether reasonable grounds exist for the grant of a civil aid certificate. Appeal from refusal of a certificate lies to an area committee. A person resident in England or Wales desiring legal aid should apply for a certificate to the appropriate area director for the area in which he or she resides; if resident elsewhere application should be made to an area director in London. If a certificate is granted, the applicant may select his/her solicitor, and, if necessary, counsel from a panel. The costs of the assisted person's solicitor and counsel will be paid out of the legal aid fund. When, however, damages or property are recovered or preserved by the assisted person, the legal aid fund has a charge over them in respect of these costs less any contribution towards costs recovered from the unsuccessful party. In matrimonial cases, maintenance is exempt, as is the first £2,500 of any property settlement. The court may order that the costs of a successful unassisted party shall be paid out of the legal aid fund.

In an urgent case, e.g. domestic violence or to restrain the kidnapping abroad of a child, legal aid may be granted without the applicant's means being fully investigated beforehand. If on a full examination later he/she is found financially ineligible he/she is liable to pay all the costs incurred on his/her behalf.

Legal Advice and Assistance

The scheme is governed by the Legal Aid Act 1988.

Under the Legal Advice and Assistance Scheme a client may obtain such advice or assistance as is normally provided by a solicitor. If necessary the advice of a barrister may be obtained, but, with the exception of domestic proceedings in a magistrates' court and certain other proceedings (*see* below), the scheme does not extend to taking any step in any proceedings before any court or tribunal. Where legal aid is available for civil proceedings (*see* above) or in criminal cases (*see* below) the scheme covers work done in making application for such legal aid.

A person (other than one receiving advice and assistance at a police station or from a duty solicitor) is eligible for advice or assistance under the scheme provided his/her disposable capital and his/her disposable income do not exceed limits in force from time to time or if he/she is eligible for Income Support or Family Credit. In calculating disposable income, income tax and National Insurance contributions are deducted. For a married man or person with children or other dependants further deductions will be made from both income and capital. It is intended that the financial limits shall approximate to those applying for legal aid in civil proceedings (*see* above). Except when they are separated or have conflicting interests the means of husband and wife or cohabiting couple will be aggregated for the purpose of determining financial eligibility. As in the case of legal aid, depending on his/her means, a person may be called upon to pay a contribution towards the costs of work done for him/her. Particulars may be obtained from a solicitor, the Law Society or a Citizens' Advice Bureau.

A solicitor cannot do more than two hours' work, or three hours' in the case of divorce, etc., without leave of the area legal aid committee. The solicitor's costs are paid out of the client's contribution and any monies recovered in respect of costs or damages from another party (although this may be waived by leave

of the area committee in cases of hardship) and the balance will be paid by the legal aid fund.

The Act also extends the scheme to cover the costs of a solicitor who is present within the precincts of a magistrates' court or county court and is requested by the court to advise or represent a person who is in need of help.

In April 1980 the scheme was enlarged to cover the cost of representation in domestic proceedings in a magistrates' court. It has since been extended to cover the representation of patients before Mental Health Review Tribunals. Subject to financial eligibility limits, application is made to the area or local committee for 'approval of assistance by way of representation' which will replace legal aid for such proceedings. However, the two-hour limit referred to above will not apply. An applicant who is outside the financial limits but eligible for legal aid will still have to apply for a legal aid certificate as before. Free advice and assistance, and assistance by way of representation from a duty solicitor, is also available in limited circumstances to persons appearing before a magistrates' court charged with a criminal offence.

In January 1986 the scheme was further extended to provide free advice and assistance to all suspects detained at a police station, whether arrested or merely helping police with their enquiries, and free representation for all arrested persons who are the subject of an application for a warrant of further detention under the Police and Criminal Evidence Act 1984. Such persons may instruct a solicitor of their choice or take advantage of the duty solicitor scheme which has now been extended to cover police stations.

Criminal Proceedings

The Legal Aid Act 1988 provides for legal aid in criminal proceedings, and for children and parents in care proceedings and related applications under the Children and Young Persons Act 1969. A criminal court (e.g. magistrates' court, Crown Court) has power to order legal aid to be granted where it appears desirable to do so in the interests of justice. The court shall make an order in certain cases, e.g. where a person is committed for trial on a charge of murder. However, the court may not make an order unless it appears to the court that the person's disposable income and capital are such that he/she requires assistance in meeting the costs of the particular proceedings in question. Application should be made to the appropriate court where proceedings are to take place.

An applicant shall be required to make a contribution towards the costs of his/her case if his/her disposable income and capital exceed certain prescribed limits. Persons in receipt of Income Support are automatically exempt. In order to ascertain the amount of this contribution an applicant will have to produce written evidence of his/her means. Investigation of means will be carried out by the court. Any person who falls into arrears with the payment of contribution is liable to have the order revoked.

Any practising barrister or solicitor may act for a legally aided person in criminal proceedings unless excluded by reason of misconduct. In general, where legal aid is given it will normally include representation by both counsel and solicitor. However, in connection with magistrates' courts, representation will be by solicitor alone unless the offence is a serious offence.

Where any doubt arises about the grant of a legal aid order that doubt is to be resolved in favour of the applicant. The court also has power to amend or revoke a legal aid order. Legal aid may also be granted in connection with appellate proceedings, e.g. on appeal to the Criminal Division of the Court of Appeal under the Criminal Appeal Act 1968.

SCOTLAND

Legal aid in Scotland is now governed by the Legal Aid (Scotland) Act 1986 and the Regulations made thereunder. This Act established the Scottish Legal Aid Board which has the general function of securing that legal aid and legal advice and assistance are available in accordance with the Act, and of administering the Scottish Legal Aid Fund.

Civil Proceedings

Civil legal aid is available in relation to civil proceedings in the House of Lords in appeals from the Court of Session, in the Court of Session, the Lands Valuation Appeal Court, the Scottish Land Court, the Sheriff Court, the Lands Tribunal for Scotland, the Employment Appeals Tribunal and to the European Court of Human Rights. Civil legal aid is granted if on application to the Board, the Board is satisfied that there is *probabilis causa litigandi* and it is reasonable in the particular circumstances of the case that legal aid should be awarded. As in England eligibility and any contribution required from an applicant is dependent on their disposable income and disposable capital. Information on current financial limits can be obtained from the Scottish Legal Aid Board, a solicitor, or a Citizens' Advice Bureau.

A person believing himself to be eligible may instruct any solicitor of his/her own choice. If a court action is not immediately contemplated application will be made for legal advice and assistance which operates in a similar manner to the legal advice and assistance scheme in England. If proceedings are contemplated then a formal application for civil legal aid will be made and there are special provisions for emergency applications in appropriate circumstances.

If proceedings are decided against a person in receipt of legal aid the court shall determine a reasonable sum in the circumstances as an appropriate award of expenses to be made against the applicant. The court may only make an award out of the fund if proceedings were instituted by the legally assisted person and the court is satisfied that the resisting party would suffer severe financial hardship unless the order is made, and the court is satisfied that in all the circumstances it is just and equitable that an award be made. If monies are recovered by a legally assisted person these fall to be paid to the Scottish Legal Aid Board who will then determine the appropriate level of contribution from the sums received which should be made to the expenses of their litigation.

Criminal Proceedings

Legal aid in criminal causes is also administered under the Legal Aid (Scotland) Act 1986. The procedure for application for criminal legal aid is dependent on the circumstances of each case. In serious cases heard before a jury under solemn procedure it is for the court to decide whether to grant legal aid. Applications for legal aid must normally be made on the prescribed forms to the clerk of the court in question and an applicant is required to provide therein particulars of the merits of his/her case and his/her financial circumstances. In summary criminal causes, however, the procedure is dependent on whether the applicant is in custody; if so he/she is entitled to automatic free legal aid from the duty solicitor. If the applicant is not in custody and wishes to plead guilty he/she is ineligible for full legal aid but may be entitled to criminal legal advice and assistance and in some circumstances may qualify for assistance by way of representation which will enable his/her solicitor to appear and make a plea in mitigation on his/her behalf. If he is not in custody and wishes to plead not guilty he can apply to the Scottish Legal Aid Board for criminal legal aid on the prescribed form not later than fourteen days after the first court appearance at which he made the plea and legal aid shall only be granted if the Board is satisfied that the accused cannot meet the expenses of the case without undue hardship and that it is in the interest of justice as defined by the 1986 Act.

TOWN AND COUNTRY PLANNING

The Town and Country Planning Act 1990 (consolidating earlier Acts) contains far-reaching provisions affecting the liberty of an owner of land to develop and use it as he will. A person has generally to get planning permission from the local planning authority before carrying out any development on his land.

Development is deemed to be:—

(a) Carrying out of building, engineering, mining or other operations.

(b) Making a material change in use.

It is expressly provided that if one dwelling-house is converted into two or more dwelling-houses, this involves a material change in use.

It is not deemed to be 'development' if:—

(a) Maintaining, improving or altering the interior of a building, provided there is no material change to the exterior, with the exception that any expansion, or works begun for the expansion, of a building below ground level constitutes development.

(b) Changing the use of property within the curtilage of a dwelling-house for a purpose incidental to the use of the dwelling-house as such. (It will, however, be development if building operations are carried out.)

Application can be made to the local planning authority to determine whether or not an operation or change of use constitutes development.

Planning Permission

Application for planning permission is not always necessary, as the Secretary of State may make Development Orders giving general permission for a specified type of development, e.g. enlargement of a dwelling-house (including erection of a garage), so long as the cubic content of the original dwelling (external measurement) is not exceeded by more than 70 cubic metres or 15 per cent, whichever is greater, subject to a maximum of 115 cubic metres. However, in the case of a terraced house, the limitation is 50 cubic metres or 10 per cent, whichever is the greater, subject to the maximum of 115 cubic metres.

Appeal against refusal of permission lies to the Secretary of State and from his decision, in limited circumstances, to the High Court. If the result of the appeal is unsatisfactory, an applicant may in certain circumstances require the local authority to purchase the land.

SCOTLAND

The Town and Country Planning (Scotland) Act 1972 consolidates the statute law relating to town and country planning in Scotland.

The uses of buildings are classified by the Town

and Country Planning (Use Classes) (Scotland) Order 1988. Changes in use prior to December 31, 1984 are immune from enforcement proceedings.

Development normally requires to be commenced within five years from the date of granting permission.

The 1972 Act contains provisions for an appeal to the Secretary of State against the refusal of planning permission. The decision of the Secretary of State is final.

Sections 87 and 92 of the Local Government, Planning and Land Act 1980 contain important provisions on planning applications and, unlike certain parts of this Act, extend to Scotland.

VOTERS' QUALIFICATIONS

The franchise is governed by the Representation of the People Acts 1983 and 1985. Those entitled to vote as electors at a parliamentary election in any constituency are all persons resident there on the qualifying date who, at that date and on the date of the poll are Commonwealth citizens or citizens of the Republic of Ireland and not subject to any legal incapacity to vote and who on the date of the poll are at least 18 years of age. However, a person is not entitled to vote at a parliamentary election in any constituency in Northern Ireland unless he/she was resident in Northern Ireland during the whole of the period of three months ending on the qualifying date for that election. Also, no person can use his/her vote unless he/she is on the register of electors kept for the constituency. A person who is of voting age on the date of the poll at a parliamentary or local government election is entitled to vote, whether or not he/she was of voting age on the qualifying date. Accordingly, a qualified person will be entitled to be registered in a register of parliamentary electors or a register of local government electors if he/she will attain voting age within twelve months from the date on which the register is required to be published. Subject to certain conditions, the 1985 Act extends the franchise to British citizens overseas.

The register is prepared by the Registration Officer in each constituency in Great Britain. It is the registration officer's duty to have a house-to-house or other official inquiry made as to the persons entitled to be registered and to publish preliminary electors lists showing the persons appearing to him/her to be entitled to be registered. Any person whose name is omitted may claim registration, and any person on the list may object to the inclusion therein of other persons' names; the Registration Officer determines the claims and objections.

Voters at a parliamentary or local government election must generally vote in person at the allotted polling station, except for those entitled to vote by post or at any polling station, and those for whom proxies have been appointed. Certain people can apply to be treated as absent voters at a parliamentary election and thus able to vote by post—among these are registered service voters, those unable by reason of blindness or other physical incapacity to go in person to the polling station, and those unable to go in person from their qualifying address to the polling station without making a journey by air or sea.

Unless entitled to vote by post, a person registered as a service voter may vote by proxy at a parliamentary or local government election. A proxy may also be appointed by a registered elector, where the registration officer is satisfied that the applicant's circumstances on the date of the poll are likely to be such that he cannot reasonably be expected to vote in person at the polling station allotted to him. The appointment of a person to vote as proxy at parliamentary elections has effect also for the purposes of local government elections.

THE PROBATION SERVICE

England and Wales

The Probation Service is employed in each area (56 in total) by an independent committee of justices and it provides a professional social work agency in the courts, with responsibility for a wide range of duties which include: (a) a social enquiry service for the criminal courts; (b) provision of a range of non-custodial measures involving the supervision of offenders in the community; (c) supervisory aftercare for offenders released from custody, together with social work in penal establishments and help for the families of those serving sentences; (d) an enquiry, conciliation and supervision service in the divorce and domestic courts; (e) support for and promotion of preventive and containment measures in the community designed to reduce the level of crime and domestic breakdown. It is a direct grant service funded 80 per cent from the Home Office and 20 per cent from the relevant local authority.

Its national representative bodies are:

(i) The Central Council of Probation Committees, 38 Belgrave Square, London SW1X 8NT (Tel: 071–245 9364). *Secretary*, I. Miles;

(ii) The Association of Chief Officers of Probation, 20–30 Lawefield Lane, Wakefield WF2 8SP (Tel: 0924–361156). *Secretary*, W. R. Weston; and

(iii) The National Association of Probation Officers, 3–4 Chivalry Road, Battersea, London SW11 1HT (Tel: 071–223 4887). *Gen. Secretary*, W. Beaumont.

Scotland

The probationary service in Scotland is a statutory duty of local authorities under s. 27 of the Social Work (Scotland) Act 1968. Social workers have to supervise and provide advice, guidance and assistance to those persons living in their area who are subject to a court's supervision order. This is done by social workers as part of their normal duties and not by a separate probationary staff.

NATIONAL INSURANCE AND RELATED CASH BENEFITS

The State insurance and assistance schemes, comprising schemes of national insurance and industrial injuries insurance, national assistance, and non-contributory old age pensions came into force from July 5, 1948. The Ministry of Social Security Act, 1966, replaced national assistance and non-contributory old age pensions with a scheme of non-contributory benefits, termed supplementary allowances and pensions, and subsequent measures relating to social security provision in Great Britain, were consolidated by the Social Security Act, 1975; the Social Security (Consequential Provisions) Act, 1975; and the Industrial Injuries and Diseases (Old Cases) Act, 1975. Corresponding measures were passed for Northern Ireland. The Social Security Pensions Act, 1975, introduced a new State pensions scheme, which came into force on April 6, 1978, and the graduated pension scheme 1961–1975 has been wound up, existing rights being preserved. The Pensioners' Payments and Social Security Act, 1979, provided for a £10 bonus for pensioners in 1979 and for the payment of a bonus in succeeding years at levels then to be determined. The Child Benefit Act, 1975, replaced family allowances (introduced 1946) with child benefit and one parent benefit.

Some of the above legislation has been superseded by the provisions of the Social Security Act, 1986, passed in July 1986 and introduced at various dates since.

NATIONAL INSURANCE SCHEME

The National Insurance scheme operates under the Social Security Acts, 1975 to 1988, and orders and regulations made thereunder. The scheme is financed by contributions payable by earners, employers and others (such as non-employed persons, paying voluntary contributions). It provides the funds required for paying benefits payable under the Social Security Acts out of the National Insurance Fund and not out of other public money; for the making of payments towards the cost of the National Health Service and into the Redundancy and Maternity Pay Funds; and for paying benefit under the Industrial Injuries and Diseases (Old Cases) Act, 1975. The yearly Treasury supplement to the National Insurance Fund was abolished in April 1989.

CONTRIBUTIONS

Contributions are of four classes:

Class 1 contributions are earnings-related, based on a percentage of the employee's earnings.

(a) *primary Class 1* contributions are payable by employed earners and office-holders over age 16 with gross earnings at or above the lower earnings limit of £46·00 per week. For those with gross earnings at or above this level, contributions are payable on *all* earnings up to an upper limit of £350 per week. 'Gross earnings' include overtime pay, commission, bonus, etc., without deduction of any superannuation contributions.

Women who marry for the first time no longer have a right to elect not to pay the full contribution rate. Married women and widows who before May 12, 1977, elected not to pay contributions at the full rate retain the right to pay a reduced rate over the same earnings range, which covers industrial injuries benefits and a contribution to the National Health Service. They lose this right if, after April 5, 1978, there are two consecutive tax years in which they have no earnings on which primary Class 1 contributions are payable and in which they have not been at any time self-employed earners. No primary contributions are due on earnings paid for a period on or after the employee's pension age, even when retirement is deferred.

(b) *secondary Class 1* contributions are payable by employers of employed earners, and by the appropriate authorities in the case of office-holders. On Oct. 6, 1985, the upper earnings limit for employers' contributions was abolished and secondary contributions are payable on *all* the employee's earnings if they reach or exceed £46·00 per week.

Primary contributions are deducted from earnings by the employer, and are paid, together with the employer's contributions, to the Inland Revenue along with income tax collected under the PAYE system. On Oct. 6, 1985 several lower percentage rates of contribution for lower paid employees and their employers were introduced.

Class 2 contributions are flat-rate, paid weekly by self-employed earners over age 16. Those with earnings below £2,350 a year for the tax year 1989–90 can apply for exception from liability to pay Class 2 contributions. People who while self-employed are excepted from liability to pay contributions on the grounds of small earnings may pay either Class 2 or Class 3 contributions voluntarily. Self-employed earners (whether or not they pay Class 2 contributions) may also be liable to pay Class 4 contributions based on profits or gains within certain limits. There are special rules for those who are concurrently employed and self-employed. Married women and widows can no longer choose not to pay Class 2 contributions. Those who elected not to pay Class 2 contributions before May 12, 1977, retain the right until there is a period of two consecutive tax years after April 5, 1978 in which they were not at any time either self-employed earners or had earnings on which primary Class 1 contributions were payable.

Class 2 contributions may be paid by direct debit through a bank or National Giro account or by stamping a contribution card.

Class 3 contributions are voluntary flat-rate contributions payable by persons over school-leaving age who would otherwise be unable to qualify for retirement pension and certain other benefits because they have an insufficient record of Class 1 or Class 2 contributions. Married women and widows who on or before May 11, 1977, elected not to pay Class 1 (full rate) or Class 2 contributions cannot pay Class 3 contributions while they retain this right.

Payment may be made by stamping a contribution card or by direct debit through a bank Giro account.

Class 4 contributions are payable by self-employed earners, whether or not they pay Class 2 contributions, on annual profits or gains from a trade, profession or vocation chargeable to income tax under Schedule D, where these fall between £5,450 and £18,200 a year. The maximum Class 4 contribution, payable on profits or gains of £18,200 or more, is £803·25.

Class 4 contributions are generally assessed and collected by the Inland Revenue along with Schedule D income tax. Self-employed persons under 16, or who at the beginning of a tax year are over pension age even when retirement is deferred, are not liable to pay Class 4 contributions. There are special rules for people who have more than one job, or who pay Class 1 contributions on earnings which are chargeable to income tax under Schedule D.

Regulations state the cases in which earners may be excepted from liability to pay contributions, and the conditions upon which contributions are credited to persons who are excepted. Leaflet NI 208 is obtainable from local social security offices.

The Secretary of State for Social Services is empowered by the Social Security Acts to alter certain rates of contributions by order approved by both Houses of Parliament, and is required by the same enactments to make annual reviews of the general level of earnings in order to determine whether such an order should be made.

For the period April 6, 1989 to Oct. 4, 1989 the earnings brackets determining Class 1 contributions were:

	Weekly earnings £
a	0 — 43·00
b	43·00— 74·99
c	75·00—114·99
d	115·00—164·99
e	165·00—325·00
f	over 325·00

Contribution rates for the period April 6, 1989 to Oct. 4, 1989 were:

Class 1 contributions—not contracted out

Earnings bracket	Percentage of reckonable income		
	Employee's rate standard reduced		Employer's rate
a	0	0	0
b	5	3·85	5
c	7	3·85	7
d	9	3·85	9
e	9	3·85	10·45
f	9*	3·85*	10·45

* to a maximum of £325 per week.

Class 1 contributions—contracted out
(see also p. 1046)

Employee's rates

Earnings bracket	On first £43·00		On earnings from £43·00–£325·00	
	standard	reduced	standard	reduced
a	0	0	0	0
b	5	3·85	3·00	3·85
c	7	3·85	5·00	3·85
d, e, f	9	3·85	7·00	3·85

Employer's rates

Earnings bracket	On first £43·00	On earnings from £43·00–£325·00	On any earnings over £325·00
a	0	0	0
b	5	1·2	0
c	7	3·2	0
d	9	5·2	0
e	10·45	6·65	0
f	10·45	6·65	10·45

	Weekly flat rate
Class 2 contributions	£4·25
Class 3 contributions	£4·15

	Percentage of profits or gains
Class 4 contributions	6·3

From Oct. 5, 1989 there was a change in the assessment of National Insurance contributions for employees. Earnings brackets for employees' contributions were abolished and replaced by a new lower contribution rate on earnings up to and including the lower earnings limit and at a main percentage rate on earnings between the lower earnings limit up to and including the employees' upper earnings limit.

Where earnings were paid or were due to be paid before Oct. 5, 1989, employees' contributions continued to be paid at 5, 7, and 9 per cent (plus the

corresponding lower contracted out rates if appropriate) depending on the earnings bracket.

Where earnings were paid or were due to be paid on or after Oct. 5, 1989, employees' contributions were paid at 2 per cent of earnings at the lower earnings limit (£46·00 a week or equivalent) plus 9 per cent (not contracted out) or 7 per cent (contracted out) of earnings between the lower earnings limit up to and including the employees' upper earnings limit (£350·00 a week or equivalent). Employees contributing at the reduced rate continue to pay contributions at 3·85 per cent on all earnings up to and including the employees' upper earnings limit.

Employees earning less than the lower earnings limit continue not to pay any contributions.

There was no change in the assessment of employers' contributions.

THE STATE EARNINGS RELATED PENSION SCHEME (SERPS)

The Social Security Pensions Act, 1975, which came into force in April, 1978, aims to reduce reliance upon means-tested benefit in old age, in widowhood and in chronic ill-health by providing better pensions; to ensure that occupational pension schemes which are contracted out of part of the State scheme fulfil the conditions of a good scheme; that pensions are adequately protected against inflation; and that in both the State and occupational schemes men and women are treated equally. Retirement, widow's and invalidity pensions under the new scheme started to be paid in April 1979. Since April 6, 1979, flat-rate retirement and other State pensions have been augmented for employed earners by additional pensions related to earnings, but it will be twenty years before these additional pensions become payable at the full rate.

Under the scheme, retirement, invalidity and widow's pensions for employees are related to the earnings on which national insurance contributions have been paid. For employees of either sex with a complete insurance record the scheme provides a category A retirement pension in two parts, a basic and an additional pension. The basic pension corresponds to the old personal flat-rate national insurance pension. The additional pension is 1·25 per cent of average earnings between the lower weekly earnings limit for Class 1 contribution liability and the upper earnings limit for each year of such earnings under the scheme, and will thus build up to 25 per cent in twenty years.

The additional pension will be calculated in a different way for individuals who reach pension age after April 6, 1999. The changes are to be phased in over 10 years. From 2010 a lifetime's earnings will be included in the calculation and for years from 1988–89 onwards the accrual rate on these surplus earnings will be 20 per cent. The accrual rate on surplus earnings for the years from 1978–79 to 1987–88 will remain at 25 per cent.

Actual earnings are to be revalued in terms of the earnings level current in the last complete tax year before pension age (or death or incapacity). Both components of pensions in payment will be uprated annually in line with the movement of prices. Graduated retirement pensions in payment, and rights to such pensions earned by people who are still working, will be brought into the annual review of benefits.

Self-employed persons pay contributions towards the basic pension. The non-employed and employees with earnings below the lower limit may contribute voluntarily for basic pension. Although no primary Class 1 contributions or Class 2 or Class 4 contributions are payable by persons who work beyond pension age (65 for men, 60 for women), the employer's liability for secondary Class 1 contributions continues if earnings are at or above the lower earnings limit. Class 4 contributions are still payable up to the end of the tax year during which pension age is reached.

Widows will get the whole of any additional pensions earned by their husbands with their widowed mother's allowances or widow's pensions; and can add to the retirement pensions earned by their own contributions any additional pensions earned by their husbands up to the maximum payable on one person's contributions. Men whose wives die when they are both over pension age can add together their own and their wives' pension rights in the same way as widows. Among the steps taken to give women equal treatment in benefit provision, the State scheme permits years of home responsibilities to reduce the number of qualifying years (since 1978) needed for retirement pension, widowed mother's allowance and widow's pension; and the 'half-test' by which a married woman who married before age 55 could not qualify for a Category A retirement pension unless she had contributed on earnings at the basic level in at least half the years between marriage and pension age has been abolished with effect from Dec. 22, 1984. The range of short-term social security benefits and industrial injury benefits under the Social Security Act, 1975, continues with only minor changes.

Contracted-Out and Personal Pension Schemes

Members of occupational pension schemes which meet the standards laid down in the Social Security Pensions Act, 1975, can be contracted-out of the earnings related part of the state scheme relating to retirement and widows' benefits. Regulations made under the Act require employers to consult employees and their organizations and inform them of their intention to contract out. (Leaflets relating to pensions and guidance for employers about contracting-out are available from local social security offices.) The Act also contains provisions ensuring equal access to membership of schemes for men and women.

Until April 6, 1988, occupational pension schemes could only contract out if they promised a pension that was related to earnings. These are known as contracted-out salary related schemes. They must provide a pension that is not less than the guaranteed minimum pension (GMP), which is broadly equivalent to the state earnings related pension. However, new options have been introduced by the Social Security Act, 1986. Since April 6, 1988, occupational pension schemes which promise a minimum level of contributions have also been able to contract out. These are known as contracted-out money purchase schemes. They provide a pension based on the value of the fund built up in the scheme.

In addition, since July 1988 employees whose employers do not provide a pension scheme have been able to start their own personal pension instead of staying in the state earnings related pension scheme. Since April 6, 1988, this choice has been open to all employees even if their employer does have a pension scheme. A personal pension, like a contracted-out money purchase scheme, provides a pension based on the value of the fund built up in the scheme.

The decision on whether or not an occupational pension scheme may become contracted-out lies with the Occupational Pension Board, an independent statutory body who have a general responsibility for supervising contracting-out. They also consider and approve personal pension schemes which can be used instead of state additional pension.

The State earnings related pension payable to a member of a contracted-out salary related scheme, or his widow, will be reduced by the amount of GMP payable (which in the case of a widow must be at least half of the late husband's GMP entitlement). Members of contracted-out money purchase schemes and personal pension schemes, or their widows, have no GMP entitlement as such. But the state earnings related pension payable will be reduced by an amount equivalent to a GMP (or widow's GMP).

Since April 6, 1988 contracted-out salary related schemes must also provide a widower's GMP which must be at least half of the late wife's GMP entitlement built up from April 6, 1988. (A scheme need not provide entitlement to a GMP for widowers of earners dying before April 1989.) Contracted-out money purchase schemes and personal pension schemes must provide half-rate widower's benefit.

In contracted-out schemes, both the employee and the employer pay the full ordinary rate of contribution on the first £43·00 (1989–90 figure) of earnings but earnings above that amount attract a lower rate of contribution from the employee, and from the employer where the employee's earnings are under £350·00; where the employee's earnings exceed this amount, the full ordinary rate of contribution is payable only by the employer and the employee has no liability for contributions on these earnings (*see also* p. 1045).

An employee who chooses a personal pension in place of SERPS or their employer's pension scheme must pay National Insurance contributions at the full ordinary rate (the employer's share must also be paid at the same rate). The DSS pays the difference between the lower contracted-out rate and the full ordinary rate directly into the personal pension scheme.

FINANCE

The National Insurance Fund receives all social security contributions (less only the National Health Service and Redundancy Fund and Maternity Pay Fund allocations and the National Insurance Surcharge for taxation purposes) together with the Consolidated Fund supplement; and it bears the cost of all contributory benefits provided by the Social Security Acts and the cost of administration.

Approximate receipts and payments of the National Insurance Fund for the year ended March 31, 1988, were as follows:

Receipts	£'000
Balance, April 1, 1987................	5,706,966
Contributions under the Social Security Acts (net of SSP)	24,564,489
Consolidated Fund Supplement	2,135,000
Income from Investments	596,395
Other receipts	39,847
	33,042,697

Payments	£'000	£'000
Benefit:—		
Unemployment benefit ..	1,467,928	
Sickness benefit	193,001	
Invalidity benefit	2,968,405	
Maternity allowance ...	50,746	
Widow's benefit	839,250	
Guardian's allowance and child's special allowance	1,434	
Retirement pension	18,648,391	
Death grant	2,608	

Payments	£'000	£'000
Industrial injuries benefits	—	
Disablement benefits....	453,386	
Death benefit	56,492	
Other industrial injury benefits	4,224	
Pensioners' lump sum payments	107,000	
Payments in lieu of benefit forgone	—	
		24,792,865
Transfers to Northern Ireland		155,000
Administration		802,000
Other payments		4,746
Write offs	—	
Balance, March 31, 1988		7,287,620
		33,042,697

NOTE.—There have been changes to the National Insurance Fund. Payments will no longer be paid into surcharges or the Maternity Pay Fund. However, residual payments are still being paid in respect of late paid contributions for premium years.

BENEFITS

The benefits payable under the Social Security Acts are as follows:

Contributory Benefits:

> Unemployment benefit.
> Sickness benefit.
> Invalidity pension and allowance.
> Maternity allowance.
> Widow's benefit, comprising widow's payment, widowed mother's allowance and widow's pension.
> Retirement pensions, categories A and B.

Non-contributory Benefits:

> Child benefit.
> One parent benefit.
> Guardian's allowance.
> Invalid care allowance.
> Attendance allowance.
> Severe disablement allowance.
> Mobility allowance.
> Retirement pensions, categories C and D.
> Income Support.
> Family Credit.
> Social Fund.

Benefits for Industrial Injuries, Disablement and Death.

Leaflets relating to the various benefits are obtainable from local social security offices.

The Social Security Acts empower the Secretary of State to increase certain rates of benefit by order approved by both Houses of Parliament, and require him to increase certain rates by such an order if an annual review shows that they have not retained their value in relation to the general level of prices obtaining in Great Britain as measured by the Retail Price Index.

The latest order providing for increases in benefit rates took effect from the week commencing April 9, 1990. It did not apply to all benefits.

CONTRIBUTORY BENEFITS

Entitlement to contributory benefits depends on contribution conditions being satisfied either by the claimant or by some other person (depending on the kind of benefit). The class or classes of contribution which for this purpose are relevant to each benefit are as follows:

Short-term benefits

Unemployment benefit	Class 1
Sickness benefit	Class 1 or 2
Maternity allowance	Class 1 or 2
Widow's payment	Class 1, 2 or 3

Other benefits

Widowed mother's allowance	
Widow's pension	
Category A retirement pension	Class 1, 2 or 3
Category B retirement pension	
Invalidity benefit	Class 1 or 2

The system of contribution conditions relates to yearly levels of earnings on which contributions have been paid. The contribution conditions for different benefits are set out in summary form in leaflets available at local social security offices.

Unemployment Benefit

Benefit is payable in a period of interruption of employment for up to 312 days (a year, excluding Sundays). Spells of unemployment and sickness not separated by more than 8 weeks count as one period of interruption of employment. A person who has exhausted benefit requalifies when he has again worked as an employed earner for at least 16 hours a week for 13 weeks. These weeks need not be consecutive but must generally fall within 26 weeks prior to the date of the claim (effective from Oct. 1989).

Disqualifications.—There are disqualifications from receiving benefit, e.g. for a period not exceeding 26 weeks if a person has lost his employment through his misconduct, or has voluntarily left his employment without just cause, or has, without good cause, refused an offer of suitable employment or training.

Sickness Benefit

Sickness benefit is payable for up to 28 weeks of sickness in a period of interruption of employment and is then replaced by invalidity benefit (*see* below).

Disqualifications.—There are disqualifications from receiving sickness or invalidity benefit for a period not exceeding six weeks if a person has become incapable of work through his own misconduct or if he fails without good cause to attend for or submit himself to prescribed medical or other examination or treatment, or observe prescribed rules of behaviour.

Since April 6, 1986, employers are responsible for paying Statutory Sick Pay (SSP) to their employees for up to 28 weeks of sickness in any period of incapacity for work. SSP replaces the employee's entitlement to State Sickness Benefit which is not payable as long as any SSP liability remains. SSP is subject to PAYE and to NI deductions. Employers can recover the SSP they have paid out and can also withhold an extra amount to compensate themselves for the NI contributions they have paid on SSP from the payments of NI they make each month to the Collector of Taxes. Employees who cannot get SSP can claim State Sickness Benefit instead.

Invalidity Benefit

Normally, after 28 weeks of sickness, sickness benefit, or SSP where the underlying conditions for sickness benefit are satisfied, is replaced by an invalidity pension. In addition an invalidity allowance is payable if incapacity for work begins more than five years before pension age. The allowance varies according to the age on falling sick, and if still in payment at pension age will continue as an addition to retirement pension. From Sept. 16, 1985 invalidity allowance has been reduced or withdrawn completely if there is entitlement to an additional earnings-related pension and/or a guaranteed minimum pension.

Maternity Benefit

Statutory maternity pay (SMP) is administered by employers but there is still a state maternity allowance scheme for women who are self-employed or otherwise do not qualify for SMP.

In general, employers pay SMP to pregnant women who have been employed by them for at least six months and earned at least the lower earnings limit for the payment of NI contributions. For those who have been employed for at least two years, payment of SMP for the first six weeks is related to earnings, followed by up to twelve weeks at a standard rate of £39·25. Those who have been employed for at least six months but less than two years receive payment at standard rate only for the 18 weeks. Part-time working women also qualify for the earnings-related element if employed for at least five years. Women have some choice in deciding when to begin maternity leave but SMP is not payable for any week in which work is done.

A woman may qualify for maternity allowance (MA) if she has been working and paying contributions at the full rate for at least 26 weeks in the 52-week period which ends 15 weeks before the baby is due. She also has an element of choice in deciding when to stop work and receive MA, which is not payable for any period she works.

Widow's Benefits

Only the late husband's contributions of any class count for widow's benefit in any of its three forms.

Widow's Payment.—May be received by a woman who at her husband's death is under 60, or whose husband was not entitled to a Category A retirement pension when he died.

Widowed Mother's Allowance.—Payable to a widow if she is receiving child benefit for one of her children; if her husband was receiving child benefit; or if she is expecting her husband's baby.

Widow's Pension.—A widow may receive this pension if aged 45 or over at the time of her husband's death or when her widowed mother's allowance ends. If aged 55 or over she will receive the full widow's pension rate.

Widow's benefit of any form ceases upon re-marriage.

Retirement Pension

Categories A and B

A *Category A pension* is payable for life to men or women on their own contributions if they are over pension age (65 for a man and 60 for a woman).

Where a person defers making a claim at 65 (60 for a woman) or later opts to be treated as if he/she had not made a claim, and does not draw a Category A pension, the weekly rate of pension is increased, when he or she finally makes a claim or reaches the age of 70 (65 for a woman), in respect of weeks when pension is foregone during the five years after reaching minimum pension age. Details of the increase in the rate of pension due to deferred retirement are given in leaflet NP46, available at social security offices. If a married man defers his own Category A pension then his wife has to defer receiving her Category B pension based on his contribution record. During this time she earns increments to the Category B pension, which is payable to her (and not her husband) when they both claim their pensions.

A *Category B pension* is normally payable for life to a woman on her husband's contributions when he has claimed, or is over 70, and has qualified for his own Category A pension, and she has reached 60 and

retired from regular work or has reached 65. It is also payable on widowhood after 60 whether or not the late husband had retired and qualified for his own pension. The weekly pension is payable at the rate of the increase for a wife while the husband is alive, and at the single person's rate on widowhood after 60. Where a woman is widowed before she reaches 60, a Category B pension is paid to her on reaching 60 at the same weekly rate as her widow's pension if she claims. If a woman qualifies for a pension of each category she receives whichever pension is the larger. Details of the increase in the rate of pension due to deferred retirement are given in leaflet NP46, available at social security offices.

The earnings rule which stated that a man aged 65 to 70, or a woman aged 60 to 65, who has qualified for pension would have it reduced if he or she earned more than a certain amount was abolished on Oct. 1, 1989. Where an adult dependant is living with the claimant, an Adult Dependants Allowance will only be payable if the dependant's earnings do not exceed the standard rate of unemployment benefit for a single person under pensionable age (*see below*). For the purpose of the dependency rule only, earnings will include payments by way of occupational pension. The earnings of a separated spouse affect the increase of retirement pension if they exceed £28·20 a week.

Unemployment, sickness or invalidity benefit is payable to men between 65 and 70 and women between 60 and 65 who have not claimed their retirement pension and who would have been entitled to a retirement pension if they had claimed at pension age. This applies in the case of sickness and invalidity benefit if incapacity for work is the result of an industrial accident or prescribed disease. These rates of benefit for people over pension age are shown in leaflet NI 196. A retirement pension will be increased by the amount of any invalidity allowance the pensioner was getting within the period of 8 weeks and one day before reaching minimum pension age but this will be offset against any Additional Pension or Guaranteed Minimum Pension. An age addition of 25p per week is payable if a retirement pensioner is aged 80 or over. (For attendance and invalidity care allowance, *see* Non-contributory Benefits).

Graduated Pension

The graduated pension scheme under which national insurance contributions and retirement pensions were graduated within specified limits, according to earnings, was discontinued in April, 1975, under the Social Security Act, 1975. Any graduated pension which an employed person over 18 and under 70 (65 for a woman) had earned by paying graduated contributions between April 6, 1961, when the scheme started and April 5, 1975, will be paid when the contributor claims their retirement pension, or at 70 (65 for a woman), in addition to any retirement pension for which he or she qualifies.

Graduated pension is at the rate of £6·14 a week for each 'unit' of graduated contributions paid by the employee (half a unit or more counts as a whole unit). A unit of contributions is £7·50 for men, and £9·00 for women, of graduated contributions paid.

A wife can get a graduated pension in return for her own graduated contributions, but not for her husband's. A widow gets a graduated addition to her retirement pension equal to half of any graduated additions earned by her late husband, plus any additions earned by her own graduated contributions. If a person defers making a claim beyond 65 (60 for a woman), entitlement may be increased by one seventh of a penny per £1 of its weekly rate for each complete week of deferred retirement, as long as the retirement is deferred for a minimum of seven weeks.

Rates of Benefits
(from week commencing April 9, 1990)

	Weekly rate £
Unemployment Benefit—standard rate	
Person under pension age	37·35
Increase for wife/other adult dependant	23·05
Person over pension age*	46·90
Increase for wife/other adult dependant	28·20
Sickness Benefit—standard rate	
Person under pension age	35·70
Increase for wife/other adult dependant	22·10
Person over pension age*	45·00
Increase for wife/other adult dependant	27·00
Invalidity Pension*	
Person (under or over pension age)....	46·90
Increase for wife or adult dependant	28·20
Invalidity Allowance (maximum amounts payable)	
higher rate	10·00
middle rate	6·20
lower rate	3·10
Maternity Allowance................	35·70
Widow's Payment (lump sum)	1,000·00
Widowed Mother's Allowance* and Widow's Pension*.................	46·90
Retirement pension*—*categories A and B*	
Single person	46·90
Increase for wife or adult dependant	28·20

Earnings limit for retirement pensioners (abolished from Oct. 1, 1989).

* These benefits attract an increase for each dependent child (in addition to child benefit) of £9·65.

NON-CONTRIBUTORY BENEFITS

Child Benefit

Child benefit is payable for virtually all children aged under 16, and for those aged 16–18 who are studying full-time up to and including A-Level or equivalent standard. It is also payable for a short period if the child has left school recently and is registered for work or a Youth Training Scheme.

One Parent Benefit

This benefit is paid to a person responsible for bringing up one or more children on his/her own. It is a flat rate non means-tested benefit payable for the first or only child.

Guardian's Allowance

Where the parents of a child are dead, the person who has the child in his family may claim a guardian's allowance in addition to child benefit. The allowance in exceptional circumstances, is payable on the death of only one parent.

Invalid Care Allowance

Invalid care allowance is payable to persons of working age, who are not gainfully employed because they are regularly and substantially engaged in caring for a severely disabled person who is receiving attendance allowance or constant attendance allowance with either a war or services pension, industrial disablement workman's compensation, or an allowance under the Pneumoconiosis, Byssinosis and Miscellaneous Diseases Benefit Scheme.

Mobility Allowance

The allowance is, subject to certain conditions, payable to persons who are suffering from such physical disablement that they are likely to remain unable, or virtually unable, to walk for at least a year. It can be claimed by persons between the ages of 5 and 65 (for this purpose a claim may be made up to 12 months from that birthday) and may be retained to age 80.

Severe Disablement Allowance

Persons of working age who have been continuously incapable of work for a period of at least 28 weeks but who do not qualify for a contributory invalidity pension may be entitled to severe disablement allowance. People who first become incapable of work after their 20th birthday must be at least 80 per cent disabled.

Attendance Allowance

Attendance allowance is payable to the severely disabled. Entitlement is determined by the Attendance Allowance Board or by a doctor acting on the Board's behalf. The full rate is paid to those in need of a great deal of attention or supervision both by day and by night. The allowance is paid at the lower rate to those whose need for attention or supervision arises either by day or by night. There is a six-month qualifying period.

Non-contributory Retirement Pension
Categories C and D

A *Category C pension* is provided, subject to a residence test, for persons who were over pensionable age on July 5, 1948, and for women whose husbands are so entitled if they are over pension age, with increases for adult and child dependants. A *Category D pension* is provided for others when they reach 80 if they are not already getting a retirement pension of any category or if they are getting that pension at less than these rates. An age addition of 25p per week is payable if persons entitled to retirement pension are aged 80 or over.

Rates of Benefits
(from week commencing April 9, 1990)

	Weekly rate £
Child Benefit (per child).............	7·25
One Parent Benefit	
First or only child of certain lone parents........................	5·60
Guardian's Allowance	9·65
Severe Disablement Allowance*	28·20
Increase for wife/other adult dependant	15·65
Mobility Allowance	26·25
Invalid Care Allowance*	28·20
Increase for wife/other adult dependant	16·85
Attendance Allowance	
higher rate	37·55
lower rate	25·05
Retirement Pension—Categories C* and D.	
Single person	28·20
Increase for wife/other adult dependant	16·85
(not payable with Category D pension)	

*These benefits attract an increase for each dependent child (in addition to child benefit) of £9·65.

INCOME SUPPORT

Income Support is a benefit for those whose income is inadequate and who are unemployed; over 60; bringing up children alone; unable to work or working only part-time through sickness or disability; or staying at home to care for a disabled relative. Except in special cases Income Support is not available to those who work for more than 24 hours per week or who have a partner who works for more than 24 hours per week. Income Support is not payable if the claimant, or claimant and partner, have capital or savings in excess of £8,000. The rate of benefits is affected by possession of capital or savings in excess of £3,000 and may be affected by a claimant's earnings. Sums payable depend on fixed allowances laid down by law for people in different circumstances. Special rates apply for people living in board and lodging, hostels, residential care or nursing homes. Details are available from local social security offices. Income Support is payable via post offices, either by order book or, for the unemployed, by girocheque. Applications for Income Support are made on form SB1, available from post offices; Income Support claim forms, available from social security offices; or on form B1 (for the unemployed), available from unemployment benefit offices. If both partners are entitled to Income Support, either may claim it. People receiving Income Support will be able to receive Housing Benefit, help with mortgage or home loan interest and help with health care. They may also be eligible for help with exceptional expenses, from the Social Fund. Leaflet SB20 gives a detailed explanation of Income Support.

INCOME SUPPORT PREMIUMS

Income Support Premiums are additional weekly payments for those with special needs. People qualifying for more than one premium will normally only receive the highest single premium for which they qualify. However Family Premium, Disabled Child's Premium and Severe Disability Premium are payable in addition to other premiums.

People with children qualify for a Family Premium if they have at least one child; a Disabled Child's Premium if they have a child who receives Attendance Allowance or Mobility Allowance or is registered blind; or a Lone Parent Premium if they are bringing up one or more children alone.

Long-term sick or disabled people qualify for a Disability Premium if they or their partner are receiving certain benefits because they are disabled or cannot work; are registered blind; or have been sending in doctor's statements for at least 28 weeks stating inability to work through sickness. If they are in receipt of Attendance Allowance, without anyone receiving Invalid Care Allowance for looking after them, they qualify for a Severe Disability Premium in addition to a Disability Premium.

People qualify for a Pensioner Premium if they or their partner are aged between 60 and 79, and for a Higher Pensioner Premium if they or their partner are aged 80 or over. A Higher Pensioner Premium is also payable to people aged between 60 and 79 who receive Attendance Allowance, Mobility Allowance, Invalidity Benefit or Severe Disablement Allowance, or who are registered blind. A Higher Pensioner Premium may be paid as well as a Severe Disability Premium.

Rates of Benefit
(from week commencing April 9, 1990)

	Weekly rate £
Income Support	
Single people	
aged 16–17	21·90
aged 18—24	28·80
aged 25 and over	36·70
aged 18 and over and a single parent	36·70
Couples	
both under 18	43·80
one or both aged 18 or over	57·60
For each child in a family	
under 11	12·35
aged 11–15	18·25
aged 16–17*	21·90
aged 18 and over*	28·80

* if in full-time education up to A level or equivalent standard.

Premiums	
Family Premium	7·35
Disabled Child's Premium	7·35
Lone Parent Premium	4·10
Disability Premium	
Single	15·40
Couple	22·10
Severe Disability Premium	
Single	28·20
Couple (one person qualified)	28·20
Couple (both qualified)	56·40
Pensioner Premium	
Single	11·80
Couple	17·95
Higher Pensioner Premium	
Single	17·05
Couple	24·25
Enhanced Pensioner Premium (from Oct. 1989)	
Single	2·60
Couple	3·65

(payable to pensioners aged between 75 and 79 in addition to Pensioner Premium).

FAMILY CREDIT

Family Credit is a tax-free benefit for working families with children. It is not a loan and is not repayable. To qualify, a family must include at least one child under 16 (under 19 if in full-time education up to A level or equivalent standard), and the claimant, or partner, must be working for at least 24 hours per week. It does not matter which partner is working and they may be employed or self-employed. The right to Family Credit does not depend on NI contributions and the same rates of benefit are paid to one and two parent families. Family Credit is not payable if the claimant, or claimant and partner, have capital or savings in excess of £8,000. The rate of benefit is affected if capital or savings in excess of £3,000 are held. The rate of benefit payable depends upon the claimant's (and partner's) net income (excluding Child Benefit), number of children, and children's ages. Family Credit is paid for 26 weeks and the amount payable will usually remain the same throughout this period, regardless of change of circumstances. Payment is made weekly via post offices or four-weekly directly into a bank or building society account. Applications for Family Credit are made on form FC1, obtainable together with a Family Credit Claim pack at a post office or social security office. In two parent families the woman should claim.

Rates of Benefit
(from week commencing April 9, 1990)

	Weekly rate £

The maximum amount will be payable where net income is no more than £57·60 per week. Where net income exceeds that amount, the maximum credit is reduced by 70 per cent of the excess and the result is the Family Credit payable. The maximum rate consists of:

Adult credit (for one or two parents)....................	36·35
plus for each child aged:	
under 11..........................	8·25
11–15..............................	14·15
16–17..............................	17·80
18................................	25·10

THE SOCIAL FUND

The Social Fund helps people with expenses which are difficult to meet from regular income. Regulated Maternity, Funeral and Cold Weather payments are decided by Adjudication Officers and are not cash-limited. Discretionary Community Care Grants, and Budgeting and Crisis Loans are decided by Social Fund Officers and come out of a yearly budget which, except for a contingency reserve, is allocated to local offices (1990–91, grants £63 million; loans £152m; reserve £2m).

Regulated payments

Maternity Payments.— A flat rate payment of £100 for each baby expected, born or adopted. It is payable to people on Income Support and Family Credit and is non-repayable.

Funeral Payments.—Payable for reasonable funeral expenses incurred by people receiving Income Support, Family Credit, Housing Benefit or Community Charge Rebate. It is recoverable from the estate of the deceased.

Cold Weather Payments.—£5 for each seven-day period of cold weather. Paid to people on Income Support who are pensioners, disabled or parents with a child under 5. It is non-repayable.

Discretionary payments

Community Care Grants.—They are intended to help people on Income Support to move into the community or avoid institutional care; ease exceptional pressures on families; and/or meet certain essential travelling expenses. They are usually non-repayable.

Budgeting Loans.—These are interest-free loans to people who have been receiving Income Support for at least six months, for intermittent expenses that may be difficult to budget for.

Crisis Loans.—These are interest-free loans to anyone, whether receiving benefit or not, who are without resources in an emergency, where there is no other means of preventing serious risk or damage to health or safety.

Loans are normally repaid over a period of up to 78 weeks at between 5 and 15 per cent of Income Support (less housing costs), depending on other commitments. Savings over £500 (£1,000 for people aged 60 or over) are taken into account for Cold Weather, Maternity and Funeral Payments, Community Care Grants and Budgeting Loans. All savings are taken into account for crisis loans. For regulated payment there is a right of appeal to an independent Social Security Appeal and thereafter to a Social Security Commissioner. For discretionary payments there is a review system where persons can ask for a review

at the local office with a further right of review to an independent Social Fund Inspector.

DETERMINATION OF CLAIMS AND QUESTIONS

With a few exceptions, claims and questions relating to Social Security benefits are decided by statutory authorities who act independently of the Department of Social Security and Department of Employment. The first of the statutory authorities, the Adjudication Officer, determines entitlement to benefit. A claimant who is dissatisfied with that decision has the right of appeal to a Social Security Appeal Tribunal. There is a further right of appeal to a Social Security Commissioner against the Tribunal's decision but leave to appeal must first be obtained. Appeals to the Commissioner must be on a point of law. Provision is also made for the determination of certain questions by the Secretary of State for Social Services.

Disablement questions are decided by adjudicating medical authorities or Medical Appeal Tribunals. Appeal to the Commissioner against a tribunal's decision is with leave and on a point of law only.

Leaflet NI 246 which is available from social security offices, explains how to appeal, and leaflet NI260 is a guide to reviews and appeals.

INDUSTRIAL INJURIES, DISABLEMENT AND DEATH BENEFITS

The Industrial Injuries scheme, administered under the Social Security Act 1975 and subsequent Acts and Regulations, provides a range of benefits designed to compensate for disablement resulting from an industrial accident (i.e. an accident arising out of and in the course of an employed earner's employment) or from a prescribed disease due to the nature of a person's employment. Rates of benefit are increased periodically.

Determination of Claims and Questions.—Provision is made for the determination of certain questions by the Secretary of State for Social Security, and of 'disablement questions' by a medical board (or a single doctor) or, on appeal, by a medical appeal tribunal. An appeal on a point of law against a medical appeal tribunal decision is determined by the Social Security Commissioner. Claims for benefit and certain questions arising in connection with a claim for or award of benefit (e.g. whether the accident arose out of and in the course of the employment) are determined by an adjudication officer appointed by the Secretary of State, or a Social Security Appeal Tribunal, or in certain circumstances, on further appeal, by the Commissioners.

Special schemes under the Industrial Injuries and Diseases (Old Cases) Act 1975 provide supplementary allowances to those entitled to receive weekly payments of workmen's compensation for loss of earnings due to injury at work, or disease contracted during employment before July 5, 1948 when the Industrial Injuries scheme was introduced. Other schemes under the Act provide allowances to those who contracted slowly developing diseases during employment before July 1948 where neither workmen's compensation nor Industrial Injuries Benefits are payable. A lump sum death benefit of up to £300 may also be payable to a dependant of such a person.

Benefits

Disablement Benefit is normally payable 15 weeks (90 days) after the date of accident or onset of disease if the employed earner suffers from loss of physical or mental faculty such that the resulting disablement is assessed at not less than 14 per cent. The amount of disablement benefit payable varies according to the degree of disablement (in the form of a percentage) assessed by an adjudicating medical authority or medical appeal tribunal.

Disablement assessed at less than 14 per cent does not normally attract basic benefit except for certain chest diseases. A weekly pension is payable where the assessment of disablement is between 14 and 100 per cent (assessments of 14 to 19 per cent are payable at the 20 per cent rate). Payment can be made for a limited period or for life.

The basic rates are applicable to adults and to juveniles entitled to an increase for a child or adult dependant; other juveniles receive lower rates.

Basic rates of pension are not related to the pensioner's loss of earning power, and are payable whether he is in work or not. If disablement is assessed at one per cent or more, loss of earnings may be compensated by a reduced earnings allowance. This may be paid even if basic disablement pension is not paid because disablement is assessed at less than 14 per cent, providing there is a current disablement assessment of at least 1 per cent. However, reduced earnings allowance cannot be paid where the date of the accident or the onset of a prescribed disease was on or after Oct. 1, 1990. There is provision also for increases of pension if the pensioner requires constant attendance or if his disablement is exceptionally severe. A pensioner may draw SSP, sickness or invalidity benefit as appropriate, in addition to disablement pension, during spells of incapacity for work.

Death Benefit, in the form of a pension, is available for women widowed before April 11, 1988. The amount of pension depends on the widow's circumstances at the date of the death and not upon the deceased's earnings.

Regulations impose certain obligations on claimants and beneficiaries and on employers, including, in the case of claimants for disablement benefit, that of submitting themselves for medical examination.

Rates of Benefits
(from April 9, 1990)

	Weekly rate £
Disablement Benefit/Pension	
Degree of disablement—100 per cent.	76·60
90	68·94
80	61·28
70	53·62
60	45·96
50	38·30
40	30·64
30	22·98
20	15·32
Unemployability supplement*	46·90
Addition for adult dependant (subject to earnings rule)	28·20
Reduced earnings allowance (maximum)	30·64
Constant Attendance allowance (normal maximum rate)	30·70
Exceptionally severe disablement allowance	30·70
Industrial death benefit widow's pension*	
Higher permanent rate	46·90
Lower permanent rate	14·07

* These benefits attract an increase for each dependent child (in addition to child benefit) of £9·65.

WAR PENSIONS

War pensions are awarded under The Naval, Military and Air Forces, Etc. (Disablement and Death) Service Pensions Order 1983, which was a consolidation of the previous Royal Warrants, Orders in Council and Orders by Her Majesty.

The DSS awards war pensions to members of HM Armed Forces in respect of the periods Aug. 4, 1914 to Sept. 30, 1921 and subsequent to Sept. 3, 1939 (including present members of the armed forces). The DSS also has special schemes for the Merchant Navy, Naval Auxiliary personnel, the Ulster Defence Regiment, civil defence volunteers, civilians, Home Guard, Polish armed forces under British command and Polish resettlement forces.

War pensions for the period Oct. 1, 1921 to Sept. 2, 1939 are dealt with by the Ministry of Defence who are also responsible for the Armed Forces Pension Scheme.

ELIGIBILITY AND GENERAL PROVISIONS

War disablement pension is awarded for the disabling effects of any injury, wound or disease which is attributable to, or aggravated by, conditions of service in the armed forces. It cannot be paid until the serviceman has left the armed forces.

Disablement is assessed by comparison of the disabled person's condition with that of a normal, healthy person of the same age and sex, without taking into account the disabled person's earnings or occupation, and is expressed on a percentage scale up to 100 per cent. Disablement above 20 per cent, for which a pension is awarded, is assessed in steps of 10 per cent. Maximum assessment does not necessarily imply total incapacity. For assessment of less than 20 per cent a lump sum is payable.

Dependency allowance. A 100 per cent disabled pensioner may receive an allowance of 60p a week for his wife or dependent child. Where disablement is less than 100 per cent the allowance is proportionate to the degree of disablement.

War widows pension is awarded where death occurs as a result of service. Where a war disablement pensioner was receiving constant attendance allowance at the time of his death, or would have been receiving it if he were not in hospital, his widow has automatic entitlement to a war widow's pension, regardless of the cause of death.

Additional allowances are payable for dependent children, in addition to child benefit.

A reduced weekly rate is payable to war widows below the rank of Lieutenant-Colonel who are under the age of 40, without children and capable of maintaining themselves. This is increased to the standard rate at age 40.

Rank additions to disablement and widows pensions. Rank additions may be paid with war pensions where the rank held was above that of private (or equivalent).

Claims.—Where a claim is made no later than 7 years after the termination of service, the claimant does not have to prove that the disablement or death on which the claim is based is related to service and receives the benefit of any reasonable doubt. Where a claim is made more than 7 years after the termination of service the claimant has to show that disablement or death is related to service. However, the claim succeeds if reliable evidence is produced which raises a reasonable doubt whether disablement or death is related to service. There is no time limit for making a claim for war pension.

SUPPLEMENTARY ALLOWANCES

A number of supplementary allowances may be awarded to a war pensioner which are intended to meet the various needs which may result from disablement or death and take account of its particular effect on the pensioner. Decisions on supplementary allowances are made on a discretionary basis on behalf of the Secretary of State and there is no provision for a statutory right of appeal against them. However, war pensioners may discuss any aspect of their pension position with their local War Pensions Committees, which may be able to arrange help or make representations to the war pensions branch of the DSS.

Unemployability supplement, with additional allowances for dependants, may be paid to a war pensioner whose pensioned disablement is so serious as to make him unemployable. In addition, an invalidity allowance may be payable if the incapacity for work began more than 5 years before normal retirement age.

Allowance for lowered standard of occupation may be awarded to a partially disabled pensioner whose pensioned disablement permanently prevents him from following his pre-service occupation and from doing another job of equivalent financial standard. The allowance, together with the basic war disablement pension, must not exceed pension at the 100 per cent rate.

Constant attendance allowance may be awarded to a war pensioner who is so severely handicapped by the nature of his pensioned disablement, assessed at not less than 80 per cent, that he must depend to a greater or lesser extent upon regular attendance of a personal nature. There are four rates of the allowance and these vary according to the amount of time attendance is needed.

Exceptionally severe disablement allowance is paid to pensioners who are receiving constant attendance allowance on a permanent basis at either of the two highest rates.

Severe disablement occupational allowance is paid to those pensioners who qualify for constant attendance allowance at either of the two highest rates and who, despite their handicap, are normally in employment. This allowance is not payable if the pensioner is in receipt of unemployability supplement.

Comforts allowance is payable at one of two rates. The higher rate is paid to those pensioners who are receiving both constant attendance allowance and unemployability supplement. When only one of these allowances is in payment the lower rate of comforts allowance is normally paid, but the higher rate can be paid under certain conditions where only constant attendance allowance is in payment.

Clothing allowance may be awarded where the pensioned disablement causes exceptional wear and tear of clothing. It is payable at two rates, depending on the degree of wear and tear caused.

Mobility supplement is intended to help those war pensioners who because of their pensioned disablement are unable, or virtually unable, to walk; also those with assessment of over 80 per cent for blindness and 80 per cent or more for deafness and who, because of the combined effects of those conditions, are unable to walk to any intended or required destination out of doors without the assistance of another person.

Treatment allowance may be paid to a pensioner receiving medical treatment in hospital or at home if the treatment is for the pensioned disablement, is necessary because of the continuing effects of service, and is of a kind which prevents the pensioner from working for more than seven days, or would do so if he was not unemployed or had not retired from work.

The allowance replaces the disablement pension and is paid at the 100 per cent rate.

Part Time Treatment Allowance may be payable for pensioners whose treatment prevents them from working for less than seven days.

Age allowance may be awarded to those war pensioners aged 65 or over whose war disablement is assessed at 40 per cent or more. It is payable at four rates, depending on the degree of disablement.

Widow's age allowance is paid at three different rates according to age (65–69, 70–79 and over 80).

Widow's child's allowance may be paid in addition to child benefit.

Rent allowance may be paid to a widow who receives a war widow's pension and maintains a home for a child eligible for an allowance.

Education allowance may be payable to a war disablement pensioner or war widow in respect of a dependent child if the DSS is satisfied that the education is suitable for the child and that the family circumstances are such as to require an allowance.

Temporary allowance for widows may be payable in the form of a special allowance for the first 26 weeks of widowhood for widows of war pensioners who received constant attendance allowance or unemployability supplement. After 26 weeks the widow will get any war widow's pension or national insurance widow's benefit to which she is entitled.

Funeral grant may be payable where the pensioner dies as a result of his pensioned disablement, or he died in hospital while having treatment for that disability, or was getting constant attendance allowance at the time of his death. Claims should be made within three months of the funeral.

WAR PENSIONERS ABROAD

The DSS is responsible for the payment of war pensions, and provision of necessary treatment for accepted disablement, to pensioners who reside overseas. They receive the same pension rates as war pensioners in this country and benefit from the same annual upratings.

WAR PENSIONERS AND SOCIAL SECURITY BENEFITS

When a war disablement pensioner is sick, unemployed or retired, the appropriate social security benefits are paid in addition to the war pension, unless he is entitled to unemployability supplement or severe disablement occupational allowance instead.

Any sickness, invalidity, unemployment benefit or retirement pension for which a war widow qualifies on her own contributions, and any graduated retirement benefit, or additional earnings related pension inherited from her husband, can be paid in addition to her war widow's pension or temporary allowance. A war pensioner or war widow who claims Income Support or Family Credit has the first £10 of pension disregarded. A similar provision operates for housing benefit and community charge relief; but the local authority may, at its discretion, disregard any or all of the balance. A special tax free Christmas bonus of £10.00 is payable to war disablement pensioners who are in receipt of unemployability supplement, constant attendance allowance, have retired, or are aged over 70 (65 for women); and to all war widows who do not otherwise receive this payment.

PENSIONS APPEAL TRIBUNALS

There are independent Pensions Appeal Tribunals which hear appeals against the decisions of the DSS on entitlement, and assessment of disablement, in respect of 1939 War and subsequent service cases. There are now no rights of appeal in the 1914 War disablement cases, the great majority of which were given final assessment in the 1920s with a 12 months right of appeal at the time. An appeal by a 1914 war widow must be made within twelve months of the date on which the rejection of the claim is notified.

WAR PENSIONERS WELFARE SERVICE

The DSS operates a war pensioners welfare service to advise and assist war pensioners and their widows on any matters affecting their welfare. Welfare officers are attached to War Pensioners' Welfare Offices located in the major towns, and work closely with central and local Government agencies as well as the various ex-service organizations. The service is available on call to any war pensioner or widow who needs it. In addition the service takes the initiative in arranging regular visits in certain cases.

Rates of War Pensions and Allowances
(from week commencing April 9, 1990)

	Weekly rates £
War Disablement pension	
(for Private or equivalent rank)	
Degree of disablement—	
100 per cent	76.60
90 per cent	68.94
80 per cent	61.28
70 per cent	53.62
60 per cent	45.96
50 per cent	38.30
40 per cent	30.64
30 per cent	22.98
20 per cent	15.32
Unemployability supplement	
Personal allowance	49.80
Increase for wife/other adult dependant	28.20
Increase for child	9.65
Allowance for lowered standard of	
occupation (maximum)	30.64
Widow's pension	
(widow of Private or equivalent rank)	
Standard rate	60.95
Increase for child	13.40
Childless widow under 40	14.07
Widow's age allowance	
Age—65–69	7.00
70–79	13.50
80 and over	20.00

The current rates of all War Pensions and Allowances are listed in leaflet MPL154 'Rates of War Pensions and Allowances' which is obtainable from War Pensioners Welfare Offices or from The Leaflets Unit, PO Box 21, Stanmore, Middx. HA7 1AY.

NATIONAL HEALTH SERVICE
(and Local Authority Personal Social Services)

The National Health Service came into being on July 5, 1948, as a result of the National Health Service Act 1946. The Act placed a duty on the Secretary of State for Social Services to promote the establishment in England and Wales of a comprehensive Health Service designed to secure improvement in the mental and physical health of the people and the prevention, diagnosis and treatment of illness. The Secretary of State for Wales administers the National Health Service in Wales. There are separate Acts for Scotland and Northern Ireland, where the Health Services are run on very similar lines and the respective Secretaries of State are responsible to Parliament.

The National Health Service covers a comprehensive range of hospital, specialist, family practitioner (medical, dental, ophthalmic and pharmaceutical), artificial limb and appliance, ambulance, and community health services. Everyone normally resident in this country is entitled to use any of these services, there are no contribution conditions and the charges made (except those for amenity beds) are reduced or waived in cases of hardship. In addition the Secretary of State for Social Services is responsible under the Local Authority Social Services Act 1970 for the provision by local authorities of social services for the elderly, the disabled, those with mental disorders and for families and children.

The 1980 Health Services Act led to major changes in the structure of the Health Service. Since April 1982, District Health Authorities (DHAs) are responsible for the operational management of health services and for planning within regional and national strategic guidelines. There are 190 DHAs in England and nine in Wales. Each DHA is required to arrange its services into units of management at hospital and community services level, and as many decisions as possible are delegated to unit level. Four of the London postgraduate teaching hospitals are now managed by DHAs (and eight are managed by special health authorities). Arrangements for the Family Doctor Service are administered by Family Health Services Authorities—90 in England and eight in Wales. FHSAs also contribute to the planning of health services.

The 14 Regional Health Authorities (RHAs) in England are responsible for regional planning, the allocation of resources to District Authorities, and the promotion of national policies and priorities. Performance review meetings are held annually between each hospital unit and its DHA, each DHA and its RHA, and between each RHA and Department of Health Ministers, thereby strengthening Authorities' accountability to Parliament, whilst respecting the essentially locally-based nature of decision making. Professional advisory machinery incorporated within the structure ensures that Health Authorities and their staffs make decisions in the full knowledge of expert opinion.

The NHS is financed mainly from taxation and the cost met from moneys voted by Parliament. In the United Kingdom this will amount to £29·1 billion in 1990–91. The Department of Health makes capital and revenue allocations to the RHAs and from these the RHAs meet the cost of their own services and make allocations to DHAs as well as funding Community Health Councils.

The Government published a White Paper in January 1989 setting out proposals to improve the quality and efficiency of health services; extend patient choice; and enhance the Service's responsiveness to its consumers. The reforms will be introduced on a phased basis depending on Parliamentary approval of the necessary legislation.

THE HEALTH SERVICES
Family Doctor Service

In England and Wales the Family Doctor Service (or General Medical Services) is organized by 98 Family Health Services Authorities which also organize the general dental, pharmaceutical and ophthalmic services for their areas. There is a Family Health Services Authority for one or more District Health Authorities. In Wales the chairman and non-executive members are appointed by the Secretary of State. In England the chairman is appointed by the Secretary of State and the non-executive members by the Regional Health Authority. There are nine non-executive members—a general medical practitioner, a general dental practitioner, a community pharmacist, a nurse and five lay members.

Any doctor may take part in the Family Doctor Scheme (provided the area in which he wishes to practise has not already an adequate number of doctors) and about 29,000 general practitioners in England and Wales do so. They may at the same time have private fee-paying patients. Family doctors are paid for their Health Service work in accordance with a scheme of remuneration which includes *inter alia* a basic practice allowance, capitation fees, reimbursement of certain practice expenses and payments for 'out of hours' work.

Everyone aged 16 or over can choose their doctor (parents or guardians choose for children under 16) and the doctor is also free to accept a person or not as he or she chooses. A person may change their doctor if they wish, by going to the surgery of a general practioner of their choice who is willing to accept them, and either handing in their medical card to register or filling in a form. When people are away from home they can still use the Family Doctor Service if they ask to be treated as 'temporary residents', and in an emergency, if a person's own doctor is not available, any doctor in the service will give treatment and advice.

Patients are treated either in the Doctor's surgery or, when necessary, at home. Doctors may prescribe for their patients all drugs and medicines which are medically necessary for their treatment and also a certain number of surgical appliances (the more elaborate being provided through hospitals).

Dental Service

Dentists, like doctors, may take part in the Service and may also have private patients. About 14,500 of the dentists available for general practice in England provide NHS general dental services. They are responsible to the Family Health Services Authorities in whose areas they provide services.

Patients are free to go to any dentist taking part in the Service and willing to accept them. Dentists receive payment for items of treatment for individual patients, instead of the capitation fee received by doctors.

Patients are asked to pay three-quarters of the cost of NHS dental treatment. The maximum charge for a course of treatment is £150. There is no charge for arrest of bleeding, repairs to dentures, home visits by the dentist or re-opening a surgery in an emergency (in these two cases payment will be for treatment given in the normal way). The following are exempt from dental charges:

(i) young people under 18;
(ii) full time students under 19;
(iii) expectant mothers who were pregnant when accepted for treatment;

(iv) women who have had a child in the previous 12 months.

People receiving Income Support or Family Credit, and members of the same family as someone receiving Income Support or Family Credit, are automatically entitled to full remission of charges.

Leaflet AB11 available from post offices and leaflet D11 available from local social security offices explain how other people on a low income can, depending on their financial circumstances, get free treatment or help with charges.

Pharmaceutical Service

Patients may obtain medicines, appliances and oral contraceptives prescribed under the NHS from any pharmacy whose owner has entered into arrangements with the Family Health Services Authority to provide this service. Almost all pharmacy owners have done so and displays notices that they dispense under the NHS; the number of these pharmacies in England and Wales at the end of 1988 was about 10,400. There are also some appliance suppliers who only provide special appliances. In country areas where access to a pharmacy may be difficult, patients may be able to obtain medicines etc. from their doctor.

Except for contraceptives (for which there is no charge), a charge of £3·05 is payable for each item supplied unless the patient is exempt and the declaration on the back of the prescription form is completed. Exemptions cover:

(i) children under 16;
(ii) young people under 19 and still in full-time education;
(iii) men aged 65 and over;
(iv) women aged 60 and over;
(v) pregnant women;
(vi) mothers who have had a baby within the last 12 months;
(vii) people suffering from certain medical conditions;
(viii) people who receive Income Support or Family Credit;
(ix) people on low income;
(x) war pensioners (for their accepted disablements).

Prepayment certificates (£15·80 valid for four months, £43·50 valid for a year) may be purchased by those patients not entitled to exemption who require frequent prescriptions. Further information about the exemption and prepayment arrangements is given in leaflet P11.

General Ophthalmic Services

General Ophthalmic Services, which are administered by Family Practitioner Committees, form part of the ophthalmic services available under the National Health Service. The NHS sight test is available free to children under 16, full-time students under the age of 19, those people and their partners in receipt of Income Support and Family Credit, people prescribed complex lenses, the registered blind and partially sighted, diagnosed diabetic and glaucoma patients, and close relatives aged 40 or over of diagnosed glaucoma patients. Those on a low income may qualify for help with the cost.

Certain groups are automatically entitled to help with the purchase of glasses under an NHS voucher scheme: children under 16; full-time students under 19; people who are themselves or whose partners are in receipt of Income Support or Family Credit, people wearing certain complex lenses and people whose spectacles are lost or damaged as a result of their disability, injury or illness. The value of the voucher depends on the lenses required. Vouchers may be used to help pay for the glasses or contact lenses of

the patient's choice. People with a low income may claim help on form AG1. Glasses or contact lenses should not be purchased until the result of a claim is known as no refunds can be given. Leaflet G11 gives further details.

Diagnosis and specialist treatment of eye conditions is available through the Hospital Eye Service as well as the provision of glasses of a special type. Testing of sight may be carried out by any ophthalmic medical practitioner or ophthalmic optician and can cost up to £10. The optician must hand the prescription, and a voucher if eligible, to the patient who can take this to any supplier of glasses of his choice to have dispensed. However, only registered opticians can supply glasses to children and to people registered as blind or partially sighted.

Primary Health Care Services

Primary health care services include the general medical, dental, ophthalmic and pharmaceutical services and the family doctor service. They also include community services run by district health authorities, health centres and clinics, family planning outside the hospital service, and preventive activities in the community including vaccination, immunization and fluoridation. The district nursing and health visiting services include community psychiatric nursing for mentally ill people living outside hospital, and school nursing for the health surveillance of school children of all ages; ante- and post-natal care and chiropody are also an integral part of the primary health care service.

Community Child Health Services

Pre-school services, usually at child health clinics, provide regular surveillance of children's physical, mental and emotional health and development, and advice to parents on their children's health and welfare. The School Health Service provides for the medical and dental examination of schoolchildren, and advises the local education authority, the school, the parents and the pupil of any health factors which may require special consideration during the pupil's school life.

Hospitals and Other Services

The Secretary of State for Health has a duty to provide, to such extent as he/she considers necessary to meet all reasonable requirements, hospital and other accommodation; medical, dental, nursing and ambulance services; other facilities for the care of expectant and nursing mothers and young children; facilities for the prevention of illness and the care and after-care of persons suffering from illness; and such other services as are required for the diagnosis and treatment of illness. Rehabilitation services (occupational therapy, physiotherapy and speech therapy) may also be provided for those who need it and surgical and medical appliances are supplied in appropriate cases.

Specialists and consultants who take part in the Service can engage in private practice, including the treatment of their private patients in NHS hospitals.

In a number of hospitals accommodation is available for the treatment of private in-patients who undertake to pay the full costs of hospital accommodation and services and (usually) separate medical fees to a specialist as well. The amount of the medical fees is a matter for agreement between doctor and patient. Hospital charges for private resident patients are determined by District Health Authorities either on a local basis or in line with a central 'model' list.

Certain hospitals have accommodation in single rooms or small wards which, if not required for patients who need privacy for medical reasons, may be made available to patients who desire it as an amenity. In such cases the patients are treated in every other respect as National Health patients.

There is no charge for drugs supplied to National Health hospital in-patients but out-patients pay £3·05 per item unless they are exempt.

With certain exceptions, hospital out-patients have to pay fixed charges for dentures, contact lenses and certain appliances. Glasses may be obtained either from the hospital or an optician and the charge will be related to the type of lens prescribed and the choice of frame.

Local Authority Personal Social Services

Local authorities are responsible for the organization, management and administration of the personal social services and each authority has a Director of Social Services and a Social Services Committee responsible for the social services functions placed upon them by the Local Authority Social Services Act 1970.

POSTAL SERVICES

On October 1, 1969 the Post Office ceased to be a government department. The responsibility for running postal services was transferred to a public authority called the Post Office, which also administered telecommunications in the United Kingdom. The British Telecommunications Act 1981 (which also separated the postal and telecommunications functions) gave the Secretary of State for Trade and Industry powers to suspend the monopoly of the Post Office in certain areas and to issue licences to other bodies to provide an alternative service. Non-Post Office bodies are now permitted to transfer mail between document exchanges and to deliver letters, provided that a minimum fee of £1 per letter is charged. Charitable organizations are allowed to carry and deliver Christmas and New Year cards.

INLAND POSTAL SERVICES AND REGULATIONS

Inland Letter Post Rates

Not over	1st Class	2nd Class
60 g	22p	17p
100 g	33p	27p
150 g	41p	32p
200 g	49p	38p
250 g	51p	46p
300 g	68p	55p
350 g	78p	63p
400 g	88p	71p
450 g	98p	79p
500 g	£1.10	87p
600 g	£1.35	£1.05
700 g	£1.60	£1.25
750 g	£1.70	£1.30 (max)
800 g	£1.80	
900 g	£1.95	
1,000 g	£2.10	
Each extra 250 g or part thereof	55p	

Postcards travel at the same rates.

Stamps

There is a two-tier postal delivery system in the UK with 1st class letters normally being delivered the following day and 2nd class post within two days.

Postage stamps are sold in values of 1p, 2p, 3p, 4p, 5p, 10p, 15p, 17p, 22p, 24p, 27p, 29p, 30p, 32p, 34p, 37p, 50p, 75p, £1, £1.50, £2.00, and £5.00.

Books of stamps costing 50p or £1 are available from electronic vending machines at some main post offices. At post office counters books are sold containing 10 first class stamps (£2.20) and 10 second class stamps (£1.70). Rolls of 17p and 22p stamps are also sold. Mixed value rolls are only available on special order from post offices. The sale of postage stamps has been extended to outlets other than post offices, including stationers and newsagents.

Prepaid Stationery

Aerogrammes to all destinations, 32p.

Forces Aerogrammes, 17p.

Registered Letter Envelopes, printed with a £1.75 stamp (£1.55 for registration and 20p for postage), come in three sizes.

G, 156 × 95mm	= £1.85
H, 203 × 120mm	= £1.90
K, 292 × 152mm	= £2.00

Printed postage stamps cut from envelopes, postcards, newspaper wrappers etc. may be used as stamps in payment of postage, provided that they are not imperfect or defaced.

Postal Orders

Postal Orders (British pattern) are issued and paid at nearly all post offices in the UK. They are also paid in the Irish Republic, and issued and/or paid in many other countries overseas.

Postal orders are printed with a counterfoil for denominations of 25p, 30p, 40p, 50p, 60p, 70p, 80p, 90p, and £1, followed by £1 steps to £10, and £20. Postage stamps not exceeding two in number may be affixed in the space provided to increase the value of the postal order by up to 9p.

Charges (in addition to the value of the postal order): Up to £1 = 25p; £2–£10 = 44p; £20 = 68p.

The name of the payee must be inserted on the postal order. If not presented within six months of the last day of the month of issue, orders must be sent to the local head postmaster (in London, the district head postmaster) to ascertain whether the order may still be paid.

Other Services

Cash on Delivery Service.—(Inland, excluding Irish Republic and HM ships). A trade charge (amount to be collected) up to £350 can, under certain conditions, be collected from addresses and remitted to the sender of a parcel containing an invoice. Invoice values of over £50 are only collectable at Post Office premises.

Charge per parcel (exclusive of postage and registration): Customers under contract = 85p; other customers = £1.15; COD enquiry = 85p.

Certificate of Posting.—Issued free on request at time of posting.

Compensation.—(Inland only). Compensation up to a maximum of £22 may be paid where it can be shown that a letter or parcel was damaged or lost in the post. The onus of making up properly any parcel sent by post lies with the sender. The Post Office does not accept any responsibility for loss arising from faulty packing. No compensation may be claimed for injury or damage to a parcel unless the item was registered and covered by consequential loss insurance.

Newspaper Post.—Copies of newspapers registered at the Post Office may be posted by the publisher or their agents in wrappers open at both ends, in unsealed envelopes approved by the Post Office, or without covers and tied by string which can be removed without cutting. Wrappers and envelopes must be prominently marked 'newspaper post' in the top left-hand corner. No writing or additional printing is permitted, other than the words 'with compliments', name and address of sender, request for return if undeliverable and a reference to a page. Items receive 1st class letter service.

Newspapers posted by the public, or supplements to registered newspapers despatched apart from their ordinary publications, are transmitted under the conditions governing the 1st or 2nd class letter services.

Prohibited Articles.—Prohibitions include offensive or dangerous articles, packets likely to impede Post Office sorters, and certain kinds of advertisement.

Recorded Delivery.—The recorded delivery service provides a record of posting and delivery of inland letters. No compensation is available for money or jewellery sent by this service. Charge: 28p; advice of delivery: a further 29p.

Redirection.—(i) By agent of addressee.—Mail other than parcels, business reply and freepost items may be reposted free not later than the day after delivery (not counting Sundays and public holidays) if unopened and if original addressee's name is unobscured. Parcels may be redirected free of charge within the same time limits only if the original and substituted address are in the same local parcel delivery area (or within the London postal area). Registered packets, which must be taken to a post office, are re-registered free only up to the day after delivery.

(ii) By the Post Office.—Requests for redirection of mail should be made on printed forms obtainable from the Post Office and must be signed by the person to whom the letters are to be addressed. A fee is payable for each different surname on the application form.

Charges: Up to 1 calendar month = £3.25; Up to 3 calendar months = £7.25; Up to 12 calendar months = £17.50; Up to 12 calendar months where redirection has already been in operation for 12 months or more = £60.00.

Registration.—(Inland 1st class letters only). All packets intended for registration must be handed to the post office and a certificate of posting obtained.

Compensation in respect of money is given only if money is sent by registered letter post in one of the special envelopes sold officially (*see* **Prepaid Stationery**). Compensation cannot be paid in the case of any packet containing anything not legally transmissible by post. Compensation is paid for fragile articles only if they have been adequately packed. No compensation is paid for deterioration due to delay of perishable articles or for damage to exceptionally fragile articles. Information about charges and compensation rates is available from the local head postmaster (in London, the district head postmaster). Advice of delivery: a further 29p at time of posting.

Undelivered Mail.—Undelivered mail is returned to the sender provided the return address is indicated either on the outside of the envelope or inside. If the sender's address is not available, items not containing property are destroyed. If the packet contains something of value it is retained for up to three months. Exceptionally, items in the minimum weight step on which a rebate of postage has been allowed are destroyed unopened unless there is a return address shown on the outside of the cover. In addition, undeliverable 2nd class mail which contains newspapers, magazines or commercial advertising is destroyed.

Unpaid Mail.—All unpaid or underpaid letters are treated as 2nd class mail. The recipient is charged the amount of underpayment plus 13p per item. The same rates apply to parcels.

SPECIAL DELIVERY SERVICES

Datapost.—A guaranteed service for the delivery of documents and packages: (i) Datapost Sameday offers same-day collection and delivery in many areas; (ii) Datapost Overnight offers next day delivery nationwide. Items may be collected or handed in at post offices. There are also Datapost links with a number of overseas countries.

Express Delivery.—This service is by special messenger from the office of delivery and is available to or from the Isle of Man or the Channel Islands. Charge (in addition to postage): £1.85.

Royal Mail Special Delivery.—This service offers special messenger treatment, where necessary, to ensure next day delivery of 1st class letters and packets. The fee of £1.85 is refunded if next working day delivery is not achieved, provided that items are posted before latest recommended posting times.

Swiftair.—Express delivery of air mail letters and packets anywhere in the world. Items normally arrive at least one day in advance of normal air mail. Charge (in addition to postage): £1.85.

OVERSEAS POSTAL SERVICES AND REGULATIONS

Overseas Surface Mail Rates

Letters and Postcards

Not over		Not over	
20 g	26p	450 g	£2.15
60 g	43p	500 g	£2.36
100 g	63p	750 g	£3.53
150 g	84p	1,000 g	£4.60
200 g	£1.05	1,250 g	£5.58
250 g	£1.26	1,500 g	£6.56
300 g	£1.47	1,750 g	£7.31
350 g	£1.73	2,000 g	£8.45
400 g	£1.94		

Airmail Letter Rates

Europe: Letters and Postcards

Not over		Not over	
20 g	22p	400 g	£1.94
20 g non EC	26p	450 g	£2.15
60 g	43p	500 g	£2.36
100 g	63p	750 g	£3.53
150 g	84p	1,000 g	£4.60
200 g	£1.05	1,250 g	£5.58
250 g	£1.26	1,500 g	£6.56
300 g	£1.47	1,750 g	£7.31
350 g	£1.73	2,000 g	£8.45

Outside Europe: Letters

	Not over 10 g	Each extra 10 g
Zone A	53p	17p
Zone B	53p	17p
Zone C	57p	21p

(For Airmail Letter Zones outside Europe, *see* pp. 1063–5).

Other Services

Cash on Delivery.—(Applicable to parcels only, but not to all countries, nor to British naval, military and RAF forces serving overseas.) A charge starting at £2.70 per parcel must be prepaid in addition to the postage for outward parcels. For inward parcels the delivery fee is 80p. The trade charge (amount to be collected) may not exceed £1,500 but to most non-European countries the limit is lower. The addressee has also to pay on delivery, besides Customs charges if any, a further charge which is not prepayable. If the trade charge cannot be collected, special rules apply for undeliverable COD parcels.

Compensation.—If a certificate of posting is produced, compensation may be given for loss or damage in the UK to uninsured parcels to or from most overseas countries. No compensation will be paid for any loss or damage due to the action of the Queen's Enemies.

Export Restrictions.—Under Department of Trade and Industry regulations the exportation of some goods by post is prohibited except under

Department of Trade licence. Enquiries should be addressed to the Export Data Branch, Overseas Trade Divisions, Department of Trade and Industry, 1 Victoria Street, London, SW1H 0ET (Tel. 071-215 5000).

Insurance.—Packets containing valuable papers, documents or articles such as jewellery can be insured as letters, or as parcels if the country of destination does not accept dutiable goods in the letter post. For HM ships abroad and also members of the Army and RAF overseas using BFPO numbers, parcels only are insurable up to £140 at a fee of £1.20.

Charges: Cover up to £150 = £1.75; up to £300 = £1.95; up to £450 = £2.20; up to £600 = £2.50; to a limit of £3.85 for £1,500 coverage.

International Reply Coupons.—Coupons are used to prepay replies to letters. They are exchangeable abroad for stamps representing the minimum surface mail letter rate from the country concerned to the UK. Charge: 60p each.

Poste Restante.—(Solely for the convenience of travellers and for three months only in any one town). A packet may be addressed to any post office, except town sub-offices, and should have the words 'Poste Restante' or 'to be called for' in the address. Redirection from a Poste Restante is undertaken for up to three months. Letters at a seaport for an expected ship are kept for two months: otherwise letters are kept for two weeks, or for one month if originating from abroad. At the end of this period

mail is treated as undeliverable, unless bearing a request for return.

Registration.—(Except for parcels and printed paper items posted in bulk). Registration is available to all countries except the British Indian Ocean Territory and the Republic of the Maldives. No compensation is payable for loss or damage to valuable articles sent in an unregistered letter. Charge in addition to postage: £1.75.

Small Packets Post.—This service permits the transmission of goods up to 1 kg to all countries, in the same mails as printed papers. (NB To Australia, Bhutan, Bolivia, Myanmar (Burma), Colombia, Cuba and Papua New Guinea there is a limit of 500 g). Packets must be packed to enable examination by the Post Office. Registration is allowed but not insurance. A customs declaration is required.

Instructions for the disposal of undelivered packets must be given at the time of posting. A parcel which cannot be delivered will be returned to the sender at his expense.

Small Packets Post Rates

Not over		Not over	
100 g	42p	400 g	£1.15
150 g	52p	450 g	£1.26
200 g	64p	500 g	£1.36
250 g	75p	750 g	£1.83
300 g	87p	1,000 g	£2.29
350 g	£1.06		

WEATHERCALL SERVICE

To obtain local weather forecasts, dial the prefix code 0898 500 followed by the appropriate regional code.

Greater London	401
Kent, Surrey and Sussex	402
Dorset, Hampshire and IOW	403
Devon and Cornwall	404
Wiltshire, Glos., Avon and Somerset	405
Berks., Bucks. and Oxfordshire	406
Beds., Herts. and Essex	407
Norfolk, Suffolk and Cambridgeshire	408
West, Mid and South Glamorgan and Gwent	409
Salop, Hereford and Worcester	410
Central Midlands	411
East Midlands	412
Lincolnshire and Humberside	413
Dyfed and Powys	414
Gwynedd and Clwyd	415
North West England	416
W. and S. Yorkshire and Yorkshire Dales	417
North East England	418
Cumbria and the Lake District	419
South West Scotland	420
West Central Scotland	421
Edinburgh, S. Fife, Lothian and Borders	422
East Central Scotland	423
Grampian and East Highlands	424
North West Scotland	425
Caithness, Orkney and Shetland	426
Northern Ireland	427
Five-day national forecast	430

MARINECALL SERVICE

To obtain information about weather conditions up to twelve miles off the coast, dial the prefix code 0898 500, followed by the appropriate area code.

Scotland North	451
Scotland East	452
North East	453
East	454
Anglia	455
Channel East	456
Mid-Channel	457
South West	458
Bristol Channel	459
Wales	460
North West	461
Clyde	462
Caledonia	463
Minch	464
Ulster	465

PUBLIC TELECOMMUNICATIONS SERVICES

Under the British Telecommunications Act 1981 the functions of the Post Office were divided between two separate organizations. The Post Office retained control of postal services and British Telecom was created to provide a telecommunications service. The Act also provided for a limited relaxation of the telecommunications monopoly. This was further advanced by the Telecommunications Act 1984, which removed British Telecom's monopoly on running the public telecommunications system. British Telecom was privatized as a public limited company in 1984.

The Telecommunications Act 1984 also established the Office of Telecommunications (Oftel) as the independent regulatory body for the telecommunications industry. (*See* also **Government and Public Offices.**)

Public Telecommunications Operators

There are three licensed fixed link Public Telecommunications Operators (PTOs) in the UK: British Telecom (BT), Mercury Communications Ltd. and Kingston Communications (Hull) PLC. In 1988 the Government announced its intention to license up to six other operators to provide one-way satellite communications systems; during 1989, three of these operators were granted temporary licences and the Government announced that such operators could offer services throughout Europe, rather than in the UK only, as previously indicated. In November 1990, the Government began a formal review of the two major fixed link operators as part of a wider review of UK telecommunications provision and competition arrangements.

British Telecom's obligations under its operating licence include the provision of (i) a universal telecommunications service; (ii) a service in rural areas; and (iii) essential services, such as public call boxes and emergency services.

Mercury Communications is licensed to provide national and international telephone services for residential and business customers. These services utilize the digital network created by Mercury. Mercury can also provide the following services: (i) public payphone services; (ii) national and international telex; (iii) international packet data services; (iv) electronic messaging (electronic mail and access to telex via a personal computer); (v) data network services; and (vi) nationwide radiopaging.

Private Telephone Services

There are over 260 private telephone companies which offer information on a variety of subjects such as the weather, stock market analysis, horoscopes, etc., on the British Telecom network. Other services are also now available on Mercury's network

The lines and equipment are provided by British Telecom under condition that services adhere to the codes of practice of the Independent Committee for the Supervision of Standards of Telephone Information Practice. All services are charged at 44p per minute (peak and standard rate) or 33p per minute (cheap rate).

Mobile Telephone Systems

Cellular telephone network systems, in existence since 1985, allow calls to be made to and from mobile telephones. The two companies licensed by the Department of Trade and Industry to provide competing cellular telephone systems are Cellnet, jointly owned by BT and Securicor, and Racal Vodafone Ltd., owned by the Racal Electronics Group. Cellular phones can be identified by the number prefixes 0860 or 0836 and calls to them are charged at the 'm' rate.

INLAND TELEPHONES

Since December 1986 an individual customer can install an extension telephone socket or apparatus in their own home without the need to buy the items from any of the licensed Public Telecommunications Operators. It is necessary to possess a special style of master-socket which must be supplied by the public network operator. Although an individual need not buy or rent an apparatus from a PTO, a telephone bought from a retail outlet must be of an approved standard compatible with the public network (indicated by a green disc on the label).

British Telecom Charges

Exchange line rentals	Per quarter (excl. VAT)
Residential, exclusive............	£17.13
Business, exclusive	£27.75

Telephone apparatus rental	
Residential	from £3.80
Business	from £4.70
Private payphone	from £32.17

Exchange line connection and take-over charges (incl. VAT)

	Residential	Business
New customer	£148.65	£162.70
Removing customer	£127.40	£141.68
Take-over of existing lines	£22.60	£22.60

Local and dialled national calls are charged in 4.4p units when made from ordinary lines and in 10p units when made from payphones. All charges are subject to VAT except those from payphones which are VAT inclusive. VAT charges on ordinary lines are calculated as a percentage of the total quarterly bill.

The length of time per unit depends on the distance of the call and the time of day:

Local rate*
'a' rate = up to 35 miles (56 km).
'b1' rate = frequently used routes over 35 miles (56 km).
'b' rate = over 35 miles (56 km) (incl. Channel Islands and Isle of Man).
'm' rate = dialled calls to mobile phones.
* Greater London has an exceptionally large 'local' call area.

Peak rate: Monday to Friday, 9am–1pm.
Standard rate: Monday to Friday, 8am–9am and 1pm–6pm.
Cheap rate: Monday to Friday, 6pm–8am. All day Saturday and Sunday and also Christmas Day, Boxing Day and New Year's Day.

Dialled Call Unit Charge
(incl. VAT)

	1 min	3 mins
Local rate		
Peak	5p	15p
Standard	5p	15p
Cheap	5p	5p
'a' rate		
Peak	15p	35p
Standard	10p	30p
Cheap	5p	15p

'b1' rate		
Peak	15p	40p
Standard	10p	30p
Cheap	10p	20p
'b' rate		
Peak	20p	51p
Standard	15p	40p
Cheap	10p	25p
'm' rate		
Peak	40p	£1.16
Standard	40p	£1.16
Cheap	25p	76p

Prefixed call charges

0800 = free.
0345 = charged at the local rate.
0860 and 0898 = charged at 'm' rate (and some 0836 calls also).

Operator-Connected Calls

Operator-connected calls from ordinary lines are generally subject to a three-minute minimum charge (and thereafter by the minute) which varies with distance and time of day. Operator-connected calls from payphones are charged in three-minute periods at the payphone tariff. For calls that have to be placed through the operator because a dialled call has failed, the charge is equivalent to the dialled rate, subject normally to the three-minute minimum.

Higher charges apply to other operator-connected calls, including special services calls and those to mobile phones, the Irish Republic and the Channel Islands.

Phonecards

Phonecards to the value of £2, £4, £10, and £20 are available from post offices and other outlets for use in specially designated public telephone boxes. Each phonecard unit is equivalent to a 10p coin in a payphone.

Special public payphones at major railway stations and airports also accept commercial credit cards.

INTERNATIONAL TELEPHONES

All UK customers have access to International Direct Dialling (IDD) and can dial direct to numbers on most exchanges in 200 countries worldwide. Details about how to make calls are given in dialling code information and in the International Telephone Guide.

For countries without IDD, calls have to be made through the International Operator. All operator-connected calls are subject to a three-minute minimum charge. Thereafter the call is charged by the minute.

Countries which can be called on IDD fall into one of 13 International Charge Bands depending on location. Charges in each band also vary according to the time of day; cheap rate dialled calls are available to all countries at certain times, but there is no reduced rate for operator-connected calls. Details of current international telephone charges can be obtained from the International Operator.

(For International Dialling Codes, *see* pp. 1063–65.)

OTHER TELECOMMUNICATIONS SERVICES

Telex Service.—There are now 208 countries that can be reached by the British Telecom telex service from the UK, over 200 of them by direct dialling.

For most customers, direct dialled calls to international destinations are charged in six-second units.

Units cost between 2.3p and 13.2p depending upon the country called. Calls via the British Telecom operator are charged in one-minute steps with a three-minute minimum, plus a surcharge of £1.30 a call. Operator-connected calls are charged at between 51p and £1.60 a minute depending upon the country called.

Calls made via British Telecom's Telex Plus store and forward facility attract normal telex charges and a handling charge of 13p for inland delivered messages and 30p for international delivered messages.

Telemessage.—Telemessages can be sent by telephone or telex within the UK for 'hard copy' delivery the next working day, including Saturdays. To achieve this, a telemessage must be telephoned/ telexed before 10pm Monday to Saturday (7pm Sundays and Bank Holidays). Dial 100 (190 in London, Birmingham and Glasgow) and ask for the Telemessage Service or see the telex directory for codes.

A Telemessage costs £5 for the first 50 words and £2.75 for each subsequent group of 50 words. The name and address are free. A sender's copy costs 85p. A selection of cards is available for special occasions at 80p per card. All prices are subject to VAT.

International Telemessage.—Telemessage is also available to the USA. For next working day delivery a telemessage must be filed by 10pm UK time Monday to Saturday (7pm Sundays and Bank Holidays). US addresses must include the ZIP code. Charges are £7.25 for the first 50 words and £3.60 for each subsequent group of 50 words. The name and address are free but all charges are subject to VAT.

BRITISH TELECOM SERVICES

Operator Services—100
For difficulties
For the following call services: alarm calls (booking charge £2.15); advice of duration and charge (charge 75p); charge card calls (charge 25p); fixed time calls (charge £1.75); freefone calls; international personal calls (charge £2.15–£4.30); transferred charge calls (charge 40p); subscriber controlled transfer. (All charges exclude VAT)

International Operator—155

Directory Enquries:-
For numbers in the London postal area, 142.
For numbers outside the London postal area including the Irish Republic, 192.

International Directory Enquiries—153

Emergency Services—999
Services include: fire service; police service; ambulance service; coastguard; lifeboat; cave rescue; mountain rescue.

Faults—151

Telemessage—100 (190 in London, Birmingham and Glasgow).

International Telemessage—100 (190 in London, Birmingham and Glasgow). The service is only available to the USA.

International Telegrams—100 (190 in London, Birmingham and Glasgow). The service is available worldwide.

Maritime Services—100. Includes Ship's Telegram Service and Ship's Telephone Service.

BT Inmarsat Satellite Service—155

All other call enquiries—191

INTERNATIONAL POST AND TELEPHONE CODES

The table below includes airmail letter zones for countries outside Europe (A, B or C). Destinations to which European airmail letter rates apply are indicated by *e*, or by *ec* for European Community destinations (*see* p. 1059).

International dialling codes are composed of *four* elements which are dialled in sequence: (i) the international code (from the UK this is always 010); (ii) the country code (*see* list below); (iii) the area code; (iv) the customer's number. Calls to some countries (indicated by † below) must be made via the international operator.

Country	Airmail zone	IDD code from UK	IDD code to UK
Afghanistan	B	†	†
Albania	e	†	†
Algeria	A	010 213	00*p*44
Andorra	ec	010 33 628	0*p*44
Angola	B	010 244	
Anguilla	B	010 1 809	001 44
Antigua and Barbuda	B	010 1 809	011 44
Argentina	B	010 54	00 44
Aruba	B	010 297	†
Ascension Island	B	010 247	
Australia	C	010 61	00 11 44
Austria	e	010 43	00 44
Azores	ec	010 351	00 44
Bahamas	B	010 1 809	011 44
Bahrain	A	010 973	0 44
Bangladesh	B	010 880	00 44
Barbados	B	010 1 809	011 44
Belgium	ec	010 32	00*p*44*
Belize	B	010 501	
Benin	B	010 229	00 44
Bermuda	B	010 1 809	1 44
Bhutan	B	010 975	†
Bolivia	B	010 591	00 44
Botswana	B	010 267	00 44
Brazil	B	010 55	00 44
British Virgin Islands	B	010 1 809 49	011 44
Brunei	B	010 673	00 44
Bulgaria	e	010 359	00 44
Burkina	B	010 226	
Burma/Myanmar	B	010 95	†
Burundi	B	010 257	90 44
Cambodia	B	†	†
Cameroon	B	010 237	00 44
Canada	B	010 1	011 44
Canary Islands	ec	010 34	07*p*44
Cape Verde	e	010 238	†
Cayman Islands	B	010 1 809	0 44
Central African Republic	B	010 236	†
Chad	B	010 235	†
Chile	B	010 56	00 44
China	C	010 86	00 44
Colombia	B	010 57	90 44
Comoros	B	†	†
Congo	B	010 242	00 44
Cook Islands	C	010 682	00 44
Costa Rica	B	010 506	00 44
Côte d'Ivoire	B	010 225	00 44
Cuba	B	010 53	
Cyprus	e	010 357	00 44
Czechoslovakia	e	010 42	00 44
Denmark	ec	010 45	009 44
Djibouti	A	010 253	00 44
Dominica	B	010 1 809	011 44
Dominican Republic	B	010 1 809	†
Ecuador	B	010 593	00 44
Egypt	A	010 20	00 44
Equatorial Guinea	B	010 240	†
Ethiopia	A	010 251	
Falkland Islands	B	010 500	01 44
Faroe Islands	e	010 298	009 44
Fiji	C	010 679	05 44
Finland	e	010 358	990 44
France	ec	010 33	19*p*44°

e Europe. *ec* European Community. † Calls must be made via the international operator. *p* A pause in dialling is necessary whilst waiting for a second tone. * *p* only in Bruges, Ostende and Veurne. ° The second tone may not always be audible.

Country	Airmail zone	IDD code from UK	IDD code to UK
French Guiana	B	010 594	†
French Polynesia	C	010 689	00 44
Gabon	B	010 241	00 44
The Gambia	B	010 220	00 44
Germany, East	e	010 37	000 44§
Germany, West	ec	010 49	00 44
Ghana	B	010 233	
Gibraltar	ec	010 350	00 44
Greece	ec	010 30	00 44
Greenland	e	010 299	009 44
Grenada	B	010 1 809	011 44
Guadeloupe	B	010 590	†
Guam	C	010 671	00 44
Guatemala	B	010 502	00 44
Guinea	B	010 224	†
Guinea-Bissau	B	010 245	†
Guyana	B	010 592	011 44
Haiti	B	010 509	†
Honduras	B	010 504	00 44
Hong Kong	B	010 852	001 44
Hungary	e	010 36	00 44
Iceland	e	010 354	90 44
India	B	010 91	00 44
Indonesia	B	010 62	00 44
Iran	A	010 98	00 44
Iraq	A	010 964	00 44
Ireland, Republic of	ec	010 353	
Dublin		0001	
Israel	A	010 972	00 44
Italy	ec	010 39	00 44
Jamaica	B	010 1 809	†
Japan	C	010 81	001 44
Jordan	A	010 962	00 44 varies
Kenya	B	010 254	000 44
Kiribati	C	010 686	†
Korea, North	C	010 850	†
Korea, South	C	010 82	001 44
Kuwait	A	010 965	00 44
Laos	B	†	†
Lebanon	A	010 961	00 44
Lesotho	B	010 266	00 44
Liberia	B	010 231	00 44
Libya	A	010 218	00 44
Liechtenstein	e	010 41 75	00 44
Luxembourg	ec	010 352	00 44
Macao	B	010 853	00 44
Madagascar	B	010 261	†
Madeira	ec	010 351 91	00 44*
Malawi	B	010 265	101 44
Malaysia	B	010 60	00 44
Maldives	B	010 960	
Mali	B	010 223	†
Malta	e	010 356	00 44
Martinique	B	010 596	†
Mauritania	B	010 222	†
Mauritius	B	010 230	
Mexico	B	010 52	98 44
Monaco	ec	010 33 93	19p44
Mongolia	C	†	†
Montserrat	B	010 1 809	†
Morocco	A	010 212	00p44
Mozambique	B	010 258	†
Namibia	B	010 264	091 44
Nauru	C	010 674	00 44
Nepal	B	010 977	00 44
Netherlands	ec	010 31	09p44
Netherlands Antilles	B	010 599	00 44
New Caledonia	C	010 687	00 44
New Zealand	C	010 64	00 44
Nicaragua	B	010 505	00 44
Niger	B	010 227	00 44

e Europe. *ec* European Community. † Calls must be made via the international operator. *p* A pause in dialling is necessary whilst waiting for a second tone. § From Berlin, Cottbus, Erfurt, Frankfurt (Oder), Gera, Halle/ Salle, Leipzig, Magdeburg, Neubrandenburg and Suhl, dial 06 44. * Varies in some areas.

Country	Airmail zone	IDD code from UK	IDD code to UK
Nigeria	B	010 234	009 44
Norfolk Island	C	010 672	
Norway	e	010 47	095 44
Oman	A	010 968	00 44
Pakistan	B	010 92	00 44
Panama	C	010 507	00 44
Papua New Guinea	C	010 675	31 44
Paraguay	B	010 595	002 or 003 44
Peru	B	010 51	00 44
Philippines	C	010 63	00 44
Poland	e	010 48	0p044
Portugal	ec	010 351	00 44
Puerto Rico	B	010 1 809	135 44
Qatar	A	010 974	044
Réunion	B	010 262	19p44
Romania	e	010 40	
Rwanda	B	010 250	†
St Helena	B	010 290	†
St. Kitts and Nevis	B	010 1 809	†
St. Lucia	B	010 1 809	0 44
St. Pierre and Miquelon	B	010 508	†
St. Vincent and the Grenadines	B	010 1 809	0 44
El Salvador	B	010 503	00 44
Samoa, American	C	010 684	144
San Marino	ec	010 39 549	00 44
São Tomé and Príncipe	B	010 239	†
Saudi Arabia	A	010 966	00 44
Senegal	B	010 221	00p44
Seychelles	B	010 248	0 44
Sierra Leone	B	010 232	†
Singapore	B	010 65	005 44
Solomon Islands	C	010 677	00 44
Somalia	B	010 252	†
South Africa	B	010 27	09 44
Spain	ec	010 34	07p44
Sri Lanka	B	010 94	00 44
Sudan	A	010 249	†
Suriname	B	010 597	001 44
Swaziland	B	010 268	00 44
Sweden	e	010 46	009 44p
Switzerland	e	010 41	00 44
Syria	A	010 963	00 44
Taiwan	C	010 886	002 44
Tanzania	B	010 255	†
Thailand	B	010 66	001 44
Togo	B	010 228	
Tonga	C	010 676	0 44
Trinidad and Tobago	B	010 1 809	01 44
Tristan da Cunha	B	†	
Tunisia	A	010 216	00 44
Turkey	e	010 90	9p944
Turks and Caicos Islands	B	010 1 809 946	†
Tuvalu	C	†	†
Uganda	B	010 256	†
United Arab Emirates	A	010 971	00 44
Uruguay	B	010 598	00 44
USA	B	010 1	011 44
Alaska		010 1 907	
Hawaii		010 1 808	
USSR	e	010 7	810 44
Vanuatu	C	010 678	†
Vatican City State	ec	010 39 66982	
Venezuela	B	010 58	00 44
Vietnam	B	010 84	†
Virgin Islands (US)	B	010 1 809	011 44
Western Samoa	C	010 685	†
Yemen, North	A	010 967	00 44
Yemen, South	A	010 969	00 44
Yugoslavia	e	010 38	99 44
Zaire	B	010 243	00 44
Zambia	B	010 260	00 44
Zimbabwe	B	010 263	110 44

e Europe. *ec* European Community. † Calls must be made via the international operator. *p* A pause in dialling is necessary whilst waiting for a second tone.

SUMMARY OF SPORT 1989–90

COMMONWEALTH GAMES 1990

Held at Auckland, New Zealand, Jan. 24–Feb. 3

ATHLETICS

Men

100m	L. Christie (England)	9.93s
200m	M. Adam (England)	20.10s
400m	D. Clark (Australia)	44.60s
800m	S. Tirop (Kenya)	1m 45.98s
1,500m	P. Elliott (England)	3m 33.39s
5,000m	A. Lloyd (Australia)	13m 24.86s
10,000m	E. Martin (England)	28m 08·57s
Marathon	D. Wakiihuri (Kenya)	2h 10m 27s
30km walk	G. Leblanc (Canada)	2h 08m 28s
3,000m steeplechase	J. Kariuki (Kenya)	8m 20·64s
110m hurdles	C. Jackson (Wales)	13·08s
400m hurdles	K. Akabusi (England)	48·89s
4 × 100m relay	England	38·67s
4 × 400m relay	Kenya	3m 02·48s
High jump	N. Saunders (Bermuda)	2·36m
Pole vault	S. Arkell (Australia)	5·35m
Long jump	Y. Alli (Nigeria)	8·39m
Triple jump	M. Hadjiandreou (Cyprus)	16·95m
Shot	S. Williams (England)	18·54m
Discus	A. Olukoju (Nigeria)	62·62m
Hammer	S. Carlin (Australia)	75·66m
Javelin	S. Backley (England)	86·02m
Decathlon	M. Smith (Canada)	8,525pts

Women

100m	M. Ottey (Jamaica)	11·02s
200m	M. Ottey (Jamaica)	22·76s
400m	F. Yusuf (Nigeria)	51·08s
800m	D. Edwards (England)	2m 00·25s
1,500m	A. Chalmers (Canada)	4m 08·41s
3,000m	A. Chalmers (Canada)	8m 38·38s
10,000m	E. McColgan (Scotland)	32m 23·56s
Marathon	L. Martin (Australia)	2h 25m 28s
10km walk	K. Saxby (Australia)	45m 03s
100m hurdles	K. Morley (Wales)	12·91s
400m hurdles	S. Gunnell (England)	55·38s
4 × 100m relay	Australia	43·87s
4 × 400m relay	England	3m 28·08s
High jump	T. Murray (NZ)	1·88m
Long jump	J. Flemming (Australia)	6.78m
Shot	M. Augee (England)	18·48m
Discus	L.-M. Vizaniari (Australia)	56·38m
Javelin	T. Sanderson (England)	65·72m
Heptathlon	J. Flemming (Australia)	6,695pts

BADMINTON

Men's singles	Rashid Sidek (Malaysia)
Men's doubles	Malaysia
Women's singles	F. Smith (England)
Women's doubles	England
Mixed doubles	Hong Kong
Team event	England

BOWLS

Men's singles	R. Parrella (Australia)
Men's pairs	Australia
Men's fours	Scotland
Women's singles	G. Tau (Papua New Guinea)
Women's pairs	New Zealand
Women's fours	Australia

BOXING

Light-flyweight	J. Juko (Uganda)
Flyweight	W. McCullough (N. Ireland)
Bantamweight	S. Mohammed (Nigeria)
Featherweight	J. Irwin (England)
Lightweight	G. Nyakana (Uganda)
Light-welterweight	C. Kane (Scotland)
Welterweight	D. Defiagbon (Nigeria)
Light-middleweight	R. Woodhall (England)
Middleweight	C. Johnson (Canada)
Light-heavyweight	J. Akhasamba (Kenya)
Heavyweight	G. Onyango (Kenya)
Super-heavyweight	M. Kenny (NZ)

CYCLING

Men

1,000m sprint	G. Neiwand (Australia)	
1,000m ind. time trial	M. Vinnicombe (Australia)	1m 05·572s
4,000m ind. pursuit	G. Anderson (NZ)	4m 44·610s

4,000m team pursuit	New Zealand	4m 22·760s
10 miles scratch	G. Anderson (NZ)	19m 44·20s
50km points race	R. Burns (Australia)	81 pts
100km team time trial	New Zealand	2h 06m 46·55s
173km road race	G. Miller (NZ)	4h 34m 00·19s

Women

1,000m sprint	L. Jones (Wales)	
3,000m ind. pursuit	M. Harris (NZ)	3m 54·670s
72km road race	K. Watt (Australia)	1h 55m 11·60s

GYMNASTICS

Men

All-round	C. Hibbert (Canada)	57·950 pts
Team	Canada	171·80 pts
Floor exercises	N. Thomas (England)	9·750 pts
Pommel horse	B. Dowrick (Australia)	9·825 pts
Rings	C. Hibbert (Canada)	9·775 pts
Vault	J. May (England)	9·625 pts
Parallel bars	C. Hibbert (Canada)	9·800 pts
High bar	{ A. Nolet (Canada) } { C. Hibbert (Canada) }	9·850 pts

Women

All-round	L. Strong (Canada)	38·912 pts
Team	Canada	116·784 pts
Vault	N. Jenkins (NZ)	9·712 pts
Asymmetric bars	M. Allen (Australia)	9·875 pts
Beam	L. Strong (Canada)	9·850 pts
Floor exercises	L. Strong (Canada)	9·887 pts

Women's Rhythmic

All-round	M. Fuzesi (Canada)	37·65 pts
Ball	M. Gimotea (Canada)	9·450 pts
Hoop	M. Fuzesi (Canada)	9·400 pts
Ribbon	M. Fuzesi (Canada)	9·400 pts
Rope	A. Walker (NZ)	9·300 pts

JUDO

Men		**Women**	
Under 60kg	C. Finney (England)	*Under 48 kg*	K. Briggs (England)
Under 65kg	B. Cooper (NZ)	*Under 51 kg*	S. Rendle (England)
Under 71kg	R. Stone (England)	*Under 56 kg*	L. Cusack (Scotland)
Under 78kg	D. Southby (England)	*Under 61 kg*	D. Bell (England)
Under 86kg	D. White (England)	*Under 66 kg*	S. Mills (England)
Under 95kg	R. Stevens (England)	*Under 72 kg*	J. Morris (England)
Over 95kg	E. Gordon (England)	*Over 72 kg*	S. Lee (England)
Open	E. Gordon (England)	*Open*	S. Lee (England)

SHOOTING

Individual

Free pistol	P. Adams (Australia)	554 pts
Air pistol	B. Sandstrom (Australia)	580 pts
Rapid fire pistol	A. Breton (Guernsey)	583 pts
Centre-fire pistol	A. Pandit (India)	583 pts
Air rifle	G. Lorion (Canada)	583 pts
Smallbore rifle-prone	R. Harvey (NZ)	591 pts
Smallbore rifle-3 positions	M. Klepp (Canada)	1,157 pts
Fullbore rifle	C. Mallett (Jersey)	394 pts
Running boar	C. Robertson (Australia)	539 pts
Shotgun skeet	K. Harman (England)	187 pts
Shotgun trench	J. Maxwell (Australia)	184 pts

Pairs

Free pistol	Australia	1,106 pts
Air pistol	Bangladesh	1,138 pts
Rapid fire pistol	Australia	1,153 pts
Centre-fire pistol	Australia	1,155 pts
Air rifle	Canada	1,163 pts
Smallbore rifle-prone	New Zealand	1,185 pts
Smallbore rifle—3 positions	Canada	2,272 pts
Fullbore rifle	England	580 pts
Running boar	New Zealand	1,091 pts
Shotgun skeet	Scotland	189 pts
Shotgun trench	England	181 pts

SWIMMING AND DIVING

Men

50m freestyle	A. Baildon (Australia)	22·76s
100m freestyle	A. Baildon (Australia)	49·80s
200m freestyle	M. Roberts (Australia)	1m 49·58s
400m freestyle	I. Brown (Australia)	3m 49·91s
1,500m freestyle	G. Housman (Australia)	14m 55·25s
100m backstroke	M. Tewksbury (Canada)	56·07s
200m backstroke	G. Anderson (Canada)	2m 01·69s
100m breaststroke	A. Moorhouse (England)	1m 01·49s
200m breaststroke	J. Cleveland (Canada)	2m 14·96s
100m butterfly	A. Baildon (Australia)	53·98s
200m butterfly	A. Mosse (NZ)	1m 57·33s
200m ind. medley	G. Anderson (Canada)	2m 02·94s
400m ind. medley	R. Bruce (Australia)	4m 20·26s
4 × 100m freestyle	Australia	3m 20·05s
4 × 200m freestyle	Australia	7m 21·17s
4 × 100m medley	Canada	3m 42·25s
1m springboard	R. Butler (Australia)	583·65 pts
3m springboard	C. Rogerson (Australia)	594·84 pts
Highboard	R. Morgan (Wales)	639·84 pts

Women

50m freestyle	L. Curry (Australia)	25·80s
100m freestyle	K. Van Wirdum (Australia)	56·48s
200m freestyle	H. Lewis (Australia)	2m 00·79s
400m freestyle	H. Lewis (Australia)	4m 08·89s
800m freestyle	J. McDonald (Australia)	8m 30·27s
100m backstroke	N. Livingstone (Australia)	1m 02·46s
200m backstroke	A. Simcic (NZ)	2m 12·32s
100m breaststroke	K. Duggan (Canada)	1m 10·74s
200m breaststroke	N. Giguere (Canada)	2m 32·16s
100m butterfly	L. Curry (Australia)	1m 00·66s
200m butterfly	H. Lewis (Australia)	2m 11·15s
200m ind. medley	N. Sweetnam (Canada)	2m 15·61s
400m ind. medley	H. Lewis (Australia)	4m 42·65s
4 × 100m freestyle	Australia	3m 46·85s
4 × 200m freestyle	Australia	8m 08·95s
4 × 100m medley	Australia	4m 10·87s
1m springboard	M. De Piero (Canada)	443·28 pts
3m springboard	J. Donnet (Australia)	491·79 pts
Highboard	A. Dacyshyn (Canada)	391·68 pts

Synchronized Swimming

Solo	S. Frechette (Canada)	196·680 pts
Duet	Canada	191·230 pts

WEIGHTLIFTING

52kg

Snatch	C. Raghavan (India)	105kg
Clean & jerk	C. Raghavan (India)	127·5kg
Combined	C. Raghavan (India)	232·5kg

56kg

Snatch	R. Punnuswamy (India)	110kg
Clean & jerk	R. Punnuswamy (India)	137·5kg
Combined	R. Punnuswamy (India)	247·5kg

60kg

Snatch	M. Stephen (Nauru)	112·5kg
Clean & jerk	P. Chandra Sharma (India)	145kg
Combined	P. Chandra Sharma (India)	257·5kg

67·5kg

Snatch	P. Sharma (India)	130kg
Clean & jerk	P. Sharma (India)	165kg
Combined	P. Sharma (India)	295kg

75kg

Snatch	K. Mondal (India)	135kg
Clean & jerk	R. Laycock (Australia)	177·5kg
Combined	R. Laycock (Australia)	310kg

82·5kg

Snatch	D. Morgan (Wales)	155kg
Clean & jerk	D. Morgan (Wales)	192·5kg
Combined	D. Morgan (Wales)	347·5kg

90kg

Snatch	D. Dawkins (England)	162·5kg
Clean & jerk	D. Dawkins (England)	195kg

Combined	D. Dawkins (England)	357·5kg
100kg		
Snatch	A. Saxton (England)	165kg
Clean & jerk	A. Saxton (England)	197·5kg
Combined	A. Saxton (England)	362·5kg
110kg		
Snatch	M. Thomas (England)	160kg
Clean & jerk	M. Thomas (England)	197·5kg
Combined	M. Thomas (England)	357·5kg
Over 110kg		
Snatch	A. Davies (Wales)	180kg
Clean & jerk	A. Davies (Wales)	222·5kg
Combined	A. Davies (Wales)	402·5kg

RECORDS

ATHLETICS

WORLD RECORDS
(as at August 31, 1990)

(All the world records given below have been accepted by the International Amateur Athletic Federation except those marked with an asterisk* which are awaiting homologation.)

Fully automatic timing to 1/100th second is mandatory up to and including 400 metres. For distances up to and including 10,000 metres records will be accepted to 1/100th second if timed automatically, and to 1/10th if hand timing is used.

MEN'S EVENTS
Running

Distances	h	m	Time s	Name	Nation	Year
100 metres			9·92	C. Lewis	USA	1988
200 metres			19·72	P. Mennea	Italy	1979
400 metres			43·29	H. Reynolds	USA	1988
800 metres		1	41·73	S. Coe	GB	1981
1,000 metres		2	12·18	S. Coe	GB	1981
1,500 metres		3	29·46	S. Aouita	Morocco	1985
1 mile		3	46·32	S. Cram	GB	1985
2,000 metres		4	50·81	S. Aouita	Morocco	1987
3,000 metres		7	29·45	S. Aouita	Morocco	1989
5,000 metres		12	58·39	S. Aouita	Morocco	1987
10,000 metres		27	08·23	A. Barrios	Mexico	1989
20,000 metres		57	18·4	Dion. Castro	Portugal	1990
20,944 metres (13 miles 24 yards 2 feet)	1	00	00·0	J. Hermens	Netherlands	1976
25,000 metres	1	13	55·8	T. Seko	Japan	1981
30,000 metres	1	29	18·8	T. Seko	Japan	1981
110 metres hurdles (3 ft 6 in)			12·92	R. Kingdom	USA	1989
400 metres hurdles (3 ft 0 in)			47·02	E. Moses	USA	1983
3,000 metres steeplechase		8	05·35	P. Koech	Kenya	1989

Relay Racing

Distance	m	Time s	Nation	Year
4 × 100 metres		37·79*	France	1990
4 × 200 metres	1	19·38	Santa Monica TC	1989
4 × 400 metres	2	56·16	USA	1968
4 × 800 metres	7	03·89	GB	1982
4 × 1,500 metres	14	38·8	FRG	1977

Jumping and Throwing

	metres	ft	in	Name	Nation	Year
High jump	2·44	8	0	J. Sotomayor	Cuba	1989
Pole vault	6·06	19	10¼	S. Bubka	USSR	1988
Long jump	8·90	29	2½	R. Beamon	USA	1968
Triple jump	17·97	58	11½	W. Banks	USA	1985
Shot	23·12*	75	10¼	R. Barnes	USA	1990
Discus	74·08	243	0	J. Schult	GDR	1986
Hammer	86·74	284	7	Y. Sedykh	USSR	1986
Javelin†	90·98*	298	6	S. Backley	GB	1990
Decathlon‡	8,847 pts.			D. Thompson	GB	1984

† New type of javelin now in force
‡ Ten events comprising 100 m, long jump, shot, high jump, 400 m, 110 m hurdles, discus, pole vault, javelin, 1500 m.

Walking (Track)

Distance	Time			Name	Nation	Year
	h	m	s			
20,000 metres	1	18	40	E. Canto	Mexico	1984
28,565 metres						
(17 miles 1319 yards)	2	00	00·0	M. Damilano	Italy	1985
30,000 metres	2	06	07·3	M. Damilano	Italy	1985
50,000 metres	3	41	39·00	R. Gonzalez	Mexico	1979

WOMEN'S EVENTS

Running

Distance	Time		Name	Nation	Year
	m	s			
100 metres		10·49	F. Griffith-Joyner	USA	1988
200 metres		21·34	F. Griffith-Joyner	USA	1988
400 metres		47·60	M. Koch	GDR	1985
800 metres	1	53·28	J. Kratochvilova	Czechoslovakia	1983
1,500 metres	3	52·47	T. Kazankina	USSR	1980
1 mile	4	15·61	P. Ivan	Romania	1989
3,000 metres	8	22·62	T. Kazankina	USSR	1984
5,000 metres	14	37·33	I. Kristiansen	Norway	1986
10,000 metres	30	13·74	I. Kristiansen	Norway	1986
100 metres hurdles (2 ft 9 in)		12·21	Y. Donkova	Bulgaria	1988
400 metres hurdles (2 ft 6 in)		52·94	M. Stepanova	USSR	1986

Relays

Distance	Time		Nation	Year
	m	s		
4 × 100 metres		41·37	GDR	1985
4 × 200 metres	1	28·15	GDR	1980
4 × 400 metres	3	15·17	USSR	1988
4 × 800 metres	7	50·17	USSR	1984

Jumping and Throwing

	metres	ft	in	Name	Nation	Year
High jump	2·09	6	10¼	S. Kostadinova	Bulgaria	1987
Long jump	7·52	24	8¼	G. Chistiakova	USSR	1988
Shot	22·63	74	3	N. Lisovskaya	USSR	1987
Discus	76·80	252	0	G. Reinsch	GDR	1988
Javelin	80·00	262	5	P. Felke	GDR	1988
Heptathlon†	7,291 pts.			J. Joyner–Kersee	USA	1988

†Seven events comprising 100m hurdles, shot, high jump, 200m, long jump, javelin, 800m.

UNITED KINGDOM (NATIONAL) RECORDS
(as at Sept. 1, 1990)
(Records set anywhere by athletes eligible to represent Great Britain and Northern Ireland)

Men

Distance	Time	Name	Year		Event	Time/Mark	Name	Year
100 metres	9.97s	L. Christie	1988		*Hurdles*			
200 metres	20.09s	J. Regis	1988		110 metres	13.08s	C. Jackson	1990
400 metres	44.50s	D. Redmond	1987		400 metres	47.92s	K. Akabusi	1990
800 metres	1m 41.73s	S. Coe	1981					
1,000 metres	2m 12.18s	S. Coe	1981		*Relay*			
1,500 metres	3m 29.67s	S. Coe	1985		4 × 100 metres	37.98s	GB team	1990
1 mile	3m 46.32s	S. Cram	1985		4 × 200 metres	1m 21.29s	GB team	1989
2,000 metres	4m 51.39s	S. Cram	1985		4 × 400 metres	2m 58.22s	GB team	1990
3,000 metres	7m 32.79s	D. Moorcroft	1982		4 × 800 metres	7m 03.89s	GB team	1982
5,000 metres	13m 00.41s	D. Moorcroft	1982		High jump	2.34m (7ft 8in)	D. Grant	1989
10,000 metres	27m 23.06s	E. Martin	1988		Pole vault	5.65m (18ft 6½in)	K. Stock	1981
20,000 metres	57m 28.7s	C. Thackery	1990		Long jump	8.23m (27ft 0in)	L. Davies	1968
20,855 metres	1h	C. Thackery	1990		Triple jump	17.57m (57ft 7¼in)	K. Connor	1982
25,000 metres	1h 15m 22.6s	R. Hill	1965		Shot	21.68m (71ft 1¼in)	G. Capes	1980
30,000 metres	1h 31m 30.4s	J. Alder	1970		Discus	64.32m (211ft 0in)	W. Tancred	1974
					Hammer	77.54m (254ft 5in)	M. Girvan	1984
Steeplechase					Javelin	90.98m (298ft 6in)	S. Backley	1990
3,000 metres	8m 07.96s	M. Rowland	1988		Decathlon	8,847 points*	D. Thompson	1984

Walking (track)

20,000 metres	1h 23m 26.5s	I. McCombie	1990
30,000 metres	2h 19m 18s	C. Maddocks	1984
50,000 metres	4h 05m 44.6s	P. Blagg .	1990
2 hours	16 miles 315 yards	R. Wallwork	1971

Women

100 metres	11.10s	K. Cook	1981
200 metres	22.10s	K. Cook	1984
400 metres	49.43s	K. Cook	1984
800 metres	1m 57.42s	K. Wade	1985
1,500 metres	3m 59.96s	Z. Budd	1985
1 mile	4m 17.57s	Z. Budd	1985
3,000 metres	8m 28.83s	Z. Budd	1985
5,000 metres	14m 48.07s	Z. Budd	1985
10,000 metres	31m 06.99s	E. McColgan	1988

Hurdles

100 metres	12,82s	S. Gunnell	1988
400 metres	54.03s	S. Gunnell	1988

Relay

4 × 100 metres	42.43s	GB team	1980
4 × 200 metres	1m 31.57s	GB team	1977
4 × 400 metres	3m 24.78s	GB team	1990
4 × 800 metres	8m 23.8s	GB team	1971
High jump	1.95m (6ft 4½in)	D. Elliott	1982
Long jump	6.90m (22ft 7½in)	B. Kinch	1983
Shot	19.36m (63ft 6½in)	J. Oakes	1988
Discus	67.48m (221ft 5in)	M. Ritchie	1981
Javelin	77.44m (254ft 1in)	F. Whitbread	1986
Heptathlon	6,623 points	J. Simpson	1986

SWIMMING

WORLD RECORDS
(as at August 31, 1990)

Men

100 metres freestyle.—M. Biondi (USA), 48·42s
200 metres freestyle.—G. Lamberti (Italy), 1m 46·69s
400 metres freestyle.—U. Dassler (GDR), 3m 46·95s
800 metres freestyle.—V. Salnikov (USSR), 7m 50·64s
1,500 metres freestyle.—V. Salnikov (USSR), 14m 54·76s
100 metres breaststroke.—A. Moorhouse (GB), 1m 01·49s
200 metres breaststroke.—M. Borrowman (USA), 2m 11·53s
100 metres butterfly.—P. Morales (USA), 52·84s
200 metres butterfly.—M. Gross (FRG), 1m 56·24s
100 metres backstroke.—D. Berkoff (USA), 54·51s
200 metres backstroke.—I. Polyanski (USSR), 1m 58·14s
200 metres medley.—D. Wharton (USA), 2m 00·11s
400 metres medley.—T. Darnyi (Hungary) 4m 14·75s
4 × 100 metres freestyle relay.—USA, 3m 16·53s
4 × 200 metres freestyle relay.—USA, 7m 12·51s
4 × 100 metres medley relay.—USA, 3m 36·93s

Women

100 metres freestyle.—K. Otto (GDR), 54·73s
200 metres freestyle.—H. Friedrich (GDR), 1m 57·55s
400 metres freestyle.—J. Evans (USA), 4m 03·85s
800 metres freestyle.—J. Evans (USA), 8m 16·22s
1,500 metres freestyle.—J. Evans (USA), 15m 52·10s
100 metres breaststroke.—S. Hörner (GDR), 1m 07·91s
200 metres breaststroke.—S. Hörner (GDR), 2m 26·71s
100 metres butterfly.—M. Meagher (USA), 57·93s

200 metres butterfly.—M. Meagher (USA), 2m 05·96s
100 metres backstroke.—I. Kleber (GDR), 1m 00·59s
200 metres backstroke.—B. Mitchell (USA), 2m 08·60s
200 metres medley.—U. Geweniger (GDR), 2m 11·73s
400 metres medley.—P. Schneider (GDR), 4m 36·10s
4 × 100 metres freestyle relay.—GDR, 3m 40·57s
4 × 200 metres freestyle relay.—GDR, 7m 55·47s
4 × 100 metres medley relay.—GDR, 4m 03·69s

WEIGHTLIFTING
WORLD RECORDS (TOTALS)
(as at August 31, 1990)

Class	Kg		
52 kg	270	S. Marinov (Bulgaria)	1988
56 kg	300	N. Shalamanov (Bulgaria)	1984
60 kg	342·5	N. Suleymanoglu (Turkey)	1988
67·5 kg	355	M. Petrov (Bulgaria)	1987
75 kg	382·5	A. Varbanov (Bulgaria)	1988
82·5 kg	405	Y. Vardanyan (USSR)	1984
90 kg	422·5	V. Solodov (USSR)	1984
100 kg	440	Y. Zakharevich (USSR)	1983
110 kg	455	Y. Zakharevich (USSR)	1988
Over 110 kg	475	L. Taranenko (USSR)	1988

RESULTS

ALPINE SKIING

WORLD CUP 1989–90

Men
Downhill.—H. Hoeflehner (Austria), 166 pts.
Slalom.—A. Bittner (W. Germany), 150 pts.
Giant Slalom.—O. K. Furuseth (Norway), 96 pts.
Super Giant Slalom.—P. Zurbriggen (Switzerland), 98 pts.
Overall.—P. Zurbriggen (Switzerland), 357 pts.

Women
Downhill.—K. Gutensohn-Knopf (W. Germany), 110 pts.
Slalom.—V. Schneider (Switzerland), 125 pts.
Giant Slalom.—A. Wachter (Austria), 133 pts.

Super Giant Slalom.—C. Merle (France), 99 pts.
Overall.—P. Kronberger (Austria), 341 pts.
Nations Cup.—1. Austria; 2. Switzerland; 3. W. Germany.

AMERICAN FOOTBALL, 1990

XXIV American Superbowl (New Orleans, Jan. 28).—
San Francisco 49ers beat Denver Broncos 55–10.
Coca Cola League final (Crystal Palace, Aug. 4).—
Manchester Spartans beat Northants. Storm 27–25.
American Bowl V (Wembley, Aug. 5).—New Orleans Saints beat Los Angeles Raiders 17–10.

ANGLING

NATIONAL COARSE CHAMPIONSHIPS

Year	Venue	No. of teams	Individual Winner	Weight kg	Team Winners	Points	Division
1989	R. Severn	76	B. Wickens (Isfield & DAC)	39·910	Reading & District	705	1
,,	R. Huntspill	78	E. Warner (Colchester APS)	21·210	DELCAC	722	2
,,	R. Trent	75	A. K. Bunting (Grantham AA)	16·050	Tipton & District	751	3
,,	Oxford Canal	70	K. Huggins (East Grinstead AS)	2·900	Highfield AS	696	4
,,	16 & 40 Foot Drains	107	M. Shaw (Tonbridge A & FPS)	39·540	Silstar Goldthorpe	1018	5
,,	Lancaster Canal	47	J. Rowland (Smithies Tackle)	5·190	Disley & New Mills	466	Jnr

ASSOCIATION FOOTBALL 1989–90

League Competitions

ENGLAND AND WALES

Division 1.—1. Liverpool, 79 pts; 2. Aston Villa, 70 pts. *Relegated*, Sheffield Wednesday, 43 pts; Charlton Athletic, 30 pts; Millwall, 26 pts.
Division 2.—1. Leeds Utd., 85 pts; 2. Sheffield Utd., 85 pts. *Third promotion place:* won in playoff by Swindon Town but Swindon Town remains in Division 2 as penalty for illegal payments to players (*see* **Events of the Year—Sport**) and Sunderland promoted. *Relegated*, Bournemouth, 48 pts; Bradford City, 41 pts; Stoke City, 37 pts.
Division 3.—1. Bristol Rovers, 93 pts; 2. Bristol City, 91 pts. *Third promotion place:* Notts County. *Relegated*, Cardiff City, 50 pts; Northampton Town, 47 pts; Blackpool, 46 pts; Walsall, 41 pts.
Division 4.—1. Exeter, 89 pts; 2. Grimsby Town, 79 pts; 3. Southend Utd., 75 pts. *Fourth promotion place:* Cambridge Utd. *Relegated to GM Vauxhall Conference*, Colchester Utd.
GM Vauxhall Conference.—*Promoted*, Darlington, 87 pts. *Relegated*, Chorley, 45 pts; Farnborough, 42 pts; Enfield, 36 pts.

SCOTLAND

Premier Division.—1. Rangers, 51 pts; 2. Aberdeen, 44 pts. *Relegated*, Dundee, 24 pts.
Division 1.—1. St. Johnstone, 58 pts (*promoted*); 2. Aidrie, 54 pts. *Relegated*, Albion, 27 pts; Alloa, 25 pts.
Division 2.—1. Brechin City, 49 pts; 2. Kilmarnock, 48 pts (*promoted*).

Cup Competitions

ENGLAND

FA Cup final (Wembley, May 12).—Manchester Utd. 3, Crystal Palace 3 a.e.t. *Replay* (May 17).—Manchester Utd. beat Crystal Palace 1–0.
Littlewoods Cup final.—Nottingham Forest beat Oldham Athletic 1–0.
Zenith Data Systems Cup final.—Chelsea beat Middlesbrough 1–0.
Leyland Daf Cup final.—Tranmere Rovers beat Bristol Rovers 2–1.
FA Vase final.—Yeading beat Bridlington Town 1–0.
FA Trophy final.—Barrow beat Leek 3–0.
Arthur Dunn Cup final.—Old Chigwellians beat Old Reptonians 3–2.
Women's FA Cup final.—Doncaster Belles beat Friends of Fulham 1–0.

WALES

Welsh Cup final.—Hereford beat Wrexham 2–1.

SCOTLAND

Scottish FA Cup final (Hampden, May 12).—Aberdeen 0, Celtic 0. Aberdeen won 9–8 on penalties.
Skol Cup final.—Aberdeen beat Rangers 2–1 a.e.t.

EUROPE

European Cup final (Vienna).—AC Milan beat Benfica 1–0.
European Cup-Winners Cup final (Gothenberg).—Sampdoria beat Anderlecht 2–0 a.e.t.
UEFA Cup final.— Juventus beat Fiorentina 3–1 on agg.

Rous Cup 1990.—Cancelled.
Charity Shield 1989.—Liverpool beat Arsenal 1–0.

Internationals

1989			
Nov.	15	Wembley:	England 0, Italy 0.
Dec.	13	Wembley:	England 2, Yugoslavia 1.
1990			
Mar.	27	Belfast:	N. Ireland 2, Norway 3.
Mar.	28	Wembley:	England 1, Brazil 0.
		Dublin:	Rep. of Ireland 1, Wales 0.
		Hampden:	Scotland 1, Argentina 0.
Apr.	25	Wembley:	England 4, Czechoslovakia 2.
		Stockholm:	Sweden 4, Wales 2.
		Hampden:	Scotland 0, E. Germany 1.
May	15	Wembley:	England 1, Denmark 0.
May	16	Aberdeen:	Scotland 1, Egypt 3.
May	18	Belfast:	N. Ireland 1, Uruguay 0.
May	19	Hampden:	Scotland 1, Poland 1.
May	20	Cardiff:	Wales 1, Costa Rica 0.
May	22	Wembley:	England 1, Uruguay 2.
May	28	Valetta:	Malta 1, Scotland 2.
June	2	Tunis:	Tunisia 1, England 1.

World Cup
(Qualifying Round)

1989			
Oct.	11	Katowice:	Poland 0, England 0.
		Cardiff:	Wales 1, Netherlands 2.
		Paris:	France 3, Scotland 0.
		Dublin:	Rep. of Ireland 3, N. Ireland 0.
Nov.	15	Cologne:	W. Germany 2, Wales 1.
		Hampden:	Scotland 1, Norway 1.

WORLD CUP 1990
(Italy, June 8–July 8)

First Round

Group A.—Italy, 6 pts; Czechoslovakia, 4 pts; Austria, 2 pts; USA, 0 pt.

Group B.—Cameroon, 4 pts; Romania, 3 pts; Argentina, 3 pts; USSR, 2 pts.

Group C.—Brazil, 6 pts; Costa Rica, 4 pts; Scotland, 2 pts; Sweden, 0 pt.

Group D.—W. Germany, 5 pts; Yugoslavia, 4 pts; Colombia, 3 pts; UAE, 0 pts.

Group E.—Spain, 5 pts; Belgium, 4 pts; Uruguay, 3 pts; S. Korea, 0 pts.

Group F.—England, 4 pts; Rep. of Ireland, 3 pts; Netherlands, 3 pts; Egypt, 2 pts.

Second Round

Cameroon v. Colombia, 2–1; Czechoslovakia v. Costa Rica, 4–1; Brazil v. Argentina, 0–1; W. Germany v. Netherlands, 2–1; Rep. of Ireland v. Romania, 0–0 (5–4 on penalties); Italy v. Uruguay, 2–0; Spain v. Yugoslavia, 1–2; England v. Belgium, 1–0.

Quarter-Finals

Argentina v. Yugoslavia, 0–0 (3–2 on penalties); Rep. of Ireland v. Italy, 0–1; Czechoslovakia v. W. Germany, 0–1; Cameroon v. England, 2–3.

Semi-Finals

Argentina v. Italy, 1–1 (4–3 on penalties); England v. W. Germany, 1–1 (3–4 on penalties).

Third-Place Playoff

Italy v. England, 2–1.

Final

Argentina v. W. Germany, 0–1.

ATHLETICS, 1990

National Cross-Country Championships (Women)

Held at Rickmansworth, February 17, 1990

		min.	sec.
1.	A. Whitcombe (Parkside)	19	03
2.	L. Adam (Stevenage)	19	14
3.	A. Wyeth (Parkside)	19	26
	Team result: 1. Parkside		70 pts.

National Cross-Country Championships (Men)

Held at Leeds, Feburary 24, 1990

		min.	sec.
1.	R. Nerurkar (Bingley)	44	56
2.	P. Taylor (Copeland)	45	23
3.	S. Tunstall (Preston)	45	34
	Team result: 1. Valli		200 pts.

United Kingdom v. East Germany (Indoors)

Held at Glasgow, February 23, 1990

Men's Events

metres		min.	sec.
60—L. Christie (UK)			6·61
200—M. Adam (UK)			20·97
400—T. Schoenlebe (GDR)			45·92
800—T. McKean (UK)		1	46·86
1,500—P. Elliott (UK)		3	46·79
3,000—U. Pflugner (GDR)		7	53·47
60 hurdles—A. Jarrett (UK)			7·64
5,000 walk—A. Noack (GDR)		18	56·27
4 × 200 relay—United Kingdom		1	22·99

	metres
High jump—D. Grant (UK)	2·26
Pole vault—A. Ashurst (UK)	5·20
Long jump—S. Faulkner (UK)	7·93
Triple jump—J. Herbert (UK)	16·43
Shot—S. Buder (GDR)	20·06

UK 88 pts, East Germany 61 pts.

Women's Events

metres	min.	sec.
60—S. Moller (GDR)		7·27
200—S. Gunther (GDR)		23·90
400—L. Keogh (UK)		52·87
800—C. Wachtel (GDR)	2	02·49
1,500—E. Keissling (GDR)	4	28·44
3,000—A. Hahmann (GDR)	9	07·52
60 hurdles—J. Agyepong (UK)		8·12
3,000 walk—B. Anders (GDR)	12	38·34
4 × 200 relay—East Germany	1	33·83

	metres
High jump—B. Voros (GDR)	1·91
Long jump—H. Radtke (GDR)	6·76
Shot—G. Hammer (GDR)	19·35

East Germany 79·5 pts, UK 46·5 pts.

European Indoor Championships

Held at Glasgow, March 3–4, 1990

Men's Events

metres		min.	sec.
60—L. Christie (UK)			6·56
200—S. Floris (Italy)			21·01
400—N. Dobeleit (FRG)			46·08
800—T. McKean (UK)		1	46·22
1,500—J.-P. Herold (GDR)		3	44·39
3,000—E. Dubus (France)		7	53·94
60 hurdles—I. Kazanov (USSR)			7·52
5,000 walk—M. Shchennikov (USSR)		19	00·62

	metres
High jump—A. Partyka (Poland)	2·33
Pole vault—R. Gataullin (USSR)	5·80
Long jump—D. Haaf (FRG)	8·11
Triple jump—I. Lapshin (USSR)	17·14
Shot—K. Bodenmöller (Austria)	21·03

Women's Events

metres		min.	sec.
60—U. Sarvari (FRG)			7·10
200—U. Sarvari (FRG)			22·96
400—M. Shonina (USSR)			51·22
800—L. Gurina (USSR)		2	01·63
1,500—D. Melinte (Romania)		4	09·73
3,000—E. van Hulst (Neth.)		8	57·28
60 hurdles—L. Narozhilenko (USSR)			7·74
3,000 walk—B. Anders (GDR)		11	59·36

	metres
High jump—H. Henkel (FRG)	2·00
Long jump—G. Chistiakova (USSR)	6·85
Shot—C. Losch (FRG)	20·64

AAA/WAAA Indoor Championships

Held at Cosford, March 9–10, 1990

Men's Events

metres		min.	sec.
60—L. Christie (TVH)			6·61
200—M. Adam (Belgrave)			21·25
400—D. Harris (USA)			46·73
800—T. McKean (Bellshill)		1	46·49
1,500—K. Cheruiyot (Kenya)		3	44·12
3,000—R. Denmark (Gateshead)		7	54·41
60 hurdles—C. Jackson (Cardiff)			7·43

	metres
High jump—N. Saunders (Bermuda) ..	2·25
Pole vault—A. Ashurst (Sale)	5·20
Long jump—S. Faulkner (Birchfield) ..	8·03
Triple jump—F. Agyepong	
(Shaftesbury)	16·05
Shot—P. Edwards (RAF)	17·79

Women's Events

	metres	min.	sec.
60—B. Kinch (Hounslow)			7·26
200—M. Ottey (Jamaica)			23·07
400—S. Guise (Birchfield)			55·24
800—D. Gandy (Hounslow)		2	07·65
1,500—D. Gunning (Swindon)		4	27·55
3,000—D. Peel (Crawley)		9	45·00
60 *hurdles*—J. Agyepong (Shaftesbury)			8·16

	metres
High jump—J. Bennett (Epsom &	
Ewell)	1·92
Long jump—K. Hagger (Essex Ladies) .	6·28
Shot—J. Oakes (Croydon)	18·55

UK Cross-Country Trials

Held at Glasgow, March 11, 1990

Men	min.	sec.
1. A. Passey (Bromsgrove)	32	46
2. D. McNeilly (Willowdale)	32	59
3. P. Taylor (Copeland)	33	04
Women		
1. A. Wallace (Torbay)	15	18
2. S. McGeorge (Brighton)	15	20
3. A. Wyeth (Parkside)	15	25
Junior Men		
1. A. Pearson (Longwood)	23	25
2. M. Campbell (Winchester)	23	45
3. S. Green (Stretford)	23	51
Junior Women		
1. A. Whitcombe (Parkside)	14	36
2. G. Stacey (Bromley)...............	14	55
3. A. Duke (Mandale)................	15	04

National 10 Mile Road Walk (Men)

Held at Southend, March 17, 1990

	hr.	min.	sec.
1. I. McCombie (Cambridge H.) ..	1	08	36
2. P. Blagg (Cambridge H.)	1	11	43
3. D. Thorn (Coventry)	1	13	22
Team result: 1. Cambridge Harriers, 41 pts.			

National 10km Road Walk (Women)

Held at Southend, March 17, 1990

	min.	sec.
1. B. Sworowski (Sheffield)	46	40
2. M. Walsh (Ireland)................	49	11
3. H. Elleker (Sheffield)	49	29
Team result: 1. Sheffield, 7 pts.		

UK v. USA v. USSR (Indoors)

Held at Cosford, March 18, 1990

Men's Events

metres	min.	sec.
60—L. Christie (UK).................		6·59
200—M. Adam (UK)		21·03
400—A. Valmon (USA)		46·37
800—M. Steele (UK)	1	48·37
1 mile—E. Slowikowski (USA)	4	12·81
3,000—R. Denmark (UK)	8	05·02

60 *hurdles*—T. Dees (USA)			7·46
5,000 *walk*—M. Shchennikov (USSR)..		19	45·28
4×400 *relay*—USA		3	10·83
			metres
High jump—D. Grank (UK)			2·25
Pole vault—I. Trandenkov (USSR)			5·55
Long jump—G. McKee (USA)			8·02
Triple jump—V. Sokov (USSR)			16·97
Shot—V. Lykho (USSR)..............			21·16
35lb weight—K. Flax (USA)			20·34

USA 121 pts, UK 100 pts, USSR 93 pts.

IAAF World Cross-Country Championships

Held at Aix-les-Bains, France, March 24, 1990

Men (12,200 m)	min.	sec.
1. K. Skah (Morocco)	34	21
2. M. Tanui (Kenya)...................	34	21
3. J. Korir (Kenya)...................	34	22
Team result: 1. Kenya		42 pts.
2. Ethiopia		96 pts.
3. Spain		176 pts.
Women (6,000 m)	min.	sec.
1. L. Jennings (USA)	19	21
2. A. Dias (Portugal)	19	33
3. E. Romanova (USSR)................	19	33
Team result: 1. USSR		37 pts.
2. Ethiopia		75 pts.
3. Portugal		80 pts.
Junior Men (8,000 m)	min.	sec.
1. K. Kororia (Kenya)	22	13
2. R. Chelimo (Kenya)	22	14
3. B. Fita (Ethiopia)	22	24
Team result: 1. Kenya		12 pts.
2. Ethiopia		27 pts.
3. Italy		85 pts.
Junior Women (4,400 m)	min.	sec.
1. Shixiang Liu (China)................	14	19
2. Qinglan Yan (China)	14	20
3. S. Chepkemei (Kenya)	14	22
Team result: 1. Kenya		19 pts.
2. Japan		45 pts.
3. China		68 pts.

London Marathon

Held April 22, 1990

Men	hr.	min.	sec.
1. A. Hutton (UK)................	2	10	10
2. S. Bettiol (Italy)	2	10	40
3. J. Romera (Spain).............	2	10	48
Women	hr.	min.	sec.
1. W. Panfil (Poland)	2	26	31
2. F. Larrieu-Smith (USA)	2	28	01
3. L. Weidenbach (USA)	2	28	15

National 20km Road Walk (Men)

Held at Leicester, May 12, 1990

	hr.	min.	sec.
1. S. Martingale (York)	1	27	37
2. Q. Moreno (Colombia)	1	28	33
3. J. Ball (Steyning)	1	30	44
Team result: Splott, 31 pts.			

National 15km Road Walk (Women)

Held at Leicester, May 12, 1990

	hr.	min.	sec.
1. B. Sworowski (Sheffield)	1	12	36
2. H. Elleker (Sheffield)	1	18	01
3. V. Lupton (Sheffield)	1	18	02
Team result: Sheffield, 6 pts.			

UK v. West Germany v. Italy v. Hungary
(Field only)

Held at Southampton, May 27, 1990

Men		metres
Shot—K. Konya (FRG)		19·25
Discus—W. Schmidt (FRG)		63·60
Hammer—T. Gecsek (Hungary)		77·00
Javelin—A. Linden (FRG)		75·92
Women		
Shot—S. Storp (FRG)		19·84
Discus—U. Kreutel (FRG)		60·24
Javelin—K. Hartai (Hungary)		62·36

West Germany 100 pts, Hungary 68 pts,
Italy 48 pts, UK 43 pts.

UK v. Italy v. International Select
(Field only)

Held at Southampton, May 27, 1990

Men		metres
High jump—B. Reilly (UK)		2·27
Pole vault—M. Andreini (Italy)		5·20
Long jump—S. Faulkner (UK)		7·79
Triple jump—D. Badinelli (Italy)		16·38
Women		
High jump—B. Fiammengo (Italy)		1·84
Long jump—M. Berkeley (UK)		6·32

Italy 54 pts, UK 51 pts,
International Select 25 pts.

United Kingdom Championships

Held at Cardiff, June 2–3, 1990

Men's Events

metres	min.	sec.
100—L. Christie (TVH)		10·13
200—A. Mafe (London Irish)		21·13
400—R. Black (Team Solent)		45·63
800—D. Sharpe (Gateshead)	1	51·46
1,500—N. Horsfield (Newport)	3	48·39
3,000—G. Turnbull (Valli)	8	11·35
5,000—S. Mugglestone (Oxford Univ.)	13	43·70
3,000 *steeplechase*—K. Penney (Haringey)	8	50·90
110 *hurdles*—C. Jackson (Cardiff)		13·10
400 *hurdles*—K. Akabusi (Team Solent)		51·50
10,000 *walk*—I. McCombie (Cambridge H.)	41	16·00

	metres
High jump—D. Grant (Haringey)	2·25
Pole vault—A. Ashurst (Sale)	5·30
Long jump—K. Liddington (Birchfield)	7·62
Triple jump—F. Agyepong (Shaftesbury)	16·06
Shot—P. Edwards (RAF)	18·57
Discus—P. Mardle (Wolverhampton)	57·02
Hammer—P. Head (Newham)	71·64
Javelin—S. Backley (Cambridge H.)	88·46

Women's Events

metres	min.	sec.
100—S. Short (Torfaen)		11·36
200—P. Smith (Wolverhampton)		23·97
400—D. Edwards (Sale)		54·32
800—H. Thorpe (Cambridge H.)	2	05·52
1,500—J. Wyeth (Parkside)	4	20·40
3,000—A. Wallace (Torbay)	9	08·10
100 *hurdles*—K. Morley (Cardiff)		13·16

400 *hurdles*—C. Sugden (Stretford)		57·52
5,000 *walk*—B. Sworowski (Sheffield)	22	31·59

	metres
High jump—J. Bennett (Epsom & Ewell)	1·84
Long jump—M. Berkeley (Shaftesbury)	6·17
Triple jump—M. Griffith (Windsor)	12·94
Shot—M. Augee (Bromley)	19·03
Discus—J. McKernan (Lisburn)	55·36
Javelin—S. Gibson (Nottingham)	58·32

RWA National 35km Walk

Held at York, June 9, 1990

	hr.	min.	sec.
1. L. Morton (Sheffield)	2	50	50
2. G. Brown (Steyning)	2	58	35
3. S. Phillips (Ilford)	2	58	58

Team result: 1. Sheffield 35 pts.

RWA National 5,000m Walk (Women)

Held at York, June 9, 1990

	min.	sec.
1. L. Langford (Wolverhampton)	22	24
2. H. Elleker (Sheffield)	23	05
3. V. Lupton (Sheffield)	23	11

Team result: 1. Sheffield 34 pts.

UK v. Kenya v. USA

Held at Portsmouth, June 22, 1990

Men's Events (Track only)

metres	min.	sec.
100—L. Christie (UK)		9·95
200—J. Regis (UK)		20·52
400—T. Simon (USA)		45·86
800—M. Everett (USA)	1	46·33
1 *mile*—J. Gladwin (UK)	4	02·87
3,000—J. Gregorek (USA)	7	52·72
5,000—S. Mugglestone (UK)	13	33·67
3,000 *steeplechase*—J. Kariuki (Kenya)	8	30·12
110 *hurdles*—R. Kingdom (USA)		13·11
400 *hurdles*—K. Akabusi (UK)		50·10
4 × 100 *relay*—USA		40·25
4 × 400 *relay*—United Kingdom	3	05·25

USA 94 pts, UK 86 pts, Kenya 63 pts.

UK v. USA

Held at Portsmouth, June 22, 1990

Women's Events (Field only)

	metres
High jump—J. Wohlschlag (USA)	1·95
Long jump—F. May (UK)	6·68
Shot—J. Oakes (UK)	18·88
Discus—L. Barnes (USA)	55·30
Javelin—D. Mayhew (USA)	63·42

USA 63 pts, UK 47 pts.

UK v. Canada v. East Germany

Held at Gateshead, June 29, 1990

Men's Events

metres	min.	sec.
100—L. Christie (UK)		10·35
200—L. Christie (UK)		20·69
400—R. Black (UK)		45·61

				min.	sec.
800—T. McKean (UK)				1	46·98
1,500—H. Fuhlbrugge (GDR)				3	45·61
3,000—J. Nuttall (UK)				7	58·39
5,000—E. Martin (UK)				13	39·01
3,000 *steeplechase*—G. Fell (UK)				8	33·32
110 *hurdles*—C. Jackson (UK)					13·53
400 *hurdles*—K. Akabusi (UK)					49·22
10,000 *walk*—G. Leblanc (Canada)				39	26·02
4 × 100 *relay*—United Kingdom					39·38
4 × 400 *relay*—United Kingdom				3	04·48

	metres
High jump—G. Parsons (UK)	2·24
Pole vault—C. Pietz (GDR)	5·40
Long jump—S. Faulkner (UK)	8·02
Triple jump—V. Mai (GDR)	17·13
Shot—U. Timmermann (GDR)	20·67
Discus—J. Schult (GDR)	62·32
Hammer—G. Rodehau (GDR)	74·40
Javelin—S. Backley (UK)	87·22

UK 181 pts, East Germany 159 pts, Canada 100 pts.

Women's Events

metres		min.	sec.
100—K. Krabbe (GDR)			11·52
200—S. Gunther (GDR)			23·46
400—G. Breuer (GDR)			51·03
800—C. Wachtel (GDR)		1	59·54
1,500—Y. Mai (GDR)		4	10·13
3,000—K. Ullrich (GDR)		9	06·25
100 *hurdles*—C. Oschkenat (GDR)			13·29
400 *hurdles*—P. Krug (GDR)			55·65
5,000 *walk*—B. Anders (GDR)		21	42·02
4 × 100 *relay*—East Germany			43·06
4 × 400 *relay*—East Germany		3	29·67

	metres
High jump—H. Balck (GDR)	1·87
Long jump—H. Radtke (GDR)	6·92
Shot—A. Kumbernuss (GDR)	20·26
Discus—I. Wyludda (GDR)	67·10
Javelin—K. Forkel (GDR)	65·98

East Germany 169·5 pts, UK 107 pts, Canada 55·5 pts.

RWA 50km Walk

Held at Sutton Coldfield, July 14, 1990

		hr.	min.	sec.
1. C. Berwick (Leicester)		4	33	23
2. C. Thomson (Sarnia)		4	40	56
3. R. Dobson (Ilford)		4	41	31
Team: 1. Sheffield				

AAA/WAAA Championships

Held at Birmingham, August 3–4, 1990

Men's Events

metres		min.	sec.
100—C. Smith (USA)			10·21
200—J. Regis (Belgrave)			20·28
400—H. Burnett (Jamaica)			45·52
800—W. Tanui (Kenya)		1	44·14
1,500—N. Horsfield (Newport)		3	44·70
3,000—J. Walker (NZ)		8	05·01
5,000—E. Martin (Basildon)		13	32·07
3,000 *steeplechase*—P. Barkutwo (Kenya)		8	22·22
110 *hurdles*—C. Jackson (Cardiff)			13·23
400 *hurdles*—N. Page (USA)			50·06
10,000 *walk*—M. Easton (Surrey)		41	32·80

	metres
High jump—D. Grant (Haringey)	2·28
Pole vault—P. Benavides (USA)	5·30
Long jump—S. Faulkner (Birchfield)	8·05
Triple jump—J. Herbert (Haringey)	16·61
Shot—P. Edwards (RAF)	19·00
Discus—A. Ekoku (Belgrave)	57·58

Hammer—P. Head (Newham)		72·68
Javelin—M. Hill (Leeds)		81·22

Held at Gateshead, June 29, 1990

		min.	sec.
10,000m—R. Nerurkar (Bingley)		28	05·16

Women's Events

metres		min.	sec.
100—S. Douglas (Milton Keynes)			11·38
200—J. Stoute (Essex)			23·07
400—L. Leatherwood (USA)			51·62
800—A. Williams (Sale)		2	03·45
1,500—C. Cahill (Gateshead)		4	12·54
3,000—Y. Murray (Edinburgh)		8	48·21
100 *hurdles*—L.-A. Skeete (Swindon)			13·03
400 *hurdles*—G. Retchakan (Thurrock)			57·14
5,000 *walk*—B. Sworowski (Sheffield)		22	23·35

	metres
High jump—L. Haggett (Croydon)	1·88
Long jump—F. May (Derby)	6·66
Shot—J. Oakes (Croydon)	18·63
Discus—L.-M. Vizaniari (Australia)	57·22
Javelin—T. Sanderson (Hounslow)	58·42

Held at Portsmouth, June 22, 1990

		min.	sec.
10,000m—A. Wallace (Torbay)		32	51·17

European Championships

Held at Split, Yugoslavia, Aug. 27–Sept. 1, 1990

Men's Events

metres		hr.	min.	sec.
100—L. Christie (UK)				10·00
200—J. Regis (UK)				20·11
400—R. Black (UK)				45·08
800—T. McKean (UK)			1	44·76
1,500—J.-P. Herold (GDR)			3	38·25
5,000—S. Antibo (Italy)			13	22·00
10,000—S. Antibo (Italy)			27	41·27
Marathon—G. Bordin (Italy)		2	14	02
3,000 *steeplechase*—F. Panetta (Italy)			8	12·66
110 *hurdles*—C. Jackson (UK)				13·18
400 *hurdles*—K. Akabusi (UK)				47·92
20km *walk*—P. Blazeck (Czech.)		1	22	05
50km *walk*—A. Perlov (USSR)		3	54	36
4 × 100 *relay*—France				37·79
4 × 400 *relay*—United Kingdom		2	58	22

	metres
High jump—D. Topic (Yugoslavia)	2·34
Pole vault—R. Gataullin (USSR)	5·85
Long jump—D. Haaf (FRG)	8·25
Triple jump—L. Voloshin (USSR)	17·74
Shot—U. Timmermann (GDR)	21·32
Discus—J. Schult (GDR)	64·58
Hammer—I. Astapkovich (USSR)	84·14
Javelin—S. Backley (UK)	87·30
Decathlon—C. Plaziat (France)	8,574 pts.

Women's Events

metres		hr.	min.	sec.
100—K. Krabbe (GDR)				10·89
200—K. Krabbe (GDR)				21·95
400—G. Breuer (GDR)				49·50
800—S. Wodars (GDR)			1	55·87
1,500—S. Pajkic (Yugoslavia)			4	08·12
3,000—Y. Murray (UK)			8	43·06
10,000—Y. Romanova (USSR)			31	46·83

	hr.	min.	sec.
Marathon—R. Mota (Portugal) ..	2	31	27
100 *hurdles*—M. Ewanje-Epee (France)...................			12·79
10km *walk*—A.-R. Sidotti (Italy) .		44	00
400 *hurdles*—T. Ledovskaya (USSR)....................			53·62
4 × 100 *relay*—GDR			41·68
4 × 400 *relay*—GDR		3	21·02

	metres
High jump—H. Henkel (FRG) ...	1·99
Long jump—H. Drechsler (GDR) .	7·30
Shot—A. Kumbernuss (GDR)....	20·38
Discus—I. Wyludda (GDR)	68·46
Javelin—P. Alafrantti (Finland) .	67·68
Heptathlon—S. Braun (FRG)	6,688 pts.

BADMINTON, 1989–90

English National Championships
(Crawley, Dec. 1989)

Men's Singles.—D Hall.
Women's Singles.—F. Smith.
Men's Doubles.—M. Brown and A. Goode.
Women's Doubles.—G. Clark and G. Gowers.
Mixed Doubles.—Miss G. Clark and A. Goode.

All-England Championships
(Wembley)

Men's Singles.—Zhao Jianhua (China).
Women's Singles.—Susi Susanti (Indonesia).
Men's Doubles.—Park Joo Bong and Kim Moon Soo (S. Korea).
Women's Doubles.—Chung Myung Hee and Hwang Hye Young (S. Korea).
Mixed Doubles.—Park Joo Bong and Miss Chung Myung Hee (S. Korea).

BASKETBALL, 1989–90

Men's

NatWest Trophy.—Kingston beat Manchester Giants 86–77.
National Cup.—Kingston beat Sunderland 103–78.
Premier League.—Kingston, 44 pts.
National Basketball League.—Oldham.

Women's

National Cup.—Sheffield Hatters beat Brixton Lady Topcats 64–46.
National League.—Avon Northampton.

BOWLS, 1989–90

National Championships
(Worthing)

Fours final.—Bath (Somerset) beat Mansfield Colliery (Notts.) 20–13.
Triples final.—Cheltenham (Glos.) beat Welford-on-Avon (Warks.) 18–16.
Pairs final.—Wymondham Dell (Norfolk) beat West Ealing (Middx.) 19–15.
Singles final.—A. Allcock (Cheltenham, Glos.) beat K. E. Smith (Denham, Bucks.) 25–12.

World Indoor Championship.—J. Price (Wales).
World Indoor Pairs Championship.—D. Bryant and A. Allcock (England).
British Isles Indoor Singles Championship.—G. Robertson (Scotland).
UK Indoor Singles Championship.—D. Bryant (England).

World Fours Champions.—Ireland.
World Singles Champion.—D. Bryant (England).
Middleton Cup (Inter-County Championship) final.—Yorkshire beat Dorset 136–113.

BOXING, 1989–90

Amateur Boxing Association
(ABA) Championship Winners

Super-heavy (91 + kg).—K. McCormack.
Heavy (91kg).—K. Inglis.
Light-heavy (81kg).—J. McCluskey.
Middle (75kg).—S. Wilson.
Light-middle (71kg).—T. Taylor.
Welter (67kg).—A. Carew.
Light-welter (63.5kg).—J. Pender.
Light (60kg).—P. Gallagher.
Feather (57kg).—B. Carr.
Bantam (54kg).—P. Lloyd.
Fly (51kg).—J. Armour.
Light-fly (48kg).—N. Tooley.

PROFESSIONAL BOXING
(as at August 30, 1990)

World Boxing Council (WBC) Champions

Heavy.—B. Douglas (USA).
Cruiser.—M. Duran (Italy).
Light-heavy.—D. Andries (GB).
Super-middle.—vacant.
Middle.—vacant.
Super-welter.—T. Norris (USA).
Welter.—M. Blocker (USA).
Super-light.—J. C. Chavez (Mexico).
Light.—P. Whitaker (USA).
Super-feather.—vacant.
Feather.—M. Villasana (Mexico).
Super-bantam.—P. Banke (USA).
Bantam.—R. Perez (Mexico).
Super-fly.—S. Moon (Korea).
Fly.—S. Chitalada (Thailand).
Light-fly.—H. Gonzalez (Mexico).
Straw.—H. Ohashi (Japan).

World Boxing Association (WBA) Champions

Heavy.—B. Douglas (USA).
Cruiser.—R. Daniels (USA).
Light-heavy.—V. Hill (USA).
Super-middle.—C. Tiozzo (France).
Middle.—M. McCallum (Jamaica/USA).
Super-welter.—J. Jackson (Virgin Is.).
Welter.—A. Davis (USA).
Super-light.—L. Garza (USA).
Light.—P. Whitaker (GB).
Super-feather.—B. Mitchell (S. Africa).
Feather.—A. Esparragoza (Venezuela).
Super-bantam.—J. Salud (USA).
Bantam.—L. Espinoza (Philippines).
Super-fly.—K. Galaxy (Thailand).
Fly.—Y. Lee (Korea).
Light-fly.—Yuh Myung Woo (Korea).
Straw.—Bong-Jun Kim (Korea).

International Boxing Federation (IBF) Champions

Heavy.—B. Douglas (USA).
Cruiser.—J. Lampkin (USA).
Light-heavy.—C. Williams (USA).
Super-middle.—L. Holmes (USA).
Middle.—M. Nunn (USA).
Super-welter.—G. F. Rosi (Italy).
Welter.—S. Brown (USA).
Super-light.—J. Chavez (Mexico).
Light.—P. Whitaker (USA).
Super-feather.—T. Lopez (USA).
Feather.—J. Paez (Mexico).

Super-bantam.—W. Ncita (S. Africa).
Bantam.—O. Canizales (USA).
Super-fly.—R. Quiroga (USA).
Fly.—D. McAuley (GB).
Light-fly.—M. Carbajal (USA).
Straw.—F. L. Lookmingkwan (Thailand).

BRITISH CHAMPIONS

Heavy.—G. Mason.
Cruiser.—J. Nelson.
Light-heavy.—T. Collins.
Middle.—H. Graham.
Light-middle.—G. Stretch.
Welter.—K. Laing.
Light-welter.—vacant.
Light.—S. Boyle.
Super-feather.—J. Jacobs.
Feather.—S. Murphy.
Bantam.—B. Hardy.
Fly.—P. Clinton.

COMMONWEALTH CHAMPIONS

Heavy.—D. Williams (GB).
Cruiser.—D. Angol (GB).
Light-heavy.—G. Waters (Australia).
Super-middle.—L. Lafaro (Australia).
Middle.—M. Watson (GB).
Light-middle.—T. Waters (Australia).
Welter.—D. Boucher (Canada).
Light-welter.—T. Ekubia (GB).
Light.—C. Crook (GB).
Super-feather.—M. Reefer (GB).
Feather.—M. Napunyi (Kenya).
Bantam.—R. Minus (Bahamas).
Fly.—A. Kotei (Ghana).

EUROPEAN CHAMPIONS

Heavy.—J. Chanet (France).
Cruiser.—vacant.
Light-heavy.—T. Collins (GB).
Super-middle.—M. Galvano (Italy).
Middle.—S. Kalambay (Italy).
Light-middle.—G. Dele (France).
Welter.—K. Laing (GB).
Light-welter.—P. Barratt (GB).
Light.—P. Diaz (Spain).
Super-feather.—D. Londas (France).
Feather.—P. Hodkinson (GB).
Bantam.—vacant.
Fly.—P. Clinton (GB).

(The above information was supplied
by *Boxing Weekly*.)

CRICKET, 1989–90

TEST MATCHES

Pakistan v. India, 1989

First Test (Karachi, Nov. 15–20).—Drawn. Pakistan 409 and 305 for 5 dec.; India 262 and 303 for 3.

Second Test (Faisalabad, Nov. 23–28).—Drawn. India 288 and 398 for 7; Pakistan 423 for 9 dec.

Third Test (Lahore, Dec. 1–6).—Drawn. India 509 all out; Pakistan 699 for 5.

Fourth Test (Sialkot, Dec. 9–14).—Drawn. India 324 and 234 for 7; Pakistan 250.

Australia v. New Zealand, 1989–90

First Test (Perth, Nov. 24–28).—Drawn. Australia 521 for 9 dec.; New Zealand 231 and 322 for 7.

Second Test (Wellington, March 15–19).—New Zealand won by 9 wickets. Australia 110 and 269; New Zealand 202 and 181 for 1.

Australia v. Sri Lanka, 1989

First Test (Brisbane, Dec. 8–12).—Drawn. Australia 367 and 375 for 6; Sri Lanka 418.

Second Test (Hobart, Dec. 16–20).—Australia won by 173 runs. Australia 224 and 513 for 5 dec.; Sri Lanka 216 and 348.

Australia v. Pakistan, 1990

First Test (Melbourne, Jan. 12–16).—Australia won by 92 runs. Australia 223 and 312 for 8 dec.; Pakistan 107 and 336.

Second Test (Adelaide, Jan. 19–23).—Drawn. Pakistan 257 and 387 for 9 dec.; Australia 341 and 233 for 6.

Third Test (Sydney, Feb. 3–8).—Drawn. Pakistan 199; Australia 176 for 2.

New Zealand v. India, 1990

First Test (Christchurch, Feb. 2–5).—New Zealand won by 10 wickets. New Zealand 459 and 2 for no wicket; India 164 and 296.

Second Test (Napier, Feb. 10–12).—Drawn. India 358 for 9 dec.; New Zealand 178 for 1.

Third Test (Auckland, Feb. 22–26).—Drawn. New Zealand 391 and 483 for 5 dec.; India 482 and 149 for no wicket.

West Indies v. England, 1990

First Test (Kingston, Jamaica, Feb. 24–March 1).—England won by 9 wickets. West Indies 164 and 240; England 364 and 41 for 1.

Second Test (Georgetown, Guyana, March 10–15).—Match abandoned.

Third Test (Port of Spain, Trinidad, March 23–28).—Drawn. West Indies 199 and 239; England 288 and 120 for 5.

Fourth Test (Bridgetown, Barbados, April 5–10).—West Indies won by 164 runs. West Indies 446 and 267 for 8 dec.; England 358 and 191.

Fifth Test (St. John's, Antigua, April 12–17).—West Indies won by an innings and 32 runs. England 260 and 154; West Indies 446.

England v. New Zealand, 1990

First Test (Trent Bridge, June 7–12).—Drawn. New Zealand 208 and 36 for 2; England 345 for 9 dec.

Second Test (Lord's, June 21–26).—Drawn. England 334 and 272 for 4 dec.; New Zealand 462 for 9 dec.

Third Test (Edgbaston, July 5–10).—England won by 114 runs. England 435 and 158; New Zealand 249 and 230.

England v. India, 1990

First Test (Lord's, July 26–31).—England won by 247 runs. England 653 for 4 dec. and 272 for 4 dec.; India 454 and 224.

Second Test (Old Trafford, Aug. 9–14).—Drawn. England 519 and 320 for 4 dec.; India 432 and 343 for 6.

Third Test (The Oval, Aug. 23–28).—Drawn. India 606 for 9 dec.; England 340 and 477 for 4 dec.

ONE-DAY INTERNATIONALS

West Indies v. England, 1990

Port of Spain, Feb. 14.—Match abandoned after rain stopped play. West Indies 208 for 8; England 26 for 1.

Port of Spain, Feb. 17.—Match abandoned after rain stopped play. West Indies 13 for no wicket.

Kingston, March 3.—West Indies won by 3 wickets. England 214 for 8; West Indies 216 for 7.

Georgetown, March 7.—West Indies won by 6 wickets. England 188 for 8; West Indies 191 for 4 wickets.

*Georgetown, March 15.—West Indies won by 7 wickets. England 166 for 9 wickets; West Indies 167 for 3 wickets.

Bridgetown, April 3.—West Indies won by 4 wickets. England 214 for 3 wickets; West Indies 217 for 6 wickets.

West Indies win series 3–0.

* unofficial match.

England v. New Zealand, 1990
(Texaco Trophy)

Headingley (May 23).—New Zealand won by 4 wickets. England 295 for 6 wickets; New Zealand 298 for 6 wickets.

The Oval (May 25).—England won by 6 wickets. New Zealand 212 for 6 wickets; England 213 for 4 wickets.

England win Texaco Trophy on faster run rate.

England v. India, 1990
(Texaco Trophy)

Headingley (July 18).—India won by 6 wickets. England 229; India 233 for 4 wickets.

Trent Bridge (July 20).—India won by 5 wickets. England 281; India 282 for 5 wickets.

India won Texaco Trophy 2–0.

INTERNATIONAL CUPS

Nehru Cup 1989.—Pakistan.
World Series Cup 1990.—Australia.
ICC Cup 1990.—Zimbabwe.

England v. New Zealand, 1990 (Averages)

ENGLAND BATTING

Batsmen	I	NO	R	HS	Av.
M. A. Atherton ...	5	0	357	151	71·40
G. A. Gooch	5	0	306	154	61·20
G. C. Small	4	2	84	44*	42·00
A. J. Lamb	5	1	129	84*	32·25
R. A. Smith	5	0	152	64	30·40
A. J. Stewart	5	0	147	54	29·40
P. A. J. DeFreitas .	2	0	52	38	26·00
R. C. Russell	4	0	84	43	21·00
N. H. Fairbrother .	5	1	59	33*	14·75
E. E. Hemmings ...	4	1	33	20	11·00
D. E. Malcolm	4	2	4	4*	2·00

Played in one match: C. C. Lewis, 32, 1.
*Not Out.

BOWLING

Bowlers	O	M	R	W	Av.
D. E. Malcolm	118·4	38	269	15	17·93
E. E. Hemmings ...	107·3	44	215	10	21·50
P. A. J. DeFreitas .	59·4	9	175	6	29·16
C. C. Lewis	41·0	8	127	4	31·75
G. C. Small	104·0	27	290	5	58·00

Also bowled: M. A. Atherton, 10-6-17-0; G. A. Gooch, 13-7-25-0.

NEW ZEALAND BATTING

Batsmen	I	NO	R	HS	Av.
T. J. Franklin	5	1	227	101	56·75
J. G. Wright	5	0	177	98	35·40
I. D. S. Smith	2	1	29	27	29·00
M. J. Greatbatch ..	4	0	115	47	28·75
A. H. Jones	5	0	143	49	28·60
R. J. Hadlee	4	0	107	86	26·75
M. D. Crowe	4	0	96	59	24·00
M. C. Snedden	4	2	36	21*	18·00
K. R. Rutherford ..	3	0	47	29	15·66
J. G. Bracewell	4	0	57	28	14·25
D. K. Morrison	5	2	9	6	3·00

Played in one match: M. W. Priest, 26; A. C. Parore, 12*, 20.
*Not out.

BOWLING

Bowlers	O	M	R	W	Av.
R. J. Hadlee	133·5	24	384	16	24·00
J. G. Bracewell	148·0	41	400	12	33·33
M. C. Snedden	101·0	30	264	6	44·00
D. K. Morrison	85·4	15	351	7	50·14

Also bowled: M. W. Priest, 12-4-26-1; A. H. Jones, 13-3-42-1; K. R. Rutherford, 3-0-18-0.

England v. India, 1990 (Averages)

ENGLAND BATTING

Batsmen	I	NO	R	HS	Av.
R. A. Smith	6	4	361	121*	180·50
G. A. Gooch	6	0	752	333	125·33
D. I. Gower	6	2	291	157*	72·75
M. A. Atherton ...	6	0	378	131	63·00
A. J. Lamb	6	0	364	139	60·66
N. F. Williams	1	0	38	38	38·00
E. E. Hemmings ..	2	0	70	51	35·00
R. C. Russell	3	1	59	35	29·50
D. E. Malcolm	2	1	28	15*	28·00
J. E. Morris	5	2	71	32	23·66
C. C. Lewis	1	0	3	3	3·00
A. R. C. Fraser	2	0	1	1	0·50

*Not out.

BOWLING

Bowlers	O	M	R	W	Av.
A. R. C. Fraser	159·1	41	460	16	28·75
E. E. Hemmings ...	137·2	26	454	11	41·27
C. C. Lewis	65·0	8	281	5	56·20
D. E. Malcolm	110·0	16	436	7	62·28
G. A. Gooch	18·0	4	70	1	70·00
N. F. Williams	41·0	5	148	2	74·00
M. A. Atherton ...	28·0	3	161	1	161·00

INDIA BATTING

Batsmen	I	NO	R	HS	Av.
M. Azharuddin ...	5	0	426	179	85·20
R. J. Shastri	5	0	336	187	67·20
S. R. Tendulkar ...	5	1	245	119*	61·25
Kapil Dev	5	1	220	110	55·00
S. V. Manjrekar ...	5	0	216	93	43·20
M. Prabhakar	5	1	132	67*	33·00
D. B. Vengsarkar ..	5	0	158	52	31·60
K. S. More	4	1	91	61*	30·33
S. K. Sharma	2	0	38	38	19·00
N. D. Hirwani	4	3	17	15*	17·00
A. Wasson	1	0	15	15	15·00
N. S. Sidhu	5	0	56	30	11·20
A. R. Kumble	1	0	2	2	2·00

*Not out.

BOWLING

Bowlers	O	M	R	W	Av.
A. R. Kumble	60·0	10	170	3	56·66
A. Wasson	37·0	5	173	3	57·66
Kapil Dev	128·0	23	445	7	63·57
N. D. Hirwani	212·0	41	586	9	65·11
S. K. Sharma	48·0	5	197	3	65·66
M. Prabhakar	155·0	28	554	8	69·25
R. J. Shastri	95·5	6	341	2	170·50

County Championship Table, 1990

Order for 1989 in brackets	Played	Won	Lost	Drawn	Bonus Btg.	Bonus Blng.	Points
Middlesex (3)	22	10	1	11	73	55	288
Essex (2)	22	8	2	12	73	56	257
Hampshire (6)	22	8	4	10	67	48	243
Worcestershire (1)	22	7	1	14	70	58	240
Warwickshire (8)	22	7	7	8	55	64	231
Lancashire (4)	22	6	3	13	65	56	217
Leicestershire (13)	22	6	7	9	61	53	210
Glamorgan (17)	22	5	6	11	64	48	192
Surrey (12)†	22	4	3	15	54	64	190
Yorkshire (16)	22	5	9	8	52	55	187
Northamptonshire (5) ..	22	4	9	9	61	60	185
Derbyshire (7)*	22	6	7	9	58	52	181
Gloucestershire (9)	22	4	7	11	51	58	173
Nottinghamshire (11) ..	22	4	8	10	51	58	173
Somerset (14)	22	3	4	15	73	45	166
Kent (15)	22	3	6	13	69	35	152
Sussex (10)	22	3	9	10	51	44	143

† Surrey was awarded 8 pts for batting last in a drawn match in which the scores finished level.
* Derbyshire had 25 pts deducted for a sub-standard pitch.

Other Results, 1990

Benson and Hedges Cup final.—Lancashire beat Worcestershire by 69 runs. Lancashire 241 for 8 wickets; Worcestershire 172 all out.
NatWest Trophy final.—Lancashire beat Northamptonshire by 7 wickets. Northants. 171; Lancashire 173 for 3.
Refuge Assurance Sunday League Champions.—Derbyshire.
Refuge Assurance Cup.—Middlesex beat Derbyshire by 5 wickets. Derbyshire 197 for 7 wickets; Middlesex 201 for 5 wickets.
Holt Cup (Minor Counties knockout final).—Buckinghamshire beat Lincolnshire by 16 runs. Buckinghamshire 227 for 7 wickets; Lincolnshire 211 for 9 wickets.

Minor Counties Championship final.—Hertfordshire beat Berkshire by 7 wickets. Berkshire 171 for 5; Hertfordshire 172 for 3.
National Club Championship final.—Blackpool beat Cheam by 3 wickets. Cheam 193 for 8; Blackpool 194 for 7.
National Village Championship final.—Goatacre (Wilts.) beat Dunstall (Staffs.) by 50 runs. Goatacre 267 for 5; Dunstall 217 for 5.
Universities.—Drawn. Oxford University 269 for 8 dec.; Cambridge University 146.

BATTING AND BOWLING AVERAGES
First Class Batting Averages, 1990

Batsmen	I	NO	R	HS	Av.
G. A. Gooch	30	3	2,746	333	101·70
G. A. Hick	35	9	2,347	252*	90·26
T. M. Moody	15	2	1,163	168	89·46
A. N. Aymes	8	4	317	75*	79·25
†M. Azharuddin	11	1	770	179	77·00
D. M. Ward	34	7	2,072	263	76·74
M. E. Waugh	33	6	2,072	207*	76·74
S. J. Cook.........	41	7	2,608	313*	76·70
B. R. Hardie	17	7	728	125	72·80
M. A. Atherton ...	31	4	1,924	191	71·25
P. A. De Silva ...	12	4	563	221*	70·37
N. H. Fairbrother .	32	7	1,740	366	69·60
D. J. Bicknell	23	4	1,317	186	69·31
M. A. Crawley	14	3	762	105*	69·27
D. L. Haynes	39	5	2,346	255*	69·00
R. A. Smith	30	8	1,454	181	66·09
†R. J. Shastri	11	1	644	187	64·40
R. J. Bailey	39	8	1,987	204*	64·09
A. J. Lamb	29	4	1,596	235	63·84
†S. R. Tendulkar ..	19	4	945	119*	63·00
I. V. A. Richards ..	28	5	1,425	164*	61·95
N. R. Taylor	37	5	1,979	204	61·84
C. L. Smith	38	7	1,886	148	60·83
R. J. Harden	31	7	1,460	104*	60·83
A. R. Butcher	41	5	2,116	151*	58·77

† Includes tourists.
* Not out.

First Class Bowling Averages, 1990

Bowlers	O	M	R	W	Av.
I. R. Bishop	407·3	92	1,124	59	19·05
M. D. Marshall...	554·2	141	1,381	72	19·18
D. J. Millns	206·4	36	662	31	21·35
V. J. Wells	85·0	19	257	12	21·41
O. H. Mortensen .	316·2	91	785	35	22·42
C. E. L. Ambrose .	503·4	127	1,413	61	23·16
Waqar Younis ...	423·0	70	1,357	57	23·80
†R. J. Hadlee	201·5	39	586	24	24·41
M. W. Alleyne ...	112·0	29	391	16	24·43
P. A. Smith	148·5	34	497	20	24·85
N. A. Foster	819·2	175	2,502	94	26·61
†M. Madurasinghe .	176·2	28	560	21	26·66
A. R. C. Fraser ...	596·0	144	1,533	57	26·89
M. P. Bicknell ...	671·1	157	1,827	67	27·26
†G. F. Labrooy ...	111·0	13	440	16	27·50
G. J. Parsons	304·5	77	963	35	27·51
†M. C. Snedden ...	231·5	56	633	23	27·52
J. E. Benjamin ...	388·3	68	1,205	43	28·02
C. A. Walsh	611·1	107	2,022	72	28·08
R. K. Illingworth .	875·5	280	2,122	75	28·29
D. J. Capel	234·0	51	711	25	28·44
D. A. Reeve......	377·4	110	940	33	28·48
T. A. Merrick	184·3	45	488	17	28·70
M. A. Feltham ...	349·4	61	1,150	40	28·75
T. A. Munton	827·1	199	2,254	78	28·89

† Includes tourists.

CYCLING, 1989–90

Tour of Spain.— M. Giovannetti (Italy).
Giro d'Italia.—G. Bugno (Italy).
Milk Race.—S. Sutton (Australia.)
Tour de France.—G. LeMond (USA).
Tour of Britain.—M. Dernies (Belgium).
Nissan Classic.—E. Breukink (Netherlands).

World Professional Road Race Championship.—R. Dhaenens (Belgium).
British Professional Road Race Championship.—C. Sturgess.
British Amateur Road Race Championship.—S. Hempsall.
Scottish Provident League.—D. Rayner (Banana–Falcon).
World Professional Cyclo-Cross Championship.—H. Baars (Netherlands).
World Amateur Cyclo-Cross Championship.—A. Buesser (Switzerland).
Women's World Road Race Championship.—C. Marsal (France).
Women's National Road Race Championship.—M. Purvis.

EQUESTRIANISM, 1989–90

Show Jumping

World Cup final (Dortmund)
1. J. Whitaker on Henderson Milton (GB).
2. P. Durand on Jappeloup (France).
3. F. Sloothaak on Optiebeurs Walzerkoenig (W. Germany).

British Jumping Derby (Hickstead)
1. J. Turi on Vital (GB).
2. N. Skelton on Alan Paul Apollo (GB).
3eq. H. Godignon on Moet & Chandon Quidam (France).
   H. Godignon on Prince (France).
   M. Whitaker on Henderson Montana (GB).

Three-day Eventing

Badminton Horse Trials
1. Mrs. N. McIrvine on Middle Road (GB).
2. B. Tait on Messiah (NZ).
3. Miss M. Thomson on King Boris (GB).

British Open Horse Trials (Gatcombe Park)
1. Miss M. Thomson on King Boris (GB).
2. Miss P. Nolan on Sir Barnaby (GB).
3. C. Hunnable on Parisian (GB).

Burghley Horse Trials
1. M. Todd on Face The Music (NZ).
2. Miss M. Thomson on King Cuthbert (GB).
3. R. Walker on Jacana (GB).

World Three-day Event Championship
(Stockholm)

Individual
1. B. Tait on Messiah (NZ).
2. I. Stark on Murphy Himself (GB).
3. B. Davidson on Pirate Lion (USA).

Team
1. New Zealand.
2. Great Britain.
3. West Germany.

World Equestrian Games
(Stockholm)

Carriage Driving
Individual.—A. Aarts (Netherlands).
Team.—Netherlands.

Dressage
Individual.—Miss N. Uphoff on Rembrandt (W. Germany).
Team.—West Germany.

Endurance Riding
Individual.—Ms B. Hart on RO Grand Sultan (USA).
Team.—Great Britain.

Show Jumping
Individual.—E. Navet on Malesan Quito de Baussy (France).
Team.—France.

Vaulting
Individual (men).—M. Lehner (W. Germany).
Individual (women).—S. Bernhard (W. Germany).
Team.—Switzerland.

ETON FIVES, 1990

Amateur Championship (Kinnaird Cup).—B. C. Matthews and J. Reynolds.
NatWest County Championship.—North London.
Holmwoods Schools' Championships.—Highgate.
Alan Barber Cup.—Old Cholmeleians.
League Championship (Douglas Keeble Cup).—The Village Club.

FENCING 1989–90

British Championships:
Foil.—W. Gosbee.
Epée.—R. Johnson.
Sabre.—I. Williams (London Thames).
Ladies' Foil.—F. McIntosh (Salle Paul).
Ladies' Epée.—N. Twig (Chelsea and Westminster).
Sporting Record Cup.—Hemel Hempstead.
Savage Shield.—cancelled.
Martin Edmunds Cup.—Salle Paul.
Challenge Martini International Epée.—E. Strecki (France).

GOLF, 1989–90

MEN'S CHAMPIONSHIPS
The Major Championships 1990

US Masters (Augusta, Georgia; April 5–8).—N. Faldo (GB) and R. Floyd (US) tied with 278. N. Faldo won playoff at second extra hole.
US Open (Medinah, Chicago; June 14–18).—H. Irwin (US) and M. Donald (US) tied with 280. H. Irwin won playoff.
The Open (St. Andrews; July 19–22).—N. Faldo (GB), 270.
US PGA Championship (Birmingham, Alabama; Aug. 9–12).—W. Grady (Australia), 282.

European PGA Tour, 1989

German Masters (Stuttgart).—B. Langer (W. Germany), 276.
World Matchplay (Wentworth).—N. Faldo (GB).
Portuguese Open (Quinto do Lago).—C. Montgomerie (Scotland), 264.
Volvo Masters (Valderrama, Spain).—R. Rafferty (GB), 282.
European Order of Merit 1989.—1. R. Rafferty (GB & Ireland); 2. J.-M. Olazábal (Spain); 3. C. Parry (Australia).

European PGA Tour, 1990

Atlantic Open (Oporto, Portugal).—S. McAllister (GB), 288.
Desert Classic (Dubai).—E. Darcy (Ireland), 276.

Mediterranean Open (Las Brisas, Spain).—I. Woosnam (GB), 210.

Majorca Open.—S. Ballesteros (Spain), 269.

Tenerife Open.—V. Fernández (Argentina), 282.

Volvo Open (Florence).—E. Romero (Argentina), 265.

AGF Open (Montpellier).—B. Ogle (Australia), 278.

El Bosque Open (Valencia, Spain).—Vijay Singh (Fiji), 278.

Cannes Open.—M. McNulty (Zimbabwe), 280.

Madrid Open.—B. Langer (W. Germany), 270.

Spanish Open (Madrid).—R. Davis (Australia), 277.

International Open (St. Mellion, Plymouth).—J.-M. Olazábal (Spain), 279.

Belgian Open (Brussels).—O. Sellberg (Sweden), 272.

Italian Open (Milan).—R. Boxall (GB), 267.

PGA Championship (Wentworth).—M. Harwood (Australia), 271.

Dunhill British Masters (Woburn).—M. James (GB), 270.

Scandinavian Open (Stockholm).—C. Stadler (USA), 268.

Irish Open (Portmarnock).—J.-M. Olazábal (Spain), 282.

French Open (Paris).—P. Walton (Ire), 275.

Monte Carlo Open.—I. Woosnam (GB), 258.

Scottish Open (Gleneagles).—I. Woosnam (GB), 269.

119th Open Championship (St. Andrews).—N. Faldo (GB), 270.

Dutch Open (Zandvoort).—S. McAllister (GB), 274.

PLM Open (Malmo, Sweden).—R. Rafferty (GB), 270.

English Open (The Belfry).—M. James (GB) and S. Torrance (GB) tied on 284. M. James won play-off.

German Open (Dusseldorf).—M. McNulty (Zimbabwe), 270.

European Masters—Swiss Open (Crans-sur-Sierre).—R. Rafferty (GB), 267.

European Open (Sunningdale).—P. Senior (Australia), 267.

Lancôme Trophy (Paris).—J.-M. Olazábal (Spain), 269.

World Matchplay (Wentworth).—I. Woosnam (GB).

International Open (Munich).—P. Azinger (USA) and D. Feherty (GB) tied on 277. Azinger won playoff at first extra hole.

Grand Prix (Chepstow).—I. Woosnam (GB), 271.

German Masters (Stuttgart).—S. Torrance (GB), 272.

Amateur Championships

President's Putter (Rye).—G. Wuollet.

Halford Hewitt Cup (for schools) (Deal).—Tonbridge beat Malvern, 3–2.

Berkshire Trophy (The Berkshire).—J. O'Shea, 271.

Welsh Open (Pyle & Kenfig).—G. Houston, 288.

Brabazon Trophy (English Open) (Burnham & Berrow).—*Equal 1.* O. Edmond (France), 287; G. Evans (GB), 287.

English Open (Bridgnorth & Enville).—N. Paul, 217.

British Amateur Championship (Muirfield).—R. Muntz (Netherlands).

Lytham Trophy (Royal Lytham & St. Anne's).—G.Evans, 291.

English Amateur (Woodhall Spa).—I. Garbutt.

Scottish Amateur (Gullane).—C. Everett.

Welsh Amateur (Prestatyn).—A. Barnett.

Universities.—Cambridge beat Oxford 11–4.

Team Events

RYDER CUP (The Belfry, Sept. 22–24, 1989).—Great Britain and Europe drew with the USA, 14–14.

WOMEN'S CHAMPIONSHIPS

US Women's Open (Duluth, Georgia).— E. King (US), 284.

WPG European Tour, 1990

Valextra Classic (Rome).—F. Descampe (Belgium), 279.

Ford Ladies Classic (Woburn).—M.-L. de Lorenzi (France), 284.

Hennessy Ladies' Cup (Paris).—T. Johnson (GB), 285.

European Tour Classic (Tytherington, Cheshire).—T. Abitbol (Spain), 213.

Bonmont Ladies' Classic (Geneva).—E. Orley (Switzerland), 289.

European Masters (Brussels).—K. Lunn (Australia), 285.

Ladies' Classic (Dusseldorf).—D. Barnard (GB), 278.

Ladies' Charity Classic (Stoke Pages).—L. Maritz (S. Africa) and A. Nicholas (GB) tied on 275. L. Maritz won playoff at first extra hole.

Eastleigh Classic (Eastleigh).—T. Johnson (GB), 249.

Women's British Open (Woburn).—H. Alfredsson (Sweden) and J. Hill (Zimbabwe) tied on 288. H. Alfredsson won playoff at fourth extra hole.

Ladies' German Open (Munich).—A. Okamoto (Japan), C. Rarick (USA) and L. Maritz (S. Africa) tied on 274. A. Okamoto won playoff.

Haninge Ladies' Open (Stockholm).—D. Reid (GB), 291.

Celebrity Classic (Reading).—A. Nicholas (GB), 275.

TEC Players' Championship (Wolverhampton).—A. Jones (Australia), 281.

Ladies' European Open (Kingswood, Surrey).—T. Johnson (GB), 276.

Trophée International (Paris).—C. Dibnah (Australia), 284.

Italian Ladies' Open (Lake Garda).—F. Descampe (Belgium), 282.

Amateur Championships

Welsh Championship (Ashburnham).—S. Roberts.

Scottish Championship (Machrihanish).—E. Farquharson.

English Championship (Rye).—A. Uzielli.

British Open Championship (Dunbar).—J. Hall.

Welsh Open (Newport).—L. Hackney.

English Strokeplay Championship (Saunton).—K. Tebbet, 299.

British Strokeplay Championship (Strathaven).—V. Thomas, 287.

Team Championships

Curtis Cup (Bernardsville, New Jersey, USA).—USA beat Great Britain and Ireland 14–4.

Home Internationals (Hunstanton).—Scotland.

GREYHOUND RACING, 1989–90

Television Trophy (Walthamstow).—Shropshire Lass.

Grand National (Birmingham).—Gizma Pasha.

Greyhound Derby (Wimbledon).—Slippy Blue.

Scurry Gold Cup (Catford).—Ready Rubbed.

GYMNASTICS, 1989

MEN'S

British Men's Champion, N. Thomas.

British Men's Individual Apparatus Champions:

  Floor, J. May.

  Pommel Horse, N. Thomas.

  Rings, M. Bone.

  Vault, N. Thomas.

  Parallel Bars, D. Cox.

  High Bar, M. Campbell.

British Men's Team Champions (Adam Shield), Liverpool School of Physical Education.

WOMEN'S

British Women's Champion, S. Mercer.
British Women's Individual Apparatus Champions:
  Vault, L. Reading.
  Asymmetric Bars, S. Mercer.
  Beam, N. Mainwaring.
  Floor, S. Mercer.
British Rhythmics Champion, A. Sands (Coventry).
British Women's Open Club Team Champions, Camberley.

Leading Breeders, 1989

	Value
Hamdan Al-Maktoum	£834,623
Kentucky Select Bloodstock	400,180
HH Aga Khan	392,672
Juddmonte Farms	390,530
Ovidstown Investments Ltd	277,924
R. F. Johnson Houghton	229,302
Peter Burrell Trust	223,761
Charles Rowe (USA)	184,162
Mrs. R. B. Kennard	182,309
Darley Stud Management	171,631

HOCKEY, 1989–90

MEN

World Cup (Lahore).—Netherlands.
Champions Trophy 1989.—Australia.
Home Countries Indoor.—England.
County Championship final.—Middlesex beat Yorkshire 2–1 a.e.t.
National League.—Hounslow.
National Club Championship final.—Havant beat Hounslow 3–2.
National Indoor Club Championship final.—St. Albans beat Stourport 4–3.
Universities.—Cambridge beat Oxford 4–2.

WOMEN

World Cup (Sydney).—Netherlands.
Typhoo Tea Cup.—England 0, Netherlands 0. Netherlands won 4–3 on penalties.
Home Countries Indoor Tournament.—England.
County Championship.—Lancashire beat Kent.
National Club Championship.—Sutton Coldfield beat Hightown 1–0.
National League.—Slough.
National Indoor Club Championship final.—Ipswich beat Hightown 4–3.

Winning Sires, 1989

	Horses	Races won	Value
Blushing Groom (1974) by Red God	35	24	£1,007,619
Sadler's Wells (1981) by Northern Dancer	43	41	847,945
Nureyev (1977) by Northern Dancer	40	35	796,165
Danzig (1977) by Northern Dancer	31	31	790,864
Caerleon (1980) by Nijinsky	63	49	715,099
Ile de Bourbon (1975) by Nijinsky	41	27	587,860
Alleged (1974) by Hoist the Flag	27	29	491,759
Alydar (1975) by Raise a Native	9	10	470,322
Known Fact (1977) by In Reality	46	28	437,186
Habitat (1966) by Sir Gaylord	50	37	432,026

HORSERACING, 1989–90

Horseracing in Great Britain is under the control of THE JOCKEY CLUB (incorporating the National Hunt Committee), 42 Portman Square, London, W1H 0EN. Stewards are: Marquess of Hartington (*Senior Steward*); Viscount Chelsea (*Deputy Senior Steward*); Col. A. H. Parker Bowles; Sir John Barlow; Maj. M. C. Wyatt; Col. Sir Piers Bengough.

Winning Owners, 1989

Sheikh Mohammed	£1,296,032
Hamdan Al-Maktoum	1,222,192
K. Abdulla	683,577
Maktoum Al-Maktoum	484,688
HH Aga Khan	484,581
Mana Al-Maktoum	397,606
Sir Gordon White	337,712
Charles A. B. St. George	250,069
Athos Christodoulou	213,795

Winning Trainers, 1989

M. Stoute	£1,469,158
H. Cecil	1,175,041
Major W. Hern	1,096,211
G. Harwood	1,070,813
L. Cumani	822,022
B. Hills	479,669
D. Elsworth	418,001
R. Hannon	352,506
J. Tree	323,203
A. Scott	314,285

Winning Flat Jockeys, 1989

	1st	2nd	3rd	Unpl.	Total Mts.
P. Eddery	171	126	91	450	838
S. Cauthen	163	92	65	341	661
W. Carson	137	126	122	482	867
R. Cochrane	121	97	85	379	682
M. Roberts	106	105	88	512	811
W. Swinburn	94	92	91	375	652
M. Birch	91	61	75	462	689
D. McKeown	86	77	63	496	722
J. Reid	84	71	69	363	587
G. Duffield	77	65	63	471	676

Winning National Hunt Jockeys 1989–90

	1st	2nd	3rd	Unpl.	Total Mts.
P. Scudamore	170	79	45	229	523
R. Dunwoody	102	102	84	316	604
G. McCourt	100	58	54	223	435
C. Grant	94	68	57	206	425
M. Dwyer	75	54	47	203	379
H. Davies	60	52	39	255	406
M. Pitman	57	38	17	79	191
S. Smith Eccles	56	28	20	115	219
J. Osborne	53	39	31	153	276
M. Perrett	52	28	22	126	228

(The above statistics are the copyright of
The Sporting Life.)

THE CLASSICS
One Thousand Guineas (1814)
(Rowley Mile, Newmarket. For three year old fillies)

Year	Winner	Owner	Jockey	Trainer	No. of Runners
1987	Miesque	S. Niarchos	F. Head	F. Boutin	14
1988	Ravinella	E. Aland	G. Moore	Mrs. C. Head	12
1989	Musical Bliss	Sheikh Mohammed	W. Swinburn ...	M. Stoute.......	7
1990	Salsabil	H. Al-Maktoum ...	W. Carson	J. Dunlop	10

Two Thousand Guineas (1809)
(Rowley Mile, Newmarket. For three year olds)

Year	Winner	Owner	Jockey	Trainer	No. of Runners
1987	Don't Forget Me	J. Horgan	W. Carson	R. Hannon......	13
1988	Doyoun	HH Aga Khan	W. Swinburn ...	M. Stoute.......	9
1989	Nashwan	H. Al-Maktoum ..	W. Carson	R. Hern	14
1990	Tirol	J. Horgan	M. Kinane......	R. Hannon......	14

Record time: 1 minute 35·84 seconds, 1990.

The Derby (1780)
(Epsom, 1½ miles. For three year olds)

The first winner was Sir Charles Bunbury's Diomed in 1780. The owners with the record number of winners are Lord Egremont, who won in 1782, 1804, 1805, 1807, 1826 (also won 5 Oaks); and the late Aga Khan, who won in 1930, 1935, 1936, 1948, 1952 (also won 2 Oaks). Other winning owners are: Duke of Grafton (1802, 1809, 1810, 1815); Mr. J. Bowes (1835, 1843, 1852, 1853); Sir J. Hawley (1851, 1858, 1859, 1868); the 1st Duke of Westminster (1880, 1882, 1886, 1899); Sir Victor Sassoon (1953, 1957, 1958, 1960).

Record times are: 2 min. 33·80 sec. by Mahmoud in 1936; 2 min. 33·84 sec. by Kahyasi in 1988; 2 min. 33·9 sec. by Reference Point in 1987.

The Derby was run at Newmarket from 1915–18 and from 1940–45.

Year	Winner	Owner	Jockey	Trainer	No. of Runners
1987	Reference Point.....	L. Freedman	S. Cauthen	H. Cecil	19
1988	Kahyasi	HH Aga Khan	R. Cochrane	L. Cumani	14
1989	Nashwan	H. Al-Maktoum ..	W. Carson	R. Hern	12
1990	Quest for Fame......	K. Abdulla........	P. Eddery.......	R. Charlton	18

The Oaks (1779)
(Epsom, 1½ miles. For three year old fillies)

Year	Winner	Owner	Jockey	Trainer	No. of Runners
1987	Unite	Sheikh Mohammed	W. Swinburn ...	M. Stoute.......	11
1988	Diminuendo	Sheikh Mohammed	S. Cauthen	H. Cecil	11
1989	Aliysa..............	HH Aga Khan	W. Swinburn ...	M. Stoute.......	9
1990	Salsabil	H. Al-Maktoum ...	W. Carson	J.Dunlop	8

St. Leger (1776)
(Doncaster, 1 m. 6f., 127 yd. For three year olds)

Year	Winner	Owner	Jockey	Trainer	No. of Runners
1987	Reference Point.....	L. Freedman	S. Cauthen	H. Cecil	7
1988	Minster Son	Lady Beaverbrook.	W. Carson	N. Graham	6
1989	Michelozzo	C. St. George......	S. Cauthen	H. Cecil	8
1990	Snurge	M. Abib	R. Quinn	P. Cole	8

The 1989 St. Leger was run at Ayr on Sept. 23 after the course at Doncaster was ruled unsatisfactory.

Cesarewitch (1839)
(Newmarket, 2¼ miles)

1987	Private Audition	5y	7st 7lb
1988	Nomadic Way	3y	7st 9lb
1989	Double Dutch	5y	9st 10lb

Champion Stakes (1877)
(Newmarket, 1¼ miles)

1987	Triptych	5y	9st
1988	Indian Skimmer	4y	9st
1989	Legal Case	3y	8st 10lb

Cheltenham Gold Cup (1924)*
(about 3¼ miles)

1987	The Thinker	9y	12st
1988	Charter Party	10y	12st
1989	Desert Orchid	10y	12st
1990	Norton's Coin	9y	12st

Lincoln Handicap (1965)
(Doncaster, 1 mile)

1987	Star of a Gunner	7y	8st 8lb
1988	Cuvee Charlie	4y	7st 13lb
1989	Fact Finder	5y	7st 9lb
1990	Evichstar	6y	7st 10lb

Grand National (1837)*
(Liverpool, about 4 miles, 856 yds)

1987	Maori Venture	11y	10st 13lb
1988	Rhyme 'N' Reason	9y	11st
1989	Little Polveir	12y	10st
1990	Mr. Frisk	11y	10st 6lb

Record times: 8 min. 47·8 sec. by Mr. Frisk in 1990; 9 min. 1·9 sec. by Red Rum in 1973.

Irish Grand National (1870)*
(Fairyhouse, 3 miles)

1987	Brittany Boy	8y	10st 10lb
1988	Perris Valley	7y	10st
1989	Maid of Money	7y	11st 6lb
1990	Desert Orchid	11y	12st

European Free Handicap (1929)
(Newmarket, 7 furlongs. Three year olds)

1987	Noble Minstrel		9st 7lb
1988	Lapierre		9st 1lb
1989	Danehill		9st 1lb
1990	Anshan		9st 7lb

Jockey Club Stakes (1894)
(Newmarket, 1½ miles)

1987	Phardante	5y	8st 12lb
1988	Almaarad	4y	8st 5lb
1989	Unfwain	4y	8st 10lb
1990	Roseate Tern	4y	8st 9lb

Chester Cup (1824)
(Chester, 2¼ miles, 77 yd.)

1987	Just David	4y	9st 8lb
1988	Old Hubert	7y	7st 8lb
1989	Grey Salute	6y	8st 7lb
1990	Travelling Light	4y	9st 1lb

Coronation Cup (1902)
(Epsom, about 1½ miles)

1987	Triptych	5y	8st 11lb
1988	Triptych	6y	8st 11lb
1989	Sheriff's Star	4y	9st
1990	In The Wings	4y	9st

Coventry Stakes (1890)
(Ascot, 6 furlongs. Two year olds)

1987	Always Fair		8st 13lb
1988	High Estate		8st 13lb
1989	Rock City		8st 13lb
1990	Mac's Imp		8st 13lb

Ascot Gold Cup (1807)
(Ascot, 2½ miles)

1987	Paean	4y	9st
1988	Sadeem	5y	9st
1989	Sadeem	6y	9st
1990	Ashal	4y	9st

Irish Sweeps Derby (1866)
(Curragh, 1½ miles. Three year olds)

1987	Sir Harry Lewis		
1988	Kahyasi		9st
1989	Old Vic		9st
1990	Salsabil		8st 11lb

Eclipse Stakes (1886)
(Sandown, 1¼ miles)

1987	Mtoto	4y	9st 7lb
1988	Mtoto	5y	9st 7lb
1989	Nashwan	3y	8st 8lb
1990	Elmaamul	3y	8st 10lb

King George VI and Queen Elizabeth Diamond Stakes (1952)
(Ascot, 1½ miles)

1987	Reference Point	3y	8st 8lb
1988	Mtoto	5y	9st 7lb
1989	Nashwan	3y	8st 8lb
1990	Belmez	3y	8st 9lb

Goodwood Cup (1812)
(Goodwood, about 2m., 5f.)

1987	Sergeyevich	3y	7st
1988	Sadeem	5y	9st 7lb
1989	Mazzacano	4y	9st
1990	Lucky Moon	3y	7st 10lb

Gimcrack Stakes (1846)
(York, 6 furlongs. Two year old colts)

1987	Reprimand		9st
1988	Sharp 'N' Early		9st
1989	Rock City		9st 3lb
1990	Mujtahid		9st 3lb

Middle Park Stakes (1866)
(Newmarket, 6 furlongs. Two year old colts)

1987	Gallic League		9st
1988	Mon Tresor		9st
1989	Balla Cove		9st
1990	Lycius		9st

Cambridgeshire Handicap (1839)
(Newmarket, 1m., 1f.)

1987	Balthus		8st 1lb
1988	Quinlan Terry	3y	8st 5lb
1989	Rambo's Hall	4y	8st 6lb
1990	Risen Moon	3y	8st 9lb

Prix de L'Arc de Triomphe (1920)
(Longchamp, 1½ mile)

1987	Trempolino	3y	8st 11lb
1988	Tony Bin	5y	9st 4lb
1989	Carroll House	4y	9st 4lb
1990	Saumarez	3y	8st 11lb

*National Hunt

ICE SKATING, 1989–90

British Championships

(Basingstoke, Nov. 1989)

Men's Figure.—S. Cousins.
Women's Figure.—Miss E. Murdoch.
Pairs.—Miss C. Peake and A. Naylor.
Ice Dance.—Miss L. Burton and A. Place.

European Championships

(Leningrad, Feb. 1990)

Men's Figures.—V. Petrenko (USSR).
Women's Figures.—Miss C. Leistner (W. Germany).
Pairs.—Miss E. Gordeyeva and S. Grinkov (USSR).
Ice Dance.—Miss M. Klimova and S. Ponomarenko (USSR).

World Championships

(Halifax, Nova Scotia, March 1990)

Men's Figures.—K. Browning (Canada).
Women's Figures.—Miss J. Trenary (USA).
Pairs.—Miss E. Gordeyeva and S. Grinkov (USSR).
Ice Dance.—Miss M. Klimova and S. Ponomarenko (USSR).

JUDO

British Championships

(Crystal Palace, Nov. 1989)

MEN'S

Heavyweight (over 95kg), E. Gordon.
Light Heavyweight (95kg), N. Kokotaylo.
Middleweight (86kg), D. White.
Light Middleweight (78kg), F. Davis.
Lightweight (71kg), S. Ravenscroft.
Featherweight (65kg), O. Pinnock.
Bantamweight (60kg), C. Finney.

WOMEN'S

Light Heavyweight (72kg), A. Lucitt.
Middleweight (66kg), K. Howey.
Light Middleweight (61kg), L. Hancock.
Lightweight (56kg), N. Fairbrother.
Featherweight (52kg), S. Tedder.
Bantamweight (48kg), A. Mohamoodally.

LAWN TENNIS, 1989–90

MAJOR CHAMPIONSHIPS 1990

Australian Open Championships (Melbourne)

Men's Singles.—I. Lendl (Czechoslovakia) beat S. Edberg (Sweden) 4–6, 7–6, 5–2; Edberg retired injured.
Women's Singles.—Miss S. Graf (W. Germany) beat Miss M. J. Fernandez (USA) 6–3, 6–4.
Men's Doubles.—P. Aldrich and D. Visser (S. Africa) beat G. Connell and G. Michibata (Canada) 6–4, 4–6, 6–1, 6–4.
Women's Doubles.—Miss H. Sukova and Miss J. Novotna (Czechoslovakia) beat Miss P. Fendick and Miss M. J. Fernandez (USA) 7–6, 7–6.

French Open Championships (Paris)

Men's Singles.—A. Gomez (Ecuador) beat A. Agassi (USA) 6–3, 2–6, 6–4, 6–4.
Women's Singles.—Miss M. Seles (Yugoslavia) beat Miss S. Graf (W. Germany) 7–6, 6–4.
Men's Doubles.—S. Casal and E. Sanchez (Spain) beat G. Ivanisevic (Yugoslavia) and P. Korda (Czechoslovakia) 7–5, 6–3.

Women's Doubles.—Miss J. Novotna and Miss H. Sukova (Czechoslovakia) beat Miss L. Savchenko and Miss N. Zvereva (USSR) 6–4, 7–5.
Mixed Doubles.—Miss A. Sánchez Vicario (Spain) and J. Lozano (Mexico) beat Miss N. Provis (Australia) and D. Visser (S. Africa) 7–6, 7–6.

All England Championships (Wimbledon)

Men's Singles.—S. Edberg (Sweden) beat B. Becker (W. Germany) 6–2, 6–2, 3–6, 3–6, 6–4.
Women's Singles.—Miss M. Navratilova (USA) beat Ms Z. Garrison (USA) 6–4, 6–1.
Men's Doubles.—R. Leach and J. Pugh (USA) beat P. Aldrich and D. Visser (S. Africa) 7–6, 7–6, 7–6.
Women's Doubles.—Miss J. Novotna and Miss H. Sukova (Czechoslovakia) beat Miss K. Jordan (USA) and Miss P. D. Smylie (Australia) 6–3, 6–4.
Mixed Doubles.—Ms Z. Garrison and R. Leach (USA) beat Miss P. D. Smylie (Australia) and J. B. Fitzgerald (Australia) 7–5, 6–2.

US Open Championships (New York)

Men's Singles.—P. Sampras (USA) beat A. Agassi (USA), 6–4, 6–3, 6–2.
Women's Singles.—G. Sabatini (Argentina) beat S. Graf (W. Germany) 6–2, 7–6.
Men's Doubles.—P. Aldrich and D. Visser (S. Africa) beat P. Annacone and D. Wheaton (USA) 6–2, 7–6, 6–2.
Women's Doubles.—G. Fernandez and M. Navratilova (USA) beat J. Novotna and H. Sukova (Czechoslovakia) 6–2, 6–4.
Mixed Doubles.—Miss E. Smyllie and T. Woodbridge (Australia) beat Miss N. Zvereva (USSR) and J. Pugh (USA) 6–4, 6–2.

TEAM CHAMPIONSHIPS

Davis Cup 1989.—West Germany beat Sweden 3–2.
Federation Cup 1990 (Atlanta, USA).—USA beat USSR 2–1.
Wightman Cup 1990.—Cancelled.
Prudential County Cup 1990.—*Men,* Surrey; *Women,* Surrey.

MOTOR CYCLING, 1990

500 cc Grand Prix, 1990

Japanese (Suzuka).—W. Rainey (Yamaha).
United States (Laguna Seca, California).—W. Rainey (Yamaha).
Spanish (Jerez).—W. Gardner (Honda).
Italian (Misano).—W. Rainey (Yamaha).
West German (Nurburgring).—K. Schwantz (Suzuki).
Austrian (Salzburg).—K. Schwantz (Suzuki).
Yugoslav (Rijeka).—W. Rainey (Yamaha).
Dutch (Assen).—K. Schwantz (Suzuki).
Belgian (Spa Francorchamps).—W. Rainey (Yamaha).
French (Le Mans).—K. Schwantz (Suzuki).
British (Donington Park).—K. Schwantz (Suzuki).
Swedish (Anderstorp).—W. Rainey (Yamaha).
Czech (Brno).—W. Rainey (Yamaha).
Hungarian (Budapest).—M. Doohan (Honda).
Australian (Phillip Island).—W. Gardner (Honda).

Senior Manx Grand Prix.—S. Beck (Honda).
Senior TT, Isle of Man.—C. Fogarty (Honda).
Junior TT, Isle of Man.—I. Lougher (Yamaha).

MOTOR RACING, 1989–90

Formula One Grand Prix, 1989

Japanese (Suzuka).—1. A. Nannini (Benetton); 2. R. Patrese (Williams); 3. T. Boutsen (Williams).
Australian (Adelaide).—1. T. Boutsen (Williams); 2. A. Nannini (Benetton); 3. R. Patrese (Williams).

Drivers' Championship winner 1989.—A. Prost (McLaren), 76 pts.
Constructors' Championship winner 1989.—McLaren Honda, 141 pts.

Formula One Grand Prix, 1990

United States (Phoenix).—1. A. Senna (McLaren); 2. J. Alesi (Tyrrell); 3. T. Boutsen (Williams).
Brazilian (Sao Paulo).—1. A. Prost (Ferrari); 2. G. Berger (McLaren); 3. A. Senna (McLaren).
San Marino (Imola).—1. R. Patrese (Williams); 2. G. Berger (McLaren); 3. A. Nannini (Benetton).
Monaco (Monte Carlo).—1. A. Senna (McLaren); 2. J. Alesi (Tyrrell); 3. G. Berger (McLaren).
Canadian (Montreal).—1. A. Senna (McLaren); 2. N. Piquet (Benetton); 3. N. Mansell (Ferrari).
Mexican (Mexico City).—1. A. Prost (Ferrari); 2. N. Mansell (Ferrari); 3. G. Berger (McLaren).
French (Le Castellet).—1. A. Prost (Ferrari); 2. I. Capelli (Leyton House); 3. A. Senna (McLaren).
British (Silverstone).—1. A. Prost (Ferrari); 2. T. Boutsen (Williams); 3. A. Senna (McLaren).
West German (Hockenheim).—1. A. Senna (McLaren); 2. A. Nannini (Benetton); 3. G. Berger (McLaren).
Hungarian (Budapest).—1. T. Boutsen (Williams); 2. A. Senna (McLaren); 3. N. Piquet (Benetton).
Belgian (Spa-Francorchamps).—1. A. Senna (McLaren); 2. A. Prost (Ferrari); G. Berger (McLaren).
Italian (Monza).—1. A. Senna (McLaren); 2. A. Prost (Ferrari); 3. G. Berger (McLaren).
Portuguese (Estoril).—1. N. Mansell (Ferrari); 2. A. Senna (McLaren); 3. A. Prost (Ferrari).
Spanish (Jerez).—1. A. Prost (Ferrari); 2. N. Mansell (Ferrari); 3. A. Nannini (Benetton).

MOTOR RALLYING

Lombard RAC Rally, 1989.—P. Airikkala and R. McNamee (Mitsubishi).
Paris/Dakar Trans-Sahara Rally.—A. Vatanen (Finland) (Peugeot).
Monte Carlo Rally.—D. Auriol (France) (Lancia).
Safari Rally.—B. Waldegaard (Toyota).
Circuit of Ireland Rally.—D. Llewellin (Toyota).
Indianapolis 500.—A. Luyendyk (Lola–Chevrolet).
Le Mans 24-hour.—J. Nielsen (Denmark), P. Cobb (US) and M. Brundle (GB) (Jaguar).
Birmingham Super-Prix.—E. van de Poele (Belgium) (Reynard–Cosworth).

NETBALL, 1989–90

Internationals

1989
Nov. 25 Middlesbrough: England 80, Scotland 18.
1990
Feb. 3 Glasgow: Scotland 28, England 69.
    17 Poole: England 43, Wales 30.

Inter-County Championship.—Middlesex beat Bedfordshire 10–9.
National Clubs Championship.—New Cambell beat Linden 49–43.

POLO, 1990

Prince of Wales's Trophy.—Tramontana beat Champagne-Pommery 10–9.
Queen's Cup final.—Santa Fe beat Rosamundo 12–7.
Gold Cup (British Championship).—Hildon beat Cowdray Park 10–9.
Coronation Cup.—England beat France 6–5.
Silver Jubilee Cup.—Ellerston White beat Hurlingham Association 5–4.

Warwickshire Cup.—Ellerston White beat Hildon 9–7.
Cowdray Challenge Cup.—Rosamundo beat Santa Fe 5½–4.

RACKETS, 1989–90

World Singles Champion.—J. Male.
World Doubles Championship.—J. Male and J. Prenn beat S. Hazell and N. Smith 8–5.
Amateur Singles Championship.—W. Boone beat J. Prenn 3–0.
Amateur Doubles Championship.—J. Prenn and J. Male beat M. and C. Hue Williams, 4–1.
Professional Singles Championship.—S. Hazell beat N. Smith 3–2.
British Open Singles Championship.—N. Smith beat W. Boone 4–0.
British Open Doubles Championship.—J. Prenn and J. Male beat N. Smith and S. Hazell 4–1.
Noel Bruce Cup.—Eton (W. Boone and M. Hue Williams) beat Harrow (J. Prenn and C. Hue Williams) 4–2.
Public Schools Doubles Championship.—Clifton (J. Crane and M. Windows) beat Eton (J. Larken and A. Smith-Bingham) 4–2.
Universities.—Cambridge beat Oxford 3–0.

REAL TENNIS, 1989–90

World Singles Champion.—W. Davies.

Professional Singles Championship.—L. Deuchar beat D. Johnson 3–0.

Professional Doubles Championship.—P. Brake and C. Bray beat N. Wood and P. Mears 2–0.

Amateur Singles Championship.—J. Male beat J. Snow 3–0.

Amateur Doubles Championship.—M. Happell and J. Male beat M. McMurrugh and J. Snow 3–1.

British Open Singles Championship.—L. Deuchar beat C. Ronaldson 3–0.

British Open Doubles Championship.—W. Davies and L. Deuchar beat K. Sheldon and J. Howell 3–0.

British Open Ladies Singles.—S. Jones beat A. Warren-Piper 2–0.

Henry Leaf Cup final.—Radley (J. Male and J. Snow) beat Winchester (A. Lovell and P. Seabrook) 2–0.

Universities.—Oxford beat Cambridge 4–2.

ROWING, 1990

Henley Royal Regatta, 1990

Grand Challenge Cup.—Hansa Dortmund (W. Germany) beat Leander and University of London by 2 lengths.
Ladies' Challenge Plate.—Harvard University (USA) beat University of London by 3¼ lengths.
Henley Prize.—Imperial College, London beat Trinity College, Dublin (Ire) by 1¼ lengths.
Visitors' Cup.—University of London A beat Goldie, not rowed out.
Thames Challenge Cup.—Nottinghamshire County beat Harvard University A (USA) by 2 lengths.
Stewards' Challenge Cup.—Star Club and Leander A beat Star Club and Leander B by 4¼ lengths.
Queen Mother Challenge Cup.—Danmarks Rocenter Roklub (Denmark) beat ASR Nereus and Skadi (Netherlands) by half a length.
Princess Elizabeth Cup.—Eton College beat Westminster School by two-thirds of a length.
Prince Philip Cup.—Hansa Dortmund (W. Germany) beat Levski Spartak (Bulgaria) by 4 lengths.

Silver Goblets and Nickall's Challenge Cup.—K. S. Sinzinger and H. Bauer (Heeresportverein Kapsch Linz, Austria) beat M. P. Cross (Thames Tradesmen's) and T. J. C. Foster (Star Club) by 1 ft.

Wyfold Cup.—London RC A beat Nottinghamshire County by 1¼ lengths.

Britannia Challenge Cup.—University College, Galway (Ire) beat Cappoquin (Ire) by 2 lengths.

Double Sculls Cup.—A. C. Rudkin (Tideway Scullers' School) and A. P. S. Kittermaster (Barclay's Bank) beat M. B. Alloway and C. F. Williams (Tideway Scullers' School) by 1¼ lengths.

Diamond Challenge Sculls.—E. F. M. Verdonk (Koru, NZ) beat W. van Belleghem (Brugges Trimm-en, Belgium) by three-quarters of a length.

National Championships 1990

(Holme Pierrepont)

MEN

Coxed pairs.—Thames Tradesmen's.
Coxless pairs.—Lea/London University.
Coxed fours.—Lea A.
Coxless fours.—Nottingham County.
Single sculls.—S. Larkin (Nottingham County).
Double sculls.—Molesey.
Quad sculls.—Upper Thames A.
Eights.—Nottingham County.

WOMEN

Coxless pairs.—GB Squad B.
Coxless fours.—GB Squad.
Coxed fours.—University of London.
Single sculls.—P. Reid (GB Squad).
Double sculls.—GB Squad.
Quad sculls.—Tideway Scullers A.
Eights.—Cambridge University A.

The 136th University Boat Race

(Putney-Mortlake, 4 m. 1 f. 180 yds.)

Oxford beat Cambridge by 2¼ lengths, 7s.

(Cambridge have won 69 times, Oxford 66 and there has been 1 dead-heat. The record time is the 16 m 45 s rowed by Oxford in 1984.)

Women's Boat Race.—Cambridge beat Oxford by 3¼ lengths, 7m. 17s.

Other Rowing Events

Oxford Torpids.—Oriel.
Cambridge Lents.—*Men*, Lady Margaret; *Women*, Emmanuel.
Oxford Summer Eights.—*Men*, University College; *Women*, Somerville.
Cambridge Mays.—*Men*, Downing; *Women*, Emmanuel.
Head of the River.—*Men*, Great Britain National Squad; *Women*, Thames A.
Doggett's Coat and Badge (*Estab.* 1715, 276th race, *London Bridge-Chelsea*, 4½ miles).—S. Collins.

RUGBY FIVES, 1989–90

National Schools' Championships.—*Singles:* I. Ford (St. Dunstan's). *Doubles:* St. Dunstan's.

RUGBY LEAGUE, 1989–90

International Matches

1989
Oct. 21 Old Trafford: Gt. Britain 16, New Zealand 24.
28 Elland Road: Gt. Britain 26, New Zealand 6.
Nov. 11 Wigan: Gt. Britain 10, New Zealand 6.
1990
Mar. 18 Perpignan: France 4, Gt. Britain 8.
Apr. 7 Headingley: Gt. Britain 18, France 25.
May 27 Goroka: Papua New Guinea 20, Gt. Britain 18.

Jun. 3 Port Moresby: Papua New Guinea 8, Gt. Britain 40.
24 Palmerston North: New Zealand 10, Gt. Britain 11.
July 8 Auckland: New Zealand 14, Gt. Britain 16.
15 Christchurch: New Zealand 21, Gt. Britain 18.

Domestic Competitions

Rugby League Challenge Cup final (Wembley, April 28).—Wigan beat Warrington 36–14.
Premiership Trophy final (Old Trafford, May 13).—Widnes beat Bradford Northern 28–6.
Division 2 Premiership final.—Oldham beat Hull KR 30–29.
Stones Bitter Championship.—Wigan.
Division 2 Championship.—Hull KR.
Regal Trophy final (Headingley, Jan. 13).—Wigan beat Halifax 24–12.
Lancashire Cup.—Warrington beat Oldham 24–16.
Yorkshire Cup.—Bradford Northern beat Featherstone Rovers 20–14.
Universities.—Cambridge beat Oxford 20–15.

AMATEUR RUGBY LEAGUE, 1989–90

County Championship.—Cumbria.
National Inter-League Shield Competitions.—
Open Age.—Humberside.
Under 19.—St. Helens.
Under 17.—Leeds.
National Cup Competitions.—
Open Age.—Egremont Rangers.
Under 19.—Leigh MW.
National League Champions.—Dudley Hill.
National League Challenge Cup Winners.—Wigan St. Patricks.

RUGBY UNION, 1989–90

International Matches

1989
Oct. 28 Edinburgh: Scotland 38, Fiji 17.
Nov. 4 Cardiff: Wales 9, New Zealand 34.
Twickenham: England 58, Fiji 23.
18 Dublin: Ireland 6, New Zealand 23.
1990
Jan. 20 Twickenham: England 23, Ireland 0.
Cardiff: Wales 19, France 29.
Feb. 3 Dublin: Ireland 10, Scotland 13.
Paris: France 7, England 26.
17 Twickenham: England 34, Wales 6.
Edinburgh: Scotland 21, France 0.
Mar. 3 Cardiff: Wales 9, Scotland 13.
Paris: France 31, Ireland 12.
17 Edinburgh: Scotland 3, England 7.
24 Dublin: Ireland 14, Wales 8.
Jun. 2 Windhoek: Namibia 9, Wales 18.
9 Windhoek: Namibia 30, Wales 34.
16 Dunedin: New Zealand 31, Scotland 16.
23 Auckland: New Zealand 21, Scotland 18.
July 28 Buenos Aires: Argentina 12, England 25.
Aug. 4 Buenos Aires: Argentina 15, England 13.

Five Nations' Championship 1990

	P	W	D	L	Pts.		Total
					F	A	
Scotland	4	4	0	0	60	26	8
England	4	3	0	1	90	27	6
France	4	2	0	2	67	78	4
Ireland	4	1	0	3	36	81	2
Wales	4	0	0	4	42	90	0

Domestic Competitions

Division 1 Club Champions.—Wasps.
Division 2 Club Champions.—Northampton.
Division 3 Club Champions.—London Scottish.
County Championship final.—Lancashire beat Middlesex 32–9.
Pilkington Cup final (Twickenham, May 5).—Bath beat Gloucester 48–6.
Welsh Cup final.—Neath beat Bridgend 16–10.
Hospitals' Cup final.—St. Mary's beat The London 9–6.
Services Championship.—Army beat Royal Navy 16–7; RAF beat Royal Navy 22–14; Army beat RAF 32–14.
Universities, 1989.—Cambridge beat Oxford 22–13.
Middlesex Sevens.—Harlequins beat Rosslyn Park 26–10.
Women's Rugby Union Cup final.—Wasps beat Richmond 10–3.

SHOOTING

Bisley, 121st NRA, 1990

Queen's Prize.—1. J. P. S. Bloomfield, 293 pts; 2. W. W. Baldwin, 293 pts; 3. A. Marion, 290 pts.
Prince of Wales Prize.—1. Miss T. J. Fitzsimons, 75.14 pts; 2. D. G. P. Vamplew, 75.14 pts; 3. D. M. McArthur, 75.13 pts.
Land Rover Grand Aggregate.—1. A. Marion, 654 pts.; 2. H. J. Orpen-Smellie, 654 pts.; 3. J. D. Warburton, 653 pts.
St. George's Vase.—1. A. Ringer, 149 pts; 2. P. Papasideris, 149 pts; 3. G. T. Pern, 148 pts.
All Comers Aggregate.—1. D. G. M. Coleman, 321 pts; 2. M. S. Merry, 320 pts; 3. J. H. Carmichael, 319 pts.
National Trophy.—1. England, 2,040 pts; 2. Ireland 2,004 pts; 3. Scotland, 1,998 pts.
Kolapore Cup.—1. Great Britain, 1,178·164 pts; 2. Canada, 1,178·160 pts; 3. Australia, 1,157 pts.
Chancellor's Challenge Plate.—1. Cambridge University, 1,141·129 pts; 2. Oxford University, 1,111·88 pts.
Musketeers Cup.—1. London University, 582·72 pts; 2. Southampton University, 576 pts.
Vizianagram Trophy.—1. House of Lords, 795·37 pts; 2. House of Commons, 763·22 pts.
County Long-Range Championship.—1. Hertfordshire, 279 pts; 2. Aberdeenshire, 275 pts; 3. Devon, 274 pts.
MacKinnon Challenge Cup.—1. Canada, 1,145 pts; 2. England, 1,137 pts; 3. New Zealand, 1,119 pts.

Clay Pigeon Shooting, 1990

International Cup (Down-the-Line).—England, 7,337/7,500.
British Open Down-the-Line Championship.—I. Jones, 100/299.
Mackintosh Trophy.—Canada, 7,371/7,500.
British Open Skeet Championship.—J. Munday, 100+25.
British Open Sporting Championship.—G. Phillips, 93/100.
Coronation Cup.—J. Winn.

SNOOKER AND BILLIARDS, 1989–90

World Professional Snooker Championship.—S. Hendry beat J. White 18–12.
World Matchplay Championship.—J. White beat J. Parrott 18–9.
World Team Cup.—Canada beat N. Ireland 9–5.
Benson and Hedges Masters Snooker Tournament.—S. Hendry beat J. Parrott by 9–4.
UK Professional Snooker Championship.—S. Hendry beat S. Davis 16–12.

British Open Snooker Championship.—R. Chaperon (Canada) beat A. Higgins (N. Ireland) 10–8.
Mercantile Credit Classic.—S. James beat W. King 10–6.
World Amateur Snooker Championship 1989.—K. Doherty (Rep. of Ireland) beat J. Birch (England) 11–2.
Women's UK Snooker Championship.—A. Fisher beat S. Hillyard 5–0.
World Professional Billiards Champion.—M. Russell (GB).
World Amateur Billiards Championship.—M. Kothari (India), 2,890.
UK Billiards Championship.—M. Russell (England) beat J. Murphy (England) 1,478–1,058.
British Open Billiards Championship.—P. Gilchrist beat N. Dagley 1,166–1,008.

SPEEDWAY, 1989–90

British Champion 1990.—K. Tatum (Coventry).
British League Riders' Champion 1990.—S. Moran (Belle Vue).
British League Champions 1989.—Oxford.
Gold Cup 1990.—Bradford.
Knock-Out Cup Winners 1989.—Cradley Heath.
World Individual Speedway Championship (World Final).—P. Jonsson (Sweden).
World Pairs Speedway Championship.—H. Nielson and J. O. Pedersen (Denmark).
World Team Speedway Championship.—USA.

SQUASH RACKETS, 1989–90
MEN

World Open Championship 1989.—Jansher Khan (Pakistan) beat C. Dittmar (Australia) 3–2.
World Team Championship.—Australia.
European Club Championship.—Lambs Club (England).
British Open Championship.—Jahangir Khan (Pakistan) beat R. Martin (Australia), 3–0.
National Championship.—D. Harris beat B. Beeson 3–2.

WOMEN

World Open Championship 1989.—Miss M. Le Moignan (GB) beat Miss S. Devoy (NZ) 3–1.
World Team Championship.—England.
European Club Championship.—Richmond Town (England).
British Open Championship.—Miss S. Devoy (NZ) beat Mrs S. Horner 3–1.
National Championship.—Miss L. Soutter beat Mrs S. Horner 3–0.

SWIMMING, 1990

National Swimming Championships, 1990
(Coventry, July)

Men

50m freestyle.—N. Sanders (NZ).
100m freestyle.—J. Steel (NZ).
200m freestyle.—P. Howe (Birmingham).
400m freestyle.—P. Howe (Birmingham).
1,500m freestyle.—I. Wilson (Sunderland).
100m breaststroke.—A. Moorhouse (Leeds).
200m breaststroke.—N. Gillingham (Birmingham).
100m butterfly.—N. Sanders (NZ).
200m butterfly.—P. Howe (Birmingham).
100m backstroke.—M. Harris (Barnet).
200m backstroke.—T. Deutsch (Hungary).
200m medley.—G. Robins (Portsmouth).

400m medley.—J. Munro (NZ).
4 × 100m freestyle relay.—Barnet Copthall.
4 × 100m medley relay.—Leeds.

Women

50m freestyle.—C. Woodcock (Barnet).
100m freestyle.—K. Pickering (Ipswich).
200m freestyle.—K. Pickering (Ipswich).
400m freestyle.—K. Mellor (Sheffield).
800m freestyle.—K. Mellor (Sheffield).
100m breaststroke.—L. Hooiveld (Leeds).
200m breaststroke.—S. Brownsdon (Wigan).
100m butterfly.—M. Scarborough (Portsmouth).
200m butterfly.—M. Scarborough (Portsmouth).
100m backstroke.—S. Page (Wigan).
200m backstroke.—A. Simcic (NZ).
200m medley.—Z. Long (Beckenham).
400m medley.—Z. Long (Beckenham).
4 × 100m freestyle relay.—Portsmouth Northsea.
4 × 100m medley relay.—City of Southampton.

TABLE TENNIS, 1990

English National Championships
(Oldham)

Men's Singles.—D. Douglas beat C. Prean, 3–2.
Women's Singles.—Miss F. Elliot beat Miss A. Holt 3–1.
Men's Doubles.—A. Cooke and D. Douglas beat S. Andrew and N. Mason 2–0.
Women's Doubles.—Miss F. Elliot and Mrs. L. Lomas beat Miss A. Gordon and Miss A. Holt 2–1.
Mixed Doubles.—S. Andrew and Miss F. Elliot beat J. Holland and Miss J. Billington 2–0.

YACHTING, 1989–90

America's Cup 1988
(San Diego, USA)

Final.—The defender *Stars and Stripes* (USA) beat the challenger *New Zealand* (NZ) by 2–0. In March 1989 a court ruling decided that *New Zealand* should be declared the winner after the disqualification of *Stars and Stripes* for being a catamaran, a design contrary to the rules of the America's Cup. A series of appeals led to the decision being reversed a number of times but the dispute was finally settled in April 1990 when the New York State Court found in favour of *Stars and Stripes*.

Whitbread Round the World Yacht Race
(Sept. 1989–May 1990)

Division 1
1. *Steinlager 2* in 128 days, 9 hrs., 40 mins.
2. *Fisher & Paykel*, 129 days, 21 hrs., 18 mins.
3. *Merit*, 130 days, 10 hrs., 10 mins.

Division 2
Equity and Law, 148 days, 23 hrs., 50 mins.

Division 3
1. *L'Esprit de Liberté*, 164 days, 21 hrs., 36 mins.
2. *Maiden*, 167 days, 3 hrs., 6 mins.
3. *Schlussel von Bremen*, 167 days, 19 hrs., 7 mins.

Cruiser Division.
1. *Creighton Naturally*, 162 days, 6 hrs., 34 mins.
2. *With Integrity*, 170 days, 16 hrs., 19 mins.

Globe Yachting Challenge non-stop single-handed round-the-world race (Nov. 26, 1989–March 1990).—Titouan Lamazou (*Ecureuil d'Aquitaine*) in 109 days, 8 hours, 48 minutes.

Transatlantic Two-Handed Yacht Race 1990.—J. Maurel and M. Desjoyeaux (*Elf Aquitaine*) in 10 days, 23 hours, 15 minutes.

Admiral's Cup 1989.—Great Britain (*Jamarella/ Juno/Indulgence*), 748 pts.

Fastnet Race 1989.—R. Short (USA) *Great News*.

OXFORD AND CAMBRIDGE
Principal Events and Winners, 1989–90

Event (with date of first meeting)	Summary of Results			Results 1989–90
	Ox.	Camb.	Drawn	
Athletics (1864)	59	50	7	Oxford
Boat Race (1829)	66	69	1	Oxford
Cricket (1827)	46	54	45	Drawn
Football—				
Association (1873–4)	39	45	22	Drawn
Rugby (1871–2)	46	49	13	Camb.
Golf (1878)	39	55	5	Camb.
Hockey (1890)	28	43	16	Camb.

Other University Events and Winners, 1989–90

Cross Country	Oxford
Rackets	Cambridge
Real Tennis	Oxford
Rugby League	Cambridge
Shooting (small bore rifle)	Cambridge
Squash Rackets	Oxford

SPORTS REPRESENTATIVE BODIES

Angling.—NATIONAL ANGLERS' COUNCIL, 11 Cowgate, Peterborough PE1 1LZ. *Exec. Dir.*, P. H. Tombleson, OBE; NATIONAL FEDERATION OF ANGLERS, Halliday House, 2 Wilson Street, Derby DE1 1PG. *Chief Admin. Officer*, K. E. Watkins.

Association Football.—THE FOOTBALL ASSOCIATION, 16 Lancaster Gate, W2 3LW. *Chief Exec.*, R. H. G. Kelly.

Athletics.—AMATEUR ATHLETIC ASSOCIATION, Edgbaston House, 3 Duchess Place, Hagley Road, Birmingham B16 8NM. *Gen. Sec.*, M. A. Farrell.
—WOMEN'S AMATEUR ATHLETIC ASSOCIATION, Francis House, Francis Street, SW1P 1DE. *Hon. Sec.*, Miss M. Hartman, CBE.

Badminton.—BADMINTON ASSOCIATION OF ENGLAND, National Badminton Centre, Loughton Lodge, Bradwell Road, Milton Keynes MK8 9LA. *Chief Exec.*, G. Snowdon.

Basket Ball.—ENGLISH BASKET BALL ASSOCIATION, Calomax House, Lupton Avenue, Leeds LS9 6EE. *Sec.*, M. D. Welch.

Billiards.—BILLIARDS AND SNOOKER CONTROL COUNCIL, Coronet House, Queen Street, Leeds LS1 2TN. *Chair.*, S. Brooke.

Bobsleigh.—BRITISH BOBSLEIGH ASSOCIATION, Springfield House, 7 Woodstock Road, Coulsdon, Surrey CR5 3HS. *Sec.*, P. Pruszynski.

Bowls.—ENGLISH BOWLING ASSOCIATION, Lyndhurst Road, Worthing, W. Sussex BN11 2AZ. *Sec.*, D. W. Johnson.
—ENGLISH INDOOR BOWLING ASSOCIATION, *Sec.*, B. Telfer. 290A Barking Road, E6 3BA.

Boxing.—AMATEUR BOXING ASSOCIATION OF ENGLAND, Francis House, Francis Street, SW1P 1DE.—*Hon. Sec.*, J. H. Lewis.
—BRITISH BOXING BOARD OF CONTROL, 70 Vauxhall Bridge Road, SW1V 2RP.—*Gen. Sec.*, J. Morris.

Canoeing.—BRITISH CANOE UNION, Adbolton Lane, West Bridgford, Nottingham NG2 5AS. *Dir.*, T. J. Bailey.

Cricket.—MCC, Lords, NW8 8QN. *Pres.* Sir Denys Roberts, KBE, QC; *Sec.*, Lt.-Col. J. R. Stephenson, OBE.
—TEST AND COUNTY CRICKET BOARD, Lord's, NW8 8QZ. *Chairman* (1990–91), W. R. F. Chamberlain; *Chief Exec.*, A. C. Smith.
—CRICKET COUNCIL, Lord's, NW8 8QN. *Chairman*, W. R. F. Chamberlain; *Sec.*, A. C. Smith.

Croquet.—CROQUET ASSOCIATION, c/o The Hurlingham Club, Ranelagh Gardens, SW6 3PR. *Sec.*, B. C. Macmillan.

Cycling.—BRITISH CYCLING FEDERATION, 36 Rockingham Road, Kettering, Northants. NN16 8HG. *Chief Exec.*, J. Hendry.
—ROAD TIME TRIALS COUNCIL, Dallacre, Mill Road, Yarwell, Peterborough PE8 6PS. *Sec.*, D. E. Roberts.

Eton Fives.—ETON FIVES ASSOCIATION.—*Hon. Sec.*, M. P. Powell, Grafton Cottage, Bentley, Farnham, Surrey GU10 5HY.

Fencing.—AMATEUR FENCING ASSOCIATION, 83 Perham Road, W14 9SP. *Sec.*, Miss G. Kenneally.

Golf.—ROYAL AND ANCIENT GOLF CLUB, St. Andrews, Fife KY16 9JD. *Sec.*, M. F. Bonallack, OBE.
—LADIES' GOLF UNION, The Scores, St. Andrews, Fife KY16 9AT.—*Administrator*, Mrs A. Robertson.

Gymnastics.—BRITISH AMATEUR GYMNASTICS ASSOCIATION, Thames Valley College (Block D), Wellington Street, Slough, Berks. SL1 1XT. *Dir.*, A. L. Murdock.

Hockey.—HOCKEY ASSOCIATION, 16 Northdown Street, N1 9BG. *Chief Exec.*, S. P. Baines.
— ALL ENGLAND WOMEN'S HOCKEY ASSOCIATION, 51 High Street, Shrewsbury SY1 1ST. *Sec.*, Miss T. Morris.

Horse-racing.—THE JOCKEY CLUB (incorporating National Hunt Committee), 42 Portman Square, W1H 0EN. *Chief Exec.*, C. J. M. Haines.

Judo.—BRITISH JUDO ASSOCIATION, 16 Upper Woburn Place, WC1H 0QH. *Gen. Sec.*, Miss G. M. Kenneally.

Lacrosse.—ENGLISH LACROSSE UNION, *Hon. Sec.*, R. Balls, 70 High Road, Rayleigh, Essex SS6 7AD.
— ALL ENGLAND WOMEN'S LACROSSE ASSOCIATION, Francis House, Francis Street, SW1P 1DE.

Lawn Tennis.—LAWN TENNIS ASSOCIATION, The Queen's Club, W14 9EG. *Sec.*, J. C. U. James.
— INTERNATIONAL TENNIS FEDERATION, Palliser Road, W14 9EN. *Gen. Sec.*, M. Davies.

Lugeing.—THE GREAT BRITAIN LUGE ASSOCIATION, 43 Wimpole Street, W1M 7AF. *President*, R. L. Liversedge.

Motor Cycling.—AUTO-CYCLE UNION, Miller House, Corporation Street, Rugby, Warwicks. CV21 2DN. *Sec. Gen.*, D. G. Coleman.

Netball.—ALL ENGLAND NETBALL ASSOCIATION, Francis House, Francis Street, SW1P 1DE. *Chief Exec.*, Mrs E. M. Nicholl.

Olympics.—BRITISH OLYMPIC ASSOCIATION, 1 Wandsworth Plain, SW18 1EH. *Gen. Sec.*, R. Palmer, OBE.

Polo.—THE HURLINGHAM POLO ASSOCIATION, Winterlake, Kirtlington, Oxford OX5 3HG. *Hon. Sec.*, J. W. M. Crisp.

Rifle Shooting.—NATIONAL RIFLE ASSOCIATION, Bisley Camp, Brookwood, Woking, Surrey GU24 0PB. *Chief Exec.*, S. Ewing.
—NATIONAL SMALL-BORE RIFLE ASSOCIATION, Lord Roberts House, Bisley Camp, Brookwood, Woking GU24 0NP. *Sec.*, Gp. Capt. D. King, MBE.

Rowing.—AMATEUR ROWING ASSOCIATION, The Priory, 6 Lower Mall, W6 9DJ. *Exec. Sec.*, I. W. Pratt.

Rugby Football.—THE RUGBY FOOTBALL UNION, Whitton Road, Twickenham TW1 1DZ. *Sec.*, D. E. Wood.
— THE RUGBY FOOTBALL LEAGUE, 180 Chapeltown Road, Leeds LS7 4HT. *Chief Exec.*, D. S. Oxley, OBE.
— BRITISH AMATEUR RUGBY LEAGUE ASSOCIATION, West Yorkshire House, 4 New North Parade, Huddersfield HD1 5JP. *Administr.*, M. F. Oldroyd.

Skating.—NATIONAL SKATING ASSOCIATION OF GREAT BRITAIN, 15–27 Gee Street, EC1V 3RE. *Pres.*, C. J. L. Jones, OBE.

Skiing.—BRITISH SKI FEDERATION, Brocades House, Pyrford Road, West Byfleet, Surrey KT14 6RA. *Chairman*, T. Fitzpatrick.

Speedway.—THE SPEEDWAY CONTROL BOARD, 57 Villa Crescent, Bulkington, Nuneaton CV12 9NF. *Manager*, J. Eglese.

Squash Rackets.—SQUASH RACKETS ASSOCIATION, Westpoint, 33–34 Worple Way, W3 0RQ. *Chief Exec.*, R. I. Morris.

Swimming.—AMATEUR SWIMMING ASSOCIATION, Harold Fern House, Derby Square, Loughborough, Leics. LE11 0AL. *Sec.*, D. A. Reeves.

Table Tennis.—ENGLISH TABLE TENNIS ASSOCIATION, Queensbury House, Havelock Road, Hastings TN34 1HF. *Chief Exec.*, E. J. Wallbutton.

Walking.—RACE WALKING ASSOCIATION. *Gen. Sec.*, J. F. Keowm, 30 Maxwell Gardens, Orpington, Kent BR6 9QS.

Weightlifting.—BRITISH AMATEUR WEIGHTLIFTERS ASSOCIATION. *Hon. Sec.*, W. Holland, OBE, 3 Iffley Turn, Oxford OX4 4DU.

Wrestling.—ENGLISH OLYMPIC WRESTLING ASSOCIATION, 16 Choir Street, Cambridge Industrial Estate, Salford M7 9ZD. *Sec.*, H. I. Jacob, OBE.

Yachting.—ROYAL YACHTING ASSOCIATION, RYA House, Romsey Road, Eastleigh, Hants. SO5 4YA. *Sec. Gen.*, R. Duchesne, OBE.

THE OLYMPIC GAMES

The modern Olympic Games have been held as follows:

I	Athens, Greece	1896
II	Paris, France	1900
III	St. Louis, USA	1904
IV	London, Britain	1908
V	Stockholm, Sweden	1912
VII	Antwerp, Belgium	1920
VIII	Paris, France	1924
IX	Amsterdam, Netherlands	1928
X	Los Angeles, USA	1932
XI	Berlin, Germany	1936
XIV	London, Britain	1948
XV	Helsinki, Finland	1952
XVI	Melbourne, Australia	1956
XVII	Rome, Italy	1960
XVIII	Tokyo, Japan	1964
XIX	Mexico City, Mexico	1968
XX	Munich, West Germany	1972
XXI	Montreal, Canada	1976
XXII	Moscow, USSR	1980
XXIII	Los Angeles, USA	1984
XXIV	Seoul, South Korea	1988
XXV	Barcelona, Spain	1992

The following Games were scheduled but did not take place owing to World Wars:

VI	Berlin, Germany	1916
XII	Tokyo, Japan, then Helsinki, Finland	1940
XIII	London, Britain	1944

WINTER OLYMPIC GAMES

I	Chamonix, France	1924
II	St. Moritz, Switzerland	1928
III	Lake Placid, USA	1932
IV	Garmisch-Partenkirchen, Germany	1936
V	St. Moritz, Switzerland	1948
VI	Oslo, Norway	1952
VII	Cortina d'Ampezzo, Italy	1956
VIII	Squaw Valley, USA	1960
IX	Innsbruck, Austria	1964
X	Grenoble, France	1968
XI	Sapporo, Japan	1972
XII	Innsbruck, Austria	1976
XIII	Lake Placid, USA	1980
XIV	Sarajevo, Yugoslavia	1984
XV	Calgary, Canada	1988
XVI	Albertville, France	1992
XVII	Lillehammer, Norway	1994

THE COMMONWEALTH GAMES

The Games were originally called the British Empire Games. From 1954 to 1966 the Games were known as the British Empire and Commonwealth Games, and from 1970 to 1974 as the British Commonwealth Games. Since 1978 the Games have been called the Commonwealth Games.

British Empire Games

I	Hamilton, Canada	1930
II	London, England	1934
III	Sydney, Australia	1938
IV	Auckland, New Zealand	1950

British Empire and Commonwealth Games

V	Vancouver, Canada	1954
VI	Cardiff, Wales	1958
VII	Perth, Australia	1962
VIII	Kingston, Jamaica	1966

British Commonwealth Games

IX	Edinburgh, Scotland	1970
X	Christchurch, New Zealand	1974

Commonwealth Games

XI	Edmonton, Canada	1978
XII	Brisbane, Australia	1982
XIII	Edinburgh, Scotland	1986
XIV	Auckland, New Zealand	1990
XV	Victoria, Canada	1994

WORLD CUP

Venue	Winners	
Uruguay	Uruguay	1930
Italy	Italy	1934
France	Italy	1938
Brazil	Uruguay	1950
Switzerland	West Germany	1954
Sweden	Brazil	1958
Chile	Brazil	1962
England	England	1966
Mexico	Brazil	1970
West Germany	West Germany	1974
Argentina	Argentina	1978
Spain	Italy	1982
Mexico	Argentina	1986
Italy	West Germany	1990

THE NOBEL PRIZES

For prize winners for the years 1901–1986, *see* earlier editions of WHITAKER'S ALMANACK.

The Nobel Prizes are awarded each year from the income of a trust fund established by the Swedish scientist Alfred Nobel, the inventor of dynamite, who died on December 10, 1896, leaving a fortune of £1,750,000. The prizes are awarded to those who have contributed most to the common good in the domain of:

(*a*) Physics, awarded by the Royal Swedish Academy of Sciences;
(*b*) Chemistry, awarded by the Royal Swedish Academy of Sciences;
(*c*) Physiology or Medicine, awarded by the Karolinska Institute;
(*d*) Literature, awarded by the Swedish Academy of Arts;
(*e*) Peace, awarded by a five-person committee elected by the Norwegian Storting;
(*f*) Economic Sciences (instituted 1969), awarded by the Royal Swedish Academy of Sciences.

The first awards were made in 1901 on the fifth anniversary of Nobel's death. The prizes are awarded every year on December 10, the anniversary of Nobel's death.

The Trust is administered by the board of directors of the Nobel Foundation, Stockholm, consisting of five members and three deputy members. The Swedish Government appoints a chairman and a deputy chairman, the remaining members being appointed by the awarding authorities.

Prize	1987	1988	1989
PHYSICS	Dr. J. G. Bednorz (W. German) Dr. K. A. Müller (Swiss)	Dr. L. Lederman (American) Dr. M. Schwartz (American) Dr. J. Steinberger (American)	Prof. N. Ramsey (American) Prof. H. Dehmelt (American) Prof. W. Paul (W. German)
CHEMISTRY	Prof. D. Cram (American) Prof. J.-M. Lehn (French) C. J. Pedersen (American)	Dr. J. Deisenhofer (W. German) Dr. R. Huber (W. German) Dr. H. Michel (W. German)	Prof. T. Cech (American) Prof. S. Altman (American)
PHYSIOLOGY OR MEDICINE	S. Tonegawa (Japanese)	Sir James Black (British) Dr. G. Elion (American) Dr. G. Hitchings (American)	Prof. J. M. Bishop (American) Prof. H. E. Varmus (American)
LITERATURE	J. Brodsky (American)	N. Mahfouz (Egyptian)	C. José Cela (Spanish)
PEACE	Pres. O. Arias (Costa Rican)	United Nations peacekeeping forces	HH the Dalai Lama of Tibet (Tibetan)
ECONOMICS	Prof. R. M. Solow (American)	Prof. M. Allais (French)	T. Haavelmo (Norwegian)

The awards have been distributed as follows:

PHYSICS.—American 53; British 20; German 19 (before 1948, 11; W. German 8); French 9; Russian 7; Dutch 6; Swedish 4; Austrian 3; Danish 3; Italian 3; Japanese 3; Chinese 2; Swiss 2; Indian 1; Irish 1; Pakistani 1.

CHEMISTRY.—American 35; German 27 (before 1948, 17; W. German 10); British 23; French 7; Swedish 4; Swiss 4; Canadian 2; Dutch 2; Argentinian 1; Austrian 1; Belgian 1; Czech 1; Finnish 1; Hungarian 1; Italian 1; Japanese 1; Norwegian 1; Russian 1.

PHYSIOLOGY/MEDICINE.—American 65; British 22; German 12 (before 1948, 8; W. German 4); French 7; Swedish 7; Danish 5; Swiss 5; Austrian 4; Belgian 4; Italian 3; Australian 2; Canadian 2; Dutch 2; Hungarian 2; Russian 2; Argentinian 1; Japanese 1; Portuguese 1; S. African 1; Spanish 1.

LITERATURE.—French 12; American 9; British 8; Swedish 7; German 6 (before 1948, 5; W. German 1); Italian 5; Spanish 5; Danish 3; Norwegian 3; Russian 3; Chilean 2; Greek 2; Irish 2; Polish 2; Swiss 2; Australian 1; Belgian 1; Colombian 1; Czech 1; Egyptian 1; Finnish 1; Guatemalan 1; Icelandic 1; Indian 1; Israeli 1; Japanese 1; Nigerian 1; Yugoslav 1; Stateless 1.

PEACE.—American 17; Institutions 16; British 9; French 9; Swedish 5; German 4 (before 1948, 3; W. German 1); Belgian 3; Swiss 3; Argentinian 2; Austrian 2; Norwegian 2; S. African 2; Canadian 1; Costa Rican 1; Danish 1; Dutch 1; Egyptian 1; Irish 1; Israeli 1; Italian 1; Japanese 1; Mexican 1; Polish 1; Russian 1; Tibetan 1; Vietnamese 1; Yugoslav 1.

ECONOMICS.—American 15; British 5; Norwegian 2; Swedish 2; Dutch 1; French 1; Russian 1.

BOOKS PUBLISHED IN GREAT BRITAIN IN 1989

This table shows the books published in 1989 with the number of new editions, translations and limited editions. Books and pamphlets priced at less than 15p have been omitted, as are also all Government publications except the more important issued by HMSO.

Classification	Total	Reprints and new editions	Translations	Limited editions
Aeronautics	218	36	2	—
Agriculture and Forestry	537	106	8	—
Architecture	439	89	13	—
Art	1,757	276	69	6
Astronomy	146	28	2	—
Bibliography and Library Economy	621	110	1	—
Biography	2,150	602	81	7
Chemistry and Physics	1,068	154	30	—
Children's Books	6,217	1,537	192	3
Commerce	1,818	484	10	2
Customs, Costumes, Folklore	217	49	7	2
Domestic Science	860	244	11	—
Education	1,499	279	3	—
Engineering	1,416	327	15	—
Entertainment	614	140	20	—
Fiction	7,221	3,560	321	8
General	838	152	9	—
Geography and Archaeology	718	238	14	—
Geology and Meteorology	313	56	4	—
History	2,205	487	63	1
Humour	262	31	1	—
Industry	600	129	6	—
Language	749	194	7	2
Law and Public Administration	2,438	603	19	—
Literature	1,816	273	69	1
Mathematics	1,554	324	35	—
Medical Science	3,238	718	31	1
Military Science	457	126	3	1
Music	469	130	17	—
Natural Sciences	1,361	233	11	1
Occultism	481	114	15	1
Philosophy	729	127	69	—
Photography	287	30	4	2
Plays	388	109	43	—
Poetry	898	104	83	13
Political Science and Economics	4,444	852	52	—
Psychology	1,014	199	20	—
Religion and Theology	2,186	329	157	1
School Textbooks	1,751	254	21	2
Science, General	153	22	1	—
Sociology	1,468	214	30	—
Sports and Outdoor Games	913	242	5	3
Stockbreeding	321	75	6	1
Trade	697	165	1	—
Travel and Guidebooks	1,396	535	17	1
Wireless and Television	253	67	—	—
Total	61,195	15,153	1,598	59

BOOK PRODUCTION AND BOOK EXPORTS

The following figures for book production and exports are issued by the Department of Trade and Industry.

Year	Total value of books produced in UK £ million	Total value of books exported from UK £ million	Year	Total value of books produced in UK £ million	Total value of books exported from UK £ million
1975	342·4	138·6	1984	937·2	307·3
1980	666·9	213·7	1985	1044·0	340·9
1981	738·0	234·5	1986	1068·3	315·4
1982	759·1	232·8	1987	1191·2	342·2
1983	831·9	261·1	1988 (provisional)	1296·3	358·8

LITERATURE 1989–90

The controversy over Salman Rushdie's *The Satanic Verses* remained unresolved, with the author still in hiding under armed guard. The *fatwa* (religious decree) that sentenced him to death for blasphemy against Islam was reaffirmed by Ayatollah Khamenei, successor to Ayatollah Khomeini as spiritual leader of Iran. *A Satanic Affair: Salman Rushdie and the Rage of Islam* by Malise Ruthven attempted to put the whole affair into perspective by examining the Muslim religion, politics and sensibilities.

Rushdie broke his silence about the controversy in a 7,000 word article in the *Independent on Sunday* entitled 'In Good Faith', which was his justification for *The Satanic Verses*. He said, 'Fiction was a way of creating the sort of distance from actuality that I felt would prevent offence being taken'. He appealed to 'ordinary, decent fair-minded Muslims' to reconsider the work; 'the way forward might be found through mutual recognition of mutual pain'. He also wrote, 'I honestly believe there isn't a sentence I can't justify'.

Rushdie's thoughts about the controversy were also conveyed in the Herbert Read Memorial Lecture. His speech was entitled 'Is Nothing Sacred?' and was delivered on his behalf by Harold Pinter at the Institute of Contemporary Arts. 'We have been witnessing an attack upon a particular work of fiction that is also an attack upon the very ideas of the novel form, an attack of such bewildering ferocity that it has become necessary to restate what is most precious about the art of literature.'

The Booker

The 21st Booker Prize for Fiction was awarded to Kazuo Ishiguro for *The Remains of the Day*. The prize money in 1989 was increased from £15,000 to £20,000. David Lodge, chairman of the judges (and a finalist in 1988 with *Nice Work*), commended Ishiguro's work as 'a cunningly structured and beautifully paced performance. *The Remains of the Day* renders with humour and pathos a memorable character, and explores the vexed themes of class, tradition and duty. It was narrowly preferred, but universally admired.'

The novel tells the story of Stevens, former butler to Lord Darlington, an aristocrat whom he had served loyally. Stevens begins not only to appreciate the defects in his master's character, but also to realize that he has been diminished by serving such a man. During his West Country holiday, Stevens visits Miss Kenton, former housekeeper at Darlington Hall, and realizes that he has also passed up his only chance of happiness. 'I gave my best to Lord Darlington. I gave him the very best I had to give, and now—well—I find I do not have a great deal more left to give.' At the end of his trip of personal and emotional discovery, Stevens achieves a degree of self-realization: 'I should cease looking back so much . . . I should adopt a more positive outlook and try to make the best of what remains of my day'.

Ishiguro's previous novel, *An Artist of the Floating World*, had won the Whitbread Prize.

Booker Shortlist

Rose Tremain's *Restoration* is the story of Robert Merivel, son of the glove-maker to King Charles II, and Court Physician to the King's spaniel, Bibillou. Merivel is devoted to the monarch, who makes him 'paper groom' to one of his mistresses, Celia Clemence, and dispatches him to Norfolk with an estate and knighthood. Merivel makes the mistake of falling in love with his wife, thus incurring the king's displeasure. The novel wittily and convincingly relates Merivel's career, his work in a Quaker-run asylum, and his return to London at the time of the Plague and the Great Fire. Merivel eventually achieves his own spiritual restoration during the historical period of that name.

John Banville's *The Book of Evidence* is the story of a murderer. Rogue aristocrat Freddie Montgomery returns to his mother's home in Ireland in need of funds and while trying to steal a painting, kidnaps and kills a housemaid. His belated attempt to make some sense of his life is exquisitely written. Sybille Bedford's *Jigsaw—An Unsentimental Education*, described as 'a biographical novel', is her first for 20 years. It describes the life of a young girl abroad and in Bloomsbury between the wars. James Kelman's *A Disaffection* is the story of Patrick Doyle, a teacher at a Glasgow comprehensive school, who becomes increasingly bitter about his life. The final shortlisted book was Margaret Attwood's *Cat's Eye*, about an artist in Canada for a retrospective exhibition of her work who revisits and remembers the scenes of her childhood.

Consolation

Tremain's *Restoration*, while unsuccessful in the Booker, was chosen as the *Sunday Express* Book of the Year, for which she received £20,000. Roald Dahl, who chaired the judging panel, used the prize-giving ceremony to attack the Whitbread and Booker awards; Booker winners were chosen 'more for their literary eloquence than their entertainment value', he asserted. His remarks may have helped drum up some publicity for an award that had hitherto been largely ignored outside its own book pages.

Richest Prize

John Banville's work was also recognized beyond the Booker. *The Book of Evidence* became the first recipient of the most valuable prize for a single work, the Guinness Peat Aviation Award for a work by a writer from Ireland. The prize, worth IR£50,000, is presented every three years. A shortlist of five works was selected, from which Graham Greene was asked to choose the winner. Some confusion was caused by his reported wish to award the prize to a book not on the shortlist, a move apparently not excluded by the terms of the prize. In the end, however, Banville's work was selected from the shortlist and an extra award, of IR£20,000, was made to Vincent McDonnell for *The Broken Commandment*.

Whitbread

The 1989 Whitbread Book of the Year was *Coleridge: Early Visions*, the first of two volumes of biography by Richard Holmes. He received £20,250 for the overall prize, plus £1,750 for winning the biography category. His critical and personal life of the poetic genius, critic and philosopher was widely praised. Holmes said that he wished to demonstrate 'what made Coleridge—for all his extravagant panoply of faults—such an extraordinary man, such an extraordinary mind. If Coleridge does not leap out of these pages—brilliant, animated, endlessly provoking—and invade your imagination (as he has done mine), then I have failed to do him justice.' The general consensus was that he had succeeded triumphantly. Brenda Maddox, one of the Whitbread judges, said of the book, 'It is a most vivid reconstruction, so that you can see, and hear, and smell Coleridge. Sometimes he smells terrible.'

Winner of the novel category of the Whitbread was Lindsay Clarke's *The Chymical Wedding*, although there was some controversy in the judging which led to a premature announcement that Alexander Stuart's *The War Zone* had been chosen. Michael Donaghy's *Shibboleth* won the poetry section, James Hamilton-Paterson's *Gerontius* was judged best first novel and Hugh Scott's *Why Weeps the Brogan?* best children's novel.

Other awards

The David Higham Prize for a first work of fiction, worth £1,000, was awarded to Timothy O'Grady for *Motherland*. The Emil/Kurt Maschler Award (£1,000) went to Martin Waddell and Barbara Firth for *The Park in the Dark*. The *Guardian* Fiction Prize (£1,000) was won by Carol Lake for *Rosehill: Portraits from a Midlands City*.

The first *Irish Times* and Aer Lingus Award for International Fiction was won by Don De Lillo for *Libra*, who received £25,000, while a £10,000 award for Irish Literature was given to Frank Ronan for *The Men Who Loved Evelyn Cotton*. The NCR Book Award for Non-Fiction was presented to Simon Schama for *Citizens: A Chronicle of the French Revolution* (£25,000). Awards of £1,500 each were awarded to the other shortlisted works: *The Godwins and the Shelleys* by William St Clair, *C. S. Lewis* by A. N. Wilson and *Pity the Nation: Lebanon at Risk* by Robert Fisk.

Claire Harman received the John Llewellyn Rhys Prize of £5,000 for *Sylvia Townsend Warner*. The Boots Romantic Novel of the Year Award went to Reay Tannahill for *Passing Glory*, while Robert MacLiam Wilson received the Betty Trask Award, worth £16,000, for *Ripley Bogle*. Betty Trask awards of £3,000 were also presented to Elizabeth Chadwick for *The Wild Hunt*, Rosemary Cohen for *No Strange Land* and Nicholas Shakespeare for *The Vision of Elena Silves*. Shakespeare also received a Somerset Maugham Award of £5,000 for his book, with further awards going to Mark Hudson for *Our Grandmothers' Drums* and Sam North for *The Automatic Man*.

Cholmondeley Awards for Poetry, worth £2,500, were presented to Kingsley Amis, Elaine Feinstein and Michael O'Neill. Eric Gregory Poetry Awards worth £5,000 were presented to Nicholas Drake, Maggie Hannan and William Park, with awards of £4,000 to Jonathan Davidson, Lavinia Greenlaw and Don Paterson. A new award, the £5,000 McKitterick Prize for a first novel by a writer aged over 40, was introduced. The first recipient was Simon Mawer for *Chimera*.

Janet Frame received the £10,000 Commonwealth Writers Prize for *The Carpathians*, while Bonnie Burnard received £1,000 for best first book for her collection of short stories entitled *Women of Influence*. The Duff Cooper Memorial Prize was won by Ian Gibson for *Federico Garcia: A Life*.

Nobel Prize

The 1989 Nobel Prize for Literature was awarded to the Spanish writer Camilo José Cela. The award, worth nearly £290,000, is for the 'person who shall have produced in the field of literature the most outstanding work of an idealistic tendency'. Cela is a member of the Spanish Royal Academy and well considered in Spain, though he is not generally regarded as Spain's major living writer. He has not published any works of great significance recently; his best-known books are *The Family of Pascal Duarte* (1942) and *The Beehive* (1950). The prestigious French Prix Goncourt was won by Jean Vautrin for *Un grand pas vers le Bon Dieu*, a family saga set in Louisiana at the turn of the 19th century.

Great Lives

The second volume of Michael Holroyd's biography of George Bernard Shaw has been published. The first, *The Search for Love*, covered the first 42 years of his life up to his marriage. *The Pursuit of Power* covers the next twenty years, a period in which he wrote *Man and Superman*, *Major Barbara* and *Pygmalion*. Holroyd has been working on the project for fifteen years, and he presents a convincing portrait of a brilliant man who was obsessed with his own genius. Shaw was eccentric, pursuing interests ranging from socialism to his phonetic alphabet, and he was frequently foolish; he declared that the traffic in the Strand made it more dangerous than the Somme. The second volume (of three) takes Shaw to the end of the First World War, a period which saw a sharp decline in his popularity with the publication of his *Common Sense about the War*. Shaw 'wanted power, he wanted knowledge, and by changing the environment he wanted to father a new generation of men and women'.

Bitter Fame: A Life of Sylvia Plath by Anne Stevenson exposes the darker side of the brilliant young American poet, who killed herself soon after the publication of her only novel, *The Bell Jar*. Plath, who was married to the English poet Ted Hughes (now the Poet Laureate), has generated a critical industry since her suicide; Linda Wagner-Martin's recent life showed how the death of her father when she was aged eight left a void that was never subsequently filled. Stevenson's book shows other aspects of her character, such as her 'gift of malice' against former friends to whom she frequently meted out harsh treatment. Plath was 'a complex, completely self-absorbed, stubbornly ambitious American, whose outer shell of bright capability contained a seething core of inexplicable fury'.

The latest subject of a biography by A. N. Wilson, who has previously written about Scott, Milton, Belloc and Tolstoy, was C. S. Lewis. With the recent television adaptations of *The Chronicles of Narnia*, and a play, *Shadowlands*, about his marriage late in life to an American admirer of his work, a new assessment of his life and work may have seemed appropriate. In *C. S. Lewis*, Wilson gives a sound account of Lewis's career and the development of his religious beliefs, without adding greatly to the sum of knowledge about a man who 'plumbed the irrational depths of childhood and religion'. Wilson speculates that Lewis's long relationship with a friend's mother, Mrs Moore, who was 25 years older than him, was a physical one, rather than the fulfilment of a pledge made in wartime. This suggestion provoked some controversy.

Father and Son

In his latest novel, *London Fields*, Martin Amis continues his obsession with the age of nuclear weapons, the threat of which he feels has dominated life since the 1950s. The story, set in 1999, concerns an American writer, Samson Young, who thinks he is dying from a terminal illness. He is also suffering from writer's block, and he comes to London intending to write a work of journalism. He takes over the flat of an English author, Mark Asprey, and finds himself in the middle of a real-life drama which leads to the murder of *femme fatale* Nicola Six. The plot is complicated and confusing, weighed down with allegory. Amis has a weakness for characters with obvious names; like John Self in *Money*, Keith Talent and Guy Clinch are wittily drawn but hardly exist outside the scheme of the plot, which concerns an Earth gone mad in the face of a 'cathartic nuclear strike'.

Kingsley Amis's characters in *The Folks that Live on the Hill* are concerned with the problems of everyday life. Harry Caldecote, a retired librarian who is twice divorced, lives with his widowed sister Clare and her dog Towser in Shepherd's Hill, north London. The novel deals with the large circle of relations that Harry has acquired—his son Piers, his stepdaughter Bunty from his second marriage, his brother Freddie with his domineering wife Desiree—and with Harry's efforts to resolve their professional and personal crises. The novel is written in Amis's usual acerbic style.

A. S. Byatt's *Possession* is a cleverly written story about the search by two academics for the truth about a secret love affair between two Victorian writers. Penelope Lively explored a similar idea recently in *According to Mark*. Byatt's epigraph is taken from Hawthorne: 'an attempt to connect a bygone time with the very present that is flitting away from us'. The story opens with the discovery by researcher Roland Michell of a letter from Randolph Henry Ash, famous Victorian man of letters, to Christabel La Motte, a little known poet whose work is being reconsidered in feminist circles. With Dr Maud Bailey, Michell discovers the truth

about a secret love affair between Ash and La Motte. The novel is cleverly constructed around the poems, letters and stories of the pair.

Margaret Drabble, Antonia Byatt's sister, has written *A Natural Curiosity* as a sequel to *The Radiant Way*. In an author's note, Drabble said that she felt that the earlier story 'was in some way unfinished, that it had asked questions it had not answered, and introduced people who had hardly been allowed to speak'. However, many critics felt her characters were unconvincing, and her story about contemporary England, set in the town of Northam, was uninspiring and over-written: 'not a bad country, but mean, cold, ugly, divided, tired, clapped-out post-imperial, post-industrial slagheap covered in polystyrene hamburger cartons.' Some felt that the novel demonstrated a lack of thought disguised by an excess of verbiage.

Vandalism

Robert Nye's *The Memoirs of Lord Byron* sympathetically and skilfully recreated the poet's lost autobiography. Byron entrusted his own memoirs to Thomas Moore. They were 'memoranda and not confessions', he said, 'I must not compromise other people'. In one of the greatest acts of literary vandalism, they were burned within a month of his death at the Albermarle Street offices of his publisher, John Murray. Nye is convincing in his version of Byron's life, particularly over the difficult subject of his relationship with his half-sister Augusta, and captures his style and tone to perfection.

Brian Moore's *Lies of Silence* is a tautly constructed thriller set in Northern Ireland. Michael Dillon is the manager of a Belfast hotel. Unhappily married, he is about to tell his wife that he is leaving her for his mistress when IRA terrorists break into his home. Dillon is instructed to drive his car, containing a bomb, to his hotel, where a Protestant religious leader called Pottinger is about to speak. If he fails to fulfil the task, his wife will be killed. Dillon's dilemma, set against the difficulties that arise through the Government policy of media censorship in Northern Ireland, are handled with skill in an effective thriller.

In *The Innocent* by Ian McEwan, a Post Office technician called Leonard Marnham is sent to Berlin to help the Americans. The novel is set in 1955, at the height of the Cold War, and is based on an actual espionage plan, codenamed Operation Gold, which was disclosed to the Soviet Union by the double agent George Blake. In the novel, a 'G. Blake' lives in the flat below Marnham's. The world of spying is contrasted with Marnham's private life as he is drawn into a passionate affair with an older German woman. *The Innocent* is a powerful, well written work, although a long and gruesome section dealing with murder and the dismemberment of a body tends to overshadow the rest of the book.

Iris Murdoch's *The Message to the Planet* is a long, densely characterized work about human relationships and the search for the meaning of life. In the novel, Alfred Ludens pursues the once brilliant mathematician and philosopher Marcus Vallar in the belief that Vallar can reveal the ultimate truth to him, 'a great new meaning, a meaning for all mankind'.

Umberto Eco, a professor at the University of Bologna, followed his best-selling medieval detective story *The Name of the Rose* with *Foucault's Pendulum*. The novel is a learned but enjoyable thriller about the search for the Templars' master-plan to control the world, narrated by Casaubon, editor in a Milan publishing house.

Adam Dalgliesh, poet and detective, makes a welcome reappearance in P. D. James's *Devices and Desires*. Dalgliesh is on holiday in Norfolk, where he has been left a windmill and an inheritance by an aunt. He becomes involved in tracking down a serial killer known as the Norfolk whistler. The plot becomes complicated when Hilary Robarts, acting administration officer at Larksoken nuclear power station, is killed. The delineation of character and resolution of the plot are handled with P. D. James's customary skill.

Dick Francis's latest thriller is *Straight*, in which Derek Franklin, a steeplechase jockey, takes over the precious stones business of his elder brother who is killed in an accident. Franklin discovers that a large consignment of diamonds ordered by his brother before his death is missing. As he unlocks the secrets of the business, Franklin also learns about his deceased brother's private life, including his mistress. In death, he learns to know the brother he had never really known in life. The novel is well written and, as usual, Francis's style appears simple and straightforward, but conceals much skill in the plotting and execution.

A Time to Dance by Melvyn Bragg is the story of a retired bank manager in his mid-50s, who lives with his invalid wife in a small town in Cumbria. The novel is written in the form of a letter to an 18-year-old girl with whom he falls in love, and Bragg sensitively explores the relationship. D. M. Thomas's *Lying Together* concludes his 'Russian Nights' sequence of five novels, and deals with his familiar themes of improvisational story-telling and sexual fantasy. Paul Sayer's first novel, *The Comfort of Madness*, won the Whitbread Prize; his study of a catatonic man living in a twilight world was highly praised. His second novel, *Howling at the Moon*, also deals with insanity. It tells the story of Michael Crumly, who disintegrates mentally after his wife tells him that she is pregnant. Once again, Sayer handles difficult themes with skill and perception.

American fiction

Vineland is Thomas Pynchon's first novel for 17 years, and only his fourth in 27 years. Pynchon is notoriously reclusive, believing that he should be judged by his work and not his life, and his latest work attracted much critical attention. The novel opens in 1984 with Zoyd Wheeler, an ageing hippy, preparing to jump through a plate-glass window in front of television cameras in order to prove his insanity and requalify for his annual mental disability allowance. Pynchon's world is that of the abnormal and the eccentric, dominated by conspiracies and politics, and one in which the power of technology and television has destroyed American individuality. The novel can be criticized for weak

plotting or unconvincing characterization, but bears the unmistakable touch of Pynchon's talent.

William Wharton is a distinctive novelist, highly praised for previous novels such as *Birdy* and *Pride*. He is also an acclaimed artist, although he paints under another name and keeps the two sides of his creative talent separate. His latest novel, *Franky Furbo*, is a fantastical story about a magical fox who travels through time and possesses supernatural powers. The story is quirky and humorous, beautifully written and wholly convincing.

Billy Bathgate is the latest work by E. L. Doctorow, author of *Ragtime*. The hero is a reformed gangster who reflects on his life from the time he joined a New York gang in the 1930s, becoming the protégé of 'Dutch Schultz', until the present when he has put himself through college on the money he earned through crime.

Gore Vidal's *Hollywood: A Novel of the Twenties* is the fifth in his 'biography' of the United States of America which began with *Burr*. The novel opens in 1917 as America is about to enter the First World War, closing with the death of Warren Harding in 1923. Throughout, Vidal contrasts the political world with the growth of Hollywood, which is mapped out through the rise of Caroline Sandford (who appeared in *Empire*), who rises from being a publisher to film star and studio mogul.

Reference

A new volume of *The Dictionary of National Biography* was published. Edited by Lord Blake and C. S. Nicholls, it covers the lives of 380 distinguished people who died between the years 1981 and 1985. The publishers decided to produce a volume covering only five years, as opposed to the usual ten, because of 'public pressure for the Supplements to appear more frequently'. Among lives included in this issue are R. A. Butler, Diana Dors (denounced by an earlier Archbishop of Canterbury as 'a wayward hussy'), 'Bomber' Harris, John Betjeman, J. B. Priestley and Philip Larkin.

The eighth edition of *The Concise Oxford Dictionary* brought up-to-date a popular and much used work of linguistic reference. It was first produced in 1911, edited by the Fowler brothers, whose object was 'to present as vivid a picture as the small dictionary could be made to give of the English that was being spoken and written at the time'. The current editor, Robert Allen, acknowledging that the COD is an institution, said in his introduction that he was 'faced, essentially, with the task of producing a dictionary for the 1990s without making it totally unrecognizable as the Concise'. The new edition contains some 20,000 new entries in its 1,450 pages, with a total of 120,000 headwords and 190,000 definitions.

Other books of note published during the year included: *Lawrence of Arabia: The Authorised Biography of T. E. Lawrence* by Jeremy Wilson; *The Oxford Book of Humorous Prose* edited by Frank Muir; *Wolfwatching* by Ted Hughes; *New Selected Poems 1966–1987* by Seamus Heaney; *Reinventing Shakespeare: A Cultural History from the Restoration to the Present* by Gary Taylor; *A Peace to End All*

Peace: Creating the Modern Middle East 1914–1922 by David Fromkin; *The Time of My Life* by Denis Healey; *Against the Tide: Diaries 1973–1976* by Tony Benn; *Brief Lives* by Anita Brookner; *Fludd* by Hilary Mantel; *A Question of Loyalties* by Alan Massie; *The Trick of It* by Michael Frayn; *Sexing the Cherry* by Jeanette Winterson; *Baden-Powell* by Tim Jeal; *Chicago Loop* by Paul Theroux; *Lady's Maid* by Margaret Forster; and *The Gate of Angels* by Penelope Fitzgerald.

Public Lending Right

The seventh annual payment to authors under the Public Lending Right scheme was made in January 1990. Of 17,594 authors registered under the scheme, payments totalling £3,072,000 were made to 14,149 authors: 63 received the maximum payment of £6,000 (compared with 67 in 1988); 27 received between £5,000 and £5,999; 155 authors, £2,500–£4,999; 417 authors, £1,000–£2,499; 559 authors, £500–£999; 3,119 authors, £100–£499; 9,960 authors, £1–99; 3,294 registered authors received no payment under the scheme. Catherine Cookson was the novelist most in demand, with 32 titles in the top 100. Agatha Christie, who does not qualify for PLR because she died before the scheme started, was the second most borrowed author, although none of her titles individually was included in the top 100.

BOOKER PRIZEWINNERS

The finalists for the 1990 prize are:

Amongst Women—John McGahern (Faber); *An Awfully Big Adventure*—Beryl Bainbridge (Duckworth); *The Gate of Angels*—Penelope Fitzgerald (Collins); *Lies of Silence*—Brian Moore (Bloomsbury); *Possession*—A. S. Byatt (Chatto & Windus); *Solomon Gursky Was Here*—Mordecai Richler (Chatto & Windus).

POETS LAUREATE

TELEVISION 1989–90

Following the publication of the Government's White Paper *Broadcasting in the '90s* in November 1988, the whole future of broadcasting in Britain was under review. The Broadcasting Bill was included in the Queen's Speech opening the 1989–90 session of Parliament, the occasion of the first televised broadcast of the proceedings of the House of Commons.

The Broadcasting Bill was published on December 7, 1989. It included 12 Schedules and 167 clauses. The main provisions, as detailed in the White Paper, are intended to provide more choice for the public, by encouraging competition among broadcasters, without compromising programme quality. Provisions include replacing the independent television companies by Channel 3 from 1993. Licences would be awarded to regionally based companies on the basis of 'the highest qualifying cash bid', but a 'quality threshold' would have to be passed. A new body, the Independent Television Commission, is proposed, to replace both the Independent Broadcasting Authority and the Cable Authority. It would have responsibility for enforcing licence conditions and rules of ownership of the television and cable companies.

The Bill includes a provision to place the Broadcasting Standards Council on a statutory footing. It would be required to draft and maintain a code of practice on the portrayal of violence and sex on TV, to monitor programmes and to deal with complaints on standards. The BBC and ITV companies would lose their monopoly on programme listings in *Radio Times* and *TV Times*, and the BBC would take over responsibility from the Post Office for collecting its licence fee.

Proposals also include a new channel, to be known as Channel 5, which will be established in 1992. It would cover approximately 70 per cent of the country. The licence would be put out to competitive tender, subject also to a quality threshold. Local television stations could be established, using either microwave transmission or cable. Channel 4 would be able to sell its own airtime, but would be protected by a 'safety net' of finance from the ITV companies if its revenue fell below 14 per cent of their income.

Broadcasting Bill

There was much initial criticism of the Bill, both within and outside Parliament. However, David Mellor, the Home Office Minister with responsibility for broadcasting, indicated that he expected the proposals to undergo radical revision before reaching the statute book. During the committee stage in the Commons, Mr Mellor's willingness to amend the Bill won widespread praise. In particular, he reconsidered proposals that would have removed the obligation on companies winning the next round of ITV franchises to include religious programmes in their schedules. The Government also considered amendments to a provision that would have prevented religious organizations from owning television channels, a clause which had been included because financial and sex scandals in the USA had brought such services into disrepute. As originally drafted, the Independent Television Commission

would not have been able to grant licences to 'organizations whose objectives are wholly or mainly of a religious nature'.

There was also concern over a provision in the Bill to allow television rights to major sporting events to be sold to the highest bidder. This would end the system whereby BBC and ITV both have the right to screen 'prestige' events such as the FA Cup, Wimbledon, the Olympic Games and the Grand National. A successful bid by a satellite company would restrict viewing to those who had purchased dedicated receiving equipment. There was a strong feeling that such events should not be shown exclusively on subscription or 'pay as you view' services.

While the Broadcasting Bill was being considered by Parliament, a survey conducted by National Opinion Poll on behalf of Channel 4's *Media Show* indicated that the majority of television viewers were either not bothered, or only a little concerned, if television companies could no longer afford to make top quality drama programmes; they also wished to retain the *status quo* for awarding ITV franchises.

Local service

In April 1990, Granada Television carried out an experiment in a Lancashire village, to gauge public reaction to the wide range of television services that are now available to the viewing public. Homes were provided with cable services that enabled them to receive 30 channels in addition to the four BBC and ITV services. The experiment was monitored by Manchester University's European Institute for the Media, with support from the Government, the IBA, the ITV Association and European Community institutions. A community television channel established for the purpose of the trial proved particularly popular.

The Government proposed to limit cross-interests between satellite broadcasters and those with terrestrial media interests. A report by the National Economic Research Associates claimed that the proposals were inflexible and threatened competition. The report was commissioned by W. H. Smith TV, which owns a 75 per cent stake in two European satellite channels as well as 21 per cent of Yorkshire Television, which just exceeds the limit proposed by the Home Secretary. British Satellite Broadcasting (BSB), felt that Sky Television, its rival extraterrestrial broadcasting service, had an unfair advantage, in that Sky's proprietor Rupert Murdoch is able to promote it heavily through his News International newspapers. The chief executive of BSB, Anthony Simonds-Gooding, questioned 'the extent to which it is proper to let the commercial interests of a company influence news selection in any media outlet which it owns'.

Sport for all?

The question of televising major sporting events focused attention on the new era of competition that had been opened up by the Government. The BBC considers that it has a duty to screen major sporting events as part of its public service broadcasting role. When ITV has exercised its right to show 'prestige' events, the BBC has usually emerged with higher viewing figures. The introduction of satellite broadcasters has altered the balance significantly, however. Long before BSB began transmitting, it entered jointly into an agreement with the BBC and the Football Association to screen FA cup matches and England home internationals, while ITV agreed a costly deal with the Football League.

The England cricket tour of the West Indies in the winter of 1989–90 was also the subject of dispute. In the past, television coverage of England tours in the Caribbean has been limited. Sky Television, however, decided to show ball-by-ball coverage of the Test series on the Sky One channel. The programmes were provided by Trans World International and the BBC was provided with edited highlights for showing after the close of play. Independent Television News, however, could not reach agreement for news coverage of the series. ITN were asked to pay £50,000 for news rights, and offered only £15,000. They were, therefore, unable to provide any news coverage in their main bulletins.

The BBC's monopoly of the Wimbledon tennis championships was also under threat. ITV offered five times more than the BBC for British rights to the event. However, the All England Club and the Lawn Tennis Association renewed their contract with the BBC. BSB reached an agreement to show extended Wimbledon highlights. The BBC lost out, however, on two cricket competitions. BSB secured exclusive rights to screen the Benson and Hedges Cup, and Sky Television to cover the Sunday Refuge Assurance League, reportedly for substantially more than the BBC paid the previous year.

Televising the Commons

After inordinate delay, and in spite of the successful experiment of televising proceedings in the House of Lords, Members of Parliament agreed in 1989 to the televising of proceedings of the House of Commons. Although the select committee published its rule governing the introduction of cameras in April 1989, transmission did not begin until November 1989. After broadcasting the Queen's Speech, both BBC2 and Ch4 televised the debate that followed in the House of Commons, while Sky broadcast continuous coverage of proceedings on an experimental basis.

In spite of the reservations of many in the House, including the Prime Minister, the initial reaction to admitting the television cameras was largely favourable. After the novelty had worn off, it appeared both natural and reasonable that the workings of both Houses of Parliament should be accessible to the public through the medium of television. It soon became apparent that early guidelines, such as restricting the cameras to head and shoulder shots of Members of Parliament while speaking, needed to be modified. Had they been strictly complied with, they would have had the effect of suggesting that Neil Kinnock, the Leader of the Opposition, was in danger of losing his balance, due to his practice of leaning forward on to the Despatch box while speaking. *The Times* commented in a leader: 'For the great majority

of people who have never seen the Commons at work, and for those who know it only through vocal snippets on television or from the confused hubbub of Question Time on radio, the first opportunity to see the Commons as they are made riveting television. On a more serious level, the televising of Parliament should enhance the value of the citizens' right to choose between the rivals for his voting affections by this addition to their sources of information. Even the considerable entertainment potential in broadcast parliamentary proceedings has a place in the quality of life.'

After the first two months, the rules were relaxed to permit the showing of 'reaction' shots of MPs and Ministers who were referred to by speakers. It was also decided to permit wide-angle shots to show the reactions of groups of MPs.

Eight months after the experiment began, the Commons select committee concluded that the televising of the Commons should continue. A study carried out by the Institute of Communication Studies at Leeds University on behalf of the select committee said that, 'Broadcast reporting of parliamentary proceedings has been extensive, serious, responsible, balanced in many respects, even at times creative.' However, a survey by Aston University on behalf of the House of Commons Broadcasting Unit said that 'it has not excited the public or changed their attitudes very much, except to make them a bit more negative in how they see MPs.'

Launch of BSB

British Satellite Broadcasting began broadcasting on April 29, 1990. Its launch was deliberately low-key, with its five channels being unveiled a day at a time. The chief executive, Anthony Simonds-Good-ing, said, 'We intend to honour what is best in British broadcasting whilst broadening choice and giving greater power to the viewer. BSB is in the best traditions of British enterprise. It is ambitious, innovative, committed to quality and based upon a long-term view of investment.' He hoped to make it 'the third force in British broadcasting'.

BSB represents £1.3 billion in investment, and it needs to attract a great many viewers before the companies financing it can hope to see a return on their money. Its launch was delayed for seven months because of problems in developing the receiving equipment, by which time its rival, Sky, had had over a year in which to establish itself before BSB could compete. Because of the shortage of 'squarials' for receiving BSB, the company was forced to delay its advertising campaign, to avoid raising expectations that it was unable to satisfy. Although it made the service available to 500,000 cable subscribers a month before the official launch, BSB was aware that until sufficient receivers were available (at a cost of between £300 and £370), it would face an uphill battle to establish itself.

BSB's five channels consist of the Power Station, which offers 18 hours of pop and rock music, youth programmes and alternative comedy; Galaxy, the entertainment channel, including drama, children's programmes, soap operas and chat shows; the Now Channel, 'The Channel for Living', with a news magazine, environmental programmes, political discussion, information and women's programmes, and at weekends the performing arts; the Movie Channel, with seven feature films each day from its library of 2,500 films (on which it has spent over £350 million) plus independent British feature films, on which it has invested £12 million; and the Sports Channel, which shows football, tennis, cricket, golf and other sports.

BSB commissioned a new science fiction soap opera, to be screened three times a week. It has committed itself to 150 episodes of the series, *Jupiter's Moon*, set in the year AD 2050 on the planetoid Callisto. BSB also reached an agreement with the actors' union Equity, which allows BSB to show old BBC programmes for a one-off payment to the actors in the cast, in return for its commitment to investing in British-made programmes. BSB has already bought programmes such as *Dr Who, Porridge* and *Steptoe and Son* from the BBC.

In January 1990 BSB announced a refinancing package, which involved raising a further £900 million from its main investors, in addition to the £400 million already spent. One of its main shareholders, the Alan Bond Corporation of Australia, which purchased the stake originally held by the Virgin Group, underwent financial difficulties which saw the value of its stake drop from 35 per cent to 7.5 per cent because it was unable to take up its rights during the refinancing package. The company was unable to sell its stake to a party agreeable to the other shareholders, after which it issued a writ against them.

Broadcasting standards

The Broadcasting Standards Council was set up by the Government in 1988 with Lord Rees-Mogg as chairman. The BSC is felt to be unnecessary by the broadcasting bodies, while the Labour Party has promised to disband it if Labour comes to power. However, the Council, strongly supported by the Prime Minister, will be placed on a statutory footing under the provisions of the Broadcasting Bill.

The Council is something of an anomaly, with no powers to preview programmes or to enforce standards. The Home Secretary, Douglas Hurd, said that the Council's role would be to act as 'a focus for public concern', particularly in relation to the portrayal of sex and violence on television and radio. It would assist broadcasters in matters of 'taste and decency', but would not replace existing bodies, such as the Broadcasting Complaints Commission.

The BSC published its first annual report in November 1989. At the same time, it issued its code of practice, which it based on 'best practice' within the broadcasting industry. The council said that it was particularly concerned to protect children and felt that the idea of a 'watershed', before which time material unsuitable for children should not be screened, was important.

The BSC disclosed the results of a survey it had undertaken on viewers' attitudes to television. 'Almost seven out of ten parents with children of school age claimed to have turned off the television, or turned to another channel, as a result of seeing an unsuitable programme', it said. 'These are not isolated incidents; over four in ten parents claim that they turn off or over at least once a month. Adults are themselves disturbed or upset by occasional television programmes. One-quarter of the population declared they had been disgusted by something which they had watched on television in the previous month.'

The BSC announced that it would set up viewers' panels to monitor radio and television programmes and to report each week on programme trends and offensive material. The council also said that it would hold a series of meetings with parents, teachers and television executives 'to consider questions of parental responsibility for their children's viewing and the wider issue of the responsibilities borne by the broadcasters and by society'.

In January, the BBC announced that it would be spending up to £100,000 on a survey to examine how television treated sex, violence, bad language and minority groups. The research will be undertaken by Dr Guy Cumberbatch, head of the Communications Research Department at Aston University, and will look at all four television channels. By carrying out its own research, the BBC hopes to be better able to defend itself against criticism by the BSC at a later date.

The BBC

In October 1989, the chairman of the BBC, Marmaduke Hussey, attacked the Government over its ban on interviews with spokesmen of Sinn Fein, the IRA and other proscribed organizations in Northern Ireland: 'All of us in the BBC share the nation's outrage at the cowardly and murderous attacks of the IRA', he said. 'I happen to believe the Government has set a very dangerous precedent by preventing us interviewing directly members of a legally recognized political party who have been elected to Parliament or local councils.' An appeal against the ban by journalists was later upheld by the Court of Appeal.

Speaking at the Royal Television Society's convention in Cambridge, the director-general of the BBC, Michael Checkland, said that the BBC intended to set up a new company to develop the concept of nighttime subscription services. These services provide programmes which are transmitted at night in scrambled form for reception and decoding on adapted VCR equipment. A financial service was planned for 1990 to follow the service for doctors already in existence. Unfortunately, due to technical and financial problems, that service, operated by British Medical Television, closed down in January. It was reported that it only had 4,000 subscribers, and owed the BBC £500,000. Nevertheless, the BBC hopes to continue with the concept.

Mr Checkland warned, however, that subscription services were a means of raising extra money for the BBC, not a possible substitute for the licence fee. 'Public service broadcasting has to be available to all, wherever people live and whatever their circumstances. Subscription is a market mechanism that simply cannot apply to all', he said.

In January, the BBC announced cuts in staff as part of a major reorganization. Although staffing reductions were not enumerated, it is expected that thousands of jobs will disappear in the 1990s, partly through natural wastage but also through cuts in production staff to meet the Government's target of 25 per cent of BBC programmes being provided by independent producers. Plans to open a £200 million radio centre in west London were scrapped, the Radio Orchestra is to be disbanded and head office staff reduced by 10 per cent. It was estimated that the measures would lead to savings of £75 million a year by 1993.

In June the BBC said that it was seeking to raise finance in the City of London to enable it to launch a world television news service in 1991. Programmes would be distributed around the world by satellite and would probably include advertising. John Tusa, managing director of the BBC World Service, said: 'We intend that this new television news service will reflect both the international agenda and the analytical approach to news for which the World Service has been famous since it began radio broadcasting more than fifty years ago.'

One of the more controversial programmes screened by the Corporation during the year was Dennis Potter's *Blackeyes*, which he adapted from his own novel and, for the first time, directed as well. The four-part drama series featured Gina Bellman as a model who is exploited by all those with whom she deals. The series operated on many levels, with a mixture of fantasy and reality. Potter said it was about 'how men manipulate women, how women are obliged to counter-manipulate, and how that, in turn, damages men as well as women'. Although the BBC received only 40 complaints about the sexual content of the series, it was criticized by many who felt that Potter was guilty of the manipulation he was attacking.

BBC 2 screened the Indian adaptation of the Hindu epic *The Mahabharata* in 93 episodes. The series had been a huge success in India, with regular audiences of 115 million viewers.

Independent companies

After the relaxation of IBA guidelines on sponsorship of programmes, PowerGen, one of the generating companies formed from the Central Electricity Generating Board, announced in September 1989 that it would be sponsoring weather forecasts at the end of the ITN news bulletins, at a cost of nearly £2 million. The money is shared between International Weather Productions, which provides the service on behalf of the Met Office, and the independent television companies. The arrangement was initially for one year, with an option to renew until the current ITV franchises expire in December 1992.

The new guidelines caused some confusion, however. A series produced for children, called *The Magic Mirror*, was made by Ragdoll Productions with finance from Kelloggs, the breakfast cereals company, after both the BBC and ITV declined to put up money for it. The IBA banned the series after viewing two of the 13 animated films, on the grounds that it contained excessive advertising for Kelloggs in the opening sequences. The IBA ruled that, in future, independent programme makers should have the support of an ITV company or Channel 4 before

making a programme funded by a sponsor. The Independent Programme Producers' Association said that this rule threatened their programming and was potentially disastrous. 'It completely undermines the notion of the independent producer. It ties the independent producer to the broadcaster'. Anne Wood, producer of the series said, 'It is crucial for every independent to be able to seek legitimate sources of funding from sponsors for programmes, such as children's shows, which ITV companies are very reluctant to back. This decision threatens the viability of independents in the market-place.'

In March the IBA issued new guidelines on sponsorship, indicating which types of programmes could be sponsored and which could not, and the credits that were permissible. The Broadcasting Bill will allow all programmes except news and current affairs to be sponsored. Presentation of the Football World Cup on ITV was sponsored by the other generating company, National Power, at a cost of £2 million. PowerGen's sponsorship of the weather forecasts was reported to have significantly increased public awareness of the company. The BBC also became involved with sponsored broadcasting, with outside support for the British Design Awards and the Young Musician of the Year competition.

TVS, the largest programme provider to the ITV network outside the 'big five' of Thames, London Weekend, Central, Yorkshire and Granada, experienced major problems over its purchase of the American company, MTM, for which it paid £190 million as part of a policy of diversification. Although MTM was responsible for successful programmes such as *Lou Grant* and *Hill St Blues*, and possessed an extensive library of programmes, it experienced a severe drop in its profitability which caused the share price of TVS to drop. Thames, which reported a 27 per cent increase in pre-tax profits, later experienced difficulties over its purchase of the US Reeves Communications group, an independent producer, for which it paid £57 million. It announced a downturn in half-year profits to June.

Channel 4

At the Royal Television Society Conference in Edinburgh in September 1989, the Home Secretary, Douglas Hurd, announced changes to the new financial arrangements for Channel 4, which will have the effect of enabling the company to retain more of any surplus it earns above the safety net figure of 14 per cent of ITV companies' revenues. When the new system comes into force, half of sums in excess of the 14 per cent figure will go to ITV, with the remainder being divided equally between Channel 4's reserves and investment in future programming.

Channel 4's winter schedule included the British television premiers of 16 feature films originally made for the cinema with financial support from Channel 4. The channel also screened a major series on women's cinema, *Women Call the Shots*, which included 28 feature films. *Channel 4 Daily*, its breakfast show which was launched in April 1989, was reported to have lost £4 million of its first year budget of £11 million. Viewing figures were around

200,000 a day, some 4 per cent of the total audience, except for Sundays, when programmes aimed at children attracted an audience of 2.6 million. Channel 4 revamped its morning programmes to attract a younger viewing audience. Later in the year, Channel 4 showed a series of documentaries and films about the Soviet Union. Its *A TV Dante* was a bold and imaginative attempt to interpret the classic poet of Italian literature for the television screen.

Television news

With the future of independent television uncertain during progress of the Broadcasting Bill through Parliament, the future ownership of Independent Television News could not be settled. The Government wishes the news provider for the new Channel 3 companies to be decided on the basis of quality, not cost, and the contract to be awarded by the Independent Television Commission. The ITC could choose two news providers if this does not prejudice or undermine the quality of the news provided. If two news companies were licensed, Channel 3 companies would be able to choose which service they use. There would be an obligation on Channels 3, 4 and 5 to provide high-quality news during peak viewing periods, and news on Channel 3 would have to be broadcast at the same time in all regions.

The new arrangements were considered to put ITN in a strong position. The company has provided news services for ITV since 1955, and has established a sound reputation for its news programmes. However, the ITV companies were reluctant to give up control of ITN; the Broadcasting Bill requires that 51 per cent of its shares be placed in new ownership. Sir Alastair Burnet, senior news-reader and a director of the board of ITN, resigned from the board in February because of the dispute with ITV over ITN's future ownership. The ITN board, which is dominated by the ITV companies, supported proposals by the IBA that they should retain two-thirds of the shares in ITN.

Channel 5

The Government intended that the proposed new Channel 5 should begin broadcasting in 1993. However, it seems likely that the new service will be delayed for up to two years, and there were doubts about its viability. Channel 5 would only cover 70 per cent of the country, and many areas, such as the south of England and large areas of Wales and Scotland, would not be able to receive it because of the need to avoid interference with broadcasts from France, Ireland and Belgium. Channel 5 would be offered as a single franchise but the other ITV franchises would have to be awarded first, so that companies unsuccessful in tendering for Channel 3 licences could bid for Channel 5. The Government refused to finance the network of transmitters that would be required by Channel 5 in advance of the tender being awarded, on the grounds that the franchise holder should decide the transmission system. The IBA believes that this decision could delay the service by up to two years, although the Home Office feels it would be less: 'The time advantage gained by starting work on a transmitter system now does not outweigh the possibility that a Channel 5

franchisee might regret having some of the decisions about a transmitter network taken away from him.'

A more serious obstacle to the success of the putative new station was the Government's requirement that the cost of retuning television sets and video recorders to receive Channel 5 (which would be necessary to avoid interference) would have to be met by the franchise holder. This would impose a severe financial burden on the channel, which would have to raise its income either through advertising or through subscription.

There was also uncertainty over what sort of service Channel 5 would be expected to provide. The Government has suggested that it should offer a national service for most of its programmes, with a network of small companies providing a balance of local services.

Sky's limit

In November 1989 Sky Television celebrated its one-millionth subscriber. The service, which was launched in February 1989, aimed to be in 1.5 million homes by January 1990. Of its one million customers, 365,000 receive transmissions via satellite dishes and 635,000 through the cable network. Rupert Murdoch, executive chairman of Sky, said, 'Satellite television has gone faster than the introduction of any other electronic product in history, faster than television when it came in, faster than colour television, faster than when the VCRs came in with stereo sound.'

However, it was estimated that Sky was losing £2 million a week. Mr Murdoch said that he would give it five years to become profitable, otherwise he would either sell it or close it down. Sky launched a major promotion offering a package of satellite dish, with decoding equipment, installation cost and maintenance for a weekly payment of £4.49. It hoped thereby to attract customers who had been put off by the capital investment needed to obtain a satellite dish. From February 1990, the Sky Movie Channel was scrambled and only available on subscription at a cost of just under £10 a month.

Sky scored a major coup with its transmission of the England and West Indies test series in the Caribbean because of the unexpectedly good performance by the England team. Two surveys also showed that satellite services were making inroads into the land-based stations because of the choice they offer.

Cable

In September 1989 the Cable Authority expressed concern at the failure of six companies that had been awarded franchises to provide cable services. In July 1990 it warned that companies would lose their franchise unless they secured the necessary licence. The Authority hopes that all of the 135 franchises in Britain will be cabled by 1996.

ITV programmes

ITV attempted to match the success of BBC's Australian import *Neighbours* by making its own twice-weekly soap opera. *Families*, starring Malcolm Stoddart, was filmed in both Britain and Australia. Granada invested £75,000 in researching the series before filming began in the hope of avoiding a repeat of the failure of its earlier soap *Albion Market*. The company invested £3 million in the initial 104 episodes; if *Families* proves successful in an afternoon slot, it is hoped to move the programme to evening viewing at a later date.

Yorkshire Television made a drama documentary based on the 'shoot to kill' controversy in Northern Ireland. The four-hour programme featured Jack Shepherd as John Stalker. However, it was not shown by Ulster Television on legal advice. Sir John Hermon, former chief constable of the Royal Ulster Constabulary, who was portrayed in the programme by T. P. McKenna, said that the programme was not truthful, was damaging to the credibility of the RUC and gave succour to terrorists. Granada Television's *Who Bombed Birmingham?* questioned the convictions of those alleged to have carried out the Birmingham pub bombings. Based on the research of Chris Mullin, MP, the programme claimed to have located and identified those who actually carried out the bombing. In August 1990, the Home Secretary referred the case back to the Court of Appeal.

A programme in Central TV's *The Cook Report* criticized the work of the World Wide Fund for Nature. It was approved by the IBA and broadcast in spite of complaints by the Fund, backed by its president the Duke of Edinburgh, that the programme was a travesty of the Fund's work.

Awards

In the American Emmy Awards ceremony in November 1989, Channel 4's *Traffik* was named best drama, Yorkshire's *Four Hours in My Lai* was best documentary, the BBC's *Red Dwarf* best comedy and *Gwen, A Juliet Remembered* best arts documentary.

Rowan Atkinson won the Golden Rose of Montreux for his comedy mime programme *Mr Bean*, which was directed by John Howard Davies for Thames Television. The programme also won the City of Montreux Comedy Award and the International Press Special Prize for Television Achievement. Atkinson also won the awards for best comedy and best light entertainment at the British Academy of Film and Television Awards. John Thaw won the BAFTA award for best actor for *Inspector Morse* and Diana Rigg best actress for *Mother Love*. Best single drama was *The Accountant* and best light entertainment series *Clive James on the '80s*. Best comedy series was *Blackadder goes Forth*, and the best news or outside broadcast coverage award went to BBC News for coverage of the Tiananmen Square killings. Kate Adie received the Richard Dimbleby Award for her reports from Peking about the killings. She also received the Judges' Award from the Royal Television Society Journalism Awards for an outstanding contribution to the advancement of television journalism.

FILM AND VIDEO CERTIFICATES

The British Board of Film Classification issues the following categories of film certificates:

U   Universal: suitable for all.
PG   Parental Guidance: some scenes may be unsuitable for young children.
12   Passed only for persons of twelve years and over.
15   Passed only for persons of fifteen years and over.
18   Passed only for persons of eighteen years and over.
R18   For Restricted Distribution Only (through specially licensed cinemas or sex shops to which no one under the age of eighteen is admitted).

The classifications of video tapes differ slightly:

U   Universal: suitable for all.
Uc   Universal: particularly suitable for children.
PG   Parental Guidance: general viewing, but some scenes may be unsuitable for young children.
15   Suitable only for persons of 15 years and over.
18   Suitable only for persons of 18 years and over.
R18   Restricted: to be supplied only in licensed sex shops to persons of not less than 18 years.

FILM AND CINEMA, 1989–90

The British film industry in 1989 was in decline; barely 40 feature films were made during the year, compared with around 70 a year in the mid 1980s. Investment in British films has dropped from a peak of £270 million in 1986 to £126 million in 1988. The British Screen Advisory Council launched an inquiry into the crisis and criticized the Government for its lack of support for the film industry.

The Government's contribution to the film industry amounts to some £3 million a year: £1.5 million is given to British Screen Finance, £1 million to the British Film Institute's production fund, and £500,000 for script development. The ending of tax incentives for film production and the abolition of the Eady levy on cinema takings has contributed to the decline. The French Government invests some £70 million a year in the French film industry, while the West German Government gives £25 million to its native film industry. Another problem in the United Kingdom is the lack of continuity in ministerial responsibility. The film industry is only one of a large number of responsibilities attached to the position of Under Secretary of State for Industry and Consumer Affairs; ten different people have held this portfolio since 1979.

In June 1990, a deputation of leading film industry figures visited Downing Street to discuss with the Prime Minister the problems facing the film industry. The Prime Minister promised that the Government would provide £5 million over the following three years to assist British producers seeking to enter into European co-productions. She also said that a working party, to be chaired by the Secretary of State for Trade and Industry, would be set up to consider the financing of the industry.

Driving Miss Daisy

At the 62nd Academy Awards (Oscars) ceremony of the US Academy of Motion Picture Arts and Sciences, the award for best picture went to *Driving Miss Daisy*. The film, nominated in nine categories, received a total of four Oscars. Adapted by Alfred Uhry from his own play and directed by Bruce Beresford, the film told the story of an elderly Jewish widow and her relationship with her black chauffeur, Hoke, over a period of 25 years. This delightful and unsentimental tale was preferred to Oliver Stone's *Born on the Fourth of July*, Peter Weir's *Dead Poets Society*, Phil Alden Robinson's *Field of Dreams*, and Jim Sheridan's *My Left Foot*.

British-born Jessica Tandy won the best actress award for her role as Miss Daisy, at 80 the oldest winner of an Oscar. Alfred Uhry won the Oscar for best adapted screenplay; the film also won the award for best make-up. Surprisingly, Bruce Beresford was not nominated as best director, an almost unprecedented omission.

Daniel Day-Lewis won the award for best actor for *My Left Foot*, directed by Jim Sheridan. His moving portrayal of Irish writer and painter Christy Brown, who was crippled by cerebral palsy, was widely praised. The film was made in Ireland for less than £2 million and financed by Granada Television. Brenda Fricker, who played Christy's mother, was voted best supporting actress. Denzel Washington was best supporting actor for *Glory*, which also received the awards for cinematography (Freddie Francis) and for sound.

Oliver Stone's *Born on the Fourth of July* won the award for best direction. Stone won this award in 1987 for *Platoon*, a film based on his experiences during the Vietnam war, for which he spent ten years trying to raise funding. *Born on the Fourth of July* was another uncompromising and factually-based film about Vietnam which Stone first tried to film in 1978. The film was based on a book by Ron Kovic, who was paralysed in the war. When Stone's first attempt to film the book collapsed, he promised Kovic that he would return to the story one day. When Stone eventually got the project off the ground, Kovic helped to write the screenplay. The Kovic character was played in the film by Tom Cruise, who gave a powerful performance. *Born on the Fourth of July* also won the Academy award for film editing.

Peter Weir's *Dead Poets Society* featured Robin Williams as an unconventional, inspirational English teacher at a private boys' college in Vermont in 1959. His motto is *carpe diem* (seize the day), and, against the wishes of the school, he teaches his pupils to enjoy literature, explore ideas and question conventions. A group of boys form a society dedicated to midnight poetry readings in a cave, but the film ends in tragedy when one pupil, whose interest in acting is thwarted by his father, commits suicide. Tom Schulman won the Oscar for best original screenplay.

Cinema Paradiso won the award for best foreign film, completing a remarkable run of success for a film that was savaged by critics in Italy when it was first released. Giuseppe Tornatore's nostalgic look at the golden age of cinema in a small Sicilian town also won the Grand Prix at Cannes in 1989. It featured Jacques Perrin, Philippe Noiret and Salvatore Cascio.

Phyllis Dalton won the award for best costume design for Kenneth Branagh's *Henry V*; the best documentary feature award went to *Common Threads: Stories from the Quilt*; best documentary short subject, *The Johnstown Flood*; best animated short film, *Balance*; best live action short film, *Work Experience*; and best visual effects, *The Abyss*. A special Oscar was presented to Akira Kurosawa, Japanese director of *The Seven Samurai* and *Rashomon*, on his 80th birthday.

British Awards

At the British Academy of Film and Television Awards, *Dead Poets Society* was judged best film. Daniel Day-Lewis won the best actor award for *My Left Foot*, and Ray McAnally was posthumously voted best supporting actor for his role in the same film, Pauline Collins was named best actress for *Shirley Valentine* and Kenneth Branagh won the best director award for *Henry V*. Best screenplay went to Christopher Hampton for *Dangerous Liaisons*.

Branagh's *Henry V* drew inevitable comparisons with Laurence Olivier's wartime version of the same film. Branagh said, 'The more I thought about it, the more convinced I became that there was a play to be reclaimed from jingoism and World War Two associations'. His was a darker, more intimate film than Olivier's, and concentrated on the full horror of battle. Although Branagh drew inevitable criticism for daring to follow in Olivier's footsteps, the film was generally well received. Branagh adapted Shakespeare's play, directed the film and starred as Henry. A distinguished cast included Paul Schofield as the King of France, Derek Jacobi as Chorus, Ian Holm as Fluellen, Richard Briers as Bardolph and Judi Dench as Mistress Quickly.

Shirley Valentine was developed for the cinema by Willy Russell from his widely praised play for a solo performer. Directed by Lewis Gilbert, with whom Russell collaborated on *Educating Rita* a few years earlier, the film featured a fine performance from Pauline Collins as the housewife from Wallasey who finds freedom from domestic drudgery on a fortnight's holiday in Mykonos. Tom Conti and Bernard Hill were excellent in supporting roles.

Latest Krays

One of the more controversial films of the year was *The Krays*, the story of the East End gangsters of the 1960s who are still serving prison sentences for murder. Directed by Peter Medak, Philip Ridley's intelligent script avoided glorifying violence and largely concentrated on the twins' relationship with their mother Violet, played by Billie Whitelaw. Reggie and Ronnie Kray were portrayed by Gary and Martin Kemp.

Peter Greenaway's films, from the enigmatic *The Draughtsman's Contract* to *Drowning by Numbers*, are both highly original and highly provocative. His latest film, *The Cook, the Thief, His Wife and Her Lover*, is no exception, being violent and revolting. A black comedy with an anti-materialistic stance, the film is set in a hellish restaurant. Greenaway himself describes the film as 'a classic Revenge Tragedy out of "The Theatre of Blood", with a great obsession in human corporeality'. A strong cast was led by Alan Howard, Michael Gambon and Helen Mirren. Costumes were by the French designer Jean-Paul Gaultier.

Alan Ayckbourn's play about an amateur dramatic company's trials and tribulations, *A Chorus of Disapproval*, was adapted for the screen by the playwright in association with the film director Michael Winner. Jeremy Irons played Guy Jones, who joins the company 'to have fun and meet friends', only to become involved in the backstage intrigues of its members. Anthony Hopkins played the producer, Dafydd Ap Llewellyn, and the cast also included Prunella Scales, Jenny Seagrove, Richard Briers and Lionel Jefferies.

Tom Sharpe's novel *Wilt*, a farce about an unsuccessful polytechnic lecturer suspected of murdering his wife, was adapted for the screen by Andrew Marshall and David Renwick. Although the film starred the comedians Griff Rhys Jones and Mel Smith, uninspired direction by Michael Tuchner failed to improve on the puerile humour of the novel.

Ken Russell had a great success in 1969 with his adaptation of D. H. Lawrence's *Women In Love*, the story of Ursula and Gudrun Brangwen. Russell's latest film *The Rainbow*, based on Lawrence's novel of the same name, concentrates on the early life of Ursula, played by Sammi Davis, and in particular her relationship with her teacher Winifred Inger (played by Amanda Donohue) and the soldier Anton Skrebensky (played by Paul McGann). The cast also featured Glenda Jackson, who starred in *Women In Love*, and David Hemmings.

Terry Jones's *Erik the Viking* was based on the promising idea of a Viking leader (played by Tim Robbins) trying to dissuade his men from following their traditional pursuits of rape and pillage. However, despite a fine performance as Halfdan the Black from John Cleese and some amusing moments, the idea was not sustained. The film featured cameo performances from Mickey Rooney, Eartha Kitt and Freddie Jones.

Martin Amis's first novel, *The Rachel Papers*, was adapted for the screen and directed by Damian Harris. Dexter Fletcher starred in the film as Charles Highway, who keeps computer files on his romantic affairs, with Ione Skye as Rachel, the object of his affections. *Queen of Hearts* was a whimsical and highly enjoyable film set in London's Italian Community. Made for only £2 million, the film is narrated by ten-year-old Eddie, played by Ian Hawkes, and tells the story of Eddie's parents, Rosa and Danilo, who eloped from Tuscany in order to marry. Eddie's memories are unreliable, poetic and laced with fantasy: 'That's my story. It's up to you if you want to believe it or not, but it's all true—at least, that's the way I remember it'. Directed by John Amiel from a screenplay by Tony Grisoni, the excellent cast included Vittorio Duse, Joseph Long and Anita Zagaria.

Dick Tracy

Following the huge success of *Batman*, which took over $150 million in its first three weeks in America, the latest comic strip derived blockbuster from the United States was the Walt Disney Company's *Dick Tracy*. Produced and directed by Warren Beatty, who also starred in the title role, the film was based on the popular cartoon strip of the 1930s about a legendary detective. The film was reported to have cost some $30 million to produce, with a similar amount being spent on promotion. Beatty's failure to promote his previous pet project, *Reds*, was considered to have harmed that film at the box office. The reclusive star gave extensive interviews after critical reaction to *Dick Tracy* was lukewarm.

Unlike *Batman*, the *Dick Tracy* cartoon strip is unfamiliar to the younger generation in the USA and virtually unknown in Britain. However, the film's publicity exploited the appearance of popular singer Madonna in the role of Breathless Mahoney, which widened the film's appeal. The pre-publicity and hype that precede films like *Batman* and *Dick Tracy* tend to obscure whatever merit they possess. *Batman* is a dark and brooding film with an undercurrent of menace that transcends its comicbook beginnings. *Dick Tracy*, in contrast, exploits its cartoon origins on the screen. Filmed in the same primary colours used in the original cartoon drawings, its stylized presentation of characters reinforces the impression of fantasy. Al Pacino played the criminal mastermind Big Boy, with Dustin Hoffman (who appeared with Beatty in the disastrous *Ishtar*) as Mumbles, and Mandy Patinkin as 88 Keys, the piano player. Stephen Sondheim wrote the music and the film was designed by Richard Sylbert.

Back to the box office

American studios continued their obsession with sequels. Directing the follow-up to his hugely successful *Back to the Future*, Robert Zemeckis found that he had too much material for one film. Accordingly, two films were made and released at intervals during the year. Parts II and III continued the time travels of Marty McFly, played again by Michael J. Fox, with Christopher Lloyd as the eccentric Doc Brown. Part II is confusing, with frequent time changes and a limp ending pointing too obviously towards the concluding part of the saga. Part III is set largely in the Wild West in 1885 and enjoys some gentle humour at the expense of Hollywood and cowboy films.

Ghostbusters 2 lacks the freshness of the original film, in which the team of Bill Murray, Dan Aykroyd and Harold Ramis saved New York from supernatural forces. In the second film the team rescues the city from being overwhelmed by a river of ectoplasmic slime. Directed by Ivan Reitman, the script was written by Aykroyd and Ramis. *Gremlins 2: The New Batch* continues the story of the Mugwumps, lovable furry creatures which turn into Gremlins if they are fed at night or become wet. Directed by Joe Dante, the film features excellent special effects from Rick Baker and is full of witty and satiric touches. Other sequels released during the year include *The Fly II*, directed by Chris Walas, *Die Hard 2*, starring Bruce Willis, and *Lethal Weapon 2* starring Mel Gibson.

Total Recall

One of the major successes of the year was *Total Recall*, an intelligent but brutal science fiction fantasy starring Arnold Schwarzenegger. He played Doug Quaid, a construction worker who is haunted by dreams of life on the planet Mars. Quaid visits a company called Recall Incorporated which offers holidays trips through implanting experiences into the mind. However, the operation goes wrong and disturbs a previous implant of which Quaid was unaware. It quickly becomes difficult to distinguish between fact and fantasy. The film is convoluted but clever. The stunning sets, along with Schwarzenegger's $10 million fee, accounted for much of the $70 million production budget. The film took $100 million at the box office in its first two months of release in the USA. Based on a story by Philip K. Dick, it was directed by Paul Verhoeven. The cast also included Sharon Stone, Rachel Ticotin and Ronny Cox.

Clint Eastwood starred in and directed *White Hunter Black Death*. The film is an adaptation of Peter Viertel's novel based on a trip to Africa with the legendary director John Huston during script research and the filming of *The African Queen*. The story concerns Huston's obsession with killing an elephant before he would finish making the film. Eastwood was widely praised for his performance.

Taped

Steven Soderbergh's first feature, *Sex, lies and videotape*, which he both wrote and directed, was the surprise winner of the Palme d'Or at the 1989 Cannes Film Festival. A complex film, which Soderbergh described as 'emotionally autobiographical', it features James Spader as a character who suffers from impotence, which he is only able to overcome by viewing videotapes of women talking about their love lives. Soderbergh shot the film in just five weeks at a cost of only $1.2 million. It proved to be an impressive and accomplished debut which sensitively and wittily examines and illuminates contemporary issues. Soderbergh sees video as 'a way of distancing ourselves, anaesthetizing our responses. People seem afraid to come out and say what they mean.' Unfortunately, the percipience of the Cannes jury was not matched by the American Academy, which failed to recognize the film in any category. The cast also included Andie MacDowell, Peter Gallagher and Laura San Giacomo.

Stephen Spielberg's *Always* is a remake of Dalton Trumbo's 1942 film *A Guy Named Joe*, about a fighter pilot who is killed in action and returns as a ghost to guide the inexperienced pilot with whom his former girlfriend has fallen in love. In *Always* the story has been updated and the pilots fight forest fires rather than enemy aircraft, which diminishes the dramatic impact somewhat. Nevertheless, the film is well constructed and filmed, with a good performance from Richard Dreyfuss in the role originally played by Spencer Tracy. He is well supported by Audrey Hepburn, Holly Hunter and Brad Johnson.

Roland Joffe's *The Shadow Makers* was originally released in the USA as *Fat Man and Little Boy*, the nicknames given to the two atomic bombs dropped on the Japanese cities of Hiroshima and Nagasaki. However, in spite of the change of name, the film was not successful in America. It tells the story of the development of the atomic bomb, an operation code-named the Manhattan Project, through two of the main personalities involved. Dwight Schultz played J. Robert Oppenheimer, the physicist in charge, who began to have doubts about the morality of what he was doing, and Paul Newman played General Leslie Groves, the soldier with whom Oppenheimer was in frequent conflict.

Hubert Selby's novel about low life in New York was a literary *cause célèbre* in the 1960s and was prosecuted for obscenity in Great Britain. *Last Exit to Brooklyn* has now been brought to the screen, with a screenplay by Desmond Nakano and directed by Uli Edel. Although some of the brutality and grimness of the novel had to be omitted to ensure that the film received a certificate, it is still true in spirit to Selby's original. The screenplay also retains the episodic structure of the novel, using the linking device of a strike to give coherence and structure to the different stories of the novel. The cast included Jennifer Jason Leigh as Tra La La, Stephen Lang as union leader Harry Black and Burt Young as Big Joe.

Vietnam

Apart from Stone's *Born on the Fourth of July*, several other films dealt with the Vietnam war and its aftermath. Brian de Palma's *Casualties of War* was adapted from a true story by Daniel Lang about an American patrol which captured, raped and killed a Vietnamese girl. Michael J. Fox played Eriksson, the soldier who refuses to become involved and later turns in his fellow soldiers to the authorities. Sean Penn was the young sergeant, Meserve, who instigates the incident. Norman Jewison's *In Country* starred Emily Lloyd as a teenage girl determined to find out everything she can about her father, who was killed in Vietnam before she was born. Bruce Willis played her uncle Emmett, a man still haunted by memories of the war. Emily Lloyd also starred in *Chicago Joe and the Showgirl* with Kiefer Sutherland. Directed by Bernard Rose, the film was based on an incident in the Second World War, in which an American soldier in London joined with an English showgirl to commit a senseless murder.

Ridley Scott's *Black Rain* starred Michael Douglas as a New York policeman sent to Japan to escort a criminal back to America. The clash of cultures is effectively handled, with Douglas's brash character contrasted with the methodical Ken Takakura as his Japanese opposite number. The Japanese officer eventually adopts the unorthodox techniques of the American to ensure that justice is done. The film was stylishly filmed in Osaka, with the rain-soaked neon-lit streets an impressive backdrop for the violent action. Shoehei Imamura also released a film called *Black Rain*. The Japanese film is an adaptation of a novel by Masuji Ibusi about the daughter of a peasant family who is stricken by radiation sickness after passing through Hiroshima following the fall of the atomic bomb.

The Fabulous Baker Boys was an enjoyable romantic comedy, written and directed by Steve Kloves in an impressive feature debut. It starred brothers Jeff and Beau Bridges as a small-time and fading piano act whose careers are boosted when they take on a singer, Susie Diamond, brilliantly played by Michelle Pfeiffer. Rob Reiner's *When Harry Met Sally* was a charming and intelligent comedy, which starred Billy Crystal and Meg Ryan as a couple whose relationship gradually develops over a period of eleven years. The script was written by Nora Ephron.

Bear facts

Jean-Jacques Annaud's *The Bear* is a remarkable wildlife film. The director developed the film from a simple outline: 'An orphaned bear cub. A huge, solitary bear. Two hunters. The animal's point of view'. A well-deserved success in Europe, it was made without any cruelty to the animals involved. The only questionable aspect of the film was the way it imbued dangerous wild creatures with human thoughts and instincts.

Polish director Kryzysztof Kieslowski's *Dekalog* consists of ten 50-minute television films which interpret the Ten Commandments through their relevance to modern morality and dilemmas. In return for funding from the Polish Ministry of Culture, Kieslowski agreed to expand two of the pieces into feature-length versions. These were released as *A Short Film Above Love*, about a young

man's obsession with a woman in a neighbouring apartment, and *A Short Film About Killing*, an uncompromising and brutal account of a murder followed by judicial execution.

One of the more remarkable films to emanate from the Soviet Union since *glasnost* permitted some artistic freedom is Stanislav Govorukhin's *You Can't Live Like This*. A damning indictment of the Soviet system since the Revolution, the film is based on the premise that 'Ours is a society that was built on an unpunished crime', the murder of the Tsar and his family.

Akira Kurosawa's *Dreams* consists of eight short pieces, including his visions of childhood and a tribute to Van Gogh. Kurosawa is as widely revered outside Japan as in his native country, an appreciation which was signified by the award of his honorary Oscar. Now in his eighties, Kurosawa's career has received a well-deserved boost through the attentions of leading Hollywood filmmakers. *Dreams* was presented by Steven Spielberg.

Costa-Gavras's *Music Box* featured Armin Mueller-Stahl as Laszlo, a Hungarian living in Chicago who is tried for crimes allegedly committed during the war. Jessica Lange played his daughter, a lawyer who defends her father but comes to question his innocence.

Festivals

At the 46th Venice Film Festival, Dame Peggy Ashcroft and Geraldine James shared the award for best actress for their roles in *She's Been Away*, a film directed by Sir Peter Hall and produced by BBC Television. Written by Stephen Poliakoff, it featured Ashcroft as an old lady who goes to live with her nephew and his wife after almost a lifetime spent in a mental institution. The best actor prize was shared by Marcello Mastroianni and Massimo Troissi, who played father and son in Ettore Scola's *What's the Time?* The Golden Lion was awarded to *City of Sorrows* by Hou Xiaoxian, a family saga set in Taiwan.

The 33rd London Film Festival included some 140 full-length features over 17 days. It opened with Ron Howard's *Parenthood*, a comedy starring Steven Martin and Tom Hulce. The Thames Silent film was Harold Lloyd's 1923 classic, *Safety Last*, in which the comic genius climbs up the side of a departmental store. Carl Davis wrote a new score for the film. Also shown were a colour-restored print of *The Thief of Baghdad*, and Cecil B. de Mille's story of Nero, *Sign of the Cross*, which was made in 1932 and in which Charles Laughton starred as Nero, with Claudette Colbert as Poppaea. The print included scenes that had been cut by the censors when the film was first released. Also shown was Euzhan Palcy's drama about apartheid in South Africa, *A Dry White Season*. The film is based on Andre Brink's novel and starred Donald Sutherland as a white schoolteacher whose black gardener's son is killed in the Soweto riots. In his fight for justice, the teacher has to face the full implications of the political situation in his country. The film features a cameo performance from Marlon Brando as a civil rights lawyer.

The Berlin Film Festival celebrated the reunion of

the city with shows in both east and west and the showing of many films that had previously been banned in the east. The Golden Bear was awarded jointly to *Larks on a String*, Jiri Menzel's Czechoslovakian film from 1968 about Stalinist 're-education' of the bourgeoisie, and to Costa-Gavras's *Music Box*. Michael Verhoven was awarded the prize for best director for *The Frightful Girl*, and best acting awards were shared by Jessica Tandy and Morgan Freeman for *Driving Miss Daisy*.

The Cannes Film Festival in 1989 rejected both *Henry V* and *My Left Foot* for the competition. At the 1990 Festival Ken Loach's controversial thriller set in Northern Ireland, *Hidden Agenda*, received the Special Jury Prize. American director David Lynch won the Palme d'Or for *Wild at Heart*, which featured Nicholas Cage and Laura Dern being pursued by killers in the American south. Gerard Depardieu won the best actor award for *Cyrano de Bergerac*, and Krystyna Janda was best actress for her role in *Interrogation* as a singer arrested and imprisoned during the Stalinist purges in 1951. Directed by Richard Bugajski, the film has been banned in Poland

since 1981 because of its harsh portrayal of prison conditions.

Other films released during the year included: *Steel Magnolias*, directed by Herbert Ross, featuring Sally Field, Shirley MacLaine, Dolly Parton and Olympia Dukakis; *Look Who's Talking*, written and directed by Amy Heckerling, with Kirstie Alley, John Travolta and Bruce Willis; *Sea of Love*, directed by Harold Becker, with Al Pacino and Ellen Barkin; *Honey, I Shrunk the Kids*, directed by Joe Johnson, with Rick Moranis and Matt Frewer; *Celia*, directed by Ann Turner, with Rebecca Smart and Maryanne Fahey; *Leningrad Cowboys Go America*, directed by Aki Kaurismaki; *Young Einstein*, directed by and starring Yahoo Serious; *Talk Radio*, directed by Oliver Stone, with Eric Bogosian and Ellen Greene; *Earth Girls Are Easy*, directed by Julien Temple, with Jeff Goldblum and Geena Davies; *Where the Heart Is*, directed by John Boorman, with Dabney Coleman, Uma Thirman and Christopher Plummer; and *Diamond Skulls*, directed by Nick Broomfield, with Gabriel Byrne, Amanda Donohue and Michael Hordern.

THE ACADEMY AWARDS 1989

Best Picture.—*Driving Miss Daisy*.
Best Director.—Oliver Stone, *Born on the Fourth of July*.
Best Actor.—Daniel Day-Lewis, *My Left Foot*.
Best Actress.—Jessica Tandy, *Driving Miss Daisy*.
Best Supporting Actor.—Denzel Washington, *Glory*.
Best Supporting Actress.—Brenda Fricker, *My Left Foot*.
Best Original Screenplay.—Tom Schulman, *Dead Poets Society*.
Best Adapted Screenplay.—Alfred Uhry, *Driving Miss Daisy*.
Best Foreign Language.—*Cinema Paradise*, Italy.
Best Original Score.—Alan Menken, *The Little Mermaid*.
Best Original Song.—Alan Menken and Howard Ashman, 'Under the Sea', *The Little Mermaid*.
Best Cinematography.—Freddie Francis, *Glory*.
Best Art Direction.—Anton Furst and Peter Young, *Batman*.

Best Costume Design.—Phyllis Dalton, *Henry V*.
Best Film Editing.—David Brenner and Joe Hutshing, *Born on the Fourth of July*.
Best Sound.—Donald O. Mitchell, Gregg C. Rudloff, Elliot Tyson, Russel Williams II, *Glory*.
Best Sound Effects Editing.—Ben Burtt and Richard Hymns, *Indiana Jones and the Last Crusade*.
Best Visual Effects.—John Bruno, Dennis Muren, Hoyt Yeatman, Dennis Skotak, *The Abyss*.
Best Make-up.—Manlio Rocchetti, Lynn Barber, Kevin Haney, *Driving Miss Daisy*.
Best Animated Short.—Christoph and Wolfgang Lauenstein, *Balance*.
Best Short Documentary.—Charles Guggenheim, *The Johnstown Flood*.
Best Documentary Feature.—Robert Epstein and Bill Couturie, *Common Threads: Stories from the Quilt*.
Best Live Action Short.—James Hendrie, *Work Experience*.
Honorary Award.—Akira Kurosawa.

DRAMA 1989–90

The Royal Shakespeare Company announced in February 1990 that its two London stages at the Barbican will be closed from November 1990 until March 1991 because of its continuing financial crisis. The RSC estimated that this would save £1·3 million, at a time when it faces a deficit of over £1 million for the second year running. The company projected that the deficit would rise to £2·9 million without drastic measures. The RSC pointed out that in the 1984 review of its finances, it had been found to be well managed but 'palpably underfunded'. The review had recommended that the RSC's subsidy should be raised to a proper level and its real value be maintained in future years. However, the second part of the recommendation had not been carried out and the level of public subsidy has dropped from 44 per cent of income to its current level of 30 per cent. In spite of substantial private sector sponsorship, increased transfer income (including £1 million a year from *Les Misérables*) and cutting back the number of theatres used from six in 1987 to four in 1990, there is a shortfall of £2·2 million in the company's income.

The Government announced that the arts would receive an extra 12 per cent in funding this year, allowing the Arts Council to increase the RSC's grant to £6 million for 1990. However, the increase in real terms was only 3·3 per cent or about £180,000, enough to underwrite one production. Terry Hands, outgoing artistic director of the company, said that the decision to close the Barbican stages was 'immensely painful'. 'We have long been proud of our association with the City of London . . . but there was no choice. In business terms it all makes sense, but not in cultural terms.'

Royal Insurance announced that it would continue its sponsorship of the RSC, and increased its funding from £1·1 million for 1988–90 to £2·1 million for 1991–3. The money will be used primarily to help fund the RSC's regional tour and to expand the 'armchair proms' outside London and Stratford. Royal Insurance will also sponsor the RSC's tour of Europe with *Les Liaisons Dangereuses*, which opened in Glasgow in July 1990 before visiting five other European countries. The Royal Insurance deal is a record amount of sponsorship for any performing arts company in Britain. When announcing the sponsorship, Royal Insurance called on the Government to pay off the deficits of all Britain's main arts companies to enable them to 'carry on with their proper artistic function'. Base funding for the arts should come from ticket sales and government subsidy, not from sponsorship. Peter Palumbo, chairman of the Arts Council, supported this view, saying that, 'Sponsorship should provide additional resources for the development of new projects and initiatives. Arts Council subsidy and box office must remain the RSC's core funding. We continue to press upon the Government the need to increase the grant-in-aid sufficiently to enable us to put such important companies as the RSC on a secure financial footing.'

In February 1990, it was announced that Adrian Noble will succeed Terry Hands as artistic director of the RSC in March 1991. Mr Noble appointed Michael Attenborough as executive producer and deputy director, with special resonsibility for new writing, marketing, and social and physical environment. Genista McIntosh was appointed to take charge of casting, planning and training. The posts of associate director, held by Bill Alexander, Ron Daniels, Barry Kyle and John Caird at present, will be dispensed with.

For his last season with the company Terry Hands announced 'the smallest output the RSC has done in a single year', with 19 productions in total, compared with 27 the previous season and 32 in 1988. There are ten productions in Stratford, compared with 15 the previous year; the third Stratford theatre, The Other Place, remains closed for redevelopment. There are also fewer transfers to London, and the two companies of actors have been reduced by one-third to 65 each at Stratford and the Barbican. A scheduled production based on the book of Genesis, *Children of Eden*, was cancelled, although John Caird continued to develop the musical epic in the private sector.

At Stratford, notable Shakespearian productions included *Coriolanus*, with Charles Dance taking the leading role, his first stage role for seven years, and Barbara Jefford as his mother Volumnia. Also much praised was Ian Judge's production of *The Comedy of Errors*, with Desmond Barrit and Graham Turner, respectively, playing both Antipholus and Dromio parts. The Memorial Theatre also presented Jerome Kern's and Oscar Hammerstein's *Show Boat*, the result of the RSC's collaboration with Opera North (*see* **Opera** summary for production details).

The Swan presented the premiere of Peter Flannery's *Singer*, 'a modern Jacobean tragi-comedy'. Antony Sher played Peter Singer, a Polish Jew who survives the horrors of Auschwitz to become a crooked property tycoon in London, and who later develops a social conscience. The play sold out in Stratford and on the company's Newcastle visit, before moving to the Barbican. After a successful run in the Pit, *Singer* transferred to the main stage, where it confirmed its status as a major new work.

The Last Days of Don Juan was adapted by Nick Dear from *El Burlador de Sevilla*, written in 1630 by Tirso de Molina. This is the first recorded version of the Don Juan story; Linus Roache played the inveterate seducer who finally receives his just rewards. The production was well received, although Dear's decision to change the sex of Don Juan's servant to a female was felt, in spite of a fine performance from Sally Dexter, to have reduced some of the dramatic impact by failing to provide the necessary counterpoint to Don Juan.

At the Barbican, the RSC enjoyed success with its adaptation of Anthony Burgess's *A Clockwork Orange—2004*. Although lacking some of the impact of Stanley Kubrick's film of the same novella, Ron Daniels's production had a strong leading performance from Phil Daniels as Alex. The impressive set was designed by Richard Hudson, choreography was by Arlene Phillips and music by the Edge and Bono of U2. The show transferred to the Royalty.

The Barbican Pit premiered a number of new plays, including Stephen Poliakoff's *Playing with Trains*, with Michael Pennington as a British inventor trying to prevent British inventions and discoveries going abroad. Paula Milne's *Earwig* concerned the world of television soap opera and the use of a computer to calculate audience ratings. *A Dream of People* by Michael Hastings was the directing debut of Janet Suzman; it concerns Claude Godber, played by Peter McEnery, a civil servant who rebels against the lack of compassion in modern Britain.

National Theatre

The National Theatre, whose grant was raised by the Arts Council to £8·9 million in 1990, embarked on a major tour, with Ian McKellen as *Richard III* and Brian Cox as *King Lear* going on the road in autumn 1990 after 67 performances at the Lyttelton. International Theatre productions included the Moscow Arts production of *Uncle Vanya*, directed by Oleg Yefremov and featuring Innokenti Smoktunovski, who had last performed in London in 1966. The Tokyo Ninagawa Company presented *Suicide for Love* by Matsuyo Akimoto, a Japanese play based on two 18th century puppet plays. The English commentary was spoken by Vanessa Redgrave.

Richard Eyre's production of *Hamlet* was dogged by misfortune towards the end of its run. Daniel Day-Lewis had to leave the production with seven of the 72 performances remaining as he was suffering from exhaustion. Ian Charleson took over, even though he was already ill with AIDS, from which he died soon afterwards. In the Cottesloe, *Ma Rainey's Black Bottom* was the first British production of a play by the Pulitzer Prize-winning American playwright August Wilson. Set in 1927 in a Chicago studio, it used the recording of a song called 'Black Bottom' by the legendary blues singer Ma Rainey to expose the economic exploitation of black performers. Howard Davies's production featured Carol Woods-Coleman as Ma Rainey, with Hugh Quarshie and Clarke Peters as two of the session musicians.

Martin Sherman's *Bent*, a modern classic, received a welcome revival at the Lyttelton. First staged at the Royal Court in 1979, this powerful drama about homosexuality and the triumph of the human spirit had lost none of its impact. Ian McKellen repeated his role as Max, with Michael Cashman taking the part of Horst. *Bent* later transferred from the National to the Garrick.

David Hare's new play, *Racing Demon*, is a thoughtful and well-crafted drama about the Church of England. It concerns four clergymen trying to make sense of their mission, of good in an evil world, and the loss of spirituality. Directed by Richard Eyre, the play has a strong cast led by Oliver Ford Davies and including Michael Bryant, Richard Pasco, and David Bamber. The play proved to be a sell-out on the Cottesloe stage and achieved an unprecedented transfer to the main Olivier auditorium.

The Lyttelton presented Stephen Soldheim's *Sunday in the Park with George*. This ran for 15 months on Broadway after opening in 1984 but no commercial management in London was prepared to risk staging it. Inspired by the great *pointilliste* painting *A Sunday Afternoon on the Island of La Grande Jatte* by Seurat, Sondheim's study of art and the creative process was not wholly convincing.

Arthur Miller's 75th birthday was marked by a number of productions, including one of *The Crucible* at the Olivier. Written in 1953, this powerful drama about the 17th century Salem witch trials has always been much more than an indictment of the McCarthy era, and Howard Davies's production brought out the power and tragedy of the work. The Cottesloe also gave the London premiere of Miller's *After the Fall*. Written in 1964, the play was regarded at the time as a thinly-veiled autobiographical account of Miller's marriage to Marilyn Monroe. Michael Blakemore, directing his first National production for 14 years, played down the parallels by casting the black actress Josette Simon in the role of Maggie. Simon and James Laurenson gave highly-praised performances in the leading roles.

Tony Harrison adapted the remaining fragment of a lost satyr play by Sophocles about the invention of the lyre to create *The Trackers of Oxyrhynchus*, an absorbing and stimulating drama. The play has only been performed once since the 5th century BC, when the National Theatre presented a version at Delphi. It featured Jack Shepherd and Barrie Rutter as Grenfell and Hunt, the papyrologists who discovered the fragment in 1907, who are transformed into Apollo and Silenus to enact the story.

The production of Bertolt Brecht's *The Good Person of Sichuan* was Deborah Warner's directing debut at the National. Fiona Shaw played Shen Te, the prostitute blessed by the gods but hounded by her neighbours. *Man, Beast and Virtue* by Pirandello was a flop when first staged in 1919 in Milan. It gave offence with its story about an unfaithful wife, pregnant by her tutor, who needs to entice her sea-captain husband to bed when he returns home for one night, even though they have been celibate for years. Directed by William Gaskill, the production was the first staging in the UK since 1958. Ibsen's verse drama *Peer Gynt* was produced at the Olivier by Declan Donnellan and Nick Ormerod, the directing and design team of Cheek by Jowl. Ibsen had not intended the play to be performed and the work is a difficult one to stage. The imaginative and inventive production overcame many of the difficulties inherent in the play and the main reservation of most critics was the decision to split the role of Peer Gynt between two actors: Peter Morrissey played the younger Peer and Stephen Moore the older man. This device was felt to interrupt the development of the character. Also well received was Peter Wood's revival of Sheridan's *The School for Scandal*, which marked the welcome return to the British stage of John Neville, in the role of Sir Peter Teazle.

Musical ups and downs

Once again, the year was dominated by news of costly musical productions, most of which failed to make the grade. The undoubted success of the season was *Miss Saigon*, a version of the *Madam Butterfly* story set at the time of the fall of Vietnam. Although too obviously contrived for some tastes, this tale of an American soldier's love for a Vietnamese girl proved to have found the magic formula. Although it cost £3 million to stage, advance bookings exceeded £4·5 million. The music was written by Claude-Michel Schonberg, with lyrics by Richard Maltby jun.

and Alain Boublil. Nicholas Hytner directed, and the impressive staging, which included the last helicopter flight from Saigon and a huge statue of Ho Chi Minh, was by John Napier.

The proposal to mount a Broadway production of *Miss Saigon* led to a clash between the producers of the show and the American actors' union Equity. Although the show had taken some $23 million in advance bookings, American Equity refused to accept that Jonathan Pryce should recreate his starring role as the Eurasian pimp, on the grounds that the role should be played by an Asian actor. Cameron Mackintosh, producer of the show, immediately cancelled the whole production, forcing a rapid climbdown by the union.

Less successful was *King*, a musical based on the life of Martin Luther King. The production was dogged by controversy, disputes and adverse publicity. The opening of the musical was twice postponed, it went through four scriptwriters and three directors, and at one stage King's widow Caretta withdrew her support, claiming that it trivialized her husband's life. There were also arguments over whether white actors and writers could fully understand and appreciate King's 'black identity'. After experiencing probably more problems than any other show in the West End, the £3 million production took barely £100,000 in advance bookings and the show closed after six weeks.

Another stage disaster was *Bernadette*, the so-called people's musical. The story of the saint of Lourdes reached the West End on a wave of emotion and sentiment, and £700,000 provided by 2,000 'angels'. However, Maureen and Gwyn Hughes's trite lyrics and anodyne treatment were a critical disaster and failed to draw audiences. It closed within two months.

Someone Like You was conceived and co-written by Petula Clark, who also starred in this musical love story set in West Virginia after the American Civil War. It closed after five weeks, forcing impresario Harold Fielding into liquidation. Two years previously Fielding had lost £3 million on *Ziegfeld*. Anthony Newley revived his 30-year-old musical *Stop the World I Want to Get Off*, co-written with Lesley Bricusse. Newley recreated his role as Mr. Littlechap, the teaboy who marries the boss's daughter, but the show's charm had worn thin over the years and it failed to make any impact. Also unsuccessful was Trevor Nunn's production of *The Baker's Wife*, a comedy musical by Joseph Stein and Stephen Schwartz. Based on the book by Marcel Pagnol, it featured Alun Armstrong as the baker who stops baking when his wife runs off with an admirer. It closed after a six-week run at the Phoenix.

Ian Dury's *Apples*, at the Royal Court, was a rock musical that veered uneasily between satire and sentimentality in its vision of London life seen through the eyes of tabloid journalist Byline Brown (played by Dury). More successful was *Buddy*, Plymouth Theatre Royal's celebration of the life and music of Buddy Holly which came to the Victoria Palace, London. A surprise musical success was *Return to the Forbidden Planet*, 'Shakespeare's forgotten Rock and Roll masterpiece', which combines *The Tempest* with the 1950s B-movie *Forbidden Planet* to produce a funny and vibrant space opera. Written and directed by Bob Carlton, the show was the unexpected winner of the Laurence Olivier Award for best musical, beating *Miss Saigon*. The production opened at the Belgrade Theatre, Coventry before its transfer to the Cambridge Theatre, London.

Low life

One of the season's major successes was Keith Waterhouse's *Jeffrey Bernard is Unwell*. Based on the 'Low Life' articles of *Spectator* columnist Jeffrey Bernard, the play wittily reviewed his life and managed to say much about the human condition. The role was brilliantly created by Peter O'Toole; after he left the production the part was taken over equally successfully first by Tom Conti and then by James Bolam.

Richard Harris made a triumphant return to the stage in Pirandello's *Henry IV*. Although the production was dogged by problems and disagreements, which saw director David Thacker leaving over 'artistic differences' and Sarah Miles withdrawing through exhaustion, its delayed London opening eventually went ahead to widespread acclaim. Harris, as the man who suffers concussion while dressed as Henry IV for a pageant and then believes he is the monarch, was convincing in a notoriously difficult role.

Samuel Beckett adapted *Krapp's Last Tape* specially for David Warrilow, exploiting the actor's knowledge of mime to pare down the text. The play was coupled with Beckett's *Catastrophe* (written in 1982 and dedicated to Vaclav Havel) in its Riverside Studios production which transferred from the Leicester Haymarket. The political upheaval in eastern Europe has seen Havel himself transformed from dissident and frequently imprisoned playwright to President of Czechoslovakia. To mark this there were productions of his *Vanek Plays* at the Lyric Studio, while his 'zany mightmare comedy' *Temptation*, which updates the Faust story, played at the Westminster.

Following the success of *Noises Off*, Michael Frayn's *Look Look* was eagerly awaited. However, while his earlier study of backstage dramas worked brilliantly, Frayn's attempt in *Look Look* to make a play about front of house dramas failed to gel, for author, cast, critics and audience. The second part of the play was thoroughly confusing.

Vanilla by Jane Stanton-Hitchcock was a weak contemporary drama about the Marcos regime in the Philippines. A fine cast (led by Joanna Lumley) was wasted on a weak plot laced with poor jokes and unsubtle caricatures. Most surprising was the involvement of Harold Pinter as director.

Ben Elton's *Gasping*, a modern satire about the privatization of air starring Hugh Laurie and Bernard Hill, was a popular success. Although the satire was heavy-handed at times, the concept of 'designer air' was just plausible enough and the jokes frequent enough to carry the day.

Simon Gray's *Hidden Laughter* covers the lives of an English family over ten years at their Devon country cottage. Concerning 'the possibilities of faith for the modern Englishman', it featured Peter Barkworth as the local vicar, and Felicity Kendal as a novelist whose marriage to a successful literary agent falls apart as she achieves her own literary ambitions.

Ronald Harwood's *Another Time* starred Albert Finney as an unsuccessful Jew in South Africa whose son is a musical prodigy. In the second act, set 35 years later, Finney played the son, boycotting a proposed concert tour of South Africa in spite of his mother's desire for him to return triumphant to his homeland. Alan Ayckbourn's 35th play, *Man of the Moment*, featured Peter Bowles as a former bank robber turned media personality who is brought face to face for a television show with the bank clerk who stopped him during a raid. The clerk was brilliantly played by Michael Gambon. Ayckbourn's *Absurd Person Singular* was revived at the Whitehall in his own Scarborough production, while his new play, *Body Language*, a black comedy about head swapping, premiered at Scarborough.

Stop press

Jeffrey Archer's first play, *Beyond Reasonable Doubt*, enjoyed a successful West End run. However, his second play, *Exclusive*, which covered seven days in the life of the *Chronicle* newspaper, was a critical and popular disaster. Damning reviews of its try-out in Bath preceded it to London, where they were largely confirmed; the scheduled 18-month run lasted barely three. Although thoroughly researched, the cardboard characters and wooden plot proved too big a handicap. Alex McCowen played a senior reporter whose job was under threat from a young upstart, while Paul Scofield seemed to have little heart for the role of the newspaper editor.

The vacancy at the Strand Theatre caused by the demise of *Exclusive* was filled by David Mamet's *A Life in the Theatre*, which transferred after a successful run at the Haymarket Theatre Royal. Mamet's 'English piece' was a funny and moving two-hander with excellent performances from Denholm Elliott as a fading actor past his prime and Samuel West as the rising star.

William Nicholson adapted for the stage his BAFTA award-winning television play *Shadowlands*, the story of the love affair between C. S. Lewis and his American admirer Joy Davidman. Nigel Hawthorne and Jane Lapotaire played the lead roles in Elijah Moshinsky's production.

The Almeida theatre is currently enjoying a new lease of life under the joint artistic directorship of Ian McDiarmid and Jonathan Kent. The small Islington theatre was built in 1837 as a meeting-place for 'some gentlemen of literary and scientific attainments' in the locality, and has had a varied history. It was the venue for the British stage premiere of Howard Barker's *Scenes from an Execution*. Barker's play featured Glenda Jackson as Galactia, a woman artist in 16th century Venice who is commissioned to paint a picture of the Battle of Lepanto to commemorate the victory of Christianity over the Moors. Her unromantic vision of war brings about her gradual estrangement from her family and friends and leads to her imprisonment. Jackson played the role in the original radio version of the play five years previously. Barker's *Seven Lears* was per-

formed at the Royal Court by the Wrestling School Group of actors, who were formed specifically to produce his work.

The Almeida also presented Ibsen's final work *When We Dead Waken*, in a translation by David Rudkin. This was the first London production for some 45 years of Ibsen's 'epilogue to a life's work'. The leading Norwegian actor Espen Skjønberg took the part of the sculptor Rubek who returns to Norway late in life and is reunited with Irena (played by Claire Bloom), the woman who had inspired his great work.

Peter Hall's company produced a much-acclaimed version of Ibsen's *The Wild Duck*. Featuring Alex Jennings as Hjalmar and David Threlfall as Gregers, the production toured for eight weeks before opening at the Phoenix. David Thacker continued the Young Vic's special relationship with Arthur Miller, producing both *The Price* (rehearsals of which the playwright attended) and his little-known first play, *The Man Who Had All the Luck*. The latter play, written in 1944, ran for four performances in New York; Miller has revised it many times since, most recently in 1988. The Young Vic co-produced it with the Bristol Old Vic.

Other notable productions included Adrian Noble's production of Chekhov's *Three Sisters*, which featured sisters Sinead, Sorcha and Niamh Cusack, as well as their father Cyril; after opening at the Gate Theatre, Dublin, the play moved to the Royal Court. Glenda Jackson played the lead in Brecht's *Mother Courage* in a production by Philip Prowse that opened at the Glasgow Citizens' Theatre before moving to the Mermaid in London. David Freeman's seven-hour version of *Morte d'Arthur* used two venues, the Lyric Hammersmith and St Paul's Church, to present Malory's Arthurian legend. At the Old Vic, two Corneille plays, both translated by Ranjit Bolt, were presented: Jonathan Miller directed *The Liar*, starring Alex Jennings, and *The Illusion* was directed by Richard Jones. At the same venue, Derek Jacobi played the title role in Jean-Paul Sartre's *Kean, or Disorder and Genius*, an enjoyable account of the great 19th century actor.

Theatres

In October 1989 it was announced that the site of the Globe Theatre had been located during exploratory excavations by the Museum of London (*see* Archaeology summary). This discovery, following the discovery of remains of the Rose in 1988, provides a unique opportunity to obtain information about the size and design of Elizabethan stages. Sam Wanamaker, founder of the International Shakespeare Globe Trust which is constructing a replica of the Globe in Southwark, said that work on the replica would cease in order to accommodate any changes needed to the design. 'We now know that we have found the Elizabethans' Shaftesbury Avenue,' he commented.

Fire destroyed the interior of the Savoy Theatre in February 1990. Built in 1881 by Richard d'Oyly Carte with the money he made from Gilbert and Sullivan's *Patience*, the theatre premiered many of the pair's works. It also funded the building of the famous hotel next door in 1889. In 1907, under Harley Granville Barker, it began a successful association with the works of George Bernard Shaw. The auditorium was rebuilt in 1929 to the designs of Basil Ionides and its Art Deco interior, 'suffused with light', is a serious loss. However, as the theatre is a Grade I listed building, it must be restored to its original condition.

The Dominion in Tottenham Court Road was threatened with closure and redevelopment as a hotel and office block. Built in 1929, the theatre is one of the largest in London, with 2,700 seats. The future of the Young Vic is also in doubt; with a substantial deficit and in urgent need of repair work to meet local authority requirements, the theatre needs to raise at least £100,000 to remain open.

On a happier note, the West Yorkshire Playhouse in Leeds opened in March 1990 with John O'Keefe's *Wild Oats*, featuring Reece Dinsdale. The building, on the site of the demolished Quarry Hill flats, contains two stages: the Quarry Theatre, which seats 750 people in 14 rows in a 90° arc, and the smaller Courtyard Theatre, a galleried rectangle with flexible seating for up to 350 people. The artistic director is Jude Kelly.

Awards

In the London Evening Standard Drama Awards for 1989, best play was *Ghetto* by Joshua Sobol; best actor, Ian McKellen (Iago in *Othello*); best actress, Felicity Kendal (*Much Ado About Nothing* and *Ivanov*); best comedy was Alan Ayckbourn's *Henceforward*; best musical, *Miss Saigon*; best director, Nicholas Hytner (*Miss Saigon* and *Ghetto*); most promising playwright, Stephen Jeffreys (*Valued Friends*). Stephen Sondheim received a special award.

The Laurence Olivier Awards, made by the Society of West End Theatres, went to: best play, *Racing Demon* by David Hare; best actor, Oliver Ford Davies (*Racing Demon*); best supporting actor, Michael Bryant (*Racing Demon*, *Hamlet* and *The Voysey Inheritance*); best actress, Fiona Shaw (*The Good Person of Sichuan*, *Electra* and *As You Like It*); best musical actor, Jonathan Pryce (*Miss Saigon*); best musical actress, Lea Salonga (*Miss Saigon*); best musical, *Return to the Forbidden Planet*; most promising newcomer, Jeremy Northam (*The Voysey Inheritance*); best designer, Bob Crowley (*Ma Rainey's Black Bottom*, *Hedda Gabler*, *Ghetto* and *The Plantagenets*); best director, Michael Bogdanov (*The Wars of the Roses*); Observer award for outstanding achievement, Declan Donnellan (*Fuente Ovejuna*); best comedy, Alan Bennett (*Single Spies*); best comic performance, Michael Gambon (*Man of the Moment*).

In the *Plays & Players* London Critics Awards 1989, best musical was *Miss Saigon*; best actor, Ian McKellen (*Othello*); best actress, Fiona Shaw (*Electra*, *As You Like it* and *The Good Person of Sichuan*); best supporting actor, Simon Russell Beale (*Some Americans Abroad* and *The Man of Mode*) and Michael Bryant (*Hamlet*); best supporting actress, Zoe Wanamaker (*Othello*); best director, Nicholas Hytner (*Miss Saigon*, *Ghetto* and *The Tempest*); best designer, John Napier (*Miss Saigon*). The award for best new play

was shared after four plays received the same number of votes: *Ghetto* by Joshua Sobol, *Singer* by Peter Flannery, *Some Americans Abroad* by Richard Nelson, and *Valued Friends* by Stephen Jeffreys.

PRODUCTIONS

London productions between September 1, 1989, and August 15, 1990, included the following:

ALDWYCH: WC2. (1989) Oct. 24. *The Cherry Orchard* by Anton Chekhov (translated by Michael Frayn), with Judi Dench, Ronald Pickup, Bernard Hill, Michael Gough, Nicholas Farrell, Tom Watts and Miranda Foster, directed by Sam Mendes, designed by Paul Farnsworth. (1990) April 17. *Look Look* by Michael Frayn, with Stephen Fry, Robin Bailey, Margaret Courtenay and Gabrielle Drake, directed by Mike Ockrent, designed by Carl Toms, lighting by David Hersey.

ALMEIDA: Almeida Street, N1. (1989) Sept. 13. Shakespeare's *King Lear* with Richard Haddon-Haines, Desmond Barrit, Patrick Miller and Amanda Root, dir. by Cicely Berry, des. by Chris Dyer (RSC season). Sept. 19. *Kissing the Pope* by Nick Darke, with Christian Dixon, Mark Hadfield, Edward Peel and Richard Bremner, dir. by Roger Michell. Sept. 28. *H.I.D.* (*Hess is Dead*) by Howard Brenton, with David Calder, Pip Donaghy, Penny Downie, Polly Walker and Diane Fletcher, dir. by Danny Boyle. Nov. 28. *Lady Betty* by Declan Donnellan, with Sally Dexter, Gerard O'Hare and Ray McBride, dir. by Declan Donnellan, des. by Nick Ormerod (Cheek by Jowl prodn.). (1990). Jan. 9. *Scenes from an Execution* by Howard Barker, with Glenda Jackson, Jonathan Hyde and Kevin McNally, dir. by Ian McDiarmid, des. by David Fielding. Feb. 20. *When We Dead Awaken* by Henrik Ibsen (trans. by David Rudkin), with Espen Skjönberg, Claire Bloom, Suzanne Burden and Miles Anderson, dir. by Jonathan Kent, des. by Peter J. Davison. March 29. *Volpone* by Ben Jonson, with Ian McDiarmid, Denis Lawson, Philip Locke, Marc Warren and Cyril Shaps, dir. by Nicholas Hytner, des. by Mark Thompson. May 14. *Desire* by David Lan, with Vicky Licorish, Marcia Myrie, Louis Mahoney and Cyril Nri, dir. by Andrei Serban, des. by Richard Hudson.

APOLLO: Shaftesbury Avenue, W1. (1989) Oct. 17. *Jeffrey Bernard Is Unwell* by Keith Waterhouse, with Peter O'Toole, Sarah Berger, Annabel Leventon, Timothy Ackroyd and Royce Mills, dir. by Ned Sherrin, des. by John Gunter.

BARBICAN: EC2. (1989) Sept. 21. *The Master Builder* by Henrik Ibsen, with John Wood, Joanne Pearce, Alfred Burke, Geraldine Alexander and Marjorie Yates, dir. by Adrian Noble, des. by Richard Hudson. Nov. 20. Shakespeare's *Hamlet*, with Mark Rylance, Clare Higgins, Rebecca Saire and Peter Wight, dir. by Ron Daniels, des. by Antony McDonald. Dec. 4. Shakespeare's *A Midsummer Night's Dream*, with John Carlisle, Clare Higgins, Amanda Bellamy, Richard McCabe, Sarah Crowden, Paul Lacoux, Stephens Simms and David Troughton, dir. by John Caird, des. by Sue Blane. (1990) Feb. 6. *A Clockwork Orange—2004* by Anthony Burgess, with Phil Daniels, John Hannah, Linda Spurrier, Mark Brignall and Patrick Brennan, dir. by Ron Daniels, des. by Richard Hudson, music by the Edge and Bono (U2), chor. by Arlene Phillips. March 30. Shakespeare's *All's Well That Ends Well*, with Gwen Watford, Patricia Kerrigan, Hugh Ross, Bruce Alexander and Paul Venables, dir. by Barry Kyle, des. by Chris Dyer. April 11. Shakespeare's *As You Like It*, with Sophie Thompson, Jerome Flynn, Mark Williams, Gillian Bevan, Clifford Rose and Hugh Ross, dir. by John

Caird, des. by Ultz. May 2. Shakespeare's *Coriolanus*, with Charles Dance, Barbara Jefford, Joe Melia, Geoffrey Freshwater, Malcolm Storry and Joseph O'Conor, dir. by Terry Hands with John Barton, des. by Christopher Morley. July 12. *Singer* by Peter Flannery (transferred from the Pit). July 19. *Barbarians* by Maxim Gorky (trans. by Jeremy Brooks and Kitty Hunter-Blair), with Stephen Boxer, Peter Egan, Mick Ford, Barbara Jefford, Joe Melia and Louise Jameson, dir. by David Jones, des. by Tazeena Firth.

BARBICAN PIT: (1989). Sept. 27. *Mary and Lizzie* by Frank McGuinness, with Lesley Sharp, Maureen Beattie, Simon Russell Beale, Simon Dormandy, Robert Demeger and Nicholas Woodeson, dir. by Sarah Pia Anderson. Nov. 20. *Dr. Faustus* by Christopher Marlowe, with Gerard Murphy and David Bradley, dir. by Barry Kyle, des. by Ashley Martin-Davies. Nov. 29. *Playing with Trains* by Stephen Poliakoff, with Michael Pennington, Simon Russell Beale and Lesley Sharp, dir. by Ron Daniels, des. by KitSurrey. Dec. 13. Shakespeare's *Romeo and Juliet*, with Mark Rylance and Georgia Slowe, dir. by Terry Hands, des. by Farrah. (1990) Jan. 30. *Have* by Julius Hay, with Estelle Kohler, Naomi Wirthner, Rob Heyland and John Ramm, dir. by Janice Honeyman, des. by Johan Engels. March 28. *Singer* by Peter Flannery, with Antony Sher, Malcolm Storry, Mick Ford and Joe Melia, dir. by Terry Hands, des. by Sanja Jurca Avci. April 12. Shakespeare's *Pericles*, with Rob Edwards, Suzan Sylvester, Rudolph Walker, Sally Edwards, dir. by David Thacker, des. by Fran Thompson. May 1. *The Duchess of Malfi* by John Webster, with Harriet Walter, Mick Ford, Stephen Boxer, Bruce Alexander and Russell Dixon, dir. by Bill Alexander, des. by Fotini Dimou. July 12. *Earwig* by Paula Milne, with Lisa Harrow, Peter Birrel, Ian Driver, Clive Russell and Sally Edwards, dir. by Ron Daniels, des. by Ralph Kiltai and Sue Formston. July 19. *A Dream of People* by Michael Hastings, with Peter McEnery, Clifford Rose, Judy Parfitt and Helen Ryan, dir. by Janet Suzman, des. by Johan Engels.

BUSH: Shepherd's Bush Green, W12. (1990) March 2. *Jackets 2* by Edward Bond, with Tom Hudson, William Whymper and Steve Ullathorne, dir. by Nick Philippou, des. by Anthony Lamble (Leicester Haymarket Outreach Prodn.).

CAMBRIDGE: Earlham Street, Cambridge Circus, WC2. (1989) Sept. 18. *Return to the Forbidden Planet*, written and dir. by Bob Carlton, with Nicky Furre, Kraig Thornber, Matthew Devitt and Allison Harding (Belgrade Theatre, Coventry, prodn.).

COMEDY: Panton Street, WC2. (1989) Dec. 19. *Noël and Gertie* by Sheridan Morley, with Simon Cadell and Patricia Hodge, dir. by Alan Strachan, des. by Carl Toms.

DOMINION: Tottenham Court Road, WC1. (1990) June 21. *Bernadette* by Maureen and Gwyn Hughes, with Natalie Wright, dir. by Ernest Maxin, des. by Martin Collins.

GARRICK: Charing Cross Road, WC2. (1989) Oct. 4. *Paris Match* by Jean Poiret, with Siân Phillips, Sheila Steafel, Stephen Moore and Leslie Ash, dir. by Christopher Renshaw, des. by Douglas Heap. Nov. 29. *Our Country's Good* by Timberlake Wertenbaker (Royal Court prodn.). (1990) March 6. *Bent* by Martin Sherman (National Theatre prodn.).

GATE: Pembridge Road, W11. (1990) Feb. 19. *A Confederacy of Dunces* by John Kennedy Toole, adapted by and featuring Kerry Shale, dir. by John Abbott. May 25. *Punishment Without Revenge* by Lope de Vega, with Paul Mooney, Sara Mair-Thomas and David Sumner, dir. by Laurence Boswell.

GLOBE: Shaftesbury Avenue, W1. (1990) Feb. 14. *Man of the Moment* by Alan Ayckbourn, with Michael Gambon, Peter Bowles, Diane Bull, Samantha Bond and Shirley-Anne Selby, dir. by Alan Ayckbourn, des. by Roger Glossop.

GREENWICH: Croom's Hill, SE10. (1989) Oct. 16. *The Talk of the Steamie* by Tony Roper, with Myra McFadyen, Julia McCarthy, Judy Sweeney and Emma Dingwall, dir. by Alex Norton, des. by Sally Crabb. (1990) June 28. *A Single Man* by Christopher Isherwood (adapted by Michael Michaelian), with Alec McCowen, Rosemary Martin, Neil Roberts and Barbara Barnes, dir. by Waris Hussein.

HAMPSTEAD: Swiss Cottage, NW3. (1989) Aug. 29. *The Water Engine* by David Mamet, with Nick Dunning, Stephen Boxer and Peter Whitman, dir. by Robin Lefevre, des. by Robin Don. Dec. 15. *Treats* by Christopher Hampton, with Tom Conti, Julia Ormond and Peter Capaldi, dir. by Geraldine McEwan. (1990) Jan. 22. *Valued Friends* by Stephen Jeffreys, with Michael Angelis, Josie Lawrence, Jimmy Mulville and Louisa Rix. March 7. *Saint Oscar* by Terry Eagleton, with Stephen Rea, Eileen Pollock, Seamus Moran and Brendan Gleeson, dir. by Trevor Griffiths, des. by Bob Crowley. April 19. *The Awakening* by Julian Garner, with Linda Bassett, Paul Copley, Con O'Neill and Gabrielle Reidy, dir. by John Dove. May 29. *Burn This* by Lanford Wilson, with John Malkovich, Juliet Stevenson, Lou Liberatore and Michael Simpkins, dir. by Robert Allan Ackerman. June 13. *Sugar Hill Blues* by Kevin Hood, with Liza Sadovy, Pauline Black, Simon Slater and Okon Jones, dir. by Ted Craig.

HAYMARKET THEATRE ROYAL: SW1. (1989) Oct. 31. *A life in the Theatre* by David Mamet, with Denholm Elliott and Samuel West, dir. by Bill Bryden. Dec. 13. *London Assurance* by Dion Boucicault, with Paul Eddington, Angela Thorne and Sarah Woodward, dir. by Sam Mendes, des. by Daphne Dare (Chichester Festival prodn.). (1990) June 1. *Gasping* by Ben Elton, with Hugh Laurie, Bernard Hill, Simon Mattacks and Jaye Griffiths, dir. by Bob Spiers, des. by Terry Parsons.

LILIAN BAYLIS: Sadler's Wells, EC1. (1990) June 5. *Sara* by G. E. Lessing, with Rachel Joyce, Sheila Gish, Raad Rawi and Daniel Thorndike, dir. by Declan Donnellan, des. by Nick Ormerod (Cheek by Jowl prodn.).

LONDON PALLADIUM: Argyll Street, W1. (1990) March 26. *The Pirates of Penzance* by Gilbert and Sullivan, with Paul Nicholas, Bonnie Langford, Simon Browne and Frank Thornton, dir. by Peter Walker. July 25. *Show Boat* by Jerome Kern and Oscar Hammerstein II, dir. by Ian Judge (RSC and Opera North prodn.).

LYRIC: Hammersmith, W6. (1989) Oct. 17. *Faith, Hope and Charity* by Ödön von Horváth with Wilhelm Lukas Kristi (trans. by Christopher Hampton), with Julia Ormond and Stephen Boxer, dir. by Heribert Sasse, des. by Santiago del Corral. Dec. 21. *Thark* by Ben Travers, with Griff Rhys Jones, Dinsdale Landen, Hugh Lloyd, Sonia Ritter and Helen Lindsay, dir. by Peter James. (1990) April 24. *Glory!* by Felix Cross, with Adjoa Andoh, Alan Cook and Oscar James, dir. by Earl Warner, des. by Vonnie Roudette (Temba prodn.). July 19. *Morte d'Arthur*, dramatized and dir. by David Freeman, with Jacques Bourgaux, David Hobbs, Mark Lewis Jones, Belinda Davison, Lucinda Galloway and Katharine Roger, des. by David Roger.

LYRIC—STUDIO: Hammersmith, W6. (1990) Jan. 18. *In Pursuit of the English* by Katie Campbell, with Sheila Reid, Melanie Jessop, Pippa Guard and

Richard Avery, dir. by Matthew Francis. Feb. 17. *Hangover Square* by Fidelis Morgan, with Dudley Sutton, Celia Imrie, Anne Lambton and Ian Reddington, dir. by Caroline Sherman. March 5. *The Vanek Plays* by Vaclav Havel, with John Peters, Simon Mattacks, Louise Bangay and Tom Knight, dir. by Peter Casterton. April 17. *Crux* by April de Angelis, with Kathy Burke, Christina Jones, Anna Keaveney and David Mallinson, dir. by Saffron Myers, des. by Catherine Armstrong (Paines Plough prodn.).

LYRIC: Shaftesbury Avenue, W1. (1989) Oct. 19. *Stop the World I Want to Get Off* by Anthony Newley and Lesley Bricusse, featuring and dir. by Anthony Newley, with Rhonda Burchmore, des. by Mark Hinton. Dec. 1. *Prin* by Andrew Davies (transferred from Lyric, Hammersmith). (1990) March. *Bus Stop* by William Inge, with Jerry Hall, Shaun Cassidy and David Healy, dir. by Phil Oesterman, des. by Tim Goodchild. May 16. *Vanilla* by Jane Stanton Hitchcock, with Joanna Lumley, Siân Phillips, Gwen Humble, Ron Cook, Charlotte Cornwell and Greg Hicks, dir. by Harold Pinter, des. by Hayden Griffin.

MERMAID: Puddle Dock, Blackfriars, EC4. (1990) March 20. *How Steeple Sinderby Wanderers Won the FA Cup* by J. L. Carr (adapted by Christopher Lillicrap and Mike Fields), with Phil Croft, Karen Davies and Justine Midda, dir. by Mike Fields. July 4. *Mother Courage* by Bertolt Brecht (trans. from Glasgow Citizens' Theatre).

NATIONAL THEATRE: South Bank, SE1. COTTESLOE: (1989) Sept. 7. *Man, Beast and Virtue* by Pirandello (adapted by Charles Wood), with Marion Bailey, Terence Rigby and Trevor Eve, dir. by William Gaskill, des. by Annie Smart. Oct. 25. *Ma Rainey's Black Bottom* by August Wilson, with Carol Woods-Coleman, Hugh Quarshie, William Hoyland, George Harris, Tommy Eytle and Clarke Peters, dir. by Howard Davies, des. by Bob Crowley, music by Neil McArthur. (1990) Feb. 1. *Racing Demon* by David Hare, with David Bamber, Michael Bryant, Stella Gonet, Barbara Leigh-Hunt, Oliver Ford Davies, Richard Pasco and Adam Kotz, dir. by Richard Eyre, des. by Bob Crowley. March 29. *Abingdon Square* by Maria Irene Fornes, with Philip Voss, Annabelle Apsion, Pearce Quigley and Christopher Eccleston, dir. by Nancy Meckler, des. by Lucy Weller. April 18. *Tartuffe* by Molière, with Bhasker, Ayub Khan Din, Shelley King, Nizwar Karanj and Yogesh Bhatt, dir. by Jatinder Verma, des. by Magdalen Rubalcava (Tara Arts prodn.). May 9. *Berenice* by Racine (trans. by Neil Bartlett), with Lindsay Duncan, David Haig, Owen Teale and Kevin O'Donohoe, dir. by Tim Albery, des. by Antony McDonald. June 15. *After the Fall* by Arthur Miller, with James Laurenson, Josette Simon, Lois Baxter, Shelley Thompson and Garrick Hagon, dir. by Michael Blakemore, des. by Hayden Griffin. Aug. *Piano* by Trevor Griffiths, with Penelope Wilton, Geoffrey Palmer, Oliver Cotton, Basil Henson, Philip Voss and Stephen Rea, dir. by Howard Davies, des. by Ashley Martin-Davis.

LYTTLETON: (1989) Sept. 14. *Uncle Vanya* by Anton Chekov, with Innokenti Smoktunovski, dir. by Oleg Yefremov, des. by V. Ya Levental, (Moscow Arts Theatre Co.). Oct. 9. *Suicide for Love* by Matsuyo Akimoto, dir. by Yukio Ninagawa (Tokyo Ninagawa Co.). Nov. 7. *Salome* by Oscar Wilde, with Steven Berkoff, Katharine Schlesinger, Carmen Du Sautoy and Rory Edwards, dir. by Steven Berkoff, des. by Robert Ballagh (Gate Theatre, Dublin, prodn.). Nov. 10. *The Beaux' Strategem* by George Farquhar, with Brenda Blethyn, Allan Corduner, Harold Innocent, Paul Mooney and Marc Sinden, dir. by Peter Wood, des. by Peter J. Davison (joint prodn. with Belgrade Theatre, Coventry). Dec. 7. *Whale* by David Holman, with Peter Caffrey, Maggie Steed and Toyah

Wilcox, dir. by Tim Supple, des. by Ashley Martin-Davis. (1990) Jan. 5. *Bent* by Martin Sherman with Ian McKellen, Michael Cashman, Paul Rhys and Robert Eddison, dir. by Sean Mathias, des. by Michael Vale. March 15. *Sunday in the Park with George* by Stephen Sondheim and James Lapine, with Philip Quast, Maria Friedman, Nyree Dawn Porter and Gary Raymond, dir. by Steven Pimlott, des. by Tom Cairns, mus. dir. by Jeremy Sams, chor. by Aletta Collins. July 25. Shakespeare's *Richard III* with Ian McKellen, Susan Engel, Eve Matheson, Clare Higgins, Peter Jeffrey and Brian Cox, dir. by Richard Eyre, des. by Bob Crowley. July 26. Shakespeare's *King Lear* with Brian Cox, Ian McKellen, Susan Engel, Clare Higgins, Eve Matheson, David Bradley, Derek Hutchinson and Peter Jeffrey, dir. by Deborah Warner, des. by Hildegard Bechtler.

OLIVIER: (1989) Nov. 28. *The Good Person of Sichuan* by Bertolt Brecht (trans. by Michael Hoffman), with Fiona Shaw, Bill Paterson, Moira Charles and Alison Peebles, dir. by Deborah Warner, des. by Sue Blane. (1990) Feb. 28. *Peer Gynt* by Henrik Ibsen (adapted by Kenneth McLeish), with Stephen Moore, David Morrissey, Philip Voss, Alison Peebles, Sara Mair-Thomas, Meera Syal and Mona Hammond, dir. by Declan Donnellan, des. by Nick Ormerod. March 27. *The Trackers of Oxyrhynchus*, trans., adapted and dir. by Tony Harrison, with Jack Shepherd, Barrie Rutter and Brian Glover, des. by Jocelyn Herbert. April 24. *The School for Scandal* by R. B. Sheridan, with John Neville, Jane Asher, Denis Quilley, Prunella Scales, Diana Hardcastle, Jeremy Northam and Alfred Lynch, dir. by Peter Wood, des. by John Gunter. May 31. *The Crucible* by Arthur Miller, with Tom Wilkinson, Zoë Wanamaker, Clare Holman, Michael Bryant, Julia Ford, David Burke and Oliver Cotton, dir. by Howard Davies, des. by William Dudley. Aug. 2. *Racing Demon* by David Hare (trans. from Cottesloe).

NEW END: Hampstead, NW3. (1989) Oct. 5. *The Devil and Stepashka* by Claire Booker, with David Beckett, Terence Budd, Miriam Cooper and Penelope Asquith, dir. by David Gillies.

OLD VIC: The Cut, SE1. (1989) Nov. 21. Shakespeare's *Hamlet*, with Daniel Webb, Andrew Jarvis, Anne White and Veronica Smart, dir. by Yur Lyubimov (Leicester Haymarket prodn.). Dec. 7. *The Liar* by Corneille (trans. by Ranjit Bolt), with Alex Jennings, Christine Kavanagh and Desmond Barrit, dir. by Jonathan Miller, des. by Peter J. Davison. (1990) March 29. *Marya* by Isaac Babel (trans. by Michael Glenny and Harold Shukman, adapted by Christopher Hampton), with Robert Demeger, Allan Corduner, Julie Legrand and Sylvestra le Touzel, dir. by Roger Michell, des. by William Dudley. June 12. *The Illusion* by Corneille (trans. by Ranjit Bolt), with Clive Swift, Sylvestra le Touzel, Duncan Bell and Siân Thomas, dir. by Richard Jones, des. by Nigel Lowery. July 31. *Kean* by Jean-Paul Sartre (trans. by Frank Hauser), with Derek Jacobi, Eleanor David, Nicholas Farrell, Ian McNeice and Sarah Woodward, dir. by Sam Mendes, des. by Simon Higlett.

OPEN AIR: Regent's Park, NW1. (1990) May 29. Shakespeare's *Much Ado About Nothing*, with Karl Johnson, Susan Tracy, Martin Clunes, Tilly Blackwood, Patrick O'Connell and John Hart Dyke, dir. by Lindsay Posner, des. by Julian McGowan. June 13. Shakespeare's *Julius Caesar*, with Patrick O'Connell, Martin Clunes, Des McAleer and Pip Donaghy, dir. by Caroline Smith, des. by Michael Holt. July 23. *The Fantasticks*, book and lyrics by Tom Jones, music by Harvey Schmidt, with Roy Hudd, Emma Amos, Anthony Barclay, Anthony O'Donnell and Erick Ray Evans, dir. by Ian Talbot, des. by Paul Farnsworth.

PHOENIX: Charing Cross Road, WC2. (1989) Nov. 27. *The Baker's Wife*, book by Joseph Stein, music and lyrics by Stephen Schwarz, with Alun Armstrong, Sharon Lee Hill, James Villiers, George Raistrick and Jill Martin, dir. by Trevor Nunn, des. by John Napier. (1990) Jan. 20. *Salome* by Oscar Wilde (trans. from Lyttelton). May 17. *The Wild Duck* by Henrik Ibsen (trans. by Peter Hall and Inga-Stina Ewbank), with David Threlfall, Nichola Mc-Auliffe, Alex Jennings, Maria Miles, Lionel Jefferies, Alan Dobie and Terence Rigby, dir. by Peter Hall, des. by John Bury.

PICCADILLY: Denman Street, W1. (1989) Oct. 10. *A Little Night Music*, music and lyrics by Stephen Sondheim, book by Hugh Wheeler, with Dorothy Tutin, Peter McEnery, Susan Hampshire, Eric Flynn and Lila Kedrova, dir. by Ian Judge, des. by Mark Thompson. (1990) April 23. *King*, music by Richard Blackford, lyrics by Maya Angelou and Alistair Beaton, book by Ron Milner and Lonne Elder, with Simon Estes, Cynthia Haymon, Godfrey James, Ray Shell and Clarke Peters, dir. by Clarke Peters, des. by Timothy O'Brien, mus. dir. by Fiz Shapur, chor. by Dianne McIntyre. July 16. *The Rocky Horror Show* by Richard O'Brien, with Adrian Edmondson, Tim McInnerny, Gina Bellman and Adam Caine, dir. by Robin Lefevre, des. by Robin Don.

PLAYHOUSE: Northumberland Avenue, WC2. (1989) Sept. 6. *Boswell for the Defence* by Patrick Edgeworth, with Leo McKern, dir. by Frank Hauser, des. by Kristian Fredrickson. (1990) Jan. 16. *Diversions and Delights* by John Gay, with Donald Sinden. March 29. *Never the Sinner* by John Logan, with Joss Ackland, Julian Glover, Denis O'Hare and Ben Daniels.

QUEEN'S: Shaftesbury Avenue, W1. (1989) Oct. 23. *Shadowlands* by William Nicholson, with Nigel Hawthorne and Jane Lapotaire, dir. by Elijah Moshinsky, des. by Mark Thompson.

RIVERSIDE STUDIOS: Hammersmith, W6. (1990) Jan. 11. *Krapp's Last Tape/Catastrophe* by Samuel Beckett, with Tom Knight, Christina Paul and David Warrilow, dir. by Antoni Libera (Leicester Haymarket prodn.). Feb. 26. *Say Hallelujah* by Jimi Rand, with Anthony Lorriette, Stephan Kalipha, Herbert Norville and Basil Otoin.

ROYAL COURT: Sloane Square, W1. (1989) Sept. 26. *The Astronomer's Garden* by Kevin Hood, with John Arnatt, Charlotte Attenborough, Emily Richard and Robin Sachs, dir. by Ted Craig, des. by Michael Pavelka. Oct. 17. *Apples* by Ian Dury and Mickey Gallagher, with Ian Dury, Jessie Birdsall, Pam Ferris and Bob Goody, dir. by Simon Curtis, des. by Richard Hudson. (1990) Jan. 5. *Seven Lears* by Howard Barker, with Nicholas le Prevost, Tricia Kelly, Philippa Vafadari and Jemma Redgrave, dir. by Kenny Ireland. Feb. 13. *My Heart's a Suitcase* by Clare McIntyre, with Frances Barber, Sylvestra le Touzel and Anna Patrick, dir. by Max Stafford-Clark, des. by Annabelle Temple. April 4. *Beside Herself* by Sarah Daniels, with Marion Bailey, Nick Dunning, Dinah Stabb, Julia Hills and Tenniel Evans, dir. by Jules Wright, des. by Jenny Tiramani (co-prodn. with Women's Playhouse Trust). May 11. *In the Ruins* by Nick Dear, with Patrick Malahide, dir. by Paul Unwin, des. by Annabelle Temple. July 24. *Three Sisters* by Anton Chekov, with Sinead Cusack, Sorcha Cusack, Niamh Cusack, Cyril Cusack, Nicky Henson and Lesley Manville, dir. by Adrian Noble, des. by Bob Crowley (Dublin Gate Theatre prodn.).

ROYALTY: Kingsway, WC2. (1990) April 23. *A Clockwork Orange—2004* by Anthony Burgess (trans. from Barbican).

STRAND: Aldwych, WC2. (1989) Sept. 19. *Exclusive* by Jeffrey Archer, with Paul Scofield, Eileen Atkins, Alec McCowen and Steven Pacey, dir. by Michael Rudman, des. by Timothy O'Brien. Dec. 13. *A Life in the Theatre* by David Mamet (trans. from Haymarket Theatre Royal). (1990) March 22. *Someone Like You*, lyrics by Petula Clark and Dee Shipman, book by Robin Midgley and Fay Weldon, with Petula Clark, Dave Willetts and Clive Carter, dir. by Robin Midgley, des. by Tim Goodchild, mus. dir. by Kenny Clayton.

THEATRE ROYAL: Drury Lane, WC2. (1989) Sept. 20. *Miss Saigon*, music by Claude-Michel Schonberg, lyrics by Richard Maltby jun. and Alain Boublil, with Jonathan Pryce, Simon Bowman, Lea Salonga, dir. by Nicholas Hytner, des. by John Napier, chor. by Bob Avian.

THEATRE ROYAL: Stratford East, E15. (1989) Oct. 24. *Rent Party* by Alan Plater, with Louis Emerick, Polly Hemingway and John Turner, dir. by Philip Hedley, des. by Robin Don. (1990) March 14. *Revolting Peasants* by Patrick Prior, with Bill Thomas, Alan Cowan and Yvonne Edgell, dir. by Jeff Teare. April 19. *Not Fade Away* by Barry Keeffe, with Miriam Karlin, Paul Barber and Angela Bruce, dir. by Philip Hedley.

TRICYCLE: Kilburn High Road, NW6. (1990) May 8. *Fashion* by Doug Lucie, with Paul Freeman, Jim Carter and Robin Soans, dir. by Michael Attenborough, des. by Michael Pavelka. July 12. *Remembrance* by Derek Walcott, with Norman Beaton and Mabel Jordan, dir. by Anton Phillips.

VAUDEVILLE: Strand, WC2. (1989) Sept. 19. *Re:Joyce!* with Maureen Lipman and Denis King, dir. by Alan Strachan. Dec. 4. *Barnaby and the Old Boys* by Keith Baxter, with Jill Gascoigne, Robert Gwilym, Brian Croucher, Jennifer Hilary, Deborah Norton and Keith Baxter, dir. by Toby Robertson, des. by Douglas Heap (Nuffield Theatre, Southampton prodn.). (1990) Feb. 19. *Exchange* by Yuri Trifonov (trans. by Michael Frayn), with Martin Jarvis, Doreen Mantle and Rosalind Ayres, dir. by Patrick Sandford, des. by Tanya McCallin. June 12. *Hidden Laughter* by Simon Gray, with Felicity Kendal, Peter Barkworth, Richard Vernon and Kevin McNally, dir. by Simon Gray, des. by Robin Don.

VICTORIA PALACE: SW1. (1989) Oct. 12. *Buddy* by Alan James, with Paul Hipp, Gareth Marks, David Howarth and David Bardsley, dir. by Rob Bettinson, des. by Andy Walmsley (Plymouth Theatre Royal prodn.).

WESTMINSTER: Palace Street, SW1. (1990) June 6. *Temptation* by Vaclav Havel (trans. by George Theiner), with Sylvester McCoy, Rula Lenska, Frank Middlemass and Aden Gillett, dir. by James Roose-Evans, des. by Bruno Santini and Mike Roberts.

WHITEHALL: SW1. (1990) May 15. *Absurd Person Singular*, written and dir. by Alan Ayckbourn, with Richard Kane, Lavinia Bertram, Donald Douglas and Moira Redmond, des. by Michael Holt (Stephen Joseph Theatre, Scarborough, prodn.).

WYNDHAM'S: Charing Cross Road, WC2. (1989) Sept. 25. *Another Time* by Ronald Harwood, with Albert Finney, Janet Suzman, Sara Kestelman, David de Keyser and Christien Anholt, dir. by Elijah Moshinsky, des. by Saul Radomsky. (1990) April 18. *Abracadaver* by Allan Scott and David Ambrose, with Frank Langella, Elizabeth Bennett and Miriam Cyr, dir. by Richard Oliver, des. by Terry Parsons. May 23. *Henry IV* by Pirandello (trans. by John Wardle and Robert Rietty), with Richard Harris, Ian Hogg, Harold Innocent and Isla Blair, dir. by Val May, des. by Tim Goodchild.

YOUNG VIC: 66 The Cut, SE1. (1990) Feb. 7. *The Price* by Arthur Miller, with David Calder, Alan MacNaughtan, Marjorie Yates and Bob Peck, dir. by David Thacker, des. by Fran Thompson. June 14. *Anna Christie* by Eugene O'Neill, with Natasha Richardson, John Woodvine, Marjorie Yates and David Herlihy, dir. by David Thacker, des. by Shelagh Keegan. Aug. *The Man Who Had All the Luck* by Arthur Miller, with Iain Glen, Rudi Davies, Christopher Ettridge and Barry Stanton, dir. by Paul Unwin, des. by Sally Crabb, music by Andy Sheppard.

Productions outside London included the following:

STRATFORD MEMORIAL THEATRE: (Royal Shakespeare Company) (1989) Sept. 13. *As You Like It* with Sophie Thompson, Gillian Bevan, Clifford Rose, Hugh Ross, Mark Williams and Jerome Flynn, dir. by John Caird, des. by Ultz. Oct. 10. *All's Well that Ends Well* with Gwen Watford, Patricia Kerrigan, Hugh Ross, Paul Venables, Bruce Alexander and Clifford Rose, dir. by Barry Kyle, des. by Chris Dyer. Dec. 5. *Coriolanus* with Charles Dance, Barbara Jefford, Joe Melia, Malcolm Storry, Joseph O'Conor and Geoffrey Freshwater, dir. by Terry Hands with John Barton, des. by Christopher Morley. (1990) Feb. 13. *Show Boat* by Jerome Kern and Oscar Hammerstein II, dir. by Ian Judge (co-prodn. with Opera North). April 5. *Much Ado About Nothing* with Roger Allam, Susan Fleetwood, Alex Kingston, Vincent Regan, John McAndrew, John Carlisle and George Raistrick, dir. by Bill Alexander, des. by Kit Surrey. April 25. *The Comedy of Errors* with Desmond Barrit, Graham Turner, David Waller, David Killick and Estelle Kohler, dir. by Ian Judge, des. by Mark Thompson. July 11. *King Lear* with John Wood, Estelle Kohler, Alex Kingston, Sally Dexter, Norman Rodway, David Troughton, Linda Kerr Scott and Linus Roache, dir. by Nicholas Hytner, des. by David Fielding.

THE SWAN: (1989) Sept. 6. *Pericles* with Nigel Terry, Suzan Sylvester, Rudolph Walker and Sally Edwards, dir. by David Thacker, des. by Fran Thompson. Sept. 27. *Singer* by Peter Flannery, with Antony Sher, Joe Melia, Malcolm Storry and Mick Ford, dir. by Terry Hands, des. by Sanja Jurca Avci, music by Ilona Sekacz. Dec. 6. *The Duchess of Malfi* by John Webster, with Harriet Walter, Nigel Terry, Mick Ford, Russell Dixon and Bruce Alexander, dir. by Bill Alexander, des. by Fotini Dimou. (1990) March 28. *The Last Days of Don Juan* by Tirso de Mølina (adapted by Nick Dear), with Linus Roache, Sally Dexter, Ciaran Hinds, Paterson Joseph, Catherine White and Sylvester Morand, dir. by Danny Boyle, des. by Kandis Cook. April 26. *Troilus and Cressida* with Amanda Root, Ralph Fiennes, Simon Russell Beale, Alfred Burke, David Troughton, Norman Rodway and Ciaran Hinds, dir. by Sam Mendes, des. by Anthony Ward. June 27. *Edward II* by Christopher Marlowe, with Simon Russell Beale,

Katy Behean, Grant Thatcher, Ciaran Hinds, David Killick and John Warnaby, dir. by Gerard Murphy, des. by Sandy Powell.

CHICHESTER FESTIVAL: (1990) May 2. Shakespeare's *The Merry Wives of Windsor*, with Penelope Keith, Bill Maynard, Barbara Ferris, Brian Matthew, Richard Moore and Phyllida Law, dir. by Michael Rudman, des. by Hugh Durrant. May 23. *The Power and the Glory* by Graham Greene (adapted by Denis Cannan), with Edward Petherbridge, Penny Downie, Alan Howard, Peter Guinness, John Turner and Jeffery Wickham, dir. by Tim Luscombe, des. by Paul Farnsworth. July 9. *The Silver King* by Henry Arthur Jones and Henry Herman, with Alan Howard, Jessica Turner, Lucy Baker, Richard Moore and Garry Cooper, dir. by Peter Wood, des. by Carl Toms. July 30. *Rumours* by Neil Simon, with Simon Ward, Una Stubbs.

EDINBURGH: ROYAL LYCEUM: (1989) Sept. *Volpone* by Ben Johnson, with Dudley Sutton, Paul Spence and Victoria Hardcastle, dir. by Hugh Hodgart, des. by Gregory Smith.

GLASGOW: CITIZENS': (1990) May. *Mother Courage* by Bertolt Brecht, with Glenda Jackson, Jane Bertish and Laurance Rudic, dir. by Philip Prowse.

LEICESTER: HAYMARKET STUDIO: (1990) Jan. 25. *The Naked* by Luigi Pirandello (trans. by Diane Cilento), with Stephen Caro, Kevin Costello and Fenella Fielding, dir. by Simon Usher, des. by Anthony Lamble.

MANCHESTER: ROYAL EXCHANGE: (1989) Sept. 14. *The Parasol* by Anton Chekhov (adapted by Frank Dunai), with Simon Cadell and Maggie O'Neill, dir. by Tim Luscombe, des. by Anthony Ward. Oct. 26. *Winding the Ball* by Alex Finlayson, with Lisa Eichhorn, Gordon Case, Roberta Taylor, Ian Bartholomew and Trevor Cooper, dir. by Gregory Hersov. Dec. 21. *She Stoops to Conquer* by Oliver Goldsmith, with Una Stubbs, Ewan Hooper, Karen Drury and Andy Serkis, dir. by James Maxwell, des. by David Millard. (1990) Feb. 8. Shakespeare's *The Winter's Tale*, with Sean Baker, Barbara Marten, Myra McFadyen, Adrian Lester and Claire Hackett, dir. by Phyllida Lloyd. March 23. *The Crucible* by Arthur Miller, with Barry Foster, David Allister, Theresa Boden, David Schofield, Rosalind Bennett and Eleanor David, dir. by Gregory Hersov, des. by Michael Holt, Chris Parry and Alastair Goolden. May 10. *The School for Scandal* by R. B. Sheridan, with Kelly Hunter, Anne Lambton, Deborah Norton, Peter Darling, Ian Bartholomew, Trevor Baxter and John Nettleton, dir. by Phillida Lloyd.

SCARBOROUGH: STEPHEN JOSEPH THEATRE: (1990) May 21. *Body Language* by Alan Ayckbourn, with Lia Williams, Tam Hoskyns, Peter Forbes, Nigel Anthony and Cecily Hobbs, dir. by Alan Ayckbourn.

OPERA, 1989–90

In his 1989 Autumn statement, the Chancellor of the Exchequer announced a 12·5 per cent increase in the Government grant to the arts. As a result the Arts Council was able to offer a rise of 11 per cent to the Royal Opera and to English National Opera. In addition, Opera North, Scottish Opera, Glyndebourne Touring Opera and Opera 80 were offered 8 per cent extra in funding for touring purposes. However, finance continued to be a major difficulty for many companies. Kent Opera, reprieved in January 1988, was finally axed by the Arts Council, which announced the withdrawal of its funding from December 1989 only days after the appointment had been announced of the new artistic director, Ivan Fischer. Consequently, the advertised performances of Kent Opera's production of *King Priam* at Covent Garden, intended as an 85th birthday tribute to Sir Michael Tippett, did not take place.

After considerable modification, the Royal Opera's £175 million redevelopment scheme in Covent Garden was finally approved by Westminster City Council. The work will take about three years, resulting in the closure of the opera house between 1993 and 1996. Artistically, the Royal Opera earned rather better notices in 1989–90 than in the past two or three seasons. Owing to differences between the conductor, Bernard Haitink, and the producer, Yuri Lyubimov, the *Ring* cycle begun the previous season with *Das Rheingold* was cancelled and another production, staged by Götz Friedrich, was borrowed from the Deutsche Oper, Berlin. Reviews of *Die Walküre*, which opened the season, were cautious in tone, most reviewers preferring to wait for the complete cycle before committing themselves. The other new productions at Covent Garden were given varied receptions: *Médée, Idomeneo* and *La Cenerentola* were generally condemned; *Prince Igor, Elektra* and *Guillaume Tell* on the whole won praise, while *The Cunning Little Vixen* (sung in English) sent audiences and critics alike into raptures.

Clarissa

English National Opera scored a higher ratio of success to failure. The world premiere of *Clarissa*, second in the company's series of British opera commissions, won considerable respect. Robin Holloway began his opera, an adaptation of the novel by Samuel Richardson, some 14 years ago, but has managed to keep the original inspiration behind his composition at white heat. A gripping production by David Pountney saw to it that tension was never allowed to sag. Two new stagings of Verdi operas, *A Masked Ball* and *Macbeth*, produced by David Alden and Pountney respectively, received mixed verdicts from the critics, but were both extremely popular with the public. David Freeman's staging of *The Return of Ulysses* was generally admired, but did not have quite the overwhelming effect of his previous production for ENO of Monteverdi's *Orfeo*. Despite an excellent performance and the veneration felt by Berlioz by Shakespeare, *Beatrice and Benedict* was found a little disappointing. At the end of the London season, English National Opera went on a three-week tour of the USSR. The opening in Kiev, timed to coincide with the trade and cultural exhibition

'British Days in the USSR', was followed by visits to Moscow and Leningrad. The three operas taken by the company—Nicholas Hytner's award-winning production of *Xerxes*, the new *Macbeth* and Jonathan Miller's staging of *The Turn of the Screw*—were rapturously received by the Soviet audiences.

Opera North, who managed to balance their budget for the third year running, announced the appointment of Paul Daniel to succeed David Lloyd Jones as musical director. The company scored heavily with two British first performances: *Jérusalem*, Verdi's reworking of his early opera *I lombardi*, and *Masquerade* by the Danish composer Carl Nielsen, which was mounted as part of the Leeds Festival. Both these productions were highly acclaimed. Even greater praise was lavished on Ian Judge's staging of *Show Boat*, the Jerome Kern musical, a co-production with the Royal Shakespeare Company. After an initial triumph in Leeds, *Show Boat* played at Stratford-upon-Avon and was later transferred to the London Palladium.

Scottish Opera also did well by Verdi, offering a vigorous production of *La forza del destino* with the original prelude and the original version of the final scene, not heard in Britain since 1867. Glasgow, cultural capital of Europe for 1990, played host to the Bolshoi Opera from Moscow in August. To accommodate two of the company's large-scale operas, *Mlada* by Rimsky Korsakov and *The Maid of Orleans* by Tchaikovsky, the Exhibition Centre was converted into a vast theatre. When the Bolshoi moved to the Edinburgh Festival later in the month, the only opera that they were able to present was Prokofiev's *Betrothal in a Monastery*, as no suitable venue for the larger productions was available.

Tornrak

Welsh National Opera boasted a world premiere in *Tornrak* by John Metcalf, jointly commissioned and co-produced by WNO and the Banff Centre, Alberta. Set partly in the Canadian Arctic and partly in nineteenth-century Britain, *Tornrak* compares the noble simplicity of the Inuit (Eskimo) heroine, executed for stealing sheep to feed starving children, with the corruption of a so-called civilized society. Metcalf's score includes themes from Inuit music and examples of Inuit throat-singing. Together with the Musician's Union, WNO commissioned a survey into the salaries of opera musicians. It was discovered that the value of earnings of musicians in opera companies had fallen, not only relative to the salaries of other white-collar workers, but relative to those of musicians in symphony orchestras. Singers in British regional companies are not well paid, either, and according to Brian McMaster, managing director of WNO, the present 'very lively and innovative scene in opera is being maintained at the expense of the artists who create what is seen on the stage'.

Glyndebourne was the scene of unusual controversy. The production of *Die Zauberflöte* by the American director Peter Sellars, which opened the season, aroused a storm of loud and persistent booing, something never heard before in the Sussex opera house. The booing of producers and set designers is not unknown in British opera houses. Both Covent

Garden and the London Coliseum have at times resounded with hostile demonstrations of this sort; but Glyndebourne has not. The factors that particularly annoyed the audience in this case were the setting, the environs of a Los Angeles freeway during the drug-based culture of the 1960s, and the excision of all the dialogue. This was replaced partly by sign language and partly by mid-titles, flashed in neon across the centre of the two-level set. The reviews were predictably awful; a number of traditionally-minded Glyndebourne patrons returned their tickets. At subsequent performances, however, audience reaction, after the first gasp of surprise as the curtain rose, was generally good and word got around that this was one of the most interesting and original productions seen at Glyndebourne for many years. The returned tickets were all rapidly resold. There was one serious consequence. Sir Peter Hall resigned from his position as artistic director because, he claimed, he was not consulted by the management about the cutting of the dialogue and did not discover it until two days before the opening night, presumably at the dress rehearsal. As the decision to cut the dialogue had been made in February and *Die Zauberflöte* opened on May 21, this was hardly the most convincing of reasons.

Hall himself was responsible for the widely admired staging of *New Year*, Sir Michael Tippett's new opera (jointly commissioned by Houston Grand Opera, who gave the premiere last season, Glyndebourne and the BBC), which received its first British performance at the 1990 festival. A space opera, *New Year* has a rich and exhilarating score that it is almost impossible to believe was written by a composer in his eighties. A most important feature of the production was the tremendously energetic choreography of Bill T. Jones.

Festival surprises

Many of the more interesting operatic events of the season were presented by the smaller companies and festivals. The world premiere of *The Intelligence Park* by Gerald Barry (an Irish composer born in 1952) was the most notable event of the 1990 Almeida Festival, held in July. An opera-within-an-opera, *The Intelligence Park* takes place in eighteenth-century Dublin. A composer who has lost his source of inspiration becomes wholly obsessed with the castrato who teaches his fiancée singing. Only after these two have eloped together is the composer's creativity restored. Barry's score, a fascinating mixture of baroque, classical and contemporary elements, is extremely accomplished. At Buxton towards the end of July, the discovery of the festival was *Le Huron* by André Grétry, first produced in 1768 and now receiving its British premiere. Based on Voltaire's novella *L'Ingénu*, the Huron, who has been brought up as a Canadian Indian, travels to France to discover his real parentage. Voltaire's tale ends tragically; Grétry's version, being an *opéra comique*, has the happy ending that is obligatory to the genre. The Buxton production, cleverly and very funnily staged by Jamie Hayes, updated the period to 1914 and set the action at Chatsworth House (not far from Buxton), so that the Huron becomes the long-lost nephew of the Duke of Devonshire. The Ameri-

can Indian theme reappeared in Opera Anglia's staging of *The Cherokee* by Stephen Storace (brother of Nancy Storace, the first Susanna in *Le nozze di Figaro*) at the Queen Elizabeth Hall, London in August. Earlier, in June, the now well-established London International Opera Festival included the first British performance of Zbigniew Rudzinski's chamber opera *Mannekins* at The Place. This delightful work, in which the dummies in a tailor's establishment come to life, deserves wider recognition. The BBC paid its birthday homage to Sir Michael Tippett with a promenade concert at the Albert Hall of *The Ice Break*. The soprano Heather Harper, making her farewell appearance in London, sang Nadia, the role she had created with the Royal Opera at Covent Garden in 1977.

Losses

The operatic world was saddened by the death of Dame Eva Turner, the Lancashire-born dramatic soprano, who died in London on June 16, in her 98th year. Eva Turner is best remembered for her magnificent performances in the title role of *Turandot*, which she sang at La Scala, Milan, as well as at Covent Garden and many other theatres during the 1920s and 1930s. She was also a very fine Brünnhilde and Isolde, a compelling Aida and a fiery Donna Anna in *Don Giovanni*. After her retirement from the opera stage, she became a teacher of high reputation. Three other well-known British sopranos—Amy Shuard, Gwyneth Jones and Pauline Tinsley—studied Turandot with her before singing the part themselves. Dame Eva continued to teach, to lecture and to attend performances of opera until well into her nineties.

Elizabeth Harwood, the British soprano who also died in June 1990, aged only 52 years, had a much shorter, though very distinguished career. She sang with Sadler's Wells Opera (later English National Opera), at Covent Garden and at Glyndebourne, in a repertory ranging from Mozart and Rossini to Verdi and Richard Strauss. She also appeared frequently at the Salzburg Festival, where she sang her Mozart roles: Donna Elvira, Countess Almaviva, Fiordiligi and Constanze. Her last appearance, as the Marschallin in *Der Rosenkavalier* in 1982 at Glyndebourne, was unbearably poignant.

Sir John Pritchard, a conductor whose career was bound up with Glyndebourne for over thirty years, died at San Francisco on December 5, 1989, aged 68. Pritchard first worked at Glyndebourne in 1947, as a repetiteur. In 1949 he became the chorus master and the following year assistant conductor to Fritz Busch, making an unscheduled debut in 1951 conducting *Don Giovanni* when Busch became ill. From 1969 to 1978 John Pritchard was musical director at Glyndebourne; he then moved to Cologne, to Brussels, and finally to San Francisco. He made his Covent Garden debut in 1952, conducting *Un ballo in maschera*; he conducted the premieres of Britten's *Gloriana* (1953), and Tippett's *Midsummer Marriage* (1955) and *King Priam* (Coventry, 1962). His operatic repertory included Donizetti, Bellini, Verdi and Puccini, as well as Tchaikovsky, Berlioz, Bizet and Richard Strauss; but it is as a deeply sympathetic interpreter of Mozart that he will be best remembered.

Sir Lennox Berkeley, whose large musical output contained one full-length and three shorter operas, died on December 26, 1989, at the age of 86. *Nelson*, which was produced at Sadler's Wells in 1953, achieved a certain success, but by far his most popular stage work was the one-act *A Dinner Engagement*, first given at Aldeburgh in 1954 and revived many times since. Although Paul Dehn's libretto, which deals with the domestic troubles of an ex-ambassador and his wife faced with the difficulty of life without servants, has dated, the music remains fresh and full of interest. Berkeley's other short pieces, *Ruth* (1956) and *The Castaway* (1967), were less successful, although they both contain some fine music. The Earl of Drogheda, chairman of the Royal Opera, Covent Garden from 1958 to 1974, also died in December, aged 79. During the period of his chairmanship, Lord Drogheda worked indefatigably on behalf of the Royal Opera, helping to transform the company from one of merely parochial standards to one of high international reputation. Whether that reputation can be maintained into the last decade of the twentieth century remains to be seen.

PRODUCTIONS

In the summaries of the company activities shown below, the dates in brackets indicate the year that the current production entered the company's repertory.

ROYAL OPERA (1946)
Royal Opera House, Covent Garden, WC2E 9DD

Productions from the repertory were *Rigoletto* (1988), *Peter Grimes* (1975), *Der Freischütz* (1977), *Otello* (1987), *Don Pasquale* (1973). *L'elisir d'amore* (1975), *Die Meistersinger von Nürnberg* (1969), *Il trovatore* (1989), *La Bohème* (1974) and *Arabella* (1965).

New productions were:
Sept. 27, 1989. **Die Walküre** (Wagner). *Conductor*, Bernard Haitink; *producer*, Götz Friedrich; *designer*, Peter Sykora.
Siegmund, René Kollo; *Sieglinde*, Gabriele Schnaut; *Hunding*, John Tomlinson; *Wotan*, James Morris; *Brünnhilde*, Gwyneth Jones; *Fricka*, Helga Dernesch.

Nov. 6, 1989. **Médée** (Cherubini). *Conductor*, Mark Ermler; *producer*, Mike Ashman; *designer*, Bernard Culshaw.
Médée, Rosalind Plowright; *Jason*, Alexei Steblianko; *Dircé* (*Glauce*), Renée Fleming; *Créon*, Robert Lloyd; *Néris*, Claire Powell.

Nov. 27, 1989. **Idomeneo** (Mozart). *Conductor*, Jeffrey Tate; *producer*, Johannes Schaaf; *designers*, Hans Schavernoch (*set*), Lore Haas (*costumes*).
Idomeneo, Philip Langridge; *Idamante*, Ann Murray; *Ilia*, Sylvia McNair; *Elettra*, Elizabeth Connell; *Arbace*, Robert Tear.

Feb. 1. **Prince Igor** (Borodin). *Conductor*, Bernard Haitink; *producer*, Andrei Serban; *designers*, Liviu Ciulei (*set*), Deirdre Clancy (*costumes*).
Igor, Sergei Leiferkus; *Yaroslavna*, Anna Tomowa-Sintow; *Vladimir*, Alexei Steblianko; *Galitsky*, Nicola Ghiuselev; *Konchak*, Paata Burchuladze; *Konchakovna*, Elena Zaremba.

March 3. **Elektra** (R. Strauss). *Conductor*, Georg Solti; *producer*, Götz Friedrich; *designers*, Hans Schavernoch (*set*), Lore Haas (*costumes*).
Elektra, Eva Marton; *Chrysothemis*, Nadine Se-

cunde; *Clytemnestra*, Marjana Lipovšek; *Orestes*, Robert Hale; *Aegisthus*, Robert Tear.

April 24. **La Cenerentola** (Rossini). *Conductor*, Carlo Rizzi; *producer*, Michael Hampe; *designer*, Mauro Pagano.
Ramiro, Deon van der Walt; *Dandini*, François Le Roux; *Don Magnifico*, Claudio Desderi; *Clorinda*, Daniela Lojarro; *Tisbe*, Eirian James; *Angelina*, Agnes Baltsa; *Alidoro*, Donald Maxwell.

June 7. **The Cunning Little Vixen** (Janacek). *Conductor*, Simon Rattle; *producer*, Bill Bryden; *designer*, William Dudley.
Vixen Sharp-Ears, Lillian Watson; *Schoolteacher*, Robert Tear; *Forester*, Thomas Allen; *Fox*, Diana Montague; *Parson/Badger*, Gwynne Howell; *Harašta*, William Shimmell.

June 29. **Guillaume Tell** (Rossini). *Conductor*, Michel Plasson; *producer*, John Cox; *designers*, Robin Wagner (*set*), Liz da Costa (*costumes*).
Tell, Gregory Yurisich; *Hedwige*, Eva Podles; *Jemmy*, Linda Kitchen; *Arnold*, Chris Merritt; *Mathilde*, Lella Cuberli; *Gesler*, Stafford Dean.

ENGLISH NATIONAL OPERA (1931)
London Coliseum, St Martin's Lane, WC2N 4ES

Productions from the repertory were *The Magic Flute* (1988), *Katya Kabanova* (1973), *Madam Butterfly* (1984), *Hansel and Gretel* (1987), *Faust* (1985), *La traviata* (1988), *The Mikado* (1986), *The Gambler* (1983), *Ariadne auf Naxos* (1983) and *The Marriage of Figaro* (1978).

New productions were:
Sept. 14, 1989. **A Masked Ball** (Verdi). *Conductor*, Mark Elder; *producer*, David Alden; *designer*, David Fielding.
Gustavus, Arthur Davies; *Amelia*, Janice Cairns; *Ankarström*, Jonathan Summers; *Oscar*, Lesley Garrett; *Arvidson*, Linda Finnie.

Oct. 17, 1989. **Street Scene** (Weill), a co-production with Scottish Opera. *Conductor*, Carl Davis; *producer*, David Pountney; *designer*, David Fielding
Anna Maurrant, Kristine Ciesinski; *Frank Maurrant*, Richard Van Allen; *Rose Maurrant*, Janis Kelly; *Sam Kaplan*, Bonaventura Bottone.

Nov. 8, 1989. **The Return of Ulysses** (Monteverdi), a co-production with Opera North. *Conductor*, Paul Daniel; *producer*, David Freeman; *designer*, David Roger.
Ulysses, Anthony Rolfe Johnson; *Penelope*, Jean Rigby; *Minerva*, Sally Burgess; *Telemachus*, Laurence Dale.

Dec. 6, 1989. **The Love for Three Oranges** (Prokofiev), a co-production with Opera North. *Conductor*, David Atherton; *producer*, Richard Jones; *designers*, the Brothers Quay (*set*), Sue Blane (*costumes*).
King of Clubs, Peter Rose; *Prince*, Alan Woodrow; *Truffaldino*, Bonaventura Bottone; *Leandro*, Donald Maxwell; *Fata Morgana*, Jane Eaglen; *Ninetta*, Lesley Garrett.

Jan. 25. **Beatrice and Benedict** (Berlioz). *Conductor*, Mark Elder; *producer*, Tim Albery; *designers*, Tom Cairns and Antony McDonald.
Beatrice, Ann Murray; *Benedict*, Philip Langridge; *Hero*, Anne Dawson; *Ursula*, Jean Rigby; *Somarone*, Eric Shilling.

April 5. **Macbeth** (Verdi). *Conductor*, Mark Elder; *producer*, David Pountney; *designer*, Stefanos Lazaridis.
Macbeth, Jonathan Summers; *Banquo*, John Con-

nell; Lady Macbeth, Kristine Ciesinski; *Macduff,* Edmund Barham; *Malcolm,* Anthony Mee.

May 18. The world premiere of **Clarissa** (Holloway). *Conductor,* Oliver Knussen; *producer,* David Pountney; *designer,* David Fielding.

Clarissa, Vivian Tiernery; *Lovelace,* Graeme Matheson-Bruce; *Anna Howe,* Rose Mannion.

Xerxes, The Turn of the Screw and *Macbeth* were toured to Kiev, Moscow and Leningrad during June 1990.

WELSH NATIONAL OPERA (1946)
John Streeet, Cardiff CF1 4SP

Productions from the repertory were *Lucia di Lammermoor* (1986), *The Bartered Bride* (1982), *Così fan tutte* (1985), *The Barber of Seville* (1986) and *Otello* (1986).

New productions were:

Sept. 16, 1989. **Der Freischütz** (Weber). *Conductor,* Peter Hirsch; *producer,* André Engel; *designers,* Nick Rieti (*set*), Elizabeth Neumuller (*costumes*).

Agathe, Rita Cullis; *Aennchen,* Eirian Davies; *Max,* Joseph Evans; *Kaspar,* Richard Paul Fink; *Kuno,* Ian Comboy; *Hermit/Samiel,* Geoffrey Moses.

March 1. **Der Rosenkavalier** (R. Strauss), a co-production with Australian Opera. *Conductor,* Charles Mackerras; *producer,* Wolfgang Weber; *designer* Carl Friedrich Oberle.

Marschallin, Rita Cullis; *Oktavian,* Constance Fee; *Sophie,* Amanda Roocroft; *Baron Ochs,* Donald Adams; *Faninal,* Barry Mora; *Italian singer,* Peter Bronder.

May 19. The world premiere of **Tornrak** (Metcalf), a co-production with the Banff Centre for the Arts, Alberta. *Conductor,* Richard Armstrong; *producer,* Mike Ashman; *designers,* Bernard Culshaw (*set*), John Pennoyer (*costumes*).

Arthur, David Owen; *Milak,* Penelope Walker; *Sir Charles Keighley,* Glenville Hargreaves.

Performances of the repertory were given at the New Theatre, Cardiff, and on tour at Birmingham, Oxford, Southampton, Bristol, Swansea, Liverpool, Manchester and at the Dominion Theatre, London.

SCOTTISH OPERA
Theatre Royal, Hope Street, Glasgow G2 3QA

Productions from the repertory were *The Marriage of Figaro* (1986), *Jenufa* (1977), *Die Fledermaus* (1988), *Oedipus Rex* (1989) and *Madama Butterfly* (1987).

New productions were:

Sept. 19, 1989. **The Merry Widow** (Léhar). *Conductor,* John Pryce-Jones; *producer,* Di Trevis; *designer,* Bunny Christie.

Hanna Glawari, Suzanne Murphy; *Valencienne,* Deborah Stuart Roberts; *Danilo,* Simon Keenlyside; *Camille,* Jorge Pita; *Baron Mirko Zeta,* Peter Knapp.

Jan. 24. **Duke Bluebeard's Castle** (Bartok), given as a double-bill with *Oedipus Rex. Conductor,* Vachtang Matchavariani; *producer* and *designer,* Stefanos Lazaridis.

Bluebeard, Monte Jaffe; *Judith,* Kathryn Harries.

Feb. 13. **La forza del destino** (Verdi). *Conductor,* John Mauceri; *producer,* Elijah Moshinsky; *designer,* Michael Yeargan.

Leonora, Andrea Gruber; *Don Alvaro,* Stefano Algieri; *Don Carlo,* Vladimir Chernov; *Preziosilla,* Della Jones; *Padre Guardiano,* Alexander Morosov; *Fra Melitone,* Nicholas Folwell.

April 25. **Salome** (R. Strauss), co-production with Welsh National Opera. *Conductor,* John Mauceri;

producer, André Engel; *designers,* Nick Rieti (*set*), Elizabeth Neumuller (*costumes*).

Salome, Cynthia Makris; *Herodias,* Elizabeth Vaughan; *Herod,* Eduardo Alvares; *Narraboth,* Bonaventura Bottone; *Jokanaan,* Greer Grimsley.

May 19. **Così fan tutte.** *Conductor,* Peter Hirsch; *producer,* Jürgen Gosch; *designer,* Nina Ritter.

Fiordiligi, Jane Englen; *Dorabella,* Clare Shearer; *Ferrando,* Thomas Randle; *Guglielmo,* Simon Keenlyside; *Despina,* Nan Christie; *Don Alfonso,* Terence Sharpe.

Performances were given at the Theatre Royal, Glasgow, and on tour at Edinburgh, Newcastle, Aberdeen, Inverness and Liverpool.

OPERA NORTH
Grand Theatre, New Briggate, Leeds LS1 6NZ

Productions from the repertory were *The Love for Three Oranges* (1988), *Tosca* (1988), *La finta giardiniera* (1989), *The Barber of Seville* (1985) and *Orpheus and Eurydice* (1984).

New productions were:

Sept. 23, 1989. **Peter Grimes** (Britten). *Conductor,* David Lloyd-Jones; *producer,* Ronald Eyre; *designer,* Mark Thompson.

Peter Grimes, John Treleaven; *Ellen Orford,* Marie Slorach; *Balstrode,* Malcolm Donnelly; *Auntie,* Anne Collins; *Bob Boles,* Peter Bodenham; *Ned Keene,* Peter Savidge.

Dec. 8, 1989. **Show Boat** (Kern), a co-production with the Royal Shakespeare Company. *Conductor,* Graeme Jenkins; *producer,* Ian Judge; *designers,* Russell Craig (*set*), Alexander Reid (*costumes*).

Magnolia/Kim, Linda Kitchen; *Julie,* Sally Burgess; *Queenie,* Carla Burns; *Joe,* Bruce Hubbard; *Ravenal,* Peter Savidge.

Jan. 11. **Don Pasquale** (Donizetti). *Conductor,* David Lloyd-Jones; *producer,* Patrick Mason; *designer,* Joe Vanek.

Norina, Juliet Booth; *Ernesto,* Adrian Martin; *Malatesta,* Robert Hayward; *Don Pasquale,* Andrew Shore.

March 31. The British premiere of **Jérusalem** (Verdi). *Conductor,* Paul Daniel; *producer,* Pierre Audi; *designers,* Michael Simon (*set*), Jorge Jara (*costumes*).

Gaston, Arthur Davies; *Hélène,* Janice Cairns; *Count of Toulouse,* Keith Latham; *Roger,* José Garcia.

April 12. **L'Heure éspagnole** (Ravel) in a double-bill with **Gianni Schicchi** (Puccini). *Conductor,* David Lloyd-Jones; *producer,* Martin Duncan; *designer,* Tom Cairns.

Concepcion, Louise Winter; *Gonzalve,* Harry Nicoll; *Ramiro,* Jason Howard; *Don Inigo Gomez,* Andrew Shore.

Gianni Schicchi, Andrew Shore; *Lauretta,* Juliet Booth; *Rinuccio,* David Maxwell-Anderson; *Zita,* Linda Ormiston.

June 23. The British professional premiere of **Masquerade** (Nielsen), in conjunction with the Leeds Festival. *Conductor,* Elgar Howarth; *producer,* Helena Kaut-Howson; *designer,* Lez Brotherston.

Leander, Paul Nilon; *Henrik,* Geoffrey Dolton; *Jeronimus,* Clive Bayley; *Magdelone,* Meriel Dickinson; *Leonora,* Mary Hegarty; *Pernille,* Llyndall Trotman; *Leonard,* Paul Wade.

Performances were also given on tour in Manchester, Nottingham, Hull and York. *Show Boat* was performed at the Royal Shakespeare Theatre, Stratford-upon-Avon, and at the London Palladium.

GLYNDEBOURNE FESTIVAL OPERA (1934)
Glyndebourne, Lewes, Sussex BN8 5UU

The 1990 Festival ran from May 21 to August 22. Four of the productions were revivals: *Albert Herring* (1985), *Kat'a Kabanova* (1988), *Capriccio* (1973) and *Falstaff* (1988).

The new productions were:

May 21. **Die Zauberflöte** (Mozart). *Conductor*, Lothar Zagrosek; *producer*, Peter Sellars; *designers*, Adrianne Lobel (*set*), Duna Ramicova (*costumes*).

Tamino, Kurt Streit; *Pamina*, Ai-Lan Zhu; *Queen of Night*, Hellen Kwon; *Sarastro*, Mark Doss; *Papageno*, James Maddalena; *Monostatos*, Howard Haskin; *Speaker*, Alistair Miles; *Papagena*, Alison Hagley.

July 1. The British premiere of **New Year** (Tippett), a co-production with Houston Grand Opera and the BBC. *Conductor*, Andrew Davis; *producer*, Peter Hall; *designer*, Alison Chitty.

Jo Ann, Helen Field; *Donny*, Krister St Hill; *Pelegrin*, Philip Langridge; *Regan*, Richetta Manager; *Nan*, Jane Shaulis; *Merlin*, James Maddalena; *Presenter*, Nigel Robson.

The Glyndebourne Touring Opera performed *Die Zauberflöte*, *Fidelio* and *New Year* at Glyndebourne, Glasgow, Oxford, Manchester, Birmingham, Southampton and Plymouth between October and December 1990.

OPERA 80 (1980)

Performances of *Lucia di Lammermoor* and *The Merry Widow* were toured to Swindon, Cheltenham, Weston-super-Mare, Exeter, Barnstaple, Yeovil, Poole, Southend, Reading, Crawley, Ipswich, Lincoln, Preston, Carlisle, Ulverston, Scunthorpe, Buxton, Basildon, Brighton, Cambridge and Sadler's Wells Theatre, London, between February and June 1990.

OPERA NORTHERN IRELAND
Grand Opera House, Belfast

Sept. 15. **Don Giovanni** (Mozart). *Conductor*, Kenneth Montgomery; *producer*, Seamus McGrenera; *designer*, George Souglides.

Don Giovanni, Nicolas Rivenq; *Leporello*, Huub Claessens; *Donna Anna*, Elizabeth Collier; *Donna Elvira*, Riona Bradley; *Don Ottavio*, Kim Begley; *Zerlina*, Deborah Rees; *Masetto*, Paul Parfitt; *Commendatore*, Paul Nemeer.

Sept. 16. **Faust** (Gounod). *Conductor*, Stephen Barlow; *producer*, Bliss Hebert; *designer*, Allen Charles Klein.

Faust, Stephen Smith; *Mephistopheles*, Frederic Vassar; *Marguerite*, Joanne Kolomyjec; *Valentine*, Didier Henry; *Siebel*, Kate McCarney; *Marthe*, Therese Feighan.

March 3. **Die Fledermaus** (J. Strauss), borrowed from Welsh National Opera, re-staged by Tim Coleman.

MASTERS OF THE QUEEN'S/KING'S MUSIC

	Apptd.
Nicholas Lanier	1626
Louis Grabu	1666
Nicholas Staggins	1674
John Eccles	1700
Maurice Greene	1735
William Boyce	1755
John Stanley	1779
Sir William Parsons	1786
William Shield	1817
Christian Kramer	1829

	Apptd.
François (Franz) Cramer	1834
George Frederick Anderson	1848
Sir William George Cusins	1870
Sir Walter Parratt	1893
Sir Edward Elgar	1924
Sir Henry Walford Davies	1934
Sir Arnold Bax	1942
Sir Arthur Bliss	1953
Malcolm Williamson	1975

DANCE 1989–90

English National Ballet celebrated its 40th anniversary in 1990, but the abrupt sacking in January 1990 of its artistic director, Peter Schaufuss, was hardly an auspicious beginning to the year. 'Irreconcilable differences' between Schaufuss and the new chairman of the ENB board, Lady Harlech, were cited as the reason for his dismissal. The company's financial situation was believed to be at the root of the problem. After an unsuccessful season at London's Dominion Theatre in June 1989, ENB's deficit had grown to £350,000. The Arts Council, of which Lady Harlech was at that time a member, had promised the company a 12 per cent increase in funding for 1990–91 on condition that the deficit be reduced. Schaufuss' artistic policies were deemed to be inappropriate in the circumstances, and personality clashes and factions also played their part. It was later announced that the Hungarian-born director of the Cincinnati Ballet, Ivan Nagy, would replace Schaufuss in September 1990.

The controversy was regarded in the dance world as symptomatic of the problems besetting all British dance companies, who find themselves having to give priority to fund-raising and securing sponsorship. Financial and executive directors increasingly hold sway over artistic directors. This has recently been the case at the Scottish Ballet, and it is not only a British phenomenon: American Ballet Theatre's director Mikhail Baryshnikov walked out on the company after a series of rows, declaring 'Nothing is ever too expensive if it furthers the repertoire and artistic standards of a ballet company'. This idealistic opinion is not widely shared by those responsible for running and funding companies.

Nevertheless, the dance department of the Arts Council has been given a 17 per cent rise in funding for 1990–91 (to £13·5 million), and the Royal Opera House is to receive an extra 11 per cent (taking its total grant to £15·2 million). The news was welcomed, though the grant was felt to be insufficient to compensate for years of under-funding. The Royal Opera House seems to be heading for a clash with the Arts Council over its decision to budget for a deficit of £2 million for the 1989–90 season, taking its total deficit to £5·3 million. There is also widespread concern over the planned reorganization of the Arts Council, which will result in regional arts associations taking over responsibility for allocating grants, while the Arts Council will become an overall policy-making body as well as retaining the funding of major national companies. This proposal led to the resignation in March of the Arts Council's secretary-general, Luke Rittner.

Funding, or lack of it, was part of the problem behind a pay dispute at the Royal Opera House which culminated in the Royal Ballet dancers going on strike, several performances being cancelled, and the co-production of *Prince Igor* with the Royal Opera losing its planned new choreography by David Bintley. The dispute was settled in time to save Kenneth MacMillan's new production of *The Prince of the Pagodas*, and a ballet committee of about 13 people, drawn from all ranks of the company, has been formed to hold regular talks with the management of the Royal Opera House.

The Prince of the Pagodas had its Royal Gala premiere four days before MacMillan's 60th birthday. It is his first full-length ballet for eight years, and was seen in some quarters as marking a rapprochement between MacMillan and the company of which he is officially principal choreographer and which he directed from 1970–77. Since the disastrous reception of his *Isadora* in 1981, MacMillan has created only four ballets for the company. However, many of his earlier works have continued in the repertoire and the 1989–90 season included revivals of *Song of the Earth*, *Gloria*, *Requiem*, and *My Brother, My Sisters*, as a 60th birthday tribute to the choreographer. Undoubtedly the event of the season, though, was *The Prince of the Pagodas*.

MacMillan had long been attracted by Benjamin Britten's score for the original production by John Cranko in 1957, but found the original scenario dramatically unconvincing. He enlisted the help of the writer Colin Thubron in producing a more coherent adaptation of the scenario. In the leading role of Princess Rose MacMillan cast the youngest soloist in the company, Darcey Bussell; her success in the role saw her immediate promotion to principal dancer. The ballet was well received by audiences; critical reaction was mixed, as has often been the case with MacMillan's works. On the one hand, there was praise for the choreographer's 'radiantly open and classically beautiful writing . . . A grand achievement'; on the other, the reflection that 'dramatic cogency is what the production sadly lacks'. These judgements notwithstanding, *The Prince of the Pagodas* is an ambitious and important addition to the Royal Ballet's repertoire.

The rest of the Royal Ballet's season was unusually unpredictable; several new works which had been announced failed to materialize, while unscheduled additions appeared on several other programmes. Sylvie Guillem, the company's principal guest artist and somewhat controversial star, continued to attract enormous attention. This may be rivalled in the coming season by the arrival of Irek Mukhamedov, formerly the Bolshoi's leading male dancer, who unexpectedly signed a five-year contract with the Royal Ballet at the end of the season. One of the youngest principal dancers in the company, Viviana Durante, won the Evening Standard Ballet Award for the consistently high standard of her dancing. Jonathan Cope and Maria Almeida, on the other hand, have both 'retired' from dancing while still in their mid-twenties, giving as their reason the high level of mental and physical stress involved in dance as a career. Another sad loss, to the Royal Ballet and other dance companies, was the death of the conductor Ashley Lawrence. He showed a sympathy for the art rare among conductors, and his dedication and musicianship earned him wide respect and popularity.

The Royal Ballet's sister company gave its last performances under the name of the Sadler's Wells Royal Ballet. In autumn 1990 it relocates to Birmingham, taking the name the Birmingham Royal Ballet. In what has been described as 'the arts coup of the decade', Birmingham City Council persuaded the company to adopt the Birmingham Hippodrome as its new base. The council has offered the company £1 million additional funding over three years, a sum which the Arts Council will match. The theatre offers excellent facilities and the company will have its own purpose-built headquarters, on which the council has spent £4 million. Many of the dancers have moved to Birmingham with the company, although one of its most popular ballerinas, Margaret Barbieri, decided to retire; she had been a member of the company for 24 years and was especially praised for her interpretation of Giselle. A leading young dancer, Roland Price, also left the company; he joined the Boston Ballet, but like Barbieri will return to the Birmingham Royal Ballet as a guest artist.

As the company embarks on a new and promising phase of its existence, it has also had to say farewell to Dame Peggy van Praagh, who died in Australia in January. Although known as assistant director (under Dame Ninette de Valois) from 1946-55, van Praagh was in fact responsible for the day-to-day running of the then Sadler's Wells Theatre Ballet, which was formed to replace the Sadler's Wells Ballet when that company moved to the Royal Opera House after the Second World War. She gave early opportunities to both Kenneth MacMillan and John Cranko and established the company as a considerable force in its own right, helped by such dancers as Svetlana Beriosova, Nadia Nerina and David Blair.

Various plans to improve facilities for dance companies in London (including visiting companies) are still under discussion. One plan involves building a new improved Sadler's Wells Theatre on the same site in Islington. The theatre has agreed with Thames Water, which owns the site next door to it, that joint redevelopment plans for the site be prepared. As the land would be worth more as part of a high quality development including a theatre, it seems possible that funds for the new theatre could be forthcoming without the need for public subsidy or great sponsorship and fund-raising efforts. A 2,200 seat theatre is envisaged (with the possibility of adapting it for smaller companies), with a large stage, good backstage and front-of-house facilities, and space for a national centre for dance. Opposition is expected, however, to the idea of demolishing the present theatre with its historic and sentimental associations. Other schemes for increasing venues for dance include a new 2,500 seat theatre near the Old Vic, and the refurbishment of the Lyceum and Dominion Theatres and the Roundhouse in north London. These are all still at various stages of negotiation.

Two smaller classical companies, Northern Ballet Theatre and London City Ballet, continue to give a large number of performances throughout the United Kingdom, struggling all the time to keep afloat in the face of mounting costs. Northern Ballet has now received a guarantee that funding from the Arts Council will continue, though this is conditional on assurances from local authorities in West Yorkshire of their financial support when the company moves to Halifax from Manchester in August 1990. At the same time as this move across the Pennines, York-

shire-born ballerina Elaine McDonald, former principal dancer with the Scottish Ballet, is to join the Northern Ballet company as associate artistic director. A new production of Giselle by the company's artistic director, Christopher Gable, received its premiere in Sheffield in February and was subsequently performed at Sadler's Wells in London, together with a triple bill of new works.

London City Ballet gave two seasons at Sadler's Wells. Formed in 1978, this company, under the directorship of Harold King, states that its aim is 'to make classical ballet accessible and to provide ballet of quality at affordable prices'. It receives no Arts Council funding apart from a touring subsidy, relying on business sponsorship, fund-raising and box office income. A new full-length production this season, *La traviata*, to Verdi's music and with choreography by Andre Prokovsky, has proved to be a popular success.

The world of contemporary dance, according to some reports, is suffering a decline in popularity. Rambert Dance Company is, nevertheless, enjoying a period of critical success under the artistic direction of Richard Alston. It was awarded the 1989 Prudential Award for the Arts, worth £75,000, in addition to the £25,000 prize it had already received as the winner of the dance section of the competition. The company's style and repertoire are increasingly influenced by the works of Siobhan Davies and of Alston himself; the dancers are rigorous and confident, and the company as a whole has established a strong identity and sense of purpose since Alston took over four years ago. London Contemporary Dance Theatre, on the other hand, is still in a period of transition. Its new artistic director, Dan Wagoner, has yet to make a strong impression on the company, which has been going through an unfocused, uninspiring period of late. It received acclaim, however, for its new work by Kim Brandstrup, *Orfeo*, which was awarded the Laurence Olivier Award for Outstanding Achievement in Dance.

The annual Dance Umbrella season (the world's largest festival of contemporary dance) ran for six weeks in autumn 1989, with performances in five London theatres and also in smaller venues throughout the United Kingdom. Val Bourne, the organizer of Dance Umbrella since its inception in 1978, was the 1989 winner of the Digital Dance Premier Award for someone judged to have made an outstanding contribution to current British dance. The 1989 Umbrella season had a French emphasis in recognition of the bicentenary of the French Revolution. Five leading French contemporary dance companies took part. There were also programmes of works by young British choreographers, and new works by some of the leading lights in British contemporary dance: the Siobhan Davies Company, the Cholmondeleys, Second Stride, Laurie Booth and others. There was also a season at Sadler's Wells Theatre by the Merce Cunningham Dance Company in autumn 1989. Merce Cunningham has had an enormous influence on the development of modern dance, in his native USA and throughout the world, since he formed his first company in 1953. He began his association with the composer John Cage in the early 1940s, and together they have proposed radical innovations in musical and choreographic composition (for example, the independence of dance and music in a work, and the use of chance processes).

The Place Theatre, London, under the direction of John Ashford, has also been the recipient of a major award (the 1990 Prudential Award for Dance), in recognition of the successful and adventurous seasons of contemporary dance which have been held there recently. In addition to its activities in London, the theatre has also worked in collaboration with Glasgow's Mayfest festival, helping to bring major international contemporary dance companies to Britain. Another initiative, which has so far benefited mainly the world of contemporary dance, is the Arts Council's scheme to encourage creative collaboration between dance and music. The Arts Council set up the 'Composers for Dance' scheme four years ago, with a budget of £30,000. Applications can be made by choreographers or companies wanting to commission a work involving new music from a particular composer; in the 1989–90 season, beneficiaries included Jonathan Burrows (a member of the Royal Ballet), working with Matteo Fargion, and Ian Spink of Second Stride, working with Judith Weir.

Two long-awaited visitors to the United Kingdom in the 1989–90 season were the Paul Taylor Dance Company and American Ballet Theatre (ABT), both from New York. Paul Taylor's last London season was 16 years ago and ABT have not performed here since 1977; both seasons were therefore major events in the dance world. Paul Taylor has been a dominant

influence in both American and European dance for over 30 years. From 1955–62 he was a soloist with the Martha Graham Dance Company, while at the same time presenting his own work in concerts in both the USA and Europe. He also worked with the two great American choreographers George Balanchine and Merce Cunningham. His company has performed all over the world and has gained a reputation for outstanding musicality, imagination, vitality and humour.

American Ballet Theatre is one of the world's leading classical companies. Founded in 1940, its original aim was to build up a repertoire of the best works from ballet history as well as commissioning a steady flow of new American works. This, fundamentally, remains its policy today. For many years the company was known for presenting and promoting star dancers, and this culminated in the appointment of Mikhail Baryshnikov as artistic director in 1980. Baryshnikov gradually led the company away from its emphasis on 'stars' and towards a more cohesive company style, as well as working in close collaboration with modern choreographers such as Twyla Tharp. His acrimonious departure from ABT in 1989 leaves the company once more at a turning point.

One of the reasons for the long absence from London of the Paul Taylor Dance Company and ABT has been the non-availability of a suitable venue; even if only one of the schemes mentioned above comes to fruition, this situation could be a problem of the past.

PRODUCTIONS

ROYAL BALLET (1931)
Royal Opera House, Covent Garden, WC2E 9DD

World premières:
The Prince of the Pagodas (Dec. 7, 1989). *Choreography*, Kenneth MacMillan; *score*, Benjamin Britten; *design*, Nicholas Georgiadis; *scenario*, Colin Thubron after John Cranko.

Cast: *Princess Rose*, Darcey Bussell; *The Prince*, Jonathan Cope; *Pricess Epine*, Fiona Chadwick; *Emperor*, Anthony Dowell; *The Fool*, Tetsuya Kumakawa.

Farewell—a *pas de deux* from *Winter Dreams* (July 19). *Choreography*, Kenneth MacMillan; *music*, Tchaikovsky; *costumes*, Peter Farmer; *dancers*, Darcey Bussell and Irek Mukhamedov.

The Planets (Aug. 1). *Choreography*, David Bintley; *music*, Holst; *scenery*, Ralph Koltai; *costumes*, Sue Blane.

Enclosure (Aug. 1). *Choreography*, William Tuckett; *music*, Alban Berg; *design*, Stephen Meaha. The leading role was taken by Dana Fouras.

Company première:
Other Dances (Oct. 6, 1989). *Choreography*, Jerome Robbins (1976); *costumes*, Santo Loquasto; *dancers*, Sylvie Guillem and Laurent Hilaire.

Full-length ballets from the repertoire performed during the season: *La Bayadère* (Makarova after Petipa, 1980); *Swan Lake* (Petipa/Ivanov, prod. Dowell, 1987); *Cinderella* (Ashton, 1948); *La Fille mal gardée* (Ashton, 1960); *Giselle* (Petipa after Coralli/Perrot, prod. Wright, 1985); *Romeo and Juliet* (MacMillan, 1965), including a gala performance on May 30 as a tribute to Dame Margot Fonteyn.

One-act ballets from the repertoire were: *Rubies (Capriccio for Piano and Orchestra)* (Balanchine); *Piano* (Page); *Requiem* (MacMillan); *A Wedding Bouquet* (Ashton); *My Brother, My Sisters* (MacMillan); *Frankenstein, the Modern Prometheus* (Eagling); *Polovtsian Dances* from *Prince Igor* (co-production with the Royal Opera) (Fokine); *Laurentia pas de six* (Chaboukiani); *Galanteries* (Bintley); *Pursuit* (Page); *Gloria* (MacMillan); *A Month in the Country* (Ashton); *Song of the Earth* (MacMillan); *'Still Life' at the Penguin Café* (Bintley).

Tours: Birmingham Hippodrome and Palace Theatre, Manchester (Feb.–March) with *The Prince of the Pagodas* and *La Bayadère*. A planned tour of the USA in July 1990 was cancelled because the necessary sponsorship was not forthcoming.

SADLER'S WELLS ROYAL BALLET (1946)
Royal Opera House, Covent Garden WC2E 9DD

World premières:
Meridian of Youth (April 24). *Choreography*, Vincent Redmon; *music*, Bartók; *design*, Claudia Mayer. The cast was led by Joseph Cipolla and Marion Tait.

Game (May 4). *Choreography*, William Tuckett; *music*, Debussy; *design*, Stephen Meaha. The leading roles were taken by Kevin O'Hare, Bonnie Moore and Tony Fabre.

Inscape (June 1). *Choreography*, Graham Lustig; *score*, Peter McGowan; *design*, Henk Schut. The central role was taken by Kevin O'Hare.

Company première:
Divertimento No. 15 (Oct. 13, 1989). *Choreography*, George Balanchine (1956); *music*, Mozart; *design*,

Peter Farmer. The first cast included Miyako Yoshida and Petter Jacobsson.

Full-length ballets from the repertoire performed during the season: *Hobson's Choice* (Bintley, 1989); *Swan Lake* (Petipa/Ivanov, additional choreography by Wright, 1980); *The Two Pigeons* (Ashton, 1961); *La Fille mal gardée* (Ashton, 1960).

One-act ballets and *pas de deux* from the repertoire were: *The Dream* (Ashton); *Façade* (Ashton); *Solitaire* (MacMillan); *Flowers of the Forest* (Bintley); *Don Quixote pas de deux* (Petipa); *Danses concertantes* (MacMillan); *Las Hermanas* (MacMillan); *Paramour* (Lustig); *These and Variations* (Balanchine); *Elite Syncopations* (MacMillan), *Les Sylphides* (Fokine); *Auras* (Redmon); *Those Unheard* (Tuckett); *Allegri Diversi* (Bintley); *Tchaikovsky pas de deux* (Balanchine); *Valses nobles et sentimentales* (Ashton) (one performance on April 24 as a tribute to Dame Peggy van Praagh).

In addition to two seasons at Sadler's Wells Theatre, London, and two at the Birmingham Hippodrome, performances were given in Bristol, Leeds, Oxford, Southampton, Northampton, Eastbourne, Canterbury, Plymouth and Liverpool. The company also undertook a five-week tour of New Zealand in Feb.–March, with *Swan Lake, Theme and Variations, The Dream* and *Elite Syncopations.*

ENGLISH NATIONAL BALLET (1950)
(formerly London Festival Ballet)
Markova House, 39 Jay Mews, SW7 2ES

World premières:
Symphony in Three Movements (Nov. 27, 1989). *Choreography*, Christpher Bruce; *music*, Stravinsky; *design*, Nadine Baylis. The cast at the premiere included Josephine Jewkes and Alessandro Iacopini.

Dancing Ledge (July 18). *Choreography*, Siobhan Davies; *music*, John Adams; *designs*, David Buckland. The cast at the première included Janette Mulligan and Martin James.

Company première:
The Moor's Pavane (Dec. 1, 1989, Athens). *Choreography*, José Limón (1949); *music*, Purcell; *costumes*, P. Lawrence. The first cast was Diego Ciavatti, Johnny Eliasen, Lynn Seymour and Marguerite Donelle.

Full-length ballets from the repertoire performed during the season: *Coppélia* (Hynd, 1985); *Swan Lake* (Petipa/Ivanov, additional choreography by Ashton, prod. Makarova, 1988); *Romeo and Juliet* (Ashton, 1955); *The Nutcracker* (Schaufuss, 1986); *Onegin* (Cranko, 1965).

One-act ballets and *pas de deux* from the repertoire were: *Anastasia* (MacMillan); *Etudes* (Lander); *Echoing of Trumpets* (Tudor); *Bolero* (Béjart); *Les Sylphides* (Fokine); *Apollo* (Balanchine); *Aureole* (Paul Taylor); *Land* (Bruce); *Flower Festival pas de deux* (Bournonville); *Swansong* (Bruce); *Three Preludes* (Stevenson); *Song of a Wayfarer* (Béjart).

The company gave performances in London at the Royal Festival Hall and the London Coliseum, and toured to Newcastle, Manchester, Bradford, Birmingham, Bristol, Plymouth, Nottingham, Southampton and Liverpool.

A small-scale tour in spring 1990 visited Bury St. Edmunds, Exeter, Malvern, Ulverston, Basildon, Worthing, Cambridge, Yeovil, Swindon and Scunthorpe. The repertoire included the first British showing of *The Moor's Pavane; Aureole; Flower Festival pas de deux*; and *Swansong.*

The company also visited Athens (Dec. 1989), taking *The Moor's Pavane, Apollo, Land, Three Preludes* and *Song of a Wayfarer*; Rotterdam (June), performing *Swansong, Anastasia* and *Symphony in Three Movements*; and Amman, Jordan (July), performing

Les Sylphides, The Moor's Pavane and *Coppélia* Act 3.

A 40th Anniversary Gala was held at the Royal Albert Hall, London, on March 27. The programme included excerpts from *Swan Lake, Romeo and Juliet, Onegin* and *Symphony in Three Movements*, and complete performances of *Bolero* and *Etudes.* Dancers included Fernando Bujones, Michael Clark, Richard Cragun, Carla Fracci, Sylvie Guillem, Marcia Haydée, Ekaterina Maximova, Maya Plisetskaya and Vladimir Vasiliev.

RAMBERT DANCE COMPANY (1926)
94 Chiswick High Road, W4 1SH.

World premières:
Currulao (Feb. 9). (The first Frederick Ashton memorial commission). *Choreography*, Ashley Page; *music*, Orlando Gough; *costumes*, John Galliano.

Dealing With Shadows (March 14). *Choreography*, Richard Alston; *music*, Mozart; *clothes*, English Eccentrics.

Longevity (March 21). *Choreography*, Gary Lambert; *text*, Martin Luther King; *dancers*, Colin Poole and Gary Lambert.

Signature (May 24). Choreography, Siobhan Davies; *score*, Kevin Volans; *design*, Kate Whiteford.

Company première:
Doubles (Jan. 30). *Choreography*, Merce Cunningham (1984); *music*, Takehisa Kosugi; *design*, Mark Lancaster.

Works from the repertoire performed during the season: *Calm* (Evelyn, 1989); *Septet* (Cunningham, 1953); *Dark Elegies* (Tudor, 1937); *Soldat* (Page, 1988); *Cinema* (Alston, 1989); *Sounding* (Davies, 1989); *Hymnos* (Alston, 1988); *Pulau Dewata* (Alston, 1989); *Opal Loop* (Brown, 1980); *Strong Language* (Alston, 1987); *Embrace Tiger and Return to Mountain* (Tetley, 1968); *Embarque* (Davies, 1988).

The company performed in Dublin, Manchester, Leicester, Oxford, Glasgow, Newcastle, Birmingham, Mold, York, London (Sadler's Wells), Brighton and Bristol. It also visited Rimini, Italy, in April, Larnaca, Cyprus, in July, and Ankara, Turkey, in May; works performed were *Dealing With Shadows, Embarque, Strong Language, Septet* and *Embrace Tiger and Return to Mountain.*

LONDON CONTEMPORARY DANCE THEATRE (1967)
The Place, 17 Duke's Road, WC1H 9AB.

World premières:
Orfeo (Oct. 4, 1989). *Choreography*, Kim Brandstrup; *music*, Ian Dearden; *design*, Craig Givens. The leading roles were taken by Tracey Fitzgerald, David Hughes, Jonathan Lunn and Kenneth Tharp.

Ace of Spaces (Oct. 18, 1989). *Choreography and costumes*, Darshan Singh Bhuller; *music*, Samuel Barber/Barrington Pheloung; *set*, Robert Cohan.

Turtles All the Way Down (Oct. 18, 1989). *Choreography*, Dan Wagoner; *music*, Aaron Copland; *design*, Kit Reading.

Goes Without Saying (Oct. 24, 1989). *Choreography*, Jonathan Lunn; *music*, Orlando Gough; *design*, Peter Mumford.

Doppelgänger (Oct. 26, 1989). *Choreography and costumes*, Jonathan Lunn; *music*, Philip Glass; *dancers*, Darshan Singh Bhuller and Aletta Collins.

On March 6 in Northampton a new work choreographed by Kenneth Tharp was premiered by the Northamptonshire Dance Group. A season of new choreography was presented at The Place Theatre, London (April 18–21), including works by Aletta Collins (*It's Gonna Rain*), Kim Brandstrup (*The*

Dybbuk) and Joann Fregalette-Jansen (*Noon Talk on Millionth Street*).

Company premières:

To Comfort Ghosts (Oct. 4, 1989). *Choreography*, Dan Wagoner (1988); *music*, Shostakovich; *costumes*, William Ivey Long.

Flee As a Bird (March 5). *Choreography*, Dan Wagoner (1986); *music*, traditional ragtime/jazz; *costumes*, Candice Donnelly.

Works from the repertoire performed during the season: *Metamorphoses* (Cohan, 1989); *Interlock* (Bhuller, 1988); *Arden Court* (Paul Taylor, 1981).

The company gave performances in Southampton, Plymouth, Warwick, Bristol, Leeds, Cardiff, London (Sadler's Wells Theatre and The Place), Northampton, Hexham, Oxford, Newcastle, Glasgow and Canterbury. It also toured the USSR (the first major British modern dance company to do so) for 12 days in June–July, visiting Kiev and Moscow and performing works including *Arden Court*, *Orfeo*, *To Comfort Ghosts* and *Turtles All the Way Down*. The company then visited Czechoslovakia.

THE SCOTTISH BALLET (1956)
261 West Princes Street, Glasgow G4 9EE.

World premières:
In May, during Glasgow's Mayfest celebrations, the company presented a programme of new works at the Tramway. The programme included **Zwei Gesänge**, with choreography by Massimo Moricone and music by Brahms; **Sun and Steele**, also choreographed by Moricone; **Pretty Ugly**, with choreography by Amanda Miller; and **Aquarelle**, with choreography by Michel Rahn. The company won a 'Scotland on Sunday Mayfest Award' for this programme.

A new work by Janet Smith entitled **Loose Connections** was premiered by the company on June 12 at the Clan Donald Centre, Armadale, Isle of Skye. The music was by Chris Bensted.

Company premières:
Scotch Symphony (March 16). *Choreography*, George Balanchine (1952); *music*, Mendelssohn; *set*, H. Armistead (backcloth by John Cunningham); *costumes*, after Karinska and David Ffolkes. The central roles were danced by Linda Packer and Vincent Hantam.

Grand pas from *Paquita* (March 16). *Choreography*, Petipa (1881), staged by Oleg and Yelena Vinogradov; *music*, Minkus; *costumes and set*, Oleg Vinogradov. The dancers included Rebecca Fletcher and Robert Hampton.

Who Cares? (March 16). *Choreography*, George Balanchine (1970); *music*, Gershwin; *costumes*, Chas Haines. The dancers at the première included Clare French and Robert Hampton.

Full-length ballets from the repertoire performed during the season: *La Sylphide* (Bournonville, 1973); *Peter Pan* (Lustig, 1989).

One-act ballets and *pas de deux* from the repertoire were: *Chéri* (Darrell); *Grand pas des Fiancées* (Carter); *The Prisoners* (Darrell); *Petrushka* (Vinogradov); *Symphony in D* (Kylian); *Othello* (Darrell); *Belong* (*pas de deux* from *What to do Till the Messiah Cometh*, Vesak).

The company also performed a set of divertissements from the repertoire of the Kirov Ballet, mounted by Oleg Vinogradov. The divertissements included a *pas de trois* from *The Fairy Doll* (Nikolai and Sergei Legat); the *pas de six* from *La Esmeralda* (Bourmeister); the *pas de six* from *La Vivandière* (Saint-Léon); and the *pas de trois* from *Paquita* (Petipa).

The company performed in Glasgow, Edinburgh, Aberdeen, Tain, Wick, Brora, Nairn, Darlington, Canterbury, Newcastle and Hull. It also undertook a small-scale tour to other venues in Scotland and venues in Wales and Northern Ireland in May–June, performing *Othello*, *Zwei Gesänge*, *Belong*, *Paquita pas de six* and *La Esmeralda pas de six*.

ARCHITECTURE 1989–90

THE DOME, DONCASTER
Architect: Faulkner Browns

The leisure industry has in recent years given rise to increasingly complex and exotic structures housing all manner of leisure and sports-orientated activities. Few of these can compare with the recently completed and quite extraordinary building located within a new leisure park on the eastern edge of Doncaster. The decision to proceed with such a large and complex project was the result of a lengthy analysis of the prospects for industry and employment in the area at a time when the traditional basis for this, coal-mining, was in decline, and a period of economic and social depression could be anticipated. Doncaster Metropolitan Borough Council came to the conclusion that they needed to introduce a new industry that would improve Doncaster's image, enhance the perceived quality of life in the town by providing new social amenities, and create the right atmosphere for attracting new investment and industry.

The Council already owned a 320-acre disused site on the eastern edge of Doncaster and it was decided to create there a large mixed-use park offering the widest possible range of leisure and tourism-based attractions. The centrepiece of the whole project is the Dome. This opened in the autumn of 1989, but work on the site will continue for several years as other landscaping and development projects are completed.

In terms of the range of activities housed under one roof, the Dome is one of the most ambitious centres yet attempted. The designers have risen to the challenge of organizing a plethora of different shapes, forms and activities with a stunning concept that gives all these disparate elements a unified and coherent architectural form. Among the activities accommodated are a free-form swimming-pool, a new concept in ice rinks, a sports hall, a bowls rink, squash courts, fitness and health suites, a snooker room, and the usual array of cafés, bars, spectator facilities and the centre's administration offices.

The architects have organized the plan on an axial basis, with the four major areas, swimming-pool, ice rink, sports hall and bowls hall, arranged around a central circulation spine. The spine develops into a huge circular atrium space at the centre of the building. This is the focal point for all activities, acting as a kind of hinge between the massive circular form of the swimming-pool and ice rink areas to the west, and the rectangular form of the sports and bowls halls paired together at the east end. The notional line of the central circulation spine continues in a curving extension at the east end, the 'tail of the dragon' as it were, which houses the five squash courts, administration and services plant.

The main entrance is sited at the west end of the circulation spine, leading into a pedestrian mall which bisects the semi-circular areas devoted to the swimming-pool and ice rinks. Public access is permitted unhindered through this zone and right into the central atrium or 'forum', a device to encourage casual visitors further into the centre and, by giving

enticing glimpses of the activities within, to tempt customers into joining in. Glazing along the mall gives views over the swimming-pools and ice rinks, and at one point a pair of brightly coloured flume tubes coil overhead on their sinuous path to the plunge pool. The swimming-pool can boast 24 different water features. The pool itself comprises six free-form pools linked together in a semi-circle but on different levels, a device which enables different user groups to be separated and enjoy a degree of privacy within the ambience of a larger space. Hovering over the pools, flying saucer fashion, is a health suite, featuring an Irish/Roman sauna, approached by an aerial gangway from the spectator gallery. The ice rink area has adopted some of the free-form principles of the pools. It is laid out as two separate rinks at different levels linked by gently sloping ramps that enable skaters to pass from one to the other without leaving the ice.

The more rigid requirements of the sports and bowls halls has inevitably resulted in a less dynamic interplay of spaces in the east half of the building. The rectangular volumes of the major areas back on to a central core accommodating changing and lavatory facilities, fitness training rooms and a snooker room.

At the centre of all this activity lies the forum, a dramatic, futuristic architectural statement providing the most memorable visual image of the whole centre. It is in the form of a solid masonry drum, 30 metres in diameter and 19 metres high, inside which a smaller secondary circle of masonry colums supports an upper level drum topped by a domed rooflight. The curved walls of the drum are punctuated by a number of openings leading into the various areas of the centre and out into the park. At first floor level a sophisticated metal and glass walkway circles the space, supported on chunky cylindrical masonry columns. The transition between the inner ring of masonry columns and the high-level drum is effected by means of a transfer into steel stub columns and corbels supporting an I-section ring beam below the masonry drum. Virtually all the exposed steel members, here and in the main concourse, are perforated with large regular holes, like a gigantic Meccano kit, adding decoration and lightening the visual effect. The metal work is either painted white or has a polished chrome finish.

The masonry walls employ a specially developed polished masonry block, in grey and cream colours. Two-course high bands of these colours are used throughout to break up the large areas of solid wall and avoid the need for applied decoration. The blocks are a wet-cast masonry using dolomite aggregates, and they are machine-polished on the exposed face to give a similar appearance to marble or granite. Terrazzo, in a pattern of grey and white squares, is used for the main floor area. The overall effect is startling and grandiose, like a gigantic stage-set for a play of the future. The Dome has become a destination in its own right since the centre opened; it hosts fashion shows, music recitals and exhibitions, as well as doubling as a theatre foyer when plays are put on in the events hall.

The external form of the building and the varied uses of structural forms and materials is intended to relate to the broader concepts underlying the planning strategy for the park. The north elevation is handled in a contained and formal way, in response to the adjacent line of the park boundary. To the south, the same component structural elements are handled in a much more diffuse, informal and fragmented manner, extending beyond the plane of the building like 'fingers' into the surrounding landscape. The structural framework is of steel construction. Much play is made of the decorative and dramatic possibilities inherent in the massive triangulated steel lattice beams spanning the major spaces from the central structural spine. On the curving north elevation these trusses are sliced off at the point of intersection with the external wall and at the same angle. The load is transferred to a single steel column by means of a corbelled column-head constructed from three perforated steel members, recalling the similar corbels used within the central forum. The bays between the columns are infilled with panels of banded masonry and a border of curtain wall glazing to produce a controlled and formal elevational design.

The south elevation is composed from the same structural components, but here the resolution of roof plane and trusses on to load-bearing columns is separated from the walls of the spaces behind to produce a fragmented profile of considerable complexity. The steel lattice beams sail beyond the external wall to be supported on free-standing columns clad in banded masonry. As on the north side, their triangular forms project through the overall roof plane like giant ribs. The free-standing columns have a corbelled masonry capping which supports a triangular open capital, each apex picking up one of the downstand legs at the end of the truss. It is an imaginative detail handled with great confidence and contributes to a level of structural exhibitionism rarely seen in public buildings these days.

The 33-month building programme commenced in November 1986 after a three-year concept and design development period which covered the strategy for the leisure park as a whole. Work finished in August 1989 for a total cost of just under £19 million. Further projects are envisaged for the completion of the park in years to come. For those who follow, the Dome has set the highest possible standards of design, combining a mastery of building technology and an almost outrageous inventiveness to produce a unique building that should do much to enhance Doncaster's future prospects.

HEADQUARTERS OF THE RMC GROUP, THORPE, SURREY

Architect: Edward Cullinan Architects
Landscape Architect: Derek Lovejoy & Partners

For the new international headquarters of a large commercial group, this is a remarkably self-effacing example of modern office design, being largely concealed beneath one of the largest roof gardens in Europe. A major influence in the choice of this design approach was the location of the site, which is just

inside the M25 motorway at Thorpe, Surrey, and right in the heart of London's green belt. The site was owned by the RMC Group as part of its gravel-bed holdings and the buildings on the site had previously been used as training centre. Despite the obvious problems associated with green belt development, RMC decided that this should be the site for their new headquarters building. The design concept was therefore developed to smooth the path as far as possible. Approval was received from the Department of the Environment inspector after a public inquiry in 1986, following an appeal against refusal of planning permission on principle by the local authority.

In response to the green belt location, and mindful of the views of the site from nearby St Ann's Hill, it was decided to retain all the existing trees, to keep three historic buildings already on the site but to clear away all superfluous and unsightly additions, and to arrange all the new office and ancillary accommodation in a predominantly single storey structure covered with extensive roof gardens. The unusual emphasis on the landscape component within the scheme and the large floor area resulting from the single storey layout generated a need for several internal courtyards to provide daylight. Consequently, the internal office spaces benefit from a relationship with the carefully landscaped outer world so close that in many instances they seem to merge completely.

The new building fills in the area of the site between the three retained historic buildings and links them together physically. On the western edge of the complex is Eastley End House, a three storey Georgian building internally decorated in full period style, which is for the use of the RMC directors. This has been extended on the south side in similar period style with a new circular dining-room wing at first floor level. A short distance to the south lies Meadlake House, a two storey brick-built stable block converted into residential units for staff on training courses. This too has been extended in a vernacular style with the addition of two wings which return at right angles to form a wide shallow U-shaped block enclosing a court. The ends of the wings are accentuated with a new staircase tower where they adjoin the existing building. The two extended historic buildings form the western boundary of the complex from which spring the new single storey offices in long wings which enclose three open courtyards and are covered by the roof gardens. The layout of the office wings and courtyards is developed on a strongly axial basis. The two major axes to north and south align with the central bays of the original buildings, and a third is centred on the new dining-room extension to Eastley End House.

Each of the major east-west axes forms the centre line of a courtyard with offices ranged either side. The spacious and formal northern courtyard reflects the character of Eastley End House and is laid out with trees and shrubs bordering a lawn and central pool. The equally large southern courtyard is less formal, with a lawn fronting Meadlake House. Where this courtyard narrows between the slightly angled façades of the offices, it is sub-divided by hedges into smaller gardens designed to give privacy to the adjacent offices. The third courtyard is smaller, narrow and designed as a complete contrast, being paved with cream coloured tiles and featuring a granite water channel connecting small fountains at the ends with a central pool.

The office accommodation is designed to enjoy as close a relationship as possible with its setting, obtaining as much natural light as possible and relying on natural ventilation, not air-conditioning. The offices are set out within a 6m × 3m module on a 6m × 6m structural grid. A completely glazed external wall to each unit incorporates a full-height sliding door for summertime ventilation and a small hopper for use at other times.

The office zone teminates on a long north-south corridor which forms the outer edge of the reception, dining and leisure facilities. These are also arranged around a central axis, this one running north-south and crossing the other axes at key points. The approach to the building is from the north along this main axis. Visitors arrive at a circular courtyard with a central fountain marking the crossing point of the axis with that from Eastley End Court. At this point an opening in the circular courtyard wall provides a glimpse of the north courtyard and the pool in front of Eastley End House.

The entrance is marked by the only two-storey section of the new building, where a cruciform-plan executive dining pavilion at first floor level sits over the reception foyer, two squash courts and the staff dining area. The reception area coincides with the third, central axis through the widest wing of the office accommodation. The entrance into the offices is to one side and framed by two glass-sided squash courts, while the axis continues on the opposite side through the centre of a white concrete spiral staircase leading to the first floor dining-rooms. These are lit by clerestory windows and by fully glazed sections at the centres on the main axes, and look out over the landscaped roof, conveying the feeling of a garden pavilion.

Continuing past the reception area on the main entrance axis, the axial route is terminated by a substantial indoor swimming-pool. From here the view extends over the pool, through the angled bay of the glazed end wall and out over a wide expanse of lake. The vista is framed by the semi-circular profile of a new brick-arched pedestrian bridge. The existing lake has been extended as part of the landscape design and in an imaginative stroke has been brought right up to the new building, creating a direct visual link with the internal pool. The route continues around and past the swimming-pool to a coffee area next to a lecture room. From this point a third axial view is obtained across the pool and out into Meadlake Court, with the central bay of Meadlake House at the far end.

The main north-south axial route combines the functions of office reception area and social heart of the complex. The treatment of space and the cool, white ambience create a relaxed feeling more akin to a smart country club than a formal office building. The organization of functions around these principal axes and cross-axes gives the building a strong

underlying sense of structure and order that echoes the symmetry embodied in the historic buildings, but at no time is the effect rigid. Views constantly change, space and light are carefully modulated to produce a varied and picturesque architectural experience. The complex runs out at the south-east corner beyond the swimming pool, where it links in with the third existing building, The Grange. This is an Arts and Crafts period house which now contains training rooms, offices and a social centre. The Grange extends away from the new building to be almost entirely free standing in its parkland setting.

Aside from the confident and masterful control of planning, the design has benefited from considerable expertise in landscaping, and the contribution of the landscape architects must be recognized. At a number of points, such as along the north boundary where the enclosing brick walls curve in and out to avoid the mature trees, the existing landscape has exerted a direct influence on the building form. Elsewhere in the new courtyard and roof garden areas, the space is defined and structured by areas of lawn, hedges, geometric planting beds, pergolas and areas of hard landscaping. At the edges of the roof gardens the planting is closely related to the visible external structure of the offices. Long planting troughs supported behind exposed vierendeel trusses contain clipped yew hedges and, marking the structural bay positions in the offices below, small spherical clipped holly bushes housed in circular pots are supported between pairs of free-standing, white-painted steel columns. The planting acts as a natural balustrade picking up the rhythm of the office layout and structure.

A number of features are designed into the roofscape, such as a pergola which conceals air inlets and outlets for the offices, and a raised diamond shaped platform, or belvedere, above the projecting window of the swimming-pool which gives views out over the lake to St Ann's Hill. The floor of this area is paved in black and white squares like a chessboard, and the over-sized modernistic bright red and white metal chess pieces in the adjacent roof garden are cowls concealing ductwork and extract vents.

The design of this fascinating building works on many layers. On the one hand there is a sense of architectural humour and a respect for classical symmetry in the underlying axial structure, and on the other, there is a predisposition to the picturesque in the sequence of spaces and views and the degree of asymmetry. Underlying all is the recognition of the need to provide a sociable and humane working environment for the office users and a completed building that enhances the qualities of the green belt. To combine all this in a building of considerable integrity and distinction is a great achievement on the part of all concerned.

HALL OF RESIDENCE, PEMBROKE COLLEGE, OXFORD
Architect: Maguire & Co.

Many of the best examples of modern architecture are to be found within the precincts of the universities of Oxford and Cambridge. It can be no accident that many of these have arisen as a result of these institutions' policy of limited architectural competitions. The newly completed student hall of residence at Pembroke College, Oxford (to be known as the Sir Geoffrey Arthur Building), is the result of an architectural competition held in 1986. The hall was offically opened in June 1990.

The design of the winning entry of Robert Maguire and Keith Murray Architects in many ways favoured the traditional pattern for student accommodation: two quadrangles, east and west, of two and three storey buildings, forming a secure 'wall' around the site, with a single point of public access controlled from the porter's lodge. The northern edge of the building follows the curving line of the river bank which forms one edge of the site. Despite its attractive riverside setting on the rural outskirts of Oxford, the site posed several demanding environmental problems, being the former location of the city's gas works. This operation had left the ground polluted and special measures were required for any new buildings.

The solution adopted was to raise the ground floor of the building throughout and provide a ventilated undercroft to deal with the possible release of gases. The raising of the accommodation over this substantial base proved to be an excellent means of improving the security of the accommodation, particularly at ground floor level where the level of the windows are well above the head height of any people passing outside. Ensuring adequate privacy and security for students has become an increasingly critical aspect of the design of college residences and was an important component of the design brief. The layout of the plan, with its single entry point, also reflects the need to control and supervise those gaining access to the building.

The main point of entry is provided by a break in the continuity of the 'wall' where the southern wing of the East Quad extends beyond the line of the main east wing, which is separated into two overlapping sections. A long, gently inclined flight of brick steps rises against the eastern façade from the brick paved forecourt, leading up through the gap at the re-entrant corner past the porter's office and into the corner of the East Quad. In the East Quad a stone flagged perimeter pathway surrounds a large grassed sunken garden, the main area of which is at the original site level.

The accommodation includes 96 study bedrooms arranged, in the traditional manner of undergraduate rooms, with access from the staircases. Each of the 14 staircases gives access to six rooms at ground and first floor levels, with a communal kitchen, common room and bathroom at second floor level. A number of graduate flats are also provided, together with a dining room and bar, a gymnasium, a small pavilion containing music practice rooms, and on the east side at first floor level the Rockefeller room, which leads out into an open loggia overlooking the entry forecourt.

The treatment of the external façades also echoes traditional collegiate architecture, but in a simple, straightforward style befitting its contemporary date and devoid of any superfluous decoration. Built within an extremely tight budget, the building adopts the mellow, honey-coloured tones of traditional Cotswold stonework. However, the external walls are constructed not of natural stone but from a special cast-masonry blockwork, with precast window surrounds and dressings in similar lighter-coloured material. The blockwork is given some of the visual quality of natural stonework by the use of large and small blocks in alternating courses, the larger blocks being twice the height and twice the length of the smaller blocks. The windows are simple, glazed sash windows in natural oak, which is being allowed to weather to an attractive silver grey colour. The simple punched window openings are grouped in twos, threes and fours to modulate the rhythm of the openings within the predominantly solid external walls.

Though mainly two storeys in height, the walls rise to three storeys at the corners. Here, projecting bays step forward from the main building line, forming tower-like features which break through the main roof plane and are capped by hipped and pyramidal roof forms. The roofing material is a natural, dark grey Spanish slate, its broad expanses punctuated by the larger tower elements and intermediate triangular dormer windows lighting the second floor rooms within the roof space. Smaller semi-circular variants of the projecting bays add further interest at key points, such as overlooking the entry forecourt and as a 'hinge' point on the north elevation. Though the overall building form is essentially simple and traditional, the interrupted eaves lines, the varied roofscape and the patterns of window openings all make this a lively composition, crisply and economically detailed and clearly modern in outlook. Indeed, there are so few overt stylistic references to earlier periods that the heavily rusticated central columns supporting the lintels over the covered passageway between the East and West Quads look rather out of place; the alternating cubes and drums of each successive course recall some of the more Mannerist classical column styles.

However, the building is definitely not Mannerist. Though it eschews the technological sophistication of many Modern movement masterpieces, it stands as a thoroughly modern building, solid and dignified. It will doubtless mellow gracefully over the years as it provides a peaceful, secure and high quality environment for future generations of students.

ST ENOCH CENTRE, GLASGOW
Archiects: GMW Partnership in association with Reiach and Hall

One of the largest buildings to be erected in Scotland in recent times, the St Enoch Centre treads the thin line between architecture and engineering with flair and confidence, its bold and simple forms made all the more impressive by virtue of the complexity and awesome scale of the structure. Built on the site of the St Enoch railway terminus and hotel, the new centre clearly owes a visual debt to the high glazed arches of the old train shed, and may also be seen as reflecting the vigorous engineering and shipbuilding traditions of Glasgow.

Viewed from across the Clyde the centre resembles a gigantic greenhouse. Vast, sloping surfaces of glazing terminate in a long 'backbone' of pyramidal rooflights, and sweep down at low level to form wide projecting canopies over the entrances. The centre is reputed to be the largest glazed enclosure in Europe. Located on a 6·5 hectare site to the south and east of Argyll Street and St Enoch's Square, it is ringed on three sides by traditional Glasgow commercial terraces. But it makes no apologies for its modernistic style where it breaks through for the principal entrance points in Argyll Street and St Enoch's Square, where its scale could not be further removed from the charming Jacobean style of the St Enoch travel centre.

Like all large new shopping centres, easy access by car is of critical importance for its commercial success. Here, the car-park assumes its natural location at the heart of the building, providing an opportunity for a dramatic entry point and generating good circulation for the pedestrian malls which wrap around two sides. The pitched glazed greenhouse structure turns out to be more of a huge lean-to conservatory, the solid central mass of the 750-car-park block supporting a dramatic array of sloping triangulated trusses, under the L-shaped glazed envelope.

The main structure spans 40 metres, with sloping lattice trusses at 14·4 metre centres supported on 1 metre diameter steel columns around the perimeter, and rising to a maximum height of 32 metres above mall level. These major trusses are linked by lattice purlins. Pairs of trusses are also supported at the upper level from columns placed centrally between them by means of triangulated 'tree-heads' which sprout pairs of inclined triangulated lattice truss supports. These coincide with the corners of the row of pyramid lantern rooflights which form the articulated ridge profile seen from a distance, and which also act as ventilators.

All the structural elements are painted white, in the glasshouse tradition, and this helps to lighten what would otherwise be an overwhelmingly complex roof structure. The glazing system, covering 26,000 square metres, was specially developed to meet a particularly onerous set of performance criteria; it is required to cope with the expected movement of a huge supporting structure, as well as the problems of intense sunlight and the worst of Scotland's winter weather. The glazing employs single sheet 6mm toughened and heat-sealed glass, and the system also incorporates computer-controlled motorized internal solar blinds to prevent direct sunlight falling on the shopping malls. Natural ventilation is provided by a series of vents around the perimeter base which draw in cooler air as warm air rises to be extracted from the roof level pyramid ventilators.

For all the height and drama of the internal spaces, however, the shopping activities are confined to just two lower levels. There are some seventy shop units fronting the malls at ground and first floor levels, with an ice rink and 450-seat Food Court area located at the corner of the L-shaped malls. Split-level seating areas enable diners to watch the antics on the ice rink or peruse the long views down the main

malls. The views are enlivened by the projecting balconies and bridge links of the upper mall and a vast internal trellised planting structure supported from the blank walls of the seven-level multi-storey car-park. Pairs of glass-sided wall-climber lifts shuttle up and down inside glass tubes at the corners of the car-park block, ferrying shoppers down from their cars to the malls below and providing exciting views of the activity far below and the visual drama of the roof above.

Cars enter the centre on the south side via a circular ramp from which the carriageways develop into bridges suspended from trussed pylons. The roadway passes through the glazed envelope and enters a mirror-glazed tube which spans right across the shopping malls and enters the lowest level of the central car-park block. The mirror glazing is deceptive, however, because the sides of the tube are in fact one-way glass. Unbeknown to shoppers below, those arriving by car have the rather strange experience of gazing down on the interiors unnoticed, the upper surface of the tube being clear-glazed to permit views of the roof.

Despite the extensive areas of glazing and the dominant feeling of light and airiness, one is not aware of significant views out to surrounding buildings or streets. With sightlines enclosed by the shop units at both pedestrian levels, the space focuses in upon itself and one is left to contemplate the sky and the intricate spider's web of steel latticework overhead.

The sloping roof concept is the single dominating architectural idea of the entire complex and has been implemented with skill and determination. While undeniably impressive in its scale and detailing, it is at the same time the one element that fails to impress in its relationship with the surrounding townscape of Glasgow's city centre. It is perhaps least successful in the short but violent intrusion into the sober street elevations of Argyll Street. Here the treatment of the shopfronts and the entrance tucked to one side lacks the clarity, precision and flair that are essential if the very literally expressed cutting edge of technology is not to appear impersonal, crude and overscaled. As it is, the mechanistic appearance, allied to the receding form of the sloping glazing, creates an uneasy relationship between new and old.

Despite this the designers deserve great credit for having the courage to design a major new retail centre in a historic setting without resorting to the current vogue for superficial pastiche. It is perhaps because so few are permitted to explore truly contemporary solutions that questions of scale, proportion and appropriateness for the context are still being explored.

The building cost in the region of £60 million and is a major project for the developers, the Church Commissioners for England and Sears Property, Glasgow. However, with a solid location in the retail heartland of Argyll and Buchanan Streets, its commercial success seems assured. Glasgow's shoppers have acquired another handsome internal street space to complement the earlier Princes Square development (*see* Architecture summary, **Whita-**

ker's Almanack 1989), yet one which offers an interesting contrast of scale and style.

IMPERIUM BUILDING, READING
Architect: Bennetts Associates

Designed as a landmark building for a key site on the route into Reading from the M4 Motorway, this crisp, new, white, consciously modern building exemplifies the best qualities to be found in the integration of office and light industry uses that characterized the emergence of high-tech companies during the 1980s. The building is sited to exploit its future position next to the new A33 relief road (which has yet to be constructed). It is set close to the line of the new road, with its main entrance elevation overlooking the site of a major roundabout.

From the start the architects sought to achieve a building form of great clarity and simplicity. This has been accomplished with a layout of elements that is immediately intelligible to the visitor, and sufficient attention to visual complexity, detailing and use of quality materials to provide an interesting aesthetic experience. With little inspiration to be gained from its immediate context, the architectural appearance evolved largely from the building's internal organization and its relationship with the new road.

From the main entrance, the content and layout of the building is immediately apparent; two parallel wings of office accommodation on three floors enclosing a central atrium. The office wings are clad in a white panelled proprietary cladding system. Their relative solidity contrasts with the openness and transparency of the central atrium, which has a glazed roof and a fully glazed end wall incorporating the main entrance doors. The office floors are 18 metres deep, and provide clear open space uninterrupted by circulation or service cores, with a single row of columns at 7·5 metre centres dividing the 18 metre depth into a 12 metre span externally and 6 metres facing into the atrium. The 6 metre bays either side of the atrium are expressed on the shorter front and rear elevations. The four main escape staircases are pulled forwards from the elevations and enclosed in solid cylindrical towers defining and emphasizing the entrance. These central zones of the building have flat roofs, with simple box-like plant rooms over them. The 12 metre spans of the outer office zones are expressed on the short elevations by means of barrel-vaulted roof forms, though unfortunately these are not expressed internally. The central atrium has a simple shallow-pitched glazed roof rising above the general eaves or cornice line. Thus the organization of the internal plan and structure is clearly reflected on the external elevations, enabling the building to be easily 'read' on arrival.

This perception is assisted by the treatment of the site and the access routes into the building. One of the disappointing aspects of many modern business parks and 'green field' developments is the tendency for buildings to be surrounded and dominated by acres of intrusive car-parking. At the Imperium Building 430 car-parking spaces were required to satisfy the needs of the occupants, calculated at the rate of one space for every 205 square feet of the 106,000 square feet total net office space. Positive steps were needed, therefore, to integrate the car-parks so as to minimize their visual intrusion and benefit the outlook of the building users as well as the public image of the building itself.

The solution adopted has been to raise the level of the ground floor some 2 metres above the general site level. This allows 130 cars to be parked directly beneath the building and also provides a covered basement drop-off point. The remainder of the car-parking is outside but substantially below the level of the ground floor office windows. With the building located at the corner of the site and grass embankments along the line of the new road, the car-parks are much less conspicuous to passers-by and will be further screened as a formal landscaping scheme of American oaks and Hornbeam hedges grows to maturity.

A long sloping path lined by seven mature horse-chestnut trees leads from the car-park towards the main entrance. As it passes the first of the front pair of stair towers, the ground falls away and the path becomes a steel bridge crossing a pool with a waterfall. An abrupt change of direction brings the visitor directly on to the axial line of the central atrium and the main entrance doors. This device adds drama to the approach and emphasizes the raised floor level of the building in its landscape setting, an effect which is enhanced by the decision to clad the basement level in dark brick, leaving the white panelled cladding floating delicately above.

As is often the case with speculative building, the atrium is the only internal space fully fitted out in an architectural style sympathetic to the general character of the building, the office floors being very much at the mercy of the tenants' fitting-out programmes. In the atrium natural materials have been used to enhance the feeling of quality already generated by the carefully engineered horizontal panels of the glazed screen at the entrance, and the spatial interest created by the three-storey space, open staircases and glazed lift. Panels of American oak mirror the glass and metal panels of the exterior cladding system, and the floor is paved with slabs of Jura limestone with a Genoa slate surround.

Simple rectangular buildings clad in proprietary systems can easily become repetitive in their elevations. Here, however, the long elevations in particular are helped by differences in floor height and modulation that imply a hierarchy and progression of spaces through the building that are not entirely apparent from the inside but are significant externally. The ground floor has a slightly higher storey height, 3·05 metres instead of 2·7 metres, and has three horizontal bands of glazing, compared to the two bands at first floor level. It is designed for heavier loadings and has the option of additional air-conditioning capacity, so that it could function as a computer suite, a 'clean' area, or for storage of manufactured components. The top storey has a much closer rhythm of vertical sub-divisions and appears more like an attic storey of windows than curtain walling. This feature is accentuated by the face of the cladding being slightly recessed behind the main plane of the façade, and by the continuous lines of the projecting sill below and the eaves or cornice above. The three floors each have an identity and an order as a group, and contrast happily in their whiteness, lightness and delicacy with the heavy brick and concrete base.

Construction work lasted for 18 months and the building was completed in March 1990 for a total cost of £9·4 million. The developer, Speyhawk, has good reason to be satisfied with its investment. The Imperium Building demonstrates that with sufficient care and commitment on the part of clients and designers alike, relatively simple and straightforward buildings can be elevated into works of architectural delight.

ARCHAEOLOGY 1989–90

Globe Theatre excavation

The investigation of part of the site of the Globe Theatre was not accompanied by the same intensity of public debate which characterized the investigation of the Rose Theatre only a matter of a few months previously. The reasons may be, first, that the owners of the site of the Globe Theatre, Hanson PLC, demonstrated a commitment to the investigation and treatment of the remains of the theatre, not least by funding the excavation; and second, the remains of the Globe Theatre were scheduled as an ancient monument on December 13, 1989.

The excavation of the Globe theatre is described in *London Archaeologist*, Spring 1990, Volume 6, Number 6. The report explains how the Museum of London's Department of Greater London Archaeology worked on the site between July 3 and October 16, 1989. The area involved lies to the east of Southwark Bridge Road and south of Park Street and revealed only a small part of the Globe Theatre, approximately 12m × 9m (40ft × 30ft). The archaeologists found part of the north-east section of the theatre and revealed three parallel wall foundations, two of brick and one of chalk and timber. 'The central chalk and timber foundation, which is of a solid mortared construction, would have supported the outer gallery wall of the first theatre. No trace of the inner gallery wall of the earlier theatre has been found, but a short length of the substantial brick and mortar foundation for the inner gallery wall of the second survives. The bottom brick course of the outer gallery wall of the second Globe was supported on the foundation for the first outer wall. Brick cross walls added at the time of the construction of the later theatre extend to the east and link with other brick walls, which may well belong to an outside staircase/turret. The gap in the easternmost wall may be an entrance to the theatre. Partially overlying one of the two cross walls between the inner and outer gallery walls of the second theatre are patches of crushed hazelnut shells and silt, remains of the internal floor surfaces. Lying on top of this flooring was a farthing of Charles I (1625–42). Abutting the eastern edge of the outer wall are the remains of the exterior gravel metalling where people may have stood before entering the theatre for a performance. The build-up of material which covered the remains of the Globe is probably the debris from the destruction and levelling of the second Globe in 1644. It consisted primarily of 17th-century brick and tiles, but included pottery and clay pipes.'

Although only about 5 per cent of the Globe was uncovered—much more probably still lies under Anchor Terrace to the west—archaeologists can already begin to make comparisons with the Rose Theatre found nearby. For example, both had hazelnut flooring and their gallery walls were similar distances apart. The main difference so far seems to be that 'The Rose had mainly chalk foundations, which may have supported brick work and then timber, while the Globe's foundations were of chalk with timber for the first theatre and mostly of brick for the second.'

The archaeological record is likely to be of great importance in interpreting the history of the Globe, because so little is known from other sources. It is described as 'this wooden O' in the prologue to Shakespeare's *Henry V*, and there is a view by C. J. Visscher published in 1616 showing a three-storey gallery, octagonal in shape and sloping inwards from the top, while a later view by Wenceslas Hollar, drawn in 1630 and published in 1647, depicts a squat, circular theatre. It is known that the Globe was built in the spring of 1599, after the construction of the Rose in 1587 and the Swan in 1596. The report in *London Archaeologist* notes that: 'The cost of both of the lease on the Globe estate and of construction was divided, one half being met by Cuthbert and Richard Burbage, William Kempe, Augustine Phillips, Thomas Pope and William Shakespeare. The Globe was constructed by a carpenter, Peter Streete, using timbers from the dismantled theatre which had been built in Shoreditch in 1576 by the Burbage family. The Globe soon became one of the most popular theatres of the day. Many leading dramatists, including Ben Jonson, Thomas Dekker and William Shakespeare, wrote works especially for it. It was the Globe that saw the first performances of (amongst others), *Hamlet*, *Othello*, *King Lear*, and *Macbeth*, with Richard Burbage in the title roles.' By the time it was pulled down on Cromwell's orders in 1644, the Globe had already been rebuilt since it caught fire and was destroyed as a result of a cannon being fired during the first performance of Shakespeare's *Henry VIII* on June 29, 1613.

The Icklingham Bronzes

'One of the biggest archaeological storms in recent years' was how the *British Archaeological News* for November 1989 described the events surrounding the illegal removal (i.e., without the permission either of the landowner or the Secretary of State) from a scheduled ancient monument at Weatherhill Farm, Icklingham, Suffolk, of a hoard of sixteen Romano-British bronzes in 1982. These subsequently appeared for sale in New York in 1989, having previously been purchased in Switzerland. 'The finest specimen, a bronze cheetah inlaid with silver had been offered for sale to the Getty Museum in California for $600,000.' It is reported that the owner of the land from which the bronzes had been taken, and therefore the lawful owner of the items in question, Mr. John Browning, wished to regain possession of his property, although other proposals for its future had been made. However, he failed in his efforts to get any assistance in his quest, from the Government, through the Office of Arts and Libraries. It is argued that the main reason for this is that successive UK governments have failed to ratify the 1970 Unesco Convention on the Means of Prohibiting and Preventing the Illicit Import, Export, and Transfer of Ownership of Cultural Property.

If progress was not possible on the international front, then action could still be taken under English law by a resolute landowner and local constabulary. In the words of *British Archaeological News*: 'It is clear that a whole series of offences have been committed in this case. Under the 1979 Act it is an offence to use a metal detector on a protected site or to remove material from it without the permission of the Secretary of State, whilst no archaeological material from the soil of Britain may be exported without an export licence. No such permission was granted nor was any application made for an export licence. Since Mr. Browning as the owner of the land has title to any material in the soil, an offence will have been committed under the Theft Act by virtue of the material having been removed without his consent.' It was reported that the Suffolk Police had arrested six people who were charged and released on bail in connection with offences under the Ancient Monuments and Archaeological Areas Act 1979, while the January 1990 issue of *British Archaeological News* reports that: 'Two treasure hunters caught on the scheduled site at Icklingham (Suffolk) with Roman and Medieval coins in their pockets were fined £350 for theft and £150 for unauthorized use of metal detectors and had their detectors confiscated by Mildenhall Magistrates on 13th November. A third man admitted stealing coins and was also fined £350. This brings to thirteen the number of people brought to trial by the owner of the site, Mr. John Browning.'

Colchester Roman Church

Most archaeological excavation is undertaken in advance of development of some kind, whether it be road building, office construction or new homes. However interesting the discoveries, unless they can be removed to a museum, they are usually swept away in the ensuing development. Therefore, it is worth remarking upon an occasion when the discoveries are retained, consolidated and open to the public. In late September 1989 representatives of various Christian denominations gathered together to mark the opening to the public of the remains of what is believed to be a Roman church in Colchester, Essex. The project is described in an article in *Church Archaeology*, Number 120, June 1990, in which it is noted that the church lies very close to the new police station. In the course of preparing the ground, two cemeteries of Roman date were investigated, the second overlying the first. This second cemetery was for Christians, whereas the first one had been for pagans, and probably dated to the early part of the fourth century. 'The graves were east-west with the heads to the west, and were laid out in tightly-packed rows which, as the number of burials grew, crept over and gradually obliterated the graves of the first cemetery'. Now the church was at one corner of the cemetery and is described as being 'a long narrow building, oriented east-west, to which an apse was added at the east end in a secondary phase. The building was divided by a wooden screen: two rows of posts run down the eastern half, forming aisles. It was built between AD 320–340 and was contemporary with the second cemetery. However it was altered during its life in substantial ways. The apse was a later addition, the west wall had been rebuilt and the internal plan had been radically modified by the insertion of substantial posts.' Although it is difficult, so it is explained, to be absolutely certain that this building was a church because no proof such as Christian wall paintings or the use of chi-rho monogram were found, nevertheless the plan of the building and its association with the cemetery suggest that this is the most likely explanation. It is further explained that 'Some grave-like pits at the eastern end of the church may have been the burial place of important local Christians. Finds from the site included hundreds of 4th century coins and five complete oil lamps—hinting perhaps that the interior was rather dark? There was also extraordinary evidence that funerary and/or commemorative meals may have taken place in the church: there were two iron vessels—one of them a frying pan, while the animal bones contained an abnormally high number of bird and young pig remains.'

Roman Britain

An extensive summary of work carried out on sites of the Roman period is contained in *Britannia*, Volume XX for 1989. It is not possible here to do justice to the vast range of sites investigated, not least along the line of Hadrian's Wall and in London, but it should be noted that in West Glamorgan the excavation of Loughor Fort which started in 1987 has been completed and the results collated with those from earlier seasons. It is reported that a total of 18 Roman phases was identified, with six representing major construction. It is thought that the fort was founded in about AD 75 and partly abandoned

by about AD 130, although there is limited evidence for late 3rd-century occupation. In Durham, it is noted that at Piercebridge 'a large quantity of votive objects and pottery was recovered by divers at the site of the Roman bridge over the Tees, they included coins ranging from AD 70 to 350, brooches, rings, figurines and bronze pins, together with pottery of first- to fourth-century date'. In Greater Manchester the excavation of the fortlet at Castleshaw Fort was completed and it is noted that 'Although examination of the undisturbed features was not permitted, recovery of the plan is now virtually complete. Except for a stone hypocaust, all the buildings were of timber and consisted of a number of workshops, a courtyard-building and a granary of a size more suitable for a fort than a fortlet. In a second phase the granary had been enlarged to the north with an additional row of posts.'

Coin hoards of the Roman period continue to be recovered. For example, at Wishaw, Warwickshire, it is reported that 'a hoard of 197 antoniniani, Gallienus to Tetrichus II, was recovered by metal-detector in the base of a grey storage jar and spread by the plough. The vicinity of the find has yielded tiles, seven brooches, second- to fourth-century pottery and traces of bronze-working'. The remains of what appears to be another scattered hoard of twelve denarii, Flavian to late Antonine, was also found in the area. At Cottenham in Cambridgeshire a hoard of 5,084 3rd-century coins was reported, while at Baylham in Suffolk a scattered hoard of 33 coins, all of Carausius, apart from one of the early third century, was found by a metal-detector user. Also found by chance at Bampton in Oxfordshire was 'a limestone altar with a round-headed niche containing a relief of Fortuna holding a cornucopia' which was ploughed up badly damaged. In the same county, at Bowling Green Farm, Stanford in the Vale, 'the fourth-century settlement previously recorded was found to overlie an earlier villa within the ditched enclosure; the ditch of this yielded second-century pottery, burnt grain and painted plaster. Almost all of the 300 coins from the overlying settlement are issues of AD 348–368 and include a substantial number of copies.'

Road construction was the reason for the discovery at Wavendon Gate, Walton, Bucks., of 13 second-century cremations in both pottery and glass vessels. 'Grave-goods included a tinned bronze mirror. Later excavations showed the cemetery to lie within a ditched enclosure measuring *c.*140 by 100m, which also contained numerous post-holes, pits and ditches. To the north lay a polygonal Iron Age enclosure and round houses defined by penannular ditches. A small group of later cremations lay 200m to the south-east.'

At Harlow Temple in Essex the reinvestigation of the forecourt of the Romano-Celtic temple over three seasons 'has revealed an underlying circular Iron Age building 13m in diameter and a number of adjacent post-holes: 595 Celtic coins were recovered, mainly of Cunobelin, the great majority within or close to the structure. Other finds included brooches and a bronze chape. Post-conquest finds included a crude stone relief of a warrior god and the head of a cult statue of Minerva ... together with a bronze votive leaf, three iron spearheads, horse bits and a miniature pewter cup.' In the same county archaeological excavations in advance of the development of Stansted Airport led to the discovery at Duckend Farm that 'a complex series of late Roman ditches was cut through an earlier cremation cemetery. Fourteen burials ranging from the late Iron Age to the 2nd century included four which were richly furnished, one yielding several complete pots, bone and bronze bridal-fittings, and the bronze mounts of a casket.' At Duckend car park 'topsoil-stripping revealed ditches of late Iron Age and Roman date and two cobbled areas. Further south lay over 30 cremation burials ranging from the middle of the first century BC to the mid-second century AD. Several were richly furnished. One, perhaps of a male, yielded five bronze vessels including an engraved and silver-inlaid flagon, five glass vessels, a colour-coated beaker, an iron knife and a "carrot" amphora. The cremation had been placed on a metal tray within an iron-bound casket. Nearby was a possibly female cremation, also placed in a casket with iron fittings and accompanied by five Samian vessels with other pottery, two glass vessels, bronze jewellery, a pair of sandals and a rectangular mirror.'

Among the many extensive discoveries in London, mention should be made of the scatter of over 500 forger's coin moulds, some of which were for late third-century low-denomination bronzes, recovered during excavations at 85 London Wall and 53 New Broad Street. At numbers 19–25 Old Bailey, up to seven kilns were reported but only one in such a state as to suggest the manufacture of fine pottery. These kilns were replaced by 'a large octagonal building, probably a Romano-Celtic temple. It was 16m in diameter with a surrounding ambulatory 3·75m wide; robbing was complete, but red-painted plaster, rag-stones and *opus signinum* survived. Later the site was occupied by a large masonry building containing at least nine rooms. This had been reconstructed once, and later a hypocaust was added. A coin of 335–41 was found in the demolition-deposit.' In Holborn, at Barnard's Inn, 'in the south part of the site early gravel-pits were refilled in the first and second centuries, and there were three burials of the second to fourth centuries lying east of a N.–S. ditch and possible fence. In the centre of the site the sequence was similar. One cremation was contained in a Verulamium-region face-pot, and another lay in a cist of six bricks; an inhumation had a necklace of 66 jet beads, a jet finger-ring and a bone pin.'

At Northview Hospital, Purton, Wiltshire, 'part of a probably walled cemetery was examined; 30m of the south boundary wall was seen. Of six inhumations of the third and fourth centuries two were in large limestone coffins, one of them with a lead lining and occupying a large grave-pit surrounded by a wall 18m in diameter, as if for a tumulus. A cremation was buried in a limestone ossuary 1m square containing a circular lead cannister decorated with bead-and-reel at the rim and two opposing St. Andrew's crosses separated by scallop-shell decoration. Within this was a blue glass vessel containing the ashes.' Perhaps one of the most unusual discoveries of the year was at East Wear Bay, Folkestone, Kent, where 'over 130 green sand quernstones, both upper and lower, in various stages of manufacture have been recovered from the beach below the villa site on East Cliff. They derive from a low gault cliff where in 1974 excavation revealed stratified deposits, one of which was composed entirely of greensand chippings associated with querns and first-century pottery. The discoveries indicate a quern-factory, originating perhaps in the late Iron Age, using material from the Folkestone Beds which outcrop at the south end of the beach.'

Medieval Period

An extensive survey of work relating to the medieval period was published in *Medieval Archaeology*, Volume XXXIII, for 1989. Amongst the important excavations may be noted work at the Round Tower of Windsor Castle, Berkshire, where 'on January 28, 1988 movement of the foundations of the Round Tower occurred causing cracks in external and internal walls of the W. side of the Tower. A soil survey of the motte and the Tower foundations was carried out to determine the cause and nature of the

movement.' It is reported that 'geotechnical analysis of the test data shows that the motte is an inadequate base for the Tower, and that further movement may occur; it is therefore proposed that the foundation be strengthened, with underpinning of the walls and piling of the motte. This will be preceded by archaeological evaluation of the interior of the shell keep, both of the surviving 14th-century wooden interior structure and of the stratigraphy of the motte summit, followed by full excavation where necessary.'

In Cambridgeshire, at Barrington, 'a report of Saxon remains led to the excavation of two skeletons. One was accompanied by a knife and shield, the other by two gilded saucer brooches, blue glass and amber beads, and an iron and silver buckle. Many other Saxon artefacts have been found in plough soil by a metal detector. Attempts to purchase the field to protect the extensive cemetery have so far failed.' In Carlisle, Cumbria, excavations at the Cathedral Treasury outside the west end of the Cathedral revealed a Saxon cemetery. 'Forty-one inhumations were recovered, representing at least three phases of burial. An important group of artefacts was recovered from the cemetery, including buckles, strap-ends and a pendant whetstone. Most were of 10th-century date, though earlier origins for the graveyard are suggested by a 9th-century strap-end and a radio-carbon date of AD 750 ± 70 from a skeleton excavated in 1985. The foundations for the N. wall and N. arcade of the Cathedral nave cut the cemetery. The nave was partially destroyed during the Civil War. The most important medieval find was a small jet crucifix probably dating from the second half of the 13th century.'

At Little Holland Church in Essex, development enabled archaeologists to locate its remains, although it was previously thought to have been completely destroyed. 'The ground-plan was found to survive almost intact, and four building periods were identi-fied. The first, dated tentatively to the 11th/12th century, consisted of a single-celled, absidal-ended church measuring 13·4 × 6m. This was later (12th/13th century) lengthened by some 4m and divided off into nave and chancel. Subsequently (13th/14th century) both W. and E. walls were rebuilt, and the apsidal E. end squared off. This work was in mortared local septaria stone, whereas the previous periods were in unmortared septaria. The final alteration was the addition of diagonal buttresses to the E. wall (15th/16th century). Documentary references give a demolition date for the church of *c.* 1659.' Also in Essex, at Southend, investigations into numbers 269–71 Victoria Avenue suggest that two dwellings with a cartway through the centre to provide access to the rear had originally, before the 18th century, been a central hall with cross-walls. 'Documentary research is continuing but it is suggested that the original hall and cross-wings were built as a yeoman's house between AD 1450–70 with subsequent alterations.' In north-west Essex, at Priors Hall, Widdington, 'recent work on the Hall, formerly known as Stone Hall and reputed to be 13th century in origin, has established that it incorporates a substantial stone building of Saxon date. The building appears to have been a two-celled structure. . . . It seems most likely that this building was a church, perhaps associated with the pre-Conquest manor which was granted to the Abbey of St. Valery in Picardy after 1066.'

In London at 54–66 Carter Lane, 1–3 Pilgrim Street, and 29–33 Ludgate Hill, archaeologists discovered that 'the earliest features on site were the truncated pits and portions of the ditches of a Norman period (1050–1200) fortress (perhaps Montfichet's Tower). . . . this fortress was probably a motte and bailey complex on Ludgate Hill inside the city walls. The fortress was defended by ditches on three sides approximately in line with modern streets (N., Ludgate Hill; E., probably Creed Lane; S., Carter Lane) and with the city wall on the fourth side. The fortress is recorded as being in ruins by 1272, and in either 1274 or 1276 the Dominicans acquired it as a stone quarry to provide materials to help build their new friary nearby. The later S. ditch was systematically infilled (date 1150–1350), then used as part of the friary cemetery. Sixty articulated inhumations were excavated on the present site, thirteen in a mass grave, two in a double grave and the rest were single burials. Twenty-five had evidence of wooden coffins; there was also one lead coffin. There were five possibly empty or unused graves. The overall plan of the graves showed a regular layout. Finds from the grave fills indicate a 13th- or 14th-century date; two graves may be as late as *c.* 1500. Several of the medieval burials were accompanied by grave-goods, in the form of built-fittings, pins, a spindle-whorl and a "prunted" glass beaker.'

Also in London, at 85 London Wall and 53 New Broad Street, investigations exposed lengths of the standing city wall. The medieval face of the wall utilized reworked Roman core blocks of ragstone and tiles and the medieval core used new materials such as flint and chalk. The wall is preserved as a scheduled ancient monument and a panel exposing the face of the medieval wall is to be left uncovered for public inspection.' At the Royal Mint site in East Smithfield excavations were completed on the site of the Cistercian Abbey of St. Mary Graces which was founded in 1350, and the Royal Navy Victualling Yard founded in 1560. 'Excavations of the E. end of the church, the chapter house, the N. end of the infirmary and the W. alley of the cloisters was completed. Within the church 133 burials were found. A number of possible chapels were identified S. of the choir and presbytery. Several areas of tiled floor were examined within the church and the chapter house.'

In the High Street, Andover, Hants., important work was done on the timber framed buildings. At 84A High Street it was suggested that the property 'was perhaps built after the fire that destroyed much of the Upper High Street area of Andover in 1435. The ground floor may have been a trading area with living quarters in the two bay hall upstairs.' Numbers 89–91 High Street and 2 Chantry Way were formerly part of the Angel Inn built for Winchester College in 1444. 'This area of Andover was destroyed by fire in 1435, and the land was known as "Niggesland", no doubt because of its black, burnt appearance. The "Angel" is of a particular interest and importance because the carpenters' accounts survive at Winchester College. They describe the scantlings of the timber to be used, the layout, and details of the construction, such as the scissor brace in the great hall. The latter feature still survives.'

At Worcester, in Powick Lane, evidence was found of a 15th-century bronze foundry. 'Evidence for the foundry comprised a number of wall lines, the most substantial of sandstone, later rebuilt with roof tile, fronting Powick Lane. Units extending back from this wall line comprised limestone post-pads and sandstone, limestone and tile sill foundations. Within and outside these units were numerous casting pits, ranging in size from 1·5m to 3m in diameter. Each pit appeared to have been used for several castings, and all were back-filled with ceramic mould fragments and slag (one pit contained over 1 ton of ceramic mould fragments). Preliminary analysis of the ceramic moulds suggest that both bells and cauldrons were being cast on site. However, the presence of small stone crucibles and a variety of small stone mould fragments together with numerous pins, studs, twists of copper wire and several rings, brooches, clasps and candlesticks (mould fragments

for the latter having been recovered) suggests that the industry was diverse.'

In Hertfordshire at Green Lane, Norton, Letchworth, excavations revealed traces of cellared or sunken-featured buildings. 'The features clearly belong to several phases, and pottery from them suggests a period of occupation from *c.*650–*c.*1200 AD. The earliest phase may be contemporary with a small, scattered inhumation cemetery discovered 200m to the S. in Blackhorse Road in the 1960s. It is possible that the settlement is a 'lost' settlement of one hide adjacent to Norton and called *Rodenhanger* in a charter of Ethelred II.' In Kent archaeologists have been investigating the Euro-Tunnel Terminal site at Newington/Folkestone in advance of ground works. It is reported that, as well as the discovery of major sites, numerous pre-Conquest and medieval finds have been revealed.

At Aynho, Northamptonshire, work during the construction of the M40 motorway extension led to the recovery of Saxon pottery from a surface deposit overlying earlier features and in part infilling the top of a Roman ditch. The assemblage represents a minimum of 14 vessels which can be attributed to a short phase during the period from the mid-5th to early-6th century. In Norfolk excavations at Westwick Street, Norwich, helped interpret the development of the city. 'Urban development in this western part of the city is now more clearly understood with growth on St. Benedict's Street in the 11th century probably preceding that on Westwick Street in the 12th century. Medieval occupation was exclusively industrial, a large number of pits and burnt deposits being recorded. It seems probable that these were all associated with the cloth finishing industry, notably dyeing, which was predominant on this street. Large quantities of artefacts were recovered including carding-combs, spindle whorls and heckle teeth.'

In Ipswich, excavations at Butter Market and St. Stephen's Lane in advance of a shopping centre development revealed that 'the earliest activity consisted of an inhumation cemetery dating from the 7th–8th centuries which probably extended in all directions outside the excavated area. Of the 70 or so burials surviving, some were in coffins, some in chamber graves and some were surrounded by small ring ditches. The cemetery illustrates the changeover from pagan to Christian burial practices, ranging from a burial of the earlier 7th century with seax, scabbard, spear, shield and palm cups to burials with no grave goods at all. In the early 9th century two streets, established N.–S., across the disused cemetery, were lined with buildings of individual post-hole construction, with sunken featured buildings to their rear. Intensive craft activity is associated with the 9th-century occupation including an Ipswich ware potter, a bronze-smith, and a bone/antler worker.' At Bosham in East Sussex Holy Trinity Church Tower, which appears on the Bayeaux Tapestry, was recorded while under repair.

Particularly important excavations have been undertaken in Waterford in the Republic of Ireland and it is reported that 'finds from the excavations number *c.*100,000 objects. There is a substantial assemblage of 12 types of coarse pottery from the 11th- to early 12th-century levels. Wares imported from NW France, Ham Green (Bristol) and N. Wiltshire occur extensively in 12th-century levels. Cross reference with dendrochronological dates would indicate that Ham Green ware was imported as early as AD 1140. Other finds from the late Viking Age (11th- to early 12th-century) include several gaming pieces for a peg-board, lead weights, bronze stick pins, a complete decorated leather sword scabbard and a highly ornate silver and gold foil kite-shaped brooch. Excellent preservation conditions in the Viking defensive ditch ensured the preservation of large amounts of textiles, leather and animal bone. There were also vast quantities of sawn antler waste from comb making. The range of pottery from 13th-to 14th century levels is very diverse. Wares from Bristol, N. Wiltshire, the Saintonge area and NW France are well represented, while there is also pottery in smaller quantities from the Rhineland region. The organic finds include a range of well-preserved wooden and bone objects, as well as textiles and leather. Amongst the metal finds is an intricate gilt bronze bracelet, and a highly decorated 13th-century gold annular brooch.'

Post-Medieval Period

A comprehensive summary of work relating to post-medieval Britain may be found in *Post-Medieval Archaeology*, Volume 23 for 1989. Amongst the investigations undertaken may be noted that in London at St. Bartholomew the Great churchyard where a pit adjacent to the wall of the 14th century Lady Chapel was found to contain '1,857 18th-century pipe-clay wig curlers from at least 60 different moulds'.

At Moyne in Co. Mayo, excavations carried out in the graveyard produced large quantities of clay pipes. 'Many of these finds are wake pipes, i.e. small, thin-walled pipes, which are commonly found on or in graves in Western Galway and Co. Mayo. They are probably derived from Dutch pipes; several examples bear a crude version of the arms of Gouda on the spur. They were probably manufactured at the Knockcroghery factory in Co. Roscommon, and perhaps also in Galway City, in the early 19th century.'

A quite different kind of industry was investigated at The Breach, Ditchfield, Hampshire, where field-work 'identified a rare example of an early 17th-century sea pond at Hillhead where the Neon estuary enters the sea. Such features are recorded by classical writers and they had been suspected in medieval and post-medieval England. This is the first extant example recorded. The Breach is a large artificial pond cut out of the side of the Neon estuary. It is currently about 2 acres in extent and is protected from the open sea by a wall constructed by the Earl of Southampton in the early 17th century. The Breach is first mentioned in 1607, and was the object of a dispute in the 1740s. These records explain how the pond operates as a simple form of tidal trap, with the fish entering on the rising tide when they can be confined to the pond by the subsequent blocking of the entrance. A sketch plan drawn in 1745 shows hatches through which the fish enter the estuary and the pond.' The alum industry is another that has received the attention of archaeologists and at Ravenscar in North Yorkshire it has been shown that at the 17th- to 19th-century Peak Alum Works 'much of the 19th-century processing plant and parts of the 18th-century Alum Factory survive above ground, together with the Manager's House, a 19th-century horizontal wheel house and an early 19th-century lime-kiln. Parts of the 17th-century factory appear to have been incorporated into later buildings. The site retains a largely undisturbed stratification.'

Much work continues to be done on the Civil War period; for example, at the ABC Cinema redevelop-ment site in Exeter 'two main phases of Civil War features were identified in the excavation, these have been assigned to documented periods of activity on defences in 1642–3 and 1644–6'. An excavation in Southgate Street in Gloucester 'revealed the demolition levels of a house probably deliberately fired prior to the siege of 10th August 1643 (when all the buildings in suburbs were destroyed by the defenders in order to prevent them being used as cover by the advancing Royalists). The remains of two possible Royalist sapping operations were also excavated.' Military works of a later period were investigated at Tilbury Fort in Essex, at Portsmouth in Hampshire, and at the Citadel in Hull. At Newcastle upon Tyne it is reported that two substantial stretches of the town wall 'were found to have been completely rebuilt after the Civil War siege of 1644, and part of a mine crater at one of the reconstructed breaches was excavated'.

Among the excavations undertaken in London was one at 86–96 Cannon Street which revealed that 'a chalk-line well over 5m deep was backfilled in the early 18th century, and contains some 30 complete wine bottles, some 30 pharmaceutical jars, and about 50 albarelli.' Excavations at 9 Cloak Lane in the area of the Skinner's Hall kitchen led to the recovery from rubbish pits of 'an array of faunal remains, including hair, eel, duck and other wild birds.' At 35–45 New Broad Street 'finds include a large assemblage of post-medieval kitchen vessels, a cloth seal, a silver half groat of 1561–77, and a highly decorated bone handle of late 16th- or early 17th-century date with Renaissance motifs.' In Lambeth, at 19 Albert Embankment, excavations 'uncovered a ceramic mould for the production of clay pipes, dated typologically to the early 17th century; it is the first of its kind to be found which dates to before the 18th century. Quantities of dumped wasters and kiln furniture from the nearby tin-glazed earthenware kilns and later stoneware factory were found, together with a 19th-century kiln probably for ceramic manufacture.' On the Victoria Embankment excavations at the City of London Boys School demonstrated that the N.–S. walls of the Duke's Theatre appear to have been incorporated into a range of 18th century buildings, although the theatre itself was demolished in 1709. The theatre's significance was that it was 'one of the first theatres in England to separate the audience from the stage by a proscenium arch'. It was designed either by Sir Christopher Wren or Robert Hooke, and opened in 1671.

In King's Lynn, Norfolk, at 9 Stonegate Street 'removal of a later fireplace in this late 18th-century terraced house, formerly standing on the bank of the Millfleet, revealed a collection of 237 delftware tiles depicting naval scenes, sea monsters, etc. This is believed to be one of the largest finds of delftware tiles *in situ* made in the region.' In Northampton at the Angel Hotel an iron stone-lined well was examined and a selection of 18th century finds recovered. 'An inn is shown occupying the site on a map of 1747 and the finds confirm the long history of association with an hotel or public house. Out of 26 pottery vessels, 19 are drinking mugs, while 47 fragments of glass include 37 pieces from wine bottles and 6 from decorated wine glasses. Other finds comprise a series of bowls of clay tobacco pipes dated to *c.*1730–1800, and a silver threepenny piece of James II.'

SCIENCE AND DISCOVERY 1989-90

Ant antibodies.—Ants play no part in pollinating flowers although bees and wasps, close relatives to the ants, play a major part. This puzzled Andrew Beattie of Macquarie University in Sydney, Australia, and prompted him to study more than a dozen species of ants. He found that pollen dies when it touches the body of an ant. In every species he studied, Beattie found that secretion from the metapleural glands at the rear of the ant's thorax kills the pollen. On examination, the secretion was found to be an antibiotic, metapleurin, which prevents fungi and bacteria from growing on the ant's body. In addition to protecting the ant, it has the property of making the pollen less able to germinate and so the pollen dies. Beattie found that the one species of ant which lacks the metapleural gland is an important pollinator. This particular species of ant is known to pollinate up to half the population of a common orchid found in southern Australia.

Medical studies have shown that although most of the bacteria are unaffected by the antibiotics, metapleurin is highly effective against some strains of a common bacterium *Staphylococcus aureus* that are resistant to other antibiotics. Trials in a Sydney hospital have shown that these antibiotics are effective against a wide range of organisms, especially fungi, that cause diseases in humans. For example, they kill *Candida albicans*, the fungus which causes 'thrush', an infection of the mucous membranes. Pharmaceutical companies have shown interest in the results for, in addition to its success against *C. albicans*, metapleurin has been effective in the treatment of infections of the skin and internal tissues.

Bamboo's strange behaviour.—Bamboo has a strange life-cycle which is not fully understood at present. Whether a particular species grows individually or in huge forests, the plants all flower at the same time, regardless of the stage any individual plant has reached. Then all the plants die, leaving a carpet of seed to start the next cycle. No one knows why this happens and no one has explained why the growth cycle can vary in a limited way. Bamboo can flower every 15, 30, 60 or 120 years, these times forming a geometric series.

Because of its versatility, bamboo is used by approximately a quarter of the Earth's population, as a building material, for furniture making or as food for livestock. It is valuable fodder, providing as much as four times more protein than other grasses. The sudden dying of a whole plantation or forest presents huge problems.

Scientists at the National Chemical Laboratory in Pune, India, may have achieved a breakthrough in understanding the life cycle. They have succeeded in making bamboo shoots flower in the laboratory. The scientists fed the young shoots a concentrated mixture of minerals, vitamins, sugar, coconut milk and hormones. As the seedlings grew, cuttings were taken from them and fed with the same mixture as before. After this process had been repeated three times over a period of a few weeks, the shoots flowered and the experimenters were able to harvest the seeds.

Under normal conditions it would have been at least 15 years before the bamboo flowered. The work opens up the possibility of developing hybrids and strains which would flower after only one year. Bamboo could then be cultivated in the normal way.

There are over 500 species of bamboo. One is particularly important as a food for the pandas in China. They are very fussy eaters and the sudden dying of their favourite food creates tremendous problems. The development of a hybrid acceptable to the pandas would have other benefits for the country's economy.

Bird that smells like a cow.—In 1886 naturalists discovered a bird which smelled like fresh cow manure and it was named the stinkbird, *Opishocomus hoatzin*. A hundred years later scientists from the United States, Venezuela and Scotland studied the gut of the bird in detail and found it to have a stomach similar, broadly speaking, to that of a cow. The hoatzin is a small bird weighing about 750 grams which lives in a region stretching from Guyana to Brazil. It is one of the few birds that eats nothing but leaves. To digest these and remove the toxic compounds that many leaves contain, the bird employs 'foregut fermentation', similar to ruminants and some other mammals. It is the only bird known to ferment food in its foregut, the oesophagus and crop. It selects very carefully what it eats, the most nutritious plants and new growths, and digests the leaves efficiently with the help of microbes in its gut. To maximize digestion, the bird can hold its food in the gut for as long as 43 hours. The hoatzin is, however, a very poor flier. Its breastbone, where the flight muscles are attached, is very small, its growth apparently having been suppressed by the development of a very large stomach. Scientists are of the opinion that its loss of flying skills and the novel method of digestion may explain some unusual features of its anatomy and behaviour. For instance, young hoatzins have functional claws on the first and second digits of their wings, similar to those of the *Archaeopteryx*; the claws are used to climb trees. Hoatzins also fling themselves into water when threatened by a predator.

Cradling a baby.—Eighty per cent of women, regardless of whether they are right- or left-handed, hold a baby against the left-hand side of their bodies. John Manning and Andrew Chamberlain of Liverpool University believe that they have found the reason for this. They wondered originally whether this instinct was unique to humans but their research revealed that it is also common to chimpanzees and gorillas. According to the investigators, this indicates that the behaviour originated in the common ancestor of the African apes and humans. If this is the case, the instinct predates the development of the bias towards righthandedness which is unique to humans.

There have been in the past many theories to explain the left-handed cradling but none has been really satisfactory. At one time it was thought that the heartbeat is localized on the left-hand side of humans. However, the beats are caused by the closure of valves which are situated in the centre of the chest. Observational evidence has shown this theory to be untenable.

Research in the 1960s and 1970s suggested that the noise of the heartbeat will quieten a baby but it has been shown since that other sounds are just as effective. Manning and Chamberlain believe that the explanation lies in terms of the way the brain is organized. It has been known for a long time that the two halves of the brain do not have identical uses, a phenomenon known as lateralization. In humans the right side of the brain specializes in decoding information which has emotional significance. Much of the information from the left eye and ear is processed on the right side of the brain and so the mother is better equipped to interpret emotion if the baby is cradled on her left-hand side. In addition, because there is evidence that lateralization also applies to facial expressions, left-handed cradling has advantages for the infant, allowing it to see the left-hand and more emotionally expressive side of the mother's face.

Crop circles.—Much has been written in recent years about the cause of circles which suddenly appear in fields of growing crops, but little of it has had a scientific basis. Now, however, the witnessing of the formation of a crop circle suggests that the features are a natural weather phenomenon.

In the *Journal of Meteorology*, Terence Meaden of the Circles Effect Research Group describes the formation of a crop circle, as witnessed by Ray Barnes in a field near Westbury, Wiltshire, in 1982. Barnes reported that he saw a wavefront propagating through the heads of a cereal crop at about 50 miles per hour along a path that was slightly curved. The advancing wavefront suddenly swept round in a clockwise direction, creating a circle about 75ft in radius in about four seconds. Barnes said that the corn rustled as it fell. He also reported a hissing sound. The sky was clearing after a thunderstorm and it was still raining slightly. Meaden suggests that a spinning column of air with its axis parallel to the ground caused the wavefront seen advancing across the field. When this vortex tilted slightly the wavefront traced out a circle, in the same manner as a spinning top.

Vortices have been known to develop on the lee of isolated hills, but the one seen by Barnes was on the windward side. This does not provide too strong an objection to the theory because different patterns of vortices can arise from a combination of the shape of the land and the wind speed. Objections to the theory have been raised by sceptics who claim that because of air turbulence the edges of the circle should be irregular whereas the boundary was abrupt. However, Meaden suggests that sharp margins could develop because the air in the vortex could be ionized to make a plasma.

Dating the past.—The traditional way of dating the past is by using radio-carbon techniques. This method assumes that the ratio of carbon-14 to the more common isotope carbon-12 found in the atmosphere remains a constant, but this assumption was found to be invalid because the rate at which carbon-14 forms can vary because of bombardment by energetic particles from space. The time-scale was then calibrated against growth rings in living trees and ancient wood to produce a reliable method going back for about 11,000 years.

This time-scale can now be reliably pushed back to 30,000 years as a result of work carried out on corals from the Caribbean island of Barbados. The new scale is based on the measurement of the amount of uranium and thorium in the coral. The uranium-thorium dates obtained by Edouard Bard and colleagues of the Lamont-Doherty Geological Observatory match closely the tree-ring dates for the past 11,000 years but can be extrapolated back as far as 30,000 years. The new scale also enables a specific date to be placed on information derived from radio-carbon dating methods. Carbon dating can be used to show relative ages and timing of events but now more accurate dates can be assigned.

The new time-scale can be used for studies of past climatic changes and changes in the sea level at the end of the last ice age. Its use in conjunction with the carbon dating method has revealed that there was more carbon-14 in the upper atmosphere in the past, either because the solar wind was stronger or because the Earth's magnetic field was weaker. However, studies on the distribution of the carbon isotopes in sediments taken from shallow water and deep water have shown that the distribution has changed little over the years. One explanation for this could be that the distribution of carbon between the atmosphere and the oceans was different in the past.

Dinosaur extinction theory.—Although not accepted by all scientists, the theory that the extinction of the dinosaurs was the result of an asteroid impact 65 million years ago has been strengthened by new evidence obtained by American geologists. Evidence has been put forward suggesting that the crater near Manson, Iowa, is the impact point. However, although the age is correct, the size of the crater (35km diameter) suggests that the impact that caused it was too small to have produced such powerful effects. In 1984 Alan Hildebrand and William Boynton, planetary scientists from the University of Arizona, started searching for evidence of impacts in the Caribbean and two new sites have now been suggested. An impact at sea would have generated a tsunami (a huge destructive wave) so the search was for unusual deposits. In 1988 Hildebrand and Boynton found features which had the appearance they would expect to be produced within 1,000km of an impact. Subsequent research revealed other features. One location, the Big Boulder Bed in Cuba, which is a deposit up to 450 metres thick, contains boulders as large as 12 metres. Bruce Bohor of the US Geological Survey and Russell Seitz of Cambridge, Mass., have suggested that the impact point is in an area just south of Cuba near to the Isle of Pines and that the crater was about 225km in diameter. Hildebrand, however, is of the opinion that the impact point was 1,000km farther south, just off the coast of Colombia.

He reports that seismic profiles show a buried structure about 300km in diameter. He has also studied rocks from the end of the Cretaceous period in southern Haiti and has found shocked quartz, high iridium content and glassy beads thought to be tektites.

The geology of the Caribbean region is very complex and there are many questions to be answered before this work is accepted generally. Eugene Shoemaker of the US Geological Survey believes that there were two impacts at the end of the Cretaceous period and that they formed two layers. The upper one, he believes, was caused by the impact at Manson and the lower one is associated with the new discoveries. Alternatively, he thinks it possible that the actual impact site might have been subducted beneath South America by the movement of lithospheric plates.

Dinosaur's eggs exposed.—A rockfall in Romania has exposed an outcrop of red, silty clay in which were found 14 dinosaur eggs. The rockfall occurred in the northern part of the Hateg Basin of Transylvania, about 4·5km east of the town of Vălioara. The rocks were of late Cretaceous age, laid down about 65 million years ago. The eggs were the first dinosaur eggs to be found in Romania.

The eggs, although distorted to varying degrees, are basically sub-spherical in shape and were found lying in clusters in four linear rows, each cluster containing either two or four eggs. Two particular clusters containing two and four eggs were separated by a distance of 0·5 metres. The diameters of the eggs were about 150mm and the thickness of the egg-shells varied between 2·3mm and 2·4mm. Eight of the eggs were well-preserved with their lower surfaces almost complete, although their upper surfaces were cracked and eroded. Fragments of shell from the upper surfaces were found in the surrounding sediment. No skeletal remains were found.

The clay in which the eggs were found is sandwiched between iron-rich marls. Analysis of the clay has shown that it contains fine volcanic ash. The external surface of the eggs is irregularly tuberculated (i.e. covered with small projections) and the air canals between the tubercles are filled with calcite. The problem at the moment is to identify the animal that laid the eggs. Although the Hateg fauna includes many types of dinosaur, the size of the eggs indicates that they must have been fairly large. It is thought likely that the parents were sauropod dinosaurs (herbivorous) and a provisional name of *Magyarosaurus* has been suggested.

Early man a scavenger.—There has been much debate over the years about whether early hominids, such as *Homo habilis*, obtained meat by scavenging or hunting, or by both methods. Research carried out by John Cavallo and Robert Blumenshine of Rutgers University in New Brunswick suggests that the most likely method was scavenging from supplies left in trees by animals such as leopards. Leopards have a habit of storing their kill high in trees where it will be safe from lions and hyenas.

Cavallo and Blumenshine observed leopard behaviour in the Serengeti National Park in Tanzania.

They found that leopards often abandon temporarily a partially-eaten kill or even a complete animal which they have taken up into a tree. The scientists found that the leopards would desert the food for several hours and move out of sight of the tree. Sometimes it took two or more days to eat the kill completely.

Early hominids could climb trees quite easily and were active during the day. It is believed, therefore, that food left in trees by leopards could have provided man with a regular supply of meat and marrow, without the effort needed for hunting. The fact that leopards tend to use the same tree time and time again would have made the scavenging even easier. However, scavenging would not have been completely without effort or danger, as leopards will attack intruders. There is evidence of scavenging, particularly at a cave in Sterkfontein, South Africa. Archaeologists examining hominid sites, including the Olduvai gorge, Tanzania, have found evidence of flesh being removed from bones with sharp stone tools. It was thought that the hominids had scavenged the meat from lion and hyena kills. The weakness in this argument is that such opportunities would have been rare; the large carnivores usually eat up the complete carcass immediately. The new investigations show that the early hominids probably relied for their protein on opportunistic scavenging.

Faintest galaxy identified.—One of the problems troubling astronomers at present is estimating the amount of dark matter in our own galaxy. A satisfactory solution would provide information on the way galaxies are formed. It is hoped that the discovery of the faintest galaxy so far detected, right next to the Milky Way, will help to clarify the problem.

Astronomers at Cambridge, using a computerized plate measuring machine, have been scanning photographs of the sky taken by the Schmidt telescope in Australia. They discovered a group of very faint stars in the constellation Sextans. Further study of this group has revealed that they are actually the brighter stars in a galaxy a mere 300,000 light years distant. The galaxy is in fact so dim that it cannot be seen visually on the photographic plate. The total brightness of the galaxy is about 100,000 times the brightness of the Sun. This is quite small; some of the stars in the Milky Way, such as the bright star Rigel in the constellation Orion, individually emit more light.

This faint galaxy will now come under close scrutiny using the large William Herschel telescope at La Palma, Canary Islands. By studying the spectra of individual stars it is hoped to be able to determine the galaxy's speed and motion. This, together with the data collected from the six other dwarf spherical galaxies orbiting the Milky Way, may provide information on the gravitational pull of our galaxy and hence its mass. This will indicate, amongst other things, the amount of dark matter present.

The Cambridge team has so far scanned photographs covering about a quarter of the sky and the possibility of discovering more of these objects is quite good. It may be that they are so common that most of the mass of the universe is to be found in dwarf galaxies and this may explain the constitution of the mass of the universe.

The first Australians.

—Until recently it was thought that man first arrived on Australian soil about 40,000 years ago. However, research by Richard Roberts of the University of Wollongong and Rhys Jones and Mike Smith of the Australian National University has shown that the first arrivals took place some 20,000 years earlier. They obtained this new date from a study of the occupation of a rock shelter known as Malakunanja which lies at the foot of the Arnhem Land escarpment in the Kakadu National Park in the Northern Territories.

The technique used to obtain the date was based on the measure of the thermoluminescence of grains of quartz occurring in layers where stone artefacts had been identified. Thermoluminescence is the release of light by previously irradiated phosphors upon subsequent reheating; the intensity of the thermoluminescence in this case depended on how long ago the sand grains were last exposed to sunlight. Amongst the oldest stone artefacts were pieces of ground haematite, yellow ochre and a grindstone, suggesting that these early occupants decorated themselves in a similar way to the later Aboriginals.

The earlier date for the arrival of man in Australia presents several major problems. Until this discovery there was no evidence that *Homo sapiens* lived in south-east Asia 60,000 years ago. Fossil human remains of this age have been found in Africa and the Near East, but the oldest in the regions around Australia have dated from about 30,000 years ago. One possibility, although it is thought unlikely, is that the earlier arrivals were late representatives of *Homo erectus*, who were known to have lived in Java and mainland Asia for the previous 900,000 years.

Another problem is the manner in which these early arrivals reached the Australian mainland. If they came by sea they must have been capable of building rafts or canoes and must have had the skill to navigate at sea for journeys of up to 400km. These feats would indicate that they were *Homo sapiens*. The sea level was about 30 metres below the present-day level 60,000 years ago, falling to 40 metres 40,000 years ago and to 120 metres some 20,000 years ago. At this time New Guinea was joined to Australia by a wide land bridge. Similarly Java, Borneo and the Philippines were joined to the Malay peninsula. There was, however, a cold spell between 60,000 and 70,000 years ago when the sea level dropped to between 60 and 70 metres below the present-day level. It is possible that this was the time when the early arrivals reached the mainland.

Gamma ray bursts.

—Over the last twenty years astronomers have recorded many hundred short bursts of gamma rays from space, from directions which do not correspond to known astronomical objects. These bursts have such high energies that they must have been generated in regions where conditions are abnormal. Studies carried out by Soviet scientists indicate that the source could be the passage of a comet through the magnetic field of a neutron star. Information collected from the *Vega* and *Giotto* probes to Halley's comet have shown that comets in general are about 60 times more massive than previously thought. This means that faint comets, which are far more numerous than bright ones, should be sufficiently massive to produce bursts of gamma rays. Originally it was thought that it would be necessary for a comet actually to hit a neutron star, but the likelihood of this happening frequently is considered to be too remote to explain the frequency of the bursts. According to I. G. Mitrofanov and R. Z. Sagdeev of the Space Institute, Moscow, it is not necessary for a comet to hit the star. The Soviet team has shown that as the comet nucleus passes through the star's magnetic field, intense electric currents are generated in the comet, causing it to vaporize. The ionized material generated by the vaporization short-circuits the magnetic field and in doing so generates the gamma ray bursts which have been observed.

Sagdeev thinks that most of the gamma ray bursts are caused by cometary nuclei from interstellar space that happen to pass unrelated neutron stars. The reoccurrence of bursts from a single source is thought to be caused by comets from the cloud of comets which surround the star, similar to the Oort cloud which surrounds the Sun. If this idea is found to be correct, astronomers will be able to use comets as a method of understanding the magnetosphere of neutron stars.

The Iranian earthquake.

—Iran lies in a particularly sensitive area as far as earthquakes are concerned. It lies along the belt of mountains stretching from the Alps to the Himalayas which has been formed by the movement of tectonic plates. In the east the Indian continental crust has been pushed under the Asian land mass to form the Himalayas, but further west along the belt the position is far more complex. In the region around Iran pieces of the Earth's crust are jostling against each other, leading to frequent earthquakes. In addition, the tectonic plate containing the Arabian peninsula is moving at a rate of about 16mm a year in a north-northeasterly direction.

During the last twelve years Iran has suffered 12 tremors of magnitude 7 or greater but the one that occurred in the early hours of June 21, 1990 was the largest on record for the area. It registered 7·7 on the Richter scale and was centred on the edge of the Caspian Sea, just north of Rasht. This region lies farther north than the Zagros Mountains, the area that experiences most of the severe tremors. One of the reasons why this earthquake caused so much damage is that it originated in the crust at a much shallower depth than usual, only 10km below the surface. Roger Clark, a seismologist at Leeds University, commented that there are about four or five tremors of this intensity each year and one or two occur in the Alpine-Himalayan mountain belt. About a quarter of these are shallow, so it is possible for such an event to occur every two to three years.

This particular earthquake has presented seismologists with unusual problems. They are not sure what type of fault caused the tremor because the seismometers around the world did not give a clear indication of the vibrations at the start of the event. It is thought, therefore, that two or more tremors happened close together in rapid succession. The shallowness of the focus was responsible for the considerable damage recorded and for the huge loss of life. It is thought that over 40,000 people were killed, 100,000 injured and half a million left homeless. About twelve hours after the earthquake, an aftershock killed another 20 and caused fresh landslides, hampering rescue teams.

Krypton atom clusters.—Krypton is one of the inert gases which, in general, do not combine with other inert gas atoms or other elements to form compounds. Recent work carried out by Paul Lethbridge and Tony Stace of Sussex University has shown how krypton atoms can combine together to form clusters and then fall back to their original state. The importance of this kind of study lies in the understanding of the mechanisms used by catalysts.

Krypton gas was passed into a vacuum through a hole only 200 micrometres in diameter. This process cooled the gas atoms so that when they collided with other krypton atoms, the weak van de Waals' forces were strong enough to hold them together. The scientists were able to make a wide range of clusters containing between 10 and 340 atoms. They then ionized the clusters with an electron beam and studied the positive ions using a mass spectrometer. This analysis was quite complicated, requiring the use of a computer, because krypton exists in six naturally occurring isotopes, each having a different mass.

Chemical theory favours the production of clusters based on three-dimensional structures known as Mackay icosahedra, with 13, 55, 147, 309, 561 and 923 atoms. The icosahedral structure has 20 regular faces, and the numbers correspond to the number of atoms required to produce a closed shell. The investigators showed that they had produced clusters with 147 and 309 atoms, which correspond to three and four layered closed shells.

Although the gaseous form can take these unusual structures, in the solid state they always have a face-centred cubic structure. The possible transition stage between these two extremes is of great interest and the scientists believe that this may be possible with clusters having about 2,000 atoms; work is proceeding along these lines. Also of importance is the possibility that metal atoms may behave in a similar way. If this is shown to be the case it may disclose new types of catalytic activity. Catalysis is a surface phenomenon and the large surface area of these clusters could provide the ideal conditions for chemical reactions.

Largest known prime number.—Often in scientific research the discovery of some abstruse fact does not, in the first instance, seem of great importance and it is subsequent work that reveals the true importance of the discovery. Such is the case with the announcement by John Brown and fellow researchers at the Amdahl Corporation in Sunnyvale, California, that they had calculated the largest

known prime number, one with 65,087 digits, after more than a year of computation. A prime number is one that cannot be divided by any number other than 1 and the number itself without leaving a remainder.

Research into prime numbers started with Euclid, who demonstrated that there were an infinite number of them. Very little work was done in this field until the availability of high capacity computers. In 1952 the highest known prime number had 157 digits; this had increased to 6,533 digits by 1978. The new prime announced by the Amdahl researchers has 37 more digits than the previous record holder, which was discovered by David Slowinski of Cray Research in La Habra, California. The new prime was found by first selecting 350,000 possible candidates. These were tested to make sure that they were not divisible by any of the several billion smaller primes; this left 7,000 possibilities. Each was tested initially at the rate of one every 80 minutes, though by modifying their techniques the mathematicians reduced this to one every 33 minutes. One of the team, Sergio Zarantonello, commented that this new prime is of interest to mathematicians because it has a different form. It was found by raising 2 to the power 216,193, multiplying by 391, 581 and then subtracting 1.

The finding of large prime numbers is useful because the techniques of number theory used in calculating them have applications in other scientific fields where it is necessary to devise methods of carrying out large numbers of calculations in the most efficient manner.

Lemur discovered.—A few years ago Bernard Meier, a West German zoologist, discovered a new species of primate in the rainforest of Madagascar, the golden bamboo lemur *Hapalemur aureus*. He continued to explore the forest and in the northern part of the island in spring 1989 located a hairy-eared lemur, *Allocebus trikolis*, which had been thought to be extinct. The hairy-eared lemur is one of the smallest primates, being only 30cm long, including the tail, and weighing only 80 grams.

The species was discovered in 1875 by Albert Gunther in a collection of preserved animals sent to Europe. Andre Peyrieras, a French entomologist was given a live specimen in 1964 but he assumed it to be an unusual specimen of the lesser mouse lemur. When it died he preserved it and sent it to the Museum of Natural History in Paris. The only other people to have seen a live hairy-eared lemur were the inhabitants of the rainforest.

Meier visited Madagascar in spring 1989 to make a documentary film about the aye-aye, a type of lemur which was thought until recently to be extinct. He concentrated his searches near to Mananara, a town on the north-east coast and at each village he asked the inhabitants to describe and draw all the lemurs they had seen. In one of the villages an old man told Meier of an animal which fitted the description of the hairy-eared dwarf lemur. A search in the area failed to find it. On the way back to base, one was seen but only for a few seconds. At the time Meier was suffering from malaria and blood poisoning in his right foot and was unable to follow up the find. On his next expedition to the area he was successful, thanks mainly to a dog which discovered a burrow used by hairy-eared dwarf lemurs. One was caught, measured and photographed, and then released. Meier's colleagues later caught further specimens.

The new discoveries emphasize the importance of Madagascar from a biological point of view. Having been isolated for the last 60 million years, it has evolved independently, producing unique plants and animals.

Mapping the Great Attractor.—Several years ago a group of American astronomers put forward an explanation for the huge perturbation observed in the general outflow of galaxies on which the theories for the expansion of the universe are based. This disturbance in what is called the Hubble flow manifests itself as a streaming of all the galaxies in our region of the universe in the general direction of the Hydra-Centaurus super-cluster of galaxies, situated about 150 million light years away. This concentration of mass has been termed the Great Attractor and has an estimated mass equivalent to tens of thousands of galaxies.

The initial measurements of the galactic motions carried out by Alan Dressler of the Carnegie Institution of Washington and Sandra Faber of the University of California at Santa Cruz, were limited to those galaxies lying this side of the attractive force. However, in 1988 they extended their measurements to galaxy motions through the centre of the Great Attractor and beyond. The new observations included spiral galaxies as well as elliptical. On the near side of the Great Attractor the number of galaxies studied increased fivefold, all showing that they were being attracted to the centre of the region. Those galaxies at the centre were found to have very little motion relative to our own Milky Way galaxy, while those situated on the far side showed motions lower than that expected for an even expansion of the universe.

Although the existence of the Great Attractor is more or less accepted, the main problem lies in trying to explain its constitution. Although visible galaxies can account for some of the mass, most of the mass must be in a form of dark matter. Many astronomers claim that 90 per cent of the mass of the universe is in this form, although recent discoveries have thrown doubt on this.

Mathematical proofs computerized.—Many of the problems confronting the mathematician involve series where it is required to find the sum to a finite number of terms or even to infinity. Such a problem arises when computing the probability of an event. This is carried out by finding a simple formula for the sum, known as a combinatorial identity. Quite often the proof of such an identity requires pages of *ad hoc* arguments. These long-winded proofs may now be a thing of the past. Doron Zeilberger of Drexel University and Herbert Wilf of the University of Pennsylvania have developed a computer-based method, a computer language called Macsyma which operates on mathematical symbols instead of on numbers.

Mathematically a combinatorial identity is an equation that says that there are two different ways of counting a set of objects, one complicated, involving the addition of each term in the sum, and the other a simple formula. The problem in the past has been the difficulty of proving that both sides of the equation are in fact equal. For each identity mathematicians find a so-called proof certificate, a rational function $R(n,k)$ of two integer variables that satisfies certain boundary conditions. Using Macsyma Zeilberger and Wilf have programmed the complete procedure for finding the proof certificate. Once this has been determined it is possible to construct an ordinary paper and pencil proof by checking that certain simple conditions are satisfied. The team has produced a theoretical foundation to this work. Wilf also applied the Macsyma procedures to 60 identities. In 54 cases he was able to obtain a proof of the identity. The fact that procedures work in a majority of cases shows that they are on the right lines.

Meteorites from the Moon.—Evidence that a particular type of meteorite found in the Antarctic originated from the planet Mars has led to speculation that meteorites could also have landed from the Moon. In theory any object larger than 100 metres which struck the Moon could eject material at velocities greater than 2·4km per second, the lunar escape velocity. From a study of the size and number of craters on the lunar surface it has been estimated that such an event has occurred about three times in a million years during the Moon's recent history. Any rocks ejected from the Moon would not travel directly to the Earth but go into orbit round the Earth for a period of just under a million years to about 10 million years. It is possible to estimate the age of the rocks and how long they remained in orbit. Helium, argon and xenon are produced in the rocks by natural radiation and the amount present gives an indication of the age of the rock. Whilst in orbit, the rocks are bombarded by cosmic rays to produce other isotopes, the amount produced being an indication of the time spent in orbit. Once the rock has landed the reactions proceed in a different way and so an estimate of the time spent on the Earth's surface can be made.

Otto Eugster of the University of Bern, Switzerland, claims that five of the meteorites found in the Antarctic came from two lunar impact craters. Three of the five samples appear to have arrived at about the same time, about 75,000 years ago. Another is much older, arriving about 170,000 years ago. The fifth specimen is thought to have arrived less than 100,000 years ago. However, there are large differences in the times spent in orbit. Three of the rocks appear to have been first exposed on the Moon by an impact 16 million years ago and then blasted into space about 11 million years later. The other two are thought to have been exposed to cosmic rays on the lunar surface for hundreds of millions of years before being ejected. They made the journey to the Earth very quickly, in about 200,000 years. The composition of the meteorites suggests that they came from different parts of the Moon.

Missing interstellar link.—Many of the molecules that have been identified in space are the result of chemical reactions which could not be substantiated by scientists because they were unable to identify a molecule which would make the reactions possible. This difficulty has now been overcome as a result of work carried out by French and Canadian astronomers using the Canada-France-Hawaii telescope on Mauna Kea.

The astronomers were looking at the infra-red spectrum from two regions of high magnetic activity in Jupiter's atmosphere for the presence of molecular hydrogen. The spectral lines for the molecule were found but in addition the spectrum contained a complicated series of unexplained lines. Work carried out at many establishments identified these lines as belonging to the molecule H_3^+. It is the first time that this particular molecule has been identified from space and the discovery has confirmed the suspicion that H_3^+ is the missing link for the chemical reactions mentioned above.

The discovery of extraterrestrial H_3^+ is important for several reasons. It radiates at frequencies which are convenient for astronomical observations of gas clouds in our own galaxy because the spectral lines are not dimmed by interstellar dust. Also, although molecular hydrogen may be more plentiful, the radiation it emits is faint and difficult to record. The ability to record the presence of H_3^+ within hydrogen molecule clouds will permit more accurate distribution maps to be obtained. The intensity of the H_3^+ lines is over a billion times stronger than those of molecular hydrogen, molecule for molecule. This opens up the possibility of identifying the presence of H_3^+ in other more distant galaxies. In addition, the discovery may be useful to cosmologists because it may help in obtaining a better value for the deuterium (heavy hydrogen) to hydrogen ratio. This value was fixed in the Big Bang and determining it more precisely would give more information about the history of the universe.

New pulsar upsets theory.—The accepted theory about pulsars is that they are rapidly spinning neutron stars, emitting light as a series of rapid pulses. These pulses are seen in the same way as we see a lighthouse's beam as it swings round the horizon. For a pulsar to be recognized as such it has to be orientated in a special way so that the beam passes through the solar system. In the case of a newly discovered pulsar PSR 0021-72A, it is difficult to apply this model. The pulsar is spinning every 4·5 milliseconds and is one of ten very rapidly spinning pulsars located in globular clusters, in which millions of stars are clustered together in a spherical mass.

It is thought that rapidly spinning pulsars are produced in binary systems, with material from one component being captured by its companion neutron star. This infalling material will make the star rotate faster, just as ice skaters do when they draw in their arms. Analysis of the light from this new pulsar indicates that it is a member of a binary system orbiting its companion every 32 minutes. Scientists in Australia have calculated that the orbital plane is virtually at right angles to the line of sight to the

pulsar, which, according to current theory, should make it impossible to observe the pulses. Statistically such an orientation should occur once in every 45,000 binary pulsars. Currently only 13 binary pulsars are known. It has been suggested that the orbit is highly elliptical as the result of a collision of the system with another star, producing a situation in which the pulsar's spin axis is at right angles to its orbital plane.

It is estimated that the pulsar is about 1·4 times the mass of the Sun and the companion star, a white dwarf, about 0·8 that of the Sun. If these estimates are correct the pulsar should precess (wobble) with a period of about eight years, due to an effect called spin-orbit coupling predicted by the general theory of relativity. If this effect is observed, it will provide further proof of the accuracy of the general theory of relativity.

New quasar puzzle.—Quasars are the most luminous objects in the universe, shining with as much light as thousands of galaxies even though they cannot be much larger in size than the solar system. A quasar has a red shift characteristic of very remote objects. The red shift, or recessional velocity, of a distant galaxy or quasar is a measure of the expansion of the universe.

Current ideas about the formation and evolution of the universe may have to revised drastically in the light of the recent discovery of a quasar with a red shift of 4·73 (which breaks the previous record of 4·43 recorded two years ago). A red shift of 4·73 indicates that the universe had condensed out of the void between 1 and 1·5 thousand million years after the Big Bang. This implies that even at that early stage, the universe was 'lumpy'. This new object existed when the universe was only about one sixth of its present size. It seems to have the same properties as the other 16 known quasars with red shifts greater than 4, although as a group they look different from the nearer quasars.

The reported lumpiness is in contrast to other results which indicate that matter was distributed smoothly in the early universe. At present it is difficult to see how such concentration of matter could have been formed from such an even distribution of matter. An even greater problem for the cosmologist is the discovery by Margaret Geller and John Huchra of the Harvard-Smithsonian Center for Astrophysics, of a 'great wall', a system of thousands of galaxies in the form of a membrane some 500 million light years across. This, together with the new distant quasars, has had a marked effect on the theories of the abundance of cold dark matter, although other scientists think that more information is needed before theories are revised. The questions might be clarified when the Hubble space telescope becomes fully operational. Further clarification should come from the results from the Cosmic Background Explorer (COBE) satellite designed specifically to investigate cosmic radiation thought to be the remnants of the Big Bang.

Oldest Dinosaur.—Argentinian scientists have found in the Andes a 230 million year old dinosaur fossil, the oldest known dinosaur on record. The fossil is nearly complete and is of a bipedal carnivore which would have stood just over 2 metres high and weighed more than 100 kilograms. The expedition, led by Alfredo Monetta of the University of San Juan, found two nearly complete specimens in sandstone deposits by a river. The dinosaur has been named *Herrerasaurus* after Victorino Herrera, an amateur fossil collector who discovered the first fragmentary bones some years ago.

Herrerasaurus was an active predator running on its hindlegs. Its front limbs were short but had long claws and semi-opposable thumbs for grasping its prey. It was lightly built and had a long bird-like skull. The skeleton was so well-preserved that tiny earbones and plates in the iris of the eyes showed in the rocks. The fragments discovered earlier had also been found in the same deposits.

Dinosaurs evolved during the Triassic period between 200 and 250 million years ago. Protodinosaurs, which were like long-legged crocodiles, lived in the early Triassic. Towards the end of the Triassic period dinosaurs split into two distinct families, the 'bird-hipped' ornithischians such as the stegosaurs, and the lizard-hipped saurischians, of which *Tyrannosaurus* is an example. *Herrerasaurus* is believed to have been closely related to the primitive dinosaurs but not a direct ancestor of the later dinosaurs. It had many primitive dinosaurian features but it also had advanced features such as a dual-hinged jaw, which allowed the creature to hold its prey more tightly. This feature did not appear in other dinosaurs until 50 million years later, which suggests that it was a member of an evolutionary sidebranch. Work is still proceeding on extracting the fossil from the rocks. When this has been completed the whole skeleton will be displayed at the San Juan Museum.

Origin of life on Earth.—The way in which life developed on this planet has taxed scientists for a long time. Amino acids and other simple organic compounds have been synthesized under conditions which are thought to have existed on the Earth some four thousand million years ago, at a time when the Earth had an atmosphere of methane, nitrogen and water. Much of this early work was carried out by Harold Urey of the United States in the 1950s.

Recent work carried out by Cyril Ponnamperuma at the University of Maryland has extended Urey's work. By passing electrical discharges through a model of the Earth's primitive atmosphere, Ponnamperuma has produced molecules similar to small proteins, these molecules acting like biological enzymes. Prior to this latest work Ponnamperuma and his colleagues had produced polymers containing chains of between five and ten amino acids. They claimed at the time that these polymers could have been the beginnings of the proteins necessary for life. In their latest work, they tried to discover whether or not these polymers acted like enzymes. They discovered that there was a link between some of the compounds and those associated with respiration. Also of interest was that this association could be obtained alone or in the presence of the metals copper and zinc.

The discovery is of fundamental importance because it could help to explain how life developed on Earth. It suggests that enzyme-like molecules existed before any biological organisms evolved; therefore living cells could have refined chemical processes that existed long before living creatures started to evolve. It also shows a possible route for the evolution of living material from inorganic compounds.

Pioneer probes update.—The *Pioneer 10* probe, the first spacecraft to leave the solar system, is now travelling through interstellar space. It is sending back data about background light in our galaxy and the universe in general. One of the main problems affecting observations made from the Earth and its immediate surroundings is zodiacal light, the background light within the solar system. This is a faint glow caused by sunlight scattered by the disc of dust which envelopes the planetary orbits. It is estimated that 40 per cent of the light received at the telescope is from this disc of dust. The *Pioneer* observations are uncontaminated by background light and their quality allows astronomers to investigate background radiation to a degree impossible from points within the solar system.

The *Pioneer 11* probe is now in the vicinity of the orbit of Neptune. It is also providing data about background light because at the distance from the Sun of Neptune's orbit, the intensity of zodiacal light has fallen to a negligible level.

The light from the photomultipliers on the spacecraft has been analysed by Gary Toller of NASA's Goddard Space Flight Center. He found that the non-solar system light is generated from several sources. About 82 per cent is starlight from stars too faint to be seen with the naked eye. Much of the remainder comes from the scattering of light from stars within our galaxy by interstellar dust. A small contribution, about 0·6 per cent, comes from sources beyond our galaxy. This information, combined with other observations, has enabled the position of the Sun above the plane of the galaxy to be found to a much greater accuracy. The Sun's position is now put at about 40 light years above the plane.

Pole Star evolving.—Polaris, the Pole Star, lies very near to the north celestial pole and so is famous for its use in finding the direction of geographical north. To astronomers, however, it was just an interesting variable star. Studies carried out during the 19th century showed that the star belonged to a class of stars known as the Cepheids, variable stars that change in brightness with absolute precision over a precise period; the brightness of Polaris was found to vary regularly over a period of about four hours. It is believed that it has been pulsating regularly for about 40,000 years. However, observations carried out in 1987 by astronomers at the University of Vancouver, British Columbia, indicated that these pulsations were dying out and subsequent observations have confirmed this. It therefore appears that Polaris has reached a critical point in its evolution.

Current theory indicates that the slow vibrations exhibited by Cepheids are maintained by the energy which is trapped below the surface of the star in a layer of ionized helium. These vibrations die down as the star expands, causing the surface to cool. When the helium layer sinks too deep within the star, the pulsations cease. It has been predicted that these pulsations should gradually die down within a period of ten years. Prior to the 1980s the surface of Polaris pulsated in and out at about 5km per second but in the early 1980s it was suggested that this value had fallen. The observers at British Columbia in 1987 found a value of only 1·5km per second. Subsequent observations have shown that the velocity has been falling continually and had reached a value of only 0·5km per second by February 1990. The Canadian team predicts that Polaris will stop pulsating completely by 1992.

The behaviour of Polaris has provided evidence that the theory for the pulsations of Cepheid variables is more or less correct. Detailed study over the next few years should enable astronomers to refine the theory. The theory is of great importance to both astronomers and cosmologists because these variables are used in distant galaxies as one of the main methods of estimating distances.

The rings of Neptune.—More information has been released about the data collected from *Voyager 2* when it flew past Neptune in the summer of 1989. Of particular interest is the ring system around the planet. As the probe approached the planet, two narrow rings could be seen, 53,200km and 62,900km distant from the planet. The outer ring contained three regions which were much brighter than the rest of the ring and these were labelled arcs. After passing Neptune, the cameras on board *Voyager 2* looked back towards the Sun and located a third, broader, ring only 41,900km from the centre of the planet, and also a very faint sheet of material stretching down to the surface of the planet from half-way between the outer two rings. Whereas the third ring had a width of 1,700km, the outer ring was no more than 15km wide, although the photopolari-meter identified a faint region just outside the ring, giving a total width of about 50km.

The structure of this ring is similar to that of the F-ring of Saturn and of two of the rings around Uranus. Of the six new moons found round Neptune, 1989N4 orbits 1,000km inside the ring and therefore acts as a shepherd. This is also the case with the moons shepherding the F-ring of Saturn and the rings around Uranus. The existence of the arcs has still not been satisfactorily explained.

Although the ring systems of Uranus and Neptune appear similar, there are significant differences. The mass of the material in Neptune's ring system is only 0·0001 that of the ring system surrounding Uranus. Both systems lie within the Roche limit, the minimum distance at which a moon can travel around its planet without disintegrating. Neptune has five satellites within the limit, whereas Uranus has nine but they are only about half the size of Neptune's satellites. Up to 75 per cent of the material in the two narrow rings of Neptune is in the form of microscopic dust, but only about 1 per cent of the corresponding rings of Uranus is dust. It is estimated that if all the

material from the rings and satellites within the Roche limit of Saturn, Uranus and Neptune was collected, it would form a single body with diameters of 390, 150 and 260km respectively.

Star's surface observed.—The stars are so far away that even in the largest telescopes they appear as points of light. In theory, with the largest telescopes it should be possible to see details on the surface of the larger stars but the image is blurred due to the atmosphere.

Some years ago John Baldwin and Peter Warner of the Cavendish Laboratory at Cambridge developed a novel way of reducing this blurring. They covered the telescope mirror with a solid mask which had holes in it so that light could only reach a few small patches of the mirror. The different beams were combined to form characteristic interference patterns which were then converted back to the image of the star, in a manner similar to that used by radio astronomers when combining signals from several radio telescopes.

The first star to have its diameter measured by this interferometric technique was the red giant Betelgeuse which lies in the constellation Orion. At a distance of 500 light years, Betelgeuse is one of the nearest red giants and one of the largest. Although it has an apparent diameter of only 50 milliarcseconds, it is 500 times the size of the Sun. If placed in the position of the Sun, even the orbit of Mars would lie beneath its surface.

The technique was used on the 4·2 metre William Herschel telescope at La Palma in the Canary Islands. Betelgeuse appeared as a single star with a brighter patch towards one side. The discovery confirms a theoretical prediction made by American astronomers that red giants contain just a few very large convection cells where energy bubbles up from inside the star. In stars like the Sun, pressure increases rapidly with depth and so the convection currents which carry energy from the interior of the star to layers just below the surface are relatively small. In red giants the pressure changes are much more gradual with depth, and so the convection cells are much larger.

The observation also ruled out the suggestion that there was a companion star which was responsible for some of the variation of light received from Betelgeuse.

Stinging nettle and fungi.—Willem Broekaert and colleagues at the Catholic University, Leuven, Belgium, have been carrying out research on stinging nettles and their work may open the way to producing crops that are resistant to some types of fungi. Their work has concentrated on lectins, proteins that recognize and bind to specific sugar molecules. Some lectins are toxic and their presence in seeds helps to protect the seeds from being eaten by animals. A lectin found in wheatgerm binds to the polysaccharide chitin. Chitin is chemically resistant and makes up the shells of crustaceans and the exoskeletons of insects. Chitin is also a component of the thick wall of many fungi. It is thought, therefore, that the chitin-bonding lectin in wheatgerm protects the wheat seedlings from fungal attack.

What is unusual about the stinging nettle is that it is the adult plant, not the seeds, that produces lectins. Broekaert and his colleagues have managed to extract from the nettle another lectin that bonds to chitin. They found that in the rhizome (the underground stem of the plant) the protein was present at about ten times the level needed to block the growth of fungi. They found that the lectin was concentrated in the outer layers of the rhizomes and the roots and not in the stem or leaves. It is thought that the nettle lectin may be able to penetrate deep into the cell walls of the invading fungus, thus interfering with its growth.

The small size of the lectin molecule makes it particularly useful in genetic engineering, where work is being carried out on new strains of crops that are resistant to fungi.

Sunspots and cosmic rays.—The 11-year cycle of sunspot activity is well documented, although not fully understood. It has been found in the past that during times of maximum sunspot activity the intensity of cosmic rays reaching the Earth's surface has fallen due to what is called the Forbush decrease. At such times the solar wind, streams of solar particles, tends to deflect cosmic rays from deep space, leaving just those originating from the Sun. These cosmic rays consist of high energy sub-atomic particles, mainly protons. They have been monitored continuously for over a quarter of a century. In the second half of 1989 more were detected even though the Sun is currently at the maximum sunspot stage. This increase could be associated with the gradual increase in solar activity that has been going on for the last 400 years, but the current peak in cosmic rays cannot be due solely to the normal 11-year solar activity cycle because the current maximum is by no means the strongest recorded.

Nevertheless, short periods of spot activity have reached levels rivalling the levels in the 1977–79 maximum, the most active maximum recorded. During the last six months of 1989 the average flux of solar particles reaching the Earth's surface was the highest ever recorded in a six-month period. Increases in cosmic rays are referred to as ground level events (GLE). Six such events were detected by scientists at the University of Calgary, and a further event was recorded at another station.

These events can have a considerable effect on communications, electrical power grids and satellites. For example, one such peak caused an electrical blackout in Quebec in spite of the use of many circuit breakers to protect the network from power surges induced by the geomagnetic storm. During the 1958 maximum, Sweden lost its national electric grid for several days. There is also evidence that increasing solar activity may be linked to small increases in the Sun's surface temperature, which may have a similar effect on the Earth.

Three particle families.—In October 1989 physicists at CERN, the European laboratory for particle physics, announced that they were almost certain that only three families of neutrinos exist in the universe. The possibility of there being more than three is considered to be less than one chance in fifty. This result was based on the first set of experiments on CERN's new particle accelerator, the Large Electron Positron (LEP). The three families of neutrinos are thought to be associated with electrons, muons and tau particles. The physicists also announced that they had observed 11,000 collisions between electrons and positrons to produce $Z°$ particles, and had been able to calculate the $Z°$ particle's mass as 91·10 gigaelectron volts (GeV, i.e. 91·10 thousand million electron volts) with an error of 0·06 GeV. The first $Z°$ particle was observed on August 14, 1989.

The announcement by CERN came a day after physicists from Stanford University, California, had announced a similar but less precise result. The Europeans accused the American team of jumping the gun with inferior results because the Stanford team had based their figures on only 500 $Z°$ particles. This accusation was strongly denied, the Stanford team claiming that they had detected the $Z°$ particle the previous April. However, there is no doubt that any discoveries which depend on a high degree of statistical significance will come from the CERN group.

$Z°$ particles are produced when a stream of electrons collide head on with a beam of positrons, particles with the same mass as electrons but having a positive charge. The beams had a variable known energy of about 45 GeV. The particles were detected by four different detectors and there had been some speculation as to which of these detectors would provide the most accurate information. The team running the most successful detector claimed that their results indicated the number of families of neutrinos to be 3·27, plus or minus 0·3. This result makes the chance of there being more than three families less than 2 per cent.

Track dated accurately.—A few years ago a 1,000 metre long wooden track over the Somerset Levels was identified as the oldest known man-made track in Europe. At the time estimates for its age ranged between 4000 and 3800 BC. The archaeologists could not be more precise because there was a gap in the tree-ring chronology for English oak for the period between 4165 and 3807 BC; nor was it possible to link the patterns of the rings in the wood used in making the track with the tree-ring chronology for western Europe. The controlling chronology, based on oak from Ireland and Germany, goes back for more than 7,000 years and any local chronology that matches a section of it provides an accurate date for the age of the wood. It can be observed from the tree-ring patterns that trees grow by varying amounts each year. This variation provides a unique link by matching patterns where they overlap with the reference patterns in older wood.

The gap in the English oak chronology has been filled recently by dates from timber found in Humberside and Lancashire. British archaeologists now have a continuous reference scale from 4989 to 381 BC which provides an accurate method of dating prehistoric sites in Britain. Jennifer Hillam and colleagues at the University of Sheffield and Queen's University, Belfast, together with John and Bryony Coles of the Somerset Levels Project, have used this latest technique to give a precise date of 3807/3806 BC as the date the timber was felled to make the track. Research carried out by the Coles suggests that the track was built very quickly, although the amount of wood used was considerable. They estimate that the structure contained over 4,000 metres of planks supported on a substructure involving a further 2,000 metres of wood and 6,000 pegs.

Volcanic activity in the solar system.—The *Voyager* space probes passed the planet Jupiter and its satellites between 1979 and 1981. The probes recorded signs of volcanic activity in Io, the innermost of the four large Galilean satellites. Since then Io has been monitored closely to see if such activity could be seen or at least recorded, from earth-based observatories. Success came in 1989 when astronomers at NASA's Infra-red Telescope facility in Hawaii started testing a new infra-red camera known as Protocam.

It is very difficult to observe detail on the surface of Io because it is such a small object, only 1·2 arcseconds across when viewed from the Earth. The new camera is able to record details as small as 0·4 arcsecond, one third of the apparent diameter of Io. The astronomers used a wavelength of 3·8 micrometres and were able to locate Loki, the large volcano recorded by the *Voyager* space probes, as a bright spot against the darker disc of Io. Computer processing of the data to increase the contrast has revealed another bright spot on Io, only a twentieth of the brightness of Loki and situated on the opposite face of the satellite. Subsequent analysis of the signals showed that this was neither a flaw in the camera's electronics nor due to the effect of the Earth's atmosphere, but another volcano.

Volcanic activity on Io is believed to be produced by tidal forces caused by the nearness of Jupiter and the difference between the gravitational force of Jupiter on the near side and the far side of the satellite. By monitoring the satellite regularly, astronomers will be able to learn how much molten magma (molten rock, including dissolved water and other gases) is available on Io at any time. Astronomers will also be able to determine whether these outbursts of activity are a continuous process or just isolated events.

In August 1989 *Voyager 2* photographed an eruption on the surface of Triton, the largest of Neptune's moons. The photographs showed particles that had been thrown high into the thin atmosphere of the moon. Cameras on board *Voyager* had earlier recorded dark patches on the bright south polar region. It was thought that these patches might be the results of geyser activity in the recent geological past but it was not clear whether or not this activity was continuing. The latest photograph confirms that the activity is still present.

By studying a series of pictures stereoscopically, investigators were able to show that the plume of particles rose to a height of 8km above the surface of Triton. After rising vertically the plume drifted westwards in the atmospheric winds for about 150km. It is thought that the plume originated when pressurized nitrogen rose from beneath the surface and escaped through a vent, carrying ice particles upwards. The dark appearance of the patches on the south polar region is thought to be due to the ice crystals being bombarded by particles from space, particularly the solar wind.

Triton is the fourth body in the solar system known to be active volcanically, the others being Io, the Earth and Venus. More is known of activity on Venus now that astronomers have mapped in detail four areas, using the large Arecibo radio telescope in Puerto Rico. In the lowland plains the astronomers found dozens of small vents which have spewed lava to create lava flows without forming cones. The large number and distribution of these vents implies that volcanic activity in the plains is an important evolutionary process. The studies show that there are relatively few impact craters on the plains compared with the number on the uplands, suggesting that the plains are relatively new features.

Whale with feet.—A team of American scientists led by Philip Gingerich of the University of Michigan have found a fossilized whale with rudimentary legs. The team believes that the fossil could be the missing link between the stage when whales walked on their hind legs and when they entered the sea and lived a fully aquatic life.

The animal, known as *Basiliosaurus*, was a large serpent-like creature which lived about 40 million years ago, in the middle of the Eocene epoch. It is classed as a member of the *Archaeoceti*, the ancient whales. The remains were discovered at Zeuglodon valley in the northern Egyptian desert. Gingerich and his team mapped the skeletons and parts of 243 specimens of *Basiliosaurus isis* and 77 smaller archaeocetes. The *Basiliosaurus isis* lived in shallow water. It had two small hind feet and a functional pelvis. The long bone of the leg (femur) faced forward and lay completely within the body wall. The rest of the leg, outside the body, pointed backwards with the ankle extended and the foot facing upwards. It is thought that this was the resting position. Considering the size of the creature, the limbs would have been virtually useless for swimming and they certainly could not have supported the weight of the body out of water. The condition of the joints and the fact that there are fittings for powerful muscles indicate that the limbs had some use. In addition, the knee had a powerful locking mechanism. It is thought that the legs may have acted as guides during copulation.

Modern whales have functional forelimbs which are used as fins. They do have rudimentary hind limbs that do not protrude from the body, and a remnant pelvic bone anchoring the reproductive organs.

CONSERVATION AND HERITAGE 1989–90

THE NATURAL ENVIRONMENT

Badgers.—Badgers have joined the small group of wild mammals whose national distribution and status are known in great detail (the others are red deer, the seals and the greater horseshoe bat), thanks to a four-year survey recently completed by Bristol University. The badger survey, which was funded by the Nature Conservancy Council and the Mammal Society, used a method pioneered by the Institute of Terrestrial Ecology. It found approximately 43,000 badger social groups scattered throughout Great Britain, comprising some 250,000 individuals. About 105,000 cubs are born each year.

The survey found that interference to badger setts in the form of hole-blocking or digging is widespread, affecting one sett in six. An estimated 9,000 badgers each year are dug out and killed by the terrier dogs of badger-baiters. In areas where baiting is particularly prevalent, such as South Yorkshire, specially designed concrete setts have been built to offer the animals some security. About 47,000 badgers a year are road casualties. In some areas badgers also face cage-trapping by the Ministry of Agriculture in an attempt to control the incidence of bovine tuberculosis, of which badgers are believed to be carriers.

The main influences on badger numbers, however, are overall changes in land-use, especially the replacement of beef and dairy farms by cereals, and the expansion of towns and cities. Badgers rarely survive long in new towns, and their well-documented decline in southern Essex is probably due to urbanization. Badgers flourish best in woods and forests, including conifer plantations, and in well-grazed pasture where short grass enables them to forage in the surface soil for earthworms. Few badgers live on arable land and the badger population may decline severely in the Midlands if, as currently predicted, many farms replace beef with cereal crops. Badgers are already scarce in predominantly arable East Anglia.

The survey provides a base-line for monitoring future changes in badger numbers. It also provides detailed local information against which potential threats from disturbance, persecution and disease control operations can be evaluated. It is proposed to repeat the survey every few years.

The Cairngorms.—For nearly a decade the future of the northern slopes of the Cairngorms has been in dispute. On the one hand are those who want to expand downhill skiing and boost the local economy, but development is opposed by others who argue that this area, with its pine forests, corries, snow-beds and rare animal and plant communities, should be safeguarded against any development that would damage it (*see also* p. 1157 of **Whitaker's Almanack 1990**). After a public inquiry in 1981, the Secretary of State for Scotland ruled against a proposal to extend ski-tows, access roads and other building works from the existing site on the northern slopes of Cairngorm into Lurcher's Gully and two neighbouring corries. The plan has been revived by Highland Regional Council, who included a modified version of the proposal as a recommendation in their structure plan, published in October 1989. Approval by the Secretary of State would allow a major expansion of ski-related development at Cairngorm and its sister hills.

Objectors to the development proposal organized an international 'Save the Cairngorms' campaign. They emphasized the biological diversity of the area, pointing out that Lurcher's Gully is the best example in the Highlands of an unhindered natural zonation from the high tops down to lochs and pine forest, including a rare example of the phenomenon known as *krummholz*— a wood of wind-pruned dwarf trees. The 'Save the Cairngorms' campaign marshalled an impressive breadth of support from leading scientists and mountain users. A total of 7,100 objections were made to the Secretary of State (Malcolm Rifkind), compared with 135 in favour of the proposals.

In June 1990 Mr. Rifkind rejected any development at Lurcher's Gully. It is believed that, apart from the weight of scientific evidence and opinion, he was influenced by forecasts of climatic warming which place a question-mark over the long-term future of Scottish skiing. His decision is likely to have important implications for the whole of the Cairngorms, which has been earmarked as a possible World Heritage Site.

The Environment Protection Bill.—Last year the Government announced that it intended to break up the present Nature Conservancy Council (NCC) to form three national agencies for England, Scotland and Wales. In Scotland and Wales the functions of the NCC and the Countryside Commission will merge and the new bodies come under the control of the Scottish and Welsh Offices. The enabling legislation was introduced in November 1989 as part of the Environmental Protection Bill (popularly known as the Green Bill), which also includes measures to tackle air pollution, to control pollution and to control the release of genetically modified organisms.

The near-unanimous view of the scientific and conservation world, as well as of the NCC itself, is that devolving nature conservation will lead to serious inconsistencies in standards and performance between the new agencies. In response to this the Secretary of State for the Environment (Christopher Patten) agreed to set up an independent Joint Committee to provide a common science base and a national overview on nature conservation matters. The Joint Committee is to have an independent chairman, Sir Fred Holliday, but no enforcement powers. The appointment of chairmen to head the three new agencies was announced in January 1990: the chairman for England is the Earl of Cranbrook, an influential and well-respected conservationist; for Scotland Magnus Magnusson, the television personality and president of the RSPB; and for Wales Michael Griffith, a landowner prominent in Welsh countryside affairs.

The Government's proposals have been criticized for their lack of forethought by virtually every conservation body in Britain, although they were welcomed by many farming, forestry and development interests, especially in Scotland. The Bill was given a rough ride in both Houses of Parliament, and it will be surprising if it reaches its final stages without substantial amendment. It is already clear that the changes will considerably increase expenditure, with four bodies instead of one. The gain to conservation is not yet apparent. Concern remains that the measures will lead in Scotland and Wales to a watering down of existing landscape and nature conservation policies by powerful vested interests.

January storms.—The strong gales in January 1990 were comparable in intensity with those of October 1987. The gales caused widespread damage to trees, woods and plantations in the West Country, parts of Wales, the south coast and the Midlands. The gales were followed by severe flooding along the west and south coasts from overflowing rivers and powerful tidal surges produced by strong onshore winds. The gales affected a larger part of Britain than in 1987, but as broadleaved trees were not in leaf their impact was more selective. Close-packed conifer plantations have little resistance to strong winds and the damage was considerable in places like the New Forest. The Forestry Commission estimated its loss at 3 million trees. Isolated trees in parks also fell victim; about 4,500 trees belonging to the National Trust were toppled in Devon and Cornwall alone. In general it was top-heavy trees with shallow roots, like beech, that were blown over, while most native trees in woods escaped serious damage. Old pollard trees of great beauty and landscape significance were often shredded or toppled; the famous great yew in Selborne churchyard was a victim and The Vyne in Hampshire lost thousands of trees. The Government is aiding storm-damaged parks and properties with a number of measures, the first of which was a £1 million grant towards tree-planting.

Not all the effects of the gales are negative ones. In terms of nature conservation, the gales have done as much good as harm; many a neglected wood has received a spectacular thinning at the hand of nature, bringing renewed warmth and light to the woodland floor and the best displays of woodland flowers seen for years. And lessons have been learnt from the experiences of 1987 when, for instance, damage was caused to woods by heavy machinery running over wet soil during clearing-up operations. In the long term the gales may have an effect on forestry policy. If such winds presage a change to a more violent and unpredictable climate, forestry policy, which currently favours trees such as conifers and beech which are the most vulnerable to strong winds, will have to be rethought.

Marine pollution.—Environment ministers from the countries bordering the North Sea met at The Hague in March 1990 for the third North Sea Conference. The meeting reflected the growing international realization that the pollution of the North Sea cannot continue indefinitely without the toxic chemicals being poured into it sooner or later making their presence felt. The last North Sea conference in 1987 proposed to clean up the North Sea by halving discharges of dangerous chemicals over the following ten years. At The Hague conference governments agreed to reduce discharges of 37 types of toxic chemical, including cadmium, mercury and lead, by half or more by 1995, and to destroy their stocks of polychlorinated biphenyls (PCBs), a persistent toxin which is stored in the body tissues of sea birds and seals). Britain agreed to stop the dumping of 'hazardous wastes' by 1992 and to stop dumping sewage sludge in the North Sea by 1998. The British Environment Secretary (Christopher Patten) insisted, however, that Britain could reserve the right to dispose of radioactive waste in the North Sea, a practice condemned by the other participating countries.

Mr. Patten also expressed concern about the status of dolphins and porpoises in coastal waters. In Britain eleven species of cetaceans are regularly seen; all of these are afforded complete protection under the Wildlife and Countryside Act and commercial whaling has been prohibited since 1934. There is particular concern about the bottle-nosed dolphin, now found mainly in the Moray Firth, where there are about 25 resident individuals, and in Cardigan Bay where there is another small resident population. Dolphins and porpoises in British waters contain high levels of PCBs and other persistent chemicals in their tissues, but it is not known whether this or other factors, such as overfishing or entanglement in nets, is responsible for the observed decline of the dolphin. Long-term study of whales and dolphins is difficult and expensive, but Mr. Patten indicated that government support would be given for new protective measures.

There were three serious oil spillages during the year. In the worst oil pollution incident in south-west England since the *Torrey Canyon* in 1967, 1,000 tonnes of oil blew ashore after the tanker *Rose Bay* collided with a trawler fourteen miles off the south Devon coast. Rock pools and beaches between Plymouth and Dartmouth and the Erme estuary were polluted by oil, but co-operation between wildlife authorities and coastguards minimized the damage from the oil and also from the chemical cleaning techniques, the over-zealous use of these sometimes causing more harm to wildlife than the oil itself. There were also major spillages in enclosed waters at Southampton Water and the River Mersey. The Mersey incident resulted from a pipeline breaking and spurting oil into the estuary, oiling thousands of seabirds. Shell UK was prosecuted by the newly-established National Rivers Authority, and was found guilty of failing to monitor the ageing pipeline adequately and fined £1 million.

Peatlands in danger.—A campaign to highlight the plight of Britain's dwindling number of lowland peat bogs was launched in March 1990 by the Royal Society for Nature Conservation in association with other conservation bodies. Since 1945, lowland peat has been systematically stripped away by commercial companies like Fisons and ICI, the main suppliers of garden peat. In many cases planning permission for peat extraction was given many years ago and legally overrides any later statutory protection for peatlands. Important areas under threat include Thorne Moors and Hatfield Moors near Doncaster, the

Somerset Levels and Whixall Moss in Shropshire. Conservationists estimate that if the current extraction rate of two million tonnes of peat a year continues, all lowland peat outside nature reserves will be exhausted in twenty years' time. The problem is exacerbated by fires, which burned 405 hectares of Thorne Moors in 1989.

Peat is a non-renewable resource; even wet, active bogs regenerate by only two millimetres per year. Conservationists are promoting alternatives to peat, such as wood chippings and compost, and advocating a national strategy for peatland conservation. A peatland protection charter has already been signed by several local authorities, water companies and the National Rivers Authority, and the aims of the campaign have been supported by the Prince of Wales. The Peat Producers Association, which represents the major companies, recently issued a code of practice advising producers to co-operate more closely with conservation bodies. However, the Association's claim that Britain has enough peat resources for everyone fails to distinguish between upland and lowland peat, which have quite different ecologies. The only real solution, according to the Peatlands in Danger campaign, is for the planning permissions for peat extraction in threatened areas to be bought out or revoked by the Secretary of State for the Environment. Such action has already been taken by the Federal Republic of Germany to safeguard its own dwindling lowland peat bogs.

Rainham Marshes.—Planning permission to develop Rainham Marshes, one of London's last wild open spaces, has been granted to MCA Enterprises International and the Rank Organization. The development will include film studios, a theme park, hotels, housing and industrial units and a shopping centre and will cover over 1,650 acres along the north bank of the River Thames in the boroughs of Havering and Thurrock. Most of the land is part of the Inner Thames Marshes Site of Special Scientific Interest (SSSI), an area of grazing marsh intersected by dykes and used by thousands of wildfowl in winter. The brackish water conditions support rare plants and invertebrates.

The Secretary of State for the Environment decided against calling in the proposal for his consideration. The Government is keen for the development to take place in London rather than at a rival site near Paris, and is offering incentives to the developers worth up to $250 million. Other bodies are also interested in developing the site; Havering Borough Council wishes to reclaim 230 acres of the marsh as a site for industrial units, and the Department of Transport wants to build a road across it.

The developers have offered to set aside 428 acres—about a third of the SSSI—as a nature reserve. However, environmentalists fear that wildlife considerations will not have a significant impact on the development plans.

Roads to prosperity.—The Government's road-building plans were outlined in the 1989 White Paper *Roads to Prosperity.* This included proposals to spend £12 billion to widen or build 1,500 miles of trunk roads and motorways over the next decade in response to Government forecasts of the future volume of road traffic. After examining the proposals, leading environmental groups published their response *'Roads to Ruin'*, which points out that road construction on this scale will entail considerable loss of attractive countryside and irreplaceable wildlife habitat. Some 163 Sites of Special Scientific Interest are likely to be damaged, and a doubling of the present number of cars will contribute to the pollution caused by car exhaust emissions. The environmentalists proposed an integrated approach to transport with a greater emphasis on public transport, especially in cities.

Current road-building proposals affecting wildlife habitats and areas of scenic beauty are numerous. The Transport Department has approved a 400-foot wide motorway cutting through an SSSI and Area of Outstanding Natural Beauty at Twyford Down near Winchester, rejecting the alternative of a tunnel on the grounds of cost. A rejection of alternatives on similar grounds means that Oxleas Wood, one of the best-preserved ancient woods in the London area, will be cut in half by a major road linking the east London river crossing with the M2 motorway. A dual carriageway threatens downland near Dover, and plans for a trans-Pennine scheme will mar the Woodland Pass, a popular beauty spot between Manchester and Sheffield. The National Trust now sees roads as the biggest threat to its supposedly protected landscapes, gardens, parks and monuments. The Transport Department make much of tree-planting on motorway embankments to reduce noise and emphasize the value of motorway embankments as 'linear nature reserves'. However, these measures do not compensate for or restore the destruction of habitats in the path of new roads.

THE BUILT ENVIRONMENT

Architectural Awards.—The Royal Institute of British Architects confers awards annually for work on conversions and new buildings sensitively slotted into historic townscapes. The national award winners announced in January 1990 included the adaptation of Billingsgate Market (Richard Rogers) (*see* Architecture summary, **Whitaker's Almanack 1990**); the new Court of Justice at Truro (Evans and Shalev) (ibid.); the rotunda which serves as a cutlery factory for David Mellor at Hathersage, Derbyshire (Michael Hopkins and Partners); the Ecotechnology Centre at Cranfield, Bedfordshire (Chamberlin Powell Bon and Woods); Haward House, London NW5 (van Heyningen and Haward); Kings Meadow, Chester (Aukett Associates); Millpond, Devon, a house created from a derelict woollen mill with 'detailing and craftsmanship of the highest order' (Alan van der Steen Associates); New Court Offices and Library at Ledbury, Herefordshire (William G. McMorran); Richmond House, Whitehall, incorporating Richmond Terrace (the Property Services Agency and William Whitfield); the TSB at St. Andrew's, Fife (Nicoll Russell Studio); and the Tate Gallery at Albert Dock, Liverpool (Stirling, Wilford and Associates) (*see* Architecture summary, **Whitaker's Almanack 1989**).

The Civic Trust Awards, announced in December, are broader in their coverage of general environmental improvements but this year were more exclusive geographically, covering only London and eight large English and Scottish conurbations. Recipients of the Civic Trust awards included the spectacular flood-lighting of a number of buildings in Glasgow; the new shopping centre in the centre of Bolton (*see* Architecture summary, **Whitaker's Almanack 1990**); the conversion of mill buildings at Bury, Lancashire, into flats; the adaptation of a derelict barn at Gunthwaite Top, Barnsley, into houses; the Farm Museum Interpretation Centre at Sandwell Park Farm, West Midlands; and the new Church of St. Lazar, Birmingham, by the architect Predrag Rislich.

Europa Nostra announced the winners of its 1989 awards in January 1990. From over 200 entries, 40 awards were made and no less than 21 of these went to projects in the United Kingdom. Two Medals of Honour come to Britain: for the restoration of the packhorse route over the Sty Head Pass at Borrow-dale, Cumbria, and for the conservation of Chester. Winners of the Diplomas of Merit included the restoration of the 18th century Chinese Temple at Amesbury Abbey, Wiltshire; the restoration of the House of Dun, near Montrose, by William Adam; the conversion of Callaly Castle in Northumberland for multiple residential use; the enhancement of the village of Gracehill, founded in 1761, at Ballymena, Northern Ireland; the new shopping centre at Bolton; the conversion of the mid-19th century Thermal Baths at Buxton, Derbyshire, to provide shopping arcades and a restaurant; the conservation programme in central Cheltenham; the refurbish-ment of the Town Bridge at Leatherhead, Surrey; the conservation in London of Spencer House, St. James's, the Michelin House, Fulham, and Whiteleys Department Store, Bayswater; the conversion of the old waterside railway station at Londonderry, North-ern Ireland; the restoration of the bell tower at St. Mary the Virgin, Pembridge, IOW; and the recon-struction of the south transept of York Minster after the fire in 1984.

In 1990 the Society for the Protection of Ancient Buildings announced the establishment of the John Betjeman Memorial Award. This is to be awarded annually 'for repair to the fabric of buildings in use as churches and chapels in England and Wales'.

Church Heritage Centres.—A campaign has been launched to establish a National Nonconformist Heritage Centre. The leader of the campaign is the Rev. Timothy Royds, Minister of the United Re-formed Church at Rothwell, Northamptonshire (build 1735, listed Grade II*), which it is envisaged would be the location of the centre. At present it is not possible to visit one building or collection which covers the full range of Nonconformist history. Other churches have already taken similar steps. The Roman Catholic Church's history is illustrated at the Bar Convent Museum at 17 Blossom Street, York. The Jewish Museum in the former Spanish and Portuguese Synagogue at Cheetham, Manchester, opened in 1984, and the Welsh Nonconformist Mu-seum, in a former Wesleyan Chapel at Dre'r-ddol between Aberystwyth and Machynnlleth, is run as an outpost of the Welsh Folk Museum. There are museums of Methodism in the crypt of the City Road Chapel, London, at Wesley's home in Epworth, Lincolnshire, purchased by the World Methodist Council in 1954, and at the New Room at Bristol (1748).

Conservation Courses.—The successful repair of historic buildings depends on the skills of those in charge. The past year saw the establishment of the National Historical Building Crafts Institute in Lincoln and of a new course run by the Royal Institution of Chartered Surveyors to train survey-ors in conservation principles. An Appeal was launched by the Society for the Protection of Ancient Buildings to raise money to endow scholarships to allow young architects, surveyors and others from related professions, to study the conservation and repair of historic buildings through practical involve-ment and personal experience.

A new reference and training centre for masonry conservation was opened in May 1990. The Lime Centre, based at the Long Barn, Morestead, Winches-ter, was founded by Bob Bennett, a masonry consult-ant. The Centre offers courses on all aspects of the use of lime, from slaking, preparing lime mortars and lime washes, to practical application in brick, stone, flint and cob. Courses on masonry cleaning and conservation will also be held. Plans for the future include a store of aggregates, a mortar library for reference and matching, and new workshop facilities.

Historic Buildings.—The famous 18th century landscape gardens at Stowe, in Buckinghamshire, are of European significance, both for the 37 temples and garden buildings designed by men such as Capability Brown, Vanbrugh, Gibbs and Kent, and for the flora and fauna of the woodlands and lakes. Stow School took over the estate in 1923, saving it and all the buildings from demolition and develop-ment. The School has a good record in maintaining the garden but the financial burden for the future would have proved very daunting. The School continues to own and occupy the house but the gardens have been transferred to the ownership of the National Trust. The Trust already owned the Oxford Avenue at Stow and held covenants over a part of the garden.

A financial package for a ten-year programme of restoration work and for endowment funding has been put together after an anonymous benefactor came forward with an offer of £2 million. The National Heritage Memorial Fund has contributed a further grant of £4·5 million. The restoration pro-gramme commenced immediately and will be grant-aided by English Heritage. The repair of the Corin-thian Arch will be undertaken by the Landmark Trust. The National Trust itself needs to raise a further £1 million and has launched a special appeal. A small exhibition in the Temple of Concord and Victory in the gardens will explain the programme of work as it proceeds.

Just as the future of Stowe became secure, another National Trust property, Uppark in West Sussex, suffered a serious fire. The 17th century house, designed by Talman, was gutted by the fire, which began in the roof. The attic and first floor were destroyed, although most of the contents on the ground floor were saved. Among the contents salvaged were the state bed with its silk damask hangings, and all but one of the paintings, including a celebrated set of 12 pictures by Arthur Devis and nine early portraits by Pompeo Batoni. Two 18th century chandeliers were among the items lost, together with fine 18th century plasterwork and ceilings. The Trust announced in October 1989 that the restoration would proceed, an operation that may take up to 10 years.

Berry Pomeroy Castle, near Totnes, Devon, now opened by English Heritage, opened to the public for the first time in April 1990. Although taken into care as long ago as 1977, excavation and consolidation has proved a lengthy process. Berry Pomeroy Castle is a late medieval fortified house which was remodelled by the Protector Somerset to serve as his base in the West Country. It was left unfinished at his execution in 1552 and the whole site was abandoned at the end of the 17th century. For the first time for many years the late 15th century wall painting in the gatehouse has been exposed and careful unearthing has revealed the remains of Somerset's grand classical loggia.

The Queen's House, Greenwich, has re-opened in 1990 after a multi-million pound restoration and reconstruction which began in 1984. The paintings originally commissioned for the ceiling of the hall at the Queen's House are now at Marlborough House. In order to restore the hall of the Queen's House to its original appearance, laser analysis and computer reconstruction of the originals at Marlborough House was used to create reproductions in oil paint for the Queen's House.

Moves are afoot to reconstruct the country's last surviving Georgian grandstand, at the former Richmond racecourse in North Yorkshire. It is to be restored, at a cost of more than £1½ million, with the assistance of English Heritage and the Vivat Trust. The grandstand was built in 1775 and is probably by Carr of York. Following the closure of the racecourse in 1891, the building fell into decay and its upper storeys were demolished in the late 1960s. Stones from the stand remained on the site because the Richmond Burgage Pasture Committee refused to allow the old Richmond Borough Council to transport the material across the racecourse. As a result, about 90 per cent of the stone from the upper storey remains in dismantled state on the site. It is hoped to stage a fund-raising race meeting in 1991 to commemorate the centenary of the last races.

Historical Monuments.—The Royal Commission on the Historical Monuments of England continues to expand its work. Among new projects is a national inventory of war memorials, in concert with the Imperial War Museum, and a pilot study of non-Anglican places of worship in Islington, in preparation for a fuller London-wide assessment in partnership with English Heritage. Also in partnership with English Heritage, the Commission is to compile guidelines for the listing of textile mills.

The National Buildings Record (formerly the National Monuments Record) contains the most comprehensive collection of illustrative material of historic buildings in the country. It celebrates its 50th anniversary in 1991 and this is to be commemorated with an exhibition. In Northern Ireland illustrative material of historic buildings is to be collected for the first time. The Department of the Environment for Northern Ireland announced early in 1990 the establishment of a National Buildings Record for Ulster, to act as a much needed centre for photographs and drawings related to historic buildings.

Laws and reports.—The past year saw the passing of three measures with relevance to architectural conservation; the Care of Cathedrals Measure, which provides for greater outside control over works to cathedrals, and two planning Acts. The Town and Country Planning Act 1990 consolidates the provisions of previous legislation and separates certain clauses of the 1971 Act into a self-contained piece of legislation, the Planning (Listed Buildings and Conservation Areas) Act 1990. This Act consolidates provisions relating to special controls in respect of buildings and areas of special architectural and historic interest.

The Government does propose changes in law although at the time of writing the much heralded White Paper on the Environment had yet to be published. Also promised is a discussion paper on 'fixtures and fittings' in historic buildings. Concern about these has been prompted in large measure by the furore over the alienation from the temple at Woburn Abbey of Canova's statue of the Three Graces, which the temple was built to house.

Other proposals mooted by the Department of the Environment include a ban on the designation, cancellation or modification of conservation areas, other than during the preparation of development plans (which normally takes place only every ten years); limitations on 'planning gain', the system under which permissions for development are granted provided that the applicant makes a financial contribution or otherwise assists a worthy project in the area; and the introduction of a charge for lodging planning appeals ranging from £100 to £4,000.

The report by Richard Wilding on the working of the Redundant Churches Fund, commissioned jointly by the Department of the Environment and the Church Commissioners, was published in 1990. It found generally in favour of the Fund, although urging a change of name to the Church Heritage Trust. It also recommended changes in the methods of funding and greater caution over the number and quality of churches vested in the Fund, which at present cares for 250 disused Anglican churches.

Listed buildings.—By the end of June 1990 the total of listed buildings in England stood at 435,243, an increase of some 4,000 on the year before. Of these 6,065 are in the Grade I category.

In the course of the year it was announced that a review of 379 urban sets of lists identified as deficient by English Heritage is to be funded by the Department of the Environment. The reassessment should be complete by 1992. A review, however, is not the same as a thorough resurvey, which implies an inspection inside and out of every building. The funding could not run to resurveying all the buildings concerned.

The 4,000 additions to the lists made in the course of the year have afforded protection to a great range of structures. One listing was of an early 19th century peat shed at Bowles Farmhouse, Melchet Park, Plaitford, Hants. A timber-framed structure, the shed was filled with peat through the high-level door and the peat was then removed as needed from the front door. Another unusual listing was the Llanstinan Bridge at Scleddau, Dyfed, said to date from 1602. This is described as 'an unaltered bridge of primitive construction with slightly corbelled drystone abutments and longer stones used for lintels over the centre of the arch, an extremely rare, possibly unique, example of ancient bridge building technology'. Other non-domestic listings include the former stables and forge at Joliffe Yard, London Road, North Merstham, Surrey, erected in 1803–05 as part of the terminus of the Surrey Iron Railway; 38 and 39 Corve Street, Ludlow, a late 18th century building which includes in its upper storey a completely weatherboarded front thought to be a rare survival of the louvred ventilation system used for drying skins in glovers' workshops; The Dome, Marine Parade, Worthing, an early 'multifunctional leisure complex', dating from 1911; Harker's Studio, Queens Row, London SE17 (1904), the workshop of Joseph Harker, one of the most important theatrical scene painters of his day; the Mappin Terraces at Regent's Park Zoo, 'an early and ingenious example of reinforced concrete construction'; the Queen's Arms, Green Lane, Patricroft, Eccles (1828), which may be considered the first railway pub in the world; the purpose-built lifeboat house (1862) at the Point car park, Teignmouth, Devon; and the public library at Brentwood in Essex. This was originally built between 1844 and 1851 to house the local constabulary, making it one of the earliest police stations in England which can be positively identified.

Listed farm buildings include the remarkably complete 18th century bakehouse at Peaches Farmhouse, Cirencester Road, Minchinhampton, Glos.; a beehive pigsty at Peacock Farm, Rhes-y-Cae, Halkyn, Clwyd, an oval animal shelter constructed to the ancient corbelled technique, with rubble walls and 'vaults', now partly dismantled; and a rare staddle threshing barn (dated 1806) at Williamstrip Farm, Coln St. Aldwyns in the Cotswolds.

Listed domestic buildings include 6 Scarrob Beck at Erpingham, Norfolk, a 16th century cottage important for its brick mullion windows rendered to simulate stone; 224 The Cedars, Henwick Road, Worcester, described as 'a remarkably complete Victorian villa altered only by modern plumbing in the upper rooms, retaining a basement with full domestic fittings, butter pantry, housekeeper's room, kitchen, scullery, wine cellar and laundry with copper and boiler'; the Garden House at 16 St. Giles Street, Oxford, which incorporates the model of the 1737 Gibbs design for the Radcliffe Camera; and the only surviving example in the Blackpool district of an 18th century Fylde cobble-built farmhouse, Walkers Hill Farmhouse, at Midgeland Road. One of the more unusual domestic listings is a former railway carriage now used as a dwelling at Hayle, Cornwall.

The carriage seems to have travelled the length of the country to perform its new role, having been built for the Cumbrian Railways Company.

Listed buildings under threat.—In 1989 application was made to demolish 459 listed buildings in England and Wales. This was the lowest number of applications for over six years.

The more important buildings threatened included Oakhill Park, Accrington, Lancs, a gentleman's villa of 1815 in the centre of the local municipal park; Hardwick House, Southam Road, Banbury, Oxon, a Grade II* listed house of the 16th and 17th centuries (application withdrawn); the great mill chimney (1854) at Bridgefoot, Belper, Derbys.; the rare circular horse exercise ring (1819) at Belvoir Castle, Leics. (application refused); the Belgrave Chapel, Darwen, Lancs., designed by Edward Walters in 1847 with a spectacular west front; Nos 3–7 Bradley Road, Donnington, Shrops., a late 18th century example of 'barracks housing' where male workers at Ironbridge were housed during the week before returning to their families at the weekend; the dovecote at Easton Neston House, Northants.; the former Wesleyan chapel at Hartlepool (1873), which has an impressive portico; Ingress Abbey, Greenhithe, Kent (1833); Nos 79–85 Essex Road, Islington, which have rare late 17th century interiors; the Lieutenant Governor's House in Jersey, apparently designed with some advice from Sir John Soane; and St. Jude's Church, Southsea (1851).

The question mark over plans for the Channel Tunnel rail link precluded applications to demolish in Kent. The rejection by the House of Commons of Clause 19 of the Bill providing for the construction of the Channel Tunnel terminal at Kings Cross has given back to the planning authorities the right to decide the fate of a number of listed buildings, most notably the Great Northern Hotel, threatened by the development for the Kings Cross-St. Pancras area.

One of the greatest controversies of the year arose from the application by the businessman Peter Palumbo to demolish nine listed buildings in the centre of the City of London. Demolition is proposed to allow the construction of a new building by James Stirling. The case reached the courts after the decision by the Secretary of State for the Environment of the time (Nicholas Ridley) to grant the necessary permissions. SAVE Britain's Heritage challenged the legality of the Environment Secretary's decision in the High Court, losing the first round but obtaining a favourable judgment in the Court of Appeal. At the time of writing Mr Palumbo had received leave to appeal to the House of Lords, with a hearing expected in January 1991.

Demolition applications were not the only threat to listed buildings in 1990. The gales in January 1990 caused widespread damage, affecting a greater number of historic buildings than the storm in October 1987. Twenty listed buildings, most of them barns, were destroyed or damaged beyond repair, and the Ecclesiastical Insurance Office received over 4,000 claims for damage to churches.

Museums.—Many inner city regeneration schemes, particularly those sponsored by the Urban

Development Corporations, are attracted to the idea of museums as 'flagships'. The Corporation recently appointed for the Lower Don Valley at Sheffield is considering housing a Museum of the North within the valley. It is actively canvassing a number of museum administrators, particularly the owners of the Royal Armouries Collection, of which only a small part is on show in the Tower of London.

In Barrow-in-Furness plans are progressing for the creation of a Dock Maritime Museum. Barrow is renowned for shipbuilding and the museum will be located within a 19th century repair dock, to be covered by a roof supported on steel A-frames. Exhibits will range from submarines and airships to yachts.

A further section of Chatham's historic Dockyard is now open to the public. Restoration work has been completed on the Dockyard's Master House and Mould Loft of 1753. The building was originally used for the construction of masts and templates for 18th century warships; now a live exhibition has been installed to give visitors an impression of the sights, sounds and smells of the Dockyard activities by leading them through the life of a shipwright's apprentice in the 1750s.

What must be London's smallest museum has opened within the redundant ticket office at Arnos Grove station, on the Piccadilly Underground line. Within the little rotunda is the first publicly available display of the work of Charles Holden, the architect of Arnos Grove and of many of the most distinctive stations owned by London Transport.

A Museum of Church Treasures and Artefacts opened in April 1990 at Winchester Cathedral; it is situated in the South Transept Triforium. Exhibits include what is described as 'the only complete piece of late Saxon glass surviving in Britain' (with a possible rival, it must be said, at Jarrow), the Winchester Madonna (1480), and the chair on which Queen Mary Tudor sat during her marriage to Philip II of Spain, which took place at the cathedral in 1554.

The National Heritage Memorial Fund.—In 1988–89 the National Heritage Memorial Fund made grants of some £12,000,000, bringing the total donated since its foundation in April 1980 to £103,000,000. As ever, the definition of 'heritage' is catholic.

The Fund gave £2,735,200 towards the setting up of a charitable trust to secure the future of Paxton House, Berwick, and its collection of Chippendale furniture. A grant of £215,000 was made towards the purchase by the Victoria and Albert Museum of the marble bust of James Gibbs by Rysbrack. This was presented to the Church of St. Martin-in-the-Fields, Gibbs' most famous London commission, in 1885 and recently sold by the parish church council. The Fund also assisted the purchase by Birmingham City Museum and Art Gallery of one of the Klismos Chairs. These are believed to have been designed for Soho House, Birmingham, a property acquired by Matthew Boulton in 1761 and subsequently altered with the help of James and Samuel Wyatt. The chair may be the design of Thomas Hope.

Other schemes grant-aided during the year included the resiting at Bradford Industrial Museum of three pairs of 1870s back-to-back terraced houses; the purchase of John Constable's *Somerset House*, an oil sketch of 1819, by the Royal Academy; the acquisition by the Grosvenor Museum, Chester, of 12 items of church silver from four redundant churches which stood, or originally stood, within 100 yards of the museum; the purchase by the Arkwright Society of the last section of the major mill complex at Cromford, Derbyshire, not in its possession; the acquisition by the National Trust of the antique sculpture comprising 29 marble busts and eight marble bas-relief panels incorporated in the mid-18th century into four remodelled rooms at Farnborough Hall, Warwickshire; the deposition within the East Sussex County Council Record Office of the Figg Archive of plans and maps of the county covering the years between 1746 and the early 1850s; the safeguarding by the University of London Library of the collection of 600 original theatre designs by members of the Grieve family of scene painters, dating from the 1820s; the repair of the great William Hill organ (1905) in Pearson's church of All Saints, Hove, E. Sussex; the conservation of five memorials within Kinneff Old Church, near Aberdeen; the purchase by the Hunterian Art Gallery of designs by Charles Rennie Mackintosh; and the return to Marble Hill House, Twickenham, of the last of five paintings by Panini dating from 1738 which were set into the walls of the Great Room until their removal at the turn of the century.

ASTRONOMERS ROYAL

John Flamsteed, first Astronomer Royal	1675–1719	Sir William Christie	1881–1910
Edmund Halley	1720–1742	Sir Frank Dyson	1910–1933
James Bradley	1742–1762	Sir Harold Jones	1933–1955
Nathaniel Bliss	1762–1764	Sir Richard Woolley	1955–1971
Nevil Maskelyne	1765–1811	Sir Martin Ryle	1972–1982
John Pond	1811–1835	Prof. Sir Francis Graham Smith	1982–
Sir George Airy	1835–1881		

NATIONAL PARKS
England and Wales

The ten National Parks of England and Wales were established in the 1950s under the provisions of the National Parks and Access to the Countryside Act 1949. The National Parks were set up to conserve and protect scenic landscapes from inappropriate development and to provide access to the land for public enjoyment.

The Countryside Commission is the statutory body which has the power to designate National Parks. The designation of National Parks in England is considered and confirmed by the Secretary of State for the Environment, and the designation of National Parks in Wales by the Secretary of State for Wales. The designation of a National Park does not affect the ownership of the land, nor does it remove the rights of the local community. Although the parks are administered through local government, the vast majority of the land is owned by private landowners (74 per cent) or by other bodies like the National Trust (7 per cent) and the Forestry Commission (7 per cent). The National Park Authorities own only 2·3 per cent of the land in the National Parks.

Under the Local Government Act 1972, National Park Authorities (NPAs) are the authorities responsible for park administration. They also influence land use and development, and deal with planning applications.

Two-thirds of the members of each authority are appointed by the county and district councils within whose boundaries the parks lie. One-third of the members are appointed by the Secretary of State for the Environment or the Secretary of State for Wales with advice from the Countryside Commission.

In the Peak District and the Lake District the NPAs are special boards: the Peak Park Joint Planning Board and the Lake District Special Planning Board. These are autonomous authorities which are financially independent, unlike the authorities in the other eight parks which are county council committees. The NPAs appoint the National Park Officer for the National Park they administer.

Central government provides 75 per cent of the funding for the parks through the National Park Supplementary Grant. The remaining 25 per cent is supplied by the local authorities concerned. Forecast expenditure for 1989–90 was £17,417,650.

The Countryside Commission has stated that other areas are regarded as being worthy of National Parks status. A special statutory authority was established in 1989 to develop, conserve and manage the Norfolk and Suffolk Broads (see p. 304). The other area considered worthy of designation is the New Forest and it has been the subject of a consultative report to decide upon its future.

The National Parks in England and Wales are:

Brecon Beacons (519 sq. miles/1,344 sq. km).—Designated in 1957, the park lies in Powys (66 per cent), Dyfed, Gwent and Mid Glamorgan. The park is centred on the Beacons, Pen y Fan, Corn Du and Cribyn, but also includes the valley of the Usk, the Black Mountains to the east and the Black Mountain to the west.

There are information centres at Brecon, Craig-y-nos Country Park, Abergavenny and Llandovery, a study centre at Danywenallt and a day visitor centre near Libanus.

Information Office, 7 Glamorgan Street, Brecon, Powys LD3 7DP. (Tel. 0874-4437). *National Park Officer*, M. Beresford.

Dartmoor (365 sq. miles/945 sq. km).—Designated

in 1951, Dartmoor lies wholly in Devon. Dartmoor consists of moorland and rocky granite tors, and is rich in prehistoric remains.

There are information centres at Newbridge, Tavistock, Bovey Tracey, Steps Bridge, Princetown and Postbridge.

Information Office, Parke, Haytor Road, Bovey Tracey, Devon TQ13 9JQ. (Tel. 0626-832093). *National Park Officer*, I. Mercer.

Exmoor (265 sq. miles/686 sq. km).—Designated in 1954, Exmoor lies in Somerset (71 per cent) and Devon. Exmoor is a moorland plateau inhabited by wild ponies and red deer. There are many ancient remains and burial mounds.

There are information centres at Lynmouth, County Gate, Dulverton and Combe Martin.

Information Office, Exmoor House, Dulverton, Somerset TA22 9HL. (Tel. 0398-23665). *National Park Officer*, K. Bungay.

Lake District (885 sq. miles/2,292 sq. km).—Designated in 1951, the Lake District lies wholly in Cumbria. The Lake District includes England's highest mountains (Scafell Pike, Helvellyn and Skiddaw) but it is most famous for its glaciated lakes.

There are information centres at Keswick, Waterhead, Hawkshead, Seatoller, Bowness, Grasmere, Coniston, Glenridding and Pooley Bridge, an information van at Gosforth and a park centre at Brockhole, Windermere.

Information Office, Busher Walk, Kendal, Cumbria LA9 4RH. (Tel. 0539-24555). *National Park Officer*, J. Toothill.

Northumberland (398 sq. miles/1,031 sq. km).—Designated in 1956, the Northumberland National Park lies wholly in Northumberland. The park is an area of hill country stretching from Hadrian's Wall to the Scottish Border.

There are information centres at Ingram, Once Brewed, Rothbury, Housesteads, Harbottle and Kielder, and an information caravan at Cawfields.

Information Office, Eastburn, South Park, Hexham, Northumberland NE46 1BS. (Tel. 0434-605555). *National Park Officer*, T. Macdonald.

North York Moors (553 sq. miles/1,433 sq. km).—Designated in 1952, the North York Moors lie in North Yorkshire (96 per cent) and Cleveland. The park consists of woodland and moorland, and includes the Hambleton Hills and the Cleveland Way.

There are information centres at Danby, Pickering, Sutton Bank, Ravenscar, Helmsley and Hutton-le-Hole, and a day study centre at Danby.

Information Office, The Old Vicarage, Bondgate, Helmsley, York YO6 5BP. (Tel. 0439-70657). *National Park Officer*, D. Statham.

Peak District (542 sq. miles/1,404 sq. km).—Designated in 1951, the Peak District lies in Derbyshire (64 per cent), Staffordshire, South Yorkshire, Cheshire, West Yorkshire and Greater Manchester. The Peak District is composed of the gritstone moors of the 'dark peak' and the limestone dales of the 'white peak'.

There are information centres at Bakewell, Edale, Fairholmes and Castleton, and information points in the Goyt Valley and at Hartington.

Information Office, Aldern House, Baslow Road, Bakewell, Derbyshire DE4 1AE. (Tel. 062 981-4321). *National Park Officer*, M. Dower.

Pembrokeshire Coast (225 sq. miles/583 sq. km).—Designated in 1952, the Pembrokeshire Coast National Park lies wholly in Dyfed. The park consists of cliffs, open moorland and Skomer Island.

There are information centres at Tenby, St. David's, Pembroke, Newport, Kilgetty, Haverford-west and Broad Haven.

Information Office, County Offices, Haverfordwest, Dyfed SA61 1QZ. (Tel. 0437-4591). *National Park Officer*, N. Wheeler.

Snowdonia (838 sq. miles/2,171 sq. km).—Designated in 1951, Snowdonia lies wholly in Gwynedd. It is an area of deep valleys and rugged mountains in northern Wales.

There are information centres at Aberdovey, Bala, Betws y Coed, Blaenau Ffestiniog, Conwy, Harlech, Dolgellau and Llanberis.

Information Office, Penrhyndeudraeth, Gwynedd LL48 6LS. (Tel. 0766-770274). *National Park Officer*, A. Jones.

Yorkshire Dales (680 sq. miles/1,762 sq. km).—Designated in 1954, the Yorkshire Dales National Park lies in North Yorkshire (88 per cent) and Cumbria. The Yorkshire Dales are composed primarily of limestone overlaid in places by millstone grit. The three peaks of Ingleborough, Whernside and Pen-y-Ghent are within the park.

There are information centres at Clapham, Grassington, Hawes, Aysgarth Falls, Malham and Sedbergh.

Information Office, Yorebridge House, Bainbridge, Leyburn, North Yorkshire DL8 3BP. (Tel. 0969-50456). *National Park Officer*, R. Harvey.

Scotland and Northern Ireland

The National Parks and Access to the Countryside Act 1949 dealt only with England and Wales and made no provision for Scotland or Northern Ireland. Although there are no national parks in these two countries, there is power to designate them in Northern Ireland under the Amenity Lands Act 1965 and the Nature Conservation and Amenity Lands Order (Northern Ireland) 1985; and in 1989 the Scottish Office asked the Countryside Commission for Scotland to report on whether national parks should be designated in Scotland.

AREAS OF OUTSTANDING NATURAL BEAUTY

England and Wales

Under the National Parks and Access to the Countryside Act 1949, provision was made for the designation of Areas of Outstanding Natural Beauty (AONBs) by the Countryside Commission. The Countryside Act 1968 further defines the role of AONBs, suggesting that they should show due regard for the interests of other land users, such as agriculture and forestry groups. Designations in England are confirmed by the Secretary of State for the Environment and those in Wales by the Secretary of State for Wales.

Although less emphasis is placed upon the provision of open-air enjoyment for the public than in the national parks, AONBs are seen as areas which are no less beautiful and require the same degree of protection to conserve and enhance the natural beauty of the countryside. This includes protecting flora and fauna, geographical and other landscape features.

In AONBs planning and management responsibilities are split between county and district councils (there are 16 which cross county boundaries). Finance for the AONBs is provided by grant-aid.

Thirty-eight Areas of Outstanding Natural Beauty have been designated since 1956. They are (with dates of foundation):

Anglesey (1967) (83 sq. miles/215 sq. km).—The designated area extends along the entire coastline of the island, except for breaks around the urban areas and in the vicinity of Wylfa.

Arnside and Silverdale (1972) (29 sq. miles/75 sq. km).—The area embraces the upper half of Morecambe Bay, the Kent estuary, and includes extensive tidal flats in the Bay.

Cannock Chase (1958) (26 sq. miles/68 sq. km).—An area of high heathland in Staffordshire. Deer continue to roam over the Chase.

Chichester Harbour (1964) (29 sq. miles/75 sq. km).—The area extends from Hayling Island to Apuldram and includes Thorney Island.

Chilterns (1965) (325 sq. miles/833 sq. km).—Chalk downlands running from South Oxfordshire north-eastwards to Bedfordshire, including the outlying group of hills beyond Luton.

Clwydian Range (1985) (60 sq. miles/156 sq. km).—A prominent ridge extending southwards from Prestatyn on the North Wales coast. Offas's Dyke runs along the crest of the Range.

Cornwall (1959; Camel Estuary 1983) (370 sq. miles/957 sq. km).—A number of separate areas including Bodmin Moor; most of the Land's End peninsula; the coast between St. Michael's Mount and St. Austell (with Falmouth omitted); the Fowey Estuary; in north Cornwall most of the coast to Bedruthan Steps and between Perranporth and Godrevy Towans, plus the Camel Estuary.

Cotswolds (1966) (582 sq. miles/1,507 sq. km).—The area of limestone hills above the Vales of Gloucester and Evesham.

Cranborne Chase and West Wiltshire Downs (1983) (371 sq. miles/960 sq. km).—A chalkland area covering parts of Wiltshire, Dorset, Hampshire and Somerset, including the wooded remnants of the ancient Chase.

Dedham Vale (1970; extended 1978) (28 sq. miles/72 sq. km).—The area bordering Essex and Suffolk, where John Constable painted.

East Devon (1963) (103 sq. miles/267 sq. km).—The coastline between Exmouth and Lyme Regis, with Sidmouth, Beer and Seaton omitted. Inland Gittisham Hill, East Hill and Woodbury and Aylebeare Commons are included.

North Devon (1960) (66 sq. miles/171 sq. km).—Includes most of the North Devon coastline, from just north of Bude to the boundary of the Exmoor National Park.

South Devon (1960) (128 sq. miles/332 sq. km).—Includes the coast between Bolt Head and Bolt Tail, Salcombe, Slapton Sands and Dartmouth, and the estuaries and valleys of the Yealm, Erme, Avon and Dart.

Dorset (1959) (400 sq. miles/1,036 sq. km).—The coastline between Lyme Regis and Poole, with the Isle of Portland and Weymouth omitted, stretching inland to include the Purbeck Hills and the downs of Hardy country.

Forest of Bowland (1964) (310 sq. miles/803 sq. km).—A moorland area mostly in Lancashire running westward from the River Ribble, with a small outlying area east of the Ribble which includes Pendle Hill.

Gower (1956) (73 sq. miles/189 sq. km).—A peninsula in West Glamorgan, South Wales, known for its coastline.

East Hampshire (1962) (151 sq. miles/391 sq. km).— A chalkland area stretching from the outskirts of Winchester to the Sussex border at a distance of about 10 miles inland.

South Hampshire Coast (1967) (30 sq. miles/78 sq. km).—14 miles of coastline between Hurst Castle and Calshot Castle, extending inland up the Beaulieu River for about six miles.

High Weald (1983) (560 sq. miles/1,450 sq. km).— The area covers parts of East and West Sussex, Kent and Surrey. It is predominantly wooded, and includes larger heathland areas like Ashdown Forest, the remnants of the old Wealden forests.

Howardian Hills (1987) (79 sq. miles/205 sq. km).— Wooded hills which rise above the Vales of York and Pickering.

Kent Downs (1968) (326 sq. miles/845 sq. km).— Running east and south-east from the Surrey border near Westerham to the coast near Dover and Folkestone, with a coastal outlier at South Foreland and a narrow strip of the old sea cliff escarpment west of Hythe overlooking Romney Marsh.

Lincolnshire Wolds (1973) (216 sq. miles/560 sq. km).—The area extends in a south-east direction from Laceby and Caistor in the north to the region of Spilsby, about ten miles west of the coast.

Lleyn (1957) (60 sq. miles/155 sq. km).—An isolated peninsula in Gwynedd, North Wales.

Malvern Hills (1959) (40 sq. miles/104 sq. km).— The whole range of the Malvern Hills in the county of Hereford and Worcester, just touching Gloucestershire.

Mendip Hills (1972) (80 sq. miles/206 sq. km).— Comprising over half of the Mendip Hills, the area stretches from Bleadon Hill to the A39 road north of Wells and includes Cheddar Gorge and Wookey Hole.

Norfolk Coast (1968) (174 sq. miles/450 sq. km).— An almost continuous coastal strip three to five miles in depth from Hunstanton to Bacton, with a further small strip between Sea Palling and Winterton-on-Sea. The area includes part of the Sandringham Estate.

North Pennines (1988) (779 sq. miles/1,998 sq. km).

Northumberland Coast (1958) (50 sq. miles/129 sq. km).—Stretches from just south of Berwick to Amble and includes Holy Island and the Farne Islands.

Quantock Hills (1957) (38 sq. miles/99 sq. km).—A range of sandstone hills in Somerset.

Isles of Scilly (1976) (6 sq. miles/16 sq. km).—About 140 islands and skerries in the Scillies group of which only five are inhabited. There are a number of Sites of Special Scientific Interest.

Shropshire Hills (1959) (300 sq. miles/777 sq. km).— Most of south-west Shropshire between the Welsh border and the boundary with Hereford and Worcester, including the region around Clun, the area of the Stiperstones, the Long Mynd and Wenlock Edge, with the tongues of land running north-east to the Wrekin and south towards Ludlow.

Solway Coast (1964) (41 sq. miles/107 sq. km).—A stretch of coastline in Cumbria from Maryport to the estuaries of the Rivers Eden and Esk (with Silloth omitted) backed by the Solway Plain.

Suffolk Coast and Heaths (1970) (151 sq. miles/ 391 sq. km).—The area includes 38 miles of coastline and parts of the Stour and Orwell estuaries, while the Deben, Alde and Blyth flow through it.

Surrey Hills (1958) (160 sq. miles/414 sq. km).—An area of hills to the east and south of Guildford, including the Hog's Back and the ridge of the North Downs.

Sussex Downs (1966) (379 sq. miles/981 sq. km).— The area includes the chalk escarpment of the South Downs from Beachy Head to the Hampshire border, and stretches down to the coast between Eastbourne and Seaford.

North Wessex Downs (1972) (671 sq. miles/1,738 sq. km).—An upland area in Hampshire, Wiltshire, Oxfordshire and Berkshire, bounded by the Marlborough and Lambourn Downs in the west and the Chiltern Hills in the east. Salisbury Plain forms the southern limit of what is so far the largest area designated.

Isle of Wight (1963) (73 sq. miles/189 sq. km).—A number of separate areas comprising stretches of coastline, the Yar Valley, the high downland behind Ventnor and the chalk ridge which runs from Newport to Culver Cliff and Foreland.

Wye Valley (1971) (125 sq. miles/325 sq. km).—The river valley running through the counties of Gwent, Gloucestershire and Hereford and Worcester.

Proposals for further designations include: the Tamar and Tavy Valleys, Devon/Cornwall; the Blackdown Hills, Devon/Somerset; the Berwyn Mountains, mid-Wales; and the Nidderdale Moors, N. Yorkshire.

Northern Ireland

The Department of the Environment for Northern Ireland, with advice from the Council for Nature Conservation and the Countryside, designates Areas of Outstanding Natural Beauty in Northern Ireland. At present there are nine and these cover a total area of approximately 695,166 acres (282,395 hectares).

Antrim Coast and Glens, Co. Antrim (174,452 acres/ 70,600 ha).

Causeway Coast, Co. Antrim (10,008 acres/4,050 ha).

Lagan Valley, Co. Down (5,119 acres/2,072 ha).

Lecale Coast, Co. Down (7,679 acres/3,108 ha).

Mourne, Co. Down (140,876 acres/57,012 ha).

North Derry, Co. Londonderry (31,999 acres/12,950 ha)

South Armagh, Co. Armagh (31,999 acres/12,950 ha).

Sperrin, Co. Tyrone/Co. Londonderry (249,585 acres/ 101,006 ha).

Strangford Lough, Co. Down (46,077 acres/ 18,647 ha).

NATIONAL SCENIC AREAS

No Areas of Outstanding Natural Beauty are designated in Scotland. However, National Scenic Areas have a broadly equivalent status.

The Countryside Commission for Scotland recognizes areas of national scenic significance. At present there are 40, covering a total area of 2,513,748 acres (1,017,300 ha).

Development within National Scenic Areas is dealt with by the local planning authority, who are required to consult with the Countryside Commission for Scotland for certain categories of development within these areas. Land management uses can also be modified in the interest of scenic conservation. The Secretary of State for Scotland has limited powers of intervention should a planning authority and the Countryside Commission for Scotland disagree.

	acres	ha			acres	ha
Border				**Orkney Islands**		
Eildon and Leaderfoot	8,896	3,600		Hoy and West Mainland ...	36,571	14,800
Upper Tweeddale	30,393	12,300				
				Shetland Islands		
Central				Shetland	38,548	15,600
Loch Lomond*	34,347	13,900				
Loch Rannoch and Glen				**Strathclyde**		
Lyon*	3,212	1,300		Ben Nevis and Glen Coe* ..	43,242	17,500
The Trossachs	11,367	4,600		Jura	53,868	21,800
				Knapdale	48,926	19,800
Dumfries and Galloway				Kyles of Bute	10,872	4,400
East Stewartry Coast	12,849	5,200		Loch Lomond*	74,871	30,300
Fleet Valley	13,096	5,300		Loch na Keal, Isle of Mull ..	31,382	12,700
Nith Estuary	22,980	9,300		Lynn of Lorn	11,861	4,800
				Scarba, Lunga and the		
Grampian				Garvellachs	4,695	1,900
The Cairngorm Mountains*	73,636	29,800				
Deeside and Lochnagar* ...	79,566	32,200		**Tayside**		
				Ben Nevis and Glen Coe* ..	11,119	4,500
Highland				Deeside and Lochnagar* ...	19,274	7,800
Assynt-Coigach	222,884	90,200		Loch Rannoch and Glen		
Ben Nevis and Glen Coe* ..	171,982	69,600		Lyon*	116,384	47,100
The Cairngorm Mountains*	92,415	37,400		Loch Tummel	22,733	9,200
The Cuillin Hills	54,115	21,900		River Earn	7,413	3,000
Dornoch Firth	18,532	7,500		River Tay	13,838	5,600
Glen Affric	47,690	19,300				
Glen Strathfarrar	9,390	3,800		**Western Isles**		
Kintail	40,277	16,300		St. Kilda	2,224	900
Knoydart	97,604	39,500		South Lewis, Harris and		
Kyle of Tongue	45,713	18,500		North Uist	268,351	108,600
Loch Shiel	33,111	13,400		South Uist Machair	15,073	6,100
Morar, Moidart and						
Ardnamurchan	39,289	15,900		**Total**	2,513,748	1,017,300
North-west Sutherland	50,655	20,500				
The Small Isles	38,300	15,500				
Trotternish	12,355	5,000				
Wester Ross	359,036	145,300		*National Scenic Areas in more than one region		

PERIODS OF GESTATION OR INCUBATION

The table shows approximate periods of gestation or incubation for some common animals and birds. In some cases the periods may vary and where doubt arises professional advice should be sought.

Species	Shortest period (days)	Usual period (days)	Longest period (days)	Species	Shortest period (days)	Usual period (days)	Longest period (days)
Human	240	273	313	Duck	28	28	32
Horse	305	336	340	Chicken	20	21	22
Cow	273	280	294	Pigeon	17	18	19
Goat	147	151	155	Canary	12	14	14
Sheep	140	147–50	160	Guinea Pig	63	—	70
Pig	109	112	125	Mouse	18	—	19
Dog	55	63	70	Rat	21		24
Cat	53	56	63	Elephant		21–22 months	
Rabbit	30	32	35				
Goose	28	30	32	Zebra		56 weeks	
Turkey	25	28	28	Camel		45 weeks	

NATURE CONSERVATION AREAS

SITES OF SPECIAL SCIENTIFIC INTEREST

Site of Special Scientific Interest (SSSI) is a legal designation applied to land in England, Scotland or Wales which the Nature Conservancy Council (NCC) identifies as being of special interest because of its flora, fauna, geological or physiographical features. In some cases, SSSI are managed as nature reserves.

The NCC must notify its intention to declare the land of special interest to the local planning authority, the water and drainage authority, every owner/occupier of the land, and the Secretary of State for the Environment (or Secretary of State for Scotland or for Wales where applicable). Forestry and agricultural departments must also be notified.

Objections to the designation of SSSI can be made and ultimately heard at a full meeting of the NCC Council. As a last resort the NCC can purchase a site.

The protection of most sites depends on the co-operation of individual landowners and occupiers. Occupiers must consult the NCC and gain written consent before they can undertake certain listed activities on the site.

As at March 31, 1990 there were 5,435 SSSI in Britain, covering 4,234,841 acres (1,713,840 hectares).

	No.	Acres	Hectares
England	3,404	1,846,140	747,133
Scotland	1,262	1,929,367	780,815
Wales	769	459,333	185,892

Northern Ireland

In Northern Ireland 25 Areas of Special Scientific Interest (ASSIs) have been established by the Department of the Environment for Northern Ireland. These cover a total area of 16,450 acres (6,660 hectares).

NATIONAL NATURE RESERVES

National Nature Reserves are defined in the National Parks and Access to the Countryside Act 1949 as land designated for the study and preservation of flora and fauna, or of geological or physiographical features.

The NCC can designate as a National Nature Reserve land which is being managed as a nature reserve under an agreement with the NCC; land held and managed by the NCC; or land held and managed as a nature reserve by another approved body. The NCC can turn to the appropriate Secretary of State to impose by-laws for the protection of the reserves from undesirable development.

As at March 31, 1990 there were 235 National Nature Reserves in Britain, covering 411,048 acres (166,351 hectares).

	No.	Acres	Hectares
England	121	102,081	41,312
Scotland	68	277,344	112,241
Wales	46	31,623	12,798

Northern Ireland

National Nature Reserves are established and managed by the Department of the Environment for Northern Ireland, with advice from the Council for Nature Conservation and the Countryside. There are 44 National Nature Reserves covering 10,789 acres (4,368 hectares).

LOCAL NATURE RESERVES

Local Nature Reserves are defined in the National Parks and Access to the Countryside Act 1949 as land designated for the study and preservation of flora and fauna, or of geological or physiographical features. The Act gives local authorities in England and Wales and district councils in Scotland the power to acquire, declare and manage local nature reserves in consultation with the Nature Conservancy Council. Conservation trusts can also own and manage non-statutory local nature reserves.

As at March 31, 1990 there were 195 designated Local Nature Reserve areas in Britain, covering 35,555 acres (14,389 hectares).

	No.	Acres	Hectares
England	175	26,103	10,564
Scotland	6	6,643	2,688
Wales	14	2,809	1,137

An additional 7.79 km of linear trails are designated as LNRs.

FOREST NATURE RESERVES

The Forestry Commission has created Forest Nature Reserves from conservation sites within the Commission's estate. These are like other nature reserves in that their purpose is to protect and conserve special forms of natural habitat, flora and fauna existing in forested areas.

The Forestry Commission has 340 SSSI on its estates and has chosen 46 as Forest Nature Reserves. They extend in size from under 124 acres (50 hectares) to 1,236 acres (500 hectares). The largest include the Black Wood of Rannoch, by Loch Rannoch; Cannop Valley Oakwoods, Forest of Dean; Culbin Forest, near Forres; Glen Affric, near Fort Augustus; Kylerhea, Skye; Pembrey, Carmarthen Bay; Starr Forest, in Galloway Forest Park; Wyre Forest, near Kidderminster.

Northern Ireland

There are 36 Forest Nature Reserves in Northern Ireland, covering 4,346 acres (1,759 hectares). They are designated and administered by the Forest Service, a division of the Department of Agriculture for Northern Ireland.

MARINE NATURE RESERVES

The Wildlife and Countryside Act 1981 gave the Secretary of State for the Environment (and the Secretaries of State for Wales and for Scotland where appropriate) power to designate Marine Nature Reserves and the Nature Conservancy Council powers to select and manage these reserves. Interested parties at a local and at a national level are consulted prior to the confirmation of an area.

Marine Nature Reserves provide protection for marine flora and fauna and geological and physiographical features on land covered by tidal waters up to and including the limit of territorial waters. Reserves also provide opportunities for study and research.

Lundy, in the Bristol Channel, became the first statutory Marine Nature Reserve in November 1986. Skomer, Dyfed, was designated in July 1990. Other areas proposed for designation as reserves are: the Isles of Scilly; the Menai Strait; Bardsey Island and part of the Lleyn peninsula, Gwynedd; Loch Sween, Strathclyde; St. Abb's Head, Berwickshire.

A number of non-statutory marine reserves have been set up by conservation groups.

HISTORIC MONUMENTS

England

A select list of monuments under the control of English Heritage.

Charges for admission represent the figures obtaining in 1990–91. Concessionary rates are available for children etc.

Annual membership passes are available at £12·50 for adults, £9 for pensioners and £6 for children upon application to English Heritage Membership Dept., PO Box 1BB, W1A 1BB.

Standard hours of opening (marked *) are as follows:

Good Friday or April 1 (whichever is earlier)–Sept. 30   Daily 10–6
Oct. 1–Maundy Thursday or
April 1 (whichever is earlier)   Tues.–Sun. 10–4

Monuments not marked * open Good Friday–Sept. only.

All monuments are closed on Christmas Eve, Christmas Day, Boxing Day and New Year's Day. Some smaller sites may close for the lunch-hour, which is normally 1–2 p.m. During the winter season, many monuments are closed on Mondays.

BATTLE ABBEY, E. Sussex. £1·70*. Remains of the abbey founded by William the Conqueror on the site of the Battle of Hastings.

BEESTON CASTLE, Cheshire. £1.40*. Thirteenth-century inner ward with gatehouse and towers, and considerable remains of large outer ward.

BOLSOVER CASTLE, Derbyshire. £1.40*. Notable for its exceptionally interesting 17th century buildings.

BOSCOBEL HOUSE, Shropshire. £1.90*. Timber-framed early 17th century hunting lodge with later alterations. Charles II's 'Royal Oak' is nearby.

BRINKBURN PRIORY, Northumberland. 85p. A house of Augustinian canons; the church (c.1200, repaired in 1858) and parts of the cloister buildings survive.

BROUGHAM CASTLE, Cumbria. 85p*. Extensive remains of the 13th century keep, and of other buildings of periods up to the 17th century.

BYLAND ABBEY, North Yorkshire. 85p*. Considerable remains of church and conventual buildings date from the abbey's foundation in 1177 by the Cistercians.

CARISBROOKE CASTLE, Isle of Wight. £2.30*. Norman castle, the prison of Charles I from 1647–1648.

CARLISLE CASTLE, Cumbria. £1.40*. Medieval castle, prison of Mary Queen of Scots. Inner and outer wards enclosing a 12th century keep.

CASTLE ACRE PRIORY, Norfolk. £1.15*. Extensive remains include the 12th century church and the prior's lodgings.

CASTLE RISING CASTLE, Norfolk. 85p*. A 12th century keep standing in a massive earthwork with its gatehouse and bridge.

CHESTERS ROMAN FORT, Northumberland. £1.40*. Fine example of a bath house.

CHYSAUSTER ANCIENT VILLAGE, Cornwall. 85p*. Romano–Cornish village, 2nd and 3rd century AD, probably on a late Iron Age site.

CLEEVE ABBEY, Somerset. £1.15*. Much of the claustral buildings survive including timber-roofed frater, but only foundations of the church.

CORBRIDGE ROMAN SITE, Northumberland. £1.40*. Excavations have revealed the central area of a Roman town and successive military bases.

DEAL CASTLE, Kent. £1.15*. The largest and most complete of the forts erected by Henry VIII for coastal defence.

DOVER CASTLE, Kent. £3.00*. One of the strongest British castles, with Roman, Saxon and Norman features.

DUNSTANBURGH CASTLE, Northumberland. 85p*. The 14th century castle standing on a cliff above the sea has a substantial gatehouse-keep.

FARLEIGH HUNGERFORD CASTLE, Somerset. 85p*. Late 14th century castle of two courts. The chapel contains fine tomb of Sir Thomas Hungerford.

FARNHAM CASTLE KEEP, Surrey. £1.15. Built by the Bishops of Winchester, the motte of the castle is enclosed by a large 12th century shell keep. Foundations of a Norman tower.

FINCHALE PRIORY, Durham. 85p* (free in winter). Benedictine priory on banks of River Wear with considerable 13th century remains.

FRAMLINGHAM CASTLE, Suffolk. £1.15*. Impressive castle (c.1200) with high curtain walls enclosing a poorhouse of 1639.

FURNESS ABBEY, Cumbria. £1.40*. Founded in 1123 by Stephen, afterwards King of England; extensive remains of church and conventual buildings.

GOODRICH CASTLE, Hereford and Worcester. £1.15*. Extensive remains of 13th and 14th century castle incorporating 12th century keep.

GRIMES GRAVES, Norfolk. 85p*. Extensive group of flint mines dating from the Neolithic period. Several shafts can be inspected.

HAILES ABBEY, Gloucestershire. £1.15*. Ruins of a Cistercian monastery founded in 1246. Museum contains some fine architectural fragments.

HELMSLEY CASTLE, North Yorkshire. £1.15*. Twelfth century keep and curtain wall with 16th century domestic buildings. Spectacular earthwork defences.

HOUSESTEADS ROMAN FORT, Northumberland. £1.40*. Excavation has exposed this infantry fort on Hadrian's Wall with its extra-mural civilian settlement.

KENILWORTH CASTLE, Warwickshire. £1.15*. One of the most extensive castles in Britain, showing many styles of building from 1155 to 1649.

LANERCOST PRIORY, Cumbria. 60p. The nave of the Augustinian priory church, c.1166, is still used and there are remains of other claustral buildings.

LINDISFARNE PRIORY, Northumberland. £1.40* (subject to tide). The bishopric of the Northumbrian Kingdom destroyed by the Danes; re-established in 11th century as a Benedictine priory, now ruined.

LULLINGSTONE ROMAN VILLA, Kent. £1.15*. A large villa occupied through much of the Roman period; fine mosaics.

MIDDLEHAM CASTLE, North Yorkshire. 85p*. Childhood home of Richard III. The 12th century keep stands within later fortifications and domestic buildings.

MOUNT GRACE PRIORY, North Yorkshire. £1.40*. Carthusian monastery, founded 1398, with remains of monastic buildings.

NETLEY ABBEY, Hampshire. 85p* (weekends only in winter). Extensive remains of Cistercian abbey, founded 1239, with ruined Tudor house.

OLD SARUM, Wiltshire. 85p*. Large earthworks enclosing the excavated remains of the castle and the first Salisbury cathedral, begun in 1078.

ORFORD CASTLE, Suffolk. £1.15*. Circular keep of c.1170 and remains of coastal defence castle built by Henry II.

PENDENNIS CASTLE, Cornwall. £1.40*. Well-preserved castle erected by Henry VIII for coastal defence.

PEVENSEY CASTLE, East Sussex. £1.15*. Walls of a 4th century Roman fort enclosing remains of an 11th century castle.

PEVERIL CASTLE, Derbyshire. 85p*. In a picturesque and nearly impregnable position, this 12th century castle is defended on two sides by precipitous rocks.

PORTCHESTER CASTLE, Hampshire. £1.15*. Walls of a late Roman fort enclosing a Norman keep and an Augustinian priory church.

RECULVER TOWERS and ROMAN FORT, Kent. Remains of Saxon and Norman church with 12th century towers, standing in a Roman fort.

RICHBOROUGH CASTLE, Kent. 85p*. The landing-site of the Claudian invasion in 43 AD, with massive 3rd century stone walls.

RICHMOND CASTLE, North Yorkshire. £1.15*. This 12th century keep, with 11th century curtain wall and gatehouse, commands Swaledale.

RIEVAULX ABBEY, North Yorkshire. £1.40*. Founded c.1132. Extensive remains include an early Cistercian nave and fine 13th century choir and claustral buildings.

ROCHESTER CASTLE, Kent. £1.15*. Eleventh century castle partly founded on the Roman city wall, with a square keep of c.1130.

ST. AUGUSTINE'S ABBEY, Kent. 85p*. Remains of Benedictine monastery, with Norman church, on site of abbey founded by St. Augustine in 598.

ST. MAWES CASTLE, Cornwall. 85p*. Coastal defence castle built by Henry VIII consisting of central tower and three bastions.

SCARBOROUGH CASTLE, North Yorkshire. £1.15*. Remains of 12th century keep and curtain walls dominating the town.

STONEHENGE, Wiltshire. £1.70*. Prehistoric monument consisting of a series of concentric stone circles surrounded by a ditch and bank.

TILBURY FORT, Essex. £1.15*. One of Henry VIII's coastal forts, extended by Charles II.

TINTAGEL CASTLE, Cornwall. £1.40*. 12th century castle on cliff top. Dark Age settlement site.

TYNEMOUTH PRIORY and CASTLE, Tyne and Wear. 85p*. Remains of a Benedictine priory, founded 1090, on Saxon monastic site. Coastal batteries with reconstructed First World War magazine.

WALMER CASTLE, Kent. £1.70*. (Closed when Lord Warden is in residence.) One of Henry VIII's coastal defence castles, now the residence of the Lord Warden of the Cinque Ports.

WARKWORTH CASTLE, Northumberland. 85p*. 15th century keep amidst earlier ruins with a 14th century hermitage upstream.

WHITBY ABBEY, North Yorkshire. 85p*. 13th and 14th century Benedictine church on site of monastery founded in 657.

WROXETER ROMAN CITY, Shropshire. 85p*. The 2nd century public baths and part of the forum remain of the Roman town of Viroconium.

Wales

A select list of monuments under the control of Cadw: Welsh Historic Monuments. Charges for admission (subject to alteration) are given below. Concessionary rates are available for children, etc.
Standard hours of admission:

	Weekdays	Sundays
March 15–Oct. 15	9.30–6.30	2.00–6.30
Oct. 16–March 14	9.30–4.00	2.00–4.00

All monuments are closed on Christmas Eve, Christmas Day, Boxing Day and New Year's Day.

BEAUMARIS CASTLE, Anglesey, Gwynedd. £1.25. The finest example of the concentrically planned castle in Britain, it is still almost intact.

CAERLEON ROMAN AMPHITHEATRE, Gwent. £1. Late 1st century oval arena surrounded by bank for spectators.

CAERLEON ROMAN FORTRESS BATHS, Gwent. £1. Rare example of a legionary bath-house.

CAERNARFON CASTLE, Gwynedd. £2.50. Family Ticket £6. The most important of the Edwardian castles, built together with the town wall between 1283 and 1330.

CAERPHILLY CASTLE, Mid-Glamorgan. £1.25. Concentrically planned castle (c.1270) notable for its great scale and use of water defences.

CASTELL COCH, S. Glamorgan. £1.50. Rebuilt 1875–90 on medieval foundations.

CHEPSTOW CASTLE, Gwent. £1. Fine rectangular keep in the middle of extensive fortifications.

CONWY CASTLE, Gwynedd. £1.50. Built by Edward I to guard the Conway ferry.

CRICCIETH CASTLE, Gwynedd. £1.50. A native Welsh castle of the early 13th century, much altered by Edward I.

DENBIGH CASTLE, Clwyd. £1. The remains of the castle, which dates from 1282–1322, include an unusual triangular gatehouse.

HARLECH CASTLE, Gwynedd. £1.50. Well preserved Edwardian castle with a concentric plan sited on a rocky outcrop above the former shore-line.

RAGLAN CASTLE, Gwent. £1.25. Extensive remains of 15th century castle with moated hexagonal keep.

ST. DAVID'S, BISHOP'S PALACE, Dyfed. £1.50. Extensive remains of principal residence of Bishop of St. David's dating from 1280–1350.

TINTERN ABBEY, Gwent. £1.50. Extensive remains of 13th century church and conventual buildings of this Cistercian monastery.

TRETOWER COURT, Powys. £1.25. Medieval house with remains of castle nearby.

Scotland

A select list of monuments under the control of Historic Buildings and Monuments, Scottish Development Department.
Charges for admission are those obtaining in 1990. Except where indicated differently, charges are adults 60p, concessions (con.) 30p.
Standard hours of opening (marked S.) are as follows:

	Weekdays	Sundays
April–Sept.	9.30–7.00	2.00–7.00
Oct.–March	9.30–4.00	2.00–4.00

Monuments open at any reasonable time are indicated by A.

ABERLEMNO, Tayside. A. Closed in winter. Adm. free. Four Pictish stones.

ANTONINE WALL, Central and Strathclyde Regions. A. Adm. free.

ARNOL BLACKHOUSE, Western Isles. S. Closed Sun. Traditional Hebridean dwelling.

BONAWE, Strathclyde. S. Closed in winter. Mid-18th century iron-furnace. £1, con. 50p.

BROCH OF BIRSAY, Orkney. S. Closed Mon., Tues. a.m. in winter. Remains of the Norse period.

BROWN AND WHITE CATERTHUNS, Tayside. A. Adm. free. Iron Age hill forts.

CAERLAVEROCK CASTLE, Dumfries and Galloway. S.

CAIRNPAPPLE HILL, Lothian. S. Closed in winter. A prehistoric ritual complex and Bronze Age cairn.

CALLANISH, Western Isles. A. Adm. free. Standing Stones.

CAMSTER CAIRNS, Highland. A. Adm. free.

CLAVA CAIRNS, Highland. A. Adm. free.

DRYBURGH ABBEY, Borders. S. £1.20, con. 60p.

EARLS AND BISHOPS PALACES, Kirkwall, Orkney. S. Closed in winter.

EDINBURGH CASTLE, including Scottish National War Memorial, Scottish United Services Museum and Historic Apartments. Open winter: Jan. 4–March 31 and Oct. 1–Dec. 31, Mon.–Sat. 9.30–4.20, Sun. 12.30–3.35. Summer: April 1–Sept. 30, Mon.–Sat. 9.30–5.05, Sun. 11–5.05. Alterations may be made to opening hours during the Tattoo, State and Military events. Adm. to War Memorial, free; to all other areas £2.20, con. £1.10, Family Ticket £5.

EDZELL CASTLE, Tayside. S. Closed Tues., Thurs. a.m. £1, con. 50p.

ELGIN CATHEDRAL, Grampian. S.

FORT GEORGE, Highland. S. £1.75, con. 85p.

GLASGOW CATHEDRAL, Strathclyde. S. Adm. free.

GLENELG BROCHS, Highland. A. Adm. free.

HERMITAGE CASTLE, Borders. S.

HUNTLY CASTLE, Grampian. S.

JARLSHOF, Shetland. S. Closed Tues., Wed. p.m. in winter. Remains of villages from Bronze Age to Viking times.

JEDBURGH ABBEY, Borders. S. Closed Thurs. p.m. and Fri. in winter. £1.20, con. 60p.

KELSO ABBEY, Borders. S. Adm. free.

LINLITHGOW PALACE, Lothian. S. £1, con. 50p.

LOANHEAD STONE CIRCLE, Grampian. A. Adm. free.

MAES HOWE, Orkney. S. £1, con. 50p. Prehistoric tomb.

MEIGLE MUSEUM, Tayside. S. Closed Sun. Pictish stones.

MELROSE ABBEY, Borders. S. £1.20, con. 60p.

MOUSA BROCH, Shetland. A. Adm. free.

NETHER LARGIE CAIRNS, Strathclyde. A. Adm. free.

NEW ABBEY CORN MILL, Dumfries and Galloway. S. Closed Wed. p.m., Thurs.

RING OF BROGAR, Orkney. A. Adm. free.

RUTHWELL CROSS, Dumfries and Galloway. A. Adm. free.

ST. ANDREWS' CASTLE AND CATHEDRAL, Fife. S.

SKARA BRAE, Orkney. S. £1.20, con. 60p. Prehistoric village.

SMAILHOLM TOWER, Borders. S. Closed in winter.

STIRLING CASTLE, Central. Open winter: Jan. 4–March 31 and Oct. 1–Dec. 31, Mon.–Sat. 9.30–4.20, Sun. 12.30–3.35; summer: April 1–Sept. 30, Mon.–Sat. 9.30–5.15, Sun. 10.30–4.45. £1·75, con. 85p, Family Ticket £4.50.

TANTALLON CASTLE, Lothian. S. £1, con. 50p. Closed Wed., Thurs. a.m. in winter.

THREAVE CASTLE, Dumfries and Galloway. S. Adm. 60p, con. 30p, including ferry.

HOUSES OPEN TO THE PUBLIC

Dates of opening and admission fees shown are those which obtained in 1990, and are subject to modification. Specific opening hours are not given but may be checked by telephone. Most houses have concessionary rates for certain categories of visitor.

Space permits only a selection of some of the more noteworthy houses in the UK which are open to the public. (*Property of the National Trust; Adm. admission; PM. = open in afternoons only).

A LA RONDE, Exmouth.—Good Friday–Oct. 31 daily. Tel. 0395–265514.

ALNWICK CASTLE, Northumberland.—April 29–Oct. 5 daily (not Sat. except July–Aug.). Open Bank Hol. weekends. Adm. £2.20. Tel. 0665–510777.

ALTHORP, Northampton.—Daily (not Christmas). Adm. £2.75, Weds. £3.75 (Connoisseurs' Day). Gardens 50p.

*ANGLESEY ABBEY, Cambs.—March 31–Oct. 14 (not Good Friday). PM. Adm. £4. Gardens only Adm. £1.50. Tel. 0223–811200.

ARUNDEL CASTLE, W. Sussex.—April 21–Oct. 26 daily (not Sat.). PM. Adm. charge. Tel. 0903–883136.

*BASILDON PARK, Berks.—April–Oct. (not Mon. except Bank Hols; not Good Friday). Adm. £2.50. Grounds £1. Tel. 0734–843040.

BEAULIEU, Hants.—Daily (not Christmas). Tel. 0590–612345. (see also page 1170).

*BELTON HOUSE, Grantham.—April–Oct. Wed.-Sun. and Bank Hol. Mons. (not Good Friday). PM. Adm. £3.20. Tel. 0476–66116.

BELVOIR CASTLE, nr. Grantham.—March 17–Oct. 7 daily (not Mon. except Bank Hols.) Rest of Oct., Sat. and Sun. only. Adm. £2.80. Tel. 0476–870262.

BERKELEY CASTLE, Glos.—April, Sept. daily (not Mon. except Bank Hols.). PM only except May–Aug., Tues.–Sat. and Bank Hols. Oct. Sun. only. Adm. charge. Tel. 0453–810332.

BLAIR CASTLE, Tayside.—April–Oct. 26 daily (Sun. April, May and Oct PM.). Adm. £3. Tel. 079 681–207.

BLENHEIM PALACE, Oxon.—Mid-March–Oct. 31 daily. Adm. charge. Tel. 0993–811325.

BOUGHTON HOUSE, Northants.—July 28–Aug. 30 daily. Grounds (excl. Gardens) daily (not Fri.) April 28–Sept. 30. PM. Adm. £3, Grounds only, £1. Tel. 0536–515731.

BOWHILL, Selkirk.—House July 1–July 31 daily; Grounds April 28–Aug. 28 (not Fri.). daily PM. Adm. £3, Grounds only, £1. Tel. 0750–20732.

BROADLANDS, Hants.—April 12–Sept. 30 daily (not Fri. until Aug.). Adm. £4. Tel. 0794–516878.

BRONTË PARSONAGE, Haworth, West Yorks.—Daily, April–Sept. (not Christmas or Jan. 22–Feb. 9). Adm. £1.30. Tel. 0535–42323.

BROUGHTON CASTLE, Oxon.—May 20–Sept. 12 Wed., Sun. (also Thurs. in July and Aug.) and Bank Hol. Suns and Mons. PM. Adm. £2.30. Tel. 0295–262624.

*BUCKLAND ABBEY, Devon.—April 1–end Oct. daily. Nov.–March Wed., Sat., Sun. PM. Adm. £3.20. Tel. 0822–853607.

BURGHLEY HOUSE, Stamford.—Good Friday–Oct. 7 (closed Sept. 8) daily. Adm. £3.30. Tel. 0780–52451.

*CALKE ABBEY, Derbyshire.—April 1–end Oct., Sat.–Wed. PM. Adm. £3.50. Tel. 0332–863822.

CARDIFF CASTLE.—Daily (not Christmas, New Year). Adm. £2.75, Grounds £1.50. Tel. 0222–822086.

CARLYLE'S HOUSE, Chelsea, London.—April–end Oct. Wed.–Sun. and Bank Hol. Mons. (not Good Friday). Adm.£2. Tel. 071–352 7087.

*CASTLE COOLE, Enniskillen.—Easter period, daily; June, July, Aug. daily (not Thurs.); Sat., Sun. and Bank Hols. in April, May, Sept. PM. Adm. £2, Grounds April–Sept. free. Tel. 0365–22690.

*CASTLE DROGO, Devon.—April 1–end Oct. daily. Adm. £3.40. Grounds £1.50. Tel. 06473–3306.

CASTLE HOWARD, N. Yorks.—March 22–Nov. 4, daily. Adm. £4.50. Tel. 065384–333.

CAWDOR CASTLE, Inverness.—May–Oct. 7, daily. Adm. £2.90, Grounds £1.40. Tel. 06677–615.

*CHARTWELL, Kent.—Open three days each week. Times vary. Adm. £3.30, Grounds £1.70. Tel. 0732–866368.

CHATSWORTH, Derbyshire.—March 25–Oct. 28 daily. Grounds March 25–Sept. 30, daily. Adm. charge. Tel. 0246–582204.

CHICHELEY HALL, Newport Pagnell.—April 13–May 27, Aug. 5–Sept. 30 Sun. and Bank Hols. PM. Adm. £2.50. Tel. 023065–252.

*CLIVEDEN, Maidenhead.—House, April 1–Oct. 28, Thurs. and Sun. PM. Gardens March–Dec. daily. Adm. £2.50, £1 extra for House. Tel. 0628–605069.

*COMPTON CASTLE, nr. Paignton.—April 2–end Oct. Mon., Wed., Thurs. daily. Adm. £1.80. Tel. 0803–872112.

*CROFT CASTLE, Herefordshire.—Easter Bank Hol. weekend, May–Sept. Wed.–Sun., Bank Hol. Mons., April and Oct. weekends. PM. Adm. £2.20. Tel. 056885–246.

DICKENS HOUSE, London, WC1.—Daily (not Sun. and Bank Hols.). Adm. £1.50. Tel. 071–405 2127.

DR. JOHNSON'S HOUSE, London, EC4.—Daily (not Sun. and Bank Hols.). Adm. charge. Tel. 071–353 3745.

DOWN HOUSE, Downe, Kent.—March–Jan. 31 (not Christmas), not Mon. (except Bank Hols.) or Fri. PM. Adm. £1·50. Tel. 0689–59119.

DRUMLANRIG CASTLE, Dumfries.—May 5–Aug. 19, daily (not Thurs.). Grounds open April 28–end Sept. Adm. £3, Grounds only £1. Tel. 0848–30248.

HADDON HALL, Derbyshire.—April–Sept. 30. Tues.–Sun., and Bank Hols. Closed Sun. in July and Aug. (except Bank Hol. weekends). Adm. £2.80. Tel. 0629–812855.

HAM HOUSE, Richmond, Surrey.—Daily (not Mon., except Bank Hols.; not Good Friday, Christmas, New Year or May 1). Adm. £2, Grounds free. Tel. 081–940 1950.

*HARDWICK HALL, Derbyshire.—April 1–Sept. 16. House Wed., Thurs., Sat., Sun., Bank Hol. Mons. Garden daily to end Oct. (not Good Friday). PM. Adm. £4.30, Garden only, £1.50. Tel. 0246–850430.

HAREWOOD HOUSE, Leeds.—Easter–Oct. daily. Sun. only, Feb., March, and Nov. Adm. charge. Tel. 0532–886225.

HATFIELD HOUSE, Herts.—March 25–Oct. 14 daily (not Mon. except Bank Hols., not Good Friday). PM. except Bank Hols. Grounds, times vary. Adm. £3.50. Tel. 0707–262823.

HEVER CASTLE, Kent.—March 27–Nov. 4, daily PM, except Grounds. Adm. charge. Tel. 0732–865224.

HOLKER HALL, Cumbria.—Easter Sun.–last Sun. in Oct. daily (not Sat.). Adm. charge. Tel. 05395–58328.

HOLKHAM HALL, Norfolk.—Late May–Sept. Sun.–Thurs. and Easter, Spring and Summer Bank Holidays. PM, except Bank Hols. Adm. £2. Tel. 0328–710227.

HOPETOUN HOUSE, nr. Edinburgh.—April 13–Sept. 30, daily. Adm. £2.80. Tel. 031–331 2451.

HOUGHTON HALL, Norfolk.—Easter Sun.–Sept. 30, Sun., Thurs. and Bank Hols. PM. Adm. £3. Tel. 048–522 569.

*HUGHENDEN MANOR, High Wycombe.—April–end Oct. (not Good Friday), Wed.–Sun. and Bank Hol. Mons. PM. March, weekends only. Adm. £2.50. Tel. 0494–32580.

INVERARAY CASTLE, Argyll.—1st Sat. in April–2nd Sun. in Oct. daily (not Fri., except July–Aug.), Sun., PM. Woods open all year. Tel. 0499–2203.

JANE AUSTEN'S HOUSE, Chawton, Hants.—April–Oct. daily, Jan. and Feb. weekends, Nov., Dec. and March, Wed.–Sun. (not Christmas). Adm. £1. Tel. 0420–83262.

KEATS HOUSE, Hampstead, London.—All year, daily, PM (except Sat.). (Not Christmas, New Year, Good Friday, Easter Eve., May 7.) Adm. free. Tel. 071–435 2062.

KELMSCOTT MANOR, nr. Lechlade, Glos.—April–Sept., Wed. only. Other days by written application. Adm. £3.50.

*KINGSTON LACY HOUSE, Dorset.—April–Nov. 4, PM. Sat.–Wed. Adm. £4, Grounds only £1.20. Tel. 0202–883402.

KNEBWORTH HOUSE, Herts.—April 7–May 20, Sat., Sun., School and Bank Hols., May 26–Sept. 9 daily (not Mon.). PM. Weekends only to Oct. 1. Adm. £3.50, Grounds only, £2. Tel. 0438–812661.

*KNOLE, Kent.—March 24–Oct. Wed.–Sat. and Bank Hol. Mons. Sun., PM. Adm. £2.50. Tel. 0732–450608.

LEEDS CASTLE, Kent.—April 1–end Oct. daily. Nov.–March, weekends only. Adm. charge. Tel. 0622–765400.

*LITTLE MORETON HALL, Cheshire.—April 14–Sept. 30, except Bank Hols. daily (not Tues.), March 3–April 8 and Oct., weekends only. PM. Adm. £2. Weekends and Bank Hols. £2.50. Tel. 0260–272018.

LONGLEAT HOUSE, Warminster.—Easter–Sept. daily (not Christmas). Safari Park mid-March–Oct. Adm. charge. Tel. 09853–551.

LUTON HOO, Beds.—April 12–Oct. 14, daily, PM (not Mon. except Bank Hols.). Adm. £3.50. Tel. 0582–22955.

MARBLE HILL HOUSE, Twickenham, Middx.—All year, daily (not Dec. 24, 25). Adm. free. Tel. 081–892 5115.

MICHELHAM PRIORY, E. Sussex.—March 25–Oct. 31 daily. Nov., Feb. and March, Sun. only. Adm. £2.50. Tel. 0323–844224.

*MONTACUTE HOUSE, Yeovil.—April 1–Nov. 4 daily (not Tues.). Grounds open all year. Adm. £3.50, Grounds only £1.50. Tel. 0935–823289.

*MOUNT STEWART, Co. Down.—Times vary. Adm. House, Garden, Temple £3, Garden and Temple only £2.50. Tel. 024774–387.

OSBORNE HOUSE, IOW.—Good Friday–Oct. 31 daily. Adm. £3.20. Tel. 0983–200022.

OSTERLEY PARK HOUSE, Isleworth, Middx.—Daily (not Mon., May 1, Good Friday, Dec. 24–28, Jan. 1). Adm. £2, Grounds free. Tel. 081–560 3918.

*PENRHYN CASTLE, Bangor.—April 1–Nov. 4 daily (not Tues.) PM, except July–Aug. Adm. £2.80. Tel. 0243–353084.

PENSHURST PLACE, Kent.—April 3–Sept. 30 daily (not Mon. except Bank Hols.) PM. Adm. charge. Tel. 0892–870307.

*PETWORTH HOUSE, W. Sussex.—April 1–end Oct. Tues.–Sun., Bank Hol. Mons., Good Friday. PM. Adm. £3. Tel. 0798–42207.

PORTMEIRION, Gwynedd.—March–Jan. daily. Adm. charge. Tel. 0766–770457.

POWDERHAM CASTLE, Exeter.—May 27–Sept. 13 Sun.–Thurs. PM. Adm. charge. Tel. 0626–890243.

*POWIS CASTLE, Powys.—April 1–June 30, Sept. 1–

Nov. 4 Wed.–Sun. and Bank Hol. Mons.; July and Aug. daily (not Mon. except Bank Hol.). Nov. 11–March 31 Sun., PM. Adm. charge. Tel. 0938–4336.

RABY CASTLE, Durham.—Easter (Sat.–Wed.), May 2–June 30 Wed. and Sun., July–Sept. daily (not Sat.). Also Bank Hol. Sat.–Tues., PM. Adm. £2.25. Tel. 0833–60202.

RAGLEY HALL, Warks.—April 14–Sept. 30 daily (not Mon., Fri.), PM. Open Bank Hols. Adm. £3.50. Tel. 0789–762090.

ROCKINGHAM CASTLE, Corby.—Easter Sunday–Sept. 30, Sun., Thurs., (also Bank Hol. Mon. and Tues. and Tues. in Aug.), PM. Adm. £2.70, Gardens only £1.40. Tel. 0536–770240.

*RUFFORD OLD HALL, Lancashire—April 1–Nov. 4 daily (not Fri.), PM. Adm. £2. Tel. 0704–821254.

SANDRINGHAM, Norfolk.—April 29–Sept. 30 (closed July 16–Aug. 4) Mon.–Thurs.; Sun. PM. Closed when Royal Family in residence. Adm. £2.20. Tel. 0553–772675.

SCONE PALACE, Perth.—April 23–Oct. 16, daily. Sun., PM. Adm. £3. Tel. 0738–52300.

SHERBORNE CASTLE, Dorset.—Easter Sat.–end Sept. Thurs., Sat., Sun. and Bank Hol. Mons. PM. Adm. charge. Tel. 0935–813182.

*SHUGBOROUGH, Staffs.—March 31–Dec. 22, daily. Adm. £5 (House, Museum, Farm; House only, £2). Tel. 0889–881388.

SKIPTON CASTLE, N. Yorks.—Open all year (not Christmas Day). Daily. (Sun., PM). Adm. £1.80. Tel. 0756–792442.

*SMALLHYTHE PLACE, Kent.—April–end Oct. Sat.–Wed. PM. Open Good Friday. Adm. £1.70. Tel. 05806–2334.

STANFORD HALL, Leics.—Easter Saturday–end Sept. Thurs. (July and Aug. only), Sat., Sun., Bank Hols. (Mon. and Tues.). PM. Adm. £2.30. Tel. 0788–860250.

STONELEIGH ABBEY, Warks.—Open by prior appointment only, Mon.–Fri. Tel. 0926–52116.

STONOR PARK, Oxon.—April Sun. only, May–Sept. Wed., Thurs., Sun. (also Sat. in Aug.). Open Bank Hol. Mons., PM. Adm. £2. Tel. 049163–587.

*STOURHEAD, Wilts.—April 1–Nov.4, Sat.–Wed. PM. Adm. £2.50. Gardens all year, daily. Adm. House £3, Garden £3. Tel. 0747–840348.

STRATFIELD SAYE HOUSE, Reading.—May 1–last Sun. in Sept. daily (not Fri.). Grounds March–Oct. daily, Nov.–Feb. weekends only. Adm. charge. Tel. 0256–882882.

SUDELEY CASTLE, Glos.—April–Oct. daily, PM. Adm. £3.75. Tel. 0242–602308.

SULGRAVE MANOR, Northants.—March–Dec. 31, daily (not Wed.), Closed Christmas. Adm. £2. Tel. 029576–205.

SYON HOUSE, Brentford, Middx.—April 1–Sept. 29 Sun.–Thurs., and Sun. in Oct. PM. Adm. charge. Tel. 081–560 0881.

*TRERICE, Cornwall.—April 1–end Oct. daily. Adm. £2.80. Tel. 0637–875404.

TYN-Y-RHOS HALL, and Shrine of St. George, Shropshire—May–end Sept. Sun. PM. Morning prayers 11. Adm. £1. Tel. 0691–777898.

WARWICK CASTLE.—Daily (not Christmas Day). Adm. charge. Tel. 0926–495421.

WILTON HOUSE, Wilts.—April 10–Oct. 14, Tues–Sat. and Bank Hol. Mons., Sun. PM. Adm. £3.80. Tel. 0722–743641.

WOBURN ABBEY, Beds.—April 2–Oct. 28 daily. Dec. 30–April 1, weekends only. Adm. £4.50. Tel. 0525–290666.

MUSEUMS AND ART GALLERIES OUTSIDE LONDON

(For National Art Galleries and Museums in London and Merseyside Museums, *see* Index.)

(Adm. admission; con. concessionary rates)

Barnard Castle, Co. Durham.—*The Bowes Museum*. Important collections of British and European fine art, from medieval period to 19th century. Fine porcelain and glass, tapestries and furniture. Music and costume galleries. English period rooms from Elizabeth I to Victoria; French decorative arts of 18th and 19th centuries; local antiquities. Temporary exhibitions. Open weekdays: May–Sept., 10–5.30, March, April, Oct., 10–5, Nov.–Feb., 10–4. Sun.: 2–5 (summer); 2–4 (winter). Adm. £1·60, con. 80p.

Bath.—*Roman Baths Museum*. Roman Baths complex of 1st century AD. Open daily, 9–6. Adm. (including adjoining 18th century Pump Room), £3.25, con. £1.50. *Museum of Costume*, Assembly Rooms. Fashion from 16th century to date. Closed for repairs until 1991. *American Museum in Britain*, Claverton Manor. American decorative arts from late 17th to mid 19th centuries. Open April 1–Oct. 30, daily (not Mon.), 2–5, Bank Hol. Mons. and preceding Suns. 11–5. During winter only on application. Adm. charge. *Victoria Art Gallery*, Bridge Street. Open Mon.–Fri. 10–6, Sat. 10–5. Closed Sun., Bank Hols. Adm. free.

Beamish.—*North of England Open Air Museum*, Beamish, Co. Durham. Re-creates Northern life c.1900. Local buildings have been rebuilt and furnished, including the Town with houses, shops, etc., the Colliery Village, the Railway Station and Home Farm complete with agricultural machinery, animals and exhibitions. Open daily (not Mon. in winter): summer 10–6, winter 10–5.

Beaulieu.—*National Motor Museum*. Displays of vehicles dating from 1895 to present day. Open daily (not Christmas Day), 10–6 (winter, 10–5). Adm. charge.

Belfast.—*Ulster Museum*, Botanic Gardens. Collections of Irish antiquities, natural and local history, fine and applied arts. Open Mon.–Fri. 10–5, Sat. 1–5, Sun. 2–5. *Ulster Folk and Transport Museum*, Holywood. Indoor and outdoor exhibits. Open Oct.–April, weekdays 11–5, Sun. 2–5 (May–Sept. 11–6, Sun. 2–6). May–June (Wed. only) 11–9. Adm. £2, con. £1. *Transport Museum*, Holywood and Witham Street. History of land, sea and air transport in Ireland. Holywood site—open as for Folk Museum. Witham Street site open weekdays 10–5. Adm. 60p, children 40p, other con. 20p. Special arrangements over Christmas and Easter.

Beverley, N. Humberside.—*Museum of Army Transport*. Exhibits include field workshop, amphibious assault landing, railway section and aircraft. Open 10–5. Closed Christmas period and Mon., Nov.–Feb. Adm. charge.

Birmingham.—*City Museum and Art Gallery*. British and European masters from 14th to 20th centuries (particularly Pre-Raphaelites), sculpture, European gold, silver and jewellery, metalwork, glass, pottery and porcelain, furniture, textiles and costume, archaeology, local and natural history. Open Mon.–Sat. 9.30–5, Sun. 2–5. Closed Christmas Day, Boxing Day, and New Year's Day. Adm. free.

Museum of Science and Industry, Newhall Street. From the Industrial Revolution to the present; many working machines. Open Mon.–Sat. 9.30–5, Sun. 2–5. Adm. free. Also *Aston Hall, Blakesley Hall, Birmingham Nature Centre, Sarehole Mill*, and *Weoley Castle*.

Bradford.—*Cartwright Hall*, Lister Park. British 19th and 20th century fine art. *Bolling Hall*, off Wakefield Road, a furnished period house, mainly

17th and 18th century. *Industrial Museum*, Moorside Road, illustrates the local industries and transport in an old mill, with mill owner's house. *Cliffe Castle*, Keighley. Natural and local history, minerals and gem display, and period rooms. *Manor House*, Ilkley. Archaeology, local history and contemporary fine art. Open 10–5 (April–Sept. 10–6, except Industrial Museum). Closed Good Friday, Christmas Day, Boxing Day and Mon. (except Bank Hols.). Adm. free.

Brighton.—*The Royal Pavilion, Palace of George IV*. Chinoiserie interiors with much of the original furniture. Open daily 10–5 (June–Sept. 10–6). Closed Christmas Day and Boxing Day. Adm. £2.80.

Museum and Art Gallery, Church Street. Old master paintings; Willett pottery and porcelain collection, 20th century art and furniture, ethnography, archaeology, local history, musical instruments, costume gallery. Open Tues.–Sat. 10–5.45, Sun. 2–5. Closed Mons, Christmas Day, Boxing Day, Good Friday and Jan. 1. Adm. free.

Preston Manor, Preston Park. Thomas-Stanford: Macquoid bequests of English period furniture, china and silver. Servants quarters. Open Tues.–Sun. and Bank Hol. Mons. 10–5. Adm. £2. Closed Christmas Day, Boxing Day, Good Friday. Gardens open daily. Adm. free.

The Grange, Art Gallery and Museum, Rottingdean. Sussex Room, Kipling Room and collections of National Toy Museum. Open Mon., Thurs., Sat. 10–5, Tues. and Fri. 10–1, 2–5, Sun. 2–5. Closed Christmas Day, Boxing Day, Good Friday, Wed. and Jan. 1. Adm. free.

The Booth Museum of Natural History, Dyke Road. Open 10–5, Sun. 2–5. Closed Christmas Day, Boxing Day, Good Friday, Thurs. and Jan. 1. Adm. free.

Bristol.—*City Museum and Art Gallery*. Collections include Egyptology, ethnography, Bristol ceramics and the Bristol school of artists, silver, French paintings and Chinese ceramics. Glass collection. Open daily, 10–5. *Bristol Industrial Museum*, Prince's Wharf. Collections connected with the Bristol region's industrial history, including an early working model railway and Bristol-built aero-engines. Open Sat.-Wed. 10–1, 2–5. *Maritime Heritage Centre*, open daily 10–6 (winter 10–5). Adm. free. Includes SS *Great Britain*. Adm. charge. *National Life-boat Museum*, Prince's Wharf, Wapping Road. Open daily 10.30–4.30. Adm. charge. Also *Red Lodge, Blaise Castle House Museum, Kings Weston Roman Villa, Georgian House* and *St. Nicholas Church Museum*.

Cambridge.—*Fitzwilliam Museum*. Egyptian, Greek, Near Eastern and Roman antiquities, coins and medals, medieval manuscripts, paintings and drawings, prints, sculpture, Oriental and Occidental fans, pottery and porcelain, textiles, arms and armour, medieval and renaissance objects of art, and a library. Open Tues.–Sat., Lower Galleries 10–2, Upper Galleries 2–5; Sun. 2.15–5. Closed Dec. 24–Jan. 1, Good Friday, Mons. incl. May Day Bank Hol. but not Easter and Bank Hol. Mons. Adm. free.

Canterbury.—*Royal Museum and Art Gallery*, and *Buffs Regimental Museum*. Archaeology, porcelain, prints and pictures. Open Mon.–Sat. 10–5. Adm. free. *Canterbury Heritage*, a museum of the city's history in the medieval Poor Priest's Hospital, Stour Street. Open Mon.–Sat. 10.30–5, Sun. (June–Oct.) 1.30–5. Adm. £1.20, con. 90p. *Roman Mosaic Museum*. Closed for redevelopment. *West Gate Museum*. Arms and armour and display of city gate-house with battlements. Re-opening 1991.

Carlisle.—*Tullie House Museum and Art Gallery,* Castle Street. Collections of archaeology, natural and social history, fine and decorative arts in Jacobean house with Victorian and modern extensions. *Guildhall,* Greenmarket. Civic and Guild history and artefacts. Contact Tullie House Museum for information.

Chester.—*Grosvenor Museum,* Grosvenor Street. Roman antiquities from legionary fortress; natural history, art and folk-life. Open weekdays 10.30–5, Sun. 2–5. *The Georgian House,* Castle Street. Period room displays, costume and musical instruments. Open weekdays, 10.30–5, Sun., 2–5. *King Charles Tower* on City Walls. Civil War displays. Open daily (summer), weekends (winter), times vary. Adm. charge.

Colchester.—*Colchester Castle.* Local archaeological antiquities, especially from Roman Colchester. Tours of Roman vaults, castle walls, chapel and prisons, weekends April-Sept. and weekdays July-Aug. Open Mon.–Sat. 10–5, Sun. April–Sept. 2–5. Closed Good Friday and Christmas period. Adm. £1, con. 50p. *Hollytrees Museum.* 18th and 19th century costume, toys and social history. Open Mon.–Sat. 10–5. Closed Good Friday and Christmas period. Adm. free. *Natural History Museum,* All Saints Church. Open as Hollytrees. *Social History Museum,* Holy Trinity Church. Domestic life and crafts. Open as Hollytrees. *Tymperleys Clock Museum.* Open Mon.–Sat., April–Oct. 10–5. Adm. 50p, con. 25p.

Coventry.—*Herbert Art Gallery and Museum,* Jordan Well. Archaeology, natural and local history, fine and decorative arts. Open weekdays 10–5.30, Sun. 2–5. Closed Good Friday and Christmas period. *Museum of British Road Transport,* St. Agnes Lane, Hales Street. Open daily 10–5, April–Sept; Oct.–March, Fri., Sat. and Sun. only. Adm. £1.50, con. 75p. *Lunt Roman Fort,* Baginton. June–Sept., 12–6 (closed Mon. and Thurs.). Adm. £1, con. 25p. *Whitefriars Museum.* Open Thurs., Fri., Sat., and some Bank Hols., 10–5.

Crich, Nr. Matlock, Derbyshire—*National Tramway Museum.* Open-air working museum. Open April–Oct. weekends and Bank Hols. 10–6.30. May–Sept., open daily (not Fri. except during school holidays) 10–5.30.

Derby.—*Museum and Art Gallery,* The Strand. Archaeology, military, social history, natural history, paintings by Joseph Wright of Derby, Derby porcelain. Open Mon. 11–5, Tues.–Sat. 10–5, Sun. and Bank Hols. 2–5. *Industrial Museum,* Silk Mill, Full Street. Rolls-Royce collection of aero engines, a railway engineering gallery. Open as above. Adm. 30p. *Pickford's House,* Friargate. 18th and 19th century period room settings, social history, decorative arts, costume and textiles. Open as above. Adm. 30p.

Dorchester.—*Dorset County Museum.* Geology, archaeology, local and natural history and rural crafts of Dorset. Collection of Thomas Hardy's manuscripts, books, notebooks, drawings, etc. Open Mon.–Sat. 10–5, closed Christmas Day, Boxing Day and Good Friday. Adm. £1.50, con. 75p.

Durham.—*Light Infantry Museum and Arts Centre.* Display of County regiment's 200-year history, arts and crafts exhibitions. Open weekdays (except Mon.) 10–5, Sun. and Bank Hol. Mon. 2–5. Closed Christmas Day and Boxing Day. Adm. 65p, con. 30p. *Oriental Museum,* The University. Collections ranging from Ancient Egypt to China and Japan. Open weekdays: 9.30–5. Weekends: Nov.–Feb. closed; March–Oct. Sat. 9.30–5, Sun. 2–5. *Cathedral Treasury.* Relics of St. Cuthbert, church plate, medieval seals, manuscripts and vestments. Open

weekdays 10–4.30, Sun. 2–4.30. Adm. 60p, con. 10p. *Old Fulling Mill Museum.* Archaeological material from local excavations. Open Nov.–March, daily 12.30–3, April–Oct., daily 11–4. Adm. 50p, con. 25p.

Edinburgh.—*City Art Centre,* 2 Market Street. Late 19th and 20th century art, mostly Scottish, and temporary exhibitions. Open weekdays 10–5 (June–Sept. 10–6). Adm. free. *People's Story, Canongate Tolbooth,* Canongate. Courthouse and prison, now museum of Edinburgh life. Open weekdays 10–5 (June–Sept. 10–6). Adm. free. *Huntly House,* Canongate. Local history, collections of Edinburgh silver, glass and Scottish pottery. Open weekdays 10–5 (June–Sept. 10–6). Adm. free. *Lady Stair's House,* Lawnmarket. Mon.–Sat. 10–5 (June–Sept. 10–6). *Lauriston Castle,* Cramond Road South. April–Oct. daily (except Fri.), 11–5; Nov.–March, weekends only. *Museum of Childhood,* High Street. Open weekdays 10–5 (June–Sept. 10–6). Adm. free.

Exeter.—*Exeter Maritime Museum,* The Haven. Collection of working boats. Open daily 10–5 (July–Aug. 10–6). Adm. charge. *Royal Albert Memorial Museum and Art Gallery,* Queen Street. Fine art, Exeter silver, ceramics, ethnography, natural and local history. Open Tues.–Sat. and some Suns. in summer, 10–5.30. Adm. free. *Underground Passages,* High Street. Medieval water supply. *Rougemont House Museum.* Costume displayed in Georgian rooms. Castle Street. Open Mon.–Sat. 10–5. *St. Nicholas' Priory.* Norman priory. Open Tues.–Sat. 10–5.30.

Fort William.—*West Highland Museum,* Cameron Square. Historical, natural history and folk exhibits, including those of the 1745 Rising. Daily (except Sun.) 10–5; June and Sept. 9.30–5.30; July and Aug. 9.30–9.

Glasgow.—*Art Gallery and Museum,* Kelvingrove. Old Masters, 19th century French paintings, archaeology and natural history, collection of armour. *People's Palace,* Glasgow Green. History of city from 1175 to present. *The Burrell Collection,* Pollok Park. Textiles, furniture, ceramics, stained glass, silver and paintings, especially 19th century French. *Pollok House,* Pollok Park. Spanish paintings, furniture, silver, ceramics. *Haggs Castle Museum,* St. Andrews Drive. Children's museum with activity workshops. *Provand's Lordship,* Castle Street. Oldest house in Glasgow, period furniture displays. *Rutherglen Museum,* King Street. History of former royal burgh of Rutherglen. *Museum of Transport,* Kelvin Hall. All open daily, times vary. Adm. free. Also *McLellan Galleries,* Sauchiehall Street. Major exhibition venue for large-scale temporary exhibitions. Adm. charge.

Hull.—*Ferens Art Gallery.* European art, especially Dutch 17th century, British portraits from 17th–20th centuries, Humberside marine paintings, contemporary art and changing exhibitions. *Wilberforce House.* Jacobean merchant's house, birthplace of Wilberforce; slavery relics, period furniture, costume and ceramics. *Streetlife.* Museum of Transport; public service vehicles from the stage-coach to the last surviving Hull tram. *Hull and East Riding Museum.* Archæology and transport; includes the iron-age Hasholme Boat. *Town Docks Museum.* Whaling, fishing, trawling, ships and shipping. *Old Grammar School.* Hull's oldest secular building with city history displays. *Spurn Lightship,* built 1927, restored 1986. Closed Mon. and Tues. in winter. All open Mon.–Sat. 10–5, Sun. 1.30–4.30.

Huntingdon.—*Cromwell Museum.* Remaining portion of the 12th century Hospital of St. John; portraits of Cromwell, his family and Parliamentary notables, and Cromwelliana. Open April–Oct. Tues.–Fri. 11–5, Sat, Sun. 11–4; Nov.–March, Tues.–Fri. 2–

5, Sat. 11–4, Sun. 2–4. Closed Bank Hols. other than Good Friday. Adm. free.

Ipswich.—*Ipswich Museum*. Suffolk geology, archaeology, natural history and ethnology. Temporary exhibitions. Open Mon.–Sat. 10–5. Closed Bank Hols. *Christchurch Mansion*. Tudor house containing furniture, Suffolk portraits, English porcelain, pottery and glass. *Wolsey Art Gallery*. Collections of paintings (local artists, Gainsborough, Constable), modern prints, sculpture. Open Mon.–Sat. 10–5, Sun. 2.30–4.30. Closed Good Friday, Dec. 24, 25, 26.

Leeds.—*City Art Gallery*. English watercolours. British and European painting, modern sculpture, Henry Moore gallery, Print Room. Open weekdays, 10–6, Suns., 2–5.

Temple Newsam House. Tudor/Jacobean house, furnished in style of 17th and 18th centuries; silver, European porcelain and pottery, pictures, etc. Open daily (except Mon.) 10.30–6.15, Weds. (May–Sept.) 10.30–8.30, all Bank Hols. (except Christmas). Adm. 65p, con. 30p. *Lotherton Hall*, Gascoigne art and silver collection, oriental gallery, costume collection, 19th century furniture, ceramics; park and gardens. Open daily (except Mon.) 10.30–6.15, Thurs. (May–Sept.) 10.30–8.30, all Bank Hols. (except Christmas). Adm. 65p, con. 30p. *Abbey House Museum*. Folk museum including three full-sized streets. Open Oct.–March weekdays 10–5, Sun. 2–5 (April–Sept. 2–6). *Industrial Museum*. Open April–Sept. Tues.–Sat. 10–5, Sun. 2–5 (Oct.–March 2–4). Open Bank Hols. *City Museum*. Geology, archaeology, ethnography and natural history. Open Tues.–Fri. 9.30–5.30, Sat. 9.30–4.

Leicester.—*Leicestershire Museum and Art Gallery*, New Walk. Natural history, geology, Egyptology, 18th–20th century English paintings, ceramics, silver. *Newarke Houses*, The Newarke. Social history of Leicestershire from 1500 AD, musical instruments, local clocks. *Jewry Wall Museum*, St. Nicholas Circle. Archaeology, Roman Jewry Wall and Baths, mosaics. *Belgrave Hall*, Church Road. Queen Anne house with furniture and garden, coaches and agricultural collection. *Museum of the Royal Leicestershire Regiment*, Oxford Street. *Museum of Technology*, Corporation Road. Knitting industry and Power galleries. Horse-drawn and motor vehicles, beam engines. *Wygston's House Museum of Costume*, Applegate. Costume from 1789–present. All museums open weekdays 10–5.30, Sun. 2–5.30. Closed Christmas Day, Boxing Day and Good Friday.

Lewes.—*Museum of Sussex Archaeology*, Barbican House, near Castle. Open weekdays, 10–5.30, Sun. (April–Oct.) 11–5.30. Adm. (including Castle) £2.50, con. £1.25. *Anne of Cleves House*, Southover. Local history and folk museum. Open April–Oct., weekdays 10–5.30, Sun. 2–5.30. Adm. £1.50, con. 75p.

Lincoln.—*Usher Gallery*. Watches, miniatures, porcelain, silver, etc., Peter de Wint collection of oils and watercolours, Lincolnshire topographical drawings, *personalia* associated with Tennyson family. Open weekdays 10–5.30, Sun. 2.30–5. *City and County Museum*, The Greyfriars. Geology, natural history and archaeology of Lincolnshire. Open weekdays 10–5.30, Sun. 2.30–5. *Museum of Lincolnshire Life*. Covers the last 200 years; large agricultural collection. Open weekdays 10–5.30, Sun. 2–5.30. *National Cycle Museum*, Brayford Wharf North. Vintage cycles. Open Easter–Oct. 10–5 daily; Oct.–Easter Fri., Sat., and Sun. 10–5.

Manchester.—*City Art Galleries*, Mosley Street and Princess Street. Old Masters, Turner, Pre-Raphaelites; sculpture, porcelain, silver. Changing exhibitions. Times vary. *Whitworth Art Gallery*, University of Manchester, Oxford Road. Watercol-

ours, drawings, prints, textiles and wallpaper collections, 20th century British art. Mon.–Sat. 10–5 (Thurs. 10–9), closed Suns, Good Friday and Christmas week. Adm. free. *Museum of Science and Industry*, Liverpool Road, Castlefield. Working machinery and displays in world's oldest passenger railway station. Open daily 10–5. *Gallery of English Costume*, Platt Hall, Rusholme. Exhibits from 16th century to present. Times vary. Also *Heaton Hall*, Prestwich, *Wythenshawe Hall*, Northenden and *Fletcher Moss Museum*, Didsbury. Times vary.

Newcastle upon Tyne.—*Laing Art Gallery*, Higham Place. Fine art from 17th century, pottery, glass, silver and metalwork. Open Tues.–Fri. 10–5.30, Sat. 10–4.30, Sun. 2.30–5.30. *Castle Keep*, St. Nicholas Street. Oct.–March, Tues.–Sun. 9.30–4 (April–Sept. 9.30–5). *Trinity Maritime Centre* and *Trinity House*, Broad Chare. Centre open April–Oct. daily 11–4; Nov.–March, by arrangement. Trinity House April–Nov. (chapel and entrance hall only; tour of house by appointment.) *Military Vehicle Museum*, Exhibition Park. Open daily 10–4.30. *Museum of Science and Engineering*, West Blandford Square. Tues.–Fri. 10–5.30, Sat. 10–4. *Newburn Hall Motor Museum*, Townfield Gdns. Tues.–Sat. 10–8, Sun. 10–6.

Newmarket.—*National Horseracing Museum*. Five galleries of displays relating to horseracing, horses and people connected with the sport. Equine Tours. Open March 26–Dec. 8, Tues.–Sat. 10–5, Sun. 2–5. Closed Mon. except Aug. and Bank Hols. Adm. £2, con. £1/50p.

Norwich.—*Castle Museum*. Exhibits of art (including Norwich School), archaeology, natural history, silver and glass. Open, Mon.–Sat., 10–5, Sun. 2–5. *Strangers' Hall*, Charing Cross. Medieval mansion with period room settings from Tudor to Victorian times, toy display and costumes. Open Mon.–Sat. 10–5. *Bridewell Museum of Local Industries*, Bridewell Alley. Open Mon.–Sat. 10–5. *St. Peter Hungate Church Museum*, Princes Street. 15th century church used for display of church art and antiquities. Open Mon.–Sat. 10–5.

Nottingham.—*Castle Museum and Art Gallery*. English and Dutch paintings and drawings 17th–20th centuries, ceramics, silver, glass, medieval alabaster carvings, local archaeological displays, classical, oriental and ethnographical antiquities, the regimental collection of the Sherwood Foresters. Conducted tours of Mortimer's Hole Caves. Open summer, 10–5.45, winter, 10–4.45. Closed Christmas Day. Adm. free, small charge on Sun. and Bank Hols. *Industrial Museum*, Wollaton Park. Lacemaking machinery, steam engines, transport. Open April–Sept. Mon.–Sat. 10–6, Sun. 2–6; Oct.–April, Thurs., Sat. 10–4.30, Sun. 1.30–4.30. Closed Christmas Day. Adm. free, small charge on Sun. and Bank Hols. *Canal Museum*, Canal Street. History of local canals and rivers. Open Easter–Oct. Wed.–Sat. 10–5.45, Sun. 1–5.45; Oct.–Easter, Wed.–Sat. 1–5, Sun. 1–5. Adm. free. *Natural History Museum*, Wollaton Hall. Tudor building and park. Open summer 10–7, Sun. 2–5; winter 10–dusk (Sun. 1.30–4.30). Closed Christmas Day. Adm. free except Sun. and Bank Hols. *Castlegate Museum of Costumes and Textiles*. Open daily 10–5. Closed Christmas Day. Adm. free. *Brewhouse Yard Museum*, Castle Boulevard. Everyday life from the 17th century to present. Open daily 10–5. Adm. free. Closed Christmas Day. *Green's Mill and Science Centre*, Sneinton. Working windmill and museum with displays about George Green. Open Wed.–Sun. 10–5. Closed Christmas Day. Adm. free. Also *The Lace Hall* and *Robin Hood Centre*.

Oakham, *Rutland County Museum*, Catmos Street.—Archaeology, local history, craft tools and agricultural implements. Open Tues.-Sat. 10–5, Sun. (April–Oct.) 2–5, and Bank Hol. Mons.

Oxford, *Ashmolean Museum,* Beaumont Street.— The University's collections of European and Oriental fine and applied arts, Classical and Near-Eastern archaeology and Numismatics. Open Tues.-Sat. 10–4, Sun. 2–4. Bank Hol. Mons. 2–5. Adm. free.

Plymouth.—*City Museum and Art Gallery,* Drake Circus. Fine art including Reynolds' portraits, Plymouth porcelain, archaeology, local and natural history. Tues.-Sat. 10–5.30, Sun. 2–5. Also Bank Holiday Mons. Adm. free. *Elizabethan House,* 32 New Street. *Merchant's House,* 33 St. Andrew's Street. 16th century. *The Dome,* the Hoe. Maritime history museum.

Portsmouth.—*City Museum and Art Gallery,* Museum Road. *Cumberland House Natural Science Museum and Butterfly House,* Eastern Parade. *Southsea Castle and Museum,* Clarence Esplanade. *D-Day Museum,* Clarence Esplanade. All open daily 10.30–5.30, except Dec. 24–26. Adm. charge. *Charles Dickens' Birthplace Museum,* Old Commercial Road. Open March 1–Oct. 31, daily 10.30–5.30. Adm. charge. *Eastney Pumping Station,* Henderson Road. Open April–Sept. daily 1.30–5.30; Oct.–March 1st Sun. of month. Adm. charge. *Naval Heritage Area.* Tells the story of the Royal Navy using Henry VIII's *Mary Rose,* HMS *Victory* and the Victorian ironclad, HMS *Warrior* (1860). *Royal Naval Museum.* Open daily (except Christmas Day). Adm. charge.

St. Albans.—*Museum of St. Alban,* Hatfield Road. Story of St. Albans since Roman times. Open weekdays 10–5. Adm. free. *Verulamium Museum,* St. Michael's. Iron Age and Roman Verulamium including wall plasters, jewellery, mosaics. Open weekdays 10–5.30, Sun. 2–5.30. Closes 4 Nov.–Feb. Adm. £1.20, con. 60p.

Sheffield.—*City Museum, Weston Park.* Includes the Bateman Collection of antiquities from Peak District, cutlery and old Sheffield plate, local geology and wildlife. *Mappin Art Gallery,* Weston Park. Paintings and sculpture of 18th–20th centuries (mainly British School) and contemporary works. *Abbeydale Industrial Hamlet,* Abbeydale Road South. A late 18th–early 19th century scythe and steel works with associated housing. *Kelham Island Industrial Museum. Shepherd Wheel,* Whiteley Wood. Waterpowered cutlery grinding establishment. *Bishops' House,* Meersbrook Park. Museum of local history. Opening times vary.

Stoke-on-Trent.—*City Museum and Art Gallery,* Bethesda Street, Hanley. Major ceramic collections. Open daily 10–5, Sun. 2–5. *Chatterley Whitfield Mining Museum,* Tunstall. Guided tours underground. *Gladstone Pottery Museum,* Longton. A working Victorian pottery.

Pottery Factory Tours are available at the following: *Minton,* London Road, Stoke; *Royal Doulton,* Nile Street, Burslem; *Spode,* Church Street, Stoke; *Beswick,* Gold Street; *Royal Grafton China,* Marlborough Road, Longton; *Coalport,* Park Street, Fenton and *Wedgwood's* at Barlaston.

Stratford-upon-Avon.—*Shakespeare's Birthplace.* Period furniture, rare books, MSS and memorabilia; new Shakespeare Centre nearby. *Anne Hathaway's Cottage,* Shottery. Home of Shakespeare's wife. *Mary Arden's House,* Wilmcote. Tudor farmhouse home of Shakespeare's mother. *New Place,* where Shakespeare died. *Hall's Croft.* Shakespeare's daughter's home. *Grammar School* attended by Shakespeare. *Royal Shakespeare Theatre.* Burnt down 1926, rebuilt 1932. New *Swan Theatre,* opened in 1986.

Styal.—*Quarry Bank Mill,* Cheshire. History of the cotton industry, weaving demonstrations. Giant iron waterwheel. Restored Apprentice House. Open all year. Closed Mon. Oct.–March. Open Bank Hols. Adm. £3.75, con. £2.75.

Winchester.—*City Museum.* Weekdays 10–5, Sun. 2–5 (closed Mon. in winter). *Cathedral Library* and *Triforium Gallery.* Illuminated manuscripts, sculpture, wood- and metalwork from 12th–19th centuries. Times vary. Closed Mon. morning and Suns. Adm. charge. *Cathedral Treasury.* Exhibition of silverware. Open May–Sept. daily 2.30–4.30. Adm. charge.

Worcester.—*City Museum and Art Gallery.* Natural history of Worcestershire, changing art exhibitions; also military museum. Open Mon.–Wed., Fri. 9.30–6, Sat. 9.30–5. Closed Thurs., Sun. *The Commandery,* Sidbury. Civil War Centre, costume, industrial history. Weekdays 10.30–5, Sun. 2–5. *Tudor House Museum,* Friar Street. Local history. Mon.–Wed., Fri., Sat. 10.30–5. *Dyson Perrins Museum and Royal Worcester Porcelain Works,* Severn Street. Mon. to Fri. 9.30–5, Sat. 10–5.

York.—*Castle Museum.* Everyday life of the last three centuries. Open weekdays 9.30–5.30, Sun. 10–5.30 (closes 6.30 April–Oct.). Adm. £3, con. £1.50. *Jorvik Viking Centre,* Coppergate. Reconstruction of Viking York. Open daily. Adm. £3, con. £1.50. *Yorkshire Museum and Gardens,* Museum Street, Roman Life gallery, archaeology, decorative arts, geology, natural history. Open weekdays 10–5, Sun. 1–5. Adm. charge. Gardens, Roman, Anglian and medieval ruins. Open weekdays 7.30–dusk (summer 7.30–8), Sun. 10–dusk. *The York Story,* Castlegate. Open weekdays 10–5, Sun. 1–5. Adm. 80p, con. 40p. *Art Gallery,* Exhibition Square. European paintings, 14th–20th century; watercolours and prints of Yorkshire; modern English stoneware pottery. Open weekdays 10–5, Sun. 2.30–5. Adm. free *Treasurer's House* (National Trust). Chapter House Street. Open April–Oct. 10.30–5 (closed Good Friday). Adm. charge.

WILDLIFE CONSERVATION

PROTECTED SPECIES

The Wildlife and Countryside Act 1981 gives legal protection to a wide range of wild plants and animals.

Animals, etc.

Under Schedule 5 of the Act it is normally an offence to kill, injure, take, possess or sell any of the animals mentioned below (whether alive or dead) and to disturb its place of shelter and protection or to destroy that place.

* Adder (*Vipera berus*)
Anemone, Ivell's Sea (*Edwardsia ivelli*)
Anemone, Startlet Sea (*Nematosella vectensis*)
Apus (*Triops cancriformis*)
Bat, Horseshoe (*Rhinolophidae*, all species)
Bat, Typical (*Vespertilionidae*, all species)
Beetle, Rainbow Leaf (*Chrysolina cerealis*)
Beetle, Violet Click (*Limoniscus violaceus*)
Burbot (*Lota lota*)
* Butterfly, Adonis Blue (*Lysandra bellargus*)
* Butterfly, Black Hairstreak (*Strymonidia pruni*)
* Butterfly, Brown Hairstreak (*Thecla betulae*)
* Butterfly, Chalkhill Blue (*Lysandra coridon*)
* Butterfly, Chequered Skipper (*Carterocephalus palaemon*)
* Butterfly, Duke of Burgundy Fritillary (*Hamearis lucina*)
* Butterfly, Glanville Fritillary (*Melitaea cinxia*)
Butterfly, Heath Fritillary (*Mellicta athalia* (or *Melitaea athalia*))
* Butterfly, High Brown Fritillary (*Argynnis adippe*)
Butterfly, Large Blue (*Maculinea arion*)
* Butterfly, Large Copper (*Lycaena dispar*)
* Butterfly, Large Heath (*Coenonympha tullia*)
* Butterfly, Large Tortoiseshell (*Nymphalis polychloros*)
* Butterfly, Lulworth Skipper (*Thymelicus acteon*)
* Butterfly, Marsh Fritillary (*Eurodryas aurinia*)
* Butterfly, Mountain Ringlet (*Erebia epiphron*)
* Butterfly, Northern Brown Argus (*Aricia artaxerxes*)
* Butterfly, Pearl-bordered Fritillary (*Boloria euphrosyne*)
* Butterfly, Purple Emperor (*Apatura iris*)
* Butterfly, Silver Spotted Skipper (*Hesperia comma*)
* Butterfly, Silver-studded Blue (*Plebejus argus*)
* Butterfly, Small Blue (*Cupido minimus*)
Butterfly, Swallowtail (*Papilio machaon*)
* Butterfly, White Letter Hairstreak (*Stymonida w-album*)
* Butterfly, Wood White (*Leptidea sinapis*)
Cat, Wild (*Felis silvestris*)
Cicada, New Forest (*Cicadetta montana*)
** Crayfish, Atlantic Stream (*Austropotamobius pallipes*)
Cricket, Field (*Gryllus campestris*)
Cricket, Mole (*Gryllotalpa gryllotalpa*)
Dolphin (*Cetacea*)
Dormouse (*Muscardinus avellanarius*)
Dragonfly, Norfolk Aeshna (*Aeshna isosceles*)
* Frog, Common (*Rana temporaria*)
Grasshopper, Wart-biter (*Decticus verrucivorus*)
Leech, Medicinal (*Hirudo medicinalis*)
Lizard, Sand (*Lacerta agilis*)
† Lizard, Viviparous(*Lacerta vivipara*)
Marten, Pine (*Martes martes*)

Moth, Barberry Carpet (*Pareulype berberata*)
Moth, Black-veined (*Siona lineata* (or *Idaea lineata*))
Moth, Essex Emerald (*Thetidia smaragdaria*)
Moth, New Forest Burnet (*Zygaena viciae*)
Moth, Reddish Buff (*Acosmetia caliginosa*)
Moth, Viper's Bugloss (*Hadena irregularis*)
Newt, Great Crested (or Warty) (*Triturus cristatus*)
* Newt, Palmate (*Triturus helveticus*)
* Newt, Smooth (*Triturus vulgaris*)
Otter, Common (*Lutra lutra*)
Porpoise (*Cetacea*)
Sandworm, Lagoon (*Armandia cirrhosa*)
Sea-Mat, Trembling (*Victorella pavida*)
Shrimp, Fairy (*Chirocephalus diaphanus*)
Shrimp, Lagoon Sand (*Gammarus insensibilis*)
† Slow-worm (*Anguis fragilis*)
Snail, Glutinous (*Myxas glutinosa*)
Snail, Sandbowl (*Catinella arenaria*)
† Snake, Grass (*Natrix natrix* (*Natrix helvetica*))
Snake, Smooth (*Coronella austriaca*)
Spider, Fen Raft (*Dolomedes plantarius*)
Spider, Ladybird (*Eresus niger*)
Squirrel, Red (*Sciurus vulgaris*)
* Toad, Common (*Bufo bufo*)
Toad, Natterjack (*Bufo calamita*)
Turtle, Marine (*Dermochelyidae* and *Cheloniidae*, all species)
Vendace (*Coregonus albula*)
Walrus (*Odobenus rosmarus*)
Whale (*Cetacea*)
Whitefish (*Coregonus lavaretus*)

Plants

Under Schedule 8 of the Wildlife and Countryside Act, it is normally an offence to pick, uproot, sell or destroy any of the plants mentioned below and, unless authorized, to uproot any wild plant.

Adder's tongue, Least (*Ophioglossum lusitanicum*)
Alison, Small (*Alyssum alyssoides*)
Broomrape, Bedstraw (*Orobanche caryophyllacea*)
Broomrape, Oxtongue (*Orobanche loricata*)
Broomrape, Thistle (*Orobanche reticulata*)
Cabbage, Lundy (*Rhynchosinapis wrightii*)
Calamint, Wood (*Calamintha sylvatica*)
Catchfly, Alpine (*Lychnis alpina*)
Cinquefoil, Rock (*Potentilla rupestris*)
Club-rush, Triangular (*Scirpus triquetrus*)
Colt's-foot, Purple (*Homogyne alpina*)
Cotoneaster, Wild (*Cotoneaster integerrimus*)
Cottongrass, Slender (*Eriophorum gracile*)
Cow-wheat, Field (*Melampyrum arvense*)
Crocus, Sand (*Romulea columnae*)
Cudweed, Jersey (*Gnaphalium luteoalbum*)
Cudweed, Red-tipped (*Filago lutescens*)
Diapensia (*Diapensia lapponica*)
Eryngo, Field (*Eryngium campestre*)
Fern, Dickie's bladder (*Cystopteris dickieana*)
Fern, Killarney (*Trichomanes speciosum*)
Fleabane, Alpine (*Erigeron borealis*)
Fleabane, Small (*Pulicaria vulgaris*)
Galingale, Brown (*Cyperus fuscus*)
Gentian, Alpine (*Gentiana nivalis*)
Gentian, Fringed (*Gentianella ciliata*)
Gentian, Spring (*Gentiana verna*)
Germander, Cut-leaved (*Teucrium botrys*)
Germander, Water (*Teucrium scordium*)
Gladiolus, Wild (*Gladiolus illyricus*)
Goosefoot, Stinking (*Chenopodium vulvaria*)
Grass-poly (*Lythrum hyssopifolia*)
Hare's-ear, Sickle-leaved (*Bupleurum falcatum*)
Hare's-ear, Small (*Bupleurum baldense*)

---

* the offence relates to 'sale' only.
** the offence relates to 'taking' and 'sale' only.
† the offence relates to 'killing, injuring and sale'.

Hawk's-beard, Stinking (*Crepis foetida*)
Heath, Blue (*Phyllodoce caerulea*)
Helleborine, Red (*Cephalanthera rubra*)
Helleborine, Young's (*Epipactis youngiana*)
Horsetail, Branched (*Equisetum ramosissimum*)
Hound's-tongue, Green (*Cynoglossum germanicum*)
Knawel, Perennial (*Scleranthus perennis*)
Knotgrass, Sea (*Polygonum maritimum*)
Lady's-slipper (*Cypripedium calceolus*)
Lavender, Sea (*Limonium paradoxum*) (*Limonium recurvum*)
Leek, Round-headed (*Allium sphaerocephalon*)
Lettuce, Least (*Lactuca saligna*)
Lily, Snowdon (*Lloydia serotina*)
Marsh-mallow, Rough (*Althaea hirsuta*)
Marshwort, Creeping (*Apium repens*)
Milk-parsley, Cambridge (*Selinum carvifolia*)
Naiad, Holly-leaved (*Najas marina*)
Orchid, Early Spider (*Ophrys sphegodes*)
Orchid, Fen (*Liparis loeselii*)
Orchid, Ghost (*Epipogium aphyllum*)
Orchid, Late Spider (*Ophrys fuciflora*)
Orchid, Lizard (*Himantoglossum hircinum*)
Orchid, Military (*Orchis militaris*)
Orchid, Monkey (*Orchis simia*)
Pear, Plymouth (*Pyrus cordata*)
Pennyroyal (*Mentha pulegium*)
Pigmyweed (*Crassula aquatica*)
Pink, Cheddar (*Dianthus gratianopolitanus*)
Pink, Childling (*Petroraghia nanteuilii*)
Ragwort, Fen (*Senecio paludosus*)
Ramping-fumitory, Martin's (*Fumaria martinii*)
Restharrow, Small (*Ononis reclinata*)
Rock-cress, Alpine (*Arabis alpina*)
Rock-cress, Bristol (*Arabis stricta*)
Sandwort, Norwegian (*Arenaria norvegica*)
Sandwort, Teesdale (*Minuartia stricta*)
Saxifrage, Drooping (*Saxifraga cernua*)
Saxifrage, Tufted (*Saxifraga cespitosa*)
Solomon's-seal, Whorled (*Polygonatum verticillatum*)
Sow-thistle, Alpine (*Cicerbita alpina*)
Spearwort, Adder's-tongue (*Ranunculus ophioglossifolius*)
Speedwell, Fingered (*Veronica triphyllos*)
Speedwell, Spiked (*Veronica spicata*)
Spurge, Purple (*Euphorbia peplis*)
Star-of-Bethlehem, Early (*Gagea bohemica*)
Starfruit (*Damasonium alisma*)
Stonewort, Foxtail (*Lamprothamnium papulosum*)
Strapwort (*Corrigiola litoralis*)
Violet, Fen (*Viola persicifolia*)
Viper's-grass (*Scorzonera humilis*)
Water-plantain, Ribbon-leaved (*Alisma gramineum*)
Wood-sedge, Starved (*Carex depauperata*)
Woodsia, Alpine (*Woodsia alpina*)
Woodsia, Oblong (*Woodsia ilvensis*)
Wormwood, Field (*Artemisia campestris*)
Woundwort, Downy (*Stachys germanica*)
Woundwort, Limestone (*Stachys alpina*)
Yellow-rattle, Greater (*Rhinanthus serotinus*)

Wild Birds

The Wildlife and Countryside Act, 1981, lays down a close season for wild birds (other than game birds) from February 1 to August 31 inclusive, each year. Exceptions to these dates are made for:

Capercaillie and (except Scotland) *Woodcock*—Feb. 1–Sept. 30.
Snipe—Feb. 1–Aug. 11.
Wild Duck and *Wild Goose* (below high water mark)—Feb. 21–Aug. 31.

Birds which may be killed or taken outside the close season (except on Sundays and on Christmas Day in Scotland, and on Sundays in prescribed areas of England and Wales) are the above-named and coot,

certain wild duck (gadwall, goldeneye, mallard, pintail, pochard, shoveler, teal, tufted duck, wigeon), certain wild geese (Canada, greylag, pink-footed, white-fronted (in England and Wales only)), moorhen, golden plover and woodcock.

Certain wild birds may be killed or taken at any time by authorized persons—crow, collared dove, gull (great and lesser black-backed or herring), jackdaw, jay, magpie, pigeon (feral or wood), rook, sparrow (house), and starling.

All other British birds are fully protected by law throughout the year.

CLOSE SEASONS AND TIMES
Game Birds

In each case the dates are inclusive:—

Black Game–Dec. 11–Aug. 19 (Aug. 31 in Somerset, Devon, and New Forest).
*Grouse–Dec. 11–Aug. 11.
*Partridge–Feb. 2–Aug. 31.
*Pheasant–Feb. 2–Sept. 30.
*Ptarmigan–(Scotland only) Dec. 11–Aug. 11.

It is also unlawful in England and Wales to kill the game marked * above on a Sunday or Christmas Day.

Hunting and Ground Game

There is no statutory close-time for fox-hunting or rabbit-shooting, nor for hares; but by an Act passed in 1892 the *sale* of hares or leverets in Great Britain is prohibited from March 1 to July 31 inclusive under a penalty of £1. November 1 is the recognized date for the opening of the fox-hunting season, which continues till the following April.

Deer

The statutory close seasons for deer (all dates inclusive) are:

	England and Wales	Scotland
Fallow deer		
Male	May 1–July 31	May 1–July 31
Female	Mar. 1–Oct. 31	Feb. 16–Oct. 20
Red deer		
Male	May 1–July 31	Oct. 21–June 30
Female	Mar. 1–Oct. 31	Feb. 16–Oct. 20
Roe deer		
Male	Nov. 1–Mar. 31	Oct. 21–Mar. 31
Female	Mar. 1–Oct. 31	April 1–Oct. 31
Sika deer		
Male	May 1–July 31	Oct. 21–June 30
Female	Mar. 1–Oct. 31	Feb. 16–Oct. 20
Red/Sika hybrids		
Male	—	Oct. 21–June 30
Female	—	Feb. 16–Oct. 20

Angling

Close seasons (dates inclusive) are:
Coarse fishing.—Yorkshire, last day in Feb.–May 31; South West, none; rest of country, March 15–June 15.
Game fishing.—Trout, Oct. 1–last day of Feb.*; Salmon, Nov. 1–Jan. 31*.

* The above dates are statutory close times. Particularly with salmon, migratory trout and trout, close seasons vary in accordance with water authority local by-laws. In all cases, it is best to check with the water authority concerned.

HALLMARKS ON GOLD, SILVER AND PLATINUM WARES
London (Goldsmiths' Hall) Date Letters
From 1498

Description	Period	Description	Period
Black letter, small	1498–9 to 1517–8	Roman letter, small ...	1739–40 to 1755–6
Lombardic	1518–9 ,, 1537–8	Old English, capitals ..	1756–7 ,, 1775–6
Roman and other capitals	1538–9 ,, 1557–8	Roman letter, small ...	1776–7 ,, 1795–6
Black letter, small	1558–9 ,, 1577–8	Roman letter, capitals .	1796–7 ,, 1815–6
Roman letter, capitals .	1578–9 ,, 1597–8	Roman letter, small ...	1816–7 ,, 1835–6
Lombardic, external cusps	1598–9 ,, 1617–8	Old English, capitals ..	1836–7 ,, 1855–6
Italic letter, small	1618–9 ,, 1637–8	Old English, small	1856–7 ,, 1875–6
Court hand	1638–9 ,, 1657–8	Roman letter, capitals [A to M *square* shield N to Z as shown]	1876–7 ,, 1895–6
Black letter, capitals ..	1658–9 ,, 1677–8	Roman letter, small ...	1896–7 ,, 1915–6
Black letter, small	1678–9 ,, 1696–7	Black letter, small	1916–7 ,, 1935–6
Court hand	1697 ,, 1715–6	Roman letter, capitals .	1936–7 ,, 1955–6
Roman letter, capitals	1716–7 ,, 1735–6	Italic letter, small	1956–7 ,, 1974
Roman letter, small ...	1736–7 ,, 1738–9	Italic letter, capitals ..	1975 ,, ...

Hallmarks are the symbols stamped on gold, silver, or platinum articles to indicate that they have been chemically tested and that they conform to one of the legal standards. With certain exceptions, all gold, silver, or platinum articles are required by law to be hallmarked before they are offered for sale. Hallmarking was instituted in 1300 under a statute of Edward I.

Normally a complete modern hallmark consists of four symbols—the maker's mark or sponsor's mark, assay office mark, standard mark and date letter. Additional marks have been authorized from time to time.

Maker's Mark.—Instituted in 1363, the maker's mark was originally a device such as a bird or fleur-de-lis and now consists invariably of the initial letters of the name or names of the maker or sponsor, or of the firm.

Assay Office Mark.—The existing assay offices and their distinguishing marks are:—

LONDON (Goldsmiths' Hall, EC2V 8AQ).
A leopard's head (uncrowned from 1300 to 1478–9, when it became crowned until 1821, since when it has been uncrowned). From 1697 to 1974 a lion's head erased was used on silver of the higher (Britannia) standard.

BIRMINGHAM (Newhall Street, B3 1SB). An anchor
SHEFFIELD (137 Portobello Street, S1 4DS) . . A rose
EDINBURGH (9 Granton Road, EH5 3QJ) . . A castle

Offices formerly existed in other towns, e.g. Chester, Glasgow, Newcastle, Exeter, York and Norwich, each having its own distinguishing mark.

Standard Mark.—Instituted in 1544. The current legal standards and their marks are as follows:—

SILVER.—Sterling silver (92·5 per cent silver) is marked by English assay offices with a *lion passant* and by the Edinburgh Assay Office with a *lion rampant*. A full-length figure of *Britannia* was impressed on silver of a higher standard (95·84 per cent silver) between 1697 and 1720 and this mark is still used occasionally by all British assay offices.

GOLD.—Since 1975 gold articles are marked with a crown followed by the millesimal figure for the standard, i.e. 916 for 22 carat, 750 for 18 carat, 585 for 14 carat and 375 for 9 carat.

PLATINUM.—Hallmarking of platinum articles began in 1975. The only standard permitted contains at least 95 per cent platinum.

    PLATINUM

Date Letter.—Instituted in 1478. The date letter denotes the year in which an article was assayed and hallmarked. Each alphabetical cycle has a distinctive style of lettering or shape of shield. The date letters were different at the various assay offices and the particular office must be established from the assay office mark before reference is made to tables of date letters. Specimen shields and letters used by the

London Office on silver articles in each period from 1498 to date are shown on the previous page. The same letters are found on gold articles but the surrounding shield may differ. Since January 1, 1975 each Office has used the same style of date letter and shield for all articles.

OTHER MARKS

Duty Mark.—In 1784 an additional mark of the reigning sovereign's head was introduced to signify that the excise duty had been paid. The mark became obsolete on the abolition of the duty in 1890.

Commemorative Marks.—There are three other marks to commemorate special events, the Silver Jubilee of King George V and Queen Mary in 1935, the Coronation of Queen Elizabeth II in 1953 and her Silver Jubilee in 1977.

Foreign Wares.—Since 1842 foreign wares imported into Great Britain have been required to be hallmarked before sale. The marks consist of the importer's mark, a special assay office mark (*see* below), the figures denoting fineness and the annual date letter. The current assay office marks for foreign wares are as follows:—

LONDON.—The sign of the Constellation Leo.
BIRMINGHAM.—Equilateral triangle.
SHEFFIELD.—The sign of the Constellation Libra.
EDINBURGH.—St. Andrew's Cross.

Common Control Mark.—Special marks at authorized Assay Offices of the signatory countries of the International Convention (United Kingdom, Austria, Denmark, Finland, Ireland, Portugal, Norway, Sweden and Switzerland) are legally recognized in the United Kingdom as approved hallmarks. These marks consist of a sponsor's mark, a common control mark, a fineness mark (arabic numerals showing the standard in parts per thousand) and an assay office mark. There is no date letter.

WEIGHTS AND MEASURES

SI UNITS

The Système International d'Unités (SI) is an international and coherent system of units devised to meet all known needs for measurement in science and technology. The system was adopted by the 11th Conférence Générale des Poids et. Mesures (CGPM) in 1960. The British Standards describing the essential features of the International System of Units are *Specifications for SI Units* (BS 5555:1981) and *Conversion Factors and Tables* (BS 350, Part 1:1974).

The system consists of seven base units and the derived units formed as products or quotients of various powers of the base units. Together the base units and the derived units make up the coherent system of units. In the UK the SI base units, and almost all important derived units, are realized at the National Physical Laboratory and disseminated through the National Measurement System.

Base Units

Metre (m) = unit of length

Kilogram (kg) = unit of mass

Second (s) = unit of time

Ampere (A) = unit of electric current

Kelvin (K) = unit of thermodynamic temperature

Mole (mol) = unit of amount of substance

Candela (cd) = unit of luminous intensity

Derived Units

For some of the derived SI units, special names and symbols exist; those approved by the CGPM are listed below.

Hertz (Hz) = unit of frequency

Newton (N) = unit of force

Pascal (Pa) = unit of pressure, stress

Joule (J) = unit of energy, work, quantity of heat

Watt (W) = unit of power, radiant flux

Coulomb (C) = unit of electric charge, quantity of electricity

Volt (V) = unit of electric potential, potential difference, electromotive force

Farad (F) = unit of electric capacitance

Ohm (Ω) = unit of electric resistance

Siemens (S) = unit of electric conductance

Weber (Wb) = unit of magnetic flux

Tesla (T) = unit of magnetic flux density

Henry (H) = unit of inductance

Degree Celsius (°C) = unit of Celsius temperature

Lumen (lm) = unit of luminous flux

Lux (lx) = unit of illuminance

Becquerel (Bq) = unit of activity (of a radionuclide)

Gray (Gy) = unit of absorbed dose, specific energy imparted, kerma, absorbed dose index

Sievert (Sv) = unit of dose equivalent, dose equivalent index

Supplementary Units

The derived units include, as a special case, the supplementary units which may be treated as dimensionless within the SI.

Radian (rad) = unit of plane angle
Steradian (sr) = unit of solid angle

Other derived units are expressed in terms of base units and/or supplementary units. Some of the more commonly-used derived units are the following:

Unit of area = square metre (m^2)

Unit of volume = cubic metre (m^3)

Unit of velocity = metre per second (m s^{-1})

Unit of acceleration = metre per second squared (m s^{-2})

Unit of density = kilogram per cubic metre (kg m^{-3})

Unit of momentum = kilogram metre per second (kg m s^{-1})

Unit of magnetic field = ampere per metre (A m^{-1})

Unit of surface tension = newton per metre (N m^{-1})

Unit of dynamic viscosity = pascal second (Pa s)

Unit of heat capacity = joule per kelvin (J K^{-1})

Unit of specific heat capacity = joule per kilogram kelvin (J kg^{-1} K^{-1})

Unit of heat flux density, irradiance = watt per square metre (W m^{-2})

Unit of thermal conductivity = watt per metre kelvin (W m^{-1} K^{-1})

Unit of electric field strength = volt per metre (V m^{-1})

Unit of luminance = candela per square metre (cd m^{-2})

SI Prefixes

Decimal multiples and submultiples of the SI units are indicated by SI prefixes. These are as follows:

multiples	submultiples
exa (E) $\times 10^{18}$	deci (d) $\times 10^{-1}$
peta (P) $\times 10^{15}$	centi (c) $\times 10^{-2}$
tera (T) $\times 10^{12}$	milli (m) $\times 10^{-3}$
giga (G) $\times 10^{9}$	micro (μ) $\times 10^{-6}$
mega (M) $\times 10^{6}$	nano (n) $\times 10^{-9}$
kilo (k) $\times 10^{3}$	pico (p) $\times 10^{-12}$
hecto (h) $\times 10^{2}$	femto (f) $\times 10^{-15}$
deca (da) $\times 10$	atto (a) $\times 10^{-18}$

UK UNITS

The legal measures for the United Kingdom are enacted in the Weights and Measures Act 1985. The United Kingdom primary standards are the **yard** or the **metre** as the unit of measurement of length, and the **pound** or the **kilogram** as the unit of measurement of mass. Other units of measurement are defined by reference to the primary standards.

Responsibility for the maintenance of the primary standards and for the determination or redetermination of their value rests with the Secretary of State for Trade and Industry.

The definition of the UK primary standards is as follows:

YARD = 0·9144 metre

METRE is the length of the path travelled by light in vacuum during a time interval of 1/299 792 458 of a second.

POUND = 0·453 592 37 kilogram

KILOGRAM is equal to the mass of the international prototype of the kilogram

The following list shows the definitions of measures set out in Schedule 1 of the Weights and Measures Act 1985.

Measurement of Length

Imperial Units
Mile = 1760 yards
YARD (yd) = 0·9144 metre
Foot (ft) = 1/3 yard
Inch (in) = 1/36 yard

Metric Units
Kilometre (km) = 1000 metres
METRE (m) is the length of the path travelled by light in vacuum during a time interval of 1/299 792 458 of a second
Decimetre (dm) = 1/10 metre
Centimetre (cm) = 1/100 metre
Millimetre (mm) = 1/1000 metre

Measurement of Area

Imperial Units
Acre = 4840 square yards
SQUARE YARD = a superficial area equal to that of a square each side of which measures one yard
Square foot = 1/9 square yard

Metric Units
Hectare (ha) = 100 ares
Decare = 10 ares
Are (a) = 100 square metres
SQUARE METRE = a superficial area equal to that of a square each side of which measures one metre
Square decimetre = 1/100 square metre
Square centimetre = 1/100 square decimetre
Square millimetre = 1/100 square centimetre

Measurement of Volume

Metric Units
CUBIC METRE (m^3) = a volume equal to that of a cube each edge of which measures one metre
Cubic decimetre = 1/1000 cubic metre
Cubic centimetre (cc) = 1/1000 cubic decimetre
Hectolitre = 100 litres
LITRE = a cubic decimetre
Decilitre = 1/10 litre
Centilitre = 1/100 litre
Millilitre = 1/1000 litre

Measurement of Capacity

Imperial Units
GALLON = 4·546 09 cubic decimetres
Quart = 1/4 gallon
Pint (pt) = 1/2 quart
Gill = 1/4 pint
Fluid ounce (fl oz) = 1/20 pint

Metric Units
Hectolitre (hl) = 100 litres
LITRE (l or L) = a cubic decimetre
Decilitre (dl) = 1/10 litre
Centilitre (cl) = 1/100 litre
Millilitre (ml) = 1/1000 litre

Measurement of Mass or Weight

Imperial Units
POUND (lb) = 0·453 592 37 kilogram
Ounce (oz) = 1/16 pound
*Ounce troy = 12/175 pound

Metric Units
Tonne, metric ton (t) = 1000 kilograms
KILOGRAM (kg) is the unit of mass; it is equal to the mass of the international prototype of the kilogram
Hectogram (hg) = 1/10 kilogram
Gram (g) = 1/1000 kilogram

**Carat (metric) = 1/5 gram
Milligram (mg) = 1/1000 gram

*used only for transactions in gold, silver or other precious metals, and articles made therefrom.
**used only for transactions in precious stones or pearls.

Certain units of measurement may no longer be used for trade although the measure may still be used, e.g. it is legal to sell a 112 lb quantity of a commodity but it must be referred to in invoices, etc., as 112 lb, not as 1 cwt. These units are defined as follows:

Measurement of Length

Furlong = 220 yards
Chain = 22 yards

Measurement of Area

Square mile = 640 acres
Rood = 1210 square yards
Square inch = 1/144 square foot

Measurement of Volume

Cubic yard = a volume equal to that of a cube each edge of which measures one yard
Cubic foot = 1/27 cubic yard
Cubic inch = 1/1728 cubic foot

Measurement of Capacity

Bushel = 8 gallons
Peck = 2 gallons
Fluid drachm = 1/8 fluid ounce
Minim (min) = 1/60 fluid drachm

Measurement of Mass or Weight

Ton = 2240 pounds
Hundredweight (cwt) = 112 pounds
Cental = 100 pounds
Quarter = 28 pounds
Stone = 14 pounds
Dram (dr) = 1/16 ounce
Grain (gr) = 1/7000 pound
Pennyweight (dwt) = 24 grains
Ounce apothecaries = 480 grains
Drachm (ʒ1) = 1/8 ounce apothecaries
Scruple(ɂ)1) = 1/3 drachm

Metric ton = 1000 kilograms
Quintal (q) = 100 kilograms

Measurement of Electricity

Units of measurement of electricity are defined by the Weights and Measures Act 1985, as follows:

An AMPERE (A) is that constant current which, if maintained in two straight parallel conductors of infinite length, of negligible circular cross-section and placed 1 metre apart in vacuum, would produce between these conductors a force equal to 2×10^{-7} newton per metre of length.

An OHM (Ω) is the electric resistance between two points of a conductor when a constant potential difference of 1 volt, applied between the two points, produces in the conductor a current of 1 ampere, the conductor not being the seat of any electromotive force.

A VOLT (V) is the difference of electric potential between two points of a conducting wire carrying a constant current of 1 ampere when the power dissipated between these points is equal to 1 watt.

A WATT (W) is the power which in one second gives rise to energy of 1 joule

Kilowatt (kW) = 1,000 watts

Megawatt (MW) = one million watts

WATER MEASURES
(approximate)

1 cubic foot = 62·32 lb

1 gallon = 10 lb

1 cubic cm = 1 gram

1000 cubic cm = 1 litre; 1 kilogram

1 cubic metre = 1000 litres; 1000 kg; 1 tonne

An inch of rain on the surface of an acre (43560 sq. ft) = 3630 cubic ft = 100·992 tons

Cisterns: A cistern 4 × 2½ feet and 3 feet deep will hold brimful 186·963 gallons, weighing 1869·63 lbs in addition to its own weight

Water for Ships

Kilderkin = 18 gallons

Barrel = 36 gallons

Puncheon = 72 gallons

Butt = 110 gallons

Tun = 210 gallons

Wine Measures

Under the Weights and Measures (Intoxicating Liquor) Order 1988, still wines may be pre-packed only in the following quantities: 10, 25, 37·5, 50 and 75 cl; 1, 1·5, 2, 3, 5, 6, 9 and 10 litres. In addition, the 18·7 cl size is permitted for consumption on board aircraft and ships.

The Intoxicating Liquor Order also provides that, with effect from January 1, 1991, sparkling wines (including champagne) may be pre-packed only in the following quantities: 12·5, 20, 37·5 and 75 cl; 1·5, 3, 4·5, 6 and 9 litres. From January 1, 1992, spirits and liqueurs may be pre-packed only in the following quantities: 2, 3, 4, 5, 7·1, 10, 20, 35, 50 and 70 cl; 1, 1·5, 2, 2·5, 3 and 4·5 litres.

Bottles of Wine

Traditional equivalents in standard champagne bottles:

Magnum = 2 bottles

Jeroboam = 4 bottles

Rehoboam = 6 bottles

Methuselah = 8 bottles

Salmanazar = 12 bottles

Balthazar = 16 bottles

Nebuchadnezzar = 20 bottles

A quarter of a bottle is known as a *nip.*

An eighth of a bottle is known as a *baby.*

ANGULAR OR CIRCULAR MEASURES

60 seconds (″) = 1 minute (′)

60 minutes = 1 degree (°)

90 degrees = 1 right angle or quadrant

Diameter of circle × 3·141 6 = circumference

Diameter squared × 0·7854 = area of circle

Diameter squared × 3·141 6 = surface of sphere

Diameter cubed × 0·523 = solidity of sphere

One degree of circumference × 57·3 = radius*

Diameter of cylinder × 3·141 6; product by length or height, gives the surface

Diameter squared × 0·7854; product by length or height, gives solid content.

* Or, one radian (the angle subtended at the centre of a circle by an arc of the circumference equal in length to the radius) = 57·3 degrees.

MILLION, BILLION, ETC.

Value in the United Kingdom

Million . . . . thousand × thousand (10^6)

Billion . . . . million × million (10^{12})

Trillion . . . . million × billion (10^{18})

Quadrillion . . . . million × trillion (10^{24})

The American usage of billion (i.e. 10^9) is increasingly common, and is now universally used by statisticians.

Value in USA

Million . . . . thousand × thousand (10^6)

Billion . . . . thousand × million (10^9)

Trillion . . . . million × million (10^{12})

Quadrillion . . . . million × billion US (10^{15})

NAUTICAL MEASURES

Distance at sea is measured in nautical miles. The British standard nautical mile was 6080 feet (the length of a minute of an arc of a great circle of the earth, rounded off to a mean value to allow for the length varying at different latitudes). This measure has been obsolete since 1970 when the international nautical mile of 1852 metres was adopted by the Hydrographic Department of the Ministry of Defence as a result of a recommendation by the International Hydrographic Bureau.

The cable (600 feet or 100 fathoms) was a measure approximately one tenth of a nautical mile. Such distances are now expressed in decimal parts of a sea mile or in metres.

Soundings at sea were recorded in fathoms (6 feet). Depths are now expressed in metres on new Admiralty charts.

Speed

Speed is measured in nautical miles per hour, called knots. A ship moving at the rate of 30 nautical miles per hour is said to be doing 30 knots.

Knots	m.p.h.	Knots	m.p.h.
1	1·1515	9	10·3636
2	2·3030	10	11·5151
3	3·4545	15	17·2727
4	4·6060	20	23·0303
5	5·7575	25	28·7878
6	6·9090	30	34·5454
7	8·0606	35	40·3030
8	9·2121	40	46·0606

Tonnage

The tonnage of a vessel is measured in tons of 100 cubic feet.

Gross tonnage = the total volume of all the enclosed spaces of a vessel

Net tonnage = gross tonnage less deductions for crew space, engine room, water ballast and other spaces not used for passengers or cargo

DISTANCE OF THE HORIZON

The limit of distance to which one can see varies with the height of the spectator. The greatest distance at which an object on the surface of the sea, or of a level plain, can be seen by a person whose eyes are at a height of five feet from the same level is nearly three miles. At a height of 20 feet the range is increased to nearly six miles, and an approximate rule for finding the range of vision for small heights is to increase the square root of the number of feet that the eye is above the level surface by a third of itself. The result is the distance of the horizon in miles, but is slightly in excess of that in the table below, which is computed by a more precise formula. The table may be used conversely to show the distance of an object of given height that is just visible from a point on the surface of the earth or sea. Refraction is taken into account both in the approximate rule and in the table.

At a height of	the range is
5 ft	2·9 miles
20 „	5·9 „
50 „	9·3 „
100 „	13·2 „
500 „	29·5 „
1,000 „	41·6 „
2,000 „	58·9 „
3,000 „	72·1 „
4,000 „	83·3 „
5,000 „	93·1 „
20,000 „	186·2 „

THERMOMETER COMPARISONS

The Celsius scale is the SI name for the Centigrade scale.

$$C = (F - 32) \div 1·8$$
$$F = (C \times 1·8) + 32$$

Comparison between Scales of Celsius and Fahrenheit

°C	°F	°C	°F	°C	°F
100	212	60	140	20	68
99	210·2	59	138·2	19	66·2
98	208·4	58	136·4	18	64·4
97	206·6	57	134·6	17	62·6
96	204·8	56	132·8	16	60·8
95	203	55	131	15	59
94	201·2	54	129·2	14	57·2
93	199·4	53	127·4	13	55·4
92	197·6	52	125·6	12	53·6
91	195·8	51	123·8	11	51·8
90	194	50	122	10	50
89	192·2	49	120·2	9	48·2
88	190·4	48	118·4	8	46·4
87	188·6	47	116·6	7	44·6
86	186·8	46	114·8	6	42·8
85	185	45	113	5	41
84	183·2	44	111·2	4	39·2
83	181·4	43	109·4	3	37·4
82	179·6	42	107·6	2	35·6
81	177·8	41	105·8	1	33·8
80	176	40	104	zero	32
79	174·2	39	102·2	− 1	30·2
78	172·4	38	100·4	− 2	28·4
77	170·6	37	98·6	− 3	26·6
76	168·8	36	96·8	− 4	24·8
75	167	35	95	− 5	23
74	165·2	34	93·2	− 6	21·2
73	163·4	33	91·4	− 7	19·4
72	161·6	32	89·6	− 8	17·6
71	159·8	31	87·8	− 9	15·8
70	158	30	86	−10	14
69	156·2	29	84·2	−11	12·2
68	154·4	28	82·4	−12	10·4
67	152·6	27	80·6	−13	8·6
66	150·8	26	78·8	−14	6·8
65	149	25	77	−15	5
64	147·2	24	75·2	−16	3·2
63	145·4	23	73·4	−17	1·4
62	143·6	22	71·6	−18	0·4
61	141·8	21	69·8	−19	−2·2

NOTE:—The normal temperature of the human body is 36·9 °C or 98·4 °F. Freezing point = 0 °C = 32 °F. Boiling point = 99·974 °C (on adoption of a new International Temperature Scale, ITS–90, from January 1, 1990) = 212 °F.

On the kelvin temperature scale, kelvin = 1/273·16 of the triple point of water (i.e. where ice, water and water vapour are in equilibrium). Absolute zero is zero K, the freezing point of water is 273·15 K and the boiling point is 373·124 K.

PAPER MEASURES

Writing Paper	Printing Paper
480 sheets = 1 ream	516 sheets = 1 ream
24 sheets = 1 quire	2 reams = 1 bundle
20 quires = 1 ream	5 bundles = 1 bale

Sizes of Writing and Drawing Papers

	inches		inches
Emperor......	72 ×48	Copy or Draft .	20 ×16
Antiquarian ..	53 ×31	Demy	20 ×15½
Double		Post	19 ×15¼
Elephant ...	40 ×27	Pinched Post .	18½ ×14½
Grand Eagle ..	42 ×28¾	Foolscap......	17 ×13½
Atlas.........	34 ×26	Double	
Colombier	34½ ×23½	Foolscap....	26½ ×16½
Imperial......	30 ×22	Double Post..	30½ ×19
Elephant	28 ×23	Double Large	
Cartridge.....	26 ×21	Post	33 ×21
Super Royal ..	27 ×19	Double Demy .	31 ×20
Royal	24 ×19	Brief.........	16½ ×13½
Medium	22 ×17½	Pott	15 ×12½
Large Post....	21 ×16½		

Sizes of Printing Papers

	inches		inches
Foolscap......	17 ×13½	Double Large	
Double		Post	33 ×21
Foolscap....	27 ×17	Demy	22½ ×17½
Quad Foolscap	34 ×27	Double Demy .	35 ×22½
Crown	20 ×15	Quad Demy ...	45 ×35
Double Crown	30 ×20	Music Demy ..	20 ×15½
Quad Crown ..	40 ×30	Medium	23 ×18
Double Quad		Royal	25 ×20
Crown	60 ×40	Super Royal ..	27½ ×20½
Post	19½ ×15½	Elephant	28 ×23
Double Post..	31½ ×19½	Imperial......	30 ×22

Sizes of Brown Papers

	inches		inches
Casing	46 ×36	Imperial Cap..	29 ×22
Double		Haven Cap ...	26 ×21
Imperial....	45 ×29	Bag Cap	24 ×19½
Elephant	34 ×24	Kent Cap	21 ×18
Double Four			
Pound......	31 ×21		

INTERNATIONAL PAPER SIZES

The basis of the international series of paper sizes is a rectangle having an area of one square metre, the sides of which are in the proportion of 1 : √2. The proportions 1 : √2 have a geometrical relationship, the side and diagonal of any square being in this proportion. The effect of this arrangement is that if the area of the sheet of paper is doubled or halved, the shorter side and the longer side of the new sheet are still in the same proportion 1 : √2. This feature is useful where photographic enlargement or reduction is used, as the proportions remain the same.

Description of the A series is by capital A followed by a figure. The basic size has the description A0 and the higher the figure following the letter, the greater is the number of sub-divisions and therefore the smaller the sheet. Half A0 is A1 and half A1 is A2.

Where larger dimensions are required the A is *preceded* by a figure. Thus 2A means twice the size A0; 4A is four times the size of A0.

Subsidiary Series.—A series of B sizes has been devised for use in exceptional circumstances when sizes intermediate between any two adjacent sizes of the A series are needed.

In addition there is a series of C sizes which is used much less. A is for magazines and books, B for posters, wall charts and other large items, C for envelopes particularly where it is necessary for an envelope (in C series) to fit into another envelope. The size recommended for business correspondence is A4.

Long Sizes.—Long sizes (DL) are obtainable by dividing any appropriate sizes from the two series above into three, four or eight equal parts parallel with the shorter side in such a manner that the proportions mentioned in paragraph two (above) are not maintained, the ratio between the longer and the shorter sides being greater than $\sqrt{2}$:1. In practice long sizes should be produced from the A series only.

It is an essential feature of these series that the dimensions are of the trimmed or finished size.

A Series

	mm		mm
A0	841 × 1189	A6	105 × 148
A1	594 × 841	A7	74 × 105
A2	420 × 594	A8	52 × 74
A3	297 × 420	A9	37 × 52
A4	210 × 297	A10	26 × 37
A5	148 × 210		

B Series

	mm		mm
B0	1000 × 1414	B6	125 × 176
B1	707 × 1000	B7	88 × 125
B2	500 × 707	B8	62 × 88
B3	353 × 500	B9	44 × 62
B4	250 × 353	B10	31 × 44
B5	176 × 250		

C Series

	mm
C4	324 × 229
C5	229 × 162
C6	114 × 162

DL

	mm
DL	110 × 220

SIZES OF BOUND BOOKS

The book sizes most commonly used are listed below. Approximate centimetre equivalents are also shown. International sizes are converted to their nearest imperial size (e.g. A4=D4; A5=D8).

		inches	cm
Crown 32mo	C32	2½ × 3¾	6 × 9
Crown 16mo	C16	3¾ × 5	9 × 13
Foolscap 8vo	F8	4½ × 6¾	11 × 17
Demy 16mo	D16	4⅜ × 5⅞	11 × 14
Crown 8vo	C8	5 × 7½	13 × 19
Demy 8vo	D8	5⅝ × 8¾	14 × 22
Medium 8vo	M8	5½ × 9	15 × 23
Royal 8vo	R8	6¼ × 10	16 × 25
Super Royal 8vo	suR8	6¾ × 10	17 × 25
Foolscap 4to	F4	6½ × 8¼	17 × 22
Crown 4to	C4	7½ × 10	19 × 25
Imperial 8vo	Imp8	7½ × 11	19 × 28
Demy 4to	D4	8¾ × 11¼	22 × 29
Royal 4to	R4	10 × 12½	25 × 31
Super Royal 4to	suR4	10 × 13½	25 × 34
Crown Folio	Cfol	10 × 15	25 × 38
Imperial Folio	Impfol	11 × 15	28 × 38

Folio means a sheet folded in half, *quarto* (4to) folded into four, *octavo* (8vo) folded into eight. Books are usually bound up in sheets of 16 or 32 pages. Octavo books are generally printed 64 pages at a time—32 pages on each side of a sheet of quad.

A TABLE OF THE NUMBER OF DAYS FROM ANY DAY IN ONE MONTH TO THE SAME IN ANY OTHER MONTH IN ORDINARY YEARS

	Jan.	Feb.	Mar.	April	May	June	July	Aug.	Sept.	Oct.	Nov.	Dec.
January	365	31	59	90	120	151	181	212	243	273	304	334
February	334	365	28	59	89	120	150	181	212	242	273	303
March	306	337	365	31	61	92	122	153	184	214	245	275
April	275	306	334	365	30	61	91	122	153	183	214	244
May	245	276	304	335	365	31	61	92	123	153	184	214
June	214	245	273	304	334	365	30	61	92	122	153	183
July	184	215	243	274	304	335	365	31	62	92	123	153
August	153	184	212	243	273	304	334	365	31	61	92	122
September	122	153	181	212	242	273	303	334	365	30	61	91
October	92	123	151	182	212	243	273	304	335	365	31	61
November	61	92	120	151	181	212	242	273	304	334	365	30
December	31	62	90	121	151	182	212	243	274	304	335	365

CONVERSION TABLES FOR WEIGHTS AND MEASURES

NOTE.—The central figures in heavy type represent either of the two columns beside them, as the case may be.
Examples:—1 centimetre = 0·394 inch and 1 inch = 2·540 centimetres. 1 metre = 1·094 yards and 1 yard = 0·914 metre. 1 kilometre = 0·621 mile and 1 mile = 1·609 kilometres.

Length / Area / Volume / Weight (Mass)

Centi-metres		Inches	Square Centi-metres		Square Inches	Cubic Centi-metres		Cubic Inches	Kilo-grams		Pounds
2·540	1	0·394	6·452	1	0·155	16·387	1	0·061	0·454	1	2·205
5·080	2	0·787	12·903	2	0·310	32·774	2	0·122	0·907	2	4·409
7·620	3	1·181	19·355	3	0·465	49·161	3	0·183	1·361	3	6·614
10·160	4	1·575	25·806	4	0·620	65·548	4	0·244	1·814	4	8·819
12·700	5	1·969	32·258	5	0·775	81·936	5	0·305	2·268	5	11·023
15·240	6	2·362	38·710	6	0·930	98·323	6	0·366	2·722	6	13·228
17·780	7	2·756	45·161	7	1·085	114·710	7	0·427	3·175	7	15·432
20·320	8	3·150	51·613	8	1·240	131·097	8	0·488	3·629	8	17·637
22·860	9	3·543	58·064	9	1·395	147·484	9	0·549	4·082	9	19·842
25·400	10	3·937	64·516	10	1·550	163·871	10	0·610	4·536	10	22·046
50·800	20	7·874	129·032	20	3·100	327·742	20	1·220	9·072	20	44·092
76·200	30	11·811	193·548	30	4·650	491·613	30	1·831	13·608	30	66·139
101·600	40	15·748	258·064	40	6·200	655·484	40	2·441	18·144	40	88·185
127·000	50	19·685	322·580	50	7·750	819·355	50	3·051	22·680	50	110·231
152·400	60	23·622	387·096	60	9·300	983·226	60	3·661	27·216	60	132·277
177·800	70	27·559	451·612	70	10·850	1147·097	70	4·272	31·752	70	154·324
203·200	80	31·496	516·128	80	12·400	1310·968	80	4·882	36·287	80	176·370
228·600	90	35·433	580·644	90	13·950	1474·839	90	5·492	40·823	90	198·416
254·000	100	39·370	645·160	100	15·500	1638·710	100	6·102	45·359	100	220·464

Metres		Yards	Square Metres		Square Yards	Cubic Metres		Cubic Yards	Metric Tonnes		Tons (UK)
0·914	1	1·094	0·836	1	1·196	0·765	1	1·308	1·016	1	0·984
1·829	2	2·187	1·672	2	2·392	1·529	2	2·616	2·032	2	1·968
2·743	3	3·281	2·508	3	3·588	2·294	3	3·924	3·048	3	2·953
3·658	4	4·374	3·345	4	4·784	3·058	4	5·232	4·064	4	3·937
4·572	5	5·468	4·181	5	5·980	3·823	5	6·540	5·080	5	4·921
5·486	6	6·562	5·017	6	7·176	4·587	6	7·848	6·096	6	5·905
6·401	7	7·655	5·853	7	8·372	5·352	7	9·156	7·112	7	6·889
7·315	8	8·749	6·689	8	9·568	6·116	8	10·464	8·128	8	7·874
8·230	9	9·843	7·525	9	10·764	6·881	9	11·772	9·144	9	8·858
9·144	10	10·936	8·361	10	11·960	7·646	10	13·080	10·161	10	9·842
18·288	20	21·872	16·723	20	23·920	15·291	20	26·159	20·321	20	19·684
27·432	30	32·808	25·084	30	35·880	22·937	30	39·239	30·481	30	29·526
36·576	40	43·745	33·445	40	47·840	30·582	40	52·318	40·642	40	39·368
45·720	50	54·681	41·806	50	59·799	38·228	50	65·398	50·802	50	49·210
54·864	60	65·617	50·168	60	71·759	45·873	60	78·477	60·963	60	59·052
64·008	70	76·553	58·529	70	83·719	53·519	70	91·557	71·123	70	68·894
73·152	80	87·489	66·890	80	95·679	61·164	80	104·636	81·284	80	78·737
82·296	90	98·425	75·251	90	107·639	68·810	90	117·716	91·444	90	88·579
91·440	100	109·361	83·613	100	119·599	76·455	100	130·795	101·605	100	98·421

Kilo-metres		Miles	Hectares		Acres	Litres		Gallons	Metric Tonnes		Tons (US)
1·609	1	0·621	0·405	1	2·471	4·546	1	0·220	0·907	1	1·102
3·219	2	1·243	0·809	2	4·942	9·092	2	0·440	1·814	2	2·205
4·828	3	1·864	1·214	3	7·413	13·638	3	0·660	2·722	3	3·305
6·437	4	2·485	1·619	4	9·844	18·184	4	0·880	3·629	4	4·409
8·047	5	3·107	2·023	5	12·355	22·730	5	1·100	4·536	5	5·521
9·656	6	3·728	2·428	6	14·826	27·276	6	1·320	5·443	6	6·614
11·265	7	4·350	2·833	7	17·297	31·822	7	1·540	6·350	7	7·716
12·875	8	4·971	3·327	8	19·769	36·368	8	1·760	7·257	8	8·818
14·484	9	5·592	3·642	9	22·240	40·914	9	1·980	8·165	9	9·921
16·093	10	6·214	4·047	10	24·711	45·460	10	2·200	9·072	10	11·023
32·187	20	12·427	8·094	20	49·421	90·919	20	4·400	18·144	20	22·046
48·280	30	18·641	12·140	30	74·132	136·379	30	6·599	27·216	30	33·069
64·374	40	24·855	16·187	40	98·842	181·839	40	8·799	36·287	40	44·092
80·467	50	31·069	20·234	50	123·555	227·298	50	10·999	45·359	50	55·116
96·561	60	37·282	24·281	60	148·263	272·758	60	13·199	54·431	60	66·139
112·654	70	43·496	28·328	70	172·974	318·217	70	15·398	63·503	70	77·162
128·748	80	49·710	32·375	80	197·684	363·677	80	17·598	72·575	80	88·185
144·841	90	55·923	36·422	90	222·395	409·137	90	19·798	81·647	90	99·208
160·934	100	62·137	40·469	100	247·105	454·596	100	21·998	90·719	100	110·231

DIARY OF EVENTS IN 1991

The Sports Council has designated 1991 the Year of Sport.

SHOWS, PAGEANTS AND EXHIBITIONS

Jan. 3–13	London International Boat Show	Earls Court, London
Jan. 9–12	Cruft's Dog Show	National Exhibition Centre, Birmingham
March 14–April 7	*Daily Mail* Ideal Home Exhibition	Earls Court, London
March 24–26	London International Book Fair	Olympia, London
May 8–12	Royal Windsor Horse Show	Home Park, Windsor
May 23–24	Chelsea Flower Show	Royal Hospital, Chelsea, London
June 15	Trooping the Colour	Horse Guards Parade, London
July 1–4	Royal International Agricultural Show	Stoneleigh, Kenilworth, Warks.
July 10–27	Royal Tournament	Earls Court, London
Aug. 2–24	Edinburgh Military Tattoo	Edinburgh Castle
Aug. 8	Battle of Flowers	Jersey
Sept. 7	Braemar Royal Highland Gathering	Braemar, Grampian
Sept. 13–21	Southampton International Boat Show	Mayflower Park, Southampton
Nov. 3	London to Brighton Veteran Car Run	Hyde Park to Brighton
Nov. 9	Lord Mayor's Procession and Show	City of London
Dec. 1–5	Royal Smithfield Show and Agricultural Machinery Exhibition	Earls Court, London

MUSIC AND DRAMA FESTIVALS

May 21–Aug. 23	Glyndebourne Festival Opera season	Glyndebourne, Lewes, E. Sussex
May 24–June 9	Bath International Festival	Bath, Avon
May–Sept.	Chichester Festival Theatre season	Chichester, W. Sussex
June 7–23	Aldeburgh Festival of Music and Arts	Aldeburgh, Suffolk
July 19–Sept. 14	Promenade Concerts season	Royal Albert Hall, London
July 20–Aug. 11	Buxton Festival	Buxton, Derbyshire
Aug. 3–10	Royal National Eisteddfod of Wales	Bro Delyn, Mold
Aug. 11–31	Edinburgh International Festival	Edinburgh
Aug. 18–23	Three Choirs Festival	Hereford
Nov. 8–25	London International Film Festival	London

HORSE RACING

March 14	Cheltenham Gold Cup	Cheltenham
March 23	Lincoln Handicap	Doncaster
April 6	Grand National	Aintree
May 2	One Thousand Guineas	Newmarket
May 4	Two Thousand Guineas	Newmarket
June 5	The Derby	Epsom
June 6	Coronation Cup	Epsom
June 8	The Oaks	Epsom
June 18–21	Royal Ascot	Ascot
July 27	King George VI and Queen Elizabeth Diamond Stakes	Ascot
Sept. 14	St. Leger	Doncaster
Oct. 5	Cambridgeshire	Newmarket
Oct. 19	Cesarewitch	Newmarket

OTHER SPORTS

Jan. 19	Rugby Union: Wales v. England	Cardiff Arms Park
Feb. 2	Rugby Union: Scotland v. Wales	Murrayfield, Edinburgh
Feb. 16	Rugby Union: England v. Scotland	Twickenham, London
April 21	London Marathon	London
May 2–5	Badminton Horse Trials	Badminton, Avon
May 18	Football: FA Cup Final	Wembley Stadium, London
May 27–June 7	International TT Motorcycle Races	Isle of Man
June 24–July 7	Lawn Tennis Championships	Wimbledon, London
July 3–7	Henley Royal Regatta	Henley-on-Thames
July 11–25	World Student Games	Sheffield
July 18–21	Golf: Open Championship	Royal Birkdale, Southport
Aug. 3–11	Cowes Week	Cowes, Isle of Wight
Sept. 10–15	Golf: British Amateur Championship	Ganton, Scarborough North Cliff
Oct. 7–12	Horse of the Year Show	Wembley Arena, London
Nov. 2	Rugby Union: World Cup Final	Twickenham, London

The horse racing fixtures are the copyright of The Jockey Club.

INDEX

INDEX

ARTHRITIS RESEARCH

If Timmy could write a Will, he would probably leave something to us.

You see, he's an arthritis sufferer. He's one of about 15,000 children in our country today who, along with over 8 million people of all other ages, are seriously affected by the disease. And, young as he is, Timmy knows we're his only hope.

We are the Arthritis and Rheumatism Council, the only UK charity financing medical research into all aspects of arthritis. Currently, we spend over £11 million annually on our research and legacies are a major source of our income. We rely entirely on voluntary contributions, receive no State aid whatsoever and spend a mere 2½p in the £ on administration.

We've made many advances in treatment through our research, but as yet there's no cure. With your help, though, we'll find one. Please do what Timmy would do: remember us in your Will.

You'd be helping us achieve the goal of ensuring future generations of Timmy's don't have to suffer this dreadful disease. Talk to your solicitor today; or alternatively, complete and return the coupon below for our Legacy leaflet.

THE ARTHRITIS AND RHEUMATISM COUNCIL FOR RESEARCH

Working to find an earlier cure

THE ARTHRITIS AND RHEUMATISM COUNCIL FOR RESEARCH
41 Eagle Street, London WC1R 4AR. Tel: 071-405 8572

Assured of Care

for the rest of their lives

For 90 years Princess Christian Homes, Knaphill, Surrey have been offering family-type care to elderly single and widowed men who might otherwise spend their declining years in loneliness and difficulty.

Now, among the ex-service community as in the rest of the population, the number of frail elderly is increasing, and the informal care which the Homes can at present give is not enough.

THE FORCES HELP SOCIETY therefore plans to build a new wing, to be called the Lord Roberts Wing, to enable those among the present residents, and others who may enter, with special needs for care, to be looked after by a sufficient number of fully trained staff, in a compact, well-equipped care unit with all its own facilities.

**Please help us to care in their old age
for those who served us so well**

THE FORCES HELP SOCIETY & LORD ROBERTS WORKSHOPS
122 Brompton Road, London SW3 1JE   Tel: 071-589 3243   Fax: 071-584 0676
Registered Charity No. 209753

NEAR TO HOME

We have a new home – a generous gift which will help us to look after more elderly people. It is a happy place – a real Friends of the Elderly home from home.

Please help us to provide for the many aspects of care and attention so important to the old and frail. Many of us lead longer, contented lives today but for some there is an unacceptable price to pay in loneliness and need.

We have been looking after the elderly since 1905 and now have twelve residential homes. Here men and women from professional backgrounds find security and freedom, for the rest of their lives, with nursing care when needed. Friends of the Elderly also give financial help to old people from all backgrounds who wish to stay in their own homes.

We all face old age, one way or another. Ours is a cause very near to home. Please be a Friend and make a covenant or remember us in your will.

Write today with a donation and enquiry to:

The General Secretary,
Friends of the Elderly (Dept.   WA),
42 Ebury Street,
LONDON SW1W 0LZ.

FRIENDS OF THE ELDERLY
and Gentlefolk's help

Registered charity number: 226064

PD

NOBODY KNOWS WHAT CAUSES IT.

NOBODY KNOWS HOW TO CURE IT.

AND, WORST OF ALL...

NOBODY KNOWS IF <u>YOU</u> ARE GOING TO GET IT.

We're asking everybody to help us find a breakthrough

Parkinson's Disease can be *anybody's* disease. You can help to make it *nobody's* disease. Men and women all over the world suffer from this disabling condition. Researchers need your help. So do more than 100,000 sufferers in this country alone.

Please send a donation, a covenant or leave us a legacy. You can even phone your donation by Access or Visa to 071-383 3513.

YOU CAN'T IMAGINE WHAT IT'S LIKE TO LIVE WITH

PARKINSON'S DISEASE

Parkinson's Disease Society
22 Upper Woburn Place. London WC1H 0RA. Tel: 071-383 3513
Patron: HRH The Princess of Wales

THE GARDENER'S ROYAL BENEVOLENT SOCIETY

Bridge House, 139 Kingston Road
Leatherhead, Surrey KT22 7NT

A Happy Retirement for Gardeners

Please help us to provide nursing, residential and sheltered accommodation,
pensions, special grants and holidays by donations, deeds of covenant or
legacies.

TEL: 0372 373962

VITAL MEDICAL RESEARCH IS FUNDED BY
The HUMANE RESEARCH TRUST

HELPS PEOPLE SAVES ANIMALS

- ° **No living animals are used**
- ° **It is more relevant to man,**
- ° **Cheaper, More Efficient, Quicker!**

Grants have been given in Universities, Hospitals and Centres of
Healing all over the UK for work on many diseases.
The following are three of many on-going programmes:

BRAIN CANCER - *Institute of Psychiatry LONDON*
we need £12,000 a year for three years,
KIDNEY DISEASE - *University of Strathclyde*
we need £20,000 a year for three years
CATARACTS _ *University of East Anglia*
we need £20,000 a year for 4 years

We rely entirely on voluntary funding, please ask us for information:-

National H/Q BROOK HOUSE*(WH91)*
29 Bramhall Lane South, BRAMHALL, Cheshire SK7 2DN
Telephone 061-439-8041 Fax 160 439 3713 Registered Charity No.267779

SOCIETY FOR THE ASSISTANCE OF LADIES IN REDUCED CIRCUMSTANCES

Founded by the late Miss Edith Smallwood

Charity Registration No. 205798

* The Society exists to provide financial help to elderly ladies (above retirement age) of British Nationality living alone on low incomes, domiciled in the British Isles.

* We welcome enquiries from those wishing to assist us in our work or from those who may need our help.

Further information and a Preliminary Application Form may be obtained from:-

The Secretary, S.A.L.R.C. (W)
Lancaster House, 25 Hornyold Road,
Malvern, Worcs WR14 1QQ

SO MUCH STILL TO BE DONE

for the hundreds of elderly people from all parts of the country—lonely, living in distressing circumstances—who are waiting and hoping that we can accommodate them soon in self-contained flatlets of their own.

Time for them is running out fast!

We have the skill, experience and desire to provide still more self-contained flatlets, where the elderly can live independent, secure and comfortable lives.

But tomorrow may be too late. We need your help now.

Only the unceasing flow of legacies, gifts and covenants will enable us to continue to provide this vital housing need.

PLEASE REMEMBER US AND THE ELDERLY IN YOUR WILL

The Secretary (W.A.),

FELLOWSHIP HOUSES TRUST,

Clock House, Byfleet,
Weybridge, Surrey.

Telephone: Byfleet 43172

Registered Charity No. 205786   Registered Housing Association No. L1821

A LEGACY MEANS A LOT TO THE LIMBLESS

We come from two World Wars, Korea, Kenya, Malaya, Aden, Cyprus, Ulster, The Falklands and all those areas of turmoil where peace must be restored.

Now, disabled and mainly aged, we must look to you for help. Please help by helping our Association.

BLESMA looks after the limbless from all the Services. It helps to overcome the shock of losing arms, or legs or an eye. And, for the severely handicapped, it provides Residential Homes where they can live in peace and dignity.

Help the disabled by helping BLESMA with a donation now or a legacy in the future. We promise you that not one penny will be wasted.

PLEASE GIVE TO THOSE WHO GAVE

Give to those who gave—please
Donations and information: The Chairman, National Appeal Committee, BLESMA, Midland Bank PLC, 60 West Smithfield, London EC1A 9DX

BLESMA
BRITISH LIMBLESS
EX-SERVICE MEN'S ASSOCIATION

THE FIRST STEP
by a recent, young double amputee

THE MALCOLM SARGENT CANCER FUND FOR CHILDREN

The Fund gives practical help to children suffering from cancer, leukaemia or Hodgkin's disease and over 1000 new cases are accepted each year.

A Senior Social Worker from Coventry writes:

"Without doubt, I would award the Malcolm Sargent Cancer Fund for Children the award for being the most effective, generous and helpful charity. I could not have asked or imagined such a swift response to my application for a grant for Liam."

Donations please to:

MALCOLM SARGENT CANCER FUND FOR CHILDREN

Miss Sylvia Darley, General Administrator, 14 Abingdon Road, London, W8 6AF   *Or if you live in Scotland to:*

Miss Venetia Fane, Drumwhill, Mossdale, by Castle Douglas, Kirkcudbrightshire, DG7 2NL.

Alexandra Rose Day

Founded in 1912, as the nation's first Flag Day, this much loved charity continues to-day, as it began, to make it possible for voluntary organisations caring for the aged, the young, the sick and the disabled to raise funds for themselves by taking part in Alexandra Rose Day, keeping at least 80% of the monies that they raise.

In addition, Alexandra Rose Day administers a Trust Fund set up to provide emergency help to "people caring" charities facing financial crisis. Funding comes from social events organised by Alexandra Rose Day, individual donations, and a percentage of the return from the Flag Day.

For further information please contact:
Mrs. Gillian Greenwood, National Director
Alexandra Rose Day, 1 Castelnau, Barnes
London SW13 9RP
Telephone: 081 748 4824

THE BRITISH POLIO FELLOWSHIP

*(The Infantile Paralysis Fellowship, registered as a charity in accordance with the
National Assistance Act 1948)*

THE NATIONAL VOLUNTARY ORGANISATION FOR
THE POLIO DISABLED

(Patron: Lavinia, Duchess of Norfolk, C.B.E.)

- Founded in 1939, the Fellowship has helped thousands of polio victims to live
a fuller life and to cope with their disabilities.

- Polio is no respecter of persons; it has stricken the physically strong of all age
groups and from different walks of life.

- The Fellowship's work in caring for all polio victims knows no barriers and helps
all who have suffered from polio.

- Over £400,000 spent annually on welfare grants, aids, residential care, etc. Can
you help—by donation? covenanted gift? or by legacy? Please write to:

**BELL CLOSE, WEST END ROAD, RUISLIP, MIDDX.
HA4 6LP**

Telephone: 0895 675515

INDEX TO ADVERTISEMENTS

OCCURRENCES DURING PRINTING

EVENTS

Sept. 1. The Prince of Wales underwent a second operation on his broken right arm. The first group of British hostages returned from Iraq. **2.** A five-nation West African peace-keeping force was reported to have taken control of Monrovia, capital of Liberia. **3.** The TUC conference opened in Blackpool. President Siad Barre of Somalia sacked the government and appointed Muhammad Madar as the new prime minister. The secretary-general of the League of Arab States, Chedli Klibi, resigned. **4.** The prime minister of New Zealand, Geoffrey Palmer, resigned and was replaced by Michael Moore; a general election was called for Oct. 27. **6.** The House of Commons re-assembled for a two-day emergency debate on the Gulf crisis. Provincial elections in Ontario, Canada, were won by the New Democratic Party. **7.** Michael Forsyth resigned as chairman of the Scottish Conservative Party and was replaced by Lord Sanderson of Bowden, who relinquished his post as Minister of State at the Scottish Office. Mr. Forsyth was promoted from Under-Secretary to Minister of State at the Scottish Office. **8.** In China Li Peng was replaced by Chen Jinhua as Minister in Charge of the State Commission for Restructuring the Economy. **9.** A seven-hour summit meeting about the Gulf crisis was held in Helsinki between President Bush and President Gorbachov. President Samuel Doe of Liberia was captured by rebels; it was later reported that he had been killed. **10.** The National Union of Rail, Maritime and Transport Workers came into existence after the merger of the NUR and the NUS. Iran and Iraq agreed to resume diplomatic ties. Benazir Bhutto, the deposed prime minister of Pakistan, was formally charged with abuse of power during her 20 months in office. **11.** The official report into the Lockerbie disaster was published. Mongolia's Great Hural appointed Dash Byambasuren prime minister. **12.** The treaty on the final settlement with respect to Germany, clearing the way for German reunification, was signed in Moscow by the USSR, USA, Britain, France, and East and West Germany. In provincial elections in Manitoba, Canada, the Conservatives were returned to power with a slim majority. **14.** Iraqi soldiers in Kuwait forced their way into French, Canadian, Dutch and Belgian diplomatic premises, abducting or detaining several people. President Gorbachov's programme for reforming the Soviet economy in 500 days was outlined to the Soviet parliament. **15.** The Social and Liberal Democrat conference opened in Blackpool. **16.** Gabon held its first multi-party elections. **17.** European Community foreign ministers agreed to expel Iraqi military diplomatic staff and limit the freedom of movement of other embassy staff, in retaliation for the raids on western embassies in Kuwait. Britain announced its intention of expelling two military attachés, six support staff and 23 non-diplomats. The Chief of Staff of the US Air Force, Gen. Michael Dugan, was dismissed after discussing, in an interview with the *Washington Post*, US military options in the event of war with Iraq. **18.** The International Olympic Committee voted to stage the 1996 Olympic Games in Atlanta, USA. Air

Vice-Marshal Sir Peter Terry was shot and wounded by the IRA at his home near Stafford. **19.** The Scottish National Party conference opened in Perth. The Iraqi government announced that it would impound the assets in Iraq of those countries which have frozen Iraqi money and property. **20.** The East German Volkskammer and the West German Bundestag voted to accept the unification treaty. The Dutch Agriculture Minister, Gerrit Braks, resigned. **21.** Iraq expelled the military attachés of all European embassies in Baghdad, and imposed restrictions on the movement of remaining western diplomats. The USA expelled three Iraqi diplomats. **22.** The Green Party conference opened in Wolverhampton. Saudi Arabia expelled Iraqi, Jordanian and Yemeni diplomats, and cut off oil supplies to Jordan. **23.** Hor Nam Hong was appointed Foreign Minister of Cambodia. **24.** President von Weisäcker of West Germany signed the treaty making official the reunification of East and West Germany. East Germany formally left the Warsaw Pact. The Supreme Soviet of the USSR granted President Gorbachov further executive powers, including the power to rule by decree, to enable him to implement plans to reform the Soviet economy. **25.** The United Nations Security Council adopted resolution 670, imposing an air blockade of Iraq. Sir Jack Lyons, the fourth man convicted in the Guinness affair, was fined £3 million. **27.** The Labour candidate, Eddie O'Hara, won the Knowsley South by-election. The Queen approved the creation of eight additional seats in Canada's Senate. **29.** The Labour Party conference opened in Blackpool. **30.** Rwanda was invaded by a force of Rwandan exiles backed by the Rwandan Patriotic Front.

Oct. 1. Lt.-Gen. Sir Peter de la Billière was appointed commander of British forces in the Middle East. **2.** The USSR agreed to hold formal independence talks with Lithuania. A presidential election in Poland on Nov. 25 was announced. There was a government reshuffle in France. **3.** East and West Germany were unified as one country, with Berlin as the capital. The unified state has adopted the flag and national anthem of West Germany. Germany became a member of NATO. Federal, state and local elections took place in Brazil. **4.** Rebel troops in the Philippines launched a separatist insurrection in Mindanao. **5.** Interest rates went down by 1 per cent. The Malaysian parliament was dissolved and a general election called for November. **8.** Britain joined the European exchange rate mechanism. **9.** The Conservative Party conference opened in Bournemouth.

APPOINTMENTS

Royal Household

Lord Cavendish to be a Lord in Waiting. M. C. G. Peat to be Director of Finance and Property Services in HM Household.

Parliament, etc.

Michael Forsyth, MP, to be a Minister of State at the Scottish Office in place of Lord Sanderson of Bowden.
Lord Cavendish to be a Lord in Waiting.

Lord Sanderson of Bowden to be chairman of the Scottish Conservative Party.

A. Salmond, MP, to be National Convener of the Scottish National Party in place of G. Wilson.

Eddie O'Hara (Lab.) elected MP for Knowsley South.

Government Offices

A. Chancellor to be a Commissioner of English Heritage.

L. Briggs to be curator of the Tate Gallery, Liverpool.

Law Courts

Joyanne Bracewell, QC, to be a Justice of the High Court (Family Division).

The Hon. Mr. Justice Thomas to transfer from the Family Division to the Queen's Bench Division.

G. Penrose to be a Senator of the College of Justice in place of Lord Dunpark, who is retiring.

Churches

R. Gray, QC, to be Chancellor of the diocese of Southwark.

M. Njue to be Bishop of the new diocese of Embu in Kenya.

Foreign Countries

David H. Souter to be an Associate Justice of the Supreme Court of the USA.

September

2. Robert Holmes à Court, Australian businessman, aged 52.
3. Sir Eric Smith, CBE, FRS, aged 81.
4. Irene Dunne, film actress, aged 88.
5. Lord Caradon (formerly Sir Hugh Foot), aged 82.
—. Allen Adams, MP, Labour MP for Paisley North since 1979, aged 44.
6. Sir Leonard Hutton, cricketer, aged 74.
7. A. J. P. Taylor, historian, aged 84.
8. Denys Watkins-Pitchford ('BB'), aged 85.
10. Samuel Doe, president of Liberia, aged 40.
12. Athene Seyler, CBE, actress, aged 101.
22. Lord Swann, FRS, aged 70.
26. Alberto Moravia, Italian writer, aged 82.
29. Baroness Portal of Hungerford, aged 67.
—. William Dring, RA, artist, aged 86.
30. Patrick White, Australian novelist, aged 78.
—. 5th Baron Annaly, aged 63.

October

1. General Curtis LeMay, aged 83.
4. Jill Bennett, actress, aged 58.
—. Avis Bunnage, actress, aged 67.
7. Sheik Rashid bin Said al-Maktoum, ruler of Dubai and vice-president and prime minister of the United Arab Emirates.